The NIV™

# Interlinear Hebrew-English Old Testament

The NIV™

# Interlinear Hebrew-English Old Testament

## Four Volumes in One
## Genesis–Malachi

Edited by
John R. Kohlenberger III

ZondervanPublishingHouse
*Academic and Professional Books*
*Grand Rapids, Michigan*
*A Division of* HarperCollins*Publishers*

THE NIV INTERLINEAR HEBREW-ENGLISH OLD TESTAMENT


Requests for information should be addressed to:
Academic and Professional Books
Zondervan Publishing House
1415 Lake Drive, S.E., Grand Rapids, Michigan 49506

**Library of Congress Cataloging in Publication Data**

Bible. O.T. Hebrew. 1987.
The NIV interlinear Hebrew-English Old Testament.

Reprint. Originally published: Grand Rapids: Zondervan, c1979–c1985. With new introd.
"Genesis-Malachi."
Bibliography: p.
1. Bible. O.T.—Interlinear translations, English. I. Kohlenberber, John R. II. Bible. O.T. English. New International. 1987. III. Title. IV. Title: Interlinear Hebrew-English Old Testament.

BS715 1987 220.4'4 87–3356

ISBN 0–310–44220–6



*Printed in the United States of America*

91 92 93 94 95 / AK / 11 10 9 8 7 6

This edition is printed on acid-free paper and meets the American National Standards Institute Z39.48 standard.

# CONTENTS

## VOLUME FOUR

# ACKNOWLEDGMENTS

Five years of labor, 1574 pages of Hebrew text, and 2290 pages of translation went into the four-volume *NIV Interlinear Hebrew-English Old Testament*, now available in this one-volume edition. Of course, those five years involved more than my own labors. I am thankful, therefore, for the opportunity to publicly acknowledge those whose names do not appear on the cover, those without whose involvement this volume would not be what it is.

I must first thank the Zondervan Corporation for committing this project to me in the first place. Although together we have produced nine reference books and two study Bibles in the past eight years, the publisher took a chance on a complete unknown when this project began in 1978. Thanks to John Van Diest of the Christian Supply Centers and to Kin Millen, then of Zondervan, who first put me in touch with the publisher. Special thanks go to those who worked as editors on the original four-volume set—Bob DeVries, Paul Hillman, Doris Rikkers, and Stan Gundry—for their exceptional patience, encouragement, and support.

For granting permission to use their exceptional texts as the bases for this work, thanks to the International Bible Society for their New International Version and to the Deutsche Bibelstiftung Stuttgart for their *Biblia Hebraica Stuttgartensia*.

Recognition must go to the exceptional work of the typesetters: Deutsche Bibelstiftung Stuttgart for setting the Hebrew Text, Auto-Graphics for setting the NIV marginal text, SeTyp for setting the interlinear translation, and my parents (John and Doris) for their help and technical advice. With deep gratitude for the tedious and exacting work of putting each Hebrew word in its proper place relative to the translation, I thank R. Burwell Davis, Rosalie Donais, and Linda Schley, though I must single out Jeanne and Ralph Kunselman for doing the majority of the work on volumes 3 and 4. I also acknowledge the immense contributions of the late John Hemmingsen to the production and proofreading of volumes 1 and 2.

For proofreading the translation and biblical texts, special thanks to Paul Jesclard, who worked on volume 2, and especially to Dr. Ronald Youngboood of the NIV Committee on Bible Translation, who worked on volumes 3 and 4. They must not be criticized for any of the tendencies or mistakes in this work, for that is my responsibility, but they must be credited for the hundreds of places in which their suggestions improved the text.

I also extend my gratitude to the people who helped put me together—the faculties of Multonomah School of the Bible and Western Conservative

Baptist Seminary. I must single out two from Western—Dr. Ronald B. Allen and Dr. Ralph Alexander—who taught me to read Hebrew and to love the Old Testament and one from Multnomah—Dr. E. W. Goodrick—who has been my mentor, co-author, and dear friend and without whose encouragement I would not have taken this direction in biblical studies.

Again, I must single out the man who made this set and my current career possible. More than any other individual, Dr. Robert K. DeVries—whose faith in an unknown kid from the wild northwest, and whose commitment to and support of this project, made this entire set a reality. To my good friend Bob I dedicated volume 4.

As this set grew, so did my family. I dedicated volume 1 to wife Carolyn, volume 2 to daughter Sarah Natanya, and volume 3 to son Joshua David. Although I worked on these books at home, I was not always "at home." But they regularly pulled me back to reality, so that I was never "gone" for long. I lovingly thank them and praise God for their remarkable patience and encouragement.

# HOW TO USE THIS VOLUME

This preintroductory section is designed to acquaint English Bible students and beginning language students with the value and use of this (or any other) interlinear work by describing what it is, what it can do, and what it cannot do. The introduction that follows presents in more detail a technical discussion of the Hebrew text and the translation techniques underlying the interlinear version and is directed to those already familiar with the basics of Hebrew grammar and textual criticism.

## WHAT IT IS

As the title states, an interlinear Hebrew-English Old Testament is a book that interlines Hebrew with English; that is, it provides a line of English translation for each line of Hebrew. Furthermore, it matches these lines word-for-word so that each Hebrew word has a representative word or phrase translating it into English.

This interlinear is difficult to read as a line because Hebrew reads right to left whereas English reads left to right. In the past, interlinears have written their English lines right to left, thus making the English reader read backwards. In this interlinear, on the other hand, each multiple-word phrase that translates a single Hebrew word is written normally in English—left to right—so that when the interlinear is used to read Hebrew a word at a time, its English rendering reads as English should. For example, in Genesis 12:2, the Hebrew word וַאֲבָרֶכְךָ in traditional interlinears would be rendered "you bless will I and," but in this volume it is "and-I-will-bless-you."

An interlinear *should* be read a word at a time, not as a version. No passage in one language can be translated into another language consistently word by word and still make the best sense. Anyone who has studied a foreign language knows that. Thus, for an interlinear to accurately represent the Hebrew (or Greek, for the New Testament), it must not represent itself as a version by itself. In most other Old or New Testament interlinears, words are numbered so they may be read in proper English order, and many words are supplied in brackets or italics because they are needed in English but do not come directly from the original language. This interlinear was *not* constructed in that way. Instead, a specific rendering is given for each Hebrew word. By comparing the sum total of these English words and phrases with the version in the margin, the reader can see the sort of give and take that must go on in order to express in proper English idiom the sentences generated by these words.

This brings us closer to defining what an interlinear is. It is a sourcebook for word studies and for the study of Hebrew. It is a source for word studies because the reader can work from the New International Version (NIV), which parallels the interlinear text, and thus discover the Hebrew word that underlies the key words of the text. It is a source for the study of Hebrew because it provides an English translation for every Hebrew word; so the student of Hebrew can read large portions of the text without constant reference to dictionaries or grammar books. These processes will be explained further in the next section.

### What It Can Do

Because it is based on the NIV, and the NIV is contained on the same page as the interlinear text, one can read from the major words of the English text into the interlinear text and find the Hebrew word that will begin a word study. Needless to say, if you do not know the Hebrew alphabet, this book will be of little value to you. Thus, I have included a chart of the alphabet and vowels with pronunciation as a bare-bones minimum of knowledge necessary to work with this text. It would be of great value, however, if you were to dabble in a beginning Hebrew grammar or, better yet, to learn the essentials of Hebrew sounds and grammar from E. W. Goodrick's *Do It Yourself Hebrew and Greek* (Portland: Multnomah, 1976; Grand Rapids; Zondervan, 1979). Goodrick's book has a companion cassette that pronounces all Hebrew sounds and slowly reads through the first two chapters of Genesis to apply the basic sounds to the actual words of the text.

Suppose you are reading "The Song of Moses" in Exodus 15 and you see the footnote in verse 4 that says the Hebrew meaning of the name *Red Sea* is really the "Sea of Reeds." As you look over to the interlinear text, you do not even find the word *red*. The last word in verse 4 is "Reed," its corresponding Hebrew word being סוּף. If this is not enough information for you, you will want to take the next step of going to Hebrew dictionaries (or lexicons) and *The Englishman's Hebrew and Chaldee Concordance of the Old Testament* (Grand Rapids: Zondervan, 1970).

Before you can use these tools, you will have to know the root form of the word. Hebrew (and Greek) words change their forms in many ways, depending on how they are used in a sentence, but the dictionaries list only the most basic form of each word. The book that will give you this form is called *The Analytical Hebrew and Chaldee Lexicon*, 2nd ed. (Grand Rapids: Zondervan, 1970). We find the form סוּף on page 574 and notice that it is indeed already in its basic form, for there is a definition after it (note that this is the word in the second column [a noun], not the word in brackets in the first column [a verb]). The definitions given include "seaweed," "sedge," "reed," "rush," and "bulrush," besides the proper name

"Red Sea." If you go further and look in a larger lexicon like that of Brown, Driver, and Briggs (BDB)—and you should!—you will discover that the word never refers to the color red at all; it is used only of water plants and of the "arms" of the Red Sea—the gulfs of Suez and Akaba. BDB explains that the term *Red Sea* comes from the *Greek* translation of the Old Testament, for the Greeks called these bodies of water by their color, not by their vegetation.

In addition to checking dictionary definitions, you can do your own inductive study by looking at every verse in which a word occurs. Every occurrence of the word סוּף, for example, is listed on page 872 of the *Englishman's Concordance*. After looking them all up, you will see that whenever the word is not used of the Red Sea, it refers to reeds or water plants in general. This does not mean you cannot refer to this body of water as the Red Sea; it simply means that you know the basis for the footnote in the NIV and can explain to someone else what the Hebrew word means. Goodrick's book, mentioned earlier, will not only teach you how to sound out Hebrew words; it will also teach you how to do this kind of word study in both Hebrew and Greek.

This interlinear can help someone learn the Hebrew language, because it is a grammatically literal translation, allowing the Hebrew text to be read without constant reference to lexicons and grammars. When the reader is unable to immediately identify the form or determine the meaning of a word, a mere glance at the English translation will show if it is a noun or a verb, a participle or an imperative, singular or plural, or whatever, besides giving its definition. By comparing the interlinear rendering with the NIV, the reader will also see how the form functions, for sometimes the form in which Hebrew casts a word or phrase is changed in order to make good sense in English.

For example, the first word in Exodus 20:8, זָכוֹר, being an infinitive, is translated in the interlinear as "to-remember." But in the NIV it is rendered as an imperative, "Remember." The student would then understand (or discover in a grammar) that this infinitive is an "imperitival infinitive," an emphatic way of expressing a command. The difference in form between the interlinear translation and that of the NIV does not mean that the NIV is neither literal nor accurate; rather, a change in grammatical form was felt necessary in order to express the same idea in each language.

## What It Cannot Do

This brings us to the third section: what an interlinear cannot do. First, it cannot be used by itself to "correct" or criticize a *real* translation. By "real translation" I mean one that was made for English-speaking people to read in normal English idiom, such as the NIV. As we saw in the preceding example, the form of grammar and even the number and order of words used in an expression may change from one language to another. Because the interlinear supplies only a word-for-word grammatically literal equivalence, it cannot be used as a normal English translation. It is a sort of half-way point between the Hebrew original and its idiomatic English rendering. So, the English Bible student cannot use the interlinear *grammatically* as he can *lexcially* (that is, as a source for word studies).

Second, in respect to word studies, the interlinear translation cannot fully and exactly express the Hebrew in every instance. It can give a definition for a word in its context but cannot provide a commentary on all of the subtle nuances and meanings of that word. For this, one must consult lexicons and concordances. With the help of a concordance one can examine any word in every location in which it appears in Scripture, and with the lexicon he can obtain categorized definitions and even commentary on key passages. We have already seen this process in regard to the Red Sea.

Third, the interlinear cannot be an independent source of exegesis or interpretation. For example, בְּרֵאשִׁית, the first word in Genesis 1:1, is translated "in-beginning" (because there is no definite article present in the Hebrew), but this does not mean it should be interpreted as speaking of *a* beginning (i.e., one among many). An article is required in English—whether "a" or "the"—even though the Hebrew has none, and the NIV has interpreted this verse to refer to *the* beginning (as have most other English versions). That decision cannot be challenged and refuted solely on the rendering of the Hebrew word in the interlinear.

Similarly, in Isaiah 7:14, because the NIV translators chose "the virgin" to translate the Hebrew word הָעַלְמָה, the interlinear translation reflects this choice rather than using "the young woman," which might be the better option linguistically, contextually, and theologically. This "proves" only that the NIV agrees with the word choice of some versions—e.g., King James Version, Living Bible, New American Standard Bible—as opposed to the choice of other versions—e.g., Good News Bible, Jerusalem Bible, and Revised Standard Version. It does not prove that הָעַלְמָה means "the virgin."

In summary, the English Bible student can use this volume to locate and begin to study words in lexicons, concordances, and linguistically based commentaries and even to glean a little information about Hebrew grammar by observing the style of translation. The student of Hebrew can use it more fully, as a companion to translation that provides both form and function and as a pedagogue to lead him to a better reading knowledge of Hebrew—even to the point where he outgrows the book altogether.

The introduction that follows explains more fully to the student of Hebrew how to use the interlinear as a help in understanding grammar. It does so by pointing out the techniques of translation that express the forms of the words. A careful reading of the introduction will give the student a better understanding of the book and a fuller, more satisfying use of it. At the end of the introduction is a list of books basic to the study of Hebrew and of the biblical languages in general.

## The Hebrew Alphabet and Vowel System

The following table lists the alphabet in order, giving both pronunciation value (as used in modern Hebrew) and transliteration value (that is, the way reference books represent the letters in English characters).

| Form | Final Form | Transliteration | Name | Pronounced as in: |
|---|---|---|---|---|
| א | | ʾ | ʾAleph | (silent) |
| בּ (ב) | | b (bh or ḇ) | Beth | *b*all (*v*ery) |
| גּ (ג) | | g (gh or ḡ) | Gimel | *g*one (same)* |
| דּ (ד) | | d (dh or ḏ) | Daleth | *d*og (same)* |
| ה | | h | He | *h*at |
| ו | | w or v | Vav | *v*ery |
| ז | | z | Zayin | *z*eal |
| ח | | ḥ or ch | Heth | Ba*ch* (the composer) |
| ט | | ṭ | Teth | *t*en |
| י | | y | Yodh | *y*et |
| כּ (כ) | ך | k (kh or ḵ) | Kaph | *k*ing (like ח) |
| ל | | l | Lamedh | *l*ong |
| מ | ם | m | Mem | *m*en |
| נ | ן | n | Nun | *n*ew |
| ס | | s | Samech | *s*ign |
| ע | | ʿ | ʿAyin | (silent) |
| פּ (פ) | ף | p (ph or p̄) | Pe | *p*ea (*ph*one) |
| צ | ץ | ṣ or ts | Tsadhe | hi*ts* |
| ק | | q | Qoph | uni*q*ue |
| ר | | r | Resh | *r*un |
| שׂ | | ś | Sin | *s*o |
| שׁ | | š or sh | Shin | *sh*ip |
| תּ (ת) | | t (th or ṯ) | Tav | *t*oe (same)* |

*Modern Hebrew does not distinguish the variant forms of the consonant in pronunciation.

The following charts give the pronunciation value as used in modern Hebrew:

| Hebrew Long Vowel | Name | Translit-eration | Sounds Like |
|---|---|---|---|
| ָ | qamets | ā | f*a*ther |
| ֵ | tsere | ē | th*ey* |
| ִי | hireq yodh | î | mach*i*ne |
| וֹ or ֹ | holem | ô or ō | r*o*ll |
| וּ | shureq | û | t*u*ne |

| Hebrew Short Vowel | Name | Translit-eration | Sounds Like |
|---|---|---|---|
| ַ | pathah | a | f*a*ther |
| ֶ | seghol | e | m*e*t |
| ִ | hireq | i | p*i*n |
| ָ | qamets hatuph | o | r*o*ll |
| ֻ | qibbuts | u | t*u*ne |

The following half vowels require only a fraction of the effort put into pronouncing the regular vowels, much as the *e* in "the" in the phrase "the bee."

| Hebrew | Name | Translit-eration | Pronunciation Value |
|---|---|---|---|
| ְ | shewa | $^{e}$ | half an "eh" sound, or silent |
| ֲ | hateph pathah | $^{a}$ | half an "ah" sound |
| ֱ | hateph seghol | $^{e}$ | half an "eh" sound |
| ֳ | hateph qamets | $^{o}$ | half an "oh" sound |

# INTRODUCTION

*The NIV Interlinear Hebrew-English Old Testament* (NIVIHEOT) combinies the best available Hebrew text and English version, bridged with a grammatically literal, word-for-word translation to meet the needs of English Bible students as well as those of both beginning and intermediate students of Hebrew. As the interlinear translation is based on the vocabulary of the New International Version (NIV), the English Bible student may use the NIVIHEOT to identify the Hebrew word or phrase underlying any portion of his English text, thereby providing himself with the material for word studies or interaction with linguistically based commentaries. For formal studies, the NIVIHEOT provides a word-for-word translation; this is of great help in learning Hebrew, because it permits one to read large portions of text without constant reference to lexicons and grammars. In addition, this translation is grammatically literal—a feature not found in any previous interlinear translation—which aids in the identification of nominal and verbal inflection, the first step of exegesis. The following discussion details these and other features characteristic of the Hebrew, English, and interlinear texts.

## The Contents and the Canons

As is clear from the table of contents, this interlinear follows (as do most versions) the Greek canonical order, not the Hebrew order, of Old Testament books. This order was chosen because the work is based on the New International Version. Moreover, most Hebrew tools for the English reader or the beginning/intermediate student of Hebrew are also arranged according to the Greek order—e.g., *The Englishman's Hebrew and Chaldee Concordance of the Old Testament* (Grand Rapids: Zondervan, 1970) and Einspahr's *Index to Brown, Driver and Briggs Hebrew Lexicon*, rev. ed. (Chicago: Moody, 1977); thus, having chosen this order, the NIVIHEOT will be more useful in conjunction with them. This one-volume edition has adopted the pagination of the four-volume set rather than repaginate the contents of volumes 2–4 (Joshua–Malachi).

When the contents of the two arrangements are compared, however, it is apparent that the NIVIHEOT also complements the Hebrew order in its larger divisions (see Table 1). Volume 1 (Genesis–Deuteronomy) is equivalent to the Hebrew Torah. Volume 2 (Joshua–2 Kings) contains the Former Prophets with the addition of Ruth. Volume 3 (1 Chronicles–Song of Songs) contains the Writings (not including Ruth, Lamentations, and Daniel). Volume 4 (Isaiah–Malachi) contains the Latter Prophets (with the addition of Lamentations and Daniel). Thus the order 1-2-4-3 approxi-

### TABLE 1
## THE OLD TESTAMENT CANON

**GREEK CANONICAL ORDER**

I. THE PENTATEUCH
- A. Genesis
- B. Exodus
- C. Leviticus
- D. Numbers
- E. Deuteronomy

II. THE HISTORICAL BOOKS
- A. Joshua
- B. Judges
- C. Ruth
- D. 1 and 2 Samuel
- E. 1 and 2 Kings
- F. 1 and 2 Chronicles
- G. Ezra
- H. Nehemiah
- I. Esther

III. THE BOOKS OF POETRY AND WISDOM
- A. Job
- B. Psalms
- C. Proverbs
- D. Ecclesiates
- E. Song of Songs

IV. THE PROPHETS
- A. The Major Prophets
  1. Isaiah
  2. Jeremiah and Lamentations
  3. Ezekiel
  4. Daniel
- B. The Minor Prophets
  1. Hosea
  2. Joel
  3. Amos
  4. Obadiah
  5. Jonah
  6. Micah
  7. Nahum
  8. Habakkuk
  9. Zephaniah
  10. Haggai
  11. Zechariah
  12. Malachi

**HEBREW CANONICAL ORDER**

I. THE TORAH
- A. Genesis
- B. Exodus
- C. Leviticus
- D. Numbers
- E. Deuteronomy

II. THE PROPHETS
- A. The Former Prophets
  1. Joshua
  2. Judges
  3. 1 and 2 Samuel
  4. 1 and 2 Kings
- B. The Latter Prophets
  1. Isaiah
  2. Jeremiah
  3. Ezekiel
  4. The Twelve
     - a. Hosea
     - b. Joel
     - c. Amos
     - d. Obadiah
     - e. Jonah
     - f. Micah
     - g. Nahum
     - h. Habakkuk
     - i. Zephaniah
     - j. Haggai
     - k. Zechariah
     - l. Malachi

III. THE WRITINGS
- A. The Books of Truth
  1. Psalms
  2. Job
  3. Proverbs
- B. The Scrolls
  1. Ruth
  2. Song of Songs
  3. Ecclesiastes
  4. Lamentations
  5. Esther
- C. The Rest
  1. Daniel
  2. Ezra-Nehemiah
  3. 1 and 2 Chronicles

mates the divisions—though not the internal order—of the Hebrew canon.

## The Hebrew Text

In contrast to the New Testament, where the best approximation of the original text is produced through the careful collation and evaluation of the thousands of available Greek manuscripts, the Old Testament is predominantly represented by one type of text (commonly known as the Masoretic Text [MT]), which has very few significant variations. As a result, all printed texts of the Hebrew Old Testament are virtually identical. Even in the critical editions produced in this century, deviations from the basic MT are not incorporated into the text but appear in footnotes. However, the existence of readings differing from the MT—as found in such early recensions and versions as the Samaritan Pentateuch, the Targums, the Septuagint and other Greek translations, the Syriac Peshitta, and the Latin Vulgate—as well as the existence of some untranslatable readings in the MT, prompt even conservative scholars to carefully suggest some changes in the Hebrew text.

In the desire to represent the basic MT, as well as to provide material for limited textual criticism, the NIVIHEOT uses as its Hebrew text the *Biblia Hebraica Stuttgartensia* (BHS), which reproduces the Leningrad Codex B19a (L), considered the oldest dated MS of the complete Hebrew Bible. Deviations from the text of B19a (L) in the NIVIHEOT are very few and conservative (in contrast to the textual footnotes of BHS, which are not reproduced), and these changes are based only on the translations and footnotes of the NIV, as follows:

1) When the NIV adds to the MT, the suggested emendation and translation are entered into the text in brackets [ ] and are discussed in a footnote (e.g., Gen. 4:8).

2) When, based on versions, the NIV presents an alternative reading in the text, the conjectured Hebrew reading is printed in a footnote (e.g., Gen. 47:21).

3) When, again based on the versions, the NIV suggests an alternative spelling of a proper name or place-name (whether reproduced in the text or suggested in the footnotes), the conjectured Hebrew reading is *not* supplied (e.g., Gen. 10:4). Readers wishing to see the suggested alternate spelling may consult the critical notes of BHS.

4) When in the footnotes (not in the text) the NIV suggests alternate readings from the versions, the conjectured Hebrew reading is *not* supplied (e.g., Gen. 1:26). Again, consult BHS.

5) There are many readings in B19a (L) that do not exactly agree with the majority of the Masoretic tradition. Most of these differences are idiosyncrasies of vowel pointing and the use of the *dagesh*. In the desire to represent the majority tradition, all such divergences in spelling noted in BHS are corrected in footnotes (e.g., Gen. 2:18).

The ancient textual variants noted with the MT—which occurred when the reading in the text (*Kethib*, "which is written") was corrected for the proper pronunication or spelling by a reading in the margin (*Qere*, "read!")—are indicated by the small circle (°) over the *Kethib* form. The *Qere* form is given in a footnote with its verse number preceded by the small circle. When more than one type of footnote appears on a page, the *Kethib-Qere* is always at the bottom of the page (e.g., Num. 12:3). The exception to this occurs when the *Qere* form is a different word or word division than the Kethib. In this case, a translation is supplied beneath the footnote (e.g., Gen. 30:11).

Four forms in the Hebrew Bible are always pronounced differently from the way they are pointed, yet are not noted as *Kethib-Qere*. These so-called *Qere perpetua* are as follows:

1) יהוה ("Yahweh," the proper name of God) is written either יְהוָה, pointed with the vowels of אֲדֹנָי ("Lord"), or יֱהוִה, pointed with the vowels of אֱלֹהִים ("God"), and it is to be pronounced as the word whose vowels it borrows. This deliberate mispointing was an effort by the scribes to make the name of God unpronounceable and thus to keep it from being taken in vain (Exod. 20:7; Lev. 24:11). This device was misinterpreted in 1520 by one Galatinus who mixed the vowels of אֲדֹנָי with the consonants of יהוה, thus producing the hybrid form *Jehovah*, which has remained with us to this day.

2) הִוא occurs throughout the Pentateuch in place of הִיא, the normal spelling of the third person, feminine, singular pronoun ("she"). There is no clear explanation for this.

3) יִשָּׂשכָר ("Issachar") is consistently spelled in this unpronounceable form, the background of which is a mystery.

4) יְרוּשָׁלַםִ ("Jerusalem") is the normal spelling of יְרוּשָׁלַיִם.

Although the *Kethib-Qere* and the *Qere perpetua* are included in the NIVIHEOT as normal features of the MT, textual notes are included only because of alternate readings in the NIV. . Textual criticism—Greek or Hebrew—is the domain of the scholar and should not be dabbled in by beginning, intermediate, or even advanced students. For further discussion, the reader is referred to the excellent introduction and bibliography to Old Testament textual criticism by Bruce Waltke that appears in volume 1 of *The Expositor's Bible Commentary* (Grand Rapids: Zondervan, 1979).

## The English Text

The NIVIHEOT reproduces in the margin the text of the NIV, complete with its special indentations, section headings, and footnotes. The reason for the choice of the NIV is twofold. First, the desire to make this interlinear a lasting standard necessitated the choice of the Hebrew and English texts most likely to remain standards. Second, the character of both the translation and the format of the NIV makes it a superior marginal text. Because it is fluid and idiomatic, yet accurate and dignified, the NIV provides a superb model of expressing in good colloquial English the thought forms generated by a word-for-word translation of the Hebrew. Further, the structure of the text, often as significant as the grammar, is displayed by the special indentations and paragraphing that make more apparent the literary forms of poetry, letters, lists, and so forth, reminding the student that the text is woven into a unified and flowing whole and is not simply a collection of words.

The introduction prepared by the Committee on Bible Translation follows this introduction and explains more fully the presuppositions, goals, and methods underlying the translation and publication of the NIV. For further and more detailed insights into the NIV, see *The NIV: The Making of a Contemporary Translation* (Grand Rapids: Zondervan, 1986).

## The Interlinear Text

As previously mentioned, the interlinear text is based on the vocabulary of the NIV and is grammatically literal. In this regard, the NIVIHEOT presents a unique concept in interlinear translation. The interlinear translator is usually quite independent, choosing not only the vocabulary of his version but also the verbal and nominal forms into which they are cast. The result is a translation that is literal in the sense that it gives an English equivalent for every word of the original (if indeed *literal* means "word-for-word") but not literal in grammatical form (if *literal* also means matching each inflection of the original with a consistent approximation of that inflection in English). Thus, all interlinear translations contain English singulars translating plurals and vice versa, verbs translating nouns, finite verbs translating infinitives and participles, and so forth, so that the text will make better sense to the reader of English. Even when this idiomatic translation is corrected by the grammatically literal rendering supplied in brackets, the impression remains that the interlinear rendering is the most accurate rendering possible, whereas in reality it is just another version, not necessarily more accurate or less accurate than any other English version.

In fact, sometimes a good idiomatic translation can be as accurate as an interlinear translation, for, as any linguist will testify, no two languages are completely identical in word meanings and grammatical structures. Thus, accuracy in translation depends on "dynamic equivalence": the process by which the *meanings* and *impacts* generated by the words and grammar of the original language are reproduced in the words and grammar of the receptor language best suited to recreate these meanings and impacts. In some cases a word-for-word translation produces the best dynamic equivalence, but in other instances this effect must be generated through idiomatic rendering.

This does not preclude the role of the interlinear translation, for the meaning of the original language must first be discovered through the careful study of words and grammar before this meaning may be recast into the words and grammar of the receptor language. With this in mind, the NIVIHEOT attempts to supply this grammatically and lexically literal link between the words of the Hebrew text and the skillfully cast idioms of the NIV. The following discussion presents the format and features of the interlinear translation.

*Word Choice and Word Order*

**Word Choice**

Words have little meaning outside of the contexts in which they are used. Thus, the translator must see the whole context of a word before he can accurately render it with one of its many potential definitions. The NIV is the product of many brilliant scholars working many hours to establish the best contextual lexical choices; so it would be presumptuous to alter their word choices simply for the sake of novelty or to provide new synonyms. The vocabulary of the interlinear text, then, is taken from the NIV in most cases.

There are six types of exceptions to this general policy. As far as three of them are concerned, it need only be said that exceptions occur when the limits of space in the interlinear text require a shorter word or phrase (e.g., "unleavened bread" instead of "bread made without yeast"), when Hebrew words are combined to produce a single English reading (e.g., "sons of Israel" instead of "Israelites"), and when the English renders the Hebrew with an idiom that cannot be matched word-for-word (e.g., "he lifted his eyes" instead of "he looked up"). This wording does not imply that it is the only viable option for any context; the thorough student will want to consult the standard lexicons of biblical Hebrew for more detailed discussion of words, idioms, and difficult readings. Although the words are taken from the NIV, the grammatical form of these words is determined strictly by the Hebrew form, as detailed below.

A fourth type of exception involves the name of God. The proper name of God (יהוה) is translated "LORD" in the NIV and most other English versions. The NIVIHEOT consistently renders this name as "Yahweh."

This is the spelling and pronunciation generally acknowledged by Bible scholars. Further, according to Scripture, this is God's special name, and it has no direct connection with the idea of lordship. Thus the use of the name Yahweh is a major—and, I think, meaningful—exception to the NIV.

Throughout the prophets, the NIV translates the compound name or title יְהוָה צְבָאוֹת as "the LORD Almighty." The NIVIHEOT has it as "Yahweh of Hosts" (e.g., Isa. 1:9). The NIV follows the dominant Greek translation of the second word, *παντοκράτωρ*; the NIVIHEOT renders it according to the dominant meaning of the Hebrew root, "host" or "army." This also distinguishes it from שַׁדַּי (e.g., in Joel 1:15), which the NIV consistently translates also as "Almighty."

These exceptions were not made because of dissatisfaction with the NIV translation. Rather, they were made to translate each name and title of God uniquely and consistently, for the benefit of any reader who undertakes this immensely valuable and rewarding word/name study.

A fifth area of departure from the NIV involves the so-called cognate accusative, a major characteristic of Hebrew style. This occurs when a verb takes as its object a noun of the same root as itself, as in Jonah 1:16, where it is said that the sailors "feared a great fear" (NIV: "greatly feared"). In some places, the NIV renders the object as a noun from a different root than that of the verb. The NIVIHEOT maintains the same English root for both to point out the Hebrew style. For another example, in Ezekiel 32:10, where the NIV reads "shudder with horror," the the NIVIHEOT reads "they-will-shudder . . . shuddering."

Sixth—and similar to the fifth exception—is the fact that, in a few places, the NIVIHEOT maintains a consistent translation for a key term, though the NIV may use a range of synonyms. For example, the root רצה is used throughout Ezekiel 34 and is variously translated by the NIV as "to shepherd," "care for," "feed," and "tend." The NIVIHEOT points out the Hebrew repetition by repeating the translation "to shepherd" throughout.

Again, these exceptions are very few. They are not intended as an indictment of the NIV. They are intended to distinguish the names and titles of God for the attentive reader and to point out a major aspect of Hebrew style to the language student.

### Word Order

The word order presents great difficulty because Hebrew reads right-to-left while English reads left-to-right. This problem is further complicated by the need to render most Hebrew words with more than one English word. Thus, all previous interlinears have forced the English reader not only to read the word-for-word translation backwards but also to read the phrases used to translate individual Hebrew words backwards. Whereas the first situation is unavoidable in an interlinear, the second is unnecessary. Why should the reader be made to read the translation of the word וְשָׁמַעְתָּ as "hear shall you and," when the phrase could be put in normal order "and you shall hear"? The NIVIHEOT chooses the latter format, believing that most readers will be reading the Hebrew one word at a time and would therefore prefer to read its translation in proper English word order.

A further difficulty found in most interlinears—especially the few that have appeared for portions of the Old Testament—is determining where the translation for one word ends and the translation for the next begins. To eliminate this confusion, the NIVIHEOT connects all the English words used to translate any one Hebrew word with hyphens. The example above appears as "and-you-shall-hear."

With these two features in the format—giving the translation of each Hebrew word in proper English word order and connecting multiple words with hyphens—the NIVIHEOT should prove to be the easiest to read of all existing interlinear translations of the Old Testament.

*Translation Techniques*

Although this introduction is not intended as a primer for Hebrew grammar, the attempt to maintain grammatical literalness demands that the elements of Hebrew grammar be discussed in relation to the way they affect the translation. Underlying the following description is the presupposition that no English words will be supplied that are not direct translations of a Hebrew word and its inflected form. The NIV text given in the margin will provide the reader with English words necessary to construct a good translation—e.g., the indefinite article (a, an), which does not occur in Hebrew but is required in English. In this way the student can see where even literal translation necessarily involves a degree of interpretation. Also, no punctuation is provided in the interlinear text except to indicate interrogative pronouns and particles and the imperative form of verbs.

**The Nominal System**

*Nouns in General.* Hebrew nouns are rendered as English nouns unless the Hebrew nouns are also used as adjectives. In the latter case they are rendered as adjectives. Only proper names (e.g., Jacob), place-names (e.g., Canaan), and titles of God (e.g., Holy One) are capitalized.

*Number.* Hebrew singulars are rendered as singulars, even when the noun is a collective (e.g., Gen. 6:1, הָאָדָם, "the man" rather than "the men"). Hebrew duals are usually rendered simply as plurals, unless the dual demands the use of the number two (e.g., Exod. 25:10, אַמָּתַיִם, "two cubits"). Hebrew plurals are translated as plurals. If the plural is a fixed form denoting a singular object, it may be rendered as a singular (e.g., Gen. 1:1, אֱלֹהִים, "God").

*Gender*. Although English has gender distinctions in certain nouns—e.g., the female counterparts of the male *actor, waiter*, and *god* are the *actress, waitress*, and *goddess*—gender is not a universal feature of the language. Thus, gender will be seen consistently only in the pronouns and the verbal system, discussed below.

*Case*. Case endings existed in Hebrew older than that of the MT, but no case endings have survived in our existing manuscripts. Since case is therefore determined by context rather than by inflection, no special translation device is used to distinguish nominative, genitive, or accusative, even if the context demands an English preposition (e.g., Gen. 2:7, עָפָר, "dust" rather than "from the dust"). The NIV text will be of great value in providing the prepositions needed for good English translation when no preposition exists in the Hebrew context.

*Absolute and construct structure*. Possession and other genitive functions are expressed by the construct structure. The word in construct in Hebrew is indicated in the translation by the use of the word *of* as a suffix (e.g., Gen. 12:15, בֵּית פַּרְעֹה, "house-of Pharaoh"). When the inflection of a word does not change to indicate it is in construct, the Masoretic accentuation becomes the guide. But as it is not always an absolute determinant, many "judgment calls" in relation to this grammatical structure had to be made, and criticisms and corrections are welcomed. (See *Article* below.)

*Adjectives*. Adjectives are rendered in the same way as nouns in regard to number and gender. Plurality is indicated by the addition of the word *ones* (e.g., Gen. 1:16, הַמְּאֹרֹת הַגְּדֹלִים, "the-lights the-great-ones").

*Article*. The Hebrew article is always translated by the English definite article (see example of Gen. 1:16 above). It is translated everywhere it appears, even when not needed in English (e.g., Gen. 22:9, הָאֱלֹהִים, "the-God"). It is never supplied in translation where it does not occur in Hebrew. As words in construct do not take the article, even when they are considered definite by being in construct to a proper name or a noun with the article, the English article is not supplied in translation (e.g., Gen. 1:2, וְרוּחַ אֱלֹהִים, "and-Spirit-of" not "and-the-Spirit-of").

*Numerals*. Numerals are simply translated as numbers, whether ordinal or cardinal, without indication of gender.

*Pronouns*. Pronouns are consistently rendered according to person, number, and gender. Since Hebrew, unlike English, has no neuter gender, inanimate objects are referred to as "he" or "she," not as "it." Although this will sound foreign to English ears (e.g., Gen. 1:12), this gender distinction will often aid in the identification of a subject with its verb or a noun with its modifier, as they will share the same gender. In the translation, moreover, pronominal suffixes are suffixed to the word they modify (e.g., Gen. 6:18, בְּרִיתִי, "covenant-of-me"). Because no special pronouns are used in Hebrew to refer to God and because such reference is often a matter of interpretation, no pronouns are capitalized.

As English does not distinguish between second person masculine and feminine, singular and plural (using "you" for all four forms), or between third person plural, masculine and feminine (referring to both as "they"), the interlinear makes no differentation either. To introduce another typeface or to resort to archaic English (e.g., "ye" and "thee") would draw undue attention to this matter and possibly confuse those unfamiliar with Hebrew. But for those who have not memorized these pronouns and wish to see the difference, the following chart shows all the possible spellings of these pronouns, both independent and suffixed:

| | Independent | Suffixed |
|---|---|---|
| Second masc. sing. | אָתָּה, אַתָּה | ךָ׳, כָה׳ |
| Second fem. sing. | אָתְּ, אַתְּ | ךְ׳ |
| Second masc. plur. | אַתֶּם | כֶם׳ |
| Second fem. plur. | אַתֵּן, אַתֶּן, אַתֵּנָה | כֶן׳ |
| Third masc. plur. | הֵמָּה, הֵם | מוֹ׳, ם׳, הֶם׳ |
| Third fem. plur. | הֵנָּה, הֵן | נָה׳, ן, הֵן׳, הֶן׳ |

*Demonstratives.* Demonstratives are translated consistently as to number, but gender is not indicated.

*Interrogatives.* As interrogatives introduce a question, they are always followed by a question mark, whether they are independent words (e.g., Gen. 4:9, אֵי, "where?") or the prefix הֲ (e.g., Gen. 4:7, הֲלוֹא, "not?").

*Relatives.* The Hebrew relatives אֲשֶׁר and (rarely) זוּ are translated by the English relative pronouns "that," "which," and "who." If אֲשֶׁר expresses the idea of place, it is rendered "where."

### The Verbal System

*Stem, or theme.* The eight (or nine, counting Qal passive) Hebrew stems, or themes, have not been distinguished in translation. Their influence on verbs is seen, however, in the way in which the words are rendered (e.g., Lev. 11:36, יִטְמָא, "he-is unclean" [Qal]; 11:43a, תְּטַמְּאוּ, "you-make-yourselves-unclean" [Hithpa'el]; and 43b, וְנִטְמֵתֶם, "or-you-be-made-unclean" [Niphal]). Since this is not adequate material for parsing, the student who has not memorized the basic vowel patterns of the verbal system should consult the *Analytical Hebrew and Chaldee Lexicon*, 2nd ed. (Grand Rapids: Zondervan, 1970) when in doubt about the inflection of a verb—or about any other part of speech for that matter.

*Person, number, and gender.* The person, number, and gender of all finite verbs are indicated by the use of pronouns as subjects, even when the subject is expressed by means of a noun or independent pronoun (e.g., Gen. 1:1, בָּרָא אֱלֹהִים, "he-created God."). The possibility of confusing the expressed subject with the object of the verb is usually eliminated by pronouns or the definite direct object indicator (see אֵת below). If these prove inadequate, consult the NIV translation.

Again, there is the problem of distinguishing second person, masculine and feminine, singular and plural, as well as third person plural, masculine and feminine (see *Pronouns* above). Most questions should be answered by consulting the *Analytical Lexicon* or the following chart, which lists all the perfect and imperfect preformative and afformative indicators used consistently in all themes to distinguish person, number, and gender.

| | PERFECT | | IMPERFECT | |
|---|---|---|---|---|
| | Singular | Plural | Singular | Plural |
| 3rd masc. | (none) | ''וּ | י'' | י''וּ |
| 3rd fem. | ''ָה | ''וּ | ת'' | ת''נָה |
| 2nd masc. | ''תָּ | ''תֶּם | ת'' | ת''וּ |
| 2nd fem. | ''תְּ | ''תֶּן | ת''ִי | ת''נָה |
| 1st com. | ''תִּי | ''נוּ | א'' | נ'' |

*Tense, or aspect, and mood.* Because the two major tenses, or aspects—perfect and imperfect—overlap so greatly in both time orientation and function, they are not distinguished in translation. The chart above or the *Analytical Lexicon* should prove sufficient for this distinction. The tense and the function expressed in the NIV have been used to translate this element of verbal inflection. However, in the interlinear text, simple past and simple present forms have consistently been used in place of perfective or continual forms in order to save space and to eliminate the confusion of a finite verb with a participle or infinitive (e.g., Gen. 2:21, וַיִּישָׁן, "and-he-slept," rather than "and-while-he-was-sleeping").

Jussive and cohortative forms are often indistinguishable from the imperfect; therefore the NIV serves as the guide in rendering these forms by their English counterparts (e.g., Gen. 33:15, אֶמְצָא־חֵן, "let-me-find favor").

Imperative forms are indicated by an exclamation mark (e.g., Gen. 12:1, לֶךְ, "go!") but are not distinguished as to number or gender. As the imperative uses the same afformatives as the imperfect, the chart above or the *Analytical Lexicon* will serve to make the necessary distinctions.

There is a further difficulty with stative verbs—verbs expressing a state of being rather than an activity—when they are inflected as Qal perfect, third person, masculine gender, singular number. In this form they are spelled exactly the same as their cognate adjectives and nouns. In choosing between these two possibilities, Lisowsky's *Kondordanz zum Herbraischen Alten Testamentum* (Stuttgart: Württembergische Bibelanstalt, 1958) has generally been followed (e.g., Lev. 5:2, טָמֵא, "unclean"; 11:25, וְטָמֵא, "and-he-will-be-unclean").

*Infinitives.* The infinitives, absolute and construct, are always prefixed with *to* in translation but are not distinguished (e.g., Gen. 2:17, מוֹת, "to-die"; cf. Gen. 25:32, לָמוּת, "to-die"). The preposition ל, often prefixed to the infinitive construct, does not receive an additional *to* in translation, as seen in the previous example.

*Participles.* Participles are translated by English participles that end in *-ing* (e.g., Gen. 1:2, מְרַחֶפֶת, "hovering"). However, in the case of most passive participles and of words that do not have a participial form in English, the word *being* is used as a helper (e.g., Exod. 39:9, כָּפוּל, "being-doubled"). Gender is not indicated, but plurals are rendered with the addition of the word *ones* (e.g., Exod. 25:20, סֹכְכִים, "ones-overshadowing").

There are two difficulties in regard to participles. First, many participial forms in Hebrew have become fixed as substantives (e.g., Gen. 14:18, כֹהֵן, "priest") and are therefore rendered as nouns, though they could have been rendered as participles. Unfortunately, the lexicons are not in total agreement as to when a participle ceases to be a verbal noun and becomes a noun proper; therefore, in such instances I have often used my own judgment, well aware that my decisions will not be universally accepted. Second, not all English words ending in *-ing* are participles (e.g., Gen. 1:1, בְּרֵאשִׁית, "in-beginning"). When in doubt in either situation, consult the *Analytical Lexicon.*

**Particles**

*Prepositions.* Prepositions—prefixed or independent—are always translated, whether or not they are necessary in English (e.g., Gen. 27:27, וַיִּשַּׁק־לוֹ, "and-he-kissed on-him"). The exception to this (the ל prefixed to the infinitive construct) has been mentioned above. Some prepositions are fixed forms compounded from several Hebrew words but rendered with one term (e.g., Lev. 1:3, לִפְנֵי, "before"). The *Analytical Lexicon* will sort out the components, if needed.

*Adverbs.* Adverbs of manner or place are simply rendered with the words chosen by the NIV translators.

*Negatives.* Negatives are always rendered with "no" or "not." The substantive אַיִן is often rendered as a quasi-verb (e.g., Gen. 37:29, אֵין, "he-was-not").

*Conjunctions.* Conjunctions are usually rendered as in the NIV. The conjunction אִם is rendered as a negative when it appears in an abbreviated oath formula (e.g., Gen. 14:23, וְאִם־אֶקַּח, "and-not I-will-accept"), the full oath being something like, "May God punish me *if* I accept anything from you." As in the case of prepositions, although more rarely, some compounded conjunctions must be translated as a unit (e.g., Gen. 18:5, כִּי־עַל־כֵּן, "because").

*Other particles and parts of speech.* The specialized translations of some parts of speech (listed in alphabetical order) deserve attention.

אֵת, the definite direct object indicator, is never translated. When standing independently, it is rendered with three asterisks (***, e.g., Gen. 1:1). When prefixed or suffixed, only those components to which it is affixed are translated (e.g., Gen. 1:1, וְאֵת, "and"; Gen. 2:3, אֹתוֹ, "him").

ָה, the directive suffix, is translated as a preposition (e.g., Gen. 12:10, מִצְרַיְמָה, "to-Egypt").

הֵן, הִנֵּה, the interjection, is translated "see!" (e.g., Gen. 24:13).

יֵשׁ, the particle of existence (counter to אַיִן), is usually translated as a quasi-verb (e.g., Gen. 44:20, "he-is").

נָא is used to intensify, or make more politely formal, the cohortative, the jussive, the imperative, and some particles. It is always translated "now!" because the distinction between intensity and politeness is not always easy to determine.

### The Aramaic of Ezra, Jeremiah, and Daniel

Most of the Old Testament is in Hebrew, but a few passages (Ezra 4:8–6:18; 7:12–26; Jer. 10:11; and Dan. 2:4–7:28) are in Aramaic, a close cognate language. Translation techniques used in the NIVIHEOT to identify Aramaic parts of speech and inflection are identical to those used for Hebrew, with one major exception.

Unlike Hebrew, which has two "states" of nominal inflection, Aramaic has three. The *absolute* and *construct* states correspond to their equivalents in Hebrew, and thus they correspond also in the way in which they are translated in this volume. The third—the *emphatic*, or *determined*, state—corresponds to a Hebrew noun with the definite article prefixed (in fact, some scholars argue that this state should rather be considered a suffixed article), and thus it is translated by means of the definite article in English—for example, the absolute state (טְעֵם, "order," Ezra 4:21), the construct state (טַעַם, "command-of," 6:14), and the emphatic, or determined, state (טַעְמָא, "the-order," 4:21).

For further information on the orthography, inflection, and syntax of biblical Aramaic, I have found Alger F. Johns, *A Short Grammar of Biblical Aramaic* (Berrien Springs, Mich.: Andrews University Press, 1963), more clearly written than the standard beginning grammar of Franz Rosenthal, *A Grammar of Biblical Aramaic* (Wiesbaden: Otto Harrasowitz, 1961). The Aramaic section (pp. 1078–1118) of Brown, Driver, and Briggs, *Hebrew and*

*English Lexicon of the Old Testament* (Oxford: Oxford University Press, 1907), is most complete and helpful in its treatment of the inflection and definition of the Aramaic of Ezra, while the Aramaic section (pp. 1045–1138) by Walter Baumgartner in *Lexicon in Veteris Testamenti Libros* (Leiden: Brill; Grand Rapids: Eerdmans, 1953) is more up-to-date in etymology and bibliography.

## Select Bibliography

### *General*

de Waard, Jan, and Nida, Eguene A. *From One Language to Another.* Nashville: Nelson, 1986.

> Subtitled "Functional Equivalence in Bible Translating," this is a more technical discussion of translation technique for a more scholarly reader.

Glassman, Eugene H. *The Translation Debate*. Downers Grove: InterVarsity, 1981.

> This book illustrates the necessity of dynamic equivalence in translation, written for the general reader.

Goodrick, Edward W. *Do-it-Yourself Hebrew and Greek.* Portland: Multnomah, 1976; Grand Rapids: Zondervan, 1979.

> This book introduces the student to both biblical languages by providing information and exercises in the use of lexicons, grammars, interlinears, and other resources for linguistic study.

Silva, Moisés. *Biblical Words and Their Meaning*. Grand Rapids: Zondervan, 1983.

> This volume is an important introduction to the problems of understanding the meaning and significance of biblical words, especially when those words are crucial to exegesis and theology.

### *Grammars*

Gesenius, Wilhelm; Kautzsch, E.; and Cowley, A. E. *Gesenius' Hebrew Grammar*. 2nd English ed. London: Oxford University Press, 1910.

> This encyclopedic work is the finest advanced grammar in English and, despite its age, is still the final word in matters of inflection, syntax, and interpretation.

LaSor, William Sanford. *Handbook of Biblical Hebrew.* Grand Rapids: Eerdmans, 1979.

An excellent and demanding beginning grammar, this will take the student far beyond the level of most other grammars. It is also keyed to the advanced grammar of Gesenius, Kautzsch, and Cowley (see above) for further study.

Mansoor, Menahem. *Biblical Hebrew: Step by Step* (2nd ed. 1980) and *Volume 2: Readings From the Book of Genesis* (3rd ed. 1984). Grand Rapids, Baker.

These two volumes are valuable for self-study of Hebrew, as answer keys are available for both. They are also used as textbooks for an accredited correspondence course from the University of Wisconsin (Madison).

Williams, Ronald J. *Hebrew Syntax: An Outline*. 2nd ed. Toronto: University of Toronto Press, 1976.

This linguistically up-to-date grammar is valuable on the intermediate and advanced levels for dealing with the potential interpretations of word inflection and syntax.

*Lexicons*

Botterweck, G. Johannes, and Ringgren, Helmer. *Theological Dictionary of the Old Testament*. 4 vols. Grand Rapids: Eerdmans, 1974–78.

This set, projected for ten volumes of which five are in print in English, combines lexicography with a full examination of the cognate languages to give lengthy expositions on significant words in the Old Testament. Although liberal in theological orientation, it is a rich source of data for the student of any theological persuasion.

Brown, Francis; Driver, S. R.; and Briggs, Charles A. *A Hebrew and English Lexicon of the Old Testament*. London: Oxford University Press, 1968.

This lexicon, though dated and difficult to use, is the finest lexicon for the classification of its definitions and the thoroughness of its biblical references.

Harris, R. Laird; Archer, Gleason L.; and Waltke, Bruce K. *Theological Wordbook of the Old Testament*. Chicago: Moody, 1980.

This two-volume set, arranged in Hebrew alphabetical order and keyed to the numbering system of Strong's *Concordance*, gives definitions for the entire Hebrew and Aramaic vocabulary of the Old Testament and fuller articles for words of theological significance.

Koehler, Ludwig, and Baumgartner, Walter. *Lexicon in Veteris Testamenti Libros*. Leiden: E. J. Brill, 1953, with *Supplementum*, 1958.

This two-volume work, available also from William B. Eerdmans Publishing Company, is the most up-to-date of Hebrew lexicons in English, though its definitions are translated from the German original and are awkward at times. William Holladay had produced an abridged reworking of this set under the title *A Concise Hebrew and Aramaic Lexicon of the Old Testament* (Grand Rapids: Eerdmans, 1971)—an edition that may prove more useful for beginning students. For those who read German, a third edition is in process and exists in two fascicles (1967 א–טבח and 1974 טבח–נבט) available from Brill.

*Analytical and Readers Lexicons*

Armstrong, Terry A.; Busby, Douglas L.; and Carr, Cyril F. *A Reader's Hebrew-English Lexicon of the Old Testament*. Grand Rapids: Zondervan (Vol. 1, 1980; Vol. 2, 1982; Vol. 3, 1986; Vol. 4, 1987).

Arranged verse-by-verse in biblical order, this four-volume set assists the reader of the Hebrew text by providing the lexical spellings and definitions for every word that occurs less than fifty times.

Beall, Todd S., and Banks, William A. *Old Testament Parsing Guide: Genesis to Esther*. Chicago: Moody Press, 1986.

Arranged verse-by-verse in biblical order, this projected two-volume set assists the analysis of the Hebrew text by parsing and defining every verb in the Old Testament.

Einspahr, Bruce. *Index to Brown, Driver & Briggs Hebrew Lexicon*. Rev. ed. Chicago: Moody Press, 1977.

Arranged verse-by-verse in biblical order, this volume provides a Scripture index to every word treated in the BDB Lexicon, and thus it can also function as a reader's lexicon.

Wigram, George. *Analytical Hebrew and Chaldee Lexicon*. 1848. Reprint. Grand Rapids: Zondervan, 1970.

Dated in definitions, etymology, and terminology, this volume is still valuable for its parsing of every word in the Masoretic Text and for its summary of Hebrew grammar.

*Commentaries*

Critical/exegetical commentaries often provide the most relevant and thorough lexical, grammatical, and text-critical information on any passage of the biblical text. Brevard Childs' *Old Testament Books for Pastor and Teacher* (Philadelphia: Westminster, 1977) contains a fine annotated list of the best titles for each book of the Bible. I will not duplicate his recommendations but will comment on several sets that contain most of the best critical commentaries.

Two classic sets were completed before the discovery of the Dead Sea Scrolls and of several important cognate semitic languages, but they remain valuable for their thorough treatments of grammatical and lexical difficulties. Keil and Delitzsch's *Commentary on the Old Testament* (reprint, Grand Rapids: Eerdmans), is more conservative in its approach to text and interpretation. *The International Critical Commentary* (Edinburgh: T&T Clark; Philadelphia: Fortress) is more thorough in content and more liberal in its presuppositions and methodology.

Four as yet incomplete sets are more up-to-date in resources and methodology. *The Anchor Bible* (Garden City: Doubleday) has long been a favorite of translators and was one of my constant companions in preparing the NIVIHEOT. *The Westminster Old Testament Library* (Philadelphia: Westminster) and *Hermenia* (Philadelphia: Fortress) combine translations of well-received German works with original volumes, providing linguistic, critical, and theological insights. The more recent *Word Biblical Commentary* (Waco: Word) brings cutting-edge evangelical scholarship to the text.

Though expository in nature and intended for a more general reader, *The New International Commentary on the Old Testament* (Grand Rapids: Eerdmans) and *The Expositor's Bible Commentary* (Grand Rapids: Zondervan) are also useful for translation and exegesis.

# NIV PREFACE

The New International Version is a completely new translation of the Holy Bible made by over a hundred scholars working directly from the best available Hebrew, Aramaic and Greek texts. It had its beginning in 1965 when, after several years of exploratory study by committees from the Christian Reformed Church and the National Association of Evangelicals, a group of scholars met at Palos Heights, Illinois, and concurred in the need for a new translation of the Bible in contemporary English. This group, though not made up of official church representatives, was transdenominational. Its conclusion was endorsed by a large number of leaders from many denominations who met in Chicago in 1966.

Responsibility for the new version was delegated by the Palos Heights group to a self-governing body of fifteen, the Committee on Bible Translation, composed for the most part of biblical scholars from colleges, universities and seminaries. In 1967 the New York Bible Society (now the International Bible Society) generously undertook the financial sponsorship of the project—a sponsorship that made it possible to enlist the help of many distinguished scholars. The fact that participants from the United States, Great Britain, Canada, Australia and New Zealand worked together gave the project its international scope. That they were from many denominations—including Anglican, Assemblies of God, Baptist, Brethren, Christian Reformed, Church of Christ, Evangelical Free, Lutheran, Mennonite, Methodist, Nazarene, Presbyterian, Wesleyan and other churches—helped to safeguard the translation from sectarian bias.

How it was made helps to give the New International Version its distinctiveness. The translation of each book was assigned to a team of scholars. Next, one of the Intermediate Editorial Committees revised the initial translation, with constant reference to the Hebrew, Aramaic or Greek. Their work then went to one of the General Editorial Committees, which checked it in detail and made another thorough revision. This revision in turn was carefully reviewed by the Committee on Bible Translation, which made further changes and then released the final version for publication. In this way the entire Bible underwent three revisions, during each of which the translation was examined for its faithfulness to the original languages and for its English style.

All this involved many thousands of hours of research and discussion regarding the meaning of the texts and the precise way of putting them into English. It may well be that no other translation has been made by a more thorough process of review and revision from committee to committee than this one.

From the beginning of the project, the Committee on Bible Translation held to certain goals for the New International Version: that it would be an accurate translation and one that would have clarity and literary quality and so prove suitable for public and private reading, teaching preaching, memorizing and liturgical use. The Committee also sought to preserve some measure of continuity with the long tradition of translating the Scriptures into English.

In working toward these goals, the translators were united in their commitment to the authority and infallibility of the Bible as God's Word in written form. They believe that it contains the divine answer to the deepest needs of humanity, that it sheds unique light on our path in a dark world, and that it sets forth the way to our eternal well-being.

The first concern of the translators has been the accuracy of the translation and its fidelity to the thought of the biblical writers. They have weighed the significance of the lexical and grammatical details of the Hebrew, Aramaic and Greek texts. At the same time, they have striven for more than a word-for-word translation. Because thought patterns and syntax differ from language to language, faithful communication of the meaning of the writers of the Bible demands frequent modifications in sentence structure and constant regard for the contextual meanings of words.

A sensitive feeling for style does not always accompany scholarship. Accordingly the Committee on Bible Translation submitted the developing version to a number of stylistic consultants. Two of them read every book of both Old and New Testaments twice—once before and once after the last major revision—and made invaluable suggestions. Samples of the translation were tested for clarity and ease of reading by various kinds of people—young and old, highly educated and less well educated, ministers and laymen.

Concern for clear and natural English—that the New International Version should be idiomatic but not idiosyncratic, contemporary but not dated—motivated the translators and consultants. At the same time, they tried to reflect the differing styles of the biblical writers. In view of the international use of English, the translators sought to avoid obvious Americanisms on the one hand and obvious Anglicisms on the other. A British edition reflects the comparatively few differences of significant idiom and of spelling.

As for the traditional pronouns "thou," "thee," and "thine" in reference to the Deity, the translators judged that to use these archaisms (along with the old verb forms such as "doest,"wouldest" and "hadst") would violate accuracy in translation. Neither Hebrew, Aramaic nor Greek uses special pronouns for the persons of the Godhead. A present-day translation is not enhanced by forms that in the time of the King James Version were used in everyday speech, whether referring to God or man.

For the Old Testament the standard Hebrew text, the Masoretic Text as published in the latest editions of *Biblia Hebraica,* was used throughout. The Dead Sea Scrolls contain material bearing on an earlier stage of the Hebrew text. They were consulted, as were the Samaritan [entateuch and the ancient scribal traditions relating to textual changes. Sometimes a variant Hebrew reading in the margin of the Masoretic Text was followed instead of the text itself. Such instances, being variants within the Masoretic tradition, are not specified by footnotes. In rare cases, words in the consonantal text were divided differently from the way they appear in the Masoretic Text. Footnotes indicate this. The translators also consulted the more important early versions—the Septuagint; Symmachus and Theodotion; the Vulgate; the Syriac Peshitta; the Targums; and for the Psalms the *Juxta Hebraica* of Jerome. Readings from these versions were occasionally followed where the Masoretic Text seemed doubtful and where accepted principles of textual criticism showed that one or more of these textual witnesses appeared to provide the correct reading. Such instances are footnoted. Sometimes vowel letters and vowel signs did not, in the judgment of the translators, represent the correct vowels for the original consonantal text. Accordingly some words were read with a different set of vowels. These instances are usually not indicated by footnotes.

The Greek text used in translating the New Testament was an eclectic one. No other piece of ancient literature has such an abundance of manuscript witnesses as does the New Testament. Where existing manuscripts differ, the translators made their choice of readings according to accepted principles of New Testament textual criticism. Footnotes call attention to places where there was uncertainty about what the original text was. The best current printed texts of the Greek New Testament were used.

There is a sense in which the work of translation is never wholly finished. This applies to all great literature and uniquely so to the Bible. In 1973 the New Testament in the New International Version was published. Since then, suggestions for corrections and revisions have been received from various sources. The Committee on Bible Translation carefully considered the suggestions and adopted a number of them. These are incorporated in the first printing of the entire Bible in 1978. Additional revisions were made by the Committee on Bible Translation in 1983 and appear in printings after that date.

As in other ancient documents, the precise meaning of the biblical texts is sometimes uncertain. This is more often the case with the Hebrew and Aramaic texts than with the Greek text. Although archaeological and linguistic discoveries in this century aid in understanding difficult passages, some uncertainties remain. The more significant of these have been called to the reader's attention in the footnotes.

In regard to the divine name *YHWH*, commonly referred to as the *Tetragrammaton*, the translators adopted the device used in most English versions of rendering that name as "LORD" in capital letters to distinguish it from *Adonai*, another Hebrew word rendered "Lord," for which small letters are used. Whenever the two names stand together in the Old Testament as a compound name of God, they are rendered "Sovereign LORD."

Because for most readers today the phrase "the LORD of hosts" and "God of hosts" have little meaning, this version renders them "the LORD Almighty" and "God Almighty." These renderings convey the sense of the Hebrew, namely, "he who is sovereign over all the 'hosts' (powers) in heaven and on earth, especially over the 'hosts' (armies) of Israel." For readers unacquainted with Hebrew this does not make clear the distinction between *Sabaoth* ("hosts" or "Almighty") and *Shaddai* (which can also be translated "Almighty"), but the latter occurs infrequently and is always footnoted. When *Adonai* and *YHWH Sabaoth* occur together, they are rendered "the Lord, the LORD Almighty."

As for other proper nouns, the familiar spellings of the King James Version are generally retained. Names traditionally spelled with 'ch," except where it is final, are usually spelled in this translation with "k" or "c," since the biblical languages do not have the sound that "ch" frequently indicates in English—for example, in *chant*. For well-known names such as Zechariah, however, the traditional spelling has been retained. Variation in the spelling of names in the original languages has usually not been indicated. Where a person or place has two or more different names in the Hebrew, Aramaic or Greek texts, the more familiar one has generally been used, with footnotes where needed.

To achieve clarity the translators sometimes supplied words not in the original texts but required by the context. If there was uncertainty about such material, it is enclosed in brackets. Also for the sake of clarity or style, nouns, including some proper nouns, are sometimes substituted for pronouns, and vice versa. And though the Hebrew writers often shifted back and forth between first, second and third personal pronouns without change of antecedent, this translation often makes them uniform, in accordance with English style and without the use of footnotes.

Poetical passages are printed as poetry, that is, with indentation of lines and with separate stanzas. These are generally designed to reflect the structure of Hebrew poetry. This poetry is normally characterized by parallelism in balanced lines. Most of the poetry in the Bible is in the Old Testament, and scholars differ regarding the scansion of Hebrew lines. The translators determined the stanza divisions for the most part by analysis of the subject matter. The stanzas therefore serve as poetic paragraphs.

As an aid to the reader, italicized sectional headings are inserted in most of the books. They are not to be regarded as part of the NIV text, are not for oral reading, and are not intended to dictate the interpretation of the sections they head.

The footnotes in this version are of several kinds, most of which need no explanation. Those giving alternative translations begin with "Or" and generally introduce the alternative with the last word preceding it in the text, except when it is a single-word alternative; in poetry quoted in a footnote a slant mark indicates a line division. Footnotes introduced by "Or" do not have uniform significance. In some cases two possible translations were considered to have about equal validity. In other cases, though the translators were convinced that the translation in the text was correct, they judged that another interpretation was possible and of sufficient importance to be represented in a footnote.

In the New Testament, footnotes that refer to uncertainty regarding the original texts are introduced by "Some manuscripts" or similar expressions. In the Old Testament, evidence for the reading chosen is given first and evidence for the alternative is added after a semicolon (for example: Septuagint; Hebrew *father*). in such notes the term "Hebrew" refers to the Masoretic Text.

It should be noted that minerals, flora and fauna, architectural details, articles of clothing and jewelry, musical instruments and other articles cannot always be identified with precision. Also measures of capacity in the biblical period are particularly uncertain (see the table of weights and measures following the text).

Like all translations of the Bible, made as they are by imperfect man, this one undoubtedly falls short of its goals. Yet we are grateful to God for the extent to which he had enabled us to realize these goals and for the strength he has given us and our colleagues to complete our task. We offer this version of the Bible to him in whose name and for whose glory it has been made. We pray that it will lead many into a better understanding of the Holy Scriptures and a fuller knowledge of Jesus Christ the incarnate Word, of whom the Scriptures so faithfully testify.

*The Committee on Bible Translation*

June 1978
(Revised August 1983)

Names of the translators and editors may be secured
from the International Bible Society,
translation sponsors of the NIV,
144 Tices Lane, East Brunswick, New Jersey 08816 USA

The NIV

# Interlinear Hebrew-English Old Testament

## Volume One
## Genesis–Deuteronomy

בְּרֵאשִׁית בָּרָא אֱלֹהִים אֵת הַשָּׁמַיִם וְאֵת הָאָרֶץ׃
the-earth and the-heavens *** God he-created in-beginning (1:1)

וְהָאָרֶץ הָיְתָה תֹהוּ וָבֹהוּ וְחֹשֶׁךְ עַל־פְּנֵי
surface-of over and-darkness and-empty formless she-was now-the-earth (2)

תְהוֹם וְרוּחַ אֱלֹהִים מְרַחֶפֶת עַל־פְּנֵי הַמָּיִם׃ וַיֹּאמֶר
and-he-said (3) the-waters surface-of over hovering God and-spirit-of deep

אֱלֹהִים יְהִי אוֹר וַיְהִי־אוֹר׃ וַיַּרְא אֱלֹהִים אֶת־הָאוֹר כִּי־
that the-light *** God and-he-saw (4) light and-he-was light let-him-be God

טוֹב וַיַּבְדֵּל אֱלֹהִים בֵּין הָאוֹר וּבֵין הַחֹשֶׁךְ׃
the-darkness and-between the-light between God and-he-separated good

וַיִּקְרָא אֱלֹהִים ׀ לָאוֹר יוֹם וְלַחֹשֶׁךְ קָרָא לָיְלָה
night he-called and-to-the-darkness day to-the-light God and-he-called (5)

וַיְהִי־עֶרֶב וַיְהִי־בֹקֶר יוֹם אֶחָד׃ וַיֹּאמֶר אֱלֹהִים
God and-he-said (6) first day morning and-he-was evening and-he-was

יְהִי רָקִיעַ בְּתוֹךְ הַמָּיִם וִיהִי מַבְדִּיל בֵּין
between separating and-let-him-be the-waters between expanse let-him-be

מַיִם לָמָיִם׃ וַיַּעַשׂ אֱלֹהִים אֶת־הָרָקִיעַ וַיַּבְדֵּל
and-he-separated the-expanse *** God so-he-made (7) from-the-waters waters

בֵּין הַמַּיִם אֲשֶׁר מִתַּחַת לָרָקִיעַ וּבֵין הַמַּיִם
the-waters and-between to-the-expanse from-under which the-waters between

אֲשֶׁר מֵעַל לָרָקִיעַ וַיְהִי־כֵן׃ וַיִּקְרָא אֱלֹהִים
God and-he-called (8) so and-he-was to-the-expanse from-above which

לָרָקִיעַ שָׁמָיִם וַיְהִי־עֶרֶב וַיְהִי־בֹקֶר יוֹם שֵׁנִי׃
second day morning and-he-was evening and-he-was sky to-the-expanse

וַיֹּאמֶר אֱלֹהִים יִקָּווּ הַמַּיִם מִתַּחַת הַשָּׁמַיִם אֶל־
to the-sky from-under the-waters let-them-be-gathered God and-he-said (9)

מָקוֹם אֶחָד וְתֵרָאֶה הַיַּבָּשָׁה וַיְהִי־כֵן׃ וַיִּקְרָא
and-he-called (10) so and-he-was the-dry-ground and-let-her-appear one place

אֱלֹהִים ׀ לַיַּבָּשָׁה אֶרֶץ וּלְמִקְוֵה הַמַּיִם קָרָא יַמִּים
seas he-called the-waters and-to-gathering-of land to-the-dry-ground God

וַיַּרְא אֱלֹהִים כִּי־טוֹב׃ וַיֹּאמֶר אֱלֹהִים תַּדְשֵׁא הָאָרֶץ
the-earth let-her-produce God then-he-said (11) good that God and-he-saw

דֶּשֶׁא עֵשֶׂב מַזְרִיעַ זֶרַע עֵץ פְּרִי עֹשֶׂה פְּרִי לְמִינוֹ
to-kind-of-him fruit bearing fruit tree seed seed-bearing plant vegetation

אֲשֶׁר זַרְעוֹ־בוֹ עַל־הָאָרֶץ וַיְהִי־כֵן׃ וַתּוֹצֵא
and-she-produced (12) so and-he-was the-land on in-him seed-of-him which

הָאָרֶץ דֶּשֶׁא עֵשֶׂב מַזְרִיעַ זֶרַע לְמִינֵהוּ וְעֵץ
and-tree to-kind-of-him seed seed-bearing plant vegetation the-land

*The Beginning*

1 In the beginning God
created the heavens and
the earth. [2]Now the earth
was[a] formless and empty,
darkness was over the surface of the deep, and the
Spirit of God was hovering
over the waters.
[3]And God said, "Let there be
light," and there was light.
[4]God saw that the light was
good, and he separated the
light from the darkness.
[5]God called the light "day"
and the darkness he called
"night." And there was
evening, and there was
morning—the first day.
[6]And God said, "Let there be
an expanse between the
waters to separate water
from water." [7]So God
made the expanse and sep-
arated the water under the
expanse from the water
above it. And it was so.
[8]God called the expanse
"sky." And there was eve-
ning, and there was morn-
ing—the second day.
[9]And God said, "Let the water
under the sky be gathered
to one place, and let dry
ground appear." And it
was so. [10]God called the dry
ground "land," and the
gathered waters he called
"seas." And God saw that
it was good.
[11]Then God said, "Let the
land produce vegetation:
seed-bearing plants and
trees on the land that bear
fruit with seed in it, according to their various
kinds." And it was so.
[12]The land produced vegetation: plants bearing seed
according to their kinds
and trees bearing fruit

[a]2 Or possibly *became*

עֹשֶׂה פְּרִי אֲשֶׁר זַרְעוֹ־בוֹ לְמִינֵהוּ וַיַּרְא אֱלֹהִים
God and-he-saw to-kind-of-him in-him seed-of-him which fruit bearing

כִּי־טוֹב׃ וַיְהִי־עֶרֶב וַיְהִי־בֹקֶר יוֹם שְׁלִישִׁי׃
third day morning and-he-was evening and-he-was (13) good that

וַיֹּאמֶר אֱלֹהִים יְהִי מְאֹרֹת בִּרְקִיעַ הַשָּׁמַיִם לְהַבְדִּיל
to-separate the-sky in-expanse-of lights let-him-be God and-he-said (14)

בֵּין הַיּוֹם וּבֵין הַלָּיְלָה וְהָיוּ לְאֹתֹת וּלְמוֹעֲדִים
and-for-seasons as-signs and-let-them-be the-night and-between the-day between

וּלְיָמִים וְשָׁנִים׃ וְהָיוּ לִמְאוֹרֹת בִּרְקִיעַ הַשָּׁמַיִם
the-sky in-expanse-of for-lights and-let-them-be (15) and-years and-for-days

לְהָאִיר עַל־הָאָרֶץ וַיְהִי־כֵן׃ וַיַּעַשׂ אֱלֹהִים אֶת־שְׁנֵי
two-of *** God and-he-made (16) so and-he-was the-earth on to-give-light

הַמְּאֹרֹת הַגְּדֹלִים אֶת־הַמָּאוֹר הַגָּדֹל לְמֶמְשֶׁלֶת הַיּוֹם
the-day for-governing-of the-great the-light *** the-great-ones the-lights

וְאֶת־הַמָּאוֹר הַקָּטֹן לְמֶמְשֶׁלֶת הַלַּיְלָה וְאֵת הַכּוֹכָבִים׃
the-stars also the-night for-governing-of the-less the-light and

וַיִּתֵּן אֹתָם אֱלֹהִים בִּרְקִיעַ הַשָּׁמָיִם לְהָאִיר עַל־הָאָרֶץ׃
the-earth on to-give-light the-sky in-expanse-of God them and-he-set (17)

וְלִמְשֹׁל בַּיּוֹם וּבַלַּיְלָה וּֽלֲהַבְדִּיל בֵּין
between and-to-separate and-over-the-night over-the-day and-to-govern (18)

הָאוֹר וּבֵין הַחֹשֶׁךְ וַיַּרְא אֱלֹהִים כִּי־טוֹב׃ וַיְהִי־
and-he-was (19) good that God and-he-saw the-darkness and-between the-light

עֶרֶב וַיְהִי־בֹקֶר יוֹם רְבִיעִי׃ וַיֹּאמֶר אֱלֹהִים יִשְׁרְצוּ
let-them-teem God and-he-said (20) fourth day morning and-he-was evening

הַמַּיִם שֶׁרֶץ נֶפֶשׁ חַיָּה וְעוֹף יְעוֹפֵף עַל־הָאָרֶץ
the-earth above let-him-fly and-bird living breath-of creature the-waters

עַל־פְּנֵי רְקִיעַ הַשָּׁמָיִם׃ וַיִּבְרָא אֱלֹהִים אֶת־הַתַּנִּינִם
the-sea-creatures *** God so-he-created (21) the-sky expanse-of face-of across

הַגְּדֹלִים וְאֵת כָּל־נֶפֶשׁ הַחַיָּה הָרֹמֶשֶׂת אֲשֶׁר שָׁרְצוּ
they-teem which the-moving the-living breath-of every-of and the-great-ones

הַמַּיִם לְמִינֵהֶם וְאֵת כָּל־עוֹף כָּנָף לְמִינֵהוּ
to-kind-of-him wing bird-of every-of and to-kind-of-them the-waters

וַיַּרְא אֱלֹהִים כִּי־טוֹב׃ וַיְבָרֶךְ אֹתָם אֱלֹהִים לֵאמֹר פְּרוּ
be-fruitful! to-say God them and-he-blessed (22) good that God and-he-saw

וּרְבוּ וּמִלְאוּ אֶת־הַמַּיִם בַּיַּמִּים וְהָעוֹף יִרֶב
let-him-increase and-the-bird in-the-seas the-waters *** and-fill! and-increase!

בָּאָרֶץ׃ וַיְהִי־עֶרֶב וַיְהִי־בֹקֶר יוֹם חֲמִישִׁי׃ וַיֹּאמֶר
and-he-said (24) fifth day morning and-he-was evening and-he-was (23) on-the-earth

with seed in it according
to their kinds. And God
saw that it was good.
[13]And there was evening,
and there was morning—
the third day.
[14]And God said, "Let there be
lights in the expanse of the
sky to separate the day
from the night, and let
them serve as signs to
mark seasons and days
and years, [15]and let them
be lights in the expanse of
the sky to give light on the
earth." And it was so.
[16]God made two great
lights—the greater light to
govern the day and the
lesser light to govern the
night. He also made the
stars. [17]God set them in the
expanse of the sky to give
light on the earth, [18]to govern the day and the night,
and to separate light from
darkness. And God saw
that it was good. [19]And
there was evening, and
there was morning—the
fourth day.
[20]And God said, "Let the water
teem with living creatures,
and let birds fly above the
earth across the expanse of
the sky." [21]So God created
the great creatures of the
sea and every living and
moving thing with which
the water teems, according
to their kinds, and every
winged bird according to
its kind. And God saw that
it was good. [22]God blessed
them and said, "Be fruitful
and increase in number
and fill the water in the
seas, and let the birds increase on the earth." [23]And
there was evening, and
there was morning—the
fifth day.

אֱלֹהִים תּוֹצֵא הָאָרֶץ נֶפֶשׁ חַיָּה לְמִינָהּ בְּהֵמָה
livestock to-kind-of-her living creature-of the-land let-her-produce God

וָרֶמֶשׂ וְחַיְתוֹ־ אֶרֶץ לְמִינָהּ וַיְהִי־ כֵן׃ וַיַּעַשׂ
and-he-made (25) so and-he-was to-kind-of-her earth and-animal-of and-crawler

אֱלֹהִים אֶת־ חַיַּת הָאָרֶץ לְמִינָהּ וְאֶת־ הַבְּהֵמָה לְמִינָהּ
to-kind-of-her the-livestock and to-kind-of-her the-earth animal-of *** God

וְאֵת כָּל־ רֶמֶשׂ הָאֲדָמָה לְמִינֵהוּ וַיַּרְא אֱלֹהִים כִּי־טוֹב׃
good that God and-he-saw to-kind-of-him the-ground crawler-of every-of and

וַיֹּאמֶר אֱלֹהִים נַעֲשֶׂה אָדָם בְּצַלְמֵנוּ כִּדְמוּתֵנוּ
in-likeness-of-us in-image-of-us man let-us-make God then-he-said (26)

וְיִרְדּוּ בִדְגַת הַיָּם וּבְעוֹף הַשָּׁמַיִם
the-air and-over-bird-of the-sea over-fish-of and-let-them-rule

וּבַבְּהֵמָה וּבְכָל־ הָאָרֶץ וּבְכָל־ הָרֶמֶשׂ
the-crawler and-over-every-of the-earth and-over-all-of and-over-the-livestock

הָרֹמֵשׂ עַל־ הָאָרֶץ׃ וַיִּבְרָא אֱלֹהִים ׀ אֶת־ הָאָדָם
the-man *** God so-he-created (27) the-ground along the-one-crawling

בְּצַלְמוֹ בְּצֶלֶם אֱלֹהִים בָּרָא אֹתוֹ זָכָר וּנְקֵבָה בָּרָא
he-created and-female male him he-created God in-image-of in-image-of-him

אֹתָם׃ וַיְבָרֶךְ אֹתָם אֱלֹהִים וַיֹּאמֶר לָהֶם אֱלֹהִים פְּרוּ
be-fruitful! God to-them and-he-said God them and-he-blessed (28) them

וּרְבוּ וּמִלְאוּ אֶת־ הָאָרֶץ וְכִבְשֻׁהָ וּרְדוּ בִּדְגַת
over-fish-of and-rule! and-subdue-her! the-earth *** and-fill! and-increase!

הַיָּם וּבְעוֹף הַשָּׁמַיִם וּבְכָל־ חַיָּה הָרֹמֶשֶׂת עַל־
on the-one-crawling living and-over-every-of the-air and-over-bird-of the-sea

הָאָרֶץ׃ וַיֹּאמֶר אֱלֹהִים הִנֵּה נָתַתִּי לָכֶם אֶת־ כָּל־ עֵשֶׂב ׀ זֹרֵעַ
seed-bearing plant every-of *** to-you I-give see! God then-he-said (29) the-ground

זֶרַע אֲשֶׁר עַל־ פְּנֵי כָל־ הָאָרֶץ וְאֶת־ כָּל־ הָעֵץ אֲשֶׁר־ בּוֹ
in-it which the-tree every-of and the-earth whole-of face-of on which seed

פְרִי־ עֵץ זֹרֵעַ זָרַע לָכֶם יִהְיֶה לְאָכְלָה׃ וּלְכָל־
and-to-every-of (30) for-food he-will-be for-you seed seeding tree fruit-of

חַיַּת הָאָרֶץ וּלְכָל־ עוֹף הַשָּׁמַיִם וּלְכֹל ׀ רוֹמֵשׂ
crawling-one and-to-every-of the-air bird-of and-to-every-of the-earth beast-of

עַל־ הָאָרֶץ אֲשֶׁר־ בּוֹ נֶפֶשׁ חַיָּה אֶת־ כָּל־ יֶרֶק עֵשֶׂב לְאָכְלָה
for-food plant green every-of *** life breath-of in-him which the-ground on

וַיְהִי־ כֵן׃ וַיַּרְא אֱלֹהִים אֶת־כָּל־ אֲשֶׁר עָשָׂה וְהִנֵּה־ טוֹב מְאֹד
very good and-see! he-made that all-of *** God and-he-saw (31) so and-he-was

וַיְהִי־ עֶרֶב וַיְהִי־ בֹקֶר יוֹם הַשִּׁשִּׁי׃ וַיְכֻלּוּ
thus-they-were-done (2:1) the-sixth day-of morning and-he-was evening and-he-was

24 And God said, "Let the land
produce living creatures
according to their kinds:
livestock, creatures that
move along the ground,
and wild animals, each according to its kind." And it
was so. 25 God made the
wild animals according to
their kinds, the livestock
according to their kinds,
and all the creatures that
move along the ground ac-
cording to their kinds.
And God saw that it was
good.

26 Then God said, "Let us
make man in our image, in
our likeness, and let them
rule over the fish of the sea
and the birds of the air,
over the livestock, over all
the earth,[b] and over all the
creatures that move along
the ground."

27 So God created man in his
own image,
in the image of God he
created him;
male and female he
created them.

28 God blessed them and
said to them, "Be fruitful
and increase in number;
fill the earth and subdue it.
Rule over the fish of the
sea and the birds of the air
and over every living creature that moves on the
ground."

29 Then God said, "I give
you every seed-bearing
plant on the face of the
whole earth and every tree
that has fruit with seed in
it. They will be yours for
food. 30 And to all the beasts
of the earth and all the
birds of the air and all the
creatures that move on the
ground—everything that
has the breath of life in
it—I give every green plant
for food." And it was so.

31 God saw all that he had
made, and it was very
good. And there was eve-
ning, and there was morn-
ing—the sixth day.

[b]26 Hebrew; Syriac *all the wild animals*

הַשָּׁמַיִם וְהָאָרֶץ וְכָל־ צְבָאָם׃ וַיְכַל אֱלֹהִים
God and-he-finished (2) array-of-them and-all-of and-the-earth the-heavens

בַּיּוֹם הַשְּׁבִיעִי מְלַאכְתּוֹ אֲשֶׁר עָשָׂה וַיִּשְׁבֹּת בַּיּוֹם
on-the-day and-he-rested he-did which work-of-him the-seventh by-the-day

הַשְּׁבִיעִי מִכָּל־ מְלַאכְתּוֹ אֲשֶׁר עָשָׂה׃ וַיְבָרֶךְ אֱלֹהִים אֶת־
*** God and-he-blessed (3) he-did which work-of-him from-all-of the-seventh

יוֹם הַשְּׁבִיעִי וַיְקַדֵּשׁ אֹתוֹ כִּי בוֹ שָׁבַת מִכָּל־
from-all-of he-rested on-him because him and-he-made-holy the-seventh day-of

מְלַאכְתּוֹ אֲשֶׁר־ בָּרָא אֱלֹהִים לַעֲשׂוֹת׃ אֵלֶּה תוֹלְדוֹת הַשָּׁמַיִם
the-heavens generations-of these (4) to-do God he-created that work-of-him

וְהָאָרֶץ בְּהִבָּרְאָם בְּיוֹם עֲשׂוֹת יְהוָה אֱלֹהִים אֶרֶץ וְשָׁמָיִם׃
and-heavens earth God Yahweh to-make in-day when-to-be-created-them and-the-earth

וְכֹל ׀ שִׂיחַ הַשָּׂדֶה טֶרֶם יִהְיֶה בָאָרֶץ וְכָל־
and-any-of on-the-earth he-appeared not-yet the-field shrub-of and-any-of (5)

עֵשֶׂב הַשָּׂדֶה טֶרֶם יִצְמָח כִּי לֹא הִמְטִיר יְהוָה אֱלֹהִים עַל־
on God Yahweh he-sent-rain not for he-sprung-up not-yet the-field plant-of

הָאָרֶץ וְאָדָם אַיִן לַעֲבֹד אֶת־ הָאֲדָמָה׃ וְאֵד יַעֲלֶה
he-came-up but-stream (6) the-ground *** to-work was-not and-man the-earth

מִן־ הָאָרֶץ וְהִשְׁקָה אֶת־ כָּל־ פְּנֵי־ הָאֲדָמָה׃
the-ground surface-of whole-of *** and-he-watered the-earth from

וַיִּיצֶר יְהוָה אֱלֹהִים אֶת־ הָאָדָם עָפָר מִן־ הָאֲדָמָה וַיִּפַּח
and-he-breathed the-ground from dust the-man *** God Yahweh and-he-formed (7)

בְּאַפָּיו נִשְׁמַת חַיִּים וַיְהִי הָאָדָם לְנֶפֶשׁ חַיָּה׃
living into-being the-man and-he-became life breath-of into-nostrils-of-him

וַיִּטַּע יְהוָה אֱלֹהִים גַּן־ בְּעֵדֶן מִקֶּדֶם וַיָּשֶׂם שָׁם אֶת־
*** there and-he-put in-east in-Eden garden God Yahweh now-he-planted (8)

הָאָדָם אֲשֶׁר יָצָר׃ וַיַּצְמַח יְהוָה אֱלֹהִים מִן־ הָאֲדָמָה
the-ground from God Yahweh and-he-made-grow (9) he-formed whom the-man

כָּל־ עֵץ נֶחְמָד לְמַרְאֶה וְטוֹב לְמַאֲכָל וְעֵץ הַחַיִּים
the-life and-tree-of for-food and-good to-sight being-pleasant tree every-of

בְּתוֹךְ הַגָּן וְעֵץ הַדַּעַת טוֹב וָרָע׃ וְנָהָר
and-river (10) and-evil good the-knowledge and-tree-of the-garden in-middle-of

יֹצֵא מֵעֵדֶן לְהַשְׁקוֹת אֶת־ הַגָּן וּמִשָּׁם יִפָּרֵד
he-divided and-from-there the-garden *** to-water from-Eden flowing

וְהָיָה לְאַרְבָּעָה רָאשִׁים׃ שֵׁם הָאֶחָד פִּישׁוֹן הוּא הַסֹּבֵב
the-one-winding he Pishon the-first name-of (11) headstreams to-four and-he-became

אֵת כָּל־ אֶרֶץ הַחֲוִילָה אֲשֶׁר־ שָׁם הַזָּהָב׃ וּזֲהַב הָאָרֶץ
the-land and-gold-of (12) the-gold there where the-Havilah land-of all-of ***

2 Thus the heavens and the earth were completed in all their vast array.

2 By the seventh day God had finished the work he had been doing; so on the seventh day he rested from all his work.
3 And God blessed the seventh day and made it holy, because on it he rested[c] from all the work of creating that he had done.

*Adam and Eve*

4 This is the account of the heavens and the earth when they were created.

When the LORD God made the earth and the heavens,
5 no shrub of the field had yet appeared on the earth[d] and no plant of the field had yet sprung up; the LORD God had not sent rain on the earth[d] and there was no man to work the ground,
6 but streams[e] came up from the earth and watered the whole surface of the ground.
7 And the LORD God formed man[f] from the dust of the ground and breathed into his nostrils the breath of life, and man became a living being.
8 Now the LORD God had planted a garden in the east, in Eden; and there he put the man he had formed.
9 And the LORD God made all kinds of trees grow out of the ground—trees that were pleasing to the eye and good for food. In the middle of the garden were the tree of life and the tree of the knowledge of good and evil.
10 A river watering the garden flowed from Eden, and from there it divided; it had four headstreams.
11 The name of the first is the Pishon; it winds through the entire land of Havilah, where there is gold.
12 (The gold of that land is

[c] 3 Or *ceased* [d] 5 Or *land;* also in verse 6
[e] 6 Or *mist*
[f] 7 The Hebrew for *man (adam)* sounds like and may be related to the Hebrew for *ground (adamah);* it is also the name *Adam* (see Gen. 2:20).

הַהִוא טֹוב שָׁם הַבְּדֹלַח וְאֶבֶן הַשֹּׁהַם׃ וְשֵׁם־ הַנָּהָר
the-river and-name-of (13) the-onyx and-stone-of the-resin there good the-that

הַשֵּׁנִי גִּיחֹון הוּא הַסֹּובֵב אֵת כָּל־ אֶרֶץ כּוּשׁ׃ וְשֵׁם
and-name-of (14) Cush land-of all-of *** the-one-winding he Gihon the-second

הַנָּהָר הַשְּׁלִישִׁי חִדֶּקֶל הוּא הַהֹלֵךְ קִדְמַת אַשּׁוּר וְהַנָּהָר
and-the-river Asshur east-of the-one-running he Tigris the-third the-river

הָרְבִיעִי הוּא פְרָת׃ וַיִּקַּח יְהוָה אֱלֹהִים אֶת־הָאָדָם וַיַּנִּחֵהוּ
and-he-put-him the-man *** God Yahweh and-he-took (15) Euphrates he the-fourth

בְגַן־ עֵדֶן לְעָבְדָהּ וּלְשָׁמְרָהּ׃ וַיְצַו יְהוָה
Yahweh and-he-commanded (16) and-to-care-for-her to-work-her Eden in-garden-of

אֱלֹהִים עַל־הָאָדָם לֵאמֹר מִכֹּל עֵץ־ הַגָּן אָכֹל תֹּאכֵל׃
you-may-eat to-eat the-garden tree-of from-any-of to-say the-man to God

וּמֵעֵץ הַדַּעַת טֹוב וָרָע לֹא תֹאכַל מִמֶּנּוּ כִּי
for from-him you-must-eat not and-evil good the-knowledge but-from-tree-of (17)

בְּיֹום אֲכָלְךָ מִמֶּנּוּ מֹות תָּמוּת׃ וַיֹּאמֶר יְהוָה אֱלֹהִים
God Yahweh and-he-said (18) you-will-die to-die from-him to-eat-you in-day-of

לֹא־ טֹוב הֱיֹות הָאָדָם לְבַדֹּו אֶעֱשֶׂה־* לֹּו עֵזֶר כְּנֶגְדֹּו׃
to-suit-him helper for-him I-will-make alone the-man to-be good not

וַיִּצֶר יְהוָה אֱלֹהִים מִן־ הָאֲדָמָה כָּל־ חַיַּת הַשָּׂדֶה
the-field beast-of every-of the-ground from God Yahweh now-he-formed (19)

וְאֵת כָּל־ עֹוף הַשָּׁמַיִם וַיָּבֵא אֶל־ הָאָדָם לִרְאֹות מַה־
what to-see the-man to and-he-brought the-air bird-of every-of and

יִּקְרָא־ לֹו וְכֹל אֲשֶׁר יִקְרָא־ לֹו הָאָדָם נֶפֶשׁ חַיָּה
living creature the-man to-him he-named which and-all to-him he-would-name

הוּא שְׁמֹו׃ וַיִּקְרָא הָאָדָם שֵׁמֹות לְכָל־ הַבְּהֵמָה
the-livestock to-all-of names the-man so-he-named (20) name-of-him that

וּלְעֹוף הַשָּׁמַיִם וּלְכֹל חַיַּת הַשָּׂדֶה וּלְאָדָם לֹא־
not but-for-Adam the-field beast-of and-to-every-of the-air and-to-bird-of

מָצָא עֵזֶר כְּנֶגְדֹּו׃ וַיַּפֵּל יְהוָה אֱלֹהִים ׀ תַּרְדֵּמָה עַל־
upon deep-sleep God Yahweh so-he-made-fall (21) to-suit-him helper he-found

הָאָדָם וַיִּישָׁן וַיִּקַּח אַחַת מִצַּלְעֹתָיו וַיִּסְגֹּר בָּשָׂר
flesh and-he-closed from-ribs-of-him one-of and-he-took and-he-slept the-man

תַּחְתֶּנָּה׃ וַיִּבֶן יְהוָה אֱלֹהִים ׀ אֶת־הַצֵּלָע אֲשֶׁר־ לָקַח מִן־
from he-took which the-rib *** God Yahweh then-he-made (22) place-of-her

הָאָדָם לְאִשָּׁה וַיְבִאֶהָ אֶל־ הָאָדָם׃ וַיֹּאמֶר הָאָדָם
the-man and-he-said (23) the-man to and-he-brought-her into-woman the-man

זֹאת הַפַּעַם עֶצֶם מֵעֲצָמַי וּבָשָׂר מִבְּשָׂרִי לְזֹאת
to-this from-flesh-of-me and-flesh from-bones-of-me bone the-now this

good; aromatic resin[g] and
onyx are also there.) [13]The
name of the second river is the
Gihon; it winds through the
entire land of Cush.[h] [14]The
name of the third river is the
Tigris; it runs along the east
side of Asshur. And the fourth
river is the Euphrates.

[15]The LORD God took the
man and put him in the Garden of Eden to work it and
take care of it. [16]And the LORD
God commanded the man,
"You are free to eat from any
tree in the garden; [17]but you
must not eat from the tree of
the knowledge of good and
evil, for when you eat of it you
will surely die."

[18]The LORD God said, "It is
not good for the man to be
alone. I will make a helper
suitable for him."

[19]Now the LORD God had
formed out of the ground all
the beasts of the field and all
the birds of the air. He
brought them to the man to
see what he would name
them; and whatever the man
called each living creature,
that was its name. [20]So the
man gave names to all the
livestock, the birds of the air
and all the beasts of the field.
But for Adam[i] no suitable
helper was found. [21]So the
LORD God caused the man to
fall into a deep sleep; and
while he was sleeping, he took
one of the man's ribs[j] and
closed up the place with flesh.
[22]Then the LORD God made a
woman from the rib[k] he had
taken out of the man, and he
brought her to the man.

[23]The man said,

"This is now bone of my
bones
and flesh of my flesh;

g12 Or *good; pearls*
h13 Possibly southeast Mesopotamia
i20 Or *man*
j21 Or *took part of the man's side*
k22 Or *part*

*18 Most mss have no *mappiq* in the *he* (הָ).

יִקָּרֵא אִשָּׁה כִּי מֵאִישׁ לֻקֳחָה־זֹּאת׃ עַל־כֵּן
this for (24) this she-was-taken from-man for woman he-shall-be-called

יַעֲזָב־אִישׁ אֶת־אָבִיו וְאֶת־אִמּוֹ וְדָבַק
and-he-will-unite mother-of-him and father-of-him *** man he-will-leave

בְּאִשְׁתּוֹ וְהָיוּ לְבָשָׂר אֶחָד׃ וַיִּהְיוּ שְׁנֵיהֶם
both-of-them and-they-were (25) one as-flesh and-they-will-be to-wife-of-him

עֲרוּמִּים הָאָדָם וְאִשְׁתּוֹ וְלֹא יִתְבֹּשָׁשׁוּ׃ וְהַנָּחָשׁ
now-the-serpent (3:1) they-felt-shame and-not and-wife-of-him the-man naked-ones

הָיָה עָרוּם מִכֹּל חַיַּת הַשָּׂדֶה אֲשֶׁר עָשָׂה יְהוָה אֱלֹהִים
God Yahweh he-made which the-field animal-of more-than-all-of crafty he-was

וַיֹּאמֶר אֶל־הָאִשָּׁה אַף כִּי־אָמַר אֱלֹהִים לֹא תֹאכְלוּ מִכֹּל
from-any-of you-must-eat not God he-said really indeed the-woman to and-he-said

עֵץ הַגָּן׃ וַתֹּאמֶר הָאִשָּׁה אֶל־הַנָּחָשׁ מִפְּרִי
from-fruit-of the-serpent to the-woman and-she-said (2) the-garden tree-of

עֵץ־הַגָּן נֹאכֵל׃ וּמִפְּרִי הָעֵץ אֲשֶׁר בְּתוֹךְ־
in-middle-of that the-tree but-from-fruit-of (3) we-may-eat the-garden tree-of

הַגָּן אָמַר אֱלֹהִים לֹא תֹאכְלוּ מִמֶּנּוּ וְלֹא תִגְּעוּ
you-must-touch and-not from-him you-must-eat not God he-said the-garden

בּוֹ פֶּן־תְּמֻתוּן׃ וַיֹּאמֶר הַנָּחָשׁ אֶל־הָאִשָּׁה לֹא־מוֹת
to-die not the-woman to the-serpent and-he-said (4) you-will-die or on-him

תְּמֻתוּן׃ כִּי יֹדֵעַ אֱלֹהִים כִּי בְּיוֹם אֲכָלְכֶם מִמֶּנּוּ
from-him to-eat-you in-day that God knowing for (5) you-will-die

וְנִפְקְחוּ עֵינֵיכֶם וִהְיִיתֶם כֵּאלֹהִים יֹדְעֵי טוֹב
good knowing-of like-God and-you-will-be eyes-of-you and-they-will-be-opened

וָרָע׃ וַתֵּרֶא הָאִשָּׁה כִּי טוֹב הָעֵץ לְמַאֲכָל וְכִי
and-that for-food the-tree good that the-woman and-she-saw (6) and-evil

תַאֲוָה־הוּא לָעֵינַיִם וְנֶחְמָד הָעֵץ לְהַשְׂכִּיל וַתִּקַּח
and-she-took to-gain-wisdom the-tree and-being-desirable to-the-eyes he pleasant

מִפִּרְיוֹ וַתֹּאכַל וַתִּתֵּן גַּם־לְאִישָׁהּ עִמָּהּ
with-her to-husband-of-her also and-she-gave and-she-ate from-fruit-of-him

וַיֹּאכַל׃ וַתִּפָּקַחְנָה עֵינֵי שְׁנֵיהֶם וַיֵּדְעוּ כִּי
that and-they-realized both-of-them eyes-of and-they-were-opened (7) and-he-ate

עֵירֻמִּם הֵם וַיִּתְפְּרוּ עֲלֵה תְאֵנָה וַיַּעֲשׂוּ לָהֶם
for-themselves and-they-made fig leaf-of and-they-sewed they naked-ones

חֲגֹרֹת׃ וַיִּשְׁמְעוּ אֶת־קוֹל יְהוָה אֱלֹהִים מִתְהַלֵּךְ בַּגָּן
in-the-garden walking God Yahweh sound-of *** then-they-heard (8) coverings

לְרוּחַ הַיּוֹם וַיִּתְחַבֵּא הָאָדָם וְאִשְׁתּוֹ מִפְּנֵי יְהוָה אֱלֹהִים
God Yahweh from-face-of and-wife-of-him the-man and-he-hid the-day in-cool-of

she shall be called
'woman,[l]'
for she was taken out of
man."

[24]For this reason a man will
leave his father and mother
and be united to his wife, and
they will become one flesh.
[25]The man and his wife were
both naked, and they felt no
shame.

*The Fall of Man*

3 Now the serpent was
more crafty than any of
the wild animals the LORD God
had made. He said to the
woman, "Did God really say,
'You must not eat from any
tree in the garden'?"
[2]The woman said to the serpent, "We may eat fruit from
the trees in the garden, [3]but
God did say, 'You must not eat
fruit from the tree that is in the
middle of the garden, and you
must not touch it, or you will
die.'"
[4]"You will not surely die,"
the serpent said to the woman.
[5]"For God knows that when
you eat of it your eyes will be
opened, and you will be like
God, knowing good and evil."
[6]When the woman saw that
the fruit of the tree was good
for food and pleasing to the
eye, and also desirable for
gaining wisdom, she took
some and ate it. She also gave
some to her husband, who
was with her, and he ate it.
[7]Then the eyes of both of them
were opened, and they realized they were naked; so they
sewed fig leaves together and
made coverings for them-
selves.
[8]Then the man and his wife
heard the sound of the LORD
God as he was walking in the
garden in the cool of the day,
and they hid from the LORD

[l]23 The Hebrew for *woman* sounds like the Hebrew for *man*.

בְּתוֹךְ עֵץ הַגָּן׃ וַיִּקְרָא יְהוָה אֱלֹהִים אֶל־הָאָדָם וַיֹּאמֶר
and-he-said the-man to God Yahweh but-he-called (9) the-garden tree-of among

לוֹ אַיֶּכָּה׃ וַיֹּאמֶר אֶת־ קֹלְךָ שָׁמַעְתִּי בַּגָּן
in-the-garden I-heard sound-of-you *** and-he-answered (10) where-you? to-him

וָאִירָא כִּי־עֵירֹם אָנֹכִי וָאֵחָבֵא׃ וַיֹּאמֶר מִי הִגִּיד לְךָ
to-you he-told who? and-he-said (11) so-I-hid I naked because and-I-was-afraid

כִּי עֵירֹם אָתָּה הֲמִן־ הָעֵץ אֲשֶׁר צִוִּיתִיךָ לְבִלְתִּי אֲכָל־ מִמֶּנּוּ
from-him to-eat not I-commanded-you that the-tree from? you naked that

אָכָלְתָּ׃ וַיֹּאמֶר הָאָדָם הָאִשָּׁה אֲשֶׁר נָתַתָּה עִמָּדִי הִוא נָתְנָה־
she-gave she with-me you-put whom the-woman the-man and-he-said (12) you-ate

לִּי מִן־ הָעֵץ וָאֹכֵל׃ וַיֹּאמֶר יְהוָה אֱלֹהִים לָאִשָּׁה מַה־
what? to-the-woman God Yahweh and-he-said (13) and-I-ate the-tree from to-me

זֹּאת עָשִׂית וַתֹּאמֶר הָאִשָּׁה הַנָּחָשׁ הִשִּׁיאַנִי וָאֹכֵל׃
and-I-ate he-deceived-me the-serpent the-woman and-she-said you-did this

וַיֹּאמֶר יְהוָה אֱלֹהִים ׀ אֶל־הַנָּחָשׁ כִּי עָשִׂיתָ זֹּאת אָרוּר
being-cursed this you-did because the-serpent to God Yahweh and-he-said (14)

אַתָּה מִכָּל־ הַבְּהֵמָה וּמִכֹּל חַיַּת הַשָּׂדֶה עַל־ גְּחֹנְךָ
belly-of-you on the-field animal-of and-above-all the-livestock above-all-of you

תֵלֵךְ וְעָפָר תֹּאכַל כָּל־ יְמֵי חַיֶּיךָ׃ וְאֵיבָה ׀
and-enmity (15) life-of-you days-of all-of you-will-eat and-dust you-will-crawl

אָשִׁית בֵּינְךָ וּבֵין הָאִשָּׁה וּבֵין זַרְעֲךָ
offspring-of-you and-between the-woman and-between between-you I-will-put

וּבֵין זַרְעָהּ הוּא יְשׁוּפְךָ רֹאשׁ וְאַתָּה תְּשׁוּפֶנּוּ
you-will-strike-him and-you head he-will-crush-you he offspring-of-her and-between

עָקֵב׃ אֶל ־ הָאִשָּׁה אָמַר הַרְבָּה אַרְבֶּה עִצְּבוֹנֵךְ
pain-of-you I-will-increase to-increase he-said the-woman to (16) heel

וְהֵרֹנֵךְ בְּעֶצֶב תֵּלְדִי בָנִים וְאֶל־ אִישֵׁךְ
husband-of-you and-to children you-will-bear in-pain and-childbearing-of-you

תְּשׁוּקָתֵךְ וְהוּא יִמְשָׁל־ בָּךְ׃ וּלְאָדָם אָמַר כִּי
because he-said and-to-Adam (17) over-you he-will-rule and-he desire-of-you

שָׁמַעְתָּ לְקוֹל אִשְׁתֶּךָ וַתֹּאכַל מִן־ הָעֵץ אֲשֶׁר
which the-tree from and-you-ate wife-of-you to-voice-of you-listened

צִוִּיתִיךָ לֵאמֹר לֹא תֹאכַל מִמֶּנּוּ אֲרוּרָה הָאֲדָמָה
the-ground being-cursed from-him you-must-eat not to-say I-commanded-you

בַּעֲבוּרֶךָ בְּעִצָּבוֹן תֹּאכֲלֶנָּה כֹּל יְמֵי חַיֶּיךָ׃
life-of-you days-of all-of you-will-eat-her by-painful-toil because-of-you

וְקוֹץ וְדַרְדַּר תַּצְמִיחַ לָךְ וְאָכַלְתָּ אֶת־ עֵשֶׂב
plant-of *** and-you-will-eat for-you she-will-produce and-thistle and-thorn (18)

God among the trees of the garden. 9 But the LORD God called to the man, "Where are you?"

10 He answered, "I heard you in the garden, and I was afraid because I was naked; so I hid."

11 And he said, "Who told you that you were naked? Have you eaten from the tree that I commanded you not to eat from?"

12 The man said, "The woman you put here with me—she gave me some fruit from the tree, and I ate it."

13 Then the LORD God said to the woman, "What is this you have done?"

The woman said, "The serpent deceived me, and I ate."

14 So the LORD God said to the serpent, "Because you have done this,

"Cursed are you above all
the livestock
and all the wild animals!
You will crawl on your
belly
and you will eat dust
all the days of your life.
15 And I will put enmity
between you and the
woman,
and between your
offspring[m] and hers;
he will crush[n] your head,
and you will strike his
heel."

16 To the woman he said,

"I will greatly increase
your pains in
childbearing;
with pain you will give
birth to children.
Your desire will be for your
husband,
and he will rule over
you."

17 To Adam he said, "Because you listened to your wife and ate from the tree about which I commanded you, 'You must not eat of it,'

"Cursed is the ground
because of you;
through painful toil you
will eat of it
all the days of your life.
18 It will produce thorns and
thistles for you,
and you will eat the
plants of the field.

m15 Or *seed* n15 Or *strike*

הַשָּׂדֶה׃ בְּזֵעַת אַפֶּיךָ תֹּאכַל לֶחֶם עַד שׁוּבְךָ
to-return-you until food you-will-eat brow-of-you by-sweat-of (19) the-field

אֶל־הָאֲדָמָה כִּי מִמֶּנָּה לֻקָּחְתָּ כִּי־עָפָר אַתָּה וְאֶל־עָפָר
dust and-to you dust for you-were-taken from-her since the-ground to

תָּשׁוּב׃ וַיִּקְרָא הָאָדָם שֵׁם אִשְׁתּוֹ חַוָּה כִּי הִוא
she because Eve wife-of-him name-of the-man and-he-named (20) you-will-return

הָיְתָה אֵם כָּל־חָי׃ וַיַּעַשׂ יְהוָה אֱלֹהִים לְאָדָם
for-Adam God Yahweh and-he-made (21) living all-of mother-of she-would-be

וּלְאִשְׁתּוֹ כָּתְנוֹת עוֹר וַיַּלְבִּשֵׁם׃ וַיֹּאמֶר ׀
and-he-said (22) and-he-clothed-them skin garments-of and-for-wife-of-him

יְהוָה אֱלֹהִים הֵן הָאָדָם הָיָה כְּאַחַד מִמֶּנּוּ לָדַעַת טוֹב וָרָע
and-evil good to-know from-us like-one-of he-became the-man see! God Yahweh

וְעַתָּה ׀ פֶּן־יִשְׁלַח יָדוֹ וְלָקַח גַּם מֵעֵץ הַחַיִּים
the-life from-tree-of also and-he-take hand-of-him he-reach-out lest and-now

וְאָכַל וָחַי לְעֹלָם׃ וַיְשַׁלְּחֵהוּ יְהוָה אֱלֹהִים מִגַּן־
from-garden-of God Yahweh so-he-sent-him (23) for-ever and-he-live and-he-eat

עֵדֶן לַעֲבֹד אֶת־הָאֲדָמָה אֲשֶׁר לֻקַּח מִשָּׁם׃ וַיְגָרֶשׁ
and-he-drove-out (24) from-there he-was-taken which the-ground *** to-work Eden

אֶת־הָאָדָם וַיַּשְׁכֵּן מִקֶּדֶם לְגַן־עֵדֶן אֶת־הַכְּרֻבִים וְאֵת
and the-cherubim *** Eden to-garden-of on-east and-he-placed the-man ***

לַהַט הַחֶרֶב הַמִּתְהַפֶּכֶת לִשְׁמֹר אֶת־דֶּרֶךְ עֵץ הַחַיִּים׃
the-life tree-of way-of *** to-guard the-one-flashing-around the-sword flame-of

וְהָאָדָם יָדַע אֶת־חַוָּה אִשְׁתּוֹ וַתַּהַר וַתֵּלֶד
and-she-bore and-she-conceived wife-of-him Eve *** he-knew and-the-man (4:1)

אֶת־קַיִן וַתֹּאמֶר קָנִיתִי אִישׁ אֶת־יְהוָה׃ וַתֹּסֶף
and-she-continued (2) Yahweh with man I-brought-forth and-she-said Cain ***

לָלֶדֶת אֶת־אָחִיו אֶת־הָבֶל וַיְהִי־הֶבֶל רֹעֵה צֹאן וְקַיִן
and-Cain flock keeping-of Abel now-he-was Abel *** brother-of-him *** to-bear

הָיָה עֹבֵד אֲדָמָה׃ וַיְהִי מִקֵּץ יָמִים וַיָּבֵא קַיִן
Cain and-he-brought days in-course-of and-he-was (3) soil working-of he-was

מִפְּרִי הָאֲדָמָה מִנְחָה לַיהוָה׃ וְהֶבֶל הֵבִיא גַם־הוּא
he also he-brought but-Abel (4) to-Yahweh offering the-soil from-fruit-of

מִבְּכֹרוֹת צֹאנוֹ וּמֵחֶלְבֵהֶן וַיִּשַׁע יְהוָה
Yahweh and-he-had-favor and-from-fat-of-them flock-of-him from-firstborn-of

אֶל־הֶבֶל וְאֶל־מִנְחָתוֹ׃ וְאֶל־קַיִן וְאֶל־מִנְחָתוֹ לֹא
not offering-of-him and-on Cain but-on (5) offering-of-him and-on Abel on

שָׁעָה וַיִּחַר לְקַיִן מְאֹד וַיִּפְּלוּ פָּנָיו׃
faces-of-him and-they-were-downcast very to-Cain so-he-was-angry he-had-favor

[19]By the sweat of your brow
you will eat your food
until you return to the
ground,
since from it you were
taken;
for dust you are
and to dust you will
return."

[20]Adam[o] named his wife Eve,[p] because she would become the mother of all the living.

[21]The LORD God made garments of skin for Adam and his wife and clothed them.
[22]And the LORD God said, "The man has now become like one of us, knowing good and evil. He must not be allowed to reach out his hand and take also from the tree of life and eat, and live forever." [23]So the LORD God banished him from the Garden of Eden to work the ground from which he had been taken. [24]After he drove the man out, he placed on the east side[q] of the Garden of Eden cherubim and a flaming sword flashing back and forth to guard the way to the tree of life.

*Cain and Abel*

4 Adam[o] lay with his wife Eve, and she conceived and gave birth to Cain.[r] She said, "With the help of the LORD I have brought forth[s] a man." [2]Later she gave birth to his brother Abel.

Now Abel kept flocks, and Cain worked the soil. [3]In the course of time Cain brought some of the fruits of the soil as an offering to the LORD. [4]But Abel brought fat portions from some of the firstborn of his flock. The LORD looked with favor on Abel and his offering, [5]but on Cain and his offering he did not look with favor. So Cain was very angry, and his face was downcast.

[o]20,1 Or *The man* [p]20 *Eve* means *living.*
[q]24 Or *placed in front*
[r]1 *Cain* sounds like the Hebrew for *brought forth* or *acquired.*
[s]1 Or *have acquired*

וַיֹּאמֶר יְהוָה אֶל־קָיִן לָמָּה חָרָה לָךְ וְלָמָּה
and-why? to-you is-he-angry why? Cain to Yahweh then-he-said (6)

נָפְלוּ פָנֶיךָ׃ הֲלוֹא אִם־תֵּיטִיב שְׂאֵת
to-be-accepted you-do-right if not? (7) faces-of-you are-they-downcast

וְאִם לֹא תֵיטִיב לַפֶּתַח חַטָּאת רֹבֵץ וְאֵלֶיךָ תְּשׁוּקָתוֹ
desire-of-him and-for-you crouching sin at-the-door you-do-right not but-if

וְאַתָּה תִּמְשָׁל־בּוֹ׃ וַיֹּאמֶר קַיִן אֶל־הֶבֶל אָחִיו
brother-of-him Abel to Cain now-he-said (8) over-him you-must-master but-you

[ נֵלְכָה הַשָּׂדֶה ]* וַיְהִי בִּהְיוֹתָם בַּשָּׂדֶה
in-the-field while-to-be-them and-he-was *[the-field let-us-go]

וַיָּקָם קַיִן אֶל־הֶבֶל אָחִיו וַיַּהַרְגֵהוּ׃ וַיֹּאמֶר
and-he-said (9) and-he-killed-him brother-of-him Abel at Cain and-he-attacked

יְהוָה אֶל־קַיִן אֵי הֶבֶל אָחִיךָ וַיֹּאמֶר לֹא יָדַעְתִּי
I-know not and-he-replied brother-of-you Abel where? Cain to Yahweh

הֲשֹׁמֵר אָחִי אָנֹכִי׃ וַיֹּאמֶר מֶה עָשִׂיתָ קוֹל
voice-of you-did what? and-he-said (10) I brother-of-me keeping-of?

דְּמֵי אָחִיךָ צֹעֲקִים אֵלַי מִן־הָאֲדָמָה׃ וְעַתָּה
and-now (11) the-ground from to-me ones-crying brother-of-you bloods-of

אָרוּר אָתָּה מִן־הָאֲדָמָה אֲשֶׁר פָּצְתָה אֶת־פִּיהָ לָקַחַת
to-receive mouth-of-her *** she-opened which the-ground from you being-cursed

אֶת־דְּמֵי אָחִיךָ מִיָּדֶךָ׃ כִּי תַעֲבֹד אֶת־הָאֲדָמָה
the-ground *** you-work when (12) from-hand-of-you brother-of-you bloods-of ***

לֹא־תֹסֵף תֵּת־כֹּחָהּ לָךְ נָע וָנָד
and-wandering being-restless to-you crop-of-her to-yield she-will-continue not

תִּהְיֶה בָאָרֶץ׃ וַיֹּאמֶר קַיִן אֶל־יְהוָה גָּדוֹל עֲוֹנִי
punishment-of-me more Yahweh to Cain and-he-said (13) on-the-earth you-will-be

מִנְּשֹׂא׃ הֵן גֵּרַשְׁתָּ אֹתִי הַיּוֹם מֵעַל פְּנֵי הָאֲדָמָה
the-land face-of from-on today me you-drive see! (14) than-to-bear

וּמִפָּנֶיךָ אֶסָּתֵר וְהָיִיתִי נָע
being-restless and-I-will-be I-will-be-hidden and-from-presence-of-you

וָנָד בָּאָרֶץ וְהָיָה כָל־מֹצְאִי יַהַרְגֵנִי׃
he-will-kill-me one-finding-me every-of and-he-will-be on-the-earth and-wandering

וַיֹּאמֶר לוֹ יְהוָה לָכֵן כָּל־הֹרֵג קַיִן שִׁבְעָתַיִם
seven-times Cain killing every-of not-so Yahweh to-him but-he-said (15)

יֻקָּם וַיָּשֶׂם יְהוָה לְקַיִן אוֹת לְבִלְתִּי הַכּוֹת־אֹתוֹ
him to-kill not mark on-Cain Yahweh then-he-put he-will-suffer-vengeance

כָּל־מֹצְאוֹ׃ וַיֵּצֵא קַיִן מִלִּפְנֵי יְהוָה
Yahweh from-presence-of Cain so-he-went-out (16) finding-him every-of

6Then the LORD said to Cain,
"Why are you angry? Why is
your face downcast? 7If you do
what is right, will you not be
accepted? But if you do not do
what is right, sin is crouching
at your door; it desires to have
you, but you must master it."
8Now Cain said to his brother Abel, "Let's go out to the
field."[t] And while they were
in the field, Cain attacked his
brother Abel and killed him.
9Then the LORD said to Cain,
"Where is your brother Abel?"
"I don't know," he replied.
"Am I my brother's keeper?"
10The LORD said, "What have
you done? Listen! Your brother's blood cries out to me from
the ground. 11Now you are under a curse and driven from
the ground, which opened its
mouth to receive your brother's blood from your hand.
12When you work the ground,
it will no longer yield its crops
for you. You will be a restless
wanderer on the earth."
13Cain said to the LORD, "My
punishment is more than I
can bear. 14Today you are driving me from the land, and I
will be hidden from your presence; I will be a restless wanderer on the earth, and whoever finds me will kill me."
15But the LORD said to him,
"Not so[u]; if anyone kills Cain,
he will suffer vengeance seven
times over." Then the LORD
put a mark on Cain so that no
one who found him would kill
him. 16So Cain went out from
the LORD's presence and lived

[t]8 Samaritan Pentateuch, Septuagint, Vulgate and Syriac; Masoretic Text does not have *"Let's go out to the field."*
[u]15 Septuagint, Vulgate and Syriac; Hebrew *Very well*

*8 This Hebrew reading and translation is conjectured on the basis of the early versions listed above in note *t*.

וַיֵּשֶׁב בְּאֶרֶץ־ נוֹד קִדְמַת־ עֵדֶן׃ וַיֵּדַע קַיִן אֶת־ אִשְׁתּוֹ
wife-of-him *** Cain and-he-knew (17) Eden east-of Nod in-land-of and-he-lived

וַתַּהַר וַתֵּלֶד אֶת־ חֲנוֹךְ וַיְהִי בֹּנֶה עִיר
city building and-he-was Enoch *** and-she-bore and-she-became-pregnant

וַיִּקְרָא שֵׁם הָעִיר כְּשֵׁם בְּנוֹ חֲנוֹךְ׃ וַיִּוָּלֵד
and-he-was-born (18) Enoch son-of-him after-name-of the-city name-of and-he-called

לַחֲנוֹךְ אֶת־עִירָד וְעִירָד יָלַד אֶת־ מְחוּיָאֵל וּמְחִיָּיאֵל יָלַד
he-fathered and-Mehujael Mehujael *** he-fathered and-Irad Irad *** to-Enoch

אֶת־ מְתוּשָׁאֵל וּמְתוּשָׁאֵל יָלַד אֶת־ לָמֶךְ׃ וַיִּקַּח־
and-he-married (19) Lamech *** he-fathered and-Methushael Methushael ***

לוֹ לֶמֶךְ שְׁתֵּי נָשִׁים שֵׁם הָאַחַת עָדָה וְשֵׁם הַשֵּׁנִית
the-second and-name-of Adah the-one name-of women two-of Lamech for-him

צִלָּה׃ וַתֵּלֶד עָדָה אֶת־ יָבָל הוּא הָיָה אֲבִי יֹשֵׁב אֹהֶל
tent living-of father-of he-was he Jabal *** Adah and-she-bore (20) Zillah

וּמִקְנֶה׃ וְשֵׁם אָחִיו יוּבָל הוּא הָיָה אֲבִי
father-of he-was he Jubal brother-of-him and-name-of (21) and-livestock-raiser

כָּל־ תֹּפֵשׂ כִּנּוֹר וְעוּגָב׃ וְצִלָּה גַם־הִוא יָלְדָה אֶת־תּוּבַל
Tubal *** she-bore she also and-Zillah (22) and-flute harp playing-of every-of

קַיִן לֹטֵשׁ כָּל־ חֹרֵשׁ נְחֹשֶׁת וּבַרְזֶל וַאֲחוֹת תּוּבַל־ קַיִן
Cain Tubal and-sister-of and-iron bronze tooling-of every-of forging Cain

נַעֲמָה׃ וַיֹּאמֶר לֶמֶךְ לְנָשָׁיו עָדָה וְצִלָּה שְׁמַעַן קוֹלִי
voice-of-me listen! and-Zillah Adah to-wives-of-him Lamech and-he-said (23) Naamah

נְשֵׁי לֶמֶךְ הַאְזֵנָּה אִמְרָתִי כִּי אִישׁ הָרַגְתִּי לְפִצְעִי וְיֶלֶד
and-youth for-wound-of-me I-killed man for word-of-me hear! Lamech wives-of

לְחַבֻּרָתִי׃ כִּי שִׁבְעָתַיִם יֻקַּם־ קָיִן וְלֶמֶךְ שִׁבְעִים
seventy then-Lamech Cain he-is-avenged seven-times if (24) for-injury-of-me

וְשִׁבְעָה׃ וַיֵּדַע אָדָם עוֹד אֶת־ אִשְׁתּוֹ וַתֵּלֶד בֵּן
son and-she-bore wife-of-him *** again Adam and-he-knew (25) and-seven

וַתִּקְרָא אֶת־ שְׁמוֹ שֵׁת כִּי שָׁת־ לִי אֱלֹהִים זֶרַע אַחֵר
another child God to-me he-granted for Seth name-of-him *** and-she-called

תַּחַת הֶבֶל כִּי הֲרָגוֹ קָיִן׃ וּלְשֵׁת גַּם־הוּא יֻלַּד־
he-was-born he also and-to-Seth (26) Cain he-killed-him since Abel in-place-of

בֵּן וַיִּקְרָא אֶת־ שְׁמוֹ אֱנוֹשׁ אָז הוּחַל לִקְרֹא בְּשֵׁם
on-name-of to-call he-began then Enosh name-of-him *** and-he-called son

יְהוָה׃ זֶה סֵפֶר תּוֹלְדֹת אָדָם בְּיוֹם בְּרֹא אֱלֹהִים אָדָם בִּדְמוּת
in-likeness-of man God to-create in-day Adam lines-of account-of this (5:1) Yahweh

אֱלֹהִים עָשָׂה אֹתוֹ׃ זָכָר וּנְקֵבָה בְּרָאָם וַיְבָרֶךְ אֹתָם
them and-he-blessed he-created-them and-female male (2) him he-made God

in the land of Nod,[v] east of
Eden.
17 Cain lay with his wife, and
she became pregnant and
gave birth to Enoch. Cain was
then building a city, and he
named it after his son Enoch.
18 To Enoch was born Irad, and
Irad was the father of Mehujael, and Mehujael was the father of Methushael, and Methushael was the father of Lamech.
19 Lamech married two
women, one named Adah and
the other Zillah.
20 Adah gave
birth to Jabal; he was the father of those who live in tents
and raise livestock.
21 His
brother's name was Jubal; he
was the father of all who play
the harp and flute.
22 Zillah also
had a son, Tubal-Cain, who
forged all kinds of tools out of[w]
bronze and iron. Tubal-Cain's
sister was Naamah.
23 Lamech said to his wives,

"Adah and Zillah, listen to me;
wives of Lamech, hear my words.
I have killed[x] a man for wounding me,
a young man for injuring me.
24 If Cain is avenged seven times,
then Lamech seventy-seven times."

25 Adam lay with his wife
again, and she gave birth to a
son and named him Seth,[y]
saying, "God has granted me
another child in place of Abel,
since Cain killed him."
26 Seth
also had a son, and he named
him Enosh.
At that time men began to
call on[z] the name of the LORD.

*From Adam to Noah*

5 This is the written account
of Adam's line.

When God created man, he
made him in the likeness of
God.
2 He created them male
and female; at the time they
were created, he blessed them

[v] 16 *Nod* means *wandering* (see verses 12 and 14).
[w] 22 Or *who instructed all who work in*
[x] 23 Or *I will kill*
[y] 25 *Seth* probably means *granted.*
[z] 26 Or *to proclaim*

וַיִּקְרָא אֶת־ שְׁמָם אָדָם בְּיוֹם הִבָּרְאָם׃
to-be-created-them in-day man name-of-them *** and-he-called

(3) וַיְחִי אָדָם שְׁלֹשִׁים וּמְאַת שָׁנָה וַיּוֹלֶד
and-he-fathered year and-hundred-of thirty Adam and-he-lived (3)

בִּדְמוּתוֹ כְּצַלְמוֹ וַיִּקְרָא אֶת־ שְׁמוֹ שֵׁת׃
Seth name-of-him *** and-he-called in-image-of-him in-likeness-of-him

(4) וַיִּהְיוּ יְמֵי־ אָדָם אַחֲרֵי הוֹלִידוֹ אֶת־ שֵׁת שְׁמֹנֶה מֵאֹת
hundreds eight Seth *** to-father-him after Adam days-of and-they-were (4)

שָׁנָה וַיּוֹלֶד בָּנִים וּבָנוֹת׃ (5) וַיִּהְיוּ כָּל־ יְמֵי
days-of all-of and-they-were (5) and-daughters sons and-he-fathered year

אָדָם אֲשֶׁר־ חַי תְּשַׁע מֵאוֹת שָׁנָה וּשְׁלֹשִׁים שָׁנָה וַיָּמֹת׃
then-he-died year and-thirty year hundreds nine life which Adam

(6) וַיְחִי־ שֵׁת חָמֵשׁ שָׁנִים וּמְאַת שָׁנָה וַיּוֹלֶד אֶת־
*** and-he-fathered year and-hundred years five Seth and-he-lived (6)

אֱנוֹשׁ׃ (7) וַיְחִי־ שֵׁת אַחֲרֵי הוֹלִידוֹ אֶת־ אֱנוֹשׁ שֶׁבַע שָׁנִים
years seven Enosh *** to-father-him after Seth and-he-lived (7) Enosh

וּשְׁמֹנֶה מֵאוֹת שָׁנָה וַיּוֹלֶד בָּנִים וּבָנוֹת׃
and-daughters sons and-he-fathered year hundreds and-eight

(8) וַיִּהְיוּ כָּל־ יְמֵי־ שֵׁת שְׁתֵּים עֶשְׂרֵה שָׁנָה וּתְשַׁע מֵאוֹת שָׁנָה
year hundreds and-nine year ten two Seth days-of all-of and-they-were (8)

וַיָּמֹת׃ (9) וַיְחִי אֱנוֹשׁ תִּשְׁעִים שָׁנָה וַיּוֹלֶד אֶת־ קֵינָן׃
Kenan *** and-he-fathered year ninety Enosh and-he-lived (9) then-he-died

(10) וַיְחִי אֱנוֹשׁ אַחֲרֵי הוֹלִידוֹ אֶת־ קֵינָן חֲמֵשׁ עֶשְׂרֵה שָׁנָה
year ten five Kenan *** to-father-him after Enosh and-he-lived (10)

וּשְׁמֹנֶה מֵאוֹת שָׁנָה וַיּוֹלֶד בָּנִים וּבָנוֹת׃
and-daughters sons and-he-fathered year hundreds and-eight

(11) וַיִּהְיוּ כָּל־ יְמֵי אֱנוֹשׁ חָמֵשׁ שָׁנִים וּתְשַׁע מֵאוֹת שָׁנָה
year hundreds and-nine years five Enosh days-of all-of and-they-were (11)

וַיָּמֹת׃ (12) וַיְחִי קֵינָן שִׁבְעִים שָׁנָה וַיּוֹלֶד אֶת־
*** and-he-fathered year seventy Kenan and-he-lived (12) then-he-died

מַהֲלַלְאֵל׃ (13) וַיְחִי קֵינָן אַחֲרֵי הוֹלִידוֹ אֶת־מַהֲלַלְאֵל אַרְבָּעִים
forty Mahalalel *** to-father-him after Kenan and-he-lived (13) Mahalalel

שָׁנָה וּשְׁמֹנֶה מֵאוֹת שָׁנָה וַיּוֹלֶד בָּנִים וּבָנוֹת׃
and-daughters sons and-he-fathered year hundreds and-eight year

(14) וַיִּהְיוּ כָּל־ יְמֵי קֵינָן עֶשֶׂר שָׁנִים וּתְשַׁע מֵאוֹת שָׁנָה
year hundreds and-nine years ten Kenan days-of all-of and-they-were (14)

וַיָּמֹת׃ (15) וַיְחִי מַהֲלַלְאֵל חָמֵשׁ שָׁנִים וְשִׁשִּׁים שָׁנָה
year and-sixty years five Mahalalel and-he-lived (15) then-he-died

and called them "man.[a]"
[3]When Adam had lived 130
years, he had a son in his own
likeness, in his own image;
and he named him Seth. [4]Af-
ter Seth was born, Adam lived
800 years and had other sons
and daughters. [5]Altogether,
Adam lived 930 years, and
then he died.
[6]When Seth had lived 105
years, he became the father[b] of
Enosh. [7]And after he became
the father of Enosh, Seth lived
807 years and had other sons
and daughters. [8]Altogether,
Seth lived 912 years, and then
he died.
[9]When Enosh had lived 90
years, he became the father of
Kenan. [10]And after he became
the father of Kenan, Enosh
lived 815 years and had other
sons and daughters. [11]Alto-
gether, Enosh lived 905 years,
and then he died.
[12]When Kenan had lived 70
years, he became the father of
Mahalalel. [13]And after he
became the father of Mahalalel, Kenan lived 840 years and
had other sons and daughters.
[14]Altogether, Kenan lived 910
years, and then he died.
[15]When Mahalalel had lived

[a]2 Hebrew *adam*
[b]6 *Father* may mean *ancestor*; also in verses 7-26.

וַיּ֖וֹלֶד אֶת־ יָ֑רֶד׃ וַֽיְחִ֣י מַֽהֲלַלְאֵ֗ל אַֽחֲרֵי֙ הוֹלִיד֣וֹ
to-father-him after Mahalalel and-he-lived (16) Jared *** and-he-fathered

אֶת־ יֶ֔רֶד שְׁלֹשִׁ֣ים שָׁנָ֔ה וּשְׁמֹנֶ֥ה מֵא֖וֹת שָׁנָ֑ה וַיּ֥וֹלֶד בָּנִ֖ים
sons and-he-fathered year hundreds and-eight year thirty Jared ***

וּבָנֽוֹת׃ וַיִּֽהְיוּ֙ כָּל־ יְמֵ֣י מַֽהֲלַלְאֵ֔ל חָמֵ֤שׁ וְתִשְׁעִים֙
and-ninety five Mahalalel days-of all-of and-they-were (17) and-daughters

שָׁנָ֔ה וּשְׁמֹנֶ֥ה מֵא֖וֹת שָׁנָ֑ה וַיָּמֹֽת׃ וַֽיְחִי־ יֶ֕רֶד שְׁתַּ֧יִם
two Jared and-he-lived (18) and-he-died year hundreds and-eight year

וְשִׁשִּׁ֛ים שָׁנָ֖ה וּמְאַ֣ת שָׁנָ֑ה וַיּ֖וֹלֶד אֶת־ חֲנֽוֹךְ׃ וַֽיְחִי־
and-he-lived (19) Enoch *** and-he-fathered year and-hundred-of year and-sixty

יֶ֗רֶד אַֽחֲרֵי֙ הוֹלִיד֣וֹ אֶת־ חֲנ֔וֹךְ שְׁמֹנֶ֥ה מֵא֖וֹת שָׁנָ֑ה וַיּ֥וֹלֶד בָּנִ֖ים
sons and-he-fathered year hundreds eight Enoch *** to-father-him after Jared

וּבָנֽוֹת׃ וַיִּֽהְיוּ֙ כָּל־ יְמֵי־ יֶ֔רֶד שְׁתַּ֤יִם וְשִׁשִּׁים֙ שָׁנָ֔ה
year and-sixty two Jared days-of all-of and-they-were (20) and-daughters

וּתְשַׁ֥ע מֵא֖וֹת שָׁנָ֑ה וַיָּמֹֽת׃ וַֽיְחִ֣י חֲנ֔וֹךְ חָמֵ֥שׁ וְשִׁשִּׁ֖ים
and-sixty five Enoch and-he-lived (21) then-he-died year hundreds and-nine

שָׁנָ֑ה וַיּ֖וֹלֶד אֶת־ מְתוּשָֽׁלַח׃ וַיִּתְהַלֵּ֨ךְ חֲנ֜וֹךְ אֶת־הָֽאֱלֹהִ֗ים אַֽחֲרֵי֙
after the-God with Enoch and-he-walked (22) Methuselah *** and-he-fathered year

הוֹלִיד֣וֹ אֶת־ מְתוּשֶׁ֔לַח שְׁלֹ֥שׁ מֵא֖וֹת שָׁנָ֑ה וַיּ֥וֹלֶד בָּנִ֖ים
sons and-he-fathered year hundreds three Methuselah *** to-father-him

וּבָנֽוֹת׃ וַיְהִ֖י כָּל־ יְמֵ֣י חֲנ֑וֹךְ חָמֵ֤שׁ וְשִׁשִּׁים֙ שָׁנָ֔ה
year and-sixty five Enoch days-of all-of and-he-was (23) and-daughters

וּשְׁלֹ֥שׁ מֵא֖וֹת שָׁנָֽה׃ וַיִּתְהַלֵּ֥ךְ חֲנ֖וֹךְ אֶת־הָֽאֱלֹהִ֑ים וְאֵינֶ֕נּוּ
then-he-was-not the-God with Enoch and-he-walked (24) year hundreds and-three

כִּֽי־ לָקַ֥ח אֹת֖וֹ אֱלֹהִֽים׃ וַֽיְחִ֣י מְתוּשֶׁ֔לַח שֶׁ֧בַע וּשְׁמֹנִ֛ים שָׁנָ֖ה
year and-eighty seven Methuselah and-he-lived (25) God him he-took because

וּמְאַ֣ת שָׁנָ֑ה וַיּ֖וֹלֶד אֶת־ לָֽמֶךְ׃ וַֽיְחִ֣י מְתוּשֶׁ֗לַח
Methuselah and-he-lived (26) Lamech *** and-he-fathered year and-hundred-of

אַֽחֲרֵי֙ הוֹלִיד֣וֹ אֶת־ לֶ֔מֶךְ שְׁתַּ֤יִם וּשְׁמוֹנִים֙ שָׁנָ֔ה וּשְׁבַ֥ע מֵא֖וֹת שָׁנָ֑ה
year hundreds and-seven year and-eighty two Lamech *** to-father-him after

וַיּ֥וֹלֶד בָּנִ֖ים וּבָנֽוֹת׃ וַיִּֽהְיוּ֙ כָּל־ יְמֵ֣י
days-of all-of and-they-were (27) and-daughters sons and-he-fathered

מְתוּשֶׁ֔לַח תֵּ֤שַׁע וְשִׁשִּׁים֙ שָׁנָ֔ה וּתְשַׁ֥ע מֵא֖וֹת שָׁנָ֑ה וַיָּמֹֽת׃
then-he-died year hundreds and-nine year and-sixty nine Methuselah

וַֽיְחִי־ לֶ֕מֶךְ שְׁתַּ֧יִם וּשְׁמֹנִ֛ים שָׁנָ֖ה וּמְאַ֣ת שָׁנָ֑ה וַיּ֖וֹלֶד
and-he-fathered year and-hundred-of year and-eighty two Lamech and-he-lived (28)

בֵּֽן׃ וַיִּקְרָ֧א אֶת־ שְׁמ֛וֹ נֹ֖חַ לֵאמֹ֑ר זֶ֞ה יְנַחֲמֵ֤נוּ
he-will-comfort-us this to-say Noah name-of-him *** and-he-called (29) son

65 years, he became the father
of Jared. 16 And after he became
the father of Jared, Mahalalel
lived 830 years and had other
sons and daughters. 17 Altogether, Mahalalel lived 895
years, and then he died.
18 When Jared had lived 162
years, he became the father of
Enoch. 19 And after he became
the father of Enoch, Jared
lived 800 years and had other
sons and daughters. 20 Altogether, Jared lived 962 years,
and then he died.
21 When Enoch had lived 65
years, he became the father of
Methuselah. 22 And after he
became the father of Me-
thuselah, Enoch walked with
God 300 years and had other
sons and daughters. 23 Altogether, Enoch lived 365 years.
24 Enoch walked with God;
then he was no more, because
God took him away.
25 When Methuselah had
lived 187 years, he became the
father of Lamech. 26 And after
he became the father of Lamech, Methuselah lived 782
years and had other sons and
daughters. 27 Altogether, Methuselah lived 969 years, and
then he died.
28 When Lamech had lived
182 years, he had a son. 29 He
named him Noah[c] and said,

[c]29 *Noah* sounds like the Hebrew for *comfort.*

מִמַּעֲשֵׂנוּ וּמֵעִצְּבוֹן יָדֵינוּ מִן־ הָאֲדָמָה אֲשֶׁר אֵרְרָהּ
he-cursed-her which the-ground from hands-of-us and-in-toil-of in-labors-of-us

יְהוָה׃ וַיְחִי־ לֶמֶךְ אַחֲרֵי הוֹלִידוֹ אֶת־ נֹחַ חָמֵשׁ וְתִשְׁעִים
and-ninety five Noah *** to-father-him after Lamech and-he-lived (30) Yahweh

שָׁנָה וַחֲמֵשׁ מֵאֹת שָׁנָה וַיּוֹלֶד בָּנִים וּבָנוֹת׃ וַיְהִי
and-he-was (31) and-daughters sons and-he-fathered year hundreds and-five year

כָּל־ יְמֵי־ לֶמֶךְ שֶׁבַע וְשִׁבְעִים שָׁנָה וּשְׁבַע מֵאוֹת שָׁנָה
year hundreds and-seven year and-seventy seven Lamech days-of all-of

וַיָּמֹת׃ וַיְהִי־ נֹחַ בֶּן־ חֲמֵשׁ מֵאוֹת שָׁנָה וַיּוֹלֶד
and-he-fathered year hundreds five son-of Noah and-he-was (32) then-he-died

נֹחַ אֶת־ שֵׁם אֶת־ חָם וְאֶת־ יָפֶת׃ וַיְהִי כִּי־ הֵחֵל הָאָדָם
the-man he-began when and-he-was (6:1) Japheth and Ham *** Shem *** Noah

לָרֹב עַל־ פְּנֵי הָאֲדָמָה וּבָנוֹת יֻלְּדוּ לָהֶם׃
to-them they-were-born and-daughters the-earth face-of on to-increase

וַיִּרְאוּ בְנֵי־ הָאֱלֹהִים אֶת־ בְּנוֹת הָאָדָם כִּי טֹבֹת
beautiful-ones that the-man daughters-of *** the-God sons-of and-they-saw (2)

הֵנָּה וַיִּקְחוּ לָהֶם נָשִׁים מִכֹּל אֲשֶׁר בָּחָרוּ׃ וַיֹּאמֶר
then-he-said (3) they-chose whom from-any wives for-them and-they-took they

יְהוָה לֹא־ יָדוֹן רוּחִי בָאָדָם לְעֹלָם בְּשַׁגַּם הוּא
he for-indeed for-ever with-the-man spirit-of-me he-will-contend not Yahweh

בָשָׂר וְהָיוּ יָמָיו מֵאָה וְעֶשְׂרִים שָׁנָה׃ הַנְּפִלִים
the-Nephilim (4) year and-twenty hundred days-of-him and-they-will-be mortal

הָיוּ בָאָרֶץ בַּיָּמִים הָהֵם וְגַם אַחֲרֵי־ כֵן אֲשֶׁר
when then after and-also the-those in-the-days on-the-earth they-were

יָבֹאוּ בְּנֵי הָאֱלֹהִים אֶל־ בְּנוֹת הָאָדָם וְיָלְדוּ לָהֶם הֵמָּה
they to-them and-they-bore the-man daughters-of to the-God sons-of they-went

הַגִּבֹּרִים אֲשֶׁר מֵעוֹלָם אַנְשֵׁי הַשֵּׁם׃ וַיַּרְא יְהוָה כִּי רַבָּה
great how Yahweh and-he-saw (5) the-name men-of of-old which the-heroes

רָעַת הָאָדָם בָּאָרֶץ וְכָל־ יֵצֶר מַחְשְׁבֹת
thoughts-of inclination-of and-every-of on-the-earth the-man wickedness-of

לִבּוֹ רַק רַע כָּל־ הַיּוֹם׃ וַיִּנָּחֶם יְהוָה כִּי־
that Yahweh and-he-was-grieved (6) the-day all-of evil only heart-of-him

עָשָׂה אֶת־ הָאָדָם בָּאָרֶץ וַיִּתְעַצֵּב אֶל־ לִבּוֹ׃ וַיֹּאמֶר
so-he-said (7) heart-of-him to and-he-hurt on-the-earth the-man *** he-made

יְהוָה אֶמְחֶה אֶת־ הָאָדָם אֲשֶׁר־ בָּרָאתִי מֵעַל פְּנֵי הָאֲדָמָה
the-earth face-of from-on I-created whom the-man *** I-will-wipe-away Yahweh

מֵאָדָם עַד־ בְּהֵמָה עַד־ רֶמֶשׂ וְעַד־ עוֹף הַשָּׁמַיִם כִּי נִחַמְתִּי כִּי
that I-am-grieved for the-air bird-of and-to crawler to animal to from-man

"He will comfort us in the labor and painful toil of our hands caused by the ground the LORD has cursed." [30]After Noah was born, Lamech lived 595 years and had other sons and daughters. [31]Altogether, Lamech lived 777 years, and then he died.

[32]After Noah was 500 years old, he became the father of Shem, Ham and Japheth.

*The Flood*

6 When men began to increase in number on the earth and daughters were born to them, [2]the sons of God saw that the daughters of men were beautiful, and they married any of them they chose. [3]Then the LORD said, "My Spirit will not contend with[d] man forever, for he is mortal; his days will be a hundred and twenty years."

[4]The Nephilim were on the earth in those days—and also afterward—when the sons of God went to the daughters of men and had children by them. They were the heroes of old, men of renown.

[5]The LORD saw how great man's wickedness on the earth had become, and that every inclination of the thoughts of his heart was only evil all the time. [6]The LORD was grieved that he had made man on the earth, and his heart was filled with pain. [7]So the LORD said, "I will wipe mankind, whom I have created, from the face of the earth—men and animals, and creatures that move along the ground, and birds of the air—for I am grieved that I have

[d]3 Or *My spirit will not remain in*

עֲשִׂיתִֽם׃ וְנֹחַ מָצָא חֵן בְּעֵינֵי יְהוָה׃ אֵלֶּה תּוֹלְדֹת
lines-of these (9) Yahweh in-eyes-of favor he-found but-Noah (8) I-made-them

נֹחַ נֹחַ אִישׁ צַדִּיק תָּמִים הָיָה בְּדֹרֹתָיו אֶת־הָאֱלֹהִים
the-God with in-contemporaries-of-him he-was blameless righteous man Noah Noah

הִֽתְהַלֶּךְ־ נֹחַ׃ וַיּוֹלֶד נֹחַ שְׁלֹשָׁה בָנִים אֶת־ שֵׁם אֶת־ חָם וְאֶת־
and Ham *** Shem *** sons three Noah and-he-fathered (10) Noah he-walked

יָפֶת׃ וַתִּשָּׁחֵת הָאָרֶץ לִפְנֵי הָאֱלֹהִים וַתִּמָּלֵא
and-she-was-full the-God in-face-of the-earth now-she-was-corrupt (11) Japheth

הָאָרֶץ חָמָס׃ וַיַּרְא אֱלֹהִים אֶת־ הָאָרֶץ וְהִנֵּה נִשְׁחָתָה
she-was-corrupt and-see! the-earth *** God and-he-saw (12) violence the-earth

כִּֽי־ הִשְׁחִית כָּל־ בָּשָׂר אֶת־ דַּרְכּוֹ עַל־ הָאָרֶץ׃ וַיֹּאמֶר
so-he-said (13) the-earth on way-of-him *** person every-of he-corrupted for

אֱלֹהִים לְנֹחַ קֵץ כָּל־ בָּשָׂר בָּא לְפָנַי כִּֽי־ מָלְאָה
she-is-filled for before-me coming person every-of end-of to-Noah God

הָאָרֶץ חָמָס מִפְּנֵיהֶם וְהִנְנִי מַשְׁחִיתָם אֶת־ הָאָרֶץ׃
the-earth with destroying-them so-now-I from-face-of-them violence the-earth

עֲשֵׂה לְךָ תֵּבַת עֲצֵי־ גֹפֶר קִנִּים תַּעֲשֶׂה אֶת־הַתֵּבָה
the-ark *** you-make rooms cypress woods-of ark-of for-you make! (14)

וְכָפַרְתָּ אֹתָהּ מִבַּיִת וּמִחוּץ בַּכֹּפֶר׃ וְזֶה אֲשֶׁר תַּעֲשֶׂה
you-build how and-this (15) with-the-pitch and-outside on-inside her and-you-coat

אֹתָהּ שְׁלֹשׁ מֵאוֹת אַמָּה אֹרֶךְ הַתֵּבָה חֲמִשִּׁים אַמָּה רָחְבָּהּ
width-of-her cubit fifty the-ark length-of cubit hundreds three-of her

וּשְׁלֹשִׁים אַמָּה קוֹמָתָהּ׃ צֹהַר ׀ תַּעֲשֶׂה לַתֵּבָה וְאֶל־ אַמָּה
cubit and-to for-the-ark you-make roof (16) height-of-her cubit and-thirty

תְּכַלֶּנָּה* מִלְמַעְלָה וּפֶתַח הַתֵּבָה בְּצִדָּהּ תָּשִׂים
you-put in-side-of-her the-ark and-door-of from-above you-finish-her

תַּחְתִּיִּם שְׁנִיִּם וּשְׁלִשִׁים תַּעֲשֶׂהָ׃ וַאֲנִי הִנְנִי מֵבִיא
bringing now-I and-I (17) you-make and-third-ones second-ones lower-ones

אֶת־ הַמַּבּוּל מַיִם עַל־ הָאָרֶץ לְשַׁחֵת כָּל־ בָּשָׂר אֲשֶׁר־
that creature every-of to-destroy the-earth on waters the-flood-of ***

בּוֹ רוּחַ חַיִּים מִתַּחַת הַשָּׁמָיִם כֹּל אֲשֶׁר־ בָּאָרֶץ
on-the-earth that everything the-heavens from-under life breath-of in-him

יִגְוָע׃ וַהֲקִמֹתִי אֶת־ בְּרִיתִי אִתָּךְ
with-you covenant-of-me *** but-I-will-establish (18) he-will-perish

וּבָאתָ אֶל־הַתֵּבָה אַתָּה וּבָנֶיךָ וְאִשְׁתְּךָ וּנְשֵׁי־
and-wives-of and-wife-of-you and-sons-of-you you the-ark to and-you-will-enter

בָנֶיךָ אִתָּךְ׃ וּמִכָּל־ הָחַי מִכָּל־ בָּשָׂר
creature from-every-of the-living and-from-all-of (19) with-you sons-of-you

made them." [8]But Noah found favor in the eyes of the LORD.

[9]This is the account of Noah.

Noah was a righteous man, blameless among the people of his time, and he walked with God. [10]Noah had three sons: Shem, Ham and Japheth.

[11]Now the earth was corrupt in God's sight and was full of violence. [12]God saw how corrupt the earth had become, for all the people on earth had corrupted their ways. [13]So God said to Noah, "I am going to put an end to all people, for the earth is filled with violence because of them. I am surely going to destroy both them and the earth. [14]So make yourself an ark of cypress[e] wood; make rooms in it and coat it with pitch inside and out. [15]This is how you are to build it: The ark is to be 450 feet long, 75 feet wide and 45 feet high.[f] [16]Make a roof for it and finish[g] the ark to within 18 inches[h] of the top. Put a door in the side of the ark and make lower, middle and upper decks. [17]I am going to bring floodwaters on the earth to destroy all life under the heavens, every creature that has the breath of life in it. Everything on earth will perish. [18]But I will establish my covenant with you, and you will enter the ark—you and your sons and your wife and your sons' wives with you. [19]You

[e]14 The meaning of the Hebrew for this word is uncertain.
[f]15 Hebrew *300 cubits long, 50 cubits wide and 30 cubits high* (about 140 meters long, 23 meters wide and 13.5 meters high)
[g]16 Or *Make an opening for light by finishing*
[h]16 Hebrew *a cubit* (about 0.5 meter)

*16 Most mss have *dagesh* in the *lamed* (לּ–).

שְׁנַיִם מִכֹּל תָּבִיא אֶל־הַתֵּבָה לְהַחֲיֹת אִתָּךְ זָכָר וּנְקֵבָה
and-female male with-you to-keep-alive the-ark to you-shall-bring from-all two

יִהְיוּ׃ מֵהָעוֹף לְמִינֵהוּ וּמִן־הַבְּהֵמָה לְמִינָהּ
to-kind-of-her the-animal and-from to-kind-of-him from-the-bird (20) they-shall-be

מִכֹּל רֶמֶשׂ הָאֲדָמָה לְמִינֵהוּ שְׁנַיִם מִכֹּל יָבֹאוּ
they-will-come from-all two to-kind-of-him the-ground crawler-of from-every-of

אֵלֶיךָ לְהַחֲיוֹת׃ וְאַתָּה קַח־לְךָ מִכָּל־מַאֲכָל אֲשֶׁר
that food from-every-of for-you take! and-you (21) to-keep-alive to-you

יֵאָכֵל וְאָסַפְתָּ אֵלֶיךָ וְהָיָה לְךָ וְלָהֶם לְאָכְלָה׃
as-food and-for-them for-you and-he-is for-you and-you-store he-is-eaten

וַיַּעַשׂ נֹחַ כְּכֹל אֲשֶׁר צִוָּה אֹתוֹ אֱלֹהִים כֵּן עָשָׂה׃
he-did so God him he-commanded that as-all Noah so-he-did (22)

וַיֹּאמֶר יְהוָה לְנֹחַ בֹּא־אַתָּה וְכָל־בֵּיתְךָ אֶל־הַתֵּבָה
the-ark into family-of-you and-whole-of you go! to-Noah Yahweh then-he-said (7:1)

כִּי־אֹתְךָ רָאִיתִי צַדִּיק לְפָנַי בַּדּוֹר הַזֶּה׃ מִכֹּל ׀
from-every-of (2) the-this in-the-generation before-me righteous I-found you for

הַבְּהֵמָה הַטְּהוֹרָה תִּקַּח־לְךָ שִׁבְעָה שִׁבְעָה אִישׁ וְאִשְׁתּוֹ
and-mate-of-him male seven seven with-you you-take the-clean the-animal

וּמִן־הַבְּהֵמָה אֲשֶׁר לֹא טְהֹרָה הִוא שְׁנַיִם אִישׁ וְאִשְׁתּוֹ׃ גַּם
also (3) and-mate-of-him male two she clean not that the-animal and-from

מֵעוֹף הַשָּׁמַיִם שִׁבְעָה שִׁבְעָה זָכָר וּנְקֵבָה לְחַיּוֹת זֶרַע עַל־
on kind to-keep-alive and-female male seven seven the-air from-bird-of

פְּנֵי כָל־הָאָרֶץ׃ כִּי לְיָמִים עוֹד שִׁבְעָה אָנֹכִי מַמְטִיר עַל־
on sending-rain I seven from-now to-days for (4) the-earth all-of face-of

הָאָרֶץ אַרְבָּעִים יוֹם וְאַרְבָּעִים לָיְלָה וּמָחִיתִי אֶת־כָּל־
every-of *** and-I-will-wipe-away night and-forty day forty the-earth

הַיְקוּם אֲשֶׁר עָשִׂיתִי מֵעַל פְּנֵי הָאֲדָמָה׃ וַיַּעַשׂ נֹחַ כְּכֹל
as-all Noah and-he-did (5) the-earth face-of from-on I-made that creature

אֲשֶׁר־צִוָּהוּ יְהוָה׃ וְנֹחַ בֶּן־שֵׁשׁ מֵאוֹת שָׁנָה
year hundreds six son-of and-Noah (6) Yahweh he-commanded-him that

וְהַמַּבּוּל הָיָה מַיִם עַל־הָאָרֶץ׃ וַיָּבֹא נֹחַ
Noah and-he-entered (7) the-earth on waters he-was and-the-flood

וּבָנָיו וְאִשְׁתּוֹ וּנְשֵׁי־בָנָיו אִתּוֹ אֶל־
into with-him sons-of-him and-wives-of and-wife-of-him and-sons-of-him

הַתֵּבָה מִפְּנֵי מֵי הַמַּבּוּל׃ מִן־הַבְּהֵמָה הַטְּהוֹרָה
the-clean the-animal from (8) the-flood waters-of from-face-of the-ark

וּמִן־הַבְּהֵמָה אֲשֶׁר אֵינֶנָּה טְהֹרָה וּמִן־הָעוֹף וְכֹל אֲשֶׁר־
that and-all the-bird and-from clean she-is-not that the-animal and-from

are to bring into the ark two of all living creatures, male and female, to keep them alive with you. [20]Two of every kind of bird, of every kind of animal and of every kind of creature that moves along the ground will come to you to be kept alive. [21]You are to take every kind of food that is to be eaten and store it away as food for you and for them."

[22]Noah did everything just as God commanded him.

7 The LORD then said to Noah, "Go into the ark, you and your whole family, because I have found you righteous in this generation. [2]Take with you seven[i] of every kind of clean animal, a male and its mate, and two of every kind of unclean animal, a male and its mate, [3]and also seven of every kind of bird, male and female, to keep their various kinds alive throughout the earth. [4]Seven days from now I will send rain on the earth for forty days and forty nights, and I will wipe from the face of the earth every living creature I have made."

[5]And Noah did all that the LORD commanded him.

[6]Noah was six hundred years old when the floodwaters came on the earth. [7]And Noah and his sons and his wife and his sons' wives entered the ark to escape the waters of the flood. [8]Pairs of clean and unclean animals, of birds and of all creatures that move

[i]2 Or *seven pairs*; also in verse 3

רֹמֵשׂ עַל־ הָאֲדָמָה׃ שְׁנַיִם שְׁנַיִם בָּאוּ אֶל־ נֹחַ אֶל־הַתֵּבָה זָכָר
male the-ark to Noah to they-came pair pair (9) the-ground on moving

וּנְקֵבָה כַּאֲשֶׁר צִוָּה אֱלֹהִים אֶת־ נֹחַ׃ וַיְהִי לְשִׁבְעַת
after-seven-of and-he-was (10) Noah *** God he-commanded just-as and-female

הַיָּמִים וּמֵי הַמַּבּוּל הָיוּ עַל־ הָאָרֶץ׃ בִּשְׁנַת
in-year-of (11) the-earth on they-came the-flood and-waters-of the-days

שֵׁשׁ־ מֵאוֹת שָׁנָה לְחַיֵּי־ נֹחַ בַּחֹדֶשׁ הַשֵּׁנִי בְּשִׁבְעָה־עָשָׂר יוֹם
day ten on-seven the-second in-the-month Noah to-life-of year hundreds six

לַחֹדֶשׁ בַּיּוֹם הַזֶּה נִבְקְעוּ כָּל־ מַעְיְנֹת תְּהוֹם רַבָּה
great deep springs-of all-of they-burst the-that on-the-day to-the-month

וַאֲרֻבֹּת הַשָּׁמַיִם נִפְתָּחוּ׃ וַיְהִי הַגֶּשֶׁם עַל־
on the-rain and-he-fell (12) they-were-opened the-heavens and-floodgates-of

הָאָרֶץ אַרְבָּעִים יוֹם וְאַרְבָּעִים לָיְלָה׃ בְּעֶצֶם הַיּוֹם הַזֶּה
the-that the-day on-very-of (13) night and-forty day forty the-earth

בָּא נֹחַ וְשֵׁם־ וְחָם וָיֶפֶת בְּנֵי־ נֹחַ וְאֵשֶׁת נֹחַ
Noah and-wife-of Noah sons-of and-Japheth and-Ham and-Shem Noah he-entered

וּשְׁלֹשֶׁת נְשֵׁי־ בָנָיו אִתָּם אֶל־ הַתֵּבָה׃ הֵמָּה
they (14) the-ark into with-them sons-of-him wives-of and-three-of

וְכָל־ הַחַיָּה לְמִינָהּ וְכָל־ הַבְּהֵמָה
the-livestock and-every-of to-kind-of-her the-animal and-every-of

לְמִינָהּ וְכָל־ הָרֶמֶשׂ הָרֹמֵשׂ עַל־ הָאָרֶץ
the-ground on the-one-crawling the-crawler and-every-of to-kind-of-her

לְמִינֵהוּ וְכָל־ הָעוֹף לְמִינֵהוּ כֹּל צִפּוֹר כָּל־ כָּנָף׃
wing every-of bird every-of to-kind-of-him the-bird and-every-of to-kind-of-him

וַיָּבֹאוּ אֶל־ נֹחַ אֶל־ הַתֵּבָה שְׁנַיִם שְׁנַיִם מִכָּל־ הַבָּשָׂר
the-creature from-every-of pair pair the-ark into Noah to and-they-came (15)

אֲשֶׁר־ בּוֹ רוּחַ חַיִּים׃ וְהַבָּאִים זָכָר וּנְקֵבָה
and-female male and-the-ones-going-in (16) life breath-of in-him that

מִכָּל־ בָּשָׂר בָּאוּ כַּאֲשֶׁר צִוָּה אֹתוֹ אֱלֹהִים וַיִּסְגֹּר
then-he-shut-in God him he-commanded just-as they-came creature from-every-of

יְהוָה בַּעֲדוֹ׃ וַיְהִי הַמַּבּוּל אַרְבָּעִים יוֹם עַל־ הָאָרֶץ
the-earth on day forty the-flood and-he-came (17) after-him Yahweh

וַיִּרְבּוּ הַמַּיִם וַיִּשְׂאוּ אֶת־ הַתֵּבָה וַתָּרָם
and-she-rose the-ark *** and-they-lifted the-waters and-they-increased

מֵעַל הָאָרֶץ׃ וַיִּגְבְּרוּ הַמַּיִם וַיִּרְבּוּ מְאֹד
greatly and-they-increased the-waters and-they-rose (18) the-earth from-on

עַל־ הָאָרֶץ וַתֵּלֶךְ הַתֵּבָה עַל־ פְּנֵי הַמָּיִם׃
the-waters surface-of on the-ark and-she-floated the-earth on

along the ground, 9male and
female, came to Noah and entered the ark, as God had commanded Noah. 10And after the
seven days the floodwaters
came on the earth.

11In the six hundredth year
of Noah's life, on the seventeenth day of the second
month—on that day all the
springs of the great deep burst
forth, and the floodgates of the
heavens were opened. 12And
rain fell on the earth forty
days and forty nights.

13On that very day Noah and
his sons, Shem, Ham and
Japheth, together with his
wife and the wives of his three
sons, entered the ark. 14They
had with them every wild animal according to its kind, all
livestock according to their
kinds, every creature that
moves along the ground according to its kind and every
bird according to its kind,
everything with wings. 15Pairs
of all creatures that have the
breath of life in them came to
Noah and entered the ark.
16The animals going in were
male and female of every living thing, as God had commanded Noah. Then the LORD
shut him in.

17For forty days the flood
kept coming on the earth, and
as the waters increased they
lifted the ark high above the
earth. 18The waters rose and
increased greatly on the earth,
and the ark floated on the surface of the water. 19They rose

וְהַמַּיִם גָּבְרוּ מְאֹד מְאֹד עַל־הָאָרֶץ וַיְכֻסּוּ
and-they-were-covered the-earth on greatly greatly they-rose and-the-waters (19)

כָּל־הֶהָרִים הַגְּבֹהִים אֲשֶׁר־תַּחַת כָּל־הַשָּׁמָיִם׃
the-heavens entire-of under that the-high-ones the-mountains all-of

חֲמֵשׁ עֶשְׂרֵה אַמָּה מִלְמַעְלָה גָּבְרוּ הַמָּיִם וַיְכֻסּוּ
and-they-were-covered the-waters they-rose from-above cubit ten five (20)

הֶהָרִים׃ וַיִּגְוַע כָּל־בָּשָׂר ׀ הָרֹמֵשׂ עַל־
on the-one-crawling creature every-of and-he-perished (21) the-mountains

הָאָרֶץ בָּעוֹף וּבַבְּהֵמָה וּבַחַיָּה
and-with-the-animal and-with-the-livestock with-the-bird the-earth

וּבְכָל־הַשֶּׁרֶץ הַשֹּׁרֵץ עַל־הָאָרֶץ וְכֹל
and-every-of the-earth on the-one-swarming the-swarmer and-with-every-of

הָאָדָם׃ כֹּל אֲשֶׁר נִשְׁמַת־רוּחַ חַיִּים בְּאַפָּיו
in-nostrils-of-him life spirit-of breath-of that everything (22) the-mankind

מִכֹּל אֲשֶׁר בֶּחָרָבָה מֵתוּ׃ וַיִּמַח אֶת־כָּל־
every-of *** and-he-was-wiped-out (23) they-died on-the-dry-land that from-everything

הַיְקוּם ׀ אֲשֶׁר ׀ עַל־פְּנֵי הָאֲדָמָה מֵאָדָם עַד־בְּהֵמָה עַד־רֶמֶשׂ וְעַד־
and-to crawler to animal to from-man the-earth face-of on that the-living

עוֹף הַשָּׁמַיִם וַיִּמָּחוּ מִן־הָאָרֶץ וַיִּשָּׁאֶר* אַךְ־
only and-he-was-left the-earth from and-they-were-wiped-out the-air bird-of

נֹחַ וַאֲשֶׁר אִתּוֹ בַּתֵּבָה׃ וַיִּגְבְּרוּ הַמַּיִם עַל־
over the-waters and-they-flooded (24) in-the-ark with-him and-whom Noah

הָאָרֶץ חֲמִשִּׁים וּמְאַת יוֹם׃ וַיִּזְכֹּר אֱלֹהִים אֶת־נֹחַ וְאֵת
and Noah *** God but-he-remembered (8:1) day and-hundred-of fifty the-earth

כָּל־הַחַיָּה וְאֶת־כָּל־הַבְּהֵמָה אֲשֶׁר אִתּוֹ בַּתֵּבָה
on-the-ark with-him that the-livestock every-of and the-animal every-of

וַיַּעֲבֵר אֱלֹהִים רוּחַ עַל־הָאָרֶץ וַיָּשֹׁכּוּ הַמָּיִם׃
the-waters and-they-receded the-earth over wind God and-he-sent

וַיִּסָּכְרוּ מַעְיְנֹת תְּהוֹם וַאֲרֻבֹּת הַשָּׁמָיִם
the-heavens and-floodgates-of deep springs-of and-they-were-closed (2)

וַיִּכָּלֵא הַגֶּשֶׁם מִן־הַשָּׁמָיִם׃ וַיָּשֻׁבוּ הַמַּיִם
the-waters and-they-receded (3) the-sky from the-rain and-he-stopped

מֵעַל הָאָרֶץ הָלוֹךְ וָשׁוֹב וַיַּחְסְרוּ הַמַּיִם
the-waters and-they-went-down and-to-recede to-continue the-earth from-on

מִקְצֵה חֲמִשִּׁים וּמְאַת יוֹם׃ וַתָּנַח הַתֵּבָה בַּחֹדֶשׁ
on-the-month the-ark and-she-rested (4) day and-hundred-of fifty at-end-of

הַשְּׁבִיעִי בְּשִׁבְעָה־עָשָׂר יוֹם לַחֹדֶשׁ עַל הָרֵי אֲרָרָט׃
Ararat mountains-of on to-the-month day ten in-seven the-seventh

greatly on the earth, and all
the high mountains under the
entire heavens were covered.
[20]The waters rose and covered
the mountains to a depth of
more than twenty feet.[j, k]
[21]Every living thing that
moved on the earth perished—
birds, livestock, wild animals,
all the creatures that swarm
over the earth, and all mankind. [22]Everything on dry land
that had the breath of life in its
nostrils died. [23]Every living
thing on the face of the earth
was wiped out; men and animals and the creatures that
move along the ground and
the birds of the air were wiped
from the earth. Only Noah
was left, and those with him
in the ark.

[24]The waters flooded the
earth for a hundred and fifty
days.

8 But God remembered
Noah and all the wild animals and the livestock that
were with him in the ark, and
he sent a wind over the earth
and the waters receded. [2]Now
the springs of the deep and the
floodgates of the heavens had
been closed, and the rain had
stopped falling from the sky.
[3]The water receded steadily
from the earth. At the end of
the hundred and fifty days the
water had gone down, [4]and on
the seventeenth day of the
seventh month the ark came
to rest on the mountains of

j20 Hebrew *fifteen cubits* (about 6.9 meters)
k20 Or *rose more than twenty feet, and the mountains were covered*

*23 Most mss have *dagesh* in the *yod* (וַיִּ).

וְהַמַּיִם הָיוּ הָלוֹךְ וְחָסוֹר עַד הַחֹדֶשׁ
the-month until and-to-recede to-continue they-were and-the-waters (5)

הָעֲשִׂירִי בָּעֲשִׂירִי בְּאֶחָד לַחֹדֶשׁ נִרְאוּ רָאשֵׁי
tops-of they-became-visible to-the-month on-first on-the-tenth the-tenth

הֶהָרִים׃ וַיְהִי מִקֵּץ אַרְבָּעִים יוֹם וַיִּפְתַּח נֹחַ אֶת־
*** Noah and-he-opened day forty at-end-of and-he-was (6) the-mountains

חַלּוֹן הַתֵּבָה אֲשֶׁר עָשָׂה׃ וַיְשַׁלַּח אֶת־ הָעֹרֵב וַיֵּצֵא
and-he-went the-raven *** then-he-sent (7) he-made that the-ark window-of

יָצוֹא וָשׁוֹב עַד־ יְבֹשֶׁת הַמַּיִם מֵעַל הָאָרֶץ׃
the-earth from-on the-waters to-dry until and-to-return to-go-out

וַיְשַׁלַּח אֶת־ הַיּוֹנָה מֵאִתּוֹ לִרְאוֹת הֲקַלּוּ הַמַּיִם
the-waters they-receded? to-see from-with-him the-dove *** then-he-sent (8)

מֵעַל פְּנֵי הָאֲדָמָה׃ וְלֹא־ מָצְאָה הַיּוֹנָה מָנוֹחַ
place the-dove she-found but-not (9) the-ground surface-of from-on

לְכַף־ רַגְלָהּ וַתָּשָׁב אֵלָיו אֶל־ הַתֵּבָה כִּי־ מַיִם עַל־
over waters for the-ark to to-him so-she-returned foot-of-her for-sole-of

פְּנֵי כָל־ הָאָרֶץ וַיִּשְׁלַח יָדוֹ וַיִּקָּחֶהָ
and-he-took-her hand-of-him and-he-reached the-earth all-of surface-of

וַיָּבֵא אֹתָהּ אֵלָיו אֶל־ הַתֵּבָה׃ וַיָּחֶל עוֹד שִׁבְעַת
seven-of yet and-he-waited (10) the-ark to to-him her and-he-brought

יָמִים אֲחֵרִים וַיֹּסֶף שַׁלַּח אֶת־ הַיּוֹנָה מִן־ הַתֵּבָה׃
the-ark from the-dove *** to-send and-he-repeated more-ones days

וַתָּבֹא אֵלָיו הַיּוֹנָה לְעֵת עֶרֶב וְהִנֵּה עֲלֵה־
leaf-of and-see! evening in-time-of the-dove to-him when-she-returned (11)

זַיִת טָרָף בְּפִיהָ וַיֵּדַע נֹחַ כִּי־ קַלּוּ
they-receded that Noah then-he-knew in-beak-of-her freshly-plucked olive

הַמַּיִם מֵעַל הָאָרֶץ׃ וַיִּיָּחֶל עוֹד שִׁבְעַת יָמִים אֲחֵרִים
more-ones days seven-of yet and-he-waited (12) the-earth from-on the-waters

וַיְשַׁלַּח אֶת־ הַיּוֹנָה וְלֹא־ יָסְפָה שׁוּב־ אֵלָיו עוֹד׃
again to-him to-return she-repeated and-not the-dove *** and-he-sent

וַיְהִי בְּאַחַת וְשֵׁשׁ־ מֵאוֹת שָׁנָה בָּרִאשׁוֹן בְּאֶחָד
on-first on-the-first year hundreds and-six on-first and-he-was (13)

לַחֹדֶשׁ חָרְבוּ הַמַּיִם מֵעַל הָאָרֶץ וַיָּסַר נֹחַ
Noah and-he-removed the-earth from-on the-waters they-dried-up to-the-month

אֶת־ מִכְסֵה הַתֵּבָה וַיַּרְא וְהִנֵּה חָרְבוּ פְּנֵי
surfaces-of they-were-dry and-see! and-he-looked the-ark covering-of ***

הָאֲדָמָה׃ וּבַחֹדֶשׁ הַשֵּׁנִי בְּשִׁבְעָה וְעֶשְׂרִים יוֹם
day and-twenty on-seven the-second and-by-the-month (14) the-ground

Ararat. [5]The waters continued
to recede until the tenth
month, and on the first day of
the tenth month the tops of
the mountains became visible.
[6]After forty days Noah
opened the window he had
made in the ark [7]and sent out
a raven, and it kept flying back
and forth until the water had
dried up from the earth. [8]Then
he sent out a dove to see if the
water had receded from the
surface of the ground. [9]But the
dove could find no place to set
its feet because there was
water over all the surface of
the earth; so it returned to
Noah in the ark. He reached
out his hand and took the
dove and brought it back to
himself in the ark. [10]He waited
seven more days and again
sent out the dove from the ark.
[11]When the dove returned to
him in the evening, there in
its beak was a freshly plucked
olive leaf! Then Noah knew
that the water had receded
from the earth. [12]He waited
seven more days and sent the
dove out again, but this time it
did not return to him.
[13]By the first day of the first
month of Noah's six hundred
and first year, the water had
dried up from the earth. Noah
then removed the covering
from the ark and saw that the
surface of the ground was dry.
[14]By the twenty-seventh day
of the second month the earth

לַחֹדֶשׁ יָבְשָׁה הָאָרֶץ׃ וַיְדַבֵּר אֱלֹהִים אֶל־ נֹחַ לֵאמֹר׃
to-say Noah to God then-he-said (15) the-earth she-was-dry to-the-month

צֵא מִן־ הַתֵּבָה אַתָּה וְאִשְׁתְּךָ וּבָנֶיךָ וּנְשֵׁי־
and-wives-of and-sons-of-you and-wife-of-you you the-ark from come-out! (16)

בָנֶיךָ אִתָּךְ׃ כָּל־ הַחַיָּה אֲשֶׁר־ אִתְּךָ מִכָּל־
from-every-of with-you that the-living every-of (17) with-you sons-of-you

בָּשָׂר בָּעוֹף וּבַבְּהֵמָה וּבְכָל־ הָרֶמֶשׂ
the-crawler and-with-every-of and-with-the-animal with-the-bird creature

הָרֹמֵשׂ עַל־ הָאָרֶץ הַוְצֵא° אִתָּךְ וְשָׁרְצוּ
so-they-can-multiply with-you bring-out! the-ground on the-one-crawling

בָאָרֶץ וּפָרוּ וְרָבוּ עַל־ הָאָרֶץ׃
the-earth upon and-they-increase and-they-be-fruitful on-the-earth

וַיֵּצֵא־ נֹחַ וּבָנָיו וְאִשְׁתּוֹ וּנְשֵׁי־ בָנָיו
sons-of-him and-wives-of and-wife-of-him and-sons-of-him Noah so-he-came-out (18)

אִתּוֹ׃ כָּל־ הַחַיָּה כָּל־ הָרֶמֶשׂ וְכָל־ הָעוֹף
the-bird and-every-of the-crawler every-of the-animal every-of (19) with-him

כֹּל רוֹמֵשׂ עַל־ הָאָרֶץ לְמִשְׁפְּחֹתֵיהֶם יָצְאוּ מִן־ הַתֵּבָה׃
the-ark from they-came by-kinds-of-them the-earth on moving every-of

וַיִּבֶן נֹחַ מִזְבֵּחַ לַיהוָה וַיִּקַּח מִכֹּל | הַבְּהֵמָה
the-animal from-every-of and-he-took to-Yahweh altar Noah then-he-built (20)

הַטְּהוֹרָה וּמִכֹּל הָעוֹף הַטָּהֹר וַיַּעַל
and-he-sacrificed the-clean the-bird and-from-every-of the-clean

עֹלֹת בַּמִּזְבֵּחַ׃ וַיָּרַח יְהוָה אֶת־ רֵיחַ הַנִּיחֹחַ
the-pleasant aroma-of *** Yahweh and-he-smelled (21) on-the-altar burnt-offerings

וַיֹּאמֶר יְהוָה אֶל־ לִבּוֹ לֹא־ אֹסִף לְקַלֵּל עוֹד אֶת־
*** again to-curse I-will-repeat not heart-of-him in Yahweh and-he-said

הָאֲדָמָה בַּעֲבוּר הָאָדָם כִּי יֵצֶר לֵב הָאָדָם רַע
evil the-man heart-of inclination-of though the-man because-of the-ground

מִנְּעֻרָיו וְלֹא־ אֹסִף עוֹד לְהַכּוֹת אֶת־ כָּל־
every-of *** to-destroy again I-will-repeat and-not from-childhood-of-him

חַי כַּאֲשֶׁר עָשִׂיתִי׃ עֹד כָּל־ יְמֵי הָאָרֶץ זֶרַע וְקָצִיר
and-harvest seedtime the-earth days-of all-of while (22) I-did just-as living

וְקֹר וָחֹם וְקַיִץ וָחֹרֶף וְיוֹם וָלַיְלָה לֹא יִשְׁבֹּתוּ׃
they-will-cease never and-night and-day and-winter and-summer and-heat and-cold

וַיְבָרֶךְ אֱלֹהִים אֶת־ נֹחַ וְאֶת־ בָּנָיו וַיֹּאמֶר לָהֶם
to-them and-he-said sons-of-him and Noah *** God then-he-blessed (9:1)

פְּרוּ וּרְבוּ וּמִלְאוּ אֶת־ הָאָרֶץ׃ וּמוֹרַאֲכֶם
and-fear-of-you (2) the-earth *** and-fill! and-increase! be-fruitful!

was completely dry.

15Then God said to Noah, 16"Come out of the ark, you and your wife and your sons and their wives. 17Bring out every kind of living creature that is with you—the birds, the animals, and all the creatures that move along the ground—so they can multiply on the earth and be fruitful and increase in number upon it."

18So Noah came out, together with his sons and his wife and his sons' wives. 19All the animals and all the creatures that move along the ground and all the birds—everything that moves on the earth—came out of the ark, one kind after another.

20Then Noah built an altar to the LORD and, taking some of all the clean animals and clean birds, he sacrificed burnt offerings on it. 21The LORD smelled the pleasing aroma and said in his heart: "Never again will I curse the ground because of man, even though[l] every inclination of his heart is evil from childhood. And never again will I destroy all living creatures, as I have done.

22"As long as the earth endures,
seedtime and harvest,
cold and heat,
summer and winter,
day and night
will never cease."

*God's Covenant With Noah*

9 Then God blessed Noah and his sons, saying to them, "Be fruitful and increase in number and fill the earth. 2The fear and dread of

l21 Or *man, for*

°17 ק היצא

וְחִתְּכֶם יִהְיֶה עַל כָּל־ חַיַּת הָאָרֶץ וְעַל כָּל־
every-of and-upon the-earth beast-of every-of upon he-will-be and-dread-of-you

עוֹף הַשָּׁמַיִם בְּכֹל אֲשֶׁר תִּרְמֹשׂ הָאֲדָמָה וּבְכָל־ דְּגֵי
fishes-of and-on-all-of the-ground she-moves that on-every the-air bird-of

הַיָּם בְּיֶדְכֶם נִתָּנוּ׃ (3) כָּל־ רֶמֶשׂ אֲשֶׁר הוּא־ חַי
lives he that crawler every-of (3) they-are-given into-hand-of-you the-sea

לָכֶם יִהְיֶה לְאָכְלָה כְּיֶרֶק עֵשֶׂב נָתַתִּי לָכֶם אֶת־ כֹּל׃
everything *** to-you I-gave plant as-green for-food he-will-be to-you

(4) אַךְ־ בָּשָׂר בְּנַפְשׁוֹ דָמוֹ לֹא תֹאכֵלוּ׃ (5) וְאַךְ
and-surely (5) you-must-eat not blood-of-him with-life-of-him meat but (4)

אֶת־ דִּמְכֶם לְנַפְשֹׁתֵיכֶם אֶדְרֹשׁ מִיַּד כָּל־ חַיָּה
animal every-of from-hand-of I-will-demand for-lives-of-you blood-of-you ***

אֶדְרְשֶׁנּוּ וּמִיַּד הָאָדָם מִיַּד אִישׁ אָחִיו
fellow-of-him man from-hand-of the-man and-from-hand-of I-will-demand-him

אֶדְרֹשׁ אֶת־ נֶפֶשׁ הָאָדָם׃ (6) שֹׁפֵךְ דַּם הָאָדָם בָּאָדָם
by-the-man the-man blood-of one-shedding (6) the-man life-of *** I-will-demand

דָּמוֹ יִשָּׁפֵךְ כִּי בְּצֶלֶם אֱלֹהִים עָשָׂה אֶת־ הָאָדָם׃
the-man *** he-made God in-image-of for he-shall-be-shed blood-of-him

(7) וְאַתֶּם פְּרוּ וּרְבוּ שִׁרְצוּ בָאָרֶץ וּרְבוּ־
and-increase! on-the-earth multiply! and-increase! be-fruitful! and-you (7)

בָהּ׃ (8) וַיֹּאמֶר אֱלֹהִים אֶל־ נֹחַ וְאֶל־ בָּנָיו אִתּוֹ לֵאמֹר׃
to-say with-him sons-of-him and-to Noah to God then-he-said (8) on-her

(9) וַאֲנִי הִנְנִי מֵקִים אֶת־ בְּרִיתִי אִתְּכֶם וְאֶת־
and-with with-you covenant-of-me *** establishing see!-I now-I (9)

זַרְעֲכֶם אַחֲרֵיכֶם׃ (10) וְאֵת כָּל־ נֶפֶשׁ הַחַיָּה אֲשֶׁר
that the-creature living-of every-of and-with (10) after-you descendants-of-you

אִתְּכֶם בָּעוֹף בַּבְּהֵמָה וּבְכָל־ חַיַּת
animal-of and-with-every-of with-the-livestock with-the-bird with-you

הָאָרֶץ אִתְּכֶם מִכֹּל יֹצְאֵי הַתֵּבָה לְכֹל
with-every-of the-ark ones-coming-out-of with-all-of with-you the-earth

חַיַּת הָאָרֶץ׃ (11) וַהֲקִמֹתִי אֶת־ בְּרִיתִי אִתְּכֶם
with-you covenant-of-me *** and-I-establish (11) the-earth creature-of

וְלֹא־ יִכָּרֵת כָּל־ בָּשָׂר עוֹד מִמֵּי הַמַּבּוּל וְלֹא־
and-not the-flood by-waters-of ever life all-of he-will-be-cut-off and-not

יִהְיֶה עוֹד מַבּוּל לְשַׁחֵת הָאָרֶץ׃ (12) וַיֹּאמֶר אֱלֹהִים זֹאת אוֹת־
sign-of this God and-he-said (12) the-earth to-destroy flood ever he-will-be

הַבְּרִית אֲשֶׁר־אֲנִי נֹתֵן בֵּינִי וּבֵינֵיכֶם וּבֵין כָּל־
every-of and-between and-between-you between-me making I that the-covenant

---

you will fall upon all the beasts of the earth and all the birds of the air, upon every creature that moves along the ground, and upon all the fish of the sea; they are given into your hands. [3]Everything that lives and moves will be food for you. Just as I gave you the green plants, I now give you everything.

[4]"But you must not eat meat that has its lifeblood still in it. [5]And for your lifeblood I will surely demand an accounting. I will demand an accounting from every animal. And from each man, too, I will demand an accounting for the life of his fellow man.

[6]"Whoever sheds the blood of man,
by man shall his blood be shed;
for in the image of God has God made man.

[7]As for you, be fruitful and increase in number; multiply on the earth and increase upon it."

[8]Then God said to Noah and to his sons with him: [9]"I now establish my covenant with you and with your descendants after you [10]and with every living creature that was with you—the birds, the livestock and all the wild animals, all those that came out of the ark with you—every living creature on earth. [11]I establish my covenant with you: Never again will all life be cut off by the waters of a flood; never again will there be a flood to destroy the earth."

[12]And God said, "This is the sign of the covenant I am making between me and you

נֶפֶשׁ חַיָּה אֲשֶׁר אִתְּכֶם לְדֹרֹת עוֹלָם׃ אֶת־ קַשְׁתִּי
rainbow-of-me *** (13) to-come for-generations with-you that creature living

נָתַתִּי בֶּעָנָן וְהָיְתָה לְאוֹת בְּרִית בֵּינִי וּבֵין
and-between between-me covenant for-sign-of and-she-will-be in-the-cloud I-set

הָאָרֶץ׃ וְהָיָה בְּעַנְנִי עָנָן עַל־ הָאָרֶץ
the-earth over cloud when-to-bring-me and-he-will-be (14) the-earth

וְנִרְאֲתָה הַקֶּשֶׁת בֶּעָנָן׃ וְזָכַרְתִּי אֶת־
*** and-I-will-remember (15) in-the-cloud the-rainbow and-she-appears

בְּרִיתִי אֲשֶׁר בֵּינִי וּבֵינֵיכֶם וּבֵין כָּל־ נֶפֶשׁ
living every-of and-between and-between-you between-me that covenant-of-me

חַיָּה בְּכָל־ בָּשָׂר וְלֹא־ יִהְיֶה עוֹד הַמַּיִם לְמַבּוּל
for-flood the-waters again he-will-become and-not kind with-every-of creature

לְשַׁחֵת כָּל־ בָּשָׂר׃ וְהָיְתָה הַקֶּשֶׁת בֶּעָנָן וּרְאִיתִיהָ
and-I-see-her in-the-cloud the-rainbow when-she-is (16) life all-of to-destroy

לִזְכֹּר בְּרִית עוֹלָם בֵּין אֱלֹהִים וּבֵין כָּל־ נֶפֶשׁ
living every-of and-between God between everlasting covenant to-remember

חַיָּה בְּכָל־ בָּשָׂר אֲשֶׁר עַל־ הָאָרֶץ׃ וַיֹּאמֶר אֱלֹהִים אֶל־ נֹחַ
Noah to God so-he-said (17) the-earth on that kind with-every-of creature

זֹאת אוֹת־ הַבְּרִית אֲשֶׁר הֲקִמֹתִי בֵּינִי וּבֵין כָּל־
all-of and-between between-me I-established that the-covenant sign-of this

בָּשָׂר אֲשֶׁר עַל־הָאָרֶץ׃ וַיִּהְיוּ בְנֵי־ נֹחַ הַיֹּצְאִים מִן־
from the-ones-coming Noah sons-of and-they-were (18) the-earth on that life

הַתֵּבָה שֵׁם וְחָם וָיָפֶת וְחָם הוּא אֲבִי כְנָעַן׃ שְׁלֹשָׁה
three (19) Canaan father-of he and-Ham and-Japheth and-Ham Shem the-ark

אֵלֶּה בְּנֵי־ נֹחַ וּמֵאֵלֶּה נָפְצָה כָל־ הָאָרֶץ׃
the-earth all-of she-was-populated and-from-these Noah sons-of these

וַיָּחֶל נֹחַ אִישׁ הָאֲדָמָה וַיִּטַּע כָּרֶם׃
vineyard and-he-planted the-soil man-of Noah and-he-proceeded (20)

וַיֵּשְׁתְּ מִן־ הַיַּיִן וַיִּשְׁכָּר וַיִּתְגַּל בְּתוֹךְ
inside and-he-lay-uncovered and-he-became-drunk the-wine from when-he-drank (21)

אָהֳלֹה׃ וַיַּרְא חָם אֲבִי כְנַעַן אֵת עֶרְוַת אָבִיו
father-of-him nakedness-of *** Canaan father-of Ham and-he-saw (22) tent-of-him

וַיַּגֵּד לִשְׁנֵי־ אֶחָיו בַּחוּץ׃ וַיִּקַּח שֵׁם
Shem but-he-took (23) on-the-outside brothers-of-him to-two-of and-he-told

וָיֶפֶת אֶת־ הַשִּׂמְלָה וַיָּשִׂימוּ עַל־ שְׁכֶם שְׁנֵיהֶם
two-of-them shoulder-of across and-they-laid the-garment *** and-Japheth

וַיֵּלְכוּ אֲחֹרַנִּית וַיְכַסּוּ אֵת עֶרְוַת אֲבִיהֶם
father-of-them nakedness-of *** and-they-covered backward and-they-walked

°21 ק אהלו

and every living creature with you, a covenant for all generations to come: 13I have set my rainbow in the clouds, and it will be the sign of the covenant between me and the earth. 14Whenever I bring clouds over the earth and the rainbow appears in the clouds, 15I will remember my covenant between me and you and all living creatures of every kind. Never again will the waters become a flood to destroy all life. 16Whenever the rainbow appears in the clouds, I will see it and remember the everlasting covenant between God and all living creatures of every kind on the earth."

17So God said to Noah, "This is the sign of the covenant I have established between me and all life on the earth."

### *The Sons of Noah*

18The sons of Noah who came out of the ark were Shem, Ham and Japheth. (Ham was the father of Canaan.) 19These were the three sons of Noah, and from them came the people who were scattered over the earth.

20Noah, a man of the soil, proceeded[m] to plant a vineyard. 21When he drank some of its wine, he became drunk and lay uncovered inside his tent. 22Ham, the father of Canaan, saw his father's nakedness and told his two brothers outside. 23But Shem and Japheth took a garment and laid it across their shoulders; then they walked in backward and covered their father's

m20 *Or soil, was the first*

| | | | | | |
|---|---|---|---|---|---|
| רָאוּ׃ | לֹא | אֲבִיהֶם | וְעֶרְוַת | אֲחֹרַנִּית | וּפְנֵיהֶם |
| they-saw | not | father-of-them | and-nakedness-of | backward | and-faces-of-them |

| | | | | | | | |
|---|---|---|---|---|---|---|---|
| עָשָׂה־ | אֲשֶׁר־ | אֵת | וַיֵּדַע | מִיֵּינוֹ | נֹחַ | וַיִּיקֶץ | |
| he-did | what | *** | and-he-found-out | from-wine-of-him | Noah | when-he-awoke | (24) |

| | | | | | | | |
|---|---|---|---|---|---|---|---|
| עֶבֶד | כְּנָעַן | אָרוּר | וַיֹּאמֶר | | הַקָּטָן׃ | בְּנוֹ | לוֹ |
| slave-of | Canaan | being-cursed | and-he-said | (25) | the-young | son-of-him | to-him |

| | | | | | | |
|---|---|---|---|---|---|---|
| יְהוָה | בָּרוּךְ | וַיֹּאמֶר | | לְאֶחָיו׃ | יִהְיֶה | עֲבָדִים |
| Yahweh | being-blessed | also-he-said | (26) | to-brothers-of-him | he-will-be | slaves |

| | | | | | | | | |
|---|---|---|---|---|---|---|---|---|
| אֱלֹהִים | יַפְתְּ | | לָמוֹ׃ | עֶבֶד | כְנַעַן | וִיהִי | שֵׁם | אֱלֹהֵי |
| God | may-he-enlarge | (27) | to-him | slave | Canaan | and-may-he-be | Shem | God-of |

| | | | | | | |
|---|---|---|---|---|---|---|
| עֶבֶד | כְנַעַן | וִיהִי | שֵׁם | בְּאָהֳלֵי־ | וְיִשְׁכֹּן | לְיֶפֶת |
| slave | Canaan | and-may-he-be | Shem | in-tents-of | and-may-he-live | to-Japheth |

| | | | | | | | | | |
|---|---|---|---|---|---|---|---|---|---|
| וַחֲמִשִּׁים | שָׁנָה | מֵאוֹת | שְׁלֹשׁ | הַמַּבּוּל | אַחַר | נֹחַ | וַיְחִי־ | | לָמוֹ׃ |
| and-fifty | year | hundreds | three | the-flood | after | Noah | and-he-lived | (28) | to-him |

| | | | | | | | | | |
|---|---|---|---|---|---|---|---|---|---|
| וַחֲמִשִּׁים | שָׁנָה | מֵאוֹת | תְּשַׁע | נֹחַ | יְמֵי־ | כָּל־ | וַיִּהְיוּ | | שָׁנָה׃ |
| and-fifty | year | hundreds | nine | Noah | days-of | all-of | and-they-were | (29) | year |

| | | | | | | | | | |
|---|---|---|---|---|---|---|---|---|---|
| וָיָפֶת | חָם | שֵׁם | נֹחַ | בְּנֵי־ | תּוֹלְדֹת | וְאֵלֶּה | | וַיָּמֹת׃ | שָׁנָה |
| and-Japheth | Ham | Shem | Noah | sons-of | lines-of | and-these | (10:1) | then-he-died | year |

| | | | | | | | | |
|---|---|---|---|---|---|---|---|---|
| גֹּמֶר | יֶפֶת | בְּנֵי | | הַמַּבּוּל׃ | אַחַר | בָּנִים | לָהֶם | וַיִּוָּלְדוּ |
| Gomer | Japheth | sons-of | (2) | the-flood | after | sons | to-them | and-they-were-born |

| | | | | | | | |
|---|---|---|---|---|---|---|---|
| וּבְנֵי | | וְתִירָס׃ | וּמֶשֶׁךְ | וְתֻבָל | וְיָוָן | וּמָדַי | וּמָגוֹג |
| and-sons-of | (3) | and-Tiras | and-Meshech | and-Tubal | and-Javan | and-Madai | and-Magog |

| | | | | | | | |
|---|---|---|---|---|---|---|---|
| אֱלִישָׁה | יָוָן | וּבְנֵי | | וְתֹגַרְמָה׃ | וְרִיפַת | אַשְׁכְּנַז | גֹּמֶר |
| Elishah | Javan | and-sons-of | (4) | and-Togarmah | and-Riphath | Ashkenaz | Gomer |

| | | | | | | |
|---|---|---|---|---|---|---|
| אִיֵּי | נִפְרְדוּ | מֵאֵלֶּה | | וְדֹדָנִים׃ | כִּתִּים | וְתַרְשִׁישׁ |
| maritime-ones-of | they-spread | from-these | (5) | and-Dodanim | Kittim | and-Tarshish |

| | | | | |
|---|---|---|---|---|
| לְמִשְׁפְּחֹתָם | לִלְשֹׁנוֹ | אִישׁ | בְּאַרְצֹתָם | הַגּוֹיִם |
| by-clans-of-them | with-language-of-him | each | into-territories-of-them | the-peoples |

| | | | | | | | |
|---|---|---|---|---|---|---|---|
| וּכְנָעַן׃ | וּפוּט | וּמִצְרַיִם | כּוּשׁ | חָם | וּבְנֵי | | בְּגוֹיֵהֶם׃ |
| and-Canaan | and-Put | and-Mizraim | Cush | Ham | and-sons-of | (6) | within-nations-of-them |

| | | | | | | | |
|---|---|---|---|---|---|---|---|
| וְסַבְתְּכָא | וְרַעְמָה | וְסַבְתָּה | וַחֲוִילָה | סְבָא | כּוּשׁ | וּבְנֵי | |
| and-Sabtecah | and-Raamah | and-Sabtah | and-Havilah | Seba | Cush | and-sons-of | (7) |

| | | | | | | | | | |
|---|---|---|---|---|---|---|---|---|---|
| הוּא | נִמְרֹד | אֶת־ | יָלַד | וְכוּשׁ | | וּדְדָן׃ | שְׁבָא | רַעְמָה | וּבְנֵי |
| he | Nimrod | *** | he-fathered | and-Cush | (8) | and-Dedan | Sheba | Raamah | and-sons-of |

| | | | | | | | | | |
|---|---|---|---|---|---|---|---|---|---|
| לִפְנֵי | צַיִד | גִבֹּר־ | הָיָה | הוּא־ | | בָּאָרֶץ׃ | גִּבֹּר | לִהְיוֹת | הֵחֵל |
| before | hunter | mighty | he-was | he | (9) | on-the-earth | mighty | to-be | he-was-first |

| | | | | | | | | |
|---|---|---|---|---|---|---|---|---|
| יְהוָה׃ | לִפְנֵי | צַיִד | גִּבּוֹר | כְּנִמְרֹד | יֵאָמַר | כֵּן | עַל־ | יְהוָה |
| Yahweh | before | hunter | mighty | like-Nimrod | he-is-said | this | for | Yahweh |

nakedness. Their faces were
turned the other way so that
they would not see their father's nakedness.
[24]When Noah awoke from
his wine and found out what
his youngest son had done to
him, [25]he said,

"Cursed be Canaan!
The lowest of slaves
will he be to his
brothers."

[26]He also said,

"Blessed be the LORD, the
God of Shem!
May Canaan be the slave
of Shem.[n]
[27]May God extend the
territory of Japheth[o];
may Japheth live in the
tents of Shem,
and may Canaan be his[p]
slave."

[28]After the flood Noah lived
350 years. [29]Altogether, Noah
lived 950 years, and then he
died.

*The Table of Nations*

10 This is the account of
Shem, Ham and
Japheth, Noah's sons, who
themselves had sons after the
flood.

*The Japhethites*

[2]The sons[q] of Japheth:
Gomer, Magog, Madai,
Javan, Tubal, Meshech
and Tiras.
[3]The sons of Gomer:
Ashkenaz, Riphath and
Togarmah.
[4]The sons of Javan:
Elishah, Tarshish, the
Kittim and the Roda-
nim.[r] [5](From these the
maritime peoples spread
out into their territories
by their clans within
their nations, each with
its own language.)

*The Hamites*

[6]The sons of Ham:
Cush, Mizraim,[s] Put and
Canaan.
[7]The sons of Cush:
Seba, Havilah, Sabtah,
Raamah and Sabtecah.
The sons of Raamah:
Sheba and Dedan.

[8]Cush was the father[t] of
Nimrod, who grew to be a
mighty warrior on the earth.
[9]He was a mighty hunter before the LORD; that is why it is
said, "Like Nimrod, a mighty

[n]26 Or *be his slave*
[o]27 *Japheth* sounds like the Hebrew for *extend.* [p]27 Or *their*
[q]2 *Sons* may mean *descendants* or *successors* or *nations;* also in verses 3, 4, 6, 7, 20-23, 29 and 31.
[r]4 Some manuscripts of the Masoretic Text and Samaritan Pentateuch (see also Septuagint and 1 Chron. 1:7); most manuscripts of the Masoretic Text *Dodanim*
[s]6 That is, Egypt; also in verse 13
[t]8 *Father* may mean *ancestor* or *predecessor* or *founder;* also in verses 13, 15, 24 and 26.

וַתְּהִי רֵאשִׁית מַמְלַכְתּוֹ בָּבֶל וְאֶרֶךְ וְאַכַּד
and-Akkad and-Erech Babylon kingdom-of-him first-of and-she-was (10)

וְכַלְנֵה בְּאֶרֶץ שִׁנְעָר׃ מִן־ הָאָרֶץ הַהִוא יָצָא אַשּׁוּר
Assyria he-went-to the-that the-land from (11) Shinar in-land-of and-Calneh

וַיִּבֶן אֶת־ נִינְוֵה וְאֶת־ רְחֹבֹת עִיר וְאֶת־כָּלַח׃ וְאֶת־ רֶסֶן בֵּין
between Resen and (12) Calah and Ir Rehoboth and Ninevah *** and-he-built

נִינְוֵה וּבֵין כָּלַח הִוא הָעִיר הַגְּדֹלָה׃ וּמִצְרַיִם יָלַד
he-fathered and-Mizraim (13) the-great the-city that Calah and-between Nineveh

אֶת־לוּדִים וְאֶת־ עֲנָמִים וְאֶת־ לְהָבִים וְאֶת־ נַפְתֻּחִים׃ וְאֶת־ פַּתְרֻסִים
Pathrusites and (14) Naphtuhites and Lehabites and Anamites and Ludites ***

וְאֶת־ כַּסְלֻחִים אֲשֶׁר יָצְאוּ מִשָּׁם פְּלִשְׁתִּים וְאֶת־ כַּפְתֹּרִים׃
Caphtorites and Philistines from-there they-came whom Casluhites and

וּכְנַעַן יָלַד אֶת־ צִידֹן בְּכֹרוֹ וְאֶת־ חֵת׃ וְאֶת־
and (16) Hittite and firstborn-of-him Sidon *** he-fathered and-Canaan (15)

הַיְבוּסִי וְאֶת־ הָאֱמֹרִי וְאֵת הַגִּרְגָּשִׁי׃ וְאֶת־ הַחִוִּי וְאֶת־
and the-Hivite and (17) the-Girgashite and the-Amorite and the-Jebusite

הָעַרְקִי וְאֶת־ הַסִּינִי׃ וְאֶת־ הָאַרְוָדִי וְאֶת־ הַצְּמָרִי וְאֶת־
and the-Zemarite and the-Arvadite and (18) the-Sinite and the-Arkite

הַחֲמָתִי וְאַחַר נָפֹצוּ מִשְׁפְּחוֹת הַכְּנַעֲנִי׃ וַיְהִי
and-he-was (19) the-Canaanite clans-of they-scattered and-later the-Hamathite

גְּבוּל הַכְּנַעֲנִי מִצִּידֹן בֹּאֲכָה גְרָרָה עַד־ עַזָּה בֹּאֲכָה
to-go-you Gaza as-far-as to-Gerar to-go-you from-Sidon the-Canaanite border-of

סְדֹמָה וַעֲמֹרָה וְאַדְמָה וּצְבֹיִם עַד־ לָשַׁע׃ אֵלֶּה
these (20) Lasha as-far-as and-Zeboiim and-Admah and-Gomorrah to-Sodom

בְנֵי־ חָם לְמִשְׁפְּחֹתָם לִלְשֹׁנֹתָם בְּאַרְצֹתָם
in-territories-of-them by-languages-of-them by-clans-of-them Ham sons-of

בְּגוֹיֵהֶם׃ וּלְשֵׁם יֻלַּד גַּם־ הוּא אֲבִי כָּל־ בְּנֵי־
sons-of all-of father-of he also he-was-born and-to-Shem (21) in-nations-of-them

עֵבֶר אֲחִי יֶפֶת הַגָּדוֹל׃ בְּנֵי שֵׁם עֵילָם וְאַשּׁוּר
and-Asshur Elam Shem sons-of (22) the-older Japheth brother-of Eber

וְאַרְפַּכְשַׁד וְלוּד וַאֲרָם׃ וּבְנֵי אֲרָם עוּץ וְחוּל וְגֶתֶר
and-Gether and-Hul Uz Aram and-sons-of (23) and-Aram and-Lud and-Arphaxad

וָמַשׁ׃ וְאַרְפַּכְשַׁד יָלַד אֶת־ שָׁלַח וְשֶׁלַח יָלַד אֶת־
*** he-fathered and-Shelah Shelah *** he-fathered and-Arphaxad (24) and-Mash

עֵבֶר׃ וּלְעֵבֶר יֻלַּד שְׁנֵי בָנִים שֵׁם הָאֶחָד פֶּלֶג כִּי
because Peleg the-one name-of sons two-of he-was-born and-to-Eber (25) Eber

בְיָמָיו נִפְלְגָה הָאָרֶץ וְשֵׁם אָחִיו יָקְטָן׃
Joktan brother-of-him and-name-of the-earth she-was-divided in-days-of-him

---

hunter before the LORD." [10]The first centers of his kingdom were Babylon, Erech, Akkad and Calneh, in[u] Shinar.[v] [11]From that land he went to Assyria, where he built Nineveh, Rehoboth Ir,[w] Calah [12]and Resen, which is between Nineveh and Calah; that is the great city.

[13]Mizraim was the father of
the Ludites, Anamites,
Lehabites, Naphtuhites,
[14]Pathrusites, Casluhites
(from whom the Philistines came) and Caphtorites.

[15]Canaan was the father of
Sidon his firstborn,[x] and
of the Hittites, [16]Jebusites, Amorites, Girgashites, [17]Hivites, Arkites,
Sinites, [18]Arvadites,
Zemarites and Hamathites.

Later the Canaanite clans scattered [19]and the borders of Canaan reached from Sidon toward Gerar as far as Gaza, and then toward Sodom, Gomorrah, Admah and Zeboiim, as far as Lasha.

[20]These are the descendants of Ham by their clans and languages, in their territories and nations.

*The Semites*

[21]Sons were also born to Shem, whose older brother was[y] Japheth; Shem was the ancestor of all the sons of Eber.

[22]The sons of Shem:
Elam, Asshur, Arphaxad,
Lud and Aram.
[23]The sons of Aram:
Uz, Hul, Gether and Meshech.[z]
[24]Arphaxad was the father
of[a] Shelah,
and Shelah the father of
Eber.
[25]Two sons were born to
Eber:
One was named Peleg,[b]
because in his time the
earth was divided; his
brother was named Joktan.

[u]10 Or *Erech and Akkad—all of them in*
[v]10 That is, Babylonia
[w]11 Or *Nineveh with its city squares*
[x]15 Or *of the Sidonians, the foremost*
[y]21 Or *Shem, the older brother of*
[z]23 Septuagint (see also 1 Chron. 1:17); Hebrew *Mash*
[a]24 Hebrew; Septuagint *father of Cainan, and Cainan was the father of*
[b]25 *Peleg* means *division.*

וְיָקְטָן יָלַד אֶת־אַלְמוֹדָד וְאֶת־שָׁלֶף וְאֶת־חֲצַרְמָוֶת וְאֶת־
and Hazarmaveth and Sheleph and Almodad *** he-fathered and-Joktan (26)

יָרַח׃ וְאֶת־הֲדוֹרָם וְאֶת־אוּזָל וְאֶת־דִּקְלָה׃ וְאֶת־עוֹבָל וְאֶת־אֲבִימָאֵל וְאֶת־
and Abimael and Obal and (28) Diklah and Uzal and Hadoram and (27) Jerah

שְׁבָא׃ וְאֶת־אוֹפִר וְאֶת־חֲוִילָה וְאֶת־יוֹבָב כָּל־אֵלֶּה בְּנֵי יָקְטָן׃
Joktan sons-of these all-of Jobab and Havilah and Ophir and (29) Sheba

וַיְהִי מוֹשָׁבָם מִמֵּשָׁא בֹּאֲכָה סְפָרָה הַר
hill-country-of to-Sephar to-go-you from-Mesha region-of-them and-he-was (30)

הַקֶּדֶם׃ אֵלֶּה בְנֵי־שֵׁם לְמִשְׁפְּחֹתָם לִלְשֹׁנֹתָם
by-languages-of-them by-clans-of-them Shem sons-of these (31) the-east

בְּאַרְצֹתָם לְגוֹיֵהֶם׃ אֵלֶּה מִשְׁפְּחֹת בְּנֵי־נֹחַ
Noah sons-of clans-of these (32) by-nations-of-them in-territories-of-them

לְתוֹלְדֹתָם בְּגוֹיֵהֶם וּמֵאֵלֶּה נִפְרְדוּ הַגּוֹיִם
the-nations they-spread-out and-from-these in-nations-of-them by-lines-of-them

בָּאָרֶץ אַחַר הַמַּבּוּל׃ וַיְהִי כָל־הָאָרֶץ שָׂפָה אֶחָת
one language the-earth all-of now-he-had (11:1) the-flood after on-the-earth

וּדְבָרִים אֲחָדִים׃ וַיְהִי בְּנָסְעָם מִקֶּדֶם וַיִּמְצְאוּ
and-they-found to-east as-to-move-them and-he-was (2) common-ones and-words

בִקְעָה בְּאֶרֶץ שִׁנְעָר וַיֵּשְׁבוּ שָׁם׃ וַיֹּאמְרוּ אִישׁ אֶל־
to each and-they-said (3) there and-they-settled Shinar in-land-of plain

רֵעֵהוּ הָבָה נִלְבְּנָה לְבֵנִים וְנִשְׂרְפָה לִשְׂרֵפָה וַתְּהִי
and-she-was with-fire and-let-us-bake bricks let-us-make come! fellow-of-him

לָהֶם הַלְּבֵנָה לְאָבֶן וְהַחֵמָר הָיָה לָהֶם לַחֹמֶר׃
instead-of-mortar to-them he-was and-the-tar instead-of-stone the-brick to-them

וַיֹּאמְרוּ הָבָה ׀ נִבְנֶה־לָּנוּ עִיר וּמִגְדָּל וְרֹאשׁוֹ
and-top-of-him and-tower city for-us let-us-build come! then-they-said (4)

בַשָּׁמַיִם וְנַעֲשֶׂה־לָּנוּ שֵׁם פֶּן־נָפוּץ עַל־פְּנֵי
face-of over we-be-scattered lest name for-us so-let-us-make in-the-heavens

כָל־הָאָרֶץ׃ וַיֵּרֶד יְהוָה לִרְאֹת אֶת־הָעִיר וְאֶת־
and the-city *** to-see Yahweh but-he-came-down (5) the-earth whole-of

הַמִּגְדָּל אֲשֶׁר בָּנוּ בְּנֵי הָאָדָם׃ וַיֹּאמֶר יְהוָה הֵן עַם
people see! Yahweh and-he-said (6) the-man sons-of they-built that the-tower

אֶחָד וְשָׂפָה אַחַת לְכֻלָּם וְזֶה הַחִלָּם לַעֲשׂוֹת וְעַתָּה
then-now to-do to-begin-them and-this to-all-of-them same and-language one

לֹא־יִבָּצֵר מֵהֶם כֹּל אֲשֶׁר יָזְמוּ לַעֲשׂוֹת׃ הָבָה
come! (7) to-do they-plan that all for-them he-is-impossible nothing

נֵרְדָה וְנָבְלָה שָׁם שְׂפָתָם אֲשֶׁר לֹא
not so language-of-them there and-let-us-confuse let-us-go-down

26Joktan was the father of
Almodad, Sheleph,
Hazarmaveth, Jerah,
27Hadoram, Uzal, Diklah,
28Obal, Abimael, Sheba,
29Ophir, Havilah and
Jobab. All these were
sons of Joktan.

30The region where they lived
stretched from Mesha toward
Sephar, in the eastern hill
country.
31These are the sons of Shem
by their clans and languages,
in their territories and nations.

32These are the clans of
Noah's sons, according to
their lines of descent, within
their nations. From these the
nations spread out over the
earth after the flood.

*The Tower of Babel*

11 Now the whole world
had one language and
a common speech. 2As men
moved eastward,[c] they found
a plain in Shinar[d] and settled
there.
3They said to each other,
"Come, let's make bricks and
bake them thoroughly." They
used brick instead of stone,
and tar instead of mortar.
4Then they said, "Come, let us
build ourselves a city, with a
tower that reaches to the heavens, so that we may make a
name for ourselves and not be
scattered over the face of the
whole earth."
5But the LORD came down to
see the city and the tower that
the men were building. 6The
LORD said, "If as one people
speaking the same language
they have begun to do this,
then nothing they plan to do
will be impossible for them.
7Come, let us go down and
confuse their language so they

[c]2 Or *from the east;* or *in the east*
[d]2 That is, Babylonia

יִשְׁמְעוּ אִישׁ שְׂפַת רֵעֵהוּ׃ וַיָּפֶץ יְהוָה
Yahweh so-he-scattered (8) fellow-of-him language-of one they-will-understand

אֹתָם מִשָּׁם עַל־ פְּנֵי כָל־ הָאָרֶץ וַיַּחְדְּלוּ לִבְנֹת
to-build and-they-stopped the-earth all-of face-of over from-there them

הָעִיר׃ עַל־ כֵּן קָרָא שְׁמָהּ בָּבֶל כִּי־ שָׁם בָּלַל
he-confused there because Babel name-of-her he-calls this for (9) the-city

יְהוָה שְׂפַת כָּל־ הָאָרֶץ וּמִשָּׁם הֱפִיצָם יְהוָה
Yahweh he-scattered-them and-from-there the-earth whole-of language-of Yahweh

עַל־ פְּנֵי כָּל־ הָאָרֶץ׃ אֵלֶּה תּוֹלְדֹת שֵׁם שֵׁם בֶּן־
son-of Shem Shem lines-of these (10) the-earth whole-of face-of over

מְאַת שָׁנָה וַיּוֹלֶד אֶת־אַרְפַּכְשָׁד שְׁנָתַיִם אַחַר הַמַּבּוּל׃ וַיְחִי־
and-he-lived (11) the-flood after two Arphaxad *** and-he-fathered year hundred-of

שֵׁם אַחֲרֵי הוֹלִידוֹ אֶת־אַרְפַּכְשָׁד חֲמֵשׁ מֵאוֹת שָׁנָה וַיּוֹלֶד
and-he-fathered year hundreds five Arphaxad *** to-father-him after Shem

בָּנִים וּבָנוֹת׃ וְאַרְפַּכְשַׁד חַי חָמֵשׁ וּשְׁלֹשִׁים שָׁנָה וַיּוֹלֶד
and-he-fathered year and-thirty five life and-Arphaxad (12) and-daughters sons

אֶת־ שָׁלַח׃ וַיְחִי אַרְפַּכְשַׁד אַחֲרֵי הוֹלִידוֹ אֶת־ שֶׁלַח שָׁלֹשׁ
three Shelah *** to-father-him after Arphaxad and-he-lived (13) Shelah ***

שָׁנִים וְאַרְבַּע מֵאוֹת שָׁנָה וַיּוֹלֶד בָּנִים וּבָנוֹת׃ וְשֶׁלַח
and-Shelah (14) and-daughters sons and-he-fathered year hundreds and-four years

חַי שְׁלֹשִׁים שָׁנָה וַיּוֹלֶד אֶת־ עֵבֶר׃ וַיְחִי־ שֶׁלַח אַחֲרֵי
after Shelah and-he-lived (15) Eber *** and-he-fathered year thirty life

הוֹלִידוֹ אֶת־ עֵבֶר שָׁלֹשׁ שָׁנִים וְאַרְבַּע מֵאוֹת שָׁנָה וַיּוֹלֶד
and-he-fathered year hundreds and-four years three Eber *** to-father-him

בָּנִים וּבָנוֹת׃ וַיְחִי־ עֵבֶר אַרְבַּע וּשְׁלֹשִׁים שָׁנָה וַיּוֹלֶד
and-he-fathered year and-thirty four Eber and-he-lived (16) and-daughters sons

אֶת־ פָּלֶג׃ וַיְחִי־ עֵבֶר אַחֲרֵי הוֹלִידוֹ אֶת־ פֶּלֶג שְׁלֹשִׁים שָׁנָה
year thirty Peleg *** to-father-him after Eber and-he-lived (17) Peleg ***

וְאַרְבַּע מֵאוֹת שָׁנָה וַיּוֹלֶד בָּנִים וּבָנוֹת׃ וַיְחִי־
and-he-lived (18) and-daughters sons and-he-fathered year hundreds and-four

פֶלֶג שְׁלֹשִׁים שָׁנָה וַיּוֹלֶד אֶת־ רְעוּ׃ וַיְחִי־ פֶלֶג אַחֲרֵי
after Peleg and-he-lived (19) Reu *** and-he-fathered year thirty Peleg

הוֹלִידוֹ אֶת־ רְעוּ תֵּשַׁע שָׁנִים וּמָאתַיִם שָׁנָה וַיּוֹלֶד בָּנִים
sons and-he-fathered year and-two-hundred years nine Reu *** to-father-him

וּבָנוֹת׃ וַיְחִי רְעוּ שְׁתַּיִם וּשְׁלֹשִׁים שָׁנָה וַיּוֹלֶד אֶת־
*** and-he-fathered year and-thirty two Reu and-he-lived (20) and-daughters

שְׂרוּג׃ וַיְחִי רְעוּ אַחֲרֵי הוֹלִידוֹ אֶת־ שְׂרוּג שֶׁבַע שָׁנִים
years seven Serug *** to-father-him after Reu and-he-lived (21) Serug

will not understand each other."

8 So the LORD scattered them from there over all the earth, and they stopped building the city. 9 That is why it was called Babel[e]—because there the LORD confused the language of the whole world. From there the LORD scattered them over the face of the whole earth.

*From Shem to Abram*

10 This is the account of Shem.

Two years after the flood, when Shem was 100 years old, he became the father[f] of Arphaxad. 11 And after he became the father of Arphaxad, Shem lived 500 years and had other sons and daughters.

12 When Arphaxad had lived 35 years, he became the father of Shelah. 13 And after he became the father of Shelah, Arphaxad lived 403 years and had other sons and daughters.[g]

14 When Shelah had lived 30 years, he became the father of Eber. 15 And after he became the father of Eber, Shelah lived 403 years and had other sons and daughters.

16 When Eber had lived 34 years, he became the father of Peleg. 17 And after he became the father of Peleg, Eber lived 430 years and had other sons and daughters.

18 When Peleg had lived 30 years, he became the father of Reu. 19 And after he became the father of Reu, Peleg lived 209 years and had other sons and daughters.

20 When Reu had lived 32 years, he became the father of Serug. 21 And after he became the father of Serug, Reu lived

[e] 9 That is, Babylon; *Babel* sounds like the Hebrew for *confused*.

[f] 10 *Father* may mean *ancestor*; also in verses 11-25.

[g] 12,13 Hebrew; Septuagint (see also Gen. 10:24 and Luke 3:35, 36) *35 years, he became the father of Cainan. 13 And after he became the father of Cainan, Arphaxad lived 430 years and had other sons and daughters. When Cainan had lived 130 years, he became the father of Shelah. And after he became the father of Shelah, Cainan lived 330 years and had other sons and daughters*

וּמָאתַיִם שָׁנָה וַיּוֹלֶד בָּנִים וּבָנוֹת׃ וַיְחִי
and-he-lived (22) and-daughters sons and-he-fathered year and-two-hundred

שְׂרוּג שְׁלֹשִׁים שָׁנָה וַיּוֹלֶד אֶת־ נָחוֹר׃ וַיְחִי שְׂרוּג אַחֲרֵי
after Serug and-he-lived (23) Nahor *** and-he-fathered year thirty Serug

הוֹלִידוֹ אֶת־ נָחוֹר מָאתַיִם שָׁנָה וַיּוֹלֶד בָּנִים וּבָנוֹת׃
and-daughters sons and-he-fathered year two-hundred Nahor *** to-father-him

וַיְחִי נָחוֹר תֵּשַׁע וְעֶשְׂרִים שָׁנָה וַיּוֹלֶד אֶת־ תָּרַח׃
Terah *** and-he-fathered year and-twenty nine Nahor and-he-lived (24)

וַיְחִי נָחוֹר אַחֲרֵי הוֹלִידוֹ אֶת־ תֶּרַח תְּשַׁע־עֶשְׂרֵה שָׁנָה
year ten nine Terah *** to-father-him after Nahor and-he-lived (25)

וּמְאַת שָׁנָה וַיּוֹלֶד בָּנִים וּבָנוֹת׃ וַיְחִי־
and-he-lived (26) and-daughters sons and-he-fathered year and-hundred-of

תֶרַח שִׁבְעִים שָׁנָה וַיּוֹלֶד אֶת־ אַבְרָם אֶת־ נָחוֹר וְאֶת־ הָרָן׃
Haran and Nahor *** Abram *** and-he-fathered year seventy Terah

וְאֵלֶּה תּוֹלְדֹת תֶּרַח תֶּרַח הוֹלִיד אֶת־ אַבְרָם אֶת־ נָחוֹר וְאֶת־
and Nahor *** Abram *** he-fathered Terah Terah lines-of and-these (27)

הָרָן וְהָרָן הוֹלִיד אֶת־לוֹט׃ וַיָּמָת הָרָן עַל־ פְּנֵי תֶּרַח
Terah life-of in Haran and-he-died (28) Lot *** he-fathered and-Haran Haran

אָבִיו בְּאֶרֶץ מוֹלַדְתּוֹ בְּאוּר כַּשְׂדִּים׃ וַיִּקַּח
and-he-took (29) Chaldeans in-Ur-of birth-of-him in-land-of father-of-him

אַבְרָם וְנָחוֹר לָהֶם נָשִׁים שֵׁם אֵשֶׁת־ אַבְרָם שָׂרָי וְשֵׁם אֵשֶׁת־
wife-of and-name-of Sarai Abram wife-of name-of wives to-them and-Nahor Abram

נָחוֹר מִלְכָּה בַּת־ הָרָן אֲבִי־ מִלְכָּה וַאֲבִי יִסְכָּה׃
Iscah and-father-of Milcah father-of Haran daughter-of Milcah Nahor

וַתְּהִי שָׂרַי עֲקָרָה אֵין לָהּ וָלָד׃ וַיִּקַּח תֶּרַח אֶת־
*** Terah and-he-took (31) child to-her not barren Sarai now-she-was (30)

אַבְרָם בְּנוֹ וְאֶת־לוֹט בֶּן־ הָרָן בֶּן־ בְּנוֹ וְאֵת שָׂרַי
Sarai and son-of-him son-of Haran son-of Lot and son-of-him Abram

כַּלָּתוֹ אֵשֶׁת אַבְרָם בְּנוֹ וַיֵּצְאוּ אִתָּם
together and-they-set-out son-of-him Abram wife-of daughters-in-law-of-him

מֵאוּר כַּשְׂדִּים לָלֶכֶת אַרְצָה כְּנַעַן וַיָּבֹאוּ עַד־ חָרָן
Haran to but-they-came Canaan to-land to-go Chaldeans from-Ur-of

וַיֵּשְׁבוּ שָׁם׃ וַיִּהְיוּ יְמֵי־ תֶרַח חָמֵשׁ שָׁנִים
years five Terah days-of and-they-were (32) there and-they-settled

וּמָאתַיִם שָׁנָה וַיָּמָת תֶּרַח בְּחָרָן׃ וַיֹּאמֶר יְהוָה
Yahweh and-he-said (12:1) in-Haran Terah and-he-died year and-two-hundred

אֶל־ אַבְרָם לֶךְ־ לְךָ מֵאַרְצְךָ וּמִמּוֹלַדְתְּךָ
and-from-people-of-you from-country-of-you for-you leave! Abram to

207 years and had other sons and daughters.
22When Serug had lived 30 years, he became the father of
Nahor. 23And after he became the father of Nahor, Serug lived 200 years and had other sons and daughters.
24When Nahor had lived 29 years, he became the father of
Terah. 25And after he became the father of Terah, Nahor lived 119 years and had other sons and daughters.
26After Terah had lived 70 years, he became the father of Abram, Nahor and Haran.

27This is the account of Terah.

Terah became the father of Abram, Nahor and Haran. And Haran became the father
of Lot. 28While his father Terah was still alive, Haran died in Ur of the Chaldeans, in the
land of his birth. 29Abram and Nahor both married. The name of Abram's wife was Sarai, and the name of Nahor's wife was Milcah; she was the daughter of Haran, the father of both Milcah and
Iscah. 30Now Sarai was barren; she had no children.
31Terah took his son Abram, his grandson Lot son of Haran, and his daughter-in-law Sarai, the wife of his son Abram, and together they set out from Ur of the Chaldeans to go to Canaan. But when they came to Haran, they settled there.
32Terah lived 205 years, and he died in Haran.

*The Call of Abram*

12 The LORD had said to Abram, "Leave your country, your people and your

וּמִבֵּית אָבִיךָ אֶל־הָאָרֶץ אֲשֶׁר אַרְאֶךָּ׃

I-will-show-you that the-land to father-of-you and-from-house-of

(2) וְאֶעֶשְׂךָ לְגוֹי גָּדוֹל וַאֲבָרֶכְךָ וַאֲגַדְּלָה

and-I-will-make-great and-I-will-bless-you great into-nation and-I-will-make-you (2)

שְׁמֶךָ וֶהְיֵה בְּרָכָה׃ (3) וַאֲבָרְכָה מְבָרְכֶיךָ

ones-blessing-you and-I-will-bless (3) blessing and-be! name-of-you

וּמְקַלֶּלְךָ אָאֹר וְנִבְרְכוּ בְךָ כֹּל

all-of through-you and-they-will-be-blessed I-will-curse and-one-cursing-you

מִשְׁפְּחֹת הָאֲדָמָה׃ (4) וַיֵּלֶךְ אַבְרָם כַּאֲשֶׁר דִּבֶּר אֵלָיו יְהוָה

Yahweh to-him he-told just-as Abram so-he-left (4) the-earth peoples-of

וַיֵּלֶךְ אִתּוֹ לוֹט וְאַבְרָם בֶּן־חָמֵשׁ שָׁנִים וְשִׁבְעִים שָׁנָה

year and-seventy years five son-of and-Abram Lot with-him and-he-went

בְּצֵאתוֹ מֵחָרָן׃ (5) וַיִּקַּח אַבְרָם אֶת־שָׂרַי אִשְׁתּוֹ וְאֶת־לוֹט

Lot and wife-of-him Sarai *** Abram and-he-took (5) from-Haran when-to-go-him

בֶּן־אָחִיו וְאֶת־כָּל־רְכוּשָׁם אֲשֶׁר רָכָשׁוּ

they-accumulated that possessions-of-them all-of and brother-of-him son-of

וְאֶת־הַנֶּפֶשׁ אֲשֶׁר־עָשׂוּ בְחָרָן וַיֵּצְאוּ לָלֶכֶת אַרְצָה

to-land to-go and-they-set-out in-Haran they-acquired that the-people and

כְּנַעַן וַיָּבֹאוּ אַרְצָה כְּנָעַן׃ (6) וַיַּעֲבֹר אַבְרָם בָּאָרֶץ

in-the-land Abram and-he-traveled (6) Canaan in-land and-they-arrived Canaan

עַד מְקוֹם שְׁכֶם עַד אֵלוֹן מוֹרֶה וְהַכְּנַעֲנִי אָז בָּאָרֶץ׃

in-the-land then and-the-Canaanite Moreh tree-of to Shechem site-of as-far-as

(7) וַיֵּרָא יְהוָה אֶל־אַבְרָם וַיֹּאמֶר לְזַרְעֲךָ אֶתֵּן

I-will-give to-offspring-of-you and-he-said Abram to Yahweh but-he-appeared (7)

אֶת־הָאָרֶץ הַזֹּאת וַיִּבֶן שָׁם מִזְבֵּחַ לַיהוָה הַנִּרְאֶה

the-one-appearing to-Yahweh altar there so-he-built the-this the-land ***

אֵלָיו׃ (8) וַיַּעְתֵּק מִשָּׁם הָהָרָה מִקֶּדֶם לְבֵית־אֵל

El to-Beth on-east to-the-hill from-there and-he-went-on (8) to-him

וַיֵּט אָהֳלֹה בֵּית־אֵל מִיָּם וְהָעַי מִקֶּדֶם וַיִּבֶן־

and-he-built on-east and-the-Ai on-west El Beth tent-of-him and-he-pitched

שָׁם מִזְבֵּחַ לַיהוָה וַיִּקְרָא בְּשֵׁם יְהוָה׃ (9) וַיִּסַּע

then-he-set-out (9) Yahweh on-name-of and-he-called to-Yahweh altar there

אַבְרָם הָלוֹךְ וְנָסוֹעַ הַנֶּגְבָּה׃ (10) וַיְהִי רָעָב בָּאָרֶץ

in-the-land famine and-he-was (10) to-the-Negev and-to-continue to-go Abram

וַיֵּרֶד אַבְרָם מִצְרַיְמָה לָגוּר שָׁם כִּי־כָבֵד הָרָעָב

the-famine he-was-severe because there to-live to-Egypt Abram and-he-went-down

בָּאָרֶץ׃ (11) וַיְהִי כַּאֲשֶׁר הִקְרִיב לָבוֹא מִצְרָיְמָה

into-Egypt to-enter he-was-about just-as and-he-was (11) in-the-land

°8 ק אהלו

father's household and go to
the land I will show you.

[2]"I will make you into a
great nation
and I will bless you;
I will make your name
great,
and you will be a
blessing.
[3]I will bless those who bless
you,
and whoever curses you I
will curse;
and all peoples on earth
will be blessed through
you."

[4]So Abram left, as the LORD
had told him; and Lot went
with him. Abram was seventy-five years old when he set
out from Haran. [5]He took his
wife Sarai, his nephew Lot, all
the possessions they had accumulated and the people they
had acquired in Haran, and
they set out for the land of Canaan, and they arrived there.
[6]Abram traveled through the
land as far as the site of the
great tree of Moreh at Shechem. The Canaanites were
then in the land, [7]but the LORD
appeared to Abram and said,
"To your offspring[h] I will give
this land." So he built an altar
there to the LORD, who had appeared to him.
[8]From there he went on
toward the hills east of Bethel
and pitched his tent, with
Bethel on the west and Ai on
the east. There he built an altar
to the LORD and called on the
name of the LORD. [9]Then
Abram set out and continued
toward the Negev.

*Abram in Egypt*

[10]Now there was a famine in
the land, and Abram went
down to Egypt to live there for
a while because the famine
was severe. [11]As he was about
to enter Egypt, he said to his

[h]7 *Or seed*

וַיֹּאמֶר אֶל־ שָׂרַי אִשְׁתּוֹ הִנֵּה־ נָא יָדַעְתִּי כִּי אִשָּׁה יְפַת־מַרְאֶה
sight beautiful-of woman that I-know now! see! wife-of-him Sarai to and-he-said

אָתְּ׃ וְהָיָה כִּי־ יִרְאוּ אֹתָךְ הַמִּצְרִים וְאָמְרוּ
and-they-will-say the-Egyptians you they-see when and-he-will-be (12) you

אִשְׁתּוֹ זֹאת וְהָרְגוּ אֹתִי וְאֹתָךְ יְחַיּוּ׃ אִמְרִי־ נָא
now! say! (13) they-will-let-live but-you me and-they-will-kill this wife-of-him

אֲחֹתִי אָתְּ לְמַעַן יִיטַב־ לִי בַעֲבוּרֵךְ
for-sake-of-you for-me he-will-be-well so-that you sister-of-me

וְחָיְתָה נַפְשִׁי בִּגְלָלֵךְ׃ וַיְהִי כְּבוֹא
as-to-come and-he-was (14) on-account-of-you life-of-me and-she-will-be-spared

אַבְרָם מִצְרָיְמָה וַיִּרְאוּ הַמִּצְרִים אֶת־ הָאִשָּׁה כִּי־ יָפָה הִוא
she beautiful that the-woman *** the-Egyptians and-they-saw to-Egypt Abram

מְאֹד׃ וַיִּרְאוּ אֹתָהּ שָׂרֵי פַרְעֹה וַיְהַלְלוּ אֹתָהּ אֶל־
to her and-they-praised Pharaoh officials-of her when-they-saw (15) very

פַּרְעֹה וַתֻּקַּח הָאִשָּׁה בֵּית פַּרְעֹה׃ וּלְאַבְרָם
and-for-Abram (16) Pharaoh palace-of the-woman and-she-was-taken Pharaoh

הֵיטִיב בַּעֲבוּרָהּ וַיְהִי־ לוֹ צֹאן־ וּבָקָר
and-cattle sheep to-him and-he-was for-sake-of-her he-treated-well

וַחֲמֹרִים וַעֲבָדִים וּשְׁפָחֹת וַאֲתֹנֹת וּגְמַלִּים׃
and-camels and-female-donkeys and-maidservants and-menservants and-donkeys

וַיְנַגַּע יְהוָה ׀ אֶת־ פַּרְעֹה נְגָעִים גְּדֹלִים וְאֶת־
and serious-ones diseases Pharaoh *** Yahweh but-he-inflicted (17)

בֵּיתוֹ עַל־ דְּבַר שָׂרַי אֵשֶׁת אַבְרָם׃ וַיִּקְרָא
and-he-summoned (18) Abram wife-of Sarai reason-of for household-of-him

פַרְעֹה לְאַבְרָם וַיֹּאמֶר מַה־ זֹּאת עָשִׂיתָ לִּי לָמָּה לֹא־ הִגַּדְתָּ
you-tell not why? to-me you-did this what? and-he-said for-Abram Pharaoh

לִּי כִּי אִשְׁתְּךָ הִוא׃ לָמָה אָמַרְתָּ אֲחֹתִי הִוא וָאֶקַּח אֹתָהּ
her so-I-took she sister-of-me you-say why? (19) she wife-of-you that to-me

לִי לְאִשָּׁה וְעַתָּה הִנֵּה אִשְׁתְּךָ קַח וָלֵךְ׃ וַיְצַו
and-he-gave-orders (20) and-go! take! wife-of-you see! and-now for-wife to-me

עָלָיו פַּרְעֹה אֲנָשִׁים וַיְשַׁלְּחוּ אֹתוֹ וְאֶת־ אִשְׁתּוֹ וְאֶת־ כָּל־ אֲשֶׁר־
that everything and wife-of-him and him and-they-sent men Pharaoh about-him

לוֹ׃ וַיַּעַל אַבְרָם מִמִּצְרַיִם הוּא וְאִשְׁתּוֹ וְכָל־
and-everything and-wife-of-him he from-Egypt Abram so-he-went-up (13:1) to-him

אֲשֶׁר־ לוֹ וְלוֹט עִמּוֹ הַנֶּגְבָּה׃ וְאַבְרָם כָּבֵד
he-became-wealthy and-Abram (2) to-the-Negev with-him and-Lot to-him that

מְאֹד בַּמִּקְנֶה בַּכֶּסֶף וּבַזָּהָב׃ וַיֵּלֶךְ
and-he-went (3) and-in-the-gold in-the-silver in-the-livestock very

wife Sarai, "I know what a beautiful woman you are. [12]When the Egyptians see you, they will say, 'This is his wife.' Then they will kill me but will let you live. [13]Say you are my sister, so that I will be treated well for your sake and my life will be spared because of you."

[14]When Abram came to Egypt, the Egyptians saw that she was a very beautiful woman. [15]And when Pharaoh's officials saw her, they praised her to Pharaoh, and she was taken into his palace. [16]He treated Abram well for her sake, and Abram acquired sheep and cattle, male and female donkeys, menservants and maidservants, and camels.

[17]But the LORD inflicted serious diseases on Pharaoh and his household because of Abram's wife Sarai. [18]So Pharaoh summoned Abram. "What have you done to me?" he said. "Why didn't you tell me she was your wife? [19]Why did you say, 'She is my sister,' so that I took her to be my wife? Now then, here is your wife. Take her and go!" [20]Then Pharaoh gave orders about Abram to his men, and they sent him on his way, with his wife and everything he had.

### *Abram and Lot Separate*

13 So Abram went up from Egypt to the Negev, with his wife and everything he had, and Lot went with him. [2]Abram had become very wealthy in livestock and in silver and gold.

לְמַסָּעָיו מִנֶּגֶב וְעַד־בֵּית־אֵל עַד־הַמָּקוֹם אֲשֶׁר־הָיָה שָׁם
there he-was where the-place to El Beth and-to from-Negev on-journeys-of-him

אָהֳלֹה בַּתְּחִלָּה בֵּין בֵּית־אֵל וּבֵין הָעָי׃ אֶל־מְקוֹם
place-of to (4) the-Ai and-between El Beth between at-the-first tent-of-him

הַמִּזְבֵּחַ אֲשֶׁר־עָשָׂה שָׁם בָּרִאשֹׁנָה וַיִּקְרָא שָׁם אַבְרָם
Abram there and-he-called at-the-first there he-built that the-altar

בְּשֵׁם יְהוָה׃ וְגַם־לְלוֹט הַהֹלֵךְ אֶת־אַבְרָם הָיָה צֹאן־
flock he-was Abram with the-one-moving to-Lot and-also (5) Yahweh on-name-of

וּבָקָר וְאֹהָלִים׃ וְלֹא־נָשָׂא אֹתָם הָאָרֶץ לָשֶׁבֶת
to-stay the-land them he-could-support but-not (6) and-tents and-herd

יַחְדָּו כִּי־הָיָה רְכוּשָׁם רָב וְלֹא יָכְלוּ לָשֶׁבֶת
to-stay they-were-able that-not great possession-of-them he-was for together

יַחְדָּו׃ וַיְהִי־רִיב בֵּין רֹעֵי מִקְנֵה־אַבְרָם
Abram herd-of ones-tending-of between quarrel and-he-rose (7) together

וּבֵין רֹעֵי מִקְנֵה־לוֹט וְהַכְּנַעֲנִי וְהַפְּרִזִּי
and-the-Perizzite and-the-Canaanite Lot herd-of ones-tending-of and-between

אָז יֹשֵׁב בָּאָרֶץ׃ וַיֹּאמֶר אַבְרָם אֶל־לוֹט אַל־נָא תְהִי מְרִיבָה
quarrel let-her-be now! not Lot to Abram so-he-said (8) in-the-land living then

בֵּינִי וּבֵינֶךָ וּבֵין רֹעַי וּבֵין
and-between ones-tending-of-me and-between and-between-you between-me

רֹעֶיךָ כִּי־אֲנָשִׁים אַחִים אֲנָחְנוּ׃ הֲלֹא כָל־הָאָרֶץ לְפָנֶיךָ
before-you the-land whole-of not? (9) we brothers men for ones-tending-of-you

הִפָּרֶד נָא מֵעָלָי אִם־הַשְּׂמֹאל וְאֵימִנָה וְאִם־הַיָּמִין
the-right and-if then-I-will-go-right the-left if from-me now! part-company!

וְאַשְׂמְאִילָה׃ וַיִּשָּׂא־לוֹט אֶת־עֵינָיו וַיַּרְא אֶת־
*** and-he-saw eyes-of-him *** Lot and-he-lifted (10) then-I-will-go-left

כָּל־כִּכַּר הַיַּרְדֵּן כִּי כֻלָּהּ מַשְׁקֶה לִפְנֵי ׀ שַׁחֵת
to-destroy before well-watered all-of-her that the-Jordan plain-of whole-of

יְהוָה אֶת־סְדֹם וְאֶת־עֲמֹרָה כְּגַן־יְהוָה כְּאֶרֶץ מִצְרַיִם
Egypt like-land-of Yahweh like-garden-of Gomorrah and Sodom *** Yahweh

בֹּאֲכָה צֹעַר׃ וַיִּבְחַר־לוֹ לוֹט אֵת כָּל־כִּכַּר הַיַּרְדֵּן
the-Jordan plain-of whole-of *** Lot for-him so-he-chose (11) Zoar to-go-you

וַיִּסַּע לוֹט מִקֶּדֶם וַיִּפָּרְדוּ אִישׁ מֵעַל אָחִיו׃ אַבְרָם
Abram (12) brother-of-him from each and-they-parted to-east Lot and-he-set-out

יָשַׁב בְּאֶרֶץ־כְּנָעַן וְלוֹט יָשַׁב בְּעָרֵי הַכִּכָּר
the-plain among-cities-of he-lived and-Lot Canaan in-land-of he-lived

וַיֶּאֱהַל עַד־סְדֹם׃ וְאַנְשֵׁי סְדֹם רָעִים וְחַטָּאִים
and-sinners wicked-ones Sodom now-men-of (13) Sodom near and-he-pitched-tent

3From the Negev he went
from place to place until he
came to Bethel, to the place between Bethel and Ai where his
tent had been earlier 4and
where he had first built an altar. There Abram called on the
name of the LORD.

5Now Lot, who was moving
about with Abram, also had
flocks and herds and tents.
6But the land could not support them while they stayed
together, for their possessions
were so great that they were
not able to stay together. 7And
quarreling arose between
Abram's herdsmen and the
herdsmen of Lot. The Canaanites and Perizzites were also
living in the land at that time.

8So Abram said to Lot, "Let's
not have any quarreling between you and me, or between
your herdsmen and mine, for
we are brothers. 9Is not the
whole land before you? Let's
part company. If you go to the
left, I'll go to the right; if you
go to the right, I'll go to the
left."

10Lot looked up and saw that
the whole plain of the Jordan
was well watered, like the garden of the LORD, like the land
of Egypt, toward Zoar. (This
was before the LORD destroyed
Sodom and Gomorrah.) 11So
Lot chose for himself the
whole plain of the Jordan and
set out toward the east. The
two men parted company:
12Abram lived in the land of
Canaan, while Lot lived
among the cities of the plain
and pitched his tents near
Sodom. 13Now the men of
Sodom were wicked and were

°3 ק אהלו

לַיהוָה מְאֹד׃ וַיהוָה אָמַר אֶל־אַבְרָם אַחֲרֵי הִפָּרֶד־לוֹט
Lot he-parted after Abram to he-said and-Yahweh (14) great against-Yahweh

מֵעִמּוֹ שָׂא נָא עֵינֶיךָ וּרְאֵה מִן־הַמָּקוֹם אֲשֶׁר־אַתָּה שָׁם
there you where the-place from and-look! eyes-of-you now! lift! from-with-him

צָפֹנָה וָנֶגְבָּה וָקֵדְמָה וָיָמָּה׃ כִּי אֶת־כָּל־הָאָרֶץ
the-land all-of *** for (15) and-to-west and-to-east and-to-south to-north

אֲשֶׁר־אַתָּה רֹאֶה לְךָ אֶתְּנֶנָּה וּלְזַרְעֲךָ עַד־עוֹלָם׃
ever for and-to-offspring-of-you I-will-give-her to-you seeing you that

וְשַׂמְתִּי אֶת־זַרְעֲךָ כַּעֲפַר הָאָרֶץ אֲשֶׁר ׀ אִם־
if that the-earth like-dust-of offspring-of-you *** and-I-will-make (16)

יוּכַל אִישׁ לִמְנוֹת אֶת־עֲפַר הָאָרֶץ גַּם־זַרְעֲךָ
offspring-of-you then the-earth dust-of *** to-count anyone he-could

יִמָּנֶה׃ קוּם הִתְהַלֵּךְ בָּאָרֶץ לְאָרְכָּהּ
through-length-of-her through-the-land walk! go! (17) he-could-be-counted

וּלְרָחְבָּהּ כִּי לְךָ אֶתְּנֶנָּה׃ וַיֶּאֱהַל אַבְרָם
Abram so-he-moved-tent (18) I-give-her to-you for and-through-breadth-of-her

וַיָּבֹא וַיֵּשֶׁב בְּאֵלֹנֵי מַמְרֵא אֲשֶׁר בְּחֶבְרוֹן וַיִּבֶן־
and-he-built at-Hebron that Mamre near-trees-of and-he-lived and-he-went

שָׁם מִזְבֵּחַ לַיהוָה׃ וַיְהִי בִּימֵי אַמְרָפֶל מֶלֶךְ־שִׁנְעָר
Shinar king-of Amraphel in-days-of now-he-was (14:1) to-Yahweh altar there

אַרְיוֹךְ מֶלֶךְ אֶלָּסָר כְּדָרְלָעֹמֶר מֶלֶךְ עֵילָם וְתִדְעָל מֶלֶךְ גּוֹיִם׃
Goiim king-of and-Tidal Elam king-of Kedorlaomer Ellasar king-of Arioch

עָשׂוּ מִלְחָמָה אֶת־בֶּרַע מֶלֶךְ סְדֹם וְאֶת־בִּרְשַׁע מֶלֶךְ עֲמֹרָה
Gomorrah king-of Birsha and-with Sodom king-of Bera with war they-made (2)

שִׁנְאָב ׀ מֶלֶךְ אַדְמָה וְשֶׁמְאֵבֶר מֶלֶךְ צְבֹיִים וּמֶלֶךְ בֶּלַע הִיא־צֹעַר׃
Zoar that Bela and-king-of Zeboiim king-of and-Shemeber Admah king-of Shinab

כָּל־אֵלֶּה חָבְרוּ אֶל־עֵמֶק הַשִּׂדִּים הוּא יָם
sea-of that the-Siddim valley-of in they-joined-forces these all-of (3)

הַמֶּלַח׃ שְׁתֵּים עֶשְׂרֵה שָׁנָה עָבְדוּ אֶת־כְּדָרְלָעֹמֶר וּשְׁלֹשׁ־עֶשְׂרֵה שָׁנָה
year ten but-three Kedorlaomer *** they-served year ten two (4) the-salt

מָרָדוּ׃ וּבְאַרְבַּע עֶשְׂרֵה שָׁנָה בָּא כְדָרְלָעֹמֶר וְהַמְּלָכִים
and-the-kings Kedorlaomer he-went year ten and-in-four (5) they-rebelled

אֲשֶׁר אִתּוֹ וַיַּכּוּ אֶת־רְפָאִים בְּעַשְׁתְּרֹת קַרְנַיִם וְאֶת־
and Karnaim in-Ashteroth Rephaites *** and-they-defeated with-him that

הַזּוּזִים בְּהָם וְאֵת הָאֵימִים בְּשָׁוֵה קִרְיָתָיִם׃ וְאֶת־הַחֹרִי
the-Horite and (6) Kiriathaim in-Shaveh the-Emites and in-Ham the-Zuzites

בְּהַרְרָם שֵׂעִיר עַד אֵיל פָּארָן אֲשֶׁר עַל־הַמִּדְבָּר׃
the-desert near that Paran El as-far-as Seir on-hill-of-them

°2 ק צבוים

sinning greatly against the
LORD.
[14]The LORD said to Abram after Lot had parted from him,
"Lift up your eyes from where
you are and look north and
south, east and west. [15]All the
land that you see I will give to
you and your offspring[i] forever. [16]I will make your offspring
like the dust of the earth, so
that if anyone could count the
dust, then your offspring
could be counted. [17]Go, walk
through the length and
breadth of the land, for I am
giving it to you."
[18]So Abram moved his tents
and went to live near the great
trees of Mamre at Hebron,
where he built an altar to the
LORD.

### *Abram Rescues Lot*

14 At this time Amraphel
king of Shinar,[j] Arioch
king of Ellasar, Kedorlaomer
king of Elam and Tidal king of
Goiim [2]went to war against
Bera king of Sodom, Birsha
king of Gomorrah, Shinab
king of Admah, Shemeber
king of Zeboiim, and the king
of Bela (that is, Zoar). [3]All
these latter kings joined forces
in the Valley of Siddim (the
Salt Sea[k]). [4]For twelve years
they had been subject to Kedorlaomer, but in the thirteenth
year they rebelled.
[5]In the fourteenth year, Kedorlaomer and the kings allied
with him went out and de-
feated the Rephaites in Ash-
teroth Karnaim, the Zuzites in
Ham, the Emites in Shaveh
Kiriathaim [6]and the Horites in
the hill country of Seir, as far
as El Paran near the desert.

[i]15 Or *seed*; also in verse 16
[j]1 That is, Babylonia; also in verse 9
[k]3 That is, the Dead Sea

וַיָּשֻׁבוּ וַיָּבֹאוּ אֶל־עֵין מִשְׁפָּט הִוא קָדֵשׁ וַיַּכּוּ
and-they-conquered Kadesh that Mishpat En to and-they-went then-they-turned (7)

אֶת־כָּל־שְׂדֵה הָעֲמָלֵקִי וְגַם אֶת־הָאֱמֹרִי
the-Amorite *** as-well-as the-Amalekite territory-of whole-of ***

הַיֹּשֵׁב בְּחַצְצֹן תָּמָר׃ וַיֵּצֵא מֶלֶךְ־סְדֹם
Sodom king-of then-he-marched-out (8) Tamar in-Hazezon the-one-living

וּמֶלֶךְ עֲמֹרָה וּמֶלֶךְ אַדְמָה וּמֶלֶךְ צְבֹיִים° וּמֶלֶךְ בֶּלַע
Bela and-king-of Zeboiim and-king-of Admah and-king-of Gomorrah and-king-of

הִוא־צֹעַר וַיַּעַרְכוּ אִתָּם מִלְחָמָה בְּעֵמֶק הַשִּׂדִּים׃ אֵת
against (9) the-Siddim in-valley-of battle with-them and-they-joined Zoar that

כְּדָרְלָעֹמֶר מֶלֶךְ עֵילָם וְתִדְעָל מֶלֶךְ גּוֹיִם וְאַמְרָפֶל מֶלֶךְ שִׁנְעָר
Shinar king-of and-Amraphel Goiim king-of and-Tidal Elam king-of Kedorlaomer

וְאַרְיוֹךְ מֶלֶךְ אֶלָּסָר אַרְבָּעָה מְלָכִים אֶת־הַחֲמִשָּׁה׃ וְעֵמֶק
now-valley-of (10) the-five against kings four Ellasar king-of and-Arioch

הַשִׂדִּים* בֶּאֱרֹת בֶּאֱרֹת חֵמָר וַיָּנֻסוּ מֶלֶךְ־סְדֹם וַעֲמֹרָה
and-Gomorrah Sodom king-of when-they-fled tar pits-of pits the-Siddim

וַיִּפְּלוּ־שָׁמָּה וְהַנִּשְׁאָרִים הֶרָה נָּסוּ׃
they-fled to-hill and-the-ones-remaining into-there and-they-fell

וַיִּקְחוּ אֶת־כָּל־רְכֻשׁ סְדֹם וַעֲמֹרָה וְאֶת־כָּל־
all-of and and-Gomorrah Sodom goods-of all-of *** and-they-seized (11)

אָכְלָם וַיֵּלֵכוּ׃ וַיִּקְחוּ אֶת־לוֹט וְאֶת־
and Lot *** and-they-carried-off (12) then-they-left food-of-them

רְכֻשׁוֹ בֶּן־אֲחִי אַבְרָם וַיֵּלֵכוּ וְהוּא יֹשֵׁב
living since-he and-they-left Abram brother-of son-of possession-of-him

בִּסְדֹם׃ וַיָּבֹא הַפָּלִיט וַיַּגֵּד לְאַבְרָם הָעִבְרִי
the-Hebrew to-Abram and-he-reported the-escapee and-he-came (13) in-Sodom

וְהוּא שֹׁכֵן בְּאֵלֹנֵי מַמְרֵא הָאֱמֹרִי אֲחִי אֶשְׁכֹּל וַאֲחִי
and-brother-of Eshcol brother-of the-Amorite Mamre near-trees-of living now-he

עָנֵר וְהֵם בַּעֲלֵי בְרִית־אַבְרָם׃ וַיִּשְׁמַע אַבְרָם כִּי
that Abram when-he-heard (14) Abram covenant-of owners-of and-these Aner

נִשְׁבָּה אָחִיו וַיָּרֶק אֶת־חֲנִיכָיו
trained-men-of-him *** and-he-called-out relative-of-him he-was-captive

יְלִידֵי בֵיתוֹ שְׁמֹנָה עָשָׂר וּשְׁלֹשׁ מֵאוֹת וַיִּרְדֹּף
and-he-pursued hundreds and-three ten eight household-of-him born-ones-of

עַד־דָּן׃ וַיֵּחָלֵק עֲלֵיהֶם ׀ לַיְלָה הוּא וַעֲבָדָיו
and-servants-of-him he night against-them and-he-divided (15) Dan as-far-as

וַיַּכֵּם וַיִּרְדְּפֵם עַד־חוֹבָה אֲשֶׁר מִשְּׂמֹאל
to-north that Hobah as-far-as and-he-pursued-them and-he-routed-them

7Then they turned back and
went to En Mishpat (that is,
Kadesh), and they conquered
the whole territory of the
Amalekites, as well as the Amorites who were living in
Hazezon Tamar.
8Then the king of Sodom,
the king of Gomorrah, the
king of Admah, the king of Zeboiim and the king of Bela
(that is, Zoar) marched out and
drew up their battle lines in
the Valley of Siddim 9against
Kedorlaomer king of Elam, Tidal king of Goiim, Amraphel
king of Shinar and Arioch
king of Ellasar—four kings
against five. 10Now the Valley
of Siddim was full of tar pits,
and when the kings of Sodom
and Gomorrah fled, some of
the men fell into them and the
rest fled to the hills. 11The four
kings seized all the goods of
Sodom and Gomorrah and all
their food; then they went
away. 12They also carried off
Abram's nephew Lot and his
possessions, since he was living in Sodom.
13One who had escaped
came and reported this to
Abram the Hebrew. Now
Abram was living near the
great trees of Mamre the Amorite, a brother[l] of Eshcol and
Aner, all of whom were allied
with Abram. 14When Abram
heard that his relative had
been taken captive, he called
out the 318 trained men born
in his household and went in
pursuit as far as Dan. 15During
the night Abram divided his
men to attack them and he
routed them, pursuing them
as far as Hobah, north of

[l]13 Or *a relative;* or *an ally*

*10 Most mss have *dagesh* in the *sin* (הַשּׂ).

°8 ק צבוים

לְדַמָּשֶׂק׃ וַיָּשֶׁב אֵת כָּל־ הָרְכֻשׁ וְגַם אֶת־ לוֹט
Lot *** and-also the-goods all-of *** and-he-recovered (16) to-Damascus

אָחִיו וּרְכֻשׁוֹ הֵשִׁיב וְגַם אֶת־ הַנָּשִׁים
the-women *** and-also he-brought-back and-possession-of-him relative-of-him

וְאֶת־ הָעָם׃ וַיֵּצֵא־ מֶלֶךְ סְדֹם לִקְרָאתוֹ אַחֲרֵי
after to-meet-him Sodom king-of and-he-came-out (17) the-people and

שׁוּבוֹ מֵהַכּוֹת אֶת־ כְּדָר־לָעֹמֶר וְאֶת־ הַמְּלָכִים אֲשֶׁר אִתּוֹ אֶל־
in with-him that the-kings and Kedorlaomer *** from-to-defeat to-return-him

עֵמֶק שָׁוֵה הוּא עֵמֶק הַמֶּלֶךְ׃ וּמַלְכִּי־צֶדֶק מֶלֶךְ
king-of then-Melchizedek (18) the-king valley-of that Shaveh valley-of

שָׁלֵם הוֹצִיא לֶחֶם וָיָיִן וְהוּא כֹהֵן לְאֵל עֶלְיוֹן׃
Most-High to-God priest now-he and-wine bread he-brought-out Salem

וַיְבָרְכֵהוּ וַיֹּאמַר בָּרוּךְ אַבְרָם לְאֵל עֶלְיוֹן
Most-High by-God Abram being-blessed and-he-said and-he-blessed-him (19)

קֹנֵה שָׁמַיִם וָאָרֶץ׃ וּבָרוּךְ אֵל עֶלְיוֹן אֲשֶׁר־
who Most-High God and-being-blessed (20) and-earth heaven creating-of

מִגֵּן צָרֶיךָ בְּיָדֶךָ וַיִּתֶּן־ לוֹ מַעֲשֵׂר
tenth to-him then-he-gave into-hand-of-you enemies-of-you he-delivered

מִכֹּל׃ וַיֹּאמֶר מֶלֶךְ־ סְדֹם אֶל־אַבְרָם תֶּן־ לִי הַנֶּפֶשׁ
the-people to-me give! Abram to Sodom king-of and-he-said (21) from-everything

וְהָרְכֻשׁ קַח־ לָךְ׃ וַיֹּאמֶר אַבְרָם אֶל־ מֶלֶךְ סְדֹם הֲרִמֹתִי
I-raised Sodom king-of to Abram but-he-said (2) for-you keep! and-the-goods

יָדִי אֶל־ יְהוָה אֵל עֶלְיוֹן קֹנֵה שָׁמַיִם וָאָרֶץ׃ אִם־
that (23) and-earth heaven creating-of Most-High God Yahweh to hand-of-me

מִחוּט וְעַד שְׂרוֹךְ־ נַעַל וְאִם־ אֶקַּח מִכָּל־ אֲשֶׁר־
that from-anything I-will-accept and-not sandal thong-of or-even even-thread

לָךְ וְלֹא תֹאמַר אֲנִי הֶעֱשַׁרְתִּי אֶת־אַבְרָם׃ בִּלְעָדַי רַק
but nothing-to-me (24) Abram *** I-made-rich I you-will-say so-never to-you

אֲשֶׁר אָכְלוּ הַנְּעָרִים וְחֵלֶק הָאֲנָשִׁים אֲשֶׁר הָלְכוּ אִתִּי עָנֵר
Aner with-me they-went who the-men and-share-of the-men they-ate what

אֶשְׁכֹּל וּמַמְרֵא הֵם יִקְחוּ חֶלְקָם׃ אַחַר ׀ הַדְּבָרִים
the-events after (15:1) share-of-them let-them-have they and-Mamre Eshcol

הָאֵלֶּה הָיָה דְבַר־ יְהוָה אֶל־אַבְרָם בַּמַּחֲזֶה לֵאמֹר אַל־ תִּירָא
you-fear not to-say in-the-vision Abram to Yahweh word-of he-came the-these

אַבְרָם אָנֹכִי מָגֵן לָךְ שְׂכָרְךָ הַרְבֵּה מְאֹד׃ וַיֹּאמֶר אַבְרָם אֲדֹנָי
Lord Abram but-he-said (2) very to-be-great reward-of-you to-you shield I Abram

יְהוִה מַה־ תִּתֶּן־ לִי וְאָנֹכִי הוֹלֵךְ עֲרִירִי וּבֶן־
and-son-of childless to-remain since-I to-me you-will-give what? Yahweh

Damascus. [16]He recovered all
the goods and brought back
his relative Lot and his possessions, together with the
women and the other people.
[17]After Abram returned from
defeating Kedorlaomer and
the kings allied with him, the
king of Sodom came out to
meet him in the Valley of Shaveh (that is, the King's Valley).
[18]Then Melchizedek king of
Salem[m] brought out bread and
wine. He was priest of God
Most High, [19]and he blessed
Abram, saying,

"Blessed be Abram by God
Most High,
Creator[n] of heaven and
earth.
[20]And blessed be[o] God Most
High,
who delivered your
enemies into your
hand."

Then Abram gave him a tenth
of everything.
[21]The king of Sodom said to
Abram, "Give me the people
and keep the goods for yourself."
[22]But Abram said to the king
of Sodom, "I have raised my
hand to the LORD, God Most
High, Creator of heaven and
earth, and have taken an oath
[23]that I will accept nothing belonging to you, not even a
thread or the thong of a sandal, so that you will never be
able to say, 'I made Abram
rich.' [24]I will accept nothing
but what my men have eaten
and the share that belongs to
the men who went with me—
to Aner, Eshcol and Mamre.
Let them have their share."

### *God's Covenant With Abram*

15 After this, the word of
the LORD came to
Abram in a vision:

"Do not be afraid, Abram.
I am your shield,[p]
your very great reward.[q]"

[2]But Abram said, "O Sovereign LORD, what can you give
me since I remain childless

[m]18 That is, Jerusalem
[n]19 Or *Possessor;* also in verse 22
[o]20 Or *And praise be to*
[p]1 Or *sovereign*
[q]1 Or *shield; / your reward will be very great*

מֶשֶׁק בֵּיתִי הוּא דַּמֶּשֶׂק אֱלִיעֶזֶר׃ וַיֹּאמֶר אַבְרָם הֵן
see! Abram and-he-said (3) Eliezer Damascus he estate-of-me inheritance-of

לִי לֹא נָתַתָּה זָרַע וְהִנֵּה בֶן־ בֵּיתִי יוֹרֵשׁ אֹתִי׃
me being-heir household-of-me servant-of and-see! child you-gave not to-me

וְהִנֵּה דְבַר־ יְהוָה אֵלָיו לֵאמֹר לֹא יִירָשְׁךָ זֶה
this he-will-be-heir-of-you not to-say to-him Yahweh word-of and-see! (4)

כִּי־ אִם אֲשֶׁר יֵצֵא מִמֵּעֶיךָ הוּא יִירָשֶׁךָ׃
he-will-be-heir-of-you he from-body-of-you he-will-come who rather but

וַיּוֹצֵא אֹתוֹ הַחוּצָה וַיֹּאמֶר הַבֶּט־ נָא הַשָּׁמַיְמָה וּסְפֹר
and-count! at-the-heavens now! look! and-he-said to-the-outside him and-he-took (5)

הַכּוֹכָבִים אִם־ תּוּכַל לִסְפֹּר אֹתָם וַיֹּאמֶר לוֹ כֹּה יִהְיֶה
he-shall-be so to-him then-he-said them to-count you-can if the-stars

זַרְעֶךָ׃ וְהֶאֱמִן בַּיהוָה וַיַּחְשְׁבֶהָ לּוֹ
to-him and-he-credited-her in-Yahweh and-he-believed (6) offspring-of-you

צְדָקָה׃ וַיֹּאמֶר אֵלָיו אֲנִי יְהוָה אֲשֶׁר הוֹצֵאתִיךָ מֵאוּר
from-Ur-of I-brought-you who Yahweh I to-him also-he-said (7) righteousness

כַּשְׂדִּים לָתֶת לְךָ אֶת־ הָאָרֶץ הַזֹּאת לְרִשְׁתָּהּ׃ וַיֹּאמַר
but-he-said (8) to-possess-her the-this the-land *** to-you to-give Chaldeans

אֲדֹנָי יֱהוִה בַּמָּה אֵדַע כִּי אִירָשֶׁנָּה׃ וַיֹּאמֶר אֵלָיו
to-him so-he-said (9) I-will-possess-her that I-can-know how? Yahweh Lord

קְחָה לִי עֶגְלָה מְשֻׁלֶּשֶׁת וְעֵז מְשֻׁלֶּשֶׁת
being-three-years-old and-goat being-three-years-old heifer to-me bring!

וְאַיִל מְשֻׁלָּשׁ וְתֹר וְגוֹזָל׃ וַיִּקַּח־ לוֹ
to-him so-he-brought (10) and-pigeon and-dove being-three-years-old and-ram

אֶת־ כָּל־ אֵלֶּה וַיְבַתֵּר אֹתָם בַּתָּוֶךְ וַיִּתֵּן אִישׁ־
each and-he-arranged in-the-middle them and-he-cut-in-two these all-of ***

בִּתְרוֹ לִקְרַאת רֵעֵהוּ וְאֶת־ הַצִּפֹּר* לֹא בָתָר׃
he-cut-in-half not the-bird but other-of-him to-be-opposite half-of-him

וַיֵּרֶד הָעַיִט עַל־ הַפְּגָרִים וַיַּשֵּׁב
but-he-drive-away the-carcasses on the-bird-of-prey then-he-came-down (11)

אֹתָם אַבְרָם׃ וַיְהִי הַשֶּׁמֶשׁ לָבוֹא וְתַרְדֵּמָה נָפְלָה עַל־ אַבְרָם
Abram on she-fell and-deep-sleep to-set the-sun as-he-was (12) Abram them

וְהִנֵּה אֵימָה חֲשֵׁכָה גְדֹלָה נֹפֶלֶת עָלָיו׃ וַיֹּאמֶר לְאַבְרָם
to-Abram then-he-said (13) over-him coming great darkness dreadful and-see!

יָדֹעַ תֵּדַע כִּי־ גֵר ׀ יִהְיֶה זַרְעֲךָ בְּאֶרֶץ לֹא
not in-country descendant-of-you he-will-be stranger that you-know to-know

לָהֶם וַעֲבָדוּם וְעִנּוּ אֹתָם אַרְבַּע מֵאוֹת
hundreds four them and-they-will-mistreat and-they-will-serve-them to-them

and the one who will inherit[r]
my estate is Eliezer of Damascus?" 3And Abram said, "You
have given me no children; so
a servant in my household
will be my heir."
4Then the word of the LORD
came to him: "This man will
not be your heir, but a son
coming from your own body
will be your heir." 5He took
him outside and said, "Look
up at the heavens and count
the stars—if indeed you can
count them." Then he said to
him, "So shall your offspring
be."
6Abram believed the LORD,
and he credited it to him as
righteousness.
7He also said to him, "I am
the LORD, who brought you
out of Ur of the Chaldeans to
give you this land to take
possession of it."
8But Abram said, "O Sovereign LORD, how can I know
that I will gain possession of
it?"
9So the LORD said to him,
"Bring me a heifer, a goat and
a ram, each three years old,
along with a dove and a young
pigeon."
10Abram brought all these to
him, cut them in two and arranged the halves opposite
each other; the birds, however, he did not cut in half.
11Then birds of prey came
down on the carcasses, but
Abram drove them away.
12As the sun was setting,
Abram fell into a deep sleep,
and a thick and dreadful darkness came over him. 13Then
the LORD said to him, "Know
for certain that your descendants will be strangers in a
country not their own, and
they will be enslaved and mistreated four hundred years.

[r]2 The meaning of the Hebrew for this phrase is uncertain.

*10 Most mss have *dagesh* in the *tsade* (הצ׳).

שָׁנָה׃ וְגַם אֶת־הַגּוֹי אֲשֶׁר יַעֲבֹדוּ דָּן אָנֹכִי וְאַחֲרֵי־
and-after I punishing they-serve that the-nation *** but-indeed (14) year

כֵן יֵצְאוּ בִּרְכֻשׁ גָּדוֹל׃ וְאַתָּה תָּבוֹא אֶל־
to you-will-go but-you (15) great with-possession they-will-come-out that

אֲבֹתֶיךָ בְּשָׁלוֹם תִּקָּבֵר בְּשֵׂיבָה טוֹבָה׃ וְדוֹר
and-generation (16) good at-old-age you-will-be-buried in-peace fathers-of-you

רְבִיעִי יָשׁוּבוּ הֵנָּה כִּי לֹא־שָׁלֵם עֲוֺן הָאֱמֹרִי עַד־הֵנָּה׃
here to the-Amorite sin-of full not for here they-will-come-back fourth

וַיְהִי הַשֶּׁמֶשׁ בָּאָה וַעֲלָטָה הָיָה וְהִנֵּה תַנּוּר עָשָׁן
smoke fire-pot and-see! he-fell and-darkness he-set the-sun and-he-was (17)

וְלַפִּיד אֵשׁ אֲשֶׁר עָבַר בֵּין הַגְּזָרִים הָאֵלֶּה׃ בַּיּוֹם
on-the-day (18) the-these the-pieces between he-passed that blaze and-torch

הַהוּא כָּרַת יְהוָה אֶת־אַבְרָם בְּרִית לֵאמֹר לְזַרְעֲךָ נָתַתִּי
I-give to-descendant-of-you to-say covenant Abram with Yahweh he-made the-that

אֶת־הָאָרֶץ הַזֹּאת מִנְּהַר מִצְרַיִם עַד־הַנָּהָר הַגָּדֹל נְהַר־
river-of the-great the-river to Egypt from-river-of the-this the-land ***

פְּרָת׃ אֶת־הַקֵּינִי וְאֶת־הַקְּנִזִּי וְאֵת הַקַּדְמֹנִי׃ וְאֶת־
and (20) the-Kadmonite and the-Kenizzite and the-Kenite *** (19) Euphrates

הַחִתִּי וְאֶת־הַפְּרִזִּי וְאֶת־הָרְפָאִים׃ וְאֶת־הָאֱמֹרִי וְאֶת־
and the-Amorite and (21) the-Rephaites and the-Perizzite and the-Hittite

הַכְּנַעֲנִי וְאֶת־הַגִּרְגָּשִׁי וְאֶת־הַיְבוּסִי׃ וְשָׂרַי אֵשֶׁת
wife-of now-Sarai (16:1) the-Jebusite and the-Girgashite and the-Canaanite

אַבְרָם לֹא יָלְדָה לוֹ וְלָהּ שִׁפְחָה מִצְרִית וּשְׁמָהּ
and-name-of-her Egyptian maidservant but-to-her for-him she-bore not Abram

הָגָר׃ וַתֹּאמֶר שָׂרַי אֶל־אַבְרָם הִנֵּה־נָא עֲצָרַנִי יְהוָה מִלֶּדֶת
from-to-bear Yahweh he-kept-me now! see! Abram to Sarai so-she-said (2) Hagar

בֹּא־נָא אֶל־שִׁפְחָתִי אוּלַי אִבָּנֶה מִמֶּנָּה*
through-her I-can-build-family perhaps maidservant-of-me to now! go!

וַיִּשְׁמַע אַבְרָם לְקוֹל שָׂרָי׃ וַתִּקַּח שָׂרַי אֵשֶׁת־אַבְרָם
Abram wife-of Sarai so-she-took (3) Sarai to-voice-of Abram and-he-listened

אֶת־הָגָר הַמִּצְרִית שִׁפְחָתָהּ מִקֵּץ עֶשֶׂר שָׁנִים לְשֶׁבֶת אַבְרָם
Abram to-live years ten at-end-of maidservant-of-her the-Egyptian Hagar ***

בְּאֶרֶץ כְּנָעַן וַתִּתֵּן אֹתָהּ לְאַבְרָם אִישָׁהּ לוֹ לְאִשָּׁה׃
as-wife to-him husband-of-her to-Abram her and-she-gave Canaan in-land-of

וַיָּבֹא אֶל־הָגָר וַתַּהַר וַתֵּרֶא כִּי הָרָתָה
she-was-pregnant that when-she-saw and-she-conceived Hagar to and-he-went (4)

וַתֵּקַל גְּבִרְתָּהּ בְּעֵינֶיהָ׃ וַתֹּאמֶר שָׂרַי אֶל־
to Sarai so-she-said (5) with-eyes-of-her mistress-of-her then-she-despised

[14]But I will punish the nation they serve as slaves, and afterward they will come out with great possessions. [15]You, however, will go to your fathers in peace and be buried at a good old age. [16]In the fourth generation your descendants will come back here, for the sin of the Amorites has not yet reached its full measure."

[17]When the sun had set and darkness had fallen, a smoking fire pot with a blazing torch appeared and passed between the pieces. [18]On that day the LORD made a covenant with Abram and said, "To your descendants I give this land, from the river[s] of Egypt to the great river, the Euphrates— [19]the land of the Kenites, Kenizzites, Kadmonites, [20]Hittites, Perizzites, Rephaites, [21]Amorites, Canaanites, Girgashites and Jebusites."

*Hagar and Ishmael*

16 Now Sarai, Abram's wife, had borne him no children. But she had an Egyptian maidservant named Hagar; [2]so she said to Abram, "The LORD has kept me from having children. Go, sleep with my maidservant; perhaps I can build a family through her."

Abram agreed to what Sarai said. [3]So after Abram had been living in Canaan ten years, Sarai his wife took her Egyptian maidservant Hagar and gave her to her husband to be his wife. [4]He slept with Hagar, and she conceived.

When she knew she was pregnant, she began to despise her mistress. [5]Then Sarai

[s]18 Or *Wadi*

*2 Most mss have *segol* under the second *mem* (מִמֶּ).

אַבְרָם חֲמָסִי עָלֶיךָ אָנֹכִי נָתַתִּי שִׁפְחָתִי בְּחֵיקֶךָ וַתֵּרֶא
now-she-sees in-arm-of-you servant-of-me I-put I upon-you wrong-to-me Abram

כִּי הָרָתָה וָאֵקַל בְּעֵינֶיהָ יִשְׁפֹּט יְהוָה
Yahweh may-he-judge in-eyes-of-her and-I-am-despised she-is-pregnant that

בֵּינִי וּבֵינֶיךָ׃ וַיֹּאמֶר אַבְרָם אֶל־שָׂרַי הִנֵּה שִׁפְחָתֵךְ
servant-of-you see! Sarai to Abram so-he-said (6) and-between-you between-me

בְּיָדֵךְ עֲשִׂי־לָהּ הַטּוֹב בְּעֵינָיִךְ וַתְּעַנֶּהָ
then-she-mistreated-her in-eyes-of-you the-good with-her do! in-hands-of-you

שָׂרַי וַתִּבְרַח מִפָּנֶיהָ׃ וַיִּמְצָאָהּ מַלְאַךְ יְהוָה עַל־
near Yahweh angel-of and-he-found-her (7) from-face-of-her so-she-fled Sarai

עֵין הַמַּיִם בַּמִּדְבָּר עַל־הָעַיִן בְּדֶרֶךְ שׁוּר׃
Shur beside-road-of the-spring near in-the-desert the-water spring-of

וַיֹּאמַר הָגָר שִׁפְחַת שָׂרַי אֵי־מִזֶּה בָאת וְאָנָה
and-where you-came from-there where? Sarai servant-of Hagar and-he-said (8)

תֵלֵכִי וַתֹּאמֶר מִפְּנֵי שָׂרַי גְּבִרְתִּי אָנֹכִי בֹּרַחַת׃
running I mistress-of-me Sarai from-face-of and-she-answered you-go

וַיֹּאמֶר לָהּ מַלְאַךְ יְהוָה שׁוּבִי אֶל־גְּבִרְתֵּךְ
mistress-of-you to go-back! Yahweh angel-of to-her then-he-told (9)

וְהִתְעַנִּי תַּחַת יָדֶיהָ׃ וַיֹּאמֶר לָהּ מַלְאַךְ יְהוָה
Yahweh angel-of to-her and-he-said (10) hands-of-her under and-submit!

הַרְבָּה אַרְבֶּה אֶת־זַרְעֵךְ וְלֹא יִסָּפֵר
he-will-be-counted so-not descendant-of-you *** I-will-increase to-increase

מֵרֹב׃ וַיֹּאמֶר לָהּ מַלְאַךְ יְהוָה הִנָּךְ הָרָה
with-child see-you! Yahweh angel-of to-her also-he-said (11) because-of-size

וְיֹלַדְתְּ בֵּן וְקָרָאת שְׁמוֹ יִשְׁמָעֵאל כִּי־שָׁמַע
he-heard for Ishmael name-of-him and-you-shall-call son and-you-will-have

יְהוָה אֶל־עָנְיֵךְ׃ וְהוּא יִהְיֶה פֶּרֶא אָדָם יָדוֹ
hand-of-him man wild-donkey-of he-will-be and-he (12) misery-of-you to Yahweh

בַכֹּל וְיַד כֹּל בּוֹ וְעַל־פְּנֵי
faces-of and-against against-him everyone and-hand-of against-everyone

כָל־אֶחָיו יִשְׁכֹּן׃ וַתִּקְרָא שֵׁם־יְהוָה
Yahweh name-of and-she-called (13) he-will-live brothers-of-him all-of

הַדֹּבֵר אֵלֶיהָ אַתָּה אֵל רֳאִי כִּי אָמְרָה הֲגַם הֲלֹם רָאִיתִי אַחֲרֵי
back-of I-saw here now? she-said for sight God-of you to-her the-one-speaking

רֹאִי׃ עַל־כֵּן קָרָא לַבְּאֵר בְּאֵר לַחַי רֹאִי הִנֵּה בֵין־
between see! Roi Lahai Beer to-the-well he-called this for (14) one-seeing-me

קָדֵשׁ וּבֵין בָּרֶד׃ וַתֵּלֶד הָגָר לְאַבְרָם בֵּן וַיִּקְרָא
and-he-gave son to-Abram Hagar so-she-bore (15) Bered and-between Kadesh

said to Abram, "You are responsible for the wrong I am suffering. I put my servant in your arms, and now that she knows she is pregnant, she despises me. May the LORD judge between you and me."

[6]"Your servant is in your hands," Abram said. "Do with her whatever you think best." Then Sarai mistreated Hagar; so she fled from her.

[7]The angel of the LORD found Hagar near a spring in the desert; it was the spring that is beside the road to Shur. [8]And he said, "Hagar, servant of Sarai, where have you come from, and where are you going?"

"I'm running away from my mistress Sarai," she answered.

[9]Then the angel of the LORD told her, "Go back to your mistress and submit to her." [10]The angel added, "I will so increase your descendants that they will be too numerous to count."

[11]The angel of the LORD also said to her:

"You are now with child
and you will have a son.
You shall name him
Ishmael,[t]
for the LORD has heard of
your misery.
[12]He will be a wild donkey
of a man;
his hand will be against
everyone
and everyone's hand
against him,
and he will live in hostility
toward[u] all his brothers."

[13]She gave this name to the LORD who spoke to her: "You are the God who sees me," for she said, "I have now seen[v] the One who sees me." [14]That is why the well was called Beer Lahai Roi[w]; it is still there, between Kadesh and Bered.

[15]So Hagar bore Abram a son, and Abram gave the

[t]11 *Ishmael* means *God hears.*
[u]12 Or *live to the east / of*
[v]13 Or *seen the back of*
[w]14 *Beer Lahai Roi* means *well of the Living One who sees me.*

אַבְרָם שֶׁם־ בְּנוֹ אֲשֶׁר־ יָלְדָה הָגָר יִשְׁמָעֵאל׃ וְאַבְרָם בֶּן־
son-of and-Abram (16) Ishmael Hagar she-bore whom son-of-him name-of Abram

שְׁמֹנִים שָׁנָה וְשֵׁשׁ שָׁנִים בְּלֶדֶת־ הָגָר אֶת־יִשְׁמָעֵאל לְאַבְרָם׃
for-Abram Ishmael *** Hagar when-to-bear years and-six year eighty

וַיְהִי אַבְרָם בֶּן־ תִּשְׁעִים שָׁנָה וְתֵשַׁע שָׁנִים וַיֵּרָא
and-he-appeared years and-nine year ninety son-of Abram when-he-was (17:1)

יְהוָה אֶל־אַבְרָם וַיֹּאמֶר אֵלָיו אֲנִי־אֵל שַׁדַּי הִתְהַלֵּךְ לְפָנַי וֶהְיֵה
and-be! before-me walk! Almighty God I to-him and-he-said Abram to Yahweh

תָמִים׃ וְאֶתְּנָה בְרִיתִי בֵּינִי וּבֵינֶךָ
and-between-you between-me covenant-of-me and-I-will-confirm (2) blameless

וְאַרְבֶּה אוֹתְךָ בִּמְאֹד מְאֹד׃ וַיִּפֹּל אַבְרָם עַל־ פָּנָיו
face-of-him on Abram and-he-fell (3) greatly greatly you and-I-will-increase

וַיְדַבֵּר אִתּוֹ אֱלֹהִים לֵאמֹר׃ אֲנִי הִנֵּה בְרִיתִי אִתָּךְ וְהָיִיתָ
now-you-will-be with-you covenant-of-me see! I (4) to-say God to-him and-he-said

לְאַב הֲמוֹן גּוֹיִם׃ וְלֹא־ יִקָּרֵא עוֹד אֶת־
*** longer he-will-be-called and-not (5) nations many-of as-father-of

שִׁמְךָ אַבְרָם וְהָיָה שִׁמְךָ אַבְרָהָם כִּי אַב־ הֲמוֹן
many-of father-of for Abraham name-of-you but-he-will-be Abram name-of-you

גּוֹיִם נְתַתִּיךָ׃ וְהִפְרֵתִי אֹתְךָ בִּמְאֹד מְאֹד
greatly greatly you and-I-will-make-fruitful (6) I-made-you nations

וּנְתַתִּיךָ לְגוֹיִם וּמְלָכִים מִמְּךָ יֵצֵאוּ׃
they-will-come from-you and-kings into-nations and-I-will-make-you

וַהֲקִמֹתִי אֶת־ בְּרִיתִי בֵּינִי וּבֵינֶךָ וּבֵין
and-between and-between-you between-me covenant-of-me *** and-I-will-establish (7)

זַרְעֲךָ אַחֲרֶיךָ לְדֹרֹתָם לִבְרִית עוֹלָם
everlasting as-covenant-of for-generations-of-them after-you descendant-of-you

לִהְיוֹת לְךָ לֵאלֹהִים וּלְזַרְעֲךָ אַחֲרֶיךָ׃ וְנָתַתִּי
and-I-will-give (8) after-you and-to-descendant-of-you as-God to-you to-be

לְךָ וּלְזַרְעֲךָ אַחֲרֶיךָ אֵת ׀ אֶרֶץ מְגֻרֶיךָ אֵת
*** journeys-of-you land-of *** after-you and-to-descendant-of-you to-you

כָּל־ אֶרֶץ כְּנַעַן לַאֲחֻזַּת עוֹלָם וְהָיִיתִי לָהֶם
to-them and-I-will-be everlasting as-possession-of Canaan land-of whole-of

לֵאלֹהִים׃ וַיֹּאמֶר אֱלֹהִים אֶל־אַבְרָהָם וְאַתָּה אֶת־ בְּרִיתִי תִשְׁמֹר
you-keep covenant-of-me *** now-you Abraham to God then-he-said (9) as-God

אַתָּה וְזַרְעֲךָ אַחֲרֶיךָ לְדֹרֹתָם׃ זֹאת
this (10) for-generations-of-them after-you and-descendant-of-you you

בְּרִיתִי אֲשֶׁר תִּשְׁמְרוּ בֵּינִי וּבֵינֵיכֶם וּבֵין
and-between and-between-you between-me you-must-keep that covenant-of-me

name Ishmael to the son she
had borne. 16Abram was
eighty-six years old when Hagar bore him Ishmael.

*The Covenant of Circumcision*

17 When Abram was
ninety-nine years old, the LORD appeared to him and said, "I am God Almighty[x]; walk before me and be blameless.
2I will confirm my covenant between me and you and will greatly increase your numbers."
3Abram fell facedown, and God said to him,
4"As for me, this is my covenant with you: You will be the father of many nations.
5No longer will you be called Abram[y]; your name will be Abraham,[z] for I have made you a father of many nations.
6I will make you very fruitful; I will make nations of you, and kings will come from you.
7I will establish my covenant as an everlasting covenant between me and you and your descendants after you for the generations to come, to be your God and the God of your descendants after you.
8The whole land of Canaan, where you are now an alien, I will give as an everlasting possession to you and your descendants after you; and I will be their God."
9Then God said to Abraham, "As for you, you must keep my covenant, you and your descendants after you for the generations to come.
10This is my covenant with you and your descendants after you, the covenant you are to keep:

x1 Hebrew *El-Shaddai*
y5 *Abram* means *exalted father.*
z5 *Abraham* means *father of many.*

זַרְעֲךָ אַחֲרֶיךָ הִמּוֹל לָכֶם כָּל־ זָכָר׃
male every-of among-you to-be-circumcised after-you descendant-of-you

(11) וּנְמַלְתֶּם אֵת בְּשַׂר עָרְלַתְכֶם וְהָיָה
and-he-will-be foreskin-of-you flesh-of *** and-you-will-be-circumcised (11)

לְאוֹת בְּרִית בֵּינִי וּבֵינֵיכֶם׃ (12) וּבֶן־ שְׁמֹנַת יָמִים
days eight-of and-son-of (12) and-between-you between-me covenant as-sign-of

יִמּוֹל לָכֶם כָּל־ זָכָר לְדֹרֹתֵיכֶם יְלִיד
born-of for-generations-of-you male every-of among-you he-must-be-circumcised

בָּיִת וּמִקְנַת־ כֶּסֶף מִכֹּל בֶּן־ נֵכָר אֲשֶׁר לֹא
not who foreigner son-of from-every-of money or-bought-of household

מִזַּרְעֲךָ הוּא׃ (13) הִמּוֹל ׀ יִמּוֹל יְלִיד
born-of he-must-be-circumcised to-be-circumcised (13) he from-offspring-of-you

בֵּיתְךָ וּמִקְנַת כַּסְפֶּךָ וְהָיְתָה בְרִיתִי
covenant-of-me so-she-will-be money-of-you or-bought-of household-of-you

בִּבְשַׂרְכֶם לִבְרִית עוֹלָם׃ (14) וְעָרֵל ׀ זָכָר אֲשֶׁר
who male but-uncircumcised (14) everlasting as-covenant-of in-flesh-of-you

לֹא־ יִמּוֹל אֶת־ בְּשַׂר עָרְלָתוֹ וְנִכְרְתָה
and-she-will-be-cut-off foreskin-of-him flesh-of *** he-is-circumcised not

הַנֶּפֶשׁ הַהִוא מֵעַמֶּיהָ אֶת־ בְּרִיתִי הֵפַר׃
he-broke covenant-of-me *** from-people-of-her the-that the-person

(15) וַיֹּאמֶר אֱלֹהִים אֶל־אַבְרָהָם שָׂרַי אִשְׁתְּךָ לֹא־תִקְרָא אֶת־ שְׁמָהּ
name-of-her *** you-call not wife-of-you Sarai Abraham to God and-he-said (15)

שָׂרָי כִּי שָׂרָה שְׁמָהּ׃ (16) וּבֵרַכְתִּי אֹתָהּ וְגַם נָתַתִּי
I-will-give and-surely her and-I-will-bless (16) name-of-her Sarah for Sarai

מִמֶּנָּה לְךָ בֵּן וּבֵרַכְתִּיהָ וְהָיְתָה לְגוֹיִם מַלְכֵי
kings-of as-nations so-she-will-be and-I-will-bless-her son to-you by-her

עַמִּים מִמֶּנָּה יִהְיוּ׃ (17) וַיִּפֹּל אַבְרָהָם עַל־ פָּנָיו
face-of-him on Abraham and-he-fell (17) they-will-come from-her peoples

וַיִּצְחָק וַיֹּאמֶר בְּלִבּוֹ הַלְּבֶן מֵאָה־ שָׁנָה יִוָּלֵד
he-will-be-born year hundred to-son-of? in-heart-him and-he-said and-he-laughed

וְאִם־ שָׂרָה הֲבַת תִּשְׁעִים שָׁנָה תֵּלֵד׃ (18) וַיֹּאמֶר אַבְרָהָם
Abraham and-he-said (18) she-will-bear year ninety daughter-of? Sarah and-if

אֶל־הָאֱלֹהִים לוּ יִשְׁמָעֵאל יִחְיֶה לְפָנֶיךָ׃ (19) וַיֹּאמֶר אֱלֹהִים אֲבָל
yes-but God then-he-said (19) before-you he-might-live Ishmael if-only the-God to

שָׂרָה אִשְׁתְּךָ יֹלֶדֶת לְךָ בֵּן וְקָרָאתָ אֶת־ שְׁמוֹ יִצְחָק
Isaac name-of-him *** and-you-will-call son for-you bearing wife-of-you Sarah

וַהֲקִמֹתִי אֶת־ בְּרִיתִי אִתּוֹ לִבְרִית עוֹלָם
everlasting as-covenant-of with-him covenant-of-me *** and-I-will-establish

Every male among you shall be circumcised. [11]You are to undergo circumcision, and it will be the sign of the covenant between me and you. [12]For the generations to come every male among you who is eight days old must be circumcised, including those born in your household or bought with money from a foreigner—those who are not your offspring. [13]Whether born in your household or bought with your money, they must be circumcised. My covenant in your flesh is to be an everlasting covenant. [14]Any uncircumcised male, who has not been circumcised in the flesh, will be cut off from his people; he has broken my covenant."

[15]God also said to Abraham, "As for Sarai your wife, you are no longer to call her Sarai; her name will be Sarah.[a] [16]I will bless her and will surely give you a son by her. I will bless her so that she will be the mother of nations; kings of peoples will come from her."

[17]Abraham fell facedown; he laughed and said to himself, "Will a son be born to a man a hundred years old? Will Sarah bear a child at the age of ninety?" [18]And Abraham said to God, "If only Ishmael might live under your blessing!"

[19]Then God said, "Yes, but your wife Sarah will bear you a son, and you will call him Isaac.[b] I will establish my covenant with him as an everlasting covenant for his descendants after him. [20]And as for

[a]15 *Sarah* means *princess.*
[b]19 *Isaac* means *he laughs.*

לְזַרְעוֹ אַחֲרָיו׃ וּלְיִשְׁמָעֵאל שְׁמַעְתִּיךָ הִנֵּה ׀

see! I-heard-you and-for-Ishmael (20) after-him for-descendant-of-him

בֵּרַכְתִּי אֹתוֹ וְהִפְרֵיתִי אֹתוֹ וְהִרְבֵּיתִי אֹתוֹ בִּמְאֹד

greatly him and-I-will-increase him and-I-will-make-fruitful him I-will-bless

מְאֹד שְׁנֵים־עָשָׂר נְשִׂיאִם יוֹלִיד וּנְתַתִּיו לְגוֹי גָּדוֹל׃

great into-nation and-I-will-make-him he-will-father rulers ten two greatly

וְאֶת־ בְּרִיתִי אָקִים אֶת־ יִצְחָק אֲשֶׁר תֵּלֵד לְךָ

to-you she-will-bear whom Isaac with I-will-establish covenant-of-me but (21)

שָׂרָה לַמּוֹעֵד הַזֶּה בַּשָּׁנָה הָאַחֶרֶת׃ וַיְכַל

when-he-finished (22) the-next in-the-year the-this by-the-time Sarah

לְדַבֵּר אִתּוֹ וַיַּעַל אֱלֹהִים מֵעַל אַבְרָהָם׃ וַיִּקַּח אַבְרָהָם

Abraham and-he-took (23) Abraham from God then-he-went-up with-him to-speak

אֶת־ יִשְׁמָעֵאל בְּנוֹ וְאֵת כָּל־ יְלִידֵי בֵיתוֹ וְאֵת כָּל־

all-of and household-of-him born-ones-of all-of and son-of-him Ishmael ***

מִקְנַת כַּסְפּוֹ כָּל־ זָכָר בְּאַנְשֵׁי בֵּית אַבְרָהָם

Abraham household-of among-men-of male every-of money-of-him bought-of

וַיָּמָל אֶת־ בְּשַׂר עָרְלָתָם בְּעֶצֶם הַיּוֹם הַזֶּה

the-that the-day on-very-of foreskin-of-them flesh-of *** and-he-circumcised

כַּאֲשֶׁר דִּבֶּר אִתּוֹ אֱלֹהִים׃ וְאַבְרָהָם בֶּן־ תִּשְׁעִים וָתֵשַׁע שָׁנָה

year and-nine ninety son-of now-Abraham (24) God him he-told just-as

בְּהִמֹּלוֹ בְּשַׂר עָרְלָתוֹ׃ וְיִשְׁמָעֵאל בְּנוֹ

son-of-him and-Ishmael (25) foreskin-of-him flesh-of when-to-be-circumcised-him

בֶּן־ שְׁלֹשׁ עֶשְׂרֵה שָׁנָה בְּהִמֹּלוֹ אֵת בְּשַׂר עָרְלָתוֹ׃

foreskin-of-him flesh-of *** when-to-be-circumcised-him year ten three son-of

בְּעֶצֶם הַיּוֹם הַזֶּה נִמּוֹל אַבְרָהָם וְיִשְׁמָעֵאל

and-Ishmael Abraham being-circumcised the-that the-day on-very-of (26)

בְּנוֹ׃ וְכָל־ אַנְשֵׁי בֵיתוֹ יְלִיד בָּיִת

household born-of household-of-him men-of and-all-of (27) son-of-him

וּמִקְנַת־ כֶּסֶף מֵאֵת בֶּן־ נֵכָר נִמֹּלוּ אִתּוֹ׃

with-him they-were-circumcised foreigner son-of from money or-bought-of

וַיֵּרָא אֵלָיו יְהוָה בְּאֵלֹנֵי מַמְרֵא וְהוּא יֹשֵׁב

sitting and-he Mamre near-trees-of Yahweh to-him and-he-appeared (18:1)

פֶּתַח־ הָאֹהֶל כְּחֹם הַיּוֹם׃ וַיִּשָּׂא עֵינָיו

eyes-of-him and-he-lifted (2) the-day in-heat-of the-tent entrance-of

וַיַּרְא וְהִנֵּה שְׁלֹשָׁה אֲנָשִׁים נִצָּבִים עָלָיו וַיַּרְא וַיָּרָץ

then-he-ran when-he-saw near-him ones-standing men three and-see! and-he-saw

לִקְרָאתָם מִפֶּתַח הָאֹהֶל וַיִּשְׁתַּחוּ אָרְצָה׃ וַיֹּאמַר

and-he-said (3) to-ground and-he-bowed the-tent from-entrance-of to-meet-them

Ishmael, I have heard you: I
will surely bless him; I will
make him fruitful and will
greatly increase his numbers.
He will be the father of twelve
rulers, and I will make him
into a great nation. [21]But my
covenant I will establish with
Isaac, whom Sarah will bear to
you by this time next year."
[22]When he had finished
speaking with Abraham, God
went up from him.
[23]On that very day Abraham
took his son Ishmael and all
those born in his household or
bought with his money, every
male in his household, and
circumcised them, as God told
him. [24]Abraham was ninety-
nine years old when he was
circumcised, [25]and his son Ishmael was thirteen; [26]Abraham
and his son Ishmael were both
circumcised on that same day.
[27]And every male in Abraham's household, including
those born in his household or
bought from a foreigner, was
circumcised with him.

*The Three Visitors*

18 The LORD appeared to
Abraham near the
great trees of Mamre while he
was sitting at the entrance to
his tent in the heat of the day.
[2]Abraham looked up and saw
three men standing nearby.
When he saw them, he hur-
ried from the entrance of his
tent to meet them and bowed
low to the ground.

אֲדֹנָי אִם־נָא מָצָאתִי חֵן בְּעֵינֶיךָ אַל־נָא תַעֲבֹר מֵעַל עַבְדֶּךָ׃
servant-of-you by you-pass now! not in-eyes-of-you favor I-found now! if my-lord

יֻקַּח־נָא מְעַט־מַיִם וְרַחֲצוּ רַגְלֵיכֶם וְהִשָּׁעֲנוּ
and-rest! feet-of-you then-wash! water little-of now! let-him-be-brought (4)

תַּחַת הָעֵץ׃ וְאֶקְחָה פַת־לֶחֶם וְסַעֲדוּ לִבְּכֶם אַחַר
then heart-of-you and-refresh! bread piece-of and-let-me-get (5) the-tree under

תַּעֲבֹרוּ כִּי־עַל־כֵּן עֲבַרְתֶּם עַל־עַבְדְּכֶם וַיֹּאמְרוּ כֵּן
very-well and-they-answered servant-of-you to you-came now-that you-go-away

תַּעֲשֶׂה כַּאֲשֶׁר דִּבַּרְתָּ׃ וַיְמַהֵר אַבְרָהָם הָאֹהֱלָה אֶל־שָׂרָה
Sarah to into-the-tent Abraham so-he-hurried (6) you-say just-as you-do

וַיֹּאמֶר מַהֲרִי שְׁלֹשׁ סְאִים קֶמַח סֹלֶת לוּשִׁי וַעֲשִׂי עֻגוֹת׃
loaves and-make! knead! fine flour seahs-of three-of be-quick! and-he-said

וְאֶל־הַבָּקָר רָץ אַבְרָהָם וַיִּקַּח בֶּן־בָּקָר רַךְ
tender herd calf-of and-he-selected Abraham he-ran the-herd and-to (7)

וָטוֹב וַיִּתֵּן אֶל־הַנַּעַר וַיְמַהֵר לַעֲשׂוֹת אֹתוֹ׃
him to-prepare and-he-hurried the-servant to and-he-gave and-choice

וַיִּקַּח חֶמְאָה וְחָלָב וּבֶן־הַבָּקָר אֲשֶׁר עָשָׂה
he-prepared that the-herd and-calf-of and-milk curd then-he-brought (8)

וַיִּתֵּן לִפְנֵיהֶם וְהוּא־עֹמֵד עֲלֵיהֶם תַּחַת הָעֵץ וַיֹּאכֵלוּ׃
as-they-ate the-tree under near-them standing and-he before-them and-he-set

וַיֹּאמְרוּ אֵלָיו אַיֵּה שָׂרָה אִשְׁתֶּךָ וַיֹּאמֶר הִנֵּה
see! and-he-said wife-of-you Sarah where? to-him and-they-asked (9)

בָאֹהֶל׃ וַיֹּאמֶר שׁוֹב אָשׁוּב אֵלֶיךָ כָּעֵת
about-the-time to-you I-will-return to-return then-he-said (10) in-the-tent

חַיָּה וְהִנֵּה־בֵן לְשָׂרָה אִשְׁתֶּךָ וְשָׂרָה שֹׁמַעַת פֶּתַח
entrance-of listening now-Sarah wife-of-you to-Sarah son and-see! spring

הָאֹהֶל וְהוּא אַחֲרָיו׃ וְאַבְרָהָם וְשָׂרָה זְקֵנִים בָּאִים
being-advanced old-ones and-Sarah now-Abraham (11) behind-him and-he the-tent

בַּיָּמִים חָדַל לִהְיוֹת לְשָׂרָה אֹרַח כַּנָּשִׁים׃
normal-to-the-women manner with-Sarah to-be he-was-past in-the-days

וַתִּצְחַק שָׂרָה בְּקִרְבָּהּ לֵאמֹר אַחֲרֵי בְלֹתִי הָיְתָה־
she-is to-be-worn-out-me after to-say to-self-of-her Sarah so-she-laughed (12)

לִּי עֶדְנָה וַאדֹנִי זָקֵן׃ וַיֹּאמֶר יְהוָה אֶל־אַבְרָהָם
Abraham to Yahweh then-he-said (13) he-is-old and-master-of-me pleasure to-me

לָמָּה זֶּה צָחֲקָה שָׂרָה לֵאמֹר הַאַף אֻמְנָם אֵלֵד וַאֲנִי זָקַנְתִּי׃
I-am-old yet-I I-will-bear really? now? to-say Sarah she-laughed this why?

הֲיִפָּלֵא מֵיְהוָה דָּבָר לַמּוֹעֵד אָשׁוּב אֵלֶיךָ
to-you I-will-return at-the-time anything for-Yahweh is-he-too-hard? (14)

3 He said, "If I have found favor in your eyes, my lord,[c] do
not pass your servant by. 4 Let
a little water be brought, and
then you may all wash your
feet and rest under this tree.
5 Let me get you something to
eat, so you can be refreshed
and then go on your way—
now that you have come to
your servant."
"Very well," they answered,
"do as you say."
6 So Abraham hurried into
the tent to Sarah. "Quick," he
said, "get three seahs[d] of fine
flour and knead it and bake
some bread."
7 Then he ran to the herd and
selected a choice, tender calf
and gave it to a servant, who
hurried to prepare it. 8 He then
brought some curds and milk
and the calf that had been prepared, and set these before
them. While they ate, he stood
near them under a tree.
9 "Where is your wife Sarah?" they asked him.
"There, in the tent," he said.
10 Then the LORD[e] said, "I will
surely return to you about this
time next year, and Sarah your
wife will have a son."
Now Sarah was listening at
the entrance to the tent, which
was behind him. 11 Abraham
and Sarah were already old
and well advanced in years,
and Sarah was past the age of
childbearing. 12 So Sarah
laughed to herself as she
thought, "After I am worn out
and my master[f] is old, will I
now have this pleasure?"
13 Then the LORD said to
Abraham, "Why did Sarah
laugh and say, 'Will I really
have a child, now that I am
old?' 14 Is anything too hard for
the LORD? I will return to you

c3 Or *O Lord*
d6 That is, probably about 20 quarts (about 22 liters)
e10 Hebrew *he*
f12 Or *husband*

כָּעֵת חַיָּה וּלְשָׂרָה בֵן׃ וַתְּכַחֵשׁ שָׂרָה ׀ לֵאמֹר לֹא
not to-say Sarah so-she-lied (15) son and-to-Sarah spring at-the-time

צָחַקְתִּי כִּי ׀ יָרֵאָה וַיֹּאמֶר ׀ לֹא כִּי צָחָקְתְּ׃
you-did-laugh indeed no but-he-said she-was-afraid for I-laughed

וַיָּקֻמוּ מִשָּׁם הָאֲנָשִׁים וַיַּשְׁקִפוּ עַל־ פְּנֵי סְדֹם
Sodom toward-of down then-they-looked the-men from-there when-they-got-up (16)

וְאַבְרָהָם הֹלֵךְ עִמָּם לְשַׁלְּחָם׃ וַיהוָה אָמָר
he-said then-Yahweh (17) to-send-off-them with-them walking and-Abraham

הַמְכַסֶּה אֲנִי מֵאַבְרָהָם אֲשֶׁר אֲנִי עֹשֶׂה׃ וְאַבְרָהָם הָיוֹ יִהְיֶה
he-will-become to-become now-Abraham (18) doing I what from-Abraham I hiding?

לְגוֹי גָּדוֹל וְעָצוּם וְנִבְרְכוּ בוֹ כֹּל
all-of through-him and-they-will-be-blessed and-powerful great to-nation

גּוֹיֵי הָאָרֶץ׃ כִּי יְדַעְתִּיו לְמַעַן אֲשֶׁר יְצַוֶּה אֶת־
*** he-will-direct that so I-chose-him for (19) the-earth nations-of

בָּנָיו וְאֶת־ בֵּיתוֹ אַחֲרָיו וְשָׁמְרוּ דֶּרֶךְ
way-of so-they-will-keep after-him household-of-him and children-of-him

יְהוָה לַעֲשׂוֹת צְדָקָה וּמִשְׁפָּט לְמַעַן הָבִיא יְהוָה עַל־אַבְרָהָם אֵת אֲשֶׁר־
what *** Abraham for Yahweh he-will-bring so-that and-just right to-do Yahweh

דִּבֶּר עָלָיו׃ וַיֹּאמֶר יְהוָה זַעֲקַת סְדֹם וַעֲמֹרָה כִּי־
so and-Gomorrah Sodom outcry-of Yahweh then-he-said (20) to-him he-promised

רָבָּה וְחַטָּאתָם כִּי כָבְדָה מְאֹד׃ אֵרֲדָה־ נָּא
now! I-will-go-down (21) very she-is-grievous so and-sin-of-them she-is-great

וְאֶרְאֶה הַכְּצַעֲקָתָהּ הַבָּאָה אֵלַי עָשׂוּ ׀
they-did to-me the-one-reaching if-according-to-outcry-of-her and-I-will-see

כָּלָה וְאִם־ לֹא אֵדָעָה׃ וַיִּפְנוּ מִשָּׁם הָאֲנָשִׁים
the-men from-there and-they-turned (22) I-will-know not and-if all

וַיֵּלְכוּ סְדֹמָה וְאַבְרָהָם עוֹדֶנּוּ עֹמֵד לִפְנֵי יְהוָה׃
Yahweh before standing remained-him but-Abraham toward-Sodom and-they-went

וַיִּגַּשׁ אַבְרָהָם וַיֹּאמַר הַאַף תִּסְפֶּה
you-will-sweep-away indeed? and-he-said Abraham then-he-approached (23)

צַדִּיק עִם־ רָשָׁע׃ אוּלַי יֵשׁ חֲמִשִּׁים צַדִּיקִם בְּתוֹךְ
in righteous-ones fifty there-are what-if (24) wicked with righteous

הָעִיר הַאַף תִּסְפֶּה וְלֹא־ תִשָּׂא לַמָּקוֹם
to-the-place you-will-spare and-not you-will-sweep-away indeed? the-city

לְמַעַן חֲמִשִּׁים הַצַּדִּיקִם אֲשֶׁר בְּקִרְבָּהּ׃ חָלִלָה לְּךָ
from-you far-be-it! (25) in-midst-of-her who the-righteous-ones fifty for-sake-of

מֵעֲשֹׂת ׀ כַּדָּבָר הַזֶּה לְהָמִית צַדִּיק עִם־ רָשָׁע וְהָיָה
and-he-be wicked with righteous to-kill the-this such-the-thing from-to-do

at the appointed time next year and Sarah will have a son."

15 Sarah was afraid, so she lied and said, "I did not laugh."

But he said, "Yes, you did laugh."

*Abraham Pleads for Sodom*

16 When the men got up to leave, they looked down toward Sodom, and Abraham walked along with them to see them on their way. 17 Then the LORD said, "Shall I hide from Abraham what I am about to do? 18 Abraham will surely become a great and powerful nation, and all nations on earth will be blessed through him. 19 For I have chosen him, so that he will direct his children and his household after him to keep the way of the LORD by doing what is right and just, so that the LORD will bring about for Abraham what he has promised him."

20 Then the LORD said, "The outcry against Sodom and Gomorrah is so great and their sin so grievous 21 that I will go down and see if what they have done is as bad as the outcry that has reached me. If not, I will know."

22 The men turned away and went toward Sodom, but Abraham remained standing before the LORD.[g] 23 Then Abraham approached him and said: "Will you sweep away the righteous with the wicked? 24 What if there are fifty righteous people in the city? Will you really sweep it away and not spare[h] the place for the sake of the fifty righteous people in it? 25 Far be it from you to do such a thing—to kill the righteous with the

g22 Masoretic Text; an ancient Hebrew scribal tradition *but the LORD remained standing before Abraham*

h24 Or *forgive*; also in verse 26

כַּצַּדִּיק כָּרָשָׁע חָלִלָה לָּךְ הֲשֹׁפֵט כָּל־
all-of one-judging-of? from-you far-be-it! as-the-wicked as-the-righteous

הָאָרֶץ לֹא יַעֲשֶׂה מִשְׁפָּט׃ וַיֹּאמֶר יְהוָה אִם־אֶמְצָא בִסְדֹם
in-Sodom I-find if Yahweh so-he-said (26) right will-he-do not the-earth

חֲמִשִּׁים צַדִּיקִם בְּתוֹךְ הָעִיר וְנָשָׂאתִי לְכָל־ הַמָּקוֹם
the-place to-whole-of then-I-will-spare the-city in righteous-ones fifty

בַּעֲבוּרָם׃ וַיַּעַן אַבְרָהָם וַיֹּאמַר הִנֵּה־ נָא הוֹאַלְתִּי
I-was-bold now! see! and-he-said Abraham then-he-answered (27) for-sake-of-them

לְדַבֵּר אֶל־אֲדֹנָי וְאָנֹכִי עָפָר וָאֵפֶר׃ אוּלַי יַחְסְרוּן חֲמִשִּׁים
the-fifty they-lacked what-if (28) and-ash dust though-I Lord to to-speak

הַצַּדִּיקִם חֲמִשָּׁה הֲתַשְׁחִית בַּחֲמִשָּׁה אֶת־ כָּל־ הָעִיר
the-city whole-of *** because-of-five will-you-destroy? five the-righteous-ones

וַיֹּאמֶר לֹא אַשְׁחִית אִם־ אֶמְצָא שָׁם אַרְבָּעִים וַחֲמִשָּׁה׃
and-five forty there I-find if I-will-destroy not and-he-said

וַיֹּסֶף עוֹד לְדַבֵּר אֵלָיו וַיֹּאמַר אוּלַי יִמָּצְאוּן
they-are-found what-if and-he-said to-him to-speak again and-he-repeated (29)

שָׁם אַרְבָּעִים וַיֹּאמֶר לֹא אֶעֱשֶׂה בַּעֲבוּר הָאַרְבָּעִים׃ וַיֹּאמֶר
and-he-said (30) the-forty for-sake-of I-will-do not and-he-said forty there

אַל־ נָא יִחַר לַאדֹנָי וַאֲדַבֵּרָה אוּלַי יִמָּצְאוּן שָׁם
there they-were-found what-if but-let-me-speak to-Lord may-he-be-angry now! not

שְׁלֹשִׁים וַיֹּאמֶר לֹא אֶעֱשֶׂה אִם־אֶמְצָא שָׁם שְׁלֹשִׁים׃ וַיֹּאמֶר
and-he-said (31) thirty there I-find if I-will-do not and-he-answered thirty

הִנֵּה־ נָא הוֹאַלְתִּי לְדַבֵּר אֶל־ אֲדֹנָי אוּלַי יִמָּצְאוּן שָׁם עֶשְׂרִים
twenty there they-were-found what-if Lord to to-speak I-was-bold now! see!

וַיֹּאמֶר לֹא אַשְׁחִית בַּעֲבוּר הָעֶשְׂרִים׃ וַיֹּאמֶר אַל־ נָא
now! not so-he-said (32) the-twenty for-sake-of I-will-destroy not and-he-said

יִחַר לַאדֹנָי וַאֲדַבְּרָה אַךְ־ הַפַּעַם אוּלַי יִמָּצְאוּן
they-are-found what-if the-once just but-let-me-speak to-Lord may-he-be-angry

שָׁם עֲשָׂרָה וַיֹּאמֶר לֹא אַשְׁחִית בַּעֲבוּר הָעֲשָׂרָה׃
the-ten for-sake-of I-will-destroy not and-he-answered ten there

וַיֵּלֶךְ יְהוָה כַּאֲשֶׁר כִּלָּה לְדַבֵּר אֶל־אַבְרָהָם וְאַבְרָהָם
and-Abraham Abraham with to-speak he-finished as-soon-as Yahweh and-he-left (33)

שָׁב לִמְקֹמוֹ׃ וַיָּבֹאוּ שְׁנֵי הַמַּלְאָכִים סְדֹמָה
at-Sodom the-angels two-of and-they-arrived (19:1) to-home-of-him he-returned

בָּעֶרֶב וְלוֹט יֹשֵׁב בְּשַׁעַר־ סְדֹם וַיַּרְא־ לוֹט
Lot when-he-saw Sodom in-gateway-of sitting and-Lot in-the-evening

וַיָּקָם לִקְרָאתָם וַיִּשְׁתַּחוּ אַפַּיִם אָרְצָה׃ וַיֹּאמֶר הִנֶּה
see! and-he-said (2) to-ground faces and-he-bowed to-meet-them then-he-got-up

wicked, treating the righteous
and the wicked alike. Far be it
from you! Will not the Judge of
all the earth do right?"
26 The LORD said, "If I find
fifty righteous people in the
city of Sodom, I will spare the
whole place for their sake."
27 Then Abraham spoke up
again: "Now that I have been
so bold as to speak to the Lord,
though I am nothing but dust
and ashes, 28 what if the number of the righteous is five less
than fifty? Will you destroy
the whole city because of five
people?"
"If I find forty-five there,"
he said, "I will not destroy it."
29 Once again he spoke to
him, "What if only forty are
found there?"
He said, "For the sake of
forty, I will not do it."
30 Then he said, "May the
Lord not be angry, but let me
speak. What if only thirty can
be found there?"
He answered, "I will not do
it if I find thirty there."
31 Abraham said, "Now that I
have been so bold as to speak
to the Lord, what if only
twenty can be found there?"
He said, "For the sake of
twenty, I will not destroy it."
32 Then he said, "May the
Lord not be angry, but let me
speak just once more. What if
only ten can be found there?"
He answered, "For the sake
of ten, I will not destroy it."
33 When the LORD had
finished speaking with Abraham, he left, and Abraham returned home.

*Sodom and Gomorrah Destroyed*

19 The two angels arrived
at Sodom in the eve-
ning, and Lot was sitting in
the gateway of the city. When
he saw them, he got up to meet
them and bowed down with
his face to the ground. 2 "My

נָא־ אֲדֹנַי סוּרוּ נָא אֶל־ בֵּית עַבְדְּכֶם וְלִינוּ וְרַחֲצוּ
and-wash! and-spend-night! servant-of-you house-of to now! turn! lords-of-me now!

רַגְלֵיכֶם וְהִשְׁכַּמְתֶּם וַהַלַכְתֶּם* לְדַרְכְּכֶם וַיֹּאמְרוּ לֹּא
no but-they-said on-way-of-you and-you-may-go then-you-may-rise feet-of-you

כִּי בָרְחוֹב נָלִין׃ (3) וַיִּפְצַר־ בָּם מְאֹד
strongly with-them but-he-persisted (3) we-will-spend-night in-the-square for

וַיָּסֻרוּ אֵלָיו וַיָּבֹאוּ אֶל־ בֵּיתוֹ וַיַּעַשׂ
and-he-prepared house-of-him to and-they-entered with-him and-they-went

לָהֶם מִשְׁתֶּה וּמַצּוֹת אָפָה וַיֹּאכֵלוּ׃ (4) טֶרֶם
before (4) and-they-ate he-baked and-bread-without-yeast meal for-them

יִשְׁכָּבוּ וְאַנְשֵׁי הָעִיר אַנְשֵׁי סְדֹם נָסַבּוּ עַל־
around they-surrounded Sodom men-of the-city now-men-of they-went-to-bed

הַבַּיִת מִנַּעַר וְעַד־ זָקֵן כָּל־ הָעָם מִקָּצֶה׃
to-last-one the-people all-of old and-to from-young the-house

(5) וַיִּקְרְאוּ אֶל־לוֹט וַיֹּאמְרוּ לוֹ אַיֵּה הָאֲנָשִׁים† אֲשֶׁר־ בָּאוּ
they-came who the-men where? to-him and-they-said Lot to and-they-called (5)

אֵלֶיךָ הַלָּיְלָה הוֹצִיאֵם אֵלֵינוּ וְנֵדְעָה אֹתָם׃ (6) וַיֵּצֵא
but-he-went (6) with-them so-we-can-have-sex to-us bring-them! the-night to-you

אֲלֵהֶם לוֹט הַפֶּתְחָה וְהַדֶּלֶת סָגַר אַחֲרָיו׃ (7) וַיֹּאמַר אַל־נָא
now! not and-he-said (7) after-him he-shut and-the-door to-the-outside Lot to-them

אַחַי תָּרֵעוּ׃ (8) הִנֵּה־ נָא לִי שְׁתֵּי בָנוֹת אֲשֶׁר לֹא־ יָדְעוּ
they-slept not who daughters two-of to-me now! see! (8) you-do-evil friends-of-me

אִישׁ אוֹצִיאָה־ נָּא אֶתְהֶן אֲלֵיכֶם וַעֲשׂוּ לָהֶן כַּטּוֹב בְּעֵינֵיכֶם
in-eyes-of-you as-the-good to-them and-you-do to-you them now! let-me-bring man

רַק לָאֲנָשִׁים הָאֵל אַל־ תַּעֲשׂוּ דָבָר כִּי־עַל־ כֵּן בָּאוּ בְּצֵל
under-shelter-of they-came for anything you-do not the-these to-the-men but

קֹרָתִי׃ (9) וַיֹּאמְרוּ גֶּשׁ־ הָלְאָה וַיֹּאמְרוּ הָאֶחָד בָּא־
he-came the-one and-they-said away get! but-they-replied (9) roof-of-me

לָגוּר וַיִּשְׁפֹּט שָׁפוֹט עַתָּה נָרַע לְךָ
to-you we-will-treat-worse now to-judge and-he-would-judge to-be-alien

מֵהֶם וַיִּפְצְרוּ בָאִישׁ בְּלוֹט מְאֹד וַיִּגְּשׁוּ
and-they-moved strongly against-Lot against-the-man and-they-pressed than-them

לִשְׁבֹּר הַדָּלֶת׃ (10) וַיִּשְׁלְחוּ הָאֲנָשִׁים אֶת־ יָדָם
hand-of-them *** the-men but-they-reached-out (10) the-door to-break-down

וַיָּבִיאוּ אֶת־ לוֹט אֲלֵיהֶם הַבָּיְתָה וְאֶת־ הַדֶּלֶת סָגָרוּ׃
they-shut the-door and into-the-house to-them Lot *** and-they-pulled

(11) וְאֶת־ הָאֲנָשִׁים אֲשֶׁר־ פֶּתַח הַבַּיִת הִכּוּ בַּסַּנְוֵרִים
with-the-blindnesses they-struck the-house door-of who the-men and (11)

lords," he said, "please turn aside to your servant's house. You can wash your feet and spend the night and then go on your way early in the morning."

"No," they answered, "we will spend the night in the square."

3 But he insisted so strongly that they did go with him and entered his house. He prepared a meal for them, baking bread without yeast, and they ate. 4 Before they had gone to bed, all the men from every part of the city of Sodom—both young and old—surrounded the house. 5 They called to Lot, "Where are the men who came to you tonight? Bring them out to us so that we can have sex with them."

6 Lot went outside to meet them and shut the door behind him 7 and said, "No, my friends. Don't do this wicked thing. 8 Look, I have two daughters who have never slept with a man. Let me bring them out to you, and you can do what you like with them. But don't do anything to these men, for they have come under the protection of my roof."

9 "Get out of our way," they replied. And they said, "This fellow came here as an alien, and now he wants to play the judge! We'll treat you worse than them." They kept bringing pressure on Lot and moved forward to break down the door.

10 But the men inside reached out and pulled Lot back into the house and shut the door. 11 Then they struck the men who were at the door of the house, young and old, with

*2 Most mss have *hateph pathah* under the *he* (וַהֲ).

†5 Most mss have *hateph pathah* under the *aleph* (הָאֲ).

מִקָּטֹ֖ן וְעַד־ גָּד֑וֹל וַיִּלְא֖וּ לִמְצֹ֥א הַפָּֽתַח׃ וַיֹּאמְר֨וּ
then-they-said (12) the-door to-find so-they-gave-up great and-to from-small

הָאֲנָשִׁ֜ים אֶל־ ל֗וֹט עֹ֚ד מִֽי־ לְךָ֣ פֹ֔ה חָתָן֙ וּבָנֶ֣יךָ
or-sons-of-you son-in-law here with-you who? else Lot to the-men

וּבְנֹתֶ֔יךָ וְכֹ֥ל אֲשֶׁר־ לְךָ֖ בָּעִ֑יר הוֹצֵ֖א מִן־הַמָּקֽוֹם׃
the-place from bring-out! in-the-city to-you who or-anyone or-daughters-of-you

כִּֽי־ מַשְׁחִתִ֣ים אֲנַ֔חְנוּ אֶת־הַמָּק֖וֹם הַזֶּ֑ה כִּֽי־ גָֽדְלָ֤ה צַעֲקָתָם֙
cry-of-them great for the-this the-place *** we ones-destroying because (13)

אֶת־ פְּנֵ֣י יְהוָ֔ה וַיְשַׁלְּחֵ֥נוּ יְהוָ֖ה לְשַׁחֲתָֽהּ׃ וַיֵּצֵ֨א
so-he-went-out (14) to-destroy-her Yahweh that-he-sent-us Yahweh face-of ***

ל֜וֹט וַיְדַבֵּ֣ר ׀ אֶל־ חֲתָנָ֣יו ׀ לֹקְחֵ֣י בְנֹתָ֗יו
daughters-of-him ones-being-pledged-of sons-in-law-of-him to and-he-spoke Lot

וַיֹּ֙אמֶר֙ ק֤וּמוּ צְּאוּ֙ מִן־ הַמָּק֣וֹם הַזֶּ֔ה כִּֽי־ מַשְׁחִ֥ית
destroying because the-this the-place from get-out! get-up! and-he-said

יְהוָ֖ה אֶת־ הָעִ֑יר וַיְהִ֥י כִמְצַחֵ֖ק בְּעֵינֵ֥י חֲתָנָֽיו׃
sons-in-law-of-him in-eyes-of as-joking but-he-was the-city *** Yahweh

וּכְמוֹ֙ הַשַּׁ֣חַר עָלָ֔ה וַיָּאִ֥יצוּ הַמַּלְאָכִ֖ים בְּל֣וֹט לֵאמֹ֑ר
to-say with-Lot the-angels then-they-urged he-came the-morning and-when (15)

קוּם֩ קַ֨ח אֶֽת־ אִשְׁתְּךָ֜ וְאֶת־ שְׁתֵּ֤י בְנֹתֶ֙יךָ֙ הַנִּמְצָאֹ֔ת
the-ones-being-here daughters-of-you two-of and wife-of-you *** take! get-up!

פֶּן־ תִּסָּפֶ֖ה בַּעֲוֺ֥ן הָעִֽיר׃ וַיִּתְמַהְמָ֓הּ ׀
when-he-hesitated (16) the-city in-punishment-of you-will-be-swept-away or

וַיַּחֲזִ֨קוּ הָאֲנָשִׁ֜ים בְּיָד֣וֹ וּבְיַד־ אִשְׁתּ֗וֹ
wife-of-him and-on-hand-of on-hand-of-him the-men then-they-grasped

וּבְיַד֙ שְׁתֵּ֣י בְנֹתָ֔יו בְּחֶמְלַ֥ת יְהוָ֖ה עָלָ֑יו
to-him Yahweh for-merciful-of daughters-of-him two-of and-on-hand-of

וַיֹּצִאֻ֥הוּ וַיַּנִּחֻ֖הוּ מִח֥וּץ לָעִֽיר׃ וַיְהִ֡י
and-he-was (17) the-city outside and-they-set-him and-they-led-him

כְהוֹצִיאָ֨ם אֹתָ֜ם הַח֗וּצָה וַיֹּ֙אמֶר֙ הִמָּלֵ֣ט עַל־ נַפְשֶׁ֔ךָ אַל־
not life-of-you for flee! that-he-said to-the-outside them as-to-bring-them

תַּבִּ֣יט אַחֲרֶ֔יךָ וְאַל־ תַּעֲמֹ֖ד בְּכָל־ הַכִּכָּ֑ר הָהָ֥רָה
to-the-hill the-plain in-anywhere-of you-stop and-not back-of-you you-look

הִמָּלֵ֖ט פֶּן־ תִּסָּפֶֽה׃ וַיֹּ֥אמֶר ל֖וֹט אֲלֵהֶ֑ם אַל־ נָ֖א אֲדֹנָֽי׃
lords-of-me now! no to-them Lot but-he-said (18) you-be-swept-away or flee!

הִנֵּה־ נָ֠א מָצָ֨א עַבְדְּךָ֜ חֵן֮ בְּעֵינֶיךָ֒ וַתַּגְדֵּ֣ל
and-you-made-great in-eyes-of-you favor servant-of-you he-found now! see! (19)

חַסְדְּךָ֗ אֲשֶׁ֤ר עָשִׂ֙יתָ֙ עִמָּדִ֔י לְהַחֲי֖וֹת אֶת־ נַפְשִׁ֑י וְאָנֹכִ֗י לֹ֤א אוּכַל֙
I-can not but-I life-of-me *** to-spare to-me you-showed that kindness-of-you

blindness so that they could not find the door.

12 The two men said to Lot, "Do you have anyone else here—sons-in-law, sons or daughters, or anyone else in the city who belongs to you? Get them out of here, 13 because we are going to destroy this place. The outcry to the LORD against its people is so great that he has sent us to destroy it."

14 So Lot went out and spoke to his sons-in-law, who were pledged to marry[i] his daughters. He said, "Hurry and get out of this place, because the LORD is about to destroy the city!" But his sons-in-law thought he was joking.

15 With the coming of dawn, the angels urged Lot, saying, "Hurry! Take your wife and your two daughters who are here, or you will be swept away when the city is punished."

16 When he hesitated, the men grasped his hand and the hands of his wife and of his two daughters and led them safely out of the city, for the LORD was merciful to them. 17 As soon as they had brought them out, one of them said, "Flee for your lives! Don't look back, and don't stop anywhere in the plain! Flee to the mountains or you will be swept away!"

18 But Lot said to them, "No, my lords,[j] please! 19 Your[k] servant has found favor in your[k] eyes, and you[k] have shown great kindness to me in sparing my life. But I can't flee to

[i] 14 Or *were married to*
[j] 18 Or *No, Lord;* or *No, my lord*
[k] 19 The Hebrew is singular.

לְהִמָּלֵט הָהָרָה פֶּן־ תִּדְבָּקַנִי הָרָעָה וָמַתִּי׃ הִנֵּה־ נָא
now! see! (20) and-I-die the-disaster she-overtake-me lest to-the-mountain to-flee

הָעִיר הַזֹּאת קְרֹבָה לָנוּס שָׁמָּה וְהִוא מִצְעָר אִמָּלְטָה נָּא שָׁמָּה
to-there now! let-me-flee small and-she to-there to-run near the-this the-town

הֲלֹא מִצְעָר הִוא וּתְחִי נַפְשִׁי׃ וַיֹּאמֶר אֵלָיו הִנֵּה
see! to-him and-he-said (21) life-of-me and-she-will-live she small not?

נָשָׂאתִי פָנֶיךָ גַּם לַדָּבָר הַזֶּה לְבִלְתִּי הָפְכִּי אֶת־
*** to-overthrow-me not the-this to-the-request also face-of-you I-will-grant

הָעִיר אֲשֶׁר דִּבַּרְתָּ׃ מַהֵר הִמָּלֵט שָׁמָּה כִּי לֹא אוּכַל לַעֲשׂוֹת
to-do I-can not because to-there flee! hurry! (22) you-speak-of that the-town

דָּבָר עַד־ בֹּאֲךָ שָׁמָּה עַל־ כֵּן קָרָא שֵׁם־ הָעִיר צוֹעַר׃
Zoar the-town name-of he-called this for to-there to-reach-you until anything

הַשֶּׁמֶשׁ יָצָא עַל־ הָאָרֶץ וְלוֹט בָּא צֹעֲרָה׃ וַיהוָה
and-Yahweh (24) to-Zoar he-reached when-Lot the-land over he-rose the-sun (23)

הִמְטִיר עַל־סְדֹם וְעַל־ עֲמֹרָה גָּפְרִית וָאֵשׁ מֵאֵת יְהוָה מִן־ הַשָּׁמָיִם׃
the-heavens from Yahweh from and-fire sulfur Gomorrah and-on Sodom on he-rained

וַיַּהֲפֹךְ אֶת־ הֶעָרִים הָאֵל וְאֵת כָּל־ הַכִּכָּר וְאֵת כָּל־
all-of and the-plain all-of and the-these the-cities *** so-he-overthrew (25)

יֹשְׁבֵי הֶעָרִים וְצֶמַח הָאֲדָמָה׃ וַתַּבֵּט
but-she-looked (26) the-land vegetation-of the-cities the-ones-living-of

אִשְׁתּוֹ מֵאַחֲרָיו וַתְּהִי נְצִיב מֶלַח׃ וַיַּשְׁכֵּם
and-he-got-up (27) salt pillar-of and-she-became behind-him wife-of-him

אַבְרָהָם בַּבֹּקֶר אֶל־ הַמָּקוֹם אֲשֶׁר־ עָמַד שָׁם אֶת־ פְּנֵי יְהוָה׃
Yahweh before *** there he-stood where the-place to in-the-morning Abraham

וַיַּשְׁקֵף עַל־ פְּנֵי סְדֹם וַעֲמֹרָה וְעַל־ כָּל־ פְּנֵי
surface-of all-of and-to and-Gomorrah Sodom toward down and-he-looked (28)

אֶרֶץ הַכִּכָּר וַיַּרְא וְהִנֵּה עָלָה קִיטֹר הָאָרֶץ כְּקִיטֹר
like-smoke-of the-land smoke-of he-rose and-see! and-he-saw the-plain land-of

הַכִּבְשָׁן׃ וַיְהִי בְּשַׁחֵת אֱלֹהִים אֶת־ עָרֵי הַכִּכָּר
the-plain cities-of *** God when-to-destroy so-he-was (29) the-furnace

וַיִּזְכֹּר אֱלֹהִים אֶת־ אַבְרָהָם וַיְשַׁלַּח אֶת־ לוֹט מִתּוֹךְ
from-midst-of Lot *** and-he-brougnt Abraham *** God that-he-remembered

הַהֲפֵכָה בַּהֲפֹךְ אֶת־ הֶעָרִים אֲשֶׁר־ יָשַׁב בָּהֵן לוֹט׃
Lot in-them he-lived where the-cities *** when-to-overthrow the-catastrophe

וַיַּעַל לוֹט מִצּוֹעַר וַיֵּשֶׁב בָּהָר וּשְׁתֵּי
and-two-of in-the-mountain and-he-settled from-Zoar Lot and-he-left (30)

בְּנֹתָיו עִמּוֹ כִּי יָרֵא לָשֶׁבֶת בְּצוֹעַר וַיֵּשֶׁב
and-he-lived in-Zoar to-stay he-was-afraid for with-him daughters-of-him

the mountains; this disaster will overtake me, and I'll die. [20]Look, here is a town near enough to run to, and it is small. Let me flee to it—it is very small, isn't it? Then my life will be spared."

[21]He said to him, "Very well, I will grant this request too; I will not overthrow the town you speak of. [22]But flee there quickly, because I cannot do anything until you reach it." (That is why the town was called Zoar.[l])

[23]By the time Lot reached Zoar, the sun had risen over the land. [24]Then the LORD rained down burning sulfur on Sodom and Gomorrah—from the LORD out of the heavens. [25]Thus he overthrew those cities and the entire plain, including all those living in the cities—and also the vegetation in the land. [26]But Lot's wife looked back and she became a pillar of salt.

[27]Early the next morning Abraham got up and returned to the place where he had stood before the LORD. [28]He looked down toward Sodom and Gomorrah, toward all the land of the plain, and he saw dense smoke rising from the land, like smoke from a furnace.

[29]So when God destroyed the cities of the plain, he remembered Abraham, and he brought Lot out of the catastrophe that overthrew the cities where Lot had lived.

*Lot and His Daughters*

[30]Lot and his two daughters left Zoar and settled in the mountains, for he was afraid to stay in Zoar. He and his two

[l]22 *Zoar* means *small.*

בַּמְּעָרָה הוּא וּשְׁתֵּי בְנֹתָיו׃ וַתֹּאמֶר הַבְּכִירָה אֶל־

to the-older now-she-said (31) daughters-of-him and-two-of he in-the-cave

הַצְּעִירָה אָבִינוּ זָקֵן וְאִישׁ אֵין בָּאָרֶץ לָבוֹא

to-lie in-the-area there-is-no and-man he-is-old father-of-us the-younger

עָלֵינוּ כְּדֶרֶךְ כָּל־ הָאָרֶץ׃ לְכָה נַשְׁקֶה אֶת־

*** let-us-make-drink come! (32) the-earth all-of as-custom-of with-us

אָבִינוּ יַיִן וְנִשְׁכְּבָה עִמּוֹ וּנְחַיֶּה מֵאָבִינוּ

by-father-of-us and-let-us-preserve with-him then-let-us-lie wine father-of-us

זָרַע׃ וַתַּשְׁקֶיןָ אֶת־ אֲבִיהֶן יַיִן בַּלַּיְלָה הוּא

that in-the-night wine father-of-them *** so-they-made-drink (33) family

וַתָּבֹא הַבְּכִירָה וַתִּשְׁכַּב אֶת־ אָבִיהָ וְלֹא־ יָדַע

he-knew and-not father-of-her with and-she-lay the-older and-she-went-in

בְּשִׁכְבָהּ וּבְקוּמָהּ׃ וַיְהִי מִמָּחֳרָת

on-next-day and-he-was (34) or-when-to-get-up-her when-to-lie-down-her

וַתֹּאמֶר הַבְּכִירָה אֶל־ הַצְּעִירָה הֵן־שָׁכַבְתִּי אֶמֶשׁ אֶת־ אָבִי

father-of-me with last-night I-lay see! the-younger to the-older that-she-said

נַשְׁקֶנּוּ יַיִן גַּם־ הַלַּיְלָה וּבֹאִי שִׁכְבִי עִמּוֹ

with-him lie! and-go! the-night also wine let-us-make-drink-him

וּנְחַיֶּה מֵאָבִינוּ זָרַע׃ וַתַּשְׁקֶיןָ גַּם

also so-they-made-drink (35) family by-father-of-us and-let-us-preserve

בַּלַּיְלָה הַהוּא אֶת־ אֲבִיהֶן יַיִן וַתָּקָם הַצְּעִירָה

the-younger and-she-went wine father-of-them *** the-that on-the-night

וַתִּשְׁכַּב עִמּוֹ וְלֹא־ יָדַע בְּשִׁכְבָהּ וּבְקֻמָהּ׃

or-when-to-get-up-her when-to-lie-down-her he-knew and-not with-him and-she-lay

וַתַּהֲרֶיןָ שְׁתֵּי בְנוֹת־ לוֹט מֵאֲבִיהֶן׃

by-father-of-them Lot daughters-of two-of so-they-became-pregnant (36)

וַתֵּלֶד הַבְּכִירָה בֵּן וַתִּקְרָא שְׁמוֹ מוֹאָב הוּא אֲבִי־

father-of he Moab name-of-him and-she-called son the-older and-she-bore (37)

מוֹאָב עַד־ הַיּוֹם׃ וְהַצְּעִירָה גַם־ הִוא יָלְדָה בֵּן וַתִּקְרָא

and-she-called son she-bore she also and-the-younger (38) the-day to Moab

שְׁמוֹ בֶּן־ עַמִּי הוּא אֲבִי בְנֵי־ עַמּוֹן עַד־ הַיּוֹם׃ וַיִּסַּע

now-he-left (20:1) the-day to Ammon sons-of father-of he Ammi Ben name-of-him

מִשָּׁם אַבְרָהָם אַרְצָה הַנֶּגֶב וַיֵּשֶׁב בֵּין־ קָדֵשׁ

Kadesh between and-he-lived the-Negev into-region Abraham from-there

וּבֵין שׁוּר וַיָּגָר בִּגְרָר׃ וַיֹּאמֶר אַבְרָהָם אֶל־ שָׂרָה

Sarah about Abraham and-he-said (2) in-Gerar and-he-stayed Shur and-between

אִשְׁתּוֹ אֲחֹתִי הִוא וַיִּשְׁלַח אֲבִימֶלֶךְ מֶלֶךְ גְּרָר וַיִּקַּח

and-he-took Gerar king-of Abimelech then-he-sent she sister-of-me wife-of-him

daughters lived in a cave. 31 One day the older daughter said to the younger, "Our father is old, and there is no man around here to lie with us, as is the custom all over the earth. 32 Let's get our father to drink wine and then lie with him and preserve our family line through our father."

33 That night they got their father to drink wine, and the older daughter went in and lay with him. He was not aware of it when she lay down or when she got up.

34 The next day the older daughter said to the younger, "Last night I lay with my father. Let's get him to drink wine again tonight, and you go in and lie with him so we can preserve our family line through our father." 35 So they got their father to drink wine that night also, and the younger daughter went and lay with him. Again he was not aware of it when she lay down or when she got up.

36 So both of Lot's daughters became pregnant by their father. 37 The older daughter had a son, and she named him Moab[m]; he is the father of the Moabites of today. 38 The younger daughter also had a son, and she named him Ben-Ammi[n]; he is the father of the Ammonites of today.

### *Abraham and Abimelech*

**20** Now Abraham moved on from there into the region of the Negev and lived between Kadesh and Shur. For a while he stayed in Gerar, 2 and there Abraham said of his wife Sarah, "She is my sister." Then Abimelech king of Gerar sent for Sarah and took her.

[m]37 *Moab* sounds like the Hebrew for *from father.*
[n]38 *Ben-Ammi* means *son of my people.*

אֶת־שָׂרָה׃ וַיָּבֹא אֱלֹהִים אֶל־אֲבִימֶלֶךְ בַּחֲלוֹם הַלָּיְלָה וַיֹּאמֶר

and-he-said the-night in-dream-of Abimelech to God but-he-came (3) Sarah ***

לוֹ הִנְּךָ מֵת עַל־הָאִשָּׁה אֲשֶׁר־לָקַחְתָּ וְהִוא

now-she you-took whom the-woman because-of being-dead see-you! to-him

בְּעֻלַת בָּעַל׃ וַאֲבִימֶלֶךְ לֹא קָרַב אֵלֶיהָ וַיֹּאמַר

and-he-said to-her he-went-near not now-Abimelech (4) husband being-married-of

אֲדֹנָי הֲגוֹי גַּם־צַדִּיק תַּהֲרֹג׃ הֲלֹא הוּא אָמַר־לִי

to-me he-said he not? (5) will-you-destroy innocent indeed nation? Lord

אֲחֹתִי הִוא וְהִיא־גַם־הִוא אָמְרָה אָחִי הוּא בְּתָם־

with-clear-of he brother-of-me she-said she also and-she she sister-of-me

לְבָבִי וּבְנִקְיֹן כַּפַּי עָשִׂיתִי זֹּאת׃ וַיֹּאמֶר

then-he-said (6) this I-did hands-of-me and-with-clean-of conscience-of-me

אֵלָיו הָאֱלֹהִים בַּחֲלֹם גַּם אָנֹכִי יָדַעְתִּי כִּי בְתָם־לְבָבְךָ

conscience-of-you with-clear-of that I-know I yes in-the-dream the-God to-him

עָשִׂיתָ זֹּאת וָאֶחְשֹׂךְ גַּם־אָנֹכִי אוֹתְךָ מֵחֲטוֹ־לִי עַל־כֵּן לֹא־

not this for against-me from-to-sin you I indeed so-I-kept this you-did

נְתַתִּיךָ לִנְגֹּעַ אֵלֶיהָ׃ וְעַתָּה הָשֵׁב אֵשֶׁת־הָאִישׁ כִּי־נָבִיא

prophet for the-man wife-of return! now-you (7) on-her to-touch I-let-you

הוּא וְיִתְפַּלֵּל בַּעַדְךָ וֶחְיֵה וְאִם־אֵינְךָ מֵשִׁיב דַּע כִּי־

that be-sure! returning not-you but-if and-live! for-you and-he-will-pray he

מוֹת תָּמוּת אַתָּה וְכָל־אֲשֶׁר־לָךְ׃ וַיַּשְׁכֵּם אֲבִימֶלֶךְ

Abimelech and-he-rose (8) to-you that and-all you you-will-die to-die

בַּבֹּקֶר וַיִּקְרָא לְכָל־עֲבָדָיו וַיְדַבֵּר אֶת־

*** and-he-told officials-of-him to-all-of and-he-summoned in-the-morning

כָּל־הַדְּבָרִים הָאֵלֶּה בְּאָזְנֵיהֶם וַיִּירְאוּ הָאֲנָשִׁים מְאֹד׃

very the-men and-they-were-afraid in-ears-of-them the-these the-things all-of

וַיִּקְרָא אֲבִימֶלֶךְ לְאַבְרָהָם וַיֹּאמֶר לוֹ מֶה־עָשִׂיתָ לָּנוּ

to-us you-did what? to-him and-he-said to-Abraham Abimelech and-he-called (9)

וּמֶה־חָטָאתִי לָךְ כִּי־הֵבֵאתָ עָלַי וְעַל־מַמְלַכְתִּי חֲטָאָה

guilt kingdom-of-me and-on on-me you-brought that to-you I-wronged and-how?

גְדֹלָה מַעֲשִׂים אֲשֶׁר לֹא־יֵעָשׂוּ עָשִׂיתָ עִמָּדִי׃ וַיֹּאמֶר

and-he-asked (10) to-me you-did they-should-be-done not that things great

אֲבִימֶלֶךְ אֶל־אַבְרָהָם מָה רָאִיתָ כִּי עָשִׂיתָ אֶת־הַדָּבָר הַזֶּה׃

the-this the-thing *** you-did that you-reasoned what? Abraham to Abimelech

וַיֹּאמֶר אַבְרָהָם כִּי אָמַרְתִּי רַק אֵין־יִרְאַת אֱלֹהִים

God fear-of there-is-no surely I-said because Abraham and-he-replied (11)

בַּמָּקוֹם הַזֶּה וַהֲרָגוּנִי עַל־דְּבַר אִשְׁתִּי׃

wife-of-me account-of on and-they-will-kill-me the-this in-the-place

3 But God came to Abimelech
in a dream one night and said
to him, "You are as good as
dead because of the woman
you have taken; she is a married woman."
4 Now Abimelech had not
gone near her, so he said,
"Lord, will you destroy an innocent nation?
5 Did he not say
to me, 'She is my sister,' and
didn't she also say, 'He is my
brother'? I have done this
with a clear conscience and
clean hands."
6 Then God said to him in the
dream, "Yes, I know you did
this with a clear conscience,
and so I have kept you from
sinning against me. That is
why I did not let you touch
her.
7 Now return the man's
wife, for he is a prophet, and
he will pray for you and you
will live. But if you do not return her, you may be sure that
you and all yours will die."
8 Early the next morning
Abimelech summoned all his
officials, and when he told
them all that had happened,
they were very much afraid.
9 Then Abimelech called Abraham in and said, "What have
you done to us? How have I
wronged you that you have
brought such great guilt upon
me and my kingdom? You
have done things to me that
should not be done."
10 And
Abimelech asked Abraham,
"What was your reason for doing this?"
11 Abraham replied, "I said to
myself, 'There is surely no fear
of God in this place, and they
will kill me because of my

וְגַם־ אָמְנָה אֲחֹתִי בַת־ אָבִי הִוא אַךְ לֹא
not though she father-of-me daughter-of sister-of-me really and-besides (12)

בַּת־ אִמִּי וַתְּהִי־ לִי לְאִשָּׁה׃ וַיְהִי כַּאֲשֶׁר
when and-he-was (13) for-wife to-me and-she-became mother-of-me daughter-of

הִתְעוּ אֹתִי אֱלֹהִים מִבֵּית אָבִי וָאֹמַר לָהּ זֶה
this to-her that-I-said father-of-me from-household-of God me he-make-wander

חַסְדֵּךְ אֲשֶׁר תַּעֲשִׂי עִמָּדִי אֶל כָּל־ הַמָּקוֹם אֲשֶׁר נָבוֹא
we-go where the-place every-of in to-me you-can-show that love-of-you

שָׁמָּה אִמְרִי־ לִי אָחִי הוּא׃ וַיִּקַּח אֲבִימֶלֶךְ צֹאן
sheep Abimelech then-he-brought (14) he brother-of-me of-me say! to-there

וּבָקָר וַעֲבָדִים וּשְׁפָחֹת וַיִּתֵּן לְאַבְרָהָם
to-Abraham and-he-gave and-female-slaves and-male-slaves and-cattle

וַיָּשֶׁב לוֹ אֵת שָׂרָה אִשְׁתּוֹ׃ וַיֹּאמֶר אֲבִימֶלֶךְ הִנֵּה
see! Abimelech and-he-said (15) wife-of-him Sarah *** to-him and-he-returned

אַרְצִי לְפָנֶיךָ בַּטּוֹב בְּעֵינֶיךָ שֵׁב׃ וּלְשָׂרָה
and-to-Sarah (16) live! to-eyes-of-you in-the-good before-you land-of-me

אָמַר הִנֵּה נָתַתִּי אֶלֶף כֶּסֶף לְאָחִיךְ הִנֵּה הוּא־ לָךְ
to-you he see! to-brother-of-you silver thousand-of I-give see! he-said

כְּסוּת עֵינַיִם לְכֹל אֲשֶׁר אִתָּךְ וְאֵת כֹּל וְנֹכָחַת׃
now-you-are-vindicated all and-before with-you who before-all eyes cover-of

וַיִּתְפַּלֵּל אַבְרָהָם אֶל־הָאֱלֹהִים וַיִּרְפָּא אֱלֹהִים אֶת־אֲבִימֶלֶךְ וְאֶת־
and Abimelech *** God and-he-healed the-God to Abraham then-he-prayed (17)

אִשְׁתּוֹ וְאַמְהֹתָיו וַיֵּלֵדוּ׃ כִּי־ עָצֹר עָצַר
he-closed to-close for (18) so-they-could-bear and-slave-girls-of-him wife-of-him

יְהוָה בְּעַד כָּל־ רֶחֶם לְבֵית אֲבִימֶלֶךְ עַל־ דְּבַר שָׂרָה
Sarah account-of on Abimelech in-household-of womb every-of up Yahweh

אֵשֶׁת אַבְרָהָם׃ וַיהוָה פָּקַד אֶת־ שָׂרָה כַּאֲשֶׁר אָמָר
he-said just-as Sarah *** he-was-gracious now-Yahweh (21:1) Abraham wife-of

וַיַּעַשׂ יְהוָה לְשָׂרָה כַּאֲשֶׁר דִּבֵּר׃ וַתַּהַר
and-she-became-pregnant (2) he-promised just-as for-Sarah Yahweh and-he-did

וַתֵּלֶד שָׂרָה לְאַבְרָהָם בֵּן לִזְקֻנָיו לַמּוֹעֵד אֲשֶׁר־
that at-the-time in-old-age-of-him son to-Abraham Sarah and-she-bore

דִּבֶּר אֹתוֹ אֱלֹהִים׃ וַיִּקְרָא אַבְרָהָם אֶת־ שֶׁם־ בְּנוֹ
son-of-him name-of *** Abraham and-he-gave (3) God him he-promised

הַנּוֹלַד־ לוֹ אֲשֶׁר־ יָלְדָה־ לּוֹ שָׂרָה יִצְחָק׃ וַיָּמָל
and-he-circumcised (4) Isaac Sarah to-him she-bore whom to-him the-one-being-born

אַבְרָהָם אֶת־יִצְחָק בְּנוֹ בֶּן־ שְׁמֹנַת יָמִים כַּאֲשֶׁר צִוָּה אֹתוֹ אֱלֹהִים׃
God him he-commanded just-as days eight son-of son-of-him Isaac *** Abraham

wife.' 12Besides, she really is
my sister, the daughter of my
father though not of my
mother; and she became my
wife. 13And when God had me
wander from my father's
household, I said to her, 'This
is how you can show your love
to me: Everywhere we go, say
of me, "He is my brother." ' "
14Then Abimelech brought
sheep and cattle and male and
female slaves and gave them
to Abraham, and he returned
Sarah his wife to him. 15And
Abimelech said, "My land is
before you; live wherever you
like."
16To Sarah he said, "I am
giving your brother a thousand shekels[o] of silver. This is
to cover the offense against
you before all who are with
you; you are completely vindicated."
17Then Abraham prayed to
God, and God healed Abimelech, his wife and his slave
girls so they could have children again, 18for the LORD had
closed up every womb in
Abimelech's household because of Abraham's wife Sarah.

*The Birth of Isaac*

21 Now the LORD was gracious to Sarah as he
had said, and the LORD did for
Sarah what he had promised.
2Sarah became pregnant and
bore a son to Abraham in his
old age, at the very time God
had promised him. 3Abraham
gave the name Isaac[p] to the
son Sarah bore him. 4When
his son Isaac was eight days
old, Abraham circumcised
him, as God commanded him.

[o] *16* That is, about 25 pounds (about 11.5 kilograms)
[p] *3* *Isaac* means *he laughs.*

וְאַבְרָהָם בֶּן־ מְאַת שָׁנָה בְּהִוָּלֶד לוֹ אֵת יִצְחָק
Isaac *** to-him when-to-be-born year hundred-of son-of now-Abraham (5)

בְּנוֹ׃ וַתֹּאמֶר שָׂרָה צְחֹק עָשָׂה לִי אֱלֹהִים כָּל־
every-of God to-me he-brought laughter Sarah and-she-said (6) son-of-him

הַשֹּׁמֵעַ יִצְחַק־ לִי׃ וַתֹּאמֶר מִי מִלֵּל
he-would-have-said who? and-she-said (7) with-me he-will-laugh the-one-hearing

לְאַבְרָהָם הֵינִיקָה בָנִים שָׂרָה כִּי־ יָלַדְתִּי בֵן לִזְקֻנָיו׃
in-old-age-of-him son I-bore yet Sarah children she-would-nurse to-Abraham

וַיִּגְדַּל הַיֶּלֶד וַיִּגָּמַל וַיַּעַשׂ אַבְרָהָם מִשְׁתֶּה גָדוֹל
great feast Abraham and-he-held and-he-was-weaned the-child and-he-grew (8)

בְּיוֹם הִגָּמֵל אֶת־ יִצְחָק׃ וַתֵּרֶא שָׂרָה אֶת־ בֶּן־ הָגָר
Hagar son-of *** Sarah but-she-was (9) Isaac *** to-be-weaned on-day-of

הַמִּצְרִית אֲשֶׁר־ יָלְדָה לְאַבְרָהָם מְצַחֵק׃ וַתֹּאמֶר לְאַבְרָהָם
to-Abraham and-she-said (10) mocking to-Abraham she-bore whom the-Egyptian

גָּרֵשׁ הָאָמָה הַזֹּאת וְאֶת־ בְּנָהּ כִּי לֹא יִירַשׁ
he-will-inherit never for son-of-her and the-that the-slave-woman get-rid-of!

בֶּן־ הָאָמָה הַזֹּאת עִם־ בְּנִי עִם־ יִצְחָק׃
Isaac with son-of-me with the-that the-slave-woman son-of

וַיֵּרַע הַדָּבָר מְאֹד בְּעֵינֵי אַבְרָהָם עַל אוֹדֹת
concerns-of for Abraham in-eyes-of greatly the-matter and-he-was-distressing (11)

בְּנוֹ׃ וַיֹּאמֶר אֱלֹהִים אֶל־ אַבְרָהָם אַל־ יֵרַע בְּעֵינֶיךָ
in-eyes-of-you he-be-distressing not Abraham to God but-he-said (12) son-of-him

עַל־ הַנַּעַר וְעַל־ אֲמָתֶךָ כֹּל אֲשֶׁר תֹּאמַר אֵלֶיךָ שָׂרָה
Sarah to-you she-tells that all maidservant-of-you and-about the-boy about

שְׁמַע בְּקֹלָהּ כִּי בְיִצְחָק יִקָּרֵא לְךָ
to-you he-will-be-reckoned through-Isaac because to-voice-of-her listen!

זָרַע׃ וְגַם אֶת־ בֶּן־ הָאָמָה לְגוֹי אֲשִׂימֶנּוּ
I-will-make-him into-nation the-maidservant son-of *** and-also (13) offspring

כִּי זַרְעֲךָ הוּא׃ וַיַּשְׁכֵּם אַבְרָהָם ׀ בַּבֹּקֶר
in-the-morning Abraham and-he-rose (14) he offspring-of-you because

וַיִּקַּח־ לֶחֶם וְחֵמַת מַיִם וַיִּתֵּן אֶל־ הָגָר שָׂם עַל־
on setting Hagar to and-he-gave waters and-skin-of food and-he-took

שִׁכְמָהּ וְאֶת־ הַיֶּלֶד וַיְשַׁלְּחֶהָ וַתֵּלֶךְ וַתֵּתַע
and-she-wandered and-she-went then-he-sent-off-her the-boy and shoulder-of-her

בְּמִדְבַּר בְּאֵר שָׁבַע׃ וַיִּכְלוּ הַמַּיִם מִן־ הַחֵמֶת
the-skin from the-waters when-they-were-gone (15) Sheba Beer in-desert-of

וַתַּשְׁלֵךְ אֶת־ הַיֶּלֶד תַּחַת אַחַד הַשִּׂיחִם׃ וַתֵּלֶךְ וַתֵּשֶׁב
and-she-sat then-she-went (16) the-bushes one-of under the-boy *** then-she-put

5 Abraham was a hundred years old when his son Isaac was born to him.

6 Sarah said, "God has brought me laughter, and everyone who hears about this will laugh with me." 7 And she added, "Who would have said to Abraham that Sarah would nurse children? Yet I have borne him a son in his old age."

*Hagar and Ishmael Sent Away*

8 The child grew and was weaned, and on the day Isaac was weaned Abraham held a great feast. 9 But Sarah saw that the son whom Hagar the Egyptian had borne to Abraham was mocking, 10 and she said to Abraham, "Get rid of that slave woman and her son, for that slave woman's son will never share in the inheritance with my son Isaac."

11 The matter distressed Abraham greatly because it concerned his son. 12 But God said to him, "Do not be so distressed about the boy and your maidservant. Listen to whatever Sarah tells you, because it is through Isaac that your offspring[q] will be reckoned. 13 I will make the son of the maidservant into a nation also, because he is your offspring."

14 Early the next morning Abraham took some food and a skin of water and gave them to Hagar. He set them on her shoulders and then sent her off with the boy. She went on her way and wandered in the desert of Beersheba.

15 When the water in the skin was gone, she put the boy under one of the bushes. 16 Then she went off and sat down

[q] 12 Or *seed*

לָהּ מִנֶּגֶד הַרְחֵק כִּמְטַחֲוֵי קֶשֶׁת כִּי אָמְרָה אַל־
not she-said for bow like-ones-shooting-of to-be-away by-near by-herself

אֶרְאֶה בְּמוֹת הַיָּלֶד וַתֵּשֶׁב מִנֶּגֶד וַתִּשָּׂא אֶת־
*** and-she-lifted by-near and-she-sat the-boy on-death-of I-can-look

קֹלָהּ וַתֵּבְךְּ׃ וַיִּשְׁמַע אֱלֹהִים אֶת־קוֹל הַנַּעַר
the-boy cry-of *** God and-he-heard (17) and-she-sobbed voice-of-her

וַיִּקְרָא מַלְאַךְ אֱלֹהִים ׀ אֶל־הָגָר מִן־הַשָּׁמַיִם וַיֹּאמֶר לָהּ מַה־
what? to-her and-he-said the-heavens from Hagar to God angel-of and-he-called

לָּךְ הָגָר אַל־תִּירְאִי כִּי־שָׁמַע אֱלֹהִים אֶל־קוֹל הַנַּעַר בַּאֲשֶׁר
as the-boy cry-of to God he-heard for you-be-afraid not Hagar with-you

הוּא־שָׁם׃ קוּמִי שְׂאִי אֶת־הַנַּעַר וְהַחֲזִיקִי אֶת־יָדֵךְ בּוֹ כִּי־
for on-him hand-of-you with and-hold! the-boy *** lift! rise! (18) there he

לְגוֹי גָּדוֹל אֲשִׂימֶנּוּ׃ וַיִּפְקַח אֱלֹהִים אֶת־עֵינֶיהָ
eyes-of-her *** God then-he-opened (19) I-will-make-him great into-nation

וַתֵּרֶא בְּאֵר מָיִם וַתֵּלֶךְ וַתְּמַלֵּא אֶת־הַחֵמֶת מַיִם
waters the-skin *** and-she-filled so-she-went waters well-of and-she-saw

וַתַּשְׁקְ אֶת־הַנָּעַר׃ וַיְהִי אֱלֹהִים אֶת־הַנַּעַר וַיִּגְדָּל
and-he-grew the-boy with God and-he-was (20) the-boy *** and-she-gave-drink

וַיֵּשֶׁב בַּמִּדְבָּר וַיְהִי רֹבֶה קַשָּׁת׃ וַיֵּשֶׁב
and-he-lived (21) bow one-shooting and-he-became in-the-desert and-he-lived

בְּמִדְבַּר פָּארָן וַתִּקַּח־לוֹ אִמּוֹ אִשָּׁה מֵאֶרֶץ מִצְרָיִם׃
Egypt from-land-of wife mother-of-him for-him and-she-got Paran in-desert-of

וַיְהִי בָּעֵת הַהִוא וַיֹּאמֶר אֲבִימֶלֶךְ וּפִיכֹל
and-Phicol Abimelech and-he-said the-that at-the-time and-he-was (22)

שַׂר־צְבָאוֹ אֶל־אַבְרָהָם לֵאמֹר אֱלֹהִים עִמְּךָ בְּכֹל אֲשֶׁר־אַתָּה
you that in-all with-you God to-say Abraham to force-of-him commander-of

עֹשֶׂה׃ וְעַתָּה הִשָּׁבְעָה לִּי בֵאלֹהִים הֵנָּה אִם־תִּשְׁקֹר
you-will-deal-falsely not here before-God to-me swear! and-now (23) doing

לִי וּלְנִינִי וּלְנֶכְדִּי כַּחֶסֶד אֲשֶׁר־
that as-the-kindness or-with-descendant-of-me or-with-child-of-me with-me

עָשִׂיתִי עִמְּךָ תַּעֲשֶׂה עִמָּדִי וְעִם־הָאָרֶץ אֲשֶׁר־גַּרְתָּה בָּהּ׃
in-her you-live that the-country and-to to-me you-show to-you I-showed

וַיֹּאמֶר אַבְרָהָם אָנֹכִי אִשָּׁבֵעַ׃ וְהוֹכִחַ אַבְרָהָם אֶת־
*** Abraham then-he-complained (25) I-swear I Abraham and-he-said (24)

אֲבִימֶלֶךְ עַל־אֹדוֹת בְּאֵר הַמַּיִם אֲשֶׁר גָּזְלוּ עַבְדֵי
servants-of they-seized that the-water well-of accounts-of on Abimelech

אֲבִימֶלֶךְ׃ וַיֹּאמֶר אֲבִימֶלֶךְ לֹא יָדַעְתִּי מִי עָשָׂה אֶת־הַדָּבָר
the-thing *** he-did who? I-know not Abimelech but-he-said (26) Abimelech

nearby, about a bowshot away, for she thought, "I cannot watch the boy die." And as she sat there nearby, she began to sob.

17God heard the boy crying, and the angel of God called to Hagar from heaven and said to her, "What is the matter, Hagar? Do not be afraid; God has heard the boy crying as he lies there. 18Lift the boy up and take him by the hand, for I will make him into a great nation."

19Then God opened her eyes and she saw a well of water. So she went and filled the skin with water and gave the boy a drink.

20God was with the boy as he grew up. He lived in the desert and became an archer. 21While he was living in the Desert of Paran, his mother got a wife for him from Egypt.

*The Treaty at Beersheba*

22At that time Abimelech and Phicol the commander of his forces said to Abraham, "God is with you in everything you do. 23Now swear to me here before God that you will not deal falsely with me or my children or my descendants. Show to me and the country where you are living as an alien the same kindness I have shown to you."

24Abraham said, "I swear it."

25Then Abraham complained to Abimelech about a well of water that Abimelech's servants had seized. 26But Abimelech said, "I don't know who has done this. You

הַזֶּה וְגַם־אַתָּה לֹא־הִגַּדְתָּ לִּי וְגַם אָנֹכִי לֹא שָׁמַעְתִּי בִּלְתִּי הַיּוֹם׃
the-day until I-heard not I and-also to-me you-told not you and-also the-this

וַיִּקַּח אַבְרָהָם צֹאן וּבָקָר וַיִּתֵּן לַאֲבִימֶלֶךְ
to-Abimelech and-he-gave and-cattle sheep Abraham so-he-brought (27)

וַיִּכְרְתוּ שְׁנֵיהֶם בְּרִית׃ וַיַּצֵּב אַבְרָהָם אֶת־שֶׁבַע
seven *** Abraham and-he-set-apart (28) treaty two-of-them and-they-made

כִּבְשֹׂת הַצֹּאן לְבַדְהֶן׃ וַיֹּאמֶר אֲבִימֶלֶךְ אֶל־אַבְרָהָם
Abraham to Abimelech and-he-asked (29) by-themselves the-flock ewe-lambs-of

מָה הֵנָּה שֶׁבַע כְּבָשֹׂת הָאֵלֶּה אֲשֶׁר הִצַּבְתָּ לְבַדָּנָה׃
by-themselves you-set-apart that the-these ewe-lambs seven these what?

וַיֹּאמֶר כִּי אֶת־שֶׁבַע כְּבָשֹׂת תִּקַּח מִיָּדִי
from-hand-of-me you-accept ewe-lambs seven *** indeed and-he-replied (30)

בַּעֲבוּר תִּהְיֶה־לִּי לְעֵדָה כִּי חָפַרְתִּי אֶת־הַבְּאֵר הַזֹּאת׃
the-this the-well *** I-dug that as-witness for-me you-may-be so-that

עַל־כֵּן קָרָא לַמָּקוֹם הַהוּא בְּאֵר שָׁבַע כִּי שָׁם
there because Sheba Beer the-that to-the-place he-called this for (31)

נִשְׁבְּעוּ שְׁנֵיהֶם׃ וַיִּכְרְתוּ בְרִית בִּבְאֵר שָׁבַע וַיָּקָם
then-he-rose Sheba at-Beer treaty so-they-made (32) two-of-them they-swore-oath

אֲבִימֶלֶךְ וּפִיכֹל שַׂר־צְבָאוֹ וַיָּשֻׁבוּ אֶל־אֶרֶץ
land-of to and-they-returned force-of-him commander-of and-Phicol Abimelech

פְּלִשְׁתִּים׃ וַיִּטַּע אֶשֶׁל בִּבְאֵר שָׁבַע וַיִּקְרָא־
and-he-called Sheba in-Beer tamarisk-tree and-he-planted (33) Philistines

שָׁם בְּשֵׁם יְהוָה אֵל עוֹלָם׃ וַיָּגָר אַבְרָהָם בְּאֶרֶץ
in-land-of Abraham and-he-stayed (34) Eternal God Yahweh upon-name-of there

פְּלִשְׁתִּים יָמִים רַבִּים׃ וַיְהִי אַחַר הַדְּבָרִים הָאֵלֶּה
the-these the-events after and-he-was (22:1) many days Philistines

וְהָאֱלֹהִים נִסָּה אֶת־אַבְרָהָם וַיֹּאמֶר אֵלָיו אַבְרָהָם וַיֹּאמֶר
and-he-replied Abraham to-him and-he-said Abraham *** he-tested that-the-God

הִנֵּנִי׃ וַיֹּאמֶר קַח־נָא אֶת־בִּנְךָ אֶת־יְחִידְךָ אֲשֶׁר־
whom only-of-you *** son-of-you *** now! take! then-he-said (2) here-I

אָהַבְתָּ אֶת־יִצְחָק וְלֶךְ־לְךָ אֶל־אֶרֶץ הַמֹּרִיָּה וְהַעֲלֵהוּ
and-sacrifice-him! the-Moriah region-of to yourself and-go! Isaac *** you-love

שָׁם לְעֹלָה עַל אַחַד הֶהָרִים אֲשֶׁר אֹמַר אֵלֶיךָ׃
to-you I-will-tell that the-mountains one-of on as-burnt-offering there

וַיַּשְׁכֵּם אַבְרָהָם בַּבֹּקֶר וַיַּחֲבֹשׁ אֶת־חֲמֹרוֹ
donkey-of-him *** and-he-saddled in-the-morning Abraham so-he-rose (3)

וַיִּקַּח אֶת־שְׁנֵי נְעָרָיו אִתּוֹ וְאֵת יִצְחָק בְּנוֹ
son-of-him Isaac and with-him servants-of-him two-of *** and-he-took

did not tell me, and I heard
about it only today."
[27]So Abraham brought sheep
and cattle and gave them to
Abimelech, and the two men
made a treaty. [28]Abraham set
apart seven ewe lambs from
the flock, [29]and Abimelech
asked Abraham, "What is the
meaning of these seven ewe
lambs you have set apart by
themselves?"
[30]He replied, "Accept these
seven lambs from my hand as
a witness that I dug this well."
[31]So that place was called
Beersheba,[r] because the two
men swore an oath there.
[32]After the treaty had been
made at Beersheba, Abime-
lech and Phicol the com-
mander of his forces returned
to the land of the Philistines.
[33]Abraham planted a tamarisk
tree in Beersheba, and there
he called upon the name of the
LORD, the Eternal God. [34]And
Abraham stayed in the land of
the Philistines for a long time.

## *Abraham Tested*

22 Some time later God
tested Abraham. He
said to him, "Abraham!"
"Here I am," he replied.
[2]Then God said, "Take your
son, your only son Isaac,
whom you love, and go to the
region of Moriah. Sacrifice
him there as a burnt offering
on one of the mountains I will
tell you about."
[3]Early the next morning
Abraham got up and saddled
his donkey. He took with him
two of his servants and his
son Isaac. When he had cut

[r]31 *Beersheba* can mean *well of seven* or *well of the oath.*

וַיְבַקַּע עֲצֵי עֹלָה וַיָּקָם וַיֵּלֶךְ אֶל־הַמָּקוֹם
the-place for and-he-set-out then-he-rose burnt-offering wood-of and-he-cut

אֲשֶׁר־אָמַר־לוֹ הָאֱלֹהִים׃ בַּיּוֹם הַשְּׁלִישִׁי וַיִּשָּׂא אַבְרָהָם
Abraham then-he-lifted the-third on-the-day (4) the-God to-him he-told that

אֶת־עֵינָיו וַיַּרְא אֶת־הַמָּקוֹם מֵרָחֹק׃ וַיֹּאמֶר אַבְרָהָם
Abraham and-he-said (5) in-distance the-place *** and-he-saw eyes-of-him ***

אֶל־נְעָרָיו שְׁבוּ־לָכֶם פֹּה עִם־הַחֲמוֹר וַאֲנִי וְהַנַּעַר
and-the-boy while-I the-donkey with here yourselves stay! servants-of-him to

נֵלְכָה עַד־כֹּה וְנִשְׁתַּחֲוֶה וְנָשׁוּבָה אֲלֵיכֶם׃
to-you and-we-will-come-back then-we-will-worship there over we-go

וַיִּקַּח אַבְרָהָם אֶת־עֲצֵי הָעֹלָה וַיָּשֶׂם עַל־
on and-he-placed the-burnt-offering wood-of *** Abraham then-he-took (6)

יִצְחָק בְּנוֹ וַיִּקַּח בְּיָדוֹ אֶת־הָאֵשׁ וְאֶת־הַמַּאֲכֶלֶת
the-knife and the-fire *** in-hand-of-him and-he-carried son-of-him Isaac

וַיֵּלְכוּ שְׁנֵיהֶם יַחְדָּו׃ וַיֹּאמֶר יִצְחָק אֶל־אַבְרָהָם
Abraham to Isaac and-he-spoke (7) together two-of-them and-they-went-on

אָבִיו וַיֹּאמֶר אָבִי וַיֹּאמֶר הִנֶּנִּי בְנִי
son-of-me here-I and-he-replied father-of-me and-he-said father-of-him

וַיֹּאמֶר הִנֵּה הָאֵשׁ וְהָעֵצִים וְאַיֵּה הַשֶּׂה לְעֹלָה׃
for-burnt-offering the-lamb but-where? and-the-wood the-fire see! and-he-said

וַיֹּאמֶר אַבְרָהָם אֱלֹהִים יִרְאֶה־לּוֹ הַשֶּׂה
the-lamb himself he-will-provide God Abraham and-he-answered (8)

לְעֹלָה בְּנִי וַיֵּלְכוּ שְׁנֵיהֶם יַחְדָּו׃
together two-of-them and-they-went-on son-of-me for-burnt-offering

וַיָּבֹאוּ אֶל־הַמָּקוֹם אֲשֶׁר אָמַר־לוֹ הָאֱלֹהִים וַיִּבֶן
and-he-built the-God to-him he-told that the-place to and-they-reached (9)

שָׁם אַבְרָהָם אֶת־הַמִּזְבֵּחַ וַיַּעֲרֹךְ אֶת־הָעֵצִים וַיַּעֲקֹד אֶת־
*** and-he-bound the-wood *** and-he-arranged the-altar *** Abraham there

יִצְחָק בְּנוֹ וַיָּשֶׂם אֹתוֹ עַל־הַמִּזְבֵּחַ מִמַּעַל לָעֵצִים׃
on-the-woods on-top the-altar on him and-he-laid son-of-him Isaac

וַיִּשְׁלַח אַבְרָהָם אֶת־יָדוֹ וַיִּקַּח אֶת־הַמַּאֲכֶלֶת לִשְׁחֹט אֶת־
*** to-slay the-knife *** and-he-took hand-of-him *** Abraham then-he-reached (10)

בְּנוֹ׃ וַיִּקְרָא אֵלָיו מַלְאַךְ יְהוָה מִן־הַשָּׁמַיִם
the-heavens from Yahweh angel-of to-him but-he-called (11) son-of-him

וַיֹּאמֶר אַבְרָהָם ׀ אַבְרָהָם וַיֹּאמֶר הִנֵּנִי׃ וַיֹּאמֶר אַל־
not and-he-said (12) here-I and-he-replied Abraham Abraham and-he-said

תִּשְׁלַח יָדְךָ אֶל־הַנַּעַר וְאַל־תַּעַשׂ לוֹ מְאוּמָה כִּי ׀ עַתָּה יָדַעְתִּי
I-know now for anything to-him you-do and-not the-boy on hand-of-you you-lay

enough wood for the burnt offering, he set out for the place God had told him about. [4]On the third day Abraham looked up and saw the place in the distance. [5]He said to his servants, "Stay here with the donkey while I and the boy go over there. We will worship and then we will come back to you."

[6]Abraham took the wood for the burnt offering and placed it on his son Isaac, and he himself carried the fire and the knife. As the two of them went on together, [7]Isaac spoke up and said to his father Abraham, "Father?"

"Yes, my son?" Abraham replied.

"The fire and wood are here," Isaac said, "but where is the lamb for the burnt offering?"

[8]Abraham answered, "God himself will provide the lamb for the burnt offering, my son." And the two of them went on together.

[9]When they reached the place God had told him about, Abraham built an altar there and arranged the wood on it. He bound his son Isaac and laid him on the altar, on top of the wood. [10]Then he reached out his hand and took the knife to slay his son. [11]But the angel of the LORD called out to him from heaven, "Abraham! Abraham!"

"Here I am," he replied.

[12]"Do not lay a hand on the boy," he said. "Do not do anything to him. Now I know that

*12 Most mss have no *dagesh* in the second *mem* ( וּמָה ).

כִּֽי־ יְרֵא אֱלֹהִים֙ אַתָּה וְלֹא חָשַׂכְתָּ אֶת־ בִּנְךָ אֶת־ יְחִידְךָ
only-of-you *** son-of-you *** you-withheld for-not you God fearing-of that

מִמֶּנִּי׃ וַיִּשָּׂא אַבְרָהָם אֶת־ עֵינָיו וַיַּרְא֙ וְהִנֵּה־
and-see! and-he-looked eyes-of-him *** Abraham and-he-lifted (13) from-me

אַיִל אַחַר נֶאֱחַז בַּסְּבַךְ בְּקַרְנָיו וַיֵּלֶךְ אַבְרָהָם֙
Abraham so-he-went by-horns-of-him in-the-thicket being-caught behind ram

וַיִּקַּח אֶת־ הָאַיִל וַיַּעֲלֵהוּ לְעֹלָה תַּחַת
instead-of as-burnt-offering and-he-sacrificed-him the-ram *** and-he-took

בְּנוֹ׃ וַיִּקְרָא אַבְרָהָם שֵׁם־ הַמָּקוֹם הַהוּא יְהוָה ׀
Yahweh the-that the-place name-of Abraham so-he-called (14) son-of-him

יִרְאֶה אֲשֶׁר֙ יֵאָמֵר הַיּוֹם בְּהַר יְהוָה יֵרָאֶה׃
he-will-be-provided Yahweh on-mountain-of the-day he-is-said as he-will-provide

וַיִּקְרָא מַלְאַךְ יְהוָה אֶל־אַבְרָהָם שֵׁנִית מִן־ הַשָּׁמָיִם׃
the-heavens from second Abraham to Yahweh angel-of and-he-called (15)

וַיֹּאמֶר בִּי נִשְׁבַּעְתִּי נְאֻם־ יְהוָה כִּי יַעַן אֲשֶׁר עָשִׂיתָ֙
you-did that because that Yahweh declares I-swear by-myself and-he-said (16)

אֶת־ הַדָּבָר הַזֶּה וְלֹא חָשַׂכְתָּ אֶת־ בִּנְךָ אֶת־ יְחִידֶךָ׃
only-of-you *** son-of-you *** you-withheld and-not the-this the-thing ***

כִּי־ בָרֵךְ אֲבָרֶכְךָ וְהַרְבָּה אַרְבֶּה אֶת־
*** I-will-increase and-to-increase I-will-bless-you to-bless surely (17)

זַרְעֲךָ֙ כְּכוֹכְבֵי הַשָּׁמַיִם וְכַחוֹל אֲשֶׁר עַל־ שְׂפַת
shore-of on that and-as-the-sand the-skies as-stars-of descendant-of-you

הַיָּם וְיִרַשׁ זַרְעֲךָ אֵת שַׁעַר אֹיְבָיו׃
being-enemies-of-him gate-of *** descendant-of-you and-he-will-possess the-sea

וְהִתְבָּרְכוּ בְזַרְעֲךָ כֹּל גּוֹיֵי הָאָרֶץ
the-earth nations-of all-of through-seed-of-you and-they-will-be-blessed (18)

עֵקֶב אֲשֶׁר שָׁמַעְתָּ בְּקֹלִי׃ וַיָּשָׁב אַבְרָהָם֙ אֶל־
to Abraham then-he-returned (19) to-voice-of-me you-obeyed that because

נְעָרָיו וַיָּקֻמוּ וַיֵּלְכוּ יַחְדָּו אֶל־ בְּאֵר שָׁבַע
Sheba Beer to together and-they-set-off and-they-rose servants-of-him

וַיֵּשֶׁב אַבְרָהָם בִּבְאֵר שָׁבַע׃ וַיְהִי אַחֲרֵי הַדְּבָרִים הָאֵלֶּה
the-these the-things after and-he-was (20) Sheba in-Beer Abraham and-he-stayed

וַיֻּגַּד לְאַבְרָהָם לֵאמֹר הִנֵּה יָלְדָה מִלְכָּה גַם־הִוא בָּנִים לְנָחוֹר
to-Nahor sons she also Milcah she-bore see! to-say to-Abraham that-he-was-told

אָחִיךָ׃ אֶת־עוּץ בְּכֹרוֹ וְאֶת־בּוּז אָחִיו וְאֶת־קְמוּאֵל
Kemuel and brother-of-him Buz and firstborn-of-him Uz *** (21) brother-of-you

אֲבִי אֲרָם׃ וְאֶת־ כֶּשֶׂד וְאֶת־ חֲזוֹ וְאֶת־פִּלְדָּשׁ וְאֶת־ יִדְלָף וְאֵת בְּתוּאֵל׃
Bethuel and Jidlaph and Pildash and Hazo and Kesed and (22) Aram father-of

you fear God, because you
have not withheld from me
your son, your only son."
13Abraham looked up and
there in a thicket he saw a
ram[s] caught by its horns. He
went over and took the ram
and sacrificed it as a burnt
offering instead of his son.
14So Abraham called that place
"The LORD will provide." And
to this day it is said, "On the
mountain of the LORD it will
be provided."
15The angel of the LORD
called to Abraham from heav-
en a second time 16and said, "I
swear by myself, declares the
LORD, that because you have
done this and have not withheld your son, your only son,
17I will surely bless you and
make your descendants as numerous as the stars in the sky
and as the sand on the seashore. Your descendants will
take possession of the cities of
their enemies, 18and through
your offspring[t] all nations on
earth will be blessed, because
you have obeyed me."
19Then Abraham returned to
his servants, and they set off
together for Beersheba. And
Abraham stayed in Beersheba.

*Nahor's Sons*

20Some time later Abraham
was told, "Milcah is also a
mother; she has borne sons to
your brother Nahor: 21Uz the
firstborn, Buz his brother,
Kemuel (the father of Aram),
22Kesed, Hazo, Pildash, Jidlaph and Bethuel." 23Bethuel

s *13* Many manuscripts of the Masoretic Text, Samaritan Pentateuch, Septuagint and Syriac; most manuscripts of the Masoretic Text *a ram behind* ⌊*him*⌋

t *18* Or *seed*

וּבְתוּאֵל יָלַד אֶת־ רִבְקָה שְׁמֹנָה אֵלֶּה יָלְדָה מִלְכָּה לְנָחוֹר
to-Nahor Milcah she-bore these eight Rebekah *** he-fathered and-Bethuel (23)

אֲחִי אַבְרָהָם׃ וּפִילַגְשׁוֹ וּשְׁמָהּ רְאוּמָה
Reumah now-name-of-her and-concubine-of-him (24) Abraham brother-of

וַתֵּלֶד גַּם־ הִוא אֶת־ טֶבַח וְאֶת־ גַּחַם וְאֶת־ תַּחַשׁ וְאֶת־ מַעֲכָה׃
Maacah and Tahash and Gaham and Tebah *** she also and-she-bore

וַיִּהְיוּ חַיֵּי שָׂרָה מֵאָה שָׁנָה וְעֶשְׂרִים שָׁנָה וְשֶׁבַע
and-seven year and-twenty year hundred Sarah lives-of and-they-were (23:1)

שָׁנִים שְׁנֵי חַיֵּי שָׂרָה׃ וַתָּמָת שָׂרָה בְּקִרְיַת אַרְבַּע הִוא
that Arba in-Kiriath Sarah and-she-died (2) Sarah lives-of years-of years

חֶבְרוֹן בְּאֶרֶץ כְּנָעַן וַיָּבֹא אַבְרָהָם לִסְפֹּד לְשָׂרָה
for-Sarah to-mourn Abraham and-he-went Canaan in-land-of Hebron

וְלִבְכֹּתָהּ׃ וַיָּקָם אַבְרָהָם מֵעַל פְּנֵי מֵתוֹ
being-dead-of-him beside-of from Abraham then-he-rose (3) and-to-weep-over-her

וַיְדַבֵּר אֶל־ בְּנֵי־ חֵת לֵאמֹר׃ גֵּר־ וְתוֹשָׁב אָנֹכִי עִמָּכֶם
among-you I and-stranger alien (4) to-say Heth sons-of to and-he-spoke

תְּנוּ לִי אֲחֻזַּת־ קֶבֶר עִמָּכֶם וְאֶקְבְּרָה מֵתִי
being-dead-of-me so-I-can-bury among-you burial property-of to-me sell!

מִלְּפָנָי׃ וַיַּעֲנוּ בְנֵי־ חֵת אֶת־ אַבְרָהָם לֵאמֹר לוֹ׃
to-him to-say Abraham to Heth sons-of and-they-replied (5) from-before-me

שְׁמָעֵנוּ ׀ אֲדֹנִי נְשִׂיא אֱלֹהִים אַתָּה בְּתוֹכֵנוּ בְּמִבְחַר קְבָרֵינוּ
tombs-of-us in-choice-of-us among-us you mighty prince-of sir-of-me listen-to-us! (6)

קְבֹר אֶת־ מֵתֶךָ אִישׁ מִמֶּנּוּ אֶת־ קִבְרוֹ לֹא־ יִכְלֶה
he-will-refuse not tomb-of-him *** from-us man being-dead-of-you *** bury!

מִמְּךָ מִקְּבֹר מֵתֶךָ׃ וַיָּקָם אַבְרָהָם וַיִּשְׁתַּחוּ
and-he-bowed Abraham then-he-rose (7) being-dead-of-you for-to-bury to-you

לְעַם־ הָאָרֶץ לִבְנֵי־ חֵת׃ וַיְדַבֵּר אִתָּם לֵאמֹר
to-say to-them and-he-said (8) Heth before-sons-of the-land before-people-of

אִם־ יֵשׁ אֶת־ נַפְשְׁכֶם לִקְבֹּר אֶת־ מֵתִי מִלְּפָנַי
from-before-me being-dead-of-me *** to-bury will-of-you in it-is if

שְׁמָעוּנִי וּפִגְעוּ־ לִי בְּעֶפְרוֹן בֶּן־ צֹחַר׃
Zohar son-of with-Ephron for-me and-intercede! listen-to-me!

וְיִתֶּן־ לִי אֶת־מְעָרַת הַמַּכְפֵּלָה אֲשֶׁר־ לוֹ אֲשֶׁר בִּקְצֵה
in-end-of which to-him which the-Machpelah cave-of *** to-me so-he-will-sell (9)

שָׂדֵהוּ בְּכֶסֶף מָלֵא יִתְּנֶנָּה לִּי בְּתוֹכְכֶם לַאֲחֻזַּת־ קָבֶר׃
burial as-site-of among-you to-me let-him-sell-her full for-price field-of-him

וְעֶפְרוֹן יֹשֵׁב בְּתוֹךְ בְּנֵי־ חֵת וַיַּעַן עֶפְרוֹן הַחִתִּי
the-Hittite Ephron and-he-replied Heth sons-of among sitting now-Ephron (10)

became the father of Rebekah. Milcah bore these eight sons to Abraham's brother Nahor. 24His concubine, whose name was Reumah, also had sons: Tebah, Gaham, Tahash and Maacah.

*The Death of Sarah*

23 Sarah lived to be a hundred and twenty-seven years old. 2She died at Kiriath Arba (that is, Hebron) in the land of Canaan, and Abraham went to mourn for Sarah and to weep over her.

3Then Abraham rose from beside his dead wife and spoke to the Hittites.[u] He said, 4"I am an alien and a stranger among you. Sell me some property for a burial site here so I can bury my dead."

5The Hittites replied to Abraham, 6"Sir, listen to us. You are a mighty prince among us. Bury your dead in the choicest of our tombs. None of us will refuse you his tomb for burying your dead."

7Then Abraham rose and bowed down before the people of the land, the Hittites. 8He said to them, "If you are willing to let me bury my dead, then listen to me and intercede with Ephron son of Zohar on my behalf 9so he will sell me the cave of Machpelah, which belongs to him and is in the end of his field. Ask him to sell it to me for the full price as a burial site among you."

10Ephron the Hittite was sitting among his people and he

[u]3 Or *the sons of Heth;* also in verses 5, 7, 10, 16, 18 and 20

אֶת־ אַבְרָהָם בְּאָזְנֵי בְנֵי־ חֵת לְכֹל בָּאֵי שַׁעַר־
gate-of ones-coming-of to-all Heth sons-of in-hearing-of Abraham ***

עִירוֹ לֵאמֹר׃ לֹא־ אֲדֹנִי שְׁמָעֵנִי הַשָּׂדֶה נָתַתִּי לָךְ
to-you I-give the-field listen-to-me! lord-of-me no (11) to-say city-of-him

וְהַמְּעָרָה אֲשֶׁר־ בּוֹ לְךָ נְתַתִּיהָ לְעֵינֵי בְנֵי־ עַמִּי
people-of-me sons-of before-eyes-of I-give-her to-you in-him that and-the-cave

נְתַתִּיהָ לָּךְ קְבֹר מֵתֶךָ׃ וַיִּשְׁתַּחוּ אַבְרָהָם לִפְנֵי
before Abraham and-he-bowed (12) being-dead-of-you bury! to-you I-give-her

עַם הָאָרֶץ׃ וַיְדַבֵּר אֶל־ עֶפְרוֹן בְּאָזְנֵי עַם־ הָאָרֶץ
the-land people-of in-hearing-of Ephron to and-he-said (13) the-land people-of

לֵאמֹר אַךְ אִם־אַתָּה לוּ שְׁמָעֵנִי נָתַתִּי כֶּסֶף הַשָּׂדֶה קַח
accept! the-field price-of I-will-pay listen-to-me! will you if now to-say

מִמֶּנִּי וְאֶקְבְּרָה אֶת־ מֵתִי שָׁמָּה׃ וַיַּעַן עֶפְרוֹן
Ephron and-he-answered (14) at-there being-dead-of-me *** so-I-can-bury from-me

אֶת־ אַבְרָהָם לֵאמֹר לוֹ׃ אֲדֹנִי שְׁמָעֵנִי אֶרֶץ אַרְבַּע מֵאֹת
hundreds-of four land listen-to-me! lord-of-me (15) to-him to-say Abraham ***

שֶׁקֶל־ כֶּסֶף בֵּינִי וּבֵינְךָ מַה־ הִוא וְאֶת־ מֵתְךָ
being-dead-of-you now that what? and-between-you between-me silver shekel-of

קְבֹר׃ וַיִּשְׁמַע אַבְרָהָם אֶל־ עֶפְרוֹן וַיִּשְׁקֹל אַבְרָהָם לְעֶפְרֹן
for-Ephron Abraham and-he-weighed Ephron with Abraham and-he-agreed (16) bury!

אֶת־ הַכֶּסֶף אֲשֶׁר דִּבֶּר בְּאָזְנֵי בְנֵי־ חֵת אַרְבַּע מֵאוֹת
hundreds-of four Heth sons-of in-hearing-of he-named that the-price ***

שֶׁקֶל כֶּסֶף עֹבֵר לַסֹּחֵר׃ וַיָּקָם ׀ שְׂדֵה
field-of so-he-was-deeded (17) to-the-ones-selling according silver shekel-of

עֶפְרוֹן אֲשֶׁר בַּמַּכְפֵּלָה אֲשֶׁר לִפְנֵי מַמְרֵא הַשָּׂדֶה וְהַמְּעָרָה אֲשֶׁר־
that and-the-cave the-field Mamre near that in-the-Machpelah that Ephron

בּוֹ וְכָל־ הָעֵץ אֲשֶׁר בַּשָּׂדֶה אֲשֶׁר בְּכָל־ גְּבֻלוֹ
border-of-him in-all-of that in-the-field that the-tree and-every-of in-him

סָבִיב׃ לְאַבְרָהָם לְמִקְנָה לְעֵינֵי בְנֵי־ חֵת בְּכֹל
before-all-of Heth sons-of in-presence-of as-property to-Abraham (18) around

בָּאֵי שַׁעַר־ עִירוֹ׃ וְאַחֲרֵי־ כֵן קָבַר אַבְרָהָם אֶת־
*** Abraham he-buried this and-after (19) city-of-him gate-of ones-coming-of

שָׂרָה אִשְׁתּוֹ אֶל־ מְעָרַת שְׂדֵה הַמַּכְפֵּלָה עַל־ פְּנֵי מַמְרֵא הִוא
which Mamre near by the-Machpelah field-of cave-of in wife-of-him Sarah

חֶבְרוֹן בְּאֶרֶץ כְּנָעַן׃ וַיָּקָם הַשָּׂדֶה וְהַמְּעָרָה אֲשֶׁר־
that and-the-cave the-field so-he-was-deeded (20) Canaan in-land-of Hebron

בּוֹ לְאַבְרָהָם לַאֲחֻזַּת־ קָבֶר מֵאֵת בְּנֵי־ חֵת׃ וְאַבְרָהָם
now-Abraham (24:1) Heth sons-of by burial as-site-of to-Abraham in-him

replied to Abraham in the hearing of all the Hittites who had come to the gate of his city. [11]"No, my lord," he said. "Listen to me; I give[v] you the field, and I give[v] you the cave that is in it. I give[v] it to you in the presence of my people. Bury your dead."

[12]Again Abraham bowed down before the people of the land [13]and he said to Ephron in their hearing, "Listen to me, if you will. I will pay the price of the field. Accept it from me so I can bury my dead there."

[14]Ephron answered Abraham, [15]"Listen to me, my lord; the land is worth four hundred shekels[w] of silver, but what is that between me and you? Bury your dead."

[16]Abraham agreed to Ephron's terms and weighed out for him the price he had named in the hearing of the Hittites: four hundred shekels of silver, according to the weight current among the merchants.

[17]So Ephron's field in Machpelah near Mamre—both the field and the cave in it, and all the trees within the borders of the field—was deeded [18]to Abraham as his property in the presence of all the Hittites who had come to the gate of the city. [19]Afterward Abraham buried his wife Sarah in the cave in the field of Machpelah near Mamre (which is at Hebron) in the land of Canaan. [20]So the field and the cave in it were deeded to Abraham by the Hittites as a burial site.

v11 Or *sell*
w15 That is, about 10 pounds (about 4.5 kilograms)

זָקֵן בָּא בַּיָּמִים וַיהוָה בֵּרַךְ אֶת־אַבְרָהָם
Abraham *** he-blessed and-Yahweh in-the-days he-was-advanced he-was-old

בַּכֹּל׃ וַיֹּאמֶר אַבְרָהָם אֶל־עַבְדּוֹ זְקַן
chief-of servant-of-him to Abraham and-he-said (2) in-the-every-way

בֵּיתוֹ הַמֹּשֵׁל בְּכָל־אֲשֶׁר־לוֹ שִׂים־נָא
now! put! to-him that over-all the-one-having-charge household-of-him

יָדְךָ תַּחַת יְרֵכִי׃ וְאַשְׁבִּיעֲךָ בַּיהוָה אֱלֹהֵי
God-of by-Yahweh and-I-want-to-swear-you (3) thigh-of-me under hand-of-you

הַשָּׁמַיִם וֵאלֹהֵי הָאָרֶץ אֲשֶׁר לֹא־תִקַּח אִשָּׁה לִבְנִי
for-son-of-me wife you-will-get not that the-earth and-God-of the-heavens

מִבְּנוֹת הַכְּנַעֲנִי אֲשֶׁר אָנֹכִי יוֹשֵׁב בְּקִרְבּוֹ׃ כִּי אֶל־
to but (4) in-midst-of-him living I whom the-Canaanite from-daughters-of

אַרְצִי וְאֶל־מוֹלַדְתִּי תֵּלֵךְ וְלָקַחְתָּ אִשָּׁה לִבְנִי
for-son-of-me wife and-you-get you-will-go relative-of-me and-to country-of-me

לְיִצְחָק׃ וַיֹּאמֶר אֵלָיו הָעֶבֶד אוּלַי לֹא־תֹאבֶה הָאִשָּׁה
the-woman she-wills not what-if? the-servant to-him and-he-asked (5) for-Isaac

לָלֶכֶת אַחֲרַי אֶל־הָאָרֶץ הַזֹּאת הֶהָשֵׁב אָשִׁיב אֶת־
*** shall-I-take-back to-take-back? the-this the-land to after-me to-come

בִּנְךָ אֶל־הָאָרֶץ אֲשֶׁר־יָצָאתָ מִשָּׁם׃ וַיֹּאמֶר אֵלָיו
to-him and-he-said (6) from-there you-came that the-country to son-of-you

אַבְרָהָם הִשָּׁמֶר לְךָ פֶּן־תָּשִׁיב אֶת־בְּנִי שָׁמָּה׃ יְהוָה׀
Yahweh (7) to-there son-of-me *** you-take that-not to-you be-sure! Abraham

אֱלֹהֵי הַשָּׁמַיִם אֲשֶׁר לְקָחַנִי מִבֵּית אָבִי וּמֵאֶרֶץ
and-from-land-of father-of-me from-house-of he-brought-me who the-heavens God-of

מוֹלַדְתִּי וַאֲשֶׁר דִּבֶּר־לִי וַאֲשֶׁר נִשְׁבַּע־לִי לֵאמֹר
to-say to-me he-swore and-who to-me he-spoke and-who relative-of-me

לְזַרְעֲךָ אֶתֵּן אֶת־הָאָרֶץ הַזֹּאת הוּא יִשְׁלַח
he-will-send he the-this the-land *** I-will-give to-offspring-of-you

מַלְאָכוֹ לְפָנֶיךָ וְלָקַחְתָּ אִשָּׁה לִבְנִי מִשָּׁם׃ וְאִם־
but-if (8) from-there for-son-of-me wife so-you-can-get before-you angel-of-him

לֹא תֹאבֶה הָאִשָּׁה לָלֶכֶת אַחֲרֶיךָ וְנִקִּיתָ מִשְּׁבֻעָתִי זֹאת
this from-oath-of-me so-you-are-free with-you to-come the-woman she-will not

רַק אֶת־בְּנִי לֹא תָשֵׁב שָׁמָּה׃ וַיָּשֶׂם הָעֶבֶד אֶת־יָדוֹ
hand-of-him *** the-servant so-he-put (9) to-there you-take not son-of-me *** only

תַּחַת יֶרֶךְ אַבְרָהָם אֲדֹנָיו וַיִּשָּׁבַע לוֹ עַל־הַדָּבָר
the-matter concerning to-him and-he-swore master-of-him Abraham thigh-of under

הַזֶּה׃ וַיִּקַּח הָעֶבֶד עֲשָׂרָה גְמַלִּים מִגְּמַלֵּי אֲדֹנָיו
master-of-him from-camels-of camels ten the-servant then-he-took (10) the-this

### *Isaac and Rebekah*

**24** Abraham was now old
and well advanced in
years, and the LORD had
blessed him in every way. [2]He
said to the chief[x] servant in
his household, the one in
charge of all that he had, "Put
your hand under my thigh. [3]I
want you to swear by the
LORD, the God of heaven and
the God of earth, that you will
not get a wife for my son from
the daughters of the Canaanites, among whom I am living,
[4]but will go to my country and
my own relatives and get a
wife for my son Isaac."
[5]The servant asked him,
"What if the woman is unwilling to come back with me to
this land? Shall I then take
your son back to the country
you came from?"
[6]"Make sure that you do not
take my son back there,"
Abraham said. [7]"The LORD,
the God of heaven, who
brought me out of my father's
household and my native land
and who spoke to me and
promised me on oath, saying,
'To your offspring[y] I will give
this land'—he will send his
angel before you so that you
can get a wife for my son from
there. [8]If the woman is unwilling to come back with you,
then you will be released from
this oath of mine. Only do not
take my son back there." [9]So
the servant put his hand under the thigh of his master
Abraham and swore an oath
to him concerning this matter.
[10]Then the servant took ten
of his master's camels and left,

[x]2 Or *oldest* [y]7 Or *seed*

וַיֵּלֶךְ וְכָל־ טוּב אֲדֹנָיו בְּיָדוֹ וַיָּקָם
and-he-rose in-hand-of-him master-of-him good-of with-all-of and-he-left

וַיֵּלֶךְ אֶל־ אֲרַם נַהֲרַיִם אֶל־ עִיר נָחוֹר׃ וַיַּבְרֵךְ
and-he-made-kneel (11) Nahor city-of to Nahariam Aram for and-he-set-out

הַגְּמַלִּים מִחוּץ לָעִיר אֶל־ בְּאֵר הַמָּיִם לְעֵת עֶרֶב
evening at-time-of the-waters well-of near to-the-city outside the-camels

לְעֵת צֵאת הַשֹּׁאֲבֹת׃ וַיֹּאמַר׀ יְהוָה אֱלֹהֵי
God-of Yahweh and-he-prayed (12) the-women-drawing-water to-go-out at-time-of

אֲדֹנִי אַבְרָהָם הַקְרֵה־ נָא לְפָנַי הַיּוֹם וַעֲשֵׂה־ חֶסֶד עִם
to kindness and-show! the-day to-me now! give-success! Abraham master-of-me

אֲדֹנִי אַבְרָהָם׃ הִנֵּה אָנֹכִי נִצָּב עַל־ עֵין הַמָּיִם
the-waters spring-of by standing I see! (13) Abraham master-of-me

וּבְנוֹת אַנְשֵׁי הָעִיר יֹצְאֹת לִשְׁאֹב מָיִם׃
waters to-draw ones-coming the-city people-of and-daughters-of

וְהָיָה הַנַּעֲרָ אֲשֶׁר אֹמַר אֵלֶיהָ הַטִּי־ נָא כַדֵּךְ
jar-of-you now! let-down! to-her I-say whom the-girl now-may-he-be (14)

וְאֶשְׁתֶּה וְאָמְרָה שְׁתֵה וְגַם־ גְּמַלֶּיךָ אַשְׁקֶה אֹתָהּ
her I-will-water camels-of-you and-also drink! and-she-says so-I-may-drink

הֹכַחְתָּ לְעַבְדְּךָ לְיִצְחָק וּבָהּ אֵדַע כִּי־ עָשִׂיתָ
you-showed that I-will-know and-by-her for-Isaac for-servant-of-you you-chose

חֶסֶד עִם־ אֲדֹנִי׃ וַיְהִי־ הוּא טֶרֶם כִּלָּה לְדַבֵּר
to-pray he-finished before this and-he-was (15) master-of-me to kindness

וְהִנֵּה רִבְקָה יֹצֵאת אֲשֶׁר יֻלְּדָה לִבְתוּאֵל בֶּן־ מִלְכָּה אֵשֶׁת
wife-of Milcah son-of to-Bethuel she-was-born whom coming Rebekah and-see!

נָחוֹר אֲחִי אַבְרָהָם וְכַדָּהּ עַל־ שִׁכְמָהּ׃ וְהַנַּעֲרָ
now-the-girl (16) shoulder-of-her on and-jar-of-her Abraham brother-of Nahor

טֹבַת מַרְאֶה מְאֹד בְּתוּלָה וְאִישׁ לֹא יְדָעָהּ וַתֵּרֶד
and-she-went-down he-knew-her no and-man virgin very sight beautiful-of

הָעַיְנָה וַתְּמַלֵּא כַדָּהּ וַתָּעַל׃ וַיָּרָץ
and-he-hurried (17) and-she-came-up jar-of-her and-she-filled to-the-spring

הָעֶבֶד לִקְרָאתָהּ וַיֹּאמֶר הַגְמִיאִינִי נָא מְעַט־ מַיִם
waters little-of now! give-me! and-he-said to-meet-her the-servant

מִכַּדֵּךְ׃ וַתֹּאמֶר שְׁתֵה אֲדֹנִי וַתְּמַהֵר
and-she-hurried lord-of-me drink! and-she-said (18) from-jar-of-you

וַתֹּרֶד כַּדָּהּ עַל־ יָדָהּ וַתַּשְׁקֵהוּ׃
and-she-gave-drink-him hand-of-her to jar-of-her and-she-lowered

וַתְּכַל לְהַשְׁקֹתוֹ וַתֹּאמֶר גַּם לִגְמַלֶּיךָ
for-camels-of-you also then-she-said to-give-drink-him when-she-finished (19)

taking with him all kinds of good things from his master. He set out for Aram Naharaim[z] and made his way to the town of Nahor. 11He had the camels kneel down near the well outside the town; it was toward evening, the time the women go out to draw water.

12Then he prayed, "O Lord, God of my master Abraham, give me success today, and show kindness to my master Abraham. 13See, I am standing beside this spring, and the daughters of the townspeople are coming out to draw water. 14May it be that when I say to a girl, 'Please let down your jar that I may have a drink,' and she says, 'Drink, and I'll water your camels too'—let her be the one you have chosen for your servant Isaac. By this I will know that you have shown kindness to my master."

15Before he had finished praying, Rebekah came out with her jar on her shoulder. She was the daughter of Bethuel son of Milcah, who was the wife of Abraham's brother Nahor. 16The girl was very beautiful, a virgin; no man had ever lain with her. She went down to the spring, filled her jar and came up again.

17The servant hurried to meet her and said, "Please give me a little water from your jar."

18"Drink, my lord," she said, and quickly lowered the jar to her hands and gave him a drink.

19After she had given him a drink, she said, "I'll draw

[z]*10* That is, Northwest Mesopotamia

אֶשְׁאָב עַד אִם־ כִּלּוּ לִשְׁתֹּת׃ וַתְּמַהֵר
and-she-hurried (20) to-drink they-finish when until I-will-draw

וַתְּעַר כַּדָּהּ אֶל־ הַשֹּׁקֶת וַתָּרָץ עוֹד אֶל־ הַבְּאֵר
the-well to back and-she-ran the-trough into jar-of-her and-she-emptied

לִשְׁאֹב וַתִּשְׁאַב לְכָל־ גְּמַלָּיו׃ וְהָאִישׁ מִשְׁתָּאֵה לָהּ
to-her watching and-the-man (21) camels-of-him for-all-of and-she-drew to-draw

מַחֲרִישׁ לָדַעַת הַהִצְלִיחַ יְהוָה דַּרְכּוֹ אִם־לֹא׃
not or journey-of-him Yahweh if-he-made-successful to-learn being-silent

וַיְהִי כַּאֲשֶׁר כִּלּוּ הַגְּמַלִּים לִשְׁתּוֹת וַיִּקַּח הָאִישׁ
the-man that-he-took to-drink the-camels they-finished just-as and-he-was (22)

נֶזֶם זָהָב בֶּקַע מִשְׁקָלוֹ וּשְׁנֵי צְמִידִים עַל־ יָדֶיהָ עֲשָׂרָה
ten arms-of-her for bracelets and-two-of weight-of-him beka gold nose-ring

זָהָב מִשְׁקָלָם׃ וַיֹּאמֶר בַּת־ מִי אַתְּ הַגִּידִי נָא לִי
to-me now! tell! you whose daughter-of and-he-said (23) weight-of-them gold

הֲיֵשׁ בֵּית־ אָבִיךְ מָקוֹם לָנוּ לָלִין׃ וַתֹּאמֶר
so-she-said (24) to-spend-night for-us room father-of-you in-house-of is-there?

אֵלָיו בַּת־ בְּתוּאֵל אָנֹכִי בֶּן־ מִלְכָּה אֲשֶׁר יָלְדָה לְנָחוֹר׃
to-Nahor she-bore whom Milcah son-of I Bethuel daughter-of to-him

וַתֹּאמֶר אֵלָיו גַּם־ תֶּבֶן גַּם־מִסְפּוֹא רַב עִמָּנוּ גַּם־ מָקוֹם
room as-well-as with-us plenty fodder also straw also to-him and-she-said (25)

לָלוּן׃ וַיִּקֹּד הָאִישׁ וַיִּשְׁתַּחוּ לַיהוָה׃
to-Yahweh and-he-worshiped the-man then-he-bowed (26) to-spend-night

וַיֹּאמֶר בָּרוּךְ יְהוָה אֱלֹהֵי אֲדֹנִי אַבְרָהָם אֲשֶׁר לֹא־
not who Abraham master-of-me God-of Yahweh being-praised and-he-said (27)

עָזַב חַסְדּוֹ וַאֲמִתּוֹ מֵעִם אֲדֹנִי אָנֹכִי
I master-of-me to and-faithfulness-of-him kindness-of-him he-abandoned

בַּדֶּרֶךְ נָחַנִי יְהוָה בֵּית אֲחֵי אֲדֹנִי׃
master-of-me relatives-of to-house-of Yahweh he-led-me on-the-journey

וַתָּרָץ הַנַּעֲרָ וַתַּגֵּד לְבֵית אִמָּהּ
mother-of-her to-household-of and-she-told the-girl and-she-ran (28)

כַּדְּבָרִים הָאֵלֶּה׃ וּלְרִבְקָה אָח וּשְׁמוֹ לָבָן
Laban and-name-of-him brother now-to-Rebekah (29) the-these about-the-things

וַיָּרָץ לָבָן אֶל־ הָאִישׁ הַחוּצָה אֶל־ הָעָיִן׃ וַיְהִי ׀
and-he-was (30) the-spring to to-the-outside the-man to Laban and-he-hurried

כִּרְאֹת אֶת־ הַנֶּזֶם וְאֶת־ הַצְּמִדִים עַל־ יְדֵי אֲחֹתוֹ
sister-of-him arms-of on the-bracelets and the-nose-ring *** as-to-see

וּכְשָׁמְעוֹ אֶת־ דִּבְרֵי רִבְקָה אֲחֹתוֹ לֵאמֹר כֹּה־ דִבֶּר
he-said what to-say sister-of-him Rebekah words-of *** and-as-to-hear-him

water for your camels too, until they have finished drinking." [20]So she quickly emptied her jar into the trough, ran back to the well to draw more water, and drew enough for all his camels. [21]Without saying a word, the man watched her closely to learn whether or not the LORD had made his journey successful.

[22]When the camels had finished drinking, the man took out a gold nose ring weighing a beka[a] and two gold bracelets weighing ten shekels.[b] [23]Then he asked, "Whose daughter are you? Please tell me, is there room in your father's house for us to spend the night?"

[24]She answered him, "I am the daughter of Bethuel, the son that Milcah bore to Nahor." [25]And she added, "We have plenty of straw and fodder, as well as room for you to spend the night."

[26]Then the man bowed down and worshiped the LORD, [27]saying, "Praise be to the LORD, the God of my master Abraham, who has not abandoned his kindness and faithfulness to my master. As for me, the LORD has led me on the journey to the house of my master's relatives."

[28]The girl ran and told her mother's household about these things. [29]Now Rebekah had a brother named Laban, and he hurried out to the man at the spring. [30]As soon as he had seen the nose ring, and the bracelets on his sister's arms, and had heard Rebekah tell what the man said to her,

[a]22 That is, about 1/5 ounce (about 5.5 grams)
[b]22 That is, about 4 ounces (about 110 grams)

אֵלַי הָאִישׁ וַיָּבֹא אֶל־הָאִישׁ וְהִנֵּה עֹמֵד עַל־הַגְּמַלִּים עַל־
near the-camels by standing and-see! the-man to that-he-went the-man to-me

הָעָיִן׃ וַיֹּאמֶר בּוֹא בְּרוּךְ יְהוָה לָמָּה תַעֲמֹד
you-stand why? Yahweh being-blessed-of come! and-he-said (31) the-spring

בַּחוּץ וְאָנֹכִי פִּנִּיתִי הַבַּיִת וּמָקוֹם לַגְּמַלִּים׃ וַיָּבֹא
so-he-went (32) for-the-camels and-place the-house I-prepared now-I out-here

הָאִישׁ הַבַּיְתָה וַיְפַתַּח הַגְּמַלִּים וַיִּתֵּן תֶּבֶן
straw and-he-brought the-camels and-he-unloaded to-the-house the-man

וּמִסְפּוֹא לַגְּמַלִּים וּמַיִם לִרְחֹץ רַגְלָיו וְרַגְלֵי הָאֲנָשִׁים
the-men and-feet-of feet-of-him to-wash and-water for-the-camels and-fodder

אֲשֶׁר אִתּוֹ׃ °וַיִּישֶׂם לְפָנָיו לֶאֱכֹל וַיֹּאמֶר לֹא אֹכַל
I-will-eat not but-he-said to-eat before-him and-he-was-set (33) with-him who

עַד אִם־דִּבַּרְתִּי דְּבָרָי וַיֹּאמֶר דַּבֵּר׃ וַיֹּאמַר עֶבֶד
servant-of so-he-said (34) tell! so-he-said words-of-me I-tell when until

אַבְרָהָם אָנֹכִי׃ וַיהוָה בֵּרַךְ אֶת־אֲדֹנִי מְאֹד וַיִּגְדָּל
and-he-is-wealthy greatly master-of-me *** he-blessed now-Yahweh (35) I Abraham

וַיִּתֶּן־לוֹ צֹאן וּבָקָר וְכֶסֶף וְזָהָב וַעֲבָדִם
and-menservants and-gold and-silver and-cattle sheep to-him and-he-gave

וּשְׁפָחֹת וּגְמַלִּים וַחֲמֹרִים׃ וַתֵּלֶד שָׂרָה אֵשֶׁת
wife-of Sarah and-she-bore (36) and-donkeys and-camels and-maidservants

אֲדֹנִי בֵן לַאדֹנִי אַחֲרֵי זִקְנָתָהּ וַיִּתֶּן־לוֹ* אֶת־כָּל־
all *** to-him and-he-gave old-age-of-her in to-master-of-me son master-of-me

אֲשֶׁר־לוֹ׃ וַיַּשְׁבִּעֵנִי אֲדֹנִי לֵאמֹר לֹא־תִקַּח אִשָּׁה
wife you-must-get not to-say master-of-me and-he-made-swear-me (37) to-him that

לִבְנִי מִבְּנוֹת הַכְּנַעֲנִי אֲשֶׁר אָנֹכִי יֹשֵׁב בְּאַרְצוֹ׃
in-land-of-him living I whom the-Canaanite from-daughters-of for-son-of-me

אִם־לֹא אֶל־בֵּית־אָבִי תֵּלֵךְ וְאֶל־מִשְׁפַּחְתִּי וְלָקַחְתָּ
and-you-get clan-of-me and-to you-go father-of-me family-of to rather but (38)

אִשָּׁה לִבְנִי׃ וָאֹמַר אֶל־אֲדֹנִי אֻלַי לֹא־תֵלֵךְ
she-comes not what-if? master-of-me to then-I-asked (39) for-son-of-me wife

הָאִשָּׁה אַחֲרָי׃ וַיֹּאמֶר אֵלָי יְהוָה אֲשֶׁר־הִתְהַלַּכְתִּי לְפָנָיו
before-him I-walk whom Yahweh to-me and-he-replied (40) after-me the-woman

יִשְׁלַח מַלְאָכוֹ אִתָּךְ וְהִצְלִיחַ דַּרְכֶּךָ
journey-of-you and-he-will-make-succeed with-you angel-of-him he-will-send

וְלָקַחְתָּ אִשָּׁה לִבְנִי מִמִּשְׁפַּחְתִּי וּמִבֵּית
and-from-family-of from-clan-of-me for-son-of-me wife so-you-can-get

אָבִי׃ אָז תִּנָּקֶה מֵאָלָתִי כִּי תָבוֹא אֶל־
to you-go when from-oath-of-me you-will-be-free then (41) father-of-me

he went out to the man and
found him standing by the
camels near the spring.
[31]"Come, you who are blessed
by the LORD," he said. "Why
are you standing out here? I
have prepared the house and a
place for the camels."
[32]So the man went to the
house, and the camels were
unloaded. Straw and fodder
were brought for the camels,
and water for him and his
men to wash their feet. [33]Then
food was set before him, but
he said, "I will not eat until I
have told you what I have to
say."
"Then tell us," ⌊Laban⌋ said.
[34]So he said, "I am Abraham's servant. [35]The LORD has
blessed my master abundantly, and he has become
wealthy. He has given him
sheep and cattle, silver and
gold, menservants and maidservants, and camels and donkeys. [36]My master's wife Sarah
has borne him a son in her[c]
old age, and he has given him
everything he owns. [37]And my
master made me swear an
oath, and said, 'You must not
get a wife for my son from the
daughters of the Canaanites,
in whose land I live, [38]but go to
my father's family and to my
own clan, and get a wife for
my son.'
[39]"Then I asked my master,
'What if the woman will not
come back with me?'
[40]"He replied, 'The LORD, before whom I have walked, will
send his angel with you and
make your journey a success,
so that you can get a wife for
my son from my own clan and
from my father's family.
[41]Then, when you go to my
clan, you will be released from

[c]36 Or *his*

*36 Most mss have no *dagesh* in the *lamed* (לוֹ).

°33 ק ויושם

מִשְׁפַּחְתִּ֑י וְאִם־ לֹ֤א יִתְּנוּ֙ לָ֔ךְ וְהָיִ֥יתָ נָקִ֖י מֵאָלָתִֽי׃
from-oath-of-me · free · and-you-will-be · to-you · they-give · not · even-if · clan-of-me

וָאָבֹ֣א הַיֹּ֔ום אֶל־ הָעָ֑יִן וָאֹמַ֕ר יְהוָה֙ אֱלֹהֵי֙ אֲדֹנִ֣י
master-of-me · God-of · Yahweh · then-I-said · the-spring · to · the-day · when-I-came · (42)

אַבְרָהָ֑ם אִם־ יֶשְׁךָ֣־ נָּא֩ מַצְלִ֨יחַ דַּרְכִּ֜י אֲשֶׁ֧ר אָנֹכִ֛י הֹלֵ֖ךְ
coming · I · that · journey-of-me · granting-success · now! · will-of-you · if · Abraham

עָלֶֽיהָ׃ הִנֵּ֛ה אָנֹכִ֥י נִצָּ֖ב עַל־ עֵ֣ין הַמָּ֑יִם וְהָיָ֤ה הָעַלְמָה֙
the-maiden · now-may-he-be · the-water · spring-of · beside · standing · I · see! · (43) · on-her

הַיֹּצֵ֣את לִשְׁאֹ֗ב וְאָמַרְתִּ֥י אֵלֶ֛יהָ הַשְׁקִֽינִי־ נָ֥א מְעַט־ מַ֖יִם
water · little-of · now! · give-drink-me! · to-her · that-I-say · to-draw · the-one-coming

מִכַּדֵּֽךְ׃ וְאָמְרָ֥ה אֵלַ֖י גַּם־ אַתָּ֣ה שְׁתֵ֔ה וְגַ֥ם
and-also · drink! · you · indeed · to-me · and-she-says · (44) · from-jar-of-you

לִגְמַלֶּ֖יךָ אֶשְׁאָ֑ב הִ֣וא הָאִשָּׁ֔ה אֲשֶׁר־ הֹכִ֥יחַ יְהוָ֖ה לְבֶן־
for-son-of · Yahweh · he-chose · whom · the-woman · she · I-will-draw · for-camels-of-you

אֲדֹנִֽי׃ אֲנִי֩ טֶ֨רֶם אֲכַלֶּ֜ה לְדַבֵּ֣ר אֶל־ לִבִּ֗י וְהִנֵּ֤ה רִבְקָה֙
Rebekah · and-see! · heart-of-me · in · to-pray · I-finished · before · I · (45) · master-of-me

יֹצֵ֗את וְכַדָּ֣הּ עַל־ שִׁכְמָ֔הּ וַתֵּ֥רֶד הָעַ֖יְנָה
to-the-spring · and-she-went-down · shoulder-of-her · on · with-jar-of-her · coming

וַתִּשְׁאָ֑ב וָאֹמַ֥ר אֵלֶ֖יהָ הַשְׁקִ֥ינִי נָֽא׃ וַתְּמַהֵ֗ר
and-she-hurried · (46) · now! · give-drink-me! · to-her · and-I-said · and-she-drew

וַתֹּ֤ורֶד כַּדָּהּ֙ מֵֽעָלֶ֔יהָ וַתֹּ֣אמֶר שְׁתֵ֔ה וְגַם־
and-also · drink! · and-she-said · from-on-her · jar-of-her · and-she-lowered

גְּמַלֶּ֖יךָ אַשְׁקֶ֑ה וָאֵ֕שְׁתְּ וְגַ֥ם הַגְּמַלִּ֖ים הִשְׁקָֽתָה׃
she-watered · the-camels · and-also · so-I-drank · I-will-water · camels-of-you

וָאֶשְׁאַ֣ל אֹתָ֗הּ וָאֹמַר֙ בַּת־ מִ֣י אַ֔תְּ וַתֹּ֗אמֶר
and-she-said · you · whom? · daughter-of · and-I-said · her · then-I-asked · (47)

בַּת־ בְּתוּאֵל֙ בֶּן־ נָחֹ֔ור אֲשֶׁ֥ר יָֽלְדָה־ לֹּ֖ו מִלְכָּ֑ה וָאָשִׂ֤ם
then-I-put · Milcah · to-him · she-bore · whom · Nahor · son-of · Bethuel · daughter-of

הַנֶּ֨זֶם֙ עַל־ אַפָּ֔הּ וְהַצְּמִידִ֖ים עַל־ יָדֶֽיהָ׃ וָאֶקֹּ֧ד
then-I-bowed · (48) · arms-of-her · on · and-the-bracelets · nose-of-her · in · the-ring

וָֽאֶשְׁתַּחֲוֶ֖ה לַֽיהוָ֑ה וָאֲבָרֵ֗ךְ אֶת־ יְהוָה֙ אֱלֹהֵי֙ אֲדֹנִ֣י
master-of-me · God-of · Yahweh · *** · and-I-praised · to-Yahweh · and-I-worshiped

אַבְרָהָ֔ם אֲשֶׁ֤ר הִנְחַ֨נִי֙ בְּדֶ֣רֶךְ אֱמֶ֔ת לָקַ֛חַת אֶת־ בַּת־ אֲחִ֥י
brother-of · granddaughter-of · *** · to-get · right · on-road-of · he-led-me · who · Abraham

אֲדֹנִ֖י לִבְנֹֽו׃ וְעַתָּ֗ה אִם־ יֶשְׁכֶ֨ם עֹשִׂ֥ים חֶ֛סֶד
kindness · ones-showing · will-of-you · if · and-now · (49) · for-son-of-him · master-of-me

וֶֽאֱמֶ֛ת אֶת־ אֲדֹנִ֖י הַגִּ֣ידוּ לִ֑י וְאִם־ לֹ֔א הַגִּ֣ידוּ לִ֔י
to-me · tell! · not · and-if · to-me · tell! · master-of-me · to · and-faithfulness

---

my oath even if they refuse to give her to you—you will be released from my oath.'

42"When I came to the spring today, I said, 'O LORD, God of my master Abraham, if you will, please grant success to the journey on which I have come. 43See, I am standing beside this spring; if a maiden comes out to draw water and I say to her, "Please let me drink a little water from your jar," 44and if she says to me, "Drink, and I'll draw water for your camels too," let her be the one the LORD has chosen for my master's son.'

45"Before I finished praying in my heart, Rebekah came out, with her jar on her shoulder. She went down to the spring and drew water, and I said to her, 'Please give me a drink.'

46"She quickly lowered her jar from her shoulder and said, 'Drink, and I'll water your camels too.' So I drank, and she watered the camels also.

47"I asked her, 'Whose daughter are you?'

"She said, 'The daughter of Bethuel son of Nahor, whom Milcah bore to him.'

"Then I put the ring in her nose and the bracelets on her arms, 48and I bowed down and worshiped the LORD. I praised the LORD, the God of my master Abraham, who had led me on the right road to get the granddaughter of my master's brother for his son. 49Now if you will show kindness and faithfulness to my master, tell me; and if not, tell me, so I

וְאֶפְנֶה עַל־יָמִין אוֹ עַל־שְׂמֹאל׃ (50) וַיַּעַן לָבָן וּבְתוּאֵל
and-Bethuel Laban and-he-answered (50) left to or right to so-I-may-turn

וַיֹּאמְרוּ מֵיְהוָה יָצָא הַדָּבָר לֹא נוּכַל דַּבֵּר אֵלֶיךָ רַע
bad to-you to-say we-can not the-thing he-comes from-Yahweh and-they-said

אוֹ־טוֹב׃ (51) הִנֵּה־רִבְקָה לְפָנֶיךָ קַח וָלֵךְ וּתְהִי אִשָּׁה
wife and-let-her-be and-go take! before-you Rebekah see! (51) good or

לְבֶן־אֲדֹנֶיךָ כַּאֲשֶׁר דִּבֶּר יְהוָה׃ (52) וַיְהִי כַּאֲשֶׁר
when and-he-was (52) Yahweh he-directed just-as master-of-you for-son-of

שָׁמַע עֶבֶד אַבְרָהָם אֶת־דִּבְרֵיהֶם וַיִּשְׁתַּחוּ אַרְצָה
to-ground that-he-bowed words-of-them *** Abraham servant-of he-heard

לַיהוָה׃ (53) וַיּוֹצֵא הָעֶבֶד כְּלֵי־כֶסֶף וּכְלֵי
and-jewelry-of silver jewelry-of the-servant and-he-brought-out (53) to-Yahweh

זָהָב וּבְגָדִים וַיִּתֵּן לְרִבְקָה וּמִגְדָּנֹת נָתַן לְאָחִיהָ
to-brother-of-her he-gave and-gifts to-Rebekah and-he-gave and-clothing gold

וּלְאִמָּהּ׃ (54) וַיֹּאכְלוּ וַיִּשְׁתּוּ הוּא וְהָאֲנָשִׁים אֲשֶׁר־
who and-the-men he and-they-drank then-they-ate (54) and-to-mother-of-her

עִמּוֹ וַיָּלִינוּ וַיָּקוּמוּ בַבֹּקֶר וַיֹּאמֶר
then-he-said in-the-morning when-they-rose and-they-spent-night with-him

שַׁלְּחֻנִי לַאדֹנִי׃ (55) וַיֹּאמֶר אָחִיהָ וְאִמָּהּ
and-mother-of-her brother-of-her but-he-replied (55) to-master-of-me send-me!

תֵּשֵׁב הַנַּעֲרָ אִתָּנוּ יָמִים אוֹ עָשׂוֹר אַחַר תֵּלֵךְ׃
you-may-go then ten about days with-us the-girl let-her-remain

וַיֹּאמֶר אֲלֵהֶם אַל־תְּאַחֲרוּ אֹתִי וַיהוָה הִצְלִיחַ דַּרְכִּי
journey-of-me he-made-succeed as-Yahweh me you-detain not to-them but-he-said (56)

שַׁלְּחוּנִי וְאֵלְכָה לַאדֹנִי׃ (57) וַיֹּאמְרוּ נִקְרָא
let-us-call then-they-said (57) to-master-of-me so-I-may-go send-me!

לַנַּעֲרָ וְנִשְׁאֲלָה אֶת־פִּיהָ׃ (58) וַיִּקְרְאוּ לְרִבְקָה
to-Rebekah to-they-called (58) mouth-of-her *** and-let-us-ask to-the-girl

וַיֹּאמְרוּ אֵלֶיהָ הֲתֵלְכִי עִם־הָאִישׁ הַזֶּה וַתֹּאמֶר
and-she-said the-this the-man with will-you-go? to-her and-they-asked

אֵלֵךְ׃ (59) וַיְשַׁלְּחוּ אֶת־רִבְקָה אֲחֹתָם וְאֶת־מֵנִקְתָּהּ
one-nursing-her and sister-of-them Rebekah *** so-they-sent (59) I-will-go

וְאֶת־עֶבֶד אַבְרָהָם וְאֶת־אֲנָשָׁיו׃ (60) וַיְבָרְכוּ אֶת־רִבְקָה
Rebekah *** and-they-blessed (60) men-of-him and Abraham servant-of and

וַיֹּאמְרוּ לָהּ אֲחֹתֵנוּ אַתְּ הֲיִי לְאַלְפֵי רְבָבָה
ten-thousand to-thousands-of increase! you sister-of-us to-her and-they-said

וְיִירַשׁ זַרְעֵךְ אֵת שַׁעַר שֹׂנְאָיו׃
ones-hating-him gate-of *** offspring-of-you and-may-he-possess

may know which way to turn."
50Laban and Bethuel answered, "This is from the LORD; we can say nothing to you one way or the other.
51Here is Rebekah; take her and go, and let her become the wife of your master's son, as the LORD has directed."
52When Abraham's servant heard what they said, he bowed down to the ground before the LORD.
53Then the servant brought out gold and silver jewelry and articles of clothing and gave them to Rebekah; he also gave costly gifts to her brother and to her mother.
54Then he and the men who were with him ate and drank and spent the night there.

When they got up the next morning, he said, "Send me on my way to my master."
55But her brother and her mother replied, "Let the girl remain with us ten days or so; then you[d] may go."
56But he said to them, "Do not detain me, now that the LORD has granted success to my journey. Send me on my way so I may go to my master."
57Then they said, "Let's call the girl and ask her about it."
58So they called Rebekah and asked her, "Will you go with this man?"

"I will go," she said.
59So they sent their sister Rebekah on her way, along with her nurse and Abraham's servant and his men.
60And they blessed Rebekah and said to her,

"Our sister, may you increase
to thousands upon thousands;
may your offspring possess
the gates of their enemies."

[d]55 Or *she*

וַתָּקָם רִבְקָה וְנַעֲרֹתֶיהָ וַתִּרְכַּבְנָה עַל־ הַגְּמַלִּים
the-camels on and-they-mounted and-maids-of-her Rebekah then-she-rose (61)

וַתֵּלַכְנָה אַחֲרֵי הָאִישׁ וַיִּקַּח הָעֶבֶד אֶת־ רִבְקָה וַיֵּלַךְ׃
and-he-left Rebekah *** the-servant so-he-took the-man after and-they-went

וְיִצְחָק בָּא מִבּוֹא בְּאֵר לַחַי רֹאִי וְהוּא יוֹשֵׁב בְּאֶרֶץ
in-land-of living for-he Roi Lahai Beer from-to-come he-came now-Isaac (62)

הַנֶּגֶב׃ וַיֵּצֵא יִצְחָק לָשׂוּחַ בַּשָּׂדֶה לִפְנוֹת עָרֶב
evening to-be in-the-field to-meditate Isaac and-he-went (63) the-Negev

וַיִּשָּׂא עֵינָיו וַיַּרְא וְהִנֵּה גְמַלִּים בָּאִים׃
ones-coming camels and-see! and-he-saw eyes-of-him and-he-lifted

וַתִּשָּׂא רִבְקָה אֶת־ עֵינֶיהָ וַתֵּרֶא אֶת־יִצְחָק וַתִּפֹּל
and-she-got-down Isaac *** and-she-saw eyes-of-her *** Rebekah and-she-lifted (64)

מֵעַל הַגָּמָל׃ וַתֹּאמֶר אֶל־ הָעֶבֶד מִי־ הָאִישׁ הַלָּזֶה
the-that the-man who? the-servant to and-she-asked (65) the-camel from-on

הַהֹלֵךְ בַּשָּׂדֶה לִקְרָאתֵנוּ וַיֹּאמֶר הָעֶבֶד הוּא
he the-servant and-he-answered to-meet-us in-the-field the-one-coming

אֲדֹנִי וַתִּקַּח הַצָּעִיף וַתִּתְכָּס׃ וַיְסַפֵּר
then-he-told (66) and-she-covered-herself the-veil so-she-took master-of-me

הָעֶבֶד לְיִצְחָק אֵת כָּל־ הַדְּבָרִים אֲשֶׁר עָשָׂה׃ וַיְבִאֶהָ
and-he-brought-her (67) he-did that the-things all-of *** to-Isaac the-servant

יִצְחָק הָאֹהֱלָה שָׂרָה אִמּוֹ וַיִּקַּח אֶת־ רִבְקָה
Rebekah *** and-he-married mother-of-him Sarah into-the-tent Isaac

וַתְּהִי־ לוֹ לְאִשָּׁה וַיֶּאֱהָבֶהָ וַיִּנָּחֵם יִצְחָק
Isaac and-he-was-comforted and-he-loved-her as-wife to-him so-she-became

אַחֲרֵי אִמּוֹ׃ וַיֹּסֶף אַבְרָהָם וַיִּקַּח אִשָּׁה
wife and-he-took Abraham and-he-added (25:1) mother-of-him after

וּשְׁמָהּ קְטוּרָה׃ וַתֵּלֶד לוֹ אֶת־ זִמְרָן וְאֶת־ יָקְשָׁן וְאֶת־
and Jokshan and Zimran *** to-him and-she-bore (2) Keturah and-name-of-her

מְדָן וְאֶת־ מִדְיָן וְאֶת־ יִשְׁבָּק וְאֶת־ שׁוּחַ׃ וְיָקְשָׁן יָלַד אֶת־ שְׁבָא
Sheba *** he-fathered and-Jokshan (3) Shuah and Ishbak and Midian and Medan

וְאֶת־ דְּדָן וּבְנֵי דְדָן הָיוּ אַשּׁוּרִם וּלְטוּשִׁים
and-Letushites Asshurites they-were Dedan and-descendants-of Dedan and

וּלְאֻמִּים׃ וּבְנֵי מִדְיָן עֵיפָה וָעֵפֶר וַחֲנֹךְ וַאֲבִידָע
and-Abida and-Hanoch and-Epher Ephah Midian and-sons-of (4) and-Leummites

וְאֶלְדָּעָה כָּל־ אֵלֶּה בְּנֵי קְטוּרָה׃ וַיִּתֵּן אַבְרָהָם אֶת־
*** Abraham and-he-left (5) Keturah descendants-of these all-of and-Eldaah

כָּל־אֲשֶׁר־ לוֹ לְיִצְחָק׃ וְלִבְנֵי הַפִּילַגְשִׁים אֲשֶׁר לְאַבְרָהָם
to-Abraham that the-concubines and-to-sons-of (6) to-Isaac to-him that all

61 Then Rebekah and her maids got ready and mounted their camels and went back with the man. So the servant took Rebekah and left.

62 Now Isaac had come from Beer Lahai Roi, for he was living in the Negev. 63 He went out to the field one evening to meditate,[e] and as he looked up, he saw camels approaching. 64 Rebekah also looked up and saw Isaac. She got down from her camel 65 and asked the servant, "Who is that man in the field coming to meet us?"

"He is my master," the servant answered. So she took her veil and covered herself.

66 Then the servant told Isaac all he had done. 67 Isaac brought her into the tent of his mother Sarah, and he married Rebekah. So she became his wife, and he loved her; and Isaac was comforted after his mother's death.

### *The Death of Abraham*

25 Abraham took[f] another wife, whose name was Keturah. 2 She bore him Zimran, Jokshan, Medan, Midian, Ishbak and Shuah. 3 Jokshan was the father of Sheba and Dedan; the descendants of Dedan were the Asshurites, the Letushites and the Leummites. 4 The sons of Midian were Ephah, Epher, Hanoch, Abida and Eldaah. All these were descendants of Keturah.

5 Abraham left everything he owned to Isaac. 6 But while he was still living, he gave gifts to the sons of his concubines and

[e]63 The meaning of the Hebrew for this word is uncertain.
[f]1 Or *had taken*

נָתַן אַבְרָהָם מַתָּנֹת וַיְשַׁלְּחֵם מֵעַל יִצְחָק בְּנוֹ בְּעוֹדֶנּוּ
while-he son-of-him Isaac away-from and-he-sent-them gifts Abraham he-gave

חַי קֵדְמָה אֶל־אֶרֶץ קֶדֶם׃ וְאֵלֶּה יְמֵי שְׁנֵי־חַיֵּי אַבְרָהָם
Abraham lives-of years-of days-of and-these (7) east land-of to to-east alive

אֲשֶׁר־חָי מְאַת שָׁנָה וְשִׁבְעִים שָׁנָה וְחָמֵשׁ שָׁנִים׃
years and-five year and-seventy year hundred-of alive that

וַיִּגְוַע וַיָּמָת אַבְרָהָם בְּשֵׂיבָה טוֹבָה זָקֵן וְשָׂבֵעַ
and-full old good at-old-age Abraham and-he-died and-he-breathed-last (8)

וַיֵּאָסֶף אֶל־עַמָּיו׃ וַיִּקְבְּרוּ אֹתוֹ יִצְחָק
Isaac him and-they-buried (9) people-of-him to and-he-was-gathered

וְיִשְׁמָעֵאל בָּנָיו אֶל־מְעָרַת הַמַּכְפֵּלָה אֶל־שְׂדֵה עֶפְרֹן בֶּן־
son-of Ephron field-of in the-Machpelah cave-of in sons-of-him and-Ishmael

צֹחַר הַחִתִּי אֲשֶׁר עַל־פְּנֵי מַמְרֵא׃ הַשָּׂדֶה אֲשֶׁר־קָנָה
he-bought that the-field (10) Mamre area-of near that the-Hittite Zohar

אַבְרָהָם מֵאֵת בְּנֵי־חֵת שָׁמָּה קֻבַּר אַבְרָהָם וְשָׂרָה אִשְׁתּוֹ׃
wife-of-him and-Sarah Abraham he-was-buried at-there Heth sons-of from Abraham

וַיְהִי אַחֲרֵי מוֹת אַבְרָהָם וַיְבָרֶךְ אֱלֹהִים אֶת־יִצְחָק
Isaac *** God that-he-blessed Abraham death-of after and-he-was (11)

בְּנוֹ וַיֵּשֶׁב יִצְחָק עִם־בְּאֵר לַחַי רֹאִי׃ וְאֵלֶּה תֹּלְדֹת
lines-of now-these (12) Roi Lahai Beer near Isaac and-he-lived son-of-him

יִשְׁמָעֵאל בֶּן־אַבְרָהָם אֲשֶׁר יָלְדָה הָגָר הַמִּצְרִית שִׁפְחַת שָׂרָה
Sarah maidservant-of the-Egyptian Hagar she-bore whom Abraham son-of Ishmael

לְאַבְרָהָם׃ וְאֵלֶּה שְׁמוֹת בְּנֵי יִשְׁמָעֵאל בִּשְׁמֹתָם
by-names-of-them Ishmael sons-of names-of and-these (13) to-Abraham

לְתוֹלְדֹתָם בְּכֹר יִשְׁמָעֵאל נְבָיֹת וְקֵדָר וְאַדְבְּאֵל
and-Adbeel and-Kedar Nebaioth Ishmael firstborn-of by-births-of-them

וּמִבְשָׂם׃ וּמִשְׁמָע וְדוּמָה וּמַשָּׂא׃ חֲדַד וְתֵימָא יְטוּר
Jetur and-Tema Hadad (15) and-Massa and-Dumah and-Mishma (14) and-Mibsam

נָפִישׁ וָקֵדְמָה׃ אֵלֶּה הֵם בְּנֵי יִשְׁמָעֵאל וְאֵלֶּה שְׁמֹתָם
names-of-them and-these Ishmael sons-of they these (16) and-Kedemah Naphish

בְּחַצְרֵיהֶם וּבְטִירֹתָם שְׁנֵים־עָשָׂר נְשִׂיאִם לְאֻמֹּתָם׃
by-tribes-of-them rulers ten two and-by-camps-of-them by-settlements-of-them

וְאֵלֶּה שְׁנֵי חַיֵּי יִשְׁמָעֵאל מְאַת שָׁנָה וּשְׁלֹשִׁים שָׁנָה
year and-thirty year hundred-of Ishmael lives-of years-of and-these (17)

וְשֶׁבַע שָׁנִים וַיִּגְוַע וַיָּמָת וַיֵּאָסֶף אֶל־
to and-he-was-gathered and-he-died and-he-breathed-last years and-seven

עַמָּיו׃ וַיִּשְׁכְּנוּ מֵחֲוִילָה עַד־שׁוּר אֲשֶׁר עַל־פְּנֵי
border-of near that Shur to from-Havilah and-they-settled (18) people-of-him

sent them away from his son Isaac to the land of the east.
7Altogether, Abraham lived a hundred and seventy-five years.
8Then Abraham breathed his last and died at a good old age, an old man and full of years; and he was gathered to his people.
9His sons Isaac and Ishmael buried him in the cave of Machpelah near Mamre, in the field of Ephron son of Zohar the Hittite,
10the field Abraham had bought from the Hittites.[g] There Abraham was buried with his wife Sarah.
11After Abraham's death, God blessed his son Isaac, who then lived near Beer Lahai Roi.

*Ishmael's Sons*

12This is the account of Abraham's son Ishmael, whom Sarah's maidservant, Hagar the Egyptian, bore to Abraham.

13These are the names of the sons of Ishmael, listed in the order of their birth: Nebaioth the firstborn of Ishmael, Kedar, Adbeel, Mibsam,
14Mishma, Dumah, Massa,
15Hadad, Tema, Jetur, Naphish and Kedemah.
16These were the sons of Ishmael, and these are the names of the twelve tribal rulers according to their settlements and camps.
17Altogether, Ishmael lived a hundred and thirty-seven years. He breathed his last and died, and he was gathered to his people.
18His descendants settled in the area from Havilah to Shur, near the border of

*g10 Or the sons of Heth*

מִצְרַיִם בֹּאֲכָה אַשּׁוּרָה עַל־ פְּנֵי כָל־ אֶחָיו נָפָל׃
he-was-hostile brothers-of-him all-of faces-of to to-Asshur to-go-you Egypt

וְאֵלֶּה תּוֹלְדֹת יִצְחָק בֶּן־ אַבְרָהָם אַבְרָהָם הוֹלִיד אֶת־ יִצְחָק׃
Isaac *** he-fathered Abraham Abraham son-of Isaac lines-of and-these (19)

וַיְהִי יִצְחָק בֶּן־ אַרְבָּעִים שָׁנָה בְּקַחְתּוֹ אֶת־ רִבְקָה
Rebekah *** when-to-take-him year forty son-of Isaac and-he-was (20)

בַּת־ בְּתוּאֵל הָאֲרַמִּי מִפַּדַּן אֲרָם אֲחוֹת לָבָן הָאֲרַמִּי
the-Aramean Laban sister-of Aram from-Paddan the-Aramean Bethuel daughter-of

לוֹ לְאִשָּׁה׃ וַיֶּעְתַּר יִצְחָק לַיהוָה לְנֹכַח אִשְׁתּוֹ
wife-of-him on-behalf-of to-Yahweh Isaac and-he-prayed (21) as-wife to-him

כִּי עֲקָרָה הִוא וַיֵּעָתֶר לוֹ יְהוָה וַתַּהַר רִבְקָה
Rebekah and-she-conceived Yahweh to-him and-he-answered-prayer she barren for

אִשְׁתּוֹ׃ וַיִּתְרֹצְצוּ הַבָּנִים בְּקִרְבָּהּ וַתֹּאמֶר אִם־ כֵּן
so if and-she-said within-her the-babies and-they-jostled (22) wife-of-him

לָמָּה זֶּה אָנֹכִי וַתֵּלֶךְ לִדְרֹשׁ אֶת־ יְהוָה׃ וַיֹּאמֶר יְהוָה לָהּ
to-her Yahweh and-he-said (23) Yahweh *** to-inquire so-she-went me this why?

שְׁנֵי גֹיִים° בְּבִטְנֵךְ וּשְׁנֵי לְאֻמִּים מִמֵּעַיִךְ
from-within-you peoples and-two-of in-womb-of-you nations two-of

יִפָּרֵדוּ וּלְאֹם מִלְאֹם יֶאֱמָץ וְרַב
and-older he-will-be-stronger than-people and-people they-will-be-separated

יַעֲבֹד צָעִיר׃ וַיִּמְלְאוּ יָמֶיהָ לָלֶדֶת
to-give-birth days-of-her when-they-were-fulfilled (24) younger he-will-serve

וְהִנֵּה תוֹמִם בְּבִטְנָהּ׃ וַיֵּצֵא הָרִאשׁוֹן אַדְמוֹנִי
red the-first and-he-came-out (25) in-womb-of-her twin-boys now-see!

כֻּלּוֹ כְּאַדֶּרֶת שֵׂעָר וַיִּקְרְאוּ שְׁמוֹ עֵשָׂו׃
Esau name-of-him so-they-called hair like-garment-of whole-of-him

וְאַחֲרֵי־ כֵן יָצָא אָחִיו וְיָדוֹ אֹחֶזֶת
grasping with-hand-of-him brother-of-him he-came-out this and-after (26)

בַּעֲקֵב עֵשָׂו וַיִּקְרָא שְׁמוֹ יַעֲקֹב וְיִצְחָק בֶּן־ שִׁשִּׁים שָׁנָה
year sixty son-of now-Isaac Jacob name-of-him so-he-called Esau on-heel-of

בְּלֶדֶת אֹתָם׃ וַיִּגְדְּלוּ הַנְּעָרִים וַיְהִי עֵשָׂו אִישׁ
man Esau and-he-became the-boys and-they-grew-up (27) them when-to-bear

יֹדֵעַ צַיִד אִישׁ שָׂדֶה וְיַעֲקֹב אִישׁ תָּם יֹשֵׁב אֹהָלִים׃
tents staying quiet man-of while-Jacob field man-of hunting being-skilled

וַיֶּאֱהַב יִצְחָק אֶת־ עֵשָׂו כִּי־ צַיִד בְּפִיו וְרִבְקָה אֹהֶבֶת
loving but-Rebekah in-taste-of-him game for Esau *** Isaac now-he-loved (28)

אֶת־ יַעֲקֹב׃ וַיָּזֶד יַעֲקֹב נָזִיד וַיָּבֹא עֵשָׂו מִן־ הַשָּׂדֶה
the-field from Esau and-he-came stew Jacob now-he-cooked (29) Jacob ***

Egypt, as you go toward Asshur. And they lived in hostility toward all their brothers.

*Jacob and Esau*

[19]This is the account of Abraham's son Isaac.

Abraham became the father of Isaac, [20]and Isaac was forty years old when he married Rebekah daughter of Bethuel the Aramean from Paddan Aram[h] and sister of Laban the Aramean.

[21]Isaac prayed to the LORD on behalf of his wife, because she was barren. The LORD answered his prayer, and his wife Rebekah became pregnant. [22]The babies jostled each other within her, and she said, "Why is this happening to me?" So she went to inquire of the LORD.

[23]The LORD said to her,

"Two nations are in your womb,
and two peoples from within you will be separated;
one people will be stronger than the other,
and the older will serve the younger."

[24]When the time came for her to give birth, there were twin boys in her womb. [25]The first to come out was red, and his whole body was like a hairy garment; so they named him Esau.[i] [26]After this, his brother came out, with his hand grasping Esau's heel; so he was named Jacob.[j] Isaac was sixty years old when Rebekah gave birth to them.

[27]The boys grew up, and Esau became a skillful hunter, a man of the open country, while Jacob was a quiet man, staying among the tents. [28]Isaac, who had a taste for wild game, loved Esau, but Rebekah loved Jacob.

[29]Once when Jacob was cooking some stew, Esau came in from the open country,

[h]20 That is, Northwest Mesopotamia
[i]25 *Esau* may mean *hairy;* he is also called Edom, which means *red.*
[j]26 *Jacob* means *he grasps the heel* (figuratively, *he deceives*).

°23 ק גוים

וְהוּא עָיֵף׃ וַיֹּאמֶר עֵשָׂו אֶל־יַעֲקֹב הַלְעִיטֵנִי נָא מִן־
some-of now! let-eat-me! Jacob to Esau and-he-said (30) famished and-he

הָאָדֹם הָאָדֹם הַזֶּה כִּי עָיֵף אָנֹכִי עַל־ כֵּן קָרָא־
he-called this for I famished for the-that the-red-stew the-red-stew

שְׁמוֹ אֱדוֹם׃ וַיֹּאמֶר יַעֲקֹב מִכְרָה כַיּוֹם אֶת־ בְּכֹרָתְךָ
birthright-of-you *** on-the-day sell! Jacob and-he-said (31) Edom name-of-him

לִי׃ וַיֹּאמֶר עֵשָׂו הִנֵּה אָנֹכִי הוֹלֵךְ לָמוּת וְלָמָּה־ זֶּה לִי בְּכֹרָה׃
birthright to-me this so-what? to-die going I see! Esau and-he-said (32) to-me

וַיֹּאמֶר יַעֲקֹב הִשָּׁבְעָה לִּי כַּיּוֹם וַיִּשָּׁבַע לוֹ וַיִּמְכֹּר
so-he-sold to-him so-he-swore on-the-day to-me swear! Jacob but-he-said (33)

אֶת־ בְּכֹרָתוֹ לְיַעֲקֹב׃ וְיַעֲקֹב נָתַן לְעֵשָׂו לֶחֶם
bread to-Esau he-gave then-Jacob (34) to-Jacob birthright-of-him ***

וּנְזִיד עֲדָשִׁים וַיֹּאכַל וַיֵּשְׁתְּ וַיָּקָם וַיֵּלַךְ
and-he-left then-he-got-up and-he-drank and-he-ate lentils and-stew-of

וַיִּבֶז עֵשָׂו אֶת־ הַבְּכֹרָה׃ וַיְהִי רָעָב בָּאָרֶץ
in-the-land famine now-he-was (26:1) the-birthright *** Esau so-he-despised

מִלְּבַד הָרָעָב הָרִאשׁוֹן אֲשֶׁר הָיָה בִּימֵי אַבְרָהָם וַיֵּלֶךְ
so-he-went Abraham in-days-of he-was that the-earlier the-famine besides

יִצְחָק אֶל־ אֲבִימֶּלֶךְ* מֶלֶךְ־ פְּלִשְׁתִּים גְּרָרָה׃ וַיֵּרָא אֵלָיו
to-him and-he-appeared (2) in-Gerar Philistines king-of Abimelech to Isaac

יְהוָה וַיֹּאמֶר אַל־ תֵּרֵד מִצְרָיְמָה שְׁכֹן בָּאָרֶץ אֲשֶׁר אֹמַר
I-tell where in-the-land live! to-Egypt you-go-down not and-he-said Yahweh

אֵלֶיךָ׃ גּוּר בָּאָרֶץ הַזֹּאת וְאֶהְיֶה עִמְּךָ וַאֲבָרְכֶךָּ
and-I-will-bless-you with-you and-I-will-be the-this in-the-land stay! (3) to-you

כִּי־ לְךָ וּלְזַרְעֲךָ אֶתֵּן אֶת־ כָּל־ הָאֲרָצֹת
the-lands all-of *** I-will-give and-to-descendant-of-you to-you for

הָאֵל וַהֲקִמֹתִי אֶת־ הַשְּׁבֻעָה אֲשֶׁר נִשְׁבַּעְתִּי לְאַבְרָהָם
to-Abraham I-swore that the-oath *** and-I-will-confirm the-these

אָבִיךָ׃ וְהִרְבֵּיתִי אֶת־ זַרְעֲךָ כְּכוֹכְבֵי
as-stars-of descendant-of-you *** and-I-will-increase (4) father-of-you

הַשָּׁמַיִם וְנָתַתִּי לְזַרְעֲךָ אֵת כָּל־ הָאֲרָצֹת הָאֵל
the-these the-lands all-of *** to-descendant-of-you and-I-will-give the-skies

וְהִתְבָּרֲכוּ בְזַרְעֲךָ כֹּל גּוֹיֵי הָאָרֶץ׃
the-earth nations-of all-of through-offspring-of-you and-they-will-be-blessed

עֵקֶב אֲשֶׁר־ שָׁמַע אַבְרָהָם בְּקֹלִי וַיִּשְׁמֹר מִשְׁמַרְתִּי
requirements-of-me and-he-kept to-voice-me Abraham he-obeyed that because (5)

מִצְוֺתַי חֻקּוֹתַי וְתוֹרֹתָי׃ וַיֵּשֶׁב יִצְחָק בִּגְרָר׃
in-Gerar Isaac so-he-stayed (6) and-laws-of-me decrees-of-me commands-of-me

famished. [30]He said to Jacob, "Quick, let me have some of that red stew! I'm famished!" (That is why he was also called Edom.[k])

[31]Jacob replied, "First sell me your birthright."

[32]"Look, I am about to die," Esau said. "What good is the birthright to me?"

[33]But Jacob said, "Swear to me first." So he swore an oath to him, selling his birthright to Jacob.

[34]Then Jacob gave Esau some bread and some lentil stew. He ate and drank, and then got up and left.

So Esau despised his birthright.

*Isaac and Abimelech*

26 Now there was a famine in the land—besides the earlier famine of Abraham's time—and Isaac went to Abimelech king of the Philistines in Gerar. [2]The LORD appeared to Isaac and said, "Do not go down to Egypt; live in the land where I tell you to live. [3]Stay in this land for a while, and I will be with you and will bless you. For to you and your descendants I will give all these lands and will confirm the oath I swore to your father Abraham. [4]I will make your descendants as numerous as the stars in the sky and will give them all these lands, and through your offspring all nations on earth will be blessed, [5]because Abraham obeyed me and kept my requirements, my commands, my decrees and my laws." [6]So Isaac stayed in Gerar.

[k]30 *Edom* means *red.*

*1 Most mss have no *dagesh* in the *mem* ( מ ).

וַיִּשְׁאֲלוּ אַנְשֵׁי הַמָּקוֹם לְאִשְׁתּוֹ וַיֹּאמֶר
then-he-said about-wife-of-him the-place men-of when-they-asked (7)

אֲחֹתִי הִוא כִּי יָרֵא לֵאמֹר אִשְׁתִּי פֶּן־ יַהַרְגֻנִי אַנְשֵׁי
men-of they-kill-me lest wife-of-me to-say he-was-afraid for she sister-of-me

הַמָּקוֹם עַל־ רִבְקָה כִּי־ טוֹבַת מַרְאֶה הִיא׃ וַיְהִי
and-he-was (8) she sight beautiful-of for Rebekah on-account-of the-place

כִּי אָרְכוּ־ לוֹ שָׁם הַיָּמִים וַיַּשְׁקֵף אֲבִימֶלֶךְ מֶלֶךְ
king-of Abimelech that-he-looked the-days there to-him they-were-long when

פְּלִשְׁתִּים בְּעַד הַחַלּוֹן וַיַּרְא וְהִנֵּה יִצְחָק מְצַחֵק אֵת
*** caressing Isaac and-see! and-he-saw the-window down-from Philistines

רִבְקָה אִשְׁתּוֹ׃ וַיִּקְרָא אֲבִימֶלֶךְ לְיִצְחָק וַיֹּאמֶר אַךְ
really and-he-said to-Isaac Abimelech and-he-summoned (9) wife-of-him Rebekah

הִנֵּה אִשְׁתְּךָ הִוא וְאֵיךְ אָמַרְתָּ אֲחֹתִי הִוא וַיֹּאמֶר אֵלָיו
to-him and-he-answered she sister-of-me you-said so-why? she wife-of-you see!

יִצְחָק כִּי אָמַרְתִּי פֶּן־ אָמוּת עָלֶיהָ׃ וַיֹּאמֶר
then-he-said (10) because-of-her I-will-die perhaps I-thought because Isaac

אֲבִימֶלֶךְ מַה־ זֹּאת עָשִׂיתָ לָּנוּ כִּמְעַט שָׁכַב אַחַד הָעָם אֶת־
with the-people one-of he-slept might-well to-us you-did this what? Abimelech

אִשְׁתֶּךָ וְהֵבֵאתָ עָלֵינוּ אָשָׁם׃ וַיְצַו אֲבִימֶלֶךְ אֶת־
*** Abimelech so-he-ordered (11) guilt upon-us and-you-brought wife-of-you

כָּל־ הָעָם לֵאמֹר הַנֹּגֵעַ בָּאִישׁ הַזֶּה
the-this on-the-man the-one-molesting to-say the-people all-of

וּבְאִשְׁתּוֹ מוֹת יוּמָת׃ וַיִּזְרַע יִצְחָק
Isaac and-he-planted-seed (12) he-will-be-killed to-kill or-on-wife-of-him

בָּאָרֶץ הַהִוא וַיִּמְצָא בַּשָּׁנָה הַהִוא מֵאָה שְׁעָרִים
times hundred the-that in-the-year and-he-reaped the-that in-the-land

וַיְבָרְכֵהוּ יְהוָה׃ וַיִּגְדַּל הָאִישׁ וַיֵּלֶךְ הָלוֹךְ
to-grow and-he-grew the-man and-he-became-rich (13) Yahweh for-he-blessed-him

וְגָדֵל עַד כִּי־ גָדַל מְאֹד׃ וַיְהִי־ לוֹ
to-him and-he-was (14) very he-became-wealthy when until more-rich

מִקְנֵה־ צֹאן וּמִקְנֵה בָקָר וַעֲבֻדָּה רַבָּה וַיְקַנְאוּ
and-they-envied many and-servant cattle and-possession-of flock possession-of

אֹתוֹ פְּלִשְׁתִּים׃ וְכָל־ הַבְּאֵרֹת אֲשֶׁר חָפְרוּ עַבְדֵי אָבִיו
father-of-him servanst-of they-dug that the-wells so-all-of (15) Philistines him

בִּימֵי אַבְרָהָם אָבִיו סִתְּמוּם פְּלִשְׁתִּים
Philistines they-stopped-up-them father-of-him Abraham in-days-of

וַיְמַלְאוּם עָפָר׃ וַיֹּאמֶר אֲבִימֶלֶךְ אֶל־ יִצְחָק לֵךְ
move-away! Isaac to Abimelech then-he-said (16) earth and-they-filled-them

7When the men of that place
asked him about his wife, he
said, "She is my sister," because he was afraid to say,
"She is my wife." He thought,
"The men of this place might
kill me on account of Rebekah,
because she is beautiful."
8When Isaac had been there
a long time, Abimelech king of
the Philistines looked down
from a window and saw Isaac
caressing his wife Rebekah.
9So Abimelech summoned
Isaac and said, "She is really
your wife! Why did you say,
'She is my sister'?"
Isaac answered him, "Be-
cause I thought I might lose
my life on account of her."
10Then Abimelech said,
"What is this you have done
to us? One of the men might
well have slept with your wife,
and you would have brought
guilt upon us."
11So Abimelech gave orders
to all the people: "Anyone
who molests this man or his
wife shall surely be put to
death."
12Isaac planted crops in that
land and the same year reaped
a hundredfold, because the
LORD blessed him. 13The man
became rich, and his wealth
continued to grow until he
became very wealthy. 14He
had so many flocks and herds
and servants that the Philistines envied him. 15So all the
wells that his father's servants
had dug in the time of his father Abraham, the Philistines
stopped up, filling them with
earth.
16Then Abimelech said to
Isaac, "Move away from us;

מֵעִמָּנוּ כִּי־ עָצַמְתָּ מִמֶּנּוּ מְאֹד׃ וַיֵּלֶךְ מִשָּׁם יִצְחָק
Isaac from-there so-he-moved (17) more than-us you-are-powerful for from-us

וַיִּחַן בְּנַחַל־ גְּרָר וַיֵּשֶׁב שָׁם׃ וַיָּשָׁב
and-he-returned (18) there and-he-settled Gerar in-valley-of and-he-camped

יִצְחָק וַיַּחְפֹּר ׀ אֶת־ בְּאֵרֹת הַמַּיִם אֲשֶׁר חָפְרוּ בִּימֵי אַבְרָהָם
Abraham in-days-of they-dug that the-water wells-of *** and-he-reopened Isaac

אָבִיו וַיְסַתְּמוּם פְּלִשְׁתִּים אַחֲרֵי מוֹת אַבְרָהָם
Abraham death-of after Philistines and-they-stopped-up-them father-of-him

וַיִּקְרָא לָהֶן שֵׁמוֹת כַּשֵּׁמֹת אֲשֶׁר־ קָרָא לָהֶן
to-them he-called that same-as-the-names names to-them and-he-called

אָבִיו׃ וַיַּחְפְּרוּ עַבְדֵי־ יִצְחָק בַּנָּחַל וַיִּמְצְאוּ־
and-they-found in-the-valley Isaac servants-of and-they-dug (19) father-of-him

שָׁם בְּאֵר מַיִם חַיִּים׃ וַיָּרִיבוּ רֹעֵי גְרָר עִם־
with Gerar ones-herding-of but-they-quarreled (20) fresh water well-of there

רֹעֵי יִצְחָק לֵאמֹר לָנוּ הַמָּיִם וַיִּקְרָא שֵׁם־ הַבְּאֵר
the-well name-of so-he-called the-water to-us to-say Isaac ones-herding-of

עֵשֶׂק כִּי הִתְעַשְּׂקוּ עִמּוֹ׃ וַיַּחְפְּרוּ בְּאֵר אַחֶרֶת
another well then-they-dug (21) with-him they-disputed for Esek

וַיָּרִיבוּ גַּם־ עָלֶיהָ וַיִּקְרָא שְׁמָהּ שִׂטְנָה׃
Sitnah name-of-her so-he-called over-her also but-they-quarreled

וַיַּעְתֵּק מִשָּׁם וַיַּחְפֹּר בְּאֵר אַחֶרֶת וְלֹא רָבוּ
they-quarreled and-not another well and-he-dug from-there so-he-moved (22)

עָלֶיהָ וַיִּקְרָא שְׁמָהּ רְחֹבוֹת וַיֹּאמֶר כִּי־ עַתָּה הִרְחִיב
he-gave-room now for and-he-said Rehoboth name-of-her so-he-called over-her

יְהוָה לָנוּ וּפָרִינוּ בָאָרֶץ׃ וַיַּעַל מִשָּׁם בְּאֵר
Beer from-there and-he-went (23) in-the-land and-we-will-flourish to-us Yahweh

שָׁבַע׃ וַיֵּרָא אֵלָיו יְהוָה בַּלַּיְלָה הַהוּא וַיֹּאמֶר
and-he-said the-that in-the-night Yahweh to-him and-he-appeared (24) Sheba

אָנֹכִי אֱלֹהֵי אַבְרָהָם אָבִיךָ אַל־ תִּירָא כִּי־ אִתְּךָ אָנֹכִי וּבֵרַכְתִּיךָ
and-I-will-bless-you I with-you for you-fear not father-of-you Abraham God-of I

וְהִרְבֵּיתִי אֶת־ זַרְעֲךָ בַּעֲבוּר אַבְרָהָם עַבְדִּי׃
servant-of-me Abraham for-sake-of descendant-of-you *** and-I-will-increase

וַיִּבֶן שָׁם מִזְבֵּחַ וַיִּקְרָא בְּשֵׁם יְהוָה וַיֶּט־
and-he-pitched Yahweh on-name-of and-he-called altar there so-he-built (25)

שָׁם אָהֳלוֹ וַיִּכְרוּ־ שָׁם עַבְדֵי־ יִצְחָק בְּאֵר׃ וַאֲבִימֶלֶךְ
and-Abimelech (26) well Isaac servants-of there and-they-dug tent-of-him there

הָלַךְ אֵלָיו מִגְּרָר וַאֲחֻזַּת מֵרֵעֵהוּ וּפִיכֹל שַׂר־
commander-of and-Phicol adviser-of-him with-Ahuzzath from-Gerar to-him he-came

you have become too powerful for us."

[17]So Isaac moved away from there and encamped in the Valley of Gerar and settled there. [18]Isaac reopened the wells that had been dug in the time of his father Abraham, which the Philistines had stopped up after Abraham died, and he gave them the same names his father had given them.

[19]Isaac's servants dug in the valley and discovered a well of fresh water there. [20]But the herdsmen of Gerar quarreled with Isaac's herdsmen and said, "The water is ours!" So he named the well Esek,[l] because they disputed with him. [21]Then they dug another well, but they quarreled over that one also; so he named it Sitnah.[m] [22]He moved on from there and dug another well, and no one quarreled over it. He named it Rehoboth,[n] saying, "Now the LORD has given us room and we will flourish in the land."

[23]From there he went up to Beersheba. [24]That night the LORD appeared to him and said, "I am the God of your father Abraham. Do not be afraid, for I am with you; I will bless you and will increase the number of your descendants for the sake of my servant Abraham."

[25]Isaac built an altar there and called on the name of the LORD. There he pitched his tent, and there his servants dug a well.

[26]Meanwhile, Abimelech had come to him from Gerar, with Ahuzzath his personal adviser and Phicol the commander of his forces. [27]Isaac

[l]20 *Esek* means *dispute.*
[m]21 *Sitnah* means *opposition.*
[n]22 *Rehoboth* means *room.*

צְבָאֽוֹ׃ וַיֹּאמֶר אֲלֵהֶם יִצְחָק מַדּוּעַ בָּאתֶם אֵלָי וְאַתֶּם
since-you to-me you-came why? Isaac to-them and-he-asked (27) force-of-him

שְׂנֵאתֶם אֹתִי וַתְּשַׁלְּחוּנִי מֵאִתְּכֶֽם׃ וַיֹּאמְרוּ
and-they-answered (28) from-you and-you-sent-me to-me you-were-hostile

רָאוֹ רָאִינוּ כִּֽי־ הָיָה יְהוָה ׀ עִמָּךְ וַנֹּאמֶר תְּהִי נָא אָלָה
oath now! let-her-be so-we-said with-you Yahweh he-was that we-saw to-see

בֵּינוֹתֵינוּ בֵּינֵינוּ וּבֵינֶךָ וְנִכְרְתָה בְרִית עִמָּֽךְ׃
with-you treaty so-let-us-make and-between-you between-us between-us

אִם־ תַּעֲשֵׂה עִמָּנוּ רָעָה כַּאֲשֶׁר לֹא נְגַעֲנוּךָ וְכַאֲשֶׁר
and-just-as we-molested-you not just-as harm to-us you-will-do not (29)

עָשִׂינוּ עִמְּךָ רַק־ טוֹב וַנְּשַׁלֵּֽחֲךָ בְּשָׁלוֹם אַתָּה עַתָּה בְּרוּךְ
being-blessed-of now you in-peace and-we-sent-you good only with-you we-did

יְהוָֽה׃ וַיַּעַשׂ לָהֶם מִשְׁתֶּה וַיֹּאכְלוּ וַיִּשְׁתּֽוּ׃
and-they-drank and-they-ate feast for-them so-he-made (30) Yahweh

וַיַּשְׁכִּימוּ בַבֹּקֶר וַיִּשָּׁבְעוּ אִישׁ לְאָחִיו
to-other-of-him man and-they-swore in-the-morning and-they-rose (31)

וַיְשַׁלְּחֵם יִצְחָק וַיֵּלְכוּ מֵאִתּוֹ בְּשָׁלֽוֹם׃ וַיְהִי ׀
and-he-was (32) in-peace from-him and-they-left Isaac and-he-sent-away-them

בַּיּוֹם הַהוּא וַיָּבֹאוּ עַבְדֵי יִצְחָק וַיַּגִּדוּ לוֹ
to-him and-they-told Isaac servants-of that-they-came the-that in-the-day

עַל־ אֹדוֹת הַבְּאֵר אֲשֶׁר חָפָרוּ וַיֹּאמְרוּ לוֹ מָצָאנוּ מָֽיִם׃
water we-found to-him and-they-said they-dug that the-well matter-of about

וַיִּקְרָא אֹתָהּ שִׁבְעָה עַל־ כֵּן שֵׁם־ הָעִיר בְּאֵר שֶׁבַע עַד הַיּוֹם
the-day to Sheba Beer the-city name-of this for Shibah her and-he-called (33)

הַזֶּֽה׃ וַיְהִי עֵשָׂו בֶּן־אַרְבָּעִים שָׁנָה וַיִּקַּח אִשָּׁה אֶת־יְהוּדִית
Judith *** wife he-took year forty son-of Esau when-he-was (34) the-this

בַּת־ בְּאֵרִי הַחִתִּי וְאֶת־ בָּשְׂמַת בַּת־ אֵילֹן הַחִתִּֽי׃
the-Hittite Elon daughter-of Basemath and the-Hittite Berri daughter-of

וַתִּהְיֶיןָ מֹרַת רוּחַ לְיִצְחָק וּלְרִבְקָֽה׃ וַיְהִי
and-he-was (27:1) and-to-Rebekah to-Isaac spirit grief-of and-they-were (35)

כִּֽי־ זָקֵן יִצְחָק וַתִּכְהֶיןָ עֵינָיו מֵרְאֹת
than-to-see eyes-of-him and-they-were-weaker Isaac he-was-old when

וַיִּקְרָא אֶת־ עֵשָׂו בְּנוֹ הַגָּדֹל וַיֹּאמֶר אֵלָיו בְּנִי
son-of-me to-him and-he-said the-older son-of-him Esau *** and-he-called

וַיֹּאמֶר אֵלָיו הִנֵּֽנִי׃ וַיֹּאמֶר הִנֵּה־נָא זָקַנְתִּי לֹא יָדַעְתִּי
I-know not I-am-old now! see! and-he-said (2) here-I to-him and-he-answered

יוֹם מוֹתִֽי׃ וְעַתָּה שָׂא־נָא כֵלֶיךָ תֶּלְיְךָ
quiver-of-you weapons-of-you now! take! and-now (3) death-of-me day-of

asked them, "Why have you come to me, since you were hostile to me and sent me away?"

28They answered, "We saw clearly that the LORD was with you; so we said, 'There ought to be a sworn agreement between us'—between us and you. Let us make a treaty with you 29that you will do us no harm, just as we did not molest you but always treated you well and sent you away in peace. And now you are blessed by the LORD."

30Isaac then made a feast for them, and they ate and drank. 31Early the next morning the men swore an oath to each other. Then Isaac sent them on their way, and they left him in peace.

32That day Isaac's servants came and told him about the well they had dug. They said, "We've found water!" 33He called it Shibah,[o] and to this day the name of the town has been Beersheba.[p]

34When Esau was forty years old, he married Judith daughter of Beeri the Hittite, and also Basemath daughter of Elon the Hittite. 35They were a source of grief to Isaac and Rebekah.

### *Jacob Gets Isaac's Blessing*

27 When Isaac was old and his eyes were so weak that he could no longer see, he called for Esau his older son and said to him, "My son."

"Here I am," he answered.

2Isaac said, "I am now an old man and don't know the day of my death. 3Now then, get your weapons—your quiver

[o]33 *Shibah* can mean *oath* or *seven*.
[p]33 *Beersheba* can mean *well of the oath* or *well of seven*.

וְקַשְׁתֶּךָ וְצֵא הַשָּׂדֶה וְצוּדָה לִּי צָיִדה׃ וַעֲשֵׂה־
and-prepare! (4) game for-me and-hunt! the-country and-go-out! and-bow-of-you

לִי מַטְעַמִּים כַּאֲשֶׁר אָהַבְתִּי וְהָבִיאָה לִּי וְאֹכֵלָה בַּעֲבוּר
so-that so-I-may-eat to-me and-bring I-like just-as tasty-foods for-me

תְּבָרֶכְךָ נַפְשִׁי בְּטֶרֶם אָמוּת׃ וְרִבְקָה שֹׁמַעַת בְּדַבֵּר
as-to-speak listening now-Rebekah (5) I-die before self-of-me she-may-bless-you

יִצְחָק אֶל־ עֵשָׂו בְּנוֹ וַיֵּלֶךְ עֵשָׂו הַשָּׂדֶה לָצוּד צַיִד
game to-hunt the-country Esau and-he-left son-of-him Esau to Isaac

לְהָבִיא׃ וְרִבְקָה אָמְרָה אֶל־ יַעֲקֹב בְּנָהּ לֵאמֹר הִנֵּה
see! to-say son-of-her Jacob to she-said and-Rebekah (6) to-bring-back

שָׁמַעְתִּי אֶת־ אָבִיךָ מְדַבֵּר אֶל־עֵשָׂו אָחִיךָ לֵאמֹר׃ הָבִיאָה
bring! (7) to-say brother-of-you Esau to saying father-of-you *** I-overheard

לִּי צַיִד וַעֲשֵׂה־ לִי מַטְעַמִּים וְאֹכֵלָה וַאֲבָרֶכְכָה
and-I-may-bless-you so-I-may-eat tasty-foods for-me and-prepare! game to-me

לִפְנֵי יְהוָה לִפְנֵי מוֹתִי׃ וְעַתָּה בְנִי שְׁמַע בְּקֹלִי
to-voice-of-me listen! son-of-me and-now (8) death-of-me before Yahweh before

לַאֲשֶׁר אֲנִי מְצַוָּה אֹתָךְ׃ לֶךְ־ נָא אֶל־ הַצֹּאן וְקַח־ לִי מִשָּׁם
from-there to-me and-bring! the-flock to now! go! (9) you telling I to-what

שְׁנֵי גְּדָיֵי עִזִּים טֹבִים וְאֶעֱשֶׂה אֹתָם מַטְעַמִּים
tasty-foods them so-I-can-prepare choice-ones goats kids-of two-of

לְאָבִיךָ כַּאֲשֶׁר אָהֵב׃ וְהֵבֵאתָ לְאָבִיךָ
to-father-of-you then-you-take (10) he-likes just-as for-father-of-you

וְאָכָל בַּעֲבֻר אֲשֶׁר יְבָרֶכְךָ לִפְנֵי מוֹתוֹ׃
death-of-him before he-may-bless-you then so-that so-he-can-eat

וַיֹּאמֶר יַעֲקֹב אֶל־רִבְקָה אִמּוֹ הֵן עֵשָׂו אָחִי אִישׁ שָׂעִר
hairy man brother-of-me Esau see! mother-of-him Rebekah to Jacob but-he-said (11)

וְאָנֹכִי אִישׁ חָלָק׃ אוּלַי יְמֻשֵּׁנִי אָבִי וְהָיִיתִי
and-I-appear father-of-me he-touches-me what-if? (12) smooth man but-I

בְעֵינָיו כִּמְתַעְתֵּעַ וְהֵבֵאתִי עָלַי קְלָלָה וְלֹא בְרָכָה׃
blessing and-not curse on-me then-I-would-bring as-tricking in-eyes-of-him

וַתֹּאמֶר לוֹ אִמּוֹ עָלַי קִלְלָתְךָ בְּנִי אַךְ
just son-of-me curse-of-you on-me mother-of-him to-him and-she-said (13)

שְׁמַע בְּקֹלִי וְלֵךְ קַח־ לִי׃ וַיֵּלֶךְ וַיִּקַּח
and-he-got so-he-went (14) for-me get! and-go! to-voice-of-me obey!

וַיָּבֵא לְאִמּוֹ וַתַּעַשׂ אִמּוֹ מַטְעַמִּים
tasty-foods mother-of-him and-she-prepared to-mother-of-him and-he-brought

כַּאֲשֶׁר אָהֵב אָבִיו׃ וַתִּקַּח רִבְקָה אֶת־ בִּגְדֵי עֵשָׂו
Esau clothes-of *** Rebekah then-she-took (15) father-of-him he-liked just-as

and bow—and go out to the
open country to hunt some
wild game for me. [4]Prepare me
the kind of tasty food I like
and bring it to me to eat, so
that I may give you my
blessing before I die."
[5]Now Rebekah was listening as Isaac spoke to his son
Esau. When Esau left for the
open country to hunt game
and bring it back, [6]Rebekah
said to her son Jacob, "Look, I
overheard your father say to
your brother Esau, [7]'Bring me
some game and prepare me
some tasty food to eat, so that
I may give you my blessing in
the presence of the LORD before I die.' [8]Now, my son, listen carefully and do what I tell
you: [9]Go out to the flock and
bring me two choice young
goats, so I can prepare some
tasty food for your father, just
the way he likes it. [10]Then take
it to your father to eat, so that
he may give you his blessing
before he dies."
[11]Jacob said to Rebekah his
mother, "But my brother Esau
is a hairy man, and I'm a man
with smooth skin. [12]What if
my father touches me? I would
appear to be tricking him and
would bring down a curse on
myself rather than a blessing."
[13]His mother said to him,
"My son, let the curse fall on
me. Just do what I say; go and
get them for me."
[14]So he went and got them
and brought them to his
mother, and she prepared
some tasty food, just the way
his father liked it. [15]Then Rebekah took the best clothes of

°3 ק ציד

בְּנָהּ הַגָּדֹל הַחֲמֻדֹת אֲשֶׁר אִתָּהּ בַּבָּיִת וַתַּלְבֵּשׁ
and-she-dressed in-the-house with-her that the-best-ones the-older son-of-her

אֶת־יַעֲקֹב בְּנָהּ הַקָּטָן׃ וְאֵת עֹרֹת גְּדָיֵי הָעִזִּים
the-goats kids-of skins-of and (16) the-younger son-of-her Jacob ***

הִלְבִּישָׁה עַל־ יָדָיו וְעַל חֶלְקַת צַוָּארָיו׃
neck-of-him smooth-part-of and-over hands-of-him over and-she-covered

וַתִּתֵּן אֶת־ הַמַּטְעַמִּים וְאֶת־ הַלֶּחֶם אֲשֶׁר עָשָׂתָה
she-made that the-bread and the-tasty-foods *** and-she-handed (17)

בְּיַד יַעֲקֹב בְּנָהּ׃ וַיָּבֹא אֶל־ אָבִיו וַיֹּאמֶר
and-he-said father-of-him to and-he-went (18) son-of-her Jacob to-hand-of

אָבִי וַיֹּאמֶר הִנֶּנִּי מִי אַתָּה בְּנִי׃ וַיֹּאמֶר
and-he-said (19) son-of-me you who? here-I and-he-answered father-of-me

יַעֲקֹב אֶל־ אָבִיו אָנֹכִי עֵשָׂו בְּכֹרֶךָ עָשִׂיתִי כַּאֲשֶׁר דִּבַּרְתָּ אֵלָי
to-me you-told just-as I-did firstborn-of-you Esau I father-of-him to Jacob

קוּם־ נָא שְׁבָה וְאָכְלָה מִצֵּידִי בַּעֲבוּר תְּבָרְכַנִּי
she-may-bless-me so-that from-game-of-me and-eat! sit-up! now! rise!

נַפְשֶׁךָ׃ וַיֹּאמֶר יִצְחָק אֶל־ בְּנוֹ מַה־ זֶּה מִהַרְתָּ
you-were-quick this how? son-of-him to Isaac but-he-asked (20) self-of-you

לִמְצֹא בְּנִי וַיֹּאמֶר כִּי הִקְרָה יְהוָה אֱלֹהֶיךָ לְפָנָי׃
to-me God-of-you Yahweh he-gave-success for and-he-replied son-of-me to-find

וַיֹּאמֶר יִצְחָק אֶל־יַעֲקֹב גְּשָׁה־ נָּא וַאֲמֻשְׁךָ בְּנִי
son-of-me so-I-can-touch-you now! come-near! Jacob to Isaac then-he-said (21)

הַאַתָּה זֶה בְּנִי עֵשָׂו אִם־לֹא׃ וַיִּגַּשׁ יַעֲקֹב אֶל־ יִצְחָק
Isaac to Jacob so-he-went-close (22) not or Esau son-of-me really whether-you

אָבִיו וַיְמֻשֵּׁהוּ וַיֹּאמֶר הַקֹּל קוֹל יַעֲקֹב
Jacob voice-of the-voice and-he-said and-he-touched-him father-of-him

וְהַיָּדַיִם יְדֵי עֵשָׂו׃ וְלֹא הִכִּירוֹ כִּי־הָיוּ
they-were for he-recognized-him and-not (23) Esau hands-of but-the-hands

יָדָיו כִּידֵי עֵשָׂו אָחִיו שְׂעִרֹת וַיְבָרְכֵהוּ׃
so-he-blessed-him hairy-ones brother-of-him Esau like-hands-of hands-of-him

וַיֹּאמֶר אַתָּה זֶה בְּנִי עֵשָׂו וַיֹּאמֶר אָנִי׃ וַיֹּאמֶר
so-he-said (25) I and-he-replied Esau son-of-me really you and-he-asked (24)

הַגִּשָׁה לִּי וְאֹכְלָה מִצֵּיד בְּנִי לְמַעַן תְּבָרֶכְךָ
she-may-bless-you so-that son-of-me from-game-of so-I-may-eat to-me bring!

נַפְשִׁי וַיַּגֶּשׁ־ לוֹ וַיֹּאכַל וַיָּבֵא לוֹ יַיִן
wine to-him and-he-brought and-he-ate to-him so-he-brought self-of-me

וַיֵּשְׁתְּ׃ וַיֹּאמֶר אֵלָיו יִצְחָק אָבִיו גְּשָׁה־ נָּא
now! come-here! father-of-him Isaac to-him then-he-said (26) and-he-drank

Esau her older son, which she
had in the house, and put
them on her younger son
Jacob. 16She also covered his
hands and the smooth part of
his neck with the goatskins.
17Then she handed to her son
Jacob the tasty food and the
bread she had made.
18He went to his father and
said, "My father."
"Yes, my son," he answered. "Who is it?"
19Jacob said to his father, "I
am Esau your firstborn. I have
done as you told me. Please sit
up and eat some of my game
so that you may give me your
blessing."
20Isaac asked his son, "How
did you find it so quickly, my
son?"
"The LORD your God gave
me success," he replied.
21Then Isaac said to Jacob,
"Come near so I can touch
you, my son, to know whether
you really are my son Esau or
not."
22Jacob went close to his father Isaac, who touched him
and said, "The voice is the
voice of Jacob, but the hands
are the hands of Esau." 23He
did not recognize him, for his
hands were hairy like those of
his brother Esau; so he blessed
him. 24"Are you really my son
Esau?" he asked.
"I am," he replied.
25Then he said, "My son,
bring me some of your game
to eat, so that I may give you
my blessing."
Jacob brought it to him and
he ate; and he brought some
wine and he drank. 26Then his
father Isaac said to him,

וּשְׁקָה־ לִּי בְּנִי׃ וַיִּגַּשׁ וַיִּשַּׁק־ לוֹ וַיָּרַח
and-he-smelled on-him and-he-kissed so-he-went (27) son-of-me on-me and-kiss!

אֶת־ רֵיחַ בְּגָדָיו וַיְבָרְכֵהוּ וַיֹּאמֶר רְאֵה רֵיחַ
smell-of see! and-he-said and-he-blessed-him clothes-of-him smell-of ***

בְּנִי כְּרֵיחַ שָׂדֶה אֲשֶׁר בֵּרֲכוֹ יְהוָה׃ וְיִתֶּן־
now-may-he-give (28) Yahweh he-blessed-him that field like-smell-of son-of-me

לְךָ הָאֱלֹהִים מִטַּל הַשָּׁמַיִם וּמִשְׁמַנֵּי הָאָרֶץ
the-earth and-from-riches-of the-heavens from-dew-of the-God to-you

וְרֹב דָּגָן וְתִירֹשׁ׃ יַעַבְדוּךָ עַמִּים
nations may-they-serve-you (29) and-new-wine grain and-abundance-of

וְיִשְׁתַּחֲוֻ לְךָ לְאֻמִּים הֱוֵה גְבִיר לְאַחֶיךָ
over-brothers-of-you lord be! peoples to-you and-may-they-bow-down

°וְיִשְׁתַּחֲוּוּ* לְךָ בְּנֵי אִמֶּךָ אֹרְרֶיךָ
ones-cursing-you mother-of-you sons-of to-you and-may-they-bow-down

אָרוּר וּמְבָרְכֶיךָ בָּרוּךְ׃ וַיְהִי כַּאֲשֶׁר
just-as and-he-was (30) being-blessed and-ones-blessing-you being-cursed

כִּלָּה יִצְחָק לְבָרֵךְ אֶת־יַעֲקֹב וַיְהִי אַךְ יָצֹא יָצָא
he-left to-leave scarcely and-he-was Jacob *** to-bless Isaac he-finished

יַעֲקֹב מֵאֵת פְּנֵי יִצְחָק אָבִיו וְעֵשָׂו אָחִיו בָּא
he-came brother-of-him that-Esau father-of-him Isaac presence-of from Jacob

מִצֵּידוֹ׃ וַיַּעַשׂ גַּם־ הוּא מַטְעַמִּים וַיָּבֵא
and-he-brought tasty-foods he also and-he-prepared (31) from-hunt-of-him

לְאָבִיו וַיֹּאמֶר לְאָבִיו יָקֻם אָבִי
father-of-me let-him-sit-up to-father-of-him and-he-said to-father-of-him

וְיֹאכַל מִצֵּיד בְּנוֹ בַּעֲבוּר תְּבָרְכַנִּי נַפְשֶׁךָ׃
self-of-you she-may-bless-me so-that son-of-him from-game-of and-let-him-eat

וַיֹּאמֶר לוֹ יִצְחָק אָבִיו מִי־ אָתָּה וַיֹּאמֶר אֲנִי
I and-he-answered you who? father-of-him Isaac to-him and-he-asked (32)

בִּנְךָ בְּכֹרְךָ עֵשָׂו׃ וַיֶּחֱרַד יִצְחָק חֲרָדָה גְּדֹלָה
great tremble Isaac and-he-trembled (33) Esau firstborn-of-you son-of-you

עַד־ מְאֹד וַיֹּאמֶר מִי־ אֵפוֹא הוּא הַצָּד־ צַיִד וַיָּבֵא
and-he-brought game the-one-hunting he then who? and-he-said violence to

לִי וָאֹכַל מִכֹּל בְּטֶרֶם תָּבוֹא וָאֲבָרְכֵהוּ גַּם־
indeed and-I-blessed-him you-came just-before from-all and-I-ate to-me

בָּרוּךְ יִהְיֶה׃ כִּשְׁמֹעַ עֵשָׂו אֶת־ דִּבְרֵי אָבִיו
father-of-him words-of *** Esau when-to-hear (34) he-will-be being-blessed

וַיִּצְעַק צְעָקָה גְּדֹלָה וּמָרָה עַד־ מְאֹד וַיֹּאמֶר לְאָבִיו
to-father-of-him and-he-said very to and-bitter loud cry then-he-cried

"Come here, my son, and kiss me."

27 So he went to him and kissed him. When Isaac caught the smell of his clothes, he blessed him and said,

"Ah, the smell of my son
is like the smell of a field
that the LORD has
blessed.
28 May God give you of
heaven's dew
and of earth's richness—
an abundance of grain
and new wine.
29 May nations serve you
and peoples bow down
to you.
Be lord over your brothers,
and may the sons of
your mother bow
down to you.
May those who curse you
be cursed
and those who bless you
be blessed."

30 After Isaac finished blessing him and Jacob had scarcely left his father's presence, his brother Esau came in from hunting. 31 He too prepared some tasty food and brought it to his father. Then he said to him, "My father, sit up and eat some of my game, so that you may give me your blessing."

32 His father Isaac asked him, "Who are you?"

"I am your son," he answered, "your firstborn, Esau."

33 Isaac trembled violently and said, "Who was it, then, that hunted game and brought it to me? I ate it just before you came and I blessed him—and indeed he will be blessed!"

34 When Esau heard his father's words, he burst out with a loud and bitter cry and said

*29 Most mss have no *dagesh* in the first *vav* ( וּ– ).

°29 ק וישתחוו

בָּרְכֵנִי גַם־ אָנִי אָבִי׃ וַיֹּאמֶר בָּא אָחִיךָ
brother-of-you he-came but-he-said (35) father-of-me me also bless-me!

בְּמִרְמָה וַיִּקַּח בִּרְכָתֶךָ׃ וַיֹּאמֶר הֲכִי קָרָא
he-called rightly? and-he-said (36) blessing-of-you and-he-took in-deceit

שְׁמוֹ יַעֲקֹב וַיַּעְקְבֵנִי זֶה פַעֲמַיִם אֶת־ בְּכֹרָתִי
birthright-of-me *** two-times this now-he-deceived-me Jacob name-of-him

לָקָח וְהִנֵּה עַתָּה לָקַח בִּרְכָתִי וַיֹּאמַר הֲלֹא־ אָצַלְתָּ
you-reserved not? then-he-asked blessing-of-me he-took now and-see! he-took

לִּי בְּרָכָה׃ וַיַּעַן יִצְחָק וַיֹּאמֶר לְעֵשָׂו הֵן גְּבִיר
lord see! to-Esau and-he-said Isaac and-he-answered (37) blessing for-me

שַׂמְתִּיו לָךְ וְאֶת־ כָּל־ אֶחָיו נָתַתִּי לוֹ לַעֲבָדִים
as-servants to-him I-made brothers-of-him all-of and over-you I-made-him

וְדָגָן וְתִירֹשׁ סְמַכְתִּיו וּלְכָה אֵפוֹא מָה אֶעֱשֶׂה בְּנִי׃
son-of-me can-I-do what? then so-for-you I-sustained-him and-new-wine and-grain

וַיֹּאמֶר עֵשָׂו אֶל־ אָבִיו הַבְרָכָה אַחַת הִוא־ לְךָ אָבִי
father-of-me to-you she one blessing? father-of-him to Esau and-he-said (38)

בָּרְכֵנִי גַם־ אָנִי אָבִי וַיִּשָּׂא עֵשָׂו קֹלוֹ וַיֵּבְךְּ׃
and-he-wept voice-of-him Esau then-he-lifted father-of-me me also bless-me!

וַיַּעַן יִצְחָק אָבִיו וַיֹּאמֶר אֵלָיו הִנֵּה מִשְׁמַנֵּי
from-riches-of see! to-him and-he-said father-of-him Isaac and-he-answered (39)

הָאָרֶץ יִהְיֶה מוֹשָׁבֶךָ וּמִטַּל הַשָּׁמַיִם מֵעָל׃
above the-heavens and-from-dew-of dwelling-of-you he-will-be the-earth

וְעַל־ חַרְבְּךָ תִחְיֶה וְאֶת־ אָחִיךָ תַּעֲבֹד
you-will-serve brother-of-you and you-will-live sword-of-you and-by (40)

וְהָיָה כַּאֲשֶׁר תָּרִיד וּפָרַקְתָּ עֻלּוֹ
yoke-of-him then-you-will-throw you-grow-restless when but-he-will-be

מֵעַל צַוָּארֶךָ׃ וַיִּשְׂטֹם עֵשָׂו אֶת־ יַעֲקֹב עַל־
because-of Jacob *** Esau and-he-held-grudge (41) neck-of-you from-off

הַבְּרָכָה אֲשֶׁר בֵּרֲכוֹ אָבִיו וַיֹּאמֶר עֵשָׂו בְּלִבּוֹ
to-himself Esau and-he-said father-of-him he-blessed-him that the-blessing

יִקְרְבוּ יְמֵי אֵבֶל אָבִי וְאַהַרְגָה אֶת־ יַעֲקֹב
Jacob *** then-I-will-kill father-of-me mourning-of days-of they-are-near

אָחִי׃ וַיֻּגַּד לְרִבְקָה אֶת־ דִּבְרֵי עֵשָׂו בְּנָהּ
son-of-her Esau words-of *** to-Rebekah but-he-was-told (42) brother-of-me

הַגָּדֹל וַתִּשְׁלַח וַתִּקְרָא לְיַעֲקֹב בְּנָהּ הַקָּטָן
the-younger son-of-her for-Jacob and-she-called so-she-sent the-older

וַתֹּאמֶר אֵלָיו הִנֵּה עֵשָׂו אָחִיךָ מִתְנַחֵם לְךָ
about-you consoling-self brother-of-you Esau see! to-him and-she-said

to his father, "Bless me—me too, my father!"

[35]But he said, "Your brother came deceitfully and took your blessing."

[36]Esau said, "Isn't he rightly named Jacob[q]? He has deceived me these two times: He took my birthright, and now he's taken my blessing!" Then he asked, "Haven't you reserved any blessing for me?"

[37]Isaac answered Esau, "I have made him lord over you and have made all his relatives his servants, and I have sustained him with grain and new wine. So what can I possibly do for you, my son?"

[38]Esau said to his father, "Do you have only one blessing, my father? Bless me too, my father!" Then Esau wept aloud.

[39]His father Isaac answered him,

"Your dwelling will be
away from the earth's richness,
away from the dew of heaven above.
[40]You will live by the sword
and you will serve your brother.
But when you grow restless,
you will throw his yoke
from off your neck."

*Jacob Flees to Laban*

[41]Esau held a grudge against Jacob because of the blessing his father had given him. He said to himself, "The days of mourning for my father are near; then I will kill my brother Jacob."

[42]When Rebekah was told what her older son Esau had said, she sent for her younger son Jacob and said to him, "Your brother Esau is consoling himself with the thought

[q]36 *Jacob* means *he grasps the heel* (figuratively, *he deceives*).

לְהָרְגֶךָ׃ וְעַתָּה בְנִי שְׁמַע בְּקֹלִי וְקוּם בְּרַח־
and-flee! and-rise! to-voice-of-me obey! son-of-me so-now (43) to-kill-you

לְךָ אֶל־ לָבָן אָחִי חָרָנָה׃ וְיָשַׁבְתָּ עִמּוֹ יָמִים
days with-him and-you-stay (44) in-Haran brother-of-me Laban to for-yourself

אֲחָדִים עַד אֲשֶׁר־ תָּשׁוּב חֲמַת אָחִיךָ׃ עַד־ שׁוּב
he-subsides when (45) brother-of-you fury-of she-subsides when until few-ones

אַף־ אָחִיךָ מִמְּךָ וְשָׁכַח אֵת אֲשֶׁר־ עָשִׂיתָ לּוֹ
to-him you-did what *** and-he-forgets from-you brother-of-you anger-of

וְשָׁלַחְתִּי וּלְקַחְתִּיךָ מִשָּׁם לָמָה אֶשְׁכַּל גַּם־
also should-I-lose why? from-there and-I-will-get-you then-I-will-send

שְׁנֵיכֶם יוֹם אֶחָד׃ וַתֹּאמֶר רִבְקָה אֶל־יִצְחָק קַצְתִּי
I-am-disgusted Isaac to Rebekah then-she-said (46) one day both-of-you

בְחַיַּי מִפְּנֵי בְּנוֹת חֵת אִם־ לֹקֵחַ יַעֲקֹב אִשָּׁה
wife Jacob taking if Heth daughters-of because-of with-life-of-me

מִבְּנוֹת־ חֵת כָּאֵלֶּה מִבְּנוֹת הָאָרֶץ לָמָּה לִּי חַיִּים׃
lives to-me what? the-land from-women-of like-these Heth from-daughters-of

וַיִּקְרָא יִצְחָק אֶל־יַעֲקֹב וַיְבָרֶךְ אֹתוֹ וַיְצַוֵּהוּ
and-he-commanded-him him and-he-blessed Jacob for Isaac so-he-called (28:1)

וַיֹּאמֶר לוֹ לֹא־ תִקַּח אִשָּׁה מִבְּנוֹת כְּנָעַן׃ קוּם לֵךְ
go! rise! (2) Canaan from-women-of wife you-take not to-him and-he-said

פַּדֶּנָה אֲרָם בֵּיתָה בְתוּאֵל אֲבִי אִמֶּךָ וְקַח־
and-take! mother-of-you father-of Bethuel to-house-of Aram to-Paddan

לְךָ מִשָּׁם אִשָּׁה מִבְּנוֹת לָבָן אֲחִי אִמֶּךָ׃
mother-of-you brother-of Laban from-daughters-of wife from-there for-yourself

וְאֵל שַׁדַּי יְבָרֵךְ אֹתְךָ וְיַפְרְךָ
and-may-he-make-fruitful-you you may-he-bless Almighty now-God (3)

וְיַרְבֶּךָ וְהָיִיתָ לִקְהַל עַמִּים׃
peoples as-community-of so-you-become and-may-he-increase-you

וְיִתֶּן־ לְךָ אֶת־ בִּרְכַּת אַבְרָהָם לְךָ וּלְזַרְעֲךָ
and-to-seed-of-you to-you Abraham blessing-of *** to-you and-may-he-give (4)

אִתָּךְ לְרִשְׁתְּךָ אֶת־ אֶרֶץ מְגֻרֶיךָ אֲשֶׁר־ נָתַן אֱלֹהִים
God he-gave that journeys-of-you land-of *** to-possess-you with-you

לְאַבְרָהָם׃ וַיִּשְׁלַח יִצְחָק אֶת־יַעֲקֹב וַיֵּלֶךְ פַּדֶּנָה אֲרָם
Aram to-Paddan and-he-went Jacob *** Isaac then-he-sent-off (5) to-Abraham

אֶל־ לָבָן בֶּן־ בְּתוּאֵל הָאֲרַמִּי אֲחִי רִבְקָה אֵם יַעֲקֹב
Jacob mother-of Rebekah brother-of the-Aramean Bethuel son-of Laban to

וְעֵשָׂו׃ וַיַּרְא עֵשָׂו כִּי־ בֵרַךְ יִצְחָק אֶת־יַעֲקֹב וְשִׁלַּח
and-he-sent Jacob *** Isaac he-blessed that Esau now-he-learned (6) and-Esau

of killing you. 43Now then, my son, do what I say: Flee at once to my brother Laban in Haran.
44Stay with him for a while until your brother's fury subsides.
45When your brother is no longer angry with you and forgets what you did to him, I'll send word for you to come back from there. Why should I lose both of you in one day?"
46Then Rebekah said to Isaac, "I'm disgusted with living because of these Hittite women. If Jacob takes a wife from among the women of this land, from Hittite women like these, my life will not be worth living."

28 So Isaac called for Jacob and blessed[r] him and commanded him: "Do not marry a Canaanite woman.
2Go at once to Paddan Aram,[s] to the house of your mother's father Bethuel. Take a wife for yourself there, from among the daughters of Laban, your mother's brother.
3May God Almighty[t] bless you and make you fruitful and increase your numbers until you become a community of peoples.
4May he give you and your descendants the blessing of Abraham, so that you may take possession of the land where you now live as an alien, the land God gave to Abraham."
5Then Isaac sent Jacob on his way, and he went to Paddan Aram, to Laban son of Bethuel the Aramean, the brother of Rebekah, who was the mother of Jacob and Esau.
6Now Esau learned that Isaac had blessed Jacob and

r1 Or *greeted*
s2 That is, Northwest Mesopotamia
t3 Hebrew *El-Shaddai*

אֹתוֹ פַּדֶּנָה אֲרָם לָקַחַת־ לוֹ מִשָּׁם אִשָּׁה בְּבָרְכוֹ אֹתוֹ
him when-to-bless-him wife from-there for-him to-take Aram to-Paddan him

וַיְצַו עָלָיו לֵאמֹר לֹא־ תִקַּח אִשָּׁה מִבְּנוֹת כְּנָעַן׃
Canaan from-women-of wife you-take not to-say to-him and-he-commanded

וַיִּשְׁמַע יַעֲקֹב אֶל־ אָבִיו וְאֶל־ אִמּוֹ וַיֵּלֶךְ
and-he-went mother-of-him and-to father-of-him to Jacob and-he-obeyed (7)

פַּדֶּנָה אֲרָם׃ וַיַּרְא עֵשָׂו כִּי רָעוֹת בְּנוֹת כְּנָעַן
Canaan women-of displeasing-ones how Esau then-he-realized (8) Aram to-Paddan

בְּעֵינֵי יִצְחָק אָבִיו׃ וַיֵּלֶךְ עֵשָׂו אֶל־יִשְׁמָעֵאל וַיִּקַּח
and-he-married Ishmael to Esau so-he-went (9) father-of-him Isaac to-eyes-of

אֶת־ מָחֲלַת ׀ בַּת־ יִשְׁמָעֵאל בֶּן־ אַבְרָהָם אֲחוֹת נְבָיוֹת עַל־
besides Nebaioth sister-of Abraham son-of Ishmael daughter-of Mahalath ***

נָשָׁיו לוֹ לְאִשָּׁה׃ וַיֵּצֵא יַעֲקֹב מִבְּאֵר שָׁבַע
Sheba from-Beer Jacob and-he-left (10) as-wife to-him wives-of-him

וַיֵּלֶךְ חָרָנָה׃ וַיִּפְגַּע בַּמָּקוֹם וַיָּלֶן
then-he-stopped to-the-place when-he-reached (11) for-Haran and-he-set-out

שָׁם כִּי־בָא הַשֶּׁמֶשׁ וַיִּקַּח מֵאַבְנֵי הַמָּקוֹם וַיָּשֶׂם
and-he-put the-place from-stones-of and-he-took the-sun he-set for there

מְרַאֲשֹׁתָיו וַיִּשְׁכַּב בַּמָּקוֹם הַהוּא׃ וַיַּחֲלֹם
and-he-dreamed (12) the-that in-the-place and-he-slept under-head-of-him

וְהִנֵּה סֻלָּם מֻצָּב אַרְצָה וְרֹאשׁוֹ מַגִּיעַ הַשָּׁמָיְמָה
to-the-heavens reaching and-top-of-him on-earth resting stairway and-see!

וְהִנֵּה מַלְאֲכֵי אֱלֹהִים עֹלִים וְיֹרְדִים בּוֹ׃ וְהִנֵּה
and-see! (13) on-him and-descending-ones ascending-ones God angels-of and-see!

יְהוָה נִצָּב עָלָיו וַיֹּאמַר אֲנִי יְהוָה אֱלֹהֵי אַבְרָהָם אָבִיךָ
father-of-you Abraham God-of Yahweh I and-he-said above-him standing Yahweh

וֵאלֹהֵי יִצְחָק הָאָרֶץ אֲשֶׁר אַתָּה שֹׁכֵב עָלֶיהָ לְךָ אֶתְּנֶנָּה
I-will-give-her to-you on-her lying you which the-land Isaac and-God-of

וּלְזַרְעֶךָ׃ וְהָיָה זַרְעֲךָ כַּעֲפַר
like-dust-of descendant-of-you and-he-will-be (14) and-to-descendant-of-you

הָאָרֶץ וּפָרַצְתָּ יָמָּה וָקֵדְמָה וְצָפֹנָה וָנֶגְבָּה
and-to-south and-to-north and-to-east to-west and-you-will-spread the-earth

וְנִבְרְכוּ בְךָ כָּל־ מִשְׁפְּחֹת הָאֲדָמָה
the-earth peoples-of all-of through-you and-they-will-be-blessed

וּבְזַרְעֶךָ׃ וְהִנֵּה אָנֹכִי עִמָּךְ וּשְׁמַרְתִּיךָ
and-I-will-watch-over-you with-you I and-see! (15) and-through-offspring-of-you

בְּכֹל אֲשֶׁר־ תֵּלֵךְ וַהֲשִׁבֹתִיךָ אֶל־הָאֲדָמָה הַזֹּאת כִּי
indeed the-this the-land to and-I-will-bring-back-you you-go where in-any-of

had sent him to Paddan Aram to take a wife from there, and that when he blessed him he commanded him, "Do not marry a Canaanite woman," [7]and that Jacob had obeyed his father and mother and had gone to Paddan Aram. [8]Esau then realized how displeasing the Canaanite women were to his father Isaac; [9]so he went to Ishmael and married Mahalath, the sister of Nebaioth and daughter of Ishmael son of Abraham, in addition to the wives he already had.

*Jacob's Dream at Bethel*

[10]Jacob left Beersheba and set out for Haran. [11]When he reached a certain place, he stopped for the night because the sun had set. Taking one of the stones there, he put it under his head and lay down to sleep. [12]He had a dream in which he saw a stairway[u] resting on the earth, with its top reaching to heaven, and the angels of God were ascending and descending on it. [13]There above it[v] stood the LORD, and he said: "I am the LORD, the God of your father Abraham and the God of Isaac. I will give you and your descendants the land on which you are lying. [14]Your descendants will be like the dust of the earth, and you will spread out to the west and to the east, to the north and to the south. All peoples on earth will be blessed through you and your offspring. [15]I am with you and will watch over you wherever you go, and I will bring you back to this land. I will not

[u]12 Or *ladder* [v]13 Or *There beside him*

לֹא אֶעֱזָבְךָ עַד אֲשֶׁר אִם־ עָשִׂיתִי אֵת אֲשֶׁר־ דִּבַּרְתִּי לָךְ׃
to-you I-promised what *** I-do when *** until I-will-leave-you not

(16) וַיִּיקַץ יַעֲקֹב מִשְּׁנָתוֹ וַיֹּאמֶר אָכֵן יֵשׁ יְהוָה
Yahweh he-is surely then-he-thought from-sleep-of-him Jacob when-he-woke (16)

בַּמָּקוֹם הַזֶּה וְאָנֹכִי לֹא יָדָעְתִּי׃ (17) וַיִּירָא וַיֹּאמַר
and-he-said and-he-was-afraid (17) I-was-aware not and-I the-this in-the-place

מַה־ נּוֹרָא הַמָּקוֹם הַזֶּה אֵין זֶה כִּי אִם־ בֵּית אֱלֹהִים
God house-of than other this not the-this the-place being-awesome how!

וְזֶה שַׁעַר הַשָּׁמָיִם׃ (18) וַיַּשְׁכֵּם יַעֲקֹב בַּבֹּקֶר וַיִּקַּח
and-he-took in-the-morning Jacob and-he-rose (18) the-heavens gate-of yes-this

אֶת־ הָאֶבֶן אֲשֶׁר־ שָׂם מְרַאֲשֹׁתָיו וַיָּשֶׂם אֹתָהּ מַצֵּבָה
pillar her and-he-set-up under-head-of-him he-placed that the-stone ***

וַיִּצֹק שֶׁמֶן עַל־ רֹאשָׁהּ׃ (19) וַיִּקְרָא אֶת־ שֵׁם־ הַמָּקוֹם
the-place name-of *** and-he-called (19) top-of-her on oil and-he-poured

הַהוּא בֵּית־אֵל וְאוּלָם לוּז שֵׁם־ הָעִיר לָרִאשֹׁנָה׃ (20) וַיִּדַּר
and-he-made (20) at-the-first the-city name-of Luz even-though El Beth the-that

יַעֲקֹב נֶדֶר לֵאמֹר אִם־ יִהְיֶה אֱלֹהִים עִמָּדִי וּשְׁמָרַנִי בַּדֶּרֶךְ
on-the-journey and-he-watches-over-me with-me God he-is if to-say vow Jacob

הַזֶּה אֲשֶׁר אָנֹכִי הוֹלֵךְ וְנָתַן־ לִי לֶחֶם לֶאֱכֹל וּבֶגֶד לִלְבֹּשׁ׃
to-wear and-clothes to-eat food to-me and-he-gives taking I that the-this

(21) וְשַׁבְתִּי בְשָׁלוֹם אֶל־ בֵּית אָבִי וְהָיָה יְהוָה
Yahweh then-he-will-be father-of-me house-of to in-safety so-I-return (21)

לִי לֵאלֹהִים׃ (22) וְהָאֶבֶן הַזֹּאת אֲשֶׁר־ שַׂמְתִּי מַצֵּבָה יִהְיֶה
he-will-be pillar I-set-up that the-this and-the-stone (22) as-God to-me

בֵּית אֱלֹהִים וְכֹל אֲשֶׁר תִּתֶּן־ לִי עַשֵּׂר אֲעַשְּׂרֶנּוּ לָךְ׃
to-you I-will-give-him to-be-tenth to-me you-give that and-all God house-of

(29:1) וַיִּשָּׂא יַעֲקֹב רַגְלָיו וַיֵּלֶךְ אַרְצָה בְנֵי־
peoples-of to-land-of and-he-continued feet-of-him Jacob and-he-lifted (29:1)

קֶדֶם׃ (2) וַיַּרְא וְהִנֵּה בְאֵר בַּשָּׂדֶה וְהִנֵּה־ שָׁם שְׁלֹשָׁה עֶדְרֵי־
flocks-of three there and-see! in-the-field well and-see! and-he-saw (2) east

צֹאן רֹבְצִים עָלֶיהָ כִּי מִן־ הַבְּאֵר הַהִוא יַשְׁקוּ
they-were-watered the-that the-well from for near-her ones-lying sheep

הָעֲדָרִים וְהָאֶבֶן גְּדֹלָה עַל־ פִּי הַבְּאֵר׃ (3) וְנֶאֶסְפוּ־
as-they-were-gathered (3) the-well mouth-of over large and-the-stone the-flocks

שָׁמָּה כָל־ הָעֲדָרִים וְגָלְלוּ אֶת־ הָאֶבֶן מֵעַל פִּי
mouth-of away-from the-stone *** then-they-rolled the-flocks all-of to-there

הַבְּאֵר וְהִשְׁקוּ אֶת־ הַצֹּאן וְהֵשִׁיבוּ אֶת־ הָאֶבֶן
the-stone *** then-they-returned the-sheep *** and-they-watered the-well

leave you until I have done what I have promised you."

[16]When Jacob awoke from his sleep, he thought, "Surely the LORD is in this place, and I was not aware of it." [17]He was afraid and said, "How awesome is this place! This is none other than the house of God; this is the gate of heaven."

[18]Early the next morning Jacob took the stone he had placed under his head and set it up as a pillar and poured oil on top of it. [19]He called that place Bethel,[w] though the city used to be called Luz.

[20]Then Jacob made a vow, saying, "If God will be with me and will watch over me on this journey I am taking and will give me food to eat and clothes to wear [21]so that I return safely to my father's house, then the LORD[x] will be my God. [22]This stone that I have set up as a pillar will be God's house, and of all that you give me I will give you a tenth."

### *Jacob Arrives in Paddan Aram*

**29** Then Jacob continued on his journey and came to the land of the eastern peoples. [2]There he saw a well in the field, with three flocks of sheep lying near it because the flocks were watered from that well. The stone over the mouth of the well was large. [3]When all the flocks were gathered there, the shepherds would roll the stone away from the well's mouth and water the sheep. Then they would return the stone to its

[w]19 *Bethel* means *house of God.*
[x]20,21 Or *Since God ... father's house, the* LORD

עַל־ פִּי הַבְּאֵר לִמְקֹמָהּ׃ וַיֹּאמֶר לָהֶם֙ יַעֲקֹב

Jacob to-them and-he-asked (4) to-place-of-her the-well mouth-of over

אַחַי מֵאַיִן אַתֶּם וַיֹּאמְרוּ מֵחָרָן אֲנָחְנוּ׃ וַיֹּאמֶר

and-he-said (5) we from-Haran and-they-replied you from-where? brothers-of-me

לָהֶם הַיְדַעְתֶּם אֶת־ לָבָן בֶּן־ נָחוֹר וַיֹּאמְרוּ יָדָעְנוּ׃

we-know and-they-answered Nahor son-of Laban *** you-know? to-them

וַיֹּאמֶר לָהֶם הֲשָׁלוֹם לוֹ וַיֹּאמְרוּ שָׁלוֹם וְהִנֵּה֙ רָחֵל

Rachel now-see! well and-they-said with-him well? to-them then-he-asked (6)

בִּתּוֹ בָּאָה עִם־ הַצֹּאן׃ וַיֹּאמֶר הֵן עוֹד֙ הַיּוֹם

the-day still see! and-he-said (7) the-sheep with coming daughter-of-him

גָּדוֹל לֹא־ עֵת הֵאָסֵף הַמִּקְנֶה הַשְׁקוּ הַצֹּאן וּלְכוּ רְעוּ׃

pasture! and-go! the-sheep water! the-flock to-be-gathered time-of not high

וַיֹּאמְרוּ֙ לֹא נוּכַל֒ עַד אֲשֶׁר יֵאָסְפוּ֙ כָּל־ הָעֲדָרִים

the-flocks all-of they-are-gathered when until we-can not but-they-replied (8)

וְגָלְלוּ֙ אֶת־ הָאֶבֶן מֵעַל פִּי הַבְּאֵר וְהִשְׁקִינוּ

then-we-will-water the-well mouth-of away-from the-stone *** and-they-roll

הַצֹּאן׃ עוֹדֶנּוּ מְדַבֵּר עִמָּם וְרָחֵל ׀ בָּאָה עִם־ הַצֹּאן֙

the-sheep with she-came then-Rachel with-them talking while-he (9) the-sheep

אֲשֶׁר לְאָבִיהָ כִּי רֹעָה הִוא׃ וַיְהִי כַּאֲשֶׁר֩ רָאָה

he-saw when and-he-was (10) she being-shepherdess for to-father-of-her that

יַעֲקֹב אֶת־ רָחֵל בַּת־ לָבָן֙ אֲחִי אִמּוֹ וְאֶת־ צֹאן

sheep-of and mother-of-him brother-of Laban daughter-of Rachel *** Jacob

לָבָן אֲחִי אִמּוֹ וַיִּגַּשׁ יַעֲקֹב וַיָּגֶל אֶת־

*** and-he-rolled Jacob then-he-went-over mother-of-him brother-of Laban

הָאֶבֶן מֵעַל֙ פִּי הַבְּאֵר וַיַּשְׁק אֶת־ צֹאן לָבָן

Laban sheep-of *** and-he-watered the-well mouth-of away-from the-stone

אֲחִי אִמּוֹ׃ וַיִּשַּׁק יַעֲקֹב לְרָחֵל וַיִּשָּׂא

and-he-lifted on-Rachel Jacob then-he-kissed (11) mother-of-him brother-of

אֶת־ קֹלוֹ וַיֵּבְךְּ׃ וַיַּגֵּד יַעֲקֹב לְרָחֵל כִּי אֲחִי

relative-of that to-Rachel Jacob and-he-told (12) and-he-wept voice-of-him ***

אָבִיהָ֙ הוּא וְכִי בֶן־ רִבְקָה הוּא וַתָּרָץ וַתַּגֵּד

and-she-told so-she-ran he Rebekah son-of and-that he father-of-her

לְאָבִיהָ׃ וַיְהִי֩ כִשְׁמֹעַ לָבָן אֶת־ שֵׁמַע ׀ יַעֲקֹב

Jacob news-of *** Laban as-soon-as-to-hear and-he-was (13) to-father-of-her

בֶּן־ אֲחֹתוֹ וַיָּרָץ לִקְרָאתוֹ֙ וַיְחַבֶּק־ לוֹ֙

on-him and-he-embraced to-meet-him that-he-ran sister-of-him son-of

וַיְנַשֶּׁק־ לוֹ וַיְבִיאֵהוּ אֶל־ בֵּיתוֹ וַיְסַפֵּר לְלָבָן

to-Laban and-he-told home-of-him to and-he-brought-him on-him and-he-kissed

place over the mouth of the well.

4Jacob asked the shepherds, "My brothers, where are you from?"

"We're from Haran," they replied.

5He said to them, "Do you know Laban, Nahor's grandson?"

"Yes, we know him," they answered.

6Then Jacob asked them, "Is he well?"

"Yes, he is," they said, "and here comes his daughter Rachel with the sheep."

7"Look," he said, "the sun is still high; it is not time for the flocks to be gathered. Water the sheep and take them back to pasture."

8"We can't," they replied, "until all the flocks are gathered and the stone has been rolled away from the mouth of the well. Then we will water the sheep."

9While he was still talking with them, Rachel came with her father's sheep, for she was a shepherdess. 10When Jacob saw Rachel daughter of Laban, his mother's brother, and Laban's sheep, he went over and rolled the stone away from the mouth of the well and watered his uncle's sheep. 11Then Jacob kissed Rachel and began to weep aloud. 12He had told Rachel that he was a relative of her father and a son of Rebekah. So she ran and told her father.

13As soon as Laban heard the news about Jacob, his sister's son, he hurried to meet him. He embraced him and kissed him and brought him to his home, and there Jacob told

אֵת כָּל־ הַדְּבָרִים הָאֵלֶּה׃ וַיֹּאמֶר לוֹ לָבָן אַךְ
indeed Laban to-him then-he-said (14) the-these the-things all-of ***

עַצְמִי וּבְשָׂרִי אָתָּה וַיֵּשֶׁב עִמּוֹ חֹדֶשׁ יָמִים׃
days month-of with-him and-he-stayed you and-flesh-of-me bone-of-me

וַיֹּאמֶר לָבָן לְיַעֲקֹב הֲכִי־ אָחִי אַתָּה וַעֲבַדְתַּנִי
should-you-serve-me you relative-of-me because? to-Jacob Laban then-he-said (15)

חִנָּם הַגִּידָה לִּי מַה־ מַּשְׂכֻּרְתֶּךָ׃ וּלְלָבָן שְׁתֵּי בָנוֹת
daughters two-of now-to-Laban (16) wage-of-you what? to-me tell! for-nothing

שֵׁם הַגְּדֹלָה לֵאָה וְשֵׁם הַקְּטַנָּה רָחֵל׃ וְעֵינֵי לֵאָה
Leah now-eyes-of (17) Rachel the-younger and-name-of Leah the-older name-of

רַכּוֹת וְרָחֵל הָיְתָה יְפַת־ תֹּאַר וִיפַת מַרְאֶה׃
appearance and-beautiful-of form lovely-of she-was but-Rachel weak-ones

וַיֶּאֱהַב יַעֲקֹב אֶת־ רָחֵל וַיֹּאמֶר אֶעֱבָדְךָ שֶׁבַע שָׁנִים
years seven I-will-serve-you and-he-said Rachel *** Jacob now-he-loved (18)

בְּרָחֵל בִּתְּךָ הַקְּטַנָּה׃ וַיֹּאמֶר לָבָן טוֹב תִּתִּי
to-give-me better Laban so-he-said (19) the-younger daughter-of-you for-Rachel

אֹתָהּ לָךְ מִתִּתִּי אֹתָהּ לְאִישׁ אַחֵר שְׁבָה עִמָּדִי׃ וַיַּעֲבֹד
so-he-served (20) with-me stay! other to-man her than-to-give-me to-you her

יַעֲקֹב בְּרָחֵל שֶׁבַע שָׁנִים וַיִּהְיוּ בְעֵינָיו כְּיָמִים אֲחָדִים
few-ones like-days in-eyes-of-him but-they-seemed years seven for-Rachel Jacob

בְּאַהֲבָתוֹ אֹתָהּ׃ וַיֹּאמֶר יַעֲקֹב אֶל־ לָבָן הָבָה אֶת־ אִשְׁתִּי
wife-of-me *** give! Laban to Jacob then-he-said (21) her because-to-love-him

כִּי מָלְאוּ יָמָי וְאָבוֹאָה אֵלֶיהָ׃ וַיֶּאֱסֹף
so-he-gathered (22) with-her and-I-would-lie days-of-me they-are-completed for

לָבָן אֶת־ כָּל־ אַנְשֵׁי הַמָּקוֹם וַיַּעַשׂ מִשְׁתֶּה׃ וַיְהִי
but-he-was (23) feast and-he-gave the-place people-of all-of *** Laban

בָעֶרֶב וַיִּקַּח אֶת־ לֵאָה בִתּוֹ וַיָּבֵא אֹתָהּ אֵלָיו
to-him her and-he-gave daughter-of-him Leah *** that-he-took in-the-evening

וַיָּבֹא אֵלֶיהָ׃ וַיִּתֵּן לָבָן לָהּ אֶת־ זִלְפָּה שִׁפְחָתוֹ
servant-of-him Zilpah *** to-her Laban and-he-gave (24) with-her and-he-lay

לְלֵאָה בִתּוֹ שִׁפְחָה׃ וַיְהִי בַבֹּקֶר וְהִנֵּה־
and-see! in-the-morning and-he-was (25) maidservant daughter-of-him to-Leah

הִוא לֵאָה וַיֹּאמֶר אֶל־ לָבָן מַה־ זֹּאת עָשִׂיתָ לִּי הֲלֹא בְרָחֵל
for-Rachel not? to-me you-did this what? Laban to so-he-said Leah she

עָבַדְתִּי עִמָּךְ וְלָמָּה רִמִּיתָנִי׃ וַיֹּאמֶר לָבָן לֹא־
not Laban and-he-replied (26) you-deceived-me so-why? for-you I-served

יֵעָשֶׂה כֵן בִּמְקוֹמֵנוּ לָתֵת הַצְּעִירָה לִפְנֵי הַבְּכִירָה׃
the-firstborn before the-younger to-give in-land-of-us so he-is-done

him all these things.
[14]Then Laban said to him, "You are my own flesh and blood."

*Jacob Marries Leah and Rachel*

After Jacob had stayed with him for a whole month,
[15]Laban said to him, "Just because you are a relative of mine, should you work for me for nothing? Tell me what your wages should be."
[16]Now Laban had two daughters; the name of the older was Leah, and the name of the younger was Rachel.
[17]Leah had weak[y] eyes, but Rachel was lovely in form, and beautiful.
[18]Jacob was in love with Rachel and said, "I'll work for you seven years in return for your younger daughter Rachel."
[19]Laban said, "It's better to give her to you than to some other man. Stay here with me."
[20]So Jacob served seven years to get Rachel, but they seemed like only a few days to him because of his love for her.
[21]Then Jacob said to Laban, "Give me my wife. My time is completed, and I want to lie with her."
[22]So Laban brought together all the people of the place and gave a feast.
[23]But when evening came, he took his daughter Leah and gave her to Jacob, and Jacob lay with her.
[24]And Laban gave his servant girl Zilpah to his daughter as her maidservant.
[25]When morning came, there was Leah! So Jacob said to Laban, "What is this you have done to me? I served you for Rachel, didn't I? Why have you deceived me?"
[26]Laban replied, "It is not our custom here to give the younger daughter in marriage before the older one.
[27]Finish

[y]17 Or *delicate*

מַלֵּא שְׁבֻעַ זֹאת וְנִתְּנָה לְךָ גַּם־אֶת־זֹאת בַּעֲבֹדָה אֲשֶׁר
that for-work other *** also to-you and-we-will-give this week-of finish! (27)

תַּעֲבֹד עִמָּדִי עוֹד שֶׁבַע־שָׁנִים אֲחֵרוֹת׃ וַיַּעַשׂ יַעֲקֹב כֵּן
so Jacob and-he-did (28) other-ones years seven for for-me you-will-do

וַיְמַלֵּא שְׁבֻעַ זֹאת וַיִּתֶּן־לוֹ אֶת־רָחֵל בִּתּוֹ
daughter-of-him Rachel *** to-him then-he-gave this week-of and-he-finished

לוֹ לְאִשָּׁה׃ וַיִּתֵּן לָבָן לְרָחֵל בִּתּוֹ אֶת־בִּלְהָה
Bilhah *** daughter-of-him to-Rachel Laban and-he-gave (29) for-wife to-him

שִׁפְחָתוֹ לָהּ לְשִׁפְחָה׃ וַיָּבֹא גַּם אֶל־רָחֵל
Rachel with also and-he-lay (30) as-maidservant to-her servant-of-him

וַיֶּאֱהַב גַּם־אֶת־רָחֵל מִלֵּאָה וַיַּעֲבֹד עִמּוֹ עוֹד שֶׁבַע־שָׁנִים
years seven for for-him and-he-worked than-Leah Rachel *** more and-he-loved

אֲחֵרוֹת׃ וַיַּרְא יְהוָה כִּי־שְׂנוּאָה לֵאָה וַיִּפְתַּח
then-he-opened Leah being-unloved that Yahweh when-he-saw (31) other-ones

אֶת־רַחְמָהּ וְרָחֵל עֲקָרָה׃ וַתַּהַר לֵאָה וַתֵּלֶד
and-she-bore Leah and-she-conceived (32) barren but-Rachel womb-of-her ***

בֵּן וַתִּקְרָא שְׁמוֹ רְאוּבֵן כִּי אָמְרָה כִּי־רָאָה יְהוָה
Yahweh he-looked because she-said for Reuben name-of-him and-she-called son

בְּעָנְיִי כִּי עַתָּה יֶאֱהָבַנִי אִישִׁי׃ וַתַּהַר
and-she-conceived (33) husband-of-me he-will-love-me now surely on-misery-of-me

עוֹד וַתֵּלֶד בֵּן וַתֹּאמֶר כִּי־שָׁמַע יְהוָה כִּי־שְׂנוּאָה
being-unloved that Yahweh he-heard because and-she-said son and-she-bore again

אָנֹכִי וַיִּתֶּן־לִי גַּם־אֶת־זֶה וַתִּקְרָא שְׁמוֹ שִׁמְעוֹן׃
Simeon name-of-him so-she-called this *** also to-me now-he-gave I

וַתַּהַר עוֹד וַתֵּלֶד בֵּן וַתֹּאמֶר עַתָּה הַפַּעַם
the-time now and-she-said son and-she-bore again and-she-conceived (34)

יִלָּוֶה אִישִׁי אֵלַי כִּי־יָלַדְתִּי לוֹ שְׁלֹשָׁה בָנִים עַל־
for sons three to-him I-bore for to-me husband-of-me he-will-become-attached

כֵּן קָרָא־שְׁמוֹ לֵוִי׃ וַתַּהַר עוֹד וַתֵּלֶד
and-she-bore again and-she-conceived (35) Levi name-of-him he-called this

בֵּן וַתֹּאמֶר הַפַּעַם אוֹדֶה אֶת־יְהוָה עַל־כֵּן קָרְאָה
she-called this for Yahweh *** I-will-praise the-time and-she-said son

שְׁמוֹ יְהוּדָה וַתַּעֲמֹד מִלֶּדֶת׃ וַתֵּרֶא רָחֵל
Rachel when-she-saw (30:1) from-to-bear then-she-stopped Judah name-of-him

כִּי לֹא יָלְדָה לְיַעֲקֹב וַתְּקַנֵּא רָחֵל בַּאֲחֹתָהּ
of-sister-of-her Rachel then-she-was-jealous to-Jacob she-bore not that

וַתֹּאמֶר אֶל־יַעֲקֹב הָבָה־לִּי בָנִים וְאִם־אַיִן מֵתָה אָנֹכִי׃ וַיִּחַר־
and-he-burned (2) I dying not and-if children to-me give! Jacob to so-she-said

out this daughter's bridal week; then we will give you the younger one also, in return for another seven years of work."

28And Jacob did so. He finished out the week with Leah, and then Laban gave him his daughter Rachel to be his wife. 29Laban gave his servant girl Bilhah to his daughter Rachel as her maidservant. 30Jacob lay with Rachel also, and he loved Rachel more than Leah. And he worked for Laban another seven years.

*Jacob's Children*

31When the LORD saw that Leah was not loved, he opened her womb, but Rachel was barren. 32Leah became pregnant and gave birth to a son. She named him Reuben,[a] for she said, "It is because the LORD has seen my misery. Surely my husband will love me now."

33She conceived again, and when she gave birth to a son she said, "Because the LORD heard that I am not loved, he gave me this one too." So she named him Simeon.[b]

34Again she conceived, and when she gave birth to a son she said, "Now at last my husband will become attached to me, because I have borne him three sons." So he was named Levi.[c]

35She conceived again, and when she gave birth to a son she said, "This time I will praise the LORD." So she named him Judah.[d] Then she stopped having children.

30 When Rachel saw that she was not bearing Jacob any children, she became jealous of her sister. So she said to Jacob, "Give me children, or I'll die!"

[a]32 *Reuben* sounds like the Hebrew for *he has seen my misery;* the name means *see, a son*
[b]33 *Simeon* probably means *one who hears*
[c]34 *Levi* sounds like and may be derived from the Hebrew for *attached.*
[d]35 *Judah* sounds like and may be derived from the Hebrew for *praise.*

אַף יַעֲקֹב בְּרָחֵל וַיֹּאמֶר הֲתַחַת אֱלֹהִים אָנֹכִי אֲשֶׁר־מָנַע מִמֵּךְ

from-you he-kept who I God in-place-of? and-he-said at-Rachel Jacob anger-of

פְּרִי־בָטֶן׃ וַתֹּאמֶר הִנֵּה אֲמָתִי בִלְהָה בֹּא אֵלֶיהָ

with-her sleep! Bilhah maidservant-of-me see! then-she-said (3) womb fruit-of

וְתֵלֵד עַל־בִּרְכַּי וְאִבָּנֶה גַם־אָנֹכִי מִמֶּנָּה׃

through-her I also so-I-can-build knees-of-me at so-she-can-bear

וַתִּתֶּן־לוֹ אֶת־בִּלְהָה שִׁפְחָתָהּ לְאִשָּׁה וַיָּבֹא אֵלֶיהָ

with-her and-he-slept as-wife servant-of-her Bilhah *** to-him so-she-gave (4)

יַעֲקֹב׃ וַתַּהַר בִּלְהָה וַתֵּלֶד לְיַעֲקֹב בֵּן׃ וַתֹּאמֶר

and-she-said (6) son to-Jacob and-she-bore Bilhah and-she-conceived (5) Jacob

רָחֵל דָּנַנִּי אֱלֹהִים וְגַם שָׁמַע בְּקֹלִי וַיִּתֶּן־

and-he-gave to-plea-of-me he-listened and-also God he-vindicated-me Rachel

לִי בֵּן עַל־כֵּן קָרְאָה שְׁמוֹ דָּן׃ וַתַּהַר עוֹד

again and-she-conceived (7) Dan name-of-him she-called this for son to-me

וַתֵּלֶד בִּלְהָה שִׁפְחַת רָחֵל בֵּן שֵׁנִי לְיַעֲקֹב׃ וַתֹּאמֶר

and-she-said (8) to-Jacob second son Rachel servant-of Bilhah and-she-bore

רָחֵל נַפְתּוּלֵי אֱלֹהִים ׀ נִפְתַּלְתִּי עִם־אֲחֹתִי גַּם־יָכֹלְתִּי

I-won indeed sister-of-me with I-struggled great-ones struggles-of Rachel

וַתִּקְרָא שְׁמוֹ נַפְתָּלִי׃ וַתֵּרֶא לֵאָה כִּי עָמְדָה

she-stopped that Leah when-she-saw (9) Naphtali name-of-him so-she-called

מִלֶּדֶת וַתִּקַּח אֶת־זִלְפָּה שִׁפְחָתָהּ וַתִּתֵּן אֹתָהּ

her and-she-gave maidservant-of-her Zilpah *** then-she-took from-to-bear

לְיַעֲקֹב לְאִשָּׁה׃ וַתֵּלֶד זִלְפָּה שִׁפְחַת לֵאָה לְיַעֲקֹב בֵּן׃

son to-Jacob Leah servant-of Zilpah and-she-bore (10) as-wife to-Jacob

וַתֹּאמֶר לֵאָה בְּגָד וַתִּקְרָא אֶת־שְׁמוֹ גָּד׃

Gad name-of-him *** so-she-called *what-good-fortune Leah then-she-said (11)

וַתֵּלֶד זִלְפָּה שִׁפְחַת לֵאָה בֵּן שֵׁנִי לְיַעֲקֹב׃ וַתֹּאמֶר

and-she-said (13) to-Jacob second son Leah servant-of Zilpah and-she-bore (12)

לֵאָה בְּאָשְׁרִי כִּי אִשְּׁרוּנִי בָּנוֹת וַתִּקְרָא אֶת־

*** so-she-called women they-will-call-happy-me now how-happy-I Leah

שְׁמוֹ אָשֵׁר׃ וַיֵּלֶךְ רְאוּבֵן בִּימֵי קְצִיר־חִטִּים

wheat harvest-of in-days-of Reuben and-he-went-out (14) Asher name-of-him

וַיִּמְצָא דוּדָאִים בַּשָּׂדֶה וַיָּבֵא אֹתָם אֶל־לֵאָה אִמּוֹ

mother-of-him Leah to them and-he-brought in-the-field mandrakes and-he-found

וַתֹּאמֶר רָחֵל אֶל־לֵאָה תְּנִי־נָא לִי מִדּוּדָאֵי בְּנֵךְ׃

son-of-you from-mandrakes-of to-me now! give! Leah to Rachel and-she-said

וַתֹּאמֶר לָהּ הַמְעַט קַחְתֵּךְ אֶת־אִישִׁי וְלָקַחַת

now-you-take husband-of-me *** to-take-you enough? to-her but-she-said (15)

2 Jacob became angry with her and said, "Am I in the place of God, who has kept you from having children?"

3 Then she said, "Here is Bilhah, my maidservant. Sleep with her so that she can bear children for me and that through her I too can build a family."

4 So she gave him her servant Bilhah as a wife. Jacob slept with her, 5 and she became pregnant and bore him a son. 6 Then Rachel said, "God has vindicated me; he has listened to my plea and given me a son." Because of this she named him Dan.[g]

7 Rachel's servant Bilhah conceived again and bore Jacob a second son. 8 Then Rachel said, "I have had a great struggle with my sister, and I have won." So she named him Naphtali.[h]

9 When Leah saw that she had stopped having children, she took her maidservant Zilpah and gave her to Jacob as a wife. 10 Leah's servant Zilpah bore Jacob a son. 11 Then Leah said, "What good fortune!"[i] So she named him Gad.[j]

12 Leah's servant Zilpah bore Jacob a second son. 13 Then Leah said, "How happy I am! The women will call me happy." So she named him Asher.[k]

14 During wheat harvest, Reuben went out into the fields and found some mandrake plants, which he brought to his mother Leah. Rachel said to Leah, "Please give me some of your son's mandrakes."

15 But she said to her, "Wasn't it enough that you took away my husband? Will

[g] 6 *Dan here means he has vindicated*
[h] 8 *Naphtali means my struggle*
[i] 11 *Or "A troop is coming!"*
[j] 11 *Gad can mean good fortune or a troop.*
[k] 13 *Asher means happy.*

°11 ק בא גד

*11 *good-fortune he-came* (*Qere* translation)

גַּם אֶת־ דּוּדָאֵי בְּנִי וַתֹּאמֶר רָחֵל לָכֵן יִשְׁכַּב
he-can-sleep very-well Rachel and-she-said son-of-me mandrakes-of *** also

עִמָּךְ הַלַּיְלָה תַּחַת דּוּדָאֵי בְנֵךְ׃ וַיָּבֹא יַעֲקֹב
Jacob when-he-came-in (16) son-of-you mandrakes-of for the-night with-you

מִן־ הַשָּׂדֶה בָּעֶרֶב וַתֵּצֵא לֵאָה לִקְרָאתוֹ וַתֹּאמֶר
and-she-said to-meet-him Leah then-she-went-out in-the-evening the-field from

אֵלַי תָּבוֹא כִּי שָׂכֹר שְׂכַרְתִּיךָ בְּדוּדָאֵי בְּנִי
son-of-me with-mandrakes-of I-hired-you to-hire for you-must-sleep with-me

וַיִּשְׁכַּב עִמָּהּ בַּלַּיְלָה הוּא׃ וַיִּשְׁמַע אֱלֹהִים אֶל־לֵאָה
Leah to God and-he-listened (17) that in-the-night with-her so-he-slept

וַתַּהַר וַתֵּלֶד לְיַעֲקֹב בֵּן חֲמִישִׁי׃ וַתֹּאמֶר לֵאָה
Leah then-she-said (18) fifth son to-Jacob and-she-bore and-she-conceived

נָתַן אֱלֹהִים שְׂכָרִי אֲשֶׁר־ נָתַתִּי שִׁפְחָתִי לְאִישִׁי
to-husband-of-me maidservant-of-me I-gave for reward-of-me God he-gave

וַתִּקְרָא שְׁמוֹ יִשָּׂשכָר׃ וַתַּהַר עוֹד לֵאָה
Leah again and-she-conceived (19) Issachar name-of-him so-she-called

וַתֵּלֶד בֵּן־ שִׁשִּׁי לְיַעֲקֹב׃* וַתֹּאמֶר לֵאָה זְבָדַנִי אֱלֹהִים ׀
God he-presented-me Leah and-she-said (20) to-Jacob sixth son and-she-bore

אֹתִי זֵבֶד טוֹב הַפַּעַם יִזְבְּלֵנִי אִישִׁי כִּי־יָלַדְתִּי לוֹ
to-him I-bore for husband-of-me he-will-honor-me the-time precious gift me

שִׁשָּׁה בָנִים וַתִּקְרָא אֶת־ שְׁמוֹ זְבֻלוּן׃ וְאַחַר יָלְדָה
she-bore and-later (21) Zebulun name-of-him *** so-she-called sons six

בַּת וַתִּקְרָא אֶת־ שְׁמָהּ דִּינָה׃ וַיִּזְכֹּר אֱלֹהִים
God then-he-remembered (22) Dinah name-of-her *** and-she-called daughter

אֶת־ רָחֵל וַיִּשְׁמַע אֵלֶיהָ אֱלֹהִים וַיִּפְתַּח אֶת־ רַחְמָהּ׃
womb-of-her *** and-he-opened God to-her and-he-listened Rachel ***

וַתַּהַר וַתֵּלֶד בֵּן וַתֹּאמֶר אָסַף אֱלֹהִים אֶת־
*** God he-took-away and-she-said son and-she-bore so-she-conceived (23)

חֶרְפָּתִי׃ וַתִּקְרָא אֶת־ שְׁמוֹ יוֹסֵף לֵאמֹר יֹסֵף
may-he-add to-say Joseph name-of-him *** so-she-called (24) disgrace-of-me

יְהוָה לִי בֵּן אַחֵר׃ וַיְהִי כַּאֲשֶׁר יָלְדָה רָחֵל אֶת־ יוֹסֵף
Joseph *** Rachel she-bore after and-he-was (25) another son to-me Yahweh

וַיֹּאמֶר יַעֲקֹב אֶל־ לָבָן שַׁלְּחֵנִי וְאֵלְכָה אֶל־ מְקוֹמִי
home-of-me to so-I-can-go sent-away-me! Laban to Jacob that-he-said

וּלְאַרְצִי׃ תְּנָה אֶת־ נָשַׁי וְאֶת־ יְלָדַי אֲשֶׁר
for-whom children-of-me and wives-of-me *** give! (26) and-to-land-of-me

עָבַדְתִּי אֹתְךָ בָּהֵן וְאֵלֵכָה כִּי אַתָּה יָדַעְתָּ אֶת־ עֲבֹדָתִי אֲשֶׁר
that work-of-me *** you-know you for and-I-will-go for-them you I-served

you take my son's mandrakes too?"

"Very well," Rachel said, "he can sleep with you tonight in return for your son's mandrakes."

[16]So when Jacob came in from the fields that evening, Leah went out to meet him. "You must sleep with me," she said. "I have hired you with my son's mandrakes." So he slept with her that night.

[17]God listened to Leah, and she became pregnant and bore Jacob a fifth son. [18]Then Leah said, "God has rewarded me for giving my maidservant to my husband." So she named him Issachar.[m]

[19]Leah conceived again and bore Jacob a sixth son. [20]Then Leah said, "God has presented me with a precious gift. This time my husband will treat me with honor, because I have borne him six sons." So she named him Zebulun.[n]

[21]Some time later she gave birth to a daughter and named her Dinah.

[22]Then God remembered Rachel; he listened to her and opened her womb. [23]She became pregnant and gave birth to a son and said, "God has taken away my disgrace." [24]She named him Joseph,[o] and said, "May the LORD add to me another son."

### *Jacob's Flocks Increase*

[25]After Rachel gave birth to Joseph, Jacob said to Laban, "Send me on my way so I can go back to my own homeland. [26]Give me my wives and children, for whom I have served you, and I will be on my way. You know how much work

[m]18 *Issachar* sounds like the Hebrew for *reward*
[n]20 *Zebulun* probably means *honor.*
[o]24 *Joseph* means *may he add.*

*19 Most mss have no *dagesh* in the *lamed* (לִ).

עֲבַדְתִּיךָ׃ (27) וַיֹּאמֶר אֵלָיו לָבָן אִם־ נָא מָצָאתִי חֵן
favor I-found now! if Laban to-him but-he-said (27) I-did-for-you

בְּעֵינֶיךָ נִחַשְׁתִּי וַיְבָרְכֵנִי יְהוָה בִּגְלָלֶךָ׃
because-of-you Yahweh that-he-blessed-me I-learned-by-divination in-eyes-of-you

(28) וַיֹּאמַר נָקְבָה שְׂכָרְךָ עָלַי וְאֶתֵּנָה׃ (29) וַיֹּאמֶר
and-he-said (29) and-I-will-pay to-me wage-of-you name! and-he-said (28)

אֵלָיו אַתָּה יָדַעְתָּ אֵת אֲשֶׁר עֲבַדְתִּיךָ וְאֵת אֲשֶׁר־ הָיָה מִקְנְךָ
stock-of-you he-fared how and I-worked-for-you how *** you-know you to-him

אִתִּי׃ (30) כִּי מְעַט אֲשֶׁר־ הָיָה לְךָ לְפָנַי וַיִּפְרֹץ
now-he-increased before-me to-you he-was that little indeed (30) with-me

לָרֹב וַיְבָרֶךְ יְהוָה אֹתְךָ לְרַגְלִי וְעַתָּה מָתַי אֶעֱשֶׂה
can-I-do when? but-now at-feet-of-me you Yahweh and-he-blessed to-be-great

גַם־ אָנֹכִי לְבֵיתִי׃ (31) וַיֹּאמֶר מָה אֶתֶּן־ לָךְ
to-you shall-I-give what? and-he-asked (31) for-household-of-me I also

וַיֹּאמֶר יַעֲקֹב לֹא־ תִתֶּן־ לִי מְאוּמָה אִם־ תַּעֲשֶׂה־ לִּי
for-me you-do but-if anything to-me you-give not Jacob and-he-replied

הַדָּבָר הַזֶּה אָשׁוּבָה אֶרְעֶה צֹאנְךָ אֶשְׁמֹר׃
I-will-watch flock-of-you I-will-tend I-will-go-on the-this the-thing

(32) אֶעֱבֹר בְּכָל־ צֹאנְךָ הַיּוֹם הָסֵר מִשָּׁם
from-there to-remove the-day flock-of-you through-all-of let-me-go (32)

כָּל־ שֶׂה ׀ נָקֹד וְטָלוּא וְכָל־ שֶׂה־ חוּם בַּכְּשָׂבִים
from-the-lambs dark sheep and-every-of or-being-spotted specked sheep every-of

וְטָלוּא וְנָקֹד בָּעִזִּים וְהָיָה שְׂכָרִי׃
wage-of-me and-he-will-be from-the-goats or-speckled and-being-spotted

(33) וְעָנְתָה־ בִּי צִדְקָתִי בְּיוֹם מָחָר כִּי־ תָבוֹא
you-check when future in-day honesty-of-me for-me and-she-will-testify (33)

עַל־ שְׂכָרִי לְפָנֶיךָ כֹּל אֲשֶׁר־ אֵינֶנּוּ נָקֹד וְטָלוּא
or-being-spotted speckled not-he that all before-you wage-of-me on

בָּעִזִּים וְחוּם בַּכְּשָׂבִים גָּנוּב הוּא אִתִּי׃
with-me he being-stolen from-the-lambs or-dark from-the-goats

(34) וַיֹּאמֶר לָבָן הֵן לוּ יְהִי כִדְבָרֶךָ׃ (35) וַיָּסַר
so-he-removed (35) as-word-of-you let-him-be now! agreed Laban so-he-said (34)

בַּיּוֹם הַהוּא אֶת־ הַתְּיָשִׁים הָעֲקֻדִּים וְהַטְּלֻאִים
or-the-being-spotted-ones the-streaked-ones the-male-goats *** the-that on-the-day

וְאֵת כָּל־ הָעִזִּים הַנְּקֻדּוֹת וְהַטְּלֻאֹת כֹּל
all or-the-being-spotted-ones the-speckled-ones the-female-goats all-of and

אֲשֶׁר־ לָבָן בּוֹ וְכָל־ חוּם בַּכְּשָׂבִים וַיִּתֵּן בְּיַד־
in-hand-of and-he-placed from-the-lambs dark and-every-of on-him white that

I've done for you."

27But Laban said to him, "If I have found favor in your eyes, please stay. I have learned by divination that[p] the LORD has blessed me because of you." 28He added, "Name your wages, and I will pay them."

29Jacob said to him, "You know how I have worked for you and how your livestock has fared under my care. 30The little you had before I came has increased greatly, and the LORD has blessed you wherever I have been. But now, when may I do something for my own household?"

31"What shall I give you?" he asked.

"Don't give me anything," Jacob replied. "But if you will do this one thing for me, I will go on tending your flocks and watching over them: 32Let me go through all your flocks today and remove from them every speckled or spotted sheep, every dark-colored lamb and every spotted or speckled goat. They will be my wages. 33And my honesty will testify for me in the future, whenever you check on the wages you have paid me. Any goat in my possession that is not speckled or spotted, or any lamb that is not dark-colored will be considered stolen."

34"Agreed," said Laban. "Let it be as you have said." 35That same day he removed all the male goats that were streaked or spotted, and all the speckled or spotted female goats (all that had white on them) and all the dark-colored lambs, and he placed them in the care of

p27 Or possibly *have become rich and*

בָּנָיו׃ וַיָּשֶׂם דֶּרֶךְ שְׁלֹשֶׁת יָמִים בֵּינוֹ וּבֵין

and-between between-him days three-of journey-of then-he-put (36) sons-of-him

יַעֲקֹב וְיַעֲקֹב רֹעֶה אֶת־ צֹאן לָבָן הַנּוֹתָרֹת׃ וַיִּקַּח־

and-he-took (37) the-ones-being-left Laban flock-of *** tending and-Jacob Jacob

לוֹ יַעֲקֹב מַקַּל לִבְנֶה לַח וְלוּז וְעֶרְמוֹן וַיְפַצֵּל

and-he-peeled and-plane and-almond fresh-cut poplar from-branch-of Jacob to-him

בָּהֵן פְּצָלוֹת לְבָנוֹת מַחְשֹׂף הַלָּבָן אֲשֶׁר עַל־ הַמַּקְלוֹת׃

the-branches in that the-white exposed white-ones stripes in-them

וַיַּצֵּג אֶת־ הַמַּקְלוֹת אֲשֶׁר פִּצֵּל בָּרְהָטִים בְּשִׁקֲתוֹת

in-troughs-of in-the-troughs he-peeled that the-branches *** then-he-placed (38)

הַמָּיִם אֲשֶׁר תָּבֹאןָ הַצֹּאן לִשְׁתּוֹת לְנֹכַח הַצֹּאן

the-flock in-front-of to-drink the-flock they-came where the-water

וַיֵּחַמְנָה בְּבֹאָן לִשְׁתּוֹת׃ וַיֶּחֱמוּ הַצֹּאן

the-flock and-they-mated (39) to-drink when-to-come-them as-they-were-in-heat

אֶל־ הַמַּקְלוֹת וַתֵּלַדְןָ הַצֹּאן עֲקֻדִּים נְקֻדִּים

speckled-ones streaked-ones the-flock and-they-bore the-branches by

וּטְלֻאִים׃ וְהַכְּשָׂבִים הִפְרִיד יַעֲקֹב וַיִּתֵּן

but-he-made Jacob he-set-apart and-the-young-ones (40) and-being-spotted-ones

פְּנֵי הַצֹּאן אֶל־ עָקֹד וְכָל־ חוּם בְּצֹאן לָבָן וַיָּשֶׁת־

thus-he-made Laban in-flock-of dark and-all-of streaked to the-flock faces-of

לוֹ עֲדָרִים לְבַדּוֹ וְלֹא שָׁתָם עַל־ צֹאן לָבָן׃

Laban flock-of with he-put-them and-not for-himself flocks for-him

וְהָיָה בְּכָל־ יַחֵם הַצֹּאן הַמְקֻשָּׁרוֹת

the-ones-being-stronger the-female to-be-in-heat when-ever and-he-was (41)

וְשָׂם יַעֲקֹב אֶת־ הַמַּקְלוֹת לְעֵינֵי הַצֹּאן בָּרְהָטִים

in-the-troughs the-animal in-front-of the-branches *** Jacob that-he-placed

לְיַחְמֶנָּה בַּמַּקְלוֹת׃ וּבְהַעֲטִיף הַצֹּאן לֹא

not the-animal but-if-to-be-weak (42) near-the-branches to-mate-them

יָשִׂים וְהָיָה הָעֲטֻפִים לְלָבָן וְהַקְּשֻׁרִים

and-the-ones-being-strong to-Laban the-ones-being-weak so-he-was he-placed

לְיַעֲקֹב׃ וַיִּפְרֹץ הָאִישׁ מְאֹד מְאֹד וַיְהִי־ לוֹ

to-him and-he-was greatly greatly the-man so-he-prospered (43) to-Jacob

צֹאן רַבּוֹת וּשְׁפָחוֹת וַעֲבָדִים וּגְמַלִּים וַחֲמֹרִים׃

and-donkeys and-camels and-menservants and-maidservants large-ones flock

וַיִּשְׁמַע אֶת־ דִּבְרֵי בְנֵי־ לָבָן לֵאמֹר לָקַח יַעֲקֹב אֵת

*** Jacob he-took to-say Laban sons-of words-of *** now-he-heard (31:1)

כָּל־ אֲשֶׁר לְאָבִינוּ וּמֵאֲשֶׁר לְאָבִינוּ עָשָׂה אֵת כָּל־

all-of *** he-gained to-father-of-us and-from-what to-father-of-us that all

his sons. [36]Then he put a three-day journey between himself and Jacob, while Jacob continued to tend the rest of Laban's flocks.

[37]Jacob, however, took fresh-cut branches from poplar, almond and plane trees and made white stripes on them by peeling the bark and exposing the white inner wood of the branches. [38]Then he placed the peeled branches in all the watering troughs, so that they would be directly in front of the flocks when they came to drink. When the flocks were in heat and came to drink, [39]they mated in front of the branches. And they bore young that were streaked or speckled or spotted. [40]Jacob set apart the young of the flock by themselves, but made the rest face the streaked and dark-colored animals that belonged to Laban. Thus he made separate flocks for himself and did not put them with Laban's animals. [41]Whenever the stronger females were in heat, Jacob would place the branches in the troughs in front of the animals so they would mate near the branches, [42]but if the animals were weak, he would not place them there. So the weak animals went to Laban and the strong ones to Jacob. [43]In this way the man grew exceedingly prosperous and came to own large flocks, and maidservants and menservants, and camels and donkeys.

*Jacob Flees From Laban*

31 Jacob heard that Laban's sons were saying, "Jacob has taken everything our father owned and has gained all this wealth

הַכָּבֹד הַזֶּה׃ וַיַּרְא יַעֲקֹב אֶת־ פְּנֵי לָבָן וְהִנֵּה
and-see! Laban attitudes-of *** Jacob and-he-noticed (2) the-this the-wealth

אֵינֶנּוּ עִמּוֹ כִּתְמוֹל שִׁלְשׁוֹם׃ וַיֹּאמֶר יְהוָה אֶל־ יַעֲקֹב שׁוּב
go-back! Jacob to Yahweh then-he-said (3) formerly as-before with-him not-he

אֶל־ אֶרֶץ אֲבוֹתֶיךָ וּלְמוֹלַדְתֶּךָ וְאֶהְיֶה עִמָּךְ׃
with-you and-I-will-be and-to-relative-of-you fathers-of-you land-of to

וַיִּשְׁלַח יַעֲקֹב וַיִּקְרָא לְרָחֵל וּלְלֵאָה הַשָּׂדֶה אֶל־
to the-field and-to-Leah to-Rachel and-he-called Jacob so-he-sent (4)

צֹאנוֹ׃ וַיֹּאמֶר לָהֶן רֹאֶה אָנֹכִי אֶת־ פְּנֵי אֲבִיכֶן
father-of-you attitudes-of *** I seeing to-them and-he-said (5) flock-of-him

כִּי־ אֵינֶנּוּ אֵלַי כִּתְמֹל שִׁלְשֹׁם וֵאלֹהֵי אָבִי הָיָה עִמָּדִי׃
with-me he-is father-of-me but-God-of formerly as-before to-me not-he that

וְאַתֵּנָה יְדַעְתֶּן כִּי בְּכָל־ כֹּחִי עָבַדְתִּי אֶת־ אֲבִיכֶן׃
father-of-you *** I-served strength-of-me with-all-of that you-know now-you (6)

וַאֲבִיכֶן הֵתֶל בִּי וְהֶחֱלִף אֶת־ מַשְׂכֻּרְתִּי
wage-of-me *** and-he-changed with-me he-cheated yet-father-of-you (7)

עֲשֶׂרֶת מֹנִים וְלֹא־ נְתָנוֹ אֱלֹהִים לְהָרַע עִמָּדִי׃ אִם־כֹּה יֹאמַר
he-said thus if (8) to-me to-do-harm God he-allowed-him but-not times ten-of

נְקֻדִּים יִהְיֶה שְׂכָרֶךָ וְיָלְדוּ כָל־ הַצֹּאן
the-flock all-of then-they-bore wage-of-you he-will-be speckled-ones

נְקֻדִּים וְאִם־ כֹּה יֹאמַר עֲקֻדִּים יִהְיֶה שְׂכָרֶךָ
wage-of-you he-will-be streaked-ones he-said thus and-if speckled-ones

וְיָלְדוּ כָל־ הַצֹּאן עֲקֻדִּים׃ וַיַּצֵּל אֱלֹהִים אֶת־ מִקְנֵה
stock-of *** God so-he-took (9) streaked-ones the-flock all-of then-they-bore

אֲבִיכֶם וַיִּתֶּן־ לִי׃ וַיְהִי בְּעֵת יַחֵם
to-breed in-season-of now-he-was (10) to-me and-he-gave father-of-you

הַצֹּאן וָאֶשָּׂא עֵינַי וָאֵרֶא בַּחֲלוֹם וְהִנֵּה הָעַתֻּדִים
the-male-goats and-see! in-dream and-I-saw eyes-of-me that-I-lifted the-flock

הָעֹלִים עַל־ הַצֹּאן עֲקֻדִּים נְקֻדִּים וּבְרֻדִּים׃
or-spotted-ones speckled-ones streaked-ones the-flock with the-ones-mating

וַיֹּאמֶר אֵלַי מַלְאַךְ הָאֱלֹהִים בַּחֲלוֹם יַעֲקֹב וָאֹמַר הִנֵּנִי׃
here-I and-I-answered Jacob in-dream the-God angel-of to-me and-he-said (11)

וַיֹּאמֶר שָׂא־ נָא עֵינֶיךָ וּרְאֵה כָּל־ הָעַתֻּדִים
the-male-goats all-of and-see! eyes-of-you now! lift! and-he-said (12)

הָעֹלִים עַל־ הַצֹּאן עֲקֻדִּים נְקֻדִּים וּבְרֻדִּים
or-spotted-ones speckled-ones streaked-ones the-flock with the-ones-mating

כִּי רָאִיתִי אֵת כָּל־אֲשֶׁר לָבָן עֹשֶׂה לָּךְ׃ אָנֹכִי הָאֵל בֵּית־אֵל אֲשֶׁר
where El Beth the-God I (13) to-you he-did Laban that all *** I-saw for

from what belonged to our father." 2And Jacob noticed that Laban's attitude toward him was not what it had been.

3Then the LORD said to Jacob, "Go back to the land of your fathers and to your relatives, and I will be with you."

4So Jacob sent word to Rachel and Leah to come out to the fields where his flocks were. 5He said to them, "I see that your father's attitude toward me is not what it was before, but the God of my father has been with me. 6You know that I've worked for your father with all my strength, 7yet your father has cheated me by changing my wages ten times. However, God has not allowed him to harm me. 8If he said, 'The speckled ones will be your wages,' then all the flocks gave birth to speckled young; and if he said, 'The streaked ones will be your wages,' then all the flocks bore streaked young. 9So God has taken away your father's livestock and has given them to me.

10"In breeding season I once had a dream in which I looked up and saw that the male goats mating with the flock were streaked, speckled or spotted. 11The angel of God said to me in the dream, 'Jacob.' I answered, 'Here I am.' 12And he said, 'Look up and see that all the male goats mating with the flock are streaked, speckled or spotted, for I have seen all that Laban has been doing to you. 13I am the God of Bethel,

מָשַׁחְתָּ שָּׁם מַצֵּבָה אֲשֶׁר נָדַרְתָּ לִּי שָׁם נֶדֶר עַתָּה קוּם צֵא
leave! rise! now! vow there to-me you-vowed where pillar there you-anointed

מִן־הָאָרֶץ הַזֹּאת וְשׁוּב אֶל־אֶרֶץ מוֹלַדְתֶּךָ׃ וַתַּעַן
so-she-replied (14) birth-of-you land-of to and-go-back! the-this the-land from

רָחֵל וְלֵאָה וַתֹּאמַרְנָה לוֹ הַעוֹד לָנוּ חֵלֶק וְנַחֲלָה
and-inheritance share to-us still? to-him and-they-said and-Leah Rachel

בְּבֵית אָבִינוּ׃ הֲלוֹא נָכְרִיּוֹת נֶחְשַׁבְנוּ לוֹ כִּי
for by-him we-are-regarded foreigners not? (15) father-of-us in-estate-of

מְכָרָנוּ וַיֹּאכַל גַּם־אָכוֹל אֶת־כַּסְפֵּנוּ׃ כִּי כָל־
all-of surely (16) pay-of-us *** to-use indeed and-he-used he-sold-us

הָעֹשֶׁר אֲשֶׁר הִצִּיל אֱלֹהִים מֵאָבִינוּ לָנוּ הוּא וּלְבָנֵינוּ
and-to-children-of-us that to-us from-father-of-us God he-took that the-wealth

וְעַתָּה כֹּל אֲשֶׁר אָמַר אֱלֹהִים אֵלֶיךָ עֲשֵׂה׃ וַיָּקָם יַעֲקֹב וַיִּשָּׂא אֶת־
*** and-he-put Jacob so-he-rose (17) do! to-you god he-told that all and-now

בָּנָיו וְאֶת־נָשָׁיו עַל־הַגְּמַלִּים׃ וַיִּנְהַג אֶת־כָּל־
all-of *** and-he-drove (18) the-camels on wives-of-him and children-of-him

מִקְנֵהוּ וְאֶת־כָּל־רְכֻשׁוֹ אֲשֶׁר רָכָשׁ מִקְנֵה
livestock-of he-accumulated that good-of-him all-of and stock-of-him

קִנְיָנוֹ אֲשֶׁר רָכַשׁ בְּפַדַּן אֲרָם לָבוֹא אֶל־יִצְחָק
Isaac to to-go Aram in-Paddan he-accumulated that possession-of-him

אָבִיו אַרְצָה כְּנָעַן׃ וְלָבָן הָלַךְ לִגְזֹז אֶת־
*** to-shear he-went when-Laban (19) Canaan to-land-of father-of-him

צֹאנוֹ וַתִּגְנֹב רָחֵל אֶת־הַתְּרָפִים אֲשֶׁר לְאָבִיהָ׃
to-father-of-her that the-gods *** Rachel then-she-stole sheep-of-him

וַיִּגְנֹב יַעֲקֹב אֶת־לֵב לָבָן הָאֲרַמִּי עַל־בְּלִי הִגִּיד
to-tell not by the-Aramean Laban heart-of *** Jacob and-he-deceived (20)

לוֹ כִּי בֹרֵחַ הוּא׃ וַיִּבְרַח הוּא וְכָל־אֲשֶׁר־לוֹ
to-him that with-all he so-he-fled (21) he running-away that to-him

וַיָּקָם וַיַּעֲבֹר אֶת־הַנָּהָר וַיָּשֶׂם אֶת־פָּנָיו
face-of-him *** and-he-headed the-river *** and-he-crossed and-he-rose

הַר הַגִּלְעָד׃ וַיֻּגַּד לְלָבָן בַּיּוֹם הַשְּׁלִישִׁי
the-third on-the-day to-Laban and-he-was-told (22) the-Gilead hill-country-of

כִּי בָרַח יַעֲקֹב׃ וַיִּקַּח אֶת־אֶחָיו עִמּוֹ וַיִּרְדֹּף
and-he-pursued with-him relatives-of-him *** so-he-took (23) Jacob he-fled that

אַחֲרָיו דֶּרֶךְ שִׁבְעַת יָמִים וַיַּדְבֵּק אֹתוֹ בְּהַר הַגִּלְעָד׃
the-Gilead in-hill-of him and-he-caught days seven-of journey-of after-him

וַיָּבֹא אֱלֹהִים אֶל־לָבָן הָאֲרַמִּי בַּחֲלֹם הַלָּיְלָה וַיֹּאמֶר
and-he-said the-night in-dream-of the-Aramean Laban to God then-he-came (24)

where you anointed a pillar and where you made a vow to me. Now leave this land at once and go back to your native land.' "

14 Then Rachel and Leah replied, "Do we still have any share in the inheritance of our father's estate? 15 Does he not regard us as foreigners? Not only has he sold us, but he has used up what was paid for us. 16 Surely all the wealth that God took away from our father belongs to us and our children. So do whatever God has told you."

17 Then Jacob put his children and his wives on camels, 18 and he drove all his livestock ahead of him, along with all the goods he had accumulated in Paddan Aram,[q] to go to his father Isaac in the land of Canaan.

19 When Laban had gone to shear his sheep, Rachel stole her father's household gods. 20 Moreover, Jacob deceived Laban the Aramean by not telling him he was running away. 21 So he fled with all he had, and crossing the River,[r] he headed for the hill country of Gilead.

*Laban Pursues Jacob*

22 On the third day Laban was told that Jacob had fled. 23 Taking his relatives with him, he pursued Jacob for seven days and caught up with him in the hill country of Gilead. 24 Then God came to Laban the Aramean in a dream at night and said to him, "Be

[q]18 That is, Northwest Mesopotamia
[r]21 That is, the Euphrates

לוֹ הִשָּׁמֶר לְךָ פֶּן־ תְּדַבֵּר עִם־ יַעֲקֹב מִטּוֹב עַד־ רָע׃
bad or either-good Jacob to you-say that-not yourself be-careful! to-him

(25) וַיַּשֵּׂג לָבָן אֶת־ יַעֲקֹב וְיַעֲקֹב תָּקַע אֶת־ אָהֳלוֹ
tent-of-him *** he-pitched now-Jacob Jacob *** Laban when-he-overtook (25)

בָּהָר וְלָבָן תָּקַע אֶת־ אֶחָיו בְּהַר
in-hill-country-of relatives-of-him with he-camped so-Laban on-the-hill

הַגִּלְעָד׃ (26) וַיֹּאמֶר לָבָן לְיַעֲקֹב מֶה עָשִׂיתָ וַתִּגְנֹב
now-you-deceived you-did what? to-Jacob Laban then-he-said (26) the-Gilead

אֶת־ לְבָבִי וַתְּנַהֵג אֶת־ בְּנֹתַי כִּשְׁבֻיוֹת
like-being-captives-of daughters-of-me *** and-you-carried-off heart-of-me ***

חָרֶב׃ (27) לָמָּה נַחְבֵּאתָ לִבְרֹחַ וַתִּגְנֹב אֹתִי וְלֹא־ הִגַּדְתָּ
you-tell and-not me and-you-deceive to-run-off you-were-secret why? (27) sword

לִּי וָאֲשַׁלֵּחֲךָ בְּשִׂמְחָה וּבְשִׁרִים בְּתֹף
with-tambourine and-with-songs with-joy so-I-could-send-away-you to-me

וּבְכִנּוֹר׃ (28) וְלֹא נְטַשְׁתַּנִי לְנַשֵּׁק לְבָנַי
on-grandchildren-of-me to-kiss you-let-me and-not (28) and-with-harp

וְלִבְנֹתָי עַתָּה הִסְכַּלְתָּ עֲשׂוֹ׃ (29) יֶשׁ־ לְאֵל יָדִי
power-of-me in it-is (29) to-do you-were-foolish now or-on-daughters-of-me

לַעֲשׂוֹת עִמָּכֶם רָע וֵאלֹהֵי אֲבִיכֶם אֶמֶשׁ ׀ אָמַר אֵלַי לֵאמֹר
to-say to-me he-spoke last-night father-of-you but-God-of harm to-you to-do

הִשָּׁמֶר לְךָ מִדַּבֵּר עִם־ יַעֲקֹב מִטּוֹב עַד־ רָע׃ (30) וְעַתָּה
and-now (30) bad nor neither-good Jacob to that-to-say yourself be-careful!

הָלֹךְ הָלַכְתָּ כִּי־ נִכְסֹף נִכְסַפְתָּה לְבֵית אָבִיךָ לָמָּה
why? father-of-you for-house-of you-longed to-long because you-went to-go

גָנַבְתָּ אֶת־ אֱלֹהָי׃ (31) וַיַּעַן יַעֲקֹב וַיֹּאמֶר לְלָבָן
to-Laban and-he-said Jacob and-he-answered (31) gods-of-me *** you-stole

כִּי יָרֵאתִי כִּי אָמַרְתִּי פֶּן־ תִּגְזֹל אֶת־
*** you-would-take-by-force that I-thought for I-was-afraid indeed

בְּנוֹתֶיךָ מֵעִמִּי׃ (32) עִם אֲשֶׁר תִּמְצָא אֶת־ אֱלֹהֶיךָ לֹא
not gods-of-you *** you-find whom with (32) from-me daughters-of-you

יִחְיֶה נֶגֶד אַחֵינוּ הַכֶּר־ לְךָ מָה עִמָּדִי וְקַח־
and-take! with-me what for-yourself see! relatives-of-us before he-shall-live

לָךְ וְלֹא־ יָדַע יַעֲקֹב כִּי רָחֵל גְּנָבָתַם׃ (33) וַיָּבֹא
so-he-went (33) she-stole-them Rachel that Jacob he-knew now-not if-yours

לָבָן בְּאֹהֶל יַעֲקֹב ׀ וּבְאֹהֶל לֵאָה וּבְאֹהֶל שְׁתֵּי
two-of and-into-tent-of Leah and-into-tent-of Jacob into-tent-of Laban

הָאֲמָהֹת וְלֹא מָצָא וַיֵּצֵא מֵאֹהֶל לֵאָה וַיָּבֹא
and-he-went Leah from-tent-of so-he-came-out he-found but-not the-maidservants

careful not to say anything to Jacob, either good or bad."

25 Jacob had pitched his tent in the hill country of Gilead when Laban overtook him, and Laban and his relatives camped there too. 26 Then Laban said to Jacob, "What have you done? You've deceived me, and you've carried off my daughters like captives in war. 27 Why did you run off secretly and deceive me? Why didn't you tell me, so I could send you away with joy and singing to the music of tambourines and harps? 28 You didn't even let me kiss my grandchildren and my daughters good-by. You have done a foolish thing. 29 I have the power to harm you; but last night the God of your father said to me, 'Be careful not to say anything to Jacob, either good or bad.' 30 Now you have gone off because you longed to return to your father's house. But why did you steal my gods?"

31 Jacob answered Laban, "I was afraid, because I thought you would take your daughters away from me by force. 32 But if you find anyone who has your gods, he shall not live. In the presence of our relatives, see for yourself whether there is anything of yours here with me; and if so, take it." Now Jacob did not know that Rachel had stolen the gods.

33 So Laban went into Jacob's tent and into Leah's tent and into the tent of the two maidservants, but he found nothing. After he came out of

בְּאֹהֶל רָחֵל׃ וְרָחֵל לָקְחָה אֶת־הַתְּרָפִים וַתְּשִׂמֵם
and-she-put-them the-gods *** she-took now-Rachel (34) Rachel into-tent-of

בְּכַר הַגָּמָל וַתֵּשֶׁב עֲלֵיהֶם וַיְמַשֵּׁשׁ לָבָן אֶת־כָּל־
all-of *** Laban and-he-searched on-them and-she-sat the-camel in-saddle-of

הָאֹהֶל וְלֹא מָצָא׃ וַתֹּאמֶר אֶל־אָבִיהָ אַל־
not father-of-her to and-she-said (35) he-found but-not the-tent

יִחַר בְּעֵינֵי אֲדֹנִי כִּי לוֹא אוּכַל לָקוּם מִפָּנֶיךָ
in-presence-of-you to-stand I-can not but lord-of-me in-eyes-of may-he-be-angry

כִּי־דֶרֶךְ נָשִׁים לִי וַיְחַפֵּשׂ וְלֹא מָצָא אֶת־הַתְּרָפִים׃
the-gods *** he-found but-not so-he-searched to-me women way-of for

וַיִּחַר לְיַעֲקֹב וַיָּרֶב בְּלָבָן וַיַּעַן יַעֲקֹב
Jacob and-he-asked at-Laban and-he-scolded to-Jacob and-he-angered (36)

וַיֹּאמֶר לְלָבָן מַה־פִּשְׁעִי מַה חַטָּאתִי כִּי דָלַקְתָּ
you-hunted that sin-of-me what? crime-of-me what? to-Laban and-he-said

אַחֲרָי׃ כִּי־מִשַּׁשְׁתָּ אֶת־כָּל־כֵּלַי מַה־מָּצָאתָ
you-found what? goods-of-me all-of *** you-searched now (37) after-me

מִכֹּל כְּלֵי־בֵיתֶךָ שִׂים כֹּה נֶגֶד אַחַי
relatives-of-me in-front-of here put! household-of-you goods-of from-any-of

וְאַחֶיךָ וְיוֹכִיחוּ בֵּין שְׁנֵינוּ׃ זֶה עֶשְׂרִים
twenty now (38) two-of-us between and-let-them-judge and-relatives-of-you

שָׁנָה אָנֹכִי עִמָּךְ רְחֵלֶיךָ וְעִזֶּיךָ לֹא שִׁכֵּלוּ וְאֵילֵי
and-rams-of they-miscarried not and-goats-of-you sheep-of-you with-you I year

צֹאנְךָ לֹא אָכָלְתִּי׃ טְרֵפָה לֹא־הֵבֵאתִי אֵלֶיךָ אָנֹכִי אֲחַטֶּנָּה
I-bore-loss-of-her I to-you I-brought not torn-animal (39) I-ate not flock-of-you

מִיָּדִי תְּבַקְשֶׁנָּה גְּנֻבְתִי יוֹם וּגְנֻבְתִי לָיְלָה׃
night or-being-stolen-of day being-stolen-of you-required-her from-hand-of-me

הָיִיתִי בַיּוֹם אֲכָלַנִי חֹרֶב וְקֶרַח בַּלָּיְלָה וַתִּדַּד
and-he-fled in-the-night and-cold heat he-consumed-me in-the-day I-was (40)

שְׁנָתִי מֵעֵינָי׃ זֶה־לִּי עֶשְׂרִים שָׁנָה בְּבֵיתֶךָ
in-household-of-you year twenty to-me this (41) from-eyes-of-me sleep-of-me

עֲבַדְתִּיךָ אַרְבַּע־עֶשְׂרֵה שָׁנָה בִּשְׁתֵּי בְנֹתֶיךָ וְשֵׁשׁ שָׁנִים
years and-six daughters-of-you for-two-of year ten four I-served-you

בְּצֹאנֶךָ וַתַּחֲלֵף אֶת־מַשְׂכֻּרְתִּי עֲשֶׂרֶת מֹנִים׃ לוּלֵי אֱלֹהֵי
God-of if-not (42) times ten wage-of-me *** and-you-changed for-flock-of-you

אָבִי אֱלֹהֵי אַבְרָהָם וּפַחַד יִצְחָק הָיָה לִי כִּי עַתָּה
now surely with-me he-was Isaac and-Fear-of Abraham God-of father-of-me

רֵיקָם שִׁלַּחְתָּנִי אֶת־עָנְיִי וְאֶת־יְגִיעַ
toil-of and hardship-of-me *** you-would-have-sent-me empty-handed

Leah's tent, he entered Rachel's tent. 34 Now Rachel had
taken the household gods and
put them inside her camel's
saddle and was sitting on
them. Laban searched through
everything in the tent but
found nothing.
35 Rachel said to her father,
"Don't be angry, my lord, that
I cannot stand up in your presence; I'm having my period."
So he searched but could not
find the household gods.
36 Jacob was angry and took
Laban to task. "What is my
crime?" he asked Laban.
"What sin have I committed
that you hunt me down?
37 Now that you have searched
through all my goods, what
have you found that belongs
to your household? Put it here
in front of your relatives and
mine, and let them judge between the two of us.
38 "I have been with you for
twenty years now. Your sheep
and goats have not miscarried,
nor have I eaten rams from
your flocks. 39 I did not bring
you animals torn by wild
beasts; I bore the loss myself.
And you demanded payment
from me for whatever was stolen by day or night. 40 This was
my situation: The heat consumed me in the daytime and
the cold at night, and sleep
fled from my eyes. 41 It was like
this for the twenty years I was
in your household. I worked
for you fourteen years for your
two daughters and six years
for your flocks, and you
changed my wages ten times.
42 If the God of my father, the
God of Abraham and the Fear
of Isaac, had not been with
me, you would surely have
sent me away empty-handed.

כַּפַּי רָאָה אֱלֹהִים וַיּוֹכַח אָמֶשׁ׃ וַיַּעַן לָבָן
Laban and-he-answered (43) last-night and-he-rebuked God he-saw hands-of-me

וַיֹּאמֶר אֶל־ יַעֲקֹב הַבָּנוֹת בְּנֹתַי וְהַבָּנִים
and-the-children daughters-of-me the-women Jacob to and-he-said

בָּנַי וְהַצֹּאן צֹאנִי וְכֹל אֲשֶׁר־ אַתָּה רֹאֶה לִי־ הוּא
he to-me seeing you that and-all flock-of-me and-the-flock children-of-me

וְלִבְנֹתַי מָה־ אֶעֱשֶׂה לָאֵלֶּה הַיּוֹם אוֹ
or the-day about-these can-I-do what? yet-about-daughters-of-me

לִבְנֵיהֶן אֲשֶׁר יָלָדוּ׃ וְעַתָּה לְכָה נִכְרְתָה בְרִית
covenant let-us-make come! so-now (44) they-bore that about-children-of-them

אֲנִי וָאָתָּה וְהָיָה לְעֵד בֵּינִי וּבֵינֶךָ׃ וַיִּקַּח
so-he-took (45) and-between-you between-me as-witness and-he-will-be and-you I

יַעֲקֹב אָבֶן וַיְרִימֶהָ מַצֵּבָה׃ וַיֹּאמֶר יַעֲקֹב לְאֶחָיו
to-relatives-of-him Jacob and-he-said (46) pillar and-he-set-up-her stone Jacob

לִקְטוּ אֲבָנִים וַיִּקְחוּ אֲבָנִים וַיַּעֲשׂוּ־ גָל וַיֹּאכְלוּ שָׁם
there and-they-ate heap and-they-made stones so-they-took stones gather!

עַל־ הַגָּל׃ וַיִּקְרָא־ לוֹ לָבָן יְגַר שָׂהֲדוּתָא וְיַעֲקֹב
and-Jacob Sahadutha Jegar Laban to-him and-he-called (47) the-heap near

קָרָא לוֹ גַּלְעֵד׃ וַיֹּאמֶר לָבָן הַגַּל הַזֶּה עֵד
witness the-this the-heap Laban and-he-said (48) Galeed to-him he-called

בֵּינִי וּבֵינְךָ הַיּוֹם עַל־ כֵּן קָרָא־ שְׁמוֹ גַּלְעֵד׃
Galeed name-of-him he-called this for the-day and-between-you between-me

וְהַמִּצְפָּה אֲשֶׁר אָמַר יִצֶף יְהוָה בֵּינִי וּבֵינֶךָ
and-between-you between-me Yahweh may-he-watch he-said for also-the-Mizpah (49)

כִּי נִסָּתֵר אִישׁ מֵרֵעֵהוּ׃ אִם־ תְּעַנֶּה אֶת־
*** you-mistreat if (50) from-other-of-him one we-are-away when

בְּנֹתַי וְאִם־ תִּקַּח נָשִׁים עַל־ בְּנֹתַי אֵין אִישׁ עִמָּנוּ
with-us man not daughters-of-me besides wives you-take or-if daughters-of-me

רְאֵה אֱלֹהִים עֵד בֵּינִי וּבֵינֶךָ׃ וַיֹּאמֶר לָבָן
Laban and-he-said (51) and-between-you between-me witness God remember!

לְיַעֲקֹב הִנֵּה ׀ הַגַּל הַזֶּה וְהִנֵּה הַמַּצֵּבָה* אֲשֶׁר יָרִיתִי בֵּינִי
between-me I-set-up that the-pillar and-see! the-this the-heap see! to-Jacob

וּבֵינֶךָ׃ עֵד הַגַּל הַזֶּה וְעֵדָה הַמַּצֵּבָה אִם־
that the-pillar and-witness the-this the-heap witness (52) and-between-you

אָנִי לֹא־ אֶעֱבֹר אֵלֶיךָ אֶת־ הַגַּל הַזֶּה וְאִם־ אַתָּה לֹא־
not you and-that the-this the-heap *** to-you I-will-go-past not I

תַעֲבֹר אֵלַי אֶת־ הַגַּל הַזֶּה וְאֶת־ הַמַּצֵּבָה הַזֹּאת לְרָעָה׃
for-harm the-this the-pillar and the-this the-heap *** to-me you-will-go-past

But God has seen my hardship and the toil of my hands, and last night he rebuked you."

43 Laban answered Jacob, "The women are my daughters, the children are my children, and the flocks are my flocks. All you see is mine. Yet what can I do today about these daughters of mine, or about the children they have borne?
44 Come now, let's make a covenant, you and I, and let it serve as a witness between us."

45 So Jacob took a stone and set it up as a pillar.
46 He said to his relatives, "Gather some stones." So they took stones and piled them in a heap, and they ate there by the heap.
47 Laban called it Jegar Sahadutha,[s] and Jacob called it Galeed.[t]

48 Laban said, "This heap is a witness between you and me today." That is why it was called Galeed.
49 It was also called Mizpah,[u] because he said, "May the LORD keep watch between you and me when we are away from each other.
50 If you mistreat my daughters or if you take any wives besides my daughters, even though no one is with us, remember that God is a witness between you and me."

51 Laban also said to Jacob, "Here is this heap, and here is this pillar I have set up between you and me.
52 This heap is a witness, and this pillar is a witness, that I will not go past this heap to your side to harm you and that you will not go past this heap and pillar to my side to harm me.
53 May

[s] 47 The Aramaic *Jegar Sahadutha* means *witness heap.*
[t] 47 The Hebrew *Galeed* means *witness heap.*
[u] 49 *Mizpah* means *watchtower.*

*51 Most mss have *dagesh* in the *mem* (הַמַּ).

אֱלֹהֵי אַבְרָהָם וֵאלֹהֵי נָחוֹר יִשְׁפְּטוּ בֵינֵינוּ אֱלֹהֵי
God-of between-us may-they-judge Nahor and-God-of Abraham God-of (53)

אֲבִיהֶם וַיִּשָּׁבַע יַעֲקֹב בְּפַחַד אָבִיו יִצְחָק׃
Isaac father-of-him by-Fear-of Jacob so-he-swore father-of-them

וַיִּזְבַּח יַעֲקֹב זֶבַח בָּהָר וַיִּקְרָא
and-he-invited in-the-hill-country sacrifice Jacob and-he-offered (54)

לְאֶחָיו לֶאֱכָל־לָחֶם וַיֹּאכְלוּ לֶחֶם וַיָּלִינוּ בָּהָר׃
on-the-hill so-they-spent-night meal so-they-ate meal to-eat to-relatives-of-him

וַיַּשְׁכֵּם לָבָן בַּבֹּקֶר וַיְנַשֵּׁק לְבָנָיו
on-grandchildren-of-him and-he-kissed in-the-morning Laban and-he-rose (32:1)*

וְלִבְנוֹתָיו וַיְבָרֶךְ אֶתְהֶם וַיֵּלֶךְ וַיָּשָׁב
and-he-returned then-he-left them and-he-blessed and-on-daughters-of-him

לָבָן לִמְקֹמוֹ׃ וְיַעֲקֹב הָלַךְ לְדַרְכּוֹ וַיִּפְגְּעוּ־בוֹ
with-him and-they-met on-way-of-him he-went and-Jacob (2) to-home-of-him Laban

מַלְאֲכֵי אֱלֹהִים׃ וַיֹּאמֶר יַעֲקֹב כַּאֲשֶׁר רָאָם מַחֲנֵה אֱלֹהִים זֶה
this God camp-of he-saw-them when Jacob and-he-said (3) God angels-of

וַיִּקְרָא שֵׁם־הַמָּקוֹם הַהוּא מַחֲנָיִם׃ וַיִּשְׁלַח יַעֲקֹב
Jacob and-he-sent (4) Mahanaim the-that the-place name-of so-he-called

מַלְאָכִים לְפָנָיו אֶל־עֵשָׂו אָחִיו אַרְצָה שֵׂעִיר שְׂדֵה אֱדוֹם׃
Edom country-of Seir to-land-of brother-of-him Esau to ahead-of-him messengers

וַיְצַו אֹתָם לֵאמֹר כֹּה תֹאמְרוּן לַאדֹנִי לְעֵשָׂו
to-Esau to-master-of-me you-will-say this to-say them and-he-instructed (5)

כֹּה אָמַר עַבְדְךָ† יַעֲקֹב עִם־לָבָן גַּרְתִּי וָאֵחַר עַד־
till and-I-remained I-stayed Laban with Jacob servant-of-you he-says this

עָתָּה׃ וַיְהִי־לִי שׁוֹר וַחֲמוֹר צֹאן וְעֶבֶד
and-menservant flock and-donkey cattle to-me and-he-is (6) now

וְשִׁפְחָה וָאֶשְׁלְחָה לְהַגִּיד לַאדֹנִי לִמְצֹא־חֵן בְּעֵינֶיךָ׃
in-eyes-of-you favor to-find to-lord-of-me to-tell and-I-sent and-maidservant

וַיָּשֻׁבוּ הַמַּלְאָכִים אֶל־יַעֲקֹב לֵאמֹר בָּאנוּ אֶל־אָחִיךָ
brother-of-you to we-went to-say Jacob to the-messengers when-they-returned (7)

אֶל־עֵשָׂו וְגַם הֹלֵךְ לִקְרָאתְךָ וְאַרְבַּע־מֵאוֹת אִישׁ עִמּוֹ׃
with-him man hundreds and-four to-meet-you coming and-now Esau to

וַיִּירָא יַעֲקֹב מְאֹד וַיֵּצֶר לוֹ וַיַּחַץ
so-he-divided himself and-he-distressed greatly Jacob and-he-was-afraid (8)

אֶת־הָעָם אֲשֶׁר־אִתּוֹ וְאֶת־הַצֹּאן וְאֶת־הַבָּקָר וְהַגְּמַלִּים
and-the-camels the-herd and the-flock and with-him that the-people ***

לִשְׁנֵי מַחֲנוֹת׃ וַיֹּאמֶר אִם־יָבוֹא עֵשָׂו אֶל־הַמַּחֲנֶה הָאַחַת
the-one the-group to Esau he-comes if and-he-thought (9) groups into-two-of

the God of Abraham and the God of Nahor, the God of their father, judge between us."

So Jacob took an oath in the name of the Fear of his father Isaac. [54]He offered a sacrifice there in the hill country and invited his relatives to a meal. After they had eaten, they spent the night there.

[55]Early the next morning Laban kissed his grandchildren and his daughters and blessed them. Then he left and returned home.

*Jacob Prepares to Meet Esau*

32 Jacob also went on his way, and the angels of God met him. [2]When Jacob saw them, he said, "This is the camp of God!" So he named that place Mahanaim.[v]

[3]Jacob sent messengers ahead of him to his brother Esau in the land of Seir, the country of Edom. [4]He instructed them: "This is what you are to say to my master Esau: 'Your servant Jacob says, I have been staying with Laban and have remained there till now. [5]I have cattle and donkeys, sheep and goats, menservants and maidservants. Now I am sending this message to my lord, that I may find favor in your eyes.' "

[6]When the messengers returned to Jacob, they said, "We went to your brother Esau, and now he is coming to meet you, and four hundred men are with him."

[7]In great fear and distress Jacob divided the people who were with him into two groups, and the flocks and herds and camels as well. [8]He thought, "If Esau comes and

[v]2 *Mahanaim* means *two camps.*

*The Hebrew numeration of chapter 32 begins with verse 55 of chapter 31 in English; thus, there is a one- verse discrepancy throughout chapter 32.

†5 Most mss have *dagesh* in the *daleth* ( ־דְּךָ ).

וְהִכָּהוּ וְהָיָה הַמַּחֲנֶה הַנִּשְׁאָר לִפְלֵיטָה׃
to-escape the-one-being-left the-group then-he-may-be and-he-attacks-him

וַיֹּאמֶר יַעֲקֹב אֱלֹהֵי אָבִי אַבְרָהָם וֵאלֹהֵי אָבִי
father-of-me and-God-of Abraham father-of-me God-of Jacob then-he-prayed (10)

יִצְחָק יְהוָה הָאֹמֵר אֵלַי שׁוּב לְאַרְצְךָ וּלְמוֹלַדְתְּךָ
to-relative-of-you to-land-of-you go-back! to-me the-one-saying Yahweh Isaac

וְאֵיטִיבָה עִמָּךְ׃ קָטֹנְתִּי מִכֹּל הַחֲסָדִים
the-kindnesses of-all-of I-am-unworthy (11) with-you and-I-will-make-prosper

וּמִכָּל־ הָאֱמֶת אֲשֶׁר עָשִׂיתָ אֶת־ עַבְדֶּךָ כִּי
only servant-of-you *** you-showed that the-faithfulness and-of-all-of

בְמַקְלִי עָבַרְתִּי אֶת־ הַיַּרְדֵּן הַזֶּה וְעַתָּה הָיִיתִי לִשְׁנֵי
as-two-of I-became but-now the-this the-Jordan *** I-crossed with-staff-of-me

מַחֲנוֹת׃ הַצִּילֵנִי נָא מִיַּד אָחִי מִיַּד עֵשָׂו כִּי־
for Esau from-hand-of brother-of-me from-hand-of now! save-me! (12) groups

יָרֵא אָנֹכִי אֹתוֹ פֶּן־ יָבוֹא וְהִכַּנִי אֵם עַל־ בָּנִים׃
children with mother and-he-will-attack-me he-will-come that him I fearing

וְאַתָּה אָמַרְתָּ הֵיטֵב אֵיטִיב עִמָּךְ וְשַׂמְתִּי
and-I-will-make with-you I-will-make-prosper to-prosper you-said but-you (13)

אֶת־ זַרְעֲךָ כְּחוֹל הַיָּם אֲשֶׁר לֹא־ יִסָּפֵר
he-can-be-counted not that the-sea like-sand-of descendant-of-you ***

מֵרֹב׃ וַיָּלֶן שָׁם בַּלַּיְלָה הַהוּא וַיִּקַּח
and-he-took the-that during-the-night there so-he-stayed (14) because-of-size

מִן־ הַבָּא בְיָדוֹ מִנְחָה לְעֵשָׂו אָחִיו׃
brother-of-him for-Esau gift in-hand-of-him the-one-being from

עִזִּים מָאתַיִם וּתְיָשִׁים עֶשְׂרִים רְחֵלִים מָאתַיִם וְאֵילִים
and-rams two-hundreds ewes twenty and-male-goats two-hundreds female-goats (15)

עֶשְׂרִים׃ גְּמַלִּים מֵינִיקוֹת וּבְנֵיהֶם שְׁלֹשִׁים פָּרוֹת אַרְבָּעִים
forty cows thirty with-young-ones-of-them being-females camels (16) twenty

וּפָרִים עֲשָׂרָה אֲתֹנֹת עֶשְׂרִים וַעְיָרִם עֲשָׂרָה׃ וַיִּתֵּן
and-he-put (17) ten and-male-donkeys twenty female-donkeys ten and-bulls

בְּיַד־ עֲבָדָיו עֵדֶר עֵדֶר לְבַדּוֹ וַיֹּאמֶר אֶל־ עֲבָדָיו
servants-of-him to and-he-said by-himself herd herd servants-of-him in-care-of

עִבְרוּ לְפָנַי וְרֶוַח תָּשִׂימוּ בֵּין עֵדֶר וּבֵין עֵדֶר׃
herd and-between herd between you-keep and-space ahead-of-me go!

וַיְצַו אֶת־ הָרִאשׁוֹן לֵאמֹר כִּי יְפָגֶשְׁךָ עֵשָׂו אָחִי
brother-of-me Esau he-meets-you when to-say the-leader *** and-he-instructed (18)

וִשְׁאֵלְךָ† לֵאמֹר לְמִי־ אַתָּה וְאָנָה תֵלֵךְ וּלְמִי אֵלֶּה
these and-to-whom? you-go and-where? you to-whom? to-say and-he-asks-you

attacks one group, the group that is left may escape."

[9]Then Jacob prayed, "O God of my father Abraham, God of my father Isaac, O LORD, who said to me, 'Go back to your country and your relatives, and I will make you prosper,' [10]I am unworthy of all the kindness and faithfulness you have shown your servant. I had only my staff when I crossed this Jordan, but now I have become two groups.[w] [11]Save me, I pray, from the hand of my brother Esau, for I am afraid he will come and attack me, and also the mothers with their children. [12]But you have said, 'I will surely make you prosper and will make your descendants like the sand of the sea, which cannot be counted.' "

[13]He spent the night there, and from what he had with him he selected a gift for his brother Esau: [14]two hundred female goats and twenty male goats, two hundred ewes and twenty rams, [15]thirty female camels with their young, forty cows and ten bulls, and twenty female donkeys and ten male donkeys. [16]He put them in the care of his servants, each herd by itself, and said to his servants, "Go ahead of me, and keep some space between the herds."

[17]He instructed the one in the lead: "When my brother Esau meets you and asks, 'To whom do you belong, and where are you going, and who owns all these animals in

w10 Or *camps*

*See the note on page 87.

†18 Most mss have *shureq* instead of *vav* with *hireq* ( וּשְׁ ).

לְפָנֶיךָ׃ וְאָמַרְתָּ לְעַבְדְּךָ לְיַעֲקֹב מִנְחָה הִוא

this gift to-Jacob to-servant-of-you then-you-say (19) ahead-of-you

שְׁלוּחָה לַאדֹנִי לְעֵשָׂו וְהִנֵּה גַם־ הוּא אַחֲרֵינוּ׃

behind-us he also and-see! to-Esau to-lord-of-me being-sent

וַיְצַו גַּם אֶת־ הַשֵּׁנִי גַּם אֶת־ הַשְּׁלִישִׁי גַּם אֶת־ כָּל־

all-of *** also the-third *** also the-second *** also and-he-instructed (20)

הַהֹלְכִים אַחֲרֵי הָעֲדָרִים לֵאמֹר כַּדָּבָר הַזֶּה תְּדַבְּרוּן

you-say the-this same-the-thing to-say the-herds after the-ones-following

אֶל־עֵשָׂו בְּמֹצַאֲכֶם אֹתוֹ׃ וַאֲמַרְתֶּם גַּם הִנֵּה עַבְדְּךָ יַעֲקֹב

Jacob servant-of-you see! also then-you-say (21) him when-meeting-you Esau to

אַחֲרֵינוּ כִּי־ אָמַר אֲכַפְּרָה פָנָיו בַּמִּנְחָה

with-the-gift face-of-him I-will-pacify he-thought for behind-us

הַהֹלֶכֶת לְפָנָי וְאַחֲרֵי־ כֵן אֶרְאֶה פָנָיו אוּלַי

perhaps face-of-him I-will-see that and-after ahead-of-me the-one-coming

יִשָּׂא פָנָי׃ וַתַּעֲבֹר הַמִּנְחָה עַל־ פָּנָיו וְהוּא

but-he face-of-him ahead the-gift so-she-went (22) face-of-me he-will-receive

לָן בַּלַּיְלָה־ הַהוּא בַּמַּחֲנֶה׃ וַיָּקָם ׀

now-he-got-up (23) in-the-camp the-that through-the-night he-stayed

בַּלַּיְלָה הוּא וַיִּקַּח אֶת־ שְׁתֵּי נָשָׁיו וְאֶת־ שְׁתֵּי

two-of and wives-of-him two-of *** and-he-took that in-the-night

שִׁפְחֹתָיו וְאֶת־אַחַד עָשָׂר יְלָדָיו וַיַּעֲבֹר אֵת מַעֲבַר יַבֹּק׃

Jabbok ford-of *** and-he-crossed sons-of-him ten one and maidservants-of-him

וַיִּקָּחֵם וַיַּעֲבִרֵם אֶת־ הַנָּחַל וַיַּעֲבֵר

and-he-sent-over the-stream *** and-he-sent-across-them and-he-took-them (24)

אֶת־אֲשֶׁר־ לוֹ†׃ וַיִּוָּתֵר יַעֲקֹב לְבַדּוֹ וַיֵּאָבֵק אִישׁ

man and-he-wrestled by-himself Jacob so-he-was-alone (25) to-him that ***

עִמּוֹ עַד עֲלוֹת הַשָּׁחַר׃ וַיַּרְא כִּי לֹא יָכֹל

he-could-overpower not that when-he-saw (26) the-dawn to-come until with-him

לוֹ וַיִּגַּע בְּכַף־ יְרֵכוֹ וַתֵּקַע כַּף־

socket-of so-she-was-wrenched hip-of-him on-socket-of then-he-touched over-him

יֶרֶךְ יַעֲקֹב בְּהֵאָבְקוֹ עִמּוֹ׃ וַיֹּאמֶר שַׁלְּחֵנִי כִּי

for let-go-me! then-he-said (27) with-him as-to-wrestle-him Jacob hip-of

עָלָה הַשָּׁחַר וַיֹּאמֶר לֹא אֲשַׁלֵּחֲךָ כִּי אִם־ בֵּרַכְתָּנִי׃

you-bless-me if unless I-will-let-go-you not but-he-replied the-dawn he-came

וַיֹּאמֶר אֵלָיו מַה־ שְּׁמֶךָ וַיֹּאמֶר יַעֲקֹב׃

Jacob and-he-answered name-of-you what? to-him so-he-asked (28)

וַיֹּאמֶר לֹא יַעֲקֹב יֵאָמֵר עוֹד שִׁמְךָ כִּי אִם־יִשְׂרָאֵל

Israel now but name-of-you longer he-will-be-called Jacob not then-he-said (29)

front of you?' [18]then you are to say, 'They belong to your servant Jacob. They are a gift sent to my lord Esau, and he is coming behind us.' "

[19]He also instructed the second, the third and all the others who followed the herds: "You are to say the same thing to Esau when you meet him. [20]And be sure to say, 'Your servant Jacob is coming behind us.' " For he thought, "I will pacify him with these gifts I am sending on ahead; later, when I see him, perhaps he will receive me." [21]So Jacob's gifts went on ahead of him, but he himself spent the night in the camp.

### *Jacob Wrestles With God*

[22]That night Jacob got up and took his two wives, his two maidservants and his eleven sons and crossed the ford of the Jabbok. [23]After he had sent them across the stream, he sent over all his possessions. [24]So Jacob was left alone, and a man wrestled with him till daybreak. [25]When the man saw that he could not overpower him, he touched the socket of Jacob's hip so that his hip was wrenched as he wrestled with the man. [26]Then the man said, "Let me go, for it is daybreak."

But Jacob replied, "I will not let you go unless you bless me."

[27]The man asked him, "What is your name?"

"Jacob," he answered.

[28]Then the man said, "Your name will no longer be Jacob, but Israel,[x] because you have

[x]28 *Israel* means *he struggles with God.*

*See the note on page 87.

†24 Most mss have *silluq* under the final word. ( לוֹ ).

כִּי־ שָׂרִיתָ עִם־אֱלֹהִים וְעִם־ אֲנָשִׁים וַתּוּכָל׃ וַיִּשְׁאַל
then-he-asked (30) and-you-overcame men and-with God with you-struggled for

יַעֲקֹב וַיֹּאמֶר הַגִּידָה־ נָּא שְׁמֶךָ וַיֹּאמֶר לָמָּה זֶּה תִּשְׁאַל
you-ask this why? but-he-replied name-of-you now! tell! and-he-said Jacob

לִשְׁמִי וַיְבָרֶךְ אֹתוֹ שָׁם׃ וַיִּקְרָא יַעֲקֹב שֵׁם
name-of Jacob so-he-called (31) there him then-he-blessed for-name-of-me

הַמָּקוֹם פְּנִיאֵל כִּי־ רָאִיתִי אֱלֹהִים פָּנִים אֶל־ פָּנִים וַתִּנָּצֵל נַפְשִׁי׃
life-of-me yet-she-was-spared face to face God I-saw for Peniel the-place

וַיִּזְרַח־ לוֹ הַשֶּׁמֶשׁ כַּאֲשֶׁר עָבַר אֶת־ פְּנוּאֵל וְהוּא צֹלֵעַ
limping and-he Penuel *** he-passed just-as the-sun above-him and-he-rose (32)

עַל־ יְרֵכוֹ׃ עַל־ כֵּן לֹא־ יֹאכְלוּ בְנֵי־ יִשְׂרָאֵל אֶת־ גִּיד
sinew-of *** Israel sons-of they-eat not this for (33) hip-of-him because-of

הַנָּשֶׁה אֲשֶׁר עַל־ כַּף הַיָּרֵךְ עַד הַיּוֹם הַזֶּה כִּי נָגַע
he-touched for the-this the-day to the-hip socket-of on that the-tendon

בְּכַף־ יֶרֶךְ יַעֲקֹב בְּגִיד הַנָּשֶׁה׃ וַיִּשָּׂא יַעֲקֹב
Jacob and-he-lifted (33:1) the-tendon on-sinew-of Jacob hip-of on-socket-of

עֵינָיו וַיַּרְא וְהִנֵּה עֵשָׂו בָּא וְעִמּוֹ אַרְבַּע מֵאוֹת אִישׁ
man hundreds four and-with-him coming Esau and-see! and-he-saw eyes-of-him

וַיַּחַץ אֶת־ הַיְלָדִים עַל־ לֵאָה וְעַל־ רָחֵל וְעַל שְׁתֵּי
two-of and-to Rachel and-to Leah to the-children *** so-he-divided

הַשְּׁפָחוֹת׃ וַיָּשֶׂם אֶת־ הַשְּׁפָחוֹת וְאֶת־ יַלְדֵיהֶן
children-of-them and the-maidservants *** and-he-put (2) the-maidservants

רִאשֹׁנָה וְאֶת־לֵאָה וִילָדֶיהָ אַחֲרֹנִים וְאֶת־ רָחֵל וְאֶת־ יוֹסֵף אַחֲרֹנִים׃
rear-ones Joseph and Rachel and next-ones and-children-of-her Leah and front

וְהוּא עָבַר לִפְנֵיהֶם וַיִּשְׁתַּחוּ אַרְצָה שֶׁבַע פְּעָמִים עַד־
as times seven to-ground and-he-bowed ahead-of-them he-went and-he (3)

גִּשְׁתּוֹ עַד־ אָחִיו׃ וַיָּרָץ עֵשָׂו לִקְרָאתוֹ
to-meet-him Esau but-he-ran (4) brother-of-him to to-approach-him

וַיְחַבְּקֵהוּ וַיִּפֹּל עַל־ צַוָּארָו וַיִּשָּׁקֵהוּ
and-he-kissed-him neck-of-him around and-he-hugged and-he-embraced-him

וַיִּבְכּוּ׃ וַיִּשָּׂא אֶת־ עֵינָיו וַיַּרְא אֶת־ הַנָּשִׁים
the-women *** and-he-saw eyes-of-him *** and-he-lifted (5) and-they-wept

וְאֶת־ הַיְלָדִים וַיֹּאמֶר מִי־ אֵלֶּה לָּךְ וַיֹּאמַר הַיְלָדִים
the-children and-he-answered with-you these who? and-he-asked the-children and

אֲשֶׁר־ חָנַן אֱלֹהִים אֶת־ עַבְדֶּךָ׃ וַתִּגַּשְׁןָ
then-they-approached (6) servant-of-you to God he-graciously-gave whom

הַשְּׁפָחוֹת הֵנָּה וְיַלְדֵיהֶן וַתִּשְׁתַּחֲוֶיןָ׃ וַתִּגַּשׁ
next-she-came (7) and-they-bowed and-children-of-them they the-maidservants

struggled with God and with men and have overcome."

29 Jacob said, "Please tell me your name."

But he replied, "Why do you ask my name?" Then he blessed him there.

30 So Jacob called the place Peniel,[y] saying, "It is because I saw God face to face, and yet my life was spared."

31 The sun rose above him as he passed Peniel,[z] and he was limping because of his hip. 32 Therefore to this day the Israelites do not eat the tendon attached to the socket of the hip, because the socket of Jacob's hip was touched near the tendon.

*Jacob Meets Esau*

33 Jacob looked up and there was Esau, coming with his four hundred men; so he divided the children among Leah, Rachel and the two maidservants. 2 He put the maidservants and their children in front, Leah and her children next, and Rachel and Joseph in the rear. 3 He himself went on ahead and bowed down to the ground seven times as he approached his brother.

4 But Esau ran to meet Jacob and embraced him; he threw his arms around his neck and kissed him. And they wept. 5 Then Esau looked up and saw the women and children. "Who are these with you?" he asked.

Jacob answered, "They are the children God has graciously given your servant."

6 Then the maidservants and their children approached and bowed down. 7 Next, Leah and

y30 *Peniel* means *face of God.*
z31 Hebrew *Penuel,* a variant of *Peniel*

*See the note on page 87.

°4 ק צואריו

גַּם־ לֵאָה וִילָדֶיהָ וַיִּשְׁתַּחֲווּ וְאַחַר נִגַּשׁ יוֹסֵף
Joseph he-approached and-last and-they-bowed and-children-of-her Leah also

וְרָחֵל וַיִּשְׁתַּחֲווּ׃ וַיֹּאמֶר מִי לְךָ כָּל־ הַמַּחֲנֶה
the-drove all-of to-you what? and-he-asked (8) and-they-bowed and-Rachel

הַזֶּה אֲשֶׁר פָּגָשְׁתִּי וַיֹּאמֶר לִמְצֹא־ חֵן בְּעֵינֵי אֲדֹנִי׃
lord-of-me in-eyes-of-you favor to-find and-he-said I-met that the-this

וַיֹּאמֶר עֵשָׂו יֶשׁ־ לִי רָב אָחִי יְהִי לְךָ
to-you let-him-stay brother-of-me plenty to-me there-is Esau but-he-said (9)

אֲשֶׁר־ לָךְ׃ וַיֹּאמֶר יַעֲקֹב אַל־ נָא אִם־ נָא מָצָאתִי חֵן
favor I-found now! if now! no Jacob but-he-said (10) to-you what

בְּעֵינֶיךָ וְלָקַחְתָּ מִנְחָתִי מִיָּדִי כִּי עַל־ כֵּן
this for indeed from-hand-of-me gift-of-me now-you-accept in-eyes-of-you

רָאִיתִי פָנֶיךָ כִּרְאֹת פְּנֵי אֱלֹהִים וַתִּרְצֵנִי׃ קַח־
accept! (11) as-you-received-me God face-of like-to-see face-of-you I-see

נָא אֶת־ בִּרְכָתִי אֲשֶׁר הֻבָאת לָךְ כִּי־ חַנַּנִי
he-is-gracious-to-me for to-you she-was-brought that present-of-me *** now!

אֱלֹהִים וְכִי יֶשׁ־ לִי־ כֹל וַיִּפְצַר־ בּוֹ וַיִּקָּח׃
so-he-accepted with-him and-he-insisted all to-me there-is and-because God

וַיֹּאמֶר נִסְעָה וְנֵלֵכָה וְאֵלְכָה לְנֶגְדֶּךָ׃
next-to-you and-I-will-go and-let-us-go let-us-travel then-he-said (12)

וַיֹּאמֶר אֵלָיו אֲדֹנִי יֹדֵעַ כִּי־ הַיְלָדִים רַכִּים
tender-ones the-children that knowing lord-of-me to-him but-he-said (13)

וְהַצֹּאן וְהַבָּקָר עָלוֹת עָלָי וּדְפָקוּם
if-they-drive-hard-them care-of-me nursing-ones and-the-cattle and-the-flock

יוֹם אֶחָד וָמֵתוּ כָּל־ הַצֹּאן׃ יַעֲבָר־ נָא
now! let-him-go-ahead (14) the-flock all-of then-they-will-die one day

אֲדֹנִי לִפְנֵי עַבְדּוֹ וַאֲנִי אֶתְנָהֲלָה לְאִטִּי לְרֶגֶל
at-pace-of with-slowness-me I-move while-I servant-of-him before lord-of-me

הַמְּלָאכָה אֲשֶׁר־ לְפָנַי וּלְרֶגֶל הַיְלָדִים עַד אֲשֶׁר־ אָבֹא אֶל־
to I-come when until the-children and-at-pace-of before-me that the-drove

אֲדֹנִי שֵׂעִירָה׃ וַיֹּאמֶר עֵשָׂו אַצִּיגָה־ נָּא עִמְּךָ מִן־
from with-you now! let-me-leave Esau so-he-said (15) at-Seir lord-of-me

הָעָם אֲשֶׁר אִתִּי וַיֹּאמֶר לָמָּה זֶּה אֶמְצָא־ חֵן בְּעֵינֵי
in-eyes-of favor let-me-find that why? but-he-asked with-me that the-people

אֲדֹנִי׃ וַיָּשָׁב בַּיּוֹם הַהוּא עֵשָׂו לְדַרְכּוֹ
on-way-of-him Esau the-that on-the-day so-he-went-back (16) lord-of-me

שֵׂעִירָה׃ וְיַעֲקֹב נָסַע סֻכֹּתָה וַיִּבֶן לוֹ בָּיִת
place for-him and-he-built to-Succoth he-went but-Jacob (17) to-Seir

her children came and bowed
down. Last of all came Joseph
and Rachel, and they too
bowed down.
8 Esau asked, "What do you
mean by all these droves I
met?"
"To find favor in your eyes,
my lord," he said.
9 But Esau said, "I already
have plenty, my brother. Keep
what you have for yourself."
10 "No, please!" said Jacob.
"If I have found favor in your
eyes, accept this gift from me.
For to see your face is like seeing the face of God, now that
you have received me favorably. 11 Please accept the
present that was brought to
you, for God has been gracious
to me and I have all I need."
And because Jacob insisted,
Esau accepted it.
12 Then Esau said, "Let us be
on our way; I'll accompany
you."
13 But Jacob said to him, "My
lord knows that the children
are tender and that I must care
for the ewes and cows that are
nursing their young. If they
are driven hard just one day,
all the animals will die. 14 So let
my lord go on ahead of his servant, while I move along
slowly at the pace of the
droves before me and that of
the children, until I come to
my lord in Seir."
15 Esau said, "Then let me
leave some of my men with
you."
"But why do that?" Jacob
asked. "Just let me find favor
in the eyes of my lord."
16 So that day Esau started on
his way back to Seir. 17 Jacob,
however, went to Succoth,
where he built a place for himself and made shelters for his

וּלְמִקְנֵהוּ עָשָׂה סֻכֹּת עַל־ כֵּן קָרָא שֵׁם־ הַמָּקוֹם
the-place name-of he-called this for shelters he-made and-for-stock-of-him

סֻכּוֹת׃ (18) וַיָּבֹא יַעֲקֹב שָׁלֵם עִיר שְׁכֶם אֲשֶׁר בְּאֶרֶץ
in-land-of that Shechem city-of safely Jacob and-he-arrived (18) Succoth

כְּנַעַן בְּבֹאוֹ מִפַּדַּן אֲרָם וַיִּחַן אֶת־ פְּנֵי הָעִיר׃
the-city sight-of *** and-he-camped Aram from-Paddan after-to-come-him Canaan

(19) וַיִּקֶן אֶת־ חֶלְקַת הַשָּׂדֶה אֲשֶׁר נָטָה־ שָׁם אָהֳלוֹ
tent-of-him there he-pitched where the-ground plot-of *** and-he-bought (19)

מִיַּד בְּנֵי־ חֲמוֹר אֲבִי שְׁכֶם בְּמֵאָה קְשִׂיטָה׃
money for-hundred Shechem father-of Hamor sons-of from-hand-of

(20) וַיַּצֶּב־ שָׁם מִזְבֵּחַ וַיִּקְרָא־ לוֹ אֵל אֱלֹהֵי יִשְׂרָאֵל׃
Israel Elohe El to-him and-he-called altar there and-he-set-up (20)

(34:1) וַתֵּצֵא דִינָה בַּת־ לֵאָה אֲשֶׁר יָלְדָה לְיַעֲקֹב
to-Jacob she-bore whom Leah daughter-of Dinah now-she-went-out (34:1)

לִרְאוֹת בִּבְנוֹת הָאָרֶץ׃ (2) וַיַּרְא אֹתָהּ שְׁכֶם בֶּן־ חֲמוֹר
Hamor son-of Shechem her and-he-saw (2) the-land with-women-of to-visit

הַחִוִּי נְשִׂיא הָאָרֶץ וַיִּקַּח אֹתָהּ וַיִּשְׁכַּב אֹתָהּ
with-her and-he-lay her and-he-took the-area ruler-of the-Hivite

וַיְעַנֶּהָ׃ (3) וַתִּדְבַּק נַפְשׁוֹ בְּדִינָה בַּת־
daughter-of to-Dinah heart-of-him and-she-was-drawn (3) and-he-violated-her

יַעֲקֹב וַיֶּאֱהַב אֶת־ הַנַּעֲרָ וַיְדַבֵּר עַל־ לֵב הַנַּעֲרָ׃
the-girl heart-of to and-he-spoke the-girl *** and-he-loved Jacob

(4) וַיֹּאמֶר שְׁכֶם אֶל־חֲמוֹר אָבִיו לֵאמֹר קַח־ לִי אֶת־הַיַּלְדָּה
the-girl *** for-me get! to-say father-of-him Hamor to Shechem and-he-said (4)

הַזֹּאת לְאִשָּׁה׃ (5) וְיַעֲקֹב שָׁמַע כִּי טִמֵּא אֶת־ דִּינָה
Dinah *** he-defiled that he-heard when-Jacob (5) as-wife the-this

בִתּוֹ וּבָנָיו הָיוּ אֶת־ מִקְנֵהוּ בַּשָּׂדֶה
in-the-field stock-of-him with they-were then-sons-of-him daughter-of-him

וְהֶחֱרִשׁ יַעֲקֹב עַד־ בֹּאָם׃ (6) וַיֵּצֵא חֲמוֹר
Hamor then-he-went-out (6) to-come-them until Jacob so-he-kept-quiet

אֲבִי־ שְׁכֶם אֶל־יַעֲקֹב לְדַבֵּר אִתּוֹ׃ (7) וּבְנֵי יַעֲקֹב בָּאוּ
they-came Jacob now-sons-of (7) with-him to-talk Jacob to Shechem father-of

מִן־ הַשָּׂדֶה כְּשָׁמְעָם וַיִּתְעַצְּבוּ הָאֲנָשִׁים
the-men and-they-were-grieved as-soon-as-to-hear-them the-field from

וַיִּחַר לָהֶם מְאֹד כִּי־ נְבָלָה עָשָׂה בְיִשְׂרָאֵל לִשְׁכַּב אֶת־
with to-lie against-Israel he-did disgrace for greatly to-them and-he-angered

בַּת־ יַעֲקֹב וְכֵן לֹא יֵעָשֶׂה׃ (8) וַיְדַבֵּר חֲמוֹר
Hamor but-he-said (8) he-should-be-done not for-this Jacob daughter-of

livestock. That is why the
place is called Succoth.[a]
18After Jacob came from Paddan Aram,[b] he arrived safely
at the[c] city of Shechem in Canaan and camped within
sight of the city. 19For a hundred pieces of silver,[d] he
bought from the sons of Hamor, the father of Shechem,
the plot of ground where he
pitched his tent. 20There he set
up an altar and called it El
Elohe Israel.[e]

*Dinah and the Shechemites*

34 Now Dinah, the
daughter Leah had
borne to Jacob, went out to
visit the women of the land.
2When Shechem son of Hamor
the Hivite, the ruler of that
area, saw her, he took her and
violated her. 3His heart was
drawn to Dinah daughter of
Jacob, and he loved the girl
and spoke tenderly to her.
4And Shechem said to his father Hamor, "Get me this girl
as my wife."
5When Jacob heard that his
daughter Dinah had been
defiled, his sons were in the
fields with his livestock; so he
kept quiet about it until they
came home.
6Then Shechem's father Hamor went out to talk with
Jacob. 7Now Jacob's sons had
come in from the fields as soon
as they heard what had happened. They were filled with
grief and fury, because Shechem had done a disgraceful
thing in[f] Israel by lying with
Jacob's daughter—a thing that
should not be done.
8But Hamor said to them,

[a]17 *Succoth* means *shelters.*
[b]18 That is, Northwest Mesopotamia
[c]18 Or *arrived at Shalem, a*
[d]19 Hebrew *hundred kesitahs;* a kesitah was a unit of money of unknown weight and value.
[e]20 *El Elohe Israel* can mean *God, the God of Israel* or *mighty is the God of Israel.*
[f]7 Or *against*

אתם לאמר שכם בני חשקה נפשו בבתכם
on-daughter-of-you heart-of-him she-is-set son-of-me Shechem to-say to-them

תנו נא אתה לו לאשה: והתחתנו אתנו בנתיכם תתנו־
give! daughters-of-you with-us intermarry! (9) as-wife to-him her now! give!

לנו ואת־ בנתינו תקחו לכם: ואתנו תשבו
you-settle and-among-us (10) for-you you-take daughters-of-us and to-us

והארץ תהיה לפניכם שבו וסחרוה והאחזו בה:
in-her and-acquire! and-trade-in-her! live! before-you she-is now-the-land

ויאמר שכם אל־ אביה* ואל־ אחיה אמצא־
let-me-find brothers-of-her and-to father-of-her to Shechem then-he-said (11)

חן בעיניכם ואשר תאמרו אלי אתן: הרבו
make-great! (12) I-will-give of-me you-ask and-whatever in-eyes-of-you favor

עלי מאד מהר ומתן ואתנה כאשר תאמרו אלי ותנו־
but-give! of-me you-ask what and-I-will-pay and-gift bride-price very for-me

לי את־ הנער לאשה: ויענו בני־ יעקב את־ שכם
Shechem *** Jacob sons-of but-they-replied (13) as-wife the-girl *** to-me

ואת־חמור אביו במרמה וידברו אשר טמא את דינה
Dinah *** he-defiled because as-they-spoke in-deceit father-of-him Hamor and

אחתם: ויאמרו אליהם לא נוכל לעשות הדבר הזה
the-this the-thing to-do we-can not to-them and-they-said (14) sister-of-them

לתת את־ אחתנו לאיש אשר־ לו ערלה כי־ חרפה הוא לנו:
to-us that disgrace for foreskin to-him who to-man sister-of-us *** to-give

אך־ בזאת נאות לכם אם תהיו כמנו להמל
to-be-circumcised like-us you-become if to-you we-will-consent on-this only (15)

לכם כל־ זכר: ונתנו את־ בנתינו לכם ואת־
and to-you daughters-of-us *** then-we-will-give (16) male every-of to-you

בנתיכם נקח־ לנו וישבנו אתכם
among-you and-we-will-settle for-us we-will-take daughters-of-you

והיינו לעם אחד: ואם־ לא תשמעו אלינו
with-us you-will-agree not but-if (17) one as-people and-we-will-become

להמול ולקחנו את־ בתנו והלכנו:
and-we-will-go daughter-of-us *** then-we-will-take to-be-circumcised

וייטבו דבריהם בעיני חמור ובעיני
and-in-eyes-of Hamor in-eyes-of words-of-them and-they-seemed-good (18)

שכם בן־ חמור: ולא־ אחר הנער לעשות הדבר
the-thing to-do the-young-man he-delayed and-not (19) Hamor son-of Shechem

כי חפץ בבת־ יעקב והוא נכבד מכל
over-all-of being-honored now-he Jacob with-daughter-of he-was-delighted for

"My son Shechem has his heart set on your daughter. Please give her to him as his wife. [9]Intermarry with us; give us your daughters and take our daughters for yourselves. [10]You can settle among us; the land is open to you. Live in it, trade[h] in it, and acquire property in it."

[11]Then Shechem said to Dinah's father and brothers, "Let me find favor in your eyes, and I will give you whatever you ask. [12]Make the price for the bride and the gift I am to bring as great as you like, and I'll pay whatever you ask me. Only give me the girl as my wife."

[13]Because their sister Dinah had been defiled, Jacob's sons replied deceitfully as they spoke to Shechem and his father Hamor. [14]They said to them, "We can't do such a thing; we can't give our sister to a man who is not circumcised. That would be a disgrace to us. [15]We will give our consent to you on one condition only: that you become like us by circumcising all your males. [16]Then we will give you our daughters and take your daughters for ourselves. We'll settle among you and become one people with you. [17]But if you will not agree to be circumcised, we'll take our sister[i] and go."

[18]Their proposal seemed good to Hamor and his son Shechem. [19]The young man, who was the most honored of all his father's household, lost no time in doing what they said, because he was delighted with Jacob's daughter. [20]So

[h]10 Or *move about freely;* also in verse 21
[i]17 Hebrew *daughter*

*11 Most mss have *qamets* under the *he* (הָ–).

בֵּית אָבִיו׃ וַיָּבֹא חֲמוֹר וּשְׁכֶם בְּנוֹ
son-of-him and-Shechem Hamor so-they-went (20) father-of-him household-of

אֶל־שַׁעַר עִירָם וַיְדַבְּרוּ אֶל־אַנְשֵׁי עִירָם לֵאמֹר׃
to-say city-of-them men-of to and-they-spoke city-of-them gate-of to

הָאֲנָשִׁים הָאֵלֶּה שְׁלֵמִים הֵם אִתָּנוּ וְיֵשְׁבוּ
so-let-them-settle with-us they friendly-ones the-these the-men (21)

בָאָרֶץ וְיִסְחֲרוּ אֹתָהּ וְהָאָרֶץ הִנֵּה רַחֲבַת־יָדַיִם
measures large-of see! now-the-land in-her and-let-them-trade in-the-land

לִפְנֵיהֶם אֶת־בְּנֹתָם נִקַּח־לָנוּ לְנָשִׁים וְאֶת־
and as-wives for-us we-can-take daughters-of-them *** before-them

בְּנֹתֵינוּ נִתֵּן לָהֶם׃ אַךְ־בְּזֹאת יֵאֹתוּ לָנוּ
to-us will-they-consent on-this only (22) to-them we-can-give daughters-of-us

הָאֲנָשִׁים לָשֶׁבֶת אִתָּנוּ לִהְיוֹת לְעַם אֶחָד בְּהִמּוֹל לָנוּ
to-us that-to-be-circumcised one as-people to-be with-us to-live the-men

כָּל־זָכָר כַּאֲשֶׁר הֵם נִמֹּלִים׃ מִקְנֵהֶם
livestock-of-them (23) ones-being-circumcised they just-as male every-of

וְקִנְיָנָם וְכָל־בְּהֶמְתָּם הֲלוֹא לָנוּ הֵם אַךְ
so they to-us not? animal-of-them and-every-of and-property-of-them

נֵאוֹתָה לָהֶם וְיֵשְׁבוּ אִתָּנוּ׃ וַיִּשְׁמְעוּ אֶל־
with so-they-agreed (24) with-us and-they-will-settle to-them let-us-consent

חֲמוֹר וְאֶל־שְׁכֶם בְּנוֹ כָּל־יֹצְאֵי שַׁעַר
gate-of ones-going-out-of every-of son-of-him Shechem and-with Hamor

עִירוֹ וַיִּמֹּלוּ כָּל־זָכָר כָּל־יֹצְאֵי
ones-going-out-of every-of male every-of and-they-were-circumcised city-of-him

שַׁעַר עִירוֹ׃ וַיְהִי בַיּוֹם הַשְּׁלִישִׁי בִּהְיוֹתָם
when-to-be-them the-third on-the-day and-he-was (25) city-of-him gate-of

כֹּאֲבִים וַיִּקְחוּ שְׁנֵי־בְנֵי־יַעֲקֹב שִׁמְעוֹן וְלֵוִי
and-Levi Simeon Jacob sons-of two-of then-they-took ones-being-in-pain

אֲחֵי דִינָה אִישׁ חַרְבּוֹ וַיָּבֹאוּ עַל־הָעִיר בֶּטַח
unsuspected the-city into and-they-came sword-of-him each Dinah brothers-of

וַיַּהַרְגוּ כָּל־זָכָר׃ וְאֶת־חֲמוֹר וְאֶת־שְׁכֶם בְּנוֹ
son-of-him Shechem and Hamor and (26) male every-of and-they-killed

הָרְגוּ לְפִי־חָרֶב וַיִּקְחוּ אֶת־דִּינָה מִבֵּית שְׁכֶם
Shechem from-house-of Dinah *** and-they-took sword with-edge-of they-killed

וַיֵּצֵאוּ׃ בְּנֵי יַעֲקֹב בָּאוּ עַל־הַחֲלָלִים וַיָּבֹזּוּ
and-they-looted the-dead-ones upon they-came Jacob sons-of (27) and-they-left

הָעִיר אֲשֶׁר טִמְּאוּ אֲחוֹתָם׃ אֶת־צֹאנָם וְאֶת־
and flock-of-them *** (28) sister-of-them they-defiled where the-city

Hamor and his son Shechem went to the gate of their city to speak to their fellow townsmen. 21 "These men are friendly toward us," they said. "Let them live in our land and trade in it; the land has plenty of room for them. We can marry their daughters and they can marry ours. 22 But the men will consent to live with us as one people only on the condition that our males be circumcised, as they themselves are. 23 Won't their livestock, their property and all their other animals become ours? So let us give our consent to them, and they will settle among us."

24 All the men who went out of the city gate agreed with Hamor and his son Shechem, and every male in the city was circumcised.

25 Three days later, while all of them were still in pain, two of Jacob's sons, Simeon and Levi, Dinah's brothers, took their swords and attacked the unsuspecting city, killing every male. 26 They put Hamor and his son Shechem to the sword and took Dinah from Shechem's house and left. 27 The sons of Jacob came upon the dead bodies and looted the city where[j] their sister had been defiled. 28 They seized their flocks and herds and

j27 Or *because*

בְּקָרָם וְאֶת־ חֲמֹרֵיהֶם* וְאֵת אֲשֶׁר־ בָּעִיר וְאֶת־ אֲשֶׁר בַּשָּׂדֶה
in-the-field what and in-the-city what and donkeys-of-them and herd-of-them

לָקָחוּ׃ וְאֶת־ כָּל־ חֵילָם וְאֶת־ כָּל־ טַפָּם֙ וְאֶת־
and child-of-them every-of and wealth-of-them all-of and (29) they-seized

נְשֵׁיהֶם שָׁבוּ וַיָּבֹזּוּ וְאֵת כָּל־ אֲשֶׁר בַּבָּיִת׃
in-the-house that all also and-they-plundered they-carried-off women-of-them

וַיֹּאמֶר יַעֲקֹב אֶל־ שִׁמְעוֹן וְאֶל־ לֵוִי֮ עֲכַרְתֶּם אֹתִי֒
on-me you-brought-trouble Levi and-to Simeon to Jacob then-he-said (30)

לְהַבְאִישֵׁנִי֙ בְּיֹשֵׁב הָאָרֶץ בַּכְּנַעֲנִי
to-the-Canaanite the-land to-one-living by-to-make-stench-of-me

וּבַפְּרִזִּי וַאֲנִי֙ מְתֵי מִסְפָּר וְנֶאֶסְפוּ עָלַי֙
against-me if-they-join number men-of now-I and-to-the-Perizzite

וְהִכּוּנִי וְנִשְׁמַדְתִּי אֲנִי וּבֵיתִי׃
and-household-of-me I then-I-will-be-destroyed and-they-attack-me

וַיֹּאמְרוּ הַכְזוֹנָה יַעֲשֶׂה אֶת־ אֲחוֹתֵנוּ׃
sister-of-us *** should-he-treat as-being-prostitute? but-they-replied (31)

וַיֹּאמֶר אֱלֹהִים֙ אֶל־יַעֲקֹב קוּם עֲלֵה בֵית־ אֵל וְשֶׁב־ שָׁם
there and-settle! El Beth go-up! rise! Jacob to God then-he-said (35:1)

וַעֲשֵׂה־ שָׁם מִזְבֵּחַ לָאֵל֙ הַנִּרְאֶה אֵלֶיךָ בְּבָרְחֲךָ†
when-to-flee-you to-you the-one-appearing to-God altar there and-build!

מִפְּנֵי עֵשָׂו אָחִיךָ׃ וַיֹּאמֶר יַעֲקֹב֙ אֶל־ בֵּיתוֹ
household-of-him to Jacob so-he-said (2) brother-of-you Esau from-face-of

וְאֶל כָּל־ אֲשֶׁר עִמּוֹ הָסִרוּ אֶת־ אֱלֹהֵי הַנֵּכָר֙ אֲשֶׁר בְּתֹכְכֶם
with-you that the-foreign gods-of *** get-rid-of! with-him who all and-to

וְהִטַּהֲרוּ וְהַחֲלִיפוּ שִׂמְלֹתֵיכֶם׃ וְנָקוּמָה
then-let-us-rise (3) clothes-of-you and-change! and-purify-yourselves!

וְנַעֲלֶה בֵּית־ אֵל וְאֶעֱשֶׂה־ שָּׁם מִזְבֵּחַ לָאֵל הָעֹנֶה
the-one-answering to-God altar there and-I-will-build El Beth and-let-us-go-up

אֹתִי֙ בְּיוֹם צָרָתִי וַיְהִי֙ עִמָּדִי בַּדֶּרֶךְ אֲשֶׁר הָלָכְתִּי׃
I-go that in-the-way with-me and-he-is distress-of-me in-day-of me

וַיִּתְּנוּ אֶל־יַעֲקֹב אֵת כָּל־ אֱלֹהֵי הַנֵּכָר֙ אֲשֶׁר בְּיָדָם
in-hand-of-them that the-foreign gods-of all-of *** Jacob to so-they-gave (4)

וְאֶת־ הַנְּזָמִים אֲשֶׁר בְּאָזְנֵיהֶם וַיִּטְמֹן אֹתָם֙ יַעֲקֹב תַּחַת הָאֵלָה
the-oak under Jacob them and-he-buried in-ears-of-them that the-rings and

אֲשֶׁר עִם־ שְׁכֶם׃ וַיִּסָּעוּ וַיְהִי ׀ חִתַּת אֱלֹהִים עַל־ הֶעָרִים֙
the-cities on God terror-of and-he-was then-they-set-out (5) Shechem at that

אֲשֶׁר֙ סְבִיבֹתֵיהֶם וְלֹא רָדְפוּ אַחֲרֵי בְּנֵי יַעֲקֹב׃ וַיָּבֹא
and-he-came (6) Jacob sons-of after they-pursued and-not around-them that

donkeys and everything else of theirs in the city and out in the fields. [29]They carried off all their wealth and all their women and children, taking as plunder everything in the houses.

[30]Then Jacob said to Simeon and Levi, "You have brought trouble on me by making me a stench to the Canaanites and Perizzites, the people living in this land. We are few in number, and if they join forces against me and attack me, I and my household will be destroyed."

[31]But they replied, "Should he have treated our sister like a prostitute?"

*Jacob Returns to Bethel*

35 Then God said to Jacob, "Go up to Bethel and settle there, and build an altar there to God, who appeared to you when you were fleeing from your brother Esau."

[2]So Jacob said to his household and to all who were with him, "Get rid of the foreign gods you have with you, and purify yourselves and change your clothes. [3]Then come, let us go up to Bethel, where I will build an altar to God, who answered me in the day of my distress and who has been with me wherever I have gone." [4]So they gave Jacob all the foreign gods they had and the rings in their ears, and Jacob buried them under the oak at Shechem. [5]Then they set out, and the terror of God fell upon the towns all around them so that no one pursued them.

*28 Most mss have no *dagesh* in the *he* (הֶם–).

†1 Most mss have additional accentuation (בְּבָרְחֲךָ).

יַעֲקֹב לוּזָה אֲשֶׁר בְּאֶרֶץ כְּנַעַן הִוא בֵּית־אֵל הוּא וְכָל־ הָעָם

the-people and-all-of he El Beth that Canaan in-land-of that to-Luz Jacob

אֲשֶׁר־ עִמּוֹ׃ וַיִּבֶן שָׁם מִזְבֵּחַ וַיִּקְרָא לַמָּקוֹם אֵל בֵּית־

Beth El to-the-place and-he-called altar there and-he-built (7) with-him who

אֵל כִּי שָׁם נִגְלוּ אֵלָיו הָאֱלֹהִים בְּבָרְחוֹ מִפְּנֵי

from-face-of when-to-flee-him the-God to-him they-were-revealed there for El

אָחִיו׃ וַתָּמָת דְּבֹרָה מֵינֶקֶת רִבְקָה

Rebekah one-nursing-of Deborah now-she-died (8) brother-of-him

וַתִּקָּבֵר מִתַּחַת לְבֵית־אֵל תַּחַת הָאַלּוֹן וַיִּקְרָא שְׁמוֹ

name-of-him so-he-called the-oak under El to-Beth below and-she-was-buried

אַלּוֹן בָּכוּת׃ וַיֵּרָא אֱלֹהִים אֶל־ יַעֲקֹב עוֹד בְּבֹאוֹ

when-to-return-him again Jacob to God and-he-appeared (9) Bacuth Allon

מִפַּדַּן אֲרָם וַיְבָרֶךְ אֹתוֹ׃ וַיֹּאמֶר־ לוֹ אֱלֹהִים שִׁמְךָ

name-of-you God to-him and-he-said (10) him and-he-blessed Aram from-Paddan

יַעֲקֹב לֹא־ יִקָּרֵא שִׁמְךָ עוֹד יַעֲקֹב כִּי אִם־יִשְׂרָאֵל יִהְיֶה

he-will-be Israel now for Jacob longer name-of-you he-will-be-called not Jacob

שְׁמֶךָ וַיִּקְרָא אֶת־ שְׁמוֹ יִשְׂרָאֵל׃ וַיֹּאמֶר לוֹ אֱלֹהִים

God to-him and-he-said (11) Israel name-of-him *** so-he-called name-of-you

אֲנִי אֵל שַׁדַּי פְּרֵה וּרְבֵה גּוֹי וּקְהַל גּוֹיִם

nations and-company-of nation and-increase! be-fruitful! Almighty God I

יִהְיֶה מִמֶּךָּ וּמְלָכִים מֵחֲלָצֶיךָ יֵצֵאוּ׃ וְאֶת־

and (12) they-will-come from-loins-of-you and-kings from-you he-will-come

הָאָרֶץ אֲשֶׁר נָתַתִּי לְאַבְרָהָם וּלְיִצְחָק לְךָ אֶתְּנֶנָּה

I-will-give-her to-you and-to-Isaac to-Abraham I-gave that the-land

וּלְזַרְעֲךָ אַחֲרֶיךָ אֶתֵּן אֶת־ הָאָרֶץ׃ וַיַּעַל

then-he-went-up (13) the-land *** I-will-give after-you and-to-descendant-of-you

מֵעָלָיו אֱלֹהִים בַּמָּקוֹם אֲשֶׁר־ דִּבֶּר אִתּוֹ׃ וַיַּצֵּב יַעֲקֹב

Jacob and-he-set-up (14) with-him he-talked where at-the-place God from-him

מַצֵּבָה בַּמָּקוֹם אֲשֶׁר־ דִּבֶּר אִתּוֹ מַצֶּבֶת אָבֶן וַיַּסֵּךְ

and-he-poured stone pillar-of with-him he-talked where at-the-place pillar

עָלֶיהָ נֶסֶךְ וַיִּצֹק עָלֶיהָ שָׁמֶן׃ וַיִּקְרָא יַעֲקֹב אֶת־

*** Jacob and-he-called (15) oil on-her and-he-poured drink-offering on-her

שֵׁם הַמָּקוֹם אֲשֶׁר דִּבֶּר אִתּוֹ שָׁם אֱלֹהִים בֵּית־אֵל׃ וַיִּסְעוּ

and-they-left (16) El Beth God there with-him he-talked where the-place name-of

מִבֵּית אֵל וַיְהִי־ עוֹד כִּבְרַת־ הָאָרֶץ לָבוֹא אֶפְרָתָה

to-Ephrath to-go the-land distance-of still and-he-was El from-Beth

וַתֵּלֶד רָחֵל וַתְּקַשׁ בְּלִדְתָּהּ׃ וַיְהִי

and-he-was (17) while-to-bear-her and-she-had-difficulty Rachel then-she-bore

6Jacob and all the people with him came to Luz (that is, Bethel) in the land of Canaan.
7There he built an altar, and he called the place El Bethel,[k] because it was there that God revealed himself to him when he was fleeing from his brother.

8Now Deborah, Rebekah's nurse, died and was buried under the oak below Bethel. So it was named Allon Bacuth.[l]

9After Jacob returned from Paddan Aram,[m] God appeared to him again and blessed him.
10God said to him, "Your name is Jacob,[n] but you will no longer be called Jacob; your name will be Israel.[o]" So he named him Israel.

11And God said to him, "I am God Almighty[p]; be fruitful and increase in number. A nation and a community of nations will come from you, and kings will come from your body.
12The land I gave to Abraham and Isaac I also give to you, and I will give this land to your descendants after you."
13Then God went up from him at the place where he had talked with him.

14Jacob set up a stone pillar at the place where God had talked with him, and he poured out a drink offering on it; he also poured oil on it.
15Jacob named the place where God had talked with him Bethel.[q]

*The Deaths of Rachel and Isaac*

16Then they moved on from Bethel. While they were still some distance from Ephrath, Rachel began to give birth and had great difficulty.
17And as

[k]7 *El Bethel* means *God of Bethel.*
[l]8 *Allon Bacuth* means *oak of weeping.*
[m]9 That is, Northwest Mesopotamia; also in verse 26
[n]10 *Jacob* means *he grasps the heel* (figuratively, *he deceives*).
[o]10 *Israel* means *he struggles with God.*
[p]11 Hebrew *El-Shaddai*
[q]15 *Bethel* means *house of God.*

בְּהַקְשֹׁתָהּ בְּלִדְתָּהּ וַתֹּאמֶר לָהּ הַמְיַלֶּדֶת
the-being-midwife to-her that-she-said as-to-bear-her as-to-have-difficulty-her

אַל־ תִּירְאִי כִּי־ גַם־ זֶה לָךְ בֵּן׃ וַיְהִי בְּצֵאת
as-to-go and-he-was (18) son to-you this another for you-be-afraid not

נַפְשָׁהּ כִּי מֵתָה וַתִּקְרָא שְׁמוֹ בֶּן־ אוֹנִי וְאָבִיו
but-father-of-him Oni Ben name-of-him that-she-called she-died for life-of-her

קָרָא־ לוֹ בִנְיָמִין׃ וַתָּמָת רָחֵל וַתִּקָּבֵר בְּדֶרֶךְ
on-way-of and-she-was-buried Rachel so-she-died (19) Benjamin to-him he-named

אֶפְרָתָה הִוא בֵּית לָחֶם׃ וַיַּצֵּב יַעֲקֹב מַצֵּבָה עַל־ קְבֻרָתָהּ
tomb-of-her over pillar Jacob and-he-set-up (20) Lehem Beth that to-Ephrath

הִוא מַצֶּבֶת קְבֻרַת־ רָחֵל עַד־ הַיּוֹם׃ וַיִּסַּע יִשְׂרָאֵל
Israel so-he-moved-on (21) the-day to Rachel tomb-of pillar-of that

וַיֵּט אָהֳלֹה מֵהָלְאָה לְמִגְדַּל־ עֵדֶר׃ וַיְהִי בִּשְׁכֹּן
as-to-live and-he-was (22) Eder to-Migdal beyond tent-of-him and-he-pitched

יִשְׂרָאֵל בָּאָרֶץ הַהִוא וַיֵּלֶךְ רְאוּבֵן וַיִּשְׁכַּב אֶת־ בִּלְהָה
Bilhah with and-he-slept Reuben that-he-went the-that in-the-region Israel

פִּילֶגֶשׁ אָבִיו וַיִּשְׁמַע יִשְׂרָאֵל וַיִּהְיוּ בְנֵי־ יַעֲקֹב
Jacob sons-of now-they-were Israel and-he-heard father-of-him concubine-of

שְׁנֵים עָשָׂר׃ בְּנֵי לֵאָה בְּכוֹר יַעֲקֹב רְאוּבֵן וְשִׁמְעוֹן וְלֵוִי
and-Levi and-Simeon Reuben Jacob firstborn-of Leah sons-of (23) ten two

וִיהוּדָה וְיִשָּׂשכָר וּזְבוּלֻן׃ בְּנֵי רָחֵל יוֹסֵף וּבִנְיָמִן׃
and-Benjamin Joseph Rachel sons-of (24) and-Zebulun and-Issachar and-Judah

וּבְנֵי בִלְהָה שִׁפְחַת רָחֵל דָּן וְנַפְתָּלִי׃
and-Naphtali Dan Rachel maidservant-of Bilhah and-sons-of (25)

וּבְנֵי זִלְפָּה שִׁפְחַת לֵאָה גָּד וְאָשֵׁר אֵלֶּה בְּנֵי יַעֲקֹב
Jacob sons-of these and-Asher Gad Leah maidservant-of Zilpah and-sons-of (26)

אֲשֶׁר יֻלַּד־ לוֹ בְּפַדַּן אֲרָם׃ וַיָּבֹא יַעֲקֹב אֶל־ יִצְחָק
Isaac to Jacob and-he-came (27) Aram in-Paddan to-him he-was-born who

אָבִיו מַמְרֵא קִרְיַת הָאַרְבַּע הִוא חֶבְרוֹן אֲשֶׁר־ גָּר־ שָׁם
there he-stayed where Hebron that the-Arba Kiriath Mamre father-of-him

אַבְרָהָם וְיִצְחָק׃ וַיִּהְיוּ יְמֵי יִצְחָק מְאַת שָׁנָה וּשְׁמֹנִים
and-eighty year hundred-of Isaac days-of and-they-were (28) and-Isaac Abraham

שָׁנָה׃ וַיִּגְוַע יִצְחָק וַיָּמָת וַיֵּאָסֶף אֶל־
to and-he-was-gathered and-he-died Isaac and-he-breathed-last (29) year

עַמָּיו זָקֵן וּשְׂבַע יָמִים וַיִּקְבְּרוּ אֹתוֹ עֵשָׂו וְיַעֲקֹב
and-Jacob Esau him and-they-buried days and-full-of old people-of-him

בָּנָיו׃ וְאֵלֶּה תֹּלְדוֹת עֵשָׂו הוּא אֱדוֹם׃ עֵשָׂו לָקַח אֶת־
*** he-took Esau (2) Edom that Esau lines-of now-these (36:1) sons-of-him

she was having great difficulty in childbirth, the midwife said to her, "Don't be afraid, for you have another son."
18 As she breathed her last—for she was dying—she named her son Ben-Oni.[r] But his father named him Benjamin.[s]
19 So Rachel died and was buried on the way to Ephrath (that is, Bethlehem). 20 Over her tomb Jacob set up a pillar, and to this day that pillar marks Rachel's tomb.
21 Israel moved on again and pitched his tent beyond Migdal Eder. 22 While Israel was living in that region, Reuben went in and slept with his father's concubine Bilhah, and Israel heard of it.

Jacob had twelve sons:
23 The sons of Leah:
Reuben the firstborn of Jacob,
Simeon, Levi, Judah, Issachar and Zebulun.
24 The sons of Rachel:
Joseph and Benjamin.
25 The sons of Rachel's maidservant Bilhah:
Dan and Naphtali.
26 The sons of Leah's maidservant Zilpah:
Gad and Asher.
These were the sons of Jacob, who were born to him in Paddan Aram.

27 Jacob came home to his father Isaac in Mamre, near Kiriath Arba (that is, Hebron), where Abraham and Isaac had stayed. 28 Isaac lived a hundred and eighty years. 29 Then he breathed his last and died and was gathered to his people, old and full of years. And his sons Esau and Jacob buried him.

*Esau's Descendants*

36 This is the account of Esau (that is, Edom).

2 Esau took his wives from

r18 *Ben-Oni* means *son of my trouble.*
s18 *Benjamin* means *son of my right hand.*

°21 ק אהלו

נָשָׁיו מִבְּנוֹת כְּנָעַן אֶת־עָדָה בַּת־ אֵילוֹן הַחִתִּי וְאֶת־
and the-Hittite Elon daughter-of Adah *** Canaan from-women-of wives-of-him

אָהֳלִיבָמָה בַּת־ עֲנָה בַּת־ צִבְעוֹן הַחִוִּי׃ וְאֶת־
and (3) the-Hittite Zibeon granddaughter-of Anah daughter-of Oholibamah

בָּשְׂמַת בַּת־ יִשְׁמָעֵאל אֲחוֹת נְבָיוֹת׃ וַתֵּלֶד עָדָה לְעֵשָׂו
to-Esau Adah and-she-bore (4) Nebaioth sister-of Ishmael daughter-of Basemath

אֶת־אֱלִיפָז וּבָשְׂמַת יָלְדָה אֶת־רְעוּאֵל׃ וְאָהֳלִיבָמָה יָלְדָה אֶת־
*** she-bore and-Oholibamah (5) Reuel *** she-bore and-Basemath Eliphaz ***

יְעִישׁ° וְאֶת־יַעְלָם וְאֶת־ קֹרַח אֵלֶּה בְּנֵי עֵשָׂו אֲשֶׁר יֻלְּדוּ־ לוֹ
to-him they-were-born who Esau sons-of these Korah and Jalam and Jeush

בְּאֶרֶץ כְּנָעַן׃ וַיִּקַּח עֵשָׂו אֶת־ נָשָׁיו וְאֶת־ בָּנָיו וְאֶת־
and sons-of-him and wives-of-him *** Esau and-he-took (6) Canaan in-land-of

בְּנֹתָיו וְאֶת־ כָּל־ נַפְשׁוֹת בֵּיתוֹ וְאֶת־ מִקְנֵהוּ וְאֶת־ כָּל־
every-of and stock-of-him and house-of-him members-of all-of and daughters-of-him

בְּהֶמְתּוֹ וְאֵת כָּל־ קִנְיָנוֹ אֲשֶׁר רָכַשׁ בְּאֶרֶץ כְּנָעַן
Canaan in-land-of he-acquired that good-of-him all-of and animal-of-him

וַיֵּלֶךְ אֶל־ אֶרֶץ מִפְּנֵי יַעֲקֹב אָחִיו׃ כִּי־ הָיָה
he-was for (7) brother-of-him Jacob from-face-of land to and-he-moved

רְכוּשָׁם רָב מִשֶּׁבֶת יַחְדָּו וְלֹא יָכְלָה אֶרֶץ
land-of he-could and-not together than-to-remain greater possession-of-them

מְגוּרֵיהֶם לָשֵׂאת אֹתָם מִפְּנֵי מִקְנֵיהֶם׃ וַיֵּשֶׁב
so-he-settled (8) stock-of-them because-of them to-support journeys-of-them

עֵשָׂו בְּהַר שֵׂעִיר עֵשָׂו הוּא אֱדוֹם׃ וְאֵלֶּה תֹּלְדוֹת עֵשָׂו
Esau lines-of now-these (9) Edom he Esau Seir in-hill-country-of Esau

אֲבִי אֱדוֹם בְּהַר שֵׂעִיר׃ אֵלֶּה שְׁמוֹת בְּנֵי־ עֵשָׂו
Esau sons-of names-of these (10) Seir in-hill-country-of Edom father-of

אֱלִיפַז בֶּן־ עָדָה אֵשֶׁת עֵשָׂו רְעוּאֵל בֶּן־ בָּשְׂמַת אֵשֶׁת עֵשָׂו׃
Esau wife-of Basemath son-of Reuel Esau wife-of Adah son-of Eliphaz

וַיִּהְיוּ בְּנֵי אֱלִיפָז תֵּימָן אוֹמָר צְפוֹ וְגַעְתָּם וּקְנַז׃
and-Kenaz and-Gatam Zepho Omar Teman Eliphaz sons-of and-they-were (11)

וְתִמְנַע ׀ הָיְתָה פִילֶגֶשׁ לֶאֱלִיפַז בֶּן־ עֵשָׂו וַתֵּלֶד
and-she-bore Esau son-of to-Eliphaz concubine she-was now-Timna (12)

לֶאֱלִיפַז אֶת־ עֲמָלֵק אֵלֶּה בְּנֵי עָדָה אֵשֶׁת עֵשָׂו׃ וְאֵלֶּה
and-these (13) Esau wife-of Adah grandsons-of these Amalek *** to-Eliphaz

בְּנֵי רְעוּאֵל נַחַת וָזֶרַח שַׁמָּה וּמִזָּה אֵלֶּה* הָיוּ בְּנֵי
grandsons-of they-were these and-Mizzah Shammah and-Zerah Nahath Reuel sons-of

בָשְׂמַת אֵשֶׁת עֵשָׂו׃ וְאֵלֶּה הָיוּ בְּנֵי אָהֳלִיבָמָה בַת־
daughter-of Oholibamah sons-of they-were and-these (14) Esau wife-of Basemath

the women of Canaan:
Adah daughter of Elon the
Hittite, and Oholibamah
daughter of Anah and
granddaughter of Zibeon
the Hivite— [3]also Basemath
daughter of Ishmael and
sister of Nebaioth.
[4]Adah bore Eliphaz to
Esau, Basemath bore Reuel,
[5]and Oholibamah bore
Jeush, Jalam and Korah.
These were the sons of
Esau, who were born to
him in Canaan.
[6]Esau took his wives and
sons and daughters and all
the members of his
household, as well as his
livestock and all his other
animals and all the goods
he had acquired in Canaan,
and moved to a land some
distance from his brother
Jacob. [7]Their possessions
were too great for them to
remain together; the land
where they were staying
could not support them
both because of their livestock. [8]So Esau (that is,
Edom) settled in the hill
country of Seir.

[9]This is the account of Esau
the father of the Edomites in
the hill country of Seir.

[10]These are the names of
Esau's sons:
Eliphaz, the son of Esau's
wife Adah, and Reuel,
the son of Esau's wife
Basemath.
[11]The sons of Eliphaz:
Teman, Omar, Zepho,
Gatam and Kenaz.
[12]Esau's son Eliphaz also
had a concubine named
Timna, who bore him
Amalek. These were
grandsons of Esau's wife
Adah.
[13]The sons of Reuel:
Nahath, Zerah, Sham-
mah and Mizzah. These
were grandsons of Esau's
wife Basemath.
[14]The sons of Esau's wife
Oholibamah daughter of

**13* Most mss have no *munah* after the *segol* ( אֵלֶּה ).

°5 ק יעוש

עֲנָה בַּת־ צִבְעוֹן אֵשֶׁת עֵשָׂו וַתֵּלֶד לְעֵשָׂו אֶת־ יְעִישׁ וְאֶת־
and Jeush *** to-Esau and-she-bore Esau wife-of Zibeon granddaughter-of Anah

יַעְלָם וְאֶת־ קֹרַח׃ אֵלֶּה אַלּוּפֵי בְנֵי־ עֵשָׂו בְּנֵי אֱלִיפַז
Eliphaz sons-of Esau descendants-of chiefs-of these (15) Korah and Jalam

בְּכוֹר עֵשָׂו אַלּוּף תֵּימָן אַלּוּף אוֹמָר אַלּוּף צְפוֹ אַלּוּף קְנַז׃ אַלּוּף
Chief (16) Kenaz Chief Zepho Chief Omar Chief Teman Chief Esau firstborn-of

קֹרַח אַלּוּף גַּעְתָּם אַלּוּף עֲמָלֵק אֵלֶּה אַלּוּפֵי אֱלִיפַז בְּאֶרֶץ אֱדוֹם אֵלֶּה
these Edom in-land-of Eliphaz chiefs-of these Amalek Chief Gatam Chief Korah

בְּנֵי עָדָה׃ וְאֵלֶּה בְּנֵי רְעוּאֵל בֶּן־ עֵשָׂו אַלּוּף נַחַת אַלּוּף
Chief Nahath Chief Esau son-of Reuel sons-of and-these (17) Adah grandsons-of

זֶרַח אַלּוּף שַׁמָּה אַלּוּף מִזָּה אֵלֶּה אַלּוּפֵי רְעוּאֵל בְּאֶרֶץ אֱדוֹם אֵלֶּה
these Edom in-land-of Reuel chiefs-of these Mizzah Chief Shammah Chief Zerah

בְּנֵי בָשְׂמַת אֵשֶׁת עֵשָׂו׃ וְאֵלֶּה בְּנֵי אָהֳלִיבָמָה אֵשֶׁת
wife-of Oholibamah sons-of and-these (18) Esau wife-of Basemath grandsons-of

עֵשָׂו אַלּוּף יְעוּשׁ אַלּוּף יַעְלָם אַלּוּף קֹרַח אֵלֶּה אַלּוּפֵי אָהֳלִיבָמָה
Oholibamah chiefs-of these Korah Chief Jalam Chief Jeush Chief Esau

בַּת־ עֲנָה אֵשֶׁת עֵשָׂו׃ אֵלֶּה בְנֵי־ עֵשָׂו וְאֵלֶּה אַלּוּפֵיהֶם
chiefs-of-them and-these Esau sons-of these (19) Esau wife-of Anah daughter-of

הוּא אֱדוֹם׃ אֵלֶּה בְנֵי־ שֵׂעִיר הַחֹרִי יֹשְׁבֵי הָאָרֶץ
the-region ones-living-of the-Horite Seir sons-of these (20) Edom that

לוֹטָן וְשׁוֹבָל וְצִבְעוֹן וַעֲנָה׃ וְדִשׁוֹן וְאֵצֶר וְדִישָׁן
and-Dishan and-Ezer and-Dishon (21) and-Anah and-Zibeon and-Shobal Lotan

אֵלֶּה אַלּוּפֵי הַחֹרִי בְּנֵי שֵׂעִיר בְּאֶרֶץ אֱדוֹם׃ וַיִּהְיוּ
and-they-were (22) Edom in-land-of Seir sons-of the-Horite chiefs-of these

בְנֵי־ לוֹטָן חֹרִי וְהֵימָם וַאֲחוֹת לוֹטָן תִּמְנָע׃ וְאֵלֶּה בְּנֵי
sons-of and-these (23) Timna Lotan now-sister-of and-Hemam Hori Lotan sons-of

שׁוֹבָל עַלְוָן וּמָנַחַת וְעֵיבָל שְׁפוֹ וְאוֹנָם׃ וְאֵלֶּה בְנֵי־
sons-of and-these (24) and-Onam Shepho and-Ebal and-Manahath Alvan Shobal

צִבְעוֹן וְאַיָּה וַעֲנָה הוּא עֲנָה אֲשֶׁר מָצָא אֶת־ הַיֵּמִם
the-hot-springs *** he-discovered who Anah this and-Anah even-Aiah Zibeon

בַּמִּדְבָּר בִּרְעֹתוֹ אֶת־ הַחֲמֹרִים לְצִבְעוֹן אָבִיו׃
father-of-him to-Zibeon the-donkeys *** while-to-graze-him in-the-desert

וְאֵלֶּה בְנֵי־ עֲנָה דִּשֹׁן וְאָהֳלִיבָמָה בַּת־ עֲנָה׃
Anah daughter-of and-Oholibamah Dishon Anah children-of and-these (25)

וְאֵלֶּה בְּנֵי דִישָׁן חֶמְדָּן וְאֶשְׁבָּן וְיִתְרָן וּכְרָן׃
and-Keran and-Ithran and-Eshban Hemdan Dishon sons-of and-these (26)

אֵלֶּה בְּנֵי־ אֵצֶר בִּלְהָן וְזַעֲוָן וַעֲקָן׃ אֵלֶּה בְנֵי־ דִישָׁן
Dishan sons-of these (28) and-Akan and-Zaavan Bilhan Ezer sons-of these (27)

Anah and granddaughter of Zibeon, whom she bore to Esau:
Jeush, Jalam and Korah.

15 These were the chiefs among Esau's descendants:
The sons of Eliphaz the firstborn of Esau:
Chiefs Teman, Omar, Zepho, Kenaz, 16 Korah,[t] Gatam and Amalek.
These were the chiefs descended from Eliphaz in Edom; they were grandsons of Adah.

17 The sons of Esau's son Reuel:
Chiefs Nahath, Zerah, Shammah and Mizzah.
These were the chiefs descended from Reuel in Edom; they were grandsons of Esau's wife Basemath.

18 The sons of Esau's wife Oholibamah:
Chiefs Jeush, Jalam and Korah. These were the chiefs descended from Esau's wife Oholibamah daughter of Anah.

19 These were the sons of Esau (that is, Edom), and these were their chiefs.

20 These were the sons of Seir the Horite, who were living in the region:
Lotan, Shobal, Zibeon, Anah, 21 Dishon, Ezer and Dishan. These sons of Seir in Edom were Horite chiefs.

22 The sons of Lotan:
Hori and Homam.[u] Timna was Lotan's sister.

23 The sons of Shobal:
Alvan, Manahath, Ebal, Shepho and Onam.

24 The sons of Zibeon:
Aiah and Anah. This is the Anah who discovered the hot springs[v] in the desert while he was grazing the donkeys of his father Zibeon.

25 The children of Anah:
Dishon and Oholibamah daughter of Anah.

26 The sons of Dishon[w]:
Hemdan, Eshban, Ithran and Keran.

27 The sons of Ezer:
Bilhan, Zaavan and Akan.

28 The sons of Dishan:

[t] 16 Masoretic Text; Samaritan Pentateuch (see also Gen. 36:11 and 1 Chron. 1:36) does not have *Korah*.
[u] 22 Hebrew *Hemam*, a variant of *Homam*
[v] 24 Vulgate; Syriac *discovered water;* the meaning of the Hebrew for this word is uncertain.
[w] 26 Hebrew *Dishan*, a variant of *Dishon*

°14 ק יעוש

עוּץ וַאֲרָן׃ אֵלֶּה אַלּוּפֵי הַחֹרִי אַלּוּף לוֹטָן אַלּוּף שׁוֹבָל אַלּוּף
Chief Shobal Chief Lotan Chief the-Horite chiefs-of these (29) and-Aran Uz

צִבְעוֹן אַלּוּף עֲנָה׃ אַלּוּף דִּשֹׁן אַלּוּף אֵצֶר אַלּוּף דִּישָׁן אֵלֶּה אַלּוּפֵי
chiefs-of these Dishan Chief Ezer Chief Dishon Chief (30) Anah Chief Zibeon

הַחֹרִי לְאַלֻּפֵיהֶם בְּאֶרֶץ שֵׂעִיר׃ וְאֵלֶּה הַמְּלָכִים אֲשֶׁר
who the-kings and-these (31) Seir in-land-of by-divisions-of-them the-Horite

מָלְכוּ בְּאֶרֶץ אֱדוֹם לִפְנֵי מְלָךְ־ מֶלֶךְ לִבְנֵי יִשְׂרָאֵל׃
Israel from-sons-of king to-reign before Edom in-land-of they-reigned

וַיִּמְלֹךְ בֶּאֱדוֹם בֶּלַע בֶּן־ בְּעוֹר וְשֵׁם עִירוֹ דִּנְהָבָה׃
Dinhabah city-of-him and-name-of Beor son-of Bela in-Edom now-he-reigned (32)

וַיָּמָת בָּלַע וַיִּמְלֹךְ תַּחְתָּיו יוֹבָב בֶּן־ זֶרַח
Zerah son-of Jobab after-him then-he-reigned Bela when-he-died (33)

מִבָּצְרָה׃ וַיָּמָת יוֹבָב וַיִּמְלֹךְ תַּחְתָּיו חֻשָׁם
Husham after-him then-he-reigned Jobab when-he-died (34) from-Bozrah

מֵאֶרֶץ הַתֵּימָנִי׃ וַיָּמָת חֻשָׁם וַיִּמְלֹךְ תַּחְתָּיו
after-him then-he-reigned Husham when-he-died (35) the-Temanite from-land-of

הֲדַד בֶּן־ בְּדַד הַמַּכֶּה אֶת־ מִדְיָן בִּשְׂדֵה מוֹאָב וְשֵׁם
and-name-of Moab in-country-of Midian *** the-one-defeating Bedad son-of Hadad

עִירוֹ עֲוִית׃ וַיָּמָת הֲדָד וַיִּמְלֹךְ תַּחְתָּיו שַׂמְלָה
Samlah after-him then-he-reigned Hadad when-he-died (36) Avith city-of-him

מִמַּשְׂרֵקָה׃ וַיָּמָת שַׂמְלָה וַיִּמְלֹךְ תַּחְתָּיו שָׁאוּל
Shaul after-him then-he-reigned Samlah when-he-died (37) from-Masrekah

מֵרְחֹבוֹת הַנָּהָר׃ וַיָּמָת שָׁאוּל וַיִּמְלֹךְ תַּחְתָּיו
after-him then-he-reigned Shaul when-he-died (38) the-river from-Rehoboth-of

בַּעַל חָנָן בֶּן־ עַכְבּוֹר׃ וַיָּמָת בַּעַל חָנָן בֶּן־ עַכְבּוֹר
Acbor son-of Hanan Baal when-he-died (39) Acbor son-of Hanan Baal

וַיִּמְלֹךְ תַּחְתָּיו הֲדַר וְשֵׁם עִירוֹ פָּעוּ וְשֵׁם
and-name-of Pau city-of-him and-name-of Hadar after-him then-he-reigned

אִשְׁתּוֹ מְהֵיטַבְאֵל בַּת־ מַטְרֵד בַּת מֵי זָהָב׃ וְאֵלֶּה
and-these (40) Zahab Me daughter-of Matred daughter-of Mehetebel wife-of-him

שְׁמוֹת אַלּוּפֵי עֵשָׂו לְמִשְׁפְּחֹתָם לִמְקֹמֹתָם בִּשְׁמֹתָם
by-names-of-them by-regions-of-them by-clans-of-them Esau chiefs-of names-of

אַלּוּף תִּמְנָע אַלּוּף עַלְוָה אַלּוּף יְתֵת׃ אַלּוּף אָהֳלִיבָמָה אַלּוּף אֵלָה אַלּוּף
Chief Elah Chief Oholibamah Chief (41) Jetheth Chief Alvah Chief Timna Chief

פִּינֹן׃ אַלּוּף קְנַז אַלּוּף תֵּימָן אַלּוּף מִבְצָר׃ אַלּוּף מַגְדִּיאֵל אַלּוּף עִירָם
Iram Chief Magdiel Chief (43) Mibzar Chief Teman Chief Kenaz Chief (42) Pinon

אֵלֶּה ׀ אַלּוּפֵי אֱדוֹם לְמֹשְׁבֹתָם בְּאֶרֶץ אֲחֻזָּתָם הוּא
this occupation-of-them in-land-of by-settlements-of-them Edom chiefs-of these

Uz and Aran.
29 These were the Horite chiefs:
Lotan, Shobal, Zibeon, Anah, 30 Dishon, Ezer and Dishan. These were the Horite chiefs, according to their divisions, in the land of Seir.

*The Rulers of Edom*

31 These were the kings who reigned in Edom before any Israelite king reigned[x]:
32 Bela son of Beor became king of Edom. His city was named Dinhabah.
33 When Bela died, Jobab son of Zerah from Bozrah succeeded him as king.
34 When Jobab died, Husham from the land of the Temanites succeeded him as king.
35 When Husham died, Hadad son of Bedad, who defeated Midian in the country of Moab, succeeded him as king. His city was named Avith.
36 When Hadad died, Samlah from Masrekah succeeded him as king.
37 When Samlah died, Shaul from Rehoboth on the river[y] succeeded him as king.
38 When Shaul died, Baal-Hanan son of Acbor succeeded him as king.
39 When Baal-Hanan son of Acbor died, Hadad[z] succeeded him as king. His city was named Pau, and his wife's name was Mehetabel daughter of Matred, the daughter of Me-Zahab.

40 These were the chiefs descended from Esau, by name, according to their clans and regions:
Timna, Alvah, Jetheth, 41 Oholibamah, Elah, Pinon, 42 Kenaz, Teman, Mibzar, 43 Magdiel and Iram. These were the chiefs of Edom, according to their settlements in the land they occupied.

x31 Or *before an Israelite king reigned over them*
y37 Or *River*
z39 Many manuscripts of the Masoretic Text, Samaritan Pentateuch and Syriac (see also 1 Chron. 1:50); most manuscripts of the Masoretic Text *Hadar*

עֵשָׂו אֲבִי אֱדוֹם׃ וַיֵּשֶׁב יַעֲקֹב בְּאֶרֶץ מְגוּרֵי
journeys-of in-land-of Jacob now-he-lived (37:1) Edom father-of Esau

אָבִיו בְּאֶרֶץ כְּנָעַן׃ אֵלֶּה ׀ תֹּלְדוֹת יַעֲקֹב יוֹסֵף בֶּן־ שְׁבַע־
seven son-of Joseph Jacob lines-of these (2) Canaan in-land-of father-of-him

עֶשְׂרֵה שָׁנָה הָיָה רֹעֶה אֶת־ אֶחָיו בַּצֹּאן וְהוּא נַעַר
young-man now-he to-the-flock brothers-of-him with tending he-was year ten

אֶת־ בְּנֵי בִלְהָה וְאֶת־בְּנֵי זִלְפָּה נְשֵׁי אָבִיו וַיָּבֵא
and-he-brought father-of-him wives-of Zilpah sons-of and Bilhah sons-of with

יוֹסֵף אֶת־ דִּבָּתָם רָעָה אֶל־ אֲבִיהֶם׃ וְיִשְׂרָאֵל אָהַב אֶת־
*** he-loved now-Israel (3) father-of-them to bad report-of-them *** Joseph

יוֹסֵף מִכָּל־ בָּנָיו כִּי־ בֶן־ זְקֻנִים הוּא לוֹ וְעָשָׂה
and-he-made to-him he old-ages son-of for sons-of-him more-than-all-of Joseph

לוֹ כְּתֹנֶת פַּסִּים׃ וַיִּרְאוּ אֶחָיו כִּי־ אֹתוֹ אָהַב
he-loved him that brothers-of-him when-they-saw (4) ornaments robe-of for-him

אֲבִיהֶם מִכָּל־ אֶחָיו וַיִּשְׂנְאוּ אֹתוֹ וְלֹא
and-not him then-they-hated brothers-of-him more-than-any-of father-of-them

יָכְלוּ דַּבְּרוֹ לְשָׁלֹם׃ וַיַּחֲלֹם יוֹסֵף חֲלוֹם
dream Joseph and-he-dreamed (5) with-kindness to-speak-to-him they-could

וַיַּגֵּד לְאֶחָיו וַיּוֹסִפוּ עוֹד שְׂנֹא אֹתוֹ׃
him to-hate more but-they-increased to-brothers-of-him and-he-told

וַיֹּאמֶר אֲלֵיהֶם שִׁמְעוּ־נָא הַחֲלוֹם הַזֶּה אֲשֶׁר חָלָמְתִּי׃
I-dreamed that the-this the-dream now! listen! to-them and-he-said (6)

וְהִנֵּה אֲנַחְנוּ מְאַלְּמִים אֲלֻמִּים בְּתוֹךְ הַשָּׂדֶה וְהִנֵּה קָמָה
she-rose and-see! the-field out-in sheaves ones-binding we now-see! (7)

אֲלֻמָּתִי וְגַם־ נִצָּבָה וְהִנֵּה תְסֻבֶּינָה אֲלֻמֹּתֵיכֶם
sheaves-of-you they-gathered-around and-see! she-stood and-also sheaf-of-me

וַתִּשְׁתַּחֲוֶיןָ לַאֲלֻמָּתִי׃ וַיֹּאמְרוּ לוֹ אֶחָיו
brothers-of-him to-him and-they-said (8) to-sheaf-of-me and-they-bowed

הֲמָלֹךְ תִּמְלֹךְ עָלֵינוּ אִם־ מָשׁוֹל תִּמְשֹׁל בָּנוּ
over-us will-you-rule to-rule really over-us will-you-reign to-reign?

וַיּוֹסִפוּ עוֹד שְׂנֹא אֹתוֹ עַל־ חֲלֹמֹתָיו וְעַל־
and-because-of dreams-of-him because-of him to-hate more and-they-increased

דְּבָרָיו׃ וַיַּחֲלֹם עוֹד חֲלוֹם אַחֵר וַיְסַפֵּר אֹתוֹ
him and-he-told another dream again then-he-dreamed (9) words-of-him

לְאֶחָיו וַיֹּאמֶר הִנֵּה חָלַמְתִּי חֲלוֹם עוֹד וְהִנֵּה הַשֶּׁמֶשׁ
the-sun and-see! again dream I-dreamed see! and-he-said to-brothers-of-him

וְהַיָּרֵחַ וְאַחַד עָשָׂר כּוֹכָבִים מִשְׁתַּחֲוִים לִי׃ וַיְסַפֵּר אֶל־
to when-he-told (10) to-me ones-bowing stars ten and-one and-the-moon

This was Esau, the father of the Edomites.

*Joseph's Dreams*

37 Jacob lived in the land where his father had stayed, the land of Canaan.

2 This is the account of Jacob.

Joseph, a young man of seventeen, was tending the flocks with his brothers, the sons of Bilhah and the sons of Zilpah, his father's wives, and he brought their father a bad report about them.
3 Now Israel loved Joseph more than any of his other sons, because he had been born to him in his old age; and he made a richly ornamented[a] robe for him. 4 When his brothers saw that their father loved him more than any of them, they hated him and could not speak a kind word to him.
5 Joseph had a dream, and when he told it to his brothers, they hated him all the more. 6 He said to them, "Listen to this dream I had: 7 We were binding sheaves of grain out in the field when suddenly my sheaf rose and stood upright, while your sheaves gathered around mine and bowed down to it."
8 His brothers said to him, "Do you intend to reign over us? Will you actually rule us?" And they hated him all the more because of his dream and what he had said.
9 Then he had another dream, and he told it to his brothers. "Listen," he said, "I had another dream, and this time the sun and moon and eleven stars were bowing down to me."
10 When he told his father as

[a]3 The meaning of the Hebrew for this word is uncertain; also in verses 23 and 32.

אָבִיו וְאֶל־ אֶחָיו וַיִּגְעַר־ בּוֹ אָבִיו
father-of-him to-him then-he-rebuked brothers-of-him and-to father-of-him

וַיֹּאמֶר לוֹ מָה הַחֲלוֹם הַזֶּה אֲשֶׁר חָלָמְתָּ הֲבוֹא
to-come? you-dreamed that the-this the-dream what? to-him and-he-said

נָבוֹא אֲנִי וְאִמְּךָ וְאַחֶיךָ לְהִשְׁתַּחֲוֹת לְךָ
before-you to-bow and-brothers-of-you and-mother-of-you I will-we-come

אָרְצָה׃ (11) וַיְקַנְאוּ־ בוֹ אֶחָיו וְאָבִיו
but-father-of-him brothers-of-him of-him and-they-were-jealous (11) to-ground

שָׁמַר אֶת־ הַדָּבָר׃ (12) וַיֵּלְכוּ אֶחָיו לִרְעוֹת
to-graze brothers-of-him now-they-went (12) the-matter *** he-kept-in-mind

אֶת־ צֹאן אֲבִיהֶם בִּשְׁכֶם׃ (13) וַיֹּאמֶר יִשְׂרָאֵל אֶל־ יוֹסֵף
Joseph to Israel and-he-said (13) near-Shechem father-of-them flock-of ***

הֲלוֹא אַחֶיךָ רֹעִים בִּשְׁכֶם לְכָה וְאֶשְׁלָחֲךָ
and-I-will-send-you come! near-Shechem ones-grazing brothers-of-you not?

אֲלֵיהֶם וַיֹּאמֶר לוֹ הִנֵּנִי׃ (14) וַיֹּאמֶר לוֹ לֶךְ־ נָא רְאֵה אֶת־
*** see! now! go! to-him so-he-said (14) here-I to-him and-he-replied to-them

שְׁלוֹם אַחֶיךָ וְאֶת־ שְׁלוֹם הַצֹּאן וַהֲשִׁבֵנִי דָּבָר
word and-bring-me! the-flock welfare-of and brothers-of-you welfare-of

וַיִּשְׁלָחֵהוּ מֵעֵמֶק חֶבְרוֹן וַיָּבֹא שְׁכֶמָה׃
to-Shechem and-he-went Hebron from-valley-of so-he-sent-him

(15) וַיִּמְצָאֵהוּ אִישׁ וְהִנֵּה תֹעֶה בַּשָּׂדֶה וַיִּשְׁאָלֵהוּ הָאִישׁ
the-man and-he-asked-him in-the-field wandering and-see! man and-he-found-him (15)

לֵאמֹר מַה־ תְּבַקֵּשׁ׃ (16) וַיֹּאמֶר אֶת־ אַחַי אָנֹכִי מְבַקֵּשׁ
looking I brothers-of-me *** and-he-replied (16) you-look-for what? to-say

הַגִּידָה־נָּא לִי אֵיפֹה הֵם רֹעִים׃ (17) וַיֹּאמֶר הָאִישׁ נָסְעוּ
they-moved the-man and-he-answered (17) grazing they where to-me now! tell!

מִזֶּה כִּי שָׁמַעְתִּי אֹמְרִים נֵלְכָה דֹּתָיְנָה וַיֵּלֶךְ יוֹסֵף אַחַר
after Joseph so-he-went to-Dothan let-us-go ones-saying I-heard for from-here

אֶחָיו וַיִּמְצָאֵם בְּדֹתָן׃ (18) וַיִּרְאוּ אֹתוֹ
him but-they-saw (18) near-Dothan and-he-found-them brothers-of-him

מֵרָחֹק וּבְטֶרֶם יִקְרַב אֲלֵיהֶם וַיִּתְנַכְּלוּ אֹתוֹ לַהֲמִיתוֹ׃
to-kill-him him then-they-plotted to-them he-reached and-before in-distance

(19) וַיֹּאמְרוּ אִישׁ אֶל־ אָחִיו הִנֵּה בַּעַל הַחֲלֹמוֹת הַלָּזֶה
the-this the-dreams lord-of see! brother-of-him to each and-they-said (19)

בָּא׃ (20) וְעַתָּה ׀ לְכוּ וְנַהַרְגֵהוּ וְנַשְׁלִכֵהוּ
and-let-us-throw-him and-let-us-kill-him come! so-now (20) he-comes

בְּאַחַד הַבֹּרוֹת וְאָמַרְנוּ חַיָּה רָעָה אֲכָלָתְהוּ
she-devoured-him ferocious animal then-we-will-say the-cisterns into-one-of

well as his brothers, his father
rebuked him and said, "What
is this dream you had? Will
your mother and I and your
brothers actually come and
bow down to the ground before you?" [11]His brothers were
jealous of him, but his father
kept the matter in mind.

*Joseph Sold by His Brothers*

[12]Now his brothers had gone
to graze their father's flocks
near Shechem, [13]and Israel
said to Joseph, "As you know,
your brothers are grazing the
flocks near Shechem. Come, I
am going to send you to
them."
"Very well," he replied.
[14]So he said to him, "Go and
see if all is well with your
brothers and with the flocks,
and bring word back to me."
So he sent him off from the
Valley of Hebron.
When Joseph arrived at Shechem, [15]a man found him
wandering around in the
fields and asked him, "What
are you looking for?"
[16]He replied, "I'm looking
for my brothers. Can you tell
me where they are grazing
their flocks?"
[17]"They have moved on
from here," the man an-
swered. "I heard them say,
'Let's go to Dothan.'"
So Joseph went after his
brothers and found them near
Dothan. [18]But they saw him in
the distance, and before he
reached them, they plotted to
kill him.
[19]"Here comes that dreamer!" they said to each other.
[20]"Come now, let's kill him
and throw him into one of
these cisterns and say that a
ferocious animal devoured

וְנִרְאֶה מַה־ יִּהְיוּ חֲלֹמֹתָיו׃ וַיִּשְׁמַע רְאוּבֵן
Reuben when-he-heard (21) dreams-of-him they-become what then-we-will-see

וַיַּצִּלֵהוּ מִיָּדָם וַיֹּאמֶר לֹא נַכֶּנּוּ נָפֶשׁ׃
life let-us-take not and-he-said from-hand-of-them then-he-rescued-him

וַיֹּאמֶר אֲלֵהֶם ׀ רְאוּבֵן אַל־ תִּשְׁפְּכוּ־ דָם הַשְׁלִיכוּ אֹתוֹ אֶל־ הַבּוֹר
the-cistern into him throw! blood you-shed not Reuben to-them and-he-said (22)

הַזֶּה אֲשֶׁר בַּמִּדְבָּר וְיָד אַל־ תִּשְׁלְחוּ־ בוֹ לְמַעַן הַצִּיל
to-rescue in-order on-him you-lay not but-hand in-the-desert that the-this

אֹתוֹ מִיָּדָם לַהֲשִׁיבוֹ אֶל־ אָבִיו׃ וַיְהִי
and-he-was (23) father-of-him to to-take-back-him from-hand-of-them him

כַּאֲשֶׁר־ בָּא יוֹסֵף אֶל־ אֶחָיו וַיַּפְשִׁיטוּ אֶת־ יוֹסֵף אֶת־
*** Joseph *** that-they-stripped brothers-of-him to Joseph he-came when

כֻּתָּנְתּוֹ אֶת־ כְּתֹנֶת הַפַּסִּים אֲשֶׁר עָלָיו׃ וַיִּקָּחֻהוּ
and-they-took-him (24) on-him that the-ornaments robe-of *** robe-of-him

וַיַּשְׁלִכוּ אֹתוֹ הַבֹּרָה וְהַבּוֹר רֵק אֵין בּוֹ מָיִם׃
water in-him not empty now-the-cistern into-the-cistern him and-they-threw

וַיֵּשְׁבוּ לֶאֱכָל־ לֶחֶם וַיִּשְׂאוּ עֵינֵיהֶם וַיִּרְאוּ
and-they-saw eyes-of-them then-they-lifted meal to-eat as-they-sat-down (25)

וְהִנֵּה אֹרְחַת יִשְׁמְעֵאלִים בָּאָה מִגִּלְעָד וּגְמַלֵּיהֶם
and-camels-of-them from-Gilead coming Ishmaelites caravan-of and-see!

נֹשְׂאִים נְכֹאת וּצְרִי וָלֹט הוֹלְכִים לְהוֹרִיד מִצְרָיְמָה׃
to-Egypt to-take-down ones-going and-myrrh and-balm spice ones-being-loaded

וַיֹּאמֶר יְהוּדָה אֶל־ אֶחָיו מַה־ בֶּצַע כִּי נַהֲרֹג אֶת־
*** we-kill if gain what? brothers-of-him to Judah and-he-said (26)

אָחִינוּ וְכִסִּינוּ אֶת־ דָּמוֹ׃ לְכוּ וְנִמְכְּרֶנּוּ
let-us-sell-him come! (27) blood-of-him *** and-we-cover brother-of-us

לַיִּשְׁמְעֵאלִים וְיָדֵנוּ אַל־ תְּהִי־ בוֹ כִּי־ אָחִינוּ
brother-of-us for on-him she-will-be not and-hand-of-us to-the-Ishmaelites

בְשָׂרֵנוּ הוּא וַיִּשְׁמְעוּ אֶחָיו׃ וַיַּעַבְרוּ אֲנָשִׁים
men when-they-came-by (28) brothers-of-him and-they-agreed he flesh-of-us

מִדְיָנִים סֹחֲרִים וַיִּמְשְׁכוּ וַיַּעֲלוּ אֶת־ יוֹסֵף מִן־
from Joseph *** and-they-lifted then-they-drew-up ones-trading Midianites

הַבּוֹר וַיִּמְכְּרוּ אֶת־ יוֹסֵף לַיִּשְׁמְעֵאלִים בְּעֶשְׂרִים כָּסֶף
silver for-twenty to-the-Ishmaelites Joseph *** and-they-sold the-cistern

וַיָּבִיאוּ אֶת־ יוֹסֵף מִצְרָיְמָה׃ וַיָּשָׁב רְאוּבֵן אֶל־ הַבּוֹר
the-cistern to Reuben when-he-returned (29) to-Egypt Joseph *** and-they-took

וְהִנֵּה אֵין־ יוֹסֵף בַּבּוֹר וַיִּקְרַע אֶת־ בְּגָדָיו׃
clothes-of-him *** then-he-tore in-the-cistern Joseph he-is-not and-see!

him. Then we'll see what comes of his dreams."

21 When Reuben heard this, he tried to rescue him from their hands. "Let's not take his life," he said. 22 "Don't shed any blood. Throw him into this cistern here in the desert, but don't lay a hand on him." Reuben said this to rescue him from them and take him back to his father.

23 So when Joseph came to his brothers, they stripped him of his robe—the richly ornamented robe he was wearing— 24 and they took him and threw him into the cistern. Now the cistern was empty; there was no water in it.

25 As they sat down to eat their meal, they looked up and saw a caravan of Ishmaelites coming from Gilead. Their camels were loaded with spices, balm and myrrh, and they were on their way to take them down to Egypt.

26 Judah said to his brothers, "What will we gain if we kill our brother and cover up his blood? 27 Come, let's sell him to the Ishmaelites and not lay our hands on him; after all, he is our brother, our own flesh and blood." His brothers agreed.

28 So when the Midianite merchants came by, his brothers pulled Joseph up out of the cistern and sold him for twenty shekels[b] of silver to the Ishmaelites, who took him to Egypt.

29 When Reuben returned to the cistern and saw that Joseph was not there, he tore his

[b] 28 That is, about 8 ounces (about 0.2 kilogram)

וַיָּשָׁב אֶל־ אֶחָיו וַיֹּאמַר הַיֶּלֶד אֵינֶנּוּ וַאֲנִי אָנָה
where? and-I not-he the-boy and-he-said brothers-of-him to so-he-went (30)

אֲנִי־בָא׃ וַיִּקְחוּ אֶת־ כְּתֹנֶת יוֹסֵף וַיִּשְׁחֲטוּ שְׂעִיר
male-of and-they-slaughtered Joseph robe-of *** then-they-got (31) turning I

עִזִּים וַיִּטְבְּלוּ אֶת־הַכֻּתֹּנֶת בַּדָּם׃ וַיְשַׁלְּחוּ אֶת־ כְּתֹנֶת
robe-of *** then-they-took (32) in-the-blood robe *** and-they-dipped goats

הַפַּסִּים וַיָּבִיאוּ אֶל־ אֲבִיהֶם וַיֹּאמְרוּ זֹאת מָצָאנוּ
we-found this and-they-said father-of-them to and-they-brought the-ornaments

הַכֶּר־ נָא הַכְּתֹנֶת בִּנְךָ הִוא אִם־לֹא׃ וַיַּכִּירָהּ
and-he-recognized-her (33) not or he son-of-you the-robe now! examine!

וַיֹּאמֶר כְּתֹנֶת בְּנִי חַיָּה רָעָה אֲכָלָתְהוּ טָרֹף
to-be-torn she-devoured-him ferocious animal son-of-me robe-of and-he-said

טֹרַף יוֹסֵף׃ וַיִּקְרַע יַעֲקֹב שִׂמְלֹתָיו וַיָּשֶׂם
and-he-put-on clothes-of-him Jacob then-he-tore (34) Joseph he-was-torn

שַׂק בְּמָתְנָיו וַיִּתְאַבֵּל עַל־ בְּנוֹ יָמִים רַבִּים׃
many days son-of-him for and-he-mourned on-loins-of-him sackcloth

וַיָּקֻמוּ כָל־ בָּנָיו וְכָל־ בְּנֹתָיו
daughters-of-him and-all-of sons-of-him all-of and-they-came (35)

לְנַחֲמוֹ וַיְמָאֵן לְהִתְנַחֵם וַיֹּאמֶר כִּי־ אֵרֵד
I-will-go-down for and-he-said to-be-comforted but-he-refused to-comfort-him

אֶל־ בְּנִי אָבֵל שְׁאֹלָה וַיֵּבְךְּ אֹתוֹ אָבִיו׃
father-of-him for-him so-he-wept to-Sheol mourning son-of-me to

וְהַמְּדָנִים מָכְרוּ אֹתוֹ אֶל־מִצְרָיִם לְפוֹטִיפַר סְרִיס פַּרְעֹה
Pharaoh official-of to-Potiphar Egypt in him they-sold now-the-Medanites (36)

שַׂר הַטַּבָּחִים׃ וַיְהִי בָּעֵת הַהִוא וַיֵּרֶד
that-he-went-down the-that at-the-time and-he-was (38:1) the-guards captain-of

יְהוּדָה מֵאֵת אֶחָיו וַיֵּט עַד־ אִישׁ עֲדֻלָּמִי
Adullamite man with and-he-stayed brothers-of-him from-with Judah

וּשְׁמוֹ חִירָה׃ וַיַּרְא־ שָׁם יְהוּדָה בַּת־ אִישׁ כְּנַעֲנִי
Canaanite man daughter-of Judah there and-he-met (2) Hirah and-name-of-him

וּשְׁמוֹ שׁוּעַ וַיִּקָּחֶהָ וַיָּבֹא אֵלֶיהָ׃
with-her and-he-lay and-he-married-her Shua and-name-of-her

וַתַּהַר וַתֵּלֶד בֵּן וַיִּקְרָא אֶת־ שְׁמוֹ עֵר׃
Er name-of-him *** and-he-called son and-she-bore and-she-conceived (3)

וַתַּהַר עוֹד וַתֵּלֶד בֵּן וַתִּקְרָא אֶת־ שְׁמוֹ
name-of-him *** and-she-called son and-she-bore again and-she-conceived (4)

אוֹנָן׃ וַתֹּסֶף עוֹד וַתֵּלֶד בֵּן וַתִּקְרָא אֶת־
*** and-she-called son and-she-bore still and-she-continued (5) Onan

clothes. [30]He went back to his brothers and said, "The boy isn't there! Where can I turn now?"

[31]Then they got Joseph's robe, slaughtered a goat and dipped the robe in the blood. [32]They took the ornamented robe back to their father and said, "We found this. Examine it to see whether it is your son's robe."

[33]He recognized it and said, "It is my son's robe! Some ferocious animal has devoured him. Joseph has surely been torn to pieces."

[34]Then Jacob tore his clothes, put on sackcloth and mourned for his son many days. [35]All his sons and daughters came to comfort him, but he refused to be comforted. "No," he said, "in mourning will I go down to the grave[c] to my son." So his father wept for him.

[36]Meanwhile, the Midianites[d] sold Joseph in Egypt to Potiphar, one of Pharaoh's officials, the captain of the guard.

*Judah and Tamar*

38 At that time, Judah left his brothers and went down to stay with a man of Adullam named Hirah. [2]There Judah met the daughter of a Canaanite man named Shua. He married her and lay with her; [3]she became pregnant and gave birth to a son, who was named Er. [4]She conceived again and gave birth to a son and named him Onan. [5]She gave birth to still another son

[c]35 Hebrew *Sheol*
[d]36 Samaritan Pentateuch, Septuagint, Vulgate and Syriac (see also verse 28); Masoretic Text *Medanites*

שְׁמוֹ שֵׁלָה וְהָיָה בִכְזִיב בְּלִדְתָּהּ אֹתוֹ׃ וַיִּקַּח
and-he-got (6) him that-to-bear-her at-Kezib now-he-was Shelah name-of-him

יְהוּדָה אִשָּׁה לְעֵר בְּכוֹרוֹ וּשְׁמָהּ תָּמָר׃ וַיְהִי עֵר
Er but-he-was (7) Tamar and-name-of-her firstborn-of-him for-Er wife Judah

בְּכוֹר יְהוּדָה רַע בְּעֵינֵי יְהוָה וַיְמִתֵהוּ יְהוָה׃
Yahweh so-he-killed-him Yahweh in-eyes-of wicked Judah firstborn-of

וַיֹּאמֶר יְהוּדָה לְאוֹנָן בֹּא אֶל־אֵשֶׁת אָחִיךָ
brother-of-you wife-of with lie! to-Onan Judah then-he-said (8)

וְיַבֵּם אֹתָהּ וְהָקֵם זֶרַע לְאָחִיךָ׃
for-brother-of-you offspring and-produce! to-her and-fulfill-duty!

וַיֵּדַע אוֹנָן כִּי לֹּא* לוֹ יִהְיֶה הַזָּרַע וְהָיָה אִם־
when so-he-was the-offspring he-would-be to-him not that Onan but-he-knew (9)

בָּא אֶל־אֵשֶׁת אָחִיו וְשִׁחֵת אַרְצָה לְבִלְתִּי
so-not on-the-ground and-he-spilled brother-of-him wife-of with he-lay

נְתָן־זֶרַע לְאָחִיו׃ וַיֵּרַע בְּעֵינֵי
in-eyes-of so-he-was-wicked (10) for-brother-of-him offspring to-produce

יְהוָה אֲשֶׁר עָשָׂה וַיָּמֶת גַּם־אֹתוֹ׃ וַיֹּאמֶר יְהוּדָה לְתָמָר
to-Tamar Judah then-he-said (11) him also so-he-killed he-did what Yahweh

כַּלָּתוֹ שְׁבִי אַלְמָנָה בֵית־אָבִיךְ עַד־יִגְדַּל
he-grows-up until father-of-you house-of widow live! daughter-in-law-of-him

שֵׁלָה בְנִי כִּי אָמַר פֶּן־יָמוּת גַּם־הוּא כְּאֶחָיו
as-brothers-of-him he also he-will-die perhaps he-thought for son-of-me Shelah

וַתֵּלֶךְ תָּמָר וַתֵּשֶׁב בֵּית אָבִיהָ׃ וַיִּרְבּוּ
and-they-were-many (12) father-of-her house-of and-she-lived Tamar so-she-went

הַיָּמִים וַתָּמָת בַּת־שׁוּעַ אֵשֶׁת־יְהוּדָה וַיִּנָּחֶם
when-he-was-comforted Judah wife-of Shua daughter-of and-she-died the-days

יְהוּדָה וַיַּעַל עַל־גֹּזְזֵי צֹאנוֹ הוּא וְחִירָה
and-Hirah he sheep-of-him ones-shearing-of to then-he-went-up Judah

רֵעֵהוּ הָעֲדֻלָּמִי תִּמְנָתָה׃ וַיֻּגַּד לְתָמָר לֵאמֹר
to-say to-Tamar and-he-was-told (13) to-Timnah the-Adullamite friend-of-him

הִנֵּה חָמִיךְ עֹלֶה תִמְנָתָה לָגֹז צֹאנוֹ׃
sheep-of-him to-shear to-Timnah going-up father-in-law-of-you see!

וַתָּסַר בִּגְדֵי אַלְמְנוּתָהּ מֵעָלֶיהָ וַתְּכַס
and-she-covered-self from-on-her widow-of-her clothes-of then-she-took-off (14)

בַּצָּעִיף וַתִּתְעַלָּף וַתֵּשֶׁב בְּפֶתַח עֵינַיִם אֲשֶׁר
which Enaim at-entrance-of then-she-sat and-she-disguised-self with-the-veil

עַל־דֶּרֶךְ תִּמְנָתָה כִּי רָאֲתָה כִּי־גָדַל שֵׁלָה וְהִוא לֹא־
not yet-she Shelah he-was-grown that she-saw for to-Timnah road on

and named him Shelah. It was at Kezib that she gave birth to him.

6Judah got a wife for Er, his firstborn, and her name was Tamar. 7But Er, Judah's firstborn, was wicked in the LORD's sight; so the LORD put him to death.

8Then Judah said to Onan, "Lie with your brother's wife and fulfill your duty to her as a brother-in-law to produce offspring for your brother." 9But Onan knew that the offspring would not be his; so whenever he lay with his brother's wife, he spilled his seed on the ground to keep from producing offspring for his brother. 10What he did was wicked in the LORD's sight; so he put him to death also.

11Judah then said to his daughter-in-law Tamar, "Live as a widow in your father's house until my son Shelah grows up." For he thought, "He may die too, just like his brothers." So Tamar went to live in her father's house.

12After a long time Judah's wife, the daughter of Shua, died. When Judah had recovered from his grief, he went up to Timnah, to the men who were shearing his sheep, and his friend Hirah the Adullamite went with him.

13When Tamar was told, "Your father-in-law is on his way to Timnah to shear his sheep," 14she took off her widow's clothes, covered herself with a veil to disguise herself, and then sat down at the entrance to Enaim, which is on the road to Timnah. For she saw that, though Shelah had now grown up, she had not

*9 Most mss have no *dagesh* in the *lamed* ( לא ).

נִתְּנָה לוֹ לְאִשָּׁה׃ וַיִּרְאֶהָ יְהוּדָה וַיַּחְשְׁבֶהָ
then-he-thought-her Judah when-he-saw-her (15) as-wife to-him she-was-given

לְזוֹנָה כִּי כִסְּתָה פָּנֶיהָ׃ וַיֵּט אֵלֶיהָ אֶל־
by to-her so-he-went (16) face-of-her she-covered for to-being-prostitute

הַדֶּרֶךְ וַיֹּאמֶר הָבָה־נָּא אָבוֹא אֵלַיִךְ כִּי לֹא יָדַע
he-realized not for with-you let-me-lie now! come! and-he-said the-roadside

כִּי כַלָּתוֹ הִוא וַתֹּאמֶר מַה־תִּתֶּן־לִּי כִּי
that to-me will-you-give what? and-she-asked she daughter-in-law-of-him that

תָבוֹא אֵלָי׃ וַיֹּאמֶר אָנֹכִי אֲשַׁלַּח גְּדִי־עִזִּים מִן־הַצֹּאן
the-flock from goats kid-of I-will-send I and-he-said (17) with-me you-may-lie

וַתֹּאמֶר אִם־תִּתֵּן עֵרָבוֹן עַד שָׁלְחֶךָ׃ וַיֹּאמֶר
and-he-said (18) to-send-you until pledge will-you-give now and-she-asked

מָה הָעֵרָבוֹן אֲשֶׁר אֶתֶּן־לָּךְ וַתֹּאמֶר חֹתָמְךָ
seal-of-you and-she-answered to-you I-should-give that the-pledge what?

וּפְתִילֶךָ וּמַטְּךָ אֲשֶׁר בְּיָדֶךָ וַיִּתֶּן־לָהּ
to-her so-he-gave in-hand-of-you that and-staff-of-you and-belt-of-you

וַיָּבֹא אֵלֶיהָ וַתַּהַר לוֹ׃ וַתָּקָם וַתֵּלֶךְ
and-she-left then-she-rose (19) by-him and-she-conceived with-her and-he-lay

וַתָּסַר צְעִיפָהּ מֵעָלֶיהָ וַתִּלְבַּשׁ בִּגְדֵי
clothes-of and-she-put-on from-on-her veil-of-her and-she-took-off

אַלְמְנוּתָהּ׃ וַיִּשְׁלַח יְהוּדָה אֶת־גְּדִי הָעִזִּים בְּיַד
by-hand-of the-goats kid-of *** Judah then-he-sent (20) widow-of-her

רֵעֵהוּ הָעֲדֻלָּמִי לָקַחַת הָעֵרָבוֹן מִיַּד הָאִשָּׁה
the-woman from-hand-of the-pledge to-get-back the-Adullamite friend-of-him

וְלֹא מְצָאָהּ׃ וַיִּשְׁאַל אֶת־אַנְשֵׁי מְקֹמָהּ לֵאמֹר אַיֵּה
where? to-say area-of-her men-of *** so-he-asked (21) he-found-her but-not

הַקְּדֵשָׁה הִוא בָעֵינַיִם עַל־הַדָּרֶךְ וַיֹּאמְרוּ לֹא־הָיְתָה
she-was not but-they-said the-road by at-the-Enaim who the-shrine-prostitute

בָזֶה קְדֵשָׁה׃ וַיָּשָׁב אֶל־יְהוּדָה וַיֹּאמֶר לֹא
not and-he-said Judah to so-he-went-back (22) shrine-prostitute at-here

מְצָאתִיהָ וְגַם אַנְשֵׁי הַמָּקוֹם אָמְרוּ לֹא־הָיְתָה בָזֶה
at-here she-was not they-said the-area men-of and-besides I-found-her

קְדֵשָׁה׃ וַיֹּאמֶר יְהוּדָה תִּקַּח־לָהּ פֶּן נִהְיֶה
we-will-be or for-her let-her-keep Judah then-he-said (23) shrine-prostitute

לָבוּז הִנֵּה שָׁלַחְתִּי הַגְּדִי הַזֶּה וְאַתָּה לֹא מְצָאתָהּ׃
you-found-her not but-you the-this the-goat I-sent see! as-laughingstock

וַיְהִי ׀ כְּמִשְׁלֹשׁ חֳדָשִׁים וַיֻּגַּד לִיהוּדָה לֵאמֹר
to-say to-Judah that-he-was-told months about-three-of and-he-was (24)

been given to him as his wife.
[15]When Judah saw her, he
thought she was a prostitute,
for she had covered her face.
[16]Not realizing that she was
his daughter-in-law, he went
over to her by the roadside
and said, "Come now, let me
sleep with you."
"And what will you give me
to sleep with you?" she asked.
[17]"I'll send you a young goat
from my flock," he said.
"Will you give me something as a pledge until you
send it?" she asked.
[18]He said, "What pledge
should I give you?"
"Your seal and its cord, and
the staff in your hand," she
answered. So he gave them to
her and slept with her, and
she became pregnant by him.
[19]After she left, she took off her
veil and put on her widow's
clothes again.
[20]Meanwhile Judah sent the
young goat by his friend the
Adullamite in order to get his
pledge back from the woman,
but he did not find her. [21]He
asked the men who lived
there, "Where is the shrine
prostitute who was beside the
road at Enaim?"
"There hasn't been any
shrine prostitute here," they
said.
[22]So he went back to Judah
and said, "I didn't find her.
Besides, the men who lived
there said, 'There hasn't been
any shrine prostitute here.' "
[23]Then Judah said, "Let her
keep what she has, or we will
become a laughingstock. After
all, I did send her this young
goat, but you didn't find her."
[24]About three months later

**16* Most mss have no *dagesh* in the *lamed* ( ל ).

זָנְתָה תָּמָר כַּלָּתֶךָ וְגַם הִנֵּה הָרָה

pregnant see! and-also daughter-in-law-of-you Tamar she-played-harlot

לִזְנוּנִים וַיֹּאמֶר יְהוּדָה הוֹצִיאוּהָ וְתִשָּׂרֵף׃

and-let-her-be-burned bring-out-her! Judah so-he-said by-prostitutions

(25) הִוא מוּצֵאת וְהִיא שָׁלְחָה אֶל־ חָמִיהָ לֵאמֹר

to-say father-in-law-of-her to she-sent then-she being-brought-out she (25)

לְאִישׁ אֲשֶׁר־ אֵלֶּה לּוֹ אָנֹכִי הָרָה וַתֹּאמֶר הַכֶּר־ נָא לְמִי הַחֹתֶמֶת

the-seal to-whom now! see! also-she-said pregnant I to-him these who by-man

וְהַפְּתִילִים וְהַמַּטֶּה הָאֵלֶּה׃ (26) וַיַּכֵּר יְהוּדָה וַיֹּאמֶר

and-he-said Judah and-he-recognized (26) the-these and-the-staff and-the-belts

צָדְקָה מִמֶּנִּי כִּי־עַל־כֵּן לֹא־ נְתַתִּיהָ לְשֵׁלָה בְנִי וְלֹא־

so-not son-of-me to-Shelah I-gave-her not because more-than-I she-is-righteous

יָסַף עוֹד לְדַעְתָּה׃ (27) וַיְהִי בְּעֵת לִדְתָּהּ

to-bear-her at-time-of and-he-was (27) to-lie-with-her again he-repeated

וְהִנֵּה תְאוֹמִים בְּבִטְנָהּ׃ (28) וַיְהִי בְלִדְתָּהּ וַיִּתֶּן־

that-he-put-out as-to-bear-her and-he-was (28) in-womb-of-her twin-boys and-see!

יָד וַתִּקַּח הַמְיַלֶּדֶת וַתִּקְשֹׁר עַל־ יָדוֹ

wrist-of-him on and-she-tied the-one-being-midwife so-she-took hand

שָׁנִי לֵאמֹר זֶה יָצָא רִאשֹׁנָה׃ (29) וַיְהִי ׀ כְּמֵשִׁיב

as-to-draw-back but-he-was (29) first he-came-out this to-say scarlet-thread

יָדוֹ וְהִנֵּה יָצָא אָחִיו וַתֹּאמֶר מַה־

this-how and-she-said brother-of-him he-came-out that-see! hand-of-him

פָּרַצְתָּ עָלֶיךָ פָּרֶץ וַיִּקְרָא שְׁמוֹ פָּרֶץ׃ (30) וְאַחַר

and-then (30) Perez name-of-him so-he-called break for-you you-broke-out

יָצָא אָחִיו אֲשֶׁר עַל־ יָדוֹ הַשָּׁנִי וַיִּקְרָא

and-he-called the-scarlet-thread wrist-of-him on who brother-of-him he-came-out

שְׁמוֹ זָרַח׃ (39:1) וְיוֹסֵף הוּרַד מִצְרָיְמָה וַיִּקְנֵהוּ

and-he-bought-him to-Egypt he-was-taken now-Joseph (39:1) Zerah name-of-him

פּוֹטִיפַר סְרִיס פַּרְעֹה שַׂר הַטַּבָּחִים אִישׁ מִצְרִי מִיַּד

from-hand-of Egyptian man the-guards captain-of Pharaoh official-of Potiphar

הַיִּשְׁמְעֵאלִים אֲשֶׁר הוֹרִדֻהוּ שָׁמָּה׃ (2) וַיְהִי יְהוָה אֶת־ יוֹסֵף

Joseph with Yahweh and-he-was (2) to-there they-took-him who the-Ishmaelites

וַיְהִי אִישׁ מַצְלִיחַ וַיְהִי בְּבֵית אֲדֹנָיו הַמִּצְרִי׃

the-Egyptian master-of-him in-house-of and-he-was prospering man and-he-was

(3) וַיַּרְא אֲדֹנָיו כִּי יְהוָה אִתּוֹ וְכֹל אֲשֶׁר־הוּא עֹשֶׂה

doing he that and-all with-him Yahweh that master-of-him and-he-saw (3)

יְהוָה מַצְלִיחַ בְּיָדוֹ׃ (4) וַיִּמְצָא יוֹסֵף חֵן

favor Joseph so-he-found (4) in-hand-of-him giving-success Yahweh

Judah was told, "Your daughter-in-law Tamar is guilty of
prostitution, and as a result
she is now pregnant."
Judah said, "Bring her out
and have her burned to
death!"
25 As she was being brought
out, she sent a message to her
father-in-law. "I am pregnant
by the man who owns these,"
she said. And she added, "See
if you recognize whose seal
and cord and staff these are."
26 Judah recognized them
and said, "She is more righteous than I, since I wouldn't
give her to my son Shelah."
And he did not sleep with her
again.
27 When the time came for
her to give birth, there were
twin boys in her womb. 28 As
she was giving birth, one of
them put out his hand; so the
midwife took a scarlet thread
and tied it on his wrist and
said, "This one came out
first." 29 But when he drew
back his hand, his brother
came out, and she said, "So
this is how you have broken
out!" And he was named
Perez.[e] 30 Then his brother,
who had the scarlet thread on
his wrist, came out and he was
given the name Zerah.[f]

### *Joseph and Potiphar's Wife*

39 Now Joseph had been
taken down to Egypt.
Potiphar, an Egyptian who
was one of Pharaoh's officials,
the captain of the guard,
bought him from the Ishmaelites who had taken him there.
2 The LORD was with Joseph
and he prospered, and he
lived in the house of his Egyptian master. 3 When his master
saw that the LORD was with
him and that the LORD gave
him success in everything he
did, 4 Joseph found favor in his

[e] 29 *Perez* means *breaking out.*
[f] 30 *Zerah* can mean *scarlet* or *brightness.*

*26 Most mss have *mappiq* in the *he* (ה–).

בְּעֵינָיו וַיְשָׁרֶת אֹתוֹ וַיַּפְקִדֵהוּ עַל־ בֵּיתוֹ
house-of-him over and-he-put-in-charge-him him so-he-attended in-eyes-of-him

וְכָל־ יֶשׁ־ לוֹ נָתַן בְּיָדוֹ׃ וַיְהִי מֵאָז
from-time and-he-was (5) to-care-of-him he-entrusted to-him that-is and-all

הִפְקִיד אֹתוֹ בְּבֵיתוֹ וְעַל כָּל־ אֲשֶׁר יֶשׁ־ לוֹ
to-him he-is that all and-over of-house-of-him him he-put-in-charge

וַיְבָרֶךְ יְהוָה אֶת־ בֵּית הַמִּצְרִי בִּגְלַל יוֹסֵף
Joseph because-of the-Egyptian household-of *** Yahweh that-he-blessed

וַיְהִי בִּרְכַּת יְהוָה בְּכָל־ אֲשֶׁר יֶשׁ־ לוֹ בַּבַּיִת
in-the-house to-him he-is that on-all Yahweh blessing-of and-he-was

וּבַשָּׂדֶה׃ וַיַּעֲזֹב כָּל־ אֲשֶׁר־ לוֹ בְּיַד־ יוֹסֵף וְלֹא־
and-not Joseph in-care-of to-him that all so-he-left (6) and-in-the-field

יָדַע אִתּוֹ מְאוּמָה כִּי אִם־ הַלֶּחֶם אֲשֶׁר־הוּא אוֹכֵל וַיְהִי
now-he-was eating he that the-food only except anything to-him he-concerned

יוֹסֵף יְפֵה־ תֹאַר וִיפֵה מַרְאֶה׃ וַיְהִי אַחַר הַדְּבָרִים
the-things after and-he-was (7) sight and-good-of build good-of Joseph

הָאֵלֶּה וַתִּשָּׂא אֵשֶׁת־ אֲדֹנָיו אֶת־ עֵינֶיהָ אֶל־ יוֹסֵף
Joseph to eyes-of-her *** master-of-him wife-of that-she-lifted the-these

וַתֹּאמֶר שִׁכְבָה עִמִּי׃ וַיְמָאֵן ׀ וַיֹּאמֶר אֶל־ אֵשֶׁת
wife-of to and-he-said but-he-refused (8) with-me lie! and-she-said

אֲדֹנָיו הֵן אֲדֹנִי לֹא־ יָדַע אִתִּי מַה־ בַּבָּיִת
in-the-house what to-him he-concerns not master-of-me see! master-of-him

וְכֹל אֲשֶׁר־ יֶשׁ־ לוֹ נָתַן בְּיָדִי׃ אֵינֶנּוּ גָדוֹל
greater not-he (9) to-care-of-me he-entrusted to-him he-is that and-all

בַּבַּיִת הַזֶּה מִמֶּנִּי וְלֹא־ חָשַׂךְ מִמֶּנִּי מְאוּמָה כִּי
except anything from-me he-withheld and-not than-me the-this in-the-house

אִם־ אוֹתָךְ בַּאֲשֶׁר אַתְּ־ אִשְׁתּוֹ וְאֵיךְ אֶעֱשֶׂה הָרָעָה
the-wicked-thing could-I-do then-how? wife-of-him you because you only

הַגְּדֹלָה הַזֹּאת וְחָטָאתִי לֵאלֹהִים׃ וַיְהִי כְּדַבְּרָהּ
though-to-speak-her and-he-was (10) against-God and-I-sin the-this the-great

אֶל־ יוֹסֵף יוֹם ׀ יוֹם וְלֹא־ שָׁמַע אֵלֶיהָ לִשְׁכַּב אֶצְלָהּ לִהְיוֹת עִמָּהּ׃
with-her to-be with-her to-lie to-her he-listened yet-not day day Joseph to

וַיְהִי כְּהַיּוֹם הַזֶּה וַיָּבֹא הַבַּיְתָה לַעֲשׂוֹת
to-attend into-the-house that-he-went the-this on-the-day now-he-was (11)

מְלַאכְתּוֹ וְאֵין אִישׁ מֵאַנְשֵׁי הַבַּיִת שָׁם בַּבָּיִת׃
in-the-house there the-house from-men-of man and-there-is-no duty-of-him

וַתִּתְפְּשֵׂהוּ בְּבִגְדוֹ לֵאמֹר שִׁכְבָה עִמִּי וַיַּעֲזֹב
but-he-left with-me lie! to-say by-cloak-of-him and-she-caught-him (12)

eyes and became his attendant. Potiphar put him in
charge of his household, and
he entrusted to his care everything he owned. 5From the
time he put him in charge of
his household and of all that
he owned, the LORD blessed
the household of the Egyptian
because of Joseph. The
blessing of the LORD was on
everything Potiphar had, both
in the house and in the field.
6So he left in Joseph's care
everything he had; with Joseph in charge, he did not
concern himself with any-
thing except the food he ate.
Now Joseph was well-built
and handsome, 7and after a
while his master's wife took
notice of Joseph and said,
"Come to bed with me!"
8But he refused. "With me in
charge," he told her, "my master does not concern himself
with anything in the house;
everything he owns he has
entrusted to my care. 9No one
is greater in this house than I
am. My master has withheld
nothing from me except you,
because you are his wife. How
then could I do such a wicked
thing and sin against God?"
10And though she spoke to Joseph day after day, he refused
to go to bed with her or even
be with her.
11One day he went into the
house to attend to his duties,
and none of the household
servants was inside. 12She
caught him by his cloak and
said, "Come to bed with me!"

בִּגְדוֹ בְּיָדָהּ וַיָּנָס וַיֵּצֵא הַחוּצָה׃
to-the-outside and-he-went and-he-ran in-hand-of-her cloak-of-him

(13) וַיְהִי כִּרְאוֹתָהּ כִּי־ עָזַב בִּגְדוֹ בְּיָדָהּ
in-hand-of-her cloak-of-him he-left that when-to-see-her and-he-was (13)

וַיָּנָס הַחוּצָה׃ (14) וַתִּקְרָא לְאַנְשֵׁי בֵיתָהּ
household-of-her to-men-of that-she-called (14) to-the-outside and-he-ran

וַתֹּאמֶר לָהֶם לֵאמֹר רְאוּ הֵבִיא לָנוּ אִישׁ עִבְרִי לְצַחֶק
to-make-sport Hebrew man to-us he-brought look! to-say to-them and-she-said

בָּנוּ בָּא אֵלַי לִשְׁכַּב עִמִּי וָאֶקְרָא בְּקוֹל גָּדוֹל׃
loud with-voice but-I-screamed with-me to-sleep to-me he-came of-us

(15) וַיְהִי כְשָׁמְעוֹ כִּי־ הֲרִימֹתִי קוֹלִי וָאֶקְרָא
and-I-screamed voice-of-me I-lifted that when-to-hear-him and-he-was (15)

וַיַּעֲזֹב בִּגְדוֹ אֶצְלִי וַיָּנָס וַיֵּצֵא הַחוּצָה׃
to-the-outside and-he-went and-he-ran with-me cloak-of-him then-he-left

(16) וַתַּנַּח בִּגְדוֹ אֶצְלָהּ עַד־ בּוֹא אֲדֹנָיו אֶל־
to masters-of-him to-come until beside-her cloak-of-him so-she-kept (16)

בֵּיתוֹ׃ (17) וַתְּדַבֵּר אֵלָיו כַּדְּבָרִים הָאֵלֶּה לֵאמֹר
to-say the-these according-to-the-words to-him then-she-told (17) home-of-him

בָּא־ אֵלַי הָעֶבֶד הָעִבְרִי אֲשֶׁר־ הֵבֵאתָ לָּנוּ לְצַחֶק בִּי׃
of-me to-make-sport to-us you-brought whom the-Hebrew the-slave to-me he-came

(18) וַיְהִי כַּהֲרִימִי קוֹלִי וָאֶקְרָא וַיַּעֲזֹב
that-he-left and-I-screamed voice-of-me as-to-raise-me and-he-was (18)

בִּגְדוֹ אֶצְלִי וַיָּנָס הַחוּצָה׃ (19) וַיְהִי כִשְׁמֹעַ
when-to-hear and-he-was (19) to-the-outside and-he-ran beside-me cloak-of-him

אֲדֹנָיו אֶת־ דִּבְרֵי אִשְׁתּוֹ אֲשֶׁר דִּבְּרָה אֵלָיו לֵאמֹר
to-say to-him she-told that wife-of-him words-of *** masters-of-him

כַּדְּבָרִים הָאֵלֶּה עָשָׂה* לִי עַבְדֶּךָ וַיִּחַר אַפּוֹ׃
anger-of-him that-he-burned slave-of-you to-me he-did the-these as-the-things

(20) וַיִּקַּח אֲדֹנֵי יוֹסֵף אֹתוֹ וַיִּתְּנֵהוּ אֶל־ בֵּית הַסֹּהַר
the-prison house-of in and-he-put-him him Joseph masters-of and-he-took (20)

מְקוֹם אֲשֶׁר־ אֲסוּרֵי° הַמֶּלֶךְ אֲסוּרִים וַיְהִי־ שָׁם
there and-he-was ones-being-confined the-king prisoners-of where place-of

בְּבֵית הַסֹּהַר׃ (21) וַיְהִי יְהוָה אֶת־ יוֹסֵף וַיֵּט
and-he-showed Joseph with Yahweh but-he-was (21) the-prison in-house-of

אֵלָיו חָסֶד וַיִּתֵּן חִנּוֹ בְּעֵינֵי שַׂר בֵּית־
house-of warden-of in-eyes-of favor-of-him and-he-granted kindness to-him

הַסֹּהַר׃ (22) וַיִּתֵּן שַׂר בֵּית־ הַסֹּהַר בְּיַד־ יוֹסֵף
Joseph in-care-of the-prison house-of warden-of so-he-put (22) the-prison

But he left his cloak in her
hand and ran out of the house.
13 When she saw that he had
left his cloak in her hand and
had run out of the house, 14 she
called her household servants.
"Look," she said to them,
"this Hebrew has been
brought to us to make sport of
us! He came in here to sleep
with me, but I screamed.
15 When he heard me scream
for help, he left his cloak beside me and ran out of the
house."
16 She kept his cloak beside
her until his master came
home. 17 Then she told him this
story: "That Hebrew slave you
brought us came to me to
make sport of me. 18 But as
soon as I screamed for help, he
left his cloak beside me and
ran out of the house."
19 When his master heard the
story his wife told him, saying, "This is how your slave
treated me," he burned with
anger. 20 Joseph's master took
him and put him in prison,
the place where the king's
prisoners were confined.
But while Joseph was there
in the prison, 21 the LORD was
with him; he showed him
kindness and granted him favor in the eyes of the prison
warden. 22 So the warden put
Joseph in charge of all those

**19* Most mss have no *mappiq* in the *he* (ָה).

°*20* ק אסירי

אֶת כָּל־ הָאֲסִירִם אֲשֶׁר בְּבֵית הַסֹּהַר וְאֵת כָּל־אֲשֶׁר עֹשִׂים
ones-doing that all and the-prison in-house-of who the-prisoners all-of ***

שָׁם הוּא הָיָה עֹשֶׂה׃ אֵין | שַׂר בֵּית־ הַסֹּהַר רֹאֶה
attending the-prison house-of warden-of he-is-not (23) doing he-was he there

אֶת־ כָּל־ מְאוּמָה בְּיָדוֹ בַּאֲשֶׁר יְהוָה אִתּוֹ וַאֲשֶׁר־הוּא
he and-what with-him Yahweh because under-care-of-him anything any-of ***

עֹשֶׂה יְהוָה מַצְלִיחַ׃ וַיְהִי אַחַר הַדְּבָרִים הָאֵלֶּה
the-these the-things after and-he-was (40:1) giving-success Yahweh doing

חָטְאוּ מַשְׁקֵה מֶלֶךְ־ מִצְרַיִם וְהָאֹפֶה לַאֲדֹנֵיהֶם
to-masters-of-them and-the-one-baking Egypt king-of cupbearer-of they-offended

לְמֶלֶךְ מִצְרָיִם׃ וַיִּקְצֹף פַּרְעֹה עַל שְׁנֵי סָרִיסָיו
officials-of-him two-of with Pharaoh and-he-was-angry (2) Egypt to-king-of

עַל שַׂר הַמַּשְׁקִים וְעַל שַׂר הָאוֹפִים׃ וַיִּתֵּן
so-he-put (3) the-ones-baking chief-of and-with the-cupbearers chief-of with

אֹתָם בְּמִשְׁמַר בֵּית שַׂר הַטַּבָּחִים* אֶל־ בֵּית הַסֹּהַר
the-prison house-of in the-guards captain-of house-of in-custody-of them

מְקוֹם אֲשֶׁר יוֹסֵף אָסוּר שָׁם׃ וַיִּפְקֹד שַׂר
captain-of and-he-assigned (4) there being-confined Joseph where place-of

הַטַּבָּחִים אֶת־ יוֹסֵף אִתָּם וַיְשָׁרֶת אֹתָם וַיִּהְיוּ יָמִים
days and-they-were them and-he-attended with-them Joseph *** the-guards

בְּמִשְׁמָר׃ וַיַּחַלְמוּ חֲלוֹם שְׁנֵיהֶם אִישׁ חֲלֹמוֹ בְּלַיְלָה
in-night dream-of-him each two-of-them dream and-they-dreamed (5) in-custody

אֶחָד אִישׁ כְּפִתְרוֹן חֲלֹמוֹ הַמַּשְׁקֶה וְהָאֹפֶה אֲשֶׁר
who and-the-one-baking the-cupbearer dream-of-him own-meaning-of each same

לְמֶלֶךְ מִצְרַיִם אֲשֶׁר אֲסוּרִים בְּבֵית הַסֹּהַר׃ וַיָּבֹא
when-he-came (6) the-prison in-house-of ones-being-held who Egypt to-king-of

אֲלֵיהֶם יוֹסֵף בַּבֹּקֶר וַיַּרְא אֹתָם וְהִנָּם זֹעֲפִים׃
being-dejected-ones and-see-them! them then-he-saw in-the-morning Joseph to-them

וַיִּשְׁאַל אֶת־ סְרִיסֵי פַרְעֹה אֲשֶׁר אִתּוֹ בְמִשְׁמַר בֵּית
house-of in-custody-of with-him who Pharaoh officials-of *** so-he-asked (7)

אֲדֹנָיו לֵאמֹר מַדּוּעַ פְּנֵיכֶם רָעִים הַיּוֹם׃ וַיֹּאמְרוּ
so-they-answered (8) the-day sad-ones faces-of-you why? to-say masters-of-him

אֵלָיו חֲלוֹם חָלַמְנוּ וּפֹתֵר אֵין אֹתוֹ וַיֹּאמֶר
and-he-said for-him there-is-not but-one-interpreting we-dreamed dream to-him

אֲלֵהֶם יוֹסֵף הֲלוֹא לֵאלֹהִים פִּתְרֹנִים סַפְּרוּ־ נָא לִי׃ וַיְסַפֵּר
so-he-told (9) to-me now! tell! interpretations to-God not? Joseph to-them

שַׂר־ הַמַּשְׁקִים אֶת־ חֲלֹמוֹ לְיוֹסֵף וַיֹּאמֶר לוֹ
to-him and-he-said to-Joseph dream-of-him *** the-cupbearers chief-of

held in the prison, and he was made responsible for all that was done there. 23The warden paid no attention to anything under Joseph's care, because the LORD was with Joseph and gave him success in whatever he did.

*The Cupbearer and the Baker*

40 Some time later, the cupbearer and the baker of the king of Egypt offended their master, the king of Egypt. 2Pharaoh was angry with his two officials, the chief cupbearer and the chief baker, 3and put them in custody in the house of the captain of the guard, in the same prison where Joseph was confined. 4The captain of the guard assigned them to Joseph, and he attended them.

After they had been in custody for some time, 5each of the two men—the cupbearer and the baker of the king of Egypt, who were being held in prison—had a dream the same night, and each dream had a meaning of its own.

6When Joseph came to them the next morning, he saw that they were dejected. 7So he asked Pharaoh's officials who were in custody with him in his master's house, "Why are your faces so sad today?"

8"We both had dreams," they answered, "but there is no one to interpret them."

Then Joseph said to them, "Do not interpretations belong to God? Tell me your dreams."

9So the chief cupbearer told Joseph his dream. He said to

*3 Most mss have *dagesh* in the *teth* (הט').

בַּחֲלוֹמִי וְהִנֵּה־ גֶפֶן לְפָנָי׃ וּבַגֶּפֶן שְׁלֹשָׁה
three and-on-the-vine (10) in-front-of-me vine now-see! in-dream-of-me

שָׂרִיגִם וְהִיא כְפֹרַחַת עָלְתָה נִצָּהּ הִבְשִׁילוּ
and-they-ripened blossom-of-her she-came budding when-she branches

אַשְׁכְּלֹתֶיהָ עֲנָבִים׃ וְכוֹס פַּרְעֹה בְּיָדִי וָאֶקַּח אֶת־
*** and-I-took in-hand-of-me Pharaoh now-cup-of (11) grapes clusters-of-her

הָעֲנָבִים וָאֶשְׂחַט אֹתָם אֶל־ כּוֹס פַּרְעֹה וָאֶתֵּן אֶת־ הַכּוֹס
the-cup *** and-I-put Pharaoh cup-of into them and-I-squeezed the-grapes

עַל־ כַּף פַּרְעֹה׃ וַיֹּאמֶר לוֹ יוֹסֵף זֶה פִּתְרֹנוֹ
meaning-of-him this Joseph to-him and-he-said (12) Pharaoh hand-of into

שְׁלֹשֶׁת הַשָּׂרִגִים שְׁלֹשֶׁת יָמִים הֵם׃ בְּעוֹד | שְׁלֹשֶׁת יָמִים יִשָּׂא
he-will-lift days three-of within (13) they days three-of branches three-of

פַרְעֹה אֶת־ רֹאשֶׁךָ וַהֲשִׁיבְךָ עַל־ כַּנֶּךָ
position-of-you to and-he-will-restore-you head-of-you *** Pharaoh

וְנָתַתָּ כוֹס־ פַּרְעֹה בְּיָדוֹ כַּמִּשְׁפָּט הָרִאשׁוֹן אֲשֶׁר
when the-former as-the-custom in-hand-of-him Pharaoh cup-of and-you-will-put

הָיִיתָ מַשְׁקֵהוּ׃ כִּי אִם־ זְכַרְתַּנִי אִתְּךָ כַּאֲשֶׁר
when with-you you-remember-me now indeed (14) cupbearer-of-him you-were

יִיטַב לָךְ וְעָשִׂיתָ־ נָּא עִמָּדִי חָסֶד וְהִזְכַּרְתַּנִי
and-you-mention-me kindness with-me now! and-you-show with-you he-goes-well

אֶל־ פַּרְעֹה וְהוֹצֵאתַנִי מִן־ הַבַּיִת הַזֶּה׃ כִּי־ גֻנֹּב
to-be-forced for (15) the-this the-prison from so-you-get-out-me Pharaoh to

גֻּנַּבְתִּי מֵאֶרֶץ הָעִבְרִים וְגַם־ פֹּה לֹא־עָשִׂיתִי מְאוּמָה כִּי־
that anything I-did not here and-even the-Hebrews from-land-of I-was-forced

שָׂמוּ אֹתִי בַּבּוֹר׃ וַיַּרְא שַׂר־ הָאֹפִים
the-ones-baking chief-of when-he-saw (16) in-the-dungeon me they-should-put

כִּי טוֹב פָּתָר וַיֹּאמֶר אֶל־ יוֹסֵף אַף־ אֲנִי בַּחֲלוֹמִי
in-dream-of-me I also Joseph to then-he-said he-interpreted favorably that

וְהִנֵּה שְׁלֹשָׁה סַלֵּי חֹרִי עַל־ רֹאשִׁי׃ וּבַסַּל
and-in-the-basket (17) head-of-me on bread baskets-of three-of and-see!

הָעֶלְיוֹן מִכֹּל מַאֲכַל פַּרְעֹה מַעֲשֵׂה אֹפֶה וְהָעוֹף אֹכֵל
eating but-the-bird one-baking work-of Pharaoh food-of from-all-of the-top

אֹתָם מִן־ הַסַּל מֵעַל רֹאשִׁי׃ וַיַּעַן יוֹסֵף וַיֹּאמֶר
and-he-said Joseph and-he-replied (18) head-of-me upon the-basket from them

זֶה פִּתְרֹנוֹ שְׁלֹשֶׁת הַסַּלִּים שְׁלֹשֶׁת יָמִים הֵם׃ בְּעוֹד |
within (19) they days three-of the-baskets three-of meaning-of-him this

שְׁלֹשֶׁת יָמִים יִשָּׂא פַרְעֹה אֶת־ רֹאשְׁךָ מֵעָלֶיךָ
from-on-you head-of-you *** Pharaoh he-will-lift-off days three-of

him, "In my dream I saw a vine in front of me, 10and on the vine were three branches. As soon as it budded, it blossomed, and its clusters ripened into grapes. 11Pharaoh's cup was in my hand, and I took the grapes, squeezed them into Pharaoh's cup and put the cup in his hand."

12"This is what it means," Joseph said to him. "The three branches are three days. 13Within three days Pharaoh will lift up your head and restore you to your position, and you will put Pharaoh's cup in his hand, just as you used to do when you were his cupbearer. 14But when all goes well with you, remember me and show me kindness; mention me to Pharaoh and get me out of this prison. 15For I was forcibly carried off from the land of the Hebrews, and even here I have done nothing to deserve being put in a dungeon."

16When the chief baker saw that Joseph had given a favorable interpretation, he said to Joseph, "I too had a dream: On my head were three baskets of bread.[g] 17In the top basket were all kinds of baked goods for Pharaoh, but the birds were eating them out of the basket on my head."

18"This is what it means," Joseph said. "The three baskets are three days. 19Within three days Pharaoh will lift off

[g]16 *Or three wicker baskets*

וְתָלָה אוֹתְךָ עַל־ עֵץ וְאָכַל הָעוֹף אֶת־ בְּשָׂרְךָ
flesh-of-you *** the-bird and-he-will-eat tree on you and-he-will-hang

מֵעָלֶיךָ׃ וַיְהִי ׀ בַּיּוֹם הַשְּׁלִישִׁי יוֹם הֻלֶּדֶת אֶת־ פַּרְעֹה
Pharaoh *** to-be-born day-of the-third on-the-day and-he-was (20) from-you

וַיַּעַשׂ מִשְׁתֶּה לְכָל־ עֲבָדָיו וַיִּשָּׂא אֶת־ רֹאשׁ ׀
head-of *** and-he-lifted officials-of-him for-all-of feast and-he-gave

שַׂר הַמַּשְׁקִים וְאֶת־ רֹאשׁ שַׂר הָאֹפִים בְּתוֹךְ
in-presence-of the-ones-baking chief-of head-of and the-cupbearers chief-of

עֲבָדָיו׃ וַיָּשֶׁב אֶת־ שַׂר הַמַּשְׁקִים עַל־
to the-cupbearers chief-of *** and-he-restored (21) officials-of-him

מַשְׁקֵהוּ וַיִּתֵּן הַכּוֹס עַל־ כַּף פַּרְעֹה׃ וְאֵת שַׂר
chief-of but (22) Pharaoh hand-of into the-cup again-he-put position-of-him

הָאֹפִים תָּלָה כַּאֲשֶׁר פָּתַר לָהֶם יוֹסֵף׃ וְלֹא־
yet-not (23) Joseph to-them he-interpreted just-as he-hanged the-ones-baking

זָכַר שַׂר־ הַמַּשְׁקִים אֶת־ יוֹסֵף וַיִּשְׁכָּחֵהוּ׃
but-he-forgot-him Joseph *** the-cupbearers chief-of he-remembered

וַיְהִי מִקֵּץ שְׁנָתַיִם יָמִים וּפַרְעֹה חֹלֵם וְהִנֵּה
and-see! dreaming that-Pharaoh full-ones two-years at-end-of and-he-was (41:1)

עֹמֵד עַל־ הַיְאֹר׃ וְהִנֵּה מִן־ הַיְאֹר עֹלֹת שֶׁבַע פָּרוֹת
cows seven ones-coming the-Nile from and-see! (2) the-Nile by standing

יְפוֹת מַרְאֶה וּבְרִיאֹת בָּשָׂר וַתִּרְעֶינָה בָּאָחוּ׃
among-the-reed and-they-grazed body and-fat-of appearance ones-sleek-of

וְהִנֵּה שֶׁבַע פָּרוֹת אֲחֵרוֹת עֹלוֹת אַחֲרֵיהֶן מִן־ הַיְאֹר
the-Nile from after-them ones-coming other-ones cows seven and-see! (3)

רָעוֹת מַרְאֶה וְדַקּוֹת בָּשָׂר וַתַּעֲמֹדְנָה אֵצֶל הַפָּרוֹת
the-cows beside and-they-stood body and-ones-gaunt-of appearance ones-ugly-of

עַל־ שְׂפַת הַיְאֹר׃ וַתֹּאכַלְנָה הַפָּרוֹת רָעוֹת הַמַּרְאֶה
the-appearance ones-ugly-of the-cows and-they-ate (4) the-Nile bank-of on

וְדַקֹּת הַבָּשָׂר אֵת שֶׁבַע הַפָּרוֹת יְפֹת הַמַּרְאֶה
the-appearance ones-sleek-of the-cows seven *** the-body and-ones-gaunt-of

וְהַבְּרִיאֹת וַיִּיקַץ פַּרְעֹה׃ וַיִּישָׁן וַיַּחֲלֹם שֵׁנִית
second and-he-dreamed and-he-slept (5) Pharaoh then-he-woke and-the-fat-ones

וְהִנֵּה ׀ שֶׁבַע שִׁבֳּלִים עֹלוֹת בְּקָנֶה אֶחָד בְּרִיאוֹת וְטֹבוֹת׃
and-good-ones fat-ones one on-stalk ones-growing heads-of-grain seven and-see!

וְהִנֵּה שֶׁבַע שִׁבֳּלִים דַּקּוֹת וּשְׁדוּפֹת
and-ones-being-scorched-of thin-ones heads-of-grain seven and-see! (6)

קָדִים צֹמְחוֹת אַחֲרֵיהֶן׃ וַתִּבְלַעְנָה הַשִּׁבֳּלִים
the-heads-of-grain and-they-swallowed (7) after-them sprouting east-winds

your head and hang you on a tree.[h] And the birds will eat away your flesh."

[20]Now the third day was Pharaoh's birthday, and he gave a feast for all his officials. He lifted up the heads of the chief cupbearer and the chief baker in the presence of his officials: [21]He restored the chief cupbearer to his position, so that he once again put the cup into Pharaoh's hand, [22]but he hanged[i] the chief baker, just as Joseph had said to them in his interpretation.

[23]The chief cupbearer, however, did not remember Joseph; he forgot him.

*Pharaoh's Dreams*

41 When two full years had passed, Pharaoh had a dream: He was standing by the Nile, [2]when out of the river there came up seven cows, sleek and fat, and they grazed among the reeds. [3]After them, seven other cows, ugly and gaunt, came up out of the Nile and stood beside those on the riverbank. [4]And the cows that were ugly and gaunt ate up the seven sleek, fat cows. Then Pharaoh woke up.

[5]He fell asleep again and had a second dream: Seven heads of grain, healthy and good, were growing on a single stalk. [6]After them, seven other heads of grain sprouted—thin and scorched by the east wind. [7]The thin heads of grain swallowed up the seven

[h]19 Or *and impale you on a pole*
[i]22 Or *impaled*

הַדַּקּוֹת אֵת שֶׁבַע הַשִּׁבֳּלִים הַבְּרִיאוֹת וְהַמְּלֵאוֹת

and-the-full-ones the-fat-ones the-heads-of-grain seven *** the-thin-ones

וַיִּיקַץ פַּרְעֹה וְהִנֵּה חֲלוֹם׃ וַיְהִי בַבֹּקֶר

in-the-morning and-he-was (8) dream and-see! Pharaoh then-he-woke

וַתִּפָּעֶם רוּחוֹ וַיִּשְׁלַח וַיִּקְרָא אֶת־ כָּל־

all-of *** and-he-called so-he-sent mind-of-him that-she-was-troubled

חַרְטֻמֵּי מִצְרַיִם וְאֶת־ כָּל־ חֲכָמֶיהָ וַיְסַפֵּר פַּרְעֹה לָהֶם

to-them Pharaoh then-he-told wise-men-of-her all-of and Egypt magicians-of

אֶת־ חֲלֹמוֹ וְאֵין־ פּוֹתֵר אוֹתָם לְפַרְעֹה׃

for-Pharaoh them one-interpreting but-there-is-no dream-of-him ***

וַיְדַבֵּר שַׂר הַמַּשְׁקִים אֶת־ פַּרְעֹה לֵאמֹר אֶת־ חֲטָאַי

faults-of-me *** to-say Pharaoh to the-cupbearers chief-of then-he-spoke (9)

אֲנִי מַזְכִּיר הַיּוֹם׃ פַּרְעֹה קָצַף עַל־ עֲבָדָיו

servants-of-him with he-was-angry Pharaoh (10) the-day remembering I

וַיִּתֵּן אֹתִי בְּמִשְׁמַר בֵּית שַׂר הַטַּבָּחִים אֹתִי וְאֵת שַׂר

chief-of and me the-guards captain-of house-of in-custody-of me and-he-put

הָאֹפִים׃ וַנַּחַלְמָה חֲלוֹם בְּלַיְלָה אֶחָד אֲנִי וָהוּא אִישׁ

each and-he I same in-night dream and-we-dreamed (11) the-ones-baking

כְּפִתְרוֹן חֲלֹמוֹ חָלָמְנוּ׃ וְשָׁם אִתָּנוּ נַעַר

young-man with-us now-there (12) we-dreamed dream-of-him own-meaning-of

עִבְרִי עֶבֶד לְשַׂר הַטַּבָּחִים וַנְּסַפֶּר־ לוֹ וַיִּפְתָּר־

and-he-interpreted to-him and-we-told the-guards to-captain-of servant Hebrew

לָנוּ אֶת־ חֲלֹמֹתֵינוּ אִישׁ כַּחֲלֹמוֹ פָּתָר׃ וַיְהִי

and-he-was (13) he-interpreted own-dream-of-him each dreams-of-us *** for-us

כַּאֲשֶׁר פָּתַר־ לָנוּ כֵּן הָיָה אֹתִי הֵשִׁיב עַל־ כַּנִּי

position-of-me to he-restored me he-happened so to-us he-interpreted just-as

וְאֹתוֹ תָלָה׃ וַיִּשְׁלַח פַּרְעֹה וַיִּקְרָא אֶת־ יוֹסֵף

Joseph *** and-he-called Pharaoh so-he-sent (14) he-hanged and-him

וַיְרִיצֻהוּ מִן־ הַבּוֹר וַיְגַלַּח וַיְחַלֵּף

and-he-changed when-he-shaved the-dungeon from and-they-brought-him

שִׂמְלֹתָיו וַיָּבֹא אֶל־ פַּרְעֹה׃ וַיֹּאמֶר פַּרְעֹה אֶל־ יוֹסֵף

Joseph to Pharoah and-he-said (15) Pharaoh before then-he-came clothes-of-him

חֲלוֹם חָלַמְתִּי וּפֹתֵר אֵין אֹתוֹ וַאֲנִי שָׁמַעְתִּי

I-heard but-I for-him there-is-not but-one-interpreting I-dreamed dream

עָלֶיךָ לֵאמֹר תִּשְׁמַע חֲלוֹם לִפְתֹּר אֹתוֹ׃ וַיַּעַן יוֹסֵף אֶת־

to Joseph and-he-replied (16) him to-interpret dream you-hear to-say of-you

פַּרְעֹה לֵאמֹר בִּלְעָדָי אֱלֹהִים יַעֲנֶה אֶת־ שְׁלוֹם פַּרְעֹה׃

Pharaoh favorably *** he-will-answer God not-in-me to-say Pharaoh

healthy, full heads. Then Pharaoh woke up; it had been a dream.

[8]In the morning his mind was troubled, so he sent for all the magicians and wise men of Egypt. Pharaoh told them his dreams, but no one could interpret them for him.

[9]Then the chief cupbearer said to Pharaoh, "Today I am reminded of my shortcomings. [10]Pharaoh was once angry with his servants, and he imprisoned me and the chief baker in the house of the captain of the guard. [11]Each of us had a dream the same night, and each dream had a meaning of its own. [12]Now a young Hebrew was there with us, a servant of the captain of the guard. We told him our dreams, and he interpreted them for us, giving each man the interpretation of his dream. [13]And things turned out exactly as he interpreted them to us: I was restored to my position, and the other man was hanged.[j]"

[14]So Pharaoh sent for Joseph, and he was quickly brought from the dungeon. When he had shaved and changed his clothes, he came before Pharaoh.

[15]Pharaoh said to Joseph, "I had a dream, and no one can interpret it. But I have heard it said of you that when you hear a dream you can interpret it."

[16]"I cannot do it," Joseph replied to Pharaoh, "but God will give Pharaoh the answer he desires."

j13 Or *impaled*

וַיְדַבֵּר פַּרְעֹה אֶל־יוֹסֵף בַּחֲלֹמִי הִנְנִי עֹמֵד עַל־שְׂפַת
bank-of on standing see-I! in-dream-of-me Joseph to Pharaoh then-he-said (17)

הַיְאֹר׃ וְהִנֵּה מִן־הַיְאֹר עֹלֹת שֶׁבַע פָּרוֹת בְּרִיאוֹת
ones-fat-of cows seven ones-coming-up the-Nile from and-see! (18) the-Nile

בָּשָׂר וִיפֹת תֹּאַר וַתִּרְעֶינָה בָּאָחוּ׃ וְהִנֵּה
then-see! (19) among-the-reed and-they-grazed form and-ones-sleek-of body

שֶׁבַע־פָּרוֹת אֲחֵרוֹת עֹלוֹת אַחֲרֵיהֶן דַּלּוֹת וְרָעוֹת
and-ones-ugly-of ones-scrawny-of after-them ones-coming-up other-ones cows seven

תֹּאַר מְאֹד וְרַקּוֹת בָּשָׂר לֹא־רָאִיתִי כָהֵנָּה בְּכָל־אֶרֶץ
land-of in-all-of such-as-these I-saw never body and-ones-lean-of very form

מִצְרַיִם לָרֹעַ׃ וַתֹּאכַלְנָה הַפָּרוֹת הָרַקּוֹת וְהָרָעוֹת אֵת
*** and-the-ugly-ones the-lean-ones the-cows and-they-ate (20) so-ugly Egypt

שֶׁבַע הַפָּרוֹת הָרִאשֹׁנוֹת הַבְּרִיאֹת׃ וַתָּבֹאנָה אֶל־קִרְבֶּנָה
midst-of-them to and-they-went (21) the-fat-ones the-first-ones the-cows seven

וְלֹא נוֹדַע כִּי־בָאוּ אֶל־קִרְבֶּנָה וּמַרְאֵיהֶן
for-appearance-of-them midst-of-them into they-went that he-could-tell but-not

רַע כַּאֲשֶׁר בַּתְּחִלָּה וָאִיקָץ׃ וָאֵרֶא בַּחֲלֹמִי וְהִנֵּה׀
and-see! in-dream-of-me then-I-saw (22) then-I-woke at-the-start just-as ugly

שֶׁבַע שִׁבֳּלִים עֹלֹת בְּקָנֶה אֶחָד מְלֵאֹת וְטֹבוֹת׃
and-good-ones full-ones single on-stalk ones-growing heads-of-grain seven

וְהִנֵּה שֶׁבַע שִׁבֳּלִים צְנֻמוֹת דַּקּוֹת
and-ones-thin ones-being-withered heads-of-grain seven then-see! (23)

שְׁדֻפוֹת קָדִים צֹמְחוֹת אַחֲרֵיהֶם׃
after-them ones-sprouting east-winds and-ones-being-scorched-of

וַתִּבְלַעְןָ הַשִּׁבֳּלִים הַדַּקֹּת אֵת שֶׁבַע הַשִּׁבֳּלִים*
the-heads-of-grain seven *** the-thin-ones the-heads-of-grain and-they-swallowed (24)

הַטֹּבוֹת וָאֹמַר אֶל־הַחַרְטֻמִּים וְאֵין מַגִּיד לִי׃
to-me explaining but-there-is-no the-magicians to and-I-told the-good-ones

וַיֹּאמֶר יוֹסֵף אֶל־פַּרְעֹה חֲלוֹם פַּרְעֹה אֶחָד הוּא אֵת אֲשֶׁר
what *** he one Pharoah dream-of Pharoah to Joseph then-he-said (25)

הָאֱלֹהִים עֹשֶׂה הִגִּיד לְפַרְעֹה׃ שֶׁבַע פָּרֹת הַטֹּבֹת שֶׁבַע שָׁנִים
years seven the-good-ones cows seven (26) to-Pharaoh he-revealed doing the-God

הֵנָּה וְשֶׁבַע הַשִּׁבֳּלִים† הַטֹּבֹת שֶׁבַע שָׁנִים הֵנָּה חֲלוֹם אֶחָד
one dream they years seven the-good-ones the-heads-of-grain and-seven they

הוּא׃ וְשֶׁבַע הַפָּרוֹת הָרַקּוֹת וְהָרָעֹת הָעֹלֹת
the-ones-coming-up and-the-ugly-ones the-lean-ones the-cows and-seven (27) he

אַחֲרֵיהֶן שֶׁבַע שָׁנִים הֵנָּה וְשֶׁבַע הַשִּׁבֳּלִים הָרֵקוֹת
the-worthless-ones the-heads-of-grain and-seven they years seven after-them

17Then Pharaoh said to Joseph, "In my dream I was standing on the bank of the Nile, 18when out of the river there came up seven cows, fat and sleek, and they grazed among the reeds. 19After them, seven other cows came up—scrawny and very ugly and lean. I had never seen such ugly cows in all the land of Egypt. 20The lean, ugly cows ate up the seven fat cows that came up first. 21But even after they ate them, no one could tell that they had done so; they looked just as ugly as before. Then I woke up.

22"In my dreams I also saw seven heads of grain, full and good, growing on a single stalk. 23After them, seven other heads sprouted—withered and thin and scorched by the east wind. 24The thin heads of grain swallowed up the seven good heads. I told this to the magicians, but none could explain it to me."

25Then Joseph said to Pharaoh, "The dreams of Pharaoh are one and the same. God has revealed to Pharaoh what he is about to do. 26The seven good cows are seven years, and the seven good heads of grain are seven years; it is one and the same dream. 27The seven lean, ugly cows that came up after they did are seven years, and so are the seven worthless heads of grain scorched by the

*24 Most mss have *pathah* under the *he* and *dagesh* in the *shin* (הַשׁ׳).

†26 Most mss have *hateph qamets* under the *beth* (׳בֳּ—).

| שְׂדֻפוֹת | הַקָּדִ֔ים | יִהְי֖וּ | שֶׁ֥בַע | שְׁנֵ֣י | רָעָ֑ב |
|---|---|---|---|---|---|
| and-ones-being-scorched-of | the-east-winds | they-are | seven | years-of | famine |

| הֽוּא | הַדָּבָ֔ר | אֲשֶׁ֥ר | דִּבַּ֖רְתִּי | אֶל־פַּרְעֹ֑ה | אֲשֶׁ֧ר | הָאֱלֹהִ֛ים | עֹשֶׂ֖ה | הֶרְאָ֥ה | אֶת־ |
|---|---|---|---|---|---|---|---|---|---|
| (28) the-thing | this | as | I-said | to Pharaoh | what | the-God | doing | he-showed | *** |

| פַּרְעֹֽה׃ | הִנֵּ֛ה | שֶׁ֥בַע | שָׁנִ֖ים | בָּא֑וֹת | שָׂבָ֥ע | גָּד֖וֹל | בְּכָל־ |
|---|---|---|---|---|---|---|---|
| (29) Pharaoh | see! | seven | years | ones-coming | abundance | great | through-all-of |

| אֶ֥רֶץ | מִצְרָֽיִם׃ | וְ֠קָמוּ | שֶׁ֣בַע | שְׁנֵ֤י | רָעָב֙ | אַחֲרֵיהֶ֔ן |
|---|---|---|---|---|---|---|
| land-of | Egypt | (30) but-they-will-come | seven | years-of | famine | after-them |

| וְנִשְׁכַּ֥ח | כָּל־ | הַשָּׂבָ֖ע | בְּאֶ֣רֶץ | מִצְרָ֑יִם |
|---|---|---|---|---|
| and-he-will-be-forgotten | all-of | the-abundance | in-land-of | Egypt |

| וְכִלָּ֥ה | הָרָעָ֖ב | אֶת־הָאָֽרֶץ׃ | וְלֹֽא־ | יִוָּדַ֤ע |
|---|---|---|---|---|
| and-he-will-ravage | the-famine | (31) *** the-land | and-not | he-will-be-remembered |

| הַשָּׂבָ֣ע | בָּאָ֔רֶץ | מִפְּנֵ֛י | הָרָעָ֥ב | הַה֖וּא | אַחֲרֵי־כֵ֑ן | כִּֽי־ |
|---|---|---|---|---|---|---|
| the-abundance | in-the-land | because-of | the-famine | the-that | after this | for |

| כָבֵ֥ד | ה֖וּא | מְאֹֽד׃ | וְעַ֨ל | הִשָּׁנ֧וֹת | הַחֲל֛וֹם | אֶל־פַּרְעֹ֖ה | פַּעֲמָ֑יִם | כִּֽי־ |
|---|---|---|---|---|---|---|---|---|
| severe | he | very | (32) and-so | to-repeat | the-dream | to Pharaoh | two-times | because |

| נָכ֤וֹן | הַדָּבָר֙ | מֵעִ֣ם | הָאֱלֹהִ֔ים | וּמְמַהֵ֥ר | הָאֱלֹהִ֖ים | לַעֲשֹׂתֽוֹ׃ |
|---|---|---|---|---|---|---|
| being-decided | the-matter | by | the-God | and-being-soon | the-God | to-do-him |

| וְעַתָּה֙ | יֵרֶ֣א | פַרְעֹ֔ה | אִ֖ישׁ | נָב֣וֹן | וְחָכָ֑ם | וִישִׁיתֵ֖הוּ |
|---|---|---|---|---|---|---|
| and-now | let-him-seek | Pharaoh | man | discerning | and-wise | and-let-him-set-him |

| עַל־ | אֶ֥רֶץ | מִצְרָֽיִם׃ | יַעֲשֶׂ֣ה | פַרְעֹ֔ה | וְיַפְקֵ֥ד |
|---|---|---|---|---|---|
| over | land-of | Egypt | (34) and-let-him-make | Pharaoh | and-let-him-appoint |

| פְּקִדִ֖ים | עַל־ | הָאָ֑רֶץ | וְחִמֵּשׁ֙ | אֶת־ | אֶ֣רֶץ | מִצְרַ֔יִם | בְּשֶׁ֖בַע |
|---|---|---|---|---|---|---|---|
| commissioners | over | the-land | and-let-him-take-fifth | *** | land-of | Egypt | in-seven |

| שְׁנֵ֥י | הַשָּׂבָֽע׃ | וְיִקְבְּצ֗וּ | אֶת־ | כָּל־ | אֹ֙כֶל֙ | הַשָּׁנִ֣ים |
|---|---|---|---|---|---|---|
| years-of | (35) the-abundance | and-they-will-collect | *** | all-of | food-of | the-years |

| הַטֹּבֹ֔ת | הַבָּאֹ֖ת | הָאֵ֣לֶּה | וְיִצְבְּרוּ־ | בָ֗ר | תַּ֣חַת |
|---|---|---|---|---|---|
| the-good-ones | the-ones-coming | the-these | and-they-will-store | grain | under |

| יַד־ | פַּרְעֹ֛ה | אֹ֥כֶל | בֶּעָרִ֖ים | וְשָׁמָֽרוּ׃ | וְהָיָ֧ה |
|---|---|---|---|---|---|
| authority-of | Pharaoh | food | in-the-cities | they-will-keep | (36) and-he-will-be |

| הָאֹ֤כֶל | לְפִקָּדוֹן֙ | לָאָ֔רֶץ | לְשֶׁ֣בַע | שְׁנֵ֣י | הָרָעָ֔ב | אֲשֶׁ֥ר |
|---|---|---|---|---|---|---|
| the-food | in-reserve | for-the-country | for-seven | years-of | the-famine | that |

| תִּהְיֶ֖יןָ | בְּאֶ֣רֶץ | מִצְרָ֑יִם | וְלֹֽא־ | תִכָּרֵ֥ת | הָאָ֖רֶץ |
|---|---|---|---|---|---|
| they-will-come | on-land-of | Egypt | so-not | she-will-be-ruined | the-country |

| בָּרָעָֽב׃ | וַיִּיטַ֥ב | הַדָּבָ֖ר | בְּעֵינֵ֣י | פַרְעֹ֑ה |
|---|---|---|---|---|
| by-the-famine | (37) and-he-seemed-good | the-plan | in-eyes-of | Pharaoh |

| וּבְעֵינֵ֖י | כָּל־ | עֲבָדָֽיו׃ | וַיֹּ֥אמֶר | פַּרְעֹ֖ה | אֶל־ |
|---|---|---|---|---|---|
| and-in-eyes-of | all-of | officials-of-him | (38) then-he-asked | Pharaoh | to |

east wind: They are seven years of famine.

28"It is just as I said to Pharaoh: God has shown Pharaoh what he is about to do. 29Seven years of great abundance are coming throughout the land of Egypt, 30but seven years of famine will follow them. Then all the abundance in Egypt will be forgotten, and the famine will ravage the land. 31The abundance in the land will not be remembered, because the famine that follows it will be so severe. 32The reason the dream was given to Pharaoh in two forms is that the matter has been firmly decided by God, and God will do it soon.

33"And now let Pharaoh look for a discerning and wise man and put him in charge of the land of Egypt. 34Let Pharaoh appoint commissioners over the land to take a fifth of the harvest of Egypt during the seven years of abundance. 35They should collect all the food of these good years that are coming and store up the grain under the authority of Pharaoh, to be kept in the cities for food. 36This food should be held in reserve for the country, to be used during the seven years of famine that will come upon Egypt, so that the country may not be ruined by the famine."

37The plan seemed good to Pharaoh and to all his officials. 38So Pharaoh asked them,

עֲבָדָיו   הֲנִמְצָא   כָזֶה   אִישׁ   אֲשֶׁר   רוּחַ   אֱלֹהִים   בּוֹ
officials-of-him / can-we-find? / like-this / man / whom / spirit-of / God / in-him

(39) וַיֹּאמֶר   פַּרְעֹה   אֶל־יוֹסֵף   אַחֲרֵי   הוֹדִיעַ   אֱלֹהִים   אוֹתְךָ   אֶת־כָּל־
then-he-said / Pharaoh / to / Joseph / since / to-show / God / to-you / *** / all-of

זֹאת   אֵין־נָבוֹן   וְחָכָם   כָּמוֹךָ:   (40) אַתָּה   תִּהְיֶה   עַל־
this / there-is-none discerning / and-wise / as-you / you / you-shall-be / over

בֵּיתִי   וְעַל־פִּיךָ   יִשַּׁק   כָּל־עַמִּי   רַק
palace-of-me / and-to order-of-you / he-will-submit / all-of people-of-me / only

הַכִּסֵּא   אֶגְדַּל   מִמֶּךָּ:   (41) וַיֹּאמֶר   פַּרְעֹה   אֶל־יוֹסֵף
the-throne / I-will-be-greater / than-you / so-he-said / Pharaoh / to / Joseph

רְאֵה   נָתַתִּי   אֹתְךָ   עַל   כָּל־אֶרֶץ   מִצְרָיִם:   (42) וַיָּסַר   פַּרְעֹה
see! / I-put-in-charge / you / over / all-of / land-of / Egypt / then-he-took / Pharaoh

אֶת־   טַבַּעְתּוֹ   מֵעַל   יָדוֹ   וַיִּתֵּן   אֹתָהּ   עַל־יַד
*** / signet-ring-of-him / from-on / finger-of-him / and-he-put / her / on / finger-of

יוֹסֵף   וַיַּלְבֵּשׁ   אֹתוֹ   בִּגְדֵי־שֵׁשׁ   וַיָּשֶׂם   רְבִד   הַזָּהָב
Joseph / and-he-dressed / him / robes-of linen / and-he-put / chain-of / the-gold

עַל־צַוָּארוֹ:   (43) וַיַּרְכֵּב   אֹתוֹ   בְּמִרְכֶּבֶת   הַמִּשְׁנֶה   אֲשֶׁר־
around neck-of-him / then-he-had-ride / him / in-chariot-of / the-second / that

לוֹ   וַיִּקְרְאוּ   לְפָנָיו   אַבְרֵךְ   וְנָתוֹן   אֹתוֹ   עַל   כָּל־
to-him / and-they-shouted / before-him / make-way! / so-to-put / him / over / all-of

אֶרֶץ   מִצְרָיִם:   (44) וַיֹּאמֶר   פַּרְעֹה   אֶל־יוֹסֵף   אֲנִי   פַרְעֹה   וּבִלְעָדֶיךָ
land-of / Egypt / then-he-said / Pharaoh / to / Joseph / I / Pharaoh / and-without-you

לֹא־יָרִים   אִישׁ   אֶת־יָדוֹ   וְאֶת־רַגְלוֹ   בְּכָל־אֶרֶץ   מִצְרָיִם:
not he-will-lift / man / *** hand-of-him / or foot-of-him / in-all-of land-of / Egypt

(45) וַיִּקְרָא   פַרְעֹה   שֵׁם־יוֹסֵף   צָפְנַת   פַּעְנֵחַ   וַיִּתֶּן־לוֹ
and-he-called / Pharaoh / name-of Joseph / Zaphenath / Paneah / and-he-gave to-him

אֶת־אָסְנַת   בַּת־פּוֹטִי   פֶרַע   כֹּהֵן   אֹן   לְאִשָּׁה   וַיֵּצֵא   יוֹסֵף
*** Asenath / daughter-of Poti / Phera / priest-of / On / as-wife / he-went / Joseph

עַל־אֶרֶץ   מִצְרָיִם:   (46) וְיוֹסֵף   בֶּן־שְׁלֹשִׁים   שָׁנָה   בְּעָמְדוֹ
throughout land-of / Egypt / now-Joseph / son-of thirty / year / when-to-serve-him

לִפְנֵי   פַּרְעֹה   מֶלֶךְ־מִצְרָיִם   וַיֵּצֵא   יוֹסֵף   מִלִּפְנֵי   פַרְעֹה
before / Pharaoh / king-of Egypt / and-he-went-out / Joseph / from-presence-of / Pharaoh

וַיַּעֲבֹר   בְּכָל־אֶרֶץ   מִצְרָיִם:   (47) וַתַּעַשׂ   הָאָרֶץ
and-he-traveled / through-all-of land-of / Egypt / and-she-produced / the-land

בְּשֶׁבַע   שְׁנֵי   הַשָּׂבָע   לִקְמָצִים:   (48) וַיִּקְבֹּץ   אֶת־
in-seven / years-of / the-abundance / by-great-amounts / and-he-collected / ***

כָּל־אֹכֶל   שֶׁבַע   שָׁנִים   אֲשֶׁר   הָיוּ   בְּאֶרֶץ   מִצְרַיִם   וַיִּתֶּן
all-of food-of / seven / years / that / they-produced / in-land-of / Egypt / and-he-put

---

"Can we find anyone like this man, one in whom is the spirit of God[k]?" **39**Then Pharaoh said to Joseph, "Since God has made all this known to you, there is no one so discerning and wise as you. **40**You shall be in charge of my palace, and all my people are to submit to your orders. Only with respect to the throne will I be greater than you."

*Joseph in Charge of Egypt*

**41**So Pharaoh said to Joseph, "I hereby put you in charge of the whole land of Egypt." **42**Then Pharaoh took his signet ring from his finger and put it on Joseph's finger. He dressed him in robes of fine linen and put a gold chain around his neck. **43**He had him ride in a chariot as his second-in-command,[l] and men shouted before him, "Make way[m]!" Thus he put him in charge of the whole land of Egypt.

**44**Then Pharaoh said to Joseph, "I am Pharaoh, but without your word no one will lift hand or foot in all Egypt." **45**Pharaoh gave Joseph the name Zaphenath-Paneah and gave him Asenath daughter of Potiphera, priest of On,[n] to be his wife. And Joseph went throughout the land of Egypt.

**46**Joseph was thirty years old when he entered the service of Pharaoh king of Egypt. And Joseph went out from Pharaoh's presence and traveled throughout Egypt. **47**During the seven years of abundance the land produced plentifully. **48**Joseph collected all the food produced in those seven years of abundance in Egypt and

---

*k38 Or of the gods*
*l43 Or in the chariot of his second-in-command; or in his second chariot*
*m43 Or Bow down*
*n45 That is, Heliopolis; also in verse 50*

*46 Most mss have *hateph pathah* under the *ayin* (וַיַּעֲבֹר).

אֹכֶל בֶּעָרִים אֹכֶל שְׂדֵה־ הָעִיר אֲשֶׁר סְבִיבֹתֶיהָ נָתַן
he-put surround-her that the-city field-of food-of in-the-cities food

בְּתוֹכָהּ׃ וַיִּצְבֹּר יוֹסֵף בָּר כְּחוֹל הַיָּם הַרְבֵּה
to-be-great the-sea like-sand-of grain Joseph and-he-stored (49) within-her

מְאֹד עַד כִּי־ חָדַל לִסְפֹּר כִּי־ אֵין מִסְפָּר׃
measurable he-is-not for to-keep-record he-stopped when until very

וּלְיוֹסֵף יֻלַּד שְׁנֵי בָנִים בְּטֶרֶם תָּבוֹא שְׁנַת הָרָעָב
the-famine year-of she-came before sons two-of he-was-born and-to-Joseph (50)

אֲשֶׁר יָלְדָה־ לּוֹ אָסְנַת בַּת־ פּוֹטִי פֶרַע כֹּהֵן אוֹן׃
On priest-of Phera Poti daughter-of Asenath to-him she-bore when

וַיִּקְרָא יוֹסֵף אֶת־ שֵׁם הַבְּכוֹר מְנַשֶּׁה כִּי־ נַשַּׁנִי
he-made-forget-me for Manasseh the-firstborn name-of *** Joseph and-he-called (51)

אֱלֹהִים אֶת־כָּל־ עֲמָלִי וְאֵת כָּל־ בֵּית אָבִי׃ וְאֵת
and (52) father-of-me household-of all-of and trouble-of-me all-of *** God

שֵׁם הַשֵּׁנִי קָרָא אֶפְרָיִם כִּי־ הִפְרַנִי אֱלֹהִים בְּאֶרֶץ
in-land-of God he-made-fruitful-me for Ephraim he-called the-second name-of

עָנְיִי׃ וַתִּכְלֶינָה שֶׁבַע שְׁנֵי הַשָּׂבָע אֲשֶׁר הָיָה
he-was that the-abundance years-of seven then-they-ended (53) suffering-of-me

בְּאֶרֶץ מִצְרָיִם׃ וַתְּחִלֶּינָה שֶׁבַע שְׁנֵי הָרָעָב לָבוֹא
to-come the-famine years-of seven and-they-began (54) Egypt in-land-of

כַּאֲשֶׁר אָמַר יוֹסֵף וַיְהִי רָעָב בְּכָל־ הָאֲרָצוֹת וּבְכָל־
but-in-whole-of the-lands in-all-of famine and-he-was Joseph he-said just-as

אֶרֶץ מִצְרַיִם הָיָה לָחֶם׃ וַתִּרְעַב כָּל־ אֶרֶץ מִצְרַיִם
Egypt land-of all-of and-she-felt-famine (55) food he-was Egypt land-of

וַיִּצְעַק הָעָם אֶל־ פַּרְעֹה לַלָּחֶם וַיֹּאמֶר פַּרְעֹה לְכָל־
to-all-of Pharaoh then-he-told for-the-food Pharaoh to the-people and-he-cried

מִצְרַיִם לְכוּ אֶל־יוֹסֵף אֲשֶׁר־ יֹאמַר לָכֶם תַּעֲשׂוּ׃ וְהָרָעָב הָיָה
he-was when-the-famine (56) you-do to-you he-tells what Joseph to go! Egypt

עַל כָּל־ פְּנֵי הָאָרֶץ וַיִּפְתַּח יוֹסֵף אֶת־ כָּל־ אֲשֶׁר
what all-of *** Joseph then-he-opened the-country surface-of all-of over

בָּהֶם וַיִּשְׁבֹּר לְמִצְרַיִם וַיֶּחֱזַק הָרָעָב בְּאֶרֶץ
in-land-of the-famine for-he-was-severe to-Egyptians and-he-sold in-them

מִצְרָיִם׃ וְכָל־ הָאָרֶץ בָּאוּ מִצְרַיְמָה לִשְׁבֹּר אֶל־ יוֹסֵף כִּי־
for Joseph from to-buy to-Egypt they-came the-world and-all-of (57) Egypt

חָזַק הָרָעָב בְּכָל־ הָאָרֶץ׃ וַיַּרְא יַעֲקֹב
Jacob when-he-learned (42:1) the-world in-all-of the-famine he-was-severe

כִּי יֶשׁ־ שֶׁבֶר בְּמִצְרָיִם וַיֹּאמֶר יַעֲקֹב לְבָנָיו לָמָּה
why? to-sons-of-him Jacob then-he-said in-Egypt grain there-is that

stored it in the cities. In each city he put the food grown in the fields surrounding it. [49]Joseph stored up huge quantities of grain, like the sand of the sea; it was so much that he stopped keeping records because it was beyond measure.

[50]Before the years of famine came, two sons were born to Joseph by Asenath daughter of Potiphera, priest of On. [51]Joseph named his firstborn Manasseh[p] and said, "It is because God has made me forget all my trouble and all my father's household." [52]The second son he named Ephraim[q] and said, "It is because God has made me fruitful in the land of my suffering."

[53]The seven years of abundance in Egypt came to an end, [54]and the seven years of famine began, just as Joseph had said. There was famine in all the other lands, but in the whole land of Egypt there was food. [55]When all Egypt began to feel the famine, the people cried to Pharaoh for food. Then Pharaoh told all the Egyptians, "Go to Joseph and do what he tells you."

[56]When the famine had spread over the whole country, Joseph opened the storehouses and sold grain to the Egyptians, for the famine was severe throughout Egypt. [57]And all the countries came to Egypt to buy grain from Joseph, because the famine was severe in all the world.

*Joseph's Brothers Go to Egypt*

**42** When Jacob learned that there was grain in Egypt, he said to his sons,

[p]51 *Manasseh* sounds like and may be derived from the Hebrew for *forget*.
[q]52 *Ephraim* sounds like the Hebrew for *twice fruitful*.

תִּתְרָאוּ׃ וַיֹּאמֶר הִנֵּה שָׁמַעְתִּי כִּי יֶשׁ־שֶׁבֶר
grain there-is that I-heard see! and-he-said (2) you-look-at-each-other

בְּמִצְרָיִם רְדוּ־שָׁמָּה וְשִׁבְרוּ־לָנוּ מִשָּׁם וְנִחְיֶה וְלֹא
and-not so-we-may-live from-there for-us and-buy! to-there go-down! in-Egypt

נָמוּת׃ וַיֵּרְדוּ אֲחֵי־יוֹסֵף עֲשָׂרָה לִשְׁבֹּר בָּר מִמִּצְרָיִם׃
from-Egypt grain to-buy ten Joseph brothers-of then-they-went-down (3) we-die

וְאֶת־בִּנְיָמִין אֲחִי יוֹסֵף לֹא־שָׁלַח יַעֲקֹב אֶת־אֶחָיו
brothers-of-him with Jacob he-sent not Joseph brother-of Benjamin but (4)

כִּי אָמַר פֶּן־יִקְרָאֶנּוּ אָסוֹן׃ וַיָּבֹאוּ בְּנֵי
sons-of so-they-went (5) harm he-might-come-to-him perhaps he-thought for

יִשְׂרָאֵל לִשְׁבֹּר בְּתוֹךְ הַבָּאִים כִּי־הָיָה הָרָעָב בְּאֶרֶץ כְּנָעַן׃
Canaan in-land-of the-famine he-was for the-ones-going among to-buy Israel

וְיוֹסֵף הוּא הַשַּׁלִּיט עַל־הָאָרֶץ הוּא הַמַּשְׁבִּיר לְכָל־
to-all-of the-one-selling he the-land over the-governor he now-Joseph (6)

עַם הָאָרֶץ וַיָּבֹאוּ אֲחֵי יוֹסֵף וַיִּשְׁתַּחֲווּ־לוֹ
to-him and-they-bowed Joseph brothers-of and-they-came the-world people-of

אַפַּיִם אָרְצָה׃ וַיַּרְא יוֹסֵף אֶת־אֶחָיו וַיַּכִּרֵם
and-he-recognized-them brothers-of-him *** Joseph and-he-saw (7) to-ground faces

וַיִּתְנַכֵּר אֲלֵיהֶם וַיְדַבֵּר אִתָּם קָשׁוֹת וַיֹּאמֶר
and-he-asked harshly to-them and-he-spoke to-them but-he-was-as-stranger

אֲלֵהֶם מֵאַיִן בָּאתֶם וַיֹּאמְרוּ מֵאֶרֶץ כְּנַעַן לִשְׁבָּר־
to-buy Canaan from-land-of and-they-replied you-come from-where? to-them

אֹכֶל׃ וַיַּכֵּר יוֹסֵף אֶת־אֶחָיו וְהֵם לֹא
not but-they brothers-of-him *** Joseph so-he-recognized (8) food

הִכִּרֻהוּ׃ וַיִּזְכֹּר יוֹסֵף אֵת הַחֲלֹמוֹת אֲשֶׁר
that the-dreams *** Joseph then-he-remembered (9) they-recognized-him

חָלַם לָהֶם וַיֹּאמֶר אֲלֵהֶם מְרַגְּלִים אַתֶּם לִרְאוֹת אֶת־
*** to-see you ones-spying to-them and-he-said about-them he-dreamed

עֶרְוַת הָאָרֶץ בָּאתֶם׃ וַיֹּאמְרוּ אֵלָיו לֹא אֲדֹנִי
lord-of-me no to-him but-they-said (10) you-came the-land weakness-of

וַעֲבָדֶיךָ בָּאוּ לִשְׁבָּר־אֹכֶל׃ כֻּלָּנוּ בְּנֵי אִישׁ־אֶחָד נָחְנוּ
we one man sons-of all-of-us (11) food to-buy they-came but-servants-of-you

כֵּנִים אֲנַחְנוּ לֹא־הָיוּ עֲבָדֶיךָ מְרַגְּלִים׃ וַיֹּאמֶר
but-he-said (12) ones-spying servants-of-you they-are not we honest-ones

אֲלֵהֶם לֹא כִּי־עֶרְוַת הָאָרֶץ בָּאתֶם לִרְאוֹת׃ וַיֹּאמְרוּ
but-they-replied (13) to-see you-came the-land weakness-of for no to-them

שְׁנֵים עָשָׂר עֲבָדֶיךָ אַחִים ׀ אֲנַחְנוּ בְּנֵי אִישׁ־אֶחָד בְּאֶרֶץ כְּנָעַן
Canaan in-land-of one man sons-of we brothers servants-of-you ten two

"Why do you just keep looking at each other?" 2He continued, "I have heard that there is grain in Egypt. Go down there and buy some for us, so that we may live and not die."

3Then ten of Joseph's brothers went down to buy grain from Egypt. 4But Jacob did not send Benjamin, Joseph's brother, with the others, because he was afraid that harm might come to him. 5So Israel's sons were among those who went to buy grain, for the famine was in the land of Canaan also.

6Now Joseph was the governor of the land, the one who sold grain to all its people. So when Joseph's brothers arrived, they bowed down to him with their faces to the ground. 7As soon as Joseph saw his brothers, he recognized them, but he pretended to be a stranger and spoke harshly to them. "Where do you come from?" he asked.

"From the land of Canaan," they replied, "to buy food."

8Although Joseph recognized his brothers, they did not recognize him. 9Then he remembered his dreams about them and said to them, "You are spies! You have come to see where our land is unprotected."

10"No, my lord," they answered. "Your servants have come to buy food. 11We are all the sons of one man. Your servants are honest men, not spies."

12"No!" he said to them. "You have come to see where our land is unprotected."

13But they replied, "Your servants were twelve brothers, the sons of one man, who lives in the land of Canaan. The

וְהִנֵּה הַקָּטֹן אֶת־ אָבִינוּ הַיּוֹם וְהָאֶחָד אֵינֶנּוּ׃
not-is-he and-the-one the-day father-of-us with the-young and-see!

וַיֹּאמֶר אֲלֵהֶם יוֹסֵף הוּא אֲשֶׁר דִּבַּרְתִּי אֲלֵכֶם לֵאמֹר מְרַגְּלִים
ones-spying to-say to-you I-told as he Joseph to-them but-he-said (14)

אַתֶּם׃ בְּזֹאת תִּבָּחֵנוּ חֵי פַרְעֹה אִם־ תֵּצְאוּ
you-will-leave not Pharaoh life-of you-will-be-tested by-this (15) you

מִזֶּה כִּי אִם־ בְּבוֹא אֲחִיכֶם הַקָּטֹן הֵנָּה׃ שִׁלְחוּ מִכֶּם
from-you send! (16) here the-young brother-of-you to-come if unless from-this

אֶחָד וְיִקַּח אֶת־ אֲחִיכֶם וְאַתֶּם הֵאָסְרוּ וְיִבָּחֲנוּ
so-they-be-tested be-in-prison! and-you brother-of-you *** and-let-him-get one

דִּבְרֵיכֶם הַאֱמֶת אִתְּכֶם וְאִם־ לֹא חֵי פַרְעֹה כִּי מְרַגְּלִים
ones-spying then Pharaoh life-of not but-if in-you whether-truth words-of-you

אַתֶּם׃ וַיֶּאֱסֹף אֹתָם אֶל־ מִשְׁמָר שְׁלֹשֶׁת יָמִים׃ וַיֹּאמֶר אֲלֵהֶם
to-them and-he-said (18) days three-of custody in them and-he-put (17) you

יוֹסֵף בַּיּוֹם הַשְּׁלִישִׁי זֹאת עֲשׂוּ וִחְיוּ אֶת־ הָאֱלֹהִים אֲנִי יָרֵא׃
fearing I the-God *** and-live! do! this the-third on-the-day Joseph

אִם־ כֵּנִים אַתֶּם אֲחִיכֶם אֶחָד יֵאָסֵר בְּבֵית
in-house-of let-him-stay one brother-of-you you honest-men if (19)

מִשְׁמַרְכֶם וְאַתֶּם לְכוּ הָבִיאוּ שֶׁבֶר רַעֲבוֹן בָּתֵּיכֶם׃
households-of-you famine-of grain take-back! go! and-you prison-of-you

וְאֶת־ אֲחִיכֶם הַקָּטֹן תָּבִיאוּ אֵלַי וְיֵאָמְנוּ
so-they-may-be-verified to-me you-bring the-young brother-of-you but (20)

דִבְרֵיכֶם וְלֹא תָמוּתוּ וַיַּעֲשׂוּ־ כֵן׃ וַיֹּאמְרוּ אִישׁ אֶל־
to each and-they-said (21) this so-they-did you-die so-not words-of-you

אָחִיו אֲבָל אֲשֵׁמִים ׀ אֲנַחְנוּ עַל־ אָחִינוּ אֲשֶׁר רָאִינוּ
we-saw whom brother-of-us because-of we punished-ones surely brother-of-him

צָרַת נַפְשׁוֹ בְּהִתְחַנְנוֹ אֵלֵינוּ וְלֹא שָׁמָעְנוּ עַל־
for we-listened but-not with-us when-to-plead-him life-of-him distress-of

כֵּן בָּאָה אֵלֵינוּ הַצָּרָה הַזֹּאת׃ וַיַּעַן רְאוּבֵן אֹתָם
to-them Reuben and-he-replied (22) the-this the-distress on-us she-came this

לֵאמֹר הֲלוֹא אָמַרְתִּי אֲלֵיכֶם ׀ לֵאמֹר אַל־ תֶּחֶטְאוּ בַיֶּלֶד וְלֹא
but-not against-the-boy you-sin not to-say to-you I-told not? to-say

שְׁמַעְתֶּם וְגַם־ דָּמוֹ הִנֵּה נִדְרָשׁ׃ וְהֵם לֹא יָדְעוּ
they-knew not now-they (23) accounting see! blood-of-him so-now you-listened

כִּי שֹׁמֵעַ יוֹסֵף כִּי הַמֵּלִיץ בֵּינֹתָם׃
between-them the-one-interpreting for Joseph understanding that

וַיִּסֹּב מֵעֲלֵיהֶם וַיֵּבְךְּ וַיָּשָׁב אֲלֵהֶם וַיְדַבֵּר
and-he-spoke to-them but-he-returned and-he-wept from-them then-he-turned (24)

youngest is now with our father, and one is no more."

14Joseph said to them, "It is just as I told you: You are spies! 15And this is how you will be tested: As surely as Pharaoh lives, you will not leave this place unless your youngest brother comes here. 16Send one of your number to get your brother; the rest of you will be kept in prison, so that your words may be tested to see if you are telling the truth. If you are not, then as surely as Pharaoh lives, you are spies!" 17And he put them all in custody for three days.

18On the third day, Joseph said to them, "Do this and you will live, for I fear God: 19If you are honest men, let one of your brothers stay here in prison, while the rest of you go and take grain back for your starving households. 20But you must bring your youngest brother to me, so that your words may be verified and that you may not die." This they proceeded to do.

21They said to one another, "Surely we are being punished because of our brother. We saw how distressed he was when he pleaded with us for his life, but we would not listen; that's why this distress has come upon us."

22Reuben replied, "Didn't I tell you not to sin against the boy? But you wouldn't listen! Now we must give an accounting for his blood." 23They did not realize that Joseph could understand them, since he was using an interpreter.

24He turned away from them and began to weep, but then turned back and spoke to them

אֱלֵהֶם וַיִּקַּח מֵאִתָּם אֶת־שִׁמְעוֹן וַיֶּאֱסֹר אֹתוֹ לְעֵינֵיהֶם׃
before-eyes-of-them him and-he-bound Simeon *** from-them and-he-took to-them

וַיְצַו יוֹסֵף וַיְמַלְאוּ אֶת־כְּלֵיהֶם בָּר וּלְהָשִׁיב
and-to-put grain bags-of-them *** and-they-filled Joseph and-he-ordered (25)

כַּסְפֵּיהֶם אִישׁ אֶל־שַׂקּוֹ וְלָתֵת לָהֶם צֵדָה לַדָּרֶךְ
for-journey provision to-them and-to-give sack-of-him in each silvers-of-them

וַיַּעַשׂ לָהֶם כֵּן׃ וַיִּשְׂאוּ אֶת־שִׁבְרָם עַל־
on grain-of-them *** so-they-loaded (26) this for-them and-he-did

חֲמֹרֵיהֶם וַיֵּלְכוּ מִשָּׁם׃ וַיִּפְתַּח הָאֶחָד אֶת־
*** the-one now-he-opened (27) from-there and-they-left donkeys-of-them

שַׂקּוֹ לָתֵת מִסְפּוֹא לַחֲמֹרוֹ בַּמָּלוֹן וַיַּרְא אֶת־
*** and-he-saw at-the-place for-donkey-of-him feed to-get sack-of-him

כַּסְפּוֹ וְהִנֵּה־הוּא בְּפִי אַמְתַּחְתּוֹ׃ וַיֹּאמֶר אֶל־
to so-he-said (28) sack-of-him in-mouth-of he now-see! silver-of-him

אֶחָיו הוּשַׁב כַּסְפִּי וְגַם הִנֵּה בְאַמְתַּחְתִּי
in-sack-of-me see! now-indeed silver-of-me he-was-returned brothers-of-him

וַיֵּצֵא לִבָּם וַיֶּחֶרְדוּ אִישׁ אֶל־אָחִיו לֵאמֹר
to-say brother-of-him with each and-they-trembled heart-of-them and-he-sank

מַה־זֹּאת עָשָׂה אֱלֹהִים לָנוּ׃ וַיָּבֹאוּ אֶל־יַעֲקֹב אֲבִיהֶם
father-of-them Jacob to when-they-came (29) to-us God he-did this what?

אַרְצָה כְּנָעַן וַיַּגִּידוּ לוֹ אֵת כָּל־הַקֹּרֹת אֹתָם
to-them the-ones-happening all-of *** to-him then-they-told Canaan in-land-of

לֵאמֹר׃ דִּבֶּר הָאִישׁ אֲדֹנֵי הָאָרֶץ אִתָּנוּ קָשׁוֹת וַיִּתֵּן
and-he-treated harshly to-us the-land lords-of the-man he-spoke (30) to-say

אֹתָנוּ כִּמְרַגְּלִים אֶת־הָאָרֶץ׃ וַנֹּאמֶר אֵלָיו כֵּנִים אֲנַחְנוּ לֹא
not we honest-men to-him but-we-said (31) the-land *** as-ones-spying us

הָיִינוּ מְרַגְּלִים׃ שְׁנֵים־עָשָׂר אֲנַחְנוּ אַחִים בְּנֵי אָבִינוּ הָאֶחָד
the-one father-of-us sons-of brothers we ten two (32) ones-spying we-are

אֵינֶנּוּ וְהַקָּטֹן הַיּוֹם אֶת־אָבִינוּ בְּאֶרֶץ כְּנָעַן׃
Canaan in-land-of father-of-us with the-day and-the-young not-is-he

וַיֹּאמֶר אֵלֵינוּ הָאִישׁ אֲדֹנֵי הָאָרֶץ בְּזֹאת אֵדַע כִּי
that I-will-know by-this the-land lords-of the-man to-us then-he-said (33)

כֵנִים אַתֶּם אֲחִיכֶם הָאֶחָד הַנִּיחוּ אִתִּי וְאֶת־רַעֲבוֹן
famine-of and with-me leave! the-one brother-of-you you honest-men

בָּתֵּיכֶם קְחוּ וָלֵכוּ׃ וְהָבִיאוּ אֶת־אֲחִיכֶם הַקָּטֹן
the-young brother-of-you *** but-bring! (34) and-go! take! houses-of-you

אֵלַי וְאֵדְעָה כִּי לֹא מְרַגְּלִים אַתֶּם כִּי כֵנִים אַתֶּם אֶת־אֲחִיכֶם
brother-of-you *** you honest-men but you ones-spying not that so-I-know to-me

again. He had Simeon taken from them and bound before their eyes.

25Joseph gave orders to fill their bags with grain, to put each man's silver back in his sack, and to give them provisions for their journey. After this was done for them, 26they loaded their grain on their donkeys and left.

27At the place where they stopped for the night one of them opened his sack to get feed for his donkey, and he saw his silver in the mouth of his sack. 28"My silver has been returned," he said to his brothers. "Here it is in my sack."

Their hearts sank and they turned to each other trembling and said, "What is this that God has done to us?"

29When they came to their father Jacob in the land of Canaan, they told him all that had happened to them. They said, 30"The man who is lord over the land spoke harshly to us and treated us as though we were spying on the land. 31But we said to him, 'We are honest men; we are not spies. 32We were twelve brothers, sons of one father. One is no more, and the youngest is now with our father in Canaan.'

33"Then the man who is lord over the land said to us, 'This is how I will know whether you are honest men: Leave one of your brothers here with me, and take food for your starving households and go. 34But bring your youngest brother to me so I will know that you are not spies but honest men. Then I will give your

אֶתֵּן לָכֶם וְאֶת־הָאָרֶץ תִּסְחָרוּ׃ וַיְהִי הֵם
they and-he-was (35) you-can-trade the-land and to-you I-will-return

מְרִיקִים שַׂקֵּיהֶם וְהִנֵּה־אִישׁ צְרוֹר־כַּסְפּוֹ בְּשַׂקּוֹ
in-sack-of-him silver-of-him pouch-of each and-see! sacks-of-them ones-emptying

וַיִּרְאוּ אֶת־צְרֹרוֹת כַּסְפֵּיהֶם הֵמָּה וַאֲבִיהֶם
and-father-of-them they silvers-of-them pouches-of *** when-they-saw

וַיִּירָאוּ׃ וַיֹּאמֶר אֲלֵהֶם יַעֲקֹב אֲבִיהֶם אֹתִי
me father-of-them Jacob to-them and-he-said (36) then-they-were-afraid

שִׁכַּלְתֶּם יוֹסֵף אֵינֶנּוּ וְשִׁמְעוֹן אֵינֶנּוּ וְאֶת־בִּנְיָמִן תִּקָּחוּ
you-would-take Benjamin and not-is-he and-Simeon not-is-he Joseph you-deprived

עָלַי הָיוּ כֻלָּנָה׃ וַיֹּאמֶר רְאוּבֵן אֶל־אָבִיו
father-of-him to Reuben then-he-said (37) all-things they-are against-me

לֵאמֹר אֶת־שְׁנֵי בָנַי תָּמִית אִם־לֹא אֲבִיאֶנּוּ אֵלֶיךָ תְּנָה
entrust! to-you I-bring-him not if you-may-kill sons-of-me two-of *** to-say

אֹתוֹ עַל־יָדִי וַאֲנִי אֲשִׁיבֶנּוּ אֵלֶיךָ׃ וַיֹּאמֶר לֹא־
not but-he-said (38) to-you I-will-bring-back-him and-I care-of-me to him

יֵרֵד בְּנִי עִמָּכֶם כִּי־אָחִיו מֵת וְהוּא
and-he he-is-dead brother-of-him for with-you son-of-me he-will-go-down

לְבַדּוֹ נִשְׁאָר וּקְרָאָהוּ אָסוֹן בַּדֶּרֶךְ אֲשֶׁר תֵּלְכוּ־בָהּ
on-her you-go that on-the-journey harm if-he-comes-to-him being-left only-he

וְהוֹרַדְתֶּם אֶת־שֵׂיבָתִי בְּיָגוֹן שְׁאוֹלָה׃
to-Sheol in-sorrow gray-head-of-me *** then-you-will-bring-down

וְהָרָעָב כָּבֵד בָּאָרֶץ׃ וַיְהִי כַּאֲשֶׁר כִּלּוּ
they-finished when so-he-was (2) in-the-land severe now-the-famine (43:1)

לֶאֱכֹל אֶת־הַשֶּׁבֶר אֲשֶׁר הֵבִיאוּ מִמִּצְרָיִם וַיֹּאמֶר אֲלֵיהֶם
to-them then-he-said from-Egypt they-brought that the-grain *** to-eat

אֲבִיהֶם שֻׁבוּ שִׁבְרוּ־לָנוּ מְעַט־אֹכֶל׃ וַיֹּאמֶר אֵלָיו
to-him but-he-said (3) food little-of for-us buy! go-back! father-of-them

יְהוּדָה לֵאמֹר הָעֵד הֵעִד בָּנוּ הָאִישׁ לֵאמֹר לֹא־תִרְאוּ פָנַי
face-of-me you-will-see not to-say the-man to-us he-warned to-warn to-say Judah

בִּלְתִּי אֲחִיכֶם אִתְּכֶם׃ אִם־יֶשְׁךָ מְשַׁלֵּחַ אֶת־אָחִינוּ
brother-of-us *** sending will-of-you if (4) with-you brother-of-you unless

אִתָּנוּ נֵרְדָה וְנִשְׁבְּרָה לְךָ אֹכֶל׃ וְאִם־אֵינְךָ
not-you but-if (5) food for-you and-we-will-buy we-will-go-down with-us

מְשַׁלֵּחַ לֹא נֵרֵד כִּי־הָאִישׁ אָמַר אֵלֵינוּ לֹא־תִרְאוּ
you-will-see not to-us he-said the-man for we-will-go-down not sending

פָנַי בִּלְתִּי אֲחִיכֶם אִתְּכֶם׃ וַיֹּאמֶר יִשְׂרָאֵל לָמָה
why? Israel and-he-asked (6) with-you brother-of-you unless face-of-me

brother back to you, and you can trade[r] in the land.' "
[35]As they were emptying their sacks, there in each man's sack was his pouch of silver! When they and their father saw the money pouches, they were frightened. [36]Their father Jacob said to them, "You have deprived me of my children. Joseph is no more and Simeon is no more, and now you want to take Benjamin. Everything is against me!"
[37]Then Reuben said to his father, "You may put both of my sons to death if I do not bring him back to you. Entrust him to my care, and I will bring him back."
[38]But Jacob said, "My son will not go down there with you; his brother is dead and he is the only one left. If harm comes to him on the journey you are taking, you will bring my gray head down to the grave[s] in sorrow."

*The Second Journey to Egypt*

43 Now the famine was still severe in the land. [2]So when they had eaten all the grain they had brought from Egypt, their father said to them, "Go back and buy us a little more food."
[3]But Judah said to him, "The man warned us solemnly, 'You will not see my face again unless your brother is with you.' [4]If you will send our brother along with us, we will go down and buy food for you. [5]But if you will not send him, we will not go down, because the man said to us, 'You will not see my face again unless your brother is with you.' "
[6]Israel asked, "Why did you

[r]34 Or *move about freely*
[s]38 Hebrew *Sheol*

הֲרֵעֹתֶם לִי לְהַגִּיד לָאִישׁ הַעוֹד לָכֶם אָח׃
brother to-you another? to-the-man to-tell to-me you-bring-trouble

וַיֹּאמְרוּ שָׁאוֹל שָׁאַל־ הָאִישׁ לָנוּ וּלְמוֹלַדְתֵּנוּ
and-about-family-of-us about-us the-man he-asked to-ask and-they-replied (7)

לֵאמֹר הַעוֹד אֲבִיכֶם חַי הֲיֵשׁ לָכֶם אָח וַנַּגֶּד־
so-we-answered brother to-you is-there? alive father-of-you still? to-say

לוֹ עַל־ פִּי הַדְּבָרִים הָאֵלֶּה הֲיָדוֹעַ נֵדַע כִּי יֹאמַר
he-would-say that could-we-know to-know? the-these the-words mouth-of on to-him

הוֹרִידוּ אֶת־ אֲחִיכֶם׃ וַיֹּאמֶר יְהוּדָה אֶל־ יִשְׂרָאֵל אָבִיו
father-of-him Israel to Judah then-he-said (8) brother-of-you *** bring-down!

שִׁלְחָה הַנַּעַר אִתִּי וְנָקוּמָה וְנֵלֵכָה וְנִחְיֶה וְלֹא
and-not so-we-may-live and-we-will-go and-we-will-rise with-me the-boy send!

נָמוּת גַּם־ אֲנַחְנוּ גַם־ אַתָּה גַּם־ טַפֵּנוּ׃ אָנֹכִי אֶעֶרְבֶנּוּ
I-guarantee-him I (9) children-of-us also you also we indeed we-die

מִיָּדִי תְּבַקְשֶׁנּוּ אִם־ לֹא הֲבִיאֹתִיו אֵלֶיךָ
to-you I-bring-back-him not if you-can-require-him from-hand-of-me

וְהִצַּגְתִּיו לְפָנֶיךָ וְחָטָאתִי לְךָ כָּל־ הַיָּמִים׃
the-days all-of before-you I-will-bear-blame before-you and-I-set-him

כִּי לוּלֵא הִתְמַהְמָהְנוּ כִּי־ עַתָּה שַׁבְנוּ זֶה פַעֲמָיִם׃
twice here we-could-have-returned now then we-had-delayed if-not for (10)

וַיֹּאמֶר אֲלֵהֶם יִשְׂרָאֵל אֲבִיהֶם אִם־כֵּן | אֵפוֹא זֹאת עֲשׂוּ קְחוּ
put! do! this then so if father-of-them Israel to-them then-he-said (11)

מִזִּמְרַת הָאָרֶץ בִּכְלֵיכֶם וְהוֹרִידוּ לָאִישׁ מִנְחָה
gift to-the-man and-take-down! in-bags-of-you the-land from-best-produce-of

מְעַט צֳרִי וּמְעַט דְּבַשׁ נְכֹאת וָלֹט בָּטְנִים וּשְׁקֵדִים׃
and-almonds pistachio-nuts and-myrrh spice honey and-little-of balm little-of

וְכֶסֶף מִשְׁנֶה קְחוּ בְיֶדְכֶם וְאֶת־ הַכֶּסֶף הַמּוּשָׁב
the-being-returned the-silver and in-hand-of-you take! twice and-silver (12)

בְּפִי אַמְתְּחֹתֵיכֶם תָּשִׁיבוּ בְיֶדְכֶם אוּלַי מִשְׁגֶּה הוּא׃
he mistake perhaps in-hand-of-you you-must-take-back sacks-of-you in-mouth-of

וְאֶת־ אֲחִיכֶם קָחוּ וְקוּמוּ שׁוּבוּ אֶל־ הָאִישׁ׃ וְאֵל
and-God (14) the-man to go-back! and-rise! take! brother-of-you and (13)

שַׁדַּי יִתֵּן לָכֶם רַחֲמִים לִפְנֵי הָאִישׁ וְשִׁלַּח לָכֶם
with-you so-he-will-send the-man before mercies to-you may-he-grant Almighty

אֶת־ אֲחִיכֶם אַחֵר וְאֶת־ בִּנְיָמִין וַאֲנִי כַּאֲשֶׁר שָׁכֹלְתִּי שָׁכָלְתִּי׃
I-am-bereaved I-am-bereaved if but-I Benjamin and other brother-of-you ***

וַיִּקְחוּ הָאֲנָשִׁים אֶת־הַמִּנְחָה הַזֹּאת וּמִשְׁנֶה־ כֶּסֶף לָקְחוּ
they-took silver and-double the-this the-gift *** the-men so-they-took (15)

bring this trouble on me by telling the man you had another brother?"

7They replied, "The man questioned us closely about ourselves and our family. 'Is your father still living?' he asked us. 'Do you have another brother?' We simply answered his questions. How were we to know he would say, 'Bring your brother down here'?"

8Then Judah said to Israel his father, "Send the boy along with me and we will go at once, so that we and you and our children may live and not die. 9I myself will guarantee his safety; you can hold me personally responsible for him. If I do not bring him back to you and set him here before you, I will bear the blame before you all my life. 10As it is, if we had not delayed, we could have gone and returned twice."

11Then their father Israel said to them, "If it must be, then do this: Put some of the best products of the land in your bags and take them down to the man as a gift—a little balm and a little honey, some spices and myrrh, some pistachio nuts and almonds. 12Take double the amount of silver with you, for you must return the silver that was put back into the mouths of your sacks. Perhaps it was a mistake. 13Take your brother also and go back to the man at once. 14And may God Almighty[t] grant you mercy before the man so that he will let your other brother and Benjamin come back with you. As for me, if I am bereaved, I am bereaved."

15So the men took the gifts

[t]14 Hebrew *El-Shaddai*

*7 Most mss have *dagesh* in the *nun* (וַנַּ).

בְּיָדָם וְאֶת־ בִּנְיָמִן וַיָּקֻמוּ וַיֵּרְדוּ מִצְרַיִם
Egypt and-they-went-down then-they-rose Benjamin and in-hand-of-them

וַיַּעַמְדוּ לִפְנֵי יוֹסֵף׃ וַיַּרְא יוֹסֵף אִתָּם אֶת־ בִּנְיָמִין
Benjamin *** with-them Joseph when-he-saw (16) Joseph before and-they-stood

וַיֹּאמֶר לַאֲשֶׁר עַל־ בֵּיתוֹ הָבֵא אֶת־ הָאֲנָשִׁים הַבָּיְתָה
to-the-house the-men *** take! house-of-him over to-whom then-he-said

וּטְבֹחַ טֶבַח וְהָכֵן כִּי אִתִּי יֹאכְלוּ הָאֲנָשִׁים
the-men they-will-eat with-me for and-prepare! animal and-slaughter!

בַּצָּהֳרָיִם׃ וַיַּעַשׂ הָאִישׁ כַּאֲשֶׁר אָמַר יוֹסֵף וַיָּבֵא הָאִישׁ
the-man and-he-took Joseph he-said just-as the-man so-he-did (17) at-the-noon

אֶת־הָאֲנָשִׁים בֵּיתָה יוֹסֵף׃ וַיִּירְאוּ הָאֲנָשִׁים כִּי
when the-men now-they-were-afraid (18) Joseph to-house-of the-men ***

הוּבְאוּ בֵּית יוֹסֵף וַיֹּאמְרוּ עַל־ דְּבַר
matter-of because-of and-they-thought Joseph house-of they-were-taken

הַכֶּסֶף הַשָּׁב בְּאַמְתְּחֹתֵינוּ בַּתְּחִלָּה אֲנַחְנוּ
we on-the-first-time into-sacks-of-us the-being-put-back the-silver

מוּבָאִים לְהִתְגֹּלֵל עָלֵינוּ וּלְהִתְנַפֵּל עָלֵינוּ וְלָקַחַת
and-to-seize over-us and-to-overpower against-us to-attack ones-being-brought

אֹתָנוּ לַעֲבָדִים וְאֶת־ חֲמֹרֵינוּ׃ וַיִּגְּשׁוּ אֶל־ הָאִישׁ אֲשֶׁר עַל־
over who the-man to so-they-went-up (19) donkeys-of-us and as-slaves us

בֵּית יוֹסֵף וַיְדַבְּרוּ אֵלָיו פֶּתַח הַבָּיִת׃ וַיֹּאמְרוּ
and-they-said (20) the-house entrance-of to-him and-they-spoke Joseph house-of

בִּי אֲדֹנִי יָרֹד יָרַדְנוּ בַּתְּחִלָּה לִשְׁבָּר־אֹכֶל׃
food to-buy on-the-first-time we-came-down to-come-down sir-of-me Oh

וַיְהִי כִּי־ בָאנוּ אֶל־ הַמָּלוֹן וַנִּפְתְּחָה אֶת־ אַמְתְּחֹתֵינוּ
sacks-of-us *** and-we-opened the-place to we-came when and-he-was (21)

וְהִנֵּה כֶסֶף־ אִישׁ בְּפִי אַמְתַּחְתּוֹ כַּסְפֵּנוּ
silver-of-us sack-of-him in-mouth-of each silver-of and-see!

בְּמִשְׁקָלוֹ וַנָּשֶׁב אֹתוֹ בְּיָדֵנוּ׃ וְכֶסֶף
and-silver (22) in-hand-of-us him so-we-brought-back in-exact-weight-of-him

אַחֵר הוֹרַדְנוּ בְיָדֵנוּ לִשְׁבָּר־אֹכֶל לֹא יָדַעְנוּ מִי־ שָׂם
he-put who we-know not food to-buy in-hand-of-us we-brought-down additional

כַּסְפֵּנוּ בְּאַמְתְּחֹתֵינוּ׃ וַיֹּאמֶר שָׁלוֹם לָכֶם אַל־ תִּירָאוּ
you-be-afraid not to-you all-right but-he-said (23) in-sacks-of-us silver-of-us

אֱלֹהֵיכֶם וֵאלֹהֵי אֲבִיכֶם נָתַן לָכֶם מַטְמוֹן בְּאַמְתְּחֹתֵיכֶם
in-sacks-of-you treasure to-you he-gave father-of-you and-God-of God-of-you

כַּסְפְּכֶם בָּא אֵלָי וַיּוֹצֵא אֲלֵהֶם אֶת־ שִׁמְעוֹן׃
Simeon *** to-them then-he-brought-out to-me he-came silver-of-you

and double the amount of silver, and Benjamin also. They hurried down to Egypt and presented themselves to Joseph.
16 When Joseph saw Benjamin with them, he said to the steward of his house, "Take these men to my house, slaughter an animal and prepare dinner; they are to eat with me at noon."

17 The man did as Joseph told him and took the men to Joseph's house.
18 Now the men were frightened when they were taken to his house. They thought, "We were brought here because of the silver that was put back into our sacks the first time. He wants to attack us and overpower us and seize us as slaves and take our donkeys."

19 So they went up to Joseph's steward and spoke to him at the entrance to the house.
20 "Please, sir," they said, "we came down here the first time to buy food.
21 But at the place where we stopped for the night we opened our sacks and each of us found his silver—the exact weight—in the mouth of his sack. So we have brought it back with us.
22 We have also brought additional silver with us to buy food. We don't know who put our silver in our sacks."

23 "It's all right," he said. "Don't be afraid. Your God and the God of your father has given you treasure in your sacks; I received your silver." Then he brought Simeon out to them.

וַיָּבֵא הָאִישׁ אֶת־הָאֲנָשִׁים בֵּיתָה יוֹסֵף וַיִּתֶּן־מַיִם
water and-he-gave Joseph into-house-of the-men *** the-man then-he-took (24)

וַיִּרְחֲצוּ רַגְלֵיהֶם וַיִּתֵּן מִסְפּוֹא לַחֲמֹרֵיהֶם׃
for-donkeys-of-them fodder and-he-provided feet-of-them and-they-washed

וַיָּכִינוּ אֶת־הַמִּנְחָה עַד־בּוֹא יוֹסֵף בַּצָּהֳרָיִם כִּי
for at-the-noon Joseph to-come for the-gift *** then-they-prepared (25)

שָׁמְעוּ כִּי־שָׁם יֹאכְלוּ לָחֶם׃ וַיָּבֹא יוֹסֵף הַבַּיְתָה
to-the-home Joseph when-he-came (26) meal they-would-eat there that they-heard

וַיָּבִיאוּ לוֹ אֶת־הַמִּנְחָה אֲשֶׁר־בְּיָדָם הַבָּיְתָה
into-the-house in-hand-of-them that the-gift *** to-him then-they-presented

וַיִּשְׁתַּחֲווּ־לוֹ אָרְצָה׃ וַיִּשְׁאַל לָהֶם לְשָׁלוֹם
about-welfare to-them and-he-asked (27) to-ground before-him and-they-bowed

וַיֹּאמֶר הֲשָׁלוֹם אֲבִיכֶם הַזָּקֵן אֲשֶׁר אֲמַרְתֶּם הַעוֹדֶנּוּ חָי׃
alive still-he? you-spoke whom the-aged father-of-you well? then-he-said

וַיֹּאמְרוּ שָׁלוֹם לְעַבְדְּךָ לְאָבִינוּ עוֹדֶנּוּ חָי
alive still-he with-father-of-us with-servant-of-you well and-they-replied (28)

וַיִּקְּדוּ וַיִּשְׁתַּחֲוֻּ*׃ וַיִּשָּׂא עֵינָיו
eyes-of-him and-he-lifted (29) and-they-bowed-low then-they-bowed-head

וַיַּרְא אֶת־בִּנְיָמִין אָחִיו בֶּן־אִמּוֹ וַיֹּאמֶר
and-he-asked mother-of-him son-of brother-of-him Benjamin *** and-he-saw

הֲזֶה אֲחִיכֶם הַקָּטֹן אֲשֶׁר אֲמַרְתֶּם אֵלָי וַיֹּאמַר אֱלֹהִים
God and-he-said to-me you-told whom the-young brother-of-you this?

יָחְנְךָ בְּנִי׃ וַיְמַהֵר יוֹסֵף כִּי־
for Joseph then-he-hurried (30) son-of-me may-he-be-gracious-to-you

נִכְמְרוּ רַחֲמָיו אֶל־אָחִיו וַיְבַקֵּשׁ לִבְכּוֹת
to-weep and-he-looked brother-of-him at compassions-of-him they-were-moved

וַיָּבֹא הַחַדְרָה וַיֵּבְךְּ שָׁמָּה׃ וַיִּרְחַץ
then-he-washed (31) at-there and-he-wept to-the-private-room so-he-went

פָּנָיו וַיֵּצֵא וַיִּתְאַפַּק וַיֹּאמֶר שִׂימוּ לָחֶם׃
food serve! and-he-said and-he-controlled-self and-he-came-out face-of-him

וַיָּשִׂימוּ לוֹ לְבַדּוֹ וְלָהֶם לְבַדָּם
by-themselves and-to-them by-himself to-him so-they-served (32)

וְלַמִּצְרִים הָאֹכְלִים אִתּוֹ לְבַדָּם כִּי לֹא יוּכְלוּן
they-could not for by-themselves with-him the-ones-eating and-to-the-Egyptians

הַמִּצְרִים לֶאֱכֹל אֶת־הָעִבְרִים לֶחֶם כִּי־תוֹעֵבָה הִוא לְמִצְרָיִם׃
to-Egyptians that destestable for food the-Hebrews with to-eat the-Egyptians

וַיֵּשְׁבוּ לְפָנָיו הַבְּכֹר כִּבְכֹרָתוֹ
according-to-age-of-him the-firstborn before-him now-they-sat (33)

24 The steward took the men
into Joseph's house, gave
them water to wash their feet
and provided fodder for their
donkeys.
25 They prepared
their gifts for Joseph's arrival
at noon, because they had
heard that they were to eat
there.
26 When Joseph came home,
they presented to him the gifts
they had brought into the
house, and they bowed down
before him to the ground.
27 He
asked them how they were,
and then he said, "How is
your aged father you told me
about? Is he still living?"
28 They replied, "Your servant our father is still alive
and well." And they bowed
low to pay him honor.
29 As he looked about and
saw his brother Benjamin, his
own mother's son, he asked,
"Is this your youngest brother, the one you told me
about?" And he said, "God be
gracious to you, my son."
30 Deeply moved at the sight of
his brother, Joseph hurried out
and looked for a place to weep.
He went into his private room
and wept there.
31 After he had washed his
face, he came out and, controlling himself, said, "Serve the
food."
32 They served him by himself, the brothers by themselves, and the Egyptians who
ate with him by themselves,
because Egyptians could not
eat with Hebrews, for that is
detestable to Egyptians.
33 The
men had been seated before
him in the order of their ages,
from the firstborn to the

*28 Most mss have the *Qere* form in the text (חוּו-).

°28 וישתחוו ק

וְהַצָּעִיר כִּצְעִרָתוֹ וַיִּתְמְהוּ הָאֲנָשִׁים

the-men and-they-were-astonished according-to-youth-of-him and-the-young

אִישׁ אֶל־ רֵעֵהוּ׃ וַיִּשָּׂא מַשְׂאֹת מֵאֵת פָּנָיו אֲלֵהֶם

to-them before-him from portions and-he-served (34) other-of-him with each

וַתֵּרֶב מַשְׂאַת בִּנְיָמִן מִמַּשְׂאֹת כֻּלָּם חָמֵשׁ

five all-of-them than-portions-of Benjamin portion-of and-she-was-greater

יָדוֹת וַיִּשְׁתּוּ וַיִּשְׁכְּרוּ עִמּוֹ׃ וַיְצַו אֶת־

*** then-he-instructed (44:1) with-him and-they-feasted so-they-drank times

אֲשֶׁר עַל־ בֵּיתוֹ לֵאמֹר מַלֵּא אֶת־ אַמְתְּחֹת הָאֲנָשִׁים אֹכֶל כַּאֲשֶׁר

as-much-as food the-men sacks-of *** fill! to-say house-of-him over whom

יוּכְלוּן שְׂאֵת וְשִׂים כֶּסֶף־ אִישׁ בְּפִי אַמְתַּחְתּוֹ׃ וְאֶת־

and (2) sack-of-him in-mouth-of each silver-of and-put! to-carry they-can

גְּבִיעִי גְּבִיעַ הַכֶּסֶף תָּשִׂים בְּפִי אַמְתַּחַת הַקָּטֹן וְאֵת

and the-young sack-of in-mouth-of you-put the-silver cup-of cup-of-me

כֶּסֶף שִׁבְרוֹ וַיַּעַשׂ כִּדְבַר יוֹסֵף אֲשֶׁר דִּבֵּר׃

he-spoke that Joseph as-word-of and-he-did grain-of-him silver-of

הַבֹּקֶר אוֹר וְהָאֲנָשִׁים שֻׁלְּחוּ הֵמָּה וַחֲמֹרֵיהֶם׃

and-donkeys-of-them they they-were-sent and-the-men light the-morning (3)

הֵם יָצְאוּ אֶת־ הָעִיר לֹא הִרְחִיקוּ וְיוֹסֵף אָמַר

he-said when-Joseph they-went-far not the-city *** they-went they (4)

לַאֲשֶׁר עַל־ בֵּיתוֹ קוּם רְדֹף אַחֲרֵי הָאֲנָשִׁים וְהִשַּׂגְתָּם

when-you-catch-them the-men after go! rise! house-of-him over to-whom

וְאָמַרְתָּ אֲלֵהֶם לָמָּה שִׁלַּמְתֶּם רָעָה תַּחַת טוֹבָה׃ הֲלוֹא זֶה אֲשֶׁר

which this not? (5) good for evil you-repaid why? to-them then-you-say

יִשְׁתֶּה אֲדֹנִי בּוֹ וְהוּא נַחֵשׁ יְנַחֵשׁ בּוֹ

with-him he-divines to-divine also-he from-him master-of-me he-drinks

הֲרֵעֹתֶם אֲשֶׁר עֲשִׂיתֶם׃ וַיַּשִּׂגֵם וַיְדַבֵּר אֲלֵהֶם

to-them then-he-said when-he-caught-them (6) you-did what you-were-wicked

אֶת־ הַדְּבָרִים הָאֵלֶּה׃ וַיֹּאמְרוּ אֵלָיו לָמָּה יְדַבֵּר אֲדֹנִי

master-of-me he-says why? to-him but-they-said (7) the-these the-words ***

כַּדְּבָרִים הָאֵלֶּה חָלִילָה לַעֲבָדֶיךָ מֵעֲשׂוֹת

from-to-do from-servants-of-you far-be-it! the-these such-the-things

כַּדָּבָר הַזֶּה׃ הֵן כֶּסֶף אֲשֶׁר מָצָאנוּ בְּפִי אַמְתְּחֹתֵינוּ

sacks-of-us in-mouth-of we-found that silver see! (8) the-that such-the-thing

הֱשִׁיבֹנוּ אֵלֶיךָ מֵאֶרֶץ כְּנָעַן וְאֵיךְ נִגְנֹב

would-we-steal so-why? Canaan from-land-of to-you we-brought-back

מִבֵּית אֲדֹנֶיךָ כֶּסֶף אוֹ זָהָב׃ אֲשֶׁר יִמָּצֵא אִתּוֹ

with-him he-is-found whom (9) gold or silver masters-of-you from-house-of

youngest; and they looked at each other in astonishment. 34When portions were served to them from Joseph's table, Benjamin's portion was five times as much as anyone else's. So they feasted and drank freely with him.

*A Silver Cup in a Sack*

44 Now Joseph gave these instructions to the steward of his house: "Fill the men's sacks with as much food as they can carry, and put each man's silver in the mouth of his sack. 2Then put my cup, the silver one, in the mouth of the youngest one's sack, along with the silver for his grain." And he did as Joseph said.

3As morning dawned, the men were sent on their way with their donkeys. 4They had not gone far from the city when Joseph said to his steward, "Go after those men at once, and when you catch up with them, say to them, 'Why have you repaid good with evil? 5Isn't this the cup my master drinks from and also uses for divination? This is a wicked thing you have done.'"

6When he caught up with them, he repeated these words to them. 7But they said to him, "Why does my lord say such things? Far be it from your servants to do anything like that! 8We even brought back to you from the land of Canaan the silver we found inside the mouths of our sacks. So why would we steal silver or gold from your master's house? 9If any of your servants is found

מֵעֲבָדֶיךָ וָמֵת וְגַם־ אֲנַחְנוּ נִהְיֶה לַאדֹנִי
to-master-of-me we-will-become we and-also now-he-will-die from-servants-of-you

לַעֲבָדִים׃ וַיֹּאמֶר גַּם־ עַתָּה כְדִבְרֵיכֶם כֶּן־ הוּא אֲשֶׁר
whom he thus as-words-of-you then very-well so-he-said (10) as-slaves

יִמָּצֵא אִתּוֹ יִהְיֶה־ לִּי עָבֶד וְאַתֶּם תִּהְיוּ נְקִיִּם׃
blameless-ones you-will-be but-you slave to-me he-will-be with-him he-is-found

וַיְמַהֲרוּ וַיּוֹרִדוּ אִישׁ אֶת־ אַמְתַּחְתּוֹ אָרְצָה
to-ground sack-of-him *** each and-they-lowered so-they-hurried (11)

וַיִּפְתְּחוּ אִישׁ אַמְתַּחְתּוֹ׃ וַיְחַפֵּשׂ בַּגָּדוֹל
with-the-oldest then-he-searched (12) sack-of-him each and-they-opened

הֵחֵל וּבַקָּטֹן כִּלָּה וַיִּמָּצֵא הַגָּבִיעַ בְּאַמְתַּחַת
in-sack-of the-cup and-he-was-found he-ended and-with-the-youngest he-began

בִּנְיָמִן׃ וַיִּקְרְעוּ שִׂמְלֹתָם וַיַּעֲמֹס אִישׁ עַל־
on each and-they-loaded clothes-of-them then-they-tore (13) Benjamin

חֲמֹרוֹ וַיָּשֻׁבוּ הָעִירָה׃ וַיָּבֹא יְהוּדָה
Judah when-he-came (14) to-the-city and-they-returned donkey-of-him

וְאֶחָיו בֵּיתָה יוֹסֵף וְהוּא עוֹדֶנּוּ שָׁם וַיִּפְּלוּ
and-they-fell there still-he now-he Joseph into-house-of and-brothers-of-him

לְפָנָיו אָרְצָה׃ וַיֹּאמֶר לָהֶם יוֹסֵף מָה־ הַמַּעֲשֶׂה הַזֶּה
the-this the-deed what? Joseph to-them and-he-said (15) to-ground before-him

אֲשֶׁר עֲשִׂיתֶם הֲלוֹא יְדַעְתֶּם כִּי־ נַחֵשׁ יְנַחֵשׁ אִישׁ אֲשֶׁר כָּמֹנִי׃
like-me who man he-divines to-divine that you-know not? you-did that

וַיֹּאמֶר יְהוּדָה מַה־ נֹּאמַר לַאדֹנִי מַה־ נְּדַבֵּר
can-we-speak what? to-lord-of-me can-we-say what? Judah and-he-replied (16)

וּמַה־ נִּצְטַדָּק הָאֱלֹהִים מָצָא אֶת־ עֲוֹן
guilt-of *** he-uncovered the-God can-we-show-innocence and-how?

עֲבָדֶיךָ הִנֶּנּוּ עֲבָדִים לַאדֹנִי גַּם־ אֲנַחְנוּ גַּם אֲשֶׁר־ נִמְצָא
he-was-found whom also we indeed to-lord-of-me slaves see-us! servants-of-you

הַגָּבִיעַ בְּיָדוֹ׃ וַיֹּאמֶר חָלִילָה לִּי מֵעֲשׂוֹת זֹאת
this from-to-do from-me far-be-it! but-he-said (17) in-hand-of-him the-cup

הָאִישׁ אֲשֶׁר נִמְצָא הַגָּבִיעַ בְּיָדוֹ הוּא יִהְיֶה־ לִּי
to-me he-will-become he in-hand-of-him the-cup he-was-found whom the-man

עָבֶד וְאַתֶּם עֲלוּ לְשָׁלוֹם אֶל־ אֲבִיכֶם׃ וַיִּגַּשׁ אֵלָיו
to-him then-he-went-up (18) father-of-you to in-peace go-back! but-you slave

יְהוּדָה וַיֹּאמֶר בִּי אֲדֹנִי יְדַבֶּר־ נָא עַבְדְּךָ דָבָר
word servant-of-you now! let-him-speak lord-of-me Oh and-he-said Judah

בְּאָזְנֵי אֲדֹנִי וְאַל־ יִחַר אַפְּךָ בְּעַבְדֶּךָ
against-servant-of-you anger-of-you let-him-burn and-not lord-of-me in-ears-of

to have it, he will die; and the
rest of us will become my
lord's slaves."
10"Very well, then," he said,
"let it be as you say. Whoever
is found to have it will become
my slave; the rest of you will
be free from blame."
11Each of them quickly lowered his sack to the ground
and opened it. 12Then the
steward proceeded to search,
beginning with the oldest and
ending with the youngest.
And the cup was found in
Benjamin's sack. 13At this,
they tore their clothes. Then
they all loaded their donkeys
and returned to the city.
14Joseph was still in the
house when Judah and his
brothers came in, and they
threw themselves to the
ground before him. 15Joseph
said to them, "What is this
you have done? Don't you
know that a man like me can
find things out by divination?"
16"What can we say to my
lord?" Judah replied. "What
can we say? How can we
prove our innocence? God has
uncovered your servants'
guilt. We are now my lord's
slaves—we ourselves and the
one who was found to have
the cup."
17But Joseph said, "Far be it
from me to do such a thing!
Only the man who was found
to have the cup will become
my slave. The rest of you, go
back to your father in peace."
18Then Judah went up to him
and said: "Please, my lord, let
your servant speak a word to
my lord. Do not be angry with

כִּי כָמוֹךָ כְּפַרְעֹה׃ אֲדֹנִי שָׁאַל אֶת־ עֲבָדָיו
servants-of-him *** he-asked lord-of-me (19) to-Pharaoh equal-you though

לֵאמֹר הֲיֵשׁ־ לָכֶם אָב אוֹ־ אָח׃ וַנֹּאמֶר אֶל־ אֲדֹנִי
lord-of-me to and-we-answered (20) brother or father to-you is-there? to-say

יֶשׁ־ לָנוּ אָב זָקֵן וְיֶלֶד זְקֻנִים קָטָן וְאָחִיו
and-brother-of-him young old-ages and-son-of old father to-us there-is

מֵת וַיִּוָּתֵר הוּא לְבַדּוֹ לְאִמּוֹ וְאָבִיו
and-father-of-him from-mother-of-him by-himself he and-he-is-left he-is-dead

אֲהֵבוֹ׃ וַתֹּאמֶר אֶל־ עֲבָדֶיךָ הוֹרִדֻהוּ אֵלָי
to-me bring-down-him! servants-of-you to then-you-said (21) he-loves-him

וְאָשִׂימָה עֵינִי עָלָיו׃ וַנֹּאמֶר אֶל־ אֲדֹנִי לֹא־ יוּכַל
he-can not lord-of-me to and-we-said (22) on-him eye-of-me so-I-can-set

הַנַּעַר לַעֲזֹב אֶת־ אָבִיו וְעָזַב אֶת־ אָבִיו וָמֵת׃
he-will-die father-of-him *** if-he-leaves father-of-him *** to-leave the-boy

וַתֹּאמֶר אֶל־ עֲבָדֶיךָ אִם־ לֹא יֵרֵד אֲחִיכֶם
brother-of-you he-comes-down not if servants-of-you to but-you-told (23)

הַקָּטֹן אִתְּכֶם לֹא תֹסִפוּן לִרְאוֹת פָּנָי׃ וַיְהִי כִּי
when and-he-was (24) face-of-me to-see you-will-again not with-you the-young

עָלִינוּ אֶל־ עַבְדְּךָ אָבִי וַנַּגֶּד־ לוֹ אֵת דִּבְרֵי
words-of *** to-him then-we-told father-of-me servant-of-you to we-went-back

אֲדֹנִי׃ וַיֹּאמֶר אָבִינוּ שֻׁבוּ שִׁבְרוּ־ לָנוּ מְעַט־ אֹכֶל׃
food little-of for-us buy! go-back! father-of-us then-he-said (25) lord-of-me

וַנֹּאמֶר לֹא נוּכַל לָרֶדֶת אִם־ יֵשׁ אָחִינוּ הַקָּטֹן
the-young brother-of-us he-is if to-go-down we-can not but-we-said (26)

אִתָּנוּ וְיָרַדְנוּ כִּי־ לֹא נוּכַל לִרְאוֹת פְּנֵי הָאִישׁ וְאָחִינוּ
if-brother-of-us the-man face-of to-see we-can not for then-we-will-go with-us

הַקָּטֹן אֵינֶנּוּ אִתָּנוּ׃ וַיֹּאמֶר עַבְדְּךָ אָבִי אֵלֵינוּ
to-us father-of-me servant-of-you then-he-said (27) with-us not-he the-young

אַתֶּם יְדַעְתֶּם כִּי שְׁנַיִם יָלְדָה־ לִּי אִשְׁתִּי׃ וַיֵּצֵא הָאֶחָד
the-one and-he-went-away (28) wife-of-me to-me she-bore two that you-know you

מֵאִתִּי וָאֹמַר אַךְ טָרֹף טֹרָף וְלֹא רְאִיתִיו עַד־ הֵנָּה׃
now until I-saw-him and-not he-was-torn to-be-torn surely and-I-said from-me

וּלְקַחְתֶּם גַּם־ אֶת־ זֶה מֵעִם פָּנַי וְקָרָהוּ אָסוֹן
harm and-he-comes-to-him presence-of-me from this *** also if-you-take (29)

וְהוֹרַדְתֶּם אֶת־ שֵׂיבָתִי בְּרָעָה שְׁאֹלָה׃ וְעַתָּה
so-now (30) to-Sheol in-misery gray-head-of-me *** then-you-will-bring-down

כְּבֹאִי אֶל־ עַבְדְּךָ אָבִי וְהַנַּעַר אֵינֶנּוּ אִתָּנוּ
with-us not-he and-the-boy father-of-me servant-of-you to when-to-go-me

your servant, though you are equal to Pharaoh himself. [19]My lord asked his servants, 'Do you have a father or a brother?' [20]And we answered, 'We have an aged father, and there is a young son born to him in his old age. His brother is dead, and he is the only one of his mother's sons left, and his father loves him.'

[21]"Then you said to your servants, 'Bring him down to me so I can see him for myself.' [22]And we said to my lord, 'The boy cannot leave his father; if he leaves him, his father will die.' [23]But you told your servants, 'Unless your youngest brother comes down with you, you will not see my face again.' [24]When we went back to your servant my father, we told him what my lord had said.

[25]"Then our father said, 'Go back and buy a little more food.' [26]But we said, 'We cannot go down. Only if our youngest brother is with us will we go. We cannot see the man's face unless our youngest brother is with us.'

[27]"Your servant my father said to us, 'You know that my wife bore me two sons. [28]One of them went away from me, and I said, "He has surely been torn to pieces." And I have not seen him since. [29]If you take this one from me too and harm comes to him, you will bring my gray head down to the grave[u] in misery.'

[30]"So now, if the boy is not with us when I go back to your servant my father and if my

[u]29 Hebrew *Sheol*; also in verse 31

וְנַפְשׁוֹ קְשׁוּרָה בְנַפְשׁוֹ׃ וְהָיָה כִּרְאוֹתוֹ
as-to-see-him then-he-will-be (31) with-life-of-him being-bound and-life-of-him

כִּי־ אֵין הַנַּעַר וָמֵת וְהוֹרִידוּ עֲבָדֶיךָ
servants-of-you and-they-will-bring then-he-will-die the-boy he-is-not that

אֶת־ שֵׂיבַת עַבְדְּךָ אָבִינוּ בְּיָגוֹן שְׁאֹלָה׃ כִּי
now (32) to-Sheol in-sorrow father-of-us servant-of-you gray-head-of ***

עַבְדְּךָ עָרַב אֶת־ הַנַּעַר מֵעִם אָבִי לֵאמֹר אִם־ לֹא
not if to-say father-of-me to the-boy *** he-guaranteed servant-of-you

אֲבִיאֶנּוּ אֵלֶיךָ וְחָטָאתִי לְאָבִי כָּל־ הַיָּמִים׃
the-days all-of before-father-of-me then-I-will-bear-blame to-you I-bring-him

וְעַתָּה יֵשֶׁב־ נָא עַבְדְּךָ תַּחַת הַנַּעַר עֶבֶד
slave the-boy in-place-of servant-of-you now! let-him-remain so-now (33)

לַאדֹנִי וְהַנַּעַר יַעַל עִם־ אֶחָיו׃ כִּי־ אֵיךְ
how? for (34) brothers-of-him with let-him-return and-the-boy to-lord-of-me

אֶעֱלֶה אֶל־ אָבִי וְהַנַּעַר אֵינֶנּוּ אִתִּי פֶּן אֶרְאֶה
I-look lest with-me not-he if-the-boy father-of-me to can-I-go-back

בָרָע אֲשֶׁר יִמְצָא אֶת־ אָבִי׃ וְלֹא־ יָכֹל
he-could then-not (45:1) father-of-me to he-would-come that on-the-misery

יוֹסֵף לְהִתְאַפֵּק לְכֹל הַנִּצָּבִים עָלָיו
to-him the-ones-attending before-all-of to-control-himself Joseph

וַיִּקְרָא הוֹצִיאוּ כָל־ אִישׁ מֵעָלָי וְלֹא־ עָמַד אִישׁ אִתּוֹ
with-him man he-stood so-not from-me man every-of make-leave! and-he-cried

בְּהִתְוַדַּע יוֹסֵף אֶל־ אֶחָיו׃ וַיִּתֵּן אֶת־
*** and-he-raised (2) brothers-of-him to Joseph when-to-make-self-known

קֹלוֹ בִּבְכִי וַיִּשְׁמְעוּ מִצְרַיִם וַיִּשְׁמַע בֵּית
house-of and-he-heard Egyptians and-they-heard in-weeping voice-of-him

פַּרְעֹה׃ וַיֹּאמֶר יוֹסֵף אֶל־ אֶחָיו אֲנִי יוֹסֵף הַעוֹד אָבִי
father-of-me still? Joseph I brothers-of-him to Joseph and-he-said (3) Pharaoh

חָי וְלֹא־ יָכְלוּ אֶחָיו לַעֲנוֹת אֹתוֹ כִּי נִבְהֲלוּ
they-were-terrified for him to-answer brothers-of-him they-could but-not alive

מִפָּנָיו׃ וַיֹּאמֶר יוֹסֵף אֶל־ אֶחָיו גְּשׁוּ־
come-close! brothers-of-him to Joseph then-he-said (4) at-presence-of-him

נָא אֵלַי וַיִּגָּשׁוּ וַיֹּאמֶר אֲנִי יוֹסֵף אֲחִיכֶם אֲשֶׁר־
whom brother-of-you Joseph I and-he-said so-they-came-close to-me now!

מְכַרְתֶּם אֹתִי מִצְרָיְמָה׃ וְעַתָּה אַל־ תֵּעָצְבוּ וְאַל־
and-not you-be-distressed not and-now (5) into-Egypt me you-sold

יִחַר בְּעֵינֵיכֶם כִּי־ מְכַרְתֶּם אֹתִי הֵנָּה כִּי לְמִחְיָה
to-save-life for here me you-sold because in-eyes-of-you let-him-be-angry

father, whose life is closely bound up with the boy's life,
31 sees that the boy isn't there, he will die. Your servants will bring the gray head of our father down to the grave in sorrow.
32 Your servant guaranteed the boy's safety to my father. I said, 'If I do not bring him back to you, I will bear the blame before you, my father, all my life!'
33 "Now then, please let your servant remain here as my lord's slave in place of the boy, and let the boy return with his brothers.
34 How can I go back to my father if the boy is not with me? No! Do not let me see the misery that would come upon my father."

*Joseph Makes Himself Known*

45 Then Joseph could no longer control himself before all his attendants, and he cried out, "Have everyone leave my presence!" So there was no one with Joseph when he made himself known to his brothers.
2 And he wept so loudly that the Egyptians heard him, and Pharaoh's household heard about it.
3 Joseph said to his brothers, "I am Joseph! Is my father still living?" But his brothers were not able to answer him, because they were terrified at his presence.
4 Then Joseph said to his brothers, "Come close to me." When they had done so, he said, "I am your brother Joseph, the one you sold into Egypt!
5 And now, do not be distressed and do not be angry with yourselves for selling me here, because it was to save

שְׁלָחַנִי אֱלֹהִים לִפְנֵיכֶם׃ כִּי־ זֶה שְׁנָתַיִם הָרָעָב בְּקֶרֶב

in-midst-of the-famine two-years now for (6) ahead-of-you God he-sent-me

הָאָרֶץ וְעוֹד חָמֵשׁ שָׁנִים אֲשֶׁר אֵין־ חָרִישׁ וְקָצִיר*׃ וַיִּשְׁלָחֵנִי אֱלֹהִים

God but-he-sent-me (7) or-harvest plowing not that years five and-next the-land

לִפְנֵיכֶם לָשׂוּם לָכֶם שְׁאֵרִית בָּאָרֶץ וּלְהַחֲיוֹת

and-to-save-life on-the-earth remnant for-you to-preserve ahead-of-you

לָכֶם לִפְלֵיטָה גְּדֹלָה׃ וְעַתָּה לֹא־ אַתֶּם שְׁלַחְתֶּם אֹתִי הֵנָּה כִּי

but here me you-sent you not so-then (8) great by-deliverance for-you

הָאֱלֹהִים וַיְשִׂימֵנִי לְאָב לְפַרְעֹה וּלְאָדוֹן לְכָל־

over-all-of and-as-lord to-Pharaoh as-father and-he-made-me the-God

בֵּיתוֹ וּמֹשֵׁל בְּכָל־ אֶרֶץ מִצְרָיִם׃ מַהֲרוּ וַעֲלוּ

and-go-back! hurry! (9) Egypt land-of over-all-of and-one-ruling house-of-him

אֶל־ אָבִי וַאֲמַרְתֶּם אֵלָיו כֹּה אָמַר בִּנְךָ יוֹסֵף שָׂמַנִי

he-made-me Joseph son-of-you he-says this to-him and-you-say father-of-me to

אֱלֹהִים לְאָדוֹן לְכָל־ מִצְרָיִם רְדָה אֵלַי אַל־ תַּעֲמֹד׃ וְיָשַׁבְתָּ

and-you-live (10) you-delay not to-me come-down! Egypt over-all-of as-lord God

בְאֶרֶץ־ גֹּשֶׁן וְהָיִיתָ קָרוֹב אֵלַי אַתָּה וּבָנֶיךָ

and-children-of-you you to-me near and-you-be Goshen in-region-of

וּבְנֵי בָנֶיךָ וְצֹאנְךָ וּבְקָרְךָ וְכָל־ אֲשֶׁר־

that and-all and-herd-of-you and-flock-of-you children-of-you and-children-of

לָךְ׃ וְכִלְכַּלְתִּי אֹתְךָ שָׁם כִּי־ עוֹד חָמֵשׁ שָׁנִים רָעָב

famine years five still for there for-you and-I-will-provide (11) to-you

פֶּן־ תִּוָּרֵשׁ אַתָּה וּבֵיתְךָ וְכָל־ אֲשֶׁר־ לָךְ׃

to-you that and-all and-house-of-you you you-will-be-destitute otherwise

וְהִנֵּה עֵינֵיכֶם רֹאוֹת וְעֵינֵי אָחִי בִנְיָמִין

Benjamin brother-of-me and-eyes-of ones-seeing eyes-of-you now-see! (12)

כִּי־ פִי הַמְדַבֵּר אֲלֵיכֶם׃ וְהִגַּדְתֶּם לְאָבִי

to-father-of-me so-you-tell (13) to-you the-one-speaking mouth-of-me really

אֶת־ כָּל־ כְּבוֹדִי בְּמִצְרַיִם וְאֵת כָּל־ אֲשֶׁר רְאִיתֶם וּמִהַרְתֶּם

then-you-hurry you-saw that all and in-Egypt honor-of-me all-of ***

וְהוֹרַדְתֶּם אֶת־ אָבִי הֵנָּה׃ וַיִּפֹּל עַל־ צַוְּארֵי

neck-of around then-he-hugged (14) here father-of-me *** and-you-bring-down

בִנְיָמִן־ אָחִיו וַיֵּבְךְּ וּבִנְיָמִן בָּכָה עַל־ צַוָּארָיו׃

neck-of-him on he-wept and-Benjamin and-he-wept brother-of-him Benjamin

וַיְנַשֵּׁק לְכָל־ אֶחָיו וַיֵּבְךְּ עֲלֵהֶם וְאַחֲרֵי

and-after over-them and-he-wept brothers-of-him on-all-of and-he-kissed (15)

כֵן דִּבְּרוּ אֶחָיו אִתּוֹ׃ וְהַקֹּל נִשְׁמַע

he-was-heard when-the-news (16) with-him brothers-of-him they-talked this

lives that God sent me ahead of you. [6]For two years now there has been famine in the land, and for the next five years there will not be plowing and reaping. [7]But God sent me ahead of you to preserve for you a remnant on earth and to save your lives by a great deliverance.[v]

[8]"So then, it was not you who sent me here, but God. He made me father to Pharaoh, lord of his entire household and ruler of all Egypt. [9]Now hurry back to my father and say to him, 'This is what your son Joseph says: God has made me lord of all Egypt. Come down to me; don't delay. [10]You shall live in the region of Goshen and be near me—you, your children and grandchildren, your flocks and herds, and all you have. [11]I will provide for you there, because five years of famine are still to come. Otherwise you and your household and all who belong to you will become destitute.'

[12]"You can see for yourselves, and so can my brother Benjamin, that it is really I who am speaking to you. [13]Tell my father about all the honor accorded me in Egypt and about everything you have seen. And bring my father down here quickly."

[14]Then he threw his arms around his brother Benjamin and wept, and Benjamin embraced him, weeping. [15]And he kissed all his brothers and wept over them. Afterward his brothers talked with him.

[16]When the news reached

v7 Or *save you as a great band of survivors*

*6 Most mss have no *dagesh* in the *tsade* ('צ—).

בֵּית פַּרְעֹה לֵאמֹר בָּאוּ אֲחֵי יוֹסֵף וַיִּיטַב
then-he-pleased Joseph brothers-of they-came to-say Pharaoh palace-of

בְּעֵינֵי פַרְעֹה וּבְעֵינֵי עֲבָדָיו׃ וַיֹּאמֶר פַּרְעֹה
Pharaoh and-he-said (17) officials-of-him and-in-eyes-of Pharaoh in-eyes-of

אֶל־ יוֹסֵף אֱמֹר אֶל־ אַחֶיךָ זֹאת עֲשׂוּ טַעֲנוּ אֶת־ בְּעִירְכֶם וּלְכוּ־
and-go! animal-of-you *** load! do! this brothers-of-you to tell! Joseph to

בֹאוּ אַרְצָה כְּנָעַן׃ וּקְחוּ אֶת־ אֲבִיכֶם וְאֶת־
and father-of-you *** and-get! (18) Canaan to-land-of return!

בָּתֵּיכֶם וּבֹאוּ אֵלָי וְאֶתְּנָה לָכֶם אֶת־ טוּב אֶרֶץ
land-of best-of *** to-you and-I-will-give to-me and-come! families-of-you

מִצְרַיִם וְאִכְלוּ אֶת־ חֵלֶב הָאָרֶץ׃ וְאַתָּה צֻוֵּיתָה זֹאת עֲשׂוּ
do! this you-are-directed and-you (19) the-land fat-of *** and-eat! Egypt

קְחוּ־ לָכֶם מֵאֶרֶץ מִצְרַיִם עֲגָלוֹת לְטַפְּכֶם וְלִנְשֵׁיכֶם
and-for-wives-of-you for-children-of-you carts Egypt from-land-of with-you take!

וּנְשָׂאתֶם אֶת־ אֲבִיכֶם וּבָאתֶם׃ וְעֵינְכֶם אַל־ תָּחֹס
you-think not and-eye-of-you (20) and-you-come father-of-you *** then-you-get

עַל־ כְּלֵיכֶם כִּי־ טוּב כָּל־ אֶרֶץ מִצְרַיִם לָכֶם הוּא׃
he to-you Egypt land-of all-of best-of for belongings-of-you about

וַיַּעֲשׂוּ־ כֵן בְּנֵי יִשְׂרָאֵל וַיִּתֵּן לָהֶם יוֹסֵף עֲגָלוֹת עַל־
as carts Joseph to-them and-he-gave Israel sons-of this so-they-did (21)

פִּי פַרְעֹה וַיִּתֵּן לָהֶם צֵדָה לַדָּרֶךְ׃
for-the-journey provision to-them and-he-gave Pharaoh command-of

לְכֻלָּם נָתַן לָאִישׁ חֲלִפוֹת שְׂמָלֹת וּלְבִנְיָמִן
but-to-Benjamin clothing changes-of to-each he-gave to-each-of-them (22)

נָתַן שְׁלֹשׁ מֵאוֹת כֶּסֶף וְחָמֵשׁ חֲלִפֹת שְׂמָלֹת׃
clothes sets-of and-five silver hundreds three-of he-gave

וּלְאָבִיו שָׁלַח כְּזֹאת עֲשָׂרָה חֲמֹרִים נֹשְׂאִים מִטּוּב
with-best-of ones-being-loaded donkeys ten as-this he-sent and-to-father-of-him (23)

מִצְרַיִם וְעֶשֶׂר אֲתֹנֹת נֹשְׂאֹת בָּר וָלֶחֶם וּמָזוֹן
and-provision and-bread grain ones-being-loaded female-donkeys and-ten Egypt

לְאָבִיו לַדָּרֶךְ׃ וַיְשַׁלַּח אֶת־ אֶחָיו
brothers-of-him *** then-he-sent (24) for-the-journey for-father-of-him

וַיֵּלֵכוּ וַיֹּאמֶר אֲלֵהֶם אַל־ תִּרְגְּזוּ בַּדָּרֶךְ׃ וַיַּעֲלוּ
so-they-left (25) on-the-way you-quarrel not to-them and-he-said and-they-left

מִמִּצְרָיִם וַיָּבֹאוּ אֶרֶץ כְּנַעַן אֶל־ יַעֲקֹב אֲבִיהֶם׃
father-of-them Jacob to Canaan land-of and-they-came from-Egypt

וַיַּגִּדוּ לוֹ לֵאמֹר עוֹד יוֹסֵף חַי וְכִי־ הוּא מֹשֵׁל
one-ruling he and-in-fact alive Joseph still to-say to-him then-they-told (26)

Pharaoh's palace that Joseph's brothers had come, Pharaoh and all his officials were pleased. [17]Pharaoh said to Joseph, "Tell your brothers, 'Do this: Load your animals and return to the land of Canaan, [18]and bring your father and your families back to me. I will give you the best of the land of Egypt and you can enjoy the fat of the land.'

[19]"You are also directed to tell them, 'Do this: Take some carts from Egypt for your children and your wives, and get your father and come. [20]Never mind about your belongings, because the best of all Egypt will be yours.' "

[21]So the sons of Israel did this. Joseph gave them carts, as Pharaoh had commanded, and he also gave them provisions for their journey. [22]To each of them he gave new clothing, but to Benjamin he gave three hundred shekels[w] of silver and five sets of clothes. [23]And this is what he sent to his father: ten donkeys loaded with the best things of Egypt, and ten female donkeys loaded with grain and bread and other provisions for his journey. [24]Then he sent his brothers away, and as they were leaving he said to them, "Don't quarrel on the way!"

[25]So they went up out of Egypt and came to their father Jacob in the land of Canaan. [26]They told him, "Joseph is still alive! In fact, he is ruler of

[w]22 That is, about 7 1/2 pounds (about 3.5 kilograms)

בְּכָל־ אֶרֶץ מִצְרָיִם וַיָּפָג לִבּוֹ כִּי לֹא־ הֶאֱמִין
he-believed not for heart-of-him but-he-was-stunned Egypt land-of over-all-of

לָהֶם׃ וַיְדַבְּרוּ אֵלָיו אֵת כָּל־ דִּבְרֵי יוֹסֵף אֲשֶׁר דִּבֶּר
he-said that Joseph words-of all-of *** to-him but-they-told (27) to-them

אֲלֵהֶם וַיַּרְא אֶת־ הָעֲגָלוֹת אֲשֶׁר־ שָׁלַח יוֹסֵף לָשֵׂאת אֹתוֹ
him to-carry Joseph he-sent that the-carts *** and-he-saw to-them

וַתְּחִי רוּחַ יַעֲקֹב אֲבִיהֶם׃ וַיֹּאמֶר יִשְׂרָאֵל רַב
enough! Israel and-he-said (28) father-of-them Jacob spirit-of and-she-revived

עוֹד־ יוֹסֵף בְּנִי חָי אֵלְכָה וְאֶרְאֶנּוּ בְּטֶרֶם אָמוּת׃
I-die before and-I-will-see-him I-will-go alive son-of-me Joseph still

וַיִּסַּע יִשְׂרָאֵל וְכָל־ אֲשֶׁר־ לוֹ וַיָּבֹא בְּאֵרָה שָּׁבַע
Sheba to-Beer and-he-went to-him that with-all Israel so-he-set-out (46:1)

וַיִּזְבַּח זְבָחִים לֵאלֹהֵי אָבִיו יִצְחָק׃ וַיֹּאמֶר
and-he-spoke (2) Isaac father-of-him to-God-of sacrifices and-he-offered

אֱלֹהִים ׀ לְיִשְׂרָאֵל בְּמַרְאֹת הַלַּיְלָה וַיֹּאמֶר יַעֲקֹב ׀ יַעֲקֹב וַיֹּאמֶר
and-he-replied Jacob Jacob and-he-said the-night in-visions-of to-Israel God

הִנֵּנִי׃ וַיֹּאמֶר אָנֹכִי הָאֵל אֱלֹהֵי אָבִיךָ אַל־ תִּירָא
you-be-afraid not father-of-you God-of the-God I and-he-said (3) here-I

מֵרְדָה מִצְרַיְמָה כִּי־ לְגוֹי גָּדוֹל אֲשִׂימְךָ שָׁם׃
there I-will-make-you great into-nation for to-Egypt from-to-go-down

אָנֹכִי אֵרֵד עִמְּךָ מִצְרַיְמָה וְאָנֹכִי אַעַלְךָ גַם־
surely I-will-bring-up-you and-I to-Egypt with-you I-will-go-down I (4)

עָלֹה וְיוֹסֵף יָשִׁית יָדוֹ עַל־ עֵינֶיךָ׃ וַיָּקָם
then-he-left (5) eyes-of-you on hand-of-him he-will-set and-Joseph to-go-up

יַעֲקֹב מִבְּאֵר שָׁבַע וַיִּשְׂאוּ בְנֵי־ יִשְׂרָאֵל אֶת־יַעֲקֹב אֲבִיהֶם
father-of-them Jacob *** Israel sons-of and-they-took Sheba from-Beer Jacob

וְאֶת־ טַפָּם וְאֶת־ נְשֵׁיהֶם בָּעֲגָלוֹת אֲשֶׁר־ שָׁלַח פַּרְעֹה
Pharaoh he-sent that in-the-carts wives-of-them and children-of-them and

לָשֵׂאת אֹתוֹ׃ וַיִּקְחוּ אֶת־ מִקְנֵיהֶם וְאֶת־ רְכוּשָׁם
possession-of-them and stock-of-them *** and-they-took (6) him to-transport

אֲשֶׁר רָכְשׁוּ בְּאֶרֶץ כְּנַעַן וַיָּבֹאוּ מִצְרָיְמָה יַעֲקֹב וְכָל־
and-all-of Jacob to-Egypt and-they-went Canaan in-land-of they-acquired that

זַרְעוֹ אִתּוֹ׃ בָּנָיו וּבְנֵי בָנָיו אִתּוֹ
with-him sons-of-him and-sons-of sons-of-him (7) with-him offspring-of-him

בְּנֹתָיו וּבְנוֹת בָּנָיו וְכָל־ זַרְעוֹ
offspring-of-him and-all-of sons-of-him and-daughters-of daughters-of-him

הֵבִיא אִתּוֹ מִצְרָיְמָה׃ וְאֵלֶּה שְׁמוֹת בְּנֵי־ יִשְׂרָאֵל הַבָּאִים
the-ones-going Israel sons-of names-of now-these (8) to-Egypt with-him he-took

all Egypt." Jacob was stunned;
he did not believe them. 27But
when they told him every-
thing Joseph had said to them,
and when he saw the carts Joseph had sent to carry him
back, the spirit of their father
Jacob revived. 28And Israel
said, "I'm convinced! My son
Joseph is still alive. I will go
and see him before I die."

### *Jacob Goes to Egypt*

46 So Israel set out with all
that was his, and when
he reached Beersheba, he
offered sacrifices to the God of
his father Isaac.

2And God spoke to Israel in
a vision at night and said,
"Jacob! Jacob!"

"Here I am," he replied.

3"I am God, the God of your
father," he said. "Do not be
afraid to go down to Egypt, for
I will make you into a great
nation there. 4I will go down
to Egypt with you, and I will
surely bring you back again.
And Joseph's own hand will
close your eyes."

5Then Jacob left Beersheba,
and Israel's sons took their father Jacob and their children
and their wives in the carts
that Pharaoh had sent to
transport him. 6They also took
with them their livestock and
the possessions they had acquired in Canaan, and Jacob
and all his offspring went to
Egypt. 7He took with him to
Egypt his sons and grandsons
and his daughters and grand-
daughters—all his offspring.

8These are the names of the

מִצְרַיְמָה יַעֲקֹב וּבָנָיו בְּכֹר יַעֲקֹב רְאוּבֵן׃ וּבְנֵי
and-sons-of (9) Reuben Jacob firstborn-of and-children-of-him Jacob to-Egypt

רְאוּבֵן חֲנוֹךְ וּפַלּוּא וְחֶצְרֹן וְכַרְמִי׃ וּבְנֵי שִׁמְעוֹן יְמוּאֵל
Jemuel Simeon and-sons-of (10) and-Carmi and-Hezron and-Pallu Hanoch Reuben

וְיָמִין וְאֹהַד וְיָכִין וְצֹחַר וְשָׁאוּל בֶּן־ הַכְּנַעֲנִית׃
the-Canaanite-woman son-of and-Shaul and-Zohar and-Jakin and-Ohad and-Jamin

וּבְנֵי לֵוִי גֵּרְשׁוֹן קְהָת וּמְרָרִי׃ וּבְנֵי יְהוּדָה עֵר
Er Judah and-sons-of (12) and-Merari Kohath Gershon Levi and-sons-of (11)

וְאוֹנָן וְשֵׁלָה וָפֶרֶץ וָזָרַח וַיָּמָת עֵר וְאוֹנָן בְּאֶרֶץ
in-land-of and-Onan Er but-he-died and-Zerah and-Perez and-Shelah and-Onan

כְּנַעַן וַיִּהְיוּ בְנֵי־ פֶרֶץ חֶצְרֹן וְחָמוּל׃ וּבְנֵי יִשָּׂשכָר
Issachar and-sons-of (13) and-Hamul Hezron Perez sons-of and-they-were Canaan

תּוֹלָע וּפֻוָּה וְיוֹב וְשִׁמְרֹן׃ וּבְנֵי זְבֻלוּן סֶרֶד וְאֵלוֹן
and-Elon Sered Zebulun and-sons-of (14) and-Shimron and-Job and-Puvah Tola

וְיַחְלְאֵל׃ אֵלֶּה ׀ בְּנֵי לֵאָה אֲשֶׁר יָלְדָה לְיַעֲקֹב בְּפַדַּן אֲרָם
Aram in-Paddan to-Jacob she-bore whom Leah sons-of these (15) and-Jahleel

וְאֵת דִּינָה בִתּוֹ כָּל־ נֶפֶשׁ בָּנָיו וּבְנוֹתָיו
and-daughters-of-him sons-of-him person all-of daughter-of-him Dinah and

שְׁלֹשִׁים וְשָׁלֹשׁ׃ וּבְנֵי גָד צִפְיוֹן וְחַגִּי שׁוּנִי וְאֶצְבֹּן עֵרִי
Eri and-Ezbon Shuni and-Haggi Ziphion Gad and-sons-of (16) and-three thirty

וַאֲרוֹדִי וְאַרְאֵלִי׃ וּבְנֵי אָשֵׁר יִמְנָה וְיִשְׁוָה וְיִשְׁוִי
and-Ishvi and-Ishvah Imnah Asher and-sons-of (17) and-Areli and-Arodi

וּבְרִיעָה וְשֶׂרַח אֲחֹתָם וּבְנֵי בְרִיעָה חֶבֶר וּמַלְכִּיאֵל׃
and-Malkiel Heber Beriah and-sons-of sister-of-them and-Serah and-Beriah

אֵלֶּה בְּנֵי זִלְפָּה אֲשֶׁר־ נָתַן לָבָן לְלֵאָה בִתּוֹ
daughter-of-him to-Leah Laban he-gave whom Zilpah sons-of these (18)

וַתֵּלֶד אֶת־ אֵלֶּה לְיַעֲקֹב שֵׁשׁ עֶשְׂרֵה נָפֶשׁ׃ בְּנֵי רָחֵל אֵשֶׁת
wife-of Rachel sons-of (19) person ten six to-Jacob these *** and-she-bore

יַעֲקֹב יוֹסֵף וּבִנְיָמִן׃ וַיִּוָּלֵד לְיוֹסֵף בְּאֶרֶץ מִצְרַיִם
Egypt in-land-of to-Joseph and-he-was-born (20) and-Benjamin Joseph Jacob

אֲשֶׁר יָלְדָה־ לּוֹ אָסְנַת בַּת־ פּוֹטִי פֶרַע כֹּהֵן אֹן אֶת־ מְנַשֶּׁה
Manasseh *** On priest-of Phera Poti daughter-of Asenath to-him she-bore whom

וְאֶת־ אֶפְרָיִם׃ וּבְנֵי בִנְיָמִן בֶּלַע וָבֶכֶר וְאַשְׁבֵּל גֵּרָא
Gera and-Ashbel and-Beker Bela Benjamin and-sons-of (21) Ephraim and

וְנַעֲמָן אֵחִי וָרֹאשׁ מֻפִּים וְחֻפִּים וָאָרְדְּ׃ אֵלֶּה בְּנֵי רָחֵל
Rachel sons-of these (22) and-Ard and-Huppim Muppim and-Rosh Ehi and-Naaman

אֲשֶׁר יֻלַּד לְיַעֲקֹב כָּל־ נֶפֶשׁ אַרְבָּעָה עָשָׂר׃ וּבְנֵי־ דָן חֻשִׁים׃
Hushim Dan and-sons-of (23) ten four person all-of to-Jacob she-bore whom

Israelites (Jacob and his descendants) who went to Egypt:

Reuben the firstborn of Jacob.
9 The sons of Reuben:
Hanoch, Pallu, Hezron and Carmi.
10 The sons of Simeon:
Jemuel, Jamin, Ohad, Jakin, Zohar and Shaul the son of a Canaanite woman.
11 The sons of Levi:
Gershon, Kohath and Merari.
12 The sons of Judah:
Er, Onan, Shelah, Perez and Zerah (but Er and Onan had died in the land of Canaan).
The sons of Perez:
Hezron and Hamul.
13 The sons of Issachar:
Tola, Puah,[x] Jashub[y] and Shimron.
14 The sons of Zebulun:
Sered, Elon and Jahleel.
15 These were the sons Leah bore to Jacob in Paddan Aram,[z] besides his daughter Dinah. These sons and daughters of his were thirty-three in all.

16 The sons of Gad:
Zephon,[a] Haggi, Shuni, Ezbon, Eri, Arodi and Areli.
17 The sons of Asher:
Imnah, Ishvah, Ishvi and Beriah.
Their sister was Serah.
The sons of Beriah:
Heber and Malkiel.
18 These were the children born to Jacob by Zilpah, whom Laban had given to his daughter Leah—sixteen in all.

19 The sons of Jacob's wife Rachel:
Joseph and Benjamin.
20 In Egypt, Manasseh and Ephraim were born to Joseph by Asenath daughter of Potiphera, priest of On.[b]
21 The sons of Benjamin:
Bela, Beker, Ashbel, Gera, Naaman, Ehi, Rosh, Muppim, Huppim and Ard.
22 These were the sons of Rachel who were born to Jacob—fourteen in all.

23 The son of Dan:
Hushim.

x13 Samaritan Pentateuch and Syriac (see also 1 Chron. 7:1); Masoretic Text *Puvah*
y13 Samaritan Pentateuch and some Septuagint manuscripts (see also Num. 26:24 and 1 Chron. 7:1); Masoretic Text *Iob*
z15 That is, Northwest Mesopotamia
a16 Samaritan Pentateuch and Septuagint (see also Num. 26:15); Masoretic Text *Ziphion*
b20 That is, Heliopolis

וּבְנֵי נַפְתָּלִי יַחְצְאֵל וְגוּנִי וְיֵצֶר וְשִׁלֵּם׃ אֵלֶּה
these (25) and-Shillem and-Jezer and-Guni Jahziel Naphtali and-sons-of (24)

בְּנֵי בִלְהָה אֲשֶׁר־ נָתַן לָבָן לְרָחֵל בִּתּוֹ וַתֵּלֶד אֶת־
*** and-she-bore daughter-of-him to-Rachel Laban he-gave whom Bilhah sons-of

אֵלֶּה לְיַעֲקֹב כָּל־ נֶפֶשׁ שִׁבְעָה׃ כָּל־ הַנֶּפֶשׁ הַבָּאָה
the-one-going the-person all-of (26) seven person all-of to-Jacob these

לְיַעֲקֹב מִצְרַיְמָה יֹצְאֵי יְרֵכוֹ מִלְּבַד נְשֵׁי בְנֵי־
sons-of wives-of apart-from body-of-him ones-coming-out-of to-Egypt with-Jacob

יַעֲקֹב כָּל־ נֶפֶשׁ שִׁשִּׁים וָשֵׁשׁ׃ וּבְנֵי יוֹסֵף אֲשֶׁר־ יֻלַּד־
he-was-born who Joseph with-sons-of (27) and-six sixty person all-of Jacob

לוֹ בְמִצְרַיִם נֶפֶשׁ שְׁנָיִם כָּל־ הַנֶּפֶשׁ לְבֵית־ יַעֲקֹב הַבָּאָה
the-one-going Jacob to-family-of the-person all-of two person in-Egypt to-him

מִצְרַיְמָה שִׁבְעִים׃ וְאֶת־ יְהוּדָה שָׁלַח לְפָנָיו אֶל־ יוֹסֵף לְהוֹרֹת
to-direct Joseph to ahead-of-him he-sent Judah and (28) seventy to-Egypt

לְפָנָיו גֹּשְׁנָה וַיָּבֹאוּ אַרְצָה גֹּשֶׁן׃
Goshen in-region-of and-they-arrived to-Goshen ahead-of-him

וַיֶּאְסֹר יוֹסֵף מֶרְכַּבְתּוֹ וַיַּעַל לִקְרַאת־יִשְׂרָאֵל
Israel to-meet and-he-went chariot-of-him Joseph and-he-made-ready (29)

אָבִיו גֹּשְׁנָה וַיֵּרָא אֵלָיו וַיִּפֹּל עַל־
around then-he-hugged to-him when-he-appeared in-Goshen father-of-him

צַוָּארָיו וַיֵּבְךְּ עַל־ צַוָּארָיו עוֹד׃ וַיֹּאמֶר יִשְׂרָאֵל אֶל־
to Israel and-he-said (30) long-time neck-of-him on and-he-wept neck-of-him

יוֹסֵף אָמוּתָה הַפָּעַם אַחֲרֵי רְאוֹתִי אֶת־ פָּנֶיךָ כִּי עוֹדְךָ חָי׃
alive still-you that face-of-you *** I-saw since the-now I-can-die Joseph

וַיֹּאמֶר יוֹסֵף אֶל־ אֶחָיו וְאֶל־ בֵּית אָבִיו
father-of-him household-of and-to brothers-of-him to Joseph then-he-said (31)

אֶעֱלֶה וְאַגִּידָה לְפַרְעֹה וְאֹמְרָה אֵלָיו אַחַי
brothers-of-me to-him and-I-will-say to-Pharaoh and-I-will-speak I-will-go-up

וּבֵית־ אָבִי אֲשֶׁר בְּאֶרֶץ־ כְּנַעַן בָּאוּ אֵלָי׃
to-me they-came Canaan in-land-of who father-of-me and-house-of

וְהָאֲנָשִׁים רֹעֵי צֹאן כִּי־ אַנְשֵׁי מִקְנֶה הָיוּ
they-are livestock tenders-of for sheep ones-herding-of now-the-men (32)

וְצֹאנָם וּבְקָרָם וְכָל־ אֲשֶׁר לָהֶם הֵבִיאוּ׃
they-brought to-them that and-all and-herd-of-them and-flock-of-them

וְהָיָה כִּי־ יִקְרָא לָכֶם פַּרְעֹה וְאָמַר מַה־
what? and-he-asks Pharaoh for-you he-calls when and-he-will-be (33)

מַּעֲשֵׂיכֶם׃ וַאֲמַרְתֶּם אַנְשֵׁי מִקְנֶה הָיוּ
they-are stock tenders-of then-you-answer (34) occupations-of-you

24 The sons of Naphtali:
Jahziel, Guni, Jezer and Shillem.
25 These were the sons born
to Jacob by Bilhah, whom Laban had given to his daughter Rachel—seven in all.

26 All those who went to
Egypt with Jacob—those who were his direct descendants, not counting his sons' wives—numbered sixty-six persons.
27 With the two sons who had
been born to Joseph in Egypt, the members of Jacob's family, which went to Egypt, were seventy in all.

28 Now Jacob sent Judah
ahead of him to Joseph to get directions to Goshen. When they arrived in the region of
Goshen, 29 Joseph had his chariot made ready and went to Goshen to meet his father Israel. As soon as Joseph appeared before him, he threw his arms around his father[c] and wept for a long time.
30 Israel said to Joseph, "Now
I am ready to die, since I have seen for myself that you are still alive."
31 Then Joseph said to his
brothers and to his father's household, "I will go up and speak to Pharaoh and will say to him, 'My brothers and my father's household, who were living in the land of Canaan, have come to me.
32 The men
are shepherds; they tend livestock, and they have brought along their flocks and herds and everything they own.'
33 When Pharaoh calls you in
and asks, 'What is your occupation?'
34 you should answer,
'Your servants have tended

c29 Hebrew *around him*

עֲבָדֶיךָ מִנְּעוּרֵינוּ וְעַד־ עַתָּה גַּם־ אֲנַחְנוּ גַּם־ אֲבֹתֵינוּ

fathers-of-us also we also now even-until from-youths-of-us servants-of-you

בַּעֲבוּר תֵּשְׁבוּ בְּאֶרֶץ גֹּשֶׁן כִּי־ תוֹעֲבַת מִצְרַיִם כָּל־

all-of Egyptians detestable-of for Goshen in-region-of you-may-settle so-that

רֹעֵה צֹאן׃ וַיָּבֹא יוֹסֵף וַיַּגֵּד לְפַרְעֹה וַיֹּאמֶר

and-he-said to-Pharaoh and-he-told Joseph so-he-went (47:1) sheep herding-of

אָבִי וְאַחַי וְצֹאנָם וּבְקָרָם וְכָל־

and-all and-herd-of-them and-flock-of-them and-brothers-of-me father-of-me

אֲשֶׁר לָהֶם בָּאוּ מֵאֶרֶץ כְּנָעַן וְהִנָּם בְּאֶרֶץ גֹּשֶׁן׃

Goshen in-region-of and-now-they Canaan from-land-of they-came to-them that

וּמִקְצֵה אֶחָיו לָקַח חֲמִשָּׁה אֲנָשִׁים וַיַּצִּגֵם

and-he-presented-them men five he-chose brothers-of-him and-from-midst-of (2)

לִפְנֵי פַרְעֹה׃ וַיֹּאמֶר פַּרְעֹה אֶל־ אֶחָיו מַה־

what? brothers-of-him to Pharaoh and-he-asked (3) Pharaoh before

מַּעֲשֵׂיכֶם וַיֹּאמְרוּ אֶל־ פַּרְעֹה רֹעֵה צֹאן עֲבָדֶיךָ

servants-of-you sheep herding-of Pharaoh to and-they-said occupations-of-you

גַּם־ אֲנַחְנוּ גַּם־ אֲבוֹתֵינוּ׃ וַיֹּאמְרוּ אֶל־ פַּרְעֹה לָגוּר

to-live-awhile Pharaoh to and-they-said (4) fathers-of-us also we also

בָּאָרֶץ בָּאנוּ כִּי־ אֵין מִרְעֶה לַצֹּאן אֲשֶׁר

that for-the-flock pasture there-is-no for we-came in-the-land

לַעֲבָדֶיךָ כִּי־ כָבֵד הָרָעָב בְּאֶרֶץ כְּנָעַן וְעַתָּה

so-now Canaan in-land-of the-famine severe for to-servants-of-you

יֵשְׁבוּ־ נָא עֲבָדֶיךָ בְּאֶרֶץ גֹּשֶׁן׃ וַיֹּאמֶר

then-he-said (5) Goshen in-region-of servants-of-you now! let-them-settle

פַּרְעֹה אֶל־ יוֹסֵף לֵאמֹר אָבִיךָ וְאַחֶיךָ בָּאוּ אֵלֶיךָ׃

to-you they-came and-brothers-of-you father-of-you to-say Joseph to Pharaoh

אֶרֶץ מִצְרַיִם לְפָנֶיךָ הִוא בְּמֵיטַב הָאָרֶץ הוֹשֵׁב אֶת־ אָבִיךָ

father-of-you *** settle! the-land in-best-of he before-you Egypt land-of (6)

וְאֶת־ אַחֶיךָ יֵשְׁבוּ בְּאֶרֶץ גֹּשֶׁן וְאִם־ יָדַעְתָּ

you-know and-if Goshen in-region-of let-them-live brothers-of-you and

וְיֶשׁ־ בָּם אַנְשֵׁי־ חַיִל וְשַׂמְתָּם

them-you-put-them special-ability men-of among-them that-there-is

שָׂרֵי מִקְנֶה עַל־ אֲשֶׁר־ לִי׃ וַיָּבֵא יוֹסֵף אֶת־יַעֲקֹב

Jacob *** Joseph then-he-brought (7) to-me what over stock ones-in-charge-of

אָבִיו וַיַּעֲמִדֵהוּ לִפְנֵי פַרְעֹה וַיְבָרֶךְ יַעֲקֹב אֶת־

*** Jacob and-he-blessed Pharaoh before and-he-presented-him father-of-him

פַּרְעֹה׃ וַיֹּאמֶר פַּרְעֹה אֶל־יַעֲקֹב כַּמָּה יְמֵי שְׁנֵי

years-of days-of how-many? Jacob to Pharaoh and-he-asked (8) Pharaoh

livestock from our boyhood on, just as our fathers did.' Then you will be allowed to settle in the region of Goshen, for all shepherds are detestable to the Egyptians."

**47** Joseph went and told Pharaoh, "My father and brothers, with their flocks and herds and everything they own, have come from the land of Canaan and are now in Goshen." [2]He chose five of his brothers and presented them before Pharaoh.

[3]Pharaoh asked the brothers, "What is your occupation?"

"Your servants are shepherds," they replied to Pharaoh, "just as our fathers were." [4]They also said to him, "We have come to live here awhile, because the famine is severe in Canaan and your servants' flocks have no pasture. So now, please let your servants settle in Goshen."

[5]Pharaoh said to Joseph, "Your father and your brothers have come to you, [6]and the land of Egypt is before you; settle your father and your brothers in the best part of the land. Let them live in Goshen. And if you know of any among them with special ability, put them in charge of my own livestock."

[7]Then Joseph brought his father Jacob in and presented him before Pharaoh. After Jacob blessed[d] Pharaoh, [8]Pharaoh asked him, "How old are you?"

[d]7 Or *greeted*

חַיֶּיךָ׃ וַיֹּאמֶר יַעֲקֹב אֶל־פַּרְעֹה יְמֵי שְׁנֵי מְגוּרַי
journeys-of-me years-of days-of Pharaoh to Jacob and-he-said (9) lives-of-you

שְׁלֹשִׁים וּמְאַת שָׁנָה מְעַט וְרָעִים הָיוּ יְמֵי שְׁנֵי
years-of days-of they-are difficult-ones few year and-hundred-of thirty

חַיַּי וְלֹא הִשִּׂיגוּ אֶת־ יְמֵי שְׁנֵי חַיֵּי אֲבֹתַי
fathers-of-me lives-of years-of days-of *** they-equal and-not lives-of-me

בִּימֵי מְגוּרֵיהֶם׃ וַיְבָרֶךְ יַעֲקֹב אֶת־ פַּרְעֹה וַיֵּצֵא
and-he-left Pharaoh *** Jacob then-he-blessed (10) journeys-of-them in-days-of

מִלִּפְנֵי פַרְעֹה׃ וַיּוֹשֵׁב יוֹסֵף אֶת־ אָבִיו וְאֶת־
and father-of-him *** Joseph so-he-settled (11) Pharaoh from-presence-of

אֶחָיו וַיִּתֵּן לָהֶם אֲחֻזָּה בְּאֶרֶץ מִצְרַיִם בְּמֵיטַב
in-best-of Egypt in-land-of property to-them and-he-gave brothers-of-him

הָאָרֶץ בְּאֶרֶץ רַעְמְסֵס כַּאֲשֶׁר צִוָּה פַרְעֹה׃
Pharaoh he-directed just-as Rameses in-district-of the-land

וַיְכַלְכֵּל יוֹסֵף אֶת־ אָבִיו וְאֶת־ אֶחָיו וְאֵת כָּל־
all-of and brothers-of-him and father-of-him *** Joseph and-he-provided (12)

בֵּית אָבִיו לֶחֶם לְפִי הַטָּף׃
the-children according-to-number-of food father-of-him household-of

וְלֶחֶם אֵין בְּכָל־ הָאָרֶץ כִּי־ כָבֵד הָרָעָב מְאֹד
very the-famine severe for the-region in-all-of there-is-no but-food (13)

וַתֵּלַהּ אֶרֶץ מִצְרַיִם וְאֶרֶץ כְּנַעַן מִפְּנֵי הָרָעָב׃
the-famine because-of Canaan and-land-of Egypt land-of and-she-wasted-away

וַיְלַקֵּט יוֹסֵף אֶת־ כָּל־ הַכֶּסֶף הַנִּמְצָא בְאֶרֶץ־
in-land-of the-being-found the-money all-of *** Joseph and-he-collected (14)

מִצְרַיִם וּבְאֶרֶץ כְּנַעַן בַּשֶּׁבֶר אֲשֶׁר־ הֵם שֹׁבְרִים וַיָּבֵא
and-he-brought ones-buying they that for-the-grain Canaan and-in-land-of Egypt

יוֹסֵף אֶת־ הַכֶּסֶף בֵּיתָה פַרְעֹה׃ וַיִּתֹּם הַכֶּסֶף
the-money when-he-was-gone (15) Pharaoh to-palace-of the-money *** Joseph

מֵאֶרֶץ מִצְרַיִם וּמֵאֶרֶץ כְּנַעַן וַיָּבֹאוּ כָל־מִצְרַיִם אֶל־
to Egypt all-of then-they-came Canaan and-from-land-of Egypt from-land-of

יוֹסֵף לֵאמֹר הָבָה־ לָּנוּ לֶחֶם וְלָמָּה נָמוּת נֶגְדֶּךָ כִּי
because before-you should-we-die now-why? food to-us give! to-say Joseph

אָפֵס כָּסֶף׃ וַיֹּאמֶר יוֹסֵף הָבוּ מִקְנֵיכֶם
cattle-of-you bring! Joseph and-he-said (16) money he-is-used-up

וְאֶתְּנָה לָכֶם בְּמִקְנֵיכֶם אִם־ אָפֵס כָּסֶף׃
money he-is-gone since for-cattle-of-you to-you and-I-will-sell

וַיָּבִיאוּ אֶת־ מִקְנֵיהֶם אֶל־יוֹסֵף וַיִּתֵּן לָהֶם יוֹסֵף לֶחֶם
food Joseph to-them and-he-gave Joseph to stock-of-them *** so-they-brought (17)

9 And Jacob said to Pharaoh, "The years of my pilgrimage are a hundred and thirty. My years have been few and difficult, and they do not equal the years of the pilgrimage of my fathers." 10 Then Jacob blessed[c] Pharaoh and went out from his presence.

11 So Joseph settled his father and his brothers in Egypt and gave them property in the best part of the land, the district of Rameses, as Pharaoh directed. 12 Joseph also provided his father and his brothers and all his father's household with food, according to the number of their children.

*Joseph and the Famine*

13 There was no food, however, in the whole region because the famine was severe; both Egypt and Canaan wasted away because of the famine. 14 Joseph collected all the money that was to be found in Egypt and Canaan in payment for the grain they were buying, and he brought it to Pharaoh's palace. 15 When the money of the people of Egypt and Canaan was gone, all Egypt came to Joseph and said, "Give us food. Why should we die before your eyes? Our money is used up."

16 "Then bring your livestock," said Joseph. "I will sell you food in exchange for your livestock, since your money is gone." 17 So they brought their livestock to Joseph, and he gave them food in exchange

[c] 10 *Or said farewell to*

בַּסּוּסִים וּבְמִקְנֵה הַצֹּאן וּבְמִקְנֵה הַבָּקָר
the-herd and-for-stock-of the-flock and-for-stock-of for-the-horses

וּבַחֲמֹרִים וַיְנַהֲלֵם בַּלֶּחֶם בְּכָל־ מִקְנֵהֶם
stock-of-them for-all-of with-the-food and-he-provided-them and-for-the-donkeys

בַּשָּׁנָה הַהִוא׃ (18) וַתִּתֹּם הַשָּׁנָה הַהִוא וַיָּבֹאוּ
then-they-came the-that the-year when-she-ended (18) the-that in-the-year

אֵלָיו בַּשָּׁנָה הַשֵּׁנִית וַיֹּאמְרוּ לוֹ לֹא־ נְכַחֵד
we-can-hide not to-him and-they-said the-second in-the-year to-him

מֵאֲדֹנִי כִּי אִם־ תַּם הַכֶּסֶף וּמִקְנֵה הַבְּהֵמָה אֶל־
to the-livestock and-herd-of the-money he-is-gone since that from-lord-of-me

אֲדֹנִי לֹא נִשְׁאַר לִפְנֵי אֲדֹנִי בִּלְתִּי אִם־ גְּוִיָּתֵנוּ
body-of-us but nothing lord-of-me before he-is-left not lord-of-me

וְאַדְמָתֵנוּ׃ (19) לָמָּה נָמוּת לְעֵינֶיךָ גַּם־ אֲנַחְנוּ גַּם
also we indeed before-eyes-of-you should-we-perish why? (19) and-land-of-us

אַדְמָתֵנוּ קְנֵה־ אֹתָנוּ וְאֶת־ אַדְמָתֵנוּ בַּלָּחֶם וְנִהְיֶה אֲנַחְנוּ
we and-we-will-be for-the-food land-of-us and us buy! land-of-us

וְאַדְמָתֵנוּ עֲבָדִים לְפַרְעֹה וְתֶן־ זֶרַע וְנִחְיֶה וְלֹא נָמוּת
we-die and-not so-we-may-live seed so-give! to-Pharaoh slaves and-land-of-us

וְהָאֲדָמָה לֹא תֵשָׁם׃ (20) וַיִּקֶן יוֹסֵף אֶת־ כָּל־ אַדְמַת
land-of all-of *** Joseph so-he-bought (20) she-be-desolate not and-the-land

מִצְרַיִם לְפַרְעֹה כִּי־ מָכְרוּ מִצְרַיִם אִישׁ שָׂדֵהוּ כִּי־ חָזַק
he-was-severe for field-of-him each Egyptians they-sold for for-Pharaoh Egypt

עֲלֵהֶם הָרָעָב וַתְּהִי הָאָרֶץ לְפַרְעֹה׃ (21) וְאֶת־ הָעָם
the-people and (21) to-Pharaoh the-land so-she-became the-famine for-them

*הֶעֱבִיר אֹתוֹ לֶעָרִים* מִקְצֵה גְבוּל־ מִצְרַיִם וְעַד־ קָצֵהוּ׃
other-of-him and-to Egypt border-of from-end-of *into-the-cities him he-moved*

(22) רַק אַדְמַת הַכֹּהֲנִים לֹא קָנָה כִּי חֹק לַכֹּהֲנִים
to-the-priests allotment for he-bought not the-priests land-of however (22)

מֵאֵת פַּרְעֹה וְאָכְלוּ אֶת־ חֻקָּם אֲשֶׁר נָתַן לָהֶם פַּרְעֹה
Pharaoh to-them he-gave that allotment-of-them *** and-they-ate Pharaoh from

עַל־ כֵּן לֹא מָכְרוּ אֶת־ אַדְמָתָם׃ (23) וַיֹּאמֶר יוֹסֵף אֶל־ הָעָם
the-people to Joseph then-he-said (23) land-of-them *** they-sold not this for

הֵן קָנִיתִי אֶתְכֶם הַיּוֹם וְאֶת־ אַדְמַתְכֶם לְפַרְעֹה הֵא־ לָכֶם זֶרַע
seed for-you here! for-Pharaoh land-of-you and the-day you I-bought see!

וּזְרַעְתֶּם אֶת־ הָאֲדָמָה׃ (24) וְהָיָה בַּתְּבוּאֹת
at-the-harvests but-he-will-be (24) the-ground *** so-you-can-plant

וּנְתַתֶּם חֲמִישִׁית לְפַרְעֹה וְאַרְבַּע הַיָּדֹת יִהְיֶה לָכֶם לְזֶרַע
as-seed-of for-you he-will-be the-parts and-four to-Pharaoh fifth that-you-give

for their horses, their sheep and goats, their cattle and donkeys. And he brought them through that year with food in exchange for all their livestock.

18When that year was over, they came to him the following year and said, "We cannot hide from our lord the fact that since our money is gone and our livestock belongs to you, there is nothing left for our lord except our bodies and our land. 19Why should we perish before your eyes—we and our land as well? Buy us and our land in exchange for food, and we with our land will be in bondage to Pharaoh. Give us seed so that we may live and not die, and that the land may not become desolate."

20So Joseph bought all the land in Egypt for Pharaoh. The Egyptians, one and all, sold their fields, because the famine was too severe for them. The land became Pharaoh's, 21and Joseph reduced the people to servitude,[f] from one end of Egypt to the other. 22However, he did not buy the land of the priests, because they received a regular allotment from Pharaoh and had food enough from the allotment Pharaoh gave them. That is why they did not sell their land.

23Joseph said to the people, "Now that I have bought you and your land today for Pharaoh, here is seed for you so you can plant the ground. 24But when the crop comes in, give a fifth of it to Pharaoh. The other four-fifths you may keep as seed for the fields and

[f]21 Samaritan Pentateuch and Septuagint (see also Vulgate); Masoretic Text *and he moved the people into the cities*

*21 הֶעֱבִיד אתו לַעֲבָדִים
*to-slaves him he-reduced*
This Hebrew text and translation is conjectured on the basis of the early versions listed above in footnote *f*.

הַשָּׂדֶה וּלְאָכְלְכֶם וְלַאֲשֶׁר בְּבָתֵּיכֶם וְלֶאֱכֹל
and-to-eat in-houses-of-you and-for-whom and-as-food-of-you the-field

לְטַפְּכֶם׃ וַיֹּאמְרוּ הֶחֱיִתָנוּ נִמְצָא־חֵן
favor may-we-find you-saved-lives-of-us and-they-said (25) for-children-of-you

בְּעֵינֵי אֲדֹנִי וְהָיִינוּ עֲבָדִים לְפַרְעֹה׃ וַיָּשֶׂם
so-he-established (26) to-Pharaoh slaves now-we-will-be lord-of-me in-eyes-of

אֹתָהּ יוֹסֵף לְחֹק עַד־הַיּוֹם הַזֶּה עַל־אַדְמַת מִצְרַיִם לְפַרְעֹה
to-Pharaoh Egypt land-of concerning the-this the-day to as-law Joseph her

לַחֹמֶשׁ רַק אַדְמַת הַכֹּהֲנִים לְבַדָּם לֹא הָיְתָה לְפַרְעֹה׃
to-Pharaoh she-became not by-themselves the-priests land-of only the-fifth

וַיֵּשֶׁב יִשְׂרָאֵל בְּאֶרֶץ מִצְרַיִם בְּאֶרֶץ גֹּשֶׁן
Goshen in-region-of Egypt in-land-of Israel now-he-settled (27)

וַיֵּאָחֲזוּ בָהּ וַיִּפְרוּ וַיִּרְבּוּ
and-they-increased and-they-were-fruitful in-her and-they-acquired-property

מְאֹד׃ וַיְחִי יַעֲקֹב בְּאֶרֶץ מִצְרַיִם שְׁבַע עֶשְׂרֵה שָׁנָה וַיְהִי
and-he-was year ten seven Egypt in-land-of Jacob and-he-lived (28) greatly

יְמֵי־יַעֲקֹב שְׁנֵי חַיָּיו שֶׁבַע שָׁנִים וְאַרְבָּעִים וּמְאַת שָׁנָה׃
year and-hundred-of and-forty years seven lives-of-him years-of Jacob days-of

וַיִּקְרְבוּ יְמֵי־יִשְׂרָאֵל לָמוּת וַיִּקְרָא ׀ לִבְנוֹ
for-son-of-him then-he-called to-die Israel days-of when-they-drew-near (29)

לְיוֹסֵף וַיֹּאמֶר לוֹ אִם־נָא מָצָאתִי חֵן בְּעֵינֶיךָ שִׂים־נָא
now! put! in-eyes-of-you favor I-found now! if to-him and-he-said for-Joseph

יָדְךָ תַּחַת יְרֵכִי וְעָשִׂיתָ עִמָּדִי חֶסֶד וֶאֱמֶת
and-faithfulness kindness to-me and-you-show thigh-of-me under hand-of-you

אַל־נָא תִקְבְּרֵנִי בְּמִצְרָיִם׃ וְשָׁכַבְתִּי עִם־אֲבֹתַי
fathers-of-me with when-I-rest (30) in-Egypt you-bury-me now! not

וּנְשָׂאתַנִי מִמִּצְרַיִם וּקְבַרְתַּנִי בִּקְבֻרָתָם וַיֹּאמַר אָנֹכִי
I and-he-said in-tomb-of-them and-you-bury-me from-Egypt then-you-carry-me

אֶעֱשֶׂה כִדְבָרֶךָ׃ וַיֹּאמֶר הִשָּׁבְעָה לִי וַיִּשָּׁבַע לוֹ
to-him and-he-swore to-me swear! then-he-said (31) as-word-of-you I-will-do

וַיִּשְׁתַּחוּ יִשְׂרָאֵל עַל־רֹאשׁ הַמִּטָּה׃ וַיְהִי אַחֲרֵי הַדְּבָרִים
the-things after and-he-was (48:1) the-bed head-of at Israel then-he-bowed

הָאֵלֶּה וַיֹּאמֶר לְיוֹסֵף הִנֵּה אָבִיךָ חֹלֶה וַיִּקַּח אֶת־
*** so-he-took being-ill father-of-you see! to-Joseph that-he-said the-these

שְׁנֵי בָנָיו עִמּוֹ אֶת־מְנַשֶּׁה וְאֶת־אֶפְרָיִם׃ וַיַּגֵּד לְיַעֲקֹב
to-Jacob and-he-told (2) Ephraim and Manasseh *** with-him sons-of-him two-of

וַיֹּאמֶר הִנֵּה בִּנְךָ יוֹסֵף בָּא אֵלֶיךָ וַיִּתְחַזֵּק יִשְׂרָאֵל
Israel and-he-strengthened to-you he-came Joseph son-of-you see! and-he-said

as food for yourselves and
your households and your
children."
25 "You have saved our
lives," they said. "May we
find favor in the eyes of our
lord; we will be in bondage to
Pharaoh."
26 So Joseph established it as
a law concerning land in
Egypt—still in force today—
that a fifth of the produce belongs to Pharaoh. It was only
the land of the priests that did
not become Pharaoh's.
27 Now the Israelites settled
in Egypt in the region of Goshen. They acquired property
there and were fruitful and increased greatly in number.
28 Jacob lived in Egypt seventeen years, and the years of his
life were a hundred and forty-
seven. 29 When the time drew
near for Israel to die, he called
for his son Joseph and said to
him, "If I have found favor in
your eyes, put your hand under my thigh and promise that
you will show me kindness
and faithfulness. Do not bury
me in Egypt, 30 but when I rest
with my fathers, carry me out
of Egypt and bury me where
they are buried."
"I will do as you say," he
said.
31 "Swear to me," he said.
Then Joseph swore to him,
and Israel worshiped as he
leaned on the top of his staff.[g]

### *Manasseh and Ephraim*

48 Some time later Joseph
was told, "Your father
is ill." So he took his two sons
Manasseh and Ephraim along
with him. 2 When Jacob was
told, "Your son Joseph has
come to you," Israel rallied his

*g31 Or Israel bowed down at the head of his bed*

וַיֵּשֶׁב עַל־ הַמִּטָּה: וַיֹּאמֶר יַעֲקֹב אֶל־ יוֹסֵף אֵל שַׁדַּי
Almighty God Joseph to Jacob and-he-said (3) the-bed on and-he-sat-up

נִרְאָה־ אֵלַי בְּלוּז בְּאֶרֶץ כְּנָעַן וַיְבָרֶךְ אֹתִי: וַיֹּאמֶר
and-he-said (4) me and-he-blessed Canaan in-land-of at-Luz to-me he-appeared

אֵלַי הִנְנִי מַפְרְךָ וְהִרְבִּיתִךָ וּנְתַתִּיךָ
and-I-will-make-you and-I-will-increase-you making-fruitful-you see-I! to-me

לִקְהַל עַמִּים וְנָתַתִּי אֶת־ הָאָרֶץ הַזֹּאת
the-this the-land *** and-I-will-give peoples into-community-of

לְזַרְעֲךָ אַחֲרֶיךָ אֲחֻזַּת עוֹלָם: וְעַתָּה שְׁנֵי־
two-of and-now (5) everlasting possession-of after-you to-descendant-of-you

בָנֶיךָ הַנּוֹלָדִים לְךָ בְּאֶרֶץ מִצְרַיִם עַד־ בֹּאִי
to-come-me before Egypt in-land-of to-you the-ones-being-born sons-of-you

אֵלֶיךָ מִצְרַיְמָה לִי־ הֵם אֶפְרַיִם וּמְנַשֶּׁה כִּרְאוּבֵן וְשִׁמְעוֹן
and-Simeon as-Reuben and-Manasseh Ephraim they to-me to-Egypt to-you

יִהְיוּ־ לִי: וּמוֹלַדְתְּךָ אֲשֶׁר־ הוֹלַדְתָּ אַחֲרֵיהֶם לְךָ
to-you after-them you-father whom but-children-of-you (6) to-me they-are

יִהְיוּ עַל שֵׁם אֲחֵיהֶם יִקָּרְאוּ
they-will-be-reckoned brothers-of-them name-of under they-are

בְּנַחֲלָתָם: וַאֲנִי | בְּבֹאִי מִפַּדָּן מֵתָה עָלַי
by-me she-died from-Paddan as-to-return-me now-I (7) in-inheritance-of-them

רָחֵל בְּאֶרֶץ כְּנַעַן בַּדֶּרֶךְ בְּעוֹד כִּבְרַת־ אֶרֶץ לָבֹא
to-go land distance-of while-still on-the-way Canaan in-land-of Rachel

אֶפְרָתָה וָאֶקְבְּרֶהָ שָּׁם בְּדֶרֶךְ אֶפְרָת הִוא בֵּית לָחֶם:
Lehem Beth that Ephrath by-road-of there so-I-buried-her to-Ephrath

וַיַּרְא יִשְׂרָאֵל אֶת־ בְּנֵי יוֹסֵף וַיֹּאמֶר מִי־ אֵלֶּה:
these who? then-he-asked Joseph sons-of *** Israel when-he-saw (8)

וַיֹּאמֶר יוֹסֵף אֶל־ אָבִיו בָּנַי הֵם אֲשֶׁר־ נָתַן־ לִי אֱלֹהִים
God to-me he-gave whom they sons-of-me father-of-him to Joseph and-he-said (9)

בָּזֶה וַיֹּאמַר קָחֶם־ נָא אֵלַי וַאֲבָרְכֵם: וְעֵינֵי
now-eyes-of (10) so-I-may-bless-them to-me now! bring-them! then-he-said at-here

יִשְׂרָאֵל כָּבְדוּ מִזֹּקֶן לֹא יוּכַל לִרְאוֹת וַיַּגֵּשׁ אֹתָם
them so-he-brought to-see he-could not from-age they-were-failing Israel

אֵלָיו וַיִּשַּׁק לָהֶם וַיְחַבֵּק לָהֶם: וַיֹּאמֶר
and-he-said (11) on-them and-he-embraced on-them and-he-kissed to-him

יִשְׂרָאֵל אֶל־יוֹסֵף רְאֹה פָנֶיךָ לֹא פִלָּלְתִּי וְהִנֵּה הֶרְאָה אֹתִי
me he-let-see but-see! I-expected not face-of-you to-see Joseph to Israel

אֱלֹהִים גַּם אֶת־ זַרְעֶךָ: וַיּוֹצֵא יוֹסֵף אֹתָם מֵעִם
from-on them Joseph then-he-removed (12) children-of-you *** also God

strength and sat up on the bed.
3 Jacob said to Joseph, "God Almighty[h] appeared to me at Luz in the land of Canaan, and there he blessed me 4 and said to me, 'I am going to make you fruitful and will increase your numbers. I will make you a community of peoples, and I will give this land as an everlasting possession to your descendants after you.'
5 "Now then, your two sons born to you in Egypt before I came to you here will be reckoned as mine; Ephraim and Manasseh will be mine, just as Reuben and Simeon are mine. 6 Any children born to you after them will be yours; in the territory they inherit they will be reckoned under the names of their brothers. 7 As I was returning from Paddan,[i] to my sorrow Rachel died in the land of Canaan while we were still on the way, a little distance from Ephrath. So I buried her there beside the road to Ephrath" (that is, Bethlehem).
8 When Israel saw the sons of Joseph, he asked, "Who are these?"
9 "They are the sons God has given me here," Joseph said to his father.
Then Israel said, "Bring them to me so I may bless them."
10 Now Israel's eyes were failing because of old age, and he could hardly see. So Joseph brought his sons close to him, and his father kissed them and embraced them.
11 Israel said to Joseph, "I never expected to see your face again, and now God has allowed me to see your children too."
12 Then Joseph removed

[h]3 Hebrew *El-Shaddai*
[i]7 That is, Northwest Mesopotamia

בִּרְכָּיו וַיִּשְׁתַּחוּ לְאַפָּיו אָרְצָה׃ וַיִּקַּח יוֹסֵף
Joseph and-he-took (13) to-ground with-face-of-him and-he-bowed knees-of-him

אֶת־ שְׁנֵיהֶם אֶת־ אֶפְרַיִם בִּימִינוֹ מִשְּׂמֹאל יִשְׂרָאֵל וְאֶת־
and Israel toward-left-of on-right-of-him Ephraim *** both-of-them ***

מְנַשֶּׁה בִשְׂמֹאלוֹ מִימִין יִשְׂרָאֵל וַיַּגֵּשׁ אֵלָיו׃
to-him and-he-brought Israel toward-right-of on-left-of-him Manasseh

וַיִּשְׁלַח יִשְׂרָאֵל אֶת־ יְמִינוֹ וַיָּשֶׁת עַל־ רֹאשׁ
head-of on and-he-put right-hand-of-him *** Israel but-he-reached (14)

אֶפְרַיִם וְהוּא הַצָּעִיר וְאֶת־ שְׂמֹאלוֹ עַל־ רֹאשׁ מְנַשֶּׁה
Manasseh head-of on left-hand-of-him and the-younger though-he Ephraim

שִׂכֵּל אֶת־ יָדָיו כִּי מְנַשֶּׁה הַבְּכוֹר׃ וַיְבָרֶךְ
and-he-blessed (15) the-firstborn Manasseh though arms-of-him *** he-crossed

אֶת־ יוֹסֵף וַיֹּאמַר הָאֱלֹהִים אֲשֶׁר הִתְהַלְּכוּ אֲבֹתַי לְפָנָיו
before-him fathers-of-me they-walked whom the-God and-he-said Joseph ***

אַבְרָהָם וְיִצְחָק הָאֱלֹהִים הָרֹעֶה אֹתִי מֵעוֹדִי עַד־ הַיּוֹם
the-day to all-life-of-me me the-one-shepherding the-God and-Isaac Abraham

הַזֶּה׃ הַמַּלְאָךְ הַגֹּאֵל אֹתִי מִכָּל־ רָע יְבָרֵךְ
may-he-bless harm from-all-of me the-one-delivering the-angel (16) the-this

אֶת־הַנְּעָרִים וְיִקָּרֵא בָהֶם שְׁמִי וְשֵׁם אֲבֹתַי
fathers-of-me and-name-of and-name-of-me on-them and-may-he-be-called the-boys ***

אַבְרָהָם וְיִצְחָק וְיִדְגּוּ לָרֹב בְּקֶרֶב הָאָרֶץ׃
the-earth in-midst-of greatly and-may-they-increase and-Isaac Abraham

וַיַּרְא יוֹסֵף כִּי־ יָשִׁית אָבִיו יַד־ יְמִינוֹ
right-of-him hand-of father-of-him he-placed that Joseph when-he-saw (17)

עַל־ רֹאשׁ אֶפְרַיִם וַיֵּרַע בְּעֵינָיו וַיִּתְמֹךְ
then-he-took-hold in-eyes-of-him and-he-was-displeasing Ephraim head-of on

יַד־ אָבִיו לְהָסִיר אֹתָהּ מֵעַל רֹאשׁ־ אֶפְרַיִם עַל־רֹאשׁ מְנַשֶּׁה׃
Manasseh head-of to Ephraim head-of from-on her to-move father-of-him hand-of

וַיֹּאמֶר יוֹסֵף אֶל־ אָבִיו לֹא־ כֵן אָבִי כִּי־ זֶה
this for father-of-me so not father-of-him to Joseph and-he-said (18)

הַבְּכֹר שִׂים יְמִינְךָ עַל־ רֹאשׁוֹ׃ וַיְמָאֵן
but-he-refused (19) head-of-him on right-hand-of-you put! the-firstborn

אָבִיו וַיֹּאמֶר יָדַעְתִּי בְנִי יָדַעְתִּי גַּם־ הוּא יִהְיֶה־
he-will-become he indeed I-know son-of-me I-know and-he-said father-of-him

לְעָם וְגַם־ הוּא יִגְדָּל וְאוּלָם אָחִיו הַקָּטֹן
the-young brother-of-him nevertheless he-will-be-great he and-also as-people

יִגְדַּל מִמֶּנּוּ וְזַרְעוֹ יִהְיֶה מְלֹא־
group-of he-will-become and-descendant-of-him than-he he-will-be-greater

them from Israel's knees and bowed down with his face to the ground. 13And Joseph took both of them, Ephraim on his right toward Israel's left hand and Manasseh on his left toward Israel's right hand, and brought them close to him. 14But Israel reached out his right hand and put it on Ephraim's head, though he was the younger, and crossing his arms, he put his left hand on Manasseh's head, even though Manasseh was the firstborn.

15Then he blessed Joseph and said,

"May the God before whom my fathers
Abraham and Isaac walked,
the God who has been my Shepherd
all my life to this day,
16the Angel who has delivered me from all harm
—may he bless these boys.
May they be called by my name
and the names of my fathers Abraham and Isaac,
and may they increase greatly
upon the earth."

17When Joseph saw his father placing his right hand on Ephraim's head he was displeased; so he took hold of his father's hand to move it from Ephraim's head to Manasseh's head. 18Joseph said to him, "No, my father, this one is the firstborn; put your right hand on his head."

19But his father refused and said, "I know, my son, I know. He too will become a people, and he too will become great. Nevertheless, his younger brother will be greater than he, and his descendants will become a group of nations."

הַגּוֹיִם׃ וַיְבָרְכֵם בַּיּוֹם הַהוּא לֵאמוֹר בְּךָ
by-you to-say the-that on-the-day and-he-blessed-them (20) the-nations

יְבָרֵךְ יִשְׂרָאֵל לֵאמֹר יְשִׂמְךָ אֱלֹהִים כְּאֶפְרַיִם וְכִמְנַשֶּׁה
and-like-Manasseh like-Ephraim God may-he-make-you to-say Israel he-will-bless

וַיָּשֶׂם אֶת־אֶפְרַיִם לִפְנֵי מְנַשֶּׁה׃ וַיֹּאמֶר יִשְׂרָאֵל אֶל־יוֹסֵף
Joseph to Israel then-he-said (21) Manasseh ahead-of Ephraim *** so-he-put

הִנֵּה אָנֹכִי מֵת וְהָיָה אֱלֹהִים עִמָּכֶם וְהֵשִׁיב אֶתְכֶם אֶל־אֶרֶץ
land-of to you and-he-will-take-back with-you God but-he-will-be dying I see!

אֲבֹתֵיכֶם׃ וַאֲנִי נָתַתִּי לְךָ שְׁכֶם אַחַד עַל־אַחֶיךָ
brothers-of-you over one portion to-you I-give and-I (22) fathers-of-you

אֲשֶׁר לָקַחְתִּי מִיַּד הָאֱמֹרִי בְּחַרְבִּי וּבְקַשְׁתִּי׃
and-with-bow-of-me with-sword-of-me the-Amorite from-hand-of I-took which

וַיִּקְרָא יַעֲקֹב אֶל־בָּנָיו וַיֹּאמֶר הֵאָסְפוּ וְאַגִּידָה
so-I-can-tell gather! and-he-said sons-of-him for Jacob then-he-called (49:1)

לָכֶם אֵת אֲשֶׁר־יִקְרָא אֶתְכֶם בְּאַחֲרִית הַיָּמִים׃ הִקָּבְצוּ
assemble! (2) the-days in-coming-of to-you he-will-happen what *** to-you

וְשִׁמְעוּ בְּנֵי יַעֲקֹב וְשִׁמְעוּ אֶל־יִשְׂרָאֵל אֲבִיכֶם׃ רְאוּבֵן
Reuben (3) father-of-you Israel to and-listen! Jacob sons-of and-listen!

בְּכֹרִי אַתָּה כֹּחִי וְרֵאשִׁית אוֹנִי יֶתֶר
excelling-of strength-of-me and-first-of might-of-me you firstborn-of-me

שְׂאֵת וְיֶתֶר עָז׃ פַּחַז כַּמַּיִם אַל־תּוֹתַר
you-will-excel not as-the-waters turbulent (4) power and-excelling-of honor

כִּי עָלִיתָ מִשְׁכְּבֵי אָבִיךָ אָז חִלַּלְתָּ יְצוּעִי עָלָה׃
he-went-up couch-of-me you-defiled then father-of-you beds-of you-went-up for

שִׁמְעוֹן וְלֵוִי אַחִים כְּלֵי חָמָס מְכֵרֹתֵיהֶם׃
swords-of-them violence weapons-of brothers and-Levi Simeon (5)

בְּסֹדָם אַל־תָּבֹא נַפְשִׁי בִּקְהָלָם אַל־
not to-assembly-of-them self-of-me let-her-enter not in-council-of-them (6)

תֵּחַד כְּבֹדִי כִּי בְאַפָּם הָרְגוּ אִישׁ
man they-killed in-anger-of-them for glory-of-me let-her-join

וּבִרְצֹנָם עִקְּרוּ־שׁוֹר׃ אָרוּר אַפָּם כִּי
so anger-of-them being-cursed (7) ox they-hamstrung and-in-pleasure-of-them

עָז וְעֶבְרָתָם כִּי קָשָׁתָה אֲחַלְּקֵם בְּיַעֲקֹב
in-Jacob I-will-scatter-them cruel so and-fury-of-them fierce

וַאֲפִיצֵם בְּיִשְׂרָאֵל׃ יְהוּדָה אַתָּה יוֹדוּךָ
they-will-praise-you you Judah (8) in-Israel and-I-will-disperse-them

אַחֶיךָ יָדְךָ בְּעֹרֶף אֹיְבֶיךָ יִשְׁתַּחֲווּ לְךָ
to-you they-will-bow ones-opposing-you on-neck-of hand-of-you brothers-of-you

20He blessed them that day and said,

"In your[j] name will Israel pronounce this blessing:
'May God make you like Ephraim and Manasseh.' "

So he put Ephraim ahead of Manasseh.
21Then Israel said to Joseph, "I am about to die, but God will be with you[k] and take you[k] back to the land of your[k] fathers. 22And to you, as one who is over your brothers, I give the ridge of land[l] I took from the Amorites with my sword and my bow."

*Jacob Blesses His Sons*

49 Then Jacob called for his sons and said: "Gather around so I can tell you what will happen to you in days to come.

2"Assemble and listen, sons of Jacob;
listen to your father Israel.

3"Reuben, you are my firstborn,
my might, the first sign of my strength,
excelling in honor, excelling in power.
4Turbulent as the waters, you will no longer excel,
for you went up onto your father's bed,
onto my couch and defiled it.

5"Simeon and Levi are brothers—
their swords[m] are weapons of violence.
6Let me not enter their council,
let me not join their assembly,
for they have killed men in their anger
and hamstrung oxen as they pleased.
7Cursed be their anger, so fierce,
and their fury, so cruel!
I will scatter them in Jacob
and disperse them in Israel.

8"Judah,[n] your brothers will praise you;
your hand will be on the neck of your enemies;
your father's sons will bow down to you.

[j]20 The Hebrew is singular.
[k]21 The Hebrew is plural.
[l]22 Or *And to you I give one portion more than to your brothers—the portion*
[m]5 The meaning of the Hebrew for this word is uncertain.
[n]8 *Judah* sounds like and may be derived from the Hebrew for *praise*.

*8 Most mss have no *dagesh* in the first *vav* (יוּ־).

בְּנֵי אָבִיךָ׃ גּוּר אַרְיֵה יְהוּדָה מִטֶּרֶף בְּנִי עָלִיתָ

you-return son-of-me from-prey Judah lion cub-of (9) father-of-you sons-of

כָּרַע רָבַץ כְּאַרְיֵה וּכְלָבִיא מִי יְקִימֶנּוּ׃ לֹא־

not (10) he-rouses-him who? and-like-lioness like-lion he-lies he-crouches

יָסוּר שֵׁבֶט מִיהוּדָה וּמְחֹקֵק מִבֵּין רַגְלָיו

feet-of-him from-between nor-ruling-staff from-Judah scepter he-will-depart

עַד כִּי־ יָבֹא שִׁילֹה וְלוֹ יִקְּהַת עַמִּים׃

peoples obedience-of and-to-him whose-he he-comes when until

אֹסְרִי לַגֶּפֶן עִירֹה וְלַשֹּׂרֵקָה בְּנִי

colt-of and-to-choicest-branch donkey-of-him to-the-vine tethering-of (11)

אֲתֹנוֹ כִּבֵּס בַּיַּיִן לְבֻשׁוֹ וּבְדַם־ עֲנָבִים

grapes and-in-blood-of garment-of-him in-the-wine he-will-wash donkey-of-him

סוּתֹה׃ חַכְלִילִי עֵינַיִם מִיָּיִן וּלְבֶן־ שִׁנַּיִם מֵחָלָב׃ זְבוּלֻן

Zebulun (13) than-milk teeth and-whiter than-wine eyes darker (12) robe-of-him

לְחוֹף יַמִּים יִשְׁכֹּן וְהוּא לְחוֹף אֳנִיֹּת וְיַרְכָתוֹ

and-border-of-him ships as-haven-of and-he he-will-live seas by-shore-of

עַל־ צִידֹן׃ יִשָּׂשכָר חֲמֹר גָּרֶם רֹבֵץ בֵּין הַמִּשְׁפְּתָיִם׃

the-two-saddlebags between lying-down strong donkey Issachar (14) Sidon up-to

וַיַּרְא מְנֻחָה כִּי טוֹב וְאֶת־ הָאָרֶץ כִּי נָעֵמָה

she-is-pleasant how the-land and good how resting-place when-he-sees (15)

וַיֵּט שִׁכְמוֹ לִסְבֹּל וַיְהִי לְמַס־

to-forced-labor and-he-will-be to-bear shoulder-of-him then-he-will-bend

עֹבֵד׃ דָּן יָדִין עַמּוֹ כְּאַחַד שִׁבְטֵי

tribes-of as-one-of people-of-him he-will-provide-justice Dan (16) submitting

יִשְׂרָאֵל׃ יְהִי־ דָן נָחָשׁ עֲלֵי־ דֶרֶךְ שְׁפִיפֹן עֲלֵי־ אֹרַח הַנֹּשֵׁךְ

the-one-biting path along viper road beside serpent Dan he-will-be (17) Israel

עִקְּבֵי־ סוּס וַיִּפֹּל רֹכְבוֹ אָחוֹר׃ לִישׁוּעָתְךָ

for-deliverance-of-you (18) backward one-riding-him so-he-tumbles horse heels-of

קִוִּיתִי יְהוָה׃ גָּד גְּדוּד יְגוּדֶנּוּ וְהוּא יָגֻד עָקֵב׃

heel he-will-attack but-he he-will-attach-him raider Gad (19) Yahweh I-look

מֵאָשֵׁר שְׁמֵנָה לַחְמוֹ וְהוּא יִתֵּן מַעֲדַנֵּי־ מֶלֶךְ׃

king delicacies-of he-will-provide and-he food-of-him rich for-Asher (20)

נַפְתָּלִי אַיָּלָה שְׁלֻחָה הַנֹּתֵן אִמְרֵי־ שָׁפֶר׃ בֵּן

son-of (22) beauty fawns-of the-one-bearing being-set-free doe Naphtali (21)

פֹּרָת יוֹסֵף בֵּן פֹּרָת עֲלֵי־ עָיִן בָּנוֹת צָעֲדָה

climbing branches spring near being-fruitful son-of Joseph being-fruitful

עֲלֵי־ שׁוּר׃ וַיְמָרְרֻהוּ וָרֹבּוּ וַיִּשְׂטְמֻהוּ

and-they-harassed-him and-they-shot and-they-attached-him (23) wall over

9You are a lion's cub, O Judah;
you return from the prey, my son.
Like a lion he crouches and lies down,
like a lioness—who dares to rouse him?
10The scepter will not depart from Judah,
nor the ruler's staff from between his feet,
until he comes to whom it belongs[o]
and the obedience of the nations is his.
11He will tether his donkey to a vine,
his colt to the choicest branch;
he will wash his garments in wine,
his robes in the blood of grapes.
12His eyes will be darker than wine,
his teeth whiter than milk.[p]
13"Zebulun will live by the seashore
and become a haven for ships;
his border will extend toward Sidon.
14"Issachar is a rawboned[q] donkey
lying down between two saddlebags.[r]
15When he sees how good is his resting place
and how pleasant is his land,
he will bend his shoulder to the burden
and submit to forced labor.
16"Dan[s] will provide justice for his people
as one of the tribes of Israel.
17Dan will be a serpent by the roadside,
a viper along the path,
that bites the horse's heels
so that its rider tumbles backward.
18"I look for your deliverance, O LORD.
19"Gad[t] will be attacked by a band of raiders,
but he will attack them at their heels.
20"Asher's food will be rich;
he will provide delicacies fit for a king.
21"Naphtali is a doe set free
that bears beautiful fawns.[u]

[o]10 Or *until Shiloh comes;* or *until he comes to whom tribute belongs*
[p]12 Or *will be dull from wine, / his teeth white from milk* [q]14 Or *strong* [r]14 Or *campfires*
[s]16 *Dan* here means *he provides justice.*
[t]19 *Gad* can mean *attack* and *band of raiders.*
[u]21 Or *free; / he utters beautiful words*

ק °10 שילו , °11a עירו , °11b סותו

בַּעֲלֵי חִצִּים׃ וַתֵּשֶׁב בְּאֵיתָן קַשְׁתּוֹ וַיָּפֹזּוּ
and-they-were-limber bow-of-him steady but-she-remained (24) arrows masters-of

זְרֹעֵי יָדָיו מִידֵי אֲבִיר יַעֲקֹב מִשָּׁם
because-of Jacob Mighty-One-of because-of-hands-of arms-of-him strong-ones-of

רֹעֶה אֶבֶן יִשְׂרָאֵל׃ מֵאֵל אָבִיךָ
father-of-you because-of-God-of (25) Israel Rock-of Shepherding-One

וְיַעְזְרֶךָּ וְאֵת שַׁדַּי וִיבָרְכֶךָּ בִּרְכֹת שָׁמַיִם מֵעָל
above heavens blessings-of for-he-blesses-you Almighty and for-he-helps-you

בִּרְכֹת תְּהוֹם רֹבֶצֶת תָּחַת בִּרְכֹת שָׁדַיִם וָרָחַם׃ בִּרְכֹת
blessings-of (26) and-womb breasts blessings-of below lying deep blessings-of

אָבִיךָ גָּבְרוּ עַל־ בִּרְכֹת הוֹרַי עַד־
ancient mountains-of blessing-of than they-are-greater father-of-you

תַּאֲוַת גִּבְעֹת עוֹלָם תִּהְיֶיןָ לְרֹאשׁ יוֹסֵף וּלְקָדְקֹד
and-on-brow-of Joseph on-head-of let-them-rest age-old hills-of bounty-of

נְזִיר אֶחָיו׃ בִּנְיָמִין זְאֵב יִטְרָף בַּבֹּקֶר
in-the-morning he-is-ravenous wolf Benjamin (27) brothers-of-him prince-of

יֹאכַל עַד וְלָעֶרֶב יְחַלֵּק שָׁלָל׃ כָּל־ אֵלֶּה
these all-of (28) plunder he-divides and-in-the-evening prey he-devours

שִׁבְטֵי יִשְׂרָאֵל שְׁנֵים עָשָׂר וְזֹאת אֲשֶׁר־ דִּבֶּר לָהֶם אֲבִיהֶם
father-of-them to-them he-said what and-this ten two Israel tribes-of

וַיְבָרֶךְ אוֹתָם אִישׁ אֲשֶׁר כְּבִרְכָתוֹ בֵּרַךְ אֹתָם׃
them he-blessed blessing-of-him whose each them when-he-blessed

וַיְצַו אוֹתָם וַיֹּאמֶר אֲלֵהֶם אֲנִי נֶאֱסָף אֶל־ עַמִּי
people-of-me to being-gathered I to-them and-he-said them and-he-instructed (29)

קִבְרוּ אֹתִי אֶל־ אֲבֹתָי אֶל־הַמְּעָרָה אֲשֶׁר בִּשְׂדֵה עֶפְרוֹן הַחִתִּי׃
the-Hittite Ephron in-field-of that the-cave in fathers-of-me with me bury!

בַּמְּעָרָה אֲשֶׁר בִּשְׂדֵה הַמַּכְפֵּלָה אֲשֶׁר עַל־ פְּנֵי־ מַמְרֵא
Mamre area-of near that the-Machpelah in-field-of which in-the-cave (30)

בְּאֶרֶץ כְּנָעַן אֲשֶׁר קָנָה אַבְרָהָם אֶת־ הַשָּׂדֶה מֵאֵת עֶפְרֹן
Ephron from the-field *** Abraham he-bought which Canaan in-land-of

הַחִתִּי לַאֲחֻזַּת־ קָבֶר׃ שָׁמָּה קָבְרוּ אֶת־ אַבְרָהָם וְאֵת
and Abraham *** they-buried at-there (31) burial as-place-of the-Hittite

שָׂרָה אִשְׁתּוֹ שָׁמָּה קָבְרוּ אֶת־ יִצְחָק וְאֵת רִבְקָה אִשְׁתּוֹ
wife-of-him Rebekah and Isaac *** they-buried at-there wife-of-him Sarah

וְשָׁמָּה קָבַרְתִּי אֶת־ לֵאָה׃ מִקְנֵה הַשָּׂדֶה וְהַמְּעָרָה אֲשֶׁר־
that and-the-cave the-field purchase-of (32) Leah *** I-buried and-at-there

בּוֹ מֵאֵת בְּנֵי־ חֵת׃ וַיְכַל יַעֲקֹב לְצַוֺּת אֶת־
*** to-instruct Jacob when-he-finished (33) Heth sons-of from in-him

22"Joseph is a fruitful vine,
a fruitful vine near a spring,
whose branches climb over a wall.[w]
23With bitterness archers attacked him;
they shot at him with hostility.
24But his bow remained steady,
his strong arms stayed[x] limber,
because of the hand of the Mighty One of Jacob,
because of the Shepherd, the Rock of Israel,
25because of your father's God, who helps you,
because of the Almighty,[y] who blesses you
with blessings of the heavens above,
blessings of the deep that lies below,
blessings of the breast and womb.
26Your father's blessings are greater
than the blessings of the ancient mountains,
than[z] the bounty of the age-old hills.
Let all these rest on the head of Joseph,
on the brow of the prince among[a] his brothers.

27"Benjamin is a ravenous wolf;
in the morning he devours the prey,
in the evening he divides the plunder."

28All these are the twelve tribes of Israel, and this is what their father said to them when he blessed them, giving each the blessing appropriate to him.

*The Death of Jacob*

29Then he gave them these instructions: "I am about to be gathered to my people. Bury me with my fathers in the cave in the field of Ephron the Hittite, 30the cave in the field of Machpelah, near Mamre in Canaan, which Abraham bought as a burial place from Ephron the Hittite, along with the field. 31There Abraham and his wife Sarah were buried, there Isaac and his wife Rebekah were buried, and there I buried Leah. 32The field and the cave in it were bought from the Hittites.[b]"
33When Jacob had finished giving instructions to his

[w]22 *Joseph is a wild colt, / a wild colt near a spring, / a wild donkey on a terraced hill*
[x]23,24 Or *archers will attack . . . will shoot . . . will remain . . . will stay*
[y]25 Hebrew *Shaddai*
[z]26 Or *of my progenitors, / as great as*
[a]26 Or *the one separated from*
[b]32 Or *the sons of Heth*

בָּנָיו וַיֶּאֱסֹף רַגְלָיו אֶל־ הַמִּטָּה וַיִּגְוַע
and-he-breathed-last the-bed into feet-of-him then-he-drew sons-of-him

וַיֵּאָסֶף אֶל־ עַמָּיו׃ וַיִּפֹּל יוֹסֵף עַל־ פְּנֵי
face-of on Joseph and-he-fell (50:1) people-of-him to and-he-was-gathered

אָבִיו וַיֵּבְךְּ עָלָיו וַיִּשַּׁק־ לוֹ׃ וַיְצַו
then-he-directed (2) on-him and-he-kissed over-him and-he-wept father-of-him

יוֹסֵף אֶת־ עֲבָדָיו אֶת־ הָרֹפְאִים לַחֲנֹט אֶת־ אָבִיו
father-of-him *** to-embalm the-ones-healing *** servants-of-him *** Joseph

וַיַּחַנְטוּ הָרֹפְאִים אֶת־ יִשְׂרָאֵל׃ וַיִּמְלְאוּ־ לוֹ אַרְבָּעִים
forty for-him and-they-took (3) Israel *** the-ones-healing so-they-embalmed

יוֹם כִּי כֵּן יִמְלְאוּ יְמֵי הַחֲנֻטִים וַיִּבְכּוּ אֹתוֹ
for-him and-they-mourned the-embalmings days-of they-required that for day

מִצְרַיִם שִׁבְעִים יוֹם׃ וַיַּעַבְרוּ יְמֵי בְכִיתוֹ וַיְדַבֵּר
then-he-said mourning-of-him days-of when-they-passed (4) day seventy Egyptians

יוֹסֵף אֶל־ בֵּית פַּרְעֹה לֵאמֹר אִם־ נָא מָצָאתִי חֵן בְּעֵינֵיכֶם
in-eyes-of-you favor I-found now! if to-say Pharaoh court-of to Joseph

דַּבְּרוּ־נָא בְּאָזְנֵי פַרְעֹה לֵאמֹר׃ אָבִי הִשְׁבִּיעַנִי
he-made-swear-me father-of-me (5) to-say Pharaoh in-ears-of now! speak!

לֵאמֹר הִנֵּה אָנֹכִי מֵת בְּקִבְרִי אֲשֶׁר כָּרִיתִי לִי בְּאֶרֶץ כְּנַעַן
Canaan in-land-of for-myself I-dug that in-tomb-of-me dying I see! to-say

שָׁמָּה תִּקְבְּרֵנִי וְעַתָּה אֶעֱלֶה־ נָּא וְאֶקְבְּרָה אֶת־ אָבִי
father-of-me *** and-let-me-bury now! let-me-go-up so-now you-bury-me at-there

וְאָשׁוּבָה׃ וַיֹּאמֶר פַּרְעֹה עֲלֵה וּקְבֹר אֶת־ אָבִיךָ
father-of-you *** and-bury! go-up! Pharaoh and-he-said (6) then-I-will-return

כַּאֲשֶׁר הִשְׁבִּיעֶךָ׃ וַיַּעַל יוֹסֵף לִקְבֹּר אֶת־ אָבִיו
father-of-him *** to-bury Joseph so-he-went-up (7) he-made-swear-you just-as

וַיַּעֲלוּ אִתּוֹ כָּל־ עַבְדֵי פַרְעֹה זִקְנֵי
dignitaries-of Pharaoh officials-of all-of with-him and-they-went-up

בֵיתוֹ וְכֹל זִקְנֵי אֶרֶץ־ מִצְרָיִם׃ וְכֹל בֵּית
house-of and-all-of (8) Egypt land-of dignitaries-of and-all-of court-of-him

יוֹסֵף וְאֶחָיו וּבֵית אָבִיו רַק טַפָּם
children-of-them only father-of-him and-house-of and-brothers-of-him Joseph

וְצֹאנָם וּבְקָרָם עָזְבוּ בְּאֶרֶץ גֹּשֶׁן׃
Goshen in-region-of they-left and-herd-of-them and-flock-of-them

וַיַּעַל עִמּוֹ גַּם־ רֶכֶב גַּם־ פָּרָשִׁים וַיְהִי הַמַּחֲנֶה
the-company so-he-was horsemen also chariot also with-him and-he-went-up (9)

כָּבֵד מְאֹד׃ וַיָּבֹאוּ עַד־ גֹּרֶן הָאָטָד אֲשֶׁר בְּעֵבֶר
near-to that the-Atad threshing-floor-of to when-they-came (10) very large

sons, he drew his feet up into the bed, breathed his last and was gathered to his people.

50 Joseph threw himself upon his father and wept over him and kissed him. 2Then Joseph directed the physicians in his service to embalm his father Israel. So the physicians embalmed him, 3taking a full forty days, for that was the time required for embalming. And the Egyptians mourned for him seventy days.

4When the days of mourning had passed, Joseph said to Pharaoh's court, "If I have found favor in your eyes, speak to Pharaoh for me. Tell him, 5'My father made me swear an oath and said, "I am about to die; bury me in the tomb I dug for myself in the land of Canaan." Now let me go up and bury my father; then I will return.' "

6Pharaoh said, "Go up and bury your father, as he made you swear to do."

7So Joseph went up to bury his father. All Pharaoh's officials accompanied him—the dignitaries of his court and all the dignitaries of Egypt—8besides all the members of Joseph's household and his brothers and those belonging to his father's household. Only their children and their flocks and herds were left in Goshen. 9Chariots and horsemen[d] also went up with him. It was a very large company.

10When they reached the threshing floor of Atad, near

[d]9 Or *charioteers*

הַיַּרְדֵּן וַיִּסְפְּדוּ־ שָׁם מִסְפֵּד גָּדוֹל וְכָבֵד מְאֹד
very and-bitter loud with-lamentation there then-they-lamented the-Jordan

וַיַּעַשׂ לְאָבִיו אֵבֶל שִׁבְעַת יָמִים׃ וַיַּרְא
when-they-saw (11) days seven-of mourning for-father-of-him and-he-observed

יוֹשֵׁב הָאָרֶץ הַכְּנַעֲנִי אֶת־ הָאֵבֶל בְּגֹרֶן
at-threshing-floor-of the-mourning *** the-Canaanite the-land one-living-of

הָאָטָד וַיֹּאמְרוּ אֵבֶל־ כָּבֵד זֶה לְמִצְרָיִם עַל־ כֵּן קָרָא
he-called this for by-Egyptians this solemn mourning then-they-said the-Atad

שְׁמָהּ אָבֵל מִצְרַיִם אֲשֶׁר בְּעֵבֶר הַיַּרְדֵּן׃ וַיַּעֲשׂוּ בָנָיו
sons-of-him so-they-did (12) the-Jordan near-to that Mizraim Abel name-of-her

לוֹ כֵּן כַּאֲשֶׁר צִוָּם׃ וַיִּשְׂאוּ אֹתוֹ בָנָיו
sons-of-him him and-they-carried (13) he-commanded-them just-as this for-him

אַרְצָה כְּנַעַן וַיִּקְבְּרוּ אֹתוֹ בִּמְעָרַת שְׂדֵה הַמַּכְפֵּלָה אֲשֶׁר
that the-Machpelah field-of in-cave-of him and-they-buried Canaan to-land-of

קָנָה אַבְרָהָם אֶת־ הַשָּׂדֶה לַאֲחֻזַּת־ קֶבֶר מֵאֵת עֶפְרֹן הַחִתִּי
the-Hittite Ephron from burial as-place-of the-field *** Abraham he-bought

עַל־ פְּנֵי מַמְרֵא׃ וַיָּשָׁב יוֹסֵף מִצְרַיְמָה הוּא וְאֶחָיו
and-brothers-of-him he to-Egypt Joseph then-he-returned (14) Mamre area-of near

וְכָל־ הָעֹלִים אִתּוֹ לִקְבֹּר אֶת־ אָבִיו אַחֲרֵי
after father-of-him *** to-bury with-him the-ones-going and-all-of

קָבְרוֹ אֶת־ אָבִיו׃ וַיִּרְאוּ אֲחֵי־ יוֹסֵף כִּי־
that Joseph brothers-of when-they-saw (15) father-of-him *** to-bury-him

מֵת אֲבִיהֶם וַיֹּאמְרוּ לוּ יִשְׂטְמֵנוּ
he-holds-grudge-against-us what-if then-they-said father-of-them he-was-dead

יוֹסֵף וְהָשֵׁב יָשִׁיב לָנוּ אֵת כָּל־ הָרָעָה אֲשֶׁר גָּמַלְנוּ אֹתוֹ׃
to-him we-did that the-wrong all-of *** to-us he-repays and-to-repay Joseph

וַיְצַוּוּ אֶל־ יוֹסֵף לֵאמֹר אָבִיךָ צִוָּה לִפְנֵי
before he-instructed father-of-you to-say Joseph to so-they-sent-word (16)

מוֹתוֹ לֵאמֹר׃ כֹּה־ תֹאמְרוּ לְיוֹסֵף אָנָּא שָׂא נָא פֶּשַׁע
sin-of now! forgive! please! to-Joseph you-say this (17) to-say to-die-him

אַחֶיךָ וְחַטָּאתָם כִּי־ רָעָה גְמָלוּךָ וְעַתָּה שָׂא
forgive! so-now they-treated-you badly so and-wrong-of-them brothers-of-you

נָא לְפֶשַׁע עַבְדֵי אֱלֹהֵי אָבִיךָ וַיֵּבְךְּ יוֹסֵף
Joseph and-he-wept father-of-you God-of servants-of to-sin-of now!

בְּדַבְּרָם אֵלָיו׃ וַיֵּלְכוּ גַּם־ אֶחָיו
brothers-of-him also then-they-came (18) to-him when-to-speak-them

וַיִּפְּלוּ לְפָנָיו וַיֹּאמְרוּ הִנֶּנּוּ לְךָ לַעֲבָדִים׃
as-slaves to-you see-us! and-they-said before-him and-they-fell

the Jordan, they lamented loudly and bitterly; and there Joseph observed a seven-day period of mourning for his father. [11]When the Canaanites who lived there saw the mourning at the threshing floor of Atad, they said, "The Egyptians are holding a solemn ceremony of mourning." That is why that place near the Jordan is called Abel Mizraim.[e]

[12]So Jacob's sons did as he had commanded them: [13]They carried him to the land of Canaan and buried him in the cave in the field of Machpelah, near Mamre, which Abraham had bought as a burial place from Ephron the Hittite, along with the field. [14]After burying his father, Joseph returned to Egypt, together with his brothers and all the others who had gone with him to bury his father.

### *Joseph Reassures His Brothers*

[15]When Joseph's brothers saw that their father was dead, they said, "What if Joseph holds a grudge against us and pays us back for all the wrongs we did to him?" [16]So they sent word to Joseph, saying, "Your father left these instructions before he died: [17]'This is what you are to say to Joseph: I ask you to forgive your brothers the sins and the wrongs they committed in treating you so badly.' Now please forgive the sins of the servants of the God of your father." When their message came to him, Joseph wept.

[18]His brothers then came and threw themselves down before him. "We are your slaves," they said.

[e]11 *Abel Mizraim* means *mourning of the Egyptians.*

וַיֹּאמֶר אֲלֵהֶם יוֹסֵף אַל־ תִּירָאוּ כִּי הֲתַחַת אֱלֹהִים אָנִי׃

I God in-place-of? for you-be-afraid not Joseph to-them but-he-said (19)

וְאַתֶּם חֲשַׁבְתֶּם עָלַי רָעָה אֱלֹהִים חֲשָׁבָהּ לְטֹבָה

for-good he-intended-her God harm against-me you-intended now-you (20)

לְמַעַן עֲשֹׂה כַּיּוֹם הַזֶּה לְהַחֲיֹת עַם־ רָב׃

many people to-keep-alive the-this as-the-day to-accomplish in-order

וְעַתָּה אַל־ תִּירָאוּ אָנֹכִי אֲכַלְכֵּל אֶתְכֶם וְאֶת־ טַפְּכֶם

children-of-you and for-you I-will-provide I you-be-afraid not so-then (21)

וַיְנַחֵם אוֹתָם וַיְדַבֵּר עַל־ לִבָּם׃ וַיֵּשֶׁב יוֹסֵף

Joseph so-he-stayed (22) heart-of-them to and-he-spoke them and-he-reassured

בְּמִצְרַיִם הוּא וּבֵית אָבִיו וַיְחִי יוֹסֵף מֵאָה וָעֶשֶׂר

and-ten hundred Joseph and-he-lived father-of-him and-family-of he in-Egypt

שָׁנִים׃ וַיַּרְא יוֹסֵף לְאֶפְרַיִם בְּנֵי שִׁלֵּשִׁים גַּם

also third-generations children-of to-Ephraim Joseph and-he-saw (23) years

בְּנֵי מָכִיר בֶּן־ מְנַשֶּׁה יֻלְּדוּ עַל־ בִּרְכֵּי יוֹסֵף׃

Joseph knees-of on they-were-born Manasseh son-of Makir children-of

וַיֹּאמֶר יוֹסֵף אֶל־ אֶחָיו אָנֹכִי מֵת וֵאלֹהִים פָּקֹד

to-aid but-God dying I brothers-of-him to Joseph then-he-said (24)

יִפְקֹד אֶתְכֶם וְהֶעֱלָה אֶתְכֶם מִן־ הָאָרֶץ הַזֹּאת אֶל־ הָאָרֶץ

the-land to the-this the-land from you and-he-will-take-up you he-will-aid

אֲשֶׁר נִשְׁבַּע לְאַבְרָהָם לְיִצְחָק וּלְיַעֲקֹב׃ וַיַּשְׁבַּע

and-he-made-swear (25) and-to-Jacob to-Isaac to-Abraham he-promised that

יוֹסֵף אֶת־ בְּנֵי יִשְׂרָאֵל לֵאמֹר פָּקֹד יִפְקֹד אֱלֹהִים אֶתְכֶם וְהַעֲלִתֶם

then-you-carry you God he-will-aid to-aid to-say Israel sons-of *** Joseph

אֶת־ עַצְמֹתַי מִזֶּה׃ וַיָּמָת יוֹסֵף בֶּן־ מֵאָה וָעֶשֶׂר

and-ten hundred son-of Joseph so-he-died (26) from-this bones-of-me ***

שָׁנִים וַיַּחַנְטוּ אֹתוֹ וַיִּישֶׂם בָּאָרוֹן בְּמִצְרָיִם׃

in-Egypt in-the-coffin and-he-was-placed him and-they-embalmed years

19 But Joseph said to them, "Don't be afraid. Am I in the place of God? 20 You intended to harm me, but God intended it for good to accomplish what is now being done, the saving of many lives. 21 So then, don't be afraid. I will provide for you and your children." And he reassured them and spoke kindly to them.

*The Death of Joseph*

22 Joseph stayed in Egypt, along with all his father's family. He lived a hundred and ten years 23 and saw the third generation of Ephraim's children. Also the children of Makir son of Manasseh were placed at birth on Joseph's knees.[f]

24 Then Joseph said to his brothers, "I am about to die. But God will surely come to your aid and take you up out of this land to the land he promised on oath to Abraham, Isaac and Jacob." 25 And Joseph made the sons of Israel swear an oath and said, "God will surely come to your aid, and then you must carry my bones up from this place."

26 So Joseph died at the age of a hundred and ten. And after they embalmed him, he was placed in a coffin in Egypt.

f23 That is, were counted as his

וְאֵלֶּה שְׁמוֹת בְּנֵי יִשְׂרָאֵל הַבָּאִים מִצְרָיְמָה אֶת
with to-Egypt the-ones-entering Israel sons-of names-of now-these (1:1)

יַעֲקֹב אִישׁ וּבֵיתוֹ בָּאוּ׃ רְאוּבֵן שִׁמְעוֹן לֵוִי וִיהוּדָה׃
and-Judah Levi Simeon Reuben (2) they-came with-family-of-him each Jacob

יִשָּׂשכָר זְבוּלֻן וּבִנְיָמִן׃ דָּן וְנַפְתָּלִי גָּד וְאָשֵׁר׃
and-Asher Gad and-Naphtali Dan (4) and-Benjamin Zebulun Issachar (3)

וַיְהִי כָּל־נֶפֶשׁ יֹצְאֵי יֶרֶךְ־יַעֲקֹב שִׁבְעִים נָפֶשׁ
person seventy Jacob body-of ones-coming-out-of person all-of and-he-was (5)

וְיוֹסֵף הָיָה בְמִצְרָיִם׃ וַיָּמָת יוֹסֵף וְכָל־אֶחָיו
brothers-of-him and-all-of Joseph now-he-died (6) in-Egypt he-was now-Joseph

וְכֹל הַדּוֹר הַהוּא׃ וּבְנֵי יִשְׂרָאֵל פָּרוּ
they-were-fruitful Israel but-sons-of (7) the-that the-generation and-all-of

וַיִּשְׁרְצוּ וַיִּרְבּוּ וַיַּעַצְמוּ בִּמְאֹד מְאֹד
greatly so-greatly and-they-grew and-they-increased and-they-multiplied

וַתִּמָּלֵא הָאָרֶץ אֹתָם׃ וַיָּקָם מֶלֶךְ־חָדָשׁ
new king then-he-came-to-power (8) with-them the-land that-she-was-filled

עַל־מִצְרָיִם אֲשֶׁר לֹא־יָדַע אֶת־יוֹסֵף׃ וַיֹּאמֶר אֶל־עַמּוֹ הִנֵּה
see! people-of-him to and-he-said (9) Joseph *** he-knew not who Egypt over

עַם בְּנֵי יִשְׂרָאֵל רַב וְעָצוּם מִמֶּנּוּ׃ הָבָה
come! (10) than-us and-powerful numerous Israel sons-of people-of

נִתְחַכְּמָה לוֹ פֶּן־יִרְבֶּה וְהָיָה כִּי־
if and-he-will-be he-will-increase or with-him we-must-deal-shrewdly

תִקְרֶאנָה מִלְחָמָה וְנוֹסַף גַּם־הוּא עַל־שֹׂנְאֵינוּ
ones-opposing-us with he indeed then-he-will-join war they-break-out

וְנִלְחַם־בָּנוּ וְעָלָה מִן־הָאָרֶץ׃
the-country from and-he-will-leave against-us and-he-will-fight

וַיָּשִׂימוּ עָלָיו שָׂרֵי מִסִּים לְמַעַן עַנֹּתוֹ
to-afflict-him in-order slaves masters-of over-him so-they-put (11)

בְּסִבְלֹתָם וַיִּבֶן עָרֵי מִסְכְּנוֹת לְפַרְעֹה אֶת־פִּתֹם
Pithom *** for-Pharaoh storages cities-of and-he-built with-labors-of-them

וְאֶת־רַעַמְסֵס׃ וְכַאֲשֶׁר יְעַנּוּ אֹתוֹ כֵּן יִרְבֶּה וְכֵן
and-more he-multiplied more him they-oppressed but-more (12) Rameses and

יִפְרֹץ וַיָּקֻצוּ מִפְּנֵי בְּנֵי יִשְׂרָאֵל׃ וַיַּעֲבִדוּ
so-they-made-work (13) Israel sons-of presence-of so-they-dreaded he-spread

מִצְרַיִם אֶת־בְּנֵי יִשְׂרָאֵל בְּפָרֶךְ׃ וַיְמָרְרוּ אֶת־
*** and-they-made-bitter (14) ruthlessly Israel sons-of *** Egyptians

חַיֵּיהֶם בַּעֲבֹדָה קָשָׁה בְּחֹמֶר וּבִלְבֵנִים וּבְכָל־עֲבֹדָה
labor and-with-all-of and-in-bricks in-mortar hard with-labor lives-of-them

*The Israelites Oppressed*

1 These are the names of the
sons of Israel who entered
Egypt with Jacob, each with
his family: 2Reuben, Simeon,
Levi and Judah; 3Issachar,
Zebulun and Benjamin; 4Dan
and Naphtali; Gad and Asher.
5The descendants of Jacob
numbered seventy[a] in all; Joseph was already in Egypt.
6Now Joseph and all his
brothers and all that generation died, 7but the Israelites
were fruitful and multiplied
greatly and became exceedingly numerous, so that the
land was filled with them.
8Then a new king, who did
not know about Joseph, came
to power in Egypt. 9"Look," he
said to his people, "the Israelites have become much too
numerous for us. 10Come, we
must deal shrewdly with them
or they will become even more
numerous and, if war breaks
out, will join our enemies,
fight against us and leave the
country."
11So they put slave masters
over them to oppress them
with forced labor, and they
built Pithom and Rameses as
store cities for Pharaoh. 12But
the more they were oppressed,
the more they multiplied and
spread; so the Egyptians came
to dread the Israelites 13and
worked them ruthlessly.
14They made their lives bitter
with hard labor in brick and
mortar and with all kinds of
work in the fields; in all their

[a]5 Masoretic Text (see also Gen. 46:27); Dead Sea Scrolls and Septuagint (see also Acts 7:14) *seventy-five*

בַּשָּׂדֶה אֵת כָּל־ עֲבֹדָתָם אֲשֶׁר־ עָבְדוּ בָהֶם בְּפָרֶךְ׃
ruthlessly with-them they-used that labor-of-them all-of *** in-the-field

וַיֹּאמֶר מֶלֶךְ מִצְרַיִם לַמְיַלְּדֹת הָעִבְרִיֹּת אֲשֶׁר
whose the-Hebrews to-the-being-midwives Egypt king-of then-he-said (15)

שֵׁם הָאַחַת שִׁפְרָה וְשֵׁם הַשֵּׁנִית פּוּעָה׃ וַיֹּאמֶר
and-he-said (16) Puah the-second and-name-of Shiphrah the-first name-of

בְּיַלֶּדְכֶן אֶת־ הָעִבְרִיּוֹת וּרְאִיתֶן עַל־
on and-you-observe the-Hebrew-women *** when-to-help-in-childbirth-you

הָאָבְנָיִם אִם־ בֵּן הוּא וַהֲמִתֶּן אֹתוֹ וְאִם־ בַּת הִיא וָחָיָה׃
then-let-him-live she girl but-if him then-you-kill he boy if the-delivery-stool

וַתִּירֶאןָ הַמְיַלְּדֹת אֶת־ הָאֱלֹהִים וְלֹא עָשׂוּ כַּאֲשֶׁר
as-what they-did and-not the-God *** the-being-midwives but-they-feared (17)

דִּבֶּר אֲלֵיהֶן מֶלֶךְ מִצְרָיִם וַתְּחַיֶּיןָ אֶת־ הַיְלָדִים׃ וַיִּקְרָא
so-he-called (18) the-boys *** but-they-let-live Egypt king-of to-them he-told

מֶלֶךְ־ מִצְרַיִם לַמְיַלְּדֹת וַיֹּאמֶר לָהֶן מַדּוּעַ עֲשִׂיתֶן
you-did why? to-them and-he-asked for-the-being-midwives Egypt king-of

הַדָּבָר הַזֶּה וַתְּחַיֶּיןָ אֶת־ הַיְלָדִים׃ וַתֹּאמַרְןָ
and-they-answered (19) the-boys *** that-you-let-live the-this the-thing

הַמְיַלְּדֹת אֶל־ פַּרְעֹה כִּי לֹא כַנָּשִׁים הַמִּצְרִיֹּת הָעִבְרִיֹּת
the-Hebrews the-Egyptians like-the-woman not now Pharaoh to the-being-midwives

כִּי־ חָיוֹת הֵנָּה בְּטֶרֶם תָּבוֹא אֲלֵהֶן הַמְיַלֶּדֶת
the-one-being-midwife to-them she-arrives before they vigorous-ones for

וְיָלָדוּ׃ וַיֵּיטֶב אֱלֹהִים לַמְיַלְּדֹת
to-the-ones-being-midwives God so-he-was-kind (20) then-they-give-birth

וַיִּרֶב הָעָם וַיַּעַצְמוּ מְאֹד׃ וַיְהִי
and-he-was (21) more and-they-became-numerous the-people and-he-increased

כִּי־ יָרְאוּ הַמְיַלְּדֹת אֶת־ הָאֱלֹהִים וַיַּעַשׂ לָהֶם
to-them that-he-gave the-God *** the-being-midwives they-feared because

בָּתִּים׃ וַיְצַו פַּרְעֹה לְכָל־ עַמּוֹ לֵאמֹר כָּל־
every-of to-say people-of-him to-all-of Pharaoh then-he-ordered (22) families

הַבֵּן הַיִּלּוֹד הַיְאֹרָה תַּשְׁלִיכֻהוּ וְכָל־ הַבַּת
the-girl but-every-of you-must-throw-him into-the-Nile the-born the-boy

תְּחַיּוּן׃ וַיֵּלֶךְ אִישׁ מִבֵּית לֵוִי וַיִּקַּח אֶת־
*** and-he-married Levi from-house-of man now-he-went (2:1) you-let-live

בַּת־ לֵוִי׃ וַתַּהַר הָאִשָּׁה וַתֵּלֶד בֵּן וַתֵּרֶא
when-she-saw son and-she-bore the-woman and-she-conceived (2) Levi daughter-of

אֹתוֹ כִּי־ טוֹב הוּא וַתִּצְפְּנֵהוּ שְׁלֹשָׁה יְרָחִים׃ וְלֹא־ יָכְלָה עוֹד
longer she-could when-not (3) months three then-she-hid-him he fine that him

hard labor the Egyptians used them ruthlessly.

[15]The king of Egypt said to the Hebrew midwives, whose names were Shiphrah and Puah, [16]"When you help the Hebrew women in childbirth and observe them on the delivery stool, if it is a boy, kill him; but if it is a girl, let her live." [17]The midwives, however, feared God and did not do what the king of Egypt had told them to do; they let the boys live. [18]Then the king of Egypt summoned the midwives and asked them, "Why have you done this? Why have you let the boys live?"

[19]The midwives answered Pharaoh, "Hebrew women are not like Egyptian women; they are vigorous and give birth before the midwives arrive."

[20]So God was kind to the midwives and the people increased and became even more numerous. [21]And because the midwives feared God, he gave them families of their own.

[22]Then Pharaoh gave this order to all his people: "Every boy that is born you must throw into the river, but let every girl live."

*The Birth of Moses*

2 Now a man of the house of Levi married a Levite woman, [2]and she became pregnant and gave birth to a son. When she saw that he was a fine child, she hid him for three months. [3]But when she could hide him no longer,

הַצְּפִינוֹ וַתִּקַּח־ לוֹ תֵּבַת גֹּמֶא וַתַּחְמְרָה
and-she-coated-her papyrus basket-of for-him then-she-got to-hide-him

בַחֵמָר וּבַזָּפֶת וַתָּשֶׂם בָּהּ אֶת־ הַיֶּלֶד
the-child *** in-her then-she-placed and-with-the-pitch with-the-tar

וַתָּשֶׂם בַּסּוּף עַל־ שְׂפַת הַיְאֹר׃ וַתֵּתַצַּב
and-she-stood (4) the-Nile bank-of along among-the-reed and-she-put

אֲחֹתוֹ מֵרָחֹק לְדֵעָה מַה־ יֵּעָשֶׂה לוֹ׃
to-him he-would-happen what to-see at-distance sister-of-him

וַתֵּרֶד בַּת־ פַּרְעֹה לִרְחֹץ עַל־הַיְאֹר וְנַעֲרֹתֶיהָ
and-maidens-of-her the-Nile in to-bathe Pharaoh daughter-of then-she-went-down (5)

הֹלְכֹת עַל־ יַד הַיְאֹר וַתֵּרֶא אֶת־ הַתֵּבָה בְּתוֹךְ הַסּוּף
the-reed among the-basket *** and-she-saw the-Nile bank-of along ones-walking

וַתִּשְׁלַח אֶת־ אֲמָתָהּ וַתִּקָּחֶהָ וַתִּפְתַּח
then-she-opened (6) and-she-got-her slave-girl-of-her *** and-she-sent

וַתִּרְאֵהוּ אֶת־ הַיֶּלֶד וְהִנֵּה־ נַעַר בֹּכֶה וַתַּחְמֹל עָלָיו
for-him and-she-felt-sorry crying child and-see! the-baby *** and-she-saw-him

וַתֹּאמֶר מִיַּלְדֵי הָעִבְרִים זֶה׃ וַתֹּאמֶר אֲחֹתוֹ
sister-of-him then-she-asked (7) this the-Hebrews from-babies-of and-she-said

אֶל־ בַּת־ פַּרְעֹה הַאֵלֵךְ וְקָרָאתִי לָךְ אִשָּׁה מֵינֶקֶת מִן
from nursing woman for-you and-I-get shall-I-go? Pharaoh daughter-of to

הָעִבְרִיֹּת וְתֵינִק לָךְ אֶת־ הַיָּלֶד׃ וַתֹּאמֶר־ לָהּ
to-her and-she-answered (8) the-baby *** for-you so-she-can-nurse the-Hebrews

בַּת־ פַּרְעֹה לֵכִי וַתֵּלֶךְ הָעַלְמָה וַתִּקְרָא אֶת־ אֵם
mother-of *** and-she-got the-girl and-she-went go! Pharaoh daughter-of

הַיָּלֶד׃ וַתֹּאמֶר לָהּ בַּת־ פַּרְעֹה הֵילִיכִי אֶת־ הַיֶּלֶד
the-baby *** take! Pharaoh daughter-of to-her and-she-said (9) the-baby

הַזֶּה וְהֵינִקִהוּ לִי וַאֲנִי אֶתֵּן אֶת־ שְׂכָרֵךְ וַתִּקַּח
so-she-took wage-of-you *** I-will-pay and-I for-me and-nurse-him! the-this

הָאִשָּׁה הַיֶּלֶד וַתְּנִיקֵהוּ׃ וַיִּגְדַּל הַיֶּלֶד
the-child when-he-grew (10) and-she-nursed-him the-baby the-woman

וַתְּבִאֵהוּ לְבַת־ פַּרְעֹה וַיְהִי־ לָהּ לְבֵן
as-son to-her and-he-became Pharaoh to-daughter-of then-she-took-him

וַתִּקְרָא שְׁמוֹ מֹשֶׁה וַתֹּאמֶר כִּי מִן־ הַמַּיִם מְשִׁיתִהוּ׃
I-drew-him the-waters from for and-she-said Moses name-of-him and-she-called

וַיְהִי ׀ בַּיָּמִים הָהֵם וַיִּגְדַּל מֹשֶׁה וַיֵּצֵא
that-he-went-out Moses when-he-grew the-these in-the-days and-he-was (11)

אֶל־ אֶחָיו וַיַּרְא בְּסִבְלֹתָם וַיַּרְא אִישׁ מִצְרִי
Egyptian man and-he-saw at-labors-of-them and-he-watched brothers-of-him among

she got a papyrus basket for him and coated it with tar and pitch. Then she placed the child in it and put it among the reeds along the bank of the Nile. [4]His sister stood at a distance to see what would happen to him.

[5]Then Pharaoh's daughter went down to the Nile to bathe, and her attendants were walking along the river bank. She saw the basket among the reeds and sent her slave girl to get it. [6]She opened it and saw the baby. He was crying, and she felt sorry for him. "This is one of the Hebrew babies," she said.

[7]Then his sister asked Pharaoh's daughter, "Shall I go and get one of the Hebrew women to nurse the baby for you?"

[8]"Yes, go," she answered. And the girl went and got the baby's mother. [9]Pharaoh's daughter said to her, "Take this baby and nurse him for me, and I will pay you." So the woman took the baby and nursed him. [10]When the child grew older, she took him to Pharaoh's daughter and he became her son. She named him Moses,[b] saying, "I drew him out of the water."

*Moses Flees to Midian*

[11]One day, after Moses had grown up, he went out to where his own people were and watched them at their hard labor. He saw an Egyptian beating a Hebrew, one of

[b]10 *Moses* sounds like the Hebrew for *draw out.*

*10 Most mss have *dagesh* in the *yod* (ויג׳).

מַכֶּה אִישׁ־ עִבְרִי מֵאֶחָיו׃ וַיִּפֶן כֹּה וָכֹה

and-that this and-he-glanced (12) from-brothers-of-him Hebrew man beating

וַיַּרְא כִּי אֵין אִישׁ וַיַּךְ אֶת־ הַמִּצְרִי וַיִּטְמְנֵהוּ

and-he-hid-him the-Egyptian *** and-he-killed man there-is-no that and-he-saw

בַּחוֹל׃ וַיֵּצֵא בַּיּוֹם הַשֵּׁנִי וְהִנֵּה שְׁנֵי־ אֲנָשִׁים

men two-of and-see! the-next on-the-day and-he-went-out (13) in-the-sand

עִבְרִים נִצִּים וַיֹּאמֶר לָרָשָׁע לָמָּה תַכֶּה

you-hit why? to-the-one-in-wrong and-he-asked ones-fighting Hebrews

רֵעֶךָ׃ וַיֹּאמֶר מִי שָׂמְךָ לְאִישׁ שַׂר וְשֹׁפֵט

and-judging ruler as-one he-made-you who? and-he-said (14) fellow-of-you

עָלֵינוּ הַלְהָרְגֵנִי אַתָּה אֹמֵר כַּאֲשֶׁר הָרַגְתָּ אֶת־ הַמִּצְרִי

the-Egyptian *** you-killed just-as thinking you to-kill-me? over-us

וַיִּירָא מֹשֶׁה וַיֹּאמַר אָכֵן נוֹדַע הַדָּבָר׃

the-thing he-is-known surely and-he-thought Moses and-he-was-afraid

וַיִּשְׁמַע פַּרְעֹה אֶת־ הַדָּבָר הַזֶּה וַיְבַקֵּשׁ לַהֲרֹג אֶת־

*** to-kill then-he-tried the-this the-thing *** Pharaoh when-he-heard (15)

מֹשֶׁה וַיִּבְרַח מֹשֶׁה מִפְּנֵי פַרְעֹה וַיֵּשֶׁב בְּאֶרֶץ־ מִדְיָן

Midian to-land-of and-he-went Pharaoh from-face-of Moses but-he-fled Moses

וַיֵּשֶׁב עַל־ הַבְּאֵר׃ וּלְכֹהֵן מִדְיָן שֶׁבַע בָּנוֹת

daughters seven Midian now-to-priest-of (16) the-well by and-he-sat

וַתָּבֹאנָה וַתִּדְלֶנָה וַתְּמַלֶּאנָה אֶת־ הָרְהָטִים לְהַשְׁקוֹת

to-water the-troughs *** and-they-filled and-they-drew and-they-came

צֹאן אֲבִיהֶן׃ וַיָּבֹאוּ הָרֹעִים וַיְגָרְשׁוּם

and-they-drove-them the-ones-herding but-they-came (17) father-of-them flock-of

וַיָּקָם מֹשֶׁה וַיּוֹשִׁעָן וַיַּשְׁקְ אֶת־ צֹאנָם׃

flock-of-them *** and-he-watered and-he-rescued-them Moses but-he-got-up

וַתָּבֹאנָה אֶל־ רְעוּאֵל אֲבִיהֶן וַיֹּאמֶר מַדּוּעַ מִהַרְתֶּן

you-are-early why? and-he-asked father-of-them Reuel to when-they-returned (18)

בֹּא הַיּוֹם׃ וַתֹּאמַרְןָ אִישׁ מִצְרִי הִצִּילָנוּ

he-rescued-us Egyptian man and-they-answered (19) the-day to-return

מִיַּד הָרֹעִים וְגַם־ דָּלֹה דָלָה לָנוּ וַיַּשְׁקְ

and-he-watered for-us he-drew to-draw and-even the-ones-herding from-hand-of

אֶת־ הַצֹּאן׃ וַיֹּאמֶר אֶל־ בְּנֹתָיו וְאַיּוֹ לָמָּה זֶּה

this why? and-where-he? daughters-of-him to and-he-asked (20) the-flock ***

עֲזַבְתֶּן אֶת־ הָאִישׁ קִרְאֶן לוֹ וְיֹאכַל לָחֶם׃ וַיּוֹאֶל

so-he-agreed (21) meal so-he-can-eat to-him invite! the-man *** you-left

מֹשֶׁה לָשֶׁבֶת אֶת־ הָאִישׁ וַיִּתֵּן אֶת־ צִפֹּרָה בִתּוֹ לְמֹשֶׁה׃

to-Moses daughter-of-him Zipporah *** and-he-gave the-man with to-stay Moses

his own people. [12]Glancing
this way and that and seeing
no one, he killed the Egyptian
and hid him in the sand. [13]The
next day he went out and saw
two Hebrews fighting. He
asked the one in the wrong,
"Why are you hitting your fellow Hebrew?"
[14]The man said, "Who made
you ruler and judge over us?
Are you thinking of killing me
as you killed the Egyptian?"
Then Moses was afraid and
thought, "What I did must
have become known."
[15]When Pharaoh heard of
this, he tried to kill Moses, but
Moses fled from Pharaoh and
went to live in Midian, where
he sat down by a well. [16]Now
a priest of Midian had seven
daughters, and they came to
draw water and fill the troughs
to water their father's flock.
[17]Some shepherds came along
and drove them away, but
Moses got up and came to
their rescue and watered their
flock.
[18]When the girls returned to
Reuel their father, he asked
them, "Why have you re-
turned so early today?"
[19]They answered, "An Egyptian rescued us from the shepherds. He even drew water for
us and watered the flock."
[20]"And where is he?" he
asked his daughters. "Why
did you leave him? Invite him
to have something to eat."
[21]Moses agreed to stay with
the man, who gave his daughter Zipporah to Moses in marriage. [22]Zipporah gave birth to

וַתֵּלֶד בֵּן וַיִּקְרָא אֶת־ שְׁמוֹ גֵּרְשֹׁם כִּי אָמַר גֵּר
alien he-said for Gershom name-of-him *** and-he-called son and-she-bore (22)

הָיִיתִי בְּאֶרֶץ נָכְרִיָּה׃ וַיְהִי בַיָּמִים הָרַבִּים הָהֵם
the-those the-many during-the-days and-he-was (23) foreign in-land I-became

וַיָּמָת מֶלֶךְ מִצְרַיִם וַיֵּאָנְחוּ בְנֵי־ יִשְׂרָאֵל מִן־ הָעֲבֹדָה
the-slavery from Israel sons-of and-they-groaned Egypt king-of that-he-died

וַיִּזְעָקוּ וַתַּעַל שַׁוְעָתָם אֶל־ הָאֱלֹהִים מִן־ הָעֲבֹדָה׃
the-slavery from the-God to cry-of-them and-she-went-up and-they-cried-out

וַיִּשְׁמַע אֱלֹהִים אֶת־ נַאֲקָתָם וַיִּזְכֹּר אֱלֹהִים אֶת־
*** God and-he-remembered groan-of-them *** God and-he-heard (24)

בְּרִיתוֹ אֶת־ אַבְרָהָם אֶת־ יִצְחָק וְאֶת־ יַעֲקֹב׃ וַיַּרְא
so-he-looked (25) Jacob and-with Isaac with Abraham with covenant-of-him

אֱלֹהִים אֶת־ בְּנֵי יִשְׂרָאֵל וַיֵּדַע אֱלֹהִים׃ וּמֹשֶׁה הָיָה
he-was now-Moses (3:1) God and-he-was-concerned Israel sons-of *** God

רֹעֶה אֶת־ צֹאן יִתְרוֹ חֹתְנוֹ כֹּהֵן מִדְיָן וַיִּנְהַג
and-he-led Midian priest-of father-in-law-of-him Jethro flock-of *** tending

אֶת־ הַצֹּאן אַחַר הַמִּדְבָּר וַיָּבֹא אֶל־ הַר הָאֱלֹהִים חֹרֵבָה׃
to-Horeb the-God mountain-of to and-he-came the-desert far-side the-flock ***

וַיֵּרָא מַלְאַךְ יְהוָה אֵלָיו בְּלַבַּת־ אֵשׁ מִתּוֹךְ
from-within fire in-flame-of to-him Yahweh angel-of and-he-appeared (2)

הַסְּנֶה וַיַּרְא וְהִנֵּה הַסְּנֶה בֹּעֵר בָּאֵשׁ וְהַסְּנֶה
yet-the-bush with-the-fire burning the-bush and-see! and-he-saw the-bush

אֵינֶנּוּ אֻכָּל׃ וַיֹּאמֶר מֹשֶׁה אָסֻרָה־ נָּא
now! I-will-go-over Moses so-he-thought (3) being-consumed not-he

וְאֶרְאֶה אֶת־ הַמַּרְאֶה הַגָּדֹל הַזֶּה מַדּוּעַ לֹא־ יִבְעַר הַסְּנֶה׃
the-bush he-burns-up not why the-this the-strange the-sight *** and-I-will-see

וַיַּרְא יְהוָה כִּי סָר לִרְאוֹת וַיִּקְרָא אֵלָיו
to-him then-he-called to-look he-went-over that Yahweh when-he-saw (4)

אֱלֹהִים מִתּוֹךְ הַסְּנֶה וַיֹּאמֶר מֹשֶׁה מֹשֶׁה וַיֹּאמֶר הִנֵּנִי׃
here-I and-he-said Moses Moses and-he-said the-bush from-within God

וַיֹּאמֶר אַל־ תִּקְרַב הֲלֹם שַׁל־ נְעָלֶיךָ מֵעַל
from-on sandals-of-you take-off! closer you-come not and-he-said (5)

רַגְלֶיךָ כִּי הַמָּקוֹם אֲשֶׁר אַתָּה עוֹמֵד עָלָיו אַדְמַת־ קֹדֶשׁ הוּא׃
he holy ground-of on-him standing you where the-place for feet-of-you

וַיֹּאמֶר אָנֹכִי אֱלֹהֵי אָבִיךָ אֱלֹהֵי אַבְרָהָם אֱלֹהֵי יִצְחָק וֵאלֹהֵי
and-God-of Isaac God-of Abraham God-of father-of-you God-of I then-he-said (6)

יַעֲקֹב וַיַּסְתֵּר מֹשֶׁה פָּנָיו כִּי יָרֵא מֵהַבִּיט אֶל־ הָאֱלֹהִים׃
the-God at from-to-look he-was-afraid for face-of-him Moses and-he-hid Jacob

a son, and Moses named him Gershom,[c] saying, "I have become an alien in a foreign land."

[23]During that long period, the king of Egypt died. The Israelites groaned in their slavery and cried out, and their cry for help because of their slavery went up to God. [24]God heard their groaning and he remembered his covenant with Abraham, with Isaac and with Jacob. [25]So God looked on the Israelites and was concerned about them.

*Moses and the Burning Bush*

3 Now Moses was tending the flock of Jethro his father-in-law, the priest of Midian, and he led the flock to the far side of the desert and came to Horeb, the mountain of God. [2]There the angel of the LORD appeared to him in flames of fire from within a bush. Moses saw that though the bush was on fire it did not burn up. [3]So Moses thought, "I will go over and see this strange sight—why the bush does not burn up."

[4]When the LORD saw that he had gone over to look, God called to him from within the bush, "Moses, Moses!"

And Moses said, "Here I am."

[5]"Do not come any closer," God said. "Take off your sandals, for the place where you are standing is holy ground." [6]Then he said, "I am the God of your father, the God of Abraham, the God of Isaac and the God of Jacob." At this, Moses hid his face, because he was afraid to look at God.

[c]22 *Gershom* sounds like the Hebrew for *an alien there.*

וַיֹּאמֶר יְהוָה רָאֹה רָאִיתִי אֶת־ עֳנִי עַמִּי אֲשֶׁר בְּמִצְרָיִם
in-Egypt who people-of-me misery-of *** I-saw to-see Yahweh and-he-said (7)

וְאֶת־ צַעֲקָתָם שָׁמַעְתִּי מִפְּנֵי נֹגְשָׂיו כִּי יָדַעְתִּי
I-am-concerned indeed ones-driving-him because-of I-heard cry-of-them and

אֶת־ מַכְאֹבָיו׃ וָאֵרֵד לְהַצִּילוֹ ׀ מִיַּד מִצְרַיִם
Egyptians from-hand-of to-rescue-him so-I-came-down (8) sufferings-of-him ***

וּלְהַעֲלֹתוֹ מִן־ הָאָרֶץ הַהִוא אֶל־ אֶרֶץ טוֹבָה וּרְחָבָה אֶל־
into and-spacious good land into the-that the-land from and-to-bring-him

אֶרֶץ זָבַת חָלָב וּדְבָשׁ אֶל־ מְקוֹם הַכְּנַעֲנִי וְהַחִתִּי
and-the-Hittite the-Canaanite home-of into and-honey milk flowing-of land

וְהָאֱמֹרִי וְהַפְּרִזִּי וְהַחִוִּי וְהַיְבוּסִי׃ וְעַתָּה
and-now (9) and-the-Jebusite and-the-Hivite and-the-Perizzite and-the-Amorite

הִנֵּה צַעֲקַת בְּנֵי־ יִשְׂרָאֵל בָּאָה אֵלָי וְגַם־ רָאִיתִי אֶת־ הַלַּחַץ
the-oppression *** I-saw and-also to-me she-reached Israel sons-of cry-of see!

אֲשֶׁר מִצְרַיִם לֹחֲצִים אֹתָם׃ וְעַתָּה לְכָה וְאֶשְׁלָחֲךָ אֶל־
to for-I-send-you go! so-now (10) them ones-oppressing Egyptians that

פַּרְעֹה וְהוֹצֵא אֶת־ עַמִּי בְנֵי־ יִשְׂרָאֵל מִמִּצְרָיִם׃ וַיֹּאמֶר
but-he-said (11) from-Egypt Israel sons-of people-of-me *** and-bring! Pharaoh

מֹשֶׁה אֶל־הָאֱלֹהִים מִי אָנֹכִי כִּי אֵלֵךְ אֶל־פַּרְעֹה וְכִי אוֹצִיא
I-should-bring and-that Pharaoh to I-should-go that I who? the-God to Moses

אֶת־ בְּנֵי יִשְׂרָאֵל מִמִּצְרָיִם׃ וַיֹּאמֶר כִּי־ אֶהְיֶה עִמָּךְ
with-you I-will-be indeed and-he-said (12) from-Egypt Israel sons-of ***

וְזֶה־ לְּךָ הָאוֹת כִּי אָנֹכִי שְׁלַחְתִּיךָ בְּהוֹצִיאֲךָ אֶת־ הָעָם
the-people *** when-to-bring-you I-sent-you I that the-sign to-you and-this

מִמִּצְרַיִם תַּעַבְדוּן אֶת־ הָאֱלֹהִים עַל הָהָר הַזֶּה׃
the-this the-mountain on the-God *** you-will-worship from-Egypt

וַיֹּאמֶר מֹשֶׁה אֶל־הָאֱלֹהִים הִנֵּה אָנֹכִי בָא אֶל־ בְּנֵי יִשְׂרָאֵל וְאָמַרְתִּי
and-I-say Israel sons-of to going I suppose the-God to Moses but-he-said (13)

לָהֶם אֱלֹהֵי אֲבוֹתֵיכֶם שְׁלָחַנִי אֲלֵיכֶם וְאָמְרוּ־ לִי מַה־
what? to-me and-they-ask to-you he-sent-me fathers-of-you God-of to-them

שְּׁמוֹ מָה אֹמַר אֲלֵהֶם׃ וַיֹּאמֶר אֱלֹהִים אֶל־מֹשֶׁה אֶהְיֶה
I-am Moses to God and-he-said (14) to-them shall-I-tell what? name-of-him

אֲשֶׁר אֶהְיֶה וַיֹּאמֶר כֹּה תֹאמַר לִבְנֵי יִשְׂרָאֵל אֶהְיֶה שְׁלָחַנִי
he-sent-me I-am Israel to-sons-of you-shall-say this and-he-said I-am who

אֲלֵיכֶם׃ וַיֹּאמֶר עוֹד אֱלֹהִים אֶל־מֹשֶׁה כֹּה־ תֹאמַר אֶל־ בְּנֵי
sons-of to you-shall-say this Moses to God also and-he-said (15) to-you

יִשְׂרָאֵל יְהוָה אֱלֹהֵי אֲבֹתֵיכֶם אֱלֹהֵי אַבְרָהָם אֱלֹהֵי יִצְחָק וֵאלֹהֵי
and-God-of Isaac God-of Abraham God-of fathers-of-you God-of Yahweh Israel

7 The LORD said, "I have indeed seen the misery of my
people in Egypt. I have heard
them crying out because of
their slave drivers, and I am
concerned about their
suffering. 8 So I have come
down to rescue them from the
hand of the Egyptians and to
bring them up out of that land
into a good and spacious land,
a land flowing with milk and
honey—the home of the Ca-
naanites, Hittites, Amorites,
Perizzites, Hivites and Jebusites. 9 And now the cry of the
Israelites has reached me, and
I have seen the way the Egyptians are oppressing them.
10 So now, go. I am sending you
to Pharaoh to bring my people
the Israelites out of Egypt."
11 But Moses said to God,
"Who am I, that I should go to
Pharaoh and bring the Israelites out of Egypt?"
12 And God said, "I will be
with you. And this will be the
sign to you that it is I who
have sent you: When you have
brought the people out of
Egypt, you[d] will worship God
on this mountain."
13 Moses said to God, "Suppose I go to the Israelites and
say to them, 'The God of your
fathers has sent me to you,'
and they ask me, 'What is his
name?' Then what shall I tell
them?"
14 God said to Moses, "I am
who I am.[e] This is what you
are to say to the Israelites: 'I
AM has sent me to you.'"
15 God also said to Moses,
"Say to the Israelites, 'The
LORD,[f] the God of your fathers—the God of Abraham,
the God of Isaac and the God

[d] 12 The Hebrew is plural.
[e] 14 Or *I will be what I will be*
[f] 15 The Hebrew for *LORD* sounds like and may be derived from the Hebrew for *I AM* in verse 14.

יַעֲקֹב שְׁלָחַנִי אֲלֵיכֶם זֶה־שְּׁמִי לְעֹלָם וְזֶה זִכְרִי
memorial-of-me and-this for-ever name-of-me this to-you he-sent-me Jacob

לְדֹר דֹּר׃ לֵךְ וְאָסַפְתָּ אֶת־זִקְנֵי יִשְׂרָאֵל
Israel elders-of *** and-you-assemble go! (16) generation for-generation

וְאָמַרְתָּ אֲלֵהֶם יְהוָה אֱלֹהֵי אֲבֹתֵיכֶם נִרְאָה אֵלַי אֱלֹהֵי
God-of to-me he-appeared fathers-of-you God-of Yahweh to-them and-you-say

אַבְרָהָם יִצְחָק וְיַעֲקֹב לֵאמֹר פָּקֹד פָּקַדְתִּי אֶתְכֶם וְאֶת־הֶעָשׂוּי
the-being-done and over-you I-watched to-watch to-say and-Jacob Isaac Abraham

לָכֶם בְּמִצְרָיִם׃ וָאֹמַר אַעֲלֶה אֶתְכֶם מֵעֳנִי מִצְרַיִם
Egypt from-misery-of you I-will-bring-up and-I-promised (17) in-Egypt to-you

אֶל־אֶרֶץ הַכְּנַעֲנִי וְהַחִתִּי וְהָאֱמֹרִי וְהַפְּרִזִּי
and-the-Perizzite and-the-Amorite and-the-Hittite the-Canaanite land-of into

וְהַחִוִּי וְהַיְבוּסִי אֶל־אֶרֶץ זָבַת חָלָב וּדְבָשׁ׃
and-honey milk flowing-of land into and-the-Jebusite and-the-Hivite

וְשָׁמְעוּ לְקֹלֶךָ וּבָאתָ אַתָּה וְזִקְנֵי
and-elders-of you than-you-will-go to-voice-of-you and-they-will-listen (18)

יִשְׂרָאֵל אֶל־מֶלֶךְ מִצְרַיִם וַאֲמַרְתֶּם אֵלָיו יְהוָה אֱלֹהֵי הָעִבְרִיִּים
the-Hebrews God-of Yahweh to-him and-you-will-say Egypt king-of to Israel

נִקְרָה עָלֵינוּ וְעַתָּה נֵלְכָה־נָּא דֶּרֶךְ שְׁלֹשֶׁת יָמִים
days three-of journey-of now! let-us-take and-now with-us he-met

בַּמִּדְבָּר וְנִזְבְּחָה לַיהוָה אֱלֹהֵינוּ׃ וַאֲנִי יָדַעְתִּי
I-know but-I (19) God-of-us to-Yahweh and-let-us-sacrifice into-the-desert

כִּי לֹא־יִתֵּן אֶתְכֶם מֶלֶךְ מִצְרַיִם לַהֲלֹךְ וְלֹא בְּיָד חֲזָקָה׃
mighty by-hand if-not to-go Egypt king-of you he-will-let not that

וְשָׁלַחְתִּי אֶת־יָדִי וְהִכֵּיתִי אֶת־מִצְרַיִם
Egyptians *** and-I-will-strike hand-of-me *** so-I-will-stretch-out (20)

בְּכֹל נִפְלְאֹתַי אֲשֶׁר אֶעֱשֶׂה בְּקִרְבּוֹ וְאַחֲרֵי־
and-after in-midst-of-him I-will-perform that being-wonders-of-me with-all-of

כֵן יְשַׁלַּח אֶתְכֶם׃ וְנָתַתִּי אֶת־חֵן הָעָם־
the-people favorable *** and-I-will-make (21) you he-will-let-go that

הַזֶּה בְּעֵינֵי מִצְרָיִם וְהָיָה כִּי תֵלֵכוּן לֹא תֵלְכוּ
you-will-go not you-leave when so-he-will-be Egyptians in-eyes-of the-this

רֵיקָם׃ וְשָׁאֲלָה אִשָּׁה מִשְּׁכֶנְתָּהּ
from-neighbor-of-her woman so-she-shall-ask (22) empty-handed

וּמִגָּרַת בֵּיתָהּ כְּלֵי־כֶסֶף וּכְלֵי זָהָב
gold and-articles-of silver articles-of house-of-her and-from-one-living-of

וּשְׂמָלֹת וְשַׂמְתֶּם עַל־בְּנֵיכֶם וְעַל־בְּנֹתֵיכֶם
daughters-of-you and-on sons-of-you on and-you-shall-put and-clothing

of Jacob—has sent me to you.' This is my name forever, the name by which I am to be remembered from generation to generation.

16"Go, assemble the elders of Israel and say to them, 'The LORD, the God of your fathers, the God of Abraham, Isaac and Jacob, appeared to me and said: I have watched over you and have seen what has been done to you in Egypt. 17And I have promised to bring you up out of your misery in Egypt into the land of the Canaanites, Hittites, Amorites, Perizzites, Hivites and Jebusites—a land flowing with milk and honey.'

18"The elders of Israel will listen to you. Then you and the elders are to go to the king of Egypt and say to him, 'The LORD, the God of the Hebrews, has met with us. Let us take a three-day journey into the desert to offer sacrifices to the LORD our God.' 19But I know that the king of Egypt will not let you go unless a mighty hand compels him. 20So I will stretch out my hand and strike the Egyptians with all the wonders that I will perform among them. After that, he will let you go.

21"And I will make the Egyptians favorably disposed toward this people, so that when you leave you will not go empty-handed. 22Every woman is to ask her neighbor and any woman living in her house for articles of silver and gold and for clothing, which you will put on your sons and

וְנִצַּלְתֶּם אֶת־ מִצְרָיִם׃ וַיַּעַן מֹשֶׁה וַיֹּאמֶר
and-he-said Moses but-he-answered (4:1) Egyptians *** so-you-will-plunder

וְהֵן לֹא־ יַאֲמִינוּ לִי וְלֹא יִשְׁמְעוּ בְּקֹלִי כִּי
but to-voice-of-me they-listen and-not in-me they-believe not but-what-if

יֹאמְרוּ לֹא־ נִרְאָה אֵלֶיךָ יְהוָה׃ וַיֹּאמֶר אֵלָיו יְהוָה
Yahweh to-him then-he-said (2) Yahweh to-you he-appeared not they-say

מַזֶּה בְיָדֶךָ וַיֹּאמֶר מַטֶּה׃ וַיֹּאמֶר הַשְׁלִיכֵהוּ
throw-him! so-he-said (3) staff and-he-replied in-hand-of-you what-that?

אַרְצָה וַיַּשְׁלִיכֵהוּ אַרְצָה וַיְהִי לְנָחָשׁ וַיָּנָס מֹשֶׁה
Moses and-he-ran into-snake and-he-became on-ground so-he-threw-him on-ground

מִפָּנָיו׃ וַיֹּאמֶר יְהוָה אֶל־ מֹשֶׁה שְׁלַח יָדְךָ
hand-of-you reach-out! Moses to Yahweh then-he-said (4) from-before-him

וֶאֱחֹז בִּזְנָבוֹ וַיִּשְׁלַח יָדוֹ וַיַּחֲזֶק בּוֹ
onto-him and-he-held hand-of-him so-he-reached by-tail-of-him and-take!

וַיְהִי לְמַטֶּה בְּכַפּוֹ׃ לְמַעַן יַאֲמִינוּ כִּי־
that they-will-believe so-that (5) in-hand-of-him into-staff and-he-turned

נִרְאָה אֵלֶיךָ יְהוָה אֱלֹהֵי אֲבֹתָם אֱלֹהֵי אַבְרָהָם אֱלֹהֵי יִצְחָק
Isaac God-of Abraham God-of fathers-of-them God-of Yahweh to-you he-appeared

וֵאלֹהֵי יַעֲקֹב׃ וַיֹּאמֶר יְהוָה לוֹ עוֹד הָבֵא־נָא יָדְךָ
hand-of-you now! put! also to-him Yahweh then-he-said (6) Jacob and-God-of

בְּחֵיקֶךָ וַיָּבֵא יָדוֹ בְּחֵיקוֹ וַיּוֹצִאָהּ
when-he-took-out-her into-cloak-of-him hand-of-him so-he-put into-cloak-of-you

וְהִנֵּה יָדוֹ מְצֹרַעַת כַּשָּׁלֶג׃ וַיֹּאמֶר הָשֵׁב
put-back! than-he-said (7) like-the-snow being-leprous hand-of-him now-see!

יָדְךָ אֶל־ חֵיקֶךָ וַיָּשֶׁב יָדוֹ אֶל־ חֵיקוֹ
cloak-of-him into hand-of-him so-he-put-back cloak-of-you into hand-of-you

וַיּוֹצִאָהּ מֵחֵיקוֹ וְהִנֵּה־ שָׁבָה
she-was-restored now-see! from-cloak-of-him when-he-took-out-her

כִּבְשָׂרוֹ׃ וְהָיָה אִם־ לֹא יַאֲמִינוּ לָךְ וְלֹא
or-not in-you they-believe not if and-he-will-be (8) like-flesh-of-him

יִשְׁמְעוּ לְקֹל הָאֹת הָרִאשׁוֹן וְהֶאֱמִינוּ
then-they-may-believe the-first the-sign to-voice-of they-pay-attention

לְקֹל הָאֹת הָאַחֲרוֹן׃ וְהָיָה אִם־ לֹא יַאֲמִינוּ
they-believe not if but-he-will-be (9) the-second the-sign in-voice-of

גַּם לִשְׁנֵי הָאֹתוֹת הָאֵלֶּה וְלֹא יִשְׁמְעוּן לְקֹלֶךָ
to-voice-of-you they-listen or-not the-these the-signs in-two-of either

וְלָקַחְתָּ מִמֵּימֵי הַיְאֹר וְשָׁפַכְתָּ הַיַּבָּשָׁה
the-dry-ground and-you-pour the-Nile from-waters-of then-you-take

daughters. And so you will plunder the Egyptians."

*Signs for Moses*

4 Moses answered, "What if they do not believe me or listen to me and say, 'The LORD did not appear to you'?"
2Then the LORD said to him, "What is that in your hand?"
"A staff," he replied.
3The LORD said, "Throw it on the ground."
Moses threw it on the ground and it became a snake, and he ran from it. 4Then the LORD said to him, "Reach out your hand and take it by the tail." So Moses reached out and took hold of the snake and it turned back into a staff in his hand. 5"This," said the LORD, "is so that they may believe that the LORD, the God of their fathers—the God of Abraham, the God of Isaac and the God of Jacob—has appeared to you."
6Then the LORD said, "Put your hand inside your cloak." So Moses put his hand into his cloak, and when he took it out, it was leprous,[g] like snow.
7"Now put it back into your cloak," he said. So Moses put his hand back into his cloak, and when he took it out, it was restored, like the rest of his flesh.
8Then the LORD said, "If they do not believe you or pay attention to the first miraculous sign, they may believe the second. 9But if they do not believe these two signs or listen to you, take some water from the Nile and pour it on the dry

g6 The Hebrew word was used for various diseases affecting the skin—not necessarily leprosy.

°2 ק מה זה

וְהָיוּ הַמַּיִם אֲשֶׁר תִּקַּח מִן־הַיְאֹר וְהָיוּ
and-they-will-become the-Nile from you-take that the-waters and-they-will-become

לְדָם בַּיַּבָּשֶׁת׃ וַיֹּאמֶר מֹשֶׁה אֶל־יְהוָה בִּי אֲדֹנָי
Lord oh! Yahweh to Moses then-he-said (10) on-the-dry-ground into-blood

לֹא אִישׁ דְּבָרִים אָנֹכִי גַּם מִתְּמוֹל גַּם מִשִּׁלְשֹׁם גַּם מֵאָז דַּבֶּרְךָ*
to-speak-you from-since nor in-past nor in-yesterday neither I words man-of not

אֶל־עַבְדֶּךָ כִּי כְבַד־פֶּה וּכְבַד לָשׁוֹן אָנֹכִי׃
I tongue and-slow-of speech slow-of but servant-of-you to

וַיֹּאמֶר יְהוָה אֵלָיו מִי שָׂם פֶּה לָאָדָם אוֹ מִי־יָשׂוּם אִלֵּם
dumb he-makes who? or to-man mouth he-gave who? to-him Yahweh and-he-said (11)

אוֹ חֵרֵשׁ אוֹ פִקֵּחַ אוֹ עִוֵּר הֲלֹא אָנֹכִי יְהוָה׃ וְעַתָּה לֵךְ וְאָנֹכִי אֶהְיֶה
I-will-be and-I go! so-now (12) Yahweh I not? blind or sight or deaf or

עִם־פִּיךָ וְהוֹרֵיתִיךָ אֲשֶׁר תְּדַבֵּר׃ וַיֹּאמֶר
but-he-said (13) you-will-say what and-I-will-teach-you mouth-of-you with

בִּי אֲדֹנָי שְׁלַח־נָא בְּיַד־תִּשְׁלָח׃ וַיִּחַר־אַף יְהוָה
Yahweh anger-of then-he-burned (14) you-send by-another now! send! Lord oh!

בְּמֹשֶׁה וַיֹּאמֶר הֲלֹא אַהֲרֹן אָחִיךָ הַלֵּוִי יָדַעְתִּי כִּי־
that I-know the-Levite brother-of-you Aaron not? and-he-said against-Moses

דַבֵּר יְדַבֵּר הוּא וְגַם הִנֵּה־הוּא יֹצֵא לִקְרָאתֶךָ וְרָאֲךָ
when-he-sees-you to-meet-you going-out he see! and-also he he-speaks to-speak

וְשָׂמַח בְּלִבּוֹ׃ וְדִבַּרְתָּ אֵלָיו וְשַׂמְתָּ
and-you-put to-him so-you-speak (15) in-heart-of-him then-he-will-be-glad

אֶת־הַדְּבָרִים בְּפִיו וְאָנֹכִי אֶהְיֶה עִם־פִּיךָ וְעִם־
and-with mouth-of-you with I-will-be and-I in-mouth-of-him the-words ***

פִּיהוּ וְהוֹרֵיתִי אֶתְכֶם אֵת אֲשֶׁר תַּעֲשׂוּן׃ וְדִבֶּר־
and-he-will-speak (16) you-will-do what *** you and-I-will-teach mouth-of-him

הוּא לְךָ אֶל־הָעָם וְהָיָה הוּא יִהְיֶה־לְּךָ לְפֶה
as-mouth to-you he-will-be he and-he-will-be the-people to for-you he

וְאַתָּה תִּהְיֶה־לּוֹ לֵאלֹהִים׃ וְאֶת־הַמַּטֶּה הַזֶּה תִּקַּח
you-take the-this the-staff but (17) as-God to-him you-will-be and-you

בְּיָדֶךָ אֲשֶׁר תַּעֲשֶׂה־בּוֹ אֶת־הָאֹתֹת׃ וַיֵּלֶךְ
then-he-went (18) the-signs *** with-him you-can-perform that in-hand-of-you

מֹשֶׁה וַיָּשָׁב׀ אֶל־יֶתֶר חֹתְנוֹ וַיֹּאמֶר לוֹ
to-him and-he-said father-in-law-of-him Jethro to and-he-returned Moses

אֵלְכָה נָּא וְאָשׁוּבָה אֶל־אַחַי אֲשֶׁר־בְּמִצְרַיִם וְאֶרְאֶה
and-let-me-see in-Egypt who people-of-me to and-let-me-return now! let-me-go

הַעוֹדָם חַיִּים וַיֹּאמֶר יִתְרוֹ לְמֹשֶׁה לֵךְ לְשָׁלוֹם׃
in-peace go! to-Moses Jethro and-he-said alive-ones if-still-them

ground. The water you take from the river will become blood on the ground."

10 Moses said to the LORD, "O Lord, I have never been eloquent, neither in the past nor since you have spoken to your servant. I am slow of speech and tongue."

11 The LORD said to him, "Who gave man his mouth? Who makes him deaf or dumb? Who gives him sight or makes him blind? Is it not I, the LORD? 12 Now go; I will help you speak and will teach you what to say."

13 But Moses said, "O Lord, please send someone else to do it."

14 Then the LORD's anger burned against Moses and he said, "What about your brother, Aaron the Levite? I know he can speak well. He is already on his way to meet you, and his heart will be glad when he sees you. 15 You shall speak to him and put words in his mouth; I will help both of you speak and will teach you what to do. 16 He will speak to the people for you, and it will be as if he were your mouth and as if you were God to him. 17 But take this staff in your hand so you can perform miraculous signs with it."

### *Moses Returns to Egypt*

18 Then Moses went back to Jethro his father-in-law and said to him, "Let me go back to my own people in Egypt to see if any of them are still alive."

Jethro said, "Go, and I wish you well."

**10* Most mss have the accent *tiphha* (ךָ֖-).

וַיֹּאמֶר יְהוָה אֶל־מֹשֶׁה בְּמִדְיָן לֵךְ שֻׁב מִצְרָיִם כִּי־מֵתוּ
they-died for Egypt return! go! in-Midian Moses to Yahweh now-he-said (19)

כָּל־הָאֲנָשִׁים הַמְבַקְשִׁים אֶת־נַפְשֶׁךָ׃ וַיִּקַּח מֹשֶׁה אֶת־
*** Moses so-he-took (20) life-of-you *** the-ones-wanting the-men all-of

אִשְׁתּוֹ וְאֶת־בָּנָיו וַיַּרְכִּבֵם עַל־הַחֲמֹר וַיָּשָׁב
and-he-went-back the-donkey on and-he-put-them sons-of-him and wife-of-him

אַרְצָה מִצְרָיִם וַיִּקַּח מֹשֶׁה אֶת־מַטֵּה הָאֱלֹהִים בְּיָדוֹ׃
in-hand-of-him the-God staff-of *** Moses and-he-took Egypt to-land-of

וַיֹּאמֶר יְהוָה אֶל־מֹשֶׁה בְּלֶכְתְּךָ לָשׁוּב מִצְרַיְמָה רְאֵה
see! to-Egypt to-return when-to-go-you Moses to Yahweh and-he-said (21)

כָּל־הַמֹּפְתִים אֲשֶׁר־שַׂמְתִּי בְיָדֶךָ וַעֲשִׂיתָם לִפְנֵי
before that-you-perform-them in-hand-of-you I-gave that the-wonders all-of

פַרְעֹה וַאֲנִי אֲחַזֵּק אֶת־לִבּוֹ וְלֹא יְשַׁלַּח אֶת־
*** he-will-let-go so-not heart-of-him *** I-will-harden but-I Pharaoh

הָעָם׃ וְאָמַרְתָּ אֶל־פַּרְעֹה כֹּה אָמַר יְהוָה בְּנִי
son-of-me Yahweh he-says this Pharaoh to then-you-say (22) the-people

בְכֹרִי יִשְׂרָאֵל׃ וָאֹמַר אֵלֶיךָ שַׁלַּח אֶת־בְּנִי
son-of-me *** let-go! to-you and-I-told (23) Israel firstborn-of-me

וְיַעַבְדֵנִי וַתְּמָאֵן לְשַׁלְּחוֹ הִנֵּה אָנֹכִי הֹרֵג אֶת־
*** killing I see! to-let-go-him but-you-refused so-he-may-worship-me

בִּנְךָ בְּכֹרֶךָ׃ וַיְהִי בַדֶּרֶךְ בַּמָּלוֹן
at-the-lodging-place on-the-way and-he-was (24) firstborn-of-you son-of-you

וַיִּפְגְּשֵׁהוּ יְהוָה וַיְבַקֵּשׁ הֲמִיתוֹ׃ וַתִּקַּח צִפֹּרָה
Zipporah but-she-took (25) to-kill-him and-he-wanted Yahweh that-he-met-him

צֹר וַתִּכְרֹת אֶת־עָרְלַת בְּנָהּ וַתַּגַּע
and-she-touched son-of-her foreskin-of *** and-she-cut-off flint-knife

לְרַגְלָיו וַתֹּאמֶר כִּי חֲתַן־דָּמִים אַתָּה לִי׃
to-me you bloods bridegroom-of surely and-she-said on-feet-of-him

וַיִּרֶף מִמֶּנּוּ אָז אָמְרָה חֲתַן דָּמִים לַמּוּלֹת׃
about-the-circumcision bloods bridegroom-of she-said then from-him so-he-left (26)

וַיֹּאמֶר יְהוָה אֶל־אַהֲרֹן לֵךְ לִקְרַאת מֹשֶׁה הַמִּדְבָּרָה וַיֵּלֶךְ
so-he-went in-the-desert Moses to-meet go! Aaron to Yahweh and-he-said (27)

וַיִּפְגְּשֵׁהוּ בְּהַר הָאֱלֹהִים וַיִּשַּׁק־לוֹ׃ וַיַּגֵּד
then-he-told (28) on-him and-he-kissed the-God at-mountain-of and-he-met-him

מֹשֶׁה לְאַהֲרֹן אֵת כָּל־דִּבְרֵי יְהוָה אֲשֶׁר שְׁלָחוֹ וְאֵת כָּל־
all-of and he-sent-him that Yahweh words-of all-of *** to-Aaron Moses

הָאֹתֹת אֲשֶׁר צִוָּהוּ׃ וַיֵּלֶךְ מֹשֶׁה וְאַהֲרֹן
and-Aaron Moses so-he-went (29) he-commanded-him that the-signs

[19]Now the LORD had said to Moses in Midian, "Go back to Egypt, for all the men who wanted to kill you are dead." [20]So Moses took his wife and sons, put them on a donkey and started back to Egypt. And he took the staff of God in his hand.

[21]The LORD said to Moses, "When you return to Egypt, see that you perform before Pharaoh all the wonders I have given you the power to do. But I will harden his heart so that he will not let the people go. [22]Then say to Pharaoh, 'This is what the LORD says: Israel is my firstborn son, [23]and I told you, "Let my son go, so he may worship me." But you refused to let him go; so I will kill your firstborn son.' "

[24]At a lodging place on the way, the LORD met Moses and was about to kill him. [25]But Zipporah took a flint knife, cut off her son's foreskin and touched ⌊Moses'⌋ feet with it.[h] "Surely you are a bridegroom of blood to me," she said. [26]So the LORD let him alone. (At that time she said "bridegroom of blood," referring to circumcision.)

[27]The LORD said to Aaron, "Go into the desert to meet Moses." So he met Moses at the mountain of God and kissed him. [28]Then Moses told Aaron everything the LORD had sent him to say, and also about all the miraculous signs he had commanded him to perform.

[29]Moses and Aaron brought

[h]25 Or *and drew near ⌊Moses'⌋ feet*

וַיַּאַסְפוּ אֶת־ כָּל־ זִקְנֵי בְּנֵי יִשְׂרָאֵל׃ וַיְדַבֵּר

and-he-told (30) Israel sons-of elders-of all-of *** and-they-assembled

אַהֲרֹן אֵת כָּל־ הַדְּבָרִים אֲשֶׁר־ דִּבֶּר יְהוָה אֶל־מֹשֶׁה וַיַּעַשׂ

and-he-performed Moses to Yahweh he-said that the-words all-of *** Aaron

הָאֹתֹת לְעֵינֵי הָעָם׃ וַיַּאֲמֵן הָעָם

the-people and-he-believed (31) the-people before-eyes-of the-signs

וַיִּשְׁמְעוּ כִּי־ פָקַד יְהוָה אֶת־ בְּנֵי יִשְׂרָאֵל וְכִי

and-that Israel sons-of *** Yahweh he-was-concerned that when-they-heard

רָאָה אֶת־ עָנְיָם וַיִּקְּדוּ וַיִּשְׁתַּחֲווּ*׃ וְאַחַר

and-afterwards (5:1) and-they-worshiped then-they-bowed misery-of-them *** he-saw

בָּאוּ מֹשֶׁה וְאַהֲרֹן וַיֹּאמְרוּ אֶל־ פַּרְעֹה כֹּה־ אָמַר יְהוָה

Yahweh he-says this Pharaoh to and-they-said and-Aaron Moses they-went

אֱלֹהֵי יִשְׂרָאֵל שַׁלַּח אֶת־ עַמִּי וְיָחֹגּוּ לִי

to-me so-they-may-hold-festival people-of-me *** let-go! Israel God-of

בַּמִּדְבָּר׃ וַיֹּאמֶר פַּרְעֹה מִי יְהוָה אֲשֶׁר אֶשְׁמַע

I-should-obey that Yahweh who? Pharaoh but-he-said (2) in-the-desert

בְּקֹלוֹ לְשַׁלַּח אֶת־יִשְׂרָאֵל לֹא יָדַעְתִּי אֶת־ יְהוָה וְגַם אֶת־יִשְׂרָאֵל

Israel *** and-so Yahweh *** I-know not Israel *** to-let-go to-voice-of-him

לֹא אֲשַׁלֵּחַ׃ וַיֹּאמְרוּ אֱלֹהֵי הָעִבְרִים נִקְרָא עָלֵינוּ

with-us he-met the-Hebrews God-of then-they-said (3) I-will-let-go not

נֵלֲכָה נָּא דֶּרֶךְ שְׁלֹשֶׁת יָמִים בַּמִּדְבָּר וְנִזְבְּחָה

and-let-us-sacrifice into-the-desert days three-of journey-of now! let-us-take

לַיהוָה אֱלֹהֵינוּ פֶּן־ יִפְגָּעֵנוּ בַּדֶּבֶר אוֹ בֶחָרֶב׃

with-the-sword or with-the-plague he-may-strike-us or God-of-us to-Yahweh

וַיֹּאמֶר אֲלֵהֶם מֶלֶךְ מִצְרַיִם לָמָּה מֹשֶׁה וְאַהֲרֹן תַּפְרִיעוּ אֶת־

*** you-take and-Aaron Moses why? Egypt king-of to-them but-he-said (4)

הָעָם מִמַּעֲשָׂיו לְכוּ לְסִבְלֹתֵיכֶם׃ וַיֹּאמֶר

then-he-said (5) to-burdens-of-you get-back! from-labors-of-him the-people

פַּרְעֹה הֵן־ רַבִּים עַתָּה עַם הָאָרֶץ וְהִשְׁבַּתֶּם אֹתָם

them and-you-stop the-land people-of now numerous-ones see! Pharaoh

מִסִּבְלֹתָם׃ וַיְצַו פַּרְעֹה בַּיּוֹם הַהוּא אֶת־

*** the-same on-the-day Pharaoh and-he-ordered (6) from-burdens-of-them

הַנֹּגְשִׂים בָּעָם וְאֶת־ שֹׁטְרָיו לֵאמֹר׃ לֹא

not (7) to-say foremen-of-him and over-the-people the-ones-driving

תֹאספוּן לָתֵת תֶּבֶן לָעָם לִלְבֹּן הַלְּבֵנִים כִּתְמוֹל

as-yesterday the-bricks to-make to-the-people straw to-supply you-continue

שִׁלְשֹׁם הֵם יֵלְכוּ וְקֹשְׁשׁוּ לָהֶם תֶּבֶן׃ וְאֶת־

but (8) straw for-themselves and-let-them-gather let-them-go they before

together all the elders of the Israelites, [30]and Aaron told them everything the LORD had said to Moses. He also performed the signs before the people, [31]and they believed. And when they heard that the LORD was concerned about them and had seen their misery, they bowed down and worshiped.

*Bricks Without Straw*

5 Afterward Moses and Aaron went to Pharaoh and said, "This is what the LORD, the God of Israel, says: 'Let my people go, so that they may hold a festival to me in the desert.' "

[2]Pharaoh said, "Who is the LORD, that I should obey him and let Israel go? I do not know the LORD and I will not let Israel go."

[3]Then they said, "The God of the Hebrews has met with us. Now let us take a three-day journey into the desert to offer sacrifices to the LORD our God, or he may strike us with plagues or with the sword."

[4]But the king of Egypt said, "Moses and Aaron, why are you taking the people away from their labor? Get back to your work!" [5]Then Pharaoh said, "Look, the people of the land are now numerous, and you are stopping them from working."

[6]That same day Pharaoh gave this order to the slave drivers and foremen in charge of the people: [7]"You are no longer to supply the people with straw for making bricks; let them go and gather their

*31 Most mss have no *dagesh* in the first *vav* (וּו־).

מַתְכֹּנֶת הַלְּבֵנִים אֲשֶׁר הֵם עֹשִׂים תְּמוֹל שִׁלְשֹׁם תָּשִׂימוּ עֲלֵיהֶם
from-them you-require before yesterday ones-making they that the-bricks number-of

לֹא תִגְרְעוּ מִמֶּנּוּ כִּי־ נִרְפִּים הֵם עַל־ כֵּן הֵם צֹעֲקִים
ones-crying they this for they being-lazy-ones for from-him you-reduce not

לֵאמֹר נֵלְכָה נִזְבְּחָה לֵאלֹהֵינוּ׃ תִּכְבַּד הָעֲבֹדָה
the-work let-her-be-hard (9) to-God-of-us let-us-sacrifice let-us-go to-say

עַל־ הָאֲנָשִׁים וְיַעֲשׂוּ־ בָהּ וְאַל־ יִשְׁעוּ בְּדִבְרֵי־
to-words-of they-will-attend and-not at-her so-they-will-work the-men for

שָׁקֶר׃ וַיֵּצְאוּ נֹגְשֵׂי הָעָם וְשֹׁטְרָיו
and-foremen-of-him the-people ones-driving-of then-they-went-out (10) lie

וַיֹּאמְרוּ אֶל־ הָעָם לֵאמֹר כֹּה אָמַר פַּרְעֹה אֵינֶנִּי נֹתֵן לָכֶם
to-you giving not-I Pharaoh he-says this to-say the-people to and-they-said

תֶּבֶן׃ אַתֶּם לְכוּ קְחוּ לָכֶם תֶּבֶן מֵאֲשֶׁר תִּמְצָאוּ כִּי אֵין
not but you-find from-where straw for-yourselves get! go! you (11) straw

נִגְרָע מֵעֲבֹדַתְכֶם דָּבָר׃ וַיָּפֶץ הָעָם
the-people so-he-scattered (12) at-all from-work-of-you being-reduced

בְּכָל־ אֶרֶץ מִצְרָיִם לְקֹשֵׁשׁ קַשׁ לַתֶּבֶן׃
for-the-straw stubble to-gather Egypt land-of over-all-of

וְהַנֹּגְשִׂים אָצִים לֵאמֹר כַּלּוּ מַעֲשֵׂיכֶם דְּבַר־
required-of work-of-you complete! to-say ones-pressing and-the-ones-driving (13)

יוֹם בְּיוֹמוֹ כַּאֲשֶׁר בִּהְיוֹת הַתֶּבֶן׃ וַיֻּכּוּ
and-they-were-beaten (14) the-straw when-to-have just-as in-day-of-him day

שֹׁטְרֵי בְּנֵי יִשְׂרָאֵל אֲשֶׁר־ שָׂמוּ עֲלֵהֶם נֹגְשֵׂי
ones-driving-of over-them they-appointed whom Israel sons-of foremen-of

פַרְעֹה לֵאמֹר מַדּוּעַ לֹא כִלִּיתֶם חָקְכֶם לִלְבֹּן כִּתְמוֹל
as-yesterday to-make-brick quota-of-you you-met not why? to-say Pharaoh

שִׁלְשֹׁם גַּם־ תְּמוֹל גַּם־ הַיּוֹם׃ וַיָּבֹאוּ שֹׁטְרֵי בְּנֵי
sons-of foremen-of then-they-went (15) the-day or yesterday either before

יִשְׂרָאֵל וַיִּצְעֲקוּ אֶל־ פַּרְעֹה לֵאמֹר לָמָּה תַעֲשֶׂה כֹה לַעֲבָדֶיךָ׃
to-servants-of-you this you-do why? to-say Pharaoh to and-they-appealed Israel

תֶּבֶן אֵין נִתָּן לַעֲבָדֶיךָ וּלְבֵנִים אֹמְרִים לָנוּ
to-us ones-telling yet-bricks to-servants-of-you being-given no straw (16)

עֲשׂוּ וְהִנֵּה עֲבָדֶיךָ מֻכִּים וְחָטָאת
but-he-is-at-fault ones-being-beaten servants-of-you and-see! make!

עַמֶּךָ׃ וַיֹּאמֶר נִרְפִּים אַתֶּם נִרְפִּים עַל־ כֵּן
this for ones-being-lazy you ones-being-lazy but-he-said (17) people-of-you

אַתֶּם אֹמְרִים נֵלְכָה נִזְבְּחָה לַיהוָה׃ וְעַתָּה לְכוּ עִבְדוּ
work! go! so-now (18) to-Yahweh let-us-sacrifice let-us-go ones-saying you

own straw. 8But require them to make the same number of bricks as before; don't reduce the quota. They are lazy; that is why they are crying out, 'Let us go and sacrifice to our God.' 9Make the work harder for the men so that they keep working and pay no attention to lies."

10Then the slave drivers and the foremen went out and said to the people, "This is what Pharaoh says: 'I will not give you any more straw. 11Go and get your own straw wherever you can find it, but your work will not be reduced at all.'" 12So the people scattered all over Egypt to gather stubble to use for straw. 13The slave drivers kept pressing them, saying, "Complete the work required of you for each day, just as when you had straw." 14The Israelite foremen appointed by Pharaoh's slave drivers were beaten and were asked, "Why haven't you met your quota of bricks yesterday or today, as before?"

15Then the Israelite foremen went and appealed to Pharaoh: "Why have you treated your servants this way? 16Your servants are given no straw, yet we are told, 'Make bricks!' Your servants are being beaten, but the fault is with your own people."

17Pharaoh said, "Lazy, that's what you are—lazy! That is why you keep saying, 'Let us go and sacrifice to the LORD.' 18Now get to work. You will

| תִּתֵּֽנּוּ׃ | לְבֵנִ֖ים | וְתֹ֥כֶן | לָכֶ֔ם | יִנָּתֵ֣ן | לֹֽא | וְתֶ֖בֶן |
|---|---|---|---|---|---|---|
| you-must-produce | bricks | yet-quota-of | to-you | he-will-be-given | not | but-straw |

| לֵאמֹ֑ר | בְּרָ֖ע | אֹתָ֛ם | יִשְׂרָאֵ֧ל | בְּנֵֽי | שֹׁטְרֵ֨י | וַיִּרְא֞וּ |
|---|---|---|---|---|---|---|
| to-say | in-trouble | they | Israel | sons-of | foremen-of | and-they-realized (19) |

| בְּיוֹמֽוֹ׃ | יֽוֹם | דְּבַר | מִלִּבְנֵיכֶ֖ם | תִגְרְע֥וּ | לֹֽא |
|---|---|---|---|---|---|
| in-day-of-him | day | required-of | from-bricks-of-you | you-can-reduce | not |

| לִקְרָאתָֽם׃ | נִצָּבִ֖ים | אַהֲרֹ֔ן | וְאֶֽת | מֹשֶׁ֣ה | אֶת | וַֽיִּפְגְּעוּ֙ |
|---|---|---|---|---|---|---|
| to-meet-them | ones-waiting | Aaron | and | Moses | *** | and-they-found (20) |

| יֵ֣רֶא | אֲלֵהֶ֔ם | וַיֹּאמְר֣וּ | פַּרְעֹֽה׃ | מֵאֵ֥ת | בְּצֵאתָ֖ם |
|---|---|---|---|---|---|
| may-he-look | to-them | and-they-said (21) | Pharaoh | from | when-to-leave-them |

| רֵיחֵ֗נוּ | אֶת | הִבְאַשְׁתֶּ֣ם | אֲשֶׁ֞ר | וְיִשְׁפֹּ֑ט | עֲלֵיכֶ֖ם | יְהוָ֛ה |
|---|---|---|---|---|---|---|
| stench-of-us | *** | you-made-stink | for | and-may-he-judge | on-you | Yahweh |

| בְּיָדָֽם׃ | חֶ֖רֶב | לָֽתֶת | עֲבָדָ֔יו | וּבְעֵינֵ֣י | פַּרְעֹה֙ | בְּעֵינֵ֤י |
|---|---|---|---|---|---|---|
| in-hand-of-them | sword | to-put | servants-of-him | and-in-eyes-of | Pharaoh | in-eyes-of |

| לָמָ֣ה | אֲדֹנָ֗י | וַיֹּאמַ֑ר | יְהוָ֖ה | אֶל | מֹשֶׁ֛ה | וַיָּ֧שָׁב | לְהָרְגֵֽנוּ׃ |
|---|---|---|---|---|---|---|---|
| why? | Lord | and-he-said | Yahweh | to | Moses | so-he-returned (22) | to-kill-us |

| שְׁלַחְתָּֽנִי׃ | זֶּ֖ה | לָ֥מָּה | הַזֶּ֔ה | לָעָ֣ם | הֲרֵעֹ֙תָה֙ |
|---|---|---|---|---|---|
| you-sent-me | this | why? | the-this | on-the-people | you-brought-trouble |

| הֵרַע֙ | בִּשְׁמֶ֔ךָ | לְדַבֵּ֣ר | פַּרְעֹה֙ | אֶל | בָ֤אתִי | וּמֵאָ֞ז |
|---|---|---|---|---|---|---|
| he-brought-trouble | in-name-of-you | to-speak | Pharaoh | to | I-went | for-ever-since (23) |

| עַמֶּֽךָ׃ | אֶת | הִצַּ֖לְתָּ | לֹֽא | וְהַצֵּ֥ל | הַזֶּ֔ה | לָעָ֣ם |
|---|---|---|---|---|---|---|
| people-of-you | *** | you-rescued | not | and-to-rescue | the-this | on-the-people |

| לְפַרְעֹֽה׃ | אֶֽעֱשֶׂ֖ה | אֲשֶׁ֥ר | תִרְאֶ֔ה | עַתָּ֣ה | מֹשֶׁ֔ה | אֶל | יְהוָה֙ | וַיֹּ֤אמֶר |
|---|---|---|---|---|---|---|---|---|
| to-Pharaoh | I-will-do | what | you-will-see | now | Moses | to | Yahweh | then-he-said (6:1) |

| חֲזָקָ֔ה | וּבְיָ֣ד | יְשַׁלְּחֵ֑ם | חֲזָקָ֖ה | בְיָ֥ד | כִּ֣י |
|---|---|---|---|---|---|
| mighty | and-because-of-hand | he-will-let-go-them | mighty | because-of-hand | for |

| מֹשֶׁ֑ה | אֶל | אֱלֹהִ֖ים | וַיְדַבֵּ֥ר | מֵאַרְצֽוֹ׃ | יְגָרְשֵׁ֖ם |
|---|---|---|---|---|---|
| Moses | to | God | and-he-spoke (2) | from-country-of-him | he-will-drive-them |

| וְאֶֽל | וְיִצְחָ֖ק | אַבְרָהָ֥ם | אֶל | וָאֵרָ֗א | יְהוָֽה׃ | אֲנִ֥י | אֵלָ֖יו | וַיֹּ֥אמֶר |
|---|---|---|---|---|---|---|---|---|
| and-to | Isaac | to | Abraham | to | and-I-appeared (3) | Yahweh | I | to-him | and-he-said |

| לָהֶֽם׃ | נוֹדַ֖עְתִּי | לֹ֥א | יְהוָ֔ה | וּשְׁמִ֣י | שַׁדָּ֑י | בְּאֵ֣ל | יַעֲקֹ֖ב |
|---|---|---|---|---|---|---|---|
| to-them | I-made-myself-known | not | Yahweh | but-name-of-me | Almighty | as-God | Jacob |

| אֶת | לָהֶ֖ם | לָתֵ֥ת | אִתָּ֔ם | בְּרִיתִי֙ | אֶת | הֲקִמֹ֤תִי | וְגַ֨ם |
|---|---|---|---|---|---|---|---|
| *** | to-them | to-give | with-them | covenant-of-me | *** | I-established | and-also (4) |

| בָּֽהּ׃ | גָּ֥רוּ | אֲשֶׁר | מְגֻרֵיהֶ֖ם | אֶ֥רֶץ | אֵ֛ת | כְּנָ֑עַן | אֶ֣רֶץ |
|---|---|---|---|---|---|---|---|
| in-her | they-lived | where | journeys-of-them | land-of | *** | Canaan | land-of |

| מִצְרַ֖יִם | אֲשֶׁ֥ר | יִשְׂרָאֵ֔ל | בְּנֵ֣י | נַאֲקַת֙ | אֶֽת | שָׁמַ֗עְתִּי | אֲנִ֣י | וְגַ֣ם |
|---|---|---|---|---|---|---|---|---|
| Egyptians | whom | Israel | sons-of | groan-of | *** | I-heard | I | and-also (5) |

---

not be given any straw, yet you must produce your full quota of bricks." [19]The Israelite foremen realized they were in trouble when they were told, "You are not to reduce the number of bricks required of you for each day." [20]When they left Pharaoh, they found Moses and Aaron waiting to meet them, [21]and they said, "May the LORD look upon you and judge you! You have made us a stench to Pharaoh and his servants and have put a sword in their hand to kill us."

*God Promises Deliverance*

[22]Moses returned to the LORD and said, "O Lord, why have you brought trouble upon this people? Is this why you sent me? [23]Ever since I went to Pharaoh to speak in your name, he has brought trouble upon this people, and you have not rescued your people at all."

**6** Then the LORD said to Moses, "Now you will see what I will do to Pharaoh: Because of my mighty hand he will let them go; because of my mighty hand he will drive them out of his country."

[2]God also said to Moses, "I am the LORD. [3]I appeared to Abraham, to Isaac and to Jacob as God Almighty,[i] but by my name the LORD[j] I did not make myself known to them.[k] [4]I also established my covenant with them to give them the land of Canaan, where they lived as aliens. [5]Moreover, I have heard the groaning of the Israelites,

*i3* Hebrew *El-Shaddai*
*j3* See note at Exodus 3:15.
*k3* Or *Almighty, and by my name the LORD did*
*I not let myself be known to them?*

*18 Most mss have no *dagesh* in the
nun (תִתֵּֽנּוּ).

מַעֲבִדִים אֹתָם וָאֶזְכֹּר אֶת־ בְּרִיתִי׃ לָכֵן אֱמֹר
say! therefore (6) covenant-of-me *** and-I-remembered them ones-enslaving

לִבְנֵי־ יִשְׂרָאֵל אֲנִי יְהוָה וְהוֹצֵאתִי אֶתְכֶם מִתַּחַת סִבְלֹת
yokes-of from-under you and-I-will-bring Yahweh I Israel to-sons-of

מִצְרַיִם וְהִצַּלְתִּי אֶתְכֶם מֵעֲבֹדָתָם וְגָאַלְתִּי אֶתְכֶם
you and-I-will-redeem from-service-of-them you and-I-will-free Egyptians

בִּזְרוֹעַ נְטוּיָה וּבִשְׁפָטִים גְּדֹלִים׃
mighty-ones and-with-acts-of-judgment being-outstretched with-arm

וְלָקַחְתִּי אֶתְכֶם לִי לְעָם וְהָיִיתִי לָכֶם לֵאלֹהִים
as-God to-you and-I-will-be as-people to-me you and-I-will-take (7)

וִידַעְתֶּם כִּי אֲנִי יְהוָה אֱלֹהֵיכֶם הַמּוֹצִיא אֶתְכֶם מִתַּחַת
from-under you the-one-bringing God-of-you Yahweh I that then-you-will-know

סִבְלוֹת מִצְרָיִם׃ וְהֵבֵאתִי אֶתְכֶם אֶל־הָאָרֶץ אֲשֶׁר נָשָׂאתִי אֶת־
*** I-lifted that the-land to you and-I-will-bring (8) Egyptians yokes-of

יָדִי לָתֵת אֹתָהּ לְאַבְרָהָם לְיִצְחָק וּלְיַעֲקֹב וְנָתַתִּי אֹתָהּ
her and-I-will-give and-to-Jacob to-Isaac to-Abraham her to-give hand-of-me

לָכֶם מוֹרָשָׁה אֲנִי יְהוָה׃ וַיְדַבֵּר מֹשֶׁה כֵּן אֶל־ בְּנֵי יִשְׂרָאֵל
Israel sons-of to this Moses and-he-reported (9) Yahweh I possession to-you

וְלֹא שָׁמְעוּ אֶל־ מֹשֶׁה מִקֹּצֶר רוּחַ וּמֵעֲבֹדָה קָשָׁה׃
cruel and-for-bondage spirit for-shortness-of Moses to they-listened but-not

וַיְדַבֵּר יְהוָה אֶל־מֹשֶׁה לֵּאמֹר׃ בֹּא דַבֵּר אֶל־פַּרְעֹה מֶלֶךְ
king-of Pharaoh to tell! go! (11) to-say Moses to Yahweh then-he-said (10)

מִצְרָיִם וִישַׁלַּח אֶת־ בְּנֵי־ יִשְׂרָאֵל מֵאַרְצוֹ׃ וַיְדַבֵּר
but-he-said (12) from-country-of-him Israel sons-of *** so-he-will-let-go Egypt

מֹשֶׁה לִפְנֵי יְהוָה לֵאמֹר הֵן בְּנֵי־ יִשְׂרָאֵל לֹא־ שָׁמְעוּ אֵלַי וְאֵיךְ
so-why? to-me they-listen not Israel sons-of see! to-say Yahweh to Moses

יִשְׁמָעֵנִי פַרְעֹה וַאֲנִי עֲרַל שְׂפָתָיִם׃ וַיְדַבֵּר
now-he-spoke (13) lips uncircumcised-of since-I Pharaoh would-he-listen-to-me

יְהוָה אֶל־ מֹשֶׁה וְאֶל־ אַהֲרֹן וַיְצַוֵּם אֶל־ בְּנֵי יִשְׂרָאֵל
Israel sons-of about and-he-commanded-them Aaron and-to Moses to Yahweh

וְאֶל־ פַּרְעֹה מֶלֶךְ מִצְרָיִם לְהוֹצִיא אֶת־ בְּנֵי־ יִשְׂרָאֵל מֵאֶרֶץ
from-land-of Israel sons-of *** to-bring Egypt king-of Pharaoh and-about

מִצְרָיִם׃ אֵלֶּה רָאשֵׁי בֵית־ אֲבֹתָם בְּנֵי רְאוּבֵן בְּכֹר
firstborn-of Reuben sons-of fathers-of-them house-of heads-of these (14) Egypt

יִשְׂרָאֵל חֲנוֹךְ וּפַלּוּא חֶצְרוֹן וְכַרְמִי אֵלֶּה מִשְׁפְּחֹת רְאוּבֵן׃ וּבְנֵי
and-sons-of (15) Reuben clans-of these and-Carmi Hezron and-Pallu Hanoch Israel

שִׁמְעוֹן יְמוּאֵל וְיָמִין וְאֹהַד וְיָכִין וְצֹחַר וְשָׁאוּל בֶּן־
son-of and-Shaul and-Zohar and-Jakin and-Ohad and-Jamin Jemuel Simeon

whom the Egyptians are en-
slaving, and I have remembered my covenant.
6 "Therefore, say to the Israelites: 'I am the LORD and I will
bring you out from under the
yoke of the Egyptians. I will
free you from being slaves to
them and will redeem you
with an outstretched arm and
with mighty acts of judgment.
7 I will take you as my own
people, and I will be your God.
Then you will know that I am
the LORD your God, who
brought you out from under
the yoke of the Egyptians.
8 And I will bring you to the
land I swore with uplifted
hand to give to Abraham, to
Isaac and to Jacob. I will give it
to you as a possession. I am
the LORD.' "
9 Moses reported this to the
Israelites, but they did not listen to him because of their
discouragement and cruel
bondage.
10 Then the LORD said to
Moses, 11 "Go, tell Pharaoh
king of Egypt to let the Israelites go out of his country."
12 But Moses said to the LORD,
"If the Israelites will not listen
to me, why would Pharaoh listen to me, since I speak with
faltering lips[m]?"

### *Family Record of Moses and Aaron*

13 Now the LORD spoke to
Moses and Aaron about the Israelites and Pharaoh king of
Egypt, and he commanded
them to bring the Israelites out
of Egypt.

14 These were the heads of
their families[n]:

The sons of Reuben the
firstborn son of Israel were
Hanoch and Pallu, Hezron
and Carmi. These were the
clans of Reuben.
15 The sons of Simeon
were Jemuel, Jamin, Ohad,
Jakin, Zohar and Shaul the

[m] 12 Hebrew *I am uncircumcised of lips*; also in verse 30
[n] 14 The Hebrew for *families* here and in verse 25 refers to units larger than clans.

הַכְּנַעֲנִית אֵלֶּה מִשְׁפְּחֹת שִׁמְעוֹן׃ וְאֵלֶּה שְׁמוֹת בְּנֵי־

sons-of names-of and-these (16) Simeon clans-of these the-Canaanite-woman

לֵוִי לְתֹלְדֹתָם גֵּרְשׁוֹן וּקְהָת וּמְרָרִי וּשְׁנֵי חַיֵּי

lives-of and-years-of and-Merari and-Kohath Gershon by-records-of-them Levi

לֵוִי שֶׁבַע וּשְׁלֹשִׁים וּמְאַת שָׁנָה׃ בְּנֵי גֵרְשׁוֹן לִבְנִי

Libni Gershon sons-of (17) year and-hundred-of and-thirty seven Levi

וְשִׁמְעִי לְמִשְׁפְּחֹתָם׃ וּבְנֵי קְהָת עַמְרָם וְיִצְהָר

and-Izhar Amram Kohath and-sons-of (18) by-clans-of-them and-Shimei

וְחֶבְרוֹן וְעֻזִּיאֵל וּשְׁנֵי חַיֵּי קְהָת שָׁלֹשׁ וּשְׁלֹשִׁים

and-thirty three Kohath lives-of and-years-of and-Uzziel and-Hebron

וּמְאַת שָׁנָה׃ וּבְנֵי מְרָרִי מַחְלִי וּמוּשִׁי אֵלֶּה מִשְׁפְּחֹת

clans-of these and-Mushi Mahli Merari and-sons-of (19) year and-hundred-of

הַלֵּוִי לְתֹלְדֹתָם׃ וַיִּקַּח עַמְרָם אֶת־ יוֹכֶבֶד

Jochebed *** Amram and-he-took (20) by-records-of-them the-Levi

דֹּדָתוֹ לוֹ לְאִשָּׁה וַתֵּלֶד לוֹ אֶת־ אַהֲרֹן וְאֶת־

and Aaron *** to-him and-she-bore for-wife to-him sister-of-father-of-him

מֹשֶׁה וּשְׁנֵי חַיֵּי עַמְרָם שֶׁבַע וּשְׁלֹשִׁים וּמְאַת שָׁנָה׃

year and-hundred-of and-thirty seven Amram lives-of and-years-of Moses

וּבְנֵי יִצְהָר קֹרַח וָנֶפֶג וְזִכְרִי׃ וּבְנֵי עֻזִּיאֵל

Uzziel and-sons-of (22) and-Zicri and-Nepheg Korah Izhar and-sons-of (21)

מִישָׁאֵל וְאֶלְצָפָן וְסִתְרִי׃ וַיִּקַּח אַהֲרֹן אֶת־אֱלִישֶׁבַע

Elisheba *** Aaron and-he-took (23) and-Sithri and-Elzaphan Mishael

בַּת־ עַמִּינָדָב אֲחוֹת נַחְשׁוֹן לוֹ לְאִשָּׁה וַתֵּלֶד לוֹ

to-him and-she-bore for-wife to-him Nahshon sister-of Amminadab daughter-of

אֶת־ נָדָב וְאֶת־אֲבִיהוּא אֶת־ אֶלְעָזָר וְאֶת־אִיתָמָר׃ וּבְנֵי קֹרַח אַסִּיר

Assir Korah and-sons-of (24) Ithamar and Eleazar *** Abihu and Nadab ***

וְאֶלְקָנָה וַאֲבִיאָסָף אֵלֶּה מִשְׁפְּחֹת הַקָּרְחִי׃ וְאֶלְעָזָר בֶּן־

son-of and-Eleazar (25) the-Korahite clans-of these and-Abiasaph and-Elkanah

אַהֲרֹן לָקַח־ לוֹ מִבְּנוֹת פּוּטִיאֵל לוֹ לְאִשָּׁה וַתֵּלֶד

and-she-bore for-wife to-him Putiel from-daughters-of to-him he-took Aaron

לוֹ אֶת־ פִּינְחָס אֵלֶּה רָאשֵׁי אֲבוֹת הַלְוִיִּם לְמִשְׁפְּחֹתָם׃

by-clans-of-them the-Levites fathers-of heads-of these Phinehas *** to-him

הוּא אַהֲרֹן וּמֹשֶׁה אֲשֶׁר אָמַר יְהוָה לָהֶם הוֹצִיאוּ אֶת־ בְּנֵי

sons-of *** bring! to-them Yahweh he-said whom and-Moses Aaron this (26)

יִשְׂרָאֵל מֵאֶרֶץ מִצְרַיִם עַל־ צִבְאֹתָם׃ הֵם הַמְדַבְּרִים

the-ones-speaking they (27) divisions-of-them by Egypt from-land-of Israel

אֶל־פַּרְעֹה מֶלֶךְ־מִצְרַיִם לְהוֹצִיא אֶת־ בְּנֵי־ יִשְׂרָאֵל מִמִּצְרַיִם הוּא מֹשֶׁה

Moses this from-Egypt Israel sons-of *** to-bring Egypt king-of Pharaoh to

son of a Canaanite woman. These were the clans of Simeon.

16These were the names of the sons of Levi according to their records: Gershon, Kohath and Merari. Levi lived 137 years.

17The sons of Gershon, by clans, were Libni and Shimei.

18The sons of Kohath were Amram, Izhar, Hebron and Uzziel. Kohath lived 133 years.

19The sons of Merari were Mahli and Mushi.

These were the clans of Levi according to their records.

20Amram married his father's sister Jochebed, who bore him Aaron and Moses. Amram lived 137 years.

21The sons of Izhar were Korah, Nepheg and Zicri.

22The sons of Uzziel were Mishael, Elzaphan and Sithri.

23Aaron married Elisheba, daughter of Amminadab and sister of Nahshon, and she bore him Nadab and Abihu, Eleazar and Ithamar.

24The sons of Korah were Assir, Elkanah and Abiasaph. These were the Korahite clans.

25Eleazar son of Aaron married one of the daughters of Putiel, and she bore him Phinehas.

These were the heads of the Levite families, clan by clan.

26It was this same Aaron and Moses to whom the LORD said, "Bring the Israelites out of Egypt by their divisions." 27They were the ones who spoke to Pharaoh king of Egypt about bringing the Israelites out of Egypt. It was the same Moses and Aaron.

וְאַהֲרֹֽן׃ וַיְהִ֗י בְּי֨וֹם דִּבֶּ֧ר יְהוָ֛ה אֶל־מֹשֶׁ֖ה בְּאֶ֥רֶץ מִצְרָֽיִם׃

Egypt in-land-of Moses to Yahweh he-spoke on-day and-he-was (28) and-Aaron

וַיְדַבֵּ֨ר יְהוָ֧ה אֶל־מֹשֶׁ֛ה לֵּאמֹ֖ר אֲנִ֣י יְהוָ֑ה דַּבֵּ֗ר אֶל־פַּרְעֹה֙ מֶ֣לֶךְ

king-of Pharaoh to tell! Yahweh I to-say Moses to Yahweh that-he-said (29)

מִצְרַ֔יִם אֵ֛ת כָּל־אֲשֶׁ֥ר אֲנִ֖י דֹּבֵ֥ר אֵלֶֽיךָ׃ וַיֹּ֥אמֶר מֹשֶׁ֖ה לִפְנֵ֣י יְהוָ֑ה הֵ֤ן

see! Yahweh to Moses but-he-said (30) to-you telling I that all *** Egypt

אֲנִי֙ עֲרַ֣ל שְׂפָתַ֔יִם וְאֵ֕יךְ יִשְׁמַ֥ע אֵלַ֖י פַּרְעֹֽה׃ וַיֹּ֤אמֶר

so-he-said (7:1) Pharaoh to-me would-he-listen so-why? lips uncircumcised-of I

יְהוָה֙ אֶל־מֹשֶׁ֔ה רְאֵ֛ה נְתַתִּ֥יךָ אֱלֹהִ֖ים לְפַרְעֹ֑ה וְאַהֲרֹ֥ן אָחִ֖יךָ

brother-of-you and-Aaron to-Pharaoh God I-made-you see! Moses to Yahweh

יִהְיֶ֥ה נְבִיאֶֽךָ׃ אַתָּ֣ה תְדַבֵּ֔ר אֵ֖ת כָּל־אֲשֶׁ֣ר אֲצַוֶּ֑ךָּ וְאַהֲרֹ֤ן

and-Aaron I-command-you that all *** you-say you (2) prophet-of-you he-is

אָחִ֙יךָ֙ יְדַבֵּ֣ר אֶל־פַּרְעֹ֔ה וְשִׁלַּ֥ח אֶת־בְּנֵֽי־יִשְׂרָאֵ֖ל

Israel sons-of *** so-he-will-let-go Pharaoh to he-will-tell brother-of-you

מֵאַרְצֽוֹ׃ וַאֲנִ֥י אַקְשֶׁ֖ה אֶת־לֵ֣ב פַּרְעֹ֑ה

Pharaoh heart-of *** I-will-harden but-I (3) from-land-of-him

וְהִרְבֵּיתִ֧י אֶת־אֹתֹתַ֛י וְאֶת־מוֹפְתַ֖י בְּאֶ֥רֶץ מִצְרָֽיִם׃

Egypt in-land-of wonders-of-me and signs-of-me *** and-I-will-multiply

וְלֹֽא־יִשְׁמַ֤ע אֲלֵכֶם֙ פַּרְעֹ֔ה וְנָתַתִּ֥י אֶת־יָדִ֖י

hand-of-me *** then-I-will-lay Pharaoh to-you he-will-listen but-not (4)

בְּמִצְרָ֑יִם וְהוֹצֵאתִ֨י אֶת־צִבְאֹתַ֜י אֶת־עַמִּ֣י בְנֵֽי־

sons-of people-of-me *** divisions-of-me *** and-I-will-bring on-Egypt

יִשְׂרָאֵל֙ מֵאֶ֣רֶץ מִצְרַ֔יִם בִּשְׁפָטִ֖ים גְּדֹלִֽים׃

mighty-ones by-acts-of-judgment Egypt from-land-of Israel

וְיָדְע֤וּ מִצְרַ֙יִם֙ כִּֽי־אֲנִ֣י יְהוָ֔ה בִּנְטֹתִ֥י אֶת־

*** when-to-stretch-out-me Yahweh I that Egyptians and-they-will-know (5)

יָדִ֖י עַל־מִצְרָ֑יִם וְהוֹצֵאתִ֥י אֶת־בְּנֵֽי־יִשְׂרָאֵ֖ל מִתּוֹכָֽם׃

from-midst-of-them Israel sons-of *** and-I-bring Egypt against hand-of-me

וַיַּ֥עַשׂ מֹשֶׁ֖ה וְאַהֲרֹ֑ן כַּאֲשֶׁ֨ר צִוָּ֧ה יְהוָ֛ה אֹתָ֖ם כֵּ֥ן

this them Yahweh he-commanded just-as and-Aaron Moses and-he-did (6)

עָשֽׂוּ׃ וּמֹשֶׁה֙ בֶּן־שְׁמֹנִ֣ים שָׁנָ֔ה וְאַהֲרֹ֕ן בֶּן־שָׁל֥שׁ וּשְׁמֹנִ֖ים

and-eighty three son-of and-Aaron year eighty son-of now-Moses (7) they-did

שָׁנָ֑ה בְּדַבְּרָ֖ם אֶל־פַּרְעֹֽה׃ וַיֹּ֣אמֶר יְהוָ֔ה אֶל־מֹשֶׁ֥ה וְאֶל־

and-to Moses to Yahweh and-he-said (8) Pharaoh to when-to-speak-them year

אַהֲרֹ֖ן לֵאמֹֽר׃ כִּי֩ יְדַבֵּ֨ר אֲלֵכֶ֤ם פַּרְעֹה֙ לֵאמֹ֔ר תְּנ֥וּ לָכֶ֖ם מוֹפֵ֑ת

miracle to-you perform! to-say Pharaoh to-you he-says when (9) to-say Aaron

וְאָמַרְתָּ֣ אֶֽל־אַהֲרֹ֗ן קַ֧ח אֶֽת־מַטְּךָ֛ וְהַשְׁלֵ֥ךְ לִפְנֵֽי־פַרְעֹ֖ה

Pharaoh before and-throw-down! staff-of-you *** take! Aaron to then-you-say

*Aaron to Speak for Moses*

28Now when the LORD spoke to Moses in Egypt, 29he said to him, "I am the LORD. Tell Pharaoh king of Egypt everything I tell you."

30But Moses said to the LORD, "Since I speak with faltering lips, why would Pharaoh listen to me?"

7 Then the LORD said to Moses, "See, I have made you like God to Pharaoh, and your brother Aaron will be your prophet. 2You are to say everything I command you, and your brother Aaron is to tell Pharaoh to let the Israelites go out of his country. 3But I will harden Pharaoh's heart, and though I multiply my miraculous signs and wonders in Egypt, 4he will not listen to you. Then I will lay my hand on Egypt and with mighty acts of judgment I will bring out my divisions, my people the Israelites. 5And the Egyptians will know that I am the LORD when I stretch out my hand against Egypt and bring the Israelites out of it."

*Moses' Staff Becomes a Snake*

6Moses and Aaron did just as the LORD commanded them. 7Moses was eighty years old and Aaron eighty-three when they spoke to Pharaoh.

8The LORD said to Moses and Aaron, 9"When Pharaoh says to you, 'Perform a miracle,' then say to Aaron, 'Take your staff and throw it down before

יְהִי לְתַנִּין׃ וַיָּבֹא מֹשֶׁה וְאַהֲרֹן אֶל־ פַּרְעֹה
Pharaoh to and-Aaron Moses so-he-went (10) into-snake he-will-become

וַיַּעֲשׂוּ* כֵן כַּאֲשֶׁר צִוָּה יְהוָה וַיַּשְׁלֵךְ אַהֲרֹן אֶת־
*** Aaron and-he-threw-down Yahweh he-commanded just-as this and-they-did

מַטֵּהוּ לִפְנֵי פַרְעֹה וְלִפְנֵי עֲבָדָיו וַיְהִי
and-he-became officials-of-him and-before Pharaoh before staff-of-him

לְתַנִּין׃ וַיִּקְרָא גַּם־ פַּרְעֹה לַחֲכָמִים
to-the-wise-men Pharaoh also then-he-summoned (11) into-snake

וְלַמְכַשְּׁפִים וַיַּעֲשׂוּ גַם־ הֵם חַרְטֻמֵּי מִצְרַיִם
Egypt magicians-of they also and-they-did and-to-the-ones-being-sorcerors

בְּלַהֲטֵיהֶם כֵּן׃ וַיַּשְׁלִיכוּ אִישׁ מַטֵּהוּ
staff-of-him each and-they-threw-down (12) same by-secret-arts-of-them

וַיִּהְיוּ לְתַנִּינִם וַיִּבְלַע מַטֵּה־ אַהֲרֹן אֶת־ מַטֹּתָם׃
staffs-of-them *** Aaron staff-of but-he-swallowed into-snakes and-they-became

וַיֶּחֱזַק לֵב פַּרְעֹה וְלֹא שָׁמַע אֲלֵהֶם כַּאֲשֶׁר
just-as to-them he-listened and-not Pharaoh heart-of yet-he-was-hard (13)

דִּבֶּר יְהוָה׃ וַיֹּאמֶר יְהוָה אֶל־ מֹשֶׁה כָּבֵד לֵב
heart-of he-is-unyielding Moses to Yahweh then-he-said (14) Yahweh he-said

פַּרְעֹה מֵאֵן לְשַׁלַּח הָעָם׃ לֵךְ אֶל־ פַּרְעֹה בַּבֹּקֶר
in-the-morning Pharaoh to go! (15) the-people to-let-go he-refuses Pharaoh

הִנֵּה יֹצֵא הַמַּיְמָה וְנִצַּבְתָּ לִקְרָאתוֹ עַל־ שְׂפַת הַיְאֹר
the-Nile bank-of on to-meet-him and-you-wait to-the-waters going-out see!

וְהַמַּטֶּה אֲשֶׁר־ נֶהְפַּךְ לְנָחָשׁ תִּקַּח בְּיָדֶךָ׃
in-hand-of-you you-take into-snake he-was-changed that and-the-staff

וְאָמַרְתָּ אֵלָיו יְהוָה אֱלֹהֵי הָעִבְרִים שְׁלָחַנִי אֵלֶיךָ לֵאמֹר
to-say to-you he-sent-me the-Hebrews God-of Yahweh to-him then-you-say (16)

שַׁלַּח אֶת־ עַמִּי וְיַעַבְדֻנִי בַּמִּדְבָּר וְהִנֵּה לֹא־
not but-see! in-the-desert so-they-may-worship-me people-of-me *** let-go!

שָׁמַעְתָּ עַד־ כֹּה׃ כֹּה אָמַר יְהוָה בְּזֹאת תֵּדַע כִּי
that you-will-know by-this Yahweh he-says this (17) now until you-listened

אֲנִי יְהוָה הִנֵּה אָנֹכִי מַכֶּה ׀ בַּמַּטֶּה אֲשֶׁר־ בְּיָדִי עַל־ הַמַּיִם
the-waters on in-hand-of-me that with-the-staff striking I see! Yahweh I

אֲשֶׁר בַּיְאֹר וְנֶהֶפְכוּ לְדָם׃ וְהַדָּגָה אֲשֶׁר־
that and-the-fish (18) into-blood and-they-will-be-changed in-the-Nile that

בַּיְאֹר תָּמוּת וּבָאַשׁ הַיְאֹר וְנִלְאוּ
and-they-will-be-unable the-Nile and-he-will-stink she-will-die in-the-Nile

מִצְרַיִם לִשְׁתּוֹת מַיִם מִן־ הַיְאֹר׃ וַיֹּאמֶר יְהוָה אֶל־ מֹשֶׁה
Moses to Yahweh and-he-said (19) the-Nile from waters to-drink Egyptians

Pharaoh,' and it will become a snake."

[10]Then Moses and Aaron went to Pharaoh and did just as the LORD commanded. Aaron threw his staff down in front of Pharaoh and his officials, and it became a snake. [11]Pharaoh then summoned wise men and sorcerers, and the Egyptian magicians also did the same things by their secret arts: [12]Each one threw down his staff and it became a snake. But Aaron's staff swallowed up their staffs. [13]Yet Pharaoh's heart became hard and he would not listen to them, just as the LORD had said.

*The Plague of Blood*

[14]Then the LORD said to Moses, "Pharaoh's heart is unyielding; he refuses to let the people go. [15]Go to Pharaoh in the morning as he goes out to the water. Wait on the bank of the Nile to meet him, and take in your hand the staff that was changed into a snake. [16]Then say to him, 'The LORD, the God of the Hebrews, has sent me to say to you: Let my people go, so that they may worship me in the desert. But until now you have not listened. [17]This is what the LORD says: By this you will know that I am the LORD: With the staff that is in my hand I will strike the water of the Nile, and it will be changed into blood. [18]The fish in the Nile will die, and the river will stink; the Egyptians will not be able to drink its water.' "

[19]The LORD said to Moses,

*10 Most mss have *hateph pathah* under the *ayin* ( וַיַּעֲשׂוּ ).

אֱמֹר אֶל־ אַהֲרֹן קַח מַטְּךָ וּנְטֵה־ יָדְךָ עַל־ מֵימֵי
waters-of over hand-of-you and-stretch! staff-of-you take! Aaron to tell!

מִצְרַיִם עַל־ נַהֲרֹתָם | עַל־ יְאֹרֵיהֶם וְעַל־ אַגְמֵיהֶם
ponds-of-them and-over canals-of-them over streams-of-them over Egypt

וְעַל כָּל־ מִקְוֵה מֵימֵיהֶם וְיִהְיוּ־ דָם
blood and-they-will-become waters-of-them reservoir-of every-of and-over

וְהָיָה דָם בְּכָל־ אֶרֶץ מִצְרַיִם וּבָעֵצִים
even-in-the-wood-buckets Egypt land-of in-all-of blood and-he-will-be

וּבָאֲבָנִים׃ וַיַּעֲשׂוּ־ כֵן מֹשֶׁה וְאַהֲרֹן כַּאֲשֶׁר | צִוָּה
he-commanded just-as and-Aaron Moses this and-they-did (20) and-in-the-stone-jars

יְהוָה וַיָּרֶם בַּמַּטֶּה וַיַּךְ אֶת־ הַמַּיִם אֲשֶׁר
that the-waters *** and-he-struck with-the-staff and-he-raised Yahweh

בַּיְאֹר לְעֵינֵי פַרְעֹה וּלְעֵינֵי עֲבָדָיו
officials-of-him and-before-eyes-of Pharaoh before-eyes-of in-the-Nile

וַיֵּהָפְכוּ כָּל־ הַמַּיִם אֲשֶׁר־ בַּיְאֹר לְדָם׃
into-blood in-the-Nile that the-waters all-of and-they-were-changed

וְהַדָּגָה אֲשֶׁר־ בַּיְאֹר מֵתָה וַיִּבְאַשׁ הַיְאֹר וְלֹא־
so-not the-Nile and-he-stunk she-died in-the-Nile that and-the-fish (21)

יָכְלוּ מִצְרַיִם לִשְׁתּוֹת מַיִם מִן־ הַיְאֹר וַיְהִי הַדָּם
the-blood and-he-was the-Nile from waters to-drink Egyptians they-could

בְּכָל־ אֶרֶץ מִצְרָיִם׃ וַיַּעֲשׂוּ־ כֵן חַרְטֻמֵּי מִצְרַיִם
Egypt magicians-of same but-they-did (22) Egypt land-of in-all-of

בְּלָטֵיהֶם וַיֶּחֱזַק לֵב־ פַּרְעֹה וְלֹא־ שָׁמַע אֲלֵהֶם
to-them he-listened and-not Pharaoh heart-of so-he-was-hard by-arts-of-them

כַּאֲשֶׁר דִּבֶּר יְהוָה׃ וַיִּפֶן פַּרְעֹה וַיָּבֹא אֶל־ בֵּיתוֹ
palace-of-him into and-he-went Pharaoh so-he-turned (23) Yahweh he-said just-as

וְלֹא־ שָׁת לִבּוֹ גַּם־ לָזֹאת׃ וַיַּחְפְּרוּ כָל־ מִצְרַיִם
Egyptians all-of and-they-dug (24) to-this even heart-of-him he-took and-not

סְבִיבֹת הַיְאֹר מַיִם לִשְׁתּוֹת כִּי לֹא יָכְלוּ לִשְׁתֹּת מִמֵּימֵי
from-waters-of to-drink they-could not for to-drink waters the-Nile along

הַיְאֹר׃ וַיִּמָּלֵא שִׁבְעַת יָמִים אַחֲרֵי הַכּוֹת־ יְהוָה אֶת־ הַיְאֹר׃
the-Nile *** Yahweh to-strike after days seven-of and-he-passed (25) the-Nile

וַיֹּאמֶר יְהוָה אֶל־ מֹשֶׁה בֹּא אֶל־ פַּרְעֹה וְאָמַרְתָּ אֵלָיו כֹּה
this to-him and-you-say Pharaoh to go! Moses to Yahweh then-he-said *(26[1])

אָמַר יְהוָה שַׁלַּח אֶת־ עַמִּי וְיַעַבְדֻנִי׃ וְאִם־
but-if (27[2]) so-they-may-worship-me people-of-me *** let-go! Yahweh he-says

מָאֵן אַתָּה לְשַׁלֵּחַ הִנֵּה אָנֹכִי נֹגֵף אֶת־ כָּל־ גְּבוּלְךָ בַּצְפַרְדְּעִים׃
with-the-frogs country-of-you all-of *** plaguing I see! to-let-go you to-refuse

"Tell Aaron, 'Take your staff and stretch out your hand over the waters of Egypt—over the streams and canals, over the ponds and all the reservoirs'—and they will turn to blood. Blood will be everywhere in Egypt, even in the wooden buckets and stone jars."

20 Moses and Aaron did just as the LORD had commanded. He raised his staff in the presence of Pharaoh and his officials and struck the water of the Nile, and all the water was changed into blood. 21 The fish in the Nile died, and the river smelled so bad that the Egyptians could not drink its water. Blood was everywhere in Egypt.

22 But the Egyptian magicians did the same things by their secret arts, and Pharaoh's heart became hard; he would not listen to Moses and Aaron, just as the LORD had said. 23 Instead, he turned and went into his palace, and did not take even this to heart. 24 And all the Egyptians dug along the Nile to get drinking water, because they could not drink the water of the river.

*The Plague of Frogs*

25 Seven days passed after the LORD struck the Nile.
8 1 Then the LORD said to Moses, "Go to Pharaoh and say to him, 'This is what the LORD says: Let my people go, so that they may worship me. 2 If you refuse to let them go, I will plague your whole country with frogs. 3 The Nile will

*The Hebrew numeration of chapter 8 begins with verse 5 in English. The number in brackets indicates the English numeration.

וְשָׁרַץ הַיְאֹר צְפַרְדְּעִים וְעָלוּ וּבָאוּ
and-they-will-go and-they-will-come-up frogs the-Nile and-he-will-teem (28[3])

בְּבֵיתֶךָ וּבַחֲדַר מִשְׁכָּבְךָ וְעַל־ מִטָּתֶךָ
bed-of-you and-onto sleep-of-you and-into-room-of into-palace-of-you

וּבְבֵית עֲבָדֶיךָ וּבְעַמֶּךָ וּבְתַנּוּרֶיךָ
and-into-ovens-of-you and-on-people-of-you officials-of-you and-into-house-of

וּבְמִשְׁאֲרוֹתֶיךָ׃ וּבְכָה וּבְעַמְּךָ
and-on-people-of-you and-on-you (29[4]) and-into-kneading-troughs-of-you

וּבְכָל־ עֲבָדֶיךָ יַעֲלוּ הַצְפַרְדְּעִים׃ וַיֹּאמֶר
then-he-said (8:1[5]) the-frogs they-will-go-up officials-of-you and-on-all-of

יְהוָה אֶל־ מֹשֶׁה אֱמֹר אֶל־ אַהֲרֹן נְטֵה אֶת־ יָדְךָ בְּמַטֶּךָ
with-staff-of-you hand-of-you *** stretch-out! Aaron to tell! Moses to Yahweh

עַל־ הַנְּהָרֹת עַל־ הַיְאֹרִים וְעַל־ הָאֲגַמִּים וְהַעַל אֶת־
*** and-make-come-up! the-ponds and-over the-canals over the-streams over

הַצְפַרְדְּעִים עַל־אֶרֶץ מִצְרָיִם׃ וַיֵּט אַהֲרֹן אֶת־ יָדוֹ עַל
over hand-of-him *** Aaron so-he-stretched (2[6]) Egypt land-of on the-frogs

מֵימֵי מִצְרָיִם וַתַּעַל הַצְּפַרְדֵּעַ וַתְּכַס אֶת־ אֶרֶץ מִצְרָיִם׃
Egypt land-of *** and-she-covered the-frog and-she-came-up Egypt waters-of

וַיַּעֲשׂוּ־ כֵן הַחַרְטֻמִּים† בְּלָטֵיהֶם וַיַּעֲלוּ
and-they-brought-up by-arts-of-them the-magicians same but-they-did (3[7])

אֶת־הַצְפַרְדְּעִים עַל־אֶרֶץ מִצְרָיִם׃ וַיִּקְרָא פַרְעֹה לְמֹשֶׁה
to-Moses Pharaoh then-he-summoned (4[8]) Egypt land-of on the-frogs ***

וּלְאַהֲרֹן וַיֹּאמֶר הַעְתִּירוּ אֶל־ יְהוָה וְיָסֵר הַצְפַרְדְּעִים מִמֶּנִּי
from-me the-frogs so-he-will-take-away Yahweh to pray! and-he-said and-to-Aaron

וּמֵעַמִּי וַאֲשַׁלְּחָה אֶת־ הָעָם וְיִזְבְּחוּ
so-they-may-sacrifice the-people *** and-I-will-let-go and-from-people-of-me

לַיהוָה׃ וַיֹּאמֶר מֹשֶׁה לְפַרְעֹה הִתְפָּאֵר עָלַי לְמָתַי ׀
as-when? for-me declare! to-Pharaoh Moses and-he-said (5[9]) to-Yahweh

אַעְתִּיר לְךָ וְלַעֲבָדֶיךָ וּלְעַמְּךָ לְהַכְרִית
to-remove and-for-people-of-you and-for-officials-of-you for-you I-pray

הַצְפַרְדְּעִים†† מִמְּךָ וּמִבָּתֶּיךָ רַק בַּיְאֹר תִּשָּׁאַרְנָה׃
they-remain in-the-Nile except and-from-houses-of-you from-you the-frogs

וַיֹּאמֶר לְמָחָר וַיֹּאמֶר כִּדְבָרְךָ לְמַעַן
so-that as-word-of-you and-he-replied on-tomorrow and-he-said (6[10])

תֵּדַע כִּי־ אֵין כַּיהוָה אֱלֹהֵינוּ׃
God-of-us like-Yahweh there-is-no-one that you-may-know

וְסָרוּ הַצְפַרְדְּעִים מִמְּךָ וּמִבָּתֶּיךָ
and-from-houses-of-you from-you the-frogs and-they-will-leave (7[11])

teem with frogs. They will come up into your palace and your bedroom and onto your bed, into the houses of your officials and on your people, and into your ovens and kneading troughs. [4]The frogs will go up on you and your people and all your officials.' "

[5]Then the LORD said to Moses, "Tell Aaron, 'Stretch out your hand with your staff over the streams and canals and ponds, and make frogs come up on the land of Egypt.' "

[6]So Aaron stretched out his hand over the waters of Egypt, and the frogs came up and covered the land. [7]But the magicians did the same things by their secret arts; they also made frogs come up on the land of Egypt.

[8]Pharaoh summoned Moses and Aaron and said, "Pray to the LORD to take the frogs away from me and my people, and I will let your people go to offer sacrifices to the LORD."

[9]Moses said to Pharaoh, "I leave to you the honor of setting the time for me to pray for you and your officials and your people that you and your houses may be rid of the frogs, except for those that remain in the Nile."

[10]"Tomorrow," Pharaoh said.

Moses replied, "It will be as you say, so that you may know there is no one like the LORD our God. [11]The frogs will leave you and your houses, your

*See the note on page 163.

†3 Most mss have *pathah* under the *beth* ( הַחַרְ' ).

††5 Most mss have *sheva* under the *tsade* ( הַצְ' ).

וּמֵעֲבָדֶיךָ וּמֵעַמֶּךָ רַק בַּיְאֹר תִּשָּׁאַרְנָה׃

they-remain in-the-Nile except and-from-people-of-you and-from-officials-of-you

(8[12]) וַיֵּצֵא מֹשֶׁה וְאַהֲרֹן מֵעִם פַּרְעֹה וַיִּצְעַק מֹשֶׁה

Moses and-he-cried-out Pharaoh from-with and-Aaron Moses and-he-left (8[12])

אֶל־ יְהוָה עַל־ דְּבַר הַצְפַרְדְּעִים אֲשֶׁר־ שָׂם לְפַרְעֹה׃

on-Pharaoh he-brought that the-frogs matter-of about Yahweh to

(9[13]) וַיַּעַשׂ יְהוָה כִּדְבַר מֹשֶׁה וַיָּמֻתוּ הַצְפַרְדְּעִים מִן־הַבָּתִּים

the-houses in the-frogs and-they-died Moses as-request-of Yahweh and-he-did (9[13])

מִן־ הַחֲצֵרֹת וּמִן־ הַשָּׂדֹת׃ (10[14]) וַיִּצְבְּרוּ אֹתָם חֳמָרִם חֳמָרִם

heaps heaps them and-they-piled (10[14]) the-fields and-in the-courtyards in

וַתִּבְאַשׁ הָאָרֶץ׃ (11[15]) וַיַּרְא פַּרְעֹה כִּי הָיְתָה הָרְוָחָה

the-relief she-was that Pharaoh when-he-saw (11[15]) the-land and-she-reeked

וְהַכְבֵּד אֶת־ לִבּוֹ וְלֹא שָׁמַע אֲלֵהֶם כַּאֲשֶׁר

just-as to-them he-listened and-not heart-of-him *** then-he-hardened

דִּבֶּר יְהוָה׃ (12[16]) וַיֹּאמֶר יְהוָה אֶל־ מֹשֶׁה אֱמֹר אֶל־ אַהֲרֹן

Aaron to tell! Moses to Yahweh then-he-said (12[16]) Yahweh he-said

נְטֵה אֶת־ מַטְּךָ וְהַךְ אֶת־ עֲפַר הָאָרֶץ

the-ground dust-of *** and-strike! staff-of-you *** stretch-out!

וְהָיָה לְכִנִּם בְּכָל־ אֶרֶץ מִצְרָיִם׃ (13[17]) וַיַּעֲשׂוּ־

so-they-did (13[17]) Egypt land-of in-all-of into-gnats and-he-will-become

כֵן וַיֵּט אַהֲרֹן אֶת־ יָדוֹ בְמַטֵּהוּ וַיַּךְ

and-he-struck with-staff-of-him hand-of-him *** Aaron and-he-stretched this

אֶת־ עֲפַר הָאָרֶץ וַתְּהִי הַכִּנָּם בָּאָדָם וּבַבְּהֵמָה

and-upon-the-animal upon-the-man the-gnat and-she-came the-ground dust-of ***

כָּל־ עֲפַר הָאָרֶץ הָיָה כִנִּים בְּכָל־ אֶרֶץ מִצְרָיִם׃

Egypt land-of in-all-of gnats he-became the-ground dust-of all-of

(14[18]) וַיַּעֲשׂוּ־ כֵן הַחַרְטֻמִּים בְּלָטֵיהֶם לְהוֹצִיא אֶת־ הַכִּנִּים

the-gnats *** to-produce by-arts-of-them the-magicians same and-they-tried (14[18])

וְלֹא יָכֹלוּ וַתְּהִי הַכִּנָּם בָּאָדָם וּבַבְּהֵמָה׃

and-on-the-animal on-the-man the-gnat and-she-was they-could but-not

(15[19]) וַיֹּאמְרוּ הַחַרְטֻמִּם אֶל־ פַּרְעֹה אֶצְבַּע אֱלֹהִים הִוא

this God finger-of Pharaoh to the-magicians so-they-said (15[19])

וַיֶּחֱזַק לֵב־ פַּרְעֹה וְלֹא־ שָׁמַע אֲלֵהֶם כַּאֲשֶׁר דִּבֶּר

he-said just-as to-them he-listened and-not Pharaoh heart-of but-he-was-hard

יְהוָה׃ (16[20]) וַיֹּאמֶר יְהוָה אֶל־ מֹשֶׁה הַשְׁכֵּם בַּבֹּקֶר

in-the-morning rise-early! Moses to Yahweh then-he-said (16[20]) Yahweh

וְהִתְיַצֵּב לִפְנֵי פַרְעֹה הִנֵּה יוֹצֵא הַמָּיְמָה וְאָמַרְתָּ אֵלָיו

to-him and-you-say to-the-waters going see! Pharaoh before and-confront!

officials and your people; they will remain only in the Nile."

12After Moses and Aaron left Pharaoh, Moses cried out to the LORD about the frogs he had brought on Pharaoh. 13And the LORD did what Moses asked. The frogs died in the houses, in the courtyards and in the fields. 14They were piled into heaps, and the land reeked of them. 15But when Pharaoh saw that there was relief, he hardened his heart and would not listen to Moses and Aaron, just as the LORD had said.

*The Plague of Gnats*

16Then the LORD said to Moses, "Tell Aaron, 'Stretch out your staff and strike the dust of the ground,' and throughout the land of Egypt the dust will become gnats." 17They did this, and when Aaron stretched out his hand with the staff and struck the dust of the ground, gnats came upon men and animals. All the dust throughout the land of Egypt became gnats. 18But when the magicians tried to produce gnats by their secret arts, they could not. And the gnats were on men and animals.

19The magicians said to Pharaoh, "This is the finger of God." But Pharaoh's heart was hard and he would not listen, just as the LORD had said.

*The Plague of Flies*

20Then the LORD said to Moses, "Get up early in the morning and confront Pharaoh as he goes to the water and say to him, 'This is what

*See the note on page 163.

כֹּה אָמַר יְהוָה שַׁלַּח עַמִּי וְיַעַבְדֻנִי׃ כִּי
but (17[21]) so-they-may-worship-me people-of-me let-go! Yahweh he-says this

אִם־ אֵינְךָ מְשַׁלֵּחַ אֶת־ עַמִּי הִנְנִי מַשְׁלִיחַ בְּךָ
on-you sending see-I! people-of-me *** letting-go not-you if

וּבַעֲבָדֶיךָ וּבְעַמְּךָ וּבְבָתֶּיךָ אֶת־
*** and-into-houses-of-you and-on-people-of-you and-on-officials-of-you

הֶעָרֹב וּמָלְאוּ בָּתֵּי מִצְרַיִם אֶת־הֶעָרֹב וְגַם הָאֲדָמָה
the-ground and-even the-fly *** Egypt houses-of and-they-will-be-full the-fly

אֲשֶׁר־ הֵם עָלֶיהָ׃ וְהִפְלֵיתִי בַּיּוֹם הַהוּא
the-that on-the-day but-I-will-deal-differently (18[22]) on-her they where

אֶת־ אֶרֶץ גֹּשֶׁן אֲשֶׁר עַמִּי עֹמֵד עָלֶיהָ לְבִלְתִּי הֱיוֹת־שָׁם עָרֹב
fly there to-be not in-her living people-of-me where Goshen land-of ***

לְמַעַן תֵּדַע כִּי אֲנִי יְהוָה בְּקֶרֶב הָאָרֶץ׃
the-land in-midst-of Yahweh I that you-will-know so-that

וְשַׂמְתִּי פְּדֻת בֵּין עַמִּי וּבֵין עַמֶּךָ
people-of-you and-between people-of-me between †distinction and-I-will-make (19[23])

לְמָחָר יִהְיֶה הָאֹת הַזֶּה׃ וַיַּעַשׂ יְהוָה כֵּן
this Yahweh and-he-did (20[24]) the-this the-sign he-will-occur on-tomorrow

וַיָּבֹא עָרֹב כָּבֵד בֵּיתָה פַרְעֹה וּבֵית עֲבָדָיו
officials-of-him and-house-of Pharaoh into-palace-of many fly and-he-came

וּבְכָל־ אֶרֶץ מִצְרַיִם תִּשָּׁחֵת הָאָרֶץ מִפְּנֵי הֶעָרֹב׃
the-fly because-of the-land she-was-ruined Egypt land-of and-in-all-of

וַיִּקְרָא פַרְעֹה אֶל־ מֹשֶׁה וּלְאַהֲרֹן וַיֹּאמֶר לְכוּ
go! and-he-said and-to-Aaron Moses to Pharaoh then-he-summoned (21[25])

זִבְחוּ לֵאלֹהֵיכֶם בָּאָרֶץ׃ וַיֹּאמֶר מֹשֶׁה לֹא
not Moses but-he-said (22[26]) in-the-land to-God-of-you sacrifice!

נָכוֹן לַעֲשׂוֹת כֵּן כִּי תּוֹעֲבַת מִצְרַיִם נִזְבַּח
we-would-sacrifice Egyptians detestable-of for this to-do he-would-be-right

לַיהוָה אֱלֹהֵינוּ הֵן נִזְבַּח אֶת־ תּוֹעֲבַת מִצְרַיִם לְעֵינֵיהֶם
in-eyes-of-them Egyptians detestable-of *** we-sacrifice if God-of-us to-Yahweh

וְלֹא יִסְקְלֻנוּ׃ דֶּרֶךְ שְׁלֹשֶׁת יָמִים נֵלֵךְ
we-must-take days three-of journey-of (23[27]) they-stone-us now-not

בַּמִּדְבָּר וְזָבַחְנוּ לַיהוָה אֱלֹהֵינוּ כַּאֲשֶׁר יֹאמַר
he-tells just-as God-of-us to-Yahweh and-we-must-sacrifice into-the-desert

אֵלֵינוּ׃ וַיֹּאמֶר פַּרְעֹה אָנֹכִי אֲשַׁלַּח אֶתְכֶם וּזְבַחְתֶּם
so-you-can-sacrifice you I-will-let-go I Pharaoh so-he-said (24[28]) to-us

לַיהוָה אֱלֹהֵיכֶם בַּמִּדְבָּר רַק הַרְחֵק לֹא־ תַרְחִיקוּ לָלֶכֶת
to-go you-must-go-far not to-go-far but in-the-desert God-of-you to-Yahweh

the LORD says: Let my people go, so that they may worship me. [21]If you do not let my people go, I will send swarms of flies on you and your officials, on your people and into your houses. The houses of the Egyptians will be full of flies, and even the ground where they are.

[22]" 'But on that day I will deal differently with the land of Goshen, where my people live; no swarms of flies will be there, so that you will know that I, the LORD, am in this land. [23]I will make a distinction° between my people and your people. This miraculous sign will occur tomorrow.' "

[24]And the LORD did this. Dense swarms of flies poured into Pharaoh's palace and into the houses of his officials, and throughout Egypt the land was ruined by the flies.

[25]Then Pharaoh summoned Moses and Aaron and said, "Go, sacrifice to your God here in the land."

[26]But Moses said, "That would not be right. The sacrifices we offer the LORD our God would be detestable to the Egyptians. And if we offer sacrifices that are detestable in their eyes, will they not stone us? [27]We must take a three-day journey into the desert to offer sacrifices to the LORD our God, as he commands us."

[28]Pharaoh said, "I will let you go to offer sacrifices to the LORD your God in the desert, but you must not go very far.

°23 Septuagint and Vulgate; Hebrew *will put a deliverance*

*See the note on page 163.

†*19* The normal definition of this Hebrew word is *deliverance.* The word translated by *distinction* suggested by the versions may be פְּלֻת.

הַעְתִּירוּ בַּעֲדִי׃ וַיֹּאמֶר מֹשֶׁה הִנֵּה אָנֹכִי יוֹצֵא מֵעִמָּךְ
from-with-you leaving I see! Moses and-he-answered (25[29]) for-me pray!

וְהַעְתַּרְתִּי אֶל־ יְהוָה וְסָר הֶעָרֹב מִפַּרְעֹה
from-Pharaoh the-fly and-he-will-leave Yahweh to and-I-will-pray

מֵעֲבָדָיו וּמֵעַמּוֹ מָחָר רַק אַל־ יֹסֵף
may-he-repeat not only tomorrow and-from-people-of-him from-officials-of-him

פַּרְעֹה הָתֵל לְבִלְתִּי שַׁלַּח אֶת־ הָעָם לִזְבֹּחַ לַיהוָה׃
to-Yahweh to-sacrifice the-people *** to-let-go not to-deceive Pharaoh

וַיֵּצֵא מֹשֶׁה מֵעִם פַּרְעֹה וַיֶּעְתַּר אֶל־ יְהוָה׃
Yahweh to and-he-prayed Pharaoh from-with Moses then-he-left (26[30])

וַיַּעַשׂ יְהוָה כִּדְבַר מֹשֶׁה וַיָּסַר הֶעָרֹב
the-fly and-he-left Moses as-request-of Yahweh and-he-did (27[31])

מִפַּרְעֹה מֵעֲבָדָיו וּמֵעַמּוֹ לֹא נִשְׁאַר
he-remained not and-from-people-of-him and-from-officials-of-him from-Pharaoh

אֶחָד׃ וַיַּכְבֵּד פַּרְעֹה אֶת־ לִבּוֹ גַּם בַּפַּעַם
on-the-time also heart-of-him *** Pharaoh but-he-hardened (28[32]) one

הַזֹּאת וְלֹא שִׁלַּח אֶת־ הָעָם׃ וַיֹּאמֶר יְהוָה אֶל־מֹשֶׁה
Moses to Yahweh then-he-said (9:1) the-people *** he-let-go and-not the-this

בֹּא אֶל־ פַּרְעֹה וְדִבַּרְתָּ אֵלָיו כֹּה־ אָמַר יְהוָה אֱלֹהֵי הָעִבְרִים
the-Hebrews God-of Yahweh he-says this to-him and-you-say Pharaoh to go!

שַׁלַּח אֶת־ עַמִּי וְיַעַבְדֻנִי׃ כִּי אִם־ מָאֵן אַתָּה
you to-refuse if but (2) so-they-may-worship-me people-of-me *** let-go!

לְשַׁלֵּחַ וְעוֹדְךָ מַחֲזִיק בָּם׃ הִנֵּה יַד־ יְהוָה הוֹיָה
bringing Yahweh hand-of see! (3) on-them holding-back and-still-you to-let-go

בְּמִקְנְךָ אֲשֶׁר בַּשָּׂדֶה בַּסּוּסִים בַּחֲמֹרִים בַּגְּמַלִּים
on-the-camels on-the-donkeys on-the-horses in-the-field that on-stock-of-you

בַּבָּקָר וּבַצֹּאן דֶּבֶר כָּבֵד מְאֹד׃ וְהִפְלָה
but-he-will-separate (4) very terrible plague and-on-the-flock on-the-cattle

יְהוָה בֵּין מִקְנֵה יִשְׂרָאֵל וּבֵין מִקְנֵה מִצְרָיִם וְלֹא יָמוּת
he-will-die so-not Egypt stock-of and-between Israel stock-of between Yahweh

מִכָּל־ לִבְנֵי יִשְׂרָאֵל דָּבָר׃ וַיָּשֶׂם יְהוָה מוֹעֵד לֵאמֹר
to-say time Yahweh and-he-set (5) animal Israel to-sons-of from-any-of

מָחָר יַעֲשֶׂה יְהוָה הַדָּבָר הַזֶּה בָּאָרֶץ׃ וַיַּעַשׂ
and-he-did (6) in-the-land the-this the-thing Yahweh he-will-do tomorrow

יְהוָה אֶת־ הַדָּבָר הַזֶּה מִמָּחֳרָת וַיָּמָת כֹּל מִקְנֵה
stock-of all-of and-he-died on-next-day the-this the-thing *** Yahweh

מִצְרָיִם וּמִמִּקְנֵה בְנֵי־ יִשְׂרָאֵל לֹא־ מֵת אֶחָד׃ וַיִּשְׁלַח
and-he-sent (7) one he-died not Israel sons-of but-from-stock-of Egyptians

Now pray for me."

29Moses answered, "As soon as I leave you, I will pray to the LORD, and tomorrow the flies will leave Pharaoh and his officials and his people. Only be sure that Pharaoh does not act deceitfully again by not letting the people go to offer sacrifices to the LORD."

30Then Moses left Pharaoh and prayed to the LORD, 31and the LORD did what Moses asked: The flies left Pharaoh and his officials and his people; not a fly remained. 32But this time also Pharaoh hardened his heart and would not let the people go.

*The Plague on Livestock*

9 Then the LORD said to Moses, "Go to Pharaoh and say to him, 'This is what the LORD, the God of the Hebrews, says: "Let my people go, so that they may worship me." 2If you refuse to let them go and continue to hold them back, 3the hand of the LORD will bring a terrible plague on your livestock in the field—on your horses and donkeys and camels and on your cattle and sheep and goats. 4But the LORD will make a distinction between the livestock of Israel and that of Egypt, so that no animal belonging to the Israelites will die.'"

5The LORD set a time and said, "Tomorrow the LORD will do this in the land." 6And the next day the LORD did it: All the livestock of the Egyptians died, but not one animal belonging to the Israelites died.

*See the note on page 163.

פַּרְעֹה וְהִנֵּה לֹא־ מֵת מִמִּקְנֵה יִשְׂרָאֵל עַד־ אֶחָד וַיִּכְבַּד
but-he-was-hard one even Israel from-stock-of he-died not and-see! Pharaoh

לֵב פַּרְעֹה וְלֹא שִׁלַּח אֶת־ הָעָם׃ וַיֹּאמֶר יְהוָה
Yahweh then-he-said (8) the-people *** he-let-go and-not Pharaoh heart-of

אֶל־ מֹשֶׁה וְאֶל־ אַהֲרֹן קְחוּ לָכֶם מְלֹא חָפְנֵיכֶם פִּיחַ כִּבְשָׁן
furnace soot-of hands-of-you full-of to-you take! Aaron and-to Moses to

וּזְרָקוֹ מֹשֶׁה הַשָּׁמַיְמָה לְעֵינֵי פַרְעֹה׃
Pharaoh before-eyes-of into-the-air Moses and-let-him-toss-him

וְהָיָה לְאָבָק עַל כָּל־ אֶרֶץ מִצְרָיִם וְהָיָה
and-he-will-be Egypt land-of all-of over into-fine-dust and-he-will-become (9)

עַל־ הָאָדָם וְעַל־ הַבְּהֵמָה לִשְׁחִין פֹּרֵחַ אֲבַעְבֻּעֹת בְּכָל־ אֶרֶץ
land-of in-all-of festers breaking-out into-boil the-animal and-on the-man on

מִצְרָיִם׃ וַיִּקְחוּ אֶת־ פִּיחַ הַכִּבְשָׁן וַיַּעַמְדוּ לִפְנֵי
before and-they-stood the-furnace soot-of *** so-they-took (10) Egypt

פַרְעֹה וַיִּזְרֹק אֹתוֹ מֹשֶׁה הַשָּׁמָיְמָה וַיְהִי שְׁחִין אֲבַעְבֻּעֹת
festers boil and-he-became into-the-air Moses him and-he-tossed Pharaoh

פֹּרֵחַ בָּאָדָם וּבַבְּהֵמָה׃ וְלֹא־ יָכְלוּ
they-could and-not (11) and-on-the-animal on-the-man breaking-out

הַחַרְטֻמִּים לַעֲמֹד לִפְנֵי מֹשֶׁה מִפְּנֵי הַשְּׁחִין כִּי־ הָיָה הַשְּׁחִין
the-boil he-was for the-boil because-of Moses before to-stand the-magicians

בַּחַרְטֻמִּם* וּבְכָל־ מִצְרָיִם׃ וַיְחַזֵּק יְהוָה אֶת־
*** Yahweh but-he-hardened (12) Egyptians and-on-all-of on-the-magicians

לֵב פַּרְעֹה וְלֹא שָׁמַע אֲלֵהֶם כַּאֲשֶׁר דִּבֶּר יְהוָה אֶל־מֹשֶׁה׃
Moses to Yahweh he-said just-as to-them he-listened and-not Pharaoh heart-of

וַיֹּאמֶר יְהוָה אֶל־ מֹשֶׁה הַשְׁכֵּם בַּבֹּקֶר וְהִתְיַצֵּב
and-confront! in-the-morning get-up-early! Moses to Yahweh then-he-said (13)

לִפְנֵי פַרְעֹה וְאָמַרְתָּ אֵלָיו כֹּה־ אָמַר יְהוָה אֱלֹהֵי הָעִבְרִים
the-Hebrews God-of Yahweh he-says this to-him and-you-say Pharaoh before

שַׁלַּח אֶת־ עַמִּי וְיַעַבְדֻנִי׃ כִּי ׀ בַּפַּעַם
on-the-time or (14) so-they-may-worship-me people-of-me *** let-go!

הַזֹּאת אֲנִי שֹׁלֵחַ אֶת־ כָּל־ מַגֵּפֹתַי אֶל־ לִבְּךָ
heart-of-you against plagues-of-me full-force-of *** sending I the-this

וּבַעֲבָדֶיךָ וּבְעַמֶּךָ בַּעֲבוּר תֵּדַע
you-may-know so-that and-against-people-of-you and-against-officials-of-you

כִּי אֵין כָּמֹנִי בְּכָל־ הָאָרֶץ׃ כִּי עַתָּה שָׁלַחְתִּי
I-could-stretch now for (15) the-earth in-all-of like-me there-is-no-one that

אֶת־ יָדִי וָאַךְ אוֹתְךָ וְאֶת־ עַמְּךָ בַּדָּבֶר
with-the-plague people-of-you and you and-I-could-strike hand-of-me ***

7 Pharaoh sent men to investigate and found that not even one of the animals of the Israelites had died. Yet his heart was unyielding and he would not let the people go.

*The Plague of Boils*

8 Then the LORD said to Moses and Aaron, "Take handfuls of soot from a furnace and have Moses toss it into the air in the presence of Pharaoh. 9 It will become fine dust over the whole land of Egypt, and festering boils will break out on men and animals throughout the land."

10 So they took soot from a furnace and stood before Pharaoh. Moses tossed it into the air, and festering boils broke out on men and animals. 11 The magicians could not stand before Moses because of the boils that were on them and on all the Egyptians. 12 But the LORD hardened Pharaoh's heart and he would not listen to Moses and Aaron, just as the LORD had said to Moses.

*The Plague of Hail*

13 Then the LORD said to Moses, "Get up early in the morning, confront Pharaoh and say to him, 'This is what the LORD, the God of the Hebrews, says: Let my people go, so that they may worship me, 14 or this time I will send the full force of my plagues against you and against your officials and your people, so you may know that there is no one like me in all the earth. 15 For by now I could have stretched out my hand and struck you and your people with a plague that would have

*11 Most mss have *pathah* under the *beth* (בַּחַ׳).

וַתִּכָּחֵד מִן־הָאָרֶץ׃ וְאוּלָם בַּעֲבוּר זֹאת
this for-purpose but-however (16) the-earth off and-you-would-be-wiped

הֶעֱמַדְתִּיךָ בַּעֲבוּר הַרְאֹתְךָ אֶת־כֹּחִי וּלְמַעַן סַפֵּר
to-proclaim and-so-that power-of-me *** to-show-you so-that I-raised-you

שְׁמִי בְּכָל־הָאָרֶץ׃ עוֹדְךָ מִסְתּוֹלֵל
setting-yourself still-you (17) the-earth in-all-of name-of-me

בְּעַמִּי לְבִלְתִּי שַׁלְּחָם׃ הִנְנִי מַמְטִיר כָּעֵת
at-the-time sending see-I! (18) to-let-go-them not against-people-of-me

מָחָר בָּרָד כָּבֵד מְאֹד אֲשֶׁר לֹא־הָיָה כָמֹהוּ בְּמִצְרַיִם לְמִן־
from in-Egypt like-him he-was never that very severe hailstorm tomorrow

הַיּוֹם הִוָּסְדָה וְעַד־עָתָּה׃ וְעַתָּה שְׁלַח הָעֵז אֶת־
*** shelter! give-order! so-now (19) now even-till to-be-founded-her the-day

מִקְנְךָ וְאֵת כָּל־אֲשֶׁר לְךָ בַּשָּׂדֶה כָּל־הָאָדָם וְהַבְּהֵמָה
and-the-animal the-man every-of in-the-field to-you that all and stock-of-you

אֲשֶׁר־יִמָּצֵא בַשָּׂדֶה וְלֹא יֵאָסֵף הַבַּיְתָה
into-the-shelter he-was-brought and-not in-the-field he-is-found that

וְיָרַד עֲלֵהֶם הַבָּרָד וָמֵתוּ׃ הַיָּרֵא
the-one-fearing (20) and-they-will-die the-hail on-them then-he-will-fall

אֶת־דְּבַר יְהוָה מֵעַבְדֵי פַּרְעֹה הֵנִיס אֶת־עֲבָדָיו
slaves-of-him *** he-brought Pharaoh from-officials-of Yahweh word-of ***

וְאֶת־מִקְנֵהוּ אֶל־הַבָּתִּים׃ וַאֲשֶׁר לֹא־שָׂם לִבּוֹ
heart-of-him he-took not but-who (21) the-shelters into stock-of-him and

אֶל־דְּבַר יְהוָה וַיַּעֲזֹב אֶת־עֲבָדָיו וְאֶת־מִקְנֵהוּ
stock-of-him and slaves-of-him *** then-he-left Yahweh word-of about

בַּשָּׂדֶה׃ וַיֹּאמֶר יְהוָה אֶל־מֹשֶׁה* נְטֵה אֶת־יָדְךָ
hand-of-you *** stretch-out! Moses to Yahweh then-he-said (22) in-the-field

עַל־הַשָּׁמַיִם וִיהִי בָרָד בְּכָל־אֶרֶץ מִצְרָיִם עַל־הָאָדָם
the-man on Egypt land-of over-all-of hail so-he-will-fall the-heavens to

וְעַל־הַבְּהֵמָה וְעַל כָּל־עֵשֶׂב הַשָּׂדֶה בְּאֶרֶץ מִצְרָיִם׃
Egypt in-land-of the-field plant-of every-of and-on the-animal and-on

וַיֵּט מֹשֶׁה אֶת־מַטֵּהוּ עַל־הַשָּׁמַיִם וַיהוָה נָתַן
he-sent and-Yahweh the-heavens to staff-of-him *** Moses so-he-stretched (23)

קֹלֹת וּבָרָד וַתִּהֲלַךְ אֵשׁ אָרְצָה וַיַּמְטֵר
so-he-rained to-ground lightning and-she-flashed-down and-hail thunders

יְהוָה בָּרָד עַל־אֶרֶץ מִצְרָיִם׃ וַיְהִי בָרָד וְאֵשׁ מִתְלַקַּחַת
flashing and-lightning hail and-he-fell (24) Egypt land-of on hail Yahweh

בְּתוֹךְ הַבָּרָד כָּבֵד מְאֹד אֲשֶׁר לֹא־הָיָה כָמֹהוּ בְּכָל־אֶרֶץ
land-of in-all-of like-him he-was never that very severe the-hail in-midst-of

wiped you off the earth. 16But I have raised you up[p] for this very purpose, that I might show you my power and that my name might be proclaimed in all the earth. 17You still set yourself against my people and will not let them go. 18Therefore, at this time tomorrow I will send the worst hailstorm that has ever fallen on Egypt, from the day it was founded till now. 19Give an order now to bring your livestock and everything you have in the field to a place of shelter, because the hail will fall on every man and animal that has not been brought in and is still out in the field, and they will die.' "

20Those officials of Pharaoh who feared the word of the LORD hurried to bring their slaves and their livestock inside. 21But those who ignored the word of the LORD left their slaves and livestock in the field.

22Then the LORD said to Moses, "Stretch out your hand toward the sky so that hail will fall all over Egypt—on men and animals and on everything growing in the fields of Egypt." 23When Moses stretched out his staff toward the sky, the LORD sent thunder and hail, and lightning flashed down to the ground. So the LORD rained hail on the land of Egypt; 24hail fell and lightning flashed back and forth. It was the worst storm

[p]16 *Or have spared you*

*22 Most mss have the accent *rebia* (מֹשֶׁה).

מִצְרַיִם מֵאָז הָיְתָה לְגוֹי׃ וַיַּךְ הַבָּרָד
the-hail and-he-struck (25) into-nation she-became since-when Egypt

בְּכָל־ אֶרֶץ מִצְרַיִם אֵת כָּל־ אֲשֶׁר בַּשָּׂדֶה מֵאָדָם וְעַד־
and-to from-man in-the-field that everything *** Egypt land-of through-all-of

בְּהֵמָה וְאֵת כָּל־ עֵשֶׂב הַשָּׂדֶה הִכָּה הַבָּרָד וְאֶת־ כָּל־
every-of and the-hail he-beat-down the-field plant-of every-of and animal

עֵץ הַשָּׂדֶה שִׁבֵּר׃ רַק בְּאֶרֶץ גֹּשֶׁן אֲשֶׁר־ שָׁם בְּנֵי
sons-of there where Goshen in-land-of only (26) he-stripped the-field tree-of

יִשְׂרָאֵל לֹא הָיָה בָּרָד׃ וַיִּשְׁלַח פַּרְעֹה וַיִּקְרָא לְמֹשֶׁה
to-Moses and-he-called Pharaoh then-he-summoned (27) hail he-was not Israel

וּלְאַהֲרֹן וַיֹּאמֶר אֲלֵהֶם חָטָאתִי הַפָּעַם יְהוָה הַצַּדִּיק וַאֲנִי
and-I the-right Yahweh the-time I-sinned to-them and-he-said and-to-Aaron

וְעַמִּי הָרְשָׁעִים׃ הַעְתִּירוּ אֶל־ יְהוָה וְרַב מִהְיֹת
from-to-be for-enough Yahweh to pray! (28) the-wrong-ones and-people-of-me

קֹלֹת אֱלֹהִים וּבָרָד וַאֲשַׁלְּחָה אֶתְכֶם וְלֹא
and-not you and-I-will-let-go and-hail mighty-ones thunders-of

תֹסִפוּן לַעֲמֹד׃ וַיֹּאמֶר אֵלָיו מֹשֶׁה כְּצֵאתִי
when-to-leave-me Moses to-him and-he-replied (29) to-stay you-will-continue

אֶת־ הָעִיר אֶפְרֹשׂ אֶת־ כַּפַּי אֶל־ יְהוָה הַקֹּלוֹת
the-thunders Yahweh to hands-of-me *** I-will-spread the-city ***

יֶחְדָּלוּן וְהַבָּרָד לֹא יִהְיֶה־ עוֹד לְמַעַן תֵּדַע
you-may-know so-that any-more he-will-be not and-the-hail they-will-stop

כִּי לַיהוָה הָאָרֶץ׃ וְאַתָּה וַעֲבָדֶיךָ יָדַעְתִּי כִּי
that I-know and-officials-of-you but-you (30) the-earth to-Yahweh that

טֶרֶם תִּירְאוּן מִפְּנֵי יְהוָה אֱלֹהִים׃ וְהַפִּשְׁתָּה וְהַשְּׂעֹרָה
and-the-barley now-the-flax (31) God Yahweh before you-fear not-yet

נֻכָּתָה כִּי הַשְּׂעֹרָה אָבִיב וְהַפִּשְׁתָּה גִּבְעֹל׃ וְהַחִטָּה
but-the-wheat (32) bloom and-the-flax head the-barley for she-was-destroyed

וְהַכֻּסֶּמֶת לֹא נֻכּוּ כִּי אֲפִילֹת הֵנָּה׃ וַיֵּצֵא
then-he-left (33) they later-ripen for they-were-destroyed not and-the-spelt

מֹשֶׁה מֵעִם פַּרְעֹה אֶת־ הָעִיר וַיִּפְרֹשׂ כַּפָּיו אֶל־ יְהוָה
Yahweh to hands-of-him and-he-spread the-city *** Pharaoh from-with Moses

וַיַּחְדְּלוּ הַקֹּלוֹת וְהַבָּרָד וּמָטָר לֹא־ נִתַּךְ אָרְצָה׃
on-land he-poured not and-rain and-the-hail the-thunders and-they-stopped

וַיַּרְא פַּרְעֹה כִּי־ חָדַל הַמָּטָר וְהַבָּרָד
and-the-hail the-rain he-stopped that Pharaoh when-he-saw (34)

וְהַקֹּלֹת וַיֹּסֶף לַחֲטֹא וַיַּכְבֵּד לִבּוֹ הוּא
he heart-of-him and-he-hardened to-sin then-he-repeated and-the-thunders

in all the land of Egypt since it had become a nation. 25Throughout Egypt hail struck everything in the fields—both men and animals; it beat down everything growing in the fields and stripped every tree. 26The only place it did not hail was the land of Goshen, where the Israelites were.

27Then Pharaoh summoned Moses and Aaron. "This time I have sinned," he said to them. "The LORD is in the right, and I and my people are in the wrong. 28Pray to the LORD, for we have had enough thunder and hail. I will let you go; you don't have to stay any longer."

29Moses replied, "When I have gone out of the city, I will spread out my hands in prayer to the LORD. The thunder will stop and there will be no more hail, so you may know that the earth is the LORD's. 30But I know that you and your officials still do not fear the LORD God."

31(The flax and barley were destroyed, since the barley had headed and the flax was in bloom. 32The wheat and spelt, however, were not destroyed, because they ripen later.)

33Then Moses left Pharaoh and went out of the city. He spread out his hands toward the LORD; the thunder and hail stopped, and the rain no longer poured down on the land. 34When Pharaoh saw that the rain and hail and thunder had stopped, he sinned again: He and his officials hardened

וַעֲבָדָיו׃ וַיֶּחֱזַק לֵב פַּרְעֹה וְלֹא שִׁלַּח
he-let-go and-not Pharaoh heart-of so-he-was-hard (35) and-officials-of-him

אֶת־ בְּנֵי יִשְׂרָאֵל כַּאֲשֶׁר דִּבֶּר יְהוָה בְּיַד־ מֹשֶׁה׃ וַיֹּאמֶר
then-he-said (10:1) Moses by-hand-of Yahweh he-said just-as Israel sons-of ***

יְהוָה אֶל־ מֹשֶׁה בֹּא אֶל־ פַּרְעֹה כִּי־ אֲנִי הִכְבַּדְתִּי אֶת־ לִבּוֹ וְאֶת־
and heart-of-him *** I-hardened I for Pharaoh to go! Moses to Yahweh

לֵב עֲבָדָיו לְמַעַן שִׁתִי אֹתֹתַי אֵלֶּה בְּקִרְבּוֹ׃
among-him these signs-of-me performing-me so-that officials-of-him heart-of

וּלְמַעַן תְּסַפֵּר בְּאָזְנֵי בִנְךָ וּבֶן־ בִּנְךָ
child-of-you and-child-of child-of-you in-ears-of you-may-tell and-that (2)

אֵת אֲשֶׁר הִתְעַלַּלְתִּי בְּמִצְרַיִם וְאֶת־ אֹתֹתַי אֲשֶׁר־ שַׂמְתִּי
I-performed how signs-of-me and with-Egyptians I-dealt-harshly how ***

בָם וִידַעְתֶּם כִּי־ אֲנִי יְהוָה׃ וַיָּבֹא מֹשֶׁה וְאַהֲרֹן
and-Aaron Moses so-he-went (3) Yahweh I that that-you-may-know among-them

אֶל־ פַּרְעֹה וַיֹּאמְרוּ אֵלָיו כֹּה־ אָמַר יְהוָה אֱלֹהֵי הָעִבְרִים עַד־
how the-Hebrews God-of Yahweh he-says this to-him and-they-said Pharaoh to

מָתַי מֵאַנְתָּ לֵעָנֹת מִפָּנָי שַׁלַּח עַמִּי
people-of-me to-let-go before-me to-humble-yourself will-you-refuse long

וְיַעַבְדֻנִי׃ כִּי אִם־ מָאֵן אַתָּה לְשַׁלֵּחַ אֶת־ עַמִּי
people-of-me *** to-let-go you to-refuse if but (4) so-they-may-worship-me

הִנְנִי מֵבִיא מָחָר אַרְבֶּה בִּגְבֻלֶךָ׃ וְכִסָּה
and-he-will-cover (5) into-country-of-you locust tomorrow bringing see-I!

אֶת־ עֵין הָאָרֶץ וְלֹא יוּכַל לִרְאֹת אֶת־ הָאָרֶץ וְאָכַל ׀
and-he-will-devour the-ground *** to-see he-can so-not the-ground face-of ***

אֶת־ יֶתֶר הַפְּלֵטָה הַנִּשְׁאֶרֶת לָכֶם מִן־ הַבָּרָד וְאָכַל
and-he-will-devour the-hail after to-you the-remaining the-remnant left-of ***

אֶת־ כָּל־ הָעֵץ הַצֹּמֵחַ לָכֶם מִן־ הַשָּׂדֶה׃ וּמָלְאוּ
and-they-will-fill (6) the-field in to-you the-one-growing the-tree every-of ***

בָתֶּיךָ וּבָתֵּי כָל־ עֲבָדֶיךָ וּבָתֵּי כָל־
all-of and-houses-of officials-of-you all-of and-houses-of houses-of-you

מִצְרַיִם אֲשֶׁר לֹא־ רָאוּ אֲבֹתֶיךָ וַאֲבוֹת אֲבֹתֶיךָ
fathers-of-you nor-fathers-of fathers-of-you they-saw not that Egyptians

מִיּוֹם הֱיוֹתָם עַל־ הָאֲדָמָה עַד הַיּוֹם הַזֶּה וַיִּפֶן
then-he-turned the-this the-day until the-land in to-settle-them from-day

וַיֵּצֵא מֵעִם פַּרְעֹה׃ וַיֹּאמְרוּ עַבְדֵי פַרְעֹה אֵלָיו
to-him Pharaoh officials-of and-they-said (7) Pharaoh from-with and-he-left

עַד־ מָתַי יִהְיֶה זֶה לָנוּ לְמוֹקֵשׁ שַׁלַּח אֶת־ הָאֲנָשִׁים
the-people *** let-go! as-snare to-us this will-he-be long how

their hearts. 35So Pharaoh's
heart was hard and he would
not let the Israelites go, just as
the LORD had said through
Moses.

*The Plague of Locusts*

10 Then the LORD said to
Moses, "Go to Pharaoh,
for I have hardened his heart
and the hearts of his officials
so that I may perform these
miraculous signs of mine
among them 2that you may tell
your children and grandchildren how I dealt harshly with
the Egyptians and how I performed my signs among them,
and that you may know that I
am the LORD."
3So Moses and Aaron went
to Pharaoh and said to him,
"This is what the LORD, the
God of the Hebrews, says:
'How long will you refuse to
humble yourself before me?
Let my people go, so that they
may worship me. 4If you
refuse to let them go, I will
bring locusts into your country tomorrow. 5They will cover
the face of the ground so that
it cannot be seen. They will
devour what little you have
left after the hail, including
every tree that is growing in
your fields. 6They will fill your
houses and those of all your
officials and all the Egyptians—something neither
your fathers nor your forefathers have ever seen from the
day they settled in this land
till now.' " Then Moses turned
and left Pharaoh.
7Pharaoh's officials said to
him, "How long will this man
be a snare to us? Let the people

וְיַֽעַבְדוּ אֶת־ יְהוָה אֱלֹהֵיהֶם הֲטֶרֶם תֵּדַע כִּי

that you-realize not-yet? God-of-them Yahweh *** so-they-may-worship

אָבְדָה מִצְרָיִם׃ וַיּוּשַׁב אֶת־ מֹשֶׁה וְאֶת־ אַהֲרֹן אֶל־

to Aaron and Moses *** so-he-was-brought-back (8) Egypt she-is-ruined

פַּרְעֹה וַיֹּאמֶר אֲלֵהֶם לְכוּ עִבְדוּ אֶת־ יְהוָה אֱלֹהֵיכֶם מִי וָמִי

and-who? who? God-of-you Yahweh *** worship! go! to-them and-he-said Pharaoh

הַהֹלְכִים׃ וַיֹּאמֶר מֹשֶׁה בִּנְעָרֵינוּ

with-young-ones-of-us Moses and-he-answered (9) the-ones-going

וּבִזְקֵנֵינוּ נֵלֵךְ בְּבָנֵינוּ וּבִבְנוֹתֵנוּ

and-with-daughters-of-us with-sons-of-us we-will-go and-with-ones-of-us

בְּצֹאנֵנוּ וּבִבְקָרֵנוּ נֵלֵךְ כִּי חַג־ יְהוָה לָנוּ׃

to-us Yahweh festival-of for we-will-go and-with-herd-of-us with-flock-of-us

וַיֹּאמֶר אֲלֵהֶם יְהִי כֵן יְהוָה עִמָּכֶם כַּאֲשֶׁר אֲשַׁלַּח אֶתְכֶם

you I-let-go if-ever with-you Yahweh so may-he-be to-them but-he-said (10)

וְאֶת־ טַפְּכֶם רְאוּ כִּי רָעָה נֶגֶד פְּנֵיכֶם׃ לֹא כֵן לְכוּ־

go! so not (11) faces-of-you before evil clearly see! children-of-you and

נָא הַגְּבָרִים וְעִבְדוּ אֶת־ יְהוָה כִּי אֹתָהּ אַתֶּם מְבַקְשִׁים

ones-requesting you she since Yahweh *** and-worship! the-men now!

וַיְגָרֶשׁ אֹתָם מֵאֵת פְּנֵי פַרְעֹה׃ וַיֹּאמֶר יְהוָה אֶל־

to Yahweh and-he-said (12) Pharaoh presence-of from them then-he-drove-out

מֹשֶׁה נְטֵה יָדְךָ עַל־ אֶרֶץ מִצְרַיִם בָּאַרְבֶּה

for-the-locust Egypt land-of over hand-of-you stretch-out! Moses

וְיַעַל עַל־ אֶרֶץ מִצְרָיִם וְיֹאכַל אֶת־ כָּל־ עֵשֶׂב

plant-of every-of *** and-he-will-devour Egypt land-of over so-he-will-swarm

הָאָרֶץ אֵת כָּל־ אֲשֶׁר הִשְׁאִיר הַבָּרָד׃ וַיֵּט מֹשֶׁה אֶת־

*** Moses so-he-stretched (13) the-hail he-left that all *** the-land

מַטֵּהוּ עַל־ אֶרֶץ מִצְרַיִם וַיהוָה נִהַג רוּחַ קָדִים

east wind-of he-made-blow and-Yahweh Egypt land-of over staff-of-him

בָּאָרֶץ כָּל־ הַיּוֹם הַהוּא וְכָל־ הַלָּיְלָה הַבֹּקֶר

the-morning the-night and-all-of the-that the-day all-of across-the-land

הָיָה וְרוּחַ הַקָּדִים נָשָׂא אֶת־ הָאַרְבֶּה׃ וַיַּעַל

and-he-invaded (14) the-locust *** he-brought the-east and-wind-of he-was

הָאַרְבֶּה עַל כָּל־ אֶרֶץ מִצְרַיִם וַיָּנַח בְּכֹל גְּבוּל מִצְרָיִם

Egypt area-of in-every-of and-he-settled Egypt land-of all-of on the-locust

כָּבֵד מְאֹד לְפָנָיו לֹא־ הָיָה כֵן אַרְבֶּה כָּמֹהוּ וְאַחֲרָיו לֹא

not and-after-him like-him locust such he-was never before-him very many

יִהְיֶה־ כֵּן׃ וַיְכַס אֶת־ עֵין כָּל־ הָאָרֶץ

the-ground all-of face-of *** and-he-covered (15) again he-will-be

go, so that they may worship
the LORD their God. Do you
not yet realize that Egypt is
ruined?"
8Then Moses and Aaron
were brought back to Pharaoh.
"Go, worship the LORD your
God," he said. "But just who
will be going?"
9Moses answered, "We will
go with our young and old,
with our sons and daughters,
and with our flocks and herds,
because we are to celebrate a
festival to the LORD."
10Pharaoh said, "The LORD
be with you—if I let you go,
along with your women and
children! Clearly you are bent
on evil.[p] 11No! Have only the
men go; and worship the
LORD, since that's what you
have been asking for." Then
Moses and Aaron were driven
out of Pharaoh's presence.
12And the LORD said to
Moses, "Stretch out your hand
over Egypt so that locusts will
swarm over the land and devour everything growing in
the fields, everything left by
the hail."
13So Moses stretched out his
staff over Egypt, and the LORD
made an east wind blow
across the land all that day and
all that night. By morning the
wind had brought the locusts;
14they invaded all Egypt and
settled down in every area of
the country in great numbers.
Never before had there been
such a plague of locusts, nor
will there ever be again.
15They covered all the ground

[p]10 Or *Be careful, trouble is in store for you!*

וַתֶּחְשַׁךְ הָאָרֶץ וַיֹּאכַל אֶת־ כָּל־ עֵשֶׂב הָאָרֶץ
the-land plant-of every-of *** and-he-devoured the-ground so-she-was-black

וְאֵת כָּל־ פְּרִי הָעֵץ אֲשֶׁר הוֹתִיר הַבָּרָד וְלֹא־ נוֹתַר
he-remained and-not the-hail he-left that the-tree fruit-of all-of and

כָּל־ יֶרֶק בָּעֵץ וּבְעֵשֶׂב הַשָּׂדֶה בְּכָל־ אֶרֶץ מִצְרָיִם׃
Egypt land-of in-all-of the-field or-on-plant-of on-the-tree green any-of

וַיְמַהֵר פַּרְעֹה לִקְרֹא לְמֹשֶׁה וּלְאַהֲרֹן וַיֹּאמֶר
and-he-said and-to-Aaron to-Moses to-summon Pharaoh and-he-hurried (16)

חָטָאתִי לַיהוָה אֱלֹהֵיכֶם וְלָכֶם׃ וְעַתָּה שָׂא נָא
now! forgive! and-now (17) and-against-you God-of-you against-Yahweh I-sinned

חַטָּאתִי אַךְ הַפַּעַם וְהַעְתִּירוּ לַיהוָה אֱלֹהֵיכֶם וְיָסֵר
so-he-will-take God-of-you to-Yahweh and-pray! the-time again sin-of-me

מֵעָלַי רַק אֶת־ הַמָּוֶת הַזֶּה׃ וַיֵּצֵא מֵעִם
from-with then-he-left (18) the-this the-deadly-plague *** also away-from-me

פַּרְעֹה וַיֶּעְתַּר אֶל־ יְהוָה׃ וַיַּהֲפֹךְ יְהוָה רוּחַ־ יָם
west wind-of Yahweh and-he-changed (19) Yahweh to and-he-prayed Pharaoh

חָזָק מְאֹד וַיִּשָּׂא אֶת־ הָאַרְבֶּה וַיִּתְקָעֵהוּ יָמָּה סּוּף
Reed into-Sea-of and-he-carried-him the-locust *** and-he-caught very strong

לֹא נִשְׁאַר אַרְבֶּה אֶחָד בְּכֹל גְּבוּל מִצְרָיִם׃ וַיְחַזֵּק
but-he-hardened (20) Egypt area-of in-any-of one locust he-was-left not

יְהוָה אֶת־ לֵב פַּרְעֹה וְלֹא שִׁלַּח אֶת־ בְּנֵי יִשְׂרָאֵל׃
Israel sons-of *** he-let-go and-not Pharaoh heart-of *** Yahweh

וַיֹּאמֶר יְהוָה אֶל־ מֹשֶׁה נְטֵה יָדְךָ עַל־ הַשָּׁמַיִם
the-heavens to hand-of-you stretch-out! Moses to Yahweh then-he-said (21)

וִיהִי חֹשֶׁךְ עַל־ אֶרֶץ מִצְרָיִם וְיָמֵשׁ חֹשֶׁךְ׃
darkness and-he-can-feel Egypt land-of over darkness so-he-will-spread

וַיֵּט מֹשֶׁה אֶת־ יָדוֹ עַל־ הַשָּׁמָיִם וַיְהִי
and-he-covered the-heavens to hand-of-him *** Moses so-he-stretched (22)

חֹשֶׁךְ־ אֲפֵלָה בְּכָל־ אֶרֶץ מִצְרַיִם שְׁלֹשֶׁת יָמִים׃ לֹא־ רָאוּ
they-saw not (23) days three-of Egypt land-of over-all-of thick darkness

אִישׁ אֶת־ אָחִיו וְלֹא־ קָמוּ אִישׁ מִתַּחְתָּיו שְׁלֹשֶׁת יָמִים
days three-of from-place-of-him any they-left and-not fellow-of-him *** any

וּלְכָל־ בְּנֵי יִשְׂרָאֵל הָיָה אוֹר בְּמוֹשְׁבֹתָם׃
in-dwellings-of-them light he-was Israel sons-of yet-to-all-of

וַיִּקְרָא פַרְעֹה אֶל־מֹשֶׁה וַיֹּאמֶר לְכוּ עִבְדוּ אֶת־ יְהוָה רַק
only Yahweh *** worship! go! and-he-said Moses to Pharaoh and-he-summoned (24)

צֹאנְכֶם וּבְקַרְכֶם יֻצָּג גַּם־ טַפְּכֶם יֵלֵךְ
he-may-go child-of-you even he-will-be-left and-herd-of-you flock-of-you

until it was black. They devoured all that was left after the hail—everything growing in the fields and the fruit on the trees. Nothing green remained on tree or plant in all the land of Egypt.

16Pharaoh quickly summoned Moses and Aaron and said, "I have sinned against the LORD your God and against you. 17Now forgive my sin once more and pray to the LORD your God to take this deadly plague away from me."

18Moses then left Pharaoh and prayed to the LORD. 19And the LORD changed the wind to a very strong west wind, which caught up the locusts and carried them into the Red Sea.[q] Not a locust was left anywhere in Egypt. 20But the LORD hardened Pharaoh's heart, and he would not let the Israelites go.

*The Plague of Darkness*

21Then the LORD said to Moses, "Stretch out your hand toward the sky so that darkness will spread over Egypt—darkness that can be felt." 22So Moses stretched out his hand toward the sky, and total darkness covered all Egypt for three days. 23No one could see anyone else or leave his place for three days. Yet all the Israelites had light in the places where they lived.

24Then Pharaoh summoned Moses and said, "Go, worship the LORD. Even your women and children may go with you; only leave your flocks and herds behind."

q19 Hebrew *Yam Suph;* that is, Sea of Reeds

עִמָּכֶם׃ וַיֹּאמֶר מֹשֶׁה גַּם־ אַתָּה תִּתֵּן בְּיָדֵנוּ

in-hand-of-us you-must-allow you also Moses but-he-said (25) with-you

זְבָחִים וְעֹלֹת וְעָשִׂינוּ לַיהוָה אֱלֹהֵינוּ׃ וְגַם־

so-also (26) God-of-us to-Yahweh so-we-may-present and-burnt-offerings sacrifices

מִקְנֵנוּ יֵלֵךְ עִמָּנוּ לֹא תִשָּׁאֵר פַּרְסָה כִּי מִמֶּנּוּ

from-him for hoof she-may-be-left not with-us he-must-go cattle-of-us

נִקַּח לַעֲבֹד אֶת־ יְהוָה אֱלֹהֵינוּ וַאֲנַחְנוּ לֹא־ נֵדַע מַה־

what we-know not and-we God-of-us Yahweh *** to-worship we-must-use

נַּעֲבֹד אֶת־ יְהוָה עַד־ בֹּאֵנוּ שָׁמָּה׃ וַיְחַזֵּק

but-he-hardened (27) to-there to-get-us until Yahweh *** we-must-offer

יְהוָה אֶת־ לֵב פַּרְעֹה וְלֹא אָבָה לְשַׁלְּחָם׃

to-let-go-them he-was-willing and-not Pharaoh heart-of *** Yahweh

וַיֹּאמֶר־ לוֹ פַּרְעֹה לֵךְ מֵעָלָי הִשָּׁמֶר לְךָ אֶל־*

not to-you make-sure! from-me go! Pharaoh to-him then-he-said (28)

תֹּסֶף רְאוֹת פָּנַי כִּי בְּיוֹם רְאֹתְךָ פָּנַי תָּמוּת׃

you-will-die face-of-me to-see-you on-day for face-of-me to-see you-repeat

וַיֹּאמֶר מֹשֶׁה כֵּן דִּבַּרְתָּ לֹא־ אֹסִף עוֹד רְאוֹת פָּנֶיךָ׃

face-of-you to-see again I-will-repeat not you-say as Moses and-he-replied (29)

וַיֹּאמֶר יְהוָה אֶל־מֹשֶׁה עוֹד נֶגַע אֶחָד אָבִיא עַל־פַּרְעֹה

Pharaoh on I-will-bring one plague again Moses to Yahweh now-he-said (11:1)

וְעַל־ מִצְרַיִם אַחֲרֵי־ כֵן יְשַׁלַּח אֶתְכֶם מִזֶּה כְּשַׁלְּחוֹ

when-to-let-go-him from-here you he-will-let-go that after Egypt and-on

כָּלָה גָּרֵשׁ יְגָרֵשׁ אֶתְכֶם מִזֶּה׃ דַּבֶּר־ נָא

now! tell! (2) from-here you he-will-drive-out to-drive-out completely

בְּאָזְנֵי הָעָם וְיִשְׁאֲלוּ אִישׁ | מֵאֵת רֵעֵהוּ וְאִשָּׁה

and-woman neighbor-of-him from man so-they-may-ask the-people in-ears-of

מֵאֵת רְעוּתָהּ כְּלֵי־ כֶסֶף וּכְלֵי זָהָב׃ וַיִּתֵּן

and-he-made (3) gold and-articles-of silver articles-of neighbor-of-her from

יְהוָה אֶת־ חֵן הָעָם בְּעֵינֵי מִצְרָיִם גַּם | הָאִישׁ מֹשֶׁה

Moses the-man also Egyptians in-eyes-of the-people favorable *** Yahweh

גָּדוֹל מְאֹד בְּאֶרֶץ מִצְרַיִם בְּעֵינֵי עַבְדֵי־ פַרְעֹה

Pharaoh officials-of in-eyes-of Egypt in-land-of highly regarded

וּבְעֵינֵי הָעָם׃ וַיֹּאמֶר מֹשֶׁה כֹּה אָמַר יְהוָה

Yahweh he-says this Moses so-he-said (4) the-people and-in-eyes-of

כַּחֲצֹת הַלַּיְלָה אֲנִי יוֹצֵא בְּתוֹךְ מִצְרָיִם׃ וּמֵת כָּל־

every-of and-he-will-die (5) Egypt throughout going I the-night about-mid-of

בְּכוֹר בְּאֶרֶץ מִצְרַיִם מִבְּכוֹר פַּרְעֹה הַיֹּשֵׁב עַל־

on the-one-sitting Pharaoh from-firstborn-of Egypt in-land-of firstborn

25But Moses said, "You must allow us to have sacrifices and burnt offerings to present to the LORD our God. 26Our livestock too must go with us; not a hoof is to be left behind. We have to use some of them in worshiping the LORD our God, and until we get there we will not know what we are to use to worship the LORD."

27But the LORD hardened Pharaoh's heart, and he was not willing to let them go. 28Pharaoh said to Moses, "Get out of my sight! Make sure you do not appear before me again! The day you see my face you will die."

29"Just as you say," Moses replied, "I will never appear before you again."

*The Plague on the Firstborn*

11 Now the LORD had said to Moses, "I will bring one more plague on Pharaoh and on Egypt. After that, he will let you go from here, and when he does, he will drive you out completely. 2Tell the people that men and women alike are to ask their neighbors for articles of silver and gold." 3(The LORD made the Egyptians favorably disposed toward the people, and Moses himself was highly regarded in Egypt by Pharaoh's officials and by the people.)

4So Moses said, "This is what the LORD says: 'About midnight I will go throughout Egypt. 5Every firstborn son in Egypt will die, from the firstborn son of Pharaoh, who

*28 Most mss have *pathah* under the *aleph* (אַל).

כִּסְאוֹ עַד בְּכוֹר הַשִּׁפְחָה אֲשֶׁר אַחַר הָרֵחָיִם וְכֹל
and-all-of the-handmill at who the-slave-girl firstborn-of to throne-of-him

בְּכוֹר בְּהֵמָה׃ וְהָיְתָה צְעָקָה גְדֹלָה בְּכָל־ אֶרֶץ
land-of through-all-of loud wail and-she-will-be (6) cattle firstborn-of

מִצְרָיִם אֲשֶׁר כָּמֹהוּ לֹא נִהְיָתָה וְכָמֹהוּ לֹא תֹסִף׃
she-will-be-again never and-like-him she-was never like-him that Egypt

וּלְכֹל ׀ בְּנֵי יִשְׂרָאֵל לֹא יֶחֱרַץ־ כֶּלֶב לְשֹׁנוֹ
tongue-of-him dog he-will-bark not Israel sons-of but-among-all-of (7)

לְמֵאִישׁ וְעַד־ בְּהֵמָה לְמַעַן תֵּדְעוּן אֲשֶׁר יַפְלֶה
he-distinguishes that you-will-know so-that animal or-at either-at-man

יְהוָה בֵּין מִצְרַיִם וּבֵין יִשְׂרָאֵל׃ וְיָרְדוּ כָל־
all-of and-they-will-come-down (8) Israel and-between Egypt between Yahweh

עֲבָדֶיךָ אֵלֶּה אֵלַי וְהִשְׁתַּחֲווּ־* לִי לֵאמֹר צֵא אַתָּה
you go! to-say to-me and-they-will-bow to-me these officials-of-you

וְכָל־ הָעָם אֲשֶׁר־ בְּרַגְלֶיךָ וְאַחֲרֵי־ כֵן אֵצֵא
I-will-leave that and-after at-feet-of-you who the-people and-all-of

וַיֵּצֵא מֵעִם־ פַּרְעֹה בָּחֳרִי־ אָף׃ וַיֹּאמֶר יְהוָה אֶל־
to Yahweh now-he-said (9) anger in-heat-of Pharaoh from-with then-he-left

מֹשֶׁה לֹא־ יִשְׁמַע אֲלֵיכֶם פַּרְעֹה לְמַעַן רְבוֹת מוֹפְתַי
wonders-of-me to-be-multiplied so-that Pharaoh to-you he-will-listen not Moses

בְּאֶרֶץ מִצְרָיִם׃ וּמֹשֶׁה וְאַהֲרֹן עָשׂוּ אֶת־ כָּל־ הַמֹּפְתִים
the-wonders all-of *** they-performed and-Aaron so-Moses (10) Egypt in-land-of

הָאֵלֶּה לִפְנֵי פַרְעֹה וַיְחַזֵּק יְהוָה אֶת־ לֵב פַּרְעֹה וְלֹא־
and-not Pharaoh heart-of *** Yahweh but-he-hardened Pharaoh before the-these

שִׁלַּח אֶת־ בְּנֵי־ יִשְׂרָאֵל מֵאַרְצוֹ׃ וַיֹּאמֶר יְהוָה
Yahweh and-he-said (12:1) from-country-of-him Israel sons-of *** he-let-go

אֶל־מֹשֶׁה וְאֶל־ אַהֲרֹן בְּאֶרֶץ מִצְרַיִם לֵאמֹר׃ הַחֹדֶשׁ הַזֶּה לָכֶם
for-you the-this the-month (2) to-say Egypt in-land-of Aaron and-to Moses to

רֹאשׁ חֳדָשִׁים רִאשׁוֹן הוּא לָכֶם לְחָדְשֵׁי הַשָּׁנָה׃ דַּבְּרוּ אֶל־
to tell! (3) the-year among-months-of for-you he first months first-of

כָּל־ עֲדַת יִשְׂרָאֵל לֵאמֹר בֶּעָשֹׂר לַחֹדֶשׁ הַזֶּה
the-this of-the-month on-the-tenth to-say Israel community-of whole-of

וְיִקְחוּ לָהֶם אִישׁ שֶׂה לְבֵית־ אָבֹת שֶׂה לַבָּיִת׃
for-the-household lamb fathers for-house-of lamb each to-them that-they-take

וְאִם־ יִמְעַט הַבַּיִת מִהְיוֹת מִשֶּׂה
whole-lamb than-to-have the-household he-is-too-small and-if (4)

וְלָקַח הוּא וּשְׁכֵנוֹ הַקָּרֹב אֶל־ בֵּיתוֹ
household-of-him with the-nearest with-neighbor-of-him he then-he-must-share

sits on the throne, to the firstborn son of the slave girl, who is at her hand mill, and all the firstborn of the cattle as well. 6There will be loud wailing throughout Egypt—worse than there has ever been or ever will be again. 7But among the Israelites not a dog will bark at any man or animal.' Then you will know that the LORD makes a distinction between Egypt and Israel. 8All these officials of yours will come to me, bowing down before me and saying, 'Go, you and all the people who follow you!' After that I will leave." Then Moses, hot with anger, left Pharaoh.

9The LORD had said to Moses, "Pharaoh will refuse to listen to you—so that my wonders may be multiplied in Egypt." 10Moses and Aaron performed all these wonders before Pharaoh, but the LORD hardened Pharaoh's heart, and he would not let the Israelites go out of his country.

*The Passover*

12 The LORD said to Moses and Aaron in Egypt, 2"This month is to be for you the first month, the first month of your year. 3Tell the whole community of Israel that on the tenth day of this month each man is to take a lamb[r] for his family, one for each household. 4If any household is too small for a whole lamb, they must share one with their nearest neighbor, having taken into account

[r]3 The Hebrew word can mean both *lamb* or *kid;* also in verse 4.

*8 Most mss have no *dagesh* in the first *vav* (וּ־).

בְּמִכְסַת נְפָשֹׁת אִישׁ לְפִי אָכְלוֹ תָּכֹסּוּ עַל־

about you-will-determine to-eat-him by-amount-of each people by-number-of

הַשֶּׂה׃ שֶׂה תָמִים זָכָר בֶּן־ שָׁנָה יִהְיֶה לָכֶם מִן־

from to-you he-must-be year son-of male without-defect lamb (5) the-lamb

הַכְּבָשִׂים וּמִן־ הָעִזִּים תִּקָּחוּ׃ וְהָיָה לָכֶם

with-you and-he-will-be (6) you-may-take the-goats or-from the-sheep

לְמִשְׁמֶרֶת עַד אַרְבָּעָה עָשָׂר יוֹם לַחֹדֶשׁ הַזֶּה וְשָׁחֲטוּ

and-they-must-slaughter the-this of-the-month day ten four until for-care

אֹתוֹ כֹּל קְהַל עֲדַת־ יִשְׂרָאֵל בֵּין הָעַרְבָּיִם׃ וְלָקְחוּ

then-they-take (7) the-twilight at Israel community-of people-of all-of him

מִן־ הַדָּם וְנָתְנוּ עַל־ שְׁתֵּי הַמְּזוּזֹת וְעַל־

and-on the-doorposts the-two-sides-of on and-they-must-put the-blood from

הַמַּשְׁקוֹף עַל הַבָּתִּים אֲשֶׁר־ יֹאכְלוּ אֹתוֹ בָּהֶם׃ וְאָכְלוּ

then-they-must-eat (8) in-them him they-eat where the-houses on the-top-post

אֶת־ הַבָּשָׂר בַּלַּיְלָה הַזֶּה צְלִי־ אֵשׁ וּמַצּוֹת

and-breads-without-yeast fire roasted-of the-that in-the-night the-meat ***

עַל־ מְרֹרִים יֹאכְלֻהוּ׃ אַל־ תֹּאכְלוּ מִמֶּנּוּ נָא וּבָשֵׁל

or-boiled raw from-him you-eat not (9) they-must-eat-him bitter-herbs with

מְבֻשָּׁל בַּמָּיִם כִּי אִם־ צְלִי־ אֵשׁ רֹאשׁוֹ עַל־

with head-of-him fire roasted-of only but in-the-water being-cooked

כְּרָעָיו וְעַל־ קִרְבּוֹ׃ וְלֹא־ תוֹתִירוּ מִמֶּנּוּ עַד־

till from-him you-leave and-not (10) inner-part-of-him and-with legs-of-him

בֹּקֶר וְהַנֹּתָר מִמֶּנּוּ עַד־ בֹּקֶר בָּאֵשׁ תִּשְׂרֹפוּ׃

you-must-burn in-the-fire morning until from-him and-the-being-left morning

וְכָכָה תֹּאכְלוּ אֹתוֹ מָתְנֵיכֶם חֲגֻרִים

being-tucked-in-ones loins-of-you him you-must-eat and-this-way (11)

נַעֲלֵיכֶם בְּרַגְלֵיכֶם וּמַקֶּלְכֶם בְּיֶדְכֶם וַאֲכַלְתֶּם

and-you-eat in-hand-of-you and-staff-of-you on-feet-of-you sandals-of-you

אֹתוֹ בְּחִפָּזוֹן פֶּסַח הוּא לַיהוָה׃ וְעָבַרְתִּי בְאֶרֶץ־

through-land-of and-I-will-pass (12) to-Yahweh he Passover in-haste him

מִצְרַיִם בַּלַּיְלָה הַזֶּה וְהִכֵּיתִי כָל־ בְּכוֹר בְּאֶרֶץ

in-land-of firstborn every-of and-I-will-strike the-that on-the-night Egypt

מִצְרַיִם מֵאָדָם וְעַד־ בְּהֵמָה וּבְכָל־ אֱלֹהֵי מִצְרַיִם אֶעֱשֶׂה

I-will-bring Egypt gods-of and-on-all-of animal even-to from-man Egypt

שְׁפָטִים אֲנִי יְהוָה׃ וְהָיָה הַדָּם לָכֶם לְאֹת עַל

on as-sign for-you the-blood and-he-will-be (13) Yahweh I judgments

הַבָּתִּים אֲשֶׁר אַתֶּם שָׁם וְרָאִיתִי אֶת־ הַדָּם וּפָסַחְתִּי עֲלֵכֶם

over-you then-I-will-pass the-blood *** when-I-see there you where the-houses

the number of people there are. You are to determine the amount of lamb needed in accordance with what each person will eat. [5]The animals you choose must be year-old males without defect, and you may take them from the sheep or the goats. [6]Take care of them until the fourteenth day of the month, when all the people of the community of Israel must slaughter them at twilight. [7]Then they are to take some of the blood and put it on the sides and tops of the doorframes of the houses where they eat the lambs. [8]That same night they are to eat the meat roasted over the fire, along with bitter herbs, and bread made without yeast. [9]Do not eat the meat raw or cooked in water, but roast it over the fire—head, legs and inner parts. [10]Do not leave any of it till morning; if some is left till morning, you must burn it. [11]This is how you are to eat it: with your cloak tucked into your belt, your sandals on your feet and your staff in your hand. Eat it in haste; it is the LORD's Passover.

[12]"On that same night I will pass through Egypt and strike down every firstborn—both men and animals—and I will bring judgment on all the gods of Egypt. I am the LORD. [13]The blood will be a sign for you on the houses where you are; and when I see the blood, I will pass over you. No destructive

וְלֹא־ יִהְיֶה בָכֶם נֶגֶף לְמַשְׁחִית בְּהַכֹּתִי בְּאֶרֶץ
on-land-of when-to-strike-me to-destroy plague among-you he-will-be and-not

מִצְרָיִם׃ וְהָיָה הַיּוֹם הַזֶּה לָכֶם לְזִכָּרוֹן וְחַגֹּתֶם
and-you-celebrate to-commemorate to-you the-this the-day and-he-is (14) Egypt

אֹתוֹ חַג לַיהוָה לְדֹרֹתֵיכֶם חֻקַּת עוֹלָם
lasting ordinance-of for-generations-of-you to-Yahweh festival him

תְּחָגֻּהוּ׃ שִׁבְעַת יָמִים מַצּוֹת תֹּאכֵלוּ אַךְ
indeed you-must-eat breads-without-yeast days seven-of (15) you-celebrate-him

בַּיּוֹם הָרִאשׁוֹן תַּשְׁבִּיתוּ שְׂאֹר* מִבָּתֵּיכֶם כִּי ׀ כָּל־ אֹכֵל
eating any-of for from-houses-of-you yeast you-remove the-first on-the-day

חָמֵץ וְנִכְרְתָה הַנֶּפֶשׁ הַהִוא מִיִּשְׂרָאֵל מִיּוֹם
from-day from-Israel the-that the-person now-she-must-be-cut-off leavened

הָרִאשֹׁן עַד־ יוֹם הַשְּׁבִעִי׃ וּבַיּוֹם הָרִאשׁוֹן מִקְרָא־
assembly the-first and-on-the-day (16) the-seventh day through the-first

קֹדֶשׁ וּבַיּוֹם הַשְּׁבִיעִי מִקְרָא־ קֹדֶשׁ יִהְיֶה לָכֶם כָּל־
any-of to-you he-will-be holy assembly the-seventh and-on-the-day holy

מְלָאכָה לֹא־ יֵעָשֶׂה בָהֶם אַךְ אֲשֶׁר יֵאָכֵל לְכָל־ נֶפֶשׁ
person by-every-of he-is-eaten what except on-them he-may-be-done not work

הוּא לְבַדּוֹ יֵעָשֶׂה לָכֶם׃ וּשְׁמַרְתֶּם אֶת־
*** and-you-celebrate (17) by-you he-may-be-done by-himself that

הַמַּצּוֹת כִּי בְּעֶצֶם הַיּוֹם הַזֶּה הוֹצֵאתִי
I-brought-out the-this the-day on-very for the-Feast-of-Unleavened-Breads

אֶת־ צִבְאוֹתֵיכֶם מֵאֶרֶץ מִצְרָיִם וּשְׁמַרְתֶּם אֶת־ הַיּוֹם הַזֶּה
the-this the-day *** so-you-celebrate Egypt from-land-of divisions-of-you ***

לְדֹרֹתֵיכֶם חֻקַּת עוֹלָם׃ בָּרִאשֹׁן בְּאַרְבָּעָה עָשָׂר
ten on-four in-the-first (18) lasting ordinance-of for-generations-of-you

יוֹם לַחֹדֶשׁ בָּעֶרֶב תֹּאכְלוּ מַצֹּת עַד יוֹם
day until breads-without-yeast you-must-eat in-the-evening of-the-month day

הָאֶחָד וְעֶשְׂרִים לַחֹדֶשׁ בָּעָרֶב׃ שִׁבְעַת יָמִים שְׂאֹר לֹא
not yeast days seven-of (19) the-evening of-the-month and-twenty the-one

יִמָּצֵא בְּבָתֵּיכֶם כִּי ׀ כָּל־ אֹכֵל מַחְמֶצֶת
leavened eating any-of for in-houses-of-you he-may-be-found

וְנִכְרְתָה הַנֶּפֶשׁ הַהִוא מֵעֲדַת יִשְׂרָאֵל
Israel from-community-of the-that the-person now-she-must-be-cut-off

בַּגֵּר וּבְאֶזְרַח הָאָרֶץ׃ כָּל־ מַחְמֶצֶת לֹא
not leavened any-of (20) the-land or-whether-born-of whether-the-alien

תֹּאכֵלוּ בְּכֹל מוֹשְׁבֹתֵיכֶם תֹּאכְלוּ מַצּוֹת׃
breads-without-yeast you-must-eat dwellings-of-you in-all-of you-may-eat

plague will touch you when I strike Egypt.

[14]"This is a day you are to commemorate; for the generations to come you shall celebrate it as a festival to the LORD—a lasting ordinance. [15]For seven days you are to eat bread made without yeast. On the first day remove the yeast from your houses, for whoever eats anything with yeast in it from the first day through the seventh must be cut off from Israel. [16]On the first day hold a sacred assembly, and another one on the seventh day. Do no work at all on these days, except to prepare food for everyone to eat—that is all you may do.

[17]"Celebrate the Feast of Unleavened Bread, because it was on this very day that I brought your divisions out of Egypt. Celebrate this day as a lasting ordinance for the generations to come. [18]In the first month you are to eat bread made without yeast, from the evening of the fourteenth day until the evening of the twenty-first day. [19]For seven days no yeast is to be found in your houses. And whoever eats anything with yeast in it must be cut off from the community of Israel, whether he is an alien or native-born. [20]Eat nothing made with yeast. Wherever you live, you must eat unleavened bread."

*15 Most mss have no *dagesh* in the *sin* (שׂאר).

וַיִּקְרָא מֹשֶׁה לְכָל־ זִקְנֵי יִשְׂרָאֵל וַיֹּאמֶר אֲלֵהֶם

to-them and-he-said Israel elders-of to-all-of Moses then-he-summoned (21)

מִשְׁכוּ וּקְחוּ לָכֶם צֹאן לְמִשְׁפְּחֹתֵיכֶם וְשַׁחֲטוּ

and-slaughter! for-families-of-you animal for-you and-take! select!

הַפָּסַח׃ וּלְקַחְתֶּם אֲגֻדַּת אֵזוֹב וּטְבַלְתֶּם בַּדָּם

in-the-blood and-you-dip hyssop bunch-of and-you-take (22) the-Passover-lamb

אֲשֶׁר־ בַּסַּף וְהִגַּעְתֶּם אֶל־ הַמַּשְׁקוֹף וְאֶל־ שְׁתֵּי

two-sides-of and-on the-top-post on and-you-put in-the-basin that

הַמְּזוּזֹת מִן־ הַדָּם אֲשֶׁר בַּסָּף וְאַתֶּם לֹא תֵצְאוּ אִישׁ

any you-must-go not and-you in-the-basin that the-blood from the-doorposts

מִפֶּתַח־ בֵּיתוֹ עַד־ בֹּקֶר׃ וְעָבַר יְהוָה לִנְגֹּף

to-strike Yahweh when-he-passes (23) morning until house-of-him from-door-of

אֶת־ מִצְרַיִם וְרָאָה אֶת־ הַדָּם עַל־ הַמַּשְׁקוֹף וְעַל

and-on the-top-post on the-blood *** then-he-will-see Egyptians ***

שְׁתֵּי הַמְּזוּזֹת וּפָסַח יְהוָה עַל־ הַפֶּתַח וְלֹא

and-not the-doorway over Yahweh and-he-will-pass the-doorposts two-sides-of

יִתֵּן הַמַּשְׁחִית לָבֹא אֶל־ בָּתֵּיכֶם לִנְגֹּף׃

to-strike houses-of-you into to-enter the-one-destroying he-will-permit

וּשְׁמַרְתֶּם אֶת־ הַדָּבָר הַזֶּה לְחָק־ לְךָ

for-you as-ordinance the-this the-instruction *** now-you-obey (24)

וּלְבָנֶיךָ עַד־ עוֹלָם׃ וְהָיָה כִּי־ תָבֹאוּ אֶל־

to you-come when and-he-will-be (25) ever for and-for-descendants-of-you

הָאָרֶץ אֲשֶׁר יִתֵּן יְהוָה לָכֶם כַּאֲשֶׁר דִּבֵּר וּשְׁמַרְתֶּם

then-you-observe he-promised just-as to-you Yahweh he-will-give that the-land

אֶת־ הָעֲבֹדָה הַזֹּאת׃ וְהָיָה כִּי־ יֹאמְרוּ אֲלֵיכֶם

to-you they-say when and-he-will-be (26) the-this the-ceremony ***

בְּנֵיכֶם מָה הָעֲבֹדָה הַזֹּאת לָכֶם׃ וַאֲמַרְתֶּם

then-you-tell (27) to-you the-this the-ceremony what? children-of-you

זֶבַח־ פֶּסַח הוּא לַיהוָה אֲשֶׁר פָּסַח עַל־ בָּתֵּי בְנֵי־

sons-of houses-of over he-passed who to-Yahweh this Passover sacrifice-of

יִשְׂרָאֵל בְּמִצְרַיִם בְּנָגְפּוֹ אֶת־ מִצְרַיִם וְאֶת־ בָּתֵּינוּ הִצִּיל

he-spared homes-of-us and Egyptians *** when-to-strike-him in-Egypt Israel

וַיִּקֹּד הָעָם וַיִּשְׁתַּחֲווּ*׃ וַיֵּלְכוּ וַיַּעֲשׂוּ

and-they-did and-they-went (28) and-they-worshiped the-people and-he-bowed

בְּנֵי יִשְׂרָאֵל כַּאֲשֶׁר צִוָּה יְהוָה אֶת־ מֹשֶׁה וְאַהֲרֹן כֵּן עָשׂוּ׃

they-did this and-Aaron Moses *** Yahweh he-commanded just-as Israel sons-of

וַיְהִי ׀ בַּחֲצִי הַלַּיְלָה וַיהוָה הִכָּה כָל־ בְּכוֹר

firstborn every-of he-struck that-Yahweh the-night at-mid-of and-he-was (29)

21 Then Moses summoned all the elders of Israel and said to them, "Go at once and select the animals for your families and slaughter the Passover lamb. 22 Take a bunch of hyssop, dip it into the blood in the basin and put some of the blood on the top and on both sides of the doorframe. Not one of you shall go out the door of his house until morning. 23 When the LORD goes through the land to strike down the Egyptians, he will see the blood on the top and sides of the doorframe and will pass over that doorway, and he will not permit the destroyer to enter your houses and strike you down.

24 "Obey these instructions as a lasting ordinance for you and your descendants. 25 When you enter the land that the LORD will give you as he promised, observe this ceremony. 26 And when your children ask you, 'What does this ceremony mean to you?' 27 then tell them, 'It is the Passover sacrifice to the LORD, who passed over the houses of the Israelites in Egypt and spared our homes when he struck down the Egyptians.' " Then the people bowed down and worshiped. 28 The Israelites did just what the LORD commanded Moses and Aaron.

29 At midnight the LORD struck down all the firstborn

*27 Most mss have no *dagesh* in the first *vav* (וּו־).

בְּאֶרֶץ מִצְרַיִם מִבְּכֹר פַּרְעֹה הַיֹּשֵׁב עַל־ כִּסְאוֹ
in-land-of Egypt from-firstborn-of Pharaoh the-one-sitting on throne-of-him

עַד בְּכוֹר הַשְּׁבִי אֲשֶׁר בְּבֵית הַבּוֹר וְכֹל
to firstborn-of the-prisoner who in-house-of the-dungeon and-every-of

בְּכוֹר בְּהֵמָה׃ (30) וַיָּקָם פַּרְעֹה לַיְלָה הוּא וְכָל־
firstborn-of animal (30) and-he-got-up Pharaoh night he and-all-of

עֲבָדָיו וְכָל־ מִצְרַיִם וַתְּהִי צְעָקָה גְדֹלָה בְּמִצְרָיִם כִּי־
officials-of-him and-all-of Egyptians and-she-was wail loud in-Egypt for

אֵין בַּיִת אֲשֶׁר אֵין־ שָׁם מֵת׃ (31) וַיִּקְרָא לְמֹשֶׁה
not house where not there being-dead (31) so-he-summoned to-Moses

וּלְאַהֲרֹן לַיְלָה וַיֹּאמֶר קוּמוּ צְּאוּ מִתּוֹךְ עַמִּי גַּם־
and-to-Aaron night and-he-said get-up! leave! from-among people-of-me indeed

אַתֶּם גַּם־ בְּנֵי יִשְׂרָאֵל וּלְכוּ עִבְדוּ אֶת־ יְהוָה כְּדַבֶּרְכֶם׃
you also sons-of Israel and-go! worship! *** Yahweh as-to-request-you

(32) גַּם־ צֹאנְכֶם גַּם־ בְּקַרְכֶם קְחוּ כַּאֲשֶׁר דִּבַּרְתֶּם וָלֵכוּ
(32) also flock-of-you also herd-of-you take! just-as you-said and-go!

וּבֵרַכְתֶּם גַּם־ אֹתִי׃ (33) וַתֶּחֱזַק מִצְרַיִם עַל־ הָעָם לְמַהֵר
and-you-bless also me (33) and-she-urged Egyptians with the-people to-hurry

לְשַׁלְּחָם מִן־ הָאָרֶץ כִּי אָמְרוּ כֻּלָּנוּ מֵתִים׃
to-leave-them from the-country for they-said all-of-us being-dead-ones

(34) וַיִּשָּׂא הָעָם אֶת־ בְּצֵקוֹ טֶרֶם יֶחְמָץ
(34) so-he-took the-people *** dough-of-him before he-was-leavened

מִשְׁאֲרֹתָם צְרֻרֹת בְּשִׂמְלֹתָם עַל־
kneading-troughs-of-them ones-being-wrapped in-clothing-of-them on

שִׁכְמָם׃ (35) וּבְנֵי־ יִשְׂרָאֵל עָשׂוּ כִּדְבַר מֹשֶׁה
shoulder-of-them (35) and-sons-of Israel they-did as-instruction-of Moses

וַיִּשְׁאֲלוּ מִמִּצְרַיִם כְּלֵי־ כֶסֶף וּכְלֵי זָהָב
and-they-asked from-Egyptians articles-of silver and-articles-of gold

וּשְׂמָלֹת׃ (36) וַיהוָה נָתַן אֶת־ חֵן הָעָם בְּעֵינֵי
and-clothing (36) now-Yahweh he-made *** favorable the-people in-eyes-of

מִצְרַיִם וַיַּשְׁאִלוּם וַיְנַצְּלוּ אֶת־ מִצְרָיִם׃
Egyptians and-they-granted-request-of-them so-they-plundered *** Egyptians

(37) וַיִּסְעוּ בְנֵי־ יִשְׂרָאֵל מֵרַעְמְסֵס סֻכֹּתָה כְּשֵׁשׁ־
(37) and-they-journeyed sons-of Israel from-Rameses to-Succoth about-six

מֵאוֹת אֶלֶף רַגְלִי הַגְּבָרִים לְבַד מִטָּף׃ (38) וְגַם־
hundreds thousand on-foot the-men beside from-children (38) and-also

עֵרֶב רַב עָלָה אִתָּם וְצֹאן וּבָקָר מִקְנֶה כָּבֵד מְאֹד׃
other-people many he-went-up with-them and-flock and-herd stock many very

in Egypt, from the firstborn of Pharaoh, who sat on the throne, to the firstborn of the prisoner, who was in the dungeon, and the firstborn of all the livestock as well.
30Pharaoh and all his officials and all the Egyptians got up during the night, and there was loud wailing in Egypt, for there was not a house without someone dead.

*The Exodus*

31During the night Pharaoh summoned Moses and Aaron and said, "Up! Leave my people, you and the Israelites! Go, worship the LORD as you have requested.
32Take your flocks and herds, as you have said, and go. And also bless me."

33The Egyptians urged the people to hurry and leave the country. "For otherwise," they said, "we will all die!"
34So the people took their dough before the yeast was added, and carried it on their shoulders in kneading troughs wrapped in clothing.
35The Israelites did as Moses instructed and asked the Egyptians for articles of silver and gold and for clothing.
36The LORD had made the Egyptians favorably disposed toward the people, and they gave them what they asked for; so they plundered the Egyptians.

37The Israelites journeyed from Rameses to Succoth. There were about six hundred thousand men on foot, besides women and children.
38Many other people went up with them, as well as large droves of livestock, both flocks and

וַיֹּאפוּ אֶת־ הַבָּצֵק אֲשֶׁר הוֹצִיאוּ מִמִּצְרַיִם עֻגֹת
cakes-of from-Egypt they-brought that the-dough *** and-they-baked (39)

מַצּוֹת כִּי לֹא חָמֵץ כִּי־ גֹרְשׁוּ מִמִּצְרַיִם
from-Egypt they-were-driven for he-had-yeast not for unleavened-breads

וְלֹא יָכְלוּ לְהִתְמַהְמֵהַּ וְגַם־ צֵדָה לֹא־ עָשׂוּ לָהֶם׃
for-themselves they-made not food and-also to-take-time they-could and-not

וּמוֹשַׁב בְּנֵי יִשְׂרָאֵל אֲשֶׁר יָשְׁבוּ בְּמִצְרָיִם שְׁלֹשִׁים שָׁנָה וְאַרְבַּע
and-four year thirty in-Egypt they-lived that Israel sons-of now-time-of (40)

מֵאוֹת שָׁנָה׃ וַיְהִי מִקֵּץ שְׁלֹשִׁים שָׁנָה וְאַרְבַּע מֵאוֹת שָׁנָה
year hundreds and-four year thirty at-end-of and-he-was (41) year hundreds

וַיְהִי בְּעֶצֶם הַיּוֹם הַזֶּה יָצְאוּ כָּל־ צִבְאוֹת יְהוָה
Yahweh divisions-of all-of they-left the-this the-day to-very and-he-was

מֵאֶרֶץ מִצְרָיִם׃ לֵיל שִׁמֻּרִים הוּא לַיהוָה לְהוֹצִיאָם
to-bring-out-them by-Yahweh that vigils night-of (42) Egypt from-land-of

מֵאֶרֶץ מִצְרַיִם הוּא־ הַלַּיְלָה הַזֶּה לַיהוָה שִׁמֻּרִים לְכָל־
by-all-of vigils to-Yahweh the-this the-night this Egypt from-land-of

בְּנֵי יִשְׂרָאֵל לְדֹרֹתָם׃ וַיֹּאמֶר יְהוָה אֶל־ מֹשֶׁה
Moses to Yahweh then-he-said (43) for-generations-of-them Israel sons-of

וְאַהֲרֹן זֹאת חֻקַּת הַפָּסַח כָּל־ בֶּן־ נֵכָר לֹא־
not foreigner son-of any-of the-Passover regulation-of this and-Aaron

יֹאכַל בּוֹ׃ וְכָל־ עֶבֶד אִישׁ מִקְנַת־ כָּסֶף
money bought-of man slave but-any-of (44) from-it he-may-eat

וּמַלְתָּה אֹתוֹ אָז יֹאכַל בּוֹ׃ תּוֹשָׁב
temporary-resident (45) from-him he-may-eat then him and-you-circumcised

וְשָׂכִיר לֹא־ יֹאכַל־ בּוֹ׃ בְּבַיִת אֶחָד יֵאָכֵל
he-must-be-eaten one in-house (46) from-him he-may-eat not or-hired-worker

לֹא־ תוֹצִיא מִן־ הַבַּיִת מִן־ הַבָּשָׂר חוּצָה וְעֶצֶם לֹא תִשְׁבְּרוּ־
you-break not and-bone to-outside the-meat from the-house from you-take not

בוֹ׃ כָּל־ עֲדַת יִשְׂרָאֵל יַעֲשׂוּ אֹתוֹ׃ וְכִי־
and-if (48) him he-must-celebrate Israel community-of whole-of (47) in-him

יָגוּר אִתְּךָ גֵּר וְעָשָׂה פֶסַח לַיהוָה הִמּוֹל
circumcise! to-Yahweh Passover and-he-would-celebrate alien with-you he-lives

לוֹ כָל־ זָכָר וְאָז יִקְרַב לַעֲשֹׂתוֹ וְהָיָה
and-he-will-be to-celebrate-him he-may-take-part and-then male every-of to-him

כְּאֶזְרַח הָאָרֶץ וְכָל־ עָרֵל לֹא־ יֹאכַל בּוֹ׃
from-him he-may-eat not uncircumcised but-any-of the-land like-born-of

תּוֹרָה אַחַת יִהְיֶה לָאֶזְרָח וְלַגֵּר הַגָּר
the-one-living and-to-the-alien to-the-native-born he-applies same law (49)

herds. 39With the dough they had brought from Egypt, they baked cakes of unleavened bread. The dough was without yeast because they had been driven out of Egypt and did not have time to prepare food for themselves.

40Now the length of time the Israelite people lived in Egypt[s] was 430 years. 41At the end of the 430 years, to the very day, all the LORD's divisions left Egypt. 42Because the LORD kept vigil that night to bring them out of Egypt, on this night all the Israelites are to keep vigil to honor the LORD for the generations to come.

*Passover Restrictions*

43The LORD said to Moses and Aaron, "These are the regulations for the Passover:

"No foreigner is to eat of it. 44Any slave you have bought may eat of it after you have circumcised him, 45but a temporary resident and a hired worker may not eat of it.

46"It must be eaten inside one house; take none of the meat outside the house. Do not break any of the bones. 47The whole community of Israel must celebrate it.

48"An alien living among you who wants to celebrate the LORD's Passover must have all the males in his household circumcised; then he may take part like one born in the land. No uncircumcised male may eat of it. 49The same law applies to the native-born and to the alien living among you."

[s]40 Masoretic Text; Samaritan Pentateuch and Septuagint *Egypt and Canaan*

בְּתוֹכְכֶֽם׃ וַֽיַּעֲשׂוּ כָּל־ בְּנֵי יִשְׂרָאֵל כַּאֲשֶׁר צִוָּה יְהוָה
Yahweh he-commanded just-as Israel sons-of all-of so-they-did (50) among-you

אֶת־ מֹשֶׁה וְאֶת־אַהֲרֹן כֵּן עָשֽׂוּ׃ וַיְהִי בְּעֶצֶם הַיּוֹם הַזֶּה
the-that the-day on-very and-he-was (51) they-did this Aaron and Moses ***

הוֹצִיא יְהוָה אֶת־ בְּנֵי יִשְׂרָאֵל מֵאֶרֶץ מִצְרַיִם עַל־ צִבְאֹתָֽם׃
divisions-of-them by Egypt from-land-of Israel sons-of *** Yahweh he-brought

וַיְדַבֵּר יְהוָה אֶל־ מֹשֶׁה לֵּאמֹֽר׃ קַדֶּשׁ־ לִי כָל־
every-of to-me consecrate! (2) to-say Moses to Yahweh then-he-said (13:1)

בְּכוֹר פֶּטֶר כָּל־ רֶחֶם בִּבְנֵי יִשְׂרָאֵל בָּאָדָם
whether-the-man Israel among-sons-of womb every-of first-of firstborn

וּבַבְּהֵמָה לִי הֽוּא׃ וַיֹּאמֶר מֹשֶׁה אֶל־ הָעָם
the-people to Moses then-he-said (3) he to-me or-whether-the-animal

זָכוֹר אֶת־ הַיּוֹם הַזֶּה אֲשֶׁר יְצָאתֶם מִמִּצְרַיִם מִבֵּית
from-house-of from-Egypt you-came-out that the-this the-day *** to-commemorate

עֲבָדִים כִּי בְּחֹזֶק יָד הוֹצִיא יְהוָה אֶתְכֶם מִזֶּה וְלֹא
so-not from-this you Yahweh he-brought-out hand with-mighty-of for slaveries

יֵאָכֵל חָמֵֽץ׃ הַיּוֹם אַתֶּם יֹצְאִים בְּחֹדֶשׁ הָאָבִֽיב׃
the-Abib in-month-of ones-leaving you the-day (4) leavened he-may-be-eaten

וְהָיָה כִי־ יְבִיאֲךָ יְהוָה אֶל־ אֶרֶץ הַֽכְּנַעֲנִי
the-Canaanite land-of into Yahweh he-brings-you when and-he-will-be (5)

וְהַֽחִתִּי וְהָאֱמֹרִי וְהַֽחִוִּי וְהַיְבוּסִי אֲשֶׁר
that and-the-Jebusite and-the-Hivite and-the-Amorite and-the-Hittite

נִשְׁבַּע לַאֲבֹתֶיךָ לָתֶת לָךְ אֶרֶץ זָבַת חָלָב וּדְבָשׁ
and-honey milk flowing-of land to-you to-give to-fathers-of-you he-swore

וְעָבַדְתָּ אֶת־ הָעֲבֹדָה הַזֹּאת בַּחֹדֶשׁ הַזֶּֽה׃ שִׁבְעַת
seven-of (6) the-this in-the-month the-this the-ceremony *** then-you-observe

יָמִים תֹּאכַל מַצֹּת וּבַיּוֹם הַשְּׁבִיעִי חַג
festival the-seventh and-on-the-day breads-without-yeast you-eat days

לַיהוָֽה׃ מַצּוֹת יֵאָכֵל אֵת שִׁבְעַת הַיָּמִים וְלֹא־
and-not the-days seven-of *** he-must-be-eaten unleavened-breads (7) to-Yahweh

יֵרָאֶה לְךָ חָמֵץ וְלֹא־ יֵרָאֶה לְךָ שְׂאֹר
yeast among-you he-may-be-seen and-not leavened among-you he-may-be-seen

בְּכָל־ גְּבֻלֶֽךָ׃ וְהִגַּדְתָּ לְבִנְךָ בַּיּוֹם
on-the-day to-son-of-you and-you-tell (8) border-of-you within-all-of

הַהוּא לֵאמֹר בַּעֲבוּר זֶה עָשָׂה יְהוָה לִי בְּצֵאתִי
when-to-come-me for-me Yahweh he-did what because-of to-say the-that

מִמִּצְרָֽיִם׃ וְהָיָה לְךָ לְאוֹת עַל־ יָֽדְךָ וּלְזִכָּרוֹן
and-as-reminder hand-of-you on as-sign for-you and-he-will-be (9) from-Egypt

50 All the Israelites did just what the LORD had commanded Moses and Aaron. 51 And on that very day the LORD brought the Israelites out of Egypt by their divisions.

*Consecration of the Firstborn*

13 The LORD said to Moses, 2 "Consecrate to me every firstborn male. The first offspring of every womb among the Israelites belongs to me, whether man or animal."

3 Then Moses said to the people, "Commemorate this day, the day you came out of Egypt, out of the land of slavery, because the LORD brought you out of it with a mighty hand. Eat nothing containing yeast. 4 Today, in the month of Abib, you are leaving. 5 When the LORD brings you into the land of the Canaanites, Hittites, Amorites, Hivites and Jebusites—the land he swore to your forefathers to give you, a land flowing with milk and honey—you are to observe this ceremony in this month: 6 For seven days eat bread made without yeast and on the seventh day hold a festival to the LORD. 7 Eat unleavened bread during those seven days; nothing with yeast in it is to be seen among you, nor shall any yeast be seen anywhere within your borders. 8 On that day tell your son, 'I do this because of what the LORD did for me when I came out of Egypt.' 9 This observance will be for you like a sign on your hand

בֵּין עֵינֶיךָ לְמַעַן תִּהְיֶה תּוֹרַת יְהוָה בְּפִיךָ כִּי
for in-mouth-of-you Yahweh law-of she-must-be that eyes-of-you between

בְּיָד חֲזָקָה הוֹצִאֲךָ יְהוָה מִמִּצְרָיִם׃ וְשָׁמַרְתָּ אֶת־
*** so-you-must-keep (10) from-Egypt Yahweh he-brought-you mighty with-hand

הַחֻקָּה הַזֹּאת לְמוֹעֲדָהּ מִיָּמִים יָמִימָה׃ וְהָיָה
and-he-will-be (11) to-days from-days at-time-of-her the-this the-ordinance

כִּי־יְבִאֲךָ יְהוָה אֶל־אֶרֶץ הַכְּנַעֲנִי כַּאֲשֶׁר נִשְׁבַּע לְךָ
to-you he-swore just-as the-Canaanite land-of to Yahweh he-brings-you after

וְלַאֲבֹתֶיךָ וּנְתָנָהּ לָךְ׃ וְהַעֲבַרְתָּ
then-you-must-give (12) to-you and-he-gives-her and-to-fathers-of-you

כָל־פֶּטֶר־רֶחֶם לַיהוָה וְכָל־פֶּטֶר | שֶׁגֶר בְּהֵמָה אֲשֶׁר
that animal born-of first-of and-every-of to-Yahweh womb first-of every-of

יִהְיֶה לְךָ הַזְּכָרִים לַיהוָה׃ וְכָל־פֶּטֶר חֲמֹר
donkey firstborn-of but-every-of (13) to-Yahweh the-males to-you he-is

תִּפְדֶּה בְשֶׂה וְאִם־לֹא תִפְדֶּה וַעֲרַפְתּוֹ
then-you-break-neck-of-him you-redeem not but-if with-lamb you-redeem

וְכֹל בְּכוֹר אָדָם בְּבָנֶיךָ תִּפְדֶּה׃ וְהָיָה
and-he-will-be (14) you-redeem among-sons-of-you man firstborn-of and-every-of

כִּי־יִשְׁאָלְךָ בִנְךָ מָחָר לֵאמֹר מַה־זֹּאת וְאָמַרְתָּ אֵלָיו
to-him then-you-say this what? to-say day-to-come son-of-you he-asks-you when

בְּחֹזֶק יָד הוֹצִיאָנוּ יְהוָה מִמִּצְרַיִם מִבֵּית עֲבָדִים׃
slaveries from-house-of from-Egypt Yahweh he-brought-us hand with-mighty-of

וַיְהִי כִּי־הִקְשָׁה פַרְעֹה לְשַׁלְּחֵנוּ וַיַּהֲרֹג יְהוָה
Yahweh then-he-killed to-let-go-us Pharaoh he-refused when and-he-was (15)

כָּל־בְּכוֹר בְּאֶרֶץ מִצְרַיִם מִבְּכֹר אָדָם וְעַד־בְּכוֹר
firstborn-of even-to man from-firstborn-of Egypt in-land-of firstborn every-of

בְּהֵמָה עַל־כֵּן אֲנִי זֹבֵחַ לַיהוָה כָּל־פֶּטֶר רֶחֶם הַזְּכָרִים
the-males womb first-of every-of to-Yahweh sacrificing I this for animal

וְכָל־בְּכוֹר בָּנַי אֶפְדֶּה׃ וְהָיָה לְאוֹת
like-sign and-he-will-be (16) I-redeem sons-of-me firstborn-of and-every-of

עַל־יָדְכָה וּלְטוֹטָפֹת בֵּין עֵינֶיךָ כִּי בְּחֹזֶק יָד
hand with-mighty-of for eyes-of-you between and-like-symbols hand-of-you on

הוֹצִיאָנוּ יְהוָה מִמִּצְרָיִם׃ וַיְהִי בְּשַׁלַּח פַּרְעֹה אֶת־
*** Pharaoh when-to-let-go and-he-was (17) from-Egypt Yahweh he-brought-us

הָעָם וְלֹא־נָחָם אֱלֹהִים דֶּרֶךְ אֶרֶץ פְּלִשְׁתִּים כִּי
though Philistines country-of road-of God he-led-them and-not the-people

קָרוֹב הוּא כִּי | אָמַר אֱלֹהִים פֶּן־יִנָּחֵם הָעָם בִּרְאֹתָם
if-to-face-them the-people he-change-mind might God he-said for that short

and a reminder on your forehead that the law of the LORD is to be on your lips. For the LORD brought you out of Egypt with his mighty hand. [10]You must keep this ordinance at the appointed time year after year.

[11]"After the LORD brings you into the land of the Canaanites and gives it to you, as he promised on oath to you and your forefathers, [12]you are to give over to the LORD the first offspring of every womb. All the firstborn males of your livestock belong to the LORD. [13]Redeem with a lamb every firstborn donkey, but if you do not redeem it, break its neck. Redeem every firstborn among your sons.

[14]"In days to come, when your son asks you, 'What does this mean?' say to him, 'With a mighty hand the LORD brought us out of Egypt, out of the land of slavery. [15]When Pharaoh stubbornly refused to let us go, the LORD killed every firstborn in Egypt, both man and animal. This is why I sacrifice to the LORD the first male offspring of every womb and redeem each of my firstborn sons.' [16]And it will be like a sign on your hand and a symbol on your forehead that the LORD brought us out of Egypt with his mighty hand."

*Crossing the Sea*

[17]When Pharaoh let the people go, God did not lead them on the road through the Philistine country, though that was shorter. For God said, "If they face war, they might change their minds and return

מִלְחָמָה וְשָׁבוּ מִצְרָיְמָה׃ וַיַּסֵּב אֱלֹהִים ׀ אֶת־ הָעָם
the-people *** God so-he-led-around (18) to-Egypt and-they-return war

דֶּרֶךְ הַמִּדְבָּר יַם־ סוּף וַחֲמֻשִׁים עָלוּ בְנֵי־ יִשְׂרָאֵל
Israel sons-of they-went-up and-ones-armed Reed Sea-of the-desert road-of

מֵאֶרֶץ מִצְרָיִם׃ וַיִּקַּח מֹשֶׁה אֶת־ עַצְמוֹת יוֹסֵף עִמּוֹ כִּי
for with-him Joseph bones-of *** Moses and-he-took (19) Egypt from-land-of

הַשְׁבֵּעַ הִשְׁבִּיעַ אֶת־ בְּנֵי יִשְׂרָאֵל לֵאמֹר פָּקֹד יִפְקֹד
he-will-aid to-aid to-say Israel sons-of *** he-made-swear to-make-swear

אֱלֹהִים אֶתְכֶם וְהַעֲלִיתֶם אֶת־ עַצְמֹתַי מִזֶּה אִתְּכֶם׃
with-you from-this bones-of-me *** then-you-must-carry you God

וַיִּסְעוּ מִסֻּכֹּת וַיַּחֲנוּ בְאֵתָם בִּקְצֵה הַמִּדְבָּר׃
the-desert on-edge-of at-Etham and-they-camped from-Succoth so-they-left (20)

וַיהוָה הֹלֵךְ לִפְנֵיהֶם יוֹמָם בְּעַמּוּד עָנָן לַנְחֹתָם
to-guide-them cloud in-pillar-of by-day ahead-of-them going now-Yahweh (21)

הַדֶּרֶךְ וְלַיְלָה בְּעַמּוּד אֵשׁ לְהָאִיר לָהֶם לָלֶכֶת יוֹמָם
by-day to-travel to-them to-give-light fire in-pillar-of and-night the-way

וָלָיְלָה׃ לֹא־ יָמִישׁ עַמּוּד הֶעָנָן יוֹמָם וְעַמּוּד הָאֵשׁ
the-fire nor-pillar-of by-day the-cloud pillar-of he-left not (22) or-night

לָיְלָה לִפְנֵי הָעָם׃ וַיְדַבֵּר יְהוָה אֶל־ מֹשֶׁה לֵּאמֹר׃
to-say Moses to Yahweh then-he-said (14:1) the-people in-front-of night

דַּבֵּר אֶל־ בְּנֵי יִשְׂרָאֵל וְיָשֻׁבוּ וְיַחֲנוּ לִפְנֵי פִּי
Pi near and-they-encamp so-they-turn-back Israel sons-of to tell! (2)

הַחִירֹת בֵּין מִגְדֹּל וּבֵין הַיָּם לִפְנֵי בַּעַל צְפֹן נִכְחוֹ
opposite-him Zephon Baal near the-sea and-between Migdol between Hahiroth

תַּחֲנוּ עַל־ הַיָּם׃ וְאָמַר פַּרְעֹה לִבְנֵי
about-sons-of Pharaoh and-he-will-think (3) the-sea by you-shall-encamp

יִשְׂרָאֵל נְבֻכִים הֵם בָּאָרֶץ סָגַר עֲלֵיהֶם הַמִּדְבָּר׃
the-desert on-them he-hemmed-in around-the-land they ones-wandering Israel

וְחִזַּקְתִּי אֶת־ לֵב־ פַּרְעֹה וְרָדַף אַחֲרֵיהֶם
after-them and-he-will-pursue Pharaoh heart-of *** and-I-will-harden (4)

וְאִכָּבְדָה בְּפַרְעֹה וּבְכָל־ חֵילוֹ
army-of-him and-through-all-of through-Pharaoh but-I-will-glorify-myself

וְיָדְעוּ מִצְרַיִם כִּי־ אֲנִי יְהוָה וַיַּעֲשׂוּ־ כֵן׃ וַיֻּגַּד
and-he-was-told (5) this so-they-did Yahweh I that Egyptians and-they-will-know

לְמֶלֶךְ מִצְרַיִם כִּי בָרַח הָעָם וַיֵּהָפֵךְ לְבַב פַּרְעֹה
Pharaoh mind-of and-he-was-changed the-people he-fled that Egypt to-king-of

וַעֲבָדָיו אֶל־ הָעָם וַיֹּאמְרוּ מַה־ זֹּאת עָשִׂינוּ כִּי־
for we-did this what? and-they-said the-people about and-officials-of-him

to Egypt." 18So God led the
people around by the desert
road toward the Red Sea.[t] The
Israelites went up out of Egypt
armed for battle.
19Moses took the bones of Joseph with him because Joseph
had made the sons of Israel
swear an oath. He had said,
"God will surely come to your
aid, and then you must carry
my bones up with you from
this place."[u]
20After leaving Succoth they
camped at Etham on the edge
of the desert. 21By day the LORD
went ahead of them in a pillar
of cloud to guide them on their
way and by night in a pillar of
fire to give them light, so that
they could travel by day or
night. 22Neither the pillar of
cloud by day nor the pillar of
fire by night left its place in
front of the people.
14 Then the LORD said to
Moses, 2"Tell the Isra-
elites to turn back and encamp
near Pi Hahiroth, between
Migdol and the sea. They are
to encamp by the sea, directly
opposite Baal Zephon. 3Phar-
aoh will think, 'The Israelites
are wandering around the
land in confusion, hemmed in
by the desert.' 4And I will
harden Pharaoh's heart, and
he will pursue them. But I will
gain glory for myself through
Pharaoh and all his army, and
the Egyptians will know that I
am the LORD." So the Israelites
did this.
5When the king of Egypt
was told that the people had
fled, Pharaoh and his officials
changed their minds about
them and said, "What have

[t]18 Hebrew *Yam Suph;* that is, Sea of Reeds
[u]19 See Genesis 50:25.

שִׁלַּחְנוּ אֶת־ יִשְׂרָאֵל מֵעָבְדֵנוּ׃ וַיֶּאְסֹר אֶת־ רִכְבּוֹ
chariot-of-him *** so-he-readied (6) from-to-serve-us Israel *** we-let-go

וְאֶת־ עַמּוֹ לָקַח עִמּוֹ׃ וַיִּקַּח שֵׁשׁ־ מֵאוֹת רֶכֶב
chariot hundreds six and-he-took (7) with-him he-took army-of-him and

בָּחוּר וְכֹל רֶכֶב מִצְרָיִם וְשָׁלִשִׁם עַל־ כֻּלּוֹ׃
each-of-him over with-officers Egypt chariot-of with-all-of being-best

וַיְחַזֵּק יְהוָה אֶת־ לֵב פַּרְעֹה מֶלֶךְ מִצְרַיִם וַיִּרְדֹּף
so-he-pursued Egypt king-of Pharaoh heart-of *** Yahweh and-he-hardened (8)

אַחֲרֵי בְּנֵי יִשְׂרָאֵל וּבְנֵי יִשְׂרָאֵל יֹצְאִים בְּיָד
with-hand ones-marching-out Israel now-sons-of Israel sons-of after

רָמָה׃ וַיִּרְדְּפוּ מִצְרַיִם אַחֲרֵיהֶם וַיַּשִּׂיגוּ
and-they-overtook after-them Egyptians so-they-pursued (9) being-boldly-lifted

אוֹתָם חֹנִים עַל־ הַיָּם כָּל־ סוּס רֶכֶב פַּרְעֹה
Pharaoh chariot-of horse-of every-of the-sea by ones-camping them

וּפָרָשָׁיו וְחֵילוֹ עַל־ פִּי הַחִירֹת לִפְנֵי בַּעַל צְפֹן׃
Zephon Baal opposite-of Hahiroth Pi near and-army-of-him and-horsemen-of-him

וּפַרְעֹה הִקְרִיב וַיִּשְׂאוּ בְנֵי־ יִשְׂרָאֵל אֶת־ עֵינֵיהֶם
eyes-of-them *** Israel sons-of then-they-lifted he-approached as-Pharaoh (10)

וְהִנֵּה מִצְרַיִם ׀ נֹסֵעַ אַחֲרֵיהֶם וַיִּירְאוּ מְאֹד
very and-they-were-terrified after-them marching Egyptians and-see!

וַיִּצְעֲקוּ בְנֵי־ יִשְׂרָאֵל אֶל־ יְהוָה׃ וַיֹּאמְרוּ אֶל־ מֹשֶׁה הֲמִבְּלִי
because? Moses to and-they-said (11) Yahweh to Israel sons-of and-they-cried

אֵין־ קְבָרִים בְּמִצְרַיִם לְקַחְתָּנוּ לָמוּת בַּמִּדְבָּר מַה־ זֹּאת עָשִׂיתָ
you-did this what? in-the-desert to-die you-brought-us in-Egypt graves no

לָּנוּ לְהוֹצִיאָנוּ מִמִּצְרָיִם׃ הֲלֹא־ זֶה הַדָּבָר אֲשֶׁר דִּבַּרְנוּ אֵלֶיךָ
to-you we-said that the-word this not? (12) from-Egypt to-bring-us to-us

בְמִצְרַיִם לֵאמֹר חֲדַל מִמֶּנּוּ וְנַעַבְדָה אֶת־ מִצְרָיִם כִּי
for Egyptians *** and-let-us-serve from-us leave-alone! to-say in-Egypt

טוֹב לָנוּ עֲבֹד אֶת־ מִצְרַיִם מִמֻּתֵנוּ בַּמִּדְבָּר׃
in-the-desert than-to-die-us Egyptians *** to-serve for-us better

וַיֹּאמֶר מֹשֶׁה אֶל־ הָעָם אַל־ תִּירָאוּ הִתְיַצְבוּ וּרְאוּ
and-see! stand-firm! you-fear not the-people to Moses and-he-answered (13)

אֶת־ יְשׁוּעַת יְהוָה אֲשֶׁר־ יַעֲשֶׂה לָכֶם הַיּוֹם כִּי אֲשֶׁר רְאִיתֶם
you-see whom for the-day to-you he-will-bring that Yahweh deliverance-of ***

אֶת־ מִצְרַיִם הַיּוֹם לֹא תֹסִפוּ לִרְאֹתָם עוֹד עַד־ עוֹלָם׃
forever to again to-see you-will-repeat not the-day Egyptians ***

יְהוָה יִלָּחֵם לָכֶם וְאַתֶּם תַּחֲרִשׁוּן׃ וַיֹּאמֶר
then-he-said (15) you-be-still and-you for-you he-will-fight Yahweh (14)

we done? We have let the Israelites go and have lost their services!" 6So he had his chariot made ready and took his army with him. 7He took six hundred of the best chariots, along with all the other chariots of Egypt, with officers over all of them. 8The LORD hardened the heart of Pharaoh king of Egypt, so that he pursued the Israelites, who were marching out boldly. 9The Egyptians—all Pharaoh's horses and chariots, horsemen[v] and troops—pursued the Israelites and overtook them as they camped by the sea near Pi Hahiroth, opposite Baal Zephon.

10As Pharaoh approached, the Israelites looked up, and there were the Egyptians, marching after them. They were terrified and cried out to the LORD. 11They said to Moses, "Was it because there were no graves in Egypt that you brought us to the desert to die? What have you done to us by bringing us out of Egypt? 12Didn't we say to you in Egypt, 'Leave us alone; let us serve the Egyptians'? It would have been better for us to serve the Egyptians than to die in the desert!"

13Moses answered the people, "Do not be afraid. Stand firm and you will see the deliverance the LORD will bring you today. The Egyptians you see today you will never see again. 14The LORD will fight for you; you need only to be still."

[v]9 Or *charioteers;* also in verses 17, 18, 23, 26 and 28

**13* Most mss have *dagesh* in the *tsade* ( צּ־ ).

יְהוָה אֶל־ מֹשֶׁה מַה־ תִּצְעַק אֵלָי דַּבֵּר אֶל־ בְּנֵי־ יִשְׂרָאֵל וְיִסָּעוּ׃
so-they-move-on Israel sons-of to tell! to-me you-cry why? Moses to Yahweh

(16) וְאַתָּה הָרֵם אֶת־ מַטְּךָ וּנְטֵה אֶת־ יָדְךָ עַל־
over hand-of-you *** and-stretch! staff-of-you *** raise! now-you (16)

הַיָּם וּבְקָעֵהוּ וְיָבֹאוּ בְנֵי־ יִשְׂרָאֵל בְּתוֹךְ הַיָּם
the-sea through Israel sons-of so-they-can-go and-divide-him! the-sea

בַּיַּבָּשָׁה׃ (17) וַאֲנִי הִנְנִי מְחַזֵּק אֶת־ לֵב מִצְרַיִם
Egyptians heart-of *** hardening see-I! and-I (17) on-the-dry-ground

וְיָבֹאוּ אַחֲרֵיהֶם וְאִכָּבְדָה בְּפַרְעֹה
through-Pharaoh and-I-will-glorify-myself after-them so-they-will-go

וּבְכָל־ חֵילוֹ בְּרִכְבּוֹ וּבְפָרָשָׁיו׃
and-through-horsemen-of-him through-chariot-of-him army-of-him and-through-all-of

(18) וְיָדְעוּ מִצְרַיִם כִּי־ אֲנִי יְהוָה בְּהִכָּבְדִי
when-to-be-glorified-me Yahweh I that Egyptians then-they-will-know (18)

בְּפַרְעֹה בְּרִכְבּוֹ וּבְפָרָשָׁיו׃
and-through-horsemen-of-him through-chariot-of-him through-Pharaoh

(19) וַיִּסַּע מַלְאַךְ הָאֱלֹהִים הַהֹלֵךְ לִפְנֵי מַחֲנֵה
army-of in-front-of the-one-traveling the-God angel-of then-he-withdrew (19)

יִשְׂרָאֵל וַיֵּלֶךְ מֵאַחֲרֵיהֶם וַיִּסַּע עַמּוּד הֶעָנָן
the-cloud pillar-of and-he-moved to-behind-them and-he-went Israel

מִפְּנֵיהֶם וַיַּעֲמֹד מֵאַחֲרֵיהֶם׃ (20) וַיָּבֹא בֵּין ׀
between and-he-came (20) at-behind-them and-he-stood from-in-front-of-them

מַחֲנֵה מִצְרַיִם וּבֵין מַחֲנֵה יִשְׂרָאֵל וַיְהִי הֶעָנָן
the-cloud and-he-brought Israel army-of and-between Egypt army-of

וְהַחֹשֶׁךְ וַיָּאֶר אֶת־ הַלָּיְלָה וְלֹא־ קָרַב
he-went-near so-not the-night *** and-he-brought-light both-the-darkness

זֶה אֶל־ זֶה כָּל־ הַלָּיְלָה׃ (21) וַיֵּט מֹשֶׁה אֶת־ יָדוֹ
hand-of-him *** Moses then-he-stretched (21) the-night all-of other to this

עַל־ הַיָּם וַיּוֹלֶךְ יְהוָה ׀ אֶת־ הַיָּם בְּרוּחַ קָדִים עַזָּה
strong east with-wind-of the-sea *** Yahweh and-he-drove-back the-sea over

כָּל־ הַלַּיְלָה וַיָּשֶׂם אֶת־ הַיָּם לֶחָרָבָה
into-the-dry-land the-sea *** and-he-turned the-night all-of

וַיִּבָּקְעוּ הַמָּיִם׃ (22) וַיָּבֹאוּ בְנֵי־ יִשְׂרָאֵל בְּתוֹךְ
through Israel sons-of and-they-went (22) the-waters and-they-were-divided

הַיָּם בַּיַּבָּשָׁה וְהַמַּיִם לָהֶם חוֹמָה מִימִינָם
on-right-of-them wall to-them and-the-waters on-the-dry-ground the-sea

וּמִשְּׂמֹאלָם׃ (23) וַיִּרְדְּפוּ מִצְרַיִם וַיָּבֹאוּ אַחֲרֵיהֶם
after-them and-they-went Egyptians and-they-pursued (23) and-on-left-of-them

15Then the LORD said to Moses, "Why are you crying out to me? Tell the Israelites to move on.
16Raise your staff and stretch out your hand over the sea to divide the water so that the Israelites can go through the sea on dry ground.
17I will harden the hearts of the Egyptians so that they will go in after them. And I will gain glory through Pharaoh and all his army, through his chariots and his horsemen.
18The Egyptians will know that I am the LORD when I gain glory through Pharaoh, his chariots and his horsemen."

19Then the angel of God, who had been traveling in front of Israel's army, withdrew and went behind them. The pillar of cloud also moved from in front and stood behind them,
20coming between the armies of Egypt and Israel. Throughout the night the cloud brought darkness to the one side and light to the other side; so neither went near the other all night long.

21Then Moses stretched out his hand over the sea, and all that night the LORD drove the sea back with a strong east wind and turned it into dry land. The waters were divided,
22and the Israelites went through the sea on dry ground, with a wall of water on their right and on their left.

23The Egyptians pursued

כֹּל סוּס פַּרְעֹה רִכְבּוֹ וּפָרָשָׁיו אֶל־תּוֹךְ
midst-of into and-horsemen-of-him chariot-of-him Pharaoh horse-of every-of

הַיָּם׃ וַיְהִי בְּאַשְׁמֹרֶת הַבֹּקֶר וַיַּשְׁקֵף יְהוָה
Yahweh that-he-looked-down the-morning in-watch-of and-he-was (24) the-sea

אֶל־מַחֲנֵה מִצְרַיִם בְּעַמּוּד אֵשׁ וְעָנָן וַיָּהָם אֶת מַחֲנֵה
army-of *** and-he-confused and-cloud fire from-pillar-of Egypt army-of at

מִצְרָיִם׃ וַיָּסַר* אֵת אֹפַן מַרְכְּבֹתָיו וַיְנַהֲגֵהוּ
so-he-drove-him chariots-of-him wheel-of *** *and-he-made-come-off (25) Egypt

בִּכְבֵדֻת וַיֹּאמֶר מִצְרַיִם אָנוּסָה מִפְּנֵי יִשְׂרָאֵל כִּי
for Israel from-before let-me-get-away Egyptians and-he-said with-difficulty

יְהוָה נִלְחָם לָהֶם בְּמִצְרָיִם† וַיֹּאמֶר יְהוָה אֶל־מֹשֶׁה
Moses to Yahweh then-he-said (26) against-Egypt for-them fighting Yahweh

נְטֵה אֶת־יָדְךָ עַל־הַיָּם וְיָשֻׁבוּ הַמַּיִם עַל־
over the-waters so-they-may-flow-back the-sea over hand-of-you *** stretch!

מִצְרַיִם עַל־רִכְבּוֹ וְעַל־פָּרָשָׁיו׃ וַיֵּט
so-he-stretched (27) horsemen-of-him and-over chariot-of-him over Egyptians

מֹשֶׁה אֶת־יָדוֹ עַל־הַיָּם וַיָּשָׁב הַיָּם לִפְנוֹת
at-to-dawn the-sea and-he-went-back the-sea over hand-of-him *** Moses

בֹּקֶר לְאֵיתָנוֹ וּמִצְרַיִם נָסִים לִקְרָאתוֹ וַיְנַעֵר
and-he-swept to-meet-him ones-fleeing and-Egyptians to-place-of-him morning

יְהוָה אֶת־מִצְרַיִם בְּתוֹךְ הַיָּם׃ וַיָּשֻׁבוּ הַמַּיִם
the-waters and-they-flowed-back (28) the-sea into Egyptians *** Yahweh

וַיְכַסּוּ אֶת־הָרֶכֶב וְאֶת־הַפָּרָשִׁים לְכֹל חֵיל פַּרְעֹה
Pharaoh army-of over-all-of the-horsemen and the-chariot *** and-they-covered

הַבָּאִים אַחֲרֵיהֶם בַּיָּם לֹא־נִשְׁאַר בָּהֶם עַד־אֶחָד׃
one even of-them he-survived not into-the-sea after-them the-ones-following

וּבְנֵי יִשְׂרָאֵל הָלְכוּ בַיַּבָּשָׁה בְּתוֹךְ הַיָּם
the-sea through on-the-dry-ground they-went Israel but-sons-of (29)

וְהַמַּיִם לָהֶם חֹמָה מִימִינָם וּמִשְּׂמֹאלָם†
and-on-left-of-them on-right-of-them wall to-them and-the-waters

וַיּוֹשַׁע יְהוָה בַּיּוֹם הַהוּא אֶת־יִשְׂרָאֵל מִיַּד מִצְרָיִם
Egyptians from-hand-of Israel *** the-that on-the-day Yahweh so-he-saved (30)

וַיַּרְא יִשְׂרָאֵל אֶת־מִצְרַיִם מֵת עַל־שְׂפַת הַיָּם׃
the-sea shore-of on being-dead Egyptians *** Israel and-he-saw

וַיַּרְא יִשְׂרָאֵל אֶת־הַיָּד הַגְּדֹלָה אֲשֶׁר עָשָׂה יְהוָה
Yahweh he-displayed that the-great the-power *** Israel when-he-saw (31)

בְּמִצְרַיִם וַיִּירְאוּ הָעָם אֶת־יְהוָה וַיַּאֲמִינוּ
and-they-trusted Yahweh *** the-people then-they-feared against-Egyptians

them, and all Pharaoh's horses and chariots and horsemen followed them into the sea.
24In the morning watch the LORD looked down from the pillar of fire and cloud at the Egyptian army and threw it into confusion.
25He made the wheels of their chariots come off[w] so that they had difficulty driving. And the Egyptians said, "Let's get away from the Israelites! The LORD is fighting for them against Egypt."

26Then the LORD said to Moses, "Stretch out your hand over the sea so that the waters may flow back over the Egyptians and their chariots and horsemen."
27Moses stretched out his hand over the sea, and at daybreak the sea went back to its place. The Egyptians were fleeing toward[x] it, and the LORD swept them into the sea.
28The water flowed back and covered the chariots and horsemen—the entire army of Pharaoh that had followed the Israelites into the sea. Not one of them survived.

29But the Israelites went through the sea on dry ground, with a wall of water on their right and on their left.
30That day the LORD saved Israel from the hands of the Egyptians, and Israel saw the Egyptians lying dead on the shore.
31And when the Israelites saw the great power the LORD displayed against the Egyptians, the people feared the LORD and

[w]25 Or *He jammed the wheels of their chariots* (see Samaritan Pentateuch, Septuagint and Syriac)

*25 וַיֶּאְסֹר, *and-he-jammed*
This Hebrew reading and translation is conjectured on the basis of the early versions listed above in note w.

†25, 29 Most mss end verses 25 and 29 with *soph pasuq* ( ׃ ).

בַּיהוָה וּבְמֹשֶׁה עַבְדּוֹ׃ אָז יָשִׁיר־מֹשֶׁה וּבְנֵי

and-sons-of Moses he-sang then (15:1) servant-of-him and-in-Moses in-Yahweh

יִשְׂרָאֵל אֶת־הַשִּׁירָה הַזֹּאת לַיהוָה וַיֹּאמְרוּ לֵאמֹר אָשִׁירָה

I-will-sing to-say and-they-said to-Yahweh the-this the-song *** Israel

לַיהוָה כִּי־גָאֹה גָּאָה סוּס וְרֹכְבוֹ רָמָה

he-hurled and-one-riding-him horse he-is-exalted to-be-exalted for to-Yahweh

בַיָּם׃ עָזִּי וְזִמְרָת יָהּ וַיְהִי־לִי לִישׁוּעָה

as-salvation to-me and-he-became Yah and-song strength-of-me (2) into-the-sea

זֶה אֵלִי וְאַנְוֵהוּ אֱלֹהֵי אָבִי וַאֲרֹמְמֶנְהוּ׃

and-I-will-exalt-him father-of-me God-of and-I-will-praise-him God-of-me this

יְהוָה אִישׁ מִלְחָמָה יְהוָה שְׁמוֹ׃ מַרְכְּבֹת פַּרְעֹה

Pharaoh chariots-of (4) name-of-him Yahweh war man-of Yahweh (3)

וְחֵילוֹ יָרָה בַיָּם וּמִבְחַר שָׁלִשָׁיו

officers-of-him and-best-of into-the-sea he-hurled and-army-of-him

טֻבְּעוּ בְיַם־סוּף׃ תְּהֹמֹת יְכַסְיֻמוּ יָרְדוּ

they-sank they-covered-them deep-waters (5) Reed in-Sea-of they-drowned

בִמְצוֹלֹת כְּמוֹ־אָבֶן׃ יְמִינְךָ יְהוָה נֶאְדָּרִי

being-majestic-of Yahweh right-hand-of-you (6) stone like to-depths

בַּכֹּחַ יְמִינְךָ יְהוָה תִּרְעַץ אוֹיֵב׃

being-enemy she-shattered Yahweh right-hand-of-you in-the-power

וּבְרֹב גְּאוֹנְךָ תַּהֲרֹס קָמֶיךָ

ones-opposing-you you-threw-down majesty-of-you and-in-greatness-of (7)

תְּשַׁלַּח חֲרֹנְךָ יֹאכְלֵמוֹ כַּקַּשׁ׃ וּבְרוּחַ

and-by-blast-of (8) like-the-stubble he-consumed-them anger-of-you you-unleased

אַפֶּיךָ נֶעֶרְמוּ מַיִם נִצְּבוּ כְמוֹ־נֵד נֹזְלִים

ones-raging wall like they-stood-firm waters they-piled-up nostrils-of-you

קָפְאוּ תְהֹמֹת בְּלֶב־יָם׃ אָמַר אוֹיֵב

being-enemy he-boasted (9) sea in-heart-of deep-waters they-congealed

אֶרְדֹּף אַשִּׂיג אֲחַלֵּק שָׁלָל תִּמְלָאֵמוֹ

she-will-gorge-on-them spoil I-will-divide I-will-overtake I-will-pursue

נַפְשִׁי אָרִיק חַרְבִּי תּוֹרִישֵׁמוֹ יָדִי׃

hand-of-me she-will-destroy-them sword-of-me I-will-draw self-of-me

נָשַׁפְתָּ בְרוּחֲךָ כִּסָּמוֹ יָם צָלֲלוּ כַּעוֹפֶרֶת

like-the-lead they-sank sea he-covered-them with-breath-of-you you-blew (10)

בַּמַּיִם אַדִּירִים׃ מִי־כָמֹכָה בָּאֵלִם יְהוָה מִי כָּמֹכָה

like-you who? Yahweh among-the-gods like-you who? (11) mighty-ones in-waters

נֶאְדָּר בַּקֹּדֶשׁ נוֹרָא תְהִלֹּת עֹשֵׂה פֶלֶא׃

wonder working glories being-awesome in-the-holiness being-majestic

put their trust in him and in Moses his servant.

*The Song of Moses*

15 Then Moses and the Israelites sang this song to the LORD:

"I will sing to the LORD,
for he is highly exalted.
The horse and its rider
he has hurled into the sea.
2 The LORD is my strength
and my song;
he has become my salvation.
He is my God, and I will praise him,
my father's God, and I will exalt him.
3 The LORD is a warrior;
the LORD is his name.
4 Pharaoh's chariots and his army
he has hurled into the sea.
The best of Pharaoh's officers
are drowned in the Red Sea.[y]
5 The deep waters have covered them;
they sank to the depths like a stone.

6 "Your right hand, O LORD,
was majestic in power.
Your right hand, O LORD,
shattered the enemy.
7 In the greatness of your majesty
you threw down those who opposed you.
You unleashed your burning anger;
it consumed them like stubble.
8 By the blast of your nostrils
the waters piled up.
The surging waters stood firm like a wall;
the deep waters congealed in the heart of the sea.

9 "The enemy boasted,
'I will pursue, I will overtake them.
I will divide the spoils;
I will gorge myself on them.
I will draw my sword
and my hand will destroy them.'
10 But you blew with your breath,
and the sea covered them.
They sank like lead
in the mighty waters.

11 "Who among the gods is like you, O LORD?
Who is like you—
majestic in holiness,
awesome in glory,

[x] 27 Or *from*
[y] 4 Hebrew *Yam Suph;* that is, Sea of Reeds; also in verse 22

נָטִיתָ יְמִינְךָ תִּבְלָעֵמוֹ אָרֶץ׃ נָחִיתָ

you-will-lead (13) earth she-swallowed-them right-hand-of-you you-stretched (12)

בְחַסְדְּךָ עַם־ זוּ גָּאָלְתָּ נֵהַלְתָּ בְעָזְּךָ

in-strength-of-you you-will-guide you-redeemed whom people in-love-of-you

אֶל־ נְוֵה קָדְשֶׁךָ׃ שָׁמְעוּ עַמִּים יִרְגָּזוּן

they-will-tremble nations they-will-hear (14) holy-of-you dwelling-of to

חִיל אָחַז יֹשְׁבֵי פְּלָשֶׁת׃ אָז נִבְהֲלוּ

they-will-be-terrified then (15) Philistia ones-living-of he-will-grip anguish

אַלּוּפֵי אֱדוֹם אֵילֵי מוֹאָב יֹאחֲזֵמוֹ רָעַד נָמֹגוּ

they-will-melt trembling he-will-seize-them Moab leaders-of Edom chiefs-of

כֹּל יֹשְׁבֵי כְנָעַן׃ תִּפֹּל עֲלֵיהֶם אֵימָתָה וָפַחַד

and-dread terror on-them she-will-fall (16) Canaan ones-living-of all-of

בִּגְדֹל זְרוֹעֲךָ יִדְּמוּ כָּאָבֶן עַד־ יַעֲבֹר

he-passes-by until as-the-stone they-will-be-still arm-of-you by-power-of

עַמְּךָ יְהוָה עַד־ יַעֲבֹר עַם־ זוּ קָנִיתָ׃

you-bought whom people he-passes-by until Yahweh people-of-you

תְּבִאֵמוֹ וְתִטָּעֵמוֹ בְּהַר

on-mountain-of and-you-will-plant-them you-will-bring-in-them (17)

נַחֲלָתְךָ מָכוֹן לְשִׁבְתְּךָ פָּעַלְתָּ יְהוָה מִקְּדָשׁ אֲדֹנָי

Lord sanctuary Yahweh you-made to-dwell-you place inheritance-of-you

כּוֹנְנוּ יָדֶיךָ׃ יְהוָה יִמְלֹךְ לְעֹלָם וָעֶד׃

and-ever for-ever he-will-reign Yahweh (18) hands-of-you they-established

כִּי בָא סוּס פַּרְעֹה בְּרִכְבּוֹ וּבְפָרָשָׁיו

and-with-horsemen-of-him with-chariot-of-him Pharaoh horse-of he-went when (19)

בַּיָּם וַיָּשֶׁב יְהוָה עֲלֵהֶם אֶת־ מֵי הַיָּם

the-sea waters-of *** over-them Yahweh then-he-brought into-the-sea

וּבְנֵי יִשְׂרָאֵל הָלְכוּ בַיַּבָּשָׁה בְּתוֹךְ הַיָּם׃

the-sea through on-the-dry-ground they-walked Israel but-sons-of

וַתִּקַּח מִרְיָם הַנְּבִיאָה אֲחוֹת אַהֲרֹן אֶת־ הַתֹּף

the-tambourine *** Aaron sister-of the-prophetess Miriam then-she-took (20)

בְּיָדָהּ וַתֵּצֶאןָ כָל־ הַנָּשִׁים אַחֲרֶיהָ בְּתֻפִּים

with-tambourines after-her the-women all-of and-they-followed in-hand-of-her

וּבִמְחֹלֹת׃ וַתַּעַן לָהֶם מִרְיָם שִׁירוּ לַיהוָה כִּי־

for to-Yahweh sing! Miriam to-them and-she-sang (21) and-with-dances

גָאֹה גָּאָה סוּס וְרֹכְבוֹ רָמָה בַיָּם׃

into-the-sea he-hurled and-one-riding-him horse he-is-exalted to-be-exalted

וַיַּסַּע מֹשֶׁה אֶת־ יִשְׂרָאֵל מִיַּם־ סוּף וַיֵּצְאוּ אֶל־

into and-they-went Reed from-Sea-of Israel *** Moses then-he-led (22)

working wonders?
12 You stretched out your right hand
and the earth swallowed them.

13 "In your unfailing love you will lead
the people you have redeemed.
In your strength you will guide them
to your holy dwelling.
14 The nations will hear and tremble;
anguish will grip the people of Philistia.
15 The chiefs of Edom will be terrified,
the leaders of Moab will be seized with trembling,
the people[z] of Canaan will melt away;
16 terror and dread will fall upon them.
By the power of your arm
they will be as still as a stone—
until your people pass by, O LORD,
until the people you bought pass by.
17 You will bring them in and plant them
on the mountain of your inheritance—
the place, O LORD, you made for your dwelling,
the sanctuary, O Lord, your hands established.
18 The LORD will reign
for ever and ever."

19 When Pharaoh's horses,
chariots and horsemen[a] went
into the sea, the LORD brought
the waters of the sea back over
them, but the Israelites walked
through the sea on dry
ground. 20 Then Miriam the
prophetess, Aaron's sister,
took a tambourine in her
hand, and all the women followed her, with tambourines
and dancing. 21 Miriam sang to
them:

"Sing to the LORD,
for he is highly exalted.
The horse and its rider
he has hurled into the sea."

*The Waters of Marah and Elim*

22 Then Moses led Israel from
the Red Sea and they went

[z]15 Or *rulers* [a]19 Or *charioteers*

מִדְבַּר־ שׁוּר וַיֵּלְכוּ שְׁלֹשֶׁת־ יָמִים בַּמִּדְבָּר וְלֹא־
and-not in-the-desert days three-of and-they-traveled Shur Desert-of

מָצְאוּ מָיִם׃ (23) וַיָּבֹאוּ מָרָתָה וְלֹא יָכְלוּ לִשְׁתֹּת
to-drink they-could but-not to-Marah and-they-came (23) waters they-found

מַיִם מִמָּרָה כִּי מָרִים הֵם עַל־ כֵּן קָרָא־ שְׁמָהּ מָרָה׃
Marah name-of-her he-called this for they bitter-ones for from-Marah waters

(24) וַיִּלֹּנוּ הָעָם עַל־ מֹשֶׁה לֵּאמֹר מַה־ נִּשְׁתֶּה׃
will-we-drink what? to-say Moses against the-people so-they-grumbled (24)

(25) וַיִּצְעַק אֶל־ יְהוָה וַיּוֹרֵהוּ יְהוָה עֵץ וַיַּשְׁלֵךְ אֶל־
into and-he-threw wood Yahweh and-he-showed-him Yahweh to then-he-cried (25)

הַמַּיִם וַיִּמְתְּקוּ הַמָּיִם שָׁם שָׂם לוֹ חֹק
decree for-him he-made there the-waters and-they-became-sweet the-waters

וּמִשְׁפָּט וְשָׁם נִסָּהוּ׃ (26) וַיֹּאמֶר אִם־ שָׁמוֹעַ תִּשְׁמַע
you-listen to-listen if and-he-said (26) he-tested-him and-there and-law

לְקוֹל יְהוָה אֱלֹהֶיךָ וְהַיָּשָׁר בְּעֵינָיו תַּעֲשֶׂה
you-do in-eyes-of-him and-the-right God-of-you Yahweh to-voice-of

וְהַאֲזַנְתָּ לְמִצְוֺתָיו וְשָׁמַרְתָּ כָּל־ חֻקָּיו כָּל־
all-of decrees-of-him all-of and-you-keep to-commands-of-him and-you-attend

הַמַּחֲלָה אֲשֶׁר־ שַׂמְתִּי בְמִצְרַיִם לֹא־ אָשִׂים עָלֶיךָ כִּי אֲנִי
I for on-you I-will-bring not on-Egyptians I-brought that the-disease

יְהוָה רֹפְאֶךָ׃ (27) וַיָּבֹאוּ אֵילִמָה וְשָׁם שְׁתֵּים עֶשְׂרֵה
ten two and-there to-Elim then-they-came (27) one-healing-you Yahweh

עֵינֹת מַיִם וְשִׁבְעִים תְּמָרִים וַיַּחֲנוּ־ שָׁם עַל־ הַמָּיִם׃
the-waters by there and-they-camped palm-trees and-seventy waters springs-of

(16:1) וַיִּסְעוּ מֵאֵילִם וַיָּבֹאוּ כָּל־ עֲדַת
community-of whole-of and-they-came from-Elim then-they-set-out (16:1)

בְּנֵי־ יִשְׂרָאֵל אֶל־ מִדְבַּר־ סִין אֲשֶׁר בֵּין־ אֵילִם וּבֵין סִינָי בַּחֲמִשָּׁה
on-five Sinai and-between Elim between which Sin Desert-of to Israel sons-of

עָשָׂר יוֹם לַחֹדֶשׁ הַשֵּׁנִי לְצֵאתָם מֵאֶרֶץ מִצְרָיִם׃
Egypt from-land-of after-to-come-out-them the-second of-the-month day ten

(2) וַיִּלִּינוּ כָּל־ עֲדַת בְּנֵי־ יִשְׂרָאֵל עַל־ מֹשֶׁה
Moses against Israel sons-of community-of whole-of and-they-grumbled (2)

וְעַל־ אַהֲרֹן בַּמִּדְבָּר׃ (3) וַיֹּאמְרוּ אֲלֵהֶם בְּנֵי יִשְׂרָאֵל
Israel sons-of to-them and-they-said (3) in-the-desert Aaron and-against

מִי־ יִתֵּן מוּתֵנוּ בְיַד־ יְהוָה בְּאֶרֶץ מִצְרַיִם בְּשִׁבְתֵּנוּ
when-to-sit-us Egypt in-land-of Yahweh by-hand-of to-die-us he-let if-only

עַל־ סִיר הַבָּשָׂר בְּאָכְלֵנוּ לֶחֶם לָשֹׂבַע כִּי־ הוֹצֵאתֶם אֹתָנוּ
us you-brought but to-fullness food when-to-eat-us the-meat pot-of around

into the Desert of Shur. For three days they traveled in the desert without finding water.
23When they came to Marah, they could not drink its water because it was bitter. (That is why the place is called Marah.[b])
24So the people grumbled against Moses, saying, "What are we to drink?"

25Then Moses cried out to the LORD, and the LORD showed him a piece of wood. He threw it into the water, and the water became sweet.

There the LORD made a decree and a law for them, and there he tested them.
26He said, "If you listen carefully to the voice of the LORD your God and do what is right in his eyes, if you pay attention to his commands and keep all his decrees, I will not bring on you any of the diseases I brought on the Egyptians, for I am the LORD who heals you."

27Then they came to Elim, where there were twelve springs and seventy palm trees, and they camped there near the water.

*Manna and Quail*

16 The whole Israelite community set out from Elim and came to the Desert of Sin, which is between Elim and Sinai, on the fifteenth day of the second month after they had come out of Egypt.
2In the desert the whole community grumbled against Moses and Aaron.
3The Israelites said to them, "If only we had died by the LORD's hand in Egypt! There we sat around pots of meat and ate all the food we wanted, but you have brought us

[b]23 *Marah* means *bitter*.

°2 ק וילונו

אֶל־ הַמִּדְבָּר הַזֶּה לְהָמִית אֶת־ כָּל־ הַקָּהָל הַזֶּה
the-this the-assembly whole-of *** to-kill the-this the-desert into

בָּרָעָב׃ וַיֹּאמֶר יְהוָה אֶל־מֹשֶׁה הִנְנִי מַמְטִיר לָכֶם לֶחֶם
bread for-you raining see-I! Moses to Yahweh then-he-said (4) with-the-hunger

מִן־ הַשָּׁמָיִם וְיָצָא הָעָם וְלָקְטוּ דְּבַר־
amount-of and-they-will-gather the-people and-he-will-go-out the-heavens from

יוֹם בְּיוֹמוֹ לְמַעַן אֲנַסֶּנּוּ הֲיֵלֵךְ בְּתוֹרָתִי
by-instruction-of-me whether-he-follows I-will-test-him in-this in-day-of-him day

אִם־לֹא׃ וְהָיָה בַּיּוֹם הַשִּׁשִּׁי וְהֵכִינוּ אֵת
*** that-they-will-prepare the-sixth on-the-day and-he-will-be (5) not or

אֲשֶׁר־ יָבִיאוּ וְהָיָה מִשְׁנֶה עַל אֲשֶׁר־ יִלְקְטוּ יוֹם ׀ יוֹם׃
day day they-gather what than twice and-he-will-be they-bring-in what

וַיֹּאמֶר מֹשֶׁה וְאַהֲרֹן אֶל־כָּל־ בְּנֵי יִשְׂרָאֵל עֶרֶב וִידַעְתֶּם
then-you-will-know evening Israel sons-of all-of to and-Aaron Moses so-he-said (6)

כִּי יְהוָה הוֹצִיא אֶתְכֶם מֵאֶרֶץ מִצְרָיִם׃ וּבֹקֶר וּרְאִיתֶם
also-you-will-see and-morning (7) Egypt from-land-of you he-brought Yahweh that

אֶת־ כְּבוֹד יְהוָה בְּשָׁמְעוֹ אֶת־ תְּלֻנֹּתֵיכֶם עַל־ יְהוָה
Yahweh against grumblings-of-you *** because-to-hear-him Yahweh glory-of ***

וְנַחְנוּ מָה כִּי תַלִּונוּ עָלֵינוּ׃ וַיֹּאמֶר מֹשֶׁה בְּתֵת
when-to-give Moses and-he-said (8) against-us you-grumble that who? and-we

יְהוָה לָכֶם בָּעֶרֶב בָּשָׂר לֶאֱכֹל וְלֶחֶם בַּבֹּקֶר לִשְׂבֹּעַ
to-satisfy in-the-morning and-bread to-eat meat in-the-evening to-you Yahweh

בִּשְׁמֹעַ יְהוָה אֶת־ תְּלֻנֹּתֵיכֶם אֲשֶׁר־ אַתֶּם מַלִּינִם
ones-grumbling you that grumblings-of-you *** Yahweh because-to-hear

עָלָיו וְנַחְנוּ מָה לֹא־ עָלֵינוּ תְלֻנֹּתֵיכֶם כִּי עַל־ יְהוָה׃
Yahweh against but grumblings-of-you against-us not who? and-we against-him

וַיֹּאמֶר מֹשֶׁה אֶל־אַהֲרֹן אֱמֹר אֶל־כָּל־ עֲדַת בְּנֵי יִשְׂרָאֵל
Israel sons-of community-of whole-of to say! Aaron to Moses then-he-told (9)

קִרְבוּ לִפְנֵי יְהוָה כִּי שָׁמַע אֵת תְּלֻנֹּתֵיכֶם׃ וַיְהִי
and-he-was (10) grumblings-of-you *** he-heard for Yahweh before come!

כְּדַבֵּר אַהֲרֹן אֶל־ כָּל־ עֲדַת בְּנֵי־ יִשְׂרָאֵל וַיִּפְנוּ
that-they-looked Israel sons-of community-of whole-of to Aaron while-to-speak

אֶל־ הַמִּדְבָּר וְהִנֵּה כְּבוֹד יְהוָה נִרְאָה בֶּעָנָן׃
in-the-cloud appearing Yahweh glory-of and-see! the-desert toward

וַיְדַבֵּר יְהוָה אֶל־ מֹשֶׁה לֵּאמֹר׃ שָׁמַעְתִּי אֶת־ תְּלוּנֹּת
grumblings-of *** I-heard (12) to-say Moses to Yahweh and-he-spoke (11)

בְּנֵי יִשְׂרָאֵל דַּבֵּר אֲלֵהֶם לֵאמֹר בֵּין הָעַרְבַּיִם תֹּאכְלוּ בָשָׂר
meat you-will-eat the-twilight at to-say to-them tell! Israel sons-of

out into this desert to starve this entire assembly to death."

4Then the LORD said to Moses, "I will rain down bread from heaven for you. The people are to go out each day and gather enough for that day. In this way I will test them and see whether they will follow my instructions. 5On the sixth day they are to prepare what they bring in, and that is to be twice as much as they gather on the other days."

6So Moses and Aaron said to all the Israelites, "In the evening you will know that it was the LORD who brought you out of Egypt, 7and in the morning you will see the glory of the LORD, because he has heard your grumbling against him. Who are we, that you should grumble against us?" 8Moses also said, "You will know that it was the LORD when he gives you meat to eat in the evening and all the bread you want in the morning, because he has heard your grumbling against him. Who are we? You are not grumbling against us, but against the LORD."

9Then Moses told Aaron, "Say to the entire Israelite community, 'Come before the LORD, for he has heard your grumbling.'"

10While Aaron was speaking to the whole Israelite community, they looked toward the desert, and there was the glory of the LORD appearing in the cloud.

11The LORD said to Moses, 12"I have heard the grumbling of the Israelites. Tell them, 'At twilight you will eat meat, and

°7 ק תלינו

וּבַבֹּקֶר תִּשְׂבְּעוּ־ לָחֶם וִידַעְתֶּם כִּי אֲנִי יְהוָה
Yahweh I that then-you-will-know bread you-will-be-filled and-in-the-morning

אֱלֹהֵיכֶם׃ וַיְהִי בָעֶרֶב וַתַּעַל הַשְּׂלָו
the-quail that-she-came in-the-evening and-he-was (13) God-of-you

וַתְּכַס אֶת־ הַמַּחֲנֶה וּבַבֹּקֶר הָיְתָה שִׁכְבַת הַטַּל
the-dew layer-of she-was and-in-the-morning the-camp *** and-she-covered

סָבִיב לַמַּחֲנֶה׃ וַתַּעַל שִׁכְבַת הַטָּל וְהִנֵּה עַל־ פְּנֵי
floor-of on then-see! the-dew layer-of when-she-went (14) to-the-camp around

הַמִּדְבָּר דַּק מְחֻסְפָּס דַּק כַּכְּפֹר עַל־ הָאָרֶץ׃ וַיִּרְאוּ
when-they-saw (15) the-ground on like-the-frost thin flaking thin the-desert

בְנֵי־ יִשְׂרָאֵל וַיֹּאמְרוּ אִישׁ אֶל־ אָחִיו מָן הוּא כִּי לֹא
not for this what? other-of-him to each then-they-said Israel sons-of

יָדְעוּ מַה־ הוּא וַיֹּאמֶר מֹשֶׁה אֲלֵהֶם הוּא הַלֶּחֶם אֲשֶׁר נָתַן
he-gave that the-bread this to-them Moses so-he-said this what they-knew

יְהוָה לָכֶם לְאָכְלָה׃ זֶה הַדָּבָר אֲשֶׁר צִוָּה יְהוָה לִקְטוּ
gather! Yahweh he-commanded that the-thing this (16) for-food to-you Yahweh

מִמֶּנּוּ אִישׁ לְפִי אָכְלוֹ עֹמֶר לַגֻּלְגֹּלֶת מִסְפַּר
number-of for-the-each omer to-eat-him by-need-of each from-him

נַפְשֹׁתֵיכֶם אִישׁ לַאֲשֶׁר בְּאָהֳלוֹ תִּקָּחוּ׃ וַיַּעֲשׂוּ־ כֵן
this so-they-did (17) you-take in-tent-of-him for-whom each persons-of-you

בְּנֵי יִשְׂרָאֵל וַיִּלְקְטוּ הַמַּרְבֶּה וְהַמַּמְעִיט׃
and-the-being-little the-being-much and-they-gathered Israel sons-of

וַיָּמֹדּוּ בָעֹמֶר וְלֹא הֶעְדִּיף הַמַּרְבֶּה
the-being-much he-had-too-much and-not by-the-omer and-they-measured (18)

וְהַמַּמְעִיט לֹא הֶחְסִיר אִישׁ לְפִי־ אָכְלוֹ
to-eat-him by-need-of each he-had-too-little not and-the-being-little

לָקָטוּ׃ וַיֹּאמֶר מֹשֶׁה אֲלֵהֶם אִישׁ אַל־ יוֹתֵר מִמֶּנּוּ
from-him he-may-keep not anyone to-them Moses then-he-said (19) they-gathered

עַד־ בֹּקֶר׃ וְלֹא־ שָׁמְעוּ אֶל־ מֹשֶׁה וַיּוֹתִרוּ אֲנָשִׁים מִמֶּנּוּ
from-him men and-they-kept Moses to they-listened but-not (20) morning until

עַד־ בֹּקֶר וַיָּרֻם תּוֹלָעִים וַיִּבְאַשׁ וַיִּקְצֹף עֲלֵהֶם
with-them so-he-was-angry and-he-smelled maggots he-became-full morning until

מֹשֶׁה׃ וַיִּלְקְטוּ אֹתוֹ בַּבֹּקֶר בַּבֹּקֶר אִישׁ
each in-the-morning in-the-morning him so-they-gathered (21) Moses

כְּפִי אָכְלוֹ וְחַם הַשֶּׁמֶשׁ וְנָמָס׃ וַיְהִי ׀
and-he-was (22) then-he-melted the-sun when-he-grew-hot to-eat-him by-need-of

בַּיּוֹם הַשִּׁשִּׁי לָקְטוּ לֶחֶם מִשְׁנֶה שְׁנֵי הָעֹמֶר לָאֶחָד
for-the-each the-omer two-of twice bread they-gathered the-sixth on-the-day

in the morning you will be filled with bread. Then you will know that I am the LORD your God.' "

13 That evening quail came and covered the camp, and in the morning there was a layer of dew around the camp.
14 When the dew was gone, thin flakes like frost on the ground appeared on the desert floor.
15 When the Israelites saw it, they said to each other, "What is it?" For they did not know what it was.

Moses said to them, "It is the bread the LORD has given you to eat.
16 This is what the LORD has commanded: 'Each one is to gather as much as he needs. Take an omer[c] for each person you have in your tent.' "

17 The Israelites did as they were told; some gathered much, some little.
18 And when they measured it by the omer, he who gathered much did not have too much, and he who gathered little did not have too little. Each one gathered as much as he needed.

19 Then Moses said to them, "No one is to keep any of it until morning."

20 However, some of them paid no attention to Moses; they kept part of it until morning, but it was full of maggots and began to smell. So Moses was angry with them.

21 Each morning everyone gathered as much as he needed, and when the sun grew hot, it melted away.
22 On the sixth day, they gathered twice as much—two omers[d] for each

[c] *16* That is, probably about 2 quarts (about 2 liters); also in verses 18, 32, 33 and 36
[d] *22* That is, probably about 4 quarts (about 4.5 liters)

וַיָּבֹאוּ כָּל־ נְשִׂיאֵי הָעֵדָה וַיַּגִּידוּ לְמֹשֶׁה׃
to-Moses and-they-reported the-community leaders-of all-of and-they-came

וַיֹּאמֶר אֲלֵהֶם הוּא אֲשֶׁר דִּבֶּר יְהוָה שַׁבָּתוֹן שַׁבַּת־
Sabbath-of day-of-rest Yahweh he-commanded what this to-them and-he-said (23)

קֹדֶשׁ לַיהוָה מָחָר אֵת אֲשֶׁר־ תֹּאפוּ אֵפוּ וְאֵת אֲשֶׁר־ תְּבַשְּׁלוּ
you-will-boil what and bake! you-will-bake what *** tomorrow to-Yahweh holy

בַּשֵּׁלוּ וְאֵת כָּל־ הָעֹדֵף הַנִּיחוּ לָכֶם לְמִשְׁמֶרֶת עַד־ הַבֹּקֶר׃
the-morning until for-keeping for-you save! the-being-left all-of and boil!

וַיַּנִּיחוּ אֹתוֹ עַד־ הַבֹּקֶר כַּאֲשֶׁר צִוָּה מֹשֶׁה וְלֹא
and-not Moses he-commanded just-as the-morning until him so-they-saved (24)

הִבְאִישׁ וְרִמָּה לֹא־ הָיְתָה בּוֹ׃ וַיֹּאמֶר מֹשֶׁה אִכְלֻהוּ
eat-him! Moses and-he-said (25) in-him she-was not and-maggot he-stank

הַיּוֹם כִּי־ שַׁבָּת הַיּוֹם לַיהוָה הַיּוֹם לֹא תִמְצָאֻהוּ
you-will-find-him not the-day to-Yahweh the-day Sabbath for the-day

בַּשָּׂדֶה׃ שֵׁשֶׁת יָמִים תִּלְקְטֻהוּ וּבַיּוֹם הַשְּׁבִיעִי
the-seventh but-on-the-day you-will-gather-him days six-of (26) on-the-ground

שַׁבָּת לֹא יִהְיֶה־ בּוֹ׃ וַיְהִי בַּיּוֹם הַשְּׁבִיעִי
the-seventh on-the-day but-he-was (27) on-him he-will-be not Sabbath

יָצְאוּ מִן־ הָעָם לִלְקֹט וְלֹא מָצָאוּ׃ וַיֹּאמֶר
then-he-said (28) they-found but-not to-gather the-people from they-went-out

יְהוָה אֶל־ מֹשֶׁה עַד־ אָנָה מֵאַנְתֶּם לִשְׁמֹר מִצְוֹתַי
commands-of-me to-keep will-you-refuse long how Moses to Yahweh

וְתוֹרֹתָי׃ רְאוּ כִּי־ יְהוָה נָתַן לָכֶם
to-you he-gave Yahweh that bear-in-mind! (29) and-instructions-of-me

הַשַּׁבָּת עַל־ כֵּן הוּא נֹתֵן לָכֶם בַּיּוֹם הַשִּׁשִּׁי לֶחֶם יוֹמָיִם
two-days bread the-sixth on-the-day to-you giving he this for the-Sabbath

שְׁבוּ ׀ אִישׁ תַּחְתָּיו אַל־ יֵצֵא אִישׁ מִמְּקֹמוֹ בַּיּוֹם
on-the-day from-place-of-him anyone he-may-go-out not place-of-him each stay!

הַשְּׁבִיעִי׃ וַיִּשְׁבְּתוּ הָעָם בַּיּוֹם הַשְּׁבִעִי׃
the-seventh on-the-day the-people so-he-rested (30) the-seventh

וַיִּקְרְאוּ בֵית־ יִשְׂרָאֵל אֶת־ שְׁמוֹ מָן וְהוּא כְּזֶרַע
like-seed-of now-he manna name-of-him *** Israel house-of and-they-called (31)

גַּד לָבָן וְטַעְמוֹ כְּצַפִּיחִת בִּדְבָשׁ׃ וַיֹּאמֶר מֹשֶׁה
Moses and-he-said (32) with-honey like-wafer and-taste-of-him white coriander

זֶה הַדָּבָר אֲשֶׁר צִוָּה יְהוָה מְלֹא הָעֹמֶר מִמֶּנּוּ לְמִשְׁמֶרֶת
to-keep from-him the-omer fullness-of Yahweh he-commanded that the-thing this

לְדֹרֹתֵיכֶם לְמַעַן ׀ יִרְאוּ אֶת־ הַלֶּחֶם אֲשֶׁר הֶאֱכַלְתִּי אֶתְכֶם
you I-fed that the-bread *** they-can-see so-that for-generations-of-you

person—and the leaders of the community came and reported this to Moses. [23]He said to them, "This is what the LORD commanded: 'Tomorrow is to be a day of rest, a holy Sabbath to the LORD. So bake what you want to bake and boil what you want to boil. Save whatever is left and keep it until morning.' "

[24]So they saved it until morning, as Moses commanded, and it did not stink or get maggots in it. [25]"Eat it today," Moses said, "because today is a Sabbath to the LORD. You will not find any of it on the ground today. [26]Six days you are to gather it, but on the seventh day, the Sabbath, there will not be any."

[27]Nevertheless, some of the people went out on the seventh day to gather it, but they found none. [28]Then the LORD said to Moses, "How long will you[e] refuse to keep my commands and my instructions? [29]Bear in mind that the LORD has given you the Sabbath; that is why on the sixth day he gives you bread for two days. Everyone is to stay where he is on the seventh day; no one is to go out." [30]So the people rested on the seventh day.

[31]The people of Israel called the bread manna.[f] It was white like coriander seed and tasted like wafers made with honey. [32]Moses said, "This is what the LORD has commanded: 'Take an omer of manna and keep it for the generations to come, so they can see the bread I gave you to eat

[e]28 The Hebrew is plural.
[f]31 *Manna* means *What is it?* (see verse 15).

במדבר בהוציאי אתכם מארץ מצרים׃ ויאמר משה
Moses so-he-said (33) Egypt from-land-of you when-to-bring-me in-the-desert

אל־ אהרן קח צנצנת אחת ותן־ שמה מלא־ העמר מן
manna the-omer fullness-of in-there and-put! one jar take! Aaron to

והנח אתו לפני יהוה למשמרת לדרתיכם׃ כאשר
just-as (34) for-generations-of-you to-keep Yahweh before him then-place!

צוה יהוה אל־ משה ויניחהו אהרן לפני העדת
the-Testimony before Aaron so-he-put-him Moses to Yahweh he-commanded

למשמרת׃ ובני ישראל אכלו את־ המן ארבעים שנה עד־
until year forty the-manna *** they-ate Israel so-sons-of (35) to-keep

באם אל־ ארץ נושבת את־ המן אכלו עד־
until they-ate the-manna *** being-settled land-of to to-come-them

באם אל־ קצה ארץ כנען׃ והעמר עשרית האיפה
the-ephah tenth-of now-the-omer (36) Canaan land-of border-of to to-come-them

הוא׃ ויסעו כל־ עדת בני־ ישראל ממדבר־
from-Desert-of Israel sons-of community-of whole-of and-they-set-out (17:1) he

סין למסעיהם על־ פי יהוה ויחנו ברפידים
at-Rephidim and-they-camped Yahweh command-of as by-travels-of-them Sin

ואין מים לשתת העם׃ וירב העם עם־
with the-people so-they-quarreled (2) the-people for-to-drink waters but-no

משה ויאמרו תנו־ לנו מים ונשתה ויאמר
but-he-replied so-we-may-drink waters to-us give! and-they-said Moses

להם משה מה־ תריבון עמדי מה־ תנסון את־ יהוה׃
Yahweh *** you-test why? with-me you-quarrel why? Moses to-them

ויצמא שם העם למים וילן העם
the-people so-he-grumbled for-the-waters the-people there but-he-was-thirsty (3)

על־ משה ויאמר למה זה העליתנו ממצרים להמית אתי
me to-kill from-Egypt you-brought-us this why? and-he-said Moses against

ואת־ בני ואת־ מקני בצמא׃ ויצעק משה
Moses then-he-cried (4) with-the-thirst stocks-of-me and children-of-me and

אל־ יהוה לאמר מה אעשה לעם הזה עוד מעט
little longer the-this with-the-people can-I-do what? to-say Yahweh to

וסקלני׃ ויאמר יהוה אל־ משה עבר לפני
ahead-of walk-on! Moses to Yahweh and-he-answered (5) and-they-will-stone-me

העם וקח אתך מזקני ישראל ומטך אשר
that and-staff-of-you Israel from-elders-of with-you and-take! the-people

הכית בו את־ היאר קח בידך והלכת׃ הנני
see-I! (6) and-you-go in-hand-of-you take! the-Nile *** with-him you-struck

in the desert when I brought
you out of Egypt.' "
33So Moses said to Aaron,
"Take a jar and put an omer of
manna in it. Then place it before the LORD to be kept for the
generations to come."
34As the LORD commanded
Moses, Aaron put the manna
in front of the Testimony, that
it might be kept. 35The Israelites ate manna forty years, until they came to a land that was
settled; they ate manna until
they reached the border of Canaan.
36(An omer is one tenth of an
ephah.)

*Water From the Rock*

17 The whole Israelite
community set out
from the Desert of Sin, traveling from place to place as the
LORD commanded. They
camped at Rephidim, but
there was no water for the
people to drink. 2So they quarreled with Moses and said,
"Give us water to drink."
Moses replied, "Why do you
quarrel with me? Why do you
put the LORD to the test?"
3But the people were thirsty
for water there, and they
grumbled against Moses. They
said, "Why did you bring us
up out of Egypt to make us and
our children and livestock die
of thirst?"
4Then Moses cried out to the
LORD, "What am I to do with
these people? They are almost
ready to stone me."
5The LORD answered Moses,
"Walk on ahead of the people.
Take with you some of the elders of Israel and take in your
hand the staff with which you
struck the Nile, and go. 6I will

עֹמֵד לְפָנֶיךָ שָּׁם ׀ עַל־ הַצּוּר בְּחֹרֵב וְהִכִּיתָ בַצּוּר
on-the-rock and-you-strike at-Horeb the-rock by there before-you standing

וְיָצְאוּ מִמֶּנּוּ מַיִם וְשָׁתָה הָעָם וַיַּעַשׂ
so-he-did the-people so-he-may-drink waters from-him and-they-will-come

כֵּן מֹשֶׁה לְעֵינֵי זִקְנֵי יִשְׂרָאֵל׃ וַיִּקְרָא שֵׁם
name-of and-he-called (7) Israel elders-of before-eyes-of Moses this

הַמָּקוֹם מַסָּה וּמְרִיבָה עַל־ רִיב ׀ בְּנֵי יִשְׂרָאֵל וְעַל
and-because Israel sons-of to-quarrel because and-Meribah Massah the-place

נַסֹּתָם אֶת־ יְהוָה לֵאמֹר הֲיֵשׁ יְהוָה בְּקִרְבֵּנוּ אִם־ אָיִן׃ וַיָּבֹא
and-he-came (8) not or among-us Yahweh is-he? to-say Yahweh *** to-test-them

עֲמָלֵק וַיִּלָּחֶם עִם־ יִשְׂרָאֵל בִּרְפִידִם׃ וַיֹּאמֶר מֹשֶׁה אֶל־
to Moses and-he-said (9) at-Rephidim Israel against and-he-attacked Amalek

יְהוֹשֻׁעַ בְּחַר־ לָנוּ אֲנָשִׁים וְצֵא הִלָּחֵם בַּעֲמָלֵק מָחָר אָנֹכִי נִצָּב
standing I tomorrow with-Amalek fight! and-go-out! men for-us choose! Joshua

עַל־ רֹאשׁ הַגִּבְעָה וּמַטֵּה הָאֱלֹהִים בְּיָדִי׃ וַיַּעַשׂ יְהוֹשֻׁעַ
Joshua so-he-did (10) in-hand-of-me the-God and-staff-of the-hill top-of on

כַּאֲשֶׁר אָמַר־ לוֹ מֹשֶׁה לְהִלָּחֵם בַּעֲמָלֵק וּמֹשֶׁה אַהֲרֹן וְחוּר
and-Hur Aaron and-Moses with-Amalek to-fight Moses to-him he-ordered just-as

עָלוּ רֹאשׁ הַגִּבְעָה׃ וְהָיָה כַּאֲשֶׁר יָרִים מֹשֶׁה
Moses he-held-up as-long-as and-he-was (11) the-hill top-of they-went

יָדוֹ וְגָבַר יִשְׂרָאֵל וְכַאֲשֶׁר יָנִיחַ יָדוֹ
hand-of-him he-lowered but-when-ever Israel then-he-won hand-of-him

וְגָבַר עֲמָלֵק׃ וִידֵי מֹשֶׁה כְּבֵדִים וַיִּקְחוּ־ אֶבֶן
stone then-they-took tired-ones Moses when-hands-of (12) Amalek then-he-won

וַיָּשִׂימוּ תַחְתָּיו וַיֵּשֶׁב עָלֶיהָ וְאַהֲרֹן וְחוּר תָּמְכוּ
they-held-up and-Hur and-Aaron on-her and-he-sat under-him and-they-put

בְיָדָיו מִזֶּה אֶחָד וּמִזֶּה אֶחָד וַיְהִי יָדָיו
hands-of-him and-he-was one and-on-that-side one on-this-side on-hands-of-him

אֱמוּנָה עַד־ בֹּא הַשָּׁמֶשׁ׃ וַיַּחֲלֹשׁ יְהוֹשֻׁעַ אֶת־עֲמָלֵק וְאֶת־
and Amalek *** Joshua so-he-overcame (13) the-sun to-set until being-steady

עַמּוֹ לְפִי־ חָרֶב׃ וַיֹּאמֶר יְהוָה אֶל־ מֹשֶׁה כְּתֹב
write! Moses to Yahweh then-he-said (14) sword with-edge-of army-of-him

זֹאת זִכָּרוֹן בַּסֵּפֶר וְשִׂים בְּאָזְנֵי יְהוֹשֻׁעַ כִּי־ מָחֹה
to-erase for Joshua in-ears-of and-tell! on-the-scroll memorial this

אֶמְחֶה אֶת־ זֵכֶר עֲמָלֵק מִתַּחַת הַשָּׁמָיִם׃ וַיִּבֶן
so-he-built (15) the-heavens from-under Amalek memory-of *** I-will-erase

מֹשֶׁה מִזְבֵּחַ וַיִּקְרָא שְׁמוֹ יְהוָה ׀ נִסִּי׃ וַיֹּאמֶר
and-he-said (16) Banner-of-me Yahweh name-of-him and-he-called altar Moses

stand there before you by the
rock at Horeb. Strike the rock,
and water will come out of it
for the people to drink." So
Moses did this in the sight of
the elders of Israel. 7And he
called the place Massah[g] and
Meribah[h] because the Israelites quarreled and because
they tested the LORD saying,
"Is the LORD among us or
not?"

*The Amalekites Defeated*

8The Amalekites came and
attacked the Israelites at Rephidim. 9Moses said to Joshua,
"Choose some of our men and
go out to fight the Amalekites.
Tomorrow I will stand on top
of the hill with the staff of God
in my hands."

10So Joshua fought the Amalekites as Moses had ordered,
and Moses, Aaron and Hur
went to the top of the hill. 11As
long as Moses held up his
hands, the Israelites were
winning, but whenever he
lowered his hands, the Amalekites were winning. 12When
Moses' hands grew tired, they
took a stone and put it under
him and he sat on it. Aaron
and Hur held his hands up—
one on one side, one on the
other—so that his hands remained steady till sunset. 13So
Joshua overcame the Amalekite army with the sword.

14Then the LORD said to
Moses, "Write this on a scroll
as something to be remem-
bered and make sure that
Joshua hears it, because I will
completely erase the memory
of the Amalekites from under
heaven."

15Moses built an altar and
called it The LORD is my Banner. 16He said, "For hands

g7 *Massah* means *testing.*
h7 *Meribah* means *quarreling.*

כִּֽי־ יָד֙ עַל־ כֵּ֣ס יָ֔הּ מִלְחָמָ֥ה לַֽיהוָ֖ה בַּעֲמָלֵ֑ק מִדֹּ֖ר
from-generation against-Amalek with-Yahweh war Yah throne-of up-to hand for

דֹּֽר׃ וַיִּשְׁמַ֞ע יִתְר֨וֹ כֹהֵ֤ן מִדְיָן֙ חֹתֵ֣ן מֹשֶׁ֔ה
Moses father-in-law-of Midian priest-of Jethro now-he-heard (18:1) generation

אֵת֩ כָּל־ אֲשֶׁ֨ר עָשָׂ֤ה אֱלֹהִים֙ לְמֹשֶׁ֔ה וּלְיִשְׂרָאֵ֖ל עַמּ֑וֹ כִּֽי־ הוֹצִ֧יא
he-brought how people-of-him and-for-Israel for-Moses God he-did that all ***

יְהוָ֛ה אֶת־ יִשְׂרָאֵ֖ל מִמִּצְרָֽיִם׃ וַיִּקַּ֗ח יִתְרוֹ֙ חֹתֵ֣ן
father-in-law-of Jethro and-he-received (2) from-Egypt Israel *** Yahweh

מֹשֶׁ֔ה אֶת־ צִפֹּרָ֖ה אֵ֣שֶׁת מֹשֶׁ֑ה אַחַ֖ר שִׁלּוּחֶֽיהָ׃ וְאֵ֖ת שְׁנֵ֣י
two-of and (3) departures-of-her after Moses wife-of Zipporah *** Moses

בָנֶ֑יהָ אֲשֶׁ֨ר שֵׁ֤ם הָֽאֶחָד֙ גֵּֽרְשֹׁ֔ם כִּ֣י אָמַ֔ר גֵּ֣ר הָיִ֔יתִי בְּאֶ֖רֶץ
in-land I-became alien he-said for Gershom the-one name-of whose sons-of-her

נָכְרִיָּֽה׃ וְשֵׁ֥ם הָאֶחָ֖ד אֱלִיעֶ֑זֶר כִּֽי־ אֱלֹהֵ֤י אָבִי֙
father-of-me God-of for Eliezer the-other and-name-of (4) foreign

בְּעֶזְרִ֔י וַיַּצִּלֵ֖נִי מֵחֶ֥רֶב פַּרְעֹֽה׃ וַיָּבֹ֞א יִתְר֨וֹ
Jethro and-he-came (5) Pharaoh from-sword-of and-he-saved-me as-helper-of-me

חֹתֵ֥ן מֹשֶׁ֛ה וּבָנָ֥יו וְאִשְׁתּ֖וֹ אֶל־ מֹשֶׁ֑ה אֶל־ הַמִּדְבָּ֗ר
the-desert in Moses to and-wife-of-him with-sons-of-him Moses father-in-law-of

אֲשֶׁר־ ה֛וּא חֹנֶ֥ה שָׁ֖ם הַ֥ר הָאֱלֹהִֽים׃ וַיֹּ֙אמֶר֙ אֶל־ מֹשֶׁ֔ה אֲנִ֛י
I Moses to and-he-said (6) the-God mountain-of there camping he where

חֹתֶנְךָ֥ יִתְר֖וֹ בָּ֣א אֵלֶ֑יךָ וְאִ֨שְׁתְּךָ֔ וּשְׁנֵ֥י
and-two-of with-wife-of-you to-you coming Jethro father-in-law-of-you

בָנֶ֖יהָ עִמָּֽהּ׃ וַיֵּצֵ֨א מֹשֶׁ֜ה לִקְרַ֣את חֹֽתְנ֗וֹ
father-in-law-of-him to-meet Moses so-he-went-out (7) with-her sons-of-her

וַיִּשְׁתַּ֙חוּ֙ וַיִּשַּׁק־ ל֔וֹ וַיִּשְׁאֲל֥וּ אִישׁ־ לְרֵעֵ֖הוּ
to-other-of-him each and-they-asked on-him and-he-kissed and-he-bowed

לְשָׁל֑וֹם וַיָּבֹ֖אוּ הָאֹֽהֱלָה׃ וַיְסַפֵּ֤ר מֹשֶׁה֙
Moses and-he-told (8) into-the-tent then-they-went about-welfare

לְחֹ֣תְנ֔וֹ אֵת֩ כָּל־ אֲשֶׁ֨ר עָשָׂ֤ה יְהוָה֙ לְפַרְעֹ֣ה וּלְמִצְרַ֔יִם
and-to-Egypt to-Pharaoh Yahweh he-did that all *** to-father-in-law-of-him

עַ֖ל אוֹדֹ֣ת יִשְׂרָאֵ֑ל אֵ֤ת כָּל־ הַתְּלָאָה֙ אֲשֶׁ֣ר מְצָאָ֣תַם בַּדֶּ֔רֶךְ
along-the-way she-met-them that the-hardship all-of *** Israel sakes-of for

וַיַּצִּלֵ֖ם יְהוָֽה׃ וַיִּ֣חַדְּ יִתְר֔וֹ עַ֚ל כָּל־
all-of about Jethro and-he-was-delighted (9) Yahweh and-he-saved-them

הַטּוֹבָ֔ה אֲשֶׁר־ עָשָׂ֥ה יְהוָ֖ה לְיִשְׂרָאֵ֑ל אֲשֶׁ֥ר הִצִּיל֖וֹ מִיַּ֥ד
from-hand-of he-rescued-him when for-Israel Yahweh he-did that the-good

מִצְרָֽיִם׃ וַיֹּאמֶר֮ יִתְרוֹ֒ בָּר֣וּךְ יְהוָ֔ה אֲשֶׁ֨ר הִצִּ֥יל אֶתְכֶ֛ם
you he-rescued who Yahweh being-praised Jethro and-he-said (10) Egyptians

were lifted up to the throne of the LORD. The[i] LORD will be at war against the Amalekites from generation to generation."

*Jethro Visits Moses*

18 Now Jethro, the priest of Midian and father-in-law of Moses, heard of everything God had done for Moses and for his people Israel, and how the LORD had brought Israel out of Egypt.

2 After Moses had sent away his wife Zipporah, his father-in-law Jethro received her 3 and her two sons. One son was named Gershom,[j] for Moses said, "I have become an alien in a foreign land"; 4 and the other was named Eliezer,[k] for he said, "My father's God was my helper; he saved me from the sword of Pharaoh."

5 Jethro, Moses' father-in-law, together with Moses' sons and wife, came to him in the desert, where he was camped near the mountain of God. 6 Jethro had sent word to him, "I, your father-in-law Jethro, am coming to you with your wife and her two sons."

7 So Moses went out to meet his father-in-law and bowed down and kissed him. They greeted each other and then went into the tent. 8 Moses told his father-in-law about everything the LORD had done to Pharaoh and the Egyptians for Israel's sake and about all the hardships they had met along the way and how the LORD had saved them.

9 Jethro was delighted to hear about all the good things the LORD had done for Israel in rescuing them from the hand of the Egyptians. 10 He said, "Praise be to the LORD, who rescued you from the hand of

i16 Or *"Because a hand was against the throne of the LORD, the*
j3 *Gershom* sounds like the Hebrew for *an alien there.*
k4 *Eliezer* means *my God is helper.*

מִיַּד מִצְרַיִם וּמִיַּד פַּרְעֹה אֲשֶׁר הִצִּיל אֶת־הָעָם
the-people *** he-rescued who Pharaoh and-from-hand-of Egyptians from-hand-of

מִתַּחַת יַד־מִצְרָיִם׃ עַתָּה יָדַעְתִּי כִּי־גָדוֹל יְהוָה מִכָּל־
than-all-of Yahweh greater that I-know now (11) Egyptians hand-of from-under

הָאֱלֹהִים כִּי בַדָּבָר אֲשֶׁר זָדוּ עֲלֵיהֶם׃
to-them they-were-arrogant when of-the-matter because the-gods

וַיִּקַּח יִתְרוֹ חֹתֵן מֹשֶׁה עֹלָה וּזְבָחִים
and-sacrifices burnt-offering Moses father-in-law-of Jethro then-he-brought (12)

לֵאלֹהִים וַיָּבֹא אַהֲרֹן וְכֹל ׀ זִקְנֵי יִשְׂרָאֵל לֶאֱכָל־לֶחֶם עִם־
with bread to-eat Israel elders-of and-all-of Aaron and-he-came to-God

חֹתֵן מֹשֶׁה לִפְנֵי הָאֱלֹהִים׃ וַיְהִי מִמָּחֳרָת
on-next-day and-he-was (13) the-God in-presence-of Moses father-in-law-of

וַיֵּשֶׁב מֹשֶׁה לִשְׁפֹּט אֶת־הָעָם וַיַּעֲמֹד הָעָם עַל־
around the-people and-they-stood the-people *** to-judge Moses that-he-sat

מֹשֶׁה מִן־הַבֹּקֶר עַד־הָעָרֶב׃ וַיַּרְא חֹתֵן
father-in-law-of when-he-saw (14) the-evening till the-morning from Moses

מֹשֶׁה אֵת כָּל־אֲשֶׁר־הוּא עֹשֶׂה לָעָם וַיֹּאמֶר מָה־הַדָּבָר
the-thing what? then-he-said for-the-people doing he that all *** Moses

הַזֶּה אֲשֶׁר אַתָּה עֹשֶׂה לָעָם מַדּוּעַ אַתָּה יוֹשֵׁב לְבַדֶּךָ
by-yourself sitting you why? for-the-people doing you that the-this

וְכָל־הָעָם נִצָּב עָלֶיךָ מִן־בֹּקֶר עַד־עָרֶב׃
evening till morning from around-you standing the-people while-all-of

וַיֹּאמֶר מֹשֶׁה לְחֹתְנוֹ כִּי־יָבֹא אֵלַי
to-me he-comes because to-father-in-law-of-him Moses then-he-answered (15)

הָעָם לִדְרֹשׁ אֱלֹהִים׃ כִּי־יִהְיֶה לָהֶם דָּבָר בָּא אֵלַי
to-me he-comes dispute with-them he-is when (16) God to-seek the-people

וְשָׁפַטְתִּי בֵּין אִישׁ וּבֵין רֵעֵהוּ וְהוֹדַעְתִּי אֶת־
*** and-I-inform fellow-of-him and-between man between and-I-decide

חֻקֵּי הָאֱלֹהִים וְאֶת־תּוֹרֹתָיו׃ וַיֹּאמֶר חֹתֵן מֹשֶׁה
Moses father-in-law-of and-he-replied (17) laws-of-him and the-God decrees-of

אֵלָיו לֹא־טוֹב הַדָּבָר אֲשֶׁר אַתָּה עֹשֶׂה׃ נָבֹל תִּבֹּל
you-will-wear-out to-wear-out (18) doing you that the-thing good not to-him

גַּם־אַתָּה גַּם־הָעָם הַזֶּה אֲשֶׁר עִמָּךְ כִּי־כָבֵד מִמְּךָ הַדָּבָר
the-work for-you too-heavy for with-you who the-this the-people and you both

לֹא־תוּכַל עֲשֹׂהוּ לְבַדֶּךָ׃ עַתָּה שְׁמַע בְּקֹלִי
to-voice-of-me listen! now (19) by-yourself to-handle-him you-can not

אִיעָצְךָ וִיהִי אֱלֹהִים עִמָּךְ הֱיֵה אַתָּה לָעָם מוּל
before for-the-people you be! with-you God and-may-he-be I-will-advise-you

the Egyptians and of Pharaoh, and who rescued the people from the hand of the Egyptians. 11 Now I know that the LORD is greater than all other gods, for he did this to those who had treated Israel arrogantly." 12 Then Jethro, Moses' father-in-law, brought a burnt offering and other sacrifices to God, and Aaron came with all the elders of Israel to eat bread with Moses' father-in-law in the presence of God.

13 The next day Moses took his seat to serve as judge for the people, and they stood around him from morning till evening. 14 When his father-in-law saw all that Moses was doing for the people, he said, "What is this you are doing for the people? Why do you alone sit as judge, while all these people stand around you from morning till evening?"

15 Moses answered him, "Because the people come to me to seek God's will. 16 Whenever they have a dispute, it is brought to me, and I decide between the parties and inform them of God's decrees and laws."

17 Moses' father-in-law replied, "What you are doing is not good. 18 You and these people who come to you will only wear yourselves out. The work is too heavy for you; you cannot handle it alone. 19 Listen now to me and I will give you some advice, and may God be with you. You must be

הָאֱלֹהִים וְהֵבֵאתָ אַתָּה אֶת־ הַדְּבָרִים אֶל־ הָאֱלֹהִים׃ וְהִזְהַרְתָּה
and-you-teach (20) the-God to the-disputes *** you and-you-bring the-God

אֶתְהֶם אֶת־ הַחֻקִּים וְאֶת־ הַתּוֹרֹת וְהוֹדַעְתָּ לָהֶם אֶת־ הַדֶּרֶךְ
the-way *** to-them and-you-show the-laws and the-decrees *** them

יֵלְכוּ בָהּ וְאֶת־ הַמַּעֲשֶׂה אֲשֶׁר יַעֲשׂוּן׃ וְאַתָּה
but-you (21) they-should-perform that the-duty and in-her they-should-live

תֶחֱזֶה מִכָּל־ הָעָם אַנְשֵׁי־ חַיִל יִרְאֵי אֱלֹהִים
God ones-fearing-of capable men-of the-people from-all-of you-select

אַנְשֵׁי אֱמֶת שֹׂנְאֵי בָצַע וְשַׂמְתָּ עֲלֵהֶם שָׂרֵי
officials-of over-them and-you-appoint bribe ones-hating-of trust men-of

אֲלָפִים שָׂרֵי מֵאוֹת שָׂרֵי חֲמִשִּׁים וְשָׂרֵי עֲשָׂרֹת׃
tens and-officials-of fifties officials-of hundreds officials-of thousands

וְשָׁפְטוּ אֶת־ הָעָם בְּכָל־ עֵת וְהָיָה
and-he-will-be time at-all-of the-people *** and-let-them-judge (22)

כָּל־ הַדָּבָר הַגָּדֹל יָבִיאוּ אֵלֶיךָ וְכָל־ הַדָּבָר
the-case but-every-of to-you they-will-bring the-difficult the-case every-of

הַקָּטֹן יִשְׁפְּטוּ־ הֵם וְהָקֵל מֵעָלֶיךָ
from-on-you so-he-will-be-lighter they they-will-decide the-simple

וְנָשְׂאוּ אִתָּךְ׃ אִם אֶת־ הַדָּבָר הַזֶּה תַּעֲשֶׂה
you-do the-this the-thing *** if (23) with-you and-they-will-share

וְצִוְּךָ אֱלֹהִים וְיָכָלְתָּ עֲמֹד וְגַם כָּל־
all-of and-also to-stand then-you-will-be-able God and-he-commands-you

הָעָם הַזֶּה עַל־ מְקֹמוֹ יָבֹא בְשָׁלוֹם׃
in-satisfaction he-will-go home-of-him to the-this the-people

וַיִּשְׁמַע מֹשֶׁה לְקוֹל חֹתְנוֹ וַיַּעַשׂ כֹּל אֲשֶׁר
that all and-he-did father-in-law-of-him to-voice-of Moses and-he-listened (24)

אָמָר׃ וַיִּבְחַר מֹשֶׁה אַנְשֵׁי־ חַיִל מִכָּל־ יִשְׂרָאֵל וַיִּתֵּן
and-he-made Israel from-all-of capable men-of Moses and-he-chose (25) he-said

אֹתָם רָאשִׁים עַל־ הָעָם שָׂרֵי אֲלָפִים שָׂרֵי מֵאוֹת
hundreds officials-of thousands officials-of the-people over leaders them

שָׂרֵי חֲמִשִּׁים וְשָׂרֵי עֲשָׂרֹת׃ וְשָׁפְטוּ אֶת־ הָעָם
the-people *** and-they-judged (26) tens and-officials-of fifties officials-of

בְּכָל־ עֵת אֶת־ הַדָּבָר הַקָּשֶׁה יְבִיאוּן אֶל־ מֹשֶׁה וְכָל־
but-every-of Moses to they-brought the-difficult the-case *** time at-all-of

הַדָּבָר הַקָּטֹן יִשְׁפּוּטוּ הֵם׃ וַיְשַׁלַּח מֹשֶׁה אֶת־
*** Moses then-he-sent (27) they they-decided the-simple the-case

חֹתְנוֹ וַיֵּלֶךְ לוֹ אֶל־ אַרְצוֹ׃ בַּחֹדֶשׁ
in-the-month (19:1) country-of-him to to-him and-he-went father-in-law-of-him

the people's representative before God and bring their disputes to him. 20 Teach them the decrees and laws, and show them the way to live and the duties they are to perform. 21 But select capable men from all the people—men who fear God, trustworthy men who hate dishonest gain—and appoint them as officials over thousands, hundreds, fifties and tens. 22 Have them serve as judges for the people at all times, but have them bring every difficult case to you; the simple cases they can decide themselves. That will make your load lighter, because they will share it with you. 23 If you do this and God so commands, you will be able to stand the strain, and all these people will go home satisfied."

24 Moses listened to his father-in-law and did everything he said. 25 He chose capable men from all Israel and made them leaders of the people, officials over thousands, hundreds, fifties and tens. 26 They served as judges for the people at all times. The difficult cases they brought to Moses, but the simple ones they decided themselves.

27 Then Moses sent his father-in-law on his way, and he returned to his own country.

הַשְּׁלִישִׁי לְצֵאת בְּנֵי־ יִשְׂרָאֵל מֵאֶרֶץ מִצְרָיִם בַּיּוֹם
on-the-day Egypt from-land-of Israel sons-of after-to-leave the-third

הַזֶּה בָּאוּ מִדְבַּר סִינָי׃ וַיִּסְעוּ מֵרְפִידִים
from-Rephidim and-they-set-out (2) Sinai Desert-of they-came the-that

וַיָּבֹאוּ מִדְבַּר סִינַי וַיַּחֲנוּ בַּמִּדְבָּר וַיִּחַן־
and-he-camped in-the-desert and-they-camped Sinai Desert-of and-they-entered

שָׁם יִשְׂרָאֵל נֶגֶד הָהָר׃ וּמֹשֶׁה עָלָה אֶל־הָאֱלֹהִים
the-God to he-went-up then-Moses (3) the-mountain in-front-of Israel there

וַיִּקְרָא אֵלָיו יְהוָה מִן־ הָהָר לֵאמֹר כֹּה תֹאמַר לְבֵית
to-house-of you-say this to-say the-mountain from Yahweh to-him and-he-called

יַעֲקֹב וְתַגֵּיד לִבְנֵי יִשְׂרָאֵל׃ אַתֶּם רְאִיתֶם אֲשֶׁר עָשִׂיתִי לְמִצְרָיִם
to-Egypt I-did what you-saw you (4) Israel to-sons-of and-you-tell Jacob

וָאֶשָּׂא אֶתְכֶם עַל־ כַּנְפֵי נְשָׁרִים וָאָבִא אֶתְכֶם אֵלָי׃ וְעַתָּה
and-now (5) to-myself you and-I-brought eagles wings-of on you and-I-carried

אִם־ שָׁמוֹעַ תִּשְׁמְעוּ בְּקֹלִי וּשְׁמַרְתֶּם אֶת־ בְּרִיתִי
covenant-of-me *** and-you-keep to-voice-of-me you-obey to-obey if

וִהְיִיתֶם לִי סְגֻלָּה מִכָּל־ הָעַמִּים כִּי־ לִי
to-me although the-nations from-all-of possession to-me then-you-will-be

כָּל־ הָאָרֶץ׃ וְאַתֶּם תִּהְיוּ־ לִי מַמְלֶכֶת כֹּהֲנִים וְגוֹי
and-nation priests kingdom-of for-me you-will-be and-you (6) the-earth all-of

קָדוֹשׁ אֵלֶּה הַדְּבָרִים אֲשֶׁר תְּדַבֵּר אֶל־ בְּנֵי יִשְׂרָאֵל׃ וַיָּבֹא
so-he-went-back (7) Israel sons-of to you-speak that the-words these holy

מֹשֶׁה וַיִּקְרָא לְזִקְנֵי הָעָם וַיָּשֶׂם לִפְנֵיהֶם אֵת
*** before-them and-he-set the-people to-elders-of and-he-summoned Moses

כָּל־ הַדְּבָרִים הָאֵלֶּה אֲשֶׁר צִוָּהוּ יְהוָה׃ וַיַּעֲנוּ
and-they-responded (8) Yahweh he-commanded-him that the-these the-words all-of

כָל־ הָעָם יַחְדָּו וַיֹּאמְרוּ כֹּל אֲשֶׁר־ דִּבֶּר יְהוָה נַעֲשֶׂה
we-will-do Yahweh he-said that all and-they-said together the-people all-of

וַיָּשֶׁב מֹשֶׁה אֶת־ דִּבְרֵי הָעָם אֶל־ יְהוָה׃ וַיֹּאמֶר
and-he-said (9) Yahweh to the-people answers-of *** Moses and-he-brought-back

יְהוָה אֶל־ מֹשֶׁה הִנֵּה אָנֹכִי בָּא אֵלֶיךָ בְּעַב הֶעָנָן בַּעֲבוּר
so-that the-cloud in-dense-of to-you coming I see! Moses to Yahweh

יִשְׁמַע הָעָם בְּדַבְּרִי עִמָּךְ וְגַם־ בְּךָ
in-you and-also with-you when-to-speak-me the-people he-will-hear

יַאֲמִינוּ לְעוֹלָם וַיַּגֵּד מֹשֶׁה אֶת־ דִּבְרֵי הָעָם אֶל־
to the-people words-of *** Moses then-he-told for-always they-will-trust

יְהוָה׃ וַיֹּאמֶר יְהוָה אֶל־ מֹשֶׁה לֵךְ אֶל־ הָעָם
the-people to go! Moses to Yahweh and-he-said (10) Yahweh

*At Mount Sinai*

19 In the third month after the Israelites left
Egypt—on the very day—they
came to the Desert of Sinai.
2After they set out from Rephidim, they entered the Desert
of Sinai, and Israel camped
there in the desert in front of
the mountain.
3Then Moses went up to
God, and the LORD called to
him from the mountain and
said, "This is what you are to
say to the house of Jacob and
what you are to tell the people
of Israel: 4'You yourselves
have seen what I did to Egypt,
and how I carried you on eagles' wings and brought you to
myself. 5Now if you obey me
fully and keep my covenant,
then out of all nations you will
be my treasured possession.
Although the whole earth is
mine, 6you will be for me a
kingdom of priests and a holy
nation.' These are the words
you are to speak to the Israelites."
7So Moses went back and
summoned the elders of the
people and set before them all
the words the LORD had commanded him to speak. 8The
people all responded together,
"We will do everything the
LORD has said." So Moses
brought their answer back to
the LORD.
9The LORD said to Moses, "I
am going to come to you in a
dense cloud, so that the people
will hear me speaking with
you and will always put their
trust in you." Then Moses told
the LORD what the people had
said.
10And the LORD said to
Moses, "Go to the people and

וְקִדַּשְׁתָּם הַיּוֹם וּמָחָר וְכִבְּסוּ שִׂמְלֹתָם׃
clothes-of-them and-let-them-wash and-tommorow the-day and-you-consecrate-them

וְהָיוּ נְכֹנִים לַיּוֹם הַשְּׁלִישִׁי כִּי ׀ בַּיּוֹם
on-the-day for the-third by-the-day ones-being-ready and-they-will-be (11)

הַשְּׁלִשִׁי יֵרֵד יְהוָה לְעֵינֵי כָל־ הָעָם עַל־
onto the-people all-of before-eyes-of Yahweh he-will-come-down the-third

הַר סִינָי׃ וְהִגְבַּלְתָּ אֶת־ הָעָם סָבִיב לֵאמֹר הִשָּׁמְרוּ
be-careful! to-say around the-people *** and-you-limit (12) Sinai Mount-of

לָכֶם עֲלוֹת בָּהָר וּנְגֹעַ בְּקָצֵהוּ כָּל־
every-of on-border-of-him or-to-touch on-the-mountain to-go-up to-you

הַנֹּגֵעַ בָּהָר מוֹת יוּמָת׃ לֹא־ תִגַּע בּוֹ
on-him you-lay not (13) he-will-die to-die on-the-mountain the-one-touching

יָד כִּי־ סָקוֹל יִסָּקֵל אוֹ־ יָרֹה יִיָּרֶה
he-will-be-shot to-he-shot or he-will-be-stoned to-be-stoned for hand

אִם־ בְּהֵמָה אִם־ אִישׁ לֹא יִחְיֶה בִּמְשֹׁךְ הַיֹּבֵל הֵמָּה
they the-trumpet when-to-blast he-shall-live not man or animal whether

יַעֲלוּ בָהָר׃ וַיֵּרֶד מֹשֶׁה מִן־ הָהָר
the-mountain from Moses and-he-came-down (14) to-the-mountain they-may-go-up

אֶל־ הָעָם וַיְקַדֵּשׁ אֶת־ הָעָם וַיְכַבְּסוּ
and-they-washed the-people *** and-he-consecrated the-people to

שִׂמְלֹתָם׃ וַיֹּאמֶר אֶל־ הָעָם הֱיוּ נְכֹנִים
ones-being-prepared be! the-people to and-he-said (15) clothes-of-them

לִשְׁלֹשֶׁת יָמִים אַל־ תִּגְּשׁוּ אֶל־ אִשָּׁה׃ וַיְהִי
and-he-was (16) woman with you-may-have-relations not days by-third-of

בַיּוֹם הַשְּׁלִישִׁי בִּהְיֹת הַבֹּקֶר וַיְהִי קֹלֹת
thunders and-he-was the-morning when-to-come the-third on-the-day

וּבְרָקִים וְעָנָן כָּבֵד עַל־ הָהָר וְקֹל שֹׁפָר חָזָק
loud trumpet and-blast-of the-mountain over thick with-cloud and-lightnings

מְאֹד וַיֶּחֱרַד כָּל־ הָעָם אֲשֶׁר בַּמַּחֲנֶה׃ וַיּוֹצֵא
and-he-led-out (17) in-the-camp that the-people all-of and-he-trembled very

מֹשֶׁה אֶת־ הָעָם לִקְרַאת הָאֱלֹהִים מִן־ הַמַּחֲנֶה וַיִּתְיַצְּבוּ בְּתַחְתִּית
at-foot-of and-they-stood the-camp from the-God to-meet the-people *** Moses

הָהָר׃ וְהַר סִינַי עָשַׁן כֻּלּוֹ מִפְּנֵי אֲשֶׁר
when because-of around-him he-had-smoke Sinai and-Mount-of (18) the-mountain

יָרַד עָלָיו יְהוָה בָּאֵשׁ וַיַּעַל עֲשָׁנוֹ
smoke-of-him and-he-billowed-up in-the-fire Yahweh on-him he-descended

כְּעֶשֶׁן הַכִּבְשָׁן וַיֶּחֱרַד כָּל־ הָהָר מְאֹד׃
violently the-mountain whole-of and-he-trembled the-furnace like-smoke-of

consecrate them today and tomorrow. Have them wash
their clothes 11and be ready by
the third day, because on that
day the LORD will come down
on Mount Sinai in the sight of
all the people. 12Put limits for
the people around the mountain and tell them, 'Be careful
that you do not go up the
mountain or touch the foot of
it. Whoever touches the
mountain shall surely be put
to death. 13He shall surely be
stoned or shot with arrows;
not a hand is to be laid on him.
Whether man or animal, he
shall not be permitted to live.'
Only when the ram's horn
sounds a long blast may they
go up to the mountain."
14After Moses had gone
down the mountain to the
people, he consecrated them,
and they washed their clothes.
15Then he said to the people,
"Prepare yourselves for the
third day. Abstain from sexual
relations."
16On the morning of the
third day there was thunder
and lightning, with a thick
cloud over the mountain, and
a very loud trumpet blast.
Everyone in the camp trembled. 17Then Moses led the
people out of the camp to meet
with God, and they stood at
the foot of the mountain.
18Mount Sinai was covered
with smoke, because the LORD
descended on it in fire. The
smoke billowed up from it like
smoke from a furnace, the
whole mountain[l] trembled violently, 19and the sound of the

[l] 18 Most Hebrew manuscripts; a few Hebrew manuscripts and Septuagint *all the people*

וַיְהִי קוֹל הַשֹּׁפָר הוֹלֵךְ וְחָזֵק מְאֹד מֹשֶׁה
Moses very and-being-loud growing the-trumpet sound-of and-he-was (19)

יְדַבֵּר וְהָאֱלֹהִים יַעֲנֶנּוּ בְקוֹל׃ וַיֵּרֶד
and-he-descended (20) with-thunder he-answered-him and-the-God he-spoke

יְהוָה עַל־ הַר סִינַי אֶל־ רֹאשׁ הָהָר וַיִּקְרָא יְהוָה לְמֹשֶׁה
to-Moses Yahweh and-he-called the-mountain top-of to Sinai Mount-of on Yahweh

אֶל־רֹאשׁ הָהָר וַיַּעַל מֹשֶׁה׃ וַיֹּאמֶר יְהוָה אֶל־ מֹשֶׁה
Moses to Yahweh and-he-said (21) Moses so-he-went-up the-mountain top-of to

רֵד הָעֵד בָּעָם פֶּן־ יֶהֶרְסוּ אֶל־ יְהוָה לִרְאוֹת
to-see Yahweh to they-force-through so-not to-the-people warn! go-down!

וְנָפַל מִמֶּנּוּ רָב׃ וְגַם הַכֹּהֲנִים הַנִּגָּשִׁים
the-ones-approaching the-priests and-even (22) many from-him and-he-perish

אֶל־ יְהוָה יִתְקַדָּשׁוּ פֶּן־ יִפְרֹץ בָּהֶם
against-them he-will-break-out or they-must-consecrate-themselves Yahweh to

יְהוָה׃ וַיֹּאמֶר מֹשֶׁה אֶל־ יְהוָה לֹא־ יוּכַל הָעָם לַעֲלֹת
to-come-up the-people he-can not Yahweh to Moses and-he-said (23) Yahweh

אֶל־ הַר סִינָי כִּי־ אַתָּה הַעֵדֹתָה בָּנוּ לֵאמֹר הַגְבֵּל אֶת־
*** put-limit! to-say to-us you-warned you for Sinai Mount-of onto

הָהָר וְקִדַּשְׁתּוֹ׃ וַיֹּאמֶר אֵלָיו יְהוָה לֶךְ־
go! Yahweh to-him then-he-said (24) and-you-make-holy-him the-mountain

רֵד וְעָלִיתָ אַתָּה וְאַהֲרֹן עִמָּךְ וְהַכֹּהֲנִים וְהָעָם
and-the-people but-the-priests with-you and-Aaron you and-you-bring-up go-down!

אַל־ יֶהֶרְסוּ לַעֲלֹת אֶל־ יְהוָה פֶּן־ יִפְרָץ־
he-will-break-out or Yahweh to to-come-up they-may-force-through not

בָּם׃ וַיֵּרֶד מֹשֶׁה אֶל־ הָעָם וַיֹּאמֶר אֲלֵהֶם׃
to-them and-he-told the-people to Moses so-he-went-down (25) against-them

וַיְדַבֵּר אֱלֹהִים אֵת כָּל־ הַדְּבָרִים הָאֵלֶּה לֵאמֹר׃ אָנֹכִי יְהוָה
Yahweh I (2) to-say the-these the-words all-of *** God and-he-spoke (20:1)

אֱלֹהֶיךָ אֲשֶׁר הוֹצֵאתִיךָ מֵאֶרֶץ מִצְרַיִם מִבֵּית עֲבָדִים׃
slaveries from-house-of Egypt from-land-of I-brought-you who God-of-you

לֹא יִהְיֶה־ לְךָ אֱלֹהִים אֲחֵרִים עַל־ פָּנָיַ* לֹא
not (4) face-of-me before other-ones gods to-you he-shall-be not (3)

תַעֲשֶׂה־ לְךָ פֶסֶל ׀ וְכָל־ תְּמוּנָה אֲשֶׁר בַּשָּׁמַיִם ׀
in-the-heavens that image or-any-of idol for-yourself you-shall-make

מִמַּעַל וַאֲשֶׁר בָּאָרֶץ מִתָּחַת וַאֲשֶׁר בַּמַּיִם ׀
in-the-waters or-that from-beneath on-the-earth or-that from-above

מִתַּחַת לָאָרֶץ לֹא־ תִשְׁתַּחֲוֶה לָהֶם וְלֹא
and-not to-them you-shall-bow not (5) to-the-earth from-below

trumpet grew louder and louder. Then Moses spoke and the voice of God answered him.[m]

[20]The LORD descended to the top of Mount Sinai and called Moses to the top of the mountain. So Moses went up [21]and the LORD said to him, "Go down and warn the people so they do not force their way through to see the LORD and many of them perish. [22]Even the priests, who approach the LORD, must consecrate themselves, or the LORD will break out against them."

[23]Moses said to the LORD, "The people cannot come up Mount Sinai, because you yourself warned us, 'Put limits around the mountain and set it apart as holy.' "

[24]The LORD replied, "Go down and bring Aaron up with you. But the priests and the people must not force their way through to come up to the LORD, or he will break out against them."

[25]So Moses went down to the people and told them.

### *The Ten Commandments*

**20** And God spoke all these words:

[2]"I am the LORD your God, who brought you out of Egypt, out of the land of slavery.

[3]"You shall have no other gods before[n] me.

[4]"You shall not make for yourself an idol in the form of anything in heaven above or on the earth beneath or in the waters below. [5]You shall not bow down to them or

[m]19 Or *and God answered him with thunder*
[n]3 Or *besides*

*3 Most mss end verse 3 with *soph pasuq* ( : ).

תַעָבְדֵם כִּי אָנֹכִי יְהוָה אֱלֹהֶיךָ אֵל קַנָּא פֹּקֵד עֲוֺן

sin-of punishing jealous God God-of-you Yahweh I for you-shall-worship-them

אָבֹת עַל־ בָּנִים עַל־ שִׁלֵּשִׁים וְעַל־ רִבֵּעִים לְשֹׂנְאָי׃

to-ones-hating-me fourth-ones and-to third-ones to children on fathers

וְעֹשֶׂה חֶסֶד לַאֲלָפִים לְאֹהֲבַי וּלְשֹׁמְרֵי

and-to-ones-keeping-of to-ones-loving-me to-thousands love but-showing (6)

מִצְוֺתָי׃ לֹא תִשָּׂא אֶת־ שֵׁם־ יְהוָה אֱלֹהֶיךָ

God-of-you Yahweh name-of *** you-shall-take not (7) commandments-of-me

לַשָּׁוְא כִּי לֹא יְנַקֶּה יְהוָה אֵת אֲשֶׁר־ יִשָּׂא אֶת־

*** he-takes who *** Yahweh he-will-hold-guiltless not for for-the-misuse

שְׁמוֹ לַשָּׁוְא׃ זָכוֹר אֶת־ יוֹם הַשַּׁבָּת

the-Sabbath day-of *** to-remember (8) for-the-misuse name-of-him

לְקַדְּשׁוֹ׃ שֵׁשֶׁת יָמִים תַּעֲבֹד וְעָשִׂיתָ כָּל־

all-of and-you-shall-do you-shall-labor days six-of (9) to-keep-holy-him

מְלַאכְתֶּךָ׃ וְיוֹם הַשְּׁבִיעִי שַׁבָּת ׀ לַיהוָה אֱלֹהֶיךָ לֹא־

not God-of-you to-Yahweh Sabbath the-seventh but-day-of (10) work-of-you

תַעֲשֶׂה כָל־ מְלָאכָה אַתָּה ׀ וּבִנְךָ־ וּבִתֶּךָ

or-daughter-of-you or-son-of-you you work any-of you-shall-do

עַבְדְּךָ וַאֲמָתְךָ וּבְהֶמְתֶּךָ וְגֵרְךָ אֲשֶׁר

who or-alien-of-you or-animal-of-you or-maidservant-of-you manservant-of-you

בִּשְׁעָרֶיךָ׃ כִּי שֵׁשֶׁת־ יָמִים עָשָׂה יְהוָה אֶת־ הַשָּׁמַיִם וְאֶת־

and the-heavens *** Yahweh he-made days six-of for (11) within-gates-of-you

הָאָרֶץ אֶת־ הַיָּם וְאֶת־ כָּל־ אֲשֶׁר־ בָּם וַיָּנַח בַּיּוֹם

on-the-day but-he-rested in-them that all and the-sea *** the-earth

הַשְּׁבִיעִי עַל־ כֵּן בֵּרַךְ יְהוָה אֶת־ יוֹם הַשַּׁבָּת

the-Sabbath day-of *** Yahweh he-blessed this for the-seventh

וַיְקַדְּשֵׁהוּ׃ כַּבֵּד אֶת־ אָבִיךָ וְאֶת־ אִמֶּךָ לְמַעַן

that mother-of-you and father-of-you *** honor! (12) and-he-made-holy-him

יַאֲרִכוּן יָמֶיךָ עַל הָאֲדָמָה אֲשֶׁר־ יְהוָה אֱלֹהֶיךָ נֹתֵן

giving God-of-you Yahweh that the-land in days-of-you they-may-be-long

לָךְ׃ לֹא תִּרְצָח׃ לֹא תִּנְאָף׃ לֹא

not (15) you-shall-commit-adultery not (14) you-shall-murder not (13) to-you

תִּגְנֹב׃ לֹא־ תַעֲנֶה בְרֵעֲךָ עֵד

testimony-of against-neighbor-of-you you-shall-give not (16) you-shall-steal

שָׁקֶר׃ לֹא תַחְמֹד בֵּית רֵעֶךָ לֹא־ תַחְמֹד

you-shall-covet not neighbor-of-you house-of you-shall-covet not (17) false

אֵשֶׁת רֵעֶךָ וְעַבְדּוֹ וַאֲמָתוֹ

or-maidservant-of-him or-manservant-of-him neighbor-of-you wife-of

worship them; for I, the LORD your God, am a jealous God, punishing the children for the sin of the fathers to the third and fourth generation of those who hate me, 6but showing love to thousands who love me and keep my commandments.

7"You shall not misuse the name of the LORD your God, for the LORD will not hold anyone guiltless who misuses his name.

8"Remember the Sabbath day by keeping it holy. 9Six days you shall labor and do all your work, 10but the seventh day is a Sabbath to the LORD your God. On it you shall not do any work, neither you, nor your son or daughter, nor your manservant or maidservant, nor your animals, nor the alien within your gates. 11For in six days the LORD made the heavens and the earth, the sea, and all that is in them, but he rested on the seventh day. Therefore the LORD blessed the Sabbath day and made it holy.

12"Honor your father and your mother, so that you may live long in the land the LORD your God is giving you.

13"You shall not murder.

14"You shall not commit adultery.

15"You shall not steal.

16"You shall not give false testimony against your neighbor.

17"You shall not covet your neighbor's house. You shall not covet your neighbor's wife, or his

וְשׁוֹרוֹ וַחֲמֹרוֹ וְכֹל אֲשֶׁר לְרֵעֶךָ׃
to-neighbor-of-you that or-anything or-donkey-of-him or-ox-of-him

(18) וְכָל־הָעָם רֹאִים אֶת־הַקּוֹלֹת וְאֶת־הַלַּפִּידִם וְאֵת
and the-lightnings and the-thunders *** ones-seeing the-people and-all-of (18)

קוֹל הַשֹּׁפָר וְאֶת־הָהָר עָשֵׁן וַיִּרְא* הָעָם
the-people *then-they-saw smoking the-mountain and the-trumpet sound-of

וַיָּנֻעוּ וַיַּעַמְדוּ מֵרָחֹק׃ (19) וַיֹּאמְרוּ אֶל־מֹשֶׁה
Moses to and-they-said (19) at-distance and-they-stayed and-they-trembled

דַּבֵּר־אַתָּה עִמָּנוּ וְנִשְׁמָעָה וְאַל־יְדַבֵּר עִמָּנוּ אֱלֹהִים
God to-us have-him-speak but-not and-we-will-listen to-us you speak!

פֶּן־נָמוּת׃ (20) וַיֹּאמֶר מֹשֶׁה אֶל־הָעָם אַל־תִּירָאוּ כִּי
for you-be-afraid not the-people to Moses so-he-said (20) we-will-die or

לְבַעֲבוּר נַסּוֹת אֶתְכֶם בָּא הָאֱלֹהִים וּבַעֲבוּר תִּהְיֶה יִרְאָתוֹ
fear-of-him she-will-be and-so-that the-God he-became you to-test in-order-to

עַל־פְּנֵיכֶם לְבִלְתִּי תֶחֱטָאוּ׃ (21) וַיַּעֲמֹד הָעָם
the-people but-they-remained (21) you-will-sin so-not faces-of-you before

מֵרָחֹק וּמֹשֶׁה נִגַּשׁ אֶל־הָעֲרָפֶל אֲשֶׁר־שָׁם הָאֱלֹהִים׃
the-God there where the-darkness to he-approached while-Moses at-distance

(22) וַיֹּאמֶר יְהוָה אֶל־מֹשֶׁה כֹּה תֹאמַר אֶל־בְּנֵי יִשְׂרָאֵל אַתֶּם רְאִיתֶם
you-saw you Israel sons-of to you-say this Moses to Yahweh then-he-said (22)

כִּי מִן־הַשָּׁמַיִם דִּבַּרְתִּי עִמָּכֶם׃ (23) לֹא תַעֲשׂוּן אִתִּי אֱלֹהֵי
gods-of alongside-me you-make not (23) to-you I-spoke the-heavens from that

כֶסֶף וֵאלֹהֵי זָהָב לֹא תַעֲשׂוּ לָכֶם׃ (24) מִזְבַּח אֲדָמָה תַּעֲשֶׂה־
you-make earth altar-of (24) for-you you-make not gold or-gods-of silver

לִּי וְזָבַחְתָּ עָלָיו אֶת־עֹלֹתֶיךָ וְאֶת־
and burnt-offerings-of-you *** on-him and-you-sacrifice for-me

שְׁלָמֶיךָ אֶת־צֹאנְךָ וְאֶת־בְּקָרֶךָ בְּכָל־
in-every-of cattle-of-you and sheep-of-you *** fellowship-offerings-of-you

הַמָּקוֹם אֲשֶׁר אַזְכִּיר אֶת־שְׁמִי אָבוֹא אֵלֶיךָ
to-you I-will-come name-of-me *** I-cause-honor where the-place

וּבֵרַכְתִּיךָ׃ (25) וְאִם־מִזְבַּח אֲבָנִים תַּעֲשֶׂה־לִּי לֹא־
not for-me you-make stones altar-of and-if (25) and-I-will-bless-you

תִבְנֶה אֶתְהֶן גָּזִית כִּי חַרְבְּךָ הֵנַפְתָּ עָלֶיהָ
on-her you-use tool-of-you if dressed-stone them you-build

וַתְּחַלְלֶהָ׃ (26) וְלֹא־תַעֲלֶה בְמַעֲלֹת עַל־מִזְבְּחִי אֲשֶׁר לֹא־
not so altar-of-me to on-steps you-go-up and-not (26) then-you-defile-her

תִגָּלֶה עֶרְוָתְךָ עָלָיו׃ (21:1) וְאֵלֶּה הַמִּשְׁפָּטִים אֲשֶׁר
that the-laws now-these (21:1) on-him nakedness-of-you she-be-exposed

---

manservant or maidservant, his ox or donkey, or anything that belongs to your neighbor."

[18]When the people saw the thunder and lightning and heard the trumpet and saw the mountain in smoke, they trembled with fear. They stayed at a distance [19]and said to Moses, "Speak to us yourself and we will listen. But do not have God speak to us or we will die."

[20]Moses said to the people, "Do not be afraid. God has come to test you, so that the fear of God will be with you to keep you from sinning."

[21]The people remained at a distance, while Moses approached the thick darkness where God was.

*Idols and Altars*

[22]Then the LORD said to Moses, "Tell the Israelites this: 'You have seen for yourselves that I have spoken to you from heaven: [23]Do not make any gods to be alongside me; do not make for yourselves gods of silver or gods of gold.

[24]" 'Make an altar of earth for me and sacrifice on it your burnt offerings and fellowship offerings,[o] your sheep and goats and your cattle. Wherever I cause my name to be honored, I will come to you and bless you. [25]If you make an altar of stones for me, do not build it with dressed stones, for you will defile it if you use a tool on it. [26]And do not go up to my altar on steps, lest your nakedness be exposed on it.'

**21** "These are the laws you are to set before them:

[o]24 Traditionally *peace offerings*

*18 וַיִּרָאוּ, *then-they-were-afraid*
This reading is conjectured by repointing the Hebrew word on the basis of the major ancient versions.

תָּשִׂים לִפְנֵיהֶם׃ כִּי תִקְנֶה עֶבֶד עִבְרִי שֵׁשׁ שָׁנִים יַעֲבֹד
he-may-serve years six Hebrew slave you-buy if (2) before-them you-set

וּבַשְּׁבִעִת יֵצֵא לַחָפְשִׁי חִנָּם׃ אִם־
if (3) without-pay to-the-freedom he-shall-go-out but-in-the-seventh

בְּגַפּוֹ יָבֹא בְּגַפּוֹ יֵצֵא אִם־ בַּעַל אִשָּׁה הוּא וְיָצְאָה
then-she-goes he wife husband-of if he-goes-free by-himself he-comes by-himself

אִשְׁתּוֹ עִמּוֹ׃ אִם־ אֲדֹנָיו יִתֶּן־ לוֹ אִשָּׁה וְיָלְדָה־
and-she-bears wife to-him he-gives masters-of-him if (4) with-him wife-of-him

לוֹ בָנִים אוֹ בָנוֹת הָאִשָּׁה וִילָדֶיהָ תִּהְיֶה לַאדֹנֶיהָ
to-masters-of-her she-is and-children-of-her the-woman daughters or sons to-him

וְהוּא יֵצֵא בְגַפּוֹ׃ וְאִם־ אָמֹר יֹאמַר הָעֶבֶד
the-servant he-declares to-declare but-if (5) by-himself he-goes-free only-he

אָהַבְתִּי אֶת־ אֲדֹנִי אֶת־ אִשְׁתִּי וְאֶת־ בָּנָי לֹא אֵצֵא
I-would-go not children-of-me and wife-of-me *** master-of-me *** I-love

חָפְשִׁי׃ וְהִגִּישׁוֹ אֲדֹנָיו אֶל־ הָאֱלֹהִים
the-judges before masters-of-him then-he-must-take-him (6) free

וְהִגִּישׁוֹ אֶל־ הַדֶּלֶת אוֹ אֶל־ הַמְּזוּזָה וְרָצַע
and-he-shall-pierce the-doorpost to or the-door to then-he-shall-take-him

אֲדֹנָיו אֶת־ אָזְנוֹ בַּמַּרְצֵעַ וַעֲבָדוֹ לְעֹלָם׃
for-life then-he-shall-serve-him with-the-awl ear-of-him *** masters-of-him

וְכִי־ יִמְכֹּר אִישׁ אֶת־ בִּתּוֹ לְאָמָה לֹא תֵצֵא
she-may-go-free not as-servant daughter-of-him *** man he-sells and-if (7)

כְּצֵאת הָעֲבָדִים׃ אִם־ רָעָה בְּעֵינֵי אֲדֹנֶיהָ
masters-of-her in-eyes-of she-displeases if (8) the-menservants as-to-go-free

אֲשֶׁר־ לֹא° יְעָדָהּ וְהֶפְדָּהּ לְעַם נָכְרִי לֹא־
not foreign to-people then-he-must-let-be-redeemed-her he-selected-her for-him who

יִמְשֹׁל לְמָכְרָהּ בְּבִגְדוֹ־ בָהּ׃ וְאִם־
and-if (9) with-her for-to-break-faith-him to-sell-her he-has-right

לִבְנוֹ יִיעָדֶנָּה כְּמִשְׁפַּט הַבָּנוֹת יַעֲשֶׂה־ לָּהּ׃
to-her he-must-grant the-daughters as-right-of he-selects-her for-son-of-him

אִם־ אַחֶרֶת יִקַּח־ לוֹ שְׁאֵרָהּ כְּסוּתָהּ
clothing-of-her food-of-her for-him he-takes another-woman if (10)

וְעֹנָתָהּ לֹא יִגְרָע׃ וְאִם־ שְׁלָשׁ־ אֵלֶּה לֹא
not these three and-if (11) he-must-deprive not and-marital-right-of-her

יַעֲשֶׂה לָהּ וְיָצְאָה חִנָּם אֵין כָּסֶף׃ מַכֵּה אִישׁ
man one-striking (12) money without free then-she-may-go to-her he-provides

וָמֵת מוֹת יוּמָת׃ וַאֲשֶׁר לֹא צָדָה וְהָאֱלֹהִים
but-the-God he-is-intentional not but-who (13) he-must-die to-die so-he-dies

°8 ק לו

*Hebrew Servants*

2"If you buy a Hebrew servant, he is to serve you for six years. But in the seventh year, he shall go free, without paying anything. 3If he comes alone, he is to go free alone; but if he has a wife when he comes, she is to go with him. 4If his master gives him a wife and she bears him sons or daughters, the woman and her children shall belong to her master, and only the man shall go free.

5"But if the servant declares, 'I love my master and my wife and children and do not want to go free,' 6then his master must take him before the judges.[p] He shall take him to the door or the doorpost and pierce his ear with an awl. Then he will be his servant for life.

7"If a man sells his daughter as a servant, she is not to go free as menservants do. 8If she does not please the master who has selected her for himself,[q] he must let her be redeemed. He has no right to sell her to foreigners, because he has broken faith with her. 9If he selects her for his son, he must grant her the rights of a daughter. 10If he marries another woman, he must not deprive the first one of her food, clothing and marital rights. 11If he does not provide her with these three things, she is to go free, without any payment of money.

*Personal Injuries*

12"Anyone who strikes a man and kills him shall surely be put to death. 13However, if he does not do it intentionally,

p6 Or *before God*
q8 Or *master so that he does not choose her*

אִנָּה לְיָדוֹ וְשַׂמְתִּי לְךָ מָקוֹם אֲשֶׁר
where place for-you then-I-will-designate into-hand-of-him he-allows

יָנוּס שָׁמָּה׃ וְכִי־ יָזִד אִישׁ עַל־ רֵעֵהוּ
fellow-of-him about man he-deliberates but-if (14) to-there he-may-flee

לְהָרְגוֹ בְעָרְמָה מֵעִם מִזְבְּחִי תִּקָּחֶנּוּ לָמוּת׃
to-kill you-take-him altar-of-me from-on by-scheme to-kill-him

וּמַכֵּה אָבִיו וְאִמּוֹ מוֹת יוּמָת׃
he-must-die to-die or-mother-of-him father-of-him and-one-attacking (15)

וְגֹנֵב אִישׁ וּמְכָרוֹ וְנִמְצָא
or-he-is-caught whether-he-sells-him another and-one-kidnapping (16)

בְיָדוֹ מוֹת יוּמָת׃ וּמְקַלֵּל אָבִיו
father-of-him and-one-cursing (17) he-must-die to-die in-hand-of-him

וְאִמּוֹ מוֹת יוּמָת׃ וְכִי־ יְרִיבֻן אֲנָשִׁים וְהִכָּה־
and-he-hits men they-quarrel and-if (18) he-must-die to-die or-mother-of-him

אִישׁ אֶת־ רֵעֵהוּ בְּאֶבֶן אוֹ בְאֶגְרֹף וְלֹא יָמוּת וְנָפַל
but-he-stays he-dies and-not with-fist or with-stone fellow-of-him *** one

לְמִשְׁכָּב׃ אִם־ יָקוּם וְהִתְהַלֵּךְ בַּחוּץ עַל־ מִשְׁעַנְתּוֹ
staff-of-him with in-the-outside and-he-walks-around he-gets-up if (19) in-bed

וְנִקָּה הַמַּכֶּה רַק שִׁבְתּוֹ יִתֵּן
he-must-pay lost-time-of-him however the-one-striking then-he-is-cleared

וְרַפֹּא יְרַפֵּא׃ וְכִי־ יַכֶּה אִישׁ אֶת־
*** man he-beats and-if (20) he-must-see-healed and-to-see-healed

עַבְדּוֹ אוֹ אֶת־ אֲמָתוֹ בַּשֵּׁבֶט וּמֵת תַּחַת
under and-he-dies with-the-rod female-slave-of-him *** or male-slave-of-him

יָדוֹ נָקֹם יִנָּקֵם׃ אַךְ אִם־ יוֹם אוֹ יוֹמַיִם
two-days or day if but (21) he-must-be-punished to-be-punished hand-of-him

יַעֲמֹד לֹא יֻקַּם כִּי כַסְפּוֹ הוּא׃ וְכִי־
and-if (22) he property-of-him since he-may-be-punished not he-gets-up

יִנָּצוּ אֲנָשִׁים וְנָגְפוּ אִשָּׁה הָרָה וְיָצְאוּ יְלָדֶיהָ
children-of-her so-they-come-out pregnant woman and-they-hit men they-fight

וְלֹא יִהְיֶה אָסוֹן עָנוֹשׁ יֵעָנֵשׁ כַּאֲשֶׁר יָשִׁית עָלָיו
from-him he-demands as-what he-must-be-fined to-be-fined injury he-is but-not

בַּעַל הָאִשָּׁה וְנָתַן בִּפְלִלִים׃ וְאִם־ אָסוֹן יִהְיֶה
he-is injury but-if (23) by-judges and-he-allows the-woman husband-of

וְנָתַתָּה נֶפֶשׁ תַּחַת נָפֶשׁ׃ עַיִן תַּחַת עַיִן שֵׁן תַּחַת שֵׁן יָד
hand tooth for tooth eye for eye (24) life for life then-you-must-take

תַּחַת יָד רֶגֶל תַּחַת רָגֶל׃ כְּוִיָּה תַּחַת כְּוִיָּה פֶּצַע תַּחַת פָּצַע חַבּוּרָה תַּחַת חַבּוּרָה׃
bruise for bruise wound for wound burn for burn (25) foot for foot hand for

but God lets it happen, he is to flee to a place I will designate. [14]But if a man schemes and kills another man deliberately, take him away from my altar and put him to death.

[15]"Anyone who attacks[r] his father or his mother must be put to death.

[16]"Anyone who kidnaps another and either sells him or still has him when he is caught must be put to death.

[17]"Anyone who curses his father or mother must be put to death.

[18]"If men quarrel and one hits the other with a stone or with his fist[s] and he does not die but is confined to bed, [19]the one who struck the blow will not be held responsible if the other gets up and walks around outside with his staff; however, he must pay the injured man for the loss of his time and see that he is completely healed.

[20]"If a man beats his male or female slave with a rod and the slave dies as a direct result, he must be punished, [21]but he is not to be punished if the slave gets up after a day or two, since the slave is his property.

[22]"If men who are fighting hit a pregnant woman and she gives birth prematurely[t] but there is no serious injury, the offender must be fined whatever the woman's husband demands and the court allows. [23]But if there is serious injury, you are to take life for life, [24]eye for eye, tooth for tooth, hand for hand, foot for foot, [25]burn for burn, wound for wound, bruise for bruise.

r15 Or *kills* s18 Or *with a tool*
t22 Or *she has a miscarriage*

וְכִי־ יַכֶּה אִישׁ אֶת־ עֵין עַבְדּוֹ אוֹ־ אֶת־ עֵין

eye-of *** or manservant-of-him eye-of *** man he-hits and-if (26)

אֲמָתוֹ וְשִׁחֲתָהּ לַחָפְשִׁי יְשַׁלְּחֶנּוּ

he-must-let-go-him to-the-freedom and-he-destroys-her maidservant-of-him

תַּחַת עֵינוֹ׃ וְאִם־ שֵׁן עַבְדּוֹ אוֹ־ שֵׁן

tooth-of or manservant-of-him tooth-of and-if (27) eye-of-him because-of

אֲמָתוֹ יַפִּיל לַחָפְשִׁי יְשַׁלְּחֶנּוּ

he-must-let-go-him to-the-freedom he-knocks-out maidservant-of-him

תַּחַת שִׁנּוֹ׃ וְכִי־ יִגַּח שׁוֹר אֶת־ אִישׁ אוֹ אֶת־ אִשָּׁה

woman *** or man *** bull he-gores and-if (28) tooth-of-him because-of

וָמֵת סָקוֹל יִסָּקֵל הַשּׁוֹר וְלֹא יֵאָכֵל

he-may-be-eaten and-not the-bull he-must-be-stoned to-be-stoned so-he-dies

אֶת־ בְּשָׂרוֹ וּבַעַל הַשּׁוֹר נָקִי׃ וְאִם שׁוֹר נַגָּח

he-gored bull but-if (29) not-liable the-bull but-owner-of meat-of-him ***

הוּא מִתְּמֹל שִׁלְשֹׁם וְהוּעַד בִּבְעָלָיו וְלֹא יִשְׁמְרֶנּוּ

he-penned-him but-not to-owner-of-him and-he-was-warned past on-yesterday he

וְהֵמִית אִישׁ אוֹ אִשָּׁה הַשּׁוֹר יִסָּקֵל וְגַם־ בְּעָלָיו

owner-of-him and-also he-must-be-stoned the-bull woman or man and-he-kills

יוּמָת׃ אִם־ כֹּפֶר יוּשַׁת עָלָיו וְנָתַן

then-he-may-pay from-him he-is-demanded payment if (30) he-must-die

פִּדְיֹן נַפְשׁוֹ כְּכֹל אֲשֶׁר־ יוּשַׁת עָלָיו׃ אוֹ־ בֵן

son if (31) from-him he-is-demanded that by-all life-of-him redemption-of

יִגָּח אוֹ־ בַת יִגָּח כַּמִּשְׁפָּט הַזֶּה יֵעָשֶׂה לּוֹ׃

to-him he-applies the-this also-the-law he-gores daughter or he-gores

אִם־ עֶבֶד יִגַּח הַשּׁוֹר אוֹ אָמָה כֶּסֶף ׀ שְׁלֹשִׁים

thirty silver-of female-slave or the-bull he-gores male-slave if (32)

שְׁקָלִים יִתֵּן לַאדֹנָיו וְהַשּׁוֹר יִסָּקֵל׃

he-must-be-stoned and-the-bull to-masters-of-him he-must-pay shekels

וְכִי־ יִפְתַּח אִישׁ בּוֹר אוֹ כִּי־ יִכְרֶה אִישׁ בֹּר וְלֹא

and-not pit man he-digs if or pit man he-uncovers and-if (33)

יְכַסֶּנּוּ וְנָפַל־ שָׁמָּה שׁוֹר אוֹ חֲמוֹר׃ בַּעַל הַבּוֹר

the-pit owner-of (34) donkey or ox into-there and-he-falls he-covers-him

יְשַׁלֵּם כֶּסֶף יָשִׁיב לִבְעָלָיו וְהַמֵּת

and-the-one-being-dead to-owners-of-him he-must-pay money he-must-pay-for-loss

יִהְיֶה־ לּוֹ׃ וְכִי־ יִגֹּף שׁוֹר־ אִישׁ אֶת־ שׁוֹר רֵעֵהוּ

fellow-of-him bull-of *** man bull-of he-injures and-if (35) to-him he-will-be

וָמֵת וּמָכְרוּ אֶת־ הַשּׁוֹר הַחַי וְחָצוּ

and-they-must-divide the-live the-bull *** then-they-must-sell so-he-dies

[26]"If a man hits a manservant or maidservant in the eye and destroys it, he must let the servant go free to compensate for the eye. [27]And if he knocks out the tooth of a manservant or maidservant, he must let the servant go free to compensate for the tooth.

[28]"If a bull gores a man or a woman to death, the bull must be stoned to death, and its meat must not be eaten. But the owner of the bull will not be held responsible. [29]If, however, the bull has had the habit of goring and the owner has been warned but has not kept it penned up and it kills a man or woman, the bull must be stoned and the owner also must be put to death. [30]However, if payment is demanded of him, he may redeem his life by paying whatever is demanded. [31]This law also applies if the bull gores a son or daughter. [32]If the bull gores a male or female slave, the owner must pay thirty shekels[u] of silver to the master of the slave, and the bull must be stoned.

[33]"If a man uncovers a pit or digs one and fails to cover it and an ox or a donkey falls into it, [34]the owner of the pit must pay for the loss; he must pay its owner, and the dead animal will be his.

[35]"If a man's bull injures the bull of another and it dies, they are to sell the live one and

[u]32 That is, about 12 ounces (about 0.3 kilogram)

אֶת־ כַּסְפּוֹ וְגַם אֶת־ הַמֵּת יֶחֱצוּן׃ אוֹ
however (36) they-must-divide the-being-dead *** and-also money-of-him ***

נוֹדַע כִּי שׁוֹר נַגָּח הוּא מִתְּמוֹל שִׁלְשֹׁם וְלֹא יִשְׁמְרֶנּוּ
he-penned-him but-not past on-yesterday he he-gored bull that being-known

בְּעָלָיו שַׁלֵּם יְשַׁלֵּם שׁוֹר תַּחַת הַשּׁוֹר וְהַמֵּת יִהְיֶה־
he-will-be and-the-being-dead the-bull for bull he-must-pay to-pay owners-of-him

לּוֹ׃ כִּי יִגְנֹב־ אִישׁ שׁוֹר אוֹ־ שֶׂה וּטְבָחוֹ אוֹ
or and-he-slaughters-him sheep or bull man he-steals if (37)* to-him

מְכָרוֹ חֲמִשָּׁה בָקָר יְשַׁלֵּם תַּחַת הַשּׁוֹר וְאַרְבַּע־ צֹאן תַּחַת
for sheep and-four the-bull for he-must-pay-back cattle five he-sells-him

הַשֶּׂה׃ אִם־ בַּמַּחְתֶּרֶת יִמָּצֵא הַגַּנָּב וְהֻכָּה
and-he-is-struck the-thief he-is-caught in-the-break-in if (22:1)* the-sheep

וָמֵת אֵין לוֹ דָּמִים׃ אִם־ זָרְחָה הַשֶּׁמֶשׁ עָלָיו דָּמִים
bloodsheds on-him the-sun he-rose if (2) bloodsheds to-him not so-he-dies

לוֹ שַׁלֵּם יְשַׁלֵּם אִם־ אֵין לוֹ וְנִמְכַּר
then-he-must-be-sold to-him nothing if he-must-restitute to-restitute to-him

בִּגְנֵבָתוֹ׃ אִם־ הִמָּצֵא תִמָּצֵא בְיָדוֹ הַגְּנֵבָה
the-stolen in-hand-of-him she-is-found to-be-found if (3) for-theft-of-him

מִשּׁוֹר עַד־ חֲמוֹר עַד־ שֶׂה חַיִּים שְׁנַיִם יְשַׁלֵּם׃ כִּי
if (4) he-must-pay-back double alive-ones sheep or donkey or whether-ox

יַבְעֶר־ אִישׁ שָׂדֶה אוֹ־ כֶרֶם וְשִׁלַּח אֶת־ בְּעִירֹה
livestock-of-him *** and-he-lets-stray vineyard or field man he-grazes

וּבִעֵר בִּשְׂדֵה אַחֵר מֵיטַב שָׂדֵהוּ וּמֵיטַב
or-from-best-of field-of-him from-best-of another in-field-of and-he-grazes

כַּרְמוֹ יְשַׁלֵּם׃ כִּי־ תֵצֵא אֵשׁ וּמָצְאָה
and-she-spreads fire she-breaks-out if (5) he-must-restitute vineyard-of-him

קֹצִים וְנֶאֱכַל גָּדִישׁ אוֹ הַקָּמָה אוֹ הַשָּׂדֶה
the-field or the-standing-grain or shock-of-grain so-he-is-burned thorns

שַׁלֵּם יְשַׁלֵּם הַמַּבְעִר אֶת־ הַבְּעֵרָה׃ כִּי־ יִתֵּן
he-gives if (6) the-fire *** the-one-starting he-must-restitute to-restitute

אִישׁ אֶל־ רֵעֵהוּ כֶּסֶף אוֹ־ כֵלִים לִשְׁמֹר וְגֻנַּב
and-he-is-stolen to-safekeep goods or money neighbor-of-him to man

מִבֵּית הָאִישׁ אִם־ יִמָּצֵא הַגַּנָּב יְשַׁלֵּם שְׁנָיִם׃
double he-must-pay-back the-thief he-is-caught if the-man from-house-of

אִם־ לֹא יִמָּצֵא הַגַּנָּב וְנִקְרַב בַּעַל־ הַבַּיִת
the-house owner-of then-he-must-appear the-thief he-is-found not if (7)

אֶל־ הָאֱלֹהִים אִם־ לֹא שָׁלַח יָדוֹ בִּמְלֶאכֶת רֵעֵהוּ׃
neighbor-of-him on-property-of hand-of-him he-laid not whether the-judges before

divide both the money and the dead animal equally.
36 However, if it was known that the bull had the habit of goring, yet the owner did not keep it penned up, the owner must pay, animal for animal, and the dead animal will be his.

*Protection of Property*

22 "If a man steals an ox or a sheep and slaughters it or sells it, he must pay back five head of cattle for the ox and four sheep for the sheep.
2 "If a thief is caught breaking in and is struck so that he dies, the defender is not guilty of bloodshed; 3 but if it happens[v] after sunrise, he is guilty of bloodshed.

"A thief must certainly make restitution, but if he has nothing, he must be sold to pay for his theft.
4 "If the stolen animal is found alive in his possession—whether ox or donkey or sheep—he must pay back double.
5 "If a man grazes his livestock in a field or vineyard and lets them stray and they graze in another man's field, he must make restitution from the best of his own field or vineyard.
6 "If a fire breaks out and spreads into thornbushes so that it burns shocks of grain or standing grain or the whole field, the one who started the fire must make restitution.
7 "If a man gives his neighbor silver or goods for safekeeping and they are stolen from the neighbor's house, the thief, if he is caught, must pay back double. 8 But if the thief is not found, the owner of the house must appear before the judges[w] to determine whether he has laid his hands on the other man's property. 9 In all

v3 Or *if he strikes him*
w8 Or *before God*; also in verse 9

***The Hebrew numeration of chapter 22 begins with verse 2 of the English numeration; thus, there is a one-verse discrepancy throughout the chapter.**

°4 ק בעירו

עַל־ כָּל־ דְּבַר־ פֶּשַׁע עַל־ שׁוֹר עַל־ חֲמוֹר עַל־ שֶׂה

sheep or donkey or ox whether illegal-possession case-of every-of in (8)

עַל־שַׂלְמָה עַל־ כָּל־ אֲבֵדָה אֲשֶׁר יֹאמַר כִּי־ הוּא זֶה עַד

before this he that he-says of-which lost-property any-of or clothing or

הָאֱלֹהִים יָבֹא דְּבַר־ שְׁנֵיהֶם אֲשֶׁר יַרְשִׁיעֻן

they-declare-guilty whom both-of-them case-of he-must-bring the-judges

אֱלֹהִים יְשַׁלֵּם שְׁנַיִם לְרֵעֵהוּ׃ כִּי־ יִתֵּן אִישׁ אֶל־

to man he-gives if (9) to-neighbor-of-him double he-must-pay-back judges

רֵעֵהוּ חֲמוֹר אוֹ־ שׁוֹר אוֹ־ שֶׂה וְכָל־ בְּהֵמָה לִשְׁמֹר

to-safekeep animal or-any-of sheep or ox or donkey neighbor-of-him

וּמֵת אוֹ־ נִשְׁבַּר אוֹ־ נִשְׁבָּה אֵין רֹאֶה׃ שְׁבֻעַת

oath-of (10) looking no-one he-is-taken-away or he-is-injured or and-he-dies

יְהוָה תִּהְיֶה בֵּין שְׁנֵיהֶם אִם־ לֹא שָׁלַח יָדוֹ

hand-of-him he-laid not that two-of-them between she-must-be Yahweh

בִּמְלֶאכֶת רֵעֵהוּ וְלָקַח בְּעָלָיו וְלֹא

and-not owners-of-him then-he-will-accept neighbor-of-him on-property-of

יְשַׁלֵּם׃ וְאִם־ גָּנֹב יִגָּנֵב מֵעִמּוֹ

from-with-him he-was-stolen to-be-stolen but-if (11) he-must-restitute

יְשַׁלֵּם לִבְעָלָיו׃ אִם־ טָרֹף יִטָּרֵף

he-was-torn to-be-torn if (12) to-owners-of-him he-must-restitute

יְבִאֵהוּ עֵד הַטְּרֵפָה לֹא יְשַׁלֵּם׃ וְכִי־

and-if (13) he-must-repay not the-torn-animal evidence he-shall-bring-him

יִשְׁאַל אִישׁ מֵעִם רֵעֵהוּ וְנִשְׁבַּר אוֹ־ מֵת

he-dies or and-he-is-injured neighbor-of-him from-with man he-borrows

בְּעָלָיו אֵין־ עִמּוֹ שַׁלֵּם יְשַׁלֵּם׃ אִם־ בְּעָלָיו

owners-of-him if (14) he-must-restitute to-restitute with-him not owners-of-him

עִמּוֹ לֹא יְשַׁלֵּם אִם־שָׂכִיר הוּא בָּא בִּשְׂכָרוֹ׃ וְכִי־

and-if (15) by-hire-of-him he-covers he hired if he-must-repay not with-him

יְפַתֶּה אִישׁ בְּתוּלָה אֲשֶׁר לֹא־ אֹרָשָׂה וְשָׁכַב עִמָּהּ מָהֹר

to-pay with-her and-he-sleeps she-is-pledged not who virgin man he-seduces

יִמְהָרֶנָּה לּוֹ לְאִשָּׁה׃ אִם־ מָאֵן יְמָאֵן

he-refuses to-refuse if (16) as-wife for-him he-must-pay-price-of-her

אָבִיהָ לְתִתָּהּ לוֹ כֶּסֶף יִשְׁקֹל כְּמֹהַר

for-bride-price-of he-must-pay money to-him to-give-her father-of-her

הַבְּתוּלֹת׃ מְכַשֵּׁפָה לֹא תְחַיֶּה׃ כָּל־

every-of (18) you-let-live not one-being-sorceress (17) the-virgins

שֹׁכֵב עִם־ בְּהֵמָה מוֹת יוּמָת׃ זֹבֵחַ

sacrificing (19) he-must-die to-die animal with having-sexual-relation

cases of illegal possession of an ox, a donkey, a sheep, a garment, or any other lost property about which somebody says, 'This is mine,' both parties are to bring their cases before the judges. The one whom the judges declare[x] guilty must pay back double to his neighbor.

[10]"If a man gives a donkey, an ox, a sheep or any other animal to his neighbor for safekeeping and it dies or is injured or is taken away while no one is looking, [11]the issue between them will be settled by the taking of an oath before the LORD that the neighbor did not lay hands on the other person's property. The owner is to accept this, and no restitution is required. [12]But if the animal was stolen from the neighbor, he must make restitution to the owner. [13]If it was torn to pieces by a wild animal, he shall bring in the remains as evidence and he will not be required to pay for the torn animal.

[14]"If a man borrows an animal from his neighbor and it is injured or dies while the owner is not present, he must make restitution. [15]But if the owner is with the animal, the borrower will not have to pay. If the animal was hired, the money paid for the hire covers the loss.

*Social Responsibility*

[16]"If a man seduces a virgin who is not pledged to be married and sleeps with her, he must pay the bride-price, and she shall be his wife. [17]If her father absolutely refuses to give her to him, he must still pay the bride-price for virgins.

[18]"Do not allow a sorceress to live.

[19]"Anyone who has sexual relations with an animal must be put to death.

[x]9 Or *whom God declares*

*See the note on page 206.

לָאֱלֹהִים יָחֳרָם בִּלְתִּי לַיהוָה לְבַדּוֹ׃ וְגֵר
and-alien (20) by-himself to-Yahweh other-than he-must-be-destroyed to-the-gods

לֹא־ תוֹנֶה וְלֹא תִלְחָצֶנּוּ כִּי־ גֵרִים הֱיִיתֶם בְּאֶרֶץ
in-land-of you-were aliens for you-oppress-him and-not you-mistreat not

מִצְרָיִם׃ כָּל־ אַלְמָנָה וְיָתוֹם לֹא תְעַנּוּן׃ אִם־
if (22) you-take-advantage not or-orphan widow any-of (21) Egypt

עַנֵּה תְעַנֶּה אֹתוֹ כִּי אִם־ צָעֹק יִצְעַק אֵלַי
to-me he-cries to-cry if then him you-take-advantage to-take-advantage

שָׁמֹעַ אֶשְׁמַע צַעֲקָתוֹ׃ וְחָרָה אַפִּי
anger-of-me and-he-will-be-aroused (23) cry-of-him I-will-hear to-hear

וְהָרַגְתִּי אֶתְכֶם בֶּחָרֶב וְהָיוּ נְשֵׁיכֶם אַלְמָנוֹת
widows wives-of-you and-they-will-become with-the-sword you and-I-will-kill

וּבְנֵיכֶם יְתֹמִים׃ אִם־ כֶּסֶף ׀ תַּלְוֶה אֶת־ עַמִּי
people-of-me *** you-lend money if (24) fatherless-ones and-children-of-you

אֶת־ הֶעָנִי עִמָּךְ לֹא־ תִהְיֶה לוֹ כְּנֹשֶׁה לֹא־
not like-one-lending-money to-him you-shall-be not among-you the-needy ***

תְשִׂימוּן עָלָיו נֶשֶׁךְ׃ אִם־ חָבֹל תַּחְבֹּל
you-take-pledge to-take-pledge if (25) interest to-him you-shall-charge

שַׂלְמַת רֵעֶךָ עַד־ בֹּא הַשֶּׁמֶשׁ תְּשִׁיבֶנּוּ לוֹ׃ כִּי
for (26) to-him you-return-him the-sun to-set when neighbor-of-you cloak-of

הִוא כְסוּתֹה° לְבַדָּהּ הִוא שִׂמְלָתוֹ לְעֹרוֹ בַּמֶּה
with-the-what? for-body-of-him cloak-of-him she only-her covering-of-him she

יִשְׁכָּב וְהָיָה כִּי־ יִצְעַק אֵלַי וְשָׁמַעְתִּי כִּי־
for then-I-will-hear to-me he-cries when and-he-will-be will-he-sleep

חַנּוּן אָנִי׃ אֱלֹהִים לֹא תְקַלֵּל וְנָשִׂיא בְעַמְּךָ לֹא
not over-people-of-you and-ruler you-blaspheme not God (27) I compassionate

תָאֹר׃ מְלֵאָתְךָ וְדִמְעֲךָ לֹא תְאַחֵר
you-hold-back not and-outflow-of-you fullness-of-you (28) you-curse

בְּכוֹר בָּנֶיךָ תִּתֶּן־ לִי׃ כֵּן־ תַּעֲשֶׂה
you-shall-do same (29) to-me you-must-give sons-of-you firstborn-of

לְשֹׁרְךָ לְצֹאנֶךָ שִׁבְעַת יָמִים יִהְיֶה עִם־
with let-him-stay days seven-of with-sheep-of-you with-cattle-of-you

אִמּוֹ בַּיּוֹם הַשְּׁמִינִי תִּתְּנוֹ־ לִי׃ וְאַנְשֵׁי־
now-men-of (30) to-me you-give-him the-eighth but-on-the-day mother-of-him

קֹדֶשׁ תִּהְיוּן לִי וּבָשָׂר בַּשָּׂדֶה טְרֵפָה לֹא תֹאכֵלוּ
you-shall-eat not torn in-the-field and-meat to-me you-must-be holy

לַכֶּלֶב תַּשְׁלִכוּן אֹתוֹ׃ לֹא תִשָּׂא שֵׁמַע שָׁוְא אַל־
not false report-of you-spread not (23:1) him you-shall-throw to-the-dog

20"Whoever sacrifices to any god other than the LORD must be destroyed.[y]

21"Do not mistreat an alien or oppress him, for you were aliens in Egypt.

22"Do not take advantage of a widow or an orphan. 23If you do and they cry out to me, I will certainly hear their cry. 24My anger will be aroused, and I will kill you with the sword; your wives will become widows and your children fatherless.

25"If you lend money to one of my people among you who is needy, do not be like a moneylender; charge him no interest.[z] 26If you take your neighbor's cloak as a pledge, return it to him by sunset, 27because his cloak is the only covering he has for his body. What else will he sleep in? When he cries out to me, I will hear, for I am compassionate.

28"Do not blaspheme God[a] or curse the ruler of your people.

29"Do not hold back offerings from your granaries or your vats.[b]

"You must give me the firstborn of your sons. 30Do the same with your cattle and your sheep. Let them stay with their mothers for seven days, but give them to me on the eighth day.

31"You are to be my holy people. So do not eat the meat of an animal torn by wild beasts; throw it to the dogs.

### *Laws of Justice and Mercy*

23 "Do not spread false reports. Do not help a

[y]20 The Hebrew term refers to the irrevocable giving over of things or persons to the LORD, often by totally destroying them.
[z]25 Or *excessive interest*
[a]28 Or *Do not revile the judges*
[b]29 The meaning of the Hebrew for this phrase is uncertain.

*See the note on page 206.

°*26* ק כסותו

תָּשֶׁת יָדְךָ עִם־ רָשָׁע לִהְיֹת עֵד חָמָס׃ לֹא־
not (2) malicious witness-of to-be wicked-man with hand-of-you you-join

תִהְיֶה אַחֲרֵי־ רַבִּים לְרָעֹת וְלֹא־ תַעֲנֶה עַל־ רִב לִנְטֹת אַחֲרֵי
with to-side court in you-testify and-not in-wrong crowds after you-go

רַבִּים לְהַטֹּת׃ וְדָל לֹא תֶהְדַּר בְּרִיבוֹ׃
in-lawsuit-of-him you-favor not and-poor (3) to-pervert-justice crowds

כִּי תִפְגַּע שׁוֹר אֹיִבְךָ אוֹ חֲמֹרוֹ תֹּעֶה
wandering donkey-of-him or being-enemy-of-you ox-of you-find if (4)

הָשֵׁב תְּשִׁיבֶנּוּ לוֹ׃ כִּי־ תִרְאֶה חֲמוֹר שֹׂנַאֲךָ
one-hating-you donkey-of you-see if (5) to-him you-take-back-him to-take-back

רֹבֵץ תַּחַת מַשָּׂאוֹ וְחָדַלְתָּ מֵעֲזֹב לוֹ עָזֹב
to-help to-him from-to-leave then-you-refrain load-of-him under lying

תַּעֲזֹב עִמּוֹ׃ לֹא תַטֶּה מִשְׁפַּט אֶבְיֹנְךָ בְּרִיבוֹ׃
in-lawsuit-of-him poor-of-you justice-of you-deny not (6) with-him you-help

מִדְּבַר־ שֶׁקֶר תִּרְחָק וְנָקִי וְצַדִּיק אַל־ תַּהֲרֹג
you-kill not or-honest and-innocent you-stay-far false from-charge-of (7)

כִּי לֹא־ אַצְדִּיק רָשָׁע׃ וְשֹׁחַד לֹא תִקָּח כִּי הַשֹּׁחַד
the-bribe for you-accept not and-bribe (8) guilty I-will-acquit not for

יְעַוֵּר פִּקְחִים וִיסַלֵּף דִּבְרֵי צַדִּיקִים׃ וְגֵר
and-alien (9) righteous-ones words-of and-he-twists those-who-see he-blinds

לֹא תִלְחָץ וְאַתֶּם יְדַעְתֶּם אֶת־ נֶפֶשׁ הַגֵּר כִּי־ גֵרִים הֱיִיתֶם
you-were aliens for the-alien feeling-of *** you-know for-you you-oppress not

בְּאֶרֶץ מִצְרָיִם׃ וְשֵׁשׁ שָׁנִים תִּזְרַע אֶת־ אַרְצֶךָ וְאָסַפְתָּ
and-you-harvest field-of-you *** you-sow years and-six (10) Egypt in-land-of

אֶת־ תְּבוּאָתָהּ׃ וְהַשְּׁבִיעִת תִּשְׁמְטֶנָּה
you-let-lie-unplowed-her but-the-seventh (11) the-crop-of-her ***

וּנְטַשְׁתָּהּ וְאָכְלוּ אֶבְיֹנֵי עַמֶּךָ
people-of-you poor-ones-of then-they-may-eat and-you-let-lie-unused-her

וְיִתְרָם תֹּאכַל חַיַּת הַשָּׂדֶה כֵּן־ תַּעֲשֶׂה
you-do same the-field animal-of she-may-eat and-leftover-of-them

לְכַרְמְךָ לְזֵיתֶךָ׃ שֵׁשֶׁת יָמִים תַּעֲשֶׂה מַעֲשֶׂיךָ
works-of-you you-do days six (12) with-olive-grove-of-you with-vineyard-of-you

וּבַיּוֹם הַשְּׁבִיעִי תִּשְׁבֹּת לְמַעַן יָנוּחַ שׁוֹרְךָ
ox-of-you he-may-rest so-that you-rest the-seventh but-on-the-day

וַחֲמֹרֶךָ וְיִנָּפֵשׁ בֶּן־ אֲמָתְךָ וְהַגֵּר׃
and-the-alien servant-of-you son-of and-he-may-be-refreshed and-donkey-of-you

וּבְכֹל אֲשֶׁר־ אָמַרְתִּי אֲלֵיכֶם תִּשָּׁמֵרוּ וְשֵׁם אֱלֹהִים
gods and-name-of you-take-care-to-do to-you I-said that and-to-all (13)

wicked man by being a malicious witness.

2 "Do not follow the crowd in doing wrong. When you give testimony in a lawsuit, do not pervert justice by siding with the crowd, 3 and do not show favoritism to a poor man in his lawsuit.

4 "If you come across your enemy's ox or donkey wandering off, be sure to take it back to him. 5 If you see the donkey of someone who hates you fallen down under its load, do not leave it there; be sure you help him with it.

6 "Do not deny justice to your poor people in their lawsuits. 7 Have nothing to do with a false charge and do not put an innocent or honest person to death, for I will not acquit the guilty.

8 "Do not accept a bribe, for a bribe blinds those who see and twists the words of the righteous.

9 "Do not oppress an alien; you yourselves know how it feels to be aliens, because you were aliens in Egypt.

*Sabbath Laws*

10 "For six years you are to sow your fields and harvest the crops, 11 but during the seventh year let the land lie unplowed and unused. Then the poor among your people may get food from it, and the wild animals may eat what they leave. Do the same with your vineyard and your olive grove.

12 "Six days do your work, but on the seventh day do not work, so that your ox and your donkey may rest and the slave born in your household, and the alien as well, may be refreshed.

13 "Be careful to do everything I have said to you. Do

אֲחֵרִים לֹא תַזְכִּירוּ לֹא יִשָּׁמַע עַל־ פִּיךָ׃
mouth-of-you in you-let-him-be-heard not you-invoke not other-ones

(14) שָׁלֹשׁ רְגָלִים תָּחֹג לִי בַּשָּׁנָה׃ (15) אֶת־ חַג
Feast-of *** (15) in-the-year to-me you-celebrate-festival times three (14)

הַמַּצּוֹת תִּשְׁמֹר שִׁבְעַת יָמִים תֹּאכַל מַצּוֹת
breads-without-yeast you-eat days seven-of you-celebrate the-Unleavened-Breads

כַּאֲשֶׁר צִוִּיתִךָ לְמוֹעֵד חֹדֶשׁ הָאָבִיב כִּי־ בוֹ
in-him for the-Abib month-of at-appointed-time I-commanded-you just-as

יָצָאתָ מִמִּצְרָיִם וְלֹא־ יֵרָאוּ פָנַי רֵיקָם׃
empty-handed before-me he-may-appear and-none from-Egypt you-came-out

(16) וְחַג הַקָּצִיר בִּכּוּרֵי מַעֲשֶׂיךָ אֲשֶׁר תִּזְרַע
you-sow that crops-of-you firstfruits-of the-Harvest and-Feast-of (16)

בַּשָּׂדֶה וְחַג הָאָסִף בְּצֵאת הַשָּׁנָה
the-year when-to-end the-Ingathering and-Feast-of in-the-field

בְּאָסְפְּךָ אֶת־ מַעֲשֶׂיךָ מִן־ הַשָּׂדֶה׃ (17) שָׁלֹשׁ פְּעָמִים
times three (17) the-field from crops-of-you *** when-to-gather-you

בַּשָּׁנָה יֵרָאֶה כָּל־ זְכוּרְךָ אֶל־ פְּנֵי הָאָדֹן ׀
the-Sovereign face-of before male-of-you every-of he-must-appear in-the-year

יְהוָה׃ (18) לֹא־ תִזְבַּח עַל־ חָמֵץ דַּם־ זִבְחִי וְלֹא־
and-not sacrifice-of-me blood-of yeast with you-offer not (18) Yahweh

יָלִין חֵלֶב־ חַגִּי עַד־ בֹּקֶר׃ (19) רֵאשִׁית בִּכּוּרֵי
firstfruits-of best-of (19) morning until offering-of-me fat-of he-may-remain

אַדְמָתְךָ תָּבִיא בֵּית יְהוָה אֱלֹהֶיךָ לֹא־ תְבַשֵּׁל גְּדִי
young-goat you-cook not God-of-you Yahweh house-of you-bring soil-of-you

בַּחֲלֵב אִמּוֹ׃ (20) הִנֵּה אָנֹכִי שֹׁלֵחַ מַלְאָךְ לְפָנֶיךָ לִשְׁמָרְךָ
to-guard-you ahead-of-you angel sending I see! (20) mother-of-him in-milk-of

בַּדָּרֶךְ וְלַהֲבִיאֲךָ אֶל־ הַמָּקוֹם אֲשֶׁר הֲכִנֹתִי׃ (21) הִשָּׁמֶר
attend! (21) I-prepared that the-place to and-to-bring-you along-the-way

מִפָּנָיו וּשְׁמַע בְּקֹלוֹ אַל־ תַּמֵּר בּוֹ כִּי לֹא
not for against-him you-rebel not to-voice-of-him and-listen! to-him

יִשָּׂא לְפִשְׁעֲכֶם כִּי שְׁמִי בְּקִרְבּוֹ׃ (22) כִּי אִם־
if now (22) in-him Name-of-me since to-rebellion-of-you he-will-forgive

שָׁמוֹעַ תִּשְׁמַע בְּקֹלוֹ וְעָשִׂיתָ כֹּל אֲשֶׁר אֲדַבֵּר
I-say that all and-you-do to-voice-of-him you-listen to-listen

וְאָיַבְתִּי אֶת־ אֹיְבֶיךָ וְצַרְתִּי אֶת־
*** and-I-will-oppose being-enemies-of-you *** then-I-will-be-enemy

צֹרְרֶיךָ׃ (23) כִּי־ יֵלֵךְ מַלְאָכִי לְפָנֶיךָ וֶהֱבִיאֲךָ
and-he-brings-you ahead-of-you angel-of-me he-goes when (23) ones-opposing-you

not invoke the names of other gods; do not let them be heard on your lips.

*The Three Annual Festivals*

[14]"Three times a year you are to celebrate a festival to me.

[15]"Celebrate the Feast of Unleavened Bread; for seven days eat bread made without yeast, as I commanded you. Do this at the appointed time in the month of Abib, for in that month you came out of Egypt.

"No one is to appear before me empty-handed.

[16]"Celebrate the Feast of Harvest with the firstfruits of the crops you sow in your field.

"Celebrate the Feast of Ingathering at the end of the year, when you gather in your crops from the field.

[17]"Three times a year all the men are to appear before the Sovereign LORD.

[18]"Do not offer the blood of a sacrifice to me along with anything containing yeast.

"The fat of my festival offerings must not be kept until morning.

[19]"Bring the best of the firstfruits of your soil to the house of the LORD your God.

"Do not cook a young goat in its mother's milk.

*God's Angel to Prepare the Way*

[20]"See, I am sending an angel ahead of you to guard you along the way and to bring you to the place I have prepared. [21]Pay attention to him and listen to what he says. Do not rebel against him; he will not forgive your rebellion, since my Name is in him. [22]If you listen carefully to what he says and do all that I say, I will be an enemy to your enemies and will oppose those who oppose you. [23]My angel will go ahead of you and bring you

אֶל־ הָאֱמֹרִי וְהַחִתִּי וְהַפְּרִזִּי וְהַכְּנַעֲנִי
and-the-Canaanite and-the-Perizzite and-the-Hittite the-Amorite into

הַחִוִּי וְהַיְבוּסִי וְהִכְחַדְתִּיו׃ לֹא־ תִשְׁתַּחֲוֶה
you-bow not (24) then-I-will-wipe-out-him and-the-Jebusite the-Hivite

לֵאלֹהֵיהֶם וְלֹא תָעָבְדֵם וְלֹא תַעֲשֶׂה
you-follow and-not you-worship-them and-not before-gods-of-them

כְּמַעֲשֵׂיהֶם כִּי הָרֵס תְּהָרְסֵם וְשַׁבֵּר תְּשַׁבֵּר
you-break and-to-break you-demolish-them to-demolish but after-practices-of-them

מַצֵּבֹתֵיהֶם׃ וַעֲבַדְתֶּם אֵת יְהוָה אֱלֹהֵיכֶם וּבֵרַךְ
and-he-will-bless God-of-you Yahweh *** but-you-worship (25) pillars-of-them

אֶת־ לַחְמְךָ וְאֶת־ מֵימֶיךָ וַהֲסִרֹתִי מַחֲלָה מִקִּרְבֶּךָ׃
from-among-you sickness and-I-will-take-away waters-of-you and food-of-you ***

לֹא תִהְיֶה מְשַׁכֵּלָה וַעֲקָרָה בְּאַרְצֶךָ אֶת־ מִסְפַּר
and-span-of *** in-land-of-you or-barren miscarrying she-will-be not (26)

יָמֶיךָ אֲמַלֵּא׃ אֶת־ אֵימָתִי אֲשַׁלַּח לְפָנֶיךָ
ahead-of-you I-will-send terror-of-me *** (27) I-will-lengthen days-of-you

וְהַמֹּתִי אֶת־ כָּל־ הָעָם אֲשֶׁר תָּבֹא בָּהֶם
against-them you-encounter that the-nation every-of *** and-I-will-confuse

וְנָתַתִּי אֶת־ כָּל־ אֹיְבֶיךָ אֵלֶיךָ עֹרֶף׃
back toward-you being-enemies-of-you all-of *** and-I-will-make

וְשָׁלַחְתִּי אֶת־ הַצִּרְעָה לְפָנֶיךָ וְגֵרְשָׁה אֶת־
*** and-she-will-drive-out ahead-of-you the-hornet *** and-I-will-send (28)

הַחִוִּי אֶת־ הַכְּנַעֲנִי וְאֶת־ הַחִתִּי מִלְּפָנֶיךָ׃ לֹא
not (29) from-before-you the-Hittite and the-Canaanite *** the-Hivite

אֲגָרְשֶׁנּוּ מִפָּנֶיךָ בְּשָׁנָה אֶחָת פֶּן־ תִּהְיֶה
she-would-become or single in-year from-before-you I-will-drive-out-him

הָאָרֶץ שְׁמָמָה וְרַבָּה עָלֶיךָ חַיַּת הַשָּׂדֶה׃ מְעַט
little (30) the-field animal-of for-you and-too-numerous desolate the-land

מְעַט אֲגָרְשֶׁנּוּ מִפָּנֶיךָ עַד אֲשֶׁר תִּפְרֶה
you-increase when until from-before-you I-will-drive-out-him little

וְנָחַלְתָּ אֶת־ הָאָרֶץ׃ וְשַׁתִּי אֶת־ גְּבֻלְךָ
border-of-you *** and-I-will-establish (31) the-land *** so-you-possess

מִיַּם־ סוּף וְעַד־ יָם פְּלִשְׁתִּים וּמִמִּדְבָּר עַד־ הַנָּהָר
the-River to and-from-desert Philistines Sea-of even-to Reed from-Sea-of

כִּי׀ אֶתֵּן בְּיֶדְכֶם אֵת יֹשְׁבֵי הָאָרֶץ
the-land ones-living-of *** into-hand-of-you I-will-give for

וְגֵרַשְׁתָּמוֹ מִפָּנֶיךָ׃ לֹא־ תִכְרֹת לָהֶם
with-them you-make not (32) from-before-you and-you-will-drive-out-them

into the land of the Amorites,
Hittites, Perizzites, Canaanites, Hivites and Jebusites,
and I will wipe them out. [24]Do
not bow down before their
gods or worship them or follow their practices. You must
demolish them and break
their sacred stones to pieces.
[25]Worship the LORD your God,
and his blessing will be on
your food and water. I will
take away sickness from
among you, [26]and none will
miscarry or be barren in your
land. I will give you a full life
span.
[27]"I will send my terror
ahead of you and throw into
confusion every nation you
encounter. I will make all your
enemies turn their backs and
run. [28]I will send the hornet
ahead of you to drive the Hivites, Canaanites and Hittites
out of your way. [29]But I will
not drive them out in a single
year, because the land would
become desolate and the wild
animals too numerous for you.
[30]Little by little I will drive
them out before you, until you
have increased enough to take
possession of the land.
[31]"I will establish your borders from the Red Sea[b] to the
Sea of the Philistines,[c] and
from the desert to the River.[d] I
will hand over to you the
people who live in the land
and you will drive them out
before you. [32]Do not make a

[b] 31 Hebrew *Yam Suph;* that is, Sea of Reeds
[c] 31 That is, the Mediterranean
[d] 31 That is, the Euphrates

וְלֵאלֹהֵיהֶם בְּרִית׃ לֹא יֵשְׁבוּ בְּאַרְצְךָ פֶּן־
or in-land-of-you let-them-live not (33) covenant or-with-gods-of-them

יַחֲטִיאוּ אֹתְךָ לִי כִּי תַעֲבֹד אֶת־ אֱלֹהֵיהֶם כִּי־
surely gods-of-them *** you-worship if against-me you they-will-cause-to-sin

יִהְיֶה לְךָ לְמוֹקֵשׁ׃ וְאֶל־ מֹשֶׁה אָמַר עֲלֵה אֶל־ יְהוָה
Yahweh to come-up! he-said Moses then-to (24:1) as-snare to-you he-will-be

אַתָּה וְאַהֲרֹן נָדָב וַאֲבִיהוּא וְשִׁבְעִים מִזִּקְנֵי יִשְׂרָאֵל
Israel from-elders-of and-seventy and-Abihu Nadab and-Aaron you

וְהִשְׁתַּחֲוִיתֶם מֵרָחֹק׃ וְנִגַּשׁ מֹשֶׁה לְבַדּוֹ אֶל־
to by-himself Moses but-he-shall-approach (2) at-distance and-you-worship

יְהוָה וְהֵם לֹא יִגָּשׁוּ וְהָעָם לֹא יַעֲלוּ
they-may-come-up not and-the-people they-may-approach not and-they Yahweh

עִמּוֹ׃ וַיָּבֹא מֹשֶׁה וַיְסַפֵּר לָעָם אֵת כָּל־ דִּבְרֵי
words-of all-of *** to-the-people and-he-told Moses when-he-went (3) with-him

יְהוָה וְאֵת כָּל־ הַמִּשְׁפָּטִים וַיַּעַן כָּל־ הָעָם קוֹל אֶחָד
one voice the-people all-of then-he-responded the-laws all-of and Yahweh

וַיֹּאמְרוּ כָּל־ הַדְּבָרִים אֲשֶׁר־ דִּבֶּר יְהוָה נַעֲשֶׂה׃ וַיִּכְתֹּב
and-he-wrote (4) we-will-do Yahweh he-said that the-things all-of and-they-said

מֹשֶׁה אֵת כָּל־ דִּבְרֵי יְהוָה וַיַּשְׁכֵּם בַּבֹּקֶר וַיִּבֶן
and-he-built in-the-morning and-he-got-up Yahweh words-of all-of *** Moses

מִזְבֵּחַ תַּחַת הָהָר וּשְׁתֵּים עֶשְׂרֵה מַצֵּבָה לִשְׁנֵים עָשָׂר שִׁבְטֵי
tribes-of ten for-two stone-pillar ten and-two the-mountain foot-of altar

יִשְׂרָאֵל׃ וַיִּשְׁלַח אֶת־ נַעֲרֵי בְּנֵי יִשְׂרָאֵל וַיַּעֲלוּ
and-they-offered Israel sons-of young-men-of *** and-he-sent (5) Israel

עֹלֹת וַיִּזְבְּחוּ זְבָחִים שְׁלָמִים לַיהוָה
to-Yahweh fellowship-offerings sacrifices and-they-sacrificed burnt-offerings

פָּרִים׃ וַיִּקַּח מֹשֶׁה חֲצִי הַדָּם וַיָּשֶׂם בָּאַגָּנֹת
in-the-bowls and-he-put the-blood half-of Moses and-he-took (6) bulls

וַחֲצִי הַדָּם זָרַק עַל־ הַמִּזְבֵּחַ׃ וַיִּקַּח סֵפֶר
Book-of then-he-took (7) the-altar against he-sprinkled the-blood and-half-of

הַבְּרִית וַיִּקְרָא בְּאָזְנֵי הָעָם וַיֹּאמְרוּ כֹּל אֲשֶׁר־
that all and-they-responded the-people in-ears-of and-he-read the-Covenant

דִּבֶּר יְהוָה נַעֲשֶׂה וְנִשְׁמָע׃ וַיִּקַּח מֹשֶׁה אֶת־ הַדָּם
the-blood *** Moses then-he-took (8) and-we-will-obey we-will-do Yahweh he-said

וַיִּזְרֹק עַל־ הָעָם וַיֹּאמֶר הִנֵּה דַם־ הַבְּרִית אֲשֶׁר
that the-covenant blood-of see! and-he-said the-people on and-he-sprinkled

כָּרַת יְהוָה עִמָּכֶם עַל כָּל־ הַדְּבָרִים הָאֵלֶּה׃
the-these the-words all-of according-to with-you Yahweh he-made

covenant with them or with
their gods. [33]Do not let them
live in your land, or they will
cause you to sin against me,
because the worship of their
gods will certainly be a snare
to you."

*The Covenant Confirmed*

**24** Then he said to Moses,
"Come up to the LORD,
you and Aaron, Nadab and
Abihu, and seventy of the elders of Israel. You are to worship at a distance, [2]but Moses
alone is to approach the LORD;
the others must not come near.
And the people may not come
up with him."
[3]When Moses went and told
the people all the LORD's words
and laws, they responded
with one voice, "Everything
the LORD has said we will do."
[4]Moses then wrote down
everything the LORD had said.
He got up early the next
morning and built an altar at
the foot of the mountain and
set up twelve stone pillars
representing the twelve tribes
of Israel. [5]Then he sent young
Israelite men, and they offered
burnt offerings and sacrificed
young bulls as fellowship
offerings[e] to the LORD. [6]Moses
took half of the blood and put
it in bowls, and the other half
he sprinkled on the altar.
[7]Then he took the Book of the
Covenant and read it to the
people. They responded, "We
will do everything the LORD
has said; we will obey."
[8]Moses then took the blood,
sprinkled it on the people and
said, "This is the blood of the
covenant that the LORD has
made with you in accordance
with all these words."

[e]5 Traditionally *peace offerings*

וַיַּעַל מֹשֶׁה וְאַהֲרֹן נָדָב וַאֲבִיהוּא וְשִׁבְעִים מִזִּקְנֵי
from-elders-of and-seventy and-Abihu Nadab and-Aaron Moses then-he-went-up (9)

יִשְׂרָאֵל׃ וַיִּרְאוּ אֵת אֱלֹהֵי יִשְׂרָאֵל וְתַחַת רַגְלָיו
feet-of-him and-under Israel God-of *** and-they-saw (10) Israel

כְּמַעֲשֵׂה לִבְנַת הַסַּפִּיר וּכְעֶצֶם הַשָּׁמַיִם לָטֹהַר׃
for-clearness the-skies and-like-very-of the-sapphire stone-of like-pavement-of

וְאֶל־ אֲצִילֵי בְּנֵי יִשְׂרָאֵל לֹא שָׁלַח יָדוֹ
hand-of-him he-raised not Israel sons-of leaders-of but-against (11)

וַיֶּחֱזוּ אֶת־ הָאֱלֹהִים וַיֹּאכְלוּ וַיִּשְׁתּוּ׃ וַיֹּאמֶר יְהוָה
Yahweh then-he-said (12) and-they-drank and-they-ate the-God *** so-they-saw

אֶל־ מֹשֶׁה עֲלֵה אֵלַי הָהָרָה וֶהְיֵה־ שָׁם וְאֶתְּנָה
and-I-will-give here and-stay! on-the-mountain to-me come-up! Moses to

לְךָ אֶת־ לֻחֹת הָאֶבֶן וְהַתּוֹרָה וְהַמִּצְוָה אֲשֶׁר כָּתַבְתִּי
I-wrote that and-the-command with-the-law the-stone tablets-of *** to-you

לְהוֹרֹתָם׃ וַיָּקָם מֹשֶׁה וִיהוֹשֻׁעַ מְשָׁרְתוֹ
one-aiding-him with-Joshua Moses so-he-set-out (13) to-instruct-them

וַיַּעַל מֹשֶׁה אֶל־ הַר הָאֱלֹהִים׃ וְאֶל־ הַזְּקֵנִים אָמַר
he-said the-elders and-to (14) the-God mountain-of on Moses and-he-went-up

שְׁבוּ־ לָנוּ בָזֶה עַד אֲשֶׁר־ נָשׁוּב אֲלֵיכֶם וְהִנֵּה אַהֲרֹן וְחוּר
and-Hur Aaron now-see! to-you we-come-back when until at-here for-us wait!

עִמָּכֶם מִי־ בַעַל דְּבָרִים יִגַּשׁ אֲלֵהֶם׃ וַיַּעַל
when-he-went-up (15) to-them he-can-go disputes involved-of whoever with-you

מֹשֶׁה אֶל־ הָהָר וַיְכַס הֶעָנָן אֶת־ הָהָר׃
the-mountain *** the-cloud then-he-covered the-mountain on Moses

וַיִּשְׁכֹּן כְּבוֹד־ יְהוָה עַל־ הַר סִינַי וַיְכַסֵּהוּ הֶעָנָן
the-cloud and-he-covered-him Sinai Mount-of on Yahweh glory-of and-he-settled (16)

שֵׁשֶׁת יָמִים וַיִּקְרָא אֶל־ מֹשֶׁה בַּיּוֹם הַשְּׁבִיעִי מִתּוֹךְ
from-within the-seventh on-the-day Moses to then-he-called days six-of

הֶעָנָן׃ וּמַרְאֵה כְּבוֹד יְהוָה כְּאֵשׁ אֹכֶלֶת
consuming like-fire Yahweh glory-of and-appearance-of (17) the-cloud

בְּרֹאשׁ הָהָר לְעֵינֵי בְּנֵי יִשְׂרָאֵל׃ וַיָּבֹא מֹשֶׁה
Moses then-he-entered (18) Israel sons-of to-eyes-of the-mountain on-top-of

בְּתוֹךְ הֶעָנָן וַיַּעַל אֶל־ הָהָר וַיְהִי מֹשֶׁה בָּהָר
on-the-mountain Moses and-he-was the-mountain on and-he-went-up the-cloud into

אַרְבָּעִים יוֹם וְאַרְבָּעִים לָיְלָה׃ וַיְדַבֵּר יְהוָה אֶל־ מֹשֶׁה לֵּאמֹר׃
to-say Moses to Yahweh and-he-spoke (25:1) night and-forty day forty

דַּבֵּר אֶל־ בְּנֵי יִשְׂרָאֵל וְיִקְחוּ־ לִי תְּרוּמָה מֵאֵת כָּל־ אִישׁ
man every-of from offering to-me so-they-bring Israel sons-of to tell! (2)

[9]Moses and Aaron, Nadab and Abihu, and the seventy elders of Israel went up [10]and saw the God of Israel. Under his feet was something like a pavement made of sapphire,[f] clear as the sky itself. [11]But God did not raise his hand against these leaders of the Israelites; they saw God, and they ate and drank.

[12]The LORD said to Moses, "Come up to me on the mountain and stay here, and I will give you the tablets of stone, with the law and commands I have written for their instruction."

[13]Then Moses set out with Joshua his aide, and Moses went up on the mountain of God. [14]He said to the elders, "Wait here for us until we come back to you. Aaron and Hur are with you, and anyone involved in a dispute can go to them."

[15]When Moses went up on the mountain, the cloud covered it, [16]and the glory of the LORD settled on Mount Sinai. For six days the cloud covered the mountain, and on the seventh day the LORD called to Moses from within the cloud. [17]To the Israelites the glory of the LORD looked like a consuming fire on top of the mountain. [18]Then Moses entered the cloud as he went on up the mountain. And he stayed on the mountain forty days and forty nights.

### *Offerings for the Tabernacle*

25 The LORD said to Moses, [2]"Tell the Israelites to bring me an offering.

f10 Or *lapis lazuli*

אֲשֶׁר יִדְּבֶנּוּ לִבּוֹ תִּקְחוּ אֶת־ תְּרוּמָתִי׃ וְזֹאת
and-this (3) offering-of-me *** you-receive heart-of-him he-prompts-him who

הַתְּרוּמָה אֲשֶׁר תִּקְחוּ מֵאִתָּם זָהָב וָכֶסֶף וּנְחֹשֶׁת׃
and-bronze and-silver gold from-them you-receive that the-offering

וּתְכֵלֶת וְאַרְגָּמָן וְתוֹלַעַת שָׁנִי וְשֵׁשׁ וְעִזִּים׃
and-goat-hairs and-fine-linen yarn and-scarlet-of and-purple and-blue (4)

וְעֹרֹת אֵילִם מְאָדָּמִים וְעֹרֹת תְּחָשִׁים וַעֲצֵי
and-woods-of sea-cows and-hides-of being-dyed-red rams and-skins-of (5)

שִׁטִּים׃ שֶׁמֶן לַמָּאֹר בְּשָׂמִים לְשֶׁמֶן הַמִּשְׁחָה
the-annointing for-oil-of spices for-the-light olive-oil (6) acacias

וְלִקְטֹרֶת הַסַּמִּים׃ אַבְנֵי־ שֹׁהַם וְאַבְנֵי
and-stones-of onyx stones-of (7) the-fragrances and-for-incense-of

מִלֻּאִים לָאֵפֹד וְלַחֹשֶׁן׃ וְעָשׂוּ
then-they-shall-make (8) and-for-the-breastpiece for-the-ephod mounted-ones

לִי מִקְדָּשׁ וְשָׁכַנְתִּי בְּתוֹכָם׃ כְּכֹל אֲשֶׁר אֲנִי מַרְאֶה
showing I that like-all (9) among-them and-I-will-dwell sanctuary for-me

אוֹתְךָ אֵת תַּבְנִית הַמִּשְׁכָּן וְאֵת תַּבְנִית כָּל־ כֵּלָיו
furnishings-of-him all-of pattern-of and the-tabernacle pattern-of *** you

וְכֵן תַּעֲשׂוּ׃ וְעָשׂוּ אֲרוֹן עֲצֵי שִׁטִּים
acacias woods-of chest-of now-they-shall-make (10) you-shall-make and-so

אַמָּתַיִם וָחֵצִי אָרְכּוֹ וְאַמָּה וָחֵצִי רָחְבּוֹ וְאַמָּה
and-cubit width-of-him and-half and-cubit length-of-him and-half two-cubits

וָחֵצִי קֹמָתוֹ׃ וְצִפִּיתָ אֹתוֹ זָהָב טָהוֹר מִבַּיִת
on-inside pure gold him then-you-overlay (11) height-of-him and-half

וּמִחוּץ תְּצַפֶּנּוּ וְעָשִׂיתָ עָלָיו זֵר זָהָב סָבִיב׃
around gold molding on-him and-you-make you-overlay-him and-on-outside

וְיָצַקְתָּ לּוֹ אַרְבַּע טַבְּעֹת זָהָב וְנָתַתָּה עַל אַרְבַּע פַּעֲמֹתָיו
feet-of-him four to and-you-fasten gold rings four for-him and-you-cast (12)

וּשְׁתֵּי טַבָּעֹת עַל־ צַלְעוֹ הָאֶחָת וּשְׁתֵּי טַבָּעֹת עַל־ צַלְעוֹ
side-of-him on rings and-two-of the-one side-of-him on rings with-two-of

הַשֵּׁנִית׃ וְעָשִׂיתָ בַדֵּי עֲצֵי שִׁטִּים וְצִפִּיתָ אֹתָם
them and-you-overlay acacias woods-of poles-of then-you-make (13) the-other

זָהָב׃ וְהֵבֵאתָ אֶת־ הַבַּדִּים בַּטַּבָּעֹת עַל צַלְעֹת הָאָרֹן
the-chest sides-of on into-the-rings the-poles *** and-you-insert (14) gold

לָשֵׂאת אֶת־ הָאָרֹן בָּהֶם׃ בְּטַבְּעֹת הָאָרֹן יִהְיוּ
they-will-remain the-chest in-rings-of (15) with-them the-chest *** to-carry

הַבַּדִּים לֹא יָסֻרוּ מִמֶּנּוּ׃ וְנָתַתָּ אֶל־ הָאָרֹן
the-chest in then-you-put (16) from-him they-may-be-removed not the-poles

You are to receive the offering for me from each man whose heart prompts him to give. 3These are the offerings you are to receive from them: gold, silver and bronze; 4blue, purple and scarlet yarn and fine linen; goat hair; 5ram skins dyed red and hides of sea cows; acacia wood; 6olive oil for the light; spices for the anointing oil and for the fragrant incense; 7and onyx stones and other gems to be mounted on the ephod and breastpiece.

8"Then have them make a sanctuary for me, and I will dwell among them. 9Make this tabernacle and all its furnishings exactly like the pattern I will show you.

*The Ark*

10"Have them make a chest of acacia wood—two and a half cubits long, a cubit and a half wide, and a cubit and a half high.[g] 11Overlay it with pure gold, both inside and out, and make a gold molding around it. 12Cast four gold rings for it and fasten them to its four feet, with two rings on one side and two rings on the other. 13Then make poles of acacia wood and overlay them with gold. 14Insert the poles into the rings on the sides of the chest to carry it. 15The poles are to remain in the rings of this ark; they are not to be removed. 16Then put in

*g*10 That is, about 3 3/4 feet (about 1.1 meters) long and 2 1/4 feet (about 0.7 meter) wide and high

אֶת הָעֵדֻת אֲשֶׁר אֶתֵּן אֵלֶיךָ׃ וְעָשִׂיתָ כַפֹּרֶת
atonement-cover then-you-make (17) to-you I-will-give which the-Testimony ***

זָהָב טָהוֹר אַמָּתַיִם וָחֵצִי אָרְכָּהּ וְאַמָּה וָחֵצִי רָחְבָּהּ׃
width-of-her and-half and-cubit length-of-her and-half two-cubits pure gold

וְעָשִׂיתָ שְׁנַיִם כְּרֻבִים זָהָב מִקְשָׁה תַּעֲשֶׂה אֹתָם מִשְּׁנֵי קְצוֹת
ends-of at-two-of them you-make hammered gold cherubim two and-you-make (18)

הַכַּפֹּרֶת׃ וַעֲשֵׂה כְּרוּב אֶחָד מִקָּצָה מִזֶּה וּכְרוּב־ אֶחָד מִקָּצָה
at-end one and-cherub at-this at-end one cherub and-make! (19) the-cover

מִזֶּה מִן־ הַכַּפֹּרֶת תַּעֲשׂוּ אֶת־ הַכְּרֻבִים עַל־ שְׁנֵי קְצוֹתָיו׃
ends-of-him two-of at the-cherubim *** you-make the-cover with at-other

וְהָיוּ הַכְּרֻבִים פֹּרְשֵׂי כְנָפַיִם לְמַעְלָה
to-upward wings ones-spreading-of the-cherubim and-they-shall-be (20)

סֹכְכִים בְּכַנְפֵיהֶם עַל־ הַכַּפֹּרֶת וּפְנֵיהֶם
and-faces-of-them the-cover over with-wings-of-them ones-overshadowing

אִישׁ אֶל־ אָחִיו אֶל־ הַכַּפֹּרֶת יִהְיוּ פְּנֵי
faces-of they-shall-be the-cover toward other-of-him toward each

הַכְּרֻבִים׃ וְנָתַתָּ אֶת־ הַכַּפֹּרֶת עַל־ הָאָרֹן מִלְמָעְלָה וְאֶל־
and-into onto-top the-ark on the-cover *** then-you-place (21) the-cherubim

הָאָרֹן תִּתֵּן אֶת־ הָעֵדֻת אֲשֶׁר אֶתֵּן אֵלֶיךָ׃
to-you I-will-give which the-Testimony *** you-put the-ark

וְנוֹעַדְתִּי לְךָ שָׁם וְדִבַּרְתִּי אִתְּךָ מֵעַל הַכַּפֹּרֶת
the-cover from-above to-you and-I-will-tell there with-you and-I-will-meet (22)

מִבֵּין שְׁנֵי הַכְּרֻבִים אֲשֶׁר עַל־ אֲרֹן הָעֵדֻת אֵת כָּל־
all *** the-Testimony ark-of over that the-cherubim two-of from-between

אֲשֶׁר אֲצַוֶּה אוֹתְךָ אֶל־ בְּנֵי יִשְׂרָאֵל׃ וְעָשִׂיתָ שֻׁלְחָן עֲצֵי
woods-of table and-you-make (23) Israel sons-of for you I-command that

שִׁטִּים אַמָּתַיִם אָרְכּוֹ וְאַמָּה רָחְבּוֹ וְאַמָּה וָחֵצִי
and-half and-cubit width-of-him and-cubit length-of-him two-cubits acacias

קֹמָתוֹ׃ וְצִפִּיתָ אֹתוֹ זָהָב טָהוֹר וְעָשִׂיתָ לּוֹ
for-him and-you-make pure gold him and-you-overlay (24) height-of-him

זֵר זָהָב סָבִיב׃ וְעָשִׂיתָ לּוֹ מִסְגֶּרֶת טֹפַח סָבִיב
around handbreadth rim-of for-him also-you-make (25) around gold molding

וְעָשִׂיתָ זֵר־ זָהָב לְמִסְגַּרְתּוֹ סָבִיב׃ וְעָשִׂיתָ לּוֹ
for-him and-you-make (26) around on-rim-of-him gold molding and-you-put

אַרְבַּע טַבְּעֹת זָהָב וְנָתַתָּ אֶת־ הַטַּבָּעֹת עַל אַרְבַּע הַפֵּאֹת אֲשֶׁר
which the-corners four to the-rings *** and-you-fasten gold rings four

לְאַרְבַּע רַגְלָיו׃ לְעֻמַּת הַמִּסְגֶּרֶת תִּהְיֶיןָ הַטַּבָּעֹת לְבָתִּים
as-holders the-rings they-shall-be the-rim close-to (27) legs-of-him at-four

the ark the Testimony, which I will give you.
17"Make an atonement cover of pure gold—two and a half cubits long and a cubit and a half wide.[i] 18And make two cherubim out of hammered gold at the ends of the cover. 19Make one cherub on one end and the second cherub on the other; make the cherubim of one piece with the cover, at the two ends. 20The cherubim are to have their wings spread upward, overshadowing the cover with them. The cherubim are to face each other, looking toward the cover. 21Place the cover on top of the ark and put in the ark the Testimony, which I will give you. 22There, above the cover between the two cherubim that are over the ark of the Testimony, I will meet with you and give you all my commands for the Israelites.

*The Table*

23"Make a table of acacia wood—two cubits long, a cubit wide and a cubit and a half high.[j] 24Overlay it with pure gold and make a gold molding around it. 25Also make around it a rim a handbreadth wide and put a gold molding on the rim. 26Make four gold rings for the table and fasten them to the four corners, where the four legs are. 27The rings are to be close to the rim to hold the

i17 That is, about 3 3/4 feet (about 1.1 meters) long and 2 1/4 feet (about 0.7 meter) wide
j23 That is, about 3 feet (about 0.9 meter) long and 1 1/2 feet (about 0.5 meter) wide and 2 1/4 feet (about 0.7 meter) high

לְבַדִּים לָשֵׂאת אֶת־ הַשֻּׁלְחָן׃ וְעָשִׂיתָ אֶת־ הַבַּדִּים עֲצֵי

woods-of the-poles *** and-you-make (28) the-table *** to-carry for-poles

שִׁטִּים וְצִפִּיתָ אֹתָם זָהָב וְנִשָּׂא־ בָם אֶת־

*** with-them and-he-shall-be-carried gold them and-you-overlay acacias

הַשֻּׁלְחָן׃ וְעָשִׂיתָ קְּעָרֹתָיו וְכַפֹּתָיו וּקְשׂוֹתָיו

and-pitchers-of-him and-ladles-of-him plates-of-him and-you-make (29) the-table

וּמְנַקִּיֹּתָיו אֲשֶׁר יֻסַּךְ בָּהֵן זָהָב טָהוֹר תַּעֲשֶׂה אֹתָם׃

them you-make pure gold with-them he-pours-offering that and-bowls-of-him

וְנָתַתָּ עַל־ הַשֻּׁלְחָן לֶחֶם פָּנִים לְפָנַי תָּמִיד׃

always before-me Presences bread-of the-table on and-you-put (30)

וְעָשִׂיתָ מְנֹרַת זָהָב טָהוֹר מִקְשָׁה תֵּעָשֶׂה

she-shall-be-made hammered pure gold lampstand-of and-you-make (31)

הַמְּנוֹרָה יְרֵכָהּ וְקָנָהּ גְּבִיעֶיהָ כַּפְתֹּרֶיהָ

buds-of-her flower-cups-of-her and-shaft-of-her base-of-her the-lampstand

וּפְרָחֶיהָ מִמֶּנָּה יִהְיוּ׃ וְשִׁשָּׁה קָנִים

branches and-six (32) they-shall-be from-her and-blossoms-of-her

יֹצְאִים מִצִּדֶּיהָ שְׁלֹשָׁה ׀ קְנֵי מְנֹרָה מִצִּדָּהּ

from-side-of-her lampstand branches-of three from-sides-of-her ones-extending

הָאֶחָד וּשְׁלֹשָׁה קְנֵי מְנֹרָה מִצִּדָּהּ הַשֵּׁנִי׃ שְׁלֹשָׁה

three (33) the-other from-side-of-her lampstand branches-of and-three the-one

גְבִעִים מְשֻׁקָּדִים בַּקָּנֶה הָאֶחָד כַּפְתֹּר וָפֶרַח וּשְׁלֹשָׁה גְבִעִים

cups and-three and-blossom bud the-one on-the-branch being-like-almonds cups

מְשֻׁקָּדִים בַּקָּנֶה הָאֶחָד כַּפְתֹּר וָפָרַח כֵּן לְשֵׁשֶׁת

for-six-of same and-blossom bud the-next on-the-branch being-like-almonds

הַקָּנִים הַיֹּצְאִים מִן־ הַמְּנֹרָה׃ וּבַמְּנֹרָה

and-on-the-lampstand (34) the-lampstand from the-ones-extending the-branches

אַרְבָּעָה גְבִעִים מְשֻׁקָּדִים כַּפְתֹּרֶיהָ וּפְרָחֶיהָ׃ וְכַפְתֹּר

and-bud (35) and-blossoms-of-her buds-of-her being-like-almonds cups four

תַּחַת שְׁנֵי הַקָּנִים מִמֶּנָּה וְכַפְתֹּר תַּחַת שְׁנֵי הַקָּנִים

the-branches pair-of under and-bud from-her the-branches pair-of under

מִמֶּנָּה וְכַפְתֹּר תַּחַת־ שְׁנֵי הַקָּנִים מִמֶּנָּה לְשֵׁשֶׁת הַקָּנִים

the-branches for-six-of from-her the-branches pair-of under and-bud from-her

הַיֹּצְאִים מִן־ הַמְּנֹרָה׃ כַּפְתֹּרֵיהֶם וּקְנֹתָם

and-branches-of-them buds-of-them (36) the-lampstand from the-ones-extending

מִמֶּנָּה יִהְיוּ כֻּלָּהּ מִקְשָׁה אַחַת זָהָב טָהוֹר׃

pure gold one-piece hammered-out all-of-her they-shall-be from-her

וְעָשִׂיתָ אֶת־ נֵרֹתֶיהָ שִׁבְעָה וְהֶעֱלָה אֶת־

*** and-he-will-be-set-up seven lamps-of-her *** then-you-make (37)

poles used in carrying the table. [28]Make the poles of acacia wood, overlay them with gold and carry the table with them. [29]And make its plates and ladles of pure gold, as well as its pitchers and bowls for the pouring out of offerings. [30]Put the bread of the Presence on this table to be before me at all times.

*The Lampstand*

[31]"Make a lampstand of pure gold and hammer it out, base and shaft; its flowerlike cups, buds and blossoms shall be of one piece with it. [32]Six branches are to extend from the sides of the lampstand—three on one side and three on the other. [33]Three cups shaped like almond flowers with buds and blossoms are to be on one branch, three on the next branch, and the same for all six branches extending from the lampstand. [34]And on the lampstand there are to be four cups shaped like almond flowers with buds and blossoms. [35]One bud shall be under the first pair of branches extending from the lampstand, a second bud under the second pair, and a third bud under the third pair—six branches in all. [36]The buds and branches shall all be of one piece with the lampstand, hammered out of pure gold.

[37]"Then make its seven lamps and set them up on it so

נֵרֹתֶיהָ וְהֵאִיר עַל־ עֵבֶר פָּנֶיהָ׃ וּמַלְקָחֶיהָ
and-trimmers-of-her (38) in-front-of-her space on so-he-will-light lamps-of-her

וּמַחְתֹּתֶיהָ זָהָב טָהוֹר׃ כִּכַּר זָהָב טָהוֹר יַעֲשֶׂה אֹתָהּ אֵת
*** her he-shall-make pure gold talent (39) pure gold and-trays-of-her

כָּל־ הַכֵּלִים הָאֵלֶּה׃ וּרְאֵה וַעֲשֵׂה בְּתַבְנִיתָם
as-pattern-of-them and-make! now-see! (40) the-these the-accessories all-of

אֲשֶׁר־אַתָּה מָרְאֶה בָּהָר׃ וְאֶת־ הַמִּשְׁכָּן תַּעֲשֶׂה עֶשֶׂר
ten you-make the-tabernacle and (26:1) on-the-mountain being-shown you that

יְרִיעֹת שֵׁשׁ מָשְׁזָר וּתְכֵלֶת וְאַרְגָּמָן וְתֹלַעַת שָׁנִי
yarn and-scarlet and-purple and-blue being-twisted fine-linen curtains

כְּרֻבִים מַעֲשֵׂה חֹשֵׁב תַּעֲשֶׂה אֹתָם׃ אֹרֶךְ ׀ הַיְרִיעָה הָאַחַת
the-each the-curtain length-of (2) them you-make being-skillful work-of cherubim

שְׁמֹנֶה וְעֶשְׂרִים בָּאַמָּה וְרֹחַב אַרְבַּע בָּאַמָּה הַיְרִיעָה
the-curtain by-the-cubit four and-width by-the-cubit and-twenty eight

הָאֶחָת מִדָּה אַחַת לְכָל־ הַיְרִיעֹת׃ חֲמֵשׁ הַיְרִיעֹת
the-curtains five-of (3) the-curtains for-all-of same size the-each

תִּהְיֶיןָ חֹבְרֹת אִשָּׁה אֶל־ אֲחֹתָהּ וְחָמֵשׁ יְרִיעֹת
curtains and-five other-of-her with each ones-being-joined they-shall-be

חֹבְרֹת אִשָּׁה אֶל־ אֲחֹתָהּ׃ וְעָשִׂיתָ לֻלְאֹת תְּכֵלֶת
blue loops-of and-you-make (4) other-of-her with each ones-being-joined

עַל שְׂפַת הַיְרִיעָה הָאֶחָת מִקָּצָה בַּחֹבָרֶת וְכֵן תַּעֲשֶׂה
you-do and-same of-the-set at-end the-one the-curtain edge-of along

בִּשְׂפַת הַיְרִיעָה הַקִּיצוֹנָה בַּמַּחְבֶּרֶת הַשֵּׁנִית׃ חֲמִשִּׁים לֻלָאֹת
loops fifty (5) the-other of-the-set the-end-one the-curtain on-edge-of

תַּעֲשֶׂה בַּיְרִיעָה הָאֶחָת וַחֲמִשִּׁים לֻלָאֹת תַּעֲשֶׂה בִּקְצֵה הַיְרִיעָה
the-curtain on-end-of you-make loops and-fity the-one on-the-curtain you-make

אֲשֶׁר בַּמַּחְבֶּרֶת הַשֵּׁנִית מַקְבִּילֹת הַלֻּלָאֹת אִשָּׁה אֶל־ אֲחֹתָהּ׃
other-of-her to each the-loops opposing the-other of-the-set that

וְעָשִׂיתָ חֲמִשִּׁים קַרְסֵי זָהָב וְחִבַּרְתָּ אֶת־ הַיְרִיעֹת אִשָּׁה
each the-curtains *** and-you-fasten gold clasps-of fifty and-you-make (6)

אֶל־ אֲחֹתָהּ בַּקְּרָסִים וְהָיָה הַמִּשְׁכָּן אֶחָד׃ וְעָשִׂיתָ
and-you-make (7) unit the-tabernacle so-he-is with-the-clasps other-of-her to

יְרִיעֹת עִזִּים לְאֹהֶל עַל־ הַמִּשְׁכָּן עַשְׁתֵּי־ עֶשְׂרֵה יְרִיעֹת
curtains ten one the-tabernacle over for-tent goat-hairs curtains-of

תַּעֲשֶׂה אֹתָם׃ אֹרֶךְ ׀ הַיְרִיעָה הָאַחַת שְׁלֹשִׁים בָּאַמָּה
by-the-cubit thirty the-each the-curtain length-of (8) them you-make

וְרֹחַב אַרְבַּע בָּאַמָּה הַיְרִיעָה הָאֶחָת מִדָּה אַחַת לְעַשְׁתֵּי עֶשְׂרֵה
ten for-one same size the-each the-curtain by-the-cubit four and-width

that they light the space in front of it. 38Its wick trimmers and trays are to be of pure gold. 39A talent[k] of pure gold is to be used for the lampstand and all these accessories. 40See that you make them according to the pattern shown you on the mountain.

*The Tabernacle*

26 "Make the tabernacle with ten curtains of finely twisted linen and blue, purple and scarlet yarn, with cherubim worked into them by a skilled craftsman. 2All the curtains are to be the same size—twenty-eight cubits long and four cubits wide.[l] 3Join five of the curtains together, and do the same with the other five. 4Make loops of blue material along the edge of the end curtain in one set, and do the same with the end curtain in the other set. 5Make fifty loops on one curtain and fifty loops on the end curtain of the other set, with the loops opposite each other. 6Then make fifty gold clasps and use them to fasten the curtains together so that the tabernacle is a unit.

7"Make curtains of goat hair for the tent over the tabernacle—eleven altogether. 8All eleven curtains are to be the same size—thirty cubits long and four cubits wide.[m] 9Join

k39 That is, about 75 pounds (about 34 kilograms)

l2 That is, about 42 feet (about 12.5 meters) long and 6 feet (about 1.8 meters) wide

m8 That is, about 45 feet (about 13.5 meters) long and 6 feet (about 1.8 meters) wide

יְרִיעֹת׃ וְחִבַּרְתָּ אֶת־ חֲמֵשׁ הַיְרִיעֹת לְבָד וְאֶת־ שֵׁשׁ
six-of and into-one the-curtains five-of *** then-you-join (9) curtains

הַיְרִיעֹת לְבָד וְכָפַלְתָּ אֶת־ הַיְרִיעָה הַשִּׁשִּׁית אֶל־ מוּל
front at the-sixth the-curtain *** then-you-fold into-one the-curtains

פְּנֵי הָאֹהֶל׃ וְעָשִׂיתָ חֲמִשִּׁים לֻלָאֹת עַל שְׂפַת הַיְרִיעָה
the-curtain edge-of along loops fifty and-you-make (10) the-tent face-of

הָאֶחָת הַקִּיצֹנָה בַּחֹבָרֶת וַחֲמִשִּׁים לֻלָאֹת עַל שְׂפַת הַיְרִיעָה
the-curtain edge-of along loops and-fifty of-the-set the-end-one the-one

הַחֹבֶרֶת הַשֵּׁנִית׃ וְעָשִׂיתָ קַרְסֵי נְחֹשֶׁת חֲמִשִּׁים וְהֵבֵאתָ אֶת־
*** and-you-put fifty bronze clasps-of and-you-make (11) the-other the-set

הַקְּרָסִים בַּלֻּלָאֹת וְחִבַּרְתָּ אֶת־ הָאֹהֶל וְהָיָה אֶחָד׃
unit so-he-is the-tent *** so-you-fasten in-the-loops the-clasps

וְסֶרַח הָעֹדֵף בִּירִיעֹת הָאֹהֶל חֲצִי הַיְרִיעָה
the-curtain half-of the-tent on-curtains-of the-being-additional and-length-of (12)

הָעֹדֶפֶת תִּסְרַח עַל אֲחֹרֵי הַמִּשְׁכָּן׃
the-tabernacle rear-of at she-will-hang-down the-being-left-over

וְהָאַמָּה מִזֶּה וְהָאַמָּה מִזֶּה בָּעֹדֵף
on-the-being-left-over on-that-side and-the-cubit on-this-side and-the-cubit (13)

בְּאֹרֶךְ יְרִיעֹת הָאֹהֶל יִהְיֶה סָרוּחַ עַל־ צִדֵּי
sides-of over hanging he-will-be the-tent curtains-of in-length-of

הַמִּשְׁכָּן מִזֶּה וּמִזֶּה לְכַסֹּתוֹ׃ וְעָשִׂיתָ
and-you-make (14) to-cover-him and-on-that-side on-this-side the-tabernacle

מִכְסֶה לָאֹהֶל עֹרֹת אֵילִם מְאָדָּמִים וּמִכְסֵה עֹרֹת
hides-of and-cover-of being-dyed-red rams skins-of for-the-tent cover

תְּחָשִׁים מִלְמָעְלָה׃ וְעָשִׂיתָ אֶת־ הַקְּרָשִׁים לַמִּשְׁכָּן עֲצֵי
woods-of for-the-tabernacle the-frames *** and-you-make (15) for-above sea-cows

שִׁטִּים עֹמְדִים׃ עֶשֶׂר אַמּוֹת אֹרֶךְ הַקָּרֶשׁ וְאַמָּה
and-cubit the-frame length-of cubits ten (16) ones-being-upright acacias

וַחֲצִי הָאַמָּה רֹחַב הַקֶּרֶשׁ הָאֶחָד׃ שְׁתֵּי יָדוֹת
projections two-of (17) the-each the-frame width-of the-cubit and-half-of

לַקֶּרֶשׁ הָאֶחָד מְשֻׁלָּבֹת אִשָּׁה אֶל־ אֲחֹתָהּ כֵּן תַּעֲשֶׂה לְכֹל
to-all-of you-do same other-of-her to each paralleling the-each in-the-frame

קַרְשֵׁי הַמִּשְׁכָּן׃ וְעָשִׂיתָ אֶת־ הַקְּרָשִׁים לַמִּשְׁכָּן
for-the-tabernacle the-frames *** and-you-make (18) the-tabernacle frames-of

עֶשְׂרִים קֶרֶשׁ לִפְאַת נֶגְבָּה תֵימָנָה׃ וְאַרְבָּעִים אַדְנֵי־ כֶסֶף תַּעֲשֶׂה
you-make silver bases-of and-forty (19) south to-south for-side-of frame twenty

תַּחַת עֶשְׂרִים הַקָּרֶשׁ שְׁנֵי אֲדָנִים תַּחַת־ הַקֶּרֶשׁ הָאֶחָד לִשְׁתֵּי
for-two-of the-each the-frame under bases two-of the-frame twenty under

five of the curtains together into one set and the other six into another set. Fold the sixth curtain double at the front of the tent. [10]Make fifty loops along the edge of the end curtain in one set and also along the edge of the end curtain in the other set. [11]Then make fifty bronze clasps and put them in the loops to fasten the tent together as a unit. [12]As for the additional length of the tent curtains, the half curtain that is left over is to hang down at the rear of the tabernacle. [13]The tent curtains will be a cubit[n] longer on both sides; what is left will hang over the sides of the tabernacle so as to cover it. [14]Make for the tent a covering of ram skins dyed red, and over that a covering of hides of sea cows.

[15]"Make upright frames of acacia wood for the tabernacle. [16]Each frame is to be ten cubits long and a cubit and a half wide,[o] [17]with two projections set parallel to each other. Make all the frames of the tabernacle in this way. [18]Make twenty frames for the south side of the tabernacle [19]and make forty silver bases to go under them—two bases for each frame, one under

[n] 13 That is, about 1 1/2 feet (about 0.5 meter)

[o] 16 That is, about 15 feet (about 4.5 meters) long and 2 1/4 feet (about 0.7 meter) wide

יְדֹתָיו וּשְׁנֵי אֲדָנִים תַּחַת־הַקֶּרֶשׁ הָאֶחָד לִשְׁתֵּי
for-two-of the-each the-frame under bases and-two-of projections-of-him

יְדֹתָיו׃ וּלְצֶלַע הַמִּשְׁכָּן הַשֵּׁנִית לִפְאַת
for-side-of the-other the-tabernacle and-for-side-of (20) projections-of-him

צָפוֹן עֶשְׂרִים קָרֶשׁ׃ וְאַרְבָּעִים אַדְנֵיהֶם כָּסֶף שְׁנֵי אֲדָנִים תַּחַת
under bases two-of silver bases-of-them and-forty (21) frame twenty north

הַקֶּרֶשׁ הָאֶחָד וּשְׁנֵי אֲדָנִים תַּחַת הַקֶּרֶשׁ הָאֶחָד׃
the-each the-frame under bases and-two-of the-each the-frame

וּלְיַרְכְּתֵי הַמִּשְׁכָּן יָמָּה תַּעֲשֶׂה שִׁשָּׁה קְרָשִׁים׃
frames six you-make west-end the-tabernacle and-for-far-ends-of (22)

וּשְׁנֵי קְרָשִׁים תַּעֲשֶׂה לִמְקֻצְעֹת הַמִּשְׁכָּן בַּיַּרְכָתָיִם׃
at-the-far-ends the-tabernacle for-corners-of you-make frames and-two-of (23)

וְיִהְיוּ תֹאֲמִים מִלְּמַטָּה וְיַחְדָּו יִהְיוּ
they-must-be and-fitted from-bottom ones-being-double and-they-must-be (24)

תַמִּים עַל־רֹאשׁוֹ אֶל־הַטַּבַּעַת הָאֶחָת כֵּן יִהְיֶה
he-shall-be same the-single the-ring into top-of-him at being-double

לִשְׁנֵיהֶם לִשְׁנֵי הַמִּקְצֹעֹת יִהְיוּ׃ וְהָיוּ
so-they-will-be (25) they-shall-be the-corners for-both-of for-both-of-them

שְׁמֹנָה קְרָשִׁים וְאַדְנֵיהֶם כֶּסֶף שִׁשָּׁה עָשָׂר אֲדָנִים שְׁנֵי אֲדָנִים תַּחַת
under bases two-of bases ten six silver and-bases-of-them frames eight

הַקֶּרֶשׁ הָאֶחָד וּשְׁנֵי אֲדָנִים תַּחַת הַקֶּרֶשׁ הָאֶחָד׃ וְעָשִׂיתָ
and-you-make (26) the-each the-frame under bases and-two-of the-each the-frame

בְרִיחִם עֲצֵי שִׁטִּים חֲמִשָּׁה לְקַרְשֵׁי צֶלַע־הַמִּשְׁכָּן הָאֶחָד׃
the-one the-tabernacle side-of for-frames-of five acacias woods-of crossbars

וַחֲמִשָּׁה בְרִיחִם לְקַרְשֵׁי צֶלַע־הַמִּשְׁכָּן הַשֵּׁנִית
the-other the-tabernacle side-of for-frames-of crossbars and-five (27)

וַחֲמִשָּׁה בְרִיחִם לְקַרְשֵׁי צֶלַע הַמִּשְׁכָּן לַיַּרְכָתַיִם
at-the-far-ends the-tabernacle side-of for-frames-of crossbars and-five

יָמָּה׃ וְהַבְּרִיחַ הַתִּיכֹן בְּתוֹךְ הַקְּרָשִׁים מַבְרִחַ מִן־
from extending the-frames middle-of the-center and-the-crossbar (28) on-west

הַקָּצֶה אֶל־הַקָּצֶה׃ וְאֶת־הַקְּרָשִׁים תְּצַפֶּה זָהָב וְאֶת־טַבְּעֹתֵיהֶם
rings-of-them and gold you-overlay the-frames and (29) the-end to the-end

תַּעֲשֶׂה זָהָב בָּתִּים לַבְּרִיחִם וְצִפִּיתָ אֶת־הַבְּרִיחִם
the-crossbars *** also-you-overlay for-the-crossbars holders gold you-make

זָהָב׃ וַהֲקֵמֹתָ אֶת־הַמִּשְׁכָּן כְּמִשְׁפָּטוֹ אֲשֶׁר הָרְאֵיתָ
you-were-shown that as-plan-of-him the-tabernacle *** now-you-set-up (30) gold

בָּהָר׃ וְעָשִׂיתָ פָרֹכֶת תְּכֵלֶת וְאַרְגָּמָן וְתוֹלַעַת שָׁנִי
yarn and-scarlet-of and-purple blue curtain and-you-make (31) on-the-mountain

each projection. [20]For the other side, the north side of the
tabernacle, make twenty
frames [21]and forty silver
bases—two under each frame.
[22]Make six frames for the far
end, that is, the west end of
the tabernacle, [23]and make
two frames for the corners at
the far end. [24]At these two corners they must be double from
the bottom all the way to the
top, and fitted into a single
ring; both shall be like that.
[25]So there will be eight frames
and sixteen silver bases—two
under each frame.

[26]"Also make crossbars of
acacia wood: five for the
frames on one side of the tabernacle, [27]five for those on the
other side, and five for the
frames on the west, at the far
end of the tabernacle. [28]The
center crossbar is to extend
from end to end at the middle
of the frames. [29]Overlay the
frames with gold and make
gold rings to hold the crossbars. Also overlay the crossbars with gold.

[30]"Set up the tabernacle according to the plan shown you
on the mountain.

[31]"Make a curtain of blue,
purple and scarlet yarn and

וְשֵׁשׁ מָשְׁזָר מַעֲשֵׂה חֹשֵׁב יַעֲשֶׂה אֹתָהּ כְּרֻבִים׃
cherubim her he-shall-make being-skilled work-of being-twisted and-fine-linen

וְנָתַתָּה אֹתָהּ עַל־אַרְבָּעָה עַמּוּדֵי שִׁטִּים מְצֻפִּים זָהָב
gold ones-being-overlaid acacias posts-of four on her and-you-hang (32)

וָוֵיהֶם זָהָב עַל־אַרְבָּעָה אַדְנֵי־כָסֶף׃ וְנָתַתָּה אֶת־הַפָּרֹכֶת
the-curtain *** and-you-hang (33) silver bases-of four on gold hooks-of-them

תַּחַת הַקְּרָסִים וְהֵבֵאתָ שָׁמָּה מִבֵּית לַפָּרֹכֶת אֵת אֲרוֹן
ark-of *** of-the-curtain at-behind there and-you-place the-clasps from

הָעֵדוּת וְהִבְדִּילָה הַפָּרֹכֶת לָכֶם בֵּין
between for-you the-curtain and-she-will-separate the-Testimony

הַקֹּדֶשׁ וּבֵין קֹדֶשׁ הַקֳּדָשִׁים׃ וְנָתַתָּ אֶת־
*** and-you-put (34) the-Holy-Places Holiest-of and-between the-Holy-Place

הַכַּפֹּרֶת עַל אֲרוֹן הָעֵדֻת בְּקֹדֶשׁ הַקֳּדָשִׁים׃
the-Holy-Places in-Holiest-of the-Testimony ark-of on the-atonement-cover

וְשַׂמְתָּ אֶת־הַשֻּׁלְחָן מִחוּץ לַפָּרֹכֶת וְאֶת־הַמְּנֹרָה
the-lampstand and of-the-curtain outside the-table *** and-you-place (35)

נֹכַח הַשֻּׁלְחָן עַל צֶלַע הַמִּשְׁכָּן תֵּימָנָה וְהַשֻּׁלְחָן תִּתֵּן
you-put and-the-table to-south the-tabernacle side-of on the-table opposite

עַל־צֶלַע צָפוֹן׃ וְעָשִׂיתָ מָסָךְ לְפֶתַח הָאֹהֶל תְּכֵלֶת
blue the-tent for-door-of curtain and-you-make (36) north side-of on

וְאַרְגָּמָן וְתוֹלַעַת שָׁנִי וְשֵׁשׁ מָשְׁזָר מַעֲשֵׂה
work-of being-twisted and-fine-linen yarn and-scarlet-of and-purple

רֹקֵם׃ וְעָשִׂיתָ לַמָּסָךְ חֲמִשָּׁה עַמּוּדֵי שִׁטִּים
acacias posts-of five for-the-curtain and-you-make (37) embroidering

וְצִפִּיתָ אֹתָם זָהָב וָוֵיהֶם זָהָב וְיָצַקְתָּ לָהֶם חֲמִשָּׁה
five for-them and-you-cast gold hooks-of-them gold them and-you-overlay

אַדְנֵי נְחֹשֶׁת׃ וְעָשִׂיתָ אֶת־הַמִּזְבֵּחַ עֲצֵי שִׁטִּים חָמֵשׁ
five acacias woods-of the-altar *** and-you-build (27:1) bronze bases-of

אַמּוֹת אֹרֶךְ וְחָמֵשׁ אַמּוֹת רֹחַב רָבוּעַ יִהְיֶה הַמִּזְבֵּחַ וְשָׁלֹשׁ
and-three the-altar he-shall-be being-square wide cubits and-five long cubits

אַמּוֹת קֹמָתוֹ׃ וְעָשִׂיתָ קַרְנֹתָיו עַל אַרְבַּע פִּנֹּתָיו
corners-of-him four at horns-of-him and-you-make (3) height-of-him cubits

מִמֶּנּוּ תִּהְיֶיןָ קַרְנֹתָיו וְצִפִּיתָ אֹתוֹ נְחֹשֶׁת׃
bronze him and-you-overlay horns-of-him they-shall-be from-him

וְעָשִׂיתָ סִּירֹתָיו לְדַשְּׁנוֹ וְיָעָיו
and-shovels-of-him to-remove-ash-of-him pots-of-him and-you-make (3)

וּמִזְרְקֹתָיו וּמִזְלְגֹתָיו וּמַחְתֹּתָיו
and-firepans-of-him and-meat-forks-of-him and-sprinkling-bowls-of-him

finely twisted linen, with cherubim worked into it by a skilled craftsman. 32Hang it with gold hooks on four posts of acacia wood overlaid with gold and standing on four silver bases. 33Hang the curtain from the clasps and place the ark of the Testimony behind the curtain. The curtain will separate the Holy Place from the Most Holy Place. 34Put the atonement cover on the ark of the Testimony in the Most Holy Place. 35Place the table outside the curtain on the north side of the tabernacle and put the lampstand opposite it on the south side.

36"For the entrance to the tent make a curtain of blue, purple and scarlet yarn and finely twisted linen—the work of an embroiderer. 37Make gold hooks for this curtain and five posts of acacia wood overlaid with gold. And cast five bronze bases for them.

### *The Altar of Burnt Offering*

27 "Build an altar of acacia wood, three cubits[p] high; it is to be square, five cubits long and five cubits wide.[q] 2Make a horn at each of the four corners, so that the horns and the altar are of one piece, and overlay the altar with bronze. 3Make all its utensils of bronze—its pots to remove the ashes, and its shovels, sprinkling bowls, meat forks and firepans.

[p]1 That is, about 4 1/2 feet (about 1.3 meters)
[q]1 That is, about 7 1/2 feet (about 2.3 meters) long and wide

לְכָל־ כֵּלָיו תַּעֲשֶׂה נְחֹשֶׁת׃ וְעָשִׂיתָ לּוֹ מִכְבָּר
grate for-him and-you-make (4) bronze you-make utensils-of-him now-all-of

מַעֲשֵׂה רֶשֶׁת נְחֹשֶׁת וְעָשִׂיתָ עַל־ הָרֶשֶׁת אַרְבַּע טַבְּעֹת נְחֹשֶׁת עַל אַרְבַּע
four at bronze rings-of four the-net on and-you-make bronze net-of work-of

קְצוֹתָיו׃ וְנָתַתָּה אֹתָהּ תַּחַת כַּרְכֹּב הַמִּזְבֵּחַ מִלְּמָטָּה וְהָיְתָה
so-she-is beneath the-altar ledge-of under her and-you-put (5) corners-of-him

הָרֶשֶׁת עַד חֲצִי הַמִּזְבֵּחַ׃ וְעָשִׂיתָ בַדִּים לַמִּזְבֵּחַ בַּדֵּי
poles-of for-the-altar poles then-you-make (6) the-altar halfway up the-net

עֲצֵי שִׁטִּים וְצִפִּיתָ אֹתָם נְחֹשֶׁת׃ וְהוּבָא
and-he-shall-be-inserted (7) bronze them and-you-overlay acacias woods-of

אֶת־ בַּדָּיו בַּטַּבָּעֹת וְהָיוּ הַבַּדִּים עַל־ שְׁתֵּי צַלְעֹת
sides-of two-of on the-poles so-they-will-be into-the-rings poles-of-him ***

הַמִּזְבֵּחַ בִּשְׂאֵת אֹתוֹ׃ נְבוּב לֻחֹת תַּעֲשֶׂה אֹתוֹ כַּאֲשֶׁר
just-as him you-make boards being-hollow-of (8) him when-to-carry the-altar

הֶרְאָה אֹתְךָ בָּהָר כֵּן יַעֲשׂוּ׃ וְעָשִׂיתָ אֵת
*** and-you-make (9) they-shall-make so on-the-mountain you he-showed

חֲצַר הַמִּשְׁכָּן לִפְאַת נֶגֶב־ תֵּימָנָה קְלָעִים לֶחָצֵר
for-the-courtyard curtains south south at-side-of the-tabernacle courtyard-of

שֵׁשׁ מָשְׁזָר מֵאָה בָאַמָּה אֹרֶךְ לַפֵּאָה הָאֶחָת׃
the-one for-the-side long by-the-cubit hundred being-twisted fine-linen

וְעַמֻּדָיו עֶשְׂרִים וְאַדְנֵיהֶם עֶשְׂרִים נְחֹשֶׁת וָוֵי
hooks-of bronze twenty and-bases-of-them twenty and-posts-of-him (10)

הָעַמֻּדִים וַחֲשֻׁקֵיהֶם כָּסֶף׃ וְכֵן לִפְאַת צָפוֹן
north for-side-of and-same (11) silver and-bands-of-them the-posts

בָּאֹרֶךְ קְלָעִים מֵאָה אֹרֶךְ וְעַמֻּדָו עֶשְׂרִים וְאַדְנֵיהֶם
and-bases-of-them twenty and-posts-of-him long hundred curtains for-the-length

עֶשְׂרִים נְחֹשֶׁת וָוֵי הָעַמֻּדִים וַחֲשֻׁקֵיהֶם כָּסֶף׃ וְרֹחַב
and-width-of (12) silver and-bands-of-them the-posts hooks-of bronze twenty

הֶחָצֵר לִפְאַת־ יָם קְלָעִים חֲמִשִּׁים אַמָּה עַמֻּדֵיהֶם עֲשָׂרָה
ten posts-of-them cubit fifty curtains west at-end-of the-courtyard

וְאַדְנֵיהֶם עֲשָׂרָה׃ וְרֹחַב הֶחָצֵר לִפְאַת קֵדְמָה
east at-end-of the-courtyard and-width-of (13) ten and-bases-of-them

מִזְרָחָה חֲמִשִּׁים אַמָּה׃ וַחֲמֵשׁ עֶשְׂרֵה אַמָּה קְלָעִים לַכָּתֵף
on-the-side curtains cubit ten and-five (14) cubit fifty toward-sunrise

עַמֻּדֵיהֶם שְׁלֹשָׁה וְאַדְנֵיהֶם שְׁלֹשָׁה׃ וְלַכָּתֵף הַשֵּׁנִית
the-other and-on-the-side (15) three and-bases-of-them three posts-of-them

חֲמֵשׁ* עֶשְׂרֵה קְלָעִים עַמֻּדֵיהֶם שְׁלֹשָׁה וְאַדְנֵיהֶם שְׁלֹשָׁה׃
three and-bases-of-them three posts-of-them curtains ten five-of

[4]Make a grating for it, a bronze network, and make a bronze ring at each of the four corners of the network. [5]Put it under the ledge of the altar so that it is halfway up the altar. [6]Make poles of acacia wood for the altar and overlay them with bronze. [7]The poles are to be inserted into the rings so they will be on two sides of the altar when it is carried. [8]Make the altar hollow, out of boards. It is to be made just as you were shown on the mountain.

*The Courtyard*

[9]"Make a courtyard for the tabernacle. The south side shall be a hundred cubits[r] long and is to have curtains of finely twisted linen, [10]with twenty posts and twenty bronze bases and with silver hooks and bands on the posts. [11]The north side shall also be a hundred cubits long and is to have curtains, with twenty posts and twenty bronze bases and with silver hooks and bands on the posts.

[12]"The west end of the courtyard shall be fifty cubits[s] wide and have curtains, with ten posts and ten bases. [13]On the east end, toward the sunrise, the courtyard shall also be fifty cubits wide. [14]Curtains fifteen cubits[t] long are to be on one side of the entrance, with three posts and three bases, [15]and curtains fifteen cubits long are to be on the other side, with three posts and three bases.

[r] *9* That is, about 150 feet (about 46 meters); also in verse 11
[s] *12* That is, about 75 feet (about 23 meters); also in verse 13
[t] *14* That is, about 22 1/2 feet (about 6.9 meters); also in verse 15

**15* Most mss have *hateph pathah* under the *beth* (חֲמֵשׁ).

°*11* ק ועמודיו

וּלְשַׁעַר הֶחָצֵר מָסָךְ ׀ עֶשְׂרִים אַמָּה תְּכֵלֶת וְאַרְגָּמָן
and-purple blue cubit twenty curtain the-courtyard and-for-entrance-of (16)

וְתוֹלַעַת שָׁנִי וְשֵׁשׁ מָשְׁזָר מַעֲשֵׂה רֹקֵם
embroidering work-of being-twisted and-fine-linen yarn and-scarlet-of

עַמֻּדֵיהֶם אַרְבָּעָה וְאַדְנֵיהֶם אַרְבָּעָה׃ כָּל־ עַמּוּדֵי הֶחָצֵר
the-courtyard posts-of all-of (17) four and-bases-of-them four posts-of-them

סָבִיב מְחֻשָּׁקִים כֶּסֶף וָוֵיהֶם כֶּסֶף וְאַדְנֵיהֶם נְחֹשֶׁת׃
bronze and-bases-of-them silver hooks-of-them silver ones-having-bands around

אֹרֶךְ הֶחָצֵר מֵאָה בָּאַמָּה וְרֹחַב ׀ חֲמִשִּׁים בַּחֲמִשִּׁים
by-the-fifty fifty and-width by-the-cubit hundred the-courtyard length-of (18)

וְקֹמָה חָמֵשׁ אַמּוֹת שֵׁשׁ מָשְׁזָר וְאַדְנֵיהֶם נְחֹשֶׁת׃
bronze with-bases-of-them being-twisted fine-linen cubits five and-height

לְכֹל כְּלֵי הַמִּשְׁכָּן בְּכֹל עֲבֹדָתוֹ
service-of-him in-every-of the-tabernacle utensils-of now-all-of (19)

וְכָל־ יְתֵדֹתָיו וְכָל־ יִתְדֹת הֶחָצֵר נְחֹשֶׁת׃
bronze the-courtyard pegs-of and-all-of tent-pegs-of-him even-all-of

וְאַתָּה תְּצַוֶּה ׀ אֶת־ בְּנֵי יִשְׂרָאֵל וְיִקְחוּ אֵלֶיךָ שֶׁמֶן
oil-of to-you so-they-bring Israel sons-of *** you-command now-you (20)

זַיִת זָךְ כָּתִית לַמָּאוֹר לְהַעֲלֹת נֵר תָּמִיד׃ בְּאֹהֶל
in-Tent-of (21) continually lamp to-burn for-the-light pressed clear olive

מוֹעֵד מִחוּץ לַפָּרֹכֶת אֲשֶׁר עַל־ הָעֵדֻת יַעֲרֹךְ אֹתוֹ
him he-shall-keep the-Testimony before that of-the-curtain outside Meeting

אַהֲרֹן וּבָנָיו מֵעֶרֶב עַד־ בֹּקֶר לִפְנֵי יְהוָה חֻקַּת
ordinance-of Yahweh before morning till from-evening and-sons-of-him Aaron

עוֹלָם לְדֹרֹתָם מֵאֵת בְּנֵי יִשְׂרָאֵל׃ וְאַתָּה הַקְרֵב
bring! now-you (28:1) Israel sons-of among for-generations-of-them lasting

אֵלֶיךָ אֶת־ אַהֲרֹן אָחִיךָ וְאֶת־ בָּנָיו אִתּוֹ מִתּוֹךְ בְּנֵי
sons-of from-among with-him sons-of-him and brother-of-you Aaron *** to-you

יִשְׂרָאֵל לְכַהֲנוֹ־ לִי אַהֲרֹן נָדָב וַאֲבִיהוּא אֶלְעָזָר וְאִיתָמָר
and-Ithamar Eleazar and-Abihu Nadab Aaron to-me to-serve-as-priest-him Israel

בְּנֵי אַהֲרֹן׃ וְעָשִׂיתָ בִגְדֵי־ קֹדֶשׁ לְאַהֲרֹן אָחִיךָ
brother-of-you for-Aaron sacred garments-of and-you-make (2) Aaron sons-of

לְכָבוֹד וּלְתִפְאָרֶת׃ וְאַתָּה תְּדַבֵּר אֶל־ כָּל־ חַכְמֵי־
ones-skilled-of all-of to you-tell and-you (3) and-for-honor for-dignity

לֵב אֲשֶׁר מִלֵּאתִיו רוּחַ חָכְמָה וְעָשׂוּ אֶת־ בִּגְדֵי אַהֲרֹן
Aaron garments-of *** that-they-make wisdom spirit-of I-gave-him whom heart

לְקַדְּשׁוֹ לְכַהֲנוֹ־ לִי׃ וְאֵלֶּה הַבְּגָדִים
the-garments and-these (4) to-me to-serve-as-priest-him to-consecrate-him

[16]"For the entrance to the courtyard, provide a curtain twenty cubits[v] long, of blue, purple and scarlet yarn and finely twisted linen—the work of an embroiderer—with four posts and four bases. [17]All the posts around the courtyard are to have silver bands and hooks, and bronze bases. [18]The courtyard shall be a hundred cubits long and fifty cubits wide,[w] with curtains of finely twisted linen five cubits[x] high, and with bronze bases. [19]All the other articles used in the service of the tabernacle, whatever their function, including all the tent pegs for it and those for the courtyard, are to be of bronze.

*Oil for the Lampstand*

[20]"Command the Israelites to bring you clear oil of pressed olives for the light so that the lamps may be kept burning. [21]In the Tent of Meeting, outside the curtain that is in front of the Testimony, Aaron and his sons are to keep the lamps burning before the LORD from evening till morning. This is to be a lasting ordinance among the Israelites for the generations to come.

*The Priestly Garments*

28 "Have Aaron your brother brought to you from among the Israelites, along with his sons Nadab and Abihu, Eleazar and Ithamar, so they may serve me as priests. [2]Make sacred garments for your brother Aaron, to give him dignity and honor. [3]Tell all the skilled men to whom I have given wisdom in such matters that they are to make garments for Aaron, for his consecration, so he may serve me as priest. [4]These are

[v]*16* That is, about 30 feet (about 9 meters)
[w]*18* That is, about 150 feet (about 46 meters) long and 75 feet (about 23 meters) wide
[x]*18* That is, about 7 1/2 feet (about 2.3 meters)

אֲשֶׁר יַעֲשׂוּ חֹשֶׁן וְאֵפוֹד וּמְעִיל וּכְתֹנֶת תַּשְׁבֵּץ מִצְנֶפֶת
turban woven and-tunic-of and-robe and-ephod breastpiece they-make that

וְאַבְנֵט וְעָשׂוּ בִגְדֵי־ קֹדֶשׁ לְאַהֲרֹן אָחִיךָ
brother-of-you for-Aaron sacred garments-of so-they-shall-make and-sash

וּלְבָנָיו לְכַהֲנוֹ־ לִי׃ וְהֵם יִקְחוּ
they-shall-use now-they (5) to-me to-serve-as-priest-him and-for-sons-of-him

אֶת־ הַזָּהָב וְאֶת־ הַתְּכֵלֶת וְאֶת־ הָאַרְגָּמָן וְאֶת־ תּוֹלַעַת הַשָּׁנִי וְאֶת־
and the-yarn scarlet-of and the-purple and the-blue and the-gold ***

הַשֵּׁשׁ׃ וְעָשׂוּ אֶת־ הָאֵפֹד זָהָב תְּכֵלֶת וְאַרְגָּמָן
and-purple blue gold the-ephod *** and-they-shall-make (6) the-fine-linen

תּוֹלַעַת שָׁנִי וְשֵׁשׁ מָשְׁזָר מַעֲשֵׂה חֹשֵׁב׃ שְׁתֵּי
two-of (7) being-skilled work-of being-twisted and-fine-linen yarn scarlet-of

כְתֵפֹת חֹבְרֹת יִהְיֶה־ לּוֹ אֶל־ שְׁנֵי
two-of on on-him he-shall-have ones-being-attached shoulder-pieces

קְצוֹתָיו וְחֻבָּר׃ וְחֵשֶׁב אֲפֻדָּתוֹ אֲשֶׁר
that ephod-of-him and-woven-part-of (8) so-being-fastened corners-of-him

עָלָיו כְּמַעֲשֵׂהוּ מִמֶּנּוּ יִהְיֶה זָהָב תְּכֵלֶת וְאַרְגָּמָן
and-purple blue gold he-shall-be from-him like-work-of-him on-him

וְתוֹלַעַת שָׁנִי וְשֵׁשׁ מָשְׁזָר׃ וְלָקַחְתָּ אֶת־
*** then-you-take (9) being-twisted and-fine-linen yarn and-scarlet-of

שְׁתֵּי אַבְנֵי־ שֹׁהַם וּפִתַּחְתָּ עֲלֵיהֶם שְׁמוֹת בְּנֵי יִשְׂרָאֵל׃
Israel sons-of names-of on-them and-you-engrave onyx stones-of two-of

שִׁשָּׁה מִשְּׁמֹתָם עַל הָאֶבֶן הָאֶחָת וְאֶת־ שְׁמוֹת הַשִּׁשָּׁה
the-six names-of and the-one the-stone on from-names-of-them six (10)

הַנּוֹתָרִים עַל־ הָאֶבֶן הַשֵּׁנִית כְּתוֹלְדֹתָם׃ מַעֲשֵׂה
work-of (11) by-births-of-them the-other the-stone on the-ones-remaining

חָרַשׁ אֶבֶן פִּתּוּחֵי חֹתָם תְּפַתַּח אֶת־ שְׁתֵּי הָאֲבָנִים עַל־
with the-stones two-of *** you-engrave seal engraves-of gem cutter-of

שְׁמֹת בְּנֵי יִשְׂרָאֵל מֻסַבֹּת מִשְׁבְּצוֹת זָהָב תַּעֲשֶׂה אֹתָם׃
them you-mount gold filigrees-of settings-of Israel sons-of names-of

וְשַׂמְתָּ אֶת־ שְׁתֵּי הָאֲבָנִים עַל כִּתְפֹת הָאֵפֹד
the-ephod shoulder-pieces-of on the-stones two-of *** and-you-fasten (12)

אַבְנֵי זִכָּרֹן לִבְנֵי יִשְׂרָאֵל וְנָשָׂא אַהֲרֹן אֶת־
*** Aaron and-he-shall-bear Israel for-sons-of memorial stones-of

שְׁמוֹתָם לִפְנֵי יְהוָה עַל־ שְׁתֵּי כְתֵפָיו לְזִכָּרֹן׃
as-memorial shoulders-of-him two-of on Yahweh before names-of-them

וְעָשִׂיתָ מִשְׁבְּצֹת זָהָב׃ וּשְׁתֵּי שַׁרְשְׁרֹת זָהָב טָהוֹר
pure gold chains-of and-two-of (14) gold filigrees-of and-you-make (13)

the garments they are to make: a breastpiece, an ephod, a robe, a woven tunic, a turban and a sash. They are to make these sacred garments for your brother Aaron and his sons, so they may serve me as priests.
5Have them use gold, and blue, purple and scarlet yarn, and fine linen.

*The Ephod*

6"Make the ephod of gold, and of blue, purple and scarlet yarn, and of finely twisted linen—the work of a skilled craftsman.
7It is to have two shoulder pieces attached to two of its corners, so it can be fastened.
8Its skillfully woven waistband is to be like it—of one piece with the ephod and made with gold, and with blue, purple and scarlet yarn, and with finely twisted linen.
9"Take two onyx stones and engrave on them the names of the sons of Israel
10in the order of their birth—six names on one stone and the remaining six on the other.
11Engrave the names of the sons of Israel on the two stones the way a gem cutter engraves a seal. Then mount the stones in gold filigree settings
12and fasten them on the shoulder pieces of the ephod as memorial stones for the sons of Israel. Aaron is to bear the names on his shoulders as a memorial before the LORD.
13Make gold filigree settings
14and two braided chains

מִגְבָּלֹת תַּעֲשֶׂה אֹתָם מַעֲשֵׂה עֲבֹת וְנָתַתָּה אֶת־שַׁרְשְׁרֹת
chains-of *** and-you-attach ropes work-of them you-make braided-ones

הָעֲבֹתֹת עַל־הַמִּשְׁבְּצֹת׃ (15) וְעָשִׂיתָ חֹשֶׁן מִשְׁפָּט
decision breastpiece-of and-you-fashion (15) the-settings to the-ropes

מַעֲשֵׂה חֹשֵׁב כְּמַעֲשֵׂה אֵפֹד תַּעֲשֶׂנּוּ זָהָב תְּכֵלֶת וְאַרְגָּמָן
and-purple blue gold you-make-him ephod like-work-of being-skilled work-of

וְתוֹלַעַת שָׁנִי וְשֵׁשׁ מָשְׁזָר תַּעֲשֶׂה אֹתוֹ׃
him you-make being-twisted and-fine-linen yarn and-scarlet-of

(16) רָבוּעַ יִהְיֶה כָּפוּל זֶרֶת אָרְכּוֹ וְזֶרֶת
and-span length-of-him span being-doubled he-shall-be being-square (16)

רָחְבּוֹ׃ (17) וּמִלֵּאתָ בוֹ מִלֻּאַת אֶבֶן אַרְבָּעָה טוּרִים אָבֶן
stone rows four stone setting-of on-him then-you-mount (17) width-of-him

טוּר אֹדֶם פִּטְדָה וּבָרֶקֶת הַטּוּר הָאֶחָד׃ (18) וְהַטּוּר הַשֵּׁנִי
the-second and-the-row (18) the-first the-row and-beryl topaz ruby row-of

נֹפֶךְ סַפִּיר וְיָהֲלֹם׃ (19) וְהַטּוּר הַשְּׁלִישִׁי לֶשֶׁם שְׁבוֹ
agate jacinth the-third and-the-row (19) and-emerald sapphire turquoise

וְאַחְלָמָה׃ (20) וְהַטּוּר הָרְבִיעִי תַּרְשִׁישׁ וְשֹׁהַם וְיָשְׁפֵה
and-jasper and-onyx chrysolite the-fourth and-the-row (20) and-amethyst

מְשֻׁבָּצִים זָהָב יִהְיוּ בְּמִלּוּאֹתָם׃ (21) וְהָאֲבָנִים
and-the-stones (21) in-settings-of-them they-shall-be gold ones-being-mounted

תִּהְיֶיןָ עַל־שְׁמֹת בְּנֵי־יִשְׂרָאֵל שְׁתֵּים עֶשְׂרֵה עַל־שְׁמֹתָם
names-of-them for ten two Israel sons-of names-of for they-shall-be

פִּתּוּחֵי חוֹתָם אִישׁ עַל־שְׁמוֹ תִּהְיֶיןָ לִשְׁנֵי עָשָׂר שָׁבֶט׃
tribe ten for-two they-shall-be name-of-him with each seal ones-engraved-of

(22) וְעָשִׂיתָ עַל־הַחֹשֶׁן שַׁרְשֹׁת גַּבְלֻת מַעֲשֵׂה עֲבֹת זָהָב
gold ropes work-of braid chains-of the-breastpiece for and-you-make (22)

טָהוֹר׃ (23) וְעָשִׂיתָ עַל־הַחֹשֶׁן שְׁתֵּי טַבְּעוֹת זָהָב וְנָתַתָּ
and-you-fasten gold rings-of two-of the-breastpiece for and-you-make (23) pure

אֶת־שְׁתֵּי הַטַּבָּעוֹת עַל־שְׁנֵי קְצוֹת הַחֹשֶׁן׃ (24) וְנָתַתָּה
and-you-fasten (24) the-breastpiece corners-of two-of to the-rings two-of ***

אֶת־שְׁתֵּי עֲבֹתֹת הַזָּהָב עַל־שְׁתֵּי הַטַּבָּעֹת אֶל־קְצוֹת הַחֹשֶׁן׃
the-breastpiece corners-of at the-rings two-of to the-gold chains-of two-of ***

(25) וְאֵת שְׁתֵּי קְצוֹת שְׁתֵּי הָעֲבֹתֹת תִּתֵּן עַל־שְׁתֵּי הַמִּשְׁבְּצוֹת
the-settings two-of to you-fasten the-chains two-of ends-of two-of and (25)

וְנָתַתָּה עַל־כִּתְפוֹת הָאֵפֹד אֶל־מוּל פָּנָיו׃
face-of-him front at the-ephod shoulder-pieces-of to and-you-attach

(26) וְעָשִׂיתָ שְׁתֵּי טַבְּעוֹת זָהָב וְשַׂמְתָּ אֹתָם עַל־שְׁנֵי
two-of to them and-you-attach gold rings-of two-of and-you-make (26)

of pure gold, like a rope, and attach the chains to the settings.

*The Breastpiece*

15“Fashion a breastpiece for making decisions—the work of a skilled craftsman. Make it like the ephod: of gold, and of blue, purple and scarlet yarn, and of finely twisted linen. 16It is to be square—a span[y] long and a span wide—and folded double. 17Then mount four rows of precious stones on it. In the first row there shall be a ruby, a topaz and a beryl; 18in the second row a turquoise, a sapphire[z] and an emerald; 19in the third row a jacinth, an agate and an amethyst; 20in the fourth row a chrysolite, an onyx and a jasper.[a] Mount them in gold filigree settings. 21There are to be twelve stones, one for each of the names of the sons of Israel, each engraved like a seal with the name of one of the twelve tribes.

22“For the breastpiece make braided chains of pure gold, like a rope. 23Make two gold rings for it and fasten them to two corners of the breastpiece. 24Fasten the two gold chains to the rings at the corners of the breastpiece, 25and the other ends of the chains to the two settings, attaching them to the shoulder pieces of the ephod at the front. 26Make two gold rings and attach them to the

y16 That is, about 9 inches (about 22 centimeters)
z18 Or *lapis lazuli*
a20 The precise identification of some of these precious stones is uncertain.

קְצוֹת הַחֹשֶׁן עַל־ שְׂפָתוֹ אֲשֶׁר אֶל־ עֵבֶר הָאֵפֹד בָּיְתָה׃
on-inside the-ephod side-of on that edge-of-him on the-breastpiece corners-of

וְעָשִׂיתָ שְׁתֵּי טַבְּעוֹת זָהָב וְנָתַתָּה אֹתָם עַל־ שְׁתֵּי
two-of to them and-you-attach gold rings-of two-of and-you-make (27)

כִתְפוֹת הָאֵפוֹד מִלְּמַטָּה מִמּוּל פָּנָיו לְעֻמַּת
by-close-of face-of-him on-front at-bottom the-ephod shoulder-pieces-of

מֶחְבַּרְתּוֹ מִמַּעַל לְחֵשֶׁב הָאֵפוֹד׃ וְיִרְכְּסוּ אֶת־
*** and-they-shall-tie (28) the-ephod to-waistband-of just-above seam-of-him

הַחֹשֶׁן °מִטַּבְּעֹתָו אֶל־ טַבְּעֹת הָאֵפֹד בִּפְתִיל תְּכֵלֶת
blue with-cord-of the-ephod rings-of to by-rings-of-him the-breastpiece

לִהְיוֹת עַל־ חֵשֶׁב הָאֵפוֹד וְלֹא־ יִזַּח הַחֹשֶׁן
the-breastpiece he-will-swing so-not the-ephod waistband-of to to-connect

מֵעַל הָאֵפוֹד׃ וְנָשָׂא אַהֲרֹן אֶת־ שְׁמוֹת בְּנֵי־ יִשְׂרָאֵל
Israel sons-of names-of *** Aaron and-he-will-bear (29) the-ephod out-from

בְּחֹשֶׁן הַמִּשְׁפָּט עַל־ לִבּוֹ בְּבֹאוֹ אֶל־
into when-to-enter-him heart-of-him over the-decision on-breastpiece-of

הַקֹּדֶשׁ לְזִכָּרֹן לִפְנֵי־ יְהוָה תָּמִיד׃ וְנָתַתָּ אֶל־
in also-you-put (30) continual Yahweh before as-memorial the-Holy-Place

חֹשֶׁן הַמִּשְׁפָּט אֶת־ הָאוּרִים וְאֶת־ הַתֻּמִּים וְהָיוּ עַל־
over so-they-may-be the-Thummim and the-Urim *** the-decision breastpiece-of

לֵב אַהֲרֹן בְּבֹאוֹ לִפְנֵי יְהוָה וְנָשָׂא אַהֲרֹן
Aaron thus-he-will-bear Yahweh presence-of when-to-enter-him Aaron heart-of

אֶת־ מִשְׁפַּט בְּנֵי־ יִשְׂרָאֵל עַל־ לִבּוֹ לִפְנֵי יְהוָה תָּמִיד׃
always Yahweh before heart-of-him over Israel sons-of decision-maker-of ***

וְעָשִׂיתָ אֶת־ מְעִיל הָאֵפוֹד כְּלִיל תְּכֵלֶת׃
blue-cloth entirely-of the-ephod robe-of *** now-you-make (31)

וְהָיָה פִי־ רֹאשׁוֹ בְּתוֹכוֹ שָׂפָה יִהְיֶה
he-shall-be edge in-center-of-him head-of-him opening-of and-he-shall-be (32)

לְפִיו סָבִיב מַעֲשֵׂה אֹרֵג כְּפִי תַחְרָא
collar like-opening-of weaving work-of around for-opening-of-him

יִהְיֶה־ לּוֹ לֹא יִקָּרֵעַ׃ וְעָשִׂיתָ עַל־ שׁוּלָיו
hems-of-him for and-you-make (33) he-will-tear not for-him he-will-be

רִמֹּנֵי תְּכֵלֶת וְאַרְגָּמָן וְתוֹלַעַת שָׁנִי עַל־ שׁוּלָיו סָבִיב
around hems-of-him for yarn and-scarlet-of and-purple blue pomegranates-of

וּפַעֲמֹנֵי זָהָב בְּתוֹכָם סָבִיב׃ פַּעֲמֹן זָהָב וְרִמּוֹן
and-pomegranate gold bell-of (34) around between-them gold with-bells-of

פַּעֲמֹן זָהָב וְרִמּוֹן עַל־ שׁוּלֵי הַמְּעִיל סָבִיב׃ וְהָיָה
and-he-must-be (35) around the-robe hems-of on and-pomegranate gold bell-of

other two corners of the breastpiece on the inside edge next to the ephod. [27]Make two more gold rings and attach them to the bottom of the shoulder pieces on the front of the ephod, close to the seam just above the waistband of the ephod. [28]The rings of the breastpiece are to be tied to the rings of the ephod with blue cord, connecting it to the waistband, so that the breastpiece will not swing out from the ephod.

[29]"Whenever Aaron enters the Holy Place, he will bear the names of the sons of Israel over his heart on the breastpiece of decision as a continuing memorial before the LORD. [30]Also put the Urim and the Thummim in the breastpiece, so they may be over Aaron's heart whenever he enters the presence of the LORD. Thus Aaron will always bear the means of making decisions for the Israelites over his heart before the LORD.

*Other Priestly Garments*

[31]"Make the robe of the ephod entirely of blue cloth, [32]with an opening for the head in its center. There shall be a woven edge like a collar[b] around this opening, so that it will not tear. [33]Make pomegranates of blue, purple and scarlet yarn around the hem of the robe, with gold bells between them. [34]The gold bells and the pomegranates are to alternate around the hem of the robe. [35]Aaron must wear it

[b]32 The meaning of the Hebrew for this word is uncertain.

°28 ק מטבעתיו

עַל־אַהֲרֹן לְשָׁרֵת וְנִשְׁמַע קוֹלוֹ בְּבֹאוֹ אֶל־
into when-to-enter-him sound-of-him and-he-will-be-heard to-minister Aaron on

הַקֹּדֶשׁ לִפְנֵי יְהוָה וּבְצֵאתוֹ וְלֹא יָמוּת׃
he-will-die so-not and-when-to-come-out-him Yahweh before the-Holy-Place

(36) וְעָשִׂיתָ צִּיץ זָהָב טָהוֹר וּפִתַּחְתָּ עָלָיו פִּתּוּחֵי
engravings-of on-him and-you-engrave pure gold plate-of and-you-make (36)

חֹתָם קֹדֶשׁ לַיהוָה׃ (37) וְשַׂמְתָּ אֹתוֹ עַל־ פְּתִיל תְּכֵלֶת וְהָיָה
and-he-will-be blue cord-of on him and-you-fasten (37) to-Yahweh holy seal

עַל־ הַמִּצְנָפֶת אֶל־ מוּל פְּנֵי־ הַמִּצְנֶפֶת יִהְיֶה׃ (38) וְהָיָה
and-he-will-be (38) he-shall-be the-turban face-of front on the-turban on

עַל־ מֵצַח אַהֲרֹן וְנָשָׂא אַהֲרֹן אֶת־ עֲוֹן הַקֳּדָשִׁים
the-sacred-gifts guilt-of *** Aaron and-he-will-bear Aaron forehead-of on

אֲשֶׁר יַקְדִּישׁוּ בְּנֵי יִשְׂרָאֵל לְכָל־ מַתְּנֹת קָדְשֵׁיהֶם
sacred-ones-of-them gifts-of among-all-of Israel sons-of they-consecrate that

וְהָיָה עַל־ מִצְחוֹ תָּמִיד לְרָצוֹן לָהֶם
for-them to-make-acceptable continually forehead-of-him on and-he-will-be

לִפְנֵי יְהוָה׃ (39) וְשִׁבַּצְתָּ הַכְּתֹנֶת שֵׁשׁ וְעָשִׂיתָ מִצְנֶפֶת
turban and-you-make fine-linen the-tunic and-you-weave (39) Yahweh before

שֵׁשׁ וְאַבְנֵט תַּעֲשֶׂה מַעֲשֵׂה רֹקֵם׃ (40) וְלִבְנֵי אַהֲרֹן
Aaron and-for-sons-of (40) embroidering work-of you-make and-sash fine-linen

תַּעֲשֶׂה כֻתֳּנֹת וְעָשִׂיתָ לָהֶם אַבְנֵטִים וּמִגְבָּעוֹת תַּעֲשֶׂה לָהֶם
for-them you-make and-headbands sashes for-them and-you-make tunics you-make

לְכָבוֹד וּלְתִפְאָרֶת׃ (41) וְהִלְבַּשְׁתָּ אֹתָם אֶת־ אַהֲרֹן אָחִיךָ
brother-of-you Aaron *** them and-you-clothe (41) and-for-honor for-dignity

וְאֶת־ בָּנָיו אִתּוֹ וּמָשַׁחְתָּ אֹתָם וּמִלֵּאתָ אֶת־ יָדָם
hand-of-them *** and-you-ordain them and-you-anoint with-him sons-of-him and

וְקִדַּשְׁתָּ אֹתָם וְכִהֲנוּ לִי׃ (42) וַעֲשֵׂה
and-make! (42) to-me so-they-may-serve-as-priests them and-you-consecrate

לָהֶם מִכְנְסֵי־ בָד לְכַסּוֹת בְּשַׂר עֶרְוָה מִמָּתְנַיִם וְעַד־
even-to from-waists naked body-of to-cover linen undergarments-of for-them

יְרֵכַיִם יִהְיוּ׃ (43) וְהָיוּ עַל־ אַהֲרֹן וְעַל־ בָּנָיו
sons-of-him and-on Aaron on and-they-must-be (43) they-shall-reach thighs

בְּבֹאָם אֶל־ אֹהֶל מוֹעֵד אוֹ בְגִשְׁתָּם אֶל־הַמִּזְבֵּחַ
the-altar to when-to-approach-them or Meeting Tent-of into when-to-enter-them

לְשָׁרֵת בַּקֹּדֶשׁ וְלֹא־ יִשְׂאוּ עָוֹן וָמֵתוּ
and-they-die guilt they-will-incur so-not in-the-Holy-Place to-minister

חֻקַּת עוֹלָם לוֹ וּלְזַרְעוֹ אַחֲרָיו׃
after-him and-for-descendant-of-him for-him lasting ordinance-of

when he ministers. The sound of the bells will be heard when he enters the Holy Place before the LORD and when he comes out, so that he will not die.

36"Make a plate of pure gold and engrave on it as on a seal: HOLY TO THE LORD. 37Fasten a blue cord to it to attach it to the turban; it is to be on the front of the turban. 38It will be on Aaron's forehead, and he will bear the guilt involved in the sacred gifts the Israelites consecrate, whatever their gifts may be. It will be on Aaron's forehead continually so that they will be acceptable to the LORD.

39"Weave the tunic of fine linen and make the turban of fine linen. The sash is to be the work of an embroiderer. 40Make tunics, sashes and headbands for Aaron's sons, to give them dignity and honor. 41After you put these clothes on your brother Aaron and his sons, anoint and ordain them. Consecrate them so they may serve me as priests.

42"Make linen undergarments as a covering for the body, reaching from the waist to the thigh. 43Aaron and his sons must wear them whenever they enter the Tent of Meeting or approach the altar to minister in the Holy Place, so that they will not incur guilt and die.

"This is to be a lasting ordinance for Aaron and his descendants.

וְזֶה הַדָּבָר אֲשֶׁר־תַּעֲשֶׂה לָהֶם לְקַדֵּשׁ אֹתָם לְכַהֵן

to-be-priest them to-consecrate to-them you-do that the-thing now-this (29:1)

לִי לְקַח פַּר אֶחָד בֶּן־בָּקָר וְאֵילִם שְׁנַיִם תְּמִימִם׃

ones-without-defect two and-rams herd young-of one bull take! to-me

וְלֶחֶם מַצּוֹת וְחַלֹּת מַצֹּת בְּלוּלֹת

ones-being-mixed without-yeasts and-cakes-of without-yeasts and-bread-of (2)

בַּשֶּׁמֶן וּרְקִיקֵי מַצּוֹת מְשֻׁחִים בַּשָּׁמֶן

with-the-oil ones-being-spread without-yeasts and-wafers-of with-the-oil

סֹלֶת חִטִּים תַּעֲשֶׂה אֹתָם׃ וְנָתַתָּ אוֹתָם עַל־סַל אֶחָד

one basket in them and-you-put (3) them you-make fine-ones flour-of

וְהִקְרַבְתָּ אֹתָם בַּסָּל וְאֶת־הַפָּר וְאֵת שְׁנֵי הָאֵילִם׃

the-rams two-of and the-bull with in-the-basket them and-you-present

וְאֶת־אַהֲרֹן וְאֶת־בָּנָיו תַּקְרִיב אֶל־פֶּתַח אֹהֶל מוֹעֵד

Meeting Tent-of entrance-of to you-bring sons-of-him and Aaron and (4)

וְרָחַצְתָּ אֹתָם בַּמָּיִם׃ וְלָקַחְתָּ אֶת־הַבְּגָדִים

the-garments *** then-you-take (5) with-the-waters them and-you-wash

וְהִלְבַּשְׁתָּ אֶת־אַהֲרֹן אֶת־הַכֻּתֹּנֶת וְאֵת מְעִיל הָאֵפֹד וְאֶת־הָאֵפֹד

the-ephod and the-ephod robe-of and the-tunic *** Aaron *** and-you-dress

וְאֶת־הַחֹשֶׁן וְאָפַדְתָּ לוֹ בְּחֵשֶׁב הָאֵפֹד׃

the-ephod by-waistband-of on-him and-you-fasten-ephod the-breastpiece and

וְשַׂמְתָּ הַמִּצְנֶפֶת עַל־רֹאשׁוֹ וְנָתַתָּ אֶת־נֵזֶר

diadem-of *** and-you-attach head-of-him on the-turban and-you-put (6)

הַקֹּדֶשׁ עַל־הַמִּצְנָפֶת׃ וְלָקַחְתָּ אֶת־שֶׁמֶן הַמִּשְׁחָה

the-anointing oil-of *** then-you-take (7) the-turban to the-sacred

וְיָצַקְתָּ עַל־רֹאשׁוֹ וּמָשַׁחְתָּ אֹתוֹ׃ וְאֶת־בָּנָיו תַּקְרִיב

you-bring sons-of-him and (8) him and-you-anoint head-of-him on and-you-pour

וְהִלְבַּשְׁתָּם כֻּתֳּנֹת׃ וְחָגַרְתָּ אֹתָם אַבְנֵט אַהֲרֹן וּבָנָיו

and-sons-of-him Aaron sash them then-you-tie (9) tunics and-you-dress-them

וְחָבַשְׁתָּ לָהֶם מִגְבָּעֹת וְהָיְתָה לָהֶם כְּהֻנָּה

priesthood for-them and-she-will-be headbands on-them and-you-put

לְחֻקַּת עוֹלָם וּמִלֵּאתָ יַד־אַהֲרֹן וְיַד־

and-hand-of Aaron hand-of so-you-shall-ordain lasting as-ordinance-of

בָּנָיו׃ וְהִקְרַבְתָּ אֶת־הַפָּר לִפְנֵי אֹהֶל מוֹעֵד

Meeting Tent-of to-front-of the-bull *** and-you-bring (10) sons-of-him

וְסָמַךְ אַהֲרֹן וּבָנָיו אֶת־יְדֵיהֶם עַל־רֹאשׁ הַפָּר׃

the-bull head-of on hands-of-them *** and-sons-of-him Aaron and-he-shall-lay

וְשָׁחַטְתָּ אֶת־הַפָּר לִפְנֵי יְהוָה פֶּתַח אֹהֶל

Tent-of entrance-of Yahweh in-presence-of the-bull *** then-you-slaughter (11)

*Consecration of the Priests*

29 "This is what you are to do to consecrate
them, so they may serve me as priests: Take a young bull and
two rams without defect. 2And
from fine wheat flour, without yeast, make bread, and cakes
mixed with oil, and wafers
spread with oil. 3Put them in a
basket and present them in
it—along with the bull and the
two rams. 4Then bring Aaron
and his sons to the entrance to
the Tent of Meeting and wash
them with water. 5Take the
garments and dress Aaron
with the tunic, the robe of the
ephod, the ephod itself and
the breastpiece. Fasten the
ephod on him by its skillfully
woven waistband. 6Put the
turban on his head and attach
the sacred diadem to the turban. 7Take the anointing oil
and anoint him by pouring it
on his head. 8Bring his sons
and dress them in tunics 9and
put headbands on them. Then
tie sashes on Aaron and his
sons.[c] The priesthood is theirs
by a lasting ordinance. In this
way you shall ordain Aaron
and his sons.

10"Bring the bull to the front
of the Tent of Meeting, and
Aaron and his sons shall lay
their hands on its head.
11Slaughter it in the LORD's
presence at the entrance to the

[c]9 Hebrew; Septuagint *on them*

מוֹעֵד׃ וְלָקַחְתָּ מִדַּם הַפָּר וְנָתַתָּה עַל־ קַרְנֹת
horns-of on and-you-put the-bull from-blood-of and-you-take (12) Meeting

הַמִּזְבֵּחַ בְּאֶצְבָּעֶךָ וְאֶת־ כָּל־ הַדָּם תִּשְׁפֹּךְ אֶל־ יְסוֹד
base-of at you-pour-out the-blood rest-of and with-finger-of-you the-altar

הַמִּזְבֵּחַ׃ וְלָקַחְתָּ אֶת־ כָּל־ הַחֵלֶב הַמְכַסֶּה אֶת־
*** the-covering the-fat all-of *** then-you-take (13) the-altar

הַקֶּרֶב וְאֵת הַיֹּתֶרֶת עַל־ הַכָּבֵד וְאֵת שְׁתֵּי הַכְּלָיֹת וְאֶת־
and the-kidneys both-of and the-liver on the-cover and the-inner-part

הַחֵלֶב אֲשֶׁר עֲלֵיהֶן וְהִקְטַרְתָּ הַמִּזְבֵּחָה׃ וְאֶת־ בְּשַׂר
flesh-of but (14) on-the-altar and-you-burn around-them that the-fat

הַפָּר וְאֶת־ עֹרוֹ וְאֶת־ פִּרְשׁוֹ תִּשְׂרֹף בָּאֵשׁ מִחוּץ
outside with-the-fire you-burn offal-of-him and hide-of-him and the-bull

לַמַּחֲנֶה חַטָּאת הוּא׃ וְאֶת־ הָאַיִל הָאֶחָד תִּקָּח
you-take the-one the-ram and (15) he sin-offering of-the-camp

וְסָמְכוּ אַהֲרֹן וּבָנָיו אֶת־ יְדֵיהֶם עַל־ רֹאשׁ הָאָיִל׃
the-ram head-of on hands-of-them *** and-sons-of-him Aaron and-they-shall-lay

וְשָׁחַטְתָּ אֶת־ הָאָיִל וְלָקַחְתָּ אֶת־ דָּמוֹ
blood-of-him *** and-you-take the-ram *** then-you-slaughter (16)

וְזָרַקְתָּ עַל־ הַמִּזְבֵּחַ סָבִיב׃ וְאֶת־ הָאַיִל תְּנַתֵּחַ
you-cut the-ram and (17) around the-altar on and-you-sprinkle

לִנְתָחָיו וְרָחַצְתָּ קִרְבּוֹ וּכְרָעָיו וְנָתַתָּ
and-you-put and-legs-of-him inner-part-of-him and-you-wash into-pieces-of-him

עַל־ נְתָחָיו וְעַל־ רֹאשׁוֹ׃ וְהִקְטַרְתָּ אֶת־ כָּל־
entire-of *** then-you-burn (18) head-of-him and-with pieces-of-him with

הָאַיִל הַמִּזְבֵּחָה עֹלָה הוּא לַיהוָה רֵיחַ נִיחוֹחַ אִשֶּׁה
by-fire pleasant aroma-of to-Yahweh he burnt-offering on-the-altar the-ram

לַיהוָה הוּא׃ וְלָקַחְתָּ אֵת הָאַיִל הַשֵּׁנִי וְסָמַךְ אַהֲרֹן
Aaron and-he-shall-lay the-other the-ram *** then-you-take (19) he to-Yahweh

וּבָנָיו אֶת־ יְדֵיהֶם עַל־ רֹאשׁ הָאָיִל׃ וְשָׁחַטְתָּ
and-you-slaughter (20) the-ram head-of on hands-of-them *** and-sons-of-him

אֶת־ הָאַיִל וְלָקַחְתָּ מִדָּמוֹ וְנָתַתָּה עַל־ תְּנוּךְ אֹזֶן
ear-of lobe-of on and-you-put from-blood-of-him and-you-take the-ram ***

אַהֲרֹן וְעַל־ תְּנוּךְ אֹזֶן בָּנָיו הַיְמָנִית וְעַל־ בֹּהֶן
thumb-of and-on the-right sons-of-him ear-of lobe-of and-on Aaron

יָדָם הַיְמָנִית וְעַל־ בֹּהֶן רַגְלָם הַיְמָנִית
the-right foot-of-them big-toe-of and-on the-right hand-of-them

וְזָרַקְתָּ אֶת־ הַדָּם עַל־ הַמִּזְבֵּחַ סָבִיב׃ וְלָקַחְתָּ
and-you-take (21) around the-altar against the-blood *** then-you-sprinkle

Tent of Meeting. [12]Take some
of the bull's blood and put it
on the horns of the altar with
your finger, and pour out the
rest of it at the base of the altar.
[13]Then take all the fat around
the inner parts, the covering
of the liver, and both kidneys
with the fat around them, and
burn them on the altar. [14]But
burn the bull's flesh and its
hide and its offal outside the
camp. It is a sin offering.

[15]"Take one of the rams, and
Aaron and his sons shall lay
their hands on its head.
[16]Slaughter it and take the
blood and sprinkle it against
the altar on all sides. [17]Cut the
ram into pieces and wash the
inner parts and the legs, putting them with the head and
the other pieces. [18]Then burn
the entire ram on the altar. It is
a burnt offering to the LORD, a
pleasing aroma, an offering
made to the LORD by fire.

[19]"Take the other ram, and
Aaron and his sons shall lay
their hands on its head.
[20]Slaughter it, take some of its
blood and put it on the lobes of
the right ears of Aaron and his
sons, on the thumbs of their
right hands, and on the big
toes of their right feet. Then
sprinkle blood against the altar on all sides. [21]And take

מִן־ הַדָּם אֲשֶׁר עַל־הַמִּזְבֵּחַ וּמִשֶּׁמֶן הַמִּשְׁחָה וְהִזֵּיתָ
and-you-sprinkle the-anointing and-from-oil-of the-altar on that the-blood from

עַל־ אַהֲרֹן וְעַל־ בְּגָדָיו וְעַל־ בָּנָיו וְעַל־ בִּגְדֵי
garments-of and-on sons-of-him and-on garments-of-him and-on Aaron on

בָנָיו אִתּוֹ וְקָדַשׁ הוּא וּבְגָדָיו
and-garments-of-him he then-he-will-be-consecrated with-him sons-of-him

וּבָנָיו וּבִגְדֵי בָנָיו אִתּוֹ׃ וְלָקַחְתָּ מִן־
from then-you-take (22) with-him sons-of-him and-garments-of and-sons-of-him

הָאַיִל הַחֵלֶב וְהָאַלְיָה וְאֶת־ הַחֵלֶב ׀ הַמְכַסֶּה אֶת־ הַקֶּרֶב
the-inner-part *** the-covering the-fat and and-the-fat-tail the-fat the-ram

וְאֵת יֹתֶרֶת הַכָּבֵד וְאֵת ׀ שְׁתֵּי הַכְּלָיֹת וְאֶת־ הַחֵלֶב אֲשֶׁר עֲלֵיהֶן
around-them that the-fat with the-kidneys both-of and the-liver cover-of and

וְאֵת שׁוֹק הַיָּמִין כִּי אֵיל מִלֻּאִים הוּא׃ וְכִכַּר לֶחֶם
bread and-loaf-of (23) this ordinations ram-of now the-right thigh-of and

אַחַת וַחַלַּת לֶחֶם שֶׁמֶן אַחַת וְרָקִיק אֶחָד מִסַּל־ הַמַּצּוֹת
the-unleavened-breads from-basket-of one and-wafer one oil bread and-cake-of one

אֲשֶׁר לִפְנֵי יְהוָה׃ וְשַׂמְתָּ הַכֹּל עַל כַּפֵּי אַהֲרֹן וְעַל כַּפֵּי
hands-of and-in Aaron hands-of in the-all and-you-put (24) Yahweh before that

בָנָיו וְהֵנַפְתָּ אֹתָם תְּנוּפָה לִפְנֵי יְהוָה׃ וְלָקַחְתָּ
then-you-take (25) Yahweh before wave-offering them and-you-wave sons-of-him

אֹתָם מִיָּדָם וְהִקְטַרְתָּ הַמִּזְבֵּחָה עַל־ הָעֹלָה
the-burnt-offering with on-the-altar and-you-burn from-hand-of-them them

לְרֵיחַ נִיחוֹחַ לִפְנֵי יְהוָה אִשֶּׁה הוּא לַיהוָה׃ וְלָקַחְתָּ
then-you-take (26) to-Yahweh he by-fire Yahweh before pleasant for-aroma-of

אֶת־ הֶחָזֶה מֵאֵיל הַמִּלֻּאִים אֲשֶׁר לְאַהֲרֹן וְהֵנַפְתָּ אֹתוֹ
him and-you-wave for-Aaron that the-ordinations from-ram-of the-breast ***

תְּנוּפָה לִפְנֵי יְהוָה וְהָיָה לְךָ לְמָנָה׃
for-share for-you and-he-will-be Yahweh before wave-offering

וְקִדַּשְׁתָּ אֵת ׀ חֲזֵה הַתְּנוּפָה וְאֵת שׁוֹק
thigh-of and the-wave-offering breast-of *** and-you-consecrate (27)

הַתְּרוּמָה אֲשֶׁר הוּנַף וַאֲשֶׁר הוּרָם מֵאֵיל
from-ram-of he-was-presented and-that he-was-waved that the-presentation

הַמִּלֻּאִים מֵאֲשֶׁר לְאַהֲרֹן וּמֵאֲשֶׁר לְבָנָיו׃
to-sons-of-him and-from-that to-Aaron from-that the-ordinations

וְהָיָה לְאַהֲרֹן וּלְבָנָיו לְחָק־ עוֹלָם מֵאֵת בְּנֵי
sons-of from perpetual share-of and-for-sons-of-him for-Aaron and-he-will-be (28)

יִשְׂרָאֵל כִּי תְרוּמָה הוּא וּתְרוּמָה יִהְיֶה מֵאֵת בְּנֵי־יִשְׂרָאֵל
Israel sons-of from he-shall-be and-contribution he contribution for Israel

some of the blood on the altar and some of the anointing oil and sprinkle it on Aaron and his garments and on his sons and their garments. Then he and his sons and their garments will be consecrated.

22"Take from this ram the fat, the fat tail, the fat around the inner parts, the covering of the liver, both kidneys with the fat around them, and the right thigh. (This is the ram for the ordination.)
23From the basket of bread made without yeast, which is before the LORD, take a loaf, and a cake made with oil, and a wafer.
24Put all these in the hands of Aaron and his sons and wave them before the LORD as a wave offering.
25Then take them from their hands and burn them on the altar along with the burnt offering for a pleasing aroma to the LORD, an offering made to the LORD by fire.
26After you take the breast of the ram for Aaron's ordination, wave it before the LORD as a wave offering, and it will be your share.

27"Consecrate those parts of the ordination ram that belong to Aaron and his sons: the breast that was waved and the thigh that was presented.
28This is always to be the regular share from the Israelites for Aaron and his sons. It is the contribution the Israelites are

מִזִּבְחֵי שַׁלְמֵיהֶם תְּרוּמָתָם לַיהוָה׃
to-Yahweh contribution-of-them fellowship-ones-of-them from-offerings-of

(29) וּבִגְדֵי הַקֹּדֶשׁ אֲשֶׁר לְאַהֲרֹן יִהְיוּ לְבָנָיו
to-sons-of-him they-will-belong to-Aaron that the-sacred and-garments-of (29)

אַחֲרָיו לְמָשְׁחָה בָהֶם וּלְמַלֵּא־ בָם אֶת־ יָדָם׃
hand-of-them *** in-them and-to-be-ordained in-them to-be-anointed after-him

(30) שִׁבְעַת יָמִים יִלְבָּשָׁם הַכֹּהֵן תַּחְתָּיו מִבָּנָיו
from-sons-of-him succeeding-him the-priest he-shall-wear-them days seven-of (30)

אֲשֶׁר יָבֹא אֶל־ אֹהֶל מוֹעֵד לְשָׁרֵת בַּקֹּדֶשׁ׃ (31) וְאֵת
and (31) in-the-Holy-Place to-minister Meeting Tent-of into he-comes when

אֵיל הַמִּלֻּאִים תִּקָּח וּבִשַּׁלְתָּ אֶת־ בְּשָׂרוֹ בְּמָקֹם
in-place meat-of-him *** and-you-cook you-take the-ordinations ram-of

קָדֹשׁ׃ (32) וְאָכַל אַהֲרֹן וּבָנָיו אֶת־ בְּשַׂר הָאַיִל וְאֶת־
and the-ram meat-of *** and-sons-of-him Aaron and-he-shall-eat (32) sacred

הַלֶּחֶם אֲשֶׁר בַּסָּל פֶּתַח אֹהֶל מוֹעֵד׃ (33) וְאָכְלוּ
and-they-shall-eat (33) Meeting Tent-of entrance-of in-the-basket that the-bread

אֹתָם אֲשֶׁר כֻּפַּר בָּהֶם לְמַלֵּא אֶת־ יָדָם לְקַדֵּשׁ
to-consecrate hand-of-them *** to-ordain by-them he-was-atoned that them

אֹתָם וְזָר לֹא־ יֹאכַל כִּי־ קֹדֶשׁ הֵם׃ (34) וְאִם־ יִוָּתֵר
he-is-left and-if (34) they sacred for he-may-eat not but-being-other them

מִבְּשַׂר הַמִּלֻּאִים וּמִן־ הַלֶּחֶם עַד־ הַבֹּקֶר וְשָׂרַפְתָּ
then-you-burn the-morning till the-bread or-from the-ordinations from-meat-of

אֶת־ הַנּוֹתָר בָּאֵשׁ לֹא יֵאָכֵל כִּי־ קֹדֶשׁ הוּא׃
he sacred for he-may-be-eaten not with-the-fire the-remaining ***

(35) וְעָשִׂיתָ לְאַהֲרֹן וּלְבָנָיו כָּכָה כְּכֹל אֲשֶׁר־
that as-everything thus and-for-sons-of-him for-Aaron so-you-do (35)

צִוִּיתִי אֹתָכָה שִׁבְעַת יָמִים תְּמַלֵּא יָדָם׃ (36) וּפַר
and-bull-of (36) hand-of-them you-ordain days seven-of you I-commanded

חַטָּאת תַּעֲשֶׂה לַיּוֹם עַל־ הַכִּפֻּרִים וְחִטֵּאתָ
and-you-purify the-atonement for each-the-day you-sacrifice the-sin-offering

עַל־ הַמִּזְבֵּחַ בְּכַפֶּרְךָ עָלָיו וּמָשַׁחְתָּ אֹתוֹ לְקַדְּשׁוֹ׃
to-consecrate-him him and-you-anoint for-him by-to-atone-you the-altar on

(37) שִׁבְעַת יָמִים תְּכַפֵּר עַל־ הַמִּזְבֵּחַ וְקִדַּשְׁתָּ אֹתוֹ
him and-you-consecrate the-altar for you-atone days seven-of (37)

וְהָיָה הַמִּזְבֵּחַ קֹדֶשׁ קָדָשִׁים כָּל־ הַנֹּגֵעַ
the-one-touching every-of the-holy-ones holiest-of the-altar then-he-will-be

בַּמִּזְבֵּחַ יִקְדָּשׁ׃ (38) וְזֶה אֲשֶׁר תַּעֲשֶׂה עַל־ הַמִּזְבֵּחַ כְּבָשִׂים
lambs the-altar on you-offer what now-this (38) he-will-be-holy on-the-altar

to make to the LORD from their fellowship offerings.[d]

29"Aaron's sacred garments will belong to his descendants so that they can be anointed and ordained in them. 30The son who succeeds him as priest and comes to the Tent of Meeting to minister in the Holy Place is to wear them seven days.

31"Take the ram for the ordination and cook the meat in a sacred place. 32At the entrance to the Tent of Meeting, Aaron and his sons are to eat the meat of the ram and the bread that is in the basket. 33They are to eat these offerings by which atonement was made for their ordination and consecration. But no one else may eat them, because they are sacred. 34And if any of the meat of the ordination ram or any bread is left over till morning, burn it up. It must not be eaten, because it is sacred.

35"Do for Aaron and his sons everything I have commanded you, taking seven days to ordain them. 36Sacrifice a bull each day as a sin offering to make atonement. Purify the altar by making atonement for it, and anoint it to consecrate it. 37For seven days make atonement for the altar and consecrate it. Then the altar will be most holy, and whatever touches it will be holy.

38"This is what you are to offer on the altar regularly

[d]28 Traditionally *peace offerings*

בְּנֵי־ שָׁנָה שְׁנַיִם לַיּוֹם תָּמִיד׃ אֶת־ הַכֶּבֶשׂ הָאֶחָד
the-one the-lamb *** (39) regularly each-the-day two one-year sons-of

תַּעֲשֶׂה בַבֹּקֶר וְאֵת הַכֶּבֶשׂ הַשֵּׁנִי תַּעֲשֶׂה בֵּין הָעַרְבָּיִם׃
the-twilight at you-offer the-other the-lamb and in-the-morning you-offer

וְעִשָּׂרֹן סֹלֶת בָּלוּל בְּשֶׁמֶן כָּתִית רֶבַע הַהִין
the-hin fourth-of pressed with-oil being-mixed fine-flour and-tenth (40)

וְנֶסֶךְ רְבִעִית הַהִין יָיִן לַכֶּבֶשׂ הָאֶחָד׃ וְאֵת
and (41) the-first with-the-lamb wine the-hin fourth-of and-drink-offering

הַכֶּבֶשׂ הַשֵּׁנִי תַּעֲשֶׂה בֵּין הָעַרְבָּיִם כְּמִנְחַת הַבֹּקֶר
the-morning as-offering-of the-twilight at you-offer the-other the-lamb

וּכְנִסְכָּהּ תַּעֲשֶׂה־ לָּהּ לְרֵיחַ נִיחֹחַ אִשֶּׁה
by-fire pleasant for-aroma-of with-her you-offer and-as-drink-offering-of-her

לַיהוָה׃ עֹלַת תָּמִיד לְדֹרֹתֵיכֶם פֶּתַח
entrance-of for-generations-of-you continual burnt-offering-of (42) to-Yahweh

אֹהֶל־ מוֹעֵד לִפְנֵי יְהוָה אֲשֶׁר אִוָּעֵד לָכֶם שָׁמָּה לְדַבֵּר
to-speak at-there with-you I-will-meet where Yahweh before Meeting Tent-of

אֵלֶיךָ שָׁם׃ וְנֹעַדְתִּי שָׁמָּה לִבְנֵי יִשְׂרָאֵל
Israel with-sons-of at-there also-I-will-meet (43) there to-you

וְנִקְדַּשׁ בִּכְבֹדִי׃ וְקִדַּשְׁתִּי אֶת־
*** so-I-will-consecrate (44) by-glory-of-me and-he-will-be-consecrated

אֹהֶל מוֹעֵד וְאֶת־ הַמִּזְבֵּחַ וְאֶת־ אַהֲרֹן וְאֶת־ בָּנָיו אֲקַדֵּשׁ
I-will-consecrate sons-of-him and Aaron and the-altar and Meeting Tent-of

לְכַהֵן לִי׃ וְשָׁכַנְתִּי בְּתוֹךְ בְּנֵי יִשְׂרָאֵל וְהָיִיתִי
and-I-will-be Israel sons-of among then-I-will-dwell (45) to-me to-be-priest

לָהֶם לֵאלֹהִים׃ וְיָדְעוּ כִּי אֲנִי יְהוָה אֱלֹהֵיהֶם אֲשֶׁר
who God-of-them Yahweh I that then-they-will-know (46) as-God to-them

הוֹצֵאתִי אֹתָם מֵאֶרֶץ מִצְרַיִם לְשָׁכְנִי בְתוֹכָם אֲנִי יְהוָה
Yahweh I among-them so-to-dwell-me Egypt from-land-of them I-brought

אֱלֹהֵיהֶם׃ וְעָשִׂיתָ מִזְבֵּחַ מִקְטַר קְטֹרֶת עֲצֵי שִׁטִּים
acacias woods-of incense burner-of altar and-you-make (30:1) God-of-them

תַּעֲשֶׂה אֹתוֹ׃ אַמָּה אָרְכּוֹ וְאַמָּה רָחְבּוֹ רָבוּעַ
being-square width-of-him and-cubit length-of-him cubit (2) him you-make

יִהְיֶה וְאַמָּתַיִם קֹמָתוֹ מִמֶּנּוּ קַרְנֹתָיו׃
horns-of-him from-him height-of-him and-two-cubits he-shall-be

וְצִפִּיתָ אֹתוֹ זָהָב טָהוֹר אֶת־ גַּגּוֹ וְאֶת־ קִירֹתָיו סָבִיב וְאֶת־
and around sides-of-him and top-of-him *** pure gold him and-you-overlay (3)

קַרְנֹתָיו וְעָשִׂיתָ לּוֹ זֵר זָהָב סָבִיב׃ וּשְׁתֵּי
and-two-of (4) around gold molding-of for-him and-you-make horns-of-him

each day: two lambs a year old. 39Offer one in the morning and the other at twilight. 40With the first lamb offer a tenth of an ephah[f] of fine flour mixed with a fourth of a hin[g] of oil from pressed olives, and a fourth of a hin of wine as a drink offering. 41Sacrifice the other lamb at twilight with the same grain offering and its drink offering as in the morning—a pleasing aroma, an offering made to the LORD by fire.

42"For the generations to come this burnt offering is to be made regularly at the entrance to the Tent of Meeting before the LORD. There I will meet you and speak to you; 43there also I will meet with the Israelites, and the place will be consecrated by my glory.

44"So I will consecrate the Tent of Meeting and the altar and will consecrate Aaron and his sons to serve me as priests. 45Then I will dwell among the Israelites and be their God. 46They will know that I am the LORD their God, who brought them out of Egypt so that I might dwell among them. I am the LORD their God.

*The Altar of Incense*

30 "Make an altar of acacia wood for burning incense. 2It is to be square, a cubit long and a cubit wide, and two cubits high[h]—its horns of one piece with it. 3Overlay the top and all the sides and the horns with pure gold, and make a gold molding

[f]40 That is, probably about 2 quarts (about 2 liters)
[g]40 That is, probably about 1 quart (about 1 liter)
[h]2 That is, about 1 1/2 feet (about 0.5 meter) long and wide and about 3 feet (about 0.9 meter) high

טַבְּעֹת זָהָב תַּעֲשֶׂה־ לּוֹ ׀ מִתַּחַת לְזֵרוֹ עַל שְׁתֵּי
two-of on to-molding-of-him for-below for-him you-make gold rings-of

צַלְעֹתָיו תַּעֲשֶׂה עַל־ שְׁנֵי צִדָּיו וְהָיָה לְבָתִּים
as-holders and-he-shall-be sides-of-him two-of on you-make sides-of-him

לְבַדִּים לָשֵׂאת אֹתוֹ בָּהֵמָּה׃ וְעָשִׂיתָ אֶת־ הַבַּדִּים עֲצֵי
woods-of the-poles *** and-you-make (5) with-them him to-carry for-poles

שִׁטִּים וְצִפִּיתָ אֹתָם זָהָב׃ וְנָתַתָּה אֹתוֹ לִפְנֵי הַפָּרֹכֶת
the-curtain in-front-of him and-you-put (6) gold them and-you-overlay acacias

אֲשֶׁר עַל־ אֲרֹן הָעֵדֻת לִפְנֵי הַכַּפֹּרֶת אֲשֶׁר עַל־
over that the-atonement-cover before the-Testimony ark-of before that

הָעֵדֻת אֲשֶׁר אִוָּעֵד לְךָ שָׁמָּה׃ וְהִקְטִיר עָלָיו
on-him and-he-must-burn (7) at-there with-you I-will-meet where the-Testimony

אַהֲרֹן קְטֹרֶת סַמִּים בַּבֹּקֶר בַּבֹּקֶר בְּהֵיטִיבוֹ
when-to-tend-him in-the-morning in-the-morning fragrances incense-of Aaron

אֶת־ הַנֵּרֹת יַקְטִירֶנָּה׃ וּבְהַעֲלֹת אַהֲרֹן אֶת־ הַנֵּרֹת
the-lamps *** Aaron and-when-to-light (8) he-must-burn-her the-lamps ***

בֵּין הָעַרְבַּיִם* יַקְטִירֶנָּה קְטֹרֶת תָּמִיד לִפְנֵי יְהוָה
Yahweh before regularly incense he-must-burn-her the-twilight at

לְדֹרֹתֵיכֶם׃ לֹא־ תַעֲלוּ עָלָיו קְטֹרֶת זָרָה
other incense-of on-him you-offer not (9) for-generations-of-you

וְעֹלָה וּמִנְחָה וְנֶסֶךְ לֹא תִסְּכוּ עָלָיו׃
on-him you-pour not and-drink-offering or-grain-offering or-burnt-offering

וְכִפֶּר אַהֲרֹן עַל־ קַרְנֹתָיו אַחַת בַּשָּׁנָה מִדַּם
from-blood-of in-the-year once horns-of-him on Aaron and-he-shall-atone (10)

חַטַּאת הַכִּפֻּרִים אַחַת בַּשָּׁנָה יְכַפֵּר עָלָיו
with-him he-shall-atone in-the-year once the-atonements sin-offering-of

לְדֹרֹתֵיכֶם קֹדֶשׁ־ קָדָשִׁים הוּא לַיהוָה׃ וַיְדַבֵּר
then-he-spoke (11) to-Yahweh this holy-ones holiest-of for-generations-of-you

יְהוָה אֶל־ מֹשֶׁה לֵּאמֹר׃ כִּי תִשָּׂא אֶת־ רֹאשׁ בְּנֵי־ יִשְׂרָאֵל
Israel sons-of census-of *** you-take when (12) to-say Moses to Yahweh

לִפְקֻדֵיהֶם וְנָתְנוּ אִישׁ כֹּפֶר נַפְשׁוֹ לַיהוָה
to-Yahweh life-of-him ransom-of each then-they-must-pay in-countings-of-them

בִּפְקֹד אֹתָם וְלֹא־ יִהְיֶה בָהֶם נֶגֶף בִּפְקֹד אֹתָם׃
them when-to-count plague on-them he-will-come then-not them when-to-count

זֶה ׀ יִתְּנוּ כָּל־ הָעֹבֵר עַל־ הַפְּקֻדִים
the-ones-being-counted to the-one-crossing every-of they-shall-give this (13)

מַחֲצִית הַשֶּׁקֶל בְּשֶׁקֶל הַקֹּדֶשׁ עֶשְׂרִים גֵּרָה הַשֶּׁקֶל
the-shekel gerah twenty the-sanctuary by-shekel-of the-shekel half-of

around it. [4]Make two gold rings for the altar below the molding—two on opposite sides—to hold the poles used to carry it. [5]Make the poles of acacia wood and overlay them with gold. [6]Put the altar in front of the curtain that is before the ark of the Testimony—before the atonement cover that is over the Testimony—where I will meet with you.

[7]"Aaron must burn fragrant incense on the altar every morning when he tends the lamps. [8]He must burn incense again when he lights the lamps at twilight so incense will burn regularly before the LORD for the generations to come. [9]Do not offer on this altar any other incense or any burnt offering or grain offering, and do not pour a drink offering on it. [10]Once a year Aaron shall make atonement on its horns. This annual atonement must be made with the blood of the atoning sin offering for the generations to come. It is most holy to the LORD."

*Atonement Money*

[11]Then the LORD said to Moses, [12]"When you take a census of the Israelites to count them, each one must pay the LORD a ransom for his life at the time he is counted. Then no plague will come on them when you number them. [13]Each one who crosses over to those already counted is to give a half shekel,[i] according to the sanctuary shekel, which weighs twenty gerahs. This

[i]13 That is, about 1/5 ounce (about 6 grams); also in verse 15

*8 Most mss have *pathah* under the *ayin* (הָעַרְ׳).

מַחֲצִית הַשֶּׁקֶל תְּרוּמָה לַיהוָה׃ כֹּל הָעֹבֵר עַל־
to the-one-crossing every-of (14) to-Yahweh offering the-shekel half-of

הַפְּקֻדִים מִבֶּן עֶשְׂרִים שָׁנָה וָמָעְלָה יִתֵּן
he-shall-give and-upward year twenty from-son-of the-ones-being-counted

תְּרוּמַת יְהוָה׃ הֶעָשִׁיר לֹא־ יַרְבֶּה וְהַדַּל לֹא
not and-the-poor he-may-give-more not the-rich (15) Yahweh offering-of

יַמְעִיט מִמַּחֲצִית הַשָּׁקֶל לָתֵת אֶת־ תְּרוּמַת יְהוָה לְכַפֵּר
to-atone Yahweh offering-of *** to-make the-shekel than-half-of he-may-give-less

עַל־ נַפְשֹׁתֵיכֶם׃ וְלָקַחְתָּ אֶת־ כֶּסֶף הַכִּפֻּרִים מֵאֵת
from the-atonements money-of *** and-you-receive (16) lives-of-you for

בְּנֵי יִשְׂרָאֵל וְנָתַתָּ אֹתוֹ עַל־ עֲבֹדַת אֹהֶל מוֹעֵד וְהָיָה
and-he-will-be Meeting Tent-of service-of for him and-you-use Israel sons-of

לִבְנֵי יִשְׂרָאֵל לְזִכָּרוֹן לִפְנֵי יְהוָה לְכַפֵּר עַל־ נַפְשֹׁתֵיכֶם׃
lives-of-you for to-atone Yahweh before as-memorial Israel for-sons-of

וַיְדַבֵּר יְהוָה אֶל־ מֹשֶׁה לֵּאמֹר׃ וְעָשִׂיתָ כִּיּוֹר נְחֹשֶׁת
bronze basin-of now-you-make (18) to-say Moses to Yahweh then-he-spoke (17)

וְכַנּוֹ נְחֹשֶׁת לְרָחְצָה וְנָתַתָּ אֹתוֹ בֵּין־ אֹהֶל מוֹעֵד
Meeting Tent-of between him and-you-place for-to-wash bronze and-stand-of-him

וּבֵין הַמִּזְבֵּחַ וְנָתַתָּ שָׁמָּה מָיִם׃ וְרָחֲצוּ
and-they-shall-wash (19) waters in-there and-you-put the-altar and-between

אַהֲרֹן וּבָנָיו מִמֶּנּוּ אֶת־ יְדֵיהֶם וְאֶת־ רַגְלֵיהֶם׃
feet-of-them and hands-of-them *** from-him and-sons-of-him Aaron

בְּבֹאָם אֶל־ אֹהֶל מוֹעֵד יִרְחֲצוּ־ מַיִם וְלֹא
so-not waters they-shall-wash Meeting Tent-of into when-to-enter-them (20)

יָמֻתוּ אוֹ בְגִשְׁתָּם אֶל־ הַמִּזְבֵּחַ לְשָׁרֵת לְהַקְטִיר
to-present to-minister the-altar to when-to-approach-them also they-will-die

אִשֶּׁה לַיהוָה׃ וְרָחֲצוּ יְדֵיהֶם
hands-of-them and-they-shall-wash (21) to-Yahweh fire-offering

וְרַגְלֵיהֶם וְלֹא יָמֻתוּ וְהָיְתָה לָהֶם חָק־
ordinance-of for-them and-she-will-be they-will-die so-not and-feet-of-them

עוֹלָם לוֹ וּלְזַרְעוֹ לְדֹרֹתָם׃
for-generations-of-them and-for-descendant-of-him for-him lasting

וַיְדַבֵּר יְהוָה אֶל־מֹשֶׁה לֵּאמֹר׃ וְאַתָּה קַח־ לְךָ בְּשָׂמִים רֹאשׁ
fine spices to-you take! now-you (23) to-say Moses to Yahweh then-he-spoke (22)

מָר־ דְּרוֹר חֲמֵשׁ מֵאוֹת וְקִנְּמָן־ בֶּשֶׂם מַחֲצִיתוֹ חֲמִשִּׁים
fifty half-of-him fragrant and-cinnamon-of hundreds five-of liquid myrrh-of

וּמָאתַיִם וּקְנֵה־ בֹשֶׂם חֲמִשִּׁים וּמָאתָיִם׃ וְקִדָּה
and-cassia (24) and-two-hundred fifty fragrant and-cane-of and-two-hundred

half shekel is an offering to the LORD. [14]All who cross over, those twenty years old or more, are to give an offering to the LORD. [15]The rich are not to give more than a half shekel and the poor are not to give less when you make the offering to the LORD to atone for your lives. [16]Receive the atonement money from the Israelites and use it for the service of the Tent of Meeting. It will be a memorial for the Israelites before the LORD, making atonement for your lives."

*Basin for Washing*

[17]Then the LORD said to Moses, [18]"Make a bronze basin, with its bronze stand, for washing. Place it between the Tent of Meeting and the altar, and put water in it. [19]Aaron and his sons are to wash their hands and feet with water from it. [20]Whenever they enter the Tent of Meeting, they shall wash with water so that they will not die. Also, when they approach the altar to minister by presenting an offering made to the LORD by fire, [21]they shall wash their hands and feet so that they will not die. This is to be a lasting ordinance for Aaron and his descendants for the generations to come."

*Anointing Oil*

[22]Then the LORD said to Moses, [23]"Take the following fine spices: 500 shekels[j] of liquid myrrh, half as much (that is, 250 shekels) of fragrant cinnamon, 250 shekels of fragrant cane, [24]500 shekels of

j23 That is, about 12 1/2 pounds (about 6 kilograms)

חֲמֵשׁ מֵאוֹת בְּשֶׁקֶל הַקֹּדֶשׁ וְשֶׁמֶן זַיִת הִין׃
hin olive and-oil-of the-sanctuary by-shekel-of hundreds five-of

וְעָשִׂיתָ אֹתוֹ שֶׁמֶן מִשְׁחַת־ קֹדֶשׁ רֹקַח מִרְקַחַת מַעֲשֵׂה
work-of fragrant blend-of sacred anointing-of oil-of him and-you-make (25)

רֹקֵחַ שֶׁמֶן מִשְׁחַת־ קֹדֶשׁ יִהְיֶה׃ וּמָשַׁחְתָּ
then-you-anoint (26) he-will-be sacred anointing-of oil-of one-perfuming

בוֹ אֶת־ אֹהֶל מוֹעֵד וְאֵת אֲרוֹן הָעֵדֻת׃ וְאֶת־ הַשֻּׁלְחָן וְאֶת־
and the-table and (27) the-Testimony ark-of and Meeting Tent-of *** with-him

כָּל־ כֵּלָיו וְאֶת־ הַמְּנֹרָה וְאֶת־ כֵּלֶיהָ וְאֵת מִזְבַּח
altar-of and accessories-of-her and the-lampstand and articles-of-him all-of

הַקְּטֹרֶת׃ וְאֶת־ מִזְבַּח הָעֹלָה וְאֶת־ כָּל־ כֵּלָיו
utensils-of-him all-of and the-burnt-offering altar-of and (28) the-incense

וְאֶת־ הַכִּיֹּר וְאֶת־ כַּנּוֹ׃ וְקִדַּשְׁתָּ אֹתָם
them so-you-shall-consecrate (29) stand-of-him and the-basin and

וְהָיוּ קֹדֶשׁ קָדָשִׁים כָּל־ הַנֹּגֵעַ בָּהֶם
on-them the-one-touching every-of holy-ones holiest-of so-they-will-be

יִקְדָּשׁ׃ וְאֶת־ אַהֲרֹן וְאֶת־ בָּנָיו תִּמְשָׁח וְקִדַּשְׁתָּ
and-you-consecrate you-anoint sons-of-him and Aaron and (30) he-will-be-holy

אֹתָם לְכַהֵן לִי׃ וְאֶל־ בְּנֵי יִשְׂרָאֵל תְּדַבֵּר לֵאמֹר שֶׁמֶן
oil-of to-say you-speak Israel sons-of and-to (31) to-me to-be-priest them

מִשְׁחַת־ קֹדֶשׁ יִהְיֶה זֶה לִי לְדֹרֹתֵיכֶם׃ עַל־ בְּשַׂר
body-of on (32) for-generations-of-you to-me this he-is sacred anointing-of

אָדָם לֹא יִיסָךְ וּבְמַתְכֻּנְתּוֹ לֹא תַעֲשׂוּ כָּמֹהוּ קֹדֶשׁ
sacred like-him you-make not and-with-formula-of-him he-shall-pour not man

הוּא קֹדֶשׁ יִהְיֶה לָכֶם׃ אִישׁ אֲשֶׁר יִרְקַח כָּמֹהוּ וַאֲשֶׁר
or-who like-him he-mixes who anyone (33) to-you he-shall-be sacred he

יִתֵּן מִמֶּנּוּ עַל־ זָר וְנִכְרַת מֵעַמָּיו׃
from-people-of-him now-he-must-be-cut-off being-outsider on from-him he-puts

וַיֹּאמֶר יְהוָה אֶל־ מֹשֶׁה קַח־ לְךָ סַמִּים נָטָף ׀ וּשְׁחֵלֶת
and-onycha gum-resin spices to-you take! Moses to Yahweh then-he-said (34)

וְחֶלְבְּנָה סַמִּים וּלְבֹנָה זַכָּה בַּד בְּבַד יִהְיֶה׃
he-shall-be for-amount amount pure and-frankincense spices and-galbanum

וְעָשִׂיתָ אֹתָהּ קְטֹרֶת רֹקַח מַעֲשֵׂה רוֹקֵחַ מְמֻלָּח טָהוֹר
pure being-salted one-perfuming work-of blend incense her and-you-make (35)

קֹדֶשׁ׃ וְשָׁחַקְתָּ מִמֶּנָּה הָדֵק וְנָתַתָּה מִמֶּנָּה
from-her and-you-place to-be-powder from-her then-you-beat (36) sacred

לִפְנֵי הָעֵדֻת בְּאֹהֶל מוֹעֵד אֲשֶׁר אִוָּעֵד לְךָ
with-you I-will-meet where Meeting in-Tent-of the-Testimony in-front-of

cassia—all according to the sanctuary shekel—and a hin[k] of olive oil. [25]Make these into a sacred anointing oil, a fragrant blend, the work of a perfumer. It will be the sacred anointing oil. [26]Then use it to anoint the Tent of Meeting, the ark of the Testimony, [27]the table and all its articles, the lampstand and its accessories, the altar of incense, [28]the altar of burnt offering and all its utensils, and the basin with its stand. [29]You shall consecrate them so they will be most holy, and whatever touches them will be holy.

[30]"Anoint Aaron and his sons and consecrate them so they may serve me as priests. [31]Say to the Israelites, 'This is to be my sacred anointing oil for the generations to come. [32]Do not pour it on men's bodies and do not make any oil with the same formula. It is sacred, and you are to consider it sacred. [33]Whoever makes perfume like it and whoever puts it on anyone other than a priest must be cut off from his people.' "

*Incense*

[34]Then the LORD said to Moses, "Take fragrant spices—gum resin, onycha and galbanum—and pure frankincense, all in equal amounts, [35]and make a fragrant blend of incense, the work of a perfumer. It is to be salted and pure and sacred. [36]Grind some of it to powder and place it in front of the Testimony in the Tent of Meeting, where I will meet

[k]*24* That is, probably about 4 quarts (about 4 liters)

שָׁמָּה קֹדֶשׁ קָדָשִׁים תִּהְיֶה לָכֶם׃ וְהַקְּטֹרֶת אֲשֶׁר
that and-the-incense (37) to-you she-shall-be holy-ones holiest-of at-there

תַּעֲשֶׂה בְּמַתְכֻּנְתָּהּ לֹא תַעֲשׂוּ לָכֶם קֹדֶשׁ תִּהְיֶה לְךָ
to-you she-is holy for-yourselves you-make not with-formula-of-her you-make

לַיהוָה׃ אִישׁ אֲשֶׁר־יַעֲשֶׂה כָמוֹהָ לְהָרִיחַ בָּהּ
from-her to-enjoy-fragrance like-her he-makes who anyone (38) to-Yahweh

וְנִכְרַת מֵעַמָּיו׃ וַיְדַבֵּר יְהוָה אֶל־
to Yahweh then-he-spoke (31:1) from-people-of-him now-he-must-be-cut-off

מֹשֶׁה לֵּאמֹר׃ רְאֵה קָרָאתִי בְשֵׁם בְּצַלְאֵל בֶּן־ אוּרִי בֶן־ חוּר
Hur son-of Uri son-of Bezalel by-name I-chose see! (2) to-say Moses

לְמַטֵּה יְהוּדָה׃ וָאֲמַלֵּא אֹתוֹ רוּחַ אֱלֹהִים בְּחָכְמָה
with-skill God Spirit-of him and-I-filled (3) Judah from-tribe-of

וּבִתְבוּנָה וּבְדַעַת וּבְכָל־ מְלָאכָה׃ לַחְשֹׁב
to-make (4) craft and-with-all-of and-with-knowledge and-with-ability

מַחֲשָׁבֹת לַעֲשׂוֹת בַּזָּהָב וּבַכֶּסֶף וּבַנְּחֹשֶׁת׃
and-in-the-bronze and-in-the-silver in-the-gold to-work artistic-designs

וּבַחֲרֹשֶׁת אֶבֶן לְמַלֹּאת וּבַחֲרֹשֶׁת עֵץ לַעֲשׂוֹת בְּכָל־
in-all-of to-engage wood and-in-cutting-of to-set stone and-in-cutting-of (5)

מְלָאכָה׃ וַאֲנִי הִנֵּה נָתַתִּי אִתּוֹ אֵת אָהֳלִיאָב בֶּן־
son-of Oholiab *** with-him I-appointed see! and-I (6) craftsmanship

אֲחִיסָמָךְ לְמַטֵּה־ דָן וּבְלֵב כָּל־ חֲכַם־ לֵב נָתַתִּי
I-gave heart skilled-of every-of and-in-heart-of Dan from-tribe-of Ahisamach

חָכְמָה וְעָשׂוּ אֵת כָּל־אֲשֶׁר צִוִּיתִךָ׃ אֵת ׀ אֹהֶל מוֹעֵד
Meeting Tent-of *** (7) I-commanded-you that all *** so-they-can-make skill

וְאֶת־ הָאָרֹן לָעֵדֻת וְאֶת־ הַכַּפֹּרֶת אֲשֶׁר עָלָיו וְאֵת כָּל־
all-of and on-him that the-atonement-cover and of-the-Testimony the-ark and

כְּלֵי הָאֹהֶל׃ וְאֶת־ הַשֻּׁלְחָן וְאֶת־ כֵּלָיו וְאֶת־ הַמְּנֹרָה
the-lampstand and articles-of-him and the-table and (8) the-Tent furnishings-of

הַטְּהֹרָה וְאֶת־ כָּל־ כֵּלֶיהָ וְאֵת מִזְבַּח הַקְּטֹרֶת׃ וְאֶת־
and (9) the-incense altar-of and accessories-of-her all-of and the-pure

מִזְבַּח הָעֹלָה וְאֶת־ כָּל־ כֵּלָיו וְאֶת־ הַכִּיּוֹר וְאֶת־
and the-basin and utensils-of-him all-of and the-burnt-offering altar-of

כַּנּוֹ׃ וְאֵת בִּגְדֵי הַשְּׂרָד וְאֶת־ בִּגְדֵי הַקֹּדֶשׁ
the-sacred garments-of and the-woven garments-of and (10) stand-of-him

לְאַהֲרֹן הַכֹּהֵן וְאֶת־ בִּגְדֵי בָנָיו לְכַהֵן׃ וְאֵת
and (11) for-to-be-priest sons-of-him garments-of and the-priest for-Aaron

שֶׁמֶן הַמִּשְׁחָה וְאֶת־ קְטֹרֶת הַסַּמִּים לַקֹּדֶשׁ כְּכֹל
as-all for-the-Holy-Place the-fragrances incense-of and the-anointing oil-of

with you. It shall be most holy to you. 37Do not make any incense with this formula for yourselves; consider it holy to the LORD. 38Whoever makes any like it to enjoy its fragrance must be cut off from his people."

*Bezalel and Oholiab*

31 Then the LORD said to Moses, 2"See, I have chosen Bezalel son of Uri, the son of Hur, of the tribe of Judah, 3and I have filled him with the Spirit of God, with skill, ability and knowledge in all kinds of crafts— 4to make artistic designs for work in gold, silver and bronze, 5to cut and set stones, to work in wood, and to engage in all kinds of craftsmanship. 6Moreover, I have appointed Oholiab son of Ahisamach, of the tribe of Dan, to help him. Also I have given skill to all the craftsmen to make everything I have commanded you: 7the Tent of Meeting, the ark of the Testimony with the atonement cover on it, and all the other furnishings of the tent— 8the table and its articles, the pure gold lampstand and all its accessories, the altar of incense, 9the altar of burnt offering and all its utensils, the basin with its stand— 10and also the woven garments, both the sacred garments for Aaron the priest and the garments for his sons when they serve as priests, 11and the anointing oil and fragrant incense for the Holy Place. They are to make

אֲשֶׁר־ צִוִּיתִךָ יַעֲשׂוּ׃ וַיֹּאמֶר יְהוָה אֶל־ מֹשֶׁה
Moses to Yahweh then-he-said (12) they-will-make I-commanded-you that

לֵּאמֹר׃ וְאַתָּה דַּבֵּר אֶל־ בְּנֵי יִשְׂרָאֵל לֵאמֹר אַךְ אֶת־ שַׁבְּתֹתַי
Sabbaths-of-me *** surely to-say Israel sons-of to speak! now-you (13) to-say

תִּשְׁמֹרוּ כִּי אוֹת הִוא בֵּינִי וּבֵינֵיכֶם
and-between-you between-me this sign for you-must-observe

לְדֹרֹתֵיכֶם לָדַעַת כִּי אֲנִי יְהוָה מְקַדִּשְׁכֶם׃
one-making-holy-you Yahweh I that to-know for-generations-of-you

וּשְׁמַרְתֶּם אֶת־ הַשַּׁבָּת כִּי קֹדֶשׁ הִוא לָכֶם מְחַלְלֶיהָ
one-desecrating-her to-you she holy for the-Sabbath *** so-you-observe (14)

מוֹת יוּמָת כִּי כָּל־ הָעֹשֶׂה בָהּ מְלָאכָה וְנִכְרְתָה
now-she-must-be-cut work on-her the-one-doing every-of also he-must-die to-die

הַנֶּפֶשׁ הַהִוא מִקֶּרֶב עַמֶּיהָ׃ שֵׁשֶׁת יָמִים יֵעָשֶׂה
he-may-be-done days six-of (15) people-of-her from-among the-that the-person

מְלָאכָה וּבַיּוֹם הַשְּׁבִיעִי שַׁבַּת שַׁבָּתוֹן קֹדֶשׁ לַיהוָה כָּל־
every-of to-Yahweh holy rest Sabbath-of the-seventh but-on-the-day work

הָעֹשֶׂה מְלָאכָה בְּיוֹם הַשַּׁבָּת מוֹת יוּמָת׃
he-must-die to-die the-Sabbath on-day-of work the-one-doing

וְשָׁמְרוּ בְנֵי־ יִשְׂרָאֵל אֶת־ הַשַּׁבָּת לַעֲשׂוֹת אֶת־
*** to-celebrate the-Sabbath *** Israel sons-of so-they-must-observe (16)

הַשַּׁבָּת לְדֹרֹתָם בְּרִית עוֹלָם׃ בֵּינִי
between-me (17) lasting covenant-of for-generations-of-them the-Sabbath

וּבֵין בְּנֵי יִשְׂרָאֵל אוֹת הִוא לְעֹלָם כִּי־ שֵׁשֶׁת יָמִים עָשָׂה יְהוָה
Yahweh he-made days six-of for for-ever she sign Israel sons-of and-between

אֶת־ הַשָּׁמַיִם וְאֶת־ הָאָרֶץ וּבַיּוֹם הַשְּׁבִיעִי שָׁבַת
he-stopped-work the-seventh and-on-the-day the-earth and the-heavens ***

וַיִּנָּפַשׁ׃ וַיִּתֵּן אֶל־ מֹשֶׁה כְּכַלֹּתוֹ לְדַבֵּר אִתּוֹ
to-him to-speak when-to-finish-him Moses to and-he-gave (18) and-he-rested

בְּהַר סִינַי שְׁנֵי לֻחֹת הָעֵדֻת לֻחֹת אֶבֶן
stone tablets-of the-Testimony tablets-of two-of Sinai on-Mount-of

כְּתֻבִים בְּאֶצְבַּע אֱלֹהִים׃ וַיַּרְא הָעָם כִּי־
that the-people when-he-saw (32:1) God by-finger-of being-inscribed

בֹשֵׁשׁ מֹשֶׁה לָרֶדֶת מִן־ הָהָר וַיִּקָּהֵל הָעָם
the-people then-he-gathered the-mountain from to-come-down Moses he-took-long

עַל־ אַהֲרֹן וַיֹּאמְרוּ אֵלָיו קוּם ׀ עֲשֵׂה־ לָנוּ אֱלֹהִים אֲשֶׁר יֵלְכוּ
they-will-go who gods for-us make! come! to-him and-they-said Aaron around

לְפָנֵינוּ כִּי־ זֶה ׀ מֹשֶׁה הָאִישׁ אֲשֶׁר הֶעֱלָנוּ מֵאֶרֶץ מִצְרָיִם
Egypt from-land-of he-brought-us who the-fellow Moses this for before-us

them just as I commanded you."

*The Sabbath*

[12]Then the LORD said to Moses, [13]"Say to the Israelites, 'You must observe my Sabbaths. This will be a sign between me and you for the generations to come, so you may know that I am the LORD, who makes you holy.[l]

[14]" 'Observe the Sabbath, because it is holy to you. Anyone who desecrates it must be put to death; whoever does any work on that day must be cut off from his people. [15]For six days work is to be done, but the seventh day is a Sabbath of rest, holy to the LORD. Whoever does any work on the Sabbath day must be put to death. [16]The Israelites are to observe the Sabbath, celebrating it for the generations to come as a lasting covenant. [17]It will be a sign between me and the Israelites forever, for in six days the LORD made the heavens and the earth, and on the seventh day he abstained from work and rested.' "

[18]When the LORD finished speaking to Moses on Mount Sinai, he gave him the two tablets of the Testimony, the tablets of stone inscribed by the finger of God.

*The Golden Calf*

32 When the people saw that Moses was so long in coming down from the mountain, they gathered around Aaron and said, "Come, make us gods[m] who will go before us. As for this fellow Moses who brought us up out of Egypt, we don't

[l]13 Or *who sanctifies you;* or *who sets you apart as holy*
[m]1 Or *a god;* also in verses 23 and 31

לֹא יָדַעְנוּ מֶה־ הָיָה לוֹ׃ וַיֹּאמֶר אֲלֵהֶם אַהֲרֹן פָּרְקוּ
take-off! Aaron to-them and-he-said (2) to-him he-happened what we-know not

נִזְמֵי הַזָּהָב אֲשֶׁר בְּאָזְנֵי נְשֵׁיכֶם בְּנֵיכֶם
sons-of-you wives-of-you in-ears-of that the-gold earrings-of

וּבְנֹתֵיכֶם וְהָבִיאוּ אֵלָי׃ וַיִּתְפָּרְקוּ כָּל־ הָעָם
the-people all-of so-they-took-off (3) to-me and-bring! and-daughters-of-you

אֶת־ נִזְמֵי הַזָּהָב אֲשֶׁר בְּאָזְנֵיהֶם וַיָּבִיאוּ אֶל־ אַהֲרֹן׃
Aaron to and-they-brought in-ears-of-them that the-gold earrings-of ***

וַיִּקַּח מִיָּדָם וַיָּצַר אֹתוֹ בַּחֶרֶט
with-the-tool him and-he-fashioned from-hand-of-them and-he-took (4)

וַיַּעֲשֵׂהוּ עֵגֶל מַסֵּכָה וַיֹּאמְרוּ אֵלֶּה אֱלֹהֶיךָ יִשְׂרָאֵל אֲשֶׁר
who Israel gods-of-you these then-they-said cast calf-of and-he-make-him

הֶעֱלוּךָ מֵאֶרֶץ מִצְרָיִם׃ וַיַּרְא אַהֲרֹן וַיִּבֶן
then-he-built Aaron when-he-saw (5) Egypt from-land-of they-brought-you

מִזְבֵּחַ לְפָנָיו וַיִּקְרָא אַהֲרֹן וַיֹּאמַר חַג לַיהוָה
to-Yahweh festival and-he-said Aaron and-he-announced in-front-of-him altar

מָחָר׃ וַיַּשְׁכִּימוּ מִמָּחֳרָת וַיַּעֲלוּ עֹלֹת
burnt-offerings and-they-sacrificed on-next-day so-they-rose-early (6) tomorrow

וַיַּגִּשׁוּ שְׁלָמִים וַיֵּשֶׁב הָעָם לֶאֱכֹל
to-eat the-people and-he-sat fellowship-offerings and-they-presented

וְשָׁתוֹ וַיָּקֻמוּ לְצַחֵק׃ וַיְדַבֵּר יְהוָה אֶל־ מֹשֶׁה לֶךְ־
go! Moses to Yahweh then-he-said (7) to-revel and-they-got-up and-to-drink

רֵד כִּי שִׁחֵת עַמְּךָ אֲשֶׁר הֶעֱלֵיתָ מֵאֶרֶץ
from-land-of you-brought whom people-of-you he-became-corrupt for descend!

מִצְרָיִם׃ סָרוּ מַהֵר מִן־ הַדֶּרֶךְ אֲשֶׁר צִוִּיתִם עָשׂוּ
they-made I-commanded-them that the-way from quickly they-turned (8) Egypt

לָהֶם עֵגֶל מַסֵּכָה וַיִּשְׁתַּחֲווּ־ לוֹ וַיִּזְבְּחוּ־ לוֹ
to-him and-they-sacrificed to-him and-they-bowed cast calf-of for-themselves

וַיֹּאמְרוּ אֵלֶּה אֱלֹהֶיךָ יִשְׂרָאֵל אֲשֶׁר הֶעֱלוּךָ מֵאֶרֶץ
from-land-of they-brought-you who Israel gods-of-you these and-they-said

מִצְרָיִם׃ וַיֹּאמֶר יְהוָה אֶל־ מֹשֶׁה רָאִיתִי אֶת־ הָעָם הַזֶּה וְהִנֵּה
and-see! the-this the-people *** I-saw Moses to Yahweh and-he-said (9) Egypt

עַם־ קְשֵׁה־ עֹרֶף הוּא׃ וְעַתָּה הַנִּיחָה לִּי וְיִחַר־
so-he-may-burn to-me leave-alone! and-now (10) he neck stiff-of people-of

אַפִּי בָהֶם וַאֲכַלֵּם וְאֶעֱשֶׂה אוֹתְךָ
you then-I-will-make so-I-may-destroy-them against-them anger-of-me

לְגוֹי גָּדוֹל׃ וַיְחַל מֹשֶׁה אֶת־ פְּנֵי יְהוָה אֱלֹהָיו
God-of-him Yahweh face-of *** Moses then-he-sought (11) great into-nation

know what has happened to
him."
2Aaron answered them,
"Take off the gold earrings
that your wives, your sons and
your daughters are wearing,
and bring them to me." 3So all
the people took off their earrings and brought them to
Aaron. 4He took what they
handed him and made it into
an idol cast in the shape of a
calf, fashioning it with a tool.
Then they said, "These are
your gods,[n] O Israel, who
brought you up out of Egypt."
5When Aaron saw this, he
built an altar in front of the
calf and announced, "Tomorrow there will be a festival to
the LORD." 6So the next day the
people rose early and sacrificed burnt offerings and
presented fellowship of-
ferings.[o] Afterward they sat
down to eat and drink and got
up to indulge in revelry.
7Then the LORD said to
Moses, "Go down, because
your people, whom you
brought up out of Egypt, have
become corrupt. 8They have
been quick to turn away from
what I commanded them and
have made themselves an idol
cast in the shape of a calf. They
have bowed down to it and
sacrificed to it and have said,
'These are your gods, O Israel,
who brought you up out of
Egypt.'
9"I have seen these people,"
the LORD said to Moses, "and
they are a stiff-necked people.
10Now leave me alone so that
my anger may burn against
them and that I may destroy
them. Then I will make you
into a great nation."
11But Moses sought the favor
of the LORD his God. "O

[n]4 Or *This is your god;* also in verse 8
[o]6 Traditionally *peace offerings*

וַיֹּאמֶר לָמָה יְהוָה יֶחֱרֶה אַפְּךָ בְּעַמֶּךָ

against-people-of-you anger-of-you should-he-burn Yahweh why? and-he-said

אֲשֶׁר הוֹצֵאתָ מֵאֶרֶץ מִצְרַיִם בְּכֹחַ גָּדוֹל וּבְיָד חֲזָקָה׃

mighty and-with-hand great with-power Egypt from-land-of you-brought whom

לָמָּה יֹאמְרוּ מִצְרַיִם לֵאמֹר בְּרָעָה הוֹצִיאָם

he-brought-them with-evil-intent to-say Egyptians should-they-say why? (12)

לַהֲרֹג אֹתָם בֶּהָרִים וּלְכַלֹּתָם מֵעַל פְּנֵי הָאֲדָמָה

the-earth face-of from-on and-to-wipe-them in-the-mountains them to-kill

שׁוּב מֵחֲרוֹן אַפֶּךָ וְהִנָּחֵם עַל־ הָרָעָה

the-disaster from and-relent! anger-of-you from-fierceness-of turn!

לְעַמֶּךָ׃ זְכֹר לְאַבְרָהָם לְיִצְחָק וּלְיִשְׂרָאֵל

and-to-Israel to-Isaac to-Abraham remember! (13) on-people-of-you

עֲבָדֶיךָ אֲשֶׁר נִשְׁבַּעְתָּ לָהֶם בָּךְ וַתְּדַבֵּר אֲלֵהֶם

to-them and-you-said by-yourself to-them you-swore whom servants-of-you

אַרְבֶּה אֶת־ זַרְעֲכֶם כְּכוֹכְבֵי הַשָּׁמָיִם וְכָל־ הָאָרֶץ

the-land and-all-of the-skies as-stars-of descendant-of-you *** I-will-increase

הַזֹּאת אֲשֶׁר אָמַרְתִּי אֶתֵּן לְזַרְעֲכֶם וְנָחֲלוּ

and-they-will-inherit to-descendant-of-you I-will-give I-promised that the-this

לְעֹלָם׃ וַיִּנָּחֶם יְהוָה עַל־ הָרָעָה אֲשֶׁר דִּבֶּר

he-threatened that the-disaster from Yahweh then-he-relented (14) for-ever

לַעֲשׂוֹת לְעַמּוֹ׃ וַיִּפֶן וַיֵּרֶד מֹשֶׁה מִן־

from Moses and-he-went-down then-he-turned (15) on-people-of-him to-bring

הָהָר וּשְׁנֵי לֻחֹת הָעֵדֻת בְּיָדוֹ לֻחֹת

tablets in-hand-of-him the-Testimony tablets-of with-two-of the-mountain

כְּתֻבִים מִשְּׁנֵי עֶבְרֵיהֶם מִזֶּה וּמִזֶּה הֵם

they and-on-that on-this sides-of-them on-both-of ones-being-inscribed

כְּתֻבִים׃ וְהַלֻּחֹת מַעֲשֵׂה אֱלֹהִים הֵמָּה וְהַמִּכְתָּב

and-the-writing they God work-of now-the-tablets (16) ones-being-inscribed

מִכְתַּב אֱלֹהִים הוּא חָרוּת עַל־ הַלֻּחֹת׃ וַיִּשְׁמַע יְהוֹשֻׁעַ

Joshua when-he-heard (17) the-tablets on being-engraved he God writing-of

אֶת־ קוֹל הָעָם בְּרֵעֹה וַיֹּאמֶר אֶל־ מֹשֶׁה קוֹל

sound-of Moses to then-he-said in-shout-of-him the-people sound-of ***

מִלְחָמָה בַּמַּחֲנֶה׃ וַיֹּאמֶר אֵין קוֹל עֲנוֹת גְּבוּרָה

victory to-shout sound-of he-is-not but-he-replied (18) in-the-camp war

וְאֵין קוֹל עֲנוֹת חֲלוּשָׁה קוֹל עַנּוֹת אָנֹכִי שֹׁמֵעַ׃

hearing I to-sing sound-of defeat to-shout sound-of and-he-is-not

וַיְהִי כַּאֲשֶׁר קָרַב אֶל־ הַמַּחֲנֶה וַיַּרְא אֶת־ הָעֵגֶל

the-calf *** and-he-saw the-camp to he-approached when and-he-was (19)

LORD," he said, "why should your anger burn against your people, whom you brought out of Egypt with great power and a mighty hand? [12]Why should the Egyptians say, 'It was with evil intent that he brought them out, to kill them in the mountains and to wipe them off the face of the earth'? Turn from your fierce anger; relent and do not bring disaster on your people. [13]Remember your servants Abraham, Isaac and Israel, to whom you swore by your own self: 'I will make your descendants as numerous as the stars in the sky and I will give your descendants all this land I promised them, and it will be their inheritance forever.' " [14]Then the LORD relented and did not bring on his people the disaster he had threatened.

[15]Moses turned and went down the mountain with the two tablets of the Testimony in his hands. They were inscribed on both sides, front and back. [16]The tablets were the work of God; the writing was the writing of God, engraved on the tablets.

[17]When Joshua heard the noise of the people shouting, he said to Moses, "There is the sound of war in the camp."

[18]Moses replied:

"It is not the sound of victory,
it is not the sound of defeat;
it is the sound of singing that I hear."

[19]When Moses approached the camp and saw the calf and

*17 Most mss have the accent *silluq* at the end of the final word ( נֶה־ ).

°17 ק ברעו

וּמְחֹלֹת וַיִּחַר־ אַף מֹשֶׁה וַיַּשְׁלֵךְ מִיָּדָו° אֶת־
*** from-hand-of-him and-he-threw Moses anger-of then-he-burned and-dances

הַלֻּחֹת וַיְשַׁבֵּר אֹתָם תַּחַת הָהָר׃ וַיִּקַּח אֶת־
*** and-he-took (20) the-mountain at-foot-of them and-he-broke the-tablets

הָעֵגֶל אֲשֶׁר עָשׂוּ וַיִּשְׂרֹף בָּאֵשׁ וַיִּטְחַן עַד אֲשֶׁר־
*** to and-he-ground in-the-fire and-he-burned they-made that the-calf

דָּק וַיִּזֶר עַל־ פְּנֵי הַמַּיִם וַיַּשְׁקְ אֶת־
*** and-he-made-drink the-waters surface-of on and-he-scattered powder

בְּנֵי יִשְׂרָאֵל׃ וַיֹּאמֶר מֹשֶׁה אֶל־ אַהֲרֹן מֶה־ עָשָׂה לְךָ
to-you he-did what? Aaron to Moses then-he-said (21) Israel sons-of

הָעָם הַזֶּה כִּי־ הֵבֵאתָ עָלָיו חֲטָאָה גְדֹלָה׃ וַיֹּאמֶר
and-he-answered (22) great sin into-him you-led that the-this the-people

אַהֲרֹן אַל־ יִחַר אַף אֲדֹנִי אַתָּה יָדַעְתָּ אֶת־ הָעָם כִּי
how the-people *** you-know you lord-of-me anger-of may-he-burn not Aaron

בְרָע הוּא׃ וַיֹּאמְרוּ לִי עֲשֵׂה־ לָנוּ אֱלֹהִים אֲשֶׁר יֵלְכוּ
they-will-go who gods for-us make! to-me and-they-said (23) he prone-to-evil

לְפָנֵינוּ כִּי־ זֶה מֹשֶׁה הָאִישׁ אֲשֶׁר הֶעֱלָנוּ מֵאֶרֶץ מִצְרַיִם
Egypt from-land-of he-brought-us who the-fellow Moses this for before-us

לֹא יָדַעְנוּ מֶה־ הָיָה לוֹ׃ וָאֹמַר לָהֶם לְמִי זָהָב
gold to-whom to-them so-I-told (24) to-him he-happened what we-know not

הִתְפָּרָקוּ וַיִּתְּנוּ־ לִי וָאַשְׁלִכֵהוּ בָאֵשׁ וַיֵּצֵא
and-he-came-out into-the-fire and-I-threw-him to-me then-they-gave take-off!

הָעֵגֶל הַזֶּה׃ וַיַּרְא מֹשֶׁה אֶת־ הָעָם כִּי פָרֻעַ הוּא
he running-wild that the-people *** Moses and-he-saw (25) the-this the-calf

כִּי־ פְרָעֹה אַהֲרֹן לְשִׁמְצָה בְּקָמֵיהֶם׃
to-ones-opposing-them into-laughingstock Aaron he-let-run-wild-him for

וַיַּעֲמֹד מֹשֶׁה בְּשַׁעַר הַמַּחֲנֶה וַיֹּאמֶר מִי לַיהוָה
for-Yahweh whoever and-he-said the-camp at-entrance-of Moses so-he-stood (26)

אֵלָי וַיֵּאָסְפוּ אֵלָיו כָּל־ בְּנֵי לֵוִי׃ וַיֹּאמֶר לָהֶם
to-them then-he-said (27) Levi sons-of all-of to-him and-they-rallied to-me

כֹּה־ אָמַר יְהוָה אֱלֹהֵי יִשְׂרָאֵל שִׂימוּ אִישׁ־ חַרְבּוֹ עַל־ יְרֵכוֹ
side-of-him to sword-of-him each strap! Israel God-of Yahweh he-says this

עִבְרוּ וָשׁוּבוּ מִשַּׁעַר לָשַׁעַר בַּמַּחֲנֶה וְהִרְגוּ אִישׁ־אֶת־
*** each and-kill! through-the-camp to-end from-end and-go-forth! go-back!

אָחִיו וְאִישׁ אֶת־ רֵעֵהוּ וְאִישׁ אֶת־ קְרֹבוֹ׃
neighbor-of-him *** and-each friend-of-him *** and-each brother-of-him

וַיַּעֲשׂוּ בְנֵי־ לֵוִי כִּדְבַר מֹשֶׁה וַיִּפֹּל מִן־ הָעָם
the-people from and-he-died Moses as-command-of Levi sons-of and-they-did (28)

the dancing, his anger burned and he threw the tablets out of his hands, breaking them to pieces at the foot of the mountain. [20]And he took the calf they had made and burned it in the fire; then he ground it to powder, scattered it on the water and made the Israelites drink it.

[21]He said to Aaron, "What did these people do to you, that you led them into such great sin?"

[22]"Do not be angry, my lord," Aaron answered. "You know how prone these people are to evil. [23]They said to me, 'Make us gods who will go before us. As for this fellow Moses who brought us up out of Egypt, we don't know what has happened to him.' [24]So I told them, 'Whoever has any gold jewelry, take it off.' Then they gave me the gold, and I threw it into the fire, and out came this calf!"

[25]Moses saw that the people were running wild and that Aaron had let them get out of control and so become a laughingstock to their enemies. [26]So he stood at the entrance to the camp and said, "Whoever is for the LORD, come to me." And all the Levites rallied to him.

[27]Then he said to them, "This is what the LORD, the God of Israel, says: 'Each man strap a sword to his side. Go back and forth through the camp from one end to the other, each killing his brother and friend and neighbor.' " [28]The Levites did as Moses commanded, and that day about

°19 ק מידיו

בַּיּוֹם הַהוּא כִּשְׁלֹשֶׁת אַלְפֵי אִישׁ׃ וַיֹּאמֶר
then-he-said (29) people thousands-of about-three-of the-that on-the-day

מֹשֶׁה מִלְאוּ יֶדְכֶם הַיּוֹם לַיהוָה כִּי אִישׁ בִּבְנוֹ
against-son-of-him each for to-Yahweh the-day hand-of-you they-set-apart Moses

וּבְאָחִיו וְלָתֵת עֲלֵיכֶם הַיּוֹם בְּרָכָה׃ וַיְהִי
and-he-was (30) blessing the-day to-you to-give and-against-brother-of-him

מִמָּחֳרָת וַיֹּאמֶר מֹשֶׁה אֶל־הָעָם אַתֶּם חֲטָאתֶם חֲטָאָה גְדֹלָה
great sin you-sinned you the-people to Moses that-he-said on-next-day

וְעַתָּה אֶעֱלֶה אֶל־יְהוָה אוּלַי אֲכַפְּרָה בְּעַד חַטַּאתְכֶם׃
sin-of-you for I-can-atone perhaps Yahweh to I-will-go-up but-now

וַיָּשָׁב מֹשֶׁה אֶל־יְהוָה וַיֹּאמַר אָנָּא חָטָא הָעָם
the-people he-sinned oh! and-he-said Yahweh to Moses so-he-went-back (31)

הַזֶּה חֲטָאָה גְדֹלָה וַיַּעֲשׂוּ לָהֶם אֱלֹהֵי זָהָב׃ וְעַתָּה
but-now (32) gold gods-of for-themselves for-they-made great sin the-this

אִם־תִּשָּׂא חַטָּאתָם וְאִם־אַיִן מְחֵנִי נָא מִסִּפְרְךָ
from-book-of-you now! blot-out-me! not but-if sin-of-them you-forgive please

אֲשֶׁר כָּתָבְתָּ׃ וַיֹּאמֶר יְהוָה אֶל־מֹשֶׁה מִי אֲשֶׁר חָטָא־
he-sinned ever who Moses to Yahweh and-he-replied (33) you-wrote that

לִי אֶמְחֶנּוּ מִסִּפְרִי׃ וְעַתָּה לֵךְ ׀ נְחֵה אֶת־
*** lead! go! and-now (34) from-book-of-me I-will-blot-out-him against-me

הָעָם אֶל אֲשֶׁר־דִּבַּרְתִּי לָךְ הִנֵּה מַלְאָכִי יֵלֵךְ לְפָנֶיךָ
before-you he-will-go angel-of-me see! to-you I-spoke where to the-people

וּבְיוֹם פָּקְדִי וּפָקַדְתִּי עֲלֵיהֶם חַטָּאתָם׃
sin-of-them on-them then-I-will-punish to-punish-me but-in-day-of

וַיִּגֹּף יְהוָה אֶת־הָעָם עַל אֲשֶׁר עָשׂוּ אֶת־הָעֵגֶל אֲשֶׁר
that the-calf with they-did what for the-people *** Yahweh then-he-plagued (35)

עָשָׂה אַהֲרֹן׃ וַיְדַבֵּר יְהוָה אֶל־מֹשֶׁה לֵךְ עֲלֵה מִזֶּה אַתָּה
you from-here leave! go! Moses to Yahweh then-he-said (33:1) Aaron he-made

וְהָעָם אֲשֶׁר הֶעֱלִיתָ מֵאֶרֶץ מִצְרָיִם אֶל־הָאָרֶץ אֲשֶׁר נִשְׁבַּעְתִּי
I-swore that the-land to Egypt from-land-of you-brought whom and-the-people

לְאַבְרָהָם לְיִצְחָק וּלְיַעֲקֹב לֵאמֹר לְזַרְעֲךָ אֶתְּנֶנָּה׃
I-will-give-her to-descendant-of-you to-say and-to-Jacob to-Isaac to-Abraham

וְשָׁלַחְתִּי לְפָנֶיךָ מַלְאָךְ וְגֵרַשְׁתִּי אֶת־הַכְּנַעֲנִי
the-Canaanite *** and-I-will-drive-out angel before-you and-I-will-send (2)

הָאֱמֹרִי וְהַחִתִּי וְהַפְּרִזִּי הַחִוִּי וְהַיְבוּסִי׃
and-the-Jebusite the-Hivite and-the-Perizzite and-the-Hittite the-Amorite

אֶל־אֶרֶץ זָבַת חָלָב וּדְבָשׁ כִּי לֹא אֶעֱלֶה בְּקִרְבְּךָ כִּי
for among-you I-will-go-up not but and-honey milk flowing-of land to (3)

three thousand of the people died. 29 Then Moses said, "You have been set apart to the LORD today, for you were against your own sons and brothers, and he has blessed you this day."

30 The next day Moses said to the people, "You have committed a great sin. But now I will go up to the LORD; perhaps I can make atonement for your sin."

31 So Moses went back to the LORD and said, "Oh, what a great sin these people have committed! They have made themselves gods of gold. 32 But now, please forgive their sin—but if not, then blot me out of the book you have written."

33 The LORD replied to Moses, "Whoever has sinned against me I will blot out of my book. 34 Now go, lead the people to the place I spoke of, and my angel will go before you. However, when the time comes for me to punish, I will punish them for their sin."

35 And the LORD struck the people with a plague because of what they did with the calf Aaron had made.

33 Then the LORD said to Moses, "Leave this place, you and the people you brought up out of Egypt, and go up to the land I promised on oath to Abraham, Isaac and Jacob, saying, 'I will give it to your descendants.' 2 I will send an angel before you and drive out the Canaanites, Amorites, Hittites, Perizzites, Hivites and Jebusites. 3 Go up to the land flowing with milk and honey. But I will not go with

עַם־ קְשֵׁה־ עֹרֶף אַתָּה פֶּן־ אֲכֶלְךָ בַּדָּרֶךְ׃ וַיִּשְׁמַע

when-he-heard (4) on-the-way I-destroy-you lest you neck stiff-of people-of

הָעָם אֶת־ הַדָּבָר הָרָע הַזֶּה וַיִּתְאַבָּלוּ וְלֹא־

and-not then-they-mourned the-this the-distressing the-word *** the-people

שָׁתוּ אִישׁ עֶדְיוֹ עָלָיו׃ וַיֹּאמֶר יְהוָה אֶל־מֹשֶׁה אֱמֹר

tell! Moses to Yahweh for-he-said (5) on-him ornament-of-him anyone they-put

אֶל־בְּנֵי־ יִשְׂרָאֵל אַתֶּם עַם־ קְשֵׁה־ עֹרֶף רֶגַע אֶחָד אֶעֱלֶה בְקִרְבְּךָ

among-you if-I-went one moment neck stiff-of people-of you Israel sons-of to

וְכִלִּיתִיךָ וְעַתָּה הוֹרֵד עֶדְיְךָ מֵעָלֶיךָ

from-on-you ornament-of-you take-off! and-now then-I-might-destroy-you

וְאֵדְעָה מָה אֶעֱשֶׂה־ לָּךְ׃ וַיִּתְנַצְּלוּ בְנֵי־

sons-of so-they-stripped-off (6) with-you I-will-do what and-I-will-decide

יִשְׂרָאֵל אֶת־ עֶדְיָם מֵהַר חוֹרֵב׃ וּמֹשֶׁה יִקַּח אֶת־

*** he-took now-Moses (7) Horeb at-Mount-of ornament-of-them *** Israel

הָאֹהֶל וְנָטָה־ לוֹ ׀ מִחוּץ לַמַּחֲנֶה הַרְחֵק מִן־

from to-be-distant of-the-camp outside for-him and-he-pitched the-tent

הַמַּחֲנֶה וְקָרָא לוֹ אֹהֶל מוֹעֵד וְהָיָה כָּל־ מְבַקֵּשׁ

inquiring every-of and-he-was meeting tent-of to-him and-he-called the-camp

יְהוָה יֵצֵא אֶל־ אֹהֶל מוֹעֵד אֲשֶׁר מִחוּץ לַמַּחֲנֶה׃ וְהָיָה

and-he-was (8) of-the-camp outside that meeting tent-of to he-went Yahweh

כְּצֵאת מֹשֶׁה אֶל־ הָאֹהֶל יָקוּמוּ כָּל־ הָעָם וְנִצְּבוּ

and-they-stood the-people all-of that-they-rose the-tent to Moses when-to-go

אִישׁ פֶּתַח אָהֳלוֹ וְהִבִּיטוּ אַחֲרֵי מֹשֶׁה עַד־ בֹּאוֹ

to-enter-him until Moses after and-they-watched tent-of-him entrance-of each

הָאֹהֱלָה׃ וְהָיָה כְּבֹא מֹשֶׁה הָאֹהֱלָה יֵרֵד

he-came-down into-the-tent Moses as-to-go and-he-was (9) into-the-tent

עַמּוּד הֶעָנָן וְעָמַד פֶּתַח הָאֹהֶל וְדִבֶּר עִם־

with and-he-spoke the-tent entrance-of and-he-stayed the-cloud pillar-of

מֹשֶׁה׃ וְרָאָה כָל־ הָעָם אֶת־ עַמּוּד הֶעָנָן עֹמֵד

standing the-cloud pillar-of *** the-people all-of when-he-saw (10) Moses

פֶּתַח הָאֹהֶל וְקָם כָּל־ הָעָם וְהִשְׁתַּחֲווּ* אִישׁ

each and-they-worshiped the-people all-of then-he-stood the-tent entrance-of

פֶּתַח אָהֳלוֹ׃ וְדִבֶּר יְהוָה אֶל־ מֹשֶׁה פָּנִים אֶל־פָּנִים

faces to faces Moses to Yahweh and-he-spoke (11) tent-of-him entrance-of

כַּאֲשֶׁר יְדַבֵּר אִישׁ אֶל־ רֵעֵהוּ וְשָׁב אֶל־ הַמַּחֲנֶה

the-camp to then-he-returned friend-of-him with man he-speaks just-as

וּמְשָׁרְתוֹ יְהוֹשֻׁעַ בִּן־ נוּן נַעַר לֹא יָמִישׁ מִתּוֹךְ הָאֹהֶל׃

the-tent from he-left not young Nun son-of Joshua but-being-aide-of-him

you, because you are a stiff-necked people and I might destroy you on the way."

4 When the people heard these distressing words, they began to mourn and no one put on any ornaments.
5 For the LORD had said to Moses, "Tell the Israelites, 'You are a stiff-necked people. If I were to go with you even for a moment, I might destroy you. Now take off your ornaments and I will decide what to do with you.' "
6 So the Israelites stripped off their ornaments at Mount Horeb.

*The Tent of Meeting*

7 Now Moses used to take a tent and pitch it outside the camp some distance away, calling it the "tent of meeting." Anyone inquiring of the LORD would go to the tent of meeting outside the camp.
8 And whenever Moses went out to the tent, all the people rose and stood at the entrances to their tents, watching Moses until he entered the tent.
9 As Moses went into the tent, the pillar of cloud would come down and stay at the entrance, while the LORD spoke with Moses.
10 Whenever the people saw the pillar of cloud standing at the entrance to the tent, they all stood and worshiped, each at the entrance to his tent.
11 The LORD would speak to Moses face to face, as a man speaks with his friend. Then Moses would return to the camp, but his young aide Joshua son of Nun did not leave the tent.

*10 Most mss have no *dagesh* in the first *vav* (וּ—).

וַיֹּאמֶר מֹשֶׁה אֶל־יְהוָה רְאֵה אַתָּה אֹמֵר אֵלַי הַעַל אֶת־הָעָם
the-people *** lead! to-me telling you see! Yahweh to Moses and-he-said (12)

הַזֶּה וְאַתָּה לֹא הוֹדַעְתַּנִי אֵת אֲשֶׁר־תִּשְׁלַח עִמִּי וְאַתָּה
and-you with-me you-will-send whom *** you-let-know-me not but-you the-this

אָמַרְתָּ יְדַעְתִּיךָ בְשֵׁם וְגַם־מָצָאתָ חֵן בְּעֵינָי׃
in-eyes-of-me favor you-found and-also by-name I-know-you you-said

וְעַתָּה אִם־נָא מָצָאתִי חֵן בְּעֵינֶיךָ הוֹדִעֵנִי נָא אֶת־דְּרָכֶךָ
way-of-you *** now! teach-me! in-eyes-of-you favor I-found now! if so-now (13)

וְאֵדָעֲךָ לְמַעַן אֶמְצָא־חֵן בְּעֵינֶיךָ וּרְאֵה כִּי
that and-remember! in-eyes-of-you favor I-may-find so-that so-I-may-know-you

עַמְּךָ הַגּוֹי הַזֶּה׃ וַיֹּאמַר פָּנַי
Presences-of-me and-he-replied (14) the-this the-nation people-of-you

יֵלֵכוּ וַהֲנִחֹתִי לָךְ׃ וַיֹּאמֶר אֵלָיו אִם־אֵין
not if to-him then-he-said (15) to-you and-I-will-give-rest they-will-go

פָּנֶיךָ הֹלְכִים אַל־תַּעֲלֵנוּ מִזֶּה׃ וּבַמֶּה ׀
and-by-the-what? (16) from-here you-send-up-us not ones-going Presences-of-you

יִוָּדַע אֵפוֹא כִּי־מָצָאתִי חֵן בְּעֵינֶיךָ אֲנִי וְעַמֶּךָ
and-people-of-you I in-eyes-of-you favor I-found that then will-he-be-known

הֲלוֹא בְּלֶכְתְּךָ עִמָּנוּ וְנִפְלֵינוּ אֲנִי וְעַמְּךָ מִכָּל־
from-all-of and-people-of-you I so-we-are-distinct with-us by-to-go-you if-not

הָעָם אֲשֶׁר עַל־פְּנֵי הָאֲדָמָה׃ וַיֹּאמֶר יְהוָה אֶל־מֹשֶׁה גַּם
indeed Moses to Yahweh and-he-said (17) the-earth face-of on that the-people

אֶת־הַדָּבָר הַזֶּה אֲשֶׁר דִּבַּרְתָּ אֶעֱשֶׂה כִּי־מָצָאתָ חֵן
favor you-found for I-will-do you-asked that the-this the-thing ***

בְּעֵינַי וָאֵדָעֲךָ בְּשֵׁם׃ וַיֹּאמַר הַרְאֵנִי נָא אֶת־
*** now! show-me! then-he-said (18) by-name and-I-know-you in-eyes-of-me

כְּבֹדֶךָ׃ וַיֹּאמֶר אֲנִי אַעֲבִיר כָּל־טוּבִי עַל־
in goodness-of-me all-of I-will-make-pass I and-he-said (19) glory-of-you

פָּנֶיךָ וְקָרָאתִי בְשֵׁם יְהוָה לְפָנֶיךָ
in-presence-of-you Yahweh by-name and-I-will-proclaim front-of-you

וְחַנֹּתִי אֶת־אֲשֶׁר אָחֹן וְרִחַמְתִּי
and-I-will-have-compassion I-will-have-mercy whom *** and-I-will-have-mercy

אֶת־אֲשֶׁר אֲרַחֵם׃ וַיֹּאמֶר לֹא תוּכַל לִרְאֹת אֶת־
*** to-see you-can not and-he-said (20) I-will-have-compassion whom ***

פָּנָי כִּי לֹא־יִרְאַנִי הָאָדָם וָחָי׃ וַיֹּאמֶר
then-he-said (21) and-he-lives the-man he-may-see-me not for face-of-me

יְהוָה הִנֵּה מָקוֹם אִתִּי וְנִצַּבְתָּ עַל־הַצּוּר׃ וְהָיָה
and-he-will-be (22) the-rock on and-you-may-stand near-me place see! Yahweh

### *Moses and the Glory of the* LORD

12 Moses said to the LORD, "You have been telling me, 'Lead these people,' but you have not let me know whom you will send with me. You have said, 'I know you by name and you have found favor with me.'
13 If I have found favor in your eyes, teach me your ways so I may know you and continue to find favor with you. Remember that this nation is your people."

14 The LORD replied, "My Presence will go with you, and I will give you rest."

15 Then Moses said to him, "If your Presence does not go with us, do not send us up from here.
16 How will anyone know that you are pleased with me and with your people unless you go with us? What else will distinguish me and your people from all the other people on the face of the earth?"

17 And the LORD said to Moses, "I will do the very thing you have asked, because I am pleased with you and I know you by name."

18 Then Moses said, "Now show me your glory."

19 And the LORD said, "I will cause all my goodness to pass in front of you, and I will proclaim my name, the LORD, in your presence. I will have mercy on whom I will have mercy, and I will have compassion on whom I will have compassion.
20 But," he said, "you cannot see my face, for no one may see me and live."

21 Then the LORD said, "There is a place near me where you may stand on a rock.
22 When

בַּעֲבֹר כְּבֹדִי וְשַׂמְתִּיךָ בְּנִקְרַת הַצּוּר

the-rock in-cleft-of then-I-will-put-you glory-of-me when-to-pass-by

וְשַׂכֹּתִי כַפִּי עָלֶיךָ עַד־ עָבְרִי׃ וַהֲסִרֹתִי

then-I-will-remove (23) to-pass-by-me until over-you hand-of-me and-I-will-put

אֶת־ כַּפִּי וְרָאִיתָ אֶת־ אֲחֹרָי וּפָנַי לֹא

not but-faces-of-me back-of-me *** and-you-will-see hand-of-me ***

יֵרָאוּ׃ וַיֹּאמֶר יְהוָה אֶל־ מֹשֶׁה פְּסָל־ לְךָ שְׁנֵי־

two-of for-you chisel! Moses to Yahweh then-he-said (34:1) they-may-be-seen

לֻחֹת אֲבָנִים כָּרִאשֹׁנִים וְכָתַבְתִּי עַל־ הַלֻּחֹת אֶת־

*** the-tablets on and-I-will-write like-the-first-ones stones tablets-of

הַדְּבָרִים אֲשֶׁר הָיוּ עַל־ הַלֻּחֹת הָרִאשֹׁנִים אֲשֶׁר שִׁבַּרְתָּ׃

you-broke which the-first-ones the-tablets on they-were that the-words

וֶהְיֵה נָכוֹן לַבֹּקֶר וְעָלִיתָ בַבֹּקֶר אֶל־

on in-the-morning then-you-come-up in-the-morning being-ready and-be! (2)

הַר סִינַי וְנִצַּבְתָּ לִי שָׁם עַל־ רֹאשׁ הָהָר׃ וְאִישׁ

but-man (3) the-mountain top-of on there to-me and-you-present Sinai Mount-of

לֹא־ יַעֲלֶה עִמָּךְ וְגַם־ אִישׁ אַל־ יֵרָא בְּכָל־

on-any-part-of he-may-be-seen not man or-even with-you he-may-come not

הָהָר גַּם־ הַצֹּאן וְהַבָּקָר אַל־ יִרְעוּ אֶל־ מוּל

front in they-may-graze not and-the-herd the-flock even the-mountain

הָהָר הַהוּא׃ וַיִּפְסֹל שְׁנֵי־ לֻחֹת אֲבָנִים

stones tablets-of two-of so-he-chiseled (4) the-this the-mountain

כָּרִאשֹׁנִים וַיַּשְׁכֵּם מֹשֶׁה בַבֹּקֶר וַיַּעַל אֶל־

on and-he-went-up in-the-morning Moses and-he-got-up like-the-first-ones

הַר סִינַי כַּאֲשֶׁר צִוָּה יְהוָה אֹתוֹ וַיִּקַּח בְּיָדוֹ

in-hand-of-him and-he-carried him Yahweh he-commanded just-as Sinai Mount-of

שְׁנֵי לֻחֹת אֲבָנִים׃ וַיֵּרֶד יְהוָה בֶּעָנָן וַיִּתְיַצֵּב

and-he-stood in-the-cloud Yahweh then-he-came-down (5) stones tablets-of two-of

עִמּוֹ שָׁם וַיִּקְרָא בְשֵׁם יְהוָה׃ וַיַּעֲבֹר יְהוָה ׀

Yahweh and-he-passed (6) Yahweh in-name-of and-he-proclaimed there with-him

עַל־ פָּנָיו וַיִּקְרָא יְהוָה ׀ יְהוָה אֵל רַחוּם וְחַנּוּן

and-gracious compassionate God Yahweh Yahweh and-he-proclaimed front-of-him by

אֶרֶךְ אַפַּיִם וְרַב־ חֶסֶד וֶאֱמֶת׃ נֹצֵר חֶסֶד

love maintaining (7) and-faithfulness love and-abundant-of angers slow-of

לָאֲלָפִים נֹשֵׂא עָוֺן וָפֶשַׁע וְחַטָּאָה

and-sin and-rebellion wickedness forgiving to-the-thousands

וְנַקֵּה לֹא יְנַקֶּה פֹּקֵד ׀ עֲוֺן אָבוֹת

fathers sin-of punishing he-will-leave-unpunished not yet-to-leave-unpunished

my glory passes by, I will put
you in a cleft in the rock and
cover you with my hand until
I have passed by. 23Then I will
remove my hand and you will
see my back; but my face must
not be seen."

*The New Stone Tablets*

34 The LORD said to
Moses, "Chisel out two
stone tablets like the first ones,
and I will write on them the
words that were on the first
tablets, which you broke. 2Be
ready in the morning, and
then come up on Mount Sinai.
Present yourself to me there
on top of the mountain. 3No
one is to come with you or be
seen anywhere on the mountain; not even the flocks and
herds may graze in front of the
mountain."

4So Moses chiseled out two
stone tablets like the first ones
and went up Mount Sinai early in the morning, as the LORD
had commanded him; and he
carried the two stone tablets in
his hands. 5Then the LORD
came down in the cloud and
stood there with him and proclaimed his name, the LORD.
6And he passed in front of
Moses, proclaiming, "The
LORD, the LORD, the compassionate and gracious God,
slow to anger, abounding in
love and faithfulness, 7main-
taining love to thousands, and
forgiving wickedness, rebellion and sin. Yet he does not
leave the guilty unpunished;

עַל־ בָּנִים֙ וְעַל־ בְּנֵי בָנִ֔ים עַל־ שִׁלֵּשִׁ֖ים וְעַל־ רִבֵּעִֽים׃
on | children | and-on | children-of | children | to | third-ones | and-to | fourth-ones

וַיְמַהֵ֖ר מֹשֶׁ֑ה וַיִּקֹּ֥ד אַ֖רְצָה וַיִּשְׁתָּֽחוּ׃
(8) and-he-hurried | Moses | and-he-bowed | to-ground | and-he-worshiped

וַיֹּ֡אמֶר אִם־ נָא֩ מָצָ֨אתִי חֵ֤ן בְּעֵינֶ֙יךָ֙ אֲדֹנָ֔י יֵֽלֶךְ־ נָ֥א
(9) and-he-said | if | now! | I-found | favor | in-eyes-of-you | Lord | let-him-go | now!

אֲדֹנָ֖י בְּקִרְבֵּ֑נוּ כִּ֤י עַם־ קְשֵׁה־ עֹ֙רֶף֙ ה֔וּא וְסָלַחְתָּ֛
Lord | with-us | although | people-of | stiff-of | neck | this | and-you-forgive

לַעֲוֺנֵ֥נוּ וּלְחַטָּאתֵ֖נוּ וּנְחַלְתָּֽנוּ׃
to-wickedness-of-us | and-to-sin-of-us | and-you-take-as-inheritance-us

וַיֹּ֗אמֶר הִנֵּ֣ה אָנֹכִי֮ כֹּרֵ֣ת בְּרִית֒ נֶ֤גֶד כָּל־ עַמְּךָ֙
(10) then-he-said | see! | I | making | covenant | before | all-of | people-of-you

אֶעֱשֶׂ֣ה נִפְלָאֹ֔ת אֲשֶׁ֛ר לֹֽא־ נִבְרְא֥וּ בְכָל־ הָאָ֖רֶץ
I-will-do | being-wonders | that | never | they-were-done | in-all-of | the-world

וּבְכָל־ הַגּוֹיִ֑ם וְרָאָ֣ה כָל־ הָ֠עָם אֲשֶׁר־ אַתָּ֨ה
or-in-any-of | the-nations | then-he-will-see | all-of | the-people | whom | you

בְקִרְבּ֜וֹ אֶת־ מַעֲשֵׂ֤ה יְהוָה֙ כִּֽי־ נוֹרָ֣א ה֔וּא אֲשֶׁ֥ר אֲנִ֖י עֹשֶׂ֥ה עִמָּֽךְ׃
among-him | *** | work-of | Yahweh | that | being-awesome | he | that | I | doing | for-you

שְׁמָ֨ר־ לְךָ֔ אֵ֛ת אֲשֶׁ֥ר אָנֹכִ֖י מְצַוְּךָ֣ הַיּ֑וֹם הִנְנִ֣י גֹרֵ֣שׁ
(11) obey! | for-you | *** | what | I | commanding-you | the-day | see-I! | driving-out

מִפָּנֶ֗יךָ אֶת־ הָאֱמֹרִי֙ וְהַֽכְּנַעֲנִ֔י וְהַֽחִתִּ֔י
from-before-you | *** | the-Amorite | and-the-Canaanite | and-the-Hittite

וְהַפְּרִזִּ֖י וְהַֽחִוִּ֥י וְהַיְבוּסִֽי׃ הִשָּׁ֣מֶר לְךָ֗
and-the-Perizzite | and-the-Hivite | and-the-Jebusite | (12) be-careful! | for-you

פֶּן־ תִּכְרֹ֤ת בְּרִית֙ לְיוֹשֵׁ֣ב הָאָ֔רֶץ אֲשֶׁ֥ר אַתָּ֖ה בָּ֣א עָלֶ֑יהָ
not | you-make | treaty | with-one-living-of | the-land | where | you | going | into-her

פֶּן־ יִהְיֶ֥ה לְמוֹקֵ֖שׁ בְּקִרְבֶּֽךָ׃ כִּ֤י אֶת־ מִזְבְּחֹתָם֙ תִּתֹּצ֔וּן
or | he-will-be | as-snare | among-you | (13) but | *** | altars-of-them | you-break-down

וְאֶת־ מַצֵּבֹתָ֖ם תְּשַׁבֵּר֑וּן וְאֶת־ אֲשֵׁרָ֖יו תִּכְרֹתֽוּן׃
and | sacred-stones-of-them | you-smash | and | Asherah-poles-of-him | you-cut-down

כִּ֛י לֹ֥א תִֽשְׁתַּחֲוֶ֖ה לְאֵ֣ל אַחֵ֑ר כִּ֤י יְהוָה֙ קַנָּ֣א שְׁמ֔וֹ אֵ֥ל
but (14) | not | you-worship | to-god | other | for | Yahweh | Jealous | name-of-him | God

קַנָּ֖א הֽוּא׃ פֶּן־ תִּכְרֹ֥ת בְּרִ֖ית לְיוֹשֵׁ֥ב הָאָ֑רֶץ
jealous | he | (15) not | you-make | treaty | with-one-living-of | the-land

וְזָנ֣וּ ׀ אַחֲרֵ֣י אֱלֹֽהֵיהֶ֗ם וְזָבְחוּ֙ לֵאלֹ֣הֵיהֶ֔ם
for-they-prostitute | to | gods-of-them | and-they-sacrifice | to-gods-of-them

וְקָרָ֣א לְךָ֔ וְאָכַלְתָּ֖ מִזִּבְחֽוֹ׃
and-he-will-invite | to-you | and-you-will-eat | from-sacrifice-of-him

---

he punishes the children and their children for the sin of the fathers to the third and fourth generation."

[8]Moses bowed to the ground at once and worshiped. [9]"O Lord, if I have found favor in your eyes," he said, "then let the Lord go with us. Although this is a stiff-necked people, forgive our wickedness and our sin, and take us as your inheritance."

[10]Then the LORD said: "I am making a covenant with you. Before all your people I will do wonders never before done in any nation in all the world. The people you live among will see how awesome is the work that I, the LORD, will do for you. [11]Obey what I command you today. I will drive out before you the Amorites, Canaanites, Hittites, Perizzites, Hivites and Jebusites. [12]Be careful not to make a treaty with those who live in the land where you are going, or they will be a snare among you. [13]Break down their altars, smash their sacred stones and cut down their Asherah poles.p [14]Do not worship any other god, for the LORD, whose name is Jealous, is a jealous God.

[15]"Be careful not to make a treaty with those who live in the land; for when they prostitute themselves to their gods and sacrifice to them, they will invite you and you will eat their sacrifices. [16]And when

p13 That is, symbols of the goddess Asherah

וְלָקַחְתָּ מִבְּנֹתָיו לְבָנֶיךָ וְזָנוּ
and-they-prostitute for-sons-of-you from-daughters-of-him when-you-choose (16)

בְנֹתָיו אַחֲרֵי אֱלֹהֵיהֶן וְהִזְנוּ אֶת־
*** then-they-will-lead-to-prostitute gods-of-them to daughters-of-him

בָּנֶיךָ אַחֲרֵי אֱלֹהֵיהֶן׃ אֱלֹהֵי מַסֵּכָה לֹא תַעֲשֶׂה־ לָּךְ׃ אֶת־
*** (18) for-you you-make not cast idols-of (17) gods-of-them to sons-of-you

חַג הַמַּצּוֹת תִּשְׁמֹר שִׁבְעַת יָמִים תֹּאכַל
you-eat days seven-of you-celebrate the-Unleavened-Breads Feast-of

מַצּוֹת אֲשֶׁר צִוִּיתִךָ לְמוֹעֵד חֹדֶשׁ הָאָבִיב
the-Abib month-of at-appointed-time I-commanded-you as breads-without-yeast

כִּי בְּחֹדֶשׁ הָאָבִיב יָצָאתָ מִמִּצְרָיִם׃ כָּל־ פֶּטֶר
firstborn-of every-of (19) from-Egypt you-came-out the-Abib in-month-of for

רֶחֶם לִי וְכָל־ מִקְנְךָ תִּזָּכָר* פֶּטֶר שׁוֹר וָשֶׂה׃
or-flock herd firstborn-of male stock-of-you and-all-of to-me womb

וּפֶטֶר חֲמוֹר תִּפְדֶּה בְשֶׂה וְאִם־ לֹא תִפְדֶּה
you-redeem not but-if with-lamb you-redeem donkey but-firstborn-of (20)

וַעֲרַפְתּוֹ כֹּל בְּכוֹר בָּנֶיךָ תִּפְדֶּה וְלֹא־
and-not you-redeem sons-of-you firstborn-of all-of then-you-break-neck-of-him

יֵרָאוּ פָנַי רֵיקָם׃ שֵׁשֶׁת יָמִים תַּעֲבֹד
you-shall-labor days six-of (21) empty-handed before-me they-shall-appear

וּבַיּוֹם הַשְּׁבִיעִי תִּשְׁבֹּת בֶּחָרִישׁ
in-the-plowing-season you-shall-rest the-seventh but-on-the-day

וּבַקָּצִיר תִּשְׁבֹּת׃ וְחַג שָׁבֻעֹת תַּעֲשֶׂה לְךָ
for-you you-celebrate Weeks and-Feast-of (22) you-must-rest and-in-the-harvest

בִּכּוּרֵי קְצִיר חִטִּים וְחַג הָאָסִיף תְּקוּפַת
turn-of the-Ingathering and-Feast-of wheats harvest-of firstfruits-of

הַשָּׁנָה׃ שָׁלֹשׁ פְּעָמִים בַּשָּׁנָה יֵרָאֶה כָּל־ זְכוּרְךָ אֶת־
*** male-of-you every-of he-must-appear in-the-year times three (23) the-year

פְּנֵי הָאָדֹן ׀ יְהוָה אֱלֹהֵי יִשְׂרָאֵל׃ כִּי־ אוֹרִישׁ גּוֹיִם
nations I-will-drive-out for (24) Israel God-of Yahweh the-Sovereign before

מִפָּנֶיךָ וְהִרְחַבְתִּי אֶת־ גְּבוּלֶךָ וְלֹא־ יַחְמֹד
he-will-covet and-not territory-of-you *** and-I-will-enlarge from-before-you

אִישׁ אֶת־ אַרְצְךָ בַּעֲלֹתְךָ לֵרָאוֹת אֶת־ פְּנֵי יְהוָה
Yahweh before *** to-appear when-to-go-up-you land-of-you *** anyone

אֱלֹהֶיךָ שָׁלֹשׁ פְּעָמִים בַּשָּׁנָה׃ לֹא־ תִשְׁחַט עַל־ חָמֵץ דַּם־
blood-of yeast with you-offer not (25) in-the-year times three God-of-you

זִבְחִי וְלֹא־ יָלִין לַבֹּקֶר זֶבַח
sacrifice-of until-the-morning he-may-remain and-not sacrifice-of-me

you choose some of their daughters as wives for your sons and those daughters prostitute themselves to their gods, they will lead your sons to do the same.
17"Do not make cast idols.
18"Celebrate the Feast of Unleavened Bread. For seven days eat bread made without yeast, as I commanded you. Do this at the appointed time in the month of Abib, for in that month you came out of Egypt.
19"The first offspring of every womb belongs to me, including all the firstborn males of your livestock, whether from herd or flock.
20Redeem the firstborn donkey with a lamb, but if you do not redeem it, break its neck. Redeem all your firstborn sons.
"No one is to appear before me empty-handed.
21"Six days you shall labor, but on the seventh day you shall rest; even during the plowing season and harvest you must rest.
22"Celebrate the Feast of Weeks with the firstfruits of the wheat harvest, and the Feast of Ingathering at the turn of the year.[q]
23Three times a year all your men are to appear before the Sovereign LORD, the God of Israel.
24I will drive out nations before you and enlarge your territory, and no one will covet your land when you go up three times each year to appear before the LORD your God.
25"Do not offer the blood of a sacrifice to me along with anything containing yeast, and do not let any of the sacrifice

[q]22 That is, in the fall

*19 It is suggested that the first letter of the Hebrew word be dropped or replaced with the definite article.

חַג הַפָּסַח׃ רֵאשִׁית בִּכּוּרֵי אַדְמָתְךָ תָּבִיא
you-bring soil-of-you firstfruits-of best-of (26) the-Passover Feast-of

בֵּית יְהוָה אֱלֹהֶיךָ לֹא־תְבַשֵּׁל גְּדִי בַּחֲלֵב אִמּוֹ׃
mother-of-him in-milk-of young-goat you-cook not God-of-you Yahweh house-of

וַיֹּאמֶר יְהוָה אֶל־מֹשֶׁה כְּתָב־לְךָ אֶת־הַדְּבָרִים הָאֵלֶּה
the-these the-words *** for-you write! Moses to Yahweh then-he-said (27)

כִּי עַל־פִּי ׀ הַדְּבָרִים הָאֵלֶּה כָּרַתִּי אִתְּךָ בְּרִית וְאֶת־
and-with covenant with-you I-made the-these the-words accord-of in for

יִשְׂרָאֵל׃ וַיְהִי־שָׁם עִם־יְהוָה אַרְבָּעִים יוֹם וְאַרְבָּעִים לַיְלָה לֶחֶם
bread night and-forty day forty Yahweh with there and-he-was (28) Israel

לֹא אָכַל וּמַיִם לֹא שָׁתָה וַיִּכְתֹּב עַל־הַלֻּחֹת אֵת דִּבְרֵי
words-of *** the-tablets on and-he-wrote he-drank not and-waters he-ate not

הַבְּרִית עֲשֶׂרֶת הַדְּבָרִים׃ וַיְהִי בְּרֶדֶת מֹשֶׁה
Moses when-to-come-down and-he-was (29) the-Commandments Ten-of the-covenant

מֵהַר סִינַי וּשְׁנֵי לֻחֹת הָעֵדֻת בְּיַד־מֹשֶׁה
Moses in-hand-of the-Testimony tablets-of with-two-of Sinai from-Mount-of

בְּרִדְתּוֹ מִן־הָהָר וּמֹשֶׁה לֹא־יָדַע כִּי
that he-was-aware not and-Moses the-mountain from when-to-come-down-him

קָרַן עוֹר פָּנָיו בְּדַבְּרוֹ אִתּוֹ׃
with-him because-to-speak-him face-of-him skin-of he-was-radiant

וַיַּרְא אַהֲרֹן וְכָל־בְּנֵי יִשְׂרָאֵל אֶת־מֹשֶׁה וְהִנֵּה
and-see! Moses *** Israel sons-of and-all-of Aaron when-he-saw (30)

קָרַן עוֹר פָּנָיו וַיִּירְאוּ מִגֶּשֶׁת
from-to-come-near then-they-were-afraid face-of-him skin-of he-was-radiant

אֵלָיו׃ וַיִּקְרָא אֲלֵהֶם מֹשֶׁה וַיָּשֻׁבוּ אֵלָיו אַהֲרֹן
Aaron to-him and-they-came-back Moses to-them but-he-called (31) to-him

וְכָל־הַנְּשִׂאִים בָּעֵדָה וַיְדַבֵּר מֹשֶׁה אֲלֵהֶם׃
to-them Moses and-he-spoke of-the-community the-leaders and-all-of

וְאַחֲרֵי־כֵן נִגְּשׁוּ כָּל־בְּנֵי יִשְׂרָאֵל וַיְצַוֵּם
and-he-commanded-them Israel sons-of all-of they-came-near this and-after (32)

אֵת כָּל־אֲשֶׁר דִּבֶּר יְהוָה אִתּוֹ בְּהַר סִינָי׃ וַיְכַל
when-he-finished (33) Sinai on-Mount-of to-him Yahweh he-said that all ***

מֹשֶׁה מִדַּבֵּר אִתָּם וַיִּתֵּן עַל־פָּנָיו מַסְוֶה׃
veil face-of-him over then-he-put with-them from-to-speak Moses

וּבְבֹא מֹשֶׁה לִפְנֵי יְהוָה לְדַבֵּר אִתּוֹ יָסִיר
he-removed with-him to-speak Yahweh to-presences-of Moses but-when-to-enter (34)

אֶת־הַמַּסְוֶה עַד־צֵאתוֹ וְיָצָא וְדִבֶּר אֶל־בְּנֵי
sons-of to then-he-told when-he-came-out to-come-out-him until the-veil ***

from the Passover Feast remain until morning.
26"Bring the best of the
firstfruits of your soil to the
house of the LORD your God.
"Do not cook a young goat
in its mother's milk."
27Then the LORD said to
Moses, "Write down these
words, for in accordance with
these words I have made a
covenant with you and with
Israel." 28Moses was there
with the LORD forty days and
forty nights without eating
bread or drinking water. And
he wrote on the tablets the
words of the covenant—the
Ten Commandments.

*The Radiant Face of Moses*

29When Moses came down
from Mount Sinai with the
two tablets of the Testimony
in his hands, he was not
aware that his face was radiant because he had spoken
with the LORD. 30When Aaron
and all the Israelites saw
Moses, his face was radiant,
and they were afraid to come
near him. 31But Moses called to
them; so Aaron and all the
leaders of the community
came back to him, and he
spoke to them. 32Afterward all
the Israelites came near him,
and he gave them all the commands the LORD had given
him on Mount Sinai.
33When Moses finished
speaking to them, he put a veil
over his face. 34But whenever
he entered the LORD's presence
to speak with him, he
removed the veil until he came
out. And when he came out
and told the Israelites what he

יִשְׂרָאֵ֔ל אֵ֖ת אֲשֶׁ֥ר יְצֻוֶּֽה׃ וְרָא֤וּ בְנֵֽי־יִשְׂרָאֵל֙ אֶת־פְּנֵ֣י

face-of *** Israel sons-of and-they-saw (35) he-was-commanded what *** Israel

מֹשֶׁ֔ה כִּ֣י קָרַ֔ן ע֖וֹר פְּנֵ֣י מֹשֶׁ֑ה וְהֵשִׁ֨יב מֹשֶׁ֤ה אֶת־

*** Moses then-he-put-back Moses face-of skin-of he-was-radiant that Moses

הַמַּסְוֶה֙ עַל־ פָּנָ֔יו עַד־ בֹּא֖וֹ לְדַבֵּ֥ר אִתּֽוֹ׃

with-him to-speak to-go-him until face-of-him over the-veil

וַיַּקְהֵ֣ל מֹשֶׁ֗ה אֶֽת־ כָּל־ עֲדַ֛ת בְּנֵ֥י־יִשְׂרָאֵ֖ל וַיֹּ֣אמֶר

and-he-said Israel sons-of community-of whole-of *** Moses and-he-assembled (35:1)

אֲלֵהֶ֑ם אֵ֚לֶּה הַדְּבָרִ֔ים אֲשֶׁר־ צִוָּ֥ה יְהוָ֖ה לַעֲשֹׂ֥ת אֹתָֽם׃ שֵׁ֣שֶׁת

six-of (2) them to-do Yahweh he-commanded that the-things these to-them

יָמִים֮ תֵּעָשֶׂ֣ה מְלָאכָה֒ וּבַיּ֣וֹם הַשְּׁבִיעִ֗י יִהְיֶ֨ה לָכֶ֥ם

for-you he-shall-be the-seventh but-on-the-day work she-may-be-done days

קֹ֛דֶשׁ שַׁבַּ֥ת שַׁבָּת֖וֹן לַיהוָ֑ה כָּל־ הָעֹשֶׂ֥ה ב֛וֹ מְלָאכָ֖ה יוּמָֽת׃

he-must-die work on-him the-one-doing every-of to-Yahweh rest Sabbath-of holy

לֹא־ תְבַעֲר֣וּ אֵ֔שׁ בְּכֹ֖ל מֹשְׁבֹתֵיכֶ֑ם בְּי֖וֹם הַשַּׁבָּֽת׃

the-Sabbath on-day-of dwellings-of-you in-any-of fire you-light not (3)

וַיֹּ֣אמֶר מֹשֶׁ֔ה אֶֽל־ כָּל־ עֲדַ֥ת בְּנֵֽי־ יִשְׂרָאֵ֖ל לֵאמֹ֑ר זֶ֣ה

this to-say Israel sons-of community-of all-of to Moses and-he-said (4)

הַדָּבָ֔ר אֲשֶׁר־ צִוָּ֥ה יְהוָ֖ה לֵאמֹֽר׃ קְח֨וּ מֵאִתְּכֶ֤ם תְּרוּמָה֙

offering from-among-you take! (5) to-say Yahweh he-commanded that the-thing

לַֽיהוָ֔ה כֹּ֚ל נְדִ֣יב לִבּ֔וֹ יְבִיאֶ֕הָ אֵ֖ת תְּרוּמַ֣ת

offering-of *** let-him-bring-her heart-of-him generous-of every-of to-Yahweh

יְהוָ֑ה זָהָ֥ב וָכֶ֖סֶף וּנְחֹֽשֶׁת׃ וּתְכֵ֧לֶת וְאַרְגָּמָ֛ן וְתוֹלַ֥עַת

and-scarlet-of and-purple and-blue (6) and-bronze and-silver gold Yahweh

שָׁנִ֖י וְשֵׁ֥שׁ וְעִזִּֽים׃ וְעֹרֹ֨ת אֵילִ֧ם מְאָדָּמִ֛ים

ones-being-dyed-red rams and-skins-of (7) and-goat-hairs and-fine-linen yarn

וְעֹרֹ֥ת תְּחָשִׁ֖ים וַעֲצֵ֥י שִׂטִּֽים*׃ וְשֶׁ֖מֶן לַמָּא֑וֹר

for-the-light and-oil (8) acacias and-woods-of sea-cows and-hides-of

וּבְשָׂמִים֙ לְשֶׁ֣מֶן הַמִּשְׁחָ֔ה וְלִקְטֹ֖רֶת הַסַּמִּֽים׃

the-fragrances and-for-incense-of the-anointing for-oil-of and-spices

וְאַבְנֵי־ שֹׁ֔הַם וְאַבְנֵ֖י מִלֻּאִ֑ים לָאֵפ֖וֹד

for-the-ephod settings and-stones-of onyx and-stones-of (9)

וְלַחֹֽשֶׁן׃ וְכָל־ חֲכַם־ לֵ֖ב בָּכֶ֑ם

among-you heart skilled-of and-all-of (10) and-for-the-breastpiece

יָבֹ֣אוּ וְיַעֲשׂ֔וּ אֵ֛ת כָּל־ אֲשֶׁ֥ר צִוָּ֖ה יְהוָֽה׃ אֶת־

*** (11) Yahweh he-commanded that all *** and-let-them-make let-them-come

הַמִּשְׁכָּ֕ן אֶֽת־ אָהֳל֖וֹ וְאֶת־ מִכְסֵ֑הוּ אֶת־ קְרָסָיו֙ וְאֶת־

and clasps-of-him *** cover-of-him and tent-of-him *** the-tabernacle

---

had been commanded, [35]they saw that his face was radiant. Then Moses would put the veil back over his face until he went in to speak with the LORD.

*Sabbath Regulations*

**35** Moses assembled the whole Israelite community and said to them, "These are the things the LORD has commanded you to do: [2]For six days, work is to be done, but the seventh day shall be your holy day, a Sabbath of rest to the LORD. Whoever does any work on it must be put to death. [3]Do not light a fire in any of your dwellings on the Sabbath day."

*Materials for the Tabernacle*

[4]Moses said to the whole Israelite community, "This is what the LORD has commanded: [5]From what you have, take an offering for the LORD. Everyone who is willing is to bring to the LORD an offering of gold, silver and bronze; [6]blue, purple and scarlet yarn and fine linen; goat hair; [7]ram skins dyed red and hides of sea cows; acacia wood; [8]olive oil for the light; spices for the anointing oil and for the fragrant incense; [9]and onyx stones and other gems to be mounted on the ephod and breastpiece.

[10]"All who are skilled among you are to come and make everything the LORD has commanded: [11]the tabernacle with its tent and its covering,

*7 Most mss have *shin* instead of *sin* (שׁטים).

קְרָשָׁיו אֶת־ בְּרִיחָו° אֶת־ עַמֻּדָיו וְאֶת־ אֲדָנָיו׃
bases-of-him and posts-of-him *** crossbars-of-him *** frames-of-him

אֶת־ הָאָרֹן וְאֶת־ בַּדָּיו אֶת־ הַכַּפֹּרֶת וְאֵת פָּרֹכֶת
curtain-of and the-atonement-cover *** poles-of-him and the-ark *** (12)

הַמָּסָךְ׃ אֶת־ הַשֻּׁלְחָן וְאֶת־ בַּדָּיו וְאֶת־ כָּל־ כֵּלָיו
articles-of-him all-of and poles-of-him and the-table *** (13) the-shield

וְאֵת לֶחֶם הַפָּנִים׃ וְאֶת־ מְנֹרַת הַמָּאוֹר וְאֶת־
and the-light lampstand-of and (14) the-Presences bread-of and

כֵּלֶיהָ וְאֶת־ נֵרֹתֶיהָ וְאֵת שֶׁמֶן הַמָּאוֹר׃ וְאֶת־ מִזְבַּח
altar-of and (15) the-light oil-of and lamps-of-her and accessories-of-her

הַקְּטֹרֶת וְאֶת־ בַּדָּיו וְאֵת שֶׁמֶן הַמִּשְׁחָה וְאֵת קְטֹרֶת
incense-of and the-anointing oil-of and poles-of-him and the-incense

הַסַּמִּים וְאֶת־ מָסַךְ הַפֶּתַח לְפֶתַח הַמִּשְׁכָּן׃
the-tabernacle at-entrance-of the-doorway curtain-of and the-fragrances

אֵת ׀ מִזְבַּח הָעֹלָה וְאֶת־ מִכְבַּר הַנְּחֹשֶׁת אֲשֶׁר־ לוֹ
for-him that the-bronze grate-of and the-burnt-offering altar-of *** (16)

אֶת־ בַּדָּיו וְאֶת־ כָּל־ כֵּלָיו אֶת־ הַכִּיֹּר וְאֶת־ כַּנּוֹ׃
stand-of-him and the-basin *** utensils-of-him all-of and poles-of-him ***

אֵת קַלְעֵי הֶחָצֵר אֶת־ עַמֻּדָיו וְאֶת־ אֲדָנֶיהָ וְאֵת
and bases-of-her and posts-of-him *** the-courtyard curtains-of *** (17)

מָסַךְ שַׁעַר הֶחָצֵר׃ אֶת־ יִתְדֹת הַמִּשְׁכָּן
the-tabernacle tent-pegs-of *** (18) the-courtyard entrance-of curtain-of

וְאֶת־יִתְדֹת הֶחָצֵר וְאֶת־ מֵיתְרֵיהֶם׃ אֶת־ בִּגְדֵי הַשְּׂרָד
the-woven garments-of *** (19) ropes-of-them and the-courtyard pegs-of and

לְשָׁרֵת בַּקֹּדֶשׁ אֶת־ בִּגְדֵי הַקֹּדֶשׁ לְאַהֲרֹן
for-Aaron the-sacred garments-of *** in-the-sanctuary for-to-minister

הַכֹּהֵן וְאֶת־ בִּגְדֵי בָנָיו לְכַהֵן׃ וַיֵּצְאוּ
then-they-left (20) for-to-be-priest sons-of-him garments-of and the-priest

כָּל־ עֲדַת בְּנֵי־ יִשְׂרָאֵל מִלִּפְנֵי מֹשֶׁה׃ וַיָּבֹאוּ
and-they-came (21) Moses from-presence-of Israel sons-of community-of whole-of

כָּל־ אִישׁ אֲשֶׁר־ נְשָׂאוֹ לִבּוֹ וְכֹל אֲשֶׁר נָדְבָה
she-moved whom and-everyone heart-of-him he-moved-him whom one every-of

רוּחוֹ אֹתוֹ הֵבִיאוּ אֶת־ תְּרוּמַת יְהוָה לִמְלֶאכֶת אֹהֶל
Tent-of for-work-of Yahweh offering-of *** they-brought him spirit-of-him

מוֹעֵד וּלְכָל־ עֲבֹדָתוֹ וּלְבִגְדֵי הַקֹּדֶשׁ׃
the-sacred and-for-garments-of service-of-him and-for-all-of Meeting

וַיָּבֹאוּ הָאֲנָשִׁים עַל־ הַנָּשִׁים כֹּל ׀ נְדִיב לֵב הֵבִיאוּ
they-brought heart willing-of all-of the-women with the-men and-they-came (22)

clasps, frames, crossbars, posts and bases; [12]the ark with its poles and the atonement cover and the curtain that shields it; [13]the table with its poles and all its articles and the bread of the Presence; [14]the lampstand that is for light with its accessories, lamps and oil for the light; [15]the altar of incense with its poles, the anointing oil and the fragrant incense; the curtain for the doorway at the entrance to the tabernacle; [16]the altar of burnt offering with its bronze grating, its poles and all its utensils; the bronze basin with its stand; [17]the curtains of the courtyard with its posts and bases, and the curtain for the entrance to the courtyard; [18]the tent pegs for the tabernacle and for the courtyard, and their ropes; [19]the woven garments worn for ministering in the sanctuary—both the sacred garments for Aaron the priest and the garments for his sons when they serve as priests."

[20]Then the whole Israelite community withdrew from Moses' presence, [21]and everyone who was willing and whose heart moved him came and brought an offering to the LORD for the work on the Tent of Meeting, for all its service, and for the sacred garments. [22]All who were willing, men and women alike, came and

°11 ק בריחיו

חָח וָנֶזֶם וְטַבַּעַת וְכוּמָז כָּל־ כְּלִי זָהָב וְכָל־
and-every-of gold jewelry-of every-of and-ornament and-ring and-earring brooch

אִישׁ אֲשֶׁר הֵנִיף תְּנוּפַת זָהָב לַיהוָה׃ וְכָל־ אִישׁ
one and-every-of (23) to-Yahweh gold wave-offering-of he-presented who one

אֲשֶׁר־ נִמְצָא אִתּוֹ תְּכֵלֶת וְאַרְגָּמָן וְתוֹלַעַת שָׁנִי וְשֵׁשׁ
or-fine-linen yarn or-scarlet-of or-purple blue with-him he-was-found who

וְעִזִּים וְעֹרֹת אֵילִם מְאָדָּמִים וְעֹרֹת תְּחָשִׁים
sea-cows or-hides-of ones-being-dyed-red rams or-skins-of or-goat-hairs

הֵבִיאוּ׃ כָּל־ מֵרִים תְּרוּמַת כֶּסֶף וּנְחֹשֶׁת
or-bronze silver offering-of ones-presenting all-of (24) they-brought

הֵבִיאוּ אֵת תְּרוּמַת יְהוָה וְכֹל אֲשֶׁר נִמְצָא אִתּוֹ
with-him he-was-found who and-everyone Yahweh offering-of *** they-brought

עֲצֵי שִׁטִּים לְכָל־ מְלֶאכֶת הָעֲבֹדָה הֵבִיאוּ׃ וְכָל־
and-every-of (25) they-brought the-work part-of for-any-of acacias woods-of

אִשָּׁה חַכְמַת־ לֵב בְּיָדֶיהָ טָווּ וַיָּבִיאוּ מַטְוֶה
product and-they-brought they-spun with-hands-of-her heart skilled-of woman

אֶת־ הַתְּכֵלֶת וְאֶת־ הָאַרְגָּמָן אֶת־ תּוֹלַעַת הַשָּׁנִי וְאֶת־ הַשֵּׁשׁ׃
the-fine-linen and the-yarn scarlet-of *** the-purple and the-blue ***

וְכָל־ הַנָּשִׁים אֲשֶׁר נָשָׂא לִבָּן אֹתָנָה בְּחָכְמָה
with-skill them heart-of-them he-moved whom the-women and-all-of (26)

טָווּ אֶת־ הָעִזִּים׃ וְהַנְּשִׂאִם הֵבִיאוּ אֵת אַבְנֵי
stones-of *** they-brought and-the-leaders (27) the-goat-hairs *** they-spun

הַשֹּׁהַם וְאֵת אַבְנֵי הַמִּלֻּאִים לָאֵפוֹד וְלַחֹשֶׁן׃
and-for-the-breastpiece for-the-ephod the-mountings stones-of and the-onyx

וְאֶת־ הַבֹּשֶׂם וְאֶת־ הַשָּׁמֶן לְמָאוֹר וּלְשֶׁמֶן הַמִּשְׁחָה
the-anointing and-for-oil-of for-light the-oil and the-spice and (28)

וְלִקְטֹרֶת הַסַּמִּים׃ כָּל־ אִישׁ וְאִשָּׁה אֲשֶׁר נָדַב
he-moved whom and-woman man every-of (29) the-fragrances and-for-incense-of

לִבָּם אֹתָם לְהָבִיא לְכָל־ הַמְּלָאכָה אֲשֶׁר צִוָּה יְהוָה
Yahweh he-commanded that the-work for-all-of to-bring them heart-of-them

לַעֲשׂוֹת בְּיַד־ מֹשֶׁה הֵבִיאוּ בְנֵי־ יִשְׂרָאֵל נְדָבָה
freewill-offering Israel sons-of they-brought Moses through-hand-of to-do

לַיהוָה׃ וַיֹּאמֶר מֹשֶׁה אֶל־ בְּנֵי יִשְׂרָאֵל רְאוּ קָרָא יְהוָה
Yahweh he-chose see! Israel sons-of to Moses then-he-said (30) to-Yahweh

בְּשֵׁם בְּצַלְאֵל בֶּן־ אוּרִי בֶן־ חוּר לְמַטֵּה יְהוּדָה׃ וַיְמַלֵּא
and-he-filled (31) Judah from-tribe-of Hur son-of Uri son-of Bezalel by-name

אֹתוֹ רוּחַ אֱלֹהִים בְּחָכְמָה בִּתְבוּנָה וּבְדַעַת וּבְכָל־מְלָאכָה׃
craft in-all-of and-with-knowledge with-ability with-skill God Spirit-of him

brought gold jewelry of all kinds: brooches, earrings, rings and ornaments. They all presented their gold as a wave offering to the LORD. [23]Everyone who had blue, purple or scarlet yarn or fine linen, or goat hair, ram skins dyed red or hides of sea cows brought them. [24]Those presenting an offering of silver or bronze brought it as an offering to the LORD, and everyone who had acacia wood for any part of the work brought it. [25]Every skilled woman spun with her hands and brought what she had spun—blue, purple or scarlet yarn or fine linen. [26]And all the women who were willing and had the skill spun the goat hair. [27]The leaders brought onyx stones and other gems to be mounted on the ephod and breastpiece. [28]They also brought spices and olive oil for the light and for the anointing oil and for the fragrant incense. [29]All the Israelite men and women who were willing brought to the LORD freewill offerings for all the work the LORD through Moses had commanded them to do.

*Bezalel and Oholiab*

[30]Then Moses said to the Israelites, "See, the LORD has chosen Bezalel son of Uri, the son of Hur, of the tribe of Judah, [31]and he has filled him with the Spirit of God, with skill, ability and knowledge in all kinds of crafts— [32]to make

וְלַחְשֹׁב מַחֲשָׁבֹת* לַעֲשֹׂת בַּזָּהָב וּבַכֶּסֶף
and-in-the-silver in-the-gold to-work artistic-designs and-to-make (32)

וּבַנְּחֹשֶׁת׃ וּבַחֲרֹשֶׁת אֶבֶן לְמַלֹּאת וּבַחֲרֹשֶׁת
and-for-cutting-of to-set stone and-for-cutting-of (33) and-in-the-bronze

עֵץ לַעֲשׂוֹת בְּכָל־ מְלֶאכֶת מַחֲשָׁבֶת׃ וּלְהוֹרֹת נָתַן
he-put and-to-teach (34) craftsmanship kind-of in-all-of to-engage wood

בְּלִבּוֹ הוּא וְאָהֳלִיאָב בֶּן־ אֲחִיסָמָךְ לְמַטֵּה־ דָן׃
Dan from-tribe-of Ahisamach son-of and-Oholiab he in-heart-of-him

מִלֵּא אֹתָם חָכְמַת־ לֵב לַעֲשׂוֹת כָּל־ מְלֶאכֶת חָרָשׁ ׀
craftsman work-of all-of to-do heart skill-of them he-filled (35)

וְחֹשֵׁב וְרֹקֵם בַּתְּכֵלֶת וּבָאַרְגָּמָן בְּתוֹלַעַת
and-in-scarlet-of and-in-the-purple in-the-blue and-embroidering and-designing

הַשָּׁנִי וּבַשֵּׁשׁ וְאֹרֵג עֹשֵׂי כָּל־מְלָאכָה
craft all-of ones-doing-of and-weaving and-in-the-fine-linen the-yarn

וְחֹשְׁבֵי מַחֲשָׁבֹת׃ וְעָשָׂה בְצַלְאֵל וְאָהֳלִיאָב
and-Oholiab Bezalel so-he-shall-do (36:1) designs and-ones-designing-of

וְכֹל ׀ אִישׁ חֲכַם־ לֵב אֲשֶׁר נָתַן יְהוָה חָכְמָה וּתְבוּנָה
and-ability skill Yahweh he-gave whom heart skilled-of person and-every-of

בָּהֵמָּה לָדַעַת לַעֲשֹׂת אֶת־ כָּל־ מְלֶאכֶת עֲבֹדַת הַקֹּדֶשׁ
the-sanctuary construction-of work-of all-of *** to-do to-know in-them

לְכֹל אֲשֶׁר־ צִוָּה יְהוָה׃ וַיִּקְרָא מֹשֶׁה אֶל־בְּצַלְאֵל
Bezalel to Moses then-he-summoned (2) Yahweh he-commanded that as-all

וְאֶל־ אָהֳלִיאָב וְאֶל כָּל־ אִישׁ חֲכַם־ לֵב אֲשֶׁר נָתַן יְהוָה
Yahweh he-gave whom heart skilled-of person every-of and-to Oholiab and-to

חָכְמָה בְּלִבּוֹ כֹּל אֲשֶׁר נְשָׂאוֹ לִבּוֹ לְקָרְבָה
to-come heart-of-him he-moved-him whom everyone in-heart-of-him ability

אֶל־הַמְּלָאכָה לַעֲשֹׂת אֹתָהּ׃ וַיִּקְחוּ מִלִּפְנֵי מֹשֶׁה אֵת כָּל־
all-of *** Moses from and-they-received (3) her to-do the-work to

הַתְּרוּמָה אֲשֶׁר הֵבִיאוּ בְּנֵי יִשְׂרָאֵל לִמְלֶאכֶת עֲבֹדַת
construction-of for-work-of Israel sons-of they-brought that the-offering

הַקֹּדֶשׁ לַעֲשֹׂת אֹתָהּ וְהֵם הֵבִיאוּ אֵלָיו עוֹד נְדָבָה
freewill-offering still to-him they-brought and-they her to-do the-sanctuary

בַּבֹּקֶר בַּבֹּקֶר׃ וַיָּבֹאוּ כָּל־ הַחֲכָמִים
the-craftsmen all-of so-they-left (4) in-the-morning in-the-morning

הָעֹשִׂים אֵת כָּל־ מְלֶאכֶת הַקֹּדֶשׁ אִישׁ־ אִישׁ מִמְּלַאכְתּוֹ
from-work-of-him each each the-sanctuary work-of all-of *** the-ones-doing

אֲשֶׁר־הֵמָּה עֹשִׂים׃ וַיֹּאמְרוּ אֶל־ מֹשֶׁה לֵּאמֹר מַרְבִּים
amounts-being-more to-say Moses to and-they-said (5) ones-doing they that

artistic designs for work in gold, silver and bronze, [33]to cut and set stones, to work in wood and to engage in all kinds of artistic craftsmanship. [34]And he has given both him and Oholiab son of Ahisamach, of the tribe of Dan, the ability to teach others. [35]He has filled them with skill to do all kinds of work as craftsmen, designers, embroiderers in blue, purple and scarlet yarn and fine linen, and weavers—all of them master craftsmen and designers.

36 [1]So Bezalel, Oholiab and every skilled person to whom the LORD has given skill and ability to know how to carry out all the work of constructing the sanctuary are to do the work just as the LORD has commanded."

[2]Then Moses summoned Bezalel and Oholiab and every skilled person to whom the LORD had given ability and who was willing to come and do the work. [3]They received from Moses all the offerings the Israelites had brought to carry out the work of constructing the sanctuary. And the people continued to bring freewill offerings morning after morning. [4]So all the skilled craftsmen who were doing all the work on the sanctuary left their work [5]and said to Moses,

*32 Most mss have *hateph pathah* under the *beth* ('מַחֲ').

הָעָם לְהָבִיא מִדֵּי הָעֲבֹדָה לַמְּלָאכָה אֲשֶׁר־צִוָּה

he-commanded that for-the-labor the-work than-need-of to-bring the-people

יְהוָה לַעֲשֹׂת אֹתָהּ׃ וַיְצַו מֹשֶׁה וַיַּעֲבִירוּ קוֹל

word and-they-sent Moses then-he-gave-order (6) her to-do Yahweh

בַּמַּחֲנֶה לֵאמֹר אִישׁ וְאִשָּׁה אַל־יַעֲשׂוּ־עוֹד מְלָאכָה

anything else they-shall-make not or-woman man to-say through-the-camp

לִתְרוּמַת הַקֹּדֶשׁ וַיִּכָּלֵא הָעָם מֵהָבִיא׃

from-to-bring the-people so-they-were-restrained the-sanctuary as-offering-of

וְהַמְּלָאכָה הָיְתָה דַיָּם לְכָל־הַמְּלָאכָה לַעֲשׂוֹת אֹתָהּ

her to-do the-work for-all-of enough-for-them she-was for-the-material (7)

וְהוֹתֵר׃ וַיַּעֲשׂוּ כָל־חֲכַם־לֵב בְּעֹשֵׂי

among-ones-doing-of heart skilled-of all-of and-they-made (8) and-to-be-more

הַמְּלָאכָה אֶת־הַמִּשְׁכָּן עֶשֶׂר יְרִיעֹת שֵׁשׁ מָשְׁזָר וּתְכֵלֶת

and-blue being-twisted fine-linen curtains ten the-tabernacle *** the-work

וְאַרְגָּמָן וְתוֹלַעַת שָׁנִי כְּרֻבִים מַעֲשֵׂה חֹשֵׁב עָשָׂה אֹתָם׃

them he-made being-skilled work-of cherubim yarn and-scarlet-of and-purple

אֹרֶךְ הַיְרִיעָה הָאַחַת שְׁמֹנֶה וְעֶשְׂרִים בָּאַמָּה וְרֹחַב

and-width by-the-cubit and-twenty eight the-each the-curtain length-of (9)

אַרְבַּע בָּאַמָּה הַיְרִיעָה הָאֶחָת מִדָּה אַחַת לְכָל־הַיְרִיעֹת׃

the-curtains for-all-of same size the-each the-curtain by-the-cubit four

וַיְחַבֵּר אֶת־חֲמֵשׁ הַיְרִיעֹת אַחַת אֶל־אֶחָת וְחָמֵשׁ יְרִיעֹת

curtains and-five other to each the-curtains five-of *** and-he-joined (10)

חִבַּר אַחַת אֶל־אֶחָת׃ וַיַּעַשׂ לֻלְאֹת תְּכֵלֶת עַל שְׂפַת

edge-of along blue loops-of then-he-made (11) other to each he-joined

הַיְרִיעָה הָאֶחָת מִקָּצָה בַּמַּחְבָּרֶת כֵּן עָשָׂה בִּשְׂפַת הַיְרִיעָה

the-curtain on-edge-of he-did same of-the-set at-end the-one the-curtain

הַקִּיצוֹנָה בַּמַּחְבֶּרֶת הַשֵּׁנִית׃ חֲמִשִּׁים לֻלָאֹת עָשָׂה בַּיְרִיעָה הָאֶחָת

the-one on-the-curtain he-made loops fifty (12) the-other in-the-set the-end

וַחֲמִשִּׁים לֻלָאֹת עָשָׂה בִּקְצֵה הַיְרִיעָה אֲשֶׁר בַּמַּחְבֶּרֶת הַשֵּׁנִית

the-other in-the-set that the-curtain on-end-of he-made loops and-fifty

מַקְבִּילֹת הַלֻּלָאֹת אַחַת אֶל־אֶחָת׃ וַיַּעַשׂ חֲמִשִּׁים קַרְסֵי

clasps-of fifty then-he-made (13) other to each the-loops ones-opposing

זָהָב וַיְחַבֵּר אֶת־הַיְרִיעֹת אַחַת אֶל־אַחַת בַּקְּרָסִים

with-the-clasps other to each the-curtains *** and-he-fastened gold

וַיְהִי הַמִּשְׁכָּן אֶחָד׃ וַיַּעַשׂ יְרִיעֹת עִזִּים לְאֹהֶל

for-tent goat-hairs curtains-of and-he-made (14) unit the-tabernacle so-he-was

עַל־הַמִּשְׁכָּן עַשְׁתֵּי־עֶשְׂרֵה יְרִיעֹת עָשָׂה אֹתָם׃ אֹרֶךְ הַיְרִיעָה

the-curtain length-of (15) them he-made curtains ten one the-tabernacle over

---

"The people are bringing more than enough for doing the work the LORD commanded to be done."

6Then Moses gave an order and they sent this word throughout the camp: "No man or woman is to make anything else as an offering for the sanctuary." And so the people were restrained from bringing more, 7because what they already had was more than enough to do all the work.

*The Tabernacle*

8All the skilled men among the workmen made the tabernacle with ten curtains of finely twisted linen and blue, purple and scarlet yarn, with cherubim worked into them by a skilled craftsman. 9All the curtains were the same size—twenty-eight cubits long and four cubits wide.[r] 10They joined five of the curtains together and did the same with the other five. 11Then they made loops of blue material along the edge of the end curtain in one set, and the same was done with the end curtain in the other set. 12They also made fifty loops on one curtain and fifty loops on the end curtain of the other set, with the loops opposite each other. 13Then they made fifty gold clasps and used them to fasten the two sets of curtains together so that the tabernacle was a unit.

14They made curtains of goat hair for the tent over the tabernacle—eleven all together.

[r] 9 That is, about 42 feet (about 12.5 meters) long and 6 feet (about 1.8 meters) wide

הָאַחַת שְׁלֹשִׁים בָּאַמָּה וְאַרְבַּע אַמּוֹת רֹחַב הַיְרִיעָה הָאֶחָת
the-each the-curtain width-of cubits and-four by-the-cubit thirty the-each

מִדָּה אַחַת לְעַשְׁתֵּי עֶשְׂרֵה יְרִיעֹת׃ וַיְחַבֵּר אֶת־חֲמֵשׁ הַיְרִיעֹת
the-curtains five-of *** and-he-joined (16) curtains ten for-one same size

לְבָד וְאֶת־שֵׁשׁ הַיְרִיעֹת לְבָד׃ וַיַּעַשׂ לֻלָאֹת חֲמִשִּׁים עַל
along fifty loops and-he-made (17) into-set the-curtains six-of and into-set

שְׂפַת הַיְרִיעָה הַקִּיצֹנָה בַּמַּחְבָּרֶת וַחֲמִשִּׁים לֻלָאֹת עָשָׂה עַל־שְׂפַת
edge-of along he-made loops and-fifty of-the-set the-end the-curtain edge-of

הַיְרִיעָה הַחֹבֶרֶת הַשֵּׁנִית׃ וַיַּעַשׂ קַרְסֵי נְחֹשֶׁת חֲמִשִּׁים
fifty bronze clasps-of and-he-made (18) the-other the-set the-curtain

לְחַבֵּר אֶת־הָאֹהֶל לִהְיֹת אֶחָד׃ וַיַּעַשׂ מִכְסֶה לָאֹהֶל
for-the-tent cover then-he-made (19) unit to-be the-tent *** to-fasten

עֹרֹת אֵילִם מְאָדָּמִים וּמִכְסֵה עֹרֹת תְּחָשִׁים מִלְמָעְלָה׃
for-above sea-cows hides-of and-cover-of ones-being-dyed-red rams skins-of

וַיַּעַשׂ אֶת־הַקְּרָשִׁים לַמִּשְׁכָּן עֲצֵי שִׁטִּים
acacias woods-of for-the-tabernacle the-frames *** and-he-made (20)

עֹמְדִים׃ עֶשֶׂר אַמֹּת אֹרֶךְ הַקָּרֶשׁ וְאַמָּה וַחֲצִי
and-half-of and-cubit the-frame length-of cubits ten (21) ones-being-upright

הָאַמָּה רֹחַב הַקֶּרֶשׁ הָאֶחָד׃ שְׁתֵּי יָדֹת לַקֶּרֶשׁ
for-the-frame projections two-of (22) the-each the-frame width-of the-cubit

הָאֶחָד מְשֻׁלָּבֹת אַחַת אֶל־אֶחָת כֵּן עָשָׂה לְכֹל קַרְשֵׁי
frames-of for-all-of he-did same other to each ones-paralleling the-each

הַמִּשְׁכָּן׃ וַיַּעַשׂ אֶת־הַקְּרָשִׁים לַמִּשְׁכָּן עֶשְׂרִים קְרָשִׁים
frames twenty for-the-tabernacle the-frames *** and-he-made (23) the-tabernacle

לִפְאַת נֶגֶב תֵּימָנָה׃ וְאַרְבָּעִים אַדְנֵי־כֶסֶף עָשָׂה תַּחַת עֶשְׂרִים
twenty under he-made silver bases-of and-forty (24) to-south south for-side-of

הַקְּרָשִׁים שְׁנֵי אֲדָנִים תַּחַת־הַקֶּרֶשׁ הָאֶחָד לִשְׁתֵּי יְדֹתָיו
projections-of-him for-two-of the-one the-frame under bases two-of the-frames

וּשְׁנֵי אֲדָנִים תַּחַת־הַקֶּרֶשׁ הָאֶחָד לִשְׁתֵּי יְדֹתָיו׃
projections-of-him for-two-of the-other the-frame under bases and-two-of

וּלְצֶלַע הַמִּשְׁכָּן הַשֵּׁנִית לִפְאַת צָפוֹן עָשָׂה
he-made north for-side-of the-other the-tabernacle and-for-side-of (25)

עֶשְׂרִים קְרָשִׁים׃ וְאַרְבָּעִים אַדְנֵיהֶם כָּסֶף שְׁנֵי אֲדָנִים תַּחַת
under bases two-of silver bases-of-them and-forty (26) frames twenty

הַקֶּרֶשׁ הָאֶחָד וּשְׁנֵי אֲדָנִים תַּחַת הַקֶּרֶשׁ הָאֶחָד׃
the-other the-frame under bases and-two-of the-one the-frame

וּלְיַרְכְּתֵי הַמִּשְׁכָּן יָמָּה עָשָׂה שִׁשָּׁה קְרָשִׁים׃ וּשְׁנֵי
and-two-of (28) frames six he-made to-west the-tabernacle and-for-far-ends-of (27)

15 All eleven curtains were the same size—thirty cubits long and four cubits wide.[t] 16 They joined five of the curtains into one set and the other six into another set. 17 Then they made fifty loops along the edge of the end curtain in one set and also along the edge of the end curtain in the other set. 18 They made fifty bronze clasps to fasten the tent together as a unit. 19 Then they made for the tent a covering of ram skins dyed red, and over that a covering of hides of sea cows.

20 They made upright frames of acacia wood for the tabernacle. 21 Each frame was ten cubits long and a cubit and a half wide,[u] 22 with two projections set parallel to each other. They made all the frames of the tabernacle in this way. 23 They made twenty frames for the south side of the tabernacle 24 and made forty silver bases to go under them—two bases for each frame, one under each projection. 25 For the other side, the north side of the tabernacle, they made twenty frames 26 and forty silver bases—two under each frame. 27 They made six frames for the far end, that is, the west end of the tabernacle, 28 and two

[t] *15* That is, about 45 feet (about 13.5 meters) long and 6 feet (about 1.8 meters) wide

[u] *21* That is, about 15 feet (about 4.5 meters) long and 2 1/4 feet (about 0.7 meter) wide

קְרָשִׁים עָשָׂה לִמְקֻצְעֹת הַמִּשְׁכָּן בַּיַּרְכָתָיִם׃ וְהָיוּ
and-they-were (29) at-the-far-ends the-tabernacle for-corners-of he-made frames

תוֹאֲמִם מִלְּמַטָּה וְיַחְדָּו יִהְיוּ תַמִּים אֶל־
at being-fitted they-were and-together from-bottom ones-being-double

רֹאשׁוֹ אֶל־ הַטַּבַּעַת הָאֶחָת כֵּן עָשָׂה לִשְׁנֵיהֶם
for-both-of-them he-made alike the-single the-ring into top-of-him

לִשְׁנֵי הַמִּקְצֹעֹת׃ וְהָיוּ שְׁמֹנָה קְרָשִׁים וְאַדְנֵיהֶם
and-bases-of-them frames eight so-they-were (30) the-corners for-both-of

כֶּסֶף שִׁשָּׁה עָשָׂר אֲדָנִים שְׁנֵי אֲדָנִים שְׁנֵי אֲדָנִים תַּחַת הַקֶּרֶשׁ הָאֶחָד׃
the-each the-frame under bases two-of bases two-of bases ten six silver

וַיַּעַשׂ בְּרִיחֵי עֲצֵי שִׁטִּים חֲמִשָּׁה לְקַרְשֵׁי צֶלַע־
side-of for-frames-of five acacias woods-of crossbars-of and-he-made (31)

הַמִּשְׁכָּן הָאֶחָת׃ וַחֲמִשָּׁה בְּרִיחִם לְקַרְשֵׁי צֶלַע־
side-of for-frames-of crossbars and-five (32) the-one the-tabernacle

הַמִּשְׁכָּן הַשֵּׁנִית וַחֲמִשָּׁה בְּרִיחִם לְקַרְשֵׁי הַמִּשְׁכָּן
the-tabernacle for-frames-of crossbars and-five the-other the-tabernacle

לַיַּרְכָתַיִם יָמָּה׃ וַיַּעַשׂ אֶת־ הַבְּרִיחַ הַתִּיכֹן
the-center the-crossbar *** and-he-made (33) to-west at-the-far-ends

לִבְרֹחַ בְּתוֹךְ הַקְּרָשִׁים מִן־ הַקָּצֶה אֶל־ הַקָּצֶה׃ וְאֶת־ הַקְּרָשִׁים
the-frames and (34) the-end to the-end from the-frames at-middle-of to-extend

צִפָּה זָהָב וְאֶת־ טַבְּעֹתָם עָשָׂה זָהָב בָּתִּים לַבְּרִיחִם
for-the-crossbars holders gold he-made rings-of-them and gold he-overlaid

וַיְצַף אֶת־ הַבְּרִיחִם זָהָב׃ וַיַּעַשׂ אֶת־ הַפָּרֹכֶת
the-curtain *** and-he-made (35) gold the-crossbars *** and-he-overlaid

תְּכֵלֶת וְאַרְגָּמָן וְתוֹלַעַת שָׁנִי וְשֵׁשׁ מָשְׁזָר מַעֲשֵׂה
work-of being-twisted and-fine-linen yarn and-scarlet-of and-purple blue

חֹשֵׁב עָשָׂה אֹתָהּ כְּרֻבִים׃ וַיַּעַשׂ לָהּ אַרְבָּעָה עַמּוּדֵי
posts-of four for-her and-he-made (36) cherubim her he-made being-skilled

שִׁטִּים וַיְצַפֵּם זָהָב וָוֵיהֶם זָהָב וַיִּצֹק לָהֶם
for-them and-he-cast gold hooks-of-them gold and-he-overlaid-them acacias

אַרְבָּעָה אַדְנֵי־ כָסֶף׃ וַיַּעַשׂ מָסָךְ לְפֶתַח הָאֹהֶל תְּכֵלֶת
blue the-tent for-entrance-of curtain and-he-made (37) silver bases-of four

וְאַרְגָּמָן וְתוֹלַעַת שָׁנִי וְשֵׁשׁ מָשְׁזָר מַעֲשֵׂה
work-of being-twisted and-fine-linen yarn and-scarlet-of and-purple

רֹקֵם׃ וְאֶת־ עַמּוּדָיו חֲמִשָּׁה וְאֶת־ וָוֵיהֶם וְצִפָּה
and-he-overlaid hooks-of-them and five posts-of-him and (38) embroidering

רָאשֵׁיהֶם וַחֲשֻׁקֵיהֶם זָהָב וְאַדְנֵיהֶם חֲמִשָּׁה נְחֹשֶׁת׃
bronze five and-bases-of-them gold and-bands-of-them tops-of-them

frames were made for the corners of the tabernacle at the far
end. 29At these two corners the
frames were double from the
bottom all the way to the top
and fitted into a single ring;
both were made alike. 30So
there were eight frames and
sixteen silver bases—two under each frame.
31They also made crossbars
of acacia wood: five for the
frames on one side of the tabernacle, 32five for those on the
other side, and five for the
frames on the west, at the far
end of the tabernacle. 33They
made the center crossbar so
that it extended from end to
end at the middle of the
frames. 34They overlaid the
frames with gold and made
gold rings to hold the crossbars. They also overlaid the
crossbars with gold.
35They made the curtain of
blue, purple and scarlet yarn
and finely twisted linen, with
cherubim worked into it by a
skilled craftsman. 36They made
four posts of acacia wood for it
and overlaid them with gold.
They made gold hooks for
them and cast their four silver
bases. 37For the entrance to the
tent they made a curtain of
blue, purple and scarlet yarn
and finely twisted linen—the
work of an embroiderer; 38and
they made five posts with
hooks for them. They overlaid
the tops of the posts and their
bands with gold and made
their five bases of bronze.

וַיַּעַשׂ בְּצַלְאֵל אֶת־הָאָרֹן עֲצֵי שִׁטִּים אַמָּתַיִם וָחֵצִי
and-half two-cubits acacias woods-of the-ark *** Bezalel and-he-made (37:1)

אָרְכּוֹ וְאַמָּה וָחֵצִי רָחְבּוֹ וְאַמָּה וָחֵצִי
and-half and-cubit width-of-him and-half and-cubit length-of-him

קֹמָתוֹ׃ וַיְצַפֵּהוּ זָהָב טָהוֹר מִבַּיִת וּמִחוּץ
and-on-outside on-inside pure gold and-he-overlaid-him (2) height-of-him

וַיַּעַשׂ לוֹ זֵר זָהָב סָבִיב׃ וַיִּצֹק לוֹ אַרְבַּע
four for-him and-he-cast (3) around gold molding-of for-him and-he-made

טַבְּעֹת זָהָב עַל אַרְבַּע פַּעֲמֹתָיו וּשְׁתֵּי טַבָּעֹת עַל־צַלְעוֹ הָאֶחָת
the-one side-of-him on rings and-two-of feet-of-him four for gold rings-of

וּשְׁתֵּי טַבָּעוֹת עַל־צַלְעוֹ הַשֵּׁנִית׃ וַיַּעַשׂ בַּדֵּי עֲצֵי
woods-of poles-of then-he-made (4) the-other side-of-him on rings and-two-of

שִׁטִּים וַיְצַף אֹתָם זָהָב׃ וַיָּבֵא אֶת־הַבַּדִּים
the-poles *** and-he-inserted (5) gold them and-he-overlaid acacias

בַּטַּבָּעֹת עַל צַלְעֹת הָאָרֹן לָשֵׂאת אֶת־הָאָרֹן׃ וַיַּעַשׂ
and-he-made (6) the-ark *** to-carry the-ark sides-of on into-the-rings

כַּפֹּרֶת זָהָב טָהוֹר אַמָּתַיִם וָחֵצִי אָרְכָּהּ וְאַמָּה וָחֵצִי
and-half and-cubit length-of-her and-half two-cubits pure gold atonement-cover

רָחְבָּהּ׃ וַיַּעַשׂ שְׁנֵי כְרֻבִים זָהָב מִקְשָׁה עָשָׂה אֹתָם
them he-made hammered gold cherubim two-of then-he-made (7) width-of-her

מִשְּׁנֵי קְצוֹת הַכַּפֹּרֶת׃ כְּרוּב־אֶחָד מִקָּצָה מִזֶּה וּכְרוּב־אֶחָד
one and-cherub on-one on-end one cherub (8) the-cover ends-of at-two-of

מִקָּצָה מִזֶּה מִן־הַכַּפֹּרֶת עָשָׂה אֶת־הַכְּרֻבִים מִשְּׁנֵי קְצוֹוֹתָו׃
ends-of-him at-two-of the-cherubim *** he-made the-cover from on-other on-end

וַיִּהְיוּ הַכְּרֻבִים° פֹּרְשֵׂי כְנָפַיִם לְמַעְלָה
upward wings ones-spreading-of the-cherubim and-they-were (9)

סֹכְכִים בְּכַנְפֵיהֶם עַל־הַכַּפֹּרֶת וּפְנֵיהֶם אִישׁ
each and-faces-of-them the-cover over with-wings-of-them ones-overshadowing

אֶל־אָחִיו אֶל־הַכַּפֹּרֶת הָיוּ פְּנֵי הַכְּרֻבִים׃
the-cherubim faces-of they-were the-cover toward other-of-him toward

וַיַּעַשׂ אֶת־הַשֻּׁלְחָן עֲצֵי שִׁטִּים אַמָּתַיִם אָרְכּוֹ
length-of-him two-cubits acacias woods-of the-table *** and-he-made (10)

וְאַמָּה רָחְבּוֹ וְאַמָּה וָחֵצִי קֹמָתוֹ׃ וַיְצַף
and-he-overlaid (11) height-of-him and-half and-cubit width-of-him and-cubit

אֹתוֹ זָהָב טָהוֹר וַיַּעַשׂ לוֹ זֵר זָהָב סָבִיב׃ וַיַּעַשׂ
and-he-made (12) around gold molding-of for-him and-he-made pure gold him

לוֹ מִסְגֶּרֶת טֹפַח סָבִיב וַיַּעַשׂ זֵר־זָהָב לְמִסְגַּרְתּוֹ
on-rim-of-him gold molding-of and-he-put around handbreadth rim-of for-him

*The Ark*

37 Bezalel made the ark of acacia wood—two and a half cubits long, a cubit and a half wide, and a cubit and a half high.[v] 2He overlaid it with pure gold, both inside and out, and made a gold molding around it. 3He cast four gold rings for it and fastened them to its four feet, with two rings on one side and two rings on the other. 4Then he made poles of acacia wood and overlaid them with gold. 5And he inserted the poles into the rings on the sides of the ark to carry it.

6He made the atonement cover of pure gold—two and a half cubits long and a cubit and a half wide.[w] 7Then he made two cherubim out of hammered gold at the ends of the cover. 8He made one cherub on one end and the second cherub on the other; at the two ends he made them of one piece with the cover. 9The cherubim had their wings spread upward, overshadowing the cover with them. The cherubim faced each other, looking toward the cover.

*The Table*

10They[x] made the table of acacia wood—two cubits long, a cubit wide, and a cubit and a half high.[y] 11Then they overlaid it with pure gold and made a gold molding around it. 12They also made around it a rim a handbreadth wide and put a gold molding on the rim.

v1 That is, about 3 3/4 feet (about 1.1 meters) long and 2 1/4 feet (about 0.7 meter) wide and high
w6 That is, about 3 3/4 feet (about 1.1 meters) long and 2 1/4 feet (about 0.7 meter) wide
x10 Or *He;* also in verses 11-29
y10 That is, about 3 feet (about 0.9 meter) long, 1 1/2 feet (about 0.5 meter) wide, and 2 1/4 feet (about 0.7 meter) high

°8 ק קצותיו

סָבִיב׃ וַיִּצֹק לוֹ אַרְבַּע טַבְּעֹת זָהָב וַיִּתֵּן אֶת־

*** and-he-fastened gold rings-of four for-him and-he-cast (13) around

הַטַּבָּעֹת עַל אַרְבַּע הַפֵּאֹת אֲשֶׁר לְאַרְבַּע רַגְלָיו׃ לְעֻמַּת

close-of (14) legs-of-him to-four-of where the-corners four-of to the-rings

הַמִּסְגֶּרֶת הָיוּ הַטַּבָּעֹת בָּתִּים לַבַּדִּים לָשֵׂאת אֶת־הַשֻּׁלְחָן׃

the-table *** to-carry for-the-poles holders the-rings they-were the-rim

וַיַּעַשׂ אֶת־הַבַּדִּים עֲצֵי שִׁטִּים וַיְצַף אֹתָם זָהָב

gold them and-he-overlaid acacias woods-of the-poles *** and-he-made (15)

לָשֵׂאת אֶת־הַשֻּׁלְחָן׃ וַיַּעַשׂ אֶת־הַכֵּלִים ׀ אֲשֶׁר עַל־הַשֻּׁלְחָן

the-table for that the-articles *** and-he-made (16) the-table *** to-carry

אֶת־קְעָרֹתָיו וְאֶת־כַּפֹּתָיו וְאֵת מְנַקִּיֹּתָיו וְאֶת־הַקְּשָׂוֹת אֲשֶׁר

that the-pitchers and bowls-of-him and ladles-of-him and plates-of-him ***

יֻסַּךְ בָּהֵן זָהָב טָהוֹר׃ וַיַּעַשׂ אֶת־הַמְּנֹרָה

the-lampstand *** and-he-made (17) pure gold from-them he-poured-offering

זָהָב טָהוֹר מִקְשָׁה עָשָׂה אֶת־הַמְּנֹרָה יְרֵכָהּ וְקָנָהּ

and-shaft-of-her base-of-her the-lampstand *** he-made hammered pure gold

גְּבִיעֶיהָ כַּפְתֹּרֶיהָ וּפְרָחֶיהָ מִמֶּנָּה הָיוּ׃ וְשִׁשָּׁה

and-six (18) they-were from-her and-blossoms-of-her buds-of-her cups-of-her

קָנִים יֹצְאִים מִצִּדֶּיהָ שְׁלֹשָׁה ׀ קְנֵי מְנֹרָה

lampstand branches-of three from-sides-of-her ones-extending branches

מִצִּדָּהּ הָאֶחָד וּשְׁלֹשָׁה קְנֵי מְנֹרָה מִצִּדָּהּ

from-side-of-her lampstand branches-of and-three the-one from-side-of-her

הַשֵּׁנִי׃ שְׁלֹשָׁה גְבִעִים מְשֻׁקָּדִים בַּקָּנֶה הָאֶחָד כַּפְתֹּר

bud the-one on-the-branch being-like-almonds cups three (19) the-other

וָפֶרַח וּשְׁלֹשָׁה גְבִעִים מְשֻׁקָּדִים בְּקָנֶה אֶחָד כַּפְתֹּר וָפָרַח

and-blossom bud next on-branch being-like-almonds cups and-three and-blossom

כֵּן לְשֵׁשֶׁת הַקָּנִים הַיֹּצְאִים מִן־הַמְּנֹרָה׃

the-lampstand from the-ones-extending the-branches for-six-of same

וּבַמְּנֹרָה אַרְבָּעָה גְבִעִים מְשֻׁקָּדִים כַּפְתֹּרֶיהָ

buds-of-her being-like-almonds cups four and-on-the-lampstand (20)

וּפְרָחֶיהָ׃ וְכַפְתֹּר תַּחַת שְׁנֵי הַקָּנִים מִמֶּנָּה וְכַפְתֹּר

and-bud from-her the-branches pair-of under and-bud (21) and-blossoms-of-her

תַּחַת שְׁנֵי הַקָּנִים מִמֶּנָּה וְכַפְתֹּר תַּחַת־שְׁנֵי הַקָּנִים

the-branches pair-of under and-bud from-her the-branches pair-of under

מִמֶּנָּה לְשֵׁשֶׁת הַקָּנִים הַיֹּצְאִים מִמֶּנָּה׃ כַּפְתֹּרֵיהֶם

buds-of-them (22) from-her the-ones-extending the-branches for-six-of from-her

וּקְנֹתָם מִמֶּנָּה הָיוּ כֻּלָּהּ מִקְשָׁה אַחַת זָהָב

gold one-piece hammered all-of-her they-were from-her and-branches-of-them

[13]They cast four gold rings for the table and fastened them to the four corners, where the four legs were. [14]The rings were put close to the rim to hold the poles used in carrying the table. [15]The poles for carrying the table were made of acacia wood and were overlaid with gold. [16]And they made from pure gold the articles for the table—its plates and ladles and bowls and its pitchers for the pouring out of drink offerings.

*The Lampstand*

[17]They made the lampstand of pure gold and hammered it out, base and shaft; its flowerlike cups, buds and blossoms were of one piece with it. [18]Six branches extended from the sides of the lampstand—three on one side and three on the other. [19]Three cups shaped like almond flowers with buds and blossoms were on one branch, three on the next branch and the same for all six branches extending from the lampstand. [20]And on the lampstand were four cups shaped like almond flowers with buds and blossoms. [21]One bud was under the first pair of branches extending from the lampstand, a second bud under the second pair, and a third bud under the third pair—six branches in all. [22]The buds and the branches were all of one piece with the lampstand, hammered out of pure gold.

טָהוֹר׃ וַיַּעַשׂ אֶת־ נֵרֹתֶיהָ שִׁבְעָה וּמַלְקָחֶיהָ
and-trimmers-of-her seven lamps-of-her *** and-he-made (23) pure

וּמַחְתֹּתֶיהָ זָהָב טָהוֹר׃ כִּכָּר זָהָב טָהוֹר עָשָׂה אֹתָהּ וְאֵת כָּל־
all-of and her he-made pure gold talent (24) pure gold and-trays-of-her

כֵּלֶיהָ׃ וַיַּעַשׂ אֶת־ מִזְבַּח הַקְּטֹרֶת עֲצֵי
woods-of the-incense altar-of *** and-he-made (25) accessories-of-her

שִׁטִּים אַמָּה אָרְכּוֹ וְאַמָּה רָחְבּוֹ רָבוּעַ וְאַמָּתַיִם
and-two-cubits being-square width-of-him and-cubit length-of-him cubit acacias

קֹמָתוֹ מִמֶּנּוּ הָיוּ קַרְנֹתָיו׃ וַיְצַף אֹתוֹ זָהָב
gold him and-he-overlaid (26) horns-of-him they-were from-him height-of-him

טָהוֹר אֶת־ גַּגּוֹ וְאֶת־ קִירֹתָיו סָבִיב וְאֶת־ קַרְנֹתָיו וַיַּעַשׂ
and-he-made horns-of-him and around sides-of-him and top-of-him *** pure

לוֹ זֵר זָהָב סָבִיב׃ וּשְׁתֵּי טַבְּעֹת זָהָב עָשָׂה־ לוֹ
for-him he-made gold rings-of and-two-of (27) around gold molding-of for-him

מִתַּחַת לְזֵרוֹ עַל שְׁתֵּי צַלְעֹתָיו עַל שְׁנֵי צִדָּיו
sides-of-him two-of on sides-of-him two-of on to-molding-of-him for-below

לְבָתִּים לְבַדִּים לָשֵׂאת אֹתוֹ בָּהֶם׃ וַיַּעַשׂ אֶת־ הַבַּדִּים
the-poles *** and-he-made (28) with-them him to-carry for-poles as-holders

עֲצֵי שִׁטִּים וַיְצַף אֹתָם זָהָב׃ וַיַּעַשׂ אֶת־ שֶׁמֶן
oil-of *** and-he-made (29) gold them and-he-overlaid acacias woods-of

הַמִּשְׁחָה קֹדֶשׁ וְאֶת־ קְטֹרֶת הַסַּמִּים טָהוֹר מַעֲשֵׂה רֹקֵחַ׃
one-perfuming work-of pure the-fragrances incense-of and sacred the-anointing

וַיַּעַשׂ אֶת־ מִזְבַּח הָעֹלָה עֲצֵי שִׁטִּים חָמֵשׁ
five acacias woods-of the-burnt-offering altar-of *** and-he-made (38:1)

אַמּוֹת אָרְכּוֹ וְחָמֵשׁ־ אַמּוֹת רָחְבּוֹ רָבוּעַ וְשָׁלֹשׁ
and-three being-square width-of-him cubits and-five length-of-him cubits

אַמּוֹת קֹמָתוֹ׃ וַיַּעַשׂ קַרְנֹתָיו עַל אַרְבַּע פִּנֹּתָיו
corners-of-him four at horns-of-him and-he-made (2) height-of-him cubits

מִמֶּנּוּ הָיוּ קַרְנֹתָיו וַיְצַף אֹתוֹ נְחֹשֶׁת׃ וַיַּעַשׂ
and-he-made (3) bronze him and-he-overlaid horns-of-him they-were from-him

אֶת־ כָּל־ כְּלֵי הַמִּזְבֵּחַ אֶת־ הַסִּירֹת וְאֶת־ הַיָּעִים וְאֶת־
and the-shovels and the-pots *** the-altar utensils-of all-of ***

הַמִּזְרָקֹת אֶת־ הַמִּזְלָגֹת וְאֶת־ הַמַּחְתֹּת כָּל־ כֵּלָיו
utensils-of-him all-of the-firepans and the-meat-forks *** the-sprinkling-bowls

עָשָׂה נְחֹשֶׁת׃ וַיַּעַשׂ לַמִּזְבֵּחַ מִכְבָּר מַעֲשֵׂה רֶשֶׁת נְחֹשֶׁת
bronze net-of work-of grate for-the-altar and-he-made (4) bronze he-made

תַּחַת כַּרְכֻּבּוֹ מִלְּמַטָּה עַד־ חֶצְיוֹ׃ וַיִּצֹק אַרְבַּע טַבָּעֹת
rings four and-he-cast (5) halfway-of-him to downward ledge-of-him under

23They made its seven lamps, as well as its wick trimmers and trays, of pure gold. 24They made the lampstand and all its accessories from one talent[z] of pure gold.

*The Altar of Incense*

25They made the altar of incense out of acacia wood. It was square, a cubit long and a cubit wide, and two cubits high[a]—its horns of one piece with it. 26They overlaid the top and all the sides and the horns with pure gold, and made a gold molding around it. 27They made two gold rings below the molding—two on opposite sides—to hold the poles used to carry it. 28They made the poles of acacia wood and overlaid them with gold.

29They also made the sacred anointing oil and the pure, fragrant incense—the work of a perfumer.

*The Altar of Burnt Offering*

38 They[b] built the altar of burnt offering of acacia wood, three cubits[c] high; it was square, five cubits long and five cubits wide.[d] 2They made a horn at each of the four corners, so that the horns and the altar were of one piece, and they overlaid the altar with bronze. 3They made all its utensils of bronze—its pots, shovels, sprinkling bowls, meat forks and firepans. 4They made a grating for the altar, a bronze network, to be under its ledge, halfway up the altar. 5They cast bronze

z24 That is, about 75 pounds (about 34 kilograms)
a25 That is, about 1 1/2 feet (about 0.5 meter) long and wide, and about 3 feet (about 0.9 meter) high
b1 Or *He;* also in verses 2-9
c1 That is, about 4 1/2 feet (about 1.3 meters)
d1 That is, about 7 1/2 feet (about 2.3 meters) long and wide

בְּאַרְבַּע הַקְּצָוֹת לְמִכְבַּר הַנְּחֹשֶׁת בָּתִּים לַבַּדִּים׃
for-the-poles holders the-bronze for-grate-of the-corners for-four-of

וַיַּעַשׂ אֶת־ הַבַּדִּים עֲצֵי שִׁטִּים וַיְצַף אֹתָם נְחֹשֶׁת׃
bronze them and-he-overlaid acacias woods-of the-poles *** and-he-made (6)

וַיָּבֵא אֶת־ הַבַּדִּים בַּטַּבָּעֹת עַל צַלְעֹת הַמִּזְבֵּחַ
the-altar sides-of on into-the-rings the-poles *** and-he-inserted (7)

לָשֵׂאת אֹתוֹ בָּהֶם נְבוּב לֻחֹת עָשָׂה אֹתוֹ׃ וַיַּעַשׂ
and-he-made (8) him he-made boards being-hollow-of with-them him to-carry

אֵת הַכִּיּוֹר נְחֹשֶׁת וְאֵת כַּנּוֹ נְחֹשֶׁת בְּמַרְאֹת הַצֹּבְאֹת
the-woman-serving from-mirrors-of bronze stand-of-him and bronze the-basin ***

אֲשֶׁר צָבְאוּ פֶּתַח אֹהֶל מוֹעֵד׃ וַיַּעַשׂ אֶת־
*** next-he-made (9) Meeting Tent-of entrance-of they-served who

הֶחָצֵר לִפְאַת ׀ נֶגֶב תֵּימָנָה קַלְעֵי הֶחָצֵר שֵׁשׁ
fine-linen the-courtyard curtains-of to-south south for-side-of the-courtyard

מָשְׁזָר מֵאָה בָּאַמָּה׃ עַמּוּדֵיהֶם עֶשְׂרִים וְאַדְנֵיהֶם
and-bases-of-them twenty posts-of-them (10) by-the-cubit hundred being-twisted

עֶשְׂרִים נְחֹשֶׁת וָוֵי הָעַמֻּדִים וַחֲשֻׁקֵיהֶם כָּסֶף׃ וְלִפְאַת
and-for-side-of (11) silver and-bands-of-them the-posts hooks-of bronze twenty

צָפוֹן מֵאָה בָּאַמָּה עַמּוּדֵיהֶם עֶשְׂרִים וְאַדְנֵיהֶם עֶשְׂרִים
twenty and-bases-of-them twenty posts-of-them by-the-cubit hundred north

נְחֹשֶׁת וָוֵי הָעַמּוּדִים וַחֲשֻׁקֵיהֶם כָּסֶף׃ וְלִפְאַת־ יָם
west and-for-side-of (12) silver and-bands-of-them the-posts hooks-of bronze

קְלָעִים חֲמִשִּׁים בָּאַמָּה עַמּוּדֵיהֶם עֲשָׂרָה וְאַדְנֵיהֶם עֲשָׂרָה וָוֵי
hooks-of ten and-bases-of-them ten posts-of-them by-the-cubit fifty curtains

הָעַמֻּדִים וַחֲשׁוּקֵיהֶם כָּסֶף׃ וְלִפְאַת קֵדְמָה מִזְרָחָה
to-east to-east and-for-side-of (13) silver and-bands-of-them the-posts

חֲמִשִּׁים אַמָּה׃ קְלָעִים חֲמֵשׁ־ עֶשְׂרֵה אַמָּה אֶל־ הַכָּתֵף עַמּוּדֵיהֶם
posts-of-them the-one-side on cubit ten five-of curtains (14) cubit fifty

שְׁלֹשָׁה וְאַדְנֵיהֶם שְׁלֹשָׁה׃ וְלַכָּתֵף הַשֵּׁנִית מִזֶּה
on-this the-other and-for-the-side (15) three and-bases-of-them three

וּמִזֶּה לְשַׁעַר הֶחָצֵר קְלָעִים חֲמֵשׁ עֶשְׂרֵה אַמָּה
cubit ten five-of curtains the-courtyard at-entrance-of and-on-that

עַמֻּדֵיהֶם שְׁלֹשָׁה וְאַדְנֵיהֶם שְׁלֹשָׁה׃ כָּל־ קַלְעֵי
curtains-of all-of (16) three and-bases-of-them three posts-of-them

הֶחָצֵר סָבִיב שֵׁשׁ מָשְׁזָר׃ וְהָאֲדָנִים לָעַמֻּדִים
for-the-posts and-the-bases (17) being-twisted fine-linen around the-courtyard

נְחֹשֶׁת וָוֵי הָעַמּוּדִים וַחֲשׁוּקֵיהֶם כֶּסֶף וְצִפּוּי
and-overlay-of silver and-bands-of-them the-posts hooks-of bronze

rings to hold the poles for the four corners of the bronze grating. [6]They made the poles of acacia wood and overlaid them with bronze. [7]They inserted the poles into the rings so they would be on the sides of the altar for carrying it. They made it hollow, out of boards.

[8]They made the bronze basin and its bronze stand from the mirrors of the women who served at the entrance to the Tent of Meeting.

*The Courtyard*

[9]Next they made the courtyard. The south side was a hundred cubits[e] long and had curtains of finely twisted linen, [10]with twenty posts and twenty bronze bases, and with silver hooks and bands on the posts. [11]The north side was also a hundred cubits long and had twenty posts and twenty bronze bases, with silver hooks and bands on the posts.

[12]The west end was fifty cubits[f] wide and had curtains, with ten posts and ten bases, with silver hooks and bands on the posts. [13]The east end, toward the sunrise, was also fifty cubits wide. [14]Curtains fifteen cubits[g] long were on one side of the entrance, with three posts and three bases, [15]and curtains fifteen cubits long were on the other side of the entrance to the courtyard, with three posts and three bases. [16]All the curtains around the courtyard were of finely twisted linen. [17]The bases for the posts were bronze. The hooks and bands on the posts were silver, and their tops were overlaid with

[e] 9 That is, about 150 feet (about 46 meters)
[f] 12 That is, about 75 feet (about 23 meters)
[g] 14 That is, about 22 1/2 feet (about 6.9 meters)

וְרָאשֵׁיהֶם כָּסֶף וְהֵם מְחֻשָּׁקִים כֶּסֶף כֹּל עַמֻּדֵי
posts-of all-of silver ones-being-banded and-they silver tops-of-them

הֶחָצֵר׃ (18) וּמָסַךְ שַׁעַר הֶחָצֵר מַעֲשֵׂה
work-of the-courtyard entrance-of and-curtain-of (18) the-courtyard

רֹקֵם תְּכֵלֶת וְאַרְגָּמָן וְתוֹלַעַת שָׁנִי וְשֵׁשׁ מָשְׁזָר
being-twisted and-fine-linen yarn and-scarlet-of and-purple blue embroidering

וְעֶשְׂרִים אַמָּה אֹרֶךְ וְקוֹמָה בְרֹחַב חָמֵשׁ אַמּוֹת לְעֻמַּת קַלְעֵי
curtains-of just-like cubits five in-width and-high long cubit and-twenty

הֶחָצֵר׃ (19) וְעַמֻּדֵיהֶם אַרְבָּעָה וְאַדְנֵיהֶם אַרְבָּעָה נְחֹשֶׁת
bronze four bases-of-them four and-posts-of-them (19) the-courtyard

וָוֵיהֶם כֶּסֶף וְצִפּוּי רָאשֵׁיהֶם וַחֲשֻׁקֵיהֶם כָּסֶף׃
silver and-bands-of-them tops-of-them and-overlay-of silver hooks-of-them

(20) וְכָל־ הַיְתֵדֹת לַמִּשְׁכָּן וְלֶחָצֵר סָבִיב
around and-for-the-courtyard for-the-tabernacle the-tent-pegs and-all-of (20)

נְחֹשֶׁת׃ (21) אֵלֶּה פְקוּדֵי הַמִּשְׁכָּן מִשְׁכַּן הָעֵדֻת אֲשֶׁר
which the-Testimony tabernacle-of the-tabernacle amounts-of these (21) bronze

פֻּקַּד עַל־ פִּי מֹשֶׁה עֲבֹדַת הַלְוִיִּם בְּיַד
under-direction-of the-Levites work-of Moses command-of at he-was-recorded

אִיתָמָר בֶּן־ אַהֲרֹן הַכֹּהֵן׃ (22) וּבְצַלְאֵל בֶּן־ אוּרִי בֶן־ חוּר
Hur son-of Uri son-of and-Bezalel (22) the-priest Aaron son-of Ithamar

לְמַטֵּה יְהוּדָה עָשָׂה אֵת כָּל־ אֲשֶׁר־ צִוָּה יְהוָה אֶת־
*** Yahweh he-commanded that everything *** he-made Judah from-tribe-of

מֹשֶׁה׃ (23) וְאִתּוֹ אָהֳלִיאָב בֶּן־ אֲחִיסָמָךְ לְמַטֵּה־ דָן חָרָשׁ
craftsman Dan from-tribe-of Ahisamach son-of Oholiab and-with-him (23) Moses

וְחֹשֵׁב וְרֹקֵם בַּתְּכֵלֶת וּבָאַרְגָּמָן
and-in-the-purple in-the-blue and-embroidering and-one-designing

וּבְתוֹלַעַת הַשָּׁנִי וּבַשֵּׁשׁ׃ (24) כָּל־ הַזָּהָב
the-gold all-of (24) and-in-the-fine-linen the-yarn and-in-scarlet-of

הֶעָשׂוּי לַמְּלָאכָה בְּכֹל מְלֶאכֶת הַקֹּדֶשׁ וַיְהִי ׀
now-he-was the-sanctuary work-of in-all-of for-the-work the-being-used

זְהַב הַתְּנוּפָה תֵּשַׁע וְעֶשְׂרִים כִּכָּר וּשְׁבַע מֵאוֹת
hundreds and-seven-of talent and-twenty nine the-wave-offering gold-of

וּשְׁלֹשִׁים שֶׁקֶל בְּשֶׁקֶל הַקֹּדֶשׁ׃ (25) וְכֶסֶף פְּקוּדֵי
countings-of and-silver-of (25) the-sanctuary by-shekel-of shekel and-thirty

הָעֵדָה מְאַת כִּכָּר וְאֶלֶף וּשְׁבַע מֵאוֹת וַחֲמִשָּׁה
and-five hundreds and-seven-of and-thousand talent hundred-of the-community

וְשִׁבְעִים שֶׁקֶל בְּשֶׁקֶל הַקֹּדֶשׁ׃ (26) בֶּקַע לַגֻּלְגֹּלֶת
per-the-person beka (26) the-sanctuary by-shekel-of shekel and-seventy

silver; so all the posts of the
courtyard had silver bands.
18The curtain for the en-
trance to the courtyard was of
blue, purple and scarlet yarn
and finely twisted linen—the
work of an embroiderer. It was
twenty cubits[h] long and, like
the curtains of the courtyard,
five cubits[i] high, 19with four
posts and four bronze bases.
Their hooks and bands were
silver, and their tops were
overlaid with silver. 20All the
tent pegs of the tabernacle and
of the surrounding courtyard
were bronze.

*The Materials Used*

21These are the amounts of
the materials used for the tabernacle, the tabernacle of the
Testimony, which were
recorded at Moses' command
by the Levites under the direction of Ithamar son of Aaron,
the priest. 22(Bezalel son of Uri,
the son of Hur, of the tribe of
Judah, made everything the
LORD commanded Moses;
23with him was Oholiab son of
Ahisamach, of the tribe of
Dan—a craftsman and design-
er, and an embroiderer in
blue, purple and scarlet yarn
and fine linen.) 24The total
amount of the gold from the
wave offering used for all the
work on the sanctuary was 29
talents and 730 shekels,[j] according to the sanctuary
shekel.
25The silver obtained from
those of the community who
were counted in the census
was 100 talents and 1,775
shekels,[k] according to the
sanctuary shekel— 26one beka

[h] *18* That is, about 30 feet (about 9 meters)
[i] *18* That is, about 7 1/2 feet (about 2.3 meters)
[j] *24* The weight of the gold was a little over one ton (about 1 metric ton).
[k] *25* The weight of the silver was a little over 3 3/4 tons (about 3.4 metric tons).

מַחֲצִית הַשֶּׁקֶל בְּשֶׁקֶל הַקֹּדֶשׁ לְכֹל הָעֹבֵר
the-ones-crossing from-every-of the-sanctuary by-shekel-of the-shekel half-of

עַל־ הַפְּקֻדִים מִבֶּן עֶשְׂרִים שָׁנָה וָמַעְלָה לְשֵׁשׁ־
for-six and-upward year twenty from-son-of the-ones-being-counted to

מֵאוֹת אֶלֶף וּשְׁלֹשֶׁת אֲלָפִים וַחֲמֵשׁ מֵאוֹת וַחֲמִשִּׁים׃
and-fifty hundreds and-five-of thousands and-three thousand hundreds

וַיְהִי מְאַת כִּכַּר הַכֶּסֶף לָצֶקֶת אֵת אַדְנֵי
bases-of *** to-cast the-silver talent-of hundred-of and-he-used (27)

הַקֹּדֶשׁ וְאֵת אַדְנֵי הַפָּרֹכֶת מְאַת אֲדָנִים לִמְאַת
from-hundred-of bases hundred-of the-curtain bases-of and the-sanctuary

הַכִּכָּר כִּכָּר לָאָדֶן׃ וְאֶת־ הָאֶלֶף וּשְׁבַע הַמֵּאוֹת
the-hundreds and-seven-of the-thousand and (28) for-the-base talent the-talent

וַחֲמִשָּׁה וְשִׁבְעִים עָשָׂה וָוִים לָעַמּוּדִים וְצִפָּה רָאשֵׁיהֶם
tops-of-them and-he-overlaid for-the-posts hooks he-made and-seventy and-five

וְחִשַּׁק אֹתָם׃ וּנְחֹשֶׁת הַתְּנוּפָה שִׁבְעִים כִּכָּר
talent seventy the-wave-offering and-bronze-of (29) them and-he-made-bands

וְאַלְפַּיִם וְאַרְבַּע־ מֵאוֹת שָׁקֶל׃ וַיַּעַשׂ בָּהּ אֶת־
*** with-her and-he-made (30) shekel hundreds and-four and-two-thousand

אַדְנֵי פֶּתַח אֹהֶל מוֹעֵד וְאֵת מִזְבַּח הַנְּחֹשֶׁת וְאֶת־ מִכְבַּר
grate-of and the-bronze altar-of and Meeting Tent-of entrance-of bases-of

הַנְּחֹשֶׁת אֲשֶׁר־ לוֹ וְאֵת כָּל־ כְּלֵי הַמִּזְבֵּחַ׃ וְאֶת־ אַדְנֵי
bases-of and (31) the-altar utensils-of all-of and for-him that the-bronze

הֶחָצֵר סָבִיב וְאֶת־ אַדְנֵי שַׁעַר הֶחָצֵר וְאֵת כָּל־
all-of and the-courtyard entrance-of bases-of and around the-courtyard

יִתְדֹת הַמִּשְׁכָּן וְאֶת־ כָּל־ יִתְדֹת הֶחָצֵר סָבִיב׃
around the-courtyard pegs-of all-of and the-tabernacle tent-pegs-of

וּמִן־ הַתְּכֵלֶת וְהָאַרְגָּמָן וְתוֹלַעַת הַשָּׁנִי עָשׂוּ
they-made the-yarn and-scarlet-of and-the-purple the-blue and-from (39:1)

בִגְדֵי־ שְׂרָד לְשָׁרֵת בַּקֹּדֶשׁ וַיַּעֲשׂוּ אֶת־ בִּגְדֵי
garments-of *** and-they-made in-the-sanctuary to-minister woven garments-of

הַקֹּדֶשׁ אֲשֶׁר לְאַהֲרֹן כַּאֲשֶׁר צִוָּה יְהוָה אֶת־ מֹשֶׁה׃
Moses *** Yahweh he-commanded just-as for-Aaron that the-sacred

וַיַּעַשׂ אֶת־ הָאֵפֹד זָהָב תְּכֵלֶת וְאַרְגָּמָן וְתוֹלַעַת שָׁנִי
yarn and-scarlet-of and-purple blue gold the-ephod *** and-he-made (2)

וְשֵׁשׁ מָשְׁזָר׃ וַיְרַקְּעוּ אֶת־ פַּחֵי הַזָּהָב
the-gold sheets-of *** and-they-hammered (3) being-twisted and-fine-linen

וְקִצֵּץ פְּתִילִם לַעֲשׂוֹת בְּתוֹךְ הַתְּכֵלֶת וּבְתוֹךְ הָאַרְגָּמָן וּבְתוֹךְ
and-into the-purple and-into the-blue into to-work strands and-he-cut

per person, that is, half a shekel,[l] according to the sanctuary shekel, from everyone who had crossed over to those counted, twenty years old or more, a total of 603,550 men. [27]The 100 talents[m] of silver were used to cast the bases for the sanctuary and for the curtain—100 bases from the 100 talents, one talent for each base. [28]They used the 1,775 shekels[n] to make the hooks for the posts, to overlay the tops of the posts, and to make their bands.

[29]The bronze from the wave offering was 70 talents and 2,400 shekels.[o] [30]They used it to make the bases for the entrance to the Tent of Meeting, the bronze altar with its bronze grating and all its utensils, [31]the bases for the surrounding courtyard and those for its entrance and all the tent pegs for the tabernacle and those for the surrounding courtyard.

### *The Priestly Garments*

39 From the blue, purple and scarlet yarn they made woven garments for ministering in the sanctuary. They also made sacred garments for Aaron, as the LORD commanded Moses.

### *The Ephod*

[2]They[p] made the ephod of gold, and of blue, purple and scarlet yarn, and of finely twisted linen. [3]They hammered out thin sheets of gold and cut strands to be worked into the blue, purple and scarlet yarn and fine linen—the

[l]26 That is, about 1/5 ounce (about 6 grams)
[m]27 That is, about 3 3/4 tons (about 3.4 metric tons)
[n]28 That is, about 45 pounds (about 20 kilograms)
[o]29 The weight of the bronze was about 2 1/2 tons (about 2.4 metric tons).
[p]2 Or *He;* also in verses 7, 8 and 22

תּוֹלַעַת הַשָּׁנִי וּבְתוֹךְ הַשֵּׁשׁ מַעֲשֵׂה חֹשֵׁב׃
one-being-skilled work-of the-fine-linen and-into the-yarn scarlet-of

כְתֵפֹת עָשׂוּ־ לוֹ חֹבְרֹת עַל־ שְׁנֵי קְצוֹוֹתָו°
corners-of-him two-of to ones-attaching for-him they-made shoulder-pieces (4)

חֻבָּר׃ וְחֵשֶׁב אֲפֻדָּתוֹ אֲשֶׁר עָלָיו מִמֶּנּוּ
from-him on-him that ephod-of-him and-woven-band-of (5) he-was-fastened

הוּא כְּמַעֲשֵׂהוּ זָהָב תְּכֵלֶת וְאַרְגָּמָן וְתוֹלַעַת שָׁנִי וְשֵׁשׁ
and-fine-linen yarn and-scarlet-of and-purple blue gold like-work-of-him he

מָשְׁזָר כַּאֲשֶׁר צִוָּה יְהוָה אֶת־ מֹשֶׁה׃ וַיַּעֲשׂוּ אֶת־
*** and-they-mounted (6) Moses *** Yahweh he-commanded just-as being-twisted

אַבְנֵי הַשֹּׁהַם מֻסַבֹּת מִשְׁבְּצֹת זָהָב מְפֻתָּחֹת
ones-being-engraved gold filigrees-of ones-being-set-of the-onyx stones-of

פִּתּוּחֵי חוֹתָם עַל־ שְׁמוֹת בְּנֵי יִשְׂרָאֵל׃ וַיָּשֶׂם אֹתָם
them and-he-fastened (7) Israel sons-of names-of with seal engravings-of

עַל כִּתְפֹת הָאֵפֹד אַבְנֵי זִכָּרוֹן לִבְנֵי יִשְׂרָאֵל כַּאֲשֶׁר
just-as Israel for-sons-of memorial stones-of the-ephod shoulder-pieces-of on

צִוָּה יְהוָה אֶת־ מֹשֶׁה׃ וַיַּעַשׂ אֶת־ הַחֹשֶׁן מַעֲשֵׂה
work-of the-breastpiece *** and-he-made (8) Moses *** Yahweh he-commanded

חֹשֵׁב כְּמַעֲשֵׂה אֵפֹד זָהָב תְּכֵלֶת וְאַרְגָּמָן וְתוֹלַעַת
and-scarlet-of and-purple blue gold ephod like-work-of one-being-skilled

שָׁנִי וְשֵׁשׁ מָשְׁזָר׃ רָבוּעַ הָיָה כָּפוּל
being-doubled he-was being-square (9) being-twisted and-fine-linen yarn

עָשׂוּ אֶת־ הַחֹשֶׁן זֶרֶת אָרְכּוֹ וְזֶרֶת רָחְבּוֹ
width-of-him and-span length-of-him span the-breastpiece *** they-made

כָּפוּל׃ וַיְמַלְאוּ־ בוֹ אַרְבָּעָה טוּרֵי אָבֶן טוּר אֹדֶם
ruby row stone rows-of four on-him and-they-mounted (10) being-doubled

פִּטְדָה וּבָרֶקֶת הַטּוּר הָאֶחָד׃ וְהַטּוּר הַשֵּׁנִי נֹפֶךְ
turquoise the-second and-the-row (11) the-first the-row and-beryl topaz

סַפִּיר וְיָהֲלֹם*׃ וְהַטּוּר הַשְּׁלִישִׁי לֶשֶׁם שְׁבוֹ וְאַחְלָמָה׃
and-amethyst agate jacinth the-third and-the-row (12) and-emerald sapphire

וְהַטּוּר הָרְבִיעִי תַּרְשִׁישׁ שֹׁהַם וְיָשְׁפֵה מוּסַבֹּת
ones-being-mounted-of and-jasper onyx chrysolite the-fourth and-the-row (13)

מִשְׁבְּצוֹת זָהָב בְּמִלֻּאֹתָם׃ וְהָאֲבָנִים עַל־ שְׁמֹת
names-of with and-the-stones (14) in-settings-of-them gold filigrees-of

בְּנֵי־ יִשְׂרָאֵל הֵנָּה שְׁתֵּים עֶשְׂרֵה עַל־ שְׁמֹתָם פִּתּוּחֵי חֹתָם אִישׁ
each seal engravings-of names-of-them with ten two they Israel sons-of

עַל־ שְׁמוֹ לִשְׁנֵים עָשָׂר שָׁבֶט׃ וַיַּעֲשׂוּ עַל־ הַחֹשֶׁן
the-breastpiece for and-they-made (15) tribe ten for-two name-of-him with

work of a skilled craftsman.
4They made shoulder pieces
for the ephod, which were attached to two of its corners, so
it could be fastened. 5Its skillfully woven waistband was
like it—of one piece with the
ephod and made with gold,
and with blue, purple and
scarlet yarn, and with finely
twisted linen, as the LORD
commanded Moses.
6They mounted the onyx
stones in gold filigree settings
and engraved them like a seal
with the names of the sons of
Israel. 7Then they fastened
them on the shoulder pieces of
the ephod as memorial stones
for the sons of Israel, as the
LORD commanded Moses.

*The Breastpiece*

8They fashioned the breastpiece—the work of a skilled
craftsman. They made it like
the ephod: of gold, and of blue,
purple and scarlet yarn, and of
finely twisted linen. 9It was
square—a span[q] long and a
span wide—and folded dou-
ble. 10Then they mounted four
rows of precious stones on it.
In the first row there was a
ruby, a topaz and a beryl; 11in
the second row a turquoise, a
sapphire[r] and an emerald; 12in
the third row a jacinth, an
agate and an amethyst; 13in
the fourth row a chrysolite, an
onyx and a jasper.[s] They were
mounted in gold filigree settings. 14There were twelve
stones, one for each of the
names of the sons of Israel,
each engraved like a seal with
the name of one of the twelve
tribes.
15For the breastpiece they

q9 That is, about 9 inches (about 22 centimeters)
r11 Or *lapis lazuli*
s13 The precise identification of some of these precious stones is uncertain.

*11 Most mss have *pathah* under the *yod* (וְיַהֲלֹם).

°4 ק קצותיו

שְׁרֹשֶׁרֶת גַּבְלֻת מַעֲשֵׂה עֲבֹת זָהָב טָהוֹר: וַיַּעֲשׂוּ שְׁתֵּי מִשְׁבְּצֹת

chains-of braid work-of rope gold pure (16) and-they-made two-of settings-of

זָהָב וּשְׁתֵּי טַבְּעֹת זָהָב וַיִּתְּנוּ אֶת שְׁתֵּי הַטַּבָּעֹת עַל

gold and-two-of rings-of gold and-they-fastened *** two-of the-rings to

שְׁנֵי קְצוֹת הַחֹשֶׁן: וַיִּתְּנוּ שְׁתֵּי הָעֲבֹתֹת

two-of corners-of the-breastpiece (17) and-they-fastened two-of the-chains

הַזָּהָב עַל שְׁתֵּי הַטַּבָּעֹת עַל קְצוֹת הַחֹשֶׁן: וְאֵת שְׁתֵּי

the-gold to two-of the-rings at corners-of the-breastpiece (18) and two-of

קְצוֹת שְׁתֵּי הָעֲבֹתֹת נָתְנוּ עַל שְׁתֵּי הַמִּשְׁבְּצֹת

ends-of two-of the-chains they-fastened to two-of the-settings

וַיִּתְּנֻם עַל כִּתְפֹת הָאֵפֹד אֶל מוּל פָּנָיו:

and-they-attached-them to shoulder-pieces-of the-ephod at front face-of-him

וַיַּעֲשׂוּ שְׁתֵּי טַבְּעֹת זָהָב וַיָּשִׂימוּ עַל שְׁנֵי

(19) and-they-made two-of rings-of gold and-they-attached to two-of

קְצוֹת הַחֹשֶׁן עַל שְׂפָתוֹ אֲשֶׁר אֶל עֵבֶר הָאֵפֹד בָּיְתָה:

corners-of the-breastpiece on edge-of-him that on side-of the-ephod inside

וַיַּעֲשׂוּ שְׁתֵּי טַבְּעֹת זָהָב וַיִּתְּנֻם עַל שְׁתֵּי

(20) then-they-made two-of rings-of gold and-they-attached-them to two-of

כִּתְפֹת הָאֵפֹד מִלְמַטָּה מִמּוּל פָּנָיו לְעֻמַּת

shoulder-pieces-of the-ephod at-bottom on-front face-of-him to-close-of

מֶחְבַּרְתּוֹ מִמַּעַל לְחֵשֶׁב הָאֵפֹד: וַיִּרְכְּסוּ אֶת

seams-of-him just-above to-waistband-of the-ephod (21) and-they-tied ***

הַחֹשֶׁן מִטַּבְּעֹתָיו אֶל טַבְּעֹת הָאֵפֹד בִּפְתִיל תְּכֵלֶת

the-breastpiece by-rings-of-him to rings-of the-ephod with-cord-of blue

לִהְיוֹת עַל חֵשֶׁב הָאֵפֹד וְלֹא יִזַּח הַחֹשֶׁן

to-connect to waistband-of the-ephod so-not he-would-swing the-breastpiece

מֵעַל הָאֵפֹד כַּאֲשֶׁר צִוָּה יְהוָה אֶת מֹשֶׁה: וַיַּעַשׂ

from-on the-ephod just-as he-commanded Yahweh *** Moses (22) and-he-made

אֶת מְעִיל הָאֵפֹד מַעֲשֵׂה אֹרֵג כְּלִיל תְּכֵלֶת: וּפִי

*** robe-of the-ephod work-of weaving entirely-of blue (23) and-opening-of

הַמְּעִיל בְּתוֹכוֹ כְּפִי תַחְרָא שָׂפָה לְפִיו

the-robe in-center-of-him like-opening-of collar and-band for-opening-of-him

סָבִיב לֹא יִקָּרֵעַ: וַיַּעֲשׂוּ עַל שׁוּלֵי הַמְּעִיל

around not he-would-tear (24) and-they-made around hems-of the-robe

רִמּוֹנֵי תְּכֵלֶת וְאַרְגָּמָן וְתוֹלַעַת שָׁנִי מָשְׁזָר:

pomegranates-of blue and-purple and-scarlet-of yarn being-twisted

וַיַּעֲשׂוּ פַעֲמֹנֵי זָהָב טָהוֹר וַיִּתְּנוּ אֶת הַפַּעֲמֹנִים בְּתוֹךְ

(25) and-they-made bells-of gold pure and-they-attached *** the-bells between

made braided chains of pure gold, like a rope. [16]They made two gold filigree settings and two gold rings, and fastened the rings to two of the corners of the breastpiece. [17]They fastened the two gold chains to the rings at the corners of the breastpiece, [18]and the other ends of the chains to the two settings, attaching them to the shoulder pieces of the ephod at the front. [19]They made two gold rings and attached them to the other two corners of the breastpiece on the inside edge next to the ephod. [20]Then they made two more gold rings and attached them to the bottom of the shoulder pieces on the front of the ephod, close to the seam just above the waistband of the ephod. [21]They tied the rings of the breastpiece to the rings of the ephod with blue cord, connecting it to the waistband so that the breastpiece would not swing out from the ephod—as the LORD commanded Moses.

## Other Priestly Garments

[22]They made the robe of the ephod entirely of blue cloth— the work of a weaver— [23]with an opening in the center of the robe like the opening of a collar,[f] and a band around this opening, so that it would not tear. [24]They made pomegranates of blue, purple and scarlet yarn and finely twisted linen around the hem of the robe. [25]And they made bells of pure gold and attached them

[f]23 The meaning of the Hebrew for this word is uncertain.

הָרִמֹּנִים עַל־ שׁוּלֵי הַמְּעִיל סָבִיב בְּתוֹךְ הָרִמֹּנִים׃
the-pomegranates between around the-robe hems-of on the-pomegranates

פַּעֲמֹן וְרִמֹּן פַּעֲמֹן וְרִמֹּן עַל־ שׁוּלֵי הַמְּעִיל סָבִיב
around the-robe hems-of on and-pomegranate bell and-pomegranate bell (26)

לְשָׁרֵת כַּאֲשֶׁר צִוָּה יְהוָה אֶת־ מֹשֶׁה׃ וַיַּעֲשׂוּ אֶת־
*** and-they-made (27) Moses *** Yahweh he-commanded just-as to-minister

הַכָּתְנֹת שֵׁשׁ מַעֲשֵׂה אֹרֵג לְאַהֲרֹן וּלְבָנָיו׃
and-for-sons-of-him for-Aaron weaving work-of fine-linen the-tunics

וְאֵת הַמִּצְנֶפֶת שֵׁשׁ וְאֶת־ פַּאֲרֵי הַמִּגְבָּעֹת שֵׁשׁ וְאֶת־
and fine-linen the-headbands hats-of and fine-linen the-turban and (28)

מִכְנְסֵי הַבָּד שֵׁשׁ מָשְׁזָר׃ וְאֶת־ הָאַבְנֵט
the-sash and (29) being-twisted fine-linen the-underwear garments-of

שֵׁשׁ מָשְׁזָר וּתְכֵלֶת וְאַרְגָּמָן וְתוֹלַעַת שָׁנִי מַעֲשֵׂה
work-of yarn and-scarlet-of and-purple and-blue being-twisted fine-linen

רֹקֵם כַּאֲשֶׁר צִוָּה יְהוָה אֶת־ מֹשֶׁה׃ וַיַּעֲשׂוּ אֶת־
*** and-they-made (30) Moses *** Yahweh he-commanded just-as embroidering

צִיץ נֵזֶר־ הַקֹּדֶשׁ זָהָב טָהוֹר וַיִּכְתְּבוּ עָלָיו מִכְתַּב
inscription-of on-him and-they-engraved pure gold the-holy diadem-of plate

פִּתּוּחֵי חוֹתָם קֹדֶשׁ לַיהוָה׃ וַיִּתְּנוּ עָלָיו פְּתִיל
cord-of to-him and-they-fastened (31) to-Yahweh holy seal engravings-of

תְּכֵלֶת לָתֵת עַל־ הַמִּצְנֶפֶת מִלְמָעְלָה כַּאֲשֶׁר צִוָּה יְהוָה אֶת־מֹשֶׁה׃
Moses *** Yahweh he-commanded just-as on-top the-turban to to-attach blue

וַתֵּכֶל כָּל־ עֲבֹדַת מִשְׁכַּן אֹהֶל מוֹעֵד וַיַּעֲשׂוּ
and-they-did Meeting Tent-of tabernacle work-of all-of so-he-completed (32)

בְּנֵי יִשְׂרָאֵל כְּכֹל אֲשֶׁר צִוָּה יְהוָה אֶת־ מֹשֶׁה כֵּן עָשׂוּ׃
they-did so Moses *** Yahweh he-commanded that as-all Israel sons-of

וַיָּבִיאוּ אֶת־ הַמִּשְׁכָּן אֶל־ מֹשֶׁה אֶת־ הָאֹהֶל וְאֶת־ כָּל־
all-of and the-tent *** Moses to the-tabernacle *** then-they-brought (33)

כֵּלָיו קְרָסָיו קְרָשָׁיו בְּרִיחָו
crossbars-of-him frames-of-him clasps-of-him furnishings-of-him

וְעַמֻּדָיו וַאֲדָנָיו׃ וְאֶת־ מִכְסֵה עוֹרֹת הָאֵילִם
the-rams skins-of cover-of and (34) and-bases-of-him and-posts-of-him

הַמְאָדָּמִים וְאֶת־ מִכְסֵה עֹרֹת הַתְּחָשִׁים וְאֵת פָּרֹכֶת
curtain-of and the-sea-cows hides-of cover-of and the-ones-being-dyed-red

הַמָּסָךְ׃ אֶת־ אֲרוֹן הָעֵדֻת וְאֶת־ בַּדָּיו וְאֵת
and poles-of-him and the-Testimony ark-of *** (35) the-shield

הַכַּפֹּרֶת׃ אֶת־ הַשֻּׁלְחָן אֶת־ כָּל־ כֵּלָיו וְאֵת
and articles-of-him all-of *** the-table *** (36) the-atonement-cover

around the hem between the
pomegranates. [26]The bells and
pomegranates alternated
around the hem of the robe to
be worn for ministering, as
the LORD commanded Moses.
[27]For Aaron and his sons,
they made tunics of fine lin-
en—the work of a weaver—
[28]and the turban of fine linen,
the linen headbands and the
undergarments of finely twisted linen. [29]The sash was of
finely twisted linen and blue,
purple and scarlet yarn—the
work of an embroiderer—as
the LORD commanded Moses.
[30]They made the plate, the
sacred diadem, out of pure
gold and engraved on it, like
an inscription on a seal: HOLY
TO THE LORD. [31]Then they fastened a blue cord to it to attach
it to the turban, as the LORD
commanded Moses.

*Moses Inspects the Tabernacle*

[32]So all the work on the tabernacle, the Tent of Meeting,
was completed. The Israelites
did everything just as the
LORD commanded Moses.
[33]Then they brought the tabernacle to Moses: the tent and all
its furnishings, its clasps,
frames, crossbars, posts and
bases; [34]the covering of ram
skins dyed red, the covering of
hides of sea cows and the
shielding curtain; [35]the ark of
the Testimony with its poles
and the atonement cover; [36]the
table with all its articles and

°33 ק בריחיו

לֶחֶם הַפָּנִים׃ אֶת־הַמְּנֹרָה הַטְּהֹרָה אֶת־נֵרֹתֶיהָ
lamps-of-her *** the-pure the-lampstand *** (37) the-Presences bread-of

נֵרֹת הַמַּעֲרָכָה וְאֶת־כָּל־כֵּלֶיהָ וְאֵת שֶׁמֶן הַמָּאוֹר׃
the-light oil-of and accessories-of-her all-of and the-row lamps-of

וְאֵת מִזְבַּח הַזָּהָב וְאֵת שֶׁמֶן הַמִּשְׁחָה וְאֵת קְטֹרֶת
incense-of and the-anointing oil-of and the-gold altar-of and (38)

הַסַּמִּים וְאֵת מָסַךְ פֶּתַח הָאֹהֶל׃ אֵת ׀ מִזְבַּח
altar-of *** (39) the-tent entrance-of curtain-of and the-fragrances

הַנְּחֹשֶׁת וְאֶת־מִכְבַּר הַנְּחֹשֶׁת אֲשֶׁר־לוֹ אֶת־בַּדָּיו וְאֶת־כָּל־
all-of and poles-of-him *** for-him that the-bronze grate-of and the-bronze

כֵּלָיו אֶת־הַכִּיֹּר וְאֶת־כַּנּוֹ׃ אֵת קַלְעֵי
curtains-of *** (40) stand-of-him and the-basin *** utensils-of-him

הֶחָצֵר אֶת־עַמֻּדֶיהָ וְאֶת־אֲדָנֶיהָ וְאֶת־הַמָּסָךְ
the-curtain and bases-of-her and posts-of-her *** the-courtyard

לְשַׁעַר הֶחָצֵר אֶת־מֵיתָרָיו וִיתֵדֹתֶיהָ וְאֵת
and and-tent-pegs-of-her ropes-of-him *** the-courtyard for-entrance-of

כָּל־כְּלֵי עֲבֹדַת הַמִּשְׁכָּן לְאֹהֶל מוֹעֵד׃ אֶת־
*** (41) Meeting for-Tent-of the-tabernacle service-of furnishings-of all-of

בִּגְדֵי הַשְּׂרָד לְשָׁרֵת בַּקֹּדֶשׁ אֶת־בִּגְדֵי הַקֹּדֶשׁ
the-sacred garments-of *** in-the-sanctuary to-minister the-woven garments-of

לְאַהֲרֹן הַכֹּהֵן וְאֶת־בִּגְדֵי בָנָיו לְכַהֵן׃ כְּכֹל
as-all (42) to-be-priest sons-of-him garments-of and the-priest for-Aaron

אֲשֶׁר־צִוָּה יְהוָה אֶת־מֹשֶׁה כֵּן עָשׂוּ בְּנֵי יִשְׂרָאֵל אֵת כָּל־
all-of *** Israel sons-of they-did thus Moses *** Yahweh he-commanded that

הָעֲבֹדָה׃ וַיַּרְא מֹשֶׁה אֶת־כָּל־הַמְּלָאכָה וְהִנֵּה עָשׂוּ
they-did and-see! the-work all-of *** Moses and-he-inspected (43) the-work

אֹתָהּ כַּאֲשֶׁר צִוָּה יְהוָה כֵּן עָשׂוּ וַיְבָרֶךְ אֹתָם מֹשֶׁה׃
Moses them so-he-blessed they-did thus Yahweh he-commanded just-as her

וַיְדַבֵּר יְהוָה אֶל־מֹשֶׁה לֵּאמֹר׃ בְּיוֹם־הַחֹדֶשׁ הָרִאשׁוֹן
the-first the-month on-day-of (2) to-say Moses to Yahweh then-he-spoke (40:1)

בְּאֶחָד לַחֹדֶשׁ תָּקִים אֶת־מִשְׁכַּן אֹהֶל מוֹעֵד׃
Meeting Tent-of tabernacle *** you-set-up of-the-month on-first

וְשַׂמְתָּ שָׁם אֵת אֲרוֹן הָעֵדוּת וְסַכֹּתָ עַל־הָאָרֹן
the-ark over and-you-shield the-Testimony ark-of *** there and-you-place (3)

אֶת־הַפָּרֹכֶת׃ וְהֵבֵאתָ אֶת־הַשֻּׁלְחָן וְעָרַכְתָּ אֶת־
*** and-you-set-out the-table *** and-you-bring-in (4) the-curtain with

עֶרְכּוֹ וְהֵבֵאתָ אֶת־הַמְּנֹרָה וְהַעֲלֵיתָ אֶת־
*** and-you-set-up the-lampstand *** then-you-bring-in material-of-him

the bread of the Presence; [37]the pure gold lampstand with its row of lamps and all its accessories, and the oil for the light; [38]the gold altar, the anointing oil, the fragrant incense, and the curtain for the entrance to the tent; [39]the bronze altar with its bronze grating, its poles and all its utensils; the basin with its stand; [40]the curtains of the courtyard with its posts and bases, and the curtain for the entrance to the courtyard; the ropes and tent pegs for the courtyard; all the furnishings for the tabernacle, the Tent of Meeting; [41]and the woven garments worn for ministering in the sanctuary, both the sacred garments for Aaron the priest and the garments for his sons when serving as priests.

[42]The Israelites had done all the work just as the LORD had commanded Moses. [43]Moses inspected the work and saw that they had done it just as the LORD had commanded. So Moses blessed them.

*Setting Up the Tabernacle*

40 Then the LORD said to Moses: [2]"Set up the tabernacle, the Tent of Meeting, on the first day of the first month. [3]Place the ark of the Testimony in it and shield the ark with the curtain. [4]Bring in the table and set out what belongs on it. Then bring in the lampstand and set up its

נֵרֹתֶיהָ׃ וְנָתַתָּה אֶת־ מִזְבַּח הַזָּהָב לִקְטֹרֶת לִפְנֵי
in-front-of of-incense the-gold altar-of *** then-you-place (5) lamps-of-her

אֲרוֹן הָעֵדֻת וְשַׂמְתָּ אֶת־ מָסַךְ הַפֶּתַח לַמִּשְׁכָּן׃
to-the-tabernacle the-entrance curtain-of *** and-you-put the-Testimony ark-of

וְנָתַתָּה אֵת מִזְבַּח הָעֹלָה לִפְנֵי פֶּתַח
entrance-of in-front-of the-burnt-offering altar-of *** then-you-place (6)

מִשְׁכַּן אֹהֶל־ מוֹעֵד׃ וְנָתַתָּ אֶת־ הַכִּיֹּר בֵּין־ אֹהֶל
Tent-of between the-basin *** and-you-place (7) Meeting Tent-of tabernacle

מוֹעֵד וּבֵין הַמִּזְבֵּחַ וְנָתַתָּ שָׁם מָיִם׃ וְשַׂמְתָּ
and-you-set-up (8) water there and-you-put the-altar and-between Meeting

אֶת־ הֶחָצֵר סָבִיב וְנָתַתָּ אֶת־ מָסַךְ שַׁעַר הֶחָצֵר׃
the-courtyard entrance-of curtain-of *** and-you-put around the-courtyard ***

וְלָקַחְתָּ אֶת־ שֶׁמֶן הַמִּשְׁחָה וּמָשַׁחְתָּ אֶת־ הַמִּשְׁכָּן
the-tabernacle *** and-you-anoint the-anointing oil-of *** then-you-take (9)

וְאֶת־כָּל־ אֲשֶׁר־ בּוֹ וְקִדַּשְׁתָּ אֹתוֹ וְאֶת־ כָּל־ כֵּלָיו
furnishings-of-him all-of and him and-you-consecrate in-him that all and

וְהָיָה קֹדֶשׁ׃ וּמָשַׁחְתָּ אֶת־ מִזְבַּח הָעֹלָה וְאֶת־
and the-burnt-offering altar-of *** then-you-anoint (10) holy and-he-will-be

כָּל־ כֵּלָיו וְקִדַּשְׁתָּ אֶת־ הַמִּזְבֵּחַ וְהָיָה
and-he-will-be the-altar *** and-you-consecrate utensils-of-him all-of

הַמִּזְבֵּחַ קֹדֶשׁ קָדָשִׁים׃ וּמָשַׁחְתָּ אֶת־ הַכִּיֹּר וְאֶת־
and the-basin *** then-you-anoint (11) holy-ones holiest-of the-altar

כַּנּוֹ וְקִדַּשְׁתָּ אֹתוֹ׃ וְהִקְרַבְתָּ אֶת־ אַהֲרֹן וְאֶת־
and Aaron *** and-you-bring (12) him and-you-consecrate stand-of-him

בָּנָיו אֶל־ פֶּתַח אֹהֶל מוֹעֵד וְרָחַצְתָּ אֹתָם בַּמָּיִם׃
with-the-waters them and-you-wash Meeting Tent-of entrance-of to sons-of-him

וְהִלְבַּשְׁתָּ אֶת־ אַהֲרֹן אֵת בִּגְדֵי הַקֹּדֶשׁ וּמָשַׁחְתָּ אֹתוֹ
him and-you-anoint the-sacred garments-of *** Aaron *** then-you-dress (13)

וְקִדַּשְׁתָּ אֹתוֹ וְכִהֵן לִי׃ וְאֶת־ בָּנָיו
sons-of-him and (14) to-me so-he-may-be-priest him and-you-consecrate

תַּקְרִיב וְהִלְבַּשְׁתָּ אֹתָם כֻּתֳּנֹת׃ וּמָשַׁחְתָּ אֹתָם כַּאֲשֶׁר
just-as them and-you-anoint (15) tunics them and-you-dress you-bring

מָשַׁחְתָּ אֶת־ אֲבִיהֶם וְכִהֲנוּ לִי וְהָיְתָה
and-she-will-be to-me so-they-may-be-priests father-of-them *** you-anointed

לִהְיֹת לָהֶם מָשְׁחָתָם לִכְהֻנַּת עוֹלָם לְדֹרֹתָם׃
for-generations-of-them continual to-priesthood-of to-anoint-them for-them to-be

וַיַּעַשׂ מֹשֶׁה כְּכֹל אֲשֶׁר צִוָּה יְהוָה אֹתוֹ כֵּן עָשָׂה׃
he-did so him Yahweh he-commanded that as-all Moses and-he-did (16)

lamps. [5]Place the gold altar of incense in front of the ark of the Testimony and put the curtain at the entrance to the tabernacle.

[6]"Place the altar of burnt offering in front of the entrance to the tabernacle, the Tent of Meeting; [7]place the basin between the Tent of Meeting and the altar and put water in it. [8]Set up the courtyard around it and put the curtain at the entrance to the courtyard.

[9]"Take the anointing oil and anoint the tabernacle and everything in it; consecrate it and all its furnishings, and it will be holy. [10]Then anoint the altar of burnt offering and all its utensils; consecrate the altar, and it will be most holy. [11]Anoint the basin and its stand and consecrate them.

[12]"Bring Aaron and his sons to the entrance to the Tent of Meeting and wash them with water. [13]Then dress Aaron in the sacred garments, anoint him and consecrate him so he may serve me as priest. [14]Bring his sons and dress them in tunics. [15]Anoint them just as you anointed their father, so they may serve me as priests. Their anointing will be to a priesthood that will continue for all generations to come." [16]Moses did everything just as the LORD commanded him.

וַיְהִי בַּחֹדֶשׁ הָרִאשׁוֹן בַּשָּׁנָה הַשֵּׁנִית בְּאֶחָד
on-first the-second in-the-year the-first on-the-month so-he-was (17)

לַחֹדֶשׁ הוּקַם הַמִּשְׁכָּן׃ וַיָּקֶם מֹשֶׁה אֶת־
*** Moses when-he-set-up (18) the-tabernacle he-was-set-up of-the-month

הַמִּשְׁכָּן וַיִּתֵּן אֶת־ אֲדָנָיו וַיָּשֶׂם אֶת־ קְרָשָׁיו
frames-of-him *** and-he-erected bases-of-him *** then-he-put the-tabernacle

וַיִּתֵּן אֶת־ בְּרִיחָיו וַיָּקֶם אֶת־ עַמּוּדָיו׃
posts-of-him *** and-he-set-up crossbars-of-him *** and-he-inserted

וַיִּפְרֹשׂ אֶת־ הָאֹהֶל עַל־ הַמִּשְׁכָּן וַיָּשֶׂם אֶת־ מִכְסֵה
cover-of *** and-he-put the-tabernacle over the-tent *** then-he-spread (19)

הָאֹהֶל עָלָיו מִלְמָעְלָה כַּאֲשֶׁר צִוָּה יְהוָה אֶת־ מֹשֶׁה׃
Moses *** Yahweh he-commanded just-as on-top over-him the-tent

וַיִּקַּח וַיִּתֵּן אֶת־ הָעֵדֻת אֶל־הָאָרֹן וַיָּשֶׂם אֶת־
*** and-he-attached the-ark in the-Testimony *** and-he-placed and-he-took (20)

הַבַּדִּים עַל־ הָאָרֹן וַיִּתֵּן אֶת־ הַכַּפֹּרֶת עַל־ הָאָרֹן מִלְמָעְלָה׃
on-top the-ark over the-cover *** and-he-put the-ark to the-poles

וַיָּבֵא אֶת־ הָאָרֹן אֶל־ הַמִּשְׁכָּן וַיָּשֶׂם אֵת פָּרֹכֶת
curtain-of *** and-he-hung the-tabernacle into the-ark *** then-he-brought (21)

הַמָּסָךְ וַיָּסֶךְ עַל אֲרוֹן הָעֵדוּת כַּאֲשֶׁר צִוָּה
he-commanded just-as the-Testimony ark-of over and-he-shielded the-shield

יְהוָה אֶת־ מֹשֶׁה׃ וַיִּתֵּן אֶת־ הַשֻּׁלְחָן בְּאֹהֶל מוֹעֵד עַל
on Meeting in-Tent-of the-table *** and-he-placed (22) Moses *** Yahweh

יֶרֶךְ הַמִּשְׁכָּן צָפֹנָה מִחוּץ לַפָּרֹכֶת׃ וַיַּעֲרֹךְ
and-he-set-out (23) of-the-curtain outside to-north the-tabernacle side-of

עָלָיו עֵרֶךְ לֶחֶם לִפְנֵי יְהוָה כַּאֲשֶׁר צִוָּה יְהוָה אֶת־ מֹשֶׁה׃
Moses *** Yahweh he-commanded just-as Yahweh before bread set-of on-him

וַיָּשֶׂם אֶת־ הַמְּנֹרָה בְּאֹהֶל מוֹעֵד נֹכַח הַשֻּׁלְחָן
the-table opposite Meeting in-Tent-of the-lampstand *** and-he-placed (24)

עַל יֶרֶךְ הַמִּשְׁכָּן נֶגְבָּה׃ וַיַּעַל הַנֵּרֹת לִפְנֵי יְהוָה
Yahweh before the-lamps and-he-set-up (25) to-south the-tabernacle side-of on

כַּאֲשֶׁר צִוָּה יְהוָה אֶת־ מֹשֶׁה׃ וַיָּשֶׂם אֶת־ מִזְבַּח הַזָּהָב
the-gold altar-of *** and-he-placed (26) Moses *** Yahweh he-commanded just-as

בְּאֹהֶל מוֹעֵד לִפְנֵי הַפָּרֹכֶת׃ וַיַּקְטֵר עָלָיו
on-him and-he-burned (27) the-curtain in-front-of Meeting in-Tent-of

קְטֹרֶת סַמִּים כַּאֲשֶׁר צִוָּה יְהוָה אֶת־ מֹשֶׁה׃ וַיָּשֶׂם
then-he-put (28) Moses *** Yahweh he-commanded just-as fragrances incense-of

אֶת־ מָסַךְ הַפֶּתַח לַמִּשְׁכָּן׃ וְאֵת מִזְבַּח הָעֹלָה
the-offering altar-of and (29) to-the-tabernacle the-entrance curtain-of ***

[17]So the tabernacle was set
up on the first day of the first
month in the second year.
[18]When Moses set up the tabernacle, he put the bases in
place, erected the frames, inserted the crossbars and set up
the posts. [19]Then he spread the
tent over the tabernacle and
put the covering over the tent,
as the LORD commanded him.
[20]He took the Testimony and
placed it in the ark, attached
the poles to the ark and put the
atonement cover over it.
[21]Then he brought the ark into
the tabernacle and hung the
shielding curtain and shielded
the ark of the Testimony, as
the LORD commanded him.
[22]Moses placed the table in
the Tent of Meeting on the
north side of the tabernacle
outside the curtain [23]and set
out the bread on it before the
LORD, as the LORD commanded
him.
[24]He placed the lampstand in
the Tent of Meeting opposite
the table on the south side of
the tabernacle [25]and set up the
lamps before the LORD, as the
LORD commanded him.
[26]Moses placed the gold altar
in the Tent of Meeting in front
of the curtain [27]and burned
fragrant incense on it, as the
LORD commanded him. [28]Then
he put up the curtain at the
entrance to the tabernacle.
[29]He set the altar of burnt

שָׂם פֶּתַח מִשְׁכַּן אֹהֶל־מוֹעֵד וַיַּעַל עָלָיו אֶת־
*** on-him and-he-offered Meeting Tent-of tabernacle entrance-of he-set

הָעֹלָה וְאֶת־הַמִּנְחָה כַּאֲשֶׁר צִוָּה יְהוָה אֶת־מֹשֶׁה׃
Moses *** Yahweh he-commanded just-as the-grain-offering and the-burnt-offering

(30) וַיָּשֶׂם אֶת־הַכִּיֹּר בֵּין־אֹהֶל מוֹעֵד וּבֵין הַמִּזְבֵּחַ
the-altar and-between Meeting Tent-of between the-basin *** and-he-placed (30)

וַיִּתֵּן שָׁמָּה מַיִם לְרָחְצָה׃ (31) וְרָחֲצוּ מִמֶּנּוּ מֹשֶׁה וְאַהֲרֹן
and-Aaron Moses in-him and-they-washed (31) to-wash waters in-there and-he-put

וּבָנָיו אֶת־יְדֵיהֶם וְאֶת־רַגְלֵיהֶם׃ (32) בְּבֹאָם
when-to-enter-them (32) feet-of-them and hands-of-them *** and-sons-of-him

אֶל־אֹהֶל מוֹעֵד וּבְקָרְבָתָם אֶל־הַמִּזְבֵּחַ יִרְחָצוּ כַּאֲשֶׁר
just-as they-washed the-altar to or-when-to-approach-them Meeting Tent-of into

צִוָּה יְהוָה אֶת־מֹשֶׁה׃ (33) וַיָּקֶם אֶת־הֶחָצֵר סָבִיב
around the-courtyard *** then-he-set-up (33) Moses *** Yahweh he-commanded

לַמִּשְׁכָּן וְלַמִּזְבֵּחַ וַיִּתֵּן אֶת־מָסַךְ שַׁעַר
entrance-of curtain-of *** and-he-put-up and-to-the-altar to-the-tabernacle

הֶחָצֵר וַיְכַל מֹשֶׁה אֶת־הַמְּלָאכָה׃ (34) וַיְכַס
then-he-covered (34) the-work *** Moses so-he-finished the-courtyard

הֶעָנָן אֶת־אֹהֶל מוֹעֵד וּכְבוֹד יְהוָה מָלֵא אֶת־
*** he-filled Yahweh and-glory-of Meeting Tent-of *** the-cloud

הַמִּשְׁכָּן׃ (35) וְלֹא־יָכֹל מֹשֶׁה לָבוֹא אֶל־אֹהֶל מוֹעֵד כִּי־
for Meeting Tent-of into to-enter Moses he-could and-not (35) the-tabernacle

שָׁכַן עָלָיו הֶעָנָן וּכְבוֹד יְהוָה מָלֵא אֶת־הַמִּשְׁכָּן׃
the-tabernacle *** he-filled Yahweh and-glory-of the-cloud on-him he-settled

(36) וּבְהֵעָלוֹת הֶעָנָן מֵעַל הַמִּשְׁכָּן יִסְעוּ בְּנֵי
sons-of they-set-out the-tabernacle from-on the-cloud and-when-to-lift (36)

יִשְׂרָאֵל בְּכֹל מַסְעֵיהֶם׃ (37) וְאִם־לֹא יֵעָלֶה הֶעָנָן
the-cloud he-lifted not but-if (37) travels-of-them in-all-of Israel

וְלֹא יִסְעוּ עַד־יוֹם הֵעָלֹתוֹ׃ (38) כִּי עֲנַן יְהוָה עַל־
over Yahweh cloud-of so (38) to-lift-him day until they-set-out then-not

הַמִּשְׁכָּן יוֹמָם וְאֵשׁ תִּהְיֶה לַיְלָה בּוֹ לְעֵינֵי כָל־
all-of before-eyes-of in-him night she-was and-fire by-day the-tabernacle

בֵּית־יִשְׂרָאֵל בְּכָל־מַסְעֵיהֶם׃
travels-of-them in-all-of Israel house-of

offering near the entrance to the tabernacle, the Tent of Meeting, and offered on it burnt offerings and grain offerings, as the LORD commanded him.

30 He placed the basin between the Tent of Meeting and the altar and put water in it for washing, 31 and Moses and Aaron and his sons used it to wash their hands and feet. 32 They washed whenever they entered the Tent of Meeting or approached the altar, as the LORD commanded Moses.

33 Then Moses set up the courtyard around the tabernacle and altar and put up the curtain at the entrance to the courtyard. And so Moses finished the work.

*The Glory of the LORD*

34 Then the cloud covered the Tent of Meeting, and the glory of the LORD filled the tabernacle. 35 Moses could not enter the Tent of Meeting because the cloud had settled upon it, and the glory of the LORD filled the tabernacle.

36 In all the travels of the Israelites, whenever the cloud lifted from above the tabernacle, they would set out; 37 but if the cloud did not lift, they did not set out—until the day it lifted. 38 So the cloud of the LORD was over the tabernacle by day, and fire was in the cloud by night, in the sight of all the house of Israel during all their travels.

וַיִּקְרָא אֶל־מֹשֶׁה וַיְדַבֵּר יְהוָה אֵלָיו מֵאֹהֶל מוֹעֵד
Meeting from-Tent-of to-him Yahweh and-he-spoke Moses to and-he-called (1:1)

לֵאמֹר׃ דַּבֵּר אֶל־בְּנֵי יִשְׂרָאֵל וְאָמַרְתָּ אֲלֵהֶם אָדָם כִּי־יַקְרִיב
he-brings when anyone to-them and-you-say Israel sons-of to speak! (2) to-say

מִכֶּם קָרְבָּן לַיהוָה מִן־הַבְּהֵמָה מִן־הַבָּקָר וּמִן־הַצֹּאן
the-flock or-from the-herd from the-animal from to-Yahweh offering from-you

תַּקְרִיבוּ אֶת־קָרְבַּנְכֶם׃ אִם־עֹלָה קָרְבָּנוֹ מִן־
from offering-of-him burnt-offering if (3) offering-of-you *** you-bring

הַבָּקָר זָכָר תָּמִים יַקְרִיבֶנּוּ אֶל־פֶּתַח אֹהֶל מוֹעֵד
Meeting Tent-of entrance-of at he-must-offer-him without-defect male the-herd

יַקְרִיב אֹתוֹ לִרְצֹנוֹ לִפְנֵי יְהוָה׃ וְסָמַךְ
and-he-must-lay (4) Yahweh before for-acceptance-of-him him he-must-present

יָדוֹ עַל רֹאשׁ הָעֹלָה וְנִרְצָה לוֹ
for-him and-he-will-be-accepted the-burnt-offering head-of on hand-of-him

לְכַפֵּר עָלָיו׃ וְשָׁחַט אֶת־בֶּן הַבָּקָר לִפְנֵי
before the-herd son-of *** then-he-must-slaughter (5) for-him to-atone

יְהוָה וְהִקְרִיבוּ בְּנֵי אַהֲרֹן הַכֹּהֲנִים אֶת־הַדָּם
the-blood *** the-priests Aaron sons-of and-they-will-bring Yahweh

וְזָרְקוּ אֶת־הַדָּם עַל־הַמִּזְבֵּחַ סָבִיב אֲשֶׁר־פֶּתַח
entrance-of at around the-altar against the-blood *** and-they-will-sprinkle

אֹהֶל מוֹעֵד׃ וְהִפְשִׁיט אֶת־הָעֹלָה וְנִתַּח
and-he-must-cut the-burnt-offering *** and-he-must-skin (6) Meeting Tent-of

אֹתָהּ לִנְתָחֶיהָ׃ וְנָתְנוּ בְּנֵי אַהֲרֹן הַכֹּהֵן אֵשׁ
fire the-priest Aaron sons-of and-they-must-put (7) into-pieces-of-her her

עַל־הַמִּזְבֵּחַ וְעָרְכוּ עֵצִים עַל־הָאֵשׁ׃ וְעָרְכוּ
and-they-shall-arrange (8) the-fire on woods and-they-must-arrange the-altar on

בְּנֵי אַהֲרֹן הַכֹּהֲנִים אֵת הַנְּתָחִים אֶת־הָרֹאשׁ וְאֶת־הַפָּדֶר עַל־
on the-fat and the-head *** the-pieces *** the-priests Aaron sons-of

הָעֵצִים אֲשֶׁר עַל־הָאֵשׁ אֲשֶׁר עַל־הַמִּזְבֵּחַ׃ וְקִרְבּוֹ
and-inner-part-of-him (9) the-altar on that the-fire on that the-woods

וּכְרָעָיו יִרְחַץ בַּמָּיִם וְהִקְטִיר הַכֹּהֵן אֶת־
*** the-priest and-he-must-burn with-the-waters he-must-wash and-legs-of-him

הַכֹּל הַמִּזְבֵּחָה עֹלָה אִשֵּׁה רֵיחַ־נִיחוֹחַ לַיהוָה׃
to-Yahweh pleasant aroma-of by-fire burnt-offering on-the-altar the-whole

וְאִם־מִן־הַצֹּאן קָרְבָּנוֹ מִן־הַכְּשָׂבִים אוֹ מִן־
from or the-sheep from offering-of-him the-flock from and-if (10)

הָעִזִּים לְעֹלָה זָכָר תָּמִים יַקְרִיבֶנּוּ׃
he-must-offer-him without-defect male for-burnt-offering the-goats

### *The Burnt Offering*

1 The LORD called to Moses and spoke to him from the Tent of Meeting. He said,
2 "Speak to the Israelites and say to them: 'When any of you brings an offering to the LORD, bring as your offering an animal from either the herd or the flock.
3 " 'If the offering is a burnt offering from the herd, he is to offer a male without defect. He must present it at the entrance to the Tent of Meeting so that it[a] will be acceptable to the LORD.
4 He is to lay his hand on the head of the burnt offering, and it will be accepted on his behalf to make atonement for him.
5 He is to slaughter the young bull before the LORD, and then Aaron's sons the priests shall bring the blood and sprinkle it against the altar on all sides at the entrance to the Tent of Meeting.
6 He is to skin the burnt offering and cut it into pieces.
7 The sons of Aaron the priest are to put fire on the altar and arrange wood on the fire.
8 Then Aaron's sons the priests shall arrange the pieces, including the head and the fat, on the burning wood that is on the altar.
9 He is to wash the inner parts and the legs with water, and the priest is to burn all of it on the altar. It is a burnt offering, an offering made by fire, an aroma pleasing to the LORD.
10 " 'If the offering is a burnt offering from the flock, from either the sheep or the goats, he is to offer a male without

[a] 3 Or *he*

וְשָׁחַט אֹתוֹ עַל יֶרֶךְ הַמִּזְבֵּחַ צָפֹנָה לִפְנֵי יְהוָה

Yahweh before to-north the-altar side-of on him and-he-must-slaughter (11)

וְזָרְקוּ בְּנֵי אַהֲרֹן הַכֹּהֲנִים אֶת־ דָּמוֹ עַל־

against blood-of-him *** the-priests Aaron sons-of and-they-shall-sprinkle

הַמִּזְבֵּחַ סָבִיב׃ וְנִתַּח אֹתוֹ לִנְתָחָיו וְאֶת־ רֹאשׁוֹ

head-of-him and into-pieces-of-him him and-he-must-cut (12) around the-altar

וְאֶת־ פִּדְרוֹ וְעָרַךְ הַכֹּהֵן אֹתָם עַל־ הָעֵצִים אֲשֶׁר עַל־

on that the-woods on them the-priest and-he-shall-arrange fat-of-him and

הָאֵשׁ אֲשֶׁר עַל־ הַמִּזְבֵּחַ׃ וְהַקֶּרֶב וְהַכְּרָעַיִם יִרְחַץ

he-must-wash and-the-legs and-the-inner-part (13) the-altar on that the-fire

בַּמָּיִם וְהִקְרִיב הַכֹּהֵן אֶת־ הַכֹּל וְהִקְטִיר

and-he-must-burn the-whole *** the-priest then-he-must-bring with-the-waters

הַמִּזְבֵּחָה עֹלָה הוּא אִשֵּׁה רֵיחַ נִיחֹחַ לַיהוָה׃

to-Yahweh pleasant aroma-of by-fire he burnt-offering on-the-altar

וְאִם מִן־ הָעוֹף עֹלָה קָרְבָּנוֹ לַיהוָה

to-Yahweh offering-of-him burnt-offering the-bird from and-if (14)

וְהִקְרִיב מִן־ הַתֹּרִים אוֹ מִן־ בְּנֵי הַיּוֹנָה אֶת־

*** the-pigeon young-ones-of from or the-doves from then-he-must-offer

קָרְבָּנוֹ׃ וְהִקְרִיבוֹ הַכֹּהֵן אֶל־ הַמִּזְבֵּחַ

the-altar to the-priest and-he-shall-bring-him (15) offering-of-him

וּמָלַק אֶת־ רֹאשׁוֹ וְהִקְטִיר הַמִּזְבֵּחָה

on-the-altar and-he-shall-burn head-of-him *** and-he-shall-wring-off

וְנִמְצָה דָמוֹ עַל קִיר הַמִּזְבֵּחַ׃

the-altar side-of on blood-of-him and-he-shall-be-drained

וְהֵסִיר אֶת־ מֻרְאָתוֹ בְּנֹצָתָהּ וְהִשְׁלִיךְ

and-he-shall-throw with-content-of-her crop-of-him *** and-he-shall-remove (16)

אֹתָהּ אֵצֶל הַמִּזְבֵּחַ קֵדְמָה אֶל־ מְקוֹם הַדָּשֶׁן׃ וְשִׁסַּע

and-he-shall-tear-open (17) the-ash place-of at to-east the-altar side-of her

אֹתוֹ בִכְנָפָיו לֹא יַבְדִּיל וְהִקְטִיר אֹתוֹ הַכֹּהֵן

the-priest him and-he-shall-burn he-shall-sever not by-wings-of-him him

הַמִּזְבֵּחָה עַל־ הָעֵצִים אֲשֶׁר עַל־ הָאֵשׁ עֹלָה הוּא אִשֵּׁה רֵיחַ

aroma-of by-fire he burnt-offering the-fire on that the-woods on on-the-altar

נִיחֹחַ לַיהוָה׃ וְנֶפֶשׁ כִּי־ תַקְרִיב קָרְבַּן מִנְחָה

grain offering-of she-brings when and-someone (2:1) to-Yahweh pleasant

לַיהוָה סֹלֶת יִהְיֶה קָרְבָּנוֹ וְיָצַק עָלֶיהָ שֶׁמֶן

oil on-her and-he-must-pour offering-of-him he-must-be fine-flour to-Yahweh

וְנָתַן עָלֶיהָ לְבֹנָה׃ וֶהֱבִיאָהּ אֶל־ בְּנֵי אַהֲרֹן

Aaron sons-of to then-he-must-take-her (2) incense on-her and-he-must-put

defect. 11He is to slaughter it at the north side of the altar before the LORD, and Aaron's sons the priests shall sprinkle its blood against the altar on all sides. 12He is to cut it into pieces, and the priest shall arrange them, including the head and the fat, on the burning wood that is on the altar. 13He is to wash the inner parts and the legs with water, and the priest is to bring all of it and burn it on the altar. It is a burnt offering, an offering made by fire, an aroma pleasing to the LORD.

14" 'If the offering to the LORD is a burnt offering of birds, he is to offer a dove or a young pigeon. 15The priest shall bring it to the altar, wring off the head and burn it on the altar; its blood shall be drained out on the side of the altar. 16He is to remove the crop with its contents[b] and throw it to the east side of the altar, where the ashes are. 17He shall tear it open by the wings, not severing it completely, and then the priest shall burn it on the wood that is on the fire on the altar. It is a burnt offering, an offering made by fire, an aroma pleasing to the LORD.

*The Grain Offering*

2 " 'When someone brings a grain offering to the LORD, his offering is to be of fine flour. He is to pour oil on it, put incense on it 2and take it to Aaron's sons the priests. The

[b]16 Or *crop and the feathers;* the meaning of the Hebrew for this word is uncertain.

הַכֹּהֲנִים וְקָמַץ מִשָּׁם מְלֹא קֻמְצוֹ מִסָּלְתָּהּ
from-flour-of-her handful-of-him full-of from-there and-he-shall-take the-priests

וּמִשַּׁמְנָהּ עַל כָּל־ לְבֹנָתָהּ וְהִקְטִיר הַכֹּהֵן
the-priest and-he-shall-burn incense-of-her all-of with and-from-oil-of-her

אֶת־ אַזְכָּרָתָהּ הַמִּזְבֵּחָה אִשֵּׁה רֵיחַ נִיחֹחַ לַיהוָה׃
to-Yahweh pleasant aroma-of by-fire on-the-altar memorial-portion-of-her ***

(3) וְהַנּוֹתֶרֶת מִן־ הַמִּנְחָה לְאַהֲרֹן וּלְבָנָיו
and-for-sons-of-him for-Aaron the-grain-offering from and-the-being-left (3)

קֹדֶשׁ קָדָשִׁים מֵאִשֵּׁי יְהוָה׃ (4) וְכִי תַקְרִב
you-bring and-if (4) Yahweh from-fire-offerings-of holy-ones holiest-of

קָרְבַּן מִנְחָה מַאֲפֵה תַנּוּר סֹלֶת חַלּוֹת מַצֹּת
without-yeast cakes-of fine-flour oven baked-of grain offering-of

בְּלוּלֹת בַּשֶּׁמֶן וּרְקִיקֵי מַצּוֹת מְשֻׁחִים
ones-being-spread without-yeast or-wafers-of with-the-oil ones-being-mixed

בַּשָּׁמֶן׃ (5) וְאִם־ מִנְחָה עַל־ הַמַּחֲבַת קָרְבָּנֶךָ
offering-of-you the-griddle on grain-offering and-if (5) with-the-oil

סֹלֶת בְּלוּלָה בַשֶּׁמֶן מַצָּה תִהְיֶה׃ (6) פָּתוֹת
to-crumble (6) she-must-be without-yeast with-the-oil being-mixed fine-flour

אֹתָהּ פִּתִּים וְיָצַקְתָּ עָלֶיהָ שָׁמֶן מִנְחָה הִוא׃ (7) וְאִם־
and-if (7) he grain-offering oil on-her and-you-pour crumbs her

מִנְחַת מַרְחֶשֶׁת קָרְבָּנֶךָ סֹלֶת בַּשֶּׁמֶן תֵּעָשֶׂה׃
she-must-be-made with-the-oil fine-flour offering-of-you pan-cooked grain-offering-of

(8) וְהֵבֵאתָ אֶת־ הַמִּנְחָה אֲשֶׁר יֵעָשֶׂה מֵאֵלֶּה
from-these he-was-made that the-grain-offering *** then-you-bring (8)

לַיהוָה וְהִקְרִיבָהּ אֶל־ הַכֹּהֵן וְהִגִּישָׁהּ אֶל־
to and-he-shall-take-her the-priest to and-he-will-present-her to-Yahweh

הַמִּזְבֵּחַ׃ (9) וְהֵרִים הַכֹּהֵן מִן־ הַמִּנְחָה אֶת־
*** grain-offering from the-priest and-he-shall-take (9) the-altar

אַזְכָּרָתָהּ וְהִקְטִיר הַמִּזְבֵּחָה אִשֵּׁה רֵיחַ
aroma-of fire-offering on-the-altar and-he-shall-burn memorial-portion-of-her

נִיחֹחַ לַיהוָה׃ (10) וְהַנּוֹתֶרֶת מִן־ הַמִּנְחָה לְאַהֲרֹן
for-Aaron the-grain-offering from and-the-being-left (10) to-Yahweh pleasant

וּלְבָנָיו קֹדֶשׁ קָדָשִׁים מֵאִשֵּׁי יְהוָה׃
Yahweh from-fire-offerings-of holy-ones holiest-of and-for-sons-of-him

(11) כָּל־ הַמִּנְחָה אֲשֶׁר תַּקְרִיבוּ לַיהוָה לֹא תֵעָשֶׂה
she-may-be-made not to-Yahweh you-bring that the-grain-offering every-of (11)

חָמֵץ כִּי כָל־ שְׂאֹר וְכָל־ דְּבַשׁ לֹא־ תַקְטִירוּ מִמֶּנּוּ אִשֶּׁה
fire-offering from-him you-may-burn not honey or-any-of yeast any-of for yeast

priest shall take a handful of
the fine flour and oil, together
with all the incense, and burn
this as a memorial portion on
the altar, an offering made by
fire, an aroma pleasing to the
LORD. 3The rest of the grain
offering belongs to Aaron and
his sons; it is a most holy part
of the offerings made to the
LORD by fire.
4" 'If you bring a grain
offering baked in an oven, it is
to consist of fine flour: cakes
made without yeast and
mixed with oil, or[c] wafers
made without yeast and
spread with oil. 5If your grain
offering is prepared on a griddle, it is to be made of fine
flour mixed with oil, and
without yeast. 6Crumble it and
pour oil on it; it is a grain
offering. 7If your grain
offering is cooked in a pan, it
is to be made of fine flour and
oil. 8Bring the grain offering
made of these things to the
LORD; present it to the priest,
who shall take it to the altar.
9He shall take out the memorial portion from the grain
offering and burn it on the altar as an offering made by fire,
an aroma pleasing to the LORD.
10The rest of the grain offering
belongs to Aaron and his sons;
it is a most holy part of the
offerings made to the LORD by
fire.
11" 'Every grain offering you
bring to the LORD must be
made without yeast, for you
are not to burn any yeast or
honey in an offering made to

[c]4 Or *and*

לַיהוָה׃ קָרְבַּן רֵאשִׁית תַּקְרִיבוּ אֹתָם לַיהוָה וְאֶל־
but-on to-Yahweh them you-may-bring firstfruit offering-of (12) to-Yahweh

הַמִּזְבֵּחַ לֹא־ יַעֲלוּ לְרֵיחַ נִיחֹחַ׃ וְכָל־
and-every-of (13) pleasant as-aroma-of they-may-be-offered not the-altar

קָרְבַּן מִנְחָתְךָ בַּמֶּלַח תִּמְלָח וְלֹא תַשְׁבִּית
you-leave-out and-not you-season with-the-salt grain-of-you offering-of

מֶלַח בְּרִית אֱלֹהֶיךָ מֵעַל מִנְחָתֶךָ עַל כָּל־
every-of to grain-offering-of-you from-in God-of-you covenant-of salt-of

קָרְבָּנְךָ תַּקְרִיב מֶלַח׃ וְאִם־ תַּקְרִיב מִנְחַת בִּכּוּרִים
firstfruits offering-of you-bring and-if (14) salt you-add offering-of-you

לַיהוָה אָבִיב קָלוּי בָּאֵשׁ גֶּרֶשׂ כַּרְמֶל תַּקְרִיב אֵת
*** you-offer new-grain crushed in-the-fire being-roasted head to-Yahweh

מִנְחַת בִּכּוּרֶיךָ׃ וְנָתַתָּ עָלֶיהָ שֶׁמֶן וְשַׂמְתָּ עָלֶיהָ
on-her and-you-put oil on-her and-you-put (15) firstfruits-of-you offering-of

לְבֹנָה מִנְחָה הִוא׃ וְהִקְטִיר הַכֹּהֵן אֶת־
*** the-priest and-he-shall-burn (16) she grain-offering incense

אַזְכָּרָתָהּ מִגִּרְשָׂהּ וּמִשַּׁמְנָהּ עַל כָּל־
all-of with and-from-oil-of-her from-grain-of-her memorial-portion-of-her

לְבֹנָתָהּ אִשֶּׁה לַיהוָה׃ וְאִם־ זֶבַח שְׁלָמִים
fellowships offering-of and-if (3:1) to-Yahweh fire-offering incense-of-her

קָרְבָּנוֹ אִם מִן־ הַבָּקָר הוּא מַקְרִיב אִם־ זָכָר אִם־נְקֵבָה
female or male whether one-offering he the-herd from if offering-of-him

תָּמִים יַקְרִיבֶנּוּ לִפְנֵי יְהוָה׃ וְסָמַךְ
and-he-must-lay (2) Yahweh before he-must-present-him without-defect

יָדוֹ עַל־ רֹאשׁ קָרְבָּנוֹ וּשְׁחָטוֹ פֶּתַח
entrance-of and-he-must-slaughter-him offering-of-him head-of on hand-of-him

אֹהֶל מוֹעֵד וְזָרְקוּ בְּנֵי אַהֲרֹן הַכֹּהֲנִים אֶת־
*** the-priests Aaron sons-of and-they-shall-sprinkle Meeting Tent-of

הַדָּם עַל־ הַמִּזְבֵּחַ סָבִיב׃ וְהִקְרִיב מִזֶּבַח
from-offering-of then-he-must-bring (3) around the-altar against the-blood

הַשְּׁלָמִים אִשֶּׁה לַיהוָה אֶת־ הַחֵלֶב הַמְכַסֶּה אֶת־
*** the-covering the-fat *** to-Yahweh fire-offering the-fellowships

הַקֶּרֶב וְאֵת כָּל־ הַחֵלֶב אֲשֶׁר עַל־ הַקֶּרֶב׃ וְאֵת שְׁתֵּי
both-of and (4) the-inner-part on that the-fat all-of and the-inner-part

הַכְּלָיֹת וְאֶת־ הַחֵלֶב אֲשֶׁר עֲלֵהֶן אֲשֶׁר עַל־ הַכְּסָלִים וְאֶת־ הַיֹּתֶרֶת
the-cover and the-loins near that around-them that the-fat and the-kidneys

עַל־ הַכָּבֵד עַל־ הַכְּלָיוֹת יְסִירֶנָּה׃ וְהִקְטִירוּ אֹתוֹ
him and-they-shall-burn (5) he-will-remove-her the-kidneys with the-liver on

the LORD by fire. [12]You may
bring them to the LORD as an
offering of the firstfruits, but
they are not to be offered on
the altar as a pleasing aroma.
[13]Season all your grain
offerings with salt. Do not
leave the salt of the covenant
of your God out of your grain
offerings; add salt to all your
offerings.

[14]" 'If you bring a grain
offering of firstfruits to the
LORD, offer crushed heads of
new grain roasted in the fire.
[15]Put oil and incense on it; it is
a grain offering. [16]The priest
shall burn the memorial portion of the crushed grain and
the oil, together with all the
incense, as an offering made
to the LORD by fire.

### *The Fellowship Offering*

3 " 'If someone's offering is
a fellowship offering,[d] and
he offers an animal from the
herd, whether male or female,
he is to present before the
LORD an animal without defect. [2]He is to lay his hand on
the head of his offering and
slaughter it at the entrance to
the Tent of Meeting. Then
Aaron's sons the priests shall
sprinkle the blood against the
altar on all sides. [3]From the fellowship offering he is to bring
a sacrifice made to the LORD by
fire: all the fat that covers the
inner parts or is connected to
them, [4]both kidneys with the
fat around them near the
loins, and the covering of the
liver, which he will remove
with the kidneys. [5]Then
Aaron's sons are to burn it on

[d]1 Traditionally *peace offering*; also in verses 3, 6 and 9

בְנֵי־ אַהֲרֹן הַמִּזְבֵּחָה עַל־ הָעֹלָה אֲשֶׁר עַל־ הָעֵצִים אֲשֶׁר
that the-woods on that the-burnt-offering upon on-the-altar Aaron sons-of

עַל־ הָאֵשׁ אִשֵּׁה רֵיחַ נִיחֹחַ לַיהוָה׃ וְאִם־ מִן־
from and-if (6) to-Yahweh pleasant aroma-of fire-offering-of the-fire on

הַצֹּאן קָרְבָּנוֹ לְזֶבַח שְׁלָמִים לַיהוָה זָכָר אוֹ
or male to-Yahweh fellowships as-offering-of offering-of-him the-flock

נְקֵבָה תָּמִים יַקְרִיבֶנּוּ׃ אִם־ כֶּשֶׂב הוּא־ מַקְרִיב אֶת־
*** one-offering he lamb if (7) he-must-offer-him without-defect female

קָרְבָּנוֹ וְהִקְרִיב אֹתוֹ לִפְנֵי יְהוָה׃ וְסָמַךְ
and-he-must-lay (8) Yahweh before him then-he-must-present offering-of-him

אֶת־ יָדוֹ עַל־ רֹאשׁ קָרְבָּנוֹ וְשָׁחַט אֹתוֹ לִפְנֵי
in-front-of him and-he-must-slaughter offering-of-him head-of on hand-of-him ***

אֹהֶל מוֹעֵד וְזָרְקוּ בְּנֵי אַהֲרֹן אֶת־ דָּמוֹ
blood-of-him *** Aaron sons-of then-they-shall-sprinkle Meeting Tent-of

עַל־ הַמִּזְבֵּחַ סָבִיב׃ וְהִקְרִיב מִזֶּבַח
from-offering-of then-he-must-bring (9) around the-altar against

הַשְּׁלָמִים אִשֶּׁה לַיהוָה חֶלְבּוֹ הָאַלְיָה תְמִימָה
entire the-fat-tail fat-of-him to-Yahweh fire-offering the-fellowships

לְעֻמַּת הֶעָצֶה יְסִירֶנָּה וְאֶת־ הַחֵלֶב הַמְכַסֶּה אֶת־
*** the-covering the-fat and he-must-cut-off-her the-backbone close-to

הַקֶּרֶב וְאֵת כָּל־ הַחֵלֶב אֲשֶׁר עַל־ הַקֶּרֶב׃ וְאֵת שְׁתֵּי
both-of and (10) the-inner-part on that the-fat all-of and the-inner-part

הַכְּלָיֹת וְאֶת־ הַחֵלֶב אֲשֶׁר עֲלֵהֶן אֲשֶׁר עַל־ הַכְּסָלִים וְאֶת־ הַיֹּתֶרֶת
the-cover and the-loins near that around-them that the-fat and the-kidneys

עַל־ הַכָּבֵד עַל־ הַכְּלָיֹת יְסִירֶנָּה׃ וְהִקְטִירוֹ
and-he-shall-burn-him (11) he-will-remove-her the-kidneys with the-liver on

הַכֹּהֵן הַמִּזְבֵּחָה לֶחֶם אִשֶּׁה לַיהוָה׃ וְאִם־ עֵז
goat and-if (12) to-Yahweh fire-offering food on-the-altar the-priest

קָרְבָּנוֹ וְהִקְרִיבוֹ לִפְנֵי יְהוָה׃ וְסָמַךְ
and-he-must-lay (13) Yahweh before then-he-must-present-him offering-of-him

אֶת־ יָדוֹ עַל־ רֹאשׁוֹ וְשָׁחַט אֹתוֹ לִפְנֵי אֹהֶל
Tent-of in-front-of him and-he-must-slaughter head-of-him on hand-of-him ***

מוֹעֵד וְזָרְקוּ בְּנֵי אַהֲרֹן אֶת־ דָּמוֹ עַל־
against blood-of-him *** Aaron sons-of then-they-shall-sprinkle Meeting

הַמִּזְבֵּחַ סָבִיב׃ וְהִקְרִיב מִמֶּנּוּ קָרְבָּנוֹ אִשֶּׁה
by-fire offering-of-him from-him then-he-must-offer (14) around the-altar

לַיהוָה אֶת־ הַחֵלֶב הַמְכַסֶּה אֶת־ הַקֶּרֶב וְאֵת כָּל־ הַחֵלֶב
the-fat all-of and the-inner-part *** the-covering the-fat *** to-Yahweh

the altar on top of the burnt offering that is on the burning wood, as an offering made by fire, an aroma pleasing to the LORD.

6 "'If he offers an animal from the flock as a fellowship offering to the LORD, he is to offer a male or female without defect. 7 If he offers a lamb, he is to present it before the LORD. 8 He is to lay his hand on the head of his offering and slaughter it in front of the Tent of Meeting. Then Aaron's sons shall sprinkle its blood against the altar on all sides. 9 From the fellowship offering he is to bring a sacrifice made to the LORD by fire: its fat, the entire fat tail cut off close to the backbone, all the fat that covers the inner parts or is connected to them, 10 both kidneys with the fat around them near the loins, and the covering of the liver, which he will remove with the kidneys. 11 The priest shall burn them on the altar as food, an offering made to the LORD by fire.

12 "'If his offering is a goat, he is to present it before the LORD. 13 He is to lay his hand on its head and slaughter it in front of the Tent of Meeting. Then Aaron's sons shall sprinkle its blood against the altar on all sides. 14 From what he offers he is to make this offering to the LORD by fire: all the fat that covers the inner

אֲשֶׁר עַל־ הַקֶּרֶב׃ וְאֵת שְׁתֵּי הַכְּלָיֹת וְאֶת־ הַחֵלֶב אֲשֶׁר
that the-fat and the-kidneys both-of and (15) the-inner-part on that

עֲלֵהֶן אֲשֶׁר עַל־ הַכְּסָלִים וְאֶת־ הַיֹּתֶרֶת עַל־ הַכָּבֵד עַל־ הַכְּלָיֹת
the-kidneys with the-liver on the-cover and the-loins near that on-them

יְסִירֶנָּה׃ וְהִקְטִירָם הַכֹּהֵן הַמִּזְבֵּחָה לֶחֶם
food on-the-altar the-priest and-he-shall-burn-them (16) he-will-remove-her

אִשֶּׁה לְרֵיחַ נִיחֹחַ כָּל־ חֵלֶב לַיהוָה׃ חֻקַּת
ordinance-of (17) to-Yahweh fat all-of pleasant for-aroma-of fire-offering

עוֹלָם לְדֹרֹתֵיכֶם בְּכֹל מוֹשְׁבֹתֵיכֶם כָּל־ חֵלֶב וְכָל־
or-any-of fat any-of dwellings-of-you in-all-of for-generations-of-you lasting

דָּם לֹא תֹאכֵלוּ׃ וַיְדַבֵּר יְהוָה אֶל־מֹשֶׁה לֵּאמֹר׃ דַּבֵּר
say! (2) to-say Moses to Yahweh and-he-spoke (4:1) you-must-eat not blood

אֶל־ בְּנֵי יִשְׂרָאֵל לֵאמֹר נֶפֶשׁ כִּי־ תֶחֱטָא בִשְׁגָגָה מִכֹּל
against-any-of with-no-intention she-sins when anyone to-say Israel sons-of to

מִצְוֺת יְהוָה אֲשֶׁר לֹא תֵעָשֶׂינָה וְעָשָׂה מֵאַחַת
against-one and-he-does they-may-be-done not that Yahweh commands-of

מֵהֵנָּה׃ אִם הַכֹּהֵן הַמָּשִׁיחַ יֶחֱטָא לְאַשְׁמַת הָעָם
the-people to-guilt-of he-sins the-anointed the-priest if (3) from-them

וְהִקְרִיב עַל חַטָּאתוֹ אֲשֶׁר חָטָא פַּר בֶּן־ בָּקָר
herd young-of bull he-sinned that sin-of-him for then-he-must-bring

תָּמִים לַיהוָה לְחַטָּאת׃ וְהֵבִיא אֶת־ הַפָּר
the-bull *** and-he-must-present (4) as-sin-offering to-Yahweh without-defect

אֶל־ פֶּתַח אֹהֶל מוֹעֵד לִפְנֵי יְהוָה וְסָמַךְ אֶת־ יָדוֹ
hand-of-him *** and-he-must-lay Yahweh before Meeting Tent-of entrance-of at

עַל־ רֹאשׁ הַפָּר וְשָׁחַט אֶת־ הַפָּר לִפְנֵי יְהוָה׃
Yahweh before the-bull *** and-he-must-slaughter the-bull head-of on

וְלָקַח הַכֹּהֵן הַמָּשִׁיחַ מִדַּם הַפָּר
the-bull from-blood-of the-anointed the-priest then-he-shall-take (5)

וְהֵבִיא אֹתוֹ אֶל־ אֹהֶל מוֹעֵד׃ וְטָבַל הַכֹּהֵן
the-priest and-he-must-dip (6) Meeting Tent-of into him and-he-shall-carry

אֶת־ אֶצְבָּעוֹ בַּדָּם וְהִזָּה מִן־ הַדָּם שֶׁבַע
seven the-blood from and-he-must-sprinkle into-the-blood finger-of-him ***

פְּעָמִים לִפְנֵי יְהוָה אֶת־ פְּנֵי פָּרֹכֶת הַקֹּדֶשׁ׃ וְנָתַן
then-he-shall-put (7) the-sanctuary curtain-of front-of *** Yahweh before times

הַכֹּהֵן מִן־ הַדָּם עַל־ קַרְנוֹת מִזְבַּח קְטֹרֶת הַסַּמִּים
the-fragrances incense-of altar-of horns-of on the-blood from the-priest

לִפְנֵי יְהוָה אֲשֶׁר בְּאֹהֶל מוֹעֵד וְאֵת ׀ כָּל־ דַּם הַפָּר
the-bull blood-of rest-of and Meeting in-Tent-of that Yahweh before

parts or is connected to them,
[15]both kidneys with the fat on
them near the loins, and the
covering of the liver, which he
will remove with the kidneys.
[16]The priest shall burn them
on the altar as food, an
offering made by fire, a pleasing aroma. All the fat is the
LORD's.
[17]" 'This is a lasting ordinance for the generations to
come, wherever you live: You
must not eat any fat or any
blood.' "

*The Sin Offering*

4 The LORD said to Moses,
[2]"Say to the Israelites:
'When anyone sins unintentionally and does what is forbidden in any of the LORD's
commands—
[3]" 'If the anointed priest
sins, bringing guilt on the
people, he must bring to the
LORD a young bull without defect as a sin offering for the sin
he has committed. [4]He is to
present the bull at the entrance to the Tent of Meeting
before the LORD. He is to lay
his hand on its head and
slaughter it before the LORD.
[5]Then the anointed priest shall
take some of the bull's blood
and carry it into the Tent of
Meeting. [6]He is to dip his
finger into the blood and
sprinkle some of it seven
times before the LORD, in front
of the curtain of the sanctuary.
[7]The priest shall then put some
of the blood on the horns of
the altar of fragrant incense
that is before the LORD in the
Tent of Meeting. The rest of

יִשְׁפֹּךְ אֶל־ יְסוֹד מִזְבַּח הָעֹלָה אֲשֶׁר־ פֶּתַח

entrance-of that the-burnt-offering altar-of base-of at he-shall-pour-out

אֹהֶל מוֹעֵד׃ וְאֶת־ כָּל־ חֵלֶב פַּר הַחַטָּאת יָרִים

he-shall-remove the-sin-offering bull-of fat-of all-of and (8) Meeting Tent-of

מִמֶּנּוּ אֶת־ הַחֵלֶב הַמְכַסֶּה עַל־ הַקֶּרֶב וְאֵת כָּל־ הַחֵלֶב אֲשֶׁר

that the-fat all-of and the-inner-part over the-cover the-fat *** from-him

עַל־ הַקֶּרֶב׃ וְאֵת שְׁתֵּי הַכְּלָיֹת וְאֶת־הַחֵלֶב אֲשֶׁר עֲלֵיהֶן אֲשֶׁר

that on-them that the-fat and the-kidneys both-of and (9) the-inner-part onto

עַל־הַכְּסָלִים וְאֶת־הַיֹּתֶרֶת עַל־ הַכָּבֵד עַל־ הַכְּלָיוֹת יְסִירֶנָּה׃

he-will-remove-her the-kidneys with the-liver over the-cover and the-loins near

כַּאֲשֶׁר יוּרַם מִשּׁוֹר זֶבַח הַשְּׁלָמִים

the-fellowship-offerings sacrifice-of from-cow-of he-is-removed just-as (10)

וְהִקְטִירָם הַכֹּהֵן עַל מִזְבַּח הָעֹלָה׃ וְאֶת־

but (11) the-burnt-offering altar-of on the-priest and-he-shall-burn-them

עוֹר הַפָּר וְאֶת־ כָּל־ בְּשָׂרוֹ עַל־ רֹאשׁוֹ וְעַל־ כְּרָעָיו

legs-of-him and-with head-of-him with flesh-of-him all-of and the-bull hide-of

וְקִרְבּוֹ וּפִרְשׁוֹ׃ וְהוֹצִיא אֶת־ כָּל־

rest-of *** now-he-must-take (12) and-offal-of-him and-inner-part-of-him

הַפָּר אֶל־ מִחוּץ לַמַּחֲנֶה אֶל־ מָקוֹם טָהוֹר אֶל־ שֶׁפֶךְ הַדֶּשֶׁן

the-ash dump-of to clean place to of-the-camp outside to the-bull

וְשָׂרַף אֹתוֹ עַל־עֵצִים בָּאֵשׁ עַל־ שֶׁפֶךְ הַדֶּשֶׁן יִשָּׂרֵף׃

he-must-be-burned the-ash dump-of at in-the-fire woods on him and-he-must-burn

וְאִם כָּל־ עֲדַת יִשְׂרָאֵל יִשְׁגּוּ

they-sin-unintentionally Israel community-of whole-of and-if (13)

וְנֶעְלַם דָּבָר מֵעֵינֵי הַקָּהָל וְעָשׂוּ אַחַת

one and-they-do the-community from-eyes-of matter but-he-is-hidden

מִכָּל־ מִצְוֺת יְהוָה אֲשֶׁר לֹא־ תֵעָשֶׂינָה וְאָשֵׁמוּ׃

then-they-are-guilty they-may-be-done not that Yahweh commands-of from-any-of

וְנוֹדְעָה הַחַטָּאת אֲשֶׁר חָטְאוּ עָלֶיהָ וְהִקְרִיבוּ

then-they-must-bring by-her they-sinned that the-sin when-she-becomes-known (14)

הַקָּהָל פַּר בֶּן־ בָּקָר לְחַטָּאת וְהֵבִיאוּ אֹתוֹ

him and-they-must-present as-sin-offering herd young-of bull-of the-assembly

לִפְנֵי אֹהֶל מוֹעֵד׃ וְסָמְכוּ זִקְנֵי הָעֵדָה אֶת־

*** the-community elders-of and-they-must-lay (15) Meeting Tent-of before

יְדֵיהֶם עַל־ רֹאשׁ הַפָּר לִפְנֵי יְהוָה וְשָׁחַט אֶת־

*** and-he-must-slaughter Yahweh before the-bull head-of on hands-of-them

הַפָּר לִפְנֵי יְהוָה׃ וְהֵבִיא הַכֹּהֵן הַמָּשִׁיחַ

the-anointed the-priest then-he-must-take (16) Yahweh before the-bull

the bull's blood he shall pour out at the base of the altar of burnt offering at the entrance to the Tent of Meeting. 8He shall remove all the fat from the bull of the sin offering—the fat that covers the inner parts or is connected to them, 9both kidneys with the fat on them near the loins, and the covering of the liver, which he will remove with the kidneys— 10just as the fat is removed from the cow[e] sacrificed as a fellowship offering.[f] Then the priest shall burn them on the altar of burnt offering. 11But the hide of the bull and all its flesh, as well as the head and legs, the inner parts and offal— 12that is, all the rest of the bull—he must take outside the camp to a place ceremonially clean, where the ashes are thrown, and burn it in a wood fire on the ash heap.

13" 'If the whole Israelite community sins unintentionally and does what is forbidden in any of the LORD's commands, even though the community is unaware of the matter, they are guilty. 14When they become aware of the sin they committed, the assembly must bring a young bull as a sin offering and present it before the Tent of Meeting. 15The elders of the community are to lay their hands on the bull's head before the LORD, and the bull shall be slaughtered before the LORD. 16Then the anointed priest is to take some

[e]10 The Hebrew word can include both male and female.
[f]10 Traditionally *peace offering;* also in verses 26, 31 and 35

מִדַּם הַפָּר אֶל־אֹהֶל מוֹעֵד׃ וְטָבַל הַכֹּהֵן
the-priest and-he-shall-dip (17) Meeting Tent-of into the-bull from-blood-of

אֶצְבָּעוֹ מִן־הַדָּם וְהִזָּה שֶׁבַע פְּעָמִים לִפְנֵי יְהוָה
Yahweh before times seven and-he-shall-sprinkle the-blood into finger-of-him

אֶת פְּנֵי הַפָּרֹכֶת׃ וּמִן־הַדָּם יִתֵּן ׀ עַל־קַרְנֹת
horns-of on he-must-put the-blood and-from (18) the-curtain front-of ***

הַמִּזְבֵּחַ אֲשֶׁר לִפְנֵי יְהוָה אֲשֶׁר בְּאֹהֶל מוֹעֵד וְאֵת כָּל־הַדָּם
the-blood rest-of and Meeting in-Tent-of that Yahweh before that the-altar

יִשְׁפֹּךְ אֶל־יְסוֹד מִזְבַּח הָעֹלָה אֲשֶׁר־פֶּתַח
entrance-of that the-burnt-offering altar-of base-of at he-shall-pour-out

אֹהֶל מוֹעֵד׃ וְאֵת כָּל־חֶלְבּוֹ יָרִים מִמֶּנּוּ
from-him he-shall-remove fat-of-him all-of and (19) Meeting Tent-of

וְהִקְטִיר הַמִּזְבֵּחָה׃ וְעָשָׂה לַפָּר כַּאֲשֶׁר
just-as with-the-bull and-he-must-do (20) on-the-altar and-he-shall-burn

עָשָׂה לְפַר הַחַטָּאת כֵּן יַעֲשֶׂה־לּוֹ
with-him he-shall-do same the-sin-offering with-bull-of he-did

וְכִפֶּר עֲלֵהֶם הַכֹּהֵן וְנִסְלַח לָהֶם׃
to-them and-he-will-be-forgiven the-priest for-them so-he-will-atone

וְהוֹצִיא אֶת־הַפָּר אֶל־מִחוּץ לַמַּחֲנֶה וְשָׂרַף
and-he-shall-burn of-the-camp outside to the-bull *** then-he-shall-take (21)

אֹתוֹ כַּאֲשֶׁר שָׂרַף אֵת הַפָּר הָרִאשׁוֹן חַטַּאת הַקָּהָל
the-community sin-offering-of the-first the-bull *** he-burned just-as him

הוּא׃ אֲשֶׁר נָשִׂיא יֶחֱטָא וְעָשָׂה אַחַת מִכָּל־מִצְוֹת יְהוָה
Yahweh commands-of from-any-of one and-he-does he-sins leader when (22) this

אֱלֹהָיו אֲשֶׁר לֹא־תֵעָשֶׂינָה בִּשְׁגָגָה וְאָשֵׁם׃
then-he-is-guilty with-no-intention they-may-be-done not that God-of-him

אוֹ־הוֹדַע אֵלָיו חַטָּאתוֹ אֲשֶׁר חָטָא בָּהּ
by-her he-sinned that sin-of-him to-him he-is-made-aware when (23)

וְהֵבִיא אֶת־קָרְבָּנוֹ שְׂעִיר עִזִּים זָכָר תָּמִים׃
without-defect male goats male-goat-of offering-of-him *** then-he-must-bring

וְסָמַךְ יָדוֹ עַל־רֹאשׁ הַשָּׂעִיר וְשָׁחַט
and-he-must-slaughter the-goat head-of on hand-of-him and-he-must-lay (24)

אֹתוֹ בִּמְקוֹם אֲשֶׁר־יִשְׁחַט אֶת־הָעֹלָה לִפְנֵי יְהוָה
Yahweh before the-burnt-offering *** he-slaughtered where at-place him

חַטָּאת הוּא׃ וְלָקַח הַכֹּהֵן מִדַּם
from-blood-of the-priest then-he-shall-take (25) he sin-offering

הַחַטָּאת בְּאֶצְבָּעוֹ וְנָתַן עַל־קַרְנֹת מִזְבַּח
altar-of horns-of on and-he-shall-put with-finger-of-him the-sin-offering

of the bull's blood into the
Tent of Meeting. 17He shall dip
his finger into the blood and
sprinkle it before the LORD
seven times in front of the curtain. 18He is to put some of the
blood on the horns of the altar
that is before the LORD in the
Tent of Meeting. The rest of
the blood he shall pour out at
the base of the altar of burnt
offering at the entrance to the
Tent of Meeting. 19He shall
remove all the fat from it and
burn it on the altar, 20and do
with this bull just as he did
with the bull for the sin
offering. In this way the priest
will make atonement for
them, and they will be forgiven. 21Then he shall take the
bull outside the camp and
burn it as he burned the first
bull. This is the sin offering for
the community.

22"'When a leader sins
unintentionally and does
what is forbidden in any of
the commands of the LORD his
God, he is guilty. 23When he is
made aware of the sin he committed, he must bring as his
offering a male goat without
defect. 24He is to lay his hand
on the goat's head and slaughter it at the place where the
burnt offering is slaughtered
before the LORD. It is a sin
offering. 25Then the priest
shall take some of the blood of
the sin offering with his finger
and put it on the horns of the

הָעֹלָה וְאֶת־ דָּמוֹ יִשְׁפֹּךְ אֶל־ יְסוֹד מִזְבַּח

altar-of base-of at he-shall-pour-out blood-of-him and the-burnt-offering

הָעֹלָה׃ וְאֶת־ כָּל־ חֶלְבּוֹ יַקְטִיר הַמִּזְבֵּחָה

on-the-altar he-shall-burn fat-of-him all-of and (26) the-burnt-offering

כְּחֵלֶב זֶבַח הַשְּׁלָמִים וְכִפֶּר עָלָיו הַכֹּהֵן

the-priest for-him so-he-will-atone the-fellowships offering-of as-fat-of

מֵחַטָּאתוֹ וְנִסְלַח לוֹ׃ וְאִם־ נֶפֶשׁ אַחַת

one member and-if (27) to-him and-he-will-be-forgiven for-sin-of-him

תֶּחֱטָא בִשְׁגָגָה מֵעַם הָאָרֶץ בַּעֲשֹׂתָהּ אַחַת

one by-to-do-her the-land from-people-of without-intention she-sins

מִמִּצְוֺת יְהוָה אֲשֶׁר לֹא־ תֵעָשֶׂינָה וְאָשֵׁם׃ אוֹ

when (28) then-he-is-guilty they-may-be-done not that Yahweh from-commands-of

הוֹדַע אֵלָיו חַטָּאתוֹ אֲשֶׁר חָטָא וְהֵבִיא

then-he-must-bring he-sinned that sin-of-him to-him he-is-made-aware

קָרְבָּנוֹ שְׂעִירַת עִזִּים תְּמִימָה נְקֵבָה עַל־ חַטָּאתוֹ

sin-of-him for female without-defect goats female-goat-of offering-of-him

אֲשֶׁר חָטָא׃ וְסָמַךְ אֶת־ יָדוֹ עַל רֹאשׁ

head-of on hand-of-him *** and-he-must-lay (29) he-sinned that

הַחַטָּאת וְשָׁחַט אֶת־ הַחַטָּאת בִּמְקוֹם

at-place-of the-sin-offering *** and-he-must-slaughter the-sin-offering

הָעֹלָה׃ וְלָקַח הַכֹּהֵן מִדָּמָהּ

from-blood-of-her the-priest then-he-must-take (30) the-burnt-offering

בְּאֶצְבָּעוֹ וְנָתַן עַל־ קַרְנֹת מִזְבַּח הָעֹלָה

the-burnt-offering altar-of horns-of on and-he-must-put with-finger-of-him

וְאֶת־ כָּל־ דָּמָהּ יִשְׁפֹּךְ אֶל־ יְסוֹד הַמִּזְבֵּחַ׃ וְאֶת־

and (31) the-altar base-of at he-must-pour-out blood-of-her rest-of and

כָּל־ חֶלְבָּהּ יָסִיר כַּאֲשֶׁר הוּסַר חֵלֶב מֵעַל

from-on fat he-is-removed just-as he-shall-remove fat-of-her all-of

זֶבַח הַשְּׁלָמִים וְהִקְטִיר הַכֹּהֵן הַמִּזְבֵּחָה

on-the-altar the-priest and-he-shall-burn the-fellowships offering-of

לְרֵיחַ נִיחֹחַ לַיהוָה וְכִפֶּר עָלָיו הַכֹּהֵן

the-priest for-him so-he-will-atone to-Yahweh pleasant as-aroma-of

וְנִסְלַח לוֹ׃ וְאִם־ כֶּבֶשׂ יָבִיא קָרְבָּנוֹ

offering-of-him he-brings lamb and-if (32) to-him and-he-will-be-forgiven

לְחַטָּאת נְקֵבָה תְמִימָה יְבִיאֶנָּה׃ וְסָמַךְ

and-he-must-lay (33) he-must-bring-her without-defect female as-sin-offering

אֶת־ יָדוֹ עַל רֹאשׁ הַחַטָּאת וְשָׁחַט אֹתָהּ

her and-he-must-slaughter the-sin-offering head-of on hand-of-him ***

altar of burnt offering and pour out the rest of the blood at the base of the altar. 26 He shall burn all the fat on the altar as he burned the fat of the fellowship offering. In this way the priest will make atonement for the man's sin, and he will be forgiven.

27 "'If a member of the community sins unintentionally and does what is forbidden in any of the LORD's commands, he is guilty. 28 When he is made aware of the sin he committed, he must bring as his offering for the sin he committed a female goat without defect. 29 He is to lay his hand on the head of the sin offering and slaughter it at the place of the burnt offering. 30 Then the priest is to take some of the blood with his finger and put it on the horns of the altar of burnt offering and pour out the rest of the blood at the base of the altar. 31 He shall remove all the fat, just as the fat is removed from the fellowship offering, and the priest shall burn it on the altar as an aroma pleasing to the LORD. In this way the priest will make atonement for him, and he will be forgiven.

32 "'If he brings a lamb as his sin offering, he is to bring a female without defect. 33 He is to lay his hand on its head and

לְחַטָּאת בִּמְקוֹם אֲשֶׁר יִשְׁחַט אֶת־ הָעֹלָה׃

the-burnt-offering *** he-slaughters where at-place as-sin-offering

וְלָקַח הַכֹּהֵן מִדַּם הַחַטָּאת

the-sin-offering from-blood-of the-priest then-he-shall-take (34)

בְּאֶצְבָּעוֹ וְנָתַן עַל־ קַרְנֹת מִזְבַּח הָעֹלָה

the-burnt-offering altar-of horns-of on and-he-shall-put with-finger-of-him

וְאֶת־ כָּל־ דָּמָהּ יִשְׁפֹּךְ אֶל־ יְסוֹד הַמִּזְבֵּחַ׃ וְאֶת־

and (35) the-altar base-of at he-shall-pour-out blood-of-her rest-of and

כָּל־ חֶלְבָּה* יָסִיר כַּאֲשֶׁר יוּסַר חֵלֶב־ הַכֶּשֶׂב

the-lamb fat-of he-is-removed just-as he-shall-remove fat-of-her all-of

מִזֶּבַח הַשְּׁלָמִים וְהִקְטִיר הַכֹּהֵן אֹתָם

them the-priest and-he-shall-burn the-fellowships from-sacrifice-of

הַמִּזְבֵּחָה עַל אִשֵּׁי יְהוָה וְכִפֶּר עָלָיו

for-him so-he-will-atone Yahweh fire-offerings-of upon on-the-altar

הַכֹּהֵן עַל־ חַטָּאתוֹ אֲשֶׁר־ חָטָא וְנִסְלַח לוֹ׃

to-him and-he-will-be-forgiven he-sinned that sin-of-him for the-priest

וְנֶפֶשׁ כִּי־ תֶחֱטָא וְשָׁמְעָה קוֹל אָלָה וְהוּא

and-he public-charge report-of when-she-hears she-sins if and-person (5:1)

עֵד אוֹ רָאָה אוֹ יָדָע אִם־ לוֹא יַגִּיד וְנָשָׂא

then-he-will-bear he-speaks-up not but he-knows or he-was or witness

עֲוֺנוֹ׃ אוֹ נֶפֶשׁ אֲשֶׁר תִּגַּע בְּכָל־ דָּבָר טָמֵא

unclean thing on-any-of she-touches who person or (2) responsibility-of-him

אוֹ בְנִבְלַת חַיָּה טְמֵאָה אוֹ בְּנִבְלַת בְּהֵמָה טְמֵאָה אוֹ

or unclean livestock on-carcass-of or unclean animal on-carcass-of whether

בְּנִבְלַת שֶׁרֶץ טָמֵא וְנֶעְלַם מִמֶּנּוּ וְהוּא טָמֵא

unclean then-he of-him and-he-is-unaware unclean creeper on-carcass-of

וְאָשֵׁם׃ אוֹ כִי יִגַּע בְּטֻמְאַת אָדָם לְכֹל

on-any-of human on-uncleanness-of he-touches if or (3) and-he-is-guilty

טֻמְאָתוֹ אֲשֶׁר יִטְמָא בָּהּ וְנֶעְלַם מִמֶּנּוּ

of-him and-he-is-unaware by-her he-would-be-unclean that uncleanness-of-him

וְהוּא יָדַע וְאָשֵׁם׃ אוֹ נֶפֶשׁ כִּי תִשָּׁבַע

she-takes-oath if person or (4) then-he-will-be-guilty he-learns when-he

לְבַטֵּא בִשְׂפָתַיִם לְהָרַע אוֹ לְהֵיטִיב לְכֹל אֲשֶׁר יְבַטֵּא

he-is-careless that in-any to-do-good or to-do-evil with-lips to-be-careless

הָאָדָם בִּשְׁבֻעָה וְנֶעְלַם מִמֶּנּוּ וְהוּא־ יָדַע

he-learns when-he of-him and-he-is-unaware with-oath the-man

וְאָשֵׁם לְאַחַת מֵאֵלֶּה׃ וְהָיָה כִי־ יֶאְשַׁם

he-is-guilty when and-he-will-be (5) of-these in-any then-he-will-be-guilty

slaughter it for a sin offering at the place where the burnt offering is slaughtered. [34]Then the priest shall take some of the blood of the sin offering with his finger and put it on the horns of the altar of burnt offering and pour out the rest of the blood at the base of the altar. [35]He shall remove all the fat, just as the fat is removed from the lamb of the fellowship offering, and the priest shall burn it on the altar on top of the offerings made to the LORD by fire. In this way the priest will make atonement for him for the sin he has committed, and he will be forgiven.

5 " 'If a person sins because he does not speak up when he hears a public charge to testify regarding something he has seen or learned about, he will be held responsible.

[2]" 'Or if a person touches anything ceremonially unclean—whether the carcasses of unclean wild animals or of unclean livestock or of unclean creatures that move along the ground—even though he is unaware of it, he has become unclean and is guilty.

[3]" 'Or if he touches human uncleanness—anything that would make him unclean—even though he is unaware of it, when he learns of it he will be guilty.

[4]" 'Or if a person thoughtlessly takes an oath to do anything, whether good or evil—in any matter one might carelessly swear about—even though he is unaware of it, in any case when he learns of it he will be guilty.

[5]" 'When anyone is guilty in

*35 Most mss have *mappiq* in the *he* (־בָּהּ).

לְאַחַת מֵאֵלֶּה וְהִתְוַדָּה אֲשֶׁר חָטָא עָלֶיהָ׃

by-her he-sinned what-way then-he-must-confess of-these in-any

וְהֵבִיא אֶת־אֲשָׁמוֹ לַיהוָה עַל חַטָּאתוֹ אֲשֶׁר חָטָא

he-sinned that sin-of-him for to-Yahweh penalty-of-him *** and-he-must-bring (6)

נְקֵבָה מִן־הַצֹּאן כִּשְׂבָּה אוֹ־שְׂעִירַת עִזִּים לְחַטָּאת

as-sin-offering goats female-goat-of or lamb the-flock from female

וְכִפֶּר עָלָיו הַכֹּהֵן מֵחַטָּאתוֹ׃ וְאִם־לֹא

not and-if (7) for-sin-of-him the-priest for-him and-he-shall-atone

תַגִּיע* יָדוֹ דֵּי שֶׂה וְהֵבִיא אֶת־אֲשָׁמוֹ

penalty-of-him *** then-he-must-bring lamb amount-of hand-of-him she-can-afford

אֲשֶׁר חָטָא שְׁתֵּי תֹרִים אוֹ־שְׁנֵי בְנֵי־יוֹנָה לַיהוָה אֶחָד

one to-Yahweh pigeon young-ones-of two-of or doves two-of he-sinned that

לְחַטָּאת וְאֶחָד לְעֹלָה׃ וְהֵבִיא אֹתָם אֶל־

to them and-he-must-bring (8) for-burnt-offering and-other for-sin-offering

הַכֹּהֵן וְהִקְרִיב אֶת־אֲשֶׁר לַחַטָּאת רִאשׁוֹנָה

first for-the-sin-offering one *** and-he-shall-offer the-priest

וּמָלַק אֶת־רֹאשׁוֹ מִמּוּל עָרְפּוֹ וְלֹא יַבְדִּיל׃

he-shall-sever but-not neck-of-him from-on head-of-him *** and-he-shall-wring

וְהִזָּה מִדַּם הַחַטָּאת עַל־קִיר הַמִּזְבֵּחַ

the-altar side-of on the-sin-offering from-blood-of and-he-shall-sprinkle (9)

וְהַנִּשְׁאָר בַּדָּם יִמָּצֵה אֶל־יְסוֹד הַמִּזְבֵּחַ

the-altar base-of at he-must-be-drained of-the-blood and-the-being-left

חַטָּאת הוּא׃ וְאֶת־הַשֵּׁנִי יַעֲשֶׂה עֹלָה

burnt-offering he-shall-offer the-other and (10) he sin-offering

כַּמִּשְׁפָּט וְכִפֶּר עָלָיו הַכֹּהֵן מֵחַטָּאתוֹ אֲשֶׁר־

that for-sin-of-him the-priest for-him and-he-shall-atone as-the-direction

חָטָא וְנִסְלַח לוֹ׃ וְאִם־לֹא תַשִּׂיג

she-can-afford not and-if (11) to-him and-he-will-be-forgiven he-sinned

יָדוֹ לִשְׁתֵּי תֹרִים אוֹ לִשְׁנֵי בְנֵי־יוֹנָה

pigeon young-ones-of for-two-of or doves for-two-of hand-of-him

וְהֵבִיא אֶת־קָרְבָּנוֹ אֲשֶׁר חָטָא עֲשִׂירִת הָאֵפָה

the-ephah tenth-of he-sinned that offering-of-him *** then-he-must-bring

סֹלֶת לְחַטָּאת לֹא־יָשִׂים עָלֶיהָ שֶׁמֶן וְלֹא־יִתֵּן עָלֶיהָ

on-her he-must-put and-not oil on-her he-must-put not for-sin-offering flour

לְבֹנָה כִּי חַטָּאת הִיא׃ וֶהֱבִיאָה† אֶל־הַכֹּהֵן

the-priest to and-he-must-bring-her (12) she sin-offering for incense

וְקָמַץ הַכֹּהֵן מִמֶּנָּה מְלוֹא קֻמְצוֹ אֶת־אַזְכָּרָתָה†

memorial-portion-of-her *** hand-of-him full-of from-her the-priest and-he-shall-take

any of these ways, he must confess in what way he has sinned [6]and, as a penalty for the sin he has committed, he must bring to the LORD a female lamb or goat from the flock as a sin offering; and the priest shall make atonement for him for his sin.

[7]" 'If he cannot afford a lamb, he is to bring two doves or two young pigeons to the LORD as a penalty for his sin—one for a sin offering and the other for a burnt offering. [8]He is to bring them to the priest, who shall first offer the one for the sin offering. He is to wring its head from its neck, not severing it completely, [9]and is to sprinkle some of the blood of the sin offering against the side of the altar; the rest of the blood must be drained out at the base of the altar. It is a sin offering. [10]The priest shall then offer the other as a burnt offering in the prescribed way and make atonement for him for the sin he has committed, and he will be forgiven.

[11]" 'If, however, he cannot afford two doves or two young pigeons, he is to bring as an offering for his sin a tenth of an ephah[g] of fine flour for a sin offering. He must not put oil or incense on it, because it is a sin offering. [12]He is to bring it to the priest, who shall take a handful of it as a memorial portion and burn it

g11 That is, probably about 2 quarts (about 2 liters)

*7 Most mss have furtive *pathah* under the *ayin* (עַ–).

†12 Most mss have *mappiq* in the *he* (הּ–).

וְהִקְטִיר הַמִּזְבֵּחָה עַל אִשֵּׁי יְהוָה חַטָּאת הִוא׃
she sin-offering Yahweh fire-offerings-of upon on-the-altar and-he-shall-burn

(13) וְכִפֶּר עָלָיו הַכֹּהֵן עַל־ חַטָּאתוֹ אֲשֶׁר־ חָטָא
he-sinned that sin-of-him for the-priest for-him so-he-shall-atone (13)

מֵאַחַת מֵאֵלֶּה וְנִסְלַח לוֹ וְהָיְתָה לַכֹּהֵן
for-the-priest and-she-will-be to-him and-he-will-be-forgiven of-these for-any

כַּמִּנְחָה׃ (14) וַיְדַבֵּר יְהוָה אֶל־מֹשֶׁה לֵּאמֹר׃ (15) נֶפֶשׁ
person (15) to-say Moses to Yahweh and-he-spoke (14) as-the-grain-offering

כִּי־ תִמְעֹל מַעַל וְחָטְאָה בִּשְׁגָגָה מִקָּדְשֵׁי
at-holy-things-of without-intention and-she-sins violation she-commits when

יְהוָה וְהֵבִיא אֶת־ אֲשָׁמוֹ לַיהוָה אַיִל תָּמִים
without-defect ram to-Yahweh penalty-of-him *** then-he-must-bring Yahweh

מִן־ הַצֹּאן בְּעֶרְכְּךָ כֶּסֶף־ שְׁקָלִים בְּשֶׁקֶל־ הַקֹּדֶשׁ
the-sanctuary as-shekel-of shekels silver of-value-of-you the-flock from

לְאָשָׁם׃ (16) וְאֵת אֲשֶׁר חָטָא מִן־ הַקֹּדֶשׁ
the-holy-things from he-neglected what and (16) for-guilt-offering

יְשַׁלֵּם וְאֶת־ חֲמִישִׁתוֹ יוֹסֵף עָלָיו וְנָתַן אֹתוֹ
him and-he-must-give to-him he-must-add fifth-of-him and he-must-restitute

לַכֹּהֵן וְהַכֹּהֵן יְכַפֵּר עָלָיו בְּאֵיל
with-ram-of for-him he-will-atone and-the-priest to-the-priest

הָאָשָׁם וְנִסְלַח לוֹ׃ (17) וְאִם־ נֶפֶשׁ כִּי
when person and-if (17) to-him and-he-will-be-forgiven the-guilt-offering

תֶחֱטָא וְעָשְׂתָה אַחַת מִכָּל־ מִצְוֹת יְהוָה אֲשֶׁר לֹא
not that Yahweh commands-of from-any-of one and-she-does she-sins

תֵעָשֶׂינָה וְלֹא־ יָדַע וְאָשֵׁם וְנָשָׂא
and-he-bears then-he-is-guilty he-knows and-not they-may-be-done

עֲוֺנוֹ׃ (18) וְהֵבִיא אַיִל תָּמִים מִן־
from without-defect ram then-he-must-bring (18) responsibility-of-him

הַצֹּאן בְּעֶרְכְּךָ לְאָשָׁם אֶל־ הַכֹּהֵן וְכִפֶּר
so-he-will-atone the-priest to as-guilt-offering of-value-of-you the-flock

עָלָיו הַכֹּהֵן עַל שִׁגְגָתוֹ אֲשֶׁר־ שָׁגָג וְהוּא לֹא־ יָדַע
he-knew not but-he he-committed that wrong-of-him for the-priest for-him

וְנִסְלַח לוֹ׃ (19) אָשָׁם הוּא אָשֹׁם
to-do-wrong he guilt-offering (19) to-him and-he-will-be-forgiven

אָשַׁם לַיהוָה׃ *(20[1]) וַיְדַבֵּר יְהוָה אֶל־ מֹשֶׁה לֵּאמֹר׃
to-say Moses to Yahweh and-he-spoke *(20[1]) against-Yahweh he-did-wrong

(21[2]) נֶפֶשׁ כִּי תֶחֱטָא וּמָעֲלָה מַעַל בַּיהוָה
against-Yahweh violation and-she-commits she-sins if person (21[2])

on the altar on top of the offerings made to the LORD by fire. It is a sin offering. 13In this way the priest will make atonement for him for any of these sins he has committed, and he will be forgiven. The rest of the offering will belong to the priest, as in the case of the grain offering.' "

*The Guilt Offering*

14The LORD said to Moses: 15"When a person commits a violation and sins unintentionally in regard to any of the LORD's holy things, he is to bring to the LORD as a penalty a ram from the flock, one without defect and of the proper value in silver, according to the sanctuary shekel.[h] It is a guilt offering. 16He must make restitution for what he has failed to do in regard to the holy things, add a fifth of the value to that and give it all to the priest, who will make atonement for him with the ram as a guilt offering, and he will be forgiven.

17"If a person sins and does what is forbidden in any of the LORD's commands, even though he does not know it, he is guilty and will be held responsible. 18He is to bring to the priest as a guilt offering a ram from the flock, one without defect and of the proper value. In this way the priest will make atonement for him for the wrong he has committed unintentionally, and he will be forgiven. 19It is a guilt offering; he has been guilty of[i] wrongdoing against the LORD."

6 The LORD said to Moses: 2"If anyone sins and is

[h]15 That is, about 2/5 ounce (about 11.5 grams)
[i]19 Or *has made full expiation for his*

*The Hebrew numeration of chapter 6 begins with verse 8 in English. The number in brackets indicates the English numeration.

וְכִחֵשׁ בַּעֲמִיתוֹ בְּפִקָּדוֹן אוֹ־ בִתְשׂוּמֶת

about-something-left-of or about-trust against-neighbor-of-him and-he-deceives

יָד אוֹ בְגָזֵל אוֹ עָשַׁק אֶת־ עֲמִיתוֹ׃ אוֹ־ מָצָא

he-finds or (22[3]) neighbor-of-him *** he-cheats or about-stolen or care

אֲבֵדָה וְכִחֶשׁ בָּהּ וְנִשְׁבַּע עַל־ שָׁקֶר עַל־ אַחַת

one about falsehood with or-he-swears about-her and-he-lies lost-property

מִכֹּל אֲשֶׁר־ יַעֲשֶׂה הָאָדָם לַחֲטֹא בָהֵנָּה׃ וְהָיָה כִּי־

when and-he-will-be (23[4]) by-them to-sin the-man he-does that of-any

יֶחֱטָא וְאָשֵׁם וְהֵשִׁיב אֶת־ הַגְּזֵלָה אֲשֶׁר

that the-stolen-thing *** that-he-must-return and-he-becomes-guilty he-sins

גָּזָל אוֹ אֶת־ הָעֹשֶׁק אֲשֶׁר עָשָׁק אוֹ אֶת־ הַפִּקָּדוֹן אֲשֶׁר הָפְקַד

he-was-left that the-trust *** or he-extorted that the-thing *** or he-stole

אִתּוֹ אוֹ אֶת־ הָאֲבֵדָה אֲשֶׁר מָצָא׃ אוֹ מִכֹּל אֲשֶׁר־

that what-ever or (24[5]) he-found that the-lost-property *** or with-him

יִשָּׁבַע עָלָיו לַשֶּׁקֶר וְשִׁלַּם אֹתוֹ בְּרֹאשׁוֹ

in-full-of-him him and-he-must-restitute with-the-falsehood about-him he-swore

וַחֲמִשִׁתָיו יֹסֵף עָלָיו לַאֲשֶׁר הוּא לוֹ יִתְּנֶנּוּ

he-must-give-him to-him he to-whom to-him he-must-add and-fifth-of-him

בְּיוֹם אַשְׁמָתוֹ׃ וְאֶת־ אֲשָׁמוֹ יָבִיא

he-must-bring penalty-of-him and (25[6]) guilt-offering-of-him on-day-of

לַיהוָה אַיִל תָּמִים מִן־ הַצֹּאן בְּעֶרְכְּךָ לְאָשָׁם

as-guilt-offering of-value-of-you the-flock from without-defect ram to-Yahweh

אֶל־ הַכֹּהֵן׃ וְכִפֶּר עָלָיו הַכֹּהֵן לִפְנֵי יְהוָה

Yahweh before the-priest for-him so-he-will-atone (26[7]) the-priest to

וְנִסְלַח לוֹ עַל־ אַחַת מִכֹּל אֲשֶׁר־ יַעֲשֶׂה לְאַשְׁמָה בָהּ׃

by-her for-guilt he-did that from-all any for to-him and-he-will-be-forgiven

וַיְדַבֵּר יְהוָה אֶל־ מֹשֶׁה לֵּאמֹר׃ צַו אֶת־ אַהֲרֹן

Aaron *** command! (2[9]) to-say Moses to Yahweh and-he-spoke (6:1[8])

וְאֶת־ בָּנָיו לֵאמֹר זֹאת תּוֹרַת הָעֹלָה הִוא

she the-burnt-offering regulation-of this to-say sons-of-him and

הָעֹלָה עַל מוֹקְדָה עַל־ הַמִּזְבֵּחַ כָּל־ הַלַּיְלָה עַד־ הַבֹּקֶר

the-morning till the-night all-of the-altar on hearth on the-burnt-offering

וְאֵשׁ הַמִּזְבֵּחַ תּוּקַד בּוֹ׃ וְלָבַשׁ

and-he-shall-put-on (3[10]) on-him she-must-burn the-altar and-fire-of

הַכֹּהֵן מִדּוֹ בַד וּמִכְנְסֵי־ בַד יִלְבַּשׁ עַל־

on he-shall-put linen and-undergarments-of linen garment-of-him the-priest

בְּשָׂרוֹ וְהֵרִים אֶת־ הַדֶּשֶׁן אֲשֶׁר תֹּאכַל הָאֵשׁ

the-fire she-consumed that the-ash *** and-he-shall-remove body-of-him

unfaithful to the LORD by deceiving his neighbor about something entrusted to him or left in his care or stolen, or if he cheats him,
3or if he finds lost property and lies about it, or if he swears falsely, or if he commits any such sin that people may do—
4when he thus sins and becomes guilty, he must return what he has stolen or taken by extortion, or what was entrusted to him, or the lost property he found,
5or whatever it was he swore falsely about. He must make restitution in full, add a fifth of the value to it and give it all to the owner on the day he presents his guilt offering.
6And as a penalty he must bring to the priest, that is, to the LORD, his guilt offering, a ram from the flock, one without defect and of the proper value.
7In this way the priest will make atonement for him before the LORD, and he will be forgiven for any of these things he did that made him guilty."

*The Burnt Offering*

8The LORD said to Moses:
9"Give Aaron and his sons this command: 'These are the regulations for the burnt offering: The burnt offering is to remain on the altar hearth throughout the night, till morning, and the fire must be kept burning on the altar.
10The priest shall then put on his linen clothes, with linen undergarments next to his body, and shall remove the ashes of the burnt offering that the fire has consumed on

*See the note on page 278.

אֶת־ הָעֹלָה עַל־ הַמִּזְבֵּחַ וְשָׂמוֹ אֵצֶל הַמִּזְבֵּחַ׃
the-altar beside and-he-shall-place-him the-altar on the-burnt-offering ***

וּפָשַׁט אֶת־ בְּגָדָיו וְלָבַשׁ בְּגָדִים
clothes and-he-shall-put-on clothes-of-him *** then-he-shall-take-off (4[11])

אֲחֵרִים וְהוֹצִיא אֶת־ הַדֶּשֶׁן אֶל־ מִחוּץ לַמַּחֲנֶה אֶל־ מָקוֹם
place to of-the-camp outside to the-ash *** and-he-shall-carry other-ones

טָהוֹר׃ וְהָאֵשׁ עַל־ הַמִּזְבֵּחַ תּוּקַד־ בּוֹ לֹא
not on-him she-must-burn the-altar on and-the-fire (5[12]) clean

תִכְבֶּה וּבִעֵר עָלֶיהָ הַכֹּהֵן עֵצִים בַּבֹּקֶר
in-the-morning woods the-priest on-her and-he-must-burn she-must-go-out

בַּבֹּקֶר וְעָרַךְ עָלֶיהָ הָעֹלָה וְהִקְטִיר
and-he-must-burn the-burnt-offering on-her and-he-must-arrange in-the-morning

עָלֶיהָ חֶלְבֵי הַשְּׁלָמִים׃ אֵשׁ תָּמִיד
continuously fire (6[13]) the-fellowship-offerings fats-of on-her

תּוּקַד עַל־ הַמִּזְבֵּחַ לֹא תִכְבֶּה†׃ וְזֹאת תּוֹרַת
regulation-of and-this (7[14]) she-must-go-out not the-altar on she-must-burn

הַמִּנְחָה הַקְרֵב אֹתָהּ בְּנֵי־ אַהֲרֹן לִפְנֵי יְהוָה אֶל־ פְּנֵי
front-of to Yahweh before Aaron sons-of her he-must-bring the-grain-offering

הַמִּזְבֵּחַ׃ וְהֵרִים מִמֶּנּוּ בְּקֻמְצוֹ מִסֹּלֶת
from-flour-of with-handful-of-him from-him and-he-must-take (8[15]) the-altar

הַמִּנְחָה וּמִשַּׁמְנָהּ וְאֵת כָּל־ הַלְּבֹנָה אֲשֶׁר עַל־
on that the-incense all-of and and-from-oil-of-her the-grain-offering

הַמִּנְחָה וְהִקְטִיר הַמִּזְבֵּחַ רֵיחַ נִיחֹחַ
pleasant aroma-of the-altar and-he-must-burn the-grain-offering

אַזְכָּרָתָהּ לַיהוָה׃ וְהַנּוֹתֶרֶת מִמֶּנָּה
from-her and-the-being-left (9[16]) to-Yahweh memorial-portion-of-her

יֹאכְלוּ אַהֲרֹן וּבָנָיו מַצּוֹת תֵּאָכֵל בְּמָקוֹם
in-place she-must-be-eaten without-yeast and-sons-of-him Aaron they-shall-eat

קָדֹשׁ בַּחֲצַר אֹהֶל־ מוֹעֵד יֹאכְלוּהָ׃ לֹא
not (10[17]) they-shall-eat-her Meeting Tent-of in-courtyard-of holy

תֵאָפֶה חָמֵץ חֶלְקָם נָתַתִּי אֹתָהּ מֵאִשָּׁי
from-fire-offerings-of-me her I-gave share-of-them yeast she-must-be-baked

קֹדֶשׁ קָדָשִׁים הִוא כַּחַטָּאת וְכָאָשָׁם׃
and-like-the-guilt-offering like-the-sin-offering she holy-ones holiest-of

כָּל־ זָכָר בִּבְנֵי אַהֲרֹן יֹאכְלֶנָּה חָק־ עוֹלָם
regular share-of he-may-eat-her Aaron among-sons-of male any-of (11[18])

לְדֹרֹתֵיכֶם מֵאִשֵּׁי יְהוָה כֹּל אֲשֶׁר־ יִגַּע
he-touches that anything Yahweh from-fire-offerings-of for-generations-of-you

the altar and place them beside the altar. 11Then he is to take off these clothes and put on others, and carry the ashes outside the camp to a place that is ceremonially clean. 12The fire on the altar must be kept burning; it must not go out. Every morning the priest is to add firewood and arrange the burnt offering on the fire and burn the fat of the fellowship offerings[j] on it. 13The fire must be kept burning on the altar continuously; it must not go out.

*The Grain Offering*

14" 'These are the regulations for the grain offering: Aaron's sons are to bring it before the LORD, in front of the altar. 15The priest is to take a handful of fine flour and oil, together with all the incense on the grain offering, and burn the memorial portion on the altar as an aroma pleasing to the LORD. 16Aaron and his sons shall eat the rest of it, but it is to be eaten without yeast in a holy place; they are to eat it in the courtyard of the Tent of Meeting. 17It must not be baked with yeast; I have given it as their share of the offerings made to me by fire. Like the sin offering and the guilt offering, it is most holy. 18Any male descendant of Aaron may eat it. It is his regular share of the offerings made to the LORD by fire for the generations to come. Whatever[k]

j12 Traditionally *peace offerings*
k18 Or *Whoever;* also in verse 27

*See the note on page 278.

†6 Most mss have *dagesh* in the *beth* (בּה–).

בָּהֶם יִקְדָּשׁ׃ וַיְדַבֵּר יְהוָה אֶל־ מֹשֶׁה לֵּאמֹר׃
to-say Moses to Yahweh and-he-spoke (12[19]) he-will-become-holy on-them

זֶה קָרְבַּן אַהֲרֹן וּבָנָיו אֲשֶׁר־ יַקְרִיבוּ
they-must-bring that and-sons-of-him Aaron offering-of this (13[20])

לַיהוָה בְּיוֹם הִמָּשַׁח אֹתוֹ עֲשִׂירִת הָאֵפָה סֹלֶת
fine-flour the-ephah tenth-of him to-be-anointed on-day to-Yahweh

מִנְחָה תָּמִיד מַחֲצִיתָהּ בַּבֹּקֶר וּמַחֲצִיתָהּ
and-half-of-her in-the-morning half-of-her regular grain-offering

בָּעָרֶב׃ עַל־ מַחֲבַת בַּשֶּׁמֶן תֵּעָשֶׂה
she-must-be-prepared with-the-oil griddle on (14[21]) in-the-evening

מֻרְבֶּכֶת תְּבִיאֶנָּה תֻּפִינֵי מִנְחַת פִּתִּים תַּקְרִיב
you-present pieces grain-offering-of ones-broken-of you-bring-her being-mixed

רֵיחַ־ נִיחֹחַ לַיהוָה׃ וְהַכֹּהֵן הַמָּשִׁיחַ תַּחְתָּיו
after-him the-anointed and-the-priest (15[22]) to-Yahweh pleasant aroma-of

מִבָּנָיו יַעֲשֶׂה אֹתָהּ חָק־ עוֹלָם לַיהוָה כָּלִיל
completely for-Yahweh regular share-of her he-shall-prepare from-sons-of-him

תָּקְטָר׃ וְכָל־ מִנְחַת כֹּהֵן כָּלִיל
completely priest grain-offering-of and-every-of (16[23]) she-must-be-burned

תִּהְיֶה לֹא תֵאָכֵל׃ וַיְדַבֵּר יְהוָה אֶל־ מֹשֶׁה
Moses to Yahweh and-he-spoke (17[24]) she-must-be-eaten not she-must-be

לֵּאמֹר׃ דַּבֵּר אֶל־ אַהֲרֹן וְאֶל־ בָּנָיו לֵאמֹר זֹאת תּוֹרַת
regulation-of this to-say sons-of-him and-to Aaron to say! (18[25]) to-say

הַחַטָּאת בִּמְקוֹם אֲשֶׁר תִּשָּׁחֵט הָעֹלָה
the-burnt-offering she-is-slaughtered where in-place the-sin-offering

תִּשָּׁחֵט הַחַטָּאת לִפְנֵי יְהוָה קֹדֶשׁ קָדָשִׁים הִוא׃
she holy-ones most-holy-of Yahweh before the-sin-offering she-is-slaughtered

הַכֹּהֵן הַמְחַטֵּא אֹתָהּ יֹאכְלֶנָּה בְּמָקוֹם קָדֹשׁ
holy in-place he-shall-eat-her her the-one-offering the-priest (19[26])

תֵּאָכֵל בַּחֲצַר אֹהֶל מוֹעֵד׃ כֹּל אֲשֶׁר־
that anything (20[27]) Meeting Tent-of in-courtyard-of she-must-be-eaten

יִגַּע בִּבְשָׂרָהּ יִקְדָּשׁ וַאֲשֶׁר יִזֶּה
he-is-spattered and-if he-will-become-holy on-flesh-of-her he-touches

מִדָּמָהּ עַל־ הַבֶּגֶד אֲשֶׁר יִזֶּה עָלֶיהָ תְּכַבֵּס
you-wash with-her he-is-spattered whatever the-garment on from-blood-of-her

בְּמָקוֹם קָדֹשׁ׃ וּכְלִי־ חֶרֶשׂ אֲשֶׁר תְּבֻשַּׁל־ בּוֹ
in-him she-is-cooked that clay and-pot-of (21[28]) holy in-place

יִשָּׁבֵר וְאִם־ בִּכְלִי נְחֹשֶׁת בֻּשָּׁלָה וּמֹרַק
he-must-be-scoured she-is-cooked bronze in-pot-of but-if he-must-be-broken

touches it will become holy.' "
19The LORD also said to Moses, 20"This is the offering Aaron and his sons are to bring to the LORD on the day he[l] is anointed: a tenth of an ephah[m] of fine flour as a regular grain offering, half of it in the morning and half in the evening. 21Prepare it with oil on a griddle; bring it well-mixed and present the grain offering broken[n] in pieces as an aroma pleasing to the LORD. 22The son who is to succeed him as anointed priest shall prepare it. It is the LORD's regular share and is to be burned completely. 23Every grain offering of a priest shall be burned completely; it must not be eaten."

*The Sin Offering*

24The LORD said to Moses, 25"Say to Aaron and his sons: 'These are the regulations for the sin offering: The sin offering is to be slaughtered before the LORD in the place the burnt offering is slaughtered; it is most holy. 26The priest who offers it shall eat it; it is to be eaten in a holy place, in the courtyard of the Tent of Meeting. 27Whatever touches any of the flesh will become holy, and if any of the blood is spattered on a garment, you must wash it in a holy place. 28The clay pot the meat is cooked in must be broken; but if it is cooked in a bronze pot, the pot is to be scoured and

[l]20 Or *each*
[m]20 That is, probably about 2 quarts (about 2 liters)
[n]21 The meaning of the Hebrew for this word is uncertain.

*See the note on page 278.

וְשֻׁטַּף בַּמָּיִם׃ כָּל־ זָכָר בַּכֹּהֲנִים
from-the-priests male any-of (22[29]) with-the-waters and-he-must-be-rinsed

יֹאכַל אֹתָהּ קֹדֶשׁ קָדָשִׁים הִוא׃ וְכָל־ חַטָּאת
sin-offering but-any-of (23[30]) she holy-ones most-holy-of her he-may-eat

אֲשֶׁר יוּבָא מִדָּמָהּ אֶל־ אֹהֶל מוֹעֵד לְכַפֵּר
to-make-atonement Meeting Tent-of into from-blood-of-her he-is-brought that

בַּקֹּדֶשׁ לֹא תֵאָכֵל בָּאֵשׁ תִּשָּׂרֵף׃
she-must-be-burned in-the-fire she-must-be-eaten not in-the-holy-place

וְזֹאת תּוֹרַת הָאָשָׁם קֹדֶשׁ קָדָשִׁים הוּא׃
he holy-ones most-holy-of the-guilt-offering regulation-of and-this (7:1)

בִּמְקוֹם אֲשֶׁר יִשְׁחֲטוּ אֶת־ הָעֹלָה יִשְׁחֲטוּ
they-must-slaughter the-burnt-offering *** they-slaughter where in-place (2)

אֶת־ הָאָשָׁם וְאֶת־ דָּמוֹ יִזְרֹק עַל־ הַמִּזְבֵּחַ
the-altar against he-must-sprinkle blood-of-him and the-guilt-offering ***

סָבִיב׃ וְאֵת כָּל־ חֶלְבּוֹ יַקְרִיב מִמֶּנּוּ אֵת הָאַלְיָה
the-fat-tail *** from-him he-shall-offer fat-of-him all-of and (3) around

וְאֶת־ הַחֵלֶב הַמְכַסֶּה אֶת־ הַקֶּרֶב׃ וְאֵת שְׁתֵּי הַכְּלָיֹת וְאֶת־
and the-kidneys both-of and (4) the-inner-part *** the-cover the-fat and

הַחֵלֶב אֲשֶׁר עֲלֵיהֶן אֲשֶׁר עַל־ הַכְּסָלִים וְאֶת־ הַיֹּתֶרֶת עַל־ הַכָּבֵד
the-liver on the-cover and the-loins near that around-them that the-fat

עַל־ הַכְּלָיֹת יְסִירֶנָּה׃ וְהִקְטִיר אֹתָם הַכֹּהֵן
the-priest them and-he-shall-burn (5) he-must-remove-her the-kidneys with

הַמִּזְבֵּחָה אִשֶּׁה לַיהוָה אָשָׁם הוּא׃ כָּל־ זָכָר
male any-of (6) he guilt-offering to-Yahweh fire-offering on-the-altar

בַּכֹּהֲנִים יֹאכְלֶנּוּ בְּמָקוֹם קָדוֹשׁ יֵאָכֵל קֹדֶשׁ
most-holy-of he-must-be-eaten holy in-place he-may-eat-him from-the-priests

קָדָשִׁים הוּא׃ כַּחַטָּאת כָּאָשָׁם תּוֹרָה אַחַת
same regulation so-the-guilt-offering as-the-sin-offering (7) he holy-ones

לָהֶם הַכֹּהֵן אֲשֶׁר יְכַפֶּר־ בּוֹ לוֹ יִהְיֶה׃ וְהַכֹּהֵן
and-the-priest (8) he-is for-him with-him he-atones who the-priest for-them

הַמַּקְרִיב אֶת־ עֹלַת אִישׁ עוֹר הָעֹלָה
the-burnt-offering hide-of anyone burnt-offering-of *** the-one-offering

אֲשֶׁר הִקְרִיב לַכֹּהֵן לוֹ יִהְיֶה׃ וְכָל־ מִנְחָה
grain-offering and-every-of (9) he-is for-him for-the-priest he-offers that

אֲשֶׁר תֵּאָפֶה בַּתַּנּוּר וְכָל־ נַעֲשָׂה בַמַּרְחֶשֶׁת וְעַל־ מַחֲבַת
griddle or-on in-the-pan being-cooked or-every-of in-the-oven she-is-baked that

לַכֹּהֵן הַמַּקְרִיב אֹתָהּ לוֹ תִהְיֶה׃ וְכָל־
and-every-of (10) she-is for-him her the-one-offering for-the-priest

rinsed with water. [29]Any male in a priest's family may eat it; it is most holy. [30]But any sin offering whose blood is brought into the Tent of Meeting to make atonement in the Holy Place must not be eaten; it must be burned.

*The Guilt Offering*

7 " 'These are the regulations for the guilt offering, which is most holy: [2]The guilt offering is to be slaughtered in the place where the burnt offering is slaughtered, and its blood is to be sprinkled against the altar on all sides. [3]All its fat shall be offered: the fat tail and the fat that covers the inner parts, [4]both kidneys with the fat around them near the loins, and the covering of the liver, which is to be removed with the kidneys. [5]The priest shall burn them on the altar as an offering made to the LORD by fire. It is a guilt offering. [6]Any male in a priest's family may eat it, but it must be eaten in a holy place; it is most holy.

[7]" 'The same law applies to both the sin offering and the guilt offering: They belong to the priest who makes atonement with them. [8]The priest who offers a burnt offering for anyone may keep its hide for himself. [9]Every grain offering baked in an oven or cooked in a pan or on a griddle belongs to the priest who offers it,

*See the note on page 278.

מִנְחָה בְלוּלָה־ בַשֶּׁמֶן וַחֲרֵבָה לְכָל־ בְּנֵי אַהֲרֹן
grain-offering being-mixed with-the-oil or-dry for-all-of sons-of Aaron

תִּהְיֶה אִישׁ כְּאָחִיו׃ (11) וְזֹאת תּוֹרַת זֶבַח
she-is each equal-with-brother-of-him (11) and-this regulation-of offering-of

הַשְּׁלָמִים אֲשֶׁר יַקְרִיב לַיהוָה׃ (12) אִם עַל־ תּוֹדָה
the-fellowships that he-may-present to-Yahweh (12) if for thankfulness

יַקְרִיבֶנּוּ וְהִקְרִיב ׀ עַל־ זֶבַח הַתּוֹדָה חַלּוֹת
he-offers-him then-he-must-offer with sacrifice-of the-thanksgiving cakes-of

מַצּוֹת בְּלוּלֹת בַּשֶּׁמֶן וּרְקִיקֵי
breads-without-yeast ones-being-mixed with-the-oil and-wafers-of

מַצּוֹת מְשֻׁחִים בַּשָּׁמֶן וְסֹלֶת מֻרְבֶּכֶת
without-yeast ones-being-spread with-the-oil and-fine-flour being-kneaded

חַלֹּת בְּלוּלֹת בַּשָּׁמֶן׃ (13) עַל־ חַלֹּת לֶחֶם חָמֵץ
cakes ones-being-mixed with-the-oil (13) with cakes-of bread without-yeast

יַקְרִיב קָרְבָּנוֹ עַל־ זֶבַח תּוֹדַת
he-must-present offering-of-him with offering-of thanksgiving-of

שְׁלָמָיו׃ (14) וְהִקְרִיב מִמֶּנּוּ אֶחָד מִכָּל־ קָרְבָּן
fellowships-of-him (14) and-he-must-bring from-him one from-every-of offering

תְּרוּמָה לַיהוָה לַכֹּהֵן הַזֹּרֵק אֶת־ דַּם
contribution to-Yahweh for-the-priest the-one-sprinkling *** blood-of

הַשְּׁלָמִים לוֹ יִהְיֶה׃ (15) וּבְשַׂר זֶבַח
the-fellowship-offerings for-him he-is (15) and-meat-of offering-of

תּוֹדַת שְׁלָמָיו בְּיוֹם קָרְבָּנוֹ יֵאָכֵל
thanksgiving-of fellowships-of-him on-day-of offering-of-him he-must-be-eaten

לֹא־ יַנִּיחַ מִמֶּנּוּ עַד־ בֹּקֶר׃ (16) וְאִם־ נֶדֶר ׀ אוֹ נְדָבָה
not he-must-leave from-him till morning (16) but-if vow or freewill

זֶבַח קָרְבָּנוֹ בְּיוֹם הַקְרִיבוֹ אֶת־ זִבְחוֹ
sacrifice-of offering-of-him on-day to-offer-him *** sacrifice-of-him

יֵאָכֵל וּמִמָּחֳרָת וְהַנּוֹתָר מִמֶּנּוּ
he-shall-be-eaten but-on-next-day also-the-being-left from-him

יֵאָכֵל׃ (17) וְהַנּוֹתָר מִבְּשַׂר הַזָּבַח בַּיּוֹם
he-may-be-eaten (17) and-the-being-left from-meat-of the-sacrifice on-the-day

הַשְּׁלִישִׁי בָּאֵשׁ יִשָּׂרֵף׃ (18) וְאִם הֵאָכֹל יֵאָכֵל
the-third in-the-fire he-must-be-burned (18) and-if to-be-eaten he-is-eaten

מִבְּשַׂר־ זֶבַח שְׁלָמָיו בַּיּוֹם הַשְּׁלִישִׁי לֹא
from-meat-of offering-of fellowships-of-him on-the-day the-third not

יֵרָצֶה הַמַּקְרִיב אֹתוֹ לֹא יֵחָשֵׁב לוֹ
he-will-be-accepted the-one-offering him not he-will-be-credited to-him

10 and every grain offering, whether mixed with oil or dry, belongs equally to all the sons of Aaron.

*The Fellowship Offering*

11 "'These are the regulations for the fellowship offering[o] a person may present to the LORD:

12 "'If he offers it as an expression of thankfulness, then along with this sacrifice of thanksgiving he is to offer cakes of bread made without yeast and mixed with oil, wafers made without yeast and spread with oil, and cakes of fine flour well-kneaded and mixed with oil. 13 Along with his fellowship offering of thanksgiving he is to present an offering with cakes of bread made with yeast. 14 He is to bring one of each kind as an offering, a contribution to the LORD; it belongs to the priest who sprinkles the blood of the fellowship offerings. 15 The meat of his fellowship offering of thanksgiving must be eaten on the day it is offered; he must leave none of it till morning.

16 "'If, however, his offering is the result of a vow or is a freewill offering, the sacrifice shall be eaten on the day he offers it, but anything left over may be eaten on the next day. 17 Any meat of the sacrifice left over till the third day must be burned up. 18 If any meat of the fellowship offering is eaten on the third day, it will not be accepted. It will not be credited to the one who offered it, for it

[o] 11 Traditionally *peace offering;* also in verses 13-37

פִּגּוּל יִהְיֶה וְהַנֶּפֶשׁ הָאֹכֶלֶת מִמֶּנּוּ עֲוֺנָהּ
responsibility-of-her from-him the-one-eating and-the-person he-is impure

תִּשָּׂא׃ וְהַבָּשָׂר אֲשֶׁר־ יִגַּע בְּכָל־ טָמֵא לֹא
not unclean on-any-of he-touches that and-the-meat (19) she-will-bear

יֵאָכֵל בָּאֵשׁ יִשָּׂרֵף וְהַבָּשָׂר כָּל־ טָהוֹר
clean anyone-of and-the-meat he-must-be-burned in-the-fire he-must-be-eaten

יֹאכַל בָּשָׂר׃ וְהַנֶּפֶשׁ אֲשֶׁר־ תֹּאכַל בָּשָׂר מִזֶּבַח
from-offering-of meat she-eats who but-the-person (20) meat he-may-eat

הַשְּׁלָמִים אֲשֶׁר לַיהוָה וְטֻמְאָתוֹ עָלָיו
on-him and-uncleanness-of-him to-Yahweh that the-fellowships

וְנִכְרְתָה הַנֶּפֶשׁ הַהִוא מֵעַמֶּיהָ׃ וְנֶפֶשׁ
and-one (21) from-people-of-her the-that the-person then-she-must-be-cut-off

כִּי־ תִגַּע בְּכָל־ טָמֵא בְּטֻמְאַת אָדָם אוֹ בִּבְהֵמָה טְמֵאָה
unclean on-animal or human on-uncleanness-of unclean on-any-of she-touches if

אוֹ בְּכָל־ שֶׁקֶץ טָמֵא וְאָכַל מִבְּשַׂר־ זֶבַח
offering-of from-meat-of and-he-eats unclean detestable on-any-of or

הַשְּׁלָמִים אֲשֶׁר לַיהוָה וְנִכְרְתָה הַנֶּפֶשׁ הַהִוא
the-that the-person then-she-must-be-off to-Yahweh that the-fellowships

מֵעַמֶּיהָ׃ וַיְדַבֵּר יְהוָה אֶל־ מֹשֶׁה לֵּאמֹר׃ דַּבֵּר אֶל־
to say! (23) to-say Moses to Yahweh and-he-spoke (22) from-people-of-her

בְּנֵי יִשְׂרָאֵל לֵאמֹר כָּל־ חֵלֶב שׁוֹר וְכֶשֶׂב וָעֵז לֹא תֹאכֵלוּ׃
you-eat not or-goat or-sheep cattle fat-of any-of to-say Israel sons-of

וְחֵלֶב נְבֵלָה וְחֵלֶב טְרֵפָה יֵעָשֶׂה לְכָל־
for-any-of he-may-be-used torn-animal and-fat-of dead-animal and-fat-of (24)

מְלָאכָה וְאָכֹל לֹא תֹאכְלֻהוּ׃ כִּי כָּל־ אֹכֵל חֵלֶב מִן־
from fat eating any-of if (25) you-must-eat-him not but-to-eat purpose

הַבְּהֵמָה אֲשֶׁר יַקְרִיב מִמֶּנָּה אִשֶּׁה לַיהוָה וְנִכְרְתָה
then-she-must-be-cut to-Yahweh fire-offering from-her he-makes that the-animal

הַנֶּפֶשׁ הָאֹכֶלֶת מֵעַמֶּיהָ׃ וְכָל־ דָּם לֹא
not blood and-any-of (26) from-people-of-her the-one-eating the-person

תֹאכְלוּ בְּכֹל מוֹשְׁבֹתֵיכֶם לָעוֹף וְלַבְּהֵמָה׃
or-from-the-animal from-the-bird dwellings-of-you in-any-of you-must-eat

כָּל־ נֶפֶשׁ אֲשֶׁר־ תֹּאכַל כָּל־ דָּם וְנִכְרְתָה
then-she-must-be-cut-off blood any-of she-eats who person any-of (27)

הַנֶּפֶשׁ הַהִוא מֵעַמֶּיהָ׃ וַיְדַבֵּר יְהוָה אֶל־ מֹשֶׁה
Moses to Yahweh and-he-spoke (28) from-people-of-her the-that the-person

לֵּאמֹר׃ דַּבֵּר אֶל־ בְּנֵי יִשְׂרָאֵל לֵאמֹר הַמַּקְרִיב אֶת־ זֶבַח
offering-of *** the-one-bringing to-say Israel sons-of to say! (29) to-say

is impure; the person who eats any of it will be held responsible.

[19]" 'Meat that touches anything ceremonially unclean must not be eaten; it must be burned up. As for other meat, anyone ceremonially clean may eat it. [20]But if anyone who is unclean eats any meat of the fellowship offering belonging to the LORD, that person must be cut off from his people. [21]If anyone touches something unclean—whether human uncleanness or an unclean animal or any unclean, detestable thing—and then eats any of the meat of the fellowship offering belonging to the LORD, that person must be cut off from his people.' "

*Eating Fat and Blood Forbidden*

[22]The LORD said to Moses, [23]"Say to the Israelites: 'Do not eat any of the fat of cattle, sheep or goats. [24]The fat of an animal found dead or torn by wild animals may be used for any other purpose, but you must not eat it. [25]Anyone who eats the fat of an animal from which an offering by fire may be[p] made to the LORD must be cut off from his people. [26]And wherever you live, you must not eat the blood of any bird or animal. [27]If anyone eats blood, that person must be cut off from his people.' "

*The Priests' Share*

[28]The LORD said to Moses, [29]"Say to the Israelites: 'Anyone who brings a fellowship

[p]25 Or *fire is*

שְׁלָמָיו לַיהוָה יָבִיא אֶת־ קָרְבָּנוֹ לַיהוָה
to-Yahweh presentation-of-him *** he-must-bring to-Yahweh fellowships-of-him

מִזֶּבַח שְׁלָמָיו׃ יָדָיו תְּבִיאֶינָה אֵת
*** they-must-bring hands-of-him (30) fellowships-of-him from-offering-of

אִשֵּׁי יְהוָה אֶת־ הַחֵלֶב עַל־ הֶחָזֶה יְבִיאֶנּוּ אֵת
*** he-must-bring-him the-breast with the-fat *** Yahweh fire-offerings-of

הֶחָזֶה לְהָנִיף אֹתוֹ תְּנוּפָה לִפְנֵי יְהוָה׃ וְהִקְטִיר
and-he-shall-burn (31) Yahweh before wave-offering him to-wave the-breast

הַכֹּהֵן אֶת־ הַחֵלֶב הַמִּזְבֵּחָה וְהָיָה הֶחָזֶה לְאַהֲרֹן
for-Aaron the-breast but-he-is on-the-altar the-fat *** the-priest

וּלְבָנָיו׃ וְאֵת שׁוֹק הַיָּמִין תִּתְּנוּ תְרוּמָה
contribution you-give the-right thigh-of and (32) and-for-sons-of-him

לַכֹּהֵן מִזִּבְחֵי שַׁלְמֵיכֶם׃ הַמַּקְרִיב אֶת־
*** the-one-offering (33) fellowships-of-you from-offerings-of to-the-priest

דַּם הַשְּׁלָמִים וְאֶת־ הַחֵלֶב מִבְּנֵי אַהֲרֹן לוֹ
for-him Aaron from-sons-of the-fat and the-fellowship-offerings blood-of

תִהְיֶה שׁוֹק הַיָּמִין לְמָנָה׃ כִּי אֶת־ חֲזֵה הַתְּנוּפָה וְאֵת ׀
and the-one-waved breast-of *** for (34) as-share the-right thigh-of she-is

שׁוֹק הַתְּרוּמָה לָקַחְתִּי מֵאֵת בְּנֵי־ יִשְׂרָאֵל מִזִּבְחֵי
from-offerings-of Israel sons-of from I-took the-presentation thigh-of

שַׁלְמֵיהֶם וָאֶתֵּן אֹתָם לְאַהֲרֹן הַכֹּהֵן וּלְבָנָיו
and-to-sons-of-him the-priest to-Aaron them and-I-gave fellowships-of-them

לְחָק־ עוֹלָם מֵאֵת בְּנֵי יִשְׂרָאֵל׃ זֹאת מִשְׁחַת אַהֲרֹן
Aaron portion-of this (35) Israel sons-of from regular as-share-of

וּמִשְׁחַת בָּנָיו מֵאִשֵּׁי יְהוָה בְּיוֹם הִקְרִיב
he-presented on-day Yahweh from-fire-offerings-of sons-of-him and-portion-of

אֹתָם לְכַהֵן לַיהוָה׃ אֲשֶׁר צִוָּה יְהוָה לָתֵת לָהֶם
to-them to-give Yahweh he-commanded that (36) to-Yahweh to-be-priest them

בְּיוֹם מָשְׁחוֹ אֹתָם מֵאֵת בְּנֵי יִשְׂרָאֵל חֻקַּת עוֹלָם
regular share-of Israel sons-of from them to-anoint-him on-day

לְדֹרֹתָם׃ זֹאת הַתּוֹרָה לָעֹלָה
for-the-burnt-offering the-regulation this (37) for-generations-of-them

לַמִּנְחָה וְלַחַטָּאת וְלָאָשָׁם
and-for-the-guilt-offering and-for-the-sin-offering for-the-grain-offering

וְלַמִּלּוּאִים וּלְזֶבַח הַשְּׁלָמִים׃ אֲשֶׁר
that (38) the-fellowships and-for-offering-of and-for-the-ordination-offerings

צִוָּה יְהוָה אֶת־ מֹשֶׁה בְּהַר סִינָי בְּיוֹם צַוֹּתוֹ אֶת־
*** to-command-him on-day Sinai on-Mount-of Moses *** Yahweh he-commanded

offering to the LORD is to bring part of it as his sacrifice to the LORD.
30 With his own hands he is to bring the offering made to the LORD by fire; he is to bring the fat, together with the breast, and wave the breast before the LORD as a wave offering.
31 The priest shall burn the fat on the altar, but the breast belongs to Aaron and his sons.
32 You are to give the right thigh of your fellowship offerings to the priest as a contribution.
33 The son of Aaron who offers the blood and the fat of the fellowship offering shall have the right thigh as his share.
34 From the fellowship offerings of the Israelites, I have taken the breast that is waved and the thigh that is presented and have given them to Aaron the priest and his sons as their regular share from the Israelites.' "

35 This is the portion of the offerings made to the LORD by fire that were allotted to Aaron and his sons on the day they were presented to serve the LORD as priests.
36 On the day they were anointed, the LORD commanded that the Israelites give this to them as their regular share for the generations to come.

37 These, then, are the regulations for the burnt offering, the grain offering, the sin offering, the guilt offering, the ordination offering and the fellowship offering,
38 which the LORD gave Moses on Mount Sinai on the day he commanded the Israelites to

בְּנֵי יִשְׂרָאֵל לְהַקְרִיב אֶת־ קָרְבְּנֵיהֶם לַיהוָה בְּמִדְבַּר סִינָי׃
Sinai in-Desert-of to-Yahweh offerings-of-them *** to-bring Israel sons-of

וַיְדַבֵּר יְהוָה אֶל־ מֹשֶׁה לֵּאמֹר׃ קַח אֶת־ אַהֲרֹן וְאֶת־
and Aaron *** bring! (2) to-say Moses to Yahweh and-he-spoke (8:1)

בָּנָיו אִתּוֹ וְאֵת הַבְּגָדִים וְאֵת שֶׁמֶן הַמִּשְׁחָה וְאֵת ׀ פַּר
bull-of and the-anointing oil-of and the-garments and with-him sons-of-him

הַחַטָּאת וְאֵת שְׁנֵי הָאֵילִים וְאֵת סַל הַמַּצּוֹת׃
the-breads-without-yeast basket-of and the-rams two-of and the-sin-offering

וְאֵת כָּל־ הָעֵדָה הַקְהֵל אֶל־ פֶּתַח אֹהֶל מוֹעֵד׃
Meeting Tent-of entrance-of at gather! the-assembly all-of and (3)

וַיַּעַשׂ מֹשֶׁה כַּאֲשֶׁר צִוָּה יְהוָה אֹתוֹ וַתִּקָּהֵל
and-she-gathered him Yahweh he-commanded just-as Moses and-he-did (4)

הָעֵדָה אֶל־ פֶּתַח אֹהֶל מוֹעֵד׃ וַיֹּאמֶר מֹשֶׁה אֶל־
to Moses and-he-said (5) Meeting Tent-of entrance-of at the-assembly

הָעֵדָה זֶה הַדָּבָר אֲשֶׁר־ צִוָּה יְהוָה לַעֲשׂוֹת׃ וַיַּקְרֵב
then-he-brought (6) to-do Yahweh he-commanded that the-thing this the-assembly

מֹשֶׁה אֶת־ אַהֲרֹן וְאֶת־ בָּנָיו וַיִּרְחַץ אֹתָם בַּמָּיִם׃
with-the-waters them and-he-washed sons-of-him and Aaron *** Moses

וַיִּתֵּן עָלָיו אֶת־ הַכֻּתֹּנֶת וַיַּחְגֹּר אֹתוֹ בָּאַבְנֵט
with-the-sash him and-he-tied the-tunic *** on-him and-he-put (7)

וַיַּלְבֵּשׁ אֹתוֹ אֶת־הַמְּעִיל וַיִּתֵּן עָלָיו אֶת־ הָאֵפֹד וַיַּחְגֹּר
and-he-tied the-ephod *** on-him and-he-put the-robe *** him and-he-clothed

אֹתוֹ בְּחֵשֶׁב הָאֵפֹד וַיֶּאְפֹּד לוֹ בּוֹ׃ וַיָּשֶׂם
and-he-put (8) by-him on-him so-he-was-fastened the-ephod by-waistband-of him

עָלָיו אֶת־ הַחֹשֶׁן וַיִּתֵּן אֶל־ הַחֹשֶׁן אֶת־ הָאוּרִים וְאֶת־
and the-Urim *** the-breastpiece in and-he-put the-breastpiece *** on-him

הַתֻּמִּים׃ וַיָּשֶׂם אֶת־הַמִּצְנֶפֶת עַל־ רֹאשׁוֹ וַיָּשֶׂם עַל־
on and-he-set head-of-him on the-turban *** then-he-placed (9) the-Thummim

הַמִּצְנֶפֶת אֶל־ מוּל פָּנָיו אֵת צִיץ הַזָּהָב נֵזֶר הַקֹּדֶשׁ
the-sacred diadem-of the-gold plate-of *** face-of-him front-of on the-turban

כַּאֲשֶׁר צִוָּה יְהוָה אֶת־ מֹשֶׁה׃ וַיִּקַּח מֹשֶׁה אֶת־ שֶׁמֶן
oil-of *** Moses then-he-took (10) Moses *** Yahweh he-commanded just-as

הַמִּשְׁחָה וַיִּמְשַׁח אֶת־ הַמִּשְׁכָּן וְאֶת־ כָּל־ אֲשֶׁר־ בּוֹ
in-him that everything and the-tabernacle *** and-he-anointed the-anointing

וַיְקַדֵּשׁ אֹתָם׃ וַיַּז מִמֶּנּוּ עַל־הַמִּזְבֵּחַ שֶׁבַע פְּעָמִים
times seven the-altar on from-him and-he-sprinkled (11) them so-he-consecrated

וַיִּמְשַׁח אֶת־ הַמִּזְבֵּחַ וְאֶת־ כָּל־ כֵּלָיו וְאֶת־ הַכִּיֹּר וְאֶת־
and the-basin and utensils-of-him all-of and the-altar *** and-he-anointed

bring their offerings to the LORD, in the Desert of Sinai.

### *The Ordination of Aaron and His Sons*

**8** The LORD said to Moses, 2"Bring Aaron and his sons, their garments, the anointing oil, the bull for the sin offering, the two rams and the basket containing bread made without yeast, 3and gather the entire assembly at the entrance to the Tent of Meeting." 4Moses did as the LORD commanded him, and the assembly gathered at the entrance to the Tent of Meeting.

5Moses said to the assembly, "This is what the LORD has commanded to be done." 6Then Moses brought Aaron and his sons forward and washed them with water. 7He put the tunic on Aaron, tied the sash around him, clothed him with the robe and put the ephod on him. He also tied the ephod to him by its skillfully woven waistband; so it was fastened on him. 8He placed the breastpiece on him and put the Urim and Thummim in the breastpiece. 9Then he placed the turban on Aaron's head and set the gold plate, the sacred diadem, on the front of it, as the LORD commanded Moses.

10Then Moses took the anointing oil and anointed the tabernacle and everything in it, and so consecrated them. 11He sprinkled some of the oil on the altar seven times, anointing the altar and all its utensils and the basin with its

כַּנּ֖וֹ לְקַדְּשָֽׁם׃ וַיִּצֹק֙ מִשֶּׁ֣מֶן הַמִּשְׁחָ֔ה
the-anointing from-oil-of and-he-poured (12) to-consecrate-them stand-of-him

עַ֖ל רֹ֣אשׁ אַהֲרֹ֑ן וַיִּמְשַׁ֥ח אֹת֖וֹ לְקַדְּשֽׁוֹ׃ וַיַּקְרֵ֨ב
then-he-brought (13) to-consecrate-him him and-he-anointed Aaron head-of on

מֹשֶׁ֜ה אֶת־ בְּנֵ֣י אַהֲרֹ֗ן וַיַּלְבִּשֵׁ֤ם כֻּתֳּנֹת֙ וַיַּחְגֹּ֤ר אֹתָם֙
them and-he-tied-around tunics and-he-put-on-them Aaron sons-of *** Moses

אַבְנֵ֔ט וַיַּחֲבֹ֥שׁ לָהֶ֖ם מִגְבָּע֑וֹת כַּאֲשֶׁ֛ר צִוָּ֥ה יְהוָ֖ה אֶת־ מֹשֶֽׁה׃
Moses *** Yahweh he-commanded just-as headbands on-them and-he-put sash

וַיַּגֵּ֕שׁ אֵ֖ת פַּ֣ר הַֽחַטָּ֑את וַיִּסְמֹ֨ךְ אַהֲרֹ֤ן
Aaron and-he-laid the-sin-offering bull-of *** then-he-presented (14)

וּבָנָיו֙ אֶת־ יְדֵיהֶ֔ם עַל־ רֹ֖אשׁ פַּ֥ר הַֽחַטָּֽאת׃
the-sin-offering bull-of head-of on hands-of-them *** and-sons-of-him

וַיִּשְׁחָ֗ט וַיִּקַּ֨ח מֹשֶׁ֥ה אֶת־ הַדָּ֛ם וַיִּתֵּ֨ן עַל־ קַרְנ֤וֹת
horns-of on and-he-put the-blood *** Moses and-he-took and-he-slaughtered (15)

הַמִּזְבֵּ֙חַ֙ סָבִ֙יב֙ בְּאֶצְבָּע֔וֹ וַיְחַטֵּ֖א אֶת־ הַמִּזְבֵּ֑חַ וְאֶת־
and the-altar *** and-he-purified with-finger-of-him around the-altar

הַדָּ֗ם יָצַק֙ אֶל־ יְס֣וֹד הַמִּזְבֵּ֔חַ וַיְקַדְּשֵׁ֖הוּ לְכַפֵּ֥ר
to-atone so-he-consecrated-him the-altar base-of at he-poured the-blood

עָלָֽיו׃ וַיִּקַּ֗ח אֶֽת־ כָּל־ הַחֵ֘לֶב֮ אֲשֶׁ֣ר עַל־ הַקֶּ֒רֶב֒ וְאֵ֨ת
and the-inner-part around that the-fat all-of *** and-he-took (16) for-him

יֹתֶ֣רֶת הַכָּבֵ֔ד וְאֶת־ שְׁתֵּ֥י הַכְּלָיֹ֖ת וְאֶֽת־ חֶלְבְּהֶ֑ן וַיַּקְטֵ֥ר
and-he-burned fat-of-them and the-kidneys both-of and the-liver cover-of

מֹשֶׁ֖ה הַמִּזְבֵּֽחָה׃ וְאֶת־ הַפָּ֤ר וְאֶת־ עֹרוֹ֙ וְאֶת־ בְּשָׂר֣וֹ וְאֶת־
and flesh-of-him and hide-of-him and the-bull but (17) on-the-altar Moses

פִּרְשׁ֔וֹ שָׂרַ֣ף בָּאֵ֔שׁ מִח֖וּץ לַֽמַּחֲנֶ֑ה כַּאֲשֶׁ֛ר צִוָּ֥ה
he-commanded just-as of-the-camp outside in-the-fire he-burned offal-of-him

יְהוָ֖ה אֶת־ מֹשֶֽׁה׃ וַיַּקְרֵ֕ב אֵ֖ת אֵ֣יל הָעֹלָ֑ה
the-burnt-offering ram-of *** then-he-presented (18) Moses *** Yahweh

וַיִּסְמְכ֞וּ אַהֲרֹ֧ן וּבָנָ֛יו אֶת־ יְדֵיהֶ֖ם עַל־ רֹ֥אשׁ הָאָֽיִל׃
the-ram head-of on hands-of-them *** and-sons-of-him Aaron and-they-laid

וַיִּשְׁחָ֑ט וַיִּזְרֹ֨ק מֹשֶׁ֧ה אֶת־ הַדָּ֛ם עַל־ הַמִּזְבֵּ֖חַ
the-altar on the-blood *** Moses and-he-sprinkled and-he-slaughtered (19)

סָבִֽיב׃ וְאֶת־ הָאַ֕יִל נִתַּ֖ח לִנְתָחָ֑יו וַיַּקְטֵ֤ר מֹשֶׁה֙ אֶת־
*** Moses and-he-burned into-pieces-of-him he-cut the-ram and (20) around

הָרֹ֔אשׁ וְאֶת־ הַנְּתָחִ֖ים וְאֶת־ הַפָּֽדֶר׃ וְאֶת־ הַקֶּ֥רֶב וְאֶת־ הַכְּרָעַ֖יִם
the-legs and the-inner-part and (21) the-fat and the-pieces and the-head

רָחַ֣ץ בַּמָּ֑יִם וַיַּקְטֵ֨ר מֹשֶׁ֜ה אֶת־ כָּל־ הָאַ֙יִל֙
the-ram whole-of *** Moses and-he-burned with-the-waters he-washed

stand, to consecrate them.
12 He poured some of the anointing oil on Aaron's head and anointed him to consecrate him.
13 Then he brought Aaron's sons forward, put tunics on them, tied sashes around them and put headbands on them, as the LORD commanded Moses.

14 He then presented the bull for the sin offering, and Aaron and his sons laid their hands on its head.
15 Moses slaughtered the bull and took some of the blood, and with his finger he put it on all the horns of the altar to purify the altar. He poured out the rest of the blood at the base of the altar. So he consecrated it to make atonement for it.
16 Moses also took all the fat around the inner parts, the covering of the liver, and both kidneys and their fat, and burned it on the altar.
17 But the bull with its hide and its flesh and its offal he burned up outside the camp, as the LORD commanded Moses.

18 He then presented the ram for the burnt offering, and Aaron and his sons laid their hands on its head.
19 Then Moses slaughtered the ram and sprinkled the blood against the altar on all sides.
20 He cut the ram into pieces and burned the head, the pieces and the fat.
21 He washed the inner parts and the legs with water and burned the whole ram on the

הַמִּזְבֵּחָה עֹלָה הוּא לְרֵיחַ־ נִיחֹחַ אִשֶּׁה הוּא

he fire-offering pleasant as-aroma-of he burnt-offering on-the-altar

לַיהוָה כַּאֲשֶׁר צִוָּה יְהוָה אֶת־ מֹשֶׁה׃ וַיַּקְרֵב אֶת־

*** then-he-presented (22) Moses *** Yahweh he-commanded just-as to-Yahweh

הָאַיִל הַשֵּׁנִי אֵיל הַמִּלֻּאִים וַיִּסְמְכוּ אַהֲרֹן וּבָנָיו

and-sons-of-him Aaron and-they-laid the-ordinations ram-of the-other the-ram

אֶת־ יְדֵיהֶם עַל־ רֹאשׁ הָאָיִל׃ וַיִּשְׁחָט ׀ וַיִּקַּח

and-he-took then-he-slaughtered (23) the-ram head-of on hands-of-them ***

מֹשֶׁה מִדָּמוֹ וַיִּתֵּן עַל־ תְּנוּךְ אֹזֶן־ אַהֲרֹן הַיְמָנִית וְעַל־

and-on the-right Aaron ear-of lobe-of on and-he-put from-blood-of-him Moses

בֹּהֶן יָדוֹ הַיְמָנִית וְעַל־ בֹּהֶן רַגְלוֹ הַיְמָנִית׃

the-right foot-of-him big-toe-of and-on the-right hand-of-him thumb-of

וַיַּקְרֵב אֶת־ בְּנֵי אַהֲרֹן וַיִּתֵּן מֹשֶׁה מִן־ הַדָּם עַל־

on the-blood from Moses and-he-put Aaron sons-of *** and-he-brought (24)

תְּנוּךְ אָזְנָם הַיְמָנִית וְעַל־ בֹּהֶן יָדָם הַיְמָנִית וְעַל־

and-on the-right hand-of-them thumb-of and-on the-right ear-of-them lobe-of

בֹּהֶן רַגְלָם הַיְמָנִית וַיִּזְרֹק מֹשֶׁה אֶת־ הַדָּם

the-blood *** Moses then-he-sprinkled the-right foot-of-them big-toe-of

עַל־ הַמִּזְבֵּחַ סָבִיב׃ וַיִּקַּח אֶת־ הַחֵלֶב וְאֶת־ הָאַלְיָה וְאֶת־

and the-fat-tail and the-fat *** and-he-took (25) around the-altar against

כָּל־ הַחֵלֶב אֲשֶׁר עַל־ הַקֶּרֶב וְאֵת יֹתֶרֶת הַכָּבֵד וְאֶת־ שְׁתֵּי

both-of and the-liver cover-of and the-inner-part around that the-fat all-of

הַכְּלָיֹת וְאֶת־ חֶלְבְּהֶן וְאֵת שׁוֹק הַיָּמִין׃ וּמִסַּל

then-from-basket-of (26) the-right thigh-of and fat-of-them and the-kidneys

הַמַּצּוֹת אֲשֶׁר ׀ לִפְנֵי יְהוָה לָקַח חַלַּת מַצָּה אַחַת

one bread cake-of he-took Yahweh before that the-breads-without-yeast

וְחַלַּת לֶחֶם שֶׁמֶן אַחַת וְרָקִיק אֶחָד וַיָּשֶׂם עַל־ הַחֲלָבִים

the-fat-portions on and-he-put one and-wafer one oil bread and-cake-of

וְעַל שׁוֹק הַיָּמִין׃ וַיִּתֵּן אֶת־ הַכֹּל עַל כַּפֵּי אַהֲרֹן

Aaron hands-of on the-all *** and-he-put (27) the-right thigh-of and-on

וְעַל כַּפֵּי בָנָיו וַיָּנֶף אֹתָם תְּנוּפָה לִפְנֵי יְהוָה׃

Yahweh before wave-offering them and-he-waved sons-of-him hands-of and-on

וַיִּקַּח מֹשֶׁה אֹתָם מֵעַל כַּפֵּיהֶם וַיַּקְטֵר הַמִּזְבֵּחָה

on-the-altar and-he-burned hands-of-them from-on them Moses then-he-took (28)

עַל־ הָעֹלָה מִלֻּאִים הֵם לְרֵיחַ נִיחֹחַ

pleasant as-aroma-of they ordination-offerings the-burnt-offering upon

אִשֶּׁה הוּא לַיהוָה׃ וַיִּקַּח מֹשֶׁה אֶת־ הֶחָזֶה

the-breast *** Moses and-he-took (29) to-Yahweh he fire-offering

altar as a burnt offering, a pleasing aroma, an offering made to the LORD by fire, as the LORD commanded Moses.

[22]He then presented the other ram, the ram for the ordination, and Aaron and his sons laid their hands on its head. [23]Moses slaughtered the ram and took some of its blood and put it on the lobe of Aaron's right ear, on the thumb of his right hand and on the big toe of his right foot. [24]Moses also brought Aaron's sons forward and put some of the blood on the lobes of their right ears, on the thumbs of their right hands and on the big toes of their right feet. Then he sprinkled blood against the altar on all sides. [25]He took the fat, the fat tail, all the fat around the inner parts, the covering of the liver, both kidneys and their fat and the right thigh. [26]Then from the basket of bread made without yeast, which was before the LORD, he took a cake of bread, and one made with oil, and a wafer; he put these on the fat portions and on the right thigh. [27]He put all these in the hands of Aaron and his sons and waved them before the LORD as a wave offering. [28]Then Moses took them from their hands and burned them on the altar on top of the burnt offering as an ordination offering, a pleasing aroma, an offering made to the LORD by fire. [29]He also took the breast—

וַיְנִיפֵהוּ תְנוּפָה לִפְנֵי יְהוָה מֵאֵיל הַמִּלֻּאִים
the-ordinations from-ram-of Yahweh before wave-offering and-he-waved-him

לְמֹשֶׁה הָיָה לְמָנָה כַּאֲשֶׁר צִוָּה יְהוָה אֶת־ מֹשֶׁה׃
Moses *** Yahweh he-commanded just-as as-share he-was for-Moses

וַיִּקַּח מֹשֶׁה מִשֶּׁמֶן הַמִּשְׁחָה וּמִן־ הַדָּם אֲשֶׁר עַל־
on that the-blood and-from the-anointing from-oil-of Moses then-he-took (30)

הַמִּזְבֵּחַ וַיַּז עַל־ אַהֲרֹן עַל־ בְּגָדָיו וְעַל־ בָּנָיו
sons-of-him and-on garments-of-him on Aaron on and-he-sprinkled the-altar

וְעַל־ בִּגְדֵי בָנָיו אִתּוֹ וַיְקַדֵּשׁ אֶת־ אַהֲרֹן אֶת־
*** Aaron *** so-he-consecrated with-him sons-of-him garments-of and-on

בְּגָדָיו וְאֶת־ בָּנָיו וְאֶת־ בִּגְדֵי בָנָיו אִתּוֹ׃
with-him sons-of-him garments-of and sons-of-him and garments-of-him

וַיֹּאמֶר מֹשֶׁה אֶל־ אַהֲרֹן וְאֶל־ בָּנָיו בַּשְּׁלוּ אֶת־ הַבָּשָׂר
the-meat *** cook! sons-of-him and-to Aaron to Moses then-he-said (31)

פֶּתַח אֹהֶל מוֹעֵד וְשָׁם תֹּאכְלוּ אֹתוֹ וְאֶת־ הַלֶּחֶם אֲשֶׁר
that the-bread and him you-eat and-there Meeting Tent-of entrance-of

בְּסַל הַמִּלֻּאִים כַּאֲשֶׁר צִוֵּיתִי לֵאמֹר אַהֲרֹן
Aaron to-say I-commanded just-as the-ordination-offerings in-basket-of

וּבָנָיו יֹאכְלֻהוּ׃ וְהַנּוֹתָר בַּבָּשָׂר
of-the-meat and-the-being-left (32) they-shall-eat-him and-sons-of-him

וּבַלָּחֶם בָּאֵשׁ תִּשְׂרֹפוּ׃ וּמִפֶּתַח אֹהֶל
Tent-of and-from-entrance-of (33) you-burn in-the-fire and-of-the-bread

מוֹעֵד לֹא תֵצְאוּ שִׁבְעַת יָמִים עַד יוֹם מְלֹאת יְמֵי
days-of to-complete day until days seven-of you-leave not Meeting

מִלֻּאֵיכֶם כִּי שִׁבְעַת יָמִים יְמַלֵּא אֶת־ יֶדְכֶם׃
hand-of-you *** he-will-fill days seven-of for ordinations-of-you

כַּאֲשֶׁר עָשָׂה בַּיּוֹם הַזֶּה צִוָּה יְהוָה לַעֲשֹׂת לְכַפֵּר
to-atone to-do Yahweh he-commanded the-this on-the-day he-did just-as (34)

עֲלֵיכֶם׃ וּפֶתַח אֹהֶל מוֹעֵד תֵּשְׁבוּ יוֹמָם וָלַיְלָה
and-night by-day you-stay Meeting Tent-of and-entrance-of (35) for-you

שִׁבְעַת יָמִים וּשְׁמַרְתֶּם אֶת־ מִשְׁמֶרֶת יְהוָה וְלֹא תָמוּתוּ כִּי־ כֵן
this for you-die so-not Yahweh requirement-of *** and-you-do days seven-of

צֻוֵּיתִי׃ וַיַּעַשׂ אַהֲרֹן וּבָנָיו אֵת כָּל־ הַדְּבָרִים
the-things all-of *** and-sons-of-him Aaron so-he-did (36) I-was-commanded

אֲשֶׁר־ צִוָּה יְהוָה בְּיַד־ מֹשֶׁה׃ וַיְהִי בַּיּוֹם
on-the-day and-he-was (9:1) Moses by-hand-of Yahweh he-commanded that

הַשְּׁמִינִי קָרָא מֹשֶׁה לְאַהֲרֹן וּלְבָנָיו וּלְזִקְנֵי
and-to-elders-of and-to-sons-of-him to-Aaron Moses he-summoned the-eighth

Moses' share of the ordination ram—and waved it before the LORD as a wave offering, as the LORD commanded Moses.

[30]Then Moses took some of the anointing oil and some of the blood from the altar and sprinkled them on Aaron and his garments and on his sons and their garments. So he consecrated Aaron and his garments and his sons and their garments.

[31]Moses then said to Aaron and his sons, "Cook the meat at the entrance to the Tent of Meeting and eat it there with the bread from the basket of ordination offerings, as I commanded, saying,[q] 'Aaron and his sons are to eat it.' [32]Then burn up the rest of the meat and the bread. [33]Do not leave the entrance to the Tent of Meeting for seven days, until the days of your ordination are completed, for your ordination will last seven days. [34]What has been done today was commanded by the LORD to make atonement for you. [35]You must stay at the entrance to the Tent of Meeting day and night for seven days and do what the LORD requires, so you will not die; for that is what I have been commanded." [36]So Aaron and his sons did everything the LORD commanded through Moses.

### *The Priests Begin Their Ministry*

9 On the eighth day Moses summoned Aaron and his sons and the elders of Israel.

[q]31 Or *I was commanded:*

יִשְׂרָאֵל׃ וַיֹּאמֶר אֶל־אַהֲרֹן קַח־לְךָ עֵגֶל בֶּן־בָּקָר
herd young-of calf for-you take! Aaron to and-he-said (2) Israel

לְחַטָּאת וְאַיִל לְעֹלָה תְּמִימִם וְהַקְרֵב
and-present! without-defect for-burnt-offering and-ram for-sin-offering

לִפְנֵי יְהוָה׃ וְאֶל־בְּנֵי יִשְׂרָאֵל תְּדַבֵּר לֵאמֹר קְחוּ שְׂעִיר־
male-goat-of take! to-say you-say Israel sons-of then-to (3) Yahweh before

עִזִּים לְחַטָּאת וְעֵגֶל וָכֶבֶשׂ בְּנֵי־שָׁנָה תְּמִימִם
without-defect year sons-of and-lamb and-calf for-sin-offering goats

לְעֹלָה׃ וְשׁוֹר וָאַיִל לִשְׁלָמִים לִזְבֹּחַ
to-sacrifice for-fellowship-offerings and-ram and-cow (4) for-burnt-offering

לִפְנֵי יְהוָה וּמִנְחָה בְּלוּלָה בַשָּׁמֶן כִּי הַיּוֹם יְהוָה
Yahweh the-day for with-the-oil being-mixed and-grain-offering Yahweh before

נִרְאָה אֲלֵיכֶם׃ וַיִּקְחוּ אֵת אֲשֶׁר צִוָּה מֹשֶׁה אֶל־
to Moses he-commanded what *** so-they-took (5) to-you he-will-appear

פְּנֵי אֹהֶל מוֹעֵד וַיִּקְרְבוּ כָּל־הָעֵדָה וַיַּעַמְדוּ
and-they-stood the-assembly all-of and-they-came-near Meeting Tent-of front-of

לִפְנֵי יְהוָה׃ וַיֹּאמֶר מֹשֶׁה זֶה הַדָּבָר אֲשֶׁר־צִוָּה
he-commanded that the-thing this Moses then-he-said (6) Yahweh before

יְהוָה תַּעֲשׂוּ וְיֵרָא אֲלֵיכֶם כְּבוֹד יְהוָה׃ וַיֹּאמֶר
and-he-said (7) Yahweh glory-of to-you so-he-may-appear you-must-do Yahweh

מֹשֶׁה אֶל־אַהֲרֹן קְרַב אֶל־הַמִּזְבֵּחַ וַעֲשֵׂה אֶת־חַטָּאתְךָ
sin-offering-of-you *** and-sacrifice! the-altar to come! Aaron to Moses

וְאֶת־עֹלָתֶךָ וְכַפֵּר בַּעַדְךָ וּבְעַד הָעָם וַעֲשֵׂה
and-sacrifice! the-people and-for for-you and-atone! burnt-offering-of-you and

אֶת־קָרְבַּן הָעָם וְכַפֵּר בַּעֲדָם כַּאֲשֶׁר צִוָּה יְהוָה׃
Yahweh he-commanded just-as for-them and-atone! the-people offering-of ***

וַיִּקְרַב אַהֲרֹן אֶל־הַמִּזְבֵּחַ וַיִּשְׁחַט אֶת־עֵגֶל
calf-of *** and-he-slaughtered the-altar to Aaron so-he-came (8)

הַחַטָּאת אֲשֶׁר־לוֹ׃ וַיַּקְרִבוּ בְּנֵי אַהֲרֹן אֶת־
*** Aaron sons-of and-they-brought (9) for-him that the-sin-offering

הַדָּם אֵלָיו וַיִּטְבֹּל אֶצְבָּעוֹ בַּדָּם וַיִּתֵּן עַל־
on and-he-put into-the-blood finger-of-him and-he-dipped to-him the-blood

קַרְנוֹת הַמִּזְבֵּחַ וְאֶת־הַדָּם יָצַק אֶל־יְסוֹד הַמִּזְבֵּחַ׃ וְאֶת־
and (10) the-altar base-of at he-poured-out the-blood and the-altar horns-of

הַחֵלֶב וְאֶת־הַכְּלָיֹת וְאֶת־הַיֹּתֶרֶת מִן־הַכָּבֵד מִן־הַחַטָּאת
the-sin-offering from the-liver from the-cover and the-kidneys and the-fat

הִקְטִיר הַמִּזְבֵּחָה כַּאֲשֶׁר צִוָּה יְהוָה אֶת־מֹשֶׁה׃ וְאֶת־
and (11) Moses *** Yahweh he-commanded just-as on-the-altar he-burned

2He said to Aaron, "Take a bull calf for your sin offering and a ram for your burnt offering, both without defect, and present them before the LORD. 3Then say to the Israelites: 'Take a male goat for a sin offering, a calf and a lamb—both a year old and without defect—for a burnt offering, 4and a cow[r] and a ram for a fellowship offering[s] to sacrifice before the LORD, together with a grain offering mixed with oil. For today the LORD will appear to you.' "

5They took the things Moses commanded to the front of the Tent of Meeting, and the entire assembly came near and stood before the LORD. 6Then Moses said, "This is what the LORD has commanded you to do, so that the glory of the LORD may appear to you."

7Moses said to Aaron, "Come to the altar and sacrifice your sin offering and your burnt offering and make atonement for yourself and the people; sacrifice the offering that is for the people and make atonement for them, as the LORD has commanded."

8So Aaron came to the altar and slaughtered the calf as a sin offering for himself. 9His sons brought the blood to him, and he dipped his finger into the blood and put it on the horns of the altar; the rest of the blood he poured out at the base of the altar. 10On the altar he burned the fat, the kidneys and the covering of the liver from the sin offering, as the LORD commanded Moses; 11the

r4 The Hebrew word can include both male and female; also in verses 18 and 19.
s4 Traditionally *peace offering;* also in verses 18 and 22

הַבָּשָׂר וְאֶת־ הָעוֹר שָׂרַף בָּאֵשׁ מִחוּץ לַמַּחֲנֶה׃
of-the-camp outside in-the-fire he-burned the-hide and the-flesh

(12) וַיִּשְׁחַט אֶת־ הָעֹלָה וַיַּמְצִאוּ בְּנֵי אַהֲרֹן
Aaron sons-of and-they-handled the-burnt-offering *** then-he-slaughtered (12)

אֵלָיו אֶת־ הַדָּם וַיִּזְרְקֵהוּ עַל־ הַמִּזְבֵּחַ סָבִיב׃
around the-altar against and-he-sprinkled-him the-blood *** to-him

(13) וְאֶת־ הָעֹלָה הִמְצִיאוּ אֵלָיו לִנְתָחֶיהָ וְאֶת־הָרֹאשׁ
the-head and by-pieces-of-her to-him they-handed the-burnt-offering and (13)

וַיַּקְטֵר עַל־ הַמִּזְבֵּחַ׃ (14) וַיִּרְחַץ אֶת־ הַקֶּרֶב וְאֶת־
and the-inner-part *** and-he-washed (14) the-altar on and-he-burned

הַכְּרָעָיִם וַיַּקְטֵר עַל־ הָעֹלָה הַמִּזְבֵּחָה׃
on-the-altar the-burnt-offering upon and-he-burned the-legs

(15) וַיַּקְרֵב אֵת קָרְבַּן הָעָם וַיִּקַּח אֶת־ שְׂעִיר
goat-of *** and-he-took the-people offering-of *** then-he-brought (15)

הַחַטָּאת אֲשֶׁר לָעָם וַיִּשְׁחָטֵהוּ וַיְחַטְּאֵהוּ
and-he-offered-him and-he-slaughtered-him for-the-people that the-sin-offering

כָּרִאשׁוֹן׃ (16) וַיַּקְרֵב אֶת־ הָעֹלָה וַיַּעֲשֶׂהָ
and-he-offered-her the-burnt-offering *** and-he-brought (16) as-the-first

כַּמִּשְׁפָּט׃ (17) וַיַּקְרֵב אֶת־ הַמִּנְחָה וַיְמַלֵּא
and-he-filled the-grain-offering *** and-he-brought (17) as-the-prescription

כַפּוֹ מִמֶּנָּה וַיַּקְטֵר עַל־ הַמִּזְבֵּחַ מִלְּבַד עֹלַת
offering-of in-addition-to the-altar on and-he-burned from-her hand-of-him

הַבֹּקֶר׃ (18) וַיִּשְׁחַט אֶת־ הַשּׁוֹר וְאֶת־ הָאַיִל זֶבַח
offering-of the-ram and the-cow *** and-he-slaughtered (18) the-morning

הַשְּׁלָמִים אֲשֶׁר לָעָם וַיַּמְצִאוּ בְּנֵי אַהֲרֹן אֶת־
*** Aaron sons-of and-they-handed for-the-people that the-fellowships

הַדָּם אֵלָיו וַיִּזְרְקֵהוּ עַל־ הַמִּזְבֵּחַ סָבִיב׃ (19) וְאֶת־
but (19) around the-altar against and-he-sprinkled-him to-him the-blood

הַחֲלָבִים מִן־ הַשּׁוֹר וּמִן־ הָאַיִל הָאַלְיָה וְהַמְכַסֶּה
and-the-fat-layer the-fat-tail the-ram and-from the-cow from the-fat-portions

וְהַכְּלָיֹת וְיֹתֶרֶת הַכָּבֵד׃ (20) וַיָּשִׂימוּ אֶת־ הַחֲלָבִים
the-fat-portions *** and-they-laid (20) the-liver and-cover-of and-the-kidneys

עַל־ הֶחָזוֹת וַיַּקְטֵר הַחֲלָבִים הַמִּזְבֵּחָה׃ (21) וְאֵת
and (21) on-the-altar the-fat-portions and-he-burned the-breasts on

הֶחָזוֹת וְאֵת שׁוֹק הַיָּמִין הֵנִיף אַהֲרֹן תְּנוּפָה לִפְנֵי
before wave-offering Aaron he-waved the-right thigh-of and the-breasts

יְהוָה כַּאֲשֶׁר צִוָּה מֹשֶׁה׃ (22) וַיִּשָּׂא אַהֲרֹן אֶת־ יָדָו
hands-of-him *** Aaron then-he-lifted (22) Moses he-commanded just-as Yahweh

°22 ק ידיו

flesh and the hide he burned up outside the camp.

[12]Then he slaughtered the burnt offering. His sons handed him the blood, and he sprinkled it against the altar on all sides. [13]They handed him the burnt offering piece by piece, including the head, and he burned them on the altar. [14]He washed the inner parts and the legs and burned them on top of the burnt offering on the altar.

[15]Aaron then brought the offering that was for the people. He took the goat for the people's sin offering and slaughtered it and offered it for a sin offering as he did with the first one.

[16]He brought the burnt offering and offered it in the prescribed way. [17]He also brought the grain offering, took a handful of it and burned it on the altar in addition to the morning's burnt offering.

[18]He slaughtered the cow and the ram as the fellowship offering for the people. His sons handed him the blood, and he sprinkled it against the altar on all sides. [19]But the fat portions of the cow and the ram—the fat tail, the layer of fat, the kidneys and the covering of the liver— [20]these they laid on the breasts, and then Aaron burned the fat on the altar. [21]Aaron waved the breasts and the right thigh before the LORD as a wave offering, as Moses commanded.

[22]Then Aaron lifted his

אֶל־ הָעָם וַיְבָרְכֵם וַיֵּרֶד מֵעֲשֹׂת

from-to-sacrifice and-he-stepped-down and-he-blessed-them the-people toward

הַחַטָּאת וְהָעֹלָה וְהַשְּׁלָמִים׃

and-the-fellowship-offerings and-the-burnt-offering the-sin-offering

וַיָּבֹא מֹשֶׁה וְאַהֲרֹן אֶל־ אֹהֶל מוֹעֵד וַיֵּצְאוּ

when-they-came-out Meeting Tent-of into and-Aaron Moses then-he-went (23)

וַיְבָרְכוּ אֶת־ הָעָם וַיֵּרָא כְבוֹד־ יְהוָה אֶל־ כָּל־

all-of to Yahweh glory-of and-he-appeared the-people *** then-they-blessed

הָעָם׃ וַתֵּצֵא אֵשׁ מִלִּפְנֵי יְהוָה וַתֹּאכַל

and-she-consumed Yahweh from-presence-of fire and-she-came-out (24) the-people

עַל־ הַמִּזְבֵּחַ אֶת־ הָעֹלָה וְאֶת־ הַחֲלָבִים וַיַּרְא כָּל־

all-of when-he-saw the-fat-portions and the-burnt-offering *** the-altar on

הָעָם וַיָּרֹנּוּ וַיִּפְּלוּ עַל־ פְּנֵיהֶם׃

faces-of-them on and-they-fell then-they-shouted the-people

וַיִּקְחוּ בְנֵי־ אַהֲרֹן נָדָב וַאֲבִיהוּא אִישׁ מַחְתָּתוֹ וַיִּתְּנוּ

and-they-put censer-of-him each and-Abihu Nadab Aaron sons-of and-they-took (10:1)

בָהֵן אֵשׁ וַיָּשִׂימוּ עָלֶיהָ קְטֹרֶת וַיַּקְרִבוּ לִפְנֵי יְהוָה

Yahweh before and-they-offered incense to-her and-they-added fire in-them

אֵשׁ זָרָה אֲשֶׁר לֹא צִוָּה אֹתָם׃ וַתֵּצֵא אֵשׁ

fire so-she-came-out (2) them he-commanded not that unauthorized fire

מִלִּפְנֵי יְהוָה וַתֹּאכַל אוֹתָם וַיָּמֻתוּ לִפְנֵי יְהוָה׃

Yahweh before and-they-died them and-she-consumed Yahweh from-presence-of

וַיֹּאמֶר מֹשֶׁה אֶל־ אַהֲרֹן הוּא אֲשֶׁר־ דִּבֶּר יְהוָה ׀ לֵאמֹר

to-say Yahweh he-spoke what this Aaron to Moses then-he-said (3)

בִּקְרֹבַי אֶקָּדֵשׁ וְעַל־ פְּנֵי כָל־ הָעָם

the-people all-of sight-of and-in I-will-show-myself-holy among-ones-near-me

אֶכָּבֵד וַיִּדֹּם אַהֲרֹן׃ וַיִּקְרָא מֹשֶׁה אֶל־

to Moses and-he-summoned (4) Aaron and-he-was-silent I-will-be-honored

מִישָׁאֵל וְאֶל אֶלְצָפָן בְּנֵי עֻזִּיאֵל דֹּד אַהֲרֹן וַיֹּאמֶר אֲלֵהֶם

to-them and-he-said Aaron uncle-of Uzziel sons-of Elzaphan and-to Mishael

קִרְבוּ שְׂאוּ אֶת־ אֲחֵיכֶם מֵאֵת פְּנֵי־ הַקֹּדֶשׁ אֶל־ מִחוּץ

outside to the-sanctuary front-of from cousins-of-you *** carry! come!

לַמַּחֲנֶה׃ וַיִּקְרְבוּ וַיִּשָּׂאֻם בְּכֻתֳּנֹתָם אֶל־

to in-tunics-of-them and-they-carried-them so-they-came (5) of-the-camp

מִחוּץ לַמַּחֲנֶה כַּאֲשֶׁר דִּבֶּר מֹשֶׁה׃ וַיֹּאמֶר מֹשֶׁה אֶל־

to Moses then-he-said (6) Moses he-commanded just-as of-the-camp outside

אַהֲרֹן וּלְאֶלְעָזָר וּלְאִיתָמָר ׀ בָּנָיו רָאשֵׁיכֶם אַל־ תִּפְרָעוּ ׀

you-uncover not heads-of-you sons-of-him and-to-Ithamar and-to-Eleazar Aaron

hands toward the people and blessed them. And having sacrificed the sin offering, the burnt offering and the fellowship offering, he stepped down.

[23]Moses and Aaron then went into the Tent of Meeting. When they came out, they blessed the people; and the glory of the LORD appeared to all the people. [24]Fire came out from the presence of the LORD and consumed the burnt offering and the fat portions on the altar. And when all the people saw it, they shouted for joy and fell facedown.

*The Death of Nadab and Abihu*

10 Aaron's sons Nadab and Abihu took their censers, put fire in them and added incense; and they offered unauthorized fire before the LORD, contrary to his command. [2]So fire came out from the presence of the LORD and consumed them, and they died before the LORD. [3]Moses then said to Aaron, "This is what the LORD spoke of when he said:

"'Among those who
approach me
I will show myself holy;
in the sight of all the
people
I will be honored.'"

Aaron remained silent.

[4]Moses summoned Mishael and Elzaphan, sons of Aaron's uncle Uzziel, and said to them, "Come here; carry your cousins outside the camp, away from the front of the sanctuary." [5]So they came and carried them, still in their tunics, outside the camp, as Moses ordered.

[6]Then Moses said to Aaron and his sons Eleazar and Ithamar, "Do not let your hair become unkempt,[l] and do not

[l] 6 Or *Do not uncover your heads*

וּבִגְדֵיכֶם לֹא־ תִפְרֹמוּ וְלֹא תָמֻתוּ וְעַל כָּל־
whole-of and-with you-die so-not you-tear not and-clothes-of-you

הָעֵדָה יִקְצֹף וַאֲחֵיכֶם כָּל־ בֵּית יִשְׂרָאֵל
Israel house-of all-of but-relatives-of-you he-will-be-angry the-community

יִבְכּוּ אֶת־ הַשְּׂרֵפָה אֲשֶׁר שָׂרַף יְהוָה׃
Yahweh he-burned whom the-burnt-one *** they-may-mourn

וּמִפֶּתַח אֹהֶל מוֹעֵד לֹא תֵצְאוּ פֶּן־ תָּמֻתוּ כִּי־
because you-will-die or you-leave not Meeting Tent-of and-from-entrance-of (7)

שֶׁמֶן מִשְׁחַת יְהוָה עֲלֵיכֶם וַיַּעֲשׂוּ כִּדְבַר מֹשֶׁה׃
Moses as-word-of so-they-did on-you Yahweh anointing-of oil-of

וַיְדַבֵּר יְהוָה אֶל־אַהֲרֹן לֵאמֹר׃ יַיִן וְשֵׁכָר אַל־
not or-fermented-drink wine (9) to-say Aaron to Yahweh then-he-spoke (8)

תֵּשְׁתְּ ׀ אַתָּה ׀ וּבָנֶיךָ אִתָּךְ בְּבֹאֲכֶם אֶל־ אֹהֶל מוֹעֵד
Meeting Tent-of into when-to-go-you with-you and-sons-of-you you you-drink

וְלֹא תָמֻתוּ חֻקַּת עוֹלָם לְדֹרֹתֵיכֶם׃
for-generations-of-you lasting ordinance-of you-die so-not

וּלֲהַבְדִּיל בֵּין הַקֹּדֶשׁ וּבֵין הַחֹל וּבֵין
and-between the-profane and-between the-holy between and-to-distinguish (10)

הַטָּמֵא וּבֵין הַטָּהוֹר׃ וּלְהוֹרֹת אֶת־ בְּנֵי יִשְׂרָאֵל אֵת
*** Israel sons-of *** and-to-teach (11) the-clean and-between the-unclean

כָּל־ הַחֻקִּים אֲשֶׁר דִּבֶּר יְהוָה אֲלֵיהֶם בְּיַד־ מֹשֶׁה׃
Moses by-hand-of to-them Yahweh he-gave that the-decrees all-of

וַיְדַבֵּר מֹשֶׁה אֶל־אַהֲרֹן וְאֶל אֶלְעָזָר וְאֶל־ אִיתָמָר ׀ בָּנָיו
sons-of-him Ithamar and-to Eleazar and-to Aaron to Moses then-he-spoke (12)

הַנּוֹתָרִים קְחוּ אֶת־ הַמִּנְחָה הַנּוֹתֶרֶת
the-being-left the-grain-offering *** take! the-ones-remaining

מֵאִשֵּׁי יְהוָה וְאִכְלוּהָ מַצּוֹת אֵצֶל הַמִּזְבֵּחַ
the-altar beside without-yeast and-eat-her! Yahweh from-fire-offerings-of

כִּי קֹדֶשׁ קָדָשִׁים הִוא׃ וַאֲכַלְתֶּם אֹתָהּ בְּמָקוֹם קָדֹשׁ כִּי
for holy in-place her and-you-eat (13) she holy-ones most-holy-of for

חָקְךָ וְחָק־ בָּנֶיךָ הִוא מֵאִשֵּׁי יְהוָה כִּי־
for Yahweh from-fire-offerings-of she sons-of-you and-share-of share-of-you

כֵן צֻוֵּיתִי׃ וְאֵת חֲזֵה הַתְּנוּפָה וְאֵת ׀ שׁוֹק הַתְּרוּמָה
the-presentation thigh-of and the-waved breast-of but (14) I-was-commanded so

תֹּאכְלוּ בְּמָקוֹם טָהוֹר אַתָּה וּבָנֶיךָ וּבְנֹתֶיךָ אִתָּךְ
with-you and-daughters-of-you and-sons-of-you you clean in-place you-eat

כִּי־ חָקְךָ וְחָק־ בָּנֶיךָ נִתְּנוּ מִזִּבְחֵי
from-offerings-of they-are-given children-of-you and-share-of share-of-you for

tear your clothes, or you will die and the LORD will be angry with the whole community. But your relatives, all the house of Israel, may mourn for those the LORD has destroyed by fire. 7Do not leave the entrance to the Tent of Meeting or you will die, because the LORD's anointing oil is on you." So they did as Moses said.

8Then the LORD said to Aaron, 9"You and your sons are not to drink wine or other fermented drink whenever you go into the Tent of Meeting, or you will die. This is a lasting ordinance for the generations to come. 10You must distinguish between the holy and the profane, between the unclean and the clean, 11and you must teach the Israelites all the decrees the LORD has given them through Moses."

12Moses said to Aaron and his remaining sons, Eleazar and Ithamar, "Take the grain offering left over from the offerings made to the LORD by fire and eat it prepared without yeast beside the altar, for it is most holy. 13Eat it in a holy place, because it is your share and your sons' share of the offerings made to the LORD by fire; for so I have been commanded. 14But you and your sons and your daughters may eat the breast that was waved and the thigh that was presented. Eat them in a ceremonially clean place; they have been given to you and your children as your share of

שַׁלְמֵי בְּנֵי יִשְׂרָאֵל׃ שׁוֹק הַתְּרוּמָה וַחֲזֵה
and-breast-of the-presentation thigh-of (15) Israel sons-of fellowships-of

הַתְּנוּפָה עַל אִשֵּׁי הַחֲלָבִים יָבִיאוּ לְהָנִיף
to-wave they-must-bring the-fat-portions fire-offerings-of with the-waved

תְּנוּפָה לִפְנֵי יְהוָה וְהָיָה לְךָ וּלְבָנֶיךָ
and-for-children-of-you for-you and-he-will-be Yahweh before wave-offering

אִתְּךָ לְחָק־ עוֹלָם כַּאֲשֶׁר צִוָּה יְהוָה׃ וְאֵת׀ שְׂעִיר
goat-of and (16) Yahweh he-commanded just-as regular as-share-of with-you

הַחַטָּאת דָּרֹשׁ דָּרַשׁ מֹשֶׁה וְהִנֵּה שֹׂרָף
he-was-burned and-see! Moses he-inquired to-inquire the-sin-offering

וַיִּקְצֹף עַל־ אֶלְעָזָר וְעַל־ אִיתָמָר בְּנֵי אַהֲרֹן הַנּוֹתָרִם
the-ones-remaining Aaron sons-of Ithamar and-with Eleazar with so-he-was-angry

לֵאמֹר׃ מַדּוּעַ לֹא־ אֲכַלְתֶּם אֶת־ הַחַטָּאת בִּמְקוֹם הַקֹּדֶשׁ
the-sanctuary in-area-of the-sin-offering *** you-ate not why? (17) to-say

כִּי קֹדֶשׁ קָדָשִׁים הִוא וְאֹתָהּ׀ נָתַן לָכֶם לָשֵׂאת אֶת־
*** to-take-away to-you he-gave and-her she holy-ones most-holy-of for

עֲוֺן הָעֵדָה לְכַפֵּר עֲלֵיהֶם לִפְנֵי יְהוָה׃ הֵן לֹא־
not since (18) Yahweh before for-them to-atone the-community guilt-of

הוּבָא אֶת־ דָּמָהּ אֶל־ הַקֹּדֶשׁ פְּנִימָה אָכוֹל
to-eat inside the-Holy-Place into blood-of-her *** he-was-taken

תֹּאכְלוּ אֹתָהּ בַּקֹּדֶשׁ כַּאֲשֶׁר צִוֵּיתִי׃
I-commanded just-as in-the-sanctuary her you-should-have-eaten

וַיְדַבֵּר אַהֲרֹן אֶל־ מֹשֶׁה הֵן הַיּוֹם הִקְרִיבוּ אֶת־
*** they-sacrificed the-day see! Moses to Aaron and-he-replied (19)

חַטָּאתָם וְאֶת־ עֹלָתָם לִפְנֵי יְהוָה
Yahweh before burnt-offering-of-them and sin-offering-of-them

וַתִּקְרֶאנָה אֹתִי כָּאֵלֶּה וְאָכַלְתִּי חַטָּאת הַיּוֹם
the-day sin-offering if-I-ate such-as-the-these to-me but-they-happened

הַיִּיטַב בְּעֵינֵי יְהוָה׃ וַיִּשְׁמַע מֹשֶׁה
Moses when-he-heard (20) Yahweh in-eyes-of would-he-be-pleased?

וַיִּיטַב בְּעֵינָיו׃ וַיְדַבֵּר יְהוָה אֶל־ מֹשֶׁה
Moses to Yahweh and-he-spoke (11:1) in-eyes-of-him then-he-was-satisfied

וְאֶל־ אַהֲרֹן לֵאמֹר אֲלֵהֶם׃ דַּבְּרוּ אֶל־ בְּנֵי יִשְׂרָאֵל לֵאמֹר זֹאת הַחַיָּה
the-animal this to-say Israel sons-of to say! (2) to-them to-say Aaron and-to

אֲשֶׁר תֹּאכְלוּ מִכָּל־ הַבְּהֵמָה אֲשֶׁר עַל־ הָאָרֶץ׃ כֹּל׀
any-of (3) the-land on that the-animal from-all-of you-may-eat that

מַפְרֶסֶת פַּרְסָה וְשֹׁסַעַת שֶׁסַע פְּרָסֹת מַעֲלַת גֵּרָה בַּבְּהֵמָה
among-the-animal cud chewing-of hoofs division-of and-dividing hoof splitting

the Israelites' fellowship offerings.[u] [15]The thigh that was presented and the breast that was waved must be brought with the fat portions of the offerings made by fire, to be waved before the LORD as a wave offering. This will be the regular share for you and your children, as the LORD has commanded."

[16]When Moses inquired about the goat of the sin offering and found that it had been burned up, he was angry with Eleazar and Ithamar, Aaron's remaining sons, and asked, [17]"Why didn't you eat the sin offering in the sanctuary area? It is most holy; it was given to you to take away the guilt of the community by making atonement for them before the LORD. [18]Since its blood was not taken into the Holy Place, you should have eaten the goat in the sanctuary area, as I commanded."

[19]Aaron replied to Moses, "Today they sacrificed their sin offering and their burnt offering before the LORD, but such things as this have happened to me. Would the LORD have been pleased if I had eaten the sin offering today?" [20]When Moses heard this, he was satisfied.

### *Clean and Unclean Food*

**11** The LORD said to Moses and Aaron, [2]"Say to the Israelites: 'Of all the animals that live on land, these are the ones you may eat: [3]You may eat any animal that has a split hoof completely divided and that chews the cud.

[u]14 Traditionally *peace offerings*

אֹתָהּ תֹּאכֵלוּ׃ אַךְ אֶת־ זֶה לֹא תֹאכְלוּ מִמַּעֲלֵי
from-ones-chewing-of you-must-eat not this *** only (4) you-may-eat her

הַגֵּרָה וּמִמַּפְרִיסֵי הַפַּרְסָה אֶת־ הַגָּמָל כִּי־ מַעֲלֵה
chewing-of though the-camel *** the-hoof and-from-ones-splitting-of the-cud

גֵרָה הוּא וּפַרְסָה אֵינֶנּוּ מַפְרִיס טָמֵא הוּא לָכֶם׃ וְאֶת־ הַשָּׁפָן כִּי־
though the-coney and (5) for-you he unclean splitting not-he but-hoof he cud

מַעֲלֵה גֵרָה הוּא וּפַרְסָה לֹא יַפְרִיס טָמֵא הוּא לָכֶם׃ וְאֶת־
and (6) for-you he unclean he-splits not but-hoof he cud chewing-of

הָאַרְנֶבֶת כִּי־ מַעֲלַת גֵּרָה הִוא וּפַרְסָה לֹא הִפְרִיסָה טְמֵאָה הִוא
she unclean she-splits not but-hoof she cud chewing-of though the-rabbit

לָכֶם׃ וְאֶת־ הַחֲזִיר כִּי־ מַפְרִיס פַּרְסָה הוּא וְשֹׁסַע שֶׁסַע
division-of and-dividing he hoof splitting though the-pig and (7) for-you

פַּרְסָה וְהוּא גֵּרָה לֹא־ יִגָּר טָמֵא הוּא לָכֶם׃ מִבְּשָׂרָם לֹא
not from-meat-of-them (8) for-you he unclean he-chews not cud but-he hoof

תֹאכֵלוּ וּבְנִבְלָתָם לֹא תִגָּעוּ טְמֵאִים הֵם לָכֶם׃
for-you they unclean-ones you-must-touch not or-on-carcass-of-them you-must-eat

אֶת־ זֶה תֹּאכְלוּ מִכֹּל אֲשֶׁר בַּמָּיִם כֹּל אֲשֶׁר־ לוֹ סְנַפִּיר
fin to-him that any in-the-waters that from-all you-may-eat this *** (9)

וְקַשְׂקֶשֶׂת בַּמַּיִם בַּיַּמִּים וּבַנְּחָלִים אֹתָם תֹּאכֵלוּ׃
you-may-eat them and-in-the-streams in-the-seas in-the-waters and-scale

וְכֹל אֲשֶׁר אֵין־ לוֹ סְנַפִּיר וְקַשְׂקֶשֶׂת בַּיַּמִּים וּבַנְּחָלִים
or-in-the-streams in-the-seas or-scale fin to-him not that but-any (10)

מִכֹּל שֶׁרֶץ הַמַּיִם וּמִכֹּל נֶפֶשׁ הַחַיָּה
the-living creature-of or-among-every-of the-waters swarmer-of among-every-of

אֲשֶׁר בַּמָּיִם שֶׁקֶץ הֵם לָכֶם׃ וְשֶׁקֶץ יִהְיוּ
they-are since-detestable (11) to-you they detestable in-the-waters that

לָכֶם מִבְּשָׂרָם לֹא תֹאכֵלוּ וְאֶת־ נִבְלָתָם תְּשַׁקֵּצוּ׃
you-must-detest carcass-of-them and you-must-eat not from-meat-of-them to-you

כֹּל אֲשֶׁר אֵין־ לוֹ סְנַפִּיר וְקַשְׂקֶשֶׂת בַּמָּיִם שֶׁקֶץ הוּא לָכֶם׃
to-you he detestable in-the-waters or-scale fin to-him not that any (12)

וְאֶת־ אֵלֶּה תְּשַׁקְּצוּ מִן־ הָעוֹף לֹא יֵאָכְלוּ
they-must-be-eaten not the-bird among you-must-detest these and (13)

שֶׁקֶץ הֵם אֶת־ הַנֶּשֶׁר וְאֶת־ הַפֶּרֶס וְאֵת הָעָזְנִיָּה׃
the-black-vulture and the-vulture and the-eagle *** they detestable

וְאֶת־ הַדָּאָה וְאֶת־ הָאַיָּה לְמִינָהּ׃ אֵת כָּל־
any-of *** (15) any-kind-of-her the-black-kite and the-red-kite and (14)

עֹרֵב לְמִינוֹ׃ וְאֵת בַּת הַיַּעֲנָה וְאֶת־ הַתַּחְמָס
the-screech-owl and the-horned-owl daughter-of and (16) by-kind-of-him raven

4" 'There are some that only chew the cud or only have a split hoof, but you must not eat them. The camel, though it chews the cud, does not have a split hoof; it is ceremonially unclean for you. 5The coney,[v] though it chews the cud, does not have a split hoof; it is unclean for you. 6The rabbit, though it chews the cud, does not have a split hoof; it is unclean for you. 7And the pig, though it has a split hoof completely divided, does not chew the cud; it is unclean for you. 8You must not eat their meat or touch their carcasses; they are unclean for you.

9" 'Of all the creatures living in the water of the seas and the streams, you may eat any that have fins and scales. 10But all creatures in the seas or streams that do not have fins and scales—whether among all the swarming things or among all the other living creatures in the water—you are to detest. 11And since you are to detest them, you must not eat their meat and you must detest their carcasses. 12Anything living in the water that does not have fins and scales is to be detestable to you.

13" 'These are the birds you are to detest and not eat because they are detestable: the eagle, the vulture, the black vulture, 14the red kite, any kind of black kite, 15any kind of raven, 16the horned owl, the

[v]5 That is, the hyrax or rock badger

וְאֶת־ הַשַּׁחַף וְאֶת־ הַנֵּץ לְמִינֵהוּ׃ וְאֶת־ הַכּוֹס וְאֶת־
and the-little-owl and (17) any-kind-of-him the-hawk and the-gull and

הַשָּׁלָךְ וְאֶת־ הַיַּנְשׁוּף׃ וְאֶת־ הַתִּנְשֶׁמֶת וְאֶת־ הַקָּאָת
the-desert-owl and the-white-owl and (18) the-great-owl and the-cormorant

וְאֶת־ הָרָחָם׃ וְאֵת הַחֲסִידָה הָאֲנָפָה לְמִינָהּ וְאֶת־ הַדּוּכִיפַת
the-hoopoe and any-kind-of-her the-heron the-stork and (19) the-osprey and

וְאֶת־ הָעֲטַלֵּף׃ כֹּל שֶׁרֶץ הָעוֹף הַהֹלֵךְ עַל־אַרְבַּע
four on the-one-walking the-flyer insect-of any-of (20) the-bat and

שֶׁקֶץ הוּא לָכֶם׃ אַךְ אֶת־ זֶה תֹּאכְלוּ מִכֹּל
from-every-of you-may-eat this *** however (21) to-you he detestable

שֶׁרֶץ הָעוֹף הַהֹלֵךְ עַל־אַרְבַּע אֲשֶׁר־ °לֹא כְרָעַיִם מִמַּעַל
from-above legs to-him that four on the-one-walking the-wing insect-of

לְרַגְלָיו לְנַתֵּר בָּהֵן עַל־ הָאָרֶץ׃ אֶת־ אֵלֶּה מֵהֶם
from-them these *** (22) the-ground on with-them to-hop to-feet-of-him

תֹּאכֵלוּ אֶת־ הָאַרְבֶּה לְמִינוֹ וְאֶת־ הַסָּלְעָם לְמִינֵהוּ
any-kind-of-him the-katydid and any-kind-of-him the-locust *** you-may-eat

וְאֶת־ הַחַרְגֹּל לְמִינֵהוּ וְאֶת־ הֶחָגָב לְמִינֵהוּ׃
any-kind-of-him the-grasshopper and any-kind-of-him the-cricket and

וְכֹל שֶׁרֶץ הָעוֹף אֲשֶׁר־ לוֹ אַרְבַּע רַגְלָיִם שֶׁקֶץ הוּא
he detestable feet four to-him that the-wing insect-of but-every-of (23)

לָכֶם׃ וּלְאֵלֶּה תִּטַּמָּאוּ כָּל־ הַנֹּגֵעַ
the-one-touching every-of you-will-become-unclean and-by-these (24) to-you

בְּנִבְלָתָם יִטְמָא עַד־ הָעָרֶב׃ וְכָל־
and-every-of (25) the-evening till he-will-be-unclean on-carcass-of-them

הַנֹּשֵׂא מִנִּבְלָתָם יְכַבֵּס בְּגָדָיו
clothes-of-him he-must-wash on-carcass-of-them the-one-picking-up

וְטָמֵא עַד־ הָעָרֶב׃ לְכָל־ הַבְּהֵמָה אֲשֶׁר
that the-animal to-every-of (26) the-evening till and-he-will-be-unclean

הִוא מַפְרֶסֶת פַּרְסָה וְשֶׁסַע ׀ אֵינֶנָּה שֹׁסַעַת וְגֵרָה אֵינֶנָּה מַעֲלָה
chewing not-she or-cud dividing not-she but-division hoof splitting she

טְמֵאִים הֵם לָכֶם כָּל־ הַנֹּגֵעַ בָּהֶם יִטְמָא׃
he-will-be-unclean on-them the-one-touching every-of to-you they unclean-ones

וְכֹל ׀ הוֹלֵךְ עַל־ כַּפָּיו בְּכָל־ הַחַיָּה
the-animal among-all-of paws-of-him on one-walking and-every-of (27)

הַהֹלֶכֶת עַל־אַרְבַּע טְמֵאִים הֵם לָכֶם כָּל־ הַנֹּגֵעַ
the-one-touching every-of to-you they unclean-ones four on the-one-walking

בְּנִבְלָתָם יִטְמָא עַד־ הָעָרֶב׃ וְהַנֹּשֵׂא
the-one-picking-up (28) the-evening till he-will-be-unclean on-carcass-of-them

screech owl, the gull, any kind of hawk, [17]the little owl, the cormorant, the great owl, [18]the white owl, the desert owl, the osprey, [19]the stork, any kind of heron, the hoopoe and the bat.[w]

[20]" 'All flying insects that walk on all fours are to be detestable to you. [21]There are, however, some winged creatures that walk on all fours that you may eat: those that have jointed legs for hopping on the ground. [22]Of these you may eat any kind of locust, katydid, cricket or grasshopper. [23]But all other winged creatures that have four legs you are to detest.

[24]" 'You will make yourselves unclean by these; whoever touches their carcasses will be unclean till evening. [25]Whoever picks up one of their carcasses must wash his clothes, and he will be unclean till evening.

[26]" 'Every animal that has a split hoof not completely divided or that does not chew the cud is unclean for you; whoever touches ⌞the carcass of⌟ any of them will be unclean. [27]Of all the animals that walk on all fours, those that walk on their paws are unclean for you; whoever touches their carcasses will be unclean till evening. [28]Anyone

*w19* The precise identification of some of the birds, insects and animals in this chapter is uncertain.

°21 ק לו

אֶת־ נִבְלָתָם יְכַבֵּס בְּגָדָיו וְטָמֵא עַד־
till and-he-will-be-unclean clothes-of-him he-must-wash carcass-of-them ***

הָעָרֶב טְמֵאִים הֵמָּה לָכֶם׃ וְזֶה לָכֶם הַטָּמֵא
the-unclean to-you and-this (29) to-you they unclean-ones the-evening

בַּשֶּׁרֶץ הַשֹּׁרֵץ עַל־ הָאָרֶץ הַחֹלֶד וְהָעַכְבָּר
and-the-rat the-weasel the-ground on the-one-moving among-the-creeper

וְהַצָּב לְמִינֵהוּ׃ וְהָאֲנָקָה וְהַכֹּחַ
and-the-monitor-lizard and-the-gecko (30) any-kind-of-him and-the-great-lizard

וְהַלְּטָאָה וְהַחֹמֶט וְהַתִּנְשָׁמֶת׃ אֵלֶּה
these (31) and-the-chameleon and-the-skink and-the-wall-lizard

הַטְּמֵאִים לָכֶם בְּכָל־ הַשָּׁרֶץ כָּל־ הַנֹּגֵעַ
the-one-touching every-of the-creeper among-all-of for-you the-unclean-ones

בָּהֶם בְּמֹתָם יִטְמָא עַד־ הָעָרֶב׃ וְכֹל
and-anything (32) the-evening till he-will-be-unclean when-to-die-them on-them

אֲשֶׁר־ יִפֹּל־ עָלָיו מֵהֶם ׀ בְּמֹתָם יִטְמָא מִכָּל־
if-any-of he-will-be-unclean when-to-die-them from-them on-him he-falls that

כְּלִי־ עֵץ אוֹ בֶגֶד אוֹ־ עוֹר אוֹ שָׂק כָּל־ כְּלִי אֲשֶׁר־
that article any-of sackcloth or hide or cloth or wood article-of

יֵעָשֶׂה מְלָאכָה בָּהֶם בַּמַּיִם יוּבָא
he-must-be-put in-the-waters with-them work he-may-be-done

וְטָמֵא עַד־ הָעֶרֶב וְטָהֵר׃ וְכָל־
but-any-of (33) then-he-will-be-clean the-evening till and-he-will-be-unclean

כְּלִי־ חֶרֶשׂ אֲשֶׁר־ יִפֹּל מֵהֶם אֶל־ תּוֹכוֹ כֹּל אֲשֶׁר
that everything inside-of-him into from-them he-falls that clay pot-of

בְּתוֹכוֹ יִטְמָא וְאֹתוֹ תִשְׁבֹּרוּ׃ מִכָּל־
from-any-of (34) you-must-break and-him he-will-be-unclean inside-of-him

הָאֹכֶל אֲשֶׁר יֵאָכֵל אֲשֶׁר יָבוֹא עָלָיו מַיִם יִטְמָא
he-is-unclean waters onto-him he-comes that he-could-be-eaten that the-food

וְכָל־ מַשְׁקֶה אֲשֶׁר יִשָּׁתֶה בְּכָל־ כְּלִי יִטְמָא׃
he-is-unclean pot from-any-of he-could-be-drunk that liquid and-any-of

וְכֹל אֲשֶׁר־ יִפֹּל מִנִּבְלָתָם ׀ עָלָיו יִטְמָא
he-is-unclean on-him from-carcass-of-them he-falls that and-anything (35)

תַּנּוּר וְכִירַיִם יֻתָּץ טְמֵאִים הֵם וּטְמֵאִים יִהְיוּ
they-are and-unclean-ones they unclean-ones he-must-be-broken or-pot oven

לָכֶם׃ אַךְ מַעְיָן וּבוֹר מִקְוֵה־ מַיִם יִהְיֶה
he-remains waters collector-of or-cistern-of spring however (36) to-you

טָהוֹר וְנֹגֵעַ בְּנִבְלָתָם יִטְמָא׃ וְכִי יִפֹּל
he-falls but-if (37) he-is-unclean on-carcass-of-them but-one-touching clean

who picks up their carcasses must wash his clothes, and he will be unclean till evening. They are unclean for you.

29" 'Of the animals that move about on the ground, these are unclean for you: the weasel, the rat, any kind of great lizard, 30the gecko, the monitor lizard, the wall lizard, the skink and the chameleon. 31Of all those that move along the ground, these are unclean for you. Whoever touches them when they are dead will be unclean till evening. 32When one of them dies and falls on something, that article, whatever its use, will be unclean, whether it is made of wood, cloth, hide or sackcloth. Put it in water; it will be unclean till evening, and then it will be clean. 33If one of them falls into a clay pot, everything in it will be unclean, and you must break the pot. 34Any food that could be eaten but has water on it from such a pot is unclean, and any liquid that could be drunk from it is unclean. 35Anything that one of their carcasses falls on becomes unclean; an oven or cooking pot must be broken up. They are unclean, and you are to regard them as unclean. 36A spring, however, or a cistern for collecting water remains clean, but anyone who touches one of these carcasses is unclean. 37If a carcass falls

מִנִּבְלָתָם עַל־ כָּל־ זֶרַע זֵרוּעַ אֲשֶׁר יִזָּרֵעַ טָהוֹר

clean he-will-be-planted that plant seed-of any-of on from-carcass-of-them

הוּא׃ וְכִי יֻתַּן־ מַיִם עַל־ זֶרַע וְנָפַל מִנִּבְלָתָם

from-carcass-of-them and-he-falls seed on waters he-was-put but-if (38) he

עָלָיו טָמֵא הוּא לָכֶם׃ וְכִי יָמוּת מִן־ הַבְּהֵמָה אֲשֶׁר־הִיא

she that the-animal from he-dies and-if (39) for-you he unclean on-him

לָכֶם לְאָכְלָה הַנֹּגֵעַ בְּנִבְלָתָהּ יִטְמָא עַד־

till he-will-be-unclean on-carcass-of-her the-one-touching for-food to-you

הָעָרֶב׃ וְהָאֹכֵל מִנִּבְלָתָהּ יְכַבֵּס

he-must-wash from-carcass-of-her and-the-one-eating (40) the-evening

בְּגָדָיו וְטָמֵא עַד־ הָעָרֶב וְהַנֹּשֵׂא

and-the-one-picking-up the-evening till and-he-will-be-unclean clothes-of-him

אֶת־ נִבְלָתָהּ יְכַבֵּס בְּגָדָיו וְטָמֵא עַד־

till and-he-will-be-unclean clothes-of-him he-must-wash carcass-of-her ***

הָעָרֶב׃ וְכָל־ הַשֶּׁרֶץ הַשֹּׁרֵץ עַל־ הָאָרֶץ

the-ground on the-one-moving the-creature and-every-of (41) the-evening

שֶׁקֶץ הוּא לֹא יֵאָכֵל׃ כֹּל הוֹלֵךְ עַל־ גָּחוֹן וְכֹל ׀

or-any-of belly on moving any-of (42) he-may-be-eaten not he detestable

הוֹלֵךְ עַל־אַרְבַּע עַד כָּל־ מַרְבֵּה רַגְלַיִם לְכָל־ הַשֶּׁרֶץ הַשֹּׁרֵץ

the-one-moving the-creature of-any-of feet many-of any-of or four on moving

עַל־ הָאָרֶץ לֹא תֹאכְלוּם כִּי־ שֶׁקֶץ הֵם׃ אַל־ תְּשַׁקְּצוּ

you-defile not (43) they detestable for you-may-eat-them not the-ground on

אֶת־ נַפְשֹׁתֵיכֶם בְּכָל־ הַשֶּׁרֶץ הַשֹּׁרֵץ וְלֹא

and-not the-one-creeping the-creature by-any-of selves-of-you ***

תִטַּמְּאוּ בָּהֶם וְנִטְמֵתֶם בָּם׃ כִּי

for (44) by-them or-you-be-made-unclean by-them you-make-yourselves-unclean

אֲנִי יְהוָה אֱלֹהֵיכֶם וְהִתְקַדִּשְׁתֶּם וִהְיִיתֶם קְדֹשִׁים כִּי

for holy-ones and-you-be so-you-consecrate-yourselves God-of-you Yahweh I

קָדוֹשׁ אָנִי וְלֹא תְטַמְּאוּ אֶת־ נַפְשֹׁתֵיכֶם בְּכָל־ הַשֶּׁרֶץ

the-creature by-any-of selves-of-you *** you-make-unclean so-not I holy

הָרֹמֵשׂ עַל־ הָאָרֶץ׃ כִּי ׀ אֲנִי יְהוָה הַמַּעֲלֶה אֶתְכֶם

you the-one-bringing Yahweh I for (45) the-ground on the-one-moving

מֵאֶרֶץ מִצְרַיִם לִהְיֹת לָכֶם לֵאלֹהִים וִהְיִיתֶם קְדֹשִׁים כִּי קָדוֹשׁ אָנִי׃

I holy for holy-ones so-you-be as-God for-you to-be Egypt from-land-of

זֹאת תּוֹרַת הַבְּהֵמָה וְהָעוֹף וְכֹל נֶפֶשׁ

thing-of and-every-of and-the-bird the-animal regulation-of this (46)

הַחַיָּה הָרֹמֶשֶׂת בַּמָּיִם וּלְכָל־ נֶפֶשׁ

creature and-for-every-of in-the-waters the-one-moving the-living

on any seeds that are to be
planted, they remain clean.
38 But if water has been put on
the seed and a carcass falls on
it, it is unclean for you.
39 " 'If an animal that you are
allowed to eat dies, anyone
who touches the carcass will
be unclean till evening. 40 Anyone who eats some of the carcass must wash his clothes,
and he will be unclean till evening. Anyone who picks up
the carcass must wash his
clothes, and he will be unclean
till evening.
41 " 'Every creature that
moves about on the ground is
detestable; it is not to be eaten.
42 You are not to eat any creature that moves about on the
ground, whether it moves on
its belly or walks on all fours or
on many feet; it is detestable.
43 Do not defile yourselves by
any of these creatures. Do not
make yourselves unclean by
means of them or be made unclean by them. 44 I am the LORD
your God; consecrate yourselves and be holy, because I
am holy. Do not make yourselves unclean by any creature
that moves about on the
ground. 45 I am the LORD who
brought you up out of Egypt to
be your God; therefore be
holy, because I am holy.
46 " 'These are the regulations
concerning animals, birds,
every living thing that moves
in the water and every creature that moves about on the

הַשֹּׁרֶצֶת עַל־ הָאָרֶץ׃ לְהַבְדִּיל בֵּין הַטָּמֵא
the-unclean between to-distinguish (47) the-ground on the-one-moving

וּבֵין הַטָּהֹר וּבֵין הַחַיָּה הַנֶּאֱכֶלֶת וּבֵין
and-between the-being-edible the-creature and-between the-clean and-between

הַחַיָּה אֲשֶׁר לֹא תֵאָכֵל׃ וַיְדַבֵּר יְהוָה אֶל־ מֹשֶׁה
Moses to Yahweh and-he-spoke (12:1) she-may-be-eaten not that the-creature

לֵּאמֹר׃ דַּבֵּר אֶל־ בְּנֵי יִשְׂרָאֵל לֵאמֹר אִשָּׁה כִּי תַזְרִיעַ
she-conceives when woman to-say Israel sons-of to say! (2) to-say

וְיָלְדָה זָכָר וְטָמְאָה שִׁבְעַת יָמִים כִּימֵי
as-days-of days seven-of then-she-will-be-unclean son and-she-bears

נִדַּת דְּוֺתָהּ תִּטְמָא׃ וּבַיּוֹם הַשְּׁמִינִי
the-eighth and-on-the-day (3) she-is-unclean monthly-of-her period-of

יִמּוֹל בְּשַׂר עָרְלָתוֹ׃ וּשְׁלֹשִׁים יוֹם וּשְׁלֹשֶׁת
and-three-of day and-thirty (4) foreskin-of-him skin-of he-must-be-circumcised

יָמִים תֵּשֵׁב בִּדְמֵי טָהֳרָה בְּכָל־ קֹדֶשׁ לֹא־
not sacred on-any-of purification in-bloods-of she-must-wait days

תִגָּע וְאֶל־ הַמִּקְדָּשׁ לֹא תָבֹא עַד־ מְלֹאת יְמֵי
days-of to-be-over until she-must-go not the-sanctuary or-to she-must-touch

טָהֳרָהּ׃ וְאִם־ נְקֵבָה תֵלֵד וְטָמְאָה
then-she-will-be-unclean she-bears daughter and-if (5) purification-of-her

שְׁבֻעַיִם כְּנִדָּתָהּ וְשִׁשִּׁים יוֹם וְשֵׁשֶׁת יָמִים תֵּשֵׁב עַל־
until she-must-wait days and-six-of day and-sixty as-period-of-her two-weeks

דְּמֵי טָהֳרָה׃ וּבִמְלֹאת ׀ יְמֵי טָהֳרָהּ
purification-of-her days-of and-when-to-be-over (6) purification bloods-of

לְבֵן אוֹ לְבַת תָּבִיא כֶּבֶשׂ בֶּן־ שְׁנָתוֹ
year-of-him son-of lamb she-must-bring for-daughter or for-son

לְעֹלָה וּבֶן־ יוֹנָה אוֹ־ תֹר לְחַטָּאת אֶל־
to for-sin-offering dove or pigeon and-young-of for-burnt-offering

פֶּתַח אֹהֶל־ מוֹעֵד אֶל־ הַכֹּהֵן׃ וְהִקְרִיבוֹ לִפְנֵי
before and-he-shall-offer-him (7) the-priest to Meeting Tent-of entrance-of

יְהוָה וְכִפֶּר עָלֶיהָ וְטָהֲרָה מִמְּקֹר
from-flow-of then-she-will-be-clean for-her and-he-shall-atone Yahweh

דָּמֶיהָ זֹאת תּוֹרַת הַיֹּלֶדֶת לַזָּכָר אוֹ
or to-the-boy the-one-giving-birth regulation-of this bloods-of-her

לַנְּקֵבָה׃ וְאִם־ לֹא תִמְצָא יָדָהּ דֵּי שֶׂה
lamb price-of hand-of-her she-can-afford not but-if (8) to-the-girl

וְלָקְחָה שְׁתֵּי־ תֹרִים אוֹ שְׁנֵי בְּנֵי יוֹנָה אֶחָד
one pigeon young-ones-of two-of or doves two-of then-she-must-bring

ground. 47You must distinguish between the unclean and the clean, between living creatures that may be eaten and those that may not be eaten.' "

*Purification After Childbirth*

12 The LORD said to Moses, 2"Say to the Israelites: 'A woman who becomes pregnant and gives birth to a son will be ceremonially unclean for seven days, just as she is unclean during her monthly period.
3On the eighth day the boy is to be circumcised. 4Then the woman must wait thirty-three days to be purified from her bleeding. She must not touch anything sacred or go to the sanctuary until the days of her purification are over. 5If she gives birth to a daughter, for two weeks the woman will be unclean, as in her period. Then she must wait sixty-six days to be purified from her bleeding.

6" 'When the days of her purification for a son or daughter are over, she is to bring to the priest at the entrance to the Tent of Meeting a year-old lamb for a burnt offering and a young pigeon or a dove for a sin offering. 7He shall offer them before the LORD to make atonement for her, and then she will be ceremonially clean from her flow of blood. These are the regulations for the woman who gives birth to a boy or a girl.

8" 'If she cannot afford a lamb, she is to bring two doves or two young pigeons,

לְעֹלָה וְאֶחָד לְחַטָּאת וְכִפֶּר עָלֶיהָ

for-her so-he-will-atone for-sin-offering and-one for-burnt-offering

הַכֹּהֵן וְטָהֵרָה׃ וַיְדַבֵּר יְהוָה אֶל־ מֹשֶׁה וְאֶל־

and-to Moses to Yahweh and-he-spoke (13:1) and-she-will-be-clean the-priest

אַהֲרֹן לֵאמֹר׃ אָדָם כִּי־ יִהְיֶה בְעוֹר־ בְּשָׂרוֹ שְׂאֵת אוֹ־

or swelling flesh-of-him on-skin-of he-has when anyone (2) to-say Aaron

סַפַּחַת אוֹ בַהֶרֶת וְהָיָה בְעוֹר־ בְּשָׂרוֹ לְנֶגַע

to-infection-of flesh-of-him on-skin-of and-he-may-become bright-spot or rash

צָרָעַת וְהוּבָא אֶל־ אַהֲרֹן הַכֹּהֵן אוֹ אֶל־אַחַד

one to or the-priest Aaron to then-he-must-be-brought skin-disease

מִבָּנָיו הַכֹּהֲנִים׃ וְרָאָה הַכֹּהֵן אֶת־ הַנֶּגַע

the-sore *** the-priest and-he-must-examine (3) the-priests from-sons-of-him

בְּעוֹר־ הַבָּשָׂר וְשֵׂעָר בַּנֶּגַע הָפַךְ ׀ לָבָן וּמַרְאֵה

or-appearance-of white he-turned in-the-sore if-hair the-flesh on-skin-of

הַנֶּגַע עָמֹק מֵעוֹר בְּשָׂרוֹ נֶגַע צָרַעַת הוּא

he skin-disease infection-of flesh-of-him than-skin-of deeper the-sore

וְרָאָהוּ הַכֹּהֵן וְטִמֵּא אֹתוֹ׃ וְאִם־

but-if (4) him then-he-shall-pronounce-unclean the-priest when-he-examines-him

בַּהֶרֶת לְבָנָה הִוא בְּעוֹר בְּשָׂרוֹ וְעָמֹק אֵין־ מַרְאֶהָ

appearance-of-her he-is-not and-deeper flesh-of-him in-skin-of she white spot

מִן־ הָעוֹר וּשְׂעָרָה לֹא־ הָפַךְ לָבָן וְהִסְגִּיר הַכֹּהֵן

the-priest then-he-must-isolate while he-turned not and-hair the-skin than

אֶת־ הַנֶּגַע שִׁבְעַת יָמִים׃ וְרָאָהוּ הַכֹּהֵן

the-priest and-he-must-examine-him (5) days seven-of the-infected-person ***

בַּיּוֹם הַשְּׁבִיעִי וְהִנֵּה הַנֶּגַע עָמַד בְּעֵינָיו

in-eyes-of-him he-is-unchanged the-infection and-if the-seventh on-the-day

לֹא־ פָשָׂה הַנֶּגַע בָּעוֹר וְהִסְגִּירוֹ הַכֹּהֵן

the-priest then-he-must-isolate-him in-the-skin the-infection he-spread not

שִׁבְעַת יָמִים שֵׁנִית׃ וְרָאָה הַכֹּהֵן אֹתוֹ בַּיּוֹם

on-the-day him the-priest and-he-must-examine (6) another days seven-of

הַשְּׁבִיעִי שֵׁנִית וְהִנֵּה כֵּהָה הַנֶּגַע וְלֹא־ פָשָׂה

he-spread and-not the-infection he-faded and-if again the-seventh

הַנֶּגַע בָּעוֹר וְטִהֲרוֹ הַכֹּהֵן מִסְפַּחַת

rash the-priest then-he-shall-pronounce-clean-him in-the-skin the-infection

הִיא וְכִבֶּס בְּגָדָיו וְטָהֵר׃ וְאִם־ פָּשֹׂה

to-spread but-if (7) and-he-will-be-clean clothes-of-him and-he-must-wash he

תִפְשֶׂה הַמִּסְפַּחַת בָּעוֹר אַחֲרֵי הֵרָאֹתוֹ אֶל־ הַכֹּהֵן

the-priest to to-be-shown-him after in-the-skin the-rash she-spread

one for a burnt offering and the other for a sin offering. In this way the priest will make atonement for her, and she will be clean.' "

*Regulations About Infectious Skin Diseases*

13 The LORD said to Moses and Aaron, 2"When anyone has a swelling or a rash or a bright spot on his skin that may become an infectious skin disease,[x] he must be brought to Aaron the priest or to one of his sons[y] who is a priest. 3The priest is to examine the sore on his skin, and if the hair in the sore has turned white and the sore appears to be more than skin deep,[z] it is an infectious skin disease. When the priest examines him, he shall pronounce him ceremonially unclean. 4If the spot on his skin is white but does not appear to be more than skin deep and the hair in it has not turned white, the priest is to put the infected person in isolation for seven days. 5On the seventh day the priest is to examine him, and if he sees that the sore is unchanged and has not spread in the skin, he is to keep him in isolation another seven days. 6On the seventh day the priest is to examine him again, and if the sore has faded and has not spread in the skin, the priest shall pronounce him clean; it is only a rash. The man must wash his clothes, and he will be clean. 7But if the rash does spread in his skin after he has shown himself to the priest to be pronounced

[x]2 Traditionally *leprosy;* the Hebrew word was used for various diseases affecting the skin—not necessarily leprosy; also elsewhere in this chapter.
[y]2 Or *descendants*
[z]3 Or *be lower than the rest of the skin;* also elsewhere in this chapter

לְטָהֳרָתוֹ וְנִרְאָה שֵׁנִית אֶל־ הַכֹּהֵן׃
the-priest before again then-he-must-appear for-purification-of-him

(8) וְרָאָה הַכֹּהֵן וְהִנֵּה פָּשְׂתָה הַמִּסְפַּחַת בָּעוֹר
in-the-skin the-rash she-spread and-if the-priest and-he-must-examine (8)

וְטִמְּאוֹ הַכֹּהֵן צָרַעַת הִוא׃
she infectious-disease the-priest then-he-shall-pronounce-unclean-him

(9) נֶגַע צָרַעַת כִּי תִהְיֶה בְּאָדָם וְהוּבָא
then-he-must-be-brought on-anyone she-is when skin-disease infection-of (9)

אֶל־ הַכֹּהֵן׃ (10) וְרָאָה הַכֹּהֵן וְהִנֵּה שְׂאֵת־ לְבָנָה
white swelling and-if the-priest and-he-must-examine (10) the-priest to

בָּעוֹר וְהִיא הָפְכָה שֵׂעָר לָבָן וּמִחְיַת בָּשָׂר חַי
raw flesh and-spot-of white hair she-turned and-she in-the-skin

בַּשְׂאֵת׃ (11) צָרַעַת נוֹשֶׁנֶת הִוא בְּעוֹר בְּשָׂרוֹ
flesh-of-him in-skin-of she being-chronic skin-disease (11) in-the-swelling

וְטִמְּאוֹ הַכֹּהֵן לֹא יַסְגִּרֶנּוּ כִּי
for he-must-isolate-him not the-priest and-he-shall-pronounce-unclean-him

טָמֵא הוּא׃ (12) וְאִם־ פָּרוֹחַ תִּפְרַח הַצָּרַעַת בָּעוֹר
over-the-skin the-disease she-breaks-out to-break-out and-if (12) he unclean

וְכִסְּתָה הַצָּרַעַת אֵת כָּל־ עוֹר הַנֶּגַע
the-infected-person skin-of all-of *** the-disease and-she-covers

מֵרֹאשׁוֹ וְעַד־ רַגְלָיו לְכָל־ מַרְאֵה עֵינֵי הַכֹּהֵן׃
the-priest eyes-of sight-of in-all-of feet-of-him even-to from-head-of-him

(13) וְרָאָה הַכֹּהֵן וְהִנֵּה כִסְּתָה הַצָּרַעַת אֶת־ כָּל־
all-of *** the-disease she-covers and-if the-priest and-he-must-examine (13)

בְּשָׂרוֹ וְטִהַר אֶת־ הַנֶּגַע כֻּלּוֹ
all-of-him the-infected-person *** then-he-shall-pronounce-clean body-of-him

הָפַךְ לָבָן טָהוֹר הוּא׃ (14) וּבְיוֹם הֵרָאוֹת בּוֹ בָּשָׂר חַי
raw flesh on-him to-appear but-on-day (14) he clean white he-turned

יִטְמָא׃ (15) וְרָאָה הַכֹּהֵן אֶת־ הַבָּשָׂר הַחַי
the-raw the-flesh *** the-priest when-he-sees (15) he-will-be-unclean

וְטִמְּאוֹ הַבָּשָׂר הַחַי טָמֵא הוּא
he unclean the-raw the-flesh then-he-shall-pronounce-unclean-him

צָרַעַת הוּא׃ (16) אוֹ כִי יָשׁוּב הַבָּשָׂר הַחַי וְנֶהְפַּךְ
and-he-turns the-raw the-flesh he-changes if but (16) he infectious-disease

לְלָבָן וּבָא אֶל־ הַכֹּהֵן׃ (17) וְרָאָהוּ
and-he-must-examine-him (17) the-priest to then-he-must-go to-white

הַכֹּהֵן וְהִנֵּה נֶהְפַּךְ הַנֶּגַע לְלָבָן וְטִהַר
then-he-shall-pronounce-clean to-white the-sore he-turned and-if the-priest

clean, he must appear before the priest again. [8]The priest is to examine him, and if the rash has spread in the skin, he shall pronounce him unclean; it is an infectious disease.

[9]"When anyone has an infectious skin disease, he must be brought to the priest. [10]The priest is to examine him, and if there is a white swelling in the skin that has turned the hair white and if there is raw flesh in the swelling, [11]it is a chronic skin disease and the priest shall pronounce him unclean. He is not to put him in isolation, because he is already unclean.

[12]"If the disease breaks out all over his skin and, so far as the priest can see, it covers all the skin of the infected person from head to foot, [13]the priest is to examine him, and if the disease has covered his whole body, he shall pronounce that person clean. Since it has all turned white, he is clean. [14]But whenever raw flesh appears on him, he will be unclean. [15]When the priest sees the raw flesh, he shall pronounce him unclean. The raw flesh is unclean; he has an infectious disease. [16]Should the raw flesh change and turn white, he must go to the priest. [17]The priest is to examine him, and if the sores have turned white, the priest shall pronounce the

הַכֹּהֵ֖ן אֶת־הַנֶּ֑גַע טָה֖וֹר הֽוּא׃ וּבָשָׂ֕ר כִּֽי־יִהְיֶ֥ה בֽוֹ־

on-him he-has when and-body (18) he clean the-infected-person *** the-priest

בְעֹר֖וֹ שְׁחִ֑ין וְנִרְפָּֽא׃ וְהָיָ֞ה בִּמְק֤וֹם הַשְּׁחִין֙

the-boil in-place-of and-he-appears (19) and-he-heals boil skin-of-him

שְׂאֵ֣ת לְבָנָ֔ה א֖וֹ בַהֶ֣רֶת לְבָנָ֣ה אֲדַמְדָּ֑מֶת וְנִרְאָ֖ה אֶל־הַכֹּהֵֽן׃

the-priest to then-he-must-appear reddish white spot or white swelling

וְרָאָ֣ה הַכֹּהֵ֗ן וְהִנֵּ֤ה מַרְאֶ֙הָ֙ שָׁפָ֣ל מִן־

than deeper appearance-of-her and-if the-priest and-he-must-examine (20)

הָע֔וֹר וּשְׂעָרָ֖הּ הָפַ֣ךְ לָבָ֑ן וְטִמְּא֧וֹ

then-he-shall-pronounce-unclean-him white he-turned and-hair-of-her the-skin

הַכֹּהֵ֛ן נֶֽגַע־צָרַ֥עַת הִ֖וא בַּשְּׁחִ֥ין פָּרָֽחָה׃

she-broke-out after-the-boil she skin-disease infection-of the-priest

וְאִ֣ם ׀ יִרְאֶ֣נָּה הַכֹּהֵ֗ן וְהִנֵּ֤ה אֵֽין־בָּהּ֙ שֵׂעָ֣ר לָבָ֔ן

white hair in-her not and-if the-priest he-examines-her but-if (21)

וּשְׁפָלָ֥ה אֵינֶ֛נָּה מִן־הָע֖וֹר וְהִ֣יא כֵהָ֑ה וְהִסְגִּיר֥וֹ

then-he-shall-isolate-him faded and-she the-skin than is-not-she and-deeper

הַכֹּהֵ֖ן שִׁבְעַ֥ת יָמִֽים׃ וְאִם־פָּשֹׂ֥ה תִפְשֶׂ֖ה בָּע֑וֹר

in-the-skin she-spreads to-spread but-if (22) days seven-of the-priest

וְטִמֵּ֧א הַכֹּהֵ֛ן אֹת֖וֹ נֶ֥גַע הִֽוא׃ וְאִם־

but-if (23) she infection him the-priest then-he-shall-pronounce-unclean

תַּחְתֶּ֜יהָ תַּעֲמֹ֤ד הַבַּהֶ֙רֶת֙ לֹ֣א פָשָׂ֔תָה צָרֶ֥בֶת הַשְּׁחִ֖ין הִ֑וא

she the-boil scar-of she-spread not the-spot she-stays in-place-of-her

וְטִהֲר֖וֹ הַכֹּהֵֽן׃ א֣וֹ בָשָׂ֔ר כִּֽי־יִהְיֶ֥ה

he-has when body or (24) the-priest and-he-shall-pronounce-clean-him

בְעֹר֖וֹ מִכְוַת־אֵ֑שׁ וְהָֽיְתָ֞ה מִחְיַ֣ת הַמִּכְוָ֗ה בַּהֶ֛רֶת לְבָנָ֥ה

white spot the-burn raw-flesh-of and-she-appears fire burn-of skin-of-him

אֲדַמְדֶּ֖מֶת א֥וֹ לְבָנָֽה׃ וְרָאָ֣ה אֹתָ֣הּ הַכֹּהֵ֡ן וְהִנֵּ֣ה נֶהְפַּךְ֩

he-turned and-if the-priest her and-he-must-examine (25) white or reddish

שֵׂעָ֨ר לָבָ֜ן בַּבַּהֶ֗רֶת וּמַרְאֶ֙הָ֙ עָמֹ֣ק מִן־הָע֔וֹר צָרַ֣עַת

infection the-skin than deeper and-appearance-of-her in-the-spot white hair

הִ֔וא בַּמִּכְוָ֖ה פָּרָ֑חָה וְטִמֵּ֤א אֹתוֹ֙ הַכֹּהֵ֔ן

the-priest him and-he-shall-pronounce-unclean she-broke-out in-the-burn she

נֶ֥גַע צָרַ֖עַת הִֽוא׃ וְאִ֣ם ׀ יִרְאֶ֣נָּה הַכֹּהֵ֗ן וְהִנֵּ֤ה

and-if the-priest he-examines-her but-if (26) she skin-disease infection-of

אֵֽין־בַּבַּהֶ֙רֶת֙* שֵׂעָ֣ר לָבָ֔ן וּשְׁפָלָ֖ה אֵינֶ֣נָּה מִן־הָע֑וֹר

the-skin than is-not-she and-deeper white hair in-the-spot there-is-no

וְהִ֣וא כֵהָ֔ה וְהִסְגִּיר֥וֹ הַכֹּהֵ֖ן שִׁבְעַ֥ת יָמִֽים׃

days seven-of the-priest then-he-must-isolate-him faded and-she

infected person clean; then he will be clean.

[18]"When someone has a boil on his skin and it heals, [19]and in the place where the boil was, a white swelling or reddish-white spot appears, he must present himself to the priest. [20]The priest is to examine it, and if it appears to be more than skin deep and the hair in it has turned white, the priest shall pronounce him unclean. It is an infectious skin disease that has broken out where the boil was. [21]But if, when the priest examines it, there is no white hair in it and it is not more than skin deep and has faded, then the priest is to put him in isolation for seven days. [22]If it is spreading in the skin, the priest shall pronounce him unclean; it is infectious. [23]But if the spot is unchanged and has not spread, it is only a scar from the boil, and the priest shall pronounce him clean.

[24]"When someone has a burn on his skin and a reddish-white or white spot appears in the raw flesh of the burn, [25]the priest is to examine the spot, and if the hair in it has turned white, and it appears to be more than skin deep, it is an infectious disease that has broken out in the burn. The priest shall pronounce him unclean; it is an infectious skin disease. [26]But if the priest examines it and there is no white hair in the spot and if it is not more than skin deep and has faded, then the priest is to put him in isolation for seven days. [27]On the

*26 Most mss have *pathah* under the second *beth* ( 'בַּבַּ ).

וְרָאָהוּ הַכֹּהֵן בַּיּוֹם הַשְּׁבִיעִי אִם־ פָּשֹׂה
to-spread if the-seventh on-the-day the-priest and-he-must-examine-him (27)

תִפְשֶׂה בָּעוֹר וְטִמֵּא הַכֹּהֵן אֹתוֹ
him the-priest and-he-shall-pronounce-unclean in-the-skin she-spreads

נֶגַע צָרַעַת הִוא׃ וְאִם־ תַּחְתֶּיהָ תַעֲמֹד הַבַּהֶרֶת
the-spot she-stays in-place-of-her but-if (28) she skin-disease infection-of

לֹא־ פָשְׂתָה בָעוֹר וְהִוא כֵהָה שְׂאֵת הַמִּכְוָה הִוא
she the-burn swelling-of faded and-she in-the-skin she-spread not

וְטִהֲרוֹ הַכֹּהֵן כִּי־ צָרֶבֶת הַמִּכְוָה הִוא׃
she the-burn scar-of for the-priest and-he-shall-pronounce-clean-him

וְאִישׁ אוֹ אִשָּׁה כִּי־ יִהְיֶה בוֹ נָגַע בְּרֹאשׁ אוֹ בְזָקָן׃
on-chin or on-head sore on-him he-has if woman or and-man (29)

וְרָאָה הַכֹּהֵן אֶת־ הַנֶּגַע וְהִנֵּה מַרְאֵהוּ
appearance-of-him and-if the-sore *** the-priest then-he-must-examine (30)

עָמֹק מִן־ הָעוֹר וּבוֹ שֵׂעָר צָהֹב דָּק וְטִמֵּא
then-he-shall-call-unclean thin yellow hair and-in-him the-skin than deeper

אֹתוֹ הַכֹּהֵן נֶתֶק הוּא צָרַעַת הָרֹאשׁ אוֹ הַזָּקָן הוּא׃ וְכִי־
but-if (31) he the-chin or the-head infection-of he itch the-priest him

יִרְאֶה הַכֹּהֵן אֶת־ נֶגַע הַנֶּתֶק וְהִנֵּה אֵין מַרְאֵהוּ
appearance-of-him not and-if the-sore infection-of *** the-priest he-examines

עָמֹק מִן־ הָעוֹר וְשֵׂעָר שָׁחֹר אֵין בּוֹ וְהִסְגִּיר
then-he-must-isolate in-him not black and-hair the-skin than deeper

הַכֹּהֵן אֶת־ נֶגַע הַנֶּתֶק שִׁבְעַת יָמִים׃ וְרָאָה
and-he-must-examine (32) days seven-of the-sore one-infected-of *** the-priest

הַכֹּהֵן אֶת־ הַנֶּגַע בַּיּוֹם הַשְּׁבִיעִי וְהִנֵּה לֹא־ פָשָׂה הַנֶּתֶק
the-itch he-spread not and-if the-seventh on-the-day the-sore *** the-priest

וְלֹא־ הָיָה בוֹ שֵׂעָר צָהֹב וּמַרְאֵה הַנֶּתֶק אֵין עָמֹק מִן־
than deeper not the-itch and-appearance-of yellow hair in-him he-is and-not

הָעוֹר׃ וְהִתְגַּלָּח וְאֶת־ הַנֶּתֶק לֹא יְגַלֵּחַ
he-must-be-shaved not the-itch but and-he-must-be-shaved (33) the-skin

וְהִסְגִּיר הַכֹּהֵן אֶת־ הַנֶּתֶק שִׁבְעַת יָמִים שֵׁנִית׃
another days seven-of the-one-infected *** the-priest and-he-must-isolate

וְרָאָה הַכֹּהֵן אֶת־ הַנֶּתֶק בַּיּוֹם הַשְּׁבִיעִי
the-seventh on-the-day the-itch *** the-priest and-he-must-examine (34)

וְהִנֵּה לֹא־ פָשָׂה הַנֶּתֶק בָּעוֹר וּמַרְאֵהוּ אֵינֶנּוּ
not-is-he and-appearance-of-him in-the-skin the-itch he-spread not and-if

עָמֹק מִן־ הָעוֹר וְטִהַר אֹתוֹ הַכֹּהֵן
the-priest him then-he-shall-pronounce-clean the-skin than deeper

seventh day the priest is to examine him, and if it is spreading in the skin, the priest shall pronounce him unclean; it is an infectious skin disease. [28]If, however, the spot is unchanged and has not spread in the skin but has faded, it is a swelling from the burn, and the priest shall pronounce him clean; it is only a scar from the burn.

[29]"If a man or woman has a sore on the head or on the chin, [30]the priest is to examine the sore, and if it appears to be more than skin deep and the hair in it is yellow and thin, the priest shall pronounce that person unclean; it is an itch, an infectious disease of the head or chin. [31]But if, when the priest examines this kind of sore, it does not seem to be more than skin deep and there is no black hair in it, then the priest is to put the infected person in isolation for seven days. [32]On the seventh day the priest is to examine the sore, and if the itch has not spread and there is no yellow hair in it and it does not appear to be more than skin deep, [33]he must be shaved except for the diseased area, and the priest is to keep him in isolation another seven days. [34]On the seventh day the priest is to examine the itch and if it has not spread in the skin and appears to be no more than skin deep, the priest shall pronounce him

וְכִבֶּס בְּגָדָיו וְטָהֵר׃ וְאִם־ פָּשֹׂה
to-spread but-if (35) and-he-will-be-clean clothes-of-him and-he-must-wash

יִפְשֶׂה הַנֶּתֶק בָּעוֹר אַחֲרֵי טָהֳרָתוֹ׃
purification-of-him after in-the-skin the-itch he-spreads

(36) וְרָאָהוּ הַכֹּהֵן וְהִנֵּה פָּשָׂה הַנֶּתֶק בָּעוֹר לֹא־
not in-the-skin the-itch he-spread and-if the-priest and-he-must-examine-him (36)

יְבַקֵּר הַכֹּהֵן לַשֵּׂעָר הַצָּהֹב טָמֵא הוּא׃ (37) וְאִם־
but-if (37) he unclean the-yellow for-the-hair the-priest he-need-look

בְּעֵינָיו עָמַד הַנֶּתֶק וְשֵׂעָר שָׁחֹר צָמַח־ בּוֹ
in-him he-grew black and-hair the-itch he-is-unchanged to-eyes-of-him

נִרְפָּא הַנֶּתֶק טָהוֹר הוּא וְטִהֲרוֹ הַכֹּהֵן׃
the-priest and-he-shall-pronounce-clean-him he clean the-itch he-is-healed

(38) וְאִישׁ אוֹ־ אִשָּׁה כִּי־ יִהְיֶה בְעוֹר־ בְּשָׂרָם בֶּהָרֹת בֶּהָרֹת
spots spots flesh-of-them on-skin-of he-is when woman or and-man (38)

לְבָנֹת׃ (39) וְרָאָה הַכֹּהֵן וְהִנֵּה בְעוֹר־ בְּשָׂרָם
flesh-of-them on-skin-of and-if the-priest and-he-must-examine (39) white-ones

בֶּהָרֹת כֵּהוֹת לְבָנֹת בֹּהַק הוּא פָּרַח בָּעוֹר טָהוֹר הוּא׃
he clean on-the-skin he-broke-out he rash white-ones dull-ones spots

(40) וְאִישׁ כִּי יִמָּרֵט רֹאשׁוֹ קֵרֵחַ הוּא טָהוֹר הוּא׃ (41) וְאִם
and-if (41) he clean he bald hair-of-him he-lost when and-man (40)

מִפְּאַת פָּנָיו יִמָּרֵט רֹאשׁוֹ גִּבֵּחַ הוּא טָהוֹר הוּא׃
he clean he bald-of-forehead hair-of-him he-lost head-of-him from-front-of

(42) וְכִי־ יִהְיֶה בַקָּרַחַת אוֹ בַגַּבַּחַת נֶגַע לָבָן
white sore on-the-bald-forehead or on-the-bald-head he-is but-if (42)

אֲדַמְדָּם צָרַעַת פֹּרַחַת הִוא בְּקָרַחְתּוֹ אוֹ בְגַבַּחְתּוֹ׃
on-forehead-of-him or on-head-of-him she breaking-out infection reddish

(43) וְרָאָה אֹתוֹ הַכֹּהֵן וְהִנֵּה שְׂאֵת־ הַנֶּגַע לְבָנָה
white the-sore swelling-of and-if the-priest him and-he-must-examine (43)

אֲדַמְדֶּמֶת בְּקָרַחְתּוֹ אוֹ בְגַבַּחְתּוֹ כְּמַרְאֵה צָרַעַת
infection-of like-appearance-of on-forehead-of-him or on-head-of-him reddish

עוֹר בָּשָׂר׃ (44) אִישׁ־ צָרוּעַ הוּא טָמֵא הוּא טַמֵּא
to-pronounce-unclean he unclean he being-diseased man (44) flesh skin-of

יְטַמְּאֶנּוּ הַכֹּהֵן בְּרֹאשׁוֹ נִגְעוֹ׃
sore-of-him for-head-of-him the-priest he-shall-pronounce-unclean-him

(45) וְהַצָּרוּעַ אֲשֶׁר־ בּוֹ הַנֶּגַע בְּגָדָיו
clothes-of-him the-infection on-him that and-the-one-being-diseased (45)

יִהְיוּ פְרֻמִים וְרֹאשׁוֹ יִהְיֶה פָרוּעַ וְעַל־
and-on being-unkempt he-must-be and-hair-of-him ones-being-torn they-must-be

clean. He must wash his clothes, and he will be clean. [35]But if the itch does spread in the skin after he is pronounced clean, [36]the priest is to examine him, and if the itch has spread in the skin, the priest does not need to look for yellow hair; the person is unclean. [37]If, however, in his judgment it is unchanged and black hair has grown in it, the itch is healed. He is clean, and the priest shall pronounce him clean.

[38]"When a man or woman has white spots on the skin, [39]the priest is to examine them, and if the spots are dull white, it is a harmless rash that has broken out on the skin; that person is clean.

[40]"When a man has lost his hair and is bald, he is clean. [41]If he has lost his hair from the front of his scalp and has a bald forehead, he is clean. [42]But if he has a reddish-white sore on his bald head or forehead, it is an infectious disease breaking out on his head or forehead. [43]The priest is to examine him and, if the swollen sore on his head or forehead is reddish-white like an infectious skin disease, [44]the man is diseased and is unclean. The priest shall pronounce him unclean because of the sore on his head.

[45]"The person with such an infectious disease must wear torn clothes, let his hair be unkempt,[a] cover the lower part of

[a]45 Or *clothes, uncover his head*

שָׂפָם יַעְטֶה וְטָמֵא ׀ טָמֵא יִקְרָא׃ כָּל־ יְמֵי

days-of all-of (46) he-must-cry unclean and-unclean he-must-cover lower-face

אֲשֶׁר הַנֶּגַע בּוֹ יִטְמָא טָמֵא הוּא בָּדָד יֵשֵׁב

he-must-live alone he unclean he-is-unclean on-him the-infection that

מִחוּץ לַמַּחֲנֶה מוֹשָׁבוֹ׃ וְהַבֶּגֶד כִּי־ יִהְיֶה בוֹ

on-him he-is if now-the-clothing (47) dwelling-of-him of-the-camp outside

נֶגַע צָרָעַת בְּבֶגֶד צֶמֶר אוֹ בְּבֶגֶד פִּשְׁתִּים׃ אוֹ

or (48) linens on-clothing-of or wool on-clothing-of mildew contamination-of

בִשְׁתִי אוֹ בְעֵרֶב לַפִּשְׁתִּים וְלַצָּמֶר אוֹ בְעוֹר אוֹ

or on-leather or or-of-the-wool of-the-linens on-knitted or on-woven

בְּכָל־ מְלֶאכֶת עוֹר׃ וְהָיָה הַנֶּגַע יְרַקְרַק ׀ אוֹ

or greenish the-contamination and-he-is (49) leather product-of on-any-of

אֲדַמְדָּם בַּבֶּגֶד אוֹ בָעוֹר אוֹ־ בַשְּׁתִי אוֹ־ בָעֵרֶב

in-the-knitted or in-the-woven or in-the-leather or in-the-clothing reddish

אוֹ בְכָל־ כְּלִי־ עוֹר נֶגַע צָרַעַת הוּא

he mildew contamination-of leather article-of in-any-of or

וְהָרְאָה אֶת־ הַכֹּהֵן׃ וְרָאָה הַכֹּהֵן אֶת־

*** the-priest and-he-must-examine (50) the-priest *** and-he-must-be-shown

הַנֶּגַע וְהִסְגִּיר אֶת־ הַנֶּגַע שִׁבְעַת יָמִים׃

days seven-of the-affected-article *** and-he-must-isolate the-mildew

וְרָאָה אֶת־ הַנֶּגַע בַּיּוֹם הַשְּׁבִיעִי כִּי־ פָשָׂה

he-spread if the-seventh on-the-day the-mildew *** and-he-must-examine (51)

הַנֶּגַע בַּבֶּגֶד אוֹ־ בַשְּׁתִי אוֹ־ בָעֵרֶב אוֹ בָעוֹר

in-the-leather or in-the-knitted or in-the-woven or in-the-clothing the-mildew

לְכֹל אֲשֶׁר־ יֵעָשֶׂה הָעוֹר לִמְלָאכָה צָרַעַת מַמְאֶרֶת

destroying mildew-of for-use the-leather he-may-be-used that for-anything

הַנֶּגַע טָמֵא הוּא׃ וְשָׂרַף אֶת־ הַבֶּגֶד אוֹ אֶת־

*** or the-clothing *** and-he-must-burn (52) he unclean the-contamination

הַשְּׁתִי ׀ אוֹ אֶת־ הָעֵרֶב בַּצֶּמֶר אוֹ בַפִּשְׁתִּים אוֹ אֶת־ כָּל־

any-of *** or of-the-linens or of-the-wool the-knitted *** or the-woven

כְּלִי הָעוֹר אֲשֶׁר־ יִהְיֶה בוֹ הַנָּגַע כִּי־ צָרַעַת

mildew-of for the-contamination in-him he-is that the-leather article-of

מַמְאֶרֶת הִוא בָּאֵשׁ תִּשָּׂרֵף׃ וְאִם יִרְאֶה

he-examines but-if (53) she-must-be-burned in-the-fire she destroying

הַכֹּהֵן וְהִנֵּה לֹא־ פָשָׂה הַנֶּגַע בַּבֶּגֶד אוֹ בַשְּׁתִי

in-the-woven or in-the-clothing the-mildew he-spread not and-see! the-priest

אוֹ בָעֵרֶב אוֹ בְּכָל־ כְּלִי־ עוֹר׃ וְצִוָּה

then-he-shall-order (54) leather article-of in-any-of or in-the-knitted or

his face and cry out, 'Unclean! Unclean!' [46]As long as he has the infection he remains unclean. He must live alone; he must live outside the camp.

*Regulations About Mildew*

[47]"If any clothing is contaminated with mildew—any woolen or linen clothing, [48]any woven or knitted material of linen or wool, any leather or anything made of leather— [49]and if the contamination in the clothing, or leather, or woven or knitted material, or any leather article, is greenish or reddish, it is a spreading mildew and must be shown to the priest. [50]The priest is to examine the mildew and isolate the affected article for seven days. [51]On the seventh day he is to examine it, and if the mildew has spread in the clothing, or the woven or knitted material, or the leather, whatever its use, it is a destructive mildew; the article is unclean. [52]He must burn up the clothing, or the woven or knitted material of wool or linen, or any leather article that has the contamination in it, because the mildew is destructive; the article must be burned up.

[53]"But if, when the priest examines it, the mildew has not spread in the clothing, or the woven or knitted material, or the leather article, [54]he shall

הַכֹּהֵן וְכִבְּסוּ אֵת אֲשֶׁר־ בּוֹ הַנָּגַע

the-contamination on-him what *** and-they-shall-wash the-priest

וְהִסְגִּירוֹ שִׁבְעַת־ יָמִים שֵׁנִית׃ וְרָאָה

and-he-must-examine (55) another days seven-of and-he-must-isolate-him

הַכֹּהֵן אַחֲרֵי ׀ הֻכַּבֵּס אֶת־ הַנֶּגַע וְהִנֵּה לֹא־ הָפַךְ

he-changed not and-if the-affected-article *** he-was-washed after the-priest

הַנֶּגַע אֶת־ עֵינוֹ וְהַנֶּגַע לֹא־ פָשָׂה טָמֵא הוּא

he unclean he-spread not though-the-mildew appearance-of-him *** the-mildew

בָּאֵשׁ תִּשְׂרְפֶנּוּ פְּחֶתֶת הִוא בְּקָרַחְתּוֹ אוֹ בְגַבַּחְתּוֹ׃

on-front-of-him or on-back-of-him she mildew you-must-burn-him with-the-fire

וְאִם רָאָה הַכֹּהֵן וְהִנֵּה כֵּהָה הַנֶּגַע אַחֲרֵי

after the-mildew he-faded and-if the-priest he-examines but-if (56)

הֻכַּבֵּס אֹתוֹ וְקָרַע אֹתוֹ מִן־ הַבֶּגֶד אוֹ מִן־ הָעוֹר

the-leather from or the-clothing from him then-he-must-tear him he-was-washed

אוֹ מִן־ הַשְּׁתִי אוֹ מִן־ הָעֵרֶב׃ וְאִם־ תֵּרָאֶה עוֹד

again she-reappears but-if (57) the-knitted from or the-woven from or

בַּבֶּגֶד אוֹ־ בַשְּׁתִי אוֹ־ בָעֵרֶב אוֹ בְכָל־ כְּלִי־

article-of in-any-of or in-the-knitted or in-the-woven or in-the-clothing

עוֹר פֹּרַחַת הִוא בָּאֵשׁ תִּשְׂרְפֶנּוּ אֵת אֲשֶׁר־ בּוֹ

in-him what *** you-must-burn-him with-the-fire she spreading leather

הַנָּגַע׃ וְהַבֶּגֶד אוֹ־ הַשְּׁתִי אוֹ־ הָעֵרֶב אוֹ־ כָל־

any-of or the-knitted or the-woven or and-the-clothing (58) the-mildew

כְּלִי הָעוֹר אֲשֶׁר תְּכַבֵּס וְסָר מֵהֶם הַנָּגַע

the-mildew from-them and-he-left you-washed that the-leather article-of

וְכֻבַּס שֵׁנִית וְטָהֵר׃ זֹאת תּוֹרַת

regulation-of this (59) and-he-will-be-clean again then-he-must-be-washed

נֶגַע־ צָרַעַת בֶּגֶד הַצֶּמֶר ׀ אוֹ הַפִּשְׁתִּים אוֹ הַשְּׁתִי אוֹ

or the-woven or the-linens or the-wool clothing-of mildew contamination-of

הָעֵרֶב אוֹ כָּל־ כְּלִי־ עוֹר לְטַהֲרוֹ אוֹ

or to-pronounce-clean-him leather article-of any-of or the-knitted

לְטַמְּאוֹ׃ וַיְדַבֵּר יְהוָה אֶל־ מֹשֶׁה לֵּאמֹר׃ זֹאת

this (2) to-say Moses to Yahweh and-he-spoke (14:1) to-pronounce-unclean-him

תִּהְיֶה תּוֹרַת הַמְּצֹרָע בְּיוֹם טָהֳרָתוֹ

cleansing-of-him on-day-of the-one-being-diseased regulaion-of she-is

וְהוּבָא אֶל־ הַכֹּהֵן׃ וְיָצָא הַכֹּהֵן אֶל־ מִחוּץ

outside to the-priest and-he-shall-go (3) the-priest to when-he-is-brought

לַמַּחֲנֶה וְרָאָה הַכֹּהֵן וְהִנֵּה נִרְפָּא נֶגַע־

infection-of he-is-healed and-if the-priest and-he-shall-examine of-the-camp

order that the contaminated article be washed. Then he is to isolate it for another seven days. [55]After the affected article has been washed, the priest is to examine it, and if the mildew has not changed its appearance, even though it has not spread, it is unclean. Burn it with fire, whether the mildew has affected one side or the other. [56]If, when the priest examines it, the mildew has faded after the article has been washed, he is to tear the contaminated part out of the clothing, or the leather, or the woven or knitted material. [57]But if it reappears in the clothing, or in the woven or knitted material, or in the leather article, it is spreading, and whatever has the mildew must be burned with fire. [58]The clothing, or the woven or knitted material, or any leather article that has been washed and is rid of the mildew, must be washed again, and it will be clean."

[59]These are the regulations concerning contamination by mildew in woolen or linen clothing, woven or knitted material, or any leather article, for pronouncing them clean or unclean.

*Cleansing From Infectious Skin Diseases*

**14** The LORD said to Moses, [2]"These are the regulations for the diseased person at the time of his ceremonial cleansing, when he is brought to the priest: [3]The priest is to go outside the camp and examine him. If the person has been healed of his

הַצָּרַעַת מִן־ הַצָּרוּעַ׃ (4) וְצִוָּה הַכֹּהֵן
the-priest and-he-shall-order (4) the-one-being-diseased from the-skin-disease

וְלָקַח לַמִּטַּהֵר שְׁתֵּי־ צִפֳּרִים חַיּוֹת
live-ones birds two-of for-the-one-being-cleansed and-he-shall-bring

טְהֹרוֹת וְעֵץ אֶרֶז וּשְׁנִי תוֹלַעַת וְאֵזֹב׃
and-hyssop scarlet and-yarn-of cedar and-wood-of clean-ones

(5) וְצִוָּה הַכֹּהֵן וְשָׁחַט אֶת־ הַצִּפּוֹר הָאֶחָת אֶל־
in the-one the-bird *** and-he-shall-kill the-priest then-he-shall-order (5)

כְּלִי־ חֶרֶשׂ עַל־ מַיִם חַיִּים׃ (6) אֶת־ הַצִּפֹּר הַחַיָּה יִקַּח
he-shall-take the-live the-bird *** (6) fresh-ones waters over clay pot-of

אֹתָהּ וְאֶת־ עֵץ הָאֶרֶז וְאֶת־ שְׁנִי הַתּוֹלַעַת וְאֶת־ הָאֵזֹב
the-hyssop and the-scarlet yarn-of and the-cedar wood-of and her

וְטָבַל אוֹתָם וְאֵת ׀ הַצִּפֹּר הַחַיָּה בְּדַם הַצִּפֹּר
the-bird into-blood-of the-live the-bird with them and-he-shall-dip

הַשְּׁחֻטָה עַל הַמַּיִם הַחַיִּים׃ (7) וְהִזָּה
and-he-shall-sprinkle (7) the-fresh-ones the-waters over the-one-being-killed

עַל הַמִּטַּהֵר מִן־ הַצָּרַעַת שֶׁבַע פְּעָמִים
times seven the-infection from the-one-being-cleansed on

וְטִהֲרוֹ וְשִׁלַּח אֶת־ הַצִּפֹּר הַחַיָּה
the-live the-bird *** then-he-shall-release and-he-shall-pronounce-clean-him

עַל־ פְּנֵי הַשָּׂדֶה׃ (8) וְכִבֶּס הַמִּטַּהֵר אֶת־
*** the-one-being-cleansed and-he-must-wash (8) the-field surface-of over

בְּגָדָיו וְגִלַּח אֶת־ כָּל־ שְׂעָרוֹ וְרָחַץ
and-he-must-bathe hair-of-him all-of *** and-he-must-shave clothes-of-him

בַּמַּיִם וְטָהֵר וְאַחַר יָבוֹא אֶל־ הַמַּחֲנֶה
the-camp into he-may-come and-after then-he-will-be-clean in-the-waters

וְיָשַׁב מִחוּץ לְאָהֳלוֹ שִׁבְעַת יָמִים׃ (9) וְהָיָה
and-he-will-be (9) days seven-of of-tent-of-him outside but-he-must-stay

בַיּוֹם הַשְּׁבִיעִי יְגַלַּח אֶת־ כָּל־ שְׂעָרוֹ אֶת־ רֹאשׁוֹ
head-of-him *** hair-of-him all-of *** he-must-shave the-seventh on-the-day

וְאֶת־ זְקָנוֹ וְאֵת גַּבֹּת עֵינָיו וְאֶת־ כָּל־ שְׂעָרוֹ
hair-of-him rest-of and eyes-of-him brows-of and beard-of-him and

יְגַלֵּחַ וְכִבֶּס אֶת־ בְּגָדָיו וְרָחַץ אֶת־
*** and-he-must-bathe clothes-of-him *** and-he-must-wash he-must-shave

בְּשָׂרוֹ בַּמַּיִם וְטָהֵר׃ (10) וּבַיּוֹם הַשְּׁמִינִי
the-eighth and-on-the-day (10) and-he-will-be-clean in-the-waters body-of-him

יִקַּח שְׁנֵי־ כְבָשִׂים תְּמִימִם וְכַבְשָׂה אַחַת
one and-female-lamb ones-without-blemish male-lambs two-of he-must-bring

infectious skin disease,[a] [4]the priest shall order that two live clean birds and some cedar wood, scarlet yarn and hyssop be brought for the one to be cleansed. [5]Then the priest shall order that one of the birds be killed over fresh water in a clay pot. [6]He is then to take the live bird and dip it, together with the cedar wood, the scarlet yarn and the hyssop, into the blood of the bird that was killed over the fresh water. [7]Seven times he shall sprinkle the one to be cleansed of the infectious disease and pronounce him clean. Then he is to release the live bird in the open fields.

[8]"The person to be cleansed must wash his clothes, shave off all his hair and bathe with water; then he will be ceremonially clean. After this he may come into the camp, but he must stay outside his tent for seven days. [9]On the seventh day he must shave off all his hair; he must shave his head, his beard, his eyebrows and the rest of his hair. He must wash his clothes and bathe himself with water, and he will be clean.

[10]"On the eighth day he must bring two male lambs and one ewe lamb a year old, each without defect, along

[a]3 Traditionally *leprosy;* the Hebrew word was used for various diseases affecting the skin—not necessarily leprosy; also elsewhere in this chapter.

בַּת־ שְׁנָתָהּ תְּמִימָה וּשְׁלֹשָׁה עֶשְׂרֹנִים סֹלֶת
fine-flour tenths and-three without-defect year-of-her daughter-of

מִנְחָה בְּלוּלָה בַשֶּׁמֶן וְלֹג אֶחָד שָׁמֶן׃
oil one and-log with-the-oil being-mixed grain-offering

וְהֶעֱמִיד הַכֹּהֵן הַמְטַהֵר אֵת הָאִישׁ
the-man *** the-one-pronouncing-clean the-priest and-he-shall-present (11)

הַמִּטַּהֵר וְאֹתָם לִפְנֵי יְהוָה פֶּתַח אֹהֶל מוֹעֵד׃
Meeting Tent-of entrance-of Yahweh before with-them the-one-being-cleansed

וְלָקַח הַכֹּהֵן אֶת־ הַכֶּבֶשׂ הָאֶחָד
the-one the-male-lamb *** the-priest then-he-shall-take (12)

וְהִקְרִיב אֹתוֹ לְאָשָׁם וְאֶת־ לֹג הַשָּׁמֶן וְהֵנִיף
and-he-shall-wave the-oil log-of with as-guilt-offering him and-he-shall-offer

אֹתָם תְּנוּפָה לִפְנֵי יְהוָה׃ וְשָׁחַט אֶת־ הַכֶּבֶשׂ
the-lamb *** and-he-must-slaughter (13) Yahweh before wave-offering them

בִּמְקוֹם אֲשֶׁר יִשְׁחַט אֶת־ הַחַטָּאת וְאֶת־ הָעֹלָה
the-burnt-offering and the-sin-offering *** he-slaughters where in-place-of

בִּמְקוֹם הַקֹּדֶשׁ כִּי כַּחַטָּאת הָאָשָׁם הוּא
he the-guilt-offering like-the-sin-offering for the-holy in-place-of

לַכֹּהֵן קֹדֶשׁ קָדָשִׁים הוּא׃ וְלָקַח הַכֹּהֵן
the-priest and-he-must-take (14) he holy-ones most-holy-of for-the-priest

מִדַּם הָאָשָׁם וְנָתַן הַכֹּהֵן עַל־ תְּנוּךְ
lobe-of on the-priest and-he-must-put the-guilt-offering from-blood-of

אֹזֶן הַמִּטַּהֵר הַיְמָנִית וְעַל־ בֹּהֶן יָדוֹ הַיְמָנִית
the-right hand-of-him thumb-of and-on the-right the-one-being-cleansed ear-of

וְעַל־ בֹּהֶן רַגְלוֹ הַיְמָנִית׃ וְלָקַח הַכֹּהֵן
the-priest and-he-shall-take (15) the-right foot-of-him big-toe-of and-on

מִלֹּג הַשֶּׁמֶן וְיָצַק עַל־ כַּף הַכֹּהֵן הַשְּׂמָאלִית׃
the-left the-priest palm-of in and-he-shall-pour the-oil from-log-of

וְטָבַל הַכֹּהֵן אֶת־ אֶצְבָּעוֹ הַיְמָנִית מִן־ הַשֶּׁמֶן
the-oil into the-right finger-of-him *** the-priest and-he-shall-dip (16)

אֲשֶׁר עַל־ כַּפּוֹ הַשְּׂמָאלִית וְהִזָּה מִן־ הַשֶּׁמֶן
the-oil from and-he-shall-sprinkle the-left palm-of-him in that

בְּאֶצְבָּעוֹ שֶׁבַע פְּעָמִים לִפְנֵי יְהוָה׃ וּמִיֶּתֶר
and-from-remainder-of (17) Yahweh before times seven with-finger-of-him

הַשֶּׁמֶן אֲשֶׁר עַל־ כַּפּוֹ יִתֵּן הַכֹּהֵן עַל־ תְּנוּךְ אֹזֶן
ear-of lobe-of on the-priest he-shall-put palm-of-him in that the-oil

הַמִּטַּהֵר הַיְמָנִית וְעַל־ בֹּהֶן יָדוֹ הַיְמָנִית
the-right hand-of-him thumb-of and-on the-right the-one-being-cleansed

with three-tenths of an
ephah[b] of fine flour mixed
with oil for a grain offering,
and one log[c] of oil. 11 The priest
who pronounces him clean
shall present both the one to
be cleansed and his offerings
before the LORD at the entrance to the Tent of Meeting.
12 "Then the priest is to take
one of the male lambs and
offer it as a guilt offering,
along with the log of oil; he
shall wave them before the
LORD as a wave offering. 13 He
is to slaughter the lamb in the
holy place where the sin
offering and the burnt offering
are slaughtered. Like the sin
offering, the guilt offering belongs to the priest; it is most
holy. 14 The priest is to take
some of the blood of the guilt
offering and put it on the lobe
of the right ear of the one to be
cleansed, on the thumb of his
right hand and on the big toe
of his right foot. 15 The priest
shall then take some of the log
of oil, pour it in the palm of his
own left hand, 16 dip his right
forefinger into the oil in his
palm, and with his finger
sprinkle some of it before the
LORD seven times. 17 The priest
is to put some of the oil remaining in his palm on the
lobe of the right ear of the one
to be cleansed, on the thumb
of his right hand and on the

[b] 10 That is, probably about 6 quarts (about 6.5 liters)
[c] 10 That is, probably about 2/3 pint (about 0.3 liter); also in verses 12, 15, 21 and 24

וְעַל־ בֹּהֶן רַגְלוֹ הַיְמָנִית עַל דַּם הָאָשָׁם׃
the-guilt-offering blood-of upon the-right foot-of-him big-toe-of and-on

(18) וְהַנּוֹתָר בַּשֶּׁמֶן אֲשֶׁר עַל־ כַּף הַכֹּהֵן יִתֵּן
he-shall-put the-priest palm-of in that of-the-oil and-the-remaining (18)

עַל־ רֹאשׁ הַמִּטַּהֵר וְכִפֶּר עָלָיו הַכֹּהֵן
the-priest for-him and-he-shall-atone the-one-being-cleansed head-of on

לִפְנֵי יְהוָה׃ (19) וְעָשָׂה הַכֹּהֵן אֶת־ הַחַטָּאת
the-sin-offering *** the-priest then-he-must-sacrifice (19) Yahweh before

וְכִפֶּר עַל־ הַמִּטַּהֵר מִטֻּמְאָתוֹ
from-uncleanness-of-him the-one-being-cleansed for and-he-shall-atone

וְאַחַר יִשְׁחַט אֶת־ הָעֹלָה׃ (20) וְהֶעֱלָה
and-he-shall-offer (20) the-burnt-offering *** he-shall-slaughter and-after

הַכֹּהֵן אֶת־ הָעֹלָה וְאֶת־ הַמִּנְחָה הַמִּזְבֵּחָה
on-the-altar the-grain-offering with the-burnt-offering *** the-priest

וְכִפֶּר עָלָיו הַכֹּהֵן וְטָהֵר׃ (21) וְאִם־ דַּל
poor but-if (21) and-he-will-be-clean the-priest for-him and-he-shall-atone

הוּא וְאֵין יָדוֹ מַשֶּׂגֶת וְלָקַח כֶּבֶשׂ אֶחָד
one male-lamb then-he-must-take affording hand-of-him and-not he

אָשָׁם לִתְנוּפָה לְכַפֵּר עָלָיו וְעִשָּׂרוֹן סֹלֶת אֶחָד
one fine-flour and-tenth for-him to-atone as-wave-offering guilt-offering

בָּלוּל בַּשֶּׁמֶן לְמִנְחָה וְלֹג שָׁמֶן׃ (22) וּשְׁתֵּי
and-two-of (22) oil and-log-of for-grain-offering with-the-oil being-mixed

תֹרִים אוֹ שְׁנֵי בְּנֵי יוֹנָה אֲשֶׁר תַּשִּׂיג יָדוֹ
hand-of-him she-can-afford which pigeon young-ones-of two-of or doves

וְהָיָה אֶחָד חַטָּאת וְהָאֶחָד עֹלָה׃
burnt-offering and-the-other sin-offering one and-he-will-be

(23) וְהֵבִיא אֹתָם בַּיּוֹם הַשְּׁמִינִי לְטָהֳרָתוֹ אֶל־
to for-cleansing-of-him the-eighth on-the-day them and-he-must-bring (23)

הַכֹּהֵן אֶל־ פֶּתַח אֹהֶל־ מוֹעֵד לִפְנֵי יְהוָה׃ (24) וְלָקַח
and-he-must-take (24) Yahweh before Meeting Tent-of entrance-of at the-priest

הַכֹּהֵן אֶת־ כֶּבֶשׂ הָאָשָׁם וְאֶת־ לֹג הַשֶּׁמֶן וְהֵנִיף
and-he-must-wave the-oil log-of with the-guilt-offering lamb-of *** the-priest

אֹתָם הַכֹּהֵן תְּנוּפָה לִפְנֵי יְהוָה׃ (25) וְשָׁחַט אֶת־
*** and-he-shall-slaughter (25) Yahweh before wave-offering the-priest them

כֶּבֶשׂ הָאָשָׁם וְלָקַח הַכֹּהֵן מִדַּם
from-blood-of the-priest and-he-must-take the-guilt-offering lamb-of

הָאָשָׁם וְנָתַן עַל־ תְּנוּךְ אֹזֶן־ הַמִּטַּהֵר
the-one-being-cleansed ear-of lobe-of on and-he-must-put the-guilt-offering

big toe of his right foot, on top of the blood of the guilt offering. [18]The rest of the oil in his palm the priest shall put on the head of the one to be cleansed and make atonement for him before the LORD.

[19]"Then the priest is to sacrifice the sin offering and make atonement for the one to be cleansed from his uncleanness. After that, the priest shall slaughter the burnt offering [20]and offer it on the altar, together with the grain offering, and make atonement for him, and he will be clean.

[21]"If, however, he is poor and cannot afford these, he must take one male lamb as a guilt offering to be waved to make atonement for him, together with a tenth of an ephah[d] of fine flour mixed with oil for a grain offering, a log of oil, [22]and two doves or two young pigeons, which he can afford, one for a sin offering and the other for a burnt offering.

[23]"On the eighth day he must bring them for his cleansing to the priest at the entrance to the Tent of Meeting, before the LORD. [24]The priest is to take the lamb for the guilt offering, together with the log of oil, and wave them before the LORD as a wave offering. [25]He shall slaughter the lamb for the guilt offering and take some of its blood and put it on the lobe of the right ear of the one to be

[d]21 That is, probably about 2 quarts (about 2 liters)

הַיְמָנִית וְעַל־בֹּהֶן יָדוֹ הַיְמָנִית וְעַל־בֹּהֶן רַגְלוֹ
foot-of-him big-toe-of and-on the-right hand-of-him thumb-of and-on the-right

הַיְמָנִית׃ וּמִן־הַשֶּׁמֶן יִצֹק הַכֹּהֵן עַל־כַּף
palm-of into the-priest he-must-pour the-oil and-from (26) the-right

הַכֹּהֵן הַשְּׂמָאלִית׃ וְהִזָּה הַכֹּהֵן בְּאֶצְבָּעוֹ
with-finger-of-him the-priest and-he-must-sprinkle (27) the-left the-priest

הַיְמָנִית מִן־הַשֶּׁמֶן אֲשֶׁר עַל־כַּפּוֹ הַשְּׂמָאלִית שֶׁבַע פְּעָמִים לִפְנֵי
before times seven the-left palm-of-him in that the-oil from the-right

יְהוָה׃ וְנָתַן הַכֹּהֵן מִן־הַשֶּׁמֶן ׀ אֲשֶׁר עַל־כַּפּוֹ עַל־
on palm-of-him in that the-oil from the-priest and-he-must-put (28) Yahweh

תְּנוּךְ אֹזֶן הַמִּטַּהֵר הַיְמָנִית וְעַל־בֹּהֶן יָדוֹ
hand-of-him thumb-of and-on the-right the-one-being-cleansed ear-of lobe-of

הַיְמָנִית וְעַל־בֹּהֶן רַגְלוֹ הַיְמָנִית עַל־מְקוֹם דַּם
blood-of place-of on the-right foot-of-him big-toe-of and-on the-right

הָאָשָׁם׃ וְהַנּוֹתָר מִן־הַשֶּׁמֶן אֲשֶׁר עַל־כַּף
palm-of in that the-oil from and-the-remaining (29) the-guilt-offering

הַכֹּהֵן יִתֵּן עַל־רֹאשׁ הַמִּטַּהֵר לְכַפֵּר עָלָיו
for-him to-atone the-one-being-cleansed head-of on he-shall-put the-priest

לִפְנֵי יְהוָה׃ וְעָשָׂה אֶת־הָאֶחָד מִן־הַתֹּרִים אוֹ
or the-doves from the-one *** then-he-shall-sacrifice (30) Yahweh before

מִן־בְּנֵי הַיּוֹנָה מֵאֲשֶׁר תַּשִּׂיג יָדוֹ׃ אֵת
*** (31) hand-of-him she-can-afford from-which the-pigeon young-ones-of from

אֲשֶׁר־תַּשִּׂיג יָדוֹ אֶת־הָאֶחָד חַטָּאת וְאֶת־הָאֶחָד
the-other and sin-offering the-one *** hand-of-him she-can-afford which

עֹלָה עַל־הַמִּנְחָה וְכִפֶּר הַכֹּהֵן עַל
for the-priest so-he-will-atone the-grain-offering with burnt-offering

הַמִּטַּהֵר לִפְנֵי יְהוָה׃ זֹאת תּוֹרַת אֲשֶׁר־בּוֹ
on-him who regulation-of this (32) Yahweh before the-one-being-cleansed

נֶגַע צָרָעַת אֲשֶׁר לֹא־תַשִּׂיג יָדוֹ
hand-of-him she-can-afford not who skin-disease infection-of

בְּטָהֳרָתוֹ׃ וַיְדַבֵּר יְהוָה אֶל־מֹשֶׁה וְאֶל־אַהֲרֹן לֵאמֹר׃
to-say Aaron and-to Moses to Yahweh and-he-spoke (33) for-cleansing-of-him

כִּי תָבֹאוּ אֶל־אֶרֶץ כְּנַעַן אֲשֶׁר אֲנִי נֹתֵן לָכֶם לַאֲחֻזָּה
as-possession to-you giving I which Canaan land-of into you-enter when (34)

וְנָתַתִּי נֶגַע צָרַעַת בְּבֵית אֶרֶץ אֲחֻזַּתְכֶם׃
possession-of-you land-of in-house-of spreading mildew-of and-I-put

וּבָא אֲשֶׁר־לוֹ הַבַּיִת וְהִגִּיד לַכֹּהֵן
to-the-priest and-he-must-tell the-house to-him who then-he-must-go (35)

cleansed, on the thumb of his
right hand and on the big toe
of his right foot. 26 The priest is
to pour some of the oil into the
palm of his own left hand,
27 and with his right forefinger
sprinkle some of the oil from
his palm seven times before
the LORD. 28 Some of the oil in
his palm he is to put on the
same places he put the blood
of the guilt offering—on the
lobe of the right ear of the one
to be cleansed, on the thumb
of his right hand and on the
big toe of his right foot. 29 The
rest of the oil in his palm the
priest shall put on the head of
the one to be cleansed, to
make atonement for him before the LORD. 30 Then he shall
sacrifice the doves or the
young pigeons, which the person can afford, 31 one[e] as a sin
offering and the other as a
burnt offering, together with
the grain offering. In this way
the priest will make atonement before the LORD on behalf of the one to be cleansed."
32 These are the regulations for
anyone who has an infectious
skin disease and who cannot
afford the regular offerings for
his cleansing.

### *Cleansing From Mildew*

33 The LORD said to Moses
and Aaron, 34 "When you enter
the land of Canaan, which I
am giving you as your possession, and I put a spreading
mildew in a house in that
land, 35 the owner of the house
must go and tell the priest, 'I

[e]31 Hebrew [31]*such as the person can afford, one*

לֵאמֹר כְּנֶגַע נִרְאָה לִי בַּבָּיִת׃ וְצִוָּה
and-he-must-order (36) in-the-house to-me he-appeared like-mildew to-say

הַכֹּהֵן וּפִנּוּ אֶת־ הַבַּיִת בְּטֶרֶם יָבֹא הַכֹּהֵן
the-priest he-goes-in before the-house *** and-they-must-empty the-priest

לִרְאוֹת אֶת־ הַנֶּגַע וְלֹא יִטְמָא כָּל־ אֲשֶׁר
that anything he-will-pronounce-unclean so-not the-mildew *** to-examine

בַּבָּיִת וְאַחַר כֵּן יָבֹא הַכֹּהֵן לִרְאוֹת אֶת־ הַבָּיִת׃
the-house *** to-examine the-priest he-must-go-in this and-after in-the-house

וְרָאָה אֶת־ הַנֶּגַע וְהִנֵּה הַנֶּגַע בְּקִירֹת
on-walls-of the-mildew and-if the-mildew *** and-he-must-examine (37)

הַבַּיִת שְׁקַעֲרוּרֹת יְרַקְרַקֹּת אוֹ אֲדַמְדַּמֹּת וּמַרְאֵיהֶן
and-appearance-of-them reddish-ones or greenish-ones depressions the-house

שָׁפָל מִן־ הַקִּיר׃ וְיָצָא הַכֹּהֵן מִן־ הַבַּיִת
the-house from the-priest then-he-shall-go-out (38) the-wall than deeper

אֶל־ פֶּתַח הַבָּיִת וְהִסְגִּיר אֶת־ הַבַּיִת שִׁבְעַת יָמִים׃
days seven-of the-house *** and-he-shall-close the-house entrance-of at

וְשָׁב הַכֹּהֵן בַּיּוֹם הַשְּׁבִיעִי
the-seventh on-the-day the-priest and-he-shall-return (39)

וְרָאָה וְהִנֵּה פָּשָׂה הַנֶּגַע בְּקִירֹת הַבָּיִת׃
the-house on-walls-of the-mildew he-spread and-if and-he-shall-inspect

וְצִוָּה הַכֹּהֵן וְחִלְּצוּ אֶת־ הָאֲבָנִים
the-stones *** and-they-must-tear-out the-priest then-he-must-order (40)

אֲשֶׁר בָּהֵן הַנָּגַע וְהִשְׁלִיכוּ אֶתְהֶן אֶל־ מִחוּץ לָעִיר
of-the-town outside to them and-they-must-throw the-mildew on-them that

אֶל־ מָקוֹם טָמֵא׃ וְאֶת־ הַבַּיִת יַקְצִעַ מִבַּיִת סָבִיב
around on-inside he-must-scrape the-house and (41) unclean place to

וְשָׁפְכוּ אֶת־ הֶעָפָר אֲשֶׁר הִקְצוּ אֶל־ מִחוּץ
outside to they-scrape-off that the-material *** and-they-must-dump

לָעִיר אֶל־ מָקוֹם טָמֵא׃ וְלָקְחוּ אֲבָנִים אֲחֵרוֹת
other-ones stones then-they-must-take (42) unclean place into of-the-town

וְהֵבִיאוּ אֶל־ תַּחַת הָאֲבָנִים וְעָפָר אַחֵר יִקַּח
he-must-take new and-clay the-stones place-of in and-they-must-replace

וְטָח אֶת־ הַבָּיִת׃ וְאִם־ יָשׁוּב הַנֶּגַע
the-mildew he-reappears but-if (43) the-house *** and-he-must-plaster

וּפָרַח בַּבַּיִת אַחַר חִלֵּץ אֶת־ הָאֲבָנִים וְאַחֲרֵי
and-after the-stones *** he-tears-out after in-the-house and-he-spreads

הַקְצוֹת אֶת־ הַבַּיִת וְאַחֲרֵי הִטּוֹחַ׃ וּבָא
then-he-must-go (44) to-be-plastered and-after the-house *** to-scrape-off

have seen something that looks like mildew in my house.' [36]The priest is to order the house to be emptied before he goes in to examine the mildew, so that nothing in the house will be pronounced unclean. After this the priest is to go in and inspect the house. [37]He is to examine the mildew on the walls, and if it has greenish or reddish depressions that appear to be deeper than the surface of the wall, [38]the priest shall go out of the house and at the entrance close up the house for seven days. [39]On the seventh day the priest shall return to inspect the house. If the mildew has spread on the walls, [40]he is to order that the contaminated stones be torn out and thrown into an unclean place outside the town. [41]He must have all the inside walls of the house scraped and the material that is scraped off dumped into an unclean place outside the town. [42]Then they are to take other stones to replace these and take new clay and plaster the house.

[43]"If the mildew reappears in the house after the stones have been torn out and the house scraped and plastered,

הַכֹּהֵן וְרָאָה וְהִנֵּה פָּשָׂה הַנֶּגַע בַּבָּיִת
in-the-house the-mildew he-spread and-if and-he-must-examine the-priest

צָרַעַת מַמְאֶרֶת הִוא בַּבַּיִת טָמֵא הוּא׃ וְנָתַץ אֶת־
*** and-he-must-tear-down (45) he unclean in-the-house she destroying mildew

הַבַּיִת אֶת־ אֲבָנָיו וְאֶת־ עֵצָיו וְאֵת כָּל־ עֲפַר
plaster-of all-of and timbers-of-him and stones-of-him *** the-house

הַבַּיִת וְהוֹצִיא אֶל־ מִחוּץ לָעִיר אֶל־ מָקוֹם טָמֵא׃
unclean place to of-the-town outside to and-he-must-take the-house

וְהַבָּא אֶל־ הַבַּיִת כָּל־ יְמֵי הִסְגִּיר אֹתוֹ
him he-closes days-of any-of the-house into and-the-one-going (46)

יִטְמָא עַד־ הָעָרֶב׃ וְהַשֹּׁכֵב בַּבַּיִת
in-the-house and-the-one-sleeping (47) the-evening until he-will-be-unclean

יְכַבֵּס אֶת־ בְּגָדָיו וְהָאֹכֵל בַּבַּיִת יְכַבֵּס
he-must-wash in-the-house and-the-one-eating clothes-of-him *** he-must-wash

אֶת־ בְּגָדָיו׃ וְאִם־ בֹּא יָבֹא הַכֹּהֵן וְרָאָה
and-he-examines the-priest he-comes to-come but-if (48) clothes-of-him ***

וְהִנֵּה לֹא־ פָשָׂה הַנֶּגַע בַּבַּיִת אַחֲרֵי הִטֹּחַ אֶת־
*** to-be-plastered after in-the-house the-mildew he-spread not and-if

הַבָּיִת וְטִהַר הַכֹּהֵן אֶת־ הַבַּיִת כִּי
for the-house *** the-priest then-he-shall-pronounce-clean the-house

נִרְפָּא הַנָּגַע׃ וְלָקַח לְחַטֵּא אֶת־ הַבַּיִת שְׁתֵּי
two-of the-house *** to-purify and-he-must-take (49) the-mildew he-is-gone

צִפֳּרִים וְעֵץ אֶרֶז וּשְׁנִי תוֹלַעַת וְאֵזֹב׃
and-hyssop scarlet and-yarn-of cedar and-wood-of birds

וְשָׁחַט אֶת־ הַצִּפֹּר הָאֶחָת אֶל־ כְּלִי־ חֶרֶשׂ עַל־ מַיִם חַיִּים׃
fresh-ones waters over clay pot-of in the-one the-bird *** and-he-shall-kill (50)

וְלָקַח אֶת־ עֵץ־ הָאֶרֶז וְאֶת־ הָאֵזֹב וְאֵת ׀ שְׁנִי
yarn-of and the-hyssop and the-cedar wood-of *** then-he-must-take (51)

הַתּוֹלַעַת וְאֵת הַצִּפֹּר הַחַיָּה וְטָבַל אֹתָם בְּדַם הַצִּפֹּר
the-bird into-blood-of them and-he-must-dip the-live the-bird and the-scarlet

הַשְּׁחוּטָה וּבַמַּיִם הַחַיִּים וְהִזָּה
and-he-must-sprinkle the-fresh-ones and-in-the-waters the-one-being-killed

אֶל־ הַבַּיִת שֶׁבַע פְּעָמִים׃ וְחִטֵּא אֶת־ הַבַּיִת בְּדַם
with-blood-of the-house *** and-he-shall-purify (52) times seven the-house on

הַצִּפּוֹר וּבַמַּיִם הַחַיִּים וּבַצִּפֹּר הַחַיָּה
the-live and-with-the-bird the-fresh-ones and-with-the-waters the-bird

וּבְעֵץ הָאֶרֶז וּבָאֵזֹב וּבִשְׁנִי הַתּוֹלָעַת׃
the-scarlet and-with-yarn-of and-with-the-hyssop the-cedar and-with-wood-of

44 the priest is to go and examine it and, if the mildew has spread in the house, it is a destructive mildew; the house is unclean. 45 It must be torn down—its stones, timbers and all the plaster—and taken out of the town to an unclean place.

46 "Anyone who goes into the house while it is closed up will be unclean till evening. 47 Anyone who sleeps or eats in the house must wash his clothes.

48 "But if the priest comes to examine it and the mildew has not spread after the house has been plastered, he shall pronounce the house clean, because the mildew is gone. 49 To purify the house he is to take two birds and some cedar wood, scarlet yarn and hyssop. 50 He shall kill one of the birds over fresh water in a clay pot. 51 Then he is to take the cedar wood, the hyssop, the scarlet yarn and the live bird, dip them into the blood of the dead bird and the fresh water, and sprinkle the house seven times. 52 He shall purify the house with the bird's blood, the fresh water, the live bird, the cedar wood, the hyssop and the scarlet yarn. 53 Then he

וְשִׁלַּח אֶת־ הַצִּפֹּר הַחַיָּה אֶל־ מִחוּץ לָעִיר אֶל־
over of-the-town outside at the-live the-bird *** then-he-must-release (53)

פְּנֵי הַשָּׂדֶה וְכִפֶּר עַל־ הַבַּיִת וְטָהֵר׃
and-he-will-be-clean the-house for so-he-will-atone the-field surface-of

זֹאת הַתּוֹרָה לְכָל־ נֶגַע הַצָּרָעַת
the-skin-disease infection-of for-any-of the-regulation this (54)

וְלַנֶּתֶק׃ וּלְצָרַעַת הַבֶּגֶד וְלַבָּיִת׃
or-in-the-house the-clothing for-mildew-of (55) and-for-the-itch

וְלַשְׂאֵת וְלַסַּפַּחַת וְלַבֶּהָרֶת׃
and-for-the-bright-spot and-for-the-rash and-for-the-swelling (56)

לְהוֹרֹת בְּיוֹם הַטָּמֵא וּבְיוֹם הַטָּהֹר זֹאת
this the-clean or-day-of the-unclean on-day-of to-determine (57)

תּוֹרַת הַצָּרָעַת׃ וַיְדַבֵּר יְהוָה אֶל־ מֹשֶׁה וְאֶל־ אַהֲרֹן
Aaron and-to Moses to Yahweh and-he-spoke (15:1) the-infection regulation-of

לֵאמֹר׃ דַּבְּרוּ אֶל־ בְּנֵי יִשְׂרָאֵל וַאֲמַרְתֶּם אֲלֵהֶם אִישׁ אִישׁ כִּי יִהְיֶה
he-has when any man to-them and-you-say Israel sons-of to speak! (2) to-say

זָב מִבְּשָׂרוֹ זוֹבוֹ טָמֵא הוּא׃ וְזֹאת
whether-this (3) he unclean discharge-of-him from-body-of-him discharging

תִּהְיֶה טֻמְאָתוֹ בְּזוֹבוֹ רָר בְּשָׂרוֹ אֶת־
*** body-of-him he-lets-flow in-discharge-of-him uncleanness-of-him she-is

זוֹבוֹ אוֹ־ הֶחְתִּים בְּשָׂרוֹ מִזּוֹבוֹ
from-discharge-of-him body-of-him he-blocks or discharge-of-him

טֻמְאָתוֹ הִוא׃ כָּל־ הַמִּשְׁכָּב אֲשֶׁר יִשְׁכַּב עָלָיו
on-him he-lies which the-bed any-of (4) she uncleanness-of-him

הַזָּב יִטְמָא וְכָל־ הַכְּלִי אֲשֶׁר־ יֵשֵׁב
he-sits which the-thing and-any-of he-will-be-unclean the-one-discharging

עָלָיו יִטְמָא׃ וְאִישׁ אֲשֶׁר יִגַּע בְּמִשְׁכָּבוֹ
on-bed-of-him he-touches who and-anyone (5) he-will-be-unclean on-him

יְכַבֵּס בְּגָדָיו וְרָחַץ בַּמַּיִם
with-the-waters and-he-must-bathe clothes-of-him he-must-wash

וְטָמֵא עַד־ הָעָרֶב׃ וְהַיֹּשֵׁב עַל־ הַכְּלִי
the-thing on and-the-one-sitting (6) the-evening till and-he-will-be-unclean

אֲשֶׁר־ יֵשֵׁב עָלָיו הַזָּב יְכַבֵּס בְּגָדָיו
clothes-of-him he-must-wash the-one-discharging on-him he-sat that

וְרָחַץ בַּמַּיִם וְטָמֵא עַד־ הָעָרֶב׃
the-evening till and-he-will-be-unclean with-the-waters and-he-must-bathe

וְהַנֹּגֵעַ בִּבְשַׂר הַזָּב יְכַבֵּס
he-must-wash the-one-discharging on-body-of and-the-one-touching (7)

is to release the live bird in the open fields outside the town. In this way he will make atonement for the house, and it will be clean."

[54]These are the regulations for any infectious skin disease, for an itch, [55]for mildew in clothing or in a house, [56]and for a swelling, a rash or a bright spot, [57]to determine when something is clean or unclean.

These are the regulations for infectious skin diseases and mildew.

*Discharges Causing Uncleanness*

15 The LORD said to Moses and Aaron, [2]"Speak to the Israelites and say to them: 'When any man has a bodily discharge, the discharge is unclean. [3]Whether it continues flowing from his body or is blocked, it will make him unclean. This is how his discharge will bring about uncleanness:

[4]" 'Any bed the man with a discharge lies on will be unclean, and anything he sits on will be unclean. [5]Anyone who touches his bed must wash his clothes and bathe with water, and he will be unclean till evening. [6]Whoever sits on anything that the man with a discharge sat on must wash his clothes and bathe with water, and he will be unclean till evening.

[7]" 'Whoever touches the man who has a discharge

בְּגָדָיו וְרָחַץ בַּמַּיִם וְטָמֵא עַד־
till and-he-will-be-unclean with-the-waters and-he-must-bathe clothes-of-him

הָעָרֶב׃ (8) וְכִי־ יָרֹק הַזָּב בַּטָּהוֹר
on-the-clean the-one-discharging to-spit and-if (8) the-evening

וְכִבֶּס בְּגָדָיו וְרָחַץ בַּמַּיִם
with-the-waters and-he-must-bathe clothes-of-him then-he-must-wash

וְטָמֵא עַד־ הָעָרֶב׃ (9) וְכָל־ הַמֶּרְכָּב אֲשֶׁר
that the-seat and-every-of (9) the-evening till and-he-will-be-unclean

יִרְכַּב עָלָיו הַזָּב יִטְמָא׃ (10) וְכָל־
and-every-of (10) he-will-be-unclean the-one-discharging on-him he-rides

הַנֹּגֵעַ בְּכֹל אֲשֶׁר יִהְיֶה תַחְתָּיו יִטְמָא עַד־
till he-will-be-unclean under-him he-was that on-anything the-one-touching

הָעָרֶב וְהַנּוֹשֵׂא אוֹתָם יְכַבֵּס בְּגָדָיו
clothes-of-him he-must-wash them and-the-one-picking-up the-evening

וְרָחַץ בַּמַּיִם וְטָמֵא עַד־ הָעָרֶב׃
the-evening till and-he-will-be-unclean with-the-waters and-he-must-bathe

(11) וְכֹל אֲשֶׁר יִגַּע־ בּוֹ הַזָּב וְיָדָיו
and-hands-of-him the-one-discharging on-him he-touches who and-anyone (11)

לֹא־ שָׁטַף בַּמָּיִם וְכִבֶּס בְּגָדָיו
clothes-of-him then-he-must-wash with-the-waters he-rinsed not

וְרָחַץ בַּמַּיִם וְטָמֵא עַד־ הָעָרֶב׃
the-evening till and-he-will-be-unclean with-the-waters and-he-must-bathe

(12) וּכְלִי־ חֶרֶשׂ אֲשֶׁר־ יִגַּע־ בּוֹ הַזָּב
the-one-discharging on-him he-touches that clay and-pot-of (12)

יִשָּׁבֵר וְכָל־ כְּלִי־ עֵץ יִשָּׁטֵף בַּמָּיִם׃
with-the-waters he-must-be-rinsed wood article-of and-any-of he-must-be-broken

(13) וְכִי־ יִטְהַר הַזָּב מִזּוֹבוֹ
from-discharge-of-him the-one-discharging he-is-cleansed and-when (13)

וְסָפַר לוֹ שִׁבְעַת יָמִים לְטָהֳרָתוֹ וְכִבֶּס
and-he-must-wash for-cleansing-of-him days seven-of to-him then-he-must-count

בְּגָדָיו וְרָחַץ בְּשָׂרוֹ בְּמַיִם חַיִּים
fresh-ones with-waters body-of-him and-he-must-bathe clothes-of-him

וְטָהֵר׃ (14) וּבַיּוֹם הַשְּׁמִינִי יִקַּח־ לוֹ
to-him he-must-take the-eighth and-on-the-day (14) and-he-will-be-clean

שְׁתֵּי תֹרִים אוֹ שְׁנֵי בְּנֵי יוֹנָה וּבָא ׀ לִפְנֵי יְהוָה
Yahweh before and-he-must-come pigeon young-ones-of two-of or doves two-of

אֶל־ פֶּתַח אֹהֶל מוֹעֵד וּנְתָנָם אֶל־ הַכֹּהֵן׃
the-priest to and-he-must-give-them Meeting Tent-of entrance-of to

must wash his clothes and
bathe with water, and he will
be unclean till evening.
8" 'If the man with the discharge spits on someone who
is clean, that person must
wash his clothes and bathe
with water, and he will be unclean till evening.
9" 'Everything the man sits
on when riding will be unclean, 10and whoever touches
any of the things that were
under him will be unclean till
evening; whoever picks up
those things must wash his
clothes and bathe with water,
and he will be unclean till evening.
11" 'Anyone the man with a
discharge touches without
rinsing his hands with water
must wash his clothes and
bathe with water, and he will
be unclean till evening.
12" 'A clay pot that the man
touches must be broken, and
any wooden article is to be
rinsed with water.
13" 'When a man is cleansed
from his discharge, he is to
count off seven days for his
ceremonial cleansing; he must
wash his clothes and bathe
himself with fresh water, and
he will be clean. 14On the
eighth day he must take two
doves or two young pigeons
and come before the LORD to
the entrance to the Tent of
Meeting and give them to the

וְעָשָׂה אֹתָם הַכֹּהֵן אֶחָד חַטָּאת וְהָאֶחָד
and-the-other sin-offering one the-priest them then-he-must-sacrifice (15)

עֹלָה וְכִפֶּר עָלָיו הַכֹּהֵן לִפְנֵי יְהוָה
Yahweh before the-priest for-him so-he-will-atone burnt-offering

מִזּוֹבוֹ׃ וְאִישׁ כִּי־ תֵצֵא מִמֶּנּוּ שִׁכְבַת־ זָרַע
semen emission-of from-him she-goes when and-man (16) for-discharge-of-him

וְרָחַץ בַּמַּיִם אֶת־ כָּל־ בְּשָׂרוֹ
body-of-him whole-of *** with-the-waters then-he-must-bathe

וְטָמֵא עַד־ הָעָרֶב׃ וְכָל־ בֶּגֶד וְכָל־
or-any-of clothing and-any-of (17) the-evening till and-he-will-be-unclean

עוֹר אֲשֶׁר־ יִהְיֶה עָלָיו שִׁכְבַת־ זָרַע וְכֻבַּס
then-he-must-be-washed semen emission-of on-him he-has that leather

בַּמַּיִם וְטָמֵא עַד־ הָעָרֶב׃ וְאִשָּׁה אֲשֶׁר
when and-woman (18) the-evening till and-he-will-be-unclean with-the-waters

יִשְׁכַּב אִישׁ אֹתָהּ שִׁכְבַת־ זָרַע וְרָחֲצוּ בַמַּיִם
with-the-waters then-they-must-bathe semen emission-of with-her man he-lies

וְטָמְאוּ עַד־ הָעָרֶב׃ וְאִשָּׁה כִּי־ תִהְיֶה
she-has when and-woman (19) the-evening till and-they-will-be-unclean

זָבָה דָּם יִהְיֶה זֹבָהּ בִּבְשָׂרָהּ שִׁבְעַת יָמִים תִּהְיֶה
she-is days seven-of from-body-of-her flow-of-her he-is blood flowing

בְנִדָּתָהּ וְכָל־ הַנֹּגֵעַ בָּהּ יִטְמָא
he-will-be-unclean on-her the-one-touching and-any-of in-impurity-of-her

עַד־ הָעָרֶב׃ וְכֹל אֲשֶׁר תִּשְׁכַּב עָלָיו בְּנִדָּתָהּ
during-period-of-her on-him she-lies that and-anything (20) the-evening till

יִטְמָא וְכֹל אֲשֶׁר־ תֵּשֵׁב עָלָיו יִטְמָא׃
he-will-be-unclean on-him she-sits that and-anything he-will-be-unclean

וְכָל־ הַנֹּגֵעַ בְּמִשְׁכָּבָהּ יְכַבֵּס בְּגָדָיו
clothes-of-him he-must-wash on-bed-of-her the-one-touching and-any-of (21)

וְרָחַץ בַּמַּיִם וְטָמֵא עַד־ הָעָרֶב׃
the-evening till and-he-will-be-unclean with-the-waters and-he-must-bathe

וְכָל־ הַנֹּגֵעַ בְּכָל־ כְּלִי אֲשֶׁר־ תֵּשֵׁב עָלָיו
on-him she-sat that thing on-any-of the-one-touching and-any-of (22)

יְכַבֵּס בְּגָדָיו וְרָחַץ בַּמַּיִם
with-the-waters and-he-must-bathe clothes-of-him he-must-wash

וְטָמֵא עַד־ הָעָרֶב׃ וְאִם עַל־הַמִּשְׁכָּב הוּא אוֹ עַל־
on or he the-bed on whether-if (23) the-evening till and-he-will-be-unclean

הַכְּלִי אֲשֶׁר־הִוא יֹשֶׁבֶת־ עָלָיו בְּנָגְעוֹ־ בוֹ יִטְמָא
he-will-be-unclean on-him when-to-touch-him on-him sitting she that the-thing

priest. 15 The priest is to sacrifice them, the one for a sin
offering and the other for a
burnt offering. In this way he
will make atonement before
the LORD for the man because
of his discharge.
16 "'When a man has an
emission of semen, he must
bathe his whole body with
water, and he will be unclean
till evening. 17 Any clothing or
leather that has semen on it
must be washed with water,
and it will be unclean till evening. 18 When a man lies with
a woman and there is an emission of semen, both must
bathe with water, and they
will be unclean till evening.
19 "'When a woman has her
regular flow of blood, the impurity of her monthly period
will last seven days, and anyone who touches her will be
unclean till evening.
20 "'Anything she lies on
during her period will be unclean, and anything she sits
on will be unclean. 21 Whoever
touches her bed must wash his
clothes and bathe with water,
and he will be unclean till evening. 22 Whoever touches anything she sits on must wash
his clothes and bathe with
water, and he will be unclean
till evening. 23 Whether it is the
bed or anything she was sitting on, when anyone touches
it, he will be unclean till evening.

עַד־ הָעָרֶב׃ וְאִם שָׁכֹב יִשְׁכַּב אִישׁ אֹתָהּ וּתְהִי
and-she-is with-her man he-lies to-lie and-if (24) the-evening till

נִדָּתָהּ עָלָיו וְטָמֵא שִׁבְעַת יָמִים וְכָל־ הַמִּשְׁכָּב
the-bed and-any-of days seven-of then-he-will-be-unclean on-him flow-of-her

אֲשֶׁר־ יִשְׁכַּב עָלָיו יִטְמָא׃ וְאִשָּׁה כִּי־ יָזוּב
he-discharges when and-woman (25) he-will-be-unclean on-him he-lies that

זוֹב דָּמָהּ יָמִים רַבִּים בְּלֹא עֶת־ נִדָּתָהּ אוֹ כִי־
when or period-of-her time-of and-not many days blood-of-her discharge-of

תָזוּב עַל־ נִדָּתָהּ כָּל־ יְמֵי זוֹב טֻמְאָתָהּ
uncleanness-of-her flow-of days-of all-of period-of-her beyond she-discharges

כִּימֵי נִדָּתָהּ תִּהְיֶה טְמֵאָה הִוא׃ כָּל־ הַמִּשְׁכָּב אֲשֶׁר־
that the-bed any-of (26) she unclean she-is period-of-her as-days-of

תִּשְׁכַּב עָלָיו כָּל־ יְמֵי זוֹבָהּ כְּמִשְׁכַּב נִדָּתָהּ
period-of-her as-bed-of discharge-of-her days-of all-of on-him she-lies

יִהְיֶה־ לָּהּ וְכָל־ הַכְּלִי אֲשֶׁר תֵּשֵׁב עָלָיו טָמֵא יִהְיֶה
he-will-be unclean on-him she-sits that the-thing and-any-of to-her he-is

כְּטֻמְאַת נִדָּתָהּ׃ וְכָל־ הַנּוֹגֵעַ בָּם
on-them the-one-touching and-any-of (27) period-of-her as-uncleanness-of

יִטְמָא וְכִבֶּס בְּגָדָיו וְרָחַץ
and-he-must-bathe clothes-of-him and-he-must-wash he-will-be-unclean

בַּמַּיִם וְטָמֵא עַד־ הָעָרֶב׃ וְאִם־
and-when (28) the-evening till and-he-will-be-unclean with-the-waters

טָהֲרָה מִזּוֹבָהּ וְסָפְרָה לָּהּ שִׁבְעַת
seven-of to-her then-she-must-count from-discharge-of-her she-is-cleansed

יָמִים וְאַחַר תִּטְהָר׃ וּבַיּוֹם הַשְּׁמִינִי תִּקַּח־
she-must-take the-eighth and-on-the-day (29) she-will-be-unclean and-after days

לָהּ שְׁתֵּי תֹרִים אוֹ שְׁנֵי בְּנֵי יוֹנָה וְהֵבִיאָה אוֹתָם
them and-she-must-bring pigeon young-ones-of two-of or doves two-of to-her

אֶל־ הַכֹּהֵן אֶל־ פֶּתַח אֹהֶל מוֹעֵד׃ וְעָשָׂה
and-he-must-sacrifice (30) Meeting Tent-of entrance-of at the-priest to

הַכֹּהֵן אֶת־ הָאֶחָד חַטָּאת וְאֶת־ הָאֶחָד עֹלָה
burnt-offering the-other and sin-offering the-one *** the-priest

וְכִפֶּר עָלֶיהָ הַכֹּהֵן לִפְנֵי יְהוָה מִזּוֹב
for-discharge-of Yahweh before the-priest for-her so-he-will-atone

טֻמְאָתָהּ׃ וְהִזַּרְתֶּם אֶת־ בְּנֵי־ יִשְׂרָאֵל
Israel sons-of *** and-you-must-separate (31) uncleanness-of-her

מִטֻּמְאָתָם וְלֹא יָמֻתוּ בְּטֻמְאָתָם
in-uncleanness-of-them they-will-die so-not from-uncleanness-of-them

24" 'If a man lies with her and her monthly flow touches him, he will be unclean for seven days; any bed he lies on will be unclean.

25" 'When a woman has a discharge of blood for many days at a time other than her monthly period or has a discharge that continues beyond her period, she will be unclean as long as she has the discharge, just as in the days of her period. 26Any bed she lies on while her discharge continues will be unclean, as is her bed during her monthly period, and anything she sits on will be unclean, as during her period. 27Whoever touches them will be unclean; he must wash his clothes and bathe with water, and he will be unclean till evening.

28" 'When she is cleansed from her discharge, she must count off seven days, and after that she will be ceremonially clean. 29On the eighth day she must take two doves or two young pigeons and bring them to the priest at the entrance to the Tent of Meeting. 30The priest is to sacrifice one for a sin offering and the other for a burnt offering. In this way he will make atonement for her before the LORD for the uncleanness of her discharge.

31" 'You must keep the Israelites separate from things that make them unclean, so they will not die in their uncleanness for defiling my

בְּטַמְּאָם אֶת־ מִשְׁכָּנִי אֲשֶׁר בְּתוֹכָם׃ זֹאת
this (32) among-them which dwelling-of-me *** when-to-defile-them

תּוֹרַת הַזָּב וַאֲשֶׁר תֵּצֵא מִמֶּנּוּ שִׁכְבַת־
emission-of from-him she-goes and-whoever the-one-discharging regulation-of

זֶרַע לְטָמְאָה־ בָהּ׃ וְהַדָּוָה בְּנִדָּתָהּ
in-period-of-her and-the-woman (33) by-her to-be-made-unclean semen

וְהַזָּב אֶת־ זוֹבוֹ לַזָּכָר וְלַנְּקֵבָה
and-for-the-woman for-the-man discharge-of-him *** and-the-one-discharging

וּלְאִישׁ אֲשֶׁר יִשְׁכַּב עִם־ טְמֵאָה׃ וַיְדַבֵּר יְהוָה אֶל־
to Yahweh and-he-spoke (16:1) unclean-woman with he-lies who and-for-man

מֹשֶׁה אַחֲרֵי מוֹת שְׁנֵי בְּנֵי אַהֲרֹן בְּקָרְבָתָם לִפְנֵי־ יְהוָה
Yahweh before when-to-approach-them Aaron sons-of two-of to-die after Moses

וַיָּמֻתוּ׃ וַיֹּאמֶר יְהוָה אֶל־ מֹשֶׁה דַּבֵּר אֶל־ אַהֲרֹן אָחִיךָ
brother-of-you Aaron to tell! Moses to Yahweh and-he-said (2) and-they-died

וְאַל־ יָבֹא בְכָל־ עֵת אֶל־ הַקֹּדֶשׁ מִבֵּית
behind the-Most-Holy-Place into time at-any-of he-may-come that-not

לַפָּרֹכֶת אֶל־ פְּנֵי הַכַּפֹּרֶת אֲשֶׁר עַל־ הָאָרֹן וְלֹא
so-not the-ark on that the-atonement-cover front-of in to-the-curtain

יָמוּת כִּי בֶּעָנָן אֵרָאֶה עַל־ הַכַּפֹּרֶת׃ בְּזֹאת
as-this (3) the-atonement-cover over I-appear in-the-cloud for he-will-die

יָבֹא אַהֲרֹן אֶל־ הַקֹּדֶשׁ בְּפַר בֶּן־ בָּקָר לְחַטָּאת
for-sin-offering herd young-of with-bull the-sanctuary into Aaron he-may-enter

וְאַיִל לְעֹלָה׃ כְּתֹנֶת־ בַּד קֹדֶשׁ יִלְבָּשׁ
he-must-put-on sacred linen tunic-of (4) for-burnt-offering and-ram

וּמִכְנְסֵי־ בַד יִהְיוּ עַל־ בְּשָׂרוֹ וּבְאַבְנֵט
and-with-sash-of body-of-him next-to they-must-be linen and-undergarments-of

בַּד יַחְגֹּר וּבְמִצְנֶפֶת בַּד יִצְנֹף בִּגְדֵי־
garments-of he-must-put-on linen and-with-turban-of he-must-tie linen

קֹדֶשׁ הֵם וְרָחַץ בַּמַּיִם אֶת־ בְּשָׂרוֹ
body-of-him *** with-the-waters so-he-must-bathe these sacred

וּלְבֵשָׁם׃ וּמֵאֵת עֲדַת בְּנֵי יִשְׂרָאֵל יִקַּח
he-must-take Israel sons-of community-of and-from (5) before-he-puts-on-them

שְׁנֵי־ שְׂעִירֵי עִזִּים לְחַטָּאת וְאַיִל אֶחָד לְעֹלָה׃
for-burnt-offering one and-ram for-sin-offering goats male-goats-of two-of

וְהִקְרִיב אַהֲרֹן אֶת־ פַּר הַחַטָּאת אֲשֶׁר־ לוֹ
for-him that the-sin-offering bull-of *** Aaron and-he-must-offer (6)

וְכִפֶּר בַּעֲדוֹ וּבְעַד בֵּיתוֹ׃ וְלָקַח
then-he-must-take (7) household-of-him and-for for-himself so-he-will-atone

dwelling place, which is among them.' "

32 These are the regulations for a man with a discharge, for anyone made unclean by an emission of semen, 33 for a woman in her monthly period, for a man or a woman with a discharge, and for a man who lies with a woman who is ceremonially unclean.

*The Day of Atonement*

**16** The LORD spoke to Moses after the death of the two sons of Aaron who died when they approached the LORD. 2 The LORD said to Moses: "Tell your brother Aaron not to come whenever he chooses into the Most Holy Place behind the curtain in front of the atonement cover on the ark, or else he will die, because I appear in the cloud over the atonement cover.

3 "This is how Aaron is to enter the sanctuary area: with a young bull for a sin offering and a ram for a burnt offering. 4 He is to put on the sacred linen tunic, with linen undergarments next to his body; he is to tie the linen sash around him and put on the linen turban. These are sacred garments; so he must bathe himself with water before he puts them on. 5 From the Israelite community he is to take two male goats for a sin offering and a ram for a burnt offering.

6 "Aaron is to offer the bull for his own sin offering to make atonement for himself and his household. 7 Then he is

f31 Or *my tabernacle*

אֶת־ שְׁנֵי הַשְּׂעִירִם וְהֶעֱמִיד אֹתָם לִפְנֵי יְהוָה פֶּתַח

entrance-of Yahweh before them and-he-must-present the-goats two-of ***

אֹהֶל מוֹעֵד׃ וְנָתַן אַהֲרֹן עַל־ שְׁנֵי הַשְּׂעִירִם גֹּרָלוֹת גּוֹרָל

lot lots the-goats two-of for Aaron and-he-must-cast (8) Meeting Tent-of

אֶחָד לַיהוָה וְגוֹרָל אֶחָד לַעֲזָאזֵל׃ וְהִקְרִיב אַהֲרֹן

Aaron and-he-shall-bring (9) for-the-scapegoat other and-lot for-Yahweh one

אֶת־ הַשָּׂעִיר אֲשֶׁר עָלָה עָלָיו הַגּוֹרָל לַיהוָה וְעָשָׂהוּ

and-he-shall-sacrifice-him for-Yahweh the-lot for-him he-falls that the-goat ***

חַטָּאת׃ וְהַשָּׂעִיר אֲשֶׁר עָלָה עָלָיו הַגּוֹרָל לַעֲזָאזֵל

as-the-scapegoat the-lot for-him he-fell that but-the-goat (10) sin-offering

יָעֳמַד־ חַי לִפְנֵי יְהוָה לְכַפֵּר עָלָיו לְשַׁלַּח אֹתוֹ

him by-to-send for-him to-atone Yahweh before alive he-shall-be-presented

לַעֲזָאזֵל הַמִּדְבָּרָה׃ וְהִקְרִיב אַהֲרֹן אֶת־ פַּר

bull-of *** Aaron and-he-shall-bring (11) into-the-desert as-the-scapegoat

הַחַטָּאת אֲשֶׁר־ לוֹ וְכִפֶּר בַּעֲדוֹ וּבְעַד

and-for for-himself and-he-shall-atone for-him that the-sin-offering

בֵּיתוֹ וְשָׁחַט אֶת־ פַּר הַחַטָּאת אֲשֶׁר־

that the-sin-offering bull-of *** and-he-shall-slaughter household-of-him

לוֹ׃ וְלָקַח מְלֹא־ הַמַּחְתָּה גַּחֲלֵי־ אֵשׁ מֵעַל

from-on fire coals-of the-censer full-of and-he-must-take (12) for-him

הַמִּזְבֵּחַ מִלִּפְנֵי יְהוָה וּמְלֹא חָפְנָיו קְטֹרֶת

incense-of two-hands-of-him and-full-of Yahweh from-before the-altar

סַמִּים דַּקָּה וְהֵבִיא מִבֵּית לַפָּרֹכֶת׃ וְנָתַן

and-he-must-put (13) to-the-curtain behind and-he-must-take ground fragrances

אֶת־ הַקְּטֹרֶת עַל־ הָאֵשׁ לִפְנֵי יְהוָה וְכִסָּה ׀ עֲנַן

smoke-of and-he-will-conceal Yahweh before the-fire on the-incense ***

הַקְּטֹרֶת אֶת־ הַכַּפֹּרֶת אֲשֶׁר עַל־ הָעֵדוּת וְלֹא

so-not the-Testimony above that the-atonement-cover *** the-incense

יָמוּת׃ וְלָקַח מִדַּם הַפָּר וְהִזָּה

and-he-must-sprinkle the-bull from-blood-of and-he-must-take (14) he-will-die

בְאֶצְבָּעוֹ עַל־ פְּנֵי הַכַּפֹּרֶת קֵדְמָה וְלִפְנֵי

and-before in-front the-atonement-cover front-of on with-finger-of-him

הַכַּפֹּרֶת יַזֶּה שֶׁבַע־ פְּעָמִים מִן־ הַדָּם

the-blood from times seven he-shall-sprinkle the-atonement-cover

בְּאֶצְבָּעוֹ׃ וְשָׁחַט אֶת־ שְׂעִיר הַחַטָּאת

the-sin-offering goat-of *** then-he-shall-slaughter (15) with-finger-of-him

אֲשֶׁר לָעָם וְהֵבִיא אֶת־ דָּמוֹ אֶל־ מִבֵּית לַפָּרֹכֶת

of-the-curtain behind to blood-of-him *** and-he-must-take for-the-people that

to take the two goats and present them before the LORD at the entrance to the Tent of Meeting. 8He is to cast lots for the two goats—one lot for the LORD and the other for the scapegoat.[g] 9Aaron shall bring the goat whose lot falls to the LORD and sacrifice it for a sin offering. 10But the goat chosen by lot as the scapegoat shall be presented alive before the LORD to be used for making atonement by sending it into the desert as a scapegoat.

11"Aaron shall bring the bull for his own sin offering to make atonement for himself and his household, and he is to slaughter the bull for his own sin offering. 12He is to take a censer full of burning coals from the altar before the LORD and two handfuls of finely ground fragrant incense and take them behind the curtain. 13He is to put the incense on the fire before the LORD, and the smoke of the incense will conceal the atonement cover above the Testimony, so that he will not die. 14He is to take some of the bull's blood and with his finger sprinkle it on the front of the atonement cover; then he shall sprinkle some of it with his finger seven times before the atonement cover.

15"He shall then slaughter the goat for the sin offering for the people and take its blood behind the curtain and do

g8 That is, the goat of removal; Hebrew *azazel;* also in verses 10 and 26

וְעָשָׂה אֶת־ דָּמוֹ כַּאֲשֶׁר עָשָׂה לְדַם הַפָּר
the-bull with-blood-of he-did just-as blood-of-him with and-he-must-do

וְהִזָּה אֹתוֹ עַל־ הַכַּפֹּרֶת וְלִפְנֵי הַכַּפֹּרֶת׃
the-cover and-in-front-of the-atonement-cover on him and-he-shall-sprinkle

וְכִפֶּר עַל־ הַקֹּדֶשׁ מִטֻּמְאֹת בְּנֵי
sons-of for-uncleannesses-of the-Most-Holy-Place for so-he-will-atone (16)

יִשְׂרָאֵל וּמִפִּשְׁעֵיהֶם לְכָל־ חַטֹּאתָם וְכֵן יַעֲשֶׂה
he-must-do and-same sins-of-them for-all-of and-for-rebellions-of-them Israel

לְאֹהֶל מוֹעֵד הַשֹּׁכֵן אִתָּם בְּתוֹךְ טֻמְאֹתָם׃
uncleannesses-of-them in-midst-of among-them the-staying Meeting for-Tent-of

וְכָל־ אָדָם לֹא־ יִהְיֶה ׀ בְּאֹהֶל מוֹעֵד בְּבֹאוֹ
when-to-go-in-him Meeting in-Tent-of he-may-be not person and-any-of (17)

לְכַפֵּר בַּקֹּדֶשׁ עַד־ צֵאתוֹ וְכִפֶּר
and-he-atoned to-come-out-him until in-the-Most-Holy-Place to-atone

בַּעֲדוֹ וּבְעַד בֵּיתוֹ וּבְעַד כָּל־ קְהַל יִשְׂרָאֵל׃
Israel community-of whole-of and-for household-of-him and-for for-himself

וְיָצָא אֶל־ הַמִּזְבֵּחַ אֲשֶׁר לִפְנֵי־ יְהוָה וְכִפֶּר
and-he-shall-atone Yahweh before that the-altar to then-he-shall-come-out (18)

עָלָיו וְלָקַח מִדַּם הַפָּר וּמִדַּם הַשָּׂעִיר
the-goat and-from-blood-of the-bull from-blood-of and-he-shall-take for-him

וְנָתַן עַל־ קַרְנוֹת הַמִּזְבֵּחַ סָבִיב׃ וְהִזָּה
and-he-shall-sprinkle (19) around the-altar horns-of on and-he-shall-put

עָלָיו מִן־ הַדָּם בְּאֶצְבָּעוֹ שֶׁבַע פְּעָמִים וְטִהֲרוֹ
and-he-shall-cleanse-him times seven with-finger-of-him the-blood from on-him

וְקִדְּשׁוֹ מִטֻּמְאֹת בְּנֵי יִשְׂרָאֵל׃
Israel sons-of from-uncleannesses-of and-he-shall-consecrate-him

וְכִלָּה מִכַּפֵּר אֶת־ הַקֹּדֶשׁ וְאֶת־ אֹהֶל
Tent-of and the-Most-Holy-Place *** from-to-atone when-he-finishes (20)

מוֹעֵד וְאֶת־ הַמִּזְבֵּחַ וְהִקְרִיב אֶת־ הַשָּׂעִיר הֶחָי׃
the-live the-goat *** then-he-shall-bring the-altar and Meeting

וְסָמַךְ אַהֲרֹן אֶת־ שְׁתֵּי יָדָו עַל רֹאשׁ הַשָּׂעִיר
the-goat head-of on hands-of-him both-of *** Aaron and-he-shall-lay (21)

הַחַי וְהִתְוַדָּה עָלָיו אֶת־ כָּל־ עֲוֹנֹת בְּנֵי
sons-of wickednesses-of all-of *** over-him and-he-shall-confess the-live

יִשְׂרָאֵל וְאֶת־ כָּל־ פִּשְׁעֵיהֶם לְכָל־ חַטֹּאתָם וְנָתַן
and-he-shall-put sins-of-them for-all-of rebellions-of-them all-of and Israel

אֹתָם עַל־ רֹאשׁ הַשָּׂעִיר וְשִׁלַּח בְּיַד־ אִישׁ עִתִּי
appointed man in-care-of then-he-shall-send the-goat head-of on them

°21 ק ידיו

with it as he did with the
bull's blood: He shall sprinkle
it on the atonement cover and
in front of it. 16 In this way he
will make atonement for the
Most Holy Place because of the
uncleanness and rebellion of
the Israelites, whatever their
sins have been. He is to do the
same for the Tent of Meeting,
which is among them in the
midst of their uncleanness.
17 No one is to be in the Tent of
Meeting from the time Aaron
goes in to make atonement in
the Most Holy Place until he
comes out, having made
atonement for himself, his
household and the whole
community of Israel.
18 "Then he shall come out to
the altar that is before the
LORD and make atonement for
it. He shall take some of the
bull's blood and some of the
goat's blood and put it on all
the horns of the altar. 19 He
shall sprinkle some of the
blood on it with his finger sev-
en times to cleanse it and to
consecrate it from the uncleanness of the Israelites.
20 "When Aaron has finished
making atonement for the
Most Holy Place, the Tent of
Meeting and the altar, he shall
bring forward the live goat.
21 He is to lay both hands on
the head of the live goat and
confess over it all the wickedness and rebellion of the Israelites—all their sins—and put
them on the goat's head. He
shall send the goat away into
the desert in the care of a man
appointed for the task. 22 The

הַמִּדְבָּֽרָה׃ וְנָשָׂא הַשָּׂעִיר עָלָיו אֶת־ כָּל־
all-of *** on-him the-goat and-he-will-carry (22) into-the-desert

עֲוֺנֹתָם אֶל־ אֶרֶץ גְּזֵרָה וְשִׁלַּח אֶת־ הַשָּׂעִיר בַּמִּדְבָּֽר׃
in-the-desert the-goat *** and-he-shall-release solitary place to sins-of-them

וּבָא אַהֲרֹן אֶל־ אֹהֶל מוֹעֵד וּפָשַׁט אֶת־
*** and-he-must-take-off Meeting Tent-of into Aaron then-he-must-go (23)

בִּגְדֵי הַבָּד אֲשֶׁר לָבַשׁ בְּבֹאוֹ אֶל־ הַקֹּדֶשׁ
the-Most-Holy-Place into before-to-go-him he-put-on that the-linen garments-of

וְהִנִּיחָם שָׁם׃ וְרָחַץ אֶת־ בְּשָׂרוֹ
body-of-him *** and-he-shall-bathe (24) there and-he-must-leave-them

בַמַּיִם בְּמָקוֹם קָדוֹשׁ וְלָבַשׁ אֶת־ בְּגָדָיו
garments-of-him *** then-he-shall-put-on holy in-place with-the-waters

וְיָצָא וְעָשָׂה אֶת־ עֹלָתוֹ
burnt-offering-of-him *** and-he-shall-sacrifice and-he-shall-come-out

וְאֶת־ עֹלַת הָעָם וְכִפֶּר בַּעֲדוֹ וּבְעַד
and-for for-him and-he-shall-atone the-people burnt-offering-of and

הָעָם׃ וְאֵת חֵלֶב הַחַטָּאת יַקְטִיר הַמִּזְבֵּֽחָה׃
on-the-altar he-shall-burn the-sin-offering fat-of also (25) the-people

וְהַמְשַׁלֵּחַ אֶת־ הַשָּׂעִיר לַעֲזָאזֵל יְכַבֵּס
he-must-wash as-the-scapegoat the-goat *** and-the-one-releasing (26)

בְּגָדָיו וְרָחַץ אֶת־ בְּשָׂרוֹ בַּמָּיִם וְאַחֲרֵי־
and-after with-the-waters body-of-him *** and-he-must-bathe clothes-of-him

כֵן יָבוֹא אֶל־ הַמַּחֲנֶה׃ וְאֵת פַּר הַחַטָּאת וְאֵת ׀ שְׂעִיר
goat-of and the-sin-offering bull-of and (27) the-camp into he-may-come this

הַחַטָּאת אֲשֶׁר הוּבָא אֶת־ דָּמָם לְכַפֵּר
to-atone blood-of-them *** he-was-brought that the-sin-offering

בַּקֹּדֶשׁ יוֹצִיא אֶל־ מִחוּץ לַמַּחֲנֶה
of-the-camp outside to he-must-take into-the-Most-Holy-Place

וְשָׂרְפוּ בָאֵשׁ אֶת־ עֹרֹתָם וְאֶת־ בְּשָׂרָם וְאֶת־
and flesh-of-them and hides-of-them *** in-the-fire and-they-must-burn

פִּרְשָׁם׃ וְהַשֹּׂרֵף אֹתָם יְכַבֵּס בְּגָדָיו
clothes-of-him he-must-wash them and-the-one-burning (28) offal-of-them

וְרָחַץ אֶת־ בְּשָׂרוֹ בַּמָּיִם וְאַחֲרֵי־ כֵן יָבוֹא
he-may-come this and-after with-the-waters body-of-him *** and-he-must-bathe

אֶל־ הַמַּחֲנֶה׃ וְהָיְתָה לָכֶם לְחֻקַּת עוֹלָם
lasting as-ordinance-of for-you and-he-shall-be (29) the-camp into

בַּחֹדֶשׁ הַשְּׁבִיעִי בֶּעָשׂוֹר לַחֹדֶשׁ תְּעַנּוּ אֶת־
*** you-must-deny of-the-month on-the-tenth the-seventh in-the-month

goat will carry on itself all their sins to a solitary place; and the man shall release it in the desert.

23"Then Aaron is to go into the Tent of Meeting and take off the linen garments he put on before he entered the Most Holy Place, and he is to leave them there. 24He shall bathe himself with water in a holy place and put on his regular garments. Then he shall come out and sacrifice the burnt offering for himself and the burnt offering for the people, to make atonement for himself and for the people. 25He shall also burn the fat of the sin offering on the altar.

26"The man who releases the goat as a scapegoat must wash his clothes and bathe himself with water; afterward he may come into the camp. 27The bull and the goat for the sin offerings, whose blood was brought into the Most Holy Place to make atonement, must be taken outside the camp; their hides, flesh and offal are to be burned up. 28The man who burns them must wash his clothes and bathe himself with water; afterward he may come into the camp.

29"This is to be a lasting ordinance for you: On the tenth day of the seventh month you must deny yourselves[h] and

[h]29 Or *must fast;* also in verse 31

נַפְשֹׁתֵיכֶם וְכָל־ מְלָאכָה לֹא תַעֲשׂוּ הָאֶזְרָח וְהַגֵּר
or-the-alien the-native you-may-do not work and-any-of selves-of-you

הַגָּר בְּתוֹכְכֶם׃ כִּי־ בַיּוֹם הַזֶּה יְכַפֵּר עֲלֵיכֶם
for-you he-will-atone the-this on-the-day for (30) among-you the-one-living

לְטַהֵר אֶתְכֶם מִכֹּל חַטֹּאתֵיכֶם לִפְנֵי יְהוָה תִּטְהָרוּ׃
you-will-be-clean Yahweh before sins-of-you from-all-of you to-cleanse

שַׁבַּת שַׁבָּתוֹן הִיא לָכֶם וְעִנִּיתֶם אֶת־ נַפְשֹׁתֵיכֶם
selves-of-you *** and-you-must-deny to-you she rest sabbath-of (31)

חֻקַּת עוֹלָם׃ וְכִפֶּר הַכֹּהֵן אֲשֶׁר־ יִמְשַׁח אֹתוֹ
him he-anointed whom the-priest and-he-must-atone (32) lasting ordinance-of

וַאֲשֶׁר יְמַלֵּא אֶת־ יָדוֹ לְכַהֵן תַּחַת אָבִיו
father-of-him after to-be-priest hand-of-him *** he-ordained and-whom

וְלָבַשׁ אֶת־ בִּגְדֵי הַבָּד בִּגְדֵי הַקֹּדֶשׁ׃
the-sacred garments-of the-linen garments-of *** and-he-must-put-on

וְכִפֶּר אֶת־ מִקְדַּשׁ הַקֹּדֶשׁ וְאֶת־ אֹהֶל
Tent-of and the-Holy-Place Most-Holy-of *** and-he-must-atone (33)

מוֹעֵד וְאֶת־ הַמִּזְבֵּחַ יְכַפֵּר וְעַל הַכֹּהֲנִים וְעַל־ כָּל־
all-of and-for the-priests and-for he-must-atone the-altar and Meeting

עַם הַקָּהָל יְכַפֵּר׃ וְהָיְתָה־ זֹּאת לָכֶם
for-you this and-she-will-be (34) he-must-atone the-community people-of

לְחֻקַּת עוֹלָם לְכַפֵּר עַל־ בְּנֵי יִשְׂרָאֵל מִכָּל־ חַטֹּאתָם
sins-of-them for-all-of Israel sons-of for to-atone lasting for-ordinance-of

אַחַת בַּשָּׁנָה וַיַּעַשׂ כַּאֲשֶׁר צִוָּה יְהוָה אֶת־ מֹשֶׁה׃
Moses *** Yahweh he-commanded just-as and-he-did in-the-year once

וַיְדַבֵּר יְהוָה אֶל־ מֹשֶׁה לֵּאמֹר׃ דַּבֵּר אֶל־אַהֲרֹן וְאֶל־
and-to Aaron to speak! (2) to-say Moses to Yahweh and-he-spoke (17:1)

בָּנָיו וְאֶל כָּל־ בְּנֵי יִשְׂרָאֵל וְאָמַרְתָּ אֲלֵיהֶם זֶה הַדָּבָר
the-thing this to-them and-you-say Israel sons-of all-of and-to sons-of-him

אֲשֶׁר־ צִוָּה יְהוָה לֵאמֹר׃ אִישׁ אִישׁ מִבֵּית יִשְׂרָאֵל אֲשֶׁר
who Israel from-house-of any man (3) to-say Yahweh he-commanded that

יִשְׁחַט שׁוֹר אוֹ־ כֶשֶׂב אוֹ־ עֵז בַּמַּחֲנֶה אוֹ אֲשֶׁר יִשְׁחַט מִחוּץ
outside he-sacrifices who or in-the-camp goat or lamb or cow he-sacrifices

לַמַּחֲנֶה׃ וְאֶל־ פֶּתַח אֹהֶל מוֹעֵד לֹא הֱבִיאוֹ
he-brings-him not Meeting Tent-of entrance-of and-to (4) of-the-camp

לְהַקְרִיב קָרְבָּן לַיהוָה לִפְנֵי מִשְׁכַּן יְהוָה דָּם
bloodshed Yahweh tabernacle-of in-front-of to-Yahweh offering to-present

יֵחָשֵׁב לָאִישׁ הַהוּא דָּם שָׁפָךְ וְנִכְרַת
and-he-must-be-cut-off he-shed blood the-that to-the-man he-is-considered

not do any work—whether native-born or an alien living among you— 30because on this day atonement will be made for you, to cleanse you. Then, before the LORD, you will be clean from all your sins. 31It is a sabbath of rest, and you must deny yourselves; it is a lasting ordinance. 32The priest who is anointed and ordained to succeed his father as high priest is to make atonement. He is to put on the sacred linen garments 33and make atonement for the Most Holy Place, for the Tent of Meeting and the altar, and for the priests and all the people of the community.

34"This is to be a lasting ordinance for you: Atonement is to be made once a year for all the sins of the Israelites."

And it was done, as the LORD commanded Moses.

## *Eating Blood Forbidden*

17 The LORD said to Moses, 2"Speak to Aaron and his sons and to all the Israelites and say to them: 'This is what the LORD has commanded: 3Any Israelite who sacrifices a cow,[i] a lamb or a goat in the camp or outside of it 4instead of bringing it to the entrance to the Tent of Meeting to present it as an offering to the LORD in front of the tabernacle of the LORD—that man shall be considered guilty of bloodshed; he has shed blood and must be cut off

[i]3 The Hebrew word can include both male and female.

הָאִישׁ הַהוּא מִקֶּרֶב עַמּוֹ׃ לְמַעַן אֲשֶׁר יָבִיאוּ
they-will-bring *** so-that (5) people-of-him from-among the-that the-man

בְּנֵי יִשְׂרָאֵל אֶת־ זִבְחֵיהֶם אֲשֶׁר הֵם זֹבְחִים עַל־ פְּנֵי
face-of in ones-making they that sacrifices-of-them *** Israel sons-of

הַשָּׂדֶה וֶהֱבִיאֻם לַיהוָה אֶל־ פֶּתַח אֹהֶל מוֹעֵד
Meeting Tent-of entrance-of at to-Yahweh now-they-must-bring-them the-field

אֶל־ הַכֹּהֵן וְזָבְחוּ זִבְחֵי שְׁלָמִים לַיהוָה
to-Yahweh fellowships offerings-of and-they-must-sacrifice the-priest to

אוֹתָם׃ וְזָרַק הַכֹּהֵן אֶת־ הַדָּם עַל־ מִזְבַּח
altar-of against the-blood *** the-priest and-he-must-sprinkle (6) them

יְהוָה פֶּתַח אֹהֶל מוֹעֵד וְהִקְטִיר הַחֵלֶב לְרֵיחַ
as-aroma-of the-fat and-he-must-burn Meeting Tent-of entrance-of Yahweh

נִיחֹחַ לַיהוָה׃ וְלֹא־ יִזְבְּחוּ עוֹד אֶת־
*** any-longer they-must-offer but-not (7) to-Yahweh pleasant

זִבְחֵיהֶם לַשְּׂעִירִם אֲשֶׁר הֵם זֹנִים אַחֲרֵיהֶם
to-them ones-prostituting they whom to-the-goat-idols sacrifices-of-them

חֻקַּת עוֹלָם תִּהְיֶה־ זֹּאת לָהֶם לְדֹרֹתָם׃
for-generations-of-them for-them this she-will-be lasting ordinance-of

וַאֲלֵהֶם תֹּאמַר אִישׁ אִישׁ מִבֵּית יִשְׂרָאֵל וּמִן־ הַגֵּר אֲשֶׁר־
who the-alien or-from Israel from-house-of any man you-say and-to-them (8)

יָגוּר בְּתוֹכָם אֲשֶׁר־ יַעֲלֶה עֹלָה אוֹ־ זָבַח׃ וְאֶל־
and-to (9) sacrifice or burnt-offering he-offers who among-them he-lives

פֶּתַח אֹהֶל מוֹעֵד לֹא יְבִיאֶנּוּ לַעֲשׂוֹת אֹתוֹ לַיהוָה
to-Yahweh him to-sacrifice he-brings-him not Meeting Tent-of entrance-of

וְנִכְרַת הָאִישׁ הַהוּא מֵעַמָּיו׃ וְאִישׁ אִישׁ
any and-man (10) from-people-of-him the-that the-man then-he-must-be-cut-off

מִבֵּית יִשְׂרָאֵל וּמִן־ הַגֵּר הַגָּר בְּתוֹכָם אֲשֶׁר יֹאכַל
he-eats who among-them the-one-living the-alien or-from Israel from-house-of

כָּל־ דָּם וְנָתַתִּי פָנַי בַּנֶּפֶשׁ הָאֹכֶלֶת
the-one-eating against-the-person faces-of-me then-I-will-set blood any-of

אֶת־ הַדָּם וְהִכְרַתִּי אֹתָהּ מִקֶּרֶב עַמָּהּ׃ כִּי
for (11) people-of-her from-among her and-I-will-cut-off the-blood ***

נֶפֶשׁ הַבָּשָׂר בַּדָּם הִוא וַאֲנִי נְתַתִּיו לָכֶם עַל־ הַמִּזְבֵּחַ
the-altar on to-you I-gave-him and-I she in-the-blood the-creature life-of

לְכַפֵּר עַל־ נַפְשֹׁתֵיכֶם כִּי־ הַדָּם הוּא בַּנֶּפֶשׁ יְכַפֵּר׃ עַל־
for (12) he-atones for-the-life he the-blood for selves-of-you for to-atone

כֵּן אָמַרְתִּי לִבְנֵי יִשְׂרָאֵל כָּל־ נֶפֶשׁ מִכֶּם לֹא־ תֹאכַל דָּם
blood she-may-eat not from-you person any-of Israel to-sons-of I-say this

from his people. 5This is so the Israelites will bring to the LORD the sacrifices they are now making in the open fields. They must bring them to the priest, that is, to the LORD, at the entrance to the Tent of Meeting and sacrifice them as fellowship offerings.[j]
6The priest is to sprinkle the blood against the altar of the LORD at the entrance to the Tent of Meeting and burn the fat as an aroma pleasing to the LORD. 7They must no longer offer any of their sacrifices to the goat idols[k] to whom they prostitute themselves. This is to be a lasting ordinance for them and for the generations to come.'
8"Say to them: 'Any Israelite or any alien living among them who offers a burnt offering or sacrifice 9and does not bring it to the entrance to the Tent of Meeting to sacrifice it to the LORD—that man must be cut off from his people.
10" 'Any Israelite or any alien living among them who eats any blood—I will set my face against that person who eats blood and will cut him off from his people. 11For the life of a creature is in the blood, and I have given it to you to make atonement for yourselves on the altar; it is the blood that makes atonement for one's life. 12Therefore I say to the Israelites, "None of you may eat blood, nor may an

j5 Traditionally *peace offerings*
k7 Or *demons*

וְהַגֵּר הַגָּר בְּתוֹכְכֶם לֹא־יֹאכַל דָּם׃ וְאִישׁ אִישׁ
any and-man (13) blood he-may-eat not among-you the-one-living nor-the-alien

מִבְּנֵי יִשְׂרָאֵל וּמִן־הַגֵּר הַגָּר בְּתוֹכָם אֲשֶׁר יָצוּד
he-hunts who among-them the-one-living the-alien or-from Israel from-sons-of

צֵיד חַיָּה אוֹ־עוֹף אֲשֶׁר יֵאָכֵל וְשָׁפַךְ אֶת־דָּמוֹ
blood-of-him *** then-he-must-drain he-may-be-eaten that bird or wild animal

וְכִסָּהוּ בֶּעָפָר׃ כִּי־נֶפֶשׁ כָּל־בָּשָׂר
creature every-of life-of for (14) with-the-earth and-he-must-cover-him

דָּמוֹ בְנַפְשׁוֹ הוּא וָאֹמַר לִבְנֵי יִשְׂרָאֵל דַּם כָּל־
any-of blood-of Israel to-sons-of so-I-said he in-life-of-him blood-of-him

בָּשָׂר לֹא תֹאכֵלוּ כִּי נֶפֶשׁ כָּל־בָּשָׂר דָּמוֹ הִוא
she blood-of-him creature every-of life-of for you-must-eat not creature

כָּל־אֹכְלָיו יִכָּרֵת׃ וְכָל־נֶפֶשׁ אֲשֶׁר תֹּאכַל
she-eats who person and-any-of (15) he-must-be-cut-off ones-eating-him all-of

נְבֵלָה וּטְרֵפָה בָּאֶזְרָח וּבַגֵּר וְכִבֶּס
then-he-must-wash or-the-alien whether-the-native or-torn-animal carcass

בְּגָדָיו וְרָחַץ בַּמַּיִם וְטָמֵא עַד־
till and-he-will-be-unclean with-the-waters and-he-must-bathe clothes-of-him

הָעֶרֶב וְטָהֵר׃ וְאִם לֹא יְכַבֵּס וּבְשָׂרוֹ
and-body-of-him he-washes not but-if (16) then-he-will-be-clean the-evening

לֹא יִרְחָץ וְנָשָׂא עֲוֹנוֹ׃ וַיְדַבֵּר
and-he-spoke (18:1) responsibility-of-him then-he-will-bear he-bathes not

יְהוָה אֶל־מֹשֶׁה לֵּאמֹר׃ דַּבֵּר אֶל־בְּנֵי יִשְׂרָאֵל וְאָמַרְתָּ אֲלֵהֶם אֲנִי
I to-them and-you-say Israel sons-of to speak! (2) to-say Moses to Yahweh

יְהוָה אֱלֹהֵיכֶם׃ כְּמַעֲשֵׂה אֶרֶץ־מִצְרַיִם אֲשֶׁר יְשַׁבְתֶּם־בָּהּ לֹא
not in-her you-lived where Egypt land-of as-action-of (3) God-of-you Yahweh

תַעֲשׂוּ וּכְמַעֲשֵׂה אֶרֶץ־כְּנַעַן אֲשֶׁר אֲנִי מֵבִיא אֶתְכֶם שָׁמָּה
to-there you bringing I where Canaan land-of and-as-action-of you-must-do

לֹא תַעֲשׂוּ וּבְחֻקֹּתֵיהֶם לֹא תֵלֵכוּ׃ אֶת־
*** (4) you-must-follow not and-to-practices-of-them you-must-do not

מִשְׁפָּטַי תַּעֲשׂוּ וְאֶת־חֻקֹּתַי תִּשְׁמְרוּ לָלֶכֶת
to-follow you-must-be-careful decrees-of-me and you-must-obey laws-of-me

בָּהֶם אֲנִי יְהוָה אֱלֹהֵיכֶם׃ וּשְׁמַרְתֶּם אֶת־חֻקֹּתַי וְאֶת־
and decrees-of-me *** now-you-keep (5) God-of-you Yahweh I after-them

מִשְׁפָּטַי אֲשֶׁר יַעֲשֶׂה אֹתָם הָאָדָם וָחַי בָּהֶם אֲנִי יְהוָה׃
Yahweh I by-them also-he-will-live the-man them he-obeys who laws-of-me

אִישׁ אִישׁ אֶל־כָּל־שְׁאֵר בְּשָׂרוֹ לֹא תִקְרְבוּ לְגַלּוֹת
to-expose you-may-approach not body-of-him relative-of any-of to any man (6)

alien living among you eat blood."

13" 'Any Israelite or any alien living among you who hunts any animal or bird that may be eaten must drain out the blood and cover it with earth, 14because the life of every creature is its blood. That is why I have said to the Israelites, "You must not eat the blood of any creature, because the life of every creature is its blood; anyone who eats it must be cut off."

15" 'Anyone, whether native-born or alien, who eats anything found dead or torn by wild animals must wash his clothes and bathe with water, and he will be unclean till evening; then he will be clean. 16But if he does not wash his clothes and bathe himself, he will be held responsible.' "

*Unlawful Sexual Relations*

18 The LORD said to Moses, 2"Speak to the Israelites and say to them: 'I am the LORD your God. 3You must not do as they do in Egypt, where you used to live, and you must not do as they do in the land of Canaan, where I am bringing you. Do not follow their practices. 4You must obey my laws and be careful to follow my decrees. I am the LORD your God. 5Keep my decrees and laws, for the man who obeys them will live by them. I am the LORD.

6" 'No one is to approach any close relative to have sexual relations. I am the LORD.

עֶרְוָה אֲנִי יְהוָה׃ עֶרְוַת אָבִיךָ וְעֶרְוַת
or-nakedness-of father-of-you nakedness-of (7) Yahweh I nakedness

אִמְּךָ לֹא תְגַלֵּה אִמְּךָ הִוא לֹא תְגַלֶּה עֶרְוָתָהּ׃
nakedness-of-her you-expose not she mother-of-you you-expose not mother-of-you

עֶרְוַת אֵשֶׁת־ אָבִיךָ לֹא תְגַלֵּה עֶרְוַת
nakedness-of you-expose not father-of-you wife-of nakedness-of (8)

אָבִיךָ הִוא׃ עֶרְוַת אֲחוֹתְךָ בַת־ אָבִיךָ
father-of-you daughter-of sister-of-you nakedness-of (9) she father-of-you

אוֹ בַת־ אִמֶּךָ מוֹלֶדֶת בַּיִת אוֹ מוֹלֶדֶת חוּץ לֹא
not elsewhere born-of or home born-of mother-of-you daughter-of or

תְגַלֶּה עֶרְוָתָן׃ עֶרְוַת בַּת־ בִּנְךָ אוֹ
or son-of-you daughter-of nakedness-of (10) nakedness-of-them you-expose

בַת־ בִּתְּךָ לֹא תְגַלֶּה עֶרְוָתָן כִּי
for nakedness-of-them you-expose not daughter-of-you daughter-of

עֶרְוָתְךָ הֵנָּה׃ עֶרְוַת בַּת־ אֵשֶׁת אָבִיךָ
father-of-you wife-of daughter-of nakedness-of (11) they nakedness-of-you

מוֹלֶדֶת אָבִיךָ אֲחוֹתְךָ הִוא לֹא תְגַלֶּה עֶרְוָתָהּ׃
nakedness-of-her you-expose not she sister-of-you father-of-you born-of

עֶרְוַת אֲחוֹת־ אָבִיךָ לֹא תְגַלֵּה שְׁאֵר
close-relative-of you-expose not father-of-you sister-of nakedness-of (12)

אָבִיךָ הִוא׃ עֶרְוַת אֲחוֹת־ אִמְּךָ לֹא תְגַלֵּה
you-expose not mother-of-you sister-of nakedness-of (13) she father-of-you

כִּי־ שְׁאֵר אִמְּךָ הִוא׃ עֶרְוַת אֲחִי־
brother-of nakedness-of (14) she mother-of-you close-relative-of for

אָבִיךָ לֹא תְגַלֵּה אֶל־ אִשְׁתּוֹ לֹא תִקְרָב דֹּדָתְךָ הִוא׃
she aunt-of-you you-approach not wife-of-him by you-expose not father-of-you

עֶרְוַת כַּלָּתְךָ לֹא תְגַלֵּה אֵשֶׁת בִּנְךָ
son-of-you wife-of you-expose not daughter-in-law-of-you nakedness-of (15)

הִוא לֹא תְגַלֶּה עֶרְוָתָהּ׃ עֶרְוַת אֵשֶׁת־ אָחִיךָ
brother-of-you wife-of nakedness-of (16) nakedness-of-her you-expose not she

לֹא תְגַלֵּה עֶרְוַת אָחִיךָ הִוא׃ עֶרְוַת אִשָּׁה
woman nakedness-of (17) she brother-of-you nakedness-of you-expose not

וּבִתָּהּ לֹא תְגַלֵּה אֶת־ בַּת־ בְּנָהּ וְאֶת־ בַּת־
daughter-of or son-of-her daughter-of *** you-expose not and-daughter-of-her

בִּתָּהּ לֹא תִקַּח לְגַלּוֹת עֶרְוָתָהּ שַׁאֲרָה הֵנָּה
they close-relative nakedness-of-her to-expose you-take not daughter-of-her

זִמָּה הִוא וְאִשָּׁה אֶל־ אֲחֹתָהּ לֹא תִקָּח לִצְרֹר
to-be-rival you-marry not sister-of-her with and-woman (18) that wickedness

[7]"'Do not dishonor your father by having sexual relations with your mother. She is your mother; do not have relations with her.

[8]"'Do not have sexual relations with your father's wife; that would dishonor your father.

[9]"'Do not have sexual relations with your sister, either your father's daughter or your mother's daughter, whether she was born in the same home or elsewhere.

[10]"'Do not have sexual relations with your son's daughter or your daughter's daughter; that would dishonor you.

[11]"'Do not have sexual relations with the daughter of your father's wife, born to your father; she is your sister.

[12]"'Do not have sexual relations with your father's sister; she is your father's close relative.

[13]"'Do not have sexual relations with your mother's sister, because she is your mother's close relative.

[14]"'Do not dishonor your father's brother by approaching his wife to have sexual relations; she is your aunt.

[15]"'Do not have sexual relations with your daughter-in-law. She is your son's wife; do not have relations with her.

[16]"'Do not have sexual relations with your brother's wife; that would dishonor your brother.

[17]"'Do not have sexual relations with both a woman and her daughter. Do not have sexual relations with either her son's daughter or her daughter's daughter; they are her close relatives. That is wickedness.

[18]"'Do not take your wife's sister as a rival wife and have

לְגַלּוֹת עֶרְוָתָהּ עָלֶיהָ בְּחַיֶּיהָ׃ וְאֶל־אִשָּׁה
woman and-to (19) while-alive-her with-her nakedness-of-her to-expose

בְּנִדַּת טֻמְאָתָהּ לֹא תִקְרַב לְגַלּוֹת עֶרְוָתָהּ׃
nakedness-of-her to-expose you-approach not uncleanness-of-her in-period-of

וְאֶל־אֵשֶׁת עֲמִיתְךָ לֹא־תִתֵּן שְׁכָבְתְּךָ לְזָרַע
of-semen emission-of-you you-give not neighbor-of-you wife-of and-to (20)

לְטָמְאָה־בָהּ׃ וּמִזַּרְעֲךָ לֹא־תִתֵּן לְהַעֲבִיר
to-sacrifice you-give not and-from-children-of-you (21) with-her to-defile

לַמֹּלֶךְ וְלֹא תְחַלֵּל אֶת־שֵׁם אֱלֹהֶיךָ אֲנִי יְהוָה׃
Yahweh I God-of-you name-of *** you-must-profane for-not to-the-Molech

וְאֶת־זָכָר לֹא תִשְׁכַּב מִשְׁכְּבֵי אִשָּׁה תּוֹעֵבָה הִוא׃
that detestable woman ones-who-lie-of you-lie-with not man and (22)

וּבְכָל־בְּהֵמָה לֹא־תִתֵּן שְׁכָבְתְּךָ לְטָמְאָה־בָהּ
with-her to-defile emission-of-you you-give not animal and-with-any-of (23)

וְאִשָּׁה לֹא־תַעֲמֹד לִפְנֵי בְהֵמָה לְרִבְעָהּ תֶּבֶל
perversion to-have-relation-with-her animal to she-must-present not and-woman

הוּא׃ אַל־תִּטַּמְּאוּ בְּכָל־אֵלֶּה כִּי בְכָל־אֵלֶּה
these in-all-of for these in-any-of you-defile-yourselves not (24) that

נִטְמְאוּ הַגּוֹיִם אֲשֶׁר־אֲנִי מְשַׁלֵּחַ מִפְּנֵיכֶם׃
from-before-you driving-you I that the-nations they-became-defiled

וַתִּטְמָא הָאָרֶץ וָאֶפְקֹד עֲוֺנָהּ עָלֶיהָ
on-her sin-of-her so-I-punished the-land even-she-was-defiled (25)

וַתָּקִא הָאָרֶץ אֶת־יֹשְׁבֶיהָ׃ וּשְׁמַרְתֶּם אַתֶּם
you but-you-keep (26) ones-inhabiting-her *** the-land and-she-vomited-out

אֶת־חֻקֹּתַי וְאֶת־מִשְׁפָּטַי וְלֹא תַעֲשׂוּ מִכֹּל הַתּוֹעֵבֹת
the-abominations from-any-of you-do and-not laws-of-me and decrees-of-me ***

הָאֵלֶּה הָאֶזְרָח וְהַגֵּר הַגָּר בְּתוֹכְכֶם׃ כִּי אֶת־
*** for (27) among-you the-one-living or-the-alien the-native the-these

כָּל־הַתּוֹעֵבֹת הָאֵל עָשׂוּ אַנְשֵׁי־הָאָרֶץ אֲשֶׁר לִפְנֵיכֶם
before-you who the-land people-of they-did the-these the-abominations all-of

וַתִּטְמָא הָאָרֶץ׃ וְלֹא־תָקִיא הָאָרֶץ אֶתְכֶם
you the-land she-vomit-out so-not (28) the-land and-she-became-defiled

בְּטַמַּאֲכֶם אֹתָהּ כַּאֲשֶׁר קָאָה אֶת־הַגּוֹי אֲשֶׁר לִפְנֵיכֶם׃
before-you that the-nation *** she-vomited-out just-as her when-to-defile-you

כִּי כָּל־אֲשֶׁר יַעֲשֶׂה מִכֹּל הַתּוֹעֵבוֹת הָאֵלֶּה
the-these the-abominations from-any-of he-does who everyone indeed (29)

וְנִכְרְתוּ הַנְּפָשׁוֹת הָעֹשֹׂת מִקֶּרֶב עַמָּם׃
people-of-them from-among the-ones-doing the-persons then-they-must-be-cut-off

sexual relations with her while your wife is living.

19 " 'Do not approach a woman to have sexual relations during the uncleanness of her monthly period.

20 " 'Do not have intercourse with your neighbor's wife and defile yourself with her.

21 " 'Do not give any of your children to be sacrificed[l] to Molech, for you must not profane the name of your God. I am the LORD.

22 " 'Do not lie with a man as one lies with a woman; that is detestable.

23 " 'Do not have sexual relations with an animal and defile yourself with it. A woman must not present herself to an animal to have sexual relations with it; that is a perversion.

24 " 'Do not defile yourselves in any of these ways, because this is how the nations that I am going to drive out before you became defiled. 25 Even the land was defiled; so I punished it for its sin, and the land vomited out its inhabitants. 26 But you must keep my decrees and my laws. The native-born and the aliens living among you must not do any of these detestable things, 27 for all these things were done by the people who lived in the land before you, and the land became defiled. 28 And if you defile the land, it will vomit you out as it vomited out the nations that were before you.

29 " 'Everyone who does any of these detestable things—such persons must be cut off from their people. 30 Keep my

[l]21 Or *to be passed through* ⌊*the fire*⌋

וּשְׁמַרְתֶּם אֶת־ מִשְׁמַרְתִּי לְבִלְתִּי עֲשׂוֹת מֵחֻקּוֹת
from-customs-of to-follow not requirement-of-me *** so-you-keep (30)

הַתּוֹעֵבֹת אֲשֶׁר נַעֲשׂוּ לִפְנֵיכֶם וְלֹא
and-not before-you they-were-practiced that the-detestable-ones

תִטַּמְּאוּ בָּהֶם אֲנִי יְהוָה אֱלֹהֵיכֶם׃ וַיְדַבֵּר
and-he-spoke (19:1) God-of-you Yahweh I with-them you-defile-yourselves

יְהוָה אֶל־ מֹשֶׁה לֵּאמֹר דַּבֵּר אֶל־ כָּל־ עֲדַת בְּנֵי־ יִשְׂרָאֵל
Israel sons-of assembly-of entire-of to speak! (2) to-say Moses to Yahweh

וְאָמַרְתָּ אֲלֵהֶם קְדֹשִׁים תִּהְיוּ כִּי קָדוֹשׁ אֲנִי יְהוָה אֱלֹהֵיכֶם׃
God-of-you Yahweh I holy for you-must-be holy-ones to-them and-you-say

אִישׁ אִמּוֹ וְאָבִיו תִּירָאוּ וְאֶת־ שַׁבְּתֹתַי
Sabbaths-of-me and you-must-respect and-father-of-him mother-of-him each (3)

תִּשְׁמֹרוּ אֲנִי יְהוָה אֱלֹהֵיכֶם׃ אַל־ תִּפְנוּ אֶל־הָאֱלִילִם וֵאלֹהֵי
or-gods-of the-idols to you-turn not (4) God-of-you Yahweh I you-must-observe

מַסֵּכָה לֹא תַעֲשׂוּ לָכֶם אֲנִי יְהוָה אֱלֹהֵיכֶם׃ וְכִי
and-when (5) God-of-you Yahweh I for-you you-make not cast-metal

תִזְבְּחוּ זֶבַח שְׁלָמִים לַיהוָה לִרְצֹנְכֶם
to-be-accepted-for-you to-Yahweh fellowships offering-of you-sacrifice

תִּזְבָּחֻהוּ׃ בְּיוֹם זִבְחֲכֶם יֵאָכֵל
he-must-be-eaten sacrifice-of-you on-day-of (6) you-sacrifice-him

וּמִמָּחֳרָת וְהַנּוֹתָר עַד־ יוֹם הַשְּׁלִישִׁי בָּאֵשׁ
with-the-fire the-third day-of until and-the-remaining or-on-next-day

יִשָּׂרֵף׃ וְאִם הֵאָכֹל יֵאָכֵל בַּיּוֹם הַשְּׁלִישִׁי
the-third on-the-day he-is-eaten to-be-eaten and-if (7) he-must-be-burned

פִּגּוּל הוּא לֹא יֵרָצֶה׃ וְאֹכְלָיו עֲוֺנוֹ
responsibility-of-him and-ones-eating-him (8) he-will-be-accepted not he impure

יִשָּׂא כִּי־ אֶת־ קֹדֶשׁ יְהוָה חִלֵּל וְנִכְרְתָה
and-she-must-be-cut-off he-desecrated Yahweh holy-of *** for he-will-bear

הַנֶּפֶשׁ הַהִוא מֵעַמֶּיהָ׃ וּבְקֻצְרְכֶם אֶת־ קְצִיר
harvest-of *** and-when-to-reap-you (9) from-people-of-her the-that the-person

אַרְצְכֶם לֹא תְכַלֶּה פְּאַת שָׂדְךָ לִקְצֹר וְלֶקֶט
and-gleaning-of to-reap field-of-you corner-of you-complete not land-of-you

קְצִירְךָ לֹא תְלַקֵּט׃ וְכַרְמְךָ לֹא תְעוֹלֵל
you-pick-twice not and-vineyard-of-you (10) you-gather not harvest-of-you

וּפֶרֶט כַּרְמְךָ לֹא תְלַקֵּט לֶעָנִי
for-the-poor you-pick-up not vineyard-of-you and-fallen-grape-of

וְלַגֵּר תַּעֲזֹב אֹתָם אֲנִי יְהוָה אֱלֹהֵיכֶם׃ לֹא תִּגְנֹבוּ
you-steal not (11) God-of-you Yahweh I them you-leave and-for-the-alien

requirements and do not follow any of the detestable customs that were practiced before you came and do not defile yourselves with them. I am the LORD your God.' "

*Various Laws*

19 The LORD said to
Moses, [2]"Speak to the
entire assembly of Israel and
say to them: 'Be holy because
I, the LORD your God, am holy.
[3]" 'Each of you must respect
his mother and father, and
you must observe my Sabbaths. I am the LORD your God.
[4]" 'Do not turn to idols or
make gods of cast metal for
yourselves. I am the LORD your
God.
[5]" 'When you sacrifice a fellowship offering[m] to the LORD,
sacrifice it in such a way that
it will be accepted on your behalf. [6]It shall be eaten on the
day you sacrifice it or on the
next day; anything left over
until the third day must be
burned up. [7]If any of it is eaten
on the third day, it is impure
and will not be accepted.
[8]Whoever eats it will be held
responsible because he has
desecrated what is holy to the
LORD; that person must be cut
off from his people.
[9]" 'When you reap the harvest of your land, do not reap
to the very edges of your field
or gather the gleanings of your
harvest. [10]Do not go over your
vineyard a second time or pick
up the grapes that have fallen.
Leave them for the poor and
the alien. I am the LORD your
God.
[11]" 'Do not steal.

[m]5 Traditionally *peace offering*

וְלֹא־ תְכַחֲשׁוּ וְלֹא־ תְשַׁקְּרוּ אִישׁ בַּעֲמִיתוֹ׃ וְלֹא־
and-not (12) against-fellow-of-him man you-deceive and-not you-lie and-not

תִשָּׁבְעוּ בִשְׁמִי לַשָּׁקֶר וְחִלַּלְתָּ אֶת־ שֵׁם
name-of *** so-you-profane with-the-falsehood by-name-of-me you-swear

אֱלֹהֶיךָ אֲנִי יְהוָה׃ לֹא־ תַעֲשֹׁק אֶת־ רֵעֲךָ וְלֹא תִגְזֹל
you-rob or-not neighbor-of-you *** you-defraud not (13) Yahweh I God-of-you

לֹא־ תָלִין פְּעֻלַּת שָׂכִיר אִתְּךָ עַד־ בֹּקֶר׃ לֹא־ תְקַלֵּל
you-curse not (14) morning until with-you hired-man wage-of you-hold-back not

חֵרֵשׁ וְלִפְנֵי עִוֵּר לֹא תִתֵּן מִכְשֹׁל וְיָרֵאתָ
but-you-fear stumbling-block you-put not blind or-in-front-of deaf

מֵּאֱלֹהֶיךָ אֲנִי יְהוָה׃ לֹא־ תַעֲשׂוּ עָוֶל בַּמִּשְׁפָּט לֹא־
not of-the-justice perversion you-do not (15) Yahweh I to-God-of-you

תִשָּׂא פְנֵי־ דָל וְלֹא תֶהְדַּר פְּנֵי גָדוֹל בְּצֶדֶק תִּשְׁפֹּט
you-judge in-fairness great face-of you-favor or-not poor face-of you-lift

עֲמִיתֶךָ׃ לֹא־ תֵלֵךְ רָכִיל בְּעַמֶּיךָ לֹא תַעֲמֹד
you-stand not among-people-of-you slander you-go not (16) neighbor-of-you

עַל־ דַּם רֵעֶךָ אֲנִי יְהוָה׃ לֹא־ תִשְׂנָא אֶת־ אָחִיךָ
brother-of-you *** you-hate not (17) Yahweh I neighbor-of-you blood-of against

בִּלְבָבֶךָ הוֹכֵחַ תּוֹכִיחַ אֶת־ עֲמִיתֶךָ וְלֹא־ תִשָּׂא
you-share so-not neighbor-of-you *** you-rebuke to-rebuke in-heart-of-you

עָלָיו חֵטְא׃ לֹא־ תִקֹּם וְלֹא־ תִטֹּר אֶת־ בְּנֵי
sons-of *** you-bear-grudge or-not you-seek-revenge not (18) guilt with-him

עַמֶּךָ וְאָהַבְתָּ לְרֵעֲךָ כָּמוֹךָ אֲנִי יְהוָה׃ אֶת־
*** (19) Yahweh I as-yourself to-neighbor-of-you but-you-love people-of-you

חֻקֹּתַי תִּשְׁמֹרוּ בְּהֶמְתְּךָ לֹא־ תַרְבִּיעַ כִּלְאַיִם שָׂדְךָ
field-of-you two-kinds you-mate not animal-of-you you-keep decrees-of-me

לֹא־ תִזְרַע כִּלְאָיִם וּבֶגֶד כִּלְאַיִם שַׁעַטְנֵז לֹא יַעֲלֶה
you-wear not woven two-kinds and-clothing two-kinds you-plant-seed not

עָלֶיךָ׃ וְאִישׁ כִּי־ יִשְׁכַּב אֶת־ אִשָּׁה שִׁכְבַת־ זֶרַע וְהִוא
and-she semen emission-of woman with he-sleeps if and-man (20) on-you

שִׁפְחָה נֶחֱרֶפֶת לְאִישׁ וְהָפְדֵּה לֹא נִפְדָּתָה
she-was-ransomed not but-to-be-ransomed to-another being-promised slave-girl

אוֹ חֻפְשָׁה לֹא נִתַּן־ לָהּ בִּקֹּרֶת תִּהְיֶה לֹא יוּמְתוּ
they-must-die not she-must-be punishment to-her he-was-given not freedom or

כִּי־ לֹא חֻפָּשָׁה׃ וְהֵבִיא אֶת־ אֲשָׁמוֹ לַיהוָה אֶל־
to to-Yahweh guilt-offering-of-him *** but-he-must-bring (21) free not for

פֶּתַח אֹהֶל מוֹעֵד אֵיל אָשָׁם׃ וְכִפֶּר
and-he-shall-atone (22) guilt-offering ram-of Meeting Tent-of entrance-of

" 'Do not lie.

" 'Do not deceive one another.

12 " 'Do not swear falsely by my name and so profane the name of your God. I am the LORD.

13 " 'Do not defraud your neighbor or rob him.

" 'Do not hold back the wages of a hired man overnight.

14 " 'Do not curse the deaf or put a stumbling block in front of the blind, but fear your God. I am the LORD.

15 " 'Do not pervert justice; do not show partiality to the poor or favoritism to the great, but judge your neighbor fairly.

16 " 'Do not go about spreading slander among your people.

" 'Do not do anything that endangers your neighbor's life. I am the LORD.

17 " 'Do not hate your brother in your heart. Rebuke your neighbor frankly so you will not share in his guilt.

18 " 'Do not seek revenge or bear a grudge against one of your people, but love your neighbor as yourself. I am the LORD.

19 " 'Keep my decrees.

" 'Do not mate different kinds of animals.

" 'Do not plant your field with two kinds of seed.

" 'Do not wear clothing woven of two kinds of material.

20 " 'If a man sleeps with a woman who is a slave girl promised to another man but who has not been ransomed or given her freedom, there must be due punishment. Yet they are not to be put to death, because she had not been freed. 21 The man, however, must bring a ram to the entrance to the Tent of Meeting for a guilt offering to the LORD.

עָלָיו הַכֹּהֵן בְּאֵיל הָאָשָׁם לִפְנֵי יְהוָה עַל־
for Yahweh before the-guilt-offering with-ram-of the-priest for-him

חַטָּאתוֹ אֲשֶׁר חָטָא וְנִסְלַח לוֹ מֵחַטָּאתוֹ
from-sin-of-him to-him and-he-will-be-forgiven he-sinned that sin-of-him

אֲשֶׁר חָטָא׃ (23) וְכִי־ תָבֹאוּ אֶל־ הָאָרֶץ וּנְטַעְתֶּם כָּל־
any-of and-you-plant the-land into you-enter and-when (23) he-sinned that

עֵץ מַאֲכָל וַעֲרַלְתֶּם עָרְלָתוֹ אֶת־ פִּרְיוֹ
fruit-of-him *** uncircumcised-him then-you-regard-forbidden fruit tree-of

שָׁלֹשׁ שָׁנִים יִהְיֶה לָכֶם עֲרֵלִים לֹא יֵאָכֵל׃
he-must-be-eaten not ones-uncircumcised to-you he-will-be years three

(24) וּבַשָּׁנָה הָרְבִיעִת יִהְיֶה כָּל־ פִּרְיוֹ קֹדֶשׁ
holy fruit-of-him all-of he-will-be the-fourth and-in-the-year (24)

הִלּוּלִים לַיהוָה׃ (25) וּבַשָּׁנָה הַחֲמִישִׁת תֹּאכְלוּ אֶת־
*** you-may-eat the-fifth but-in-the-year (25) to-Yahweh praise-offerings

פִּרְיוֹ לְהוֹסִיף לָכֶם תְּבוּאָתוֹ אֲנִי יְהוָה אֱלֹהֵיכֶם׃ (26) לֹא
not (26) God-of-you Yahweh I harvest-of-him for-you to-increase fruit-of-him

תֹאכְלוּ עַל־ הַדָּם לֹא תְנַחֲשׁוּ וְלֹא תְעוֹנֵנוּ׃
you-practice-sorcery or-not you-practice-divination not the-blood with you-eat

(27) לֹא תַקִּפוּ פְּאַת רֹאשְׁכֶם וְלֹא תַשְׁחִית אֵת פְּאַת
edge-of *** you-clip-off or-not head-of-you side-of you-cut-hair not (27)

זְקָנֶךָ׃ (28) וְשֶׂרֶט לָנֶפֶשׁ לֹא תִתְּנוּ בִּבְשַׂרְכֶם
in-body-of-you you-cut not for-the-dead and-cut (28) beard-of-you

וּכְתֹבֶת קַעֲקַע לֹא תִתְּנוּ בָּכֶם אֲנִי יְהוָה׃ (29) אַל־ תְּחַלֵּל אֶת־
*** you-degrade not (29) Yahweh I on-you you-put not tattoo and-mark-of

בִּתְּךָ לְהַזְנוֹתָהּ וְלֹא־ תִזְנֶה הָאָרֶץ
the-land she-become-prostitute so-not to-make-prostitute-her daughter-of-you

וּמָלְאָה הָאָרֶץ זִמָּה׃ (30) אֶת־ שַׁבְּתֹתַי תִּשְׁמֹרוּ
you-observe Sabbaths-of-me *** (30) wickedness the-land and-she-be-filled

וּמִקְדָּשִׁי תִּירָאוּ אֲנִי יְהוָה׃ (31) אַל־ תִּפְנוּ אֶל־ הָאֹבֹת
the-mediums to you-turn not (31) Yahweh I you-revere and-sanctuary-of-me

וְאֶל־ הַיִּדְּעֹנִים אַל־ תְּבַקְשׁוּ לְטָמְאָה בָהֶם אֲנִי יְהוָה אֱלֹהֵיכֶם׃
God-of-you Yahweh I by-them to-be-defiled you-seek not the-spiritists or-to

(32) מִפְּנֵי שֵׂיבָה תָּקוּם וְהָדַרְתָּ פְּנֵי זָקֵן
elderly presence-of and-you-respect you-rise aged in-presence-of (32)

וְיָרֵאתָ מֵּאֱלֹהֶיךָ אֲנִי יְהוָה׃ (33) וְכִי־ יָגוּר אִתְּךָ
with-you he-lives and-when (33) Yahweh I for-God-of-you and-you-revere

גֵּר בְּאַרְצְכֶם לֹא תוֹנוּ אֹתוֹ׃ (34) כְּאֶזְרָח מִכֶּם יִהְיֶה
he-must-be from-you as-native (34) him you-mistreat not in-land-of-you alien

22 With the ram of the guilt
offering the priest is to make
atonement for him before the
LORD for the sin he has committed, and his sin will be forgiven.
23 "'When you enter the land
and plant any kind of fruit
tree, regard its fruit as forbidden.[n] For three years you
are to consider it forbidden[n]; it
must not be eaten. 24 In the
fourth year all its fruit will be
holy, an offering of praise to
the LORD. 25 But in the fifth year
you may eat its fruit. In this
way your harvest will be increased. I am the LORD your
God.
26 "'Do not eat any meat
with the blood still in it.
"'Do not practice divina-
tion or sorcery.
27 "'Do not cut the hair at the
sides of your head or clip off
the edges of your beard.
28 "'Do not cut your bodies
for the dead or put tattoo
marks on yourselves. I am the
LORD.
29 "'Do not degrade your
daughter by making her a
prostitute, or the land will turn
to prostitution and be filled
with wickedness.
30 "'Observe my Sabbaths
and have reverence for my
sanctuary. I am the LORD.
31 "'Do not turn to mediums
or seek out spiritists, for you
will be defiled by them. I am
the LORD your God.
32 "'Rise in the presence of
the aged, show respect for the
elderly and revere your God. I
am the LORD.
33 "'When an alien lives
with you in your land, do not
mistreat him. 34 The alien living with you must be treated
as one of your native-born.

[n]23 Hebrew *uncircumcised*

לָכֶם הַגֵּר ׀ הַגָּר אִתְּכֶם וְאָהַבְתָּ לוֹ כָּמוֹךָ כִּי־

for as-yourself to-him and-you-love with-you the-one-living the-alien to-you

גֵרִים הֱיִיתֶם בְּאֶרֶץ מִצְרָיִם אֲנִי יְהוָה אֱלֹהֵיכֶם׃ לֹא־ תַעֲשׂוּ

you-use not (35) God-of-you Yahweh I Egypt in-land-of you-were aliens

עָוֶל בַּמִּשְׁפָּט בַּמִּדָּה בַּמִּשְׁקָל וּבַמְּשׂוּרָה׃

or-for-the-quantity for-the-weight for-the-length in-the-measure dishonesty

מֹאזְנֵי צֶדֶק אַבְנֵי־ צֶדֶק אֵיפַת צֶדֶק וְהִין צֶדֶק

honest and-hin-of honest ephah-of honest weights-of honest scales-of (36)

יִהְיֶה לָכֶם אֲנִי יְהוָה אֱלֹהֵיכֶם אֲשֶׁר־הוֹצֵאתִי אֶתְכֶם מֵאֶרֶץ מִצְרָיִם׃

Egypt from-land-of you I-brought who God-of-you Yahweh I to-you he-must-be

וּשְׁמַרְתֶּם אֶת־ כָּל־ חֻקֹּתַי וְאֶת־ כָּל־ מִשְׁפָּטַי וַעֲשִׂיתֶם

and-you-do laws-of-me all-of and decrees-of-me all-of *** and-you-keep (37)

אֹתָם אֲנִי יְהוָה׃ וַיְדַבֵּר יְהוָה אֶל־ מֹשֶׁה לֵּאמֹר׃ וְאֶל־ בְּנֵי

sons-of now-to (2) to-say Moses to Yahweh and-he-spoke (20:1) Yahweh I them

יִשְׂרָאֵל תֹּאמַר אִישׁ אִישׁ מִבְּנֵי יִשְׂרָאֵל וּמִן־ הַגֵּר ׀ הַגָּר

the-one-living the-alien or-from Israel from-sons-of any man you-say Israel

בְּיִשְׂרָאֵל אֲשֶׁר יִתֵּן מִזַּרְעוֹ לַמֹּלֶךְ מוֹת יוּמָת

he-must-die to-die to-the-Molech from-child-of-him he-gives who in-Israel

עַם הָאָרֶץ יִרְגְּמֻהוּ בָאָבֶן׃ וַאֲנִי אֶתֵּן

I-will-set and-I (3) with-the-stone they-must-stone-him the-land people-of

אֶת־ פָּנַי בָּאִישׁ הַהוּא וְהִכְרַתִּי אֹתוֹ מִקֶּרֶב

from-among him and-I-will-cut the-that against-the-man faces-of-me ***

עַמּוֹ כִּי מִזַּרְעוֹ נָתַן לַמֹּלֶךְ לְמַעַן טַמֵּא

to-defile so-that to-the-Molech he-gave from-child-of-him for people-of-him

אֶת־ מִקְדָּשִׁי וּלְחַלֵּל אֶת־ שֵׁם קָדְשִׁי׃ וְאִם

and-if (4) holy-of-me name-of *** and-to-profane sanctuary-of-me ***

הַעְלֵם יַעְלִימוּ עַם הָאָרֶץ אֶת־ עֵינֵיהֶם מִן־ הָאִישׁ הַהוּא

the-that the-man from eyes-of-them *** the-land people-of they-close to-close

בְּתִתּוֹ מִזַּרְעוֹ לַמֹּלֶךְ לְבִלְתִּי הָמִית אֹתוֹ׃

him to-put-to-death not to-the-Molech from-child-of-him when-to-give-him

וְשַׂמְתִּי אֲנִי אֶת־ פָּנַי בָּאִישׁ הַהוּא

the-that against-the-man faces-of-me *** I then-I-will-set (5)

וּבְמִשְׁפַּחְתּוֹ וְהִכְרַתִּי אֹתוֹ וְאֵת ׀ כָּל־ הַזֹּנִים

the-ones-prostituting all-of and him and-I-will-cut and-against-family-of-him

אַחֲרָיו לִזְנוֹת אַחֲרֵי הַמֹּלֶךְ מִקֶּרֶב עַמָּם׃

people-of-them from-among the-Molech to to-prostitute with-him

וְהַנֶּפֶשׁ אֲשֶׁר תִּפְנֶה אֶל־ הָאֹבֹת וְאֶל־ הַיִּדְּעֹנִים

the-spiritists and-to the-mediums to she-turns who and-the-person (6)

Love him as yourself, for you
were aliens in Egypt. I am the
LORD your God.
35" 'Do not use dishonest
standards when measuring
length, weight or quantity.
36Use honest scales and honest
weights, an honest ephah[o]
and an honest hin.[p] I am the
LORD your God, who brought
you out of Egypt.
37" 'Keep all my decrees and
all my laws and follow them. I
am the LORD.' "

*Punishments for Sin*

20 The LORD said to
Moses, 2"Say to the Is-
raelites: 'Any Israelite or any
alien living in Israel who
gives[q] any of his children to
Molech must be put to death.
The people of the community
are to stone him. 3I will set my
face against that man and I
will cut him off from his
people; for by giving his children to Molech, he has defiled
my sanctuary and profaned
my holy name. 4If the people
of the community close their
eyes when that man gives one
of his children to Molech and
they fail to put him to death, 5I
will set my face against that
man and his family and will
cut off from their people both
him and all who follow him in
prostituting themselves to
Molech.
6" 'I will set my face against
the person who turns to mediums and spiritists to prostitute

o36 An ephah was a dry measure.
p36 A hin was a liquid measure.
q2 Or *sacrifices;* also in verses 3 and 4

לִזְנוֹת אַחֲרֵיהֶם וְנָתַתִּי אֶת־ פָּנַי בַּנֶּפֶשׁ
against-the-person faces-of-me *** also-I-will-set after-them to-prostitute

הַהִוא וְהִכְרַתִּי אֹתוֹ מִקֶּרֶב עַמּוֹ׃ וְהִתְקַדִּשְׁתֶּם
so-you-consecrate-selves (7) people-of-him from-among him and-I-will-cut the-that

וִהְיִיתֶם קְדֹשִׁים כִּי אֲנִי יְהוָה אֱלֹהֵיכֶם׃ וּשְׁמַרְתֶּם אֶת־
*** and-you-keep (8) God-of-you Yahweh I for holy-ones and-you-be

חֻקֹּתַי וַעֲשִׂיתֶם אֹתָם אֲנִי יְהוָה מְקַדִּשְׁכֶם׃ כִּי־ אִישׁ
man if (9) one-making-holy-you Yahweh I them and-you-follow decrees-of-me

אִישׁ אֲשֶׁר יְקַלֵּל אֶת־ אָבִיו וְאֶת־ אִמּוֹ מוֹת יוּמָת
he-must-die to-die mother-of-him or father-of-him *** he-curses who any

אָבִיו וְאִמּוֹ קִלֵּל דָּמָיו בּוֹ׃ וְאִישׁ
and-man (10) on-him bloods-of-him he-cursed or-mother-of-him father-of-him

אֲשֶׁר יִנְאַף אֶת־ אֵשֶׁת אִישׁ אֲשֶׁר יִנְאַף אֶת־
with he-commits-adultery who another wife-of with he-commits-adultery who

אֵשֶׁת רֵעֵהוּ מוֹת־ יוּמַת הַנֹּאֵף
the-man-committing-adultery he-must-die to-die neighbor-of-him wife-of

וְהַנֹּאָפֶת׃ וְאִישׁ אֲשֶׁר יִשְׁכַּב אֶת־ אֵשֶׁת
wife-of with he-sleeps who and-man (11) and-the-woman-committing-adultery

אָבִיו עֶרְוַת אָבִיו גִּלָּה מוֹת־ יוּמְתוּ
they-must-die to-die he-exposed father-of-him nakedness-of father-of-him

שְׁנֵיהֶם דְּמֵיהֶם בָּם׃ וְאִישׁ אֲשֶׁר יִשְׁכַּב אֶת־
with he-sleeps who and-man (12) on-them bloods-of-them both-of-them

כַּלָּתוֹ מוֹת יוּמְתוּ שְׁנֵיהֶם תֶּבֶל עָשׂוּ
they-did perversion both-of-them they-must-die to-die daughter-in-law-of-him

דְּמֵיהֶם בָּם׃ וְאִישׁ אֲשֶׁר יִשְׁכַּב אֶת־ זָכָר מִשְׁכְּבֵי אִשָּׁה
woman lyings-of man with he-lies who and-man (13) on-them bloods-of-them

תּוֹעֵבָה עָשׂוּ שְׁנֵיהֶם מוֹת יוּמָתוּ דְּמֵיהֶם בָּם׃
on-them bloods-of-them they-must-die to-die both-of-them they-did detestable

וְאִישׁ אֲשֶׁר יִקַּח אֶת־ אִשָּׁה וְאֶת־ אִמָּהּ זִמָּה הִוא
this wicked mother-of-her and woman *** he-marries who and-man (14)

בָּאֵשׁ יִשְׂרְפוּ אֹתוֹ וְאֶתְהֶן וְלֹא־ תִהְיֶה זִמָּה
wickedness she-will-be so-not and-them him they-must-burn in-the-fire

בְּתוֹכְכֶם׃ וְאִישׁ אֲשֶׁר יִתֵּן שְׁכָבְתּוֹ בִּבְהֵמָה מוֹת
to-die to-animal emission-of-him he-gives who and-man (15) among-you

יוּמָת וְאֶת־ הַבְּהֵמָה תַּהֲרֹגוּ׃ וְאִשָּׁה אֲשֶׁר תִּקְרַב
she-approaches who and-woman (16) you-must-kill the-animal and he-must-die

אֶל־ כָּל־ בְּהֵמָה לְרִבְעָה אֹתָהּ וְהָרַגְתָּ אֶת־ הָאִשָּׁה
the-woman *** then-you-must-kill with-her to-have-relation animal any-of to

himself by following them, and I will cut him off from his people.

7" 'Consecrate yourselves and be holy, because I am the LORD your God. 8Keep my decrees and follow them. I am the LORD, who makes you holy.[r]

9" 'If anyone curses his father or mother, he must be put to death. He has cursed his father or his mother, and his blood will be on his own head.

10" 'If a man commits adultery with another man's wife—with the wife of his neighbor—both the adulterer and the adulteress must be put to death.

11" 'If a man sleeps with his father's wife, he has dishonored his father. Both the man and the woman must be put to death; their blood will be on their own heads.

12" 'If a man sleeps with his daughter-in-law, both of them must be put to death. What they have done is a perversion; their blood will be on their own heads.

13" 'If a man lies with a man as one lies with a woman, both of them have done what is detestable. They must be put to death; their blood will be on their own heads.

14" 'If a man marries both a woman and her mother, it is wicked. Both he and they must be burned in the fire, so that no wickedness will be among you.

15" 'If a man has sexual relations with an animal, he must be put to death, and you must kill the animal.

16" 'If a woman approaches an animal to have sexual relations with it, kill both the

r8 *Or who sanctifies you; or who sets you apart as holy*

וְאֶת־הַבְּהֵמָה מוֹת יוּמָתוּ דְּמֵיהֶם בָּם׃ וְאִישׁ אֲשֶׁר־
who and-man (17) on-them bloods-of-them they-must-die to-die the-animal and

יִקַּח אֶת־ אֲחֹתוֹ בַּת־ אָבִיו אוֹ בַת־
daughter-of or father-of-him daughter-of sister-of-him *** he-marries

אִמּוֹ וְרָאָה אֶת־ עֶרְוָתָהּ וְהִיא־ תִרְאֶה אֶת־
*** she-sees and-she nakedness-of-her *** and-he-sees mother-of-him

עֶרְוָתוֹ חֶסֶד הוּא וְנִכְרְתוּ לְעֵינֵי
before-eyes-of and-they-must-be-cut-off this disgrace nakedness-of-him

בְּנֵי עַמָּם עֶרְוַת אֲחֹתוֹ גִּלָּה עֲוֹנוֹ
guilt-of-him he-exposed sister-of-him nakedness-of people-of-them sons-of

יִשָּׂא׃ וְאִישׁ אֲשֶׁר־ יִשְׁכַּב אֶת־ אִשָּׁה דָּוָה וְגִלָּה אֶת־
*** and-he-exposes period woman with he-lies who and-man (18) he-must-bear

עֶרְוָתָהּ אֶת־ מְקֹרָהּ הֶעֱרָה וְהִיא גִּלְּתָה אֶת־
*** she-uncovered also-she he-uncovered flow-of-her *** nakedness-of-her

מְקוֹר דָּמֶיהָ וְנִכְרְתוּ שְׁנֵיהֶם מִקֶּרֶב
from-among both-of-them and-they-must-be-cut-off bloods-of-her flow-of

עַמָּם׃ וְעֶרְוַת אֲחוֹת אִמְּךָ וַאֲחוֹת
or-sister-of mother-of-you sister-of and-nakedness-of (19) people-of-them

אָבִיךָ לֹא תְגַלֵּה כִּי אֶת־ שְׁאֵרוֹ הֶעֱרָה
he-would-dishonor close-relative-of-him *** for you-expose not father-of-you

עֲוֹנָם יִשָּׂאוּ׃ וְאִישׁ אֲשֶׁר יִשְׁכַּב אֶת־
with he-sleeps who and-man (20) they-would-bear responsibility-of-them

דֹּדָתוֹ עֶרְוַת דֹּדוֹ גִּלָּה חֶטְאָם יִשָּׂאוּ
they-will-bear guilt-of-them he-exposed uncle-of-him nakedness-of aunt-of-him

עֲרִירִים יָמֻתוּ׃ וְאִישׁ אֲשֶׁר יִקַּח אֶת־ אֵשֶׁת
wife-of *** he-marries who and-man (21) they-will-die ones-childless

אָחִיו נִדָּה הִוא עֶרְוַת אָחִיו גִּלָּה
he-exposed brother-of-him nakedness-of this impurity brother-of-him

עֲרִירִים יִהְיוּ׃ וּשְׁמַרְתֶּם אֶת־ כָּל־ חֻקֹּתַי וְאֶת־
and decrees-of-me all-of *** now-you-keep (22) they-will-be ones-childless

כָּל־ מִשְׁפָּטַי וַעֲשִׂיתֶם אֹתָם וְלֹא־ תָקִיא אֶתְכֶם הָאָרֶץ
the-land you she-will-vomit-out so-not them and-you-follow laws-of-me all-of

אֲשֶׁר אֲנִי מֵבִיא אֶתְכֶם שָׁמָּה לָשֶׁבֶת בָּהּ׃ וְלֹא תֵלְכוּ
you-live and-not (23) in-her to-live to-there you bringing I where

בְּחֻקֹּת הַגּוֹי אֲשֶׁר־אֲנִי מְשַׁלֵּחַ מִפְּנֵיכֶם כִּי אֶת־ כָּל־ אֵלֶּה
these all-of *** for from-before-you driving I that the-nation as-custom-of

עָשׂוּ וָאָקֻץ בָּם׃ וָאֹמַר לָכֶם אַתֶּם
them to-you but-I-said (24) against-them and-I-abhorred they-did

woman and the animal. They must be put to death; their blood will be on their own heads.

17" 'If a man marries his sister, the daughter of either his father or his mother, and they have sexual relations, it is a disgrace. They must be cut off before the eyes of their people. He has dishonored his sister and will be held responsible.

18" 'If a man lies with a woman during her monthly period and has sexual relations with her, he has exposed the source of her flow, and she has also uncovered it. Both of them must be cut off from their people.

19" 'Do not have sexual relations with the sister of either your mother or your father, for that would dishonor a close relative; both of you would be held responsible.

20" 'If a man sleeps with his aunt, he has dishonored his uncle. They will be held responsible; they will die childless.

21" 'If a man marries his brother's wife, it is an act of impurity; he has dishonored his brother. They will be childless.

22" 'Keep all my decrees and laws and follow them, so that the land where I am bringing you to live may not vomit you out. 23You must not live according to the customs of the nations I am going to drive out before you. Because they did all these things, I abhorred them. 24But I said to you, "You

תִּירְשׁוּ אֶת־ אַדְמָתָם וַאֲנִי אֶתְּנֶנָּה לָכֶם לָרֶשֶׁת
to-inherit to-you I-will-give-her and-I land-of-them *** you-will-possess

אֹתָהּ אֶרֶץ זָבַת חָלָב וּדְבָשׁ אֲנִי יְהוָה אֱלֹהֵיכֶם אֲשֶׁר־
who God-of-you Yahweh I and-honey milk flowing-of land her

הִבְדַּלְתִּי אֶתְכֶם מִן־ הָעַמִּים׃ וְהִבְדַּלְתֶּם בֵּין־ הַבְּהֵמָה
the-animal between so-you-distinguish (25) the-nations from you I-set-apart

הַטְּהֹרָה לַטְּמֵאָה וּבֵין־ הָעוֹף הַטָּמֵא לַטָּהֹר
from-the-clean the-unclean the-bird and-between from-the-unclean the-clean

וְלֹא־ תְשַׁקְּצוּ אֶת־ נַפְשֹׁתֵיכֶם בַּבְּהֵמָה וּבָעוֹף
or-by-the-bird by-the-animal selves-of-you *** you-defile and-not

וּבְכֹל אֲשֶׁר תִּרְמֹשׂ הָאֲדָמָה אֲשֶׁר־ הִבְדַּלְתִּי לָכֶם
for-you I-set-apart which the-ground she-moves that or-by-anything

לְטַמֵּא׃ וִהְיִיתֶם לִי קְדֹשִׁים כִּי קָדוֹשׁ אֲנִי יְהוָה
Yahweh I holy for holy-ones to-me now-you-must-be (26) to-be-unclean

וָאַבְדִּל אֶתְכֶם מִן־ הָעַמִּים לִהְיוֹת לִי׃ וְאִישׁ אוֹ־ אִשָּׁה כִּי־
if woman or now-man (27) for-me to-be the-nations from you and-I-set-apart

יִהְיֶה בָהֶם אוֹב אוֹ יִדְּעֹנִי מוֹת יוּמָתוּ בָּאֶבֶן
with-the-stone they-must-die to-die spiritist or medium among-them he-is

יִרְגְּמוּ אֹתָם דְּמֵיהֶם בָּם׃ וַיֹּאמֶר יְהוָה אֶל־
to Yahweh and-he-said (21:1) on-them bloods-of-them them they-must-stone

מֹשֶׁה אֱמֹר אֶל־ הַכֹּהֲנִים בְּנֵי אַהֲרֹן וְאָמַרְתָּ אֲלֵהֶם לְנֶפֶשׁ לֹא־
not to-self to-them and-you-say Aaron sons-of the-priests to speak! Moses

יִטַּמָּא בְּעַמָּיו׃ כִּי אִם־ לִשְׁאֵרוֹ
for-relative-of-him if except (2) for-people-of-him he-must-make-unclean

הַקָּרֹב אֵלָיו לְאִמּוֹ וּלְאָבִיו וְלִבְנוֹ
or-for-son-of-him or-for-father-of-him for-mother-of-him to-him the-one-close

וּלְבִתּוֹ וּלְאָחִיו׃ וְלַאֲחֹתוֹ
or-for-sister-of-him (3) or-for-brother-of-him or-for-daughter-of-him

הַבְּתוּלָה הַקְּרוֹבָה אֵלָיו אֲשֶׁר לֹא־ הָיְתָה לְאִישׁ לָהּ
for-her to-husband she-is not who on-him the-one-dependent the-unmarried

יִטַּמָּא׃ לֹא יִטַּמָּא בַּעַל
leader he-must-make-self-unclean not (4) he-may-make-self-unclean

בְּעַמָּיו לְהֵחַלּוֹ׃ לֹא־ יִקְרְחָה קָרְחָה
baldness they-must-shave not (5) to-defile-himself among-people-of-him

בְּרֹאשָׁם וּפְאַת זְקָנָם לֹא יְגַלֵּחוּ
they-must-shave-off not beard-of-them or-edge-of on-head-of-them

וּבִבְשָׂרָם לֹא יִשְׂרְטוּ שָׂרָטֶת׃ קְדֹשִׁים יִהְיוּ
they-must-be holy-ones (6) cut they-must-cut not or-in-body-of-them

°5 ק יקרחו

will possess their land; I will
give it to you as an inheritance, a land flowing with
milk and honey." I am the
LORD your God, who has set
you apart from the nations.
25" 'You must therefore
make a distinction between
clean and unclean animals
and between unclean and
clean birds. Do not defile
yourselves by any animal or
bird or anything that moves
along the ground—those
which I have set apart as unclean for you.
26You are to be
holy to me[s] because I, the
LORD, am holy, and I have set
you apart from the nations to
be my own.
27" 'A man or woman who is
a medium or spiritist among
you must be put to death. You
are to stone them; their blood
will be on their own heads.' "

### *Rules for Priests*

21 The LORD said to
Moses, "Speak to the
priests, the sons of Aaron, and
say to them: 'A priest must not
make himself ceremonially
unclean for any of his people
who die,
2except for a close
relative, such as his mother or
father, his son or daughter, his
brother,
3or an unmarried sister who is dependent on him
since she has no husband—for
her he may make himself unclean.
4He must not make himself unclean for people related
to him by marriage,[t] and so
defile himself.
5" 'Priests must not shave
their heads or shave off the
edges of their beards or cut
their bodies.
6They must be

s26 Or *be my holy ones*
t4 Or *unclean as a leader among his people*

לֵאלֹהֵיהֶם וְלֹא יְחַלְּלוּ שֵׁם אֱלֹהֵיהֶם כִּי אֶת־
*** for God-of-them name-of they-must-profane and-not to-God-of-them

אִשֵּׁי יְהוָה לֶחֶם אֱלֹהֵיהֶם הֵם מַקְרִיבִם
ones-presenting they God-of-them food-of Yahweh fire-offerings-of

וְהָיוּ קֹדֶשׁ׃ אִשָּׁה זֹנָה וַחֲלָלָה לֹא יִקָּחוּ
they-must-marry not and-defiled prostitute woman (7) holy so-they-must-be

וְאִשָּׁה גְּרוּשָׁה מֵאִישָׁהּ לֹא יִקָּחוּ כִּי־קָדֹשׁ
holy for they-must-marry not from-husband-of-her being-divorced or-woman

הוּא לֵאלֹהָיו׃ וְקִדַּשְׁתּוֹ כִּי־אֶת־לֶחֶם אֱלֹהֶיךָ הוּא
he God-of-you food-of *** for and-you-regard-holy-him (8) to-God-of-him he

מַקְרִיב קָדֹשׁ יִהְיֶה־לָּךְ כִּי קָדוֹשׁ אֲנִי יְהוָה מְקַדִּשְׁכֶם׃
one-making-holy-you Yahweh I holy for to-you he-must-be holy offering

וּבַת אִישׁ כֹּהֵן כִּי תֵחֵל לִזְנוֹת אֶת־
*** to-be-prostitute she-defiles-self if priest man and-daughter-of (9)

אָבִיהָ הִיא מְחַלֶּלֶת בָּאֵשׁ תִּשָּׂרֵף׃
she-must-be-burned in-the-fire disgracing she father-of-her

וְהַכֹּהֵן הַגָּדוֹל מֵאֶחָיו אֲשֶׁר־יוּצַק עַל־
on he-was-poured who among-brothers-of-him the-high and-the-priest (10)

רֹאשׁוֹ ׀ שֶׁמֶן הַמִּשְׁחָה וּמִלֵּא אֶת־יָדוֹ לִלְבֹּשׁ
to-wear hand-of-him *** and-he-ordained the-anointing oil-of head-of-him

אֶת־הַבְּגָדִים אֶת־רֹאשׁוֹ לֹא יִפְרָע וּבְגָדָיו
or-clothes-of-him he-must-let-be-unkempt not hair-of-him *** the-garments ***

לֹא יִפְרֹם׃ וְעַל כָּל־נַפְשֹׁת מֵת לֹא יָבֹא
he-must-go not dead bodies-of any-of and-to (11) he-must-tear not

לְאָבִיו וּלְאִמּוֹ לֹא יִטַּמָּא׃
he-must-make-self-unclean not or-for-mother-of-him for-father-of-him

וּמִן־הַמִּקְדָּשׁ לֹא יֵצֵא וְלֹא יְחַלֵּל אֵת
*** he-must-desecrate or-not he-must-leave not the-sanctuary nor-from (12)

מִקְדַּשׁ אֱלֹהָיו כִּי נֵזֶר שֶׁמֶן מִשְׁחַת אֱלֹהָיו עָלָיו
on-him God-of-him anointing-of oil-of dedicated for God-of-him sanctuary-of

אֲנִי יְהוָה׃ וְהוּא אִשָּׁה בִבְתוּלֶיהָ יִקָּח׃ אַלְמָנָה
widow (14) he-must-marry in-virginity-of-her woman and-he (13) Yahweh I

וּגְרוּשָׁה וַחֲלָלָה זֹנָה אֶת־אֵלֶּה לֹא יִקָּח כִּי
but he-must-marry not these *** prostitute or-defiled or-being-divorced

אִם־בְּתוּלָה מֵעַמָּיו יִקַּח אִשָּׁה׃ וְלֹא־יְחַלֵּל
he-will-defile so-not (15) wife he-may-marry from-people-of-him virgin only

זַרְעוֹ בְּעַמָּיו כִּי אֲנִי יְהוָה מְקַדְּשׁוֹ׃
one-making-holy-him Yahweh I for among-people-of-him offspring-of-him

holy to their God and must not
profane the name of their God.
Because they present the
offerings made to the LORD by
fire, the food of their God, they
are to be holy.
7 " 'They must not marry
women defiled by prostitution
or divorced from their husbands, because priests are
holy to their God. 8 Regard
them as holy, because they
offer up the food of your God.
Consider them holy, because I
the LORD, who makes you
holy,[u] am holy.
9 " 'If a priest's daughter
defiles herself by becoming a
prostitute, she disgraces her
father; she must be burned in
the fire.
10 " 'The high priest, the one
among his brothers who has
had the anointing oil poured
on his head and who has been
ordained to wear the priestly
garments, must not let his hair
become unkempt[v] or tear his
clothes. 11 He must not enter a
place where there is a dead
body. He must not make himself unclean, even for his father or mother, 12 nor leave the
sanctuary of his God or desecrate it, because he has been
dedicated by the anointing oil
of his God. I am the LORD.
13 " 'The woman he marries
must be a virgin. 14 He must
not marry a widow, a divorced
woman, or a woman defiled
by prostitution, but only a virgin from his own people, 15 so
he will not defile his offspring
among his people. I am the
LORD, who makes him
holy.[w] "

[u] 8 Or *who sanctifies you;* or *who sets you apart as holy*
[v] 10 Or *not uncover his head*
[w] 15 Or *who sanctifies him;* or *who sets him apart as holy*

וַיְדַבֵּר יְהוָה אֶל־מֹשֶׁה לֵּאמֹר׃ דַּבֵּר אֶל־אַהֲרֹן לֵאמֹר אִישׁ
man to-say Aaron to say! (17) to-say Moses to Yahweh and-he-spoke (16)

מִזַּרְעֲךָ לְדֹרֹתָם אֲשֶׁר יִהְיֶה בוֹ מוּם
defect on-him he-has who for-generations-of-them from-descendant-of-you

לֹא יִקְרַב לְהַקְרִיב לֶחֶם אֱלֹהָיו׃ כִּי כָל־אִישׁ
man any-of indeed (18) God-of-him food-of to-offer he-may-come-near not

אֲשֶׁר־בּוֹ מוּם לֹא יִקְרָב אִישׁ עִוֵּר אוֹ פִסֵּחַ אוֹ חָרֻם
being-disfigured or lame or blind man he-may-come-near not defect on-him who

אוֹ שָׂרוּעַ׃ אוֹ אִישׁ אֲשֶׁר־יִהְיֶה בוֹ שֶׁבֶר רָגֶל אוֹ שֶׁבֶר
crippled or foot crippled on-him he-has who man or (19) being-deformed or

יָד׃ אוֹ־גִבֵּן אוֹ־דַק אוֹ תְּבַלֻּל בְּעֵינוֹ אוֹ גָרָב
fester or in-eye-of-him defective or dwarfed or hunchbacked or (20) hand

אוֹ יַלֶּפֶת אוֹ מְרוֹחַ אָשֶׁךְ׃ כָּל־אִישׁ אֲשֶׁר־בּוֹ מוּם
defect on-him who man any-of (21) testicle damaged-of or running-sore or

מִזֶּרַע אַהֲרֹן הַכֹּהֵן לֹא יִגַּשׁ לְהַקְרִיב אֶת־
*** to-present he-may-come-near not the-priest Aaron from-descendant-of

אִשֵּׁי יְהוָה מוּם בּוֹ אֵת לֶחֶם אֱלֹהָיו לֹא
not God-of-him food-of *** on-him defect Yahweh fire-offerings-of

יִגַּשׁ לְהַקְרִיב׃ לֶחֶם אֱלֹהָיו מִקָּדְשֵׁי
from-most-holy-ones-of God-of-him food-of (22) to-offer he-must-come-near

הַקֳּדָשִׁים וּמִן־הַקֳּדָשִׁים יֹאכֵל׃ אַךְ אֶל־הַפָּרֹכֶת לֹא
not the-curtain to yet (23) he-may-eat the-holy-ones and-from the-holy-ones

יָבֹא וְאֶל־הַמִּזְבֵּחַ לֹא יִגַּשׁ כִּי־מוּם בּוֹ וְלֹא
so-not on-him defect for he-must-approach not the-altar or-to he-must-go

יְחַלֵּל אֶת־מִקְדָּשַׁי כִּי אֲנִי יְהוָה מְקַדְּשָׁם׃
one-making-holy-them Yahweh I for sanctuaries-of-me *** he-will-desecrate

וַיְדַבֵּר מֹשֶׁה אֶל־אַהֲרֹן וְאֶל־בָּנָיו וְאֶל־כָּל־בְּנֵי
sons-of all-of and-to sons-of-him and-to Aaron to Moses so-he-told (24)

יִשְׂרָאֵל׃ וַיְדַבֵּר יְהוָה אֶל־מֹשֶׁה לֵּאמֹר׃ דַּבֵּר אֶל־אַהֲרֹן וְאֶל־
and-to Aaron to tell! (2) to-say Moses to Yahweh and-he-spoke (22:1) Israel

בָּנָיו וְיִנָּזְרוּ מִקָּדְשֵׁי בְנֵי־יִשְׂרָאֵל
Israel sons-of for-sacred-offerings-of that-they-must-respect sons-of-him

וְלֹא יְחַלְּלוּ אֶת־שֵׁם קָדְשִׁי אֲשֶׁר הֵם מַקְדִּשִׁים לִי
to-me consecrating they that holy-of-me name-of *** they-will-profane so-not

אֲנִי יְהוָה׃ אֱמֹר אֲלֵהֶם לְדֹרֹתֵיכֶם כָּל־אִישׁ ׀ אֲשֶׁר־יִקְרַב
he-comes-near who man any-of for-generations-of-you to-them say! (3) Yahweh I

מִכָּל־זַרְעֲכֶם אֶל־הַקֳּדָשִׁים אֲשֶׁר יַקְדִּישׁוּ
they-consecrate that the-sacred-offerings to descendant-of-you from-any-of

[16]The LORD said to Moses, [17]"Say to Aaron: 'For the generations to come none of your descendants who has a defect may come near to offer the food of his God. [18]No man who has any defect may come near: no man who is blind or lame, disfigured or deformed; [19]no man with a crippled foot or hand, [20]or who is hunchbacked or dwarfed, or who has any eye defect, or who has festering or running sores or damaged testicles. [21]No descendant of Aaron the priest who has any defect is to come near to present the offerings made to the LORD by fire. He has a defect; he must not come near to offer the food of his God. [22]He may eat the most holy food of his God, as well as the holy food; [23]yet because of his defect, he must not go near the curtain or approach the altar, and so desecrate my sanctuary. I am the LORD, who makes them holy.[x]' "

[24]So Moses told this to Aaron and his sons and to all the Israelites.

22 The LORD said to Moses, [2]"Tell Aaron and his sons to treat with respect the sacred offerings the Israelites consecrate to me, so they will not profane my holy name. I am the LORD.

[3]"Say to them: 'For the generations to come, if any of your descendants is ceremonially unclean and yet comes near the sacred offerings that the Israelites consecrate to the

[x]23 Or *who sanctifies them*; or *who sets them apart as holy*

בְּנֵי־ יִשְׂרָאֵל לַיהוָה וְטֻמְאָתוֹ עָלָיו וְנִכְרְתָה
then-she-must-be-cut on-him yet-uncleanness-of-him to-Yahweh Israel sons-of

הַנֶּפֶשׁ הַהִוא מִלְּפָנַי אֲנִי יְהוָה׃ אִישׁ אִישׁ מִזֶּרַע
from-seed-of any man (4) Yahweh I from-presence-of-me the-that the-person

אַהֲרֹן וְהוּא צָרוּעַ אוֹ זָב בַּקֳּדָשִׁים לֹא יֹאכַל
he-may-eat not from-the-sacred-offerings discharge or infection and-he Aaron

עַד אֲשֶׁר יִטְהָר וְהַנֹּגֵעַ בְּכָל־ טְמֵא־ נֶפֶשׁ
body unclean-of on-any-of and-the-one-touching he-is-cleansed when until

אוֹ אִישׁ אֲשֶׁר־ תֵּצֵא מִמֶּנּוּ שִׁכְבַת־ זָרַע׃ אוֹ־ אִישׁ אֲשֶׁר יִגַּע
he-touches who man or (5) semen emission-of from-him she-comes-out who man or

בְּכָל־ שֶׁרֶץ אֲשֶׁר יִטְמָא־ לוֹ אוֹ בְאָדָם אֲשֶׁר יִטְמָא־
he-is-unclean who on-man or by-him he-is-unclean that crawler on-any-of

לוֹ לְכֹל טֻמְאָתוֹ׃ נֶפֶשׁ אֲשֶׁר תִּגַּע־ בּוֹ
on-him she-touches who person (6) uncleanness-of-him for-any-of by-him

וְטָמְאָה עַד־ הָעָרֶב וְלֹא יֹאכַל מִן־
from he-must-eat and-not the-evening till then-she-will-be-unclean

הַקֳּדָשִׁים כִּי אִם־ רָחַץ בְּשָׂרוֹ בַּמָּיִם׃
with-the-waters body-of-him he-bathed if unless the-sacred-offerings

וּבָא הַשֶּׁמֶשׁ וְטָהֵר וְאַחַר יֹאכַל
he-may-eat and-after then-he-will-be-clean the-sun when-he-goes-down (7)

מִן־ הַקֳּדָשִׁים כִּי לַחְמוֹ הוּא׃ נְבֵלָה וּטְרֵפָה
or-torn-animal corpse (8) this food-of-him for the-sacred-offerings from

לֹא יֹאכַל לְטָמְאָה־ בָהּ אֲנִי יְהוָה׃ וְשָׁמְרוּ
now-they-must-keep (9) Yahweh I by-her to-become-unclean he-must-eat not

אֶת־ מִשְׁמַרְתִּי וְלֹא־ יִשְׂאוּ עָלָיו חֵטְא וּמֵתוּ בוֹ
for-him or-they-die guilt for-him they-bear so-not requirement-of-me ***

כִּי יְחַלְּלֻהוּ אֲנִי יְהוָה מְקַדְּשָׁם׃ וְכָל־ זָר
outsider but-any-of (10) one-making-holy-them Yahweh I they-scorned-him for

לֹא־ יֹאכַל קֹדֶשׁ תּוֹשַׁב כֹּהֵן וְשָׂכִיר לֹא־ יֹאכַל
he-may-eat not or-hired-worker priest guest-of sacred-offering he-may-eat not

קֹדֶשׁ׃ וְכֹהֵן כִּי־ יִקְנֶה נֶפֶשׁ קִנְיַן כַּסְפּוֹ הוּא
he money-of-him bought-of slave he-buys if but-priest (11) sacred-offering

יֹאכַל בּוֹ וִילִיד בֵּיתוֹ הֵם יֹאכְלוּ
they-may-eat they household-of-him or-born-of with-him he-may-eat

בְּלַחְמוֹ׃ וּבַת־ כֹּהֵן כִּי תִהְיֶה לְאִישׁ זָר
outsider to-man she-marries if priest and-daughter-of (12) of-food-of-him

הִוא בִּתְרוּמַת הַקֳּדָשִׁים לֹא תֹאכֵל׃ וּבַת־
but-daughter-of (13) she-may-eat not the-sacred-ones of-contribution-of she

LORD, that person must be cut off from my presence. I am the LORD.

4 "'If a descendant of Aaron has an infectious skin disease[y] or a bodily discharge, he may not eat the sacred offerings until he is cleansed. He will also be unclean if he touches something defiled by a corpse or by anyone who has an emission of semen, 5 or if he touches any crawling thing that makes him unclean, or any person who makes him unclean, whatever the uncleanness may be. 6 The one who touches any such thing will be unclean till evening. He must not eat any of the sacred offerings unless he has bathed himself with water. 7 When the sun goes down, he will be clean, and after that he may eat the sacred offerings, for they are his food. 8 He must not eat anything found dead or torn by wild animals, and so become unclean through it. I am the LORD.

9 "'The priests are to keep my requirements so that they do not become guilty and die for treating them with contempt. I am the LORD, who makes them holy.[z]

10 "'No one outside a priest's family may eat the sacred offering, nor may the guest of a priest or his hired worker eat it. 11 But if a priest buys a slave with money, or if a slave is born in his household, that slave may eat his food. 12 If a priest's daughter marries anyone other than a priest, she may not eat any of the sacred contributions. 13 But if a

y4 Traditionally *leprosy;* the Hebrew word was used for various diseases affecting the skin—not necessarily leprosy.
z9 Or *who sanctifies them;* or *who sets them apart as holy;* also in verse 16

כֹּהֵן כִּי תִהְיֶה אַלְמָנָה וּגְרוּשָׁה וְזֶרַע אֵין לָהּ
to-her he-is-not yet-child or-being-divorced widow she-becomes if priest

וְשָׁבָה אֶל־ בֵּית אָבִיהָ כִּנְעוּרֶיהָ מִלֶּחֶם
from-food-of as-youths-of-her father-of-her house-of to and-she-returns

אָבִיהָ תֹּאכֵל וְכָל־ זָר לֹא־ יֹאכַל בּוֹ׃
of-him he-may-eat not outsider but-any-of she-may-eat father-of-her

וְאִישׁ כִּי־ יֹאכַל קֹדֶשׁ בִּשְׁגָגָה וְיָסַף
then-he-must-add by-mistake sacred-offering he-eats if and-anyone (14)

חֲמִשִׁיתוֹ עָלָיו וְנָתַן לַכֹּהֵן אֶת־ הַקֹּדֶשׁ׃
the-offering *** to-the-priest and-he-must-restitute to-him fifth-of-him

וְלֹא יְחַלְּלוּ אֶת־ קָדְשֵׁי בְּנֵי יִשְׂרָאֵל אֵת
*** Israel sons-of sacred-offerings-of *** they-must-desecrate and-not (15)

אֲשֶׁר־ יָרִימוּ לַיהוָה׃ וְהִשִּׂיאוּ אוֹתָם עֲוֹן אַשְׁמָה
payment guilt-of on-them so-they-bring (16) to-Yahweh they-present that

בְּאָכְלָם אֶת־ קָדְשֵׁיהֶם כִּי אֲנִי יְהוָה מְקַדְּשָׁם׃
one-making-holy-them Yahweh I for sacred-offerings-of-them *** by-to-eat-them

וַיְדַבֵּר יְהוָה אֶל־ מֹשֶׁה לֵּאמֹר׃ דַּבֵּר אֶל־ אַהֲרֹן וְאֶל־
and-to Aaron to speak! (18) to-say Moses to Yahweh and-he-spoke (17)

בָּנָיו וְאֶל כָּל־ בְּנֵי יִשְׂרָאֵל וְאָמַרְתָּ אֲלֵהֶם אִישׁ אִישׁ
any man to-them and-you-say Israel sons-of all-of and-to sons-of-him

מִבֵּית יִשְׂרָאֵל וּמִן־ הַגֵּר בְּיִשְׂרָאֵל אֲשֶׁר יַקְרִיב קָרְבָּנוֹ
gift-of-him he-presents who in-Israel the-alien or-from Israel from-house-of

לְכָל־ נִדְרֵיהֶם וּלְכָל־ נִדְבוֹתָם אֲשֶׁר־
that freewill-offerings-of-them or-for-any-of vows-of-them for-any-of

יַקְרִיבוּ לַיהוָה לְעֹלָה׃ לִרְצֹנְכֶם
for-acceptance-of-you (19) as-burnt-offering to-Yahweh they-present

תָּמִים זָכָר בַּבָּקָר בַּכְּשָׂבִים וּבָעִזִּים׃
or-from-the-goats from-the-sheep from-the-cattle male without-defect

כֹּל אֲשֶׁר־ בּוֹ מוּם לֹא תַקְרִיבוּ כִּי־ לֹא לְרָצוֹן
for-acceptance not for you-bring not defect on-him that anything (20)

יִהְיֶה לָכֶם׃ וְאִישׁ כִּי־ יַקְרִיב זֶבַח־ שְׁלָמִים
fellowships offering-of he-brings when and-anyone (21) for-you he-will-be

לַיהוָה לְפַלֵּא־ נֶדֶר אוֹ לִנְדָבָה בַבָּקָר אוֹ
or from-the-herd as-freewill-offering or vow to-fulfill to-Yahweh

בַצֹּאן תָּמִים יִהְיֶה לְרָצוֹן כָּל־ מוּם לֹא
not blemish any-of for-acceptance he-must-be without-defect from-the-flock

יִהְיֶה־ בּוֹ׃ עַוֶּרֶת אוֹ שָׁבוּר אוֹ־ חָרוּץ אוֹ־ יַבֶּלֶת אוֹ
or with-wart or maimed or being-injured or blind (22) on-him he-must-be

priest's daughter becomes a widow or is divorced, yet has no children, and she returns to live in her father's house as in her youth, she may eat of her father's food. No unauthorized person, however, may eat any of it.

14"'If anyone eats a sacred offering by mistake, he must make restitution to the priest for the offering and add a fifth of the value to it. 15The priests must not desecrate the sacred offerings the Israelites present to the LORD 16by allowing them to eat the sacred offerings and so bring upon them guilt requiring payment. I am the LORD, who makes them holy.'"

*Unacceptable Sacrifices*

17The LORD said to Moses, 18"Speak to Aaron and his sons and to all the Israelites and say to them: 'If any of you—either an Israelite or an alien living in Israel—presents a gift for a burnt offering to the LORD, either to fulfill a vow or as a freewill offering, 19you must present a male without defect from the cattle, sheep or goats in order that it may be accepted on your behalf. 20Do not bring anything with a defect, because it will not be accepted on your behalf. 21When anyone brings from the herd or flock a fellowship offering[a] to the LORD to fulfill a special vow or as a freewill offering, it must be without defect or blemish to be acceptable. 22Do not offer to the LORD the blind, the injured or the maimed, or

[a]21 Traditionally *peace offering*

גָרָב אוֹ יַלֶּפֶת לֹא־ תַקְרִיבוּ אֵלֶּה לַיהוָה וְאִשֶּׁה
and-fire-offering to-Yahweh these you-offer not running-sore or with-fester

לֹא־ תִתְּנוּ מֵהֶם עַל־ הַמִּזְבֵּחַ לַיהוָה׃ וְשׁוֹר וָשֶׂה
or-sheep but-cow (23) to-Yahweh the-altar on from-these you-make not

שָׂרוּעַ וְקָלוּט נְדָבָה תַּעֲשֶׂה אֹתוֹ
him you-may-present freewill-offering or-being-stunted being-deformed

וּלְנֶדֶר לֹא יֵרָצֶה׃ וּמָעוּךְ וְכָתוּת
or-being-crushed but-being-bruised (24) he-will-be-accepted not but-for-vow

וְנָתוּק וְכָרוּת לֹא תַקְרִיבוּ לַיהוָה וּבְאַרְצְכֶם
and-in-land-of-you to-Yahweh you-must-offer not or-being-cut or-being-torn

לֹא תַעֲשׂוּ׃ וּמִיַּד בֶּן־ נֵכָר לֹא תַקְרִיבוּ
you-must-offer not foreigner son-of and-from-hand-of (25) you-must-do not

אֶת־ לֶחֶם אֱלֹהֵיכֶם מִכָּל־ אֵלֶּה כִּי מָשְׁחָתָם בָּהֶם
on-them deformity-of-them for these from-any-of God-of-you food-of ***

מוּם בָּם לֹא יֵרָצוּ לָכֶם׃ וַיְדַבֵּר יְהוָה
Yahweh and-he-spoke (26) for-you they-will-be-accepted not on-them defect

אֶל־ מֹשֶׁה לֵּאמֹר׃ שׁוֹר אוֹ־ כֶשֶׂב אוֹ־ עֵז כִּי יִוָּלֵד וְהָיָה
then-he-must-be he-is-born when goat or sheep or cow (27) to-say Moses to

שִׁבְעַת יָמִים תַּחַת אִמּוֹ וּמִיּוֹם הַשְּׁמִינִי וָהָלְאָה
and-on the-eighth and-from-day mother-of-him with days seven-of

יֵרָצֶה לְקָרְבַּן אִשֶּׁה לַיהוָה׃ וְשׁוֹר אוֹ־ שֶׂה
sheep or but-cow (28) to-Yahweh fire as-offering-of he-will-be-acceptable

אֹתוֹ וְאֶת־ בְּנוֹ לֹא תִשְׁחֲטוּ בְּיוֹם אֶחָד׃ וְכִי־
and-when (29) same on-day you-slaughter not young-of-him with him

תִזְבְּחוּ זֶבַח־ תּוֹדָה לַיהוָה לִרְצֹנְכֶם
for-acceptance-of-you to-Yahweh thanksgiving offering-of you-sacrifice

תִּזְבָּחוּ׃ בַּיּוֹם הַהוּא יֵאָכֵל לֹא־ תוֹתִירוּ
you-leave not he-must-be-eaten the-same on-the-day (30) you-sacrifice

מִמֶּנּוּ עַד־ בֹּקֶר אֲנִי יְהוָה׃ וּשְׁמַרְתֶּם מִצְוֹתַי
commandments-of-me so-you-keep (31) Yahweh I morning till from-him

וַעֲשִׂיתֶם אֹתָם אֲנִי יְהוָה׃ וְלֹא תְחַלְּלוּ אֶת־ שֵׁם
name-of *** you-profane and-not (32) Yahweh I them and-you-follow

קָדְשִׁי וְנִקְדַּשְׁתִּי בְּתוֹךְ בְּנֵי יִשְׂרָאֵל אֲנִי יְהוָה
Yahweh I Israel sons-of by for-I-must-be-acknowledged-as-holy holy-of-me

מְקַדִּשְׁכֶם׃ הַמּוֹצִיא אֶתְכֶם מֵאֶרֶץ מִצְרַיִם לִהְיוֹת
to-be Egypt from-land-of you the-one-bringing (33) one-making-holy-you

לָכֶם לֵאלֹהִים אֲנִי יְהוָה׃ וַיְדַבֵּר יְהוָה אֶל־ מֹשֶׁה לֵּאמֹר׃
to-say Moses to Yahweh and-he-spoke (23:1) Yahweh I as-God for-you

anything with warts or festering or running sores. Do not place any of these on the altar as an offering made to the LORD by fire. [23]You may, however, present as a freewill offering a cow[b] or a sheep that is deformed or stunted, but it will not be accepted in fulfillment of a vow. [24]You must not offer to the LORD an animal whose testicles are bruised, crushed, torn or cut. You must not do this in your own land, [25]and you must not accept such animals from the hand of a foreigner and offer them as the food of your God. They will not be accepted on your behalf, because they are deformed and have defects.' "

[26]The LORD said to Moses, [27]"When a cow, a sheep or a goat is born, it is to remain with its mother for seven days. From the eighth day on, it will be acceptable as an offering made to the LORD by fire. [28]Do not slaughter a cow or a sheep and its young on the same day.

[29]"When you sacrifice an offering of thanksgiving to the LORD, sacrifice it in such a way that it will be accepted on your behalf. [30]It must be eaten that same day; leave none of it till morning. I am the LORD.

[31]"Keep my commands and follow them. I am the LORD. [32]Do not profane my holy name. I must be acknowledged as holy by the Israelites. I am the LORD, who makes[c] you holy[d] [33]and who brought you out of Egypt to be your God. I am the LORD."

23 The LORD said to Moses, [2]"Speak to the

[b]23 The Hebrew word can include both male and female; also in verse 27.
[c]32 Or *made*
[d]32 Or *who sanctifies you*; or *who sets you apart as holy*

דַּבֵּ֞ר אֶל־ בְּנֵ֤י יִשְׂרָאֵל֙ וְאָמַרְתָּ֣ אֲלֵהֶ֔ם מוֹעֲדֵ֣י יְהוָ֔ה אֲשֶׁר־
which   Yahweh   feasts-of   to-them   and-you-say   Israel   sons-of   to   speak!   (2)

תִּקְרְא֥וּ אֹתָ֖ם מִקְרָאֵ֣י קֹ֑דֶשׁ אֵ֥לֶּה הֵ֖ם מוֹעֲדָֽי׃ שֵׁ֖שֶׁת
six-of   (3)   feasts-of-me   they   these   sacred   assemblies-of   them   you-must-proclaim

יָמִים֮ תֵּעָשֶׂ֣ה מְלָאכָה֒ וּבַיּ֣וֹם הַשְּׁבִיעִ֗י שַׁבַּ֤ת שַׁבָּתוֹן֙
rest   Sabbath-of   the-seventh   but-on-the-day   work   she-must-be-done   days

מִקְרָא־ קֹ֔דֶשׁ כָּל־ מְלָאכָ֖ה לֹ֣א תַעֲשׂ֑וּ שַׁבָּ֥ת הִ֛וא לַיהוָ֖ה
to-Yahweh   this   Sabbath   you-may-do   not   work   any-of   sacred   assembly-of

בְּכֹ֖ל מֽוֹשְׁבֹתֵיכֶֽם׃ אֵ֚לֶּה מוֹעֲדֵ֣י יְהוָ֔ה מִקְרָאֵ֖י קֹ֑דֶשׁ
sacred   assemblies-of   Yahweh   feasts-of   these   (4)   dwellings-of-you   in-all-of

אֲשֶׁר־ תִּקְרְא֥וּ אֹתָ֖ם בְּמוֹעֲדָֽם׃ בַּחֹ֣דֶשׁ הָרִאשׁ֗וֹן
the-first   in-the-month   (5)   at-times-of-them   them   you-must-proclaim   that

בְּאַרְבָּעָ֥ה עָשָׂ֛ר לַחֹ֖דֶשׁ בֵּ֣ין הָעַרְבָּ֑יִם פֶּ֖סַח לַיהוָֽה׃
to-Yahweh   Passover   the-twilights   at   of-the-month   ten   on-four

וּבַחֲמִשָּׁ֨ה עָשָׂ֥ר יוֹם֙ לַחֹ֣דֶשׁ הַזֶּ֔ה חַ֥ג הַמַּצּ֖וֹת
the-Unleavened-Breads   Feast-of   the-that   of-the-month   day   ten   and-on-five   (6)

לַיהוָ֑ה שִׁבְעַ֥ת יָמִ֖ים מַצּ֥וֹת תֹּאכֵֽלוּ׃ בַּיּוֹם֙
on-the-day   (7)   you-must-eat   unleavened-breads   days   seven-of   to-Yahweh

הָרִאשׁ֔וֹן מִקְרָא־ קֹ֖דֶשׁ יִהְיֶ֣ה לָכֶ֑ם כָּל־ מְלֶ֥אכֶת עֲבֹדָ֖ה לֹ֥א
not   regular   work-of   any-of   for-you   he-must-be   sacred   assembly-of   the-first

תַעֲשֽׂוּ׃ וְהִקְרַבְתֶּ֥ם אִשֶּׁ֛ה לַיהוָ֖ה שִׁבְעַ֣ת יָמִ֑ים
days   seven-of   to-Yahweh   fire-offering   and-you-present   (8)   you-must-do

בַּיּ֤וֹם הַשְּׁבִיעִי֙ מִקְרָא־ קֹ֔דֶשׁ כָּל־ מְלֶ֥אכֶת עֲבֹדָ֖ה לֹ֥א
not   regular   work-of   any-of   sacred   assembly-of   the-seventh   on-the-day

תַעֲשֽׂוּ׃ וַיְדַבֵּ֥ר יְהוָ֖ה אֶל־ מֹשֶׁ֥ה לֵּאמֹֽר׃ דַּבֵּ֞ר אֶל־ בְּנֵ֤י
sons-of   to   speak!   (10)   to-say   Moses   to   Yahweh   and-he-spoke   (9)   you-must-do

יִשְׂרָאֵל֙ וְאָמַרְתָּ֣ אֲלֵהֶ֔ם כִּֽי־ תָבֹ֣אוּ אֶל־ הָאָ֗רֶץ אֲשֶׁ֤ר אֲנִי֙ נֹתֵ֣ן לָכֶ֔ם
to-you   giving   I   that   the-land   into   you-enter   when   to-them   and-you-say   Israel

וּקְצַרְתֶּ֖ם אֶת־ קְצִירָ֑הּ וַהֲבֵאתֶ֥ם אֶת־ עֹ֛מֶר רֵאשִׁ֥ית
first-of   sheaf-of   ***   then-you-bring   harvest-of-her   ***   and-you-reap

קְצִירְכֶ֖ם אֶל־ הַכֹּהֵֽן׃ וְהֵנִ֧יף אֶת־ הָעֹ֛מֶר לִפְנֵ֥י
before   the-sheaf   ***   and-he-must-wave   (11)   the-priest   to   harvest-of-you

יְהוָ֖ה לִֽרְצֹנְכֶ֑ם מִֽמָּחֳרַת֙ הַשַּׁבָּ֔ת יְנִיפֶ֖נּוּ
he-must-wave-him   the-Sabbath   on-day-after-of   for-acceptance-of-you   Yahweh

הַכֹּהֵֽן׃ וַעֲשִׂיתֶ֕ם בְּי֥וֹם הֲנִֽיפְכֶ֖ם אֶת־ הָעֹ֑מֶר
the-sheaf   ***   to-wave-you   on-day   and-you-must-sacrifice   (12)   the-priest

כֶּ֣בֶשׂ תָּמִ֧ים בֶּן־ שְׁנָת֛וֹ לְעֹלָ֖ה לַיהוָֽה׃
to-Yahweh   as-burnt-offering   year-of-him   son-of   without-defect   lamb

Israelites and say to them: 'These are my appointed feasts, the appointed feasts of the LORD, which you are to proclaim as sacred assemblies.

### The Sabbath

3'' 'There are six days when you may work, but the seventh day is a Sabbath of rest, a day of sacred assembly. You are not to do any work; wherever you live, it is a Sabbath to the LORD.

### The Passover and Unleavened Bread

4'' 'These are the LORD's appointed feasts, the sacred assemblies you are to proclaim at their appointed times: 5The LORD's Passover begins at twilight on the fourteenth day of the first month. 6On the fifteenth day of that month the LORD's Feast of Unleavened Bread begins; for seven days you must eat bread made without yeast. 7On the first day hold a sacred assembly and do no regular work. 8For seven days present an offering made to the LORD by fire. And on the seventh day hold a sacred assembly and do no regular work.' ''

### Firstfruits

9The LORD said to Moses, 10''Speak to the Israelites and say to them: 'When you enter the land I am going to give you and you reap its harvest, bring to the priest a sheaf of the first grain you harvest. 11He is to wave the sheaf before the LORD so it will be accepted on your behalf; the priest is to wave it on the day after the Sabbath. 12On the day you wave the sheaf, you must sacrifice as a burnt offering to the LORD a lamb a year old without

וּמִנְחָתוֹ שְׁנֵי עֶשְׂרֹנִים סֹלֶת בְּלוּלָה בַשֶּׁמֶן

with-the-oil being-mixed fine-flour tenths two-of with-grain-offering-him (13)

אִשֶּׁה לַיהוָה רֵיחַ נִיחֹחַ וְנִסְכֹּה יַיִן רְבִיעִת

fourth-of wine and-drink-offering-of-him pleasant aroma-of to-Yahweh fire-offering

הַהִין׃ וְלֶחֶם וְקָלִי וְכַרְמֶל לֹא תֹאכְלוּ עַד־

until you-must-eat not or-new-grain or-roasted-grain and-bread (14) the-hin

עֶצֶם הַיּוֹם הַזֶּה עַד הֲבִיאֲכֶם אֶת־ קָרְבַּן אֱלֹהֵיכֶם

God-of-you offering-of *** to-bring-you until the-that the-day very-of

חֻקַּת עוֹלָם לְדֹרֹתֵיכֶם בְּכֹל מֹשְׁבֹתֵיכֶם׃

dwellings-of-you in-all-of for-generations-of-you lasting ordinance-of

וּסְפַרְתֶּם לָכֶם מִמָּחֳרַת הַשַּׁבָּת מִיּוֹם

from-day the-Sabbath from-day-after-of to-you then-you-count (15)

הֲבִיאֲכֶם אֶת־ עֹמֶר הַתְּנוּפָה שֶׁבַע שַׁבָּתוֹת תְּמִימֹת תִּהְיֶינָה׃

they-must-be full-ones weeks seven the-wave-offering sheaf-of *** to-bring-you

עַד מִמָּחֳרַת הַשַּׁבָּת הַשְּׁבִיעִת תִּסְפְּרוּ חֲמִשִּׁים יוֹם

day fifty you-count the-seventh the-Sabbath to-day-after-of up (16)

וְהִקְרַבְתֶּם מִנְחָה חֲדָשָׁה לַיהוָה׃ מִמּוֹשְׁבֹתֵיכֶם

from-dwellings-of-you (17) to-Yahweh new grain-offering then-you-present

תָּבִיאּוּ | לֶחֶם תְּנוּפָה שְׁתַּיִם שְׁנֵי עֶשְׂרֹנִים סֹלֶת תִּהְיֶינָה

they-must-be fine-flour tenths two-of two wave-offering bread you-bring

חָמֵץ תֵּאָפֶינָה בִּכּוּרִים לַיהוָה׃ וְהִקְרַבְתֶּם עַל־

with and-you-present (18) to-Yahweh firstfruits they-must-be-baked yeast

הַלֶּחֶם שִׁבְעַת כְּבָשִׂים תְּמִימִם בְּנֵי שָׁנָה וּפַר

and-bull year sons-of ones-without-defect male-lambs seven-of the-bread

בֶּן־ בָּקָר אֶחָד וְאֵילִם שְׁנָיִם יִהְיוּ עֹלָה לַיהוָה

to-Yahweh burnt-offering they-will-be two and-rams one herd young-of

וּמִנְחָתָם וְנִסְכֵּיהֶם אִשֵּׁה רֵיחַ־

aroma-of fire-offering and-drink-offerings-of-them with-grain-offering-of-them

נִיחֹחַ לַיהוָה׃ וַעֲשִׂיתֶם שְׂעִיר־ עִזִּים אֶחָד

one goats male-goat-of then-you-sacrifice (19) to-Yahweh pleasant

לְחַטָּאת וּשְׁנֵי כְבָשִׂים בְּנֵי שָׁנָה לְזֶבַח שְׁלָמִים׃

fellowships for-offering-of year sons-of lambs and-two-of for-sin-offering

וְהֵנִיף הַכֹּהֵן | אֹתָם עַל לֶחֶם הַבִּכּוּרִים

the-firstfruits bread-of with them the-priest and-he-must-wave (20)

תְּנוּפָה לִפְנֵי יְהוָה עַל־ שְׁנֵי כְּבָשִׂים קֹדֶשׁ יִהְיוּ

they-are sacred-offering lambs two-of with Yahweh before wave-offering

לַיהוָה לַכֹּהֵן׃ וּקְרָאתֶם בְּעֶצֶם | הַיּוֹם הַזֶּה

the-that the-day on-same-of and-you-must-proclaim (21) for-the-priest to-Yahweh

defect, 13together with its grain offering of two-tenths of an ephah[f] of fine flour mixed with oil—an offering made to the LORD by fire, a pleasing aroma—and its drink offering of a fourth of a hin[g] of wine. 14You must not eat any bread, or roasted or new grain, until the very day you bring this offering to your God. This is to be a lasting ordinance for the generations to come, wherever you live.

*Feast of Weeks*

15" 'From the day after the Sabbath, the day you brought the sheaf of the wave offering, count off seven full weeks. 16Count off fifty days up to the day after the seventh Sabbath, and then present an offering of new grain to the LORD. 17From wherever you live, bring two loaves made of two-tenths of an ephah of fine flour, baked with yeast, as a wave offering of firstfruits to the LORD. 18Present with this bread seven male lambs, each a year old and without defect, one young bull and two rams. They will be a burnt offering to the LORD, together with their grain offerings and drink offerings—an offering made by fire, an aroma pleasing to the LORD. 19Then sacrifice one male goat for a sin offering and two lambs, each a year old, for a fellowship offering.[h] 20The priest is to wave the two lambs before the LORD as a wave offering, together with the bread of the firstfruits. They are a sacred offering to the LORD for the priest. 21On that same day you are to proclaim a sacred assembly and

[f] 13 That is, probably about 4 quarts (about 4.5 liters); also in verse 17
[g] 13 That is, probably about 1 quart (about 1 liter)
[h] 19 Traditionally *peace offering*

°13 ק ונסכו

מִקְרָא־ קֹדֶשׁ יִהְיֶה לָכֶם כָּל־ מְלֶאכֶת עֲבֹדָה לֹא תַעֲשׂוּ
you-must-do not regular work-of any-of for-you he-will-be sacred assembly-of

חֻקַּת עוֹלָם בְּכָל־ מוֹשְׁבֹתֵיכֶם לְדֹרֹתֵיכֶם׃
for-generations-of-you dwellings-of-you in-all-of lasting ordinance-of

וּבְקֻצְרְכֶם אֶת־ קְצִיר אַרְצְכֶם לֹא־ תְכַלֶּה פְּאַת
edge-of you-reap not land-of-you harvest-of *** and-when-to-reap-you (22)

שָׂדְךָ בְּקֻצְרֶךָ וְלֶקֶט קְצִירְךָ לֹא תְלַקֵּט
you-glean not harvest-of-you and-gleaning-of when-to-harvest-you field-of-you

לֶעָנִי וְלַגֵּר תַּעֲזֹב אֹתָם אֲנִי יְהוָה אֱלֹהֵיכֶם׃
God-of-you Yahweh I them you-leave and-for-the-alien for-the-poor

וַיְדַבֵּר יְהוָה אֶל־מֹשֶׁה לֵּאמֹר׃ דַּבֵּר אֶל־ בְּנֵי יִשְׂרָאֵל לֵאמֹר
to-say Israel sons-of to say! (24) to-say Moses to Yahweh then-he-spoke (23)

בַּחֹדֶשׁ הַשְּׁבִיעִי בְּאֶחָד לַחֹדֶשׁ יִהְיֶה לָכֶם שַׁבָּתוֹן
day-of-rest to-you he-will-be of-the-month on-first the-seventh in-the-month

זִכְרוֹן תְּרוּעָה מִקְרָא־ קֹדֶשׁ׃ כָּל־ מְלֶאכֶת עֲבֹדָה
regular work-of any-of (25) sacred assembly-of trumpet-blast commemoration-of

לֹא תַעֲשׂוּ וְהִקְרַבְתֶּם אִשֶּׁה לַיהוָה׃ וַיְדַבֵּר יְהוָה
Yahweh and-he-spoke (26) to-Yahweh fire-offering but-you-present you-do not

אֶל־ מֹשֶׁה לֵּאמֹר׃ אַךְ בֶּעָשׂוֹר לַחֹדֶשׁ הַשְּׁבִיעִי הַזֶּה
the-this the-seventh of-the-month on-the-tenth also (27) to-say Moses to

יוֹם הַכִּפֻּרִים הוּא מִקְרָא־ קֹדֶשׁ יִהְיֶה לָכֶם וְעִנִּיתֶם
and-you-deny for-you he-must-be sacred assembly-of he the-Atonements Day-of

אֶת־ נַפְשֹׁתֵיכֶם וְהִקְרַבְתֶּם אִשֶּׁה לַיהוָה׃ וְכָל־
and-any-of (28) to-Yahweh fire-offering and-you-present selves-of-you ***

מְלָאכָה לֹא תַעֲשׂוּ בְּעֶצֶם הַיּוֹם הַזֶּה כִּי יוֹם כִּפֻּרִים הוּא
he Atonements Day-of for the-that the-day on-same-of you-do not work

לְכַפֵּר עֲלֵיכֶם לִפְנֵי יְהוָה אֱלֹהֵיכֶם׃ כִּי כָל־ הַנֶּפֶשׁ אֲשֶׁר
who the-person any-of indeed (29) God-of-you Yahweh before for-you to-atone

לֹא־ תְעֻנֶּה בְּעֶצֶם הַיּוֹם הַזֶּה וְנִכְרְתָה
then-she-must-be-cut-off the-that the-day on-same-of she-denies-self not

מֵעַמֶּיהָ׃ וְכָל־ הַנֶּפֶשׁ אֲשֶׁר תַּעֲשֶׂה כָּל־ מְלָאכָה
work any-of she-does who the-person and-any-of (30) from-people-of-her

בְּעֶצֶם הַיּוֹם הַזֶּה וְהַאֲבַדְתִּי אֶת־ הַנֶּפֶשׁ הַהִוא
the-that the-person *** then-I-will-destroy the-that the-day on-same-of

מִקֶּרֶב עַמָּהּ׃ כָּל־ מְלָאכָה לֹא תַעֲשׂוּ חֻקַּת
ordinance-of you-shall-do not work any-of (31) people-of-her from-among

עוֹלָם לְדֹרֹתֵיכֶם בְּכֹל מֹשְׁבֹתֵיכֶם׃ שַׁבַּת
sabbath-of (32) dwellings-of-you in-all-of for-generations-of-you lasting

do no regular work. This is to be a lasting ordinance for the generations to come, wherever you live.
22 " 'When you reap the harvest of your land, do not reap to the very edges of your field or gather the gleanings of your harvest. Leave them for the poor and the alien. I am the LORD your God.' "

*Feast of Trumpets*

23 The LORD said to Moses,
24 "Say to the Israelites: 'On the first day of the seventh month you are to have a day of rest, a sacred assembly commemorated with trumpet blasts.
25 Do no regular work, but present an offering made to the LORD by fire.' "

*Day of Atonement*

26 The LORD said to Moses,
27 "The tenth day of this seventh month is the Day of Atonement. Hold a sacred assembly and deny yourselves,[i] and present an offering made to the LORD by fire.
28 Do no work on that day, because it is the Day of Atonement, when atonement is made for you before the LORD your God.
29 Anyone who does not deny himself on that day must be cut off from his people.
30 I will destroy from among his people anyone who does any work on that day.
31 You shall do no work at all. This is to be a lasting ordinance for the generations to come, wherever you

[i] 27 Or *and fast;* also in verses 29 and 32

שַׁבָּתוֹן הוּא לָכֶם וְעִנִּיתֶם אֶת־ נַפְשֹׁתֵיכֶם בְּתִשְׁעָה לַחֹדֶשׁ
of-the-month on-ninth selves-of-you *** and-you-must-deny for-you this rest

בָּעֶרֶב מֵעֶרֶב עַד־ עֶרֶב תִּשְׁבְּתוּ שַׁבַּתְּכֶם׃
sabbath-of-you you-must-observe evening until from-evening in-the-evening

וַיְדַבֵּר יְהוָה אֶל־ מֹשֶׁה לֵּאמֹר׃ דַּבֵּר אֶל־בְּנֵי יִשְׂרָאֵל לֵאמֹר
to-say Israel sons-of to say! (34) to-say Moses to Yahweh and-he-spoke (33)

בַּחֲמִשָּׁה עָשָׂר יוֹם לַחֹדֶשׁ הַשְּׁבִיעִי הַזֶּה חַג הַסֻּכּוֹת
the-Tabernacles Feast-of the-this the-seventh of-the-month day ten on-five

שִׁבְעַת יָמִים לַיהוָה׃ בַּיּוֹם הָרִאשׁוֹן מִקְרָא־ קֹדֶשׁ כָּל־
any-of sacred assembly-of the-first on-the-day (35) to-Yahweh days seven-of

מְלֶאכֶת עֲבֹדָה לֹא תַעֲשׂוּ׃ שִׁבְעַת יָמִים תַּקְרִיבוּ אִשֶּׁה
fire-offering you-present days seven-of (36) you-do not regular work-of

לַיהוָה בַּיּוֹם הַשְּׁמִינִי מִקְרָא־ קֹדֶשׁ יִהְיֶה לָכֶם
for-you he-must-be sacred assembly-of the-eighth on-the-day to-Yahweh

וְהִקְרַבְתֶּם אִשֶּׁה לַיהוָה עֲצֶרֶת הִוא כָּל־ מְלֶאכֶת
work-of any-of she closing-assembly to-Yahweh fire-offering and-you-present

עֲבֹדָה לֹא תַעֲשׂוּ׃ אֵלֶּה מוֹעֲדֵי יְהוָה אֲשֶׁר־ תִּקְרְאוּ אֹתָם
them you-must-proclaim which Yahweh feasts-of these (37) you-do not regular

מִקְרָאֵי קֹדֶשׁ לְהַקְרִיב אִשֶּׁה לַיהוָה עֹלָה
burnt-offering to-Yahweh fire-offering to-bring sacred assemblies-of

וּמִנְחָה זֶבַח וּנְסָכִים דְּבַר־ יוֹם
day requirement-of and-drink-offerings sacrifice and-grain-offering

בְּיוֹמוֹ׃ מִלְּבַד שַׁבְּתֹת יְהוָה וּמִלְּבַד
and-in-addition-to Yahweh Sabbaths-of in-addition-to (38) for-day-of-him

מַתְּנוֹתֵיכֶם וּמִלְּבַד כָּל־ נִדְרֵיכֶם וּמִלְּבַד כָּל־
any-of and-in-addition-to vows-of-you any-of and-in-addition-to gifts-of-you

נִדְבוֹתֵיכֶם אֲשֶׁר תִּתְּנוּ לַיהוָה׃ אַךְ בַּחֲמִשָּׁה עָשָׂר יוֹם
day ten on-five so (39) to-Yahweh you-give that freewill-offerings-of-you

לַחֹדֶשׁ הַשְּׁבִיעִי בְּאָסְפְּכֶם אֶת־ תְּבוּאַת הָאָרֶץ
the-land crop-of *** after-to-gather-you the-seventh of-the-month

תָּחֹגּוּ אֶת־ חַג־ יְהוָה שִׁבְעַת יָמִים בַּיּוֹם הָרִאשׁוֹן
the-first on-the-day days seven-of Yahweh festival-of *** you-celebrate

שַׁבָּתוֹן וּבַיּוֹם הַשְּׁמִינִי שַׁבָּתוֹן׃ וּלְקַחְתֶּם לָכֶם
for-you and-you-take (40) day-of-rest the-eighth and-on-the-day day-of-rest

בַּיּוֹם הָרִאשׁוֹן פְּרִי עֵץ הָדָר כַּפֹּת תְּמָרִים וַעֲנַף
and-branch-of palms fronds-of choice tree fruit-of the-first on-the-day

עֵץ־ עָבֹת וְעַרְבֵי־ נָחַל וּשְׂמַחְתֶּם לִפְנֵי יְהוָה אֱלֹהֵיכֶם
God-of-you Yahweh before and-you-rejoice stream and-poplars-of leafy tree

live. 32It is a sabbath of rest for you, and you must deny yourselves. From the evening of the ninth day of the month until the following evening you are to observe your sabbath."

*Feast of Tabernacles*

33The LORD said to Moses, 34"Say to the Israelites: 'On the fifteenth day of the seventh month the LORD's Feast of Tabernacles begins, and it lasts for seven days. 35The first day is a sacred assembly; do no regular work. 36For seven days present offerings made to the LORD by fire, and on the eighth day hold a sacred assembly and present an offering made to the LORD by fire. It is the closing assembly; do no regular work.

37(" 'These are the LORD's appointed feasts, which you are to proclaim as sacred assemblies for bringing offerings made to the LORD by fire—the burnt offerings and grain offerings, sacrifices and drink offerings required for each day. 38These offerings are in addition to those for the LORD's Sabbaths and[i] in addition to your gifts and whatever you have vowed and all the freewill offerings you give to the LORD.)

39" 'So beginning with the fifteenth day of the seventh month, after you have gathered the crops of the land, celebrate the festival to the LORD for seven days; the first day is a day of rest, and the eighth day also is a day of rest. 40On the first day you are to take choice fruit from the trees, and palm fronds, leafy branches and poplars, and rejoice before the LORD your God for

i38 Or *These feasts are in addition to the LORD's Sabbaths, and these offerings are*

שִׁבְעַת יָמִים׃ וְחַגֹּתֶם אֹתוֹ חַג לַיהוָה שִׁבְעַת יָמִים
days seven-of to-Yahweh festival him and-you-celebrate (41) days seven-of

בַּשָּׁנָה חֻקַּת עוֹלָם לְדֹרֹתֵיכֶם בַּחֹדֶשׁ
in-the-month for-generations-of-you lasting ordinance-of in-the-year

הַשְּׁבִיעִי תָּחֹגּוּ אֹתוֹ׃ בַּסֻּכֹּת תֵּשְׁבוּ שִׁבְעַת יָמִים
days seven-of you-live in-the-booths (42) him you-celebrate the-seventh

כָּל־ הָאֶזְרָח בְּיִשְׂרָאֵל יֵשְׁבוּ בַּסֻּכֹּת׃ לְמַעַן
so-that (43) in-the-booths he-must-live in-Israel the-native every-of

יֵדְעוּ דֹרֹתֵיכֶם כִּי בַסֻּכּוֹת הוֹשַׁבְתִּי אֶת־ בְּנֵי
sons-of *** I-made-live in-the-booths that descendants-of-you they-will-know

יִשְׂרָאֵל בְּהוֹצִיאִי אוֹתָם מֵאֶרֶץ מִצְרַיִם אֲנִי יְהוָה אֱלֹהֵיכֶם׃
God-of-you Yahweh I Egypt from-land-of them when-to-bring-me Israel

וַיְדַבֵּר מֹשֶׁה אֶת־ מֹעֲדֵי יְהוָה אֶל־ בְּנֵי יִשְׂרָאֵל׃
Israel sons-of to Yahweh feasts-of *** Moses so-he-announced (44)

וַיְדַבֵּר יְהוָה אֶל־מֹשֶׁה לֵּאמֹר׃ צַו אֶת־ בְּנֵי יִשְׂרָאֵל
Israel sons-of *** command! (2) to-say Moses to Yahweh and-he-spoke (24:1)

וְיִקְחוּ אֵלֶיךָ שֶׁמֶן זַיִת זָךְ כָּתִית לַמָּאוֹר לְהַעֲלֹת נֵר
lamp to-burn for-the-light pressed clear olive oil-of to-you so-they-bring

תָּמִיד׃ מִחוּץ לְפָרֹכֶת הָעֵדֻת בְּאֹהֶל מוֹעֵד
Meeting in-Tent-of the-Testimony of-curtain-of outside (3) continually

יַעֲרֹךְ אֹתוֹ אַהֲרֹן מֵעֶרֶב עַד־ בֹּקֶר לִפְנֵי יְהוָה תָּמִיד
continually Yahweh before morning till from-evening Aaron him he-must-tend

חֻקַּת עוֹלָם לְדֹרֹתֵיכֶם׃ עַל הַמְּנֹרָה הַטְּהֹרָה
the-pure-gold the-lampstand on (4) for-generations-of-you lasting ordinance-of

יַעֲרֹךְ אֶת־ הַנֵּרוֹת לִפְנֵי יְהוָה תָּמִיד׃ וְלָקַחְתָּ
and-you-take (5) continually Yahweh before the-lamps *** he-must-tend

סֹלֶת וְאָפִיתָ אֹתָהּ שְׁתֵּים עֶשְׂרֵה חַלּוֹת שְׁנֵי עֶשְׂרֹנִים יִהְיֶה
he-shall-be tenths two-of loaves ten two her and-you-bake fine-flour

הַחַלָּה הָאֶחָת׃ וְשַׂמְתָּ אוֹתָם שְׁתַּיִם מַעֲרָכוֹת שֵׁשׁ הַמַּעֲרָכֶת עַל הַשֻּׁלְחָן
the-table on the-row six-of rows two them and-you-set (6) the-each the-loaf

הַטָּהֹר לִפְנֵי יְהוָה׃ וְנָתַתָּ עַל־ הַמַּעֲרֶכֶת לְבֹנָה זַכָּה
pure incense the-row along and-you-put (7) Yahweh before the-pure-gold

וְהָיְתָה לַלֶּחֶם לְאַזְכָּרָה אִשֶּׁה לַיהוָה׃
to-Yahweh fire-offering as-memorial-portion for-the-bread and-she-will-be

בְּיוֹם הַשַּׁבָּת בְּיוֹם הַשַּׁבָּת יַעַרְכֶנּוּ לִפְנֵי
before he-must-set-him the-Sabbath on-day-of the-Sabbath on-day-of (8)

יְהוָה תָּמִיד מֵאֵת בְּנֵי־ יִשְׂרָאֵל בְּרִית עוֹלָם׃
lasting covenant Israel sons-of on-behalf-of continually Yahweh

seven days. 41Celebrate this as
a festival to the LORD for seven
days each year. This is to be a
lasting ordinance for the generations to come; celebrate it
in the seventh month. 42Live
in booths for seven days: All
native-born Israelites are to
live in booths 43so your descendants will know that I had
the Israelites live in booths
when I brought them out of
Egypt. I am the LORD your
God.' "
44So Moses announced to the
Israelites the appointed feasts
of the LORD.

### *Oil and Bread Set Before the LORD*

24 The LORD said to
Moses, 2"Command
the Israelites to bring you clear
oil of pressed olives for the
light so that the lamps may be
kept burning continually.
3Outside the curtain of the
Testimony in the Tent of
Meeting, Aaron is to tend the
lamps before the LORD from
evening till morning, continually. This is to be a lasting ordinance for the generations to
come. 4The lamps on the pure
gold lampstand before the
LORD must be tended continually.
5"Take fine flour and bake
twelve loaves of bread, using
two-tenths of an ephah[k] for
each loaf. 6Set them in two
rows, six in each row, on the
table of pure gold before the
LORD. 7Along each row put
some pure incense as a
memorial portion to represent
the bread and to be an offering
made to the LORD by fire. 8This
bread is to be set out before the
LORD regularly, Sabbath after
Sabbath, on behalf of the Israelites, as a lasting covenant. 9It

[k]5 That is, probably about 4 quarts (about 4.5 liters)

וְהָיְתָה לְאַהֲרֹן וּלְבָנָיו וַאֲכָלֻהוּ בְּמָקוֹם
in-place and-they-must-eat-him and-for-sons-of-him for-Aaron and-she-is (9)

קָדֹשׁ כִּי קֹדֶשׁ קָדָשִׁים הוּא לוֹ מֵאִשֵּׁי יְהוָה
Yahweh from-fire-offerings-of for-him he holy-ones most-holy-of for holy

חָק־ עוֹלָם׃ וַיֵּצֵא בֶּן־ אִשָּׁה יִשְׂרְאֵלִית וְהוּא בֶּן־
son-of and-he Israelite woman son-of now-he-went-out (10) regular share-of

אִישׁ מִצְרִי בְּתוֹךְ בְּנֵי יִשְׂרָאֵל וַיִּנָּצוּ בַּמַּחֲנֶה בֶּן
son-of in-the-camp and-they-fought Israel sons-of among Egyptian man

הַיִּשְׂרְאֵלִית וְאִישׁ הַיִּשְׂרְאֵלִי׃ וַיִּקֹּב בֶּן־
son-of and-he-blasphemed (11) the-Israelite and-man the-Israelite-woman

הָאִשָּׁה הַיִּשְׂרְאֵלִית אֶת־ הַשֵּׁם וַיְקַלֵּל וַיָּבִיאוּ אֹתוֹ אֶל־
to him so-they-brought and-he-cursed the-Name *** the-Israelite the-woman

מֹשֶׁה וְשֵׁם אִמּוֹ שְׁלֹמִית בַּת־ דִּבְרִי לְמַטֵּה־
from-tribe-of Dibri daughter-of Shelomith mother-of-him now-name-of Moses

דָן׃ וַיַּנִּיחֻהוּ בַּמִּשְׁמָר לִפְרֹשׁ לָהֶם עַל־ פִּי
will-of about to-them to-be-clear in-the-custody and-they-put-him (12) Dan

יְהוָה׃ וַיְדַבֵּר יְהוָה אֶל־ מֹשֶׁה לֵּאמֹר׃ הוֹצֵא אֶת־
*** take! (14) to-say Moses to Yahweh then-he-said (13) Yahweh

הַמְקַלֵּל אֶל־ מִחוּץ לַמַּחֲנֶה וְסָמְכוּ כָל־
all-of and-they-must-lay of-the-camp outside to the-one-blaspheming

הַשֹּׁמְעִים אֶת־ יְדֵיהֶם עַל־ רֹאשׁוֹ וְרָגְמוּ אֹתוֹ
him and-they-must-stone head-of-him on hands-of-them *** the-ones-hearing

כָּל־ הָעֵדָה׃ וְאֶל־ בְּנֵי יִשְׂרָאֵל תְּדַבֵּר לֵאמֹר אִישׁ אִישׁ
any man to-say you-say Israel sons-of and-to (15) the-assembly entire-of

כִּי־ יְקַלֵּל אֱלֹהָיו וְנָשָׂא חֶטְאוֹ׃
responsibility-of-him then-he-must-bear God-of-him he-curses if

וְנֹקֵב שֵׁם־ יְהוָה מוֹת יוּמָת רָגוֹם
to-stone he-must-die to-die Yahweh name-of and-one-blaspheming (16)

יִרְגְּמוּ־ בוֹ כָּל־ הָעֵדָה כַּגֵּר כָּאֶזְרָח
or-the-native whether-the-alien the-assembly entire-of on-him they-must-stone

בְּנָקְבוֹ־ שֵׁם יוּמָת׃ וְאִישׁ כִּי יַכֶּה כָּל־
any-of he-takes if and-anyone (17) he-must-die Name when-to-blaspheme-him

נֶפֶשׁ אָדָם מוֹת יוּמָת׃ וּמַכֵּה נֶפֶשׁ־ בְּהֵמָה
animal life-of and-one-taking (18) he-must-die to-die human life-of

יְשַׁלְּמֶנָּה נֶפֶשׁ תַּחַת נָפֶשׁ׃ וְאִישׁ כִּי־ יִתֵּן מוּם
injury he-gives if and-anyone (19) life for life he-must-restitute-her

בַּעֲמִיתוֹ כַּאֲשֶׁר עָשָׂה כֵּן יֵעָשֶׂה לּוֹ׃ שֶׁבֶר
fracture (20) to-him he-must-be-done so he-did just-as to-neighbor-of-him

belongs to Aaron and his sons, who are to eat it in a holy place, because it is a most holy part of their regular share of the offerings made to the LORD by fire."

*A Blasphemer Stoned*

[10]Now the son of an Israelite mother and an Egyptian father went out among the Israelites, and a fight broke out in the camp between him and an Israelite. [11]The son of the Israelite woman blasphemed the name of the LORD with a curse; so they brought him to Moses. (His mother's name was Shelomith, the daughter of Dibri the Danite.) [12]They put him in custody until the will of the LORD should be made clear to them.

[13]Then the LORD said to Moses: [14]"Take the blasphemer outside the camp. All those who heard him are to lay their hands on his head, and the entire assembly is to stone him. [15]Say to the Israelites: 'If anyone curses his God, he will be held responsible; [16]anyone who blasphemes the name of the LORD must be put to death. The entire assembly must stone him. Whether an alien or native-born, when he blasphemes the Name, he must be put to death.

[17]" 'If anyone takes the life of a human being, he must be put to death. [18]Anyone who takes the life of someone's animal must make restitution—life for life. [19]If anyone injures his neighbor, whatever he has done must be done to him:

תַּחַת שֶׁבֶר עַיִן תַּחַת עַיִן שֵׁן תַּחַת שֵׁן כַּאֲשֶׁר יִתֵּן מוּם בָּאָדָם

to-the-other injury he-gave just-as tooth for tooth eye for eye fracture for

כֵּן יִנָּתֶן בּוֹ׃ וּמַכֵּה בְהֵמָה יְשַׁלְּמֶנָּה

he-must-restitute-her animal and-one-killing (21) to-him he-must-be-given so

וּמַכֵּה אָדָם יוּמָת׃ מִשְׁפַּט אֶחָד יִהְיֶה לָכֶם כַּגֵּר

for-the-alien to-you he-must-be same law (22) he-must-die man but-one-killing

כָּאֶזְרָח יִהְיֶה כִּי אֲנִי יְהוָה אֱלֹהֵיכֶם׃ וַיְדַבֵּר מֹשֶׁה

Moses then-he-spoke (23) God-of-you Yahweh I for he-must-be for-the-native

אֶל־בְּנֵי יִשְׂרָאֵל וַיּוֹצִיאוּ אֶת־הַמְקַלֵּל אֶל־מִחוּץ

outside to the-one-blaspheming *** and-they-took Israel sons-of to

לַמַּחֲנֶה וַיִּרְגְּמוּ אֹתוֹ אָבֶן וּבְנֵי־יִשְׂרָאֵל עָשׂוּ כַּאֲשֶׁר

just-as they-did Israel so-sons-of stone him and-they-stoned of-the-camp

צִוָּה יְהוָה אֶת־מֹשֶׁה׃ וַיְדַבֵּר יְהוָה אֶל־מֹשֶׁה בְּהַר

on-Mount-of Moses to Yahweh and-he-spoke (25:1) Moses *** Yahweh he-commanded

סִינַי לֵאמֹר׃ דַּבֵּר אֶל־בְּנֵי יִשְׂרָאֵל וְאָמַרְתָּ אֲלֵהֶם כִּי תָבֹאוּ

you-enter when to-them and-you-say Israel sons-of to speak! (2) to-say Sinai

אֶל־הָאָרֶץ אֲשֶׁר אֲנִי נֹתֵן לָכֶם וְשָׁבְתָה הָאָרֶץ שַׁבָּת

sabbath the-land then-she-must-observe to-you giving I that the-land into

לַיהוָה׃ שֵׁשׁ שָׁנִים תִּזְרַע שָׂדֶךָ וְשֵׁשׁ שָׁנִים תִּזְמֹר

you-prune years and-six field-of-you you-sow years six (3) to-Yahweh

כַּרְמֶךָ וְאָסַפְתָּ אֶת־תְּבוּאָתָהּ׃ וּבַשָּׁנָה הַשְּׁבִיעִת

the-seventh but-in-the-year (4) crop-of-her *** and-you-gather vineyard-of-you

שַׁבַּת שַׁבָּתוֹן יִהְיֶה לָאָרֶץ שַׁבָּת לַיהוָה שָׂדְךָ לֹא

not field-of-you to-Yahweh sabbath for-the-land he-must-be rest sabbath-of

תִזְרָע וְכַרְמְךָ לֹא תִזְמֹר׃ אֵת סְפִיחַ

spontaneous-growth-of *** (5) you-prune not and-vineyard-of-you you-sow

קְצִירְךָ לֹא תִקְצוֹר וְאֶת־עִנְּבֵי נְזִירֶךָ לֹא תִבְצֹר

you-harvest not untended-vine-of-you grapes-of and you-reap not crop-of-you

שְׁנַת שַׁבָּתוֹן יִהְיֶה לָאָרֶץ׃ וְהָיְתָה שַׁבַּת הָאָרֶץ

the-land sabbath-of and-she-will-be (6) for-the-land he-must-be rest year-of

לָכֶם לְאָכְלָה לְךָ וּלְעַבְדְּךָ וְלַאֲמָתֶךָ

and-for-maidservant-of-you and-for-manservant-of-you for-you for-food for-you

וְלִשְׂכִירְךָ וּלְתוֹשָׁבְךָ הַגָּרִים עִמָּךְ׃

among-you the-ones-living and-for-guest-of-you and-for-hired-worker-of-you

וְלִבְהֶמְתְּךָ וְלַחַיָּה אֲשֶׁר בְּאַרְצֶךָ תִּהְיֶה

she-will-be in-land-of-you that and-for-wild-animal and-for-stock-of-you (7)

כָל־תְּבוּאָתָהּ לֶאֱכֹל׃ וְסָפַרְתָּ לְךָ שֶׁבַע שַׁבְּתֹת

sabbaths-of seven for-you and-you-count (8) to-eat produce-of-her all-of

20fracture for fracture, eye for eye, tooth for tooth. As he has injured the other, so he is to be injured. 21Whoever kills an animal must make restitution, but whoever kills a man must be put to death. 22You are to have the same law for the alien and the native-born. I am the LORD your God.' "

23Then Moses spoke to the Israelites, and they took the blasphemer outside the camp and stoned him. The Israelites did as the LORD commanded Moses.

*The Sabbatical Year*

25 The LORD said to Moses on Mount Sinai, 2"Speak to the Israelites and say to them: 'When you enter the land I am going to give you, the land itself must observe a sabbath to the LORD. 3For six years sow your fields, and for six years prune your vineyards and gather their crops. 4But in the seventh year the land is to have a sabbath of rest, a sabbath to the LORD. Do not sow your fields or prune your vineyards. 5Do not reap what grows of itself or harvest the grapes of your untended vines. The land is to have a year of rest. 6Whatever the land yields during the sabbath year will be food for you—for yourself, your manservant and maidservant, and the hired worker and temporary resident who live among you, 7as well as for your livestock and the wild animals in your land. Whatever the land produces may be eaten.

*The Year of Jubilee*

8" 'Count off seven sabbaths

שָׁנִים שֶׁבַע שָׁנִים שֶׁבַע פְּעָמִים וְהָיוּ לְךָ יְמֵי שֶׁבַע שַׁבְּתֹת
sabbaths-of seven days-of to-you so-they-are times seven years seven years

הַשָּׁנִים תֵּשַׁע וְאַרְבָּעִים שָׁנָה׃ וְהַעֲבַרְתָּ שׁוֹפַר תְּרוּעָה
sound trumpet then-you-have-sounded (9) year and-forty nine the-years

בַּחֹדֶשׁ הַשְּׁבִעִי בֶּעָשׂוֹר לַחֹדֶשׁ בְּיוֹם הַכִּפֻּרִים
the-Atonements on-Day-of of-the-month on-the-tenth the-seventh in-the-month

תַּעֲבִירוּ שׁוֹפָר בְּכָל־ אַרְצְכֶם׃ וְקִדַּשְׁתֶּם אֵת
*** and-you-consecrate (10) land-of-you through-all-of trumpet you-sound

שְׁנַת הַחֲמִשִּׁים שָׁנָה וּקְרָאתֶם דְּרוֹר בָּאָרֶץ
through-the-land liberty and-you-proclaim year the-fiftieth year-of

לְכָל־ יֹשְׁבֶיהָ יוֹבֵל הִוא תִּהְיֶה לָכֶם
for-you she-shall-be this jubilee ones-inhabiting-her to-all-of

וְשַׁבְתֶּם אִישׁ אֶל־ אֲחֻזָּתוֹ וְאִישׁ אֶל־ מִשְׁפַּחְתּוֹ
clan-of-him to and-each family-property-of-him to each and-you-must-return

תָּשֻׁבוּ׃ יוֹבֵל הִוא שְׁנַת הַחֲמִשִּׁים שָׁנָה תִּהְיֶה
she-shall-be year the-fiftieth year-of this jubilee (11) you-must-return

לָכֶם לֹא תִזְרָעוּ וְלֹא תִקְצְרוּ אֶת־ סְפִיחֶיהָ וְלֹא
and-not spontaneous-growth-of-her *** you-reap and-not you-sow not for-you

תִבְצְרוּ אֶת־ נְזִרֶיהָ׃ כִּי יוֹבֵל הִוא קֹדֶשׁ תִּהְיֶה
she-must-be holy this jubilee for (12) untended-vines-of-her *** you-harvest

לָכֶם מִן־ הַשָּׂדֶה תֹּאכְלוּ אֶת־ תְּבוּאָתָהּ׃ בִּשְׁנַת הַיּוֹבֵל
the-Jubilee in-Year-of (13) produce-of-her *** you-eat the-field from for-you

הַזֹּאת תָּשֻׁבוּ אִישׁ אֶל־ אֲחֻזָּתוֹ׃ וְכִי־ תִמְכְּרוּ מִמְכָּר
land you-sell and-if (14) property-of-him to each you-return the-this

לַעֲמִיתֶךָ אוֹ קָנֹה מִיַּד עֲמִיתֶךָ אַל־
not countryman-of-you from-hand-of to-buy or to-countryman-of-you

תּוֹנוּ אִישׁ אֶת־ אָחִיו׃ בְּמִסְפַּר שָׁנִים אַחַר
since years by-number-of (15) other-of-him *** each you-take-advantage

הַיּוֹבֵל תִּקְנֶה מֵאֵת עֲמִיתֶךָ בְּמִסְפַּר שְׁנֵי־ תְבוּאֹת
harvests years-of by-number-of countryman-of-you from you-buy the-Jubilee

יִמְכָּר־ לָךְ׃ לְפִי ׀ רֹב הַשָּׁנִים תַּרְבֶּה
you-increase the-years many-of on-account-of (16) to-you he-must-sell

מִקְנָתוֹ וּלְפִי מְעֹט הַשָּׁנִים תַּמְעִיט מִקְנָתוֹ
price-of-him you-decrease the-years few-of and-on-account-of price-of-him

כִּי מִסְפַּר תְּבוּאֹת הוּא מֹכֵר לָךְ׃ וְלֹא תוֹנוּ אִישׁ
each you-take-advantage and-not (17) to-you selling he crops number-of for

אֶת־ עֲמִיתוֹ וְיָרֵאתָ מֵּאֱלֹהֶיךָ כִּי אֲנִי יְהוָה אֱלֹהֵיכֶם׃
God-of-you Yahweh I for to-God-of-you but-you-fear countryman-of-him ***

of years—seven times seven years—so that the seven sabbaths of years amount to a period of forty-nine years. [9]Then have the trumpet sounded everywhere on the tenth day of the seventh month; on the Day of Atonement sound the trumpet throughout your land. [10]Consecrate the fiftieth year and proclaim liberty throughout the land to all its inhabitants. It shall be a jubilee for you; each one of you is to return to his family property and each to his own clan. [11]The fiftieth year shall be a jubilee for you; do not sow and do not reap what grows of itself or harvest the untended vines. [12]For it is a jubilee and is to be holy for you; eat only what is taken directly from the fields.

[13]" 'In this Year of Jubilee everyone is to return to his own property.

[14]" 'If you sell land to one of your countrymen or buy any from him, do not take advantage of each other. [15]You are to buy from your countryman on the basis of the number of years since the Jubilee. And he is to sell to you on the basis of the number of years left for harvesting crops. [16]When the years are many, you are to increase the price, and when the years are few, you are to decrease the price, because what he is really selling you is the number of crops. [17]Do not take advantage of each other, but fear your God. I am the LORD your God.

וַעֲשִׂיתֶם אֶת־ חֻקֹּתַי וְאֶת־ מִשְׁפָּטַי תִּשְׁמְרוּ
you-be-careful laws-of-me and decrees-of-me *** and-you-follow (18)

וַעֲשִׂיתֶם אֹתָם וִישַׁבְתֶּם עַל־ הָאָרֶץ לָבֶטַח׃ וְנָתְנָה
and-she-will-yield (19) in-safety the-land in and-you-will-live them and-you-do

הָאָרֶץ פִּרְיָהּ וַאֲכַלְתֶּם לָשֹׂבַע וִישַׁבְתֶּם
and-you-will-live to-fullness and-you-will-eat fruit-of-her the-land

לָבֶטַח עָלֶיהָ׃ וְכִי תֹאמְרוּ מַה־ נֹּאכַל בַּשָּׁנָה
in-the-year will-we-eat what? you-ask and-if (20) in-her in-safety

הַשְּׁבִיעִת הֵן לֹא נִזְרָע וְלֹא נֶאֱסֹף אֶת־ תְּבוּאָתֵנוּ׃
crop-of-us *** we-harvest or-not we-plant not if the-seventh

וְצִוִּיתִי אֶת־ בִּרְכָתִי לָכֶם בַּשָּׁנָה הַשִּׁשִּׁית
the-sixth in-the-year to-you blessing-of-me *** now-I-will-send (21)

וְעָשָׂת אֶת־ הַתְּבוּאָה לִשְׁלֹשׁ הַשָּׁנִים׃ וּזְרַעְתֶּם
while-you-plant (22) the-years for-three-of the-crop *** and-she-will-yield

אֵת הַשָּׁנָה הַשְּׁמִינִת וַאֲכַלְתֶּם מִן־ הַתְּבוּאָה יָשָׁן עַד ׀ הַשָּׁנָה
the-year until old the-crop from then-you-will-eat the-eighth the-year ***

הַתְּשִׁיעִת עַד־ בּוֹא תְּבוּאָתָהּ תֹּאכְלוּ יָשָׁן׃ וְהָאָרֶץ
and-the-land (23) old you-will-eat harvest-of-her to-come-in until the-ninth

לֹא תִמָּכֵר לִצְמִתֻת כִּי־ לִי הָאָרֶץ כִּי־ גֵרִים וְתוֹשָׁבִים
and-tenants aliens for the-land to-me for to-permanence she-must-be-sold not

אַתֶּם עִמָּדִי׃ וּבְכֹל אֶרֶץ אֲחֻזַּתְכֶם גְּאֻלָּה
redemption possession-of-you country-of and-through-all-of (24) to-me you

תִּתְּנוּ לָאָרֶץ׃ כִּי־ יָמוּךְ אָחִיךָ
countryman-of-you he-becomes-poor if (25) for-the-land you-must-provide

וּמָכַר מֵאֲחֻזָּתוֹ וּבָא גֹאֲלוֹ
one-redeeming-him then-he-must-come from-property-of-him and-he-sells

הַקָּרֹב אֵלָיו וְגָאַל אֵת מִמְכַּר אָחִיו׃
countryman-of-him sold-of *** and-he-must-redeem to-him the-one-near

וְאִישׁ כִּי לֹא יִהְיֶה־ לּוֹ גֹּאֵל וְהִשִּׂיגָה יָדוֹ
hand-of-him and-he-prospers one-redeeming to-him he-is not if and-man (26)

וּמָצָא כְּדֵי גְאֻלָּתוֹ׃ וְחִשַּׁב
and-he-must-determine (27) redemption-of-him as-sufficient-of and-he-acquires

אֶת־ שְׁנֵי מִמְכָּרוֹ וְהֵשִׁיב אֶת־ הָעֹדֵף לָאִישׁ
to-the-man the-remaining *** and-he-must-refund value-of-him years-of ***

אֲשֶׁר מָכַר־ לוֹ וְשָׁב לַאֲחֻזָּתוֹ׃ וְאִם לֹא־
not but-if (28) to-property-of-him then-he-can-go-back to-him he-sold whom

מָצְאָה יָדוֹ דֵּי הָשִׁיב לוֹ וְהָיָה
then-he-will-remain to-him to-repay means hand-of-him she-acquires

18" 'Follow my decrees and
be careful to obey my laws,
and you will live safely in the
land. 19Then the land will yield
its fruit, and you will eat your
fill and live there in safety.
20You may ask, "What will we
eat in the seventh year if we
do not plant or harvest our
crops?" 21I will send you such
a blessing in the sixth year
that the land will yield enough
for three years. 22While you
plant during the eighth year,
you will eat from the old crop
and will continue to eat from
it until the harvest of the
ninth year comes in.

23" 'The land must not be
sold permanently, because the
land is mine and you are but
aliens and my tenants.
24Throughout the country that
you hold as a possession, you
must provide for the redemption of the land.

25" 'If one of your countrymen becomes poor and sells
some of his property, his nearest relative is to come and redeem what his countryman
has sold. 26If, however, a man
has no one to redeem it for
him but he himself prospers
and acquires sufficient means
to redeem it, 27he is to determine the value for the years
since he sold it and refund the
balance to the man to whom
he sold it; he can then go back
to his own property. 28But if he
does not acquire the means to
repay him, what he sold will

מִמְכָּרוֹ בְּיַד הַקֹּנֶה אֹתוֹ עַד שְׁנַת הַיּוֹבֵל
the-Jubilee Year-of until him the-one-buying in-possession-of sold-of-him

וְיָצָא בַּיֹּבֵל וְשָׁב לַאֲחֻזָּתוֹ׃
to-property-of-him and-he-can-go-back in-the-Jubilee then-he-will-return

(29) וְאִישׁ כִּי־ יִמְכֹּר בֵּית־ מוֹשַׁב עִיר חוֹמָה וְהָיְתָה
then-he-retains wall city-of dwelling-of house-of he-sells if and-man (29)

גְּאֻלָּתוֹ עַד־ תֹּם שְׁנַת מִמְכָּרוֹ יָמִים תִּהְיֶה
she-may-be times sale-of-him year-of to-end until redemption-of-him

גְּאֻלָּתוֹ׃ (30) וְאִם לֹא־ יִגָּאֵל עַד־ מְלֹאת לוֹ שָׁנָה
year by-him to-pass before he-is-redeemed not but-if (30) redemption-of-him

תְמִימָה וְקָם הַבַּיִת אֲשֶׁר־ בָּעִיר אֲשֶׁר־ לֹא° חֹמָה
wall to-him that in-the-city that the-house then-he-shall-belong full

לַצְּמִיתֻת לַקֹּנֶה אֹתוֹ לְדֹרֹתָיו לֹא
not for-descendants-of-him him to-the-one-buying for-the-permanence

יֵצֵא בַּיֹּבֵל׃ (31) וּבָתֵּי הַחֲצֵרִים אֲשֶׁר אֵין־
he-is-not that the-villages but-houses-of (31) in-the-Jubilee he-must-return

לָהֶם חֹמָה סָבִיב עַל־ שְׂדֵה הָאָרֶץ יֵחָשֵׁב
they-must-be-considered the-country open-field-of in around wall to-them

גְּאֻלָּה תִּהְיֶה־ לּוֹ וּבַיֹּבֵל יֵצֵא׃
he-must-return and-in-the-Jubilee for-him she-will-be redemption

(32) וְעָרֵי הַלְוִיִּם בָּתֵּי עָרֵי אֲחֻזָּתָם
possession-of-them towns-of houses-of the-Levites and-towns-of (32)

גְּאֻלַּת עוֹלָם תִּהְיֶה לַלְוִיִּם׃ (33) וַאֲשֶׁר יִגְאַל
he-may-redeem so-that (33) for-the-Levites she-is continual redemption-of

מִן־ הַלְוִיִּם וְיָצָא מִמְכַּר־ בַּיִת וְעִיר אֲחֻזָּתוֹ
holding-of-them in-town-of house sold-of and-he-must-return the-Levites from

בַּיֹּבֵל כִּי בָתֵּי עָרֵי הַלְוִיִּם הִוא אֲחֻזָּתָם
property-of-them this the-Levites towns-of houses-of for in-the-Jubilee

בְּתוֹךְ בְּנֵי יִשְׂרָאֵל׃ (34) וּשְׂדֵה מִגְרַשׁ עָרֵיהֶם לֹא
not towns-of-them pasture-of but-land-of (34) Israel sons-of among

יִמָּכֵר כִּי־ אֲחֻזַּת עוֹלָם הוּא לָהֶם׃ (35) וְכִי־
and-if (35) to-them he permanent possession-of for he-must-be-sold

יָמוּךְ אָחִיךָ וּמָטָה יָדוֹ
hand-of-him and-she-cannot-support countryman-of-you he-becomes-poor

עִמָּךְ וְהֶחֱזַקְתָּ בּוֹ גֵּר וְתוֹשָׁב וָחַי
so-he-can-live or-temporary-resident alien to-him then-you-help among-you

עִמָּךְ׃ (36) אַל־ תִּקַּח מֵאִתּוֹ נֶשֶׁךְ וְתַרְבִּית וְיָרֵאתָ
but-you-fear or-usury interest from-him you-take not (36) among-you

°30 ק לו

remain in the possession of the buyer until the Year of Jubilee. It will be returned in the Jubilee, and he can then go back to his property.

29" 'If a man sells a house in a walled city, he retains the right of redemption a full year after its sale. During that time he may redeem it. 30If it is not redeemed before a full year has passed, the house in the walled city shall belong permanently to the buyer and his descendants. It is not to be returned in the Jubilee. 31But houses in villages without walls around them are to be considered as open country. They can be redeemed, and they are to be returned in the Jubilee.

32" 'The Levites always have the right to redeem their houses in the Levitical towns, which they possess. 33So the property of the Levites is redeemable—that is, a house sold in any town they hold—and is to be returned in the Jubilee, because the houses in the towns of the Levites are their property among the Israelites. 34But the pastureland belonging to their towns must not be sold; it is their permanent possession.

35" 'If one of your countrymen becomes poor and is unable to support himself among you, help him as you would an alien or a temporary resident, so he can continue to live among you. 36Do not take interest of any kind[l] from him,

[l]36 Or *take exorbitant interest*

מֵאֱלֹהֶ֑יךָ וְחֵ֥י אָחִ֖יךָ עִמָּֽךְ׃ אֶֽת־ כַּסְפְּךָ֔
money-of-you *** (37) among-you countryman-of-you so-he-may-live to-God-of-you

לֹא־ תִתֵּ֥ן ל֖וֹ בְּנֶ֑שֶׁךְ וּבְמַרְבִּ֖ית לֹא־ תִתֵּ֥ן אָכְלֶֽךָ׃
food-of-you you-sell not or-at-profit at-interest to-him you-lend not

(38) אֲנִ֗י יְהוָה֙ אֱלֹ֣הֵיכֶ֔ם אֲשֶׁר־הוֹצֵ֥אתִי אֶתְכֶ֖ם מֵאֶ֣רֶץ מִצְרָ֑יִם לָתֵ֤ת לָכֶם֙
to-you to-give Egypt from-land-of you I-brought who God-of-you Yahweh I (38)

אֶת־ אֶ֣רֶץ כְּנַ֔עַן לִהְי֥וֹת לָכֶ֖ם לֵאלֹהִֽים׃ (39) וְכִֽי־ יָמ֥וּךְ
he-becomes-poor and-if (39) as-God to-you to-be Canaan land-of ***

אָחִ֛יךָ עִמָּ֖ךְ וְנִמְכַּר־ לָ֑ךְ לֹֽא־ תַעֲבֹ֥ד
you-give-work not to-you and-he-sells-self among-you countryman-of-you

בּ֖וֹ עֲבֹ֥דַת עָֽבֶד׃ (40) כְּשָׂכִ֥יר כְּתוֹשָׁ֖ב יִהְיֶ֣ה
he-must-be as-temporary-resident as-hired-worker (40) slave work-of to-him

עִמָּ֑ךְ עַד־ שְׁנַ֥ת הַיֹּבֵ֖ל יַעֲבֹ֥ד עִמָּֽךְ׃ (41) וְיָצָא֙
and-he-must-leave (41) for-you he-will-work the-Jubilee Year-of until among-you

מֵֽעִמָּ֔ךְ ה֖וּא וּבָנָ֣יו עִמּ֑וֹ וְשָׁב֙ אֶל־
to and-he-will-go-back with-him and-children-of-him he from-among-you

מִשְׁפַּחְתּ֔וֹ וְאֶל־ אֲחֻזַּ֥ת אֲבֹתָ֖יו יָשֽׁוּב׃ (42) כִּֽי־
for (42) he-will-go-back forefathers-of-him property-of and-to clan-of-him

עֲבָדַ֣י הֵ֔ם אֲשֶׁר־ הוֹצֵ֥אתִי אֹתָ֖ם מֵאֶ֣רֶץ מִצְרָ֑יִם לֹ֥א
not Egypt from-land-of them I-brought whom they servants-of-me

יִמָּכְר֖וּ מִמְכֶּ֥רֶת עָֽבֶד׃ (43) לֹא־ תִרְדֶּ֥ה ב֖וֹ בְּפָ֑רֶךְ
with-ruthlessness over-him you-rule not (43) slave sale-of they-must-be-sold

וְיָרֵ֖אתָ מֵאֱלֹהֶֽיךָ׃ (44) וְעַבְדְּךָ֥ וַאֲמָתְךָ֖
and-female-slave-of-you now-male-slave-of-you (44) to-God-of-you but-you-fear

אֲשֶׁ֣ר יִהְיוּ־ לָ֑ךְ מֵאֵ֣ת הַגּוֹיִ֗ם אֲשֶׁר֙ סְבִיבֹ֣תֵיכֶ֔ם מֵהֶ֥ם
from-them ones-around-you that the-nations from to-you they-are who

תִּקְנ֖וּ עֶ֥בֶד וְאָמָֽה׃ (45) וְגַ֡ם מִבְּנֵי֩
from-children-of and-also (45) and-female-slave male-slave you-buy

הַתּוֹשָׁבִ֨ים הַגָּרִ֤ים עִמָּכֶם֙ מֵהֶ֣ם תִּקְנ֔וּ
you-may-buy from-them among-you the-ones-living the-temporary-residents

וּמִמִּשְׁפַּחְתָּם֙ אֲשֶׁ֣ר עִמָּכֶ֔ם אֲשֶׁ֥ר הוֹלִ֖ידוּ בְּאַרְצְכֶ֑ם
in-country-of-you they-bear whom among-you that and-from-clan-of-them

וְהָי֥וּ לָכֶ֖ם לַאֲחֻזָּֽה׃ (46) וְהִתְנַחַלְתֶּ֨ם* אֹתָ֜ם
them and-you-can-will (46) as-property to-you and-they-will-become

לִבְנֵיכֶ֤ם אַחֲרֵיכֶם֙ לָרֶ֣שֶׁת אֲחֻזָּ֔ה לְעֹלָ֖ם בָּהֶ֣ם
of-them for-life property as-inheritance-of after-you to-children-of-you

תַּעֲבֹ֑דוּ וּבְאַחֵיכֶ֣ם בְּנֵֽי־ יִשְׂרָאֵ֗ל אִ֚ישׁ
man Israel sons-of but-over-fellows-of-you you-can-make-slave

but fear your God, so that your countryman may continue to live among you. [37]You must not lend him money at interest or sell him food at a profit. [38]I am the LORD your God, who brought you out of Egypt to give you the land of Canaan and to be your God.

[39]"'If one of your countrymen becomes poor among you and sells himself to you, do not make him work as a slave. [40]He is to be treated as a hired worker or a temporary resident among you; he is to work for you until the Year of Jubilee. [41]Then he and his children are to be released, and he will go back to his own clan and to the property of his forefathers. [42]Because the Israelites are my servants, whom I brought out of Egypt, they must not be sold as slaves. [43]Do not rule over them ruthlessly, but fear your God.

[44]"'Your male and female slaves are to come from the nations around you; from them you may buy slaves. [45]You may also buy some of the temporary residents living among you and members of their clans born in your country, and they will become your property. [46]You can will them to your children as inherited property and can make them slaves for life, but you must

*46 Most mss have *pathah* under the *heth* ('נַחַ־).

בְּאָחִיו לֹא־ תִרְדֶּה בּוֹ בְּפֶרֶךְ׃ וְכִי
and-if (47) with-ruthlessness over-him you-must-rule not over-fellow-of-him

תַשִּׂיג יַד גֵּר וְתוֹשָׁב עִמָּךְ
among-you or-temporary-resident alien hand-of she-becomes-rich

וּמָךְ אָחִיךָ עִמּוֹ וְנִמְכַּר לְגֵר
to-alien and-he-sells-self with-him countryman-of-you and-he-becomes-poor

תּוֹשָׁב עִמָּךְ אוֹ לְעֵקֶר מִשְׁפַּחַת גֵּר׃ אַחֲרֵי נִמְכַּר
he-sells-self after (48) alien clan-of to-member-of or among-you resident

גְּאֻלָּה תִּהְיֶה־ לּוֹ אֶחָד מֵאֶחָיו יִגְאָלֶנּוּ׃
he-may-redeem-him from-relatives-of-him one for-him she-remains redemption

אוֹ־ דֹדוֹ אוֹ בֶן־ דֹּדוֹ יִגְאָלֶנּוּ אוֹ־
or he-may-redeem-him uncle-of-him son-of or uncle-of-him or (49)

מִשְּׁאֵר בְּשָׂרוֹ מִמִּשְׁפַּחְתּוֹ יִגְאָלֶנּוּ אוֹ־
or he-may-redeem-him from-clan-of-him flesh-of-him from-relative-of

הִשִּׂיגָה יָדוֹ וְנִגְאָל׃ וְחִשַּׁב
then-he-must-count (50) then-he-may-redeem-self hand-of-him she-prospers

עִם־ קֹנֵהוּ מִשְּׁנַת הִמָּכְרוֹ לוֹ עַד שְׁנַת
Year-of up-to to-him to-be-sold-him from-year-of one-buying-him with

הַיֹּבֵל וְהָיָה כֶּסֶף מִמְכָּרוֹ בְּמִסְפַּר שָׁנִים
years on-number-of release-of-him price-of and-he-will-be the-Jubilee

כִּימֵי שָׂכִיר יִהְיֶה עִמּוֹ׃ אִם־ עוֹד רַבּוֹת בַּשָּׁנִים
of-the-years many yet if (51) with-him he-would-be hired-man as-days-of

לְפִיהֶן יָשִׁיב גְּאֻלָּתוֹ מִכֶּסֶף מִקְנָתוֹ׃
purchase-of-him from-price-of redemption-of-him he-must-pay on-account-of-them

וְאִם־ מְעַט נִשְׁאַר בַּשָּׁנִים עַד־ שְׁנַת הַיֹּבֵל
the-Jubilee Year-of until of-the-years he-remains few but-if (52)

וְחִשַּׁב־ לוֹ כְּפִי שָׁנָיו יָשִׁיב אֶת־
*** and-he-must-pay years-of-him on-account-of for-him then-he-must-compute

גְּאֻלָּתוֹ׃ כִּשְׂכִיר שָׁנָה בְּשָׁנָה יִהְיֶה עִמּוֹ לֹא־
not to-him he-must-be by-year year as-hired-man-of (53) redemption-of-him

יִרְדֶּנּוּ בְּפֶרֶךְ לְעֵינֶיךָ׃ וְאִם־ לֹא
not even-if (54) before-eyes-of-you with-ruthlessness he-must-rule-him

יִגָּאֵל בְּאֵלֶּה וְיָצָא בִּשְׁנַת הַיֹּבֵל הוּא
he the-Jubilee in-Year-of then-he-must-go-out by-these he-is-redeemed

וּבָנָיו עִמּוֹ׃ כִּי־ לִי בְנֵי־ יִשְׂרָאֵל עֲבָדִים
servants Israel sons-of to-me for (55) with-him and-children-of-him

עֲבָדַי הֵם אֲשֶׁר־ הוֹצֵאתִי אוֹתָם מֵאֶרֶץ מִצְרָיִם אֲנִי יְהוָה
Yahweh I Egypt from-land-of them I-brought whom they servants-of-me

not rule over your fellow Israelites ruthlessly.

47" 'If an alien or a temporary resident among you becomes rich and one of your countrymen becomes poor and sells himself to the alien living among you or to a member of the alien's clan, 48he retains the right of redemption after he has sold himself. One of his relatives may redeem him: 49An uncle or a cousin or any blood relative in his clan may redeem him. Or if he prospers, he may redeem himself. 50He and his buyer are to count the time from the year he sold himself up to the Year of Jubilee. The price for his release is to be based on the rate paid to a hired man for that number of years. 51If many years remain, he must pay for his redemption a larger share of the price paid for him. 52If only a few years remain until the Year of Jubilee, he is to compute that and pay for his redemption accordingly. 53He is to be treated as a man hired from year to year; you must see to it that his owner does not rule over him ruthlessly.

54" 'Even if he is not redeemed in any of these ways, he and his children are to be released in the Year of Jubilee, 55for the Israelites belong to me as servants. They are my servants, whom I brought out of Egypt. I am the LORD your

אֱלֹהֵיכֶם׃ לֹא־ תַעֲשׂוּ לָכֶם אֱלִילִם וּפֶסֶל וּמַצֵּבָה לֹא־
not or-sacred-stone or-image idols for-you you-make not (26:1) God-of-you

תָקִימוּ לָכֶם וְאֶבֶן מַשְׂכִּית לֹא תִתְּנוּ בְּאַרְצְכֶם לְהִשְׁתַּחֲוֺת
to-bow-down in-land-of-you you-place not carved and-stone for-you you-set-up

עָלֶיהָ כִּי אֲנִי יְהוָה אֱלֹהֵיכֶם׃ אֶת־ שַׁבְּתֹתַי תִּשְׁמֹרוּ
you-observe Sabbaths-of-me *** (2) God-of-you Yahweh I for before-her

וּמִקְדָּשִׁי תִּירָאוּ אֲנִי יְהוָה׃ אִם־ בְּחֻקֹּתַי תֵּלֵכוּ
you-follow to-decrees-of-me if (3) Yahweh I you-revere and-sanctuary-of-me

וְאֶת־ מִצְוֺתַי תִּשְׁמְרוּ וַעֲשִׂיתֶם אֹתָם׃ וְנָתַתִּי
then-I-will-send (4) them and-you-obey you-are-careful commands-of-me and

גִשְׁמֵיכֶם בְּעִתָּם וְנָתְנָה הָאָרֶץ יְבוּלָהּ
crop-of-her the-earth and-she-will-yield in-season-of-them rains-of-you

וְעֵץ הַשָּׂדֶה יִתֵּן פִּרְיוֹ׃ וְהִשִּׂיג
and-he-will-continue (5) fruit-of-him he-will-yield the-field and-tree-of

לָכֶם דַּיִשׁ אֶת־ בָּצִיר וּבָצִיר יַשִּׂיג אֶת־
*** he-will-continue and-grape-harvest grape-harvest *** threshing for-you

זָרַע וַאֲכַלְתֶּם לַחְמְכֶם לָשֹׂבַע וִישַׁבְתֶּם
and-you-will-live to-satisfaction food-of-you and-you-will-eat planting

לָבֶטַח בְּאַרְצְכֶם׃ וְנָתַתִּי שָׁלוֹם בָּאָרֶץ
in-the-land peace and-I-will-grant (6) in-land-of-you in-safety

וּשְׁכַבְתֶּם וְאֵין מַחֲרִיד וְהִשְׁבַּתִּי חַיָּה
beast and-I-will-remove making-afraid and-no-one and-you-will-lie-down

רָעָה מִן־ הָאָרֶץ וְחֶרֶב לֹא־ תַעֲבֹר בְּאַרְצְכֶם׃
through-country-of-you she-will-pass not and-sword the-land from savage

וּרְדַפְתֶּם אֶת־ אֹיְבֵיכֶם וְנָפְלוּ לִפְנֵיכֶם
before-you and-they-will-fall being-enemies-of-you *** and-you-will-pursue (7)

לֶחָרֶב וְרָדְפוּ מִכֶּם חֲמִשָּׁה מֵאָה וּמֵאָה
and-hundred hundred five from-you and-they-will-chase (8) by-the-sword

מִכֶּם רְבָבָה יִרְדֹּפוּ וְנָפְלוּ אֹיְבֵיכֶם
being-enemies-of-you and-they-will-fall they-will-chase ten-thousand from-you

לִפְנֵיכֶם לֶחָרֶב׃ וּפָנִיתִי אֲלֵיכֶם וְהִפְרֵיתִי
and-I-will-make-fruitful on-you and-I-will-look (9) by-the-sword before-you

אֶתְכֶם וְהִרְבֵּיתִי אֶתְכֶם וַהֲקִימֹתִי אֶת־ בְּרִיתִי אִתְּכֶם׃
with-you covenant-of-me *** and-I-will-keep you and-I-will-increase you

וַאֲכַלְתֶּם יָשָׁן נוֹשָׁן וְיָשָׁן מִפְּנֵי חָדָשׁ
new for-presence-of and-old being-old old-harvest and-you-will-eat (10)

תּוֹצִיאוּ׃ וְנָתַתִּי מִשְׁכָּנִי בְּתוֹכְכֶם וְלֹא־
and-not in-midst-of-you dwelling-of-me and-I-will-put (11) you-will-move-out

God.

*Reward for Obedience*

26 " 'Do not make idols or
set up an image or a sa-
cred stone for yourselves, and
do not place a carved stone in
your land to bow down before
it. I am the LORD your God.
2" 'Observe my Sabbaths
and have reverence for my
sanctuary. I am the LORD.
3" 'If you follow my decrees
and are careful to obey my
commands, 4I will send you
rain in its season, and the
ground will yield its crops and
the trees of the field their fruit.
5Your threshing will continue
until grape harvest and the
grape harvest will continue
until planting, and you will
eat all the food you want and
live in safety in your land.
6" 'I will grant peace in the
land, and you will lie down
and no one will make you
afraid. I will remove savage
beasts from the land, and the
sword will not pass through
your country. 7You will pursue
your enemies, and they will
fall by the sword before you.
8Five of you will chase a hundred, and a hundred of you
will chase ten thousand, and
your enemies will fall by the
sword before you.
9" 'I will look on you with
favor and make you fruitful
and increase your numbers,
and I will keep my covenant
with you. 10You will still be
eating last year's harvest
when you will have to move it
out to make room for the new.
11I will put my dwelling place[m]

[m] 11 Or *my tabernacle*

תִגְעַל נַפְשִׁי אֶתְכֶם׃ וְהִתְהַלַּכְתִּי בְּתוֹכְכֶם
in-midst-of-you and-I-will-walk (12) you spirit-of-me she-will-abhor

וְהָיִיתִי לָכֶם לֵאלֹהִים וְאַתֶּם תִּהְיוּ־ לִי לְעָם׃ אֲנִי
I (13) as-people to-me you-will-be and-you as-God to-you and-I-will-be

יְהוָה אֱלֹהֵיכֶם אֲשֶׁר הוֹצֵאתִי אֶתְכֶם מֵאֶרֶץ מִצְרַיִם מִהְיֹת לָהֶם
to-them from-to-be Egypt from-land-of you I-brought who God-of-you Yahweh

עֲבָדִים וָאֶשְׁבֹּר מֹטֹת עֻלְּכֶם וָאוֹלֵךְ אֶתְכֶם קוֹמְמִיּוּת׃
head-held-high you and-I-made-walk yoke-of-you bars-of and-I-broke slaves

וְאִם־ לֹא תִשְׁמְעוּ לִי וְלֹא תַעֲשׂוּ אֵת כָּל־
all-of *** you-carry-out and-not to-me you-listen not but-if (14)

הַמִּצְוֹת הָאֵלֶּה׃ וְאִם־ בְּחֻקֹּתַי תִּמְאָסוּ וְאִם אֶת־
*** and-if you-reject to-decrees-of-me and-if (15) the-these the-commands

מִשְׁפָּטַי תִּגְעַל נַפְשְׁכֶם לְבִלְתִּי עֲשׂוֹת אֶת־ כָּל־ מִצְוֹתַי
commands-of-me all-of *** to-carry-out not spirit-of-you she-abhors laws-of-me

לְהַפְרְכֶם אֶת־ בְּרִיתִי׃ אַף־ אֲנִי אֶעֱשֶׂה־ זֹּאת לָכֶם
to-you this I-will-do I then (16) covenant-of-me *** to-violate-you

וְהִפְקַדְתִּי עֲלֵיכֶם בֶּהָלָה אֶת־ הַשַּׁחֶפֶת וְאֶת־ הַקַּדַּחַת
the-fever and the-wasting-disease *** sudden-terror upon-you now-I-will-bring

מְכַלּוֹת עֵינַיִם וּמְדִיבֹת נָפֶשׁ וּזְרַעְתֶּם לָרִיק
in-vain and-you-will-plant life and-ones-draining eyes ones-destroying

זַרְעֲכֶם וַאֲכָלֻהוּ אֹיְבֵיכֶם׃ וְנָתַתִּי
and-I-will-set (17) being-enemies-of-you for-they-will-eat-him seed-of-you

פָנַי בָּכֶם וְנִגַּפְתֶּם לִפְנֵי אֹיְבֵיכֶם
being-enemies-of-you by so-you-will-be-defeated against-you faces-of-me

וְרָדוּ בָכֶם שֹׂנְאֵיכֶם וְנַסְתֶּם וְאֵין־
when-he-is-not and-you-will-flee ones-hating-you over-you and-they-will-rule

רֹדֵף אֶתְכֶם׃ וְאִם־ עַד־ אֵלֶּה לֹא תִשְׁמְעוּ לִי
to-me you-will-listen not these after and-if (18) you one-pursuing

וְיָסַפְתִּי לְיַסְּרָה אֶתְכֶם שֶׁבַע עַל־ חַטֹּאתֵיכֶם׃
sins-of-you for seven-time you to-punish then-I-will-continue

וְשָׁבַרְתִּי אֶת־ גְּאוֹן עֻזְּכֶם וְנָתַתִּי אֶת־
*** and-I-will-make stubborn-of-you pride-of *** and-I-will-break-down (19)

שְׁמֵיכֶם כַּבַּרְזֶל וְאֶת־ אַרְצְכֶם כַּנְּחֻשָׁה׃
like-the-bronze ground-of-you and like-the-iron skies-of-you

וְתַם לָרִיק כֹּחֲכֶם וְלֹא־ תִתֵּן
she-will-yield for-not strength-of-you in-vain and-he-will-be-spent (20)

אַרְצְכֶם אֶת־ יְבוּלָהּ וְעֵץ הָאָרֶץ לֹא יִתֵּן פִּרְיוֹ׃
fruit-of-him he-will-yield not the-land and-tree-of crop-of-her *** soil-of-you

among you, and I will not abhor you. [12]I will walk among you and be your God, and you will be my people. [13]I am the LORD your God, who brought you out of Egypt so that you would no longer be slaves to the Egyptians; I broke the bars of your yoke and enabled you to walk with heads held high.

*Punishment for Disobedience*

[14]" 'But if you will not listen to me and carry out all these commands, [15]and if you reject my decrees and abhor my laws and fail to carry out all my commands and so violate my covenant, [16]then I will do this to you: I will bring upon you sudden terror, wasting diseases and fever that will destroy your sight and drain away your life. You will plant seed in vain, because your enemies will eat it. [17]I will set my face against you so that you will be defeated by your enemies; those who hate you will rule over you, and you will flee even when no one is pursuing you.

[18]" 'If after all this you will not listen to me, I will punish you for your sins seven times over. [19]I will break down your stubborn pride and make the sky above you like iron and the ground beneath you like bronze. [20]Your strength will be spent in vain, because your soil will not yield its crops, nor will the trees of the land yield their fruit.

וְאִם־ תֵּלְכוּ עִמִּי קֶרִי וְלֹא תֹאבוּ לִשְׁמֹעַ לִי
to-me to-listen you-will and-not hostile toward-me you-remain and-if (21)

וְיָסַפְתִּי עֲלֵיכֶם מַכָּה שֶׁבַע כְּחַטֹּאתֵיכֶם׃
according-to-sins-of-you seven-time affliction on-you then-I-will-multiply

וְהִשְׁלַחְתִּי בָכֶם אֶת־ חַיַּת הַשָּׂדֶה
the-field animal-of *** against-you and-I-will-send (22)

וְשִׁכְּלָה אֶתְכֶם וְהִכְרִיתָה אֶת־ בְּהֶמְתְּכֶם
cattle-of-you *** and-she-will-destroy you and-she-will-make-childless

וְהִמְעִיטָה אֶתְכֶם וְנָשַׁמּוּ דַּרְכֵיכֶם׃ וְאִם־
and-if (23) roads-of-you that-they-will-be-deserted you and-she-will-make-few

בְּאֵלֶּה לֹא תִוָּסְרוּ לִי וַהֲלַכְתֶּם עִמִּי קֶרִי׃
hostile toward-me and-you-continue to-me you-are-corrected not after-these

וְהָלַכְתִּי אַף־ אֲנִי עִמָּכֶם בְּקֶרִי וְהִכֵּיתִי
and-I-will-afflict with-hostility against-you I indeed then-I-will-come (24)

אֶתְכֶם גַּם־אָנִי שֶׁבַע עַל־ חַטֹּאתֵיכֶם׃ וְהֵבֵאתִי עֲלֵיכֶם חֶרֶב
sword upon-you and-I-will-bring (25) sins-of-you for seven-time I also you

נֹקֶמֶת נְקַם־ בְּרִית וְנֶאֱסַפְתֶּם אֶל־ עָרֵיכֶם
cities-of-you into when-you-withdraw covenant vengeance-of avenging

וְשִׁלַּחְתִּי דֶבֶר בְּתוֹכְכֶם וְנִתַּתֶּם בְּיַד־
into-hand-of and-you-will-be-given in-midst-of-you plague then-I-will-send

אוֹיֵב׃ בְּשִׁבְרִי לָכֶם מַטֵּה־ לֶחֶם
bread supply-of from-you when-to-cut-off-me (26) being-enemy

וְאָפוּ עֶשֶׂר נָשִׁים לַחְמְכֶם בְּתַנּוּר אֶחָד וְהֵשִׁיבוּ
and-they-will-dole-out one in-oven bread-of-you women ten then-they-will-bake

לַחְמְכֶם בַּמִּשְׁקָל וַאֲכַלְתֶּם וְלֹא תִשְׂבָּעוּ׃
you-will-be-satisfied but-not and-you-will-eat by-the-weight bread-of-you

וְאִם־ בְּזֹאת לֹא תִשְׁמְעוּ לִי וַהֲלַכְתֶּם עִמִּי
toward-me and-you-continue to-me you-listen not after-this and-if (27)

בְּקֶרִי׃ וְהָלַכְתִּי עִמָּכֶם בַּחֲמַת־ קֶרִי
hostility in-anger-of toward-you then-I-will-continue (28) in-hostility

וְיִסַּרְתִּי אֶתְכֶם אַף־ אָנִי שֶׁבַע עַל־ חַטֹּאתֵיכֶם׃
sins-of-you for seven-time I indeed you and-I-will-punish

וַאֲכַלְתֶּם בְּשַׂר בְּנֵיכֶם וּבְשַׂר בְּנֹתֵיכֶם
daughters-of-you and-flesh-of sons-of-you flesh-of and-you-will-eat (29)

תֹּאכֵלוּ׃ וְהִשְׁמַדְתִּי אֶת־ בָּמֹתֵיכֶם וְהִכְרַתִּי
and-I-will-cut high-places-of-you *** and-I-will-destroy (30) you-will-eat

אֶת־ חַמָּנֵיכֶם וְנָתַתִּי אֶת־ פִּגְרֵיכֶם עַל־
on dead-bodies-of-you *** and-I-will-pile incense-altars-of-you ***

21" 'If you remain hostile
toward me and refuse to listen
to me, I will multiply your
afflictions seven times over, as
your sins deserve.
22 I will send
wild animals against you, and
they will rob you of your children, destroy your cattle and
make you so few in number
that your roads will be deserted.
23" 'If in spite of these things
you do not accept my correction but continue to be hostile
toward me,
24 I myself will be
hostile toward you and will
afflict you for your sins seven
times over.
25 And I will bring
the sword upon you to avenge
the breaking of the covenant.
When you withdraw into your
cities, I will send a plague
among you, and you will be
given into enemy hands.
26 When I cut off your supply of
bread, ten women will be able
to bake your bread in one
oven, and they will dole out
the bread by weight. You will
eat, but you will not be satisfied.
27" 'If in spite of this you still
do not listen to me but continue to be hostile toward me,
28 then in my anger I will be
hostile toward you, and I myself will punish you for your
sins seven times over.
29 You
will eat the flesh of your sons
and the flesh of your daughters.
30 I will destroy your high
places, cut down your incense
altars and pile your dead bodies on the lifeless forms of

פִּגְרֵי גִּלּוּלֵיכֶם וְגָעֲלָה נַפְשִׁי אֶתְכֶם׃

you spirit-of-me and-she-will-abhor idols-of-you lifeless-forms-of

וְנָתַתִּי אֶת־ עָרֵיכֶם חָרְבָּה וַהֲשִׁמּוֹתִי אֶת־

*** and-I-will-lay-waste ruin cities-of-you *** and-I-will-turn (31)

מִקְדְּשֵׁיכֶם וְלֹא אָרִיחַ בְּרֵיחַ נִיחֹחֲכֶם׃

pleasant-of-you in-aroma-of I-will-delight and-not sanctuaries-of-you

וַהֲשִׁמֹּתִי אֲנִי אֶת־ הָאָרֶץ וְשָׁמְמוּ עָלֶיהָ

at-her so-they-will-be-appalled the-land *** I and-I-will-lay-waste (32)

אֹיְבֵיכֶם הַיֹּשְׁבִים בָּהּ׃ וְאֶתְכֶם אֱזָרֶה

I-will-scatter and-you (33) in-her the-ones-living being-enemies-of-you

בַגּוֹיִם וַהֲרִיקֹתִי אַחֲרֵיכֶם חָרֶב וְהָיְתָה אַרְצְכֶם

land-of-you and-she-will-be sword after-you and-I-will-draw among-the-nations

שְׁמָמָה וְעָרֵיכֶם יִהְיוּ חָרְבָּה׃ אָז תִּרְצֶה הָאָרֶץ

the-land she-will-enjoy then (34) ruin they-will-be and-cities-of-you waste

אֶת־ שַׁבְּתֹתֶיהָ כֹּל יְמֵי הָשַּׁמָּה וְאַתֶּם בְּאֶרֶץ

in-country-of and-you the-desolation days-of all-of sabbaths-of-her ***

אֹיְבֵיכֶם אָז תִּשְׁבַּת הָאָרֶץ וְהִרְצָת אֶת־

*** and-she-will-enjoy the-land she-will-rest then being-enemies-of-you

שַׁבְּתֹתֶיהָ׃ כָּל־ יְמֵי הָשַּׁמָּה תִּשְׁבֹּת אֵת

*** she-will-have-rest the-desolation days-of all-of (35) sabbaths-of-her

אֲשֶׁר לֹא־ שָׁבְתָה בְּשַׁבְּתֹתֵיכֶם בְּשִׁבְתְּכֶם עָלֶיהָ׃

on-her when-to-live-you during-sabbaths-of-you she-rested not that

וְהַנִּשְׁאָרִים בָּכֶם וְהֵבֵאתִי מֹרֶךְ בִּלְבָבָם

in-heart-of-them fear then-I-will-bring from-you and-the-ones-being-left (36)

בְּאַרְצֹת אֹיְבֵיהֶם וְרָדַף אֹתָם קוֹל

sound-of them and-he-will-put-to-flight being-enemies-of-them in-lands-of

עָלֶה נִדָּף וְנָסוּ מְנֻסַת־ חֶרֶב וְנָפְלוּ

and-they-will-fall sword flight-of and-they-will-run being-blown leaf

וְאֵין רֹדֵף׃ וְכָשְׁלוּ אִישׁ־ בְּאָחִיו

over-other-of-him one and-they-will-stumble (37) pursuing but-he-is-not

כְּמִפְּנֵי־ חֶרֶב וְרֹדֵף אָיִן וְלֹא־ תִהְיֶה לָכֶם

for-you she-will-be so-not he-is-not but-pursuing sword as-from-edges-of

תְּקוּמָה לִפְנֵי אֹיְבֵיכֶם׃ וַאֲבַדְתֶּם

and-you-will-perish (38) being-enemies-of-you before standing-place

בַּגּוֹיִם וְאָכְלָה אֶתְכֶם אֶרֶץ אֹיְבֵיכֶם׃

being-enemies-of-you land-of you and-she-will-devour among-the-nations

וְהַנִּשְׁאָרִים בָּכֶם יִמַּקּוּ בַּעֲוֹנָם

for-sin-of-them they-will-waste-away from-you and-the-ones-being-left (39)

your idols, and I will abhor
you. 31 I will turn your cities
into ruins and lay waste your
sanctuaries, and I will take no
delight in the pleasing aroma
of your offerings. 32 I will lay
waste the land, so that your
enemies who live there will be
appalled. 33 I will scatter you
among the nations and will
draw out my sword and pursue you. Your land will be laid
waste, and your cities will lie
in ruins. 34 Then the land will
enjoy its sabbath years all the
time that it lies desolate and
you are in the country of your
enemies; then the land will
rest and enjoy its sabbaths.
35 All the time that it lies desolate, the land will have the rest
it did not have during the sabbaths you lived in it.

36 " 'As for those of you who
are left, I will make their
hearts so fearful in the lands of
their enemies that the sound
of a wind-blown leaf will put
them to flight. They will run as
though fleeing from the
sword, and they will fall, even
though no one is pursuing
them. 37 They will stumble over
one another as though fleeing
from the sword, even though
no one is pursuing them. So
you will not be able to stand
before your enemies. 38 You
will perish among the nations;
the land of your enemies will
devour you. 39 Those of you
who are left will waste away

בְּאַרְצֹת אֹיְבֵיכֶם וְאַף בַּעֲוֹנֹת אֲבֹתָם
fathers-of-them for-sins-of and-also being-enemies-of-you in-lands-of

אִתָּם יִמָּקּוּ׃ (40) וְהִתְוַדּוּ אֶת־ עֲוֹנָם וְאֶת־
and sin-of-them *** if-they-confess (40) they-will-waste-away with-them

עֲוֹן אֲבֹתָם בְּמַעֲלָם אֲשֶׁר מָעֲלוּ־
they-were-treacherous when for-treachery-of-them fathers-of-them sin-of

בִי וְאַף אֲשֶׁר־ הָלְכוּ עִמִּי בְּקֶרִי׃ (41) אַף־
then (41) with-hostility toward-me they-continued when and-also against-me

אֲנִי אֵלֵךְ עִמָּם בְּקֶרִי וְהֵבֵאתִי אֹתָם בְּאֶרֶץ
into-land-of them so-I-sent with-hostility toward-them I-continued I

אֹיְבֵיהֶם אוֹ־ אָז יִכָּנַע לְבָבָם הֶעָרֵל
the-uncircumcised heart-of-them he-is-humbled when then being-enemies-of-them

וְאָז יִרְצוּ אֶת־ עֲוֹנָם׃ (42) וְזָכַרְתִּי אֶת־ בְּרִיתִי
covenant-of-me *** then-I-will-remember (42) sin-of-them *** they-pay and-when

יַעֲקוֹב וְאַף אֶת־ בְּרִיתִי יִצְחָק וְאַף אֶת־ בְּרִיתִי אַבְרָהָם
Abraham covenant-of-me *** and-also Isaac covenant-of-me *** and-also Jacob

אֶזְכֹּר וְהָאָרֶץ אֶזְכֹּר׃ (43) וְהָאָרֶץ
for-the-land (43) I-will-remember and-the-land I-will-remember

תֵּעָזֵב מֵהֶם וְתִרֶץ אֶת־ שַׁבְּתֹתֶיהָ
sabbaths-of-her *** and-she-will-enjoy by-them she-will-be-deserted

בָּהְשַׁמָּה מֵהֶם וְהֵם יִרְצוּ אֶת־ עֲוֹנָם
sin-of-them *** they-will-pay and-they without-them when-to-be-desolate

יַעַן וּבְיַעַן בְּמִשְׁפָּטַי מָאָסוּ וְאֶת־ חֻקֹּתַי גָּעֲלָה
she-abhored decrees-of-me and they-rejected to-laws-of-me yes-because because

נַפְשָׁם׃ (44) וְאַף־ גַּם־ זֹאת בִּהְיוֹתָם בְּאֶרֶץ
in-land-of when-to-be-them this in-spite-of and-yet (44) spirit-of-them

אֹיְבֵיהֶם לֹא־ מְאַסְתִּים וְלֹא־ גְעַלְתִּים
I-will-abhor-them or-not I-will-reject-them not being-enemies-of-them

לְכַלֹּתָם לְהָפֵר בְּרִיתִי אִתָּם כִּי אֲנִי יְהוָה אֱלֹהֵיהֶם׃
God-of-them Yahweh I for with-them covenant-of-me to-break to-destroy-them

(45) וְזָכַרְתִּי לָהֶם בְּרִית רִאשֹׁנִים אֲשֶׁר הוֹצֵאתִי־ אֹתָם
them I-brought whom ancestors covenant-of for-them but-I-will-remember (45)

מֵאֶרֶץ מִצְרַיִם לְעֵינֵי הַגּוֹיִם לִהְיֹת לָהֶם לֵאלֹהִים אֲנִי יְהוָה׃
Yahweh I as-God to-them to-be the-nations in-eyes-of Egypt from-land-of

(46) אֵלֶּה הַחֻקִּים וְהַמִּשְׁפָּטִים וְהַתּוֹרֹת אֲשֶׁר נָתַן
he-established that and-the-regulations and-the-laws the-decrees these (46)

יְהוָה בֵּינוֹ וּבֵין בְּנֵי יִשְׂרָאֵל בְּהַר סִינַי בְּיַד־
by-hand-of Sinai on-Mount-of Israel sons-of and-between between-him Yahweh

in the lands of their enemies because of their sins; also because of their fathers' sins they will waste away.

40 "'But if they will confess their sins and the sins of their fathers—their treachery against me and their hostility toward me, 41 which made me hostile toward them so that I sent them into the land of their enemies—then when their uncircumcised hearts are humbled and they pay for their sin, 42 I will remember my covenant with Jacob and my covenant with Isaac and my covenant with Abraham, and I will remember the land. 43 For the land will be deserted by them and will enjoy its sabbaths while it lies desolate without them. They will pay for their sins because they rejected my laws and abhorred my decrees. 44 Yet in spite of this, when they are in the land of their enemies, I will not reject them or abhor them so as to destroy them completely, breaking my covenant with them. I am the LORD their God. 45 But for their sake I will remember the covenant with their ancestors whom I brought out of Egypt in the sight of the nations to be their God. I am the LORD.'"

46 These are the decrees, the laws and the regulations that the LORD established on Mount Sinai between himself and the Israelites through Moses.

מֹשֶֽׁה׃ וַיְדַבֵּ֥ר יְהוָ֖ה אֶל־מֹשֶׁ֥ה לֵּאמֹֽר׃ דַּבֵּ֞ר אֶל־בְּנֵ֤י
sons-of to speak! (2) to-say Moses to Yahweh and-he-spoke (27:1) Moses

יִשְׂרָאֵל֙ וְאָמַרְתָּ֣ אֲלֵהֶ֔ם אִ֕ישׁ כִּ֥י יַפְלִ֖א נֶ֑דֶר בְּעֶרְכְּךָ֥ נְפָשֹׁ֖ת
persons by-value-of-you vow he-makes who anyone to-them and-you-say Israel

לַיהוָֽה׃ וְהָיָ֤ה עֶרְכְּךָ֙ הַזָּכָ֔ר מִבֶּן֙ עֶשְׂרִ֣ים שָׁנָ֔ה
year twenty from-son-of the-male value-of-you then-he-must-be (3) to-Yahweh

וְעַ֖ד בֶּן־שִׁשִּׁ֣ים שָׁנָ֑ה וְהָיָ֣ה עֶרְכְּךָ֗ חֲמִשִּׁ֛ים שֶׁ֥קֶל כֶּ֖סֶף
silver shekel-of fifty value-of-you then-he-must-be year sixty son-of even-to

בְּשֶׁ֥קֶל הַקֹּֽדֶשׁ׃ וְאִם־נְקֵבָ֖ה הִ֑וא וְהָיָ֥ה עֶרְכְּךָ֖
value-of-you then-he-must-be she female and-if (4) the-sanctuary by-shekel-of

שְׁלֹשִׁ֥ים שָֽׁקֶל׃ וְאִ֨ם מִבֶּן־חָמֵ֜שׁ שָׁנִ֗ים וְעַד֙ בֶּן־עֶשְׂרִ֣ים שָׁנָ֔ה
year twenty son-of even-to years five from-son-of and-if (5) shekel thirty

וְהָיָ֥ה עֶרְכְּךָ֛ הַזָּכָ֖ר עֶשְׂרִ֣ים שְׁקָלִ֑ים וְלַנְּקֵבָ֖ה עֲשֶׂ֥רֶת
ten and-for-the-female shekels twenty the-male value-of-you then-he-must-be

שְׁקָלִֽים׃ וְאִ֨ם מִבֶּן־חֹ֜דֶשׁ וְעַד֙ בֶּן־חָמֵ֣שׁ שָׁנִ֔ים וְהָיָ֣ה
he-must-be years five son-of even-to month from-son-of and-if (6) shekels

עֶרְכְּךָ֗ הַזָּכָ֔ר חֲמִשָּׁ֥ה שְׁקָלִ֖ים כָּ֑סֶף וְלַנְּקֵבָ֣ה עֶרְכְּךָ֔
value-of-you and-for-the-female silver shekels five the-male value-of-you

שְׁלֹ֥שֶׁת שְׁקָלִ֖ים כָּֽסֶף׃ וְאִם֩ מִבֶּן־שִׁשִּׁ֨ים שָׁנָ֤ה וָמַ֙עְלָה֙ אִם־זָכָ֔ר
male if or-more year sixty from-son-of and-if (7) silver shekels three

וְהָיָ֣ה עֶרְכְּךָ֔ חֲמִשָּׁ֥ה עָשָׂ֖ר שָׁ֑קֶל וְלַנְּקֵבָ֖ה עֲשָׂרָ֥ה שְׁקָלִֽים׃
shekels ten and-for-the-female shekel ten five value-of-you he-must-be

וְאִם־מָ֥ךְ הוּא֙ מֵֽעֶרְכֶּ֔ךָ וְהֶֽעֱמִידוֹ֙ לִפְנֵ֣י
to then-he-must-present-him than-value-of-you he being-poor and-if (8)

הַכֹּהֵ֔ן וְהֶעֱרִ֥יךְ אֹת֖וֹ הַכֹּהֵ֑ן עַל־פִּ֗י אֲשֶׁ֤ר תַּשִּׂיג֙
she-can-afford that amount for the-priest him and-he-will-set-value the-priest

יַ֣ד הַנֹּדֵ֔ר יַעֲרִיכֶ֖נּוּ הַכֹּהֵֽן׃ וְאִם־
and-if (9) the-priest he-will-set-value-of-him the-one-making-vow hand-of

בְּהֵמָ֔ה אֲשֶׁ֨ר יַקְרִ֧יבוּ מִמֶּ֛נָּה קָרְבָּ֖ן לַיהוָ֑ה כֹּל֩ אֲשֶׁ֨ר יִתֵּ֥ן
he-is-given that anything to-Yahweh offering from-her they-vowed that animal

מִמֶּ֛נּוּ לַיהוָ֖ה יִֽהְיֶה־קֹּֽדֶשׁ׃ לֹ֣א יַחֲלִיפֶ֗נּוּ וְלֹֽא־
or-not he-must-exchange-him not (10) holy he-becomes to-Yahweh from-him

יָמִ֥יר אֹת֛וֹ ט֥וֹב בְּרָ֖ע אוֹ־רַ֣ע בְּט֑וֹב וְאִם־הָמֵ֨ר
to-substitute and-if for-good bad or for-bad good him he-must-substitute

יָמִ֤יר בְּהֵמָה֙ בִּבְהֵמָ֔ה וְהָיָה־ה֥וּא וּתְמוּרָת֖וֹ
and-substitute-of-him he then-he-becomes for-animal animal he-substitutes

יִהְיֶה־קֹּֽדֶשׁ׃ וְאִם֙ כָּל־בְּהֵמָ֣ה טְמֵאָ֔ה אֲשֶׁ֛ר לֹא־יַקְרִ֥יבוּ
they-should-present not that unclean animal any-of and-if (11) holy he-becomes

*Redeeming What Is the LORD's*

27 The LORD said to Moses, 2"Speak to the Israelites and say to them: 'If anyone makes a special vow to dedicate persons to the LORD by giving equivalent values, 3set the value of a male between the ages of twenty and sixty at fifty shekels[n] of silver, according to the sanctuary shekel[o]; 4and if it is a female, set her value at thirty shekels.[p] 5If it is a person between the ages of five and twenty, set the value of a male at twenty shekels[q] and of a female at ten shekels.[r] 6If it is a person between one month and five years, set the value of a male at five shekels[s] of silver and that of a female at three shekels[t] of silver. 7If it is a person sixty years old or more, set the value of a male at fifteen shekels[u] and of a female at ten shekels. 8If anyone making the vow is too poor to pay the specified amount, he is to present the person to the priest, who will set the value for him according to what the man making the vow can afford.

9" 'If what he vowed is an animal that is acceptable as an offering to the LORD, such an animal given to the LORD becomes holy. 10He must not exchange it or substitute a good one for a bad one, or a bad one for a good one; if he should substitute one animal for another, both it and the substitute become holy. 11If what he vowed is a ceremonially unclean animal—one that is not acceptable as an offering

[n]3 That is, about 1 1/4 pounds (about 0.6 kilogram); also in verse 16
[o]3 That is, about 2/5 ounce (about 11.5 grams); also in verse 25
[p]4 That is, about 12 ounces (about 0.3 kilogram)
[q]5 That is, about 8 ounces (about 0.2 kilogram)
[r]5 That is, about 4 ounces (about 110 grams); also in verse 7
[s]6 That is, about 2 ounces (about 55 grams)
[t]6 That is, about 1 1/4 ounces (about 35 grams)
[u]7 That is, about 6 ounces (about 170 grams)

מִמֶּנָּה קָרְבָּן לַיהוָה וְהֶעֱמִיד אֶת־ הַבְּהֵמָה לִפְנֵי הַכֹּהֵן׃
the-priest to the-animal *** then-he-must-present to-Yahweh offering from-her

וְהֶעֱרִיךְ הַכֹּהֵן אֹתָהּ בֵּין טוֹב וּבֵין רָע
bad or-as good as her the-priest then-he-will-judge-quality (12)

כְּעֶרְכְּךָ הַכֹּהֵן כֵּן יִהְיֶה׃ וְאִם־ גָּאֹל
to-redeem and-if (13) he-will-be that the-priest as-value-of-you

יִגְאָלֶנָּה וְיָסַף חֲמִישִׁתוֹ עַל־ עֶרְכֶּךָ׃ וְאִישׁ
and-man (14) value-of-you to fifth-of-him then-he-must-add he-redeems-her

כִּי־ יַקְדִּשׁ אֶת־ בֵּיתוֹ קֹדֶשׁ לַיהוָה וְהֶעֱרִיכוֹ
then-he-must-evaluate-him to-Yahweh holy house-of-him *** he-dedicates if

הַכֹּהֵן בֵּין טוֹב וּבֵין רָע כַּאֲשֶׁר יַעֲרִיךְ אֹתוֹ הַכֹּהֵן כֵּן
so the-priest him he-sets-value just-as bad or-as good as the-priest

יָקוּם׃ וְאִם־ הַמַּקְדִּישׁ יִגְאַל אֶת־ בֵּיתוֹ
house-of-him *** he-redeems the-one-dedicating and-if (15) he-will-remain

וְיָסַף חֲמִישִׁית כֶּסֶף־ עֶרְכְּךָ עָלָיו וְהָיָה
then-he-will-become to-him value-of-you price-of fifth then-he-must-add

לוֹ׃ וְאִם ׀ מִשְּׂדֵה אֲחֻזָּתוֹ יַקְדִּישׁ אִישׁ
man he-dedicates family-property-of-him from-land-of and-if (16) to-him

לַיהוָה וְהָיָה עֶרְכְּךָ לְפִי זַרְעוֹ זֶרַע
seed-of seed-of-him as-amount-of value-of-you then-he-must-be to-Yahweh

חֹמֶר שְׂעֹרִים בַּחֲמִשִּׁים שֶׁקֶל כָּסֶף׃ אִם־ מִשְּׁנַת הַיֹּבֵל
the-Jubilee in-Year-of if (17) silver shekel-of for-fifty barleys homer-of

יַקְדִּישׁ שָׂדֵהוּ כְּעֶרְכְּךָ יָקוּם׃ וְאִם־ אַחַר
after but-if (18) he-remains at-value-of-you field-of-him he-dedicates

הַיֹּבֵל יַקְדִּישׁ שָׂדֵהוּ וְחִשַּׁב־ לוֹ
for-him then-he-will-determine field-of-him he-dedicates the-Jubilee

הַכֹּהֵן אֶת־ הַכֶּסֶף עַל־ פִּי הַשָּׁנִים הַנּוֹתָרֹת עַד
until the-ones-remaining the-years number-of by the-price *** the-priest

שְׁנַת הַיֹּבֵל וְנִגְרַע מֵעֶרְכֶּךָ׃ וְאִם־
and-if (19) from-value-of-you and-he-will-be-reduced the-Jubilee Year-of

גָּאֹל יִגְאַל אֶת־ הַשָּׂדֶה הַמַּקְדִּישׁ אֹתוֹ וְיָסַף
then-he-must-add him the-one-dedicating the-field *** he-redeems to-redeem

חֲמִשִׁית כֶּסֶף־ עֶרְכְּךָ עָלָיו וְקָם לוֹ׃ וְאִם־
but-if (20) to-him and-he-will-be-again to-him value-of-you price-of fifth

לֹא יִגְאַל אֶת־ הַשָּׂדֶה וְאִם־ מָכַר אֶת־ הַשָּׂדֶה לְאִישׁ אַחֵר
else to-someone the-field *** he-sold or-if the-field *** he-redeems not

לֹא יִגָּאֵל עוֹד׃ וְהָיָה הַשָּׂדֶה
the-field and-he-will-become (21) ever he-can-be-redeemed not

to the LORD—the animal must be presented to the priest, [12]who will judge its quality as good or bad. Whatever value the priest then sets, that is what it will be. [13]If the owner wishes to redeem the animal, he must add a fifth to its value.

[14]" 'If a man dedicates his house as something holy to the LORD, the priest will judge its quality as good or bad. Whatever value the priest then sets, so it will remain. [15]If the man who dedicates his house redeems it, he must add a fifth to its value, and the house will again become his.

[16]" 'If a man dedicates to the LORD part of his family land, its value is to be set according to the amount of seed required for it—fifty shekels of silver to a homer[v] of barley seed. [17]If he dedicates his field during the Year of Jubilee, the value that has been set remains. [18]But if he dedicates his field after the Jubilee, the priest will determine the value according to the number of years that remain until the next Year of Jubilee, and its set value will be reduced. [19]If the man who dedicates the field wishes to redeem it, he must add a fifth to its value, and the field will again become his. [20]If, however, he does not redeem the field, or if he has sold it to someone else, it can never be redeemed. [21]When the field is

[v]16 That is, probably about 6 bushels (about 220 liters)

בְּצֵאתוֹ בַּיֹּבֵל קֹדֶשׁ לַיהוָה כִּשְׂדֵה הַחֵרֶם
the-devotion like-field-of to-Yahweh holy in-the-Jubilee when-to-go-out-him

לַכֹּהֵן תִּהְיֶה אֲחֻזָּתוֹ׃ וְאִם אֶת־ שְׂדֵה
field-of *** and-if (22) property-of-him she-will-become for-the-priest

מִקְנָתוֹ אֲשֶׁר לֹא מִשְּׂדֵה אֲחֻזָּתוֹ יַקְדִּישׁ
he-dedicates family-property-of-him from-land-of not that purchase-of-him

לַיהוָה׃ וְחִשַּׁב־ לוֹ הַכֹּהֵן אֵת מִכְסַת
price-of *** the-priest for-him then-he-will-determine (23) to-Yahweh

הָעֶרְכְּךָ עַד שְׁנַת הַיֹּבֵל וְנָתַן אֶת־ הָעֶרְכְּךָ
the-value-of-you *** and-he-must-pay the-Jubilee Year-of to the-value-of-you

בַּיּוֹם הַהוּא קֹדֶשׁ לַיהוָה׃ בִּשְׁנַת הַיּוֹבֵל יָשׁוּב
he-will-revert the-Jubilee in-Year-of (24) to-Yahweh holy the-that on-the-day

הַשָּׂדֶה לַאֲשֶׁר קָנָהוּ מֵאִתּוֹ לַאֲשֶׁר־ לוֹ אֲחֻזַּת
possession-of to-him to-whom from-him he-bought-him to-whom the-field

הָאָרֶץ׃ וְכָל־ עֶרְכְּךָ יִהְיֶה בְּשֶׁקֶל הַקֹּדֶשׁ
the-sanctuary by-shekel-of he-must-be value-of-you and-every-of (25) the-land

עֶשְׂרִים גֵּרָה יִהְיֶה הַשָּׁקֶל׃ אַךְ־ בְּכוֹר אֲשֶׁר־ יְבֻכַּר
he-belongs that firstborn however (26) the-shekel he-must-be gerah twenty

לַיהוָה בִּבְהֵמָה לֹא־ יַקְדִּישׁ אִישׁ אֹתוֹ אִם־ שׁוֹר אִם־ שֶׂה
sheep or cow whether him anyone he-may-dedicate not of-animal to-Yahweh

לַיהוָה הוּא׃ וְאִם בַּבְּהֵמָה הַטְּמֵאָה וּפָדָה
then-he-may-buy-back the-unclean of-the-animal now-if (27) he to-Yahweh

בְעֶרְכֶּךָ וְיָסַף חֲמִשִׁתוֹ עָלָיו וְאִם־ לֹא יִגָּאֵל
he-is-redeemed not but-if to-him fifth-of-him and-he-must-add at-value-of-you

וְנִמְכַּר בְּעֶרְכֶּךָ׃ אַךְ־ כָּל־ חֵרֶם אֲשֶׁר
that devoted any-of but (28) at-value-of-you then-he-must-be-sold

יַחֲרִם אִישׁ לַיהוָה מִכָּל־ אֲשֶׁר־ לוֹ מֵאָדָם וּבְהֵמָה
or-animal whether-man to-him that from-anything to-Yahweh man he-devoted

וּמִשְּׂדֵה אֲחֻזָּתוֹ לֹא יִמָּכֵר וְלֹא
or-not he-may-be-sold not family-property-of-him or-from-land-of

יִגָּאֵל כָּל־ חֵרֶם קֹדֶשׁ־ קָדָשִׁים הוּא לַיהוָה׃
to-Yahweh he holy-things most-holy-of devoted every-of he-may-be-redeemed

כָּל־ חֵרֶם אֲשֶׁר יָחֳרַם מִן־ הָאָדָם לֹא יִפָּדֶה
he-may-be-ransomed not the-man from he-was-devoted that devoted any-of (29)

מוֹת יוּמָת׃ וְכָל־ מַעְשַׂר הָאָרֶץ מִזֶּרַע
whether-grain-of the-land tithe-of and-every-of (30) he-must-die to-die

הָאָרֶץ מִפְּרִי הָעֵץ לַיהוָה הוּא קֹדֶשׁ לַיהוָה׃ וְאִם־
and-if (31) to-Yahweh holy he to-Yahweh the-tree or-fruit-of the-soil

released in the Jubilee, it will become holy, like a field devoted to the LORD; it will become the property of the priests.[w]

22 'If a man dedicates to the LORD a field he has bought, which is not part of his family land, 23 the priest will determine its value up to the Year of Jubilee, and the man must pay its value on that day as something holy to the LORD. 24 In the Year of Jubilee the field will revert to the person from whom he bought it, the one whose land it was. 25 Every value is to be set according to the sanctuary shekel, twenty gerahs to the shekel.

26 'No one, however, may dedicate the firstborn of an animal, since the firstborn already belongs to the LORD; whether a cow[x] or a sheep, it is the LORD's. 27 If it is one of the unclean animals, he may buy it back at its set value, adding a fifth of the value to it. If he does not redeem it, it is to be sold at its set value.

28 'But nothing that a man owns and devotes[y] to the LORD—whether man or animal or family land—may be sold or redeemed; everything so devoted is most holy to the LORD.

29 'No person devoted to destruction[z] may be ransomed; he must be put to death.

30 'A tithe of everything from the land, whether grain from the soil or fruit from the trees, belongs to the LORD; it is

w21 *Or priest*
x26 The Hebrew word can include both male and female.
y28 The Hebrew term refers to the irrevocable giving over of things or persons to the LORD.
z29 The Hebrew term refers to the irrevocable giving over of things or persons to the LORD, often by totally destroying them.

גָּאֹל יִגְאַל אִישׁ מִמַּעַשְׂרוֹ חֲמִשִׁיתוֹ יֹסֵף עָלָיו׃
to-him he-must-add fifth-of-him from-tithe-of-him man he-redeems to-redeem

(32) וְכָל־ מַעְשַׂר בָּקָר וָצֹאן כֹּל אֲשֶׁר־ יַעֲבֹר תַּחַת
under he-passes that everything and-flock herd tithe-of and-entire-of (32)

הַשָּׁבֶט הָעֲשִׂירִי יִהְיֶה־ קֹּדֶשׁ לַיהוָה׃ (33) לֹא יְבַקֵּר בֵּין־
as he-must-pick-out not (33) to-Yahweh holy he-will-be the-tenth the-rod

טוֹב לָרַע וְלֹא יְמִירֶנּוּ וְאִם־ הָמֵר
to-substitute and-if he-must-substitute-him or-not from-the-bad good

יְמִירֶנּוּ וְהָיָה־ הוּא וּתְמוּרָתוֹ יִהְיֶה־ קֹּדֶשׁ
holy he-becomes and-substitute-of-him he then-he-becomes he-substitutes-him

לֹא יִגָּאֵל׃ (34) אֵלֶּה הַמִּצְוֺת אֲשֶׁר צִוָּה יְהוָה אֶת־
*** Yahweh he-commanded that the-commands these (34) he-can-be-redeemed not

מֹשֶׁה אֶל־ בְּנֵי יִשְׂרָאֵל בְּהַר סִינָי׃
Sinai on-Mount-of Israel sons-of for Moses

holy to the LORD. [31]If a man redeems any of his tithe, he must add a fifth of the value to it. [32]The entire tithe of the herd and flock—every tenth animal that passes under the shepherd's rod—will be holy to the LORD. [33]He must not pick out the good from the bad or make any substitution. If he does make a substitution, both the animal and its substitute become holy and cannot be redeemed.' "

[34]These are the commands the LORD gave Moses on Mount Sinai for the Israelites.

וַיְדַבֵּר יְהוָה אֶל־ מֹשֶׁה בְּמִדְבַּר סִינַי בְּאֹהֶל מוֹעֵד
Meeting in-Tent-of Sinai in-Desert-of Moses to Yahweh and-he-spoke (1:1)

בְּאֶחָד לַחֹדֶשׁ הַשֵּׁנִי בַּשָּׁנָה הַשֵּׁנִית לְצֵאתָם
after-to-come-out-them the-second in-the-year the-second of-the-month on-first

מֵאֶרֶץ מִצְרַיִם לֵאמֹר׃ שְׂאוּ אֶת־ רֹאשׁ כָּל־ עֲדַת
community-of whole-of census-of *** take! (2) to-say Egypt from-land-of

בְּנֵי־ יִשְׂרָאֵל לְמִשְׁפְּחֹתָם לְבֵית אֲבֹתָם בְּמִסְפַּר שֵׁמוֹת
names by-list-of fathers-of-them by-house-of by-clans-of-them Israel sons-of

כָּל־ זָכָר לְגֻלְגְּלֹתָם׃ מִבֶּן עֶשְׂרִים שָׁנָה וָמַעְלָה כָּל־
all-of or-more year twenty from-son-of (3) by-heads-of-them male every-of

יֹצֵא צָבָא בְּיִשְׂרָאֵל תִּפְקְדוּ אֹתָם לְצִבְאֹתָם אַתָּה
you by-divisions-of-them them you-must-number in-Israel army serving

וְאַהֲרֹן׃ וְאִתְּכֶם יִהְיוּ אִישׁ אִישׁ לַמַּטֶּה אִישׁ רֹאשׁ
head each from-the-tribe one man he-must-be and-with-you (4) and-Aaron

לְבֵית־ אֲבֹתָיו הוּא׃ וְאֵלֶּה שְׁמוֹת הָאֲנָשִׁים אֲשֶׁר
who the-men names-of now-these (5) he fathers-of-him of-house-of

יַעַמְדוּ אִתְּכֶם לִרְאוּבֵן אֱלִיצוּר בֶּן־ שְׁדֵיאוּר׃ לְשִׁמְעוֹן
from-Simeon (6) Shedeur son-of Elizur from-Reuben with-you they-will-assist

שְׁלֻמִיאֵל בֶּן־ צוּרִישַׁדָּי׃ לִיהוּדָה נַחְשׁוֹן בֶּן־ עַמִּינָדָב׃
Amminadab son-of Nahshon from-Judah (7) Zurishaddai son-of Shelumiel

לְיִשָּׂשכָר נְתַנְאֵל בֶּן־ צוּעָר׃ לִזְבוּלֻן אֱלִיאָב בֶּן־ חֵלֹן׃
Helon son-of Eliab from-Zebulun (9) Zuar son-of Nethanel from-Issachar (8)

לִבְנֵי יוֹסֵף לְאֶפְרַיִם אֱלִישָׁמָע בֶּן־ עַמִּיהוּד לִמְנַשֶּׁה
from-Manasseh Ammihud son-of Elishama from-Ephraim Joseph from-sons-of (10)

גַּמְלִיאֵל בֶּן־ פְּדָהצוּר׃ לְבִנְיָמִן אֲבִידָן בֶּן־ גִּדְעֹנִי׃
Gideoni son-of Abidan from-Benjamin (11) Pedahzur son-of Gamaliel

לְדָן אֲחִיעֶזֶר בֶּן־ עַמִּישַׁדָּי׃ לְאָשֵׁר פַּגְעִיאֵל בֶּן־ עָכְרָן׃
Ocran son-of Pagiel from-Asher (13) Ammishaddai son-of Ahiezer from-Dan (12)

לְגָד אֶלְיָסָף בֶּן־ דְּעוּאֵל׃ לְנַפְתָּלִי אֲחִירַע בֶּן־ עֵינָן׃
Enan son-of Ahira from-Naphtali (15) Deuel son-of Eliasaph from-Gad (14)

אֵלֶּה קְרִיאֵי הָעֵדָה נְשִׂיאֵי מַטּוֹת
tribes-of leaders-of the-community ones-being-appointed-of these (16)

אֲבוֹתָם רָאשֵׁי אַלְפֵי יִשְׂרָאֵל הֵם׃ וַיִּקַּח מֹשֶׁה
Moses and-he-took (17) they Israel clans-of heads-of ancestors-of-them

וְאַהֲרֹן אֵת הָאֲנָשִׁים הָאֵלֶּה אֲשֶׁר נִקְּבוּ בְּשֵׁמוֹת׃ וְאֵת
and (18) by-names they-were-given whom the-these the-men *** and-Aaron

כָּל־ הָעֵדָה הִקְהִילוּ בְּאֶחָד לַחֹדֶשׁ הַשֵּׁנִי
the-second of-the-month on-first they-called-together the-community whole-of

°16 ק קרואי

*The Census*

1 The LORD spoke to Moses in the Tent of Meeting in the Desert of Sinai on the first day of the second month of the second year after the Israelites came out of Egypt. He said: [2]"Take a census of the whole Israelite community by their clans and families, listing every man by name, one by one. [3]You and Aaron are to number by their divisions all the men in Israel twenty years old or more who are able to serve in the army. [4]One man from each tribe, each the head of his family, is to help you. [5]These are the names of the men who are to assist you:

from Reuben, Elizur son of Shedeur;
[6]from Simeon, Shelumiel son of Zurishaddai;
[7]from Judah, Nahshon son of Amminadab;
[8]from Issachar, Nethanel son of Zuar;
[9]from Zebulun, Eliab son of Helon;
[10]from the sons of Joseph:
from Ephraim, Elishama son of Ammihud;
from Manasseh, Gamaliel son of Pedahzur;
[11]from Benjamin, Abidan son of Gideoni;
[12]from Dan, Ahiezer son of Ammishaddai;
[13]from Asher, Pagiel son of Ocran;
[14]from Gad, Eliasaph son of Deuel;
[15]from Naphtali, Ahira son of Enan."

[16]These were the men appointed from the community, the leaders of their ancestral tribes. They were the heads of the clans of Israel.

[17]Moses and Aaron took these men whose names had been given, [18]and they called the whole community together on the first day of the second month. The people

וַיִּתְיַלְדוּ עַל־ מִשְׁפְּחֹתָם לְבֵית אֲבֹתָם
fathers-of-them by-house-of clans-of-them by and-they-indicated-ancestry

בְּמִסְפַּר שֵׁמוֹת מִבֶּן עֶשְׂרִים שָׁנָה וָמַעְלָה לְגֻלְגְּלֹתָם׃
by-heads-of-them or-more year twenty from-son-of names by-list-of

כַּאֲשֶׁר צִוָּה יְהוָה אֶת־ מֹשֶׁה וַיִּפְקְדֵם בְּמִדְבַּר
in-Desert-of so-he-counted-them Moses *** Yahweh he-commanded just-as (19)

סִינָי׃ וַיִּהְיוּ בְנֵי־ רְאוּבֵן בְּכֹר יִשְׂרָאֵל תּוֹלְדֹתָם
records-of-them Israel firstborn-of Reuben sons-of and-they-were (20) Sinai

לְמִשְׁפְּחֹתָם לְבֵית אֲבֹתָם בְּמִסְפַּר שֵׁמוֹת לְגֻלְגְּלֹתָם
by-heads-of-them names by-list-of fathers-of-them by-house-of by-clans-of-them

כָּל־ זָכָר מִבֶּן עֶשְׂרִים שָׁנָה וָמַעְלָה כֹּל יֹצֵא צָבָא׃
army serving all-of or-more year twenty from-son-of male every-of

פְּקֻדֵיהֶם לְמַטֵּה רְאוּבֵן שִׁשָּׁה וְאַרְבָּעִים אֶלֶף וַחֲמֵשׁ
and-five-of thousand and-forty six Reuben from-tribe-of numberings-of-them (21)

מֵאוֹת׃ לִבְנֵי שִׁמְעוֹן תּוֹלְדֹתָם לְמִשְׁפְּחֹתָם
by-clans-of-them records-of-them Simeon from-sons-of (22) hundreds

לְבֵית אֲבֹתָם פְּקֻדָיו בְּמִסְפַּר שֵׁמוֹת לְגֻלְגְּלֹתָם
by-heads-of-them names by-list-of countings-of-him fathers-of-them by-house-of

כָּל־ זָכָר מִבֶּן עֶשְׂרִים שָׁנָה וָמַעְלָה כֹּל יֹצֵא צָבָא׃
army serving all-of or-more year twenty from-son-of male every-of

פְּקֻדֵיהֶם לְמַטֵּה שִׁמְעוֹן תִּשְׁעָה וַחֲמִשִּׁים אֶלֶף
thousand and-fifty nine Simeon from-tribe-of numberings-of-them (23)

וּשְׁלֹשׁ מֵאוֹת׃ לִבְנֵי גָד תּוֹלְדֹתָם לְמִשְׁפְּחֹתָם
by-clans-of-them records-of-them Gad from-sons-of (24) hundreds and-three-of

לְבֵית אֲבֹתָם בְּמִסְפַּר שֵׁמוֹת מִבֶּן עֶשְׂרִים שָׁנָה וָמַעְלָה
or-more year twenty from-son-of names by-list-of fathers-of-them by-house-of

כֹּל יֹצֵא צָבָא׃ פְּקֻדֵיהֶם לְמַטֵּה גָד חֲמִשָּׁה
five Gad from-tribe-of numberings-of-them (25) army serving all-of

וְאַרְבָּעִים אֶלֶף וְשֵׁשׁ מֵאוֹת וַחֲמִשִּׁים׃ לִבְנֵי יְהוּדָה
Judah from-sons-of (26) and-fifty hundreds and-six thousand and-forty

תּוֹלְדֹתָם לְמִשְׁפְּחֹתָם לְבֵית אֲבֹתָם בְּמִסְפַּר
by-list-of fathers-of-them by-house-of by-clans-of-them records-of-them

שֵׁמֹת מִבֶּן עֶשְׂרִים שָׁנָה וָמַעְלָה כֹּל יֹצֵא צָבָא׃
army serving all-of or-more year twenty from-son-of names

פְּקֻדֵיהֶם לְמַטֵּה יְהוּדָה אַרְבָּעָה וְשִׁבְעִים אֶלֶף
thousand and-seventy four Judah from-tribe-of numberings-of-them (27)

וְשֵׁשׁ מֵאוֹת׃ לִבְנֵי יִשָּׂשכָר תּוֹלְדֹתָם לְמִשְׁפְּחֹתָם
by-clans-of-them records-of-them Issachar from-sons-of (28) hundreds and-six

indicated their ancestry by their clans and families, and the men twenty years old or more were listed by name, one by one, [19]as the LORD commanded Moses. And so he counted them in the Desert of Sinai:

[20]From the descendants of Reuben the firstborn son of Israel:

All the men twenty years old or more who were able to serve in the army were listed by name, one by one, according to the records of their clans and families. [21]The number from the tribe of Reuben was 46,500.

[22]From the descendants of Simeon:

All the men twenty years old or more who were able to serve in the army were counted and listed by name, one by one, according to the records of their clans and families. [23]The number from the tribe of Simeon was 59,300.

[24]From the descendants of Gad:

All the men twenty years old or more who were able to serve in the army were listed by name, according to the records of their clans and families. [25]The number from the tribe of Gad was 45,650.

[26]From the descendants of Judah:

All the men twenty years old or more who were able to serve in the army were listed by name, according to the records of their clans and families. [27]The number from the tribe of Judah was 74,600.

[28]From the descendants of Issachar:

לְבֵית אֲבֹתָם בְּמִסְפַּר שֵׁמֹת מִבֶּן עֶשְׂרִים שָׁנָה וָמַעְלָה
or-more year twenty from-son-of names by-list-of fathers-of-them by-house-of

כֹּל יֹצֵא צָבָא׃ (29) פְּקֻדֵיהֶם לְמַטֵּה יִשָּׂשכָר אַרְבָּעָה
four Issachar from-tribe-of numberings-of-them (29) army serving all-of

וַחֲמִשִּׁים אֶלֶף וְאַרְבַּע מֵאוֹת׃ (30) לִבְנֵי זְבוּלֻן תּוֹלְדֹתָם
records-of-them Zebulun from-sons-of (30) hundreds and-four thousand and-fifty

לְמִשְׁפְּחֹתָם לְבֵית אֲבֹתָם בְּמִסְפַּר שֵׁמֹת מִבֶּן
from-son-of names by-list-of fathers-of-them by-house-of by-clans-of-them

עֶשְׂרִים שָׁנָה וָמַעְלָה כֹּל יֹצֵא צָבָא׃ (31) פְּקֻדֵיהֶם לְמַטֵּה
from-tribe-of numberings-of-them (31) army serving all-of or-more year twenty

זְבוּלֻן שִׁבְעָה וַחֲמִשִּׁים אֶלֶף וְאַרְבַּע מֵאוֹת׃ (32) לִבְנֵי יוֹסֵף
Joseph from-sons-of (32) hundreds and-four thousand and-fifty seven Zebulun

לִבְנֵי אֶפְרַיִם תּוֹלְדֹתָם לְמִשְׁפְּחֹתָם לְבֵית
by-house-of by-clans-of-them records-of-them Ephraim from-sons-of

אֲבֹתָם בְּמִסְפַּר שֵׁמֹת מִבֶּן עֶשְׂרִים שָׁנָה וָמַעְלָה כֹּל
all-of or-more year twenty from-son-of names by-list-of fathers-of-them

יֹצֵא צָבָא׃ (33) פְּקֻדֵיהֶם לְמַטֵּה אֶפְרָיִם אַרְבָּעִים אֶלֶף
thousand forty Ephraim from-tribe-of numberings-of-them (33) army serving

וַחֲמֵשׁ מֵאוֹת׃ (34) לִבְנֵי מְנַשֶּׁה תּוֹלְדֹתָם
records-of-them Manasseh from-sons-of (34) hundreds and-five-of

לְמִשְׁפְּחֹתָם לְבֵית אֲבֹתָם בְּמִסְפַּר שֵׁמוֹת מִבֶּן
from-son-of names by-list-of fathers-of-them by-house-of by-clans-of-them

עֶשְׂרִים שָׁנָה וָמַעְלָה כֹּל יֹצֵא צָבָא׃ (35) פְּקֻדֵיהֶם לְמַטֵּה
from-tribe-of numberings-of-them (35) army serving all-of or-more year twenty

מְנַשֶּׁה שְׁנַיִם וּשְׁלֹשִׁים אֶלֶף וּמָאתָיִם׃ (36) לִבְנֵי בִנְיָמִן
Benjamin from-sons-of (36) and-two-hundreds thousand and-thirty two Manasseh

תּוֹלְדֹתָם לְמִשְׁפְּחֹתָם לְבֵית אֲבֹתָם בְּמִסְפַּר
by-list-of fathers-of-them by-house-of by-clans-of-them records-of-them

שֵׁמֹת מִבֶּן עֶשְׂרִים שָׁנָה וָמַעְלָה כֹּל יֹצֵא צָבָא׃
army serving all-of or-more year twenty from-son-of names

(37) פְּקֻדֵיהֶם לְמַטֵּה בִנְיָמִן חֲמִשָּׁה וּשְׁלֹשִׁים אֶלֶף
thousand and-thirty five Benjamin from-tribe-of numberings-of-them (37)

וְאַרְבַּע מֵאוֹת׃ (38) לִבְנֵי דָן תּוֹלְדֹתָם לְמִשְׁפְּחֹתָם
by-clans-of-them records-of-them Dan from-sons-of (38) hundreds and-four

לְבֵית אֲבֹתָם בְּמִסְפַּר שֵׁמֹת מִבֶּן עֶשְׂרִים שָׁנָה וָמַעְלָה
or-more year twenty from-son-of names by-list-of fathers-of-them by-house-of

כֹּל יֹצֵא צָבָא׃ (39) פְּקֻדֵיהֶם לְמַטֵּה דָן שְׁנַיִם וְשִׁשִּׁים
and-sixty two Dan from-tribe-of numberings-of-them (39) army serving all-of

All the men twenty years old or more who were able to serve in the army were listed by name, according to the records of their clans and families.
29 The number from the tribe of Issachar was 54,400.

30 From the descendants of Zebulun:
All the men twenty years old or more who were able to serve in the army were listed by name, according to the records of their clans and families.
31 The number from the tribe of Zebulun was 57,400.

32 From the sons of Joseph:
From the descendants of Ephraim:
All the men twenty years old or more who were able to serve in the army were listed by name, according to the records of their clans and families.
33 The number from the tribe of Ephraim was 40,500.

34 From the descendants of Manasseh:
All the men twenty years old or more who were able to serve in the army were listed by name, according to the records of their clans and families.
35 The number from the tribe of Manasseh was 32,200.

36 From the descendants of Benjamin:
All the men twenty years old or more who were able to serve in the army were listed by name, according to the records of their clans and families.
37 The number from the tribe of Benjamin was 35,400.

38 From the descendants of Dan:
All the men twenty years old or more who were able to serve in the army were listed by name, according to the records of their clans and families.
39 The number from the tribe of Dan was 62,700.

אֶלֶף וּשְׁבַע מֵאוֹת׃ (40) לִבְנֵי אָשֵׁר תּוֹלְדֹתָם
records-of-them Asher from-sons-of (40) hundreds and-seven-of thousand

לְמִשְׁפְּחֹתָם לְבֵית אֲבֹתָם בְּמִסְפַּר שֵׁמֹת מִבֶּן
from-son-of names by-list-of fathers-of-them by-house-of by-clans-of-them

עֶשְׂרִים שָׁנָה וָמַעְלָה כֹּל יֹצֵא צָבָא׃ (41) פְּקֻדֵיהֶם לְמַטֵּה
from-tribe-of numberings-of-them (41) army serving all-of or-more year twenty

אָשֵׁר אֶחָד וְאַרְבָּעִים אֶלֶף וַחֲמֵשׁ מֵאוֹת׃ (42) בְּנֵי נַפְתָּלִי
Naphtali sons-of (42) hundreds and-five-of thousand and-forty one Asher

תּוֹלְדֹתָם לְמִשְׁפְּחֹתָם לְבֵית אֲבֹתָם בְּמִסְפַּר
by-list-of fathers-of-them by-house-of by-clans-of-them records-of-them

שֵׁמֹת מִבֶּן עֶשְׂרִים שָׁנָה וָמַעְלָה כֹּל יֹצֵא צָבָא׃
army serving all-of or-more year twenty from-son-of names

(43) פְּקֻדֵיהֶם לְמַטֵּה נַפְתָּלִי שְׁלֹשָׁה וַחֲמִשִּׁים אֶלֶף
thousand and-fifty three Naphtali from-tribe-of numberings-of-them (43)

וְאַרְבַּע מֵאוֹת׃ (44) אֵלֶּה הַפְּקֻדִים אֲשֶׁר פָּקַד מֹשֶׁה
Moses he-counted whom the-ones-being-counted these (44) hundreds and-four

וְאַהֲרֹן וּנְשִׂיאֵי יִשְׂרָאֵל שְׁנֵים עָשָׂר אִישׁ אִישׁ־ אֶחָד לְבֵית־
from-house-of one each man ten two Israel and-leaders-of and-Aaron

אֲבֹתָיו הָיוּ׃ (45) וַיִּהְיוּ כָּל־ פְּקוּדֵי
ones-being-counted-of all-of and-they-were (45) they-were fathers-of-him

בְנֵי־ יִשְׂרָאֵל לְבֵית אֲבֹתָם מִבֶּן עֶשְׂרִים שָׁנָה וָמַעְלָה
or-more year twenty from-son-of fathers-of-them by-house-of Israel sons-of

כָּל־ יֹצֵא צָבָא בְּיִשְׂרָאֵל׃ (46) וַיִּהְיוּ כָּל־ הַפְּקֻדִים
the-numberings total-of and-they-were (46) in-Israel army serving all-of

שֵׁשׁ־ מֵאוֹת אֶלֶף וּשְׁלֹשֶׁת אֲלָפִים וַחֲמֵשׁ מֵאוֹת וַחֲמִשִּׁים׃
and-fifty hundreds and-five-of thousands and-three thousand hundreds six

(47) וְהַלְוִיִּם לְמַטֵּה אֲבֹתָם לֹא הָתְפָּקְדוּ
they-were-counted not fathers-of-them by-tribe-of now-the-Levites (47)

בְּתוֹכָם׃ (48) וַיְדַבֵּר יְהוָה אֶל־ מֹשֶׁה לֵּאמֹר׃ (49) אַךְ אֶת־ מַטֵּה
tribe-of *** indeed (49) to-say Moses to Yahweh and-he-spoke (48) with-them

לֵוִי לֹא תִפְקֹד וְאֶת־ רֹאשָׁם לֹא תִשָּׂא בְּתוֹךְ בְּנֵי
sons-of with you-must-take not census-of-them or you-must-count not Levi

יִשְׂרָאֵל׃ (50) וְאַתָּה הַפְקֵד אֶת־ הַלְוִיִּם עַל־ מִשְׁכַּן הָעֵדֻת
the-Testimony tabernacle-of over the-Levites *** appoint! but-you (50) Israel

וְעַל כָּל־ כֵּלָיו וְעַל כָּל־ אֲשֶׁר־ לוֹ הֵמָּה
they to-him that all and-over furnishings-of-him all-of and-over

יִשְׂאוּ אֶת־ הַמִּשְׁכָּן וְאֶת־ כָּל־ כֵּלָיו וְהֵם
and-they furnishings-of-him all-of and the-tabernacle *** they-must-carry

40 From the descendants of Asher:
All the men twenty years old or more who were able to serve in the army were listed by name, according to the records of their clans and families.
41 The number from the tribe of Asher was 41,500.

42 From the descendants of Naphtali:
All the men twenty years old or more who were able to serve in the army were listed by name, according to the records of their clans and families.
43 The number from the tribe of Naphtali was 53,400.

44 These were the men counted by Moses and Aaron and the twelve leaders of Israel, each one representing his family. 45 All the Israelites twenty years old or more who were able to serve in Israel's army were counted according to their families. 46 The total number was 603,550.

47 The families of the tribe of Levi, however, were not counted along with the others. 48 The LORD had said to Moses: 49 "You must not count the tribe of Levi or include them in the census of the other Israelites. 50 Instead, appoint the Levites to be in charge of the tabernacle of the Testimony—over all its furnishings and everything belonging to it. They are to carry the tabernacle and all its furnishings;

| | | | |
|---|---|---|---|
| יְשָׁרְתֻ֫הוּ | וְסָבִ֥יב | לַמִּשְׁכָּ֖ן | יַחֲנֽוּ׃ |
| they-must-care-for-him | and-around | to-the-tabernacle | they-must-encamp |

| | | | | |
|---|---|---|---|---|
| (51) | וּבִנְסֹ֙עַ֙ | הַמִּשְׁכָּ֔ן | יוֹרִ֣ידוּ | אֹת֖וֹ הַלְוִיִּ֑ם |
| | and-when-to-move | the-tabernacle | they-must-take-down | him  the-Levites |

| | | | |
|---|---|---|---|
| וּבַחֲנֹת֙ | הַמִּשְׁכָּ֔ן | יָקִ֥ימוּ | אֹת֖וֹ הַלְוִיִּ֑ם |
| and-when-to-camp | the-tabernacle | they-must-set-up | him  the-Levites |

| | | | | | |
|---|---|---|---|---|---|
| וְהַזָּ֥ר | הַקָּרֵ֖ב | יוּמָֽת׃ | (52) | וְחָנ֖וּ | בְּנֵ֣י |
| but-the-outsider | the-one-near | he-must-die | | and-they-must-encamp | sons-of |

| | | | | | | |
|---|---|---|---|---|---|---|
| יִשְׂרָאֵ֖ל אִ֣ישׁ | עַֽל־ | מַחֲנֵ֑הוּ | וְאִ֥ישׁ | עַל־ | דִּגְל֖וֹ | לְצִבְאֹתָֽם׃ |
| Israel  each | in | camp-of-him | and-each | under | standard-of-him | by-divisions-of-them |

| | | | | |
|---|---|---|---|---|
| (53) | וְהַלְוִיִּ֞ם | יַחֲנ֤וּ | סָבִיב֙ | לְמִשְׁכַּ֣ן |
| | but-the-Levites | they-must-encamp | around | to-tabernacle-of |

| | | | | | | | |
|---|---|---|---|---|---|---|---|
| הָעֵדֻ֗ת | וְלֹֽא־ | יִהְיֶ֤ה | קֶ֙צֶף֙ | עַל־ | עֲדַ֖ת | בְּנֵ֣י יִשְׂרָאֵ֑ל |
| the-Testimony | so-not | he-will-fall | wrath | on | community-of | sons-of  Israel |

| | | | | | |
|---|---|---|---|---|---|
| וְשָׁמְרוּ֙ | הַלְוִיִּ֔ם | אֶת־ | מִשְׁמֶ֖רֶת | מִשְׁכַּ֥ן | הָעֵדֽוּת׃ |
| and-they-are-responsible | the-Levites | *** | care-of | tabernacle-of | the-Testimony |

| | | | | | | | |
|---|---|---|---|---|---|---|---|
| (54) | וַֽיַּעֲשׂ֖וּ | בְּנֵ֣י יִשְׂרָאֵ֑ל | כְּ֠כֹל | אֲשֶׁ֨ר | צִוָּ֧ה | יְהוָ֛ה | אֶת־ מֹשֶׁ֖ה |
| | so-they-did | sons-of  Israel | as-all | that | he-commanded | Yahweh | ***  Moses |

| | | | | | | | |
|---|---|---|---|---|---|---|---|
| כֵּ֥ן עָשֽׂוּ׃ | (2:1) | וַיְדַבֵּ֣ר | יְהוָ֔ה | אֶל־ מֹשֶׁ֥ה | וְאֶֽל־ אַהֲרֹ֖ן | לֵאמֹֽר׃ | (2) אִ֣ישׁ |
| so  they-did | | and-he-spoke | Yahweh | to  Moses | and-to  Aaron | to-say | (2) each |

| | | | | | |
|---|---|---|---|---|---|
| עַל־ | דִּגְל֤וֹ | בְאֹתֹת֙ | לְבֵ֣ית | אֲבֹתָ֔ם | יַחֲנ֖וּ |
| under | standard-of-him | with-banners | of-house-of | fathers-of-them | they-must-camp |

| | | | | | | |
|---|---|---|---|---|---|---|
| בְּנֵ֣י יִשְׂרָאֵ֑ל | מִנֶּ֕גֶד | סָבִ֥יב | לְאֹֽהֶל־ | מוֹעֵ֖ד | יַחֲנֽוּ׃ |
| sons-of  Israel | at-distance | around | to-Tent-of | Meeting | they-must-camp |

| | | | | | | |
|---|---|---|---|---|---|---|
| (3) | וְהַֽחֹנִים֙ | קֵ֣דְמָה | מִזְרָ֔חָה | דֶּ֛גֶל | מַחֲנֵ֥ה יְהוּדָ֖ה |
| | and-the-ones-camping | on-east | toward-sunrise | standard-of | camp-of  Judah |

| | | | | | | |
|---|---|---|---|---|---|---|
| לְצִבְאֹתָ֑ם | וְנָשִׂיא֙ | לִבְנֵ֣י | יְהוּדָ֔ה | נַחְשׁ֖וֹן | בֶּן־ | עַמִּינָדָֽב׃ |
| by-divisions-of-them | now-leader | of-people-of | Judah | Nahshon | son-of | Amminadab |

| | | | | | |
|---|---|---|---|---|---|
| (4) | וּצְבָא֖וֹ | וּפְקֻדֵיהֶ֑ם | אַרְבָּעָ֧ה וְשִׁבְעִ֛ים | אֶ֖לֶף |
| | and-division-of-him | and-numberings-of-them | four  and-seventy | thousand |

| | | | | | | |
|---|---|---|---|---|---|---|
| וְשֵׁ֥שׁ | מֵאֽוֹת׃ | (5) | וְהַחֹנִ֥ים | עָלָ֖יו | מַטֵּ֣ה | יִשָּׂשכָ֑ר |
| and-six | hundreds | | and-the-ones-camping | next-to-him | tribe-of | Issachar |

| | | | | | | |
|---|---|---|---|---|---|---|
| וְנָשִׂ֕יא | לִבְנֵ֖י | יִשָּׂשכָ֑ר | נְתַנְאֵ֖ל | בֶּן־ | צוּעָֽר׃ | (6) וּצְבָא֖וֹ |
| and-leader | of-people-of | Issachar | Nethanel | son-of | Zuar | (6) and-division-of-him |

| | | | | | | |
|---|---|---|---|---|---|---|
| וּפְקֻדָ֑יו | אַרְבָּעָ֧ה וַחֲמִשִּׁ֛ים | אֶ֖לֶף | וְאַרְבַּ֥ע | מֵאֽוֹת׃ | (7) | מַטֵּ֣ה |
| and-numberings-of-him | four  and-fifty | thousand | and-four | hundreds | | tribe-of |

| | | | | | | |
|---|---|---|---|---|---|---|
| זְבוּלֻ֑ן | וְנָשִׂיא֙ | לִבְנֵ֣י | זְבוּלֻ֔ן | אֱלִיאָ֖ב | בֶּן־ | חֵלֹֽן׃ |
| Zebulun | and-leader | of-people-of | Zebulun | Eliab | son-of | Helon |

they are to take care of it and encamp around it. [51]Whenever the tabernacle is to move, the Levites are to take it down, and whenever the tabernacle is to be set up, the Levites shall do it. Anyone else who goes near it shall be put to death. [52]The Israelites are to set up their tents by divisions, each man in his own camp under his own standard. [53]The Levites, however, are to set up their tents around the tabernacle of the Testimony so that wrath will not fall on the Israelite community. The Levites are to be responsible for the care of the tabernacle of the Testimony."

[54]The Israelites did all this just as the LORD commanded Moses.

*The Arrangement of the Tribal Camps*

2 The LORD said to Moses and Aaron: [2]"The Israelites are to camp around the Tent of Meeting some distance from it, each man under his standard with the banners of his family."

[3]On the east, toward the sunrise, the divisions of the camp of Judah are to encamp under their standard. The leader of the people of Judah is Nahshon son of Amminadab. [4]His division numbers 74,600.

[5]The tribe of Issachar will camp next to them. The leader of the people of Issachar is Nethanel son of Zuar. [6]His division numbers 54,400.

[7]The tribe of Zebulun will be next. The leader of the people of Zebulun is Eliab son of Helon. [8]His division

(8) וּצְבָאוֹ וּפְקֻדָיו שִׁבְעָה וַחֲמִשִּׁים אֶלֶף
thousand and-fifty seven and-numberings-of-him and-division-of-him (8)

וְאַרְבַּע מֵאוֹת׃ (9) כָּל־ הַפְּקֻדִים לְמַחֲנֵה יְהוּדָה
Judah to-camp-of the-ones-being-numbered all-of (9) hundreds and-four

מְאַת אֶלֶף וּשְׁמֹנִים אֶלֶף וְשֵׁשֶׁת־ אֲלָפִים וְאַרְבַּע־
and-four thousands and-six-of thousand and-eighty thousand hundred-of

מֵאוֹת לְצִבְאֹתָם רִאשֹׁנָה יִסָּעוּ׃ (10) דֶּגֶל
standard-of (10) they-will-set-out first by-divisions-of-them hundreds

מַחֲנֵה רְאוּבֵן תֵּימָנָה לְצִבְאֹתָם וְנָשִׂיא לִבְנֵי רְאוּבֵן
Reuben of-people-of and-leader by-divisions-of-them on-south Reuben camp-of

אֱלִיצוּר בֶּן־ שְׁדֵיאוּר׃ (11) וּצְבָאוֹ וּפְקֻדָיו שִׁשָּׁה
six and-numberings-of-him and-division-of-him (11) Shedeur son-of Elizur

וְאַרְבָּעִים אֶלֶף וַחֲמֵשׁ מֵאוֹת׃ (12) וְהַחוֹנִם עָלָיו
next-to-him and-the-ones-camping (12) hundreds and-five-of thousand and-forty

מַטֵּה שִׁמְעוֹן וְנָשִׂיא לִבְנֵי שִׁמְעוֹן שְׁלֻמִיאֵל בֶּן־ צוּרִי־ שַׁדָּי׃
Shaddai Zuri son-of Shelumiel Simeon of-people-of and-leader Simeon tribe-of

(13) וּצְבָאוֹ וּפְקֻדֵיהֶם תִּשְׁעָה וַחֲמִשִּׁים אֶלֶף
thousand and-fifty nine and-numberings-of-them division-of-him (13)

וּשְׁלֹשׁ מֵאוֹת׃ (14) וְמַטֵּה* גָּד וְנָשִׂיא לִבְנֵי גָד
Gad of-people-of and-leader Gad and-tribe-of (14) hundreds and-three-of

אֶלְיָסָף בֶּן־ רְעוּאֵל׃ (15) וּצְבָאוֹ וּפְקֻדֵיהֶם חֲמִשָּׁה
five and-numberings-of-them and-division-of-him (15) Reuel son-of Eliasaph

וְאַרְבָּעִים אֶלֶף וְשֵׁשׁ מֵאוֹת וַחֲמִשִּׁים׃ (16) כָּל־ הַפְּקֻדִים
the-numberings all-of (16) and-fifty hundreds and-six thousand and-forty

לְמַחֲנֵה רְאוּבֵן מְאַת אֶלֶף וְאֶחָד וַחֲמִשִּׁים אֶלֶף וְאַרְבַּע־
and-four thousand and-fifty and-one thousand hundred-of Reuben to-camp-of

מֵאוֹת וַחֲמִשִּׁים לְצִבְאֹתָם וּשְׁנִיִּם יִסָּעוּ׃
they-will-set-out and-second-ones by-divisions-of-them and-fifty hundreds

(17) וְנָסַע אֹהֶל־ מוֹעֵד מַחֲנֵה הַלְוִיִּם בְּתוֹךְ
in-middle-of the-Levites camp-of Meeting Tent-of then-he-will-set-out (17)

הַמַּחֲנֹת כַּאֲשֶׁר יַחֲנוּ כֵּן יִסָּעוּ אִישׁ עַל־ יָדוֹ
place-of-him in each they-will-set-out same they-encamp just-as the-camps

לְדִגְלֵיהֶם׃ (18) דֶּגֶל מַחֲנֵה אֶפְרַיִם לְצִבְאֹתָם
by-divisions-of-them Ephraim camp-of standard-of (18) under-standards-of-them

יָמָּה וְנָשִׂיא לִבְנֵי אֶפְרַיִם אֱלִישָׁמָע בֶּן־ עַמִּיהוּד׃
Ammihud son-of Elishama Ephraim of-people-of and-leader on-west

(19) וּצְבָאוֹ וּפְקֻדֵיהֶם אַרְבָּעִים אֶלֶף וַחֲמֵשׁ
and-five-of thousand forty and-numberings-of-them and-division-of-him (19)

numbers 57,400.
[9]All the men assigned to
the camp of Judah, according
to their divisions, number
186,400. They will set
out first.

[10]On the south will be the
divisions of the camp of
Reuben under their standard.
The leader of the
people of Reuben is Elizur
son of Shedeur. [11]His division
numbers 46,500.
[12]The tribe of Simeon will
camp next to them. The
leader of the people of
Simeon is Shelumiel son of
Zurishaddai. [13]His division
numbers 59,300.
[14]The tribe of Gad will be
next. The leader of the
people of Gad is Eliasaph
son of Deuel.[a] [15]His division
numbers 45,650.
[16]All the men assigned to
the camp of Reuben, according
to their divisions,
number 151,450. They will
set out second.

[17]Then the Tent of Meeting
and the camp of the Levites
will set out in the middle
of the camps. They will
set out in the same order as
they encamp, each in his
own place under his standard.

[18]On the west will be the
divisions of the camp of
Ephraim under their standard.
The leader of the
people of Ephraim is Elishama
son of Ammihud.
[19]His division numbers 40,500.

[a]*14* Many manuscripts of the Masoretic Text, Samaritan Pentateuch and Vulgate (see also Num. 1:14); most manuscripts of the Masoretic Text *Reuel*

**14* Most mss have *shureq* instead of *vav* with *sheva* ( וּמ' ).

מֵאֽוֹת׃ (20) וְעָלָיו מַטֵּה מְנַשֶּׁה וְנָשִׂיא לִבְנֵי
of-people-of · and-leader · Manasseh · tribe-of · and-next-to-him · (20) · hundreds

מְנַשֶּׁה גַּמְלִיאֵל בֶּן־ (21) פְּדָהצֽוּר׃ וּצְבָאֽוֹ
and-division-of-him · (21) · Pedahzur · son-of · Gamaliel · Manasseh

וּפְקֻדֵיהֶם שְׁנַיִם וּשְׁלֹשִׁים אֶלֶף וּמָאתָֽיִם׃
and-two-hundreds · thousand · and-thirty · two · and-numberings-of-them

וּמַטֵּה בִנְיָמִן וְנָשִׂיא לִבְנֵי בִנְיָמִן אֲבִידָן בֶּן־
son-of · Abidan · Benjamin · of-people-of · and-leader · Benjamin · and-tribe-of · (22)

גִּדְעֹנִֽי׃ (23) וּצְבָאֽוֹ וּפְקֻדֵיהֶם חֲמִשָּׁה וּשְׁלֹשִׁים
and-thirty · five · and-numberings-of-them · and-division-of-him · (23) · Gideoni

אֶלֶף וְאַרְבַּע מֵאֽוֹת׃ (24) כָּל־ הַפְּקֻדִים לְמַחֲנֵה
to-camp-of · the-ones-being-numbered · all-of · (24) · hundreds · and-four · thousand

אֶפְרַיִם מְאַת אֶלֶף וּשְׁמֹנַת־ אֲלָפִים וּמֵאָה
and-hundred · thousands · and-eight-of · thousand · hundred-of · Ephraim

לְצִבְאֹתָם וּשְׁלִשִׁים יִסָּֽעוּ׃ (25) דֶּגֶל מַחֲנֵה
camp-of · standard-of · (25) · they-will-set-out · and-third-ones · by-divisions-of-them

דָן צָפֹנָה לְצִבְאֹתָם וְנָשִׂיא לִבְנֵי דָן אֲחִיעֶזֶר
Ahiezer · Dan · of-people-of · and-leader · by-divisions-of-them · on-north · Dan

בֶּן־ עַמִּֽישַׁדָּֽי׃ (26) וּצְבָאֽוֹ וּפְקֻדֵיהֶם שְׁנַיִם
two · and-numberings-of-them · and-division-of-him · (26) · Ammishaddai · son-of

וְשִׁשִּׁים אֶלֶף וּשְׁבַע מֵאֽוֹת׃ (27) וְהַחֹנִים
and-the-ones-camping · (27) · hundreds · and-seven-of · thousand · and-sixty

עָלָיו מַטֵּה אָשֵׁר וְנָשִׂיא לִבְנֵי אָשֵׁר פַּגְעִיאֵל בֶּן־ עָכְרָֽן׃
Ocran · son-of · Pagiel · Asher · of-people-of · and-leader · Asher · tribe-of · next-to-him

וּצְבָאֽוֹ וּפְקֻדֵיהֶם אֶחָד וְאַרְבָּעִים אֶלֶף
thousand · and-forty · one · and-numberings-of-them · and-division-of-him · (28)

וַחֲמֵשׁ מֵאֽוֹת׃ (29) וּמַטֵּה נַפְתָּלִי וְנָשִׂיא לִבְנֵי
of-people-of · and-leader · Naphtali · and-tribe-of · (29) · hundreds · and-five-of

נַפְתָּלִי אֲחִירַע בֶּן־ עֵינָֽן׃ (30) וּצְבָאֽוֹ וּפְקֻדֵיהֶם
and-numberings-of-them · and-division-of-him · (30) · Enan · son-of · Ahira · Naphtali

שְׁלֹשָׁה וַחֲמִשִּׁים אֶלֶף וְאַרְבַּע מֵאֽוֹת׃ (31) כָּל־ הַפְּקֻדִים
the-ones-being-numbered · all-of · (31) · hundreds · and-four · thousand · and-fifty · three

לְמַחֲנֵה דָן מְאַת אֶלֶף וְשִׁבְעָה וַחֲמִשִּׁים אֶלֶף וְשֵׁשׁ
and-six · thousand · and-fifty · and-seven · thousand · hundred-of · Dan · to-camp-of

מֵאֽוֹת לָאַחֲרֹנָה יִסְעוּ לְדִגְלֵיהֶֽם׃ (32) אֵלֶּה
these · (32) · under-standards-of-them · they-will-set-out · as-the-last · hundreds

פְּקוּדֵי בְנֵי יִשְׂרָאֵל לְבֵית אֲבֹתָם כָּל־ פְּקוּדֵי
numberings-of · all-of · fathers-of-them · by-house-of · Israel · sons-of · countings-of

[20]The tribe of Manasseh will be next to them. The leader of the people of Manasseh is Gamaliel son of Pedahzur. [21]His division numbers 32,200.

[22]The tribe of Benjamin will be next. The leader of the people of Benjamin is Abidan son of Gideoni. [23]His division numbers 35,400.

[24]All the men assigned to the camp of Ephraim, according to their divisions, number 108,100. They will set out third.

[25]On the north will be the divisions of the camp of Dan, under their standard. The leader of the people of Dan is Ahiezer son of Ammishaddai. [26]His division numbers 62,700.

[27]The tribe of Asher will camp next to them. The leader of the people of Asher is Pagiel son of Ocran. [28]His division numbers 41,500.

[29]The tribe of Naphtali will be next. The leader of the people of Naphtali is Ahira son of Enan. [30]His division numbers 53,400.

[31]All the men assigned to the camp of Dan number 157,600. They will set out last, under their standards.

[32]These are the Israelites, counted according to their families. All those in the

הַמַּחֲנֹת֙ לְצִבְאֹתָ֔ם שֵׁשׁ־ מֵא֥וֹת אֶ֗לֶף וּשְׁלֹ֧שֶׁת אֲלָפִ֛ים
the-camps　by-divisions-of-them　six　hundreds　thousand　and-three　thousands

וַחֲמֵ֥שׁ מֵא֖וֹת וַחֲמִשִּֽׁים׃ וְהַ֨לְוִיִּ֔ם לֹ֣א הָתְפָּקְד֔וּ
and-five-of　hundreds　and-fifty　(33)　but-the-Levites　not　they-were-counted

בְּת֖וֹךְ בְּנֵ֣י יִשְׂרָאֵ֑ל כַּאֲשֶׁ֛ר צִוָּ֥ה יְהוָ֖ה אֶת־ מֹשֶֽׁה׃ וַֽיַּעֲשׂ֖וּ
with　sons-of　Israel　just-as　he-commanded　Yahweh　***　Moses　(34)　so-they-did

בְּנֵ֣י יִשְׂרָאֵ֑ל כְּ֠כֹל אֲשֶׁר־ צִוָּ֨ה יְהוָ֜ה אֶת־ מֹשֶׁ֗ה כֵּ֚ן חָנ֣וּ
sons-of　Israel　as-all　that　he-commanded　Yahweh　***　Moses　so　they-encamped

לְדִגְלֵיהֶ֔ם וְכֵ֣ן נָסָ֔עוּ אִ֥ישׁ לְמִשְׁפְּחֹתָ֖יו עַל־
under-standards-of-them　and-so　they-set-out　each　with-clans-of-him　with

בֵּ֣ית אֲבֹתָֽיו׃ וְאֵ֛לֶּה תּוֹלְדֹ֥ת אַהֲרֹ֖ן וּמֹשֶׁ֑ה בְּי֗וֹם
house-of　fathers-of-him　(3:1)　now-these　accounts-of　Aaron　and-Moses　on-day

דִּבֶּ֧ר יְהוָ֛ה אֶת־ מֹשֶׁ֖ה בְּהַ֣ר סִינָֽי׃ וְאֵ֛לֶּה שְׁמ֥וֹת בְּנֵֽי־
he-talked　Yahweh　***　Moses　on-Mount-of　Sinai　(2)　and-these　names-of　sons-of

אַהֲרֹ֖ן הַבְּכ֣וֹר ׀ נָדָ֑ב וַאֲבִיה֕וּא אֶלְעָזָ֖ר וְאִֽיתָמָֽר׃ אֵ֗לֶּה שְׁמוֹת֙
Aaron　the-firstborn　Nadab　and-Abihu　Eleazar　and-Ithamar　(3)　these　names-of

בְּנֵ֤י אַהֲרֹן֙ הַכֹּהֲנִ֣ים הַמְּשֻׁחִ֔ים אֲשֶׁר־ מִלֵּ֥א יָדָ֖ם
sons-of　Aaron　the-priests　the-ones-being-anointed　whom　he-ordained　hand-of-them

לְכַהֵֽן׃ וַיָּ֣מָת נָדָ֣ב וַאֲבִיה֡וּא לִפְנֵ֣י יְהוָ֡ה בְּהַקְרִבָם֩
to-be-priest　(4)　but-he-died　Nadab　and-Abihu　before　Yahweh　when-to-offer-them

אֵ֨שׁ זָרָ֜ה לִפְנֵ֤י יְהוָה֙ בְּמִדְבַּ֣ר סִינַ֔י וּבָנִ֖ים לֹא־ הָי֣וּ
fire　unauthorized　before　Yahweh　in-Desert-of　Sinai　and-sons　not　they-were

לָהֶ֑ם וַיְכַהֵ֤ן אֶלְעָזָר֙ וְאִ֣יתָמָ֔ר עַל־ פְּנֵ֖י אַהֲרֹ֥ן
to-them　so-he-was-priest　Eleazar　and-Ithamar　during　presence-of　Aaron

אֲבִיהֶֽם׃ וַיְדַבֵּ֥ר יְהוָ֖ה אֶל־ מֹשֶׁ֥ה לֵּאמֹֽר׃ הַקְרֵב֙ אֶת־
father-of-them　(5)　and-he-spoke　Yahweh　to　Moses　to-say　(6)　bring!　***

מַטֵּ֣ה לֵוִ֔י וְהַֽעֲמַדְתָּ֣ אֹת֔וֹ לִפְנֵ֖י אַהֲרֹ֣ן הַכֹּהֵ֑ן וְשֵׁרְת֖וּ
tribe-of　Levi　and-you-present　him　before　Aaron　the-priest　so-they-may-assist

אֹתֽוֹ׃ וְשָׁמְר֣וּ אֶת־ מִשְׁמַרְתּ֗וֹ וְאֶת־ מִשְׁמֶ֙רֶת֙ כָּל־
him　(7)　and-they-must-perform　***　duty-of-him　and　duty-of　whole-of

הָ֣עֵדָ֔ה לִפְנֵ֖י אֹ֣הֶל מוֹעֵ֑ד לַעֲבֹ֖ד אֶת־ עֲבֹדַ֥ת הַמִּשְׁכָּֽן׃
the-community　at　Tent-of　Meeting　to-do　***　work-of　the-tabernacle

וְשָׁמְר֗וּ אֶֽת־ כָּל־ כְּלֵי֙ אֹ֣הֶל מוֹעֵ֔ד וְאֶ֨ת־
and-they-must-take-care　(8)　***　all-of　furnishings-of　Tent-of　Meeting　and

מִשְׁמֶ֙רֶת֙ בְּנֵ֣י יִשְׂרָאֵ֔ל לַעֲבֹ֖ד אֶת־ עֲבֹדַ֣ת הַמִּשְׁכָּֽן׃ וְנָתַתָּה֙
obligation-of　sons-of　Israel　to-do　***　work-of　the-tabernacle　(9)　so-you-give

אֶת־ הַלְוִיִּ֔ם לְאַהֲרֹ֖ן וּלְבָנָ֑יו נְתוּנִ֨ם נְתוּנִ֥ם
***　the-Levites　to-Aaron　and-to-sons-of-him　ones-being-given　ones-being-given

---

camps, by their divisions, number 603,550. [33]The Levites, however, were not counted along with the other Israelites, as the LORD commanded Moses.

[34]So the Israelites did everything the LORD commanded Moses; that is the way they encamped under their standards, and that is the way they set out, each with his clan and family.

*The Levites*

**3** This is the account of the family of Aaron and Moses at the time the LORD talked with Moses on Mount Sinai.

[2]The names of the sons of Aaron were Nadab the firstborn and Abihu, Eleazar and Ithamar. [3]Those were the names of Aaron's sons, the anointed priests, who were ordained to serve as priests. [4]Nadab and Abihu, however, fell dead before the LORD when they made an offering with unauthorized fire before him in the Desert of Sinai. They had no sons; so only Eleazar and Ithamar served as priests during the lifetime of their father Aaron.

[5]The LORD said to Moses, [6]"Bring the tribe of Levi and present them to Aaron the priest to assist him. [7]They are to perform duties for him and for the whole community at the Tent of Meeting by doing the work of the tabernacle. [8]They are to take care of all the furnishings of the Tent of Meeting, fulfilling the obligations of the Israelites by doing the work of the tabernacle. [9]Give the Levites to Aaron and his sons; they are the Israelites who are to be given wholly to

הֵמָּה לוֹ מֵאֵת בְּנֵי יִשְׂרָאֵל׃ וְאֶת־אַהֲרֹן וְאֶת־בָּנָיו תִּפְקֹד
you-appoint sons-of-him and Aaron and (10) Israel sons-of from to-him they

וְשָׁמְרוּ אֶת־כְּהֻנָּתָם וְהַזָּר הַקָּרֵב
the-one-near but-the-outsider priesthood-of-them *** so-they-serve

יוּמָת׃ וַיְדַבֵּר יְהוָה אֶל־מֹשֶׁה לֵּאמֹר וַאֲנִי הִנֵּה לָקַחְתִּי
I-took see! now-I (12) to-say Moses to Yahweh and-he-spoke (11) he-must-die

אֶת־הַלְוִיִּם מִתּוֹךְ בְּנֵי יִשְׂרָאֵל תַּחַת כָּל־בְּכוֹר
firstborn all-of in-place-of Israel sons-of from-among the-Levites ***

פֶּטֶר רֶחֶם מִבְּנֵי יִשְׂרָאֵל וְהָיוּ לִי הַלְוִיִּם׃ כִּי
for (13) the-Levites to-me so-they-are Israel from-sons-of womb opener-of

לִי כָּל־בְּכוֹר בְּיוֹם הַכֹּתִי כָל־בְּכוֹר בְּאֶרֶץ
in-land-of firstborn all-of to-strike-down-me on-day firstborn all-of to-me

מִצְרַיִם הִקְדַּשְׁתִּי לִי כָל־בְּכוֹר בְּיִשְׂרָאֵל מֵאָדָם עַד־בְּהֵמָה
animal or whether-man in-Israel firstborn every-of for-me I-set-apart Egypt

לִי יִהְיוּ אֲנִי יְהוָה׃ וַיְדַבֵּר יְהוָה אֶל־מֹשֶׁה בְמִדְבַּר
in-Desert-of Moses to Yahweh and-he-spoke (14) Yahweh I they-are for-me

סִינַי לֵאמֹר׃ פְּקֹד אֶת־בְּנֵי לֵוִי לְבֵית אֲבֹתָם
fathers-of-them by-house-of Levi sons-of *** count! (15) to-say Sinai

לְמִשְׁפְּחֹתָם כָּל־זָכָר מִבֶּן־חֹדֶשׁ וָמַעְלָה תִּפְקְדֵם׃
you-count-them or-more month from-son-of male every-of by-clans-of-them

וַיִּפְקֹד אֹתָם מֹשֶׁה עַל־פִּי יְהוָה כַּאֲשֶׁר צֻוָּה׃
he-was-commanded just-as Yahweh word-of at Moses them so-he-counted (16)

וַיִּהְיוּ־אֵלֶּה בְנֵי־לֵוִי בִּשְׁמֹתָם גֵּרְשׁוֹן וּקְהָת
and-Kohath Gershon by-names-of-them Levi sons-of these and-they-were (17)

וּמְרָרִי׃ וְאֵלֶּה שְׁמוֹת בְּנֵי־גֵרְשׁוֹן לְמִשְׁפְּחֹתָם לִבְנִי
Libni by-clans-of-them Gershon sons-of names-of and-these (18) and-Merari

וְשִׁמְעִי׃ וּבְנֵי קְהָת לְמִשְׁפְּחֹתָם עַמְרָם וְיִצְהָר חֶבְרוֹן
Hebron and-Izhar Amram by-clans-of-them Kohath and-sons-of (19) and-Shimei

וְעֻזִּיאֵל׃ וּבְנֵי מְרָרִי לְמִשְׁפְּחֹתָם מַחְלִי וּמוּשִׁי אֵלֶּה
these and-Mushi Mahli by-clans-of-them Merari and-sons-of (20) and-Uzziel

הֵם מִשְׁפְּחֹת הַלֵּוִי לְבֵית אֲבֹתָם׃ לְגֵרְשׁוֹן
to-Gershon (21) fathers-of-them by-house-of the-Levites clans-of they

מִשְׁפַּחַת הַלִּבְנִי וּמִשְׁפַּחַת הַשִּׁמְעִי אֵלֶּה הֵם מִשְׁפְּחֹת
clans-of they these the-Shimeite and-clan-of the-Libnite clan-of

הַגֵּרְשֻׁנִּי׃ פְּקֻדֵיהֶם בְּמִסְפַּר כָּל־זָכָר מִבֶּן־
from-son-of male every-of by-count-of numberings-of-them (22) the-Gershonite

חֹדֶשׁ וָמַעְלָה פְּקֻדֵיהֶם שִׁבְעַת אֲלָפִים וַחֲמֵשׁ מֵאוֹת׃
hundreds and-five-of thousands seven-of numberings-of-them or-more month

him.[b] [10]Appoint Aaron and his sons to serve as priests; anyone else who approaches the sanctuary must be put to death."

[11]The LORD also said to Moses, [12]"I have taken the Levites from among the Israelites in place of the first male offspring of every Israelite woman. The Levites are mine, [13]for all the firstborn are mine. When I struck down all the firstborn in Egypt, I set apart for myself every firstborn in Israel, whether man or animal. They are to be mine. I am the LORD."

[14]The LORD said to Moses in the Desert of Sinai, [15]"Count the Levites by their families and clans. Count every male a month old or more." [16]So Moses counted them, as he was commanded by the word of the LORD.

[17]These were the names of the sons of Levi:
Gershon, Kohath and Merari.
[18]These were the names of the Gershonite clans:
Libni and Shimei.
[19]The Kohathite clans:
Amram, Izhar, Hebron and Uzziel.
[20]The Merarite clans:
Mahli and Mushi.
These were the Levite clans, according to their families.

[21]To Gershon belonged the clans of the Libnites and Shimeites; these were the Gershonite clans. [22]The number of all the males a month old or more who were counted was

[b]9 Most manuscripts of the Masoretic Text; some manuscripts of the Masoretic Text, Samaritan Pentateuch and Septuagint (see also Num. 8:16) *to me*

*9 Some mss and the versions above in note *b* read לִי, *to-me.*

מִשְׁפְּחֹת הַגֵּרְשֻׁנִּי אַחֲרֵי הַמִּשְׁכָּן יַחֲנוּ יָמָּה׃
(23) clans-of the-Gershonite behind the-tabernacle they-camped on-west

וּנְשִׂיא בֵית־ אָב לַגֵּרְשֻׁנִּי אֶלְיָסָף בֶּן־ לָאֵל׃
(24) and-leader-of house-of father of-the-Gershonite Eliasaph son-of Lael

וּמִשְׁמֶרֶת בְּנֵי־ גֵרְשׁוֹן בְּאֹהֶל מוֹעֵד הַמִּשְׁכָּן
(25) and-responsibility-of sons-of Gershon at-Tent-of Meeting the-tabernacle

וְהָאֹהֶל מִכְסֵהוּ וּמָסַךְ פֶּתַח אֹהֶל מוֹעֵד׃
and-the-tent covering-of-him and-curtain-of entrance-of Tent-of Meeting

וְקַלְעֵי הֶחָצֵר וְאֶת־ מָסַךְ פֶּתַח הֶחָצֵר
(26) and-curtains-of the-courtyard and curtain-of entrance-of the-courtyard

אֲשֶׁר עַל־ הַמִּשְׁכָּן וְעַל־ הַמִּזְבֵּחַ סָבִיב וְאֵת מֵיתָרָיו לְכֹל
that for the-tabernacle and-for the-altar around and ropes-of-him for-all-of

עֲבֹדָתוֹ׃ וְלִקְהָת מִשְׁפַּחַת הָעַמְרָמִי וּמִשְׁפַּחַת הַיִּצְהָרִי
use-of-him (27) and-to-Kohath clan-of the-Amramite and-clan-of the-Izharite

וּמִשְׁפַּחַת הַחֶבְרֹנִי וּמִשְׁפַּחַת הָעָזִּיאֵלִי אֵלֶּה הֵם מִשְׁפְּחֹת
and-clan-of the-Hebronite and-clan-of the-Uzzielite these they clans-of

הַקְּהָתִי׃ בְּמִסְפַּר כָּל־ זָכָר מִבֶּן־ חֹדֶשׁ וָמָעְלָה
the-Kohathite (28) by-number-of every-of male from-son-of month or-more

שְׁמֹנַת אֲלָפִים וְשֵׁשׁ מֵאוֹת שֹׁמְרֵי מִשְׁמֶרֶת
eight thousands and-six hundreds ones-caring-of responsibility-of

הַקֹּדֶשׁ׃ מִשְׁפְּחֹת בְּנֵי־ קְהָת יַחֲנוּ עַל יֶרֶךְ
the-sanctuary (29) clans-of sons-of Kohath they-camped on side-of

הַמִּשְׁכָּן תֵּימָנָה׃ וּנְשִׂיא בֵית־ אָב לְמִשְׁפְּחֹת
the-tabernacle on-south (30) and-leader-of house-of father of-clans-of

הַקְּהָתִי אֱלִיצָפָן בֶּן־ עֻזִּיאֵל׃ וּמִשְׁמַרְתָּם הָאָרֹן
the-Kohathite Elizaphan son-of Uzziel (31) and-responsibility-of-them the-ark

וְהַשֻּׁלְחָן וְהַמְּנֹרָה וְהַמִּזְבְּחֹת וּכְלֵי הַקֹּדֶשׁ
and-the-table and-the-lampstand and-the-altars and-articles-of the-sanctuary

אֲשֶׁר יְשָׁרְתוּ בָּהֶם וְהַמָּסָךְ וְכֹל עֲבֹדָתוֹ׃
that they-minister with-them and-the-curtain and-all-of use-of-him

וּנְשִׂיא נְשִׂיאֵי הַלֵּוִי אֶלְעָזָר בֶּן־ אַהֲרֹן הַכֹּהֵן
(32) and-leader-of leaders-of the-Levite Eleazar son-of Aaron the-priest

פְּקֻדַּת שֹׁמְרֵי מִשְׁמֶרֶת הַקֹּדֶשׁ׃
being-appointed-of ones-caring-of responsibility-of the-sanctuary

לִמְרָרִי מִשְׁפַּחַת הַמַּחְלִי וּמִשְׁפַּחַת הַמּוּשִׁי אֵלֶּה הֵם
(33) to-Merari clan-of the-Mahlite and-clan-of the-Mushite these they

מִשְׁפְּחֹת מְרָרִי׃ וּפְקֻדֵיהֶם בְּמִסְפַּר כָּל־ זָכָר
clans-of Merarite (34) and-numberings-of-them by-count-of every-of male

7,500. [23]The Gershonite clans were to camp on the west, behind the tabernacle. [24]The leader of the families of the Gershonites was Eliasaph son of Lael. [25]At the Tent of Meeting the Gershonites were responsible for the care of the tabernacle and tent, its coverings, the curtain at the entrance to the Tent of Meeting, [26]the curtains of the courtyard, the curtain at the entrance to the courtyard surrounding the tabernacle and altar, and the ropes—and everything related to their use.

[27]To Kohath belonged the clans of the Amramites, Izharites, Hebronites and Uzzielites; these were the Kohathite clans. [28]The number of all the males a month old or more was 8,600.[c] The Kohathites were responsible for the care of the sanctuary. [29]The Kohathite clans were to camp on the south side of the tabernacle. [30]The leader of the families of the Kohathite clans was Elizaphan son of Uzziel. [31]They were responsible for the care of the ark, the table, the lampstand, the altars, the articles of the sanctuary used in ministering, the curtain, and everything related to their use. [32]The chief leader of the Levites was Eleazar son of Aaron, the priest. He was appointed over those who were responsible for the care of the sanctuary.

[33]To Merari belonged the clans of the Mahlites and the Mushites; these were the Merarite clans. [34]The number of all

[c]28 Hebrew; some Septuagint manuscripts *8,300*

מִבֶּן־ חֹדֶשׁ וָמָעְלָה שֵׁשֶׁת אֲלָפִים וּמָאתָיִם׃ וּנְשִׂיא
and-leader-of (35) and-two-hundreds thousands six-of or-more month from-son-of

בֵית־ אָב לְמִשְׁפְּחֹת מְרָרִי צוּרִיאֵל בֶּן־ אֲבִיחָיִל עַל יֶרֶךְ
side-of on Abihail son-of Zuriel Merari of-clans-of father house-of

הַמִּשְׁכָּן יַחֲנוּ צָפֹנָה׃ וּפְקֻדַּת מִשְׁמֶרֶת
care-of and-being-appointed-of (36) on-north they-camped the-tabernacle

בְּנֵי מְרָרִי קַרְשֵׁי הַמִּשְׁכָּן וּבְרִיחָיו וְעַמֻּדָיו
and-posts-of-him and-crossbars-of-him the-tabernacle frames-of Merari sons-of

וַאֲדָנָיו וְכָל־ כֵּלָיו וְכֹל עֲבֹדָתוֹ׃
use-of-him and-all-of equipments-of-him and-all-of and-bases-of-him

וְעַמֻּדֵי הֶחָצֵר סָבִיב וְאַדְנֵיהֶם וִיתֵדֹתָם
and-pegs-of-them and-bases-of-them around the-courtyard and-posts-of (37)

וּמֵיתְרֵיהֶם׃ וְהַחֹנִים לִפְנֵי הַמִּשְׁכָּן
the-tabernacle in-front-of and-the-ones-camping (38) and-ropes-of-them

קֵדְמָה לִפְנֵי אֹהֶל־ מוֹעֵד ׀ מִזְרָחָה מֹשֶׁה ׀ וְאַהֲרֹן
and-Aaron Moses toward-sunrise Meeting Tent-of in-front-of on-east

וּבָנָיו שֹׁמְרִים מִשְׁמֶרֶת הַמִּקְדָּשׁ לְמִשְׁמֶרֶת
on-behalf-of the-sanctuary care-of ones-being-responsible and-sons-of-him

בְּנֵי יִשְׂרָאֵל וְהַזָּר הַקָּרֵב יוּמָת׃ כָּל־
total-of (39) he-must-die the-one-near but-the-outsider Israel sons-of

פְּקוּדֵי הַלְוִיִּם אֲשֶׁר פָּקַד מֹשֶׁה וְאַהֲרֹן עַל־ פִּי
command-of at and-Aaron Moses he-counted that the-Levites numberings-of

יְהוָה לְמִשְׁפְּחֹתָם כָּל־ זָכָר מִבֶּן־ חֹדֶשׁ וָמַעְלָה שְׁנַיִם
two or-more month from-son-of male every-of by-clans-of-them Yahweh

וְעֶשְׂרִים אָלֶף׃ וַיֹּאמֶר יְהוָה אֶל־ מֹשֶׁה פְּקֹד כָּל־
every-of count! Moses to Yahweh then-he-said (40) thousand and-twenty

בְּכֹר זָכָר לִבְנֵי יִשְׂרָאֵל מִבֶּן־ חֹדֶשׁ וָמָעְלָה וְשָׂא אֵת
*** and-make! or-more month from-son-of Israel of-sons-of male firstborn-of

מִסְפַּר שְׁמֹתָם׃ וְלָקַחְתָּ אֶת־ הַלְוִיִּם לִי אֲנִי יְהוָה
Yahweh I for-me the-Levites *** and-you-take (41) names-of-them list-of

תַּחַת כָּל־ בְּכֹר בִּבְנֵי יִשְׂרָאֵל וְאֵת בֶּהֱמַת הַלְוִיִּם
the-Levites stock-of and Israel from-sons-of firstborn all-of in-place-of

תַּחַת כָּל־ בְּכוֹר בְּבֶהֱמַת בְּנֵי יִשְׂרָאֵל׃ וַיִּפְקֹד
so-he-counted (42) Israel sons-of from-stock-of firstborn all-of in-place-of

מֹשֶׁה כַּאֲשֶׁר צִוָּה יְהוָה אֹתוֹ אֶת־ כָּל־ בְּכֹר בִּבְנֵי יִשְׂרָאֵל׃
Israel of-sons-of firstborn all-of *** him Yahweh he-commanded just-as Moses

וַיְהִי כָל־ בְּכוֹר זָכָר בְּמִסְפַּר שֵׁמוֹת מִבֶּן־
from-son-of names by-list-of male firstborn-of total-of and-he-was (43)

the males a month old or more who were counted was 6,200. [35]The leader of the families of the Merarite clans was Zuriel son of Abihail; they were to camp on the north side of the tabernacle. [36]The Merarites were appointed to take care of the frames of the tabernacle, its crossbars, posts, bases, all its equipment, and everything related to their use, [37]as well as the posts of the surrounding courtyard with their bases, tent pegs and ropes.

[38]Moses and Aaron and his sons were to camp to the east of the tabernacle, toward the sunrise, in front of the Tent of Meeting. They were responsible for the care of the sanctuary on behalf of the Israelites. Anyone else who approached the sanctuary was to be put to death.

[39]The total number of Levites counted at the LORD's command by Moses and Aaron according to their clans, including every male a month old or more, was 22,000.

[40]The LORD said to Moses, "Count all the firstborn Israelite males who are a month old or more and make a list of their names. [41]Take the Levites for me in place of all the firstborn of the Israelites, and the livestock of the Levites in place of all the firstborn of the livestock of the Israelites. I am the LORD."

[42]So Moses counted all the firstborn of the Israelites, as the LORD commanded him. [43]The total number of firstborn males a month old or more,

חֹדֶשׁ וָמַעְלָה לִפְקֻדֵיהֶם שְׁנַיִם וְעֶשְׂרִים אֶלֶף שְׁלֹשָׁה וְשִׁבְעִים
and-seventy three thousand and-twenty two by-numberings-of-them or-more month

וּמָאתָיִם׃ וַיְדַבֵּר יְהוָה אֶל־מֹשֶׁה לֵּאמֹר׃ קַח אֶת־
*** take! (45) to-say Moses to Yahweh and-he-spoke (44) and-two-hundreds

הַלְוִיִּם תַּחַת כָּל־ בְּכוֹר בִּבְנֵי יִשְׂרָאֵל וְאֶת־ בֶּהֱמַת
stock-of and Israel of-sons-of firstborn all-of in-place-of the-Levites

הַלְוִיִּם תַּחַת בְּהֶמְתָּם וְהָיוּ־ לִי הַלְוִיִּם אֲנִי
I the-Levites for-me and-they-will-be stock-of-them in-place-of the-Levites

יְהוָה׃ וְאֵת פְּדוּיֵי הַשְּׁלֹשָׁה וְהַשִּׁבְעִים וְהַמָּאתָיִם
and-the-two-hundreds and-the-seventy the-three redemptions-of and (46) Yahweh

הָעֹדְפִים עַל־ הַלְוִיִּם מִבְּכוֹר בְּנֵי יִשְׂרָאֵל׃
Israel sons-of from-firstborn-of the-Levites over the-ones-exceeding

וְלָקַחְתָּ חֲמֵשֶׁת חֲמֵשֶׁת שְׁקָלִים לַגֻּלְגֹּלֶת בְּשֶׁקֶל
by-shekel-of for-the-each shekels five-of five-of and-you-collect (47)

הַקֹּדֶשׁ תִּקָּח עֶשְׂרִים גֵּרָה הַשָּׁקֶל׃ וְנָתַתָּה
then-you-give (48) the-shekel gerah twenty you-collect the-sanctuary

הַכֶּסֶף לְאַהֲרֹן וּלְבָנָיו פְּדוּיֵי הָעֹדְפִים
the-ones-exceeding redemptions-of and-to-sons-of-him to-Aaron the-money

בָּהֶם׃ וַיִּקַּח מֹשֶׁה אֵת כֶּסֶף הַפִּדְיוֹם מֵאֵת
from the-redemption money-of *** Moses so-he-collected (49) over-them

הָעֹדְפִים עַל פְּדוּיֵי הַלְוִיִּם׃ מֵאֵת בְּכוֹר
firstborn-of from (50) the-Levites redemptions-of over the-ones-exceeding

בְּנֵי יִשְׂרָאֵל לָקַח אֶת־ הַכֶּסֶף חֲמִשָּׁה וְשִׁשִּׁים וּשְׁלֹשׁ מֵאוֹת
hundreds and-three and-sixty five the-money *** he-collected Israel sons-of

וָאֶלֶף בְּשֶׁקֶל הַקֹּדֶשׁ׃ וַיִּתֵּן מֹשֶׁה אֶת־ כֶּסֶף
money-of *** Moses and-he-gave (51) the-sanctuary by-shekel-of and-thousand

הַפְּדֻיִם לְאַהֲרֹן וּלְבָנָיו עַל־ פִּי יְהוָה כַּאֲשֶׁר
just-as Yahweh word-of by and-to-sons-of-him to-Aaron the-redemptions

צִוָּה יְהוָה אֶת־ מֹשֶׁה׃ וַיְדַבֵּר יְהוָה אֶל־ מֹשֶׁה וְאֶל־
and-to Moses to Yahweh and-he-spoke (4:1) Moses *** Yahweh he-commanded

אַהֲרֹן לֵאמֹר׃ נָשֹׂא אֶת־ רֹאשׁ בְּנֵי קְהָת מִתּוֹךְ בְּנֵי לֵוִי
Levi sons-of from-among Kohath sons-of census-of *** to-take (2) to-say Aaron

לְמִשְׁפְּחֹתָם לְבֵית אֲבֹתָם׃ מִבֶּן שְׁלֹשִׁים שָׁנָה
year thirty from-son-of (3) fathers-of-them by-house-of by-clans-of-them

וָמַעְלָה וְעַד בֶּן־ חֲמִשִּׁים שָׁנָה כָּל־ בָּא לַצָּבָא לַעֲשׂוֹת מְלָאכָה
work to-do for-the-service coming all-of year fifty son-of even-to or-more

בְּאֹהֶל מוֹעֵד׃ זֹאת עֲבֹדַת בְּנֵי־ קְהָת בְּאֹהֶל מוֹעֵד
Meeting in-Tent-of Kohath sons-of work-of this (4) Meeting in-Tent-of

listed by name, was 22,273.

[44]The LORD also said to Moses, [45]"Take the Levites in place of all the firstborn of Israel, and the livestock of the Levites in place of their livestock. The Levites are to be mine. I am the LORD. [46]To redeem the 273 firstborn Israelites who exceed the number of the Levites, [47]collect five shekels[d] for each one, according to the sanctuary shekel, which weighs twenty gerahs. [48]Give the money for the redemption of the additional Israelites to Aaron and his sons."

[49]So Moses collected the redemption money from those who exceeded the number redeemed by the Levites. [50]From the firstborn of the Israelites he collected silver weighing 1,365 shekels,[e] according to the sanctuary shekel. [51]Moses gave the redemption money to Aaron and his sons, as he was commanded by the word of the LORD.

*The Kohathites*

**4** The LORD said to Moses and Aaron: [2]"Take a census of the Kohathite branch of the Levites by their clans and families. [3]Count all the men from thirty to fifty years of age who come to serve in the work in the Tent of Meeting.

[4]"This is the work of the Kohathites in the Tent of Meeting: the care of the most holy

[d]47 That is, about 2 ounces (about 55 grams)
[e]50 That is, about 35 pounds (about 15.5 kilograms)

| קֹדֶשׁ | הַקֳּדָשִׁים: | וּבָא | אַהֲרֹן | וּבָנָיו֯ |
|---|---|---|---|---|
| most-holy-of | the-holy-things | then-he-must-go-in (5) | Aaron | and-sons-of-him |

| בִּנְסֹעַ | הַמַּחֲנֶה | וְהוֹרִ֫דוּ | אֶת־ | פָּרֹכֶת | הַמָּסָ֔ךְ |
|---|---|---|---|---|---|
| when-to-move | the-camp | and-they-must-take-down | *** | curtain-of | the-shield |

| וְכִסּוּ־ | בָהּ | אֵת | אֲרֹן | הָעֵדֻת: | וְנָתְנוּ |
|---|---|---|---|---|---|
| and-they-must-cover | with-her | *** | ark-of | the-Testimony (6) | then-they-must-put |

| עָלָיו | כְּסוּי | ע֣וֹר | תַּ֔חַשׁ | וּפָרְשׂוּ | בֶגֶד־ | כְּלִיל |
|---|---|---|---|---|---|---|
| over-him | cover-of | hide-of | sea-cow | and-they-must-spread | cloth-of | solid-of |

| תְּכֵלֶת | מִלְמָ֑עְלָה | וְשָׂמ֖וּ | בַּדָּיו: | וְעַל | שֻׁלְחַ֣ן |
|---|---|---|---|---|---|
| blue | over-top | and-they-must-put-in-place | poles-of-him (7) | and-over | table-of |

| הַפָּנִים֙ | יִפְרְשׂוּ֙ | בֶּ֣גֶד | תְּכֵ֔לֶת | וְנָתְנ֣וּ | עָלָ֗יו | אֶת־ |
|---|---|---|---|---|---|---|
| the-Presences | they-must-spread | cloth-of | blue | and-they-must-put | on-him | *** |

| הַקְּעָרֹ֤ת | וְאֶת־ | הַכַּפֹּת֙ | וְאֶת־ | הַמְּנַקִּיֹּ֔ת | וְאֵת֙ | קְשׂ֖וֹת | הַנָּ֑סֶךְ |
|---|---|---|---|---|---|---|---|
| the-plates | and | the-ladles | and | the-bowls | and | jars-of | the-drink-offering |

| וְלֶ֥חֶם | הַתָּמִ֖יד | עָלָ֥יו | יִהְיֶֽה: | וּפָרְשׂ֣וּ |
|---|---|---|---|---|
| and-bread-of | the-continual | on-him | he-remains (8) | and-they-must-spread |

| עֲלֵיהֶ֗ם | בֶּ֚גֶד | תּוֹלַ֣עַת | שָׁנִ֔י | וְכִסּ֣וּ | אֹת֔וֹ | בְּמִכְסֵ֖ה |
|---|---|---|---|---|---|---|
| over-them | cloth-of | scarlet-of | scarlet | and-they-must-cover | him | with-cover-of |

| ע֣וֹר | תָּ֑חַשׁ | וְשָׂמ֖וּ | אֶת־ | בַּדָּֽיו: |
|---|---|---|---|---|
| hide-of | sea-cow | and-they-must-put-in-place | *** | poles-of-him |

| וְלָקְח֣וּ | בֶּ֤גֶד | תְּכֵ֙לֶת֙ | וְכִסּ֔וּ | אֶת־ | מְנֹרַ֥ת |
|---|---|---|---|---|---|
| and-they-must-take (9) | cloth-of | blue | and-they-must-cover | *** | lampstand-of |

| הַמָּא֖וֹר | וְאֶת־ | נֵרֹתֶ֑יהָ | וְאֶת־ | מַלְקָחֶ֙יהָ֙ | וְאֶת־ | מַחְתֹּתֶ֔יהָ | וְאֵת֙ |
|---|---|---|---|---|---|---|---|
| the-light | and | lamps-of-her | and | wick-trimmers-of-her | and | trays-of-her | and |

| כָּל־ | כְּלֵ֣י | שַׁמְנָ֔הּ | אֲשֶׁ֥ר | יְשָׁרְתוּ־ | לָ֖הּ | בָּהֶֽם: |
|---|---|---|---|---|---|---|
| all-of | jars-of | oil-of-her | that | they-supply | to-her | with-them |

| וְנָתְנ֤וּ | אֹתָהּ֙ | וְאֶת־ | כָּל־ | כֵּלֶ֔יהָ | אֶל־ | מִכְסֵ֖ה | ע֣וֹר |
|---|---|---|---|---|---|---|---|
| and-they-must-wrap (10) | her | and | all-of | accessories-of-her | in | cover-of | hide-of |

| תָּ֑חַשׁ | וְנָתְנ֖וּ | עַל־ | הַמּֽוֹט: | וְעַ֣ל | מִזְבַּ֣ח |
|---|---|---|---|---|---|
| sea-cow | and-they-must-put | on | the-carrying-frame (11) | and-over | altar-of |

| הַזָּהָ֗ב | יִפְרְשׂוּ֙ | בֶּ֣גֶד | תְּכֵ֔לֶת | וְכִסּ֣וּ | אֹת֔וֹ | בְּמִכְסֵ֖ה |
|---|---|---|---|---|---|---|
| the-gold | they-must-spread | cloth-of | blue | and-they-must-cover | him | with-cover-of |

| ע֣וֹר | תָּ֑חַשׁ | וְשָׂמ֖וּ | אֶת־ | בַּדָּֽיו: |
|---|---|---|---|---|
| hide-of | sea-cow | and-they-must-put-in-place | *** | poles-of-him |

| וְלָקְחוּ֩ | אֶת־ | כָּל־ | כְּלֵ֨י | הַשָּׁרֵ֜ת | אֲשֶׁ֧ר | יְשָׁרְתוּ־ |
|---|---|---|---|---|---|---|
| and-they-must-take (12) | *** | all-of | articles-of | the-ministry | that | they-minister |

| בָ֣ם | בַּקֹּ֗דֶשׁ | וְנָֽתְנוּ֙ | אֶל־ | בֶּ֣גֶד | תְּכֵ֔לֶת |
|---|---|---|---|---|---|
| with-them | in-the-sanctuary | and-they-must-wrap | in | cloth-of | blue |

things. [5]When the camp is to move, Aaron and his sons are to go in and take down the shielding curtain and cover the ark of the Testimony with it. [6]Then they are to cover this with hides of sea cows, spread a cloth of solid blue over that and put the poles in place.

[7]"Over the table of the Presence they are to spread a blue cloth and put on it the plates, ladles and bowls, and the jars for drink offerings; the bread that is continually there is to remain on it. [8]Over these they are to spread a scarlet cloth, cover that with hides of sea cows and put its poles in place.

[9]"They are to take a blue cloth and cover the lampstand that is for light, together with its lamps, its wick trimmers and trays, and all its jars for the oil used to supply it. [10]Then they are to wrap it and all its accessories in a covering of hides of sea cows and put it on a carrying frame.

[11]"Over the gold altar they are to spread a blue cloth and cover that with hides of sea cows and put its poles in place.

[12]"They are to take all the articles used for ministering in the sanctuary, wrap them in a blue cloth, cover that with

וְכִסּוּ אוֹתָם בְּמִכְסֵה עוֹר תָּחַשׁ וְנָתְנוּ עַל־

on and-they-must-put sea-cow hide-of with-cover-of them and-they-must-cover

הַמּוֹט׃ וְדִשְּׁנוּ אֶת־הַמִּזְבֵּחַ

the-altar *** and-they-must-remove-ash (13) the-carrying-frame

וּפָרְשׂוּ עָלָיו בֶּגֶד אַרְגָּמָן׃ וְנָתְנוּ

then-they-must-place (14) purple cloth-of over-him and-they-must-spread

עָלָיו אֶת־כָּל־כֵּלָיו אֲשֶׁר יְשָׁרְתוּ עָלָיו בָּהֶם אֶת־

*** with-them at-him they-minister that utensils-of-him all-of *** on-him

הַמַּחְתֹּת אֶת־הַמִּזְלָגֹת וְאֶת־הַיָּעִים וְאֶת־הַמִּזְרָקֹת

the-sprinkling-bowls and the-shovels and the-meatforks *** the-firepans

כֹּל כְּלֵי הַמִּזְבֵּחַ וּפָרְשׂוּ עָלָיו כְּסוּי עוֹר

hide-of cover-of over-him and-they-must-spread the-altar utensils-of all-of

תַּחַשׁ וְשָׂמוּ בַדָּיו׃ וְכִלָּה אַהֲרֹן־

Aaron when-he-finishes (15) poles-of-him and-they-must-put-in-place sea-cow

וּבָנָיו לְכַסֹּת אֶת־הַקֹּדֶשׁ וְאֶת־כָּל־כְּלֵי הַקֹּדֶשׁ

the-holy articles-of all-of and the-holy-thing *** to-cover and-sons-of-him

בִּנְסֹעַ הַמַּחֲנֶה וְאַחֲרֵי־כֵן יָבֹאוּ בְנֵי־קְהָת לָשֵׂאת

to-carry Kohath sons-of they-must-come this then-after the-camp when-to-move

וְלֹא־יִגְּעוּ אֶל־הַקֹּדֶשׁ וָמֵתוּ אֵלֶּה מַשָּׂא בְנֵי־

sons-of burden-of these or-they-will-die the-holy on they-must-touch but-not

קְהָת בְּאֹהֶל מוֹעֵד׃ וּפְקֻדַּת אֶלְעָזָר ׀ בֶּן־אַהֲרֹן הַכֹּהֵן

the-priest Aaron son-of Eleazar now-charge-of (16) Meeting in-Tent-of Kohath

שֶׁמֶן הַמָּאוֹר וּקְטֹרֶת הַסַּמִּים וּמִנְחַת

and-grain-offering-of the-fragrances and-incense-of the-light oil-of

הַתָּמִיד וְשֶׁמֶן הַמִּשְׁחָה פְּקֻדַּת כָּל־הַמִּשְׁכָּן

the-tabernacle entire-of charge-of the-anointing and-oil-of the-regular

וְכָל־אֲשֶׁר־בּוֹ בְּקֹדֶשׁ וּבְכֵלָיו׃ וַיְדַבֵּר

and-he-spoke (17) and-of-articles-of-him of-holy-thing in-him that and-all

יְהוָה אֶל־מֹשֶׁה וְאֶל־אַהֲרֹן לֵאמֹר׃ אַל־תַּכְרִיתוּ אֶת־שֵׁבֶט

tribe-of *** you-cut-off not (18) to-say Aaron and-to Moses to Yahweh

מִשְׁפְּחֹת הַקְּהָתִי מִתּוֹךְ הַלְוִיִּם׃ וְזֹאת ׀ עֲשׂוּ לָהֶם

for-them do! and-this (19) the-Levites from-among the-Kohathite clans-of

וְחָיוּ וְלֹא יָמֻתוּ בְּגִשְׁתָּם אֶת־קֹדֶשׁ

most-holy-of *** when-to-come-near-them they-die and-not so-they-may-live

הַקֳּדָשִׁים אַהֲרֹן וּבָנָיו יָבֹאוּ וְשָׂמוּ אוֹתָם

them and-they-must-assign they-must-go and-sons-of-him Aaron the-holy-things

אִישׁ אִישׁ עַל־עֲבֹדָתוֹ וְאֶל־מַשָּׂאוֹ׃ וְלֹא־יָבֹאוּ

they-must-go-in but-not (20) burden-of-him and-to work-of-him to each man

hides of sea cows and put
them on a carrying frame.
13"They are to remove the
ashes from the bronze altar
and spread a purple cloth over
it. 14Then they are to place on
it all the utensils used for ministering at the altar, including
the firepans, meat forks, shovels and sprinkling bowls. Over
it they are to spread a covering
of hides of sea cows and put its
poles in place.
15"After Aaron and his sons
have finished covering the
holy furnishings and all the
holy articles, and when the
camp is ready to move, the
Kohathites are to come to do
the carrying. But they must
not touch the holy things or
they will die. The Kohathites
are to carry those things that
are in the Tent of Meeting.
16"Eleazar son of Aaron, the
priest, is to have charge of the
oil for the light, the fragrant
incense, the regular grain
offering and the anointing oil.
He is to be in charge of the
entire tabernacle and everything in it, including its holy
furnishings and articles."
17The LORD said to Moses
and Aaron, 18"See that the Kohathite tribal clans are not cut
off from the Levites. 19So that
they may live and not die
when they come near the most
holy things, do this for them:
Aaron and his sons are to go
into the sanctuary and assign
to each man his work and
what he is to carry. 20But the

לִרְאוֹת כְּבַלַּע אֶת־ הַקֹּדֶשׁ וָמֵתוּ׃
or-they-will-die the-holy-thing *** even-to-be-momentary to-look

(21) וַיְדַבֵּר יְהוָה אֶל־ מֹשֶׁה לֵּאמֹר׃ (22) נָשֹׂא אֶת־ רֹאשׁ בְּנֵי
sons-of census-of *** to-take (22) to-say Moses to Yahweh and-he-spoke (21)

גֵרְשׁוֹן גַּם־ הֵם לְבֵית אֲבֹתָם לְמִשְׁפְּחֹתָם׃ (23) מִבֶּן
from-son-of (23) by-clans-of-them fathers-of-them by-house-of them also Gershon

שְׁלֹשִׁים שָׁנָה וָמַעְלָה עַד בֶּן־ חֲמִשִּׁים שָׁנָה תִּפְקֹד אוֹתָם כָּל־
every-of them you-count year fifty son-of to or-more year thirty

הַבָּא לִצְבֹא צָבָא לַעֲבֹד עֲבֹדָה בְּאֹהֶל מוֹעֵד׃ (24) זֹאת
this (24) Meeting at-Tent-of work to-work service to-serve the-one-coming

עֲבֹדַת מִשְׁפְּחֹת הַגֵּרְשֻׁנִּי לַעֲבֹד וּלְמַשָּׂא׃ (25) וְנָשְׂאוּ
now-they-must-carry (25) and-as-burden to-work the-Gershonite clans-of service-of

אֶת־ יְרִיעֹת הַמִּשְׁכָּן וְאֶת־ אֹהֶל מוֹעֵד מִכְסֵּהוּ וּמִכְסֵה
and-cover-of cover-of-him Meeting Tent-of and the-tabernacle curtains-of ***

הַתַּחַשׁ אֲשֶׁר־ עָלָיו מִלְמָעְלָה וְאֶת־ מָסַךְ פֶּתַח אֹהֶל מוֹעֵד׃
Meeting Tent-of entrance-of curtain-of and outer over-him that the-sea-cow

(26) וְאֵת קַלְעֵי הֶחָצֵר וְאֶת־ מָסַךְ | פֶּתַח | שַׁעַר
gate-of entrance-of curtain-of and the-courtyard curtains-of and (26)

הֶחָצֵר אֲשֶׁר עַל־ הַמִּשְׁכָּן וְעַל־ הַמִּזְבֵּחַ סָבִיב
surrounding the-altar and-around the-tabernacle around that the-courtyard

וְאֵת מֵיתְרֵיהֶם וְאֶת־ כָּל־ כְּלֵי עֲבֹדָתָם וְאֵת כָּל־אֲשֶׁר
that all and service-of-them equipments-of all-of and ropes-of-them and

יֵעָשֶׂה לָהֶם וְעָבָדוּ׃ (27) עַל־ פִּי אַהֲרֹן
Aaron direction-of under (27) then-they-must-do with-them he-must-be-done

וּבָנָיו תִּהְיֶה כָּל־ עֲבֹדַת בְּנֵי הַגֵּרְשֻׁנִּי
the-Gershonite sons-of service-of all-of she-must-be-done and-sons-of-him

לְכָל־ מַשָּׂאָם וּלְכֹל עֲבֹדָתָם
work-of-them or-whether-all-of burden-of-them whether-all-of

וּפְקַדְתֶּם עֲלֵהֶם בְּמִשְׁמֶרֶת אֵת כָּל־ מַשָּׂאָם׃
burden-of-them all-of *** as-responsibility to-them and-you-shall-assign

(28) זֹאת עֲבֹדַת מִשְׁפְּחֹת בְּנֵי הַגֵּרְשֻׁנִּי בְּאֹהֶל מוֹעֵד
Meeting at-Tent-of the-Gershonite sons-of clans-of service-of this (28)

וּמִשְׁמַרְתָּם בְּיַד אִיתָמָר בֶּן־ אַהֲרֹן הַכֹּהֵן׃
the-priest Aaron son-of Ithamar under-direction-of and-duty-of-them

(29) בְּנֵי מְרָרִי לְמִשְׁפְּחֹתָם לְבֵית־ אֲבֹתָם תִּפְקֹד
you-count fathers-of-them by-house-of by-clans-of-them Merari sons-of (29)

אֹתָם׃ (30) מִבֶּן שְׁלֹשִׁים שָׁנָה וָמַעְלָה וְעַד בֶּן־ חֲמִשִּׁים שָׁנָה
year fifty son-of even-to or-more year thirty from-son-of (30) them

Kohathites must not go in to look at the holy things, even for a moment, or they will die."

*The Gershonites*

21The LORD said to Moses, 22"Take a census also of the Gershonites by their families and clans. 23Count all the men from thirty to fifty years of age who come to serve in the work at the Tent of Meeting.

24"This is the service of the Gershonite clans as they work and carry burdens: 25They are to carry the curtains of the tabernacle, the Tent of Meeting, its covering and the outer covering of hides of sea cows, the curtains for the entrance to the Tent of Meeting, 26the curtains of the courtyard surrounding the tabernacle and altar, the curtain for the entrance, the ropes and all the equipment used in its service. The Gershonites are to do all that needs to be done with these things. 27All their service, whether carrying or doing other work, is to be done under the direction of Aaron and his sons. You shall assign to them as their responsibility all they are to carry. 28This is the service of the Gershonite clans at the Tent of Meeting. Their duties are to be under the direction of Ithamar son of Aaron, the priest.

*The Merarites*

29"Count the Merarites by their clans and families. 30Count all the men from thirty to fifty years of age who

תִּפְקְדֻם כָּל־ הַבָּא לַצָּבָא לַעֲבֹד אֶת־ עֲבֹדַת
work-of *** to-work to-the-service the-one-coming all-of you-count-them

אֹהֶל מוֹעֵד׃ (31) וְזֹאת מִשְׁמֶרֶת מַשָּׂאָם לְכָל־ עֲבֹדָתָם
service-of-them in-all-of burden-of-them duty-of and-this (31) Meeting Tent-of

בְּאֹהֶל מוֹעֵד קַרְשֵׁי הַמִּשְׁכָּן וּבְרִיחָיו
and-crossbars-of-him the-tabernacle frames-of Meeting at-Tent-of

וְעַמּוּדָיו וַאֲדָנָיו׃ (32) וְעַמּוּדֵי הֶחָצֵר סָבִיב
around the-courtyard and-posts-of (32) and-bases-of-him and-posts-of-him

וְאַדְנֵיהֶם וִיתֵדֹתָם וּמֵיתְרֵיהֶם לְכָל־
for-all-of and-ropes-of-them and-tent-pegs-of-them and-bases-of-them

כְּלֵיהֶם וּלְכֹל עֲבֹדָתָם וּבְשֵׁמֹת תִּפְקְדוּ אֶת־
*** you-assign and-by-names use-of-them and-for-all-of equipments-of-them

כְּלֵי מִשְׁמֶרֶת מַשָּׂאָם׃ (33) זֹאת עֲבֹדַת מִשְׁפְּחֹת בְּנֵי
sons-of clans-of service-of this (33) burden-of-them duty-of things-of

מְרָרִי לְכָל־ עֲבֹדָתָם בְּאֹהֶל מוֹעֵד בְּיַד אִיתָמָר
Ithamar under-direction-of Meeting at-Tent-of work-of-them for-all-of Merari

בֶּן־ אַהֲרֹן הַכֹּהֵן׃ (34) וַיִּפְקֹד מֹשֶׁה וְאַהֲרֹן וּנְשִׂיאֵי
and-leaders-of and-Aaron Moses so-he-counted (34) the-priest Aaron son-of

הָעֵדָה אֶת־ בְּנֵי הַקְּהָתִי לְמִשְׁפְּחֹתָם וּלְבֵית
and-by-house-of by-clans-of-them the-Kohathite sons-of *** the-community

אֲבֹתָם׃ (35) מִבֶּן שְׁלֹשִׁים שָׁנָה וָמַעְלָה וְעַד בֶּן־חֲמִשִּׁים
fifty son-of even-to or-more year thirty from-son-of (35) fathers-of-them

שָׁנָה כָּל־ הַבָּא לַצָּבָא לַעֲבֹדָה בְּאֹהֶל מוֹעֵד׃
Meeting in-Tent-of in-work to-the-service the-one-coming every-of year

(36) וַיִּהְיוּ פְקֻדֵיהֶם לְמִשְׁפְּחֹתָם אַלְפַּיִם שְׁבַע
seven-of two-thousands by-clans-of-them countings-of-them and-they-were (36)

מֵאוֹת וַחֲמִשִּׁים׃ (37) אֵלֶּה פְקוּדֵי מִשְׁפְּחֹת הַקְּהָתִי
the-Kohathite clans-of ones-being-totaled-of these (37) and-fifty hundreds

כָּל־ הָעֹבֵד בְּאֹהֶל מוֹעֵד אֲשֶׁר פָּקַד מֹשֶׁה וְאַהֲרֹן
and-Aaron Moses he-counted whom Meeting in-Tent-of the-one-serving every-of

עַל־ פִּי יְהוָה בְּיַד־ מֹשֶׁה׃ (38) וּפְקוּדֵי בְּנֵי גֵּרְשׁוֹן
Gershon sons-of and-countings-of (38) Moses by-hand-of Yahweh command-of at

לְמִשְׁפְּחוֹתָם וּלְבֵית אֲבֹתָם׃ (39) מִבֶּן שְׁלֹשִׁים
thirty from-son-of (39) fathers-of-them and-by-house-of by-clans-of-them

שָׁנָה וָמַעְלָה וְעַד בֶּן־ חֲמִשִּׁים שָׁנָה כָּל־ הַבָּא לַצָּבָא
to-the-service the-one-coming every-of year fifty son-of even-to or-more year

לַעֲבֹדָה בְּאֹהֶל מוֹעֵד׃ (40) וַיִּהְיוּ פְּקֻדֵיהֶם
countings-of-them and-they-were (40) Meeting at-Tent-of in-work

come to serve in the work at the Tent of Meeting. [31]This is their duty as they perform service at the Tent of Meeting: to carry the frames of the tabernacle, its crossbars, posts and bases, [32]as well as the posts of the surrounding courtyard with their bases, tent pegs, ropes, all their equipment and everything related to their use. Assign to each man the specific things he is to carry. [33]This is the service of the Merarite clans as they work at the Tent of Meeting under the direction of Ithamar son of Aaron, the priest."

*The Numbering of the Levite Clans*

[34]Moses, Aaron and the leaders of the community counted the Kohathites by their clans and families. [35]All the men from thirty to fifty years of age who came to serve in the work in the Tent of Meeting, [36]counted by clans, were 2,750. [37]This was the total of all those in the Kohathite clans who served in the Tent of Meeting. Moses and Aaron counted them according to the LORD's command through Moses.

[38]The Gershonites were counted by their clans and families. [39]All the men from thirty to fifty years of age who came to serve in the work at the Tent of Meeting, [40]counted

לְמִשְׁפְּחֹתָם לְבֵית אֲבֹתָם אַלְפַּיִם וְשֵׁשׁ מֵאוֹת
hundreds and-six two-thousands fathers-of-them by-house-of by-clans-of-them

וּשְׁלֹשִׁים׃ אֵלֶּה פְקוּדֵי מִשְׁפְּחֹת בְּנֵי גֵרְשׁוֹן כָּל־
every-of Gershon sons-of clans-of ones-being-totaled-of these (41) and-thirty

הָעֹבֵד בְּאֹהֶל מוֹעֵד אֲשֶׁר פָּקַד מֹשֶׁה וְאַהֲרֹן עַל־
at and-Aaron Moses he-counted whom Meeting at-Tent-of the-one-serving

פִּי יְהוָה׃ וּפְקוּדֵי מִשְׁפְּחֹת בְּנֵי מְרָרִי
Merari sons-of clans-of and-countings-of (42) Yahweh command-of

לְמִשְׁפְּחֹתָם לְבֵית אֲבֹתָם׃ מִבֶּן שְׁלֹשִׁים שָׁנָה
year thirty from-son-of (43) fathers-of-them by-house-of by-clans-of-them

וָמַעְלָה וְעַד בֶּן־ חֲמִשִּׁים שָׁנָה כָּל־ הַבָּא לַצָּבָא
to-the-service the-one-coming every-of year fifty son-of even-to or-more

לַעֲבֹדָה בְּאֹהֶל מוֹעֵד׃ וַיִּהְיוּ פְקֻדֵיהֶם
countings-of-them and-they-were (44) Meeting at-Tent-of in-work

לְמִשְׁפְּחֹתָם שְׁלֹשֶׁת אֲלָפִים וּמָאתָיִם׃ אֵלֶּה פְקוּדֵי
totalings-of these (45) and-two-hundreds thousands three by-clans-of-them

מִשְׁפְּחֹת בְּנֵי מְרָרִי אֲשֶׁר פָּקַד מֹשֶׁה וְאַהֲרֹן עַל־ פִּי יְהוָה
Yahweh command-of at and-Aaron Moses he-counted whom Merari sons-of clans-of

בְּיַד־ מֹשֶׁה׃ כָּל־ הַפְּקֻדִים אֲשֶׁר פָּקַד מֹשֶׁה
Moses he-counted whom the-ones-being-counted all-of (46) Moses by-hand-of

וְאַהֲרֹן וּנְשִׂאֵי יִשְׂרָאֵל אֶת־ הַלְוִיִּם לְמִשְׁפְּחֹתָם
by-clans-of-them the-Levites *** Israel and-leaders-of and-Aaron

וּלְבֵית אֲבֹתָם׃ מִבֶּן שְׁלֹשִׁים שָׁנָה וָמַעְלָה וְעַד
even-to or-more year thirty from-son-of (47) fathers-of-them and-by-house-of

בֶּן־ חֲמִשִּׁים שָׁנָה כָּל־ הַבָּא לַעֲבֹד עֲבֹדַת עֲבֹדָה וַעֲבֹדַת
and-work-of service work-of to-do the-one-coming every-of year fifty son-of

מַשָּׂא בְּאֹהֶל מוֹעֵד׃ וַיִּהְיוּ פְּקֻדֵיהֶם שְׁמֹנַת
eight-of numberings-of-them and-they-were (48) Meeting at-Tent-of carrying

אֲלָפִים וַחֲמֵשׁ מֵאוֹת וּשְׁמֹנִים׃ עַל־ פִּי יְהוָה
Yahweh command-of at (49) and-eighty hundreds and-five-of thousands

פָּקַד אוֹתָם בְּיַד־ מֹשֶׁה אִישׁ אִישׁ עַל־ עֲבֹדָתוֹ וְעַל־ מַשָּׂאוֹ
burden-of-him and-to work-of-him to each man Moses by-hand-of them he-counted

וּפְקֻדָיו אֲשֶׁר־ צִוָּה יְהוָה אֶת־ מֹשֶׁה׃
Moses *** Yahweh he-commanded as so-ones-being-counted-of-him

וַיְדַבֵּר יְהוָה אֶל־ מֹשֶׁה לֵּאמֹר׃ צַו אֶת־ בְּנֵי יִשְׂרָאֵל
Israel sons-of *** command! (2) to-say Moses to Yahweh and-he-spoke (5:1)

וִישַׁלְּחוּ מִן־ הַמַּחֲנֶה כָּל־ צָרוּעַ וְכָל־ זָב
discharging or-any-of being-infected any-of the-camp from so-they-send

by their clans and families,
were 2,630. 41This was the total of those in the Gershonite
clans who served at the Tent
of Meeting. Moses and Aaron
counted them according to the
LORD's command.
42The Merarites were counted by their clans and families.
43All the men from thirty to
fifty years of age who came to
serve in the work at the Tent
of Meeting, 44counted by their
clans, were 3,200. 45This was
the total of those in the Merarite clans. Moses and Aaron
counted them according to the
LORD's command through
Moses.
46So Moses, Aaron and the
leaders of Israel counted all the
Levites by their clans and
families. 47All the men from
thirty to fifty years of age who
came to do the work of serving
and carrying the Tent of Meeting 48numbered 8,580. 49At the
LORD's command through
Moses, each was assigned his
work and told what to carry.
Thus they were counted, as
the LORD commanded Moses.

### *The Purity of the Camp*

5 The LORD said to Moses,
2"Command the Israelites
to send away from the camp
anyone who has an infectious
skin disease[f] or a discharge of

f2 Traditionally *leprosy;* the Hebrew word was used for various diseases affecting the skin—not necessarily leprosy.

וְכֹל טָמֵא לָנָֽפֶשׁ׃ מִזָּכָר עַד־נְקֵבָה תְּשַׁלֵּחוּ אֶל־

to you-send-away-him female to from-male (3) from-body unclean or-any-of

מִחוּץ לַֽמַּחֲנֶה תְּשַׁלְּחוּם וְלֹא יְטַמְּאוּ אֶת־ מַחֲנֵיהֶם

camps-of-them *** they-defile so-not you-send-away-them of-the-camp outside

אֲשֶׁר אֲנִי שֹׁכֵן בְּתוֹכָם׃ וַיַּעֲשׂוּ־ כֵן בְּנֵי יִשְׂרָאֵל

Israel sons-of this and-they-did (4) among-them dwelling I where

וַיְשַׁלְּחוּ אוֹתָם אֶל־ מִחוּץ לַֽמַּחֲנֶה כַּאֲשֶׁר דִּבֶּר יְהוָה אֶל־

to Yahweh he-commanded just-as of-the-camp outside to them and-they-sent

מֹשֶׁה כֵּן עָשׂוּ בְּנֵי יִשְׂרָאֵל׃ וַיְדַבֵּר יְהוָה אֶל־מֹשֶׁה לֵּאמֹר׃

to-say Moses to Yahweh and-he-spoke (5) Israel sons-of they-did so Moses

דַּבֵּר אֶל־ בְּנֵי יִשְׂרָאֵל אִישׁ אֽוֹ־ אִשָּׁה כִּי יַעֲשׂוּ מִכָּל־

from-any-of they-commit when woman or man Israel sons-of to say! (6)

חַטֹּאת הָֽאָדָם לִמְעֹל מַעַל בַּיהוָה

to-Yahweh he-is-unfaithful to-be-unfaithful the-mankind wrongs-of

וְאָשְׁמָה הַנֶּפֶשׁ הַהִוא׃ וְהִתְוַדּוּ אֶת־

*** and-they-must-confess (7) the-that the-person and-she-is-guity

חַטָּאתָם אֲשֶׁר עָשׂוּ וְהֵשִׁיב אֶת־ אֲשָׁמוֹ

wrong-of-him *** and-he-must-restitute they-committed that sin-of-them

בְּרֹאשׁוֹ וַחֲמִישִׁתוֹ יֹסֵף עָלָיו וְנָתַן לַאֲשֶׁר

to-whom and-he-must-give to-him he-must-add and-fifth-of-him on-head-of-him

אָשָׁם לוֹ׃ וְאִם־ אֵין לָאִישׁ גֹּאֵל

relative-being-close to-the-person he-is-not but-if (8) to-him he-wronged

לְהָשִׁיב הָאָשָׁם אֵלָיו הָאָשָׁם הַמּוּשָׁב לַיהוָה

to-Yahweh the-being-restored the-wrong to-him the-wrong to-restitute

לַכֹּהֵן מִלְּבַד אֵיל הַכִּפֻּרִים אֲשֶׁר יְכַפֶּר־ בּוֹ

with-him he-atones which the-atonements ram-of along-with to-the-priest

עָלָיו׃ וְכָל־ תְּרוּמָה לְכָל־ קָדְשֵׁי בְנֵי־

sons-of sacred-ones-of from-all-of contribution and-every-of (9) for-him

יִשְׂרָאֵל אֲשֶׁר־ יַקְרִיבוּ לַכֹּהֵן לוֹ יִהְיֶה׃ וְאִישׁ אֶת־

*** and-man (10) he-is for-him to-the-priest they-bring that Israel

קֳדָשָׁיו לוֹ יִהְיוּ אִישׁ אֲשֶׁר־ יִתֵּן לַכֹּהֵן לוֹ

for-him to-the-priest he-gives what man they-are to-him sacred-gifts-of-him

יִהְיֶה׃ וַיְדַבֵּר יְהוָה אֶל־ מֹשֶׁה לֵּאמֹר׃ דַּבֵּר אֶל־ בְּנֵי

sons-of to speak! (12) to-say Moses to Yahweh and-he-spoke (11) he-is

יִשְׂרָאֵל וְאָמַרְתָּ אֲלֵהֶם אִישׁ אִישׁ כִּי־ תִשְׂטֶה אִשְׁתּוֹ

wife-of-him she-goes-astray if any man to-them and-you-say Israel

וּמָעֲלָה בוֹ מָעַל׃ וְשָׁכַב אִישׁ אֹתָהּ

with-her man and-he-sleeps (13) unfaithfulness to-him and-she-is-unfaithful

any kind, or who is ceremonially unclean because of a dead body. 3Send away male and female alike; send them outside the camp so they will not defile their camp, where I dwell among them." 4The Israelites did this; they sent them outside the camp. They did just as the LORD had instructed Moses.

### *The Test for an Unfaithful Wife*

5The LORD said to Moses, 6"Say to the Israelites: 'When a man or woman wrongs another in any way[h] and so is unfaithful to the LORD, that person is guilty 7and must confess the sin he has committed. He must make full restitution for his wrong, add one fifth to it and give it all to the person he has wronged. 8But if that person has no close relative to whom restitution can be made for the wrong, the restitution belongs to the LORD and must be given to the priest, along with the ram with which atonement is made for him. 9All the sacred contributions the Israelites bring to a priest will belong to him. 10Each man's sacred gifts are his own, but what he gives to the priest will belong to the priest.' "

11Then the LORD said to Moses, 12"Speak to the Israelites and say to them: 'If a man's wife goes astray and is unfaithful to him 13by sleeping

[h]6 Or *woman commits any wrong common to mankind*

שִׁכְבַת־ זֶרַע וְנֶעְלַם מֵעֵינֵי אִישָׁהּ
husband-of-her from-eyes-of and-he-is-hidden semen emission-of

וְנִסְתְּרָה וְהִיא נִטְמָאָה וְעֵד אֵין בָּהּ
against-her he-is-not and-witness she-is-impure also-she and-she-is-undetected

וְהִוא לֹא נִתְפָּשָׂה׃ וְעָבַר עָלָיו רוּחַ־ קִנְאָה
jealousy feeling-of over-him and-he-comes (14) she-was-caught not and-she

וְקִנֵּא אֶת־ אִשְׁתּוֹ וְהִוא נִטְמָאָה אוֹ־ עָבַר עָלָיו
over-him he-comes or she-is-impure and-she wife-of-him *** and-he-suspects

רוּחַ־ קִנְאָה וְקִנֵּא אֶת־ אִשְׁתּוֹ וְהִיא לֹא נִטְמָאָה׃
she-is-impure not but-she wife-of-him *** and-he-suspects jealousy feeling-of

וְהֵבִיא הָאִישׁ אֶת־ אִשְׁתּוֹ אֶל־ הַכֹּהֵן וְהֵבִיא
and-he-must-take the-priest to wife-of-him *** the-man then-he-must-take (15)

אֶת־ קָרְבָּנָהּ עָלֶיהָ עֲשִׂירִת הָאֵיפָה קֶמַח שְׂעֹרִים לֹא־
not barleys flour-of the-ephah tenth-of for-her offering-of-her ***

יִצֹק עָלָיו שֶׁמֶן וְלֹא־ יִתֵּן עָלָיו לְבֹנָה כִּי־ מִנְחַת
offering-of for incense on-him he-must-put or-not oil on-him he-must-pour

קְנָאֹת הוּא מִנְחַת זִכָּרוֹן מַזְכֶּרֶת עָוֺן׃
guilt drawing-attention reminder offering-of he jealousies

וְהִקְרִיב אֹתָהּ הַכֹּהֵן וְהֶעֱמִדָהּ לִפְנֵי יְהוָה׃
Yahweh before and-he-shall-stand-her the-priest her and-he-shall-bring (16)

וְלָקַח הַכֹּהֵן מַיִם קְדֹשִׁים בִּכְלִי־ חָרֶשׂ וּמִן־
and-from clay in-jar-of holy-ones waters the-priest then-he-shall-take (17)

הֶעָפָר אֲשֶׁר יִהְיֶה בְּקַרְקַע הַמִּשְׁכָּן יִקַּח הַכֹּהֵן
the-priest he-shall-take the-tabernacle on-floor-of he-is that the-dust

וְנָתַן אֶל־ הַמָּיִם׃ וְהֶעֱמִיד הַכֹּהֵן אֶת־
*** the-priest and-he-shall-stand (18) the-waters into and-he-shall-put

הָאִשָּׁה לִפְנֵי יְהוָה וּפָרַע אֶת־ רֹאשׁ הָאִשָּׁה
the-woman hair-of *** and-he-shall-loosen Yahweh before the-woman

וְנָתַן עַל־ כַּפֶּיהָ אֵת מִנְחַת הַזִּכָּרוֹן מִנְחַת
offering-of the-reminder offering-of *** hands-of-her in and-he-shall-place

קְנָאֹת הִוא וּבְיַד הַכֹּהֵן יִהְיוּ מֵי הַמָּרִים
the-bitter-ones waters-of they-are the-priest and-in-hand-of she jealousies

הַמְאָרְרִים׃ וְהִשְׁבִּיעַ אֹתָהּ הַכֹּהֵן
the-priest her then-he-shall-put-under-oath (19) the-ones-bringing-curse

וְאָמַר אֶל־ הָאִשָּׁה אִם־ לֹא שָׁכַב אִישׁ אֹתָךְ וְאִם־ לֹא
not and-if with-you man he-slept not if the-woman to and-he-shall-say

שָׂטִית טֻמְאָה תַּחַת אִישֵׁךְ הִנָּקִי מִמֵּי
by-waters-of be-unharmed! husband-of-you under impure you-went-astray

with another man, and this is hidden from her husband and her impurity is undetected (since there is no witness against her and she has not been caught in the act), 14and if feelings of jealousy come over her husband and he suspects his wife and she is impure—or if he is jealous and suspects her even though she is not impure— 15then he is to take his wife to the priest. He must also take an offering of a tenth of an ephah[i] of barley flour on her behalf. He must not pour oil on it or put incense on it, because it is a grain offering for jealousy, a reminder offering to draw attention to guilt.

16" 'The priest shall bring her and have her stand before the LORD. 17Then he shall take some holy water in a clay jar and put some dust from the tabernacle floor into the water. 18After the priest has had the woman stand before the LORD, he shall loosen her hair and place in her hands the reminder offering, the grain offering for jealousy, while he himself holds the bitter water that brings a curse. 19Then the priest shall put the woman under oath and say to her, "If no other man has slept with you and you have not gone astray and become impure while married to your husband, may this bitter water that brings a

[i]15 That is, probably about 2 quarts (about 2 liters)

הַמָּרִים הַמְאָרְרִים הָאֵלֶּה׃ (20) וְאַתְּ כִּי
the-bitter-ones the-ones-bringing-curse the-these (20) but-you if

שָׂטִית תַּחַת אִישֵׁךְ וְכִי נִטְמֵאת וַיִּתֵּן
you-went-astray under husband-of-you and-if you-defiled-self and-he-gave

אִישׁ בָּךְ אֶת־ שְׁכָבְתּוֹ מִבַּלְעֲדֵי אִישֵׁךְ׃
man to-you *** emission-of-him other-than husband-of-you

(21) וְהִשְׁבִּיעַ הַכֹּהֵן אֶת־ הָאִשָּׁה בִּשְׁבֻעַת
(21) then-he-must-put-under-oath the-priest *** the-woman under-curse-of

הָאָלָה וְאָמַר הַכֹּהֵן לָאִשָּׁה יִתֵּן יְהוָה אוֹתָךְ
the-oath and-he-shall-say the-priest to-the-woman may-he-make Yahweh you

לְאָלָה וְלִשְׁבֻעָה בְּתוֹךְ עַמֵּךְ בְּתֵת יְהוָה אֶת־
as-curse and-as-denounced among people-of-you when-to-cause Yahweh ***

יְרֵכֵךְ נֹפֶלֶת וְאֶת־ בִּטְנֵךְ צָבָה׃ (22) וּבָאוּ
thigh-of-you wasting-away and abdomen-of-you swollen (22) and-may-they-enter

הַמַּיִם הַמְאָרְרִים הָאֵלֶּה בְּמֵעַיִךְ לַצְבּוֹת
the-waters the-ones-bringing-curse the-these into-body-of-you to-make-swell

בֶּטֶן וְלַנְפִּל יָרֵךְ וְאָמְרָה הָאִשָּׁה אָמֵן | אָמֵן׃
abdomen and-to-waste-away thigh then-she-must-say the-woman so-be-it so-be-it

(23) וְכָתַב אֶת־ הָאָלֹת הָאֵלֶּה הַכֹּהֵן בַּסֵּפֶר
(23) and-he-must-write *** the-curses the-these the-priest on-the-scroll

וּמָחָה אֶל־ מֵי הַמָּרִים׃ (24) וְהִשְׁקָה
then-he-must-wash into waters-of the-bitter-ones (24) then-he-shall-have-drink

אֶת־ הָאִשָּׁה אֶת־ מֵי הַמָּרִים הַמְאָרְרִים
*** the-woman *** waters-of the-bitter-ones the-ones-bringing-curse

וּבָאוּ בָהּ הַמַּיִם הַמְאָרְרִים לְמָרִים׃
and-they-will-enter into-her the-waters the-ones-bringing-curse as-bitter-ones

(25) וְלָקַח הַכֹּהֵן מִיַּד הָאִשָּׁה אֵת מִנְחַת
(25) then-he-must-take the-priest from-hand-of the-woman *** offering-of

הַקְּנָאֹת וְהֵנִיף אֶת־ הַמִּנְחָה לִפְנֵי יְהוָה וְהִקְרִיב
the-jealousies and-he-must-wave *** the-offering before Yahweh and-he-must-bring

אֹתָהּ אֶל־ הַמִּזְבֵּחַ׃ (26) וְקָמַץ הַכֹּהֵן מִן־ הַמִּנְחָה
her to the-altar (26) then-he-must-take-handful the-priest from the-offering

אֶת־ אַזְכָּרָתָהּ וְהִקְטִיר הַמִּזְבֵּחָה וְאַחַר
*** memorial-offering-of-her and-he-must-burn on-the-altar and-after

יַשְׁקֶה אֶת־ הָאִשָּׁה אֶת־ הַמָּיִם׃ (27) וְהִשְׁקָהּ
he-must-have-drink *** the-woman *** the-waters (27) when-he-makes-drink-her

אֶת־ הַמַּיִם וְהָיְתָה אִם־ נִטְמְאָה וַתִּמְעֹל
*** the-waters then-she-will-be if she-defiled-self and-she-was-unfaithful

curse not harm you. [20]But if you have gone astray while married to your husband and you have defiled yourself by sleeping with a man other than your husband"— [21]here the priest is to put the woman under this curse of the oath—"may the LORD cause your people to curse and denounce you when he causes your thigh to waste away and your abdomen to swell.[j] [22]May this water that brings a curse enter your body so that your abdomen swells and your thigh wastes away.[k]"

" 'Then the woman is to say, "So be it."

[23]" 'The priest is to write these curses on a scroll and then wash them off into the bitter water. [24]He shall have the woman drink the bitter water that brings a curse, and this water will enter her and cause bitter suffering. [25]The priest is to take from her hands the grain offering for jealousy, wave it before the LORD and bring it to the altar. [26]The priest is then to take a handful of the grain offering as a memorial offering and burn it on the altar; after that, he is to have the woman drink the water. [27]If she has defiled herself and been unfaithful to her husband, then when she is made to drink the water that

j21 *Or causes you to have a miscarrying womb and barrenness*

k22 *Or body and cause you to be barren and have a miscarrying womb*

מַעַל בְּאִישָׁהּ וּבָאוּ בָהּ הַמַּיִם
the-waters into-her then-they-will-enter to-husband-of-her unfaithfulness

הַמְאָרְרִים לְמָרִים וְצָבְתָה בִטְנָהּ
abdomen-of-her and-she-will-swell as-bitter-ones the-ones-bringing-curse

וְנָפְלָה יְרֵכָהּ וְהָיְתָה הָאִשָּׁה לְאָלָה
as-curse the-woman and-she-will-become thigh-of-her and-she-will-waste-away

בְּקֶרֶב עַמָּהּ׃ וְאִם־ לֹא נִטְמְאָה הָאִשָּׁה
the-woman she-defiled-self not but-if (28) people-of-her in-midst-of

וּטְהֹרָה הִוא וְנִקְּתָה וְנִזְרְעָה זָרַע׃ זֹאת
this (29) child and-she-will-bear then-she-will-be-guiltless she and-clean

תּוֹרַת הַקְּנָאֹת אֲשֶׁר תִּשְׂטֶה אִשָּׁה תַּחַת אִישָׁהּ
husband-of-her under woman she-goes-astray when the-jealousies law-of

וְנִטְמָאָה׃ אוֹ אִישׁ אֲשֶׁר תַּעֲבֹר עָלָיו רוּחַ קִנְאָה
jealousy feeling-of over-him she-comes when man or (30) and-she-defiles-self

וְקִנֵּא אֶת־ אִשְׁתּוֹ וְהֶעֱמִיד אֶת־ הָאִשָּׁה לִפְנֵי
before the-woman *** and-he-must-stand wife-of-him *** and-he-suspects

יְהוָה וְעָשָׂה לָהּ הַכֹּהֵן אֵת כָּל־ הַתּוֹרָה הַזֹּאת׃
the-this the-law entire-of *** the-priest to-her and-he-must-apply Yahweh

וְנִקָּה הָאִישׁ מֵעָוֹן וְהָאִשָּׁה הַהִוא
the-that but-the-woman of-wrong the-husband then-he-will-be-innocent (31)

תִּשָּׂא אֶת־ עֲוֹנָהּ׃ וַיְדַבֵּר יְהוָה אֶל־ מֹשֶׁה לֵּאמֹר׃
to-say Moses to Yahweh and-he-spoke (6:1) sin-of-her *** she-will-bear

דַּבֵּר אֶל־ בְּנֵי יִשְׂרָאֵל וְאָמַרְתָּ אֲלֵהֶם אִישׁ אוֹ־ אִשָּׁה כִּי יַפְלִא
he-desires if woman or man to-them and-you-say Israel sons-of to speak! (2)

לִנְדֹּר נֶדֶר נָזִיר לְהַזִּיר לַיהוָה׃ מִיַּיִן
from-wine (3) to-Yahweh to-be-separate Nazirite vow-of to-vow

וְשֵׁכָר יַזִּיר חֹמֶץ יַיִן וְחֹמֶץ
or-vinegar-of wine vinegar-of he-must-abstain or-fermented-drink

שֵׁכָר לֹא יִשְׁתֶּה וְכָל־ מִשְׁרַת עֲנָבִים לֹא
not grapes juice-of and-any-of he-must-drink not fermented-drink

יִשְׁתֶּה וַעֲנָבִים לַחִים וִיבֵשִׁים לֹא יֹאכֵל׃ כֹּל
all-of (4) he-must-eat not or-dry-ones moist-ones and-grapes he-must-drink

יְמֵי נִזְרוֹ מִכֹּל אֲשֶׁר יֵעָשֶׂה מִגֶּפֶן
from-vine-of he-is-made that from-anything Nazirite-vow-of-him days-of

הַיַּיִן מֵחַרְצַנִּים וְעַד־ זָג לֹא יֹאכֵל׃ כָּל־ יְמֵי נֶדֶר
vow-of days-of all-of (5) he-must-eat not skin or-even from-seeds the-wine

נִזְרוֹ תַּעַר לֹא־ יַעֲבֹר עַל־ רֹאשׁוֹ עַד־ מְלֹאת
to-be-over until head-of-him on he-may-come not razor Nazirite-of-him

brings a curse, it will go into her and cause bitter suffering; her abdomen will swell and her thigh waste away,[l] and she will become accursed among her people. [28]If, however, the woman has not defiled herself and is free from impurity, she will be cleared of guilt and will be able to have children.

[29]" 'This, then, is the law of jealousy when a woman goes astray and defiles herself while married to her husband, [30]or when feelings of jealousy come over a man because he suspects his wife. The priest is to have her stand before the LORD and is to apply this entire law to her. [31]The husband will be innocent of any wrongdoing, but the woman will bear the consequences of her sin.' "

*The Nazirite*

6 The LORD said to Moses, [2]"Speak to the Israelites and say to them: 'If a man or woman wants to make a special vow, a vow of separation to the LORD as a Nazirite, [3]he must abstain from wine and other fermented drink and must not drink vinegar made from wine or from other fermented drink. He must not drink grape juice or eat grapes or raisins. [4]As long as he is a Nazirite, he must not eat anything that comes from the grapevine, not even the seeds or skins.

[5]" 'During the entire period of his vow of separation no razor may be used on his head.

[l]27 Or *suffering; she will have barrenness and a miscarrying womb*

הַיָּמִם אֲשֶׁר־ יַזִּיר לַיהוָה קָדֹשׁ יִהְיֶה גַּדֵּל פֶּרַע
lock-of to-be-long he-must-be holy to-Yahweh he-is-separate that the-days

שְׂעַר רֹאשׁוֹ׃ כָּל־ יְמֵי הַזִּרוֹ לַיהוָה עַל־
near to-Yahweh to-be-separate-him days-of all-of (6) head-of-him hair-of

נֶפֶשׁ מֵת לֹא יָבֹא׃ לְאָבִיו וּלְאִמּוֹ
or-for-mother-of-him for-father-of-him (7) he-must-go not dead body

לְאָחִיו וּלְאַחֹתוֹ לֹא־ יִטַּמָּא לָהֶם
for-them he-must-become-unclean not or-for-sister-of-him for-brother-of-him

בְּמֹתָם כִּי נֵזֶר אֱלֹהָיו עַל־ רֹאשׁוֹ׃ כֹּל יְמֵי
days-of all-of (8) head-of-him on God-of-him separation-of for if-to-die-them

נִזְרוֹ קָדֹשׁ הוּא לַיהוָה׃ וְכִי־ יָמוּת מֵת
one-dying he-dies and-if (9) to-Yahweh he consecrated separation-of-him

עָלָיו בְּפֶתַע פִּתְאֹם וְטִמֵּא רֹאשׁ נִזְרוֹ
dedication-of-him hair-of and-he-defiles suddenly with-suddenness by-him

וְגִלַּח רֹאשׁוֹ בְּיוֹם טָהֳרָתוֹ בַּיּוֹם
on-the-day cleansing-of-him on-day-of head-of-him then-he-must-shave

הַשְּׁבִיעִי יְגַלְּחֶנּוּ׃ וּבַיּוֹם הַשְּׁמִינִי יָבֹא
he-must-bring the-eighth and-on-the-day (10) he-must-shave-him the-seventh

שְׁתֵּי תֹרִים אוֹ שְׁנֵי בְּנֵי יוֹנָה אֶל־ הַכֹּהֵן אֶל־ פֶּתַח
entrance-of at the-priest to pigeon young-ones-of two-of or doves two-of

אֹהֶל מוֹעֵד׃ וְעָשָׂה הַכֹּהֵן אֶחָד לְחַטָּאת
as-sin-offering one the-priest and-he-must-offer (11) Meeting Tent-of

וְאֶחָד לְעֹלָה וְכִפֶּר עָלָיו מֵאֲשֶׁר חָטָא עַל־
by he-sinned because for-him and-he-will-atone as-burnt-offering and-other

הַנָּפֶשׁ וְקִדַּשׁ אֶת־ רֹאשׁוֹ בַּיּוֹם הַהוּא׃
the-same on-the-day head-of-him *** and-he-must-consecrate the-body

וְהִזִּיר לַיהוָה אֶת־ יְמֵי נִזְרוֹ
separation-of-him days-of *** to-Yahweh and-he-must-be-dedicated (12)

וְהֵבִיא כֶּבֶשׂ בֶּן־ שְׁנָתוֹ לְאָשָׁם וְהַיָּמִים
and-the-days as-guilt-offering year-of-him son-of lamb and-he-must-bring

הָרִאשֹׁנִים יִפְּלוּ כִּי טָמֵא נִזְרוֹ׃
separation-of-him defiled for they-do-not-count the-previous-ones

וְזֹאת תּוֹרַת הַנָּזִיר בְּיוֹם מְלֹאת יְמֵי
days-of to-be-over in-day-of the-Nazirite law-of now-this (13)

נִזְרוֹ יָבִיא אֹתוֹ אֶל־ פֶּתַח אֹהֶל מוֹעֵד׃
Meeting Tent-of entrance-of to him he-must-bring separation-of-him

וְהִקְרִיב אֶת־ קָרְבָּנוֹ לַיהוָה כֶּבֶשׂ[9] בֶּן־
son-of lamb to-Yahweh offering-of-him *** and-he-must-present (14)

He must be holy until the period of his separation to the LORD is over; he must let the hair of his head grow long. [6]Throughout the period of his separation to the LORD he must not go near a dead body. [7]Even if his own father or mother or brother or sister dies, he must not make himself ceremonially unclean on account of them, because the symbol of his separation to God is on his head. [8]Throughout the period of his separation he is consecrated to the LORD.

[9]" 'If someone dies suddenly in his presence, thus defiling the hair he has dedicated, he must shave his head on the day of his cleansing—the seventh day. [10]Then on the eighth day he must bring two doves or two young pigeons to the priest at the entrance to the Tent of Meeting. [11]The priest is to offer one as a sin offering and the other as a burnt offering to make atonement for him because he sinned by being in the presence of the dead body. That same day he is to consecrate his head. [12]He must dedicate himself to the LORD for the period of his separation and must bring a year-old male lamb as a guilt offering. The previous days do not count, because he became defiled during his separation.

[13]" 'Now this is the law for the Nazirite when the period of his separation is over. He is to be brought to the entrance to the Tent of Meeting. [14]There he is to present his offerings to the LORD: a year-old male lamb

שְׁנָתוֹ תָּמִים אֶחָד לְעֹלָה וְכַבְשָׂה אַחַת
year-of-him without-defect one for-burnt-offering and-ewe-lamb one

בַּת־ שְׁנָתָהּ תְּמִימָה לְחַטָּאת וְאַיִל־ אֶחָד
daughter-of year-of-her without-defect for-sin-offering and-ram one

תָּמִים לִשְׁלָמִים׃ וְסַל מַצּוֹת
without-defect for-fellowship-offerings (15) and-basket-of unleavened-breads

סֹלֶת חַלֹּת בְּלוּלֹת בַּשֶּׁמֶן וּרְקִיקֵי
fine-flour cakes-of ones-being-mixed with-the-oil and-wafers-of

מַצּוֹת מְשֻׁחִים בַּשָּׁמֶן וּמִנְחָתָם
unleavened-breads ones-being-spread with-the-oil and-grain-offering-of-them

וְנִסְכֵּיהֶם׃ וְהִקְרִיב הַכֹּהֵן לִפְנֵי
and-drink-offerings-of-them (16) and-he-must-present the-priest before

יְהוָה וְעָשָׂה אֶת־ חַטָּאתוֹ וְאֶת־ עֹלָתוֹ׃
Yahweh and-he-must-make *** sin-offering-of-him and burnt-offering-of-him

וְאֶת־ הָאַיִל יַעֲשֶׂה זֶבַח שְׁלָמִים לַיהוָה עַל
(17) and the-ram he-must-sacrifice offering-of fellowships to-Yahweh with

סַל הַמַּצּוֹת וְעָשָׂה הַכֹּהֵן אֶת־
basket-of the-unleavened-breads and-he-must-present the-priest ***

מִנְחָתוֹ וְאֶת־ נִסְכּוֹ׃ וְגִלַּח
grain-offering-of-him and drink-offering-of-him (18) then-he-must-shave

הַנָּזִיר פֶּתַח אֹהֶל מוֹעֵד אֶת־ רֹאשׁ נִזְרוֹ
the-Nazirite entrance-of Tent-of Meeting *** hair-of dedication-of-him

וְלָקַח אֶת־ שְׂעַר רֹאשׁ נִזְרוֹ וְנָתַן עַל־
and-he-must-take *** hair-of head-of dedication-of-him and-he-must-put in

הָאֵשׁ אֲשֶׁר־ תַּחַת זֶבַח הַשְּׁלָמִים׃
the-fire that under sacrifice-of the-fellowship-offerings

וְלָקַח הַכֹּהֵן אֶת־ הַזְּרֹעַ בְּשֵׁלָה מִן־ הָאַיִל
(19) then-he-must-take the-priest *** the-shoulder boiled from the-ram

וְחַלַּת מַצָּה אַחַת מִן־ הַסַּל וּרְקִיק מַצָּה אֶחָד
and-cake-of without-yeast one from the-basket and-wafer-of without-yeast one

וְנָתַן עַל־ כַּפֵּי הַנָּזִיר אַחַר הִתְגַּלְּחוֹ אֶת־
and-he-must-place in hands-of the-Nazirite after to-shave-him ***

נִזְרוֹ׃ וְהֵנִיף אוֹתָם הַכֹּהֵן ׀ תְּנוּפָה
dedicated-hair-of-him (20) and-he-must-wave them the-priest wave-offering

לִפְנֵי יְהוָה קֹדֶשׁ הוּא לַכֹּהֵן עַל חֲזֵה הַתְּנוּפָה
before Yahweh holy he for-the-priest with breast-of the-wave-offering

וְעַל שׁוֹק הַתְּרוּמָה וְאַחַר יִשְׁתֶּה הַנָּזִיר יָיִן׃
and-with thigh-of the-presentation and-after he-may-drink the-Nazirite wine

without defect for a burnt offering, a year-old ewe lamb without defect for a sin offering, a ram without defect for a fellowship offering,[m] 15together with their grain offerings and drink offerings, and a basket of bread made without yeast—cakes made of fine flour mixed with oil, and wafers spread with oil.

16" 'The priest is to present them before the LORD and make the sin offering and the burnt offering. 17He is to present the basket of unleavened bread and is to sacrifice the ram as a fellowship offering to the LORD, together with its grain offering and drink offering.

18" 'Then at the entrance to the Tent of Meeting, the Nazirite must shave off the hair that he dedicated. He is to take the hair and put it in the fire that is under the sacrifice of the fellowship offering.

19" 'After the Nazirite has shaved off the hair of his dedication, the priest is to place in his hands a boiled shoulder of the ram, and a cake and a wafer from the basket, both made without yeast. 20The priest shall then wave them before the LORD as a wave offering; they are holy and belong to the priest, together with the breast that was waved and the thigh that was presented. After that, the Nazirite may drink wine.

m14 Traditionally *peace offering;* also in verses 17 and 18

זֹאת תּוֹרַת הַנָּזִיר אֲשֶׁר יִדֹּר קָרְבָּנוֹ לַיהוָה עַל־
with to-Yahweh offering-of-him he-vows who the-Nazirite law-of this (21)

נִזְרוֹ מִלְּבַד אֲשֶׁר־תַּשִּׂיג יָדוֹ כְּפִי
in-accord-of hand-of-him she-can-afford what apart-from separation-of-him

נִדְרוֹ אֲשֶׁר יִדֹּר כֵּן יַעֲשֶׂה עַל תּוֹרַת נִזְרוֹ׃
Nazirite-vow-of-him law-of as he-must-fulfill so he-vowed that vow-of-him

וַיְדַבֵּר יְהוָה אֶל־מֹשֶׁה לֵּאמֹר׃ דַּבֵּר אֶל־אַהֲרֹן וְאֶל־
and-to Aaron to tell! (23) to-say Moses to Yahweh and-he-spoke (22)

בָּנָיו לֵאמֹר כֹּה תְבָרְכוּ אֶת־בְּנֵי יִשְׂרָאֵל אָמוֹר לָהֶם׃
to-them to-say Israel sons-of *** you-shall-bless thus to-say sons-of-him

יְבָרֶכְךָ יְהוָה וְיִשְׁמְרֶךָ׃ יָאֵר
may-he-make-shine (26) and-may-he-keep-you Yahweh may-he-bless-you (24)

יְהוָה׀ פָּנָיו אֵלֶיךָ וִיחֻנֶּךָּ׃ יִשָּׂא
may-he-turn (26) and-may-he-be-gracious-to-you on-you faces-of-him Yahweh

יְהוָה׀ פָּנָיו אֵלֶיךָ וְיָשֵׂם לְךָ שָׁלוֹם׃
peace to-you may-he-give toward-you faces-of-him Yahweh

וְשָׂמוּ אֶת־שְׁמִי עַל־בְּנֵי יִשְׂרָאֵל וַאֲנִי אֲבָרְכֵם׃
I-will-bless-them and-I Israel sons-of on name-of-me *** so-they-will-put (27)

וַיְהִי בְּיוֹם כַּלּוֹת מֹשֶׁה לְהָקִים אֶת־הַמִּשְׁכָּן
the-tabernacle *** to-set-up Moses to-finish on-day and-he-was (7:1)

וַיִּמְשַׁח אֹתוֹ וַיְקַדֵּשׁ אֹתוֹ וְאֶת־כָּל־כֵּלָיו וְאֶת־
and furnishings-of-him all-of and him and-he-consecrated him and-he-anointed

הַמִּזְבֵּחַ וְאֶת־כָּל־כֵּלָיו וַיִּמְשָׁחֵם וַיְקַדֵּשׁ
and-he-consecrated and-he-anointed-them utensils-of-him all-of and the-altar

אֹתָם׃ וַיַּקְרִיבוּ נְשִׂיאֵי יִשְׂרָאֵל רָאשֵׁי בֵּית
house-of heads-of Israel leaders-of then-they-made-offering (2) them

אֲבֹתָם הֵם נְשִׂיאֵי הַמַּטֹּת הֵם הָעֹמְדִים עַל־
over the-ones-being-in-charge they the-tribes leaders-of they fathers-of-them

הַפְּקֻדִים׃ וַיָּבִיאוּ אֶת־קָרְבָּנָם לִפְנֵי יְהוָה שֵׁשׁ־
six-of Yahweh before gift-of-them *** and-they-brought (3) the-ones-counted

עֶגְלֹת צָב וּשְׁנֵי עָשָׂר בָּקָר עֲגָלָה עַל־שְׁנֵי הַנְּשִׂאִים וְשׁוֹר
and-ox the-leaders two-of from cart ox ten and-two-of covered carts-of

לְאֶחָד וַיַּקְרִיבוּ אוֹתָם לִפְנֵי הַמִּשְׁכָּן׃ וַיֹּאמֶר
and-he-spoke (4) the-tabernacle before them and-they-presented from-each

יְהוָה אֶל־מֹשֶׁה לֵּאמֹר׃ קַח מֵאִתָּם וְהָיוּ לַעֲבֹד אֶת־עֲבֹדַת
work-of *** to-do so-they-may-be from-them accept! (5) to-say Moses to Yahweh

אֹהֶל מוֹעֵד וְנָתַתָּה אוֹתָם אֶל־הַלְוִיִּם אִישׁ כְּפִי
as-requirement-of each the-Levites to them and-you-give Meeting Tent-of

21" 'This is the law of the
Nazirite who vows his
offering to the LORD in accordance with his separation, in
addition to whatever else he
can afford. He must fulfill the
vow he has made, according to
the law of the Nazirite.' "

*The Priestly Blessing*

22The LORD said to Moses,
23"Tell Aaron and his sons,
'This is how you are to bless
the Israelites. Say to them:

24" ' "The LORD bless you
and keep you;
25the LORD make his face
shine upon you
and be gracious to you;
26the LORD turn his face
toward you
and give you peace." '

27"So they will put my name
on the Israelites, and I will
bless them."

*Offerings at the Dedication of the Tabernacle*

7 When Moses finished setting up the tabernacle, he
anointed it and consecrated it
and all its furnishings. He also
anointed and consecrated the
altar and all its utensils. 2Then
the leaders of Israel, the heads
of families who were the tribal
leaders in charge of those who
were counted, made offerings.
3They brought as their gifts
before the LORD six covered
carts and twelve oxen—an ox
from each leader and a cart
from every two. These they
presented before the tabernacle.
4The LORD said to Moses,
5"Accept these from them, that
they may be used in the work
at the Tent of Meeting. Give
them to the Levites as each

עֲבֹדָתוֹ׃ וַיִּקַּח מֹשֶׁה אֶת־הָעֲגָלֹת וְאֶת־הַבָּקָר וַיִּתֵּן אוֹתָם

them and-he-gave the-ox and the-carts *** Moses so-he-took (6) work-of-him

אֶל־הַלְוִיִּם׃ אֵת ׀ שְׁתֵּי הָעֲגָלוֹת וְאֵת אַרְבַּעַת הַבָּקָר נָתַן

he-gave the-ox four-of and the-carts two-of *** (7) the-Levites to

לִבְנֵי גֵרְשׁוֹן כְּפִי עֲבֹדָתָם׃ וְאֵת ׀ אַרְבַּע הָעֲגָלֹת

the-carts four-of and (8) work-of-them as-requirement-of Gershon to-sons-of

וְאֵת שְׁמֹנַת הַבָּקָר נָתַן לִבְנֵי מְרָרִי כְּפִי עֲבֹדָתָם

work-of-them as-requirement-of Merari to-sons-of he-gave the-ox eight-of and

בְּיַד אִיתָמָר בֶּן־אַהֲרֹן הַכֹּהֵן׃ וְלִבְנֵי קְהָת

Kohath but-to-sons-of (9) the-priest Aaron son-of Ithamar under-direction-of

לֹא נָתָן כִּי־עֲבֹדַת הַקֹּדֶשׁ עֲלֵהֶם בַּכָּתֵף

on-the-shoulder on-them the-holy-thing responsibility-of for he-gave not

יִשָּׂאוּ׃ וַיַּקְרִיבוּ הַנְּשִׂאִים אֵת חֲנֻכַּת הַמִּזְבֵּחַ

the-altar dedication-of *** the-leaders and-they-brought (10) they-carry

בְּיוֹם הִמָּשַׁח אֹתוֹ וַיַּקְרִיבוּ הַנְּשִׂיאִם אֶת־קָרְבָּנָם

offering-of-them *** the-leaders and-they-presented him to-be-anointed on-day

לִפְנֵי הַמִּזְבֵּחַ׃ וַיֹּאמֶר יְהוָה אֶל־מֹשֶׁה נָשִׂיא אֶחָד לַיּוֹם

each-the-day one leader Moses to Yahweh for-he-said (11) the-altar before

נָשִׂיא אֶחָד לַיּוֹם יַקְרִיבוּ אֶת־קָרְבָּנָם

offering-of-them *** they-must-bring each-the-day one leader

לַחֲנֻכַּת הַמִּזְבֵּחַ׃ וַיְהִי הַמַּקְרִיב בַּיּוֹם

on-the-day the-one-bringing and-he-was (12) the-altar for-dedication-of

הָרִאשׁוֹן אֶת־קָרְבָּנוֹ נַחְשׁוֹן בֶּן־עַמִּינָדָב לְמַטֵּה יְהוּדָה׃

Judah from-tribe-of Amminadab son-of Nahshon offering-of-him *** the-first

וְקָרְבָּנוֹ קַעֲרַת־כֶּסֶף אַחַת שְׁלֹשִׁים וּמֵאָה מִשְׁקָלָהּ

weight-of-her and-hundred thirty one silver plate-of and-offering-of-him (13)

מִזְרָק אֶחָד כֶּסֶף שִׁבְעִים שֶׁקֶל בְּשֶׁקֶל הַקֹּדֶשׁ

the-sanctuary by-shekel-of shekel seventy silver one sprinkling-bowl

שְׁנֵיהֶם ׀ מְלֵאִים סֹלֶת בְּלוּלָה בַשֶּׁמֶן לְמִנְחָה׃

as-grain-offering with-the-oil being-mixed fine-flour ones-filled both-of-them

כַּף אַחַת עֲשָׂרָה זָהָב מְלֵאָה קְטֹרֶת׃ פַּר אֶחָד בֶּן־בָּקָר אַיִל

ram herd young-of one bull (15) incense filled gold ten one ladle (14)

אֶחָד כֶּבֶשׂ־אֶחָד בֶּן־שְׁנָתוֹ לְעֹלָה׃ שְׂעִיר־עִזִּים

goats male-goat-of (16) for-burnt-offering year-of-him son-of one lamb one

אֶחָד לְחַטָּאת׃ וּלְזֶבַח הַשְּׁלָמִים בָּקָר

ox the-fellowship-offerings and-as-sacrifice-of (17) for-sin-offering one

שְׁנַיִם אֵילִם חֲמִשָּׁה עַתֻּדִים חֲמִשָּׁה כְּבָשִׂים בְּנֵי־שָׁנָה חֲמִשָּׁה זֶה קָרְבַּן

offering-of this five year sons-of lambs five male-goats five rams two

man's work requires."
6So Moses took the carts and
oxen and gave them to the Levites. 7He gave two carts and
four oxen to the Gershonites,
as their work required, 8and
he gave four carts and eight
oxen to the Merarites, as their
work required. They were all
under the direction of Ithamar
son of Aaron, the priest. 9But
Moses did not give any to the
Kohathites, because they were
to carry on their shoulders the
holy things, for which they
were responsible.
10When the altar was anointed, the leaders brought their
offerings for its dedication
and presented them before the
altar. 11For the LORD had said
to Moses, "Each day one leader is to bring his offering for
the dedication of the altar."

12The one who brought his
offering on the first day was
Nahshon son of Amminadab
of the tribe of Judah.
13His offering was one silver plate weighing a hun-
dred and thirty shekels,[n]
and one silver sprinkling
bowl weighing seventy
shekels,[o] both according to
the sanctuary shekel, each
filled with fine flour mixed
with oil as a grain offering;
14one gold ladle weighing
ten shekels,[p] filled with incense; 15one young bull,
one ram and one male lamb
a year old, for a burnt
offering; 16one male goat for
a sin offering; 17and two
oxen, five rams, five male
goats and five male lambs a
year old, to be sacrificed as
a fellowship offering.[q] This

[n]13 That is, about 3 1/4 pounds (about 1.5 kilograms); also elsewhere in this chapter
[o]13 That is, about 1 3/4 pounds (about 0.8 kilogram); also elsewhere in this chapter
[p]14 That is, about 4 ounces (about 110 grams); also elsewhere in this chapter
[q]17 Traditionally *peace offering*; also elsewhere in this chapter

נַחְשׁוֹן בֶּן־עַמִּינָדָב׃ בַּיּוֹם הַשֵּׁנִי הִקְרִיב נְתַנְאֵל
Nethanel he-brought the-second on-the-day (18) Amminadab son-of Nahshon

בֶּן־צוּעָר נְשִׂיא יִשָּׂשכָר׃ הִקְרִב אֶת־קָרְבָּנוֹ קַעֲרַת־
plate-of offering-of-him *** he-brought (19) Issachar leader-of Zuar son-of

כֶּסֶף אַחַת שְׁלֹשִׁים וּמֵאָה מִשְׁקָלָהּ מִזְרָק אֶחָד כֶּסֶף
silver one sprinkling-bowl weight-of-her and-hundred thirty one silver

שִׁבְעִים שֶׁקֶל בְּשֶׁקֶל הַקֹּדֶשׁ שְׁנֵיהֶם ׀ מְלֵאִים סֹלֶת
fine-flour ones-filled both-of-them the-sanctuary by-shekel-of shekel seventy

בְּלוּלָה בַשֶּׁמֶן לְמִנְחָה׃ כַּף אַחַת עֲשָׂרָה זָהָב מְלֵאָה
filled gold ten one ladle (20) as-grain-offering with-the-oil being-mixed

קְטֹרֶת׃ פַּר אֶחָד בֶּן־בָּקָר אַיִל אֶחָד כֶּבֶשׂ־אֶחָד בֶּן־שְׁנָתוֹ
year-of-him son-of one lamb one ram herd son-of one bull (21) incense

לְעֹלָה׃ שְׂעִיר־עִזִּים אֶחָד לְחַטָּאת׃
for-sin-offering one goats male-goat-of (22) for-burnt-offering

וּלְזֶבַח הַשְּׁלָמִים בָּקָר שְׁנַיִם אֵילִם חֲמִשָּׁה
five rams two ox the-fellowship-offerings and-for-sacrifice-of (23)

עַתּוּדִים חֲמִשָּׁה כְּבָשִׂים בְּנֵי־שָׁנָה חֲמִשָּׁה זֶה קָרְבַּן נְתַנְאֵל בֶּן־
son-of Nethanel offering-of this five year sons-of lambs five male-goats

צוּעָר׃ בַּיּוֹם הַשְּׁלִישִׁי נָשִׂיא לִבְנֵי זְבוּלֻן אֱלִיאָב בֶּן־חֵלֹן׃
Helon son-of Eliab Zebulun of-sons-of leader the-third on-the-day (24) Zuar

קָרְבָּנוֹ קַעֲרַת־כֶּסֶף אַחַת שְׁלֹשִׁים וּמֵאָה מִשְׁקָלָהּ
weight-of-her and-hundred thirty one silver plate-of offering-of-him (25)

מִזְרָק אֶחָד כֶּסֶף שִׁבְעִים שֶׁקֶל בְּשֶׁקֶל הַקֹּדֶשׁ
the-sanctuary by-shekel-of shekel seventy silver one sprinkling-bowl

שְׁנֵיהֶם ׀ מְלֵאִים סֹלֶת בְּלוּלָה בַשֶּׁמֶן לְמִנְחָה׃
as-grain-offering with-the-oil being-mixed fine-flour ones-filled both-of-them

כַּף אַחַת עֲשָׂרָה זָהָב מְלֵאָה קְטֹרֶת׃ פַּר אֶחָד בֶּן־בָּקָר אַיִל
ram herd young-of one bull (27) incense filled gold ten one ladle (26)

אֶחָד כֶּבֶשׂ־אֶחָד בֶּן־שְׁנָתוֹ לְעֹלָה׃ שְׂעִיר־עִזִּים
goats male-goat-of (28) for-burnt-offering year-of-him son-of one lamb one

אֶחָד לְחַטָּאת׃ וּלְזֶבַח הַשְּׁלָמִים בָּקָר
ox the-fellowship-offerings and-for-sacrifice-of (29) for-sin-offering one

שְׁנַיִם אֵילִם חֲמִשָּׁה עַתֻּדִים חֲמִשָּׁה כְּבָשִׂים בְּנֵי־שָׁנָה חֲמִשָּׁה זֶה קָרְבַּן
offering-of this five year sons-of lambs five male-goats five rams two

אֱלִיאָב בֶּן־חֵלֹן׃ בַּיּוֹם הָרְבִיעִי נָשִׂיא לִבְנֵי רְאוּבֵן
Reuben of-sons-of leader the-fourth on-the-day (30) Helon son-of Eliab

אֱלִיצוּר בֶּן־שְׁדֵיאוּר׃ קָרְבָּנוֹ קַעֲרַת־כֶּסֶף אַחַת שְׁלֹשִׁים
thirty one silver plate-of offering-of-him (31) Shedeur son-of Elizur

was the offering of Nah-
shon son of Amminadab.

[18]On the second day Nethanel
son of Zuar, the leader of Issachar, brought his offering.
[19]The offering he brought
was one silver plate weighing a hundred and thirty
shekels, and one silver
sprinkling bowl weighing
seventy shekels, both ac-
cording to the sanctuary
shekel, each filled with fine
flour mixed with oil as a
grain offering; [20]one gold
ladle weighing ten shekels,
filled with incense; [21]one
young bull, one ram and
one male lamb a year old,
for a burnt offering; [22]one
male goat for a sin offering;
[23]and two oxen, five rams,
five male goats and five
male lambs a year old, to be
sacrificed as a fellowship
offering. This was the
offering of Nethanel son of
Zuar.

[24]On the third day, Eliab son
of Helon, the leader of the
people of Zebulun, brought
his offering.
[25]His offering was one silver plate weighing a hun-
dred and thirty shekels,
and one silver sprinkling
bowl weighing seventy
shekels, both according to
the sanctuary shekel, each
filled with fine flour mixed
with oil as a grain offering;
[26]one gold ladle weighing
ten shekels, filled with incense; [27]one young bull,
one ram and one male lamb
a year old, for a burnt
offering; [28]one male goat for
a sin offering; [29]and two
oxen, five rams, five male
goats and five male lambs a
year old, to be sacrificed as
a fellowship offering. This
was the offering of Eliab
son of Helon.

[30]On the fourth day Elizur son
of Shedeur, the leader of the
people of Reuben, brought his
offering.
[31]His offering was one silver plate weighing a hun-
dred and thirty shekels,

וּמֵאָה֙ מִשְׁקָלָהּ֙ מִזְרָק אֶחָד֙ כֶּסֶף שִׁבְעִים שֶׁקֶל

shekel seventy silver one sprinkling-bowl weight-of-her and-hundred

בְּשֶׁקֶל הַקֹּדֶשׁ שְׁנֵיהֶם ׀ מְלֵאִים סֹלֶת בְּלוּלָה

being-mixed fine-flour ones-filled both-of-them the-sanctuary by-shekel-of

בַשֶּׁמֶן לְמִנְחָה׃ כַּף אַחַת עֲשָׂרָה זָהָב מְלֵאָה קְטֹרֶת

incense filled gold ten one ladle (32) as-grain-offering with-the-oil

(33) פַּר אֶחָד בֶּן־ בָּקָר אַיִל אֶחָד כֶּבֶשׂ־אֶחָד בֶּן־ שְׁנָתוֹ

year-of-him son-of one lamb one ram herd young-of one bull (33)

לְעֹלָה׃ שְׂעִיר־ עִזִּים אֶחָד לְחַטָּאת׃

for-sin-offering one goats male-goat-of (34) for-burnt-offering

וּלְזֶבַח הַשְּׁלָמִים֙ בָּקָר שְׁנַיִם֙ אֵילִם חֲמִשָּׁה֙

five rams two ox the-fellowship-offerings and-for-sacrifice-of (35)

עַתֻּדִים חֲמִשָּׁה כְּבָשִׂים בְּנֵי־ שָׁנָה חֲמִשָּׁה זֶה קָרְבַּן אֱלִיצוּר בֶּן־

son-of Elizur offering-of this five year sons-of lambs five male-goats

שְׁדֵיאוּר׃ בַּיּוֹם֙ הַחֲמִישִׁי נָשִׂיא לִבְנֵי שִׁמְעוֹן שְׁלֻמִיאֵל בֶּן־

son-of Shelumiel Simeon of-sons-of leader the-fifth on-the-day (36) Shedeur

צוּרִישַׁדָּי׃ קָרְבָּנוֹ קַעֲרַת־ כֶּסֶף אַחַת שְׁלֹשִׁים וּמֵאָה֙

and-hundred thirty one silver plate-of offering-of-him (37) Zurishaddai

מִשְׁקָלָהּ֙ מִזְרָק אֶחָד֙ כֶּסֶף שִׁבְעִים שֶׁקֶל בְּשֶׁקֶל

by-shekel-of shekel seventy silver one sprinkling-bowl weight-of-her

הַקֹּדֶשׁ שְׁנֵיהֶם ׀ מְלֵאִים סֹלֶת בְּלוּלָה בַשֶּׁמֶן

with-the-oil being-mixed fine-flour ones-filled both-of-them the-sanctuary

לְמִנְחָה׃ כַּף אַחַת עֲשָׂרָה זָהָב מְלֵאָה קְטֹרֶת׃ פַּר אֶחָד

one bull (39) incense filled gold ten one ladle (38) as-grain-offering

בֶּן־ בָּקָר אַיִל אֶחָד כֶּבֶשׂ־אֶחָד בֶּן־ שְׁנָתוֹ לְעֹלָה׃

for-burnt-offering year-of-him son-of one lamb one ram herd young-of

שְׂעִיר־ עִזִּים אֶחָד לְחַטָּאת וּלְזֶבַח

and-for-sacrifice-of (41) for-sin-offering one goats male-goat-of (40)

הַשְּׁלָמִים֙ בָּקָר שְׁנַיִם֙ אֵילִם חֲמִשָּׁה֙ עַתֻּדִים חֲמִשָּׁה כְּבָשִׂים בְּנֵי־

sons-of lambs five male-goats five rams two ox the-fellowship-offerings

שָׁנָה חֲמִשָּׁה זֶה קָרְבַּן שְׁלֻמִיאֵל בֶּן־ צוּרִישַׁדָּי׃ בַּיּוֹם֙

on-the-day (42) Zurishaddai son-of Shelumiel offering-of this five year

הַשִּׁשִּׁי נָשִׂיא לִבְנֵי גָד אֶלְיָסָף בֶּן־ דְּעוּאֵל׃ קָרְבָּנוֹ

offering-of-him (43) Deuel son-of Eliasaph Gad of-sons-of leader the-sixth

קַעֲרַת־ כֶּסֶף אַחַת שְׁלֹשִׁים וּמֵאָה֙ מִשְׁקָלָהּ֙ מִזְרָק אֶחָד֙

one sprinkling-bowl weight-of-her and-hundred thirty one silver plate-of

כֶּסֶף שִׁבְעִים שֶׁקֶל בְּשֶׁקֶל הַקֹּדֶשׁ שְׁנֵיהֶם ׀ מְלֵאִים

ones-filled both-of-them the-sanctuary by-shekel-of shekel seventy silver

and one silver sprinkling bowl weighing seventy shekels, both according to the sanctuary shekel, each filled with fine flour mixed with oil as a grain offering; 32one gold ladle weighing ten shekels, filled with incense; 33one young bull, one ram and one male lamb a year old, for a burnt offering; 34one male goat for a sin offering; 35and two oxen, five rams, five male goats and five male lambs a year old, to be sacrificed as a fellowship offering. This was the offering of Elizur son of Shedeur.

36On the fifth day Shelumiel son of Zurishaddai, the leader of the people of Simeon, brought his offering.

37His offering was one silver plate weighing a hundred and thirty shekels, and one silver sprinkling bowl weighing seventy shekels, both according to the sanctuary shekel, each filled with fine flour mixed with oil as a grain offering; 38one gold ladle weighing ten shekels, filled with incense; 39one young bull, one ram and one male lamb a year old, for a burnt offering; 40one male goat for a sin offering; 41and two oxen, five rams, five male goats and five male lambs a year old, to be sacrificed as a fellowship offering. This was the offering of Shelumiel son of Zurishaddai.

42On the sixth day Eliasaph son of Deuel, the leader of the people of Gad, brought his offering.

43His offering was one silver plate weighing a hundred and thirty shekels, and one silver sprinkling bowl weighing seventy shekels, both according to the sanctuary shekel, each

סֹלֶת בְּלוּלָה בַשֶּׁמֶן לְמִנְחָה׃ כַּף אַחַת עֲשָׂרָה
ten one ladle (44) as-grain-offering with-the-oil being-mixed fine-flour

זָהָב מְלֵאָה קְטֹרֶת׃ פַּר אֶחָד בֶּן־בָּקָר אַיִל אֶחָד כֶּבֶשׂ־אֶחָד בֶּן־
son-of one lamb one ram herd young-of one bull (45) incense filled gold

שְׁנָתוֹ לְעֹלָה׃ שְׂעִיר־עִזִּים אֶחָד לְחַטָּאת׃
for-sin-offering one goats male-goat-of (46) for-burnt-offering year-of-him

וּלְזֶבַח הַשְּׁלָמִים בָּקָר שְׁנַיִם אֵילִם חֲמִשָּׁה
five rams two ox the-fellowship-offerings and-for-sacrifice-of (47)

עַתֻּדִים חֲמִשָּׁה כְּבָשִׂים בְּנֵי־שָׁנָה חֲמִשָּׁה זֶה קָרְבַּן אֶלְיָסָף בֶּן־
son-of Eliasaph offering-of this five year sons-of lambs five male-goats

דְּעוּאֵל׃ בַּיּוֹם הַשְּׁבִיעִי נָשִׂיא לִבְנֵי אֶפְרָיִם אֱלִישָׁמָע בֶּן־
son-of Elishama Ephraim of-sons-of leader the-seventh on-the-day (48) Deuel

עַמִּיהוּד׃ קָרְבָּנוֹ קַעֲרַת־כֶּסֶף אַחַת שְׁלֹשִׁים וּמֵאָה
and-hundred thirty one silver plate-of offering-of-him (49) Ammihud

מִשְׁקָלָהּ מִזְרָק אֶחָד כֶּסֶף שִׁבְעִים שֶׁקֶל בְּשֶׁקֶל
by-shekel-of shekel seventy silver one sprinkling-bowl weight-of-her

הַקֹּדֶשׁ שְׁנֵיהֶם ׀ מְלֵאִים סֹלֶת בְּלוּלָה בַשֶּׁמֶן
with-the-oil being-mixed fine-flour ones-filled both-of-them the-sanctuary

לְמִנְחָה׃ כַּף אַחַת עֲשָׂרָה זָהָב מְלֵאָה קְטֹרֶת׃ פַּר אֶחָד
one bull (51) incense filled gold ten one ladle (50) as-grain-offering

בֶּן־בָּקָר אַיִל אֶחָד כֶּבֶשׂ־אֶחָד בֶּן־שְׁנָתוֹ לְעֹלָה׃
for-burnt-offering year-of-him son-of one lamb one ram herd young-of

שְׂעִיר־עִזִּים אֶחָד לְחַטָּאת׃ וּלְזֶבַח
and-for-sacrifice-of (53) for-sin-offering one goats male-goat-of (52)

הַשְּׁלָמִים בָּקָר שְׁנַיִם אֵילִם חֲמִשָּׁה עַתֻּדִים חֲמִשָּׁה כְּבָשִׂים בְּנֵי־
sons-of lambs five male-goats five rams two ox the-fellowship-offerings

שָׁנָה חֲמִשָּׁה זֶה קָרְבַּן אֱלִישָׁמָע בֶּן־עַמִּיהוּד׃ בַּיּוֹם
on-the-day (54) Ammihud son-of Elishama offering-of this five year

הַשְּׁמִינִי נָשִׂיא לִבְנֵי מְנַשֶּׁה גַּמְלִיאֵל בֶּן־פְּדָה־צוּר׃
Zur Pedah son-of Gamaliel Manasseh of-sons-of leader the-eighth

קָרְבָּנוֹ קַעֲרַת־כֶּסֶף אַחַת שְׁלֹשִׁים וּמֵאָה מִשְׁקָלָהּ
weight-of-her and-hundred thirty one silver plate-of offering-of-him (55)

מִזְרָק אֶחָד כֶּסֶף שִׁבְעִים שֶׁקֶל בְּשֶׁקֶל הַקֹּדֶשׁ
the-sanctuary by-shekel-of shekel seventy silver one sprinkling-bowl

שְׁנֵיהֶם ׀ מְלֵאִים סֹלֶת בְּלוּלָה בַשֶּׁמֶן לְמִנְחָה *
as-grain-offering with-the-oil being-mixed fine-flour ones-filled both-of-them

כַּף אַחַת עֲשָׂרָה זָהָב מְלֵאָה קְטֹרֶת׃ פַּר אֶחָד בֶּן־בָּקָר אַיִל
ram herd young-of one bull (57) incense filled gold ten one ladle (56)

filled with fine flour mixed with oil as a grain offering; [44]one gold ladle weighing ten shekels, filled with incense; [45]one young bull, one ram and one male lamb a year old, for a burnt offering; [46]one male goat for a sin offering; [47]and two oxen, five rams, five male goats and five male lambs a year old, to be sacrificed as a fellowship offering. This was the offering of Eliasaph son of Deuel.

[48]On the seventh day Elishama son of Ammihud, the leader of the people of Ephraim, brought his offering.

[49]His offering was one silver plate weighing a hundred and thirty shekels, and one silver sprinkling bowl weighing seventy shekels, both according to the sanctuary shekel, each filled with fine flour mixed with oil as a grain offering; [50]one gold ladle weighing ten shekels, filled with incense; [51]one young bull, one ram and one male lamb a year old, for a burnt offering; [52]one male goat for a sin offering; [53]and two oxen, five rams, five male goats and five male lambs a year old, to be sacrificed as a fellowship offering. This was the offering of Elishama son of Ammihud.

[54]On the eighth day Gamaliel son of Pedahzur, the leader of the people of Manasseh, brought his offering.

[55]His offering was one silver plate weighing a hundred and thirty shekels, and one silver sprinkling bowl weighing seventy shekels, both according to the sanctuary shekel, each filled with fine flour mixed with oil as a grain offering; [56]one gold ladle weighing ten shekels, filled with incense; [57]one young bull,

*55 Most mss end verse 55 with *soph pasuq* ( ׃ ).

אֶחָד כֶּבֶשׂ־אֶחָד בֶּן־ שְׁנָתוֹ לְעֹלָה׃ שְׂעִיר עִזִּים
goats male-goat-of (58) for-burnt-offering year-of-him son-of one lamb one

אֶחָד לְחַטָּאת׃ וּלְזֶבַח הַשְּׁלָמִים בָּקָר
ox the-fellowship-offerings and-for-sacrifice-of (59) for-sin-offering one

שְׁנַיִם אֵילִם חֲמִשָּׁה עַתֻּדִים חֲמִשָּׁה כְּבָשִׂים בְּנֵי־ שָׁנָה חֲמִשָּׁה זֶה קָרְבַּן
offering-of this five year sons-of lambs five male-goats five rams two

גַּמְלִיאֵל בֶּן־ פְּדָה־ צוּר׃ בַּיּוֹם הַתְּשִׁיעִי נָשִׂיא לִבְנֵי
of-sons-of leader the-ninth on-the-day (60) Zur Pedah son-of Gamaliel

בִנְיָמִן אֲבִידָן בֶּן־ גִּדְעֹנִי׃ קָרְבָּנוֹ קַעֲרַת־ כֶּסֶף אַחַת
one silver plate-of offering-of-him (61) Gideoni son-of Abidan Benjamin

שְׁלֹשִׁים וּמֵאָה מִשְׁקָלָהּ מִזְרָק אֶחָד כֶּסֶף שִׁבְעִים שֶׁקֶל
shekel seventy silver one sprinkling-bowl weight-of-her and-hundred thirty

בְּשֶׁקֶל הַקֹּדֶשׁ שְׁנֵיהֶם ׀ מְלֵאִים סֹלֶת בְּלוּלָה
being-mixed fine-flour ones-filled both-of-them the-sanctuary by-shekel-of

בַשֶּׁמֶן לְמִנְחָה׃ כַּף אַחַת עֲשָׂרָה זָהָב מְלֵאָה קְטֹרֶת׃
incense filled gold ten one ladle (62) as-grain-offering with-the-oil

פַּר אֶחָד בֶּן־ בָּקָר אַיִל אֶחָד כֶּבֶשׂ־ אֶחָד בֶּן־ שְׁנָתוֹ
year-of-him son-of one lamb one ram herd young-of one bull (63)

לְעֹלָה׃ שְׂעִיר־ עִזִּים אֶחָד לְחַטָּאת׃
for-sin-offering one goats male-goat-of (64) for-burnt-offering

וּלְזֶבַח הַשְּׁלָמִים בָּקָר שְׁנַיִם אֵילִם חֲמִשָּׁה
five rams two ox the-fellowship-offerings and-for-sacrifice-of (65)

עַתֻּדִים חֲמִשָּׁה כְּבָשִׂים בְּנֵי־ שָׁנָה חֲמִשָּׁה זֶה קָרְבַּן אֲבִידָן בֶּן־
son-of Abidan offering-of this five year sons-of lambs five male-goats

גִּדְעֹנִי׃ בַּיּוֹם הָעֲשִׂירִי נָשִׂיא לִבְנֵי דָן אֲחִיעֶזֶר בֶּן־
son-of Ahiezer Dan of-sons-of leader the-tenth on-the-day (66) Gideoni

עַמִּישַׁדָּי׃ קָרְבָּנוֹ קַעֲרַת־ כֶּסֶף אַחַת שְׁלֹשִׁים וּמֵאָה
and-hundred thirty one silver plate-of offering-of-him (67) Ammishaddai

מִשְׁקָלָהּ מִזְרָק אֶחָד כֶּסֶף שִׁבְעִים שֶׁקֶל בְּשֶׁקֶל
by-shekel-of shekel seventy silver one sprinkling-bowl weight-of-her

הַקֹּדֶשׁ שְׁנֵיהֶם ׀ מְלֵאִים סֹלֶת בְּלוּלָה בַשֶּׁמֶן
with-the-oil being-mixed fine-flour ones-filled both-of-them the-sanctuary

לְמִנְחָה׃ כַּף אַחַת עֲשָׂרָה זָהָב מְלֵאָה קְטֹרֶת * פַּר אֶחָד
one bull (69) incense filled gold ten one ladle (68) as-grain-offering

בֶּן־ בָּקָר אַיִל אֶחָד כֶּבֶשׂ־ אֶחָד בֶּן־ שְׁנָתוֹ לְעֹלָה׃
for-burnt-offering year-of-him son-of one lamb one ram herd young-of

שְׂעִיר־ עִזִּים אֶחָד לְחַטָּאת׃ וּלְזֶבַח
and-for-sacrifice-of (71) for-sin-offering one goats male-goat-of (70)

one ram and one male lamb
a year old, for a burnt
offering; [58]one male goat for
a sin offering; [59]and two
oxen, five rams, five male
goats and five male lambs a
year old, to be sacrificed as
a fellowship offering. This
was the offering of Gamaliel son of Pedahzur.

[60]On the ninth day Abidan
son of Gideoni, the leader of
the people of Benjamin,
brought his offering.
[61]His offering was one silver plate weighing a hun-
dred and thirty shekels,
and one silver sprinkling
bowl weighing seventy
shekels, both according to
the sanctuary shekel, each
filled with fine flour mixed
with oil as a grain offering;
[62]one gold ladle weighing
ten shekels, filled with incense; [63]one young bull,
one ram and one male lamb
a year old, for a burnt
offering; [64]one male goat for
a sin offering; [65]and two
oxen, five rams, five male
goats and five male lambs a
year old, to be sacrificed as
a fellowship offering. This
was the offering of Abidan
son of Gideoni.

[66]On the tenth day Ahiezer
son of Ammishaddai, the
leader of the people of Dan,
brought his offering.
[67]His offering was one silver plate weighing a hun-
dred and thirty shekels,
and one silver sprinkling
bowl weighing seventy
shekels, both according to
the sanctuary shekel, each
filled with fine flour mixed
with oil as a grain offering;
[68]one gold ladle weighing
ten shekels, filled with incense; [69]one young bull,
one ram and one male lamb
a year old, for a burnt
offering; [70]one male goat for
a sin offering; [71]and two

*68 Most mss end verse 68 with *soph pasuq* ( : ).

הַשְּׁלָמִים בָּקָר שְׁנַיִם אֵילִם חֲמִשָּׁה עַתֻּדִים חֲמִשָּׁה כְּבָשִׂים בְּנֵי־
sons-of lambs five male-goats five rams two ox the-fellowship-offerings

שָׁנָה חֲמִשָּׁה זֶה קָרְבַּן אֲחִיעֶזֶר בֶּן־ עַמִּישַׁדָּי׃ בְּיוֹם עַשְׁתֵּי עָשָׂר
ten one on-day (72) Ammishaddai son-of Ahiezer offering-of this five year

יוֹם נָשִׂיא לִבְנֵי אָשֵׁר פַּגְעִיאֵל בֶּן־ עָכְרָן׃ קָרְבָּנוֹ
offering-of-him (73) Ocran son-of Pagiel Asher of-sons-of leader day

קַעֲרַת־ כֶּסֶף אַחַת שְׁלֹשִׁים וּמֵאָה מִשְׁקָלָהּ מִזְרָק אֶחָד
one sprinkling-bowl weight-of-her and-hundred thirty one silver plate-of

כֶּסֶף שִׁבְעִים שֶׁקֶל בְּשֶׁקֶל הַקֹּדֶשׁ שְׁנֵיהֶם ׀ מְלֵאִים
ones-filled both-of-them the-sanctuary by-shekel-of shekel seventy silver

סֹלֶת בְּלוּלָה בַשֶּׁמֶן לְמִנְחָה׃ כַּף אַחַת עֲשָׂרָה
ten one ladle (74) as-grain-offering with-the-oil being-mixed fine-flour

זָהָב מְלֵאָה קְטֹרֶת׃ פַּר אֶחָד בֶּן־ בָּקָר אַיִל אֶחָד כֶּבֶשׂ־אֶחָד בֶּן־
son-of one lamb one ram herd young-of one bull (75) incense filled gold

שְׁנָתוֹ לְעֹלָה׃ שְׂעִיר־ עִזִּים אֶחָד לְחַטָּאת׃
for-sin-offering one goats male-goat-of (76) for-burnt-offeirng year-of-him

וּלְזֶבַח הַשְּׁלָמִים בָּקָר שְׁנַיִם אֵילִם חֲמִשָּׁה
five rams two ox the-fellowship-offerings and-for-sacrifice-of (77)

עַתֻּדִים חֲמִשָּׁה כְּבָשִׂים בְּנֵי־ שָׁנָה חֲמִשָּׁה זֶה קָרְבַּן פַּגְעִיאֵל בֶּן־
son-of Pagiel offering-of this five year sons-of lambs five male-goats

עָכְרָן׃ בְּיוֹם שְׁנֵים עָשָׂר יוֹם נָשִׂיא לִבְנֵי נַפְתָּלִי אֲחִירַע בֶּן־ עֵינָן׃
Enan son-of Ahira Naphtali of-sons-of leader day ten two on-day (78) Ocran

קָרְבָּנוֹ קַעֲרַת־ כֶּסֶף אַחַת שְׁלֹשִׁים וּמֵאָה מִשְׁקָלָהּ
weight-of-her and-hundred thirty one silver plate-of offering-of-him (79)

מִזְרָק אֶחָד כֶּסֶף שִׁבְעִים שֶׁקֶל בְּשֶׁקֶל הַקֹּדֶשׁ
the-sanctuary by-shekel-of shekel seventy silver one sprinkling-bowl

שְׁנֵיהֶם ׀ מְלֵאִים סֹלֶת בְּלוּלָה בַשֶּׁמֶן לְמִנְחָה׃
as-grain-offering with-the-oil being-mixed fine-flour ones-filled both-of-them

כַּף אַחַת עֲשָׂרָה זָהָב מְלֵאָה קְטֹרֶת׃ פַּר אֶחָד בֶּן־ בָּקָר אַיִל
ram herd young-of one bull (81) incense filled gold ten one ladle (80)

אֶחָד כֶּבֶשׂ־אֶחָד בֶּן־ שְׁנָתוֹ לְעֹלָה׃ שְׂעִיר־ עִזִּים
goats male-goat-of (82) for-burnt-offering year-of-him son-of one lamb one

אֶחָד לְחַטָּאת׃ וּלְזֶבַח הַשְּׁלָמִים בָּקָר
ox the-fellowship-offerings and-for-sacrifice-of (83) for-sin-offering one

שְׁנַיִם אֵילִם חֲמִשָּׁה עַתֻּדִים חֲמִשָּׁה כְּבָשִׂים בְּנֵי־ שָׁנָה חֲמִשָּׁה זֶה קָרְבַּן
offering-of this five year sons-of lambs five male-goats five rams two

אֲחִירַע בֶּן־ עֵינָן׃ זֹאת ׀ חֲנֻכַּת הַמִּזְבֵּחַ בְּיוֹם
on-day the-altar dedication-offering-of this (84) Enan son-of Ahira

oxen, five rams, five male goats and five male lambs a year old, to be sacrificed as a fellowship offering. This was the offering of Ahiezer son of Ammishaddai.

72On the eleventh day Pagiel son of Ocran, the leader of the people of Asher, brought his offering.

73His offering was one silver plate weighing a hundred and thirty shekels, and one silver sprinkling bowl weighing seventy shekels, both according to the sanctuary shekel, each filled with fine flour mixed with oil as a grain offering; 74one gold ladle weighing ten shekels, filled with incense; 75one young bull, one ram and one male lamb a year old, for a burnt offering; 76one male goat for a sin offering; 77and two oxen, five rams, five male goats and five male lambs a year old, to be sacrificed as a fellowship offering. This was the offering of Pagiel son of Ocran.

78On the twelfth day Ahira son of Enan, the leader of the people of Naphtali, brought his offering.

79His offering was one silver plate weighing a hundred and thirty shekels, and one silver sprinkling bowl weighing seventy shekels, both according to the sanctuary shekel, each filled with fine flour mixed with oil as a grain offering; 80one gold ladle weighing ten shekels, filled with incense; 81one young bull, one ram and one male lamb a year old, for a burnt offering; 82one male goat for a sin offering; 83and two oxen, five rams, five male goats and five male lambs a year old, to be sacrificed as a fellowship offering. This was the offering of Ahira son of Enan.

84These were the offerings of the Israelite leaders for the dedication of the altar when it

המשח אתו מאת נשיאי ישראל קערת כסף שתים עשרה
ten two silver plates-of Israel leaders-of from him to-be-anointed

מזרקי־ כסף שנים עשר כפות זהב שתים עשרה: שלשים
thirty (85) ten two gold ladles-of ten two silver sprinkling-bowls-of

ומאה הקערה האחת כסף ושבעים המזרק
the-sprinkling-bowl and-seventy silver the-each the-plate and-hundred

האחד כל כסף הכלים אלפים וארבע־ מאות
hundreds and-four two-thousands the-dishes silver-of all-of the-each

בשקל הקדש: כפות זהב שתים־עשרה מלאת קטרת
incense ones-filled ten two gold ladles-of (86) the-sanctuary by-shekel-of

עשרה עשרה הכף בשקל הקדש כל־ זהב הכפות
the-ladles gold-of all-of the-sanctuary by-shekel-of the-ladle ten ten

עשרים ומאה: כל־ הבקר לעלה שנים עשר
ten two for-burnt-offering the-animal total-of (87) and-hundred twenty

פרים אילם שנים־עשר כבשים בני־ שנה שנים עשר ומנחתם
and-grain-offering-of-them ten two year sons-of lambs ten two rams bulls

ושעירי עזים שנים עשר לחטאת: וכל בקר |
animal-of and-total-of (88) for-sin-offering ten two goats and-male-goats-of

זבח השלמים עשרים וארבעה פרים אילם ששים
sixty rams bulls and-four twenty the-fellowship-offerings sacrifice-of

עתדים ששים כבשים בני־ שנה ששים זאת חנכת
dedication-offering-of this sixty year sons-of lambs sixty male-goats

המזבח אחרי המשח אתו: ובבא משה אל־ אהל
Tent-of into Moses and-when-to-enter (89) him to-be-anointed after the-altar

מועד לדבר אתו וישמע את־ הקול מדבר אליו
to-him speaking the-voice *** then-he-heard with-him to-speak Meeting

מעל הכפרת אשר על־ ארן העדת מבין
from-between the-Testimony ark-of on that the-atonement-cover from-above

שני הכרבים וידבר אליו: וידבר יהוה אל־
to Yahweh and-he-spoke (8:1) with-him and-he-spoke the-cherubim two-of

משה לאמר: דבר אל־אהרן ואמרת אליו בהעלתך את־
*** when-to-set-up-you to-him and-you-say Aaron to speak! (2) to-say Moses

הנרת אל־ מול פני המנורה יאירו שבעת הנרות:
the-lamps seven-of they-must-light the-lampstand front-of area on the-lamps

ויעש כן אהרן אל־מול פני המנורה העלה נרתיה
lamps-of-her he-set-up the-lampstand front-of area on Aaron so and-he-did (3)

כאשר צוה יהוה את־ משה: וזה מעשה המנרה
the-lampstand make-up-of and-this (4) Moses *** Yahweh he-commanded just-as

was anointed: twelve silver plates, twelve silver sprinkling bowls and twelve gold ladles. 85Each silver plate weighed a hundred and thirty shekels, and each sprinkling bowl seventy shekels. Altogether, the silver dishes weighed two thousand four hundred shekels,[r] according to the sanctuary shekel. 86The twelve gold ladles filled with incense weighed ten shekels each, according to the sanctuary shekel. Altogether, the gold ladles weighed a hundred and twenty shekels.[s] 87The total number of animals for the burnt offering came to twelve young bulls, twelve rams and twelve male lambs a year old, together with their grain offering. Twelve male goats were used for the sin offering. 88The total number of animals for the sacrifice of the fellowship offering came to twenty-four oxen, sixty rams, sixty male goats and sixty male lambs a year old. These were the offerings for the dedication of the altar after it was anointed.

89When Moses entered the Tent of Meeting to speak with the LORD, he heard the voice speaking to him from between the two cherubim above the atonement cover on the ark of the Testimony. And he spoke with him.

*Setting Up the Lamps*

8 The LORD said to Moses, 2"Speak to Aaron and say to him, 'When you set up the seven lamps, they are to light the area in front of the lampstand.' "

3Aaron did so; he set up the lamps so that they faced forward on the lampstand, just as the LORD commanded Moses. 4This is how the lampstand was made: It was made of

r85 That is, about 60 pounds (about 28 kilograms)
s86 That is, about 3 pounds (about 1.4 kilograms)

מִקְשָׁה זָהָב עַד־ יְרֵכָהּ עַד־ פִּרְחָהּ מִקְשָׁה הִוא
she hammered blossom-of-her to base-of-her from gold hammered

כַּמַּרְאֶה אֲשֶׁר הֶרְאָה יְהוָה אֶת־ מֹשֶׁה כֵּן עָשָׂה אֶת־ הַמְּנֹרָה׃
the-lampstand *** he-made so Moses *** Yahweh he-showed that like-the-pattern

(5) וַיְדַבֵּר יְהוָה אֶל־ מֹשֶׁה לֵּאמֹר׃ (6) קַח אֶת־ הַלְוִיִּם מִתּוֹךְ
from-among the-Levites *** take! (6) to-say Moses to Yahweh and-he-spoke (5)

בְּנֵי יִשְׂרָאֵל וְטִהַרְתָּ אֹתָם׃ (7) וְכֹה־ תַעֲשֶׂה לָהֶם
to-them you-do and-this (7) them and-you-make-clean Israel sons-of

לְטַהֲרָם הַזֵּה עֲלֵיהֶם מֵי חַטָּאת וְהֶעֱבִירוּ
and-they-must-shave cleansing waters-of on-them sprinkle! to-purify-them

תַעַר עַל־ כָּל־ בְּשָׂרָם וְכִבְּסוּ בִגְדֵיהֶם
clothes-of-them and-they-must-wash body-of-them whole-of over razor

וְהִטֶּהָרוּ׃ (8) וְלָקְחוּ פַּר בֶּן־ בָּקָר
herd young-of bull and-they-must-take (8) so-they-purify-selves

וּמִנְחָתוֹ סֹלֶת בְּלוּלָה בַשָּׁמֶן וּפַר־
and-bull with-the-oil being-mixed fine-flour and-grain-offering-of-him

שֵׁנִי בֶן־ בָּקָר תִּקַּח לְחַטָּאת׃ (9) וְהִקְרַבְתָּ אֶת־
*** and-you-bring (9) for-sin-offering you-take herd young-of second

הַלְוִיִּם לִפְנֵי אֹהֶל מוֹעֵד וְהִקְהַלְתָּ אֶת־ כָּל־
whole-of *** and-you-assemble Meeting Tent-of to-front-of the-Levites

עֲדַת בְּנֵי יִשְׂרָאֵל׃ (10) וְהִקְרַבְתָּ אֶת־ הַלְוִיִּם לִפְנֵי יְהוָה
Yahweh before the-Levites *** and-you-bring (10) Israel sons-of community-of

וְסָמְכוּ בְנֵי־ יִשְׂרָאֵל אֶת־ יְדֵיהֶם עַל־ הַלְוִיִּם׃
the-Levites on hands-of-them *** Israel sons-of and-they-must-lay

(11) וְהֵנִיף אַהֲרֹן אֶת־ הַלְוִיִּם תְּנוּפָה לִפְנֵי יְהוָה
Yahweh before wave-offering the-Levites *** Aaron and-he-must-present (11)

מֵאֵת בְּנֵי יִשְׂרָאֵל וְהָיוּ לַעֲבֹד אֶת־ עֲבֹדַת יְהוָה׃
Yahweh work-of *** to-work so-they-may-be Israel sons-of from

(12) וְהַלְוִיִּם יִסְמְכוּ אֶת־ יְדֵיהֶם עַל רֹאשׁ הַפָּרִים
the-bulls head-of on hands-of-them *** they-must-lay and-the-Levites (12)

וַעֲשֵׂה אֶת־ הָאֶחָד חַטָּאת וְאֶת־ הָאֶחָד עֹלָה לַיהוָה
to-Yahweh burnt-offering the-other and sin-offering the-one *** then-use!

לְכַפֵּר עַל־ הַלְוִיִּם׃ (13) וְהַעֲמַדְתָּ אֶת־ הַלְוִיִּם לִפְנֵי
in-front-of the-Levites *** and-you-have-stand (13) the-Levites for to-atone

אַהֲרֹן וְלִפְנֵי בָנָיו וְהֵנַפְתָּ אֹתָם תְּנוּפָה
wave-offering them then-you-present sons-of-him and-in-front-of Aaron

לַיהוָה׃ (14) וְהִבְדַּלְתָּ אֶת־ הַלְוִיִּם מִתּוֹךְ בְּנֵי יִשְׂרָאֵל
Israel sons-of from-among the-Levites *** so-you-set-apart (14) to-Yahweh

hammered gold—from its base to its blossoms. The lampstand was made exactly like the pattern the LORD had shown Moses.

*The Setting Apart of the Levites*

5 The LORD said to Moses: 6 "Take the Levites from among the other Israelites and make them ceremonially clean. 7 To purify them, do this: Sprinkle the water of cleansing on them; then have them shave their whole bodies and wash their clothes, and so purify themselves. 8 Have them take a young bull with its grain offering of fine flour mixed with oil; then you are to take a second young bull for a sin offering. 9 Bring the Levites to the front of the Tent of Meeting and assemble the whole Israelite community. 10 You are to bring the Levites before the LORD, and the Israelites are to lay their hands on them. 11 Aaron is to present the Levites before the LORD as a wave offering from the Israelites, so that they may be ready to do the work of the LORD.

12 "After the Levites lay their hands on the heads of the bulls, use the one for a sin offering to the LORD and the other for a burnt offering, to make atonement for the Levites. 13 Have the Levites stand in front of Aaron and his sons and then present them as a wave offering to the LORD. 14 In this way you are to set the Levites apart from the other Israelites, and the Levites will be

וְהָיוּ לִי הַלְוִיִּם׃ וְאַחֲרֵי־כֵן יָבֹאוּ
they-must-come this and-after (15) the-Levites to-me and-they-will-be

הַלְוִיִּם לַעֲבֹד אֶת־אֹהֶל מוֹעֵד וְטִהַרְתָּ אֹתָם וְהֵנַפְתָּ
and-you-present them when-you-purify Meeting Tent-of *** to-work the-Levites

אֹתָם תְּנוּפָה׃ כִּי נְתֻנִים נְתֻנִים הֵמָּה לִי
to-me they ones-being-given ones-being-given for (16) wave-offering them

מִתּוֹךְ בְּנֵי יִשְׂרָאֵל תַּחַת פִּטְרַת כָּל־רֶחֶם בְּכוֹר
firstborn-of womb every-of first-of in-place-of Israel sons-of from-among

כֹּל מִבְּנֵי יִשְׂרָאֵל לָקַחְתִּי אֹתָם לִי׃ כִּי לִי כָל־בְּכוֹר
firstborn every-of to-me for (17) for-me them I-took Israel from-sons-of all

בִּבְנֵי יִשְׂרָאֵל בָּאָדָם וּבַבְּהֵמָה בְּיוֹם הַכֹּתִי
to-strike-me on-day or-whether-the-animal whether-the-man Israel among-sons-of

כָל־בְּכוֹר בְּאֶרֶץ מִצְרַיִם הִקְדַּשְׁתִּי אֹתָם לִי׃ וָאֶקַּח
and-I-took (18) for-me them I-set-apart Egypt in-land-of firstborn all-of

אֶת־הַלְוִיִּם תַּחַת כָּל־בְּכוֹר בִּבְנֵי יִשְׂרָאֵל׃
Israel among-sons-of firstborn all-of in-place-of the-Levites ***

וָאֶתְּנָה אֶת־הַלְוִיִּם נְתֻנִים | לְאַהֲרֹן וּלְבָנָיו
and-to-sons-of-him to-Aaron ones-being-given the-Levites *** and-I-gave (19)

מִתּוֹךְ בְּנֵי יִשְׂרָאֵל לַעֲבֹד אֶת־עֲבֹדַת בְּנֵי־יִשְׂרָאֵל בְּאֹהֶל
at-Tent-of Israel sons-of work-of *** to-do Israel sons-of from-among

מוֹעֵד וּלְכַפֵּר עַל־בְּנֵי יִשְׂרָאֵל וְלֹא יִהְיֶה בִּבְנֵי
on-sons-of he-will-strike so-not Israel sons-of for and-to-atone Meeting

יִשְׂרָאֵל נֶגֶף בְּגֶשֶׁת בְּנֵי־יִשְׂרָאֵל אֶל־הַקֹּדֶשׁ׃ וַיַּעַשׂ
so-he-did (20) the-sanctuary to Israel sons-of when-to-go-near plague Israel

מֹשֶׁה וְאַהֲרֹן וְכָל־עֲדַת בְּנֵי־יִשְׂרָאֵל לַלְוִיִּם
with-the-Levites Israel sons-of community-of and-whole-of and-Aaron Moses

כְּכֹל אֲשֶׁר־צִוָּה יְהוָה אֶת־מֹשֶׁה לַלְוִיִּם כֵּן־עָשׂוּ
they-did so for-the-Levites Moses *** Yahweh he-commanded that as-all

לָהֶם בְּנֵי יִשְׂרָאֵל׃ וַיִּתְחַטְּאוּ הַלְוִיִּם
the-Levites and-they-purified-selves (21) Israel sons-of with-them

וַיְכַבְּסוּ בִּגְדֵיהֶם וַיָּנֶף אַהֲרֹן אֹתָם תְּנוּפָה
wave-offering them Aaron then-he-presented clothes-of-them and-they-washed

לִפְנֵי יְהוָה וַיְכַפֵּר עֲלֵיהֶם אַהֲרֹן לְטַהֲרָם׃ וְאַחֲרֵי־
and-after (22) to-purify-them Aaron for-them and-he-atoned Yahweh before

כֵן בָּאוּ הַלְוִיִּם לַעֲבֹד אֶת־עֲבֹדָתָם בְּאֹהֶל מוֹעֵד לִפְנֵי
before Meeting at-Tent-of work-of-them *** to-do the-Levites they-came that

אַהֲרֹן וְלִפְנֵי בָנָיו כַּאֲשֶׁר צִוָּה יְהוָה אֶת־מֹשֶׁה עַל־
for Moses *** Yahweh he-commanded just-as sons-of-him and-before Aaron

mine.

15"After you have purified the Levites and presented them as a wave offering, they are to come to do their work at the Tent of Meeting. 16They are the Israelites who are to be given wholly to me. I have taken them as my own in place of the firstborn, the first male offspring from every Israelite woman. 17Every firstborn male in Israel, whether man or animal, is mine. When I struck down all the firstborn in Egypt, I set them apart for myself. 18And I have taken the Levites in place of all the firstborn sons in Israel. 19Of all the Israelites, I have given the Levites as gifts to Aaron and his sons to do the work at the Tent of Meeting on behalf of the Israelites and to make atonement for them so that no plague will strike the Israelites when they go near the sanctuary."

20Moses, Aaron and the whole Israelite community did with the Levites just as the LORD commanded Moses. 21The Levites purified themselves and washed their clothes. Then Aaron presented them as a wave offering before the LORD and made atonement for them to purify them. 22After that, the Levites came to do their work at the Tent of Meeting under the supervision of Aaron and his sons. They did

הַלְוִיִּם כֵּן עָשׂוּ לָהֶם׃ וַיְדַבֵּר יְהוָה אֶל־מֹשֶׁה לֵּאמֹר׃
to-say Moses to Yahweh and-he-spoke (23) with-them they-did so the-Levites

זֹאת אֲשֶׁר לַלְוִיִּם מִבֶּן חָמֵשׁ וְעֶשְׂרִים שָׁנָה וָמַעְלָה
or-more year and-twenty five from-son-of for-the-Levites what this (24)

יָבוֹא לִצְבֹא צָבָא בַּעֲבֹדַת אֹהֶל מוֹעֵד׃
Meeting Tent-of in-work-of service to-take-part he-shall-come

וּמִבֶּן חֲמִשִּׁים שָׁנָה יָשׁוּב מִצְּבָא הָעֲבֹדָה
the-work from-service-of he-must-retire year fifty but-from-son-of (25)

וְלֹא יַעֲבֹד עוֹד׃ וְשֵׁרֵת אֶת־ אֶחָיו
brothers-of-him *** now-he-may-assist (26) longer he-may-work and-not

בְּאֹהֶל מוֹעֵד לִשְׁמֹר מִשְׁמֶרֶת וַעֲבֹדָה לֹא יַעֲבֹד כָּכָה תַּעֲשֶׂה
you-assign thus he-must-do not but-work duty to-perform Meeting at-Tent-of

לַלְוִיִּם בְּמִשְׁמְרֹתָם׃ וַיְדַבֵּר יְהוָה אֶל־
to Yahweh and-he-spoke (9:1) to-responsibilities-of-them to-the-Levites

מֹשֶׁה בְמִדְבַּר־ סִינַי בַּשָּׁנָה הַשֵּׁנִית לְצֵאתָם מֵאֶרֶץ
from-land-of to-come-out-them the-second in-the-year Sinai in-Desert-of Moses

מִצְרַיִם בַּחֹדֶשׁ הָרִאשׁוֹן לֵאמֹר׃ וְיַעֲשׂוּ בְנֵי־
sons-of now-they-must-celebrate (2) to-say the-first in-the-month Egypt

יִשְׂרָאֵל אֶת־ הַפָּסַח בְּמוֹעֲדוֹ׃ בְּאַרְבָּעָה עָשָׂר־יוֹם בַּחֹדֶשׁ
of-the-month day ten on-four (3) at-time-of-him the-Passover *** Israel

הַזֶּה בֵּין הָעַרְבַּיִם* תַּעֲשׂוּ אֹתוֹ בְּמוֹעֲדוֹ כְּכָל־
as-all-of at-time-of-him him you-celebrate the-twilights at the-this

חֻקֹּתָיו וּכְכָל־ מִשְׁפָּטָיו תַּעֲשׂוּ אֹתוֹ׃
him you-celebrate regulations-of-him and-as-all-of rules-of-him

וַיְדַבֵּר מֹשֶׁה אֶל־ בְּנֵי יִשְׂרָאֵל לַעֲשֹׂת הַפָּסַח׃
the-Passover to-celebrate Israel sons-of to Moses so-he-told (4)

וַיַּעֲשׂוּ אֶת־ הַפֶּסַח בָּרִאשׁוֹן בְּאַרְבָּעָה עָשָׂר יוֹם
day ten on-four in-the-first the-Passover *** so-they-celebrated (5)

לַחֹדֶשׁ בֵּין הָעַרְבַּיִם בְּמִדְבַּר סִינָי כְּכֹל אֲשֶׁר צִוָּה
he-commanded that as-all Sinai in-Desert-of the-twilights at of-the-month

יְהוָה אֶת־ מֹשֶׁה כֵּן עָשׂוּ בְּנֵי יִשְׂרָאֵל׃ וַיְהִי אֲנָשִׁים אֲשֶׁר
who men but-he-was (6) Israel sons-of they-did so Moses *** Yahweh

הָיוּ טְמֵאִים לְנֶפֶשׁ אָדָם וְלֹא־ יָכְלוּ לַעֲשֹׂת־
to-celebrate they-could so-not man by-body-of unclean-ones they-were

הַפֶּסַח בַּיּוֹם הַהוּא וַיִּקְרְבוּ לִפְנֵי מֹשֶׁה וְלִפְנֵי אַהֲרֹן
Aaron and-before Moses before so-they-came the-that on-the-day the-Passover

בַּיּוֹם הַהוּא׃ וַיֹּאמְרוּ הָאֲנָשִׁים הָהֵמָּה אֵלָיו אֲנַחְנוּ
we to-him the-these the-men and-they-said (7) the-that on-the-day

with the Levites just as the LORD commanded Moses.
[23]The LORD said to Moses, [24]"This applies to the Levites: Men twenty-five years old or more shall come to take part in the work at the Tent of Meeting, [25]but at the age of fifty, they must retire from their regular service and work no longer. [26]They may assist their brothers in performing their duties at the Tent of Meeting, but they themselves must not do the work. This, then, is how you are to assign the responsibilities of the Levites."

*The Passover*

9 The LORD spoke to Moses in the Desert of Sinai in the first month of the second year after they came out of Egypt. He said, [2]"Have the Israelites celebrate the Passover at the appointed time. [3]Celebrate it at the appointed time, at twilight on the fourteenth day of this month, in accordance with all its rules and regulations."
[4]So Moses told the Israelites to celebrate the Passover, [5]and they did so in the Desert of Sinai at twilight on the fourteenth day of the first month. The Israelites did everything just as the LORD commanded Moses.
[6]But some of them could not celebrate the Passover on that day because they were ceremonially unclean on account of a dead body. So they came to Moses and Aaron that same day [7]and said to Moses,

*3 Most mss have *pathah* under the *ayin* (הָעַר׳).

טְמֵאִים לְנֶפֶשׁ אָדָם לָמָּה נִגָּרַע לְבִלְתִּי הַקְרִב אֶת־ קָרְבַּן
offering-of *** to-present not are-we-kept why? man by-body-of unclean-ones

יְהוָה בְּמֹעֲדוֹ בְּתוֹךְ בְּנֵי יִשְׂרָאֵל׃ וַיֹּאמֶר אֲלֵהֶם מֹשֶׁה
Moses to-them and-he-answered (8) Israel sons-of with at-time-of-him Yahweh

עִמְדוּ וְאֶשְׁמְעָה מַה־ יְצַוֶּה יְהוָה לָכֶם׃ וַיְדַבֵּר
then-he-spoke (9) about-you Yahweh he-commands what and-I-will-find wait!

יְהוָה אֶל־ מֹשֶׁה לֵּאמֹר׃ דַּבֵּר אֶל־ בְּנֵי יִשְׂרָאֵל לֵאמֹר אִישׁ אִישׁ כִּי־
when any man to-say Israel sons-of to tell! (10) to-say Moses to Yahweh

יִהְיֶה־ טָמֵא ׀ לָנֶפֶשׁ אוֹ בְדֶרֶךְ רְחֹקָה לָכֶם אוֹ
or whether-you distant on-journey or by-body unclean he-is

לְדֹרֹתֵיכֶם וְעָשָׂה פֶסַח לַיהוָה׃
of-Yahweh Passover then-he-may-celebrate whether-descendants-of-you

בַּחֹדֶשׁ הַשֵּׁנִי בְּאַרְבָּעָה עָשָׂר יוֹם בֵּין הָעַרְבַּיִם
the-twilights at day ten on-four the-second in-the-month (11)

יַעֲשׂוּ אֹתוֹ עַל־ מַצּוֹת וּמְרֹרִים
and-bitter-herbs unleavened-breads with him they-must-celebrate

יֹאכְלֻהוּ׃ לֹא־ יַשְׁאִירוּ מִמֶּנּוּ עַד־ בֹּקֶר וְעֶצֶם
or-bone morning till from-him they-must-leave not (12) they-must-eat-him

לֹא יִשְׁבְּרוּ־ בוֹ כְּכָל־ חֻקַּת הַפֶּסַח
the-Passover regulation-of as-every-of in-him they-must-break not

יַעֲשׂוּ אֹתוֹ׃ וְהָאִישׁ אֲשֶׁר־ הוּא טָהוֹר וּבְדֶרֶךְ לֹא־
not and-on-journey clean he who but-the-man (13) him they-must-celebrate

הָיָה וְחָדַל לַעֲשׂוֹת הַפֶּסַח וְנִכְרְתָה הַנֶּפֶשׁ
the-person then-she-must-be-cut the-Passover to-celebrate yet-he-fails he-is

הַהִוא מֵעַמֶּיהָ כִּי ׀ קָרְבַּן יְהוָה לֹא הִקְרִיב
he-presented not Yahweh offering-of for from-people-of-her the-that

בְּמֹעֲדוֹ חֶטְאוֹ יִשָּׂא הָאִישׁ הַהוּא׃ וְכִי־
and-if (14) the-that the-man he-must-bear sin-of-him at-time-of-him

יָגוּר אִתְּכֶם גֵּר וְעָשָׂה פֶסַח לַיהוָה
of-Yahweh Passover and-he-would-celebrate alien among-you he-lives

כְּחֻקַּת הַפֶּסַח וּכְמִשְׁפָּטוֹ כֵּן יַעֲשֶׂה חֻקָּה
regulation he-must-do so and-as-rule-of-him the-Passover as-regulation-of

אַחַת יִהְיֶה לָכֶם וְלַגֵּר וּלְאֶזְרַח הָאָרֶץ׃
the-land and-for-native-of and-for-the-alien for-you he-must-be same

וּבְיוֹם הָקִים אֶת־ הַמִּשְׁכָּן כִּסָּה הֶעָנָן אֶת־
*** the-cloud he-covered the-tabernacle *** to-set-up and-on-day (15)

הַמִּשְׁכָּן לְאֹהֶל הָעֵדֻת וּבָעֶרֶב יִהְיֶה עַל־
above he-was and-from-the-evening the-Testimony over-Tent-of the-tabernacle

"We have become unclean because of a dead body, but why should we be kept from presenting the LORD's offering with the other Israelites at the appointed time?"
8 Moses answered them, "Wait until I find out what the LORD commands concerning you."
9 Then the LORD said to
Moses, 10 "Tell the Israelites: 'When any of you or your descendants are unclean because of a dead body or are away on a journey, they may still celebrate the LORD's Passover.
11 They are to celebrate it on the fourteenth day of the second month at twilight. They are to eat the lamb, together with unleavened bread and bitter
herbs. 12 They must not leave any of it till morning or break any of its bones. When they celebrate the Passover, they must follow all the regulations.
13 But if a man who is ceremonially clean and not on a journey fails to celebrate the Passover, that person must be cut off from his people because he did not present the LORD's offering at the appointed time. That man will bear the consequences of his sin.
14 " 'An alien living among you who wants to celebrate the LORD's Passover must do so in accordance with its rules and regulations. You must have the same regulations for the alien and the native-born.' "

### *The Cloud Above the Tabernacle*

15 On the day the tabernacle, the Tent of the Testimony, was set up, the cloud covered it. From evening till morning

הַמִּשְׁכָּן כְּמַרְאֵה־ אֵשׁ עַד־ בֹּקֶר׃ כֵּן יִהְיֶה תָמִיד
continually he-was so (16) morning till fire as-appearance-of the-tabernacle

הֶעָנָן יְכַסֶּנּוּ וּמַרְאֵה־ אֵשׁ לָיְלָה׃ וּלְפִי
and-at-time-of (17) night fire and-appearance-of he-covered-him the-cloud

הֵעָלֹת הֶעָנָן מֵעַל הָאֹהֶל וְאַחֲרֵי־ כֵן יִסְעוּ
they-set-out this then-after the-Tent from-above the-cloud to-be-lifted

בְּנֵי יִשְׂרָאֵל וּבִמְקוֹם אֲשֶׁר יִשְׁכָּן־ שָׁם הֶעָנָן שָׁם
there the-cloud there he-settled where and-at-place Israel sons-of

יַחֲנוּ בְּנֵי יִשְׂרָאֵל׃ עַל־ פִּי יְהוָה יִסְעוּ בְּנֵי
sons-of they-set-out Yahweh command-of at (18) Israel sons-of they-encamped

יִשְׂרָאֵל וְעַל־ פִּי יְהוָה יַחֲנוּ כָּל־ יְמֵי אֲשֶׁר יִשְׁכֹּן
he-stayed that days-of all-of they-encamped Yahweh command-of and-at Israel

הֶעָנָן עַל־ הַמִּשְׁכָּן יַחֲנוּ׃ וּבְהַאֲרִיךְ הֶעָנָן
the-cloud and-when-to-remain (19) they-encamped the-tabernacle over the-cloud

עַל־ הַמִּשְׁכָּן יָמִים רַבִּים וְשָׁמְרוּ בְנֵי־ יִשְׂרָאֵל אֶת־מִשְׁמֶרֶת
order-of *** Israel sons-of then-they-obeyed many days the-tabernacle over

יְהוָה וְלֹא יִסָּעוּ׃ וְיֵשׁ אֲשֶׁר יִהְיֶה הֶעָנָן יָמִים
days the-cloud he-stayed when and-he-was (20) they-set-out and-not Yahweh

מִסְפָּר עַל־ הַמִּשְׁכָּן עַל־ פִּי יְהוָה יַחֲנוּ וְעַל־
then-at they-encamped Yahweh command-of at the-tabernacle over few

פִּי יְהוָה יִסָּעוּ׃ וְיֵשׁ אֲשֶׁר יִהְיֶה הֶעָנָן
the-cloud he-stayed when and-he-was (21) they-set-out Yahweh command-of

מֵעֶרֶב עַד־ בֹּקֶר וְנַעֲלָה הֶעָנָן בַּבֹּקֶר
in-the-morning the-cloud when-he-was-lifted morning till from-evening

וְנָסָעוּ אוֹ יוֹמָם וָלַיְלָה וְנַעֲלָה הֶעָנָן
the-cloud when-he-was-lifted or-night by-day whether then-they-set-out

וְנָסָעוּ׃ אוֹ־ יֹמַיִם אוֹ־ חֹדֶשׁ אוֹ־ יָמִים בְּהַאֲרִיךְ
when-to-stay days or month or two-days whether (22) then-they-set-out

הֶעָנָן עַל־ הַמִּשְׁכָּן לִשְׁכֹּן עָלָיו יַחֲנוּ בְנֵי־
sons-of then-they-encamped over-him to-remain the-tabernacle over the-cloud

יִשְׂרָאֵל וְלֹא יִסָּעוּ וּבְהֵעָלֹתוֹ יִסָּעוּ׃ עַל־
at (23) they-set-out but-when-to-be-lifted-him they-set-out and-not Israel

פִּי יְהוָה יַחֲנוּ וְעַל־ פִּי יְהוָה יִסָּעוּ אֶת־
*** they-set-out Yahweh command-of and-at they-encamped Yahweh command-of

מִשְׁמֶרֶת יְהוָה שָׁמָרוּ עַל־ פִּי יְהוָה בְּיַד־ מֹשֶׁה׃
Moses by-hand-of Yahweh command-of to they-obeyed Yahweh order-of

וַיְדַבֵּר יְהוָה אֶל־ מֹשֶׁה לֵּאמֹר׃ עֲשֵׂה לְךָ שְׁתֵּי
two-of for-you make! (2) to-say Moses to Yahweh and-he-spoke (10:1)

the cloud above the tabernacle
looked like fire. 16That is how
it continued to be; the cloud
covered it, and at night it
looked like fire. 17Whenever
the cloud lifted from above the
Tent, the Israelites set out;
wherever the cloud settled, the
Israelites encamped. 18At the
LORD's command the Israelites
set out, and at his command
they encamped. As long as the
cloud stayed over the tabernacle, they remained in camp.
19When the cloud remained
over the tabernacle a long
time, the Israelites obeyed the
LORD's order and did not set
out. 20Sometimes the cloud
was over the tabernacle only a
few days; at the LORD's command they would encamp,
and then at his command they
would set out. 21Sometimes the
cloud stayed only from evening till morning, and when it
lifted in the morning, they set
out. Whether by day or by
night, whenever the cloud lifted, they set out. 22Whether the
cloud stayed over the tabernacle for two days or a month
or a year, the Israelites would
remain in camp and not set
out; but when it lifted, they
would set out. 23At the LORD's
command they encamped,
and at the LORD's command
they set out. They obeyed the
LORD's order, in accordance
with his command through
Moses.

*The Silver Trumpets*

10 The LORD said to
Moses: 2"Make two

חֲצוֹצְרֹת כֶּסֶף מִקְשָׁה תַּעֲשֶׂה אֹתָם וְהָיוּ לְךָ
for-you and-they-will-be them you-make hammered silver trumpets-of

לְמִקְרָא הָעֵדָה וּלְמַסַּע אֶת־ הַמַּחֲנוֹת׃
the-camps *** and-for-setting-out the-community for-calling-of

וְתָקְעוּ בָּהֵן וְנוֹעֲדוּ אֵלֶיךָ כָּל־
whole-of before-you then-they-must-assemble on-them when-they-sound (3)

הָעֵדָה אֶל־ פֶּתַח אֹהֶל מוֹעֵד׃ וְאִם־ בְּאַחַת יִתְקָעוּ
they-sound on-one but-if (4) Meeting Tent-of entrance-of at the-community

וְנוֹעֲדוּ אֵלֶיךָ הַנְּשִׂיאִים רָאשֵׁי אַלְפֵי יִשְׂרָאֵל׃
Israel clans-of heads-of the-leaders before-you then-they-must-assemble

וּתְקַעְתֶּם תְּרוּעָה וְנָסְעוּ הַמַּחֲנוֹת הַחֹנִים
the-ones-camping the-camps then-they-must-set-out blast when-you-sound (5)

קֵדְמָה׃ וּתְקַעְתֶּם תְּרוּעָה שֵׁנִית וְנָסְעוּ הַמַּחֲנוֹת
the-camps then-they-must-set-out second blast when-you-sound (6) on-east

הַחֹנִים תֵּימָנָה תְּרוּעָה יִתְקְעוּ לְמַסְעֵיהֶם׃
for-settings-out-of-them they-will-signal blast on-south the-ones-camping

וּבְהַקְהִיל אֶת־ הַקָּהָל תִּתְקְעוּ וְלֹא תָרִיעוּ׃
you-signal but-not you-sound the-assembly *** and-when-to-gather (7)

וּבְנֵי אַהֲרֹן הַכֹּהֲנִים יִתְקְעוּ בַּחֲצֹצְרוֹת
on-the-trumpets they-must-blow the-priests Aaron now-sons-of (8)

וְהָיוּ לָכֶם לְחֻקַּת עוֹלָם לְדֹרֹתֵיכֶם׃
for-generations-of-you lasting as-ordinance-of for-you and-they-will-be

וְכִי־ תָבֹאוּ מִלְחָמָה בְּאַרְצְכֶם עַל־ הַצַּר
the-enemy against in-land-of-you battle you-go-into and-when (9)

הַצֹּרֵר אֶתְכֶם וַהֲרֵעֹתֶם בַּחֲצֹצְרוֹת
on-the-trumpets then-you-blast you the-one-oppressing

וַנִזְכַּרְתֶּם* לִפְנֵי יְהוָה אֱלֹהֵיכֶם וְנוֹשַׁעְתֶּם
and-you-will-be-rescued God-of-you Yahweh by then-you-will-be-remembered

מֵאֹיְבֵיכֶם׃ וּבְיוֹם שִׂמְחַתְכֶם וּבְמוֹעֲדֵיכֶם
and-at-feasts-of-you joy-of-you and-on-day-of (10) from-being-enemies-of-you

וּבְרָאשֵׁי חָדְשֵׁיכֶם וּתְקַעְתֶּם בַּחֲצֹצְרֹת עַל
over on-the-trumpets then-you-sound months-of-you and-at-beginnings-of

עֹלֹתֵיכֶם וְעַל זִבְחֵי שַׁלְמֵיכֶם
fellowships-of-you offerings-of and-over burnt-offerings-of-you

וְהָיוּ לָכֶם לְזִכָּרוֹן לִפְנֵי אֱלֹהֵיכֶם אֲנִי יְהוָה אֱלֹהֵיכֶם׃
God-of-you Yahweh I God-of-you before as-memorial for-you and-they-will-be

וַיְהִי בַּשָּׁנָה הַשֵּׁנִית בַּחֹדֶשׁ הַשֵּׁנִי בְּעֶשְׂרִים
on-twenty the-second in-the-month the-second in-the-year and-he-was (11)

trumpets of hammered silver, and use them for calling the community together and for having the camps set out. [3]When both are sounded, the whole community is to assemble before you at the entrance to the Tent of Meeting. [4]If only one is sounded, the leaders—the heads of the clans of Israel—are to assemble before you. [5]When a trumpet blast is sounded, the tribes camping on the east are to set out. [6]At the sounding of a second blast, the camps on the south are to set out. The blast will be the signal for setting out. [7]To gather the assembly, blow the trumpets, but not with the same signal.

[8]"The sons of Aaron, the priests, are to blow the trumpets. This is to be a lasting ordinance for you and the generations to come. [9]When you go into battle in your own land against an enemy who is oppressing you, sound a blast on the trumpets. Then you will be remembered by the LORD your God and rescued from your enemies. [10]Also at your times of rejoicing—your appointed feasts and New Moon festivals—you are to sound the trumpets over your burnt offerings and fellowship offerings,[t] and they will be a memorial for you before your God. I am the LORD your God."

*The Israelites Leave Sinai*

[11]On the twentieth day of the second month of the second year, the cloud lifted from

[t]10 Traditionally *peace offerings*

*9 Most mss have *sheva* under the *vav* (וְ).

בַּחֹדֶשׁ נַעֲלָה הֶעָנָן מֵעַל מִשְׁכַּן הָעֵדֻת׃
the-Testimony tabernacle-of from-above the-cloud he-was-lifted of-the-month

וַיִּסְעוּ בְנֵי־יִשְׂרָאֵל לְמַסְעֵיהֶם מִמִּדְבַּר
from-Desert-of in-travels-of-them Israel sons-of then-they-set-out (12)

סִינָי וַיִּשְׁכֹּן הֶעָנָן בְּמִדְבַּר פָּארָן׃ וַיִּסְעוּ
and-they-set-out (13) Paran in-Desert-of the-cloud and-he-rested Sinai

בָּרִאשֹׁנָה עַל־פִּי יְהוָה בְּיַד־מֹשֶׁה׃ וַיִּסַּע
and-he-set-out (14) Moses by-hand-of Yahweh command-of at at-the-first

דֶּגֶל מַחֲנֵה בְנֵי־יְהוּדָה בָּרִאשֹׁנָה לְצִבְאֹתָם וְעַל־
and-over by-divisions-of-them at-the-first Judah sons-of camp-of standard-of

צְבָאוֹ נַחְשׁוֹן בֶּן־עַמִּינָדָב׃ וְעַל־צְבָא מַטֵּה
tribe-of division-of and-over (15) Amminadab son-of Nahshon division-of-him

בְּנֵי יִשָּׂשכָר* נְתַנְאֵל בֶּן־צוּעָר׃ וְעַל־צְבָא מַטֵּה
tribe-of division-of and-over (16) Zuar son-of Nethanel Issachar sons-of

בְּנֵי זְבוּלֻן אֱלִיאָב בֶּן־חֵלֹון׃ וְהוּרַד הַמִּשְׁכָּן
the-tabernacle then-he-was-taken-down (17) Helon son-of Eliab Zebulun sons-of

וְנָסְעוּ בְנֵי־גֵרְשׁוֹן וּבְנֵי מְרָרִי נֹשְׂאֵי
ones-carrying-of Merari and-sons-of Gershon sons-of and-they-set-out

הַמִּשְׁכָּן׃ וְנָסַע דֶּגֶל מַחֲנֵה רְאוּבֵן
Reuben camp-of standard-of and-he-set-out (18) the-tabernacle

לְצִבְאֹתָם וְעַל־צְבָאוֹ אֱלִיצוּר בֶּן־שְׁדֵיאוּר׃
Shedeur son-of Elizur division-of-him and-over by-divisions-of-them

וְעַל־צְבָא מַטֵּה בְּנֵי שִׁמְעוֹן שְׁלֻמִיאֵל בֶּן־צוּרִי־
Zuri son-of Shelumiel Simeon sons-of tribe-of division-of and-over (19)

שַׁדָּי׃ וְעַל־צְבָא מַטֵּה בְנֵי־גָד אֶלְיָסָף בֶּן־
son-of Eliasaph Gad sons-of tribe-of division-of and-over (20) Shaddai

דְּעוּאֵל׃ וְנָסְעוּ הַקְּהָתִים נֹשְׂאֵי הַמִּקְדָּשׁ
the-holy-thing ones-carrying-of the-Kohathites then-they-set-out (21) Deuel

וְהֵקִימוּ אֶת־הַמִּשְׁכָּן עַד־בֹּאָם׃ וְנָסַע
and-he-set-out (22) to-arrive-them before the-tabernacle *** and-they-set-up

דֶּגֶל מַחֲנֵה בְנֵי־אֶפְרַיִם לְצִבְאֹתָם וְעַל־
and-over by-divisions-of-them Ephraim sons-of camp-of standard-of

צְבָאוֹ אֱלִישָׁמָע בֶּן־עַמִּיהוּד׃ וְעַל־צְבָא מַטֵּה
tribe-of division-of and-over (23) Ammihud son-of Elishama division-of-him

בְּנֵי מְנַשֶּׁה גַּמְלִיאֵל בֶּן־פְּדָהצוּר׃ וְעַל־צְבָא מַטֵּה
tribe-of division-of and-over (24) Pedahzur son-of Gamaliel Manasseh sons-of

בְּנֵי בִנְיָמִן אֲבִידָן בֶּן־גִּדְעוֹנִי׃ וְנָסַע דֶּגֶל
standard-of and-he-set-out (25) Gideoni son-of Abidan Benjamin sons-of

above the tabernacle of the Testimony. 12Then the Israelites set out from the Desert of Sinai and traveled from place to place until the cloud came to rest in the Desert of Paran. 13They set out, this first time, at the LORD's command through Moses.

14The divisions of the camp of Judah went first, under their standard. Nahshon son of Amminadab was in command. 15Nethanel son of Zuar was over the division of the tribe of Issachar, 16and Eliab son of Helon was over the division of the tribe of Zebulun. 17Then the tabernacle was taken down, and the Gershonites and Merarites, who carried it, set out.

18The divisions of the camp of Reuben went next, under their standard. Elizur son of Shedeur was in command. 19Shelumiel son of Zurishaddai was over the division of the tribe of Simeon, 20and Eliasaph son of Deuel was over the division of the tribe of Gad. 21Then the Kohathites set out, carrying the holy things. The tabernacle was to be set up before they arrived.

22The divisions of the camp of Ephraim went next, under their standard. Elishama son of Ammihud was in command. 23Gamaliel son of Pedahzur was over the division of the tribe of Manasseh, 24and Abidan son of Gideoni was over the division of the tribe of Benjamin.

25Finally, as the rear guard

*15 Most mss have *dagesh* in the *sin* ( יִשָּׂ ).

מַחֲנֵה בְנֵי־ דָן מְאַסֵּף לְכָל־ הַמַּחֲנֹת לְצִבְאֹתָם
by-divisions-of-them the-units for-all-of being-rear-guard Dan sons-of camp-of

וְעַל־ צְבָאוֹ אֲחִיעֶזֶר בֶּן־ עַמִּי שַׁדָּי׃ וְעַל־
and-over (26) Shaddai Ammi son-of Ahiezer division-of-him and-over

צְבָא מַטֵּה בְּנֵי אָשֵׁר פַּגְעִיאֵל בֶּן־ עָכְרָן׃ וְעַל־
and-over (27) Ocran son-of Pagiel Asher sons-of tribe-of division-of

צְבָא מַטֵּה בְּנֵי נַפְתָּלִי אֲחִירַע בֶּן־ עֵינָן׃ אֵלֶּה מַסְעֵי
orders-of these (28) Enan son-of Ahira Naphtali sons-of tribe-of division-of

בְנֵי־ יִשְׂרָאֵל לְצִבְאֹתָם וַיִּסָּעוּ׃ וַיֹּאמֶר מֹשֶׁה
Moses now-he-said (29) so-they-set-out by-divisions-of-them Israel sons-of

לְחֹבָב בֶּן־ רְעוּאֵל הַמִּדְיָנִי חֹתֵן מֹשֶׁה נֹסְעִים ׀
ones-setting-out Moses father-in-law-of the-Midianite Reuel son-of to-Hobab

אֲנַחְנוּ אֶל־הַמָּקוֹם אֲשֶׁר אָמַר יְהוָה אֹתוֹ אֶתֵּן לָכֶם לְכָה אִתָּנוּ
with-us come! to-you I-will-give him Yahweh he-said which the-place for we

וְהֵטַבְנוּ לָךְ כִּי־ יְהוָה דִּבֶּר־ טוֹב עַל־יִשְׂרָאֵל׃
Israel to good he-promised Yahweh for with-you and-we-will-treat-well

וַיֹּאמֶר אֵלָיו לֹא אֵלֵךְ כִּי אִם־ אֶל־ אַרְצִי וְאֶל־
and-to land-of-me to rather for I-will-go not to-him and-he-answered (30)

מוֹלַדְתִּי אֵלֵךְ׃ וַיֹּאמֶר אַל־ נָא תַּעֲזֹב אֹתָנוּ כִּי ׀ עַל־ כֵּן
this by for us you-leave now! not but-he-said (31) I-go people-of-me

יָדַעְתָּ חֲנֹתֵנוּ בַּמִּדְבָּר וְהָיִיתָ לָּנוּ לְעֵינָיִם׃
as-eyes to-us and-you-can-be in-the-desert to-camp-us you-know

וְהָיָה כִּי־ תֵלֵךְ עִמָּנוּ וְהָיָה ׀ הַטּוֹב הַהוּא
the-that the-good then-he-will-be with-us you-come if and-he-will-be (32)

אֲשֶׁר יֵיטִיב יְהוָה עִמָּנוּ וְהֵטַבְנוּ לָךְ׃ וַיִּסְעוּ
so-they-set-out (33) with-you then-we-will-share to-us Yahweh he-gives which

מֵהַר יְהוָה דֶּרֶךְ שְׁלֹשֶׁת יָמִים וַאֲרוֹן בְּרִית־
covenant-of and-ark-of days three-of travel-of Yahweh from-mountain-of

יְהוָה נֹסֵעַ לִפְנֵיהֶם דֶּרֶךְ שְׁלֹשֶׁת יָמִים לָתוּר לָהֶם מְנוּחָה׃
rest-place for-them to-find days three-of travel-of before-them going Yahweh

וַעֲנַן יְהוָה עֲלֵיהֶם יוֹמָם בְּנָסְעָם מִן־ הַמַּחֲנֶה׃
the-camp from when-to-set-out-them by-day over-them Yahweh and-cloud-of (34)

וַיְהִי בִּנְסֹעַ הָאָרֹן וַיֹּאמֶר מֹשֶׁה קוּמָה ׀ יְהוָה
Yahweh rise-up! Moses then-he-said the-ark when-to-set-out and-he-was (35)

וְיָפֻצוּ אֹיְבֶיךָ וְיָנֻסוּ
and-may-they-flee being-enemies-of-you and-may-they-be-scattered

מְשַׂנְאֶיךָ מִפָּנֶיךָ׃ וּבְנֻחֹה יֹאמַר שׁוּבָה
return! he-said and-when-to-rest-her (36) from-before-you ones-hating-you

for all the units, the divisions of the camp of Dan set out, under their standard. Ahiezer son of Ammishaddai was in command. 26Pagiel son of Ocran was over the division of the tribe of Asher, 27and Ahira son of Enan was over the division of the tribe of Naphtali. 28This was the order of march for the Israelite divisions as they set out.

29Now Moses said to Hobab son of Reuel the Midianite, Moses' father-in-law, "We are setting out for the place about which the LORD said, 'I will give it to you.' Come with us and we will treat you well, for the LORD has promised good things to Israel."

30He answered, "No, I will not go; I am going back to my own land and my own people."

31But Moses said, "Please do not leave us. You know where we should camp in the desert, and you can be our eyes. 32If you come with us, we will share with you whatever good things the LORD gives us."

33So they set out from the mountain of the LORD and traveled for three days. The ark of the covenant of the LORD went before them during those three days to find them a place to rest. 34The cloud of the LORD was over them by day when they set out from the camp.

35Whenever the ark set out, Moses said,

"Rise up, O LORD!
May your enemies be scattered;
may your foes flee before you."

36Whenever it came to rest, he said,

יְהוָ֖ה רִבְב֥וֹת אַלְפֵ֥י יִשְׂרָאֵֽל׃ וַיְהִ֤י הָעָם֙
the-people now-he-was (11:1) Israel thousands-of multitudes-of Yahweh

כְּמִתְאֹ֣נְנִ֔ים רַ֖ע בְּאָזְנֵ֣י יְהוָ֑ה וַיִּשְׁמַ֤ע יְהוָה֙
Yahweh and-he-heard Yahweh in-hearings-of hardship as-ones-complaining

וַיִּ֣חַר אַפּ֔וֹ וַתִּבְעַר־ בָּם֙ אֵ֣שׁ יְהוָ֔ה
Yahweh fire-of among-them and-she-burned anger-of-him and-he-was-aroused

וַתֹּ֖אכַל בִּקְצֵ֥ה הַֽמַּחֲנֶֽה׃ וַיִּצְעַ֥ק הָעָ֖ם אֶל־
to the-people when-they-cried (2) the-camp at-outskirt-of and-she-consumed

מֹשֶׁ֑ה וַיִּתְפַּלֵּ֤ל מֹשֶׁה֙ אֶל־ יְהוָ֔ה וַתִּשְׁקַ֖ע הָאֵֽשׁ׃
the-fire and-she-died-out Yahweh to Moses then-he-prayed Moses

וַיִּקְרָ֛א שֵֽׁם־ הַמָּק֥וֹם הַה֖וּא תַּבְעֵרָ֑ה כִּֽי־ בָעֲרָ֥ה בָ֖ם
among-them she-burned for Taberah the-that the-place name-of so-he-called (3)

אֵ֥שׁ יְהוָֽה׃ וְהָֽאסַפְסֻף֙ אֲשֶׁ֣ר בְּקִרְבּ֔וֹ הִתְאַוּ֖וּ תַּאֲוָ֑ה
craving they-craved in-midst-of-him that and-the-rabble (4) Yahweh fire-of

וַיָּשֻׁ֣בוּ וַיִּבְכּ֗וּ גַּ֚ם בְּנֵ֣י יִשְׂרָאֵ֔ל וַיֹּ֣אמְר֔וּ מִ֥י
if-only and-they-said Israel sons-of again and-they-wailed and-they-repeated

יַאֲכִלֵ֖נוּ בָּשָֽׂר׃ זָכַ֙רְנוּ֙ אֶת־ הַדָּגָ֔ה אֲשֶׁר־ נֹאכַ֥ל בְּמִצְרַ֖יִם חִנָּ֑ם
no-cost in-Egypt we-ate that the-fish *** we-remember (5) meat we-could-eat

אֵ֣ת הַקִּשֻּׁאִ֗ים וְאֵת֙ הָֽאֲבַטִּחִ֔ים וְאֶת־ הֶחָצִ֥יר וְאֶת־ הַבְּצָלִ֖ים וְאֶת־ הַשּׁוּמִֽים׃
the-garlics and the-onions and the-leek and the-melons and the-cucumbers ***

וְעַתָּ֛ה נַפְשֵׁ֥נוּ יְבֵשָׁ֖ה אֵ֣ין כֹּ֑ל בִּלְתִּ֖י אֶל־ הַמָּ֥ן
the-manna to except anything not she-went appetite-of-us but-now (6)

עֵינֵֽינוּ׃ וְהַמָּ֕ן כִּזְרַע־ גַּ֖ד ה֑וּא וְעֵינ֖וֹ
and-look-of-him he coriander like-seed-of now-the-manna (7) eyes-of-us

כְּעֵ֥ין הַבְּדֹֽלַח׃ שָׁטוּ֩ הָעָ֨ם וְלָֽקְט֜וּ
and-they-gathered the-people they-went (8) the-resin like-look-of

וְטָחֲנ֣וּ בָרֵחַ֗יִם א֤וֹ דָכוּ֙ בַּמְּדֹכָ֔ה וּבִשְּׁלוּ֙
and-they-cooked in-the-mortar they-crushed or in-the-handmills and-they-ground

בַּפָּר֔וּר וְעָשׂ֥וּ אֹת֖וֹ עֻג֑וֹת וְהָיָ֣ה טַעְמ֔וֹ כְּטַ֖עַם
like-taste-of taste-of-him and-he-was cakes him or-they-made in-the-pot

לְשַׁ֥ד הַשָּֽׁמֶן׃ וּבְרֶ֧דֶת הַטַּ֛ל עַל־ הַֽמַּחֲנֶ֖ה לָ֑יְלָה
night the-camp on the-dew and-when-to-settle (9) the-olive-oil prepared-of

יֵרֵ֥ד הַמָּ֖ן עָלָֽיו׃ וַיִּשְׁמַ֨ע מֹשֶׁ֜ה אֶת־ הָעָ֗ם
the-people *** Moses and-he-heard (10) with-him the-manna he-came-down

בֹּכֶה֙ לְמִשְׁפְּחֹתָ֔יו אִ֖ישׁ לְפֶ֣תַח אָהֳל֑וֹ וַיִּֽחַר־
and-he-burned tent-of-him at-entrance-of each by-families-of-him wailing

אַ֤ף יְהוָה֙ מְאֹ֔ד וּבְעֵינֵ֥י מֹשֶׁ֖ה רָֽע׃ וַיֹּ֨אמֶר
and-he-asked (11) trouble Moses and-in-eyes-of exceedingly Yahweh anger-of

"Return, O LORD,
to the countless
thousands of Israel."

*Fire From the LORD*

**11** Now the people complained about their hardships in the hearing of the LORD, and when he heard them his anger was aroused. Then fire from the LORD burned among them and consumed some of the outskirts of the camp. [2]When the people cried out to Moses, he prayed to the LORD and the fire died down. [3]So that place was called Taberah,[u] because fire from the LORD had burned among them.

*Quail From the LORD*

[4]The rabble with them began to crave other food, and again the Israelites started wailing and said, "If only we had meat to eat! [5]We remember the fish we ate in Egypt at no cost—also the cucumbers, melons, leeks, onions and garlic. [6]But now we have lost our appetite; we never see anything but this manna!"

[7]The manna was like coriander seed and looked like resin. [8]The people went around gathering it, and then ground it in a handmill or crushed it in a mortar. They cooked it in a pot or made it into cakes. And it tasted like something made with olive oil. [9]When the dew settled on the camp at night, the manna also came down.

[10]Moses heard the people of every family wailing, each at the entrance to his tent. The LORD became exceedingly angry, and Moses was troubled.

[u]3 *Taberah* means *burning.*

מֹשֶׁה אֶל־ יְהוָה לָמָה הֲרֵעֹתָ לְעַבְדֶּךָ וְלָמָּה לֹא־

not and-why? on-servant-of-you you-brought-trouble why? Yahweh to Moses

מָצָתִי חֵן בְּעֵינֶיךָ לָשׂוּם אֶת־ מַשָּׂא כָּל־ הָעָם הַזֶּה

the-this the-people all-of burden-of *** to-put in-eyes-of-you favor I-found

עָלָי׃ הֶאָנֹכִי הָרִיתִי אֵת כָּל־ הָעָם הַזֶּה אִם־אָנֹכִי יְלִדְתִּיהוּ

I-bore-him I or the-this the-people all-of *** I-conceived I? (12) on-me

כִּי־ תֹאמַר אֵלַי שָׂאֵהוּ בְחֵיקֶךָ כַּאֲשֶׁר יִשָּׂא

he-carries just-as in-bosom-of-you carry-him! to-me you-tell that

הָאֹמֵן אֶת־ הַיֹּנֵק עַל הָאֲדָמָה אֲשֶׁר נִשְׁבַּעְתָּ לַאֲבֹתָיו׃

to-fathers-of-him you-promised that the-land to the-infant *** the-one-nursing

מֵאַיִן לִי בָּשָׂר לָתֵת לְכָל־ הָעָם הַזֶּה כִּי־ יִבְכּוּ

they-wail for the-this the-people to-all-of to-give meat to-me where? (13)

עָלַי לֵאמֹר תְּנָה־ לָּנוּ בָשָׂר וְנֹאכֵלָה׃ לֹא־אוּכַל אָנֹכִי לְבַדִּי

by-myself I I-can not (14) so-we-can-eat meat to-us give! to-say to-me

לָשֵׂאת אֶת־ כָּל־ הָעָם הַזֶּה כִּי כָבֵד מִמֶּנִּי׃ וְאִם־כָּכָה ׀

thus so-if (15) for-me heavy for the-this the-people all-of *** to-carry

אַתְּ־ עֹשֶׂה לִּי הָרְגֵנִי נָא הָרֹג אִם־מָצָאתִי חֵן בְּעֵינֶיךָ

in-eyes-of-you favor I-found if to-kill now! kill-me! to-me treating you

וְאַל־ אֶרְאֶה בְּרָעָתִי׃ וַיֹּאמֶר יְהוָה אֶל־ מֹשֶׁה אֶסְפָה־

bring! Moses to Yahweh and-he-said (16) to-ruin-of-me let-me-face and-not

לִּי שִׁבְעִים אִישׁ מִזִּקְנֵי יִשְׂרָאֵל אֲשֶׁר יָדַעְתָּ כִּי־ הֵם זִקְנֵי

elders-of they that you-know whom Israel from-elders-of man seventy to-me

הָעָם וְשֹׁטְרָיו וְלָקַחְתָּ אֹתָם אֶל־ אֹהֶל מוֹעֵד

Meeting Tent-of to them and-you-take and-ones-leading-him the-people

וְהִתְיַצְּבוּ שָׁם עִמָּךְ׃ וְיָרַדְתִּי וְדִבַּרְתִּי

and-I-will-speak and-I-will-come-down (17) with-you there that-they-may-stand

עִמְּךָ שָׁם וְאָצַלְתִּי מִן־ הָרוּחַ אֲשֶׁר עָלֶיךָ וְשַׂמְתִּי

and-I-will-put on-you that the-Spirit from and-I-will-take there with-you

עֲלֵיהֶם וְנָשְׂאוּ אִתְּךָ בְּמַשָּׂא הָעָם וְלֹא־

so-not the-people on-burden-of with-you and-they-will-carry on-them

תִשָּׂא אַתָּה לְבַדֶּךָ׃ וְאֶל־ הָעָם תֹּאמַר

you-tell the-people and-to (18) by-yourself you you-will-carry

הִתְקַדְּשׁוּ לְמָחָר וַאֲכַלְתֶּם בָּשָׂר כִּי בְּכִיתֶם בְּאָזְנֵי

in-ears-of you-wailed for meat when-you-eat for-tomorrow consecrate-selves!

יְהוָה לֵאמֹר מִי יַאֲכִלֵנוּ בָּשָׂר כִּי־ טוֹב לָנוּ בְּמִצְרָיִם וְנָתַן

now-he-will-give in-Egypt to-us better for meat we-ate if-only to-say Yahweh

יְהוָה לָכֶם בָּשָׂר וַאֲכַלְתֶּם׃ לֹא יוֹם אֶחָד תֹּאכְלוּן וְלֹא

or-not you-will-eat one day not (19) and-you-will-eat meat to-you Yahweh

11 He asked the LORD, "Why have you brought this trouble on your servant? What have I done to displease you that you put the burden of all these people on me? 12 Did I conceive all these people? Did I give them birth? Why do you tell me to carry them in my arms, as a nurse carries an infant, to the land you promised on oath to their forefathers? 13 Where can I get meat for all these people? They keep wailing to me, 'Give us meat to eat!' 14 I cannot carry all these people by myself; the burden is too heavy for me. 15 If this is how you are going to treat me, put me to death right now—if I have found favor in your eyes—and do not let me face my own ruin."

16 The LORD said to Moses: "Bring me seventy of Israel's elders who are known to you as leaders and officials among the people. Have them come to the Tent of Meeting, that they may stand there with you. 17 I will come down and speak with you there, and I will take of the Spirit that is on you and put the Spirit on them. They will help you carry the burden of the people so that you will not have to carry it alone.

18 "Tell the people: 'Consecrate yourselves in preparation for tomorrow, when you will eat meat. The LORD heard you when you wailed, "If only we had meat to eat! We were better off in Egypt!" Now the LORD will give you meat, and you will eat it. 19 You will not eat it for just one day, or two

יוֹמָיִם וְלֹא ׀ חֲמִשָּׁה יָמִים וְלֹא עֲשָׂרָה יָמִים וְלֹא עֶשְׂרִים יוֹם׃ עַד ׀
for (20) day twenty or-not days ten or-not days five or-not two-days

חֹדֶשׁ יָמִים עַד אֲשֶׁר־יֵצֵא מֵאַפְּכֶם וְהָיָה לָכֶם
to-you and-he-will-be from-nostril-of-you he-comes when until days month-of

לְזָרָא יַעַן כִּי־מְאַסְתֶּם אֶת־יְהוָה אֲשֶׁר בְּקִרְבְּכֶם
in-midst-of-you who Yahweh *** you-rejected that because as-loathsome

וַתִּבְכּוּ לְפָנָיו לֵאמֹר לָמָּה זֶּה יָצָאנוּ מִמִּצְרָיִם׃ וַיֹּאמֶר
but-he-said (21) from-Egypt we-left this why? to-say before-him and-you-wailed

מֹשֶׁה שֵׁשׁ־מֵאוֹת אֶלֶף רַגְלִי הָעָם אֲשֶׁר אָנֹכִי בְּקִרְבּוֹ
in-midst-of-him I that the-people on-foot thousand hundreds-of six Moses

וְאַתָּה אָמַרְתָּ בָּשָׂר אֶתֵּן לָהֶם וְאָכְלוּ חֹדֶשׁ יָמִים׃
days month-of and-they-will-eat to-them I-will-give meat you-say and-you

הֲצֹאן וּבָקָר יִשָּׁחֵט לָהֶם וּמָצָא לָהֶם
for-them would-he-be-enough for-them he-was-slaughtered and-herd if-flock (22)

אִם אֶת־כָּל־דְּגֵי הַיָּם יֵאָסֵף לָהֶם וּמָצָא
would-he-be-enough for-them he-was-caught the-sea fishes-of all-of *** if

לָהֶם׃ וַיֹּאמֶר יְהוָה אֶל־מֹשֶׁה הֲיַד יְהוָה תִּקְצָר
is-she-short Yahweh arm-of? Moses to Yahweh and-he-answered (23) for-them

עַתָּה תִרְאֶה הֲיִקְרְךָ דְבָרִי אִם־לֹא׃ וַיֵּצֵא
so-he-went (24) not or word-of-me if-he-will-come-true-for-you you-will-see now

מֹשֶׁה וַיְדַבֵּר אֶל־הָעָם אֵת דִּבְרֵי יְהוָה וַיֶּאֱסֹף שִׁבְעִים
seventy and-he-gathered Yahweh words-of *** the-people to and-he-told Moses

אִישׁ מִזִּקְנֵי הָעָם וַיַּעֲמֵד אֹתָם סְבִיבֹת הָאֹהֶל׃
the-tent ones-around them and-he-had-stand the-people from-elders-of man

וַיֵּרֶד יְהוָה ׀ בֶּעָנָן וַיְדַבֵּר אֵלָיו וַיָּאצֶל
and-he-took with-him and-he-spoke in-the-cloud Yahweh then-he-came-down (25)

מִן־הָרוּחַ אֲשֶׁר עָלָיו וַיִּתֵּן עַל־שִׁבְעִים אִישׁ הַזְּקֵנִים וַיְהִי
and-he-was the-elders man seventy on and-he-put on-him that the-Spirit from

כְּנוֹחַ עֲלֵיהֶם הָרוּחַ וַיִּתְנַבְּאוּ וְלֹא יָסָפוּ׃
they-did-again but-not then-they-prophesied the-Spirit on-them as-to-rest

וַיִּשָּׁאֲרוּ שְׁנֵי־אֲנָשִׁים ׀ בַּמַּחֲנֶה שֵׁם הָאֶחָד ׀ אֶלְדָּד
Eldad the-one name-of in-the-camp men two-of but-they-remained (26)

וְשֵׁם הַשֵּׁנִי מֵידָד וַתָּנַח עֲלֵיהֶם הָרוּחַ וְהֵמָּה
now-they the-Spirit on-them and-she-rested Medad the-other and-name-of

בַּכְּתֻבִים וְלֹא יָצְאוּ הָאֹהֱלָה וַיִּתְנַבְּאוּ
and-they-prophesied to-the-Tent they-went but-not of-the-ones-being-listed

בַּמַּחֲנֶה׃ וַיָּרָץ הַנַּעַר וַיַּגֵּד לְמֹשֶׁה וַיֹּאמַר
and-he-said to-Moses and-he-told the-young-man and-he-ran (27) in-the-camp

days, or five, ten or twenty days, [20]but for a whole month—until it comes out of your nostrils and you loathe it—because you have rejected the LORD, who is among you, and have wailed before him, saying, "Why did we ever leave Egypt?" ' "

[21]But Moses said, "Here I am among six hundred thousand men on foot, and you say, 'I will give them meat to eat for a whole month!' [22]Would they have enough if flocks and herds were slaughtered for them? Would they have enough if all the fish in the sea were caught for them?"

[23]The LORD answered Moses, "Is the LORD's arm too short? You will now see whether or not what I say will come true for you."

[24]So Moses went out and told the people what the LORD had said. He brought together seventy of their elders and had them stand around the tent. [25]Then the LORD came down in the cloud and spoke with him, and he took of the Spirit that was on him and put the Spirit on the seventy elders. When the Spirit rested on them, they prophesied, but they did not do so again.[v]

[26]However, two men, whose names were Eldad and Medad, had remained in the camp. They were listed among the elders, but did not go out to the tent. Yet the Spirit also rested on them, and they prophesied in the camp. [27]A young man ran and told Moses, "Eldad

[v]25 Or *prophesied and continued to do so*

אֶלְדָּד וּמֵידָד מִתְנַבְּאִים בַּמַּחֲנֶה׃ וַיַּעַן יְהוֹשֻׁעַ בִּן־
son-of Joshua and-he-spoke (28) in-the-camp ones-prophesying and-Medad Eldad

נוּן מְשָׁרֵת מֹשֶׁה מִבְּחֻרָיו וַיֹּאמַר אֲדֹנִי מֹשֶׁה
Moses lord-of-me and-he-said since-youths-of-him Moses one-aiding-of Nun

כְּלָאֵם׃ וַיֹּאמֶר לוֹ מֹשֶׁה הַמְקַנֵּא אַתָּה לִי וּמִי
if-only for-me you being-jealous? Moses to-him but-he-replied (29) stop-them!

יִתֵּן כָּל־ עַם יְהוָה נְבִיאִים כִּי־ יִתֵּן יְהוָה אֶת־
*** Yahweh he-would-put if prophets Yahweh people-of all-of he-would-make

רוּחוֹ עֲלֵיהֶם׃ וַיֵּאָסֵף מֹשֶׁה אֶל־ הַמַּחֲנֶה הוּא
he the-camp to Moses then-he-returned (30) on-them Spirit-of-him

וְזִקְנֵי יִשְׂרָאֵל׃ וְרוּחַ נָסַע | מֵאֵת יְהוָה וַיָּגָז
and-he-drove-in Yahweh from he-went-out now-wind (31) Israel and-elders-of

שַׂלְוִים מִן־ הַיָּם וַיִּטֹּשׁ עַל־ הַמַּחֲנֶה כְּדֶרֶךְ יוֹם כֹּה
here day about-journey-of the-camp into and-he-brought the-sea from quails

וּכְדֶרֶךְ יוֹם כֹּה סְבִיבוֹת הַמַּחֲנֶה וּכְאַמָּתַיִם
and-about-two-cubits the-camp ones-around there day and-about-journey-of

עַל־ פְּנֵי הָאָרֶץ׃ וַיָּקָם הָעָם כָּל־ הַיּוֹם
the-day all-of the-people and-he-went-out (32) the-ground surface-of above

הַהוּא וְכָל־ הַלַּיְלָה וְכֹל | יוֹם הַמָּחֳרָת וַיַּאַסְפוּ
and-they-gathered the-next day-of and-all-of the-night and-all-of the-that

אֶת־ הַשְּׂלָו הַמַּמְעִיט אָסַף עֲשָׂרָה חֳמָרִים וַיִּשְׁטְחוּ לָהֶם
to-them and-they-spread homers ten he-gathered the-being-less the-quail ***

שָׁטוֹחַ סְבִיבוֹת הַמַּחֲנֶה׃ הַבָּשָׂר עוֹדֶנּוּ בֵּין שִׁנֵּיהֶם
teeth-of-them between while-he the-meat (33) the-camp ones-around to-spread

טֶרֶם יִכָּרֵת וְאַף יְהוָה חָרָה בָעָם
against-the-people he-burned Yahweh then-anger-of he-was-consumed before

וַיַּךְ יְהוָה בָּעָם מַכָּה רַבָּה מְאֹד׃ וַיִּקְרָא
and-he-called (34) very severe plague against-the-people Yahweh and-he-struck

אֶת־ שֵׁם־ הַמָּקוֹם הַהוּא קִבְרוֹת הַתַּאֲוָה כִּי־ שָׁם קָבְרוּ אֶת־
*** they-buried there for Hattaavah Kibroth the-that the-place name-of ***

הָעָם הַמִּתְאַוִּים׃ מִקִּבְרוֹת הַתַּאֲוָה נָסְעוּ
they-traveled Hattaavah from-Kibroth (35) the-ones-craving the-people

הָעָם חֲצֵרוֹת וַיִּהְיוּ בַּחֲצֵרוֹת׃ וַתְּדַבֵּר מִרְיָם
Miriam and-she-talked (12:1) in-Hazeroth and-they-stayed Hazeroth the-people

וְאַהֲרֹן בְּמֹשֶׁה עַל־ אֹדוֹת הָאִשָּׁה הַכֻּשִׁית אֲשֶׁר לָקָח
he-married that the-Cushite the-wife reasons-of for against-Moses and-Aaron

כִּי־ אִשָּׁה כֻשִׁית לָקָח׃ וַיֹּאמְרוּ הֲרַק אַךְ־ בְּמֹשֶׁה
through-Moses indeed only? and-they-asked (2) he-married Cushite woman for

and Medad are prophesying in the camp."

28 Joshua son of Nun, who had been Moses' aide since youth, spoke up and said, "Moses, my lord, stop them!"

29 But Moses replied, "Are you jealous for my sake? I wish that all the LORD's people were prophets and that the LORD would put his Spirit on them!" 30 Then Moses and the elders of Israel returned to the camp.

31 Now a wind went out from the LORD and drove quail in from the sea. It brought them[w] down all around the camp to about three feet[x] above the ground, as far as a day's walk in any direction. 32 All that day and night and all the next day the people went out and gathered quail. No one gathered less than ten homers.[y] Then they spread them out all around the camp. 33 But while the meat was still between their teeth and before it could be consumed, the anger of the LORD burned against the people, and he struck them with a severe plague. 34 Therefore the place was named Kibroth Hattaavah,[z] because there they buried the people who had craved other food.

35 From Kibroth Hattaavah the people traveled to Hazeroth and stayed there.

### *Miriam and Aaron Oppose Moses*

**12** Miriam and Aaron began to talk against Moses because of his Cushite wife, for he had married a Cushite. 2 "Has the LORD spoken only through Moses?"

[w]31 Or *They flew*
[x]31 Hebrew *two cubits* (about 1 meter)
[y]32 That is, probably about 60 bushels (about 2.2 kiloliters)
[z]34 *Kibroth Hattaavah* means *graves of craving.*

דִּבֶּר יְהוָה הֲלֹא גַּם־ בָּנוּ דִבֵּר וַיִּשְׁמַע יְהוָה׃

Yahweh and-he-heard he-spoke through-us also not? Yahweh he-spoke

(3) וְהָאִישׁ מֹשֶׁה עָנָו מְאֹד מִכֹּל הָאָדָם אֲשֶׁר עַל־ פְּנֵי

face-of on who the-man more-than-any-of very humble Moses now-the-man (3)

הָאֲדָמָה׃ (4) וַיֹּאמֶר יְהוָה פִּתְאֹם אֶל־מֹשֶׁה וְאֶל־ אַהֲרֹן וְאֶל־ מִרְיָם

Miriam and-to Aaron and-to Moses to at-once Yahweh and-he-said (4) the-earth

צְאוּ שְׁלָשְׁתְּכֶם אֶל־ אֹהֶל מוֹעֵד וַיֵּצְאוּ שְׁלָשְׁתָּם׃

three-of-them so-they-came-out Meeting Tent-of to three-of-you come-out!

(5) וַיֵּרֶד יְהוָה בְּעַמּוּד עָנָן וַיַּעֲמֹד פֶּתַח

entrance-of and-he-stood cloud in-pillar-of Yahweh then-he-came-down (5)

הָאֹהֶל וַיִּקְרָא אַהֲרֹן וּמִרְיָם וַיֵּצְאוּ

and-they-stepped-forward and-Miriam Aaron and-he-summoned the-Tent

שְׁנֵיהֶם׃ (6) וַיֹּאמֶר שִׁמְעוּ־ נָא דְבָרָי אִם־ יִהְיֶה

he-is when words-of-me now! listen! and-he-said (6) both-of-them

נְבִיאֲכֶם יְהוָה בַּמַּרְאָה אֵלָיו אֶתְוַדָּע בַּחֲלוֹם אֲדַבֶּר־

I-speak in-dream I-reveal-myself to-him in-the-vision Yahweh prophet-of-you

בּוֹ׃ (7) לֹא־ כֵן עַבְדִּי מֹשֶׁה בְּכָל־ בֵּיתִי נֶאֱמָן

being-faithful house-of-me in-all-of Moses servant-of-me true not (7) to-him

הוּא׃ (8) פֶּה אֶל־ פֶּה אֲדַבֶּר־ בּוֹ וּמַרְאֶה וְלֹא בְחִידֹת

in-riddles and-not and-clearly with-him I-speak face to face (8) he

וּתְמֻנַת יְהוָה יַבִּיט וּמַדּוּעַ לֹא יְרֵאתֶם לְדַבֵּר

to-speak you-were-afraid not so-why? he-sees Yahweh and-form-of

בְּעַבְדִּי בְמֹשֶׁה׃ (9) וַיִּחַר אַף יְהוָה

Yahweh anger-of and-he-burned (9) against-Moses against-servant-of-me

בָּם וַיֵּלַךְ׃ (10) וְהֶעָנָן סָר מֵעַל הָאֹהֶל

the-Tent from-above he-lifted when-the-cloud (10) and-he-left against-them

וְהִנֵּה מִרְיָם מְצֹרַעַת כַּשָּׁלֶג וַיִּפֶן אַהֲרֹן אֶל־

toward Aaron and-he-turned like-the-snow being-leprous Miriam then-see!

מִרְיָם וְהִנֵּה מְצֹרָעַת׃ (11) וַיֹּאמֶר אַהֲרֹן אֶל־ מֹשֶׁה בִּי

please! Moses to Aaron and-he-said (11) being-leprous and-see! Miriam

אֲדֹנִי אַל־ נָא תָשֵׁת עָלֵינוּ חַטָּאת אֲשֶׁר נוֹאַלְנוּ וַאֲשֶׁר

and-that we-were-foolish that sin against-us you-hold now! not! lord-of-me

חָטָאנוּ׃ (12) אַל־ נָא תְהִי כַּמֵּת אֲשֶׁר בְּצֵאתוֹ

when-to-come-him that as-the-stillborn let-her-be now! not (12) we-committed

מֵרֶחֶם אִמּוֹ וַיֵּאָכֵל חֲצִי בְשָׂרוֹ׃

flesh-of-him half-of then-he-is-eaten-away mother-of-him from-womb-of

(13) וַיִּצְעַק מֹשֶׁה אֶל־ יְהוָה לֵאמֹר אֵל נָא רְפָא נָא לָהּ׃

to-her now! heal! now! God to-say Yahweh to Moses so-he-cried-out (13)

they asked. "Hasn't he also
spoken through us?" And the
LORD heard this.
[3](Now Moses was a very
humble man, more humble
than anyone else on the face
of the earth.)
[4]At once the LORD said to
Moses, Aaron and Miriam,
"Come out to the Tent of
Meeting, all three of you." So
the three of them came out.
[5]Then the LORD came down in
a pillar of cloud; he stood at
the entrance to the Tent and
summoned Aaron and Mir-
iam. When both of them
stepped forward, [6]he said,
"Listen to my words:

"When a prophet of the
LORD is among you,
I reveal myself to him in
visions,
I speak to him in
dreams.
[7]But this is not true of my
servant Moses;
he is faithful in all my
house.
[8]With him I speak face to
face,
clearly and not in
riddles;
he sees the form of the
LORD.
Why then were you not
afraid
to speak against my
servant Moses?"

[9]The anger of the LORD
burned against them, and he
left them.
[10]When the cloud lifted from
above the Tent, there stood
Miriam—leprous,[a] like snow.
Aaron turned toward her and
saw that she had leprosy;
[11]and he said to Moses,
"Please, my lord, do not hold
against us the sin we have so
foolishly committed. [12]Do not
let her be like a stillborn infant
coming from its mother's
womb with its flesh half eaten
away."
[13]So Moses cried out to the
LORD, "O God, please heal
her!"

[a]*10* The Hebrew word was used for various diseases affecting the skin—not necessarily leprosy.

*9 Most mss bind these two words with *maqqeph* (וַיִּחַר־אַף).

°3 ק עניו

וַיֹּ֨אמֶר יְהוָ֜ה אֶל־ מֹשֶׁ֗ה וְאָבִ֨יהָ֙ יָרֹ֤ק יָרַק֙
| he-spit | to-spit | if-father-of-her | Moses | to | Yahweh | and-he-replied (14) |

בְּפָנֶ֔יהָ הֲלֹ֥א תִכָּלֵ֖ם שִׁבְעַ֣ת יָמִ֑ים תִּסָּגֵ֞ר
| she-must-be-confined | days | seven-of | she-would-be-in-disgrace | not? | in-face-of-her |

שִׁבְעַ֤ת יָמִים֙ מִחוּץ֙ לַֽמַּחֲנֶ֔ה וְאַחַ֖ר תֵּאָסֵֽף׃
| she-may-be-brought-back | and-after | of-the-camp | outside | days | seven-of |

וַתִּסָּגֵ֥ר מִרְיָ֛ם מִח֥וּץ לַֽמַּחֲנֶ֖ה שִׁבְעַ֣ת יָמִ֑ים
| days | seven-of | of-the-camp | outside | Miriam | so-she-was-confined (15) |

וְהָעָם֙ לֹ֣א נָסַ֔ע עַד־ הֵאָסֵ֖ף מִרְיָֽם׃ וְאַחַ֖ר
| and-after (16) | Miriam | to-be-brought-back | till | he-moved-on | not | and-the-people |

נָסְע֥וּ הָעָ֖ם מֵחֲצֵר֑וֹת וַֽיַּחֲנ֖וּ בְּמִדְבַּ֥ר פָּארָֽן׃
| Paran | in-Desert-of | and-they-encamped | from-Hazeroth | the-people | they-left |

## Numbers 13

וַיְדַבֵּ֥ר יְהוָ֖ה אֶל־ מֹשֶׁ֥ה לֵּאמֹֽר׃ שְׁלַח־ לְךָ֣ אֲנָשִׁ֗ים
| men | for-you | send! (2) | to-say | Moses | to | Yahweh | and-he-spoke (13:1) |

וְיָתֻ֙רוּ֙ אֶת־ אֶ֣רֶץ כְּנַ֔עַן אֲשֶׁר־ אֲנִ֥י נֹתֵ֖ן לִבְנֵ֣י יִשְׂרָאֵ֑ל אִ֣ישׁ
| man | Israel | to-sons-of | giving | I | which | Canaan | land-of | *** | so-they-may-explore |

אֶחָד֩ אִ֨ישׁ אֶחָ֜ד לְמַטֵּ֤ה אֲבֹתָיו֙ תִּשְׁלָ֔חוּ כֹּ֖ל נָשִׂ֥יא בָהֶֽם׃
| from-them | leader | each | you-send-him | ancestors-of-him | from-tribe-of | one | man | one |

וַיִּשְׁלַ֨ח אֹתָ֥ם מֹשֶׁ֛ה מִמִּדְבַּ֥ר פָּארָ֖ן עַל־ פִּ֣י יְהוָ֑ה
| Yahweh | command-of | at | Paran | from-Desert-of | Moses | them | so-he-sent (3) |

כֻּלָּ֣ם אֲנָשִׁ֔ים רָאשֵׁ֥י בְנֵֽי־ יִשְׂרָאֵ֖ל הֵֽמָּה׃ וְאֵ֖לֶּה שְׁמוֹתָ֑ם
| names-of-them | and-these (4) | they | Israel | sons-of | leaders-of | men | all-of-them |

לְמַטֵּ֣ה רְאוּבֵ֔ן שַׁמּ֖וּעַ בֶּן־ זַכּֽוּר׃ לְמַטֵּ֣ה שִׁמְע֔וֹן שָׁפָ֖ט
| Shaphat | Simeon | from-tribe-of (5) | Zaccur | son-of | Shammua | Reuben | from-tribe-of |

בֶּן־ חוֹרִֽי׃ לְמַטֵּ֣ה יְהוּדָ֔ה כָּלֵ֖ב בֶּן־ יְפֻנֶּֽה׃ לְמַטֵּ֣ה
| from-tribe-of (7) | Jephunneh | son-of | Caleb | Judah | from-tribe-of (6) | Hori | son-of |

יִשָּׂשכָ֔ר יִגְאָ֖ל בֶּן־ יוֹסֵֽף׃ לְמַטֵּ֣ה אֶפְרַ֔יִם הוֹשֵׁ֖עַ בֶּן־ נֽוּן׃
| Nun | son-of | Hoshea | Ephraim | from-tribe-of (8) | Joseph | son-of | Igal | Issachar |

לְמַטֵּ֣ה בִנְיָמִ֔ן פַּלְטִ֖י בֶּן־ רָפֽוּא׃ לְמַטֵּ֣ה זְבוּלֻ֔ן
| Zebulun | from-tribe-of (10) | Raphu | son-of | Palti | Benjamin | from-tribe-of (9) |

גַּדִּיאֵ֖ל בֶּן־ סוֹדִֽי׃ לְמַטֵּ֣ה יוֹסֵ֔ף לְמַטֵּ֣ה מְנַשֶּׁ֔ה גַּדִּ֖י
| Gaddi | Manasseh | from-tribe-of | Joseph | from-tribe-of (11) | Sodi | son-of | Gaddiel |

בֶּן־ סוּסִֽי׃ לְמַטֵּ֣ה דָ֔ן עַמִּיאֵ֖ל בֶּן־ גְּמַלִּֽי׃ לְמַטֵּ֣ה
| from-tribe-of (13) | Gemalli | son-of | Ammiel | Dan | from-tribe-of (12) | Susi | son-of |

אָשֵׁ֔ר סְת֖וּר בֶּן־ מִיכָאֵֽל׃ לְמַטֵּ֣ה נַפְתָּלִ֔י נַחְבִּ֖י בֶּן־ וָפְסִֽי׃
| Vophsi | son-of | Nahbi | Naphtali | from-tribe-of (14) | Michael | son-of | Sethur | Asher |

לְמַטֵּ֣ה גָ֔ד גְּאוּאֵ֖ל בֶּן־ מָכִֽי׃ אֵ֖לֶּה שְׁמ֣וֹת הָֽאֲנָשִׁ֑ים אֲשֶׁר־
| whom | the-men | names-of | these | (16) | Maki | son-of | Geuel | Gad | from-tribe-of (15) |

---

[14]The LORD replied to Moses, "If her father had spit in her face, would she not have been in disgrace for seven days? Confine her outside the camp for seven days; after that she can be brought back." [15]So Miriam was confined outside the camp for seven days, and the people did not move on till she was brought back. [16]After that, the people left Hazeroth and encamped in the Desert of Paran.

### Exploring Canaan

13 The LORD said to Moses, [2]"Send some men to explore the land of Canaan, which I am giving to the Israelites. From each ancestral tribe send one of its leaders."

[3]So at the LORD's command Moses sent them out from the Desert of Paran. All of them were leaders of the Israelites. [4]These are their names:

from the tribe of Reuben, Shammua son of Zaccur;
[5]from the tribe of Simeon, Shaphat son of Hori;
[6]from the tribe of Judah, Caleb son of Jephunneh;
[7]from the tribe of Issachar, Igal son of Joseph;
[8]from the tribe of Ephraim, Hoshea son of Nun;
[9]from the tribe of Benjamin, Palti son of Raphu;
[10]from the tribe of Zebulun, Gaddiel son of Sodi;
[11]from the tribe of Manasseh (a tribe of Joseph), Gaddi son of Susi;
[12]from the tribe of Dan, Ammiel son of Gemalli;
[13]from the tribe of Asher, Sethur son of Michael;
[14]from the tribe of Naphtali, Nahbi son of Vophsi;
[15]from the tribe of Gad, Geuel son of Maki.

[16]These are the names of the

שָׁלַח מֹשֶׁה לָתוּר אֶת־הָאָרֶץ וַיִּקְרָא מֹשֶׁה לְהוֹשֵׁעַ בִּן־
son-of to-Hoshea Moses now-he-named the-land *** to-explore Moses he-sent

נוּן יְהוֹשֻׁעַ׃ וַיִּשְׁלַח אֹתָם מֹשֶׁה לָתוּר אֶת־ אֶרֶץ כְּנָעַן
Canaan land-of *** to-explore Moses them when-he-sent (17) Joshua Nun

וַיֹּאמֶר אֲלֵהֶם עֲלוּ זֶה בַּנֶּגֶב וַעֲלִיתֶם אֶת־
*** and-you-go-into through-the-Negev there go-up! to-them then-he-said

הָהָר׃ וּרְאִיתֶם אֶת־ הָאָרֶץ מַה־ הִוא וְאֶת־ הָעָם
the-people and she what the-land *** and-you-see (18) the-hill-country

הַיֹּשֵׁב עָלֶיהָ הֶחָזָק הוּא הֲרָפֶה הַמְעַט הוּא אִם־רָב׃ וּמָה
and-what? (19) many or he if-few or-weak he if-strong in-her the-one-living

הָאָרֶץ אֲשֶׁר־הוּא יֹשֵׁב בָּהּ הֲטוֹבָה הִוא אִם־רָעָה וּמָה הֶעָרִים אֲשֶׁר־
that the-towns and-what? bad or she good? in-her living he where the-land

הוּא יוֹשֵׁב בָּהֵנָּה הַבְּמַחֲנִים אִם בְּמִבְצָרִים׃ וּמָה
and-how? (20) with-fortifications or without-walls? in-them living he

הָאָרֶץ הַשְּׁמֵנָה הִוא אִם־ רָזָה הֲיֵשׁ־ בָּהּ עֵץ אִם־ אַיִן וְהִתְחַזַּקְתֶּם
and-you-do-best not or tree on-her is-there? poor or she fertile? the-soil

וּלְקַחְתֶּם מִפְּרִי הָאָרֶץ וְהַיָּמִים יְמֵי בִּכּוּרֵי
first-ones-of days-of for-the-days the-land from-fruit-of and-you-bring

עֲנָבִים׃ וַיַּעֲלוּ וַיָּתֻרוּ אֶת־ הָאָרֶץ מִמִּדְבַּר־
from-Desert-of the-land *** and-they-explored so-they-went-up (21) grapes

צִן עַד־ רְחֹב לְבֹא חֲמָת׃ וַיַּעֲלוּ בַנֶּגֶב
through-the-Negev and-they-went-up (22) Hamath Lebo Rehob as-far-as Zin

וַיָּבֹא עַד־חֶבְרוֹן וְשָׁם אֲחִימַן שֵׁשַׁי וְתַלְמַי יְלִידֵי
descendants-of and-Talmai Sheshai Ahiman now-there Hebron to and-he-came

הָעֲנָק וְחֶבְרוֹן שֶׁבַע שָׁנִים נִבְנְתָה לִפְנֵי צֹעַן מִצְרָיִם׃
Egypt Zoan before being-built years seven and-Hebron the-Anak

וַיָּבֹאוּ עַד־ נַחַל אֶשְׁכֹּל וַיִּכְרְתוּ מִשָּׁם זְמוֹרָה
branch from-there then-they-cut Eshcol Valley-of to when-they-reached (23)

וְאֶשְׁכּוֹל עֲנָבִים אֶחָד וַיִּשָּׂאֻהוּ בַמּוֹט בִּשְׁנָיִם וּמִן־
and-from by-two on-the-pole and-they-carried-him one grapes and-cluster-of

הָרִמֹּנִים וּמִן־ הַתְּאֵנִים׃ לַמָּקוֹם הַהוּא קָרָא
he-called the-that to-the-place (24) the-figs and-from the-pomegranates

נַחַל אֶשְׁכּוֹל עַל אֹדוֹת הָאֶשְׁכּוֹל אֲשֶׁר־ כָּרְתוּ מִשָּׁם בְּנֵי
sons-of from-there they-cut that the-cluster reasons-of for Eshcol Valley-of

יִשְׂרָאֵל׃ וַיָּשֻׁבוּ מִתּוּר הָאָרֶץ מִקֵּץ אַרְבָּעִים יוֹם׃
day forty at-end-of the-land from-to-explore and-they-returned (25) Israel

וַיֵּלְכוּ וַיָּבֹאוּ אֶל־ מֹשֶׁה וְאֶל־ אַהֲרֹן וְאֶל־
and-to Aaron and-to Moses to and-they-came-back and-they-walked (26)

men Moses sent to explore the land. (Moses gave Hoshea son of Nun the name Joshua.)

17When Moses sent them to explore Canaan, he said, "Go up through the Negev and on into the hill country. 18See what the land is like and whether the people who live there are strong or weak, few or many. 19What kind of land do they live in? Is it good or bad? What kind of towns do they live in? Are they unwalled or fortified? 20How is the soil? Is it fertile or poor? Are there trees on it or not? Do your best to bring back some of the fruit of the land." (It was the season for the first ripe grapes.)

21So they went up and explored the land from the Desert of Zin as far as Rehob, toward Lebo[b] Hamath. 22They went up through the Negev and came to Hebron, where Ahiman, Sheshai and Talmai, the descendants of Anak, lived. (Hebron had been built seven years before Zoan in Egypt.) 23When they reached the Valley of Eshcol,[c] they cut off a branch bearing a single cluster of grapes. Two of them carried it on a pole between them, along with some pomegranates and figs. 24That place was called the Valley of Eshcol because of the cluster of grapes the Israelites cut off there. 25At the end of forty days they returned from exploring the land.

*Report on the Exploration*

26They came back to Moses

[b]21 Or *toward the entrance to*
[c]23 *Eshcol* means *cluster;* also in verse 24.

כָּל־ עֲדַת בְּנֵי־ יִשְׂרָאֵל אֶל־ מִדְבַּר פָּארָן קָדֵשָׁה
at-Kadesh Paran Desert-of in Israel sons-of community-of whole-of

וַיָּשִׁיבוּ אוֹתָם דָּבָר וְאֶת־ כָּל־ הָעֵדָה וַיַּרְאוּם אֶת־
*** and-they-showed-them the-assembly whole-of and report them and-they-gave

פְּרִי הָאָרֶץ׃ וַיְסַפְּרוּ־ לוֹ וַיֹּאמְרוּ בָּאנוּ אֶל־
into we-went and-they-said to-him and-they-reported (27) the-land fruit-of

הָאָרֶץ אֲשֶׁר שְׁלַחְתָּנוּ וְגַם זָבַת חָלָב וּדְבַשׁ הִוא וְזֶה־
and-here she and-honey milk flowing-of and-indeed you-sent-us where the-land

פִּרְיָהּ׃ אֶפֶס כִּי־ עַז הָעָם הַיֹּשֵׁב בָּאָרֶץ
in-the-land the-one-living the-people powerful also but (28) fruit-of-her

וְהֶעָרִים בְּצֻרוֹת גְּדֹלֹת מְאֹד וְגַם־ יְלִדֵי
descendants-of and-even very large-ones fortified-ones and-the-cities

הָעֲנָק רָאִינוּ שָׁם׃ עֲמָלֵק יוֹשֵׁב בְּאֶרֶץ הַנֶּגֶב וְהַחִתִּי
and-the-Hittite the-Negev in-land-of living Amalek (29) there we-saw the-Anak

וְהַיְבוּסִי וְהָאֱמֹרִי יוֹשֵׁב בָּהָר וְהַכְּנַעֲנִי
and-the-Canaanite in-the-hill-country living and-the-Amorite and-the-Jebusite

יֹשֵׁב עַל־ הַיָּם וְעַל יַד הַיַּרְדֵּן׃ וַיַּהַס כָּלֵב
Caleb then-he-silenced (30) the-Jordan bank-of and-along the-sea near living

אֶת־ הָעָם אֶל־ מֹשֶׁה וַיֹּאמֶר עָלֹה נַעֲלֶה
we-should-go-up to-go-up and-he-said Moses before the-people ***

וְיָרַשְׁנוּ אֹתָהּ כִּי־ יָכוֹל נוּכַל לָהּ׃ וְהָאֲנָשִׁים אֲשֶׁר־
who but-the-men (31) with-her we-can-do to-do for her and-we-should-possess

עָלוּ עִמּוֹ אָמְרוּ לֹא נוּכַל לַעֲלוֹת אֶל־ הָעָם כִּי־
for the-people against to-attack we-can not they-said with-him they-went-up

חָזָק הוּא מִמֶּנּוּ׃ וַיּוֹצִיאוּ דִּבַּת הָאָרֶץ אֲשֶׁר
that the-land bad-report-of and-they-spread (32) than-us he stronger

תָּרוּ אֹתָהּ אֶל־ בְּנֵי יִשְׂרָאֵל לֵאמֹר הָאָרֶץ אֲשֶׁר עָבַרְנוּ
we-passed that the-land to-say Israel sons-of among her they-explored

בָהּ לָתוּר אֹתָהּ אֶרֶץ אֹכֶלֶת יוֹשְׁבֶיהָ הִוא וְכָל־
and-all she ones-living-in-her devouring land her to-explore through-her

הָעָם אֲשֶׁר־ רָאִינוּ בְתוֹכָהּ אַנְשֵׁי מִדּוֹת׃ וְשָׁם רָאִינוּ אֶת־
*** we-saw and-there (33) great-sizes men-of in-her we-saw that the-people

הַנְּפִילִים בְּנֵי עֲנָק מִן־ הַנְּפִלִים וַנְּהִי
and-we-seemed the-Nephilim from Anak descendants-of the-Nephilim

בְעֵינֵינוּ כַּחֲגָבִים וְכֵן הָיִינוּ בְּעֵינֵיהֶם׃
in-eyes-of-them we-were and-same like-grasshoppers in-eyes-of-us

וַתִּשָּׂא כָּל־ הָעֵדָה וַיִּתְּנוּ אֶת־ קוֹלָם
voice-of-them *** and-they-gave the-community all-of and-she-raised (14:1)

and Aaron and the whole Israelite community at Kadesh in the Desert of Paran. There they reported to them and to the whole assembly and showed them the fruit of the land. 27 They gave Moses this account: "We went into the land to which you sent us, and it does flow with milk and honey! Here is its fruit. 28 But the people who live there are powerful, and the cities are fortified and very large. We even saw descendants of Anak there. 29 The Amalekites live in the Negev; the Hittites, Jebusites and Amorites live in the hill country; and the Canaanites live near the sea and along the Jordan."

30 Then Caleb silenced the people before Moses and said, "We should go up and take possession of the land, for we can certainly do it."

31 But the men who had gone up with him said, "We can't attack those people; they are stronger than we are." 32 And they spread among the Israelites a bad report about the land they had explored. They said, "The land we explored devours those living in it. All the people we saw there are of great size. 33 We saw the Nephilim there (the descendants of Anak come from the Nephilim). We seemed like grasshoppers in our own eyes, and we looked the same to them."

*The People Rebel*

14 That night all the people of the community raised their voices and

וַיִּבְכּוּ הָעָם בַּלַּיְלָה הַהוּא׃ וַיִּלֹּנוּ
and-they-grumbled (2) the-that through-the-night the-people and-they-wept

עַל־ מֹשֶׁה וְעַל־ אַהֲרֹן כֹּל בְּנֵי יִשְׂרָאֵל וַיֹּאמְרוּ אֲלֵהֶם
to-them and-they-said Israel sons-of all-of Aaron and-against Moses against

כָּל־ הָעֵדָה לוּ־ מַתְנוּ בְּאֶרֶץ מִצְרַיִם אוֹ בַּמִּדְבָּר
in-the-desert or Egypt in-land-of we-died if-only the-assembly whole-of

הַזֶּה לוּ־ מָתְנוּ׃ וְלָמָה יְהוָה מֵבִיא אֹתָנוּ אֶל־הָאָרֶץ הַזֹּאת
the-this the-land to us bringing Yahweh now-why? (3) we-died if-only the-this

לִנְפֹּל בַּחֶרֶב נָשֵׁינוּ וְטַפֵּנוּ יִהְיוּ לָבַז
as-plunder they-will-be and-child-of-us wives-of-us by-the-sword to-fall

הֲלוֹא טוֹב לָנוּ שׁוּב מִצְרָיְמָה׃ וַיֹּאמְרוּ אִישׁ אֶל־ אָחִיו
other-of-him to each and-they-said (4) to-Egypt to-go-back for-us better not?

נִתְּנָה רֹאשׁ וְנָשׁוּבָה מִצְרָיְמָה׃ וַיִּפֹּל מֹשֶׁה
Moses and-he-fell (5) to-Egypt and-we-should-go-back leader we-should-choose

וְאַהֲרֹן עַל־ פְּנֵיהֶם לִפְנֵי כָּל־ קְהַל עֲדַת
assembly-of gathering-of whole-of in-front-of faces-of-them on and-Aaron

בְּנֵי יִשְׂרָאֵל׃ וִיהוֹשֻׁעַ בִּן־ נוּן וְכָלֵב בֶּן־ יְפֻנֶּה מִן־
among Jephunneh son-of and-Caleb Nun son-of and-Joshua (6) Israel sons-of

הַתָּרִים אֶת־ הָאָרֶץ קָרְעוּ בִּגְדֵיהֶם׃ וַיֹּאמְרוּ
and-they-said (7) clothes-of-them they-tore the-land *** the-ones-exploring

אֶל־ כָּל־ עֲדַת בְּנֵי־ יִשְׂרָאֵל לֵאמֹר הָאָרֶץ אֲשֶׁר עָבַרְנוּ
we-passed that the-land to-say Israel sons-of assembly-of entire-of to

בָהּ לָתוּר אֹתָהּ טוֹבָה הָאָרֶץ מְאֹד מְאֹד׃ אִם־ חָפֵץ
he-is-pleased if (8) very very the-land good her to-explore through-her

בָּנוּ יְהוָה וְהֵבִיא אֹתָנוּ אֶל־ הָאָרֶץ הַזֹּאת וּנְתָנָהּ
and-he-will-give-her the-that the-land into us then-he-will-lead Yahweh with-us

לָנוּ אֶרֶץ אֲשֶׁר־הִוא זָבַת חָלָב וּדְבָשׁ׃ אַךְ בַּיהוָה אַל־
not against-Yahweh only (9) and-honey milk flowing-of she that land to-us

תִּמְרֹדוּ וְאַתֶּם אַל־ תִּירְאוּ אֶת־ עַם הָאָרֶץ כִּי לַחְמֵנוּ הֵם
they food-of-us for the-land people-of *** you-fear not and-you you-rebel

סָר צִלָּם מֵעֲלֵיהֶם וַיהוָה אִתָּנוּ אַל־
not with-us but-Yahweh from-over-them protection-of-them he-is-gone

תִּירָאֻם׃ וַיֹּאמְרוּ כָּל־ הָעֵדָה לִרְגּוֹם אֹתָם
them to-stone the-assembly whole-of but-they-talked (10) you-fear-them

בָּאֲבָנִים וּכְבוֹד יְהוָה נִרְאָה בְּאֹהֶל מוֹעֵד אֶל־
to Meeting in-Tent-of he-appeared Yahweh then-glory-of with-the-stones

כָּל־ בְּנֵי יִשְׂרָאֵל׃ וַיֹּאמֶר יְהוָה אֶל־ מֹשֶׁה עַד־ אָנָה
when? until Moses to Yahweh and-he-said (11) Israel sons-of all-of

wept aloud. 2 All the Israelites
grumbled against Moses and
Aaron, and the whole assembly said to them, "If only we
had died in Egypt! Or in this
desert! 3 Why is the LORD
bringing us to this land only
to let us fall by the sword? Our
wives and children will be
taken as plunder. Wouldn't it
be better for us to go back to
Egypt?" 4 And they said to
each other, "We should choose
a leader and go back to Egypt."
5 Then Moses and Aaron fell
facedown in front of the
whole Israelite assembly gathered there. 6 Joshua son of Nun
and Caleb son of Jephunneh,
who were among those who
had explored the land, tore
their clothes 7 and said to the
entire Israelite assembly, "The
land we passed through and
explored is exceedingly good.
8 If the LORD is pleased with us,
he will lead us into that land,
a land flowing with milk and
honey, and will give it to us.
9 Only do not rebel against the
LORD. And do not be afraid of
the people of the land, because
we will swallow them up.
Their protection is gone, but
the LORD is with us. Do not be
afraid of them."

10 But the whole assembly
talked about stoning them.
Then the glory of the LORD appeared at the Tent of Meeting
to all the Israelites. 11 The LORD
said to Moses, "How long will

יְנַאֲצֻנִי הָעָם הַזֶּה וְעַד־ אָנָה לֹא־
not when? and-until the-this the-people will-they-treat-with-contempt-me

יַאֲמִינוּ בִי בְּכֹל הָאֹתוֹת אֲשֶׁר עָשִׂיתִי בְּקִרְבּוֹ׃
among-him I-performed that the-signs despite-all-of in-me will-they-believe

(12) אַכֶּנּוּ בַדֶּבֶר וְאוֹרִשֶׁנּוּ וְאֶעֱשֶׂה
but-I-will-make and-I-will-destroy-him with-the-plague I-will-strike-him (12)

אֹתְךָ לְגוֹי־ גָּדוֹל וְעָצוּם מִמֶּנּוּ׃ (13) וַיֹּאמֶר מֹשֶׁה אֶל־
to Moses but-he-said (13) than-him and-stronger greater into-nation you

יְהוָה וְשָׁמְעוּ מִצְרַיִם כִּי־ הֶעֱלִיתָ בְכֹחֲךָ
by-power-of-you you-brought-up that Egyptians then-they-will-hear Yahweh

אֶת־ הָעָם הַזֶּה מִקִּרְבּוֹ׃ (14) וְאָמְרוּ אֶל־
to and-they-will-tell (14) from-among-him the-this the-people ***

יוֹשֵׁב הָאָרֶץ הַזֹּאת שָׁמְעוּ כִּי־ אַתָּה יְהוָה בְּקֶרֶב
in-midst-of Yahweh you that they-heard the-this the-land one-inhabiting-of

הָעָם הַזֶּה אֲשֶׁר־עַיִן בְּעַיִן נִרְאָה ׀ אַתָּה יְהוָה וַעֲנָנְךָ
and-cloud-of-you Yahweh you he-was-seen to-eye eye that the-this the-people

עֹמֵד עֲלֵהֶם וּבְעַמֻּד עָנָן אַתָּה הֹלֵךְ לִפְנֵיהֶם יוֹמָם
by-day before-them going you cloud and-in-pillar-of over-them staying

וּבְעַמּוּד אֵשׁ לָיְלָה׃ (15) וְהֵמַתָּה אֶת־ הָעָם הַזֶּה כְּאִישׁ
as-man the-this the-people *** if-you-kill (15) night fire and-in-pillar-of

אֶחָד וְאָמְרוּ הַגּוֹיִם אֲשֶׁר־ שָׁמְעוּ אֶת־ שִׁמְעֲךָ לֵאמֹר׃
to-say report-of-you *** they-heard who the-nations then-they-will-say one

(16) מִבִּלְתִּי יְכֹלֶת יְהוָה לְהָבִיא אֶת־ הָעָם הַזֶּה אֶל־
into the-this the-people *** to-bring Yahweh to-be-able because-not (16)

הָאָרֶץ אֲשֶׁר־ נִשְׁבַּע לָהֶם וַיִּשְׁחָטֵם בַּמִּדְבָּר׃
in-the-desert then-he-slaughtered-them to-them he-promised that the-land

(17) וְעַתָּה יִגְדַּל־ נָא כֹּחַ אֲדֹנָי כַּאֲשֶׁר דִּבַּרְתָּ לֵאמֹר׃
to-say you-declared just-as Lord strength-of now! may-he-display so-now (17)

(18) יְהוָה אֶרֶךְ אַפַּיִם וְרַב־ חֶסֶד נֹשֵׂא עָוֹן וָפָשַׁע
and-rebellion sin forgiving love and-abundant-of angers slow-of Yahweh (18)

וְנַקֵּה לֹא יְנַקֶּה פֹּקֵד עֲוֹן אָבוֹת
fathers sin-of punishing he-will-leave-unpunished not yet-to-leave-unpunished

עַל־ בָּנִים עַל־ שִׁלֵּשִׁים וְעַל־ רִבֵּעִים׃ (19) סְלַח־ נָא לַעֲוֹן
to-sin-of now! forgive! (19) fourth-ones and-to third-ones to children on

הָעָם הַזֶּה כְּגֹדֶל חַסְדֶּךָ וְכַאֲשֶׁר נָשָׂאתָה
you-pardoned and-just-as love-of-you as-greatness-of the-this the-people

לָעָם הַזֶּה מִמִּצְרַיִם וְעַד־ הֵנָּה׃ (20) וַיֹּאמֶר יְהוָה
Yahweh and-he-replied (20) now and-until from-Egypt the-this to-the-people

these people treat me with contempt? How long will they refuse to believe in me, in spite of all the miraculous signs I have performed among them? 12 I will strike them down with a plague and destroy them, but I will make you into a nation greater and stronger than they."

13 Moses said to the LORD, "Then the Egyptians will hear about it! By your power you brought these people up from among them. 14 And they will tell the inhabitants of this land about it. They have already heard that you, O LORD, are with these people and that you, O LORD, have been seen face to face, that your cloud stays over them, and that you go before them in a pillar of cloud by day and a pillar of fire by night. 15 If you put these people to death all at one time, the nations who have heard this report about you will say, 16 'The LORD was not able to bring these people into the land he promised them on oath; so he slaughtered them in the desert.'

17 "Now may the Lord's strength be displayed, just as you have declared: 18 'The LORD is slow to anger, abounding in love and forgiving sin and rebellion. Yet he does not leave the guilty unpunished; he punishes the children for the sin of the fathers to the third and fourth generation.' 19 In accordance with your great love, forgive the sin of these people, just as you have pardoned them from the time they left Egypt until now."

20 The LORD replied, "I have

סָלַחְתִּי כִּדְבָרֶךָ׃ וְאוּלָם חַי־ אָנִי וְיִמָּלֵא כְבוֹד־
glory-of and-he-fills I alive but-surely (21) as-request-of-you I-forgave

יְהוָה אֶת־ כָּל־ הָאָרֶץ׃ כִּי כָל־ הָאֲנָשִׁים הָרֹאִים אֶת־
*** the-ones-seeing the-men all-of indeed (22) the-earth whole-of *** Yahweh

כְּבֹדִי וְאֶת־ אֹתֹתַי אֲשֶׁר־ עָשִׂיתִי בְמִצְרַיִם וּבַמִּדְבָּר
and-in-the-desert in-Egypt I-performed that signs-of-me and glory-of-me

וַיְנַסּוּ אֹתִי זֶה עֶשֶׂר פְּעָמִים וְלֹא שָׁמְעוּ בְּקוֹלִי׃ אִם־
not (23) to-voice-of-me they-obeyed and-not times ten now me but-they-tested

יִרְאוּ אֶת־ הָאָרֶץ אֲשֶׁר נִשְׁבַּעְתִּי לַאֲבֹתָם וְכָל־
and-all-of to-fathers-of-them I-promised that the-land *** they-will-see

מְנַאֲצַי לֹא יִרְאוּהָ׃ וְעַבְדִּי
but-servant-of-me (24) they-will-see-her not ones-treating-with-contempt-me

כָלֵב עֵקֶב הָיְתָה רוּחַ אַחֶרֶת עִמּוֹ וַיְמַלֵּא אַחֲרָי
after-me and-he-is-wholehearted in-him different spirit she-is because Caleb

וַהֲבִיאֹתִיו אֶל־ הָאָרֶץ אֲשֶׁר־ בָּא שָׁמָּה וְזַרְעוֹ
and-seed-of-him to-there he-went that the-land into then-I-will-bring-him

יוֹרִשֶׁנָּה׃ וְהָעֲמָלֵקִי וְהַכְּנַעֲנִי יוֹשֵׁב
living and-the-Canaanite now-the-Amalekite (25) he-will-inherit-her

בָּעֵמֶק מָחָר פְּנוּ וּסְעוּ לָכֶם הַמִּדְבָּר דֶּרֶךְ
route-of the-desert for-you and-set-out! turn-back! tomorrow in-the-valley

יַם־ סוּף׃ וַיְדַבֵּר יְהוָה אֶל־מֹשֶׁה וְאֶל־ אַהֲרֹן לֵאמֹר׃ עַד־
until (27) to-say Aaron and-to Moses to Yahweh and-he-said (26) Reed Sea-of

מָתַי לָעֵדָה הָרָעָה הַזֹּאת אֲשֶׁר הֵמָּה מַלִּינִים
ones-grumbling they that the-this the-wicked for-the-community when?

עָלָי אֶת־ תְּלֻנּוֹת בְּנֵי יִשְׂרָאֵל אֲשֶׁר הֵמָּה מַלִּינִים
ones-grumbling they that Israel sons-of complaints-of *** against-me

עָלַי שָׁמָעְתִּי׃ אֱמֹר אֲלֵהֶם חַי־ אָנִי נְאֻם־ יְהוָה אִם־ לֹא
surely that Yahweh declaring-of I alive to-them tell! (28) I-heard against-me

כַּאֲשֶׁר דִּבַּרְתֶּם בְּאָזְנָי כֵּן אֶעֱשֶׂה לָכֶם׃ בַּמִּדְבָּר
in-the-desert (29) to-you I-will-do so in-ears-of-me you-said just-as

הַזֶּה יִפְּלוּ פִגְרֵיכֶם וְכָל־ פְּקֻדֵיכֶם
ones-being-counted-of-you and-all-of bodies-of-you they-will-fall the-this

לְכָל־ מִסְפַּרְכֶם מִבֶּן עֶשְׂרִים שָׁנָה וָמָעְלָה אֲשֶׁר הֲלִינֹתֶם
you-grumbled who or-more year twenty from-son-of census-of-you in-every-of

עָלָי׃ אִם־ אַתֶּם תָּבֹאוּ אֶל־ הָאָרֶץ אֲשֶׁר נָשָׂאתִי אֶת־
*** I-lifted that the-land into you-will-enter you not (30) against-me

יָדִי לְשַׁכֵּן אֶתְכֶם בָּהּ כִּי אִם־ כָּלֵב בֶּן־ יְפֻנֶּה
Jephunneh son-of Caleb except only in-her you to-make-home hand-of-me

forgiven them, as you asked. [21]Nevertheless, as surely as I live and as surely as the glory of the LORD fills the whole earth, [22]not one of the men who saw my glory and the miraculous signs I performed in Egypt and in the desert but who disobeyed me and tested me ten times— [23]not one of them will ever see the land I promised on oath to their forefathers. No one who has treated me with contempt will ever see it. [24]But because my servant Caleb has a different spirit and follows me wholeheartedly, I will bring him into the land he went to, and his descendants will inherit it. [25]Since the Amalekites and Canaanites are living in the valleys, turn back tomorrow and set out toward the desert along the route to the Red Sea.[d]"

[26]The LORD said to Moses and Aaron: [27]"How long will this wicked community grumble against me? I have heard the complaints of these grumbling Israelites. [28]So tell them, 'As surely as I live, declares the LORD, I will do to you the very things I heard you say: [29]In this desert your bodies will fall—every one of you twenty years old or more who was counted in the census and who has grumbled against me. [30]Not one of you will enter the land I swore with uplifted hand to make your home, except Caleb son of Jephunneh

[d]25 Hebrew *Yam Suph;* that is, Sea of Reeds

ויהושע בן־ נון׃ (31) וטפכם אשר אמרתם לבז
and-Joshua son-of Nun (31) and-child-of-you that you-said as-plunder

יהיה והביאתי אתם וידעו את־ הארץ אשר
he-would-be now-I-will-bring-in them and-they-will-enjoy *** the-land that

מאסתם בה׃ (32) ופגריכם אתם יפלו
you-rejected against-her (32) but-bodies-of-you you they-will-fall

במדבר הזה׃ (33) ובניכם יהיו רעים
in-the-desert the-this (33) and-children-of-you they-will-be ones-herding

במדבר ארבעים שנה ונשאו את־ זנותיכם
in-the-desert forty year and-they-will-suffer *** unfaithfulnesses-of-you

עד־ תם פגריכם במדבר׃ (34) במספר הימים
until to-be-last bodies-of-you in-the-desert (34) for-number-of the-days

אשר־ תרתם את־הארץ ארבעים יום יום לשנה יום לשנה
that you-explored *** the-land forty day day for-the-year day for-the-year

תשאו את־ עונתיכם ארבעים שנה וידעתם את־
you-will-suffer *** sins-of-you forty year and-you-will-know ***

תנואתי (35) אני יהוה דברתי אם־ לא | זאת אעשה לכל־
opposition-of-me (35) I Yahweh I-spoke that surely this I-will-do to-whole-of

העדה הרעה הזאת הנועדים עלי במדבר
the-community the-wicked the-this the-ones-banding against-me in-the-desert

הזה יתמו ושם ימתו׃ (36) והאנשים אשר־
the-this they-will-meet-end and-here they-will-die (36) so-the-men whom

שלח משה לתור את־ הארץ וישבו וילונו
he-sent Moses to-explore *** the-land and-they-returned and-they-made-grumble

עליו את־ כל־ העדה להוציא דבה על־ הארץ׃
against-him *** whole-of the-community by-to-spread bad-report about the-land

(37) וימתו האנשים מוציאי דבת־ הארץ רעה
(37) so-they-died the-men ones-spreading-of report-of the-land bad

במגפה לפני יהוה׃ (38) ויהושע בן־ נון וכלב בן־
of-the-plague before Yahweh (38) only-Joshua son-of Nun and-Caleb son-of

יפנה חיו מן־ האנשים ההם ההלכים לתור את־
Jephunneh they-survived from the-men the-these the-ones-going to-explore ***

הארץ׃ (39) וידבר משה את־ הדברים האלה אל־ כל־
the-land (39) when-he-reported Moses *** the-things the-these to all-of

בני ישראל ויתאבלו העם מאד׃ (40) וישכמו
sons-of Israel then-they-mourned the-people bitterly (40) and-they-rose

בבקר ויעלו אל־ ראש־ ההר לאמר הננו
in-the-morning and-they-went-up to height-of the-hill-country to-say see-us!

and Joshua son of Nun. [31]As for your children that you said would be taken as plunder, I will bring them in to enjoy the land you have rejected. [32]But you—your bodies will fall in this desert. [33]Your children will be shepherds here for forty years, suffering for your unfaithfulness, until the last of your bodies lies in the desert. [34]For forty years—one year for each of the forty days you explored the land—you will suffer for your sins and know what it is like to have me against you.' [35]I, the LORD, have spoken, and I will surely do these things to this whole wicked community, which has banded together against me. They will meet their end in this desert; here they will die."

[36]So the men Moses had sent to explore the land, who returned and made the whole community grumble against him by spreading a bad report about it— [37]these men responsible for spreading the bad report about the land were struck down and died of a plague before the LORD. [38]Of the men who went to explore the land, only Joshua son of Nun and Caleb son of Jephunneh survived.

[39]When Moses reported this to all the Israelites, they mourned bitterly. [40]Early the next morning they went up toward the high hill country.

°36 ק וילינו

וְעָלִינוּ אֶל־הַמָּקוֹם אֲשֶׁר־אָמַר יְהוָה כִּי חָטָאנוּ׃
we-sinned indeed Yahweh he-promised that the-place to now-we-will-go-up

וַיֹּאמֶר מֹשֶׁה לָמָּה זֶּה אַתֶּם עֹבְרִים אֶת־פִּי יְהוָה
Yahweh command-of *** ones-disobeying you now why? Moses but-he-said (41)

וְהִוא לֹא תִצְלָח׃ אַל־תַּעֲלוּ כִּי אֵין יְהוָה
Yahweh he-is-not for you-go-up not (42) she-will-succeed not now-this

בְּקִרְבְּכֶם וְלֹא תִּנָּגְפוּ לִפְנֵי אֹיְבֵיכֶם׃ כִּי
for (43) being-enemies-of-you by you-will-be-defeated so-not in-midst-of-you

הָעֲמָלֵקִי וְהַכְּנַעֲנִי שָׁם לִפְנֵיכֶם וּנְפַלְתֶּם
and-you-will-fall before-faces-of-you there and-the-Canaanite the-Amalekite

בֶּחָרֶב כִּי־עַל־כֵּן שַׁבְתֶּם מֵאַחֲרֵי יְהוָה וְלֹא־יִהְיֶה
he-will-be and-not Yahweh away-from you-turned this of because by-the-sword

יְהוָה עִמָּכֶם׃ וַיַּעְפִּלוּ לַעֲלוֹת אֶל־רֹאשׁ הָהָר
the-hill-country height-of to to-go-up but-they-presumed (44) with-you Yahweh

וַאֲרוֹן בְּרִית־יְהוָה וּמֹשֶׁה לֹא־מָשׁוּ מִקֶּרֶב
from-within they-moved not and-Moses Yahweh covenant-of though-ark-of

הַמַּחֲנֶה׃ וַיֵּרֶד הָעֲמָלֵקִי וְהַכְּנַעֲנִי
and-the-Canaanite the-Amalekite then-he-came-down (45) the-camp

הַיֹּשֵׁב בָּהָר הַהוּא וַיַּכּוּם
and-they-attacked-them the-that in-the-hill-country the-one-living

וַיַּכְּתוּם עַד־הַחָרְמָה׃ וַיְדַבֵּר יְהוָה אֶל־מֹשֶׁה לֵּאמֹר׃
to-say Moses to Yahweh and-he-spoke (15:1) the-Hormah to and-they-beat-them

דַּבֵּר אֶל־בְּנֵי יִשְׂרָאֵל וְאָמַרְתָּ אֲלֵהֶם כִּי תָבֹאוּ אֶל־אֶרֶץ
land-of into you-enter after to-them and-you-say Israel sons-of to speak! (2)

מוֹשְׁבֹתֵיכֶם אֲשֶׁר אֲנִי נֹתֵן לָכֶם׃ וַעֲשִׂיתֶם אִשֶּׁה
fire-offering and-you-present (3) to-you giving I that homes-of-you

לַיהוָה עֹלָה אוֹ־זֶבַח לְפַלֵּא־נֶדֶר אוֹ בִנְדָבָה
for-freewill-offering or vow to-fulfill sacrifice or burnt-offering to-Yahweh

אוֹ בְּמֹעֲדֵיכֶם לַעֲשׂוֹת רֵיחַ נִיחֹחַ לַיהוָה מִן־הַבָּקָר
the-herd from to-Yahweh pleasant aroma-of to-present for-festivals-of-you or

אוֹ מִן־הַצֹּאן׃ וְהִקְרִיב הַמַּקְרִיב קָרְבָּנוֹ
offering-of-him the-one-bringing then-he-shall-present (4) the-flock from or

לַיהוָה מִנְחָה סֹלֶת עִשָּׂרוֹן בָּלוּל בִּרְבִעִית הַהִין
the-hin with-fourth-of being-mixed tenth fine-flour grain-offering to-Yahweh

שָׁמֶן׃ וְיַיִן לַנֶּסֶךְ רְבִיעִית הַהִין תַּעֲשֶׂה עַל־
with you-prepare the-hin fourth-of as-the-drink-offering and-wine (5) oil

הָעֹלָה אוֹ לַזָּבַח לַכֶּבֶשׂ הָאֶחָד׃ אוֹ
or (6) the-each with-the-lamb with-the-sacrifice or the-burnt-offering

"We have sinned," they said. "We will go up to the place the LORD promised."

[41]But Moses said, "Why are you disobeying the LORD's command? This will not succeed! [42]Do not go up, because the LORD is not with you. You will be defeated by your enemies, [43]for the Amalekites and Canaanites will face you there. Because you have turned away from the LORD, he will not be with you and you will fall by the sword."

[44]Nevertheless, in their presumption they went up toward the high hill country, though neither Moses nor the ark of the LORD's covenant moved from the camp. [45]Then the Amalekites and Canaanites who lived in that hill country came down and attacked them and beat them down all the way to Hormah.

*Supplementary Offerings*

**15** The LORD said to Moses, [2]"Speak to the Israelites and say to them: 'After you enter the land I am giving you as a home [3]and you present to the LORD offerings made by fire, from the herd or the flock, as an aroma pleasing to the LORD—whether burnt offerings or sacrifices, for special vows or freewill offerings or festival offerings—[4]then the one who brings his offering shall present to the LORD a grain offering of a tenth of an ephah[e] of fine flour mixed with a fourth of a hin[f] of oil. [5]With each lamb for the burnt offering or the sacrifice, prepare a fourth of a hin of wine as a drink offering.

[e]4 That is, probably about 2 quarts (about 2 liters)
[f]4 That is, probably about 1 quart (about 1 liter); also in verse 5

לָאַ֫יִל תַּעֲשֶׂה מִנְחָה סֹלֶת שְׁנֵי עֶשְׂרֹנִים בְּלוּלָה
being-mixed tenths two-of fine-flour grain-offering you-prepare with-the-ram

בַשֶּׁמֶן שְׁלִשִׁית הַהִין׃ (7) וְיַיִן לַנֶּסֶךְ שְׁלִשִׁית
third-of as-the-drink-offering and-wine (7) the-hin third-of with-the-oil

הַהִין תַּקְרִיב רֵיחַ־ נִיחֹחַ לַיהוָה׃ (8) וְכִי־ תַעֲשֶׂה בֶן־
young-of you-prepare and-when (8) to-Yahweh pleasant aroma-of you-offer the-hin

בָּקָר עֹלָה אוֹ־ זָבַח לְפַלֵּא־ נֶדֶר אוֹ־ שְׁלָמִים
fellowship-offerings or vow to-fulfill sacrifice or burnt-offering herd

לַיהוָה׃ (9) וְהִקְרִיב עַל־ בֶּן־ הַבָּקָר מִנְחָה סֹלֶת
flour grain-offering the-herd young-of with and-he-shall-bring (9) to-Yahweh

שְׁלֹשָׁה עֶשְׂרֹנִים בָּלוּל בַּשֶּׁמֶן חֲצִי הַהִין׃ (10) וְיַיִן תַּקְרִיב
you-bring and-wine (10) the-hin half-of with-the-oil being-mixed tenths three

לַנֶּסֶךְ חֲצִי הַהִין אִשֵּׁה רֵיחַ־ נִיחֹחַ
pleasant aroma-of fire-offering-of the-hin half-of as-the-drink-offering

לַיהוָה׃ (11) כָּכָה יֵעָשֶׂה לַשּׁוֹר הָאֶחָד אוֹ לָאַיִל
for-the-ram or the-each for-the-bull he-must-be-done this (11) to-Yahweh

הָאֶחָד אוֹ־ לַשֶּׂה בַכְּבָשִׂים אוֹ בָעִזִּים׃ (12) כַּמִּסְפָּר
as-the-many (12) from-the-goats or from-the-lambs for-the-young or the-each

אֲשֶׁר תַּעֲשׂוּ כָּכָה תַּעֲשׂוּ לָאֶחָד כְּמִסְפָּרָם (13) כָּל־
everyone-of (13) as-many-of-them for-the-each you-do this you-prepare that

הָאֶזְרָח יַעֲשֶׂה־ כָּכָה אֶת־ אֵלֶּה לְהַקְרִיב אִשֵּׁה רֵיחַ־
aroma-of fire-offering-of to-bring these *** this he-must-do the-native-born

נִיחֹחַ לַיהוָה׃ (14) וְכִי־ יָגוּר אִתְּכֶם גֵּר אוֹ אֲשֶׁר־
whoever or alien with-you he-lives and-when (14) to-Yahweh pleasant

בְּתוֹכְכֶם לְדֹרֹתֵיכֶם וְעָשָׂה אִשֵּׁה רֵיחַ־
aroma-of fire-offering-of and-he-presents for-generations-of-you among-you

נִיחֹחַ לַיהוָה כַּאֲשֶׁר תַּעֲשׂוּ כֵּן יַעֲשֶׂה׃ (15) הַקָּהָל חֻקָּה
rule the-community (15) he-must-do so you-do exactly-as to-Yahweh pleasant

אַחַת לָכֶם וְלַגֵּר הַגָּר חֻקַּת עוֹלָם
lasting ordinance-of the-one-living and-for-the-alien for-you same

לְדֹרֹתֵיכֶם כָּכֶם כַּגֵּר יִהְיֶה לִפְנֵי יְהוָה׃
Yahweh before he-shall-be so-the-alien as-you for-generations-of-you

(16) תּוֹרָה אַחַת וּמִשְׁפָּט אֶחָד יִהְיֶה לָכֶם וְלַגֵּר
and-to-the-alien to-you he-will-apply same and-regulation same law (16)

הַגָּר אִתְּכֶם׃ (17) וַיְדַבֵּר יְהוָה אֶל־מֹשֶׁה לֵּאמֹר׃ (18) דַּבֵּר
speak! (18) to-say Moses to Yahweh and-he-spoke (17) among-you the-one-living

אֶל־ בְּנֵי יִשְׂרָאֵל וְאָמַרְתָּ אֲלֵהֶם בְּבֹאֲכֶם אֶל־ הָאָרֶץ אֲשֶׁר
where the-land into when-to-enter-you to-them and-you-say Israel sons-of to

6" 'With a ram prepare a grain offering of two-tenths of an ephah[g] of fine flour mixed with a third of a hin[h] of oil,
7and a third of a hin of wine as a drink offering. Offer it as an aroma pleasing to the LORD.
8" 'When you prepare a young bull as a burnt offering or sacrifice, for a special vow or a fellowship offering[i] to the LORD,
9bring with the bull a grain offering of three-tenths of an ephah[j] of fine flour mixed with half a hin[k] of oil.
10Also bring half a hin of wine as a drink offering. It will be an offering made by fire, an aroma pleasing to the LORD.
11Each bull or ram, each lamb or young goat, is to be prepared in this manner.
12Do this for each one, for as many as you prepare.
13" 'Everyone who is native-born must do these things in this way when he brings an offering made by fire as an aroma pleasing to the LORD.
14For the generations to come, whenever an alien or anyone else living among you presents an offering made by fire as an aroma pleasing to the LORD, he must do exactly as you do.
15The community is to have the same rules for you and for the alien living among you; this is a lasting ordinance for the generations to come. You and the alien shall be the same before the LORD:
16The same laws and regulations will apply both to you and to the alien living among you.' "
17The LORD said to Moses,
18"Speak to the Israelites and say to them: 'When you enter the land to which I am taking

g6 That is, probably about 4 quarts (about 4.5 liters)
h6 That is, probably about 1 1/4 quarts (about 1.2 liters); also in verse 7
i8 Traditionally *peace offering*
j9 That is, probably about 6 quarts (about 6.5 liters)
k9 That is, probably about 2 quarts (about 2 liters); also in verse 10

אֲנִי מֵבִיא אֶתְכֶם שָׁמָּה׃ וְהָיָה בַּאֲכָלְכֶם מִלֶּחֶם
from-food-of when-to-eat-you and-he-will-be (19) to-there you taking I

הָאָרֶץ תָּרִימוּ תְרוּמָה לַיהוָה׃ רֵאשִׁית עֲרִסֹתֵכֶם
ground-meal-of-you first-of (20) to-Yahweh portion you-must-present the-land

חַלָּה תָּרִימוּ תְרוּמָה כִּתְרוּמַת גֹּרֶן כֵּן תָּרִימוּ אֹתָהּ׃
her you-present so threshing-floor as-offering-of offering you-present cake

מֵרֵאשִׁית עֲרִסֹתֵיכֶם תִּתְּנוּ לַיהוָה תְּרוּמָה
offering to-Yahweh you-give ground-meal-of-you from-first-of (21)

לְדֹרֹתֵיכֶם׃ וְכִי תִשְׁגּוּ וְלֹא תַעֲשׂוּ
you-keep and-not you-are-unintentional now-if (22) through-generations-of-you

אֵת כָּל־ הַמִּצְוֺת הָאֵלֶּה אֲשֶׁר־ דִּבֶּר יְהוָה אֶל־מֹשֶׁה׃ אֵת כָּל־
any *** (23) Moses to Yahweh he-gave that the-these the-commands any-of ***

אֲשֶׁר צִוָּה יְהוָה אֲלֵיכֶם בְּיַד־ מֹשֶׁה מִן־ הַיּוֹם אֲשֶׁר
that the-day from Moses by-hand-of to-you Yahweh he-commanded that

צִוָּה יְהוָה וָהָלְאָה לְדֹרֹתֵיכֶם׃ וְהָיָה אִם
if and-he-is (24) through-generations-of-you and-onwards Yahweh he-commanded

מֵעֵינֵי הָעֵדָה נֶעֶשְׂתָה לִשְׁגָגָה וְעָשׂוּ
then-they-must-offer as-unintentional he-is-done the-community from-eyes-of

כָל־ הָעֵדָה פַּר בֶּן־ בָּקָר אֶחָד לְעֹלָה לְרֵיחַ
as-aroma-of for-burnt-offering one herd young-of bull the-community whole-of

נִיחֹחַ לַיהוָה וּמִנְחָתוֹ וְנִסְכּוֹ
and-drink-offering-of-him and-grain-offering-of-him to-Yahweh pleasant

כַּמִּשְׁפָּט וּשְׂעִיר־ עִזִּים אֶחָד לְחַטָּת׃
as-sin-offering one goats and-male-goat-of as-the-prescription

וְכִפֶּר הַכֹּהֵן עַל־ כָּל־ עֲדַת בְּנֵי יִשְׂרָאֵל
Israel sons-of community-of whole-of for the-priest and-he-must-atone (25)

וְנִסְלַח לָהֶם כִּי־ שְׁגָגָה הִוא וְהֵם הֵבִיאוּ
they-brought and-they she unintentional for to-them and-he-will-be-forgiven

אֶת־ קָרְבָּנָם אִשֶּׁה לַיהוָה וְחַטָּאתָם לִפְנֵי
to and-sin-offering-of-them to-Yahweh fire-offering offering-of-them ***

יְהוָה עַל־ שִׁגְגָתָם׃ וְנִסְלַח לְכָל־ עֲדַת
community-of to-whole-of and-he-will-be-forgiven (26) wrong-of-them for Yahweh

בְּנֵי יִשְׂרָאֵל וְלַגֵּר הַגָּר בְּתוֹכָם כִּי לְכָל־
involving-all-of for among-them the-one-living and-to-the-alien Israel sons-of

הָעָם בִּשְׁגָגָה׃ וְאִם־ נֶפֶשׁ אַחַת תֶּחֱטָא
she-sins one person but-if (27) in-unintentional-wrong the-people

בִשְׁגָגָה וְהִקְרִיבָה עֵז בַּת־ שְׁנָתָהּ
year-of-her daughter-of female-goat then-she-must-bring with-no-intention

you [19]and you eat the food of
the land, present a portion as
an offering to the LORD.
[20]Present a cake from the first
of your ground meal and
present it as an offering from
the threshing floor. [21]Through-
out the generations to come
you are to give this offering to
the LORD from the first of your
ground meal.

*Offerings for Unintentional Sins*

[22]" 'Now if you unintentionally fail to keep any of these
commands the LORD gave
Moses— [23]any of the LORD's
commands to you through
him, from the day the LORD
gave them and continuing
through the generations to
come— [24]and if this is done
unintentionally without the
community being aware of it,
then the whole community is
to offer a young bull for a
burnt offering as an aroma
pleasing to the LORD, along
with its prescribed grain
offering and drink offering,
and a male goat for a sin
offering. [25]The priest is to
make atonement for the whole
Israelite community, and they
will be forgiven, for it was not
intentional and they have
brought to the LORD for their
wrong an offering made by
fire and a sin offering. [26]The
whole Israelite community
and the aliens living among
them will be forgiven, because
all the people were involved in
the unintentional wrong.
[27]" 'But if just one person
sins unintentionally, he must
bring a year-old female goat

לְחַטָּאת׃ (28) וְכִפֶּר הַכֹּהֵן עַל־ הַנֶּפֶשׁ
the-person for the-priest and-he-must-atone (28) for-sin-offering

הַשֹּׁגֶגֶת בְּחֶטְאָה בִשְׁגָגָה לִפְנֵי יְהוָה לְכַפֵּר
when-to-atone Yahweh before with-no-intention by-to-sin the-one-erring

עָלָיו וְנִסְלַח לוֹ׃ (29) הָאֶזְרָח בִּבְנֵי יִשְׂרָאֵל
Israel from-sons-of the-native (29) to-him then-he-will-be-forgiven for-him

וְלַגֵּר הַגָּר בְּתוֹכָם תּוֹרָה אַחַת יִהְיֶה לָכֶם
to-you he-applies one law among-them the-one-living and-for-the-alien

לָעֹשֶׂה בִּשְׁגָגָה׃ (30) וְהַנֶּפֶשׁ אֲשֶׁר־ תַּעֲשֶׂה ׀
she-sins who but-the-person (30) with-no-intention to-the-one-sinning

בְּיָד רָמָה מִן־ הָאֶזְרָח וּמִן־ הַגֵּר אֶת־ יְהוָה הוּא
he Yahweh *** the-alien or-whether the-native whether being-high with-hand

מְגַדֵּף וְנִכְרְתָה הַנֶּפֶשׁ הַהִוא מִקֶּרֶב עַמָּהּ׃
people-of-her from-among the-that the-person and-she-must-be-cut blaspheming

(31) כִּי דְבַר־ יְהוָה בָּזָה וְאֶת־ מִצְוָתוֹ הֵפַר
he-broke commandment-of-him and he-despised Yahweh word-of for (31)

הִכָּרֵת ׀ תִּכָּרֵת הַנֶּפֶשׁ הַהִוא עֲוֺנָה בָהּ׃
on-her guilt-of-her the-that the-person she-must-be-cut-off to-be-cut-off

(32) וַיִּהְיוּ בְנֵי־ יִשְׂרָאֵל בַּמִּדְבָּר וַיִּמְצְאוּ אִישׁ
man then-they-found in-the-desert Israel sons-of while-they-were (32)

מְקֹשֵׁשׁ עֵצִים בְּיוֹם הַשַּׁבָּת׃ (33) וַיַּקְרִיבוּ אֹתוֹ
him and-they-brought (33) the-Sabbath on-day-of woods gathering

הַמֹּצְאִים אֹתוֹ מְקֹשֵׁשׁ עֵצִים אֶל־ מֹשֶׁה וְאֶל־ אַהֲרֹן וְאֶל כָּל־
whole-of and-to Aaron and-to Moses to woods gathering him the-ones-finding

הָעֵדָה׃ (34) וַיַּנִּיחוּ אֹתוֹ בַּמִּשְׁמָר כִּי לֹא פֹרַשׁ
being-clear not for in-the-custody him and-they-kept (34) the-assembly

מַה־ יֵּעָשֶׂה לוֹ׃ (35) וַיֹּאמֶר יְהוָה אֶל־ מֹשֶׁה מוֹת
to-die Moses to Yahweh then-he-said (35) to-him he-should-be-done what

יוּמַת הָאִישׁ רָגוֹם אֹתוֹ בָאֲבָנִים כָּל־ הָעֵדָה
the-assembly whole-of with-the-stones him to-stone the-man he-must-die

מִחוּץ לַמַּחֲנֶה׃ (36) וַיֹּצִיאוּ אֹתוֹ כָּל־ הָעֵדָה אֶל־ מִחוּץ
outside to the-assembly whole-of him so-they-took (36) of-the-camp outside

לַמַּחֲנֶה וַיִּרְגְּמוּ אֹתוֹ בָּאֲבָנִים וַיָּמֹת כַּאֲשֶׁר
just-as and-he-died with-the-stones him and-they-stoned of-the-camp

צִוָּה יְהוָה אֶת־ מֹשֶׁה׃ (37) וַיֹּאמֶר יְהוָה אֶל־ מֹשֶׁה לֵּאמֹר׃
to-say Moses to Yahweh and-he-said (37) Moses *** Yahweh he-commanded

(38) דַּבֵּר אֶל־ בְּנֵי יִשְׂרָאֵל וְאָמַרְתָּ אֲלֵהֶם וְעָשׂוּ לָהֶם
for-them so-they-make to-them and-you-say Israel sons-of to speak! (38)

for a sin offering. 28 The priest
is to make atonement before
the LORD for the one who erred
by sinning unintentionally,
and when atonement has
been made for him, he will be
forgiven. 29 One and the same
law applies to everyone who
sins unintentionally, whether
he is a native-born Israelite or
an alien.

30 "'But anyone who sins
defiantly, whether native-
born or alien, blasphemes the
LORD, and that person must be
cut off from his people. 31 Because he has despised the
LORD's word and broken his
commands, that person must
surely be cut off; his guilt remains on him.'"

*The Sabbath-Breaker Put to Death*

32 While the Israelites were in
the desert, a man was found
gathering wood on the Sabbath day. 33 Those who found
him gathering wood brought
him to Moses and Aaron and
the whole assembly, 34 and
they kept him in custody, because it was not clear what
should be done to him. 35 Then
the LORD said to Moses, "The
man must die. The whole assembly must stone him outside the camp." 36 So the assembly took him outside the
camp and stoned him to
death, as the LORD com-
manded Moses.

*Tassels on Garments*

37 The LORD said to Moses,
38 "Speak to the Israelites and
say to them: 'Throughout the
generations to come you are to

צִיצִת עַל־ כַּנְפֵי בִגְדֵיהֶם לְדֹרֹתָם
through-generations-of-them garments-of-them corners-of on tassel

וְנָתְנוּ עַל־ צִיצִת הַכָּנָף פְּתִיל תְּכֵלֶת׃ וְהָיָה לָכֶם
to-you and-he-will-be (39) blue cord-of the-corner tassel-of on and-they-must-put

לְצִיצִת וּרְאִיתֶם אֹתוֹ וּזְכַרְתֶּם אֶת־ כָּל־ מִצְוֹת
commands-of all-of *** so-you-will-remember him and-you-will-see as-tassel

יְהוָה וַעֲשִׂיתֶם אֹתָם וְלֹא־ תָתֻרוּ אַחֲרֵי לְבַבְכֶם וְאַחֲרֵי
and-after heart-of-you after you-go and-not them so-you-may-obey Yahweh

עֵינֵיכֶם אֲשֶׁר־אַתֶּם זֹנִים אַחֲרֵיהֶם׃ לְמַעַן תִּזְכְּרוּ
you-will-remember then (40) after-them ones-prostituting you that eyes-of-you

וַעֲשִׂיתֶם אֶת־ כָּל־ מִצְוֹתָי וִהְיִיתֶם קְדֹשִׁים
ones-consecrated and-you-will-be commands-of-me all-of *** and-you-will-obey

לֵאלֹהֵיכֶם׃ אֲנִי יְהוָה אֱלֹהֵיכֶם אֲשֶׁר הוֹצֵאתִי אֶתְכֶם מֵאֶרֶץ
from-land-of you I-brought who God-of-you Yahweh I (41) to-God-of-you

מִצְרַיִם לִהְיוֹת לָכֶם לֵאלֹהִים אֲנִי יְהוָה אֱלֹהֵיכֶם׃ וַיִּקַּח
now-he-became-insolent (16:1) God-of-you Yahweh I as-God for-you to-be Egypt

קֹרַח בֶּן־ יִצְהָר בֶּן־ קְהָת בֶּן־ לֵוִי וְדָתָן וַאֲבִירָם בְּנֵי
sons-of and-Abiram and-Dathan Levi son-of Kohath son-of Izhar son-of Korah

אֱלִיאָב וְאוֹן בֶּן־ פֶּלֶת בְּנֵי רְאוּבֵן׃ וַיָּקֻמוּ לִפְנֵי
against and-they-rose-up (2) Reuben sons-of Peleth son-of and-On Eliab

מֹשֶׁה וַאֲנָשִׁים מִבְּנֵי־ יִשְׂרָאֵל חֲמִשִּׁים וּמָאתָיִם נְשִׂיאֵי
leaders-of and-two-hundreds fifty Israel from-sons-of and-men Moses

עֵדָה קְרִאֵי מוֹעֵד אַנְשֵׁי־ שֵׁם׃ וַיִּקָּהֲלוּ
and-they-gathered (3) name men-of council ones-appointed-of community

עַל־ מֹשֶׁה וְעַל־ אַהֲרֹן וַיֹּאמְרוּ אֲלֵהֶם רַב־ לָכֶם כִּי
for to-you too-far to-them and-they-said Aaron and-against Moses against

כָל־ הָעֵדָה כֻּלָּם קְדֹשִׁים וּבְתוֹכָם יְהוָה וּמַדּוּעַ
then-why? Yahweh and-with-them holy-ones all-of-them the-community whole-of

תִּתְנַשְּׂאוּ עַל־ קְהַל יְהוָה׃ וַיִּשְׁמַע מֹשֶׁה
Moses when-he-heard (4) Yahweh assembly-of above you-set-yourselves

וַיִּפֹּל עַל־ פָּנָיו׃ וַיְדַבֵּר אֶל־ קֹרַח וְאֶל־ כָּל־
all-of and-to Korah to then-he-said (5) face-of-him on then-he-fell

עֲדָתוֹ לֵאמֹר בֹּקֶר וְיֹדַע יְהוָה אֶת־אֲשֶׁר־ לוֹ וְאֶת־
and to-him who *** Yahweh then-he-will-show morning to-say follower-of-him

הַקָּדוֹשׁ וְהִקְרִיב אֵלָיו וְאֵת אֲשֶׁר יִבְחַר־ בּוֹ
for-him he-chooses whom and to-him and-he-will-have-come-near the-holy

יַקְרִיב אֵלָיו׃ זֹאת עֲשׂוּ קְחוּ־ לָכֶם מַחְתּוֹת קֹרַח
Korah censers for-you take! do! this (6) to-him he-will-make-come-near

make tassels on the corners of your garments, with a blue cord on each tassel. 39You will have these tassels to look at and so you will remember all the commands of the LORD, that you may obey them and not prostitute yourselves by going after the lusts of your own hearts and eyes. 40Then you will remember to obey all my commands and will be consecrated to your God. 41I am the LORD your God, who brought you out of Egypt to be your God. I am the LORD your God.'"

*Korah, Dathan and Abiram*

16 Korah son of Izhar, the son of Kohath, the son of Levi, and certain Reubenites—Dathan and Abiram, sons of Eliab, and On son of Peleth—became insolent[l] 2and rose up against Moses. With them were 250 Israelite men, well-known community leaders who had been appointed members of the council. 3They came as a group to oppose Moses and Aaron and said to them, "You have gone too far! The whole community is holy, every one of them, and the LORD is with them. Why then do you set yourselves above the LORD's assembly?"

4When Moses heard this, he fell facedown. 5Then he said to Korah and all his followers: "In the morning the LORD will show who belongs to him and who is holy, and he will have that person come near him. The man he chooses he will cause to come near him. 6You, Korah, and all your followers are to do this: Take censers

l1 Or *Peleth—took ⌞men⌟*

וְכָל־ עֲדָתוֹ׃ וּתְנוּ בָהֵן׀ אֵשׁ וְשִׂימוּ עֲלֵיהֶן קְטֹרֶת
incense in-them and-put! fire in-them and-put! (7) follower-of-him and-all-of

לִפְנֵי יְהוָה מָחָר וְהָיָה הָאִישׁ אֲשֶׁר־ יִבְחַר יְהוָה הוּא
he Yahweh he-chooses whom the-man and-he-will-be tomorrow Yahweh before

הַקָּדוֹשׁ רַב־ לָכֶם בְּנֵי לֵוִי׃ וַיֹּאמֶר מֹשֶׁה אֶל־ קֹרַח שִׁמְעוּ־
listen! Korah to Moses and-he-said (8) Levi sons-of to-you too-far the-holy

נָא בְּנֵי לֵוִי׃ הַמְעַט מִכֶּם כִּי־ הִבְדִּיל אֱלֹהֵי יִשְׂרָאֵל אֶתְכֶם
you Israel God-of he-separated that for-you enough? (9) Levi sons-of now!

מֵעֲדַת יִשְׂרָאֵל לְהַקְרִיב אֶתְכֶם אֵלָיו לַעֲבֹד אֶת־ עֲבֹדַת
work-of *** to-do to-him you to-bring-near Israel from-community-of

מִשְׁכַּן יְהוָה וְלַעֲמֹד לִפְנֵי הָעֵדָה לְשָׁרְתָם׃
to-minister-to-them the-community before and-to-stand Yahweh tabernacle-of

וַיַּקְרֵב אֹתְךָ וְאֶת־ כָּל־ אַחֶיךָ בְנֵי־ לֵוִי אִתָּךְ
with-you Levi sons-of fellows-of-you all-of and you and-he-brought-near (10)

וּבִקַּשְׁתֶּם גַּם־ כְּהֻנָּה׃ לָכֵן אַתָּה וְכָל־ עֲדָתְךָ
follower-of-you and-all-of you therefore (11) the-priesthood too but-you-seek

הַנֹּעָדִים עַל־ יְהוָה וְאַהֲרֹן מַה־ הוּא כִּי תַלּוֹנוּ
you-grumble that he who? now-Aaron Yahweh against the-ones-banding-together

עָלָיו׃ וַיִּשְׁלַח מֹשֶׁה לִקְרֹא לְדָתָן וְלַאֲבִירָם
and-to-Abiram to-Dathan to-summon Moses then-he-sent (12) against-him

בְּנֵי אֱלִיאָב וַיֹּאמְרוּ לֹא נַעֲלֶה׃ הַמְעַט כִּי הֶעֱלִיתָנוּ
you-brought-us that enough? (13) we-will-come not but-they-said Eliab sons-of

מֵאֶרֶץ זָבַת חָלָב וּדְבַשׁ לַהֲמִיתֵנוּ בַּמִּדְבָּר כִּי־
now in-the-desert to-kill-us and-honey milk flowing-of from-land

תִשְׂתָּרֵר עָלֵינוּ גַּם־ הִשְׂתָּרֵר׃ אַף לֹא אֶל־ אֶרֶץ זָבַת
flowing-of land into not moreover (14) to-lord also over-us you-would-lord

חָלָב וּדְבַשׁ הֲבִיאֹתָנוּ וַתִּתֶּן־ לָנוּ נַחֲלַת שָׂדֶה
field inheritance-of to-us nor-you-gave you-brought-us and-honey milk

וָכָרֶם הַעֵינֵי הָאֲנָשִׁים הָהֵם תְּנַקֵּר לֹא נַעֲלֶה׃
we-will-come not would-you-gouge-out the-these the-men eyes-of? or-vineyard

וַיִּחַר לְמֹשֶׁה מְאֹד וַיֹּאמֶר אֶל־ יְהוָה אַל־ תֵּפֶן
you-accept not Yahweh to and-he-said very to-Moses then-he-was-angry (15)

אֶל־ מִנְחָתָם לֹא חֲמוֹר אֶחָד מֵהֶם נָשָׂאתִי וְלֹא הֲרֵעֹתִי אֶת־
*** I-wronged or-not I-took from-them one donkey not offering-of-them to

אַחַד מֵהֶם׃ וַיֹּאמֶר מֹשֶׁה אֶל־ קֹרַח אַתָּה וְכָל־ עֲדָתְךָ
follower-of-you and-all-of you Korah to Moses and-he-said (16) from-them any

הֱיוּ לִפְנֵי יְהוָה אַתָּה וָהֵם וְאַהֲרֹן מָחָר׃ וּקְחוּ׀ אִישׁ
each and-take! (17) tomorrow and-Aaron and-they you Yahweh before appear!

°11 ק תלינו

7and tomorrow put fire and incense in them before the LORD. The man the LORD chooses will be the one who is holy. You Levites have gone too far!"

8Moses also said to Korah, "Now listen, you Levites! 9Isn't it enough for you that the God of Israel has separated you from the rest of the Israelite community and brought you near himself to do the work at the LORD's tabernacle and to stand before the community and minister to them? 10He has brought you and all your fellow Levites near himself, but now you are trying to get the priesthood too. 11It is against the LORD that you and all your followers have banded together. Who is Aaron that you should grumble against him?"

12Then Moses summoned Dathan and Abiram, the sons of Eliab. But they said, "We will not come! 13Isn't it enough that you have brought us up out of a land flowing with milk and honey to kill us in the desert? And now you also want to lord it over us? 14Moreover, you haven't brought us into a land flowing with milk and honey or given us an inheritance of fields and vineyards. Will you gouge out the eyes of[m] these men? No, we will not come!"

15Then Moses became very angry and said to the LORD, "Do not accept their offering. I have not taken so much as a donkey from them, nor have I wronged any of them."

16Moses said to Korah, "You and all your followers are to appear before the LORD tomorrow—you and they and Aaron. 17Each man is to take

[m]14 Or *you make slaves of*; or *you deceive*

מַחְתָּתוֹ וּנְתַתֶּם עֲלֵיהֶם קְטֹרֶת וְהִקְרַבְתֶּם לִפְנֵי יְהוָה
Yahweh before and-you-present incense in-them and-you-put censer-of-him

אִישׁ מַחְתָּתוֹ חֲמִשִּׁים וּמָאתַיִם מַחְתֹּת וְאַתָּה וְאַהֲרֹן אִישׁ
each and-Aaron and-you censers and-two-hundreds fifty censer-of-him each

מַחְתָּתוֹ׃ (18) וַיִּקְחוּ אִישׁ מַחְתָּתוֹ וַיִּתְּנוּ עֲלֵיהֶם אֵשׁ
fire in-them and-they-put censer-of-him each so-they-took (18) censer-of-him

וַיָּשִׂימוּ עֲלֵיהֶם קְטֹרֶת וַיַּעַמְדוּ פֶּתַח אֹהֶל מוֹעֵד
Meeting Tent-of entrance-of and-they-stood incense in-them and-they-put

וּמֹשֶׁה וְאַהֲרֹן׃ (19) וַיַּקְהֵל עֲלֵיהֶם קֹרַח אֶת־ כָּל־
all-of *** Korah opposite-them when-he-gathered (19) and-Aaron with-Moses

הָעֵדָה אֶל־ פֶּתַח אֹהֶל מוֹעֵד וַיֵּרָא כְבוֹד־
glory-of then-he-appeared Meeting Tent-of entrance-of at the-following

יְהוָה אֶל־ כָּל־ הָעֵדָה׃ (20) וַיְדַבֵּר יְהוָה אֶל־ מֹשֶׁה וְאֶל־
and-to Moses to Yahweh and-he-spoke (20) the-assembly entire-of to Yahweh

אַהֲרֹן לֵאמֹר׃ (21) הִבָּדְלוּ מִתּוֹךְ הָעֵדָה הַזֹּאת
the-this the-assembly from-among separate-yourselves! (21) to-say Aaron

וַאכַלֶּה* אֹתָם כְּרָגַע׃ (22) וַיִּפְּלוּ עַל־ פְּנֵיהֶם
faces-of-them on but-they-fell (22) at-once them so-I-can-consume

וַיֹּאמְרוּ אֵל אֱלֹהֵי הָרוּחֹת לְכָל־ בָּשָׂר הָאִישׁ אֶחָד יֶחֱטָא
he-sins one the-man mankind of-all-of the-spirits God-of God and-they-cried

וְעַל כָּל־ הָעֵדָה תִּקְצֹף׃ (23) וַיְדַבֵּר יְהוָה
Yahweh then-he-spoke (23) you-will-be-angry the-assembly entire-of but-with

אֶל־מֹשֶׁה לֵּאמֹר׃ (24) דַּבֵּר אֶל־ הָעֵדָה לֵאמֹר הֵעָלוּ מִסָּבִיב
from-around move-away! to-say the-assembly to say! (24) to-say Moses to

לְמִשְׁכַּן־ קֹרַח דָּתָן וַאֲבִירָם׃ (25) וַיָּקָם מֹשֶׁה וַיֵּלֶךְ
and-he-went Moses and-he-got-up (25) and-Abiram Dathan Korah to-tent-of

אֶל־ דָּתָן וַאֲבִירָם וַיֵּלְכוּ אַחֲרָיו זִקְנֵי יִשְׂרָאֵל׃
Israel elders-of after-him and-they-followed and-Abiram Dathan to

(26) וַיְדַבֵּר אֶל־ הָעֵדָה לֵאמֹר סוּרוּ נָא מֵעַל אָהֳלֵי
tents-of from-near now! move-back! to-say the-assembly to and-he-warned (26)

הָאֲנָשִׁים הָרְשָׁעִים הָאֵלֶּה וְאַל־ תִּגְּעוּ בְּכָל־ אֲשֶׁר לָהֶם
to-them that on-anything you-touch and-not the-these the-wicked-ones the-men

פֶּן־ תִּסָּפוּ בְּכָל־ חַטֹּאתָם׃ (27) וַיֵּעָלוּ
so-they-moved (27) sins-of-them because-of-all-of you-will-be-swept-away or

מֵעַל מִשְׁכַּן־ קֹרֶח† דָּתָן וַאֲבִירָם מִסָּבִיב וְדָתָן וַאֲבִירָם
and-Abiram now-Dathan from-around and-Abiram Dathan Korah tent-of from-near

יָצְאוּ נִצָּבִים פֶּתַח אָהֳלֵיהֶם וּנְשֵׁיהֶם
with-wives-of-them tents-of-them entrance-of ones-standing they-came-out

his censer and put incense in it—250 censers in all—and present it before the LORD. You and Aaron are to present your censers also." [18]So each man took his censer, put fire and incense in it, and stood with Moses and Aaron at the entrance to the Tent of Meeting. [19]When Korah had gathered all his followers in opposition to them at the entrance to the Tent of Meeting, the glory of the LORD appeared to the entire assembly. [20]The LORD said to Moses and Aaron, [21]"Separate yourselves from this assembly so I can put an end to them at once."

[22]But Moses and Aaron fell facedown and cried out, "O God, God of the spirits of all mankind, will you be angry with the entire assembly when only one man sins?"

[23]Then the LORD said to Moses, [24]"Say to the assembly, 'Move away from the tents of Korah, Dathan and Abiram.' "

[25]Moses got up and went to Dathan and Abiram, and the elders of Israel followed him. [26]He warned the assembly, "Move back from the tents of these wicked men! Do not touch anything belonging to them, or you will be swept away because of all their sins." [27]So they moved away from the tents of Korah, Dathan and Abiram. Dathan and Abiram had come out and were standing with their

*21 Most mss have *hateph pathah* under the *aleph* ( וַאֲ ).

†27 Most mss have *pathah* under the *resh* (קֹרַח).

וּבְנֵיהֶם וְטַפָּם׃ וַיֹּאמֶר מֹשֶׁה בְּזֹאת

by-this Moses then-he-said (28) and-little-one-of-them and-children-of-them

תֵּדְעוּן כִּי־ יְהוָה שְׁלָחַנִי לַעֲשׂוֹת אֵת כָּל־ הַמַּעֲשִׂים הָאֵלֶּה

the-these the-things all-of *** to-do he-sent-me Yahweh that you-will-know

כִּי־ לֹא מִלִּבִּי׃ אִם־ כְּמוֹת כָּל־ הָאָדָם יְמֻתוּן אֵלֶּה

these they-die the-man every-of as-to-die if (29) from-heart-of-me not that

וּפְקֻדַּת כָּל־ הָאָדָם יִפָּקֵד עֲלֵיהֶם לֹא יְהוָה

Yahweh not by-them he-is-experienced the-man every-of and-experience-of

שְׁלָחָנִי׃ וְאִם־ בְּרִיאָה יִבְרָא יְהוָה וּפָצְתָה

and-she-opens Yahweh he-brings-about new-thing but-if (30) he-sent-me

הָאֲדָמָה אֶת־ פִּיהָ וּבָלְעָה אֹתָם וְאֶת־ כָּל־ אֲשֶׁר לָהֶם

to-them that everything and them and-she-swallows mouth-of-her *** the-earth

וְיָרְדוּ חַיִּים שְׁאֹלָה וִידַעְתֶּם כִּי נִאֲצוּ

they-abhored that then-you-will-know to-Sheol alive-ones and-they-go-down

הָאֲנָשִׁים הָאֵלֶּה אֶת־ יְהוָה׃ וַיְהִי כְּכַלֹּתוֹ לְדַבֵּר אֵת

*** to-say as-to-finish-him and-he-was (31) Yahweh *** the-these the-men

כָּל־ הַדְּבָרִים הָאֵלֶּה וַתִּבָּקַע הָאֲדָמָה אֲשֶׁר תַּחְתֵּיהֶם׃

under-them that the-ground that-she-was-split the-these the-things all-of

וַתִּפְתַּח הָאָרֶץ אֶת־ פִּיהָ וַתִּבְלַע אֹתָם וְאֶת־

and them and-she-swallowed mouth-of-her *** the-earth and-she-opened (32)

בָּתֵּיהֶם וְאֵת כָּל־ הָאָדָם אֲשֶׁר לְקֹרַח וְאֵת כָּל־

all-of and with-Korah that the-man every-of and households-of-them

הָרְכוּשׁ׃ וַיֵּרְדוּ הֵם וְכָל־ אֲשֶׁר לָהֶם

to-them that and-everything they and-they-went-down (33) the-possession

חַיִּים שְׁאֹלָה וַתְּכַס עֲלֵיהֶם הָאָרֶץ וַיֹּאבְדוּ

and-they-were-gone the-earth over-them and-she-closed to-Sheol alive-ones

מִתּוֹךְ הַקָּהָל׃ וְכָל־ יִשְׂרָאֵל אֲשֶׁר סְבִיבֹתֵיהֶם

ones-around-them that Israel and-all-of (34) the-community from-among

נָסוּ לְקֹלָם כִּי אָמְרוּ פֶּן־ תִּבְלָעֵנוּ

she-will-swallow-us perhaps they-shouted for at-cry-of-them they-fled

הָאָרֶץ׃ וְאֵשׁ יָצְאָה מֵאֵת יְהוָה וַתֹּאכַל אֵת

*** and-she-consumed Yahweh from she-came-out and-fire (35) the-earth

הַחֲמִשִּׁים וּמָאתַיִם אִישׁ מַקְרִיבֵי הַקְּטֹרֶת׃

the-censers ones-offering-of man and-two-hundreds the-fifty

וַיְדַבֵּר יְהוָה אֶל־ מֹשֶׁה לֵּאמֹר׃ אֱמֹר אֶל־ אֶלְעָזָר בֶּן־

son-of Eleazar to tell! (2[37]) to-say Moses to Yahweh and-he-spoke (17:1[36])*

אַהֲרֹן הַכֹּהֵן וְיָרֵם אֶת־ הַמַּחְתֹּת מִבֵּין הַשְּׂרֵפָה

the-smoldering-remain out-of the-censers *** so-he-takes the-priest Aaron

wives, children and little ones at the entrances to their tents.

[28]Then Moses said, "This is how you will know that the LORD has sent me to do all these things and that it was not my idea: [29]If these men die a natural death and experience only what usually happens to men, then the LORD has not sent me. [30]But if the LORD brings about something totally new, and the earth opens its mouth and swallows them, with everything that belongs to them, and they go down alive into the grave,[n] then you will know that these men have treated the LORD with contempt."

[31]As soon as he finished saying all this, the ground under them split apart [32]and the earth opened its mouth and swallowed them, with their households and all Korah's men and all their possessions. [33]They went down alive into the grave, with everything they owned; the earth closed over them, and they perished and were gone from the community. [34]At their cries, all the Israelites around them fled, shouting, "The earth is going to swallow us too!"

[35]And fire came out from the LORD and consumed the 250 men who were offering the incense.

[36]The LORD said to Moses, [37]"Tell Eleazar son of Aaron, the priest, to take the censers out of the smoldering remains

[n]30 Hebrew *Sheol;* also in verse 33

*The Hebrew numeration of chapter 17 begins with verse 36 of chapter 16 in English. The number in brackets indicates the English numeration.

וְאֶת־ הָאֵשׁ זְרֵה־ הָלְאָה כִּי קָדֵשׁוּ׃ אֵת מַחְתּוֹת
censers-of *** (3[38]) they-are-holy for at-distance scatter! the-coal and

הַחַטָּאִים הָאֵלֶּה בְּנַפְשֹׁתָם וְעָשׂוּ אֹתָם
them and-they-must-make at-lives-of-them the-these the-sinners

רִקֻּעֵי פַחִים צִפּוּי לַמִּזְבֵּחַ כִּי־ הִקְרִיבֻם לִפְנֵי־
before they-presented-them for for-the-altar overlay sheets ones-hammered-of

יְהוָה וַיִּקְדָּשׁוּ וְיִהְיוּ לְאוֹת לִבְנֵי יִשְׂרָאֵל׃
Israel to-sons-of as-sign so-let-them-be and-they-became-holy Yahweh

וַיִּקַּח אֶלְעָזָר הַכֹּהֵן אֵת מַחְתּוֹת הַנְּחֹשֶׁת
the-bronze censers-of *** the-priest Eleazar so-he-collected (4[39])

אֲשֶׁר הִקְרִיבוּ הַשְּׂרֻפִים וַיְרַקְּעוּם צִפּוּי
overlay and-they-hammered-them the-ones-being-burned they-brought that

לַמִּזְבֵּחַ׃ זִכָּרוֹן לִבְנֵי יִשְׂרָאֵל לְמַעַן אֲשֶׁר לֹא־
not *** so-that Israel for-sons-of reminder (5[40]) for-the-altar

יִקְרַב אִישׁ זָר אֲשֶׁר לֹא מִזֶּרַע אַהֲרֹן הוּא לְהַקְטִיר
to-burn he Aaron from-descendant-of not who stranger man he-should-come

קְטֹרֶת לִפְנֵי יְהוָה וְלֹא־ יִהְיֶה כְקֹרַח
like-Korah he-would-become so-not Yahweh before incense

וְכַעֲדָתוֹ כַּאֲשֶׁר דִּבֶּר יְהוָה בְּיַד־ מֹשֶׁה לוֹ׃
to-him Moses by-hand-of Yahweh he-directed just-as or-like-follower-of-him

וַיִּלֹּנוּ כָּל־ עֲדַת בְּנֵי־ יִשְׂרָאֵל מִמָּחֳרָת
on-next-day Israel sons-of community-of whole-of and-they-grumbled (6[41])

עַל־ מֹשֶׁה וְעַל־ אַהֲרֹן לֵאמֹר אַתֶּם הֲמִתֶּם אֶת־ עַם יְהוָה׃
Yahweh people-of *** you-killed you to-say Aaron and-against Moses against

וַיְהִי בְּהִקָּהֵל הָעֵדָה עַל־ מֹשֶׁה וְעַל־ אַהֲרֹן
Aaron and-against Moses against the-assembly when-to-gather but-he-was (7[42])

וַיִּפְנוּ אֶל־ אֹהֶל מוֹעֵד וְהִנֵּה כִסָּהוּ הֶעָנָן
the-cloud he-covered-him and-see! Meeting Tent-of toward and-they-turned

וַיֵּרָא כְּבוֹד יְהוָה׃ וַיָּבֹא מֹשֶׁה וְאַהֲרֹן אֶל־
to and-Aaron Moses and-he-went (8[43]) Yahweh glory-of and-he-appeared

פְּנֵי אֹהֶל מוֹעֵד׃ וַיְדַבֵּר יְהוָה אֶל־ מֹשֶׁה לֵּאמֹר׃
to-say Moses to Yahweh and-he-spoke (9[44]) Meeting Tent-of front-of

הֵרֹמּוּ מִתּוֹךְ הָעֵדָה הַזֹּאת וַאֲכַלֶּה אֹתָם
them so-I-can-consume the-this the-assembly from-among get-away! (10[45])

כְּרָגַע וַיִּפְּלוּ עַל־ פְּנֵיהֶם׃ וַיֹּאמֶר מֹשֶׁה אֶל־אַהֲרֹן
Aaron to Moses then-he-said (11[46]) faces-of-them on and-they-fell at-once

קַח אֶת־ הַמַּחְתָּה וְתֶן־ עָלֶיהָ אֵשׁ מֵעַל הַמִּזְבֵּחַ וְשִׂים
and-put! the-altar from-on fire in-her and-put! the-censer *** take!

and scatter the coals some distance away, for the censers are holy— [38]the censers of the men who sinned at the cost of their lives. Hammer the censers into sheets to overlay the altar, for they were presented before the LORD and have become holy. Let them be a sign to the Israelites."

[39]So Eleazar the priest collected the bronze censers brought by those who had been burned up, and he had them hammered out to overlay the altar, [40]as the LORD directed him through Moses. This was to remind the Israelites that no one except a descendant of Aaron should come to burn incense before the LORD, or he would become like Korah and his followers.

[41]The next day the whole Israelite community grumbled against Moses and Aaron. "You have killed the LORD's people," they said.

[42]But when the assembly gathered in opposition to Moses and Aaron and turned toward the Tent of Meeting, suddenly the cloud covered it and the glory of the LORD appeared. [43]Then Moses and Aaron went to the front of the Tent of Meeting, [44]and the LORD said to Moses, [45]"Get away from this assembly so I can put an end to them at once." And they fell facedown.

[46]Then Moses said to Aaron, "Take your censer and put incense in it, along with fire

*See the note on page 417.

קְטֹרֶת וְהוֹלֵךְ מְהֵרָה אֶל־הָעֵדָה וְכַפֵּר עֲלֵיהֶם כִּי־יָצָא
he-came-out for for-them and-atone! the-assembly to hurry and-going incense

הַקֶּצֶף מִלִּפְנֵי יְהוָה הֵחֵל הַנָּגֶף׃ וַיִּקַּח אַהֲרֹן
Aaron so-he-did (12[47]) the-plague he-started Yahweh from-before the-wrath

כַּאֲשֶׁר ׀ דִּבֶּר מֹשֶׁה וַיָּרָץ אֶל־תּוֹךְ† הַקָּהָל וְהִנֵּה
and-see! the-assembly midst-of into and-he-ran Moses he-said just-as

הֵחֵל הַנֶּגֶף בָּעָם וַיִּתֵּן אֶת־הַקְּטֹרֶת
the-incense *** but-he-offered among-the-people the-plague he-started

וַיְכַפֵּר עַל־הָעָם׃ וַיַּעֲמֹד בֵּין־הַמֵּתִים
the-dead-ones between and-he-stood (13[48]) the-people for and-he-atoned

וּבֵין הַחַיִּים וַתֵּעָצַר הַמַּגֵּפָה׃ וַיִּהְיוּ
but-they-were (14[49]) the-plague and-she-stopped the-living-ones and-between

הַמֵּתִים בַּמַּגֵּפָה אַרְבָּעָה עָשָׂר אֶלֶף וּשְׁבַע מֵאוֹת
hundreds and-seven-of thousand ten four from-the-plague the-dead-ones

מִלְּבַד הַמֵּתִים עַל־דְּבַר־קֹרַח׃ וַיָּשָׁב
then-he-returned (15[50]) Korah reason-of by the-dead-ones in-addition-to

אַהֲרֹן אֶל־מֹשֶׁה אֶל־פֶּתַח אֹהֶל מוֹעֵד וְהַמַּגֵּפָה נֶעֱצָרָה׃
she-stopped for-the-plague Meeting Tent-of entrance-of at Moses to Aaron

וַיְדַבֵּר יְהוָה אֶל־מֹשֶׁה לֵּאמֹר׃ דַּבֵּר ׀ אֶל־בְּנֵי יִשְׂרָאֵל
Israel sons-of to speak! (17[2]) to-say Moses to Yahweh and-he-spoke (16[1])

וְקַח מֵאִתָּם מַטֶּה מַטֶּה לְבֵית אָב מֵאֵת כָּל־
each-of from father from-house-of staff staff from-them and-get!

נְשִׂיאֵהֶם לְבֵית אֲבֹתָם שְׁנֵים עָשָׂר מַטּוֹת אִישׁ אֶת־
*** each staffs ten two fathers-of-them by-house-of leader-of-them

שְׁמוֹ תִּכְתֹּב עַל־מַטֵּהוּ׃ וְאֵת שֵׁם אַהֲרֹן תִּכְתֹּב
you-write Aaron name-of and (18[3]) staff-of-him on you-write name-of-him

עַל־מַטֵּה לֵוִי כִּי מַטֶּה אֶחָד לְרֹאשׁ בֵּית אֲבוֹתָם׃
fathers-of-them house-of for-head-of one staff for Levi staff-of on

וְהִנַּחְתָּם בְּאֹהֶל מוֹעֵד לִפְנֵי הָעֵדוּת אֲשֶׁר
where the-Testimony in-front-of Meeting in-Tent-of then-you-place-them (19[4])

אִוָּעֵד לָכֶם שָׁמָּה׃ וְהָיָה הָאִישׁ אֲשֶׁר אֶבְחַר־בּוֹ
to-him I-choose whom the-man and-he-will-be (20[5]) at-there with-you I-meet

מַטֵּהוּ יִפְרָח וַהֲשִׁכֹּתִי מֵעָלַי אֶת־תְּלֻנּוֹת
grumblings-of *** from-with-me and-I-will-rid he-will-sprout staff-of-him

בְּנֵי יִשְׂרָאֵל אֲשֶׁר הֵם מַלִּינִם עֲלֵיכֶם׃ וַיְדַבֵּר מֹשֶׁה
Moses so-he-spoke (21[6]) against-you ones-grumbling they that Israel sons-of

אֶל־בְּנֵי יִשְׂרָאֵל וַיִּתְּנוּ אֵלָיו ׀ כָּל־נְשִׂיאֵיהֶם מַטֶּה
staff leaders-of-them each-of to-him and-they-gave Israel sons-of to

from the altar, and hurry to the assembly to make atonement for them. Wrath has come out from the LORD; the plague has started." [47]So Aaron did as Moses said, and ran into the midst of the assembly. The plague had already started among the people, but Aaron offered the incense and made atonement for them. [48]He stood between the living and the dead, and the plague stopped. [49]But 14,700 people died from the plague, in addition to those who had died because of Korah. [50]Then Aaron returned to Moses at the entrance to the Tent of Meeting, for the plague had stopped.

*The Budding of Aaron's Staff*

17 The LORD said to Moses, [2]"Speak to the Israelites and get twelve staffs from them, one from the leader of each of their ancestral tribes. Write the name of each man on his staff. [3]On the staff of Levi write Aaron's name, for there must be one staff for the head of each ancestral tribe. [4]Place them in the Tent of Meeting in front of the Testimony, where I meet with you. [5]The staff belonging to the man I choose will sprout, and I will rid myself of this constant grumbling against you by the Israelites."

[6]So Moses spoke to the Israelites, and their leaders gave him twelve staffs, one for the

*See the note on page 417.

†12 Most mss have *sheva* in the *kaph* (תּוֹךְ).

לְנָשִׂיא אֶחָד מַטֶּה לְנָשִׂיא אֶחָד לְבֵית אֲבֹתָם שְׁנֵים עָשָׂר
ten two fathers-of-them of-house-of each for-leader staff each for-leader

מַטּוֹת וּמַטֵּה אַהֲרֹן בְּתוֹךְ מַטּוֹתָם׃ וַיַּנַּח
and-he-placed (22[7]) staffs-of-them in-among Aaron and-staff-of staffs

מֹשֶׁה אֶת־הַמַּטֹּת לִפְנֵי יְהוָה בְּאֹהֶל הָעֵדֻת׃ וַיְהִי
and-he-was (23[8]) the-Testimony in-Tent-of Yahweh before the-staffs *** Moses

מִמָּחֳרָת וַיָּבֹא מֹשֶׁה אֶל־אֹהֶל הָעֵדוּת וְהִנֵּה
and-see! the-Testimony Tent-of into Moses that-he-entered on-next-day

פָּרַח מַטֵּה־אַהֲרֹן לְבֵית לֵוִי וַיֹּצֵא פֶרַח
sprout and-he-put-out Levi from-house-of Aaron staff-of he-sprouted

וַיָּצֵץ צִיץ וַיִּגְמֹל שְׁקֵדִים׃ וַיֹּצֵא
then-he-brought (24[9]) almonds and-he-produced blossom and-he-blossomed

מֹשֶׁה אֶת־כָּל־הַמַּטֹּת מִלִּפְנֵי יְהוָה אֶל־כָּל־בְּנֵי יִשְׂרָאֵל
Israel sons-of all-of to Yahweh from-presence-of the-staffs all-of *** Moses

וַיִּרְאוּ וַיִּקְחוּ אִישׁ מַטֵּהוּ׃ וַיֹּאמֶר יְהוָה
Yahweh and-he-said (25[10]) staff-of-him each and-they-took and-they-looked

אֶל־מֹשֶׁה הָשֵׁב אֶת־מַטֵּה אַהֲרֹן לִפְנֵי הָעֵדוּת לְמִשְׁמֶרֶת
to-keep the-Testimony in-front-of Aaron staff-of *** put-back! Moses to

לְאוֹת לִבְנֵי־מֶרִי וּתְכַל תְּלוּנֹּתָם
grumblings-of-them and-she-will-put-end rebellion to-sons-of as-sign

מֵעָלַי וְלֹא יָמֻתוּ׃ וַיַּעַשׂ מֹשֶׁה כַּאֲשֶׁר
just-as Moses and-he-did (26[11]) they-will-die so-not from-against-me

צִוָּה יְהוָה אֹתוֹ כֵּן עָשָׂה׃ וַיֹּאמְרוּ בְּנֵי יִשְׂרָאֵל
Israel sons-of and-they-said (27[12]) he-did so him Yahweh he-commanded

אֶל־מֹשֶׁה לֵאמֹר הֵן גָּוַעְנוּ אָבַדְנוּ כֻּלָּנוּ אָבָדְנוּ׃
we-are-lost all-of-us we-are-lost we-will-die see! to-say Moses to

כֹּל הַקָּרֵב ׀ הַקָּרֵב אֶל־מִשְׁכַּן יְהוָה יָמוּת
he-will-die Yahweh tabernacle-of to the-one-near the-one-near any-of (28[13])

הַאִם תַּמְנוּ לִגְוֺעַ׃ וַיֹּאמֶר יְהוָה אֶל־אַהֲרֹן אַתָּה
you Aaron to Yahweh and-he-said (18:1) to-die all-of-us indeed?

וּבָנֶיךָ וּבֵית־אָבִיךָ אִתָּךְ תִּשְׂאוּ אֶת־
*** you-must-bear with-you father-of-you and-house-of and-sons-of-you

עֲוֺן הַמִּקְדָּשׁ וְאַתָּה וּבָנֶיךָ אִתָּךְ
with-you and-sons-of-you and-you the-sanctuary responsibility-of

תִּשְׂאוּ אֶת־עֲוֺן כְּהֻנַּתְכֶם׃ וְגַם אֶת־
*** and-also (2) priesthood-of-you responsibility-of *** you-must-bear

אַחֶיךָ מַטֵּה לֵוִי שֵׁבֶט אָבִיךָ הַקְרֵב אִתָּךְ
with-you , bring! father-of-you tribe-of Levi tribe-of brothers-of-you

leader of each of their ancestral tribes, and Aaron's staff was among them. [7]Moses placed the staffs before the LORD in the Tent of the Testimony.

[8]The next day Moses entered the Tent of the Testimony and saw that Aaron's staff, which represented the house of Levi, had not only sprouted but had budded, blossomed and produced almonds. [9]Then Moses brought out all the staffs from the LORD's presence to all the Israelites. They looked at them, and each man took his own staff.

[10]The LORD said to Moses, "Put back Aaron's staff in front of the Testimony, to be kept as a sign to the rebellious. This will put an end to their grumbling against me, so that they will not die." [11]Moses did just as the LORD commanded him.

[12]The Israelites said to Moses, "We will die! We are lost, we are all lost! [13]Anyone who even comes near the tabernacle of the LORD will die. Are we all going to die?"

*Duties of Priests and Levites*

18 The LORD said to Aaron, "You, your sons and your father's family are to bear the responsibility for offenses against the sanctuary, and you and your sons alone are to bear the responsibility for offenses against the priesthood. [2]Bring your fellow Levites from your ancestral

*See the note on page 417.

וְיִלָּווּ עָלֶיךָ וִישָׁרְתוּךָ וְאַתָּה וּבָנֶיךָ
and-sons-of-you both-you and-they-may-assist-you with-you so-they-may-join

אִתָּךְ לִפְנֵי אֹהֶל הָעֵדֻת׃ וְשָׁמְרוּ
they-must-be-responsible (3) the-Testimony Tent-of before with-you

מִשְׁמַרְתְּךָ וּמִשְׁמֶרֶת כָּל־ הָאֹהֶל אַךְ אֶל־ כְּלֵי הַקֹּדֶשׁ
the-sanctuary furnishings-of to only the-Tent all-of and-duty-of duty-of-you

וְאֶל־ הַמִּזְבֵּחַ לֹא יִקְרָבוּ וְלֹא־ יָמֻתוּ גַם־ הֵם גַּם־אַתֶּם׃
you and they both they-die so-not they-must-go-near not the-altar or-to

וְנִלְווּ עָלֶיךָ וְשָׁמְרוּ אֶת־מִשְׁמֶרֶת אֹהֶל
Tent-of care-of *** and-they-must-be-responsible with-you and-they-must-join (4)

מוֹעֵד לְכֹל עֲבֹדַת הָאֹהֶל וְזָר לֹא־ יִקְרַב אֲלֵיכֶם׃
to-you he-may-come-near not but-outsider the-Tent work-of for-all-of Meeting

וּשְׁמַרְתֶּם אֵת מִשְׁמֶרֶת הַקֹּדֶשׁ וְאֵת מִשְׁמֶרֶת הַמִּזְבֵּחַ
the-altar care-of and the-sanctuary care-of *** and-you-are-responsible (5)

וְלֹא־ יִהְיֶה עוֹד קֶצֶף עַל־ בְּנֵי יִשְׂרָאֵל׃ וַאֲנִי הִנֵּה לָקַחְתִּי
I-selected see! now-I (6) Israel sons-of on wrath again he-will-fall so-not

אֶת־ אֲחֵיכֶם הַלְוִיִּם מִתּוֹךְ בְּנֵי יִשְׂרָאֵל לָכֶם מַתָּנָה
gift for-you Israel sons-of from-among the-Levites fellows-of-you ***

נְתֻנִים לַיהוָה לַעֲבֹד אֶת־עֲבֹדַת אֹהֶל מוֹעֵד׃ וְאַתָּה
but-you (7) Meeting Tent-of work-of *** to-do to-Yahweh ones-being-dedicated

וּבָנֶיךָ אִתְּךָ תִּשְׁמְרוּ אֶת־ כְּהֻנַּתְכֶם לְכָל־
with-every-of priesthood-of-you *** you-serve with-you and-sons-of-you

דְּבַר הַמִּזְבֵּחַ וּלְמִבֵּית לַפָּרֹכֶת וַעֲבַדְתֶּם עֲבֹדַת
service-of so-you-serve of-the-curtain and-from-inside the-altar thing-of

מַתָּנָה אֶתֵּן אֶת־ כְּהֻנַּתְכֶם וְהַזָּר הַקָּרֵב יוּמָת׃
he-must-die the-one-near but-the-outsider priesthood-of-you *** I-give gift

וַיְדַבֵּר יְהוָה אֶל־אַהֲרֹן וַאֲנִי הִנֵּה נָתַתִּי לְךָ אֶת־ מִשְׁמֶרֶת
charge-of *** to-you I-put see! now-I Aaron to Yahweh then-he-said (8)

תְּרוּמֹתָי לְכָל־ קָדְשֵׁי בְנֵי־ יִשְׂרָאֵל לְךָ
to-you Israel sons-of holy-things-of from-all-of presentations-of-me

נְתַתִּים לְמָשְׁחָה וּלְבָנֶיךָ לְחָק־ עוֹלָם׃ זֶה־
this (9) regular as-share-of and-to-sons-of-you as-portion I-give-them

יִהְיֶה לְךָ מִקֹּדֶשׁ הַקֳּדָשִׁים מִן־ הָאֵשׁ כָּל־
every-of the-fire from the-holy-things from-most-holy-of for-you he-will-be

קָרְבָּנָם לְכָל־ מִנְחָתָם וּלְכָל־
and-from-every-of grain-offering-of-them from-every-of gift-of-them

חַטָּאתָם וּלְכָל־ אֲשָׁמָם אֲשֶׁר יָשִׁיבוּ
they-bring that guilt-offering-of-them and-from-every-of sin-offering-of-them

tribe to join you and assist you
when you and your sons minister before the Tent of the
Testimony. 3They are to be responsible to you and are to
perform all the duties of the
Tent, but they must not go
near the furnishings of the
sanctuary or the altar, or both
they and you will die. 4They
are to join you and be responsible for the care of the Tent of
Meeting—all the work at the
Tent—and no one else may
come near where you are.
5"You are to be responsible
for the care of the sanctuary
and the altar, so that wrath
will not fall on the Israelites
again. 6I myself have selected
your fellow Levites from
among the Israelites as a gift to
you, dedicated to the LORD to
do the work at the Tent of
Meeting. 7But only you and
your sons may serve as priests
in connection with every-
thing at the altar and inside
the curtain. I am giving you
the service of the priesthood
as a gift. Anyone else who
comes near the sanctuary
must be put to death."

*Offerings for Priests and Levites*

8Then the LORD said to
Aaron, "I myself have put you
in charge of the offerings
presented to me; all the holy
offerings the Israelites give me
I give to you and your sons as
your portion and regular
share. 9You are to have the
part of the most holy offerings
that is kept from the fire. From
all the gifts they bring me as

לִי קֹדֶשׁ קָדָשִׁים לְךָ הוּא וּלְבָנֶיךָ׃
and-for-sons-of-you he for-you holy-things most-holy-of to-me

בְּקֹדֶשׁ הַקֳּדָשִׁים תֹּאכְלֶנּוּ כָּל־זָכָר יֹאכַל
he-shall-eat male every-of you-eat-him the-holy-things as-most-holy-of (10)

אֹתוֹ קֹדֶשׁ יִהְיֶה־לָּךְ׃ וְזֶה־לְּךָ תְּרוּמַת מַתָּנָם
gift-of-them set-aside-of for-you also-this (11) to-you he-must-be holy him

לְכָל־תְּנוּפֹת בְּנֵי יִשְׂרָאֵל לְךָ נְתַתִּים
I-give-them to-you Israel sons-of wave-offerings-of from-all-of

וּלְבָנֶיךָ וְלִבְנֹתֶיךָ אִתְּךָ לְחָק־עוֹלָם
regular as-share-of with-you and-to-daughters-of-you and-to-sons-of-you

כָּל־טָהוֹר בְּבֵיתְךָ יֹאכַל אֹתוֹ׃ כֹּל חֵלֶב
finest-of all-of (12) him he-may-eat in-household-of-you clean everyone-of

יִצְהָר וְכָל־חֵלֶב תִּירוֹשׁ וְדָגָן רֵאשִׁיתָם אֲשֶׁר־
that firstfruit-of-them and-grain new-wine finest-of and-all-of olive-oil

יִתְּנוּ לַיהוָה לְךָ נְתַתִּים׃ בִּכּוּרֵי כָּל־אֲשֶׁר
that all firstfruits-of (13) I-give-them to-you to-Yahweh they-give

בְּאַרְצָם אֲשֶׁר־יָבִיאוּ לַיהוָה לְךָ יִהְיֶה כָּל־
everyone-of he-will-be for-you to-Yahweh they-bring that in-land-of-them

טָהוֹר בְּבֵיתְךָ יֹאכְלֶנּוּ׃ כָּל־חֵרֶם בְּיִשְׂרָאֵל
in-Israel devoted every-of (14) he-may-eat-him in-household-of-you clean

לְךָ יִהְיֶה׃ כָּל־פֶּטֶר רֶחֶם לְכָל־בָּשָׂר אֲשֶׁר־
that flesh from-all-of womb first-of every-of (15) he-will-be for-you

יַקְרִיבוּ לַיהוָה בָּאָדָם וּבַבְּהֵמָה יִהְיֶה־לָּךְ אַךְ ׀
but for-you he-is and-also-the-animal both-the-man to-Yahweh they-offer

פָּדֹה תִפְדֶּה אֵת בְּכוֹר הָאָדָם וְאֵת בְּכוֹר־הַבְּהֵמָה
the-animal firstborn-of and the-man firstborn-of *** you-must-redeem to-redeem

הַטְּמֵאָה תִּפְדֶּה׃ וּפְדוּיָו מִבֶּן־
when-son-of and-redemption-price-of-him (16) you-must-redeem the-unclean

חֹדֶשׁ תִּפְדֶּה בְּעֶרְכְּךָ כֶּסֶף חֲמֵשֶׁת שְׁקָלִים בְּשֶׁקֶל
by-shekel-of shekels five-of silver at-price-of-you you-must-redeem month

הַקֹּדֶשׁ עֶשְׂרִים גֵּרָה הוּא׃ אַךְ בְּכוֹר־שׁוֹר אוֹ־בְכוֹר כֶּשֶׂב
sheep firstborn-of or ox firstborn-of but (17) he gerah twenty the-sanctuary

אוֹ־בְכוֹר עֵז לֹא תִפְדֶּה קֹדֶשׁ הֵם אֶת־דָּמָם
blood-of-them *** they holy you-must-redeem not goat firstborn-of or

תִּזְרֹק עַל־הַמִּזְבֵּחַ וְאֶת־חֶלְבָּם תַּקְטִיר אִשֶּׁה לְרֵיחַ
as-aroma fire-offering you-burn fat-of-them and the-altar on you-sprinkle

נִיחֹחַ לַיהוָה׃ וּבְשָׂרָם יִהְיֶה־לָּךְ כַּחֲזֵה
as-breast-of for-you he-is and-meat-of-them (18) to-Yahweh pleasant

most holy offerings, whether grain or sin or guilt offerings, that part belongs to you and your sons. 10 Eat it as something most holy; every male shall eat it. You must regard it as holy.

11 "This also is yours: whatever is set aside from the gifts of all the wave offerings of the Israelites. I give this to you and your sons and daughters as your regular share. Everyone in your household who is ceremonially clean may eat it.

12 "I give you all the finest olive oil and all the finest new wine and grain they give the LORD as the firstfruits of their harvest. 13 All the land's firstfruits that they bring to the LORD will be yours. Everyone in your household who is ceremonially clean may eat it.

14 "Everything in Israel that is devoted[o] to the LORD is yours. 15 The first offspring of every womb, both man and animal, that is offered to the LORD is yours. But you must redeem every firstborn son and every firstborn male of unclean animals. 16 When they are a month old, you must redeem them at the redemption price set at five shekels[p] of silver, according to the sanctuary shekel, which weighs twenty gerahs.

17 "But you must not redeem the firstborn of an ox, a sheep or a goat; they are holy. Sprinkle their blood on the altar and burn their fat as an offering made by fire, an aroma pleasing to the LORD. 18 Their meat is to be yours, just as the breast

[o]14 The Hebrew term refers to the irrevocable giving over of things or persons to the LORD, often by totally destroying them.
[p]16 That is, about 2 ounces (about 55 grams)

הַתְּנוּפָה וּכְשׁוֹק הַיָּמִין לְךָ יִהְיֶה׃ כֹּל ׀
all-of (19) he-is for-you the-right and-as-thigh-of the-wave-offering

תְּרוּמֹת הַקֳּדָשִׁים אֲשֶׁר יָרִימוּ בְנֵי־ יִשְׂרָאֵל
Israel sons-of they-present that the-holy-ones offerings-set-aside-of

לַיהוָה נָתַתִּי לְךָ וּלְבָנֶיךָ וְלִבְנֹתֶיךָ אִתְּךָ
with-you and-to-daughters-of-you and-to-sons-of-you to-you I-give to-Yahweh

לְחָק־ עוֹלָם בְּרִית מֶלַח עוֹלָם הִוא לִפְנֵי יְהוָה לְךָ
for-you Yahweh before she everlasting salt covenant-of regular as-share-of

וּלְזַרְעֲךָ אִתָּךְ׃ וַיֹּאמֶר יְהוָה אֶל־ אַהֲרֹן
Aaron to Yahweh and-he-said (20) with-you and-for-offspring-of-you

בְּאַרְצָם לֹא תִנְחָל וְחֵלֶק לֹא־ יִהְיֶה לְךָ
for-you he-will-be not and-share you-will-inherit not in-land-of-them

בְּתוֹכָם אֲנִי חֶלְקְךָ וְנַחֲלָתְךָ בְּתוֹךְ בְּנֵי יִשְׂרָאֵל׃
Israel sons-of among and-inheritance-of-you portion-of-you I among-them

וְלִבְנֵי לֵוִי הִנֵּה נָתַתִּי כָּל־ מַעֲשֵׂר בְּיִשְׂרָאֵל לְנַחֲלָה
as-inheritance in-Israel tithe all-of I-give see! Levi and-to-sons-of (21)

חֵלֶף עֲבֹדָתָם אֲשֶׁר־ הֵם עֹבְדִים אֶת־ עֲבֹדַת אֹהֶל מוֹעֵד׃
Meeting Tent-of service-of *** ones-doing they that work-of-them return-of

וְלֹא־ יִקְרְבוּ עוֹד בְּנֵי יִשְׂרָאֵל אֶל־ אֹהֶל מוֹעֵד
Meeting Tent-of to Israel sons-of ever they-must-come-near and-not (22)

לָשֵׂאת חֵטְא לָמוּת׃ וְעָבַד הַלֵּוִי הוּא אֶת־ עֲבֹדַת אֹהֶל
Tent-of work-of *** he the-Levite now-he-must-do (23) to-die sin to-bear

מוֹעֵד וְהֵם יִשְׂאוּ עֲוֺנָם חֻקַּת עוֹלָם
lasting ordinance-of offense-of-them they-will-bear and-they Meeting

לְדֹרֹתֵיכֶם וּבְתוֹךְ בְּנֵי יִשְׂרָאֵל לֹא יִנְחֲלוּ
they-will-receive not Israel sons-of but-among for-generations-of-you

נַחֲלָה׃ כִּי אֶת־ מַעְשַׂר בְּנֵי־ יִשְׂרָאֵל אֲשֶׁר יָרִימוּ
they-present that Israel sons-of tithe-of *** instead (24) inheritance

לַיהוָה תְּרוּמָה נָתַתִּי לַלְוִיִּם לְנַחֲלָה עַל־ כֵּן אָמַרְתִּי
I-said this for as-inheritance to-the-Levites I-give offering to-Yahweh

לָהֶם בְּתוֹךְ בְּנֵי יִשְׂרָאֵל לֹא יִנְחֲלוּ נַחֲלָה׃
inheritance they-will-receive not Israel sons-of among about-them

וַיְדַבֵּר יְהוָה אֶל־ מֹשֶׁה לֵּאמֹר׃ וְאֶל־ הַלְוִיִּם תְּדַבֵּר
you-speak the-Levites now-to (26) to-say Moses to Yahweh and-he-spoke (25)

וְאָמַרְתָּ אֲלֵהֶם כִּי־ תִקְחוּ מֵאֵת בְּנֵי־ יִשְׂרָאֵל אֶת־ הַמַּעֲשֵׂר אֲשֶׁר
that the-tithe *** Israel sons-of from you-receive when to-them and-you-say

נָתַתִּי לָכֶם מֵאִתָּם בְּנַחֲלַתְכֶם וַהֲרֵמֹתֶם מִמֶּנּוּ
from-him then-you-must-present as-inheritance-of-you from-them to-you I-give

of the wave offering and the right thigh are yours. [19]Whatever is set aside from the holy offerings the Israelites present to the LORD I give to you and your sons and daughters as your regular share. It is an everlasting covenant of salt before the LORD for both you and your offspring."

[20]The LORD said to Aaron, "You will have no inheritance in their land, nor will you have any share among them; I am your share and your inheritance among the Israelites.

[21]"I give to the Levites all the tithes in Israel as their inheritance in return for the work they do while serving at the Tent of Meeting. [22]From now on the Israelites must not go near the Tent of Meeting, or they will bear the consequences of their sin and will die. [23]It is the Levites who are to do the work at the Tent of Meeting and bear the responsibility for offenses against it. This is a lasting ordinance for the generations to come. They will receive no inheritance among the Israelites. [24]Instead, I give to the Levites as their inheritance the tithes that the Israelites present as an offering to the LORD. That is why I said concerning them: 'They will have no inheritance among the Israelites.' "

[25]The LORD said to Moses, [26]"Speak to the Levites and say to them: 'When you receive from the Israelites the tithe I give you as your inheritance, you must present a tenth of

תְּרוּמַת יְהוָה מַעֲשֵׂר מִן־ הַמַּעֲשֵׂר׃ וְנֶחְשַׁב לָכֶם
to-you and-he-will-be-reckoned (27) the-tithe from tenth Yahweh offering-of

תְּרוּמַתְכֶם כַּדָּגָן מִן־ הַגֹּרֶן וְכַמְלֵאָה
or-as-the-fullness the-threshing-floor from as-the-grain offering-of-you

מִן־ הַיָּקֶב׃ כֵּן תָּרִימוּ גַם־ אַתֶּם תְּרוּמַת יְהוָה
Yahweh offering-of you also you-will-present thus (28) the-winepress from

מִכֹּל מַעְשְׂרֹתֵיכֶם אֲשֶׁר תִּקְחוּ מֵאֵת בְּנֵי יִשְׂרָאֵל וּנְתַתֶּם
and-you-must-give Israel sons-of from you-receive that tithes-of-you from-all-of

מִמֶּנּוּ אֶת־ תְּרוּמַת יְהוָה לְאַהֲרֹן הַכֹּהֵן׃ מִכֹּל
from-all-of (29) the-priest to-Aaron Yahweh portion-of *** from-him

מַתְּנֹתֵיכֶם תָּרִימוּ אֵת כָּל־ תְּרוּמַת יְהוָה מִכָּל־
from-all-of Yahweh portion-of every-of *** you-must-present gifts-of-you

חֶלְבּוֹ אֶת־ מִקְדְּשׁוֹ מִמֶּנּוּ׃ וְאָמַרְתָּ אֲלֵהֶם
to-them and-you-say (30) from-him holy-part-of-him *** best-of-him

בַּהֲרִימְכֶם אֶת־ חֶלְבּוֹ מִמֶּנּוּ וְנֶחְשַׁב
then-he-will-be-reckoned from-him best-of-him *** when-to-present-you

לַלְוִיִּם כִּתְבוּאַת גֹּרֶן וְכִתְבוּאַת יָקֶב׃
winepress and-as-product-of threshing-floor as-product-of to-the-Levites

וַאֲכַלְתֶּם אֹתוֹ בְּכָל־ מָקוֹם אַתֶּם וּבֵיתְכֶם כִּי־ שָׂכָר
wage for and-household-of-you you place in-any-of him and-you-may-eat (31)

הוּא לָכֶם חֵלֶף עֲבֹדַתְכֶם בְּאֹהֶל מוֹעֵד׃ וְלֹא־ תִשְׂאוּ
you-will-bear and-not (32) Meeting at-Tent-of work-of-you return-of for-you he

עָלָיו חֵטְא בַּהֲרִימְכֶם אֶת־ חֶלְבּוֹ מִמֶּנּוּ וְאֶת־
and from-him best-of-him *** when-to-present-you guilt because-of-him

קָדְשֵׁי בְנֵי־ יִשְׂרָאֵל לֹא תְחַלְּלוּ וְלֹא תָמוּתוּ׃
you-will-die and-not you-will-defile not Israel sons-of holy-things-of

וַיְדַבֵּר יְהוָה אֶל־ מֹשֶׁה וְאֶל־ אַהֲרֹן לֵאמֹר׃ זֹאת
this (2) to-say Aaron and-to Moses to Yahweh and-he-spoke (19:1)

חֻקַּת הַתּוֹרָה אֲשֶׁר־ צִוָּה יְהוָה לֵאמֹר דַּבֵּר ׀ אֶל־ בְּנֵי
sons-of to tell! to-say Yahweh he-commanded that the-law requirement-of

יִשְׂרָאֵל וְיִקְחוּ אֵלֶיךָ פָרָה אֲדֻמָּה תְּמִימָה אֲשֶׁר אֵין־ בָּהּ
on-her he-is-not that without-defect red heifer to-you so-they-bring Israel

מוּם אֲשֶׁר לֹא־ עָלָה עָלֶיהָ עֹל׃ וּנְתַתֶּם אֹתָהּ אֶל־ אֶלְעָזָר
Eleazar to her then-you-give (3) yoke on-her he-was-on never that blemish

הַכֹּהֵן וְהוֹצִיא אֹתָהּ אֶל־ מִחוּץ לַמַּחֲנֶה וְשָׁחַט
and-he-will-slaughter of-the-camp outside to her and-he-will-take the-priest

אֹתָהּ לְפָנָיו׃ וְלָקַח אֶלְעָזָר הַכֹּהֵן
the-priest Eleazar then-he-must-take (4) in-presence-of-him her

that tithe as the LORD's offering. [27]Your offering will be reckoned to you as grain from the threshing floor or juice from the winepress. [28]In this way you also will present an offering to the LORD from all the tithes you receive from the Israelites. From these tithes you must give the LORD's portion to Aaron the priest. [29]You must present as the LORD's portion the best and holiest part of everything given to you.'

[30]"Say to the Levites: 'When you present the best part, it will be reckoned to you as the product of the threshing floor or the winepress. [31]You and your households may eat the rest of it anywhere, for it is your wages for your work at the Tent of Meeting. [32]By presenting the best part of it you will not be guilty in this matter; then you will not defile the holy offerings of the Israelites, and you will not die.' "

*The Water of Cleansing*

19 The LORD said to Moses and Aaron: [2]"This is a requirement of the law that the LORD has commanded: Tell the Israelites to bring you a red heifer without defect or blemish and that has never been under a yoke. [3]Give it to Eleazar the priest; it is to be taken outside the camp and slaughtered in his presence. [4]Then Eleazar the priest is to

מִדָּמָהּ בְּאֶצְבָּעוֹ וְהִזָּה אֶל־ נֹכַח פְּנֵי
face-of front toward and-he-must-sprinkle on-finger-of-him from-blood-of-her

אֹהֶל־ מוֹעֵד מִדָּמָהּ שֶׁבַע פְּעָמִים׃ וְשָׂרַף אֶת־
*** and-he-must-burn (5) times seven from-blood-of-her Meeting Tent-of

הַפָּרָה לְעֵינָיו אֶת עֹרָהּ וְאֶת־ בְּשָׂרָהּ וְאֶת־
and flesh-of-her and hide-of-her *** before-eyes-of-him the-heifer

דָּמָהּ עַל־ פִּרְשָׁהּ יִשְׂרֹף׃ וְלָקַח הַכֹּהֵן
the-priest and-he-must-take (6) he-must-burn offal-of-her with blood-of-her

עֵץ אֶרֶז וְאֵזוֹב וּשְׁנִי תוֹלַעַת וְהִשְׁלִיךְ אֶל־ תּוֹךְ
midst-of onto and-he-must-throw scarlet and-wool-of and-hyssop cedar wood-of

שְׂרֵפַת הַפָּרָה׃ וְכִבֶּס בְּגָדָיו הַכֹּהֵן
the-priest clothes-of-him then-he-must-wash (7) the-heifer burning-of

וְרָחַץ בְּשָׂרוֹ בַּמַּיִם וְאַחַר יָבוֹא אֶל־
into he-may-come then-after with-the-waters body-of-him and-he-must-bathe

הַמַּחֲנֶה וְטָמֵא הַכֹּהֵן עַד־ הָעָרֶב׃
the-evening till the-priest but-he-will-be-unclean the-camp

וְהַשֹּׂרֵף אֹתָהּ יְכַבֵּס בְּגָדָיו בַּמַּיִם
with-the-waters clothes-of-him he-must-wash her and-the-one-burning (8)

וְרָחַץ בְּשָׂרוֹ בַּמָּיִם וְטָמֵא עַד־
till and-he-will-be-unclean with-the-waters body-of-him and-he-must-bathe

הָעָרֶב׃ וְאָסַף ׀ אִישׁ טָהוֹר אֵת אֵפֶר הַפָּרָה
the-heifer ash-of *** clean man and-he-shall-gather (9) the-evening

וְהִנִּיחַ מִחוּץ לַמַּחֲנֶה בְּמָקוֹם טָהוֹר וְהָיְתָה
and-she-shall-be clean in-place of-the-camp outside and-he-shall-put

לַעֲדַת בְּנֵי־ יִשְׂרָאֵל לְמִשְׁמֶרֶת לְמֵי נִדָּה
cleansing in-waters-of for-use Israel sons-of for-community-of

חַטָּאת הִוא׃ וְכִבֶּס הָאֹסֵף אֶת־ אֵפֶר
ash-of *** the-one-gathering and-he-must-wash (10) she sin-purification

הַפָּרָה אֶת־ בְּגָדָיו וְטָמֵא עַד־ הָעָרֶב
the-evening till and-he-will-be-unclean clothes-of-him *** the-heifer

וְהָיְתָה לִבְנֵי יִשְׂרָאֵל וְלַגֵּר הַגָּר בְּתוֹכָם
among-them the-one-living and-for-the-alien Israel for-sons-of and-she-will-be

לְחֻקַּת עוֹלָם׃ הַנֹּגֵעַ בְּמֵת לְכָל־
on-any-of on-dead-body and-the-one-touching (11) lasting as-ordinance-of

נֶפֶשׁ אָדָם וְטָמֵא שִׁבְעַת יָמִים׃ הוּא יִתְחַטָּא־
he-must-purify he (12) days seven-of then-he-will-be-unclean man body-of

בוֹ בַּיּוֹם הַשְּׁלִישִׁי וּבַיּוֹם הַשְּׁבִיעִי יִטְהָר
he-will-be-clean the-seventh and-on-the-day the-third on-the-day for-himself

take some of its blood on his finger and sprinkle it seven times toward the front of the
Tent of Meeting. [5]While he
watches, the heifer is to be burned—its hide, flesh, blood
and offal. [6]The priest is to take some cedar wood, hyssop and scarlet wool and throw them
onto the burning heifer. [7]After
that, the priest must wash his clothes and bathe himself with water. He may then come into the camp, but he will be ceremonially unclean
till evening. [8]The man who
burns it must also wash his clothes and bathe with water, and he too will be unclean till evening.
[9]"A man who is clean shall gather up the ashes of the heifer and put them in a ceremonially clean place outside the camp. They shall be kept by the Israelite community for use in the water of cleansing; it is for purification
from sin. [10]The man who gathers up the ashes of the heifer must also wash his clothes, and he too will be unclean till evening. This will be a lasting ordinance both for the Israelites and for the aliens living among them.
[11]"Whoever touches the dead body of anyone will be
unclean for seven days. [12]He
must purify himself with the water on the third day and on the seventh day; then he will

וְאִם־ לֹא יִתְחַטָּא בַּיּוֹם הַשְּׁלִישִׁי וּבַיּוֹם הַשְּׁבִיעִי
the-seventh and-on-the-day the-third on-the-day he-purifies-self not but-if

לֹא יִטְהָר׃ כָּל־ הַנֹּגֵעַ בְּמֵת בְּנֶפֶשׁ
on-body-of on-dead-body the-one-touching every-of (13) he-will-be-clean not

הָאָדָם אֲשֶׁר־ יָמוּת וְלֹא יִתְחַטָּא אֶת־ מִשְׁכַּן יְהוָה
Yahweh tabernacle-of *** he-purifies-self and-not he-died that the-man

טִמֵּא וְנִכְרְתָה הַנֶּפֶשׁ הַהִוא מִיִּשְׂרָאֵל כִּי מֵי
waters-of for from-Israel the-that the-person and-she-must-be-cut he-defiles

נִדָּה לֹא־ זֹרַק עָלָיו טָמֵא יִהְיֶה עוֹד טֻמְאָתוֹ
uncleanness-of-him still he-is unclean on-him he-was-sprinkled not cleansing

בוֹ׃ זֹאת הַתּוֹרָה אָדָם כִּי־ יָמוּת בְּאֹהֶל כָּל־ הַבָּא
the-one-entering any-of in-tent he-dies when person the-law this (14) on-him

אֶל־ הָאֹהֶל וְכָל־ אֲשֶׁר בָּאֹהֶל יִטְמָא שִׁבְעַת יָמִים׃
days seven-of he-will-be-unclean in-the-tent who and-anyone the-tent into

וְכֹל כְּלִי פָתוּחַ אֲשֶׁר אֵין־ צָמִיד פָּתִיל
one-fastened lid he-is-not that being-open container-of and-every-of (15)

עָלָיו טָמֵא הוּא׃ וְכֹל אֲשֶׁר־ יִגַּע עַל־ פְּנֵי הַשָּׂדֶה
the-field surface-of in he-touches who and-anyone (16) he unclean on-him

בַּחֲלַל־ חֶרֶב אוֹ בְמֵת אוֹ־ בְעֶצֶם אָדָם אוֹ בְקָבֶר
on-grave or human on-bone-of or on-dead-body or sword on-one-killed-of

יִטְמָא שִׁבְעַת יָמִים׃ וְלָקְחוּ לַטָּמֵא
for-the-unclean-one then-they-must-take (17) days seven-of he-will-be-unclean

מֵעֲפַר שְׂרֵפַת הַחַטָּאת וְנָתַן עָלָיו
on-him and-he-must-pour the-purification-offering burnt-of from-ash-of

מַיִם חַיִּים אֶל־ כֶּלִי׃ וְלָקַח אֵזוֹב וְטָבַל
and-he-must-dip hyssop then-he-must-take (18) jar into fresh-ones waters

בַּמַּיִם אִישׁ טָהוֹר וְהִזָּה עַל־ הָאֹהֶל וְעַל־ כָּל־
all-of and-on the-tent on and-he-must-sprinkle clean man in-the-waters

הַכֵּלִים וְעַל־ הַנְּפָשׁוֹת אֲשֶׁר הָיוּ־ שָׁם וְעַל־
and-on there they-were who the-people and-on the-furnishings

הַנֹּגֵעַ בַּעֶצֶם אוֹ בֶחָלָל אוֹ בַמֵּת אוֹ
or on-the-dead-body or on-the-one-killed or on-the-bone the-one-touching

בַקָּבֶר׃ וְהִזָּה הַטָּהֹר עַל־ הַטָּמֵא
the-unclean-one on the-clean-one and-he-must-sprinkle (19) on-the-grave

בַּיּוֹם הַשְּׁלִישִׁי וּבַיּוֹם הַשְּׁבִיעִי וְחִטְּאוֹ
and-he-must-purify-him the-seventh and-on-the-day the-third on-the-day

בַּיּוֹם הַשְּׁבִיעִי וְכִבֶּס בְּגָדָיו וְרָחַץ
and-he-must-bathe clothes-of-him and-he-must-wash the-seventh on-the-day

be clean. But if he does not
purify himself on the third
and seventh days, he will not
be clean. [13]Whoever touches
the dead body of anyone and
fails to purify himself defiles
the LORD's tabernacle. That
person must be cut off from Israel. Because the water of
cleansing has not been sprinkled on him, he is unclean; his
uncleanness remains on him.
[14]"This is the law that applies when a person dies in a
tent: Anyone who enters the
tent and anyone who is in it
will be unclean for seven days,
[15]and every open container
without a lid fastened on it
will be unclean.
[16]"Anyone out in the open
who touches someone who
has been killed with a sword
or someone who has died a
natural death, or anyone who
touches a human bone or a
grave, will be unclean for seven days.
[17]"For the unclean person,
put some ashes from the
burned purification offering
into a jar and pour fresh water
over them. [18]Then a man who
is ceremonially clean is to take
some hyssop, dip it in the
water and sprinkle the tent
and all the furnishings and
the people who were there. He
must also sprinkle anyone
who has touched a human
bone or a grave or someone
who has been killed or someone who has died a natural
death. [19]The man who is clean
is to sprinkle the unclean person on the third and seventh
days, and on the seventh day
he is to purify him. The person
being cleansed must wash his
clothes and bathe with water,

בַּמַּיִם וְטָהֵר בָּעָרֶב׃ וְאִישׁ אֲשֶׁר־
who but-person (20) in-the-evening and-he-will-be-clean with-the-waters

יִטְמָא וְלֹא יִתְחַטָּא וְנִכְרְתָה הַנֶּפֶשׁ
the-person then-she-must-be-cut-off he-purifies-self and-not he-is-unclean

הַהִוא מִתּוֹךְ הַקָּהָל כִּי אֶת־ מִקְדַּשׁ יְהוָה טִמֵּא
he-defiled Yahweh tabernacle-of *** for the-community from-among the-that

מֵי נִדָּה לֹא־ זֹרַק עָלָיו טָמֵא הוּא׃ וְהָיְתָה
now-she-is (21) he unclean on-him he-was-sprinkled not cleansing waters-of

לָהֶם לְחֻקַּת עוֹלָם וּמַזֵּה מֵי־
waters-of and-the-one-sprinkling lasting as-ordinance-of for-them

הַנִּדָּה יְכַבֵּס בְּגָדָיו וְהַנֹּגֵעַ בְּמֵי
on-waters-of and-the-one-touching clothes-of-him he-must-wash the-cleansing

הַנִּדָּה יִטְמָא עַד־ הָעָרֶב׃ וְכֹל אֲשֶׁר־
that and-anything (22) the-evening till he-will-be-unclean the-cleansing

יִגַּע־ בּוֹ הַטָּמֵא יִטְמָא וְהַנֶּפֶשׁ
and-the-person he-becomes-unclean the-unclean-one on-him he-touches

הַנֹּגַעַת תִּטְמָא עַד־ הָעָרֶב׃ וַיָּבֹאוּ
now-they-arrived (20:1) the-evening till she-becomes-unclean the-one-touching

בְנֵי־ יִשְׂרָאֵל כָּל־ הָעֵדָה מִדְבַּר־ צִן בַּחֹדֶשׁ הָרִאשׁוֹן
the-first in-the-month Zin Desert-of the-community whole-of Israel sons-of

וַיֵּשֶׁב הָעָם בְּקָדֵשׁ וַתָּמָת שָׁם מִרְיָם
Miriam there and-she-died at-Kadesh the-people and-he-stayed

וַתִּקָּבֵר שָׁם׃ וְלֹא־ הָיָה מַיִם לָעֵדָה
for-the-community waters he-was now-not (2) there and-she-was-buried

וַיִּקָּהֲלוּ עַל־ מֹשֶׁה וְעַל־ אַהֲרֹן׃ וַיָּרֶב
and-he-quarreled (3) Aaron and-against Moses against and-they-gathered

הָעָם עִם־ מֹשֶׁה וַיֹּאמְרוּ לֵאמֹר וְלוּ גָוַעְנוּ בִּגְוַע
when-to-die we-died if-only! to-say and-they-said Moses with the-people

אַחֵינוּ לִפְנֵי יְהוָה׃ וְלָמָה הֲבֵאתֶם אֶת־ קְהַל יְהוָה
Yahweh community-of *** you-brought now-why? (4) Yahweh before brothers-of-us

אֶל־ הַמִּדְבָּר הַזֶּה לָמוּת שָׁם אֲנַחְנוּ וּבְעִירֵנוּ׃ וְלָמָה
and-why? (5) and-livestock-of-us we here to-die the-this the-desert into

הֶעֱלִיתֻנוּ מִמִּצְרַיִם לְהָבִיא אֹתָנוּ אֶל־ הַמָּקוֹם הָרָע הַזֶּה
the-this the-terrible the-place to us to-bring from-Egypt you-brought-us

לֹא ׀ מְקוֹם זֶרַע וּתְאֵנָה וְגֶפֶן וְרִמּוֹן וּמַיִם אַיִן
there-is-no and-waters or-pomegranate or-grapevine or-fig grain place-of no

לִשְׁתּוֹת׃ וַיָּבֹא מֹשֶׁה וְאַהֲרֹן מִפְּנֵי הַקָּהָל אֶל־
to the-assembly from-before and-Aaron Moses so-he-went (6) to-drink

and that evening he will be clean. [20]But if a person who is unclean does not purify himself, he must be cut off from the community, because he has defiled the sanctuary of the LORD. The water of cleansing has not been sprinkled on him, and he is unclean. [21]This is a lasting ordinance for them.

"The man who sprinkles the water of cleansing must also wash his clothes, and anyone who touches the water of cleansing will be unclean till evening. [22]Anything that an unclean person touches becomes unclean, and anyone who touches it becomes unclean till evening."

*Water From the Rock*

20 In the first month the whole Israelite community arrived at the Desert of Zin, and they stayed at Kadesh. There Miriam died and was buried.

[2]Now there was no water for the community, and the people gathered in opposition to Moses and Aaron. [3]They quarreled with Moses and said, "If only we had died when our brothers fell dead before the LORD! [4]Why did you bring the LORD's community into this desert, that we and our livestock should die here? [5]Why did you bring us up out of Egypt to this terrible place? It has no grain or figs, grapevines or pomegranates. And there is no water to drink!"

[6]Moses and Aaron went

| | | | | | |
|---|---|---|---|---|---|
| פֶּ֫תַח | אֹֽהֶל | מוֹעֵד֮ | וַיִּפְּל֣וּ | עַל־ פְּנֵיהֶ֒ם | וַיֵּרָ֤א |
| entrance-of | Tent-of | Meeting | and-they-fell | on faces-of-them | and-he-appeared |

| | | | | |
|---|---|---|---|---|
| כְּבוֹד־ | יְהוָ֖ה | אֲלֵיהֶֽם: | וַיְדַבֵּ֥ר | יְהוָ֖ה אֶל־ מֹשֶׁ֥ה לֵּאמֹֽר: קַ֣ח |
| glory-of | Yahweh | to-them (7) | and-he-spoke | Yahweh to Moses to-say (8) take! |

| | | | | | |
|---|---|---|---|---|---|
| אֶת־ הַמַּטֶּ֗ה | וְהַקְהֵ֤ל | אֶת־ הָעֵדָה֙ | אַתָּה֙ | וְאַהֲרֹ֣ן | אָחִ֔יךָ |
| *** the-staff | and-gather! | *** the-assembly | you | and-Aaron | brother-of-you |

| | | | | | |
|---|---|---|---|---|---|
| וְדִבַּרְתֶּ֧ם | אֶל־ הַסֶּ֛לַע | לְעֵינֵיהֶ֖ם | וְנָתַ֣ן | | |
| and-you-speak | to the-rock | before-eyes-of-them | and-he-will-pour-out | | |

| | | | | | |
|---|---|---|---|---|---|
| מֵימָ֑יו | וְהוֹצֵאתָ֙ | לָהֶ֥ם | מַ֙יִם֙ | מִן־ | הַסֶּ֔לַע |
| waters-of-him | so-you-will-bring | for-them | waters | from | the-rock |

| | | | | | |
|---|---|---|---|---|---|
| וְהִשְׁקִיתָ֥ | אֶת־ הָעֵדָ֖ה | וְאֶת־ | בְּעִירָֽם: | וַיִּקַּ֥ח | |
| and-you-will-give-drink | *** the-community | and | livestock-of-them (9) | so-he-took | |

| | | | | | |
|---|---|---|---|---|---|
| מֹשֶׁ֛ה | אֶת־ הַמַּטֶּ֖ה | מִלִּפְנֵ֣י | יְהוָ֑ה | כַּאֲשֶׁ֖ר | צִוָּֽהוּ: |
| Moses | *** the-staff | from-presence-of | Yahweh | just-as | he-commanded-him |

| | | | | | | |
|---|---|---|---|---|---|---|
| וַיַּקְהִ֜לוּ | מֹשֶׁ֧ה | וְאַהֲרֹ֛ן | אֶת־ הַקָּהָ֖ל | אֶל־ פְּנֵ֣י | הַסָּ֑לַע | |
| and-they-gathered (10) | Moses | and-Aaron | *** the-assembly | in front-of | the-rock | |

| | | | | | | |
|---|---|---|---|---|---|---|
| וַיֹּ֣אמֶר | לָהֶ֔ם | שִׁמְעוּ־ נָ֖א | הַמֹּרִ֑ים | הֲמִן־ | הַסֶּ֣לַע | הַזֶּ֔ה |
| and-he-said | to-them | listen! now! | the-ones-rebelling | from? | the-rock | the-this |

| | | | | | | |
|---|---|---|---|---|---|---|
| נוֹצִ֥יא | לָכֶ֖ם | מָֽיִם: | וַיָּ֙רֶם֙ | מֹשֶׁ֣ה | אֶת־ | יָד֔וֹ |
| must-we-bring | for-you | waters (11) | then-he-raised | Moses | *** | arm-of-him |

| | | | | | | |
|---|---|---|---|---|---|---|
| וַיַּ֧ךְ | אֶת־ הַסֶּ֛לַע | בְּמַטֵּ֖הוּ | פַּעֲמָ֑יִם | וַיֵּצְאוּ֙ | מַ֣יִם | |
| and-he-struck | *** the-rock | with-staff-of-him | twice | and-they-gushed-out | waters | |

| | | | | | | |
|---|---|---|---|---|---|---|
| רַבִּ֔ים | וַתֵּ֥שְׁתְּ | הָעֵדָ֖ה | וּבְעִירָֽם: | וַיֹּ֣אמֶר | | |
| many | and-she-drank | the-community | and-livestock-of-them (12) | but-he-said | | |

| | | | | | | |
|---|---|---|---|---|---|---|
| יְהוָה֮ | אֶל־ מֹשֶׁ֣ה וְאֶֽל־ אַהֲרֹן֒ | יַ֚עַן | לֹא־ הֶאֱמַנְתֶּ֣ם | בִּ֔י | לְהַ֨קְדִּישֵׁ֔נִי | |
| Yahweh | to Moses and-to Aaron | because | not you-trusted | in-me | to-honor-as-holy-me | |

| | | | | | | |
|---|---|---|---|---|---|---|
| לְעֵינֵ֖י | בְּנֵ֣י | יִשְׂרָאֵ֑ל | לָכֵ֗ן | לֹ֤א | תָבִ֙יאוּ֙ | אֶת־ הַקָּהָ֣ל |
| before-eyes-of | sons-of | Israel | therefore | not | you-will-bring | *** the-assembly |

| | | | | | | |
|---|---|---|---|---|---|---|
| הַזֶּ֔ה | אֶל־ הָאָ֖רֶץ | אֲשֶׁר־ | נָתַ֣תִּי | לָהֶֽם: | הֵ֚מָּה | מֵ֣י מְרִיבָ֔ה |
| the-this | into the-land | that | I-give | to-them (13) | these | waters-of Meribah |

| | | | | | | |
|---|---|---|---|---|---|---|
| אֲשֶׁר־ | רָב֥וּ | בְנֵֽי־ | יִשְׂרָאֵ֖ל | אֶת־ יְהוָ֑ה | וַיִּקָּדֵ֖שׁ | |
| where | they-quarreled | sons-of | Israel | *** Yahweh | and-he-showed-himself-holy | |

| | | | | | | |
|---|---|---|---|---|---|---|
| בָּֽם: | וַיִּשְׁלַ֨ח | מֹשֶׁ֧ה | מַלְאָכִ֛ים | מִקָּדֵ֖שׁ | אֶל־ מֶ֥לֶךְ | אֱד֑וֹם |
| among-them (14) | and-he-sent | Moses | messengers | from-Kadesh | to king-of | Edom |

| | | | | | | |
|---|---|---|---|---|---|---|
| כֹּ֤ה | אָמַר֙ | אָחִ֣יךָ | יִשְׂרָאֵ֔ל | אַתָּ֣ה יָדַ֔עְתָּ | אֵ֥ת כָּל־ | הַתְּלָאָ֖ה אֲשֶׁ֥ר |
| this | he-says | brother-of-you | Israel | you you-know | *** all-of | the-hardship that |

| | | | | | |
|---|---|---|---|---|---|
| מְצָאָֽתְנוּ: | וַיֵּרְד֤וּ | אֲבֹתֵ֙ינוּ֙ | מִצְרַ֔יְמָה | וַנֵּ֥שֶׁב | |
| she-came-on-us (15) | they-went-down | fathers-of-us | into-Egypt | and-we-lived | |

from the assembly to the entrance to the Tent of Meeting and fell facedown, and the glory of the LORD appeared to them. 7The LORD said to Moses, 8"Take the staff, and you and your brother Aaron gather the assembly together. Speak to that rock before their eyes and it will pour out its water. You will bring water out of the rock for the community so they and their livestock can drink."

9So Moses took the staff from the LORD's presence, just as he commanded him. 10He and Aaron gathered the assembly together in front of the rock and Moses said to them, "Listen, you rebels, must we bring you water out of this rock?" 11Then Moses raised his arm and struck the rock twice with his staff. Water gushed out, and the community and their livestock drank.

12But the LORD said to Moses and Aaron, "Because you did not trust in me enough to honor me as holy in the sight of the Israelites, you will not bring this community into the land I give them."

13These were the waters of Meribah,*q* where the Israelites quarreled with the LORD and where he showed himself holy among them.

*Edom Denies Israel Passage*

14Moses sent messengers from Kadesh to the king of Edom, saying:

"This is what your brother Israel says: You know about all the hardships that have come upon us. 15Our forefathers went down into Egypt, and we lived there

*q13 Meribah means quarreling.*

בְּמִצְרַ֗יִם יָמִ֣ים רַבִּ֔ים וַיָּרֵ֥עוּ לָ֛נוּ מִצְרַ֖יִם וְלַאֲבֹתֵֽינוּ׃
in-Egypt | days | many | and-they-mistreated | to-us | Egyptians | and-to-fathers-of-us

(16) וַנִּצְעַ֤ק אֶל־יְהוָה֙ וַיִּשְׁמַ֣ע קֹלֵ֔נוּ וַיִּשְׁלַ֣ח מַלְאָ֔ךְ
(16) but-we-cried | to | Yahweh | and-he-heard | cry-of-us | and-he-sent | angel

וַיֹּצִאֵ֖נוּ מִמִּצְרָ֑יִם וְהִנֵּה֙ אֲנַ֣חְנוּ בְקָדֵ֔שׁ עִ֖יר קְצֵ֥ה
and-he-brought-us | from-Egypt | now-see! | we | at-Kadesh | town | edge-of

גְּבוּלֶֽךָ׃ (17) נַעְבְּרָה־נָּ֣א בְאַרְצֶ֗ךָ לֹ֤א נַעֲבֹר֙
territory-of-you | (17) | let-us-pass | now! | through-country-of-you | not | we-will-go

בְּשָׂדֶ֣ה וּבְכֶ֔רֶם וְלֹ֥א נִשְׁתֶּ֖ה מֵ֣י בְאֵ֑ר
through-field | or-through-vineyard | and-not | we-will-drink | waters-of | well

דֶּ֧רֶךְ הַמֶּ֣לֶךְ נֵלֵ֗ךְ לֹ֤א נִטֶּה֙ יָמִ֣ין וּשְׂמֹ֔אול עַ֥ד אֲשֶׁר־
highway-of | the-king | we-will-travel | not | we-will-turn | right | or-left | until | when

נַעֲבֹ֖ר גְּבוּלֶֽךָ׃ (18) וַיֹּ֤אמֶר אֵלָיו֙ אֱד֔וֹם לֹ֥א
we-passed-through | territory-of-you | (18) | but-he-answered | to-him | Edom | not

תַעֲבֹ֖ר בִּ֑י פֶּן־בַּחֶ֖רֶב אֵצֵ֥א לִקְרָאתֶֽךָ׃
you-may-pass | through-me | or | with-the-sword | I-will-march-out | to-attack-you

(19) וַיֹּאמְר֨וּ אֵלָ֜יו בְּנֵֽי־יִשְׂרָאֵ֗ל בַּֽמְסִלָּ֣ה נַעֲלֶ֔ה
(19) | and-they-replied | to-him | sons-of | Israel | on-the-main-road | we-will-go

וְאִם־מֵימֶ֤יךָ נִשְׁתֶּה֙ אֲנִ֣י וּמִקְנַ֔י וְנָתַ֖תִּי
and-if | waters-of-you | we-drink | I | or-livestock-of-me | then-I-will-pay

מִכְרָ֑ם רַ֛ק אֵ֥ין דָּבָ֖ר בְּרַגְלַ֥י אֶעֱבֹֽרָה׃
price-of-them | only | nothing | else | on-feet-of-me | I-will-pass-through

(20) וַיֹּ֖אמֶר לֹ֣א תַעֲבֹ֑ר וַיֵּצֵ֤א אֱדוֹם֙
(20) | but-he-answered | not | you-may-pass-through | then-he-came-out | Edom

לִקְרָאת֔וֹ בְּעַ֥ם כָּבֵ֖ד וּבְיָ֥ד חֲזָקָֽה׃ (21) וַיְמָאֵ֣ן ׀
to-oppose-him | with-army | large | and-with-hand | powerful | (21) | since-he-refused

אֱד֗וֹם נְתֹן֙ אֶת־יִשְׂרָאֵ֔ל עֲבֹ֖ר בִּגְבֻל֑וֹ וַיֵּ֥ט יִשְׂרָאֵ֖ל
Edom | to-let | *** | Israel | to-go | through-territory-him | and-he-turned | Israel

מֵעָלָֽיו׃ (22) וַיִּסְע֣וּ מִקָּדֵ֔שׁ וַיָּבֹ֥אוּ בְנֵֽי־יִשְׂרָאֵ֛ל
from-near-him | (22) | and-they-set-out | from-Kadesh | and-they-came | sons-of | Israel

כָּל־הָעֵדָ֖ה הֹ֣ר הָהָֽר׃ (23) וַיֹּ֧אמֶר יְהוָ֛ה אֶל־מֹשֶׁ֥ה
whole-of | the-community | Hor | the-Mount | (23) | and-he-said | Yahweh | to | Moses

וְאֶֽל־אַהֲרֹ֛ן בְּהֹ֥ר הָהָ֖ר עַל־גְּב֥וּל אֶ֥רֶץ אֱד֖וֹם לֵאמֹֽר׃
and-to | Aaron | at-Hor | the-Mount | near | border-of | land-of | Edom | to-say

יֵאָסֵ֤ף אַהֲרֹן֙ אֶל־עַמָּ֔יו כִּ֣י לֹ֤א יָבֹא֙ אֶל־
(24) | he-will-be-gathered | Aaron | to | people-of-him | for | not | he-will-enter | into

הָאָ֔רֶץ אֲשֶׁ֥ר נָתַ֖תִּי לִבְנֵ֣י יִשְׂרָאֵ֑ל עַ֛ל אֲשֶׁר־מְרִיתֶ֥ם אֶת־
the-land | that | I-give | to-sons-of | Israel | because | that | you-rebelled | ***

many years. The Egyptians mistreated us and our fathers, 16but when we cried out to the LORD, he heard our cry and sent an angel and brought us out of Egypt.

"Now we are here at Kadesh, a town on the edge of your territory. 17Please let us pass through your country. We will not go through any field or vineyard, or drink water from any well. We will travel along the king's highway and not turn to the right or to the left until we have passed through your territory."

18But Edom answered:

"You may not pass through here; if you try, we will march out and attack you with the sword."

19The Israelites replied:

"We will go along the main road, and if we or our livestock drink any of your water, we will pay for it. We only want to pass through on foot—nothing else."

20Again they answered:

"You may not pass through."

Then Edom came out against them with a large and powerful army. 21Since Edom refused to let them go through their territory, Israel turned away from them.

*The Death of Aaron*

22The whole Israelite community set out from Kadesh and came to Mount Hor. 23At Mount Hor, near the border of Edom, the LORD said to Moses and Aaron, 24"Aaron will be gathered to his people. He will not enter the land I give the Israelites, because both of you rebelled against my command

פִּי לְמֵי מְרִיבָה׃ קַח אֶת־אַהֲרֹן וְאֶת־אֶלְעָזָר בְּנוֹ
son-of-him Eleazar and Aaron *** get! (25) Meribah at-waters-of command-of-me

וְהַעַל אֹתָם הֹר הָהָר׃ וְהַפְשֵׁט אֶת־אַהֲרֹן אֶת־בְּגָדָיו
garments-of-him *** Aaron *** and-remove! (26) the-Mount Hor them and-take-up!

וְהִלְבַּשְׁתָּם אֶת־אֶלְעָזָר בְּנוֹ וְאַהֲרֹן יֵאָסֵף
he-will-be-gathered and-Aaron son-of-him Eleazar *** and-you-put-on-them

וּמֵת שָׁם׃ וַיַּעַשׂ מֹשֶׁה כַּאֲשֶׁר צִוָּה יְהוָה
Yahweh he-commanded just-as Moses and-he-did (27) there and-he-will-die

וַיַּעֲלוּ אֶל־הֹר הָהָר לְעֵינֵי כָּל־הָעֵדָה׃
the-community whole-of before-eyes-of the-Mount Hor onto and-they-went-up

וַיַּפְשֵׁט מֹשֶׁה אֶת־אַהֲרֹן אֶת־בְּגָדָיו וַיַּלְבֵּשׁ אֹתָם
them and-he-put-on garments-of-him *** Aaron *** Moses and-he-removed (28)

אֶת־אֶלְעָזָר בְּנוֹ וַיָּמָת אַהֲרֹן שָׁם בְּרֹאשׁ הָהָר
the-mountain on-top-of there Aaron and-he-died son-of-him Eleazar ***

וַיֵּרֶד מֹשֶׁה וְאֶלְעָזָר מִן־הָהָר׃ וַיִּרְאוּ
when-they-learned (29) the-mountain from and-Eleazar Moses then-he-came-down

כָּל־הָעֵדָה כִּי גָוַע אַהֲרֹן וַיִּבְכּוּ אֶת־אַהֲרֹן שְׁלֹשִׁים
thirty Aaron *** then-they-mourned Aaron he-died that the-community whole-of

יוֹם כֹּל בֵּית יִשְׂרָאֵל׃ וַיִּשְׁמַע הַכְּנַעֲנִי מֶלֶךְ־עֲרָד
Arad king-of the-Canaanite when-he-heard (21:1) Israel house-of entire-of day

יֹשֵׁב הַנֶּגֶב כִּי בָּא יִשְׂרָאֵל דֶּרֶךְ הָאֲתָרִים וַיִּלָּחֶם
then-he-attacked the-Atharim road-of Israel he-comes that the-Negev living-of

בְּיִשְׂרָאֵל וַיִּשְׁבְּ ׀ מִמֶּנּוּ שֶׁבִי׃ וַיִּדַּר יִשְׂרָאֵל נֶדֶר
vow Israel and-he-vowed (2) captive from-him and-he-captured against-Israel

לַיהוָה וַיֹּאמַר אִם־נָתֹן תִּתֵּן אֶת־הָעָם הַזֶּה
the-this the-people *** you-deliver to-deliver if and-he-said to-Yahweh

בְּיָדִי וְהַחֲרַמְתִּי אֶת־עָרֵיהֶם׃ וַיִּשְׁמַע
and-he-listened (3) cities-of-them *** then-I-will-destroy into-hand-of-me

יְהוָה בְּקוֹל יִשְׂרָאֵל וַיִּתֵּן אֶת־הַכְּנַעֲנִי וַיַּחֲרֵם
and-he-destroyed the-Canaanite *** and-he-gave-over Israel to-plea-of Yahweh

אֶתְהֶם וְאֶת־עָרֵיהֶם וַיִּקְרָא שֵׁם־הַמָּקוֹם חָרְמָה׃
Hormah the-place name-of so-he-called towns-of-them and them

וַיִּסְעוּ מֵהֹר הָהָר דֶּרֶךְ יַם־סוּף לִסְבֹב
to-go-around Reed Sea-of route-of the-Mount from-Hor and-they-travelled (4)

אֶת־אֶרֶץ אֱדוֹם וַתִּקְצַר נֶפֶשׁ־הָעָם בַּדָּרֶךְ׃
on-the-way the-people spirit-of but-she-grew-impatient Edom land-of ***

וַיְדַבֵּר הָעָם בֵּאלֹהִים וּבְמֹשֶׁה לָמָה הֶעֱלִיתֻנוּ
you-brought-us why? and-against-Moses against-God the-people and-he-spoke (5)

at the waters of Meribah. [25]Get Aaron and his son Eleazar and take them up Mount Hor. [26]Remove Aaron's garments and put them on his son Eleazar, for Aaron will be gathered to his people; he will die there."

[27]Moses did as the LORD commanded: They went up Mount Hor in the sight of the whole community. [28]Moses removed Aaron's garments and put them on his son Eleazar. And Aaron died there on top of the mountain. Then Moses and Eleazar came down from the mountain, [29]and when the whole community learned that Aaron had died, the entire house of Israel mourned for him thirty days.

*Arad Destroyed*

21 When the Canaanite king of Arad, who lived in the Negev, heard that Israel was coming along the road to Atharim, he attacked the Israelites and captured some of them. [2]Then Israel made this vow to the LORD: "If you will deliver these people into our hands, we will totally destroy[r] their cities." [3]The LORD listened to Israel's plea and gave the Canaanites over to them. They completely destroyed them and their towns; so the place was named Hormah.[s]

*The Bronze Snake*

[4]They traveled from Mount Hor along the route to the Red Sea,[t] to go around Edom. But the people grew impatient on the way; [5]they spoke against God and against Moses, and said, "Why have you brought

[r]2 The Hebrew term refers to the irrevocable giving over of things or persons to the LORD, often by totally destroying them; also in verse 3.
[s]3 *Hormah* means *destruction*.
[t]4 Hebrew *Yam Suph*; that is, Sea of Reeds

מִמִּצְרַיִם לָמוּת בַּמִּדְבָּר כִּי אֵין לֶחֶם וְאֵין מַיִם
waters and-there-is-no bread there-is-no for in-the-desert to-die from-Egypt

וְנַפְשֵׁנוּ קָצָה בַּלֶּחֶם הַקְּלֹקֵל׃ וַיְשַׁלַּח
then-he-sent (6) the-miserable against-the-food she-detests and-spirit-of-us

יְהוָה בָּעָם אֵת הַנְּחָשִׁים הַשְּׂרָפִים וַיְנַשְּׁכוּ אֶת־
*** and-they-bit the-venomous-ones the-snakes *** among-the-people Yahweh

הָעָם וַיָּמָת עַם־ רָב מִיִּשְׂרָאֵל׃ וַיָּבֹא הָעָם אֶל־
to the-people and-he-came (7) from-Israel many people and-he-died the-people

מֹשֶׁה וַיֹּאמְרוּ חָטָאנוּ כִּי־ דִבַּרְנוּ בַיהוָה וָבָךְ
and-against-you against-Yahweh we-spoke when we-sinned and-they-said Moses

הִתְפַּלֵּל אֶל־יְהוָה וְיָסֵר מֵעָלֵינוּ אֶת־ הַנָּחָשׁ וַיִּתְפַּלֵּל
so-he-prayed the-snake *** away-from-us so-he-will-take Yahweh to pray!

מֹשֶׁה בְּעַד הָעָם׃ וַיֹּאמֶר יְהוָה אֶל־מֹשֶׁה עֲשֵׂה לְךָ שָׂרָף
snake for-you make! Moses to Yahweh and-he-said (8) the-people for Moses

וְשִׂים אֹתוֹ עַל־ נֵס וְהָיָה כָּל־ הַנָּשׁוּךְ וְרָאָה
when-he-sees the-one-being-bitten any-of and-he-will-be pole on him and-put!

אֹתוֹ וָחָי׃ וַיַּעַשׂ מֹשֶׁה נְחַשׁ נְחֹשֶׁת וַיְשִׂמֵהוּ
and-he-put-him bronze snake-of Moses so-he-made (9) then-he-will-live him

עַל־ הַנֵּס וְהָיָה אִם־ נָשַׁךְ הַנָּחָשׁ אֶת־ אִישׁ וְהִבִּיט אֶל־
at and-he-looked anyone *** the-snake he-bit when and-he-was the-pole on

נְחַשׁ הַנְּחֹשֶׁת וָחָי׃ וַיִּסְעוּ בְּנֵי יִשְׂרָאֵל
Israel sons-of and-they-moved-on (10) then-he-lived the-bronze snake-of

וַיַּחֲנוּ בְּאֹבֹת׃ וַיִּסְעוּ מֵאֹבֹת וַיַּחֲנוּ
and-they-camped from-Oboth then-they-set-out (11) at-Oboth and-they-camped

בְּעִיֵּי הָעֲבָרִים בַּמִּדְבָּר אֲשֶׁר עַל־ פְּנֵי מוֹאָב מִמִּזְרַח הַשָּׁמֶשׁ׃
the-sun toward-rise-of Moab face-of to that in-the-desert the-Abarim in-Iye

מִשָּׁם נָסָעוּ וַיַּחֲנוּ בְּנַחַל זָרֶד׃
Zered in-Valley-of and-they-camped they-moved-on from-there (12)

מִשָּׁם נָסָעוּ וַיַּחֲנוּ מֵעֵבֶר אַרְנוֹן אֲשֶׁר
which Arnon along-side and-they-camped they-set-out from-there (13)

בַּמִּדְבָּר הַיֹּצֵא מִגְּבוּל הָאֱמֹרִי כִּי אַרְנוֹן
Arnon also the-Amorite into-territory-of the-one-extending in-the-desert

גְּבוּל מוֹאָב בֵּין מוֹאָב וּבֵין הָאֱמֹרִי׃ עַל־ כֵּן יֵאָמַר
he-is-said this for (14) the-Amorite and-between Moab between Moab border-of

בְּסֵפֶר מִלְחֲמֹת יְהוָה אֶת־ וָהֵב בְּסוּפָה וְאֶת־ הַנְּחָלִים אַרְנוֹן׃
Arnon the-ravines and in-Suphah Waheb *** Yahweh Wars-of in-Book-of

וְאֶשֶׁד הַנְּחָלִים אֲשֶׁר נָטָה לְשֶׁבֶת עָר וְנִשְׁעַן
and-he-lies Ar to-site-of he-leads that the-ravines and-slope-of (15)

us up out of Egypt to die in the desert? There is no bread! There is no water! And we detest this miserable food!"

6 Then the LORD sent venomous snakes among them; they bit the people and many Israelites died. 7 The people came to Moses and said, "We sinned when we spoke against the LORD and against you. Pray that the LORD will take the snakes away from us." So Moses prayed for the people.

8 The LORD said to Moses, "Make a snake and put it up on a pole; anyone who is bitten can look at it and live." 9 So Moses made a bronze snake and put it up on a pole. Then when anyone was bitten by a snake and looked at the bronze snake, he lived.

*The Journey to Moab*

10 The Israelites moved on and camped at Oboth. 11 Then they set out from Oboth and camped in Iye Abarim, in the desert that faces Moab toward the sunrise. 12 From there they moved on and camped in the Zered Valley. 13 They set out from there and camped alongside the Arnon, which is in the desert extending into Amorite territory. The Arnon is the border of Moab, between Moab and the Amorites. 14 That is why the Book of the Wars of the LORD says:

"... Waheb in Suphah[u]
and the ravines,
the Arnon 15 and[v] the
slopes of the ravines
that lead to the site of Ar

[u] 14 The meaning of the Hebrew for this phrase is uncertain.
[v] 14,15 Or *"I have been given from Suphah and the ravines / of the Arnon* 15 *to*

לִגְבוּל מוֹאָב׃ (16) וּמִשָּׁם בְּאֵרָה הִוא הַבְּאֵר אֲשֶׁר אָמַר
he-said where the-well this to-Beer and-from-there (16) Moab along-border-of

יְהוָה לְמֹשֶׁה אֱסֹף אֶת־ הָעָם וְאֶתְּנָה לָהֶם מָיִם׃
waters to-them and-I-will-give the-people *** gather! to-Moses Yahweh

(17) אָז יָשִׁיר יִשְׂרָאֵל אֶת־ הַשִּׁירָה הַזֹּאת עֲלִי בְאֵר עֱנוּ־
sing! well spring-up! the-this the-song *** Israel he-sang then (17)

לָהּ׃ (18) בְּאֵר חֲפָרוּהָ שָׂרִים כָּרוּהָ נְדִיבֵי הָעָם
the-people nobles-of they-sank-her princes they-dug-her well (18) about-her

בִּמְחֹקֵק בְּמִשְׁעֲנֹתָם וּמִמִּדְבָּר מַתָּנָה׃
Mattanah then-from-desert with-staffs-of-them with-scepter

(19) וּמִמַּתָּנָה נַחֲלִיאֵל וּמִנַּחֲלִיאֵל בָּמוֹת׃ (20) וּמִבָּמוֹת
and-from-Bamoth (20) Bamoth and-from-Nahaliel Nahaliel and-from-Mattanah (19)

הַגַּיְא אֲשֶׁר בִּשְׂדֵה מוֹאָב רֹאשׁ הַפִּסְגָּה וְנִשְׁקָפָה עַל־
to and-she-overlooks the-Pisgah top-of Moab in-field-of that the-valley

פְּנֵי הַיְשִׁימֹן׃ (21) וַיִּשְׁלַח יִשְׂרָאֵל מַלְאָכִים אֶל־ סִיחֹן מֶלֶךְ־
king-of Sihon to messengers Israel and-he-sent (21) the-wasteland face-of

הָאֱמֹרִי לֵאמֹר׃ (22) אֶעְבְּרָה בְאַרְצֶךָ לֹא נִטֶּה
we-will-turn not through-country-of-you let-me-pass (22) to-say the-Amorite

בְּשָׂדֶה וּבְכֶרֶם לֹא נִשְׁתֶּה מֵי בְאֵר בְּדֶרֶךְ
along-highway-of well waters-of we-will-drink not or-into-vineyard into-field

הַמֶּלֶךְ נֵלֵךְ עַד אֲשֶׁר־ נַעֲבֹר גְּבֻלֶךָ׃ (23) וְלֹא־
but-not (23) territory-of-you we-passed when until we-will-travel the-king

נָתַן סִיחֹן אֶת־ יִשְׂרָאֵל עֲבֹר בִּגְבֻלוֹ וַיֶּאֱסֹף
and-he-mustered through-territory-of-him to-pass Israel *** Sihon he-let

סִיחֹן אֶת־ כָּל־ עַמּוֹ וַיֵּצֵא לִקְרַאת יִשְׂרָאֵל
Israel to-oppose and-he-marched-out army-of-him entire-of *** Sihon

הַמִּדְבָּרָה וַיָּבֹא יָהְצָה וַיִּלָּחֶם בְּיִשְׂרָאֵל׃
with-Israel then-he-fought to-Jahaz when-he-came into-the-desert

(24) וַיַּכֵּהוּ יִשְׂרָאֵל לְפִי־ חָרֶב וַיִּירַשׁ אֶת־
*** and-he-took-over sword with-edge-of Israel but-he-struck-him (24)

אַרְצוֹ מֵאַרְנֹן עַד־ יַבֹּק עַד־ בְּנֵי עַמּוֹן כִּי עַז
fortified for Ammon sons-of as-far-as Jabbok to from-Arnon land-of-him

גְּבוּל בְּנֵי עַמּוֹן׃ (25) וַיִּקַּח יִשְׂרָאֵל אֵת כָּל־ הֶעָרִים
the-cities all-of *** Israel and-he-captured (25) Ammon sons-of border-of

הָאֵלֶּה וַיֵּשֶׁב יִשְׂרָאֵל בְּכָל־ עָרֵי הָאֱמֹרִי בְּחֶשְׁבּוֹן
in-Heshbon the-Amorite cities-of in-all-of Israel and-he-occupied the-these

וּבְכָל־ בְּנֹתֶיהָ׃ (26) כִּי חֶשְׁבּוֹן עִיר סִיחֹן מֶלֶךְ
king-of Sihon city-of Heshbon now (26) settlements-of-her and-in-all-of

and lie along the border
of Moab."

[16]From there they continued on to Beer, the well where the LORD said to Moses, "Gather the people together and I will give them water."

[17]Then Israel sang this song:

"Spring up, O well!
Sing about it,
[18]about the well that the princes dug,
that the nobles of the people sank—
the nobles with scepters and staffs."

Then they went from the desert to Mattanah, [19]from Mattanah to Nahaliel, from Nahaliel to Bamoth, [20]and from Bamoth to the valley in Moab where the top of Pisgah overlooks the wasteland.

*Defeat of Sihon and Og*

[21]Israel sent messengers to say to Sihon king of the Amorites:

[22]"Let us pass through your country. We will not turn aside into any field or vineyard, or drink water from any well. We will travel along the king's highway until we have passed through your territory."

[23]But Sihon would not let Israel pass through his territory. He mustered his entire army and marched out into the desert against Israel. When he reached Jahaz, he fought with Israel. [24]Israel, however, put him to the sword and took over his land from the Arnon to the Jabbok, but only as far as the Ammonites, because their border was fortified. [25]Israel captured all the cities of the Amorites and occupied them, including Heshbon and all its surrounding settlements. [26]Heshbon was the city of Sihon king of the Amorites,

הָאֱמֹרִי הִוא וְהוּא נִלְחַם בְּמֶלֶךְ מוֹאָב הָרִאשׁוֹן וַיִּקַּח
and-he-took the-former Moab against-king-of he-fought now-he she the-Amorite

אֶת־ כָּל־ אַרְצוֹ מִיָּדוֹ עַד־ אַרְנֹן׃ עַל־ כֵּן
this for (27) Arnon as-far-as from-hand-of-him land-of-him all-of ***

יֹאמְרוּ הַמֹּשְׁלִים בֹּאוּ חֶשְׁבּוֹן תִּבָּנֶה
let-her-be-rebuilt Heshbon come! the-ones-making-poem they-say

וְתִכּוֹנֵן עִיר סִיחוֹן׃ כִּי־ אֵשׁ יָצְאָה מֵחֶשְׁבּוֹן
from-Heshbon she-went-out fire for (28) Sihon city-of and-let-her-be-restored

לֶהָבָה מִקִּרְיַת סִיחֹן אָכְלָה עָר מוֹאָב בַּעֲלֵי בָּמוֹת
heights-of citizens-of Moab Ar-of she-consumed Sihon from-city-of blaze

אַרְנֹן׃ אוֹי־ לְךָ מוֹאָב אָבַדְתָּ עַם־ כְּמוֹשׁ נָתַן
he-gave-up Chemosh people-of you-are-destroyed Moab to-you woe! (29) Arnon

בָּנָיו פְּלֵיטִם וּבְנֹתָיו בַּשְּׁבִית לְמֶלֶךְ אֱמֹרִי
Amorite to-king-of as-the-captive and-daughters-of-him fugitives sons-of-him

סִיחוֹן׃ וַנִּירָם אָבַד חֶשְׁבּוֹן עַד־ דִּיבֹן
Dibon to Heshbon he-is-destroyed but-we-overthrew-them (30) Sihon

וַנַּשִּׁים עַד־ נֹפַח אֲשֶׁר עַד־מֵידְבָא׃ וַיֵּשֶׁב
so-he-settled (31) Medeba to that Nophah as-far-as and-we-demolished-them

יִשְׂרָאֵל בְּאֶרֶץ הָאֱמֹרִי׃ וַיִּשְׁלַח מֹשֶׁה לְרַגֵּל אֶת־ יַעְזֵר
Jazer *** to-spy Moses and-he-sent (32) the-Amorite in-land-of Israel

וַיִּלְכְּדוּ בְּנֹתֶיהָ וַיִּירֶשׁ° אֶת־ הָאֱמֹרִי אֲשֶׁר־
who the-Amorite *** and-he-drove-out settlements-of-her and-they-captured

שָׁם׃ וַיִּפְנוּ וַיַּעֲלוּ דֶּרֶךְ הַבָּשָׁן
the-Bashan road-of and-they-went-up then-they-turned (33) there

וַיֵּצֵא עוֹג מֶלֶךְ־ הַבָּשָׁן לִקְרָאתָם הוּא וְכָל־
and-whole-of he to-meet-them the-Bashan king-of Og and-he-marched-out

עַמּוֹ לַמִּלְחָמָה אֶדְרֶעִי׃ וַיֹּאמֶר יְהוָה אֶל־ מֹשֶׁה אַל־
not Moses to Yahweh and-he-said (34) Edrei in-the-battle army-of-him

תִּירָא אֹתוֹ כִּי בְיָדְךָ נָתַתִּי אֹתוֹ וְאֶת־ כָּל־ עַמּוֹ וְאֶת־
and army-of-him whole-of and him I-gave into-hand-of-you for him you-fear

אַרְצוֹ וְעָשִׂיתָ לּוֹ כַּאֲשֶׁר עָשִׂיתָ לְסִיחֹן מֶלֶךְ הָאֱמֹרִי
the-Amorite king-of to-Sihon you-did just-as to-him so-you-do land-of-him

אֲשֶׁר יוֹשֵׁב בְּחֶשְׁבּוֹן׃ וַיַּכּוּ אֹתוֹ וְאֶת־ בָּנָיו וְאֶת־ כָּל־
whole-of and sons-of-him and him so-they-struck (35) in-Heshbon reigning who

עַמּוֹ עַד־ בִּלְתִּי הִשְׁאִיר־ לוֹ שָׂרִיד וַיִּירְשׁוּ אֶת־
*** and-they-possessed survivor to-him he-left not until army-of-him

אַרְצוֹ׃ וַיִּסְעוּ בְּנֵי יִשְׂרָאֵל וַיַּחֲנוּ
and-they-camped Israel sons-of then-they-traveled (22:1) land-of-him

°32 ק ויורש

who had fought against the former king of Moab and had taken from him all his land as far as the Arnon.
27That is why the poets say:

"Come to Heshbon and let
it be rebuilt;
let Sihon's city be
restored.
28"Fire went out from
Heshbon,
a blaze from the city of
Sihon.
It consumed Ar of Moab,
the citizens of Arnon's
heights.
29Woe to you, O Moab!
You are destroyed, O
people of Chemosh!
He has given up his sons
as fugitives
and his daughters as
captives
to Sihon king of the
Amorites.
30"But we have overthrown
them;
Heshbon is destroyed all
the way to Dibon.
We have demolished them
as far as Nophah,
which extends to
Medeba."

31So Israel settled in the land of the Amorites.
32After Moses had sent spies to Jazer, the Israelites captured its surrounding settlements and drove out the Amorites who were there.
33Then they turned and went up along the road toward Bashan, and Og king of Bashan and his whole army marched out to meet them in battle at Edrei.
34The LORD said to Moses, "Do not be afraid of him, for I have handed him over to you, with his whole army and his land. Do to him what you did to Sihon king of the Amorites, who reigned in Heshbon."
35So they struck him down, together with his sons and his whole army, leaving them no survivors. And they took possession of his land.

*Balak Summons Balaam*

22 Then the Israelites traveled to the plains of

בְּעַרְבוֹת מוֹאָב מֵעֵבֶר לְיַרְדֵּן יְרֵחוֹ׃ וַיַּרְא בָּלָק בֶּן־
son-of Balak now-he-saw (2) Jericho of-Jordan-of along-side Moab in-plains-of

צִפּוֹר אֵת כָּל־אֲשֶׁר־עָשָׂה יִשְׂרָאֵל לָאֱמֹרִי׃ וַיָּגָר
and-he-was-terrified (3) to-the-Amorite Israel he-did that all *** Zippor

מוֹאָב מִפְּנֵי הָעָם מְאֹד כִּי רַב־הוּא וַיָּקָץ מוֹאָב
Moab and-he-was-filled-with-dread he many for very the-people because-of Moab

מִפְּנֵי בְּנֵי יִשְׂרָאֵל׃ וַיֹּאמֶר מוֹאָב אֶל־זִקְנֵי מִדְיָן עַתָּה
now Midian elders-of to Moab and-he-said (4) Israel sons-of because-of

יְלַחֲכוּ הַקָּהָל אֶת־כָּל־סְבִיבֹתֵינוּ כִּלְחֹךְ הַשּׁוֹר
the-ox as-to-lick things-around-us all-of *** the-horde they-will-lick-up

אֵת יֶרֶק הַשָּׂדֶה וּבָלָק בֶּן־צִפּוֹר מֶלֶךְ לְמוֹאָב בָּעֵת
at-the-time of-Moab king Zippor son-of now-Balak the-field grass-of ***

הַהִוא׃ וַיִּשְׁלַח מַלְאָכִים אֶל־בִּלְעָם בֶּן־בְּעוֹר פְּתוֹרָה אֲשֶׁר
that at-Pethor Beor son-of Balaam to messengers and-he-sent (5) the-that

עַל־הַנָּהָר אֶרֶץ בְּנֵי־עַמּוֹ לִקְרֹא־לוֹ לֵאמֹר הִנֵּה
see! to-say to-him to-summon people-of-him sons-of land-of the-River near

עַם יָצָא מִמִּצְרַיִם הִנֵּה כִסָּה אֶת־עֵין הָאָרֶץ וְהוּא
and-he the-land face-of *** he-covers see! from-Egypt he-came people

יֹשֵׁב מִמֻּלִי׃ וְעַתָּה לְכָה־נָּא אָרָה־לִּי אֶת־הָעָם
the-people *** for-me curse! now! come! and-now (6) next-to-me settling

הַזֶּה כִּי־עָצוּם הוּא מִמֶּנִּי אוּלַי אוּכַל נַכֶּה־
to-defeat I-will-be-able perhaps for-me he too-powerful for the-this

בּוֹ וַאֲגָרְשֶׁנּוּ מִן־הָאָרֶץ כִּי יָדַעְתִּי אֵת אֲשֶׁר־
whom *** I-know for the-country from and-I-will-drive-him against-him

תְּבָרֵךְ מְבֹרָךְ וַאֲשֶׁר תָּאֹר יוּאָר׃ וַיֵּלְכוּ
and-they-left (7) he-is-cursed you-curse and-whom being-blessed you-bless

זִקְנֵי מוֹאָב וְזִקְנֵי מִדְיָן וּקְסָמִים בְּיָדָם
in-hand-of-them and-divination-fees Midian and-elders-of Moab elders-of

וַיָּבֹאוּ אֶל־בִּלְעָם וַיְדַבְּרוּ אֵלָיו דִּבְרֵי בָלָק׃ וַיֹּאמֶר
and-he-said (8) Balak words-of to-him then-they-told Balaam to when-they-came

אֲלֵיהֶם לִינוּ פֹה הַלַּיְלָה וַהֲשִׁבֹתִי אֶתְכֶם דָּבָר כַּאֲשֶׁר
just-as answer you and-I-will-bring the-night here spend-night! to-them

יְדַבֵּר יְהוָה אֵלָי וַיֵּשְׁבוּ שָׂרֵי־מוֹאָב עִם־בִּלְעָם׃
Balaam with Moab princes-of so-they-stayed to-me Yahweh he-gives

וַיָּבֹא אֱלֹהִים אֶל־בִּלְעָם וַיֹּאמֶר מִי הָאֲנָשִׁים הָאֵלֶּה עִמָּךְ׃
with-you the-these the-men who? and-he-asked Balaam to God and-he-came (9)

וַיֹּאמֶר בִּלְעָם אֶל־הָאֱלֹהִים בָּלָק בֶּן־צִפֹּר מֶלֶךְ מוֹאָב שָׁלַח
he-sent Moab king-of Zippor son-of Balak the-God to Balaam and-he-said (10)

Moab and camped along the
Jordan across from Jericho.[w]
2 Now Balak son of Zippor
saw all that Israel had done to
the Amorites, 3 and Moab was
terrified because there were so
many people. Indeed, Moab
was filled with dread because
of the Israelites.
4 The Moabites said to the elders of Midian, "This horde is
going to lick up everything
around us, as an ox licks up
the grass of the field."
So Balak son of Zippor, who
was king of Moab at that time,
5 sent messengers to summon
Balaam son of Beor, who was
at Pethor, near the River,[x] in
his native land. Balak said:

"A people has come out
of Egypt; they cover the
face of the land and have
settled next to me. 6 Now
come and put a curse on
these people, because they
are too powerful for me.
Perhaps then I will be able
to defeat them and drive
them out of the country.
For I know that those you
bless are blessed, and those
you curse are cursed."

7 The elders of Moab and
Midian left, taking with them
the fee for divination. When
they came to Balaam, they told
him what Balak had said.
8 "Spend the night here," Balaam said to them, "and I will
bring you back the answer the
LORD gives me." So the Moabite princes stayed with him.
9 God came to Balaam and
asked, "Who are these men
with you?"
10 Balaam said to God, "Balak
son of Zippor, king of Moab,

[w] 1 Hebrew *Jordan of Jericho*; possibly an ancient name for the Jordan River
[x] 5 That is, the Euphrates

אֵלַ֑י ׀ הִנֵּ֤ה הָעָם֙ הַיֹּצֵ֣א מִמִּצְרַ֔יִם וַיְכַ֖ס אֶת־
to-me (11) see! the-people the-one-coming from-Egypt and-he-covers ***

עֵ֣ין הָאָ֑רֶץ עַתָּ֗ה לְכָ֤ה קָֽבָה־לִּי֙ אֹת֔וֹ אוּלַ֥י אוּכַ֛ל
face-of the-land now come! curse! for-me him perhaps I-will-be-able

לְהִלָּ֥חֶם בּ֖וֹ וְגֵרַשְׁתִּֽיו׃ (12) וַיֹּ֤אמֶר אֱלֹהִים֙ אֶל־
to-fight against-him and-I-will-drive-away-him (12) but-he-said God to

בִּלְעָ֔ם לֹ֥א תֵלֵ֖ךְ עִמָּהֶ֑ם לֹ֤א תָאֹר֙ אֶת־הָעָ֔ם כִּ֥י בָר֖וּךְ
Balaam not you-go with-them not you-curse *** the-people for being-blessed

ה֥וּא׃ (13) וַיָּ֤קָם בִּלְעָם֙ בַּבֹּ֔קֶר וַיֹּ֨אמֶר֙ אֶל־שָׂרֵ֣י בָלָ֔ק
he (13) so-he-got-up Balaam in-the-morning and-he-said to princes-of Balak

לְכ֖וּ אֶל־אַרְצְכֶ֑ם כִּ֚י מֵאֵ֣ן יְהוָ֔ה לְתִתִּ֖י לַהֲלֹ֥ךְ עִמָּכֶֽם׃
go-back! to country-of-you for he-refused Yahweh to-let-me to-go with-you

(14) וַיָּק֙וּמוּ֙ שָׂרֵ֣י מוֹאָ֔ב וַיָּבֹ֖אוּ אֶל־בָּלָ֑ק וַיֹּ֣אמְר֔וּ
(14) so-they-got-up princes-of Moab and-they-returned to Balak and-they-said

מֵאֵ֥ן בִּלְעָ֖ם הֲלֹ֥ךְ עִמָּֽנוּ׃ (15) וַיֹּ֥סֶף ע֖וֹד בָּלָ֑ק שְׁלֹ֣חַ
he-refused Balaam to-come with-us (15) then-he-repeated again Balak to-send

שָׂרִ֔ים רַבִּ֥ים וְנִכְבָּדִ֖ים מֵאֵֽלֶּה׃
princes ones-numerous and-ones-being-distinguished more-than-these

(16) וַיָּבֹ֖אוּ אֶל־בִּלְעָ֑ם וַיֹּ֣אמְרוּ ל֗וֹ כֹּ֤ה אָמַר֙ בָּלָ֣ק בֶּן־
(16) and-they-came to Balaam and-they-said to-him this he-says Balak son-of

צִפּ֔וֹר אַל־נָ֥א תִמָּנַ֖ע מֵהֲלֹ֣ךְ אֵלָ֑י׃ (17) כִּֽי־כַבֵּ֤ד
Zippor not now! you-be-kept from-to-come to-me (17) for to-reward

אֲכַבֶּדְךָ֙ מְאֹ֔ד וְכֹ֛ל אֲשֶׁר־תֹּאמַ֥ר אֵלַ֖י אֶֽעֱשֶׂ֑ה וּלְכָה־
I-will-reward-you handsomely and-all that you-say to-me I-will-do so-come!

נָּא֙ קָֽבָה־לִּ֔י אֵ֖ת הָעָ֥ם הַזֶּֽה׃ (18) וַיַּ֣עַן בִּלְעָ֗ם
now! curse! for-me *** the-people the-this (18) but-he-answered Balaam

וַיֹּ֙אמֶר֙ אֶל־עַבְדֵ֣י בָלָ֔ק אִם־יִתֶּן־לִ֥י בָלָ֖ק מְלֹ֣א
and-he-said to servants-of Balak if he-gave to-me Balak filled-of

בֵית֑וֹ כֶּ֖סֶף וְזָהָ֑ב לֹ֣א אוּכַ֗ל לַעֲבֹר֙ אֶת־פִּ֣י יְהוָ֔ה
palace-of-him silver and-gold not I-could to-go-beyond *** command-of Yahweh

אֱלֹהָ֔י לַעֲשׂ֥וֹת קְטַנָּ֖ה א֥וֹ גְדוֹלָֽה׃ (19) וְעַתָּ֗ה שְׁב֨וּ נָ֥א בָזֶ֛ה גַּם־אַתֶּ֖ם
God-of-me to-do small or great (19) and-now stay! now! at-here you also

הַלָּ֑יְלָה וְאֵ֣דְעָ֔ה מַה־יֹּסֵ֥ף יְהוָ֖ה דַּבֵּ֥ר עִמִּֽי׃
the-night and-I-will-find-out what he-will-add Yahweh to-tell to-me

(20) וַיָּבֹ֨א אֱלֹהִ֥ים ׀ אֶל־בִּלְעָם֮ לַיְלָה֒ וַיֹּ֣אמֶר ל֗וֹ אִם־לִקְרֹ֤א
(20) and-he-came God to Balaam night and-he-said to-him since to-summon

לְךָ֙ בָּ֣אוּ הָאֲנָשִׁ֔ים ק֖וּם לֵ֣ךְ אִתָּ֑ם וְאַ֗ךְ אֶת־הַדָּבָ֛ר אֲשֶׁר־
to-you they-came the-men rise! go! with-them but-only *** the-thing that

sent me this message: [11]"A people that has come out of Egypt covers the face of the land. Now come and put a curse on them for me. Perhaps then I will be able to fight them and drive them away.'"

[12]But God said to Balaam, "Do not go with them. You must not put a curse on those people, because they are blessed."

[13]The next morning Balaam got up and said to Balak's princes, "Go back to your own country, for the LORD has refused to let me go with you."

[14]So the Moabite princes returned to Balak and said, "Balaam refused to come with us."

[15]Then Balak sent other princes, more numerous and more distinguished than the first. [16]They came to Balaam and said:

"This is what Balak son of Zippor says: Do not let anything keep you from coming to me, [17]because I will reward you handsomely and do whatever you say. Come and put a curse on these people for me."

[18]But Balaam answered them, "Even if Balak gave me his palace filled with silver and gold, I could not do anything great or small to go beyond the command of the LORD my God. [19]Now stay here tonight as the others did, and I will find out what else the LORD will tell me."

[20]That night God came to Balaam and said, "Since these men have come to summon you, go with them, but do only

אֲדַבֵּר אֵלֶיךָ אֹתוֹ תַעֲשֶׂה׃ וַיָּקָם בִּלְעָם בַּבֹּקֶר
in-the-morning Balaam and-he-got-up (21) you-do him to-you I-tell

וַיַּחֲבֹשׁ אֶת־ אֲתֹנוֹ וַיֵּלֶךְ עִם־ שָׂרֵי מוֹאָב׃
Moab princes-of with and-he-went donkey-of-him *** and-he-saddled

וַיִּחַר־ אַף אֱלֹהִים כִּי־ הוֹלֵךְ הוּא וַיִּתְיַצֵּב מַלְאַךְ יְהוָה
Yahweh angel-of and-he-stood he going when God anger-of but-he-burned (22)

בַּדֶּרֶךְ לְשָׂטָן לוֹ וְהוּא רֹכֵב עַל־ אֲתֹנוֹ וּשְׁנֵי
and-two-of donkey-of-him on riding and-he against-him as-opposer in-the-road

נְעָרָיו עִמּוֹ׃ וַתֵּרֶא הָאָתוֹן אֶת־ מַלְאַךְ יְהוָה
Yahweh angel-of *** the-donkey when-she-saw (23) with-him servants-of-him

נִצָּב בַּדֶּרֶךְ וְחַרְבּוֹ שְׁלוּפָה בְּיָדוֹ
in-hand-of-him being-drawn and-sword-of-him in-the-road standing

וַתֵּט הָאָתוֹן מִן־ הַדֶּרֶךְ וַתֵּלֶךְ בַּשָּׂדֶה
into-the-field and-she-went the-road off the-donkey then-she-turned

וַיַּךְ בִּלְעָם אֶת־ הָאָתוֹן לְהַטֹּתָהּ הַדָּרֶךְ׃ וַיַּעֲמֹד
then-he-stood (24) the-road to-get-back-her the-donkey *** Balaam and-he-beat

מַלְאַךְ יְהוָה בְּמִשְׁעוֹל הַכְּרָמִים גָּדֵר מִזֶּה וְגָדֵר
and-wall on-this-side wall the-vineyards in-narrow-path-of Yahweh angel-of

מִזֶּה׃ וַתֵּרֶא הָאָתוֹן אֶת־ מַלְאַךְ יְהוָה
Yahweh angel-of *** the-donkey when-she-saw (25) on-that-side

וַתִּלָּחֵץ אֶל־ הַקִּיר וַתִּלְחַץ אֶת־ רֶגֶל בִּלְעָם אֶל־
against Balaam foot-of *** and-she-crushed the-wall to then-she-pressed-close

הַקִּיר וַיֹּסֶף לְהַכֹּתָהּ׃ וַיּוֹסֶף מַלְאַךְ־ יְהוָה
Yahweh angel-of then-he-repeated (26) to-beat-her so-he-repeated the-wall

עֲבוֹר וַיַּעֲמֹד בְּמָקוֹם צָר אֲשֶׁר אֵין־ דֶּרֶךְ לִנְטוֹת יָמִין
right to-turn room there-is-no where narrow in-place and-he-stood to-move

וּשְׂמֹאול׃ וַתֵּרֶא הָאָתוֹן אֶת־ מַלְאַךְ יְהוָה וַתִּרְבַּץ
then-she-lay-down Yahweh angel-of *** the-donkey when-she-saw (27) or-left

תַּחַת בִּלְעָם וַיִּחַר־ אַף בִּלְעָם וַיַּךְ אֶת־ הָאָתוֹן
the-donkey *** and-he-beat Balaam anger-of and-he-burned Balaam under

בַּמַּקֵּל׃ וַיִּפְתַּח יְהוָה אֶת־ פִּי הָאָתוֹן
the-donkey mouth-of *** Yahweh then-he-opened (28) with-the-staff

וַתֹּאמֶר לְבִלְעָם מֶה־ עָשִׂיתִי לְךָ כִּי הִכִּיתַנִי זֶה שָׁלֹשׁ רְגָלִים׃
times three this you-beat-me that to-you I-did what? to-Balaam and-she-said

וַיֹּאמֶר בִּלְעָם לָאָתוֹן כִּי הִתְעַלַּלְתְּ בִּי לוּ
if of-me you-made-fool because to-the-donkey Balaam and-he-answered (29)

יֶשׁ־ חֶרֶב בְּיָדִי כִּי עַתָּה הֲרַגְתִּיךְ׃ וַתֹּאמֶר
and-she-said (30) I-would-kill-you now then in-hand-of-me sword he-was

what I tell you."

*Balaam's Donkey*

21 Balaam got up in the morning, saddled his donkey and went with the princes of Moab. 22 But God was very angry when he went, and the angel of the LORD stood in the road to oppose him. Balaam was riding on his donkey, and his two servants were with him. 23 When the donkey saw the angel of the LORD standing in the road with a drawn sword in his hand, she turned off the road into a field. Balaam beat her to get her back on the road.

24 Then the angel of the LORD stood in a narrow path between two vineyards, with walls on both sides. 25 When the donkey saw the angel of the LORD, she pressed close to the wall, crushing Balaam's foot against it. So he beat her again.

26 Then the angel of the LORD moved on ahead and stood in a narrow place where there was no room to turn, either to the right or to the left. 27 When the donkey saw the angel of the LORD, she lay down under Balaam, and he was angry and beat her with his staff. 28 Then the LORD opened the donkey's mouth, and she said to Balaam, "What have I done to you to make you beat me these three times?"

29 Balaam answered the donkey, "You have made a fool of me! If I had a sword in my hand, I would kill you right now."

הָאָתוֹן אֶל־ בִּלְעָם הֲלוֹא אָנֹכִי אֲתֹנְךָ אֲשֶׁר־ רָכַבְתָּ עָלַי
on-me you-ride which donkey-of-you I not? Balaam to the-donkey

מֵעוֹדְךָ עַד־ הַיּוֹם הַזֶּה הַהַסְכֵּן הִסְכַּנְתִּי לַעֲשׂוֹת לְךָ
to-you to-do I-made-habit to-make-habit? the-this the-day to as-always-you

כֹּה וַיֹּאמֶר לֹא׃ וַיְגַל יְהוָה אֶת־ עֵינֵי בִלְעָם וַיַּרְא
and-he-saw Balaam eyes-of *** Yahweh then-he-opened (31) no and-he-said this

אֶת־ מַלְאַךְ יְהוָה נִצָּב בַּדֶּרֶךְ וְחַרְבּוֹ שְׁלֻפָה
being-drawn and-sword-of-him in-the-road standing Yahweh angel-of ***

בְּיָדוֹ וַיִּקֹּד וַיִּשְׁתַּחוּ לְאַפָּיו׃ וַיֹּאמֶר
and-he-asked (32) to-faces-of-him and-he-fell so-he-bowed in-hand-of-him

אֵלָיו מַלְאַךְ יְהוָה עַל־ מָה הִכִּיתָ אֶת־ אֲתֹנְךָ זֶה שָׁלוֹשׁ רְגָלִים
times three this donkey-of-you *** you-beat why? for Yahweh angel-of to-him

הִנֵּה אָנֹכִי יָצָאתִי לְשָׂטָן כִּי־ יָרַט הַדֶּרֶךְ לְנֶגְדִּי׃
before-me the-path he-is-reckless for as-opposer I-came I see!

וַתִּרְאַנִי הָאָתוֹן וַתֵּט לְפָנַי זֶה שָׁלֹשׁ רְגָלִים
times three this away-from-me and-she-turned the-donkey and-she-saw-me (33)

אוּלַי נָטְתָה מִפָּנַי כִּי עַתָּה גַּם־ אֹתְכָה הָרַגְתִּי
I-would-have-killed you indeed now then away-from-me she-turned if-not

וְאוֹתָהּ הֶחֱיֵיתִי׃ וַיֹּאמֶר בִּלְעָם אֶל־ מַלְאַךְ יְהוָה
Yahweh angel-of to Balaam and-he-said (34) I-would-have-spared but-her

חָטָאתִי כִּי לֹא יָדַעְתִּי כִּי אַתָּה נִצָּב לִקְרָאתִי בַּדָּרֶךְ
in-the-road to-oppose-me standing you that I-realized not for I-sinned

וְעַתָּה אִם־ רַע בְּעֵינֶיךָ אָשׁוּבָה לִּי׃ וַיֹּאמֶר
and-he-said (35) to-me I-will-go-back in-eyes-of-you displeasing if so-now

מַלְאַךְ יְהוָה אֶל־בִּלְעָם לֵךְ עִם־ הָאֲנָשִׁים וְאֶפֶס אֶת־ הַדָּבָר אֲשֶׁר־
that the-message *** but-only the-men with go! Balaam to Yahweh angel-of

אֲדַבֵּר אֵלֶיךָ אֹתוֹ תְדַבֵּר וַיֵּלֶךְ בִּלְעָם עִם־ שָׂרֵי בָלָק׃
Balak princes-of with Balaam so-he-went you-speak him to-you I-tell

וַיִּשְׁמַע בָּלָק כִּי בָא בִלְעָם וַיֵּצֵא לִקְרָאתוֹ
to-meet-him then-he-went-out Balaam he-comes that Balak when-he-heard (36)

אֶל־ עִיר מוֹאָב אֲשֶׁר עַל־ גְּבוּל אַרְנֹן אֲשֶׁר בִּקְצֵה הַגְּבוּל׃
the-territory at-edge-of that Arnon border-of on that Moab town-of at

וַיֹּאמֶר בָּלָק אֶל־בִּלְעָם הֲלֹא שָׁלֹחַ שָׁלַחְתִּי אֵלֶיךָ לִקְרֹא־ לָךְ
to-you to-summon to-you I-sent to-send not? Balaam to Balak and-he-said (37)

לָמָּה לֹא־ הָלַכְתָּ אֵלָי הַאֻמְנָם לֹא אוּכַל כַּבְּדֶךָ׃ וַיֹּאמֶר
and-he-said (38) to-reward-you I-am-able not really? to-me you-came not why?

בִלְעָם אֶל־ בָּלָק הִנֵּה־ בָאתִי אֵלֶיךָ עַתָּה הֲיָכֹל אוּכַל דַּבֵּר
to-say I-am-able to-be-able? now to-you I-came see! Balak to Balaam

30 The donkey said to Balaam,
"Am I not your own donkey,
which you have always ridden, to this day? Have I been
in the habit of doing this to
you?"
"No," he said.
31 Then the LORD opened Balaam's eyes, and he saw the
angel of the LORD standing in
the road with his sword
drawn. So he bowed low and
fell facedown.
32 The angel of the LORD
asked him, "Why have you
beaten your donkey these
three times? I have come here
to oppose you because your
path is a reckless one before
me.[y] 33 The donkey saw me and
turned away from me these
three times. If she had not
turned away, I would cer-
tainly have killed you by now,
but I would have spared her."
34 Balaam said to the angel of
the LORD, "I have sinned. I did
not realize you were standing
in the road to oppose me. Now
if you are displeased, I will go
back."
35 The angel of the LORD said
to Balaam, "Go with the men,
but speak only what I tell
you." So Balaam went with
the princes of Balak.
36 When Balak heard that Balaam was coming, he went out
to meet him at the Moabite
town on the Arnon border, at
the edge of his territory.
37 Balak said to Balaam, "Did I
not send you an urgent summons? Why didn't you come
to me? Am I really not able to
reward you?"
38 "Well, I have come to you
now," Balaam replied. "But

y32 The meaning of the Hebrew for this clause is uncertain.

מְאוּמָה הַדָּבָר אֲשֶׁר יָשִׂים אֱלֹהִים בְּפִי אֹתוֹ אֲדַבֵּר׃
I-must-speak him in-mouth-of-me God he-puts that the-message anything

(39) וַיֵּלֶךְ בִּלְעָם עִם־ בָּלָק וַיָּבֹאוּ קִרְיַת חֻצוֹת׃
Huzoth Kiriath and-they-went Balak with Balaam then-he-went (39)

(40) וַיִּזְבַּח בָּלָק בָּקָר וָצֹאן וַיְשַׁלַּח לְבִלְעָם
to-Balaam and-he-gave and-sheep cattle Balak and-he-sacrificed (40)

וְלַשָּׂרִים אֲשֶׁר אִתּוֹ׃ (41) וַיְהִי בַבֹּקֶר וַיִּקַּח
that-he-took in-the-morning and-he-was (41) with-him who and-to-the-princes

בָּלָק אֶת־ בִּלְעָם וַיַּעֲלֵהוּ בָּמוֹת בָּעַל וַיַּרְא מִשָּׁם
from-there and-he-saw Baal Bamoth and-he-took-up-him Balaam *** Balak

קְצֵה הָעָם׃ (23:1) וַיֹּאמֶר בִּלְעָם אֶל־ בָּלָק בְּנֵה־ לִי בָזֶה
at-here for-me build! Balak to Balaam and-he-said (23:1) the-people part-of

שִׁבְעָה מִזְבְּחֹת וְהָכֵן לִי בָּזֶה שִׁבְעָה פָרִים וְשִׁבְעָה אֵילִים׃
rams and-seven bulls seven at-here for-me and-prepare! altars seven

(2) וַיַּעַשׂ בָּלָק כַּאֲשֶׁר דִּבֶּר בִּלְעָם וַיַּעַל בָּלָק וּבִלְעָם
and-Balaam Balak and-he-offered Balaam he-said just-as Balak so-he-did (2)

פַּר וָאַיִל בַּמִּזְבֵּחַ׃ (3) וַיֹּאמֶר בִּלְעָם לְבָלָק הִתְיַצֵּב עַל־
beside stay! to-Balak Balaam then-he-said (3) on-the-altar and-ram bull

עֹלָתֶךָ וְאֵלְכָה אוּלַי יִקָּרֶה יְהוָה לִקְרָאתִי
to-meet-me Yahweh he-will-come perhaps and-I-will-go offering-of-you

וּדְבַר מַה־ יַּרְאֵנִי וְהִגַּדְתִּי לָךְ וַיֵּלֶךְ
then-he-went to-you then-I-will-tell he-reveals-to-me whatever and-message-of

שֶׁפִי׃ (4) וַיִּקָּר אֱלֹהִים אֶל־ בִּלְעָם וַיֹּאמֶר אֵלָיו אֶת־ שִׁבְעַת
seven-of *** to-him and-he-said Balaam with God and-he-met (4) barren-height

הַמִּזְבְּחֹת עָרַכְתִּי וָאַעַל פַּר וָאַיִל בַּמִּזְבֵּחַ׃ (5) וַיָּשֶׂם
and-he-put (5) on-the-altar and-ram bull and-I-offered I-prepared the-altars

יְהוָה דָּבָר בְּפִי בִלְעָם וַיֹּאמֶר שׁוּב אֶל־ בָּלָק וְכֹה
and-this Balak to go-back! and-he-said Balaam in-mouth-of message Yahweh

תְדַבֵּר׃ (6) וַיָּשָׁב אֵלָיו וְהִנֵּה נִצָּב עַל־ עֹלָתוֹ
offering-of-him beside standing and-see! to-him so-he-went-back (6) you-speak

הוּא וְכָל־ שָׂרֵי מוֹאָב׃ (7) וַיִּשָּׂא מְשָׁלוֹ וַיֹּאמַר
and-he-said oracle-of-him then-he-uttered (7) Moab princes-of and-all-of he

מִן־ אֲרָם יַנְחֵנִי בָלָק מֶלֶךְ־ מוֹאָב מֵהַרְרֵי־ קֶדֶם לְכָה
come! east from-mountains-of Moab king-of Balak he-brought-me Aram from

אָרָה־ לִּי יַעֲקֹב וּלְכָה זֹעֲמָה יִשְׂרָאֵל׃ (8) מָה אֶקֹּב לֹא
not can-I-curse how? (8) Israel denounce! and-come! Jacob for-me curse!

קַבֹּה אֵל וּמָה אֶזְעֹם לֹא זָעַם יְהוָה׃ (9) כִּי־
for (9) Yahweh he-denounced not can-I-denounce and-how? God he-cursed-him

can I say just anything? I must speak only what God puts in my mouth."

[39]Then Balaam went with Balak to Kiriath Huzoth. [40]Balak sacrificed cattle and sheep, and gave some to Balaam and the princes who were with him. [41]The next morning Balak took Balaam up to Bamoth Baal, and from there he saw part of the people.

*Balaam's First Oracle*

**23** Balaam said, "Build me seven altars here, and prepare seven bulls and seven rams for me." [2]Balak did as Balaam said, and the two of them offered a bull and a ram on each altar.

[3]Then Balaam said to Balak, "Stay here beside your offering while I go aside. Perhaps the LORD will come to meet with me. Whatever he reveals to me I will tell you." Then he went off to a barren height.

[4]God met with him, and Balaam said, "I have prepared seven altars, and on each altar I have offered a bull and a ram."

[5]The LORD put a message in Balaam's mouth and said, "Go back to Balak and give him this message."

[6]So he went back to him and found him standing beside his offering, with all the princes of Moab. [7]Then Balaam uttered his oracle:

"Balak brought me from
 Aram,
the king of Moab from
 the eastern mountains.
'Come,' he said, 'curse
 Jacob for me;
come, denounce Israel.'
[8]How can I curse
 those whom God has not
 cursed?
How can I denounce
 those whom the LORD
 has not denounced?

מֵרֹאשׁ צֻרִים אֶרְאֶנּוּ וּמִגְּבָעוֹת אֲשׁוּרֶנּוּ הֶן־ עָם

people see! I-view-him and-from-heights I-see-him rocky-ones from-peak-of

לְבָדָד יִשְׁכֹּן וּבַגּוֹיִם לֹא יִתְחַשָּׁב׃ מִי מָנָה

he-can-count who? (10) he-considers-self not and-of-the-nations he-lives apart

עֲפַר יַעֲקֹב וּמִסְפָּר אֶת־ רֹבַע יִשְׂרָאֵל תָּמֹת נַפְשִׁי

life-of-me let-her-die Israel fourth-of *** or-number Jacob dust-of

מוֹת יְשָׁרִים וּתְהִי אַחֲרִיתִי כָּמֹהוּ׃ וַיֹּאמֶר

and-he-said (11) like-of-him end-of-me and-may-she-be righteous-ones death-of

בָּלָק אֶל־בִּלְעָם מֶה עָשִׂיתָ לִי לָקֹב אֹיְבַי לְקַחְתִּיךָ

I-brought-you being-enemies-of-me to-curse to-me you-did what? Balaam to Balak

וְהִנֵּה בֵּרַכְתָּ בָרֵךְ׃ וַיַּעַן וַיֹּאמַר הֲלֹא אֵת

*** not? and-he-said and-he-answered (12) to-bless you-blessed but-see!

אֲשֶׁר יָשִׂים יְהוָה בְּפִי אֹתוֹ אֶשְׁמֹר לְדַבֵּר׃ וַיֹּאמֶר

then-he-said (13) to-speak I-must him in-mouth-of-me Yahweh he-puts what

אֵלָיו בָּלָק לְךָ־ נָּא אִתִּי אֶל־מָקוֹם אַחֵר אֲשֶׁר תִּרְאֶנּוּ

you-can-see-him where another place to with-me now! come! Balak to-him

מִשָּׁם אֶפֶס קָצֵהוּ תִרְאֶה וְכֻלּוֹ לֹא תִרְאֶה

you-will-see not but-all-of-him you-will-see part-of-him only from-there

וְקָבְנוֹ־ לִי מִשָּׁם׃ וַיִּקָּחֵהוּ שְׂדֵה צֹפִים אֶל־

on Zophim field-of so-he-took-him (14) from-there for-me and-curse-him!

רֹאשׁ הַפִּסְגָּה וַיִּבֶן שִׁבְעָה מִזְבְּחֹת וַיַּעַל פָּר וָאַיִל

and-ram bull and-he-offered altars seven and-he-built the-Pisgah top-of

בַּמִּזְבֵּחַ׃ וַיֹּאמֶר אֶל־בָּלָק הִתְיַצֵּב כֹּה עַל־ עֹלָתֶךָ

offering-of-you beside here stay! Balak to and-he-said (15) on-the-altar

וְאָנֹכִי אִקָּרֶה כֹּה׃ וַיִּקָּר יְהוָה אֶל־ בִּלְעָם וַיָּשֶׂם דָּבָר

message and-he-put Balaam with Yahweh and-he-met (16) there I-meet while-I

בְּפִיו וַיֹּאמֶר שׁוּב אֶל־בָּלָק וְכֹה תְדַבֵּר׃ וַיָּבֹא

so-he-went (17) you-speak and-this Balak to go-back! and-he-said in-mouth-of-him

אֵלָיו וְהִנּוֹ נִצָּב עַל־ עֹלָתוֹ וְשָׂרֵי מוֹאָב

Moab and-princes-of offering-of-him beside standing and-see-he! to-him

אִתּוֹ וַיֹּאמֶר לוֹ בָּלָק מַה־ דִּבֶּר יְהוָה׃ וַיִּשָּׂא

then-he-uttered (18) Yahweh he-said what? Balak to-him and-he-asked with-him

מְשָׁלוֹ וַיֹּאמַר קוּם בָּלָק וּשֲׁמָע הַאֲזִינָה עָדַי בְּנוֹ

son-of-him to-me hear! and-listen! Balak arise! and-he-said oracle-of-him

צִפֹּר׃ לֹא אִישׁ אֵל וִיכַזֵּב וּבֶן־ אָדָם וְיִתְנֶחָם

that-he-changes-mind man nor-son-of that-he-lies God man not (19) Zippor

הַהוּא אָמַר וְלֹא יַעֲשֶׂה וְדִבֶּר וְלֹא יְקִימֶנָּה׃

he-fulfills-her and-not or-he-promises he-acts and-not he-speaks he?

°13 ק לכה

9From the rocky peaks I see
them,
from the heights I view
them.
I see a people who live
apart
and do not consider
themselves one of the
nations.
10Who can count the dust of
Jacob
or number the fourth
part of Israel?
Let me die the death of the
righteous,
and may my end be like
theirs!"

11Balak said to Balaam, "What have you done to me? I brought you to curse my enemies, but you have done nothing but bless them!"

12He answered, "Must I not speak what the LORD puts in my mouth?"

*Balaam's Second Oracle*

13Then Balak said to him, "Come with me to another place where you can see them; you will see only a part but not all of them. And from there, curse them for me."
14So he took him to the field of Zophim on the top of Pisgah, and there he built seven altars and offered a bull and a ram on each altar.

15Balaam said to Balak, "Stay here beside your offering while I meet with him over there."

16The LORD met with Balaam and put a message in his mouth and said, "Go back to Balak and give him this message."

17So he went to him and found him standing beside his offering, with the princes of Moab. Balak asked him, "What did the LORD say?"

18Then he uttered his oracle:

"Arise, Balak, and listen;
hear me, son of Zippor.
19God is not a man, that he
should lie,
nor a son of man, that
he should change his
mind.
Does he speak and then
not act?
Does he promise and not
fulfill?

הִנֵּה בָרֵךְ לָקָחְתִּי וּבֵרֵךְ וְלֹא אֲשִׁיבֶנָּה׃
I-can-change-her and-not now-he-blessed I-received to-bless see! (20)

לֹא־הִבִּיט אָוֶן בְּיַעֲקֹב וְלֹא־רָאָה עָמָל בְּיִשְׂרָאֵל
in-Israel misery he-observes and-not in-Jacob misfortune he-sees not (21)

יְהוָה אֱלֹהָיו עִמּוֹ וּתְרוּעַת מֶלֶךְ בּוֹ׃ אֵל מוֹצִיאָם
bringing-them God (22) among-him King and-shout-of with-him God-of-him Yahweh

מִמִּצְרָיִם כְּתוֹעֲפֹת רְאֵם לוֹ׃ כִּי לֹא־נַחַשׁ בְּיַעֲקֹב
against-Jacob sorcery no indeed (23) to-him wild-ox as-strengths-of from-Egypt

וְלֹא־קֶסֶם בְּיִשְׂרָאֵל כָּעֵת יֵאָמֵר לְיַעֲקֹב
of-Jacob he-will-be-said at-the-now against-Israel divination and-no

וּלְיִשְׂרָאֵל מַה־פָּעַל אֵל׃ הֶן־עָם כְּלָבִיא יָקוּם
he-rises like-lioness people see! (24) God he-did what! and-of-Israel

וְכַאֲרִי יִתְנַשָּׂא לֹא יִשְׁכַּב עַד־יֹאכַל טֶרֶף וְדַם־
and-blood-of prey he-devours till he-rests not he-rouses-self and-like-lion

חֲלָלִים יִשְׁתֶּה׃ וַיֹּאמֶר בָּלָק אֶל־בִּלְעָם גַּם־קֹב לֹא
not to-curse at-all Balaam to Balak then-he-said (25) he-drinks victims

תִקֳּבֶנּוּ גַּם־בָּרֵךְ לֹא תְבָרְכֶנּוּ׃ וַיַּעַן בִּלְעָם
Balaam and-he-answered (26) you-bless-him not to-bless at-all you-curse-him

וַיֹּאמֶר אֶל־בָּלָק הֲלֹא דִּבַּרְתִּי אֵלֶיךָ לֵאמֹר כֹּל אֲשֶׁר־יְדַבֵּר יְהוָה
Yahweh he-says that all to-say to-you I-told not? Balak to and-he-said

אֹתוֹ אֶעֱשֶׂה׃ וַיֹּאמֶר בָּלָק אֶל־בִּלְעָם לְכָה־נָּא אֶקָּחֲךָ אֶל־
to let-me-take-you now! come! Balaam to Balak then-he-said (27) I-must-do him

מָקוֹם אַחֵר אוּלַי יִישַׁר בְּעֵינֵי הָאֱלֹהִים וְקַבֹּתוֹ
and-you-may-curse-him the-God in-eyes-of he-will-please perhaps another place

לִי מִשָּׁם׃ וַיִּקַּח בָּלָק אֶת־בִּלְעָם רֹאשׁ הַפְּעוֹר
the-Peor top-of Balaam *** Balak and-he-took (28) from-there for-me

הַנִּשְׁקָף עַל־פְּנֵי הַיְשִׁימֹן׃ וַיֹּאמֶר בִּלְעָם אֶל־
to Balaam and-he-said (29) the-wasteland face-of to the-one-overlooking

בָּלָק בְּנֵה־לִי בָזֶה שִׁבְעָה מִזְבְּחֹת וְהָכֵן לִי בָּזֶה שִׁבְעָה
seven at-here for-me and-prepare! altars seven at-here for-me build! Balak

פָרִים וְשִׁבְעָה אֵילִים׃ וַיַּעַשׂ בָּלָק כַּאֲשֶׁר אָמַר בִּלְעָם
Balaam he-said just-as Balak so-he-did (30) rams and-seven bulls

וַיַּעַל פַּר וָאַיִל בַּמִּזְבֵּחַ׃ וַיַּרְא בִּלְעָם כִּי
that Balaam when-he-saw (24:1) on-the-altar and-ram bull and-he-offered

טוֹב בְּעֵינֵי יְהוָה לְבָרֵךְ אֶת־יִשְׂרָאֵל וְלֹא־הָלַךְ כְּפַעַם־
as-time he-resorted then-not Israel *** to-bless Yahweh in-eyes-of pleasing

בְּפַעַם לִקְרַאת נְחָשִׁים וַיָּשֶׁת אֶל־הַמִּדְבָּר פָּנָיו׃
faces-of-him the-desert toward but-he-turned sorceries to-use at-time

20 I have received a command
to bless;
he has blessed, and I
cannot change it.

21 "No misfortune is seen in
Jacob,
no misery observed in
Israel.
The LORD their God is with
them;
the shout of the King is
among them.
22 God brought them out of
Egypt;
they have the strength of
a wild ox.
23 There is no sorcery against
Jacob,
no divination against
Israel.
It will now be said of Jacob
and of Israel, 'See what
God has done!'
24 The people rise like a
lioness;
they rouse themselves
like a lion
that does not rest till he
devours his prey
and drinks the blood of
his victims."

25 Then Balak said to Balaam, "Neither curse them at all nor bless them at all!"
26 Balaam answered, "Did I not tell you I must do whatever the LORD says?"

*Balaam's Third Oracle*

27 Then Balak said to Balaam, "Come, let me take you to another place. Perhaps it will please God to let you curse them for me from there."
28 And Balak took Balaam to the top of Peor, overlooking the wasteland.
29 Balaam said, "Build me seven altars here, and prepare seven bulls and seven rams for me."
30 Balak did as Balaam had said, and offered a bull and a ram on each altar.

24 Now when Balaam saw that it pleased the LORD to bless Israel, he did not resort to sorcery as at other times, but turned his face

וַיִּשָּׂא בִלְעָם אֶת־ עֵינָיו וַיַּרְא אֶת־יִשְׂרָאֵל שֹׁכֵן
camping Israel *** and-he-saw eyes-of-him *** Balaam when-he-lifted (2)

לִשְׁבָטָיו וַתְּהִי עָלָיו רוּחַ אֱלֹהִים׃ וַיִּשָּׂא
and-he-uttered (3) God Spirit-of on-him then-she-came by-tribes-of-him

מְשָׁלוֹ וַיֹּאמַר נְאֻם בִּלְעָם בְּנוֹ בְעֹר וּנְאֻם
and-oracle-of Beor son-of-him Balaam oracle-of and-he-said oracle-of-him

הַגֶּבֶר שְׁתֻם הָעָיִן׃ נְאֻם שֹׁמֵעַ אִמְרֵי־ אֵל
God words-of one-hearing oracle-of (4) the-eye seeing-clearly-of the-man

אֲשֶׁר מַחֲזֵה שַׁדַּי יֶחֱזֶה נֹפֵל וּגְלוּי עֵינָיִם׃ מַה־
how! (5) eyes and-being-open-of prostrating he-sees Almighty vision-of who

טֹּבוּ אֹהָלֶיךָ יַעֲקֹב מִשְׁכְּנֹתֶיךָ יִשְׂרָאֵל׃ כִּנְחָלִים
like-valleys (6) Israel dwellings-of-you Jacob tents-of-you they-are-beautiful

נִטָּיוּ כְּגַנֹּת עֲלֵי נָהָר כַּאֲהָלִים נָטַע יְהוָה
Yahweh he-plants like-aloes river beside like-gardens they-spread-out

כַּאֲרָזִים עֲלֵי־ מָיִם׃ יִזַּל־ מַיִם מִדָּלְיָו
from-buckets-of-him waters he-will-flow (7) waters beside like-cedars

וְזַרְעוֹ בְּמַיִם רַבִּים וְיָרֹם מֵאֲגַג
than-Agag and-he-will-be-greater abundant-ones with-waters and-seed-of-him

מַלְכּוֹ וְתִנַּשֵּׂא מַלְכֻתוֹ׃ אֵל מוֹצִיאוֹ
bringing-him God (8) kingdom-of-him and-she-will-be-exalted king-of-him

מִמִּצְרַיִם כְּתוֹעֲפֹת רְאֵם לוֹ יֹאכַל גּוֹיִם צָרָיו
ones-hostile-to-him nations he-devours to-him wild-ox as-strengths-of from-Egypt

וְעַצְמֹתֵיהֶם יְגָרֵם וְחִצָּיו יִמְחָץ׃
he-will-pierce and-arrows-of-him he-will-break and-bones-of-them

כָּרַע שָׁכַב כַּאֲרִי וּכְלָבִיא מִי יְקִימֶנּוּ
he-rouses-him who? and-like-lioness like-lion he-lies he-crouches (9)

מְבָרֲכֶיךָ בָרוּךְ וְאֹרְרֶיךָ אָרוּר׃
being-cursed but-one-cursing-you being-blessed one-blessing-you

וַיִּחַר־ אַף בָּלָק אֶל־ בִּלְעָם וַיִּסְפֹּק אֶת־
*** and-he-struck-together Balaam against Balak anger-of then-he-burned (10)

כַּפָּיו וַיֹּאמֶר בָּלָק אֶל־ בִּלְעָם לָקֹב אֹיְבַי
being-enemies-of-me to-curse Balaam to Balak and-he-said hands-of-him

קְרָאתִיךָ וְהִנֵּה בֵּרַכְתָּ בָרֵךְ זֶה שָׁלֹשׁ פְּעָמִים׃ וְעַתָּה
so-now (11) times three this to-bless you-blessed but-see! I-summoned-you

בְּרַח־ לְךָ אֶל־ מְקוֹמֶךָ אָמַרְתִּי כַּבֵּד אֲכַבֶּדְךָ וְהִנֵּה
but-see! I-would-reward-you to-reward I-said home-of-you to go! leave!

מְנָעֲךָ יְהוָה מִכָּבוֹד׃ וַיֹּאמֶר בִּלְעָם אֶל־בָּלָק הֲלֹא
not? Balak to Balaam and-he-answered (12) from-reward Yahweh he-kept-you

toward the desert. [2]When Balaam looked out and saw Israel encamped tribe by tribe, the Spirit of God came upon him [3]and he uttered his oracle:

"The oracle of Balaam son of Beor,
the oracle of one whose eye sees clearly,
[4]the oracle of one who hears the words of God,
who sees a vision from the Almighty,[z]
who falls prostrate, and whose eyes are opened:

[5]"How beautiful are your tents, O Jacob,
your dwelling places, O Israel!

[6]"Like valleys they spread out,
like gardens beside a river,
like aloes planted by the LORD,
like cedars beside the waters.
[7]Water will flow from their buckets;
their seed will have abundant water.

"Their king will be greater than Agag;
their kingdom will be exalted.

[8]"God brought them out of Egypt;
they have the strength of a wild ox.
They devour hostile nations
and break their bones in pieces;
with their arrows they pierce them.
[9]Like a lion they crouch and lie down,
like a lioness—who dares to rouse them?

"May those who bless you be blessed
and those who curse you be cursed!"

[10]Then Balak's anger burned against Balaam. He struck his hands together and said to him, "I summoned you to curse my enemies, but you have blessed them these three times. [11]Now leave at once and go home! I said I would reward you handsomely, but the LORD has kept you from being rewarded."

[12]Balaam answered Balak,

[z]4 Hebrew *Shaddai*; also in verse 16

גַּם אֶל־ מַלְאָכֶיךָ אֲשֶׁר־ שָׁלַחְתָּ אֵלַי דִּבַּרְתִּי לֵאמֹר׃ אִם־ יִתֶּן־
he-gave if (13) to-say I-told to-me you-sent whom messengers-of-you to indeed

לִי בָלָק מְלֹא בֵיתוֹ כֶּסֶף וְזָהָב לֹא אוּכַל לַעֲבֹר
to-go-beyond I-could not and-gold silver palace-of-him filled-of Balak to-me

אֶת־ פִּי יְהוָה לַעֲשׂוֹת טוֹבָה אוֹ רָעָה מִלִּבִּי אֲשֶׁר־יְדַבֵּר יְהוָה
Yahweh he-says what from-heart-of-me bad or good to-do Yahweh command-of ***

אֹתוֹ אֲדַבֵּר׃ וְעַתָּה הִנְנִי הוֹלֵךְ לְעַמִּי לְכָה אִיעָצְךָ
let-me-warn-you come! to-people-of-me going see-I! and-now (14) I-must-say him

אֲשֶׁר יַעֲשֶׂה הָעָם הַזֶּה לְעַמְּךָ בְּאַחֲרִית הַיָּמִים׃
the-days in-coming-of to-people-of-you the-this the-people he-will-do what

וַיִּשָּׂא מְשָׁלוֹ וַיֹּאמַר נְאֻם בִּלְעָם בְּנוֹ
son-of-him Balaam oracle-of and-he-said oracle-of-him then-he-uttered (15)

בְעֹר וּנְאֻם הַגֶּבֶר שְׁתֻם הָעָיִן׃ נְאֻם
oracle-of (16) the-eye seeing-clearly-of the-man and-oracle-of Beor

שֹׁמֵעַ אִמְרֵי־ אֵל וְיֹדֵעַ דַּעַת עֶלְיוֹן מַחֲזֵה
vision-of Most-High knowledge-of and-one-knowing God words-of one-hearing

שַׁדַּי יֶחֱזֶה נֹפֵל וּגְלוּי עֵינָיִם׃ אֶרְאֶנּוּ וְלֹא
but-not I-see-him (17) eyes and-being-open-of prostrating he-sees Almighty

עַתָּה אֲשׁוּרֶנּוּ וְלֹא קָרוֹב דָּרַךְ כּוֹכָב מִיַּעֲקֹב וְקָם
and-he-will-rise from-Jacob star he-will-come near but-not I-behold-him now

שֵׁבֶט מִיִּשְׂרָאֵל וּמָחַץ פַּאֲתֵי מוֹאָב וְקַרְקַר כָּל־
all-of and-skull-of Moab foreheads-of and-he-will-crush from-Israel scepter

בְּנֵי־ שֵׁת׃ וְהָיָה אֱדוֹם יְרֵשָׁה וְהָיָה יְרֵשָׁה
conquered and-he-will-be conquered Edom and-he-will-be (18) Sheth sons-of

שֵׂעִיר אֹיְבָיו וְיִשְׂרָאֵל עֹשֶׂה חָיִל׃ וְיֵרְדְּ
and-he-will-rule (19) strong growing but-Israel being-enemy-of-him Seir

מִיַּעֲקֹב וְהֶאֱבִיד שָׂרִיד מֵעִיר׃ וַיַּרְא אֶת־ עֲמָלֵק
Amalek *** then-he-saw (20) of-city survivor and-he-will-destroy from-Jacob

וַיִּשָּׂא מְשָׁלוֹ וַיֹּאמַר רֵאשִׁית גּוֹיִם עֲמָלֵק
Amalek nations first-of and-he-said oracle-of-him and-he-uttered

וְאַחֲרִיתוֹ עֲדֵי אֹבֵד׃ וַיַּרְא אֶת־ הַקֵּינִי וַיִּשָּׂא
and-he-uttered the-Kenite *** then-he-saw (21) being-ruin to but-last-of-him

מְשָׁלוֹ וַיֹּאמַר אֵיתָן מוֹשָׁבֶךָ וְשִׂים בַּסֶּלַע
in-the-rock and-he-is-set dwelling-of-you secure and-he-said oracle-of-him

קִנֶּךָ׃ כִּי אִם־ יִהְיֶה לְבָעֵר קָיִן עַד־ מָה אַשּׁוּר
Asshur when at Kenite to-be-destroyed he-will-be yet but (22) nest-of-you

תִּשְׁבֶּךָּ׃ וַיִּשָּׂא מְשָׁלוֹ וַיֹּאמַר אוֹי מִי
who? ah! and-he-said oracle-of-him then-he-uttered (23) she-captures-you

"Did I not tell the messengers you sent me, [13]'Even if Balak gave me his palace filled with silver and gold, I could not do anything of my own accord, good or bad, to go beyond the command of the LORD—and I must say only what the LORD says'? [14]Now I am going back to my people, but come, let me warn you of what this people will do to your people in days to come."

*Balaam's Fourth Oracle*

[15]Then he uttered his oracle:

"The oracle of Balaam son of Beor,
the oracle of one whose eye sees clearly,
[16]the oracle of one who hears the words of God,
who has knowledge from the Most High,
who sees a vision from the Almighty,
who falls prostrate, and whose eyes are opened:

[17]"I see him, but not now;
I behold him, but not near.
A star will come out of Jacob;
a scepter will rise out of Israel.
He will crush the foreheads of Moab,
the skulls[a] of[b] all the sons of Sheth.[c]
[18]Edom will be conquered;
Seir, his enemy, will be conquered,
but Israel will grow strong.
[19]A ruler will come out of Jacob
and destroy the survivors of the city."

*Balaam's Final Oracles*

[20]Then Balaam saw Amalek and uttered his oracle:

"Amalek was first among the nations,
but he will come to ruin at last."

[21]Then he saw the Kenites and uttered his oracle:

"Your dwelling place is secure,
your nest is set in a rock;
[22]yet you Kenites will be destroyed
when Asshur takes you captive."

[23]Then he uttered his oracle:

[a]17 Samaritan Pentateuch (see also Jer. 48:45); the meaning of the word in the Masoretic Text is uncertain.
[b]17 Or possibly *Moab, / batter*
[c]17 Or *all the noisy boasters*

יִחְיֶה מִשֻּׂמוֹ אֵל׃ וְצִים מִיַּד כִּתִּים

Kittim from-shore-of and-ships (24) God when-to-do-him he-can-live

וְעִנּוּ אַשּׁוּר וְעִנּוּ־ עֵבֶר וְגַם־ הוּא עֲדֵי

to he but-also Eber and-they-will-subdue Asshur and-they-will-subdue

אֹבֵד׃ וַיָּקָם בִּלְעָם וַיֵּלֶךְ וַיָּשָׁב

and-he-returned and-he-went Balaam then-he-got-up (25) being-ruin

לִמְקֹמוֹ וְגַם־ בָּלָק הָלַךְ לְדַרְכּוֹ׃ וַיֵּשֶׁב

and-he-stayed (25:1) on-way-of-him he-went Balak and-also to-home-of-him

יִשְׂרָאֵל בַּשִּׁטִּים וַיָּחֶל הָעָם לִזְנוֹת אֶל־

with to-be-sexually-immoral the-people and-he-began in-the-Shittim Israel

בְּנוֹת מוֹאָב׃ וַתִּקְרֶאןָ לָעָם לְזִבְחֵי אֱלֹהֵיהֶן

gods-of-them to-sacrifices-of to-the-people and-they-invited (2) Moab women-of

וַיֹּאכַל הָעָם וַיִּשְׁתַּחֲווּ לֵאלֹהֵיהֶן׃ וַיִּצָּמֶד

so-he-joined (3) before-gods-of-them and-they-bowed the-people and-he-ate

יִשְׂרָאֵל לְבַעַל פְּעוֹר וַיִּחַר־ אַף יְהוָה בְּיִשְׂרָאֵל׃

against-Israel Yahweh anger-of and-he-burned Peor to-Baal-of Israel

וַיֹּאמֶר יְהוָה אֶל־ מֹשֶׁה קַח אֶת־ כָּל־ רָאשֵׁי הָעָם

the-people leaders-of all-of *** take! Moses to Yahweh and-he-said (4)

וְהוֹקַע אוֹתָם לַיהוָה נֶגֶד הַשָּׁמֶשׁ וְיָשֹׁב חֲרוֹן

fierce-anger-of so-he-may-turn the-daylight in before-Yahweh them and-kill!

אַף־ יְהוָה מִיִּשְׂרָאֵל׃ וַיֹּאמֶר מֹשֶׁה אֶל־ שֹׁפְטֵי יִשְׂרָאֵל

Israel ones-judging-of to Moses so-he-said (5) from-Israel Yahweh anger-of

הִרְגוּ אִישׁ אֲנָשָׁיו הַנִּצְמָדִים לְבַעַל פְּעוֹר׃ וְהִנֵּה אִישׁ

one then-see! (6) Peor to-Baal-of the-ones-joining men-of-him each kill!

מִבְּנֵי יִשְׂרָאֵל בָּא וַיַּקְרֵב אֶל־ אֶחָיו אֶת־

*** brothers-of-him to and-he-brought coming Israel from-sons-of

הַמִּדְיָנִית לְעֵינֵי מֹשֶׁה וּלְעֵינֵי כָּל־

whole-of and-before-eyes-of Moses before-eyes-of the-Midianite-woman

עֲדַת בְּנֵי־ יִשְׂרָאֵל וְהֵמָּה בֹכִים פֶּתַח אֹהֶל

Tent-of entrance-of ones-weeping while-they Israel sons-of the-assembly-of

מוֹעֵד׃ וַיַּרְא פִּינְחָס בֶּן־ אֶלְעָזָר בֶּן־ אַהֲרֹן הַכֹּהֵן

the-priest Aaron son-of Eleazar son-of Phinehas when-he-saw (7) Meeting

וַיָּקָם מִתּוֹךְ הָעֵדָה וַיִּקַּח רֹמַח בְּיָדוֹ׃

in-hand-of-him spear and-he-took the-assembly from-among then-he-left

וַיָּבֹא אַחַר אִישׁ־ יִשְׂרָאֵל אֶל־ הַקֻּבָּה וַיִּדְקֹר

and-he-drove-through the-tent into Israel man-of after and-he-went (8)

אֶת־ שְׁנֵיהֶם אֵת אִישׁ יִשְׂרָאֵל וְאֶת־ הָאִשָּׁה אֶל־ קֳבָתָהּ

body-of-her into the-woman and Israel man-of *** both-of-them ***

"Ah, who can live when
God does this?[e]
24 Ships will come from the
shores of Kittim;
they will subdue Asshur
and Eber,
but they too will come to
ruin."

25 Then Balaam got up and returned home and Balak went his own way.

*Moab Seduces Israel*

25 While Israel was staying in Shittim, the men began to indulge in sexual immorality with Moabite women, 2 who invited them to the sacrifices to their gods. The people ate and bowed down before these gods. 3 So Israel joined in worshiping the Baal of Peor. And the LORD's anger burned against them.

4 The LORD said to Moses, "Take all the leaders of these people, kill them and expose them in broad daylight before the LORD, so that the LORD's fierce anger may turn away from Israel."

5 So Moses said to Israel's judges, "Each of you must put to death those of your men who have joined in worshiping the Baal of Peor."

6 Then an Israelite man brought to his family a Midianite woman right before the eyes of Moses and the whole assembly of Israel while they were weeping at the entrance to the Tent of Meeting. 7 When Phinehas son of Eleazar, the son of Aaron, the priest, saw this, he left the assembly, took a spear in his hand 8 and followed the Israelite into the tent. He drove the spear through both of them—through the Israelite and into the woman's body. Then the

[e]23 Masoretic Text; with a different word division of the Hebrew *A people will gather from the north.*

*2 Most mss have no *dagesh* in the first *vav* (וּחוּ־).

וַתֵּעָצַר הַמַּגֵּפָה מֵעַל בְּנֵי יִשְׂרָאֵל׃ וַיִּהְיוּ
but-they-were (9) Israel sons-of from-against the-plague then-she-was-stopped

הַמֵּתִים בַּמַּגֵּפָה אַרְבָּעָה וְעֶשְׂרִים אָלֶף׃ וַיְדַבֵּר יְהוָה
Yahweh and-he-spoke (10) thousand and-twenty four in-the-plague the-ones-dead

אֶל־מֹשֶׁה לֵּאמֹר׃ פִּינְחָס בֶּן־אֶלְעָזָר בֶּן־אַהֲרֹן הַכֹּהֵן
the-priest Aaron son-of Eleazar son-of Phinehas (11) to-say Moses to

הֵשִׁיב אֶת־חֲמָתִי מֵעַל בְּנֵי־יִשְׂרָאֵל בְּקַנְאוֹ
when-to-be-zealous-him Israel sons-of from-against anger-of-me *** he-turned

אֶת־קִנְאָתִי בְּתוֹכָם וְלֹא־כִלִּיתִי אֶת־בְּנֵי־יִשְׂרָאֵל בְּקִנְאָתִי׃
in-zeal-of-me Israel sons-of *** I-put-end so-not among-them zeal-of-me with

לָכֵן אֱמֹר הִנְנִי נֹתֵן לוֹ אֶת־בְּרִיתִי שָׁלוֹם׃
peace covenant-of-me *** with-him making see-I! tell! therefore (12)

וְהָיְתָה לּוֹ וּלְזַרְעוֹ אַחֲרָיו בְּרִית
covenant-of after-him and-for-descendant-of-him for-him and-she-will-be (13)

כְּהֻנַּת עוֹלָם תַּחַת אֲשֶׁר קִנֵּא לֵאלֹהָיו וַיְכַפֵּר
and-he-atoned for-God-of-him he-was-zealous that because lasting priesthood-of

עַל־בְּנֵי יִשְׂרָאֵל׃ וְשֵׁם אִישׁ יִשְׂרָאֵל הַמֻּכֶּה אֲשֶׁר
that the-one-being-killed Israel man-of now-name-of (14) Israel sons-of for

הֻכָּה אֶת־הַמִּדְיָנִית זִמְרִי בֶּן־סָלוּא נְשִׂיא בֵית־
house-of leader-of Salu son-of Zimri the-Midianite-woman with he-was-killed

אָב לַשִּׁמְעֹנִי׃ וְשֵׁם הָאִשָּׁה הַמֻּכָּה
the-one-being-killed the-woman and-name-of (15) of-the-Simeonite father

הַמִּדְיָנִית כָּזְבִּי בַת־צוּר רֹאשׁ אֻמּוֹת בֵּית־אָב
father house-of tribes-of chief-of Zur daughter-of Cozbi the-Midianite

בְּמִדְיָן הוּא׃ וַיְדַבֵּר יְהוָה אֶל־מֹשֶׁה לֵּאמֹר׃ צָרוֹר אֶת־
*** to-be-enemy (17) to-say Moses to Yahweh and-he-spoke (16) he in-Midian

הַמִּדְיָנִים וְהִכִּיתֶם אוֹתָם׃ כִּי צֹרְרִים הֵם לָכֶם
to-you they being-enemies for (18) them and-you-kill the-Midianites

בְּנִכְלֵיהֶם אֲשֶׁר־נִכְּלוּ לָכֶם עַל־דְּבַר־פְּעוֹר וְעַל־
and-in Peor affair-of in to-you they-deceived when in-deceptions-of-them

דְּבַר כָּזְבִּי בַת־נְשִׂיא מִדְיָן אֲחֹתָם הַמֻּכָּה
the-being-killed sister-of-them Midian leader-of daughter-of Cozbi affair-of

בְיוֹם־הַמַּגֵּפָה עַל־דְּבַר־פְּעוֹר׃ וַיְהִי אַחֲרֵי הַמַּגֵּפָה
the-plague after and-he-was (19)* Peor result-of as the-plague on-day-of

וַיֹּאמֶר יְהוָה אֶל־מֹשֶׁה וְאֶל אֶלְעָזָר בֶּן־אַהֲרֹן הַכֹּהֵן
the-priest Aaron son-of Eleazar and-to Moses to Yahweh and-he-said (26:1)

לֵאמֹר׃ שְׂאוּ אֶת־רֹאשׁ ׀ כָּל־עֲדַת בְּנֵי־יִשְׂרָאֵל
Israel sons-of community-of whole-of census-of *** take! (2) to-say

plague against the Israelites was stopped; [9]but those who died in the plague numbered 24,000.

[10]The LORD said to Moses, [11]"Phinehas son of Eleazar, the son of Aaron, the priest, has turned my anger away from the Israelites; for he was as zealous as I am for my honor among them, so that in my zeal I did not put an end to them. [12]Therefore tell him I am making my covenant of peace with him. [13]He and his descendants will have a covenant of a lasting priesthood, because he was zealous for the honor of his God and made atonement for the Israelites."

[14]The name of the Israelite who was killed with the Midianite woman was Zimri son of Salu, the leader of a Simeonite family. [15]And the name of the Midianite woman who was put to death was Cozbi daughter of Zur, a tribal chief of a Midianite family.

[16]The LORD said to Moses, [17]"Treat the Midianites as enemies and kill them, [18]because they treated you as enemies when they deceived you in the affair of Peor and their sister Cozbi, the daughter of a Midianite leader, the woman who was killed when the plague came as a result of Peor."

*The Second Census*

**26** After the plague the LORD said to Moses and Eleazar son of Aaron, the priest, [2]"Take a census of the whole Israelite community by

*19 Verse 19 in Hebrew corresponds to the first three words of verse 1 of chapter 26 in the English.

מִבֶּן עֶשְׂרִים שָׁנָה וָמַעְלָה לְבֵית אֲבֹתָם כָּל־יֹצֵא
serving every-of fathers-of-them by-house-of or-more year twenty from-son-of

צָבָא בְּיִשְׂרָאֵל׃ וַיְדַבֵּר מֹשֶׁה וְאֶלְעָזָר הַכֹּהֵן אֹתָם
with-them the-priest and-Eleazar Moses and-he-spoke (3) in-Israel army

בְּעַרְבֹת מוֹאָב עַל־יַרְדֵּן יְרֵחוֹ לֵאמֹר׃ מִבֶּן עֶשְׂרִים שָׁנָה
year twenty from-son-of (4) to-say Jericho Jordan-of by Moab on-plains-of

וָמָעְלָה כַּאֲשֶׁר צִוָּה יְהוָה אֶת־מֹשֶׁה וּבְנֵי יִשְׂרָאֵל
Israel and-sons-of Moses *** Yahweh he-commanded just-as or-more

הַיֹּצְאִים מֵאֶרֶץ מִצְרָיִם׃ רְאוּבֵן בְּכוֹר יִשְׂרָאֵל בְּנֵי
sons-of Israel firstborn-of Reuben (5) Egypt from-land-of the-ones-coming

רְאוּבֵן חֲנוֹךְ מִשְׁפַּחַת הַחֲנֹכִי לְפַלּוּא מִשְׁפַּחַת הַפַּלֻּאִי׃
the-Palluite clan-of through-Pallu the-Hanochite clan-of Hanoch Reuben

לְחֶצְרֹן מִשְׁפַּחַת הַחֶצְרוֹנִי לְכַרְמִי מִשְׁפַּחַת הַכַּרְמִי׃
the-Carmite clan-of through-Carmi the-Hezronite clan-of through-Hezron (6)

אֵלֶּה מִשְׁפְּחֹת הָראוּבֵנִי* וַיִּהְיוּ פְקֻדֵיהֶם שְׁלֹשָׁה
three numberings-of-them and-they-were the-Reubenite clans-of these (7)

וְאַרְבָּעִים אֶלֶף וּשְׁבַע מֵאוֹת וּשְׁלֹשִׁים׃ וּבְנֵי פַלּוּא
Pallu and-sons-of (8) and-thirty hundreds and-seven-of thousand and-forty

אֱלִיאָב׃ וּבְנֵי אֱלִיאָב נְמוּאֵל וְדָתָן וַאֲבִירָם הוּא־דָתָן
Dathan this and-Abiram and-Dathan Nemuel Eliab and-sons-of (9) Eliab

וַאֲבִירָם קְרוֹאֵי° הָעֵדָה אֲשֶׁר הִצּוּ עַל־מֹשֶׁה
Moses against they-rebelled who the-community officials-of and-Abiram

וְעַל־אַהֲרֹן בַּעֲדַת־קֹרַח בְּהַצֹּתָם עַל־יְהוָה׃
Yahweh against when-to-rebel-them Korah among-follower-of Aaron and-against

וַתִּפְתַּח הָאָרֶץ אֶת־פִּיהָ וַתִּבְלַע אֹתָם וְאֶת־
and them and-she-swallowed mouth-of-her *** the-earth and-she-opened (10)

קֹרַח בְּמוֹת הָעֵדָה בַּאֲכֹל הָאֵשׁ אֵת חֲמִשִּׁים
fifty *** the-fire when-to-devour the-follower when-to-die Korah

וּמָאתַיִם אִישׁ וַיִּהְיוּ לְנֵס׃ וּבְנֵי־קֹרַח לֹא־
not Korah but-sons-of (11) as-warning and-they-served man and-two-hundreds

מֵתוּ׃ בְּנֵי שִׁמְעוֹן לְמִשְׁפְּחֹתָם לִנְמוּאֵל מִשְׁפַּחַת
clan-of through-Nemuel by-clans-of-them Simeon sons-of (12) they-died-out

הַנְּמוּאֵלִי לְיָמִין מִשְׁפַּחַת הַיָּמִינִי לְיָכִין מִשְׁפַּחַת
clan-of through-Jakin the-Jaminite clan-of through-Jamin the-Nemuelite

הַיָּכִינִי׃ לְזֶרַח מִשְׁפַּחַת הַזַּרְחִי לְשָׁאוּל מִשְׁפַּחַת
clan-of through-Shaul the-Zerahite clan-of through-Zerah (13) the-Jakinite

הַשָּׁאוּלִי׃ אֵלֶּה מִשְׁפְּחֹת הַשִּׁמְעֹנִי שְׁנַיִם וְעֶשְׂרִים אֶלֶף
thousand and-twenty two the-Simeonite clans-of these (14) the-Shaulite

families—all those twenty years old or more who are able to serve in the army of Israel." [3]So on the plains of Moab by the Jordan across from Jericho,[f] Moses and Eleazar the priest spoke with them and said, [4]"Take a census of the men twenty years old or more, as the LORD commanded Moses."

These were the Israelites who came out of Egypt:

[5]The descendants of Reuben, the firstborn son of Israel, were:
- through Hanoch, the Hanochite clan;
- through Pallu, the Palluite clan;
- [6]through Hezron, the Hezronite clan;
- through Carmi, the Carmite clan.

[7]These were the clans of Reuben; those numbered were 43,730.

[8]The son of Pallu was Eliab, [9]and the sons of Eliab were Nemuel, Dathan and Abiram. The same Dathan and Abiram were the community officials who rebelled against Moses and Aaron and were among Korah's followers when they rebelled against the LORD. [10]The earth opened its mouth and swallowed them along with Korah, whose followers died when the fire devoured the 250 men. And they served as a warning sign. [11]The line of Korah, however, did not die out.

[12]The descendants of Simeon by their clans were:
- through Nemuel, the Nemuelite clan;
- through Jamin, the Jaminite clan;
- through Jakin, the Jakinite clan;
- [13]through Zerah, the Zerahite clan;
- through Shaul, the Shaulite clan.

[14]These were the clans of Simeon; there were 22,200 men.

f3 Hebrew *Jordan of Jericho;* possibly an ancient name for the Jordan River; also in verse 63

*7 Most mss have no *qibbuts* under the *resh* (הָרְאוּ׳).

°9 ק קריאי

וּמָאתָ֑יִם׃ (15) בְּנֵ֣י גָד֮ לְמִשְׁפְּחֹתָם֒ לִצְפ֗וֹן מִשְׁפַּ֙חַת֙
clan-of through-Zephon by-clans-of-them Gad sons-of (15) and-two-hundreds

הַצְּפוֹנִ֔י לְחַגִּ֕י מִשְׁפַּ֖חַת הַֽחַגִּ֑י לְשׁוּנִ֕י מִשְׁפַּ֖חַת
clan-of through-Shuni the-Haggite clan-of through-Haggi the-Zephonite

הַשּׁוּנִֽי׃ (16) לְאָזְנִ֕י מִשְׁפַּ֖חַת הָֽאָזְנִ֑י לְעֵרִ֕י מִשְׁפַּ֖חַת הָעֵרִֽי׃
the-Erite clan-of through-Eri the-Oznite clan-of through-Ozni (16) the-Shunite

(17) לַאֲר֕וֹד מִשְׁפַּ֖חַת הָאֲרוֹדִ֑י לְאַ֨רְאֵלִ֔י מִשְׁפַּ֖חַת הָאַרְאֵלִֽי׃
the-Arelite clan-of through-Areli the-Arodite clan-of through-Arod (17)

(18) אֵ֛לֶּה מִשְׁפְּחֹ֥ת בְּנֵי־גָ֖ד לִפְקֻדֵיהֶ֑ם אַרְבָּעִ֥ים אֶ֖לֶף
thousand forty by-numberings-of-them Gad sons-of clans-of these (18)

וַחֲמֵ֥שׁ מֵאֽוֹת׃ (19) בְּנֵ֥י יְהוּדָ֖ה עֵ֣ר וְאוֹנָ֑ן וַיָּ֥מָת עֵ֛ר וְאוֹנָ֖ן
and-Onan Er but-he-died and-Onan Er Judah sons-of (19) hundreds and-five-of

בְּאֶ֥רֶץ כְּנָֽעַן׃ (20) וַיִּהְי֣וּ בְנֵֽי־יְהוּדָה֮ לְמִשְׁפְּחֹתָם֒
by-clans-of-them Judah sons-of and-they-were (20) Canaan in-land-of

לְשֵׁלָ֗ה מִשְׁפַּ֙חַת֙ הַשֵּׁ֣לָנִ֔י לְפֶ֕רֶץ מִשְׁפַּ֖חַת הַפַּרְצִ֑י
the-Perezite clan-of through-Perez the-Shelanite clan-of through-Shelah

לְזֶ֕רַח מִשְׁפַּ֖חַת הַזַּרְחִֽי׃ (21) וַיִּהְי֣וּ בְנֵי־פֶ֔רֶץ
Perez sons-of and-they-were (21) the-Zerahite clan-of through-Zerah

לְחֶצְרֹ֕ן מִשְׁפַּ֖חַת הַֽחֶצְרֹנִ֑י לְחָמ֕וּל מִשְׁפַּ֖חַת הֶחָמוּלִֽי׃
the-Hamulite clan-of through-Hamul the-Hezronite clan-of through-Hezron

(22) אֵ֛לֶּה מִשְׁפְּחֹ֥ת יְהוּדָ֖ה לִפְקֻדֵיהֶ֑ם שִׁשָּׁ֧ה וְשִׁבְעִ֛ים אֶ֖לֶף
thousand and-seventy six by-numberings-of-them Judah clans-of these (22)

וַחֲמֵ֥שׁ מֵאֽוֹת׃ (23) בְּנֵ֤י יִשָּׂשכָר֙ לְמִשְׁפְּחֹתָ֔ם תּוֹלָ֕ע מִשְׁפַּ֖חַת
clan-of Tola by-clans-of-them Issachar sons-of (23) hundreds and-five-of

הַתּֽוֹלָעִ֑י לְפֻוָ֕ה מִשְׁפַּ֖חַת הַפּוּנִֽי׃ (24) לְיָשׁ֕וּב מִשְׁפַּ֖חַת
clan-of through-Jashub (24) the-Punite clan-of through-Puvah the-Tolaite

הַיָּשֻׁבִ֑י לְשִׁמְרֹ֕ן מִשְׁפַּ֖חַת הַשִּׁמְרֹנִֽי׃ (25) אֵ֛לֶּה מִשְׁפְּחֹ֥ת
clans-of these (25) the-Shimronite clan-of through-Shimron the-Jashubite

יִשָּׂשכָ֖ר לִפְקֻדֵיהֶ֑ם אַרְבָּעָ֧ה וְשִׁשִּׁ֛ים אֶ֖לֶף וּשְׁלֹ֥שׁ מֵאֽוֹת׃
hundreds and-three-of thousand and-sixty four by-numberings-of-them Issachar

(26) בְּנֵ֤י זְבוּלֻן֙ לְמִשְׁפְּחֹתָ֔ם לְסֶ֕רֶד מִשְׁפַּ֙חַת֙ הַסַּרְדִּ֔י
the-Seredite clan-of through-Sered by-clans-of-them Zebulun sons-of (26)

לְאֵל֕וֹן מִשְׁפַּ֖חַת הָאֵלֹנִ֑י לְיַ֨חְלְאֵ֔ל מִשְׁפַּ֖חַת הַיַּחְלְאֵלִֽי׃
the-Jahleelite clan-of through-Jahleel the-Elonite clan-of through-Elon

(27) אֵ֛לֶּה מִשְׁפְּחֹ֥ת הַזְּבוּלֹנִ֖י לִפְקֻדֵיהֶ֑ם שִׁשִּׁ֥ים אֶ֖לֶף
thousand sixty by-numberings-of-them the-Zebulunite clans-of these (27)

וַחֲמֵ֥שׁ מֵאֽוֹת׃ (28) בְּנֵ֥י יוֹסֵ֖ף לְמִשְׁפְּחֹתָ֑ם מְנַשֶּׁ֖ה וְאֶפְרָֽיִם׃
and-Ephraim Manasseh by-clans-of-them Joseph sons-of (28) hundreds and-five-of

15The descendants of Gad by their clans were:
through Zephon, the Zephonite clan;
through Haggi, the Haggite clan;
through Shuni, the Shunite clan;
16through Ozni, the Oznite clan;
through Eri, the Erite clan;
17through Arodi,[g] the Arodite clan;
through Areli, the Arelite clan.
18These were the clans of Gad; those numbered were 40,500.

19Er and Onan were sons of Judah, but they died in Canaan.
20The descendants of Judah by their clans were:
through Shelah, the Shelanite clan;
through Perez, the Perezite clan;
through Zerah, the Zerahite clan.
21The descendants of Perez were:
through Hezron, the Hezronite clan;
through Hamul, the Hamulite clan.
22These were the clans of Judah; those numbered were 76,500.

23The descendants of Issachar by their clans were:
through Tola, the Tolaite clan;
through Puah, the Puite[h] clan;
24through Jashub, the Jashubite clan;
through Shimron, the Shimronite clan.
25These were the clans of Issachar; those numbered were 64,300.

26The descendants of Zebulun by their clans were:
through Sered, the Seredite clan;
through Elon, the Elonite clan;
through Jahleel, the Jahleelite clan.
27These were the clans of Zebulun; those numbered were 60,500.

28The descendants of Joseph by their clans through Manasseh and Ephraim were:

[g]17 Samaritan Pentateuch and Syriac (see also Gen. 46:16); Masoretic Text *Arod*
[h]23 Samaritan Pentateuch, Septuagint, Vulgate and Syriac (see also 1 Chron. 7:1); Masoretic Text *through Puvah, the Punite*

בְּנֵי מְנַשֶּׁה לְמָכִיר מִשְׁפַּחַת הַמָּכִירִי וּמָכִיר
now-Makir the-Makirite clan-of through-Makir Manasseh sons-of (29)

הוֹלִיד אֶת־ גִּלְעָד לְגִלְעָד מִשְׁפַּחַת הַגִּלְעָדִי׃ אֵלֶּה
these (30) the-Gileadite clan-of through-Gilead Gilead *** he-fathered

בְּנֵי גִלְעָד אִיעֶזֶר מִשְׁפַּחַת הָאִיעֶזְרִי לְחֵלֶק מִשְׁפַּחַת הַחֶלְקִי׃
the-Helekite clan-of through-Helek the-Iezerite clan-of Iezer Gilead sons-of

וְאַשְׂרִיאֵל מִשְׁפַּחַת הָאַשְׂרְאֵלִי וְשֶׁכֶם מִשְׁפַּחַת הַשִּׁכְמִי׃
the-Shechemite clan-of and-Shechem the-Asrielite clan-of and-Asriel (31)

וּשְׁמִידָע מִשְׁפַּחַת הַשְּׁמִידָעִי וְחֵפֶר מִשְׁפַּחַת הַחֶפְרִי׃
the-Hepherite clan-of and-Hepher the-Shemidaite clan-of and-Shemida (32)

וּצְלָפְחָד בֶּן־ חֵפֶר לֹא־ הָיוּ לוֹ בָּנִים כִּי אִם־ בָּנוֹת
daughters only but sons to-him they-were not Hepher son-of now-Zelophehad (33)

וְשֵׁם בְּנוֹת צְלָפְחָד מַחְלָה וְנֹעָה חָגְלָה מִלְכָּה וְתִרְצָה׃
and-Tirzah Milcah Hoglah and-Noah Mahlah Zelophehad daughters-of and-name-of

אֵלֶּה מִשְׁפְּחֹת מְנַשֶּׁה וּפְקֻדֵיהֶם שְׁנַיִם וַחֲמִשִּׁים אֶלֶף
thousand and-fifty two and-numberings-of-them Manasseh clans-of these (34)

וּשְׁבַע מֵאוֹת׃ אֵלֶּה בְנֵי־ אֶפְרַיִם לְמִשְׁפְּחֹתָם
by-clans-of-them Ephraim sons-of these (35) hundreds and-seven-of

לְשׁוּתֶלַח מִשְׁפַּחַת הַשֻּׁתַלְחִי לְבֶכֶר מִשְׁפַּחַת הַבַּכְרִי
the-Bekerite clan-of through-Beker the-Shuthelahite clan-of through-Shuthelah

לְתַחַן מִשְׁפַּחַת הַתַּחֲנִי׃ וְאֵלֶּה בְּנֵי שׁוּתָלַח
Shuthelah sons-of and-these (36) the-Tahanite clan-of through-Tahan

לְעֵרָן מִשְׁפַּחַת הָעֵרָנִי׃ אֵלֶּה מִשְׁפְּחֹת בְּנֵי־ אֶפְרַיִם
Ephraim sons-of clans-of these (37) the-Eranite clan-of through-Eran

לִפְקֻדֵיהֶם שְׁנַיִם וּשְׁלֹשִׁים אֶלֶף וַחֲמֵשׁ מֵאוֹת אֵלֶּה
these hundreds and-five-of thousand and-thirty two by-numberings-of-them

בְנֵי־ יוֹסֵף לְמִשְׁפְּחֹתָם׃ בְּנֵי בִנְיָמִן לְמִשְׁפְּחֹתָם
by-clans-of-them Benjamin sons-of (38) by-clans-of-them Joseph sons-of

לְבֶלַע מִשְׁפַּחַת הַבַּלְעִי לְאַשְׁבֵּל מִשְׁפַּחַת הָאַשְׁבֵּלִי
the-Ashbelite clan-of through-Ashbel the-Belaite clan-of through-Bela

לַאֲחִירָם מִשְׁפַּחַת הָאֲחִירָמִי׃ לִשְׁפוּפָם מִשְׁפַּחַת
clan-of through-Shephupham (39) the-Ahiramite clan-of through-Ahiram

הַשּׁוּפָמִי לְחוּפָם מִשְׁפַּחַת הַחוּפָמִי׃ וַיִּהְיוּ
and-they-were (40) the-Huphamite clan-of through-Hupham the-Shuphamite

בְנֵי־ בֶלַע אַרְדְּ וְנַעֲמָן מִשְׁפַּחַת הָאַרְדִּי לְנַעֲמָן מִשְׁפַּחַת
clan-of through-Naaman the-Ardite clan-of and-Naaman Ard Bela sons-of

הַנַּעֲמִי׃ אֵלֶּה בְנֵי־ בִנְיָמִן לְמִשְׁפְּחֹתָם וּפְקֻדֵיהֶם
and-numberings-of-them by-clans-of-them Benjamin sons-of these (41) the-Naamite

29 The descendants of Manasseh:
through Makir, the Makirite clan (Makir was the father of Gilead);
through Gilead, the Gileadite clan.

30 These were the descendants of Gilead:
through Iezer, the Iezerite clan;
through Helek, the Helekite clan;
31 through Asriel, the Asrielite clan;
through Shechem, the Shechemite clan;
32 through Shemida, the Shemidaite clan;
through Hepher, the Hepherite clan.
33 (Zelophehad son of Hepher had no sons; he had only daughters, whose names were Mahlah, Noah, Hoglah, Milcah and Tirzah.)

34 These were the clans of Manasseh; those numbered were 52,700.

35 These were the descendants of Ephraim by their clans:
through Shuthelah, the Shuthelahite clan;
through Beker, the Bekerite clan;
through Tahan, the Tahanite clan.
36 These were the descendants of Shuthelah:
through Eran, the Eranite clan.
37 These were the clans of Ephraim; those numbered were 32,500.

These were the descendants of Joseph by their clans.

38 The descendants of Benjamin by their clans were:
through Bela, the Belaite clan;
through Ashbel, the Ashbelite clan;
through Ahiram, the Ahiramite clan;
39 through Shupham,[j] the Shuphamite clan;
through Hupham, the Huphamite clan.
40 The descendants of Bela through Ard and Naaman were:
through Ard,[k] the Ardite clan;
through Naaman, the Naamite clan.
41 These were the clans of Benjamin; those numbered were

[j] 39 A few manuscripts of the Masoretic Text, Samaritan Pentateuch, Septuagint, Vulgate and Syriac; most manuscripts of the Masoretic Text *Shephupham*

[k] 40 Samaritan Pentateuch, some Septuagint manuscripts and Vulgate; Masoretic Text does not have *through Ard,*

חֲמִשָּׁה וְאַרְבָּעִים אֶלֶף וְשֵׁשׁ מֵאוֹת׃ (42) אֵלֶּה בְנֵי־דָן
five and-forty thousand and-six hundreds (42) these sons-of Dan

לְמִשְׁפְּחֹתָם לְשׁוּחָם מִשְׁפַּחַת הַשּׁוּחָמִי אֵלֶּה מִשְׁפְּחֹת דָּן
by-clans-of-them through-Shuham clan-of the-Shuhamite these clans-of Dan

לְמִשְׁפְּחֹתָם׃ (43) כָּל־מִשְׁפְּחֹת הַשּׁוּחָמִי לִפְקֻדֵיהֶם
by-clans-of-them (43) all-of clans-of the-Shuhamite by-numberings-of-them

אַרְבָּעָה וְשִׁשִּׁים אֶלֶף וְאַרְבַּע מֵאוֹת׃ (44) בְּנֵי אָשֵׁר לְמִשְׁפְּחֹתָם
four and-sixty thousand and-four hundreds (44) sons-of Asher by-clans-of-them

לְיִמְנָה מִשְׁפַּחַת הַיִּמְנָה לְיִשְׁוִי מִשְׁפַּחַת הַיִּשְׁוִי
through-Imnah clan-of the-Imnite through-Ishvi clan-of the-Ishvite

לִבְרִיעָה מִשְׁפַּחַת הַבְּרִיעִי׃ (45) לִבְנֵי בְרִיעָה לְחֶבֶר
through-Beriah clan-of the-Beriite (45) through-sons-of Beriah through-Heber

מִשְׁפַּחַת הַחֶבְרִי לְמַלְכִּיאֵל מִשְׁפַּחַת הַמַּלְכִּיאֵלִי׃ (46) וְשֵׁם
clan-of the-Heberite through-Malkiel clan-of the-Malkielite (46) now-name-of

בַּת־אָשֵׁר שָׂרַח׃ (47) אֵלֶּה מִשְׁפְּחֹת בְּנֵי־אָשֵׁר לִפְקֻדֵיהֶם
daughter-of Asher Serah (47) these clans-of sons-of Asher by-numberings-of-them

שְׁלֹשָׁה וַחֲמִשִּׁים אֶלֶף וְאַרְבַּע מֵאוֹת׃ (48) בְּנֵי נַפְתָּלִי
three and-fifty thousand and-four hundreds (48) sons-of Naphtali

לְמִשְׁפְּחֹתָם לְיַחְצְאֵל מִשְׁפַּחַת הַיַּחְצְאֵלִי לְגוּנִי מִשְׁפַּחַת
by-clans-of-them through-Jahzeel clan-of the-Jahzeelite through-Guni clan-of

הַגּוּנִי׃ (49) לְיֵצֶר מִשְׁפַּחַת הַיִּצְרִי לְשִׁלֵּם מִשְׁפַּחַת
the-Gunite (49) through-Jezer clan-of the-Jezerite through-Shillem clan-of

הַשִּׁלֵּמִי׃ (50) אֵלֶּה מִשְׁפְּחֹת נַפְתָּלִי לְמִשְׁפְּחֹתָם
the-Shillemite (50) these clans-of Naphtali by-clans-of-them

וּפְקֻדֵיהֶם חֲמִשָּׁה וְאַרְבָּעִים אֶלֶף וְאַרְבַּע מֵאוֹת׃ (51) אֵלֶּה
and-numberings-of-them five and-forty thousand and-four hundreds (51) these

פְּקוּדֵי בְּנֵי יִשְׂרָאֵל שֵׁשׁ־מֵאוֹת אֶלֶף וָאָלֶף שְׁבַע
numberings-of sons-of Israel six hundreds thousand and-thousand seven-of

מֵאוֹת וּשְׁלֹשִׁים׃ (52) וַיְדַבֵּר יְהוָה אֶל־מֹשֶׁה לֵּאמֹר׃ (53) לָאֵלֶּה
hundreds and-thirty (52) and-he-spoke Yahweh to Moses to-say (53) to-these

תֵּחָלֵק הָאָרֶץ בְּנַחֲלָה בְּמִסְפַּר שֵׁמוֹת׃
she-must-be-allotted the-land as-inheritance by-number-of names

(54) לָרַב תַּרְבֶּה נַחֲלָתוֹ וְלַמְעַט
(54) to-the-large you-make-large inheritance-of-him and-to-the-small

תַּמְעִיט נַחֲלָתוֹ אִישׁ לְפִי פְקֻדָיו
you-make-small inheritance-of-him each by-amount-of numberings-of-him

יֻתַּן נַחֲלָתוֹ׃ (55) אַךְ־בְּגוֹרָל יֵחָלֵק
he-must-receive inheritance-of-him (55) only by-lot he-must-be-distributed

45,600.

42 These were the descendants of Dan by their clans:
through Shuham, the Shuhamite clan.
These were the clans of Dan:
43 All of them were Shuhamite clans; and those numbered were 64,400.

44 The descendants of Asher by their clans were:
through Imnah, the Imnite clan;
through Ishvi, the Ishvite clan;
through Beriah, the Beriite clan;
45 and through the descendants of Beriah:
through Heber, the Heberite clan;
through Malkiel, the Malkielite clan.
46 (Asher had a daughter named Serah.)
47 These were the clans of Asher; those numbered were 53,400.

48 The descendants of Naphtali by their clans were:
through Jahzeel, the Jahzeelite clan;
through Guni, the Gunite clan;
49 through Jezer, the Jezerite clan;
through Shillem, the Shillemite clan.
50 These were the clans of Naphtali; those numbered were 45,400.

51 The total number of the men of Israel was 601,730.

52 The LORD said to Moses, 53 "The land is to be allotted to them as an inheritance based on the number of names. 54 To a larger group give a larger inheritance, and to a smaller group a smaller one; each is to receive its inheritance according to the number of those listed. 55 Be sure that the land is distributed by lot. What each

אֶת־ הָאָרֶץ לִשְׁמוֹת מַטּוֹת־ אֲבֹתָם יִנְחָלוּ׃
they-will-inherit fathers-of-them tribes-of by-names-of the-land ***

עַל־ פִּי הַגּוֹרָל תֵּחָלֵק נַחֲלָתוֹ בֵּין
among inheritance-of-him he-must-be-distributed the-lot decision-of by (56)

רַב לִמְעָט׃ וְאֵלֶּה פְקוּדֵי הַלֵּוִי לְמִשְׁפְּחֹתָם
by-clans-of-them the-Levite numberings-of and-these (57) among-small large

לְגֵרְשׁוֹן מִשְׁפַּחַת הַגֵּרְשֻׁנִּי לִקְהָת מִשְׁפַּחַת הַקְּהָתִי
the-Kohathite clan-of through-Kohath the-Gershonite clan-of through-Gershon

לִמְרָרִי מִשְׁפַּחַת הַמְּרָרִי׃ אֵלֶּה׀ מִשְׁפְּחֹת לֵוִי מִשְׁפַּחַת
clan-of Levi clans-of these (58) the-Merarite clan-of through-Merari

הַלִּבְנִי מִשְׁפַּחַת הַחֶבְרֹנִי מִשְׁפַּחַת הַמַּחְלִי מִשְׁפַּחַת הַמּוּשִׁי
the-Mushite clan-of the-Mahlite clan-of the-Hebronite clan-of the-Libnite

מִשְׁפַּחַת הַקָּרְחִי וּקְהָת הוֹלִד אֶת־ עַמְרָם׃ וְשֵׁם׀
and-name-of (59) Amram *** he-fathered now-Kohath the-Korahite clan-of

אֵשֶׁת עַמְרָם יוֹכֶבֶד בַּת־ לֵוִי אֲשֶׁר יָלְדָה אֹתָהּ לְלֵוִי בְּמִצְרָיִם
in-Egypt to-Levi her she-bore whom Levi daughter-of Jochebed Amram wife-of

וַתֵּלֶד לְעַמְרָם אֶת־ אַהֲרֹן וְאֶת־ מֹשֶׁה וְאֵת מִרְיָם אֲחֹתָם׃
sister-of-them Miriam and Moses and Aaron *** to-Amram and-she-bore

וַיִּוָּלֵד לְאַהֲרֹן אֶת־ נָדָב וְאֶת־אֲבִיהוּא אֶת־אֶלְעָזָר וְאֶת־אִיתָמָר׃
Ithamar and Eleazar *** Abihu and Nadab *** to-Aaron and-he-was-born (60)

וַיָּמָת נָדָב וַאֲבִיהוּא בְּהַקְרִיבָם אֵשׁ־ זָרָה
unauthorized fire-of when-to-offer-them and-Abihu Nadab but-he-died (61)

לִפְנֵי יְהוָה׃ וַיִּהְיוּ פְקֻדֵיהֶם שְׁלֹשָׁה וְעֶשְׂרִים אֶלֶף
thousand and-twenty three numberings-of-them and-they-were (62) Yahweh before

כָּל־ זָכָר מִבֶּן־ חֹדֶשׁ וָמָעְלָה כִּי׀ לֹא הָתְפָּקְדוּ בְּתוֹךְ
along-with they-were-counted not for or-more month from-son-of male every-of

בְּנֵי יִשְׂרָאֵל כִּי לֹא־ נִתַּן לָהֶם נַחֲלָה בְּתוֹךְ בְּנֵי יִשְׂרָאֵל׃
Israel sons-of among inheritance to-them he-gave not for Israel sons-of

אֵלֶּה פְּקוּדֵי מֹשֶׁה וְאֶלְעָזָר הַכֹּהֵן אֲשֶׁר פָּקְדוּ אֶת־
*** they-counted when the-priest and-Eleazar Moses countings-of these (63)

בְּנֵי יִשְׂרָאֵל בְּעַרְבֹת מוֹאָב עַל יַרְדֵּן יְרֵחוֹ׃ וּבְאֵלֶּה
and-among-these (64) Jericho Jordan-of by Moab on-plains-of Israel sons-of

לֹא־ הָיָה אִישׁ מִפְּקוּדֵי מֹשֶׁה וְאַהֲרֹן הַכֹּהֵן אֲשֶׁר
when the-priest and-Aaron Moses from-numberings-of man he-was not

פָּקְדוּ אֶת־ בְּנֵי יִשְׂרָאֵל בְּמִדְבַּר סִינָי׃ כִּי־ אָמַר יְהוָה
Yahweh he-told for (65) Sinai in-Desert-of Israel sons-of *** they-counted

לָהֶם מוֹת יָמֻתוּ בַּמִּדְבָּר וְלֹא־ נוֹתַר מֵהֶם
from-them being-left and-not in-the-desert they-would-die to-die to-them

group inherits will be according to the names for its ancestral tribe. 56Each inheritance is to be distributed by lot among the larger and smaller groups."

57These were the Levites who were counted by their clans:
through Gershon, the Gershonite clan;
through Kohath, the Kohathite clan;
through Merari, the Merarite clan.
58These also were Levite clans:
the Libnite clan,
the Hebronite clan,
the Mahlite clan,
the Mushite clan,
the Korahite clan.
(Kohath was the forefather of Amram; 59the name of Amram's wife was Jochebed, a descendant of Levi, who was born to the Levites[l] in Egypt. To Amram she bore Aaron, Moses and their sister Miriam. 60Aaron was the father of Nadab and Abihu, Eleazar and Ithamar. 61But Nadab and Abihu died when they made an offering before the LORD with unauthorized fire.)

62All the male Levites a month old or more numbered 23,000. They were not counted along with the other Israelites because they received no inheritance among them.

63These are the ones counted by Moses and Eleazar the priest when they counted the Israelites on the plains of Moab by the Jordan across from Jericho. 64Not one of them was among those counted by Moses and Aaron the priest when they counted the Israelites in the Desert of Sinai. 65For the LORD had told those Israelites they would surely die in the desert, and not one of them was left except

[l]59 *Or Jochebed, a daughter of Levi, who was born to Levi*

אִישׁ כִּי אִם־כָּלֵב בֶּן־יְפֻנֶּה וִיהוֹשֻׁעַ בִּן־נוּן׃
Nun son-of and-Joshua Jephunneh son-of Caleb only except one

וַתִּקְרַבְנָה בְּנוֹת צְלָפְחָד בֶּן־חֵפֶר בֶּן־גִּלְעָד
Gilead son-of Hepher son-of Zelophehad daughters-of now-they-approached (27:1)

בֶּן־מָכִיר בֶּן־מְנַשֶּׁה לְמִשְׁפְּחֹת מְנַשֶּׁה בֶן־יוֹסֵף וְאֵלֶּה
and-these Joseph son-of Manasseh of-clans-of Manasseh son-of Makir son-of

שְׁמוֹת בְּנֹתָיו מַחְלָה נֹעָה וְחָגְלָה וּמִלְכָּה וְתִרְצָה׃
and-Tirzah and-Milcah and-Hoglah Noah Mahlah daughters-of-him names-of

וַתַּעֲמֹדְנָה לִפְנֵי מֹשֶׁה וְלִפְנֵי אֶלְעָזָר הַכֹּהֵן וְלִפְנֵי
and-before the-priest Eleazar and-before Moses before and-they-stood (2)

הַנְּשִׂיאִם וְכָל־הָעֵדָה פֶּתַח אֹהֶל־מוֹעֵד לֵאמֹר׃
to-say Meeting Tent-of entrance-of the-assembly and-whole-of the-leaders

אָבִינוּ מֵת בַּמִּדְבָּר וְהוּא לֹא־הָיָה בְּתוֹךְ הָעֵדָה
the-follower among he-was not now-he in-the-desert he-died father-of-us (3)

הַנּוֹעָדִים עַל־יְהוָה בַּעֲדַת־קֹרַח כִּי־בְחֶטְאוֹ
for-sin-of-him but Korah among-follower-of Yahweh against the-ones-banding

מֵת וּבָנִים לֹא־הָיוּ לוֹ׃ לָמָּה יִגָּרַע שֵׁם־
name-of should-he-disappear why? (4) to-him they-were not and-sons he-died

אָבִינוּ מִתּוֹךְ מִשְׁפַּחְתּוֹ כִּי אֵין לוֹ בֵּן תְּנָה־לָּנוּ
to-us give! son to-him not because clan-of-him from-among father-of-us

אֲחֻזָּה בְּתוֹךְ אֲחֵי אָבִינוּ׃ וַיַּקְרֵב מֹשֶׁה אֶת־
*** Moses so-he-brought (5) father-of-us relatives-of among property

מִשְׁפָּטָן לִפְנֵי יְהוָה׃ וַיֹּאמֶר יְהוָה אֶל־מֹשֶׁה לֵּאמֹר׃ כֵּן
right (7) to-say Moses to Yahweh and-he-said (6) Yahweh before case-of-them

בְּנוֹת צְלָפְחָד דֹּבְרֹת נָתֹן תִּתֵּן לָהֶם אֲחֻזַּת
property-of to-them you-give to-give ones-saying Zelophehad daughters-of

נַחֲלָה בְּתוֹךְ אֲחֵי אֲבִיהֶם וְהַעֲבַרְתָּ אֶת־נַחֲלַת
inheritance-of *** and-you-turn father-of-them relatives-of among inheritance

אֲבִיהֶן לָהֶן׃ וְאֶל־בְּנֵי יִשְׂרָאֵל תְּדַבֵּר לֵאמֹר אִישׁ כִּי־
if man to-say you-speak Israel sons-of and-to (8) to-them father-of-them

יָמוּת וּבֵן אֵין לוֹ וְהַעֲבַרְתֶּם אֶת־נַחֲלָתוֹ
inheritance-of-him *** then-you-turn to-him not and-son he-dies

לְבִתּוֹ׃ וְאִם־אֵין לוֹ בַּת וּנְתַתֶּם אֶת־
*** then-you-give daughter to-him not and-if (9) to-daughter-of-him

נַחֲלָתוֹ לְאֶחָיו׃ וְאִם־אֵין לוֹ אַחִים
brothers to-him not and-if (10) to-brothers-of-him inheritance-of-him

וּנְתַתֶּם אֶת־נַחֲלָתוֹ לַאֲחֵי אָבִיו׃ וְאִם־
and-if (11) father-of-him to-brothers-of inheritance-of-him *** then-you-give

Caleb son of Jephunneh and Joshua son of Nun.

*Zelophehad's Daughters*

27 The daughters of Zelophehad son of Hepher, the son of Gilead, the son of Makir, the son of Manasseh, belonged to the clans of Manasseh son of Joseph. The names of the daughters were Mahlah, Noah, Hoglah, Milcah and Tirzah. They
approached [2]the entrance to the Tent of Meeting and stood before Moses, Eleazar the priest, the leaders and the whole assembly, and said,
[3]"Our father died in the desert. He was not among Korah's followers, who banded together against the LORD, but he died for his own sin and left no sons. [4]Why should
our father's name disappear from his clan because he had no son? Give us property among our father's relatives."
[5]So Moses brought their case
before the LORD [6]and the LORD
said to him, [7]"What Zelophehad's daughters are saying is right. You must certainly give them property as an inheritance among their father's relatives and turn their father's inheritance over to them.
[8]"Say to the Israelites, 'If a man dies and leaves no son, turn his inheritance over to his daughter. [9]If he has no
daughter, give his inheritance to his brothers. [10]If he has no
brothers, give his inheritance to his father's brothers. [11]If his

אֵ֣ין אַחִים֮ לְאָבִיו֒ וּנְתַתֶּ֣ם אֶת־ נַחֲלָת֗וֹ
inheritance-of-him *** then-you-give to-father-of-him brothers not

לִשְׁאֵר֗וֹ הַקָּרֹ֥ב אֵלָ֛יו מִמִּשְׁפַּחְתּ֖וֹ וְיָרַ֣שׁ אֹתָ֑הּ
her that-he-may-possess in-clan-of-him to-him the-one-near to-relative-of-him

וְהָ֨יְתָ֜ה לִבְנֵ֤י יִשְׂרָאֵל֙ לְחֻקַּ֣ת מִשְׁפָּ֔ט כַּאֲשֶׁ֛ר צִוָּ֥ה
he-commanded just-as legal as-requirement-of Israel for-sons-of now-she-must-be

יְהוָ֖ה אֶת־ מֹשֶֽׁה׃ וַיֹּ֤אמֶר יְהוָה֙ אֶל־ מֹשֶׁ֔ה עֲלֵ֛ה אֶל־ הַ֥ר
mountain-of on go-up! Moses to Yahweh then-he-said (12) Moses *** Yahweh

הָעֲבָרִ֖ים הַזֶּ֑ה וּרְאֵה֙ אֶת־ הָאָ֔רֶץ אֲשֶׁ֥ר נָתַ֖תִּי לִבְנֵ֥י יִשְׂרָאֵֽל׃
Israel to-sons-of I-gave that the-land *** and-see! the-this the-Abarim

וְרָאִ֣יתָה אֹתָ֔הּ וְנֶאֱסַפְתָּ֥ אֶל־ עַמֶּ֖יךָ גַּם־אָ֑תָּה
you also people-of-you to then-you-will-be-gathered her when-you-see (13)

כַּאֲשֶׁ֥ר נֶאֱסַ֖ף אַהֲרֹ֥ן אָחִֽיךָ׃ כַּאֲשֶׁ֨ר מְרִיתֶ֜ם
you-disobeyed just-as (14) brother-of-you Aaron he-was-gathered just-as

פִּ֜י בְּמִדְבַּר־ צִ֗ן בִּמְרִיבַת֙ הָֽעֵדָ֔ה לְהַקְדִּישֵׁ֥נִי
to-honor-as-holy-me the-community in-rebellion-of Zin in-Desert-of command-of-me

בַמַּ֖יִם לְעֵינֵיהֶ֑ם הֵ֛ם מֵֽי־ מְרִיבַ֥ת קָדֵ֖שׁ
Kadesh-of Meribah-of waters-of these before-eyes-of-them at-the-waters

מִדְבַּר־ צִֽן׃ וַיְדַבֵּ֣ר מֹשֶׁ֔ה אֶל־ יְהוָ֖ה לֵאמֹֽר׃ יִפְקֹ֣ד
may-he-appoint (16) to-say Yahweh to Moses and-he-spoke (15) Zin Desert-of

יְהוָ֔ה אֱלֹהֵ֥י הָרוּחֹ֖ת לְכָל־ בָּשָׂ֑ר אִ֖ישׁ עַל־ הָעֵדָֽה׃ אֲשֶׁר־
who (17) the-community over man mankind of-all-of the-spirits God-of Yahweh

יֵצֵ֣א לִפְנֵיהֶ֗ם וַאֲשֶׁ֤ר יָבֹא֙ לִפְנֵיהֶ֔ם וַאֲשֶׁ֥ר
and-who before-them he-will-come-in and-who before-them he-will-go-out

יוֹצִיאֵ֖ם וַאֲשֶׁ֣ר יְבִיאֵ֑ם וְלֹ֤א תִהְיֶה֙
she-will-be so-not he-will-bring-in-them and-who he-will-lead-out-them

עֲדַ֣ת יְהוָ֔ה כַּצֹּ֕אן אֲשֶׁ֥ר אֵין־ לָהֶ֖ם רֹעֶֽה׃ וַיֹּ֨אמֶר
so-he-said (18) one-herding to-them not that like-the-sheep Yahweh people-of

יְהוָ֤ה אֶל־מֹשֶׁה֙ קַח־ לְךָ֙ אֶת־יְהוֹשֻׁ֣עַ בִּן־ נ֔וּן אִ֖ישׁ אֲשֶׁר־ ר֣וּחַ בּ֑וֹ
in-him spirit whom man Nun son-of Joshua *** to-you take! Moses to Yahweh

וְסָמַכְתָּ֥ אֶת־ יָדְךָ֖ עָלָֽיו׃ וְהַעֲמַדְתָּ֣ אֹת֗וֹ לִפְנֵי֙ אֶלְעָזָ֣ר
Eleazar before him and-you-stand (19) on-him hand-of-you *** and-you-lay

הַכֹּהֵ֔ן וְלִפְנֵ֖י כָּל־ הָעֵדָ֑ה וְצִוִּיתָ֥ה אֹת֖וֹ
him and-you-commission the-assembly entire-of and-before the-priest

לְעֵינֵיהֶֽם׃ וְנָתַתָּ֥ה מֵהוֹדְךָ֖ עָלָ֑יו לְמַ֣עַן
so-that to-him from-authority-of-you and-you-give (20) before-eyes-of-them

יִשְׁמְע֔וּ כָּל־ עֲדַ֖ת בְּנֵ֥י יִשְׂרָאֵֽל׃ וְלִפְנֵ֨י אֶלְעָזָ֤ר
Eleazar and-before (21) Israel sons-of community-of whole-of they-will-obey

father had no brothers, give his inheritance to the nearest relative in his clan, that he may possess it. This is to be a legal requirement for the Israelites, as the LORD commanded Moses.' "

*Joshua to Succeed Moses*

12Then the LORD said to Moses, "Go up this mountain in the Abarim range and see the land I have given the Israelites. 13After you have seen it, you too will be gathered to your people, as your brother Aaron was, 14for when the community rebelled at the waters in the Desert of Zin, both of you disobeyed my command to honor me as holy before their eyes." (These were the waters of Meribah in Kadesh, in the Desert of Zin.)

15Moses said to the LORD, 16"May the LORD, the God of the spirits of all mankind, appoint a man over this community 17to go out and come in before them, one who will lead them out and bring them in, so the LORD's people will not be like sheep without a shepherd."

18So the LORD said to Moses, "Take Joshua son of Nun, a man in whom is the spirit,[m] and lay your hand on him. 19Have him stand before Eleazar the priest and the entire assembly and commission him in their presence. 20Give him some of your authority so the whole Israelite community will obey him. 21He is to stand

[m]18 Or *Spirit*

הַכֹּהֵן יַעֲמֹד וְשָׁאַל לוֹ בְּמִשְׁפַּט הָאוּרִים
the-Urim from-decision-of for-him and-he-will-obtain he-must-stand the-priest

לִפְנֵי יְהוָה עַל־ פִּיו יֵצְאוּ וְעַל־ פִּיו
command-of-him and-at they-will-go-out command-of-him at Yahweh before

יָבֹאוּ הוּא וְכָל־ בְּנֵי־ יִשְׂרָאֵל אִתּוֹ וְכָל־
and-entire-of with-him Israel sons-of and-all-of he they-will-come-in

הָעֵדָה׃ וַיַּעַשׂ מֹשֶׁה כַּאֲשֶׁר צִוָּה יְהוָה אֹתוֹ
him Yahweh he-commanded just-as Moses so-he-did (22) the-community

וַיִּקַּח אֶת־ יְהוֹשֻׁעַ וַיַּעֲמִדֵהוּ לִפְנֵי אֶלְעָזָר הַכֹּהֵן וְלִפְנֵי
and-before the-priest Eleazar before and-he-stood-him Joshua *** and-he-took

כָּל־ הָעֵדָה׃ וַיִּסְמֹךְ אֶת־ יָדָיו עָלָיו
on-him hands-of-him *** then-he-laid (23) the-assembly whole-of

וַיְצַוֵּהוּ כַּאֲשֶׁר דִּבֶּר יְהוָה בְּיַד־ מֹשֶׁה׃
Moses by-hand-of Yahweh he-instructed just-as and-he-commissioned-him

וַיְדַבֵּר יְהוָה אֶל־מֹשֶׁה לֵּאמֹר׃ צַו אֶת־ בְּנֵי יִשְׂרָאֵל
Israel sons-of *** command! (2) to-say Moses to Yahweh and-he-spoke (28:1)

וְאָמַרְתָּ אֲלֵהֶם אֶת־ קָרְבָּנִי לַחְמִי לְאִשַּׁי
for-fire-offerings-of-me food-of-me offering-of-me *** to-them and-you-say

רֵיחַ נִיחֹחִי תִּשְׁמְרוּ לְהַקְרִיב לִי בְּמוֹעֲדוֹ׃
at-time-of-him to-me to-present you-see pleasant-of-me aroma-of

וְאָמַרְתָּ לָהֶם זֶה הָאִשֶּׁה אֲשֶׁר תַּקְרִיבוּ
you-must-present that the-fire-offering this to-them and-you-say (3)

לַיהוָה כְּבָשִׂים בְּנֵי־ שָׁנָה תְמִימִם שְׁנַיִם לַיּוֹם
for-the-day two ones-without-defect year sons-of lambs to-Yahweh

עֹלָה תָמִיד׃ אֶת־ הַכֶּבֶשׂ אֶחָד תַּעֲשֶׂה בַבֹּקֶר וְאֵת
and in-the-morning you-prepare one the-lamb *** (4) regular burnt-offering

הַכֶּבֶשׂ הַשֵּׁנִי תַּעֲשֶׂה בֵּין הָעַרְבָּיִם׃ וַעֲשִׂירִית הָאֵיפָה
the-ephah and-tenth-of (5) the-twilights at you-prepare the-other the-lamb

סֹלֶת לְמִנְחָה בְּלוּלָה בְּשֶׁמֶן כָּתִית רְבִיעִת הַהִין׃
the-hin fourth-of pressed with-oil being-mixed for-grain-offering fine-flour

עֹלַת תָּמִיד הָעֲשֻׂיָה בְּהַר סִינַי
Sinai at-Mount-of the-one-being-instituted regular burnt-offering-of (6)

לְרֵיחַ נִיחֹחַ אִשֶּׁה לַיהוָה׃ וְנִסְכּוֹ
and-drink-offering-of-him (7) to-Yahweh fire-offering pleasant as-aroma-of

רְבִיעִת הַהִין לַכֶּבֶשׂ הָאֶחָד בַּקֹּדֶשׁ הַסֵּךְ
pour-out! at-the-sanctuary the-each with-the-lamb the-hin fourth-of

נֶסֶךְ שֵׁכָר לַיהוָה׃ וְאֵת הַכֶּבֶשׂ הַשֵּׁנִי
the-second the-lamb and (8) to-Yahweh fermented-drink drink-offering

before Eleazar the priest, who will obtain decisions for him by inquiring of the Urim before the LORD. At his command he and the entire community of the Israelites will go out, and at his command they will come in."

22 Moses did as the LORD commanded him. He took Joshua and had him stand before Eleazar the priest and the whole assembly. 23 Then he laid his hands on him and commissioned him, as the LORD instructed through Moses.

*Daily Offerings*

28 The LORD said to Moses, 2 "Give this command to the Israelites and say to them: 'See that you present to me at the appointed time the food for my offerings made by fire, as an aroma pleasing to me.' 3 Say to them: 'This is the offering made by fire that you are to present to the LORD: two lambs a year old without defect, as a regular burnt offering each day. 4 Prepare one lamb in the morning and the other at twilight, 5 together with a grain offering of a tenth of an ephah[n] of fine flour mixed with a fourth of a hin[o] of oil from pressed olives. 6 This is the regular burnt offering instituted at Mount Sinai as a pleasing aroma, an offering made to the LORD by fire. 7 The accompanying drink offering is to be a fourth of a hin of fermented drink with each lamb. Pour out the drink offering to the LORD at the sanctuary. 8 Prepare the second

[n] 5 That is, probably about 2 quarts (about 2 liters); also in verses 13, 21 and 29
[o] 5 That is, probably about 1 quart (about 1 liter); also in verses 7 and 14

תַּעֲשֶׂה בֵּין הָעַרְבַּיִם כְּמִנְחַת הַבֹּקֶר
the-morning as-grain-offering-of the-twilights at you-prepare

וּכְנִסְכּוֹ תַּעֲשֶׂה אִשֵּׁה רֵיחַ נִיחֹחַ
pleasant aroma-of fire-offering you-prepare and-as-drink-offering-of-him

לַיהוָה׃ (9) וּבְיוֹם הַשַּׁבָּת שְׁנֵי־כְבָשִׂים בְּנֵי־שָׁנָה תְּמִימִם
ones-defectless year sons-of lambs two-of the-Sabbath on-day-of (9) to-Yahweh

וּשְׁנֵי עֶשְׂרֹנִים סֹלֶת מִנְחָה בְּלוּלָה בַשֶּׁמֶן
with-the-oil being-mixed grain-offering fine-flour tenths and-two-of

וְנִסְכּוֹ׃ (10) עֹלַת שַׁבַּת בְּשַׁבַּתּוֹ
on-Sabbath-of-him Sabbath burnt-offering-of (10) and-drink-offering-of-him

עַל־ עֹלַת הַתָּמִיד וְנִסְכָּהּ׃ (11) וּבְרָאשֵׁי
and-on-firsts-of (11) and-drink-offering-of-her the-regular burnt-offering-of beside

חָדְשֵׁיכֶם תַּקְרִיבוּ עֹלָה לַיהוָה פָּרִים בְּנֵי־ בָקָר
herd young-ones-of bulls to-Yahweh burnt-offering you-present months-of-you

שְׁנַיִם וְאַיִל אֶחָד כְּבָשִׂים בְּנֵי־ שָׁנָה שִׁבְעָה תְּמִימִם׃
ones-without-defect seven year sons-of and-male-lambs one and-ram two

(12) וּשְׁלֹשָׁה עֶשְׂרֹנִים סֹלֶת מִנְחָה בְּלוּלָה בַשֶּׁמֶן
with-the-oil being-mixed grain-offering fine-flour tenths and-three (12)

לַפָּר הָאֶחָד וּשְׁנֵי עֶשְׂרֹנִים סֹלֶת מִנְחָה בְּלוּלָה
being-mixed grain-offering fine-flour tenths and-two-of the-each with-the-bull

בַשֶּׁמֶן לָאַיִל הָאֶחָד׃ (13) וְעִשָּׂרֹן עִשָּׂרוֹן סֹלֶת מִנְחָה
grain-offering flour tenth and-tenth (13) the-each with-the-ram with-the-oil

בְּלוּלָה בַשֶּׁמֶן לַכֶּבֶשׂ הָאֶחָד עֹלָה רֵיחַ
aroma-of burnt-offering the-each with-the-lamb with-the-oil being-mixed

נִיחֹחַ אִשֶּׁה לַיהוָה׃ (14) וְנִסְכֵּיהֶם חֲצִי
half-of and-drink-offerings-of-them (14) to-Yahweh fire-offering pleasant

הַהִין יִהְיֶה לַפָּר וּשְׁלִישִׁת הַהִין לָאַיִל
with-the-ram the-hin and-third-of with-the-bull he-must-be the-hin

וּרְבִיעִת הַהִין לַכֶּבֶשׂ יָיִן זֹאת עֹלַת חֹדֶשׁ
month burnt-offering-of this wine with-the-lamb the-hin and-fourth-of

בְּחָדְשׁוֹ לְחָדְשֵׁי הַשָּׁנָה׃ (15) וּשְׂעִיר עִזִּים אֶחָד
one goats and-male-goat-of (15) the-year at-new-moons-of in-month-of-him

לְחַטָּאת לַיהוָה עַל־ עֹלַת הַתָּמִיד יֵעָשֶׂה
he-must-be-made the-regular burnt-offering-of beside to-Yahweh as-sin-offering

וְנִסְכּוֹ׃ (16) וּבַחֹדֶשׁ הָרִאשׁוֹן בְּאַרְבָּעָה עָשָׂר יוֹם
day ten on-four the-first and-on-the-month (16) with-drink-offering-of-him

לַחֹדֶשׁ פֶּסַח לַיהוָה׃ (17) וּבַחֲמִשָּׁה עָשָׂר יוֹם לַחֹדֶשׁ
of-the-month day ten and-on-five (17) to-Yahweh Passover of-the-month

lamb at twilight, along with the same kind of grain offering and drink offering that you prepare in the morning. This is an offering made by fire, an aroma pleasing to the LORD.

*Sabbath Offerings*

9 " 'On the Sabbath day, make an offering of two lambs a year old without defect, together with its drink offering and a grain offering of two-tenths of an ephah[p] of fine flour mixed with oil.
10 This is the burnt offering for every Sabbath, in addition to the regular burnt offering and its drink offering.

*Monthly Offerings*

11 " 'On the first of every month, present to the LORD a burnt offering of two young bulls, one ram and seven male lambs a year old, all without defect.
12 With each bull there is to be a grain offering of three-tenths of an ephah[q] of fine flour mixed with oil; with the ram, a grain offering of two-tenths of an ephah of fine flour mixed with oil;
13 and with each lamb, a grain offering of a tenth of an ephah of fine flour mixed with oil. This is for a burnt offering, a pleasing aroma, an offering made to the LORD by fire.
14 With each bull there is to be a drink offering of half a hin[r] of wine; with the ram, a third of a hin[s]; and with each lamb, a fourth of a hin. This is the monthly burnt offering to be made at each new moon during the year.
15 Besides the regular burnt offering with its drink offering, one male goat is to be presented to the LORD as a sin offering.

*The Passover*

16 " 'On the fourteenth day of the first month the LORD's Passover is to be held.
17 On the fifteenth day of this month

[p]9 That is, probably about 4 quarts (about 4.5 liters); also in verses 12, 20 and 28
[q]12 That is, probably about 6 quarts (about 6.5 liters); also in verses 20 and 28
[r]14 That is, probably about 2 quarts (about 2 liters)
[s]14 That is, probably about 1 1/4 quarts (about 1.2 liters)

הַזֶּה חָג שִׁבְעַת יָמִים מַצּוֹת יֵאָכֵל׃
he-must-be-eaten breads-without-yeast days seven-of festival the-this

בַּיּוֹם הָרִאשׁוֹן מִקְרָא־ קֹדֶשׁ כָּל־ מְלֶאכֶת עֲבֹדָה לֹא
not regular work-of any-of sacred assembly-of the-first on-the-day (18)

תַעֲשׂוּ׃ וְהִקְרַבְתֶּם אִשֶּׁה עֹלָה לַיהוָה פָּרִים
bulls to-Yahweh burnt-offering fire-offering and-you-present (19) you-do

בְּנֵי־ בָקָר שְׁנַיִם וְאַיִל אֶחָד וְשִׁבְעָה כְבָשִׂים בְּנֵי שָׁנָה
year sons-of male-lambs and-seven one and-ram two herd young-ones-of

תְּמִימִם יִהְיוּ לָכֶם׃ וּמִנְחָתָם
and-grain-offering-of-them (20) to-you they-must-be ones-without-defect

סֹלֶת בְּלוּלָה בַשָּׁמֶן שְׁלֹשָׁה עֶשְׂרֹנִים לַפָּר וּשְׁנֵי עֶשְׂרֹנִים
tenths and-two-of with-the-bull tenths three with-the-oil being-mixed flour

לָאַיִל תַּעֲשׂוּ׃ עִשָּׂרוֹן עִשָּׂרוֹן תַּעֲשֶׂה לַכֶּבֶשׂ הָאֶחָד
the-each with-the-lamb you-prepare tenth tenth (21) you-prepare with-the-ram

לְשִׁבְעַת הַכְּבָשִׂים׃ וּשְׂעִיר חַטָּאת אֶחָד לְכַפֵּר עֲלֵיכֶם׃
for-you to-atone one sin-offering and-goat-of (22) the-lambs with-seven-of

מִלְּבַד עֹלַת הַבֹּקֶר אֲשֶׁר לְעֹלַת
for-burnt-offering-of that the-morning burnt-offering-of in-addition-to (23)

הַתָּמִיד תַּעֲשׂוּ אֶת־ אֵלֶּה׃ כָּאֵלֶּה תַּעֲשׂוּ לַיּוֹם
by-the-day you-prepare as-the-these (24) these *** you-prepare the-regular

שִׁבְעַת יָמִים לֶחֶם אִשֵּׁה רֵיחַ־ נִיחֹחַ לַיהוָה עַל־
beside to-Yahweh pleasant aroma-of fire-offering-of food-of days seven-of

עוֹלַת הַתָּמִיד יֵעָשֶׂה וְנִסְכּוֹ׃
and-drink-offering-of-him he-must-be-prepared the-regular burnt-offering-of

וּבַיּוֹם הַשְּׁבִיעִי מִקְרָא־ קֹדֶשׁ יִהְיֶה לָכֶם כָּל־
any-of for-you he-must-be sacred assembly-of the-seventh and-on-the-day (25)

מְלֶאכֶת עֲבֹדָה לֹא תַעֲשׂוּ׃ וּבְיוֹם הַבִּכּוּרִים
the-firstfruits and-on-day-of (26) you-do not regular work-of

בְּהַקְרִיבְכֶם מִנְחָה חֲדָשָׁה לַיהוָה בְּשָׁבֻעֹתֵיכֶם
during-Feast-of-Weeks-of-you to-Yahweh new grain-offering when-to-present-you

מִקְרָא־ קֹדֶשׁ יִהְיֶה לָכֶם כָּל־ מְלֶאכֶת עֲבֹדָה לֹא תַעֲשׂוּ׃
you-do not regular work-of any-of for-you he-must-be sacred assembly-of

וְהִקְרַבְתֶּם עוֹלָה לְרֵיחַ נִיחֹחַ לַיהוָה פָּרִים
bulls to-Yahweh pleasant as-aroma-of burnt-offering and-you-present (27)

בְּנֵי־ בָקָר שְׁנַיִם אַיִל אֶחָד שִׁבְעָה כְבָשִׂים בְּנֵי שָׁנָה׃
year sons-of male-lambs seven one ram two herd young-ones-of

וּמִנְחָתָם סֹלֶת בְּלוּלָה בַשָּׁמֶן שְׁלֹשָׁה עֶשְׂרֹנִים
tenths three with-the-oil being-mixed flour and-grain-offering-of-them (28)

there is to be a festival; for seven days eat bread made without yeast.
18On the first day hold a sacred assembly and do no regular work.
19Present to the LORD an offering made by fire, a burnt offering of two young bulls, one ram and seven male lambs a year old, all without defect.
20With each bull prepare a grain offering of three-tenths of an ephah of fine flour mixed with oil; with the ram, two-tenths;
21and with each of the seven lambs, one-tenth.
22Include one male goat as a sin offering to make atonement for you.
23Prepare these in addition to the regular morning burnt offering.
24In this way prepare the food for the offering made by fire every day for seven days as an aroma pleasing to the LORD; it is to be prepared in addition to the regular burnt offering and its drink offering.
25On the seventh day hold a sacred assembly and do no regular work.

*Feast of Weeks*

26" 'On the day of firstfruits, when you present to the LORD an offering of new grain during the Feast of Weeks, hold a sacred assembly and do no regular work.
27Present a burnt offering of two young bulls, one ram and seven male lambs a year old as an aroma pleasing to the LORD.
28With each bull there is to be a grain offering of three-tenths of an ephah of fine flour mixed with

לַפָּר הָאֶחָד שְׁנֵי עֶשְׂרֹנִים לָאַיִל הָאֶחָד׃ עִשָּׂרוֹן עִשָּׂרוֹן

tenth tenth (29) the-each with-the-ram tenths two-of the-each with-the-bull

לַכֶּבֶשׂ הָאֶחָד לְשִׁבְעַת הַכְּבָשִׂים׃ שְׂעִיר עִזִּים אֶחָד

one goats male-goat-of (30) the-lambs with-seven-of the-each with-the-lamb

לְכַפֵּר עֲלֵיכֶם׃ מִלְּבַד עֹלַת הַתָּמִיד

the-regular burnt-offering-of in-addition-to (31) for-you to-atone

וּמִנְחָתוֹ תַּעֲשׂוּ תְּמִימִם יִהְיוּ־לָכֶם

to-you they-must-be ones-without-defect you-prepare and-grain-offering-of-him

וְנִסְכֵּיהֶם׃ וּבַחֹדֶשׁ הַשְּׁבִיעִי בְּאֶחָד

on-first the-seventh and-in-the-month (29:1) with-drink-offerings-of-them

לַחֹדֶשׁ מִקְרָא־קֹדֶשׁ יִהְיֶה לָכֶם כָּל־מְלֶאכֶת עֲבֹדָה

regular work-of any-of for-you he-must-be sacred assembly-of of-the-month

לֹא תַעֲשׂוּ יוֹם תְּרוּעָה יִהְיֶה לָכֶם׃ וַעֲשִׂיתֶם

and-you-prepare (2) for-you he-is trumpet-sound day-of you-do not

עֹלָה לְרֵיחַ נִיחֹחַ לַיהוָה פַּר בֶּן־בָּקָר אֶחָד אַיִל אֶחָד

one ram one herd young-of bull to-Yahweh pleasant as-aroma-of burnt-offering

כְּבָשִׂים בְּנֵי־שָׁנָה שִׁבְעָה תְּמִימִם׃ וּמִנְחָתָם

and-grain-offering-of-them (3) ones-without-defect seven year sons-of lambs

סֹלֶת בְּלוּלָה בַשָּׁמֶן שְׁלֹשָׁה עֶשְׂרֹנִים לַפָּר שְׁנֵי עֶשְׂרֹנִים

tenths two-of with-the-bull tenths three with-the-oil being-mixed fine-flour

לָאָיִל׃ וְעִשָּׂרוֹן אֶחָד לַכֶּבֶשׂ הָאֶחָד לְשִׁבְעַת הַכְּבָשִׂים׃

the-lambs with-seven-of the-each with-the-lamb one and-tenth (4) with-the-ram

וּשְׂעִיר־עִזִּים אֶחָד חַטָּאת לְכַפֵּר עֲלֵיכֶם׃ מִלְּבַד

in-addition-to (6) for-you to-atone sin-offering one goats and-male-goat-of (5)

עֹלַת הַחֹדֶשׁ וּמִנְחָתָהּ וְעֹלַת

and-burnt-offering-of and-grain-offering-of-her the-month burnt-offering-of

הַתָּמִיד וּמִנְחָתָהּ וְנִסְכֵּיהֶם

and-drink-offerings-of-them and-grain-offering-of-her the-regular

כְּמִשְׁפָּטָם לְרֵיחַ נִיחֹחַ אִשֶּׁה לַיהוָה׃

to-Yahweh fire-offering pleasant for-aroma-of as-specified-of-them

וּבֶעָשׂוֹר לַחֹדֶשׁ הַשְּׁבִיעִי הַזֶּה מִקְרָא־קֹדֶשׁ

sacred assembly-of the-this the-seventh of-the-month and-on-tenth (7)

יִהְיֶה לָכֶם וְעִנִּיתֶם אֶת־נַפְשֹׁתֵיכֶם כָּל־מְלָאכָה לֹא תַעֲשׂוּ׃

you-do not work any-of selves-of-you *** and-you-must-deny for-you he-must-be

וְהִקְרַבְתֶּם עֹלָה לַיהוָה רֵיחַ נִיחֹחַ פַּר בֶּן־

young-of bull pleasant aroma-of to-Yahweh burnt-offering and-you-present (8)

בָּקָר אֶחָד אַיִל אֶחָד כְּבָשִׂים בְּנֵי־שָׁנָה שִׁבְעָה תְּמִימִם יִהְיוּ

they-must-be ones-without-defect seven year sons-of lambs one ram one herd

---

oil; with the ram, two-tenths; [29]and with each of the seven lambs, one-tenth. [30]Include one male goat to make atonement for you. [31]Prepare these together with their drink offerings, in addition to the regular burnt offering and its grain offering. Be sure the animals are without defect.

*Feast of Trumpets*

29 "'On the first day of the seventh month hold a sacred assembly and do no regular work. It is a day for you to sound the trumpets. [2]As an aroma pleasing to the LORD, prepare a burnt offering of one young bull, one ram and seven male lambs a year old, all without defect. [3]With the bull prepare a grain offering of three-tenths of an ephah[t] of fine flour mixed with oil; with the ram, two-tenths[u]; [4]and with each of the seven lambs, one-tenth.[v] [5]Include one male goat as a sin offering to make atonement for you. [6]These are in addition to the monthly and daily burnt offerings with their grain offerings and drink offerings as specified. They are offerings made to the LORD by fire—a pleasing aroma.

*Day of Atonement*

[7]"'On the tenth day of this seventh month hold a sacred assembly. You must deny yourselves[w] and do no work. [8]Present as an aroma pleasing to the LORD a burnt offering of one young bull, one ram and seven male lambs a year old, all without defect. [9]With the

[t]3 That is, probably about 6 quarts (about 6.5 liters); also in verses 9 and 14
[u]3 That is, probably about 4 quarts (about 4.5 liters); also in verses 9 and 14
[v]4 That is, probably about 2 quarts (about 2 liters); also in verses 10 and 15
[w]7 Or *must fast*

לָכֶם׃ וּמִנְחָתָם סֹלֶת בְּלוּלָה בַשָּׁמֶן שְׁלֹשָׁה
three with-the-oil being-mixed flour and-grain-offering-of-them (9) to-you

עֶשְׂרֹנִים לַפָּר שְׁנֵי עֶשְׂרֹנִים לָאָיִל הָאֶחָד׃ עִשָּׂרוֹן עִשָּׂרוֹן
tenth tenth (10) the-one with-the-ram tenths two-of with-the-bull tenths

לַכֶּבֶשׂ הָאֶחָד לְשִׁבְעַת הַכְּבָשִׂים׃ שְׂעִיר־ עִזִּים אֶחָד
one goats male-goat-of (11) the-lambs for-seven-of the-each with-the-lamb

חַטָּאת מִלְּבַד חַטַּאת הַכִּפֻּרִים וְעֹלַת
and-burnt-offering-of the-atonements sin-offering-of in-addition-to sin-offering

הַתָּמִיד וּמִנְחָתָהּ וְנִסְכֵּיהֶם׃
and-drink-offerings-of-them and-grain-offering-of-her the-regular

וּבַחֲמִשָּׁה עָשָׂר יוֹם לַחֹדֶשׁ הַשְּׁבִיעִי מִקְרָא־ קֹדֶשׁ
sacred assembly-of the-seventh of-the-month day ten and-on-five (12)

יִהְיֶה לָכֶם כָּל־ מְלֶאכֶת עֲבֹדָה לֹא תַעֲשׂוּ וְחַגֹּתֶם חַג
festival and-you-celebrate you-do not regular work-of any-of for-you he-must-be

לַיהוָה שִׁבְעַת יָמִים׃ וְהִקְרַבְתֶּם עֹלָה אִשֵּׁה
fire-offering-of burnt-offering and-you-present (13) days seven-of to-Yahweh

רֵיחַ נִיחֹחַ לַיהוָה פָּרִים בְּנֵי־ בָקָר שְׁלֹשָׁה עָשָׂר אֵילִם שְׁנָיִם
two rams ten three herd young-ones-of bulls to-Yahweh pleasant aroma-of

כְּבָשִׂים בְּנֵי־ שָׁנָה אַרְבָּעָה עָשָׂר תְּמִימִם יִהְיוּ׃
they-must-be ones-without-defect ten four year sons-of male-lambs

וּמִנְחָתָם סֹלֶת בְּלוּלָה בַשָּׁמֶן שְׁלֹשָׁה עֶשְׂרֹנִים
tenths three with-the-oil being-mixed flour and-grain-offering-of-them (14)

לַפָּר הָאֶחָד לִשְׁלֹשָׁה עָשָׂר פָּרִים שְׁנֵי עֶשְׂרֹנִים לָאַיִל
with-the-ram tenths two-of bulls ten with-three the-each with-the-bull

הָאֶחָד לִשְׁנֵי הָאֵילִם׃ וְעִשָּׂרוֹן עִשָּׂרוֹן לַכֶּבֶשׂ הָאֶחָד
the-each with-the-lamb tenth and-tenth (15) the-rams with-two-of the-each

לְאַרְבָּעָה עָשָׂר כְּבָשִׂים׃ וּשְׂעִיר־ עִזִּים אֶחָד חַטָּאת מִלְּבַד
in-addition-to sin-offering one goats and-male-goat-of (16) lambs ten with-four

עֹלַת הַתָּמִיד מִנְחָתָהּ וְנִסְכָּהּ׃
and-drink-offering-of-her grain-offering-of-her the-regular burnt-offering-of

וּבַיּוֹם הַשֵּׁנִי פָּרִים בְּנֵי־ בָקָר שְׁנֵים עָשָׂר אֵילִם שְׁנָיִם
two rams ten two herd young-ones-of bulls the-second and-on-the-day (17)

כְּבָשִׂים בְּנֵי־ שָׁנָה אַרְבָּעָה עָשָׂר תְּמִימִם׃ וּמִנְחָתָם
and-grain-offering-of-them (18) ones-without-defect ten four year sons-of lambs

וְנִסְכֵּיהֶם לַפָּרִים לָאֵילִם וְלַכְּבָשִׂים
and-with-the-lambs with-the-rams with-the-bulls and-drink-offerings-of-them

בְּמִסְפָּרָם כַּמִּשְׁפָּט׃ וּשְׂעִיר־ עִזִּים אֶחָד חַטָּאת
sin-offering one goats and-male-goat-of (19) as-the-rule by-number-of-them

bull prepare a grain offering of three-tenths of an ephah of fine flour mixed with oil; with the ram, two-tenths; [10]and with each of the seven lambs, one-tenth. [11]Include one male goat as a sin offering, in addition to the sin offering for atonement and the regular burnt offering with its grain offering, and their drink offerings.

*Feast of Tabernacles*

[12]" 'On the fifteenth day of the seventh month, hold a sacred assembly and do no regular work. Celebrate a festival to the Lord for seven days. [13]Present an offering made by fire as an aroma pleasing to the Lord, a burnt offering of thirteen young bulls, two rams and fourteen male lambs a year old, all without defect. [14]With each of the thirteen bulls prepare a grain offering of three-tenths of an ephah of fine flour mixed with oil; with each of the two rams, two-tenths; [15]and with each of the fourteen lambs, one-tenth. [16]Include one male goat as a sin offering, in addition to the regular burnt offering with its grain offering and drink offering.

[17]" 'On the second day prepare twelve young bulls, two rams and fourteen male lambs a year old, all without defect. [18]With the bulls, rams and lambs, prepare their grain offerings and drink offerings according to the number specified. [19]Include one male

מִלְּבַד עֹלַת הַתָּמִיד וּמִנְחָתָהּ
and-grain-offering-of-her the-regular burnt-offering-of in-addition-to

וְנִסְכֵּיהֶם׃ (20) וּבַיּוֹם הַשְּׁלִישִׁי פָּרִים עַשְׁתֵּי־עָשָׂר
ten one bulls the-third and-on-the-day (20) and-drink-offerings-of-them

אֵילִם שְׁנָיִם כְּבָשִׂים בְּנֵי־ שָׁנָה אַרְבָּעָה עָשָׂר תְּמִימִם׃
ones-without-defect ten four year sons-of lambs two rams

(21) וּמִנְחָתָם וְנִסְכֵּיהֶם לַפָּרִים
with-the-bulls and-drink-offerings-of-them and-grain-offering-of-them (21)

לָאֵילִם וְלַכְּבָשִׂים בְּמִסְפָּרָם כַּמִּשְׁפָּט׃
as-the-specified by-number-of-them and-with-the-lambs with-the-rams

(22) וּשְׂעִיר חַטָּאת אֶחָד מִלְּבַד עֹלַת
burnt-offering-of in-addition-to one sin-offering and-male-goat-of (22)

הַתָּמִיד וּמִנְחָתָהּ וְנִסְכָּהּ׃
and-drink-offering-of-her and-grain-offering-of-her the-regular

(23) וּבַיּוֹם הָרְבִיעִי פָּרִים עֲשָׂרָה אֵילִם שְׁנָיִם כְּבָשִׂים בְּנֵי־ שָׁנָה
year sons-of lambs two rams ten bulls the-fourth and-on-the-day (23)

אַרְבָּעָה עָשָׂר תְּמִימִם׃ (24) מִנְחָתָם
grain-offering-of-them (24) ones-without-defect ten four

וְנִסְכֵּיהֶם לַפָּרִים לָאֵילִם וְלַכְּבָשִׂים
and-with-the-lambs with-the-rams with-the-bulls and-drink-offerings-of-them

בְּמִסְפָּרָם כַּמִּשְׁפָּט׃ (25) וּשְׂעִיר־ עִזִּים אֶחָד חַטָּאת
sin-offering one goats and-male-goat-of (25) as-the-rule by-number-of-them

מִלְּבַד עֹלַת הַתָּמִיד מִנְחָתָהּ
grain-offering-of-her the-regular burnt-offering-of in-addition-to

וְנִסְכָּהּ׃ (26) וּבַיּוֹם הַחֲמִישִׁי פָּרִים תִּשְׁעָה אֵילִם
rams nine bulls the-fifth and-on-the-day (26) and-drink-offering-of-her

שְׁנָיִם כְּבָשִׂים בְּנֵי־ שָׁנָה אַרְבָּעָה עָשָׂר תְּמִימִם׃
ones-without-defect ten four year sons-of lambs two

(27) וּמִנְחָתָם וְנִסְכֵּיהֶם לַפָּרִים
with-the-bulls and-drink-offerings-of-them and-grain-offering-of-them (27)

לָאֵילִם וְלַכְּבָשִׂים בְּמִסְפָּרָם כַּמִּשְׁפָּט׃
as-the-specified by-number-of-them and-with-the-lambs with-the-rams

(28) וּשְׂעִיר חַטָּאת אֶחָד מִלְּבַד עֹלַת הַתָּמִיד
the-regular burnt-offering-of in-addition-to one sin-offering and-goat-of (28)

וּמִנְחָתָהּ וְנִסְכָּהּ׃ (29) וּבַיּוֹם
and-on-the-day (29) and-drink-offering-of-her and-grain-offering-of-her

הַשִּׁשִּׁי פָּרִים שְׁמֹנָה אֵילִם שְׁנָיִם כְּבָשִׂים בְּנֵי־ שָׁנָה אַרְבָּעָה עָשָׂר
ten four year sons-of lambs two rams eight bulls the-sixth

goat as a sin offering, in addition to the regular burnt offering with its grain offering, and their drink offerings.
20 " 'On the third day prepare eleven bulls, two rams and fourteen male lambs a year old, all without defect.
21 With the bulls, rams and lambs, prepare their grain offerings and drink offerings according to the number specified.
22 Include one male goat as a sin offering, in addition to the regular burnt offering with its grain offering and drink offering.
23 " 'On the fourth day prepare ten bulls, two rams and fourteen male lambs a year old, all without defect.
24 With the bulls, rams and lambs, prepare their grain offerings and drink offerings according to the number specified.
25 Include one male goat as a sin offering, in addition to the regular burnt offering with its grain offering and drink offering.
26 " 'On the fifth day prepare nine bulls, two rams and fourteen male lambs a year old, all without defect.
27 With the bulls, rams and lambs, prepare their grain offerings and drink offerings according to the number specified.
28 Include one male goat as a sin offering, in addition to the regular burnt offering with its grain offering and drink offering.
29 " 'On the sixth day prepare eight bulls, two rams and fourteen male lambs a year old, all

תְּמִימִם׃ וּמִנְחָתָם וְנִסְכֵּיהֶם
and-drink-offerings-of-them and-grain-offering-of-them (30) ones-without-defect

לַפָּרִים לָאֵילִם וְלַכְּבָשִׂים בְּמִסְפָּרָם כַּמִּשְׁפָּט׃
as-the-rule by-number-of-them and-with-the-lambs with-the-rams with-the-bulls

וּשְׂעִיר חַטָּאת אֶחָד מִלְּבַד עֹלַת הַתָּמִיד
the-regular burnt-offering-of in-addition-to one sin-offering and-goat-of (31)

מִנְחָתָהּ וּנְסָכֶיהָ׃ וּבַיּוֹם הַשְּׁבִיעִי
the-seventh and-on-the-day (32) and-drink-offering-of-her grain-offering-of-her

פָּרִים שִׁבְעָה אֵילִם שְׁנָיִם כְּבָשִׂים בְּנֵי־ שָׁנָה אַרְבָּעָה עָשָׂר תְּמִימִם׃
ones-without-defect ten four year sons-of lambs two rams seven bulls

וּמִנְחָתָם וְנִסְכֵּהֶם לַפָּרִים
with-the-bulls and-drink-offerings-of-them and-grain-offering-of-them (33)

לָאֵילִם וְלַכְּבָשִׂים בְּמִסְפָּרָם כְּמִשְׁפָּטָם׃
as-specified-of-them by-number-of-them and-with-the-lambs with-the-rams

וּשְׂעִיר חַטָּאת אֶחָד מִלְּבַד עֹלַת הַתָּמִיד
the-regular burnt-offering-of in-addition-to one sin-offering and-goat-of (34)

מִנְחָתָהּ וְנִסְכָּהּ׃ בַּיּוֹם הַשְּׁמִינִי
the-eighth on-the-day (35) and-drink-offering-of-her grain-offering-of-her

עֲצֶרֶת תִּהְיֶה לָכֶם כָּל־ מְלֶאכֶת עֲבֹדָה לֹא תַעֲשׂוּ׃
you-do not regular work-of any-of for-you she-must-be assembly

וְהִקְרַבְתֶּם עֹלָה אִשֵּׁה רֵיחַ נִיחֹחַ
pleasant aroma-of fire-offering-of burnt-offering and-you-present (36)

לַיהוָה פַּר אֶחָד אַיִל אֶחָד כְּבָשִׂים בְּנֵי־ שָׁנָה שִׁבְעָה תְּמִימִם׃
ones-without-defect seven year sons-of lambs one ram one bull to-Yahweh

מִנְחָתָם וְנִסְכֵּיהֶם לַפָּר
with-the-bull and-drink-offerings-of-them grain-offering-of-them (37)

לָאַיִל וְלַכְּבָשִׂים בְּמִסְפָּרָם כַּמִּשְׁפָּט׃ וּשְׂעִיר
and-goat-of (38) as-the-rule by-number-of-them and-with-the-lambs with-the-ram

חַטָּאת אֶחָד מִלְּבַד עֹלַת הַתָּמִיד
the-regular burnt-offering-of in-addition-to one sin-offering

וּמִנְחָתָהּ וְנִסְכָּהּ׃ אֵלֶּה תַּעֲשׂוּ
you-prepare these (39) and-drink-offering-of-her and-grain-offering-of-her

לַיהוָה בְּמוֹעֲדֵיכֶם לְבַד מִנִּדְרֵיכֶם
from-vows-of-you addition-to at-feasts-of-you for-Yahweh

וְנִדְבֹתֵיכֶם לְעֹלֹתֵיכֶם
with-burnt-offerings-of-you and-freewill-offerings-of-you

וּלְמִנְחֹתֵיכֶם וּלְנִסְכֵּיכֶם
and-with-drink-offerings-of-you and-with-grain-offerings-of-you

without defect. 30 With the
bulls, rams and lambs, prepare
their grain offerings and drink
offerings according to the
number specified. 31 Include
one male goat as a sin offering,
in addition to the regular
burnt offering with its grain
offering and drink offering.

32 " 'On the seventh day prepare seven bulls, two rams and
fourteen male lambs a year
old, all without defect. 33 With
the bulls, rams and lambs, prepare their grain offerings and
drink offerings according to
the number specified. 34 Include one male goat as a sin
offering, in addition to the
regular burnt offering with its
grain offering and drink
offering.

35 " 'On the eighth day hold
an assembly and do no regular
work. 36 Present an offering
made by fire as an aroma
pleasing to the LORD, a burnt
offering of one bull, one ram
and seven male lambs a year
old, all without defect. 37 With
the bull, the ram and the
lambs, prepare their grain
offerings and drink offerings
according to the number
specified. 38 Include one male
goat as a sin offering, in addition to the regular burnt
offering with its grain offering
and drink offering.

39 " 'In addition to what you
vow and your freewill
offerings, prepare these for the
LORD at your appointed feasts:
your burnt offerings, grain
offerings, drink offerings and
fellowship offerings.[x] ' "

[x] 39 Traditionally *peace offerings*

וּלְשַׁלְמֵיכֶם׃ וַיֹּאמֶר מֹשֶׁה אֶל־ בְּנֵי
sons-of to Moses and-he-told (30:1)* and-with-fellowship-offerings-of-you

יִשְׂרָאֵל כְּכֹל אֲשֶׁר־ צִוָּה יְהוָה אֶת־ מֹשֶׁה׃ וַיְדַבֵּר מֹשֶׁה אֶל־
to Moses and-he-spoke (2) Moses *** Yahweh he-commanded that as-all Israel

רָאשֵׁי הַמַּטּוֹת לִבְנֵי יִשְׂרָאֵל לֵאמֹר זֶה הַדָּבָר אֲשֶׁר צִוָּה
he-commands that the-thing this to-say Israel of-sons-of the-tribes heads-of

יְהוָה׃ אִישׁ כִּי־ יִדֹּר נֶדֶר לַיהוָה אוֹ־ הִשָּׁבַע שְׁבֻעָה לֶאְסֹר
to-obligate oath to-swear or to-Yahweh vow he-vows when man (3) Yahweh

אִסָּר עַל־ נַפְשׁוֹ לֹא יַחֵל דְּבָרוֹ כְּכָל־
as-every-of word-of-him he-must-break not self-of-him on pledge

הַיֹּצֵא מִפִּיו יַעֲשֶׂה׃ וְאִשָּׁה כִּי־ תִדֹּר
she-vows when and-woman (4) he-must-do from-mouth-of-him the-thing-coming

נֶדֶר לַיהוָה וְאָסְרָה אִסָּר בְּבֵית אָבִיהָ בִּנְעֻרֶיהָ׃
in-youths-of-her father-of-her in-house-of pledge or-she-obligates to-Yahweh vow

וְשָׁמַע אָבִיהָ אֶת־ נִדְרָהּ וֶאֱסָרָהּ אֲשֶׁר
which or-pledge-of-her vow-of-her *** father-of-her and-he-hears (5)

אָסְרָה עַל־ נַפְשָׁהּ וְהֶחֱרִישׁ לָהּ אָבִיהָ
father-of-her to-her but-he-says-nothing self-of-her on she-obligated

וְקָמוּ כָּל־ נְדָרֶיהָ וְכָל־ אִסָּר אֲשֶׁר־
which pledge and-every-of vows-of-her all-of then-they-will-stand

אָסְרָה עַל־ נַפְשָׁהּ יָקוּם׃ וְאִם־ הֵנִיא
he-forbids but-if (6) he-will-stand self-of-her on she-obligated

אָבִיהָ אֹתָהּ בְּיוֹם שָׁמְעוֹ כָּל־ נְדָרֶיהָ וֶאֱסָרֶיהָ
or-pledges-of-her vows-of-her all-of to-hear-him on-day her father-of-her

אֲשֶׁר־ אָסְרָה עַל־ נַפְשָׁהּ לֹא יָקוּם וַיהוָה
and-Yahweh he-will-stand not self-of-her on she-obligated which

יִסְלַח־ לָהּ כִּי־ הֵנִיא אָבִיהָ אֹתָהּ׃ וְאִם־ הָיוֹ
to-be and-if (7) her father-of-her he-forbade for from-her he-will-release

תִהְיֶה לְאִישׁ וּנְדָרֶיהָ עָלֶיהָ אוֹ מִבְטָא שְׂפָתֶיהָ
lips-of-her rash-promise-of or on-her and-vows-of-her to-husband she-is

אֲשֶׁר אָסְרָה עַל־ נַפְשָׁהּ׃ וְשָׁמַע אִישָׁהּ בְּיוֹם
on-day husband-of-her and-he-hears (8) self-of-her on she-obligated which

שָׁמְעוֹ וְהֶחֱרִישׁ לָהּ וְקָמוּ נְדָרֶיהָ
vows-of-her then-they-will-stand to-her but-he-says-nothing to-hear-him

וֶאֱסָרֶהָ אֲשֶׁר־ אָסְרָה עַל־ נַפְשָׁהּ יָקֻמוּ׃
they-will-stand self-of-her on she-obligated which or-pledges-of-her

וְאִם בְּיוֹם שְׁמֹעַ אִישָׁהּ יָנִיא אוֹתָהּ וְהֵפֵר
then-he-nullifies her he-forbids husband-of-her to-hear on-day but-if (9)

40 Moses told the Israelites all that the LORD commanded him.

*Vows*

30 Moses said to the heads of the tribes of Israel: "This is what the LORD commands: 2 When a man makes a vow to the LORD or takes an oath to obligate himself by a pledge, he must not break his word but must do everything he said.

3 "When a young woman still living in her father's house makes a vow to the LORD or obligates herself by a pledge 4 and her father hears about her vow or pledge but says nothing to her, then all her vows and every pledge by which she obligated herself will stand. 5 But if her father forbids her when he hears about it, none of her vows or the pledges by which she obligated herself will stand; the LORD will release her because her father has forbidden her.

6 "If she marries after she makes a vow or after her lips utter a rash promise by which she obligates herself 7 and her husband hears about it but says nothing to her, then her vows or the pledges by which she obligated herself will stand. 8 But if her husband forbids her when he hears about it, he nullifies the vow that

*The Hebrew numeration of chapter 30 begins with verse 40 of chapter 29 in English; thus, there is a one-verse discrepancy throughout chapter 30.

אֶת־ נִדְרָהּ אֲשֶׁר עָלֶיהָ וְאֵת מִבְטָא שְׂפָתֶיהָ אֲשֶׁר אָסְרָה
she-obligated that lips-of-her rash-promise-of or on-her that vow-of-her ***

עַל־ נַפְשָׁהּ וַיהוָה יִסְלַח־ לָהּ׃ וְנֵדֶר אַלְמָנָה
widow and-vow-of (10) from-her he-will-release and-Yahweh self-of-her on

וּגְרוּשָׁה כֹּל אֲשֶׁר־ אָסְרָה עַל־ נַפְשָׁהּ יָקוּם
he-will-bind self-of-her on she-obligates which any or-one-being-divorced

עָלֶיהָ׃ וְאִם־ בֵּית אִישָׁהּ נָדָרָה אוֹ־ אָסְרָה אִסָּר
pledge she-obligates or she-vows husband-of-her house-of and-if (11) on-her

עַל־ נַפְשָׁהּ בִּשְׁבֻעָה׃ וְשָׁמַע אִישָׁהּ וְהֶחֱרִשׁ
but-he-says-nothing husband-of-her and-he-hears (12) under-oath self-of-her on

לָהּ לֹא הֵנִיא אֹתָהּ וְקָמוּ כָּל־ נְדָרֶיהָ וְכָל־
and-every-of vows-of-her all-of then-they-will-stand her he-forbids not to-her

אִסָּר אֲשֶׁר־ אָסְרָה עַל־ נַפְשָׁהּ יָקוּם׃ וְאִם־
but-if (13) he-will-stand self-of-her on she-obligated which pledge

הָפֵר יָפֵר אֹתָם ׀ אִישָׁהּ בְּיוֹם שָׁמְעוֹ כָּל־
every-of to-hear-him on-day husband-of-her them he-nullifies to-nullify

מוֹצָא שְׂפָתֶיהָ לִנְדָרֶיהָ וּלְאִסַּר נַפְשָׁהּ לֹא
not self-of-her or-if-pledge-of if-vows-of-her lips-of-her thing-from

יָקוּם אִישָׁהּ הֲפֵרָם וַיהוָה יִסְלַח־
he-will-release and-Yahweh he-nullified-them husband-of-her he-will-stand

לָהּ׃ כָּל־ נֵדֶר וְכָל־ שְׁבֻעַת אִסָּר לְעַנֹּת נָפֶשׁ אִישָׁהּ
husband-of-her self to-deny pledge oath-of or-any-of vow any-of (14) from-her

יְקִימֶנּוּ וְאִישָׁהּ יְפֵרֶנּוּ׃ וְאִם־
but-if (15) he-may-nullify-him or-husband-of-her he-may-confirm-him

הַחֲרֵשׁ יַחֲרִישׁ לָהּ אִישָׁהּ מִיּוֹם אֶל־ יוֹם
day to from-day husband-of-her to-her he-says-nothing to-say-nothing

וְהֵקִים אֶת־ כָּל־ נְדָרֶיהָ אוֹ אֶת־ כָּל־ אֱסָרֶיהָ אֲשֶׁר
that pledges-of-her all-of *** or vows-of-her all-of *** then-he-confirms

עָלֶיהָ הֵקִים אֹתָם כִּי־ הֶחֱרִשׁ לָהּ בְּיוֹם שָׁמְעוֹ׃
to-hear-him on-day to-her he-says-nothing for them he-confirms on-her

וְאִם־ הָפֵר יָפֵר אֹתָם אַחֲרֵי שָׁמְעוֹ וְנָשָׂא
then-he-must-bear to-hear-him after them he-nullifies to-nullify but-if (16)

אֶת־ עֲוֺנָהּ׃ אֵלֶּה הַחֻקִּים אֲשֶׁר צִוָּה יְהוָה אֶת־ מֹשֶׁה
Moses *** Yahweh he-gave that the-regulations these (17) guilt-of-her ***

בֵּין אִישׁ לְאִשְׁתּוֹ בֵּין־ אָב לְבִתּוֹ בִּנְעֻרֶיהָ
in-youths-of-her to-daughter-of-him father between to-wife-of-him man between

בֵּית אָבִיהָ׃ וַיְדַבֵּר יְהוָה אֶל־ מֹשֶׁה לֵּאמֹר׃
to-say Moses to Yahweh and-he-spoke (31:1) father-of-her house-of

obligates her or the rash promise by which she obligates herself, and the LORD will release her.

9 "Any vow or obligation taken by a widow or divorced woman will be binding on her.

10 "If a woman living with her husband makes a vow or obligates herself by a pledge under oath 11 and her husband hears about it but says nothing to her and does not forbid her, then all her vows or the pledges by which she obligated herself will stand. 12 But if her husband nullifies them when he hears about them, then none of the vows or pledges that came from her lips will stand. Her husband has nullified them, and the LORD will release her. 13 Her husband may confirm or nullify any vow she makes or any sworn pledge to deny herself. 14 But if her husband says nothing to her about it from day to day, then he confirms all her vows or the pledges binding on her. He confirms them by saying nothing to her when he hears about them. 15 If, however, he nullifies them some time after he hears about them, then he is responsible for her guilt."

16 These are the regulations the LORD gave Moses concerning relationships between a man and his wife, and between a father and his young daughter still living in his house.

### *Vengeance on the Midianites*

**31** The LORD said to Moses, 2 "Take vengeance on the Midianites for

*See the note on page 459.

נְקֹם נִקְמַת בְּנֵי יִשְׂרָאֵל מֵאֵת הַמִּדְיָנִים אַחַר

afterward the-Midianites on Israel sons-of vengeance-of avenge! (2)

תֵּאָסֵף אֶל־ עַמֶּיךָ׃ וַיְדַבֵּר מֹשֶׁה אֶל־ הָעָם

the-people to Moses so-he-said (3) people-of-you to you-will-be-gathered

לֵאמֹר הֵחָלְצוּ מֵאִתְּכֶם אֲנָשִׁים לַצָּבָא וְיִהְיוּ עַל־ מִדְיָן

Midian against and-they-will-go for-the-battle men from-with-you arm! to-say

לָתֵת נִקְמַת־ יְהוָה בְּמִדְיָן׃ אֶלֶף לַמַּטֶּה

from-the-tribe thousand (4) on-Midian Yahweh vengeance-of to-carry-out

אֶלֶף לַמַּטֶּה לְכֹל מַטּוֹת יִשְׂרָאֵל תִּשְׁלְחוּ לַצָּבָא׃

into-the-battle you-send Israel tribes-of from-all-of from-the-tribe thousand

וַיִּמָּסְרוּ מֵאַלְפֵי יִשְׂרָאֵל אֶלֶף לַמַּטֶּה

from-the-tribe thousand Israel from-thousands-of so-they-were-armed (5)

שְׁנֵים־עָשָׂר אֶלֶף חֲלוּצֵי צָבָא׃ וַיִּשְׁלַח אֹתָם מֹשֶׁה

Moses them and-he-sent (6) battle ones-being-supplied-of thousand ten two

אֶלֶף לַמַּטֶּה לַצָּבָא אֹתָם וְאֶת־ פִּינְחָס בֶּן־ אֶלְעָזָר

Eleazar son-of Phinehas and them into-the-battle from-the-tribe thousand

הַכֹּהֵן לַצָּבָא וּכְלֵי הַקֹּדֶשׁ וַחֲצֹצְרוֹת

and-trumpets-of the-sanctuary and-articles-of into-the-battle the-priest

הַתְּרוּעָה בְּיָדוֹ׃ וַיִּצְבְּאוּ עַל־ מִדְיָן כַּאֲשֶׁר

just-as Midian against and-they-fought (7) in-hand-of-him the-signal

צִוָּה יְהוָה אֶת־ מֹשֶׁה וַיַּהַרְגוּ כָּל־ זָכָר׃ וְאֶת־ מַלְכֵי

kings-of and (8) man every-of and-they-killed Moses *** Yahweh he-commanded

מִדְיָן הָרְגוּ עַל־ חַלְלֵיהֶם אֶת־אֱוִי וְאֶת־רֶקֶם וְאֶת־צוּר וְאֶת־חוּר

Hur and Zur and Rekem and Evi *** victims-of-them among they-killed Midian

וְאֶת־רֶבַע חֲמֵשֶׁת מַלְכֵי מִדְיָן וְאֵת בִּלְעָם בֶּן־ בְּעוֹר הָרְגוּ

they-killed Beor son-of Balaam and Midian kings-of five-of Reba and

בֶּחָרֶב׃ וַיִּשְׁבּוּ בְנֵי־ יִשְׂרָאֵל אֶת־ נְשֵׁי מִדְיָן

Midian women-of *** Israel sons-of and-they-captured (9) with-the-sword

וְאֶת־ טַפָּם וְאֵת כָּל־ בְּהֶמְתָּם וְאֶת־ כָּל־ מִקְנֵהֶם וְאֶת־

and flock-of-them all-of and herd-of-them all-of and child-of-them and

כָּל־ חֵילָם בָּזָזוּ׃ וְאֵת כָּל־ עָרֵיהֶם

towns-of-them all-of and (10) they-plundered good-of-them all-of

בְּמוֹשְׁבֹתָם וְאֵת כָּל־ טִירֹתָם שָׂרְפוּ בָּאֵשׁ׃

with-the-fire they-burned camps-of-them all-of and among-settlements-of-them

וַיִּקְחוּ אֶת־ כָּל־ הַשָּׁלָל וְאֵת כָּל־ הַמַּלְקוֹחַ בָּאָדָם

of-the-people the-spoil all-of and the-plunder all-of *** and-they-took (11)

וּבַבְּהֵמָה׃ וַיָּבִאוּ אֶל־ מֹשֶׁה וְאֶל־ אֶלְעָזָר הַכֹּהֵן

the-priest Eleazar and-to Moses to and-they-brought (12) and-of-the-animal

the Israelites. After that, you
will be gathered to your
people."
3So Moses said to the people,
"Arm some of your men to go
to war against the Midianites
and to carry out the LORD's
vengeance on them. 4Send
into battle a thousand men
from each of the tribes of Israel." 5So twelve thousand men
armed for battle, a thousand
from each tribe, were supplied
from the clans of Israel.
6Moses sent them into battle, a
thousand from each tribe,
along with Phinehas son of
Eleazar, the priest, who took
with him articles from the
sanctuary and the trumpets
for signaling.
7They fought against Midian, as the LORD commanded
Moses, and killed every man.
8Among their victims were
Evi, Rekem, Zur, Hur and
Reba—the five kings of Midian. They also killed Balaam
son of Beor with the sword.
9The Israelites captured the
Midianite women and chil-
dren and took all the Midianite herds, flocks and goods as
plunder. 10They burned all the
towns where the Midianites
had settled, as well as all their
camps. 11They took all the
plunder and spoils, including
the people and animals, 12and
brought the captives, spoils
and plunder to Moses and

וְאֶל־ עֲדַת בְּנֵי־ יִשְׂרָאֵל אֶת־ הַשְּׁבִי וְאֶת־ הַמַּלְקוֹחַ וְאֶת־
and the-spoil and the-captive *** Israel sons-of assembly-of and-to

הַשָּׁלָל אֶל־ הַמַּחֲנֶה אֶל־ עַרְבֹת מוֹאָב אֲשֶׁר עַל־ יַרְדֵּן יְרֵחוֹ׃
Jericho Jordan-of by that Moab plains-of on the-camp at the-plunder

וַיֵּצְאוּ מֹשֶׁה וְאֶלְעָזָר הַכֹּהֵן וְכָל־ נְשִׂיאֵי
leaders-of and-all-of the-priest and-Eleazar Moses and-they-went (13)

הָעֵדָה לִקְרָאתָם אֶל־מִחוּץ לַמַּחֲנֶה׃ וַיִּקְצֹף מֹשֶׁה
Moses and-he-was-angry (14) of-the-camp outside at to-meet-them the-community

עַל פְּקוּדֵי הֶחָיִל שָׂרֵי הָאֲלָפִים וְשָׂרֵי
and-commanders-of the-thousands commanders-of the-army being-officers-of with

הַמֵּאוֹת הַבָּאִים מִצְּבָא הַמִּלְחָמָה׃ וַיֹּאמֶר
and-he-asked (15) the-war from-battle-of the-ones-returning the-hundreds

אֲלֵיהֶם מֹשֶׁה הַחִיִּיתֶם כָּל־ נְקֵבָה׃ הֵן הֵנָּה הָיוּ לִבְנֵי
to-sons-of they-came they see! (16) woman every-of you-let-live? Moses to-them

יִשְׂרָאֵל בִּדְבַר בִּלְעָם לִמְסָר־ מַעַל בַּיהוָה עַל־ דְּבַר־ פְּעוֹר
Peor matter-of in with-Yahweh away-from to-turn Balaam at-advice-of Israel

וַתְּהִי הַמַּגֵּפָה בַּעֲדַת יְהוָה׃ וְעַתָּה הִרְגוּ כָל־
every-of kill! so-now (17) Yahweh on-people-of the-plague so-she-struck

זָכָר בַּטָּף וְכָל־ אִשָּׁה יֹדַעַת אִישׁ לְמִשְׁכַּב זָכָר הֲרֹגוּ׃
kill! man to-sleep-with man knowing woman and-every-of among-the-child male

וְכֹל הַטַּף בַּנָּשִׁים אֲשֶׁר לֹא־ יָדְעוּ מִשְׁכַּב זָכָר
man sleep-with they-know not who among-the-girls the-child but-every-of (18)

הַחֲיוּ לָכֶם׃ וְאַתֶּם חֲנוּ מִחוּץ לַמַּחֲנֶה שִׁבְעַת יָמִים
days seven-of of-the-camp outside stay! and-you (19) for-you save!

כֹּל הֹרֵג נֶפֶשׁ וְכֹל ׀ נֹגֵעַ בֶּחָלָל
on-the-one-killed one-touching or-every-of anyone one-killing every-of

תִּתְחַטְּאוּ בַּיּוֹם הַשְּׁלִישִׁי וּבַיּוֹם הַשְּׁבִיעִי אַתֶּם
you the-seventh and-on-the-day the-third on-the-day you-must-purify-selves

וּשְׁבִיכֶם׃ וְכָל־ בֶּגֶד וְכָל־ כְּלִי־ עוֹר
leather thing-of and-every-of garment and-every-of (20) and-captive-of-you

וְכָל־ מַעֲשֵׂה עִזִּים וְכָל־ כְּלִי־ עֵץ תִּתְחַטָּאוּ׃
you-purify wood thing-of and-every-of goat-hairs object-of and-every-of

וַיֹּאמֶר אֶלְעָזָר הַכֹּהֵן אֶל־ אַנְשֵׁי הַצָּבָא הַבָּאִים
the-ones-going the-army men-of to the-priest Eleazar then-he-said (21)

לַמִּלְחָמָה זֹאת חֻקַּת הַתּוֹרָה אֲשֶׁר־ צִוָּה יְהוָה אֶת־מֹשֶׁה׃
Moses *** Yahweh he-gave that the-law requirement-of this into-the-battle

אַךְ אֶת־ הַזָּהָב וְאֶת־ הַכֶּסֶף אֶת־ הַנְּחֹשֶׁת אֶת־הַבַּרְזֶל אֶת־הַבְּדִיל
the-tin *** the-iron *** the-bronze *** the-silver and the-gold *** now (22)

Eleazar the priest and the Israelite assembly at their camp
on the plains of Moab, by the
Jordan across from Jericho.[y]
13 Moses, Eleazar the priest
and all the leaders of the community went to meet them
outside the camp. 14 Moses was
angry with the officers of the
army—the commanders of
thousands and commanders
of hundreds—who returned
from the battle.
15 "Have you allowed all the
women to live?" he asked
them. 16 "They were the ones
who followed Balaam's advice
and were the means of turning the Israelites away from
the LORD in what happened at
Peor, so that a plague struck
the LORD's people. 17 Now kill
all the boys. And kill every
woman who has slept with a
man, 18 but save for yourselves
every girl who has never slept
with a man.
19 "All of you who have killed
anyone or touched anyone
who was killed must stay outside the camp seven days. On
the third and seventh days
you must purify yourselves
and your captives. 20 Purify
every garment as well as
everything made of leather,
goat hair or wood."
21 Then Eleazar the priest
said to the soldiers who had
gone into battle, "This is the
requirement of the law that
the LORD gave Moses: 22 Gold,
silver, bronze, iron, tin, lead

[y]12 Hebrew *Jordan of Jericho*; possibly an ancient name for the Jordan River

וְאֶת־הָעֹפָֽרֶת׃ כָּל־ דָּבָר אֲשֶׁר־ יָבֹא בָאֵשׁ
against-the-fire he-can-withstand that thing any-of (23) the-lead and

תַּעֲבִירוּ בָאֵשׁ וְטָהֵר אַךְ בְּמֵי
with-waters-of also then-he-will-be-clean through-the-fire you-must-put

נִדָּה יִתְחַטָּא וְכֹל אֲשֶׁר לֹא־ יָבֹא
he-can-withstand not that and-anything he-must-be-purified cleansing

בָּאֵשׁ תַּעֲבִירוּ בַּמָּֽיִם׃ וְכִבַּסְתֶּם
and-you-wash (24) through-the-waters you-must-put against-the-fire

בִּגְדֵיכֶם בַּיּוֹם הַשְּׁבִיעִי וּטְהַרְתֶּם וְאַחַר
and-then and-you-will-be-clean the-seventh on-the-day clothes-of-you

תָּבֹאוּ אֶל־ הַמַּחֲנֶֽה׃ וַיֹּאמֶר יְהוָה אֶל־ מֹשֶׁה לֵּאמֹֽר׃
to-say Moses to Yahweh and-he-said (25) the-camp into you-may-come

שָׂא אֶת רֹאשׁ מַלְקוֹחַ הַשְּׁבִי בָּאָדָם וּבַבְּהֵמָה
and-of-the-animal of-the-people the-captive spoil-of amount-of *** count! (26)

אַתָּה וְאֶלְעָזָר הַכֹּהֵן וְרָאשֵׁי אֲבוֹת הָעֵדָֽה׃
the-community fathers-of and-heads-of the-priest and-Eleazar you

וְחָצִיתָ אֶת־ הַמַּלְקוֹחַ בֵּין תֹּפְשֵׂי הַמִּלְחָמָה
the-war ones-fighting-of between the-spoil *** and-you-divide (27)

הַיֹּצְאִים לַצָּבָא וּבֵין כָּל־ הָעֵדָֽה׃
the-community rest-of and-between in-the-battle the-ones-taking-part

וַהֲרֵמֹתָ מֶכֶס לַיהוָה מֵאֵת אַנְשֵׁי הַמִּלְחָמָה הַיֹּצְאִים
the-ones-going the-war men-of from to-Yahweh tribute and-you-set-apart (28)

לַצָּבָא אֶחָד נֶפֶשׁ מֵחֲמֵשׁ הַמֵּאוֹת מִן־ הָאָדָם
the-person whether the-hundreds from-five-of thing one into-the-battle

וּמִן־ הַבָּקָר וּמִן־ הַחֲמֹרִים וּמִן־ הַצֹּֽאן׃
the-flock or-whether the-donkeys or-whether the-cattle or-whether

מִמַּחֲצִיתָם תִּקָּחוּ וְנָתַתָּה לְאֶלְעָזָר הַכֹּהֵן תְּרוּמַת
part-of the-priest to-Eleazar and-you-give you-take from-half-of-them (29)

יְהוָֽה׃ וּמִמַּחֲצִת בְּנֵֽי־ יִשְׂרָאֵל תִּקַּח ׀ אֶחָד ׀ אָחֻז
being-taken one you-select Israel sons-of and-from-half-of (30) Yahweh

מִן־ הַחֲמִשִּׁים מִן־ הָאָדָם מִן־ הַבָּקָר מִן־ הַחֲמֹרִים
the-donkeys whether the-cattle whether the-person whether the-fifty from

וּמִן־ הַצֹּאן מִכָּל־ הַבְּהֵמָה וְנָתַתָּה אֹתָם לַלְוִיִּם
to-the-Levites them and-you-give the-animal from-every-of the-flock or-whether

שֹׁמְרֵי מִשְׁמֶרֶת מִשְׁכַּן יְהוָֽה׃ וַיַּעַשׂ מֹשֶׁה
Moses so-he-did (31) Yahweh tabernacle-of care-of ones-being-responsible-of

וְאֶלְעָזָר הַכֹּהֵן כַּאֲשֶׁר צִוָּה יְהוָה אֶת־ מֹשֶֽׁה׃ וַיְהִי
and-he-was (32) Moses *** Yahweh he-commanded just-as the-priest and-Eleazar

23 and anything else that can withstand fire must be put through the fire, and then it will be clean. But it must also be purified with the water of cleansing. And whatever cannot withstand fire must be put through that water. 24 On the seventh day wash your clothes and you will be clean. Then you may come into the camp."

*Dividing the Spoils*

25 The LORD said to Moses, 26 "You and Eleazar the priest and the family heads of the community are to count all the people and animals that were captured. 27 Divide the spoils between the soldiers who took part in the battle and the rest of the community. 28 From the soldiers who fought in the battle, set apart as tribute for the LORD one out of every five hundred, whether persons, cattle, donkeys, sheep or goats. 29 Take this tribute from their half share and give it to Eleazar the priest as the LORD's part. 30 From the Israelites' half, select one out of every fifty, whether persons, cattle, donkeys, sheep, goats or other animals. Give them to the Levites, who are responsible for the care of the LORD's tabernacle." 31 So Moses and Eleazar the priest did as the LORD commanded Moses.

הַמַּלְקוֹחַ יֶתֶר הַבָּז אֲשֶׁר בָּזְזוּ עַם הַצָּבָא צֹאן
sheep the-army people-of they-took that the-plunder remainder-of the-spoil

שֵׁשׁ־מֵאוֹת אֶלֶף וְשִׁבְעִים אֶלֶף וַחֲמֵשֶׁת אֲלָפִים׃ וּבָקָר
and-cattle (33) thousands and-five-of thousand and-seventy thousand hundreds six

שְׁנַיִם וְשִׁבְעִים אָלֶף׃ וַחֲמֹרִים אֶחָד וְשִׁשִּׁים אָלֶף׃
thousand and-sixty one and-donkeys (34) thousand and-seventy two

וְנֶפֶשׁ אָדָם מִן־הַנָּשִׁים אֲשֶׁר לֹא־יָדְעוּ מִשְׁכַּב זָכָר
man sleep-with they-knew not who the-women from human and-person (35)

כָּל־נֶפֶשׁ שְׁנַיִם וּשְׁלֹשִׁים אָלֶף׃ וַתְּהִי הַמֶּחֱצָה חֵלֶק
share the-half and-she-was (36) thousand and-thirty two person every-of

הַיֹּצְאִים בַּצָּבָא מִסְפַּר הַצֹּאן שְׁלֹשׁ־מֵאוֹת
hundreds three-of the-sheep number-of into-the-battle the-ones-going

אֶלֶף וּשְׁלֹשִׁים אֶלֶף וְשִׁבְעַת אֲלָפִים וַחֲמֵשׁ מֵאוֹת׃
hundreds and-five-of thousands and-seven-of thousand and-thirty thousand

וַיְהִי הַמֶּכֶס לַיהוָה מִן־הַצֹּאן שֵׁשׁ מֵאוֹת חָמֵשׁ
five hundreds six the-sheep from for-Yahweh the-tribute and-he-was (37)

וְשִׁבְעִים׃ וְהַבָּקָר שִׁשָּׁה וּשְׁלֹשִׁים אָלֶף וּמִכְסָם
and-tribute-of-them thousand and-thirty six and-the-cattle (38) and-seventy

לַיהוָה שְׁנַיִם וְשִׁבְעִים׃ וַחֲמֹרִים שְׁלֹשִׁים אֶלֶף וַחֲמֵשׁ
and-five-of thousand thirty and-donkeys (39) and-seventy two for-Yahweh

מֵאוֹת וּמִכְסָם לַיהוָה אֶחָד וְשִׁשִּׁים׃ וְנֶפֶשׁ אָדָם
human and-person (40) and-sixty one for-Yahweh and-tribute-of-them hundreds

שִׁשָּׁה עָשָׂר אָלֶף וּמִכְסָם לַיהוָה שְׁנַיִם וּשְׁלֹשִׁים נָפֶשׁ׃
person and-thirty two for-Yahweh and-tribute-of-them thousand ten six

וַיִּתֵּן מֹשֶׁה אֶת־מֶכֶס תְּרוּמַת יְהוָה לְאֶלְעָזָר הַכֹּהֵן
the-priest to-Eleazar Yahweh part-of tribute-of *** Moses and-he-gave (41)

כַּאֲשֶׁר צִוָּה יְהוָה אֶת־מֹשֶׁה׃ וּמִמַּחֲצִית בְּנֵי יִשְׂרָאֵל
Israel sons-of and-from-half-of (42) Moses *** Yahweh he-commanded just-as

אֲשֶׁר חָצָה מֹשֶׁה מִן־הָאֲנָשִׁים הַצֹּבְאִים׃ וַתְּהִי
and-she-was (43) the-ones-fighting the-men from Moses he-set-apart that

מֶחֱצַת הָעֵדָה מִן־הַצֹּאן שְׁלֹשׁ־מֵאוֹת אֶלֶף וּשְׁלֹשִׁים
and-thirty thousand hundreds three-of the-sheep from the-community half-of

אֶלֶף שִׁבְעַת אֲלָפִים וַחֲמֵשׁ מֵאוֹת׃ וּבָקָר שִׁשָּׁה
six and-cattle (44) hundreds and-five-of thousands seven-of thousand

וּשְׁלֹשִׁים אָלֶף׃ וַחֲמֹרִים שְׁלֹשִׁים אֶלֶף וַחֲמֵשׁ מֵאוֹת׃
hundreds and-five-of thousand thirty and-donkeys (45) thousand and-thirty

וְנֶפֶשׁ אָדָם שִׁשָּׁה עָשָׂר אָלֶף׃ וַיִּקַּח מֹשֶׁה מִמַּחֲצִת
from-half-of Moses and-he-selected (47) thousand ten six human and-person (46)

[32]The plunder remaining
from the spoils that the soldiers took was 675,000 sheep,
[33]72,000 cattle, [34]61,000 donkeys [35]and 32,000 women who
had never slept with a man.
[36]The half share of those
who fought in the battle was:

337,500 sheep, [37]of which the tribute for the LORD was 675;
[38]36,000 cattle, of which the tribute for the LORD was 72;
[39]30,500 donkeys, of which the tribute for the LORD was 61;
[40]16,000 people, of which the tribute for the LORD was 32.

[41]Moses gave the tribute to
Eleazar the priest as the LORD's
part, as the LORD commanded
Moses.
[42]The half belonging to the
Israelites, which Moses set
apart from that of the fighting
men— [43]the community's
half—was 337,500 sheep,
[44]36,000 cattle, [45]30,500 donkeys [46]and 16,000 people.
[47]From the Israelites' half,
Moses selected one out of

בְּנֵי־ יִשְׂרָאֵל אֶת־ הָאָחֻז אֶחָד מִן־ הַחֲמִשִּׁים מִן־ הָאָדָם
the-person from the-fifty from one the-being-taken *** Israel sons-of

וּמִן־ הַבְּהֵמָה וַיִּתֵּן אֹתָם לַלְוִיִּם שֹׁמְרֵי
ones-being-responsible-of to-the-Levites them and-he-gave the-animal and-from

מִשְׁמֶרֶת מִשְׁכַּן יְהוָה כַּאֲשֶׁר צִוָּה יְהוָה אֶת־ מֹשֶׁה׃
Moses *** Yahweh he-commanded just-as Yahweh tabernacle-of care-of

וַיִּקְרְבוּ אֶל־ מֹשֶׁה הַפְּקֻדִים אֲשֶׁר לְאַלְפֵי
over-thousands-of that the-ones-being-officers Moses to then-they-went (48)

הַצָּבָא שָׂרֵי הָאֲלָפִים וְשָׂרֵי הַמֵּאוֹת׃
the-hundreds and-commanders-of the-thousands commanders-of the-army

וַיֹּאמְרוּ אֶל־ מֹשֶׁה עֲבָדֶיךָ נָשְׂאוּ אֶת־ רֹאשׁ אַנְשֵׁי
men-of head-of *** they-counted servants-of-you Moses to and-they-said (49)

הַמִּלְחָמָה אֲשֶׁר בְּיָדֵנוּ וְלֹא־ נִפְקַד מִמֶּנּוּ אִישׁ׃
one from-him he-is-missing and-not under-command-of-us who the-war

וַנַּקְרֵב אֶת־ קָרְבַּן יְהוָה אִישׁ אֲשֶׁר מָצָא כְלִי־
article-of he-acquired that each Yahweh offering-of *** so-we-brought (50)

זָהָב אֶצְעָדָה וְצָמִיד טַבַּעַת עָגִיל וְכוּמָז לְכַפֵּר עַל־
for to-atone and-necklace earring signet-ring and-bracelet armlet gold

נַפְשֹׁתֵינוּ לִפְנֵי יְהוָה׃ וַיִּקַּח מֹשֶׁה וְאֶלְעָזָר הַכֹּהֵן
the-priest and-Eleazar Moses so-he-accepted (51) Yahweh before selves-of-us

אֶת־ הַזָּהָב מֵאִתָּם כֹּל כְּלִי מַעֲשֶׂה׃ וַיְהִי ׀ כָּל־
all-of and-he-was (52) craft article-of every-of from-with-them the-gold ***

זְהַב הַתְּרוּמָה אֲשֶׁר הֵרִימוּ לַיהוָה שִׁשָּׁה עָשָׂר אֶלֶף שְׁבַע־
seven-of thousand ten six to-Yahweh they-presented that the-gift gold-of

מֵאוֹת וַחֲמִשִּׁים שֶׁקֶל מֵאֵת שָׂרֵי הָאֲלָפִים וּמֵאֵת
and-from the-thousands commanders-of from shekel and-fifty hundreds

שָׂרֵי הַמֵּאוֹת׃ אַנְשֵׁי הַצָּבָא בָּזְזוּ אִישׁ לוֹ׃
for-him each they-plundered the-army men-of (53) the-hundreds commanders-of

וַיִּקַּח מֹשֶׁה וְאֶלְעָזָר הַכֹּהֵן אֶת־ הַזָּהָב מֵאֵת
from the-gold *** the-priest and-Eleazar Moses and-he-accepted (54)

שָׂרֵי הָאֲלָפִים וְהַמֵּאוֹת וַיָּבִאוּ אֹתוֹ אֶל־
into him and-they-brought and-the-hundreds the-thousands commanders-of

אֹהֶל מוֹעֵד זִכָּרוֹן לִבְנֵי־ יִשְׂרָאֵל לִפְנֵי יְהוָה׃ וּמִקְנֶה ׀
now-livestock (32:1) Yahweh before Israel for-sons-of memorial Meeting Tent-of

רַב הָיָה לִבְנֵי רְאוּבֵן וְלִבְנֵי־ גָד עָצוּם מְאֹד וַיִּרְאוּ
and-they-saw very large Gad and-to-sons-of Reuben to-sons-of he-was much

אֶת־ אֶרֶץ יַעְזֵר וְאֶת־ אֶרֶץ גִּלְעָד וְהִנֵּה הַמָּקוֹם מְקוֹם מִקְנֶה׃
livestock place-of the-place and-see! Gilead land-of and Jazer land-of ***

every fifty persons and animals, as the LORD commanded him, and gave them to the Levites, who were responsible for the care of the LORD's tabernacle.

48Then the officers who were over the units of the army—the commanders of thousands and commanders of hundreds—went to Moses 49and said to him, "Your servants have counted the soldiers under our command, and not one is missing. 50So we have brought as an offering to the LORD the gold articles each of us acquired—armlets, bracelets, signet rings, earrings and necklaces—to make atonement for ourselves before the LORD."

51Moses and Eleazar the priest accepted from them the gold—all the crafted articles. 52All the gold from the commanders of thousands and commanders of hundreds that Moses and Eleazar presented as a gift to the LORD weighed 16,750 shekels.[z] 53Each soldier had taken plunder for himself. 54Moses and Eleazar the priest accepted the gold from the commanders of thousands and commanders of hundreds and brought it into the Tent of Meeting as a memorial for the Israelites before the LORD.

*The Transjordan Tribes*

32 The Reubenites and Gadites, who had very large herds and flocks, saw that the lands of Jazer and Gilead were suitable for livestock.

[z]52 That is, about 420 pounds (about 190 kilograms)

וַיָּבֹאוּ בְנֵי־גָד וּבְנֵי רְאוּבֵן וַיֹּאמְרוּ אֶל־מֹשֶׁה
Moses to and-they-said Reuben and-sons-of Gad sons-of so-they-came (2)

וְאֶל־אֶלְעָזָר הַכֹּהֵן וְאֶל־נְשִׂיאֵי הָעֵדָה לֵאמֹר׃ עֲטָרוֹת
Ataroth (3) to-say the-community leaders-of and-to the-priest Eleazar and-to

וְדִיבֹן וְיַעְזֵר וְנִמְרָה וְחֶשְׁבּוֹן וְאֶלְעָלֵה וּשְׂבָם וּנְבוֹ
and-Nebo and-Sebam and-Elealeh and-Heshbon and-Nimrah and-Jazer and-Dibon

וּבְעֹן׃ הָאָרֶץ אֲשֶׁר הִכָּה יְהוָה לִפְנֵי עֲדַת יִשְׂרָאֵל אֶרֶץ
land-of Israel people-of before Yahweh he-subdued that the-land (4) and-Beon

מִקְנֶה הִוא וְלַעֲבָדֶיךָ מִקְנֶה׃ וַיֹּאמְרוּ אִם־מָצָאנוּ
we-found if and-they-said (5) livestock and-to-servants-of-you she livestock

חֵן בְּעֵינֶיךָ יֻתַּן אֶת־הָאָרֶץ הַזֹּאת לַעֲבָדֶיךָ
to-servants-of-you the-this the-land *** let-him-be-given in-eyes-of-you favor

לַאֲחֻזָּה אַל־תַּעֲבִרֵנוּ אֶת־הַיַּרְדֵּן׃ וַיֹּאמֶר מֹשֶׁה
Moses and-he-said (6) the-Jordan *** you-make-cross-us not as-possession

לִבְנֵי־גָד וְלִבְנֵי רְאוּבֵן הַאַחֵיכֶם יָבֹאוּ
shall-they-go countrymen-of-you? Reuben and-to-sons-of Gad to-sons-of

לַמִּלְחָמָה וְאַתֶּם תֵּשְׁבוּ פֹה׃ וְלָמָּה תְנוּאוּן אֶת־לֵב
heart-of *** do-you-discourage and-why? (7) here you-sit while-you to-the-war

בְּנֵי יִשְׂרָאֵל מֵעֲבֹר אֶל־הָאָרֶץ אֲשֶׁר־נָתַן לָהֶם יְהוָה׃
Yahweh to-them he-gave that the-land into from-to-go-over Israel sons-of

כֹּה עָשׂוּ אֲבֹתֵיכֶם בְּשָׁלְחִי אֹתָם מִקָּדֵשׁ בַּרְנֵעַ
Barnea from-Kadesh them when-to-send-me fathers-of-you they-did this (8)

לִרְאוֹת אֶת־הָאָרֶץ׃ וַיַּעֲלוּ עַד־נַחַל אֶשְׁכּוֹל
Eshcol Valley-of to and-they-went-up (9) the-land *** to-look-over

וַיִּרְאוּ אֶת־הָאָרֶץ וַיָּנִיאוּ אֶת־לֵב בְּנֵי יִשְׂרָאֵל
Israel sons-of heart-of *** but-they-discouraged the-land *** and-they-viewed

לְבִלְתִּי־בֹא אֶל־הָאָרֶץ אֲשֶׁר־נָתַן לָהֶם יְהוָה׃ וַיִּחַר־
and-he-aroused (10) Yahweh to-them he-gave that the-land into to-enter not

אַף יְהוָה בַּיּוֹם הַהוּא וַיִּשָּׁבַע לֵאמֹר׃ אִם־
not (11) to-say and-he-swore-oath the-that on-the-day Yahweh anger-of

יִרְאוּ הָאֲנָשִׁים הָעֹלִים מִמִּצְרַיִם מִבֶּן עֶשְׂרִים שָׁנָה
year twenty from-son-of from-Egypt the-ones-coming the-men they-will-see

וָמַעְלָה אֵת הָאֲדָמָה אֲשֶׁר נִשְׁבַּעְתִּי לְאַבְרָהָם לְיִצְחָק וּלְיַעֲקֹב כִּי
for and-to-Jacob to-Isaac to-Abraham I-promised that the-land *** or-more

לֹא־מִלְאוּ אַחֲרָי׃ בִּלְתִּי כָּלֵב בֶּן־יְפֻנֶּה
Jephunneh son-of Caleb except (12) after-me they-were-wholehearted not

הַקְּנִזִּי וִיהוֹשֻׁעַ בִּן־נוּן כִּי מִלְאוּ אַחֲרֵי יְהוָה׃
Yahweh after they-were-wholehearted for Nun son-of and-Joshua the-Kenizzite

2So they came to Moses and Eleazar the priest and to the leaders of the community, and said, 3"Ataroth, Dibon, Jazer, Nimrah, Heshbon, Elealeh, Sebam, Nebo and Beon— 4the land the LORD subdued before the people of Israel—are suitable for livestock, and your servants have livestock. 5If we have found favor in your eyes," they said, "let this land be given to your servants as our possession. Do not make us cross the Jordan."

6Moses said to the Gadites and Reubenites, "Shall your countrymen go to war while you sit here? 7Why do you discourage the Israelites from going over into the land the LORD has given them? 8This is what your fathers did when I sent them from Kadesh Barnea to look over the land. 9After they went up to the Valley of Eshcol and viewed the land, they discouraged the Israelites from entering the land the LORD had given them. 10The LORD's anger was aroused that day and he swore this oath: 11'Because they have not followed me wholeheartedly, not one of the men twenty years old or more who came up out of Egypt will see the land I promised on oath to Abraham, Isaac and Jacob— 12not one except Caleb son of Jephunneh the Kenizzite and Joshua son of Nun, for they followed the LORD wholeheartedly.' 13The

°7 ק תניאון

וַיִּחַר־ אַף יְהוָה בְּיִשְׂרָאֵל וַיְנִעֵם
and-he-made-wander-them against-Israel Yahweh anger-of and-he-burned (13)

בַּמִּדְבָּר אַרְבָּעִים שָׁנָה עַד־ תֹּם כָּל־ הַדּוֹר הָעֹשֶׂה
the-one-doing the-generation whole-of to-be-gone until year forty in-the-desert

הָרַע בְּעֵינֵי יְהוָה׃ וְהִנֵּה קַמְתֶּם תַּחַת אֲבֹתֵיכֶם
fathers-of-you in-place-of you-stand and-see! (14) Yahweh in-eyes-of the-evil

תַּרְבּוּת אֲנָשִׁים חַטָּאִים לִסְפּוֹת עוֹד עַל חֲרוֹן אַף־ יְהוָה אֶל־
against Yahweh anger-of wrath-of to more to-add sinners men brood-of

יִשְׂרָאֵל׃ כִּי תְשׁוּבֻן מֵאַחֲרָיו וְיָסַף עוֹד
again he-will-repeat from-after-him you-turn-away if (15) Israel

לְהַנִּיחוֹ בַּמִּדְבָּר וְשִׁחַתֶּם לְכָל־ הָעָם הַזֶּה׃
the-this the-people to-all-of and-you-will-destroy in-the-desert to-leave-him

וַיִּגְּשׁוּ אֵלָיו וַיֹּאמְרוּ גִּדְרֹת צֹאן נִבְנֶה
we-would-build flock pens-of and-they-said to-him then-they-came-up (16)

לְמִקְנֵנוּ פֹּה וְעָרִים לְטַפֵּנוּ׃ וַאֲנַחְנוּ נֵחָלֵץ
we-will-arm-selves but-we (17) for-child-of-us and-cities here for-stock-of-us

חֻשִׁים לִפְנֵי בְּנֵי יִשְׂרָאֵל עַד אֲשֶׁר אִם־ הֲבִיאֹנֻם
we-brought-them when that until Israel sons-of ahead-of ones-being-ready

אֶל־ מְקוֹמָם וְיָשַׁב טַפֵּנוּ בְּעָרֵי הַמִּבְצָר
the-fortification in-cities-of child-of-us but-he-will-live place-of-them to

מִפְּנֵי יֹשְׁבֵי הָאָרֶץ׃ לֹא נָשׁוּב אֶל־
to we-will-return not (18) the-land ones-inhabiting-of from-presence-of

בָּתֵּינוּ עַד הִתְנַחֵל בְּנֵי יִשְׂרָאֵל אִישׁ נַחֲלָתוֹ׃ כִּי
now (19) inheritance-of-him each Israel sons-of he-received until homes-of-us

לֹא נִנְחַל אִתָּם מֵעֵבֶר לַיַּרְדֵּן וָהָלְאָה כִּי בָאָה
she-came for and-beyond of-the-Jordan on-side with-them we-will-inherit not

נַחֲלָתֵנוּ אֵלֵינוּ מֵעֵבֶר הַיַּרְדֵּן מִזְרָחָה׃ וַיֹּאמֶר
then-he-said (20) on-east the-Jordan on-side-of to-us inheritance-of-us

אֲלֵיהֶם מֹשֶׁה אִם־ תַּעֲשׂוּן אֶת־ הַדָּבָר הַזֶּה אִם־ תֵּחָלְצוּ
you-will-arm-selves if the-this the-thing *** you-will-do if Moses to-them

לִפְנֵי יְהוָה לַמִּלְחָמָה׃ וְעָבַר לָכֶם כָּל־
every-of of-you and-he-will-go-over (21) for-the-battle Yahweh before

חָלוּץ אֶת־ הַיַּרְדֵּן לִפְנֵי יְהוָה עַד הוֹרִישׁוֹ אֶת־
*** to-drive-him until Yahweh before the-Jordan *** one-being-armed

אֹיְבָיו מִפָּנָיו׃ וְנִכְבְּשָׁה הָאָרֶץ לִפְנֵי
before the-land when-she-is-subdued (22) from-before-him being-enemies-of-him

יְהוָה וְאַחַר תָּשֻׁבוּ וִהְיִיתֶם נְקִיִּם מֵיְהוָה
from-Yahweh free-ones and-you-will-be you-may-return then-after Yahweh

LORD'S anger burned against Israel and he made them wander in the desert forty years, until the whole generation of those who had done evil in his sight was gone.

[14]"And here you are, a brood of sinners, standing in the place of your fathers and making the LORD even more angry with Israel. [15]If you turn away from following him, he will again leave all this people in the desert, and you will be the cause of their destruction."

[16]Then they came up to him and said, "We would like to build pens here for our livestock and cities for our women and children. [17]But we are ready to arm ourselves and go ahead of the Israelites until we have brought them to their place. Meanwhile our women and children will live in fortified cities, for protection from the inhabitants of the land. [18]We will not return to our homes until every Israelite has received his inheritance. [19]We will not receive any inheritance with them on the other side of the Jordan, because our inheritance has come to us on the east side of the Jordan."

[20]Then Moses said to them, "If you will do this—if you will arm yourselves before the LORD for battle, [21]and if all of you will go armed over the Jordan before the LORD until he has driven his enemies out before him— [22]then when the land is subdued before the LORD, you may return and be free from your obligation to

וּמִיִּשְׂרָאֵל וְהָיְתָה הָאָרֶץ הַזֹּאת לָכֶם לַאֲחֻזָּה
as-possession for-you the-this the-land and-she-will-be and-from-Israel

לִפְנֵי יְהוָה׃ וְאִם־ לֹא תַעֲשׂוּן כֵּן הִנֵּה חֲטָאתֶם לַיהוָה
against-Yahweh you-sin see! this you-do not but-if (23) Yahweh before

וּדְעוּ חַטַּאתְכֶם אֲשֶׁר תִּמְצָא אֶתְכֶם׃ בְּנוּ־ לָכֶם
for-you build! (24) you she-will-find-out that sin-of-you and-be-sure!

עָרִים לְטַפְּכֶם וּגְדֵרֹת לְצֹנַאֲכֶם וְהַיֹּצֵא
but-the-thing-coming for-flock-of-you and-pens for-child-of-you cities

מִפִּיכֶם תַּעֲשׂוּ׃ וַיֹּאמֶר בְּנֵי־ גָד וּבְנֵי רְאוּבֵן
Reuben and-sons-of Gad sons-of and-he-spoke (25) you-do from-mouth-of-you

אֶל־ מֹשֶׁה לֵאמֹר עֲבָדֶיךָ יַעֲשׂוּ כַּאֲשֶׁר אֲדֹנִי מְצַוֶּה׃
commanding lord-of-me just-as they-will-do servants-of-you to-say Moses to

טַפֵּנוּ נָשֵׁינוּ מִקְנֵנוּ וְכָל־ בְּהֶמְתֵּנוּ יִהְיוּ־
they-will-stay herd-of-us and-all-of flock-of-us wives-of-us child-of-us (26)

שָׁם בְּעָרֵי הַגִּלְעָד׃ וַעֲבָדֶיךָ יַעַבְרוּ
they-will-cross-over but-servants-of-you (27) the-Gilead in-cities-of here

כָּל־ חֲלוּץ צָבָא לִפְנֵי יְהוָה לַמִּלְחָמָה כַּאֲשֶׁר
just-as to-the-fight Yahweh before battle one-being-armed-of every-of

אֲדֹנִי דֹּבֵר׃ וַיְצַו לָהֶם מֹשֶׁה אֵת אֶלְעָזָר הַכֹּהֵן
the-priest Eleazar *** Moses about-them then-he-ordered (28) saying lord-of-me

וְאֵת יְהוֹשֻׁעַ בִּן־ נוּן וְאֶת־ רָאשֵׁי אֲבוֹת הַמַּטּוֹת לִבְנֵי יִשְׂרָאֵל׃
Israel of-sons-of the-tribes fathers-of heads-of and Nun son-of Joshua and

וַיֹּאמֶר מֹשֶׁה אֲלֵהֶם אִם־ יַעַבְרוּ בְנֵי־ גָד וּבְנֵי־
and-sons-of Gad sons-of they-cross-over if to-them Moses and-he-said (29)

רְאוּבֵן ׀ אִתְּכֶם אֶת־ הַיַּרְדֵּן כָּל־ חָלוּץ לַמִּלְחָמָה
for-the-battle one-being-armed every-of the-Jordan *** with-you Reuben

לִפְנֵי יְהוָה וְנִכְבְּשָׁה הָאָרֶץ לִפְנֵיכֶם וּנְתַתֶּם לָהֶם
to-them then-you-give before-you the-land when-she-is-subdued Yahweh before

אֶת־ אֶרֶץ הַגִּלְעָד לַאֲחֻזָּה׃ וְאִם־ לֹא יַעַבְרוּ
they-cross-over not but-if (30) as-possession the-Gilead land-of ***

חֲלוּצִים אִתְּכֶם וְנֹאחֲזוּ בְתֹכְכֶם בְּאֶרֶץ כְּנָעַן׃
Canaan in-land-of with-you then-they-must-possess with-you ones-being-armed

וַיַּעֲנוּ בְנֵי־ גָד וּבְנֵי רְאוּבֵן לֵאמֹר אֵת אֲשֶׁר
what *** to-say Reuben and-sons-of Gad sons-of and-they-answered (31)

דִּבֶּר יְהוָה אֶל־ עֲבָדֶיךָ כֵּן נַעֲשֶׂה׃ נַחְנוּ נַעֲבֹר
we-will-cross-over we (32) we-will-do so servants-of-you to Yahweh he-said

חֲלוּצִים לִפְנֵי יְהוָה אֶרֶץ כְּנָעַן וְאִתָּנוּ אֲחֻזַּת
property-of but-for-us Canaan land-of Yahweh before ones-being-armed

the LORD and to Israel. And this land will be your possession before the LORD.

23 "But if you fail to do this, you will be sinning against the LORD; and you may be sure that your sin will find you out. 24 Build cities for your women and children, and pens for your flocks, but do what you have promised."

25 The Gadites and Reubenites said to Moses, "We your servants will do as our lord commands. 26 Our children and wives, our flocks and herds will remain here in the cities of Gilead. 27 But your servants, every man armed for battle, will cross over to fight before the LORD, just as our lord says."

28 Then Moses gave orders about them to Eleazar the priest and Joshua son of Nun and to the family heads of the Israelite tribes. 29 He said to them, "If the Gadites and Reubenites, every man armed for battle, cross over the Jordan with you before the LORD, then when the land is subdued before you, give them the land of Gilead as their possession. 30 But if they do not cross over with you armed, they must accept their possession with you in Canaan."

31 The Gadites and Reubenites answered, "Your servants will do what the LORD has said. 32 We will cross over before the LORD into Canaan

נַחֲלָתֵנוּ מֵעֵבֶר לַיַּרְדֵּן׃ וַיִּתֵּן לָהֶם ׀ מֹשֶׁה
Moses to-them then-he-gave (33) of-the-Jordan on-this-side inheritance-of-us

לִבְנֵי־ גָד וְלִבְנֵי רְאוּבֵן וְלַחֲצִי ׀ שֵׁבֶט ׀ מְנַשֶּׁה בֶן־
son-of Manasseh tribe-of and-to-half-of Reuben and-to-sons-of Gad to-sons-of

יוֹסֵף אֶת־ מַמְלֶכֶת סִיחֹן מֶלֶךְ הָאֱמֹרִי וְאֶת־ מַמְלֶכֶת עוֹג מֶלֶךְ
king-of Og kingdom-of and the-Amorite king-of Sihon kingdom-of *** Joseph

הַבָּשָׁן הָאָרֶץ לְעָרֶיהָ בִּגְבֻלֹת עָרֵי הָאָרֶץ
the-land cities-of in-territories with-cities-of-her the-land the-Bashan

סָבִיב׃ וַיִּבְנוּ בְנֵי־ גָד אֶת־ דִּיבֹן וְאֶת־עֲטָרֹת וְאֵת עֲרֹעֵר׃
Aroer and Ataroth and Dibon *** Gad sons-of so-they-built-up (34) around

וְאֶת־עַטְרֹת שׁוֹפָן וְאֶת־יַעְזֵר וְיָגְבְּהָה׃ וְאֶת־בֵּית נִמְרָה וְאֶת־
and Nimrah Beth and (36) and-Jogbehah Jazer and Shophan Atroth and (35)

בֵּית הָרָן עָרֵי מִבְצָר וְגִדְרֹת צֹאן׃ וּבְנֵי רְאוּבֵן
Reuben and-sons-of (37) flock and-pens-of fortified cities-of Haran Beth

בָּנוּ אֶת־ חֶשְׁבּוֹן וְאֶת־אֶלְעָלֵא וְאֵת קִרְיָתָיִם׃ וְאֶת־ נְבוֹ וְאֶת־
and Nebo and (38) Kiriathaim and Elealeh and Heshbon *** they-rebuilt

בַּעַל מְעוֹן מוּסַבֹּת שֵׁם וְאֶת־שִׂבְמָה וַיִּקְרְאוּ בְשֵׁמֹת אֶת־
*** by-names and-they-called Sibmah and name ones-being-changed-of Meon Baal

שְׁמוֹת הֶעָרִים אֲשֶׁר בָּנוּ׃ וַיֵּלְכוּ בְּנֵי מָכִיר
Makir sons-of and-they-went (39) they-rebuilt that the-cities names-of

בֶּן־ מְנַשֶּׁה גִּלְעָדָה וַיִּלְכְּדֻהָ וַיּוֹרֶשׁ אֶת־
*** and-he-drove-out and-they-captured-her to-Gilead Manasseh son-of

הָאֱמֹרִי אֲשֶׁר־ בָּהּ׃ וַיִּתֵּן מֹשֶׁה אֶת־ הַגִּלְעָד לְמָכִיר
to-Makir the-Gilead *** Moses so-he-gave (40) in-her that the-Amorite

בֶּן־ מְנַשֶּׁה וַיֵּשֶׁב בָּהּ׃ וְיָאִיר בֶּן־ מְנַשֶּׁה הָלַךְ
he-went Manasseh son-of and-Jair (41) in-her and-he-settled Manasseh son-of

וַיִּלְכֹּד אֶת־ חַוֹּתֵיהֶם וַיִּקְרָא אֶתְהֶן חַוֹּת יָאִיר׃
Jair Havvoth them and-he-called settlements-of-them *** and-he-captured

וְנֹבַח הָלַךְ וַיִּלְכֹּד אֶת־ קְנָת וְאֶת־ בְּנֹתֶיהָ
settlements-of-her and Kenath *** and-he-captured he-went and-Nobah (42)

וַיִּקְרָא לָה נֹבַח בִּשְׁמוֹ׃ אֵלֶּה מַסְעֵי
journeys-of these (33:1) after-name-of-him Nobah to-her and-he-called

בְנֵי־ יִשְׂרָאֵל אֲשֶׁר יָצְאוּ מֵאֶרֶץ מִצְרַיִם לְצִבְאֹתָם
by-divisions-of-them Egypt from-land-of they-came-out when Israel sons-of

בְּיַד־ מֹשֶׁה וְאַהֲרֹן׃ וַיִּכְתֹּב מֹשֶׁה אֶת־ מוֹצָאֵיהֶם
stages-of-them *** Moses and-he-recorded (2) and-Aaron Moses under-hand-of

לְמַסְעֵיהֶם עַל־ פִּי יְהוָה וְאֵלֶּה מַסְעֵיהֶם
journeys-of-them and-these Yahweh command-of at in-journeys-of-them

armed, but the property we inherit will be on this side of the Jordan."

33Then Moses gave to the Gadites, the Reubenites and the half-tribe of Manasseh son of Joseph the kingdom of Sihon king of the Amorites and the kingdom of Og king of Bashan—the whole land with its cities and the territory around them.

34The Gadites built up Dibon, Ataroth, Aroer, 35Atroth Shophan, Jazer, Jogbehah, 36Beth Nimrah and Beth Haran as fortified cities, and built pens for their flocks. 37And the Reubenites rebuilt Heshbon, Elealeh and Kiriathaim, 38as well as Nebo and Baal Meon (these names were changed) and Sibmah. They gave names to the cities they rebuilt.

39The descendants of Makir son of Manasseh went to Gilead, captured it and drove out the Amorites who were there. 40So Moses gave Gilead to the Makirites, the descendants of Manasseh, and they settled there. 41Jair, a descendant of Manasseh, captured their settlements and called them Havvoth Jair.[a] 42And Nobah captured Kenath and its surrounding settlements and called it Nobah after himself.

*Stages in Israel's Journey*

33 Here are the stages in the journey of the Israelites when they came out of Egypt by divisions under the leadership of Moses and Aaron. 2At the LORD's command Moses recorded the stages in their journey. This is

[a]41 *Or them the settlements of Jair*

לְמוֹצָאֵיהֶם׃ (3) וַיִּסְעוּ מֵרַעְמְסֵס בַּחֹדֶשׁ הָרִאשׁוֹן
the-first in-the-month from-Rameses now-they-set-out (3) by-stages-of-them

בַּחֲמִשָּׁה עָשָׂר יוֹם לַחֹדֶשׁ הָרִאשׁוֹן מִמָּחֳרַת הַפֶּסַח
the-Passover on-day-after-of the-first of-the-month day ten on-five

יָצְאוּ בְנֵי־יִשְׂרָאֵל בְּיָד רָמָה לְעֵינֵי כָּל־
all-of before-eyes-of being-lifted with-hand Israel sons-of they-marched-out

מִצְרָיִם׃ (4) וּמִצְרַיִם מְקַבְּרִים אֵת אֲשֶׁר הִכָּה יְהוָה
Yahweh he-struck-down whom *** ones-burying now-Egyptians (4) Egyptians

בָּהֶם כָּל־ בְּכוֹר וּבֵאלֹהֵיהֶם עָשָׂה יְהוָה
Yahweh he-brought and-on-gods-of-them firstborn every-of among-them

שְׁפָטִים׃ (5) וַיִּסְעוּ בְנֵי־ יִשְׂרָאֵל מֵרַעְמְסֵס וַיַּחֲנוּ
and-they-camped from-Rameses Israel sons-of and-they-left (5) judgments

בְּסֻכֹּת׃ (6) וַיִּסְעוּ מִסֻּכֹּת וַיַּחֲנוּ בְאֵתָם אֲשֶׁר
that at-Etham and-they-camped from-Succoth and-they-left (6) at-Succoth

בִּקְצֵה הַמִּדְבָּר׃ (7) וַיִּסְעוּ מֵאֵתָם וַיָּשָׁב עַל־
to and-they-turned-back from-Etham and-they-left (7) the-desert on-edge-of

פִּי הַחִירֹת אֲשֶׁר עַל־ פְּנֵי בַּעַל צְפוֹן וַיַּחֲנוּ לִפְנֵי מִגְדֹּל׃
Midgol near and-they-camped Zephon Baal east-of to that Hahiroth Pi

(8) וַיִּסְעוּ מִפְּנֵי הַחִירֹת וַיַּעַבְרוּ בְתוֹךְ־ הַיָּם
the-sea through and-they-passed Hahiroth from-before and-they-left (8)

הַמִּדְבָּרָה וַיֵּלְכוּ דֶּרֶךְ שְׁלֹשֶׁת יָמִים בְּמִדְבַּר
in-Desert-of days three-of journey-of and-they-traveled into-the-desert

אֵתָם וַיַּחֲנוּ בְּמָרָה׃ (9) וַיִּסְעוּ מִמָּרָה וַיָּבֹאוּ
and-they-went from-Marah and-they-left (9) at-Marah and-they-camped Etham

אֵילִמָה וּבְאֵילִם שְׁתֵּים עֶשְׂרֵה עֵינֹת מַיִם וְשִׁבְעִים תְּמָרִים
palm-trees and-seventy waters springs-of ten two now-in-Elim to-Elim

וַיַּחֲנוּ־ שָׁם׃ (10) וַיִּסְעוּ מֵאֵילִם וַיַּחֲנוּ עַל־ יַם־
Sea-of by and-they-camped from-Elim and-they-left (10) there and-they-camped

סוּף׃ (11) וַיִּסְעוּ מִיַּם־ סוּף וַיַּחֲנוּ בְּמִדְבַּר־
in-Desert-of and-they-camped Reed from-Sea-of and-they-left (11) Reed

סִין׃ (12) וַיִּסְעוּ מִמִּדְבַּר־ סִין וַיַּחֲנוּ בְּדָפְקָה׃
at-Dophkah and-they-camped Sin from-Desert-of and-they-left (12) Sin

(13) וַיִּסְעוּ מִדָּפְקָה וַיַּחֲנוּ בְּאָלוּשׁ׃ (14) וַיִּסְעוּ
and-they-left (14) at-Alush and-they-camped from-Dophkah and-they-left (13)

מֵאָלוּשׁ וַיַּחֲנוּ בִּרְפִידִם וְלֹא־ הָיָה שָׁם מַיִם
waters there he-was and-not at-Rephidim and-they-camped from-Alush

לָעָם לִשְׁתּוֹת׃ (15) וַיִּסְעוּ מֵרְפִידִם וַיַּחֲנוּ
and-they-camped from-Rephidim and-they-left (15) to-drink for-the-people

their journey by stages:
3The Israelites set out
from Rameses on the
fifteenth day of the first
month, the day after the
Passover. They marched
out boldly in full view of all
the Egyptians, 4who were
burying all their firstborn,
whom the LORD had struck
down among them; for the
LORD had brought judg-
ment on their gods.
5The Israelites left
Rameses and camped at
Succoth.
6They left Succoth and
camped at Etham, on the
edge of the desert.
7They left Etham, turned
back to Pi Hahiroth, to the
east of Baal Zephon, and
camped near Migdol.
8They left Pi Hahiroth[b]
and passed through the sea
into the desert, and when
they had traveled for three
days in the Desert of
Etham, they camped at
Marah.
9They left Marah and
went to Elim, where there
were twelve springs and
seventy palm trees, and
they camped there.
10They left Elim and
camped by the Red Sea.[c]
11They left the Red Sea
and camped in the Desert
of Sin.
12They left the Desert of
Sin and camped at Doph-
kah.
13They left Dophkah and
camped at Alush.
14They left Alush and
camped at Rephidim,
where there was no water
for the people to drink.
15They left Rephidim and

[b]8 Many manuscripts of the Masoretic Text, Samaritan Pentateuch and Vulgate; most manuscripts of the Masoretic Text *left from before Hahiroth*

[c]10 Hebrew *Yam Suph;* that is, Sea of Reeds; also in verse 11

בְּמִדְבַּר סִינָי׃ (16) וַיִּסְעוּ מִמִּדְבַּר סִינָי וַיַּחֲנוּ
and-they-camped Sinai from-Desert-of and-they-left (16) Sinai in-Desert-of

בְּקִבְרֹת הַתַּאֲוָה׃ (17) וַיִּסְעוּ מִקִּבְרֹת הַתַּאֲוָה וַיַּחֲנוּ
and-they-camped Hattaavah from-Kibroth and-they-left (17) Hattaavah at-Kibroth

בַּחֲצֵרֹת׃ (18) וַיִּסְעוּ מֵחֲצֵרֹת וַיַּחֲנוּ בְּרִתְמָה׃
at-Rithmah and-they-camped from-Hazeroth and-they-left (18) at-Hazeroth

(19) וַיִּסְעוּ מֵרִתְמָה וַיַּחֲנוּ בְּרִמֹּן פָּרֶץ׃
Perez at-Rimmon and-they-camped from-Rithmah and-they-left (19)

(20) וַיִּסְעוּ מֵרִמֹּן פָּרֶץ וַיַּחֲנוּ בְּלִבְנָה׃
at-Libnah and-they-camped Perez from-Rimmon and-they-left (20)

(21) וַיִּסְעוּ מִלִּבְנָה וַיַּחֲנוּ בְּרִסָּה׃ (22) וַיִּסְעוּ
and-they-left (22) at-Rissah and-they-camped from-Libnah and-they-left (21)

מֵרִסָּה וַיַּחֲנוּ בִּקְהֵלָתָה׃ (23) וַיִּסְעוּ מִקְּהֵלָתָה
from-Kehelathah and-they-left (23) at-Kehelathah and-they-camped from-Rissah

וַיַּחֲנוּ בְּהַר־שָׁפֶר׃ (24) וַיִּסְעוּ מֵהַר־שָׁפֶר
Shepher from-Mount-of and-they-left (24) Shepher at-Mount-of and-they-camped

וַיַּחֲנוּ בַּחֲרָדָה׃ (25) וַיִּסְעוּ מֵחֲרָדָה וַיַּחֲנוּ
and-they-camped from-Haradah and-they-left (25) at-Haradah and-they-camped

בְּמַקְהֵלֹת׃ (26) וַיִּסְעוּ מִמַּקְהֵלֹת וַיַּחֲנוּ בְּתָחַת׃
at-Tahath and-they-camped from-Makheloth and-they-left (26) at-Makheloth

(27) וַיִּסְעוּ מִתָּחַת וַיַּחֲנוּ בְּתָרַח׃ (28) וַיִּסְעוּ
and-they-left (28) at-Terah and-they-camped from-Tahath and-they-left (27)

מִתָּרַח וַיַּחֲנוּ בְּמִתְקָה׃ (29) וַיִּסְעוּ מִמִּתְקָה
from-Mithcah and-they-left (29) at-Mithcah and-they-camped from-Terah

וַיַּחֲנוּ בְּחַשְׁמֹנָה׃ (30) וַיִּסְעוּ מֵחַשְׁמֹנָה וַיַּחֲנוּ
and-they-camped from-Hashmonah and-they-left (30) at-Hashmonah and-they-camped

בְּמֹסֵרוֹת׃ (31) וַיִּסְעוּ מִמֹּסֵרוֹת וַיַּחֲנוּ בִּבְנֵי יַעֲקָן׃
Jaakan at-Bene and-they-camped from-Moseroth and-they-left (31) at-Moseroth

(32) וַיִּסְעוּ מִבְּנֵי יַעֲקָן וַיַּחֲנוּ בְּחֹר הַגִּדְגָּד׃
Haggidgad and-Hor and-they-camped Jaakan from-Bene and-they-left (32)

(33) וַיִּסְעוּ מֵחֹר הַגִּדְגָּד וַיַּחֲנוּ בְּיָטְבָתָה׃
at-Jotbathah and-they-camped Haggidgad from-Hor and-they-left (33)

(34) וַיִּסְעוּ מִיָּטְבָתָה וַיַּחֲנוּ בְּעַבְרֹנָה׃ (35) וַיִּסְעוּ
and-they-left (35) at-Abronah and-they-camped from-Jotbathah and-they-left (34)

מֵעַבְרֹנָה וַיַּחֲנוּ בְּעֶצְיֹן גָּבֶר׃ (36) וַיִּסְעוּ מֵעֶצְיֹן
from-Ezion and-they-left (36) Geber at-Ezion and-they-camped from-Abronah

גָּבֶר וַיַּחֲנוּ בְמִדְבַּר־צִן הִוא קָדֵשׁ׃ (37) וַיִּסְעוּ
and-they-left (37) Kadesh that Zin in-Desert-of and-they-camped Geber

camped in the Desert of Sinai.
16 They left the Desert of Sinai and camped at Kibroth Hattaavah.
17 They left Kibroth Hattaavah and camped at Hazeroth.
18 They left Hazeroth and camped at Rithmah.
19 They left Rithmah and camped at Rimmon Perez.
20 They left Rimmon Perez and camped at Libnah.
21 They left Libnah and camped at Rissah.
22 They left Rissah and camped at Kehelathah.
23 They left Kehelathah and camped at Mount Shepher.
24 They left Mount Shepher and camped at Haradah.
25 They left Haradah and camped at Makheloth.
26 They left Makheloth and camped at Tahath.
27 They left Tahath and camped at Terah.
28 They left Terah and camped at Mithcah.
29 They left Mithcah and camped at Hashmonah.
30 They left Hashmonah and camped at Moseroth.
31 They left Moseroth and camped at Bene Jaakan.
32 They left Bene Jaakan and camped at Hor Haggidgad.
33 They left Hor Haggidgad and camped at Jotbathah.
34 They left Jotbathah and camped at Abronah.
35 They left Abronah and camped at Ezion Geber.
36 They left Ezion Geber and camped at Kadesh, in the Desert of Zin.
37 They left Kadesh and

מִקָּדֵשׁ וַיַּחֲנוּ בְּהֹר הָהָר בִּקְצֵה אֶרֶץ אֱדוֹם׃
Edom land-of on-border-of the-Mount at-Hor and-they-camped from-Kadesh

וַיַּעַל אַהֲרֹן הַכֹּהֵן אֶל־הֹר הָהָר עַל־פִּי יְהוָה
Yahweh command-of at the-Mount Hor on the-priest Aaron and-he-went-up (38)

וַיָּמָת שָׁם בִּשְׁנַת הָאַרְבָּעִים לְצֵאת בְּנֵי־יִשְׂרָאֵל מֵאֶרֶץ
from-land-of Israel sons-of to-come the-fortieth in-year-of there and-he-died

מִצְרַיִם בַּחֹדֶשׁ הַחֲמִישִׁי בְּאֶחָד לַחֹדֶשׁ׃ וְאַהֲרֹן בֶּן־
son-of now-Aaron (39) of-the-month on-first the-fifth in-the-month Egypt

שָׁלֹשׁ וְעֶשְׂרִים וּמְאַת שָׁנָה בְּמֹתוֹ בְּהֹר הָהָר׃
the-Mount on-Hor when-to-die-him year and-hundred-of and-twenty three

וַיִּשְׁמַע הַכְּנַעֲנִי מֶלֶךְ עֲרָד וְהוּא־יֹשֵׁב בַּנֶּגֶב
in-the-Negev living now-he Arad king-of the-Canaanite and-he-heard (40)

בְּאֶרֶץ כְּנָעַן בְּבֹא בְּנֵי יִשְׂרָאֵל׃ וַיִּסְעוּ מֵהֹר
from-Hor and-they-left (41) Israel sons-of that-to-come Canaan in-land-of

הָהָר וַיַּחֲנוּ בְּצַלְמֹנָה׃ וַיִּסְעוּ מִצַּלְמֹנָה
from-Zalmonah and-they-left (42) at-Zalmonah and-they-camped the-Mount

וַיַּחֲנוּ בְּפוּנֹן׃ וַיִּסְעוּ מִפּוּנֹן וַיַּחֲנוּ
and-they-camped from-Punon and-they-left (43) at-Punon and-they-camped

בְּאֹבֹת׃ וַיִּסְעוּ מֵאֹבֹת וַיַּחֲנוּ בְּעִיֵּי הָעֲבָרִים
the-Abarim at-Iye and-they-camped from-Oboth and-they-left (44) at-Oboth

בִּגְבוּל מוֹאָב׃ וַיִּסְעוּ מֵעִיִּים וַיַּחֲנוּ בְּדִיבֹן גָּד׃
Gad at-Dibon and-they-camped from-Iyim and-they-left (45) Moab on-border-of

וַיִּסְעוּ מִדִּיבֹן גָּד וַיַּחֲנוּ בְּעַלְמֹן דִּבְלָתָיְמָה׃
at-Diblathaim at-Almon and-they-camped Gad from-Dibon and-they-left (46)

וַיִּסְעוּ מֵעַלְמֹן דִּבְלָתָיְמָה וַיַּחֲנוּ בְּהָרֵי
in-mountains-of and-they-camped at-Diblathaim from-Almon and-they-left (47)

הָעֲבָרִים לִפְנֵי נְבוֹ׃ וַיִּסְעוּ מֵהָרֵי הָעֲבָרִים
the-Abarim from-mountains-of and-they-left (48) Nebo near the-Abarim

וַיַּחֲנוּ בְּעַרְבֹת מוֹאָב עַל יַרְדֵּן יְרֵחוֹ׃ וַיַּחֲנוּ
and-they-camped (49) Jericho Jordan-of by Moab on-plains-of and-they-camped

עַל־הַיַּרְדֵּן מִבֵּית הַיְשִׁמֹת עַד אָבֵל הַשִּׁטִּים בְּעַרְבֹת
in-plains-of the-Shittim Abel to the-Jeshimoth from-Beth the-Jordan along

מוֹאָב׃ וַיְדַבֵּר יְהוָה אֶל־מֹשֶׁה בְּעַרְבֹת מוֹאָב עַל־יַרְדֵּן
Jordan-of by Moab on-plains-of Moses to Yahweh and-he-spoke (50) Moab

יְרֵחוֹ לֵאמֹר׃ דַּבֵּר אֶל־בְּנֵי יִשְׂרָאֵל וְאָמַרְתָּ אֲלֵהֶם כִּי אַתֶּם
you when to-them and-you-say Israel sons-of to speak! (51) to-say Jericho

עֹבְרִים אֶת־הַיַּרְדֵּן אֶל־אֶרֶץ כְּנָעַן׃ וְהוֹרַשְׁתֶּם אֶת־
*** then-you-drive-out (52) Canaan land-of into the-Jordan *** ones-crossing

camped at Mount Hor, on
the border of Edom. 38At the
LORD's command Aaron the
priest went up Mount Hor,
where he died on the first
day of the fifth month of
the fortieth year after the
Israelites came out of
Egypt. 39Aaron was a hun-
dred and twenty-three
years old when he died on
Mount Hor.
40The Canaanite king of
Arad, who lived in the
Negev of Canaan, heard
that the Israelites were
coming.
41They left Mount Hor
and camped at Zalmonah.
42They left Zalmonah and
camped at Punon.
43They left Punon and
camped at Oboth.
44They left Oboth and
camped at Iye Abarim, on
the border of Moab.
45They left Iyim[d] and
camped at Dibon Gad.
46They left Dibon Gad
and camped at Almon Di-
blathaim.
47They left Almon Dibla-
thaim and camped in the
mountains of Abarim, near
Nebo.
48They left the mountains
of Abarim and camped on
the plains of Moab by the
Jordan across from Jericho.[e]
49There on the plains of
Moab they camped along
the Jordan from Beth Je-
shimoth to Abel Shittim.

50On the plains of Moab by
the Jordan across from Jericho
the LORD said to Moses,
51"Speak to the Israelites and
say to them: 'When you cross
the Jordan into Canaan,
52drive out all the inhabitants

[d]45 That is, Iye Abarim
[e]48 Hebrew *Jordan of Jericho*; possibly an ancient name for the Jordan River; also in verse 50

כָּל־ יֹשְׁבֵי הָאָרֶץ מִפְּנֵיכֶם וְאִבַּדְתֶּם אֵת כָּל־

all-of *** and-you-destroy from-before-you the-land ones-inhabiting-of all-of

מַשְׂכִּיֹּתָם וְאֵת כָּל־ צַלְמֵי מַסֵּכֹתָם תְּאַבֵּדוּ וְאֵת

and you-destroy cast-ones-of-them idols-of all-of and carved-images-of-them

כָּל־ בָּמוֹתָם תַּשְׁמִידוּ׃ וְהוֹרַשְׁתֶּם אֶת־ הָאָרֶץ

the-land *** and-you-possess (53) you-demolish high-places-of-them all-of

וִישַׁבְתֶּם־ בָּהּ כִּי לָכֶם נָתַתִּי אֶת־ הָאָרֶץ לָרֶשֶׁת אֹתָהּ׃

her to-possess the-land *** I-gave to-you for in-her and-you-settle

וְהִתְנַחַלְתֶּם אֶת־ הָאָרֶץ בְּגוֹרָל לְמִשְׁפְּחֹתֵיכֶם לָרַב

to-the-large by-clans-of-you by-lot the-land *** and-you-distribute (54)

תַּרְבּוּ אֶת־ נַחֲלָתוֹ וְלַמְעַט תַּמְעִיט אֶת־

*** you-make-small and-to-the-small inheritance-of-him *** you-make-large

נַחֲלָתוֹ אֶל אֲשֶׁר־ יֵצֵא לוֹ שָׁמָּה הַגּוֹרָל לוֹ יִהְיֶה

he-will-be to-him the-lot at-there to-him he-falls whom to inheritance-of-him

לְמַטּוֹת אֲבֹתֵיכֶם תִּתְנֶחָלוּ׃ וְאִם־ לֹא תוֹרִישׁוּ אֶת־

*** you-drive-out not but-if (55) you-distribute fathers-of-you by-tribes-of

יֹשְׁבֵי הָאָרֶץ מִפְּנֵיכֶם וְהָיָה אֲשֶׁר תּוֹתִירוּ

you-let-remain whom then-he-will-be from-before-you the-land ones-inhabiting-of

מֵהֶם לְשִׂכִּים בְּעֵינֵיכֶם וְלִצְנִינִם בְּצִדֵּיכֶם

in-sides-of-you and-as-thorns in-eyes-of-you as-barbs from-them

וְצָרְרוּ אֶתְכֶם עַל־ הָאָרֶץ אֲשֶׁר אַתֶּם יֹשְׁבִים בָּהּ׃

in-her ones-living you where the-land in you and-they-will-trouble

וְהָיָה כַּאֲשֶׁר דִּמִּיתִי לַעֲשׂוֹת לָהֶם אֶעֱשֶׂה לָכֶם׃

to-you I-will-do to-them to-do I-plan just-as then-he-will-be (56)

וַיְדַבֵּר יְהוָה אֶל־מֹשֶׁה לֵּאמֹר׃ צַו אֶת־ בְּנֵי יִשְׂרָאֵל

Israel sons-of *** command! (2) to-say Moses to Yahweh and-he-spoke (34:1)

וְאָמַרְתָּ אֲלֵהֶם כִּי־ אַתֶּם בָּאִים אֶל־ הָאָרֶץ כְּנָעַן זֹאת הָאָרֶץ

the-land this Canaan the-land into ones-entering you when to-them and-you-say

אֲשֶׁר תִּפֹּל לָכֶם בְּנַחֲלָה אֶרֶץ כְּנַעַן לִגְבֻלֹתֶיהָ׃

by-boundaries-of-her Canaan land-of as-inheritance to-you she-will-fall that

וְהָיָה לָכֶם פְּאַת־ נֶגֶב מִמִּדְבַּר־ צִן עַל־ יְדֵי

borders-of along Zin from-Desert-of south side-of to-you and-he-will-be (3)

אֱדוֹם וְהָיָה לָכֶם גְּבוּל נֶגֶב מִקְצֵה יַם־ הַמֶּלַח קֵדְמָה׃

on-east the-Salt Sea-of end-of south border-of to-you and-he-will-be Edom

וְנָסַב לָכֶם הַגְּבוּל מִנֶּגֶב לְמַעֲלֵה עַקְרַבִּים

Scorpions of-Pass-of on-south the-border to-you and-he-will-cross (4)

וְעָבַר צִנָה וְהָיָה תּוֹצְאֹתָיו מִנֶּגֶב לְקָדֵשׁ

of-Kadesh on-south ends-of-him and-they-will-go to-Zin and-he-will-continue

°4 ק והיו

of the land before you. Destroy all their carved images and their cast idols, and demolish all their high places. [53]Take possession of the land and settle in it, for I have given you the land to possess. [54]Distribute the land by lot, according to your clans. To a larger group give a larger inheritance, and to a smaller group a smaller one. Whatever falls to them by lot will be theirs. Distribute it according to your ancestral tribes.

[55]" 'But if you do not drive out the inhabitants of the land, those you allow to remain will become barbs in your eyes and thorns in your sides. They will give you trouble in the land where you will live. [56]And then I will do to you what I plan to do to them.' "

*Boundaries of Canaan*

**34** The LORD said to Moses, [2]"Command the Israelites and say to them: 'When you enter Canaan, the land that will be allotted to you as an inheritance will have these boundaries:

[3]" 'Your southern side will include some of the Desert of Zin along the border of Edom. On the east, your southern boundary will start from the end of the Salt Sea,[f] [4]cross south of Scorpion[g] Pass, continue on to Zin and go south of

f3 That is, the Dead Sea; also in verse 12
g4 Hebrew *Akrabbim*

בַּרְנֵעַ וְיָצָא חֲצַר־אַדָּר וְעָבַר עַצְמֹנָה׃ וְנָסַב
and-he-will-turn (5) to-Azmon and-he-will-go Addar Hazar then-he-will-go Barnea

הַגְּבוּל מֵעַצְמוֹן נַחְלָה מִצְרָיִם וְהָיוּ תוֹצְאֹתָיו
ends-of-him and-they-will-be Egypt to-Wadi-of from-Azmon the-border

הַיָּמָּה׃ וּגְבוּל יָם וְהָיָה לָכֶם הַיָּם הַגָּדוֹל
the-Great the-Sea to-you now-he-will-be west and-boundary-of (6) at-the-Sea

וּגְבוּל זֶה־ יִהְיֶה לָכֶם גְּבוּל יָם׃ וְזֶה־ יִהְיֶה
he-will-be and-this (7) west boundary-of to-you he-will-be this and-coast

לָכֶם גְּבוּל צָפוֹן מִן־ הַיָּם הַגָּדֹל תְּתָאוּ לָכֶם הֹר
Hor for-you you-run-line the-Great the-Sea from north boundary-of to-you

הָהָר׃ מֵהֹר הָהָר תְּתָאוּ לְבֹא חֲמָת וְהָיוּ
then-they-will-go Hamath Lebo you-run-line the-Mount from-Hor (8) the-Mount

תּוֹצְאֹת הַגְּבֻל צְדָדָה׃ וְיָצָא הַגְּבֻל זִפְרֹנָה
to-Ziphron the-border and-he-will-continue (9) to-Zedad the-boundary ends-of

וְהָיוּ תוֹצְאֹתָיו חֲצַר עֵינָן זֶה־ יִהְיֶה לָכֶם גְּבוּל
boundary-of to-you he-will-be this Enan Hazar ends-of-him and-they-will-go

צָפוֹן׃ וְהִתְאַוִּיתֶם לָכֶם לִגְבוּל קֵדְמָה מֵחֲצַר עֵינָן
Enan from-Hazar on-east for-boundary for-you and-you-run-line (10) north

שְׁפָמָה׃ וְיָרַד הַגְּבֻל מִשְּׁפָם הָרִבְלָה
the-Riblah from-Shepham the-boundary and-he-will-go-down (11) to-Shepham

מִקֶּדֶם לָעָיִן וְיָרַד הַגְּבֻל וּמָחָה עַל־
along and-he-will-go the-boundary and-he-will-continue of-the-Ain on-east

כֶּתֶף יָם־ כִּנֶּרֶת קֵדְמָה׃ וְיָרַד הַגְּבוּל
the-boundary then-he-will-go-down (12) on-east Kinnereth Sea-of slope-of

הַיַּרְדֵּנָה וְהָיוּ תוֹצְאֹתָיו יָם הַמֶּלַח זֹאת תִּהְיֶה
she-will-be this the-Salt Sea-of ends-of-him and-he-will-be along-the-Jordan

לָכֶם הָאָרֶץ לִגְבֻלֹתֶיהָ סָבִיב׃ וַיְצַו מֹשֶׁה
Moses and-he-commanded (13) around with-boundaries-of-her the-land to-you

אֶת־ בְּנֵי יִשְׂרָאֵל לֵאמֹר זֹאת הָאָרֶץ אֲשֶׁר תִּתְנַחֲלוּ אֹתָהּ בְּגוֹרָל
by-lot her you-must-assign that the-land this to-say Israel sons-of ***

אֲשֶׁר צִוָּה יְהוָה לָתֵת לְתִשְׁעַת הַמַּטּוֹת וַחֲצִי הַמַּטֶּה׃
the-tribe and-half-of the-tribes to-nine-of to-give Yahweh he-ordered that

כִּי לָקְחוּ מַטֵּה בְנֵי הָראוּבֵנִי לְבֵית
by-house-of the-Reubenite sons-of tribe-of they-received for (14)

אֲבֹתָם וּמַטֵּה בְנֵי־ הַגָּדִי לְבֵית אֲבֹתָם
fathers-of-them by-house-of the-Gadite sons-of and-tribe-of fathers-of-them

וַחֲצִי מַטֵּה מְנַשֶּׁה לָקְחוּ נַחֲלָתָם׃ שְׁנֵי
two-of (15) inheritance-of-them they-received Manasseh tribe-of and-half-of

Kadesh Barnea. Then it will go
to Hazar Addar and over to
Azmon, 5where it will turn,
join the Wadi of Egypt and
end at the Sea.[h]
6" 'Your western boundary
will be the coast of the Great
Sea. This will be your boundary on the west.
7" 'For your northern
boundary, run a line from the
Great Sea to Mount Hor 8and
from Mount Hor to Lebo[i]
Hamath. Then the boundary
will go to Zedad, 9continue to
Ziphron and end at Hazar
Enan. This will be your
boundary on the north.
10" 'For your eastern boundary, run a line from Hazar
Enan to Shepham. 11The
boundary will go down from
Shepham to Riblah on the east
side of Ain and continue
along the slopes east of the Sea
of Kinnereth.[j] 12Then the
boundary will go down along
the Jordan and end at the Salt
Sea.
" 'This will be your land,
with its boundaries on every
side.' "
13Moses commanded the Is-
raelites: "Assign this land by
lot as an inheritance. The LORD
has ordered that it be given to
the nine and a half tribes, 14be-
cause the families of the tribe
of Reuben, the tribe of Gad
and the half-tribe of Manasseh have received their inheritance. 15These two and a half

[h]5 That is, the Mediterranean; also in verses 6 and 7
[i]8 Or *to the entrance to*
[j]11 That is, Galilee

הַמַּטּוֹת וַחֲצִי הַמַּטֶּה לָקְחוּ נַחֲלָתָם מֵעֵבֶר
on-side inheritance-of-them they-received the-tribe and-half-of the-tribes

לְיַרְדֵּן יְרֵחוֹ קֵדְמָה מִזְרָחָה׃ וַיְדַבֵּר יְהוָה אֶל־
to Yahweh and-he-spoke (16) toward-sunrise on-east Jericho of-Jordan-of

מֹשֶׁה לֵּאמֹר׃ אֵלֶּה שְׁמוֹת הָאֲנָשִׁים אֲשֶׁר־ יִנְחֲלוּ לָכֶם אֶת־
*** for-you they-will-assign who the-men names-of these (17) to-say Moses

הָאָרֶץ אֶלְעָזָר הַכֹּהֵן וִיהוֹשֻׁעַ בִּן־ נוּן׃ וְנָשִׂיא אֶחָד נָשִׂיא
leader one and-leader (18) Nun son-of and-Joshua the-priest Eleazar the-land

אֶחָד מִמַּטֶּה תִּקְחוּ לִנְחֹל אֶת־ הָאָרֶץ׃ וְאֵלֶּה שְׁמוֹת
names-of and-these (19) the-land *** to-assign you-appoint from-tribe one

הָאֲנָשִׁים לְמַטֵּה יְהוּדָה כָּלֵב בֶּן־ יְפֻנֶּה׃ וּלְמַטֵּה
and-from-tribe-of (20) Jephunneh son-of Caleb Judah from-tribe-of the-men

בְּנֵי שִׁמְעוֹן שְׁמוּאֵל בֶּן־ עַמִּיהוּד׃ לְמַטֵּה בִּנְיָמִן אֱלִידָד
Elidad Benjamin from-tribe-of (21) Ammihud son-of Shemuel Simeon sons-of

בֶּן־ כִּסְלוֹן׃ וּלְמַטֵּה בְנֵי־ דָן נָשִׂיא בֻּקִּי בֶּן־ יָגְלִי׃
Jogli son-of Bukki leader Dan sons-of and-from-tribe-of (22) Kislon son-of

לִבְנֵי יוֹסֵף לְמַטֵּה בְנֵי־ מְנַשֶּׁה נָשִׂיא חַנִּיאֵל
Hanniel leader Manasseh sons-of from-tribe-of Joseph from-sons-of (23)

בֶּן־ אֵפֹד׃ וּלְמַטֵּה בְנֵי־ אֶפְרַיִם נָשִׂיא קְמוּאֵל בֶּן־
son-of Kemuel leader Ephraim sons-of and-from-tribe-of (24) Ephod son-of

שִׁפְטָן׃ וּלְמַטֵּה בְנֵי־ זְבוּלֻן נָשִׂיא אֱלִיצָפָן בֶּן־
son-of Elizaphan leader Zebulun sons-of and-from-tribe-of (25) Shiphtan

פַּרְנָךְ׃ וּלְמַטֵּה בְנֵי־ יִשָּׂשכָר* נָשִׂיא פַּלְטִיאֵל בֶּן־ עַזָּן׃
Azzan son-of Paltiel leader Issachar sons-of and-from-tribe-of (26) Parnach

וּלְמַטֵּה בְנֵי־ אָשֵׁר נָשִׂיא אֲחִיהוּד בֶּן־ שְׁלֹמִי׃
Shelomi son-of Ahihud leader Asher sons-of and-from-tribe-of (27)

וּלְמַטֵּה בְנֵי־ נַפְתָּלִי נָשִׂיא פְּדַהְאֵל בֶּן־ עַמִּיהוּד׃
Ammihud son-of Pedahel leader Naphtali sons-of and-from-tribe-of (28)

אֵלֶּה אֲשֶׁר צִוָּה יְהוָה לְנַחֵל אֶת־ בְּנֵי־ יִשְׂרָאֵל בְּאֶרֶץ
in-land-of Israel sons-of *** to-assign Yahweh he-commanded whom these (29)

כְּנָעַן׃ וַיְדַבֵּר יְהוָה אֶל־ מֹשֶׁה בְּעַרְבֹת מוֹאָב עַל־ יַרְדֵּן
Jordan-of by Moab on-plains-of Moses to Yahweh and-he-spoke (35:1) Canaan

יְרֵחוֹ לֵאמֹר׃ צַו אֶת־ בְּנֵי יִשְׂרָאֵל וְנָתְנוּ לַלְוִיִּם
to-the-Levites so-they-give Israel sons-of *** command! (2) to-say Jericho

מִנַּחֲלַת אֲחֻזָּתָם עָרִים לָשָׁבֶת וּמִגְרָשׁ לֶעָרִים
by-the-towns and-pasture to-live towns possession-of-them from-inheritance-of

סְבִיבֹתֵיהֶם תִּתְּנוּ לַלְוִיִּם׃ וְהָיוּ הֶעָרִים
the-towns then-they-will-be (3) to-the-Levites they-must-give ones-around-them

tribes have received their inheritance on the east side of the Jordan of Jericho,[k] toward the sunrise."

[16]The LORD said to Moses, [17]"These are the names of the men who are to assign the land for you as an inheritance: Eleazar the priest and Joshua son of Nun. [18]And appoint one leader from each tribe to help assign the land. [19]These are their names:

Caleb son of Jephunneh,
from the tribe of Judah;
[20]Shemuel son of Ammihud,
from the tribe of Simeon;
[21]Elidad son of Kislon,
from the tribe of Benjamin;
[22]Bukki son of Jogli,
the leader from the tribe of Dan;
[23]Hanniel son of Ephod,
the leader from the tribe of Manasseh son of Joseph;
[24]Kemuel son of Shiphtan,
the leader from the tribe of Ephraim son of Joseph;
[25]Elizaphan son of Parnach,
the leader from the tribe of Zebulun;
[26]Paltiel son of Azzan,
the leader from the tribe of Issachar;
[27]Ahihud son of Shelomi,
the leader from the tribe of Asher;
[28]Pedahel son of Ammihud,
the leader from the tribe of Naphtali."

[29]These are the men the LORD commanded to assign the inheritance to the Israelites in the land of Canaan.

*Towns for the Levites*

35 On the plains of Moab by the Jordan across from Jericho,[l] the LORD said to Moses, [2]"Command the Israelites to give the Levites towns to live in from the inheritance the Israelites will possess. And give them pasturelands around the towns. [3]Then they

[k]15 *Jordan of Jericho* was possibly an ancient name for the Jordan River.
[l]1 Hebrew *Jordan of Jericho;* possibly an ancient name for the Jordan River

*26 Most mss have *dagesh* in the *sin* (יִשָּׂשכָר).

לָהֶם לָשָׁבֶת וּמִגְרְשֵׁיהֶם יִהְיוּ לִבְהֶמְתָּם
for-cattle-of-them they-will-be and-pastures-of-them to-live for-them

וְלִרְכֻשָׁם וּלְכֹל חַיָּתָם׃ (4) וּמִגְרְשֵׁי
and-pasturelands-of (4) stock-of-them and-for-all-of and-for-flock-of-them

הֶעָרִים אֲשֶׁר תִּתְּנוּ לַלְוִיִּם מִקִּיר הָעִיר וָחוּצָה
and-outward the-town from-wall-of to-the-Levites you-give that the-towns

אֶלֶף אַמָּה סָבִיב׃ (5) וּמַדֹּתֶם מִחוּץ לָעִיר אֶת־פְּאַת־
side-of *** of-the-town outside and-you-measure (5) around cubit thousand

קֵדְמָה אַלְפַּיִם בָּאַמָּה וְאֶת־פְּאַת־נֶגֶב אַלְפַּיִם בָּאַמָּה
by-the-cubit two-thousand south side-of and by-the-cubit two-thousand on-east

וְאֶת־פְּאַת־יָם ׀ אַלְפַּיִם בָּאַמָּה וְאֵת פְּאַת צָפוֹן אַלְפַּיִם
two-thousand north side-of and by-the-cubit two-thousand west side-of and

בָּאַמָּה וְהָעִיר בַּתָּוֶךְ זֶה יִהְיֶה לָהֶם מִגְרְשֵׁי
pastures-of for-them he-will-be this in-the-center and-the-town by-the-cubit

הֶעָרִים׃ (6) וְאֵת הֶעָרִים אֲשֶׁר תִּתְּנוּ לַלְוִיִּם אֵת שֵׁשׁ־עָרֵי
cities-of six *** to-the-Levites you-give that the-towns and (6) the-towns

הַמִּקְלָט אֲשֶׁר תִּתְּנוּ לָנֻס שָׁמָּה הָרֹצֵחַ וַעֲלֵיהֶם
and-to-them the-one-killing to-there to-flee you-give that the-refuge

תִּתְּנוּ אַרְבָּעִים וּשְׁתַּיִם עִיר׃ (7) כָּל־הֶעָרִים אֲשֶׁר תִּתְּנוּ לַלְוִיִּם
to-the-Levites you-give that the-towns all-of (7) town and-two forty you-give

אַרְבָּעִים וּשְׁמֹנֶה עִיר אֶתְהֶן וְאֶת־מִגְרְשֵׁיהֶן׃ (8) וְהֶעָרִים אֲשֶׁר
that and-the-towns (8) pastures-of-them also with-them town and-eight forty

תִּתְּנוּ מֵאֲחֻזַּת בְּנֵי־יִשְׂרָאֵל מֵאֵת הָרַב תַּרְבּוּ
you-give-many the-many from Israel sons-of from-possession-of you-give

וּמֵאֵת הַמְעַט תַּמְעִיטוּ אִישׁ כְּפִי נַחֲלָתוֹ אֲשֶׁר
that inheritance-of-him in-proportion-of each you-give-few the-few and-from

יִנְחָלוּ יִתֵּן מֵעָרָיו לַלְוִיִּם׃ (9) וַיְדַבֵּר
and-he-spoke (9) to-the-Levites from-towns-of-him he-must-give they-inherited

יְהוָה אֶל־מֹשֶׁה לֵּאמֹר׃ (10) דַּבֵּר אֶל־בְּנֵי יִשְׂרָאֵל וְאָמַרְתָּ אֲלֵהֶם
to-them and-you-say Israel sons-of to speak! (10) to-say Moses to Yahweh

כִּי אַתֶּם עֹבְרִים אֶת־הַיַּרְדֵּן אַרְצָה כְּנָעַן׃ (11) וְהִקְרִיתֶם
then-you-select (11) Canaan into-land-of the-Jordan *** ones-crossing you when

לָכֶם עָרִים עָרֵי מִקְלָט תִּהְיֶינָה לָכֶם וְנָס שָׁמָּה
to-there and-he-may-flee for-you they-will-be refuge cities-of towns for-you

רֹצֵחַ מַכֵּה־נֶפֶשׁ בִּשְׁגָגָה׃ (12) וְהָיוּ לָכֶם
for-you and-they-will-be (12) by-accident person slaying-of one-killing

הֶעָרִים לְמִקְלָט מִגֹּאֵל וְלֹא יָמוּת הָרֹצֵחַ
the-one-killing he-may-die so-not from-one-avenging for-refuge the-cities

will have towns to live in and pasturelands for their cattle, flocks and all their other livestock.

4 "The pasturelands around the towns that you give the Levites will extend out fifteen hundred feet[m] from the town wall. 5 Outside the town, measure three thousand feet[n] on the east side, three thousand on the south side, three thousand on the west and three thousand on the north, with the town in the center. They will have this area as pastureland for the towns.

*Cities of Refuge*

6 "Six of the towns you give the Levites will be cities of refuge, to which a person who has killed someone may flee. In addition, give them forty-two other towns. 7 In all you must give the Levites forty-eight towns, together with their pasturelands. 8 The towns you give the Levites from the land the Israelites possess are to be given in proportion to the inheritance of each tribe: Take many towns from a tribe that has many, but few from one that has few."

9 Then the LORD said to Moses: 10 "Speak to the Israelites and say to them: 'When you cross the Jordan into Canaan, 11 select some towns to be your cities of refuge, to which a person who has killed someone accidentally may flee. 12 They will be places of refuge from the avenger, so that a person accused of murder may not die before he

[m]4 Hebrew *a thousand cubits* (about 450 meters)
[n]5 Hebrew *two thousand cubits* (about 900 meters)

עַד־ עָמְדוֹ לִפְנֵי הָעֵדָה לַמִּשְׁפָּט׃ וְהֶעָרִים
and-the-towns (13) for-the-trial the-assembly before to-stand-him before

אֲשֶׁר תִּתֵּנוּ שֵׁשׁ־ עָרֵי מִקְלָט תִּהְיֶינָה לָכֶם׃ אֵת | שְׁלֹשׁ
three-of *** (14) for-you they-will-be refuge cities-of six you-give that

הֶעָרִים תִּתְּנוּ מֵעֵבֶר לַיַּרְדֵּן וְאֵת שְׁלֹשׁ הֶעָרִים תִּתְּנוּ
you-give the-towns three-of and of-the-Jordan on-this-side you-give the-towns

בְּאֶרֶץ כְּנָעַן עָרֵי מִקְלָט תִּהְיֶינָה׃ לִבְנֵי יִשְׂרָאֵל
Israel for-sons-of (15) they-will-be refuge cities-of Canaan in-land-of

וְלַגֵּר וְלַתּוֹשָׁב בְּתוֹכָם תִּהְיֶינָה שֵׁשׁ־ הֶעָרִים
the-towns six they-will-be among-them and-for-the-visitor and-for-the-alien

הָאֵלֶּה לְמִקְלָט לָנוּס שָׁמָּה כָּל־ מַכֵּה־ נֶפֶשׁ
person one-killing-of every-of to-there to-flee for-refuge the-these

בִּשְׁגָגָה׃ וְאִם־ בִּכְלִי בַרְזֶל | הִכָּהוּ וַיָּמֹת
so-he-dies he-strikes-him iron with-object-of now-if (16) by-accident

רֹצֵחַ הוּא מוֹת יוּמַת הָרֹצֵחַ׃ וְאִם
or-if (17) the-one-murdering he-shall-die to-die he one-murdering

בְּאֶבֶן יָד אֲשֶׁר־ יָמוּת בָּהּ הִכָּהוּ וַיָּמֹת
so-he-dies he-strikes-him with-her he-could-kill that hand with-stone-of

רֹצֵחַ הוּא מוֹת יוּמַת הָרֹצֵחַ׃ אוֹ בִּכְלִי
with-object-of or (18) the-one-murdering he-shall-die to-die he one-murdering

עֵץ־ יָד אֲשֶׁר־ יָמוּת בּוֹ הִכָּהוּ וַיָּמֹת
so-he-dies he-strikes-him with-him he-could-kill that hand wood-of

רֹצֵחַ הוּא מוֹת יוּמַת הָרֹצֵחַ׃ גֹּאֵל
one-avenging-of (19) the-one-murdering he-shall-die to-die he one-murdering

הַדָּם הוּא יָמִית אֶת־ הָרֹצֵחַ בְּפִגְעוֹ־ בוֹ
with-him when-to-meet-him the-one-murdering *** he-shall-kill he the-blood

הוּא יְמִיתֶנּוּ׃ וְאִם־ בְּשִׂנְאָה יֶהְדָּפֶנּוּ אוֹ־ הִשְׁלִיךְ
he-throws or he-shoves-him with-malice and-if (20) he-shall-kill-him he

עָלָיו בִּצְדִיָּה וַיָּמֹת׃ אוֹ בְאֵיבָה הִכָּהוּ
he-hits-him in-hostility or (21) so-he-dies with-intention at-him

בְיָדוֹ וַיָּמֹת מוֹת־ יוּמַת הַמַּכֶּה רֹצֵחַ
one-murdering the-one-hitting he-must-die to-die so-he-dies with-fist-of-him

הוּא גֹּאֵל הַדָּם יָמִית אֶת־ הָרֹצֵחַ
the-one-murdering *** he-shall-kill the-blood one-avenging-of he

בְּפִגְעוֹ־ בוֹ׃ וְאִם־ בְּפֶתַע בְּלֹא־ אֵיבָה
hostility with-no in-suddenness but-if (22) with-him when-to-meet-him

הֲדָפוֹ אוֹ־ הִשְׁלִיךְ עָלָיו כָּל־ כְּלִי בְּלֹא צְדִיָּה׃ אוֹ
or (23) intention with-no object any-of at-him he-throws or he-shoves-him

stands trial before the assembly. 13These six towns you give
will be your cities of refuge.
14Give three on this side of the
Jordan and three in Canaan as
cities of refuge. 15These six
towns will be a place of refuge
for Israelites, aliens and any
other people living among
them, so that anyone who has
killed another accidentally can
flee there.

16" 'If a man strikes someone
with an iron object so that he
dies, he is a murderer; the
murderer shall be put to death.
17Or if anyone has a stone in
his hand that could kill, and
he strikes someone so that he
dies, he is a murderer; the
murderer shall be put to death.
18Or if anyone has a wooden
object in his hand that could
kill, and he hits someone so
that he dies, he is a murderer;
the murderer shall be put to
death. 19The avenger of blood
shall put the murderer to
death; when he meets him, he
shall put him to death. 20If
anyone with malice afore-
thought shoves another or
throws something at him intentionally so that he dies 21or
if in hostility he hits him with
his fist so that he dies, that
person shall be put to death;
he is a murderer. The avenger
of blood shall put the murderer to death when he meets
him.

22" 'But if without hostility
someone suddenly shoves another or throws something at
him unintentionally 23or,

בְכָל־ אֶבֶן אֲשֶׁר־ יָמוּת בָּהּ בְּלֹא רְאוֹת וַיַּפֵּל
and-he-drops to-see but-not with-her he-could-kill that stone with-any-of

עָלָיו וַיָּמֹת וְהוּא לֹא־ אוֹיֵב לוֹ וְלֹא מְבַקֵּשׁ
intending and-not to-him being-enemy not and-he so-he-dies on-him

רָעָתוֹ׃ וְשָׁפְטוּ הָעֵדָה בֵּין הַמַּכֶּה
the-one-killing between the-assembly then-they-must-judge (24) harm-of-him

וּבֵין גֹּאֵל הַדָּם עַל הַמִּשְׁפָּטִים הָאֵלֶּה׃
the-these the-regulations by the-blood one-avenging-of and-between

וְהִצִּילוּ הָעֵדָה אֶת־ הָרֹצֵחַ מִיַּד
from-hand-of the-one-killing *** the-assembly and-they-must-protect (25)

גֹּאֵל הַדָּם וְהֵשִׁיבוּ אֹתוֹ הָעֵדָה אֶל־ עִיר
city-of to the-assembly him and-they-must-send the-blood one-avenging-of

מִקְלָטוֹ אֲשֶׁר־ נָס שָׁמָּה וְיָשַׁב בָּהּ עַד־ מוֹת
death-of until in-her and-he-must-stay to-there he-fled that refuge-of-him

הַכֹּהֵן הַגָּדֹל אֲשֶׁר־ מָשַׁח אֹתוֹ בְּשֶׁמֶן הַקֹּדֶשׁ׃ וְאִם־
but-if (26) the-holy with-oil-of him he-anointed whom the-high the-priest

יָצֹא יֵצֵא הָרֹצֵחַ אֶת־ גְּבוּל עִיר מִקְלָטוֹ
refuge-of-him city-of limit-of *** the-one-killing he-goes-out to-go-out

אֲשֶׁר יָנוּס שָׁמָּה׃ וּמָצָא אֹתוֹ גֹּאֵל הַדָּם
the-blood one-avenging-of him and-he-finds (27) to-there he-fled that

מִחוּץ לִגְבוּל עִיר מִקְלָטוֹ וְרָצַח גֹּאֵל
one-avenging-of then-he-may-kill refuge-of-him city-of of-limit-of outside

הַדָּם אֶת־ הָרֹצֵחַ אֵין לוֹ דָּם׃ כִּי בְעִיר
in-city-of for (28) blood to-him without the-one-killing *** the-blood

מִקְלָטוֹ יֵשֵׁב עַד־ מוֹת הַכֹּהֵן הַגָּדֹל וְאַחֲרֵי
and-after the-high the-priest death-of until he-must-stay refuge-of-him

מוֹת הַכֹּהֵן הַגָּדֹל יָשׁוּב הָרֹצֵחַ אֶל־ אֶרֶץ
land-of to the-one-killing he-may-return the-high the-priest death-of

אֲחֻזָּתוֹ׃ וְהָיוּ אֵלֶּה לָכֶם לְחֻקַּת מִשְׁפָּט
legal as-requirement-of for-you these and-they-must-be (29) property-of-him

לְדֹרֹתֵיכֶם בְּכֹל מוֹשְׁבֹתֵיכֶם׃ כָּל־ מַכֵּה־
one-killing-of every-of (30) dwellings-of-you in-all-of for-generations-of-you

נֶפֶשׁ לְפִי עֵדִים יִרְצַח אֶת־ הָרֹצֵחַ וְעֵד
but-witness the-one-murdering *** he-may-kill witnesses on-testimony-of person

אֶחָד לֹא־ יַעֲנֶה בְנֶפֶשׁ לָמוּת׃ וְלֹא־ תִקְחוּ כֹפֶר
ransom you-accept and-not (31) to-die against-person he-may-testify not one

לְנֶפֶשׁ רֹצֵחַ אֲשֶׁר־הוּא רָשָׁע לָמוּת כִּי־ מוֹת יוּמָת׃
he-must-die to-die for to-die guilty he who one-murdering for-life-of

without seeing him, drops a stone on him that could kill him, and he dies, then since he was not his enemy and he did not intend to harm him, [24]the assembly must judge between him and the avenger of blood according to these regulations. [25]The assembly must protect the one accused of murder from the avenger of blood and send him back to the city of refuge to which he fled. He must stay there until the death of the high priest, who was anointed with the holy oil.

[26]" 'But if the accused ever goes outside the limits of the city of refuge to which he has fled [27]and the avenger of blood finds him outside the city, the avenger of blood may kill the accused without being guilty of murder. [28]The accused must stay in his city of refuge until the death of the high priest; only after the death of the high priest may he return to his own property.

[29]" 'These are to be legal requirements for you throughout the generations to come, wherever you live.

[30]" 'Anyone who kills a person is to be put to death as a murderer only on the testimony of witnesses. But no one is to be put to death on the testimony of only one witness.

[31]" 'Do not accept a ransom for the life of a murderer, who deserves to die. He must surely be put to death.

וְלֹֽא־ תִקְח֣וּ כֹ֔פֶר לָנ֖וּס אֶל־ עִ֣יר מִקְלָט֑וֹ לָשׁוּב֙
to-go-back refuge-of-him city-of to to-flee ransom you-accept and-not (32)

לָשֶׁ֣בֶת בָּאָ֔רֶץ עַד־ מ֖וֹת הַכֹּהֵֽן׃ וְלֹא־ תַחֲנִ֣יפוּ אֶת־
*** you-pollute and-not (33) the-priest death-of before in-the-land to-live

הָאָ֗רֶץ אֲשֶׁ֤ר אַתֶּם֙ בָּ֔הּ כִּ֣י הַדָּ֔ם ה֥וּא יַחֲנִ֖יף אֶת־ הָאָ֑רֶץ
the-land *** he-pollutes he the-blood for in-her you where the-land

וְלָאָ֣רֶץ לֹֽא־ יְכֻפַּ֗ר לַדָּם֙ אֲשֶׁ֣ר שֻׁפַּךְ־ בָּ֔הּ
on-her he-was-shed that for-the-blood he-can-be-atoned not and-for-the-land

כִּי־ אִ֖ם בְּדַ֥ם שֹׁפְכֽוֹ׃ וְלֹ֧א תְטַמֵּ֣א אֶת־ הָאָ֗רֶץ
the-land *** you-defile and-not (34) one-shedding-him by-blood-of only except

אֲשֶׁ֤ר אַתֶּם֙ יֹשְׁבִ֣ים בָּ֔הּ אֲשֶׁ֥ר אֲנִ֖י שֹׁכֵ֣ן בְּתוֹכָ֑הּ כִּ֚י אֲנִ֣י יְהוָ֔ה
Yahweh I for within-her dwelling I where in-her ones-living you where

שֹׁכֵ֕ן בְּת֖וֹךְ בְּנֵ֥י יִשְׂרָאֵֽל׃ וַֽיִּקְרְב֞וּ רָאשֵׁ֣י הָאָב֗וֹת
the-fathers heads-of and-they-came (36:1) Israel sons-of among dwelling

לְמִשְׁפַּ֤חַת בְּנֵֽי־ גִלְעָד֙ בֶּן־ מָכִ֣יר בֶּן־ מְנַשֶּׁ֔ה מִֽמִּשְׁפְּחֹ֖ת בְּנֵ֣י
sons-of from-clans-of Manasseh son-of Makir son-of Gilead sons-of of-clan-of

יוֹסֵ֑ף וַֽיְדַבְּר֞וּ לִפְנֵ֤י מֹשֶׁה֙ וְלִפְנֵ֣י הַנְּשִׂאִ֔ים רָאשֵׁ֥י אָב֖וֹת
fathers heads-of the-leaders and-before Moses before and-they-spoke Joseph

לִבְנֵ֥י יִשְׂרָאֵֽל׃ וַיֹּאמְר֗וּ אֶת־ אֲדֹנִי֙ צִוָּ֣ה יְהוָ֔ה
Yahweh he-commanded lord-of-me *** and-they-said (2) Israel of-sons-of

לָתֵת֩ אֶת־ הָאָ֧רֶץ בְּנַחֲלָ֛ה בְּגוֹרָ֖ל לִבְנֵ֣י יִשְׂרָאֵ֑ל וַֽאדֹנִי֙
and-lord-of-me Israel to-sons-of by-lot as-inheritance the-land *** to-give

צֻוָּ֣ה בַיהוָ֔ה לָתֵ֗ת אֶת־ נַחֲלַ֛ת צְלָפְחָ֥ד אָחִ֖ינוּ
brother-of-us Zelophehad inheritance-of *** to-give by-Yahweh he-was-ordered

לִבְנֹתָֽיו׃ וְ֠הָיוּ לְאֶחָ֞ד מִבְּנֵ֣י שִׁבְטֵ֣י בְנֵֽי־
sons-of tribes-of from-sons-of to-one if-they-become (3) to-daughters-of-him

יִשְׂרָאֵל֮ לְנָשִׁים֒ וְנִגְרְעָ֤ה נַחֲלָתָן֙ מִנַּחֲלַ֣ת
from-inheritance-of inheritance-of-them then-she-will-be-taken as-wives Israel

אֲבֹתֵ֔ינוּ וְנוֹסַ֕ף עַ֚ל נַחֲלַ֣ת הַמַּטֶּ֔ה אֲשֶׁ֥ר
that the-tribe inheritance-of to and-he-will-be-added fathers-of-us

תִּהְיֶ֖ינָה לָהֶ֑ם וּמִגֹּרַ֥ל נַחֲלָתֵ֖נוּ יִגָּרֵֽעַ׃
he-will-be-taken inheritance-of-us and-from-allotment-of into-them they-marry

וְאִם־ יִהְיֶ֣ה הַיֹּבֵל֮ לִבְנֵ֣י יִשְׂרָאֵל֒ וְנוֹסְפָה֙
then-she-will-be-added Israel for-sons-of the-Jubilee he-comes and-when (4)

נַחֲלָתָ֔ן עַ֚ל נַחֲלַ֣ת הַמַּטֶּ֔ה אֲשֶׁ֥ר תִּהְיֶ֖ינָה לָהֶ֑ם
into-them they-marry that the-tribe inheritance-of to inheritance-of-them

וּמִֽנַּחֲלַת֙ מַטֵּ֣ה אֲבֹתֵ֔ינוּ יִגָּרַ֖ע
he-will-be-taken fathers-of-us tribe-of and-from-inheritance-of

32" 'Do not accept a ransom for anyone who has fled to a city of refuge and so allow him to go back and live on his own land before the death of the high priest.

33" 'Do not pollute the land where you are. Bloodshed pollutes the land, and atonement cannot be made for the land on which blood has been shed, except by the blood of the one who shed it. 34Do not defile the land where you live and where I dwell, for I, the LORD, dwell among the Israelites.' "

*Inheritance of Zelophehad's Daughters*

36 The family heads of the clan of Gilead son of Makir, the son of Manasseh, who were from the clans of the descendants of Joseph, came and spoke before Moses and the leaders, the heads of the Israelite families. 2They said, "When the LORD commanded my lord to give the land as an inheritance to the Israelites by lot, he ordered you to give the inheritance of our brother Zelophehad to his daughters. 3Now suppose they marry men from other Israelite tribes; then their inheritance will be taken from our ancestral inheritance and added to that of the tribe they marry into. And so part of the inheritance allotted to us will be taken away. 4When the Year of Jubilee for the Israelites comes, their inheritance will be added to that of the tribe into which they marry, and their property will be taken from the tribal inheritance of our forefathers."

נַחֲלָתָן׃    (5)   וַיְצַ֤ו   מֹשֶׁה֙   אֶת־   בְּנֵ֣י   יִשְׂרָאֵ֔ל   עַל־   פִּ֖י

inheritance-of-them    (5)   so-he-ordered   Moses   ***   sons-of   Israel   at   command-of

יְהוָ֖ה   לֵאמֹ֑ר   כֵּ֛ן   מַטֵּ֥ה   בְנֵֽי־   יוֹסֵ֖ף   דֹּבְרִֽים׃   (6)   זֶ֣ה   הַדָּבָ֗ר

Yahweh   to-say   right   tribe-of   sons-of   Joseph   ones-saying   (6)   this   the-thing

אֲשֶׁר־   צִוָּ֣ה   יְהוָ֗ה   לִבְנ֣וֹת   צְלָפְחָד֮   לֵאמֹ֒ר   לַטּ֣וֹב

that   he-commands   Yahweh   for-daughters-of   Zelophehad   to-say   to-the-one-pleasant

בְּעֵינֵיהֶ֖ם   תִּהְיֶ֣ינָה   לְנָשִׁ֑ים   אַ֗ךְ   לְמִשְׁפַּ֛חַת   מַטֵּ֥ה

in-eyes-of-them   they-may-become   as-wives   as-long-as   in-clan-of   tribe-of

אֲבִיהֶ֖ם   תִּהְיֶ֥ינָה   לְנָשִֽׁים׃   (7)   וְלֹֽא־   תִסֹּ֤ב   נַחֲלָה֙

father-of-them   they-become   as-wives   (7)   and-not   she-may-pass   inheritance

לִבְנֵ֣י   יִשְׂרָאֵ֔ל   מִמַּטֶּ֖ה   אֶל־   מַטֶּ֑ה   כִּ֣י   אִ֗ישׁ   בְּנַחֲלַת֙   מַטֵּ֣ה

among-sons-of   Israel   from-tribe   to   tribe   for   each   to-inheritance-of   tribe-of

אֲבֹתָ֔יו   יִדְבְּק֖וּ   בְּנֵ֥י   יִשְׂרָאֵֽל׃   (8)   וְכָל־   בַּ֞ת

fathers-of-him   they-shall-keep   sons-of   Israel   (8)   and-every-of   daughter

יֹרֶ֣שֶׁת   נַחֲלָ֗ה   מִמַּטּוֹת֙   בְּנֵ֣י   יִשְׂרָאֵ֔ל   לְאֶחָ֕ד   מִמִּשְׁפַּ֥חַת   מַטֵּ֖ה

inheriting   land   in-tribes-of   sons-of   Israel   to-one   in-clan-of   tribe-of

אָבִ֖יהָ   תִּהְיֶ֣ה   לְאִשָּׁ֑ה   לְמַ֗עַן   יִֽירְשׁוּ֙   בְּנֵ֣י   יִשְׂרָאֵ֔ל

father-of-her   she-must-be   as-wife   so-that   they-will-possess   sons-of   Israel

אִ֖ישׁ   נַחֲלַ֣ת   אֲבֹתָ֑יו׃   (9)   וְלֹֽא־   תִסֹּ֤ב   נַחֲלָה֙

each   inheritance-of   fathers-of-him   (9)   and-not   she-may-pass   inheritance

מִמַּטֶּ֖ה   לְמַטֶּ֣ה   אַחֵ֑ר   כִּי־   אִ֣ישׁ   בְּנַחֲלָת֔וֹ   יִדְבְּק֖וּ

from-tribe   to-tribe   another   for   each   to-inheritance-of-him   they-must-keep

מַטּ֖וֹת   בְּנֵ֥י   יִשְׂרָאֵֽל׃   (10)   כַּאֲשֶׁ֛ר   צִוָּ֥ה   יְהוָ֖ה   אֶת־   מֹשֶׁ֑ה   כֵּ֥ן

tribes-of   sons-of   Israel   (10)   just-as   he-commanded   Yahweh   ***   Moses   so

עָשׂ֖וּ   בְּנ֥וֹת   צְלָפְחָֽד׃   (11)   וַתִּהְיֶ֜ינָה   מַחְלָ֣ה   תִרְצָ֗ה

they-did   daughters-of   Zelophehad   (11)   and-they-became   Mahlah   Tirzah

וְחָגְלָ֧ה   וּמִלְכָּ֛ה   וְנֹעָ֖ה   בְּנ֣וֹת   צְלָפְחָ֑ד   לִבְנֵ֥י

and-Hoglah   and-Milcah   and-Noah   daughters-of   Zelophehad   to-sons-of

דֹדֵיהֶ֖ן   לְנָשִֽׁים׃   (12)   מִֽמִּשְׁפְּחֹ֛ת   בְּנֵֽי־   מְנַשֶּׁ֥ה   בֶן־   יוֹסֵ֖ף

uncles-of-them   as-wives   (12)   in-clans-of   sons-of   Manasseh   son-of   Joseph

הָי֣וּ   לְנָשִׁ֑ים   וַתְּהִי֙   נַחֲלָתָ֔ן   עַל־   מַטֵּ֖ה

they-became   as-wives   and-she-remained   inheritance-of-them   in   tribe-of

מִשְׁפַּ֥חַת   אֲבִיהֶֽן׃   (13)   אֵ֣לֶּה   הַמִּצְוֺ֤ת   וְהַמִּשְׁפָּטִים֙   אֲשֶׁ֨ר

clan-of   father-of-them   (13)   these   the-commands   and-the-regulations   that

צִוָּ֧ה   יְהוָ֛ה   בְּיַד־   מֹשֶׁ֖ה   אֶל־   בְּנֵ֣י   יִשְׂרָאֵ֑ל   בְּעַֽרְבֹ֣ת   מוֹאָ֔ב

he-gave   Yahweh   by-hand-of   Moses   to   sons-of   Israel   on-plains-of   Moab

עַ֖ל   יַרְדֵּ֥ן   יְרֵחֽוֹ׃

by   Jordan-of   Jericho

5Then at the LORD's command Moses gave this order to the Israelites: "What the tribe of the descendants of Joseph is saying is right. 6This is what the LORD commands for Zelophehad's daughters: They may marry anyone they please as long as they marry within the tribal clan of their father. 7No inheritance in Israel is to pass from tribe to tribe, for every Israelite shall keep the tribal land inherited from his forefathers. 8Every daughter who inherits land in any Israelite tribe must marry someone in her father's tribal clan, so that every Israelite will possess the inheritance of his fathers. 9No inheritance may pass from tribe to tribe, for each Israelite tribe is to keep the land it inherits."

10So Zelophehad's daughters did as the LORD commanded Moses. 11Zelophehad's daughters—Mahlah, Tirzah, Hoglah, Milcah and Noah—married their cousins on their father's side. 12They married within the clans of the descendants of Manasseh son of Joseph, and their inheritance remained in their father's clan and tribe.

13These are the commands and regulations the LORD gave through Moses to the Israelites on the plains of Moab by the Jordan across from Jericho.ᵒ

*ᵒ13 Hebrew* Jordan of Jericho; *possibly an ancient name for the Jordan River*

אֵלֶּה הַדְּבָרִים אֲשֶׁר דִּבֶּר מֹשֶׁה אֶל־ כָּל־ יִשְׂרָאֵל בְּעֵבֶר
on-east-of Israel all-of to Moses he-spoke that the-words these (1:1)

הַיַּרְדֵּן בַּמִּדְבָּר בָּעֲרָבָה מוֹל סוּף בֵּין־ פָּארָן וּבֵין־
and-between Paran between Suph opposite in-the-Arabah in-the-desert the-Jordan

תֹּפֶל וְלָבָן וַחֲצֵרֹת וְדִי זָהָב׃ אַחַד עָשָׂר יוֹם מֵחֹרֵב
from-Horeb day ten one (2) Zahab and-Di and-Hazeroth and-Laban Tophel

דֶּרֶךְ הַר־ שֵׂעִיר עַד קָדֵשׁ בַּרְנֵעַ׃ וַיְהִי בְּאַרְבָּעִים שָׁנָה בְּעַשְׁתֵּי־
in-one year in-fortieth and-he-was (3) Barnea Kadesh to Seir Mount-of road-of

עָשָׂר חֹדֶשׁ בְּאֶחָד לַחֹדֶשׁ דִּבֶּר מֹשֶׁה אֶל־ בְּנֵי יִשְׂרָאֵל
Israel sons-of to Moses he-proclaimed of-the-month on-first month ten

כְּכֹל אֲשֶׁר צִוָּה יְהוָה אֹתוֹ אֲלֵהֶם׃ אַחֲרֵי הַכֹּתוֹ אֵת
*** to-defeat-him after (4) about-them him Yahweh he-commanded that as-all

סִיחֹן מֶלֶךְ הָאֱמֹרִי אֲשֶׁר יוֹשֵׁב בְּחֶשְׁבּוֹן וְאֵת עוֹג מֶלֶךְ הַבָּשָׁן
the-Bashan king-of Og and in-Heshbon reigning who the-Amorite king-of Sihon

אֲשֶׁר־ יוֹשֵׁב בְּעַשְׁתָּרֹת בְּאֶדְרֶעִי׃ בְּעֵבֶר הַיַּרְדֵּן בְּאֶרֶץ מוֹאָב
Moab in-land-of the-Jordan on-east-of (5) at-Edrei in-Ashtaroth reigning who

הוֹאִיל מֹשֶׁה בֵּאֵר אֶת־ הַתּוֹרָה הַזֹּאת לֵאמֹר׃ יְהוָה אֱלֹהֵינוּ
God-of-us Yahweh (6) to-say the-this the-law *** he-expounded Moses he-began

דִּבֶּר אֵלֵינוּ בְּחֹרֵב לֵאמֹר רַב־ לָכֶם שֶׁבֶת בָּהָר הַזֶּה׃
the-this at-the-mountain to-stay to-you enough to-say at-Horeb to-us he-spoke

פְּנוּ ׀ וּסְעוּ לָכֶם וּבֹאוּ הַר הָאֱמֹרִי
the-Amorite hill-country-of and-go! for-you and-advance! break-camp! (7)

וְאֶל־ כָּל־ שְׁכֵנָיו בָּעֲרָבָה בָהָר וּבַשְּׁפֵלָה
and-in-the-foothill in-the-mountain in-the-Arabah neighbors-of-him all-of and-to

וּבַנֶּגֶב וּבְחוֹף הַיָּם אֶרֶץ הַכְּנַעֲנִי וְהַלְּבָנוֹן
and-the-Lebanon the-Canaanite land-of the-sea and-by-coast-of and-in-the-Negev

עַד־ הַנָּהָר הַגָּדֹל נְהַר־ פְּרָת׃ רְאֵה נָתַתִּי לִפְנֵיכֶם
before-you I-gave see! (8) Euphrates River-of the-great the-river as-far-as

אֶת־ הָאָרֶץ בֹּאוּ וּרְשׁוּ אֶת־ הָאָרֶץ אֲשֶׁר נִשְׁבַּע יְהוָה
Yahweh he-swore that the-land *** and-possess! go-in! the-land ***

לַאֲבֹתֵיכֶם לְאַבְרָהָם לְיִצְחָק וּלְיַעֲקֹב לָתֵת לָהֶם
to-them to-give and-to-Jacob to-Isaac to-Abraham to-fathers-of-you

וּלְזַרְעָם אַחֲרֵיהֶם׃ וָאֹמַר אֲלֵכֶם בָּעֵת
at-the-time to-you and-I-said (9) after-them and-to-descendant-of-them

הַהִוא לֵאמֹר לֹא־ אוּכַל לְבַדִּי שְׂאֵת אֶתְכֶם׃ יְהוָה אֱלֹהֵיכֶם
God-of-you Yahweh (10) you to-carry by-myself I-can not to-say the-that

הִרְבָּה אֶתְכֶם וְהִנְּכֶם הַיּוֹם כְּכוֹכְבֵי הַשָּׁמַיִם לָרֹב׃
for-number the-skies as-stars-of the-day so-see-you! you he-increased

*The Command to Leave Horeb*

1 These are the words
Moses spoke to all Israel in
the desert east of the Jordan—
that is, in the Arabah—opposite Suph, between Paran and
Tophel, Laban, Hazeroth and
Dizahab. 2(It takes eleven days
to go from Horeb to Kadesh
Barnea by the Mount Seir
road.)
3In the fortieth year, on the
first day of the eleventh
month, Moses proclaimed to
the Israelites all that the LORD
had commanded him con-
cerning them. 4This was after
he had defeated Sihon king of
the Amorites, who reigned in
Heshbon, and at Edrei had defeated Og king of Bashan, who
reigned in Ashtaroth.
5East of the Jordan in the territory of Moab, Moses began
to expound this law, saying:

6The LORD our God said to us
at Horeb, "You have stayed
long enough at this mountain.
7Break camp and advance into
the hill country of the Amorites; go to all the neighboring
peoples in the Arabah, in the
mountains, in the western
foothills, in the Negev and
along the seacoast, to the land
of the Canaanites and to Lebanon, as far as the great river,
the Euphrates. 8See, I have
given you this land. Go in and
take possession of the land
that the LORD swore he would
give to your fathers—to Abraham, Isaac and Jacob—and to
their descendants after them."

*The Appointment of Leaders*

9At that time I said to you,
"You are too heavy a burden
for me to carry alone. 10The
LORD your God has increased
your numbers so that today
you are as many as the stars in

יְהוָה אֱלֹהֵי אֲבוֹתֵכֶם יֹסֵף עֲלֵיכֶם כָּכֶם אֶלֶף

thousand as-you to-you may-he-increase fathers-of-you God-of Yahweh (11)

פְּעָמִים וִיבָרֵךְ אֶתְכֶם כַּאֲשֶׁר דִּבֶּר לָכֶם׃ אֵיכָה אֶשָּׂא

can-I-bear how? (12) to-you he-promised just-as you and-may-he-bless times

לְבַדִּי טָרְחֲכֶם וּמַשַּׂאֲכֶם וְרִיבְכֶם׃ הָבוּ

choose! (13) and-dispute-of-you and-burden-of-you problem-of-you by-myself

לָכֶם אֲנָשִׁים חֲכָמִים וּנְבֹנִים וִידֻעִים

and-ones-being-respected and-understanding-ones wise-ones men for-you

לְשִׁבְטֵיכֶם וַאֲשִׂימֵם בְּרָאשֵׁיכֶם׃ וַתַּעֲנוּ

and-you-answered (14) as-heads-of-you and-I-will-set-them from-tribes-of-you

אֹתִי וַתֹּאמְרוּ טוֹב־ הַדָּבָר אֲשֶׁר־ דִּבַּרְתָּ לַעֲשׂוֹת׃ וָאֶקַּח אֶת־

*** so-I-took (15) to-do you-propose that the-thing good and-you-said me

רָאשֵׁי שִׁבְטֵיכֶם אֲנָשִׁים חֲכָמִים וִידֻעִים וָאֶתֵּן

and-I-made and-ones-being-respected wise-ones men tribes-of-you leaders-of

אֹתָם רָאשִׁים עֲלֵיכֶם שָׂרֵי אֲלָפִים וְשָׂרֵי מֵאוֹת

hundreds and-commanders-of thousands commanders-of over-you authorities them

וְשָׂרֵי חֲמִשִּׁים וְשָׂרֵי עֲשָׂרֹת וְשֹׁטְרִים

and-ones-being-officers tens and-commanders-of fifties and-commanders-of

לְשִׁבְטֵיכֶם׃ וָאֲצַוֶּה אֶת־ שֹׁפְטֵיכֶם בָּעֵת הַהִוא

the-that at-the-time ones-judging-you *** and-I-charged (16) of-tribes-of-you

לֵאמֹר שָׁמֹעַ בֵּין־ אֲחֵיכֶם וּשְׁפַטְתֶּם צֶדֶק בֵּין־ אִישׁ

man between fairly and-you-judge brothers-you between to-hear to-say

וּבֵין־ אָחִיו וּבֵין גֵּרוֹ׃ לֹא־ תַכִּירוּ

you-be-partial not (17) alien-of-him or-between brother-of-him and-between

פָנִים בַּמִּשְׁפָּט כַּקָּטֹן כַּגָּדֹל תִּשְׁמָעוּן לֹא תָגוּרוּ

you-fear not you-hear as-the-great both-the-small in-the-judgment persons

מִפְּנֵי־ אִישׁ כִּי הַמִּשְׁפָּט לֵאלֹהִים הוּא וְהַדָּבָר אֲשֶׁר יִקְשֶׁה

he-is-hard that and-the-case he to-God the-judgment for any from-persons-of

מִכֶּם תַּקְרִבוּן אֵלַי וּשְׁמַעְתִּיו׃ וָאֲצַוֶּה אֶתְכֶם בָּעֵת

at-the-time you and-I-told (18) and-I-will-hear-him to-me you-bring for-you

הַהִוא אֵת כָּל־ הַדְּבָרִים אֲשֶׁר תַּעֲשׂוּן׃ וַנִּסַּע

then-we-set-out (19) you-must-do that the-things all-of *** the-that

מֵחֹרֵב וַנֵּלֶךְ אֵת כָּל־ הַמִּדְבָּר הַגָּדוֹל וְהַנּוֹרָא

and-the-being-dreadful the-vast the-desert all-of *** and-we-went from-Horeb

הַהוּא אֲשֶׁר רְאִיתֶם דֶּרֶךְ הַר הָאֱמֹרִי כַּאֲשֶׁר צִוָּה

he-commanded just-as the-Amorite hill-country-of way-of you-saw that the-that

יְהוָה אֱלֹהֵינוּ אֹתָנוּ וַנָּבֹא עַד קָדֵשׁ בַּרְנֵעַ׃ וָאֹמַר אֲלֵכֶם

to-you then-I-said (20) Barnea Kadesh to so-we-reached us God-of-us Yahweh

the sky. [11]May the LORD, the
God of your fathers, increase
you a thousand times and
bless you as he has promised!
[12]But how can I bear your
problems and your burdens
and your disputes all by myself? [13]Choose some wise,
understanding and respected
men from each of your tribes,
and I will set them over you."
[14]You answered me, "What
you propose to do is good."
[15]So I took the leading men
of your tribes, wise and respected men, and appointed
them to have authority over
you—as commanders of thousands, of hundreds, of fifties
and of tens and as tribal
officials. [16]And I charged your
judges at that time: Hear the
disputes between your brothers and judge fairly, whether
the case is between brother Israelites or between one of
them and an alien. [17]Do not
show partiality in judging;
hear both small and great
alike. Do not be afraid of any
man, for judgment belongs to
God. Bring me any case too
hard for you, and I will hear it.
[18]And at that time I told you
everything you were to do.

*Spies Sent Out*

[19]Then, as the LORD our God
commanded us, we set out
from Horeb and went toward
the hill country of the Amorites through all that vast and
dreadful desert that you have
seen, and so we reached Kadesh Barnea. [20]Then I said to

בָּאתֶם עַד־ הַר הָאֱמֹרִי אֲשֶׁר־ יְהוָה אֱלֹהֵינוּ נֹתֵן

giving God-of-us Yahweh which the-Amorite hill-country-of to you-reached

לָנוּ׃ רְאֵה נָתַן יְהוָה אֱלֹהֶיךָ לְפָנֶיךָ אֶת־ הָאָרֶץ עֲלֵה

go-up! the-land *** before-you God-of-you Yahweh he-gave see! (21) to-us

רֵשׁ כַּאֲשֶׁר דִּבֶּר יְהוָה אֱלֹהֵי אֲבֹתֶיךָ לָךְ אַל־ תִּירָא

you-fear not to-you fathers-of-you God-of Yahweh he-told just-as possess!

וְאַל־ תֵּחָת׃ וַתִּקְרְבוּן אֵלַי כֻּלְּכֶם וַתֹּאמְרוּ

and-you-said all-of-you to-me then-you-came (22) you-be-discouraged and-not

נִשְׁלְחָה אֲנָשִׁים לְפָנֵינוּ וְיַחְפְּרוּ־ לָנוּ אֶת־ הָאָרֶץ

the-land *** for-us so-they-can-spy-out ahead-of-us men let-us-send

וְיָשִׁבוּ אֹתָנוּ דָּבָר אֶת־ הַדֶּרֶךְ אֲשֶׁר נַעֲלֶה־ בָּהּ וְאֵת

and on-her we-will-go that the-route *** report us and-they-can-bring-back

הֶעָרִים אֲשֶׁר נָבֹא אֲלֵיהֶן׃ וַיִּיטַב בְּעֵינַי

in-eyes-of-me and-he-was-good (23) to-them we-will-come that the-towns

הַדָּבָר וָאֶקַּח מִכֶּם שְׁנֵים עָשָׂר אֲנָשִׁים אִישׁ אֶחָד לַשָּׁבֶט׃

from-the-tribe one man men ten two from-you so-I-selected the-idea

וַיִּפְנוּ וַיַּעֲלוּ הָהָרָה וַיָּבֹאוּ עַד־

to and-they-came the-hill-country and-they-went-up and-they-left (24)

נַחַל אֶשְׁכֹּל וַיְרַגְּלוּ אֹתָהּ׃ וַיִּקְחוּ בְיָדָם

in-hand-of-them and-they-took (25) her and-they-explored Eshcol Valley-of

מִפְּרִי הָאָרֶץ וַיּוֹרִדוּ אֵלֵינוּ וַיָּשִׁבוּ אֹתָנוּ דָבָר

report us and-they-gave to-us and-they-brought-down the-land from-fruit-of

וַיֹּאמְרוּ טוֹבָה הָאָרֶץ אֲשֶׁר־ יְהוָה אֱלֹהֵינוּ נֹתֵן לָנוּ׃ וְלֹא

but-not (26) to-us giving God-of-us Yahweh that the-land good and-they-said

אֲבִיתֶם לַעֲלֹת וַתַּמְרוּ אֶת־ פִּי יְהוָה אֱלֹהֵיכֶם׃

God-of-you Yahweh command-of *** and-you-rebelled to-go-up you-wanted

וַתֵּרָגְנוּ בְאָהֳלֵיכֶם וַתֹּאמְרוּ בְּשִׂנְאַת יְהוָה אֹתָנוּ

us Yahweh in-hate-of and-you-said in-tents-of-you and-you-grumbled (27)

הוֹצִיאָנוּ מֵאֶרֶץ מִצְרָיִם לָתֵת אֹתָנוּ בְּיַד הָאֱמֹרִי

the-Amorite into-hand-of us to-deliver Egypt from-land-of he-brought-us

לְהַשְׁמִידֵנוּ׃ אָנָה ׀ אֲנַחְנוּ עֹלִים אַחֵינוּ הֵמַסּוּ אֶת־

*** they-made-lose brothers-of-us ones-going we where? (28) to-destroy-us

לְבָבֵנוּ לֵאמֹר עַם גָּדוֹל וָרָם מִמֶּנּוּ עָרִים גְּדֹלֹת

large-ones cities than-us and-taller stronger people to-say heart-of-us

וּבְצוּרֹת בַּשָּׁמָיִם וְגַם־ בְּנֵי עֲנָקִים רָאִינוּ שָׁם׃ וָאֹמַר

then-I-said (29) there we-saw Anakites sons-of and-also to-the-skies and-walls

אֲלֵכֶם לֹא־ תַעַרְצוּן וְלֹא־ תִירְאוּן מֵהֶם׃ יְהוָה אֱלֹהֵיכֶם

God-of-you Yahweh (30) from-them you-fear and-not you-be-terrified not to-you

you, "You have reached the hill country of the Amorites, which the LORD our God is giving us. [21]See, the LORD your God has given you the land. Go up and take possession of it as the LORD, the God of your fathers, told you. Do not be afraid; do not be discouraged."

[22]Then all of you came to me and said, "Let us send men ahead to spy out the land for us and bring back a report about the route we are to take and the towns we will come to."

[23]The idea seemed good to me; so I selected twelve of you, one man from each tribe. [24]They left and went up into the hill country, and came to the Valley of Eshcol and explored it. [25]Taking with them some of the fruit of the land, they brought it down to us and reported, "It is a good land that the LORD our God is giving us."

*Rebellion Against the LORD*

[26]But you were unwilling to go up; you rebelled against the command of the LORD your God. [27]You grumbled in your tents and said, "The LORD hates us; so he brought us out of Egypt to deliver us into the hands of the Amorites to destroy us. [28]Where can we go? Our brothers have made us lose heart. They say, 'The people are stronger and taller than we are; the cities are large, with walls up to the sky. We even saw the Anakites there.' "

[29]Then I said to you, "Do not be terrified; do not be afraid of them. [30]The LORD your God,

הַהֹלֵךְ לִפְנֵיכֶם הוּא יִלָּחֵם לָכֶם כְּכֹל אֲשֶׁר עָשָׂה אִתְּכֶם

for-you he-did that as-all for-you he-will-fight he before-you the-one-going

בְּמִצְרַיִם לְעֵינֵיכֶם׃ וּבַמִּדְבָּר אֲשֶׁר רָאִיתָ אֲשֶׁר

how you-saw where and-in-the-desert (31) before-eyes-of-you in-Egypt

נְשָׂאֲךָ יְהוָה אֱלֹהֶיךָ כַּאֲשֶׁר יִשָּׂא־ אִישׁ אֶת־ בְּנוֹ

son-of-him *** man he-carries just-as God-of-you Yahweh he-carried-you

בְּכָל־ הַדֶּרֶךְ אֲשֶׁר הֲלַכְתֶּם עַד־ בֹּאֲכֶם עַד־הַמָּקוֹם הַזֶּה׃

the-this the-place to to-reach-you until you-went that the-way on-all-of

וּבַדָּבָר הַזֶּה אֵינְכֶם מַאֲמִינִם בַּיהוָה

in-Yahweh ones-trusting not-you the-this in-spite-of-the-thing (32)

אֱלֹהֵיכֶם׃ הַהֹלֵךְ לִפְנֵיכֶם בַּדֶּרֶךְ לָתוּר לָכֶם

for-you to-search on-the-journey ahead-of-you the-one-going (33) God-of-you

מָקוֹם לַחֲנֹתְכֶם בָּאֵשׁ ׀ לַיְלָה לַרְאֹתְכֶם בַּדֶּרֶךְ אֲשֶׁר תֵּלְכוּ־

you-should-go that on-the-way to-show-you night in-the-fire to-camp-you place

בָהּ וּבֶעָנָן יוֹמָם׃ וַיִּשְׁמַע יְהוָה אֶת־ קוֹל

sound-of *** Yahweh when-he-heard (34) by-day and-in-the-cloud on-her

דִּבְרֵיכֶם וַיִּקְצֹף וַיִּשָּׁבַע לֵאמֹר׃ אִם־ יִרְאֶה אִישׁ

one he-will-see not (35) to-say and-he-swore then-he-was-angry words-of-you

בָּאֲנָשִׁים הָאֵלֶּה הַדּוֹר הָרָע הַזֶּה אֵת הָאָרֶץ הַטּוֹבָה

the-good the-land *** the-this the-evil the-generation the-these of-the-men

אֲשֶׁר נִשְׁבַּעְתִּי לָתֵת לַאֲבֹתֵיכֶם׃ זוּלָתִי כָּלֵב בֶּן־

son-of Caleb excepting-me (36) to-fathers-of-you to-give I-swore that

יְפֻנֶּה הוּא יִרְאֶנָּה וְלוֹ־ אֶתֵּן אֶת־ הָאָרֶץ אֲשֶׁר

that the-land *** I-will-give and-to-him he-will-see-her he Jephunneh

דָּרַךְ־ בָּהּ וּלְבָנָיו יַעַן אֲשֶׁר מִלֵּא אַחֲרֵי

after he-was-wholehearted that because and-to-sons-of-him on-her he-sets-foot

יְהוָה׃ גַּם־ בִּי הִתְאַנַּף יְהוָה בִּגְלַלְכֶם לֵאמֹר גַּם־

also to-say because-of-you Yahweh he-became-angry with-me also (37) Yahweh

אַתָּה לֹא־ תָבֹא שָׁם׃ יְהוֹשֻׁעַ בִּן־ נוּן הָעֹמֵד לְפָנֶיךָ

to-you the-one-assisting Nun son-of Joshua (38) there you-will-enter not you

הוּא יָבֹא שָׁמָּה אֹתוֹ חַזֵּק כִּי־ הוּא יַנְחִלֶנָּה

he-will-lead-to-inherit-her he for encourage! him to-there he-will-enter he

אֶת־ יִשְׂרָאֵל׃ וְטַפְּכֶם אֲשֶׁר אֲמַרְתֶּם לָבַז יִהְיֶה

he-would-be as-captive you-said that and-little-one-of-you (39) Israel ***

וּבְנֵיכֶם אֲשֶׁר לֹא־ יָדְעוּ הַיּוֹם טוֹב וָרָע הֵמָּה יָבֹאוּ

they-will-enter they and-bad good the-day they-knew not who and-children-of-you

שָׁמָּה וְלָהֶם אֶתְּנֶנָּה וְהֵם יִירָשׁוּהָ׃

they-will-possess-her and-they I-will-give-her and-to-them to-there

who is going before you, will fight for you, as he did for you in Egypt, before your very eyes, [31]and in the desert. There you saw how the LORD your God carried you, as a father carries his son, all the way you went until you reached this place."

[32]In spite of this, you did not trust in the LORD your God, [33]who went ahead of you on your journey, in fire by night and in a cloud by day, to search out places for you to camp and to show you the way you should go.

[34]When the LORD heard what you said, he was angry and solemnly swore: [35]"Not a man of this evil generation shall see the good land I swore to give your forefathers, [36]except Caleb son of Jephunneh. He will see it, and I will give him and his descendants the land he set his feet on, because he followed the LORD wholeheartedly."

[37]Because of you the LORD became angry with me also and said, "You shall not enter it, either. [38]But your assistant, Joshua son of Nun, will enter it. Encourage him, because he will lead Israel to inherit it. [39]And the little ones that you said would be taken captive, your children who do not yet know good from bad—they will enter the land. I will give it to them and they will take possession of it. [40]But as for

וְאַתֶּם פְּנוּ לָכֶם וּסְעוּ הַמִּדְבָּרָה דֶּרֶךְ יַם־ סוּף׃
Reed Sea-of route-of to-the-desert and-set-out! to-you turn! but-you (40)

וַתַּעֲנוּ וַתֹּאמְרוּ אֵלַי חָטָאנוּ לַיהוָה אֲנַחְנוּ
we against-Yahweh we-sinned to-me and-you-said then-you-replied (41)

נַעֲלֶה וְנִלְחַמְנוּ כְּכֹל אֲשֶׁר־ צִוָּנוּ יְהוָה אֱלֹהֵינוּ
God-of-us Yahweh he-commanded-us that as-all and-we-will-fight we-will-go-up

וַתַּחְגְּרוּ אִישׁ אֶת־ כְּלֵי מִלְחַמְתּוֹ וַתָּהִינוּ לַעֲלֹת
to-go-up and-you-thought-easy war-of-him weapons-of *** each so-they-put-on

הָהָרָה׃ וַיֹּאמֶר יְהוָה אֵלַי אֱמֹר לָהֶם לֹא
not to-them tell! to-me Yahweh but-he-said (42) into-the-hill-country

תַעֲלוּ וְלֹא־ תִלָּחֲמוּ כִּי אֵינֶנִּי בְּקִרְבְּכֶם וְלֹא תִּנָּגְפוּ
you-be-defeated so-not in-midst-of-you not-I for you-fight and-not you-go-up

לִפְנֵי אֹיְבֵיכֶם׃ וָאֲדַבֵּר אֲלֵיכֶם וְלֹא שְׁמַעְתֶּם
you-listened but-not to-you so-I-told (43) being-enemies-of-you before

וַתַּמְרוּ אֶת־ פִּי יְהוָה וַתָּזִדוּ וַתַּעֲלוּ
and-you-went-up and-you-were-arrogant Yahweh command-of *** and-you-rebelled

הָהָרָה׃ וַיֵּצֵא הָאֱמֹרִי הַיֹּשֵׁב
the-one-living the-Amorite and-he-came-out (44) into-the-hill-country

בָּהָר הַהוּא לִקְרַאתְכֶם וַיִּרְדְּפוּ אֶתְכֶם כַּאֲשֶׁר תַּעֲשֶׂינָה
they-do just-as you and-they-chased to-oppose-you the-that in-the-hill

הַדְּבֹרִים וַיַּכְּתוּ אֶתְכֶם בְּשֵׂעִיר עַד־ חָרְמָה׃ וַתָּשֻׁבוּ
and-you-came-back (45) Hormah to from-Seir you and-they-beat the-bees

וַתִּבְכּוּ לִפְנֵי יְהוָה וְלֹא־ שָׁמַע יְהוָה בְּקֹלְכֶם וְלֹא
and-not to-sound-of-you Yahweh he-listened but-not Yahweh before and-you-wept

הֶאֱזִין אֲלֵיכֶם׃ וַתֵּשְׁבוּ בְקָדֵשׁ יָמִים רַבִּים כַּיָּמִים אֲשֶׁר
that as-the-days many days in-Kadesh so-you-stayed (46) to-you he-turned-ear

יְשַׁבְתֶּם׃ וַנֵּפֶן וַנִּסַּע הַמִּדְבָּרָה דֶּרֶךְ
route-of to-the-desert and-we-set-out then-we-turned-back (2:1) you-stayed

יַם־ סוּף כַּאֲשֶׁר דִּבֶּר יְהוָה אֵלָי וַנָּסָב אֶת־ הַר־
hill-of *** and-we-went-around to-me Yahweh he-directed just-as Reed Sea-of

שֵׂעִיר יָמִים רַבִּים׃ וַיֹּאמֶר יְהוָה אֵלַי לֵאמֹר׃ רַב־ לָכֶם
to-you enough (3) to-say to-me Yahweh and-he-said (2) many days Seir

סֹב אֶת־ הָהָר הַזֶּה פְּנוּ לָכֶם צָפֹנָה׃ וְאֶת־ הָעָם
the-people and (4) to-north to-you turn! the-this the-hill *** to-go-around

צַו לֵאמֹר אַתֶּם עֹבְרִים בִּגְבוּל אֲחֵיכֶם בְּנֵי־
sons-of brothers-of-you through-territory-of ones-passing you to-say order!

עֵשָׂו הַיֹּשְׁבִים בְּשֵׂעִיר וְיִירְאוּ מִכֶּם וְנִשְׁמַרְתֶּם
but-you-be-careful from-you and-they-will-fear in-Seir the-ones-living Esau

you, turn around and set out toward the desert along the route to the Red Sea.[a]"

41Then you replied, "We have sinned against the LORD. We will go up and fight, as the LORD our God commanded us." So every one of you put on his weapons, thinking it easy to go up into the hill country.

42But the LORD said to me, "Tell them, 'Do not go up and fight, because I will not be with you. You will be defeated by your enemies.'"

43So I told you, but you would not listen. You rebelled against the LORD's command and in your arrogance you marched up into the hill country. 44The Amorites who lived in those hills came out against you; they chased you like a swarm of bees and beat you down from Seir all the way to Hormah. 45You came back and wept before the LORD, but he paid no attention to your weeping and turned a deaf ear to you. 46And so you stayed in Kadesh many days—all the time you spent there.

*Wanderings in the Desert*

2 Then we turned back and set out toward the desert along the route to the Red Sea,[b] as the LORD had directed me. For a long time we made our way around the hill country of Seir.

2Then the LORD said to me, 3"You have made your way around this hill country long enough; now turn north. 4Give the people these orders: 'You are about to pass through the territory of your brothers the descendants of Esau, who live in Seir. They will be afraid of you, but be very careful. 5Do

[a]40 Hebrew *Yam Suph;* that is, Sea of Reeds
[b]1 Hebrew *Yam Suph;* that is, Sea of Reeds

מְאֹד׃ אַל־ תִּתְגָּרוּ בָם כִּי לֹא־ אֶתֵּן לָכֶם
to-you I-will-give not for with-them you-make-war not (5) very

מֵאַרְצָם עַד מִדְרַךְ כַּף־ רָגֶל כִּי־ יְרֻשָּׁה לְעֵשָׂו נָתַתִּי
I-gave of-Esau possession for foot sole-of step-of even from-land-of-them

אֶת־ הַר שֵׂעִיר׃ אֹכֶל תִּשְׁבְּרוּ מֵאִתָּם בַּכֶּסֶף
with-the-silver from-them you-buy food (6) Seir hill-country-of ***

וַאֲכַלְתֶּם וְגַם־ מַיִם תִּכְרוּ מֵאִתָּם בַּכֶּסֶף וּשְׁתִיתֶם׃
and-you-drink with-the-silver from-them you-buy waters and-also and-you-eat

כִּי יְהוָה אֱלֹהֶיךָ בֵּרַכְךָ בְּכֹל מַעֲשֵׂה יָדֶךָ
hand-of-you work-of in-all-of he-blessed-you God-of-you Yahweh for (7)

יָדַע לֶכְתְּךָ אֶת־ הַמִּדְבָּר הַגָּדֹל הַזֶּה זֶה ׀ אַרְבָּעִים שָׁנָה
year forty this the-this the-vast the-desert *** to-journey-you he-watched

יְהוָה אֱלֹהֶיךָ עִמָּךְ לֹא חָסַרְתָּ דָּבָר׃ וַנַּעֲבֹר מֵאֵת
by so-we-went-past (8) anything you-lacked not with-you God-of-you Yahweh

אַחֵינוּ בְנֵי־ עֵשָׂו הַיֹּשְׁבִים בְּשֵׂעִיר מִדֶּרֶךְ הָעֲרָבָה
the-Arabah from-road-of in-Seir the-ones-living Esau sons-of brothers-of-us

מֵאֵילַת וּמֵעֶצְיֹן גָּבֶר וַנֵּפֶן וַנַּעֲבֹר דֶּרֶךְ מִדְבַּר
desert-of road-of and-we-travelled and-we-turned Geber and-from-Ezion from-Elath

מוֹאָב׃ וַיֹּאמֶר יְהוָה אֵלַי אֶל־* תָּצַר אֶת־ מוֹאָב וְאַל־ תִּתְגָּר
you-provoke and-not Moab *** you-harass not to-me Yahweh then-he-said (9) Moab

בָּם מִלְחָמָה כִּי לֹא־ אֶתֵּן לְךָ מֵאַרְצוֹ יְרֻשָּׁה כִּי
for possession from-land-of-him to-you I-will-give not for war with-them

לִבְנֵי־ לוֹט נָתַתִּי אֶת־ עָר יְרֻשָּׁה׃ הָאֵמִים לְפָנִים יָשְׁבוּ
they-lived before the-Emites (10) possession Ar *** I-gave Lot to-sons-of

בָהּ עַם גָּדוֹל וְרַב וָרָם כַּעֲנָקִים׃ רְפָאִים
Rephaites (11) as-the-Anakites and-tall and-numerous strong people in-her

יֵחָשְׁבוּ אַף־ הֵם כָּעֲנָקִים וְהַמֹּאָבִים יִקְרְאוּ
they-called but-the-Moabites as-the-Anakites they also they-were-considered

לָהֶם אֵמִים׃ וּבְשֵׂעִיר יָשְׁבוּ הַחֹרִים לְפָנִים וּבְנֵי
but-sons-of before the-Horites they-lived and-in-Seir (12) Emites to-them

עֵשָׂו יִירָשׁוּם וַיַּשְׁמִידוּם מִפְּנֵיהֶם
from-before-them and-they-destroyed-them they-drove-out-them Esau

וַיֵּשְׁבוּ תַּחְתָּם כַּאֲשֶׁר עָשָׂה יִשְׂרָאֵל לְאֶרֶץ
in-land-of Israel he-did just-as in-place-of-them and-they-settled

יְרֻשָּׁתוֹ אֲשֶׁר־ נָתַן יְהוָה לָהֶם׃ עַתָּה קֻמוּ וְעִבְרוּ
and-cross! get-up! now (13) to-them Yahweh he-gave that possession-of-him

לָכֶם אֶת־ נַחַל זָרֶד וַנַּעֲבֹר אֶת־ נַחַל זָרֶד׃
Zered Valley-of *** so-we-crossed Zered Valley-of *** for-you

not provoke them to war, for I
will not give you any of their
land, not even enough to put
your foot on. I have given
Esau the hill country of Seir as
his own. [6]You are to pay them
in silver for the food you eat
and the water you drink.' "
[7]The LORD your God has
blessed you in all the work of
your hands. He has watched
over your journey through
this vast desert. These forty
years the LORD your God has
been with you, and you have
not lacked anything.
[8]So we went on past our
brothers the descendants of
Esau, who live in Seir. We
turned from the Arabah road,
which comes up from Elath
and Ezion Geber, and traveled
along the desert road of Moab.
[9]Then the LORD said to me,
"Do not harass the Moabites
or provoke them to war, for I
will not give you any part of
their land. I have given Ar to
the descendants of Lot as a
possession."
[10](The Emites used to live
there—a people strong and numerous, and as tall as the Anakites. [11]Like the Anakites, they
too were considered Re-
phaites, but the Moabites
called them Emites. [12]Horites
used to live in Seir, but the descendants of Esau drove them
out. They destroyed the Horites from before them and settled in their place, just as Israel
did in the land the LORD gave
them as their possession.)
[13]And the LORD said, "Now
get up and cross the Zered Valley." So we crossed the valley.

*9 Most mss have *pathah* under the *aleph* (אַל).

וְהַיָּמִים אֲשֶׁר־הָלַכְנוּ ׀ מִקָּדֵשׁ בַּרְנֵעַ עַד אֲשֶׁר־עָבַרְנוּ אֶת־
*** we-crossed when until Barnea from-Kadesh we-left that and-the-days (14)

נַחַל זֶרֶד שְׁלֹשִׁים וּשְׁמֹנֶה שָׁנָה עַד־ תֹּם כָּל־ הַדּוֹר
the-generation entire-of to-perish then year and-eight thirty Zered Valley-of

אַנְשֵׁי הַמִּלְחָמָה מִקֶּרֶב הַמַּחֲנֶה כַּאֲשֶׁר נִשְׁבַּע יְהוָה לָהֶם׃
to-them Yahweh he-swore just-as the-camp from-among the-war men-of

וְגַם יַד־ יְהוָה הָיְתָה בָּם לְהֻמָּם מִקֶּרֶב
from-among to-eliminate-them against-them she-was Yahweh hand-of and-also (15)

הַמַּחֲנֶה עַד תֻּמָּם׃ וַיְהִי כַאֲשֶׁר־ תַּמּוּ כָל־
all-of they-finished just-as was-he-was (16) to-finish-them until the-camp

אַנְשֵׁי הַמִּלְחָמָה לָמוּת מִקֶּרֶב הָעָם׃ וַיְדַבֵּר יְהוָה אֵלַי
to-me Yahweh then-he-spoke (17) the-people from-among to-die the-war men-of

לֵאמֹר׃ אַתָּה עֹבֵר הַיּוֹם אֶת־ גְּבוּל מוֹאָב אֶת־עָר׃ וְקָרַבְתָּ
when-you-come (19) Ar *** Moab border-of *** the-day passing you (18) to-say

מוּל בְּנֵי עַמּוֹן אַל־ תְּצֻרֵם וְאַל־ תִּתְגָּר בָּם כִּי לֹא־
not for with-them you-make-war and-not you-harass-them not Ammon sons-of to

אֶתֵּן מֵאֶרֶץ בְּנֵי־ עַמּוֹן לְךָ יְרֻשָּׁה כִּי לִבְנֵי־ לוֹט
Lot to-sons-of for possession to-you Ammon sons-of from-land-of I-will-give

נְתַתִּיהָ יְרֻשָּׁה׃ אֶרֶץ־ רְפָאִים תֵּחָשֵׁב אַף־ הִוא
she also she-was-considered Rephaites land-of (20) possession I-gave-her

רְפָאִים יָשְׁבוּ־ בָהּ לְפָנִים וְהָעַמֹּנִים יִקְרְאוּ לָהֶם
to-them they-called but-the-Ammonites before in-her they-lived Rephaites

זַמְזֻמִּים׃ עַם גָּדוֹל וְרַב וָרָם כָּעֲנָקִים
as-the-Anakites and-tall and-numerous strong people (21) Zamzummites

וַיַּשְׁמִידֵם יְהוָה מִפְּנֵיהֶם וַיִּירָשֻׁם
and-they-drove-out-them from-before-them Yahweh but-he-destroyed-them

וַיֵּשְׁבוּ תַחְתָּם׃ כַּאֲשֶׁר עָשָׂה לִבְנֵי עֵשָׂו
Esau for-sons-of he-did just-as (22) in-place-of-them and-they-settled

הַיֹּשְׁבִים בְּשֵׂעִיר אֲשֶׁר הִשְׁמִיד אֶת־ הַחֹרִי מִפְּנֵיהֶם
from-before-them the-Horite *** he-destroyed when in-Seir the-ones-living

וַיִּירָשֻׁם וַיֵּשְׁבוּ תַחְתָּם עַד הַיּוֹם הַזֶּה׃
the-this the-day to in-place-of-them and-they-settled and-they-drove-out-them

וְהָעַוִּים הַיֹּשְׁבִים בַּחֲצֵרִים עַד־ עַזָּה כַּפְתֹּרִים
Caphtorites Gaza as-far-as in-villages the-ones-living and-the-Avvites (23)

הַיֹּצְאִים מִכַּפְתֹּור הִשְׁמִידֻם וַיֵּשְׁבוּ
and-they-settled they-destroyed-them from-Caphtor the-ones-coming

תַחְתָּם׃ קוּמוּ סְּעוּ וְעִבְרוּ אֶת־ נַחַל אַרְנֹן רְאֵה
see! Arnon Gorge-of *** and-cross! set-out! get-up! (24) in-place-of-them

14 Thirty-eight years passed
from the time we left Kadesh
Barnea until we crossed the
Zered Valley. By then, that entire generation of fighting
men had perished from the
camp, as the LORD had sworn
to them. 15 The LORD's hand
was against them until he had
completely eliminated them
from the camp.

16 Now when the last of these
fighting men among the
people had died, 17 the LORD
said to me, 18 "Today you are to
pass by the region of Moab at
Ar. 19 When you come to the
Ammonites, do not harass
them or provoke them to war,
for I will not give you possession of any land belonging to
the Ammonites. I have given
it as a possession to the descendants of Lot."

20 (That too was considered a
land of the Rephaites, who
used to live there; but the Ammonites called them Zamzummites. 21 They were a people
strong and numerous, and as
tall as the Anakites. The LORD
destroyed them from before
the Ammonites, who drove
them out and settled in their
place. 22 The LORD had done the
same for the descendants of
Esau, who lived in Seir, when
he destroyed the Horites from
before them. They drove them
out and have lived in their
place to this day. 23 And as for
the Avvites who lived in villages as far as Gaza, the Caphtorites coming out from Caphtor[c] destroyed them and settled in their place.)

24 "Set out now and cross the

[c]23 That is, Crete

נָתַתִּי בְיָדְךָ אֶת־סִיחֹן מֶלֶךְ־חֶשְׁבּוֹן הָאֱמֹרִי וְאֶת־אַרְצוֹ
land-of-him and the-Amorite Heshbon king-of Sihon *** into-hand-of-you I-gave

הָחֵל רָשׁ וְהִתְגָּר בּוֹ מִלְחָמָה׃ הַיּוֹם הַזֶּה אָחֵל
I-will-begin the-this the-day (25) battle with-him and-fight! possess! begin!

תֵּת פַּחְדְּךָ וְיִרְאָתְךָ עַל־פְּנֵי הָעַמִּים תַּחַת כָּל־
all-of under the-nations faces-of on and-fear-of-you terror-of-you to-put

הַשָּׁמָיִם אֲשֶׁר יִשְׁמְעוּן שִׁמְעֲךָ וְרָגְזוּ
and-they-will-tremble report-of-you they-will-hear that the-heavens

וְחָלוּ מִפָּנֶיךָ׃ וָאֶשְׁלַח מַלְאָכִים
messengers and-I-sent (26) from-presence-of-you and-they-will-be-in-anguish

מִמִּדְבַּר קְדֵמוֹת אֶל־סִיחוֹן מֶלֶךְ חֶשְׁבּוֹן דִּבְרֵי שָׁלוֹם לֵאמֹר׃
to-say peace words-of Heshbon king-of Sihon to Kedemoth from-desert-of

אֶעְבְּרָה בְאַרְצֶךָ בַּדֶּרֶךְ בַּדֶּרֶךְ אֵלֵךְ
I-will-stay on-the-road on-the-road through-land-of-you let-me-pass (27)

לֹא אָסוּר יָמִין וּשְׂמֹאול׃ אֹכֶל בַּכֶּסֶף תַּשְׁבִּרֵנִי
you-sell-me for-the-silver food (28) or-left right I-will-turn not

וְאָכַלְתִּי וּמַיִם בַּכֶּסֶף תִּתֶּן־לִי וְשָׁתִיתִי רַק
only so-I-can-drink to-me you-sell for-the-silver and-waters so-I-can-eat

אֶעְבְּרָה בְרַגְלָי׃ כַּאֲשֶׁר עָשׂוּ־לִי בְּנֵי עֵשָׂו
Esau sons-of for-me they-did just-as (29) on-feet-of-me let-me-pass-through

הַיֹּשְׁבִים בְּשֵׂעִיר וְהַמּוֹאָבִים הַיֹּשְׁבִים בְּעָר עַד אֲשֶׁר־
when until in-Ar the-ones-living and-the-Moabites in-Seir the-ones-living

אֶעֱבֹר אֶת־הַיַּרְדֵּן אֶל־הָאָרֶץ אֲשֶׁר־יְהוָה אֱלֹהֵינוּ נֹתֵן לָנוּ׃
to-us giving God-of-us Yahweh that the-land to the-Jordan *** I-cross

וְלֹא אָבָה סִיחֹן מֶלֶךְ חֶשְׁבּוֹן הַעֲבִרֵנוּ בּוֹ כִּי־
for through-him to-let-pass-us Heshbon king-of Sihon he-allowed but-not (30)

הִקְשָׁה יְהוָה אֱלֹהֶיךָ אֶת־רוּחוֹ וְאִמֵּץ
and-he-made-obstinate spirit-of-him *** God-of-you Yahweh he-made-stubborn

אֶת־לְבָבוֹ לְמַעַן תִּתּוֹ בְיָדְךָ כַּיּוֹם הַזֶּה׃
the-this as-the-day into-hand-of-you to-give-him in-order heart-of-him ***

וַיֹּאמֶר יְהוָה אֵלַי רְאֵה הַחִלֹּתִי תֵּת לְפָנֶיךָ אֶת־סִיחֹן
Sihon *** before-you to-deliver I-began see! to-me Yahweh and-he-said (31)

וְאֶת־אַרְצוֹ הָחֵל רָשׁ לָרֶשֶׁת אֶת־אַרְצוֹ׃ וַיֵּצֵא
when-he-came (32) land-of-him *** to-possess conquer! begin! land-of-him and

סִיחֹן לִקְרָאתֵנוּ הוּא וְכָל־עַמּוֹ לַמִּלְחָמָה יָהְצָה׃
at-Jahaz in-the-battle army-of-him and-all-of he to-meet-us Sihon

וַיִּתְּנֵהוּ יְהוָה אֱלֹהֵינוּ לְפָנֵינוּ וַנַּךְ אֹתוֹ וְאֶת־
and him and-we-struck before-us God-of-us Yahweh then-he-delivered-him (33)

Arnon Gorge. See, I have given into your hand Sihon the Amorite, king of Heshbon, and his country. Begin to take possession of it and engage him in battle. 25This very day I will begin to put the terror and fear of you on all the nations under heaven. They will hear reports of you and will tremble and be in anguish because of you."

*Defeat of Sihon King of Heshbon*

26From the desert of Kedemoth I sent messengers to Sihon king of Heshbon offering peace and saying, 27"Let us pass through your country. We will stay on the main road; we will not turn aside to the right or to the left. 28Sell us food to eat and water to drink for their price in silver. Only let us pass through on foot—29as the descendants of Esau, who live in Seir, and the Moabites, who live in Ar, did for us—until we cross the Jordan into the land the LORD our God is giving us." 30But Sihon king of Heshbon refused to let us pass through. For the LORD your God had made his spirit stubborn and his heart obstinate in order to give him into your hands, as he has now done.

31The LORD said to me, "See, I have begun to deliver Sihon and his country over to you. Now begin to conquer and possess his land."

32When Sihon and all his army came out to meet us in battle at Jahaz, 33the LORD our God delivered him over to us

בָּנָו וְאֶת־ כָּל־ עַמּוֹ׃ וַנִּלְכֹּד אֶת־ כָּל־ עָרָיו
towns-of-him all-of *** and-we-took (34) army-of-him whole-of and sons-of-him

בָּעֵת הַהִוא וַנַּחֲרֵם אֶת־ כָּל־ עִיר מְתִם וְהַנָּשִׁים
and-the-women men city every-of *** and-we-destroyed the-that at-the-time

וְהַטָּף לֹא הִשְׁאַרְנוּ שָׂרִיד׃ רַק הַבְּהֵמָה בָּזַזְנוּ לָנוּ
for-us we-carried-off the-stock but (35) survivor we-left not and-the-child

וּשְׁלַל הֶעָרִים אֲשֶׁר לָכָדְנוּ׃ מֵעֲרֹעֵר אֲשֶׁר עַל־ שְׂפַת־
rim-of on that from-Aroer (36) we-captured that the-towns and-plunder-of

נַחַל אַרְנֹן וְהָעִיר אֲשֶׁר בַּנַּחַל וְעַד־ הַגִּלְעָד לֹא הָיְתָה
she-was not the-Gilead even-to in-the-Gorge that and-the-town Arnon Gorge-of

קִרְיָה אֲשֶׁר שָׂגְבָה מִמֶּנּוּ אֶת־ הַכֹּל נָתַן יְהוָה אֱלֹהֵינוּ
God-of-us Yahweh he-gave the-all *** for-us she-was-too-strong that town

לְפָנֵינוּ׃ רַק אֶל־ אֶרֶץ בְּנֵי־ עַמּוֹן לֹא קָרָבְתָּ כָּל־ יַד
part-of any-of you-encroached not Ammon sons-of land-of on but (37) before-us

נַחַל יַבֹּק וְעָרֵי הָהָר וְכֹל אֲשֶׁר־ צִוָּה יְהוָה
Yahweh he-commanded that and-all the-hill or-cities-of Jabbok course-of

אֱלֹהֵינוּ׃ וַנֵּפֶן וַנַּעַל דֶּרֶךְ הַבָּשָׁן וַיֵּצֵא
and-he-came the-Bashan road-of and-we-went-up next-we-turned (3:1) God-of-us

עוֹג מֶלֶךְ־ הַבָּשָׁן לִקְרָאתֵנוּ הוּא וְכָל־ עַמּוֹ לַמִּלְחָמָה
in-the-battle army-of-him and-whole-of he to-meet-us the-Bashan king-of Og

אֶדְרֶעִי׃ וַיֹּאמֶר יְהוָה אֵלַי אַל־ תִּירָא אֹתוֹ כִּי בְיָדְךָ
into-hand-of-you for him you-fear not to-me Yahweh and-he-said (2) Edrei

נָתַתִּי אֹתוֹ וְאֶת־ כָּל־ עַמּוֹ וְאֶת־ אַרְצוֹ וְעָשִׂיתָ לּוֹ
to-him so-you-do land-of-him and army-of-him whole-of and him I-handed

כַּאֲשֶׁר עָשִׂיתָ לְסִיחֹן מֶלֶךְ הָאֱמֹרִי אֲשֶׁר יוֹשֵׁב בְּחֶשְׁבּוֹן׃
in-Heshbon reigning who the-Arorite king-of to-Sihon you-did just-as

וַיִּתֵּן יְהוָה אֱלֹהֵינוּ בְּיָדֵנוּ גַּם אֶת־ עוֹג מֶלֶךְ־
king-of Og *** also into-hand-of-us God-of-us Yahweh so-he-gave (3)

הַבָּשָׁן וְאֶת־ כָּל־ עַמּוֹ וַנַּכֵּהוּ עַד־ בִּלְתִּי הִשְׁאִיר־
he-remained not until and-we-struck-him army-of-him all-of and the-Bashan

לוֹ שָׂרִיד׃ וַנִּלְכֹּד אֶת־ כָּל־ עָרָיו בָּעֵת הַהִוא
the-that at-the-time cities-of-him all-of *** and-we-took (4) survivor to-him

לֹא הָיְתָה קִרְיָה אֲשֶׁר לֹא־לָקַחְנוּ מֵאִתָּם שִׁשִּׁים עִיר כָּל־ חֶבֶל
region-of whole-of city sixty from-with-them we-took not that city she-was not

אַרְגֹּב מַמְלֶכֶת עוֹג בַּבָּשָׁן׃ כָּל־ אֵלֶּה עָרִים בְּצֻרֹת
ones-fortified cities these all-of (5) in-the-Bashan Og kingdom-of Argob

חוֹמָה גְבֹהָה דְּלָתַיִם וּבְרִיחַ לְבַד מֵעָרֵי הַפְּרָזִי הַרְבֵּה מְאֹד׃
very to-be-many the-villager from-cities-of apart and-bar gates high wall

°33 ק בניו

and we struck him down, together with his sons and his whole army. [34]At that time we took all his towns and completely destroyed[d] them—men, women and children. We left no survivors. [35]But the livestock and the plunder from the towns we had captured we carried off for ourselves. [36]From Aroer on the rim of the Arnon Gorge, and from the town in the gorge, even as far as Gilead, not one town was too strong for us. The LORD our God gave us all of them. [37]But in accordance with the command of the LORD our God, you did not encroach on any of the land of the Ammonites, neither the land along the course of the Jabbok nor that around the towns in the hills.

*Defeat of Og King of Bashan*

3 Next we turned and went up along the road toward Bashan, and Og king of Bashan with his whole army marched out to meet us in battle at Edrei. [2]The LORD said to me, "Do not be afraid of him, for I have handed him over to you with his whole army and his land. Do to him what you did to Sihon king of the Amorites, who reigned in Heshbon."

[3]So the LORD our God also gave into our hands Og king of Bashan and all his army. We struck them down, leaving no survivors. [4]At that time we took all his cities. There was not one of the sixty cities that we did not take from them—the whole region of Argob, Og's kingdom in Bashan. [5]All these cities were fortified with high walls and with gates and bars, and there were also a great many unwalled villages.

[d]34 The Hebrew term refers to the irrevocable giving over of things or persons to the LORD, often by totally destroying them.

וַנַּחֲרֵם אוֹתָם כַּאֲשֶׁר עָשִׂינוּ לְסִיחֹן מֶלֶךְ חֶשְׁבּוֹן הַחֲרֵם
to-destroy Heshbon king-of to-Sihon we-did just-as them and-we-destroyed (6)

כָּל־ עִיר מְתִם הַנָּשִׁים וְהַטָּף׃ וְכָל־ הַבְּהֵמָה
the-livestock but-all-of (7) and-the-child the-women men city every-of

וּשְׁלַל הֶעָרִים בַּזּוֹנוּ לָנוּ׃ וַנִּקַּח בָּעֵת
at-the-time so-we-took (8) for-us we-carried-off the-cities and-plunder-of

הַהִוא אֶת־ הָאָרֶץ מִיַּד שְׁנֵי מַלְכֵי הָאֱמֹרִי אֲשֶׁר בְּעֵבֶר
on-east-of who the-Amorite kings-of two-of from-hand-of the-land *** the-that

הַיַּרְדֵּן מִנַּחַל אַרְנֹן עַד־ הַר חֶרְמוֹן׃ צִידֹנִים
Sidonians (9) Hermon Mount-of as-far-as Arnon from-Gorge-of the-Jordan

יִקְרְאוּ לְחֶרְמוֹן שִׂרְיֹן וְהָאֱמֹרִי יִקְרְאוּ־ לוֹ שְׂנִיר׃ כֹּל
all-of (10) Senir to-him they-call and-the-Amorite Sirion to-Hermon they-call

עָרֵי הַמִּישֹׁר וְכָל־ הַגִּלְעָד וְכָל־ הַבָּשָׁן עַד־
as-far-as the-Bashan and-all-of the-Gilead and-all-of the-plateau towns-of

סַלְכָה וְאֶדְרֶעִי עָרֵי מַמְלֶכֶת עוֹג בַּבָּשָׁן׃ כִּי רַק־ עוֹג
Og only now (11) in-the-Bashan Og kingdom-of towns-of and-Edrei Salecah

מֶלֶךְ הַבָּשָׁן נִשְׁאַר מִיֶּתֶר הָרְפָאִים הִנֵּה עַרְשׂוֹ
bed-of-him see! the-Rephaites from-remnant-of he-was-left the-Bashan king-of

עֶרֶשׂ בַּרְזֶל הֲלֹה הִוא בְּרַבַּת בְּנֵי עַמּוֹן תֵּשַׁע אַמּוֹת אָרְכָּהּ
length-of-her cubits nine Ammon sons-of in-Rabbah-of she not? iron bed-of

וְאַרְבַּע אַמּוֹת רָחְבָּהּ בְּאַמַּת־ אִישׁ׃ וְאֶת־ הָאָרֶץ הַזֹּאת
the-this the-land and (12) man by-forearm-of width-of-her cubits and-four

יָרַשְׁנוּ בָּעֵת הַהִוא מֵעֲרֹעֵר אֲשֶׁר־עַל־ נַחַל אַרְנֹן וַחֲצִי
and-half-of Arnon Gorge-of by that from-Aroer the-that at-the-time we-took

הַר־ הַגִּלְעָד וְעָרָיו נָתַתִּי לָרְאוּבֵנִי*
to-the-Reubenite I-gave and-towns-of-him the-Gilead hill-country-of

וְלַגָּדִי׃ וְיֶתֶר הַגִּלְעָד וְכָל־ הַבָּשָׁן מַמְלֶכֶת
kingdom-of the-Bashan and-all-of the-Gilead and-rest-of (13) and-to-the-Gadite

עוֹג נָתַתִּי לַחֲצִי שֵׁבֶט הַמְנַשֶּׁה כֹּל חֶבֶל הָאַרְגֹּב
the-Argob region-of whole-of the-Manasseh tribe-of to-half-of I-gave Og

לְכָל־ הַבָּשָׁן הַהוּא יִקָּרֵא אֶרֶץ רְפָאִים׃ יָאִיר
Jair (14) Rephaites land-of he-was-called the-this the-Bashan in-all-of

בֶּן־ מְנַשֶּׁה לָקַח אֶת־ כָּל־ חֶבֶל אַרְגֹּב עַד־ גְּבוּל
border-of as-far-as Argob region-of whole-of *** he-took Manasseh son-of

הַגְּשׁוּרִי וְהַמַּעֲכָתִי וַיִּקְרָא אֹתָם עַל־ שְׁמוֹ אֶת־
*** name-of-him by them and-he-called and-the-Maacathite the-Geshurite

הַבָּשָׁן חַוֺּת יָאִיר עַד הַיּוֹם הַזֶּה׃ וּלְמָכִיר נָתַתִּי אֶת־
*** I-gave and-to-Makir (15) the-this the-day to Jair Havvoth the-Bashan

6We completely destroyed[e]
them, as we had done with Sihon king of Heshbon, destroying[e] every city—men, women and children. 7But all the livestock and the plunder from their cities we carried off for ourselves.

8So at that time we took from these two kings of the Amorites the territory east of the Jordan, from the Arnon Gorge as far as Mount Hermon. 9(Hermon is called Sirion by the Sidonians; the Amorites call it Senir.) 10We took all the towns on the plateau, and all Gilead, and all Bashan as far as Salecah and Edrei, towns of Og's kingdom in Bashan. 11(Only Og king of Bashan was left of the remnant of the Rephaites. His bed[f] was made of iron and was more than thirteen feet long and six feet wide.[g] It is still in Rabbah of the Ammonites.)

*Division of the Land*

12Of the land that we took over at that time, I gave the Reubenites and the Gadites the territory north of Aroer by the Arnon Gorge, including half the hill country of Gilead, together with its towns. 13The rest of Gilead and also all of Bashan, the kingdom of Og, I gave to the half tribe of Manasseh. (The whole region of Argob in Bashan used to be known as a land of the Rephaites.) 14Jair, a descendant of Manasseh, took the whole region of Argob as far as the border of the Geshurites and the Maacathites; it was named after him, so that to this day Bashan is called Havvoth Jair.[h] 15And I gave Gilead to Makir.

[e]6 The Hebrew term refers to the irrevocable giving over of things or persons to the LORD, often by totally destroying them.
[f]11 Or *sarcophagus*
[g]11 Hebrew *nine cubits long and four cubits wide* (about 4 meters long and 1.8 meters wide)
[h]14 Or *called the settlements of Jair*

*12 Most mss have no *qibbuts* under the *resh* (לָראוּ׳).

הַגִּלְעָד׃ וְלָרֽאוּבֵנִי וְלַגָּדִי נָתַתִּי מִן־ הַגִּלְעָד
the-Gilead from I-gave and-to-the-Gadite but-to-the-Reubenite (16) the-Gilead

וְעַד־ נַחַל אַרְנֹן תּוֹךְ הַנַּחַל וּגְבֻל וְעַד יַבֹּק הַנַּחַל
the-River Jabbok and-to also-border the-gorge middle-of Arnon Gorge-of and-to

גְּבוּל בְּנֵי עַמּוֹן׃ וְהָעֲרָבָה וְהַיַּרְדֵּן וּגְבֻל
and-border and-the-Jordan and-the-Arabah (17) Ammon sons-of border-of

מִכִּנֶּרֶת וְעַד יָם הָעֲרָבָה יָם הַמֶּלַח תַּחַת אַשְׁדֹּת
slopes-of below the-Salt Sea-of the-Arabah Sea-of even-to from-Kinnereth

הַפִּסְגָּה מִזְרָחָה׃ וָאֲצַו אֶתְכֶם בָּעֵת הַהִוא לֵאמֹר
to-say the-that at-the-time you and-I-commanded (18) on-east the-Pisgah

יְהוָה אֱלֹהֵיכֶם נָתַן לָכֶם אֶת־ הָאָרֶץ הַזֹּאת לְרִשְׁתָּהּ
to-possess-her the-this the-land *** to-you he-gave God-of-you Yahweh

חֲלוּצִים תַּעַבְרוּ לִפְנֵי אֲחֵיכֶם בְּנֵי־ יִשְׂרָאֵל כָּל־
all-of Israel sons-of brothers-of-you ahead-of you-cross-over men-being-armed

בְּנֵי־ חָיִל׃ רַק נְשֵׁיכֶם וְטַפְּכֶם וּמִקְנֵכֶם
and-stock-of-you and-child-of-you wives-of-you however (19) able men-of

יָדַעְתִּי כִּי־ מִקְנֶה רַב לָכֶם יֵשְׁבוּ בְּעָרֵיכֶם אֲשֶׁר נָתַתִּי
I-gave that in-towns-of-you they-may-stay to-you much stock that I-know

לָכֶם׃ עַד אֲשֶׁר־ יָנִיחַ יְהוָה ׀ לַאֲחֵיכֶם כָּכֶם
as-you to-brothers-of-you Yahweh he-gives-rest when until (20) to-you

וְיָרְשׁוּ גַם־ הֵם אֶת־ הָאָרֶץ אֲשֶׁר יְהוָה אֱלֹהֵיכֶם נֹתֵן
giving God-of-you Yahweh that the-land *** they also and-they-take-over

לָהֶם בְּעֵבֶר הַיַּרְדֵּן וְשַׁבְתֶּם אִישׁ לִירֻשָּׁתוֹ
to-possession-of-him each then-you-may-go-back the-Jordan on-across to-them

אֲשֶׁר נָתַתִּי לָכֶם׃ וְאֶת־יְהוֹשׁוּעַ צִוֵּיתִי בָּעֵת הַהִוא לֵאמֹר
to-say the-that at-the-time I-commanded Joshua and (21) to-you I-gave that

עֵינֶיךָ הָרֹאֹת אֵת כָּל־אֲשֶׁר עָשָׂה יְהוָה אֱלֹהֵיכֶם לִשְׁנֵי
to-two-of God-of-you Yahweh he-did that all *** the-ones-seeing eyes-of-you

הַמְּלָכִים הָאֵלֶּה כֵּן־ יַעֲשֶׂה יְהוָה לְכָל־ הַמַּמְלָכוֹת אֲשֶׁר אַתָּה
you that the-kingdoms to-all-of Yahweh he-will-do same the-these the-kings

עֹבֵר שָׁמָּה׃ לֹא תִּירָאוּם כִּי יְהוָה אֱלֹהֵיכֶם הוּא
he God-of-you Yahweh for you-fear-them not (22) to-there ones-going

הַנִּלְחָם לָכֶם׃ וָאֶתְחַנַּן אֶל־ יְהוָה בָּעֵת הַהִוא
the-that at-the-time Yahweh with and-I-pleaded (23) for-you the-one-fighting

לֵאמֹר׃ אֲדֹנָי יְהוִה אַתָּה הַחִלּוֹתָ לְהַרְאוֹת אֶת־ עַבְדְּךָ אֶת־
*** servant-of-you *** to-show you-began you Yahweh Lord (24) to-say

גָּדְלְךָ וְאֶת־ יָדְךָ הַחֲזָקָה אֲשֶׁר מִי־ אֵל בַּשָּׁמַיִם
in-the-heavens god what? for the-strong hand-of-you and greatness-of-you

16But to the Reubenites and the Gadites I gave the territory extending from Gilead down to the Arnon Gorge (the middle of the gorge being the border) and out to the Jabbok River, which is the border of the Ammonites. 17Its western border was the Jordan in the Arabah, from Kinnereth to the Sea of the Arabah (the Salt Sea[i]), below the slopes of Pisgah.

18I commanded you at that time: "The LORD your God has given you this land to take possession of it. But all your able-bodied men, armed for battle, must cross over ahead of your brother Israelites. 19However, your wives, your children and your livestock (I know you have much livestock) may stay in the towns I have given you, 20until the LORD gives rest to your brothers as he has to you, and they too have taken over the land that the LORD your God is giving them, across the Jordan. After that, each of you may go back to the possession I have given you."

### *Moses Forbidden to Cross the Jordan*

21At that time I commanded Joshua: "You have seen with your own eyes all that the LORD your God has done to these two kings. The LORD will do the same to all the kingdoms over there where you are going. 22Do not be afraid of them; the LORD your God himself will fight for you."

23At that time I pleaded with the LORD: 24"O Sovereign LORD, you have begun to show to your servant your greatness and your strong hand. For what god is there in heaven or

[i]17 That is, the Dead Sea

וּבָאָרֶץ אֲשֶׁר־ יַעֲשֶׂה כְמַעֲשֶׂיךָ וְכִגְבוּרֹתֶךָ׃
or-as-mighty-works-of-you as-deeds-of-you he-can-do who or-on-the-earth

אֶעְבְּרָה־ נָּא וְאֶרְאֶה אֶת־ הָאָרֶץ הַטּוֹבָה אֲשֶׁר בְּעֵבֶר
on-beyond that the-good the-land *** so-I-may-see now! let-me-go-over (25)

הַיַּרְדֵּן הָהָר הַטּוֹב הַזֶּה וְהַלְּבָנֹן׃
and-the-Lebanon the-that the-fine the-hill-country the-Jordan

וַיִּתְעַבֵּר יְהוָה בִּי לְמַעַנְכֶם וְלֹא שָׁמַע אֵלָי
to-me he-listened and-not because-of-you with-me Yahweh but-he-was-angry (26)

וַיֹּאמֶר יְהוָה אֵלַי רַב־ לָךְ אַל־ תּוֹסֶף דַּבֵּר אֵלַי עוֹד
anymore to-me to-speak you-repeat not to-you enough to-me Yahweh and-he-said

בַּדָּבָר הַזֶּה׃ עֲלֵה ׀ רֹאשׁ הַפִּסְגָּה וְשָׂא עֵינֶיךָ
eyes-of-you and-lift! the-Pisgah top-of go-up! (27) the-this about-the-matter

יָמָּה וְצָפֹנָה וְתֵימָנָה וּמִזְרָחָה וּרְאֵה בְעֵינֶיךָ
with-eyes-of-you and-look! and-to-east and-to-south and-to-north to-west

כִּי־ לֹא תַעֲבֹר אֶת־ הַיַּרְדֵּן הַזֶּה׃ וְצַו אֶת־
*** but-commission! (28) the-this the-Jordan *** you-will-cross not since

יְהוֹשֻׁעַ וְחַזְּקֵהוּ וְאַמְּצֵהוּ כִּי־ הוּא יַעֲבֹר לִפְנֵי
before he-will-cross he for and-strengthen-him! and-encourage-him! Joshua

הָעָם הַזֶּה וְהוּא יַנְחִיל אוֹתָם אֶת־ הָאָרֶץ אֲשֶׁר
that the-land *** them he-will-make-inherit and-he the-this the-people

תִּרְאֶה׃ וַנֵּשֶׁב בַּגָּיְא מוּל בֵּית פְּעוֹר׃ וְעַתָּה
and-now (4:1) Peor Beth near in-the-valley so-we-stayed (29) you-will-see

יִשְׂרָאֵל שְׁמַע אֶל־ הַחֻקִּים וְאֶל־ הַמִּשְׁפָּטִים אֲשֶׁר אָנֹכִי מְלַמֵּד אֶתְכֶם
you teaching I that the-laws and-to the-decrees to listen! Israel

לַעֲשׂוֹת לְמַעַן תִּחְיוּ וּבָאתֶם וִירִשְׁתֶּם אֶת־ הָאָרֶץ
the-land *** and-you-may-possess and-you-may-go-in you-may-live so-that to-do

אֲשֶׁר יְהוָה אֱלֹהֵי אֲבֹתֵיכֶם נֹתֵן לָכֶם׃ לֹא תֹסִפוּ עַל־ הַדָּבָר
the-word to you-add not (2) to-you giving fathers-of-you God-of Yahweh that

אֲשֶׁר אָנֹכִי מְצַוֶּה אֶתְכֶם וְלֹא תִגְרְעוּ מִמֶּנּוּ לִשְׁמֹר אֶת־ מִצְוֹת
commands-of *** to-keep from-him you-subtract and-not you commanding I that

יְהוָה אֱלֹהֵיכֶם אֲשֶׁר אָנֹכִי מְצַוֶּה אֶתְכֶם׃ עֵינֵיכֶם הָרֹאֹת אֵת
*** the-ones-seeing eyes-of-you (3) you giving I that God-of-you Yahweh

אֲשֶׁר־ עָשָׂה יְהוָה בְּבַעַל פְּעוֹר כִּי כָל־ הָאִישׁ אֲשֶׁר הָלַךְ אַחֲרֵי
after he-followed who the-one every-of that Peor at-Baal Yahweh he-did what

בַעַל־ פְּעוֹר הִשְׁמִידוֹ יְהוָה אֱלֹהֶיךָ מִקִּרְבֶּךָ׃ וְאַתֶּם
but-you (4) from-among-you God-of-you Yahweh he-destroyed-him Peor Baal-of

הַדְּבֵקִים בַּיהוָה אֱלֹהֵיכֶם חַיִּים כֻּלְּכֶם הַיּוֹם׃
the-day all-of-you alive-ones God-of-you to-Yahweh the-ones-holding

on earth who can do the deeds and mighty works you do? [25]Let me go over and see the good land beyond the Jordan—that fine hill country and Lebanon."

[26]But because of you the LORD was angry with me and would not listen to me. "That is enough," the LORD said. "Do not speak to me anymore about this matter. [27]Go up to the top of Pisgah and look west and north and south and east. Look at the land with your own eyes, since you are not going to cross this Jordan. [28]But commission Joshua, and encourage and strengthen him, for he will lead this people across and will cause them to inherit the land that you will see." [29]So we stayed in the valley near Beth Peor.

*Obedience Commanded*

4 Hear now, O Israel, the decrees and laws I am about to teach you. Follow them so that you may live and may go in and take possession of the land that the LORD, the God of your fathers, is giving you. [2]Do not add to what I command you and do not subtract from it, but keep the commands of the LORD your God that I give you.

[3]You saw with your own eyes what the LORD did at Baal Peor. The LORD your God destroyed from among you everyone who followed the Baal of Peor, [4]but all of you who held fast to the LORD your God are still alive today.

(5) רְאֵה ׀ לִמַּדְתִּי אֶתְכֶם חֻקִּים וּמִשְׁפָּטִים כַּאֲשֶׁר צִוַּנִי יְהוָה
Yahweh he-commanded-me just-as and-laws decrees you I-taught see! (5)

אֱלֹהָי לַעֲשׂוֹת כֵּן בְּקֶרֶב הָאָרֶץ אֲשֶׁר אַתֶּם בָּאִים שָׁמָּה
to-there ones-entering you that the-land with-in so to-do God-of-me

לְרִשְׁתָּהּ׃ (6) וּשְׁמַרְתֶּם וַעֲשִׂיתֶם כִּי הִוא חָכְמַתְכֶם
wisdom-of-you this for and-you-observe and-you-be-careful (6) to-possess-her

וּבִינַתְכֶם לְעֵינֵי הָעַמִּים אֲשֶׁר יִשְׁמְעוּן אֵת
*** they-will-hear who the-nations before-eyes-of and-understanding-of-you

כָּל־ הַחֻקִּים הָאֵלֶּה וְאָמְרוּ רַק עַם־ חָכָם
wise people surely and-they-will-say the-these the-decrees all-of

וְנָבוֹן הַגּוֹי הַגָּדוֹל הַזֶּה׃ (7) כִּי מִי־ גוֹי גָּדוֹל
great nation what? for (7) the-this the-great the-nation and-understanding

אֲשֶׁר־ לוֹ אֱלֹהִים קְרֹבִים אֵלָיו כַּיהוָה אֱלֹהֵינוּ בְּכָל־ קָרְאֵנוּ
to-pray-us when-ever-of God-of-us as-Yahweh to-him ones-near gods to-him that

אֵלָיו׃ (8) וּמִי גּוֹי גָּדוֹל אֲשֶׁר־ לוֹ חֻקִּים וּמִשְׁפָּטִים צַדִּיקִם
righteous-ones and-laws decrees to-him that great nation and-what? (8) to-him

כְּכֹל הַתּוֹרָה הַזֹּאת אֲשֶׁר אָנֹכִי נֹתֵן לִפְנֵיכֶם הַיּוֹם׃ (9) רַק
only (9) the-day before-you setting I that the-this the-law as-all-of

הִשָּׁמֶר לְךָ וּשְׁמֹר נַפְשְׁךָ מְאֹד פֶּן־ תִּשְׁכַּח אֶת־
*** you-forget so-not closely self-of-you and-watch! to-you be-careful!

הַדְּבָרִים אֲשֶׁר־ רָאוּ עֵינֶיךָ וּפֶן־ יָסוּרוּ מִלְּבָבְךָ
from-heart-of-you they-slip and-so-not eyes-of-you they-saw that the-things

כֹּל יְמֵי חַיֶּיךָ וְהוֹדַעְתָּם לְבָנֶיךָ וְלִבְנֵי
and-to-sons-of to-sons-of-you and-you-teach-them lives-of-you days-of all-of

בָנֶיךָ׃ (10) יוֹם אֲשֶׁר עָמַדְתָּ לִפְנֵי יְהוָה אֱלֹהֶיךָ בְּחֹרֵב
at-Horeb God-of-you Yahweh before you-stood that day (10) sons-of-you

בֶּאֱמֹר יְהוָה אֵלַי הַקְהֶל־ לִי אֶת־ הָעָם וְאַשְׁמִעֵם
so-I-may-tell-them the-people *** before-me assemble! to-me Yahweh when-to-say

אֶת־ דְּבָרָי אֲשֶׁר יִלְמְדוּן לְיִרְאָה אֹתִי כָּל־ הַיָּמִים אֲשֶׁר הֵם
they that the-days all-of me to-revere they-may-learn that words-of-me ***

חַיִּים עַל־ הָאֲדָמָה וְאֶת־ בְּנֵיהֶם יְלַמֵּדוּן׃ (11) וַתִּקְרְבוּן
and-you-came (11) they-may-teach children-of-them and the-land in ones-alive

וַתַּעַמְדוּן תַּחַת הָהָר וְהָהָר בֹּעֵר בָּאֵשׁ
with-the-fire blazing and-the-mountain the-mountain foot-of and-you-stood

עַד־ לֵב הַשָּׁמַיִם חֹשֶׁךְ עָנָן וַעֲרָפֶל׃ (12) וַיְדַבֵּר יְהוָה
Yahweh then-he-spoke (12) and-darkness cloud black the-heavens heart-of to

אֲלֵיכֶם מִתּוֹךְ הָאֵשׁ קוֹל דְּבָרִים אַתֶּם שֹׁמְעִים וּתְמוּנָה אֵינְכֶם
not-you but-form ones-hearing you words sound-of the-fire out-of to-you

[5]See, I have taught you decrees and laws as the LORD my God commanded me, so that you may follow them in the land you are entering to take possession of it. [6]Observe them carefully, for this will show your wisdom and understanding to the nations, who will hear about all these decrees and say, "Surely this great nation is a wise and understanding people." [7]What other nation is so great as to have their gods near them the way the LORD our God is near us whenever we pray to him? [8]And what other nation is so great as to have such righteous decrees and laws as this body of laws I am setting before you today?

[9]Only be careful, and watch yourselves closely so that you do not forget the things your eyes have seen or let them slip from your heart as long as you live. Teach them to your children and to their children after them. [10]Remember the day you stood before the LORD your God at Horeb, when he said to me, "Assemble the people before me to hear my words so that they may learn to revere me as long as they live in the land and may teach them to their children." [11]You came near and stood at the foot of the mountain while it blazed with fire to the very heavens, with black clouds and deep darkness. [12]Then the LORD spoke to you out of the fire. You heard the sound of words but saw no form; there

רֹאִים זוּלָתִי קוֹל׃ וַיַּגֵּד לָכֶם אֶת־ בְּרִיתוֹ אֲשֶׁר
that covenant-of-him *** to-you and-he-declared (13) voice only ones-seeing

צִוָּה אֶתְכֶם לַעֲשׂוֹת עֲשֶׂרֶת הַדְּבָרִים וַיִּכְתְּבֵם עַל־
on then-he-wrote-them the-commandments ten-of to-follow you he-commanded

שְׁנֵי לֻחוֹת אֲבָנִים׃ וְאֹתִי צִוָּה יְהוָה בָּעֵת הַהִוא
the-that at-the-time Yahweh he-directed and-me (14) stones tablets-of two-of

לְלַמֵּד אֶתְכֶם חֻקִּים וּמִשְׁפָּטִים לַעֲשֹׂתְכֶם אֹתָם בָּאָרֶץ אֲשֶׁר אַתֶּם
you that in-the-land them to-follow-you and-laws decrees you to-teach

עֹבְרִים שָׁמָּה לְרִשְׁתָּהּ׃ וְנִשְׁמַרְתֶּם מְאֹד
carefully and-you-watch (15) to-possess-her to-there ones-crossing

לְנַפְשֹׁתֵיכֶם כִּי לֹא רְאִיתֶם כָּל־ תְּמוּנָה בְּיוֹם דִּבֶּר יְהוָה אֲלֵיכֶם
to-you Yahweh he-spoke on-day form any-of you-saw not for to-selves-of-you

בְּחֹרֵב מִתּוֹךְ הָאֵשׁ׃ פֶּן־ תַּשְׁחִתוּן וַעֲשִׂיתֶם לָכֶם
for-you and-you-make you-become-corrupt so-not (16) the-fire out-of at-Horeb

פֶּסֶל תְּמוּנַת כָּל־ סָמֶל תַּבְנִית זָכָר אוֹ נְקֵבָה׃ תַּבְנִית כָּל־ בְּהֵמָה
animal any-of form-of (17) woman or man form-of shape any-of image-of idol

אֲשֶׁר בָּאָרֶץ תַּבְנִית כָּל־ צִפּוֹר כָּנָף אֲשֶׁר תָּעוּף בַּשָּׁמָיִם׃
in-the-skies she-flies that wing bird-of any-of form-of on-the-earth that

תַּבְנִית כָּל־ רֹמֵשׂ בָּאֲדָמָה תַּבְנִית כָּל־ דָּגָה אֲשֶׁר־
that fish any-of form-of on-the-ground one-moving any-of form-of (18)

בַּמַּיִם מִתַּחַת לָאָרֶץ׃ וּפֶן־ תִּשָּׂא עֵינֶיךָ
eyes-of-you you-lift and-so-not (19) to-the-earth at-below in-the-waters

הַשָּׁמַיְמָה וְרָאִיתָ אֶת־ הַשֶּׁמֶשׁ וְאֶת־ הַיָּרֵחַ וְאֶת־הַכּוֹכָבִים כֹּל
all-of the-stars and the-moon and the-sun *** and-you-see to-the-skies

צְבָא הַשָּׁמַיִם וְנִדַּחְתָּ וְהִשְׁתַּחֲוִיתָ לָהֶם
to-them and-you-bow-down and-you-are-enticed the-heavens array-of

וַעֲבַדְתָּם אֲשֶׁר חָלַק יְהוָה אֱלֹהֶיךָ אֹתָם לְכֹל
to-all-of them God-of-you Yahweh he-apportioned that and-you-worship-them

הָעַמִּים תַּחַת כָּל־ הַשָּׁמָיִם׃ וְאֶתְכֶם לָקַח יְהוָה וַיּוֹצִא
and-he-brought Yahweh he-took but-you (20) the-heavens all-of under the-nations

אֶתְכֶם מִכּוּר הַבַּרְזֶל מִמִּצְרָיִם לִהְיוֹת לוֹ לְעַם נַחֲלָה
inheritance as-people-of to-him to-be from-Egypt the-iron from-furnace-of your

כַּיּוֹם הַזֶּה׃ וַיהוָה הִתְאַנַּף־ בִּי עַל־ דִּבְרֵיכֶם
reasons-of-you for with-me he-was-angry but-Yahweh (21) the-this as-the-day

וַיִּשָּׁבַע לְבִלְתִּי עָבְרִי אֶת־ הַיַּרְדֵּן וּלְבִלְתִּי־ בֹא אֶל־ הָאָרֶץ
the-land into to-enter and-not the-Jordan *** to-cross-me not and-he-swore

הַטּוֹבָה אֲשֶׁר יְהוָה אֱלֹהֶיךָ נֹתֵן לְךָ נַחֲלָה׃ כִּי אָנֹכִי
I now (22) inheritance to-you giving God-of-you Yahweh that the-good

was only a voice. [13]He declared to you his covenant, the Ten Commandments, which he commanded you to follow and then wrote them on two stone tablets. [14]And the LORD directed me at that time to teach you the decrees and laws you are to follow in the land that you are crossing the Jordan to possess.

*Idolatry Forbidden*

[15]You saw no form of any kind the day the LORD spoke to you at Horeb out of the fire. Therefore watch yourselves very carefully, [16]so that you do not become corrupt and make for yourselves an idol, an image of any shape, whether formed like a man or a woman, [17]or like any animal on earth or any bird that flies in the air, [18]or like any creature that moves along the ground or any fish in the water below. [19]And when you look up to the sky and see the sun, the moon and the stars—all the heavenly array—do not be enticed into bowing down to them and worshiping things the LORD your God has apportioned to all the nations under heaven. [20]But as for you, the LORD took you and brought you out of the iron-smelting furnace, out of Egypt, to be the people of his inheritance, as you now are.

[21]The LORD was angry with me because of you, and he solemnly swore that I would not cross the Jordan and enter the good land the LORD your God is giving you as your inheritance. [22]I will die in this land;

מֵת בָּאָרֶץ הַזֹּאת אֵינֶנִּי עֹבֵר אֶת־ הַיַּרְדֵּן וְאַתֶּם עֹבְרִים
ones-crossing but-you the-Jordan *** crossing not-I the-this in-the-land dying

וִירִשְׁתֶּם אֶת־ הָאָרֶץ הַטּוֹבָה הַזֹּאת׃ הִשָּׁמְרוּ לָכֶם
to-you be-careful! (23) the-this the-good the-land *** and-you-will-possess

פֶּן־ תִּשְׁכְּחוּ אֶת־ בְּרִית יְהוָה אֱלֹהֵיכֶם אֲשֶׁר כָּרַת עִמָּכֶם
with-you he-made that God-of-you Yahweh covenant-of *** you-forget so-not

וַעֲשִׂיתֶם לָכֶם פֶּסֶל תְּמוּנַת כֹּל אֲשֶׁר צִוְּךָ יְהוָה
Yahweh he-forbade-you that anything form-of idol for-you and-you-make

אֱלֹהֶיךָ׃ כִּי יְהוָה אֱלֹהֶיךָ אֵשׁ אֹכְלָה הוּא אֵל קַנָּא׃ כִּי־
after (25) jealous God he consuming fire God-of-you Yahweh for (24) God-of-you

תוֹלִיד בָּנִים וּבְנֵי בָנִים וְנוֹשַׁנְתֶּם בָּאָרֶץ
in-the-land and-you-live children and-children-of children you-bear

וְהִשְׁחַתֶּם וַעֲשִׂיתֶם פֶּסֶל תְּמוּנַת כֹּל וַעֲשִׂיתֶם הָרַע
the-evil and-you-do anything form-of idol and-you-make if-you-become-corrupt

בְּעֵינֵי יְהוָה־ אֱלֹהֶיךָ לְהַכְעִיסוֹ׃ הַעִידֹתִי בָכֶם
against-you I-call-witness (26) to-make-angry-him God-of-you Yahweh in-eyes-of

הַיּוֹם אֶת־ הַשָּׁמַיִם וְאֶת־ הָאָרֶץ כִּי־ אָבֹד תֹּאבֵדוּן מַהֵר
quickly you-will-perish to-perish that the-earth and the-heavens *** the-day

מֵעַל הָאָרֶץ אֲשֶׁר אַתֶּם עֹבְרִים אֶת־ הַיַּרְדֵּן שָׁמָּה לְרִשְׁתָּהּ
to-possess-her to-there the-Jordan *** ones-crossing you that the-land from-on

לֹא־ תַאֲרִיכֻן יָמִים עָלֶיהָ כִּי הִשָּׁמֵד תִּשָּׁמֵדוּן׃
you-will-be-destroyed to-be-destroyed but on-her days you-will-live-long not

וְהֵפִיץ יְהוָה אֶתְכֶם בָּעַמִּים וְנִשְׁאַרְתֶּם
and-you-will-survive among-the-peoples you Yahweh and-he-will-scatter (27)

מְתֵי מִסְפָּר בַּגּוֹיִם אֲשֶׁר יְנַהֵג יְהוָה אֶתְכֶם שָׁמָּה׃
to-there you Yahweh he-will-drive which among-the-nations number few-ones-of

וַעֲבַדְתֶּם־ שָׁם אֱלֹהִים מַעֲשֵׂה יְדֵי אָדָם עֵץ וָאֶבֶן אֲשֶׁר
which and-stone wood man hands-of made-of gods there and-you-will-worship (28)

לֹא־ יִרְאוּן וְלֹא יִשְׁמְעוּן וְלֹא יֹאכְלוּן וְלֹא יְרִיחֻן׃
they-smell and-not they-eat and-not they-hear and-not they-see not

וּבִקַּשְׁתֶּם מִשָּׁם אֶת־ יְהוָה אֱלֹהֶיךָ וּמָצָאתָ כִּי
if then-you-will-find God-of-you Yahweh *** from-there if-you-seek (29)

תִדְרְשֶׁנּוּ בְּכָל־ לְבָבְךָ וּבְכָל־ נַפְשֶׁךָ׃
soul-of-you and-with-all-of heart-of-you with-all-of you-look-for-him

בַּצַּר לְךָ וּמְצָאוּךָ כֹּל הַדְּבָרִים
the-things all-of and-they-happen-to-you to-you when-the-distress (30)

הָאֵלֶּה בְּאַחֲרִית הַיָּמִים וְשַׁבְתָּ עַד־ יְהוָה אֱלֹהֶיךָ
God-of-you Yahweh to then-you-will-return the-days in-later-of the-these

I will not cross the Jordan; but you are about to cross over and take possession of that good land. 23Be careful not to forget the covenant of the LORD your God that he made with you; do not make for yourselves an idol in the form of anything the LORD your God has forbidden. 24For the LORD your God is a consuming fire, a jealous God.

25After you have had children and grandchildren and have lived in the land a long time—if you then become corrupt and make any kind of idol, doing evil in the eyes of the LORD your God and provoking him to anger, 26I call heaven and earth as witnesses against you this day that you will quickly perish from the land that you are crossing the Jordan to possess. You will not live there long but will certainly be destroyed. 27The LORD will scatter you among the peoples, and only a few of you will survive among the nations to which the LORD will drive you. 28There you will worship man-made gods of wood and stone, which cannot see or hear or eat or smell. 29But if from there you seek the LORD your God, you will find him if you look for him with all your heart and with all your soul. 30When you are in distress and all these things have happened to you, then in later days you will return to the LORD your God and obey him.

וְשָׁמַעְתָּ בְּקֹלוֹ׃ כִּי אֵל רַחוּם יְהוָה אֱלֹהֶיךָ
God-of-you Yahweh merciful God for (31) to-voice-of-him and-you-will-obey

לֹא יַרְפְּךָ וְלֹא יַשְׁחִיתֶךָ וְלֹא יִשְׁכַּח
he-will-forget and-not he-will-destroy-you and-not he-will-abandon-you not

אֶת־ בְּרִית אֲבֹתֶיךָ אֲשֶׁר נִשְׁבַּע לָהֶם׃ כִּי שְׁאַל־
ask! indeed (32) with-them he-confirmed that fathers-of-you covenant-of ***

נָא לְיָמִים רִאשֹׁנִים אֲשֶׁר־ הָיוּ לְפָנֶיךָ לְמִן־ הַיּוֹם
the-day about-from before-you they-were that former-ones about-days now!

אֲשֶׁר בָּרָא אֱלֹהִים ׀ אָדָם עַל־ הָאָרֶץ וּלְמִקְצֵה הַשָּׁמַיִם
the-heavens and-about-from-end-of the-earth on man God he-created when

וְעַד־ קְצֵה הַשָּׁמָיִם הֲנִהְיָה כַּדָּבָר הַגָּדוֹל הַזֶּה
the-this the-great like-the-thing has-he-happened? the-heavens end-of even-to

אוֹ הֲנִשְׁמַע כָּמֹהוּ׃ הֲשָׁמַע עָם קוֹל אֱלֹהִים
God voice-of people has-he-heard? (33) like-him has-he-been-heard? or

מְדַבֵּר מִתּוֹךְ־ הָאֵשׁ כַּאֲשֶׁר־ שָׁמַעְתָּ אַתָּה וַיֶּחִי׃ אוֹ ׀
or (34) and-he-lived you you-heard just-as the-fire out-of speaking

הֲנִסָּה אֱלֹהִים לָבוֹא לָקַחַת לוֹ גוֹי מִקֶּרֶב גּוֹי בְּמַסֹּת
by-tests nation out-of nation for-him to-take to-go god has-he-tried?

בְּאֹתֹת וּבְמוֹפְתִים וּבְמִלְחָמָה וּבְיָד חֲזָקָה וּבִזְרוֹעַ
and-by-arm mighty and-by-hand and-by-war and-by-wonders by-signs

נְטוּיָה וּבְמוֹרָאִים גְּדֹלִים כְּכֹל אֲשֶׁר־ עָשָׂה
he-did that like-all great-ones or-by-awesome-deeds being-outstretched

לָכֶם יְהוָה אֱלֹהֵיכֶם בְּמִצְרַיִם לְעֵינֶיךָ׃ אַתָּה הָרְאֵתָ
you-were-shown you (35) before-eyes-of-you in-Egypt God-of-you Yahweh for-you

לָדַעַת כִּי יְהוָה הוּא הָאֱלֹהִים אֵין עוֹד מִלְּבַדּוֹ׃ מִן־
from (36) besides-him other there-is-no the-God he Yahweh that to-know

הַשָּׁמַיִם הִשְׁמִיעֲךָ אֶת־ קֹלוֹ לְיַסְּרֶךָּ וְעַל־
and-on to-discipline-you voice-of-him *** he-made-hear-you the-heavens

הָאָרֶץ הֶרְאֲךָ אֶת־ אִשּׁוֹ הַגְּדוֹלָה וּדְבָרָיו שָׁמַעְתָּ
you-heard and-words-of-him the-great fire-of-him *** he-showed-you the-earth

מִתּוֹךְ הָאֵשׁ׃ וְתַחַת כִּי אָהַב אֶת־ אֲבֹתֶיךָ
fathers-of-you *** he-loved that and-because (37) the-fire from-out-of

וַיִּבְחַר בְּזַרְעוֹ אַחֲרָיו וַיּוֹצִאֲךָ
then-he-brought-you after-him in-descendant-of-him and-he-chose

בְּפָנָיו בְּכֹחוֹ הַגָּדֹל מִמִּצְרָיִם׃ לְהוֹרִישׁ
to-drive-out (38) from-Egypt the-great by-strength-of-him by-Presences-of-him

גּוֹיִם גְּדֹלִים וַעֲצֻמִים מִמְּךָ מִפָּנֶיךָ לַהֲבִיאֲךָ
to-bring-you from-before-you than-you and-stronger-ones greater-ones nations

[31]For the LORD your God is a merciful God; he will not abandon or destroy you or forget the covenant with your forefathers, which he confirmed to them by oath.

*The LORD Is God*

[32]Ask now about the former days, long before your time, from the day God created man on the earth; ask from one end of the heavens to the other. Has anything so great as this ever happened, or has anything like it ever been heard of? [33]Has any other people heard the voice of God[j] speaking out of fire, as you have, and lived? [34]Has any god ever tried to take for himself one nation out of another nation, by testings, by miraculous signs and wonders, by war, by a mighty hand and an outstretched arm, or by great and awesome deeds, like all the things the LORD your God did for you in Egypt before your very eyes?

[35]You were shown these things so that you might know that the LORD is God; besides him there is no other. [36]From heaven he made you hear his voice to discipline you. On earth he showed you his great fire, and you heard his words from out of the fire. [37]Because he loved your forefathers and chose their descendants after them, he brought you out of Egypt by his Presence and his great strength, [38]to drive out before you nations greater and stronger than you and to bring

j33 *Or of a god*

לָתֶת־ לְךָ אֶת־ אַרְצָם נַחֲלָה כַּיּוֹם הַזֶּה׃

the-this as-the-day inheritance land-of-them *** to-you to-give

וְיָדַעְתָּ הַיּוֹם וַהֲשֵׁבֹתָ אֶל־ לְבָבֶךָ כִּי יְהוָה הוּא

he Yahweh that heart-of-you to and-you-take the-day so-you-acknowledge (39)

הָאֱלֹהִים בַּשָּׁמַיִם מִמַּעַל וְעַל־ הָאָרֶץ מִתָּחַת אֵין עוֹד׃

other there-is-no at-below the-earth and-on from-above in-the-heavens the-God

וְשָׁמַרְתָּ אֶת־ חֻקָּיו וְאֶת־ מִצְוֹתָיו אֲשֶׁר אָנֹכִי מְצַוְּךָ

giving-you I which commands-of-him and decrees-of-him *** and-you-keep (40)

הַיּוֹם אֲשֶׁר יִיטַב לְךָ וּלְבָנֶיךָ אַחֲרֶיךָ

after-you and-with-children-of-you with-you he-may-go-well that the-day

וּלְמַעַן תַּאֲרִיךְ יָמִים עַל־הָאֲדָמָה אֲשֶׁר יְהוָה אֱלֹהֶיךָ נֹתֵן

giving God-of-you Yahweh that the-land in days you-may-live-long and-so-that

לְךָ כָּל־ הַיָּמִים׃ אָז יַבְדִּיל מֹשֶׁה שָׁלֹשׁ עָרִים בְּעֵבֶר

on-east-of cities three Moses he-set-aside then (41) the-days all-of to-you

הַיַּרְדֵּן מִזְרְחָה שָׁמֶשׁ׃ לָנֻס שָׁמָּה רוֹצֵחַ אֲשֶׁר יִרְצַח

he-killed who one-killing to-there to-flee (42) sun toward-rise-of the-Jordan

אֶת־ רֵעֵהוּ בִּבְלִי־ דַעַת וְהוּא לֹא־ שֹׂנֵא לוֹ

against-him having-malice not and-he knowledge without neighbor-of-him ***

מִתְּמֹול שִׁלְשֹׁום וְנָס אֶל־ אַחַת מִן־ הֶעָרִים הָאֵל

the-these the-cites from one to and-he-could-flee previously from-before

וָחָי׃ אֶת־ בֶּצֶר בַּמִּדְבָּר בְּאֶרֶץ הַמִּישֹׁר

the-plateau in-land-of in-the-desert Bezer *** (43) and-he-would-live

לָרֻאוּבֵנִי* וְאֶת־ רָאמֹת בַּגִּלְעָד לַגָּדִי וְאֶת־ גּוֹלָן

Golan and for-the-Gadite in-the-Gilead Ramoth and for-the-Reubenite

בַּבָּשָׁן לַמְנַשִּׁי׃ וְזֹאת הַתּוֹרָה אֲשֶׁר־ שָׂם מֹשֶׁה

Moses he-set that the-law and-this (44) for-the-Manassite in-the-Bashan

לִפְנֵי בְּנֵי יִשְׂרָאֵל׃ אֵלֶּה הָעֵדֹת וְהַחֻקִּים וְהַמִּשְׁפָּטִים

and-the-laws and-the-decrees the-stipulations these (45) Israel sons-of before

אֲשֶׁר דִּבֶּר מֹשֶׁה אֶל־ בְּנֵי יִשְׂרָאֵל בְּצֵאתָם מִמִּצְרָיִם׃

from-Egypt when-to-come-them Israel sons-of to Moses he-gave that

בְּעֵבֶר הַיַּרְדֵּן בַּגַּיְא מוּל בֵּית פְּעוֹר בְּאֶרֶץ סִיחֹן

Sihon in-land-of Peor Beth near in-the-valley the-Jordan on-east-of (46)

מֶלֶךְ הָאֱמֹרִי אֲשֶׁר יוֹשֵׁב בְּחֶשְׁבּוֹן אֲשֶׁר הִכָּה מֹשֶׁה וּבְנֵי

and-sons-of Moses he-defeated whom in-Heshbon reigning who the-Amorite king-of

יִשְׂרָאֵל בְּצֵאתָם מִמִּצְרָיִם׃ וַיִּירְשׁוּ אֶת־ אַרְצוֹ וְאֶת־

and land-of-him *** and-they-possessed (47) from-Egypt as-to-come-them Israel

אֶרֶץ ׀ עוֹג מֶלֶךְ־ הַבָּשָׁן שְׁנֵי מַלְכֵי הָאֱמֹרִי אֲשֶׁר בְּעֵבֶר

on-east-of who the-Amorite kings-of two-of the-Bashan king-of Og land-of

you into their land to give it to you for your inheritance, as it is today.

39 Acknowledge and take to heart this day that the LORD is God in heaven above and on the earth below. There is no other. 40 Keep his decrees and commands, which I am giving you today, so that it may go well with you and your children after you and that you may live long in the land the LORD your God gives you for all time.

*Cities of Refuge*

41 Then Moses set aside three cities east of the Jordan, 42 where anyone who had killed a person could flee if he had unintentionally killed his neighbor without malice aforethought. He could flee into one of these cities and save his life. 43 The cities were these: Bezer in the desert plateau, for the Reubenites; Ramoth in Gilead, for the Gadites; and Golan in Bashan, for the Manassites.

*Introduction to the Law*

44 This is the law Moses set before the Israelites. 45 These are the stipulations, decrees and laws Moses gave them when they came out of Egypt 46 and were in the valley near Beth Peor east of the Jordan, in the land of Sihon king of the Amorites, who reigned in Heshbon and was defeated by Moses and the Israelites as they came out of Egypt. 47 They took possession of his land and the land of Og king of Bashan, the two Amorite kings

*43 Most mss have no *qibbuts* under the *resh* (לְראוּ׳).

הַיַּרְדֵּן מִזְרַח שָׁמֶשׁ׃ מֵעֲרֹעֵר אֲשֶׁר עַל־שְׂפַת־ נַחַל אַרְנֹן וְעַד־
and-to Arnon Gorge-of rim-of on that from-Aroer (48) sun rise-of the-Jordan

הַר שִׂיאֹן הוּא חֶרְמוֹן׃ וְכָל־ הָעֲרָבָה עֵבֶר הַיַּרְדֵּן
the-Jordan east-of the-Arabah and-all-of (49) Hermon that Siyon Mount-of

מִזְרָחָה וְעַד יָם הָעֲרָבָה תַּחַת אַשְׁדֹּת הַפִּסְגָּה׃
the-Pisgah slopes-of below the-Arabah Sea-of as-far-as to-east

וַיִּקְרָא מֹשֶׁה אֶל־ כָּל־ יִשְׂרָאֵל וַיֹּאמֶר אֲלֵהֶם שְׁמַע
hear! to-them and-he-said Israel all-of to Moses and-he-summoned (5:1)

יִשְׂרָאֵל אֶת־ הַחֻקִּים וְאֶת־הַמִּשְׁפָּטִים אֲשֶׁר אָנֹכִי דֹּבֵר בְּאָזְנֵיכֶם הַיּוֹם
the-day in-ears-of-you declaring I that the-laws and the-decrees *** Israel

וּלְמַדְתֶּם אֹתָם וּשְׁמַרְתֶּם לַעֲשֹׂתָם׃ יְהוָה אֱלֹהֵינוּ
God-of-us Yahweh (2) to-follow-them and-you-be-certain them so-you-learn

כָּרַת עִמָּנוּ בְּרִית בְּחֹרֵב׃ לֹא אֶת־ אֲבֹתֵינוּ כָּרַת יְהוָה
Yahweh he-made fathers-of-us with not (3) at-Horeb covenant with-us he-made

אֶת־ הַבְּרִית הַזֹּאת כִּי אִתָּנוּ אֲנַחְנוּ אֵלֶּה פֹה הַיּוֹם כֻּלָּנוּ
all-of-us the-day here these we with-us but the-this the-covenant ***

חַיִּים׃ פָּנִים ׀ בְּפָנִים דִּבֶּר יְהוָה עִמָּכֶם בָּהָר מִתּוֹךְ
out-of on-the-mountain to-you Yahweh he-spoke to-faces faces (4) ones-alive

הָאֵשׁ׃ אָנֹכִי עֹמֵד בֵּין־ יְהוָה וּבֵינֵיכֶם בָּעֵת הַהִוא
the-that at-the-time and-between-you Yahweh between standing I (5) the-fire

לְהַגִּיד לָכֶם אֶת־ דְּבַר יְהוָה כִּי יְרֵאתֶם מִפְּנֵי
of-presence-of you-were-afraid for Yahweh word-of *** to-you to-declare

הָאֵשׁ וְלֹא־ עֲלִיתֶם בָּהָר לֵאמֹר׃ אָנֹכִי יְהוָה אֱלֹהֶיךָ
God-of-you Yahweh I (6) to-say on-the-mountain you-went-up and-not the-fire

אֲשֶׁר הוֹצֵאתִיךָ מֵאֶרֶץ מִצְרַיִם מִבֵּית עֲבָדִים׃ לֹא
not (7) slaveries from-house-of Egypt from-land-of I-brought-you who

יִהְיֶה־ לְךָ אֱלֹהִים אֲחֵרִים עַל־ פָּנָיַ׃ לֹא־ תַעֲשֶׂה־
you-shall-make not (8) faces-of-me before other-ones gods to-you he-shall-be

לְךָ פֶסֶל ׀ כָּל־ תְּמוּנָה אֲשֶׁר בַּשָּׁמַיִם ׀ מִמַּעַל וַאֲשֶׁר בָּאָרֶץ
on-the-earth or-that from-above in-the-heavens that form any-of idol for-you

מִתָּחַת וַאֲשֶׁר בַּמַּיִם ׀ מִתַּחַת לָאָרֶץ׃ לֹא־ תִשְׁתַּחֲוֶה
you-shall-bow not (9) to-the-earth at-below in-the-waters or-that at-beneath

לָהֶם וְלֹא תָעָבְדֵם כִּי אָנֹכִי יְהוָה אֱלֹהֶיךָ אֵל קַנָּא
jealous God God-of-you Yahweh I for you-shall-worship-them and-not to-them

פֹּקֵד עֲוֹן אָבוֹת עַל־ בָּנִים וְעַל־ שִׁלֵּשִׁים וְעַל־ רִבֵּעִים
fourth-ones and-to third-ones even-to children on fathers sin-of punishing

לְשֹׂנְאָי׃ וְעֹשֶׂה חֶסֶד לַאֲלָפִים לְאֹהֲבַי
to-ones-loving-me to-thousands love but-showing (10) to-ones-hating-me

east of the Jordan. 48This land extended from Aroer on the rim of the Arnon Gorge to Mount Siyon[k] (that is, Hermon), 49and included all the Arabah east of the Jordan, as far as the Sea of the Arabah,[l] below the slopes of Pisgah.

*The Ten Commandments*

5 Moses summoned all Israel and said:

Hear, O Israel, the decrees and laws I declare in your hearing today. Learn them and be sure to follow them. 2The LORD our God made a covenant with us at Horeb. 3It was not with our fathers that the LORD made this covenant, but with us, with all of us who are alive here today. 4The LORD spoke to you face to face out of the fire on the mountain. 5(At that time I stood between the LORD and you to declare to you the word of the LORD, because you were afraid of the fire and did not go up the mountain.) And he said:

6"I am the LORD your God, who brought you out of Egypt, out of the land of slavery.

7"You shall have no other gods before[m] me.

8"You shall not make for yourself an idol in the form of anything in heaven above or on the earth beneath or in the waters below. 9You shall not bow down to them or worship them; for I, the LORD your God, am a jealous God, punishing the children for the sin of the fathers to the third and fourth generation of those who hate me, 10but showing love to thousands who love me and

[k]48 Hebrew; Syriac (see also Deut. 3:9) *Sirion*
[l]49 That is, the Dead Sea
[m]7 Or *besides*

וּלְשֹׁמְרֵי מִצְוֹתָו׃ לֹא תִשָּׂא אֶת־ שֵׁם־
name-of *** you-shall-take not (11) commands-of-me and-to-ones-keeping-of

יְהוָה אֱלֹהֶיךָ לַשָּׁוְא כִּי לֹא יְנַקֶּה יְהוָה אֵת
*** Yahweh he-will-hold-guiltless not for for-the-misuse God-of-you Yahweh

אֲשֶׁר־ יִשָּׂא אֶת־ שְׁמוֹ לַשָּׁוְא׃ שָׁמוֹר אֶת־ יוֹם
day-of *** to-observe (12) for-the-misuse name-of-him *** he-takes who

הַשַּׁבָּת לְקַדְּשׁוֹ כַּאֲשֶׁר צִוְּךָ ׀ יְהוָה אֱלֹהֶיךָ
God-of-you Yahweh he-commanded-you just-as to-keep-holy-him the-Sabbath

שֵׁשֶׁת יָמִים תַּעֲבֹד וְעָשִׂיתָ כָּל־ מְלַאכְתֶּךָ׃
work-of-you all-of and-you-shall-do you-shall-labor days six-of (13)

וְיוֹם הַשְּׁבִיעִי שַׁבָּת ׀ לַיהוָה אֱלֹהֶיךָ לֹא תַעֲשֶׂה
you-shall-do not God-of-you to-Yahweh Sabbath the-seventh but-day-of (14)

כָל־ מְלָאכָה אַתָּה וּבִנְךָ־ וּבִתֶּךָ וְעַבְדְּךָ־
or-manservant-of-you or-daughter-of-you or-son-of-you you work any-of

וַאֲמָתֶךָ וְשׁוֹרְךָ וַחֲמֹרְךָ וְכָל־ בְּהֶמְתֶּךָ
animal-of-you or-any-of or-donkey-of-you or-ox-of-you or-maidservant-of-you

וְגֵרְךָ אֲשֶׁר בִּשְׁעָרֶיךָ לְמַעַן יָנוּחַ עַבְדְּךָ
manservant-of-you he-may-rest so-that within-gates-of-you who or-alien-of-you

וַאֲמָתְךָ כָּמוֹךָ׃ וְזָכַרְתָּ כִּי־ עֶבֶד הָיִיתָ ׀
you-were slave that and-you-remember (15) as-you and-maidservant-of-you

בְּאֶרֶץ מִצְרַיִם וַיֹּצִאֲךָ יְהוָה אֱלֹהֶיךָ מִשָּׁם בְּיָד
with-hand from-there God-of-you Yahweh and-he-brought-you Egypt in-land-of

חֲזָקָה וּבִזְרֹעַ נְטוּיָה עַל־ כֵּן צִוְּךָ יְהוָה
Yahweh he-commanded-you this for being-outstretched and-with-arm mighty

אֱלֹהֶיךָ לַעֲשׂוֹת אֶת־ יוֹם הַשַּׁבָּת׃ כַּבֵּד אֶת־ אָבִיךָ
father-of-you *** honor! (16) the-Sabbath day-of *** to-observe God-of-you

וְאֶת־ אִמֶּךָ כַּאֲשֶׁר צִוְּךָ יְהוָה אֱלֹהֶיךָ לְמַעַן ׀
so-that God-of-you Yahweh he-commanded-you just-as mother-of-you and

יַאֲרִיכֻן יָמֶיךָ וּלְמַעַן יִיטַב לָךְ עַל הָאֲדָמָה
the-land in with-you he-may-go-well and-so-that days-of-you they-may-be-long

אֲשֶׁר־ יְהוָה אֱלֹהֶיךָ נֹתֵן לָךְ׃ לֹא תִּרְצָח׃ וְלֹא
and-not (18) you-shall-murder not (17)* to-you giving God-of-you Yahweh that

תִּנְאָף׃ וְלֹא תִּגְנֹב׃ וְלֹא־ תַעֲנֶה
you-give and-not (20) you-shall-steal and-not (19) you-shall-commit-adultery

בְרֵעֲךָ עֵד שָׁוְא׃ וְלֹא תַחְמֹד אֵשֶׁת
wife-of you-shall-covet and-not (21) false testimony against-neighbor-of-you

רֵעֶךָ וְלֹא תִתְאַוֶּה בֵּית רֵעֶךָ שָׂדֵהוּ
land-of-him neighbor-of-you house-of you-shall-desire and-not neighbor-of-you

keep my commandments.

[11]"You shall not misuse the name of the LORD your God, for the LORD will not hold anyone guiltless who misuses his name.

[12]"Observe the Sabbath day by keeping it holy, as the LORD your God has commanded you. [13]Six days you shall labor and do all your work, [14]but the seventh day is a Sabbath to the LORD your God. On it you shall not do any work, neither you, nor your son or daughter, nor your manservant or maidservant, nor your ox, your donkey or any of your animals, nor the alien within your gates, so that your manservant and maidservant may rest, as you do. [15]Remember that you were slaves in Egypt and that the LORD your God brought you out of there with a mighty hand and an outstretched arm. Therefore the LORD your God has commanded you to observe the Sabbath day.

[16]"Honor your father and your mother, as the LORD your God has commanded you, so that you may live long and that it may go well with you in the land the LORD your God is giving you.

[17]"You shall not murder.

[18]"You shall not commit adultery.

[19]"You shall not steal.

[20]"You shall not give false testimony against your neighbor.

[21]"You shall not covet your neighbor's wife. You shall not set your desire on your neighbor's house

*Most Hebrew texts incorporate verses 17 through 20 into one verse, thus causing a three-verse discrepancy through the rest of this chapter. As BHS follows the English numeration rather than the Hebrew, so does the interlinear text.

°10 ק מצותי

וְעַבְדּוֹ וַאֲמָתוֹ שׁוֹרוֹ וַחֲמֹרוֹ
or-donkey-of-him ox-of-him or-maidservant-of-him or-manservant-of-him

וְכֹל אֲשֶׁר לְרֵעֶךָ׃ אֶת־ הַדְּבָרִים הָאֵלֶּה
the-these the-commandments *** (22) to-neighbor-of-you that or-anything

דִּבֶּר יְהוָה אֶל־ כָּל־ קְהַלְכֶם בָּהָר מִתּוֹךְ
from-out-of on-the-mountain assembly-of-you whole-of to Yahweh he-proclaimed

הָאֵשׁ הֶעָנָן וְהָעֲרָפֶל קוֹל גָּדוֹל וְלֹא יָסָף
he-added and-nothing loud voice and-the-darkness the-cloud the-fire

וַיִּכְתְּבֵם עַל־ שְׁנֵי לֻחֹת אֲבָנִים וַיִּתְּנֵם אֵלָי׃
to-me and-he-gave-them stones tablets-of two-of on and-he-wrote-them

וַיְהִי כְּשָׁמְעֲכֶם אֶת־ הַקּוֹל מִתּוֹךְ הַחֹשֶׁךְ
the-darkness from-out-of the-voice *** when-to-hear-you and-he-was (23)

וְהָהָר בֹּעֵר בָּאֵשׁ וַתִּקְרְבוּן אֵלַי כָּל־ רָאשֵׁי
leaders-of all-of to-me and-you-came with-the-fire blazing and-the-mountain

שִׁבְטֵיכֶם וְזִקְנֵיכֶם׃ וַתֹּאמְרוּ הֵן הֶרְאָנוּ יְהוָה
Yahweh he-showed-us see! and-you-said (24) and-elders-of-you tribes-of-you

אֱלֹהֵינוּ אֶת־ כְּבֹדוֹ וְאֶת־ גָּדְלוֹ וְאֶת־ קֹלוֹ שָׁמַעְנוּ
we-heard voice-of-him and majesty-of-him and glory-of-him *** God-of-us

מִתּוֹךְ הָאֵשׁ הַיּוֹם הַזֶּה רָאִינוּ כִּי־ יְדַבֵּר אֱלֹהִים אֶת־ הָאָדָם
the-man with God he-speaks that we-saw the-this the-day the-fire out-of

וָחָי׃ וְעַתָּה לָמָּה נָמוּת כִּי תֹאכְלֵנוּ הָאֵשׁ
the-fire she-will-consume-us for should-we-die why? but-now (25) yet-he-lives

הַגְּדֹלָה הַזֹּאת אִם־ יֹסְפִים ׀ אֲנַחְנוּ לִשְׁמֹעַ אֶת־ קוֹל יְהוָה
Yahweh voice-of *** to-hear we ones-continuing if the-this the-great

אֱלֹהֵינוּ עוֹד וָמָתְנוּ׃ כִּי מִי כָל־ בָּשָׂר אֲשֶׁר שָׁמַע
he-heard who mortal any-of who? for (26) then-we-will-die longer God-of-us

קוֹל אֱלֹהִים חַיִּים מְדַבֵּר מִתּוֹךְ־ הָאֵשׁ כָּמֹנוּ וַיֶּחִי׃ קְרַב
go! (27) and-he-survived as-we the-fire out-of speaking living God voice-of

אַתָּה וּשְׁמָע אֵת כָּל־ אֲשֶׁר יֹאמַר יְהוָה אֱלֹהֵינוּ וְאַתְּ ׀ תְּדַבֵּר
you-tell and-you God-of-us Yahweh he-says that all *** and-listen! you

אֵלֵינוּ אֵת כָּל־ אֲשֶׁר יְדַבֵּר יְהוָה אֱלֹהֵינוּ אֵלֶיךָ וְשָׁמַעְנוּ
and-we-will-listen to-you God-of-us Yahweh he-tells that all *** to-us

וְעָשִׂינוּ׃ וַיִּשְׁמַע יְהוָה אֶת־ קוֹל דִּבְרֵיכֶם
words-of-you sound-of *** Yahweh and-he-heard (28) and-we-will-obey

בְּדַבֶּרְכֶם אֵלָי וַיֹּאמֶר יְהוָה אֵלַי שָׁמַעְתִּי אֶת־ קוֹל
sound-of *** I-heard to-me Yahweh and-he-said to-me when-to-speak-you

דִּבְרֵי הָעָם הַזֶּה אֲשֶׁר דִּבְּרוּ אֵלֶיךָ הֵיטִיבוּ כָּל־ אֲשֶׁר
that all they-were-good to-you they-spoke that the-this the-people words-of

or land, his manservant
or maidservant, his ox or
donkey, or anything that
belongs to your neigh-
bor."

22These are the command-
ments the LORD proclaimed in
a loud voice to your whole assembly there on the mountain
from out of the fire, the cloud
and the deep darkness; and he
added nothing more. Then he
wrote them on two stone tablets and gave them to me.
23When you heard the voice
out of the darkness, while the
mountain was ablaze with
fire, all the leading men of
your tribes and your elders
came to me. 24And you said,
"The LORD our God has shown
us his glory and his majesty,
and we have heard his voice
from the fire. Today we have
seen that a man can live even
if God speaks with him. 25But
now, why should we die? This
great fire will consume us, and
we will die if we hear the voice
of the LORD our God any longer. 26For what mortal man has
ever heard the voice of the living God speaking out of fire,
as we have, and survived?
27Go near and listen to all that
the LORD our God says. Then
tell us whatever the LORD our
God tells you. We will listen
and obey."
28The LORD heard you when
you spoke to me and the LORD
said to me, "I have heard what
this people said to you. Everything they said was good.

*See the note on page 499.

דִּבֵּרוּ׃ מִי־ יִתֵּן וְהָיָה לְבָבָם זֶה

this heart-of-them and-he-would-be he-would-incline oh! (29) they-said

לָהֶם לְיִרְאָה אֹתִי וְלִשְׁמֹר אֶת־ כָּל־ מִצְוֹתַי כָּל־ הַיָּמִים

the-days all-of commands-of-me all-of *** and-to-keep me to-fear to-them

לְמַעַן יִיטַב לָהֶם וְלִבְנֵיהֶם לְעֹלָם׃

for-ever and-with-children-of-them with-them he-might-go-well so-that

לֵךְ אֱמֹר לָהֶם שׁוּבוּ לָכֶם לְאָהֳלֵיכֶם׃ וְאַתָּה פֹּה

here but-you (31) to-tents-of-you to-you return! to-them tell! go! (30)

עֲמֹד עִמָּדִי וַאֲדַבְּרָה אֵלֶיךָ אֵת כָּל־ הַמִּצְוָה וְהַחֻקִּים

and-the-decrees the-command all-of *** to-you so-I-may-give with-me stay!

וְהַמִּשְׁפָּטִים אֲשֶׁר תְּלַמְּדֵם וְעָשׂוּ בָאָרֶץ אֲשֶׁר

that in-the-land so-they-will-follow you-must-teach-them that and-the-laws

אָנֹכִי נֹתֵן לָהֶם לְרִשְׁתָּהּ׃ וּשְׁמַרְתֶּם לַעֲשׂוֹת כַּאֲשֶׁר

just-as to-do so-you-be-careful (32) to-possess-her to-them giving I

צִוָּה יְהוָה אֱלֹהֵיכֶם אֶתְכֶם לֹא תָסֻרוּ יָמִין וּשְׂמֹאל׃ בְּכָל־

in-all-of (33) or-left right you-turn not you God-of-you Yahweh he-commanded

הַדֶּרֶךְ אֲשֶׁר צִוָּה יְהוָה אֱלֹהֵיכֶם אֶתְכֶם תֵּלֵכוּ לְמַעַן תִּחְיוּן

you-may-live so-that you-walk you God-of-you Yahweh he-commanded that the-way

וְטוֹב לָכֶם וְהַאֲרַכְתֶּם יָמִים בָּאָרֶץ אֲשֶׁר תִּירָשׁוּן׃

you-will-possess that in-the-land days and-you-prolong to-you and-he-may-be-good

וְזֹאת הַמִּצְוָה הַחֻקִּים וְהַמִּשְׁפָּטִים אֲשֶׁר צִוָּה יְהוָה

Yahweh he-directed that and-the-laws the-decrees the-command and-this (6:1)

אֱלֹהֵיכֶם לְלַמֵּד אֶתְכֶם לַעֲשׂוֹת בָּאָרֶץ אֲשֶׁר אַתֶּם עֹבְרִים

ones-crossing you that in-the-land to-observe you to-teach God-of-you

שָׁמָּה לְרִשְׁתָּהּ׃ לְמַעַן תִּירָא אֶת־ יְהוָה אֱלֹהֶיךָ

God-of-you Yahweh *** you-may-fear so-that (2) to-possess-her to-there

לִשְׁמֹר אֶת־ כָּל־ חֻקֹּתָיו וּמִצְוֹתָיו אֲשֶׁר אָנֹכִי מְצַוֶּךָ

giving-you I that and-commands-of-him decrees-of-him all-of *** to-keep

אַתָּה וּבִנְךָ וּבֶן־ בִּנְךָ כֹּל יְמֵי חַיֶּיךָ

lives-of-you days-of all-of child-of-you and-child-of and-child-of-you you

וּלְמַעַן יַאֲרִכֻן יָמֶיךָ׃ וְשָׁמַעְתָּ יִשְׂרָאֵל

Israel so-you-hear (3) days-of-you they-will-be-long and-so-that

וְשָׁמַרְתָּ לַעֲשׂוֹת אֲשֶׁר יִיטַב לְךָ וַאֲשֶׁר

and-that with-you he-may-go-well that to-obey and-you-be-careful

תִּרְבּוּן מְאֹד כַּאֲשֶׁר דִּבֶּר יְהוָה אֱלֹהֵי אֲבֹתֶיךָ

fathers-of-you God-of Yahweh he-promised just-as greatly you-may-increase

לָךְ אֶרֶץ זָבַת חָלָב וּדְבָשׁ׃ שְׁמַע יִשְׂרָאֵל יְהוָה אֱלֹהֵינוּ

God-of-us Yahweh Israel hear! (4) and-honey milk flowing-of land-of to-you

29Oh, that their hearts would be inclined to fear me and keep all my commands always, so that it might go well with them and their children forever!

30"Go, tell them to return to their tents. 31But you stay here with me so that I may give you all the commands, decrees and laws you are to teach them to follow in the land I am giving them to possess."

32So be careful to do what the LORD your God has commanded you; do not turn aside to the right or to the left. 33Walk in all the way that the LORD your God has commanded you, so that you may live and prosper and prolong your days in the land that you will possess.

*Love the LORD Your God*

6 These are the commands, decrees and laws the LORD your God directed me to teach you to observe in the land that you are crossing the Jordan to possess, 2so that you, your children and their children after them may fear the LORD your God as long as you live by keeping all his decrees and commands that I give you, and so that you may enjoy long life. 3Hear, O Israel, and be careful to obey so that it may go well with you and that you may increase greatly in a land flowing with milk and honey, just as the LORD, the God of your fathers, promised you.

4Hear, O Israel: The LORD

*See the note on page 499.

יְהוָה ׀ אֶחָד׃ וְאָהַבְתָּ אֵת יְהוָה אֱלֹהֶיךָ בְּכָל־
with-all-of God-of-you Yahweh *** and-you-must-love (5) one Yahweh

לְבָבְךָ וּבְכָל־ נַפְשְׁךָ וּבְכָל־ מְאֹדֶךָ׃
strength-of-you and-with-all-of soul-of-you and-with-all-of heart-of-you

וְהָיוּ הַדְּבָרִים הָאֵלֶּה אֲשֶׁר אָנֹכִי מְצַוְּךָ הַיּוֹם עַל־
on the-day giving-you I that the-these the-commands and-they-must-be (6)

לְבָבֶךָ׃ וְשִׁנַּנְתָּם לְבָנֶיךָ וְדִבַּרְתָּ
and-you-talk on-children-of-you and-you-impress-them (7) heart-of-you

בָּם בְּשִׁבְתְּךָ בְּבֵיתֶךָ וּבְלֶכְתְּךָ בַדֶּרֶךְ
on-the-road and-when-to-walk-you in-house-of-you when-to-sit-you about-them

וּבְשָׁכְבְּךָ וּבְקוּמֶךָ׃ וּקְשַׁרְתָּם לְאוֹת
as-symbol and-you-tie-them (8) and-when-to-get-up-you and-when-to-lie-down-you

עַל־ יָדֶךָ וְהָיוּ לְטֹטָפֹת בֵּין עֵינֶיךָ׃
eyes-of-you between as-bands and-they-must-be hand-of-you on

וּכְתַבְתָּם עַל־ מְזוּזֹת בֵּיתֶךָ וּבִשְׁעָרֶיךָ׃
and-on-gates-of-you house-of-you doorframes-of on and-you-write-them (9)

וְהָיָה כִּי יְבִיאֲךָ ׀ יְהוָה אֱלֹהֶיךָ אֶל־ הָאָרֶץ אֲשֶׁר
that the-land into God-of-you Yahweh he-brings-you when and-he-will-be (10)

נִשְׁבַּע לַאֲבֹתֶיךָ לְאַבְרָהָם לְיִצְחָק וּלְיַעֲקֹב לָתֶת לָךְ
to-you to-give and-to-Jacob to-Isaac to-Abraham to-fathers-of-you he-swore

עָרִים גְּדֹלֹת וְטֹבֹת אֲשֶׁר לֹא־ בָנִיתָ׃ וּבָתִּים מְלֵאִים
ones-full and-houses (11) you-built not that and-good-ones large-ones cities

כָּל־ טוּב אֲשֶׁר לֹא־ מִלֵּאתָ וּבֹרֹת חֲצוּבִים אֲשֶׁר לֹא־חָצַבְתָּ
you-dug not that ones-being-dug and-wells you-provided not that good all-of

כְּרָמִים וְזֵיתִים אֲשֶׁר לֹא־ נָטָעְתָּ וְאָכַלְתָּ וְשָׂבָעְתָּ׃
and-you-are-sated and-you-eat you-planted not that and-olive-groves vineyards

הִשָּׁמֶר לְךָ פֶּן־ תִּשְׁכַּח אֶת־ יְהוָה אֲשֶׁר הוֹצִיאֲךָ
he-brought-you who Yahweh *** you-forget so-not to-you be-careful! (12)

מֵאֶרֶץ מִצְרַיִם מִבֵּית עֲבָדִים׃ אֶת־ יְהוָה אֱלֹהֶיךָ
God-of-you Yahweh *** (13) slaveries from-house-of Egypt from-land-of

תִּירָא וְאֹתוֹ תַעֲבֹד וּבִשְׁמוֹ תִּשָּׁבֵעַ׃ לֹא
not (14) you-take-oath and-in-name-of-him you-serve and-him you-fear

תֵלְכוּן אַחֲרֵי אֱלֹהִים אֲחֵרִים מֵאֱלֹהֵי הָעַמִּים אֲשֶׁר סְבִיבוֹתֵיכֶם׃
ones-around-you that the-peoples after-gods-of other-ones gods after you-follow

כִּי אֵל קַנָּא יְהוָה אֱלֹהֶיךָ בְּקִרְבֶּךָ פֶּן־ יֶחֱרֶה אַף־
anger-of he-burns so-not in-among-you God-of-you Yahweh jealous God for (15)

יְהוָה אֱלֹהֶיךָ בָּךְ וְהִשְׁמִידְךָ מֵעַל פְּנֵי הָאֲדָמָה׃
the-land faces-of from-on so-he-destroys-you against-you God-of-you Yahweh

our God, the LORD is one.[n] [5]Love the LORD your God with all your heart and with all your soul and with all your strength. [6]These commandments that I give you today are to be upon your hearts. [7]Impress them on your children. Talk about them when you sit at home and when you walk along the road, when you lie down and when you get up. [8]Tie them as symbols on your hands and bind them on your foreheads. [9]Write them on the doorframes of your houses and on your gates.

[10]When the LORD your God brings you into the land he swore to your fathers, to Abraham, Isaac and Jacob, to give you—a land with large, flourishing cities you did not build, [11]houses filled with all kinds of good things you did not provide, wells you did not dig, and vineyards and olive groves you did not plant—then when you eat and are satisfied, [12]be careful that you do not forget the LORD, who brought you out of Egypt, out of the land of slavery.

[13]Fear the LORD your God, serve him only and take your oaths in his name. [14]Do not follow other gods, the gods of the peoples around you; [15]for the LORD your God, who is among you, is a jealous God and his anger will burn against you, and he will destroy you from the face of the

[n]4 Or *The LORD our God is one LORD;* or *The LORD is our God, the LORD is one;* or *The LORD is our God, the LORD alone*

לֹא תְנַסּוּ אֶת־ יְהוָה אֱלֹהֵיכֶם כַּאֲשֶׁר נִסִּיתֶם בַּמַּסָּה׃
at-the-Massah you-tested just-as God-of-you Yahweh *** you-test not (16)

שָׁמוֹר תִּשְׁמְרוּן אֶת־ מִצְוֺת יְהוָה אֱלֹהֵיכֶם וְעֵדֹתָיו
and-stipulations-of-him God-of-you Yahweh commands-of *** you-keep to-keep (17)

וְחֻקָּיו אֲשֶׁר צִוָּךְ׃ וְעָשִׂיתָ הַיָּשָׁר וְהַטּוֹב
and-the-good the-right and-you-do (18) he-gave-you that and-decrees-of-him

בְּעֵינֵי יְהוָה לְמַעַן יִיטַב לָךְ וּבָאתָ
and-you-may-go-in with-you he-may-go-well so-that Yahweh in-eyes-of

וְיָרַשְׁתָּ אֶת־הָאָרֶץ הַטֹּבָה אֲשֶׁר־ נִשְׁבַּע יְהוָה לַאֲבֹתֶיךָ׃
to-fathers-of-you Yahweh he-swore that the-good the-land *** and-you-may-possess

לַהֲדֹף אֶת־ כָּל־ אֹיְבֶיךָ מִפָּנֶיךָ כַּאֲשֶׁר
just-as from-before-you being-enemines-of-you all-of *** to-thrust-out (19)

דִּבֶּר יְהוָה׃ כִּי־ יִשְׁאָלְךָ בִנְךָ מָחָר לֵאמֹר מָה
what? to-say future son-of-you he-asks-you when (20) Yahweh he-said

הָעֵדֹת וְהַחֻקִּים וְהַמִּשְׁפָּטִים אֲשֶׁר צִוָּה יְהוָה
Yahweh he-commanded that and-the-laws and-the-decrees the-stipulations

אֱלֹהֵינוּ אֶתְכֶם׃ וְאָמַרְתָּ לְבִנְךָ עֲבָדִים הָיִינוּ לְפַרְעֹה
to-Pharaoh we-were slaves to-son-of-you then-you-tell (21) you God-of-us

בְּמִצְרָיִם וַיּוֹצִיאֵנוּ יְהוָה מִמִּצְרַיִם בְּיָד חֲזָקָה׃ וַיִּתֵּן
and-he-sent (22) mighty with-hand from-Egypt Yahweh but-he-brought-us in-Egypt

יְהוָה אוֹתֹת וּמֹפְתִים גְּדֹלִים וְרָעִים ׀ בְּמִצְרַיִם בְּפַרְעֹה
on-Pharaoh on-Egypt and-terrible-ones great-ones and-wonders signs Yahweh

וּבְכָל־ בֵּיתוֹ לְעֵינֵינוּ׃ וְאוֹתָנוּ הוֹצִיא
he-brought but-us (23) before-eyes-of-us household-of-him and-on-whole-of

מִשָּׁם לְמַעַן הָבִיא אֹתָנוּ לָתֶת לָנוּ אֶת־ הָאָרֶץ אֲשֶׁר נִשְׁבַּע
he-swore that the-land *** to-us to-give us to-bring-in in-order from-there

לַאֲבֹתֵינוּ׃ וַיְצַוֵּנוּ יְהוָה לַעֲשׂוֹת אֶת־ כָּל־
all-of *** to-obey Yahweh and-he-commanded-us (24) to-fathers-of-us

הַחֻקִּים הָאֵלֶּה לְיִרְאָה אֶת־ יְהוָה אֱלֹהֵינוּ לְטוֹב לָנוּ כָּל־
all-of for-us for-good God-of-us Yahweh *** to-fear the-these the-decrees

הַיָּמִים לְחַיֹּתֵנוּ כְּהַיּוֹם הַזֶּה׃ וּצְדָקָה
and-righteousness (25) the-this as-the-day to-keep-alive-us the-days

תִּהְיֶה־ לָּנוּ כִּי־ נִשְׁמֹר לַעֲשׂוֹת אֶת־ כָּל־ הַמִּצְוָה הַזֹּאת
the-this the-law all-of *** to-obey we-are-careful if for-us she-will-be

לִפְנֵי יְהוָה אֱלֹהֵינוּ כַּאֲשֶׁר צִוָּנוּ׃ כִּי יְבִיאֲךָ
he-brings-you when (7:1) he-commanded-us just-as God-of-us Yahweh before

יְהוָה אֱלֹהֶיךָ אֶל־ הָאָרֶץ אֲשֶׁר־אַתָּה בָא־ שָׁמָּה לְרִשְׁתָּהּ
to-possess-her to-there entering you that the-land into God-of-you Yahweh

land. 16Do not test the LORD your God as you did at Massah. 17Be sure to keep the commands of the LORD your God and the stipulations and decrees he has given you. 18Do what is right and good in the LORD's sight, so that it may go well with you and you may go in and take over the good land that the LORD promised on oath to your forefathers, 19thrusting out all your enemies before you, as the LORD said.

20In the future, when your son asks you, "What is the meaning of the stipulations, decrees and laws the LORD our God has commanded you?" 21tell him: "We were slaves of Pharaoh in Egypt, but the LORD brought us out of Egypt with a mighty hand. 22Before our eyes the LORD sent miraculous signs and wonders—great and terrible—upon Egypt and Pharaoh and his whole household. 23But he brought us out from there to bring us in and give us the land that he promised on oath to our forefathers. 24The LORD commanded us to obey all these decrees and to fear the LORD our God, so that we might always prosper and be kept alive, as is the case today. 25And if we are careful to obey all this law before the LORD our God, as he has commanded us, that will be our righteousness."

*Driving Out the Nations*

7 When the LORD your God brings you into the land you are entering to possess

וְנָשַׁל גּוֹיִם־ רַבִּים ׀ מִפָּנֶיךָ הַחִתִּי וְהַגִּרְגָּשִׁי
and-the-Girgashite the-Hittite from-before-you many nations and-he-drives-out

וְהָאֱמֹרִי וְהַכְּנַעֲנִי וְהַפְּרִזִּי וְהַחִוִּי
and-the-Hivite and-the-Perizzite and-the-Canaanite and-the-Amorite

וְהַיְבוּסִי שִׁבְעָה גוֹיִם רַבִּים וַעֲצוּמִים מִמֶּךָּ׃
than-you and-ones-stronger ones-larger nations seven and-the-Jebusite

(2) וּנְתָנָם יְהוָה אֱלֹהֶיךָ לְפָנֶיךָ וְהִכִּיתָם
and-you-defeat-them before-you God-of-you Yahweh and-he-delivers-them (2)

הַחֲרֵם תַּחֲרִים אֹתָם לֹא־ תִכְרֹת לָהֶם בְּרִית וְלֹא
and-not treaty with-them you-make not them you-must-destroy to-destroy

תְחָנֵּם׃ (3) וְלֹא תִתְחַתֵּן בָּם בִּתְּךָ
daughter-of-you with-them you-intermarry and-not (3) you-show-mercy-to-them

לֹא־ תִתֵּן לִבְנוֹ וּבִתּוֹ לֹא־ תִקַּח לִבְנֶךָ׃
for-son-of-you you-take not and-daughter-of-him to-son-of-him you-give not

(4) כִּי־ יָסִיר אֶת־ בִּנְךָ מֵאַחֲרַי וְעָבְדוּ אֱלֹהִים
gods and-they-will-serve from-after-me son-of-you *** he-will-turn for (4)

אֲחֵרִים וְחָרָה אַף־ יְהוָה בָּכֶם וְהִשְׁמִידְךָ
and-he-will-destroy-you against-you Yahweh anger-of and-he-will-burn other-ones

מַהֵר׃ (5) כִּי־ אִם־ כֹּה תַעֲשׂוּ לָהֶם מִזְבְּחֹתֵיהֶם תִּתֹּצוּ
you-break-down altars-of-them to-them you-do this indeed but (5) quickly

וּמַצֵּבֹתָם תְּשַׁבֵּרוּ וַאֲשֵׁירֵהֶם תְּגַדֵּעוּן
you-cut-down and-Asherah-poles-of-them you-smash and-sacred-stones-of-them

וּפְסִילֵיהֶם תִּשְׂרְפוּן בָּאֵשׁ׃ (6) כִּי עַם קָדוֹשׁ אַתָּה לַיהוָה
to-Yahweh you holy people for (6) in-the-fire you-burn and-idols-of-them

אֱלֹהֶיךָ בְּךָ בָּחַר ׀ יְהוָה אֱלֹהֶיךָ לִהְיוֹת לוֹ לְעַם
as-people-of for-him to-be God-of-you Yahweh he-chose to-you God-of-you

סְגֻלָּה מִכֹּל הָעַמִּים אֲשֶׁר עַל־ פְּנֵי הָאֲדָמָה׃ (7) לֹא
not (7) the-earth faces-of on that the-peoples from-all-of treasure

מֵרֻבְּכֶם מִכָּל־ הָעַמִּים חָשַׁק יְהוָה
Yahweh he-set-affection the-peoples than-all-of because-to-be-numerous-you

בָּכֶם וַיִּבְחַר בָּכֶם כִּי־ אַתֶּם הַמְעַט מִכָּל־ הָעַמִּים׃ (8) כִּי
but (8) the-peoples of-all-of the-fewest you for to-you and-he-chose on-you

מֵאַהֲבַת יְהוָה אֶתְכֶם וּמִשָּׁמְרוֹ אֶת־ הַשְּׁבֻעָה
the-oath *** and-because-to-keep-him for-you Yahweh because-of-love-of

אֲשֶׁר נִשְׁבַּע לַאֲבֹתֵיכֶם הוֹצִיא יְהוָה אֶתְכֶם בְּיָד חֲזָקָה
mighty with-hand you Yahweh he-brought-out to-fathers-of-you he-swore that

וַיִּפְדְּךָ מִבֵּית עֲבָדִים מִיַּד פַּרְעֹה מֶלֶךְ־ מִצְרָיִם׃
Egypt king-of Pharaoh from-hand-of slaveries from-house-of and-he-redeemed-you

and drives out before you
many nations—the Hittites,
Girgashites, Amorites, Canaanites, Perizzites, Hivites
and Jebusites, seven nations
larger and stronger than you—
2and when the LORD your God
has delivered them over to you
and you have defeated them,
then you must destroy them
totally.[o] Make no treaty with
them, and show them no
mercy. 3Do not intermarry
with them. Do not give your
daughters to their sons or take
their daughters for your sons,
4for they will turn your sons
away from following me to
serve other gods, and the
LORD's anger will burn against
you and will quickly destroy
you. 5This is what you are to
do to them: Break down their
altars, smash their sacred
stones, cut down their
Asherah poles[p] and burn their
idols in the fire. 6For you are a
people holy to the LORD your
God. The LORD your God has
chosen you out of all the peoples on the face of the earth to
be his people, his treasured
possession.
7The LORD did not set his
affection on you and choose
you because you were more
numerous than other peoples,
for you were the fewest of all
peoples. 8But it was because
the LORD loved you and kept
the oath he swore to your
forefathers that he brought
you out with a mighty hand
and redeemed you from the
land of slavery, from the
power of Pharaoh king of

[o]2 The Hebrew term refers to the irrevocable giving over of things or persons to the LORD, often by totally destroying them; also in verse 26.
[p]5 That is, symbols of the goddess Asherah; here and elsewhere in Deuteronomy

וְיָדַעְתָּ כִּי־ יְהוָה אֱלֹהֶיךָ הוּא הָאֱלֹהִים הָאֵל הַנֶּאֱמָן
the-being-faithful the-God the-God he God-of-you Yahweh that so-you-know (9)

שֹׁמֵר הַבְּרִית וְהַחֶסֶד לְאֹהֲבָיו וּלְשֹׁמְרֵי
and-to-ones-keeping-of to-ones-loving-him and-the-love the-covenant keeping

מִצְוֺתָו לְאֶלֶף דּוֹר׃ וּמְשַׁלֵּם לְשֹׂנְאָיו
to-ones-hating-him but-repaying (10) generation to-thousand commands-of-him

אֶל־ פָּנָיו לְהַאֲבִידוֹ לֹא יְאַחֵר לְשֹׂנְאוֹ אֶל־
to to-ones-hating-him he-will-be-slow not to-destroy-him faces-of-him to

פָּנָיו יְשַׁלֶּם־ לוֹ׃ וְשָׁמַרְתָּ אֶת־ הַמִּצְוָה
the-command *** so-you-take-care (11) to-him he-will-repay faces-of-him

וְאֶת־ הַחֻקִּים וְאֶת־הַמִּשְׁפָּטִים אֲשֶׁר אָנֹכִי מְצַוְּךָ הַיּוֹם לַעֲשׂוֹתָם׃
to-follow-them the-day giving-you I that the-laws and the-decrees and

וְהָיָה ׀ עֵקֶב תִּשְׁמְעוּן אֵת הַמִּשְׁפָּטִים הָאֵלֶּה וּשְׁמַרְתֶּם
and-you-are-careful the-these the-laws *** you-attend if and-he-will-be (12)

וַעֲשִׂיתֶם אֹתָם וְשָׁמַר יְהוָה אֱלֹהֶיךָ לְךָ אֶת־
*** with-you God-of-you Yahweh then-he-will-keep them and-you-follow

הַבְּרִית וְאֶת־ הַחֶסֶד אֲשֶׁר נִשְׁבַּע לַאֲבֹתֶיךָ׃
to-fathers-of-you he-swore that the-love and the-covenant

וַאֲהֵבְךָ וּבֵרַכְךָ וְהִרְבֶּךָ
and-he-will-increase-you and-he-will-bless-you and-he-will-love-you (13)

וּבֵרַךְ פְּרִי־ בִטְנְךָ וּפְרִי־ אַדְמָתֶךָ דְּגָנְךָ
grain-of-you land-of-you and-fruit-of womb-of-you fruit-of and-he-will-bless

וְתִירֹשְׁךָ וְיִצְהָרֶךָ שְׁגַר־ אֲלָפֶיךָ וְעַשְׁתְּרֹת
and-lambs-of herds-of-you calf-of and-oil-of-you and-new-wine-of-you

צֹאנֶךָ עַל הָאֲדָמָה אֲשֶׁר־ נִשְׁבַּע לַאֲבֹתֶיךָ לָתֶת לָךְ׃
to-you to-give to-fathers-of-you he-swore that the-land in flock-of-you

בָּרוּךְ תִּהְיֶה מִכָּל־ הָעַמִּים לֹא־ יִהְיֶה
he-will-be not the-peoples more-than-any-of you-will-be being-blessed (14)

בְךָ עָקָר וַעֲקָרָה וּבִבְהֶמְתֶּךָ׃
or-among-livestock-of-you or-childless-woman childless-man among-you

וְהֵסִיר יְהוָה מִמְּךָ כָּל־ חֹלִי וְכָל־
and-all-of disease every-of from-you Yahweh and-he-will-keep-free (15)

מַדְוֵי מִצְרַיִם הָרָעִים אֲשֶׁר יָדַעְתָּ לֹא יְשִׂימָם
he-will-inflict-them not you-knew that the-horrible-ones Egypt diseases-of

בָּךְ וּנְתָנָם בְּכָל־ שֹׂנְאֶיךָ׃ וְאָכַלְתָּ
so-you-destroy (16) ones-hating-you on-all-of but-he-will-inflict-them on-you

אֶת־כָּל־ הָעַמִּים אֲשֶׁר יְהוָה אֱלֹהֶיךָ נֹתֵן לָךְ לֹא־ תָחוֹס
she-must-pity not to-you giving God-of-you Yahweh whom the-peoples all-of ***

Egypt. [9]Know therefore that the LORD your God is God; he is the faithful God, keeping his covenant of love to a thousand generations of those who love him and keep his commands. [10]But

those who hate him he will
repay to their face by
destruction;
he will not be slow to
repay to their face
those who hate him.

[11]Therefore, take care to follow the commands, decrees and laws I give you today.

[12]If you pay attention to these laws and are careful to follow them, then the LORD your God will keep his covenant of love with you, as he swore to your forefathers. [13]He will love you and bless you and increase your numbers. He will bless the fruit of your womb, the crops of your land—your grain, new wine and oil—the calves of your herds and the lambs of your flocks in the land that he swore to your forefathers to give you. [14]You will be blessed more than any other people; none of your men or women will be childless, nor any of your livestock without young. [15]The LORD will keep you free from every disease. He will not inflict on you the horrible diseases you knew in Egypt, but he will inflict them on all who hate you. [16]You must destroy all the peoples the LORD your God gives over to you. Do not look on them with pity

°9 ק מצותיו

עֵינְךָ עֲלֵיהֶם וְלֹא תַעֲבֹד אֶת־ אֱלֹהֵיהֶם כִּי־ מוֹקֵשׁ הוּא לָךְ׃
to-you that snare for gods-of-them *** you-serve and-not on-them eye-of-you

כִּי תֹאמַר בִּלְבָבְךָ רַבִּים הַגּוֹיִם הָאֵלֶּה
the-these the-nations ones-stronger in-heart-of-you you-may-say now (17)

מִמֶּנִּי אֵיכָה אוּכַל לְהוֹרִישָׁם׃ לֹא תִירָא מֵהֶם
of-them you-be-afraid not (18) to-drive-out-them can-I how? than-me

זָכֹר תִּזְכֹּר אֵת אֲשֶׁר־ עָשָׂה יְהוָה אֱלֹהֶיךָ לְפַרְעֹה
to-Pharaoh God-of-you Yahweh he-did what *** you-remember to-remember

וּלְכָל־ מִצְרָיִם׃ הַמַּסֹּת הַגְּדֹלֹת אֲשֶׁר־ רָאוּ
they-saw that the-great-ones and-the-trials (19) Egypt and-to-all-of

עֵינֶיךָ וְהָאֹתֹת וְהַמֹּפְתִים וְהַיָּד הַחֲזָקָה וְהַזְּרֹעַ
and-the-arm the-mighty and-the-hand and-the-wonders and-the-signs eyes-of-you

הַנְּטוּיָה אֲשֶׁר הוֹצִאֲךָ יְהוָה אֱלֹהֶיךָ כֵּן־
same God-of-you Yahweh he-brought-out-you which the-being-outstretched

יַעֲשֶׂה יְהוָה אֱלֹהֶיךָ לְכָל־ הָעַמִּים אֲשֶׁר־ אַתָּה יָרֵא
fearing you that the-peoples to-all-of God-of-you Yahweh he-will-do

מִפְּנֵיהֶם׃ וְגַם אֶת־ הַצִּרְעָה יְשַׁלַּח יְהוָה
Yahweh he-will-send the-hornet *** and-also (20) from-presence-of-them

אֱלֹהֶיךָ בָּם עַד־ אֲבֹד הַנִּשְׁאָרִים וְהַנִּסְתָּרִים
and-the-ones-hiding the-ones-surviving to-perish until among-them God-of-you

מִפָּנֶיךָ׃ לֹא תַעֲרֹץ מִפְּנֵיהֶם כִּי־ יְהוָה
Yahweh for from-presence-of-them you-be-terrified not (21) from-faces-of-you

אֱלֹהֶיךָ בְּקִרְבֶּךָ אֵל גָּדוֹל וְנוֹרָא׃ וְנָשַׁל
and-he-will-drive (22) and-being-awesome great God in-among-you God-of-you

יְהוָה אֱלֹהֶיךָ אֶת־ הַגּוֹיִם הָאֵל מִפָּנֶיךָ מְעַט מְעָט
little little from-before-you the-those the-nations *** God-of-you Yahweh

לֹא תוּכַל כַּלֹּתָם מַהֵר פֶּן־ תִּרְבֶּה עָלֶיךָ
around-you she-will-multiply or at-once to-eliminate-them you-can not

חַיַּת הַשָּׂדֶה׃ וּנְתָנָם יְהוָה אֱלֹהֶיךָ לְפָנֶיךָ
to-you God-of-you Yahweh but-he-will-deliver-them (23) the-field animal-of

וְהָמָם מְהוּמָה גְדֹלָה עַד הִשָּׁמְדָם׃
to-be-destroyed-them until great confusion and-he-will-confuse-them

וְנָתַן מַלְכֵיהֶם בְּיָדֶךָ וְהַאֲבַדְתָּ
and-you-will-wipe-out into-hand-of-you kings-of-them and-he-will-give (24)

אֶת־ שְׁמָם מִתַּחַת הַשָּׁמָיִם לֹא־ יִתְיַצֵּב אִישׁ
anyone he-will-stand not the-heavens from-under name-of-them ***

בְּפָנֶיךָ עַד הִשְׁמִדְךָ אֹתָם׃ פְּסִילֵי אֱלֹהֵיהֶם
gods-of-them images-of (25) them to-destroy-you when against-faces-of-you

and do not serve their gods,
for that will be a snare to you.
17You may say to yourselves,
"These nations are stronger
than we are. How can we
drive them out?" 18But do not
be afraid of them; remember
well what the LORD your God
did to Pharoah and to all
Egypt. 19You saw with your
own eyes the great trials, the
miraculous signs and won-
ders, the mighty hand and
outstretched arm, with which
the LORD your God brought
you out. The LORD your God
will do the same to all the peoples you now fear. 20Moreover,
the LORD your God will send
the hornet among them until
even the survivors who hide
from you have perished. 21Do
not be terrified by them, for
the LORD your God, who is
among you, is a great and
awesome God. 22The LORD
your God will drive out those
nations before you, little by
little. You will not be allowed
to eliminate them all at once,
or the wild animals will multiply around you. 23But the LORD
your God will deliver them
over to you, throwing them
into great confusion until they
are destroyed. 24He will give
their kings into your hand,
and you will wipe out their
names from under heaven. No
one will be able to stand up
against you; you will destroy
them. 25The images of their

תִּשְׂרְפוּן בָּאֵשׁ לֹא־תַחְמֹד כֶּסֶף וְזָהָב עֲלֵיהֶם וְלָקַחְתָּ לָךְ
for-you so-you-take on-them and-gold silver you-covet not in-the-fire you-burn

פֶּן תִּוָּקֵשׁ בּוֹ כִּי תוֹעֲבַת יְהוָה אֱלֹהֶיךָ הוּא׃
he God-of-you Yahweh detestable-of for by-him you-will-be-ensnared or

וְלֹא־תָבִיא תוֹעֵבָה אֶל־בֵּיתֶךָ וְהָיִיתָ
or-you-will-be house-of-you into detestable-thing you-bring and-not (26)

חֵרֶם כָּמֹהוּ שַׁקֵּץ ׀ תְּשַׁקְּצֶנּוּ וְתַעֵב ׀ תְּתַעֲבֶנּוּ
you-detest-him and-to-detest you-abhor-him to-abhor as-he for-destruction

כִּי־חֵרֶם הוּא׃ כָּל־הַמִּצְוָה אֲשֶׁר אָנֹכִי מְצַוְּךָ הַיּוֹם
the-day giving-you I that the-command every-of (8:1) he for-destruction for

תִּשְׁמְרוּן לַעֲשׂוֹת לְמַעַן תִּחְיוּן וּרְבִיתֶם
and-you-may-increase you-may-live so-that to-follow you-be-careful

וּבָאתֶם וִירִשְׁתֶּם אֶת־הָאָרֶץ אֲשֶׁר־נִשְׁבַּע יְהוָה
Yahweh he-promised that the-land *** and-you-may-possess and-you-may-enter

לַאֲבֹתֵיכֶם׃ וְזָכַרְתָּ אֶת־כָּל־הַדֶּרֶךְ אֲשֶׁר־הֹלִיכֲךָ
he-led-you that the-way all-of *** and-you-remember (2) to-fathers-of-you

יְהוָה אֱלֹהֶיךָ זֶה אַרְבָּעִים שָׁנָה בַּמִּדְבָּר לְמַעַן עַנֹּתְךָ
to-humble-you in-order in-the-desert year forty this God-of-you Yahweh

לְנַסֹּתְךָ לָדַעַת אֶת־אֲשֶׁר בִּלְבָבְךָ הֲתִשְׁמֹר מִצְוֹתָו אִם־לֹא׃
not or commands-of-him to-keep in-heart-of-you what *** to-know to-test-you

וַיְעַנְּךָ וַיַּרְעִבֶךָ וַיַּאֲכִלְךָ אֶת־הַמָּן
the-manna *** then-he-fed-you and-he-made-hungry-you and-he-humbled-you (3)

אֲשֶׁר לֹא־יָדַעְתָּ וְלֹא יָדְעוּן אֲבֹתֶיךָ לְמַעַן הוֹדִעֲךָ
to-teach-you in-order fathers-of-you they-knew and-not you-knew not which

כִּי לֹא עַל־הַלֶּחֶם לְבַדּוֹ יִחְיֶה הָאָדָם כִּי עַל־כָּל־מוֹצָא
thing-from every-of on but the-man he-lives by-himself the-bread on not that

פִי־יְהוָה יִחְיֶה הָאָדָם׃ שִׂמְלָתְךָ לֹא בָלְתָה
she-wore-out not clothing-of-you (4) the-man he-lives Yahweh mouth-of

מֵעָלֶיךָ וְרַגְלְךָ לֹא בָצֵקָה זֶה אַרְבָּעִים שָׁנָה׃ וְיָדַעְתָּ
so-you-know (5) year forty this she-swelled not and-foot-of-you from-on-you

עִם־לְבָבֶךָ כִּי כַּאֲשֶׁר יְיַסֵּר אִישׁ אֶת־בְּנוֹ יְהוָה
Yahweh son-of-him *** man he-disciplines just-as that heart-of-you in

אֱלֹהֶיךָ מְיַסְּרֶךָּ׃ וְשָׁמַרְתָּ אֶת־מִצְוֹת יְהוָה
Yahweh commands-of *** now-you-observe (6) disciplining-you God-of-you

אֱלֹהֶיךָ לָלֶכֶת בִּדְרָכָיו וּלְיִרְאָה אֹתוֹ׃ כִּי יְהוָה אֱלֹהֶיךָ
God-of-you Yahweh for (7) him and-to-revere in-ways-of-him to-walk God-of-you

מְבִיאֲךָ אֶל־אֶרֶץ טוֹבָה אֶרֶץ נַחֲלֵי מָיִם עֲיָנֹת וּתְהֹמֹת
and-springs pools waters streams-of land-of good land into bringing-you

°2 ק מצותיו

gods you are to burn in the fire. Do not covet the silver and gold on them, do not take it for yourselves, or you will be ensnared by it, for it is detestable to the LORD your God. [26]Do not bring a detestable thing into your house or you, like it, will be set apart for destruction. Utterly abhor and detest it, for it is set apart for destruction.

*Do Not Forget the LORD*

8 Be careful to follow every command I am giving you today, so that you may live and increase and may enter and possess the land that the LORD promised on oath to your forefathers. [2]Remember how the LORD your God led you all the way in the desert these forty years, to humble you and to test you in order to know what was in your heart, whether or not you would keep his commands. [3]He humbled you, causing you to hunger and then feeding you with manna, which neither you nor your fathers had known, to teach you that man does not live on bread alone but on every word that comes from the mouth of the LORD. [4]Your clothes did not wear out and your feet did not swell during these forty years. [5]Know then in your heart that as a man disciplines his son, so the LORD your God disciplines you.

[6]Observe the commands of the LORD your God, walking in his ways and revering him. [7]For the LORD your God is bringing you into a good land—a land with streams and pools of water, with springs

יֹצְאִים בַּבִּקְעָה וּבָהָר׃ אֶרֶץ חִטָּה וּשְׂעֹרָה
and-barley wheat land-of (8) and-into-the-hill into-the-valley ones-flowing

וְגֶפֶן וּתְאֵנָה וְרִמּוֹן אֶרֶץ־ זֵית שֶׁמֶן וּדְבָשׁ׃ אֶרֶץ
land (9) and-honey oil olive-of land-of and-pomegranate and-fig-tree and-vine

אֲשֶׁר לֹא בְמִסְכֵּנֻת תֹּאכַל־ בָּהּ לֶחֶם לֹא־ תֶחְסַר כֹּל
anything you-will-lack not bread in-her you-will-eat in-scarcity not where

בָּהּ אֶרֶץ אֲשֶׁר אֲבָנֶיהָ בַרְזֶל וּמֵהֲרָרֶיהָ תַּחְצֹב נְחֹשֶׁת׃
copper you-can-dig and-from-hills-of-her iron rocks-of-her where land in-her

וְאָכַלְתָּ וְשָׂבָעְתָּ וּבֵרַכְתָּ אֶת־ יְהוָה אֱלֹהֶיךָ
God-of-you Yahweh *** then-you-praise and-you-are-satisfied when-you-eat (10)

עַל־ הָאָרֶץ הַטֹּבָה אֲשֶׁר נָתַן־ לָךְ׃ הִשָּׁמֶר לְךָ פֶּן־
so-not to-you be-careful! (11) to-you he-gave that the-good the-land for

תִּשְׁכַּח אֶת־ יְהוָה אֱלֹהֶיךָ לְבִלְתִּי שְׁמֹר מִצְוֹתָיו
commands-of-him to-observe not God-of-you Yahweh *** you-forget

וּמִשְׁפָּטָיו וְחֻקֹּתָיו אֲשֶׁר אָנֹכִי מְצַוְּךָ הַיּוֹם׃ פֶּן־
otherwise (12) the-day giving-you I that and-decrees-of-him and-laws-of-him

תֹּאכַל וְשָׂבָעְתָּ וּבָתִּים טֹבִים תִּבְנֶה
you-build fine-ones and-houses and-you-are-satisfied when-you-eat

וְיָשָׁבְתָּ׃ וּבְקָרְךָ וְצֹאנְךָ יִרְבְּיֻן
they-grow-large and-flock-of-you and-herd-of-you (13) and-you-settle-down

וְכֶסֶף וְזָהָב יִרְבֶּה־ לָּךְ וְכֹל אֲשֶׁר־ לְךָ יִרְבֶּה׃
he-multiplies to-you that and-all to-you he-increases and-gold and-silver

וְרָם לְבָבֶךָ וְשָׁכַחְתָּ אֶת־ יְהוָה
Yahweh *** and-you-will-forget heart-of-you then-he-will-become-proud (14)

אֱלֹהֶיךָ הַמּוֹצִיאֲךָ מֵאֶרֶץ מִצְרַיִם מִבֵּית עֲבָדִים׃
slaveries from-house-of Egypt from-land-of the-one-bringing-you God-of-you

הַמּוֹלִיכֲךָ בַּמִּדְבָּר ׀ הַגָּדֹל וְהַנּוֹרָא
and-the-being-terrible the-vast through-the-desert the-one-leading-you (15)

נָחָשׁ ׀ שָׂרָף וְעַקְרָב וְצִמָּאוֹן אֲשֶׁר אֵין־ מָיִם הַמּוֹצִיא
the-one-bringing waters not where and-dry-ground and-scorpion venomous snake

לְךָ מַיִם מִצּוּר הַחַלָּמִישׁ׃ הַמַּאֲכִלְךָ מָן
manna the-one-feeding-you (16) the-hard from-rock-of waters for-you

בַּמִּדְבָּר אֲשֶׁר לֹא־ יָדְעוּן אֲבֹתֶיךָ לְמַעַן עַנֹּתְךָ
to-humble-you in-order fathers-of-you they-knew not that in-the-desert

וּלְמַעַן נַסֹּתֶךָ לְהֵיטִבְךָ בְּאַחֲרִיתֶךָ׃
in-end-of-you to-make-go-well-with-you to-test-you and-in-order

וְאָמַרְתָּ בִּלְבָבֶךָ כֹּחִי וְעֹצֶם יָדִי
hand-of-me and-strength-of power-of-me in-heart-of-you now-you-may-say (17)

flowing in the valleys and
hills; 8a land with wheat and
barley, vines and fig trees,
pomegranates, olive oil and
honey; 9a land where bread
will not be scarce and you will
lack nothing; a land where the
rocks are iron and you can dig
copper out of the hills.
10When you have eaten and
are satisfied, praise the LORD
your God for the good land he
has given you. 11Be careful that
you do not forget the LORD
your God, failing to observe
his commands, his laws and
his decrees that I am giving
you this day. 12Otherwise,
when you eat and are satisfied,
when you build fine
houses and settle down, 13and
when your herds and flocks
grow large and your silver and
gold increase and all you have
is multiplied, 14then your heart
will become proud and you
will forget the LORD your God,
who brought you out of Egypt,
out of the land of slavery. 15He
led you through the vast and
dreadful desert, that thirsty
and waterless land, with its
venomous snakes and scorpions.
He brought you water
out of hard rock. 16He gave you
manna to eat in the desert,
something your fathers had
never known, to humble and
to test you so that in the end it
might go well with you. 17You
may say to yourself, "My
power and the strength of my

עָשָׂה לִי אֶת־ הַחַיִל הַזֶּה׃ וְזָכַרְתָּ אֶת־ יְהוָה
Yahweh *** but-you-remember (18) the-this the-wealth *** for-me he-produced

אֱלֹהֶיךָ כִּי הוּא הַנֹּתֵן לְךָ כֹּחַ לַעֲשׂוֹת חָיִל לְמַעַן
in-order wealth to-produce ability to-you the-one-giving he for God-of-you

הָקִים אֶת־ בְּרִיתוֹ אֲשֶׁר־ נִשְׁבַּע לַאֲבֹתֶיךָ כַּיּוֹם
as-the-day to-fathers-of-you he-swore which covenant-of-him *** to-confirm

הַזֶּה׃ וְהָיָה אִם־ שָׁכֹחַ תִּשְׁכַּח אֶת־ יְהוָה אֱלֹהֶיךָ
God-of-you Yahweh *** you-forget to-forget if and-he-will-be (19) the-this

וְהָלַכְתָּ אַחֲרֵי אֱלֹהִים אֲחֵרִים וַעֲבַדְתָּם וְהִשְׁתַּחֲוִיתָ
and-you-bow-down and-you-worship-them other-ones gods after and-you-follow

לָהֶם הַעִדֹתִי בָכֶם הַיּוֹם כִּי אָבֹד תֹּאבֵדוּן׃
you-will-perish to-perish that the-day against-you I-testify to-them

כַּגּוֹיִם אֲשֶׁר יְהוָה מַאֲבִיד מִפְּנֵיכֶם כֵּן תֹּאבֵדוּן
you-will-perish so from-before-you destroying Yahweh that like-the-nations (20)

עֵקֶב לֹא תִשְׁמְעוּן בְּקוֹל יְהוָה אֱלֹהֵיכֶם׃ שְׁמַע יִשְׂרָאֵל אַתָּה
you Israel hear! (9:1) God-of-you Yahweh to-voice-of you-obeyed not for

עֹבֵר הַיּוֹם אֶת־ הַיַּרְדֵּן לָבֹא לָרֶשֶׁת גּוֹיִם גְּדֹלִים
ones-greater nations to-dispossess to-go-in the-Jordan *** the-day crossing

וַעֲצֻמִים מִמֶּךָּ עָרִים גְּדֹלֹת וּבְצֻרֹת בַּשָּׁמָיִם׃
to-the-skies and-walls large-ones cities than-you and-ones-stronger

עַם־ גָּדוֹל וָרָם בְּנֵי עֲנָקִים אֲשֶׁר אַתָּה יָדַעְתָּ וְאַתָּה
and-you you-know you whom Anakites sons-of and-tall strong people (2)

שָׁמַעְתָּ מִי יִתְיַצֵּב לִפְנֵי בְּנֵי עֲנָק׃ וְיָדַעְתָּ
but-you-be-assured (3) Anak sons-of against he-can-stand who? you-heard

הַיּוֹם כִּי יְהוָה אֱלֹהֶיךָ הוּא־ הָעֹבֵר לְפָנֶיךָ אֵשׁ
fire ahead-of-you the-one-crossing he God-of-you Yahweh that the-day

אֹכְלָה הוּא יַשְׁמִידֵם וְהוּא יַכְנִיעֵם לְפָנֶיךָ
before-you he-will-subdue-them and-he he-will-destroy-them he devouring

וְהוֹרַשְׁתָּם וְהַאֲבַדְתָּם מַהֵר כַּאֲשֶׁר
just-as quickly and-you-will-annihilate-them and-you-will-drive-out-them

דִּבֶּר יְהוָה לָךְ׃ אַל־ תֹּאמַר בִּלְבָבְךָ בַּהֲדֹף
after-to-drive-out in-heart-of-you you-say not (4) to-you Yahweh he-promised

יְהוָה אֱלֹהֶיךָ אֹתָם | מִלְּפָנֶיךָ לֵאמֹר בְּצִדְקָתִי
because-of-righteousness-of-me to-say from-before-you them God-of-you Yahweh

הֱבִיאַנִי יְהוָה לָרֶשֶׁת אֶת־ הָאָרֶץ הַזֹּאת וּבְרִשְׁעַת
but-for-wickedness-of the-this the-land *** to-possess Yahweh he-brought-me

הַגּוֹיִם הָאֵלֶּה יְהוָה מוֹרִישָׁם מִפָּנֶיךָ׃ לֹא
not (5) from-before-you driving-them Yahweh the-these the-nations

hands have produced this wealth for me." [18]But remember the LORD your God, for it is he who gives you the ability to produce wealth, and so confirms his covenant, which he swore to your forefathers, as it is today.

[19]If you ever forget the LORD your God and follow other gods and worship and bow down to them, I testify against you today that you will surely be destroyed. [20]Like the nations the LORD destroyed before you, so you will be destroyed for not obeying the LORD your God.

*Not Because of Israel's Righteousness*

9 Hear, O Israel. You are now about to cross the Jordan to go in and dispossess nations greater and stronger than you, with large cities that have walls up to the sky. [2]The people are strong and tall—Anakites! You know about them and have heard it said: "Who can stand up against the Anakites?" [3]But be assured today that the LORD your God is the one who goes across ahead of you like a devouring fire. He will destroy them; he will subdue them before you. And you will drive them out and annihilate them quickly, as the LORD has promised you.

[4]After the LORD your God has driven them out before you, do not say to yourself, "The LORD has brought me here to take possession of this land because of my righteousness." No, it is on account of the wickedness of these nations that the LORD is going to drive them out before you. [5]It

בְּצִדְקָתְךָ֙ וּבְיֹ֙שֶׁר֙ לְבָבְךָ֔ אַתָּ֖ה בָ֣א
for-righteousness-of-you | or-for-integrity-of | heart-of-you | you | going-in

לָרֶ֣שֶׁת אֶת־אַרְצָ֑ם כִּ֣י בְּרִשְׁעַ֣ת ׀ הַגּוֹיִ֣ם הָאֵ֗לֶּה
to-possess | *** land-of-them | but | for-wickedness-of | the-nations | the-these

יְהוָ֤ה אֱלֹהֶ֙יךָ֙ מוֹרִישָׁ֣ם מִפָּנֶ֔יךָ וּלְמַ֜עַן הָקִ֣ים
Yahweh | God-of-you | driving-them | from-before-you | and-in-order | to-accomplish

אֶת־הַדָּבָ֗ר אֲשֶׁ֨ר נִשְׁבַּ֤ע יְהוָה֙ לַאֲבֹתֶ֔יךָ לְאַבְרָהָ֥ם לְיִצְחָ֖ק
*** the-thing | that | he-swore | Yahweh | to-fathers-of-you | to-Abraham | to-Isacc

וּֽלְיַעֲקֹֽב׃ (6) וְיָ֣דַעְתָּ֔ כִּ֠י לֹ֤א בְצִדְקָֽתְךָ֙ יְהוָ֣ה
and-to-Jacob | (6) | now-you-understand | that | not | for-righteousness-of-you | Yahweh

אֱלֹהֶ֗יךָ נֹתֵ֨ן לְךָ֜ אֶת־הָאָ֧רֶץ הַטּוֹבָ֛ה הַזֹּ֖את לְרִשְׁתָּ֑הּ כִּ֥י
God-of-you | giving | to-you | *** the-land | the-good | the-this | to-possess-her | for

עַם־קְשֵׁה־עֹ֖רֶף אָֽתָּה׃ (7) זְכֹר֙ אַל־תִּשְׁכַּ֔ח אֵ֧ת אֲשֶׁר־הִקְצַ֛פְתָּ
people-of | stiff-of | neck | you | (7) | remember! | not | you-forget | *** | how | you-angered

אֶת־יְהוָ֥ה אֱלֹהֶ֖יךָ בַּמִּדְבָּ֑ר לְמִן־הַיּ֞וֹם אֲשֶׁר־יָצָ֣אתָ ׀
*** | Yahweh | God-of-you | in-the-desert | on-from | the-day | that | you-left

מֵאֶ֣רֶץ מִצְרַ֗יִם עַד־בֹּֽאֲכֶם֙ עַד־הַמָּק֣וֹם הַזֶּ֔ה מַמְרִ֥ים
from-land-of | Egypt | until | to-arrive-you | at | the-place | the-this | ones-rebelling

הֱיִיתֶ֖ם עִם־יְהוָֽה׃ (8) וּבְחֹרֵ֥ב הִקְצַפְתֶּ֖ם אֶת־יְהוָ֑ה
you-were | against | Yahweh | (8) | and-at-Horeb | you-aroused-wrath | *** | Yahweh

וַיִּתְאַנַּ֧ף יְהוָ֛ה בָּכֶ֖ם לְהַשְׁמִ֥יד אֶתְכֶֽם׃ (9) בַּעֲלֹתִ֣י
so-he-was-angry | Yahweh | with-you | to-destroy | you | (9) | when-to-go-up-me

הָהָ֗רָה לָקַ֜חַת לוּחֹ֤ת הָאֲבָנִים֙ לוּחֹ֣ת הַבְּרִ֔ית
on-the-mountain | to-receive | tablets-of | the-stones | tables-of | the-covenant

אֲשֶׁר־כָּרַ֥ת יְהוָ֖ה עִמָּכֶ֑ם וָאֵשֵׁ֣ב בָּהָ֗ר אַרְבָּעִ֥ים י֣וֹם
that | he-made | Yahweh | with-you | and-I-stayed | on-the-mountain | forty | day

וְאַרְבָּעִ֣ים לַ֔יְלָה לֶ֚חֶם לֹ֣א אָכַ֔לְתִּי וּמַ֖יִם לֹ֣א שָׁתִֽיתִי׃ (10) וַיִּתֵּ֨ן
and-forty | night | bread | not | I-ate | and-waters | not | I-drank | (10) | and-he-gave

יְהוָ֜ה אֵלַ֗י אֶת־שְׁנֵי֙ לוּחֹ֣ת הָאֲבָנִ֔ים כְּתֻבִ֖ים
Yahweh | to-me | *** | two-of | tablets-of | the-stones | ones-being-inscribed

בְּאֶצְבַּ֣ע אֱלֹהִ֑ים וַעֲלֵיהֶ֗ם כְּכָל־הַדְּבָרִ֡ים אֲשֶׁ֣ר דִּבֶּר֩
by-finger-of | God | and-on-them | as-all-of | the-commandments | that | he-proclaimed

יְהוָ֨ה עִמָּכֶ֥ם בָּהָ֛ר מִתּ֥וֹךְ הָאֵ֖שׁ בְּי֥וֹם הַקָּהָֽל׃
Yahweh | to-you | on-the-mountain | out-of | the-fire | on-day-of | the-assembly

(11) וַיְהִ֗י מִקֵּץ֙ אַרְבָּעִ֣ים י֔וֹם וְאַרְבָּעִ֖ים לָ֑יְלָה נָתַ֨ן יְהוָ֜ה אֵלַ֗י
(11) | and-he-was | at-end-of | forty | day | and-forty | night | he-gave | Yahweh | to-me

אֶת־שְׁנֵ֛י לֻחֹ֥ת הָאֲבָנִ֖ים לֻח֥וֹת הַבְּרִֽית׃ (12) וַיֹּ֤אמֶר
*** | two-of | tablets-of | the-stones | tablets-of | the-covenant | (12) | then-he-told

is not because of your right-eousness or your integrity that you are going in to take possession of their land; but on account of the wickedness of these nations, the LORD your God will drive them out before you, to accomplish what he swore to your fathers, to Abraham, Isaac and Jacob. [6]Understand, then, that it is not because of your righteous-ness that the LORD your God is giving you this good land to possess, for you are a stiff-necked people.

*The Golden Calf*

[7]Remember this and never forget how you provoked the LORD your God to anger in the desert. From the day you left Egypt until you arrived here, you have been rebellious against the LORD. [8]At Horeb you aroused the LORD's wrath so that he was angry enough to destroy you. [9]When I went up on the mountain to receive the tablets of stone, the tablets of the covenant that the LORD had made with you, I stayed on the mountain forty days and forty nights; I ate no bread and drank no water. [10]The LORD gave me two stone tablets inscribed by the finger of God. On them were all the commandments the LORD pro-claimed to you on the moun-tain out of the fire, on the day of the assembly.

[11]At the end of the forty days and forty nights, the LORD gave me the two stone tablets, the tablets of the covenant.

יְהוָה אֵלַי קוּם רֵד מַהֵר מִזֶּה כִּי שִׁחֵת
he-became-corrupt for from-here at-once go-down! rise! to-me Yahweh

עַמְּךָ אֲשֶׁר הוֹצֵאתָ מִמִּצְרָיִם סָרוּ מַהֵר מִן־ הַדֶּרֶךְ
the-way from quickly they-turned from-Egypt you-brought whom people-of-you

אֲשֶׁר צִוִּיתִם עָשׂוּ לָהֶם מַסֵּכָה׃ וַיֹּאמֶר יְהוָה
Yahweh and-he-said (13) cast-idol for-them they-made I-commanded-them that

אֵלַי לֵאמֹר רָאִיתִי אֶת־ הָעָם הַזֶּה וְהִנֵּה עַם־ קְשֵׁה־ עֹרֶף
neck stiff-of people-of and-see! the-this the-people *** I-see to-say to-me

הוּא׃ הֶרֶף מִמֶּנִּי וְאַשְׁמִידֵם וְאֶמְחֶה אֶת־
*** and-I-may-blot-out so-I-may-destroy-them from-me let-alone! (14) he

שְׁמָם מִתַּחַת הַשָּׁמָיִם וְאֶעֱשֶׂה אוֹתְךָ לְגוֹי־ עָצוּם
stronger into-nation you and-I-will-make the-heavens from-under name-of-them

וָרָב מִמֶּנּוּ׃ וָאֵפֶן וָאֵרֵד מִן־ הָהָר
the-mountain from and-I-went-down so-I-turned (15) than-him and-larger

וְהָהָר בֹּעֵר בָּאֵשׁ וּשְׁנֵי לֻחֹת הַבְּרִית
the-covenant tablets-of and-two-of with-the-fire blazing and-the-mountain

עַל שְׁתֵּי יָדָי׃ וָאֵרֶא וְהִנֵּה חֲטָאתֶם לַיהוָה
against-Yahweh you-sinned then-see! when-I-looked (16) hands-of-me two-of in

אֱלֹהֵיכֶם עֲשִׂיתֶם לָכֶם עֵגֶל מַסֵּכָה סַרְתֶּם מַהֵר מִן־
from quickly you-turned cast-idol calf for-you you-made God-of-you

הַדֶּרֶךְ אֲשֶׁר־ צִוָּה יְהוָה אֶתְכֶם׃ וָאֶתְפֹּשׂ בִּשְׁנֵי הַלֻּחֹת
the-tablets on-two-of so-I-held (17) you Yahweh he-commanded that the-way

וָאַשְׁלִכֵם מֵעַל שְׁתֵּי יָדָי וָאֲשַׁבְּרֵם לְעֵינֵיכֶם׃
before-eyes-of-you and-I-broke-them hands-of-me two-of from-in and-I-threw-them

וָאֶתְנַפַּל לִפְנֵי יְהוָה כָּרִאשֹׁנָה אַרְבָּעִים יוֹם וְאַרְבָּעִים לַיְלָה
night and-forty day forty as-the-first Yahweh before and-I-prostrated (18)

לֶחֶם לֹא אָכַלְתִּי וּמַיִם לֹא שָׁתִיתִי עַל כָּל־ חַטַּאתְכֶם אֲשֶׁר
that sin-of-you all-of because-of I-drank not and-waters I-ate not bread

חֲטָאתֶם לַעֲשׂוֹת הָרַע בְּעֵינֵי יְהוָה לְהַכְעִיסוֹ׃ כִּי
for (19) to-make-angry-him Yahweh in-eyes-of the-evil to-do you-sinned

יָגֹרְתִּי מִפְּנֵי הָאַף וְהַחֵמָה אֲשֶׁר קָצַף יְהוָה
Yahweh he-was-angry for and-the-wrath the-anger from-presences-of I-feared

עֲלֵיכֶם לְהַשְׁמִיד אֶתְכֶם וַיִּשְׁמַע יְהוָה אֵלַי גַּם בַּפַּעַם
at-the-time again to-me Yahweh but-he-listened you to-destroy with-you

הַהִוא׃ וּבְאַהֲרֹן הִתְאַנַּף יְהוָה מְאֹד לְהַשְׁמִידוֹ
to-destroy-him very Yahweh he-was-angry and-with-Aaron (20) the-that

וָאֶתְפַּלֵּל גַּם־ בְּעַד אַהֲרֹן בָּעֵת הַהִוא׃ וְאֶת־
and (21) the-that at-the-time Aaron on-behalf-of also but-I-prayed

[12]Then the LORD told me, "Go down from here at once, because your people whom you brought out of Egypt have become corrupt. They have turned away quickly from what I commanded them and have made a cast idol for themselves."

[13]And the LORD said to me, "I have seen this people, and they are a stiff-necked people indeed! [14]Let me alone, so that I may destroy them and blot out their name from under heaven. And I will make you into a nation stronger and more numerous than they."

[15]So I turned and went down from the mountain while it was ablaze with fire. And the two tablets of the covenant were in my hands.[q] [16]When I looked, I saw that you had sinned against the LORD your God; you had made for yourselves an idol cast in the shape of a calf. You had turned aside quickly from the way that the LORD had commanded you. [17]So I took the two tablets and threw them out of my hands, breaking them to pieces before your eyes.

[18]Then once again I fell prostrate before the LORD for forty days and forty nights; I ate no bread and drank no water, because of all the sin you had committed, doing what was evil in the LORD's sight and so provoking him to anger. [19]I feared the anger and wrath of the LORD, for he was angry enough with you to destroy you. But again the LORD listened to me. [20]And the LORD was angry enough with Aaron to destroy him, but at that time I prayed for Aaron too.

q15 Or *And I had the two tablets of the covenant with me, one in each hand*

חַטַּאתְכֶם אֲשֶׁר־ עֲשִׂיתֶם אֶת־ הָעֵגֶל לָקַחְתִּי וָאֶשְׂרֹף אֹתוֹ ׀

him and-I-burned I-took the-calf *** you-made that sinful-thing-of-you

בָּאֵשׁ וָאֶכֹּת אֹתוֹ טָחוֹן הֵיטֵב עַד אֲשֶׁר־ דַּק

he-was-fine when until to-be-fine to-grind him then-I-crushed in-the-fire

לְעָפָר וָאַשְׁלִךְ אֶת־ עֲפָרוֹ אֶל־ הַנַּחַל הַיֹּרֵד מִן־

from the-one-flowing the-stream into dust-of-him *** and-I-threw as-dust

הָהָר׃ וּבְתַבְעֵרָה וּבְמַסָּה וּבְקִבְרֹת הַתַּאֲוָה

Hattaavah and-at-Kibroth and-at-Massah and-at-Taberah (22) the-mountain

מַקְצִפִים הֱיִיתֶם אֶת־ יְהוָה׃ וּבִשְׁלֹחַ יְהוָה אֶתְכֶם

you Yahweh and-when-to-send (23) Yahweh *** you-were ones-angering

מִקָּדֵשׁ בַּרְנֵעַ לֵאמֹר עֲלוּ וּרְשׁוּ אֶת־ הָאָרֶץ אֲשֶׁר נָתַתִּי

I-gave that the-land *** and-possess! go-up! to-say Barnea from-Kadesh

לָכֶם וַתַּמְרוּ אֶת־ פִּי יְהוָה אֱלֹהֵיכֶם וְלֹא הֶאֱמַנְתֶּם

you-trusted and-not God-of-you Yahweh command-of *** but-you-rebelled to-you

לוֹ וְלֹא שְׁמַעְתֶּם בְּקֹלוֹ׃ מַמְרִים הֱיִיתֶם

you-were ones-rebelling (24) to-voice-of-him you-obeyed and-not in-him

עִם־ יְהוָה מִיּוֹם דַּעְתִּי אֶתְכֶם׃ וָאֶתְנַפַּל לִפְנֵי יְהוָה אֶת

*** Yahweh before and-I-lay-prostrate (25) you I-knew from-day Yahweh against

אַרְבָּעִים הַיּוֹם וְאֶת־ אַרְבָּעִים הַלַּיְלָה אֲשֶׁר הִתְנַפָּלְתִּי כִּי־ אָמַר יְהוָה

Yahweh he-said for I-lay-prostrate that the-night forty and the-day forty

לְהַשְׁמִיד אֶתְכֶם׃ וָאֶתְפַּלֵּל אֶל־ יְהוָה וָאֹמַר אֲדֹנָי יְהוִה אַל־

not Yahweh Lord and-I-said Yahweh to and-I-prayed (26) you to-destroy

תַּשְׁחֵת עַמְּךָ וְנַחֲלָתְךָ אֲשֶׁר פָּדִיתָ

you-redeemed that and-inheritance-of-you people-of-you you-destroy

בְּגָדְלֶךָ אֲשֶׁר־ הוֹצֵאתָ מִמִּצְרַיִם בְּיָד חֲזָקָה׃ זְכֹר

remember! (27) mighty with-hand from-Egypt you-brought that by-greatness-of-you

לַעֲבָדֶיךָ לְאַבְרָהָם לְיִצְחָק וּלְיַעֲקֹב אַל־ תֵּפֶן אֶל־

at you-look not and-to-Jacob to-Isaac to-Abraham to-servants-of-you

קְשִׁי הָעָם הַזֶּה וְאֶל־ רִשְׁעוֹ וְאֶל־

and-at wickedness-of-him and-at the-this the-people stubbornness-of

חַטָּאתוֹ׃ פֶּן־ יֹאמְרוּ הָאָרֶץ אֲשֶׁר הוֹצֵאתָנוּ

you-brought-us which the-country they-will-say otherwise (28) sin-of-him

מִשָּׁם מִבְּלִי יְכֹלֶת יְהוָה לַהֲבִיאָם אֶל־ הָאָרֶץ אֲשֶׁר־

that the-land into to-take-them Yahweh to-be-able because-not from-there

דִּבֶּר לָהֶם וּמִשִּׂנְאָתוֹ אוֹתָם הוֹצִיאָם

he-brought-them for-them and-because-of-hate-of-him to-them he-promised

לַהֲמִתָם בַּמִּדְבָּר׃ וְהֵם עַמְּךָ וְנַחֲלָתֶךָ

and-inheritance-of-you people-of-you but-they (29) in-the-desert to-kill-them

21 Also I took that sinful thing
of yours, the calf you had
made, and burned it in the
fire. Then I crushed it and
ground it to powder as fine as
dust and threw the dust into a
stream that flowed down the
mountain.
22 You also made the LORD
angry at Taberah, at Massah
and at Kibroth Hattaavah.
23 And when the LORD sent
you out from Kadesh Barnea,
he said, "Go up and take
possession of the land I have
given you." But you rebelled
against the command of the
LORD your God. You did not
trust him or obey him.
24 You
have been rebellious against
the LORD ever since I have
known you.
25 I lay prostrate before the
LORD those forty days and
forty nights because the LORD
had said he would destroy
you.
26 I prayed to the LORD and
said, "O Sovereign LORD, do
not destroy your people, your
own inheritance that you redeemed by your great power
and brought out of Egypt with
a mighty hand.
27 Remember
your servants Abraham, Isaac
and Jacob. Overlook the stubbornness of this people, their
wickedness and their sin.
28 Otherwise, the country from
which you brought us will say,
'Because the LORD was not able
to take them into the land he
had promised them, and because he hated them, he
brought them out to put them
to death in the desert.'
29 But
they are your people, your inheritance that you brought out

אֲשֶׁר הוֹצֵאתָ בְּכֹחֲךָ הַגָּדֹל וּבִזְרֹעֲךָ
and-by-arm-of-you the-great by-power-of-you you-brought-out that

הַנְּטוּיָה׃ (10:1) בָּעֵת הַהִוא אָמַר יְהוָה אֵלַי
to-me Yahweh he-said the-that at-the-time (10:1) the-being-outstretched

פְּסָל־ לְךָ שְׁנֵי־ לוּחֹת אֲבָנִים כָּרִאשֹׁנִים וַעֲלֵה
and-come-up! like-the-first-ones stones tablets-of two-of for-you chisel-out!

אֵלַי הָהָרָה וְעָשִׂיתָ לְּךָ אֲרוֹן עֵץ׃ (2) וְאֶכְתֹּב
and-I-will-write (2) wood chest-of for-you and-you-make on-the-mountain to-me

עַל־ הַלֻּחֹת אֶת־ הַדְּבָרִים אֲשֶׁר הָיוּ עַל־ הַלֻּחֹת הָרִאשֹׁנִים
the-first-ones the-tablets on they-were that the-words *** the-tablets on

אֲשֶׁר שִׁבַּרְתָּ וְשַׂמְתָּם בָּאָרוֹן׃ (3) וָאַעַשׂ אֲרוֹן
chest-of so-I-made (3) in-the-chest then-you-put-them you-broke which

עֲצֵי שִׁטִּים וָאֶפְסֹל שְׁנֵי־ לֻחֹת אֲבָנִים כָּרִאשֹׁנִים
like-the-first-ones stones tablets-of two-of and-I-chiseled acacias woods-of

וָאַעַל הָהָרָה וּשְׁנֵי הַלֻּחֹת בְּיָדִי׃
in-hand-of-me the-tablets and-two-of on-the-mountain and-I-went-up

(4) וַיִּכְתֹּב עַל־ הַלֻּחֹת כַּמִּכְתָּב הָרִאשׁוֹן אֵת עֲשֶׂרֶת
ten-of *** the-first as-the-writing the-tablets on and-he-wrote (4)

הַדְּבָרִים אֲשֶׁר דִּבֶּר יְהוָה אֲלֵיכֶם בָּהָר מִתּוֹךְ
out-of on-the-mountain to-you Yahweh he-proclaimed that the-commandments

הָאֵשׁ בְּיוֹם הַקָּהָל וַיִּתְּנֵם יְהוָה אֵלָי׃ (5) וָאֵפֶן
then-I-left (5) to-me Yahweh and-he-gave-them the-assembly on-day-of the-fire

וָאֵרֵד מִן־ הָהָר וָאָשִׂם אֶת־ הַלֻּחֹת בָּאָרוֹן
in-the-chest the-tablets *** and-I-put the-mountain from and-I-came-down

אֲשֶׁר עָשִׂיתִי וַיִּהְיוּ שָׁם כַּאֲשֶׁר צִוַּנִי יְהוָה׃ (6) וּבְנֵי
now-sons-of (6) Yahweh he-commanded-me just-as there and-they-are I-made that

יִשְׂרָאֵל נָסְעוּ מִבְּאֵרֹת בְּנֵי־ יַעֲקָן מוֹסֵרָה שָׁם מֵת
he-died there Moserah Jaakan sons-of from-wells-of they-travelled Israel

אַהֲרֹן וַיִּקָּבֵר שָׁם וַיְכַהֵן אֶלְעָזָר בְּנוֹ
son-of-him Eleazar then-he-became-priest there and-he-was-buried Aaron

תַּחְתָּיו׃ (7) מִשָּׁם נָסְעוּ הַגֻּדְגֹּדָה וּמִן־
and-from the-Gudgodah they-travelled from-there (7) in-place-of-him

הַגֻּדְגֹּדָה יָטְבָתָה אֶרֶץ נַחֲלֵי מָיִם׃ (8) בָּעֵת הַהִוא
the-that at-the-time (8) waters streams-of land-of Jotbathah the-Gudgodah

הִבְדִּיל יְהוָה אֶת־ שֵׁבֶט הַלֵּוִי לָשֵׂאת אֶת־ אֲרוֹן בְּרִית־
covenant-of ark-of *** to-carry the-Levi tribe-of *** Yahweh he-set-apart

יְהוָה לַעֲמֹד לִפְנֵי יְהוָה לְשָׁרְתוֹ וּלְבָרֵךְ בִּשְׁמוֹ
in-name-of-him and-to-bless to-minister-him Yahweh before to-stand Yahweh

by your great power and your outstretched arm."

*Tablets Like the First Ones*

10 At that time the LORD said to me, "Chisel out two stone tablets like the first ones and come up to me on the mountain. Also make a wooden chest.[r] 2I will write on the tablets the words that were on the first tablets, which you broke. Then you are to put them in the chest."

3So I made the ark out of acacia wood and chiseled out two stone tablets like the first ones, and I went up on the mountain with the two tablets in my hands. 4The LORD wrote on these tablets what he had written before, the Ten Commandments he had proclaimed to you on the mountain, out of the fire, on the day of the assembly. And the LORD gave them to me. 5Then I came back down the mountain and put the tablets in the ark I had made, as the LORD commanded me, and they are there now.

6(The Israelites traveled from the wells of the Jaakanites to Moserah. There Aaron died and was buried, and Eleazar his son succeeded him as priest. 7From there they traveled to Gudgodah and on to Jotbathah, a land with streams of water. 8At that time the LORD set apart the tribe of Levi to carry the ark of the covenant of the LORD, to stand before the LORD to minister and to pronounce blessings in his

r1 That is, an ark

עַד הַיּוֹם הַזֶּה׃ עַל־כֵּן לֹא־הָיָה לְלֵוִי חֵלֶק וְנַחֲלָה
or-inheritance share to-Levi he-is not this for (9) the-this the-day to

עִם־אֶחָיו יְהוָה הוּא נַחֲלָתוֹ כַּאֲשֶׁר דִּבֶּר יְהוָה
Yahweh he-told just-as inheritance-of-him he Yahweh brothers-of-him among

אֱלֹהֶיךָ לוֹ׃ וְאָנֹכִי עָמַדְתִּי בָהָר כַּיָּמִים
as-the-days on-the-mountain I-stayed now-I (10) to-him God-of-you

הָרִאשֹׁנִים אַרְבָּעִים יוֹם וְאַרְבָּעִים לַיְלָה וַיִּשְׁמַע יְהוָה אֵלַי גַּם
also to-me Yahweh and-he-listened night and-forty day forty the-first-ones

בַּפַּעַם הַהִוא לֹא־אָבָה יְהוָה הַשְׁחִיתֶךָ׃ וַיֹּאמֶר
and-he-said (11) to-destroy-you Yahweh he-willed not the-this at-the-time

יְהוָה אֵלַי קוּם לֵךְ לְמַסַּע לִפְנֵי הָעָם וְיָבֹאוּ
so-they-may-enter the-people before on-journey go! rise! to-me Yahweh

וְיִרְשׁוּ אֶת־הָאָרֶץ אֲשֶׁר־נִשְׁבַּעְתִּי לַאֲבֹתָם לָתֵת
to-give to-fathers-of-them I-swore that the-land *** and-they-may-possess

לָהֶם׃ וְעַתָּה יִשְׂרָאֵל מָה יְהוָה אֱלֹהֶיךָ שֹׁאֵל מֵעִמָּךְ כִּי
but from-you asking God-of-you Yahweh what? Israel and-now (12) to-them

אִם־לְיִרְאָה אֶת־יְהוָה אֱלֹהֶיךָ לָלֶכֶת בְּכָל־דְּרָכָיו וּלְאַהֲבָה
and-to-love ways-of-him in-all-of to-walk God-of-you Yahweh *** to-fear only

אֹתוֹ וְלַעֲבֹד אֶת־יְהוָה אֱלֹהֶיךָ בְּכָל־לְבָבְךָ
heart-of-you with-all-of God-of-you Yahweh *** and-to-serve him

וּבְכָל־נַפְשֶׁךָ׃ לִשְׁמֹר אֶת־מִצְוֺת יְהוָה וְאֶת־
and Yahweh commands-of *** to-observe (13) soul-of-you and-with-all-of

חֻקֹּתָיו אֲשֶׁר אָנֹכִי מְצַוְּךָ הַיּוֹם לְטוֹב לָךְ׃ הֵן
see! (14) for-you for-good the-day giving-you I that decrees-of-him

לַיהוָה אֱלֹהֶיךָ הַשָּׁמַיִם וּשְׁמֵי הַשָּׁמַיִם הָאָרֶץ וְכָל־
and-all the-earth the-heavens and-heavens-of the-heavens God-of-you to-Yahweh

אֲשֶׁר־בָּהּ׃ רַק בַּאֲבֹתֶיךָ חָשַׁק יְהוָה לְאַהֲבָה אוֹתָם
them to-love Yahweh he-set-affection on-fathers-of-you yet (15) in-her that

וַיִּבְחַר בְּזַרְעָם אַחֲרֵיהֶם בָּכֶם מִכָּל־הָעַמִּים
the-nations above-all-of to-you after-them to-descendant-of-them and-he-chose

כַּיּוֹם הַזֶּה׃ וּמַלְתֶּם אֵת עָרְלַת לְבַבְכֶם
heart-of-you foreskin-of *** so-you-circumcise (16) the-this as-the-day

וְעָרְפְּכֶם לֹא תַקְשׁוּ עוֹד׃ כִּי יְהוָה אֱלֹהֵיכֶם הוּא
he God-of-you Yahweh for (17) longer you-make-stiff not and-neck-of-you

אֱלֹהֵי הָאֱלֹהִים וַאֲדֹנֵי הָאֲדֹנִים הָאֵל הַגָּדֹל הַגִּבֹּר
the-mighty the-great the-God the-lords and-Lord-of the-gods God-of

וְהַנּוֹרָא אֲשֶׁר לֹא־יִשָּׂא פָנִים וְלֹא יִקַּח שֹׁחַד׃
bribe he-accepts and-not faces he-lifts not who and-the-being-awesome

name, as they still do today.
[9]That is why the Levites have
no share or inheritance
among their brothers; the
LORD is their inheritance, as
the LORD your God told them.)
[10]Now I had stayed on the
mountain forty days and
nights, as I did the first time,
and the LORD listened to me at
this time also. It was not his
will to destroy you. [11]"Go," the
LORD said to me, "and lead the
people on their way, so that
they may enter and possess
the land that I swore to their
fathers to give them."

*Fear the LORD*

[12]And now, O Israel, what
does the LORD your God ask of
you but to fear the LORD your
God, to walk in all his ways, to
love him, to serve the LORD
your God with all your heart
and with all your soul, [13]and to
observe the LORD's commands
and decrees that I am giving
you today for your own good?
[14]To the LORD your God belong the heavens, even the
highest heavens, the earth
and everything in it. [15]Yet the
LORD set his affection on your
forefathers and loved them,
and he chose you, their descendants, above all the nations, as it is today. [16]Circum-
cise your hearts, therefore,
and do not be stiff-necked any
longer. [17]For the LORD your
God is God of gods and Lord of
lords, the great God, mighty
and awesome, who shows no
partiality and accepts no

עֹשֶׂה מִשְׁפַּט יָתוֹם וְאַלְמָנָה וְאֹהֵב גֵּר לָתֶת לוֹ
to-him to-give alien and-loving and-widow fatherless cause-of defending (18)

לֶחֶם וְשִׂמְלָה׃ וַאֲהַבְתֶּם אֶת־ הַגֵּר כִּי־ גֵרִים הֱיִיתֶם
you-were aliens for the-alien *** so-you-love (19) and-clothing food

בְּאֶרֶץ מִצְרָיִם׃ אֶת־ יְהוָה אֱלֹהֶיךָ תִּירָא אֹתוֹ תַעֲבֹד
you-serve him you-fear God-of-you Yahweh *** (20) Egypt in-land-of

וּבוֹ תִדְבָּק וּבִשְׁמוֹ תִּשָּׁבֵעַ׃ הוּא
he (21) you-take-oath and-in-name-of-him you-hold-fast and-to-him

תְהִלָּתְךָ וְהוּא אֱלֹהֶיךָ אֲשֶׁר־ עָשָׂה אִתְּךָ אֶת־ הַגְּדֹלֹת
the-great-things *** for-you he-performed who God-of-you and-he praise-of-you

וְאֶת־ הַנּוֹרָאֹת הָאֵלֶּה אֲשֶׁר רָאוּ עֵינֶיךָ׃ בְּשִׁבְעִים
as-seventy (22) eyes-of-you they-saw that the-those the-ones-being-awesome and

נֶפֶשׁ יָרְדוּ אֲבֹתֶיךָ מִצְרָיְמָה וְעַתָּה שָׂמְךָ יְהוָה
Yahweh he-made-you and-now into-Egypt fathers-of-you they-went-down person

אֱלֹהֶיךָ כְּכוֹכְבֵי הַשָּׁמַיִם לָרֹב׃ וְאָהַבְתָּ אֵת יְהוָה
Yahweh *** so-you-love (11:1) for-the-number the-skies as-stars-of God-of-you

אֱלֹהֶיךָ וְשָׁמַרְתָּ מִשְׁמַרְתּוֹ וְחֻקֹּתָיו וּמִשְׁפָּטָיו
and-laws-of-him and-decrees-of-him requirement-of-him and-you-keep God-of-you

וּמִצְוֺתָיו כָּל־ הַיָּמִים׃ וִידַעְתֶּם הַיּוֹם כִּי ׀ לֹא
not that the-day and-you-remember (2) the-days all-of and-commands-of-him

אֶת־ בְּנֵיכֶם אֲשֶׁר לֹא־ יָדְעוּ וַאֲשֶׁר לֹא־ רָאוּ אֶת־
*** they-saw not and-who they-experienced not who children-of-you ***

מוּסַר יְהוָה אֱלֹהֵיכֶם אֶת־ גָּדְלוֹ אֶת־ יָדוֹ הַחֲזָקָה
the-mighty hand-of-him *** majesty-of-him *** God-of-you Yahweh discipline-of

וּזְרֹעוֹ הַנְּטוּיָה׃ וְאֶת־ אֹתֹתָיו וְאֶת־ מַעֲשָׂיו
deeds-of-him and signs-of-him and (3) the-being-outstretched and-arm-of-him

אֲשֶׁר עָשָׂה בְּתוֹךְ מִצְרַיִם לְפַרְעֹה מֶלֶךְ־ מִצְרַיִם וּלְכָל־
and-to-whole-of Egypt king-of to-Pharaoh Egypt in-midst-of he-performed that

אַרְצוֹ׃ וַאֲשֶׁר עָשָׂה לְחֵיל מִצְרַיִם לְסוּסָיו
to-horses-of-him Egypt to-army-of he-did and-what (4) country-of-him

וּלְרִכְבּוֹ אֲשֶׁר הֵצִיף אֶת־ מֵי יַם־ סוּף עַל־
over Reed Sea-of waters-of *** he-made-flow how and-to-chariot-of-him

פְּנֵיהֶם בְּרָדְפָם אַחֲרֵיכֶם וַיְאַבְּדֵם יְהוָה עַד
to Yahweh and-he-ruined-them after-you as-to-pursue-them faces-of-them

הַיּוֹם הַזֶּה׃ וַאֲשֶׁר עָשָׂה לָכֶם בַּמִּדְבָּר עַד־ בֹּאֲכֶם
to-come-you until in-the-desert for-you he-did and-what (5) the-this the-day

עַד־ הַמָּקוֹם הַזֶּה׃ וַאֲשֶׁר עָשָׂה לְדָתָן וְלַאֲבִירָם בְּנֵי
sons-of and-to-Abiram to-Dathan he-did and-what (6) the-this the-place to

bribes. [18]He defends the cause
of the fatherless and the
widow, and loves the alien,
giving him food and clothing.
[19]And you are to love those
who are aliens, for you yourselves were aliens in Egypt.
[20]Fear the LORD your God and
serve him. Hold fast to him
and take your oaths in his
name. [21]He is your praise; he is
your God, who performed for
you those great and awesome
wonders you saw with your
own eyes. [22]Your forefathers
who went down into Egypt
were seventy in all, and now
the LORD your God has made
you as numerous as the stars
in the sky.

*Love and Obey the LORD*

11 Love the LORD your
God and keep his re-
quirements, his decrees, his
laws and his commands al-
ways. [2]Remember today that
your children were not the
ones who saw and experi-
enced the discipline of the
LORD your God: his majesty,
his mighty hand, his out-
stretched arm; [3]the signs he
performed and the things he
did in the heart of Egypt, both
to Pharaoh king of Egypt and
to his whole country; [4]what he
did to the Egyptian army, to
its horses and chariots, how
he overwhelmed them with
the waters of the Red Sea[s] as
they were pursuing you, and
how the LORD brought lasting
ruin on them. [5]It was not your
children who saw what he did
for you in the desert until you
arrived at this place, [6]and
what he did to Dathan and

[s]4 Hebrew *Yam Suph;* that is, Sea of Reeds

אֱלִיאָב בֶּן־ רְאוּבֵן אֲשֶׁר פָּצְתָה הָאָרֶץ אֶת־ פִּיהָ
mouth-of-her *** the-earth she-opened when Reuben son-of Eliab

וַתִּבְלָעֵם וְאֶת־ בָּתֵּיהֶם וְאֶת־ אָהֳלֵיהֶם וְאֵת כָּל־
all-of and tents-of-them and households-of-them and and-she-swallowed-them

הַיְקוּם אֲשֶׁר בְּרַגְלֵיהֶם בְּקֶרֶב כָּל־ יִשְׂרָאֵל׃ כִּי
but (7) Israel all-of in-middle-of under-feet-of-them that the-thing

עֵינֵיכֶם הָרֹאֹת אֶת־ כָּל־ מַעֲשֵׂה יְהוָה הַגָּדֹל אֲשֶׁר עָשָׂה׃
he-did that the-great Yahweh act-of every-of *** the-ones-seeing eyes-of-you

וּשְׁמַרְתֶּם אֶת־ כָּל־ הַמִּצְוָה אֲשֶׁר אָנֹכִי מְצַוְּךָ הַיּוֹם לְמַעַן
so-that the-day giving-you I that the-command all-of *** so-you-observe (8)

תֶּחֶזְקוּ וּבָאתֶם וִירִשְׁתֶּם אֶת־ הָאָרֶץ אֲשֶׁר
that the-land *** and-you-may-possess and-you-may-go-in you-may-be-strong

אַתֶּם עֹבְרִים שָׁמָּה לְרִשְׁתָּהּ׃ וּלְמַעַן תַּאֲרִיכוּ
you-may-live-long and-so-that (9) to-possess-her to-there ones-crossing you

יָמִים עַל־ הָאֲדָמָה אֲשֶׁר נִשְׁבַּע יְהוָה לַאֲבֹתֵיכֶם לָתֵת לָהֶם
to-them to-give to-fathers-of-you Yahweh he-swore that the-land in days

וּלְזַרְעָם אֶרֶץ זָבַת חָלָב וּדְבָשׁ׃ כִּי הָאָרֶץ
the-land now (10) and-honey milk flowing-of land and-to-descendant-of-them

אֲשֶׁר אַתָּה בָא־ שָׁמָּה לְרִשְׁתָּהּ לֹא כְאֶרֶץ מִצְרַיִם הִוא
she Egypt like-land-of not to-take-over-her to-there entering you that

אֲשֶׁר יְצָאתֶם מִשָּׁם אֲשֶׁר תִּזְרַע אֶת־ זַרְעֲךָ וְהִשְׁקִיתָ
and-you-irrigated seed-of-you *** you-planted where from-there you-came which

בְרַגְלְךָ כְּגַן הַיָּרָק׃ וְהָאָרֶץ אֲשֶׁר אַתֶּם
you that but-the-land (11) the-vegetable as-garden-of by-foot-of-you

עֹבְרִים שָׁמָּה לְרִשְׁתָּהּ אֶרֶץ הָרִים וּבְקָעֹת
and-valleys mountains land-of to-possess-her to-there ones-crossing

לִמְטַר הַשָּׁמַיִם תִּשְׁתֶּה־ מָּיִם׃ אֶרֶץ אֲשֶׁר־ יְהוָה אֱלֹהֶיךָ
God-of-you Yahweh that land (12) waters she-drinks the-heavens from-rain-of

דֹּרֵשׁ אֹתָהּ תָּמִיד עֵינֵי יְהוָה אֱלֹהֶיךָ בָּהּ מֵרֵשִׁית
from-beginning-of on-her God-of-you Yahweh eyes-of continually for-her caring

הַשָּׁנָה וְעַד אַחֲרִית שָׁנָה׃ וְהָיָה אִם־ שָׁמֹעַ תִּשְׁמְעוּ אֶל־
to you-obey to-obey if so-he-will-be (13) year end-of even-to the-year

מִצְוֺתַי אֲשֶׁר אָנֹכִי מְצַוֶּה אֶתְכֶם הַיּוֹם לְאַהֲבָה אֶת־ יְהוָה אֱלֹהֵיכֶם
God-of-you Yahweh *** to-love the-day you giving I that commands-of-me

וּלְעָבְדוֹ בְּכָל־ לְבַבְכֶם וּבְכָל־ נַפְשְׁכֶם׃
soul-of-you and-with-all-of heart-of-you with-all-of and-to-serve-him

וְנָתַתִּי מְטַר־ אַרְצְכֶם בְּעִתּוֹ יוֹרֶה
autumn-rain in-season-of-him land-of-you rain-of then-I-will-send (14)

Abiram, sons of Eliab the Reubenite, when the earth opened
its mouth right in the middle
of all Israel and swallowed
them up with their
households, their tents and
every living thing that belonged to them. [7]But it was
your own eyes that saw all
these great things the LORD
has done.
[8]Observe therefore all the
commands I am giving you today, so that you may have the
strength to go in and take over
the land that you are crossing
the Jordan to possess, [9]and so
that you may live long in the
land that the LORD swore to
your forefathers to give to
them and their descendants, a
land flowing with milk and
honey. [10]The land you are entering to take over is not like
the land of Egypt, from which
you have come, where you
planted your seed and irrigat-
ed it by foot as in a vegetable
garden. [11]But the land you are
crossing the Jordan to take
possession of is a land of
mountains and valleys that
drinks rain from heaven. [12]It is
a land the LORD your God cares
for; the eyes of the LORD your
God are continually on it from
the beginning of the year to its
end.
[13]So if you faithfully obey
the commands I am giving
you today—to love the LORD
your God and to serve him
with all your heart and with
all your soul— [14]then I will
send rain on your land in its
season, both autumn and

וּמַלְקוֹשׁ וְאָסַפְתָּ דְגָנֶךָ וְתִירֹשְׁךָ

and-new-wine-of-you grain-of-you so-you-may-gather and-spring-rain

וְיִצְהָרֶךָ׃ וְנָתַתִּי עֵשֶׂב בְּשָׂדְךָ לִבְהֶמְתֶּךָ

for-cattle-of-you in-field-of-you grass and-I-will-provide (15) and-oil-of-you

וְאָכַלְתָּ וְשָׂבָעְתָּ׃ הִשָּׁמְרוּ לָכֶם פֶּן

or to-you be-careful! (16) and-you-will-be-satisfied and-you-will-eat

יִפְתֶּה לְבַבְכֶם וְסַרְתֶּם וַעֲבַדְתֶּם אֱלֹהִים

gods and-you-will-worship and-you-will-turn heart-of-you he-will-be-enticed

אֲחֵרִים וְהִשְׁתַּחֲוִיתֶם לָהֶם׃ וְחָרָה אַף־ יְהוָה

Yahweh anger-of then-he-will-burn (17) to-them and-you-will-bow other-ones

בָּכֶם וְעָצַר אֶת־ הַשָּׁמַיִם וְלֹא־ יִהְיֶה מָטָר

rain he-will-send so-not the-heavens *** and-he-will-shut against-you

וְהָאֲדָמָה לֹא תִתֵּן אֶת־ יְבוּלָהּ וַאֲבַדְתֶּם

and-you-will-perish produce-of-her *** she-will-yield not and-the-ground

מְהֵרָה מֵעַל הָאָרֶץ הַטֹּבָה אֲשֶׁר יְהוָה נֹתֵן לָכֶם׃ וְשַׂמְתֶּם

so-you-fix (18) to-you giving Yahweh that the-good the-land from-on soon

אֶת־ דְּבָרַי אֵלֶּה עַל־ לְבַבְכֶם וְעַל־ נַפְשְׁכֶם וּקְשַׁרְתֶּם אֹתָם

them and-you-tie mind-of-you and-in heart-of-you in these words-of-me ***

לְאוֹת עַל־ יֶדְכֶם וְהָיוּ לְטוֹטָפֹת בֵּין עֵינֵיכֶם׃

eyes-of-you between as-bands and-they-must-be hand-of-you on as-symbol

וְלִמַּדְתֶּם אֹתָם אֶת־ בְּנֵיכֶם לְדַבֵּר בָּם בְּשִׁבְתְּךָ

as-to-sit-you about-them to-talk children-of-you *** them and-you-teach (19)

בְּבֵיתֶךָ וּבְלֶכְתְּךָ בַדֶּרֶךְ וּבְשָׁכְבְּךָ

and-when-to-lie-down-you along-the-road and-when-to-walk-you at-home-of-you

וּבְקוּמֶךָ׃ וּכְתַבְתָּם עַל־ מְזוּזוֹת בֵּיתֶךָ

houses-of-you door-frames-of on and-you-write-them (20) and-when-to-get-up-you

וּבִשְׁעָרֶיךָ׃ לְמַעַן יִרְבּוּ יְמֵיכֶם וִימֵי

and-days-of days-of-you they-may-be-many so-that (21) and-on-gates-of-you

בְנֵיכֶם עַל הָאֲדָמָה אֲשֶׁר נִשְׁבַּע יְהוָה לַאֲבֹתֵיכֶם לָתֵת

to-give to-fathers-of-you Yahweh he-swore that the-land in children-of-you

לָהֶם כִּימֵי הַשָּׁמַיִם עַל־ הָאָרֶץ׃ כִּי אִם־ שָׁמֹר

to-observe if for (22) the-earth above the-heavens as-days-of to-them

תִּשְׁמְרוּן אֶת־ כָּל־ הַמִּצְוָה הַזֹּאת אֲשֶׁר אָנֹכִי מְצַוֶּה אֶתְכֶם לַעֲשֹׂתָהּ

to-follow-her you giving I that the-this the-command all-of *** you-observe

לְאַהֲבָה אֶת־ יְהוָה אֱלֹהֵיכֶם לָלֶכֶת בְּכָל־ דְּרָכָיו וּלְדָבְקָה־

and-to-hold-fast ways-of-him in-all-of to-walk God-of-you Yahweh *** to-love

בוֹ׃ וְהוֹרִישׁ יְהוָה אֶת־ כָּל־ הַגּוֹיִם הָאֵלֶּה

the-these the-nations all-of *** Yahweh then-he-will-drive-out (23) to-him

spring rains, so that you may
gather in your grain, new
wine and oil. [15]I will provide
grass in the fields for your cattle, and you will eat and be satisfied.
[16]Be careful, or you will be
enticed to turn away and worship other gods and bow
down to them. [17]Then the
LORD's anger will burn against
you, and he will shut the
heavens so that it will not rain
and the ground will yield no
produce, and you will soon
perish from the good land the
LORD is giving you. [18]Fix these
words of mine in your hearts
and minds; tie them as symbols on your hands and bind
them on your foreheads.
[19]Teach them to your children,
talking about them when you
sit at home and when you
walk along the road, when
you lie down and when you
get up. [20]Write them on the
doorframes of your houses
and on your gates, [21]so that
your days and the days of your
children may be many in the
land that the LORD swore to
give your forefathers, as many
as the days that the heavens
are above the earth.
[22]If you carefully observe all
these commands I am giving
you to follow—to love the LORD
your God, to walk in all his
ways and to hold fast to him—
[23]then the LORD will drive out
all these nations before you,

מִלִּפְנֵיכֶם וִירִשְׁתֶּם גּוֹיִם גְּדֹלִים וַעֲצֻמִים
and-ones-stronger ones-larger nations and-you-will-dispossess from-before-you

מִכֶּם׃ כָּל־ הַמָּקוֹם אֲשֶׁר תִּדְרֹךְ כַּף־ רַגְלְכֶם בּוֹ
on-him foot-of-you sole-of she-sets where the-place every-of (24) than-you

לָכֶם יִהְיֶה מִן־ הַמִּדְבָּר וְהַלְּבָנוֹן מִן־ הַנָּהָר נְהַר־
River-of the-River from and-the-Lebanon the-desert from he-will-be for-you

פְּרָת וְעַד הַיָּם הָאַחֲרוֹן יִהְיֶה גְּבֻלְכֶם׃ לֹא־
not (25) border-of-you he-will-be the-western the-Sea even-to Euphrates

יִתְיַצֵּב אִישׁ בִּפְנֵיכֶם פַּחְדְּכֶם וּמוֹרַאֲכֶם
and-fear-of-you terror-of-you against-faces-of-you man he-will-stand

יִתֵּן ׀ יְהוָה אֱלֹהֵיכֶם עַל־ פְּנֵי כָל־ הָאָרֶץ אֲשֶׁר תִּדְרְכוּ־
you-go wherever the-land whole-of face-of on God-of-you Yahweh he-will-put

בָהּ כַּאֲשֶׁר דִּבֶּר לָכֶם׃ רְאֵה אָנֹכִי נֹתֵן לִפְנֵיכֶם הַיּוֹם
the-day before-you setting I see! (26) to-you he-promised just-as in-her

בְּרָכָה וּקְלָלָה׃ אֶת־ הַבְּרָכָה אֲשֶׁר תִּשְׁמְעוּ אֶל־ מִצְוֹת יְהוָה
Yahweh commands-of to you-obey if the-blessing *** (27) and-curse blessing

אֱלֹהֵיכֶם אֲשֶׁר אָנֹכִי מְצַוֶּה אֶתְכֶם הַיּוֹם׃ וְהַקְּלָלָה אִם־ לֹא תִשְׁמְעוּ
you-obey not if and-the-curse (28) the-day you giving I that God-of-you

אֶל־ מִצְוֹת יְהוָה אֱלֹהֵיכֶם וְסַרְתֶּם מִן־ הַדֶּרֶךְ אֲשֶׁר אָנֹכִי
I that the-way from and-you-turn God-of-you Yahweh commands-of to

מְצַוֶּה אֶתְכֶם הַיּוֹם לָלֶכֶת אַחֲרֵי אֱלֹהִים אֲחֵרִים אֲשֶׁר לֹא־ יְדַעְתֶּם
you-knew not that other-ones gods after to-follow the-day you commanding

וְהָיָה כִּי יְבִיאֲךָ יְהוָה אֱלֹהֶיךָ אֶל־ הָאָרֶץ אֲשֶׁר־
that the-land into God-of-you Yahweh he-brings-you when and-he-will-be (29)

אַתָּה בָא־ שָׁמָּה לְרִשְׁתָּהּ וְנָתַתָּה אֶת־ הַבְּרָכָה עַל־
on the-blessing *** then-you-proclaim to-possess-her to-there entering you

הַר גְּרִזִּים וְאֶת־הַקְּלָלָה עַל־ הַר עֵיבָל׃ הֲלֹא־הֵמָּה בְּעֵבֶר
on-across they not? (30) Ebal Mount-of on the-curse and Gerizim Mount-of

הַיַּרְדֵּן אַחֲרֵי דֶּרֶךְ מְבוֹא הַשֶּׁמֶשׁ בְּאֶרֶץ הַכְּנַעֲנִי
the-Canaanite in-territory-of the-sun set-of road west-of the-Jordan

הַיֹּשֵׁב בָּעֲרָבָה מוּל הַגִּלְגָּל אֵצֶל אֵלוֹנֵי מֹרֶה׃
Moreh trees-of near the-Gilgal vicinity-of in-the-Arabah the-one-living

כִּי אַתֶּם עֹבְרִים אֶת־ הַיַּרְדֵּן לָבֹא לָרֶשֶׁת אֶת־ הָאָרֶץ
the-land *** to-possess to-enter the-Jordan *** ones-crossing you now (31)

אֲשֶׁר־ יְהוָה אֱלֹהֵיכֶם נֹתֵן לָכֶם וִירִשְׁתֶּם אֹתָהּ וִישַׁבְתֶּם־
and-you-live her when-you-take-over to-you giving God-of-you Yahweh that

בָהּ׃ וּשְׁמַרְתֶּם לַעֲשׂוֹת אֵת כָּל־ הַחֻקִּים וְאֶת־הַמִּשְׁפָּטִים
the-laws and the-decrees all-of *** to-obey then-you-be-sure (32) in-her

and you will dispossess nations larger and stronger than
you. [24]Every place where you
set your foot will be yours: from the desert to Lebanon, and from the Euphrates River to the western sea.[t] [25]No man
will be able to stand against you. The LORD your God, as he promised you, will put the terror and fear of you on the whole land, wherever you go.
[26]See, I am setting before you today a blessing and a curse—
[27]the blessing if you obey the commands of the LORD your God that I am giving you today; [28]the curse if you disobey
the commands of the LORD your God and turn from the way that I command you today by following other gods, which you have not known.
[29]When the LORD your God has brought you into the land you are entering to possess, you are to proclaim on Mount Gerizim the blessings, and on Mount Ebal the curses. [30]As
you know, these mountains are across the Jordan, west of the road,[u] toward the setting sun, near the great trees of Moreh, in the territory of those Canaanites living in the Arabah in the vicinity of Gilgal. [31]You are about to cross
the Jordan to enter and take possession of the land the LORD your God is giving you. When you have taken it over and are living there, [32]be sure
that you obey all the decrees

[t]24 That is, the Mediterranean
[u]30 Or *Jordan, westward*

אֲשֶׁר אָנֹכִי נֹתֵן לִפְנֵיכֶם הַיּוֹם׃ אֵלֶּה הַחֻקִּים וְהַמִּשְׁפָּטִים

and-the-laws the-decrees these (12:1) the-day before-you setting I that

אֲשֶׁר תִּשְׁמְרוּן לַעֲשׂוֹת בָּאָרֶץ אֲשֶׁר נָתַן יְהוָה אֱלֹהֵי

God-of Yahweh he-gave that in-the-land to-follow you-must-be-careful that

אֲבֹתֶיךָ לְךָ לְרִשְׁתָּהּ כָּל־ הַיָּמִים אֲשֶׁר־ אַתֶּם חַיִּים עַל־

in ones-alive you that the-days all-of to-possess-her to-you fathers-of-you

הָאֲדָמָה׃ אַבֵּד תְּאַבְּדוּן אֶת־ כָּל־ הַמְּקֹמוֹת אֲשֶׁר עָבְדוּ־

they-worship that the-places all-of *** you-destroy to-destroy (2) the-land

שָׁם הַגּוֹיִם אֲשֶׁר אַתֶּם יֹרְשִׁים אֹתָם אֶת־ אֱלֹהֵיהֶם עַל־

on gods-of-them *** them ones-dispossessing you that the-nations there

הֶהָרִים הָרָמִים וְעַל־ הַגְּבָעוֹת וְתַחַת כָּל־ עֵץ

tree-of every-of and-under the-hills and-on the-high-ones the-mountains

רַעֲנָן׃ וְנִתַּצְתֶּם אֶת־ מִזְבְּחֹתָם* וְשִׁבַּרְתֶּם אֶת־

*** and-you-smash altars-of-them *** and-you-break-down (3) spreading

מַצֵּבֹתָם וַאֲשֵׁרֵיהֶם תִּשְׂרְפוּן בָּאֵשׁ

in-the-fire you-burn and-Asherah-poles-of-them sacred-stones-of-them

וּפְסִילֵי אֱלֹהֵיהֶם תְּגַדֵּעוּן וְאִבַּדְתֶּם אֶת־ שְׁמָם

name-of-them *** and-you-wipe-out you-cut-down gods-of-them and-idols-of

מִן־ הַמָּקוֹם הַהוּא׃ לֹא־ תַעֲשׂוּן כֵּן לַיהוָה אֱלֹהֵיכֶם׃

God-of-you to-Yahweh same-way you-worship not (4) the-that the-place from

כִּי אִם־ אֶל־הַמָּקוֹם אֲשֶׁר־ יִבְחַר יְהוָה אֱלֹהֵיכֶם מִכָּל־

from-all-of God-of-you Yahweh he-will-choose that the-place to rather but (5)

שִׁבְטֵיכֶם לָשׂוּם אֶת־ שְׁמוֹ שָׁם לְשִׁכְנוֹ תִדְרְשׁוּ

you-seek to-dwell-him there Name-of-him *** to-put tribes-of-you

וּבָאתָ שָׁמָּה׃ וַהֲבֵאתֶם שָׁמָּה עֹלֹתֵיכֶם

burnt-offerings-of-you to-there and-you-bring (6) to-there and-you-go

וְזִבְחֵיכֶם וְאֵת מַעְשְׂרֹתֵיכֶם וְאֵת תְּרוּמַת יֶדְכֶם

hand-of-you gift-of and tithes-of-you and and-sacrifices-of-you

וְנִדְרֵיכֶם וְנִדְבֹתֵיכֶם וּבְכֹרֹת

and-ones-firstborn-of and-freewill-offerings-of-you and-things-vowed-of-you

בְּקַרְכֶם וְצֹאנְכֶם׃ וַאֲכַלְתֶּם־ שָׁם לִפְנֵי יְהוָה אֱלֹהֵיכֶם

God-of-you Yahweh before there and-you-eat (7) and-flock-of-you herd-of-you

וּשְׂמַחְתֶּם בְּכֹל מִשְׁלַח יֶדְכֶם אַתֶּם וּבָתֵּיכֶם אֲשֶׁר

for and-families-of-you you hand-of-you work-of in-every-of and-you-rejoice

בֵּרַכְךָ יְהוָה אֱלֹהֶיךָ׃ לֹא תַעֲשׂוּן כְּכֹל אֲשֶׁר אֲנַחְנוּ עֹשִׂים

ones-doing we that as-all you-do not (8) God-of-you Yahweh he-blessed-you

פֹּה הַיּוֹם אִישׁ כָּל־ הַיָּשָׁר בְּעֵינָיו׃ כִּי לֹא־

not since (9) in-eyes-of-him the-thing-fit every-of each the-day here

and laws I am setting before you today.

*The One Place of Worship*

12 These are the decrees and laws you must be careful to follow in the land that the LORD, the God of your fathers, has given you to possess—as long as you live in the land. [2]Destroy completely all the places on the high mountains and on the hills and under every spreading tree where the nations you are dispossessing worship their gods. [3]Break down their altars, smash their sacred stones and burn their Asherah poles in the fire; cut down the idols of their gods and wipe out their names from those places.

[4]You must not worship the LORD your God in their way. [5]But you are to seek the place the LORD your God will choose from among all your tribes to put his Name there for his dwelling. To that place you must go; [6]there bring your burnt offerings and sacrifices, your tithes and special gifts, what you have vowed to give and your freewill offerings, and the firstborn of your herds and flocks. [7]There, in the presence of the LORD your God, you and your families shall eat and shall rejoice in everything you have put your hand to, because the LORD your God has blessed you.

[8]You are not to do as we do here today, everyone as he sees fit, [9]since you have not

*3 Most mss have *sheva* under the […] (בְּ־).

בָּאתֶם* עַד־ עָתָּה אֶל־ הַמְּנוּחָה וְאֶל־ הַנַּחֲלָה אֲשֶׁר־ יְהוָה
Yahweh that the-inheritance and-to the-resting-place to now to you-reached

אֱלֹהֶיךָ נֹתֵן לָךְ׃ וַעֲבַרְתֶּם אֶת־ הַיַּרְדֵּן
the-Jordan *** but-you-will-cross (10) to-you giving God-of-you

וִישַׁבְתֶּם בָּאָרֶץ אֲשֶׁר־ יְהוָה אֱלֹהֵיכֶם מַנְחִיל אֶתְכֶם
you giving-inheritance God-of-you Yahweh that in-the-land and-you-will-settle

וְהֵנִיחַ לָכֶם מִכָּל־ אֹיְבֵיכֶם מִסָּבִיב
from-around being-enemies-of-you from-all-of to-you and-he-will-give-rest

וִישַׁבְתֶּם־ בֶּטַח׃ וְהָיָה הַמָּקוֹם אֲשֶׁר־ יִבְחַר
he-will-choose that the-place and-he-will-be (11) safety so-you-will-live

יְהוָה אֱלֹהֵיכֶם בּוֹ לְשַׁכֵּן שְׁמוֹ שָׁם שָׁמָּה תָבִיאוּ
you-bring to-there there Name-of-him to-make-dwell to-him God-of-you Yahweh

אֵת כָּל־ אֲשֶׁר אָנֹכִי מְצַוֶּה אֶתְכֶם עוֹלֹתֵיכֶם וְזִבְחֵיכֶם
and-sacrifices-of-you burnt-offerings-of-you you commanding I that all ***

מַעְשְׂרֹתֵיכֶם וּתְרֻמַת יֶדְכֶם וְכֹל מִבְחַר נִדְרֵיכֶם
possessions-of-you choice-of and-all-of hand-of-you and-gift-of tithes-of-you

אֲשֶׁר תִּדְּרוּ לַיהוָה׃ וּשְׂמַחְתֶּם לִפְנֵי יְהוָה אֱלֹהֵיכֶם
God-of-you Yahweh before and-you-rejoice (12) to-Yahweh you-vowed that

אַתֶּם וּבְנֵיכֶם וּבְנֹתֵיכֶם וְעַבְדֵיכֶם
and-menservants-of-you and-daughters-of-you and-sons-of-you you

וְאַמְהֹתֵיכֶם וְהַלֵּוִי אֲשֶׁר בְּשַׁעֲרֵיכֶם כִּי אֵין לוֹ
to-him not that in-gates-of-you that and-the-Levite and-maidservants-of-you

חֵלֶק וְנַחֲלָה אִתְּכֶם׃ הִשָּׁמֶר לְךָ פֶּן־ תַּעֲלֶה
you-sacrifice so-not to-you be-careful! (13) with-you or-inheritance allotment

עֹלֹתֶיךָ בְּכָל־ מָקוֹם אֲשֶׁר תִּרְאֶה׃ כִּי אִם־ בַּמָּקוֹם
at-the-place only for (14) you-see that place in-any-of burnt-offerings-of-you

אֲשֶׁר־ יִבְחַר יְהוָה בְּאַחַד שְׁבָטֶיךָ שָׁם תַּעֲלֶה
you-offer there tribes-of-you in-one-of Yahweh he-will-choose that

עֹלֹתֶיךָ וְשָׁם תַּעֲשֶׂה כֹּל אֲשֶׁר אָנֹכִי מְצַוֶּךָּ׃
commanding-you I that all you-observe and-there burnt-offerings-of-you

רַק בְּכָל־ אַוַּת נַפְשְׁךָ תִּזְבַּח ׀ וְאָכַלְתָּ
and-you-may-eat you-may-slaughter self-of-you want-of at-any-of however (15)

בָשָׂר כְּבִרְכַּת יְהוָה אֱלֹהֶיךָ אֲשֶׁר נָתַן־ לְךָ בְּכָל־
within-any-of to-you he-gives that God-of-you Yahweh as-blessing-of meat

שְׁעָרֶיךָ הַטָּמֵא וְהַטָּהוֹר יֹאכְלֶנּוּ כַּצְּבִי
gazelle he-may-eat-him and-the-clean the-unclean gates-of-you

וְכָאַיָּל׃ רַק הַדָּם לֹא תֹאכֵלוּ עַל־ הָאָרֶץ
-ground on you-must-eat not the-blood but (16) or-as-the-deer

yet reached the resting place and the inheritance the LORD your God is giving you. [10]But you will cross the Jordan and settle in the land the LORD your God is giving you as an inheritance, and he will give you rest from all your enemies around you so that you will live in safety. [11]Then to the place the LORD your God will choose as a dwelling for his Name—there you are to bring everything I command you: your burnt offerings and sacrifices, your tithes and special gifts, and all the choice possessions you have vowed to the LORD. [12]And there rejoice before the LORD your God, you, your sons and daughters, your menservants and maidservants, and the Levites from your towns, who have no allotment or inheritance of their own. [13]Be careful not to sacrifice your burnt offerings anywhere you please. [14]Offer them only at the place the LORD will choose in one of your tribes, and there observe everything I command you.

[15]Nevertheless, you may slaughter your animals in any of your towns and eat as much of the meat as you want, as if it were gazelle or deer, according to the blessing the LORD your God gives you. Both the ceremonially unclean and the clean may eat it. [16]But you must not eat the blood; pour it out on the ground like water.

*9 Most mss have no *dagesh* in the *beth* (בְ).

כַּמָּיִם׃ לֹא־ תוּכַל לֶאֱכֹל בִּשְׁעָרֶיךָ מַעְשַׂר
tithe-of within-gates-of-you to-eat you-are-able not (17) like-the-waters

דְּגָנְךָ וְתִירֹשְׁךָ וְיִצְהָרֶךָ וּבְכֹרֹת
or-ones-firstborn-of and-oil-of-you and-new-wine-of-you grain-of-you

בְּקָרְךָ וְצֹאנֶךָ וְכָל־ נְדָרֶיךָ אֲשֶׁר תִּדֹּר
you-vowed that gifts-of-you or-any-of or-flock-of-you herd-of-you

וְנִדְבֹתֶיךָ וּתְרוּמַת יָדֶךָ׃ כִּי אִם־ לִפְנֵי
before instead for (18) hand-of-you or-gift-of or-freewill-offerings-of-you

יְהוָה אֱלֹהֶיךָ תֹּאכְלֶנּוּ בַּמָּקוֹם אֲשֶׁר יִבְחַר יְהוָה
Yahweh he-will-choose that at-the-place you-eat-him God-of-you Yahweh

אֱלֹהֶיךָ בּוֹ אַתָּה וּבִנְךָ וּבִתֶּךָ וְעַבְדְּךָ
and-manservant-of-you and-daughter-of-you and-son-of-you you to-him God-of-you

וַאֲמָתֶךָ וְהַלֵּוִי אֲשֶׁר בִּשְׁעָרֶיךָ וְשָׂמַחְתָּ
and-you-rejoice in-gates-of-you that and-the-Levite and-maidservant-of-you

לִפְנֵי יְהוָה אֱלֹהֶיךָ בְּכֹל מִשְׁלַח יָדֶךָ׃ הִשָּׁמֶר
be-careful! (19) hand-of-you work-of in-every-of God-of-you Yahweh before

לְךָ פֶּן־ תַּעֲזֹב אֶת־ הַלֵּוִי כָּל־ יָמֶיךָ עַל־אַדְמָתֶךָ׃
land-of-you in days-of-you all-of the-Levite *** you-neglect so-not to-you

כִּי־ יַרְחִיב יְהוָה אֱלֹהֶיךָ אֶת־ גְּבוּלְךָ כַּאֲשֶׁר
just-as territory-of-you *** God-of-you Yahweh he-enlarges when (20)

דִּבֶּר־ לָךְ וְאָמַרְתָּ אֹכְלָה בָשָׂר כִּי־ תְאַוֶּה נַפְשְׁךָ
self-of-you she-craves for meat I-would-eat and-you-say to-you he-promised

לֶאֱכֹל בָּשָׂר בְּכָל־ אַוַּת נַפְשְׁךָ תֹּאכַל בָּשָׂר׃ כִּי־ יִרְחַק
he-is-far if (21) meat you-may-eat self-of-you want-of at-any-of meat to-eat

מִמְּךָ הַמָּקוֹם אֲשֶׁר יִבְחַר יְהוָה אֱלֹהֶיךָ לָשׂוּם שְׁמוֹ
Name-of-him to-put God-of-you Yahweh he-chooses where the-place from-you

שָׁם וְזָבַחְתָּ מִבְּקָרְךָ וּמִצֹּאנְךָ אֲשֶׁר
that or-from-flock-of-you from-herd-of-you then-you-may-slaughter there

נָתַן יְהוָה לְךָ כַּאֲשֶׁר צִוִּיתִךָ וְאָכַלְתָּ בִּשְׁעָרֶיךָ
in-gates-of-you and-you-may-eat I-commanded-you just-as to-you Yahweh he-gave

בְּכֹל אַוַּת נַפְשֶׁךָ׃ אַךְ כַּאֲשֶׁר יֵאָכֵל אֶת־ הַצְּבִי
the-gazelle *** he-is-eaten just-as only (22) self-of-you want-of as-all-of

וְאֶת־הָאַיָּל כֵּן תֹּאכְלֶנּוּ הַטָּמֵא וְהַטָּהוֹר יַחְדָּו יֹאכְלֶנּוּ׃
he-may-eat-him both and-the-clean the-unclean you-eat-him same the-deer or

רַק חֲזַק לְבִלְתִּי אֲכֹל הַדָּם כִּי הַדָּם הוּא הַנָּפֶשׁ וְלֹא־
and-not the-life he the-blood for the-blood to-eat not be-sure! but (23)

תֹאכַל הַנֶּפֶשׁ עִם־ הַבָּשָׂר׃ לֹא תֹּאכְלֶנּוּ עַל־ הָאָרֶץ
the-ground on you-must-eat-him not (24) the-meat with the-life you-must-eat

[17]You must not eat in your own towns the tithe of your grain and new wine and oil, or the firstborn of your herds and flocks, or whatever you have vowed to give, or your freewill offerings or special gifts. [18]Instead, you are to eat them in the presence of the LORD your God at the place the LORD your God will choose—you, your sons and daughters, your menservants and maidservants, and the Levites from your towns—and you are to rejoice before the LORD your God in everything you put your hand to. [19]Be careful not to neglect the Levites as long as you live in your land.

[20]When the LORD your God has enlarged your territory as he promised you, and you crave meat and say, "I would like some meat," then you may eat as much of it as you want. [21]If the place where the LORD your God chooses to put his Name is too far away from you, you may slaughter animals from the herds and flocks the LORD has given you, as I have commanded you, and in your own towns you may eat as much of them as you want. [22]Eat them as you would gazelle or deer. Both the ceremonially unclean and the clean may eat. [23]But be sure you do not eat the blood, because the blood is the life, and you must not eat the life with the meat. [24]You must not eat the blood; pour it out on the

תִּשְׁפְּכֶנּוּ כַּמָּיִם׃ לֹא תֹּאכְלֶנּוּ לְמַעַן יִיטַב
he-may-go-well so-that you-eat-him not (25) like-the-waters you-pour-him

לְךָ וּלְבָנֶיךָ אַחֲרֶיךָ כִּי־ תַעֲשֶׂה הַיָּשָׁר
the-right-thing you-will-do for after-you and-with-children-of-you with-you

בְּעֵינֵי יְהוָה׃ רַק קָדָשֶׁיךָ אֲשֶׁר־ יִהְיוּ לְךָ
to-you they-are that consecrated-things-of-you but (26) Yahweh in-eyes-of

וּנְדָרֶיךָ תִּשָּׂא וּבָאתָ אֶל־ הַמָּקוֹם אֲשֶׁר־ יִבְחַר
he-will-choose that the-place to and-you-go you-take and-things-vowed-of-you

יְהוָה׃ וְעָשִׂיתָ עֹלֹתֶיךָ הַבָּשָׂר וְהַדָּם
and-the-blood the-meat burnt-offerings-of-you and-you-present (27) Yahweh

עַל־ מִזְבַּח יְהוָה אֱלֹהֶיךָ וְדַם־ זְבָחֶיךָ יִשָּׁפֵךְ
he-must-be-poured sacrifices-of-you and-blood-of God-of-you Yahweh altar-of on

עַל־ מִזְבַּח יְהוָה אֱלֹהֶיךָ וְהַבָּשָׂר תֹּאכֵל׃ שְׁמֹר
be-careful! (28) you-may-eat but-the-meat God-of-you Yahweh altar-of beside

וְשָׁמַעְתָּ אֵת כָּל־ הַדְּבָרִים הָאֵלֶּה אֲשֶׁר אָנֹכִי מְצַוֶּךָּ לְמַעַן
so-that giving-you I that the-these the-regulations all-of *** and-you-obey

יִיטַב לְךָ וּלְבָנֶיךָ אַחֲרֶיךָ עַד־ עוֹלָם כִּי
for always for after-you and-with-children-of-you with-you he-may-go-well

תַעֲשֶׂה הַטּוֹב וְהַיָּשָׁר בְּעֵינֵי יְהוָה אֱלֹהֶיךָ׃ כִּי־
indeed (29) God-of-you Yahweh in-eyes-of and-the-right the-good you-will-do

יַכְרִית יְהוָה אֱלֹהֶיךָ אֶת־ הַגּוֹיִם אֲשֶׁר אַתָּה בָא־
invading you that the-nations *** God-of-you Yahweh he-will-cut-off

שָׁמָּה לָרֶשֶׁת אוֹתָם מִפָּנֶיךָ וְיָרַשְׁתָּ אֹתָם
them when-you-drive-out from-before-you them to-dispossess to-there

וְיָשַׁבְתָּ בְּאַרְצָם׃ הִשָּׁמֶר לְךָ פֶּן־ תִּנָּקֵשׁ
you-are-ensnared so-not to-you be-careful! (30) in-land-of-them and-you-settle

אַחֲרֵיהֶם אַחֲרֵי הִשָּׁמְדָם מִפָּנֶיךָ וּפֶן־ תִּדְרֹשׁ
you-inquire and-not from-before-you to-be-destroyed-them after after-them

לֵאלֹהֵיהֶם לֵאמֹר אֵיכָה יַעַבְדוּ הַגּוֹיִם הָאֵלֶּה אֶת־
*** the-these the-nations do-they-serve how? to-say about-gods-of-them

אֱלֹהֵיהֶם וְאֶעֱשֶׂה־ כֵּן גַּם־ אָנִי׃ לֹא־ תַעֲשֶׂה כֵן
same you-must-worship not (31) I also same now-I-will-do gods-of-them

לַיהוָה אֱלֹהֶיךָ כִּי כָל־ תּוֹעֲבַת יְהוָה אֲשֶׁר שָׂנֵא עָשׂוּ
they-do he-hates that Yahweh detestable-of all-of for God-of-you to-Yahweh

לֵאלֹהֵיהֶם כִּי גַּם אֶת־ בְּנֵיהֶם וְאֶת־ בְּנֹתֵיהֶם יִשְׂרְפוּ
they-burn daughters-of-them and sons-of-them *** even indeed for-gods-of-them

בָאֵשׁ לֵאלֹהֵיהֶם׃ אֵת כָּל־ הַדָּבָר אֲשֶׁר אָנֹכִי מְצַוֶּה
giving I that the-command all-of *** (13:1)* to-gods-of-them in-the-fire

ground like water. [25]Do not eat it, so that it may go well with you and your children after you, because you will be doing what is right in the eyes of the LORD.

[26]But take your consecrated things and whatever you have vowed to give, and go to the place the LORD will choose. [27]Present your burnt offerings on the altar of the LORD your God, both the meat and the blood. The blood of your sacrifices must be poured beside the altar of the LORD your God, but you may eat the meat. [28]Be careful to obey all these regulations I am giving you, so that it may always go well with you and your children after you, because you will be doing what is good and right in the eyes of the LORD your God.

[29]The LORD your God will cut off before you the nations you are about to invade and dispossess. But when you have driven them out and settled in their land, [30]and after they have been destroyed before you, be careful not to be ensnared by inquiring about their gods, saying, "How do these nations serve their gods? We will do the same." [31]You must not worship the LORD your God in their way, because in worshiping their gods, they do all kinds of detestable things the LORD hates. They even burn their sons and daughters in the fire as sacrifices to their gods.

[32]See that you do all I command you; do not add to it or

*The Hebrew numeration of chapter 13 begins with verse 32 of chapter 12 in English; thus, there is a one-verse discrepancy throughout chapter 13.

אֶתְכֶם אֹתוֹ תִּשְׁמְרוּ לַעֲשׂוֹת לֹא־ תֹסֵף עָלָיו וְלֹא תִגְרַע
you-take-away and-not to-him you-add not to-do you-be-careful him you

מִמֶּנּוּ׃ כִּי־ יָקוּם בְּקִרְבְּךָ נָבִיא אוֹ חֹלֵם חֲלוֹם
dream one-dreaming-of or prophet in-among-you he-appears if (2) from-him

וְנָתַן אֵלֶיךָ אוֹת אוֹ מוֹפֵת׃ וּבָא הָאוֹת
the-sign and-he-takes-place (3) wonder or sign to-you and-he-announces

וְהַמּוֹפֵת אֲשֶׁר־ דִּבֶּר אֵלֶיךָ לֵאמֹר נֵלְכָה אַחֲרֵי אֱלֹהִים אֲחֵרִים
other-ones gods after let-us-follow to-say to-you he-spoke which or-the-wonder

אֲשֶׁר לֹא־ יְדַעְתָּם וְנָעָבְדֵם׃ לֹא תִשְׁמַע אֶל־
to you-must-listen not (4) and-let-us-worship-them you-knew-them not that

דִּבְרֵי הַנָּבִיא הַהוּא אוֹ אֶל־ חוֹלֵם הַחֲלוֹם הַהוּא כִּי
for the-that the-dream one-dreaming-of to or the-that the-prophet words-of

מְנַסֶּה יְהוָה אֱלֹהֵיכֶם אֶתְכֶם לָדַעַת הֲיִשְׁכֶם אֹהֲבִים אֶת־ יְהוָה
Yahweh *** ones-loving whether-you to-find-out you God-of-you Yahweh testing

אֱלֹהֵיכֶם בְּכָל־ לְבַבְכֶם וּבְכָל־ נַפְשְׁכֶם׃ אַחֲרֵי
after (5) soul-of-you and-with-all-of heart-of-you with-all-of God-of-you

יְהוָה אֱלֹהֵיכֶם תֵּלֵכוּ וְאֹתוֹ תִירָאוּ וְאֶת־ מִצְוֹתָיו
commands-of-him and you-must-revere and-him you-must-follow God-of-you Yahweh

תִּשְׁמֹרוּ וּבְקֹלוֹ תִשְׁמָעוּ וְאֹתוֹ תַעֲבֹדוּ
you-must-serve and-him you-must-obey and-to-voice-of-him you-must-keep

וּבוֹ תִדְבָּקוּן׃ וְהַנָּבִיא הַהוּא אוֹ חֹלֵם
one-dreaming-of or the-that and-the-prophet (6) you-must-hold-fast and-to-him

הַחֲלוֹם הַהוּא יוּמָת כִּי דִבֶּר־ סָרָה עַל־ יְהוָה
Yahweh against rebellion he-preached for he-must-die the-that the-dreams

אֱלֹהֵיכֶם הַמּוֹצִיא אֶתְכֶם ׀ מֵאֶרֶץ מִצְרַיִם וְהַפֹּדְךָ
and-the-one-redeeming-you Egypt from-land-of you the-one-bringing God-of-you

מִבֵּית עֲבָדִים לְהַדִּיחֲךָ מִן־ הַדֶּרֶךְ אֲשֶׁר צִוְּךָ
he-commanded-you that the-way from to-turn-you slaveries from-house-of

יְהוָה אֱלֹהֶיךָ לָלֶכֶת בָּהּ וּבִעַרְתָּ הָרָע מִקִּרְבֶּךָ׃
from-among-you the-evil and-you-must-purge in-her to-walk God-of-you Yahweh

כִּי יְסִיתְךָ אָחִיךָ בֶן־ אִמֶּךָ אוֹ־ בִנְךָ אוֹ־
or son-of-you or mother-of-you son-of brother-of-you he-entices-you if (7)

בִתְּךָ אוֹ ׀ אֵשֶׁת חֵיקֶךָ אוֹ רֵעֲךָ אֲשֶׁר כְּנַפְשְׁךָ
as-self-of-you who friend-of-you or love-of-you wife-of or daughter-of-you

בַּסֵּתֶר לֵאמֹר נֵלְכָה וְנַעַבְדָה אֱלֹהִים אֲחֵרִים אֲשֶׁר לֹא
not that other-ones gods and-let-us-worship let-us-go to-say in-the-secret

יָדַעְתָּ אַתָּה וַאֲבֹתֶיךָ׃ מֵאֱלֹהֵי הָעַמִּים אֲשֶׁר סְבִיבֹתֵיכֶם
around-you who the-peoples from-gods-of (8) or-fathers-of-you you you-knew

take away from it.

*Worshiping Other Gods*

13 If a prophet, or one who foretells by dreams, appears among you and announces to you a miraculous sign or wonder, [2]and if the sign or wonder of which he has spoken takes place, and he says, "Let us follow other gods" (gods you have not known) "and let us worship them," [3]you must not listen to the words of that prophet or dreamer. The LORD your God is testing you to find out whether you love him with all your heart and with all your soul. [4]It is the LORD your God you must follow, and him you must revere. Keep his commands and obey him; serve him and hold fast to him. [5]That prophet or dreamer must be put to death, because he preached rebellion against the LORD your God, who brought you out of Egypt and redeemed you from the land of slavery; he has tried to turn you from the way the LORD your God commanded you to follow. You must purge the evil from among you.

[6]If your very own brother, or your son or daughter, or the wife you love, or your closest friend secretly entices you, saying, "Let us go and worship other gods" (gods that neither you nor your fathers have known, [7]gods of the peoples around you, whether near

*See the note on page 522.

הַקְּרֹבִים אֵלֶיךָ אוֹ הָרְחֹקִים מִמֶּךָּ מִקְצֵה הָאָרֶץ וְעַד־
even-to the-land from-end-of from-you the-ones-far or to-you the-ones-near

קְצֵה הָאָרֶץ׃ לֹא־תֹאבֶה לוֹ וְלֹא תִשְׁמַע אֵלָיו וְלֹא־
and-not to-him you-listen and-not to-him you-yield not (9) the-land end-of

תָחוֹס עֵינְךָ עָלָיו וְלֹא־תַחְמֹל וְלֹא־תְכַסֶּה
you-shield and-not you-spare and-not to-him eye-of-you she-must-pity

עָלָיו׃ כִּי הָרֹג תַּהַרְגֶנּוּ יָדְךָ תִּהְיֶה־בּוֹ
on-him she-must-be hand-of-you you-must-kill-him to-kill but (10) over-him

בָרִאשׁוֹנָה לַהֲמִיתוֹ וְיַד כָּל־הָעָם בָּאַחֲרֹנָה׃
as-the-next the-people all-of then-hand-of to-kill-him as-the-first

וּסְקַלְתּוֹ בָאֲבָנִים וָמֵת כִּי בִקֵּשׁ לְהַדִּיחֲךָ
to-turn-you he-tried for so-he-dies with-the-stones and-you-stone-him (11)

מֵעַל יְהוָה אֱלֹהֶיךָ הַמּוֹצִיאֲךָ מֵאֶרֶץ מִצְרַיִם
Egypt from-land-of the-one-bringing-you God-of-you Yahweh away-from

מִבֵּית עֲבָדִים׃ וְכָל־יִשְׂרָאֵל יִשְׁמְעוּ
they-will-hear Israel then-all-of (12) slaveries from-house-of

וְיִרָאוּן וְלֹא־יוֹסִפוּ לַעֲשׂוֹת כַּדָּבָר הָרָע
the-evil as-the-thing to-do they-will-repeat and-not and-they-will-be-afraid

הַזֶּה בְּקִרְבֶּךָ׃ כִּי־תִשְׁמַע בְּאַחַת עָרֶיךָ אֲשֶׁר יְהוָה
Yahweh that towns-of-you about-one-of you-hear if (13) in-among-you the-this

אֱלֹהֶיךָ נֹתֵן לְךָ לָשֶׁבֶת שָׁם לֵאמֹר׃ יָצְאוּ אֲנָשִׁים בְּנֵי־
sons-of men they-rose (14) to-say there to-live to-you giving God-of-you

בְלִיַּעַל מִקִּרְבֶּךָ וַיַּדִּיחוּ אֶת־יֹשְׁבֵי עִירָם
town-of-them ones-living-of *** and-they-led-astray from-among-you wickedness

לֵאמֹר נֵלְכָה וְנַעַבְדָה אֱלֹהִים אֲחֵרִים אֲשֶׁר לֹא־יְדַעְתֶּם׃
you-knew not that other-ones gods let-us-worship let-us-go to-say

וְדָרַשְׁתָּ וְחָקַרְתָּ וְשָׁאַלְתָּ הֵיטֵב וְהִנֵּה אֱמֶת
true and-if to-be-thorough and-you-investigate and-you-probe then-you-inquire (15)

נָכוֹן הַדָּבָר נֶעֶשְׂתָה הַתּוֹעֵבָה הַזֹּאת בְּקִרְבֶּךָ׃
in-among-you the-this the-detestable-thing she-was-done the-thing being-proved

הַכֵּה תַכֶּה אֶת־יֹשְׁבֵי הָעִיר הַהִוא לְפִי־
with-edge-of the-that the-town ones-living-of *** you-must-kill to-kill (16)

חָרֶב הַחֲרֵם אֹתָהּ וְאֶת־כָּל־אֲשֶׁר־בָּהּ וְאֶת־בְּהֶמְתָּהּ לְפִי־חָרֶב׃
sword with-edge-of stock-of-her and in-her that all and her destroy! sword

וְאֶת־כָּל־שְׁלָלָהּ תִּקְבֹּץ אֶל־תּוֹךְ רְחֹבָהּ
public-square-of-her middle-of into you-gather plunder-of-her all-of and (17)

וְשָׂרַפְתָּ בָאֵשׁ אֶת־הָעִיר וְאֶת־כָּל־שְׁלָלָהּ
plunder-of-her all-of and the-town *** with-the-fire and-you-burn

or far, from one end of the land to the other), 8do not yield to him or listen to him. Show him no pity. Do not spare him or shield him. 9You must certainly put him to death. Your hand must be the first in putting him to death, and then the hands of all the people. 10Stone him to death, because he tried to turn you away from the LORD your God, who brought you out of Egypt, out of the land of slavery. 11Then all Israel will hear and be afraid, and no one among you will do such an evil thing again.

12If you hear it said about one of the towns the LORD your God is giving you to live in 13that wicked men have arisen among you and have led the people of their town astray, saying, "Let us go and worship other gods" (gods you have not known), 14then you must inquire, probe and investigate it thoroughly. And if it is true and it has been proved that this detestable thing has been done among you, 15you must certainly put to the sword all who live in that town. Destroy it completely,[v] both its people and its livestock. 16Gather all the plunder of the town into the middle of the public square and completely burn the town and all its plunder as a whole burnt

[v]15 The Hebrew term refers to the irrevocable giving over of things or persons to the LORD, often by totally destroying them.

*See the note on page 522.

°16 ק ההיא

כָּלִיל לַיהוָה אֱלֹהֶיךָ וְהָיְתָה תֵּל עוֹלָם לֹא

not forever ruin and-she-must-remain God-of-you to-Yahweh whole-offering

תִבָּנֶה עוֹד׃ (18) וְלֹא־ יִדְבַּק בְּיָדְךָ מְאוּמָה

anything in-hand-of-you he-may-find and-not (18) ever she-must-be-rebuilt

מִן־ הַחֵרֶם לְמַעַן יָשׁוּב יְהוָה מֵחֲרוֹן אַפּוֹ

anger-of-her from-fierceness-of Yahweh he-will-turn so-that the-condemned from

וְנָתַן־ לְךָ רַחֲמִים וְרִחַמְךָ

and-he-will-have-compassion-on-you mercies to-you and-he-will-show

וְהִרְבֶּךָ כַּאֲשֶׁר נִשְׁבַּע לַאֲבֹתֶיךָ׃ (19) כִּי תִשְׁמַע

you-obey for (19) to-fathers-of-you he-swore just-as and-he-will-increase-you

בְּקוֹל יְהוָה אֱלֹהֶיךָ לִשְׁמֹר אֶת־ כָּל־ מִצְוֺתָיו אֲשֶׁר אָנֹכִי

I that commands-of-him all-of *** to-keep God-of-you Yahweh to-voice-of

מְצַוְּךָ הַיּוֹם לַעֲשׂוֹת הַיָּשָׁר בְּעֵינֵי יְהוָה אֱלֹהֶיךָ׃ (14:1) בָּנִים

sons (14:1) God-of-you Yahweh in-eyes-of the-right to-do the-day giving-you

אַתֶּם לַיהוָה אֱלֹהֵיכֶם לֹא תִתְגֹּדְדוּ וְלֹא־ תָשִׂימוּ קָרְחָה בֵּין

between bald you-shave and-not you-cut-selves not God-of-you of-Yahweh you

עֵינֵיכֶם לָמֵת׃ (2) כִּי עַם קָדוֹשׁ אַתָּה לַיהוָה אֱלֹהֶיךָ

God-of-you to-Yahweh you holy people for (2) for-the-dead eyes-of-you

וּבְךָ בָּחַר יְהוָה לִהְיוֹת לוֹ לְעַם סְגֻלָּה מִכֹּל

from-all-of treasure as-people-of for-him to-be Yahweh he-chose and-to-you

הָעַמִּים אֲשֶׁר עַל־ פְּנֵי הָאֲדָמָה׃ (3) לֹא תֹאכַל כָּל־ תּוֹעֵבָה׃

detestable-thing any-of you-eat not (3) the-earth faces-of on that the-peoples

(4) זֹאת הַבְּהֵמָה אֲשֶׁר תֹּאכֵלוּ שׁוֹר שֵׂה כְשָׂבִים וְשֵׂה עִזִּים׃

goats and-goat-of sheep sheep-of ox you-may-eat that the-animal this (4)

(5) אַיָּל וּצְבִי וְיַחְמוּר וְאַקּוֹ וְדִישֹׁן וּתְאוֹ

and-antelope and-ibex and-wild-goat and-roe-deer and-gazelle deer (5)

וָזָמֶר׃ (6) וְכָל־ בְּהֵמָה מַפְרֶסֶת פַּרְסָה וְשֹׁסַעַת

and-dividing hoof splitting animal and-any-of (6) and-mountain-sheep

שֶׁסַע שְׁתֵּי פְרָסוֹת מַעֲלַת גֵּרָה בַּבְּהֵמָה אֹתָהּ תֹּאכֵלוּ׃

you-may-eat her among-the-animal cud chewing-of hoofs two-of division

(7) אַךְ אֶת־ זֶה לֹא תֹאכְלוּ מִמַּעֲלֵי הַגֵּרָה

the-cud from-ones-chewing-of you-may-eat not this *** however (7)

וּמִמַּפְרִיסֵי הַפַּרְסָה הַשְּׁסוּעָה אֶת־ הַגָּמָל וְאֶת־

and the-camel *** the-being-divided the-hoof and-from-ones-splitting

הָאַרְנֶבֶת וְאֶת־ הַשָּׁפָן כִּי־ מַעֲלֵה גֵרָה הֵמָּה וּפַרְסָה לֹא הִפְרִיסוּ

they-split not but-hoof they cud chewing-of for the-coney and the-rabbit

טְמֵאִים הֵם לָכֶם׃ (8) וְאֶת־ הַחֲזִיר כִּי־ מַפְרִיס פַּרְסָה הוּא וְלֹא

but-not he hoof splitting for the-pig and (8) for-you they ones-unclean

offering to the LORD your God. It is to remain a ruin forever, never to be rebuilt. [17]None of those condemned things shall be found in your hands, so that the LORD will turn from his fierce anger; he will show you mercy, have compassion on you, and increase your numbers, as he promised on oath to your forefathers, [18]because you obey the LORD your God, keeping all his commands that I am giving you today and doing what is right in his eyes.

*Clean and Unclean Food*

**14** You are the children of the LORD your God. Do not cut yourselves or shave the front of your heads for the dead, [2]for you are a people holy to the LORD your God. Out of all the peoples on the face of the earth, the LORD has chosen you to be his treasured possession.

[3]Do not eat any detestable thing. [4]These are the animals you may eat: the ox, the sheep, the goat, [5]the deer, the gazelle, the roe deer, the wild goat, the ibex, the antelope and the mountain sheep.[w] [6]You may eat any animal that has a split hoof divided in two and that chews the cud. [7]However, of those that chew the cud or that have a split hoof completely divided you may not eat the camel, the rabbit or the coney.[x] Although they chew the cud, they do not have a split hoof; they are ceremonially unclean for you. [8]The pig is also unclean; although it has a split hoof, it does not chew

[w]5 The precise identification of some of the birds and animals in this chapter is uncertain.
[x]7 That is, the hyrax or rock badger

*See the note on page 522.

גֵרָה טָמֵא הוּא לָכֶם מִבְּשָׂרָם לֹא תֹאכֵלוּ וּבְנִבְלָתָם
and-on-carcass-of-them you-eat not from-meat-of-them for-you he unclean cud

לֹא תִגָּעוּ׃ אֶת־זֶה תֹּאכְלוּ מִכֹּל אֲשֶׁר בַּמָּיִם כֹּל אֲשֶׁר־
that and in-the-waters that from-all you-may-eat this *** (9) you-touch not

לוֹ סְנַפִּיר וְקַשְׂקֶשֶׂת תֹּאכֵלוּ׃ וְכֹל אֲשֶׁר אֵין־לוֹ סְנַפִּיר וְקַשְׂקֶשֶׂת
or-scale fin on-him not that and-any (10) you-may-eat or-scale fin on-him

לֹא תֹאכֵלוּ טָמֵא הוּא לָכֶם׃ כָּל־צִפּוֹר טְהֹרָה תֹּאכֵלוּ׃
you-may-eat clean bird any-of (11) for-you he unclean you-may-eat not

וְזֶה אֲשֶׁר לֹא־תֹאכְלוּ מֵהֶם הַנֶּשֶׁר וְהַפֶּרֶס
and-the-vulture the-eagle from-them you-may-eat not that but-this (12)

וְהָעָזְנִיָּה׃ וְהָרָאָה וְאֶת־הָאַיָּה וְהַדַּיָּה
and-the-falcon the-black-kite and and-the-red-kite (13) and-the-black-vulture

לְמִינָהּ׃ וְאֵת כָּל־עֹרֵב לְמִינוֹ׃ וְאֵת בַּת
daughter-of and (15) any-kind-of-him raven any-of and (14) any-kind-of-her

הַיַּעֲנָה וְאֶת־הַתַּחְמָס וְאֶת־הַשָּׁחַף וְאֶת־הַנֵּץ לְמִינֵהוּ׃
any-kind-of-him the-hawk and the-gull and the-screech-owl and the-horned-owl

אֶת־הַכּוֹס וְאֶת־הַיַּנְשׁוּף וְהַתִּנְשָׁמֶת׃ וְהַקָּאָת
the-desert-owl (17) and-the-white-owl the-great-owl and the-little-owl *** (16)

וְאֶת־הָרָחָמָה וְאֶת־הַשָּׁלָךְ׃ וְהַחֲסִידָה וְהָאֲנָפָה
and-the-heron and-the-stork (18) the-cormorant and the-osprey and

לְמִינָהּ וְהַדּוּכִיפַת וְהָעֲטַלֵּף׃ וְכֹל שֶׁרֶץ הָעוֹף
the-wing swarmer-of and-any-of (19) and-the-bat and-the-hoopoe any-kind-of-her

טָמֵא הוּא לָכֶם לֹא יֵאָכֵלוּ׃ כָּל־עוֹף טָהוֹר
clean winged-creature any-of (20) they-may-be-eaten not for-you he unclean

תֹּאכֵלוּ׃ לֹא תֹאכְלוּ כָל־נְבֵלָה לַגֵּר אֲשֶׁר־
who to-the-alien already-dead-animal any-of you-eat not (21) you-may-eat

בִּשְׁעָרֶיךָ תִּתְּנֶנָּה וַאֲכָלָהּ אוֹ מָכֹר לְנָכְרִי
to-foreigner to-sell or and-he-may-eat-her you-may-give-her in-gates-of-you

כִּי עַם קָדוֹשׁ אַתָּה לַיהוָה אֱלֹהֶיךָ לֹא־תְבַשֵּׁל גְּדִי בַּחֲלֵב
in-milk-of young-goat you-cook not God-of-you to-Yahweh you holy people but

אִמּוֹ׃ עַשֵּׂר תְּעַשֵּׂר אֵת כָּל־תְּבוּאַת
yield-of all-of *** you-give-tenth to-give-tenth (22) mother-of-him

זַרְעֶךָ הַיֹּצֵא הַשָּׂדֶה שָׁנָה שָׁנָה׃ וְאָכַלְתָּ לִפְנֵי ׀
before and-you-eat (23) year year the-field the-one-producing seed-of-you

יְהוָה אֱלֹהֶיךָ בַּמָּקוֹם אֲשֶׁר־יִבְחַר לְשַׁכֵּן שְׁמוֹ
Name-of-him to-make-dwell he-will-choose that at-the-place God-of-you Yahweh

שָׁם מַעְשַׂר דְּגָנְךָ תִּירֹשְׁךָ וְיִצְהָרֶךָ
and-oil-of-you new-wine-of-you grain-of-you tithe-of there

the cud. You are not to eat their meat or touch their carcasses.

[9]Of all the creatures living in the water, you may eat any that has fins and scales. [10]But anything that does not have fins and scales you may not eat; for you it is unclean.

[11]You may eat any clean bird. [12]But these you may not eat: the eagle, the vulture, the black vulture, [13]the red kite, the black kite, any kind of falcon, [14]any kind of raven, [15]the horned owl, the screech owl, the gull, any kind of hawk, [16]the little owl, the great owl, the white owl, [17]the desert owl, the osprey, the cormorant, [18]the stork, any kind of heron, the hoopoe and the bat.

[19]All flying insects that swarm are unclean to you; do not eat them. [20]But any winged creature that is clean you may eat.

[21]Do not eat anything you find already dead. You may give it to an alien living in any of your towns, and he may eat it, or you may sell it to a foreigner. But you are a people holy to the LORD your God.

Do not cook a young goat in its mother's milk.

*Tithes*

[22]Be sure to set aside a tenth of all that your fields produce each year. [23]Eat the tithe of your grain, new wine and oil, and the firstborn of your herds and flocks in the presence of the LORD your God at the place he will choose as a dwelling

וּבְכֹרֹת בְּקָרְךָ וְצֹאנֶךָ לְמַעַן תִּלְמַד

you-may-learn so-that and-flock-of-you herd-of-you and-ones-firstborn-of

לְיִרְאָה אֶת־ יְהוָה אֱלֹהֶיךָ כָּל־ הַיָּמִים׃ וְכִי־ יִרְבֶּה

he-is-distant but-if (24) the-days all-of God-of-you Yahweh *** to-revere

מִמְּךָ הַדֶּרֶךְ כִּי לֹא תוּכַל שְׂאֵתוֹ כִּי־ יִרְחַק מִמְּךָ

from-you he-is-far for to-carry-him you-are-able not so the-way from-you

הַמָּקוֹם אֲשֶׁר יִבְחַר יְהוָה אֱלֹהֶיךָ לָשׂוּם שְׁמוֹ שָׁם

there Name-of-him to-put God-of-you Yahweh he-will-choose that the-place

כִּי יְבָרֶכְךָ יְהוָה אֱלֹהֶיךָ׃ וְנָתַתָּה בַּכָּסֶף

for-the-silver then-you-exchange (25) God-of-you Yahweh he-blessed-you and

וְצַרְתָּ הַכֶּסֶף בְּיָדְךָ וְהָלַכְתָּ אֶל־ הַמָּקוֹם אֲשֶׁר

that the-place to and-you-go in-hand-of-you the-silver and-you-take

יִבְחַר יְהוָה אֱלֹהֶיךָ בּוֹ׃ וְנָתַתָּה הַכֶּסֶף

the-silver and-you-use (26) to-him God-of-you Yahweh he-will-choose

בְּכֹל אֲשֶׁר־ תְּאַוֶּה נַפְשְׁךָ בַּבָּקָר וּבַצֹּאן

or-of-the-flock of-the-cattle self-of-you she-likes that for-anything

וּבַיַּיִן וּבַשֵּׁכָר וּבְכֹל אֲשֶׁר תִּשְׁאָלְךָ

she-asks-you that or-of-anything or-of-the-fermented-drink or-of-the-wine

נַפְשֶׁךָ וְאָכַלְתָּ שָּׁם לִפְנֵי יְהוָה אֱלֹהֶיךָ וְשָׂמַחְתָּ אַתָּה

you and-you-rejoice God-of-you Yahweh before there then-you-eat self-of-you

וּבֵיתֶךָ׃ וְהַלֵּוִי אֲשֶׁר־ בִּשְׁעָרֶיךָ לֹא

not within-gates-of-you who and-the-Levite (27) and-household-of-you

תַעַזְבֶנּוּ כִּי אֵין לוֹ חֵלֶק וְנַחֲלָה עִמָּךְ׃

among-you or-inheritance allotment to-him not for you-neglect-him

מִקְצֵה ׀ שָׁלֹשׁ שָׁנִים תּוֹצִיא אֶת־ כָּל־ מַעְשַׂר תְּבוּאָתְךָ

produce-of-you tithe-of all-of *** you-bring years three at-end-of (28)

בַּשָּׁנָה הַהִוא וְהִנַּחְתָּ בִּשְׁעָרֶיךָ׃ וּבָא

so-he-may-come (29) in-towns-of-you and-you-store the-that of-the-year

הַלֵּוִי כִּי אֵין־ לוֹ חֵלֶק וְנַחֲלָה עִמָּךְ וְהַגֵּר

and-the-alien among-you or-inheritance allotment to-him not that the-Levite

וְהַיָּתוֹם וְהָאַלְמָנָה אֲשֶׁר בִּשְׁעָרֶיךָ וְאָכְלוּ

so-they-may-eat within-gates-of-you who and-the-widow and-the-fatherless

וְשָׂבֵעוּ לְמַעַן יְבָרֶכְךָ יְהוָה אֱלֹהֶיךָ

God-of-you Yahweh he-may-bless-you so-that and-they-may-be-satisfied

בְּכָל־ מַעֲשֵׂה יָדְךָ אֲשֶׁר תַּעֲשֶׂה׃ מִקֵּץ שֶׁבַע־ שָׁנִים

years seven-of at-end-of (15:1) you-do that hand-of-you work-of in-all-of

תַּעֲשֶׂה שְׁמִטָּה׃ וְזֶה דְּבַר הַשְּׁמִטָּה שָׁמוֹט

to-cancel the-cancel-of-debt way-of and-this (2) cancel-of-debt you-must-do

for his Name, so that you may learn to revere the LORD your God always. [24]But if that place is too distant and you have been blessed by the LORD your God and cannot carry your tithe (because the place where the LORD will choose to put his Name is so far away), [25]then exchange your tithe for silver, and take the silver with you and go to the place the LORD your God will choose. [26]Use the silver to buy whatever you like: cattle, sheep, wine or other fermented drink, or anything you wish. Then you and your household shall eat there in the presence of the LORD your God and rejoice. [27]And do not neglect the Levites living in your towns, for they have no allotment or inheritance of their own.

[28]At the end of every three years, bring all the tithes of that year's produce and store it in your towns, [29]so that the Levites (who have no allotment or inheritance of their own) and the aliens, the fatherless and the widows who live in your towns may come and eat and be satisfied, and so that the LORD your God may bless you in all the work of your hands.

*The Year for Canceling Debts*

**15** At the end of every seven years you must cancel debts. [2]This is how it is to be done: Every creditor

כָּל־ בַּעַל מַשֵּׁה יָדוֹ אֲשֶׁר יַשֶּׁה בְּרֵעֵהוּ לֹא־
not to-fellow-of-him he-loaned that hand-of-him loan-of creditor-of every-of

יִגֹּשׂ אֶת־ רֵעֵהוּ וְאֶת־ אָחִיו כִּי־ קָרָא
he-proclaimed for brother-of-him or fellow-of-him *** he-shall-require-payment

שְׁמִטָּה לַיהוָה׃ אֶת־ הַנָּכְרִי תִּגֹּשׂ
you-may-require-payment the-foreigner *** (3) of-Yahweh cancel-of-debt

וַאֲשֶׁר יִהְיֶה לְךָ אֶת־ אָחִיךָ תַּשְׁמֵט יָדֶךָ׃
hand-of-you she-must-cancel-debt brother-of-you *** to-you he-owes but-what

אֶפֶס כִּי לֹא יִהְיֶה־ בְּךָ אֶבְיוֹן כִּי־ בָרֵךְ
to-bless for poor among-you he-should-be not indeed however (4)

יְבָרֶכְךָ יְהוָה בָּאָרֶץ אֲשֶׁר יְהוָה אֱלֹהֶיךָ נֹתֵן־ לְךָ
to-you giving God-of-you Yahweh that in-the-land Yahweh he-will-bless-you

נַחֲלָה לְרִשְׁתָּהּ׃ רַק אִם־ שָׁמוֹעַ תִּשְׁמַע בְּקוֹל יְהוָה
Yahweh to-voice-of you-obey to-obey if only (5) to-possess-her inheritance

אֱלֹהֶיךָ לִשְׁמֹר לַעֲשׂוֹת אֶת־ כָּל־ הַמִּצְוָה הַזֹּאת אֲשֶׁר
that the-this the-command all-of *** to-follow to-be-careful God-of-you

אָנֹכִי מְצַוְּךָ הַיּוֹם׃ כִּי־ יְהוָה אֱלֹהֶיךָ בֵּרַכְךָ כַּאֲשֶׁר
just-as he-will-bless-you God-of-you Yahweh for (6) the-day giving-you I

דִּבֶּר־ לָךְ וְהַעֲבַטְתָּ גּוֹיִם רַבִּים וְאַתָּה לֹא תַעֲבֹט
you-will-borrow not but-you many nations and-you-will-lend to-you he-promised

וּמָשַׁלְתָּ בְּגוֹיִם רַבִּים וּבְךָ לֹא יִמְשֹׁלוּ׃ כִּי־
if (7) they-will-rule not but-over-you many over-nations and-you-will-rule

יִהְיֶה בְךָ אֶבְיוֹן מֵאַחַד אַחֶיךָ בְּאַחַד שְׁעָרֶיךָ
gates-of-you within-one-of brothers-of-you from-one-of poor among-you he-is

בְּאַרְצְךָ אֲשֶׁר־ יְהוָה אֱלֹהֶיךָ נֹתֵן לָךְ לֹא תְאַמֵּץ אֶת־
*** you-harden not to-you giving God-of-you Yahweh that in-land-of-you

לְבָבְךָ וְלֹא תִקְפֹּץ אֶת־ יָדְךָ מֵאָחִיךָ
toward-brother-of-you fist-of-you *** you-tighten and-not heart-of-you

הָאֶבְיוֹן׃ כִּי־ פָתֹחַ תִּפְתַּח אֶת־ יָדְךָ לוֹ וְהַעֲבֵט
and-to-lend to-him hand-of-you *** you-open to-open rather (8) the-poor

תַּעֲבִיטֶנּוּ דֵּי מַחְסֹרוֹ אֲשֶׁר יֶחְסַר לוֹ׃ הִשָּׁמֶר
be-careful! (9) for-him he-needs that need-of-him whatever you-lend-to-him

לְךָ פֶּן־ יִהְיֶה דָבָר עִם־ לְבָבְךָ בְלִיַּעַל לֵאמֹר קָרְבָה
she-is-near to-say wicked heart-of-you in thought he-comes so-not to-you

שְׁנַת־ הַשֶּׁבַע שְׁנַת הַשְּׁמִטָּה וְרָעָה עֵינְךָ
eye-of-you and-she-is-evil the-cancel-of-debt year-of the-seventh year-of

בְּאָחִיךָ הָאֶבְיוֹן וְלֹא תִתֵּן לוֹ וְקָרָא
then-he-may-appeal to-him you-give and-not the-needy toward-brother-of-you

shall cancel the loan he has
made to his fellow Israelite.
He shall not require payment
from his fellow Israelite or
brother, because the LORD's
time for canceling debts has
been proclaimed. 3 You may require payment from a foreigner, but you must cancel any
debt your brother owes you.
4 However, there should be no
poor among you, for in the
land the LORD your God is giving you to possess as your inheritance, he will richly bless
you, 5 if only you fully obey the
LORD your God and are careful
to follow all these commands I
am giving you today. 6 For the
LORD your God will bless you
as he has promised, and you
will lend to many nations but
will borrow from none. You
will rule over many nations
but none will rule over you.
7 If there is a poor man
among your brothers in any of
the towns of the land that the
LORD your God is giving you,
do not be hardhearted or
tightfisted toward your poor
brother. 8 Rather be openhanded and freely lend him whatever he needs. 9 Be careful not
to harbor this wicked thought:
"The seventh year, the year
for canceling debts, is near,"
so that you do not show ill will
toward your needy brother
and give him nothing. He
may then appeal to the LORD

עָלֶיךָ אֶל־ יְהוָה וְהָיָה בְךָ חֵטְא׃ נָתוֹן תִּתֵּן
you-give to-give (10) guilt on-you and-he-will-be Yahweh to against-you

לוֹ וְלֹא־ יֵרַע לְבָבְךָ בְּתִתְּךָ לוֹ כִּי
for to-him when-to-give-you heart-of-you he-must-hold-grudge and-not to-him

בִּגְלַל | הַדָּבָר הַזֶּה יְבָרֶכְךָ יְהוָה אֱלֹהֶיךָ בְּכָל־
in-all-of God-of-you Yahweh he-will-bless-you the-this the-thing because-of

מַעֲשֶׂךָ וּבְכֹל מִשְׁלַח יָדֶךָ׃ כִּי לֹא־ יֶחְדַּל
he-will-leave not for (11) hand-of-you activity-of and-in-all-of work-of-you

אֶבְיוֹן מִקֶּרֶב הָאָרֶץ עַל־ כֵּן אָנֹכִי מְצַוְּךָ לֵאמֹר פָּתֹחַ תִּפְתַּח
you-open to-open to-say commanding-you I this for the-land from-within poor

אֶת־ יָדְךָ לְאָחִיךָ לַעֲנִיֶּךָ וּלְאֶבְיֹנְךָ
and-to-needy-of-you toward-poor-of-you toward-brother-of-you hand-of-you ***

בְּאַרְצֶךָ׃ כִּי־ יִמָּכֵר לְךָ אָחִיךָ הָעִבְרִי אוֹ
or the-Hebrew-man fellow-of-you to-you he-is-sold if (12) in-land-of-you

הָעִבְרִיָּה וַעֲבָדְךָ שֵׁשׁ שָׁנִים וּבַשָּׁנָה הַשְּׁבִיעִת
the-seventh then-in-the-year years six and-he-serves-you the-Hebrew-woman

תְּשַׁלְּחֶנּוּ חָפְשִׁי מֵעִמָּךְ׃ וְכִי־ תְשַׁלְּחֶנּוּ חָפְשִׁי
free you-release-him and-when (13) from-with-you free you-must-let-go-him

מֵעִמָּךְ לֹא תְשַׁלְּחֶנּוּ רֵיקָם׃ הַעֲנֵיק תַּעֲנִיק
you-supply to-supply (14) empty-handed you-send-away-him not from-with-you

לוֹ מִצֹּאנְךָ וּמִגָּרְנְךָ וּמִיִּקְבֶךָ
and-from-wine-vat-of-you and-from-threshing-floor-of-you from-flock-of-you to-him

אֲשֶׁר בֵּרַכְךָ יְהוָה אֱלֹהֶיךָ תִּתֶּן־ לוֹ׃ וְזָכַרְתָּ
and-you-remember (15) to-him you-give God-of-you Yahweh he-blessed-you as

כִּי עֶבֶד הָיִיתָ בְּאֶרֶץ מִצְרַיִם וַיִּפְדְּךָ יְהוָה אֱלֹהֶיךָ
God-of-you Yahweh and-he-redeemed-you Egypt in-land-of you-were slave that

עַל־ כֵּן אָנֹכִי מְצַוְּךָ אֶת־ הַדָּבָר הַזֶּה הַיּוֹם׃ וְהָיָה
but-he-will-be (16) the-day the-this the-command *** giving-you I this for

כִּי־ יֹאמַר אֵלֶיךָ לֹא אֵצֵא מֵעִמָּךְ כִּי אֲהֵבְךָ וְאֶת־
and he-loves-you for from-with-you I-would-leave not to-you he-says if

בֵּיתֶךָ כִּי־ טוֹב לוֹ עִמָּךְ׃ וְלָקַחְתָּ אֶת־ הַמַּרְצֵעַ
the-awl *** then-you-take (17) with-you for-him good for family-of-you

וְנָתַתָּה בְאָזְנוֹ וּבַדֶּלֶת וְהָיָה לְךָ
for-you and-he-will-become and-into-the-door through-ear-of-him and-you-push

עֶבֶד עוֹלָם וְאַף לַאֲמָתְךָ תַּעֲשֶׂה־ כֵּן׃ לֹא־
not (18) same you-do for-maidservant-of-you and-also for-life servant

יִקְשֶׁה בְעֵינֶךָ בְּשַׁלֵּחֲךָ אֹתוֹ חָפְשִׁי מֵעִמָּךְ כִּי
for from-with-you free him when-to-send-you in-eyes-of-you he-must-be-hard

against you, and you will be
found guilty of sin. 10 Give generously to him and do so without a grudging heart; then because of this the LORD your
God will bless you in all your
work and in everything you
put your hand to. 11 There will
always be poor people in the
land. Therefore I command
you to be openhanded toward
your brothers and toward the
poor and needy in your land.

*Freeing Servants*

12 If a fellow Hebrew, a man
or a woman, is sold to you and
he serves you six years, in the
seventh year you must let him
go free. 13 And when you release him, do not send him
away empty-handed. 14 Supply
him liberally from your flock,
your threshing floor and your
winepress. Give to him as the
LORD your God has blessed
you. 15 Remember that you
were slaves in Egypt and the
LORD your God redeemed you.
That is why I give you this
command today.

16 But if your servant says to
you, "I do not want to leave
you," because he loves you
and your family and is well off
with you, 17 then take an awl
and push it through his ear
lobe into the door, and he will
become your servant for life.
Do the same for your maidservant.

18 Do not consider it a hardship to set your servant free,

מִשְׁנֶה שְׂכַר שָׂכִיר עֲבָדְךָ שֵׁשׁ שָׁנִים וּבֵרַכְךָ
and-he-will-bless-you years six he-served-you hired-hand worth-of twice

יְהוָה אֱלֹהֶיךָ בְּכֹל אֲשֶׁר תַּעֲשֶׂה׃ כָּל־ הַבְּכוֹר אֲשֶׁר
that the-firstborn every-of (19) you-do that in-all God-of-you Yahweh

יִוָּלֵד בִּבְקָרְךָ וּבְצֹאנְךָ הַזָּכָר תַּקְדִּישׁ
you-set-apart the-male and-in-flock-of-you in-herd-of-you he-is-born

לַיהוָה אֱלֹהֶיךָ לֹא תַעֲבֹד בִּבְכֹר שׁוֹרֶךָ וְלֹא
and-not ox-of-you of-firstborn-of you-make-work not God-of-you for-Yahweh

תָגֹז בְּכוֹר צֹאנֶךָ׃ לִפְנֵי יְהוָה אֱלֹהֶיךָ תֹאכְלֶנּוּ
you-eat-him God-of-you Yahweh before (20) flock-of-you firstborn-of you-shear

שָׁנָה בְשָׁנָה בַּמָּקוֹם אֲשֶׁר־ יִבְחַר יְהוָה אַתָּה וּבֵיתֶךָ׃
and-family-of-you you Yahweh he-will-choose that at-the-place by-year year

וְכִי־ יִהְיֶה בוֹ מוּם פִּסֵּחַ אוֹ עִוֵּר כֹּל מוּם רָע לֹא
not serious flaw any-of blind or lame defect on-him he-is and-if (21)

תִזְבָּחֶנּוּ לַיהוָה אֱלֹהֶיךָ׃ בִּשְׁעָרֶיךָ תֹּאכְלֶנּוּ
you-eat-him within-gates-of-you (22) God-of-you to-Yahweh you-sacrifice-him

הַטָּמֵא וְהַטָּהוֹר יַחְדָּו כַּצְּבִי וְכָאַיָּל׃ רַק אֶת־
*** but (23) or-as-the-deer as-the-gazelle both and-the-clean the-unclean

דָּמוֹ לֹא תֹאכֵל עַל־ הָאָרֶץ תִּשְׁפְּכֶנּוּ כַּמָּיִם׃
like-the-waters you-pour-out-him the-ground on you-eat not blood-of-him

שָׁמוֹר אֶת־ חֹדֶשׁ הָאָבִיב וְעָשִׂיתָ פֶּסַח לַיהוָה
of-Yahweh Passover and-you-celebrate the-Abib month-of *** to-observe (16:1)

אֱלֹהֶיךָ כִּי בְּחֹדֶשׁ הָאָבִיב הוֹצִיאֲךָ יְהוָה אֱלֹהֶיךָ
God-of-you Yahweh he-brought-you the-Abib in-month-of for God-of-you

מִמִּצְרַיִם לָיְלָה׃ וְזָבַחְתָּ פֶּסַח לַיהוָה אֱלֹהֶיךָ צֹאן
flock God-of-you to-Yahweh Passover and-you-sacrifice (2) night from-Egypt

וּבָקָר בַּמָּקוֹם אֲשֶׁר־ יִבְחַר יְהוָה לְשַׁכֵּן שְׁמוֹ
Name-of-him to-make-dwell Yahweh he-will-choose that at-the-place or-herd

שָׁם׃ לֹא־ תֹאכַל עָלָיו חָמֵץ שִׁבְעַת יָמִים תֹּאכַל־ עָלָיו
with-him you-eat days seven-of yeast with-him you-eat not (3) there

מַצּוֹת לֶחֶם עֹנִי כִּי בְחִפָּזוֹן יָצָאתָ מֵאֶרֶץ
from-land-of you-left in-haste for affliction bread-of breads-without-yeast

מִצְרַיִם לְמַעַן תִּזְכֹּר אֶת־ יוֹם צֵאתְךָ מֵאֶרֶץ מִצְרַיִם
Egypt from-land-of to-depart-you day *** you-may-remember so-that Egypt

כֹּל יְמֵי חַיֶּיךָ׃ וְלֹא־ יֵרָאֶה לְךָ שְׂאֹר
yeast with-you he-must-be-found and-not (4) lives-of-you days-of all-of

בְּכָל־ גְּבֻלְךָ שִׁבְעַת יָמִים וְלֹא־ יָלִין מִן־ הַבָּשָׂר אֲשֶׁר
that the-meat from he-may-remain and-not days seven-of land-of-you in-all-of

because his service to you these six years has been worth twice as much as that of a hired hand. And the LORD your God will bless you in everything you do.

*The Firstborn Animals*

19 Set apart for the LORD your God every firstborn male of your herds and flocks. Do not put the firstborn of your oxen to work, and do not shear the firstborn of your sheep. 20 Each year you and your family are to eat them in the presence of the LORD your God at the place he will choose. 21 If an animal has a defect, is lame or blind, or has any serious flaw, you must not sacrifice it to the LORD your God. 22 You are to eat it in your own towns. Both the ceremonially unclean and the clean may eat it, as if it were gazelle or deer. 23 But you must not eat the blood; pour it out on the ground like water.

*Passover*

16 Observe the month of Abib and celebrate the Passover of the LORD your God, because in the month of Abib he brought you out of Egypt by night. 2 Sacrifice as the Passover to the LORD your God an animal from your flock or herd at the place the LORD will choose as a dwelling for his Name. 3 Do not eat it with bread made with yeast, but for seven days eat unleavened bread, the bread of affliction, because you left Egypt in haste—so that all the days of your life you may remember the time of your departure from Egypt. 4 Let no yeast be found in your possession in all your land for seven days. Do not let any of the meat you

תִּזְבַּח בָּעֶרֶב בַּיּוֹם הָרִאשׁוֹן לַבֹּקֶר׃ לֹא
not (5) until-the-morning the-first of-the-day on-the-evening you-sacrifice

תוּכַל לִזְבֹּחַ אֶת־ הַפָּסַח בְּאַחַד שְׁעָרֶיךָ אֲשֶׁר־ יְהוָה
Yahweh that gates-of-you within-any-of the-Passover *** to-sacrifice you-can

אֱלֹהֶיךָ נֹתֵן לָךְ׃ כִּי אִם־ אֶל־ הַמָּקוֹם אֲשֶׁר־ יִבְחַר
he-will-choose that the-place in only except (6) to-you giving God-of-you

יְהוָה אֱלֹהֶיךָ לְשַׁכֵּן שְׁמוֹ שָׁם תִּזְבַּח אֶת־
*** you-must-sacrifice there Name-of-him to-make-dwell God-of-you Yahweh

הַפֶּסַח בָּעָרֶב כְּבוֹא הַשֶּׁמֶשׁ מוֹעֵד צֵאתְךָ
to-come-you anniversary the-sun when-to-go-down in-the-evening the-Passover

מִמִּצְרָיִם׃ וּבִשַּׁלְתָּ וְאָכַלְתָּ בַּמָּקוֹם אֲשֶׁר יִבְחַר
he-will-choose that at-the-place and-you-eat and-you-roast (7) from-Egypt

יְהוָה אֱלֹהֶיךָ בּוֹ וּפָנִיתָ בַבֹּקֶר וְהָלַכְתָּ
and-you-return in-the-morning then-you-go to-him God-of-you Yahweh

לְאֹהָלֶיךָ׃ שֵׁשֶׁת יָמִים תֹּאכַל מַצּוֹת וּבַיּוֹם
and-on-the-day unleavened-breads you-eat days six-of (8) to-tents-of-you

הַשְּׁבִיעִי עֲצֶרֶת לַיהוָה אֱלֹהֶיךָ לֹא תַעֲשֶׂה מְלָאכָה׃ שִׁבְעָה שָׁבֻעֹת
weeks seven (9) work you-do not God-of-you to-Yahweh assembly the-seventh

תִּסְפָּר־ לָךְ מֵהָחֵל חֶרְמֵשׁ בַּקָּמָה תָּחֵל
you-begin to-the-standing-grain sickle from-to-begin for-you you-count

לִסְפֹּר שִׁבְעָה שָׁבֻעוֹת׃ וְעָשִׂיתָ חַג שָׁבֻעוֹת לַיהוָה
to-Yahweh Weeks Feast-of then-you-celebrate (10) weeks seven to-count

אֱלֹהֶיךָ מִסַּת נִדְבַת יָדְךָ אֲשֶׁר תִּתֵּן
you-give that hand-of-you freewill-offering-of proportion-of God-of-you

כַּאֲשֶׁר יְבָרֶכְךָ יְהוָה אֱלֹהֶיךָ׃ וְשָׂמַחְתָּ לִפְנֵי ׀ יְהוָה
Yahweh before and-you-rejoice (11) God-of-you Yahweh he-blessed-you just-as

אֱלֹהֶיךָ אַתָּה וּבִנְךָ וּבִתֶּךָ וְעַבְדְּךָ
and-manservant-of-you and-daughter-of-you and-son-of-you you God-of-you

וַאֲמָתֶךָ וְהַלֵּוִי אֲשֶׁר בִּשְׁעָרֶיךָ וְהַגֵּר
and-the-alien within-gates-of-you who and-the-Levite and-maidservant-of-you

וְהַיָּתוֹם וְהָאַלְמָנָה אֲשֶׁר בְּקִרְבֶּךָ בַּמָּקוֹם אֲשֶׁר
that at-the-place in-among-you who and-the-widow and-the-fatherless

יִבְחַר יְהוָה אֱלֹהֶיךָ לְשַׁכֵּן שְׁמוֹ שָׁם׃
there Name-of-him to-make-dwell God-of-you Yahweh he-will-choose

וְזָכַרְתָּ כִּי־ עֶבֶד הָיִיתָ בְּמִצְרַיִם וְשָׁמַרְתָּ
and-you-be-careful in-Egypt you-were slave that and-you-remember (12)

וְעָשִׂיתָ אֶת־ הַחֻקִּים הָאֵלֶּה׃ חַג הַסֻּכֹּת
the-Tabernacles Feast-of (13) the-these the-decrees *** and-you-follow

sacrifice on the evening of the
first day remain until morning.
5You must not sacrifice the
Passover in any town the LORD
your God gives you 6except in
the place he will choose as a
dwelling for his Name. There
you must sacrifice the Passover in the evening, when the
sun goes down, on the anniversary[y] of your departure
from Egypt. 7Roast it and eat it
at the place the LORD your God
will choose. Then in the morning return to your tents. 8For
six days eat unleavened bread
and on the seventh day hold
an assembly to the LORD your
God and do no work.

*Feast of Weeks*

9Count off seven weeks from
the time you begin to put the
sickle to the standing grain.
10Then celebrate the Feast of
Weeks to the LORD your God
by giving a freewill offering in
proportion to the blessings the
LORD your God has given you.
11And rejoice before the LORD
your God at the place he will
choose as a dwelling for his
Name—you, your sons and
daughters, your menservants
and maidservants, the Levites
in your towns, and the aliens,
the fatherless and the widows
living among you. 12Remem-
ber that you were slaves in
Egypt, and follow carefully
these decrees.

[y]6 *Or down, at the time of day*

תַּעֲשֶׂה לְךָ שִׁבְעַת יָמִים בְּאָסְפְּךָ מִגָּרְנְךָ
from-threshing-of-you after-to-gather-you days seven-of for-you you-celebrate

וּמִיִּקְבֶךָ׃ (14) וְשָׂמַחְתָּ בְּחַגֶּךָ אַתָּה
you at-Feast-of-you and-you-rejoice (14) and-from-winepress-of-you

וּבִנְךָ וּבִתֶּךָ וְעַבְדְּךָ וַאֲמָתֶךָ
and-maidservant-of-you and-manservant-of-you and-daughter-of-you and-son-of-you

וְהַלֵּוִי וְהַגֵּר וְהַיָּתוֹם וְהָאַלְמָנָה אֲשֶׁר
who and-the-widow and-the-fatherless and-the-alien and-the-Levite

בִּשְׁעָרֶיךָ׃ (15) שִׁבְעַת יָמִים תָּחֹג לַיהוָה אֱלֹהֶיךָ
God-of-you to-Yahweh you-celebrate days seven-of (15) within-gates-of-you

בַּמָּקוֹם אֲשֶׁר־ יִבְחַר יְהוָה כִּי יְבָרֶכְךָ יְהוָה
Yahweh he-will-bless-you for Yahweh he-will-choose that at-the-place

אֱלֹהֶיךָ בְּכֹל תְּבוּאָתְךָ וּבְכֹל מַעֲשֵׂה יָדֶיךָ
hands-of-you work-of and-in-all-of harvest-of-you in-all-of God-of-you

וְהָיִיתָ אַךְ שָׂמֵחַ׃ (16) שָׁלוֹשׁ פְּעָמִים ׀ בַּשָּׁנָה יֵרָאֶה
he-must-appear in-the-year times three (16) joy complete and-you-will-have

כָל־ זְכוּרְךָ אֶת־ פְּנֵי ׀ יְהוָה אֱלֹהֶיךָ בַּמָּקוֹם אֲשֶׁר
that at-the-place God-of-you Yahweh before *** male-of-you every-of

יִבְחָר בְּחַג הַמַּצּוֹת וּבְחַג הַשָּׁבֻעוֹת
the-Weeks and-at-Feast-of the-Unleavened-Breads at-Feast-of he-will-choose

וּבְחַג הַסֻּכּוֹת וְלֹא יֵרָאֶה אֶת־ פְּנֵי יְהוָה
Yahweh before *** he-should-appear and-none the-Tabernacles and-at-Feast-of

רֵיקָם׃ (17) אִישׁ כְּמַתְּנַת יָדוֹ כְּבִרְכַּת יְהוָה
Yahweh as-blessing-of hand-of-him as-gift-of each (17) empty-handed

אֱלֹהֶיךָ אֲשֶׁר נָתַן־ לָךְ׃ (18) שֹׁפְטִים וְשֹׁטְרִים
and-ones-officiating ones-judging (18) to-you he-gave that God-of-you

תִּתֶּן־ לְךָ בְּכָל־ שְׁעָרֶיךָ אֲשֶׁר יְהוָה אֱלֹהֶיךָ נֹתֵן
giving God-of-you Yahweh that gates-of-you within-all-of for-you you-appoint

לְךָ לִשְׁבָטֶיךָ וְשָׁפְטוּ אֶת־ הָעָם מִשְׁפַּט־ צֶדֶק׃
fair judgment-of the-people *** and-they-shall-judge for-tribes-of-you to-you

(19) לֹא־ תַטֶּה מִשְׁפָּט לֹא תַכִּיר פָּנִים וְלֹא־ תִקַּח שֹׁחַד
bribe you-accept and-not faces you-regard not judgment you-pervert not (19)

כִּי הַשֹּׁחַד יְעַוֵּר עֵינֵי חֲכָמִים וִיסַלֵּף דִּבְרֵי צַדִּיקִם׃
ones-righteous words-of and-he-twists ones-wise eyes-of he-blinds the-bribe for

(20) צֶדֶק צֶדֶק תִּרְדֹּף לְמַעַן תִּחְיֶה וְיָרַשְׁתָּ אֶת־
*** and-you-may-possess you-may-live so-that you-follow justice justice (20)

הָאָרֶץ אֲשֶׁר־ יְהוָה אֱלֹהֶיךָ נֹתֵן לָךְ׃ (21) לֹא־ תִטַּע לְךָ
for-you you-set-up not (21) to-you giving God-of-you Yahweh that the-land

*Feast of Tabernacles*

[13]Celebrate the Feast of Tabernacles for seven days after you have gathered the produce of your threshing floor and your winepress. [14]Be joyful at your Feast—you, your sons and daughters, your menservants and maidservants, and the Levites, the aliens, the fatherless and the widows who live in your towns. [15]For seven days celebrate the Feast to the LORD your God at the place the LORD will choose. For the LORD your God will bless you in all your harvest and in all the work of your hands, and your joy will be complete.

[16]Three times a year all your men must appear before the LORD your God at the place he will choose: at the Feast of Unleavened Bread, the Feast of Weeks and the Feast of Tabernacles. No man should appear before the LORD empty-handed: [17]Each of you must bring a gift in proportion to the way the LORD your God has blessed you.

*Judges*

[18]Appoint judges and officials for each of your tribes in every town the LORD your God is giving you, and they shall judge the people fairly. [19]Do not pervert justice or show partiality. Do not accept a bribe, for a bribe blinds the eyes of the wise and twists the words of the righteous. [20]Follow justice and justice alone, so that you may live and possess the land the LORD your God is giving you.

*Worshiping Other Gods*

[21]Do not set up any wooden

אֲשֵׁרָה כָּל־ עֵץ אֵצֶל מִזְבַּח יְהוָה אֱלֹהֶיךָ אֲשֶׁר תַּעֲשֶׂה־
you-build that God-of-you Yahweh altar-of beside wooden any-of Asherah-pole

לָּךְ׃ וְלֹא־ תָקִים לְךָ מַצֵּבָה אֲשֶׁר שָׂנֵא יְהוָה
Yahweh he-hates that sacred-stone for-you you-erect and-not (22) for-you

אֱלֹהֶיךָ׃ לֹא־ תִזְבַּח לַיהוָה אֱלֹהֶיךָ שׁוֹר וָשֶׂה אֲשֶׁר
that or-sheep ox God-of-you to-Yahweh you-sacrifice not (17:1) God-of-you

יִהְיֶה בוֹ מוּם כֹּל דָּבָר רָע כִּי תוֹעֲבַת יְהוָה אֱלֹהֶיךָ הוּא׃
that God-of-you Yahweh detestable-of for bad flaw any-of defect on-him he-is

כִּי־ יִמָּצֵא בְקִרְבְּךָ בְּאַחַד שְׁעָרֶיךָ אֲשֶׁר־ יְהוָה
Yahweh that gates-of-you within-any-of in-among-you he-is-found if (2)

אֱלֹהֶיךָ נֹתֵן לָךְ אִישׁ אוֹ־ אִשָּׁה אֲשֶׁר יַעֲשֶׂה אֶת־ הָרַע בְּעֵינֵי
in-eyes-of the-evil *** he-does who woman or man to-you giving God-of-you

יְהוָה־ אֱלֹהֶיךָ לַעֲבֹר בְּרִיתוֹ׃ וַיֵּלֶךְ וַיַּעֲבֹד
and-he-worships and-he-goes (3) covenant-of-him to-violate God-of-you Yahweh

אֱלֹהִים אֲחֵרִים וַיִּשְׁתַּחוּ לָהֶם וְלַשֶּׁמֶשׁ ׀ אוֹ לַיָּרֵחַ אוֹ לְכָל־
to-any-of or to-the-moon or or-to-the-sun to-them and-he-bows other-ones gods

צְבָא הַשָּׁמַיִם אֲשֶׁר לֹא־ צִוִּיתִי׃ וְהֻגַּד־ לְךָ
to-you and-he-is-told (4) I-commanded not that the-heavens array-of

וְשָׁמָעְתָּ וְדָרַשְׁתָּ הֵיטֵב וְהִנֵּה אֱמֶת
true and-if to-be-thorough then-you-must-investigate and-you-heard

נָכוֹן הַדָּבָר נֶעֶשְׂתָה הַתּוֹעֵבָה הַזֹּאת בְּיִשְׂרָאֵל׃
in-Israel the-this the-detestable-thing she-was-done the-thing being-proved

וְהוֹצֵאתָ אֶת־ הָאִישׁ הַהוּא אוֹ אֶת־ הָאִשָּׁה הַהִוא אֲשֶׁר
who the-that the-woman *** or the-that the-man *** then-you-take (5)

עָשׂוּ אֶת־ הַדָּבָר הָרָע הַזֶּה אֶל־ שְׁעָרֶיךָ אֶת־ הָאִישׁ אוֹ אֶת־
*** or the-man *** gates-of-you to the-this the-evil the-deed *** they-did

הָאִשָּׁה וּסְקַלְתָּם בָּאֲבָנִים וָמֵתוּ׃ עַל־ פִּי ׀
testimony-of on (6) so-they-die with-the-stones and-you-stone-them the-woman

שְׁנַיִם עֵדִים אוֹ שְׁלֹשָׁה עֵדִים יוּמַת הַמֵּת לֹא יוּמַת
he-shall-die not the-one-dying he-shall-die witnesses three or witnesses two

עַל־ פִּי עֵד אֶחָד׃ יַד הָעֵדִים תִּהְיֶה־ בּוֹ
on-him she-must-be the-witnesses hand-of (7) one witness testimony-of on

בָרִאשֹׁנָה לַהֲמִיתוֹ וְיַד כָּל־ הָעָם בָּאַחֲרֹנָה
as-the-next the-people all-of then-hand-of to-kill-him at-the-first

וּבִעַרְתָּ הָרָע מִקִּרְבֶּךָ׃ כִּי יִפָּלֵא מִמְּךָ
for-you he-is-difficult if (8) from-among-you the-evil so-you-must-purge

דָבָר לַמִּשְׁפָּט בֵּין־ דָּם ׀ לְדָם בֵּין־ דִּין לְדִין
to-lawsuit lawsuit or to-bloodshed bloodshed whether for-the-judgment case

Asherah pole[z] beside the altar you build to the LORD your God, 22and do not erect a sacred stone, for these the LORD your God hates.

17 Do not sacrifice to the LORD your God an ox or a sheep that has any defect or flaw in it, for that would be detestable to him.

2If a man or woman living among you in one of the towns the LORD gives you is found doing evil in the eyes of the LORD your God in violation of his covenant, 3and contrary to my command has worshiped other gods, bowing down to them or to the sun or the moon or the stars of the sky, 4and this has been brought to your attention, then you must investigate it thoroughly. If it is true and it has been proved that this detestable thing has been done in Israel, 5take the man or woman who has done this evil deed to your city gate and stone that person to death. 6On the testimony of two or three witnesses a man shall be put to death, but no one shall be put to death on the testimony of only one witness. 7The hands of the witnesses must be the first in putting him to death, and then the hands of all the people. You must purge the evil from among you.

*Law Courts*

8If cases come before your courts that are too difficult for you to judge—whether bloodshed, lawsuits or assaults—

[z]21 Or *Do not plant any tree dedicated to Asherah*

וּבֵין נֶגַע לָנֶגַע דִּבְרֵי רִיבֹת בִּשְׁעָרֶיךָ וְקַמְתָּ
then-you-rise in-gates-of-you judgments cases-of to-assault assault or-whether

וְעָלִיתָ אֶל־הַמָּקוֹם אֲשֶׁר יִבְחַר יְהוָה אֱלֹהֶיךָ בּוֹ׃
to-him God-of-you Yahweh he-will-choose that the-place to and-you-go

וּבָאתָ אֶל־הַכֹּהֲנִים הַלְוִיִּם וְאֶל־הַשֹּׁפֵט אֲשֶׁר יִהְיֶה
he-is who the-one-judging and-to the-Levites the-priests to and-you-go (9)

בַּיָּמִים הָהֵם וְדָרַשְׁתָּ וְהִגִּידוּ לְךָ אֵת דְּבַר
verdict-of *** to-you and-they-will-give and-you-inquire the-those in-the-days

הַמִּשְׁפָּט׃ וְעָשִׂיתָ עַל־פִּי הַדָּבָר אֲשֶׁר
that the-decision accordance-of in and-you-must-act (10) the-judgment

יַגִּידוּ לְךָ מִן־הַמָּקוֹם הַהוּא אֲשֶׁר יִבְחַר יְהוָה
Yahweh he-will-choose which the-that the-place at to-you they-give

וְשָׁמַרְתָּ לַעֲשׂוֹת כְּכֹל אֲשֶׁר יוֹרוּךָ׃ עַל־פִּי
accordance-of in (11) they-direct-you that as-all to-do and-you-be-careful

הַתּוֹרָה אֲשֶׁר יוֹרוּךָ וְעַל־הַמִּשְׁפָּט אֲשֶׁר־יֹאמְרוּ לְךָ
to-you they-give that the-decision and-by they-teach-you that the-law

תַּעֲשֶׂה לֹא תָסוּר מִן־הַדָּבָר אֲשֶׁר־יַגִּידוּ לְךָ יָמִין וּשְׂמֹאל׃
or-left right to-you they-tell that the-thing from you-turn not you-act

וְהָאִישׁ אֲשֶׁר־יַעֲשֶׂה בְזָדוֹן לְבִלְתִּי שְׁמֹעַ אֶל־הַכֹּהֵן
the-priest to to-obey not with-contempt he-acts who and-the-man (12)

הָעֹמֵד לְשָׁרֶת שָׁם אֶת־יְהוָה אֱלֹהֶיךָ אוֹ אֶל־הַשֹּׁפֵט
the-one-judging to or God-of-you Yahweh *** there to-minister the-one-standing

וּמֵת הָאִישׁ הַהוּא וּבִעַרְתָּ הָרָע מִיִּשְׂרָאֵל׃
from-Israel the-evil so-you-must-purge the-that the-man then-he-must-die

וְכָל־הָעָם יִשְׁמְעוּ וְיִרָאוּ וְלֹא
and-not and-they-will-be-afraid they-will-hear the-people and-all-of (13)

יְזִידוּן עוֹד׃ כִּי־תָבֹא אֶל־הָאָרֶץ אֲשֶׁר יְהוָה
Yahweh that the-land into you-enter when (14) again they-will-be-contemptuous

אֱלֹהֶיךָ נֹתֵן לָךְ וִירִשְׁתָּהּ וְיָשַׁבְתָּה בָּהּ וְאָמַרְתָּ
and-you-say in-her and-you-settle and-you-possess-her to-you giving God-of-you

אָשִׂימָה עָלַי מֶלֶךְ כְּכָל־הַגּוֹיִם אֲשֶׁר סְבִיבֹתָי׃
ones-around-me that the-nations like-all-of king over-me I-will-set

שׂוֹם תָּשִׂים עָלֶיךָ מֶלֶךְ אֲשֶׁר יִבְחַר יְהוָה אֱלֹהֶיךָ
God-of-you Yahweh he-chooses whom king over-you you-appoint to-appoint (15)

בּוֹ מִקֶּרֶב אַחֶיךָ תָּשִׂים עָלֶיךָ מֶלֶךְ לֹא תוּכַל
you-can not king over-you you-appoint brothers-of-you from-among to-him

לָתֵת עָלֶיךָ אִישׁ נָכְרִי אֲשֶׁר לֹא־אָחִיךָ הוּא׃ רַק לֹא־
not moreover (16) he brother-of-you not who foreigner man over-you to-place

take them to the place the
Lord your God will choose.
[9]Go to the priests, who are Levites, and to the judge who is
in office at that time. Inquire
of them and they will give you
the verdict. [10]You must act according to the decisions they
give you at the place the Lord
will choose. Be careful to do
everything they direct you to
do. [11]Act according to the law
they teach you and the decisions they give you. Do not
turn aside from what they tell
you, to the right or to the left.
[12]The man who shows contempt for the judge or for the
priest who stands ministering
there to the Lord your God
must be put to death. You
must purge the evil from Israel. [13]All the people will hear
and be afraid, and will not be
contemptuous again.

*The King*

[14]When you enter the land
the Lord your God is giving
you and have taken possession of it and settled in it, and
you say, "Let us set a king over
us like all the nations around
us," [15]be sure to appoint over
you the king the Lord your
God chooses. He must be from
among your own brothers. Do
not place a foreigner over you,
one who is not a brother Israelite. [16]The king, moreover,

יַרְבֶּה־ לּוֹ סוּסִים וְלֹא־ יָשִׁיב אֶת־ הָעָם

the-people *** he-must-make-return and-not horses for-him he-must-increase

מִצְרַיְמָה לְמַעַן הַרְבּוֹת סוּס וַיהוָה אָמַר לָכֶם לֹא

not to-you he-told for-Yahweh horse to-get-more to-order to-Egypt

תֹסִפוּן לָשׁוּב בַּדֶּרֶךְ הַזֶּה עוֹד׃ וְלֹא

and-not (17) again the-that on-the-way to-go-back you-must-repeat

יַרְבֶּה־ לּוֹ נָשִׁים וְלֹא יָסוּר לְבָבוֹ וְכֶסֶף

and-silver heart-of-him he-strays so-not wives to-him he-must-take-many

וְזָהָב לֹא יַרְבֶּה־ לּוֹ מְאֹד׃ וְהָיָה

and-he-will-be (18) much for-him he-must-accumulate not and-gold

כְשִׁבְתּוֹ עַל כִּסֵּא מַמְלַכְתּוֹ וְכָתַב לוֹ אֶת־

*** for-him then-he-must-write kingdom-of-him throne-of on when-to-sit-him

מִשְׁנֵה הַתּוֹרָה הַזֹּאת עַל־ סֵפֶר מִלִּפְנֵי הַכֹּהֲנִים הַלְוִיִּם׃

the-Levites the-priests from-before scroll on the-this the-law copy-of

וְהָיְתָה עִמּוֹ וְקָרָא בוֹ כָּל־ יְמֵי

days-of all-of for-him and-he-must-read with-him and-she-must-be (19)

חַיָּיו לְמַעַן יִלְמַד לְיִרְאָה אֶת־ יְהוָה אֱלֹהָיו

God-of-him Yahweh *** to-revere he-may-learn so-that lives-of-him

לִשְׁמֹר אֶת־ כָּל־ דִּבְרֵי הַתּוֹרָה הַזֹּאת וְאֶת־ הַחֻקִּים הָאֵלֶּה

the-these the-decrees and the-this the-law words-of all-of *** to-be-careful

לַעֲשֹׂתָם׃ לְבִלְתִּי רוּם־ לְבָבוֹ מֵאֶחָיו וּלְבִלְתִּי

and-not over-brothers-of-him heart-of-him to-exalt not (20) to-follow-them

סוּר מִן־ הַמִּצְוָה יָמִין וּשְׂמֹאול לְמַעַן יַאֲרִיךְ יָמִים עַל־

over days he-may-lengthen so-that or-left right the-law from to-turn

מַמְלַכְתּוֹ הוּא וּבָנָיו בְּקֶרֶב יִשְׂרָאֵל׃ לֹא־ יִהְיֶה

he-shall-be not (18:1) Israel in-among and-sons-of-him he kingdom-of-him

לַכֹּהֲנִים הַלְוִיִּם כָּל־ שֵׁבֶט לֵוִי חֵלֶק וְנַחֲלָה

or-inheritance allotment Levi tribe-of whole-of the-Levites for-the-priests

עִם־ יִשְׂרָאֵל אִשֵּׁי יְהוָה וְנַחֲלָתוֹ יֹאכֵלוּן׃

they-shall-eat even-inheritance-of-him Yahweh fire-offerings-of Israel with

וְנַחֲלָה לֹא־ יִהְיֶה־ לּוֹ בְּקֶרֶב אֶחָיו יְהוָה

Yahweh brothers-of-him in-among for-him he-shall-be not and-inheritance (2)

הוּא נַחֲלָתוֹ כַּאֲשֶׁר דִּבֶּר־ לוֹ׃ וְזֶה יִהְיֶה מִשְׁפַּט

share-of he-is and-this (3) to-him he-promised just-as inheritance-of-him he

הַכֹּהֲנִים מֵאֵת הָעָם מֵאֵת זֹבְחֵי הַזֶּבַח אִם־

whether the-sacrifice ones-sacrificing-of from the-people from the-priests

שׁוֹר אִם־ שֶׂה וְנָתַן לַכֹּהֵן הַזְּרֹעַ וְהַלְּחָיַיִם

and-the-jowls the-shoulder to-the-priest now-he-must-give sheep or bull

must not acquire great numbers of horses for himself or make the people return to Egypt to get more of them, for the LORD has told you, "You are not to go back that way again." 17He must not take many wives, or his heart will be led astray. He must not accumulate large amounts of silver and gold.

18When he takes the throne of his kingdom, he is to write for himself on a scroll a copy of this law, taken from that of the priests, who are Levites. 19It is to be with him, and he is to read it all the days of his life so that he may learn to revere the LORD his God and follow carefully all the words of this law and these decrees 20and not consider himself better than his brothers and turn from the law to the right or to the left. Then he and his descendants will reign a long time over his kingdom in Israel.

*Offerings for Priests and Levites*

18 The priests, who are Levites—indeed the whole tribe of Levi—are to have no allotment or inheritance with Israel. They shall live on the offerings made to the LORD by fire, for that is their inheritance. 2They shall have no inheritance among their brothers; the LORD is their inheritance, as he promised them.

3This is the share due the priests from the people who sacrifice a bull or a sheep: the

וְהַקֵּבָה׃ (4) רֵאשִׁית דְּגָנְךָ תִּירֹשְׁךָ וְיִצְהָרֶךָ
and-oil-of-you new-wine-of-you grain-of-you first-of (4) and-the-inner-part

וְרֵאשִׁית גֵּז צֹאנְךָ תִּתֶּן־ לוֹ׃ (5) כִּי בוֹ בָּחַר
he-chose to-him for (5) to-him you-give sheep-of-you shearing-of and-first-of

יְהוָה אֱלֹהֶיךָ מִכָּל־ שְׁבָטֶיךָ לַעֲמֹד לְשָׁרֵת בְּשֵׁם־
in-name-of to-minister to-stand tribes-of-you from-all-of God-of-you Yahweh

יְהוָה הוּא וּבָנָיו כָּל־ הַיָּמִים׃ (6) וְכִי־ יָבֹא הַלֵּוִי
the-Levite he-moves and-if (6) the-days all-of and-sons-of-him he Yahweh

מֵאַחַד שְׁעָרֶיךָ מִכָּל־ יִשְׂרָאֵל אֲשֶׁר־הוּא גָּר שָׁם וּבָא
and-he-comes there living he where Israel in-any-of gates-of-you from-one-of

בְּכָל־ אַוַּת נַפְשׁוֹ אֶל־הַמָּקוֹם אֲשֶׁר־ יִבְחַר יְהוָה׃
Yahweh he-will-choose that the-place to spirit-of-him earnestness-of in-all-of

(7) וְשֵׁרֵת בְּשֵׁם יְהוָה אֱלֹהָיו כְּכָל־
like-all-of God-of-him Yahweh in-name-of then-he-may-minister (7)

אֶחָיו הַלְוִיִּם הָעֹמְדִים שָׁם לִפְנֵי יְהוָה׃
Yahweh in-presence-of there the-ones-serving the-Levites fellows-of-him

(8) חֵלֶק כְּחֵלֶק יֹאכֵלוּ לְבַד מִמְכָּרָיו עַל־
from sales-incomes-of-him even-though they-shall-share as-benefit benefit (8)

הָאָבוֹת׃ (9) כִּי אַתָּה בָּא אֶל־ הָאָרֶץ אֲשֶׁר־ יְהוָה אֱלֹהֶיךָ
God-of-you Yahweh that the-land into entering you when (9) the-families

נֹתֵן לָךְ לֹא־ תִלְמַד לַעֲשׂוֹת כְּתוֹעֲבֹת הַגּוֹיִם
the-nations as-detestable-ways-of to-imitate you-learn not to-you giving

הָהֵם׃ (10) לֹא־ יִמָּצֵא בְךָ מַעֲבִיר בְּנוֹ־
son-of-him one-sacrificing among-you let-him-be-found not (10) the-those

וּבִתּוֹ בָּאֵשׁ קֹסֵם קְסָמִים מְעוֹנֵן
practicing-sorcery divinations divining in-the-fire or-daughter-of-him

וּמְנַחֵשׁ וּמְכַשֵּׁף׃ (11) וְחֹבֵר חָבֶר
spell or-casting (11) or-engaging-in-witchcraft or-interpreting-omen

וְשֹׁאֵל אוֹב וְיִדְּעֹנִי וְדֹרֵשׁ אֶל־ הַמֵּתִים׃ (12) כִּי־
for (12) the-ones-dead to or-consulting or-spiritist medium or-inquiring

תוֹעֲבַת יְהוָה כָּל־ עֹשֵׂה אֵלֶּה וּבִגְלַל הַתּוֹעֵבֹת
the-detestable-things and-because-of these doing every-of Yahweh detestable-of

הָאֵלֶּה יְהוָה אֱלֹהֶיךָ מוֹרִישׁ אוֹתָם מִפָּנֶיךָ׃ (13) תָּמִים
blameless (13) from-before-you them driving-out God-of-you Yahweh the-these

תִּהְיֶה עִם יְהוָה אֱלֹהֶיךָ׃ (14) כִּי ׀ הַגּוֹיִם הָאֵלֶּה אֲשֶׁר
that the-these the-nations for (14) God-of-you Yahweh before you-must-be

אַתָּה יוֹרֵשׁ אוֹתָם אֶל־ מְעֹנְנִים וְאֶל־ קֹסְמִים
ones-divining and-to ones-practicing-sorcery to them dispossessing you

shoulder, the jowls and the inner parts. [4]You are to give them the firstfruits of your grain, new wine and oil, and the first wool from the shearing of your sheep, [5]for the LORD your God has chosen them and their descendants out of all your tribes to stand and minister in the LORD's name always.

[6]If a Levite moves from one of your towns anywhere in Israel where he is living, and comes in all earnestness to the place the LORD will choose, [7]he may minister in the name of the LORD his God like all his fellow Levites who serve there in the presence of the LORD. [8]He is to share equally in their benefits, even though he has received money from the sale of family possessions.

*Detestable Practices*

[9]When you enter the land the LORD your God is giving you, do not learn to imitate the detestable ways of the nations there. [10]Let no one be found among you who sacrifices his son or daughter in[a] the fire, who practices divination or sorcery, interprets omens, engages in witchcraft, [11]or casts spells, or who is a medium or spiritist or who consults the dead. [12]Anyone who does these things is detestable to the LORD, and because of these detestable practices the LORD your God will drive out those nations before you. [13]You must be blameless before the LORD your God.

*The Prophet*

[14]The nations you will dispossess listen to those who practice sorcery or divination.

[a]10 *Or who makes his son or daughter pass through*

יִשְׁמָעוּ וְאַתָּה לֹא כֵן נָתַן לְךָ יְהוָה אֱלֹהֶיךָ׃ נָבִיא
prophet (15) God-of-you Yahweh to-you he-permitted so not but-you they-listen

מִקִּרְבְּךָ מֵאַחֶיךָ כָּמֹנִי יָקִים לְךָ יְהוָה
Yahweh for-you he-will-raise-up like-me from-brothers-of-you from-among-you

אֱלֹהֶיךָ אֵלָיו תִּשְׁמָעוּן׃ כְּכֹל אֲשֶׁר־שָׁאַלְתָּ מֵעִם
from-with you-asked that as-all (16) you-must-listen to-him God-of-you

יְהוָה אֱלֹהֶיךָ בְּחֹרֵב בְּיוֹם הַקָּהָל לֵאמֹר לֹא אֹסֵף
let-me-continue not to-say the-assembly on-day-of at-Horeb God-of-you Yahweh

לִשְׁמֹעַ אֶת־קוֹל יְהוָה אֱלֹהָי וְאֶת־הָאֵשׁ הַגְּדֹלָה הַזֹּאת לֹא־
not the-this the-great the-fire and God-of-me Yahweh voice-of *** to-hear

אֶרְאֶה עוֹד וְלֹא אָמוּת׃ וַיֹּאמֶר יְהוָה אֵלָי הֵיטִיבוּ
they-are-good to-me Yahweh and-he-said (17) I-die so-not anymore let-me-see

אֲשֶׁר דִּבֵּרוּ׃ נָבִיא אָקִים לָהֶם מִקֶּרֶב אֲחֵיהֶם
brothers-of-them from-among from-them I-will-raise prophet (18) they-say what

כָּמוֹךָ וְנָתַתִּי דְבָרַי בְּפִיו וְדִבֶּר אֲלֵיהֶם
to-them and-he-will-tell in-mouth-of-him words-of-me and-I-will-put like-you

אֵת כָּל־אֲשֶׁר אֲצַוֶּנּוּ׃ וְהָיָה הָאִישׁ אֲשֶׁר לֹא־יִשְׁמַע
he-listens not who the-man and-he-will-be (19) I-command-him that all ***

אֶל־דְּבָרַי אֲשֶׁר יְדַבֵּר בִּשְׁמִי אָנֹכִי אֶדְרֹשׁ
I-will-call-account I in-name-of-me he-speaks that words-of-me to

מֵעִמּוֹ׃ אַךְ הַנָּבִיא אֲשֶׁר יָזִיד לְדַבֵּר דָּבָר בִּשְׁמִי
in-name-of-me word to-speak he-presumes who the-prophet but (20) from-with-him

אֵת אֲשֶׁר לֹא־צִוִּיתִיו לְדַבֵּר וַאֲשֶׁר יְדַבֵּר בְּשֵׁם אֱלֹהִים
gods in-name-of he-speaks or-who to-say I-commanded-him not that ***

אֲחֵרִים וּמֵת הַנָּבִיא הַהוּא׃ וְכִי תֹאמַר
you-may-say but-now (21) the-that the-prophet then-he-must-die other-ones

בִּלְבָבֶךָ אֵיכָה נֵדַע אֶת־הַדָּבָר אֲשֶׁר לֹא־דִבְּרוֹ
to-speak-him not when the-message *** can-we-know how? in-heart-of-you

יְהוָה׃ אֲשֶׁר יְדַבֵּר הַנָּבִיא בְּשֵׁם יְהוָה וְלֹא־
and-not Yahweh in-name-of the-prophet he-proclaims when (22) Yahweh

יִהְיֶה הַדָּבָר וְלֹא יָבֹא הוּא הַדָּבָר אֲשֶׁר לֹא־
not then the-thing that he-comes-true or-not the-thing he-takes-place

דִבְּרוֹ יְהוָה בְּזָדוֹן דִּבְּרוֹ הַנָּבִיא לֹא תָגוּר
you-be-afraid not the-prophet to-speak-him in-presumption Yahweh to-speak-him

מִמֶּנּוּ׃ כִּי־יַכְרִית יְהוָה אֱלֹהֶיךָ אֶת־הַגּוֹיִם אֲשֶׁר יְהוָה
Yahweh that the-nations *** God-of-you Yahweh he-destroys when (19:1) of-him

אֱלֹהֶיךָ נֹתֵן לְךָ אֶת־אַרְצָם וִירִשְׁתָּם
and-you-drive-out-them land-of-them *** to-you giving God-of-you

But as for you, the LORD your
God has not permitted you to
do so. [15]The LORD your God
will raise up for you a prophet
like me from among your own
brothers. You must listen to
him. [16]For this is what you
asked of the LORD your God at
Horeb on the day of the assembly when you said, "Let us
not hear the voice of the LORD
our God nor see this great fire
anymore, or we will die."
[17]The LORD said to me:
"What they say is good. [18]I will
raise up for them a prophet
like you from among their
brothers; I will put my words
in his mouth, and he will tell
them everything I command
him. [19]If anyone does not listen to my words that the
prophet speaks in my name, I
myself will call him to account. [20]But a prophet who
presumes to speak in my
name anything I have not
commanded him to say, or a
prophet who speaks in the
name of other gods, must be
put to death."
[21]You may say to yourselves,
"How can we know when a
message has not been spoken
by the LORD?" [22]If what a
prophet proclaims in the
name of the LORD does not
take place or come true, that is
a message the LORD has not
spoken. That prophet has
spoken presumptuously. Do
not be afraid of him.

*Cities of Refuge*

19 When the LORD your
God has destroyed the
nations whose land he is giving you, and when you have
driven them out and settled in

וִישַׁבְתָּ בְעָרֵיהֶם וּבְבָתֵּיהֶם׃ שָׁלוֹשׁ עָרִים
cities three (2) and-in-houses-of-them in-towns-of-them and-you-settle

תַּבְדִּיל לָךְ בְּתוֹךְ אַרְצְךָ אֲשֶׁר יְהוָה אֱלֹהֶיךָ נֹתֵן
giving God-of-you Yahweh that land-of-you in-center-of for-you you-set-aside

לְךָ לְרִשְׁתָּהּ׃ תָּכִין לְךָ הַדֶּרֶךְ וְשִׁלַּשְׁתָּ
and-you-divide-into-three the-road for-you you-build (3) to-possess-her to-you

אֶת־ גְּבוּל אַרְצְךָ אֲשֶׁר יַנְחִילְךָ יְהוָה אֱלֹהֶיךָ
God-of-you Yahweh he-makes-inherit-you that land-of-you boundary-of ***

וְהָיָה לָנוּס שָׁמָּה כָּל־ רֹצֵחַ׃ וְזֶה דְּבַר
rule-of and-this (4) one-killing any-of to-there to-flee so-he-will-be

הָרֹצֵחַ אֲשֶׁר־ יָנוּס שָׁמָּה וָחָי אֲשֶׁר יַכֶּה אֶת־
*** he-kills who so-he-lives to-there he-flees who the-one-killing

רֵעֵהוּ בִּבְלִי־ דַעַת וְהוּא לֹא־ שֹׂנֵא לוֹ מִתְּמֹל
on-yesterday to-him hating not and-he intention with-no neighbor-of-him

שִׁלְשֹׁם׃ וַאֲשֶׁר יָבֹא אֶת־ רֵעֵהוּ בַיַּעַר לַחְטֹב עֵצִים
woods to-cut into-the-forest neighbor-of-him with he-goes now-if (5) before

וְנִדְּחָה יָדוֹ בַגַּרְזֶן לִכְרֹת הָעֵץ וְנָשַׁל
and-he-flies-off the-tree to-fell with-the-axe hand-of-him and-she-swings

הַבַּרְזֶל מִן־ הָעֵץ וּמָצָא אֶת־ רֵעֵהוּ וָמֵת הוּא
he and-he-dies neighbor-of-him *** and-he-hits the-handle from the-head

יָנוּס אֶל־ אַחַת הֶעָרִים־ הָאֵלֶּה וָחָי׃ פֶּן־
otherwise (6) and-he-will-live the-these the-cities one-of to he-may-flee

יִרְדֹּף גֹּאֵל הַדָּם אַחֲרֵי הָרֹצֵחַ כִּי־
for the-one-killing after the-blood one-avenging-of he-might-pursue

יֵחַם לְבָבוֹ וְהִשִּׂיגוֹ כִּי־ יִרְבֶּה
he-is-too-great for and-he-might-overtake-him heart-of-him he-is-enraged

הַדֶּרֶךְ וְהִכָּהוּ נֶפֶשׁ וְלוֹ אֵין מִשְׁפַּט־מָוֶת
death judgment-of not though-to-him mortally and-he-might-strike-him the-distance

כִּי לֹא שֹׂנֵא הוּא לוֹ מִתְּמוֹל שִׁלְשׁוֹם׃ עַל־ כֵּן אָנֹכִי מְצַוְּךָ
commanding-you I this for (7) before on-yesterday to-him he hating not for

לֵאמֹר שָׁלֹשׁ עָרִים תַּבְדִּיל לָךְ׃ וְאִם־ יַרְחִיב יְהוָה
Yahweh he-enlarges and-if (8) for-you you-set-aside cities three to-say

אֱלֹהֶיךָ אֶת־ גְּבֻלְךָ כַּאֲשֶׁר נִשְׁבַּע לַאֲבֹתֶיךָ וְנָתַן
and-he-gives to-fathers-of-you he-swore just-as territory-of-you *** God-of-you

לְךָ אֶת־ כָּל־ הָאָרֶץ אֲשֶׁר דִּבֶּר לָתֵת לַאֲבֹתֶיךָ׃
to-fathers-of-you to-give he-promised that the-land whole-of *** to-you

כִּי־ תִשְׁמֹר אֶת־ כָּל־ הַמִּצְוָה הַזֹּאת לַעֲשֹׂתָהּ אֲשֶׁר
that to-follow-her the-this the-law all-of *** you-are-careful because (9)

their towns and houses, [2]then
set aside for yourselves three
cities centrally located in the
land the LORD your God is giving you to possess. [3]Build
roads to them and divide into
three parts the land the LORD
your God is giving you as an
inheritance, so that anyone
who kills a man may flee
there.

[4]This is the rule concerning
the man who kills another and
flees there to save his life—one
who kills his neighbor unintentionally, without malice
aforethought. [5]For instance, a
man may go into the forest
with his neighbor to cut wood,
and as he swings his ax to fell
a tree, the head may fly off and
hit his neighbor and kill him.
That man may flee to one of
these cities and save his life.
[6]Otherwise, the avenger of
blood might pursue him in a
rage, overtake him if the distance is too great, and kill him
even though he is not deserving of death, since he did it to
his neighbor without malice
aforethought. [7]This is why I
command you to set aside for
yourselves three cities.

[8]If the LORD your God enlarges your territory, as he
promised on oath to your
forefathers, and gives you the
whole land he promised them,
[9]because you carefully follow
all these laws I command you

אָנֹכִי מְצַוְּךָ הַיּוֹם לְאַהֲבָה אֶת־ יְהוָה אֱלֹהֶיךָ וְלָלֶכֶת
and-to-walk God-of-you Yahweh *** to-love the-day commanding-you I

בִּדְרָכָיו כָּל־ הַיָּמִים וְיָסַפְתָּ לְךָ עוֹד שָׁלֹשׁ עָרִים עַל
to cities three more for-you then-you-add the-days all-of in-ways-of-him

הַשָּׁלֹשׁ הָאֵלֶּה׃ (10) וְלֹא יִשָּׁפֵךְ דָּם נָקִי בְּקֶרֶב
in-among innocent blood he-will-be-shed so-not (10) the-these the-three

אַרְצְךָ אֲשֶׁר יְהוָה אֱלֹהֶיךָ נֹתֵן לְךָ נַחֲלָה וְהָיָה
and-he-will-be inheritance to-you giving God-of-you Yahweh that land-of-you

עָלֶיךָ דָּמִים׃ (11) וְכִי־ יִהְיֶה אִישׁ שֹׂנֵא לְרֵעֵהוּ וְאָרַב
and-he-waits to-neighbor-of-him hating man he-is but-if (11) bloodsheds on-you

לוֹ וְקָם עָלָיו וְהִכָּהוּ נֶפֶשׁ וָמֵת
and-he-dies mortally and-he-strikes-him against-him and-he-rises for-him

וְנָס אֶל־ אַחַת הֶעָרִים הָאֵל׃ (12) וְשָׁלְחוּ
then-they-shall-send (12) the-these the-cities one-of to then-he-flees

זִקְנֵי עִירוֹ וְלָקְחוּ אֹתוֹ מִשָּׁם וְנָתְנוּ
and-they-shall-give from-there him and-they-shall-bring city-of-him elders-of

אֹתוֹ בְּיַד גֹּאֵל הַדָּם וָמֵת׃ (13) לֹא־
not (13) so-he-will-die the-blood one-avenging-of into-hand-of him

תָחוֹס עֵינְךָ עָלָיו וּבִעַרְתָּ דַם־ הַנָּקִי
the-innocent blood-of so-you-must-purge to-him eye-of-you she-must-pity

מִיִּשְׂרָאֵל וְטוֹב לָךְ׃ (14) לֹא תַסִּיג גְּבוּל
boundary-stone-of you-move not (14) for-you for-good from-Israel

רֵעֲךָ אֲשֶׁר גָּבְלוּ רִאשֹׁנִים בְּנַחֲלָתְךָ אֲשֶׁר
that in-inheritance-of-you predecessors they-set-up that neighbor-of-you

תִּנְחַל בָּאָרֶץ אֲשֶׁר יְהוָה אֱלֹהֶיךָ נֹתֵן לְךָ לְרִשְׁתָּהּ׃
to-possess-her to-you giving God-of-you Yahweh that in-the-land you-receive

(15) לֹא־ יָקוּם עֵד אֶחָד בְּאִישׁ לְכָל־ עָוֹן וּלְכָל־
or-for-any-of crime for-any-of against-man one witness he-may-rise not (15)

חַטָּאת בְּכָל־ חֵטְא אֲשֶׁר יֶחֱטָא עַל־ פִּי שְׁנֵי
two-of testimony-of by he-committed that offense in-any-of offense

עֵדִים אוֹ עַל־ פִּי שְׁלֹשָׁה־ עֵדִים יָקוּם דָּבָר׃ (16) כִּי־
if (16) matter he-must-establish witnesses three testimony-of by or witnesses

יָקוּם עֵד־ חָמָס בְּאִישׁ לַעֲנוֹת בּוֹ סָרָה׃
crime against-him to-accuse against-him malicious witness he-takes-stand

(17) וְעָמְדוּ שְׁנֵי־ הָאֲנָשִׁים אֲשֶׁר־ לָהֶם הָרִיב לִפְנֵי
before the-dispute to-them who the-men two-of then-they-must-stand (17)

יְהוָה לִפְנֵי הַכֹּהֲנִים וְהַשֹּׁפְטִים אֲשֶׁר יִהְיוּ בַּיָּמִים
in-the-days they-are who and-the-ones-judging the-priests before Yahweh

today—to love the LORD your God and to walk always in his ways—then you are to set aside three more cities. [10]Do this so that innocent blood will not be shed in your land, which the LORD your God is giving you as your inheritance, and so that you will not be guilty of bloodshed.

[11]But if a man hates his neighbor and lies in wait for him, assaults and kills him, and then flees to one of these cities, [12]the elders of his town shall send for him, bring him back from the city, and hand him over to the avenger of blood to die. [13]Show him no pity. You must purge from Israel the guilt of shedding innocent blood, so that it may go well with you.

[14]Do not move your neighbor's boundary stone set up by your predecessors in the inheritance you receive in the land the LORD your God is giving you to possess.

*Witnesses*

[15]One witness is not enough to convict a man accused of any crime or offense he may have committed. A matter must be established by the testimony of two or three witnesses.

[16]If a malicious witness takes the stand to accuse a man of a crime, [17]the two men involved in the dispute must stand in the presence of the LORD before the priests and the judges who are in office at the time.

הָהֵם׃ וְדָרְשׁוּ הַשֹּׁפְטִים הֵיטֵב
to-be-thorough the-ones-judging and-they-must-investigate (18) the-those

וְהִנֵּה עֵד־ שֶׁקֶר הָעֵד שֶׁקֶר עָנָה בְאָחִיו׃
against-brother-of-him he-testifies lie the-witness liar witness-of and-if

וַעֲשִׂיתֶם לוֹ כַּאֲשֶׁר זָמַם לַעֲשׂוֹת לְאָחִיו
to-brother-of-him to-do he-intended just-as to-him then-you-do (19)

וּבִעַרְתָּ הָרָע מִקִּרְבֶּךָ׃ וְהַנִּשְׁאָרִים
and-the-ones-remaining (20) from-among-you the-evil so-you-must-purge

יִשְׁמְעוּ וְיִרָאוּ וְלֹא־ יֹסִפוּ לַעֲשׂוֹת עוֹד
again to-do they-will-repeat and-not and-they-will-be-afraid they-will-hear

כַּדָּבָר הָרָע הַזֶּה בְּקִרְבֶּךָ׃ וְלֹא תָחוֹס עֵינֶךָ
eye-of-you she-must-pity and-not (21) in-among-you the-this the-evil the-thing

נֶפֶשׁ בְּנֶפֶשׁ עַיִן בְּעַיִן שֵׁן בְּשֵׁן יָד בְּיָד רֶגֶל בְּרָגֶל׃
for-foot foot for-hand hand for-tooth tooth for-eye eye for-life life

כִּי־ תֵצֵא לַמִּלְחָמָה עַל־ אֹיְבֶךָ וְרָאִיתָ סוּס
horse and-you-see being-enemies-of-you against to-the-war you-go when (20:1)

וָרֶכֶב עַם רַב מִמְּךָ לֹא תִירָא מֵהֶם כִּי־ יְהוָה
Yahweh for of-them you-be-afraid not than-you greater army and-chariot

אֱלֹהֶיךָ עִמָּךְ הַמַּעַלְךָ מֵאֶרֶץ מִצְרָיִם׃ וְהָיָה
and-he-will-be (2) Egypt from-land-of the-one-bringing-you with-you God-of-you

כְּקָרָבְכֶם אֶל־ הַמִּלְחָמָה וְנִגַּשׁ הַכֹּהֵן
the-priest then-he-shall-come-forward the-battle into when-to-go-you

וְדִבֶּר אֶל־ הָעָם׃ וְאָמַר אֲלֵהֶם שְׁמַע יִשְׂרָאֵל
Israel hear! to-them and-he-shall-say (3) the-army to and-he-shall-address

אַתֶּם קְרֵבִים הַיּוֹם לַמִּלְחָמָה עַל־ אֹיְבֵיכֶם אַל־
not being-enemies-of-you against into-the-battle the-day ones-who-go you

יֵרַךְ לְבַבְכֶם אַל־ תִּירְאוּ וְאַל־ תַּחְפְּזוּ וְאַל־
and-not you-be-terrified and-not you-be-afraid not heart-of-you let-him-faint

תַּעַרְצוּ מִפְּנֵיהֶם׃ כִּי יְהוָה אֱלֹהֵיכֶם הַהֹלֵךְ עִמָּכֶם
with-you the-one-going God-of-you Yahweh for (4) from-before-them you-panic

לְהִלָּחֵם לָכֶם עִם־ אֹיְבֵיכֶם לְהוֹשִׁיעַ אֶתְכֶם׃
to-you to-give-victory being-enemies-of-you against for-you to-fight

וְדִבְּרוּ הַשֹּׁטְרִים אֶל־ הָעָם לֵאמֹר מִי־ הָאִישׁ
the-man any? to-say the-army to the-being-officers and-they-shall-say (5)

אֲשֶׁר בָּנָה בַיִת־ חָדָשׁ וְלֹא חֲנָכוֹ יֵלֵךְ וְיָשֹׁב
and-let-him-return let-him-go he-dedicated-him and-not new house he-built who

לְבֵיתוֹ פֶּן־ יָמוּת בַּמִּלְחָמָה וְאִישׁ אַחֵר יַחְנְכֶנּוּ׃
he-may-dedicate-him other and-man in-the-battle he-may-die or to-home-of-him

[18]The judges must make a
thorough investigation, and if
the witness proves to be a liar,
giving false testimony against
his brother, [19]then do to him
as he intended to do to his
brother. You must purge the
evil from among you. [20]The
rest of the people will hear of
this and be afraid, and never
again will such an evil thing
be done among you. [21]Show
no pity: life for life, eye for
eye, tooth for tooth, hand for
hand, foot for foot.

*Going to War*

**20** When you go to war
against your enemies
and see horses and chariots
and an army greater than
yours, do not be afraid of
them, because the LORD your
God, who brought you up out
of Egypt, will be with you.
[2]When you are about to go
into battle, the priest shall
come forward and address the
army. [3]He shall say: "Hear, O
Israel, today you are going
into battle against your enemies. Do not be faint-hearted
or afraid; do not be terrified or
give way to panic before them.
[4]For the LORD your God is the
one who goes with you to fight
for you against your enemies
to give you victory."
[5]The officers shall say to the
army: "Has anyone built a
new house and not dedicated
it? Let him go home, or he may
die in battle and someone else

וּמִי־ הָאִישׁ אֲשֶׁר־ נָטַע כֶּרֶם וְלֹא חִלְּלוֹ
he-began-to-enjoy-him and-not vineyard he-planted who the-man and-any? (6)

יֵלֵךְ וְיָשֹׁב לְבֵיתוֹ פֶּן־ יָמוּת בַּמִּלְחָמָה
in-the-battle he-may-die or to-home-of-him and-let-him-return let-him-go

וְאִישׁ אַחֵר יְחַלְּלֶנּוּ׃ וּמִי־ הָאִישׁ אֲשֶׁר־ אֵרַשׂ
he-became-pledged who the-man and-any? (7) he-may-enjoy-him other and-man

אִשָּׁה וְלֹא לְקָחָהּ יֵלֵךְ וְיָשֹׁב לְבֵיתוֹ
to-home-of-him and-let-him-return 'let-him-go he-married-her and-not woman

פֶּן־ יָמוּת בַּמִּלְחָמָה וְאִישׁ אַחֵר יִקָּחֶנָּה׃
he-may-marry-her other and-man in-the-battle he-may-die or

וְיָסְפוּ הַשֹּׁטְרִים לְדַבֵּר אֶל־ הָעָם וְאָמְרוּ
and-they-shall-say the-army to to-say the-being-officers then-they-shall-add (8)

מִי־ הָאִישׁ הַיָּרֵא וְרַךְ הַלֵּבָב יֵלֵךְ וְיָשֹׁב
and-let-him-return let-him-go the-heart or-faint-of the-afraid the-man any?

לְבֵיתוֹ וְלֹא יִמַּס אֶת־ לְבַב אֶחָיו
brothers-of-him heart-of *** he-will-trouble so-not to-home-of-him

כִּלְבָבוֹ׃ וְהָיָה כְּכַלֹּת הַשֹּׁטְרִים לְדַבֵּר
to-speak the-being-officers when-to-finish and-he-will-be (9) as-heart-of-him

אֶל־ הָעָם וּפָקְדוּ שָׂרֵי צְבָאוֹת בְּרֹאשׁ הָעָם׃
the-army at-head-of hosts commanders-of then-they-shall-appoint the-army to

כִּי־ תִקְרַב אֶל־ עִיר לְהִלָּחֵם עָלֶיהָ וְקָרָאתָ אֵלֶיהָ
to-her then-you-offer against-her to-attack city to you-march when (10)

לְשָׁלוֹם׃ וְהָיָה אִם־ שָׁלוֹם תַּעַנְךָ וּפָתְחָה לָךְ
to-you and-she-opens she-answers-you peace if and-he-will-be (11) for-peace

וְהָיָה כָּל־ הָעָם הַנִּמְצָא־ בָהּ יִהְיוּ לְךָ
for-you they-will-be in-her the-being-found the-people all-of then-he-will-be

לָמַס וַעֲבָדוּךָ׃ וְאִם־ לֹא תַשְׁלִים
she-makes-peace not but-if (12) and-they-will-serve-you for-forced-labor

עִמָּךְ וְעָשְׂתָה עִמְּךָ מִלְחָמָה וְצַרְתָּ עָלֶיהָ׃
against-her then-you-siege battle with-you and-she-engages with-you

וּנְתָנָהּ יְהוָה אֱלֹהֶיךָ בְּיָדֶךָ וְהִכִּיתָ
then-you-strike into-hand-of-you God-of-you Yahweh when-he-delivers-her (13)

אֶת־ כָּל־ זְכוּרָהּ לְפִי־ חָרֶב׃ רַק הַנָּשִׁים וְהַטַּף
and-the-child the-women only (14) sword with-edge-of man-of-her every-of ***

וְהַבְּהֵמָה וְכֹל[9] אֲשֶׁר יִהְיֶה בָעִיר כָּל־ שְׁלָלָהּ
plunder-of-her all-of in-the-city he-is that and-all and-the-stock

תָּבֹז לָךְ וְאָכַלְתָּ אֶת־ שְׁלַל אֹיְבֶיךָ
being-enemines-of-you plunder-of *** and-you-may-use for-you you-may-take

may dedicate it. [6]Has anyone planted a vineyard and not begun to enjoy it? Let him go home, or he may die in battle and someone else enjoy it. [7]Has anyone become pledged to a woman and not married her? Let him go home, or he may die in battle and someone else marry her." [8]Then the officers shall add, "Is any man afraid or faint-hearted? Let him go home so that his brothers will not become disheartened too." [9]When the officers have finished speaking to the army, they shall appoint commanders over it.

[10]When you march up to attack a city, make its people an offer of peace. [11]If they accept and open their gates, all the people in it shall be subject to forced labor and shall work for you. [12]If they refuse to make peace and they engage you in battle, lay siege to that city. [13]When the LORD your God delivers it into your hand, put to the sword all the men in it. [14]As for the women, the children, the livestock and everything else in the city, you may take these as plunder for yourselves. And you may use the

אשר נתן יהוה אלהיך לך׃ כן תעשה לכל־
to-all-of you-must-do this (15) to-you God-of-you Yahweh he-gives that

הערים הרחקת ממך מאד אשר לא־ מערי הגוים־
the-nations of-cities-of not that very from-you the-ones-distant the-cities

האלה הנה׃ רק מערי העמים האלה אשר יהוה
Yahweh that the-these the-nations of-cities-of however (16) nearby the-these

אלהיך נתן לך נחלה לא תחיה כל־
any-of you-leave-alive not inheritance to-you giving God-of-you

נשמה׃ כי־ החרם תחרימם החתי
the-Hittite you-destroy-them to-destroy but (17) breathing-thing

והאמרי הכנעני והפרזי החוי והיבוסי
and-the-Jebusite the-Hivite and-the-Perizzite the-Canaanite and-the-Amorite

כאשר צוך יהוה אלהיך׃ למען אשר לא־ ילמדו
they-teach not that in-order (18) God-of-you Yahweh he-commanded-you just-as

אתכם לעשות ככל תועבתם אשר עשו
they-do that detestable-things-of-them after-all-of to-follow you

לאלהיהם וחטאתם ליהוה אלהיכם׃ כי־ תצור
you-lay-siege when (19) God-of-you against-Yahweh so-you-sin for-gods-of-them

אל־ עיר ימים רבים להלחם עליה לתפשה לא־ תשחית את־
*** you-destroy not to-capture-her against-her to-fight many days city to

עצה לנדח עליו גרזן כי ממנו תאכל ואתו לא
not so-him you-can-eat from-him for axe to-him to-put tree-of-her

תכרת כי האדם עץ השדה לבא מפניך במצור׃
in-the-siege from-before-you to-go the-field tree-of the-man for you-cut-down

רק עץ אשר־ תדע כי־ לא־ עץ מאכל הוא אתו תשחית
you-can-use him he fruit tree-of not that you-know that tree however (20)

וכרת ובנית מצור על־ העיר אשר־ הוא עשה
making she that the-city for siege-work and-you-can-build and-you-can-cut

עמך מלחמה עד רדתה׃ כי־ ימצא חלל באדמה
in-the-land one-slain he-is-found if (21:1) to-fall-her until war against-you

אשר יהוה אלהיך נתן לך לרשתה נפל בשדה לא
not in-the-field lying to-possess-her to-you giving God-of-you Yahweh that

נודע מי הכהו׃ ויצאו זקניך
elders-of-you then-they-shall-go-out (2) he-killed-him who being-known

ושפטיך ומדדו אל־ הערים אשר סביבת
ones-around that the-towns to and-they-shall-measure and-ones-judging-you

החלל׃ והיה העיר הקרבה אל־ החלל ולקחו
that-they-shall-take the-body to the-near the-town and-he-will-be (3) the-body

plunder the LORD your God gives you from your enemies.
[15]This is how you are to treat all the cities that are at a distance from you and do not belong to the nations nearby.
[16]However, in the cities of the nations the LORD your God is giving you as an inheritance, do not leave alive anything that breathes.
[17]Completely destroy[b] them—the Hittites, Amorites, Canaanites, Perizzites, Hivites and Jebusites—as the LORD your God has commanded you.
[18]Otherwise, they will teach you to follow all the detestable things they do in worshiping their gods, and you will sin against the LORD your God.
[19]When you lay siege to a city for a long time, fighting against it to capture it, do not destroy its trees by putting an ax to them, because you can eat their fruit. Do not cut them down. Are the trees of the field men, that you should besiege them?[c]
[20]However, you may cut down trees that you know are not fruit trees and use them to build siege works until the city at war with you falls.

*Atonement for an Unsolved Murder*

21 If a man is found slain, lying in a field in the land the LORD your God is giving you to possess, and it is not known who killed him,
[2]your elders and judges shall go out and measure the distance from the body to the neighboring towns.
[3]Then the elders of the town nearest the body shall take a heifer that

[b]17 The Hebrew term refers to the irrevocable giving over of things or persons to the LORD, often by totally destroying them.
[c]19 *Or down to use in the siege, for the fruit trees are for the benefit of man.*

זִקְנֵי הָעִיר הַהִוא עֶגְלַת בָּקָר אֲשֶׁר לֹא־ עֻבַּד בָּהּ
with-her he-was-worked not that herd heifer-of the-that the-town elders-of

אֲשֶׁר לֹא־ מָשְׁכָה בְּעֹל׃ וְהוֹרִדוּ זִקְנֵי הָעִיר
the-town elders-of and-they-shall-lead (4) under-yoke she-wore not that

הַהִוא אֶת־ הָעֶגְלָה אֶל־ נַחַל אֵיתָן אֲשֶׁר לֹא־ יֵעָבֵד
he-was-plowed not that flowing-stream valley-of to the-heifer *** the-that

בּוֹ וְלֹא יִזָּרֵעַ וְעָרְפוּ־ שָׁם אֶת־ הָעֶגְלָה
the-heifer *** there and-they-shall-break-neck he-was-planted and-not in-him

בַּנָּחַל׃ וְנִגְּשׁוּ הַכֹּהֲנִים בְּנֵי לֵוִי כִּי
for Levi sons-of the-priests and-they-shall-step-forward (5) in-the-valley

בָם בָּחַר יְהוָה אֱלֹהֶיךָ לְשָׁרְתוֹ וּלְבָרֵךְ בְּשֵׁם
in-name-of and-to-bless to-minister-to-him God-of-you Yahweh he-chose to-them

יְהוָה וְעַל־ פִּיהֶם יִהְיֶה כָּל־ רִיב וְכָל־ נָגַע׃
assault and-every-of dispute every-of he-is decision-of-them and-at Yahweh

וְכֹל זִקְנֵי הָעִיר הַהִוא הַקְּרֹבִים אֶל־ הֶחָלָל
the-body to the-ones-near the-that the-city elders-of then-all-of (6)

יִרְחֲצוּ אֶת־ יְדֵיהֶם עַל־ הָעֶגְלָה הָעֲרוּפָה
the-one-having-neck-broken the-heifer over hands-of-them *** they-shall-wash

בַנָּחַל׃ וְעָנוּ וְאָמְרוּ יָדֵינוּ לֹא
not hands-of-us and-they-shall-say and-they-shall-declare (7) in-the-valley

שָׁפְכָה° אֶת־ הַדָּם הַזֶּה וְעֵינֵינוּ לֹא רָאוּ׃ כַּפֵּר
atone! (8) they-saw not and-eyes-of-us the-this the-blood *** they-shed

לְעַמְּךָ יִשְׂרָאֵל אֲשֶׁר־ פָּדִיתָ יְהוָה וְאַל־ תִּתֵּן דָּם
blood-of you-hold and-not Yahweh you-redeemed whom Israel for-people-of-you

נָקִי בְּקֶרֶב עַמְּךָ יִשְׂרָאֵל וְנִכַּפֵּר לָהֶם
for-them and-he-will-be-atoned Israel people-of-you against innocent

הַדָּם׃ וְאַתָּה תְּבַעֵר הַדָּם הַנָּקִי מִקִּרְבֶּךָ
from-among-you the-innocent the-blood you-will-purge so-you (9) the-bloodshed

כִּי־תַעֲשֶׂה הַיָּשָׁר בְּעֵינֵי יְהוָה׃ כִּי־ תֵצֵא לַמִּלְחָמָה עַל־
against to-the-war you-go when (10) Yahweh in-eyes-of the-right you-did for

אֹיְבֶיךָ וּנְתָנוֹ יְהוָה אֱלֹהֶיךָ בְּיָדֶךָ
into-hand-of-you God-of-you Yahweh and-he-delivers-him being-enemies-of-you

וְשָׁבִיתָ שִׁבְיוֹ׃ וְרָאִיתָ בַּשִּׁבְיָה אֵשֶׁת
woman-of among-the-captive and-you-notice (11) captive-of-him and-you-take

יְפַת־ תֹּאַר וְחָשַׁקְתָּ בָהּ וְלָקַחְתָּ לְךָ
to-her then-you-may-take to-her and-you-are-attracted form beautiful-of

לְאִשָּׁה׃ וַהֲבֵאתָהּ אֶל־ תּוֹךְ בֵּיתֶךָ וְגִלְּחָה
and-she-must-shave home-of-you inside-of into then-you-bring-her (12) for-wife

has never been worked and
has never worn a yoke 4and
lead her down to a valley that
has not been plowed or
planted and where there is a
flowing stream. There in the
valley they are to break the
heifer's neck. 5The priests, the
sons of Levi, shall step forward, for the LORD your God
has chosen them to minister
and to pronounce blessings in
the name of the LORD and to
decide all cases of dispute and
assault. 6Then all the elders of
the town nearest the body
shall wash their hands over
the heifer whose neck was
broken in the valley, 7and they
shall declare: "Our hands did
not shed this blood, nor did
our eyes see it done. 8Accept
this atonement for your
people Israel, whom you have
redeemed, O LORD, and do not
hold your people guilty of the
blood of an innocent man."
And the bloodshed will be
atoned for. 9So you will purge
from yourselves the guilt of
shedding innocent blood,
since you have done what is
right in the eyes of the LORD.

*Marrying a Captive Woman*

10When you go to war
against your enemies and the
LORD your God delivers them
into your hands and you take
captives, 11if you notice among
the captives a beautiful
woman and are attracted to
her, you may take her as your
wife. 12Bring her into your
home and have her shave her

°7 ק שפכו

אֶת־ רֹאשָׁהּ וְעָשְׂתָה אֶת־ צִפָּרְנֶיהָ׃ וְהֵסִירָה

and-she-must-put-aside (13) nails-of-her *** and-she-must-trim head-of-her ***

אֶת־ שִׂמְלַת שִׁבְיָהּ מֵעָלֶיהָ וְיָשְׁבָה בְּבֵיתֶךָ

in-house-of-you when-she-lived from-on-her captivity-of-her clothing-of ***

וּבָכְתָה אֶת־ אָבִיהָ וְאֶת־ אִמָּהּ יֶרַח יָמִים וְאַחַר

then-after days month-of mother-of-her and father-of-her *** and-she-mourned

כֵּן תָּבוֹא אֵלֶיהָ וּבְעַלְתָּהּ וְהָיְתָה לְךָ לְאִשָּׁה׃

as-wife to-you and-she-shall-be and-you-may-marry-her to-her you-may-go this

וְהָיָה אִם־ לֹא חָפַצְתָּ בָּהּ וְשִׁלַּחְתָּהּ

then-you-let-go-her with-her you-are-pleased not if and-he-will-be (14)

לְנַפְשָׁהּ וּמָכֹר לֹא־ תִמְכְּרֶנָּה בַּכָּסֶף לֹא־

not for-the-money you-sell-her not but-to-sell as-wish-of-her

תִתְעַמֵּר בָּהּ תַּחַת אֲשֶׁר עִנִּיתָהּ׃ כִּי־ תִהְיֶיןָ

they-are if (15) you-dishonored-her that since with-her you-treat-as-slave

לְאִישׁ שְׁתֵּי נָשִׁים הָאַחַת אֲהוּבָה וְהָאַחַת שְׂנוּאָה

being-unloved but-the-other being-loved the-one wives two-of to-man

וְיָלְדוּ־ לוֹ בָנִים הָאֲהוּבָה וְהַשְּׂנוּאָה וְהָיָה

but-he-is and-the-being-unloved the-being-loved sons to-him and-they-bear

הַבֵּן הַבְּכוֹר לַשְּׂנִיאָה׃ וְהָיָה בְּיוֹם הַנְחִילוֹ

to-will-him on-day and-he-will-be (16) of-the-unloved the-firstborn the-son

אֶת־ בָּנָיו אֵת אֲשֶׁר־ יִהְיֶה לוֹ לֹא יוּכַל לְבַכֵּר אֶת־

*** to-give-firstborn-right he-can not to-him he-is what *** sons-of-him ***

בֶּן־ הָאֲהוּבָה עַל־ פְּנֵי בֶן־ הַשְּׂנוּאָה הַבְּכֹר׃

the-firstborn the-being-unloved son-of preferences-of in the-being-loved son-of

כִּי אֶת־ הַבְּכֹר בֶּן־ הַשְּׂנוּאָה יַכִּיר

he-must-acknowledge the-being-unloved son-of the-firstborn *** for (17)

לָתֶת לוֹ פִּי שְׁנַיִם בְּכֹל אֲשֶׁר־ יִמָּצֵא לוֹ כִּי־הוּא רֵאשִׁית

first-of he for to-him he-is-found that of-all double share-of to-him to-give

אֹנוֹ לוֹ מִשְׁפַּט הַבְּכֹרָה׃ כִּי־ יִהְיֶה לְאִישׁ בֵּן

son to-man he-is if (18) the-firstborn right-of to-him strength-of-him

סוֹרֵר וּמוֹרֶה אֵינֶנּוּ שֹׁמֵעַ בְּקוֹל אָבִיו

father-of-him to-voice-of obeying not-him or-being-rebellious being-stubborn

וּבְקוֹל אִמּוֹ וְיִסְּרוּ אֹתוֹ וְלֹא יִשְׁמַע

he-listens but-not him and-they-discipline mother-of-him or-to-voice-of

אֲלֵיהֶם׃ וְתָפְשׂוּ בוֹ אָבִיו וְאִמּוֹ

and-mother-of-him father-of-him on-him then-they-shall-take-hold (19) to-them

וְהוֹצִיאוּ אֹתוֹ אֶל־ זִקְנֵי עִירוֹ וְאֶל־ שַׁעַר מְקֹמוֹ׃

place-of-him gate-of even-to town-of-him elders-of to him and-they-shall-bring

head, trim her nails [13]and put aside the clothes she was wearing when captured. After she has lived in your house and mourned her father and mother for a full month, then you may go to her and be her husband and she shall be your wife. [14]If you are not pleased with her, let her go wherever she wishes. You must not sell her or treat her as a slave, since you have dishonored her.

*The Right of the Firstborn*

[15]If a man has two wives, and he loves one but not the other, and both bear him sons but the firstborn is the son of the wife he does not love, [16]when he wills his property to his sons, he must not give the rights of the firstborn to the son of the wife he loves in preference to his actual firstborn, the son of the wife he does not love. [17]He must acknowledge the son of his unloved wife as the firstborn by giving him a double share of all he has. That son is the first sign of his father's strength. The right of the firstborn belongs to him.

*A Rebellious Son*

[18]If a man has a stubborn and rebellious son who does not obey his father and mother and will not listen to them when they discipline him, [19]his father and mother shall take hold of him and bring him to the elders at the gate of his town. [20]They shall

(20) וְאָמְרוּ אֶל־ זִקְנֵי עִירוֹ בְּנֵנוּ זֶה סוֹרֵר
being-stubborn this son-of-us town-of-him elders-of to and-they-shall-say (20)

וּמֹרֶה אֵינֶנּוּ שֹׁמֵעַ בְּקֹלֵנוּ זוֹלֵל
one-squandering to-voice-of-us listening not-him and-being-rebellious

וְסֹבֵא׃ (21) וּרְגָמֻהוּ כָּל־ אַנְשֵׁי עִירוֹ
town-of-him men-of all-of then-they-shall-stone-him (21) and-drinking

בָאֲבָנִים וָמֵת וּבִעַרְתָּ הָרָע מִקִּרְבֶּךָ וְכָל־
and-all-of from-among-you the-evil so-you-purge so-he-dies with-the-stones

יִשְׂרָאֵל יִשְׁמְעוּ וְיִרָאוּ׃ (22) וְכִי־ יִהְיֶה בְאִישׁ
to-man he-is and-if (22) and-they-will-be-afraid they-will-hear Israel

חֵטְא מִשְׁפַּט־ מָוֶת וְהוּמָת וְתָלִיתָ אֹתוֹ עַל־ עֵץ׃
tree on him and-you-hang and-he-is-killed death judgment-of guilt-of

(23) לֹא־ תָלִין נִבְלָתוֹ עַל־ הָעֵץ כִּי־ קָבוֹר תִּקְבְּרֶנּוּ
you-bury-him to-bury but the-tree on body-of-him you-leave-overnight not (23)

בַּיּוֹם הַהוּא כִּי־ קִלְלַת אֱלֹהִים תָּלוּי וְלֹא תְטַמֵּא אֶת־
*** you-desecrate and-not being-hung God curse-of for the-that on-the-day

אַדְמָתְךָ אֲשֶׁר יְהוָה אֱלֹהֶיךָ נֹתֵן לְךָ נַחֲלָה׃ (22:1) לֹא־
not (22:1) inheritance to-you giving God-of-you Yahweh that land-of-you

תִרְאֶה אֶת־ שׁוֹר אָחִיךָ אוֹ אֶת־ שֵׂיוֹ נִדָּחִים
ones-straying sheep-of-him *** or brother-of-you ox-of *** you-see

וְהִתְעַלַּמְתָּ מֵהֶם הָשֵׁב תְּשִׁיבֵם לְאָחִיךָ׃
to-brother-of-you you-take-back-them to-take-back from-them and-you-ignore

(2) וְאִם־ לֹא קָרוֹב אָחִיךָ אֵלֶיךָ וְלֹא יְדַעְתּוֹ
you-know-him or-not to-you brother-of-you near not and-if (2)

וַאֲסַפְתּוֹ אֶל־ תּוֹךְ בֵּיתֶךָ וְהָיָה עִמְּךָ עַד
until with-you and-he-will-be home-of-you inside-of to then-you-take-him

דְּרֹשׁ אָחִיךָ אֹתוֹ וַהֲשֵׁבֹתוֹ לוֹ׃ (3) וְכֵן
and-same (3) to-him then-you-give-back-him for-him brother-of-you to-look

תַּעֲשֶׂה לַחֲמֹרוֹ וְכֵן תַּעֲשֶׂה לְשִׂמְלָתוֹ וְכֵן תַּעֲשֶׂה
you-do and-same for-cloak-of-him you-do and-same for-donkey-of-him you-do

לְכָל־ אֲבֵדַת אָחִיךָ אֲשֶׁר־ תֹּאבַד מִמֶּנּוּ וּמְצָאתָהּ
and-you-find-her from-him she-is-lost that brother-of-you lost-of for-any-of

לֹא תוּכַל לְהִתְעַלֵּם׃ (4) לֹא־ תִרְאֶה אֶת־ חֲמוֹר אָחִיךָ אוֹ
or brother-of-you donkey-of *** you-see not (4) to-ignore you-can not

שׁוֹרוֹ נֹפְלִים בַּדֶּרֶךְ וְהִתְעַלַּמְתָּ מֵהֶם הָקֵם
to-help-up from-them and-you-ignore on-the-road ones-being-fallen ox-of-him

תָּקִים עִמּוֹ׃ (5) לֹא־ יִהְיֶה כְלִי־ גֶבֶר עַל־ אִשָּׁה וְלֹא־
and-not woman on man clothing-of he-shall-be not (5) with-him you-help-up

say to the elders, "This son of
ours is stubborn and rebellious. He will not obey us. He
is a profligate and a drunkard." [21]Then all the men of his
town shall stone him to death.
You must purge the evil from
among you. All Israel will hear
of it and be afraid.

*Various Laws*

[22]If a man guilty of a capital
offense is put to death and his
body is hung on a tree, [23]you
must not leave his body on the
tree overnight. Be sure to bury
him that same day, because
anyone who is hung on a tree
is under God's curse. You must
not desecrate the land the
LORD your God is giving you
as an inheritance.

22 If you see your broth-
er's ox or sheep stray-
ing, do not ignore it but be
sure to take it back to him. [2]If
the brother does not live near
you or if you do not know who
he is, take it home with you
and keep it until he comes
looking for it. Then give it
back to him. [3]Do the same if
you find your brother's donkey or his cloak or anything he
loses. Do not ignore it.

[4]If you see your brother's
donkey or his ox fallen on the
road, do not ignore it. Help
him get it to its feet.

[5]A woman must not wear
men's clothing, nor a man

יִלְבַּשׁ גֶּבֶר שִׂמְלַת אִשָּׁה כִּי תוֹעֲבַת יְהוָה אֱלֹהֶיךָ
God-of-you Yahweh detestable-of for woman clothing-of man he-shall-wear

כָּל־ עֹשֵׂה אֵלֶּה׃ כִּי יִקָּרֵא קַן־ צִפּוֹר ׀ לְפָנֶיךָ בַּדֶּרֶךְ
beside-the-road before-you bird nest-of he-is-found if (6) these doing any-of

בְּכָל־ עֵץ ׀ אוֹ עַל־ הָאָרֶץ אֶפְרֹחִים אוֹ בֵיצִים וְהָאֵם רֹבֶצֶת
sitting and-the-mother eggs or young-ones the-ground on or tree in-any-of

עַל־ הָאֶפְרֹחִים אוֹ עַל־הַבֵּיצִים לֹא־ תִקַּח הָאֵם עַל־ הַבָּנִים׃
the-young-ones with the-mother you-take not the-eggs on or the-young-ones on

שַׁלֵּחַ תְּשַׁלַּח אֶת־ הָאֵם וְאֶת־ הַבָּנִים תִּקַּח־
you-may-take the-young-ones and the-mother *** you-let-go to-let-go (7)

לָךְ לְמַעַן יִיטַב לָךְ וְהַאֲרַכְתָּ יָמִים׃ כִּי
when (8) days and-you-may-have-long with-you he-may-go-well so-that for-you

תִבְנֶה בַּיִת חָדָשׁ וְעָשִׂיתָ מַעֲקֶה לְגַגֶּךָ וְלֹא־ תָשִׂים
you-bring so-not around-roof-of-you parapet then-you-make new house you-build

דָּמִים בְּבֵיתֶךָ כִּי־ יִפֹּל הַנֹּפֵל מִמֶּנּוּ׃ לֹא־
not (9) from-him the-one-falling he-falls if on-house-of-you bloodsheds

תִזְרַע כַּרְמְךָ כִּלְאָיִם פֶּן־ תִּקְדַּשׁ הַמְלֵאָה הַזֶּרַע אֲשֶׁר
that the-seed the-crop you-defile or two-kinds vineyard-of-you you-plant

תִּזְרָע וּתְבוּאַת הַכָּרֶם׃ לֹא־ תַחֲרֹשׁ בְּשׁוֹר־
with-ox you-plow not (10) the-vineyard and-fruit-of you-planted

וּבַחֲמֹר יַחְדָּו׃ לֹא תִלְבַּשׁ שַׁעַטְנֵז צֶמֶר וּפִשְׁתִּים
and-linens wool mixed-fabric you-wear not (11) together and-with-donkey

יַחְדָּו׃ גְּדִלִים תַּעֲשֶׂה־ לָּךְ עַל־אַרְבַּע כַּנְפוֹת כְּסוּתְךָ אֲשֶׁר
that cloak-of-you corners-of four on for-you you-make tassels (12) together

תְּכַסֶּה־ בָּהּ׃ כִּי־ יִקַּח אִישׁ אִשָּׁה וּבָא אֵלֶיהָ
with-her and-he-lies wife man he-takes if (13) with-her you-cover

וּשְׂנֵאָהּ׃ וְשָׂם לָהּ עֲלִילֹת דְּבָרִים
things ones-slanderous to-her and-he-accuses (14) and-he-dislikes-her

וְהוֹצִיא עָלֶיהָ שֵׁם רָע וְאָמַר אֶת־ הָאִשָּׁה הַזֹּאת לָקַחְתִּי
I-married the-this the-woman *** and-he-says bad name to-her and-he-gives

וָאֶקְרַב אֵלֶיהָ וְלֹא־ מָצָאתִי לָהּ בְּתוּלִים׃
proofs-of-virginity with-her I-found then-not to-her when-I-approached

וְלָקַח אֲבִי הַנַּעֲרָ וְאִמָּהּ
and-mother-of-her the-girl father-of then-he-shall-take (15)

וְהוֹצִיאוּ אֶת־ בְּתוּלֵי הַנַּעֲרָ אֶל־ זִקְנֵי הָעִיר
the-town elders-of to the-girl proofs-of-virginity-of *** and-they-shall-bring

הַשָּׁעְרָה׃ וְאָמַר אֲבִי הַנַּעֲרָ אֶל־ הַזְּקֵנִים אֶת־
*** the-elders to the-girl father-of then-he-will-say (16) at-the-gate

wear women's clothing, for the LORD your God detests anyone who does this.

6 If you come across a bird's nest beside the road, either in a tree or on the ground, and the mother is sitting on the young or on the eggs, do not take the mother with the young.
7 You may take the young, but be sure to let the mother go, so that it may go well with you and you may have a long life.

8 When you build a new house, make a parapet around your roof so that you may not bring the guilt of bloodshed on your house if someone falls from the roof.

9 Do not plant two kinds of seed in your vineyard; if you do, not only the crops you plant but also the fruit of the vineyard will be defiled.[d]

10 Do not plow with an ox and a donkey yoked together.

11 Do not wear clothes of wool and linen woven together.

12 Make tassels on the four corners of the cloak you wear.

*Marriage Violations*

13 If a man takes a wife and, after lying with her, dislikes her
14 and slanders her and gives her a bad name, saying, "I married this woman, but when I approached her, I did not find proof of her virginity,"
15 then the girl's father and mother shall bring proof that she was a virgin to the town elders at the gate.
16 The girl's father will say to the elders, "I

[d]9 Or *be forfeited to the sanctuary*

°15a ק הנערה °15b, ק הנערה
°16 ק הנערה

בִּתִּי נָתַתִּי לָאִישׁ הַזֶּה לְאִשָּׁה וַיִּשְׂנָאֶהָ׃
but-he-dislikes-her as-wife the-this to-the-man I-gave daughter-of-me

וְהִנֵּה־הוּא שָׂם עֲלִילֹת דְּבָרִים לֵאמֹר לֹא־מָצָאתִי
I-found not to-say things ones-slanderous he-accused he now-see! (17)

לְבִתְּךָ בְּתוּלִים וְאֵלֶּה בְּתוּלֵי
proofs-of-virginity-of but-these proofs-of-virginity with-daughter-of-you

בִתִּי וּפָרְשׂוּ הַשִּׂמְלָה לִפְנֵי זִקְנֵי הָעִיר׃
the-town elders-of before the-cloth then-they-shall-display daughter-of-me

וְלָקְחוּ זִקְנֵי הָעִיר־הַהִוא אֶת־הָאִישׁ
the-man *** the-that the-town elders-of and-they-shall-take (18)

וְיִסְּרוּ אֹתוֹ׃ וְעָנְשׁוּ אֹתוֹ מֵאָה כֶסֶף
silver hundred him and-they-shall-fine (19) him and-they-shall-punish

וְנָתְנוּ לַאֲבִי הַנַּעֲרָה כִּי הוֹצִיא שֵׁם רָע עַל בְּתוּלַת
virgin-of to bad name he-gave for the-girl to-father-of and-they-shall-give

יִשְׂרָאֵל וְלוֹ־תִהְיֶה לְאִשָּׁה לֹא־יוּכַל לְשַׁלְּחָהּ כָּל־
all-of to-divorce-her he-can not as-wife she-will-continue and-to-him Israel

יָמָיו׃ וְאִם־אֱמֶת הָיָה הַדָּבָר הַזֶּה לֹא־נִמְצְאוּ
they-can-be-found not the-this the-charge he-is true but-if (20) days-of-him

בְתוּלִים לַנַּעֲרָ׃ וְהוֹצִיאוּ אֶת־הַנַּעֲרָ אֶל־
to the-girl *** then-they-shall-bring (21) of-the-girl proofs-of-virginity

פֶּתַח בֵּית־אָבִיהָ וּסְקָלוּהָ אַנְשֵׁי עִירָהּ
town-of-her men-of and-they-shall-stone-her father-of-her house-of door-of

בָּאֲבָנִים וָמֵתָה כִּי־עָשְׂתָה נְבָלָה בְּיִשְׂרָאֵל לִזְנוֹת
to-be-promiscuous in-Israel disgrace she-did for so-she-dies with-the-stones

בֵּית אָבִיהָ וּבִעַרְתָּ הָרָע מִקִּרְבֶּךָ׃ כִּי־
if (22) from-among-you the-evil so-you-purge father-of-her house-of

יִמָּצֵא אִישׁ שֹׁכֵב ׀ עִם־אִשָּׁה בְעֻלַת־בַּעַל וּמֵתוּ
then-they-must-die husband being-married-of woman with sleeping man he-is-found

גַּם־שְׁנֵיהֶם הָאִישׁ הַשֹּׁכֵב עִם־הָאִשָּׁה וְהָאִשָּׁה
and-the-woman the-woman with the-one-sleeping the-man both-of-them indeed

וּבִעַרְתָּ הָרָע מִיִּשְׂרָאֵל׃ כִּי יִהְיֶה נַעֲרָ בְתוּלָה מְאֹרָשָׂה
being-pledged virgin girl he-is if (23) from-Israel the-evil so-you-purge

לְאִישׁ וּמְצָאָהּ אִישׁ בָּעִיר וְשָׁכַב עִמָּהּ׃
with-her and-he-sleeps in-the-town man and-he-meets-her to-man

וְהוֹצֵאתֶם אֶת־שְׁנֵיהֶם אֶל־שַׁעַר ׀ הָעִיר הַהִוא
the-that the-town gate-of to both-of-them *** then-you-shall-take (24)

וּסְקַלְתֶּם אֹתָם בָּאֲבָנִים וָמֵתוּ אֶת־הַנַּעֲרָ עַל־
for the-girl *** so-they-die with-the-stones them and-you-shall-stone

gave my daughter in marriage to this man, but he dislikes her. [17]Now he has slandered her and said, 'I did not find your daughter to be a virgin.' But here is the proof of my daughter's virginity." Then her parents shall display the cloth before the elders of the town, [18]and the elders shall take the man and punish him. [19]They shall fine him a hundred shekels of silver[e] and give them to the girl's father, because this man has given an Israelite virgin a bad name. She shall continue to be his wife; he must not divorce her as long as he lives.

[20]If, however, the charge is true and no proof of the girl's virginity can be found, [21]she shall be brought to the door of her father's house and there the men of her town shall stone her to death. She has done a disgraceful thing in Israel by being promiscuous while still in her father's house. You must purge the evil from among you.

[22]If a man is found sleeping with another man's wife, both the man who slept with her and the woman must die. You must purge the evil from Israel.

[23]If a man happens to meet in a town a virgin pledged to be married and he sleeps with her, [24]you shall take both of them to the gate of that town and stone them to death—the

[e]19 That is, about 2 1/2 pounds (about 1 kilogram)

°20 ק הנערה °21 ,ק לנערה
°23 ק הנערה °24 , ק נערה

דבר אשר לא־ צעקה בעיר ואת־ האיש על־ דבר אשר־
that reason-of for the-man and in-the-town she-screamed not that reason-of

ענה את־ אשת רעהו ובערת הרע מקרבך׃
from-among-you the-evil so-you-purge fellow-of-him wife-of *** he-violated

ואם־ בשדה ימצא האיש את־ הנער המארשה
the-being-pledged the-girl *** the-man he-meets in-the-country but-if (25)

והחזיק־ בה האיש ושכב עמה ומת
then-he-shall-die with-her and-he-lies the-man over-her and-he-overpowers

האיש אשר־ שכב עמה לבדו׃ ולנער לא־ תעשה דבר
thing you-do not but-to-the-girl (26) only-him with-her he-lay who the-man

אין לנער חטא מות כי כאשר יקום איש על־ רעהו
neighbor-of-him against man he-rises just-as for death sin-of to-the-girl not

ורצחו נפש כן הדבר הזה׃ כי בשדה
in-the-country for (27) the-this the-case same mortally and-he-murders-him

מצאה צעקה הנער המארשה ואין מושיע
one-rescuing but-not the-being-betrothed the-girl she-screamed he-found-her

לה׃ כי־ ימצא איש נער בתולה אשר לא־ ארשה
being-pledged not who virgin girl man he-meets if (28) to-her

ותפשה ושכב עמה ונמצאו׃
and-they-are-discovered with-her and-he-lies and-he-forces-her

ונתן האיש השכב עמה לאבי הנער
the-girl to-father-of with-her the-one-lying the-man then-he-shall-pay (29)

חמשים כסף ולו־ תהיה לאשה תחת אשר ענה לא־
not he-violated-her that because as-wife she-must-be and-to-him silver fifty

יוכל שלחה כל־ ימיו׃ לא־ יקח איש את־
*** man he-must-marry not (23:1)* days-of-him all-of to-divorce-her he-can

אשת אביו ולא יגלה כנף אביו׃ לא־
not (2) father-of-him bed-of he-must-dishonor and-not father-of-him wife-of

יבא פצוע־ דכא וכרות שפכה בקהל
to-assembly-of genital of-being-cut-of crushing being-wounded-of he-may-enter

יהוה׃ לא־ יבא ממזר בקהל יהוה גם
even Yahweh to-assembly-of one-illegitimate he-may-enter not (3) Yahweh

דור עשירי לא־ יבא לו בקהל יהוה׃ לא־
not (4) Yahweh in-assembly-of of-him he-may-enter not tenth generation

יבא עמוני ומואבי בקהל יהוה גם דור עשירי
tenth generation even Yahweh to-assembly-of or-Moabite Ammonite he-may-enter

לא־ יבא להם בקהל יהוה עד־ עולם׃ על־ דבר אשר
that reason-of for (5) ever for Yahweh in-assembly-of of-them he-may-enter not

girl because she was in a town and did not scream for help, and the man because he violated another man's wife. You must purge the evil from among you.

25But if out in the country a man happens to meet a girl pledged to be married and rapes her, only the man who has done this shall die. 26Do nothing to the girl; she has committed no sin deserving death. This case is like that of someone who attacks and murders his neighbor, 27for the man found the girl out in the country, and though the betrothed girl screamed, there was no one to rescue her.

28If a man happens to meet a virgin who is not pledged to be married and rapes her and they are discovered, 29he shall pay the girl's father fifty shekels of silver.[f] He must marry the girl, for he has violated her. He can never divorce her as long as he lives.

30A man is not to marry his father's wife; he must not dishonor his father's bed.

*Exclusion From the Assembly*

23 No one who has been emasculated by crushing or cutting may enter the assembly of the LORD.

2No one born of a forbidden marriage[g] nor any of his descendants may enter the assembly of the LORD, even down to the tenth generation.

3No Ammonite or Moabite or any of his descendants may enter the assembly of the LORD, even down to the tenth generation. 4For they did not

f29 That is, about 1 1/4 pounds (about 0.6 kilogram)
g2 Or *one of illegitimate birth*

*The Hebrew numeration of chapter 23 begins with verse 30 of chapter 22 in English; thus, there is a one-verse discrepancy throughout chapter 23.

°25 ק הנערה , °26a ק לנערה
°26b ק לנערה , °27 ק הנערה
°28 ק נערה , °29 ק הנערה

לֹא־קִדְּמוּ אֶתְכֶם בַּלֶּחֶם וּבַמַּיִם בַּדֶּרֶךְ בְּצֵאתְכֶם
as-to-come-you on-the-way and-with-the-waters with-the-bread you they-met not

מִמִּצְרָיִם וַאֲשֶׁר שָׂכַר עָלֶיךָ אֶת־בִּלְעָם בֶּן־בְּעוֹר מִפְּתוֹר
from-Pethor Beor son-of Balaam *** against-you he-hired and-that from-Egypt

אֲרַם נַהֲרַיִם לְקַלְלֶךָּ׃ וְלֹא־אָבָה יְהוָה אֱלֹהֶיךָ לִשְׁמֹעַ
to-listen God-of-you Yahweh he-would but-not (6) to-curse-you Naharaim Aram

אֶל־בִּלְעָם וַיַּהֲפֹךְ יְהוָה אֱלֹהֶיךָ לְּךָ אֶת־הַקְּלָלָה לִבְרָכָה
to-blessing the-curse *** for-you God-of-you Yahweh but-he-turned Balaam to

כִּי אֲהֵבְךָ יְהוָה אֱלֹהֶיךָ׃ לֹא־תִדְרֹשׁ שְׁלֹמָם
peace-of-them you-seek not (7) God-of-you Yahweh he-loves-you for

וְטֹבָתָם כָּל־יָמֶיךָ לְעוֹלָם׃ לֹא־תְתַעֵב אֲדֹמִי כִּי
for Edomite you-abhor not (8) for-ever days-of-you all-of or-good-of-them

אָחִיךָ הוּא לֹא־תְתַעֵב מִצְרִי כִּי־גֵר הָיִיתָ בְאַרְצוֹ׃
in-land-of-him you-were alien for Egyptian you-abhor not he brother-of-you

בָּנִים אֲשֶׁר־יִוָּלְדוּ לָהֶם דּוֹר שְׁלִישִׁי יָבֹא
they-may-enter third generation to-them they-are-born that children (9)

לָהֶם בִּקְהַל יְהוָה׃ כִּי־תֵצֵא מַחֲנֶה עַל־
against camp you-set-up when (10) Yahweh to-assembly-of of-them

אֹיְבֶיךָ וְנִשְׁמַרְתָּ מִכֹּל דָּבָר רָע׃ כִּי־
if (11) impure thing from-every-of then-you-keep-away being-enemies-of-you

יִהְיֶה בְךָ אִישׁ אֲשֶׁר לֹא־יִהְיֶה טָהוֹר מִקְּרֵה־לָיְלָה וְיָצָא
then-he-must-go night from-emision-of clean he-is not who man among-you he-is

אֶל־מִחוּץ לַמַּחֲנֶה לֹא יָבֹא אֶל־תּוֹךְ הַמַּחֲנֶה׃
the-camp midst-of into he-may-enter not of-the-camp outside to

וְהָיָה לִפְנוֹת־עֶרֶב יִרְחַץ בַּמָּיִם
with-the-waters he-must-wash evening to-approach but-he-will-be (12)

וּכְבֹא הַשֶּׁמֶשׁ יָבֹא אֶל־תּוֹךְ הַמַּחֲנֶה׃ וְיָד
and-place (13) the-camp midst-of into he-may-return the-sun and-when-to-set

תִּהְיֶה לְךָ מִחוּץ לַמַּחֲנֶה וְיָצָאתָ שָׁמָּה חוּץ׃
outside to-there so-you-can-go of-the-camp outside for-you she-must-be

וְיָתֵד תִּהְיֶה לְךָ עַל־אֲזֵנֶךָ וְהָיָה
and-he-will-be equipment-of-you with for-you she-must-be and-digger (14)

בְּשִׁבְתְּךָ חוּץ וְחָפַרְתָּה בָהּ וְשַׁבְתָּ
and-you-return with-her then-you-shall-dig outside when-to-relieve-you

וְכִסִּיתָ אֶת־צֵאָתֶךָ׃ כִּי יְהוָה אֱלֹהֶיךָ מִתְהַלֵּךְ ׀
moving God-of-you Yahweh for (15) excrement-of-you *** and-you-cover

בְּקֶרֶב מַחֲנֶךָ לְהַצִּילְךָ וְלָתֵת אֹיְבֶיךָ
being-enemies-of-you and-to-deliver to-protect-you camp-of-you in-among

come to meet you with bread and water on your way when you came out of Egypt, and they hired Balaam son of Beor from Pethor in Aram Naharaim[h] to pronounce a curse on you. [5]However, the LORD your God would not listen to Balaam but turned the curse into a blessing for you, because the LORD your God loves you. [6]Do not seek peace or good relations with them as long as you live.

[7]Do not abhor an Edomite, for he is your brother. Do not abhor an Egyptian, because you lived as an alien in his country. [8]The third generation of children born to them may enter the assembly of the LORD.

### *Uncleanness in the Camp*

[9]When you are encamped against your enemies, keep away from everything impure. [10]If one of your men is unclean because of a nocturnal emission, he is to go outside the camp and stay there. [11]But as evening approaches he is to wash himself, and at sunset he may return to the camp.

[12]Designate a place outside the camp where you can go to relieve yourself. [13]As part of your equipment have something to dig with, and when you relieve yourself, dig a hole and cover up your excrement. [14]For the LORD your God moves about in your camp to protect you and to deliver your

[h]4 That is, Northwest Mesopotamia

*See the note on page 548.

לְפָנֶיךָ וְהָיָה מַחֲנֶיךָ קָדוֹשׁ וְלֹא־ יִרְאֶה בְךָ
among-you he-will-see so-not holy camps-of-you so-he-must-be before-you

עֶרְוַת דָּבָר וְשָׁב מֵאַחֲרֶיךָ׃ (16) לֹא־ תַסְגִּיר
you-hand-over not (16) away-from-you and-he-will-turn thing indecent-of

עֶבֶד אֶל־ אֲדֹנָיו אֲשֶׁר־ יִנָּצֵל אֵלֶיךָ מֵעִם אֲדֹנָיו׃
master-of-him from-with with-you he-took-refuge that master-of-him to slave

(17) עִמְּךָ יֵשֵׁב בְּקִרְבְּךָ בַּמָּקוֹם אֲשֶׁר־ יִבְחַר
he-chooses that in-the-place in-among-you let-him-live with-you (17)

בְּאַחַד שְׁעָרֶיךָ בַּטּוֹב לוֹ לֹא תּוֹנֶנּוּ׃ (18) לֹא־
not (18) you-oppress-him not to-him as-the-good gates-of-you within-any-of

תִהְיֶה קְדֵשָׁה מִבְּנוֹת יִשְׂרָאֵל וְלֹא־
and-not Israel from-daughters-of temple-prostitute she-shall-become

יִהְיֶה קָדֵשׁ מִבְּנֵי יִשְׂרָאֵל׃ (19) לֹא־ תָבִיא
you-bring not (19) Israel from-sons-of temple-prostitute he-shall-become

אֶתְנַן זוֹנָה וּמְחִיר כֶּלֶב בֵּית יְהוָה אֱלֹהֶיךָ
God-of-you Yahweh house-of dog or-hire-of female-prostitute earning-of

לְכָל־ נֶדֶר כִּי תוֹעֲבַת יְהוָה אֱלֹהֶיךָ גַּם־ שְׁנֵיהֶם׃
both-of-them indeed God-of-you Yahweh detestable-of for vow for-any-of

(20) לֹא־ תַשִּׁיךְ לְאָחִיךָ נֶשֶׁךְ כֶּסֶף נֶשֶׁךְ
interest-of money interest-of to-brother-of-you you-charge-interest not (20)

אֹכֶל נֶשֶׁךְ כָּל־ דָּבָר אֲשֶׁר יִשָּׁךְ׃ (21) לַנָּכְרִי
to-foreigner (21) he-may-earn-interest that thing any-of interest-of food

תַשִּׁיךְ וּלְאָחִיךָ לֹא תַשִּׁיךְ לְמַעַן
so-that you-charge-interest not but-to-brother-of-you you-may-charge-interest

יְבָרֶכְךָ יְהוָה אֱלֹהֶיךָ בְּכֹל מִשְׁלַח יָדֶךָ עַל־
in hand-of-you work-of in-every-of God-of-you Yahweh he-may-bless-you

הָאָרֶץ אֲשֶׁר־ אַתָּה בָא־ שָׁמָּה לְרִשְׁתָּהּ׃ (22) כִּי־ תִדֹּר נֶדֶר
vow you-vow if (22) to-possess-her to-there entering you that the-land

לַיהוָה אֱלֹהֶיךָ לֹא תְאַחֵר לְשַׁלְּמוֹ כִּי־ דָרֹשׁ
to-demand for to-pay-him you-be-slow not God-of-you to-Yahweh

יִדְרְשֶׁנּוּ יְהוָה אֱלֹהֶיךָ מֵעִמָּךְ וְהָיָה בְךָ
on-you and-he-will-be from-with-you God-of-you Yahweh he-will-demand-him

חֵטְא׃ (23) וְכִי תֶחְדַּל לִנְדֹּר לֹא־ יִהְיֶה בְךָ חֵטְא׃
guilt on-you he-will-be not from-to-vow you-refrain but-if (23) guilt

(24) מוֹצָא שְׂפָתֶיךָ תִּשְׁמֹר וְעָשִׂיתָ כַּאֲשֶׁר נָדַרְתָּ
you-vowed just-as and-you-do you-be-sure lips-of-you thing-from (24)

לַיהוָה אֱלֹהֶיךָ נְדָבָה אֲשֶׁר דִּבַּרְתָּ בְּפִיךָ׃ (25) כִּי
if (25) with-mouth-of-you you-promised that freely God-of-you to-Yahweh

enemies to you. Your camp must be holy, so that he will not see among you anything indecent and turn away from you.

*Miscellaneous Laws*

15If a slave has taken refuge with you, do not hand him over to his master. 16Let him live among you wherever he likes and in whatever town he chooses. Do not oppress him.

17No Israelite man or woman is to become a temple prostitute. 18You must not bring the earnings of a female prostitute or of a male prostitute[i] into the house of the LORD your God to pay any vow, because the LORD your God detests them both.

19Do not charge your brother interest, whether on money or food or anything else that may earn interest. 20You may charge a foreigner interest, but not a brother Israelite, so that the LORD your God may bless you in everything you put your hand to in the land you are entering to possess.

21If you make a vow to the LORD your God, do not be slow to pay it, for the LORD your God will certainly demand it of you and you will be guilty of sin. 22But if you refrain from making a vow, you will not be guilty. 23Whatever your lips utter you must be sure to do, because you made your vow freely to the LORD your God with your own mouth.

[i]18 Hebrew *of a dog*

*See the note on page 548.

תָבֹא בְּכֶרֶם רֵעֶךָ וְאָכַלְתָּ עֲנָבִים
grapes then-you-may-eat neighbor-of-you into-vineyard-of you-enter

כְּנַפְשְׁךָ שָׂבְעֶךָ וְאֶל־ כֶּלְיְךָ לֹא תִתֵּן׃ כִּי
if (26) you-put not basket-of-you but-in want-of-you as-desire-of-you

תָבֹא בְּקָמַת רֵעֶךָ וְקָטַפְתָּ מְלִילֹת
kernels then-you-may-pick neighbor-of-you into-grainfield-of you-enter

בְּיָדֶךָ וְחֶרְמֵשׁ לֹא תָנִיף עַל קָמַת רֵעֶךָ׃
neighbor-of-you standing-grain-of to you-put not but-sickle with-hand-of-you

כִּי־ יִקַּח אִישׁ אִשָּׁה וּבְעָלָהּ וְהָיָה אִם־ לֹא תִמְצָא־
she-finds not if and-he-is and-he-marries-her woman man he-takes if (24:1)

חֵן בְּעֵינָיו כִּי־ מָצָא בָהּ עֶרְוַת דָּבָר
thing indecent-of about-her he-finds because in-eyes-of-him favor

וְכָתַב לָהּ סֵפֶר כְּרִיתֻת וְנָתַן בְּיָדָהּ
in-hand-of-her and-he-gives divorce certificate-of for-her and-he-writes

וְשִׁלְּחָהּ מִבֵּיתוֹ׃ וְיָצְאָה מִבֵּיתוֹ
from-house-of-him and-she-leaves (2) from-house-of-him and-he-sends-her

וְהָלְכָה וְהָיְתָה לְאִישׁ־ אַחֵר׃ וּשְׂנֵאָהּ הָאִישׁ
the-man and-he-dislikes-her (3) another to-man and-she-becomes and-she-goes

הָאַחֲרוֹן וְכָתַב לָהּ סֵפֶר כְּרִיתֻת וְנָתַן
and-he-gives divorce certificate-of for-her and-he-writes the-second

בְּיָדָהּ וְשִׁלְּחָהּ מִבֵּיתוֹ אוֹ כִי יָמוּת הָאִישׁ
the-man he-dies if or from-house-of-him and-he-sends-her in-hand-of-her

הָאַחֲרוֹן אֲשֶׁר־ לְקָחָהּ לוֹ לְאִשָּׁה׃ לֹא־ יוּכַל
he-is-allowed not (4) as-wife for-him he-took-her that the-second

בַּעְלָהּ הָרִאשׁוֹן אֲשֶׁר־ שִׁלְּחָהּ לָשׁוּב לְקַחְתָּהּ לִהְיוֹת
to-be to-take-her to-return he-divorced-her who the-first husband-of-her

לוֹ לְאִשָּׁה אַחֲרֵי אֲשֶׁר הֻטַּמָּאָה כִּי־ תוֹעֵבָה הִוא לִפְנֵי יְהוָה
Yahweh before that detestable for she-was-defiled when after as-wife to-him

וְלֹא תַחֲטִיא אֶת־ הָאָרֶץ אֲשֶׁר יְהוָה אֱלֹהֶיךָ נֹתֵן לְךָ
to-you giving God-of-you Yahweh that the-land *** you-bring-sin so-not

נַחֲלָה׃ כִּי־ יִקַּח אִישׁ אִשָּׁה חֲדָשָׁה לֹא יֵצֵא בַּצָּבָא וְלֹא־
or-not to-the-war he-must-go not recent wife man he-takes if (5) inheritance

יַעֲבֹר עָלָיו לְכָל־ דָּבָר נָקִי יִהְיֶה לְבֵיתוֹ שָׁנָה אֶחָת
one year at-home-of-him he-must-be free duty as-any-of on-him he-must-lay

וְשִׂמַּח אֶת־ אִשְׁתּוֹ אֲשֶׁר־ לָקָח׃ לֹא־
not (6) he-married that wife-of-him *** and-he-must-bring-happiness

יַחֲבֹל רֵחַיִם וָרָכֶב כִּי־ נֶפֶשׁ הוּא חֹבֵל׃
being-security that livelihood for or-upper two-millstones you-take-as-security

24 If you enter your neighbor's vineyard, you may eat all
the grapes you want, but do
not put any in your basket. 25 If
you enter your neighbor's
grainfield, you may pick kernels with your hands, but you
must not put a sickle to his
standing grain.

24 If a man marries a
woman who becomes
displeasing to him because he
finds something indecent
about her, and he writes her a
certificate of divorce, gives it
to her and sends her from his
house, 2 and if after she leaves
his house she becomes the
wife of another man, 3 and her
second husband dislikes her
and writes her a certificate of
divorce, gives it to her and
sends her from his house, or if
he dies, 4 then her first husband, who divorced her, is not
allowed to marry her again after she has been defiled. That
would be detestable in the
eyes of the LORD. Do not bring
sin upon the land the LORD
your God is giving you as an
inheritance.

5 If a man has recently married, he must not be sent to
war or have any other duty
laid on him. For one year he is
to be free to stay at home and
bring happiness to the wife he
has married.

6 Do not take a pair of millstones—not even the upper
one—as security for a debt, because that would be taking a
man's livelihood as security.

*See the note on page 548.

כִּֽי־ יִמָּצֵא אִישׁ גֹּנֵב נֶפֶשׁ מֵאֶחָיו מִבְּנֵי יִשְׂרָאֵל
Israel from-sons-of of-brothers-of-him one kidnapping man he-is-caught if (7)

וְהִתְעַמֶּר־ בּוֹ וּמְכָרוֹ וּמֵת הַגַּנָּב
the-kidnapper then-he-must-die or-he-sells-him to-him and-he-treats-as-slave

הַהוּא וּבִעַרְתָּ הָרָע מִקִּרְבֶּךָ׃ הִשָּׁמֶר בְּנֶגַע־
about-disease-of be-careful! (8) from-among-you the-evil so-you-purge the-that

הַצָּרַעַת לִשְׁמֹר מְאֹד וְלַעֲשׂוֹת כְּכֹל אֲשֶׁר־ יוֹרוּ אֶתְכֶם
you they-instruct that as-all and-to-do very to-be-careful the-leprosy

הַכֹּהֲנִים הַלְוִיִּם כַּאֲשֶׁר צִוִּיתִם תִּשְׁמְרוּ לַעֲשׂוֹת׃
to-follow you-be-careful I-commanded-them just-as the-Levites the-priests

זָכוֹר אֵת אֲשֶׁר־ עָשָׂה יְהוָה אֱלֹהֶיךָ לְמִרְיָם בַּדֶּרֶךְ
along-the-way to-Miriam God-of-you Yahweh he-did what *** to-remember (9)

בְּצֵאתְכֶם מִמִּצְרָיִם׃ כִּֽי־ תַשֶּׁה בְרֵעֲךָ*
to-neighbor-of-you you-make-loan when (10) from-Egypt after-to-come-you

מַשַּׁאת מְאוּמָה לֹא־ תָבֹא אֶל־ בֵּיתוֹ לַעֲבֹט עֲבֹטוֹ׃
pledge-of-him to-get-pledge house-of-him into you-go not any-kind loan-of

בַּחוּץ תַּעֲמֹד וְהָאִישׁ אֲשֶׁר אַתָּה נֹשֶׁה בוֹ יוֹצִיא
let-him-bring to-him loaning you whom and-the-man you-stay on-the-outside (11)

אֵלֶיךָ אֶת־ הַעֲבוֹט הַחוּצָה׃ וְאִם־ אִישׁ עָנִי הוּא לֹא תִשְׁכַּב
you-sleep not he poor man and-if (12) to-the-outside the-pledge *** to-you

בַּעֲבֹטוֹ׃ הָשֵׁב תָּשִׁיב לוֹ אֶת־ הַעֲבוֹט כְּבֹא
as-to-set the-pledge *** to-him you-return to-return (13) with-pledge-of-him

הַשֶּׁמֶשׁ וְשָׁכַב בְּשַׂלְמָתוֹ וּבֵרְכֶךָּ וּלְךָ
and-to-you then-he-will-thank-you in-cloak-of-him so-he-may-sleep the-sun

תִּהְיֶה צְדָקָה לִפְנֵי יְהוָה אֱלֹהֶיךָ׃ לֹא־ תַעֲשֹׁק
you-take-advantage not (14) God-of-you Yahweh before righteous-act she-will-be

שָׂכִיר עָנִי וְאֶבְיוֹן מֵאַחֶיךָ אוֹ מִגֵּרְךָ אֲשֶׁר
who from-alien-of-you or from-brothers-of-you and-needy poor hired-man

בְּאַרְצְךָ בִּשְׁעָרֶיךָ׃ בְּיוֹמוֹ תִתֵּן שְׂכָרוֹ וְלֹא־
and-not wage-of-him you-pay on-day-of-him (15) in-gates-of-you in-land-of-you

תָבוֹא עָלָיו הַשֶּׁמֶשׁ כִּי עָנִי הוּא וְאֵלָיו הוּא נֹשֵׂא אֶת־ נַפְשׁוֹ
life-of-him *** basing he and-on-him he poor for the-sun on-him she-may-set

וְלֹא־ יִקְרָא עָלֶיךָ אֶל־ יְהוָה וְהָיָה בְךָ חֵטְא׃ לֹא־
not (16) guilt on-you and-he-will-be Yahweh to against-you he-may-cry so-not

יוּמְתוּ אָבוֹת עַל־ בָּנִים וּבָנִים לֹא־ יוּמְתוּ עַל־
for they-shall-die not and-children children for fathers they-shall-die

אָבוֹת אִישׁ בְּחֶטְאוֹ יוּמָתוּ׃ לֹא תַטֶּה מִשְׁפַּט
justice-of you-deprive not (17) they-shall-die for-sin-of-him each fathers

7If a man is caught kidnapping one of his brother Israelites and treats him as a slave or sells him, the kidnapper must die. You must purge the evil from among you.

8In cases of leprous[j] diseases be very careful to do exactly as the priests, who are Levites, instruct you. You must follow carefully what I have commanded them. 9Remember what the LORD your God did to Miriam along the way after you came out of Egypt.

10When you make a loan of any kind to your neighbor, do not go into his house to get what he is offering as a pledge. 11Stay outside and let the man to whom you are making the loan bring the pledge out to you. 12If the man is poor, do not go to sleep with his pledge in your possession. 13Return his cloak to him by sunset so that he may sleep in it. Then he will thank you, and it will be regarded as a righteous act in the sight of the LORD your God.

14Do not take advantage of a hired man who is poor and needy, whether he is a brother Israelite or an alien living in one of your towns. 15Pay him his wages each day before sunset, because he is poor and is counting on it. Otherwise he may cry to the LORD against you, and you will be guilty of sin.

16Fathers shall not be put to death for their children, nor children put to death for their fathers; each is to die for his own sin.

17Do not deprive the alien or

*j8* The Hebrew word was used for various diseases affecting the skin—not necessarily leprosy.

**10* Most mss have the accent *tiphhah* under the *kaph* (בְרֵעֲךָ).

גֵּר יָתוֹם וְלֹא תַחֲבֹל בֶּגֶד אַלְמָנָה׃ וְזָכַרְתָּ

and-you-remember (18) widow cloak-of you-take-pledge and-not fatherless alien

כִּי עֶבֶד הָיִיתָ בְּמִצְרַיִם וַיִּפְדְּךָ יְהוָה אֱלֹהֶיךָ מִשָּׁם

from-there God-of-you Yahweh and-he-redeemed-you in-Egypt you-were slave that

עַל־כֵּן אָנֹכִי מְצַוְּךָ לַעֲשׂוֹת אֶת־הַדָּבָר הַזֶּה׃ כִּי תִקְצֹר

you-harvest when (19) the-this the-thing *** to-do commanding-you I this for

קְצִירְךָ בְשָׂדֶךָ וְשָׁכַחְתָּ עֹמֶר בַּשָּׂדֶה לֹא

not in-the-field sheaf and-you-overlook in-field-of-you harvest-of-you

תָשׁוּב לְקַחְתּוֹ לַגֵּר לַיָּתוֹם וְלָאַלְמָנָה

and-for-the-widow for-the-fatherless for-the-alien to-get-him you-go-back

יִהְיֶה לְמַעַן יְבָרֶכְךָ יְהוָה אֱלֹהֶיךָ בְּכֹל מַעֲשֵׂה

work-of in-all-of God-of-you Yahweh he-may-bless-you so-that he-is

יָדֶיךָ׃ כִּי תַחְבֹּט זֵיתְךָ לֹא תְפַאֵר אַחֲרֶיךָ

after-you you-go-over not olive-tree-of-you you-beat when (20) hands-of-you

לַגֵּר לַיָּתוֹם וְלָאַלְמָנָה יִהְיֶה׃ כִּי תִבְצֹר

you-harvest when (21) he-is and-for-the-widow for-the-fatherless for-the-alien

כַּרְמְךָ לֹא תְעוֹלֵל אַחֲרֶיךָ לַגֵּר לַיָּתוֹם

for-the-fatherless for-the-alien after-you you-go-over-vine not vineyard-of-you

וְלָאַלְמָנָה יִהְיֶה׃ וְזָכַרְתָּ כִּי־עֶבֶד הָיִיתָ בְּאֶרֶץ

in-land-of you-were slave that and-you-remember (22) he-is and-for-the-widow

מִצְרָיִם עַל־כֵּן אָנֹכִי מְצַוְּךָ לַעֲשׂוֹת אֶת־הַדָּבָר הַזֶּה׃ כִּי־

when (25:1) the-this the-thing *** to-do commanding-you I this for Egypt

יִהְיֶה רִיב בֵּין אֲנָשִׁים וְנִגְּשׁוּ אֶל־הַמִּשְׁפָּט

the-court to then-they-must-go men between dispute he-is

וּשְׁפָטוּם וְהִצְדִּיקוּ אֶת־הַצַּדִּיק

the-innocent *** and-they-will-acquit and-they-will-judge-them

וְהִרְשִׁיעוּ אֶת־הָרָשָׁע׃ וְהָיָה אִם־בִּן

deserving-of if and-he-will-be (2) the-guilty *** and-they-will-condemn

הַכּוֹת הָרָשָׁע וְהִפִּילוֹ הַשֹּׁפֵט

the-one-judging then-he-shall-make-lie-down-him the-guilty to-beat

וְהִכָּהוּ לְפָנָיו כְּדֵי רִשְׁעָתוֹ בְּמִסְפָּר׃

in-number crime-of-him as-deserving-of before-him and-he-shall-flog-him

אַרְבָּעִים יַכֶּנּוּ לֹא יֹסִיף פֶּן־יֹסִיף

he-gives-more if he-shall-give-more not he-shall-flog-him forty (3)

לְהַכֹּתוֹ עַל־אֵלֶּה מַכָּה רַבָּה וְנִקְלָה אָחִיךָ

brother-of-you then-he-will-be-degraded many lash these than to-flog-him

לְעֵינֶיךָ׃ לֹא־תַחְסֹם שׁוֹר בְּדִישׁוֹ׃ כִּי־יֵשְׁבוּ

they-live if (5) while-to-tread-him ox you-muzzle not (4) in-eyes-of-you

the fatherless of justice, or take the cloak of the widow as a pledge. [18]Remember that you were slaves in Egypt and the LORD your God redeemed you from there. That is why I command you to do this.

[19]When you are harvesting in your field and you overlook a sheaf, do not go back to get it. Leave it for the alien, the fatherless and the widow, so that the LORD your God may bless you in all the work of your hands. [20]When you beat the olives from your trees, do not go over the branches a second time. Leave what remains for the alien, the fatherless and the widow. [21]When you harvest the grapes in your vineyard, do not go over the vines again. Leave what remains for the alien, the fatherless and the widow. [22]Remember that you were slaves in Egypt. That is why I command you to do this.

25 When men have a dispute, they are to take it to court and the judges will decide the case, acquitting the innocent and condemning the guilty. [2]If the guilty man deserves to be beaten, the judge shall make him lie down and have him flogged in his presence with the number of lashes his crime deserves, [3]but he must not give him more than forty lashes. If he is flogged more than that, your brother will be degraded in your eyes.

[4]Do not muzzle an ox while it is treading out the grain.

אַחִים יַחְדָּו וּמֵת אַחַד מֵהֶם וּבֵן אֵין־ לוֹ לֹא־
not to-him there-is-no and-son of-them one and-he-dies together brothers

תִהְיֶה אֵשֶׁת־ הַמֵּת הַחוּצָה לְאִישׁ זָר
stranger to-man on-the-outside the-one-dead widow-of she-must-marry

יְבָמָהּ יָבֹא עָלֶיהָ וּלְקָחָהּ לוֹ
to-him and-he-must-take-her to-her he-must-come brother-of-husband-to-her

לְאִשָּׁה וְיִבְּמָהּ׃ וְהָיָה הַבְּכוֹר
the-firstborn and-he-will-be (6) and-he-must-do-duty-of-brother-in-law-of-her as-wife

אֲשֶׁר תֵּלֵד יָקוּם עַל־ שֵׁם אָחִיו הַמֵּת וְלֹא־
so-not the-dead brother-of-him name-of on he-shall-carry she-bears whom

יִמָּחֶה שְׁמוֹ מִיִּשְׂרָאֵל׃ וְאִם־ לֹא יַחְפֹּץ הָאִישׁ
the-man he-wants not but-if (7) from-Israel name-of-him he-is-blotted-out

לָקַחַת אֶת־ יְבִמְתּוֹ וְעָלְתָה יְבִמְתּוֹ
wife-of-brother-of-him then-she-shall-go wife-of-brother-of-him *** to-marry

הַשַּׁעְרָה אֶל־ הַזְּקֵנִים וְאָמְרָה מֵאֵין יְבָמִי
brother-of-husband-of-me he-refuses and-she-shall-say the-elders to to-the-gate

לְהָקִים לְאָחִיו שֵׁם בְּיִשְׂרָאֵל לֹא אָבָה יַבְּמִי׃
to-fulfill-duty-to-me he-will not in-Israel name for-brother-of-him to-carry-on

וְקָרְאוּ־ לוֹ זִקְנֵי־ עִירוֹ וְדִבְּרוּ
and-they-shall-talk city-of-him elders-of for-him and-they-shall-summon (8)

אֵלָיו וְעָמַד וְאָמַר לֹא חָפַצְתִּי לְקַחְתָּהּ׃ וְנִגְּשָׁה
then-she-shall-go (9) to-marry-her I-want not and-he-says if-he-persists to-him

יְבִמְתּוֹ אֵלָיו לְעֵינֵי הַזְּקֵנִים וְחָלְצָה
and-she-shall-take-off the-elders before-eyes-of to-him widow-of-brother-of-him

נַעֲלוֹ מֵעַל רַגְלוֹ וְיָרְקָה בְּפָנָיו
in-faces-of-him and-she-shall-spit foot-of-him from-on sandal-of-him

וְעָנְתָה וְאָמְרָה כָּכָה יֵעָשֶׂה לָאִישׁ אֲשֶׁר לֹא־
not who to-the-man he-is-done this and-she-shall-say and-she-shall-speak

יִבְנֶה אֶת־ בֵּית אָחִיו׃ וְנִקְרָא
and-he-will-be-known (10) brother-of-him family-line-of *** he-will-build-up

שְׁמוֹ בְּיִשְׂרָאֵל בֵּית חֲלוּץ הַנָּעַל׃ כִּי־ יִנָּצוּ
they-fight if (11) the-sandal being-removed-of family-of in-Israel name-of-him

אֲנָשִׁים יַחְדָּו אִישׁ וְאָחִיו וְקָרְבָה אֵשֶׁת הָאֶחָד לְהַצִּיל
to-rescue the-one wife-of and-she-comes and-brother-of-him man together men

אֶת־ אִישָׁהּ מִיַּד מַכֵּהוּ וְשָׁלְחָה
and-she-reaches-out one-assaulting-him from-hand-of husband-of-her ***

יָדָהּ וְהֶחֱזִיקָה בִּמְבֻשָׁיו׃ וְקַצֹּתָה
then-you-cut-off (12) on-private-parts-of-him and-she-seizes hand-of-her

5 If brothers are living together and one of them dies without a son, his widow must not marry outside the family. Her husband's brother shall take her and marry her and fulfill the duty of a brother-in-law to her.
6 The first son she bears shall carry on the name of the dead brother so that his name will not be blotted out from Israel.

7 However, if a man does not want to marry his brother's wife, she shall go to the elders at the town gate and say, "My husband's brother refuses to carry on his brother's name in Israel. He will not fulfill the duty of a brother-in-law to me."
8 Then the elders of his town shall summon him and talk to him. If he persists in saying, "I do not want to marry her,"
9 his brother's widow shall go up to him in the presence of the elders, take off one of his sandals, spit in his face and say, "This is what is done to the man who will not build up his brother's family line."
10 That man's line shall be known in Israel as The Family of the Unsandaled.

11 If two men are fighting and the wife of one of them comes to rescue her husband from his assailant, and she reaches out and seizes him by his private parts,
12 you shall cut off

*7 Most mss have no *yod* ( מֵאֵן ).

אֶת־ כַּפָּהּ לֹא תָחוֹס עֵינֶךָ׃ לֹא־ יִהְיֶה לְךָ

to-you he-must-be not (13) eye-of-you she-must-pity not hand-of-her ***

בְּכִיסְךָ אֶבֶן וָאָבֶן גְּדוֹלָה וּקְטַנָּה׃ לֹא־ יִהְיֶה לְךָ

to-you he-must-be not (14) and-light heavy and-weight weight in-bag-of-you

בְּבֵיתְךָ אֵיפָה וְאֵיפָה גְּדוֹלָה וּקְטַנָּה׃ אֶבֶן שְׁלֵמָה

accurate weight (15) and-small large and-measure measure in-house-of-you

וָצֶדֶק יִהְיֶה־ לָּךְ אֵיפָה שְׁלֵמָה וָצֶדֶק יִהְיֶה־ לָּךְ

to-you he-must-be and-honest accurate measure to-you he-must-be and-honest

לְמַעַן יַאֲרִיכוּ יָמֶיךָ עַל הָאֲדָמָה אֲשֶׁר־ יְהוָה אֱלֹהֶיךָ

God-of-you Yahweh that the-land in days-of-you they-may-be-long so-that

נֹתֵן לָךְ׃ כִּי תוֹעֲבַת יְהוָה אֱלֹהֶיךָ כָּל־ עֹשֵׂה אֵלֶּה

these doing any-of God-of-you Yahweh detestable-of for (16) to-you giving

כֹּל עֹשֵׂה עָוֶל׃ זָכוֹר אֵת אֲשֶׁר־ עָשָׂה לְךָ עֲמָלֵק

Amalek to-you he-did what *** to-remember (17) dishonestly dealing any-of

בַּדֶּרֶךְ בְּצֵאתְכֶם מִמִּצְרָיִם׃ אֲשֶׁר קָרְךָ בַּדֶּרֶךְ

on-the-journey he-met-you when (18) from-Egypt when-to-come-you along-the-way

וַיְזַנֵּב בְּךָ כָּל־ הַנֶּחֱשָׁלִים אַחֲרֶיךָ* וְאַתָּה עָיֵף

weary and-you behind-you the-ones-lagging all-of from-you and-he-cut-off

וְיָגֵעַ וְלֹא יָרֵא אֱלֹהִים׃ וְהָיָה בְּהָנִיחַ

when-to-give-rest and-he-will-be (19) God he-feared and-not and-worn-out

יְהוָה אֱלֹהֶיךָ ׀ לְךָ מִכָּל־ אֹיְבֶיךָ מִסָּבִיב

from-around being-enemies-of-you from-all-of to-you God-of-you Yahweh

בָּאָרֶץ אֲשֶׁר יְהוָה־ אֱלֹהֶיךָ נֹתֵן לְךָ נַחֲלָה לְרִשְׁתָּהּ

to-possess-her inheritance to-you giving God-of-you Yahweh that in-the-land

תִּמְחֶה אֶת־ זֵכֶר עֲמָלֵק מִתַּחַת הַשָּׁמָיִם לֹא תִּשְׁכָּח׃

you-forget not the-heavens from-under Amalek memory-of *** you-shall-blot-out

וְהָיָה כִּי־ תָבוֹא אֶל־ הָאָרֶץ אֲשֶׁר יְהוָה אֱלֹהֶיךָ

God-of-you Yahweh that the-land into you-enter when and-he-will-be (26:1)

נֹתֵן לְךָ נַחֲלָה וִירִשְׁתָּהּ וְיָשַׁבְתָּ בָּהּ׃

in-her and-you-settle and-you-possess-her inheritance to-you giving

וְלָקַחְתָּ מֵרֵאשִׁית ׀ כָּל־ פְּרִי הָאֲדָמָה אֲשֶׁר תָּבִיא

you-produce that the-soil fruit-of all-of from-firstfruit-of then-you-take (2)

מֵאַרְצְךָ אֲשֶׁר יְהוָה אֱלֹהֶיךָ נֹתֵן לָךְ וְשַׂמְתָּ

and-you-put to-you giving God-of-you Yahweh that from-land-of-you

בַטֶּנֶא וְהָלַכְתָּ אֶל־הַמָּקוֹם אֲשֶׁר יִבְחַר יְהוָה אֱלֹהֶיךָ

God-of-you Yahweh he-will-choose that the-place to then-you-go in-the-basket

לְשַׁכֵּן שְׁמוֹ שָׁם׃ וּבָאתָ אֶל־ הַכֹּהֵן אֲשֶׁר יִהְיֶה

he-is who the-priest to and-you-go (3) there name-of-him to-make-dwell

her hand. Show her no pity.
[13]Do not have two differing weights in your bag—one heavy, one light. [14]Do not have two differing measures in your house—one large, one small. [15]You must have accurate and honest weights and measures, so that you may live long in the land the LORD your God is giving you. [16]For the LORD your God detests anyone who does these things, anyone who deals dishonestly.

[17]Remember what the Amalekites did to you along the way when you came out of Egypt. [18]When you were weary and worn out, they met you on your journey and cut off all who were lagging behind; they had no fear of God. [19]When the LORD your God gives you rest from all the enemies around you in the land he is giving you to possess as an inheritance, you shall blot out the memory of Amalek from under heaven. Do not forget!

### *Firstfruits and Tithes*

**26** When you have entered the land the LORD your God is giving you as an inheritance and have taken possession of it and settled in it, [2]take some of the firstfruits of all that you produce from the soil of the land the LORD your God is giving you and put them in a basket. Then go to the place the LORD your God will choose as a dwelling for his Name [3]and say to the

*18 Most mss have no *hateph pathah* under the *beth* (אַחֲ).

בַּיָּמִים הָהֵם וְאָמַרְתָּ אֵלָיו הִגַּדְתִּי הַיּוֹם לַיהוָה
to-Yahweh the-day I-declare to-him and-you-say the-those in-the-days

אֱלֹהֶיךָ כִּי־ בָאתִי אֶל־ הָאָרֶץ אֲשֶׁר נִשְׁבַּע יְהוָה לַאֲבֹתֵינוּ
to-fathers-of-us Yahweh he-swore that the-land into I-came that God-of-you

לָתֶת לָנוּ׃ (4) וְלָקַח הַכֹּהֵן הַטֶּנֶא מִיָּדֶךָ
from-hand-of-you the-basket the-priest and-he-shall-take (4) to-us to-give

וְהִנִּיחוֹ לִפְנֵי מִזְבַּח יְהוָה אֱלֹהֶיךָ׃ (5) וְעָנִיתָ
then-you-declare (5) God-of-you Yahweh altar-of in-front-of and-he-shall-set-him

וְאָמַרְתָּ לִפְנֵי יְהוָה אֱלֹהֶיךָ אֲרַמִּי אֹבֵד אָבִי
father-of-me wandering Aramean God-of-you Yahweh before and-you-say

וַיֵּרֶד מִצְרַיְמָה וַיָּגָר שָׁם בִּמְתֵי מְעָט וַיְהִי־
and-he-became few with-people-of there and-he-lived to-Egypt and-he-went-down

שָׁם לְגוֹי גָּדוֹל עָצוּם וָרָב׃ (6) וַיָּרֵעוּ אֹתָנוּ
us but-they-mistreated (6) and-numerous powerful great into-nation there

הַמִּצְרִים וַיְעַנּוּנוּ וַיִּתְּנוּ עָלֵינוּ עֲבֹדָה קָשָׁה׃
hard labor on-us and-they-put and-they-made-suffer-us the-Egyptians

(7) וַנִּצְעַק אֶל־ יְהוָה אֱלֹהֵי אֲבֹתֵינוּ וַיִּשְׁמַע יְהוָה אֶת־
*** Yahweh and-he-heard fathers-of-us God-of Yahweh to then-we-cried (7)

קֹלֵנוּ וַיַּרְא אֶת־ עָנְיֵנוּ וְאֶת־ עֲמָלֵנוּ וְאֶת־ לַחֲצֵנוּ׃
oppression-of-us and toil-of-us and misery-of-us *** and-he-saw voice-of-us

(8) וַיּוֹצִאֵנוּ יְהוָה מִמִּצְרַיִם בְּיָד חֲזָקָה וּבִזְרֹעַ
and-with-arm mighty with-hand from-Egypt Yahweh so-he-brought-out-us (8)

נְטוּיָה וּבְמֹרָא גָּדֹל וּבְאֹתוֹת וּבְמֹפְתִים׃
and-with-wonders and-with-signs great and-with-terror being-outstretched

(9) וַיְבִאֵנוּ אֶל־ הַמָּקוֹם הַזֶּה וַיִּתֶּן־ לָנוּ אֶת־ הָאָרֶץ
the-land *** to-us and-he-gave the-this the-place to and-he-brought-us (9)

הַזֹּאת אֶרֶץ זָבַת חָלָב וּדְבָשׁ׃ (10) וְעַתָּה הִנֵּה הֵבֵאתִי אֶת־
*** I-bring see! and-not (10) and-honey milk flowing-of land the-this

רֵאשִׁית פְּרִי הָאֲדָמָה אֲשֶׁר־ נָתַתָּה לִּי יְהוָה וְהִנַּחְתּוֹ
then-you-place-him Yahweh to-me you-gave that the-soil fruit-of first-of

לִפְנֵי יְהוָה אֱלֹהֶיךָ וְהִשְׁתַּחֲוִיתָ לִפְנֵי יְהוָה אֱלֹהֶיךָ׃
God-of-you Yahweh before and-you-bow-down God-of-you Yahweh before

(11) וְשָׂמַחְתָּ בְכָל־ הַטּוֹב אֲשֶׁר נָתַן־ לְךָ יְהוָה אֱלֹהֶיךָ
God-of-you Yahweh to-you he-gave that the-good in-all-of and-you-rejoice (11)

וּלְבֵיתֶךָ אַתָּה וְהַלֵּוִי וְהַגֵּר אֲשֶׁר בְּקִרְבֶּךָ׃
in-among-you who and-the-alien and-the-Levite you and-to-household-of-you

(12) כִּי תְכַלֶּה לַעְשֵׂר אֶת־ כָּל־ מַעְשַׂר תְּבוּאָתְךָ
produce-of-you tenth-of all-of *** to-set-aside you-finish when (12)

priest in office at the time, "I
declare today to the LORD your
God that I have come to the
land the LORD swore to our
forefathers to give us." 4The
priest shall take the basket
from your hands and set it
down in front of the altar of
the LORD your God. 5Then you
shall declare before the LORD
your God: "My father was a
wandering Aramean, and he
went down into Egypt with a
few people and lived there and
became a great nation, powerful and numerous. 6But the
Egyptians mistreated us and
made us suffer, putting us to
hard labor. 7Then we cried out
to the LORD, the God of our fathers, and the LORD heard our
voice and saw our misery, toil
and oppression. 8So the LORD
brought us out of Egypt with a
mighty hand and an out-
stretched arm, with great terror and with miraculous signs
and wonders. 9He brought us
to this place and gave us this
land, a land flowing with milk
and honey; 10and now I bring
the firstfruits of the soil that
you, O LORD, have given me."
Place the basket before the
LORD your God and bow down
before him. 11And you and the
Levites and the aliens among
you shall rejoice in all the good
things the LORD your God has
given to you and your
household.
12When you have finished
setting aside a tenth of all your

בַּשָּׁנָה הַשְּׁלִישִׁת שְׁנַת הַמַּעֲשֵׂר וְנָתַתָּה לַלֵּוִי
to-the-Levite then-you-give the-tithe year-of the-third in-the-year

לַגֵּר לַיָּתוֹם וְלָאַלְמָנָה וְאָכְלוּ בִשְׁעָרֶיךָ
in-gates-of-you so-they-may-eat and-to-the-widow to-the-fatherless to-the-alien

וְשָׂבֵעוּ׃ וְאָמַרְתָּ לִפְנֵי יְהוָה אֱלֹהֶיךָ בִּעַרְתִּי
I-removed God-of-you Yahweh before then-you-say (13) and-they-may-be-satisfied

הַקֹּדֶשׁ מִן־ הַבַּיִת וְגַם נְתַתִּיו לַלֵּוִי
to-the-Levite I-gave-him and-also the-house from the-sacred-portion

וְלַגֵּר לַיָּתוֹם וְלָאַלְמָנָה כְּכָל־ מִצְוָתְךָ
command-of-you as-all-of and-to-the-widow to-the-fatherless and-to-the-alien

אֲשֶׁר צִוִּיתָנִי לֹא־ עָבַרְתִּי מִמִּצְוֹתֶיךָ וְלֹא שָׁכָחְתִּי׃
I-forgot and-not from-commands-of-you I-turned not you-commanded-me that

לֹא־ אָכַלְתִּי בְאֹנִי מִמֶּנּוּ וְלֹא־ בִעַרְתִּי מִמֶּנּוּ
from-him I-removed and-not from-him in-mourning-of-me I-ate not (14)

בְּטָמֵא וְלֹא־ נָתַתִּי מִמֶּנּוּ לְמֵת שָׁמַעְתִּי בְּקוֹל
to-voice-of I-obeyed for-dead from-him I-offered and-not in-uncleanness

יְהוָה אֱלֹהָי עָשִׂיתִי כְּכֹל אֲשֶׁר צִוִּיתָנִי׃ הַשְׁקִיפָה
look-down! (15) you-commanded-me that as-all I-did God-of-me Yahweh

מִמְּעוֹן קָדְשְׁךָ מִן־ הַשָּׁמַיִם וּבָרֵךְ אֶת־ עַמְּךָ
people-of-you *** and-bless! the-heavens from holy-of-you from-dwelling-of

אֶת־ יִשְׂרָאֵל וְאֵת הָאֲדָמָה אֲשֶׁר נָתַתָּה לָנוּ כַּאֲשֶׁר נִשְׁבַּעְתָּ
you-promised just-as to-us you-gave that the-land and Israel ***

לַאֲבֹתֵינוּ אֶרֶץ זָבַת חָלָב וּדְבָשׁ׃ הַיּוֹם הַזֶּה יְהוָה
Yahweh the-this the-day (16) and-honey milk flowing-of land to-fathers-of-us

אֱלֹהֶיךָ מְצַוְּךָ לַעֲשׂוֹת אֶת־ הַחֻקִּים הָאֵלֶּה וְאֶת־ הַמִּשְׁפָּטִים
the-laws and the-these the-decrees *** to-follow commanding-you God-of-you

וְשָׁמַרְתָּ וְעָשִׂיתָ אוֹתָם בְּכָל־ לְבָבְךָ וּבְכָל־
and-with-all-of heart-of-you with-all-of them and-you-observe and-you-be-careful

נַפְשֶׁךָ׃ אֶת־ יְהוָה הֶאֱמַרְתָּ הַיּוֹם לִהְיוֹת לְךָ לֵאלֹהִים
as-God to-you to-be the-day you-declared Yahweh *** (17) soul-of-you

וְלָלֶכֶת בִּדְרָכָיו וְלִשְׁמֹר חֻקָּיו וּמִצְוֹתָיו
and-commands-of-him decrees-of-him and-to-keep in-ways-of-him and-to-walk

וּמִשְׁפָּטָיו וְלִשְׁמֹעַ בְּקֹלוֹ׃ וַיהוָה הֶאֱמִירְךָ
he-declared-you and-Yahweh (18) to-voice-of-him and-to-obey and-laws-of-him

הַיּוֹם לִהְיוֹת לוֹ לְעַם סְגֻלָּה כַּאֲשֶׁר דִּבֶּר־ לָךְ
to-you he-promised just-as treasure as-people-of to-him to-be the-day

וְלִשְׁמֹר כָּל־ מִצְוֹתָיו׃ וּלְתִתְּךָ עֶלְיוֹן עַל כָּל־
all-of above high and-to-set-you (19) commands-of-him all-of and-to-keep

produce in the third year, the year of the tithe, you shall give it to the Levite, the alien, the fatherless and the widow, so that they may eat in your towns and be satisfied. [13]Then say to the LORD your God: "I have removed from my house the sacred portion and have given it to the Levite, the alien, the fatherless and the widow, according to all you commanded. I have not turned aside from your commands nor have I forgotten any of them. [14]I have not eaten any of the sacred portion while I was in mourning, nor have I removed any of it while I was unclean, nor have I offered any of it to the dead. I have obeyed the LORD my God; I have done everything you commanded me. [15]Look down from heaven, your holy dwelling place, and bless your people Israel and the land you have given us as you promised on oath to our forefathers, a land flowing with milk and honey."

*Follow the LORD's Commands*

[16]The LORD your God commands you this day to follow these decrees and laws; carefully observe them with all your heart and with all your soul. [17]You have declared this day that the LORD is your God and that you will walk in his ways, that you will keep his decrees, commands and laws, and that you will obey him. [18]And the LORD has declared this day that you are his people, his treasured possession as he promised, and that you are to keep all his commands. [19]He has declared that

הַגּוֹיִם אֲשֶׁר עָשָׂה לִתְהִלָּה וּלְשֵׁם וּלְתִפְאָרֶת וְלִהְיֹתְךָ
and-to-be-you and-in-honor and-in-fame in-praise he-made that the-nations

עַם־קָדֹשׁ לַיהוָה אֱלֹהֶיךָ כַּאֲשֶׁר דִּבֵּר׃ וַיְצַו
and-he-commanded (27:1) he-promised just-as God-of-you to-Yahweh holy people

מֹשֶׁה וְזִקְנֵי יִשְׂרָאֵל אֶת־הָעָם לֵאמֹר שָׁמֹר אֶת־כָּל־
all-of *** to-keep to-say the-people *** Israel and-elders-of Moses

הַמִּצְוָה אֲשֶׁר אָנֹכִי מְצַוֶּה אֶתְכֶם הַיּוֹם׃ וְהָיָה בַּיּוֹם אֲשֶׁר
that on-the-day and-he-will-be (2) the-day you commanding I that the-command

תַּעַבְרוּ אֶת־הַיַּרְדֵּן אֶל־הָאָרֶץ אֲשֶׁר־יְהוָה אֱלֹהֶיךָ נֹתֵן לָךְ
to-you giving God-of-you Yahweh that the-land into the-Jordan *** you-cross

וַהֲקֵמֹתָ לְךָ אֲבָנִים גְּדֹלוֹת וְשַׂדְתָּ אֹתָם בַּשִּׂיד׃
with-the-plaster them and-you-coat large-ones stones for-you then-you-set-up

וְכָתַבְתָּ עֲלֵיהֶן אֶת־כָּל־דִּבְרֵי הַתּוֹרָה הַזֹּאת
the-this the-law words-of all-of *** on-them and-you-write (3)

בְּעָבְרֶךָ לְמַעַן אֲשֶׁר תָּבֹא אֶל־הָאָרֶץ אֲשֶׁר־יְהוָה אֱלֹהֶיךָ ׀
God-of-you Yahweh that the-land into you-enter when so-that when-to-cross-you

נֹתֵן לְךָ אֶרֶץ זָבַת חָלָב וּדְבַשׁ כַּאֲשֶׁר דִּבֶּר יְהוָה
Yahweh he-promised just-as and-honey milk flowing-of land to-you giving

אֱלֹהֵי־אֲבֹתֶיךָ לָךְ׃ וְהָיָה בְּעָבְרְכֶם אֶת־
*** when-to-cross-you and-he-will-be (4) to-you fathers-of-you God-of

הַיַּרְדֵּן תָּקִימוּ אֶת־הָאֲבָנִים הָאֵלֶּה אֲשֶׁר אָנֹכִי מְצַוֶּה אֶתְכֶם הַיּוֹם
the-day you commanding I that the-these the-stones *** you-set-up the-Jordan

בְּהַר עֵיבָל וְשַׂדְתָּ אוֹתָם בַּשִּׂיד׃ וּבָנִיתָ שָּׁם מִזְבֵּחַ
altar there and-you-build (5) with-the-plaster them and-you-coat Ebal on-Mount-of

לַיהוָה אֱלֹהֶיךָ מִזְבַּח אֲבָנִים לֹא־תָנִיף עֲלֵיהֶם בַּרְזֶל׃ אֲבָנִים
stones (6) iron-tool on-them you-use not stones altar-of God-of-you to-Yahweh

שְׁלֵמוֹת תִּבְנֶה אֶת־מִזְבַּח יְהוָה אֱלֹהֶיךָ וְהַעֲלִיתָ עָלָיו
on-him and-you-offer God-of-you Yahweh altar-of *** you-build natural-ones

עוֹלֹת לַיהוָה אֱלֹהֶיךָ׃ וְזָבַחְתָּ שְׁלָמִים
fellowship-offerings and-you-sacrifice (7) God-of-you to-Yahweh burnt-offerings

וְאָכַלְתָּ שָּׁם וְשָׂמַחְתָּ לִפְנֵי יְהוָה אֱלֹהֶיךָ׃ וְכָתַבְתָּ
and-you-write (8) God-of-you Yahweh before and-you-rejoice there and-you-eat

עַל־הָאֲבָנִים אֶת־כָּל־דִּבְרֵי הַתּוֹרָה הַזֹּאת בַּאֵר הֵיטֵב׃
to-be-good to-be-clear the-this the-law words-of all-of *** the-stones on

וַיְדַבֵּר מֹשֶׁה וְהַכֹּהֲנִים הַלְוִיִּם אֶל כָּל־יִשְׂרָאֵל
Israel all-of to and-the-Levites and-the-priests Moses then-he-spoke (9)

לֵאמֹר הַסְכֵּת ׀ וּשְׁמַע יִשְׂרָאֵל הַיּוֹם הַזֶּה נִהְיֵיתָ לְעָם
as-people you-became the-this the-day Israel and-listen! be-silent! to-say

he will set you in praise, fame and honor high above all the nations he has made and that you will be a people holy to the LORD your God, as he promised.

### *The Altar on Mount Ebal*

**27** Moses and the elders of Israel commanded the people: "Keep all these commands that I give you today. 2When you have crossed the Jordan into the land the LORD your God is giving you, set up some large stones and coat them with plaster. 3Write on them all the words of this law when you have crossed over to enter the land the LORD your God is giving you, a land flowing with milk and honey, just as the LORD, the God of your fathers, promised you. 4And when you have crossed the Jordan, set up these stones on Mount Ebal, as I command you today, and coat them with plaster. 5Build there an altar to the LORD your God, an altar of stones. Do not use any iron tool upon them. 6Build the altar of the LORD your God with fieldstones and offer burnt offerings on it to the LORD your God. 7Sacrifice fellowship offerings[k] there, eating them and rejoicing in the presence of the LORD your God. 8And you shall write very clearly all the words of this law on these stones you have set up."

### *Curses From Mount Ebal*

9Then Moses and the priests, who are Levites, said to all Israel, "Be silent, O Israel, and listen! You have now become the people of the LORD your

k7 Traditionally *peace offerings*

לַיהוָ֥ה אֱלֹהֶֽיךָ׃ וְשָׁ֣מַעְתָּ֔ בְּק֖וֹל יְהוָ֣ה אֱלֹהֶ֑יךָ
God-of-you Yahweh to-voice-of and-you-obey (10) God-of-you to-Yahweh

וְעָשִׂ֤יתָ אֶת־ מִצְוֺתָו֙ וְאֶת־ חֻקָּ֔יו אֲשֶׁ֛ר אָנֹכִ֥י מְצַוְּךָ֖
giving-you I that decrees-of-him and commands-of-him *** and-you-follow

הַיּֽוֹם׃ וַיְצַ֤ו מֹשֶׁה֙ אֶת־ הָעָ֔ם בַּיּ֥וֹם הַה֖וּא לֵאמֹֽר׃
to-say the-that on-the-day the-people *** Moses and-he-commanded (11) the-day

אֵ֠לֶּה יַעַמְד֞וּ לְבָרֵ֤ךְ אֶת־ הָעָם֙ עַל־ הַ֣ר גְּרִזִ֔ים
Gerizim Mount-of on the-people *** to-bless they-shall-stand these (12)

בְּעָבְרְכֶ֖ם אֶת־ הַיַּרְדֵּ֑ן שִׁמְעוֹן֙ וְלֵוִ֣י וִיהוּדָ֔ה וְיִשָּׂשכָ֖ר
and-Issachar and-Judah and-Levi Simeon the-Jordan *** when-to-cross-you

וְיוֹסֵ֥ף וּבִנְיָמִֽן׃ וְאֵ֛לֶּה יַעַמְד֥וּ עַל־ הַקְּלָלָ֖ה
the-curse for they-shall-stand and-these (13) and-Benjamin and-Joseph

בְּהַ֣ר עֵיבָ֑ל רְאוּבֵן֙ גָּ֣ד וְאָשֵׁ֔ר וּזְבוּלֻ֖ן דָּ֥ן וְנַפְתָּלִֽי׃
and-Naphtali Dan and-Zebulun and-Asher Gad Reuben Ebal on-Mount-of

וְעָנ֣וּ הַלְוִיִּ֗ם וְאָמְר֛וּ אֶל־ כָּל־ אִ֥ישׁ
person-of every-of to and-they-shall-say the-Levites and-they-shall-recite (14)

יִשְׂרָאֵ֖ל ק֥וֹל רָֽם׃ אָר֣וּר הָאִ֡ישׁ אֲשֶׁ֣ר יַעֲשֶׂה֩ פֶ֨סֶל וּמַסֵּכָ֜ה
or-cast-idol image he-makes who the-man being-cursed (15) loud voice Israel

תּוֹעֲבַ֣ת יְהוָ֗ה מַעֲשֵׂ֛ה יְדֵ֥י חָרָ֖שׁ וְשָׂ֣ם בַּסָּ֑תֶר
in-the-secret and-he-sets-up craftsman hands-of work-of Yahweh detestable-of

וְעָנ֧וּ כָל־ הָעָ֛ם וְאָמְר֖וּ אָמֵֽן׃
amen and-they-shall-say the-people all-of then-they-shall-answer

אָר֕וּר מַקְלֶ֥ה אָבִ֖יו וְאִמּ֑וֹ
or-mother-of-him father-of-him one-dishonoring being-cursed (16)

וְאָמַ֥ר כָּל־ הָעָ֖ם אָמֵֽן׃ אָר֕וּר מַסִּ֖יג
one-moving being-cursed (17) amen the-people all-of then-he-shall-say

גְּב֣וּל רֵעֵ֑הוּ וְאָמַ֥ר כָּל־ הָעָ֖ם אָמֵֽן׃
amen the-people all-of then-he-shall-say neighbor-of-him boundary-stone-of

אָר֕וּר מַשְׁגֶּ֥ה עִוֵּ֖ר בַּדָּ֑רֶךְ וְאָמַ֥ר
then-he-shall-say on-the-road blind one-leading-astray being-cursed (18)

כָּל־ הָעָ֖ם אָמֵֽן׃ אָר֗וּר מַטֶּ֛ה מִשְׁפַּ֥ט גֵּר־
alien justice-of one-withholding being-cursed (19) amen the-people all-of

יָת֖וֹם וְאַלְמָנָ֑ה וְאָמַ֥ר כָּל־ הָעָ֖ם אָמֵֽן׃ אָר֗וּר
being-cursed (20) amen the-people all-of then-he-shall-say or-widow fatherless

שֹׁכֵב֙ עִם־ אֵ֣שֶׁת אָבִ֔יו כִּ֥י גִלָּ֖ה כְּנַ֣ף אָבִ֑יו
father-of-him bed-of he-dishonors for father-of-him wife-of with one-sleeping

וְאָמַ֥ר כָּל־ הָעָ֖ם אָמֵֽן׃ אָר֗וּר שֹׁכֵב֙
one-having-relation being-cursed (21) amen the-people all-of then-he-shall-say

God. 10 Obey the LORD your
God and follow his commands
and decrees that I give you today."
11 On the same day Moses
commanded the people:
12 When you have crossed the
Jordan, these tribes shall stand
on Mount Gerizim to bless the
people: Simeon, Levi, Judah,
Issachar, Joseph and Benjamin. 13 And these tribes shall
stand on Mount Ebal to pronounce curses: Reuben, Gad,
Asher, Zebulun, Dan and
Naphtali.
14 The Levites shall recite to
all the people of Israel in a loud
voice:

15 "Cursed is the man who
carves an image or casts an
idol—a thing detestable to
the LORD, the work of the
craftsman's hands—and
sets it up in secret."
Then all the people shall
say, "Amen!"
16 "Cursed is the man who
dishonors his father or his
mother."
Then all the people shall
say, "Amen!"
17 "Cursed is the man who
moves his neighbor's
boundary stone."
Then all the people shall
say, "Amen!"
18 "Cursed is the man who
leads the blind astray on
the road."
Then all the people shall
say, "Amen!"
19 "Cursed is the man who
withholds justice from the
alien, the fatherless or the
widow."
Then all the people shall
say, "Amen!"
20 "Cursed is the man who
sleeps with his father's
wife, for he dishonors his
father's bed."
Then all the people shall
say, "Amen!"
21 "Cursed is the man who
has sexual relations with

°10 ק מצותיו

עִם־ כָּל־ בְּהֵמָה וְאָמַר כָּל־ הָעָם אָמֵן׃ אָרוּר
being-cursed (22) amen the-people all-of then-he-shall-say animal any-of with

שֹׁכֵב עִם־ אֲחֹתוֹ בַּת־ אָבִיו אוֹ בַת־
daughter-of or father-of-him daughter-of sister-of-him with one-sleeping

אִמּוֹ וְאָמַר כָּל־ הָעָם אָמֵן׃ אָרוּר
being-cursed (23) amen the-people all-of then-he-shall-say mother-of-him

שֹׁכֵב עִם־ חֹתַנְתּוֹ וְאָמַר כָּל־ הָעָם
the-people all-of then-he-shall-say mother-in-law-of-him with one-sleeping

אָמֵן׃ אָרוּר מַכֵּה רֵעֵהוּ בַּסָּתֶר
in-the-secret neighbor-of-him one-killing being-cursed (24) amen

וְאָמַר כָּל־ הָעָם אָמֵן׃ אָרוּר לֹקֵחַ
one-accepting being-cursed (25) amen the-people all-of then-he-shall-say

שֹׁחַד לְהַכּוֹת נֶפֶשׁ דַּם נָקִי וְאָמַר כָּל־ הָעָם
the-people all-of and-he-shall-say innocent blood-of person to-kill bribe

אָמֵן׃ אָרוּר אֲשֶׁר לֹא־ יָקִים אֶת־ דִּבְרֵי הַתּוֹרָה־ הַזֹּאת
the-this the-law words-of *** he-upholds not whoever being-cursed (26) amen

לַעֲשׂוֹת אוֹתָם וְאָמַר כָּל־ הָעָם אָמֵן׃ וְהָיָה
and-he-will-be (28:1) amen the-people all-of then-he-shall-say them to-carry-out

אִם־ שָׁמוֹעַ תִּשְׁמַע בְּקוֹל יְהוָה אֱלֹהֶיךָ לִשְׁמֹר לַעֲשׂוֹת
to-follow to-be-careful God-of-you Yahweh to-voice-of you-obey to-obey if

אֶת־ כָּל־ מִצְוֹתָיו אֲשֶׁר אָנֹכִי מְצַוְּךָ הַיּוֹם וּנְתָנְךָ
then-he-will-set-you the-day giving-you I that commands-of-him all-of ***

יְהוָה אֱלֹהֶיךָ עֶלְיוֹן עַל כָּל־ גּוֹיֵי הָאָרֶץ׃ וּבָאוּ
and-they-will-come (2) the-earth nations-of all-of above high God-of-you Yahweh

עָלֶיךָ כָּל־ הַבְּרָכוֹת הָאֵלֶּה וְהִשִּׂיגֻךָ כִּי
if and-they-will-accompany-you the-these the-blessings all-of upon-you

תִשְׁמַע בְּקוֹל יְהוָה אֱלֹהֶיךָ׃ בָּרוּךְ אַתָּה בָּעִיר
in-the-city you being-blessed (3) God-of-you Yahweh to-voice-of you-obey

וּבָרוּךְ אַתָּה בַּשָּׂדֶה׃ בָּרוּךְ פְּרִי־ בִטְנְךָ
womb-of-you fruit-of being-blessed (4) in-the-country you and-being-blessed

וּפְרִי אַדְמָתְךָ וּפְרִי בְהֶמְתֶּךָ שְׁגַר אֲלָפֶיךָ
herds-of-you calf-of stock-of-you and-young-of land-of-you and-crop-of

וְעַשְׁתְּרוֹת צֹאנֶךָ׃ בָּרוּךְ טַנְאֲךָ
basket-of-you being-blessed (5) flock-of-you and-lambs-of

וּמִשְׁאַרְתֶּךָ׃ בָּרוּךְ אַתָּה בְּבֹאֶךָ
when-to-come-in-you you being-blessed (6) and-kneading-trough-of-you

וּבָרוּךְ אַתָּה בְּצֵאתֶךָ׃ יִתֵּן יְהוָה אֶת־
*** Yahweh and-he-will-grant (7) when-to-go-out-you you and-being-blessed

any animal."
Then all the people shall say, "Amen!"
22"Cursed is the man who sleeps with his sister, the daughter of his father or the daughter of his mother."
Then all the people shall say, "Amen!"
23"Cursed is the man who sleeps with his mother-in-law."
Then all the people shall say, "Amen!"
24"Cursed is the man who kills his neighbor secretly."
Then all the people shall say, "Amen!"
25"Cursed is the man who accepts a bribe to kill an innocent person."
Then all the people shall say, "Amen!"
26"Cursed is the man who does not uphold the words of this law by carrying them out."
Then all the people shall say, "Amen!"

*Blessings for Obedience*

28 If you fully obey the LORD your God and carefully follow all his commands I give you today, the LORD your God will set you high above all the nations on earth.
2All these blessings will come upon you and accompany you if you obey the LORD your God:

3You will be blessed in the city and blessed in the country.
4The fruit of your womb will be blessed, and the crops of your land and the young of your livestock—the calves of your herds and the lambs of your flocks.
5Your basket and your kneading trough will be blessed.
6You will be blessed when you come in and blessed when you go out.

7The LORD will grant that the

אֹיְבֶ֙יךָ֙ הַקָּמִ֣ים עָלֶ֔יךָ נִגָּפִ֖ים לְפָנֶ֑יךָ
before-you ones-being-defeated against-you the-ones-rising being-enemies-of-you

בְּדֶ֤רֶךְ אֶחָד֙ יֵצְא֣וּ אֵלֶ֔יךָ וּבְשִׁבְעָ֥ה דְרָכִ֖ים יָנ֣וּסוּ
they-will-flee directions but-in-seven at-you they-will-come one from-direction

לְפָנֶֽיךָ׃ (8) יְצַ֨ו יְהוָ֤ה אִתְּךָ֙ אֶת־ הַבְּרָכָ֔ה בַּאֲסָמֶ֕יךָ
on-barns-of-you the-blessing *** to-you Yahweh he-will-send (8) from-you

וּבְכֹ֖ל מִשְׁלַ֣ח יָדֶ֑ךָ וּבֵ֣רַכְךָ֔ בָּאָ֕רֶץ אֲשֶׁר־
that in-the-land and-he-will-bless-you hand-of-you work-of and-on-all-of

יְהוָ֥ה אֱלֹהֶ֖יךָ נֹתֵ֥ן לָֽךְ׃ (9) יְקִימְךָ֙ יְהוָ֥ה ל֔וֹ
for-him Yahweh and-he-will-establish-you (9) to-you giving God-of-you Yahweh

לְעַ֣ם קָד֔וֹשׁ כַּאֲשֶׁ֖ר נִֽשְׁבַּֽע־ לָ֑ךְ כִּ֣י תִשְׁמֹ֗ר אֶת־ מִצְוֺת֙ יְהוָ֣ה
Yahweh commands-of *** you-keep if to-you he-promised just-as holy as-people

אֱלֹהֶ֔יךָ וְהָלַכְתָּ֖ בִּדְרָכָֽיו׃ (10) וְרָאוּ֙ כָּל־
all-of then-they-will-see (10) in-ways-of-him and-you-walk God-of-you

עַמֵּ֣י הָאָ֔רֶץ כִּ֛י שֵׁ֥ם יְהוָ֖ה נִקְרָ֣א עָלֶ֑יךָ וְיָֽרְא֖וּ
and-they-will-fear on-you he-is-called Yahweh name-of that the-earth peoples-of

מִמֶּֽךָּ׃ (11) וְהוֹתִרְךָ֤ יְהוָה֙ לְטוֹבָ֔ה בִּפְרִ֧י
in-fruit-of to-prosperity Yahweh and-he-will-grant-you (11) from-you

בִטְנְךָ֛ וּבִפְרִ֥י בְהֶמְתְּךָ֖* וּבִפְרִ֣י אַדְמָתֶ֑ךָ עַ֚ל
in ground-of-you and-in-crop-of stock-of-you and-in-young-of womb-of-you

הָאֲדָמָ֔ה אֲשֶׁ֨ר נִשְׁבַּ֧ע יְהוָ֛ה לַאֲבֹתֶ֖יךָ לָ֥תֶת לָֽךְ׃
to-you to-give to-fathers-of-you Yahweh he-swore that the-land

(12) יִפְתַּ֣ח יְהוָ֣ה ׀ לְ֠ךָ אֶת־ אוֹצָר֨וֹ הַטּ֜וֹב אֶת־
*** the-bountiful storehouse-of-him *** for-you Yahweh and-he-will-open (12)

הַשָּׁמַ֗יִם לָתֵ֤ת מְטַֽר־ אַרְצְךָ֙ בְּעִתּ֔וֹ וּלְבָרֵ֕ךְ אֵ֖ת
*** and-to-bless in-season-of-him land-of-you rain-of to-send the-heavens

כָּל־ מַעֲשֵׂ֣ה יָדֶ֑ךָ וְהִלְוִ֙יתָ֙ גּוֹיִ֣ם רַבִּ֔ים וְאַתָּ֖ה לֹ֥א
not but-you many nations and-you-will-lend hand-of-you work-of all-of

תִלְוֶֽה׃ (13) וּנְתָֽנְךָ֨ יְהוָ֤ה לְרֹאשׁ֙ וְלֹ֣א לְזָנָ֔ב
as-tail and-not as-head Yahweh and-he-will-make-you (13) you-will-borrow

וְהָיִ֙יתָ֙ רַ֣ק לְמַ֔עְלָה וְלֹ֥א תִהְיֶ֖ה לְמָ֑טָּה כִּֽי־ תִשְׁמַ֞ע אֶל־
to you-attend if at-bottom you-will-be and-not at-top always and-you-will-be

מִצְוֺ֣ת ׀ יְהוָ֣ה אֱלֹהֶ֗יךָ אֲשֶׁ֨ר אָנֹכִ֧י מְצַוְּךָ֛ הַיּ֖וֹם לִשְׁמֹ֥ר
to-be-careful the-day giving-you I that God-of-you Yahweh commands-of

וְלַעֲשֽׂוֹת׃ (14) וְלֹ֣א תָס֗וּר מִכָּל־ הַדְּבָרִ֡ים אֲשֶׁר֩ אָנֹכִ֨י מְצַוֶּ֥ה
giving I that the-commands from-any-of you-turn and-not (14) and-to-follow

אֶתְכֶ֛ם הַיּ֖וֹם יָמִ֣ין וּשְׂמֹ֑אול לָלֶ֗כֶת אַחֲרֵ֛י אֱלֹהִ֥ים אֲחֵרִ֖ים לְעָבְדָֽם׃
to-serve-them other-ones gods after to-follow or-left right the-day you

enemies who rise up against you will be defeated before you. They will come at you from one direction but flee from you in seven.
[8] The LORD will send a blessing on your barns and on everything you put your hand to. The LORD your God will bless you in the land he is giving you.
[9] The LORD will establish you as his holy people, as he promised you on oath, if you keep the commands of the LORD your God and walk in his ways. [10] Then all the peoples on earth will see that you are called by the name of the LORD, and they will fear you. [11] The LORD will grant you abundant prosperity—in the fruit of your womb, the young of your livestock and the crops of your ground—in the land he swore to your forefathers to give you.
[12] The LORD will open the heavens, the storehouse of his bounty, to send rain on your land in season and to bless all the work of your hands. You will lend to many nations but will borrow from none. [13] The LORD will make you the head, not the tail. If you pay attention to the commands of the LORD your God that I give you this day and carefully follow them, you will always be at the top, never at the bottom. [14] Do not turn aside from any of the commands I give you today, to the right or to the left, following other gods and serving them.

*11 Most mss have *segol* under the *be* (בְּהֶמ׳).

וְהָיָה אִם־ לֹא תִשְׁמַע בְּקוֹל יְהוָה אֱלֹהֶיךָ
God-of-you Yahweh to-voice-of you-obey not if but-he-will-be (15)

לִשְׁמֹר לַעֲשׂוֹת אֶת־ כָּל־ מִצְוֹתָיו וְחֻקֹּתָיו אֲשֶׁר
that and-decrees-of-him commands-of-him all-of *** to-follow to-be-careful

אָנֹכִי מְצַוְּךָ הַיּוֹם וּבָאוּ עָלֶיךָ כָּל־ הַקְּלָלוֹת הָאֵלֶּה
the-these the-curses all-of on-you then-they-will-come the-day giving-you I

וְהִשִּׂיגוּךָ׃ אָרוּר אַתָּה בָּעִיר וְאָרוּר
and-being-cursed in-the-city you being-cursed (16) and-they-will-overtake-you

אַתָּה בַּשָּׂדֶה׃ אָרוּר טַנְאֲךָ וּמִשְׁאַרְתֶּךָ׃
and-kneading-trough-of-you basket-of-you being-cursed (17) in-the-country you

אָרוּר פְּרִי־ בִטְנְךָ וּפְרִי אַדְמָתֶךָ שְׁגַר
calf-of land-of-you and-crop-of womb-of-you fruit-of being-cursed (18)

אֲלָפֶיךָ וְעַשְׁתְּרוֹת צֹאנֶךָ׃ אָרוּר אַתָּה בְּבֹאֶךָ
when-to-come-you you being-cursed (19) flock-of-you and-lambs-of herds-of-you

וְאָרוּר אַתָּה בְּצֵאתֶךָ׃ יְשַׁלַּח יְהוָה ׀ בְּךָ אֶת־
*** on-you Yahweh he-will-send (20) when-to-go-out-you you and-being-cursed

הַמְּאֵרָה אֶת־ הַמְּהוּמָה וְאֶת־ הַמִּגְעֶרֶת בְּכָל־ מִשְׁלַח יָדְךָ
hand-of-you work-of in-all-of the-rebuke and the-confusion *** the-curse

אֲשֶׁר תַּעֲשֶׂה עַד הִשָּׁמֶדְךָ וְעַד־ אֲבָדְךָ מַהֵר
suddenly to-be-ruined-you and-until to-be-destroyed-you until you-do that

מִפְּנֵי רֹעַ מַעֲלָלֶיךָ אֲשֶׁר עֲזַבְתָּנִי׃ יַדְבֵּק יְהוָה
Yahweh he-will-plague (21) you-forsook-me when deeds-of-you evil because-of

בְּךָ אֶת־ הַדָּבֶר עַד כַּלֹּתוֹ אֹתְךָ מֵעַל הָאֲדָמָה אֲשֶׁר־ אַתָּה
you that the-land from-on you to-destroy-him until the-disease *** on-you

בָא־ שָׁמָּה לְרִשְׁתָּהּ׃ יַכְּכָה יְהוָה
Yahweh he-will-strike-you (22) to-possess-her to-there entering

בַּשַּׁחֶפֶת וּבַקַּדַּחַת וּבַדַּלֶּקֶת
and-with-the-inflammation and-with-the-fever with-the-wasting-disease

וּבַחַרְחֻר וּבַחֶרֶב וּבַשִּׁדָּפוֹן וּבַיֵּרָקוֹן
and-with-the-mildew and-with-the-blight and-with-the-drought and-with-the-heat

וּרְדָפוּךָ עַד אָבְדֶךָ׃ וְהָיוּ שָׁמֶיךָ
skies-of-you and-they-will-be (23) to-perish-you until and-they-will-plague-you

אֲשֶׁר עַל־ רֹאשְׁךָ נְחֹשֶׁת וְהָאָרֶץ אֲשֶׁר־ תַּחְתֶּיךָ בַּרְזֶל׃
iron beneath-you that and-the-ground bronze head-of-you over that

יִתֵּן יְהוָה אֶת־ מְטַר אַרְצְךָ אָבָק וְעָפָר מִן־
from and-powder dust country-of-you rain-of *** Yahweh he-will-turn (24)

הַשָּׁמַיִם יֵרֵד עָלֶיךָ עַד הִשָּׁמְדָךְ׃ יִתֶּנְךָ
he-will-cause-you (25) to-be-ruined-you until on-you he-will-come-down the-skies

*Curses for Disobedience*

15However, if you do not obey the LORD your God and do not carefully follow all his commands and decrees I am giving you today, all these curses will come upon you and overtake you:

16You will be cursed in the city and cursed in the country.
17Your basket and your kneading trough will be cursed.
18The fruit of your womb will be cursed, and the crops of your land, and the calves of your herds and the lambs of your flocks.
19You will be cursed when you come in and cursed when you go out.

20The LORD will send on you curses, confusion and rebuke in everything you put your hand to, until you are destroyed and come to sudden ruin because of the evil you have done in forsaking him.[l]
21The LORD will plague you with diseases until he has destroyed you from the land you are entering to possess. 22The LORD will strike you with wasting disease, with fever and inflammation, with scorching heat and drought, with blight and mildew, which will plague you until you perish. 23The sky over your head will be bronze, the ground beneath you iron. 24The LORD will turn the rain of your country into dust and powder; it will come down from the skies until you are ruined.
25The LORD will cause you to

[l]20 Hebrew *me*

יְהוָה ׀ נִגָּף לִפְנֵי אֹיְבֶיךָ בְּדֶרֶךְ אֶחָד
Yahweh being-defeated before being-enemies-of-you from-direction one

תֵּצֵא אֵלָיו וּבְשִׁבְעָה דְרָכִים תָּנוּס לְפָנָיו
you-will-come at-him but-in-seven directions you-will-flee from-him

וְהָיִיתָ לְזַעֲוָה לְכֹל מַמְלְכוֹת הָאָרֶץ׃
and-you-will-become as-horror to-all-of kingdoms-of the-earth

(26) וְהָיְתָה נִבְלָתְךָ לְמַאֲכָל לְכָל־ עוֹף הַשָּׁמַיִם
(26) and-she-will-be carcass-of-you as-food for-every-of bird-of the-skies

וּלְבֶהֱמַת הָאָרֶץ וְאֵין מַחֲרִיד׃ (27) יַכְּכָה
and-for-beast-of the-earth and-not one-frightening (27) and-he-will-afflict-you

יְהוָה בִּשְׁחִין מִצְרַיִם וּבַעְפָלִים* וּבַגָּרָב
Yahweh with-boil-of Egypt and-with-the-tumors and-with-the-festering-sore

וּבֶחָרֶס אֲשֶׁר לֹא־ תוּכַל לְהֵרָפֵא׃ (28) יַכְּכָה
and-with-the-itch that not you-can to-be-cured (28) and-he-will-afflict-you

יְהוָה בְּשִׁגָּעוֹן וּבְעִוָּרוֹן וּבְתִמְהוֹן לֵבָב׃
Yahweh with-madness and-with-blindness and-with-confusion-of mind

(29) וְהָיִיתָ מְמַשֵּׁשׁ בַּצָּהֳרַיִם כַּאֲשֶׁר יְמַשֵּׁשׁ הָעִוֵּר
(29) and-you-will-be groping at-the-midday just-as he-gropes the-blind-man

בָּאֲפֵלָה וְלֹא תַצְלִיחַ אֶת־ דְּרָכֶיךָ וְהָיִיתָ אַךְ
in-the-dark and-not you-will-succeed *** ways-of-you and-you-will-be also

עָשׁוּק וְגָזוּל כָּל־ הַיָּמִים וְאֵין מוֹשִׁיעַ׃
being-oppressed and-being-robbed all-of the-days but-not one-rescuing

(30) אִשָּׁה תְאָרֵשׂ וְאִישׁ אַחֵר יִשְׁגָּלֶנָּה† בַּיִת
(30) woman you-will-be-pledged but-man another he-will-ravish-her house

תִּבְנֶה וְלֹא־ תֵשֵׁב בּוֹ כֶּרֶם תִּטַּע וְלֹא
you-will-build but-not you-will-live in-him vineyard you-will-plant but-not

תְּחַלְּלֶנּוּ׃ (31) שׁוֹרְךָ טָבוּחַ לְעֵינֶיךָ
you-will-begin-to-enjoy-him (31) ox-of-you being-slaughtered before-eyes-of-you

וְלֹא תֹאכַל מִמֶּנּוּ חֲמֹרְךָ גָּזוּל מִלְּפָנֶיךָ וְלֹא
but-not you-will-eat from-him donkey-of-you being-taken from-before-you and-not

יָשׁוּב לָךְ צֹאנְךָ נְתֻנוֹת לְאֹיְבֶיךָ
he-will-return to-you sheep-of-you ones-being-given to-being-enemies-of-you

וְאֵין לְךָ מוֹשִׁיעַ׃ (32) בָּנֶיךָ וּבְנֹתֶיךָ
and-not to-you one-rescuing (32) sons-of-you and-daughters-of-you

נְתֻנִים לְעַם אַחֵר וְעֵינֶיךָ רֹאוֹת
ones-being-given to-nation another and-eyes-of-you ones-watching

וְכָלוֹת אֲלֵיהֶם כָּל־ הַיּוֹם וְאֵין לְאֵל יָדֶךָ׃
and-ones-worn-out for-them all-of the-day and-not with-power hand-of-you

be defeated before your enemies. You will come at them from one direction but flee from them in seven, and you will become a thing of horror to all the kingdoms on earth. [26]Your carcasses will be food for all the birds of the air and the beasts of the earth, and there will be no one to frighten them away. [27]The LORD will afflict you with the boils of Egypt and with tumors, festering sores and the itch, from which you cannot be cured. [28]The LORD will afflict you with madness, blindness and confusion of mind. [29]At midday you will grope about like a blind man in the dark. You will be unsuccessful in everything you do; day after day you will be oppressed and robbed, with no one to rescue you.

[30]You will be pledged to be married to a woman, but another will take her and ravish her. You will build a house, but you will not live in it. You will plant a vineyard, but you will not even begin to enjoy its fruit. [31]Your ox will be slaughtered before your eyes, but you will eat none of it. Your donkey will be forcibly taken from you and will not be returned. Your sheep will be given to your enemies, and no one will rescue them. [32]Your sons and daughters will be given to another nation, and you will wear out your eyes watching for them day after day, powerless to lift a hand.

*27 The *Ketbib* and *Qere* are synonyms.

†30 The *Ketbib* is a more violent word than the *Qere*.

°27 ק ובטחרים

°30 ק ישכבנה

פְּרִי אַדְמָתְךָ וְכָל־ יְגִיעֲךָ יֹאכַל עַם אֲשֶׁר

that people he-will-eat labor-of-you and-all-of land-of-you produce-of (33)

לֹא־ יָדָעְתָּ וְהָיִיתָ רַק עָשׁוּק וְרָצוּץ כָּל־

all-of and-being-crushed being-oppressed only and-you-will-be you-know not

הַיָּמִים׃ וְהָיִיתָ מְשֻׁגָּע מִמַּרְאֵה עֵינֶיךָ

eyes-of-you from-sight-of being-driven-mad and-you-will-be (34) the-days

אֲשֶׁר תִּרְאֶה׃ יַכְּכָה יְהוָה בִּשְׁחִין רָע עַל־

on painful with-boil Yahweh and-he-will-afflict-you (35) you-see that

הַבִּרְכַּיִם וְעַל־ הַשֹּׁקַיִם אֲשֶׁר לֹא־ תוּכַל לְהֵרָפֵא מִכַּף

from-sole-of to-be-cured you-can not that the-legs and-on the-knees

רַגְלְךָ וְעַד קָדְקֳדֶךָ׃ יוֹלֵךְ יְהוָה אֹתְךָ וְאֶת־ מַלְכְּךָ

king-of-you and you Yahweh he-will-drive (36) head-of-you even-to foot-of-you

אֲשֶׁר תָּקִים עָלֶיךָ אֶל־ גּוֹי אֲשֶׁר לֹא־ יָדַעְתָּ אַתָּה וַאֲבֹתֶיךָ

or-fathers-of-you you you-know not that nation to over-you you-will-set that

וְעָבַדְתָּ שָּׁם אֱלֹהִים אֲחֵרִים עֵץ וָאָבֶן׃ וְהָיִיתָ

and-you-will-be (37) and-stone wood other-ones gods there and-you-will-worship

לְשַׁמָּה לְמָשָׁל וְלִשְׁנִינָה בְּכֹל הָעַמִּים

the-nations to-all-of and-as-object-of-ridicule as-object-of-scorn as-horror

אֲשֶׁר־ יְנַהֶגְךָ יְהוָה שָׁמָּה׃ זֶרַע רַב תּוֹצִיא

you-will-sow much seed (38) to-there Yahweh he-will-drive-you that

הַשָּׂדֶה וּמְעַט תֶּאֱסֹף כִּי יַחְסְלֶנּוּ הָאַרְבֶּה׃

the-locust he-will-devour-him for you-will-harvest but-little the-field

כְּרָמִים תִּטַּע וְעָבָדְתָּ וְיַיִן לֹא־ תִשְׁתֶּה

you-will-drink not but-wine and-you-will-cultivate you-will-plant vineyards (39)

וְלֹא תֶאֱגֹר כִּי תֹאכְלֶנּוּ הַתֹּלָעַת׃ זֵיתִים

olive-trees (40) the-worm she-will-eat-him for you-will-gather and-not

יִהְיוּ לְךָ בְּכָל־ גְּבוּלֶךָ וְשֶׁמֶן לֹא תָסוּךְ כִּי

for you-will-use not but-oil country-of-you in-all-of to-you they-will-be

יִשַּׁל זֵיתֶךָ׃ בָּנִים וּבָנוֹת תּוֹלִיד וְלֹא־

but-not you-will-bear and-daughters sons (41) olive-of-you he-will-drop-off

יִהְיוּ לָךְ כִּי יֵלְכוּ בַּשֶּׁבִי׃ כָּל־

every-of (42) into-the-captivity they-will-go for with-you they-will-stay

עֵצְךָ וּפְרִי אַדְמָתֶךָ יְיָרֵשׁ הַצְּלָצַל׃

the-locust-swarm he-will-take-over land-of-you and-crop-of tree-of-you

הַגֵּר אֲשֶׁר בְּקִרְבְּךָ יַעֲלֶה עָלֶיךָ מַעְלָה מָּעְלָה

to-higher to-higher above-you he-will-rise in-among-you who the-alien (43)

וְאַתָּה תֵרֵד מַטָּה מָּטָּה׃ הוּא יַלְוְךָ וְאַתָּה לֹא

not but-you he-will-lend-to-you he (44) lower lower you-will-sink but-you

33 A people that you do not
know will eat what your land
and labor produce, and you
will have nothing but cruel
oppression all your days. 34 The
sights you see will drive you
mad. 35 The LORD will afflict
your knees and legs with
painful boils that cannot be
cured, spreading from the
soles of your feet to the top of
your head.
36 The LORD will drive you
and the king you set over you
to a nation unknown to you or
your fathers. There you will
worship other gods, gods of
wood and stone. 37 You will
become a thing of horror and
an object of scorn and ridicule
to all the nations where the
LORD will drive you.
38 You will sow much seed in
the field but you will harvest
little, because locusts will devour it. 39 You will plant vineyards and cultivate them but
you will not drink the wine or
gather the grapes, because
worms will eat them. 40 You
will have olive trees throughout your country but you will
not use the oil, because the olives will drop off. 41 You will
have sons and daughters but
you will not keep them, because they will go into captivity. 42 Swarms of locusts will
take over all your trees and the
crops of your land.
43 The alien who lives among
you will rise above you higher
and higher, but you will sink
lower and lower. 44 He will
lend to you, but you will not

תַלְוֶנּוּ הוּא יִהְיֶה לְרֹאשׁ וְאַתָּה תִּהְיֶה לְזָנָב׃
as-tail you-will-be but-you as-head he-will-be he you-will-lend-to-him

(45) וּבָאוּ עָלֶיךָ כָּל־ הַקְּלָלוֹת הָאֵלֶּה
the-these the-curses all-of upon-you and-they-will-come (45)

וּרְדָפוּךָ וְהִשִּׂיגוּךָ עַד הִשָּׁמְדָךְ
to-be-destroyed-you until and-they-will-overtake-you and-they-will-pursue-you

כִּי־ לֹא שָׁמַעְתָּ בְּקוֹל יְהוָה אֱלֹהֶיךָ לִשְׁמֹר מִצְוֹתָיו
commands-of-him to-observe God-of+you Yahweh to-voice-of you-obeyed not for

וְחֻקֹּתָיו אֲשֶׁר צִוָּךְ׃ (46) וְהָיוּ בְךָ לְאוֹת
as-sign to-you and-they-will-be (46) he-gave-you that and-decrees-of-him

וּלְמוֹפֵת וּבְזַרְעֲךָ עַד־ עוֹלָם׃ (47) תַּחַת אֲשֶׁר לֹא־
not that because (47) forever to and-to-descendant-of-you and-as-wonder

עָבַדְתָּ אֶת־ יְהוָה אֱלֹהֶיךָ בְּשִׂמְחָה וּבְטוּב לֵבָב
heart and-with-gladness-of with-joy God-of-you Yahweh *** you-served

מֵרֹב כֹּל׃ (48) וְעָבַדְתָּ אֶת־ אֹיְבֶיךָ אֲשֶׁר
that being-enemies-of-you *** so-you-will-serve (48) great in-prosperity

יְשַׁלְּחֶנּוּ יְהוָה בָּךְ בְּרָעָב וּבְצָמָא וּבְעֵירֹם
and-in-nakedness and-in-thirst in-hunger against-you Yahweh he-sends-him

וּבְחֹסֶר כֹּל וְנָתַן עֹל בַּרְזֶל עַל־ צַוָּארֶךָ עַד
until neck-of-you on iron yoke-of and-he-will-put dire and-in-poverty

הִשְׁמִידוֹ אֹתָךְ׃ (49) יִשָּׂא יְהוָה עָלֶיךָ גּוֹי מֵרָחוֹק
from-far-away nation against-you Yahweh he-will-bring (49) you to-destroy-him

מִקְצֵה הָאָרֶץ כַּאֲשֶׁר יִדְאֶה הַנָּשֶׁר גּוֹי אֲשֶׁר לֹא־
not that nation the-eagle he-swoops-down just-as the-earth from-end-of

תִשְׁמַע לְשֹׁנוֹ׃ (50) גּוֹי עַז פָּנִים אֲשֶׁר לֹא־
not that faces fierce-of nation (50) language-of-him you-understand

יִשָּׂא פָנִים לְזָקֵן וְנַעַר לֹא יָחֹן׃ (51) וְאָכַל
and-he-will-devour (51) he-pities not and-young of-old faces he-respects

פְּרִי בְהֶמְתְּךָ וּפְרִי־ אַדְמָתְךָ עַד הִשָּׁמְדָךְ אֲשֶׁר
that to-be-destroyed-you until land-of-you and-crop-of stock-of-you young-of

לֹא־ יַשְׁאִיר לְךָ דָּגָן תִּירוֹשׁ וְיִצְהָר שְׁגַר אֲלָפֶיךָ
herds-of-you calf-of or-oil new-wine grain to-you he-will-leave not

וְעַשְׁתְּרֹת צֹאנֶךָ עַד הַאֲבִידוֹ אֹתָךְ׃ (52) וְהֵצַר
and-he-will-lay-siege (52) you to-ruin-him until flock-of-you or-lambs-of

לְךָ בְּכָל־ שְׁעָרֶיךָ עַד רֶדֶת חֹמֹתֶיךָ הַגְּבֹהוֹת
the-high-ones walls-of-you to-fall-down until gates-of-you to-all-of to-you

וְהַבְּצֻרוֹת אֲשֶׁר אַתָּה בֹּטֵחַ בָּהֵן בְּכָל־ אַרְצֶךָ
land-of-you in-all-of in-them trusting you which and-the-fortified-ones

lend to him. He will be the
head, but you will be the tail.
45All these curses will come
upon you. They will pursue
you and overtake you until
you are destroyed, because
you did not obey the LORD
your God and observe the
commands and decrees he
gave you. 46They will be a sign
and a wonder to you and your
descendants forever. 47Because
you did not serve the LORD
your God joyfully and gladly
in the time of prosperity,
48therefore in hunger and
thirst, in nakedness and dire
poverty, you will serve the
enemies the LORD sends
against you. He will put an
iron yoke on your neck until
he has destroyed you.
49The LORD will bring a nation against you from far
away, from the ends of the
earth, like an eagle swooping
down, a nation whose lan-
guage you will not under-
stand, 50a fierce-looking nation without respect for the
old or pity for the young.
51They will devour the young
of your livestock and the crops
of your land until you are destroyed. They will leave you
no grain, new wine or oil, nor
any calves of your herds or
lambs of your flocks until you
are ruined. 52They will lay
siege to all the cities throughout your land until the high
fortified walls in which you

וְהֵצַר לְךָ בְּכָל־ שְׁעָרֶיךָ בְּכָל־ אַרְצְךָ אֲשֶׁר

that land-of-you in-all-of gates-of-you to-all-of to-you and-he-will-besiege

נָתַן יְהוָה אֱלֹהֶיךָ לָךְ׃ וְאָכַלְתָּ פְרִי־ בִטְנְךָ

womb-of-you fruit-of and-you-will-eat (53) to-you God-of-you Yahweh he-gives

בְּשַׂר בָּנֶיךָ וּבְנֹתֶיךָ אֲשֶׁר נָתַן־ לְךָ יְהוָה

Yahweh to-you he-gave whom and-daughters-of-you sons-of-you flesh-of

אֱלֹהֶיךָ בְּמָצוֹר וּבְמָצוֹק אֲשֶׁר־ יָצִיק לְךָ

on-you he-inflicts that and-because-of-suffering because-of-siege God-of-you

אֹיְבֶךָ׃ הָאִישׁ הָרַךְ בְּךָ וְהֶעָנֹג מְאֹד

most and-the-sensitive among-you the-gentle the-man (54) being-enemy-of-you

תֵּרַע עֵינוֹ בְאָחִיו וּבְאֵשֶׁת חֵיקוֹ

loved-of-him and-to-wife-of to-brother-of-him eye-of-him she-will-be-evil

וּבְיֶתֶר בָּנָיו אֲשֶׁר יוֹתִיר׃ מִתֵּת ׀ לְאַחַד

to-one not-to-give (55) he-remains who children-of-him and-to-survivor-of

מֵהֶם מִבְּשַׂר בָּנָיו אֲשֶׁר יֹאכֵל מִבְּלִי הִשְׁאִיר־

he-remains because-not he-eats that children-of-him from-flesh-of of-them

לוֹ כֹּל בְּמָצוֹר וּבְמָצוֹק אֲשֶׁר יָצִיק

he-will-inflict that and-because-of-suffering because-of-siege anything to-him

לְךָ אֹיִבְךָ בְּכָל־ שְׁעָרֶיךָ׃ הָרַכָּה

the-gentle-woman (56) gates-of-you on-all-of being-enemy-of-you on-you

בְךָ וְהָעֲנֻגָּה אֲשֶׁר לֹא־ נִסְּתָה כַף־ רַגְלָהּ

foot-of-her sole-of she-would-venture not who and-the-sensitive among-you

הַצֵּג עַל־ הָאָרֶץ מֵהִתְעַנֵּג וּמֵרֹךְ תֵּרַע

she-will-be-evil and-from-gentleness from-to-be-sensitive the-ground on to-touch

עֵינָהּ בְּאִישׁ חֵיקָהּ וּבִבְנָהּ וּבְבִתָּהּ׃

and-to-daughter-of-her and-to-son-of-her loved-of-her to-husband-of eye-of-her

וּבְשִׁלְיָתָהּ הַיּוֹצֵת ׀ מִבֵּין רַגְלֶיהָ

feet-of-her from-between the-one-coming and-to-afterbirth-her (57)

וּבְבָנֶיהָ אֲשֶׁר תֵּלֵד כִּי־ תֹאכְלֵם בְּחֹסֶר־ כֹּל

great in-want she-will-eat-them for she-bears whom and-to-children-of-her

בַּסָּתֶר בְּמָצוֹר וּבְמָצוֹק אֲשֶׁר יָצִיק לְךָ

on-you he-will-inflict that and-in-distress in-siege in-the-secret

אֹיִבְךָ בִּשְׁעָרֶיךָ׃ אִם־ לֹא תִשְׁמֹר לַעֲשׂוֹת אֶת־

*** to-follow you-are-careful not if (58) on-gates-of-you being-enemy-of-you

כָּל־ דִּבְרֵי הַתּוֹרָה הַזֹּאת הַכְּתוּבִים בַּסֵּפֶר הַזֶּה

the-this in-the-book the-ones-being-written the-this the-law words-of all-of

לְיִרְאָה אֶת־ הַשֵּׁם הַנִּכְבָּד וְהַנּוֹרָא הַזֶּה אֵת

*** the-this and-the-being-awesome the-being-glorious the-name *** to-revere

trust fall down. They will besiege all the cities throughout the land the LORD your God is giving you.

53Because of the suffering that your enemy will inflict on you during the siege, you will eat the fruit of the womb, the flesh of the sons and daughters the LORD your God has given you. 54Even the most gentle and sensitive man among you will have no compassion on his own brother or the wife he loves or his surviving children, 55and he will not give to one of them any of the flesh of his children that he is eating. It will be all he has left because of the suffering your enemy will inflict on you during the siege of all your cities. 56The most gentle and sensitive woman among you—so sensitive and gentle that she would not venture to touch the ground with the sole of her foot—will begrudge the husband she loves and her own son or daughter 57the afterbirth from her womb and the children she bears. For she intends to eat them secretly during the siege and in the distress that your enemy will inflict on you in your cities.

58If you do not carefully follow all the words of this law, which are written in this book, and do not revere this glorious and awesome name—

יְהוָה אֱלֹהֶיךָ׃ וְהִפְלָא יְהוָה אֶת־ מַכֹּתְךָ וְאֵת
and plagues-of-you *** Yahweh and-he-will-make-fearful (59) God-of-you Yahweh

מַכּוֹת זַרְעֶךָ מַכּוֹת גְּדֹלוֹת וְנֶאֱמָנוֹת
and-being-prolonged-ones harsh-ones disasters descendant-of-you plagues-of

וָחֳלָיִם רָעִים וְנֶאֱמָנִים׃ וְהֵשִׁיב בְּךָ
upon-you and-he-will-bring (60) and-lingering-ones severe-ones and-illnesses

אֵת כָּל־ מַדְוֵה מִצְרַיִם אֲשֶׁר יָגֹרְתָּ מִפְּנֵיהֶם וְדָבְקוּ
and-they-will-cling from-them you-dreaded that Egypt disease-of all-of ***

בָּךְ׃ גַּם כָּל־ חֳלִי וְכָל־ מַכָּה אֲשֶׁר לֹא
not that disaster and-every-of sickness every-of also (61) to-you

כָתוּב בְּסֵפֶר הַתּוֹרָה הַזֹּאת יַעְלֵם יְהוָה עָלֶיךָ
on-you Yahweh he-will-bring-them the-this the-Law in-Book-of being-recorded

עַד הִשָּׁמְדָךְ׃ וְנִשְׁאַרְתֶּם בִּמְתֵי מְעָט תַּחַת אֲשֶׁר
that because few as-men-of and-you-will-be-left (62) to-be-destroyed-you until

הֱיִיתֶם כְּכוֹכְבֵי הַשָּׁמַיִם לָרֹב כִּי־ לֹא שָׁמַעְתָּ בְּקוֹל
to-voice-of you-obeyed not but in-number the-skies as-stars-of you-were

יְהוָה אֱלֹהֶיךָ׃ וְהָיָה כַּאֲשֶׁר־ שָׂשׂ יְהוָה עֲלֵיכֶם
about-you Yahweh he-pleased just-as and-he-will-be (63) God-of-you Yahweh

לְהֵיטִיב אֶתְכֶם וּלְהַרְבּוֹת אֶתְכֶם כֵּן יָשִׂישׂ יְהוָה עֲלֵיכֶם
about-you Yahweh he-will-please so you and-to-increase you to-make-prosper

לְהַאֲבִיד אֶתְכֶם וּלְהַשְׁמִיד אֶתְכֶם וְנִסַּחְתֶּם מֵעַל הָאֲדָמָה
the-land from-in and-you-will-be-uprooted you and-to-destroy you to-ruin

אֲשֶׁר־ אַתָּה בָא־ שָׁמָּה לְרִשְׁתָּהּ׃ וֶהֱפִיצְךָ
then-he-will-scatter-you (64) to-possess-her to-there entering you that

יְהוָה בְּכָל־ הָעַמִּים מִקְצֵה הָאָרֶץ וְעַד־ קְצֵה
end-of even-to the-earth from-end-of the-nations among-all-of Yahweh

הָאָרֶץ וְעָבַדְתָּ שָּׁם אֱלֹהִים אֲחֵרִים אֲשֶׁר לֹא־ יָדַעְתָּ אַתָּה
you you-knew not that other-ones gods there and-you-will-worship the-earth

וַאֲבֹתֶיךָ עֵץ וָאָבֶן׃ וּבַגּוֹיִם הָהֵם לֹא
not the-those and-among-the-nations (65) and-stone wood or-fathers-of-you

תַרְגִּיעַ וְלֹא־ יִהְיֶה מָנוֹחַ לְכַף־ רַגְלֶךָ
foot-of-you for-sole-of resting-place he-will-be and-not you-will-repose

וְנָתַן יְהוָה לְךָ שָׁם לֵב רַגָּז וְכִלְיוֹן עֵינַיִם
eyes and-longing anxious mind there to-you Yahweh and-he-will-give

וְדַאֲבוֹן נָפֶשׁ׃ וְהָיוּ חַיֶּיךָ תְּלֻאִים
ones-being-in-suspense lives-of-you and-you-will-live (66) heart and-despairing

לְךָ מִנֶּגֶד וּפָחַדְתָּ לַיְלָה וְיוֹמָם וְלֹא תַאֲמִין
you-will-be-sure and-not and-by-day night and-you-will-dread in-front to-you

the LORD your God— [59]the LORD will send fearful plagues on you and your descendants, harsh and prolonged disasters, and severe and lingering illnesses. [60]He will bring upon you all the diseases of Egypt that you dreaded, and they will cling to you. [61]The LORD will also bring on you every kind of sickness and disaster not recorded in this Book of the Law until you are destroyed. [62]You who were as numerous as the stars in the sky will be left but few in number, because you did not obey the LORD your God. [63]Just as it pleased the LORD to make you prosper and increase in number, so it will please him to ruin and destroy you. You will be uprooted from the land you are entering to possess.

[64]Then the LORD will scatter you among all nations, from one end of the earth to the other. There you will worship other gods—gods of wood and stone, which neither you nor your fathers have known. [65]Among those nations you will find no repose, no resting place for the sole of your foot. There the LORD will give you an anxious mind, eyes weary with longing, and a despairing heart. [66]You will live in constant suspense, filled with dread both night and day,

בְּחַיֶּיךָ׃ בַּבֹּקֶר תֹּאמַר מִֽי־ יִתֵּן
he-would-come if-only! you-will-say in-the-morning (67) of-lives-of-you

עֶרֶב וּבָעֶרֶב תֹּאמַר מִֽי־ יִתֵּן בֹּקֶר
morning he-would-come if-only! you-will-say and-in-the-evening evening

מִפַּחַד לְבָבְךָ אֲשֶׁר תִּפְחָד וּמִמַּרְאֵה עֵינֶיךָ
eyes-of-you and-from-sight-of you-will-dread that heart-of-you from-terror-of

אֲשֶׁר תִּרְאֶה׃ וֶהֱשִׁיבְךָ יְהוָה ׀ מִצְרַיִם בָּאֳנִיּוֹת
in-ships Egypt Yahweh and-he-will-send-back-you (68) you-will-see that

בַּדֶּרֶךְ אֲשֶׁר אָמַרְתִּי לְךָ לֹא־ תֹסִיף עוֹד לִרְאֹתָהּ
to-see-her again you-should-repeat not to-you I-said that on-the-journey

וְהִתְמַכַּרְתֶּם שָׁם לְאֹיְבֶיךָ לַעֲבָדִים
as-male-slaves to-being-enemies-of-you there and-you-will-sell-yourselves

וְלִשְׁפָחוֹת וְאֵין קֹנֶה׃ אֵלֶּה דִבְרֵי הַבְּרִית
the-covenant terms-of these (69)* one-buying but-not and-as-female-slaves

אֲשֶׁר־ צִוָּה יְהוָה אֶת־ מֹשֶׁה לִכְרֹת אֶת־ בְּנֵי יִשְׂרָאֵל בְּאֶרֶץ
in-land-of Israel sons-of with to-make Moses *** Yahweh he-commanded that

מוֹאָב מִלְּבַד הַבְּרִית אֲשֶׁר־ כָּרַת אִתָּם בְּחֹרֵב׃
at-Horeb with-them he-made that the-covenant in-addition-to Moab

וַיִּקְרָא מֹשֶׁה אֶל־ כָּל־ יִשְׂרָאֵל וַיֹּאמֶר אֲלֵהֶם אַתֶּם רְאִיתֶם
you-saw you to-them and-he-said Israel all-of to Moses and-he-summoned (29:1)

אֵת כָּל־אֲשֶׁר עָשָׂה יְהוָה לְעֵינֵיכֶם בְּאֶרֶץ מִצְרַיִם לְפַרְעֹה
to-Pharaoh Egypt in-land-of before-eyes-of-you Yahweh he-did that all ***

וּלְכָל־ עֲבָדָיו וּלְכָל־ אַרְצוֹ׃ הַמַּסּוֹת
the-trials (2) land-of-him and-to-all-of officials-of-him and-to-all-of

הַגְּדֹלֹת אֲשֶׁר רָאוּ עֵינֶיךָ הָאֹתֹת וְהַמֹּפְתִים
and-the-wonders the-signs eyes-of-you they-saw that the-great-ones

הַגְּדֹלִים הָהֵם׃ וְלֹא־ נָתַן יְהוָה לָכֶם לֵב לָדַעַת
to-understand mind to-you Yahweh he-gave but-not (3) the-those the-great-ones

וְעֵינַיִם לִרְאוֹת וְאָזְנַיִם לִשְׁמֹעַ עַד הַיּוֹם הַזֶּה׃ וָאוֹלֵךְ אֶתְכֶם
you when-I-led (4) the-this the-day to to-hear or-ears to-see or-eyes

אַרְבָּעִים שָׁנָה בַּמִּדְבָּר לֹא־ בָלוּ שַׂלְמֹתֵיכֶם מֵעֲלֵיכֶם
from-on-you clothes-of-you they-wore-out not through-the-desert year forty

וְנַעַלְךָ לֹא־ בָלְתָה מֵעַל רַגְלֶךָ׃ לֶחֶם לֹא אֲכַלְתֶּם
you-ate not bread (5) foot-of-you from-on she-wore-out not and-sandal-of-you

וְיַיִן וְשֵׁכָר לֹא שְׁתִיתֶם לְמַעַן תֵּדְעוּ כִּי אֲנִי
I that you-might-know so-that you-drank not or-fermented-drink and-wine

יְהוָה אֱלֹהֵיכֶם׃ וַתָּבֹאוּ אֶל־ הַמָּקוֹם הַזֶּה וַיֵּצֵא
then-he-came-out the-this the-place to when-you-reached (6) God-of-you Yahweh

never sure of your life. 67In the
morning you will say, "If only
it were evening!" and in the
evening, "If only it were
morning!"—because of the terror that will fill your hearts
and the sights that your eyes
will see. 68The LORD will send
you back in ships to Egypt on
a journey I said you should
never make again. There you
will offer yourselves for sale to
your enemies as male and
female slaves, but no one will
buy you.

*Renewal of the Covenant*

29 These are the terms of
the covenant the LORD
commanded Moses to make
with the Israelites in Moab, in
addition to the covenant he
had made with them at Horeb.
2Moses summoned all the Israelites and said to them:

Your eyes have seen all that
the LORD did in Egypt to Pharaoh, to all his officials and to
all his land. 3With your own
eyes you saw those great trials,
those miraculous signs and
great wonders. 4But to this day
the LORD has not given you a
mind that understands or eyes
that see or ears that hear.
5During the forty years that I
led you through the desert,
your clothes did not wear out,
nor did the sandals on your
feet. 6You ate no bread and
drank no wine or other fermented drink. I did this so
that you might know that I am
the LORD your God.
7When you reached this

*The Hebrew numeration of chapter 29 begins with verse 2 in English; thus, there is a one-verse discrepancy throughout the chapter.

סִיחֹן מֶֽלֶךְ־ חֶשְׁבּוֹן וְעוֹג מֶֽלֶךְ־ הַבָּשָׁן לִקְרָאתֵנוּ לַמִּלְחָמָה
in-the-fight to-meet-us the-Bashan king-of and-Og Heshbon king-of Sihon

וַנַּכֵּם׃ וַנִּקַּח אֶת־ אַרְצָם וַנִּתְּנָהּ
and-we-gave-her land-of-them *** and-we-took (7) but-we-defeated-them

לְנַחֲלָה לָרְאוּבֵנִי וְלַגָּדִי וְלַחֲצִי שֵׁבֶט
tribe-of and-to-half-of and-to-the-Gadite to-the-Reubenite as-inheritance

הַֽמְנַשִּׁי׃ וּשְׁמַרְתֶּם אֶת־ דִּבְרֵי הַבְּרִית הַזֹּאת
the-this the-covenant terms-of *** now-you-be-careful (8) the-Manassite

וַעֲשִׂיתֶם אֹתָם לְמַעַן תַּשְׂכִּילוּ אֵת כָּל־ אֲשֶׁר תַּעֲשׂוּן׃ אַתֶּם
you (9) you-do that all *** you-may-prosper so-that them and-you-follow

נִצָּבִים הַיּוֹם כֻּלְּכֶם לִפְנֵי יְהוָה אֱלֹהֵיכֶם רָאשֵׁיכֶם
leaders-of-you God-of-you Yahweh before all-of-you the-day ones-standing

שִׁבְטֵיכֶם זִקְנֵיכֶם וְשֹׁטְרֵיכֶם כֹּל אִישׁ יִשְׂרָאֵל׃
Israel man-of every-of and-being-officials-of-you elders-of-you chiefs-of-you

טַפְּכֶם נְשֵׁיכֶם וְגֵרְךָ אֲשֶׁר בְּקֶרֶב מַחֲנֶיךָ
camps-of-you in-among who and-alien-of-you wives-of-you child-of-you (10)

מֵחֹטֵב עֵצֶיךָ עַד שֹׁאֵב מֵימֶיךָ׃
waters-of-you one-drawing-of to woods-of-you from-one-cutting-of

לְעָבְרְךָ בִּבְרִית יְהוָה אֱלֹהֶיךָ וּבְאָלָתוֹ
and-into-oath-of-him God-of-you Yahweh into-covenant-of to-enter-you (11)

אֲשֶׁר יְהוָה אֱלֹהֶיךָ כֹּרֵת עִמְּךָ הַיּוֹם׃ לְמַעַן הָקִים־ אֹתְךָ
you to-confirm in-order (12) the-day with-you making God-of-you Yahweh that

הַיּוֹם ׀ לוֹ לְעָם וְהוּא יִהְיֶה־ לְּךָ לֵאלֹהִים כַּאֲשֶׁר דִּבֶּר־
he-promised just-as as-God to-you he-will-be and-he as-people to-him the-day

לָךְ וְכַאֲשֶׁר נִשְׁבַּע לַאֲבֹתֶיךָ לְאַבְרָהָם לְיִצְחָק וּֽלְיַעֲקֹב׃
and-to-Jacob to-Isaac to-Abraham to-fathers-of-you he-swore and-just-as to-you

וְלֹא אִתְּכֶם לְבַדְּכֶם אָנֹכִי כֹּרֵת אֶת־ הַבְּרִית הַזֹּאת
the-this the-covenant *** making I by-selves-of-you with-you and-not (13)

וְאֶת־הָאָלָה הַזֹּאת׃ כִּי אֶת־ אֲשֶׁר יֶשְׁנוֹ פֹּה עִמָּנוּ
with-us here there-is-him whom with indeed (14) the-this the-oath and

עֹמֵד הַיּוֹם לִפְנֵי יְהוָה אֱלֹהֵינוּ וְאֵת אֲשֶׁר אֵינֶנּוּ פֹּה
here there-is-not-him whom and-with God-of-us Yahweh before the-day standing

עִמָּנוּ הַיּוֹם׃ כִּי־ אַתֶּם יְדַעְתֶּם אֵת אֲשֶׁר־יָשַׁבְנוּ בְּאֶרֶץ מִצְרָיִם
Egypt in-land-of we-lived how *** you-know you for (15) the-day with-us

וְאֵת אֲשֶׁר־ עָבַרְנוּ בְּקֶרֶב הַגּוֹיִם אֲשֶׁר עֲבַרְתֶּם׃
you-passed-through that the-nations through-midst-of we-passed how and

וַתִּרְאוּ אֶת־ שִׁקּוּצֵיהֶם וְאֵת גִּלֻּלֵיהֶם עֵץ
wood idols-of-them and detestable-images-of-them *** and-you-saw (16)

place, Sihon king of Heshbon and Og king of Bashan came out to fight against us, but we defeated them.
8 We took their land and gave it as an inheritance to the Reubenites, the Gadites and the half-tribe of Manasseh.

9 Carefully follow the terms of this covenant, so that you may prosper in everything you do.
10 All of you are standing today in the presence of the LORD your God—your leaders and chief men, your elders and officials, and all the other men of Israel,
11 together with your children and your wives, and the aliens living in your camps who chop your wood and carry your water.
12 You are standing here in order to enter into a covenant with the LORD your God, a covenant the LORD is making with you this day and sealing with an oath,
13 to confirm you this day as his people, that he may be your God as he promised you and as he swore to your fathers, Abraham, Isaac and Jacob.
14 I am making this covenant, with its oath, not only with you
15 who are standing here with us today in the presence of the LORD our God but also with those who are not here today.

16 You yourselves know how we lived in Egypt and how we passed through the countries on the way here.
17 You saw among them their detestable images and idols of wood and

*See the note on page 568.

וָאֶבֶן כֶּסֶף וְזָהָב אֲשֶׁר עִמָּהֶם׃ פֶּן־ יֵשׁ בָּכֶם אִישׁ
man among-you there-is not (17) among-them that and-gold silver and-stone

אוֹ־ אִשָּׁה אוֹ מִשְׁפָּחָה אוֹ־שֵׁבֶט אֲשֶׁר לְבָבוֹ פֹנֶה הַיּוֹם מֵעִם
from-with the-day turning heart-of-him that tribe or clan or woman or

יְהוָה אֱלֹהֵינוּ לָלֶכֶת לַעֲבֹד אֶת־ אֱלֹהֵי הַגּוֹיִם הָהֵם פֶּן־
not the-those the-nations gods-of *** to-worship to-go God-of-us Yahweh

יֵשׁ בָּכֶם שֹׁרֶשׁ פֹּרֶה רֹאשׁ וְלַעֲנָה׃ וְהָיָה
and-he-is (18) and-bitterness poison producing root-of among-you there-is

בְּשָׁמְעוֹ אֶת־ דִּבְרֵי הָאָלָה הַזֹּאת וְהִתְבָּרֵךְ
then-he-blesses-himself the-this the-oath words-of *** when-to-hear-him

בִּלְבָבוֹ לֵאמֹר שָׁלוֹם יִהְיֶה־ לִּי כִּי בִּשְׁרִרוּת
in-stubbornness-of though to-me he-will-be safety to-say in-heart-of-him

לִבִּי אֵלֵךְ לְמַעַן סְפוֹת הָרָוָה אֶת־הַצְּמֵאָה׃ לֹא־
not (19) the-dry *** watered-land to-bring-disaster so-that I-go heart-of-me

יֹאבֶה יְהוָה סְלֹחַ לוֹ כִּי אָז יֶעְשַׁן אַף־ יְהוָה
Yahweh wrath-of he-will-burn always for to-him to-forgive Yahwh he-will-want

וְקִנְאָתוֹ בָּאִישׁ הַהוּא וְרָבְצָה בּוֹ כָּל־
all-of on-him and-she-will-fall the-that against-the-man and-zeal-of-him

הָאָלָה הַכְּתוּבָה בַּסֵּפֶר הַזֶּה וּמָחָה יְהוָה
Yahweh and-he-will-blot-out the-this in-the-book the-being-written the-curse

אֶת־ שְׁמוֹ מִתַּחַת הַשָּׁמָיִם׃ וְהִבְדִּילוֹ יְהוָה
Yahweh and-he-will-single-out-him (20) the-heavens from-under name-of-him ***

לְרָעָה מִכֹּל שִׁבְטֵי יִשְׂרָאֵל כְּכֹל אָלוֹת הַבְּרִית
the-covenant curses-of as-all-of Israel tribes-of from-all-of for-disaster

הַכְּתוּבָה בְּסֵפֶר הַתּוֹרָה הַזֶּה׃ וְאָמַר
and-he-will-say (21) the-this the-Law in-Book-of the-being-written

הַדּוֹר הָאַחֲרוֹן בְּנֵיכֶם אֲשֶׁר יָקוּמוּ מֵאַחֲרֵיכֶם
from-after-you they-follow who children-of-you the-later the-generation

וְהַנָּכְרִי אֲשֶׁר יָבֹא מֵאֶרֶץ רְחוֹקָה וְרָאוּ אֶת־
*** when-they-see distant from-land he-comes who and-the-foreigner

מַכּוֹת הָאָרֶץ הַהִוא וְאֶת־ תַּחֲלֻאֶיהָ אֲשֶׁר־ חִלָּה יְהוָה
Yahweh he-afflicted that diseases-of-her and the-this the-land calamities-of

בָּהּ׃ גָּפְרִית וָמֶלַח שְׂרֵפָה כָל־ אַרְצָהּ לֹא תִזָּרַע
she-is-planted not land-of-her all-of burnt-waste and-salt sulfur (22) on-her

וְלֹא תַצְמִחַ וְלֹא־ יַעֲלֶה בָהּ כָּל־ עֵשֶׂב כְּמַהְפֵּכַת
as-destruction-of vegetation any-of on-her she-grows and-not she-sprouts and-not

סְדֹם וַעֲמֹרָה אַדְמָה וּצְבֹיִים אֲשֶׁר הָפַךְ יְהוָה בְּאַפּוֹ
in-anger-of-him Yahweh he-overthrew which and-Zeboiim Admah and-Gomorrah Sodom

stone, of silver and gold.
18 Make sure there is no man or woman, clan or tribe among you today whose heart turns away from the LORD our God to go and worship the gods of those nations; make sure there is no root among you that produces such bitter poison.
19 When such a person hears the words of this oath, he invokes a blessing on himself and therefore thinks, "I will be safe, even though I persist in going my own way." This will bring disaster on the watered land as well as the dry.[m]
20 The LORD will never be willing to forgive him; his wrath and zeal will burn against that man. All the curses written in this book will fall upon him, and the LORD will blot out his name from under heaven.
21 The LORD will single him out from all the tribes of Israel for disaster, according to all the curses of the covenant written in this Book of the Law.
22 Your children who follow you in later generations and foreigners who come from distant lands will see the calamities that have fallen on the land and the diseases with which the LORD has afflicted it.
23 The whole land will be a burning waste of salt and sulfur—nothing planted, nothing sprouting, no vegetation growing on it. It will be like the destruction of Sodom and Gomorrah, Admah and Zeboiim, which the LORD overthrew in fierce anger.
24 All the

*m19 Or way, in order to add drunkenness to thirst."*

*See the note on page 568.

°22 ק וצבוים

וּבַחֲמָתוֹ׃ וְאָמְרוּ כָּל־ הַגּוֹיִם עַל־ מֶה עָשָׂה
he-did why? for the-nations all-of and-they-will-ask (23) and-in-wrath-of-him

יְהוָה כָּכָה לָאָרֶץ הַזֹּאת מֶה חֳרִי הָאַף הַגָּדוֹל הַזֶּה׃
the-this the-fierce the-anger burning-of why? the-this to-the-land this Yahweh

וְאָמְרוּ עַל אֲשֶׁר עָזְבוּ אֶת־ בְּרִית יְהוָה
Yahweh covenant-of *** they-abandoned that because and-they-will-answer (24)

אֱלֹהֵי אֲבֹתָם אֲשֶׁר כָּרַת עִמָּם בְּהוֹצִיאוֹ אֹתָם
them when-to-bring-him with-them he-made that fathers-of-them God-of

מֵאֶרֶץ מִצְרָיִם׃ וַיֵּלְכוּ וַיַּעַבְדוּ אֱלֹהִים אֲחֵרִים
other-ones gods and-they-worshiped and-they-went-off (25) Egypt from-land-of

וַיִּשְׁתַּחֲוּוּ† לָהֶם אֱלֹהִים אֲשֶׁר לֹא־ יְדָעוּם וְלֹא חָלַק לָהֶם׃
to-them he-gave and-not they-knew-them not that gods to-them and-they-bowed

וַיִּחַר־ אַף יְהוָה בָּאָרֶץ הַהִוא לְהָבִיא עָלֶיהָ
on-her to-bring the-this against-the-land Yahweh anger-of so-he-burned (26)

אֶת־ כָּל־ הַקְּלָלָה הַכְּתוּבָה בַּסֵּפֶר הַזֶּה׃
the-this in-the-book the-being-written the-curse all-of ***

וַיִּתְּשֵׁם יְהוָה מֵעַל אַדְמָתָם בְּאַף וּבְחֵמָה
and-in-fury in-anger land-of-them from-in Yahweh and-he-uprooted-them (27)

וּבְקֶצֶף גָּדוֹל וַיַּשְׁלִכֵם אֶל־ אֶרֶץ אַחֶרֶת כַּיּוֹם הַזֶּה׃
the-this as-the-day another land into and-he-thrust-them great and-in-wrath

הַנִּסְתָּרֹת לַיהוָה אֱלֹהֵינוּ וְהַנִּגְלֹת
but-the-things-being-revealed God-of-us to-Yahweh the-things-being-hidden (28)

לָנוּ וּלְבָנֵינוּ עַד־ עוֹלָם לַעֲשׂוֹת אֶת־ כָּל־ דִּבְרֵי הַתּוֹרָה
the-law words-of all-of *** to-follow forever to and-to-children-of-us to-us

הַזֹּאת׃ וְהָיָה כִי־ יָבֹאוּ עָלֶיךָ כָּל־ הַדְּבָרִים
the-things all-of on-you they-come when and-he-will-be (30:1) the-this

הָאֵלֶּה הַבְּרָכָה וְהַקְּלָלָה אֲשֶׁר נָתַתִּי לְפָנֶיךָ וַהֲשֵׁבֹתָ אֶל־
to and-you-take before-you I-set that and-the-curse the-blessing the-these

לְבָבֶךָ בְּכָל־ הַגּוֹיִם אֲשֶׁר הִדִּיחֲךָ יְהוָה אֱלֹהֶיךָ
God-of-you Yahweh he-disperses-you where the-nations among-all-of heart-of-you

שָׁמָּה׃ וְשַׁבְתָּ עַד־ יְהוָה אֱלֹהֶיךָ וְשָׁמַעְתָּ בְקֹלוֹ
to-voice-of-him and-you-obey God-of-you Yahweh to and-you-return (2) to-there

כְּכֹל אֲשֶׁר־ אָנֹכִי מְצַוְּךָ הַיּוֹם אַתָּה וּבָנֶיךָ בְּכָל־
with-all-of and-children-of-you you the-day commanding-you I that as-all

לְבָבְךָ וּבְכָל־ נַפְשֶׁךָ׃ וְשָׁב יְהוָה
Yahweh then-he-will-restore (3) soul-of-you and-with-all-of heart-of-you

אֱלֹהֶיךָ אֶת־ שְׁבוּתְךָ וְרִחֲמֶךָ
and-he-will-have-compassion-on-you captivity-of-you *** God-of-you

nations will ask: "Why has the LORD done this to this land? Why this fierce, burning anger?"

25 And the answer will be: "It is because this people abandoned the covenant of the LORD, the God of their fathers, the covenant he made with them when he brought them out of Egypt. 26 They went off and worshiped other gods and bowed down to them, gods they did not know, gods he had not given them. 27 Therefore the LORD's anger burned against this land, so that he brought on it all the curses written in this book. 28 In furious anger and in great wrath the LORD uprooted them from their land and thrust them into another land, as it is now."

29 The secret things belong to the LORD our God, but the things revealed belong to us and to our children forever, that we may follow all the words of this law.

### *Prosperity After Turning to the LORD*

30 When all these blessings and curses I have set before you come upon you and you take them to heart wherever the LORD your God disperses you among the nations, 2 and when you and your children return to the LORD your God and obey him with all your heart and with all your soul according to everything I command you today, 3 then the LORD your God will restore your fortunes[n] and have compassion on you and

n3 Or *will bring you back from captivity*

*See the note on page 568.

†25 Most mss have no *dagesh* in the first *vav* (וו־).

וְשָׁב וְקִבֶּצְךָ מִכָּל־ הָעַמִּים אֲשֶׁר
where the-nations from-all-of and-he-will-gather-you and-he-will-restore

הֱפִיצְךָ יְהוָה אֱלֹהֶיךָ שָׁמָּה׃ אִם־ יִהְיֶה נִדַּחֲךָ
banishing-of-you he-is if (4) to-there God-of-you Yahweh he-scattered-you

בִּקְצֵה הַשָּׁמָיִם מִשָּׁם יְקַבֶּצְךָ יְהוָה אֱלֹהֶיךָ
God-of-you Yahweh he-will-gather-you from-there the-heavens to-end-of

וּמִשָּׁם יִקָּחֶךָ׃ וֶהֱבִיאֲךָ יְהוָה
Yahweh and-he-will-bring-back-you (5) he-will-bring-back-you and-from-there

אֱלֹהֶיךָ אֶל־ הָאָרֶץ אֲשֶׁר־ יָרְשׁוּ אֲבֹתֶיךָ
fathers-of-you they-possessed that the-land to God-of-you

וִירִשְׁתָּהּ וְהֵיטִבְךָ וְהִרְבְּךָ
and-he-will-increase-you and-he-will-make-prosper-you and-you-will-possess-her

מֵאֲבֹתֶיךָ׃ וּמָל יְהוָה אֱלֹהֶיךָ אֶת־
*** God-of-you Yahweh and-he-will-circumcise (6) more-than-fathers-of-you

לְבָבְךָ וְאֶת־ לְבַב זַרְעֶךָ לְאַהֲבָה אֶת־ יְהוָה אֱלֹהֶיךָ
God-of-you Yahweh *** to-love descendant-of-you heart-of and heart-of-you

בְּכָל־ לְבָבְךָ וּבְכָל־ נַפְשְׁךָ לְמַעַן חַיֶּיךָ׃
lives-of-you so-that soul-of-you and-with-all-of heart-of-you with-all-of

וְנָתַן יְהוָה אֱלֹהֶיךָ אֵת כָּל־ הָאָלוֹת הָאֵלֶּה עַל־
on the-these the-curses all-of *** God-of-you Yahweh and-he-will-put (7)

אֹיְבֶיךָ וְעַל־ שֹׂנְאֶיךָ אֲשֶׁר רְדָפוּךָ׃
they-persecute-you who ones-hating-you and-on being-enemies-of-you

וְאַתָּה תָשׁוּב וְשָׁמַעְתָּ בְּקוֹל יְהוָה
Yahweh to-voice-of and-you-will-obey you-will-return and-you (8)

וְעָשִׂיתָ אֶת־ כָּל־ מִצְוֹתָיו אֲשֶׁר אָנֹכִי מְצַוְּךָ הַיּוֹם׃
the-day giving-you I that commands-of-him all-of *** and-you-will-follow

וְהוֹתִירְךָ יְהוָה אֱלֹהֶיךָ בְּכֹל ׀ מַעֲשֵׂה
work-of in-all-of God-of-you Yahweh then-he-will-make-prosper-you (9)

יָדֶךָ בִּפְרִי בִטְנְךָ וּבִפְרִי בְהֶמְתְּךָ וּבִפְרִי
and-in-crop-of stock-of-you and-in-young-of womb-of-you in-fruit-of hand-of-you

אַדְמָתְךָ לְטֹבָה כִּי ׀ יָשׁוּב יְהוָה לָשׂוּשׂ עָלֶיךָ לְטוֹב
to-prosperity in-you to-delight Yahweh he-will-return then for-good land-of-you

כַּאֲשֶׁר־ שָׂשׂ עַל־ אֲבֹתֶיךָ׃ כִּי תִשְׁמַע בְּקוֹל יְהוָה
Yahweh to-voice-of you-obey if (10) fathers-of-you in he-delighted just-as

אֱלֹהֶיךָ לִשְׁמֹר מִצְוֹתָיו וְחֻקֹּתָיו הַכְּתוּבָה
the-being-written and-decrees-of-him commands-of-him to-keep God-of-you

בְּסֵפֶר הַתּוֹרָה הַזֶּה כִּי תָשׁוּב אֶל־ יְהוָה אֱלֹהֶיךָ בְּכָל־
with-all-of God-of-you Yahweh to you-turn if the-this the-Law in-Book-of

gather you again from all the nations where he scattered you. [4]Even if you have been banished to the most distant land under the heavens, from there the LORD your God will gather you and bring you back. [5]He will bring you to the land that belonged to your fathers, and you will take possession of it. He will make you more prosperous and numerous than your fathers. [6]The LORD your God will circumcise your hearts and the hearts of your descendants, so that you may love him with all your heart and with all your soul, and live. [7]The LORD your God will put all these curses on your enemies who hate and persecute you. [8]You will again obey the LORD and follow all his commands I am giving you today. [9]Then the LORD your God will make you most prosperous in all the work of your hands and in the fruit of your womb, the young of your livestock and the crops of your land. The LORD will again delight in you and make you prosperous, just as he delighted in your fathers, [10]if you obey the LORD your God and keep his commands and decrees that are written in this Book of the Law and turn to the LORD your God with all

לְבָבְךָ וּבְכָל־ נַפְשֶׁךָ׃ כִּי הַמִּצְוָה הַזֹּאת אֲשֶׁר
that the-this the-command now (11) soul-of-you and-with-all-of heart-of-you

אָנֹכִי מְצַוְּךָ הַיּוֹם לֹא־ נִפְלֵאת הִוא מִמְּךָ וְלֹא רְחֹקָה
distant and-not for-you she being-too-difficult not the-day commanding-you I

הִוא׃ לֹא בַשָּׁמַיִם הִוא לֵאמֹר מִי יַעֲלֶה־ לָּנוּ
for-us he-will-ascend who? to-say she in-the-heavens not (12) she

הַשָּׁמַיְמָה וְיִקָּחֶהָ לָּנוּ וְיַשְׁמִעֵנוּ אֹתָהּ
her and-he-will-proclaim-to-us for-us so-he-will-get-her into-the-heavens

וְנַעֲשֶׂנָּה׃ וְלֹא־ מֵעֵבֶר לַיָּם הִוא לֵאמֹר מִי
who? to-say she of-the-sea on-beyond and-not (13) so-we-may-obey-her

יַעֲבָר־ לָנוּ אֶל־ עֵבֶר הַיָּם וְיִקָּחֶהָ לָּנוּ
for-us so-he-will-get-her the-sea beyond to for-us he-will-cross

וְיַשְׁמִעֵנוּ אֹתָהּ וְנַעֲשֶׂנָּה׃ כִּי־ קָרוֹב אֵלֶיךָ
to-you near for (14) so-we-may-obey-her her and-he-will-proclaim-to-us

הַדָּבָר מְאֹד בְּפִיךָ וּבִלְבָבְךָ לַעֲשֹׂתוֹ׃ רְאֵה נָתַתִּי
I-set see! (15) to-obey-him and-in-heart-of-you in-mouth-of-you very the-word

לְפָנֶיךָ הַיּוֹם אֶת־ הַחַיִּים וְאֶת־ הַטּוֹב וְאֶת־ הַמָּוֶת וְאֶת־
and the-death and the-prosperity and the-lives *** the-day before-you

הָרָע׃ אֲשֶׁר אָנֹכִי מְצַוְּךָ הַיּוֹם לְאַהֲבָה אֶת־ יְהוָה
Yahweh *** to-love the-day commanding-you I for (16) the-destruction

אֱלֹהֶיךָ לָלֶכֶת בִּדְרָכָיו וְלִשְׁמֹר מִצְוֹתָיו
commands-of-him and-to-keep in-ways-of-him to-walk God-of-you

וְחֻקֹּתָיו וּמִשְׁפָּטָיו וְחָיִיתָ וְרָבִיתָ
and-you-will-increase then-you-will-live and-laws-of-him and-decrees-of-him

וּבֵרַכְךָ יְהוָה אֱלֹהֶיךָ בָּאָרֶץ אֲשֶׁר־ אַתָּה בָא־
entering you where in-the-land God-of-you Yahweh and-he-will-bless-you

שָׁמָּה לְרִשְׁתָּהּ׃ וְאִם־ יִפְנֶה לְבָבְךָ וְלֹא
and-not heart-of-you he-turns-away but-if (17) to-possess-her to-there

תִשְׁמָע וְנִדַּחְתָּ וְהִשְׁתַּחֲוִיתָ לֵאלֹהִים אֲחֵרִים
other-ones to-gods and-you-bow-down and-you-are-drawn-away you-obey

וַעֲבַדְתָּם׃ הִגַּדְתִּי לָכֶם הַיּוֹם כִּי אָבֹד
to-be-destroyed that the-day to-you I-declare (18) and-you-worship-them

תֹּאבֵדוּן לֹא־ תַאֲרִיכֻן יָמִים עַל־ הָאֲדָמָה אֲשֶׁר אַתָּה
you that the-land in days you-will-have-long not you-will-be-destroyed

עֹבֵר אֶת־ הַיַּרְדֵּן לָבֹא שָׁמָּה לְרִשְׁתָּהּ׃ הַעִידֹתִי
I-call-witness (19) to-possess-her to-there to-enter the-Jordan *** crossing

בָכֶם הַיּוֹם אֶת־ הַשָּׁמַיִם וְאֶת־ הָאָרֶץ הַחַיִּים וְהַמָּוֶת
and-the-death the-lives the-earth and the-heavens *** the-day against-you

your heart and with all your
soul.

*The Offer of Life or Death*

11 Now what I am command-
ing you today is not too
difficult for you or beyond
your reach. 12 It is not up in
heaven, so that you have to
ask, "Who will ascend into
heaven to get it and proclaim
it to us so we may obey it?"
13 Nor is it beyond the sea, so
that you have to ask, "Who
will cross the sea to get it and
proclaim it to us so we may
obey it?" 14 No, the word is
very near you; it is in your
mouth and in your heart so
you may obey it.

15 See, I set before you today
life and prosperity, death and
destruction. 16 For I command
you today to love the LORD
your God, to walk in his ways,
and to keep his commands,
decrees and laws; then you
will live and increase, and the
LORD your God will bless you
in the land you are entering to
possess.

17 But if your heart turns
away and you are not obedient, and if you are drawn
away to bow down to other
gods and worship them, 18 I declare to you this day that you
will certainly be destroyed.
You will not live long in the
land you are crossing the Jordan to enter and possess.

19 This day I call heaven and
earth as witnesses against you
that I have set before you life

נָתַתִּי לְפָנֶיךָ הַבְּרָכָה וְהַקְּלָלָה וּבָחַרְתָּ בַּחַיִּים
to-the-lives now-you-choose and-the-curse the-blessing before-you I-set

לְמַעַן תִּחְיֶה אַתָּה וְזַרְעֶךָ׃ לְאַהֲבָה אֶת־יְהוָה אֱלֹהֶיךָ
God-of-you Yahweh *** to-love (20) and-child-of-you you you-may-live so-that

לִשְׁמֹעַ בְּקֹלוֹ וּלְדָבְקָה־בוֹ כִּי הוּא חַיֶּיךָ
lives-of-you he for to-him and-to-hold-fast to-voice-of-him to-listen

וְאֹרֶךְ יָמֶיךָ לָשֶׁבֶת עַל־הָאֲדָמָה אֲשֶׁר נִשְׁבַּע יְהוָה
Yahweh he-swore that the-land in to-dwell days-of-you and-length-of

לַאֲבֹתֶיךָ לְאַבְרָהָם לְיִצְחָק וּלְיַעֲקֹב לָתֵת לָהֶם׃
to-them to-give and-to-Jacob to-Isaac to-Abraham to-fathers-of-you

וַיֵּלֶךְ מֹשֶׁה וַיְדַבֵּר אֶת־הַדְּבָרִים הָאֵלֶּה אֶל־כָּל־
all-of to the-these the-words *** and-he-spoke Moses then-he-went-out (31:1)

יִשְׂרָאֵל׃ וַיֹּאמֶר אֲלֵהֶם בֶּן־מֵאָה וְעֶשְׂרִים שָׁנָה אָנֹכִי הַיּוֹם
the-day I year and-twenty hundred son-of to-them and-he-said (2) Israel

לֹא־אוּכַל עוֹד לָצֵאת וְלָבוֹא וַיהוָה אָמַר אֵלַי לֹא
not to-me he-said and-Yahweh and-to-come-in to-go-out longer I-am-able not

תַעֲבֹר אֶת־הַיַּרְדֵּן הַזֶּה׃ יְהוָה אֱלֹהֶיךָ הוּא ׀ עֹבֵר
crossing he God-of-you Yahweh (3) the-this the-Jordan *** you-shall-cross

לְפָנֶיךָ הוּא־יַשְׁמִיד אֶת־הַגּוֹיִם הָאֵלֶּה מִלְּפָנֶיךָ
from-before-you the-these the-nations *** he-will-destroy he ahead-of-you

וִירִשְׁתָּם יְהוֹשֻׁעַ הוּא עֹבֵר לְפָנֶיךָ כַּאֲשֶׁר דִּבֶּר
he-said just-as ahead-of-you crossing he Joshua and-you-will-possess-them

יְהוָה׃ וְעָשָׂה יְהוָה לָהֶם כַּאֲשֶׁר עָשָׂה לְסִיחוֹן וּלְעוֹג
and-to-Og to-Sihon he-did just-as to-them Yahweh and-he-will-do (4) Yahweh

מַלְכֵי הָאֱמֹרִי וּלְאַרְצָם אֲשֶׁר הִשְׁמִיד אֹתָם׃
them he-destroyed that and-to-land-of-them the-Amorite kings-of

וּנְתָנָם יְהוָה לִפְנֵיכֶם וַעֲשִׂיתֶם לָהֶם
to-them and-you-must-do over-to-you Yahweh and-he-will-deliver-them (5)

כְּכָל־הַמִּצְוָה אֲשֶׁר צִוִּיתִי אֶתְכֶם׃ חִזְקוּ וְאִמְצוּ
and-be-courageous! be-strong! (6) you I-commanded that the-command as-all-of

אַל־תִּירְאוּ וְאַל־תַּעַרְצוּ מִפְּנֵיהֶם כִּי ׀ יְהוָה אֱלֹהֶיךָ
God-of-you Yahweh for because-of-them you-be-terrified and-not you-fear not

הוּא הַהֹלֵךְ עִמָּךְ לֹא יַרְפְּךָ וְלֹא יַעַזְבֶךָּ׃
he-will-forsake-you and-not he-will-leave-you not with-you the-one-going he

וַיִּקְרָא מֹשֶׁה לִיהוֹשֻׁעַ וַיֹּאמֶר אֵלָיו לְעֵינֵי כָל־
all-of before-eyes-of to-him and-he-said to-Joshua Moses then-he-summoned (7)

יִשְׂרָאֵל חֲזַק וֶאֱמָץ כִּי אַתָּה תָּבוֹא אֶת־הָעָם
the-people with you-must-go you for and-be-courageous! be-strong! Israel

and death, blessings and curses. Now choose life, so that you and your children may live [20]and that you may love the LORD your God, listen to his voice, and hold fast to him. For the LORD is your life, and he will give you many years in the land he swore to give to your fathers, Abraham, Isaac and Jacob.

*Joshua to Succeed Moses*

31 Then Moses went out and spoke these words to all Israel: [2]"I am now a hundred and twenty years old and I am no longer able to lead you. The LORD has said to me, 'You shall not cross the Jordan.' [3]The LORD your God himself will cross over ahead of you. He will destroy these nations before you, and you will take possession of their land. Joshua also will cross over ahead of you, as the LORD said. [4]And the LORD will do to them what he did to Sihon and Og, the kings of the Amorites, whom he destroyed along with their land. [5]The LORD will deliver them to you, and you must do to them all that I have commanded you. [6]Be strong and courageous. Do not be afraid or terrified because of them, for the LORD your God goes with you; he will never leave you nor forsake you."

[7]Then Moses summoned Joshua and said to him in the presence of all Israel, "Be strong and courageous, for you must go with this people

הַזֶּה אֶל־ הָאָרֶץ אֲשֶׁר נִשְׁבַּע יְהוָה לַאֲבֹתָם לָתֵת
to-give to-fathers-of-them Yahweh he-swore that the-land into the-this

לָהֶם וְאַתָּה תַּנְחִילֶנָּה אוֹתָם׃ וַיהוָה הוּא ׀
he and-Yahweh (8) to-them you-must-divide-as-inheritance-her and-you to-them

הַהֹלֵךְ לְפָנֶיךָ הוּא יִהְיֶה עִמָּךְ לֹא יַרְפְּךָ וְלֹא
and-not he-will-leave-you not with-you he-will-be he before-you the-one-going

יַעַזְבֶךָּ לֹא תִירָא וְלֹא תֵחָת׃ וַיִּכְתֹּב
so-he-wrote (9) you-be-discouraged and-not you-fear not he-will-forsake-you

מֹשֶׁה אֶת־ הַתּוֹרָה הַזֹּאת וַיִּתְּנָהּ אֶל־ הַכֹּהֲנִים בְּנֵי לֵוִי
Levi sons-of the-priests to and-he-gave-her the-this the-law *** Moses

הַנֹּשְׂאִים אֶת־ אֲרוֹן בְּרִית יְהוָה וְאֶל־ כָּל־ זִקְנֵי
elders-of all-of and-to Yahweh covenant-of ark-of *** the-ones-carrying

יִשְׂרָאֵל׃ וַיְצַו מֹשֶׁה אוֹתָם לֵאמֹר מִקֵּץ ׀ שֶׁבַע שָׁנִים
years seven at-end-of to-say them Moses then-he-commanded (10) Israel

בְּמֹעֵד שְׁנַת הַשְּׁמִטָּה בְּחַג הַסֻּכּוֹת׃
the-Tabernacles during-Feast-of the-cancel-of-debt year-of at-time-of

בְּבוֹא כָל־ יִשְׂרָאֵל לֵרָאוֹת אֶת־ פְּנֵי יְהוָה אֱלֹהֶיךָ
God-of-you Yahweh before *** to-appear Israel all-of when-to-come (11)

בַּמָּקוֹם אֲשֶׁר יִבְחָר תִּקְרָא אֶת־ הַתּוֹרָה הַזֹּאת נֶגֶד
before the-this the-law *** you-shall-read he-will-choose that at-the-place

כָּל־ יִשְׂרָאֵל בְּאָזְנֵיהֶם׃ הַקְהֵל אֶת־ הָעָם הָאֲנָשִׁים
the-men the-people *** assemble! (12) in-ears-of-them Israel all-of

וְהַנָּשִׁים וְהַטַּף וְגֵרְךָ אֲשֶׁר בִּשְׁעָרֶיךָ לְמַעַן
so-that in-gates-of-you who and-alien-of-you and-the-child and-the-women

יִשְׁמְעוּ וּלְמַעַן יִלְמְדוּ וְיָרְאוּ אֶת־ יְהוָה
Yahweh *** so-they-will-fear they-can-learn and-so-that they-can-listen

אֱלֹהֵיכֶם וְשָׁמְרוּ לַעֲשׂוֹת אֶת־ כָּל־ דִּבְרֵי הַתּוֹרָה
the-law words-of all-of *** to-follow so-they-will-be-careful God-of-you

הַזֹּאת׃ וּבְנֵיהֶם אֲשֶׁר לֹא־ יָדְעוּ יִשְׁמְעוּ
they-must-hear they-know not who and-children-of-them (13) the-this

וְלָמְדוּ לְיִרְאָה אֶת־ יְהוָה אֱלֹהֵיכֶם כָּל־ הַיָּמִים אֲשֶׁר אַתֶּם
you that the-days all-of God-of-you Yahweh *** to-fear and-they-must-learn

חַיִּים עַל־ הָאֲדָמָה אֲשֶׁר אַתֶּם עֹבְרִים אֶת־ הַיַּרְדֵּן שָׁמָּה
to-there the-Jordan *** ones-crossing you that the-land in ones-alive

לְרִשְׁתָּהּ׃ וַיֹּאמֶר יְהוָה אֶל־ מֹשֶׁה הֵן קָרְבוּ
they-are-near see! Moses to Yahweh and-he-said (14) to-possess-her

יָמֶיךָ לָמוּת קְרָא אֶת־ יְהוֹשֻׁעַ וְהִתְיַצְּבוּ בְּאֹהֶל מוֹעֵד
Meeting at-Tent-of and-present-yourselves! Joshua *** call! do-die days-of-you

into the land that the LORD swore to their forefathers to give them, and you must divide it among them as their inheritance. 8The LORD himself goes before you and will be with you; he will never leave you nor forsake you. Do not be afraid; do not be discouraged."

*The Reading of the Law*

9So Moses wrote down this law and gave it to the priests, the sons of Levi, who carried the ark of the covenant of the LORD, and to all the elders of Israel. 10Then Moses commanded them: "At the end of every seven years, in the year for canceling debts, during the Feast of Tabernacles, 11when all Israel comes to appear before the LORD your God at the place he will choose, you shall read this law before them in their hearing. 12Assemble the people—men, women and children, and the aliens living in your towns—so they can listen and learn to fear the LORD your God and follow carefully all the words of this law. 13Their children, who do not know this law, must hear it and learn to fear the LORD your God as long as you live in the land you are crossing the Jordan to possess."

*Israel's Rebellion Predicted*

14The LORD said to Moses, "Now the day of your death is near. Call Joshua and present yourselves at the Tent of Meeting, where I will commission

וַאֲצַוֶּנּוּ וַיֵּלֶךְ מֹשֶׁה וִיהוֹשֻׁעַ וַיִּתְיַצְּבוּ
and-they-presented-selves and-Joshua Moses so-he-came and-I-will-commission-him

בְּאֹהֶל מוֹעֵד׃ וַיֵּרָא יְהוָה בָּאֹהֶל בְּעַמּוּד עָנָן
cloud in-pillar-of at-the-Tent Yahweh then-he-appeared (15) Meeting at-Tent-of

וַיַּעֲמֹד עַמּוּד הֶעָנָן עַל־ פֶּתַח הָאֹהֶל׃ וַיֹּאמֶר
and-he-said (16) the-Tent entrance-of over the-cloud pillar-of and-he-stood

יְהוָה אֶל־ מֹשֶׁה הִנְּךָ שֹׁכֵב עִם־ אֲבֹתֶיךָ וְקָם
and-he-will-rise fathers-of-you with resting see-you! Moses to Yahweh

הָעָם הַזֶּה וְזָנָה ׀ אַחֲרֵי ׀ אֱלֹהֵי נֵכַר־ הָאָרֶץ
the-land foreign-of gods-of after and-he-will-prostitute the-this the-people

אֲשֶׁר הוּא בָא־ שָׁמָּה בְּקִרְבּוֹ וַעֲזָבַנִי וְהֵפֵר
and-he-will-break and-he-will-forsake-me in-among-him to-there entering he that

אֶת־ בְּרִיתִי אֲשֶׁר כָּרַתִּי אִתּוֹ׃ וְחָרָה אַפִּי
anger-of-me and-he-will-burn (17) with-him I-made that covenant-of-me ***

בוֹ בַיּוֹם־ הַהוּא וַעֲזַבְתִּים וְהִסְתַּרְתִּי
and-I-will-hide and-I-will-forsake-them the-that on-the-day against-him

פָנַי מֵהֶם וְהָיָה לֶאֱכֹל וּמְצָאֻהוּ
and-they-will-come-on-him to-destroy and-he-will-be from-them faces-of-me

רָעוֹת רַבּוֹת וְצָרוֹת וְאָמַר בַּיּוֹם הַהוּא הֲלֹא
not? the-that on-the-day and-he-will-ask and-difficulties many disasters

עַל כִּי־ אֵין אֱלֹהַי בְּקִרְבִּי מְצָאוּנִי הָרָעוֹת
the-disasters they-came-on-me in-midst-of-me God-of-me not because for

הָאֵלֶּה׃ וְאָנֹכִי הַסְתֵּר אַסְתִּיר פָּנַי בַּיּוֹם הַהוּא
the-that on-the-day faces-of-me I-will-hide to-hide and-I (18) the-these

עַל כָּל־ הָרָעָה אֲשֶׁר עָשָׂה כִּי פָנָה אֶל־ אֱלֹהִים אֲחֵרִים׃
other-ones gods to he-turned when he-did that the-wickedness all-of for

וְעַתָּה כִּתְבוּ לָכֶם אֶת־ הַשִּׁירָה הַזֹּאת וְלַמְּדָהּ אֶת־ בְּנֵי־
sons-of *** and-teach-her! the-this the-song *** for-you write! and-now (19)

יִשְׂרָאֵל שִׂימָהּ בְּפִיהֶם לְמַעַן תִּהְיֶה־ לִּי הַשִּׁירָה הַזֹּאת
the-this the-song for-me she-may-be so-that in-mouth-of-them put-her! Israel

לְעֵד בִּבְנֵי יִשְׂרָאֵל׃ כִּי־ אֲבִיאֶנּוּ אֶל־ הָאֲדָמָה ׀
the-land into I-bring-him when (20) Israel against-sons-of as-witness

אֲשֶׁר־ נִשְׁבַּעְתִּי לַאֲבֹתָיו זָבַת חָלָב וּדְבַשׁ וְאָכַל
and-he-eats and-honey milk flowing-of to-fathers-of-him I-promised that

וְשָׂבַע וְדָשֵׁן וּפָנָה אֶל־ אֱלֹהִים אֲחֵרִים
other-ones gods to then-he-will-turn and-he-thrives and-he-is-full

וַעֲבָדוּם וְנִאֲצוּנִי וְהֵפֵר אֶת־
*** and-he-will-break and-they-will-reject-me and-they-will-worship-them

him." So Moses and Joshua came and presented themselves at the Tent of Meeting.
15Then the LORD appeared at the Tent in a pillar of cloud, and the cloud stood over the entrance to the Tent.
16And the LORD said to Moses: "You are going to rest with your fathers, and these people will soon prostitute themselves to the foreign gods of the land they are entering. They will forsake me and break the covenant I made with them.
17On that day I will become angry with them and forsake them; I will hide my face from them, and they will be destroyed. Many disasters and difficulties will come upon them, and on that day they will ask, 'Have not these disasters come upon us because our God is not with us?'
18And I will certainly hide my face on that day because of all their wickedness in turning to other gods.
19"Now write down for yourselves this song and teach it to the Israelites and have them sing it, so that it may be a witness for me against them.
20When I have brought them into the land flowing with milk and honey, the land I promised on oath to their forefathers, and when they eat their fill and thrive, they will turn to other gods and worship them, rejecting me and

בְּרִיתִֽי׃ וְהָיָ֞ה (21) כִּי־ תִמְצֶ֨אןָ אֹתֹ֜ו רָעֹ֤ות רַבֹּות֙
*covenant-of-me — (21) and-he-will-be — when — they-come — upon-him — disasters — many*

וְצָרֹ֔ות וְעָֽנְתָה֩ הַשִּׁירָ֨ה הַזֹּ֤את לְפָנָיו֙
*and-difficulties — then-she-will-testify — the-song — the-this — against-him*

לְעֵ֔ד כִּ֛י לֹ֥א תִשָּׁכַ֖ח מִפִּ֣י זַרְעֹ֑ו
*as-witness — for — not — she-will-be-forgotten — from-mouth-of — descendant-of-him*

כִּ֣י יָדַ֗עְתִּי אֶת־ יִצְרֹו֙ אֲשֶׁ֨ר ה֤וּא עֹשֶׂה֙ הַיֹּ֔ום בְּטֶ֖רֶם אֲבִיאֶ֑נּוּ
*for — I-know — *** — way-of-him — that — he — doing — the-day — even-before — I-bring-him*

אֶל־ הָאָ֖רֶץ אֲשֶׁ֣ר נִשְׁבָּ֑עְתִּי (22) וַיִּכְתֹּ֥ב מֹשֶׁ֛ה אֶת־ הַשִּׁירָ֥ה הַזֹּ֖את
*into — the-land — that — I-promised — (22) so-he-wrote — Moses — *** — the-song — the-this*

בַּיֹּ֣ום הַה֑וּא וַֽיְלַמְּדָ֖הּ אֶת־ בְּנֵ֥י יִשְׂרָאֵֽל׃ (23) וַיְצַ֞ו
*on-the-day — the-that — and-he-taught-her — *** — sons-of — Israel — (23) and-he-commanded*

אֶת־ יְהֹושֻׁ֣עַ בִּן־ נ֗וּן וַיֹּ֙אמֶר֙ חֲזַ֣ק וֶאֱמָ֔ץ כִּ֣י אַתָּ֗ה
*** — Joshua — son-of — Nun — and-he-said — be-strong! — and-be-courageous! — for — you*

תָּבִיא֙ אֶת־ בְּנֵ֣י יִשְׂרָאֵ֔ל אֶל־ הָאָ֖רֶץ אֲשֶׁר־ נִשְׁבַּ֣עְתִּי לָהֶ֑ם
*you-will-bring — *** — sons-of — Israel — into — the-land — that — I-promised — to-them*

וְאָנֹכִ֖י אֶֽהְיֶ֥ה עִמָּֽךְ׃ (24) וַיְהִ֣י ׀ כְּכַלֹּ֣ות מֹשֶׁ֗ה לִכְתֹּ֛ב אֶת־
*and-I — I-will-be — with-you — (24) and-he-was — after-to-finish — Moses — to-write — ****

דִּבְרֵ֥י הַתֹּורָֽה־ הַזֹּ֖את עַל־ סֵ֑פֶר עַ֖ד תֻּמָּֽם׃ (25) וַיְצַ֤ו
*words-of — the-law — the-this — in book — until — to-end-them — (25) then-he-commanded*

מֹשֶׁה֙ אֶת־ הַלְוִיִּ֔ם נֹ֥שְׂאֵ֛י אֲרֹ֥ון בְּרִית־ יְהוָ֖ה לֵאמֹֽר׃
*Moses — *** — the-Levites — ones-carrying-of — ark-of — covenant-of — Yahweh — to-say:*

(26) לָקֹ֗חַ אֵ֣ת סֵ֤פֶר הַתֹּורָה֙ הַזֶּ֔ה וְשַׂמְתֶּ֣ם אֹתֹ֔ו מִצַּ֛ד
*(26) to-take — *** — Book-of — the-Law — the-this — and-you-place — him — at-side-of*

אֲרֹ֥ון בְּרִית־ יְהוָ֖ה אֱלֹהֵיכֶ֑ם וְהָֽיָה־ שָׁ֥ם בְּךָ֖
*ark-of — covenant-of — Yahweh — God-of-you — and-he-will-remain — there — against-you*

לְעֵֽד׃ (27) כִּ֣י אָנֹכִ֤י יָדַ֙עְתִּי֙ אֶֽת־ מֶרְיְךָ֔ וְאֶֽת־ עָרְפְּךָ֖ הַקָּשֶׁ֑ה
*as-witness — (27) for — I — I-know — *** — rebellion-of-you — and — neck-of-you — the-stiff*

הֵ֣ן בְּעֹודֶ֨נִּי֙ חַ֤י עִמָּכֶם֙ הַיֹּ֔ום מַמְרִ֥ים הֱיִתֶ֖ם עִם־ יְהוָ֑ה
*see! — if-still-me — alive — with-you — the-day — ones-rebelling — you-are — against — Yahweh*

וְאַ֖ף כִּי־ אַחֲרֵ֥י מֹותִֽי׃ (28) הַקְהִ֣ילוּ אֵלַ֗י אֶת־
*then-how-much-more? — when — after — death-of-me — (28) assemble! — before-me — ****

כָּל־ זִקְנֵ֥י שִׁבְטֵיכֶ֖ם וְשֹׁטְרֵיכֶ֑ם וַאֲדַבְּרָ֣ה
*all-of — elders-of — tribes-of-you — and-being-officials-of-you — so-I-can-speak*

בְאָזְנֵיהֶ֗ם אֵ֤ת הַדְּבָרִים֙ הָאֵ֔לֶּה וְאָעִ֣ידָה בָּ֔ם
*in-ears-of-them — *** — the-words — the-these — so-I-can-call-witness — against-them*

אֶת־ הַשָּׁמַ֖יִם וְאֶת־ הָאָֽרֶץ׃ (29) כִּ֣י יָדַ֗עְתִּי אַחֲרֵ֤י מֹותִי֙ כִּֽי־
*** — the-heavens — and — the-earth — (29) for — I-know — after — death-of-me — that*

breaking my covenant. 21And when many disasters and difficulties come upon them, this song will testify against them, because it will not be forgotten by their descendants. I know what they are disposed to do, even before I bring them into the land I promised them on oath." 22So Moses wrote down this song that day and taught it to the Israelites.

23The LORD gave this command to Joshua son of Nun: "Be strong and courageous, for you will bring the Israelites into the land I promised them on oath, and I myself will be with you."

24After Moses finished writing in a book the words of this law from beginning to end, 25he gave this command to the Levites who carried the ark of the covenant of the LORD: 26"Take this Book of the Law and place it beside the ark of the covenant of the LORD your God. There it will remain as a witness against you. 27For I know how rebellious and stiff-necked you are. If you have been rebellious against the LORD while I am still alive and with you, how much more will you rebel after I die! 28Assemble before me all the elders of your tribes and all your officials, so that I can speak these words in their hearing and call heaven and earth to testify against them. 29For I know that after my death you are sure to become utterly corrupt and to turn from the way I have commanded you. In days to come,

הַשְׁחֵת תַּשְׁחִתוּן וְסַרְתֶּם מִן־הַדֶּרֶךְ אֲשֶׁר
that the-way from and-you-will-turn you-will-become-corrupt to-be-corrupt

צִוִּיתִי אֶתְכֶם וְקָרָאת אֶתְכֶם הָרָעָה בְּאַחֲרִית הַיָּמִים
the-days in-coming-of the-disaster on-you and-she-will-fall you I-commanded

כִּי־תַעֲשׂוּ אֶת־הָרַע בְּעֵינֵי יְהוָה לְהַכְעִיסוֹ בְּמַעֲשֵׂה
by-work-of to-anger-him Yahweh in-eyes-of the-evil *** you-will-do for

יְדֵיכֶם׃ וַיְדַבֵּר מֹשֶׁה בְּאָזְנֵי כָּל־קְהַל יִשְׂרָאֵל
Israel assembly-of all-of in-ears-of Moses and-he-recited (30) hands-of-you

אֶת־דִּבְרֵי הַשִּׁירָה הַזֹּאת עַד תֻּמָּם׃ הַאֲזִינוּ הַשָּׁמַיִם
the-heavens listen! (32:1) to-end-them until the-this the-song words-of ***

וַאֲדַבֵּרָה וְתִשְׁמַע הָאָרֶץ אִמְרֵי־פִי׃ יַעֲרֹף
let-him-fall (2) mouth-of-me words-of the-earth and-you-hear and-I-will-speak

כַּמָּטָר לִקְחִי תִּזַּל כַּטַּל אִמְרָתִי
word-of-me like-the-dew let-her-descend teaching-of-me like-the-rain

כִּשְׂעִירִם עֲלֵי־דֶשֶׁא וְכִרְבִיבִים עֲלֵי־עֵשֶׂב׃ כִּי שֵׁם
name-of for (3) plant on and-like-abundant-rains grass on like-showers

יְהוָה אֶקְרָא הָבוּ גֹדֶל לֵאלֹהֵינוּ׃ הַצּוּר תָּמִים
perfect the-Rock (4) of-God-of-us greatness praise! I-will-proclaim Yahweh

פָּעֳלוֹ כִּי כָל־דְּרָכָיו מִשְׁפָּט אֵל אֱמוּנָה וְאֵין עָוֶל
wrong and-without faithful God just ways-of-him all-of indeed work-of-him

צַדִּיק וְיָשָׁר הוּא׃ שִׁחֵת לוֹ לֹא בָּנָיו
children-of-him not toward-him he-acted-corruptly (5) he and-just upright

מוּמָם דּוֹר עִקֵּשׁ וּפְתַלְתֹּל׃ הֲ־לַיהוָה תִּגְמְלוּ־זֹאת
this you-repay to-Yahweh ? (6) and-crooked warped generation shame-of-them

עַם נָבָל וְלֹא חָכָם הֲלוֹא־הוּא אָבִיךָ קָּנֶךָ הוּא
he he-created-you Father-of-you he not? wise and-not foolish people

עָשְׂךָ וַיְכֹנְנֶךָ׃ זְכֹר יְמוֹת עוֹלָם בִּינוּ שְׁנוֹת
years-of consider! old days-of remember! (7) and-he-formed-you he-made-you

דּוֹר־וָדוֹר שְׁאַל אָבִיךָ וְיַגֵּדְךָ
and-he-will-tell-you father-of-you ask! and-generation generation

זְקֵנֶיךָ וְיֹאמְרוּ לָךְ׃ בְּהַנְחֵל
when-to-give-inheritance (8) to-you and-they-will-explain elders-of-you

עֶלְיוֹן גּוֹיִם בְּהַפְרִידוֹ בְּנֵי אָדָם יַצֵּב גְּבֻלֹת
boundaries-of he-set-up man sons-of when-to-divide-him nations Most-High

עַמִּים לְמִסְפַּר בְּנֵי יִשְׂרָאֵל׃ כִּי חֵלֶק יְהוָה עַמּוֹ
people-of-him Yahweh portion-of for (9) *Israel sons-of by-number-of peoples

יַעֲקֹב חֶבֶל נַחֲלָתוֹ׃ יִמְצָאֵהוּ בְּאֶרֶץ מִדְבָּר
desert in-land-of he-found-him (10) inheritance-of-him allotment-of Jacob

disaster will fall upon you because you will do evil in the sight of the LORD and provoke him to anger by what your hands have made."

*The Song of Moses*

30And Moses recited the words of this song from beginning to end in the hearing of the whole assembly of Israel:

**32** Listen, O heavens, and I will speak;
hear, O earth, the words of my mouth.
2Let my teaching fall like rain
and my words descend like dew,
like showers on new grass,
like abundant rain on tender plants.

3I will proclaim the name of the LORD.
Oh, praise the greatness of our God!
4He is the Rock, his works are perfect,
and all his ways are just.
A faithful God who does no wrong,
upright and just is he.

5They have acted corruptly toward him;
to their shame they are no longer his children,
but a warped and crooked generation.[n]
6Is this the way you repay the LORD,
O foolish and unwise people?
Is he not your Father, your Creator,[o]
who made you and formed you?
7Remember the days of old;
consider the generations long past.
Ask your father and he will tell you,
your elders, and they will explain to you.
8When the Most High gave the nations their inheritance,
when he divided all mankind,
he set up boundaries for the peoples
according to the number of the sons of Israel.[p]
9For the LORD's portion is his people,
Jacob his allotted inheritance.

10In a desert land he found him,

[n]5 Or *Corrupt are they and not his children, / a generation warped and twisted to their shame*
[o]6 Or *Father, who bought you*
[p]8 Masoretic Text; Dead Sea Scrolls (see also Septuagint) *sons of God*

*8 The Dead Sea Scrolls read בני אל, *God sons-of.*

וּבְתֹהוּ יְלֵל יְשִׁמֹן יְסֹבְבֶנְהוּ יְבוֹנְנֵהוּ
he-cared-for-him he-shielded-him waste and-howling and-in-barren

יִצְּרֶנְהוּ כְּאִישׁוֹן עֵינוֹ׃ כְּנֶשֶׁר יָעִיר קִנּוֹ
nest-of-him he-stirs-up like-eagle (11) eye-of-him as-pupil-of he-guarded-him

עַל־ גּוֹזָלָיו יְרַחֵף יִפְרֹשׂ כְּנָפָיו יִקָּחֵהוּ
he-catches-him wings-of-him he-spreads he-hovers young-ones-of-him over

יִשָּׂאֵהוּ עַל־ אֶבְרָתוֹ׃ יְהוָה בָּדָד יַנְחֶנּוּ וְאֵין
and-not he-led-him alone Yahweh (12) pinion-of-him on he-carries-him

עִמּוֹ אֵל נֵכָר׃ יַרְכִּבֵהוּ עַל־ בָּמֳותֵי אָרֶץ וַיֹּאכַל
and-he-ate land heights-of on he-made-ride-him (13) foreign god with-him

תְּנוּבֹת שָׂדָי וַיֵּנִקֵהוּ דְבַשׁ מִסֶּלַע וְשֶׁמֶן מֵחַלְמִישׁ
from-flinty and-oil from-rock honey-of and-he-nourished-him field fruits-of

צוּר׃ חֶמְאַת בָּקָר וַחֲלֵב צֹאן עִם־ חֵלֶב כָּרִים וְאֵילִים
and-rams lambs fat-of with flock and-milk-of herd curd-of (14) crag

בְּנֵי־ בָשָׁן וְעַתּוּדִים עִם־ חֵלֶב כִּלְיוֹת חִטָּה וְדַם־ עֵנָב
grape and-blood-of wheat kernels-of finest-of with and-goats Bashan sons-of

תִּשְׁתֶּה־ חָמֶר׃ וַיִּשְׁמַן יְשֻׁרוּן וַיִּבְעָט שָׁמַנְתָּ
you-were-filled and-he-kicked Jeshurun and-he-grew-fat (15) wine you-drank

עָבִיתָ כָּשִׂיתָ וַיִּטֹּשׁ אֱלוֹהַּ* עָשָׂהוּ
he-made-him God and-he-abandoned you-became-sleek you-became-heavy

וַיְנַבֵּל צוּר יְשֻׁעָתוֹ׃ יַקְנִאֻהוּ
they-made-jealous-him (16) Savior-of-him Rock-of and-he-rejected

בְּזָרִים בְּתוֹעֵבֹת יַכְעִיסֻהוּ׃ יִזְבְּחוּ
they-sacrificed (17) they-angered-him with-detestable-idols with-foreign-gods

לַשֵּׁדִים לֹא אֱלֹהַּ* אֱלֹהִים לֹא יְדָעוּם חֲדָשִׁים מִקָּרֹב
from-near recent-ones they-knew-them not gods God not to-the-demons

בָּאוּ לֹא שְׂעָרוּם אֲבֹתֵיכֶם׃ צוּר יְלָדְךָ
he-fathered-you Rock (18) fathers-of-you they-feared-them not they-appeared

תֶּשִׁי וַתִּשְׁכַּח אֵל מְחֹלְלֶךָ׃ וַיַּרְא יְהוָה
Yahweh and-he-saw (19) one-bearing-you God and-you-forgot you-deserted

וַיִּנְאָץ מִכַּעַס בָּנָיו וּבְנֹתָיו׃
and-daughters-of-him sons-of-him because-of-anger-of and-he-rejected

וַיֹּאמֶר אַסְתִּירָה פָנַי מֵהֶם אֶרְאֶה מָה
what I-will-see from-them faces-of-me I-will-hide and-he-said (20)

אַחֲרִיתָם כִּי דוֹר תַּהְפֻּכֹת הֵמָּה בָּנִים לֹא־ אֵמֻן
faithful not children they perverse-ones generation-of for end-of-them

בָם׃ הֵם קִנְאוּנִי בְלֹא־ אֵל כִּעֲסוּנִי
they-angered-me god by-not they-made-jealous-me they (21) among-them

in a barren and howling waste.
He shielded him and cared for him;
he guarded him as the apple of his eye,
11like an eagle that stirs up its nest
and hovers over its young,
that spreads its wings to catch them
and carries them on its pinions.
12The LORD alone led him;
no foreign god was with him.
13He made him ride on the heights of the land
and fed him with the fruit of the fields.
He nourished him with honey from the rock,
and with oil from the flinty crag,
14with curds and milk from herd and flock
and with fattened lambs and goats,
with choice rams of Bashan
and the finest kernels of wheat.
You drank the red blood of the grape.
15Jeshurun[q] grew fat and kicked;
filled with food, he became heavy and sleek.
He abandoned the God who made him
and rejected the Rock his Savior.
16They made him jealous with their foreign gods
and angered him with their detestable idols.
17They sacrificed to demons, which are not God—
gods they had not known,
gods that recently appeared,
gods your fathers did not fear.
18You deserted the Rock, who fathered you;
you forgot the God who gave you birth.
19The LORD saw this and rejected them
because he was angered by his sons and daughters.
20"I will hide my face from them," he said,
"and see what their end will be;
for they are a perverse generation,

q15 *Jeshurun* means *the upright one,* that is, Israel.

*15, 17 Most mss have *mappiq* in the *he* (הּ).

°13 ק במתי

בְּהַבְלֵיהֶם וַאֲנִי אַקְנִיאֵם בְּלֹא־ עָם
people by-not I-will-make-jealous-them so-I with-worthless-idols-of-them

בְּגוֹי נָבָל אַכְעִיסֵם׃ כִּי־ אֵשׁ קָדְחָה
she-was-kindled fire for (22) I-will-anger-them foolish by-nation

בְאַפִּי וַתִּיקַד עַד־ שְׁאוֹל תַּחְתִּית וַתֹּאכַל אֶרֶץ
earth and-she-will-devour below Sheol to and-she-burns by-wrath-of-me

וִיבֻלָהּ וַתְּלַהֵט מוֹסְדֵי הָרִים׃
mountains foundations-of and-she-will-set-afire and-harvest-of-her

אַסְפֶּה עָלֵימוֹ רָעוֹת חִצַּי אֲכַלֶּה־ בָּם׃
against-them I-will-spend arrows-of-me calamities on-them I-will-heap (23)

מְזֵי רָעָב וּלְחֻמֵי רֶשֶׁף וְקֶטֶב מְרִירִי
deadly and-plague pestilence and-ones-consuming-of famine ones-wasting-of (24)

וְשֶׁן־ בְּהֵמוֹת אֲשַׁלַּח־ בָּם עִם־ חֲמַת זֹחֲלֵי
ones-gliding-of venom-of with against-them I-will-send wild-beasts and-fang-of

עָפָר׃ מִחוּץ תְּשַׁכֶּל־ חֶרֶב וּמֵחֲדָרִים אֵימָה
terror and-in-homes sword she-will-make-childless on-outside (25) dust

גַּם־ בָּחוּר גַּם־ בְּתוּלָה יוֹנֵק עִם־ אִישׁ שֵׂיבָה׃ אָמַרְתִּי
I-said (26) gray-hair man-of with infant young-woman and young-man both

אַפְאֵיהֶם אַשְׁבִּיתָה מֵאֱנוֹשׁ זִכְרָם׃ לוּלֵי
but (27) memory-of-them from-mankind I-would-erase I-would-scatter-them

כַּעַס אוֹיֵב אָגוּר פֶּן־ יְנַכְּרוּ צָרֵימוֹ
adversary-of-them they-misunderstand lest I-dreaded being-enemy taunt-of

פֶּן־ יֹאמְרוּ יָדֵינוּ רָמָה וְלֹא יְהוָה פָּעַל כָּל־ זֹאת׃
this all-of he-did Yahweh and-not triumphing hands-of-us they-say lest

כִּי־ גוֹי אֹבַד עֵצוֹת הֵמָּה וְאֵין בָּהֶם תְּבוּנָה׃ לוּ
if! (29) discernment in-them and-not they senses lacking nation indeed (28)

חָכְמוּ יַשְׂכִּילוּ זֹאת יָבִינוּ לְאַחֲרִיתָם׃
about-end-of-them they-would-discern this they-would-understand they-were-wise

אֵיכָה יִרְדֹּף אֶחָד אֶלֶף וּשְׁנַיִם יָנִיסוּ
they-could-put-to-flight or-two thousand one could-he-chase how? (30)

רְבָבָה אִם־לֹא כִּי־ צוּרָם מְכָרָם וַיהוָה הִסְגִּירָם׃
he-gave-up-them and-Yahweh he-sold-them Rock-of-them that not if ten-thousand

כִּי לֹא כְצוּרֵנוּ צוּרָם וְאֹיְבֵינוּ פְּלִילִים׃
conceders and-being-enemies-of-us rock-of-them like-Rock-of-us not for (31)

כִּי־ מִגֶּפֶן סְדֹם גַּפְנָם וּמִשַּׁדְמֹת עֲמֹרָה
Gomorrah and-from-fields-of vine-of-them Sodom from-vine-of for (32)

עֲנָבֵמוֹ עִנְּבֵי־ רוֹשׁ אַשְׁכְּלֹת מְרֹרֹת לָמוֹ׃ חֲמַת
venom-of (33) to-them bitter-ones clusters poison grapes-of grape-of-them

children who are unfaithful.
21They made me jealous by what is no god
and angered me with their worthless idols.
I will make them envious by those who are not a people;
I will make them angry by a nation that has no understanding.
22For a fire has been kindled by my wrath,
one that burns to the realm of death[r] below.
It will devour the earth and its harvests
and set afire the foundations of the mountains.
23"I will heap calamities upon them
and spend my arrows against them.
24I will send wasting famine against them,
consuming pestilence and deadly plague;
I will send against them the fangs of wild beasts,
the venom of vipers that glide in the dust.
25In the street the sword will make them childless;
in their homes terror will reign.
Young men and young women will perish,
infants and gray-haired men.
26I said I would scatter them
and erase their memory from mankind,
27but I dreaded the taunt of the enemy,
lest the adversary misunderstand
and say, 'Our hand has triumphed;
the LORD has not done all this.' "
28They are a nation without sense,
there is no discernment in them.
29If only they were wise and would understand this
and discern what their end will be!
30How could one man chase a thousand,
or two put ten thousand to flight,
unless their Rock had sold them,
unless the LORD had given them up?
31For their rock is not like our Rock,
as even our enemies concede.
32Their vine comes from the vine of Sodom

[r]22 Hebrew *to Sheol*

תַּנִּינִם יֵינָם וְרֹאשׁ פְּתָנִים אַכְזָר׃ הֲלֹא־ הוּא
this not? (34) deadly cobras and-poison-of wine-of-them serpents

כָּמֻס עִמָּדִי חָתֻם בְּאוֹצְרֹתָי׃ לִי נָקָם
vengeance to-me (35) in-vaults-of-me being-sealed with-me being-reserved

וְשִׁלֵּם לְעֵת תָּמוּט רַגְלָם כִּי קָרוֹב יוֹם
day-of near for foot-of-them she-will-slip in-time and-repayment

אֵידָם וְחָשׁ עֲתִדֹת לָמוֹ׃ כִּי־ יָדִין יְהוָה
Yahweh he-will-judge for (36) upon-them dooms and-he-rushes disaster-of-them

עַמּוֹ וְעַל־ עֲבָדָיו יִתְנֶחָם כִּי יִרְאֶה
he-sees when he-will-have-compassion servants-of-him and-on people-of-him

כִּי־ אָזְלַת יָד וְאֶפֶס עָצוּר וְעָזוּב׃
or-being-free being-slave and-none strength she-is-gone that

וְאָמַר אֵי אֱלֹהֵימוֹ צוּר חָסָיוּ בוֹ׃
in-him they-took-refuge rock gods-of-them where? and-he-will-say (37)

אֲשֶׁר חֵלֶב זְבָחֵימוֹ יֹאכֵלוּ יִשְׁתּוּ יֵין
wine-of they-drank they-ate sacrifices-of-them fat-of who (38)

נְסִיכָם יָקוּמוּ וְיַעְזְרֻכֶם יְהִי עֲלֵיכֶם
for-you let-him-be and-let-them-help-you let-them-rise drink-offering-of-them

סִתְרָה׃ רְאוּ ׀ עַתָּה כִּי אֲנִי אֲנִי הוּא וְאֵין אֱלֹהִים עִמָּדִי אֲנִי
I besides-me gods and-there-is-no He myself I that now see! (39) shelter

אָמִית וַאֲחַיֶּה מָחַצְתִּי וַאֲנִי אֶרְפָּא וְאֵין
and-no-one I-will-heal and-I I-wounded and-I-bring-to-life I-put-to-death

מִיָּדִי מַצִּיל׃ כִּי־ אֶשָּׂא אֶל־ שָׁמַיִם יָדִי
hand-of-me heavens to I-lift indeed (40) delivering from-hand-of-me

וְאָמַרְתִּי חַי אָנֹכִי לְעֹלָם׃ אִם־ שַׁנּוֹתִי בְּרַק חַרְבִּי
sword-of-me flashing-of I-sharpen when (41) for-ever I alive and-I-declare

וְתֹאחֵז בְּמִשְׁפָּט יָדִי אָשִׁיב נָקָם
vengeance I-will-take hand-of-me in-judgment and-she-grasps

לְצָרָי וְלִמְשַׂנְאַי אֲשַׁלֵּם׃ אַשְׁכִּיר
I-will-make-drunk (42) I-will-repay and-to-ones-hating-me on-adversaries-of-me

חִצַּי מִדָּם וְחַרְבִּי תֹּאכַל בָּשָׂר מִדַּם חָלָל
slain from-blood-of flesh she-devours and-sword-of-me with-blood arrows-of-me

וְשִׁבְיָה מֵרֹאשׁ פַּרְעוֹת אוֹיֵב׃ הַרְנִינוּ גוֹיִם
nations rejoice! (43) being-enemy leaders-of from-head-of and-captive

עַמּוֹ כִּי דַם־ עֲבָדָיו יִקּוֹם וְנָקָם
and-vengeance he-will-avenge servants-of-him blood-of for * people-of-him

יָשִׁיב לְצָרָיו וְכִפֶּר אַדְמָתוֹ עַמּוֹ׃
people-of-him land-of-him and-he-will-atone on-enemies-of-him he-will-take

and from the fields of
Gomorrah.
Their grapes are filled with
poison,
and their clusters with
bitterness.
33 Their wine is the venom of
serpents,
the deadly poison of
cobras.

34 "Have I not kept this in
reserve
and sealed it in my
vaults?
35 It is mine to avenge; I will
repay.
In due time their foot
will slip;
their day of disaster is near
and their doom rushes
upon them."
36 The LORD will judge his
people
and have compassion on
his servants
when he sees their strength
is gone
and no one is left, slave
or free.
37 He will say: "Now where
are their gods,
the rock they took refuge
in,
38 the gods who ate the fat of
their sacrifices
and drank the wine of
their drink offerings?
Let them rise up to help
you!
Let them give you
shelter!
39 "See now that I myself am
He!
There is no god besides
me.
I put to death and I bring
to life,
I have wounded and I
will heal,
and no one can deliver
from my hand.
40 I lift my hand to heaven
and declare:
As surely as I live
forever,
41 when I sharpen my
flashing sword
and my hand grasps it in
judgment,
I will take vengeance on
my adversaries
and repay those who
hate me.
42 I will make my arrows
drunk with blood,
while my sword devours
flesh:
the blood of the slain and
the captives,
the heads of the enemy
leaders."

*43 והשתחוו לו (כל) אלהים
*angels (all-of) to-him and-worship!*
The Dead Sea Scrolls and Septuagint have this phrase, apparently quoted in Hebrews 1:6.

וַיָּבֹא מֹשֶׁה וַיְדַבֵּר אֶת־ כָּל־ דִּבְרֵי הַשִּׁירָה־ הַזֹּאת
the-this the-song words-of all-of *** and-he-spoke Moses and-he-came (44)

בְּאָזְנֵי הָעָם הוּא וְהוֹשֵׁעַ בִּן־ נוּן׃ וַיְכַל מֹשֶׁה
Moses when-he-finished (45) Nun son-of and-Hoshea he the-people in-ears-of

לְדַבֵּר אֶת־ כָּל־ הַדְּבָרִים הָאֵלֶּה אֶל־ כָּל־ יִשְׂרָאֵל׃ וַיֹּאמֶר
and-he-said (46) Israel all-of to the-these the-words all-of *** to-recite

אֲלֵהֶם שִׂימוּ לְבַבְכֶם לְכָל־ הַדְּבָרִים אֲשֶׁר אָנֹכִי מֵעִיד
solemnly-declaring I that the-words to-all-of heart-of-you take-to! to-them

בָּכֶם הַיּוֹם אֲשֶׁר תְּצַוֻּם אֶת־ בְּנֵיכֶם לִשְׁמֹר
to-be-careful children-of-you *** you-may-command-them that the-day to-you

לַעֲשׂוֹת אֶת־ כָּל־ דִּבְרֵי הַתּוֹרָה הַזֹּאת׃ כִּי לֹא־ דָבָר רֵק הוּא
he idle word not for (47) the-this the-law words-of all-of *** to-obey

מִכֶּם כִּי־ הוּא חַיֵּיכֶם וּבַדָּבָר הַזֶּה תַּאֲרִיכוּ
you-will-live-long the-this and-by-the-word lives-of-you he indeed for-you

יָמִים עַל־ הָאֲדָמָה אֲשֶׁר אַתֶּם עֹבְרִים אֶת־ הַיַּרְדֵּן שָׁמָּה
to-there the-Jordan *** ones-crossing you that the-land in days

לְרִשְׁתָּהּ׃ וַיְדַבֵּר יְהוָה אֶל־ מֹשֶׁה בְּעֶצֶם הַיּוֹם הַזֶּה
the-that the-day on-same Moses to Yahweh and-he-spoke (48) to-possess-her

לֵאמֹר׃ עֲלֵה אֶל־ הַר הָעֲבָרִים הַזֶּה הַר־ נְבוֹ אֲשֶׁר
that Nebo Mount-of the-this the-Abarim Range-of to go-up! (49) to-say

בְּאֶרֶץ מוֹאָב אֲשֶׁר עַל־ פְּנֵי יְרֵחוֹ וּרְאֵה אֶת־ אֶרֶץ כְּנַעַן
Canaan land-of *** and-view! Jericho faces-of across that Moab in-land-of

אֲשֶׁר אֲנִי נֹתֵן לִבְנֵי יִשְׂרָאֵל לַאֲחֻזָּה׃ וּמֻת בָּהָר
on-the-mountain and-die! (50) as-possession Israel to-sons-of giving I that

אֲשֶׁר אַתָּה עֹלֶה שָׁמָּה וְהֵאָסֵף אֶל־ עַמֶּיךָ כַּאֲשֶׁר־ מֵת
he-died just-as people-of-you to and-be-gathered! on-there climbing you that

אַהֲרֹן אָחִיךָ בְּהֹר הָהָר וַיֵּאָסֶף אֶל־ עַמָּיו׃
people-of-him to and-he-was-gathered the-Mount on-Hor brother-of-you Aaron

עַל אֲשֶׁר מְעַלְתֶּם בִּי בְּתוֹךְ בְּנֵי יִשְׂרָאֵל
Israel sons-of in-presence-of with-me you-broke-faith that because (51)

בְּמֵי־ מְרִיבַת קָדֵשׁ מִדְבַּר־ צִן עַל אֲשֶׁר לֹא־ קִדַּשְׁתֶּם
you-upheld-as-holy not that for Zin Desert-of Kadesh Meribah-of at-waters-of

אוֹתִי בְּתוֹךְ בְּנֵי יִשְׂרָאֵל׃ כִּי מִנֶּגֶד תִּרְאֶה אֶת־
*** you-will-see from-distance therefore (52) Israel sons-of among me

הָאָרֶץ וְשָׁמָּה לֹא תָבוֹא אֶל־ הָאָרֶץ אֲשֶׁר־ אֲנִי נֹתֵן
giving I that the-land into you-will-enter not but-to-there the-land

לִבְנֵי יִשְׂרָאֵל׃ וְזֹאת הַבְּרָכָה אֲשֶׁר בֵּרַךְ מֹשֶׁה אִישׁ
man-of Moses he-pronounced that the-blessing and-this (33:1) Israel to-sons-of

43Rejoice, O nations, with
his people,[r s]
for he will avenge the
blood of his servants;
he will take vengeance on
his enemies
and make atonement for
his land and people.

44Moses came with Joshua[t] son of Nun and spoke all the words of this song in the hearing of the people. 45When Moses finished reciting all these words to all Israel, 46he said to them, "Take to heart all the words I have solemnly declared to you this day, so that you may command your children to obey carefully all the words of this law. 47They are not just idle words for you—they are your life. By them you will live long in the land you are crossing the Jordan to possess."

### *Moses to Die on Mount Nebo*

48On that same day the LORD told Moses, 49"Go up into the Abarim Range to Mount Nebo in Moab, across from Jericho, and view Canaan, the land I am giving the Israelites as their own possession. 50There on the mountain that you have climbed you will die and be gathered to your people, just as your brother Aaron died on Mount Hor and was gathered to his people. 51This is because both of you broke faith with me in the presence of the Israelites at the waters of Meribah Kadesh in the Desert of Zin and because you did not uphold my holiness among the Israelites. 52Therefore, you will see the land only from a distance; you will not enter the land I am giving to the people of Israel."

### *Moses Blesses the Tribes*

33 This is the blessing that Moses the man of God pronounced on the Israelites before his death. 2He said:

[r]43 Or *Make his people rejoice, O nations*
[s]43 Masoretic Text; Dead Sea Scrolls (see also Septuagint) *people, / and let all the angels worship him /*
[t]44 Hebrew *Hoshea,* a variant of *Joshua*

הָאֱלֹהִים אֶת־ בְּנֵי יִשְׂרָאֵל לִפְנֵי מוֹתוֹ׃ וַיֹּאמַר יְהוָה
Yahweh and-he-said (2) death-of-him before Israel sons-of *** the-God

מִסִּינַי בָּא וְזָרַח מִשֵּׂעִיר לָמוֹ הוֹפִיעַ מֵהַר
from-Mount-of he-shone over-them from-Seir and-he-dawned he-came from-Sinai

פָּארָן וְאָתָה מֵרִבְבֹת קֹדֶשׁ מִימִינוֹ אֶשְׁדָּת°
*mountain-slope from-south-of-him holy-one with-myriads-of and-he-came Paran

לָמוֹ׃ אַף חֹבֵב עַמִּים כָּל־ קְדֹשָׁיו בְּיָדֶךָ
in-hand-of-you holy-ones-of-him all-of peoples one-loving surely (3) to-them

וְהֵם תֻּכּוּ לְרַגְלֶךָ יִשָּׂא מִדַּבְּרֹתֶיךָ׃
from-instructions-of-you he-receives at-foot-of-you they-bow and-they

תּוֹרָה צִוָּה־ לָנוּ מֹשֶׁה מוֹרָשָׁה קְהִלַּת יַעֲקֹב׃ וַיְהִי
and-he-was (5) Jacob assembly-of possession Moses to-us he-gave law (4)

בִישֻׁרוּן מֶלֶךְ בְּהִתְאַסֵּף רָאשֵׁי עָם יַחַד שִׁבְטֵי יִשְׂרָאֵל׃
Israel tribes-of with people leaders-of when-to-assemble king over-Jeshurun

יְחִי רְאוּבֵן וְאַל־ יָמֹת וִיהִי מְתָיו מִסְפָּר׃
few men-of-him nor-let-him-be let-him-die and-not Reuben let-him-live (6)

וְזֹאת לִיהוּדָה וַיֹּאמַר שְׁמַע יְהוָה קוֹל יְהוּדָה וְאֶל־
and-to Judah cry-of Yahweh hear! and-he-said about-Judah and-this (7)

עַמּוֹ תְּבִיאֶנּוּ יָדָיו רָב לוֹ וְעֵזֶר
and-help with-him he-defends hands-of-him you-bring-him people-of-him

מִצָּרָיו תִּהְיֶה׃ וּלְלֵוִי אָמַר תֻּמֶּיךָ
Thummim-of-you he-said and-about-Levi (8) you-be against-foes-of-him

וְאוּרֶיךָ לְאִישׁ חֲסִידֶךָ אֲשֶׁר נִסִּיתוֹ בְּמַסָּה
at-Massah you-tested-him whom favored-of-you to-man and-Urim-of-you

תְּרִיבֵהוּ עַל־ מֵי מְרִיבָה׃ הָאֹמֵר לְאָבִיו
to-father-of-him the-one-saying (9) Meribah waters-of at you-contended-with-him

וּלְאִמּוֹ לֹא רְאִיתִיו וְאֶת־ אֶחָיו לֹא הִכִּיר
he-recognized not brothers-of-him and I-regard-him not and-to-mother-of-him

וְאֶת־ בָּנָו° לֹא יָדָע כִּי שָׁמְרוּ אִמְרָתֶךָ
word-of-you they-watched-over but he-acknowledged not children-of-him or

וּבְרִיתְךָ יִנְצֹרוּ׃ יוֹרוּ מִשְׁפָּטֶיךָ לְיַעֲקֹב
to-Jacob precepts-of-you they-teach (10) they-guarded and-covenant-of-you

וְתוֹרָתְךָ לְיִשְׂרָאֵל יָשִׂימוּ קְטוֹרָה בְּאַפֶּךָ וְכָלִיל
and-offering before-face-of-you incense they-offer to-Israel and-law-of-you

עַל־ מִזְבְּחֶךָ׃ בָּרֵךְ יְהוָה חֵילוֹ וּפֹעַל יָדָיו
hands-of-him and-work-of skill-of-him Yahweh bless! (11) altar-of-you on

תִּרְצֶה מְחַץ מָתְנַיִם קָמָיו וּמְשַׂנְאָיו
and-ones-hating-him ones-rising-against-him loins smite! you-be-pleased

"The LORD came from Sinai
and dawned over them from Seir;
he shone forth from Mount Paran.
He came with[u] myriads of holy ones
from the south, from his mountain slopes.[v]
3 Surely it is you who love the people;
all the holy ones are in your hand.
At your feet they all bow down,
and from you receive instruction,
4 the law that Moses gave us,
the possession of the assembly of Jacob.
5 He was king over Jeshurun[w]
when the leaders of the people assembled,
along with the tribes of Israel.

6 "Let Reuben live and not die,
nor[x] his men be few."

7 And this he said about Judah:

"Hear, O LORD, the cry of Judah;
bring him to his people.
With his own hands he defends his cause.
Oh, be his help against his foes!"

8 About Levi he said:

"Your Thummim and Urim belong
to the man you favored.
You tested him at Massah;
you contended with him at the waters of Meribah.
9 He said of his father and mother,
'I have no regard for them.'
He did not recognize his brothers
or acknowledge his own children,
but he watched over your word
and guarded your covenant.
10 He teaches your precepts to Jacob
and your law to Israel.
He offers incense before you
and whole burnt offerings on your altar.
11 Bless all his skills, O LORD,

[u]2 Or *from*
[v]2 The meaning of the Hebrew for this phrase is uncertain.
[w]5 *Jeshurun* means *the upright one,* that is, Israel; also in verse 26.
[x]6 Or *but let*

°2 ק אש דת
*2 *law fire(-of)* [?] (*Qere* translation)

°9 ק בניו

מִן־ יְקוּמוּן (12) לְבִנְיָמִן אָמַר יְדִיד יְהוָה יִשְׁכֹּן

let-him-rest Yahweh beloved-of he-said about-Benjamin (12) they-rise not

לָבֶטַח עָלָיו חֹפֵף עָלָיו כָּל־ הַיּוֹם וּבֵין

and-between the-day all-of over-him one-shielding in-him in-security

כְּתֵפָיו שָׁכֵן׃ (13) וּלְיוֹסֵף אָמַר מְבֹרֶכֶת יְהוָה

Yahweh blessing he-said and-about-Joseph (13) he-rests shoulders-of-him

אַרְצוֹ מִמֶּגֶד שָׁמַיִם מִטָּל וּמִתְּהוֹם רֹבֶצֶת תָּחַת׃

below lying and-with-deep-water with-dew heavens with-precious-of land-of-him

(14) וּמִמֶּגֶד תְּבוּאֹת שָׁמֶשׁ וּמִמֶּגֶד גֶּרֶשׁ יְרָחִים׃

moons yield-of and-with-finest-of sun produce-of and-with-best-of (14)

(15) וּמֵרֹאשׁ הַרְרֵי־ קֶדֶם וּמִמֶּגֶד גִּבְעוֹת

hills-of and-with-fruit-of ancient mountains-of and-with-choicest-of (15)

עוֹלָם׃ (16) וּמִמֶּגֶד אֶרֶץ וּמְלֹאָהּ וּרְצוֹן

and-favor-of and-fullness-of-her earth and-with-best-of (16) everlasting

שֹׁכְנִי סְנֶה תָּבוֹאתָה לְרֹאשׁ יוֹסֵף וּלְקָדְקֹד

and-on-brow-of Joseph on-head-of you-let-rest-her burning-bush one-dwelling-of

נְזִיר אֶחָיו׃ (17) בְּכוֹר שׁוֹרוֹ הָדָר לוֹ

to-him majesty bull-of-him firstborn-of (17) brothers-of-him prince-of

וְקַרְנֵי רְאֵם קַרְנָיו בָּהֶם עַמִּים יְנַגַּח יַחְדָּו

even he-will-gore nations with-them horns-of-him wild-ox and-horns-of

אַפְסֵי־ אָרֶץ וְהֵם רִבְבוֹת אֶפְרַיִם וְהֵם אַלְפֵי מְנַשֶּׁה׃

Manasseh thousands-of so-they Ephraim ten-thousands-of so-they earth ends-of

(18) וְלִזְבוּלֻן אָמַר שְׂמַח זְבוּלֻן בְּצֵאתֶךָ

in-to-go-out-you Zebulun rejoice! he-said and-about-Zebulun (18)

וְיִשָּׂשכָר בְּאֹהָלֶיךָ׃ (19) עַמִּים הַר־ יִקְרָאוּ שָׁם

there they-will-summon mountain peoples (19) in-tents-of-you and-Issachar

יִזְבְּחוּ זִבְחֵי־ צֶדֶק כִּי שֶׁפַע יַמִּים

seas abundance-of and righteousness sacrifices-of they-will-offer

יִינָקוּ וּשְׂפֻנֵי טְמוּנֵי חוֹל׃

sand ones-being-treasured-of and-ones-being-hidden-of they-will-feast

(20) וּלְגָד אָמַר בָּרוּךְ מַרְחִיב גָּד כְּלָבִיא שָׁכֵן

he-lives like-lion Gad one-enlarging being-blessed he-said and-about-Gad (20)

וְטָרַף זְרוֹעַ אַף־ קָדְקֹד׃ (21) וַיַּרְא רֵאשִׁית לוֹ כִּי־ שָׁם

there indeed for-him best and-he-chose (21) head or arm and-he-tears

חֶלְקַת מְחֹקֵק סָפוּן וַיֵּתֵא רָאשֵׁי עָם

people heads-of when-he-assembled being-kept one-leading portion-of

צִדְקַת יְהוָה עָשָׂה וּמִשְׁפָּטָיו עִם־ יִשְׂרָאֵל׃

Israel to and-judgments-of-him he-carried-out Yahweh righteousness-of

and be pleased with the work of his hands.
Smite the loins of those who rise up against him;
strike his foes till they rise no more."

12 About Benjamin he said:

"Let the beloved of the LORD rest secure in him,
for he shields him all day long,
and the one the LORD loves rests between his shoulders."

13 About Joseph he said:

"May the LORD bless his land
with the precious dew from heaven above
and with the deep waters that lie below;
14 with the best the sun brings forth
and the finest the moon can yield;
15 with the choicest gifts of the ancient mountains
and the fruitfulness of the everlasting hills;
16 with the best gifts of the earth and its fullness
and the favor of him who dwelt in the burning bush.
Let all these rest on the head of Joseph,
on the brow of the prince among[y] his brothers.
17 In majesty he is like a firstborn bull;
his horns are the horns of a wild ox,
with them he will gore the nations,
even those at the ends of the earth.
Such are the ten thousands of Ephraim;
such are the thousands of Manasseh."

18 About Zebulun he said:

"Rejoice, Zebulun, in your going out,
and you, Issachar, in your tents.
19 They will summon peoples to the mountain
and there offer sacrifices of righteousness;
they will feast on the abundance of the seas,
on the treasures hidden in the sand."

20 About Gad he said:

"Blessed is he who enlarges Gad's domain!
Gad lives there like a lion,
tearing at arm or head.

y16 Or *of the one separated from*

וּלְדָן אָמַר דָּן גּוּר אַרְיֵה יְזַנֵּק מִן־הַבָּשָׁן׃
the-Bashan from he-springs lion cub-of Dan he-said and-about-Dan (22)

וּלְנַפְתָּלִי אָמַר נַפְתָּלִי שְׂבַע רָצוֹן וּמָלֵא
and-he-is-full favor abundant-of Naphtali he-said and-about-Naphtali (23)

בִּרְכַּת יְהוָה יָם וְדָרוֹם יְרָשָׁה׃ וּלְאָשֵׁר אָמַר
he-said and-about-Asher (24) inherit! and-south lake Yahweh blessing-of

בָּרוּךְ מִבָּנִים אָשֵׁר יְהִי רְצוּי אֶחָיו
brothers-of-him being-favored-of let-him-be Asher of-sons being-blessed

וְטֹבֵל בַּשֶּׁמֶן רַגְלוֹ׃ בַּרְזֶל וּנְחֹשֶׁת מִנְעָלֶךָ
gate-bolts-of-you and-bronze iron (25) foot-of-him in-the-oil and-bathing

וּכְיָמֶיךָ דָּבְאֶךָ׃ אֵין כָּאֵל יְשֻׁרוּן
Jeshurun like-the-God-of no-one (26) strength-of-you and-as-days-of-you

רֹכֵב שָׁמַיִם בְּעֶזְרֶךָ וּבְגַאֲוָתוֹ שְׁחָקִים׃ מְעֹנָה
refuge (27) clouds and-in-majesty-of-him in-help-of-you heavens riding

אֱלֹהֵי קֶדֶם וּמִתַּחַת זְרֹעֹת עוֹלָם וַיְגָרֶשׁ
and-he-will-drive-out everlasting arms-of and-at-under eternal God-of

מִפָּנֶיךָ אוֹיֵב וַיֹּאמֶר הַשְׁמֵד׃ וַיִּשְׁכֹּן
so-he-will-live (28) destroy! and-he-will-say being-enemy from-before-you

יִשְׂרָאֵל בֶּטַח בָּדָד עֵין יַעֲקֹב אֶל־אֶרֶץ דָּגָן וְתִירוֹשׁ אַף־
also and-new-wine grain land-of in Jacob spring-of alone safely Israel

שָׁמָיו יַעַרְפוּ־טָל׃ אַשְׁרֶיךָ יִשְׂרָאֵל מִי כָמוֹךָ עַם
people like-you who? Israel blessed-you (29) dew they-drop heavens-of-him

נוֹשַׁע בַּיהוָה מָגֵן עֶזְרֶךָ וַאֲשֶׁר־חֶרֶב גַּאֲוָתֶךָ
glorious-of-you sword and-who helper-of-you shield by-Yahweh being-saved

וְיִכָּחֲשׁוּ אֹיְבֶיךָ לָךְ וְאַתָּה עַל־
on and-you before-you being-enemies-of-you and-they-will-cower

בָּמוֹתֵימוֹ תִדְרֹךְ׃ וַיַּעַל מֹשֶׁה
Moses then-he-climbed (34:1) you-will-trample high-places-of-them

מֵעַרְבֹת מוֹאָב אֶל־הַר נְבוֹ רֹאשׁ הַפִּסְגָּה אֲשֶׁר עַל־פְּנֵי
faces-of across that the-Pisgah top-of Nebo Mount-of to Moab from-plains-of

יְרֵחוֹ וַיַּרְאֵהוּ יְהוָה אֶת־כָּל־הָאָרֶץ אֶת־הַגִּלְעָד עַד־דָּן׃
Dan to the-Gilead *** the-land whole-of *** Yahweh and-he-showed-him Jericho

וְאֵת כָּל־נַפְתָּלִי וְאֶת־אֶרֶץ אֶפְרַיִם וּמְנַשֶּׁה וְאֵת כָּל־אֶרֶץ
land-of all-of and and-Manasseh Ephraim land-of and Naphtali all-of and (2)

יְהוּדָה עַד הַיָּם הָאַחֲרוֹן׃ וְאֶת־הַנֶּגֶב וְאֶת־הַכִּכָּר בִּקְעַת
Valley-of the-region and the-Negev and (3) the-western the-sea to Judah

יְרֵחוֹ עִיר הַתְּמָרִים עַד־צֹעַר׃ וַיֹּאמֶר יְהוָה אֵלָיו זֹאת
this to-him Yahweh then-he-said (4) Zoar to the-Palms City-of Jericho

21 He chose the best land for himself;
the leader's portion was kept for him.
When the heads of the people assembled,
he carried out the LORD's righteous will,
and his judgments concerning Israel."

22 About Dan he said:

"Dan is a lion's cub,
springing out of Bashan."

23 About Naphtali he said:

"Naphtali is abounding with the favor of the LORD
and is full of his blessing;
he will inherit southward to the lake."

24 About Asher he said:

"Most blessed of sons is Asher;
let him be favored by his brothers,
and let him bathe his feet in oil.
25 The bolts of your gates will be iron and bronze,
and your strength will equal your days.

26 "There is no one like the God of Jeshurun,
who rides on the heavens to help you
and on the clouds in his majesty.
27 The eternal God is your refuge,
and underneath are the everlasting arms.
He will drive out your enemy before you,
saying, 'Destroy him!'
28 So Israel will live in safety alone;
Jacob's spring is secure
in a land of grain and new wine,
where the heavens drop dew.
29 Blessed are you, O Israel!
Who is like you,
a people saved by the LORD?
He is your shield and helper
and your glorious sword.
Your enemies will cower before you,
and you will trample down their high places.[z]"

*The Death of Moses*

34 Then Moses climbed Mount Nebo from the plains of Moab to the top of Pisgah, across from Jericho. There the LORD showed him the whole land—from Gilead

z29 Or *will tread upon your bodies*

הָאָרֶץ אֲשֶׁר נִשְׁבַּעְתִּי לְאַבְרָהָם לְיִצְחָק וּֽלְיַעֲקֹב לֵאמֹר
to-say and-to-Jacob to-Isaac to-Abraham I-promised that the-land

לְזַרְעֲךָ אֶתְּנֶנָּה הֶרְאִיתִיךָ בְעֵינֶיךָ
with-eyes-of-you I-let-see-you I-will-give-her to-descendant-of-you

וְשָׁמָּה לֹא תַעֲבֹר׃ וַיָּמָת שָׁם מֹשֶׁה עֶבֶד־
servant-of Moses there and-he-died (5) you-will-cross not but-to-there

יְהוָה בְּאֶרֶץ מוֹאָב עַל־ פִּי יְהוָה׃ וַיִּקְבֹּר אֹתוֹ בַגַּי
in-the-valley him and-he-buried (6) Yahweh saying-of as Moab in-land-of Yahweh

בְּאֶרֶץ מוֹאָב מוּל בֵּית פְּעוֹר וְלֹא־ יָדַע אִישׁ אֶת־ קְבֻרָתוֹ עַד
to grave-of-him *** man he-knows and-not Peor Beth opposite Moab in-land-of

הַיּוֹם הַזֶּה׃ וּמֹשֶׁה בֶּן־ מֵאָה וְעֶשְׂרִים שָׁנָה בְּמֹתוֹ
when-to-die-him year and-twenty hundred son-of and-Moses (7) the-this the-day

לֹא־ כָהֲתָה עֵינוֹ וְלֹא־ נָס לֵחֹה׃
strength-of-him he-was-gone and-not eye-of-him she-was-weak not

וַיִּבְכּוּ בְנֵי יִשְׂרָאֵל אֶת־ מֹשֶׁה בְּעַרְבֹת מוֹאָב שְׁלֹשִׁים יוֹם
day thirty Moab in-plains-of Moses *** Israel sons-of and-they-grieved (8)

וַיִּתְּמוּ יְמֵי בְכִי אֵבֶל מֹשֶׁה׃ וִיהוֹשֻׁעַ
now-Joshua (9) Moses mourning-of weeping-of days-of then-they-were-over

בִּן־ נוּן מָלֵא רוּחַ חָכְמָה כִּי־ סָמַךְ מֹשֶׁה אֶת־ יָדָיו
hands-of-him *** Moses he-laid for wisdom spirit-of he-was-filled Nun son-of

עָלָיו וַיִּשְׁמְעוּ אֵלָיו בְּנֵי־ יִשְׂרָאֵל וַיַּעֲשׂוּ כַּאֲשֶׁר
just-as and-they-did Israel sons-of to-him so-they-listened on-him

צִוָּה יְהוָה אֶת־ מֹשֶׁה׃ וְלֹא־ קָם נָבִיא עוֹד בְּיִשְׂרָאֵל
in-Israel since prophet he-rose and-not (10) Moses *** Yahweh he-commanded

כְּמֹשֶׁה אֲשֶׁר יְדָעוֹ יְהוָה פָּנִים אֶל־פָּנִים׃ לְכָל־ הָאֹתוֹת
the-signs with-all-of (11) faces to faces Yahweh he-knew-him whom like-Moses

וְהַמּוֹפְתִים אֲשֶׁר שְׁלָחוֹ יְהוָה לַעֲשׂוֹת בְּאֶרֶץ מִצְרָיִם לְפַרְעֹה
to-Pharaoh Egypt in-land-of to-do Yahweh he-sent-him that and-the-wonders

וּלְכָל־ עֲבָדָיו וּלְכָל־ אַרְצוֹ׃
land-of-him and-to-whole-of officials-of-him and-to-all-of

וּלְכֹל הַיָּד הַחֲזָקָה וּלְכֹל הַמּוֹרָא
the-being-awesome and-with-all-of the-mighty the-hand and-with-all-of (12)

הַגָּדוֹל אֲשֶׁר עָשָׂה מֹשֶׁה לְעֵינֵי כָּל־ יִשְׂרָאֵל׃
Israel all-of before-eyes-of Moses he-performed that the-great-deed

to Dan, 2all of Naphtali, the territory of Ephraim and Manasseh, all the land of Judah as far as the western sea,[a] 3the Negev and the whole region from the Valley of Jericho, the City of Palms, as far as Zoar. 4Then the LORD said to him, "This is the land I promised on oath to Abraham, Isaac and Jacob when I said, 'I will give it to your descendants.' I have let you see it with your eyes, but you will not cross over into it."

5And Moses the servant of the LORD died there in Moab, as the LORD had said. 6He buried him[b] in Moab, in the valley opposite Beth Peor, but to this day no one knows where his grave is. 7Moses was a hundred and twenty years old when he died, yet his eyes were not weak nor his strength gone. 8The Israelites grieved for Moses in the plains of Moab thirty days, until the time of weeping and mourning was over.

9Now Joshua son of Nun was filled with the spirit[c] of wisdom because Moses had laid his hands on him. So the Israelites listened to him and did what the LORD had commanded Moses.

10Since then, no prophet has risen in Israel like Moses, whom the LORD knew face to face, 11who did all those miraculous signs and wonders the LORD sent him to do in Egypt—to Pharaoh and to all his officials and to his whole land. 12For no one has ever shown the mighty power or performed the awesome deeds that Moses did in the sight of all Israel.

[a]2 That is, the Mediterranean
[b]6 Or *He was buried*
[c]9 Or *Spirit*

The NIV

# Interlinear Hebrew-English Old Testament

## Volume Two
## Joshua–2 Kings

וַיְהִי אַחֲרֵי מוֹת מֹשֶׁה עֶבֶד יְהוָה וַיֹּאמֶר יְהוָה

**Yahweh then-he-said Yahweh servant-of Moses death-of after and-he-was (1:1)**

אֶל־יְהוֹשֻׁעַ בִּן־נוּן מְשָׁרֵת מֹשֶׁה לֵאמֹר׃ מֹשֶׁה עַבְדִּי

**servant-of-me Moses (2) to-say Moses one-aiding-of Nun son-of Joshua to**

מֵת וְעַתָּה קוּם עֲבֹר אֶת־הַיַּרְדֵּן הַזֶּה אַתָּה וְכָל־

**and-all-of you the-this the-Jordan *** cross! get-ready! so-now he-is-dead**

הָעָם הַזֶּה אֶל־הָאָרֶץ אֲשֶׁר אָנֹכִי נֹתֵן לָהֶם לִבְנֵי יִשְׂרָאֵל׃

**Israel to-sons-of to-them giving I that the-land into the-this the-people**

כָּל־מָקוֹם אֲשֶׁר תִּדְרֹךְ כַּף־רַגְלְכֶם בּוֹ לָכֶם

**to-you on-him foot-of-you sole-of she-sets where place every-of (3)**

נְתַתִּיו כַּאֲשֶׁר דִּבַּרְתִּי אֶל־מֹשֶׁה׃ מֵהַמִּדְבָּר

**from-the-desert (4) Moses to I-promised just-as I-will-give-him**

וְהַלְּבָנוֹן הַזֶּה וְעַד־הַנָּהָר הַגָּדוֹל נְהַר־פְּרָת

**Euphrates River-of the-great the-river even-to the-this and-the-Lebanon**

כֹּל אֶרֶץ הַחִתִּים וְעַד־הַיָּם הַגָּדוֹל מְבוֹא הַשָּׁמֶשׁ

**the-sun setting-of the-Great the-Sea even-to the-Hittites country-of all-of**

יִהְיֶה גְּבוּלְכֶם׃ לֹא־יִתְיַצֵּב אִישׁ לְפָנֶיךָ כֹּל

**all-of against-you man he-will-stand not (5) territory-of-you he-will-be**

יְמֵי חַיֶּיךָ כַּאֲשֶׁר הָיִיתִי עִם־מֹשֶׁה אֶהְיֶה עִמָּךְ לֹא

**not with-you I-will-be Moses with I-was just-as lives-of-you days-of**

אַרְפְּךָ וְלֹא אֶעֶזְבֶךָּ׃ חֲזַק וֶאֱמָץ

**and-be-courageous! be-strong! (6) I-will-forsake-you and-not I-will-leave-you**

כִּי אַתָּה תַּנְחִיל אֶת־הָעָם הַזֶּה אֶת־הָאָרֶץ אֲשֶׁר־

**that the-land *** the-this the-people *** you-will-lead-to-inherit you for**

נִשְׁבַּעְתִּי לַאֲבוֹתָם לָתֵת לָהֶם׃ רַק חֲזַק

**be-strong! only (7) to-them to-give to-fathers-of-them I-swore**

וֶאֱמַץ מְאֹד לִשְׁמֹר לַעֲשׂוֹת כְּכָל־הַתּוֹרָה אֲשֶׁר

**that the-law as-all-of to-obey to-be-careful very and-be-courageous!**

צִוְּךָ מֹשֶׁה עַבְדִּי אַל־תָּסוּר מִמֶּנּוּ יָמִין וּשְׂמֹאול לְמַעַן

**so-that or-left right from-him you-turn not servant-of-me Moses he-gave-you**

תַּשְׂכִּיל בְּכֹל אֲשֶׁר תֵּלֵךְ׃ לֹא־יָמוּשׁ סֵפֶר הַתּוֹרָה

**the-Law Book-of you-let-depart not (8) you-go where in-every you-may-succeed**

הַזֶּה מִפִּיךָ וְהָגִיתָ בּוֹ יוֹמָם וָלַיְלָה לְמַעַן

**so-that and-night by-day on-him but-you-meditate from-mouth-of-you the-this**

תִּשְׁמֹר לַעֲשׂוֹת כְּכָל־הַכָּתוּב בּוֹ כִּי־אָז

**then for in-him the-being-written as-all-of to-do you-may-be-careful**

תַּצְלִיחַ אֶת־דְּרָכֶךָ וְאָז תַּשְׂכִּיל׃ הֲלוֹא

**not? (9) you-will-succeed and-then way-of-you *** you-will-prosper**

### *The LORD Commands Joshua*

1 After the death of Moses
the servant of the LORD,
the LORD said to Joshua son of
Nun, Moses' aide: 2"Moses my
servant is dead. Now then,
you and all these people, get
ready to cross the Jordan River
into the land I am about to
give to them—to the Israelites.
3I will give you every place
where you set your foot, as I
promised Moses. 4Your territory will extend from the
desert and from Lebanon to
the great river, the Euphrates—all the Hittite country—
and to the Great Sea[a] on the
west. 5No one will be able to
stand up against you all the
days of your life. As I was with
Moses, so I will be with you; I
will never leave you or forsake
you.
6"Be strong and courageous,
because you will lead these
people to inherit the land I
swore to their forefathers to
give them. 7Be strong and very
courageous. Be careful to obey
all the law my servant Moses
gave you; do not turn from it
to the right or to the left, that
you may be successful
wherever you go. 8Do not let
this Book of the Law depart
from your mouth; meditate on
it day and night, so that you
may be careful to do everything written in it. Then you
will be prosperous and successful. 9Have I not com-
manded you? Be strong and

[a]4 That is, the Mediterranean

צִוִּיתִ֗יךָ חֲזַ֣ק וֶאֱמָ֔ץ אַֽל־ תַּעֲרֹ֖ץ וְאַל־
and-not you-be-terrified not and-be-courageous! be-strong! I-commanded-you

תֵּחָ֑ת כִּ֤י עִמְּךָ֙ יְהוָ֣ה אֱלֹהֶ֔יךָ בְּכֹ֖ל אֲשֶׁ֥ר תֵּלֵֽךְ׃
you-go where in-every God-of-you Yahweh with-you for you-be-discouraged

וַיְצַ֣ו יְהוֹשֻׁ֔עַ אֶת־ שֹׁטְרֵ֥י הָעָ֖ם לֵאמֹֽר׃ עִבְר֣וּ
go! (11) to-say the-people being-officials-of *** Joshua so-he-commanded (10)

בְּקֶ֣רֶב הַֽמַּחֲנֶ֗ה וְצַוּ֤וּ אֶת־ הָעָם֙ לֵאמֹ֔ר הָכִ֥ינוּ לָכֶ֖ם
for-you get-ready! to-say the-people *** and-tell! the-camp through-midst-of

צֵידָ֑ה כִּ֞י בְּע֣וֹד ׀ שְׁלֹ֣שֶׁת יָמִ֗ים אַתֶּם֙ עֹבְרִים֙ אֶת־ הַיַּרְדֵּ֣ן הַזֶּ֔ה
the-this the-Jordan *** ones-crossing you days three-of from-now for supply

לָבוֹא֙ לָרֶ֣שֶׁת אֶת־ הָאָ֔רֶץ אֲשֶׁ֨ר יְהוָ֤ה אֱלֹֽהֵיכֶם֙ נֹתֵ֣ן לָכֶ֔ם
to-you giving God-of-you Yahweh that the-land *** to-possess to-go-in

לְרִשְׁתָּֽהּ׃ וְלָרֽאוּבֵנִי֙ וְלַגָּדִ֔י וְלַחֲצִ֖י
and-to-half-of and-to-the-Gadite but-to-the-Reubenite (12) to-possess-her

שֵׁ֣בֶט הַֽמְנַשֶּׁ֑ה אָמַ֥ר יְהוֹשֻׁ֖עַ לֵאמֹֽר׃ זָכוֹר֙ אֶת־ הַדָּבָ֔ר
the-command *** to-remember (13) to-say Joshua he-said the-Manasseh tribe-of

אֲשֶׁ֨ר צִוָּ֥ה אֶתְכֶ֛ם מֹשֶׁ֥ה עֶֽבֶד־ יְהוָ֖ה לֵאמֹ֑ר יְהוָ֤ה אֱלֹֽהֵיכֶם֙ מֵנִ֣יחַ
giving-rest God-of-you Yahweh to-say Yahweh servant-of Moses you he-gave that

לָכֶ֔ם וְנָתַ֥ן לָכֶ֖ם אֶת־ הָאָ֥רֶץ הַזֹּֽאת׃ נְשֵׁיכֶ֣ם
wives-of-you (14) the-this the-land *** to-you and-he-granted to-you

טַפְּכֶם֙ וּמִקְנֵיכֶ֔ם יֵשְׁב֕וּ בָּאָ֕רֶץ אֲשֶׁ֨ר נָתַ֥ן לָכֶ֛ם
to-you he-gave that in-the-land they-may-stay and-stocks-of-you child-of-you

מֹשֶׁ֖ה בְּעֵ֣בֶר הַיַּרְדֵּ֑ן וְאַתֶּם֩ תַּעַבְר֨וּ חֲמֻשִׁ֜ים לִפְנֵ֣י
ahead-of ones-being-armed you-must-cross but-you the-Jordan on-east-of Moses

אֲחֵיכֶ֗ם כֹּ֚ל גִּבּוֹרֵ֣י הַחַ֔יִל וַעֲזַרְתֶּ֖ם אוֹתָֽם׃ עַ֣ד
until (15) them so-you-must-help the-fight men-of all-of brothers-of-you

אֲשֶׁר־ יָנִ֣יחַ יְהוָ֣ה ׀ לַאֲחֵיכֶם֮ כָּכֶם֒ וְיָרְשׁ֣וּ גַם־
also and-they-possess as-you to-brothers-of-you Yahweh he-gives-rest when

הֵ֔מָּה אֶת־הָאָ֕רֶץ אֲשֶׁר־ יְהוָ֥ה אֱלֹהֵיכֶ֖ם נֹתֵ֣ן לָהֶ֑ם וְשַׁבְתֶּ֞ם
then-you-may-go-back to-them giving God-of-you Yahweh that the-land *** they

לְאֶ֤רֶץ יְרֻשַּׁתְכֶם֙ וִֽירִשְׁתֶּ֣ם אוֹתָ֔הּ אֲשֶׁ֣ר ׀ נָתַ֣ן לָכֶ֗ם
to-you he-gave which her and-you-may-occupy possession-of-you to-land-of

מֹשֶׁה֙ עֶ֣בֶד יְהוָ֔ה בְּעֵ֥בֶר הַיַּרְדֵּ֖ן מִזְרַ֥ח הַשָּֽׁמֶשׁ׃
the-sun rise-of the-Jordan on-east-of Yahweh servant-of Moses

וַֽיַּעֲנ֔וּ אֶת־ יְהוֹשֻׁ֖עַ לֵאמֹ֑ר כֹּ֤ל אֲשֶׁר־ צִוִּיתָ֙נוּ֙
you-commanded-us that all to-say Joshua *** then-they-answered (16)

נַעֲשֶׂ֔ה וְאֶל־ כָּל־ אֲשֶׁ֥ר תִּשְׁלָחֵ֖נוּ נֵלֵֽךְ׃ כְּכֹ֤ל אֲשֶׁר־
that as-all (17) we-will-go you-send-us that everywhere and-to we-will-do

courageous. Do not be terrified; do not be discouraged, for the LORD your God will be with you wherever you go."

10 So Joshua ordered the officers of the people: 11 "Go through the camp and tell the people, 'Get your supplies ready. Three days from now you will cross the Jordan here to go in and take possession of the land the LORD your God is giving you for your own.' "

12 But to the Reubenites, the Gadites and the half-tribe of Manasseh, Joshua said, 13 "Remember the command that Moses the servant of the LORD gave you: 'The LORD your God is giving you rest and has granted you this land.' 14 Your wives, your children and your livestock may stay in the land that Moses gave you east of the Jordan, but all your fighting men, fully armed, must cross over ahead of your brothers. You are to help your brothers 15 until the LORD gives them rest, as he has done for you, and until they too have taken possession of the land that the LORD your God is giving them. After that, you may go back and occupy your own land, which Moses the servant of the LORD gave you east of the Jordan toward the sunrise."

16 Then they answered Joshua, "Whatever you have commanded us we will do, and wherever you send us we will go. 17 Just as we fully

שָׁמַעְנוּ אֶל־ מֹשֶׁה כֵּן נִשְׁמַע אֵלֶיךָ רַק יִהְיֶה יְהוָה אֱלֹהֶיךָ
God-of-you Yahweh may-he-be only to-you we-will-obey so Moses to we-obeyed

עִמָּךְ כַּאֲשֶׁר הָיָה עִם־ מֹשֶׁה׃ כָּל־ אִישׁ אֲשֶׁר־ יַמְרֶה אֶת־
*** he-rebels who man any-of (18) Moses with he-was just-as with-you

פִּיךָ וְלֹא־ יִשְׁמַע אֶת־ דְּבָרֶיךָ לְכֹל אֲשֶׁר־
that against-anything words-of-you *** he-obeys and-not word-of-you

תְּצַוֶּנּוּ יוּמָת רַק חֲזַק וֶאֱמָץ׃
and-be-courageous! be-strong! only he-will-die you-may-command-him

וַיִּשְׁלַח יְהוֹשֻׁעַ־ בִּן־ נוּן מִן־ הַשִּׁטִּים שְׁנַיִם־אֲנָשִׁים מְרַגְּלִים
ones-spying men two the-Shittim from Nun son-of Joshua then-he-sent (2:1)

חֶרֶשׁ לֵאמֹר לְכוּ רְאוּ אֶת־ הָאָרֶץ וְאֶת־ יְרִיחוֹ וַיֵּלְכוּ
so-they-went Jericho and the-land *** look-over! go! to-say secretly

וַיָּבֹאוּ בֵּית־ אִשָּׁה זוֹנָה וּשְׁמָהּ רָחָב
Rahab and-name-of-her prostitute woman house-of and-they-entered

וַיִּשְׁכְּבוּ־ שָׁמָּה׃ וַיֵּאָמַר לְמֶלֶךְ יְרִיחוֹ לֵאמֹר הִנֵּה
see! to-say Jericho to-king-of and-he-was-told (2) at-there and-they-stayed

אֲנָשִׁים בָּאוּ הֵנָּה הַלַּיְלָה מִבְּנֵי יִשְׂרָאֵל לַחְפֹּר אֶת־הָאָרֶץ׃
the-land *** to-spy-out Israel from-sons-of the-night here they-came men

וַיִּשְׁלַח מֶלֶךְ יְרִיחוֹ אֶל־ רָחָב לֵאמֹר הוֹצִיאִי הָאֲנָשִׁים
the-men bring-out! to-say Rahab to Jericho king-of so-he-sent (3)

הַבָּאִים אֵלַיִךְ אֲשֶׁר־ בָּאוּ לְבֵיתֵךְ כִּי לַחְפֹּר אֶת־
*** to-spy-out for into-house-of-you they-entered who to-you the-ones-coming

כָּל־ הָאָרֶץ בָּאוּ׃ וַתִּקַּח הָאִשָּׁה אֶת־ שְׁנֵי הָאֲנָשִׁים
the-men two-of *** the-woman but-she-took (4) they-came the-land whole-of

וַתִּצְפְּנוֹ וַתֹּאמֶר | כֵּן בָּאוּ אֵלַי הָאֲנָשִׁים וְלֹא יָדַעְתִּי
I-knew but-not the-men to-me they-came yes and-she-said and-she-hid-him

מֵאַיִן הֵמָּה׃ וַיְהִי הַשַּׁעַר לִסְגּוֹר בַּחֹשֶׁךְ וְהָאֲנָשִׁים
and-the-men at-the-dusk to-close the-gate and-he-was (5) they from-where

יָצָאוּ לֹא יָדַעְתִּי אָנָה הָלְכוּ הָאֲנָשִׁים רִדְפוּ מַהֵר אַחֲרֵיהֶם
after-them quickly go-after! the-men they-went to-where I-know not they-left

כִּי תַשִּׂיגוּם׃ וְהִיא הֶעֱלָתַם הַגָּגָה
to-the-roof she-took-up-them but-she (6) you-may-catch-them for

וַתִּטְמְנֵם בְּפִשְׁתֵּי הָעֵץ הָעֲרֻכוֹת לָהּ עַל־
on by-her the-ones-being-laid the-stalk under-flax-of and-she-hid-them

הַגָּג׃ וְהָאֲנָשִׁים רָדְפוּ אַחֲרֵיהֶם דֶּרֶךְ הַיַּרְדֵּן עַל
to the-Jordan road-of after-them they-pursued so-the-men (7) the-roof

הַמַּעְבְּרוֹת וְהַשַּׁעַר סָגָרוּ אַחֲרֵי כַּאֲשֶׁר יָצְאוּ
they-went-out just-as after they-closed and-the-gate the-fords

obeyed Moses, so we will obey you. Only may the LORD your God be with you as he was with Moses. 18Whoever rebels against your word and does not obey your words, whatever you may command them, will be put to death. Only be strong and courageous!"

*Rahab and the Spies*

2 Then Joshua son of Nun secretly sent two spies from Shittim. "Go, look over the land," he said, "especially Jericho." So they went and entered the house of a prostitute[b] named Rahab and stayed there.

2The king of Jericho was told, "Look! Some of the Israelites have come here tonight to spy out the land." 3So the king of Jericho sent this message to Rahab, "Bring out the men who came to you and entered your house, because they have come to spy out the whole land."

4But the woman had taken the two men and hidden them. She said, "Yes, the men came to me, but I did not know where they had come from. 5At dusk, when it was time to close the city gate, the men left. I don't know which way they went. Go after them quickly. You may catch up with them." 6(But she had taken them up to the roof and hidden them under the stalks of flax she had laid out on the roof.) 7So the men set out in pursuit of the spies on the road that leads to the fords of the Jordan, and as soon as the pursuers had gone out, the gate was shut.

[b]1 Or possibly *an innkeeper*

| וְהִיא | יִשְׁכָּב֑וּן | טֶ֣רֶם | וְהֵ֖מָּה | אַחֲרֵיהֶֽם׃ | הָרֹדְפִ֔ים |
|---|---|---|---|---|---|
| then-she | they-lay-down | before | and-they | (8) after-them | the-ones-pursuing |

| עָלְתָ֖ה | עֲלֵיהֶ֣ם | עַל־ | הַגָּ֑ג | וַתֹּ֙אמֶר֙ | אֶל־הָ֣אֲנָשִׁ֔ים | יָדַ֕עְתִּי | כִּ֥י |
|---|---|---|---|---|---|---|---|
| she-went-up | to-them | on | (9) the-roof | and-she-said | to the-men | I-know | that |

| נָתַ֨ן | יְהוָ֤ה | לָכֶם֙ | אֶת־הָאָ֔רֶץ | וְכִֽי־ | נָפְלָ֤ה | אֵֽימַתְכֶם֙ | עָלֵ֔ינוּ |
|---|---|---|---|---|---|---|---|
| he-gave | Yahweh | to-you | *** the-land | and-that | she-fell | fear-of-you | on-us |

| וְכִ֥י | נָמֹ֛גוּ | כָּל־ | יֹשְׁבֵ֥י | הָאָ֖רֶץ | מִפְּנֵיכֶֽם׃ |
|---|---|---|---|---|---|
| and-that | they-melt-in-fear | all-of | ones-living-of | the-country | because-of-you |

| כִּ֣י | שָׁמַ֗עְנוּ | אֵ֤ת | אֲשֶׁר־ | הוֹבִ֤ישׁ | יְהוָה֙ | אֶת־ | מֵ֣י | יַם־ | סוּף֙ |
|---|---|---|---|---|---|---|---|---|---|
| (10) for | we-heard | *** | how | he-dried-up | Yahweh | *** | waters-of | Sea-of | Reed |

| מִפְּנֵיכֶ֔ם | בְּצֵאתְכֶ֖ם | מִמִּצְרָ֑יִם | וַאֲשֶׁ֣ר | עֲשִׂיתֶ֗ם | לִשְׁנֵ֨י |
|---|---|---|---|---|---|
| from-before-you | when-to-come-you | from-Egypt | and-what | you-did | to-two-of |

| מַלְכֵ֣י | הָאֱמֹרִ֗י | אֲשֶׁ֛ר | בְּעֵ֥בֶר | הַיַּרְדֵּ֖ן | לְסִיחֹ֣ן | וּלְע֑וֹג | אֲשֶׁ֥ר |
|---|---|---|---|---|---|---|---|
| kings-of | the-Amorite | who | on-east-of | the-Jordan | to-Sihon | and-to-Og | whom |

| הֶחֱרַמְתֶּ֖ם | אוֹתָֽם׃ | וַנִּשְׁמַע֙ | וַיִּמַּ֣ס | לְבָבֵ֔נוּ | וְלֹא־ |
|---|---|---|---|---|---|
| you-destroyed | them | (11) when-we-heard | then-he-sank | heart-of-us | and-not |

| קָ֨מָה | ע֥וֹד | ר֛וּחַ | בְּאִ֖ישׁ | מִפְּנֵיכֶ֑ם | כִּ֚י | יְהוָ֣ה | אֱלֹהֵיכֶ֔ם |
|---|---|---|---|---|---|---|---|
| she-remained | any-more | courage | in-anyone | because-of-you | for | Yahweh | God-of-you |

| ה֤וּא אֱלֹהִים֙ | בַּשָּׁמַ֣יִם | מִמַּ֔עַל | וְעַל־ | הָאָ֖רֶץ | מִתָּֽחַת׃ | וְעַתָּ֗ה הִשָּֽׁבְעוּ־ |
|---|---|---|---|---|---|---|
| God he | in-the-heavens | at-above | and-on | the-earth | at-below | (12) so-now swear! |

| נָ֥א | לִי֙ | בַּֽיהוָ֔ה | כִּי־ | עָשִׂ֥יתִי | עִמָּכֶ֖ם | חָ֑סֶד | וַעֲשִׂיתֶ֞ם |
|---|---|---|---|---|---|---|---|
| now! | to-me | by-Yahweh | because | I-showed | to-you | kindness | that-you-will-show |

| גַּם־ | אַתֶּ֗ם | עִם־ | בֵּ֤ית | אָבִי֙ | חֶ֔סֶד | וּנְתַתֶּ֥ם | לִ֖י | א֥וֹת אֱמֶֽת׃ |
|---|---|---|---|---|---|---|---|---|
| also | you | to | house-of | father-of-me | kindness | and-you-give | to-me | sign sure |

| וְהַחֲיִתֶ֞ם | אֶת־ | אָבִ֣י | וְאֶת־ | אִמִּ֗י | וְאֶת־ |
|---|---|---|---|---|---|
| that-you-will-let-live | *** | father-of-me | and | mother-of-me | and |

| אַחַי֙ | וְאֶת־ | אַחְיוֹתַ֔י | וְאֵ֖ת | כָּל־ | אֲשֶׁ֣ר | לָהֶ֑ם | וְהִצַּלְתֶּ֥ם | אֶת־ |
|---|---|---|---|---|---|---|---|---|
| brothers-of-me | and | sisters-of-me | and | all | who | to-them | and-you-will-save | *** |

| נַפְשֹׁתֵ֖ינוּ | מִמָּֽוֶת׃ | וַיֹּ֧אמְרוּ | לָ֣הּ | הָאֲנָשִׁ֗ים | נַפְשֵׁ֤נוּ | תַחְתֵּיכֶם֙ |
|---|---|---|---|---|---|---|
| lives-of-us | from-death | (14) and-they-said | to-her | the-men | life-of-us | for-you |

| לָמ֔וּת | אִ֚ם | לֹ֣א | תַגִּ֔ידוּ | אֶת־ | דְּבָרֵ֖נוּ | זֶ֑ה | וְהָיָ֗ה | בְּתֵת־ |
|---|---|---|---|---|---|---|---|---|
| to-die | if | not | you-tell | *** | deed-of-us | this | then-he-will-be | when-to-give |

| יְהוָ֥ה | לָ֙נוּ֙ | אֶת־הָאָ֔רֶץ | וְעָשִׂ֥ינוּ | עִמָּ֖ךְ | חֶ֥סֶד | וֶאֱמֶֽת׃ |
|---|---|---|---|---|---|---|
| Yahweh | to-us | *** the-land | then-we-will-treat | with-you | kindly | and-faithfully |

| וַתּוֹרִדֵ֥ם | בַּחֶ֖בֶל | בְּעַ֣ד | הַֽחַלּ֑וֹן | כִּ֤י | בֵיתָהּ֙ |
|---|---|---|---|---|---|
| (15) so-she-let-down-them | by-the-rope | through | the-window | for | house-of-her |

| בְּקִ֣יר | הַֽחוֹמָ֔ה | וּבַֽחוֹמָ֖ה | הִ֣יא | יוֹשָֽׁבֶת׃ | וַתֹּ֣אמֶר | לָהֶ֗ם |
|---|---|---|---|---|---|---|
| in-city-of | the-wall | and-in-the-wall | she | living | (16) now-she-said | to-them |

°*13* אַחִיוֹתַי

[8]Before the spies lay down for the night, she went up on the roof [9]and said to them, "I know that the LORD has given this land to you and that a great fear of you has fallen on us, so that all who live in this country are melting in fear because of you. [10]We have heard how the LORD dried up the water of the Red Sea[c] for you when you came out of Egypt, and what you did to Sihon and Og, the two kings of the Amorites east of the Jordan, whom you completely destroyed.[d] [11]When we heard of it, our hearts sank and everyone's courage failed because of you, for the LORD your God is God in heaven above and on the earth below. [12]Now then, please swear to me by the LORD that you will show kindness to my family, because I have shown kindness to you. Give me a sure sign [13]that you will spare the lives of my father and mother, my brothers and sisters, and all who belong to them, and that you will save us from death."

[14]"Our lives for your lives!" the men assured her. "If you don't tell what we are doing, we will treat you kindly and faithfully when the LORD gives us the land."

[15]So she let them down by a rope through the window, for the house she lived in was part of the city wall. [16]Now she had

*c10* Hebrew *Yam Suph;* that is, Sea of Reeds
*d10* The Hebrew term refers to the irrevocable giving over of things or persons to the LORD, often by totally destroying them.

הָהָרָה לֵּכוּ פֶּן־ יִפְגְּעוּ בָכֶם הָרֹדְפִים וְנַחְבֵּתֶם
and-you-hide-selves the-ones-pursuing to-you they-find so-not go! to-the-hill

שָׁמָּה שְׁלֹשֶׁת יָמִים עַד שׁוֹב הָרֹדְפִים וְאַחַר תֵּלְכוּ
you-go and-after the-ones-pursuing to-return until days three-of at-there

לְדַרְכְּכֶם׃ (17) וַיֹּאמְרוּ אֵלֶיהָ הָאֲנָשִׁים נְקִיִּם אֲנַחְנוּ מִשְּׁבֻעָתֵךְ
from-oath-of-us we ones-free the-men to-her and-they-said (17) on-way-of-you

הַזֶּה אֲשֶׁר הִשְׁבַּעְתָּנוּ׃ (18) הִנֵּה אֲנַחְנוּ בָאִים בָּאָרֶץ
into-the-land ones-entering we unless (18) you-made-swear-us that the-this

אֶת־ תִּקְוַת חוּט הַשָּׁנִי הַזֶּה תִּקְשְׁרִי בַּחַלּוֹן אֲשֶׁר הוֹרַדְתֵּנוּ
you-let-down-us that in-the-window you-tie this the-scarlet rope cord-of ***

בוֹ וְאֶת־ אָבִיךְ וְאֶת־ אִמֵּךְ וְאֶת־ אַחַיִךְ וְאֵת
and brother-of-you and mother-of-you and father-of-you and through-him

כָּל־ בֵּית אָבִיךְ תַּאַסְפִי אֵלַיִךְ הַבָּיְתָה׃
into-the-house with-you you-bring father-of-you house-of all-of

(19) וְהָיָה כֹּל אֲשֶׁר־ יֵצֵא מִדַּלְתֵי בֵיתֵךְ ׀
house-of-you from-doors-of he-goes-out who anyone and-he-will-be (19)

הַחוּצָה דָּמוֹ בְרֹאשׁוֹ וַאֲנַחְנוּ נְקִיִּם
ones-not-responsible and-we on-head-of-him blood-of-him into-the-street

וְכֹל אֲשֶׁר יִהְיֶה אִתָּךְ בַּבַּיִת דָּמוֹ בְרֹאשֵׁנוּ אִם־
if on-head-of-us blood-of-him in-the-house with-you he-is who but-anyone

יָד תִּהְיֶה־ בּוֹ׃ (20) וְאִם־ תַּגִּידִי אֶת־ דְּבָרֵנוּ זֶה וְהָיִינוּ
then-we-are this deed-of-us *** you-tell but-if (20) on-him she-lays hand

נְקִיִּם מִשְּׁבֻעָתֵךְ אֲשֶׁר הִשְׁבַּעְתָּנוּ׃ (21) וַתֹּאמֶר
and-she-replied (21) you-made-swear-us that from-oath-of-you ones-released

כְּדִבְרֵיכֶם כֶּן־ הוּא וַתְּשַׁלְּחֵם וַיֵּלֵכוּ וַתִּקְשֹׁר
and-she-tied and-they-departed so-she-sent-away-them he so as-words-of-you

אֶת־ תִּקְוַת הַשָּׁנִי בַּחַלּוֹן׃ (22) וַיֵּלְכוּ וַיָּבֹאוּ
then-they-went when-they-left (22) in-the-window the-scarlet cord-of ***

הָהָרָה וַיֵּשְׁבוּ שָׁם שְׁלֹשֶׁת יָמִים עַד־ שָׁבוּ
they-returned until days three-of there and-they-stayed into-the-hill

הָרֹדְפִים וַיְבַקְשׁוּ הָרֹדְפִים בְּכָל־ הַדֶּרֶךְ
the-road along-all-of the-ones-pursuing and-they-searched the-ones-pursuing

וְלֹא מָצָאוּ׃ (23) וַיָּשֻׁבוּ שְׁנֵי הָאֲנָשִׁים
the-men two-of then-they-started-back (23) they-found but-not

וַיֵּרְדוּ מֵהָהָר וַיַּעַבְרוּ וַיָּבֹאוּ אֶל־ יְהוֹשֻׁעַ
Joshua to and-they-came and-they-forded from-the-hill and-they-went-down

בִּן־ נוּן וַיְסַפְּרוּ־ לוֹ אֵת כָּל־ הַמֹּצְאוֹת אוֹתָם׃
to-them the-things-happening all-of *** to-him and-they-told Nun son-of

said to them, "Go to the hills so the pursuers will not find you. Hide yourselves there three days until they return, and then go on your way."
17 The men said to her, "This oath you made us swear will
not be binding on us 18 unless,
when we enter the land, you have tied this scarlet cord in the window through which you let us down, and unless you have brought your father and mother, your brothers and all your family into your
house. 19 If anyone goes outside your house into the street, his blood will be on his own head; we will not be responsible. As for anyone who is in the house with you, his blood will be on our head if a hand
is laid on him. 20 But if you tell
what we are doing, we will be released from the oath you made us swear."
21 "Agreed," she replied. "Let it be as you say." So she sent them away and they departed. And she tied the scarlet cord in the window.
22 When they left, they went into the hills and stayed there three days, until the pursuers had searched all along the road and returned without
finding them. 23 Then the two
men started back. They went down out of the hills, forded the river and came to Joshua son of Nun and told him everything that had happened

וַיֹּאמְרוּ אֶל־יְהוֹשֻׁעַ כִּי־ נָתַן יְהוָה בְּיָדֵנוּ אֶת־
*** into-hand-of-us Yahweh he-gave surely Joshua to and-they-said (24)

כָּל־ הָאָרֶץ וְגַם־ נָמֹגוּ כָּל־ יֹשְׁבֵי הָאָרֶץ
the-land ones-living-of all-of they-melt-in-fear and-also the-land whole-of

מִפָּנֵינוּ׃ וַיַּשְׁכֵּם יְהוֹשֻׁעַ בַּבֹּקֶר וַיִּסְעוּ
and-they-set-out in-the-morning Joshua and-he-rose (3:1) because-of-us

מֵהַשִּׁטִּים וַיָּבֹאוּ עַד־ הַיַּרְדֵּן הוּא וְכָל־ בְּנֵי יִשְׂרָאֵל
Israel sons-of and-all-of he the-Jordan to and-they-went from-the-Shittim

וַיָּלִנוּ שָׁם טֶרֶם יַעֲבֹרוּ׃ וַיְהִי מִקְצֵה
at-end-of and-he-was (2) they-crossed-over before there and-they-camped

שְׁלֹשֶׁת יָמִים וַיַּעַבְרוּ הַשֹּׁטְרִים בְּקֶרֶב הַמַּחֲנֶה׃
the-camp through-midst-of the-being-officers then-they-went days three-of

וַיְצַוּוּ אֶת־ הָעָם לֵאמֹר כִּרְאוֹתְכֶם אֵת אֲרוֹן
ark-of *** when-to-see-you to-say the-people *** and-they-ordered (3)

בְּרִית־ יְהוָה אֱלֹהֵיכֶם וְהַכֹּהֲנִים הַלְוִיִּם נֹשְׂאִים אֹתוֹ
him ones-carrying the-Levites and-the-priests God-of-you Yahweh covenant-of

וְאַתֶּם תִּסְעוּ מִמְּקוֹמְכֶם וַהֲלַכְתֶּם אַחֲרָיו׃ אַךְ ׀
but (4) after-him and-you-follow from-position-of-you you-move-out then-you

רָחוֹק יִהְיֶה בֵּינֵיכֶם וּבֵינָו כְּאַלְפַּיִם אַמָּה
cubit about-two-thousands and-between-him between-you he-must-be distance

בַּמִּדָּה אַל־ תִּקְרְבוּ אֵלָיו לְמַעַן אֲשֶׁר־ תֵּדְעוּ אֶת־ הַדֶּרֶךְ
the-way *** you-will-know then so-that to-him you-go-near not by-the-measure

אֲשֶׁר תֵּלְכוּ־ בָהּ כִּי לֹא עֲבַרְתֶּם בַּדֶּרֶךְ מִתְּמוֹל
on-yesterday on-the-way you-have-been not since on-her you-must-go which

שִׁלְשׁוֹם׃ וַיֹּאמֶר יְהוֹשֻׁעַ אֶל־ הָעָם הִתְקַדָּשׁוּ כִּי מָחָר
tomorrow for consecrated-selves! the-people to Joshua then-he-told (5) before

יַעֲשֶׂה יְהוָה בְּקִרְבְּכֶם נִפְלָאוֹת׃ וַיֹּאמֶר יְהוֹשֻׁעַ
Joshua and-he-said (6) things-being-amazing in-among-you Yahweh he-will-do

אֶל־ הַכֹּהֲנִים לֵאמֹר שְׂאוּ אֶת־ אֲרוֹן הַבְּרִית וְעִבְרוּ
and-cross-over! the-covenant ark-of *** take-up! to-say the-priests to

לִפְנֵי הָעָם וַיִּשְׂאוּ אֶת־ אֲרוֹן הַבְּרִית וַיֵּלְכוּ
and-they-went the-covenant ark-of *** so-they-took-up the-people ahead-of

לִפְנֵי הָעָם׃ וַיֹּאמֶר יְהוָה אֶל־יְהוֹשֻׁעַ הַיּוֹם הַזֶּה
the-this the-day Joshua to Yahweh and-he-said (7) the-people ahead-of

אָחֵל גַּדֶּלְךָ בְּעֵינֵי כָּל־ יִשְׂרָאֵל אֲשֶׁר יֵדְעוּן כִּי
that they-may-know that Israel all-of in-eyes-of to-exalt-you I-will-begin

כַּאֲשֶׁר הָיִיתִי עִם־ מֹשֶׁה אֶהְיֶה עִמָּךְ׃ וְאַתָּה תְּצַוֶּה אֶת־ הַכֹּהֲנִים
the-priests *** you-tell now-you (8) with-you I-am Moses with I-was just-as

°4 ק וביניו

to them. 24They said to Joshua, "The LORD has surely given the whole land into our hands; all the people are melting in fear because of us."

*Crossing the Jordan*

3 Early in the morning Joshua and all the Israelites set out from Shittim and went to the Jordan, where they camped before crossing over. 2After three days the officers went throughout the camp, 3giving orders to the people: "When you see the ark of the covenant of the LORD your God, and the priests, who are Levites, carrying it, you are to move out from your positions and follow it. 4Then you will know which way to go, since you have never been this way before. But keep a distance of about a thousand yards[e] between you and the ark; do not go near it."

5Then Joshua told the people, "Consecrate yourselves, for tomorrow the LORD will do amazing things among you."

6Joshua said to the priests, "Take up the ark of the covenant and cross over ahead of the people." So they took it up and went ahead of them.

7And the LORD said to Joshua, "Today I will begin to exalt you in the eyes of all Israel, so they may know that I am with you as I was with Moses. 8Tell the priests who carry the

e4 Hebrew *about two thousand cubits* (about 900 meters)

נֹשְׂאֵי אֲרוֹן־הַבְּרִית לֵאמֹר כְּבֹאֲכֶם עַד־קְצֵה
edge-of to when-to-reach-you to-say the-covenant ark-of ones-carrying-of

מֵי הַיַּרְדֵּן בַּיַּרְדֵּן תַּעֲמֹדוּ׃ וַיֹּאמֶר יְהוֹשֻׁעַ אֶל־
to Joshua so-he-said (9) you-stand in-the-Jordan the-Jordan waters-of

בְּנֵי יִשְׂרָאֵל גֹּשׁוּ הֵנָּה וְשִׁמְעוּ אֶת־דִּבְרֵי יְהוָה אֱלֹהֵיכֶם׃
God-of-you Yahweh words-of *** and-listen! here come! Israel sons-of

וַיֹּאמֶר יְהוֹשֻׁעַ בְּזֹאת תֵּדְעוּן כִּי אֵל חַי בְּקִרְבְּכֶם
in-among-you living God that you-will-know by-this Joshua and-he-said (10)

וְהוֹרֵשׁ יוֹרִישׁ מִפְּנֵיכֶם אֶת־הַכְּנַעֲנִי וְאֶת־
and the-Canaanite *** from-before-you he-will-drive-out and-to-drive-out

הַחִתִּי וְאֶת־הַחִוִּי וְאֶת־הַפְּרִזִּי וְאֶת־הַגִּרְגָּשִׁי
the-Girgashite and the-Perizzite and the-Hivite and the-Hittite

וְהָאֱמֹרִי וְהַיְבוּסִי׃ הִנֵּה אֲרוֹן הַבְּרִית אֲדוֹן
Lord-of the-covenant ark-of see! (11) and-the-Jebusite and-the-Amorite

כָּל־הָאָרֶץ עֹבֵר לִפְנֵיכֶם בַּיַּרְדֵּן׃ וְעַתָּה קְחוּ
choose! so-now (12) into-the-Jordan ahead-of-you going the-earth all-of

לָכֶם שְׁנֵי עָשָׂר אִישׁ מִשִּׁבְטֵי יִשְׂרָאֵל אִישׁ־אֶחָד אִישׁ־אֶחָד לַשָּׁבֶט׃
from-the-tribe one man one man Israel from-tribes-of man ten two-of for-you

וְהָיָה כְּנוֹחַ כַּפּוֹת רַגְלֵי הַכֹּהֲנִים נֹשְׂאֵי
ones-carrying-of the-priests feet-of soles-of as-to-set and-he-will-be (13)

אֲרוֹן יְהוָה אֲדוֹן כָּל־הָאָרֶץ בְּמֵי הַיַּרְדֵּן מֵי
waters-of the-Jordan in-waters-of the-earth all-of Lord-of Yahweh ark-of

הַיַּרְדֵּן יִכָּרֵתוּן הַמַּיִם הַיֹּרְדִים מִלְמָעְלָה
from-above the-ones-flowing-down the-waters they-will-be-cut-off the-Jordan

וְיַעַמְדוּ נֵד אֶחָד׃ וַיְהִי בִּנְסֹעַ הָעָם
the-people when-to-set-out and-he-was (14) one heap and-they-will-stand-up

מֵאָהֳלֵיהֶם לַעֲבֹר אֶת־הַיַּרְדֵּן וְהַכֹּהֲנִים נֹשְׂאֵי
ones-carrying-of and-the-priests the-Jordan *** to-cross from-tents-of-them

הָאָרוֹן הַבְּרִית לִפְנֵי הָעָם׃ וּכְבוֹא נֹשְׂאֵי
ones-carrying-of and-as-to-reach (15) the-people ahead-of the-covenant the-ark

הָאָרוֹן עַד־הַיַּרְדֵּן וְרַגְלֵי הַכֹּהֲנִים נֹשְׂאֵי הָאָרוֹן
the-ark ones-carrying-of the-priests and-feet-of the-Jordan to the-ark

נִטְבְּלוּ בִּקְצֵה הַמָּיִם וְהַיַּרְדֵּן מָלֵא עַל־כָּל־
all-of to he-is-full now-the-Jordan the-waters on-edge-of they-touched

גְּדוֹתָיו כֹּל יְמֵי קָצִיר׃ וַיַּעַמְדוּ הַמַּיִם
the-waters and-they-stopped (16) harvest days-of all-of banks-of-him

הַיֹּרְדִים מִלְמַעְלָה קָמוּ נֵד־אֶחָד הַרְחֵק מְאֹד
very to-be-distant one heap they-piled-up from-above the-ones-flowing-down

ark of the covenant: 'When
you reach the edge of the Jordan's waters, go and stand in
the river.' "
9 Joshua said to the Israelites,
"Come here and listen to the
words of the LORD your God.
10 This is how you will know
that the living God is among
you, and that he will certainly
drive out before you the Canaanites, Hittites, Hivites,
Perizzites, Girgashites, Amorites and Jebusites. 11 See, the
ark of the covenant of the Lord
of all the earth will go into the
Jordan ahead of you. 12 Now
then, choose twelve men from
the tribes of Israel, one from
each tribe. 13 And as soon as
the priests who carry the ark
of the LORD—the Lord of all the
earth—set foot in the Jordan,
the water flowing down-
stream will be cut off and
stand up in a heap."
14 So when the people broke
camp to cross the Jordan, the
priests carrying the ark of the
covenant went ahead of them.
15 Now the Jordan is at flood
stage all during harvest. Yet as
soon as the priests who carried
the ark reached the Jordan and
their feet touched the water's
edge, 16 the water from up-
stream stopped flowing. It
piled up in a heap a great distance away, at a town called

f16 That is, the Dead Sea

בְּאָדָם הָעִיר אֲשֶׁר מִצַּד צָרְתָן וְהַיֹּרְדִים עַל
to and-the-ones-flowing-down Zarethan in-vicinity that the-town at-Adam

יָם הָעֲרָבָה יָם־ הַמֶּלַח תַּמּוּ נִכְרָתוּ
they-were-cut-off they-were-complete the-Salt Sea-of the-Arabah Sea-of

וְהָעָם עָבְרוּ נֶגֶד יְרִיחוֹ: וַיַּעַמְדוּ
and-they-stood (17) Jericho opposite they-crossed-over so-the-people

הַכֹּהֲנִים נֹשְׂאֵי הָאָרוֹן בְּרִית־ יְהוָה בֶּחָרָבָה
on-the-dry-ground Yahweh covenant-of the-ark ones-carrying-of the-priests

בְּתוֹךְ הַיַּרְדֵּן הָכֵן וְכָל־ יִשְׂרָאֵל עֹבְרִים
ones-passing-by Israel and-all-of to-be-firm the-Jordan in-middle-of

בֶּחָרָבָה עַד אֲשֶׁר־ תַּמּוּ כָּל־ הַגּוֹי לַעֲבֹר אֶת־
*** to-cross the-nation whole-of they-completed when until on-the-dry-ground

הַיַּרְדֵּן: וַיְהִי כַּאֲשֶׁר־ תַּמּוּ כָל־ הַגּוֹי
the-nation whole-of they-finished just-as and-he-was (4:1) the-Jordan

לַעֲבוֹר אֶת־ הַיַּרְדֵּן וַיֹּאמֶר יְהוָה אֶל־ יְהוֹשֻׁעַ לֵאמֹר: קְחוּ
choose! (2) to-say Joshua to Yahweh then-he-said the-Jordan *** to-cross

לָכֶם מִן־ הָעָם שְׁנֵים עָשָׂר אֲנָשִׁים אִישׁ־אֶחָד אִישׁ־אֶחָד מִשָּׁבֶט: וְצַוּוּ
and-tell! (3) from-tribe one man one man men ten two the-people from for-you

אוֹתָם לֵאמֹר שְׂאוּ־ לָכֶם מִזֶּה מִתּוֹךְ הַיַּרְדֵּן מִמַּצַּב
from-place-of the-Jordan in-middle-of from-here for-you take-up! to-say them

רַגְלֵי הַכֹּהֲנִים הָכִין שְׁתֵּים־עֶשְׂרֵה אֲבָנִים וְהַעֲבַרְתֶּם אוֹתָם עִמָּכֶם
with-you them and-you-carry-over stones ten two to-stand the-priests feet-of

וְהִנַּחְתֶּם אוֹתָם בַּמָּלוֹן אֲשֶׁר־ תָּלִינוּ בוֹ הַלָּיְלָה:
the-night in-him you-stay where at-the-place them and-you-put-down

וַיִּקְרָא יְהוֹשֻׁעַ אֶל־ שְׁנֵים הֶעָשָׂר אִישׁ אֲשֶׁר הֵכִין
he-appointed whom man the-ten two together Joshua so-he-called (4)

מִבְּנֵי יִשְׂרָאֵל אִישׁ־אֶחָד אִישׁ־אֶחָד מִשָּׁבֶט: וַיֹּאמֶר לָהֶם
to-them and-he-said (5) from-tribe one man one man Israel from-sons-of

יְהוֹשֻׁעַ עִבְרוּ לִפְנֵי אֲרוֹן יְהוָה אֱלֹהֵיכֶם אֶל־ תּוֹךְ הַיַּרְדֵּן
the-Jordan middle-of into God-of-you Yahweh ark-of before go-over! Joshua

וְהָרִימוּ לָכֶם אִישׁ אֶבֶן אַחַת עַל־ שִׁכְמוֹ לְמִסְפַּר שִׁבְטֵי
tribes-of by-number-of shoulder-of-him on one stone each to-you and-take-up!

בְּנֵי־ יִשְׂרָאֵל: לְמַעַן תִּהְיֶה זֹאת אוֹת בְּקִרְבְּכֶם כִּי־ יִשְׁאָלוּן
they-ask when in-among-you sign this she-will-be so-that (6) Israel sons-of

בְּנֵיכֶם מָחָר לֵאמֹר מָה הָאֲבָנִים הָאֵלֶּה לָכֶם:
to-you the-these the-stones what? to-say future children-of-you

וַאֲמַרְתֶּם לָהֶם אֲשֶׁר נִכְרְתוּ מֵימֵי הַיַּרְדֵּן
the-Jordan waters-of they-were-cut-off that to-them then-you-tell (7)

Adam in the vicinity of Zarethan, while the water flowing down to the Sea of the Arabah (the Salt Sea[f]) was completely cut off. So the people crossed over opposite Jericho.
17The priests who carried the ark of the covenant of the LORD stood firm on dry ground in the middle of the Jordan, while all Israel passed by until the whole nation had completed the crossing on dry ground.

4 When the whole nation had finished crossing the Jordan, the LORD said to Joshua,
2"Choose twelve men from among the people, one from each tribe,
3and tell them to take up twelve stones from the middle of the Jordan from right where the priests stood and to carry them over with you and put them down at the place where you stay tonight."
4So Joshua called together the twelve men he had appointed from the Israelites, one from each tribe,
5and said to them, "Go over before the ark of the LORD your God into the middle of the Jordan. Each of you is to take up a stone on his shoulder, according to the number of the tribes of the Israelites,
6to serve as a sign among you. In the future, when your children ask you, 'What do these stones mean?'
7tell them that the flow of the Jordan was cut off before the

°16 ק מאדם

מִפְּנֵי֙ אֲר֣וֹן בְּרִית־ יְהוָ֔ה בְּעָבְרוֹ֙ בַּיַּרְדֵּ֔ן
over-the-Jordan when-to-cross-him Yahweh covenant-of ark-of from-before

נִכְרְת֖וּ מֵ֣י הַיַּרְדֵּ֑ן וְ֠הָיוּ הָאֲבָנִ֥ים הָאֵ֛לֶּה
the-these the-stones now-they-must-be the-Jordan waters-of they-were-cut-off

לְזִכָּר֛וֹן לִבְנֵ֥י יִשְׂרָאֵ֖ל עַד־עוֹלָֽם׃ וַיַּעֲשׂוּ־ כֵ֣ן בְּנֵֽי־ יִשְׂרָאֵ֮ל
Israel sons-of this so-they-did (8) forever to Israel to-sons-of as-memorial

כַּאֲשֶׁ֣ר צִוָּ֣ה יְהוֹשֻׁ֒עַ֒ וַיִּשְׂא֡וּ שְׁתֵּֽי־עֶשְׂרֵ֨ה אֲבָנִ֜ים מִתּ֣וֹךְ
from-middle-of stones ten two-of and-they-took Joshua he-commanded just-as

הַיַּרְדֵּ֗ן כַּאֲשֶׁ֨ר דִּבֶּ֤ר יְהוָה֙ אֶל־יְהוֹשֻׁ֔עַ לְמִסְפַּ֖ר שִׁבְטֵ֣י בְנֵֽי־
sons-of tribes-of by-number-of Joshua to Yahweh he-told just-as the-Jordan

יִשְׂרָאֵ֑ל וַיַּעֲבִר֤וּם עִמָּם֙ אֶל־ הַמָּל֔וֹן וַיַּנִּח֖וּם
and-they-put-down-them the-camp to with-them and-they-carried-them Israel

שָֽׁם׃ וּשְׁתֵּ֧ים עֶשְׂרֵ֣ה אֲבָנִ֗ים הֵקִ֣ים יְהוֹשֻׁ֘עַ֮ בְּת֣וֹךְ הַיַּרְדֵּן֒ תַּ֗חַת
at the-Jordan in-middle-of Joshua he-set-up stones ten and-two (9) there

מַצַּב֙ רַגְלֵ֣י הַכֹּהֲנִ֔ים נֹשְׂאֵ֖י אֲר֣וֹן הַבְּרִ֑ית וַיִּ֣הְיוּ
and-they-are the-covenant ark-of ones-carrying-of the-priests feet-of spot-of

שָׁ֔ם עַ֖ד הַיּ֥וֹם הַזֶּֽה׃ וְהַכֹּהֲנִ֞ים נֹשְׂאֵ֣י הָאָר֗וֹן
the-ark ones-carrying-of now-the-priests (10) the-this the-day to there

עֹמְדִים֮ בְּת֣וֹךְ הַיַּרְדֵּן֒ עַ֣ד תֹּ֣ם כָּל־ הַ֠דָּבָר
the-thing every-of to-be-done until the-Jordan in-middle-of ones-standing

אֲשֶׁר־ צִוָּ֨ה יְהוָ֜ה אֶת־יְהוֹשֻׁ֗עַ לְדַבֵּ֤ר אֶל־ הָעָם֙ כְּכֹ֥ל אֲשֶׁר־
that as-all the-people to to-speak Joshua *** Yahweh he-commanded that

צִוָּ֥ה מֹשֶׁ֖ה אֶת־ יְהוֹשֻׁ֑עַ וַיְמַהֲר֥וּ הָעָ֖ם וַֽיַּעֲבֹֽרוּ׃
and-they-came-over the-people and-they-hurried Joshua *** Moses he-directed

וַיְהִ֛י כַּאֲשֶׁר־ תַּ֥ם כָּל־ הָעָ֖ם לַעֲב֑וֹר
to-cross the-people all-of he-finished just-as and-he-was (11)

וַיַּעֲבֹ֧ר אֲרוֹן־ יְהוָ֛ה וְהַכֹּהֲנִ֖ים לִפְנֵ֥י הָעָֽם׃
the-people in-front-of and-the-priests Yahweh ark-of then-he-came-over

וַֽ֠יַּעַבְרוּ בְּנֵֽי־ רְא֨וּבֵן וּבְנֵי־ גָ֜ד וַחֲצִ֨י
and-half-of Gad and-sons-of Reuben sons-of and-they-crossed-over (12)

שֵׁ֤בֶט הַֽמְנַשֶּׁה֙ חֲמֻשִׁ֔ים לִפְנֵ֖י בְּנֵ֣י יִשְׂרָאֵ֑ל כַּאֲשֶׁ֛ר
just-as Israel sons-of in-front-of ones-being-armed the-Manasseh tribe-of

דִּבֶּ֥ר אֲלֵיהֶ֖ם מֹשֶֽׁה׃ כְּאַרְבָּעִ֥ים אֶ֖לֶף חֲלוּצֵ֣י
ones-being-armed-of thousand about-forty (13) Moses to-them he-directed

הַצָּבָ֑א עָבְר֞וּ לִפְנֵ֤י יְהוָה֙ לַמִּלְחָמָ֔ה אֶ֖ל עַֽרְב֥וֹת יְרִיחֽוֹ׃
Jericho plains-of to for-the-war Yahweh before they-crossed-over the-battle

בַּיּ֣וֹם הַה֗וּא גִּדַּ֤ל יְהוָה֙ אֶת־ יְהוֹשֻׁ֔עַ בְּעֵינֵ֖י כָּל־
all-of in-eyes-of Joshua *** Yahweh he-exalted the-that on-the-day (14)

ark of the covenant of the
LORD. When it crossed the Jordan, the waters of the Jordan
were cut off. These stones are
to be a memorial to the people
of Israel forever."
8 So the Israelites did as
Joshua commanded them.
They took twelve stones from
the middle of the Jordan, according to the number of the
tribes of the Israelites, as the
LORD had told Joshua; and
they carried them over with
them to their camp, where
they put them down. 9 Joshua
set up the twelve stones that
had been[g] in the middle of the
Jordan at the spot where the
priests who carried the ark of
the covenant had stood. And
they are there to this day.
10 Now the priests who carried the ark remained standing in the middle of the Jordan
until everything the LORD had
commanded Joshua was done
by the people, just as Moses
had directed Joshua. The
people hurried over, 11 and as
soon as all of them had
crossed, the ark of the LORD
and the priests came to the
other side while the people
watched. 12 The men of Reuben, Gad and the half-tribe of
Manasseh crossed over,
armed, in front of the Israelites, as Moses had directed
them. 13 About forty thousand
armed for battle crossed over
before the LORD to the plains
of Jericho for war.
14 That day the LORD exalted
Joshua in the sight of all Israel;

g9 Or *Joshua also set up twelve stones*

יִשְׂרָאֵל וַיִּרְאוּ אֹתוֹ כַּאֲשֶׁר יָרְאוּ אֶת־ מֹשֶׁה כָּל־ יְמֵי
days-of all-of Moses *** they-revered just-as him and-they-revered Israel

חַיָּיו׃ וַיֹּאמֶר יְהוָה אֶל־ יְהוֹשֻׁעַ לֵאמֹר׃ צַוֵּה אֶת־
*** command! (16) to-say Joshua to Yahweh then-he-said (15) lives-of-him

הַכֹּהֲנִים נֹשְׂאֵי אֲרוֹן הָעֵדוּת וְיַעֲלוּ מִן־
from so-they-come-up the-Testimony ark-of ones-carrying-of the-priests

הַיַּרְדֵּן׃ וַיְצַו יְהוֹשֻׁעַ אֶת־ הַכֹּהֲנִים לֵאמֹר עֲלוּ מִן־
from come-up! to-say the-priests *** Joshua so-he-commanded (17) the-Jordan

הַיַּרְדֵּן׃ וַיְהִי° בַּעֲלוֹת הַכֹּהֲנִים נֹשְׂאֵי אֲרוֹן
ark-of ones-carrying-of the-priests as-to-come-up and-he-was (18) the-Jordan

בְּרִית־ יְהוָה מִתּוֹךְ הַיַּרְדֵּן נִתְּקוּ כַּפּוֹת רַגְלֵי
feet-of soles-of they-moved the-Jordan from-middle-of Yahweh covenant-of

הַכֹּהֲנִים אֶל הֶחָרָבָה וַיָּשֻׁבוּ מֵי־ הַיַּרְדֵּן
the-Jordan waters-of and-they-returned the-dry-ground to the-priests

לִמְקוֹמָם וַיֵּלְכוּ כִתְמוֹל־ שִׁלְשׁוֹם עַל־ כָּל־ גְּדוֹתָיו׃
banks-of-him all-of to before as-yesterday and-they-ran to-place-of-them

וְהָעָם עָלוּ מִן־ הַיַּרְדֵּן בֶּעָשׂוֹר לַחֹדֶשׁ
of-the-month on-the-tenth the-Jordan from they-went-up so-the-people (19)

הָרִאשׁוֹן וַיַּחֲנוּ בַּגִּלְגָּל בִּקְצֵה מִזְרַח יְרִיחוֹ׃
Jericho eastern-of on-border-of at-the-Gilgal and-they-camped the-first

וְאֵת שְׁתֵּים עֶשְׂרֵה הָאֲבָנִים הָאֵלֶּה אֲשֶׁר לָקְחוּ מִן־ הַיַּרְדֵּן
the-Jordan from they-took that the-these the-stones ten two and (20)

הֵקִים יְהוֹשֻׁעַ בַּגִּלְגָּל׃ וַיֹּאמֶר אֶל־ בְּנֵי יִשְׂרָאֵל לֵאמֹר
to-say Israel sons-of to and-he-said (21) at-the-Gilgal Joshua he-set-up

אֲשֶׁר יִשְׁאָלוּן בְּנֵיכֶם מָחָר אֶת־ אֲבוֹתָם לֵאמֹר מָה
what? to-say fathers-of-them *** future descendants-of-you they-ask when

הָאֲבָנִים הָאֵלֶּה׃ וְהוֹדַעְתֶּם אֶת־ בְּנֵיכֶם לֵאמֹר
to-say descendants-of-you *** then-you-tell (22) the-these the-stones

בַּיַּבָּשָׁה עָבַר יִשְׂרָאֵל אֶת־ הַיַּרְדֵּן הַזֶּה׃ אֲשֶׁר־
for (23) the-this the-Jordan *** Israel he-crossed on-the-dry-ground

הוֹבִישׁ יְהוָה אֱלֹהֵיכֶם אֶת־ מֵי הַיַּרְדֵּן מִפְּנֵיכֶם עַד־
until from-before-you the-Jordan waters-of *** God-of-you Yahweh he-dried-up

עָבְרְכֶם כַּאֲשֶׁר עָשָׂה יְהוָה אֱלֹהֵיכֶם לְיַם־ סוּף אֲשֶׁר־
that Reed to-Sea-of God-of-you Yahweh he-did just-as to-cross-over-you

הוֹבִישׁ מִפָּנֵינוּ עַד־ עָבְרֵנוּ׃ לְמַעַן דַּעַת
to-know so-that (24) to-cross-over-us until from-before-us he-dried-up

כָּל־ עַמֵּי הָאָרֶץ אֶת־ יַד יְהוָה כִּי חֲזָקָה הִיא לְמַעַן
so-that she powerful that Yahweh hand-of *** the-earth peoples-of all-of

and they revered him all the
days of his life, just as they
had revered Moses.
15Then the LORD said to
Joshua, 16"Command the
priests carrying the ark of the
Testimony to come up out of
the Jordan."
17So Joshua commanded the
priests, "Come up out of the
Jordan."
18And the priests came up
out of the river carrying the
ark of the covenant of the
LORD. No sooner had they set
their feet on the dry ground
than the waters of the Jordan
returned to their place and ran
at flood stage as before.
19On the tenth day of the
first month the people went
up from the Jordan and
camped at Gilgal on the eastern border of Jericho. 20And
Joshua set up at Gilgal the
twelve stones they had taken
out of the Jordan. 21He said to
the Israelites, "In the future
when your descendants ask
their fathers, 'What do these
stones mean?' 22tell them, 'Israel crossed the Jordan on dry
ground.' 23For the LORD your
God dried up the Jordan before you until you had crossed
over. The LORD your God did
to the Jordan just what he had
done to the Red Sea[h] when he
dried it up before us until we
had crossed over. 24He did this
so that all the peoples of the
earth might know that the
hand of the LORD is powerful

[h]23 Hebrew *Yam Suph;* that is, Sea of Reeds

°18 ק כעלות

יְרָאתֶם אֶת־ יְהוָה אֱלֹהֵיכֶם כָּל־ הַיָּמִים׃ וַיְהִי
now-he-was (5:1) the-days all-of God-of-you Yahweh *** you-might-fear

כִשְׁמֹעַ כָּל־ מַלְכֵי הָאֱמֹרִי אֲשֶׁר בְּעֵבֶר הַיַּרְדֵּן יָמָּה
to-west the-Jordan on-side-of that the-Amorite kings-of all-of when-to-hear

וְכָל־ מַלְכֵי הַכְּנַעֲנִי אֲשֶׁר עַל־ הַיָּם אֵת אֲשֶׁר־ הוֹבִישׁ
he-dried-up how *** the-sea along that the-Canaanite kings-of and-all-of

יְהוָה אֶת־ מֵי הַיַּרְדֵּן מִפְּנֵי בְנֵי־ יִשְׂרָאֵל עַד־
until Israel sons-of from-before the-Jordan waters-of *** Yahweh

עָבְרֵנוּ° וַיִּמַּס לְבָבָם וְלֹא־ הָיָה בָם עוֹד
longer in-them he-was and-not heart-of-them then-he-sank to-cross-over-them

רוּחַ מִפְּנֵי בְּנֵי־ יִשְׂרָאֵל׃ בָּעֵת הַהִיא אָמַר יְהוָה
Yahweh he-said the-that at-the-time (2) Israel sons-of because-of courage

אֶל־יְהוֹשֻׁעַ עֲשֵׂה לְךָ חַרְבוֹת צֻרִים וְשׁוּב מֹל אֶת־ בְּנֵי־
sons-of *** circumcise! and-return! flints knives-of for-you make! Joshua to

יִשְׂרָאֵל שֵׁנִית׃ וַיַּעַשׂ־ לוֹ יְהוֹשֻׁעַ חַרְבוֹת צֻרִים וַיָּמָל
and-he-circumcised flints knives-of Joshua for-him so-he-made (3) again Israel

אֶת־ בְּנֵי יִשְׂרָאֵל אֶל־ גִּבְעַת הָעֲרָלוֹת׃ וְזֶה הַדָּבָר אֲשֶׁר־
that the-reason now-this (4) Haaraloth Gibeath at Israel sons-of ***

מָל יְהוֹשֻׁעַ כָּל־ הָעָם הַיֹּצֵא מִמִּצְרַיִם הַזְּכָרִים
the-males from-Egypt the-one-coming the-people all-of Joshua he-circumcised

כֹּל ׀ אַנְשֵׁי הַמִּלְחָמָה מֵתוּ בַמִּדְבָּר בַּדֶּרֶךְ
on-the-way in-the-desert they-died the-military men-of all-of

בְּצֵאתָם מִמִּצְרָיִם׃ כִּי־ מֻלִים הָיוּ
they-were ones-being-circumcised indeed (5) from-Egypt after-to-leave-them

כָּל־ הָעָם הַיֹּצְאִים וְכָל־ הָעָם הַיִּלֹּדִים
the-ones-born the-people but-all-of the-ones-coming-out the-people all-of

בַמִּדְבָּר בַּדֶּרֶךְ בְּצֵאתָם מִמִּצְרַיִם לֹא־
not from-Egypt when-to-come-out-them on-the-journey in-the-desert

מָלוּ׃ כִּי ׀ אַרְבָּעִים שָׁנָה הָלְכוּ בְנֵי־ יִשְׂרָאֵל
Israel sons-of they-moved-about year forty now (6) they-were-circumcised

בַּמִּדְבָּר עַד־ תֹּם כָּל־ הַגּוֹי אַנְשֵׁי הַמִּלְחָמָה
the-military men-of the-nation all-of to-die until in-the-desert

הַיֹּצְאִים מִמִּצְרַיִם אֲשֶׁר לֹא־ שָׁמְעוּ בְּקוֹל יְהוָה אֲשֶׁר
for Yahweh to-voice-of they-obeyed not since from-Egypt the-ones-coming

נִשְׁבַּע יְהוָה לָהֶם לְבִלְתִּי הַרְאוֹתָם אֶת־הָאָרֶץ אֲשֶׁר נִשְׁבַּע יְהוָה
Yahweh he-promised that the-land *** to-see-them not to-them Yahweh he-swore

לַאֲבוֹתָם לָתֶת לָנוּ אֶרֶץ זָבַת חָלָב וּדְבָשׁ׃ וְאֶת־
and (7) and-honey milk flowing-of land to-us to-give to-fathers-of-them

and so that you might always
fear the LORD your God."

*Circumcision at Gilgal*

5 Now when all the Amorite
kings west of the Jordan
and all the Canaanite kings
along the seacoast heard how
the LORD had dried up the Jordan before the Israelites until
we had crossed over, their
hearts sank and they no longer had the courage to face the
Israelites.
[2]At that time the LORD said
to Joshua, "Make flint knives
and circumcise the Israelites
again." [3]So Joshua made flint
knives and circumcised the Israelites at Gibeath Haaraloth.[i]
[4]Now this is why he did so:
All those who came out of
Egypt—all the men of military
age—died in the desert on the
way after leaving Egypt. [5]All
the people that came out had
been circumcised, but all the
people born in the desert during the journey from Egypt
had not. [6]The Israelites had
moved about in the desert
forty years until all the men
who were of military age
when they left Egypt had died,
since they had not obeyed the
LORD. For the LORD had sworn
to them that they would not
see the land that he had solemnly promised their fathers
to give us, a land flowing with
milk and honey. [7]So he raised

[i]3 *Gibeath Haaraloth* means *hill of foreskins.*

***1* The NIV here translates the *Ketbib* form; the interlinear translates the *Qere.***

°*1* ק עברם

בְּנֵיהֶם הֵקִים תַּחְתָּם אֹתָם מָל יְהוֹשֻׁעַ כִּי־
for Joshua he-circumcised them in-place-of-them he-raised-up sons-of-them

עֲרֵלִים הָיוּ כִּי לֹא־ מָלוּ אוֹתָם בַּדָּרֶךְ׃
on-the-way them they-circumcised not for they-were ones-uncircumcised

(8) וַיְהִי כַּאֲשֶׁר־ תַּמּוּ כָל־ הַגּוֹי לְהִמּוֹל
to-be-circumcised the-nation whole-of they-were-done just-as and-he-was (8)

וַיֵּשְׁבוּ תַחְתָּם בַּמַּחֲנֶה עַד חֲיוֹתָם׃
to-be-healed-them until in-the-camp in-place-of-them then-they-remained

(9) וַיֹּאמֶר יְהוָה אֶל־ יְהוֹשֻׁעַ הַיּוֹם גַּלּוֹתִי אֶת־ חֶרְפַּת
reproach-of *** I-rolled-away the-day Joshua to Yahweh then-he-said (9)

מִצְרַיִם מֵעֲלֵיכֶם וַיִּקְרָא שֵׁם הַמָּקוֹם הַהוּא גִּלְגָּל עַד הַיּוֹם
the-day to Gilgal the-that the-place name-of so-he-called from-on-you Egypt

הַזֶּה׃ (10) וַיַּחֲנוּ בְנֵי־ יִשְׂרָאֵל בַּגִּלְגָּל וַיַּעֲשׂוּ
and-they-celebrated at-the-Gilgal Israel sons-of so-they-camped (10) the-this

אֶת־ הַפֶּסַח בְּאַרְבָּעָה עָשָׂר יוֹם לַחֹדֶשׁ בָּעֶרֶב בְּעַרְבוֹת
on-plains-of in-the-evening of-the-month day ten on-four the-Passover ***

יְרִיחוֹ׃ (11) וַיֹּאכְלוּ מֵעֲבוּר הָאָרֶץ מִמָּחֳרַת
on-day-after-of the-land from-produce-of and-they-ate (11) Jericho

הַפֶּסַח מַצּוֹת וְקָלוּי בְּעֶצֶם הַיּוֹם הַזֶּה׃
the-that the-day on-very-of and-roasted-grain unleavened-breads the-Passover

(12) וַיִּשְׁבֹּת הַמָּן מִמָּחֳרָת בְּאָכְלָם מֵעֲבוּר
from-food-of when-to-eat-them on-day-after the-manna and-he-stopped (12)

הָאָרֶץ וְלֹא־ הָיָה עוֹד לִבְנֵי יִשְׂרָאֵל מָן וַיֹּאכְלוּ
but-they-ate manna Israel for-sons-of longer he-was so-not the-land

מִתְּבוּאַת אֶרֶץ כְּנַעַן בַּשָּׁנָה הַהִיא׃ (13) וַיְהִי
now-he-was (13) the-that in-the-year Canaan land-of from-produce-of

בִּהְיוֹת יְהוֹשֻׁעַ בִּירִיחוֹ וַיִּשָּׂא עֵינָיו וַיַּרְא
and-he-saw eyes-of-him that-he-lifted near-Jericho Joshua when-to-be

וְהִנֵּה־ אִישׁ עֹמֵד לְנֶגְדּוֹ וְחַרְבּוֹ שְׁלוּפָה
being-drawn and-sword-of-him in-front-of-him standing man and-see!

בְּיָדוֹ וַיֵּלֶךְ יְהוֹשֻׁעַ אֵלָיו וַיֹּאמֶר לוֹ הֲלָנוּ אַתָּה
you for-us? to-him and-he-asked to-him Joshua and-he-went in-hand-of-him

אִם־ לְצָרֵינוּ׃ (14) וַיֹּאמֶר ׀ לֹא כִּי אֲנִי שַׂר־ צְבָא־
army-of commander-of I but neither and-he-replied (14) for-enemies-of-us or

יְהוָה עַתָּה בָאתִי וַיִּפֹּל יְהוֹשֻׁעַ אֶל־ פָּנָיו אַרְצָה
to-ground faces-of-him on Joshua then-he-fell I-came now Yahweh

וַיִּשְׁתָּחוּ וַיֹּאמֶר לוֹ מָה אֲדֹנִי מְדַבֵּר אֶל־ עַבְדּוֹ׃
servant-of-him to speaking lord-of-me what? to-him and-he-asked and-he-revered

up their sons in their place, and these were the ones Joshua circumcised. They were still uncircumcised because they had not been circumcised on the way. [8]And after the whole nation had been circumcised, they remained where they were in camp until they were healed.

[9]Then the LORD said to Joshua, "Today I have rolled away the reproach of Egypt from you." So the place has been called Gilgal[j] to this day.

[10]On the evening of the fourteenth day of the month, while camped at Gilgal on the plains of Jericho, the Israelites celebrated the Passover. [11]The day after the Passover, that very day, they ate some of the produce of the land: unleavened bread and roasted grain. [12]The manna stopped the day after[k] they ate this food from the land; there was no longer any manna for the Israelites, but that year they ate of the produce of Canaan.

*The Fall of Jericho*

[13]Now when Joshua was near Jericho, he looked up and saw a man standing in front of him with a drawn sword in his hand. Joshua went up to him and asked, "Are you for us or for our enemies?"

[14]"Neither," he replied, "but as commander of the army of the LORD I have now come." Then Joshua fell facedown to the ground in reverence, and asked him, "What message does my Lord[l] have for his servant?"

[j]9 *Gilgal* sounds like the Hebrew for *roll.*
[k]12 Or *the day* [l]14 Or *lord*

וַיֹּאמֶר שַׂר־ צְבָא יְהוָה אֶל־ יְהוֹשֻׁעַ שַׁל־

take-off! Joshua to Yahweh army-of commander-of and-he-replied (15)

נַעַלְךָ מֵעַל רַגְלֶךָ כִּי הַמָּקוֹם אֲשֶׁר אַתָּה עֹמֵד עָלָיו

on-him standing you where the-place for foot-of-you from-on sandal-of-you

קֹדֶשׁ הוּא וַיַּעַשׂ יְהוֹשֻׁעַ כֵּן׃ וִירִיחוֹ סֹגֶרֶת וּמְסֻגֶּרֶת

and-being-shut being-shut now-Jericho (6:1) this Joshua so-he-did he holy

מִפְּנֵי בְּנֵי יִשְׂרָאֵל אֵין יוֹצֵא וְאֵין בָּא׃

one-coming-in and-not one-going-out not Israel sons-of because-of

וַיֹּאמֶר יְהוָה אֶל־ יְהוֹשֻׁעַ רְאֵה נָתַתִּי בְיָדְךָ אֶת־

*** into-hand-of-you I-delivered see! Joshua to Yahweh then-he-said (2)

יְרִיחוֹ וְאֶת־ מַלְכָּהּ גִּבּוֹרֵי הֶחָיִל׃ וְסַבֹּתֶם אֶת־

*** now-you-march-around (3) the-fight men-of king-of-her and Jericho

הָעִיר כָּל־ אַנְשֵׁי הַמִּלְחָמָה הַקֵּיף אֶת־ הָעִיר פַּעַם אֶחָת כֹּה

this one time the-city *** to-go-around the-armed men-of all-of the-city

תַעֲשֶׂה שֵׁשֶׁת יָמִים׃ וְשִׁבְעָה כֹהֲנִים יִשְׂאוּ שִׁבְעָה שׁוֹפְרוֹת

trumpets-of seven they-must-carry priests and-seven (4) days six-of you-do

הַיּוֹבְלִים לִפְנֵי הָאָרוֹן וּבַיּוֹם הַשְּׁבִיעִי

the-seventh and-on-the-day the-ark in-front-of the-horns-of-rams

תָּסֹבּוּ אֶת־ הָעִיר שֶׁבַע פְּעָמִים וְהַכֹּהֲנִים יִתְקְעוּ

they-must-blow and-the-priests times seven-of the-city *** you-march-around

בַּשּׁוֹפָרוֹת׃ וְהָיָה בִּמְשֹׁךְ׀ בְּקֶרֶן הַיּוֹבֵל

the-ram on-horn-of when-to-blast and-he-will-be (5) on-the-trumpets

°בְּשָׁמְעֲכֶם אֶת־ קוֹל הַשּׁוֹפָר יָרִיעוּ כָל־

all-of then-they-must-shout the-trumpet sound-of *** when-to-hear-you

הָעָם תְּרוּעָה גְדוֹלָה וְנָפְלָה חוֹמַת הָעִיר תַּחְתֶּיהָ

around-her the-city wall-of then-she-will-collapse loud shout the-people

וְעָלוּ הָעָם אִישׁ נֶגְדּוֹ׃ וַיִּקְרָא יְהוֹשֻׁעַ

Joshua so-he-called (6) straight-in-him each the-people and-they-will-go-up

בִּן־ נוּן אֶל־ הַכֹּהֲנִים וַיֹּאמֶר אֲלֵהֶם שְׂאוּ אֶת־ אֲרוֹן

ark-of *** take-up! to-them and-he-said the-priests to Nun son-of

הַבְּרִית וְשִׁבְעָה כֹהֲנִים יִשְׂאוּ שִׁבְעָה שׁוֹפְרוֹת

trumpets-of seven they-must-carry priests and-seven the-covenant

יוֹבְלִים לִפְנֵי אֲרוֹן יְהוָה׃ °וַיֹּאמְרוּ אֶל־ הָעָם

the-people to and-he-ordered (7) Yahweh ark-of in-front-of horns-of-rams

עִבְרוּ וְסֹבּוּ אֶת־ הָעִיר וְהֶחָלוּץ יַעֲבֹר

he-must-go and-the-being-armed the-city *** and-march-around! advance!

לִפְנֵי אֲרוֹן יְהוָה׃ וַיְהִי כֶּאֱמֹר יְהוֹשֻׁעַ אֶל־ הָעָם

the-people to Joshua after-to-speak and-he-was (8) Yahweh ark-of ahead-of

[15]The commander of the
LORD's army replied, "Take off
your sandals, for the place
where you are standing is
holy." And Joshua did so.
6 Now Jericho was tightly
shut up because of the Israelites. No one went out and
no one came in.
[2]Then the LORD said to
Joshua, "See, I have delivered
Jericho into your hands, along
with its king and its fighting
men. [3]March around the city
once with all the armed men.
Do this for six days. [4]Have sev-
en priests carry trumpets of
rams' horns in front of the ark.
On the seventh day, march
around the city seven times,
with the priests blowing the
trumpets. [5]When you hear
them sound a long blast on the
trumpets, have all the people
give a loud shout; then the
wall of the city will collapse
and the people will go up,
every man straight in."
[6]So Joshua son of Nun called
the priests and said to them,
"Take up the ark of the covenant of the LORD and have
seven priests carry trumpets
in front of it." [7]And he ordered
the people, "Advance! March
around the city, with the
armed guard going ahead of
the ark of the LORD."
[8]When Joshua had spoken to

°5 ק כשמעכם
°7 ק ויאמר

וְשִׁבְעָה הַכֹּהֲנִים נֹשְׂאִים שִׁבְעָה שׁוֹפְרוֹת הַיּוֹבְלִים
the-horns-of-rams trumpets-of seven ones-carrying the-priests then-seven

לִפְנֵי יְהוָה עָבְרוּ וְתָקְעוּ בַּשּׁוֹפָרוֹת וַאֲרוֹן
and-ark-of on-the-trumpets and-they-blew they-went-forward Yahweh before

בְּרִית יְהוָה הֹלֵךְ אַחֲרֵיהֶם׃ וְהֶחָלוּץ הֹלֵךְ
marching and-the-being-armed (9) after-them following Yahweh covenant-of

לִפְנֵי הַכֹּהֲנִים תֹּקְעֵו הַשּׁוֹפָרוֹת וְהַמְאַסֵּף
and-the-guarding-rear the-trumpets ones-blowing-of the-priests ahead-of

הֹלֵךְ אַחֲרֵי הָאָרוֹן הָלוֹךְ וְתָקוֹעַ בַּשּׁוֹפָרוֹת׃ וְאֶת־
but (10) on-the-trumpets and-to-sound to-follow the-ark after following

הָעָם צִוָּה יְהוֹשֻׁעַ לֵאמֹר לֹא תָרִיעוּ וְלֹא־ תַשְׁמִיעוּ
you-raise and-not you-give-war-cry not to-say Joshua he-commanded the-people

אֶת־ קוֹלְכֶם וְלֹא־ יֵצֵא מִפִּיכֶם דָּבָר עַד יוֹם
day until word from-mouth-of-you he-must-go and-not voice-of-you ***

אָמְרִי אֲלֵיכֶם הָרִיעוּ וַהֲרֵיעֹתֶם׃ וַיַּסֵּב אֲרוֹן־
ark-of so-he-had-go-around (11) then-you-shout shout! to-you to-tell-me

יְהוָה אֶת־ הָעִיר הַקֵּף פַּעַם אֶחָת וַיָּבֹאוּ הַמַּחֲנֶה
the-camp then-they-returned one time to-circle the-city *** Yahweh

וַיָּלִינוּ בַּמַּחֲנֶה׃ וַיַּשְׁכֵּם יְהוֹשֻׁעַ בַּבֹּקֶר
in-the-morning Joshua and-he-got-up (12) in-the-camp and-they-spent-night

וַיִּשְׂאוּ הַכֹּהֲנִים אֶת־ אֲרוֹן יְהוָה׃ וְשִׁבְעָה הַכֹּהֲנִים
the-priests and-seven (13) Yahweh ark-of *** the-priests and-they-took-up

נֹשְׂאִים שִׁבְעָה שׁוֹפְרוֹת הַיֹּבְלִים לִפְנֵי אֲרוֹן יְהוָה
Yahweh ark-of before the-horns-of-rams trumpets-of seven ones-carrying

הֹלְכִים הָלוֹךְ וְתָקְעוּ בַּשּׁוֹפָרוֹת וְהֶחָלוּץ
and-the-being-armed on-the-trumpets and-they-blew to-go-forward ones-going

הֹלֵךְ לִפְנֵיהֶם וְהַמְאַסֵּף הֹלֵךְ אַחֲרֵי אֲרוֹן יְהוָה
Yahweh ark-of after following and-the-guarding-rear ahead-of-them going

הוֹלֵךְ וְתָקוֹעַ בַּשּׁוֹפָרוֹת׃ וַיָּסֹבּוּ אֶת־ הָעִיר
the-city *** so-they-marched-around (14) on-the-trumpets and-to-sound to-march

בַּיּוֹם הַשֵּׁנִי פַּעַם אַחַת וַיָּשֻׁבוּ הַמַּחֲנֶה כֹּה עָשׂוּ
they-did this the-camp and-they-returned one time the-second on-the-day

שֵׁשֶׁת יָמִים׃ וַיְהִי ׀ בַּיּוֹם הַשְּׁבִיעִי וַיַּשְׁכִּמוּ
that-they-got-up the-seventh on-the-day and-he-was (15) days six-of

כַּעֲלוֹת הַשַּׁחַר וַיָּסֹבּוּ אֶת־ הָעִיר כַּמִּשְׁפָּט
as-the-manner the-city *** and-they-marched-around the-daybreak as-to-come

הַזֶּה שֶׁבַע פְּעָמִים רַק בַּיּוֹם הַהוּא סָבְבוּ אֶת־ הָעִיר
the-city *** they-circled the-that on-the-day except times seven-of the-this

the people, the seven priests carrying the seven trumpets before the LORD went forward, blowing their trumpets, and the ark of the LORD's covenant followed them. [9]The armed guard marched ahead of the priests who blew the trumpets, and the rear guard followed the ark. All this time the trumpets were sounding. [10]But Joshua had commanded the people, "Do not give a war cry, do not raise your voices, do not say a word until the day I tell you to shout. Then shout!" [11]So he had the ark of the LORD carried around the city, circling it once. Then the people returned to camp and spent the night there.

[12]Joshua got up early the next morning and the priests took up the ark of the LORD. [13]The seven priests carrying the seven trumpets went forward, marching before the ark of the LORD and blowing the trumpets. The armed men went ahead of them and the rear guard followed the ark of the LORD, while the trumpets kept sounding. [14]So on the second day they marched around the city once and returned to the camp. They did this for six days.

[15]On the seventh day, they got up at daybreak and marched around the city seven times in the same manner, except that on that day they circled the city seven times.

°9 ק תקעי
°13 ק הלוך

שֶׁבַע פְּעָמִים׃ וַיְהִי בַּפַּעַם הַשְּׁבִיעִית תָּקְעוּ
they-sounded the-seventh on-the-time and-he-was (16) times seven-of

הַכֹּהֲנִים בַּשּׁוֹפָרוֹת וַיֹּאמֶר יְהוֹשֻׁעַ אֶל־ הָעָם הָרִיעוּ
shout! the-people to Joshua and-he-commanded on-the-trumpets the-priests

כִּי־ נָתַן יְהוָה לָכֶם אֶת־ הָעִיר׃ וְהָיְתָה הָעִיר חֵרֶם הִיא
she devoted the-city and-she-is (17) the-city *** to-you Yahweh he-gave for

וְכָל־ אֲשֶׁר־ בָּהּ לַיהוָה רַק רָחָב הַזּוֹנָה תִּחְיֶה הִיא
she she-shall-live the-prostitute Rahab only to-Yahweh in-her that and-all

וְכָל־ אֲשֶׁר אִתָּהּ בַּבַּיִת כִּי הֶחְבְּאַתָה אֶת־הַמַּלְאָכִים אֲשֶׁר שָׁלָחְנוּ׃
we-sent whom the-spies *** she-hid for in-the-house with-her who and-all

וְרַק־ אַתֶּם שִׁמְרוּ מִן־ הַחֵרֶם פֶּן־
so-not the-devoted-thing from keep-away! you but-however (18)

תַּחֲרִימוּ וּלְקַחְתֶּם מִן־ הַחֵרֶם וְשַׂמְתֶּם
or-you-will-make the-devoted-thing from when-you-take you-bring-destruction

אֶת־ מַחֲנֵה יִשְׂרָאֵל לְחֵרֶם וַעֲכַרְתֶּם אוֹתוֹ׃ וְכֹל
and-all-of (19) him and-you-will-destroy for-destruction Israel camp-of ***

כֶּסֶף וְזָהָב וּכְלֵי נְחֹשֶׁת וּבַרְזֶל קֹדֶשׁ הוּא לַיהוָה
to-Yahweh he sacred and-iron bronze and-articles-of and-gold silver

אוֹצַר יְהוָה יָבוֹא׃ וַיָּרַע הָעָם
the-people and-he-shouted (20) he-must-go-in Yahweh treasury-of

וַיִּתְקְעוּ בַּשֹּׁפָרוֹת וַיְהִי כִשְׁמֹעַ הָעָם אֶת־
*** the-people when-to-hear and-he-was on-the-trumpets when-they-sounded

קוֹל הַשּׁוֹפָר וַיָּרִיעוּ הָעָם תְּרוּעָה גְדוֹלָה וַתִּפֹּל
then-she-collapsed loud shout the-people and-they-shouted the-trumpet sound-of

הַחוֹמָה תַּחְתֶּיהָ וַיַּעַל הָעָם הָעִירָה אִישׁ
each into-the-city the-people so-he-charged around-her the-wall

נֶגְדּוֹ וַיִּלְכְּדוּ אֶת־ הָעִיר׃ וַיַּחֲרִימוּ אֶת־כָּל־
all *** and-they-devoted (21) the-city *** and-they-took straight-in-him

אֲשֶׁר בָּעִיר מֵאִישׁ וְעַד־ אִשָּׁה מִנַּעַר וְעַד־ זָקֵן וְעַד
even-to old even-to from-young woman even-to from-man in-the-city that

שׁוֹר וָשֶׂה וַחֲמוֹר לְפִי־ חָרֶב׃ וְלִשְׁנַיִם הָאֲנָשִׁים
the-men and-to-two (22) sword with-edge-of and-donkey and-sheep cattle

הַמְרַגְּלִים אֶת־ הָאָרֶץ אָמַר יְהוֹשֻׁעַ בֹּאוּ בֵּית־ הָאִשָּׁה
the-woman house-of go-into! Joshua he-said the-land *** the-ones-spying

הַזּוֹנָה וְהוֹצִיאוּ מִשָּׁם אֶת־ הָאִשָּׁה וְאֶת־כָּל־אֲשֶׁר־ לָהּ
to-her who all and the-woman *** from-there and-bring-out! the-prostitute

כַּאֲשֶׁר נִשְׁבַּעְתֶּם לָהּ׃ וַיָּבֹאוּ הַנְּעָרִים
the-young-men so-they-went-in (23) with-her you-made-oath just-as

[16]The seventh time around,
when the priests sounded the
trumpet blast, Joshua commanded the people, "Shout!
For the LORD has given you the
city! [17]The city and all that is in
it are to be devoted[m] to the
LORD. Only Rahab the prostitute[n] and all who are with her
in her house shall be spared,
because she hid the spies we
sent. [18]But keep away from the
devoted things, so that you
will not bring about your own
destruction by taking any of
them. Otherwise you will
make the camp of Israel liable
to destruction and bring disaster on it. [19]All the silver and
gold and the articles of bronze
and iron are sacred to the LORD
and must go into his treasury."
[20]When the trumpets sounded, the people shouted, and at
the sound of the trumpet,
when the people gave a loud
shout, the wall collapsed; so
every man charged straight in,
and they took the city. [21]They
devoted the city to the LORD
and destroyed with the sword
every living thing in it—men
and women, young and old,
cattle, sheep and donkeys.
[22]Joshua said to the two men
who had spied out the land,
"Go into the prostitute's house
and bring her out and all who
belong to her, in accordance
with your oath to her." [23]So
the young men who had done

[m]17 The Hebrew term refers to the irrevocable giving over of things or persons to the LORD, often by totally destroying them; also in verses 18 and 21.
[n]17 Or possibly *innkeeper;* also in verses 22 and 25

המרגלים ויציאו את־ רחב ואת־ אביה ואת־
and father-of-her and Rahab *** and-they-brought-out the-ones-spying

אמה ואת־ אחיה ואת־כל־ אשר־ לה ואת כל־
entire-of and to-her who all and brothers-of-her and mother-of-her

משפחותיה הוציאו ויניחום מחוץ למחנה ישראל׃
Israel of-camp-of outside and-they-put-them they-brought-out families-of-her

(24) והעיר שרפו באש וכל־ אשר־ בה רק הכסף
the-silver but in-her that and-all in-the-fire they-burned then-the-city (24)

והזהב וכלי הנחשת והברזל נתנו אוצר
treasury-of they-put and-the-iron the-bronze and-articles-of and-the-gold

בית־ יהוה׃ (25) ואת־ רחב הזונה ואת־ בית אביה
father-of-her house-of and the-prostitute Rahab but (25) Yahweh house-of

ואת־כל־ אשר־ לה החיה יהושע ותשב בקרב ישראל עד
to Israel in-among and-she-lives Joshua he-spared to-her who all and

היום הזה כי החביאה את־המלאכים אשר־ שלח יהושע לרגל
to-spy-out Joshua he-sent whom the-spies *** she-hid for the-this the-day

את־ יריחו׃ (26) וישבע יהושע בעת ההיא לאמר
to-say the-that at-the-time Joshua and-he-pronounced-oath (26) Jericho ***

ארור האיש לפני יהוה אשר יקום ובנה את־
*** and-he-rebuilds he-undertakes who Yahweh before the-man being-cursed

העיר הזאת את־ יריחו בבכרו ייסדנה
he-will-found-her with-firstborn-of-him Jericho *** the-this the-city

ובצעירו יציב דלתיה׃ (27) ויהי יהוה
Yahweh so-he-was (27) gates-of-her he-will-set-up and-with-youngest-of-him

את־ יהושע ויהי שמעו בכל־ הארץ׃
the-land through-all-of fame-of-him and-he-spread Joshua with

(7:1) וימעלו בני־ ישראל מעל בחרם
with-the-devoted unfaithfulness Israel sons-of but-they-were-unfaithful (7:1)

ויקח עכן בן־ כרמי בן־ זבדי בן־ זרח למטה יהודה
Judah of-tribe-of Zerah son-of Zabdi son-of Carmi son-of Achan and-he-took

מן־ החרם ויחר־ אף יהוה בבני ישראל׃
Israel against-sons-of Yahweh anger-of so-he-burned the-devoted-thing from

(2) וישלח יהושע אנשים מיריחו העי אשר עם־ בית און מקדם
to-east Aven Beth near which the-Ai from-Jericho men Joshua now-he-sent (2)

לבית־ אל ויאמר אליהם לאמר עלו ורגלו את־ הארץ
the-region *** and-spy-out! go-up! to-say to-them and-he-told El of-Beth

ויעלו האנשים וירגלו את־ העי׃ (3) וישבו
when-they-returned (3) the-Ai *** and-they-spied-out the-men so-they-went-up

the spying went in and
brought out Rahab, her father
and mother and brothers and
all who belonged to her. They
brought out her entire family
and put them in a place outside the camp of Israel.
24 Then they burned the
whole city and everything in
it, but they put the silver and
gold and the articles of bronze
and iron into the treasury of
the LORD's house. 25 But Joshua
spared Rahab the prostitute,
with her family and all who
belonged to her, because she
hid the men Joshua had sent
as spies to Jericho—and she
lives among the Israelites to
this day.
26 At that time Joshua pronounced this solemn oath:
"Cursed before the LORD is the
man who undertakes to re-
build this city, Jericho:

"At the cost of his firstborn son
will he lay its foundations;
at the cost of his youngest
will he set up its gates."

27 So the LORD was with
Joshua, and his fame spread
throughout the land.

*Achan's Sin*

7 But the Israelites acted unfaithfully in regard to the
devoted things[o]; Achan son of
Carmi, the son of Zimri,[p] the
son of Zerah, of the tribe of
Judah, took some of them. So
the LORD's anger burned
against Israel.
2 Now Joshua sent men from
Jericho to Ai, which is near
Beth Aven to the east of Bethel, and told them, "Go up and
spy out the region." So the
men went up and spied out Ai.
3 When they returned to

[o]1 The Hebrew term refers to the irrevocable giving over of things or persons to the LORD, often by totally destroying them; also in verses 11, 12, 13 and 15.
[p]1 See Septuagint and 1 Chronicles 2:6; Hebrew *Zabdi;* also in verses 17 and 18.

אֶל־ יְהוֹשֻׁעַ וַיֹּאמְרוּ אֵלָיו אַל־ יַעַל כָּל־ הָעָם
the-people all-of he-must-go-up not to-him then-they-said Joshua to

כְּאַלְפַּיִם אִישׁ אוֹ כִּשְׁלֹשֶׁת אֲלָפִים אִישׁ יַעֲלוּ
they-should-go-up man thousands about-three-of or man about-two-thousands

וְיַכּוּ אֶת־ הָעָי אַל־ תְּיַגַּע־ שָׁמָּה אֶת־ כָּל־ הָעָם
the-people all-of *** at-there you-weary not the-Ai *** and-they-will-take

כִּי מְעַט הֵמָּה׃ וַיַּעֲלוּ מִן־ הָעָם שָׁמָּה כִּשְׁלֹשֶׁת
about-three-of to-there the-people from so-they-went-up (4) they few for

אֲלָפִים אִישׁ וַיָּנֻסוּ לִפְנֵי אַנְשֵׁי הָעָי׃ וַיַּכּוּ
and-they-killed (5) the-Ai men-of before but-they-were-routed man thousands

מֵהֶם אַנְשֵׁי הָעַי כִּשְׁלֹשִׁים וְשִׁשָּׁה אִישׁ וַיִּרְדְּפוּם לִפְנֵי
from and-they-chased-them man and-six about-thirty the-Ai men-of from-them

הַשַּׁעַר עַד־ הַשְּׁבָרִים וַיַּכּוּם בַּמּוֹרָד
on-the-slope and-they-struck-them the-stone-quarries as-far-as the-city-gate

וַיִּמַּס לְבַב־ הָעָם וַיְהִי לְמָיִם׃ וַיִּקְרַע
then-he-tore (6) like-waters and-he-became the-people heart-of and-he-melted

יְהוֹשֻׁעַ שִׂמְלֹתָיו וַיִּפֹּל עַל־ פָּנָיו אַרְצָה לִפְנֵי אֲרוֹן
ark-of before to-ground faces-of-him on and-he-fell clothes-of-him Joshua

יְהוָה עַד־ הָעֶרֶב הוּא וְזִקְנֵי יִשְׂרָאֵל וַיַּעֲלוּ עָפָר עַל־
on dust and-they-sprinkled Israel and-elders-of he the-evening till Yahweh

רֹאשָׁם׃ וַיֹּאמֶר יְהוֹשֻׁעַ אֲהָהּ ׀ אֲדֹנָי יְהוִה לָמָה הֵעֲבַרְתָּ
you-brought-across why? Yahweh Lord ah! Joshua and-he-said (7) head-of-them

הַעֲבִיר אֶת־ הָעָם הַזֶּה אֶת־ הַיַּרְדֵּן לָתֵת אֹתָנוּ
us to-deliver the-Jordan *** the-this the-people *** to-bring-across

בְּיַד הָאֱמֹרִי לְהַאֲבִידֵנוּ וְלוּ הוֹאַלְנוּ וַנֵּשֶׁב
and-we-stayed we-were-content if-only to-destroy-us the-Amorite into-hand-of

בְּעֵבֶר הַיַּרְדֵּן׃ בִּי אֲדֹנָי מָה אֹמַר אַחֲרֵי אֲשֶׁר הָפַךְ
he-turned that now can-I-say what? Lord oh! (8) the-Jordan on-other-side-of

יִשְׂרָאֵל עֹרֶף לִפְנֵי אֹיְבָיו׃ וְיִשְׁמְעוּ הַכְּנַעֲנִי
the-Canaanite now-they-will-hear (9) being-enemies-of-him before back Israel

וְכֹל יֹשְׁבֵי הָאָרֶץ וְנָסַבּוּ עָלֵינוּ
around-us and-they-will-surround the-country ones-living-of and-all-of

וְהִכְרִיתוּ אֶת־ שְׁמֵנוּ מִן־ הָאָרֶץ וּמַה־ תַּעֲשֶׂה
will-you-do then-what? the-earth from name-of-us *** and-they-will-wipe-out

לְשִׁמְךָ הַגָּדוֹל׃ וַיֹּאמֶר יְהוָה אֶל־ יְהוֹשֻׁעַ קֻם לָךְ
for-you stand-up! Joshua to Yahweh and-he-said (10) the-great for-name-of-you

לָמָּה זֶּה אַתָּה נֹפֵל עַל־ פָּנֶיךָ׃ חָטָא יִשְׂרָאֵל וְגַם
and-also Israel he-sinned (11) faces-of-you on being-down you this why?

Joshua, they said, "Not all the people will have to go up against Ai. Send two or three thousand men to take it and do not weary all the people, for only a few men are there." [4]So about three thousand men went up; but they were routed by the men of Ai, [5]who killed about thirty-six of them. They chased the Israelites from the city gate as far as the stone quarries[q] and struck them down on the slopes. At this the hearts of the people melted and became like water.

[6]Then Joshua tore his clothes and fell facedown to the ground before the ark of the LORD, remaining there till evening. The elders of Israel did the same, and sprinkled dust on their heads. [7]And Joshua said, "Ah, Sovereign LORD, why did you ever bring this people across the Jordan to deliver us into the hands of the Amorites to destroy us? If only we had been content to stay on the other side of the Jordan! [8]O Lord, what can I say, now that Israel has been routed by its enemies? [9]The Canaanites and the other people of the country will hear about this and they will surround us and wipe out our name from the earth. What then will you do for your own great name?"

[10]The LORD said to Joshua, "Stand up! What are you doing down on your face? [11]Israel

[q]5 Or *as far as Shebarim*

עָבְרוּ אֶת־ בְּרִיתִי אֲשֶׁר צִוִּיתִי אוֹתָם וְגַם לָקְחוּ

they-took and-also them I-commanded which covenant-of-me *** they-violated

מִן־ הַחֵרֶם וְגַם גָּנְבוּ וְגַם כִּחֲשׁוּ וְגַם

and-also they-lied and-also they-stole and-also the-devoted-thing from

שָׂמוּ בִכְלֵיהֶם׃ וְלֹא יֻכְלוּ בְּנֵי יִשְׂרָאֵל לָקוּם

to-stand Israel sons-of they-can so-not (12) with-possessions-of-them they-put

לִפְנֵי אֹיְבֵיהֶם עֹרֶף יִפְנוּ לִפְנֵי אֹיְבֵיהֶם

being-enemies-of-them before they-turn back being-enemies-of-them against

כִּי הָיוּ לְחֵרֶם לֹא אוֹסִיף לִהְיוֹת עִמָּכֶם אִם־ לֹא

not if with-you to-be I-will-continue not for-destruction they-are for

תַשְׁמִידוּ הַחֵרֶם מִקִּרְבְּכֶם׃ קֻם קַדֵּשׁ אֶת־

*** consecrate! go! (13) from-among-you the-devoted-thing you-destroy

הָעָם וְאָמַרְתָּ הִתְקַדְּשׁוּ לְמָחָר כִּי כֹה אָמַר

he-says this for for-tomorrow consecrate-yourselves! and-you-tell the-people

יְהוָה אֱלֹהֵי יִשְׂרָאֵל חֵרֶם בְּקִרְבְּךָ יִשְׂרָאֵל לֹא תוּכַל לָקוּם

to-stand you-can not Israel in-among-you devoted-thing Israel God-of Yahweh

לִפְנֵי אֹיְבֶיךָ עַד־ הֲסִירְכֶם הַחֵרֶם

the-devoted-thing to-remove-you until being-enemies-of-you against

מִקִּרְבְּכֶם׃ וְנִקְרַבְתֶּם בַּבֹּקֶר לְשִׁבְטֵיכֶם

by-tribes-of-you in-the-morning and-you-present-yourselves (14) from-among-you

וְהָיָה הַשֵּׁבֶט אֲשֶׁר־ יִלְכְּדֶנּוּ יְהוָה יִקְרַב

he-shall-come-forward Yahweh he-takes-him that the-tribe and-he-shall-be

לַמִּשְׁפָּחוֹת וְהַמִּשְׁפָּחָה אֲשֶׁר־ יִלְכְּדֶנָּה יְהוָה תִּקְרַב

she-shall-come-forward Yahweh he-takes-her that and-the-clan by-the-clans

לַבָּתִּים וְהַבַּיִת אֲשֶׁר יִלְכְּדֶנּוּ יְהוָה יִקְרַב

he-shall-come-forward Yahweh he-takes-him that and-the-family by-the-families

לַגְּבָרִים׃ וְהָיָה הַנִּלְכָּד בַּחֵרֶם

with-the-devoted-thing the-one-being-caught and-he-shall-be (15) by-the-men

יִשָּׂרֵף בָּאֵשׁ אֹתוֹ וְאֶת־ כָּל־ אֲשֶׁר־ לוֹ כִּי עָבַר

he-violated for to-him that all and him by-the-fire he-shall-be-destroyed

אֶת־ בְּרִית יְהוָה וְכִי־ עָשָׂה נְבָלָה בְּיִשְׂרָאֵל׃

in-Israel disgraceful-thing he-did and-for Yahweh covenant-of ***

וַיַּשְׁכֵּם יְהוֹשֻׁעַ בַּבֹּקֶר וַיַּקְרֵב אֶת־יִשְׂרָאֵל

Israel *** and-he-had-come-forward in-the-morning Joshua and-he-rose (16)

לִשְׁבָטָיו וַיִּלָּכֵד שֵׁבֶט יְהוּדָה׃ וַיַּקְרֵב

so-he-had-come-forward (17) Judah tribe-of and-he-was-taken by-tribes-of-him

אֶת־מִשְׁפַּחַת יְהוּדָה וַיִּלְכֹּד אֵת מִשְׁפַּחַת הַזַּרְחִי וַיַּקְרֵב

so-he-had-come-forward the-Zerahite clan-of *** and-he-took Judah clan-of ***

has sinned; they have violated my covenant, which I commanded them to keep. They have taken some of the devoted things; they have stolen, they have lied, they have put them with their own possessions. [12]That is why the Israelites cannot stand against their enemies; they turn their backs and run because they have been made liable to destruction. I will not be with you anymore unless you destroy whatever among you is devoted to destruction.

[13]"Go, consecrate the people. Tell them, 'Consecrate yourselves in preparation for tomorrow; for this is what the LORD, the God of Israel, says: That which is devoted is among you, O Israel. You cannot stand against your enemies until you remove it.

[14]" 'In the morning, present yourselves tribe by tribe. The tribe that the LORD takes shall come forward clan by clan; the clan that the LORD takes shall come forward family by family; and the family that the LORD takes shall come forward man by man. [15]He who is caught with the devoted things shall be destroyed by fire, along with all that belongs to him. He has violated the covenant of the LORD and has done a disgraceful thing in Israel!' "

[16]Early the next morning Joshua had Israel come forward by tribes, and Judah was taken. [17]The clans of Judah came forward, and he took the Zerahites. He had the clan of the Zerahites come forward by

אֶת־ מִשְׁפַּחַת הַזַּרְחִי לַגְּבָרִים וַיִּלָּכֵד זַבְדִּי׃
Zabdi and-he-was-taken by-the-families the-Zerahite clan-of ***

וַיַּקְרֵב אֶת־ בֵּיתוֹ לַגְּבָרִים וַיִּלָּכֵד
and-he-was-taken by-the-men family-of-him *** so-he-had-come-forward (18)

עָכָן בֶּן־ כַּרְמִי בֶן־ זַבְדִּי בֶּן־ זֶרַח לְמַטֵּה יְהוּדָה׃
Judah of-tribe-of Zerah son-of Zabdi son-of Carmi son-of Achan

וַיֹּאמֶר יְהוֹשֻׁעַ אֶל־ עָכָן בְּנִי שִׂים־ נָא כָבוֹד לַיהוָה
to-Yahweh glory now! give! son-of-me Achan to Joshua then-he-said (19)

אֱלֹהֵי יִשְׂרָאֵל וְתֶן־ לוֹ תוֹדָה וְהַגֶּד־ נָא לִי מֶה עָשִׂיתָ אַל־
not you-did what to-me now! and-tell! praise to-him and-give! Israel God-of

תְּכַחֵד מִמֶּנִּי׃ וַיַּעַן עָכָן אֶת־ יְהוֹשֻׁעַ וַיֹּאמַר אָמְנָה אָנֹכִי
I true and-he-said Joshua *** Achan and-he-replied (20) from-me you-hide

חָטָאתִי לַיהוָה אֱלֹהֵי יִשְׂרָאֵל וְכָזֹאת וְכָזֹאת עָשִׂיתִי׃
I-did and-as-this and-as-this Israel God-of against-Yahweh I-sinned

וָאֶרְאֶה בַשָּׁלָל אַדֶּרֶת שִׁנְעָר אַחַת טוֹבָה וּמָאתַיִם
and-two-hundreds beautiful one Shinar robe-of in-the-plunder when-I-saw (21)

שְׁקָלִים כֶּסֶף וּלְשׁוֹן זָהָב אֶחָד חֲמִשִּׁים שְׁקָלִים מִשְׁקָלוֹ
weight-of-him shekels fifty one gold and-wedge-of silver shekels

וָאֶחְמְדֵם וָאֶקָּחֵם וְהִנָּם טְמוּנִים
ones-being-hidden and-see-they! and-I-took-them then-I-coveted-them

בָּאָרֶץ בְּתוֹךְ הָאָהֳלִי וְהַכֶּסֶף תַּחְתֶּיהָ׃
under-her and-the-silver the-tent-of-me inside-of in-the-ground

וַיִּשְׁלַח יְהוֹשֻׁעַ מַלְאָכִים וַיָּרֻצוּ הָאֹהֱלָה וְהִנֵּה
and-see! to-the-tent and-they-ran messengers Joshua so-he-sent (22)

טְמוּנָה בְּאָהֳלוֹ וְהַכֶּסֶף תַּחְתֶּיהָ׃ וַיִּקָּחוּם
and-they-took-them (23) under-her and-the-silver in-tent-of-him being-hidden

מִתּוֹךְ הָאֹהֶל וַיְבִאוּם אֶל־ יְהוֹשֻׁעַ וְאֶל כָּל־ בְּנֵי
sons-of all-of and-to Joshua to and-they-brought-them the-tent from-inside-of

יִשְׂרָאֵל וַיַּצִּקֻם לִפְנֵי יְהוָה׃ וַיִּקַּח יְהוֹשֻׁעַ אֶת־
*** Joshua then-he-took (24) Yahweh before and-they-spread-out-them Israel

עָכָן בֶּן־ זֶרַח וְאֶת־ הַכֶּסֶף וְאֶת־הָאַדֶּרֶת וְאֶת־ לְשׁוֹן הַזָּהָב וְאֶת־
and the-gold wedge-of and the-robe and the-silver and Zerah son-of Achan

בָּנָיו וְאֶת־ בְּנֹתָיו וְאֶת־ שׁוֹרוֹ וְאֶת־ חֲמֹרוֹ וְאֶת־
and donkey-of-him and cattle-of-him and daughters-of-him and sons-of-him

צֹאנוֹ וְאֶת־ אָהֳלוֹ וְאֶת־כָּל־אֲשֶׁר־ לוֹ וְכָל־ יִשְׂרָאֵל עִמּוֹ
with-him Israel and-all-of to-him that all and tent-of-him and sheep-of-him

וַיַּעֲלוּ אֹתָם עֵמֶק עָכוֹר׃ וַיֹּאמֶר יְהוֹשֻׁעַ מֶה
why? Joshua and-he-said (25) Achor Valley-of them and-they-took

families, and Zimri was taken.
18Joshua had his family come
forward man by man, and
Achan son of Carmi, the son
of Zimri, the son of Zerah, of
the tribe of Judah, was taken.
19Then Joshua said to Achan,
"My son, give glory to the
LORD,[r] the God of Israel, and
give him the praise.[s] Tell me
what you have done; do not
hide it from me."
20Achan replied, "It is true! I
have sinned against the LORD,
the God of Israel. This is what
I have done: 21When I saw in
the plunder a beautiful robe
from Babylonia,[t] two hundred
shekels[u] of silver and a wedge
of gold weighing fifty
shekels,[v] I coveted them and
took them. They are hidden in
the ground inside my tent,
with the silver underneath."
22So Joshua sent messengers,
and they ran to the tent, and
there it was, hidden in his
tent, with the silver underneath. 23They took the things
from the tent, brought them to
Joshua and all the Israelites
and spread them out before
the LORD.
24Then Joshua, together with
all Israel, took Achan son of
Zerah, the silver, the robe, the
gold wedge, his sons and
daughters, his cattle, donkeys
and sheep, his tent and all that
he had, to the Valley of Achor.
25Joshua said, "Why have you

[r]19 A solemn charge to tell the truth
[s]19 Or *and confess to him*
[t]21 Hebrew *Shinar*
[u]21 That is, about 5 pounds (about 2.3 kilograms)
[v]21 That is, about 1 1/4 pounds (about 0.6 kilogram)

°21 ק וארא

בַּיּוֹם יְהוָה יַעְכָּרְךָ עֲכַרְתָּנוּ
on-the-day Yahweh he-will-bring-disaster-on-you you-brought-disaster-on-us

אֹתָם וַיִּשְׂרְפוּ אֶבֶן יִשְׂרָאֵל כָל־ אֹתוֹ וַיִּרְגְּמוּ הַזֶּה
them and-they-burned stone Israel all-of him then-they-stoned the-this

וַיָּקִימוּ בָּאֲבָנִים׃ אֹתָם וַיִּסְקְלוּ בָּאֵשׁ
and-they-heaped-up (26) with-the-stones them after-they-stoned in-the-fire

יְהוָה וַיָּשָׁב הַזֶּה הַיּוֹם עַד גָּדוֹל אֲבָנִים גַּל־ עָלָיו
Yahweh then-he-turned the-this the-day to large rocks pile-of over-him

הַהוּא הַמָּקוֹם שֵׁם קָרָא כֵּן עַל־ אַפּוֹ מֵחֲרוֹן
the-that the-place name-of he-calls this for anger-of-him from-fierceness-of

אַל־ יְהוֹשֻׁעַ אֶל־ יְהוָה וַיֹּאמֶר הַזֶּה׃ הַיּוֹם עַד עָכוֹר עֵמֶק
not Joshua to Yahweh and-he-said (8:1) the-this the-day to Achor Valley-of

עַם כָּל־ אֵת עִמְּךָ קַח תֵּחָת וְאַל־ תִּירָא
people-of all-of *** with-you take! you-be-discouraged and-not you-be-afraid

אֶת־ בְיָדְךָ נָתַתִּי רְאֵה הָעַי עֲלֵה וְקוּם הַמִּלְחָמָה
*** into-hand-of-you I-delivered see! the-Ai attack! and-go-up! the-army

אַרְצוֹ׃ וְאֶת־ עִירוֹ וְאֶת־ עַמּוֹ וְאֶת־ הָעַי מֶלֶךְ
land-of-him and city-of-him and people-of-him and the-Ai king-of

לִירִיחוֹ עָשִׂיתָ כַּאֲשֶׁר וּלְמַלְכָּהּ לָעַי וְעָשִׂיתָ
to-Jericho you-did just-as and-to-king-of-her to-the-Ai and-you-shall-do (2)

תָּבֹזּוּ וּבְהֶמְתָּהּ שְׁלָלָהּ רַק־ וּלְמַלְכָּהּ
you-may-carry-off and-stock-of-her plunder-of-her except and-to-king-of-her

מֵאַחֲרֶיהָ׃ לָעִיר אֹרֵב לְךָ שִׂים־ לָכֶם
at-behind-her for-the-city being-ambush for-you set! for-you

הָעָי לַעֲלוֹת הַמִּלְחָמָה עַם וְכָל־ יְהוֹשֻׁעַ וַיָּקָם
the-Ai to-attack the-army people-of and-all-of Joshua so-he-moved-out (3)

וַיִּשְׁלָחֵם הַחַיִל גִּבּוֹרֵי אִישׁ אֶלֶף שְׁלֹשִׁים יְהוֹשֻׁעַ וַיִּבְחַר
and-he-sent-out-them the-fight men-of man thousand thirty Joshua and-he-chose

לָעִיר אֹרְבִים אַתֶּם רְאוּ לֵאמֹר אֹתָם וַיְצַו לָיְלָה׃
against-the-city ones-ambushing you see! to-say them and-he-ordered (4) night

כֻּלְּכֶם וִהְיִיתֶם מְאֹד הָעִיר מִן־ תַּרְחִיקוּ אַל־ הָעִיר מֵאַחֲרֵי
all-of-you and-you-be very the-city from you-go-far not the-city at-behind

נִקְרַב אִתִּי אֲשֶׁר הָעָם וְכָל־ וַאֲנִי נְכֹנִים׃
we-will-advance with-me who the-people and-all-of now-I (5) ones-being-alert

כַּאֲשֶׁר לִקְרָאתֵנוּ יֵצְאוּ כִּי־ וְהָיָה הָעִיר אֶל־
just-as to-attack-us they-come-out when and-he-will-be the-city on

אַחֲרֵינוּ וְיָצְאוּ לִפְנֵיהֶם׃ וְנַסְנוּ בָּרִאשֹׁנָה
after-us and-they-will-pursue (6) before-them then-we-will-flee at-the-first

brought this disaster on us? The LORD will bring disaster on you today."

Then all Israel stoned him, and after they had stoned the rest, they burned them. [26]Over Achan they heaped up a large pile of rocks, which remains to this day. Then the LORD turned from his fierce anger. Therefore that place has been called the Valley of Achor[w] ever since.

*Ai Destroyed*

8 Then the LORD said to Joshua, "Do not be afraid; do not be discouraged. Take the whole army with you, and go up and attack Ai. For I have delivered into your hands the king of Ai, his people, his city and his land. [2]You shall do to Ai and its king as you did to Jericho and its king, except that you may carry off their plunder and livestock for yourselves. Set an ambush behind the city."

[3]So Joshua and the whole army moved out to attack Ai. He chose thirty thousand of his best fighting men and sent them out at night [4]with these orders: "Listen carefully. You are to set an ambush behind the city. Don't go very far from it. All of you be on the alert. [5]I and all those with me will advance on the city, and when the men come out against us, as they did before, we will flee from them. [6]They will pursue

w26 *Achor* means *disaster*.

*25 Most mss have *qamets* under the *kaph* (כָּ־).

עַד הַתִּיקֵנוּ אוֹתָם מִן־ הָעִיר כִּי יֹאמְרוּ נָסִים
ones-running-away they-will-say for the-city from them to-lure-us until

לְפָנֵינוּ כַּאֲשֶׁר בָּרִאשֹׁנָה וְנַסְנוּ לִפְנֵיהֶם׃ וְאַתֶּם תָּקֻמוּ
you-rise then-you (7) before-them when-we-flee at-the-first just-as before-us

מֵהָאוֹרֵב וְהוֹרַשְׁתֶּם אֶת־ הָעִיר וּנְתָנָהּ יְהוָה
Yahweh and-he-will-give-her the-city *** and-you-take from-the-being-ambush

אֱלֹהֵיכֶם בְּיֶדְכֶם׃ וְהָיָה כְּתָפְשְׂכֶם אֶת־ הָעִיר
the-city *** when-to-take-you and-he-will-be (8) into-hand-of-you God-of-you

תַּצִּיתוּ אֶת־ הָעִיר בָּאֵשׁ כִּדְבַר יְהוָה תַּעֲשׂוּ רְאוּ
see! you-do Yahweh as-command-of with-the-fire the-city *** then-you-burn

צִוִּיתִי אֶתְכֶם׃ וַיִּשְׁלָחֵם יְהוֹשֻׁעַ וַיֵּלְכוּ אֶל־ הַמַּאְרָב
the-ambush-place to and-they-went Joshua then-he-sent-them (9) you I-ordered

וַיֵּשְׁבוּ בֵּין בֵּית־ אֵל וּבֵין הָעָי מִיָּם לָעָי
of-the-Ai to-west the-Ai and-between El Beth between and-they-waited

וַיָּלֶן יְהוֹשֻׁעַ בַּלַּיְלָה הַהוּא בְּתוֹךְ הָעָם׃
the-people in-among the-that on-the-night Joshua but-he-spent-night

וַיַּשְׁכֵּם יְהוֹשֻׁעַ בַּבֹּקֶר וַיִּפְקֹד אֶת־ הָעָם
the-people *** and-he-mustered in-the-morning Joshua and-he-rose (10)

וַיַּעַל הוּא וְזִקְנֵי יִשְׂרָאֵל לִפְנֵי הָעָם הָעָי׃
the-Ai the-people before Israel and-leaders-of he and-he-marched

וְכָל־ הָעָם הַמִּלְחָמָה אֲשֶׁר אִתּוֹ עָלוּ
they-marched-up with-him that the-force the-people and-entire-of (11)

וַיִּגְּשׁוּ וַיָּבֹאוּ נֶגֶד הָעִיר וַיַּחֲנוּ
and-they-camped the-city in-front-of and-they-arrived and-they-approached

מִצְּפוֹן לָעַי וְהַגַּי בֵּינוֹ° וּבֵין־ הָעָי׃
the-Ai and-between between-him and-the-valley of-the-Ai to-north

וַיִּקַּח כַּחֲמֵשֶׁת אֲלָפִים אִישׁ וַיָּשֶׂם אוֹתָם אֹרֵב
being-ambush them and-he-set man thousands about-five-of and-he-took (12)

בֵּין בֵּית־ אֵל וּבֵין הָעַי מִיָּם לָעִיר׃ וַיָּשִׂימוּ
and-they-positioned (13) of-the-city to-west the-Ai and-between El Beth between

הָעָם אֶת־ כָּל־ הַמַּחֲנֶה אֲשֶׁר מִצְּפוֹן לָעִיר וְאֶת־ עֲקֵבוֹ
ambush-of-him and of-the-city to-north that the-camp all-of *** the-people

מִיָּם לָעִיר וַיֵּלֶךְ יְהוֹשֻׁעַ בַּלַּיְלָה הַהוּא בְּתוֹךְ הָעֵמֶק׃
the-valley into the-that on-the-night Joshua and-he-went of-the-city to-west

וַיְהִי כִּרְאוֹת מֶלֶךְ־ הָעַי וַיְמַהֲרוּ וַיַּשְׁכִּימוּ
and-they-got-up then-they-hurried the-Ai king-of when-to-see and-he-was (14)

וַיֵּצְאוּ אַנְשֵׁי־ הָעִיר לִקְרַאת־ יִשְׂרָאֵל לַמִּלְחָמָה הוּא וְכָל־
and-all-of he in-the-battle Israel to-meet the-city men-of and-they-went-out

°11 ק׳ בינו

us until we have lured them away from the city, for they will say, 'They are running away from us as they did before.' So when we flee from them, [7]you are to rise up from ambush and take the city. The LORD your God will give it into your hand. [8]When you have taken the city, set it on fire. Do what the LORD has commanded. See to it; you have my orders."

[9]Then Joshua sent them off, and they went to the place of ambush and lay in wait between Bethel and Ai, to the west of Ai—but Joshua spent that night with the people.

[10]Early the next morning Joshua mustered his men, and he and the leaders of Israel marched before them to Ai. [11]The entire force that was with him marched up and approached the city and arrived in front of it. They set up camp north of Ai, with the valley between them and the city. [12]Joshua had taken about five thousand men and set them in ambush between Bethel and Ai, to the west of the city. [13]They had the soldiers take up their positions—all those in the camp to the north of the city and the ambush to the west of it. That night Joshua went into the valley.

[14]When the king of Ai saw this, he and all the men of the city hurried out early in the

עַמּוֹ לַמּוֹעֵד לִפְנֵי הָעֲרָבָה וְהוּא לֹא יָדַע כִּי־
that he-knew not but-he the-Arabah overlooking at-the-place people-of-him

אֹרֵב לוֹ מֵאַחֲרֵי הָעִיר׃ וַיִּנָּגְעוּ
and-they-let-selves-be-driven (15) the-city at-behind against-him being-ambush

יְהוֹשֻׁעַ וְכָל־ יִשְׂרָאֵל לִפְנֵיהֶם וַיָּנֻסוּ דֶּרֶךְ הַמִּדְבָּר׃
the-desert direction-of and-they-fled before-them Israel and-all-of Joshua

וַיִּזָּעֲקוּ כָּל־ הָעָם אֲשֶׁר בָּעִיר* לִרְדֹּף אַחֲרֵיהֶם
after-them to-pursue *in-the-city who the-man all-of and-they-were-called (16)

וַיִּרְדְּפוּ אַחֲרֵי יְהוֹשֻׁעַ וַיִּנָּתְקוּ מִן־ הָעִיר׃ וְלֹא־
and-not (17) the-city from and-they-were-lured Joshua after and-they-pursued

נִשְׁאַר אִישׁ בָּעַי וּבֵית אֵל אֲשֶׁר לֹא־ יָצְאוּ אַחֲרֵי יִשְׂרָאֵל
Israel after they-went not who El or-Beth in-the-Ai man he-remained

וַיַּעַזְבוּ אֶת־ הָעִיר פְּתוּחָה וַיִּרְדְּפוּ אַחֲרֵי יִשְׂרָאֵל׃
Israel after and-they-pursued being-open the-city *** and-they-left

וַיֹּאמֶר יְהוָה אֶל־ יְהוֹשֻׁעַ נְטֵה בַּכִּידוֹן אֲשֶׁר־
that with-the-javelin hold-out! Joshua to Yahweh then-he-said (18)

בְּיָדְךָ אֶל־ הָעַי כִּי בְיָדְךָ אֶתְּנֶנָּה
I-will-deliver-her into-hand-of-you for the-Ai toward in-hand-of-you

וַיֵּט יְהוֹשֻׁעַ בַּכִּידוֹן אֲשֶׁר־ בְּיָדוֹ אֶל־ הָעִיר׃
the-city toward in-hand-of-him that with-the-javelin Joshua so-he-held-out

וְהָאוֹרֵב קָם מְהֵרָה מִמְּקוֹמוֹ וַיָּרוּצוּ
and-they-rushed from-position-of-him quickly he-rose and-the-being-ambush (19)

כִּנְטוֹת יָדוֹ וַיָּבֹאוּ הָעִיר וַיִּלְכְּדוּהָ
and-they-captured-her the-city and-they-entered hand-of-him when-to-hold-out

וַיְמַהֲרוּ וַיַּצִּיתוּ אֶת־ הָעִיר בָּאֵשׁ׃
with-the-fire the-city *** and-they-burned and-they-were-quick

וַיִּפְנוּ אַנְשֵׁי הָעַי אַחֲרֵיהֶם וַיִּרְאוּ וְהִנֵּה
and-see! and-they-looked back-of-them the-Ai men-of and-they-turned (20)

עָלָה עֲשַׁן הָעִיר הַשָּׁמַיְמָה וְלֹא־ הָיָה בָהֶם יָדַיִם
ways for-them he-was but-not against-the-skies the-city smoke-of he-rose

לָנוּס הֵנָּה וָהֵנָּה וְהָעָם הַנָּס הַמִּדְבָּר
the-desert the-one-fleeing for-the-people or-there here to-escape

נֶהְפַּךְ אֶל־ הָרוֹדֵף׃ וִיהוֹשֻׁעַ וְכָל־ יִשְׂרָאֵל
Israel and-all-of when-Joshua (21) the-one-pursuing against he-turned-back

רָאוּ כִּי־ לָכַד הָאֹרֵב אֶת־ הָעִיר וְכִי עָלָה
he-went-up and-that the-city *** the-being-ambush he-took that they-saw

עֲשַׁן הָעִיר וַיָּשֻׁבוּ וַיַּכּוּ אֶת־ אַנְשֵׁי הָעָי׃
the-Ai men-of *** and-they-attacked then-they-turned the-city smoke-of

morning to meet Israel in battle at a certain place overlooking the Arabah. But he did not know that an ambush had been set against him behind the city.
15Joshua and all Israel let themselves be driven back before them, and they fled toward the desert.
16All the men of Ai were called to pursue them, and they pursued Joshua and were lured away from the city.
17Not a man remained in Ai or Bethel who did not go after Israel. They left the city open and went in pursuit of Israel.

18Then the LORD said to Joshua, "Hold out toward Ai the javelin that is in your hand, for into your hand I will deliver the city." So Joshua held out his javelin toward Ai.
19As soon as he did this, the men in the ambush rose quickly from their position and rushed forward. They entered the city and captured it and quickly set it on fire.

20The men of Ai looked back and saw the smoke of the city rising against the sky, but they had no chance to escape in any direction, for the Israelites who had been fleeing toward the desert had turned back against their pursuers.
21For when Joshua and all Israel saw that the ambush had taken the city and that smoke was going up from the city, they turned around and attacked the men of Ai.
22The

*16 Western mss read *in-the-city* ( בָּעִיר ) with no *Qere* form; eastern mss have the *Qere in-the-Ai* ( בָּעַי ).

°16 ק בעי

וְאֵלֶּה יָצְאוּ מִן־הָעִיר לִקְרָאתָם וַיִּהְיוּ
so-they-were to-attack-them the-city from they-came-out and-these (22)

לְיִשְׂרָאֵל בַּתָּוֶךְ אֵלֶּה מִזֶּה וְאֵלֶּה מִזֶּה
on-other-side and-these on-one-side these in-the-middle by-Israel

וַיַּכּוּ אוֹתָם עַד־בִּלְתִּי הִשְׁאִיר־לוֹ שָׂרִיד וּפָלִיט׃ וְאֶת־
but (23) or-fugitive survivor to-him he-left not until them and-they-cut-down

מֶלֶךְ הָעַי תָּפְשׂוּ חָי וַיַּקְרִבוּ אֹתוֹ אֶל־יְהוֹשֻׁעַ׃ וַיְהִי
and-he-was (24) Joshua to him and-they-brought alive they-took the-Ai king-of

כְּכַלּוֹת יִשְׂרָאֵל לַהֲרֹג אֶת־ כָּל־ יֹשְׁבֵי הָעַי בַּשָּׂדֶה
in-the-field the-Ai one-living-of all-of *** to-kill Israel when-to-finish

בַּמִּדְבָּר אֲשֶׁר רְדָפוּם בּוֹ וַיִּפְּלוּ כֻלָּם
all-of-them when-they-fell into-him they-chased-them where in-the-desert

לְפִי־ חֶרֶב עַד־ תֻּמָּם וַיָּשֻׁבוּ כָל־ יִשְׂרָאֵל הָעַי
the-Ai Israel all-of then-they-returned to-finish-them when sword by-edge-of

וַיַּכּוּ אֹתָהּ לְפִי־ חָרֶב׃ וַיְהִי כָל־ הַנֹּפְלִים
the-ones-falling all-of and-he-was (25) sword with-edge-of her and-they-killed

בַּיּוֹם הַהוּא מֵאִישׁ וְעַד־ אִשָּׁה שְׁנֵים עָשָׂר אָלֶף כֹּל אַנְשֵׁי
people-of all-of thousand ten two woman even-to from-man the-that on-the-day

הָעָי׃ וִיהוֹשֻׁעַ לֹא־ הֵשִׁיב יָדוֹ אֲשֶׁר נָטָה
he-held-out that hand-of-him he-drew-back not for-Joshua (26) the-Ai

בַּכִּידוֹן עַד אֲשֶׁר הֶחֱרִים אֵת כָּל־ יֹשְׁבֵי הָעָי׃
the-Ai ones-living-of all-of *** he-destroyed when until with-the-javelin

רַק הַבְּהֵמָה וּשְׁלַל הָעִיר הַהִיא בָּזְזוּ לָהֶם
for-them they-carried-off the-this the-city and-plunder-of the-stock but (27)

יִשְׂרָאֵל כִּדְבַר יְהוָה אֲשֶׁר צִוָּה אֶת־ יְהוֹשֻׁעַ׃ וַיִּשְׂרֹף
so-he-burned (28) Joshua *** he-gave that Yahweh as-instruction-of Israel

יְהוֹשֻׁעַ אֶת־הָעָי וַיְשִׂימֶהָ תֵּל־ עוֹלָם שְׁמָמָה עַד הַיּוֹם
the-day to desolate-place permanent heap and-he-made-her the-Ai *** Joshua

הַזֶּה׃ וְאֶת־ מֶלֶךְ הָעַי תָּלָה עַל־ הָעֵץ עַד־ עֵת
time-of until the-tree on he-hung the-Ai king-of and (29) the-this

הָעָרֶב וּכְבוֹא הַשֶּׁמֶשׁ צִוָּה יְהוֹשֻׁעַ וַיֹּרִידוּ אֶת־
*** and-they-took Joshua he-ordered the-sun and-when-to-set the-evening

נִבְלָתוֹ מִן־ הָעֵץ וַיַּשְׁלִיכוּ אוֹתָהּ אֶל־ פֶּתַח שַׁעַר הָעִיר
the-city gate-of entrance-of at her and-they-threw the-tree from body-of-him

וַיָּקִימוּ עָלָיו גַּל־ אֲבָנִים גָּדוֹל עַד הַיּוֹם הַזֶּה׃ אָז
then (30) the-this the-day to large rocks pile-of over-him and-they-raised

יִבְנֶה יְהוֹשֻׁעַ מִזְבֵּחַ לַיהוָה אֱלֹהֵי יִשְׂרָאֵל בְּהַר עֵיבָל׃ כַּאֲשֶׁר
just-as (31) Ebal on-Mount-of Israel God-of to-Yahweh altar Joshua he-built

men of the ambush also came out of the city against them, so that they were caught in the middle, with Israelites on both sides. Israel cut them down, leaving them neither survivors nor fugitives. [23]But they took the king of Ai alive and brought him to Joshua.

[24]When Israel had finished killing all the men of Ai in the fields and in the desert where they had chased them, and when every one of them had been put to the sword, all the Israelites returned to Ai and killed those who were in it. [25]Twelve thousand men and women fell that day—all the people of Ai. [26]For Joshua did not draw back the hand that held out his javelin until he had destroyed[x] all who lived in Ai. [27]But Israel did carry off for themselves the livestock and plunder of this city, as the LORD had instructed Joshua.

[28]So Joshua burned Ai and made it a permanent heap of ruins, a desolate place to this day. [29]He hung the king of Ai on a tree and left him there until evening. At sunset, Joshua ordered them to take his body from the tree and throw it down at the entrance of the city gate. And they raised a large pile of rocks over it, which remains to this day.

### *The Covenant Renewed at Mount Ebal*

[30]Then Joshua built on Mount Ebal an altar to the LORD, the God of Israel, [31]as

[x]26 The Hebrew term refers to the irrevocable giving over of things or persons to the LORD, often by totally destroying them.

צִוָּה מֹשֶׁה עֶבֶד־ יְהוָה אֶת־ בְּנֵי יִשְׂרָאֵל כַּכָּתוּב
as-the-being-written Israel sons-of *** Yahweh servant-of Moses he-commanded

בְּסֵפֶר תּוֹרַת מֹשֶׁה מִזְבַּח אֲבָנִים שְׁלֵמוֹת אֲשֶׁר לֹא־ הֵנִיף עֲלֵיהֶן
on-them he-used not that uncut-ones stones altar-of Moses Law-of in-Book-of

בַּרְזֶל וַיַּעֲלוּ עָלָיו עֹלוֹת לַיהוָה וַיִּזְבְּחוּ
and-they-sacrificed to-Yahweh burnt-offerings on-him and-they-offered iron-tool

שְׁלָמִים׃ וַיִּכְתָּב־ שָׁם עַל־ הָאֲבָנִים אֵת מִשְׁנֵה תּוֹרַת
law-of copy-of *** the-stones on there and-he-wrote (32) fellowship-offerings

מֹשֶׁה אֲשֶׁר כָּתַב לִפְנֵי בְּנֵי יִשְׂרָאֵל׃ וְכָל־ יִשְׂרָאֵל
Israel and-all-of (33) Israel sons-of in-presences-of he-wrote which Moses

וּזְקֵנָיו וְשֹׁטְרִים ׀ וְשֹׁפְטָיו עֹמְדִים
ones-standing and-ones-judging-him and-being-officials and-elders-of-him

מִזֶּה ׀ וּמִזֶּה ׀ לָאָרוֹן נֶגֶד הַכֹּהֲנִים הַלְוִיִּם
the-Levites the-priests facing of-the-ark and-on-other-side on-one-side

נֹשְׂאֵי ׀ אֲרוֹן בְּרִית־ יְהוָה כַּגֵּר כָּאֶזְרָח
as-the-citizen so-the-alien Yahweh covenant-of ark-of ones-carrying-of

חֶצְיוֹ אֶל־ מוּל הַר־ גְּרִזִים וְהַחֶצְיוֹ אֶל־ מוּל
front-of in and-the-half-of-him Gerizim Mount-of front-of in half-of-him

הַר־ עֵיבָל כַּאֲשֶׁר צִוָּה מֹשֶׁה עֶבֶד־ יְהוָה לְבָרֵךְ אֶת־
*** to-bless Yahweh servant-of Moses he-commanded just-as Ebal Mount-of

הָעָם יִשְׂרָאֵל בָּרִאשֹׁנָה׃ וְאַחֲרֵי־ כֵן קָרָא אֶת־ כָּל־
all-of *** he-read this and-after (34) at-the-formerly Israel the-people

דִּבְרֵי הַתּוֹרָה הַבְּרָכָה וְהַקְּלָלָה כְּכָל־ הַכָּתוּב
the-being-written as-all-of and-the-curse the-blessing the-law words-of

בְּסֵפֶר הַתּוֹרָה׃ לֹא־ הָיָה דָבָר מִכֹּל אֲשֶׁר־ צִוָּה מֹשֶׁה אֲשֶׁר
that Moses he-commanded that of-all word he-was not (35) the-Law in-Book-of

לֹא־ קָרָא יְהוֹשֻׁעַ נֶגֶד כָּל־ קְהַל יִשְׂרָאֵל וְהַנָּשִׁים
even-the-women Israel assembly-of whole-of before Joshua he-read not

וְהַטַּף וְהַגֵּר הַהֹלֵךְ בְּקִרְבָּם׃ וַיְהִי
and-he-was (9:1) in-among-them the-one-living and-the-alien and-the-child

כִשְׁמֹעַ כָּל־ הַמְּלָכִים אֲשֶׁר בְּעֵבֶר הַיַּרְדֵּן בָּהָר
in-the-hill-country the-Jordan on-west-of who the-kings all-of when-to-hear

וּבַשְּׁפֵלָה וּבְכֹל חוֹף הַיָּם הַגָּדוֹל אֶל־ מוּל
edge-of to the-Great the-Sea coast-of and-along-entire-of and-in-the-foothill

הַלְּבָנוֹן הַחִתִּי וְהָאֱמֹרִי הַכְּנַעֲנִי הַפְּרִזִּי הַחִוִּי
the-Hivite the-Perizzite the-Canaanite and-the-Amorite the-Hittite the-Lebanon

וְהַיְבוּסִי׃ וַיִּתְקַבְּצוּ יַחְדָּו לְהִלָּחֵם עִם־ יְהוֹשֻׁעַ
Joshua against to-make-war together then-they-gathered (2) and-the-Jebusite

Moses the servant of the LORD had commanded the Israelites. He built it according to what is written in the Book of the Law of Moses—an altar of uncut stones, on which no iron tool had been used. On it they offered to the LORD burnt offerings and sacrificed fellowship offerings.[y] [32]There in the presence of the Israelites, Joshua copied on stones the law of Moses, which he had written. [33]All Israel, aliens and citizens alike, with their elders, officials and judges, were standing on both sides of the ark of the covenant of the LORD, facing those who carried it—the priests, who were Levites. Half of the people stood in front of Mount Gerizim and half of them in front of Mount Ebal, as Moses the servant of the LORD had formerly commanded when he gave instructions to bless the people of Israel.

[34]Afterward, Joshua read all the words of the law—the blessings and the curses—just as it is written in the Book of the Law. [35]There was not a word of all that Moses had commanded that Joshua did not read to the whole assembly of Israel, including the women and children, and the aliens who lived among them.

*The Gibeonite Deception*

9 Now when all the kings west of the Jordan heard about these things—those in the hill country, in the western foothills, and along the entire coast of the Great Sea[z] as far as Lebanon (the kings of the Hittites, Amorites, Canaanites, Perizzites, Hivites and Jebusites)— [2]they came together to make war against

[y]31 Traditionally *peace offerings*
[z]1 That is, the Mediterranean

*33 Most mss have *dagesh* in the *zayin* (זִּים־).

וְעִם־ יִשְׂרָאֵל פֶּה אֶחָד׃ וְיֹשְׁבֵי גִבְעוֹן שָׁמְעוּ אֵת

*** they-heard Gibeon but-ones-living-of (3) one force Israel and-against

אֲשֶׁר עָשָׂה יְהוֹשֻׁעַ לִירִיחוֹ וְלָעָי׃ וַיַּעֲשׂוּ גַם־

indeed and-they-resorted (4) and-to-the-Ai to-Jericho Joshua he-did what

הֵמָּה בְּעָרְמָה וַיֵּלְכוּ וַיִּצְטַיָּרוּ* וַיִּקְחוּ שַׂקִּים

sacks and-they-loaded *and-they-acted-as-delegation and-they-went to-ruse they

בָּלִים לַחֲמוֹרֵיהֶם וְנֹאדוֹת יַיִן בָּלִים וּמְבֻקָּעִים

and-ones-being-cracked old-ones wine and-skins-of on-donkeys-of-them ones-worn

וּמְצֹרָרִים׃ וּנְעָלוֹת בָּלוֹת וּמְטֻלָּאוֹת

and-ones-being-patched ones-worn and-sandals (5) and-ones-being-mended

בְּרַגְלֵיהֶם וּשְׂלָמוֹת בָּלוֹת עֲלֵיהֶם וְכֹל לֶחֶם

bread-of and-all-of on-them old-ones and-clothes on-feet-of-them

צֵידָם יָבֵשׁ הָיָה נִקֻּדִים׃ וַיֵּלְכוּ

then-they-went (6) ones-being-moldy he-was he-was-dry food-supply-of-them

אֶל־יְהוֹשֻׁעַ אֶל־הַמַּחֲנֶה הַגִּלְגָּל וַיֹּאמְרוּ אֵלָיו וְאֶל־ אִישׁ יִשְׂרָאֵל

Israel man-of and-to to-him and-they-said the-Gilgal the-camp in Joshua to

מֵאֶרֶץ רְחוֹקָה בָּאנוּ וְעַתָּה כִּרְתוּ־ לָנוּ בְרִית׃ וַיֹּאמְרו

and-he-said (7) treaty with-us make! and-now we-came distant from-country

אִישׁ־ יִשְׂרָאֵל אֶל־ הַחִוִּי אוּלַי בְּקִרְבִּי אַתָּה יוֹשֵׁב וְאֵיךְ

then-how? living you at-near-me perhaps the-Hivite to Israel man-of

אֶכְרָות־ לְךָ בְרִית׃ וַיֹּאמְרוּ אֶל־ יְהוֹשֻׁעַ עֲבָדֶיךָ

servants-of-you Joshua to and-they-said (8) treaty with-you can-I-make

אֲנָחְנוּ וַיֹּאמֶר אֲלֵהֶם יְהוֹשֻׁעַ מִי אַתֶּם וּמֵאַיִן תָּבֹאוּ׃

you-come and-from-where? you who? Joshua to-them but-he-asked we

וַיֹּאמְרוּ אֵלָיו מֵאֶרֶץ רְחוֹקָה מְאֹד בָּאוּ

they-came very distant from-country to-him and-they-answered (9)

עֲבָדֶיךָ לְשֵׁם יְהוָה אֱלֹהֶיךָ כִּי־ שָׁמַעְנוּ שָׁמְעוֹ

report-of-him we-heard for God-of-you Yahweh because-of-fame-of servants-of-you

וְאֵת כָּל־אֲשֶׁר עָשָׂה בְּמִצְרָיִם׃ וְאֵת ׀ כָּל־אֲשֶׁר עָשָׂה לִשְׁנֵי מַלְכֵי

kings-of to-two-of he-did that all and (10) in-Egypt he-did that all and

הָאֱמֹרִי אֲשֶׁר בְּעֵבֶר הַיַּרְדֵּן לְסִיחוֹן מֶלֶךְ חֶשְׁבּוֹן וּלְעוֹג

and-to-Og Heshbon king-of to-Sihon the-Jordan on-east-of who the-Amorite

מֶלֶךְ־ הַבָּשָׁן אֲשֶׁר בְּעַשְׁתָּרוֹת׃ וַיֹּאמְרוּ אֵלֵינוּ זְקֵינֵינוּ

elders-of-us to-us and-they-said (11) in-Ashtaroth who the-Bashan king-of

וְכָל־ יֹשְׁבֵי אַרְצֵנוּ לֵאמֹר קְחוּ בְיֶדְכֶם צֵידָה

provision in-hand-of-you take! to-say land-of-us ones-living-of and-all-of

לַדֶּרֶךְ וּלְכוּ לִקְרָאתָם וַאֲמַרְתֶּם אֲלֵיהֶם עַבְדֵיכֶם

servants-of-you to-them and-you-say to-meet-them and-go! for-the-journey

Joshua and Israel.
3However, when the people
of Gibeon heard what Joshua
had done to Jericho and Ai,
4they resorted to a ruse: They
went as a delegation whose
donkeys were loaded[a] with
worn-out sacks and old wineskins, cracked and mended.
5The men put worn and
patched sandals on their feet
and wore old clothes. All the
bread of their food supply was
dry and moldy. 6Then they
went to Joshua in the camp at
Gilgal and said to him and the
men of Israel, "We have come
from a distant country; make a
treaty with us."
7The men of Israel said to the
Hivites, "But perhaps you live
near us. How then can we
make a treaty with you?"
8"We are your servants,"
they said to Joshua.
But Joshua asked, "Who are
you and where do you come
from?"
9They answered: "Your servants have come from a very
distant country because of the
fame of the LORD your God.
For we have heard reports of
him: all that he did in Egypt,
10and all that he did to the two
kings of the Amorites east of
the Jordan—Sihon king of
Heshbon, and Og king of Bashan, who reigned in Ash-
taroth. 11And our elders and all
those living in our country
said to us, 'Take provisions for
your journey; go and meet
them and say to them, "We are

[a]4 Most Hebrew manuscripts; some Hebrew manuscripts, Vulgate and Syriac (see also Septuagint) *They prepared provisions and loaded their donkeys*

*4 Some mss and versions read *daleth* for *resh* (ידו—) as in verse 12, *and-they-prepared-provision.*

°7a ק ויאמר

°7b ק אכרת

אֲנַחְנוּ וְעַתָּה כִּרְתוּ־לָנוּ בְרִית׃ זֶה ׀ לַחְמֵנוּ חָם הִצְטַיַּדְנוּ אֹתוֹ

him we-packed warm bread-of-us this (12) treaty with-us make! so-now we

מִבָּתֵּינוּ בְּיוֹם צֵאתֵנוּ לָלֶכֶת אֲלֵיכֶם וְעַתָּה הִנֵּה יָבֵשׁ

he-is-dry see! but-now to-you to-come to-leave-us on-day at-homes-of-us

וְהָיָה נִקֻּדִים׃ וְאֵלֶּה נֹאדוֹת הַיַּיִן אֲשֶׁר מִלֵּאנוּ

we-filled that the-wine skins-of and-these (13) ones-being-moldy and-he-is

חֲדָשִׁים וְהִנֵּה הִתְבַּקָּעוּ וְאֵלֶּה שַׂלְמוֹתֵינוּ וּנְעָלֵינוּ

and-sandals-of-us clothes-of-us and-these they-are-cracked but-see! new-ones

בָּלוּ מֵרֹב הַדֶּרֶךְ מְאֹד׃ וַיִּקְחוּ הָאֲנָשִׁים

the-men so-they-sampled (14) very the-journey by-length-of they-are-worn-out

מִצֵּידָם וְאֶת־פִּי יְהוָה לֹא שָׁאָלוּ׃ וַיַּעַשׂ

then-he-made (15) they-inquired not Yahweh word-of but from-provision-of-them

לָהֶם יְהוֹשֻׁעַ שָׁלוֹם וַיִּכְרֹת לָהֶם בְּרִית לְחַיּוֹתָם

to-let-live-them treaty with-them and-he-made peace Joshua with-them

וַיִּשָּׁבְעוּ לָהֶם נְשִׂיאֵי הָעֵדָה׃ וַיְהִי

and-he-was (16) the-assembly leaders-of with-them and-they-ratified-by-oath

מִקְצֵה שְׁלֹשֶׁת יָמִים אַחֲרֵי אֲשֶׁר־כָּרְתוּ לָהֶם בְּרִית וַיִּשְׁמְעוּ

then-they-heard treaty with-them they-made when after days three-of at-end-of

כִּי־קְרֹבִים הֵם אֵלָיו וּבְקִרְבּוֹ הֵם יֹשְׁבִים׃

ones-living they and-at-near-to-him to-him they neighbors that

וַיִּסְעוּ בְנֵי־יִשְׂרָאֵל וַיָּבֹאוּ אֶל־עָרֵיהֶם בַּיּוֹם

on-the-day cities-of-them to and-they-came Israel sons-of so-they-set-out (17)

הַשְּׁלִישִׁי וְעָרֵיהֶם גִּבְעוֹן וְהַכְּפִירָה וּבְאֵרוֹת וְקִרְיַת

and-Kiriath and-Beeroth and-the-Kephirah Gibeon now-cities-of-them the-third

יְעָרִים׃ וְלֹא הִכּוּם בְּנֵי יִשְׂרָאֵל כִּי־נִשְׁבְּעוּ

they-swore-oath for Israel sons-of they-attacked-them but-not (18) Jearim

לָהֶם נְשִׂיאֵי הָעֵדָה בַּיהוָה אֱלֹהֵי יִשְׂרָאֵל וַיִּלֹּנוּ

and-they-grumbled Israel God-of by-Yahweh the-assembly leaders-of to-them

כָל־הָעֵדָה עַל־הַנְּשִׂיאִים׃ וַיֹּאמְרוּ כָל־

all-of but-they-answered (19) the-leaders against the-assembly whole-of

הַנְּשִׂיאִים אֶל־כָּל־הָעֵדָה אֲנַחְנוּ נִשְׁבַּעְנוּ לָהֶם בַּיהוָה

by-Yahweh to-them we-gave-oath we the-assembly whole-of to the-leaders

אֱלֹהֵי יִשְׂרָאֵל וְעַתָּה לֹא נוּכַל לִנְגֹּעַ בָּהֶם׃ זֹאת נַעֲשֶׂה

we-will-do this (20) on-them to-touch we-can not and-now Israel God-of

לָהֶם וְהַחֲיֵה אוֹתָם וְלֹא־יִהְיֶה עָלֵינוּ קֶצֶף עַל־הַשְּׁבוּעָה

the-oath for wrath on-us he-will-fall so-not them even-to-let-live to-them

אֲשֶׁר־נִשְׁבַּעְנוּ לָהֶם׃ וַיֹּאמְרוּ אֲלֵיהֶם הַנְּשִׂיאִים יִחְיוּ

let-them-live the-leaders to-them and-they-said (21) to-them we-swore that

your servants; make a treaty with us." ' [12]This bread of ours was warm when we packed it at home on the day we left to come to you. But now see how dry and moldy it is. [13]And these wineskins that we filled were new, but see how cracked they are. And our clothes and sandals are worn out by the very long journey."

[14]The men of Israel sampled their provisions but did not inquire of the LORD. [15]Then Joshua made a treaty of peace with them to let them live, and the leaders of the assembly ratified it by oath.

[16]Three days after they made the treaty with the Gibeonites, the Israelites heard that they were neighbors, living near them. [17]So the Israelites set out and on the third day came to their cities: Gibeon, Kephirah, Beeroth and Kiriath Jearim. [18]But the Israelites did not attack them, because the leaders of the assembly had sworn an oath to them by the LORD, the God of Israel.

The whole assembly grumbled against the leaders, [19]but all the leaders answered, "We have given them our oath by the LORD, the God of Israel, and we cannot touch them now. [20]This is what we will do to them: We will let them live, so that wrath will not fall on us for breaking the oath we swore to them." [21]They continued, "Let them live, but let

וַיִּֽהְיוּ חֹטְבֵי עֵצִים וְשֹׁאֲבֵי־מַיִם לְכָל־
for-all-of waters and-ones-carrying-of woods ones-cutting-of but-let-them-be

הָעֵדָה כַּאֲשֶׁר דִּבְּרוּ לָהֶם הַנְּשִׂיאִים׃ וַיִּקְרָא
then-he-summoned (22) the-leaders to-them they-promised just-as the-community

לָהֶם יְהוֹשֻׁעַ וַיְדַבֵּר אֲלֵיהֶם לֵאמֹר לָמָּה רִמִּיתֶם אֹתָנוּ לֵאמֹר
to-say us you-deceived why? to-say to-them and-he-said Joshua to-them

רְחוֹקִים אֲנַחְנוּ מִכֶּם מְאֹד וְאַתֶּם בְּקִרְבֵּנוּ יֹשְׁבִים׃ וְעַתָּה
and-now (23) ones-living at-near-us while-you very from-you we ones-distant

אֲרוּרִים אַתֶּם וְלֹא־יִכָּרֵת מִכֶּם עֶבֶד וְחֹטְבֵי
and-ones-cutting-of servant from-you he-will-cease and-not you ones-being-cursed

עֵצִים וְשֹׁאֲבֵי־מַיִם לְבֵית אֱלֹהָי׃ וַיַּעֲנוּ
and-they-replied (24) God-of-me for-house-of waters and-ones-carrying-of woods

אֶת־יְהוֹשֻׁעַ וַיֹּאמְרוּ כִּי הֻגֵּד הֻגַּד לַעֲבָדֶיךָ
to-servants-of-you he-was-told to-be-told clearly and-they-said Joshua ***

אֵת אֲשֶׁר צִוָּה יְהוָה אֱלֹהֶיךָ אֶת־מֹשֶׁה עַבְדּוֹ לָתֵת
to-give servant-of-him Moses *** God-of-you Yahweh he-commanded how ***

לָכֶם אֶת־כָּל־הָאָרֶץ וּלְהַשְׁמִיד אֶת־כָּל־יֹשְׁבֵי
ones-inhabiting-of all-of *** and-to-wipe-out the-land whole-of *** to-you

הָאָרֶץ מִפְּנֵיכֶם וַנִּירָא מְאֹד לְנַפְשֹׁתֵינוּ מִפְּנֵיכֶם
because-of-you for-lives-of-us greatly so-we-feared from-before-you the-land

וַנַּעֲשֵׂה אֶת־הַדָּבָר הַזֶּה׃ וְעַתָּה הִנְנוּ בְיָדֶךָ
in-hand-of-you see-we! and-now (25) the-this the-thing *** so-we-did

כַּטּוֹב וְכַיָּשָׁר בְּעֵינֶיךָ לַעֲשׂוֹת לָנוּ עֲשֵׂה׃ וַיַּעַשׂ
so-he-did (26) do! to-us to-do in-eyes-of-you and-as-the-right as-the-good

לָהֶם כֵּן וַיַּצֵּל אוֹתָם מִיַּד בְּנֵי־יִשְׂרָאֵל וְלֹא
and-not Israel sons-of from-hand-of them and-he-saved this to-them

הֲרָגוּם׃ וַיִּתְּנֵם יְהוֹשֻׁעַ בַּיּוֹם הַהוּא
the-that on-the-day Joshua and-he-made-them (27) they-killed-them

חֹטְבֵי עֵצִים וְשֹׁאֲבֵי מַיִם לָעֵדָה
for-the-community waters and-ones-carrying-of woods ones-cutting-of

וּלְמִזְבַּח יְהוָה עַד־הַיּוֹם הַזֶּה אֶל־הַמָּקוֹם אֲשֶׁר יִבְחָר׃
he-would-choose that the-place at the-this the-day to Yahweh and-for-altar-of

וַיְהִי כִשְׁמֹעַ אֲדֹנִי־צֶדֶק מֶלֶךְ יְרוּשָׁלַםִ כִּי־לָכַד
he-took that Jerusalem king-of Zedek Adoni when-to-hear now-he-was (10:1)

יְהוֹשֻׁעַ אֶת־הָעַי וַיַּחֲרִימָהּ כַּאֲשֶׁר עָשָׂה לִירִיחוֹ
to-Jericho he-did just-as and-he-destroyed-her the-Ai *** Joshua

וּלְמַלְכָּהּ כֵּן־עָשָׂה לָעַי וּלְמַלְכָּהּ וְכִי
and-that and-to-king-of-her to-the-Ai he-did same and-to-king-of-her

them be woodcutters and water carriers for the entire community." So the leaders' promise to them was kept.

22 Then Joshua summoned the Gibeonites and said, "Why did you deceive us by saying, 'We live a long way from you,' while actually you live near us? 23 You are now under a curse: You will never cease to serve as woodcutters and water carriers for the house of my God."

24 They answered Joshua, "Your servants were clearly told how the LORD your God had commanded his servant Moses to give you the whole land and to wipe out all its inhabitants from before you. So we feared for our lives because of you, and that is why we did this. 25 We are now in your hands. Do to us whatever seems good and right to you."

26 So Joshua saved them from the Israelites, and they did not kill them. 27 That day he made the Gibeonites woodcutters and water carriers for the community and for the altar of the LORD at the place the LORD would choose. And that is what they are to this day.

### *The Sun Stands Still*

10 Now Adoni-Zedek king of Jerusalem heard that Joshua had taken Ai and totally destroyed[b] it, doing to Ai and its king as he had done to Jericho and its king, and that the people of

[b]1 The Hebrew term refers to the irrevocable giving over of things or persons to the LORD, often by totally destroying them; also in verses 28, 35, 37, 39 and 40.

הִשְׁלִימוּ יֹשְׁבֵי גִבְעוֹן אֶת־ יִשְׂרָאֵל וַיִּהְיוּ

and-they-lived Israel with Gibeon ones-living-of they-made-peace-treaty

בְּקִרְבָּם׃ וַיִּירְאוּ מְאֹד כִּי עִיר גְּדוֹלָה גִּבְעוֹן

Gibeon important city for very then-they-were-alarmed (2) at-near-them

כְּאַחַת עָרֵי הַמַּמְלָכָה וְכִי הִיא גְדוֹלָה מִן־ הָעַי וְכָל־

and-all-of the-Ai than larger she and-indeed the-royal cities-of like-one-of

אֲנָשֶׁיהָ גִּבֹּרִים׃ וַיִּשְׁלַח אֲדֹנִי־ צֶדֶק מֶלֶךְ יְרוּשָׁלַםִ

Jerusalem king-of Zedek Adoni so-he-appealed (3) good-fighters men-of-her

אֶל־הוֹהָם מֶלֶךְ־ חֶבְרוֹן וְאֶל־פִּרְאָם מֶלֶךְ־ יַרְמוּת וְאֶל־ יָפִיעַ מֶלֶךְ־

king-of Japhia and-to Jarmuth king-of Piram and-to Hebron king-of Hoham to

לָכִישׁ וְאֶל־ דְּבִיר מֶלֶךְ־ עֶגְלוֹן לֵאמֹר׃ עֲלוּ־ אֵלַי וְעִזְרֻנִי

and-help-me! to-me come-up! (4) to-say Eglon king-of Debir and-to Lachish

וְנַכֶּה אֶת־ גִּבְעוֹן כִּי־ הִשְׁלִימָה אֶת־ יְהוֹשֻׁעַ וְאֶת־ בְּנֵי

sons-of and-with Joshua with she-made-peace for Gibeon *** and-we-will-attack

יִשְׂרָאֵל׃ וַיֵּאָסְפוּ וַיַּעֲלוּ חֲמֵשֶׁת ׀ מַלְכֵי הָאֱמֹרִי

the-Amorite kings-of five-of and-they-moved-up then-they-joined (5) Israel

מֶלֶךְ יְרוּשָׁלַםִ מֶלֶךְ־ חֶבְרוֹן מֶלֶךְ־ יַרְמוּת מֶלֶךְ־ לָכִישׁ מֶלֶךְ־

king-of Lachish king-of Jarmuth king-of Hebron king-of Jerusalem king-of

עֶגְלוֹן הֵם וְכָל־ מַחֲנֵיהֶם וַיַּחֲנוּ עַל־ גִּבְעוֹן

Gibeon against and-they-positioned troops-of-them and-all-of they Eglon

וַיִּלָּחֲמוּ עָלֶיהָ׃ וַיִּשְׁלְחוּ אַנְשֵׁי גִבְעוֹן אֶל־יְהוֹשֻׁעַ

Joshua to Gibeon men-of then-they-sent (6) against-her and-they-attacked

אֶל־ הַמַּחֲנֶה הַגִּלְגָּלָה לֵאמֹר אַל־ תֶּרֶף יָדֶיךָ

hands-of-you you-abandon not to-say at-the-Gilgal the-camp in

מֵעֲבָדֶיךָ עֲלֵה אֵלֵינוּ מְהֵרָה וְהוֹשִׁיעָה לָּנוּ וְעָזְרֵנוּ

and-help-us! to-us and-save! quickly to-us come-up! from-servants-of-you

כִּי נִקְבְּצוּ אֵלֵינוּ כָּל־ מַלְכֵי הָאֱמֹרִי יֹשְׁבֵי

ones-living-of the-Amorite kings-of all-of against-us they-joined for

הָהָר׃ וַיַּעַל יְהוֹשֻׁעַ מִן־ הַגִּלְגָּל הוּא וְכָל־

and-entire-of he the-Gilgal from Joshua so-he-marched-up (7) the-hill-country

עַם הַמִּלְחָמָה עִמּוֹ וְכֹל גִּבּוֹרֵי הֶחָיִל׃ וַיֹּאמֶר

and-he-said (8) the-fight men-of and-all-of with-him the-army people-of

יְהוָה אֶל־יְהוֹשֻׁעַ אַל־ תִּירָא מֵהֶם כִּי בְיָדְךָ נְתַתִּים

I-gave-them into-hand-of-you for of-them you-be-afraid not Joshua to Yahweh

לֹא־ יַעֲמֹד אִישׁ מֵהֶם בְּפָנֶיךָ׃ וַיָּבֹא אֲלֵיהֶם יְהוֹשֻׁעַ

Joshua against-them and-he-came (9) against-you of-them one he-can-stand not

פִּתְאֹם כָּל־ הַלַּיְלָה עָלָה מִן־ הַגִּלְגָּל׃ וַיְהֻמֵּם

and-he-confused-them (10) the-Gilgal from he-marched the-night all-of surprise

Gibeon had made a treaty of peace with Israel and were living near them. [2]He and his people were very much alarmed at this, because Gibeon was an important city, like one of the royal cities; it was larger than Ai, and all its men were good fighters. [3]So Adoni-Zedek king of Jerusalem appealed to Hoham king of Hebron, Piram king of Jarmuth, Japhia king of Lachish and Debir king of Eglon. [4]"Come up and help me attack Gibeon," he said, "because it has made peace with Joshua and the Israelites."

[5]Then the five kings of the Amorites—the kings of Jerusalem, Hebron, Jarmuth, Lachish and Eglon—joined forces. They moved up with all their troops and took up positions against Gibeon and attacked it.

[6]The Gibeonites then sent word to Joshua in the camp at Gilgal: "Do not abandon your servants. Come up to us quickly and save us! Help us, because all the Amorite kings from the hill country have joined forces against us."

[7]So Joshua marched up from Gilgal with his entire army, including all the best fighting men. [8]The LORD said to Joshua, "Do not be afraid of them; I have given them into your hand. Not one of them will be able to withstand you."

[9]After an all-night march from Gilgal, Joshua took them by surprise. [10]The LORD threw

יְהוָה לִפְנֵי יִשְׂרָאֵל וַיַּכֵּם מַכָּה־ גְדוֹלָה בְּגִבְעוֹן
at-Gibeon great victory and-he-defeated-them Israel before Yahweh

וַיִּרְדְּפֵם דֶּרֶךְ מַעֲלֵה בֵית־ חוֹרֹן וַיַּכֵּם עַד־
to and-he-cut-down-them Horon Beth going-up-of road-of and-he-pursued-them

עֲזֵקָה וְעַד־ מַקֵּדָה׃ וַיְהִי בְּנֻסָם מִפְּנֵי יִשְׂרָאֵל
Israel from-before as-to-flee-them and-he-was (11) Makkedah and-to Azekah

הֵם בְּמוֹרַד בֵּית־ חוֹרֹן וַיהוָה הִשְׁלִיךְ עֲלֵיהֶם אֲבָנִים
hailstones on-them he-hurled then-Yahweh Horon Beth on-road-down-of they

גְּדֹלוֹת מִן־ הַשָּׁמַיִם עַד־ עֲזֵקָה וַיָּמֻתוּ רַבִּים אֲשֶׁר־ מֵתוּ
they-died who ones-more and-they-died Azekah to the-skies from large-ones

בְּאַבְנֵי הַבָּרָד מֵאֲשֶׁר הָרְגוּ בְּנֵי יִשְׂרָאֵל בֶּחָרֶב׃
by-the-sword Israel sons-of they-killed than-whom the-hail from-stones-of

אָז יְדַבֵּר יְהוֹשֻׁעַ לַיהוָה בְּיוֹם תֵּת יְהוָה אֶת־ הָאֱמֹרִי
the-Amorite *** Yahweh to-give on-day to-Yahweh Joshua he-said then (12)

לִפְנֵי בְּנֵי יִשְׂרָאֵל וַיֹּאמֶר לְעֵינֵי יִשְׂרָאֵל שֶׁמֶשׁ בְּגִבְעוֹן
over-Gibeon sun Israel before-eyes-of and-he-said Israel sons-of over-to

דּוֹם וְיָרֵחַ בְּעֵמֶק אַיָּלוֹן׃ וַיִּדֹּם הַשֶּׁמֶשׁ
the-sun so-he-stood-still (13) Aijalon over-Valley-of and-moon stand-still!

וְיָרֵחַ עָמָד עַד־ יִקֹּם גּוֹי אֹיְבָיו הֲלֹא־
not? being-enemies-of-him nation he-avenged-self till he-stopped and-moon

הִיא כְתוּבָה עַל־ סֵפֶר הַיָּשָׁר וַיַּעֲמֹד הַשֶּׁמֶשׁ בַּחֲצִי
in-middle-of the-sun and-he-stopped the-Jashar Book-of in being-written this

הַשָּׁמַיִם וְלֹא־ אָץ לָבוֹא כְּיוֹם תָּמִים׃ וְלֹא הָיָה
he-was and-never (14) full about-day to-go-down he-hurried and-not the-skies

כַּיּוֹם הַהוּא לְפָנָיו וְאַחֲרָיו לִשְׁמֹעַ יְהוָה בְּקוֹל
to-voice-of Yahweh to-listen or-since-him before-him the-that like-the-day

אִישׁ כִּי יְהוָה נִלְחָם לְיִשְׂרָאֵל׃ וַיָּשָׁב יְהוֹשֻׁעַ
Joshua then-he-returned (15) for-Israel one-fighting Yahweh surely man

וְכָל־ יִשְׂרָאֵל עִמּוֹ אֶל־ הַמַּחֲנֶה הַגִּלְגָּלָה׃ וַיָּנֻסוּ
now-they-fled (16) at-the-Gilgal the-camp to with-him Israel and-all-of

חֲמֵשֶׁת הַמְּלָכִים הָאֵלֶּה וַיֵּחָבְאוּ בַמְּעָרָה בְּמַקֵּדָה׃
at-the-Makkedah in-the-cave and-they-hid the-these the-kings five-of

וַיֻּגַּד לִיהוֹשֻׁעַ לֵאמֹר נִמְצְאוּ חֲמֵשֶׁת הַמְּלָכִים
the-kings five-of they-were-found to-say to-Joshua when-he-was-told (17)

נֶחְבְּאִים בַּמְּעָרָה בְּמַקֵּדָה׃ וַיֹּאמֶר יְהוֹשֻׁעַ גֹּלּוּ אֲבָנִים
rocks roll! Joshua and-he-said (18) at-the-Makkedah in-the-cave ones-hiding

גְּדֹלוֹת אֶל־ פִּי הַמְּעָרָה וְהַפְקִידוּ עָלֶיהָ אֲנָשִׁים לְשָׁמְרָם׃
to-guard-them men by-her and-post! the-cave mouth-of up-to large-ones

them into confusion before Israel, who defeated them in a great victory at Gibeon. Israel pursued them along the road going up to Beth Horon and cut them down all the way to Azekah and Makkedah. [11]As they fled before Israel on the road down from Beth Horon to Azekah, the LORD hurled large hailstones down on them from the sky, and more of them died from the hailstones than were killed by the swords of the Israelites.

[12]On the day the LORD gave the Amorites over to Israel, Joshua said to the LORD in the presence of Israel:

"O sun, stand still over
Gibeon,
O moon, over the Valley
of Aijalon."
[13]So the sun stood still,
and the moon stopped,
till the nation avenged
itself on[c] its enemies,

as it is written in the Book of Jashar.

The sun stopped in the middle of the sky and delayed going down about a full day. [14]There has never been a day like it before or since, a day when the LORD listened to a man. Surely the LORD was fighting for Israel!

[15]Then Joshua returned with all Israel to the camp at Gilgal.

*Five Amorite Kings Killed*

[16]Now the five kings had fled and hidden in the cave at Makkedah. [17]When Joshua was told that the five kings had been found hiding in the cave at Makkedah, [18]he said, "Roll large rocks up to the mouth of the cave, and post some men there to guard it.

c13 Or *nation triumphed over*

וְאַתֶּם אַל־ תַּעֲמֹדוּ רִדְפוּ אַחֲרֵי אֹיְבֵיכֶם וְזִנַּבְתֶּם

and-you-attack being-enemies-of-you after pursue! you-stop not but-you (19)

אוֹתָם אַל־ תִּתְּנוּם לָבוֹא אֶל־ עָרֵיהֶם כִּי נְתָנָם יְהוָה

Yahweh he-gave-them for cities-of-them to to-reach you-let-them not them

אֱלֹהֵיכֶם בְּיֶדְכֶם׃ וַיְהִי כְּכַלּוֹת יְהוֹשֻׁעַ וּבְנֵי

and-sons-of Joshua that-to-complete so-he-was (20) into-hand-of-you God-of-you

יִשְׂרָאֵל לְהַכּוֹתָם מַכָּה גְדוֹלָה־ מְאֹד עַד־ תֻּמָּם

to-finish-them almost very great destruction to-destroy-them Israel

וְהַשְּׂרִידִים שָׂרְדוּ מֵהֶם וַיָּבֹאוּ אֶל־ עָרֵי

cities-of to and-they-reached of-them they-were-left but-the-ones-left

הַמִּבְצָר׃ וַיָּשֻׁבוּ כָל־ הָעָם אֶל־ הַמַּחֲנֶה אֶל־

to the-camp to the-army whole-of then-they-returned (21) the-fortified

יְהוֹשֻׁעַ מַקֵּדָה בְּשָׁלוֹם לֹא־ חָרַץ לִבְנֵי יִשְׂרָאֵל לְאִישׁ

against-man Israel against-sons-of he-uttered no-one in-safety Makkedah Joshua

אֶת־ לְשֹׁנוֹ׃ וַיֹּאמֶר יְהוֹשֻׁעַ פִּתְחוּ אֶת־ פִּי הַמְּעָרָה

the-cave mouth-of *** open! Joshua then-he-said (22) word-of-him ***

וְהוֹצִיאוּ אֵלַי אֶת־ חֲמֵשֶׁת הַמְּלָכִים הָאֵלֶּה מִן־ הַמְּעָרָה׃

the-cave from the-those the-kings five-of *** to-me and-bring-out!

וַיַּעֲשׂוּ כֵן וַיֹּצִיאוּ אֵלָיו אֶת־ חֲמֵשֶׁת הַמְּלָכִים

the-kings five-of *** to-him and-they-brought-out this so-they-did (23)

הָאֵלֶּה מִן־ הַמְּעָרָה אֵת׀ מֶלֶךְ יְרוּשָׁלִַם אֶת־ מֶלֶךְ חֶבְרוֹן אֶת־ מֶלֶךְ

king-of *** Hebron king-of *** Jerusalem king-of *** the-cave from the-those

יַרְמוּת אֶת־מֶלֶךְ לָכִישׁ אֶת־מֶלֶךְ עֶגְלוֹן׃ וַיְהִי כְּהוֹצִיאָם

when-to-bring-them and-he-was (24) Eglon king-of *** Lachish king-of *** Jarmuth

אֶת־הַמְּלָכִים הָאֵלֶּה אֶל־יְהוֹשֻׁעַ וַיִּקְרָא יְהוֹשֻׁעַ אֶל־ כָּל־ אִישׁ

man-of every-of to Joshua then-he-summoned Joshua to the-these the-kings ***

יִשְׂרָאֵל וַיֹּאמֶר אֶל־ קְצִינֵי אַנְשֵׁי הַמִּלְחָמָה הֶהָלְכוּא אִתּוֹ

with-him who-they-came the-army men-of commanders-of to and-he-said Israel

קִרְבוּ שִׂימוּ אֶת־ רַגְלֵיכֶם עַל־ צַוְּארֵי הַמְּלָכִים הָאֵלֶּה וַיִּקְרְבוּ

so-they-came the-these the-kings necks-of on feet-of-you *** put! come!

וַיָּשִׂימוּ אֶת־ רַגְלֵיהֶם עַל־ צַוְּארֵיהֶם׃ וַיֹּאמֶר אֲלֵיהֶם

to-them and-he-said (25) necks-of-them on feet-of-them *** and-they-placed

יְהוֹשֻׁעַ אַל־ תִּירְאוּ וְאַל־ תֵּחָתּוּ חִזְקוּ וְאִמְצוּ

and-be-courageous! be-strong! you-be-discouraged and-not you-fear not Joshua

כִּי כָכָה יַעֲשֶׂה יְהוָה לְכָל־ אֹיְבֵיכֶם אֲשֶׁר אַתֶּם

you whom being-enemies-of-you to-all-of Yahweh he-will-do this for

נִלְחָמִים אוֹתָם׃ וַיַּכֵּם יְהוֹשֻׁעַ אַחֲרֵי־ כֵן

this after Joshua then-he-struck-them (26) them ones-fighting

[19]But don't stop! Pursue your enemies, attack them from the rear and don't let them reach their cities, for the LORD your God has given them into your hand."

[20]So Joshua and the Israelites destroyed them completely—almost to a man—but the few who were left reached their fortified cities. [21]The whole army then returned safely to Joshua in the camp at Makkedah, and no one uttered a word against the Israelites.

[22]Joshua said, "Open the mouth of the cave and bring those five kings out to me." [23]So they brought the five kings out of the cave—the kings of Jerusalem, Hebron, Jarmuth, Lachish and Eglon. [24]When they had brought these kings to Joshua, he summoned all the men of Israel and said to the army commanders who had come with him, "Come here and put your feet on the necks of these kings." So they came forward and placed their feet on their necks.

[25]Joshua said to them, "Do not be afraid; do not be discouraged. Be strong and courageous. This is what the LORD will do to all the enemies you are going to fight." [26]Then Joshua struck and killed the

וַיְמִיתֵם וַיִּתְלֵם עַל חֲמִשָּׁה עֵצִים וַיִּהְיוּ תְּלוּיִם
ones-hanging and-they-were trees five on and-he-hung-them and-he-killed-them

עַל־הָעֵצִים עַד־הָעָרֶב׃ וַיְהִי לְעֵת בּוֹא הַשֶּׁמֶשׁ
the-sun to-set at-time and-he-was (27) the-evening until the-trees on

צִוָּה יְהוֹשֻׁעַ וַיֹּרִידוּם מֵעַל הָעֵצִים וַיַּשְׁלִכֻם
and-they-threw-them the-trees from-on and-they-took-down-them Joshua he-ordered

אֶל־הַמְּעָרָה אֲשֶׁר נֶחְבְּאוּ־שָׁם וַיָּשִׂמוּ אֲבָנִים גְּדֹלוֹת עַל־
at large-ones rocks and-they-placed there they-hid where the-cave into

פִּי הַמְּעָרָה עַד־עֶצֶם הַיּוֹם הַזֶּה׃ וְאֶת־מַקֵּדָה לָכַד
he-took Makkedah and (28) the-this the-day very-of to the-cave mouth-of

יְהוֹשֻׁעַ בַּיּוֹם הַהוּא וַיַּכֶּהָ לְפִי־חֶרֶב וְאֶת־מַלְכָּהּ
king-of-her and sword to-edge-of and-he-put-her the-that on-the-day Joshua

הֶחֱרִם אוֹתָם וְאֶת־כָּל־הַנֶּפֶשׁ אֲשֶׁר־בָּהּ לֹא הִשְׁאִיר שָׂרִיד
survivor he-left not in-her who the-person every-of and them he-destroyed

וַיַּעַשׂ לְמֶלֶךְ מַקֵּדָה כַּאֲשֶׁר עָשָׂה לְמֶלֶךְ יְרִיחוֹ׃
Jericho to-king-of he-did just-as Makkedah to-king-of and-he-did

וַיַּעֲבֹר יְהוֹשֻׁעַ וְכָל־יִשְׂרָאֵל עִמּוֹ מִמַּקֵּדָה
from-Makkedah with-him Israel and-all-of Joshua then-he-moved-on (29)

לִבְנָה וַיִּלָּחֶם עִם־לִבְנָה׃ וַיִּתֵּן יְהוָה גַּם־אוֹתָהּ
her also Yahweh and-he-gave (30) Libnah against and-he-attacked Libnah

בְּיַד יִשְׂרָאֵל וְאֶת־מַלְכָּהּ וַיַּכֶּהָ לְפִי־חֶרֶב וְאֶת־
and sword to-edge-of and-he-put-her king-of-her and Israel into-hand-of

כָּל־הַנֶּפֶשׁ אֲשֶׁר־בָּהּ לֹא־הִשְׁאִיר בָּהּ שָׂרִיד וַיַּעַשׂ
and-he-did survivor in-her he-left not in-her who the-person every-of

לְמַלְכָּהּ כַּאֲשֶׁר עָשָׂה לְמֶלֶךְ יְרִיחוֹ׃ וַיַּעֲבֹר
then-he-moved-on (31) Jericho to-king-of he-did just-as to-king-of-her

יְהוֹשֻׁעַ וְכָל־יִשְׂרָאֵל עִמּוֹ מִלִּבְנָה לָכִישָׁה וַיִּחַן
and-he-positioned to-Lachish from-Libnah with-him Israel and-all-of Joshua

עָלֶיהָ וַיִּלָּחֶם בָּהּ׃ וַיִּתֵּן יְהוָה אֶת־לָכִישׁ
Lachish *** Yahweh and-he-gave (32) against-her and-he-attacked against-her

בְּיַד יִשְׂרָאֵל וַיִּלְכְּדָהּ בַּיּוֹם הַשֵּׁנִי וַיַּכֶּהָ
and-he-put-her the-second on-the-day and-he-took-her Israel into-hand-of

לְפִי־חֶרֶב וְאֶת־כָּל־הַנֶּפֶשׁ אֲשֶׁר־בָּהּ כְּכֹל אֲשֶׁר־עָשָׂה
he-did that as-all in-her who the-person every-of and sword to-edge-of

לְלִבְנָה׃ אָז עָלָה הֹרָם מֶלֶךְ גֶּזֶר לַעְזֹר אֶת־לָכִישׁ
Lachish *** to-help Gezer king-of Horam he-came-up meanwhile (33) to-Libnah

וַיַּכֵּהוּ יְהוֹשֻׁעַ וְאֶת־עַמּוֹ עַד־בִּלְתִּי הִשְׁאִיר־לוֹ שָׂרִיד׃
survivor to-him he-left not until army-of-him and Joshua but-he-defeated-him

kings and hung them on five
trees, and they were left hanging on the trees until evening.
27 At sunset Joshua gave the
order and they took them
down from the trees and
threw them into the cave
where they had been hiding.
At the mouth of the cave they
placed large rocks, which are
there to this day.
28 That day Joshua took Makkedah. He put the city and its
king to the sword and totally
destroyed everyone in it. He
left no survivors. And he did
to the king of Makkedah as he
had done to the king of Jericho.

*Southern Cities Conquered*

29 Then Joshua and all Israel
with him moved on from
Makkedah to Libnah and attacked it. 30 The LORD also gave
that city and its king into Israel's hand. The city and everyone in it Joshua put to the
sword. He left no survivors
there. And he did to its king as
he had done to the king of Jericho.
31 Then Joshua and all Israel
with him moved on from Libnah to Lachish; he took up positions against it and attacked
it. 32 The LORD handed Lachish
over to Israel, and Joshua took
it on the second day. The city
and everyone in it he put to
the sword, just as he had done
to Libnah. 33 Meanwhile,
Horam king of Gezer had
come up to help Lachish, but
Joshua defeated him and his
army—until no survivors were
left.

וַיַּעֲבֹר יְהוֹשֻׁעַ וְכָל־ יִשְׂרָאֵל עִמּוֹ מִלָּכִישׁ
from-Lachish with-him Israel and-all-of Joshua then-he-moved-on (34)

עֶגְלֹנָה וַיַּחֲנוּ עָלֶיהָ וַיִּלָּחֲמוּ עָלֶיהָ׃
against-her and-they-attacked against-her and-they-positioned to-Eglon

וַיִּלְכְּדוּהָ בַּיּוֹם הַהוּא וַיַּכּוּהָ לְפִי־
to-edge-of and-they-put-her the-same on-the-day and-they-captured-her (35)

חֶרֶב וְאֵת כָּל־ הַנֶּפֶשׁ אֲשֶׁר־ בָּהּ בַּיּוֹם הַהוּא הֶחֱרִים
he-destroyed the-same on-the-day in-her who the-person every-of and sword

כְּכֹל אֲשֶׁר־ עָשָׂה לְלָכִישׁ׃ וַיַּעַל יְהוֹשֻׁעַ וְכָל־ יִשְׂרָאֵל
Israel and-all-of Joshua then-he-went-up (36) to-Lachish he-did that as-all

עִמּוֹ מֵעֶגְלוֹנָה חֶבְרוֹנָה וַיִּלָּחֲמוּ עָלֶיהָ׃
against-her and-they-attacked to-Hebron from-Eglon with-him

וַיִּלְכְּדוּהָ וַיַּכּוּהָ לְפִי־ חֶרֶב וְאֶת־ מַלְכָּהּ וְאֶת־
and king-of-her and sword to-edge-of and-they-put-her and-they-took-her (37)

כָּל־ עָרֶיהָ וְאֶת־ כָּל־ הַנֶּפֶשׁ אֲשֶׁר־ בָּהּ לֹא־ הִשְׁאִיר
he-left not in-her who the-person every-of and villages-of-her all-of

שָׂרִיד כְּכֹל אֲשֶׁר־ עָשָׂה לְעֶגְלוֹן וַיַּחֲרֵם אוֹתָהּ וְאֶת־ כָּל־
every-of and her and-he-destroyed to-Eglon he-did that as-all survivor

הַנֶּפֶשׁ אֲשֶׁר־ בָּהּ׃ וַיָּשָׁב יְהוֹשֻׁעַ וְכָל־ יִשְׂרָאֵל עִמּוֹ
with-him Israel and-all-of Joshua then-he-turned (38) in-her who the-person

דְּבִרָה וַיִּלָּחֶם עָלֶיהָ׃ וַיִּלְכְּדָהּ וְאֶת־ מַלְכָּהּ
king-of-her and and-he-took-her (39) against-her and-he-attacked to-Debir

וְאֶת־ כָּל־ עָרֶיהָ וַיַּכּוּם לְפִי־ חֶרֶב וַיַּחֲרִימוּ
and-they-destroyed sword to-edge-of and-they-put-them villages-of-her all-of and

אֶת־ כָּל־ נֶפֶשׁ אֲשֶׁר־ בָּהּ לֹא הִשְׁאִיר שָׂרִיד כַּאֲשֶׁר עָשָׂה לְחֶבְרוֹן
to-Hebron he-did just-as survivor he-left not in-her who person every-of ***

כֵּן־ עָשָׂה לִדְבִרָה וּלְמַלְכָּהּ וְכַאֲשֶׁר עָשָׂה לְלִבְנָה
to-Libnah he-did and-just-as and-to-king-of-her to-Debir he-did so

וּלְמַלְכָּהּ׃ וַיַּכֶּה יְהוֹשֻׁעַ אֶת־ כָּל־ הָאָרֶץ
the-region whole-of *** Joshua so-he-subdued (40) and-to-king-of-her

הָהָר וְהַנֶּגֶב וְהַשְּׁפֵלָה וְהָאֲשֵׁדוֹת וְאֵת כָּל־
all-of and and-the-slopes and-the-foothill and-the-Negev the-hill-country

מַלְכֵיהֶם לֹא הִשְׁאִיר שָׂרִיד וְאֵת כָּל־ הַנְּשָׁמָה הֶחֱרִים
he-destroyed the-breather every-of and survivor he-left not kings-of-them

כַּאֲשֶׁר צִוָּה יְהוָה אֱלֹהֵי יִשְׂרָאֵל׃ וַיַּכֵּם יְהוֹשֻׁעַ
Joshua and-he-subdued-them (41) Israel God-of Yahweh he-commanded just-as

מִקָּדֵשׁ בַּרְנֵעַ וְעַד־ עַזָּה וְאֵת כָּל־ אֶרֶץ גֹּשֶׁן וְעַד־ גִּבְעוֹן׃
Gibeon even-to Goshen region-of whole-of and Gaza even-to Barnea from-Kadesh

[34]Then Joshua and all Israel
with him moved on from Lachish to Eglon; they took up
positions against it and attacked it. [35]They captured it
that same day and put it to the
sword and totally destroyed
everyone in it, just as they had
done to Lachish.
[36]Then Joshua and all Israel
with him went up from Eglon
to Hebron and attacked it.
[37]They took the city and put it
to the sword, together with its
king, its villages and everyone
in it. They left no survivors.
Just as at Eglon, they totally
destroyed it and everyone in
it.
[38]Then Joshua and all Israel
with him turned around and
attacked Debir. [39]They took
the city, its king and its villages, and put them to the
sword. Everyone in it they totally destroyed. They left no
survivors. They did to Debir
and its king as they had done
to Libnah and its king and to
Hebron.
[40]So Joshua subdued the
whole region, including the
hill country, the Negev, the
western foothills and the
mountain slopes, together
with all their kings. He left no
survivors. He totally destroyed
all who breathed, just as the
LORD, the God of Israel, had
commanded. [41]Joshua subdued them from Kadesh Barnea to Gaza and from the
whole region of Goshen to

וְאֵת כָּל־ הַמְּלָכִים הָאֵלֶּה וְאֶת־ אַרְצָם לָכַד יְהוֹשֻׁעַ
Joshua he-conquered land-of-them and the-these the-kings all-of and (42)

פַּעַם אֶחָת כִּי יְהוָה אֱלֹהֵי יִשְׂרָאֵל נִלְחָם לְיִשְׂרָאֵל׃
for-Israel one-fighting Israel God-of Yahweh for one campaign

וַיָּשָׁב יְהוֹשֻׁעַ וְכָל־ יִשְׂרָאֵל עִמּוֹ אֶל־ הַמַּחֲנֶה
the-camp to with-him Israel and-all-of Joshua then-he-returned (43)

הַגִּלְגָּלָה׃ וַיְהִי כִּשְׁמֹעַ יָבִין מֶלֶךְ־ חָצוֹר וַיִּשְׁלַח
then-he-sent Hazor king-of Jabin when-to-hear and-he-was (11:1) at-the-Gilgal

אֶל־יוֹבָב מֶלֶךְ מָדוֹן וְאֶל־ מֶלֶךְ שִׁמְרוֹן וְאֶל־ מֶלֶךְ אַכְשָׁף׃
Acshaph king-of and-to Shimron king-of and-to Madon king-of Jobab to

וְאֶל־ הַמְּלָכִים אֲשֶׁר מִצְּפוֹן בָּהָר וּבָעֲרָבָה נֶגֶב
south-of and-in-the-Arabah in-the-mountain in-north-of who the-kings and-to (2)

כִּנְרוֹת וּבַשְּׁפֵלָה וּבְנָפוֹת דּוֹר מִיָּם׃ הַכְּנַעֲנִי
the-Canaanite (3) on-west Dor and-in-Naphoth and-in-the-foothill Kinnereth

מִמִּזְרָח וּמִיָּם וְהָאֱמֹרִי וְהַחִתִּי וְהַפְּרִזִּי
and-the-Perizzite and-the-Hittite and-the-Amorite and-in-west in-east

וְהַיְבוּסִי בָּהָר וְהַחִוִּי תַּחַת חֶרְמוֹן בְּאֶרֶץ
in-region-of Hermon below and-the-Hivite in-the-hill-country and-the-Jebusite

הַמִּצְפָּה׃ וַיֵּצְאוּ הֵם וְכָל־ מַחֲנֵיהֶם עִמָּם
with-them troops-of-them and-all-of they and-they-came-out (4) the-Mizpah

עַם־ רָב כַּחוֹל אֲשֶׁר עַל־ שְׂפַת־ הַיָּם לָרֹב וְסוּס
and-horse by-number the-sea shore-of on that as-the-sand numerous army

וָרֶכֶב רַב־ מְאֹד׃ וַיִּוָּעֲדוּ כֹּל הַמְּלָכִים הָאֵלֶּה
the-these the-kings all-of and-they-joined (5) large number and-chariot

וַיָּבֹאוּ וַיַּחֲנוּ יַחְדָּו אֶל־ מֵי מֵרוֹם לְהִלָּחֵם עִם־
against to-fight Merom Waters-of at together and-they-camped and-they-came

יִשְׂרָאֵל׃ וַיֹּאמֶר יְהוָה אֶל־יְהוֹשֻׁעַ אַל־ תִּירָא מִפְּנֵיהֶם כִּי־
for from-before-them you-fear not Joshua to Yahweh and-he-said (6) Israel

מָחָר כָּעֵת הַזֹּאת אָנֹכִי נֹתֵן אֶת־ כֻּלָּם חֲלָלִים לִפְנֵי
over-to ones-slain all-of-them *** handing I the-this by-the-time tomorrow

יִשְׂרָאֵל אֶת־ סוּסֵיהֶם תְּעַקֵּר וְאֶת־ מַרְכְּבֹתֵיהֶם תִּשְׂרֹף
you-burn chariots-of-them and you-hamstring horses-of-them *** Israel

בָּאֵשׁ׃ וַיָּבֹא יְהוֹשֻׁעַ וְכָל־ עַם הַמִּלְחָמָה עִמּוֹ
with-him the-battle army-of and-whole-of Joshua so-he-came (7) with-the-fire

עֲלֵיהֶם עַל־ מֵי מֵרוֹם פִּתְאֹם וַיִּפְּלוּ בָּהֶם׃
against-them and-they-attacked suddenly Merom Waters-of at against-them

וַיִּתְּנֵם יְהוָה בְּיַד־ יִשְׂרָאֵל וַיַּכּוּם
and-they-defeated-them Israel into-hand-of Yahweh and-he-gave-them (8)

Gibeon. [42]All these kings and their lands Joshua conquered in one campaign, because the LORD, the God of Israel, fought for Israel.

[43]Then Joshua returned with all Israel to the camp at Gilgal.

*Northern Kings Defeated*

**11** When Jabin king of Hazor heard of this, he sent word to Jobab king of Madon, to the kings of Shimron and Acshaph, [2]and to the northern kings who were in the mountains, in the Arabah south of Kinnereth, in the western foothills and in Naphoth Dor[d] on the west; [3]to the Canaanites in the east and west; to the Amorites, Hittites, Perizzites and Jebusites in the hill country; and to the Hivites below Hermon in the region of Mizpah. [4]They came out with all their troops and a large number of horses and chariots—a huge army, as numerous as the sand on the seashore. [5]All these kings joined forces and made camp together at the Waters of Merom, to fight against Israel.

[6]The LORD said to Joshua, "Do not be afraid of them, because by this time tomorrow I will hand all of them over to Israel, slain. You are to hamstring their horses and burn their chariots."

[7]So Joshua and his whole army came against them suddenly at the Waters of Merom and attacked them, [8]and the LORD gave them into the hand of Israel. They defeated them

[d]2 Or *in the heights of Dor*

וַיִּרְדְּפוּם עַד־צִידוֹן רַבָּה וְעַד מִשְׂרְפוֹת מַיִם וְעַד־בִּקְעַת
**Valley-of and-to Maim Misrephoth and-to Greater Sidon to and-they-pursued-them**

מִצְפֶּה מִזְרָחָה וַיַּכֻּם עַד־בִּלְתִּי הִשְׁאִיר־לָהֶם שָׂרִיד׃
**survivor to-them he-left not until and-they-defeated-them on-east Mizpah**

וַיַּעַשׂ לָהֶם יְהוֹשֻׁעַ כַּאֲשֶׁר אָמַר־לוֹ יְהוָה אֶת־
***** Yahweh to-him he-directed just-as Joshua to-them and-he-did (9)**

סוּסֵיהֶם עִקֵּר וְאֶת־מַרְכְּבֹתֵיהֶם שָׂרַף בָּאֵשׁ׃
**with-the-fire he-burned chariots-of-them and he-hamstrung horses-of-them**

וַיָּשָׁב יְהוֹשֻׁעַ בָּעֵת הַהִיא וַיִּלְכֹּד אֶת־חָצוֹר
**Hazor *** and-he-captured the-that at-the-time Joshua and-he-turned-back (10)**

וְאֶת־מַלְכָּהּ הִכָּה בֶחָרֶב כִּי־חָצוֹר לְפָנִים הִיא רֹאשׁ כָּל־
**all-of head-of she formerly Hazor for to-the-sword he-put king-of-her and**

הַמַּמְלָכוֹת הָאֵלֶּה׃ וַיַּכּוּ אֶת־כָּל־הַנֶּפֶשׁ אֲשֶׁר־בָּהּ
**in-her who the-person every-of *** and-they-put (11) the-these the-kingdoms**

לְפִי־חֶרֶב הַחֲרֵם לֹא נוֹתַר כָּל־נְשָׁמָה וְאֶת־חָצוֹר
**Hazor and breather any-of he-was-spared not to-destroy sword to-edge-of**

שָׂרַף בָּאֵשׁ׃ וְאֶת־כָּל־עָרֵי הַמְּלָכִים־הָאֵלֶּה וְאֶת־
**and the-these the-royalties cities-of all-of and (12) with-the-fire he-burned**

כָּל־מַלְכֵיהֶם לָכַד יְהוֹשֻׁעַ וַיַּכֵּם לְפִי־חֶרֶב
**sword to-edge-of and-he-put-them Joshua he-took kings-of-them all-of**

הֶחֱרִים אוֹתָם כַּאֲשֶׁר צִוָּה מֹשֶׁה עֶבֶד יְהוָה׃ רַק
**yet (13) Yahweh servant-of Moses he-commanded just-as them he-destroyed**

כָּל־הֶעָרִים הָעֹמְדוֹת עַל־תִּלָּם לֹא שְׂרָפָם
**he-burned-them not mound-of-them on the-ones-being-built the-cities any-of**

יִשְׂרָאֵל זוּלָתִי אֶת־חָצוֹר לְבַדָּהּ שָׂרַף יְהוֹשֻׁעַ׃ וְכֹל
**and-all-of (14) Joshua he-burned by-self-of-her Hazor *** except Israel**

שְׁלַל הֶעָרִים הָאֵלֶּה וְהַבְּהֵמָה בָּזְזוּ לָהֶם
**for-them they-carried-off and-the-livestock the-these the-cities plunder-of**

בְּנֵי יִשְׂרָאֵל רַק אֶת־כָּל־הָאָדָם הִכּוּ לְפִי־חֶרֶב עַד־
**until sword to-edge-of they-put the-person every-of *** but Israel sons-of**

הִשְׁמִדָם אוֹתָם לֹא הִשְׁאִירוּ כָּל־נְשָׁמָה׃ כַּאֲשֶׁר
**just-as (15) breather any-of they-spared not them he-destroyed-them**

צִוָּה יְהוָה אֶת־מֹשֶׁה עַבְדּוֹ כֵּן־צִוָּה מֹשֶׁה אֶת־
***** Moses he-commanded so servant-of-him Moses *** Yahweh he-commanded**

יְהוֹשֻׁעַ וְכֵן עָשָׂה יְהוֹשֻׁעַ לֹא־הֵסִיר דָּבָר מִכֹּל אֲשֶׁר־
**that of-all anything he-left-undone not Joshua he-did and-so Joshua**

צִוָּה יְהוָה אֶת־מֹשֶׁה׃ וַיִּקַּח יְהוֹשֻׁעַ אֶת־כָּל־הָאָרֶץ
**the-land entire-of *** Joshua so-he-took (16) Moses *** Yahweh he-commanded**

and pursued them all the way
to Greater Sidon, to Misrephoth Maim, and to the Valley
of Mizpah on the east, until no
survivors were left.
9 Joshua
did to them as the LORD had
directed: He hamstrung their
horses and burned their chariots.
10 At that time Joshua turned
back and captured Hazor and
put its king to the sword. (Hazor had been the head of all
these kingdoms.)
11 Everyone
in it they put to the sword.
They totally destroyed[e] them,
not sparing anything that
breathed, and he burned up
Hazor itself.
12 Joshua took all these royal
cities and their kings and put
them to the sword. He totally
destroyed them, as Moses the
servant of the LORD had commanded.
13 Yet Israel did not
burn any of the cities built on
their mounds—except Hazor,
which Joshua burned.
14 The
Israelites carried off for themselves all the plunder and livestock of these cities, but all the
people they put to the sword
until they completely de-
stroyed them, not sparing
anyone that breathed.
15 As the
LORD commanded his servant
Moses, so Moses commanded
Joshua, and Joshua did it; he
left nothing undone of all that
the LORD commanded Moses.
16 So Joshua took this entire

[e] *11* The Hebrew term refers to the irrevocable giving over of things or persons to the LORD, often by totally destroying them; also in verses 12, 20 and 21.

הזאת ההר ואת־ כל־ הנגב ואת כל־ ארץ
region-of whole-of and the-Negev all-of and the-hill-country the-this

הגשן ואת־ השפלה ואת־ הערבה ואת־ הר ישראל
Israel mountain-of and the-Arabah and the-foothill and the-Goshen

ושפלתה: מן־ ההר החלק העולה שעיר
Seir the-one-rising the-Halak the-Mount from (17) and-foothill-of-her

ועד־ בעל־ גד בבקעת הלבנון תחת הר־ חרמון ואת כל־
all-of and Hermon Mount-of below the-Lebanon in-Valley-of Gad Baal even-to

מלכיהם לכד ויכם וימיתם: ימים
days (18) and-he-killed-them and-he-struck-them he-captured kings-of-her

רבים עשה יהושע את־ כל־ המלכים האלה מלחמה: לא־ היתה
she-was not (19) war the-these the-kings all-of *** Joshua he-waged many

עיר אשר השלימה אל־ בני ישראל בלתי החוי ישבי
ones-living-of the-Hivite except Israel sons-of with she-made-treaty that city

גבעון את־ הכל לקחו במלחמה: כי מאת יהוה | היתה
she-was Yahweh from for (20) in-the-battle they-took the-all *** Gibeon

לחזק את־ לבם לקראת המלחמה את־ ישראל למען
so-that Israel *** the-war to-wage heart-of-them *** to-harden

החרימם לבלתי היות־ להם תחנה כי למען השמידם
to-exterminate-them so-that indeed mercy to-them to-be not to-destroy-them

כאשר צוה יהוה את־ משה: ויבא יהושע בעת
at-the-time Joshua then-he-went (21) Moses *** Yahweh he-commanded just-as

ההיא ויכרת את־ הענקים מן־ ההר מן־ חברון
Hebron from the-hill-country from the-Anakite *** and-he-destroyed the-that

מן־ דבר מן־ ענב ומכל הר יהודה ומכל
and-from-all-of Judah hill-country-of and-from-all-of Anab from Debir from

הר ישראל עם־ עריהם החרימם יהושע: לא־
not (22) Joshua he-destroyed-them cities-of-them with Israel hill-country-of

נותר ענקים בארץ בני ישראל רק בעזה בגת
in-Gath in-Gaza only Israel sons-of in-territory-of Anakites he-was-left

ובאשדוד נשארו: ויקח יהושע את־ כל־ הארץ
the-land entire-of *** Joshua so-he-took (23) they-survived and-in-Ashdod

ככל אשר דבר יהוה אל־ משה ויתנה יהושע לנחלה
as-inheritance Joshua and-he-gave-her Moses to Yahweh he-directed that as-all

לישראל כמחלקתם לשבטיהם והארץ שקטה
she-had-rest then-the-land as-tribes-of-them as-divisions-of-them to-Israel

ממלחמה: ואלה | מלכי הארץ אשר הכו בני־
sons-of they-defeated whom the-land kings-of now-these (12:1) from-war

land: the hill country, all the Negev, the whole region of Goshen, the western foothills, the Arabah and the mountains of Israel with their foothills, [17]from Mount Halak, which rises toward Seir, to Baal Gad in the Valley of Lebanon below Mount Hermon. He captured all their kings and struck them down, putting them to death. [18]Joshua waged war against all these kings for a long time. [19]Except for the Hivites living in Gibeon, not one city made a treaty of peace with the Israelites, who took them all in battle. [20]For it was the LORD himself who hardened their hearts to wage war against Israel, so that he might destroy them totally, exterminating them without mercy, as the LORD had commanded Moses.

[21]At that time Joshua went and destroyed the Anakites from the hill country: from Hebron, Debir and Anab, from all the hill country of Judah, and from all the hill country of Israel. Joshua totally destroyed them and their towns. [22]No Anakites were left in Israelite territory; only in Gaza, Gath and Ashdod did any survive. [23]So Joshua took the entire land, just as the LORD had directed Moses, and he gave it as an inheritance to Israel according to their tribal divisions.

Then the land had rest from war.

*List of Defeated Kings*

12 These are the kings of the land whom the Israelites had defeated and

יִשְׂרָאֵל וַיִּרְשׁוּ אֶת־ אַרְצָם בְּעֵבֶר הַיַּרְדֵּן

the-Jordan on-side-of territory-of-them *** and-they-took-over Israel

מִזְרְחָה הַשֶּׁמֶשׁ מִנַּחַל אַרְנוֹן עַד־ הַר חֶרְמוֹן וְכָל־

and-all-of Hermon Mount-of to Arnon from-Gorge-of the-sun toward-rise-of

הָעֲרָבָה מִזְרָחָה׃ סִיחוֹן מֶלֶךְ הָאֱמֹרִי הַיּוֹשֵׁב בְּחֶשְׁבּוֹן

in-Heshbon the-one-reigning the-Amorite king-of Sihon (2) on-east the-Arabah

מֹשֵׁל מֵעֲרוֹעֵר אֲשֶׁר עַל־ שְׂפַת־ נַחַל אַרְנוֹן וְתוֹךְ הַנַּחַל

the-gorge and-middle-of Arnon Gorge-of rim-of on that from-Aroer ruling

וַחֲצִי הַגִּלְעָד וְעַד יַבֹּק הַנַּחַל גְּבוּל בְּנֵי עַמּוֹן׃

Ammon sons-of border-of the-River Jabbok even-to the-Gilead and-half-of

וְהָעֲרָבָה עַד־ יָם כִּנְרוֹת מִזְרָחָה וְעַד יָם הָעֲרָבָה

the-Arabah Sea-of and-to on-east Kinnereth Sea-of to and-the-Arabah (3)

יָם־ הַמֶּלַח מִזְרָחָה דֶּרֶךְ בֵּית הַיְשִׁמוֹת וּמִתֵּימָן תַּחַת

below and-on-south the-Jeshimoth Beth toward on-east the-Salt Sea-of

אַשְׁדּוֹת הַפִּסְגָּה׃ וּגְבוּל עוֹג מֶלֶךְ הַבָּשָׁן מִיֶּתֶר

from-last-of the-Bashan king-of Og and-territory-of (4) the-Pisgah slopes-of

הָרְפָאִים הַיּוֹשֵׁב בְּעַשְׁתָּרוֹת וּבְאֶדְרֶעִי׃ וּמֹשֵׁל

and-ruling (5) and-in-Edrei in-Ashtaroth the-one-reigning the-Rephaites

בְּהַר חֶרְמוֹן וּבְסַלְכָה וּבְכָל־ הַבָּשָׁן עַד־ גְּבוּל

border-of to the-Bashan and-over-all-of and-over-Salecah Hermon over-Mount-of

הַגְּשׁוּרִי וְהַמַּעֲכָתִי וַחֲצִי הַגִּלְעָד גְּבוּל סִיחוֹן

Sihon border-of the-Gilead and-half-of and-the-Maacathite the-Geshurite

מֶלֶךְ־ חֶשְׁבּוֹן׃ מֹשֶׁה עֶבֶד־ יְהוָה וּבְנֵי יִשְׂרָאֵל

Israel and-sons-of Yahweh servant-of Moses (6) Heshbon king-of

הִכּוּם וַיִּתְּנָהּ מֹשֶׁה עֶבֶד־ יְהוָה יְרֻשָּׁה

possession Yahweh servant-of Moses and-he-gave-her they-conquered-them

לָרֻאוּבֵנִי וְלַגָּדִי וְלַחֲצִי שֵׁבֶט הַמְנַשֶּׁה׃

the-Manasseh tribe-of and-to-half-of and-to-the-Gadite to-the-Reubenite

וְאֵלֶּה מַלְכֵי הָאָרֶץ אֲשֶׁר הִכָּה יְהוֹשֻׁעַ וּבְנֵי יִשְׂרָאֵל

Israel and-sons-of Joshua he-conquered that the-land kings-of and-these (7)

בְּעֵבֶר הַיַּרְדֵּן יָמָּה מִבַּעַל גָּד בְּבִקְעַת הַלְּבָנוֹן וְעַד־

even-to the-Lebanon in-Valley-of Gad from-Baal to-west the-Jordan on-side-of

הָהָר הֶחָלָק הָעֹלֶה שֵׂעִירָה וַיִּתְּנָהּ יְהוֹשֻׁעַ

Joshua and-he-gave-her toward-Seir the-one-rising the-Halak the-Mount

לְשִׁבְטֵי יִשְׂרָאֵל יְרֻשָּׁה כְּמַחְלְקֹתָם׃ בָּהָר

in-the-hill-country (8) by-divisions-of-them possession Israel to-tribes-of

וּבַשְּׁפֵלָה וּבָעֲרָבָה וּבָאֲשֵׁדוֹת וּבַמִּדְבָּר

and-in-the-desert and-in-the-slopes and-in-the-Arabah and-in-the-foothill

whose territory they took over east of the Jordan, from the Arnon Gorge to Mount Hermon, including all the eastern side of the Arabah:

2 Sihon king of the Amorites, who reigned in Heshbon. He ruled from Aroer on the rim of the Arnon Gorge—from the middle of the gorge—to the Jabbok River, which is the border of the Ammonites. This included half of Gilead. 3 He also ruled over the eastern Arabah from the Sea of Kinnereth[f] to the Sea of the Arabah (the Salt Sea[g]), to Beth Jeshimoth, and then southward below the slopes of Pisgah.

4 And the territory of Og king of Bashan, one of the last of the Rephaites, who reigned in Ashtaroth and Edrei. 5 He ruled over Mount Hermon, Salecah, all of Bashan to the border of the people of Geshur and Maacah, and half of Gilead to the border of Sihon king of Heshbon.

6 Moses, the servant of the LORD, and the Israelites conquered them. And Moses the servant of the LORD gave their land to the Reubenites, the Gadites and the half-tribe of Manasseh to be their possession.

7 These are the kings of the land that Joshua and the Israelites conquered on the west side of the Jordan, from Baal Gad in the Valley of Lebanon to Mount Halak, which rises toward Seir (their lands Joshua gave as an inheritance to the tribes of Israel according to their tribal divisions— 8 the hill country, the western foothills, the Arabah, the mountain slopes, the desert and the

f3 That is, Galilee
g3 That is, the Dead Sea

*6 Most mss have no *qibbuts* under the *resh* ( לָרְאוּבֵנִי ).

וּבַנֶּגֶב הַחִתִּי הָאֱמֹרִי וְהַכְּנַעֲנִי הַפְּרִזִּי
the-Perizzite and-the-Canaanite the-Amorite the-Hittite and-in-the-Negev

הַחִוִּי וְהַיְבוּסִי׃ מֶלֶךְ יְרִיחוֹ אֶחָד מֶלֶךְ הָעַי אֲשֶׁר־
that the-Ai king-of one Jericho king-of (9) and-the-Jebusite the-Hivite

מִצַּד בֵּית־ אֵל אֶחָד׃ מֶלֶךְ יְרוּשָׁלִַם אֶחָד מֶלֶךְ חֶבְרוֹן אֶחָד׃
one Hebron king-of one Jerusalem king-of (10) one El Beth at-near

מֶלֶךְ יַרְמוּת אֶחָד מֶלֶךְ לָכִישׁ אֶחָד׃ מֶלֶךְ עֶגְלוֹן אֶחָד מֶלֶךְ
king-of one Eglon king-of (12) one Lachish king-of one Jarmuth king-of (11)

גֶּזֶר אֶחָד׃ מֶלֶךְ דְּבִר אֶחָד מֶלֶךְ גֶּדֶר אֶחָד׃ מֶלֶךְ חָרְמָה אֶחָד
one Hormah king-of (14) one Geder king-of one Debir king-of (13) one Gezer

מֶלֶךְ עֲרָד אֶחָד׃ מֶלֶךְ לִבְנָה אֶחָד מֶלֶךְ עֲדֻלָּם אֶחָד׃ מֶלֶךְ
king-of (16) one Adullam king-of one Libnah king-of (15) one Arad king-of

מַקֵּדָה אֶחָד מֶלֶךְ בֵּית־אֵל אֶחָד׃ מֶלֶךְ תַּפּוּחַ אֶחָד מֶלֶךְ חֵפֶר אֶחָד׃
one Hepher king-of one Tappuah king-of (17) one El Beth king-of one Makkedah

מֶלֶךְ אֲפֵק אֶחָד מֶלֶךְ לַשָּׁרוֹן אֶחָד׃ מֶלֶךְ מָדוֹן אֶחָד מֶלֶךְ
king-of one Madon king-of (19) one Lasharon king-of one Aphek king-of (18)

חָצוֹר אֶחָד׃ מֶלֶךְ שִׁמְרוֹן מְראוֹן אֶחָד מֶלֶךְ אַכְשָׁף אֶחָד׃ מֶלֶךְ
king-of (21) one Acshaph king-of one Meron Shimron king-of (20) one Hazor

תַּעְנַךְ אֶחָד מֶלֶךְ מְגִדּוֹ אֶחָד׃ מֶלֶךְ קֶדֶשׁ אֶחָד מֶלֶךְ־ יָקְנְעָם
Jokneam king-of one Kedesh king-of (22) one Megiddo king-of one Taanach

לַכַּרְמֶל אֶחָד׃ מֶלֶךְ דּוֹר לְנָפַת דּוֹר אֶחָד מֶלֶךְ־ גּוֹיִם לְגִלְגָּל
in-Gilgal Goyim king-of one Dor in-Naphoth Dor king-of (23) one in-the-Carmel

אֶחָד׃ מֶלֶךְ תִּרְצָה אֶחָד כָּל־מְלָכִים שְׁלֹשִׁים וְאֶחָד׃ וִיהוֹשֻׁעַ
when-Joshua (13:1) and-one thirty kings all-of one Tirzah king-of (24) one

זָקֵן בָּא בַּיָּמִים וַיֹּאמֶר יְהוָה אֵלָיו אַתָּה
you to-him Yahweh then-he-said in-the-days he-was-advanced he-was-old

זָקַנְתָּה בָּאתָ בַיָּמִים וְהָאָרֶץ נִשְׁאֲרָה הַרְבֵּה־
to-be-large she-remains and-the-land in-the-days you-are-advanced you-are-old

מְאֹד לְרִשְׁתָּהּ׃ זֹאת הָאָרֶץ הַנִּשְׁאֶרֶת כָּל־ גְּלִילוֹת
regions-of all-of the-remaining the-land this (2) to-take-over-her very

הַפְּלִשְׁתִּים וְכָל־ הַגְּשׁוּרִי׃ מִן־ הַשִּׁיחוֹר אֲשֶׁר ׀ עַל־ פְּנֵי
east-of on that the-Shihor from (3) the-Geshurite and-all-of the-Philistines

מִצְרַיִם וְעַד גְּבוּל עֶקְרוֹן צָפוֹנָה לַכְּנַעֲנִי תֵּחָשֵׁב
she-was-counted as-the-Canaanite on-north Ekron territory-of and-to Egypt

חֲמֵשֶׁת ׀ סַרְנֵי פְּלִשְׁתִּים הָעַזָּתִי וְהָאַשְׁדּוֹדִי הָאֶשְׁקְלוֹנִי
the-Ashkelonite and-the-Ashdodite the-Gazathite Philistines rulers-of five-of

הַגִּתִּי וְהָעֶקְרוֹנִי וְהָעַוִּים׃ מִתֵּימָן כָּל־ אֶרֶץ
land-of all-of from-south (4) and-the-Avvites and-the-Ekronite the-Gathite

Negev—the lands of the Hittites, Amorites, Canaanites, Perizzites, Hivites and Jebusites):

9 the king of Jericho one
the king of Ai (near Bethel) one
10 the king of Jerusalem one
the king of Hebron one
11 the king of Jarmuth one
the king of Lachish one
12 the king of Eglon one
the king of Gezer one
13 the king of Debir one
the king of Geder one
14 the king of Hormah one
the king of Arad one
15 the king of Libnah one
the king of Adullam one
16 the king of Makkedah one
the king of Bethel one
17 the king of Tappuah one
the king of Hepher one
18 the king of Aphek one
the king of Lasharon one
19 the king of Madon one
the king of Hazor one
20 the king of Shimron Meron one
the king of Acshaph one
21 the king of Taanach one
the king of Megiddo one
22 the king of Kedesh one
the king of Jokneam in Carmel one
23 the king of Dor (in Naphoth Dor[h]) one
the king of Goyim in Gilgal one
24 the king of Tirzah one
thirty-one kings in all.

*Land Still to Be Taken*

13 When Joshua was old and well advanced in years, the LORD said to him, "You are very old, and there are still very large areas of land to be taken over.

2 "This is the land that remains: all the regions of the Philistines and Geshurites:
3 from the Shihor River on the east of Egypt to the territory of Ekron on the north, all of it counted as Canaanite (the territory of the five Philistine rulers in Gaza, Ashdod, Ashkelon, Gath and Ekron—that of the Avvites);
4 from the south, all the land of the

[h] 23 Or *in the heights of Dor*

הַכְּנַעֲנִי וּמְעָרָה אֲשֶׁר לַצִּידֹנִים עַד־ אֲפֵקָה עַד
to to-Aphek as-far-as of-the-Sidonians that and-from-Arah the-Canaanite

גְּבוּל הָאֱמֹרִי׃ וְהָאָרֶץ הַגִּבְלִי וְכָל־ הַלְּבָנוֹן
the-Lebanon and-all-of the-Gebalite and-the-area (5) the-Amorite region-of

מִזְרַח הַשֶּׁמֶשׁ מִבַּעַל גָּד תַּחַת הַר־ חֶרְמוֹן עַד לְבוֹא חֲמָת׃ כָּל־
all-of (6) Hamath Lebo to Hermon Mount-of below Gad from-Baal the-sun rise-of

יֹשְׁבֵי הָהָר מִן־ הַלְּבָנוֹן עַד־ מִשְׂרְפֹת מַיִם
Maim Misrephoth to the-Lebanon from the-mountain-region ones-inhabiting-of

כָּל־ צִידֹנִים אָנֹכִי אוֹרִישֵׁם מִפְּנֵי בְּנֵי יִשְׂרָאֵל רַק
only Israel sons-of from-before I-will-drive-out-them I Sidonians all-of

הַפִּלֶהָ לְיִשְׂרָאֵל בְּנַחֲלָה כַּאֲשֶׁר צִוִּיתִיךָ׃ וְעַתָּה
and-now (7) I-instructed-you just-as for-inheritance to-Israel allocate-her!

חַלֵּק אֶת־ הָאָרֶץ הַזֹּאת בְּנַחֲלָה לְתִשְׁעַת הַשְּׁבָטִים
the-tribes among-nine-of as-inheritance the-this the-land *** divide!

וַחֲצִי הַשֵּׁבֶט הַמְנַשֶּׁה׃ עִמּוֹ הָרְאוּבֵנִי וְהַגָּדִי
and-the-Gadite the-Reubenite with-him (8) the-Manasseh the-tribe and-half-of

לָקְחוּ נַחֲלָתָם אֲשֶׁר נָתַן לָהֶם מֹשֶׁה בְּעֵבֶר
on-side-of Moses to-them he-gave that inheritance-of-them they-received

הַיַּרְדֵּן מִזְרָחָה כַּאֲשֶׁר נָתַן לָהֶם מֹשֶׁה עֶבֶד יְהוָה׃
Yahweh servant-of Moses to-them he-assigned just-as to-east the-Jordan

מֵעֲרוֹעֵר אֲשֶׁר עַל־ שְׂפַת־ נַחַל אַרְנוֹן וְהָעִיר אֲשֶׁר בְּתוֹךְ־
in-middle-of that and-the-town Arnon Gorge-of rim-of on that from-Aroer (9)

הַנַּחַל וְכָל־ הַמִּישֹׁר מֵידְבָא עַד־ דִּיבוֹן׃ וְכֹל
and-all-of (10) Dibon as-far-as Medeba the-plateau and-whole-of the-gorge

עָרֵי סִיחוֹן מֶלֶךְ הָאֱמֹרִי אֲשֶׁר מָלַךְ בְּחֶשְׁבּוֹן עַד־ גְּבוּל
border-of to in-Heshbon he-ruled who the-Amorite king-of Sihon towns-of

בְּנֵי עַמּוֹן׃ וְהַגִּלְעָד וּגְבוּל הַגְּשׁוּרִי
the-Geshurite and-territory-of and-the-Gilead (11) Ammon sons-of

וְהַמַּעֲכָתִי וְכֹל הַר חֶרְמוֹן וְכָל־ הַבָּשָׁן עַד־
as-far-as the-Bashan and-all-of Hermon Mount-of and-all-of and-the-Maacathite

סַלְכָה׃ כָּל־ מַמְלְכוּת עוֹג בַּבָּשָׁן אֲשֶׁר־ מָלַךְ בְּעַשְׁתָּרוֹת
in-Ashtaroth he-reigned who in-the-Bashan Og kingdom-of whole-of (12) Salecah

וּבְאֶדְרֶעִי הוּא נִשְׁאַר מִיֶּתֶר הָרְפָאִים וַיַּכֵּם
and-he-defeated-them the-Rephaites among-last-of he-survived he and-in-Edrei

מֹשֶׁה וַיֹּרִשֵׁם׃ וְלֹא הוֹרִישׁוּ בְּנֵי יִשְׂרָאֵל אֶת־
*** Israel sons-of they-drove-out but-not (13) and-he-took-over-them Moses

הַגְּשׁוּרִי וְאֶת־ הַמַּעֲכָתִי וַיֵּשֶׁב גְּשׁוּר וּמַעֲכָת בְּקֶרֶב
in-among and-Maacah Geshur so-he-lives the-Maacathite and the-Geshurite

Canaanites, from Arah of the Sidonians as far as Aphek, the region of the Amorites, [5]the area of the Gebalites[i]; and all Lebanon to the east, from Baal Gad below Mount Hermon to Lebo[j] Hamath.

[6]"As for all the inhabitants of the mountain regions from Lebanon to Misrephoth Maim, that is, all the Sidonians, I myself will drive them out before the Israelites. Be sure to allocate this land to Israel for an inheritance, as I have instructed you, [7]and divide it as an inheritance among the nine tribes and half of the tribe of Manasseh."

*Division of the Land East of the Jordan*

[8]The other half of Manasseh,[k] the Reubenites and the Gadites had received the inheritance that Moses had given them east of the Jordan, as he, the servant of the LORD, had assigned it to them.

[9]It extended from Aroer on the rim of the Arnon Gorge, and from the town in the middle of the gorge, and included the whole plateau of Medeba as far as Dibon, [10]and all the towns of Sihon king of the Amorites, who ruled in Heshbon, out to the border of the Ammonites. [11]It also included Gilead, the territory of the people of Geshur and Maacah, all of Mount Hermon and all Bashan as far as Salecah— [12]that is, the whole kingdom of Og in Bashan, who had reigned in Ashtaroth and Edrei and had survived as one of the last of the Rephaites. Moses had defeated them and taken over their land. [13]But the Israelites did not drive out the people of Geshur and Maacah, so they continue to live among the Israelites

[i]5 That is, the area of Byblos
[j]5 Or *to the entrance to*
[k]8 Hebrew *With it* (that is, with the other half of Manasseh)

יִשְׂרָאֵל עַד הַיּוֹם הַזֶּה׃ (14) רַק לְשֵׁבֶט הַלֵּוִי לֹא נָתַן
he-gave not the-Levite to-tribe-of but (14) the-this the-day to Israel

נַחֲלָה אִשֵּׁי יְהוָה אֱלֹהֵי יִשְׂרָאֵל הוּא נַחֲלָתוֹ
inheritance-of-him this Israel God-of Yahweh fire-offerings-of inheritance

כַּאֲשֶׁר דִּבֶּר־ לוֹ׃ (15) וַיִּתֵּן מֹשֶׁה לְמַטֵּה בְנֵי־ רְאוּבֵן
Reuben sons-of to-tribe-of Moses and-he-gave (15) to-him he-promised just-as

לְמִשְׁפְּחֹתָם׃ (16) וַיְהִי לָהֶם הַגְּבוּל מֵעֲרוֹעֵר אֲשֶׁר עַל־
on that from-Aroer the-territory to-them and-he-was (16) by-clans-of-them

שְׂפַת־ נַחַל אַרְנוֹן וְהָעִיר אֲשֶׁר בְּתוֹךְ־ הַנַּחַל וְכָל־
and-whole-of the-gorge in-middle-of that and-the-town Arnon Gorge-of rim-of

הַמִּישֹׁר עַל־ מֵידְבָא׃ (17) חֶשְׁבּוֹן וְכָל־ עָרֶיהָ אֲשֶׁר
that towns-of-her and-all-of Heshbon (17) Medeba past the-plateau

בַּמִּישֹׁר דִּיבוֹן וּבָמוֹת בַּעַל וּבֵית בַּעַל מְעוֹן׃ (18) וְיַהְצָה
and-Jahaz (18) Meon Baal and-Beth Baal and-Bamoth Dibon on-the-plateau

וּקְדֵמֹת וּמֵפָעַת׃ (19) וְקִרְיָתַיִם וְשִׂבְמָה וְצֶרֶת
and-Zereth and-Sibmah and-Kiriathaim (19) and-Mephaath and-Kedemoth

הַשַּׁחַר בְּהַר הָעֵמֶק׃ (20) וּבֵית פְּעוֹר וְאַשְׁדּוֹת הַפִּסְגָּה
the-Pisgah and-slopes-of Peor and-Beth (20) the-Valley on-hill-of the-Shahar

וּבֵית הַיְשִׁמוֹת׃ (21) וְכֹל עָרֵי הַמִּישֹׁר וְכָל־
and-entire-of the-plateau towns-of and-all-of (21) the-Jeshimoth and-Beth

מַמְלְכוּת סִיחוֹן מֶלֶךְ הָאֱמֹרִי אֲשֶׁר מָלַךְ בְּחֶשְׁבּוֹן אֲשֶׁר הִכָּה
he-defeated whom at-Heshbon he-ruled who the-Amorite king-of Sihon realm-of

מֹשֶׁה אֹתוֹ ׀ וְאֶת־ נְשִׂיאֵי מִדְיָן אֶת־ אֱוִי וְאֶת־ רֶקֶם וְאֶת־ צוּר וְאֶת־ חוּר וְאֶת־ רֶבַע
Reba and Hur and Zur and Rekem and Evi *** Midian chiefs-of and him Moses

נְסִיכֵי סִיחוֹן יֹשְׁבֵי הָאָרֶץ׃ (22) וְאֶת־ בִּלְעָם בֶּן־ בְּעוֹר
Beor son-of Balaam and (22) the-country ones-living-of Sihon princes-of

הַקּוֹסֵם הָרְגוּ בְנֵי־ יִשְׂרָאֵל בַּחֶרֶב אֶל־
beside to-the-sword Israel sons-of they-put the-one-practicing-divination

חַלְלֵיהֶם׃ (23) וַיְהִי גְּבוּל בְּנֵי רְאוּבֵן הַיַּרְדֵּן
the-Jordan Reuben sons-of boundary-of and-he-was (23) ones-slain-of-them

וּגְבוּל זֹאת נַחֲלַת בְּנֵי־ רְאוּבֵן לְמִשְׁפְּחֹתָם הֶעָרִים
the-towns by-clans-of-them Reuben sons-of inheritance-of this and-bank

וְחַצְרֵיהֶן׃ (24) וַיִּתֵּן מֹשֶׁה לְמַטֵּה־ גָד לִבְנֵי־ גָד
Gad to-sons-of Gad to-tribe-of Moses and-he-gave (24) and-villages-of-them

לְמִשְׁפְּחֹתָם׃ (25) וַיְהִי לָהֶם הַגְּבוּל יַעְזֵר וְכָל־
and-all-of Jazer the-territory to-them and-he-was (25) by-clans-of-them

עָרֵי הַגִּלְעָד וַחֲצִי אֶרֶץ בְּנֵי עַמּוֹן עַד־ עֲרוֹעֵר
Aroer as-far-as Ammon sons-of country-of and-half-of the-Gilead towns-of

to this day.

14 But to the tribe of Levi he gave no inheritance, since the offerings made by fire to the LORD, the God of Israel, are their inheritance, as he promised them.

15 This is what Moses had given to the tribe of Reuben, clan by clan:

16 The territory from Aroer on the rim of the Arnon Gorge, and from the town in the middle of the gorge, and the whole plateau past Medeba 17 to Heshbon and all its towns on the plateau, including Dibon, Bamoth Baal, Beth Baal Meon, 18 Jahaz, Kedemoth, Mephaath, 19 Kiriathaim, Sibmah, Zereth Shahar on the hill in the valley, 20 Beth Peor, the slopes of Pisgah, and Beth Jeshimoth 21—all the towns on the plateau and the entire realm of Sihon king of the Amorites, who ruled at Heshbon. Moses had defeated him and the Midianite chiefs, Evi, Rekem, Zur, Hur and Reba—princes allied with Sihon—who lived in that country. 22 In addition to those slain in battle, the Israelites had put to the sword Balaam son of Beor, who practiced divination. 23 The boundary of the Reubenites was the bank of the Jordan. These towns and their villages were the inheritance of the Reubenites, clan by clan.

24 This is what Moses had given to the tribe of Gad, clan by clan:

25 The territory of Jazer, all the towns of Gilead and half the Ammonite country

אֲשֶׁר עַל־ פְּנֵי רַבָּה׃ וּמֵחֶשְׁבּוֹן עַד־ רָמַת הַמִּצְפֶּה וּבְטֹנִים

and-Betonim the-Mizpah Ramath to and-from-Heshbon (26) Rabbah near at that

וּמִמַּחֲנַיִם עַד־ גְּבוּל לִדְבִר׃ וּבָעֵמֶק בֵּית הָרָם

Haram Beth and-in-the-valley (27) of-Debir territory to and-from-Mahanaim

וּבֵית נִמְרָה וְסֻכּוֹת וְצָפוֹן יֶתֶר מַמְלְכוּת סִיחוֹן מֶלֶךְ חֶשְׁבּוֹן

Heshbon king-of Sihon realm-of rest-of and-Zaphon and-Succoth Nimrah and-Beth

הַיַּרְדֵּן וּגְבֻל עַד־ קְצֵה יָם־ כִּנֶּרֶת עֵבֶר הַיַּרְדֵּן

the-Jordan side-of Kinnereth Sea-of end-of to and-territory the-Jordan

מִזְרָחָה׃ זֹאת נַחֲלַת בְּנֵי־ גָד לְמִשְׁפְּחֹתָם הֶעָרִים

the-towns by-clans-of-them Gad sons-of inheritance-of this (28) on-east

וְחַצְרֵיהֶם׃ וַיִּתֵּן מֹשֶׁה לַחֲצִי שֵׁבֶט מְנַשֶּׁה

Manasseh tribe-of to-half-of Moses and-he-gave (29) and-villages-of-them

וַיְהִי לַחֲצִי מַטֵּה בְנֵי־ מְנַשֶּׁה לְמִשְׁפְּחוֹתָם׃

by-clans-of-them Manasseh descendants-of family-of to-half-of and-he-was

וַיְהִי גְּבוּלָם מִמַּחֲנַיִם כָּל־ הַבָּשָׁן כָּל־

entire-of the-Bashan all-of from-Mahanaim territory-of-them and-he-was (30)

מַמְלְכוּת ׀ עוֹג מֶלֶךְ־ הַבָּשָׁן וְכָל־ חַוֹּת יָאִיר אֲשֶׁר

that Jair settlements-of and-all-of the-Bashan king-of Og realm-of

בַּבָּשָׁן שִׁשִּׁים עִיר׃ וַחֲצִי הַגִּלְעָד וְעַשְׁתָּרוֹת וְאֶדְרֶעִי

and-Edrei and-Ashtaroth the-Gilead and-half-of (31) town sixty in-the-Bashan

עָרֵי מַמְלְכוּת עוֹג בַּבָּשָׁן לִבְנֵי מָכִיר בֶּן־ מְנַשֶּׁה

Manasseh son-of Makir for-sons-of in-the-Bashan Og royalty-of cities-of

לַחֲצִי בְנֵי־ מָכִיר לְמִשְׁפְּחוֹתָם׃ אֵלֶּה אֲשֶׁר־ נִחַל

he-gave-inheritance that these (32) by-clans-of-them Makir sons-of for-half-of

מֹשֶׁה בְּעַרְבוֹת מוֹאָב מֵעֵבֶר לְיַרְדֵּן יְרִיחוֹ מִזְרָחָה׃

to-east Jericho of-Jordan-of on-across Moab in-plains-of Moses

וּלְשֵׁבֶט הַלֵּוִי לֹא־ נָתַן מֹשֶׁה נַחֲלָה יְהוָה אֱלֹהֵי

God-of Yahweh inheritance Moses he-gave not the-Levi but-to-tribe-of (33)

יִשְׂרָאֵל הוּא נַחֲלָתָם כַּאֲשֶׁר דִּבֶּר לָהֶם׃ וְאֵלֶּה

now-these (14:1) to-them he-promised just-as inheritance-of-them he Israel

אֲשֶׁר־ נָחֲלוּ בְנֵי־ יִשְׂרָאֵל בְּאֶרֶץ כְּנָעַן אֲשֶׁר נִחֲלוּ

they-allotted which Canaan in-land-of Israel sons-of they-inherited that

אוֹתָם אֶלְעָזָר הַכֹּהֵן וִיהוֹשֻׁעַ בִּן־ נוּן וְרָאשֵׁי אֲבוֹת

fathers-of and-heads-of Nun son-of and-Joshua the-priest Eleazar them

הַמַּטּוֹת לִבְנֵי יִשְׂרָאֵל׃ בְּגוֹרַל נַחֲלָתָם כַּאֲשֶׁר

just-as inheritance-of-them by-lot (2) Israel of-sons-of the-tribes

צִוָּה יְהוָה בְּיַד־ מֹשֶׁה לְתִשְׁעַת הַמַּטּוֹת וַחֲצִי

and-half-of the-tribes to-nine-of Moses by-hand-of Yahweh he-commanded

as far as Aroer, near Rabbah; [26]and from Heshbon to Ramath Mizpah and Betonim, and from Mahanaim to the territory of Debir; [27]and in the valley, Beth Haram, Beth Nimrah, Succoth and Zaphon with the rest of the realm of Sihon king of Heshbon (the east side of the Jordan, the territory up to the end of the Sea of Kinnereth[l]). [28]These towns and their villages were the inheritance of the Gadites, clan by clan.

[29]This is what Moses had given to the half-tribe of Manasseh, that is, to half the family of the descendants of Manasseh, clan by clan:

[30]The territory extending from Mahanaim and including all of Bashan, the entire realm of Og king of Bashan—all the settlements of Jair in Bashan, sixty towns, [31]half of Gilead, and Ashtaroth and Edrei (the royal cities of Og in Bashan). This was for the descendants of Makir son of Manasseh—for half of the sons of Makir, clan by clan.

[32]This is the inheritance Moses had given when he was in the plains of Moab across the Jordan east of Jericho. [33]But to the tribe of Levi, Moses had given no inheritance; the LORD, the God of Israel, is their inheritance, as he promised them.

*Division of the Land West of the Jordan*

**14** Now these are the areas the Israelites received as an inheritance in the land of Canaan, which Eleazar the priest, Joshua son of Nun and the heads of the tribal clans of Israel allotted to them. [2]Their inheritances were assigned by lot to the nine-and-a-half tribes, as the LORD had commanded through Moses.

[l]27 That is, Galilee

הַמַּטֶּה׃ כִּֽי־ נָתַן מֹשֶׁה נַחֲלַת שְׁנֵי הַמַּטּוֹת
the-tribes two-of inheritance-of Moses he-granted for (3) the-tribe

וַחֲצִי הַמַּטֶּה מֵעֵבֶר לַיַּרְדֵּן וְלַלְוִיִּם לֹא־ נָתַן
he-granted not but-to-the-Levites of-the-Jordan on-east the-tribe and-half-of

נַחֲלָה בְּתוֹכָם׃ כִּֽי־ הָיוּ בְנֵֽי־ יוֹסֵף שְׁנֵי מַטּוֹת
tribes two-of Joseph sons-of they-became for (4) in-among-them inheritance

מְנַשֶּׁה וְאֶפְרָיִם וְלֹא־ נָתְנוּ חֵלֶק לַלְוִיִּם בָּאָרֶץ כִּי
but in-the-land to-the-Levites share they-gave and-not and-Ephraim Manasseh

אִם־ עָרִים לָשֶׁבֶת וּמִגְרְשֵׁיהֶם לְמִקְנֵיהֶם וּלְקִנְיָנָם׃
and-for-herd-of-them for-flocks-of-them and-pastures-of-them to-live towns only

כַּאֲשֶׁר צִוָּה יְהוָה אֶת־ מֹשֶׁה כֵּן עָשׂוּ בְּנֵי יִשְׂרָאֵל
Israel sons-of they-did so Moses *** Yahweh he-commanded just-as (5)

וַֽיַּחְלְקוּ אֶת־ הָאָרֶץ׃ וַיִּגְּשׁוּ בְנֵֽי־ יְהוּדָה אֶל־יְהוֹשֻׁעַ
Joshua to Judah men-of now-they-approached (6) the-land *** and-they-divided

בַּגִּלְגָּל וַיֹּאמֶר אֵלָיו כָּלֵב בֶּן־ יְפֻנֶּה הַקְּנִזִּי אַתָּה
you the-Kenizzite Jephunneh son-of Caleb to-him and-he-said at-the-Gilgal

יָדַעְתָּ אֶת־ הַדָּבָר אֲשֶׁר־ דִּבֶּר יְהוָה אֶל־ מֹשֶׁה אִישׁ־הָאֱלֹהִים עַל
about the-God man-of Moses to Yahweh he-said that the-thing *** you-know

אֹדוֹתַי וְעַל אֹדוֹתֶיךָ בְּקָדֵשׁ בַּרְנֵעַ׃ בֶּן־אַרְבָּעִים
forty son-of (7) Barnea at-Kadesh because-of-you and-about because-of-me

שָׁנָה אָנֹכִי בִּשְׁלֹחַ מֹשֶׁה עֶֽבֶד־ יְהוָה אֹתִי מִקָּדֵשׁ בַּרְנֵעַ לְרַגֵּל
to-explore Barnea from-Kadesh me Yahweh servant-of Moses when-to-send I year

אֶת־ הָאָרֶץ וָאָשֵׁב אֹתוֹ דָּבָר כַּאֲשֶׁר עִם־ לְבָבִי׃
heart-of-me in just-as report him and-I-brought-back the-land ***

וְאַחַי אֲשֶׁר עָלוּ עִמִּי הִמְסִיו אֶת־ לֵב
heart-of *** they-made-melt with-me they-went-up who but-brothers-of-me (8)

הָעָם וְאָנֹכִי מִלֵּאתִי אַחֲרֵי יְהוָה אֱלֹהָי׃ וַיִּשָּׁבַע
so-he-swore (9) God-of-me Yahweh after I-was-wholehearted but-I the-people

מֹשֶׁה בַּיּוֹם הַהוּא לֵאמֹר אִם־ לֹא הָאָרֶץ אֲשֶׁר דָּרְכָה
she-walked that the-land indeed now to-say the-that on-the-day Moses

רַגְלְךָ בָּהּ לְךָ תִֽהְיֶה לְנַחֲלָה וּלְבָנֶיךָ
and-to-children-of-you as-inheritance she-will-be to-you on-her foot-of-you

עַד־עוֹלָם כִּי מִלֵּאתָ אַחֲרֵי יְהוָה אֱלֹהָי׃ וְעַתָּה הִנֵּה
see! and-now (10) God-of-me Yahweh after you-were-wholehearted for ever for

הֶחֱיָה יְהוָה ׀ אוֹתִי כַּאֲשֶׁר דִּבֶּר זֶה אַרְבָּעִים וְחָמֵשׁ שָׁנָה
year and-five forty this he-promised just-as me Yahweh he-kept-alive

מֵאָז דִּבֶּר יְהוָה אֶת־ הַדָּבָר הַזֶּה אֶל־ מֹשֶׁה אֲשֶׁר־ הָלַךְ
he-moved while Moses to the-this the-thing *** Yahweh he-said since-when

[3]Moses had granted the two-
and-a-half tribes their inheritance east of the Jordan but
had not granted the Levites an
inheritance among the rest,
[4]for the sons of Joseph had
become two tribes—Manasseh
and Ephraim. The Levites received no share of the land but
only towns to live in, with
pasturelands for their flocks
and herds. [5]So the Israelites divided the land, just as the
LORD had commanded Moses.

*Hebron Given to Caleb*

[6]Now the men of Judah approached Joshua at Gilgal, and
Caleb son of Jephunneh the
Kenizzite said to him, "You
know what the LORD said to
Moses the man of God at Kadesh Barnea about you and
me. [7]I was forty years old
when Moses the servant of the
LORD sent me from Kadesh
Barnea to explore the land.
And I brought him back a report according to my convic-
tions, [8]but my brothers who
went up with me made the
hearts of the people melt with
fear. I, however, followed the
LORD my God wholeheartedly.
[9]So on that day Moses swore to
me, 'The land on which your
feet have walked will be your
inheritance and that of your
children forever, because you
have followed the LORD my
God wholeheartedly.'[m]
[10]"Now then, just as the
LORD promised, he has kept
me alive for forty-five years
since the time he said this to
Moses, while Israel moved

[m]9 Deut. 1:36

יִשְׂרָאֵל בַּמִּדְבָּר וְעַתָּה הִנֵּה אָנֹכִי הַיּוֹם בֶּן־ חָמֵשׁ וּשְׁמוֹנִים שָׁנָה׃
year and-eighty five son-of the-day I see! so-now in-the-desert Israel

עוֹדֶנִּי הַיּוֹם חָזָק כַּאֲשֶׁר בְּיוֹם שְׁלֹחַ אוֹתִי מֹשֶׁה כְּכֹחִי
as-vigor-of-me Moses me to-send on-day just-as strong the-day still-I (11)

אָז וּכְכֹחִי עָתָּה לַמִּלְחָמָה וְלָצֵאת וְלָבוֹא׃ וְעַתָּה
so-now (12) and-to-go even-to-go-out to-the-battle now so-vigor-of-me then

תְּנָה־ לִּי אֶת־ הָהָר הַזֶּה אֲשֶׁר־ דִּבֶּר יְהוָה בַּיּוֹם
on-the-day Yahweh he-promised that the-this the-hill-country *** to-me give!

הַהוּא כִּי אַתָּה־ שָׁמַעְתָּ בַיּוֹם הַהוּא כִּי־ עֲנָקִים שָׁם וְעָרִים
and-cities there Anakites that the-that on-the-day you-heard you for the-that

גְּדֹלוֹת בְּצֻרוֹת אוּלַי יְהוָה אוֹתִי וְהוֹרַשְׁתִּים
then-I-will-drive-out-them with-me Yahweh but fortified-ones large-ones

כַּאֲשֶׁר דִּבֶּר יְהוָה׃ וַיְבָרְכֵהוּ יְהוֹשֻׁעַ וַיִּתֵּן אֶת־
*** and-he-gave Joshua then-he-blessed-him (13) Yahweh he-said just-as

חֶבְרוֹן לְכָלֵב בֶּן־ יְפֻנֶּה לְנַחֲלָה׃ עַל־ כֵּן הָיְתָה־
she-belonged this for (14) as-inheritance Jephunneh son-of to-Caleb Hebron

חֶבְרוֹן לְכָלֵב בֶּן־ יְפֻנֶּה הַקְּנִזִּי לְנַחֲלָה עַד הַיּוֹם
the-day to as-inheritance the-Kenizzite Jephunneh son-of to-Caleb Hebron

הַזֶּה יַעַן אֲשֶׁר מִלֵּא אַחֲרֵי יְהוָה אֱלֹהֵי יִשְׂרָאֵל׃
Israel God-of Yahweh after he-was-wholehearted that because the-this

וְשֵׁם חֶבְרוֹן לְפָנִים קִרְיַת אַרְבַּע הָאָדָם הַגָּדוֹל
the-greatest the-man Arba Kiriath before Hebron now-name-of (15)

בָּעֲנָקִים הוּא וְהָאָרֶץ שָׁקְטָה מִמִּלְחָמָה׃ וַיְהִי
and-he-was (15:1) from-war she-had-rest then-the-land he among-the-Anakites

הַגּוֹרָל לְמַטֵּה בְּנֵי יְהוּדָה לְמִשְׁפְּחֹתָם אֶל־ גְּבוּל
territory-of to by-clans-of-them Judah sons-of for-tribe-of the-allotment

אֱדוֹם מִדְבַּר־ צִן נֶגְבָּה מִקְצֵה תֵימָן׃ וַיְהִי לָהֶם
to-them and-he-was (2) south in-extreme-of in-south Zin Desert-of Edom

גְּבוּל נֶגֶב מִקְצֵה יָם הַמֶּלַח מִן־ הַלָּשֹׁן הַפֹּנֶה
the-one-facing the-bay from the-Salt Sea-of from-end-of south boundary-of

נֶגְבָּה׃ וְיָצָא אֶל־ מִנֶּגֶב לְמַעֲלֵה עַקְרַבִּים וְעָבַר
and-he-continued Scorpions of-Pass-of on-south at and-he-crossed (3) to-south

צִנָה וְעָלָה מִנֶּגֶב לְקָדֵשׁ בַּרְנֵעַ וְעָבַר חֶצְרוֹן
Hezron then-he-ran-past Barnea of-Kadesh to-south and-he-went to-Zin

וְעָלָה אַדָּרָה וְנָסַב הַקַּרְקָעָה׃ וְעָבַר
then-he-passed-along (4) to-the-Karka then-he-curved to-Addar then-he-went-up

עַצְמוֹנָה וְיָצָא נַחַל מִצְרַיִם וְהָיָה תֹּצְאוֹת הַגְּבוּל
the-boundary ends-of and-they-were Egypt Wadi-of and-he-joined to-Azmon

°4 ק והיו

about in the desert. So here I am today, eighty-five years old! 11I am still as strong today as the day Moses sent me out; I'm just as vigorous to go out to battle now as I was then. 12Now give me this hill country that the LORD promised me that day. You yourself heard then that the Anakites were there and their cities were large and fortified, but, the LORD helping me, I will drive them out just as he said."

13Then Joshua blessed Caleb son of Jephunneh and gave him Hebron as his inheritance. 14So Hebron has belonged to Caleb son of Jephunneh the Kenizzite ever since, because he followed the LORD, the God of Israel, wholeheartedly. 15(Hebron used to be called Kiriath Arba after Arba, who was the greatest man among the Anakites.)

Then the land had rest from war.

### *Allotment for Judah*

15 The allotment for the tribe of Judah, clan by clan, extended down to the territory of Edom, to the Desert of Zin in the extreme south.

2Their southern boundary started from the bay at the southern end of the Salt Sea,[n] 3crossed south of Scorpion[o] Pass, continued on to Zin and went over to the south of Kadesh Barnea. Then it ran past Hezron up to Addar and curved around to Karka. 4It then passed along to Azmon and joined the Wadi of Egypt,

[n]2 That is, the Dead Sea; also in verse 5
[o]3 Hebrew *Akrabbim*

יָמָּה זֶה־ יִהְיֶה לָכֶם גְּבוּל נֶגֶב׃ וּגְבוּל קֵדְמָה
to-east and-boundary-of (5) southern boundary-of for-you he-is this at-sea

יָם הַמֶּלַח עַד־ קְצֵה הַיַּרְדֵּן וּגְבוּל לִפְאַת
on-side-of and-boundary the-Jordan mouth-of as-far-as the-Salt Sea-of

צָפוֹנָה מִלְּשׁוֹן הַיָּם מִקְצֵה הַיַּרְדֵּן׃ וְעָלָה
and-he-went-up (6) the-Jordan at-mouth-of the-sea from-bay-of to-north

הַגְּבוּל בֵּית חָגְלָה וְעָבַר מִצְּפוֹן לְבֵית הָעֲרָבָה
the-Arabah of-Beth to-north and-he-continued Hoglah Beth the-boundary

וְעָלָה הַגְּבוּל אֶבֶן בֹּהַן בֶּן־ רְאוּבֵן׃ וְעָלָה
then-he-went-up (7) Reuben son-of Bohan Stone-of the-boundary and-he-went

הַגְּבוּל ׀ דְּבִרָה מֵעֵמֶק עָכוֹר וְצָפוֹנָה פֹּנֶה אֶל־ הַגִּלְגָּל
the-Gilgal to turning and-at-north Achor from-Valley-of to-Debir the-boundary

אֲשֶׁר־ נֹכַח לְמַעֲלֵה אֲדֻמִּים אֲשֶׁר מִנֶּגֶב לַנָּחַל וְעָבַר
and-he-continued of-the-gorge at-south that Adummim to-Pass-of facing which

הַגְּבוּל אֶל־ מֵי־ עֵין שֶׁמֶשׁ וְהָיוּ תֹצְאֹתָיו אֶל־עֵין רֹגֵל׃
Rogel En at ends-of-him and-they-were Shemesh En Waters-of to the-boundary

וְעָלָה הַגְּבוּל גֵּי בֶן־ הִנֹּם אֶל־ כֶּתֶף
slope-of along Hinnom Ben Valley-of the-boundary then-he-ran-up (8)

הַיְבוּסִי מִנֶּגֶב הִיא יְרוּשָׁלִָם וְעָלָה הַגְּבוּל אֶל־ רֹאשׁ
top-of to the-boundary and-he-climbed Jerusalem that on-south the-Jebusite

הָהָר אֲשֶׁר עַל־ פְּנֵי גֵי־ הִנֹּם יָמָּה אֲשֶׁר בִּקְצֵה עֵמֶק־
Valley-of at-end-of that on-west Hinnom Valley-of front-of at that the-hill

רְפָאִים צָפֹנָה׃ וְתָאַר הַגְּבוּל מֵרֹאשׁ הָהָר אֶל־
toward the-hill from-top-of the-boundary then-he-headed (9) at-north Rephaim

מַעְיַן מֵי נֶפְתּוֹחַ וְיָצָא אֶל־ עָרֵי הַר־ עֶפְרוֹן
Ephron Mount-of towns-of to and-he-came Nephtoah Waters-of spring-of

וְתָאַר הַגְּבוּל בַּעֲלָה הִיא קִרְיַת יְעָרִים׃ וְנָסַב
then-he-curved (10) Jearim Kiriath that Baalah the-boundary and-he-went

הַגְּבוּל מִבַּעֲלָה יָמָּה אֶל־ הַר שֵׂעִיר וְעָבַר אֶל־ כֶּתֶף
slope-of along and-he-ran Seir Mount-of to to-west from-Baalah the-boundary

הַר־ יְעָרִים מִצָּפוֹנָה הִיא כְסָלוֹן וְיָרַד בֵּית־ שֶׁמֶשׁ
Shemesh Beth and-he-continued-down Kesalon that on-north Jearim Mount-of

וְעָבַר תִּמְנָה׃ וְיָצָא הַגְּבוּל אֶל־ כֶּתֶף עֶקְרוֹן
Ekron slope-of to the-boundary and-he-went (11) Timnah and-he-crossed

צָפוֹנָה וְתָאַר הַגְּבוּל שִׁכְּרוֹנָה וְעָבַר הַר־
Mount-of and-he-passed-along to-Shikkeron the-boundary and-he-turned on-north

הַבַּעֲלָה וְיָצָא יַבְנְאֵל וְהָיוּ תֹּצְאוֹת הַגְּבוּל יָמָּה׃
at-sea the-boundary ends-of and-they-were Jabneel and-he-reached the-Baalah

ending at the sea. This is their[p] southern boundary.

5 The eastern boundary is the Salt Sea as far as the mouth of the Jordan.

The northern boundary started from the bay of the sea at the mouth of the Jordan, 6 went up to Beth Hoglah and continued north of Beth Arabah to the Stone of Bohan son of Reuben. 7 The boundary then went up to Debir from the Valley of Achor and turned north to Gilgal, which faces the Pass of Adummim south of the gorge. It continued along to the Waters of En Shemesh and came out at En Rogel. 8 Then it ran up the Valley of Ben Hinnom along the southern slope of the Jebusite city (that is, Jerusalem). From there it climbed to the top of the hill west of the Hinnom Valley at the northern end of the Valley of Rephaim. 9 From the hilltop the boundary headed toward the spring of the Waters of Nephtoah, came out at the towns of Mount Ephron and went down toward Baalah (that is, Kiriath Jearim). 10 Then it curved westward from Baalah to Mount Seir, ran along the northern slope of Mount Jearim (that is, Kesalon), continued down to Beth Shemesh and crossed to Timnah. 11 It went to the northern slope of Ekron, turned toward Shikkeron, passed along to Mount Baalah and reached Jabneel. The boundary ended at the sea.

p4 Hebrew *your*

וּגְבוּל יָם הַיָּמָּה הַגָּדוֹל וּגְבוּל זֶה גְּבוּל
boundary-of this and-coast the-Great to-the-Sea west and-boundary-of (12)

בְּנֵי־ יְהוּדָה סָבִיב לְמִשְׁפְּחֹתָם׃ וּלְכָלֵב בֶּן־ יְפֻנֶּה
Jephunneh son-of and-to-Caleb (13) by-clans-of-them around Judah people-of

נָתַן חֵלֶק בְּתוֹךְ בְּנֵי־ יְהוּדָה אֶל־ פִּי יְהוָה לִיהוֹשֻׁעַ
to-Joshua Yahweh command-of at Judah sons-of in-midst-of portion he-gave

אֶת־קִרְיַת אַרְבַּע אֲבִי הָעֲנָק הִיא חֶבְרוֹן׃ וַיֹּרֶשׁ
and-he-drove-out (14) Hebron that the-Anak forefather-of Arba Kiriath ***

מִשָּׁם כָּלֵב אֶת־שְׁלוֹשָׁה בְּנֵי הָעֲנָק אֶת־ שֵׁשַׁי וְאֶת־ אֲחִימַן וְאֶת־
and Ahiman and Sheshai *** the-Anak sons-of three *** Caleb from-there

תַּלְמַי יְלִידֵי הָעֲנָק׃ וַיַּעַל מִשָּׁם אֶל־
against from-there and-he-marched (15) the-Anak descendants-of Talmai

יֹשְׁבֵי דְּבִר וְשֵׁם־ דְּבִר לְפָנִים קִרְיַת־ סֵפֶר׃ וַיֹּאמֶר
and-he-said (16) Sepher Kiriath formerly Debir now-name-of Debir ones-living-of

כָּלֵב אֲשֶׁר־ יַכֶּה אֶת־ קִרְיַת־ סֵפֶר וּלְכָדָהּ
and-he-captures-her Sepher Kiriath *** he-attacks whoever Caleb

וְנָתַתִּי לוֹ אֶת־עַכְסָה בִתִּי לְאִשָּׁה׃ וַיִּלְכְּדָהּ
and-he-took-her (17) as-wife daughter-of-me Acsah *** to-him then-I-will-give

עָתְנִיאֵל בֶּן־ קְנַז אֲחִי כָלֵב וַיִּתֶּן־ לוֹ אֶת־עַכְסָה
Acsah *** to-him so-he-gave Caleb brother-of Kenaz son-of Othniel

בִתּוֹ לְאִשָּׁה׃ וַיְהִי בְּבוֹאָהּ וַתְּסִיתֵהוּ
then-she-urged-him when-to-come-her and-he-was (18) as-wife daughter-of-him

לִשְׁאוֹל מֵאֵת־ אָבִיהָ שָׂדֶה וַתִּצְנַח מֵעַל הַחֲמוֹר
the-donkey from-on when-she-got-off field father-of-her from to-ask

וַיֹּאמֶר־ לָהּ כָּלֵב מַה־ לָּךְ׃ וַתֹּאמֶר תְּנָה־ לִּי
for-me do! and-she-replied (19) for-you what? Caleb to-her then-he-asked

בְרָכָה כִּי אֶרֶץ הַנֶּגֶב נְתַתָּנִי וְנָתַתָּה לִי גֻּלֹּת
springs-of to-me also-you-give you-gave-me the-Negev land-of since favor

מָיִם וַיִּתֶּן־ לָהּ אֵת גֻּלֹּת עִלִּיּוֹת וְאֵת גֻּלֹּת תַּחְתִּיּוֹת׃
lower-ones springs-of and upper-ones springs-of *** to-her so-he-gave waters

זֹאת נַחֲלַת מַטֵּה בְנֵי־ יְהוּדָה לְמִשְׁפְּחֹתָם׃
by-clans-of-them Judah sons-of tribe-of inheritance-of this (20)

וַיִּהְיוּ הֶעָרִים מִקְצֵה לְמַטֵּה בְנֵי־ יְהוּדָה אֶל־
toward Judah sons-of of-tribe-of at-end the-towns and-they-were (21)

גְּבוּל אֱדוֹם בַּנֶּגְבָּה קַבְצְאֵל וְעֵדֶר וְיָגוּר׃ וְקִינָה
and-Kinah (22) and-Jagur and-Eder Kabzeel in-the-Negev Edom boundary-of

וְדִימוֹנָה וְעַדְעָדָה׃ וְקֶדֶשׁ וְחָצוֹר וְיִתְנָן׃ זִיף
Ziph (24) and-Ithnan and-Hazor and-Kedesh (23) and-Adadah and-Dimonah

12The western boundary
is the coastline of the Great
Sea.[q]
These are the boundaries
around the people of Judah by
their clans.

13In accordance with the
LORD's command to him,
Joshua gave to Caleb son of Je-
phunneh a portion in Judah—
Kiriath Arba, that is, Hebron.
(Arba was the forefather of
Anak.) 14From Hebron Caleb
drove out the three Anakites—
Sheshai, Ahiman and Tal-
mai—descendants of Anak.
15From there he marched
against the people living in
Debir (formerly called Kiriath
Sepher). 16And Caleb said, "I
will give my daughter Acsah
in marriage to the man who
attacks and captures Kiriath
Sepher." 17Othniel son of
Kenaz, Caleb's brother, took
it; so Caleb gave his daughter
Acsah to him in marriage.
18One day when she came to
Othniel, she urged him[r] to ask
her father for a field.
When she got off the don-
key, Caleb asked her, "What
can I do for you?"
19She replied, "Do me a
special favor. Since you have
given me land in the Negev,
give me also springs of water."
So Caleb gave her the upper
and lower springs.

20This is the inheritance of
the tribe of Judah, clan by
clan:

21The southernmost towns of
the tribe of Judah in the Negev
toward the boundary of Edom
were:
Kabzeel, Eder, Jagur,
22Kinah, Dimonah, Ada-
dah, 23Kedesh, Hazor, Ith-
nan, 24Ziph, Telem,

q12 That is, the Mediterranean; also in verse 47
r18 Hebrew and some Septuagint manuscripts; other Septuagint manuscripts (see also note at Judges 1:14) *Othniel, he urged her*

וָטֶלֶם וּבְעָלוֹת׃ וְחָצוֹר ׀ חֲדַתָּה וּקְרִיּוֹת חֶצְרוֹן הִיא חָצוֹר׃
Hazor that Hezron and-Kerioth Hadattah and-Hazor (25) and-Bealoth and-Telem

אֲמָם וּשְׁמַע וּמוֹלָדָה׃ וַחֲצַר גַּדָּה וְחֶשְׁמוֹן וּבֵית
and-Beth and-Heshmon Gaddah and-Hazar (27) and-Moladah and-Shema Amam (26)

פָּלֶט׃ וַחֲצַר שׁוּעָל וּבְאֵר שֶׁבַע וּבִזְיוֹתְיָה׃ בַּעֲלָה וְעִיִּים
and-Iim Baalah (29) and-Biziothiah Sheba and-Beer Shual and-Hazar (28) Pelet

וָעָצֶם׃ וְאֶלְתּוֹלַד וּכְסִיל וְחָרְמָה׃ וְצִקְלַג וּמַדְמַנָּה
and-Madmannah and-Ziklag (31) and-Hormah and-Kesil and-Eltolad (30) and-Ezem

וְסַנְסַנָּה׃ וּלְבָאוֹת וְשִׁלְחִים וְעַיִן וְרִמּוֹן כָּל־
total-of and-Rimmon and-Ain and-Shilhim and-Lebaoth (32) and-Sansannah

עָרִים עֶשְׂרִים וָתֵשַׁע וְחַצְרֵיהֶן׃ בַּשְּׁפֵלָה אֶשְׁתָּאוֹל
Eshtaol in-the-foothill (33) and-villages-of-them and-nine twenty towns

וְצָרְעָה וְאַשְׁנָה׃ וְזָנוֹחַ וְעֵין גַּנִּים תַּפּוּחַ וְהָעֵינָם׃
and-the-Enam Tappuah Gannim and-En and-Zanoah (34) and-Ashnah and-Zorah

יַרְמוּת וַעֲדֻלָּם שׂוֹכֹה וַעֲזֵקָה׃ וְשַׁעֲרַיִם וַעֲדִיתַיִם
and-Adithaim and-Shaaraim (36) and-Azekah Socoh and-Adullam Jarmuth (35)

וְהַגְּדֵרָה וּגְדֵרֹתָיִם עָרִים אַרְבַּע־עֶשְׂרֵה וְחַצְרֵיהֶן׃ צְנָן
Zenan (37) and-villages-of-them ten four towns or-Gederothaim and-the-Gederah

וַחֲדָשָׁה וּמִגְדַּל־ גָּד׃ וְדִלְעָן וְהַמִּצְפֶּה וְיָקְתְאֵל׃
and-Joktheel and-the-Mizpah and-Dilean (38) Gad and-Migdal and-Hadashah

לָכִישׁ וּבָצְקַת וְעֶגְלוֹן׃ וְכַבּוֹן וְלַחְמָס וְכִתְלִישׁ׃
and-Kitlish and-Lahmas and-Cabbon (40) and-Eglon and-Bozkath Lachish (39)

וּגְדֵרוֹת בֵּית־ דָּגוֹן וְנַעֲמָה וּמַקֵּדָה עָרִים שֵׁשׁ־עֶשְׂרֵה
ten six towns and-Makkedah and-Naamah Dagon Beth and-Gederoth (41)

וְחַצְרֵיהֶן׃ לִבְנָה וָעֶתֶר וְעָשָׁן׃ וְיִפְתָּח
and-Iphtah (43) and-Ashan and-Ether Libnah (42) and-villages-of-them

וְאַשְׁנָה וּנְצִיב׃ וּקְעִילָה וְאַכְזִיב וּמָרֵאשָׁה עָרִים תֵּשַׁע
nine towns and-Mareshah and-Aczib and-Keilah (44) and-Nezib and-Ashnah

וְחַצְרֵיהֶן׃ עֶקְרוֹן וּבְנֹתֶיהָ וַחֲצֵרֶיהָ׃
and-villages-of-her and-settlements-of-her Ekron (45) and-villages-of-them

מֵעֶקְרוֹן וָיָמָּה כֹּל אֲשֶׁר־עַל־ יַד אַשְׁדּוֹד וְחַצְרֵיהֶן׃
and-villages-of-them Ashdod vicinity-of in that all and-to-west from-Ekron (46)

אַשְׁדּוֹד בְּנוֹתֶיהָ וַחֲצֵרֶיהָ עַזָּה בְּנוֹתֶיהָ
settlements-of-her Gaza and-villages-of-her settlements-of-her Ashdod (47)

וַחֲצֵרֶיהָ עַד־ נַחַל מִצְרַיִם וְהַיָּם הַגָּבוֹל וּגְבוּל׃
and-coast the-Great and-the-Sea Egypt Wadi-of as-far-as and-villages-of-her

וּבָהָר שָׁמִיר וְיַתִּיר וְשׂוֹכֹה׃ וְדַנָּה
and-Dannah (49) and-Socoh and-Jattir Shamir and-in-the-hill-country (48)

Bealoth, [25]Hazor Hadattah, Kerioth Hezron (that is, Hazor), [26]Amam, Shema, Moladah, [27]Hazar Gaddah, Heshmon, Beth Pelet, [28]Hazar Shual, Beersheba, Biziothiah, [29]Baalah, Iim, Ezem, [30]Eltolad, Kesil, Hormah, [31]Ziklag, Madmannah, Sansannah, [32]Lebaoth, Shilhim, Ain and Rimmon—a total of twenty-nine towns and their villages.

[33]In the western foothills:
Eshtaol, Zorah, Ashnah, [34]Zanoah, En Gannim, Tappuah, Enam, [35]Jarmuth, Adullam, Socoh, Azekah, [36]Shaaraim, Adithaim and Gederah (or Gederothaim)[s]—fourteen towns and their villages.

[37]Zenan, Hadashah, Migdal Gad, [38]Dilean, Mizpah, Joktheel, [39]Lachish, Bozkath, Eglon, [40]Cabbon, Lahmas, Kitlish, [41]Gederoth, Beth Dagon, Naamah and Makkedah—sixteen towns and their villages.

[42]Libnah, Ether, Ashan, [43]Iphtah, Ashnah, Nezib, [44]Keilah, Aczib and Mareshah—nine towns and their villages.

[45]Ekron, with its surrounding settlements and villages; [46]west of Ekron, all that were in the vicinity of Ashdod, together with their villages; [47]Ashdod, its surrounding settlements and villages; and Gaza, its settlements and villages, as far as the Wadi of Egypt and the coastline of the Great Sea.

[48]In the hill country:
Shamir, Jattir, Socoh,

s36 Or *Gederah and Gederothaim*

°47 ק הגדול

וְקִרְיַת־ סַנָּה הִיא דְבִר׃ וַעֲנָב וְאֶשְׁתְּמֹה וְעָנִים׃
and-Anim and-Eshtemoh and-Anab (50) Debir that Sannah and-Kiriath

וְגֹשֶׁן וְחֹלֹן וְגִלֹה עָרִים אַחַת־עֶשְׂרֵה וְחַצְרֵיהֶן׃
and-villages-of-them ten one towns and-Giloh and-Holon and-Goshen (51)

אֲרַב וְרוּמָה* וְאֶשְׁעָן׃ וְיָנִים°† וּבֵית־ תַּפּוּחַ וַאֲפֵקָה׃
and-Aphekah Tappuah and-Beth and-Janim (53) and-Eshan and-Dumah Arab (52)

וְחֻמְטָה וְקִרְיַת אַרְבַּע הִיא חֶבְרוֹן וְצִיעֹר עָרִים תֵּשַׁע
nine towns and-Zior Hebron that Arba and-Kiriath and-Humtah (54)

וְחַצְרֵיהֶן׃ מָעוֹן ׀ כַּרְמֶל וָזִיף וְיוּטָּה׃ וְיִזְרְעֶאל
and-Jezreel (56) and-Juttah and-Ziph Carmel Maon (55) and-villages-of-them

וְיָקְדְעָם וְזָנוֹחַ׃ הַקַּיִן גִּבְעָה וְתִמְנָה עָרִים עֶשֶׂר
ten towns and-Timnah Gibeah the-Kain (57) and-Zanoah and-Jokdeam

וְחַצְרֵיהֶן׃ חַלְחוּל בֵּית־ צוּר וּגְדוֹר׃ וּמַעֲרָת
and-Maarath (59) and-Gedor Zur Beth Halhul (58) and-villages-of-them

וּבֵית־ עֲנוֹת וְאֶלְתְּקֹן עָרִים שֵׁשׁ וְחַצְרֵיהֶן׃ קִרְיַת־ בַּעַל
Baal Kiriath (60) and-villages-of-them six towns and-Eltekon Anoth and-Beth

הִיא קִרְיַת יְעָרִים וְהָרַבָּה עָרִים שְׁתַּיִם וְחַצְרֵיהֶן׃
and-villages-of-them two towns and-the-Rabbah Jearim Kiriath that

בַּמִּדְבָּר בֵּית הָעֲרָבָה מִדִּין וּסְכָכָה׃ וְהַנִּבְשָׁן
and-the-Nibshan (62) and-Secacah Middin the-Arabah Beth in-the-desert (61)

וְעִיר־ הַמֶּלַח וְעֵין גֶּדִי עָרִים שֵׁשׁ וְחַצְרֵיהֶן׃ וְאֶת־
but (63) and-villages-of-them six towns Gedi and-En the-Salt and-City-of

הַיְבוּסִי יוֹשְׁבֵי יְרוּשָׁלִַם לֹא־ יָכְלוּ° בְנֵי־ יְהוּדָה
Judah people-of they-could not Jerusalem ones-living-of the-Jebusite

לְהוֹרִישָׁם וַיֵּשֶׁב הַיְבוּסִי אֶת־ בְּנֵי יְהוּדָה בִּירוּשָׁלִַם
in-Jerusalem Judah people-of with the-Jebusite so-he-lives to-dislodge-them

עַד הַיּוֹם הַזֶּה׃ וַיֵּצֵא הַגּוֹרָל לִבְנֵי יוֹסֵף
Joseph for-sons-of the-allotment and-he-began (16:1) the-this the-day to

מִיַּרְדֵּן יְרִיחוֹ לְמֵי יְרִיחוֹ מִזְרָחָה הַמִּדְבָּר עֹלֶה
going-up the-desert to-east Jericho by-waters-of Jericho at-Jordan-of

מִירִיחוֹ בָּהָר בֵּית־ אֵל׃ וְיָצָא מִבֵּית־ אֵל לוּזָה
to-Luz El from-Beth and-he-went (2) El Beth into-the-hill-country from-Jericho

וְעָבַר אֶל־ גְּבוּל הָאַרְכִּי עֲטָרוֹת׃ וְיָרַד־
and-he-descended (3) Ataroth the-Arkite territory-of to and-he-crossed-over

יָמָּה אֶל־ גְּבוּל הַיַּפְלֵטִי עַד גְּבוּל בֵּית־ חוֹרֹן תַּחְתּוֹן
Lower Horon Beth region-of as-far-as the-Japhletite territory-of to to-west

וְעַד־ גֶּזֶר וְהָיוּ תֹּצְאֹתָו° יָמָּה׃ וַיִּנְחֲלוּ בְנֵי־
sons-of and-they-inherited (4) at-sea ends-of-him and-they-were Gezer and-to

49 Dannah, Kiriath Sannah
(that is, Debir), 50 Anab,
Eshtemoh, Anim, 51 Go-
shen, Holon and Giloh—
eleven towns and their villages.
52 Arab, Dumah, Eshan,
53 Janim, Beth Tappuah,
Aphekah, 54 Humtah,
Kiriath Arba (that is, Hebron) and Zior—nine
towns and their villages.
55 Maon, Carmel, Ziph,
Juttah, 56 Jezreel, Jokdeam,
Zanoah, 57 Kain, Gibeah
and Timnah—ten towns
and their villages.
58 Halhul, Beth Zur, Ge-
dor, 59 Maarath, Beth Anoth
and Eltekon—six towns
and their villages.
60 Kiriath Baal (that is,
Kiriath Jearim) and Rab-
bah—two towns and their
villages.

61 In the desert:
Beth Arabah, Middin,
Secacah, 62 Nibshan, the
City of Salt and En Gedi—
six towns and their vil-
lages.
63 Judah could not dislodge
the Jebusites, who were living
in Jerusalem; to this day the
Jebusites live there with the
people of Judah.

*Allotment for Ephraim and Manasseh*

16 The allotment for Jo-
seph began at the
Jordan of Jericho,[t] east of
the waters of Jericho, and
went up from there
through the desert into the
hill country of Bethel. 2 It
went on from Bethel (that
is, Luz),[u] crossed over to the
territory of the Arkites in
Ataroth, 3 descended westward to the territory of the
Japhletites as far as the region of Lower Beth Horon
and on to Gezer, ending at
the sea.

[t]1 *Jordan of Jericho* was possibly an ancient name for the Jordan River.
[u]2 Septuagint; Hebrew *Bethel to Luz*

*52 Most mss read *and-Dumah* ( ודומה ); L reads *and-Rumah.*

†53 Most mss have *hireq* under the *nun* and have no *dagesh* in the *yod* ( ־ִים ). The *Ketbib* form thus reads *and-Janim*, and the *Qere* reads *and-Janum.*

°53 ק וינום
°63 ק יכלו
°3 ק תצאתיו

יוֹסֵף מְנַשֶּׁה וְאֶפְרָיִם׃ וַיְהִי גְּבוּל בְּנֵי־אֶפְרַיִם

Ephraim sons-of territory-of and-he-was (5) and-Ephraim Manasseh Joseph

לְמִשְׁפְּחֹתָם וַיְהִי גְּבוּל נַחֲלָתָם מִזְרָחָה עַטְרוֹת

Ataroth in-east inheritance-of-them boundary-of and-he-was by-clans-of-them

אַדָּר עַד־בֵּית חוֹרֹן עֶלְיוֹן׃ וְיָצָא הַגְּבוּל הַיָּמָּה

to-the-sea the-boundary and-he-continued (6) Upper Horon Beth to Addar

הַמִּכְמְתָת מִצָּפוֹן וְנָסַב הַגְּבוּל מִזְרָחָה תַּאֲנַת שִׁלֹה

Shiloh Taanath to-east the-boundary and-he-curved on-north the-Micmethath

וְעָבַר אוֹתוֹ מִמִּזְרַח יָנוֹחָה׃ וְיָרַד מִיָּנוֹחָה

from-Janoah then-he-went-down (7) to-Janoah on-east him and-he-passed

עֲטָרוֹת וְנַעֲרָתָה וּפָגַע בִּירִיחוֹ וְיָצָא הַיַּרְדֵּן׃

the-Jordan and-he-came-out on-Jericho and-he-touched and-to-Naarah Ataroth

מִתַּפּוּחַ יֵלֵךְ הַגְּבוּל יָמָּה נַחַל קָנָה וְהָיוּ

and-they-were Kanah Ravine-of to-west the-border he-went from-Tappuah (8)

תֹצְאֹתָיו הַיָּמָּה זֹאת נַחֲלַת מַטֵּה בְנֵי־אֶפְרָיִם

Ephraim sons-of tribe-of inheritance-of this at-the-sea ends-of-him

לְמִשְׁפְּחֹתָם׃ וְהֶעָרִים הַמִּבְדָּלוֹת לִבְנֵי אֶפְרַיִם

Ephraim for-sons-of the-ones-set-aside and-the-towns (9) by-clans-of-them

בְּתוֹךְ נַחֲלַת בְּנֵי־מְנַשֶּׁה כָּל־הֶעָרִים וְחַצְרֵיהֶן׃

and-villages-of-them the-towns all-of Manasseh sons-of inheritance-of within

וְלֹא הוֹרִישׁוּ אֶת־הַכְּנַעֲנִי הַיּוֹשֵׁב בְּגָזֶר

in-Gezer the-one-living the-Canaanite *** they-dislodged but-not (10)

וַיֵּשֶׁב הַכְּנַעֲנִי בְּקֶרֶב אֶפְרַיִם עַד־הַיּוֹם הַזֶּה וַיְהִי

but-he-is the-this the-day to Ephraim in-among the-Canaanite so-he-lives

לְמַס־עֹבֵד׃ וַיְהִי הַגּוֹרָל לְמַטֵּה מְנַשֶּׁה

Manasseh for-tribe-of the-allotment and-he-was (17:1) working at-forced-labor

כִּי־הוּא בְּכוֹר יוֹסֵף לְמָכִיר בְּכוֹר מְנַשֶּׁה אֲבִי

ancestor-of Manasseh firstborn-of for-Makir Joseph firstborn-of he as

הַגִּלְעָד כִּי הוּא הָיָה אִישׁ מִלְחָמָה וַיְהִי־לוֹ הַגִּלְעָד

the-Gilead to-him and-he-was war man-of he-was he for the-Gilead

וְהַבָּשָׁן׃ וַיְהִי לִבְנֵי מְנַשֶּׁה הַנּוֹתָרִים

the-ones-remaining Manasseh for-people-of so-he-was (2) and-the-Bashan

לְמִשְׁפְּחֹתָם לִבְנֵי אֲבִיעֶזֶר וְלִבְנֵי־חֵלֶק

Helek and-for-people-of Abiezer for-people-of by-clans-of-them

וְלִבְנֵי אַשְׂרִיאֵל וְלִבְנֵי־שֶׁכֶם וְלִבְנֵי־חֵפֶר

Hepher and-for-people-of Shechem and-for-people-of Asriel and-for-people-of

וְלִבְנֵי שְׁמִידָע אֵלֶּה בְּנֵי מְנַשֶּׁה בֶּן־יוֹסֵף הַזְּכָרִים

the-males Joseph son-of Manasseh descendants-of these Shemida and-for-people-of

[4]So Manasseh and Ephraim, the descendants of Joseph, received their inheritance.

[5]This was the territory of Ephraim, clan by clan:

The boundary of their inheritance went from Ataroth Addar in the east to Upper Beth Horon [6]and continued to the sea. From Micmethath on the north it curved eastward to Taanath Shiloh, passing by it to Janoah on the east. [7]Then it went down from Janoah to Ataroth and Naarah, touched Jericho and came out at the Jordan. [8]From Tappuah the border went west to the Kanah Ravine and ended at the sea. This was the inheritance of the tribe of the Ephraimites, clan by clan. [9]It also included all the towns and their villages that were set aside for the Ephraimites within the inheritance of the Manassites.

[10]They did not dislodge the Canaanites living in Gezer; to this day the Canaanites live among the people of Ephraim but are required to do forced labor.

17 This was the allotment for the tribe of Manasseh as Joseph's firstborn, that is, for Makir, Manasseh's firstborn. Makir was the ancestor of the Gileadites, who had received Gilead and Bashan because the Makirites were great soldiers. [2]So this allotment was for the rest of the people of Manasseh—the clans of Abiezer, Helek, Asriel, Shechem, Hepher and Shemida. These are the other male descendants of Manasseh son of

לְמִשְׁפְּחֹתָם׃ וְלִצְלָפְחָד בֶּן־ חֵפֶר בֶּן־ גִּלְעָד בֶּן־
son-of Gilead son-of Hepher son-of now-to-Zelophehad (3) by-clans-of-them

מָכִיר בֶּן־ מְנַשֶּׁה לֹא־ הָיוּ לוֹ בָּנִים כִּי אִם־ בָּנוֹת וְאֵלֶּה
and-these daughters only but sons to-him they-were not Manasseh son-of Makir

שְׁמוֹת בְּנֹתָיו מַחְלָה וְנֹעָה חָגְלָה מִלְכָּה וְתִרְצָה׃
and-Tirzah Milcah Hoglah and-Noah Mahlah daughters-of-him names-of

וַתִּקְרַבְנָה לִפְנֵי אֶלְעָזָר הַכֹּהֵן וְלִפְנֵי ׀ יְהוֹשֻׁעַ בִּן־ נוּן
Nun son-of Joshua and-before the-priest Eleazar before and-they-went (4)

וְלִפְנֵי הַנְּשִׂיאִים לֵאמֹר יְהוָה צִוָּה אֶת־ מֹשֶׁה לָתֶת־ לָנוּ
to-us to-give Moses *** he-commanded Yahweh to-say the-leaders and-before

נַחֲלָה בְּתוֹךְ אַחֵינוּ וַיִּתֵּן לָהֶם אֶל־ פִּי יְהוָה
Yahweh command-of at to-them so-he-gave brothers-of-us in-among inheritance

נַחֲלָה בְּתוֹךְ אֲחֵי אֲבִיהֶן׃ וַיִּפְּלוּ
and-they-consisted (5) father-of-them brothers-of along-with inheritance

חַבְלֵי־ מְנַשֶּׁה עֲשָׂרָה לְבַד מֵאֶרֶץ הַגִּלְעָד וְהַבָּשָׁן
and-the-Bashan the-Gilead of-land-of besides ten Manasseh tracts-of-land-of

אֲשֶׁר מֵעֵבֶר לַיַּרְדֵּן׃ כִּי בְּנוֹת מְנַשֶּׁה נָחֲלוּ
they-received Manasseh daughters-of for (6) of-the-Jordan on-east that

נַחֲלָה בְּתוֹךְ בָּנָיו וְאֶרֶץ הַגִּלְעָד הָיְתָה
she-belonged the-Gilead and-land-of sons-of-him in-among inheritance

לִבְנֵי־ מְנַשֶּׁה הַנּוֹתָרִים׃ וַיְהִי גְבוּל־ מְנַשֶּׁה
Manasseh territory-of and-he-was (7) the-ones-remaining Manasseh to-sons-of

מֵאָשֵׁר הַמִּכְמְתָת אֲשֶׁר עַל־ פְּנֵי שְׁכֶם וְהָלַךְ הַגְּבוּל
the-boundary and-he-ran Shechem east-of to that the-Micmethath from-Asher

אֶל־ הַיָּמִין אֶל־ יֹשְׁבֵי עֵין תַּפּוּחַ׃ לִמְנַשֶּׁה הָיְתָה אֶרֶץ
land-of she-was for-Manasseh (8) Tappuah En ones-living-of to the-south to

תַּפּוּחַ וְתַפּוּחַ אֶל־ גְּבוּל מְנַשֶּׁה לִבְנֵי אֶפְרָיִם׃
Ephraim for-sons-of Manasseh boundary-of on but-Tappuah Tappuah

וְיָרַד הַגְּבוּל נַחַל קָנָה נֶגְבָּה לַנַּחַל
of-the-ravine to-south Kanah Ravine-of the-boundary then-he-continued (9)

עָרִים הָאֵלֶּה לְאֶפְרַיִם בְּתוֹךְ עָרֵי מְנַשֶּׁה וּגְבוּל
but-boundary-of Manasseh towns-of in-among to-Ephraim the-these towns

מְנַשֶּׁה מִצְּפוֹן לַנַּחַל וַיְהִי תֹצְאֹתָיו הַיָּמָּה׃
at-the-sea ends-of-him and-he-was of-the-ravine on-north Manasseh

נֶגְבָּה לְאֶפְרַיִם וְצָפוֹנָה לִמְנַשֶּׁה וַיְהִי הַיָּם
the-sea and-he-reached for-Manasseh and-on-north for-Ephraim on-south (10)

גְּבוּלוֹ וּבְאָשֵׁר יִפְגְּעוּן מִצָּפוֹן וּבְיִשָּׂשכָר מִמִּזְרָח׃
on-east and-on-Issachar on-north they-bordered and-on-Asher territory-of-him

Joseph by their clans.
[3]Now Zelophehad son of
Hepher, the son of Gilead, the
son of Makir, the son of
Manasseh, had no sons but
only daughters, whose names
were Mahlah, Noah, Hoglah,
Milcah and Tirzah. [4]They
went to Eleazar the priest,
Joshua son of Nun, and the
leaders and said, "The LORD
commanded Moses to give us
an inheritance among our
brothers." So Joshua gave
them an inheritance along
with the brothers of their father,
according to the LORD's
command. [5]Manasseh's share
consisted of ten tracts of land
besides Gilead and Bashan
east of the Jordan, [6]because the
daughters of the tribe of
Manasseh received an inheritance
among the sons. The
land of Gilead belonged to the
rest of the descendants of
Manasseh.
[7]The territory of Manasseh
extended from Asher to
Micmethath east of Shechem.
The boundary ran
southward from there to include
the people living at
En Tappuah. [8](Manasseh
had the land of Tappuah,
but Tappuah itself, on the
boundary of Manasseh, belonged
to the Ephraimites.)
[9]Then the boundary continued
south to the Kanah
Ravine. There were towns
belonging to Ephraim lying
among the towns of
Manasseh, but the boundary
of Manasseh was the
northern side of the ravine
and ended at the sea. [10]On
the south the land belonged
to Ephraim, on the north to
Manasseh. The territory of
Manasseh reached the sea
and bordered Asher on the
north and Issachar on the
east.

וַיְהִי לִמְנַשֶּׁה בְּיִשָּׂשכָר וּבְאָשֵׁר בֵּית־ שְׁאָן
Shan Beth and-within-Asher within-Issachar for-Manasseh and-he-was (11)

וּבְנוֹתֶיהָ וְיִבְלְעָם וּבְנוֹתֶיהָ וְאֶת־ יֹשְׁבֵי
ones-living-of and and-settlements-of-her and-Ibleam and-settlements-of-her

דֹאר וּבְנוֹתֶיהָ וְיֹשְׁבֵי עֵין־ דֹּר וּבְנֹתֶיהָ
and-settlements-of-her Dor En and-ones-living-of and-settlements-of-her Dor

וְיֹשְׁבֵי תַעְנַךְ וּבְנֹתֶיהָ וְיֹשְׁבֵי מְגִדּוֹ
Megiddo and-ones-living-of and-settlements-of-her Taanach and-ones-living-of

וּבְנוֹתֶיהָ שְׁלֹשֶׁת הַנָּפֶת׃ וְלֹא יָכְלוּ בְּנֵי
sons-of they-could yet-not (12) the-Naphoth third-of and-settlements-of-her

מְנַשֶּׁה לְהוֹרִישׁ אֶת־ הֶעָרִים הָאֵלֶּה וַיּוֹאֶל
for-he-was-determined the-these the-towns *** to-occupy Manasseh

הַכְּנַעֲנִי לָשֶׁבֶת בָּאָרֶץ הַזֹּאת׃ וַיְהִי כִּי
when and-he-was (13) the-that in-the-region to-live the-Canaanite

חָזְקוּ בְּנֵי יִשְׂרָאֵל וַיִּתְּנוּ אֶת־ הַכְּנַעֲנִי
the-Canaanite *** and-they-subjected Israel sons-of they-grew-stronger

לָמַס וְהוֹרֵשׁ לֹא הוֹרִישׁוֹ׃ וַיְדַבְּרוּ
and-they-said (14) he-drove-out-him not but-to-drive-out to-forced-labor

בְּנֵי יוֹסֵף אֶת־יְהוֹשֻׁעַ לֵאמֹר מַדּוּעַ נָתַתָּה לִּי נַחֲלָה גּוֹרָל
allotment inheritance to-me you-gave why? to-say Joshua *** Joseph people-of

אֶחָד וְחֶבֶל אֶחָד וַאֲנִי עַם־ רָב עַד אֲשֶׁר־ עַד־ כֹּה בֵּרְכַנִי
he-blessed-me so until now until numerous people yet-I one and-portion one

יְהוָה׃ וַיֹּאמֶר אֲלֵיהֶם יְהוֹשֻׁעַ אִם־ עַם־ רַב אַתָּה עֲלֵה
go-up! you numerous people if Joshua to-them and-he-answered (15) Yahweh

לְךָ הַיַּעְרָה וּבֵרֵאתָ לְךָ שָׁם בְּאֶרֶץ הַפְּרִזִּי
the-Perizzite in-land-of there for-you and-you-clear into-the-forest for-you

וְהָרְפָאִים כִּי־ אָץ לְךָ הַר־ אֶפְרָיִם׃
Ephraim hill-country-of for-you being-small if and-the-Rephaites

וַיֹּאמְרוּ בְּנֵי יוֹסֵף לֹא־ יִמָּצֵא לָנוּ הָהָר
the-hill-country for-us he-is-enough not Joseph people-of and-they-replied (16)

וְרֶכֶב בַּרְזֶל בְּכָל־ הַכְּנַעֲנִי הַיֹּשֵׁב בְּאֶרֶץ־
in-region-of the-one-living the-Canaanite among-all-of iron and-chariot-of

הָעֵמֶק לַאֲשֶׁר בְּבֵית־ שְׁאָן וּבְנוֹתֶיהָ וְלַאֲשֶׁר בְּעֵמֶק
in-Valley-of and-to-whom and-settlements-of-her Shan in-Beth to-whom the-plain

יִזְרְעֶאל׃ וַיֹּאמֶר יְהוֹשֻׁעַ אֶל־ בֵּית יוֹסֵף לְאֶפְרַיִם וְלִמְנַשֶּׁה
and-to-Manasseh to-Ephraim Joseph house-of to Joshua but-he-said (17) Jezreel

לֵאמֹר עַם־ רַב אַתָּה וְכֹחַ גָּדוֹל לָךְ לֹא־ יִהְיֶה לָךְ
for-you he-will-be not to-you great and-power you numerous people to-say

11 Within Issachar and
Asher, Manasseh also had
Beth Shan, Ibleam and the
people of Dor, Endor, Taanach and Megiddo, to-
gether with their surrounding settlements (the third
in the list is Naphoth[v]).
12 Yet the Manassites were not
able to occupy these towns, for
the Canaanites were determined to live in that region.
13 However, when the Israelites grew stronger, they subjected the Canaanites to forced
labor but did not drive them
out completely.
14 The people of Joseph said
to Joshua, "Why have you giv-
en us only one allotment and
one portion for an inheritance? We are a numerous
people and the LORD has
blessed us abundantly."
15 "If you are so numerous,"
Joshua answered, "and if the
hill country of Ephraim is too
small for you, go up into the
forest and clear land for yourselves there in the land of the
Perizzites and Rephaites."
16 The people of Joseph replied, "The hill country is not
enough for us, and all the Canaanites who live in the plain
have iron chariots, both those
in Beth Shan and its settlements and those in the Valley
of Jezreel."
17 But Joshua said to the
house of Joseph—to Ephraim
and Manasseh—"You are nu-
merous and very powerful.

[v] *11* That is, Naphoth Dor

גּוֹרָל אֶחָד׃ כִּי הַר יִהְיֶה־לָּךְ כִּי־יַעַר הוּא
that forest but for-you he-will-be hill-country but (18) one allotment

וּבֵרֵאתוֹ וְהָיָה לְךָ תֹּצְאֹתָיו כִּי־תוֹרִישׁ
you-drive-out indeed limits-of-him for-you and-he-will-be so-you-clear-him

אֶת־הַכְּנַעֲנִי כִּי רֶכֶב בַּרְזֶל לוֹ כִּי חָזָק הוּא׃
he strong though to-him iron chariot-of though the-Canaanite ***

וַיִּקָּהֲלוּ כָּל־עֲדַת בְּנֵי־יִשְׂרָאֵל שִׁלֹה
Shiloh Israel sons-of assembly-of whole-of and-they-gathered (18:1)

וַיַּשְׁכִּינוּ שָׁם אֶת־אֹהֶל מוֹעֵד וְהָאָרֶץ נִכְבְּשָׁה
she-was-controlled and-the-country Meeting Tent-of *** there and-they-set-up

לִפְנֵיהֶם׃ וַיִּוָּתְרוּ בִּבְנֵי יִשְׂרָאֵל אֲשֶׁר לֹא־חָלְקוּ
they-received not who Israel among-sons-of but-they-remained (2) before-them

אֶת־נַחֲלָתָם שִׁבְעָה שְׁבָטִים׃ וַיֹּאמֶר יְהוֹשֻׁעַ אֶל־בְּנֵי יִשְׂרָאֵל
Israel sons-of to Joshua so-he-said (3) tribes seven inheritance-of-them ***

עַד־אָנָה אַתֶּם מִתְרַפִּים לָבוֹא לָרֶשֶׁת אֶת־הָאָרֶץ אֲשֶׁר נָתַן
he-gave that the-land *** to-possess to-begin ones-waiting you how? long

לָכֶם יְהוָה אֱלֹהֵי אֲבוֹתֵיכֶם׃ הָבוּ לָכֶם שְׁלֹשָׁה אֲנָשִׁים
men three for-you appoint! (4) fathers-of-you God-of Yahweh to-you

לַשָּׁבֶט וְאֶשְׁלָחֵם וְיָקֻמוּ וְיִתְהַלְּכוּ
and-they-will-make-survey and-they-will-go and-I-will-send-them from-the-tribe

בָאָרֶץ וְיִכְתְּבוּ אוֹתָהּ לְפִי נַחֲלָתָם
inheritance-of-them by-portion-of about-her and-they-will-write of-the-land

וְיָבֹאוּ אֵלָי׃ וְהִתְחַלְּקוּ אֹתָהּ לְשִׁבְעָה חֲלָקִים יְהוּדָה
Judah parts into-seven her and-divide! (5) to-me then-they-will-return

יַעֲמֹד עַל־גְּבוּלוֹ מִנֶּגֶב וּבֵית יוֹסֵף
Joseph and-house-of on-south territory-of-him in he-will-remain

יַעַמְדוּ עַל־גְּבוּלָם מִצָּפוֹן׃ וְאַתֶּם תִּכְתְּבוּ
you-write-description and-you (6) on-north territory-of-them in they-will-remain

אֶת־הָאָרֶץ שִׁבְעָה חֲלָקִים וַהֲבֵאתֶם אֵלַי הֵנָּה וְיָרִיתִי לָכֶם
for-you and-I-will-cast here to-me then-you-bring parts seven the-land ***

גּוֹרָל פֹּה לִפְנֵי יְהוָה אֱלֹהֵינוּ׃ כִּי אֵין־חֵלֶק לַלְוִיִּם
for-the-Levites portion not but (7) God-of-us Yahweh in-presences-of here lot

בְּקִרְבְּכֶם כִּי־כְהֻנַּת יְהוָה נַחֲלָתוֹ וְגָד
and-Gad inheritance-of-him Yahweh priestly-service-of for in-among-you

וּרְאוּבֵן וַחֲצִי שֵׁבֶט הַמְנַשֶּׁה לָקְחוּ נַחֲלָתָם
inheritance-of-them they-received the-Manasseh tribe-of and-half-of and-Reuben

מֵעֵבֶר לַיַּרְדֵּן מִזְרָחָה אֲשֶׁר נָתַן לָהֶם מֹשֶׁה עֶבֶד יְהוָה׃
Yahweh servant-of Moses to-them he-gave that on-east of-the-Jordan on-side

You will have not only one allotment [18]but the forested hill country as well. Clear it, and its farthest limits will be yours; though the Canaanites have iron chariots and though they are strong, you can drive them out."

*Division of the Rest of the Land*

**18** The whole assembly of the Israelites gathered at Shiloh and set up the Tent of Meeting there. The country was brought under their control, [2]but there were still seven Israelite tribes who had not yet received their inheritance.

[3]So Joshua said to the Israelites: "How long will you wait before you begin to take possession of the land that the LORD, the God of your fathers, has given you? [4]Appoint three men from each tribe. I will send them out to make a survey of the land and to write a description of it, according to the inheritance of each. Then they will return to me. [5]You are to divide the land into seven parts. Judah is to remain in its territory on the south and the house of Joseph in its territory on the north. [6]After you have written descriptions of the seven parts of the land, bring them here to me and I will cast lots for you in the presence of the LORD our God. [7]The Levites, however, do not get a portion among you, because the priestly service of the LORD is their inheritance. And Gad, Reuben and the half-tribe of Manasseh have already received their inheritance on the east side of the Jordan. Moses the servant of the LORD gave it to them."

וַיָּקֻמוּ הָאֲנָשִׁים וַיֵּלֵכוּ וַיְצַו יְהוֹשֻׁעַ אֶת־
*** Joshua and-he-instructed and-they-went the-men and-they-started (8)

הַהֹלְכִים לִכְתֹּב אֶת־ הָאָרֶץ לֵאמֹר לְכוּ וְהִתְהַלְּכוּ בָאָרֶץ
of-the-land and-make-survey! go! to-say the-land *** to-map the-ones-going

וְכִתְבוּ אוֹתָהּ וְשׁוּבוּ אֵלַי וּפֹה אַשְׁלִיךְ לָכֶם גּוֹרָל
lot for-you I-will-cast and-here to-me then-return! about-her and-write!

לִפְנֵי יְהוָה בְּשִׁלֹה׃ וַיֵּלְכוּ הָאֲנָשִׁים וַיַּעַבְרוּ
and-they-went the-men so-they-left (9) at-Shiloh Yahweh in-presences-of

בָאָרֶץ וַיִּכְתְּבוּהָ לֶעָרִים לְשִׁבְעָה חֲלָקִים עַל־
on parts in-seven by-the-towns and-they-described-her through-the-land

סֵפֶר וַיָּבֹאוּ אֶל־ יְהוֹשֻׁעַ אֶל־ הַמַּחֲנֶה שִׁלֹה׃ וַיַּשְׁלֵךְ
then-he-cast (10) Shiloh the-camp in Joshua to and-they-returned scroll

לָהֶם יְהוֹשֻׁעַ גּוֹרָל בְּשִׁלֹה לִפְנֵי יְהוָה וַיְחַלֶּק־
and-he-distributed Yahweh in-presences-of in-Shiloh lot Joshua for-them

שָׁם יְהוֹשֻׁעַ אֶת־ הָאָרֶץ לִבְנֵי יִשְׂרָאֵל כְּמַחְלְקֹתָם׃
according-to-tribes-of-them Israel to-sons-of the-land *** Joshua there

וַיַּעַל גּוֹרַל מַטֵּה בְנֵי־ בִנְיָמִן לְמִשְׁפְּחֹתָם וַיֵּצֵא
and-he-lay by-clans-of-them Benjamin sons-of tribe-of lot and-he-came-up (11)

גְּבוּל גּוֹרָלָם בֵּין בְּנֵי יְהוּדָה וּבֵין בְּנֵי
sons-of and-between Judah sons-of between allotment-of-them territory-of

יוֹסֵף׃ וַיְהִי לָהֶם הַגְּבוּל לִפְאַת צָפוֹנָה מִן־
at on-north on-side-of the-boundary for-them and-he-began (12) Joseph

הַיַּרְדֵּן וְעָלָה הַגְּבוּל אֶל־ כֶּתֶף יְרִיחוֹ מִצָּפוֹן
on-north Jericho slope-of by the-boundary and-he-passed the-Jordan

וְעָלָה בָהָר יָמָּה וְהָיָה תֹּצְאֹתָיו
ends-of-him and-they-came-out to-west into-the-hill-country and-he-headed

מִדְבַּרָה בֵּית אָוֶן׃ וְעָבַר מִשָּׁם הַגְּבוּל לוּזָה אֶל־
to to-Luz the-boundary from-there and-he-crossed (13) Aven Beth at-desert-of

כֶּתֶף לוּזָה נֶגְבָּה הִיא בֵּית־ אֵל וְיָרַד הַגְּבוּל עַטְרוֹת
Ataroth the-boundary and-he-went-down El Beth that to-south to-Luz slope

אַדָּר עַל־ הָהָר אֲשֶׁר מִנֶּגֶב לְבֵית־חֹרוֹן תַּחְתּוֹן׃ וְתָאַר
and-he-turned (14) Lower Horon of-Beth on-south that the-hill on Addar

הַגְּבוּל וְנָסַב לִפְאַת־ יָם נֶגְבָּה מִן־ הָהָר אֲשֶׁר
that the-hill from to-south west along-side-of and-he-turned the-boundary

עַל־ פְּנֵי בֵית־ חֹרוֹן נֶגְבָּה וְהָיָה תֹצְאֹתָיו אֶל־ קִרְיַת־
Kiriath at ends-of-him and-they-came-out on-south Horon Beth face-of to

בַּעַל הִיא קִרְיַת יְעָרִים עִיר בְּנֵי יְהוּדָה זֹאת פְּאַת־ יָם׃
west side-of this Judah people-of town-of Jearim Kiriath that Baal

8 As the men started on their
way to map out the land,
Joshua instructed them, "Go
and make a survey of the land
and write a description of it.
Then return to me, and I will
cast lots for you here at Shiloh
in the presence of the LORD."
9 So the men left and went
through the land. They wrote
its description on a scroll,
town by town, in seven parts,
and returned to Joshua in the
camp at Shiloh. 10 Joshua then
cast lots for them in Shiloh in
the presence of the LORD, and
there he distributed the land
to the Israelites according to
their tribal divisions.

*Allotment for Benjamin*

11 The lot came up for the tribe
of Benjamin, clan by clan.
Their allotted territory lay between the tribes of Judah and
Joseph:

12 On the north side their
boundary began at the Jordan, passed the northern
slope of Jericho and headed
west into the hill country,
coming out at the desert of
Beth Aven. 13 From there it
crossed to the south slope of
Luz (that is, Bethel) and
went down to Ataroth Ad-
dar on the hill south of
Lower Beth Horon.

14 From the hill facing
Beth Horon on the south
the boundary turned south
along the western side and
came out at Kiriath Baal
(that is, Kiriath Jearim), a
town of the people of
Judah. This was the west-
ern side.

°12 ק והיו
°14 ק והיו

וּפְאַת־נֶגְבָּה מִקְצֵה קִרְיַת יְעָרִים וְיָצָא הַגְּבוּל
the-boundary and-he-began Jearim Kiriath outskirt-of at-south and-side-of (15)

יָמָּה וְיָצָא אֶל־מַעְיַן מֵי נֶפְתּוֹחַ׃ וְיָרַד
and-he-went-down (16) Nephtoah waters-of spring-of at and-he-came-out on-west

הַגְּבוּל אֶל־קְצֵה הָהָר אֲשֶׁר עַל־פְּנֵי גֵּי בֶן־הִנֹּם אֲשֶׁר
that Hinnom Ben Valley-of face-of at that the-hill foot-of to the-boundary

בְּעֵמֶק רְפָאִים צָפוֹנָה וְיָרַד גֵּי הִנֹּם אֶל־
along Hinnom Valley-of and-he-continued-down to-north Rephaim by-Valley-of

כֶּתֶף הַיְבוּסִי נֶגְבָּה וְיָרַד עֵין רֹגֵל׃ וְתָאַר
then-he-curved (17) Rogel En and-he-went on-south the-Jebusite slope-of

מִצָּפוֹן וְיָצָא עֵין שֶׁמֶשׁ וְיָצָא אֶל־גְּלִילוֹת אֲשֶׁר־נֹכַח
facing which Geliloth to and-he-continued Shemesh En and-he-went to-north

מַעֲלֵה אֲדֻמִּים וְיָרַד אֶבֶן בֹּהַן בֶּן־רְאוּבֵן׃ וְעָבַר
and-he-went (18) Reuben son-of Bohan Stone-of and-he-ran-down Adummim Pass-of

אֶל־כֶּתֶף מוּל־הָעֲרָבָה צָפוֹנָה וְיָרַד הָעֲרָבָתָה׃
into-the-Arabah and-he-continued on-north the-Arabah facing-of slope-of to

וְעָבַר הַגְּבוּל אֶל־כֶּתֶף בֵּית־חָגְלָה צָפוֹנָה
on-north Hoglah Beth slope-of to the-boundary then-he-went (19)

וְהָיָה ׀ תֹּצְאוֹתָיו הַגְּבוּל אֶל־לְשׁוֹן יָם־הַמֶּלַח צָפוֹנָה אֶל־
at on-north the-Salt Sea-of bay-of at the-boundary ends-of and-they-came-out

קְצֵה הַיַּרְדֵּן נֶגְבָּה זֶה גְּבוּל נֶגֶב׃ וְהַיַּרְדֵּן
and-the-Jordan (20) south boundary-of this in-south the-Jordan mouth-of

יִגְבֹּל־אֹתוֹ לִפְאַת־קֵדְמָה זֹאת נַחֲלַת בְּנֵי
sons-of inheritance-of this on-east on-side-of him he-formed-boundary

בִנְיָמִן לִגְבוּלֹתֶיהָ סָבִיב לְמִשְׁפְּחֹתָם׃ וְהָיוּ
and-they-were (21) for-clans-of-them around by-boundaries-of-her Benjamin

הֶעָרִים לְמַטֵּה בְּנֵי בִנְיָמִן לְמִשְׁפְּחוֹתֵיהֶם יְרִיחוֹ וּבֵית־
and-Beth Jericho by-clans-of-them Benjamin sons-of to-tribe-of the-cities

חָגְלָה וְעֵמֶק קְצִיץ׃ וּבֵית הָעֲרָבָה וּצְמָרַיִם וּבֵית־אֵל׃
El and-Beth and-Zemaraim the-Arabah and-Beth (22) Keziz and-Emek Hoglah

וְהָעַוִּים וְהַפָּרָה וְעָפְרָה׃ וּכְפַר הָעַמֹּנָי
the-Ammoni and-Kephar (24) and-Ophrah and-the-Parah and-the-Avvim (23)

וְהָעָפְנִי וָגָבַע עָרִים שְׁתֵּים־עֶשְׂרֵה וְחַצְרֵיהֶן׃ גִּבְעוֹן
Gibeon (25) and-villages-of-them ten two towns and-Geba and-the-Ophni

וְהָרָמָה וּבְאֵרוֹת׃ וְהַמִּצְפֶּה וְהַכְּפִירָה
and-the-Kephirah and-the-Mizpah (26) and-the-Beeroth and-the-Ramah

וְהַמֹּצָה׃ וְרֶקֶם וְיִרְפְּאֵל וְתַרְאֲלָה׃ וְצֵלַע הָאֶלֶף
Haeleph and-Zelah (28) and-Taralah and-Irpeel and-Rekem (27) and-the-Mozah

[15]The southern side be-
gan at the outskirts of
Kiriath Jearim on the west,
and the boundary came out
at the spring of the Waters
of Nephtoah. [16]The boundary went down to the foot
of the hill facing the Valley
of Ben Hinnom, north of
the Valley of Rephaim. It
continued down the Hin-
nom Valley along the
southern slope of the Jebusite city and so to En Rogel.
[17]It then curved north, went
to En Shemesh, continued
to Geliloth, which faces the
Pass of Adummim, and ran
down to the Stone of Bohan
son of Reuben. [18]It continued to the northern
slope of Beth Arabah[w] and
on down into the Arabah.
[19]It then went to the northern slope of Beth Hoglah
and came out at the northern bay of the Salt Sea,[x] at
the mouth of the Jordan in
the south. This was the
southern boundary.
[20]The Jordan formed the
boundary on the eastern
side.
These were the boundaries
that marked out the inheritance of the clans of Benjamin
on all sides.

[21]The tribe of Benjamin, clan
by clan, had the following cities:
Jericho, Beth Hoglah,
Emek Keziz, [22]Beth Arabah,
Zemaraim, Bethel, [23]Av-
vim, Parah, Ophrah, [24]Ke-
phar Ammoni, Ophni and
Geba—twelve towns and
their villages.
[25]Gibeon, Ramah,
Beeroth, [26]Mizpah, Ke-
phirah, Mozah, [27]Rekem,
Irpeel, Taralah, [28]Zelah, Haeleph, the Jebusite city (that

*w18* Septuagint; Hebrew *slope facing the Arabah*
*x19* That is, the Dead Sea

**24* The *Qere* reads *the-Ammonah;* the NIV has translated according to the Septuagint, reading *hireq* under the *nun* instead of *qamets* (ְ–ִ).

°*19a* ק והיו
°*19b* ק תצאות
°*24* ק העמנה

וְהַיְבוּסִי הִיא יְרוּשָׁלִַם גִּבְעַת קִרְיַת עָרִים אַרְבַּע־עֶשְׂרֵה
ten four towns Kiriath Gibeah Jerusalem that and-the-Jebusite

וְחַצְרֵיהֶן זֹאת נַחֲלַת בְּנֵי־ בִנְיָמִן לְמִשְׁפְּחֹתָם׃
for-clans-of-them Benjamin sons-of inheritance-of this and-villages-of-them

וַיֵּצֵא הַגּוֹרָל הַשֵּׁנִי לְשִׁמְעוֹן לְמַטֵּה בְנֵי־
sons-of for-tribe-of for-Simeon the-second the-lot and-he-came-out (19:1)

שִׁמְעוֹן לְמִשְׁפְּחוֹתָם וַיְהִי נַחֲלָתָם בְּתוֹךְ נַחֲלַת
territory-of within inheritance-of-them and-he-lay by-clans-of-them Simeon

בְּנֵי־ יְהוּדָה׃ וַיְהִי לָהֶם בְּנַחֲלָתָם בְּאֵר־ שֶׁבַע
Sheba Beer in-inheritance-of-them for-them and-he-was (2) Judah sons-of

וְשֶׁבַע וּמוֹלָדָה׃ וַחֲצַר שׁוּעָל וּבָלָה וָעָצֶם׃ וְאֶלְתּוֹלַד
and-Eltolad (4) and-Ezem and-Balah Shual and-Hazar (3) and-Moladah or-Sheba

וּבְתוּל וְחָרְמָה׃ וְצִקְלַג וּבֵית־ הַמַּרְכָּבוֹת וַחֲצַר סוּסָה׃
Susah and-Hazar the-Marcaboth and-Beth and-Ziklag (5) and-Hormah and-Bethul

וּבֵית לְבָאוֹת וְשָׁרוּחֶן עָרִים שְׁלֹשׁ־ עֶשְׂרֵה וְחַצְרֵיהֶן׃
and-villages-of-them ten three-of towns and-Sharuhen Lebaoth and-Beth (6)

עַיִן ׀ רִמּוֹן וָעֶתֶר וְעָשָׁן עָרִים אַרְבַּע וְחַצְרֵיהֶן׃
and-villages-of-them four towns and-Ashan and-Ether Rimmon Ain (7)

וְכָל־ הַחֲצֵרִים אֲשֶׁר סְבִיבוֹת הֶעָרִים הָאֵלֶּה עַד־
as-far-as the-these the-towns ones-around that the-villages and-all-of (8)

בַּעֲלַת בְּאֵר רָאמַת נֶגֶב זֹאת נַחֲלַת מַטֵּה בְנֵי־ שִׁמְעוֹן
Simeon sons-of tribe-of inheritance-of this Negev Ramah-of Beer Baalath

לְמִשְׁפְּחֹתָם׃ מֵחֶבֶל בְּנֵי יְהוּדָה נַחֲלַת בְּנֵי
sons-of inheritance-of Judah sons-of from-share-of (9) by-clans-of-them

שִׁמְעוֹן כִּי־ הָיָה חֵלֶק בְּנֵי־ יְהוּדָה רַב מֵהֶם וַיִּנְחֲלוּ
so-they-inherited for-them too-much Judah sons-of portion-of he-was for Simeon

בְנֵי־ שִׁמְעוֹן בְּתוֹךְ נַחֲלָתָם׃ וַיַּעַל הַגּוֹרָל
the-lot and-he-came-up (10) territory-of-them within Simeon sons-of

הַשְּׁלִישִׁי לִבְנֵי זְבוּלֻן לְמִשְׁפְּחֹתָם וַיְהִי גְּבוּל
boundary-of and-he-went by-clans-of-them Zebulun for-sons-of the-third

נַחֲלָתָם עַד־ שָׂרִיד׃ וְעָלָה גְבוּלָם ׀
boundary-of-them and-he-went (11) Sarid as-far-as inheritance-of-them

לַיָּמָּה וּמַרְעֲלָה וּפָגַע בְּדַבָּשֶׁת וּפָגַע
and-he-extended on-Dabbesheth and-he-touched and-to-Maralah to-the-west

אֶל־ הַנַּחַל אֲשֶׁר עַל־ פְּנֵי יָקְנְעָם׃ וְשָׁב מִשָּׂרִיד
from-Sarid and-he-turned (12) Jokneam areas-of near that the-ravine to

קֵדְמָה מִזְרַח הַשֶּׁמֶשׁ עַל־ גְּבוּל כִּסְלֹת תָּבֹר וְיָצָא אֶל־
to and-he-went-on Tabor Kisloth territory-of to the-sun rise-of to-east

is, Jerusalem), Gibeah and
Kiriath—fourteen towns
and their villages.
This was the inheritance of
Benjamin for its clans.

*Allotment for Simeon*

19 The second lot came
out for the tribe of
Simeon, clan by clan. Their inheritance lay within the territory of Judah. 2It included:
Beersheba (or Sheba),[y]
Moladah, 3Hazar Shual,
Balah, Ezem, 4Eltolad,
Bethul, Hormah, 5Ziklag,
Beth Marcaboth, Hazar
Susah, 6Beth Lebaoth and
Sharuhen—thirteen towns
and their villages;
7Ain, Rimmon, Ether and
Ashan—four towns and
their villages— 8and all the
villages around these
towns as far as Baalath Beer
(Ramah in the Negev).
This was the inheritance of
the tribe of the Simeonites,
clan by clan. 9The inheritance
of the Simeonites was taken
from the share of Judah, because Judah's portion was
more than they needed. So the
Simeonites received their inheritance within the territory
of Judah.

*Allotment for Zebulun*

10The third lot came up for
Zebulun, clan by clan:
The boundary of their in-
heritance went as far as Sarid. 11Going west it ran to
Maralah, touched Dab-
besheth, and extended to
the ravine near Jokneam.
12It turned east from Sarid
toward the sunrise to the
territory of Kisloth Tabor
and went on to Daberath

y2 Or *Beersheba, Sheba;* 1 Chronicles 4:28 does not have *Sheba.*

הַדָּבְרַת וְעָלָה יָפִיעַ׃ וּמִשָּׁם עָבַר קֵדְמָה
to-east he-continued then-from-there (13) Japhia and-he-went-up the-Daberath

מִזְרָחָה גִּתָּה חֵפֶר עִתָּה קָצִין וְיָצָא רִמּוֹן הַמְּתֹאָר
the-one-turning Rimmon and-he-came-out Kazin to-Eth Hepher to-Gath to-east

הַנֵּעָה׃ וְנָסַב אֹתוֹ הַגְּבוּל מִצְּפוֹן חַנָּתֹן
Hannathon on-north-of the-boundary him then-he-went-around (14) the-Neah

וְהָיוּ תֹּצְאֹתָיו גֵּי יִפְתַּח־אֵל׃ וְקַטָּת וְנַהֲלָל
and-Nahalal and-Kattath (15) El Iphtah Valley-of ends-of-him and-they-were

וְשִׁמְרוֹן וְיִדְאֲלָה וּבֵית לָחֶם עָרִים שְׁתֵּים־עֶשְׂרֵה וְחַצְרֵיהֶן׃
and-villages-of-them ten two towns Lehem and-Beth and-Idalah and-Shimron

זֹאת נַחֲלַת בְּנֵי־זְבוּלֻן לְמִשְׁפְּחוֹתָם הֶעָרִים הָאֵלֶּה
the-these the-towns clans-of-them Zebulun sons-of inheritance-of this (16)

וְחַצְרֵיהֶן׃ לְיִשָּׂשכָר יָצָא הַגּוֹרָל הָרְבִיעִי
the-fourth the-lot he-came-out for-Issachar (17) and-villages-of-them

לִבְנֵי יִשָּׂשכָר לְמִשְׁפְּחוֹתָם׃ וַיְהִי גְּבוּלָם
territory-of-them and-he-was (18) by-clans-of-them Issachar for-sons-of

יִזְרְעֶאלָה וְהַכְּסוּלֹּת וְשׁוּנֵם׃ וַחֲפָרַיִם וְשִׁיאֹן
and-Shion and-Hapharaim (19) and-Shunem and-the-Kesulloth to-Jezreel

וַאֲנָחֲרַת׃ וְהָרַבִּית וְקִשְׁיוֹן וָאָבֶץ׃ וְרֶמֶת
and-Remeth (21) and-Ebez and-Kishion and-the-Rabbith (20) and-Anaharath

וְעֵין־גַּנִּים וְעֵין חַדָּה וּבֵית פַּצֵּץ׃ וּפָגַע הַגְּבוּל
the-boundary and-he-touched (22) Pazzez and-Beth Haddah and-En Gannim and-En

בְּתָבוֹר וְשַׁחֲצוּמָה* וּבֵית שֶׁמֶשׁ וְהָיוּ תֹּצְאוֹת
ends-of and-they-were Shemesh and-Beth and-Shahazumah on-Tabor

גְּבוּלָם הַיַּרְדֵּן עָרִים שֵׁשׁ־עֶשְׂרֵה וְחַצְרֵיהֶן׃ זֹאת
this (23) and-villages-of-them ten six towns the-Jordan boundary-of-them

נַחֲלַת מַטֵּה בְנֵי־יִשָּׂשכָר לְמִשְׁפְּחֹתָם הֶעָרִים
the-towns by-clans-of-them Issachar sons-of tribe-of inheritance-of

וְחַצְרֵיהֶן׃ וַיֵּצֵא הַגּוֹרָל הַחֲמִישִׁי לְמַטֵּה
for-tribe-of the-fifth the-lot and-he-came-out (24) and-villages-of-them

בְנֵי־אָשֵׁר לְמִשְׁפְּחוֹתָם׃ וַיְהִי גְּבוּלָם חֶלְקַת
Helkath territory-of-them and-he-was (25) by-clans-of-them Asher sons-of

וַחֲלִי וָבֶטֶן וְאַכְשָׁף׃ וְאַלַּמֶּלֶךְ וְעַמְעָד וּמִשְׁאָל
and-Mishal and-Amad and-Allammelech (26) and-Acshaph and-Beten and-Hali

וּפָגַע בְּכַרְמֶל הַיָּמָּה וּבְשִׁיחוֹר לִבְנָת׃ וְשָׁב
and-he-turned (27) Libnath and-on-Shihor on-the-west on-Carmel and-he-touched

מִזְרַח הַשֶּׁמֶשׁ בֵּית דָּגֹן וּפָגַע בִּזְבֻלוּן וּבְגֵי יִפְתַּח־
Iphtah and-on-Valley-of on-Zebulun and-he-touched Dagon Beth the-sun rise-of

and up to Japhia. [13]Then it
continued eastward to Gath
Hepher and Eth Kazin; it
came out at Rimmon and
turned toward Neah.
[14]There the boundary went
around on the north to
Hannathon and ended at
the Valley of Iphtah El. [15]In-
cluded were Kattath, Na-
halal, Shimron, Idalah and
Bethlehem. There were
twelve towns and their villages.
[16]These towns and their villages were the inheritance of
Zebulun, clan by clan.

*Allotment for Issachar*

[17]The fourth lot came out for
Issachar, clan by clan. [18]Their
territory included:
Jezreel, Kesulloth, Shu-
nem, [19]Hapharaim, Shion,
Anaharath, [20]Rabbith,
Kishion, Ebez, [21]Remeth,
En Gannim, En Haddah
and Beth Pazzez. [22]The
boundary touched Tabor,
Shahazumah and Beth She-
mesh, and ended at the Jordan. There were sixteen
towns and their villages.
[23]These towns and their villages were the inheritance of
the tribe of Issachar, clan by
clan.

*Allotment for Asher*

[24]The fifth lot came out for the
tribe of Asher, clan by clan.
[25]Their territory included:
Helkath, Hali, Beten, Ac-
shaph, [26]Allammelech,
Amad and Mishal. On the
west the boundary touched
Carmel and Shihor Lib-
nath. [27]It then turned east
toward Beth Dagon,
touched Zebulun and the
Valley of Iphtah El, and

*22 Most mss have no *hireq* under the *tsade* and point the *vav* as *shureq* (צוּ—); thus, the *Kethib* reads *and-Shahazumah* and the *Qere* reads *and-Shahazimah*.

°22 ק ושחצימה

אֶל צָפוֹנָה בֵּית הָעֵמֶק וּנְעִיאֵל וְיָצָא אֶל־ כָּבוּל מִשְּׂמֹאל׃

on-left Cabul by and-he-passed and-Neiel the-Emek Beth on-north El

וְעֶבְרֹן וּרְחֹב וְחַמּוֹן וְקָנָה עַד צִידוֹן רַבָּה׃

Greater Sidon as-far-as and-Kanah and-Hammon and-Rehob and-Ebron (28)

וְשָׁב הַגְּבוּל הָרָמָה וְעַד־ עִיר מִבְצַר־ צֹר

Tyre fortified city-of and-to the-Ramah the-boundary then-he-turned (29)

וְשָׁב הַגְּבוּל חֹסָה וְיִהְיוּ° תֹצְאֹתָיו הַיָּמָּה

at-the-sea ends-of-him and-they-came-out Hosah the-boundary and-he-turned

מֵחֶבֶל אַכְזִיבָה׃ וְעֻמָה* וַאֲפֵק וּרְחֹב עָרִים עֶשְׂרִים

twenty towns and-Rehob and-Aphek and-Ummah (30) at-Aczib in-region-of

וּשְׁתַּיִם וְחַצְרֵיהֶן׃ זֹאת נַחֲלַת מַטֵּה בְנֵי־ אָשֵׁר

Asher sons-of tribe-of inheritance-of this (31) and-villages-of-them and-two

לְמִשְׁפְּחֹתָם הֶעָרִים הָאֵלֶּה וְחַצְרֵיהֶן׃ לִבְנֵי

for-sons-of (32) and-villages-of-them the-these the-towns by-clans-of-them

נַפְתָּלִי יָצָא הַגּוֹרָל הַשִּׁשִּׁי לִבְנֵי נַפְתָּלִי לְמִשְׁפְּחֹתָם׃

by-clans-of-them Naphtali for-sons-of the-sixth the-lot he-came-out Naphtali

וַיְהִי גְבוּלָם מֵחֵלֶף מֵאֵלוֹן בְּצַעֲנַנִּים

in-Zaanannim from-large-tree from-Heleph boundary-of-them and-he-went (33)

וַאֲדָמִי הַנֶּקֶב וְיַבְנְאֵל עַד־ לַקּוּם וַיְהִי תֹצְאֹתָיו הַיַּרְדֵּן׃

the-Jordan ends-of-him and-he-was Lakkum to and-Jabneel the-Nekeb and-Adami

וְשָׁב הַגְּבוּל יָמָּה אַזְנוֹת תָּבוֹר וְיָצָא מִשָּׁם

from-there and-he-came-out Tabor Aznoth to-west the-boundary and-he-ran (34)

חוּקֹקָה וּפָגַע בִּזְבֻלוּן מִנֶּגֶב וּבְאָשֵׁר פָּגַע מִיָּם

on-west he-touched and-on-Asher on-south on-Zebulun and-he-touched at-Hukkok

וּבִיהוּדָה הַיַּרְדֵּן מִזְרַח הַשָּׁמֶשׁ׃ וְעָרֵי מִבְצָר

fortified and-cities-of (35) the-sun rise-of the-Jordan and-on-Judah

הַצִּדִּים צֵר וְחַמַּת רַקַּת וְכִנָּרֶת׃ וַאֲדָמָה וְהָרָמָה

and-the-Ramah and-Adamah (36) and-Kinnereth Rakkath and-Hamath Zer the-Ziddim

וְחָצוֹר׃ וְקֶדֶשׁ וְאֶדְרֶעִי וְעֵין חָצוֹר׃ וְיִרְאוֹן וּמִגְדַּל־

and-Migdal and-Iron (38) Hazor and-En and-Edrei and-Kedesh (37) and-Hazor

אֵל חֳרֵם וּבֵית־עֲנָת וּבֵית שָׁמֶשׁ עָרִים תְּשַׁע־עֶשְׂרֵה וְחַצְרֵיהֶן׃

and-villages-of-them ten nine-of towns Shemesh and-Beth Anath and-Beth Horem El

זֹאת נַחֲלַת מַטֵּה בְנֵי־ נַפְתָּלִי לְמִשְׁפְּחֹתָם הֶעָרִים

the-towns by-clans-of-them Naphtali sons-of tribe-of inheritance-of this (39)

וְחַצְרֵיהֶן׃ לְמַטֵּה בְנֵי־ דָן לְמִשְׁפְּחֹתָם

by-clans-of-them Dan sons-of for-tribe-of (40) and-villages-of-them

יָצָא הַגּוֹרָל הַשְּׁבִיעִי׃ וַיְהִי גְּבוּל

territory-of and-he-was (41) the-seventh the-lot he-came-out

went north to Beth Emek and Neiel, passing Cabul on the left. 28It went to Abdon,[z] Rehob, Hammon and Kanah, as far as Greater Sidon. 29The boundary then turned back toward Ramah and went to the fortified city of Tyre, turned toward Hosah and came out at the sea in the region of Aczib, 30Ummah, Aphek and Rehob. There were twenty-two towns and their villages.

31These towns and their villages were the inheritance of the tribe of Asher, clan by clan.

*Allotment for Naphtali*

32The sixth lot came out for Naphtali, clan by clan:

33Their boundary went from Heleph and the large tree in Zaanannim, passing Adami Nekeb and Jabneel to Lakkum and ending at the Jordan. 34The boundary ran west through Aznoth Tabor and came out at Hukkok. It touched Zebulun on the south, Asher on the west and the Jordan[a] on the east. 35The fortified cities were Ziddim, Zer, Hammath, Rakkath, Kinnereth, 36Adamah, Ramah, Hazor, 37Kedesh, Edrei, En Hazor, 38Iron, Migdal El, Horem, Beth Anath and Beth Shemesh. There were nineteen towns and their villages.

39These towns and their villages were the inheritance of the tribe of Naphtali, clan by clan.

*Allotment for Dan*

40The seventh lot came out for the tribe of Dan, clan by clan. 41The territory of their inheritance included:

[z] *28* Some Hebrew manuscripts (see also Joshua 21:30); most Hebrew manuscripts *Ebron*
[a] *34* Septuagint; Hebrew *west, and Judah, the Jordan,*

******30* Most mss have *dagesh* in the *mem* (מ׳–).

°*29* ק והיו

נַחֲלָתָם צָרְעָה וְאֶשְׁתָּאוֹל וְעִיר שָׁמֶשׁ׃ וְשַׁעֲלַבִּין
and-Shaalabbin (42) Shemesh and-Ir and-Eshtaol Zorah inheritance-of-them

וְאַיָּלוֹן וְיִתְלָה׃ וְאֵילוֹן וְתִמְנָתָה וְעֶקְרוֹן׃ וְאֶלְתְּקֵה
and-Eltekeh (44) and-Ekron and-at-Timnah and-Elon (43) and-Ithlah and-Aijalon

וְגִבְּתוֹן וּבַעֲלָת׃ וִיהֻד וּבְנֵי־ בְרַק וְגַת־ רִמּוֹן׃
Rimmon and-Gath Berak and-Bene and-Jehud (45) and-Baalath and-Gibbethon

וּמֵי הַיַּרְקוֹן וְהָרַקּוֹן עִם־ הַגְּבוּל מוּל יָפוֹ׃
Joppa facing the-area with and-the-Rakkon the-Jarkon and-Me (46)

וַיֵּצֵא גְבוּל־ בְּנֵי־ דָן מֵהֶם וַיַּעֲלוּ
so-they-went-up from-them Dan sons-of territory-of but-he-went-out (47)

בְנֵי־ דָן וַיִּלָּחֲמוּ עִם־ לֶשֶׁם וַיִּלְכְּדוּ אוֹתָהּ | וַיַּכּוּ
and-they-put her and-they-took Leshem against and-they-attacked Dan sons-of

אוֹתָהּ לְפִי־ חֶרֶב וַיִּרְשׁוּ אוֹתָהּ וַיֵּשְׁבוּ בָהּ
in-her and-they-settled her and-they-occupied sword to-edge-of her

וַיִּקְרְאוּ לְלֶשֶׁם דָּן כְּשֵׁם דָּן אֲבִיהֶם׃ זֹאת
this (48) forefather-of-them Dan after-name-of Dan to-Leshem and-they-named

נַחֲלַת מַטֵּה בְנֵי־ דָן לְמִשְׁפְּחֹתָם הֶעָרִים הָאֵלֶּה
the-these the-towns by-clans-of-them Dan sons-of tribe-of inheritance-of

וְחַצְרֵיהֶן׃ וַיְכַלּוּ לִנְחֹל־ אֶת־ הָאָרֶץ
the-land *** to-divide when-they-finished (49) and-villages-of-them

לִגְבוּלֹתֶיהָ וַיִּתְּנוּ בְנֵי־ יִשְׂרָאֵל נַחֲלָה לִיהוֹשֻׁעַ
to-Joshua inheritance Israel sons-of then-they-gave into-portions-of-her

בִּן־ נוּן בְּתוֹכָם׃ עַל־ פִּי יְהוָה נָתְנוּ לוֹ אֶת־
*** to-him they-gave Yahweh command-of at (50) in-among-them Nun son-of

הָעִיר אֲשֶׁר שָׁאָל אֶת־ תִּמְנַת־ סֶרַח בְּהַר אֶפְרָיִם
Ephraim in-hill-country-of Serah Timnath *** he-asked-for which the-town

וַיִּבְנֶה אֶת־ הָעִיר וַיֵּשֶׁב בָּהּ׃ אֵלֶּה הַנְּחָלֹת
the-territories these (51) in-her and-he-settled the-town *** and-he-built-up

אֲשֶׁר נִחֲלוּ אֶלְעָזָר הַכֹּהֵן | וִיהוֹשֻׁעַ בִּן־ נוּן וְרָאשֵׁי
and-heads-of Nun son-of and-Joshua the-priest Eleazar they-assigned that

הָאָבוֹת לְמַטּוֹת בְּנֵי־ יִשְׂרָאֵל | בְּגוֹרָל | בְּשִׁלֹה לִפְנֵי
in-presences-of at-Shiloh by-lot Israel sons-of of-tribes-of the-fathers

יְהוָה פֶּתַח אֹהֶל מוֹעֵד וַיְכַלּוּ מֵחַלֵּק אֶת־
*** from-to-divide so-they-finished Meeting Tent-of entrance-of Yahweh

הָאָרֶץ׃ וַיְדַבֵּר יְהוָה אֶל־ יְהוֹשֻׁעַ לֵאמֹר׃ דַּבֵּר אֶל־
to tell! (2) to-say Joshua to Yahweh then-he-spoke (20:1) the-land

בְּנֵי יִשְׂרָאֵל לֵאמֹר תְּנוּ לָכֶם אֶת־ עָרֵי הַמִּקְלָט אֲשֶׁר־
as the-refuge cities-of *** for-you designate! to-say Israel sons-of

Zorah, Eshtaol, Ir Shemesh, [42]Shaalabbin, Aijalon, Ithlah, [43]Elon, Timnah, Ekron, [44]Eltekeh, Gibbethon, Baalath, [45]Jehud, Bene Berak, Gath Rimmon, [46]Me Jarkon and Rakkon, with the area facing Joppa.

[47](But the Danites had difficulty taking possession of their territory, so they went up and attacked Leshem, took it, put it to the sword and occupied it. They settled in Leshem and named it Dan after their forefather.)

[48]These towns and their villages were the inheritance of the tribe of Dan, clan by clan.

*Allotment for Joshua*

[49]When they had finished dividing the land into its allotted portions, the Israelites gave Joshua son of Nun an inheritance among them, [50]as the LORD had commanded. They gave him the town he asked for—Timnath Serah[b] in the hill country of Ephraim. And he built up the town and settled there.

[51]These are the territories that Eleazar the priest, Joshua son of Nun and the heads of the tribal clans of Israel assigned by lot at Shiloh in the presence of the LORD at the entrance to the Tent of Meeting. And so they finished dividing the land.

*Cities of Refuge*

**20** Then the LORD said to Joshua: [2]"Tell the Israelites to designate the cities of

[b]50 Also known as *Timnath Heres* (see Judges 2:9)

דִּבַּרְתִּי אֲלֵיכֶם בְּיַד־ מֹשֶׁה׃ לָנוּס שָׁמָּה רוֹצֵחַ
I-instructed to-you by-hand-of Moses (3) to-flee to-there one-killing

מַכֵּה־ נֶפֶשׁ בִּשְׁגָגָה בִּבְלִי־ דָעַת וְהָיוּ לָכֶם
one-killing-of person by-accident without intention so-they-may-be for-you

לְמִקְלָט מִגֹּאֵל הַדָּם׃ וְנָס אֶל־ אַחַת ׀
for-protection from-one-avenging-of the-blood (4) when-he-flees to one-of

מֵהֶעָרִים הָאֵלֶּה וְעָמַד פֶּתַח שַׁעַר הָעִיר
from-the-cities the-these then-he-must-stand entrance-of gate-of the-city

וְדִבֶּר בְּאָזְנֵי זִקְנֵי הָעִיר־ הַהִיא אֶת־ דְּבָרָיו
and-he-must-state in-ears-of elders-of the-city the-that *** cases-of-him

וְאָסְפוּ אֹתוֹ הָעִירָה אֲלֵיהֶם וְנָתְנוּ־ לוֹ
then-they-must-admit him into-the-city to-them and-they-must-give to-him

מָקוֹם וְיָשַׁב עִמָּם׃ וְכִי יִרְדֹּף גֹּאֵל
place so-he-can-live with-them (5) and-if he-pursues one-avenging-of

הַדָּם אַחֲרָיו וְלֹא־ יַסְגִּרוּ אֶת־ הָרֹצֵחַ
the-blood after-him then-not they-must-surrender *** the-one-killing

בְּיָדוֹ כִּי בִבְלִי־ דַעַת הִכָּה אֶת־ רֵעֵהוּ וְלֹא־
into-hand-of-him for without intention he-killed *** neighbor-of-him and-not

שֹׂנֵא הוּא לוֹ מִתְּמוֹל שִׁלְשׁוֹם׃ וְיָשַׁב ׀
having-malice he against-him on-yesterday before (6) and-he-must-stay

בָּעִיר הַהִיא עַד־ עָמְדוֹ לִפְנֵי הָעֵדָה לַמִּשְׁפָּט
in-the-city the-that until to-stand-him before the-assembly for-the-trial

עַד־ מוֹת הַכֹּהֵן הַגָּדוֹל אֲשֶׁר יִהְיֶה בַּיָּמִים הָהֵם אָז ׀
until death-of the-priest the-high who he-is in-the-days the-those then

יָשׁוּב הָרוֹצֵחַ וּבָא אֶל־ עִירוֹ וְאֶל־
he-may-go-back the-one-killing and-he-may-go to town-of-him and-to

בֵּיתוֹ אֶל־ הָעִיר אֲשֶׁר־ נָס מִשָּׁם׃ וַיַּקְדִּשׁוּ אֶת־
home-of-him in the-town which he-fled from-there (7) so-they-set-apart ***

קֶדֶשׁ בַּגָּלִיל בְּהַר נַפְתָּלִי וְאֶת־ שְׁכֶם בְּהַר
Kedesh in-the-Galilee in-hill-country-of Naphtali and Shechem in-hill-country-of

אֶפְרַיִם וְאֶת־קִרְיַת אַרְבַּע הִיא חֶבְרוֹן בְּהַר יְהוּדָה׃ וּמֵעֵבֶר
Ephraim and Kiriath Arba that Hebron in-hill-country-of Judah (8) and-on-side

לְיַרְדֵּן יְרִיחוֹ מִזְרָחָה נָתְנוּ אֶת־ בֶּצֶר בַּמִּדְבָּר
of-Jordan-of Jericho on-east they-designated *** Bezer in-the-desert

בַּמִּישֹׁר מִמַּטֵּה רְאוּבֵן וְאֶת־ רָאמֹת בַּגִּלְעָד מִמַּטֵּה־ גָד
on-the-plateau in-tribe-of Reuben and Ramoth in-the-Gilead in-tribe-of Gad

וְאֶת־ גֹּלָן בַּבָּשָׁן מִמַּטֵּה מְנַשֶּׁה׃ אֵלֶּה הָיוּ עָרֵי
and Golan in-the-Bashan in-tribe-of Manasseh (9) these they-were cities-of

refuge, as I instructed you through Moses, [3]so that anyone who kills a person accidentally and unintentionally may flee there and find protection from the avenger of blood.

[4]"When he flees to one of these cities, he is to stand in the entrance of the city gate and state his case before the elders of that city. Then they are to admit him into their city and give him a place to live with them. [5]If the avenger of blood pursues him, they must not surrender the one accused, because he killed his neighbor unintentionally and without malice aforethought. [6]He is to stay in that city until he has stood trial before the assembly and until the death of the high priest who is serving at that time. Then he may go back to his own home in the town from which he fled."

[7]So they set apart Kedesh in Galilee in the hill country of Naphtali, Shechem in the hill country of Ephraim, and Kiriath Arba (that is, Hebron) in the hill country of Judah. [8]On the east side of the Jordan of Jericho[c] they designated Bezer in the desert on the plateau in the tribe of Reuben, Ramoth in Gilead in the tribe of Gad, and Golan in Bashan in the tribe of Manasseh. [9]Any

[c]8 *Jordan of Jericho* was possibly an ancient name for the Jordan River.

°8 ק גולן

הַמּוּעָדָה לְכֹל ׀ בְּנֵי יִשְׂרָאֵל וְלַגֵּר הַגָּר
the-one-living or-for-the-alien Israel sons-of for-any-of the-designated

בְּתוֹכָם לָנוּס שָׁמָּה כָּל־ מַכֵּה־ נֶפֶשׁ בִּשְׁגָגָה
by-accident person one-killing-of any-of to-there to-flee in-among-them

וְלֹא יָמוּת בְּיַד גֹּאֵל הַדָּם עַד־
prior the-blood one-avenging-of by-hand-of he-would-be-killed so-not

עָמְדוֹ לִפְנֵי הָעֵדָה׃ וַיִּגְּשׁוּ רָאשֵׁי
heads-of now-they-approached (21:1) the-assembly before to-stand-him

אֲבוֹת הַלְוִיִּם אֶל־אֶלְעָזָר הַכֹּהֵן וְאֶל־ יְהוֹשֻׁעַ בִּן־ נוּן וְאֶל־
and-to Nun son-of Joshua and-to the-priest Eleazar to the-Levites fathers-of

רָאשֵׁי אֲבוֹת הַמַּטּוֹת לִבְנֵי יִשְׂרָאֵל׃ וַיְדַבְּרוּ אֲלֵיהֶם
to-them and-they-spoke (2) Israel of-sons-of the-tribes fathers-of heads-of

בְּשִׁלֹה בְּאֶרֶץ כְּנַעַן לֵאמֹר יְהוָה צִוָּה בְיַד־ מֹשֶׁה
Moses by-hand-of he-commanded Yahweh to-say Canaan in-land-of at-Shiloh

לָתֶת־ לָנוּ עָרִים לָשָׁבֶת וּמִגְרְשֵׁיהֶן לִבְהֶמְתֵּנוּ׃
for-livestock-of-us and-pasturelands-of-them to-live towns to-us to-give

וַיִּתְּנוּ בְנֵי־ יִשְׂרָאֵל לַלְוִיִּם מִנַּחֲלָתָם אֶל־
at from-inheritance-of-them to-the-Levites Israel sons-of so-they-gave (3)

פִּי יְהוָה אֶת־ הֶעָרִים הָאֵלֶּה וְאֶת־ מִגְרְשֵׁיהֶן׃
pasturelands-of-them and the-these the-towns *** Yahweh command-of

וַיֵּצֵא הַגּוֹרָל לְמִשְׁפְּחֹת הַקְּהָתִי וַיְהִי לִבְנֵי
for-sons-of and-he-was the-Kohathite for-clans-of the-lot and-he-came-out (4)

אַהֲרֹן הַכֹּהֵן מִן־ הַלְוִיִּם מִמַּטֵּה יְהוּדָה וּמִמַּטֵּה
and-from-tribe-of Judah from-tribe-of the-Levites from the-priest Aaron

הַשִּׁמְעֹנִי וּמִמַּטֵּה בִנְיָמִן בַּגּוֹרָל עָרִים שְׁלֹשׁ עֶשְׂרֵה׃
ten three-of towns by-the-lot Benjamin and-from-tribe-of the-Simeonite

וְלִבְנֵי קְהָת הַנּוֹתָרִים מִמִּשְׁפְּחֹת מַטֵּה־ אֶפְרַיִם
Ephraim tribe-of from-clans-of the-ones-remaining Kohath and-for-sons-of (5)

וּמִמַּטֵּה־ דָן וּמֵחֲצִי מַטֵּה מְנַשֶּׁה בַּגּוֹרָל עָרִים
towns by-the-lot Manasseh tribe-of and-from-half-of Dan and-from-tribe-of

עָשֶׂר׃ וְלִבְנֵי גֵרְשׁוֹן מִמִּשְׁפְּחוֹת מַטֵּה־ יִשָּׂשכָר
Issachar tribe-of from-clans-of Gershon and-for-sons-of (6) ten

וּמִמַּטֵּה־ אָשֵׁר וּמִמַּטֵּה נַפְתָּלִי וּמֵחֲצִי מַטֵּה
tribe-of and-from-half-of Naphtali and-from-tribe-of Asher and-from-tribe-of

מְנַשֶּׁה בַבָּשָׁן בַּגּוֹרָל עָרִים שְׁלֹשׁ עֶשְׂרֵה׃ לִבְנֵי מְרָרִי
Merari for-sons-of (7) ten three-of towns by-the-lot in-the-Bashan Manasseh

לְמִשְׁפְּחֹתָם מִמַּטֵּה רְאוּבֵן וּמִמַּטֵּה־ גָד וּמִמַּטֵּה
and-from-tribe-of Gad and-from-tribe-of Reuben from-tribe-of by-clans-of-them

of the Israelites or any alien living among them who killed someone accidentally could flee to these designated cities and not be killed by the avenger of blood prior to standing trial before the assembly.

*Towns for the Levites*

21 Now the family heads of the Levites approached Eleazar the priest, Joshua son of Nun, and the heads of the other tribal families of Israel [2]at Shiloh in Canaan and said to them, "The LORD commanded through Moses that you give us towns to live in, with pasturelands for our livestock." [3]So, as the LORD had commanded, the Israelites gave the Levites the following towns and pasturelands out of their own inheritance:

[4]The first lot came out for the Kohathites, clan by clan. The Levites who were descendants of Aaron the priest were allotted thirteen towns from the tribes of Judah, Simeon and Benjamin. [5]The rest of Kohath's descendants were allotted ten towns from the clans of the tribes of Ephraim, Dan and half of Manasseh.

[6]The descendants of Gershon were allotted thirteen towns from the clans of the tribes of Issachar, Asher, Naphtali and the half-tribe of Manasseh in Bashan.

[7]The descendants of Merari, clan by clan, received twelve towns from the tribes of Reuben, Gad and Zebulun.

זְבוּלֻ֔ן עָרִ֖ים שְׁתֵּ֥ים עֶשְׂרֵֽה׃ וַיִּתְּנ֤וּ בְנֵֽי־יִשְׂרָאֵל֙ לַלְוִיִּ֔ם אֶת־
*** to-the-Levites Israel sons-of so-they-gave (8) ten two towns Zebulun

הֶעָרִ֣ים הָאֵ֔לֶּה וְאֶת־מִגְרְשֵׁיהֶ֑ן כַּאֲשֶׁ֨ר צִוָּ֧ה יְהוָ֛ה
Yahweh he-commanded just-as pasturelands-of-them and the-these the-towns

בְּיַד־מֹשֶׁ֖ה בַּגּוֹרָֽל׃ וַֽיִּתְּנ֗וּ מִמַּטֵּה֙ בְּנֵ֣י יְהוּדָ֔ה
Judah sons-of from-tribe-of and-they-allotted (9) by-the-lot Moses by-hand-of

וּמִמַּטֵּ֖ה בְּנֵ֣י שִׁמְע֑וֹן אֵ֚ת הֶעָרִ֣ים הָאֵ֔לֶּה אֲשֶׁר־יִקְרָ֥א
he-called which the-these the-towns *** Simeon sons-of and-from-tribe-of

אֶתְהֶ֖ן בְּשֵֽׁם׃ וַֽיְהִי֙ לִבְנֵ֣י אַהֲרֹ֔ן מִמִּשְׁפְּח֥וֹת הַקְּהָתִ֖י
the-Kohathite from-clans-of Aaron to-sons-of and-he-was (10) by-name them

מִבְּנֵ֣י לֵוִ֑י כִּ֥י לָהֶ֛ם הָיָ֥ה הַגּוֹרָ֖ל רִאישֹׁנָֽה׃ וַיִּתְּנ֨וּ לָהֶ֜ם אֶת־
*** to-them and-they-gave (11) first the-lot he-fell to-them for Levi from-sons-of

קִרְיַ֨ת אַרְבַּ֜ע אֲבִ֧י הָעֲנ֛וֹק הִ֥יא חֶבְר֖וֹן בְּהַ֣ר יְהוּדָ֑ה
Judah in-hill-country-of Hebron that the-Anak forefather-of Arba Kiriath

וְאֶת־מִגְרָשֶׁ֖הָ סְבִיבֹתֶֽיהָ׃ וְאֶת־שְׂדֵ֥ה הָעִ֖יר
the-city field-of but (12) ones-surrounding-her pastureland-of-her and

וְאֶת־חֲצֵרֶ֑יהָ נָתְנ֛וּ לְכָלֵ֥ב בֶּן־יְפֻנֶּ֖ה בַּאֲחֻזָּתֽוֹ׃
as-possession-of-him Jephunneh son-of to-Caleb they-gave villages-of-her and

וְלִבְנֵ֣י ׀ אַהֲרֹ֣ן הַכֹּהֵ֗ן נָֽתְנוּ֙ אֶת־עִ֣יר מִקְלַ֣ט
refuge-of city-of *** they-gave the-priest Aaron so-to-sons-of (13)

הָרֹצֵ֔חַ אֶת־חֶבְר֖וֹן וְאֶת־מִגְרָשֶׁ֑הָ וְאֶת־לִבְנָ֖ה וְאֶת־מִגְרָשֶֽׁהָ׃
pasture-of-her and Libnah and pasture-of-her and Hebron *** the-one-killing

וְאֶת־יַתִּר֙ וְאֶת־מִגְרָשֶׁ֔הָ וְֽאֶת־אֶשְׁתְּמֹ֖עַ וְאֶת־מִגְרָשֶֽׁהָ׃ וְאֶת־
and (15) pasture-of-her and Eshtemoa and pasture-of-her and Jattir and (14)

חֹלֹן֙ וְאֶת־מִגְרָשֶׁ֔הָ וְאֶת־דְּבִ֖ר וְאֶת־מִגְרָשֶֽׁהָ׃ וְאֶת־עַ֣יִן וְאֶת־
and Ain and (16) pasture-of-her and Debir and pasture-of-her and Holon

מִגְרָשֶׁ֗הָ וְאֶת־יֻטָּה֙ וְאֶת־מִגְרָשֶׁ֔הָ אֶת־בֵּ֥ית שֶׁ֖מֶשׁ וְאֶת־
and Shemesh Beth *** pasture-of-her and Juttah and pasture-of-her

מִגְרָשֶׁ֑הָ עָרִ֣ים תֵּ֔שַׁע מֵאֵ֕ת שְׁנֵ֖י הַשְּׁבָטִ֥ים הָאֵֽלֶּה׃
the-these the-tribes two-of from nine towns pasture-of-her

וּמִמַּטֵּ֣ה בִנְיָמִ֔ן אֶת־גִּבְע֖וֹן וְאֶת־מִגְרָשֶׁ֑הָ אֶת־גֶּ֖בַע וְאֶת־
and Geba *** pasture-of-her and Gibeon *** Benjamin and-from-tribe-of (17)

מִגְרָשֶֽׁהָ׃ אֶֽת־עֲנָתוֹת֙ וְאֶת־מִגְרָשֶׁ֔הָ וְאֶת־עַלְמ֖וֹן וְאֶת־
and Almon and pasture-of-her and Anathoth *** (18) pasture-of-her

מִגְרָשֶׁ֑הָ עָרִ֖ים אַרְבַּֽע׃ כָּל־עָרֵ֥י בְנֵֽי־אַהֲרֹ֖ן הַכֹּהֲנִ֑ים
the-priests Aaron sons-of towns-of all-of (19) four towns pasture-of-her

שְׁלֹשׁ־עֶשְׂרֵ֥ה עָרִ֖ים וּמִגְרְשֵׁיהֶֽן׃ וּלְמִשְׁפְּח֤וֹת בְּנֵֽי־קְהָת֙
Kohath sons-of and-to-clans-of (20) and-pastures-of-them towns ten three-of

8So the Israelites allotted to the Levites these towns and their pasturelands, as the LORD had commanded through Moses.

9From the tribes of Judah and Simeon they allotted the following towns by name 10(these towns were assigned to the descendants of Aaron who were from the Kohathite clans of the Levites, because the first lot fell to them):

11They gave them Kiriath Arba (that is, Hebron), with its surrounding pastureland, in the hill country of Judah. (Arba was the forefather of Anak.) 12But the fields and villages around the city they had given to Caleb son of Jephunneh as his possession.

13So to the descendants of Aaron the priest they gave Hebron (a city of refuge for one accused of murder), Libnah, 14Jattir, Eshtemoa, 15Holon, Debir, 16Ain, Juttah and Beth Shemesh, together with their pasturelands—nine towns from these two tribes.

17And from the tribe of Benjamin they gave them Gibeon, Geba, 18Anathoth and Almon, together with their pasturelands—four towns.

19All the towns for the priests, the descendants of Aaron, were thirteen, together with their pasturelands.

20The rest of the Kohathite

הַלְוִיִּ֗ם הַנּוֹתָרִים֙ מִבְּנֵ֣י קְהָ֔ת וַיְהִי֙ עָרֵ֣י
towns-of and-he-was Kohath from-sons-of the-ones-remaining the-Levites

גּֽוֹרָלָ֔ם מִמַּטֵּ֖ה אֶפְרָֽיִם׃ וַיִּתְּנ֨וּ לָהֶ֜ם אֶת־
*** to-them and-they-gave (21) Ephraim from-tribe-of allotment-of-them

עִ֨יר מִקְלַ֧ט הָרֹצֵ֛חַ אֶת־ שְׁכֶ֥ם וְאֶת־ מִגְרָשֶׁ֖הָ
pasture-of-her and Shechem *** the-one-killing refuge-of city-of

בְּהַ֣ר אֶפְרָ֑יִם וְאֶת־גֶּ֖זֶר וְאֶת־ מִגְרָשֶֽׁהָ׃ וְאֶת־ קִבְצַ֨יִם֙
Kibzaim and (22) pasture-of-her and Gezer and Ephraim in-hill-country-of

וְאֶת־ מִגְרָשֶׁ֔הָ וְאֶת־ בֵּ֥ית ח֖וֹרֹן וְאֶת־ מִגְרָשֶׁ֑הָ עָרִ֖ים אַרְבַּֽע׃
four towns pasture-of-her and Horon Beth and pasture-of-her and

וּמִמַּטֵּה־ דָ֔ן אֶֽת־ אֶלְתְּקֵא וְאֶת־ מִגְרָשֶׁ֔הָ אֶֽת־ גִּבְּת֖וֹן
Gibbethon *** pasture-of-her and Eltekeh *** Dan and-from-tribe-of (23)

וְאֶת־ מִגְרָשֶֽׁהָ׃ אֶת־ אַיָּלוֹן֙ וְאֶת־ מִגְרָשֶׁ֔הָ אֶת־ גַּת־ רִמּ֖וֹן וְאֶת־
and Rimmon Gath *** pasture-of-her and Aijalon *** (24) pasture-of-her and

מִגְרָשֶׁ֑הָ עָרִ֖ים אַרְבַּֽע׃ וּמִֽמַּחֲצִית֙ מַטֵּ֣ה מְנַשֶּׁ֔ה אֶת־ תַּעְנַךְ֙
Taanach *** Manasseh tribe-of and-from-half-of (25) four towns pasture-of-her

וְאֶת־ מִגְרָשֶׁ֔הָ וְאֶת־ גַּת־ רִמּ֖וֹן וְאֶת־ מִגְרָשֶׁ֑הָ עָרִ֖ים שְׁתָּֽיִם׃ כָּל־
all-of (26) two towns pasture-of-her and Rimmon Gath and pasture-of-her and

עָרִ֥ים עֶ֖שֶׂר וּמִגְרְשֵׁיהֶ֑ן לְמִשְׁפְּח֥וֹת בְּנֵֽי־ קְהָ֖ת הַנּוֹתָרִֽים׃
the-ones-remaining Kohath sons-of to-clans-of and-pasturelands-of-them ten towns

וְלִבְנֵ֤י גֵרְשׁוֹן֙ מִמִּשְׁפְּחֹ֣ת הַלְוִיִּ֔ם מֵחֲצִ֞י מַטֵּ֣ה
tribe-of from-half-of the-Levites from-clans-of Gershon and-to-sons-of (27)

מְנַשֶּׁ֗ה אֶת־ עִיר֙ מִקְלַ֣ט הָרֹצֵ֔חַ אֶת־ גֹּלָ֥ן בַּבָּשָׁ֖ן וְאֶת־
and in-the-Bashan Golan *** the-one-killing refuge-of city-of *** Manasseh

מִגְרָשֶׁ֑הָ וְאֶת־ בְּעֶשְׁתְּרָ֥ה וְאֶת־ מִגְרָשֶׁ֖הָ עָרִ֥ים שְׁתָּֽיִם׃
two towns pasture-of-her and Be-Eshtarah and pasture-of-her

וּמִמַּטֵּ֖ה יִשָּׂשכָ֑ר אֶת־ קִשְׁי֖וֹן וְאֶת־ מִגְרָשֶׁ֔הָ אֶת־ דָּֽבְרַ֖ת
Daberath *** pasture-of-her and Kishion *** Issachar and-from-tribe-of (28)

וְאֶת־ מִגְרָשֶֽׁהָ׃ אֶת־ יַרְמוּת֙ וְאֶת־ מִגְרָשֶׁ֔הָ אֶת־ עֵ֥ין גַּנִּ֖ים וְאֶת־
and Gannim En *** pasture-of-her and Jarmuth *** (29) pasture-of-her and

מִגְרָשֶׁ֑הָ עָרִ֖ים אַרְבַּֽע׃ וּמִמַּטֵּ֣ה אָשֵׁ֔ר אֶת־ מִשְׁאָ֖ל וְאֶת־
and Mishal *** Asher and-from-tribe-of (30) four towns pasture-of-her

מִגְרָשֶׁ֑הָ אֶת־עַבְדּ֖וֹן וְאֶת־ מִגְרָשֶֽׁהָ׃ אֶת־ חֶלְקָת֙ וְאֶת־ מִגְרָשֶׁ֔הָ
pasture-of-her and Helkath *** (31) pasture-of-her and Abdon *** pasture-of-her

וְאֶת־רְחֹ֖ב וְאֶת־ מִגְרָשֶׁ֑הָ עָרִ֖ים אַרְבַּֽע׃ וּמִמַּטֵּ֨ה נַפְתָּלִ֜י אֶת־
*** Naphtali and-from-tribe-of (32) four towns pasture-of-her and Rehob and

עִ֣יר ׀ מִקְלַ֣ט הָרֹצֵ֗חַ אֶת־ קֶ֤דֶשׁ בַּגָּלִיל֙ וְאֶת־ מִגְרָשֶׁ֔הָ
pasture-of-her and in-the-Galilee Kedesh *** the-one-killing refuge-of city-of

°27 ק גולן

clans of the Levites were allotted towns from the tribe of Ephraim:
[21]In the hill country of Ephraim they were given Shechem (a city of refuge for one accused of murder) and Gezer, [22]Kibzaim and Beth Horon, together with their pasturelands—four towns.
[23]Also from the tribe of Dan they received Eltekeh, Gibbethon, [24]Aijalon and Gath Rimmon, together with their pasturelands—four towns.
[25]From half the tribe of Manasseh they received Taanach and Gath Rimmon, together with their pasturelands—two towns.
[26]All these ten towns and their pasturelands were given to the rest of the Kohathite clans.

[27]The Levite clans of the Gershonites were given:
from the half-tribe of Manasseh,
Golan in Bashan (a city of refuge for one accused of murder) and Be Eshtarah, together with their pasturelands—two towns;
[28]from the tribe of Issachar,
Kishion, Daberath, [29]Jarmuth and En Gannim, together with their pasturelands—four towns;
[30]from the tribe of Asher,
Mishal, Abdon, [31]Helkath and Rehob, together with their pasturelands—four towns;
[32]from the tribe of Naphtali,
Kedesh in Galilee (a city of refuge for one accused of

וְאֶת־חַמֹּת דֹּאר וְאֶת־מִגְרָשֶׁהָ וְאֶת־קַרְתָּן וְאֶת־מִגְרָשֶׁהָ עָרִים שָׁלֹשׁ׃
three towns pasture-of-her and Kartan and pasture-of-her and Dor Hammoth and

כָּל־עָרֵי הַגֵּרְשֻׁנִּי לְמִשְׁפְּחֹתָם שְׁלֹשׁ־עֶשְׂרֵה עִיר
town ten three-of by-clans-of-them the-Gershonite towns-of all-of (33)

וּמִגְרְשֵׁיהֶן׃ וּלְמִשְׁפְּחוֹת בְּנֵי־מְרָרִי הַלְוִיִּם
the-Levites Merari sons-of and-to-clans-of (34) and-pasturelands-of-them

הַנּוֹתָרִים מֵאֵת מַטֵּה זְבוּלֻן אֶת־יָקְנְעָם וְאֶת־מִגְרָשֶׁהָ אֶת־
*** pasture-of-her and Jokneam *** Zebulun tribe-of from the-ones-remaining

קַרְתָּה וְאֶת־מִגְרָשֶׁהָ׃ אֶת־דִּמְנָה וְאֶת־מִגְרָשֶׁהָ אֶת־נַהֲלָל וְאֶת־
and Nahalal *** pasture-of-her and Dimnah *** (35) pasture-of-her and Kartah

מִגְרָשֶׁהָ עָרִים אַרְבַּע׃ וּמִמַּטֵּה רְאוּבֵן אֶת־בֶּצֶר וְאֶת־
and Bezer *** Reuben and-from-tribe-of *(36) four towns pasture-of-her

מִגְרָשֶׁהָ וְאֶת־יַהְצָה וְאֶת־מִגְרָשֶׁהָ׃ אֶת־קְדֵמוֹת וְאֶת־
and Kedemoth *** (37) pasture-of-her and Jahaz and pasture-of-her

מִגְרָשֶׁהָ וְאֶת־מֵיפַעַת וְאֶת־מִגְרָשֶׁהָ עָרִים אַרְבַּע׃
four towns pasture-of-her and Mephaath and pasture-of-her

וּמִמַּטֵּה־גָד אֶת־עִיר מִקְלַט הָרֹצֵחַ אֶת־רָמֹת
Ramoth *** the-one-killing refuge-of city-of *** Gad and-from-tribe-of (38)

בַּגִּלְעָד וְאֶת־מִגְרָשֶׁהָ וְאֶת־מַחֲנַיִם וְאֶת־מִגְרָשֶׁהָ׃ אֶת־
*** (39) pasture-of-her and Mahanaim and pasture-of-her and in-the-Gilead

חֶשְׁבּוֹן וְאֶת־מִגְרָשֶׁהָ אֶת־יַעְזֵר וְאֶת־מִגְרָשֶׁהָ כָּל־עָרִים אַרְבַּע׃
four towns all-of pasture-of-her and Jazer *** pasture-of-her and Heshbon

כָּל־הֶעָרִים לִבְנֵי מְרָרִי לְמִשְׁפְּחֹתָם הַנּוֹתָרִים
the-ones-remaining by-clans-of-them Merari to-sons-of the-towns all-of (40)

מִמִּשְׁפְּחוֹת הַלְוִיִּם וַיְהִי גּוֹרָלָם עָרִים שְׁתֵּים עֶשְׂרֵה׃
ten two towns allotment-of-them and-he-was the-Levites from-clans-of

כֹּל עָרֵי הַלְוִיִּם בְּתוֹךְ אֲחֻזַּת בְּנֵי־יִשְׂרָאֵל עָרִים
towns Israel sons-of territory-of in-among the-Levites towns-of all-of (41)

אַרְבָּעִים וּשְׁמֹנֶה וּמִגְרְשֵׁיהֶן׃ תִּהְיֶינָה הֶעָרִים הָאֵלֶּה
the-these the-towns they-had (42) and-pasturelands-of-them and-eight forty

עִיר עִיר וּמִגְרָשֶׁיהָ סְבִיבֹתֶיהָ כֵּן לְכָל־
for-all-of true ones-surrounding-her also-pasturelands-of-her city city

הֶעָרִים הָאֵלֶּה׃ וַיִּתֵּן יְהוָה לְיִשְׂרָאֵל אֶת־כָּל־הָאָרֶץ
the-land all-of *** to-Israel Yahweh so-he-gave (43) the-these the-towns

אֲשֶׁר נִשְׁבַּע לָתֵת לַאֲבוֹתָם וַיִּרָשׁוּהָ וַיֵּשְׁבוּ
and-they-settled and-they-possessed-her to-fathers-of-them to-give he-swore that

בָהּ׃ וַיָּנַח יְהוָה לָהֶם מִסָּבִיב כְּכֹל אֲשֶׁר־נִשְׁבַּע
he-swore that as-all on-every-side to-them Yahweh and-he-gave-rest (44) in-her

murder), Hammoth Dor and Kartan, together with their pasturelands—three towns.

33 All the towns of the Gershonite clans were thirteen, together with their pasturelands.

34 The Merarite clans (the rest of the Levites) were given:
from the tribe of Zebulun, Jokneam, Kartah, 35 Dimnah and Nahalal, together with their pasturelands—four towns;
36 from the tribe of Reuben, Bezer, Jahaz, 37 Kedemoth and Mephaath, together with their pasturelands—four towns;
38 from the tribe of Gad, Ramoth in Gilead (a city of refuge for one accused of murder), Mahanaim, 39 Heshbon and Jazer, together with their pasturelands—four towns in all.
40 All the towns allotted to the Merarite clans, who were the rest of the Levites, were twelve.

41 The towns of the Levites in the territory held by the Israelites were forty-eight in all, together with their pasturelands. 42 Each of these towns had pasturelands surrounding it; this was true for all these towns.

43 So the LORD gave Israel all the land he had sworn to give

**36* Most mss and versions include verses 36 and 37, although L does not; thus BHS reproduces them from the majority MT in a reduced type. See the introduction, page xiii.

לַאֲבוֹתָם וְלֹא־ עָמַד אִישׁ בִּפְנֵיהֶם מִכָּל־
of-any-of against-faces-of-them man he-withstood and-not to-fathers-of-them

אֹיְבֵיהֶם אֵת כָּל־ אֹיְבֵיהֶם נָתַן יְהוָה
Yahweh he-gave being-enemies-of-them all-of *** being-enemies-of-them

בְּיָדָם׃ לֹא־ נָפַל דָּבָר מִכֹּל הַדָּבָר הַטּוֹב
the-good the-promise from-any-of promise he-failed not (45) into-hand-of-them

אֲשֶׁר־ דִּבֶּר יְהוָה אֶל־ בֵּית יִשְׂרָאֵל הַכֹּל בָּא׃
he-fulfilled the-every-one Israel house-of to Yahweh he-promised that

אָז יִקְרָא יְהוֹשֻׁעַ לָרֻאוּבֵנִי וְלַגָּדִי
and-to-the-Gadite to-the-Reubenite Joshua he-summoned then (22:1)

וְלַחֲצִי מַטֵּה מְנַשֶּׁה׃ וַיֹּאמֶר אֲלֵיהֶם אַתֶּם שְׁמַרְתֶּם אֵת כָּל־
all *** you-did you to-them and-he-said (2) Manasseh tribe-of and-to-half-of

אֲשֶׁר צִוָּה אֶתְכֶם מֹשֶׁה עֶבֶד יְהוָה וַתִּשְׁמְעוּ בְקוֹלִי
to-voice-of-me and-you-obeyed Yahweh servant-of Moses you he-commanded that

לְכֹל אֲשֶׁר־ צִוִּיתִי אֶתְכֶם׃ לֹא־ עֲזַבְתֶּם אֶת־ אֲחֵיכֶם
brothers-of-you *** you-deserted not (3) you I-commanded that in-everything

זֶה יָמִים רַבִּים עַד הַיּוֹם הַזֶּה וּשְׁמַרְתֶּם אֶת־ מִשְׁמֶרֶת מִצְוַת
given-of mission-of *** but-you-carried-out the-this the-day to many days this

יְהוָה אֱלֹהֵיכֶם׃ וְעַתָּה הֵנִיחַ יְהוָה אֱלֹהֵיכֶם לַאֲחֵיכֶם
to-brothers-of-you God-of-you Yahweh he-gave-rest and-now (4) God-of-you Yahweh

כַּאֲשֶׁר דִּבֶּר לָהֶם וְעַתָּה פְּנוּ וּלְכוּ לָכֶם לְאָהֳלֵיכֶם
to-homes-of-you for-you and-go! return! and-now to-them he-promised just-as

אֶל־אֶרֶץ אֲחֻזַּתְכֶם אֲשֶׁר ׀ נָתַן לָכֶם מֹשֶׁה עֶבֶד יְהוָה
Yahweh servant-of Moses to-you he-gave that possession-of-you land-of to

בְּעֵבֶר הַיַּרְדֵּן׃ רַק ׀ שִׁמְרוּ מְאֹד לַעֲשׂוֹת אֶת־ הַמִּצְוָה
the-command *** to-keep very be-careful! but (5) the-Jordan on-other-side-of

וְאֶת־הַתּוֹרָה אֲשֶׁר צִוָּה אֶתְכֶם מֹשֶׁה עֶבֶד־ יְהוָה לְאַהֲבָה אֶת־יְהוָה
Yahweh *** to-love Yahweh servant-of Moses you he-gave that the-law and

אֱלֹהֵיכֶם וְלָלֶכֶת בְּכָל־ דְּרָכָיו וְלִשְׁמֹר מִצְוֹתָיו
commands-of-him and-to-obey ways-of-him in-all-of and-to-walk God-of-you

וּלְדָבְקָה־ בוֹ וּלְעָבְדוֹ בְּכָל־ לְבַבְכֶם
heart-of-you with-all-of and-to-serve-him to-him and-to-hold-fast

וּבְכָל־ נַפְשְׁכֶם׃ וַיְבָרְכֵם יְהוֹשֻׁעַ וַיְשַׁלְּחֵם
and-he-sent-them Joshua then-he-blessed-them (6) soul-of-you and-with-all-of

וַיֵּלְכוּ אֶל־ אָהֳלֵיהֶם׃ וְלַחֲצִי ׀ שֵׁבֶט הַמְנַשֶּׁה
the-Manasseh tribe-of and-to-half-of (7) homes-of-them to and-they-went

נָתַן מֹשֶׁה בַּבָּשָׁן וּלְחֶצְיוֹ נָתַן יְהוֹשֻׁעַ עִם־
with Joshua he-gave and-to-half-of-him in-the-Bashan Moses he-gave

their forefathers, and they took possession of it and settled there. [44]The LORD gave them rest on every side, just as he had sworn to their forefathers. Not one of their enemies withstood them; the LORD handed all their enemies over to them. [45]Not one of all the LORD's good promises to the house of Israel failed; every one was fulfilled.

*Eastern Tribes Return Home*

22 Then Joshua summoned the Reubenites, the Gadites and the half-tribe of Manasseh [2]and said to them, "You have done all that Moses the servant of the LORD commanded, and you have obeyed me in everything I commanded. [3]For a long time now—to this very day—you have not deserted your brothers but have carried out the mission the LORD your God gave you. [4]Now that the LORD your God has given your brothers rest as he promised, return to your homes in the land that Moses the servant of the LORD gave you on the other side of the Jordan. [5]But be very careful to keep the commandment and the law that Moses the servant of the LORD gave you: to love the LORD your God, to walk in all his ways, to obey his commands, to hold fast to him and to serve him with all your heart and all your soul."

[6]Then Joshua blessed them and sent them away, and they went to their homes. [7](To the half-tribe of Manasseh Moses had given land in Bashan, and to the other half of the tribe

אֲחִיהֶ֖ם מֵעֵ֥בֶר הַיַּרְדֵּ֖ן יָ֑מָּה וְגַ֗ם כִּ֣י שִׁלְּחָ֧ם

he-sent-them when and-also on-west the-Jordan on-side-of brothers-of-them

יְהוֹשֻׁ֛עַ אֶל־אָהֳלֵיהֶ֖ם וַֽיְבָרְכֵֽם׃ וַיֹּ֨אמֶר אֲלֵיהֶ֜ם לֵאמֹ֗ר

to-say to-them and-he-said (8) then-he-blessed-them homes-of-them to Joshua

בִּנְכָסִ֨ים רַבִּ֜ים שׁ֣וּבוּ אֶל־אָהֳלֵיכֶ֗ם וּבְמִקְנֶ֙ה רַב־מְאֹ֔ד

very large and-with-herd homes-of-you to return! great-ones with-wealths

בְּכֶ֨סֶף וּבְזָהָ֜ב וּבִנְחֹ֧שֶׁת וּבְבַרְזֶ֛ל וּבִשְׂלָמ֖וֹת

and-with-clothes and-with-iron and-with-bronze and-with-gold with-silver

הַרְבֵּ֣ה מְאֹ֑ד חִלְק֥וּ שְׁלַל־אֹיְבֵיכֶ֖ם עִם־אֲחֵיכֶֽם׃

brothers-of-you with being-enemies-of-you plunder-of divide! very to-be-great

וַיָּשֻׁ֣בוּ וַיֵּלְכ֡וּ בְּנֵי־רְאוּבֵ֣ן וּבְנֵי־גָ֣ד וַחֲצִ֣י ׀

and-half-of Gad and-sons-of Reuben sons-of and-they-left so-they-returned (9)

שֵׁ֣בֶט הַֽמְנַשֶּׁ֗ה מֵאֵת֙ בְּנֵ֣י יִשְׂרָאֵ֔ל מִשִּׁלֹ֖ה אֲשֶׁ֣ר בְּאֶֽרֶץ־כְּנָ֑עַן

Canaan in-land-of that at-Shiloh Israel sons-of from the-Manasseh tribe-of

לָלֶ֜כֶת אֶל־אֶ֣רֶץ הַגִּלְעָ֗ד אֶל־אֶ֤רֶץ אֲחֻזָּתָם֙ אֲשֶׁ֣ר נֹֽאחֲזוּ־

they-acquired which possession-of-them land-of to the-Gilead land-of to to-go

בָ֔הּ עַל־פִּ֥י יְהוָ֖ה בְּיַד־מֹשֶֽׁה׃ וַיָּבֹ֙אוּ֙ אֶל־גְּלִיל֣וֹת

Geliloth-of to when-they-came (10) Moses by-hand-of Yahweh command-of by to-her

הַיַּרְדֵּ֔ן אֲשֶׁ֖ר בְּאֶ֣רֶץ כְּנָ֑עַן וַיִּבְנוּ֩ בְנֵי־רְאוּבֵ֨ן וּבְנֵי־

and-sons-of Reuben sons-of then-they-built Canaan in-land-of that the-Jordan

גָ֜ד וַחֲצִ֨י שֵׁ֤בֶט הַֽמְנַשֶּׁה֙ שָׁ֤ם מִזְבֵּ֙חַ֙ עַל־הַיַּרְדֵּ֔ן מִזְבֵּ֥חַ

altar the-Jordan by altar there the-Manasseh tribe-of and-half-of Gad

גָּד֖וֹל לְמַרְאֶֽה׃ וַיִּשְׁמְע֥וּ בְנֵֽי־יִשְׂרָאֵ֖ל לֵאמֹ֑ר הִנֵּ֣ה

see! to-say Israel sons-of when-they-heard (11) in-appearance imposing

בָנ֣וּ בְנֵֽי־רְאוּבֵ֣ן וּבְנֵי־גָ֡ד וַחֲצִ֨י שֵׁ֜בֶט הַֽמְנַשֶּׁ֗ה

the-Manasseh tribe-of and-half-of Gad and-sons-of Reuben sons-of they-built

אֶת־הַמִּזְבֵּ֗חַ אֶל־מוּל֙ אֶ֣רֶץ כְּנַ֔עַן אֶל־גְּלִילוֹת֙ הַיַּרְדֵּ֔ן אֶל־

on the-Jordan Geliloth-of at Canaan land-of border-of on the-altar ***

עֵ֖בֶר בְּנֵ֥י יִשְׂרָאֵֽל׃ וַֽיִּשְׁמְע֖וּ בְּנֵ֣י יִשְׂרָאֵ֑ל וַיִּקָּ֨הֲל֜וּ

then-they-gathered Israel sons-of when-they-heard (12) Israel sons-of side-of

כָּל־עֲדַ֤ת בְּנֵֽי־יִשְׂרָאֵל֙ שִׁלֹ֔ה לַעֲל֥וֹת עֲלֵיהֶ֖ם לַצָּבָֽא׃

to-the-war against-them to-go Shiloh Israel sons-of assembly-of whole-of

וַיִּשְׁלְח֣וּ בְנֵֽי־יִשְׂרָאֵ֡ל אֶל־בְּנֵֽי־רְאוּבֵ֣ן וְאֶל־בְּנֵי־גָ֡ד וְאֶל־

and-to Gad sons-of and-to Reuben sons-of to Israel sons-of so-they-sent (13)

חֲצִ֣י שֵֽׁבֶט־מְנַשֶּׁ֗ה אֶל־אֶ֣רֶץ הַגִּלְעָ֔ד אֶת־פִּינְחָ֥ס בֶּן־אֶלְעָזָ֖ר

Eleazar son-of Phinehas *** the-Gilead land-of to Manasseh tribe-of half-of

הַכֹּהֵֽן׃ וַעֲשָׂרָ֤ה נְשִׂאִים֙ עִמּ֔וֹ נָשִׂ֨יא אֶחָ֜ד נָשִׂ֤יא אֶחָד֙ לְבֵ֣ית

for-house-of one chief one chief with-him chief-men and-ten (14) the-priest

Joshua gave land on the west side of the Jordan with their brothers.) When Joshua sent them home, he blessed them,
8saying, "Return to your homes with your great wealth—with large herds of livestock, with silver, gold, bronze and iron, and a great quantity of clothing—and divide with your brothers the plunder from your enemies."
9So the Reubenites, the Gadites and the half-tribe of Manasseh left the Israelites at Shiloh in Canaan to return to Gilead, their own land, which they had acquired in accordance with the command of the LORD through Moses.
10When they came to Geliloth near the Jordan in the land of Canaan, the Reubenites, the Gadites and the half-tribe of Manasseh built an imposing altar there by the Jordan.
11And when the Israelites heard that they had built the altar on the border of Canaan at Geliloth near the Jordan on the Israelite side,
12the whole assembly of Israel gathered at Shiloh to go to war against them.
13So the Israelites sent Phinehas son of Eleazar, the priest, to the land of Gilead—to Reuben, Gad and the half-tribe of Manasseh.
14With him they sent ten of the chief men, one for each of the tribes of

°7 ק בעבר

אָב לְכֹל מַטּוֹת יִשְׂרָאֵל וְאִישׁ רֹאשׁ בֵּית־ אֲבוֹתָם
fathers-of-them house-of head-of also-each Israel tribes-of for-each-of father

הֵמָּה לְאַלְפֵי יִשְׂרָאֵל׃ וַיָּבֹאוּ אֶל־ בְּנֵי־ רְאוּבֵן וְאֶל־
and-to Reuben sons-of to when-they-went (15) Israel among-clans-of they

בְּנֵי־ גָד וְאֶל־ חֲצִי שֵׁבֶט־ מְנַשֶּׁה אֶל־ אֶרֶץ הַגִּלְעָד
the-Gilead land-of to Manasseh tribe-of half-of and-to Gad sons-of

וַיְדַבְּרוּ אִתָּם לֵאמֹר׃ כֹּה אָמְרוּ כֹּל עֲדַת יְהוָה
Yahweh assembly-of whole-of they-say this (16) to-say to-them then-they-said

מָה־ הַמַּעַל הַזֶּה אֲשֶׁר מְעַלְתֶּם בֵּאלֹהֵי יִשְׂרָאֵל
Israel with-God-of-you you-broke-faith that the-this the-breech-of-faith what?

לָשׁוּב הַיּוֹם מֵאַחֲרֵי יְהוָה בִּבְנוֹתְכֶם לָכֶם מִזְבֵּחַ
altar for-you by-to-build-you Yahweh from-after the-day to-turn-away

לִמְרָדְכֶם הַיּוֹם בַּיהוָה׃ הַמְעַט־ לָנוּ אֶת־ עֲוֺן
sin-of *** for-us not-enough? (17) against-Yahweh the-day in-to-rebel-you

פְּעוֹר אֲשֶׁר לֹא־ הִטַּהַרְנוּ מִמֶּנּוּ עַד הַיּוֹם הַזֶּה וַיְהִי
though-he-fell the-this the-day to from-him to-be-cleansed-us not that Peor

הַנֶּגֶף בַּעֲדַת יְהוָה׃ וְאַתֶּם תָּשֻׁבוּ הַיּוֹם
the-day you-turn-away and-you (18) Yahweh on-community-of the-plague

מֵאַחֲרֵי יְהוָה וְהָיָה אַתֶּם תִּמְרְדוּ הַיּוֹם בַּיהוָה
against-Yahweh the-day you-rebel you and-he-will-be Yahweh from-after

וּמָחָר אֶל־ כָּל־ עֲדַת יִשְׂרָאֵל יִקְצֹף׃ וְאַךְ
and-now (19) he-will-be-angry Israel community-of whole-of with and-tomorrow

אִם־טְמֵאָה אֶרֶץ אֲחֻזַּתְכֶם עִבְרוּ לָכֶם אֶל־ אֶרֶץ אֲחֻזַּת
possession-of land-of to for-you come-over! possession-of-you land-of defiled if

יְהוָה אֲשֶׁר שָׁכַן־ שָׁם מִשְׁכַּן יְהוָה וְהֵאָחֲזוּ בְּתוֹכֵנוּ
in-among-us and-share! Yahweh tabernacle-of there he-stands where Yahweh

וּבַיהוָה אַל־ תִּמְרֹדוּ וְאֹתָנוּ אֶל־* תִּמְרֹדוּ בִּבְנֹתְכֶם
by-to-build-you you-rebel not or-against-us you-rebel not but-against-Yahweh

לָכֶם מִזְבֵּחַ מִבַּלְעֲדֵי מִזְבַּח יְהוָה אֱלֹהֵינוּ׃ הֲלוֹא | עָכָן בֶּן־
son-of Achan not? (20) God-of-us Yahweh altar-of other-than altar for-you

זֶרַח מָעַל מַעַל בַּחֵרֶם וְעַל־ כָּל־
whole-of and-upon with-devoted-thing unfaithfulness he-acted-unfaithfully Zerah

עֲדַת יִשְׂרָאֵל הָיָה קָצֶף וְהוּא אִישׁ אֶחָד לֹא גָוַע בַּעֲוֺנוֹ׃
for-sin-of-him he-died not only man and-he wrath he-came Israel community-of

וַיַּעֲנוּ בְּנֵי־ רְאוּבֵן וּבְנֵי־ גָד וַחֲצִי שֵׁבֶט
tribe-of and-half-of Gad and-sons-of Reuben sons-of and-they-replied (21)

הַמְנַשֶּׁה וַיְדַבְּרוּ אֶת־ רָאשֵׁי אַלְפֵי יִשְׂרָאֵל׃ אֵל | אֱלֹהִים |
God Mighty-One (22) Israel clans-of heads-of *** and-they-said the-Manasseh

Israel, each the head of a family division among the Israelite clans.

[15]When they went to Gilead—to Reuben, Gad and the half-tribe of Manasseh—they said to them: [16]"The whole assembly of the LORD says: 'How could you break faith with the God of Israel like this? How could you turn away from the LORD and build yourselves an altar in rebellion against him now? [17]Was not the sin of Peor enough for us? Up to this very day we have not cleansed ourselves from that sin, even though a plague fell on the community of the LORD! [18]And are you now turning away from the LORD?

" 'If you rebel against the LORD today, tomorrow he will be angry with the whole community of Israel. [19]If the land you possess is defiled, come over to the LORD's land, where the LORD's tabernacle stands, and share the land with us. But do not rebel against the LORD or against us by building an altar for yourselves, other than the altar of the LORD our God. [20]When Achan son of Zerah acted unfaithfully regarding the devoted things,[d] did not wrath come upon the whole community of Israel? He was not the only one who died for his sin.' "

[21]Then Reuben, Gad and the half-tribe of Manasseh replied to the heads of the clans of Israel: [22]"The Mighty One, God,

[d]*20* The Hebrew term refers to the irrevocable giving over of things or persons to the LORD, often by totally destroying them.

**19* Most mss have *pathah* under the *aleph* (אַל).

יְהוָה אֵל ׀ אֱלֹהִים ׀ יְהוָה הוּא יֹדֵעַ וְיִשְׂרָאֵל הוּא יֵדָע אִם־
if let-him-know he and-Israel knowing he Yahweh God Mighty-One Yahweh

בְּמֶרֶד וְאִם־ בְּמַעַל בַּיהוָה אַל־ תּוֹשִׁיעֵנוּ הַיּוֹם הַזֶּה׃
the-this the-day you-spare-us not to-Yahweh in-disobedience or-if in-rebellion

לִבְנוֹת לָנוּ מִזְבֵּחַ לָשׁוּב מֵאַחֲרֵי יְהוָה וְאִם־לְהַעֲלוֹת
to-offer or-if Yahweh from-after to-turn-away altar for-us to-build (23)

עָלָיו עוֹלָה וּמִנְחָה וְאִם־ לַעֲשׂוֹת עָלָיו
on-him to-sacrifice or-if and-grain-offering burnt-offering on-him

זִבְחֵי שְׁלָמִים יְהוָה הוּא יְבַקֵּשׁ׃ וְאִם־
but-indeed (24) may-he-call-account himself Yahweh fellowships offerings-of

לֹא מִדְּאָגָה מִדָּבָר עָשִׂינוּ אֶת־ זֹאת לֵאמֹר מָחָר יֹאמְרוּ
they-might-say some-day to-say this *** we-did for-reason for-fear no

בְנֵיכֶם לְבָנֵינוּ לֵאמֹר מַה־ לָּכֶם וְלַיהוָה
and-with-Yahweh with-you what? to-say to-descendants-of-us descendants-of-you

אֱלֹהֵי יִשְׂרָאֵל׃ וּגְבוּל נָתַן־ יְהוָה בֵּינֵנוּ וּבֵינֵיכֶם
and-between-you between-us Yahweh he-made now-boundary (25) Israel God-of

בְּנֵי־ רְאוּבֵן וּבְנֵי־ גָד אֶת־ הַיַּרְדֵּן אֵין־ לָכֶם חֵלֶק בַּיהוָה
in-Yahweh share for-you not the-Jordan *** Gad and-sons-of Reuben sons-of

וְהִשְׁבִּיתוּ בְנֵיכֶם אֶת־ בָּנֵינוּ לְבִלְתִּי יְרֹא
to-fear not descendants-of-us *** descendants-of-you so-they-might-make-stop

אֶת־ יְהוָה׃ וַנֹּאמֶר נַעֲשֶׂה־ נָּא לָנוּ לִבְנוֹת אֶת־הַמִּזְבֵּחַ
the-altar *** to-build for-us now! let-us-get-ready so-we-said (26) Yahweh ***

לֹא לְעוֹלָה וְלֹא לְזָבַח׃ כִּי עֵד הוּא
he witness on-contrary (27) for-sacrifice and-not for-burnt-offering not

בֵּינֵינוּ וּבֵינֵיכֶם וּבֵין דֹּרוֹתֵינוּ אַחֲרֵינוּ לַעֲבֹד
to-worship after-us generations-of-us and-between and-between-you between-us

אֶת־ עֲבֹדַת יְהוָה לְפָנָיו בְּעֹלוֹתֵינוּ
with-burnt-offerings-of-us before-him Yahweh worship-of ***

וּבִזְבָחֵינוּ וּבִשְׁלָמֵינוּ וְלֹא־
then-not and-with-fellowship-offerings-of-us and-with-sacrifices-of-us

יֹאמְרוּ בְנֵיכֶם מָחָר לְבָנֵינוּ אֵין־ לָכֶם
for-you not to-descendants-of-us future descendants-of-you they-will-say

חֵלֶק בַּיהוָה׃ וַנֹּאמֶר וְהָיָה כִּי־ יֹאמְרוּ אֵלֵינוּ וְאֶל־
or-to to-us they-say if now-he-will-be and-we-said (28) in-Yahweh share

דֹּרֹתֵינוּ מָחָר וְאָמַרְנוּ רְאוּ אֶת־ תַּבְנִית מִזְבַּח
altar-of replica-of *** look! then-we-will-answer future descendants-of-us

יְהוָה אֲשֶׁר־ עָשׂוּ אֲבוֹתֵינוּ לֹא לְעוֹלָה וְלֹא
and-not for-burnt-offering not fathers-of-us they-built which Yahweh

the LORD! The Mighty One, God, the LORD! He knows! And let Israel know! If this has been in rebellion or disobedience to the LORD, do not spare us this day.
23 If we have built our own altar to turn away from the LORD and to offer burnt offerings and grain offerings, or to sacrifice fellowship offerings[e] on it, may the LORD himself call us to account.

24 "No! We did it for fear that some day your descendants might say to ours, 'What do you have to do with the LORD, the God of Israel?
25 The LORD has made the Jordan a boundary between us and you—you Reubenites and Gadites! You have no share in the LORD.' So your descendants might cause ours to stop fearing the LORD.

26 "That is why we said, 'Let us get ready and build an altar—but not for burnt offerings or sacrifices.'
27 On the contrary, it is to be a witness between us and you and the generations that follow, that we will worship the LORD at his sanctuary with our burnt offerings, sacrifices and fellowship offerings. Then in the future your descendants will not be able to say to ours, 'You have no share in the LORD.'

28 "And we said, 'If they ever say this to us, or to our descendants, we will answer: Look at the replica of the LORD's altar, which our fathers built, not for burnt offerings

[e]23 Traditionally *peace offerings;* also in verse 27

לְזֶבַח כִּי־ עֵד הוּא בֵּינֵינוּ וּבֵינֵיכֶם׃ חָלִילָה
far-be-it! (29) and-between-you between-us he witness but for-sacrifice

לָּנוּ מִמֶּנּוּ לִמְרֹד בַּיהוָה וְלָשׁוּב הַיּוֹם מֵאַחֲרֵי
from-after the-day and-to-turn-away against-Yahweh to-rebel from-him from-us

יְהוָה לִבְנוֹת מִזְבֵּחַ לְעֹלָה לְמִנְחָה וּלְזָבַח
and-for-sacrifice for-grain-offering for-burnt-offering altar to-build Yahweh

מִלְּבַד מִזְבַּח יְהוָה אֱלֹהֵינוּ אֲשֶׁר לִפְנֵי מִשְׁכָּנוֹ׃
tabernacle-of-him before that God-of-us Yahweh altar-of other-than

וַיִּשְׁמַע פִּינְחָס הַכֹּהֵן וּנְשִׂיאֵי הָעֵדָה
the-community and-leaders-of the-priest Phinehas when-he-heard (30)

וְרָאשֵׁי אַלְפֵי יִשְׂרָאֵל אֲשֶׁר אִתּוֹ אֶת־ הַדְּבָרִים אֲשֶׁר דִּבְּרוּ
they-said that the-things *** with-him who Israel clans-of even-heads-of

בְנֵי־ רְאוּבֵן וּבְנֵי־ גָד וּבְנֵי מְנַשֶּׁה וַיִּיטַב
then-he-was-pleasant Manasseh and-sons-of Gad and-sons-of Reuben sons-of

בְּעֵינֵיהֶם׃ וַיֹּאמֶר פִּינְחָס בֶּן־ אֶלְעָזָר הַכֹּהֵן אֶל־
to the-priest Eleazar son-of Phinehas and-he-said (31) in-eyes-of-them

בְּנֵי־ רְאוּבֵן וְאֶל־ בְּנֵי־ גָד וְאֶל־ בְּנֵי מְנַשֶּׁה הַיּוֹם ׀ יָדַעְנוּ
we-know the-day Manasseh sons-of and-to Gad sons-of and-to Reuben sons-of

כִּי־ בְתוֹכֵנוּ יְהוָה אֲשֶׁר לֹא־ מְעַלְתֶּם בַּיהוָה
toward-Yahweh you-acted-unfaithfully not because Yahweh in-among-us that

הַמַּעַל הַזֶּה אָז הִצַּלְתֶּם אֶת־ בְּנֵי יִשְׂרָאֵל מִיַּד
from-hand-of Israel sons-of *** you-rescued now the-this the-unfaithfulness

יְהוָה׃ וַיָּשָׁב פִּינְחָס בֶּן־ אֶלְעָזָר הַכֹּהֵן ׀ וְהַנְּשִׂיאִים
and-the-leaders the-priest Eleazar son-of Phinehas then-he-returned (32) Yahweh

מֵאֵת בְּנֵי־ רְאוּבֵן וּמֵאֵת בְּנֵי־ גָד מֵאֶרֶץ הַגִּלְעָד אֶל־ אֶרֶץ
land-of to the-Gilead in-land-of Gad sons-of and-from Reuben sons-of from

כְּנַעַן אֶל־ בְּנֵי יִשְׂרָאֵל וַיָּשִׁבוּ אוֹתָם דָּבָר׃ וַיִּיטַב
and-he-was-good (33) report them and-they-brought Israel sons-of to Canaan

הַדָּבָר בְּעֵינֵי בְּנֵי יִשְׂרָאֵל וַיְבָרְכוּ אֱלֹהִים בְּנֵי יִשְׂרָאֵל
Israel sons-of God and-they-praised Israel sons-of in-eyes-of the-report

וְלֹא אָמְרוּ לַעֲלוֹת עֲלֵיהֶם לַצָּבָא לְשַׁחֵת אֶת־ הָאָרֶץ
the-country *** to-devastate to-the-war against-them to-go they-talked and-not

אֲשֶׁר בְּנֵי־ רְאוּבֵן וּבְנֵי־ גָד יֹשְׁבִים בָּהּ׃ וַיִּקְרְאוּ
and-they-named (34) in-her ones-living Gad and-sons-of Reuben sons-of where

בְּנֵי־ רְאוּבֵן וּבְנֵי־ גָד לַמִּזְבֵּחַ כִּי עֵד הוּא בֵּינֹתֵינוּ כִּי
that between-us he witness that to-the-altar Gad and-sons-of Reuben sons-of

יְהוָה הָאֱלֹהִים׃ וַיְהִי מִיָּמִים רַבִּים אַחֲרֵי אֲשֶׁר־ הֵנִיחַ
he-gave-rest when after many after-days and-he-was (23:1) the-God Yahweh

and sacrifices, but as a witness between us and you.'

29"Far be it from us to rebel against the LORD and turn away from him today by building an altar for burnt offerings, grain offerings and sacrifices, other than the altar of the LORD our God that stands before his tabernacle."

30When Phinehas the priest and the leaders of the community—the heads of the clans of the Israelites—heard what Reuben, Gad and Manasseh had to say, they were pleased. 31And Phinehas son of Eleazar, the priest, said to Reuben, Gad and Manasseh, "Today we know that the LORD is with us, because you have not acted unfaithfully toward the LORD in this matter. Now you have rescued the Israelites from the LORD's hand."

32Then Phinehas son of Eleazar, the priest, and the leaders returned to Canaan from their meeting with the Reubenites and Gadites in Gilead and reported to the Israelites. 33They were glad to hear the report and praised God. And they talked no more about going to war against them to devastate the country where the Reubenites and the Gadites lived.

34And the Reubenites and the Gadites gave the altar this name: A WITNESS BETWEEN US THAT THE LORD IS GOD.

*Joshua's Farewell to the Leaders*

23 After a long time had passed and the LORD had given Israel rest from all

יְהוָה לְיִשְׂרָאֵל מִכָּל־ אֹיְבֵיהֶם מִסָּבִיב וִיהוֹשֻׁעַ
then-Joshua from-around being-enemies-of-them from-all-of to-Israel Yahweh

זָקֵן בָּא בַּיָּמִים׃ וַיִּקְרָא יְהוֹשֻׁעַ לְכָל־
to-all-of Joshua and-he-summoned (2) in-the-days he-was-advanced he-was-old

יִשְׂרָאֵל לִזְקֵנָיו וּלְרָאשָׁיו וּלְשֹׁפְטָיו
and-to-ones-judging-him and-to-leaders-of-him to-elders-of-him Israel

וּלְשֹׁטְרָיו וַיֹּאמֶר אֲלֵהֶם אֲנִי זָקַנְתִּי בָּאתִי
I-am-advanced I-am-old I to-them and-he-said and-to-being-officials-of-him

בַּיָּמִים׃ וְאַתֶּם רְאִיתֶם אֵת כָּל־ אֲשֶׁר עָשָׂה יְהוָה אֱלֹהֵיכֶם
God-of-you Yahweh he-did that everything *** you-saw and-you (3) in-the-days

לְכָל־ הַגּוֹיִם הָאֵלֶּה מִפְּנֵיכֶם כִּי יְהוָה אֱלֹהֵיכֶם
God-of-you Yahweh indeed for-sakes-of-you the-these the-nations to-all-of

הוּא הַנִּלְחָם לָכֶם׃ רְאוּ הִפַּלְתִּי לָכֶם אֶת־ הַגּוֹיִם
the-nations *** for-you I-allotted remember! (4) for-you the-one-fighting he

הַנִּשְׁאָרִים הָאֵלֶּה בְּנַחֲלָה לְשִׁבְטֵיכֶם מִן־ הַיַּרְדֵּן
the-Jordan between for-tribes-of-you as-inheritance the-these the-ones-remaining

וְכָל־ הַגּוֹיִם אֲשֶׁר הִכְרַתִּי וְהַיָּם הַגָּדוֹל מְבוֹא הַשָּׁמֶשׁ׃
the-sun set-of the-Great and-the-Sea I-conquered that the-nations even-all-of

וַיהוָה אֱלֹהֵיכֶם הוּא יֶהְדֳּפֵם מִפְּנֵיכֶם
from-before-you he-will-drive-out-them he God-of-you now-Yahweh (5)

וְהוֹרִישׁ אֹתָם מִלִּפְנֵיכֶם וִירִשְׁתֶּם אֶת־ אַרְצָם
land-of-them *** and-you-will-possess from-before-you them and-he-will-push-out

כַּאֲשֶׁר דִּבֶּר יְהוָה אֱלֹהֵיכֶם לָכֶם׃ וַחֲזַקְתֶּם מְאֹד
very but-you-be-strong (6) to-you God-of-you Yahweh he-promised just-as

לִשְׁמֹר וְלַעֲשׂוֹת אֵת כָּל־ הַכָּתוּב בְּסֵפֶר תּוֹרַת
Law-of in-Book-of the-being-written all-of *** and-to-obey to-be-careful

מֹשֶׁה לְבִלְתִּי סוּר־ מִמֶּנּוּ יָמִין וּשְׂמֹאול׃ לְבִלְתִּי־ בוֹא בַּגּוֹיִם
with-the-nations to-associate not (7) or-left right from-him to-turn not Moses

הָאֵלֶּה הַנִּשְׁאָרִים הָאֵלֶּה אִתְּכֶם וּבְשֵׁם אֱלֹהֵיהֶם
gods-of-them and-with-name-of among-you the-these the-ones-remaining the-these

לֹא־ תַזְכִּירוּ וְלֹא תַשְׁבִּיעוּ וְלֹא תַעַבְדוּם וְלֹא תִשְׁתַּחֲווּ
you-bow-down and-not you-serve-them and-not you-swear and-not you-invoke not

לָהֶם׃ כִּי אִם־ בַּיהוָה אֱלֹהֵיכֶם תִּדְבָּקוּ כַּאֲשֶׁר עֲשִׂיתֶם
you-did just-as you-hold-fast God-of-you to-Yahweh only but (8) to-them

עַד הַיּוֹם הַזֶּה׃ וַיּוֹרֶשׁ יְהוָה מִפְּנֵיכֶם גּוֹיִם
nations from-before-you Yahweh now-he-drove-out (9) the-this the-day until

גְּדֹלִים וַעֲצוּמִים וְאַתֶּם לֹא־ עָמַד אִישׁ בִּפְנֵיכֶם עַד
to against-you anyone he-withstood not and-you and-powerful-ones great-ones

their enemies around them, Joshua, by then old and well advanced in years, 2 summoned all Israel—their elders, leaders, judges and officials—and said to them: "I am old and well advanced in years. 3 You yourselves have seen everything the LORD your God has done to all these nations for your sake; it was the LORD your God who fought for you. 4 Remember how I have allotted as an inheritance for your tribes all the land of the nations that remain—the nations I conquered—between the Jordan and the Great Sea[f] in the west. 5 The LORD your God himself will drive them out of your way. He will push them out before you, and you will take possession of their land, as the LORD your God promised you.

6 "Be very strong; be careful to obey all that is written in the Book of the Law of Moses, without turning aside to the right or to the left. 7 Do not associate with these nations that remain among you; do not invoke the names of their gods or swear by them. You must not serve them or bow down to them. 8 But you are to hold fast to the LORD your God, as you have until now.

9 "The LORD has driven out before you great and powerful nations; to this day no one has been able to withstand you.

f4 That is, the Mediterranean

הַיּוֹם הַזֶּה׃ אִישׁ־אֶחָד מִכֶּם יִרְדָּף־אָלֶף כִּי ׀ יְהוָה אֱלֹהֵיכֶם
God-of-you Yahweh for thousand he-routs from-you one man (10) the-this the-day

הוּא הַנִּלְחָם לָכֶם כַּאֲשֶׁר דִּבֶּר לָכֶם׃ וְנִשְׁמַרְתֶּם
so-you-be-careful (11) to-you he-promised just-as for-you the-one-fighting he

מְאֹד לְנַפְשֹׁתֵיכֶם לְאַהֲבָה אֶת־יְהוָה אֱלֹהֵיכֶם׃ כִּי ׀ אִם־שׁוֹב
to-turn if but (12) God-of-you Yahweh *** to-love with-selves-of-you very

תָּשׁוּבוּ וּדְבַקְתֶּם בְּיֶתֶר הַגּוֹיִם הָאֵלֶּה
the-these the-nations with-survivor-of and-you-ally-yourselves you-turn-away

הַנִּשְׁאָרִים הָאֵלֶּה אִתְּכֶם וְהִתְחַתַּנְתֶּם בָּהֶם
with-them and-you-intermarry among-you the-these the-ones-remaining

וּבָאתֶם בָּהֶם וְהֵם בָּכֶם׃ יָדוֹעַ תֵּדְעוּ
you-be-sure to-be-sure (13) with-you and-they with-them and-you-associate

כִּי לֹא יוֹסִיף יְהוָה אֱלֹהֵיכֶם לְהוֹרִישׁ אֶת־הַגּוֹיִם
the-nations *** to-drive-out God-of-you Yahweh he-will-continue not that

הָאֵלֶּה מִלִּפְנֵיכֶם וְהָיוּ לָכֶם לְפַח וּלְמוֹקֵשׁ
and-as-trap as-snare for-you and-they-will-become from-before-you the-these

וּלְשֹׁטֵט בְּצִדֵּיכֶם וְלִצְנִנִים בְּעֵינֵיכֶם עַד־אֲבָדְכֶם
you-perish until in-eyes-of-you and-as-thorns on-backs-of-you and-as-whip

מֵעַל הָאֲדָמָה הַטּוֹבָה הַזֹּאת אֲשֶׁר נָתַן לָכֶם יְהוָה אֱלֹהֵיכֶם׃
God-of-you Yahweh to-you he-gave which the-this the-good the-land from-on

וְהִנֵּה אָנֹכִי הוֹלֵךְ הַיּוֹם בְּדֶרֶךְ כָּל־הָאָרֶץ וִידַעְתֶּם
and-you-know the-earth all-of on-way-of the-day going I now-see! (14)

בְּכָל־לְבַבְכֶם וּבְכָל־נַפְשְׁכֶם כִּי לֹא־נָפַל
he-failed not that soul-of-you and-with-all-of heart-of-you with-all-of

דָּבָר אֶחָד מִכֹּל ׀ הַדְּבָרִים הַטּוֹבִים אֲשֶׁר דִּבֶּר יְהוָה
Yahweh he-gave that the-good-ones the-promises of-all-of one promise

אֱלֹהֵיכֶם עֲלֵיכֶם הַכֹּל בָּאוּ לָכֶם לֹא־נָפַל מִמֶּנּוּ
of-him he-failed not for-you they-were-fulfilled the-all to-you God-of-you

דָּבָר אֶחָד׃ וְהָיָה כַּאֲשֶׁר־בָּא עֲלֵיכֶם כָּל־
every-of for-you he-came-true just-as but-he-will-be (15) one promise

הַדָּבָר הַטּוֹב אֲשֶׁר דִּבֶּר יְהוָה אֱלֹהֵיכֶם אֲלֵיכֶם כֵּן יָבִיא
he-will-bring so to-you God-of-you Yahweh he-gave that the-good the-promise

יְהוָה עֲלֵיכֶם אֵת כָּל־הַדָּבָר הָרָע עַד־הַשְׁמִידוֹ אוֹתְכֶם
you to-destroy-him until the-evil the-thing every-of *** on-you Yahweh

מֵעַל הָאֲדָמָה הַטּוֹבָה הַזֹּאת אֲשֶׁר נָתַן לָכֶם יְהוָה אֱלֹהֵיכֶם׃
God-of-you Yahweh to-you he-gave that the-this the-good the-land from-on

בְּעָבְרְכֶם אֶת־בְּרִית יְהוָה אֱלֹהֵיכֶם אֲשֶׁר צִוָּה
he-commanded which God-of-you Yahweh covenant-of *** if-to-violate-you (16)

10 One of you routs a thousand, because the LORD your God fights for you, just as he promised. 11 So be very careful to love the LORD your God.

12 "But if you turn away and ally yourselves with the survivors of these nations that remain among you and if you intermarry with them and associate with them, 13 then you may be sure that the LORD your God will no longer drive out these nations before you. Instead, they will become snares and traps for you, whips on your backs and thorns in your eyes, until you perish from this good land, which the LORD your God has given you.

14 "Now I am about to go the way of all the earth. You know with all your heart and soul that not one of all the good promises the LORD your God gave you has failed. Every promise has been fulfilled; not one has failed. 15 But just as every good promise of the LORD your God has come true, so the LORD will bring on you all the evil he has threatened, until he has destroyed you from this good land he has given you. 16 If you violate the covenant of the LORD your God, which he commanded

אֶתְכֶם֒ וַהֲלַכְתֶּ֗ם וַעֲבַדְתֶּם֙ אֱלֹהִ֣ים אֲחֵרִ֔ים וְהִשְׁתַּחֲוִיתֶ֖ם לָהֶ֑ם
**to-them and-you-bow-down other-ones gods and-you-serve and-you-go you**

וְחָרָ֤ה אַף־ יְהוָה֙ בָּכֶ֔ם וַאֲבַדְתֶּ֣ם מְהֵרָ֔ה
**quickly and-you-will-perish against-you Yahweh anger-of then-he-will-burn**

מֵעַל֙ הָאָ֣רֶץ הַטּוֹבָ֔ה אֲשֶׁ֖ר נָתַ֥ן לָכֶֽם׃ וַיֶּאֱסֹ֧ף*
**then-he-assembled (24:1) to-you he-gave that the-good the-land from-on**

יְהוֹשֻׁ֛עַ אֶֽת־ כָּל־ שִׁבְטֵ֥י יִשְׂרָאֵ֖ל שְׁכֶ֑מָה וַיִּקְרָא֩ לְזִקְנֵ֨י
**to-elders-of and-he-summoned at-Shechem Israel tribes-of all-of *** Joshua**

יִשְׂרָאֵ֜ל וּלְרָאשָׁ֗יו וּלְשֹֽׁפְטָיו֙ וּלְשֹׁ֣טְרָ֔יו
**and-to-being-officials-of-him and-to-ones-judging-him and-to-leaders-of-him Israel**

וַיִּֽתְיַצְּב֖וּ לִפְנֵ֥י הָאֱלֹהִֽים׃ וַיֹּ֨אמֶר יְהוֹשֻׁ֜עַ אֶל־ כָּל־
**all-of to Joshua and-he-said (2) the-God before and-they-presented-themselves**

הָעָ֗ם כֹּֽה־ אָמַ֣ר יְהוָה֮ אֱלֹהֵ֣י יִשְׂרָאֵל֒ בְּעֵ֣בֶר הַנָּהָ֗ר יָשְׁב֤וּ
**they-lived the-River at-beyond Israel God-of Yahweh he-says this the-people**

אֲבֽוֹתֵיכֶם֙ מֵֽעוֹלָ֔ם תֶּ֛רַח אֲבִ֥י אַבְרָהָ֖ם וַאֲבִ֣י נָח֑וֹר
**Nahor and-father-of Abraham father-of Terah at-long-ago fathers-of-you**

וַיַּעַבְד֖וּ אֱלֹהִ֥ים אֲחֵרִֽים׃ וָ֠אֶקַּח אֶת־ אֲבִיכֶ֤ם אֶת־
***** father-of-you *** but-I-took (3) other-ones gods and-they-worshiped**

אַבְרָהָם֙ מֵעֵ֣בֶר הַנָּהָ֔ר וָאוֹלֵ֥ךְ אוֹת֖וֹ בְּכָל־ אֶ֣רֶץ כְּנָ֑עַן
**Canaan land-of through-all-of him and-I-led the-River from-beyond Abraham**

וָאַרְבֶּה֙ אֶת־ זַרְע֔וֹ וָֽאֶתֶּן־ ל֖וֹ אֶת־ יִצְחָֽק׃
**Isaac *** to-him and-I-gave descendant-of-him *** and-I-made-many**

וָאֶתֵּ֣ן לְיִצְחָ֔ק אֶֽת־יַעֲקֹ֖ב וְאֶת־עֵשָׂ֑ו וָאֶתֵּ֨ן לְעֵשָׂ֜ו אֶת־ הַ֤ר
**mountain-of *** to-Esau and-I-gave Esau and Jacob *** to-Isaac and-I-gave (4)**

שֵׂעִיר֙ לָרֶ֣שֶׁת אוֹת֔וֹ וְיַעֲקֹ֣ב וּבָנָ֔יו יָרְד֖וּ מִצְרָֽיִם׃
**Egypt they-went-down and-sons-of-him but-Jacob him to-possess Seir**

וָאֶשְׁלַ֞ח אֶת־ מֹשֶׁ֤ה וְאֶֽת־ אַהֲרֹן֙ וָאֶגֹּ֣ף אֶת־מִצְרַ֔יִם כַּאֲשֶׁ֥ר עָשִׂ֖יתִי
**I-did by-what Egypt *** then-I-afflicted Aaron and Moses *** then-I-sent (5)**

בְּקִרְבּ֑וֹ וְאַחַ֖ר הוֹצֵ֥אתִי אֶתְכֶֽם׃ וָאוֹצִ֤יא אֶת־
***** when-I-brought-out (6) you I-brought-out and-afterward in-among-him**

אֲבוֹתֵיכֶם֙ מִמִּצְרַ֔יִם וַתָּבֹ֖אוּ הַיָּ֑מָּה וַיִּרְדְּפ֨וּ
**and-they-pursued to-the-sea then-you-came from-Egypt fathers-of-you**

מִצְרַ֜יִם אַחֲרֵ֧י אֲבוֹתֵיכֶ֛ם בְּרֶ֥כֶב וּבְפָרָשִׁ֖ים יַם־ סֽוּף׃
**Reed Sea-of and-with-horsemen with-chariot fathers-of-you after Egyptians**

וַיִּצְעֲק֣וּ אֶל־ יְהוָ֗ה וַיָּ֨שֶׂם מַאֲפֵ֜ל בֵּינֵיכֶ֣ם ׀ וּבֵ֣ין
**and-between between-you darkness and-he-put Yahweh to but-they-cried-out (7)**

הַמִּצְרִ֗ים וַיָּבֵ֨א עָלָ֤יו אֶת־ הַיָּם֙ וַיְכַסֵּ֔הוּ
**and-he-covered-him the-sea *** ʌver-him and-he-brought the-Egyptians**

you, and go and serve other gods and bow down to them, the LORD's anger will burn against you, and you will quickly perish from the good land he has given you."

*The Covenant Renewed at Shechem*

24 Then Joshua assembled
all the tribes of Israel at
Shechem. He summoned the elders, leaders, judges and officials of Israel, and they presented themselves before God.
2 Joshua said to all the people,
"This is what the LORD, the God of Israel, says: 'Long ago your forefathers, including Terah the father of Abraham and Nahor, lived beyond the River[g] and worshiped other
gods. 3 But I took your father
Abraham from the land beyond the River and led him throughout Canaan and gave him many descendants. I gave
him Isaac, 4 and to Isaac I gave
Jacob and Esau. I assigned the hill country of Seir to Esau, but Jacob and his sons went down to Egypt.
5 " 'Then I sent Moses and
Aaron, and I afflicted the Egyptians by what I did there,
and I brought you out. 6 When
I brought your fathers out of Egypt, you came to the sea, and the Egyptians pursued them with chariots and horsemen[h] as far as the Red Sea.[i]
7 But they cried to the LORD for
help, and he put darkness between you and the Egyptians; he brought the sea over them and covered them. You saw

g2 That is, the Euphrates; also in verses 3, 14 and 15
h6 Or *charioteers*
i6 Hebrew *Yam Suph;* that is, Sea of Reeds

*1 Most mss have *hateph segol* under the *aleph* (וַיֶּאֱ).

°3 ק ואַרבּה

וַתִּרְאֶינָה עֵינֵיכֶם אֵת אֲשֶׁר־עָשִׂיתִי בְּמִצְרָיִם וַתֵּשְׁבוּ
then-you-lived to-Egyptians I-did what *** eyes-of-you and-they-saw

בַּמִּדְבָּר יָמִים רַבִּים׃ וָאָבִאָה אֶתְכֶם אֶל־אֶרֶץ הָאֱמֹרִי
the-Amorite land-of to you and-I-brought (8) many days in-the-desert

הַיּוֹשֵׁב בְּעֵבֶר הַיַּרְדֵּן וַיִּלָּחֲמוּ אִתְּכֶם וָאֶתֵּן
but-I-gave against-you and-they-fought the-Jordan on-east-of the-one-living

אוֹתָם בְּיֶדְכֶם וַתִּירְשׁוּ אֶת־אַרְצָם וָאַשְׁמִידֵם
and-I-destroyed-them land-of-them *** and-you-possessed into-hand-of-you them

מִפְּנֵיכֶם׃ וַיָּקָם בָּלָק בֶּן־צִפּוֹר מֶלֶךְ מוֹאָב
Moab king-of Zippor son-of Balak when-he-prepared (9) from-before-you

וַיִּלָּחֶם בְּיִשְׂרָאֵל וַיִּשְׁלַח וַיִּקְרָא לְבִלְעָם בֶּן־
son-of for-Balaam and-he-summoned then-he-sent against-Israel and-he-fought

בְּעוֹר לְקַלֵּל אֶתְכֶם׃ וְלֹא אָבִיתִי לִשְׁמֹעַ לְבִלְעָם וַיְבָרֶךְ
so-he-blessed to-Balaam to-listen I-would but-not (10) you to-curse Beor

בָּרוֹךְ אֶתְכֶם וָאַצִּל אֶתְכֶם מִיָּדוֹ׃ וַתַּעַבְרוּ אֶת־
*** then-you-crossed (11) from-hand-of-him you and-I-delivered you to-bless

הַיַּרְדֵּן וַתָּבֹאוּ אֶל־יְרִיחוֹ וַיִּלָּחֲמוּ בָכֶם בַּעֲלֵי־
citizens-of against-you and-they-fought Jericho to and-you-came the-Jordan

יְרִיחוֹ הָאֱמֹרִי וְהַפְּרִזִּי וְהַכְּנַעֲנִי וְהַחִתִּי
and-the-Hittite and-the-Canaanite and-the-Perizzite the-Amorite Jericho

וְהַגִּרְגָּשִׁי הַחִוִּי וְהַיְבוּסִי וָאֶתֵּן אוֹתָם בְּיֶדְכֶם׃
into-hand-of-you them but-I-gave and-the-Jebusite the-Hivite and-the-Girgashite

וָאֶשְׁלַח לִפְנֵיכֶם אֶת־הַצִּרְעָה וַתְּגָרֶשׁ אוֹתָם
them and-she-drove-out the-hornet *** ahead-of-you and-I-sent (12)

מִפְּנֵיכֶם שְׁנֵי מַלְכֵי הָאֱמֹרִי לֹא בְחַרְבְּךָ וְלֹא
and-not with-sword-of-you not the-Amorite kings-of two-of from-before-you

בְקַשְׁתֶּךָ׃ וָאֶתֵּן לָכֶם אֶרֶץ אֲשֶׁר לֹא־יָגַעְתָּ בָּהּ
on-her you-toiled not which land to-you so-I-gave (13) with-bow-of-you

וְעָרִים אֲשֶׁר לֹא־בְנִיתֶם וַתֵּשְׁבוּ בָּהֶם כְּרָמִים וְזֵיתִים
and-olive-groves vineyards in-them and-you-live you-built not which and-cities

אֲשֶׁר לֹא־נְטַעְתֶּם אַתֶּם אֹכְלִים׃ וְעַתָּה יְראוּ אֶת־יְהוָה וְעִבְדוּ
and-serve! Yahweh *** fear! and-now (14) ones-eating you you-planted not that

אֹתוֹ בְּתָמִים וּבֶאֱמֶת וְהָסִירוּ אֶת־אֱלֹהִים אֲשֶׁר
that gods *** and-throw-away! and-in-faithfulness in-wholeness him

עָבְדוּ אֲבוֹתֵיכֶם בְּעֵבֶר הַנָּהָר וּבְמִצְרַיִם וְעִבְדוּ
and-serve! and-in-Egypt the-River at-beyond fathers-of-you they-worshiped

אֶת־יְהוָה׃ וְאִם רַע בְּעֵינֵיכֶם לַעֲבֹד אֶת־יְהוָה בַּחֲרוּ
choose! Yahweh *** to-serve in-eyes-of-you undesirable but-if (15) Yahweh ***

with your own eyes what I did to the Egyptians. Then you lived in the desert for a long time.
8" 'I brought you to the land of the Amorites who lived east of the Jordan. They fought against you, but I gave them into your hands. I destroyed them from before you, and you took possession of their land.
9When Balak son of Zippor, the king of Moab, prepared to fight against Israel, he sent for Balaam son of Beor to put a curse on you.
10But I would not listen to Balaam, so he blessed you again and again, and I delivered you out of his hand.
11" 'Then you crossed the Jordan and came to Jericho. The citizens of Jericho fought against you, as did also the Amorites, Perizzites, Canaanites, Hittites, Girgashites, Hivites and Jebusites, but I gave them into your hands.
12I sent the hornet ahead of you, which drove them out before you—also the two Amorite kings. You did not do it with your own sword and bow.
13So I gave you a land on which you did not toil and cities you did not build; and you live in them and eat from vineyards and olive groves that you did not plant.'
14"Now fear the LORD and serve him with all faithfulness. Throw away the gods your forefathers worshiped beyond the River and in Egypt, and serve the LORD.
15But if serving the LORD seems undesirable to you, then

°8 ק ואביא

לָכֶם הַיּוֹם אֶת־ מִי תַעֲבֹדוּן אִם אֶת־אֱלֹהִים אֲשֶׁר־ עָבְדוּ
they-served that gods *** whether you-will-serve whom *** the-day for-you

אֲבוֹתֵיכֶם אֲשֶׁר בְּעֵבֶר הַנָּהָר וְאִם אֶת־ אֱלֹהֵי הָאֱמֹרִי
the-Amorite gods-of *** or-whether the-River at-beyond when fathers-of-you

אֲשֶׁר אַתֶּם יֹשְׁבִים בְּאַרְצָם וְאָנֹכִי וּבֵיתִי נַעֲבֹד
we-will-serve and-household-of-me but-I in-land-of-them ones-living you whom

אֶת־ יְהוָה׃ וַיַּעַן הָעָם וַיֹּאמֶר חָלִילָה לָּנוּ
from-us far-be-it! and-he-said the-people then-he-answered (16) Yahweh ***

מֵעֲזֹב אֶת־ יְהוָה לַעֲבֹד אֱלֹהִים אֲחֵרִים׃ כִּי יְהוָה
Yahweh for (17) other-ones gods to-serve Yahweh *** from-to-forsake

אֱלֹהֵינוּ הוּא הַמַּעֲלֶה אֹתָנוּ וְאֶת־ אֲבוֹתֵינוּ מֵאֶרֶץ מִצְרַיִם
Egypt from-land-of fathers-of-us and us the-one-bringing-up he God-of-us

מִבֵּית עֲבָדִים וַאֲשֶׁר עָשָׂה לְעֵינֵינוּ אֶת־ הָאֹתוֹת
the-signs *** before-eyes-of-us he-performed and-who slaveries from-house-of

הַגְּדֹלוֹת הָאֵלֶּה וַיִּשְׁמְרֵנוּ בְּכָל־ הַדֶּרֶךְ אֲשֶׁר
that the-journey on-entire-of and-he-protected-us the-those the-great-ones

הָלַכְנוּ בָהּ וּבְכֹל הָעַמִּים אֲשֶׁר עָבַרְנוּ
we-traveled which the-nations and-among-all-of on-her we-traveled

בְּקִרְבָּם׃ וַיְגָרֶשׁ יְהוָה אֶת־ כָּל־ הָעַמִּים
the-nations all-of *** Yahweh and-he-drove-out (18) through-midst-of-them

וְאֶת־ הָאֱמֹרִי יֹשֵׁב הָאָרֶץ מִפָּנֵינוּ גַּם־ אֲנַחְנוּ נַעֲבֹד אֶת־
*** we-will-serve we also from-before-us the-land living-of the-Amorite and

יְהוָה כִּי־ הוּא אֱלֹהֵינוּ׃ וַיֹּאמֶר יְהוֹשֻׁעַ אֶל־ הָעָם לֹא
not the-people to Joshua then-he-said (19) God-of-us he for Yahweh

תוּכְלוּ לַעֲבֹד אֶת־ יְהוָה כִּי־ אֱלֹהִים קְדֹשִׁים הוּא אֵל־ קַנּוֹא הוּא לֹא־
not he jealous God he holy-ones God for Yahweh *** to-serve you-are-able

יִשָּׂא לְפִשְׁעֲכֶם וּלְחַטֹּאותֵיכֶם׃ כִּי תַעַזְבוּ
you-forsake if (20) and-to-sins-of-you to-rebellion-of-you he-will-forgive

אֶת־ יְהוָה וַעֲבַדְתֶּם אֱלֹהֵי נֵכָר וְשָׁב
then-he-will-turn foreign gods-of and-you-serve Yahweh ***

וְהֵרַע לָכֶם וְכִלָּה אֶתְכֶם אַחֲרֵי אֲשֶׁר־
when after you and-he-will-make-end on-you and-he-will-bring-disaster

הֵיטִיב לָכֶם׃ וַיֹּאמֶר הָעָם אֶל־יְהוֹשֻׁעַ לֹא כִּי אֶת־ יְהוָה
Yahweh *** but no Joshua to the-people but-he-said (21) to-you he-was-good

נַעֲבֹד׃ וַיֹּאמֶר יְהוֹשֻׁעַ אֶל־ הָעָם עֵדִים אַתֶּם
you witnesses the-people to Joshua then-he-said (22) we-will-serve

בָּכֶם כִּי־ אַתֶּם בְּחַרְתֶּם לָכֶם אֶת־ יְהוָה לַעֲבֹד אוֹתוֹ וַיֹּאמְרוּ
and-they-said him to-serve Yahweh *** for-you you-chose you that against-you

choose for yourselves this day whom you will serve, whether the gods your forefathers served beyond the River, or the gods of the Amorites, in whose land you are living. But as for me and my household, we will serve the LORD."
[16]Then the people answered, "Far be it from us to forsake the LORD to serve other gods!
[17]It was the LORD our God himself who brought us and our forefathers up out of Egypt, from that land of slavery, and performed those great signs before our eyes. He protected us on our entire journey and among all the nations through which we traveled. [18]And the
LORD drove out before us all the nations, including the Amorites, who lived in the land. We too will serve the LORD, because he is our God."
[19]Joshua said to the people, "You are not able to serve the LORD. He is a holy God; he is a jealous God. He will not forgive your rebellion and your sins. [20]If you forsake the LORD
and serve foreign gods, he will turn and bring disaster on you and make an end of you, after he has been good to you."
[21]But the people said to Joshua, "No! We will serve the LORD."
[22]Then Joshua said, "You are witnesses against yourselves that you have chosen to serve the LORD."

°15 ק מעבר

עֵדִֽים׃ וְעַתָּה הָסִירוּ אֶת־אֱלֹהֵי הַנֵּכָר אֲשֶׁר בְּקִרְבְּכֶם

in-among-you that the-foreign gods-of *** throw-away! then-now (23) witnesses

וְהַטּוּ אֶת־לְבַבְכֶם אֶל־יְהוָה אֱלֹהֵי יִשְׂרָאֵל׃ וַיֹּאמְרוּ

and-they-said (24) Israel God-of Yahweh to heart-of-you *** and-yield!

הָעָם אֶל־יְהוֹשֻׁעַ אֶת־יְהוָה אֱלֹהֵינוּ נַעֲבֹד וּבְקוֹלוֹ

and-to-voice-of-him we-will-serve God-of-us Yahweh *** Joshua to the-people

נִשְׁמָע׃ וַיִּכְרֹת יְהוֹשֻׁעַ בְּרִית לָעָם בַּיּוֹם

on-the-day for-the-people covenant Joshua and-he-made (25) we-will-obey

הַהוּא וַיָּשֶׂם לוֹ חֹק וּמִשְׁפָּט בִּשְׁכֶם׃ וַיִּכְתֹּב

and-he-recorded (26) at-Shechem and-law decree for-him and-he-drew-up the-that

יְהוֹשֻׁעַ אֶת־הַדְּבָרִים הָאֵלֶּה בְּסֵפֶר תּוֹרַת אֱלֹהִים וַיִּקַּח אֶבֶן

stone then-he-took God Law-of in-Book-of the-these the-things *** Joshua

גְּדוֹלָה וַיְקִימֶהָ שָּׁם תַּחַת הָאַלָּה אֲשֶׁר בְּמִקְדַּשׁ יְהוָה׃

Yahweh near-holy-place-of that the-oak under there and-he-set-up-her large

וַיֹּאמֶר יְהוֹשֻׁעַ אֶל־כָּל־הָעָם הִנֵּה הָאֶבֶן הַזֹּאת

the-this the-stone see! the-people all-of to Joshua and-he-said (27)

תִּֽהְיֶה־בָּנוּ לְעֵדָה כִּי־הִיא שָׁמְעָה אֵת כָּל־אִמְרֵי

words-of all-of *** she-heard she for as-witness against-us she-will-be

יְהוָה אֲשֶׁר דִּבֶּר עִמָּנוּ וְהָיְתָה בָכֶם לְעֵדָה פֶּן־

if as-witness against-you and-she-will-be to-us he-said that Yahweh

תְּכַחֲשׁוּן בֵּאלֹהֵיכֶם׃ וַיְשַׁלַּח יְהוֹשֻׁעַ אֶת־הָעָם

the-people *** Joshua then-he-sent-away (28) to-God-of-you you-are-untrue

אִישׁ לְנַחֲלָתוֹ׃ וַיְהִי אַחֲרֵי הַדְּבָרִים הָאֵלֶּה

the-these the-things after and-he-was (29) to-inheritance-of-him each

וַיָּמָת יְהוֹשֻׁעַ בִּן־נוּן עֶבֶד יְהוָה בֶּן־מֵאָה וָעֶשֶׂר

and-ten hundred son-of Yahweh servant-of Nun son-of Joshua that-he-died

שָׁנִים׃ וַיִּקְבְּרוּ אֹתוֹ בִּגְבוּל נַחֲלָתוֹ בְּתִמְנַת־

at-Timnath inheritance-of-him in-land-of him and-they-buried (30) years

סֶרַח אֲשֶׁר בְּהַר־אֶפְרָיִם מִצְּפוֹן לְהַר־גָּעַשׁ׃

Gaash of-Mount-of to-north Ephraim in-hill-country-of that Serah

וַיַּעֲבֹד יִשְׂרָאֵל אֶת־יְהוָה כֹּל יְמֵי יְהוֹשֻׁעַ וְכֹל ׀

and-all-of Joshua days-of all-of Yahweh *** Israel and-he-served (31)

יְמֵי הַזְּקֵנִים אֲשֶׁר הֶאֱרִיכוּ יָמִים אַחֲרֵי יְהוֹשֻׁעַ וַאֲשֶׁר

and-who Joshua after days they-outlived who the-elders days-of

יָדְעוּ אֵת כָּל־מַעֲשֵׂה יְהוָה אֲשֶׁר עָשָׂה לְיִשְׂרָאֵל׃ וְאֶת־

and (32) for-Israel he-did that Yahweh work-of all-of *** they-experienced

עַצְמוֹת יוֹסֵף אֲשֶׁר־הֶעֱלוּ בְנֵי־יִשְׂרָאֵל ׀ מִמִּצְרַיִם קָבְרוּ

they-buried from-Egypt Israel sons-of they-brought-up which Joseph bones-of

"Yes, we are witnesses," they replied.

23"Now then," said Joshua, "throw away the foreign gods that are among you and yield your hearts to the LORD, the God of Israel."

24And the people said to Joshua, "We will serve the LORD our God and obey him."

25On that day Joshua made a covenant for the people, and there at Shechem he drew up for them decrees and laws. 26And Joshua recorded these things in the Book of the Law of God. Then he took a large stone and set it up there under the oak near the holy place of the LORD.

27"See!" he said to all the people. "This stone will be a witness against us. It has heard all the words the LORD has said to us. It will be a witness against you if you are untrue to your God."

*Buried in the Promised Land*

28Then Joshua sent the people away, each to his own inheritance.

29After these things, Joshua son of Nun, the servant of the LORD, died at the age of a hundred and ten. 30And they buried him in the land of his inheritance, at Timnath Serah[j] in the hill country of Ephraim, north of Mount Gaash.

31Israel served the LORD throughout the lifetime of Joshua and of the elders who outlived him and who had experienced everything the LORD had done for Israel.

32And Joseph's bones, which the Israelites had brought up from Egypt, were buried at

j30 Also known as *Timnath Heres* (see Judges 2:9)

בִשְׁכֶם בְּחֶלְקַת הַשָּׂדֶה אֲשֶׁר קָנָה יַעֲקֹב מֵאֵת בְּנֵי־ חֲמוֹר

Hamor sons-of from Jacob he-bought that the-land in-tract-of at-Shechem

אֲבִי־ שְׁכֶם בְּמֵאָה קְשִׂיטָה וַיִּהְיוּ לִבְנֵי־ יוֹסֵף

Joseph for-sons-of and-they-became kesitah for-hundred Shechem father-of

לְנַחֲלָה׃ (33) וְאֶלְעָזָר בֶּן־ אַהֲרֹן מֵת וַיִּקְבְּרוּ אֹתוֹ

him and-they-buried he-died Aaron son-of and-Eleazar (33) as-inheritance

בְּגִבְעַת פִּינְחָס בְּנוֹ אֲשֶׁר נִתַּן־ לוֹ

to-him he-was-allotted which son-of-him Phinehas at-Gibeah-of

בְּהַר אֶפְרָיִם׃

Ephraim in-hill-country-of

Shechem in the tract of land that Jacob bought for a hundred pieces of silver[k] from the sons of Hamor, the father of Shechem. This became the inheritance of Joseph's descendants.

33 And Eleazar son of Aaron died and was buried at Gibeah, which had been allotted to his son Phinehas in the hill country of Ephraim.

[k]32 Hebrew *hundred kesitahs;* a kesitah was a unit of money of unknown weight and value.

וַיְהִי֙ אַחֲרֵי֙ מ֣וֹת יְהוֹשֻׁ֔עַ וַיִּשְׁאֲלוּ֙ בְּנֵ֣י יִשְׂרָאֵ֔ל
(1:1) and-he-was   after   death-of   Joshua   then-they-asked   sons-of   Israel

בַּיהוָ֖ה לֵאמֹ֑ר מִ֣י יַעֲלֶה־לָּ֧נוּ אֶל־הַכְּנַעֲנִ֛י בַּתְּחִלָּ֖ה
of-Yahweh   to-say   who?   will-he-go-up   for-us   against   the-Canaanite   as-the-first

לְהִלָּ֥חֶם בּֽוֹ׃ (2) וַיֹּ֣אמֶר יְהוָ֔ה יְהוּדָ֖ה יַעֲלֶ֑ה הִנֵּ֛ה נָתַ֥תִּי
to-fight   against-him   and-he-answered   Yahweh   Judah   he-must-go   see!   I-gave

אֶת־הָאָ֖רֶץ בְּיָדֽוֹ׃ (3) וַיֹּ֨אמֶר יְהוּדָ֜ה לְשִׁמְע֣וֹן אָחִ֗יו
***   the-land   into-hand-of-him   then-he-said   Judah   to-Simeon   brother-of-him

עֲלֵ֤ה אִתִּי֙ בְגֽוֹרָלִ֔י וְנִֽלָּחֲמָ֖ה בַּֽכְּנַעֲנִ֑י
come-up!   with-me   into-territory-of-me   and-we-will-fight   against-the-Canaanite

וְהָלַכְתִּ֧י גַם־אֲנִ֛י אִתְּךָ֖ בְּגוֹרָלֶ֑ךָ וַיֵּ֥לֶךְ אִתּ֖וֹ
then-I-will-go   also   I   with-you   into-territory-of-you   so-he-went   with-him

שִׁמְעֽוֹן׃ (4) וַיַּ֣עַל יְהוּדָ֔ה וַיִּתֵּ֧ן יְהוָ֛ה אֶת־הַכְּנַעֲנִ֥י
Simeon   when-he-attacked   Judah   then-he-gave   Yahweh   ***   the-Canaanite

וְהַפְּרִזִּ֖י בְּיָדָ֑ם וַיַּכּ֣וּם בְּבֶ֔זֶק עֲשֶׂ֥רֶת
and-the-Perizzite   into-hand-of-them   and-they-struck-down-them   at-Bezek   ten

אֲלָפִ֖ים אִֽישׁ׃ (5) וַֽיִּמְצְא֞וּ אֶת־אֲדֹנִ֥י בֶ֙זֶק֙ בְּבֶ֔זֶק וַיִּֽלָּחֲמ֖וּ
thousands   man   and-they-found   ***   Adoni   Bezek   at-Bezek   and-they-fought

בּ֑וֹ וַיַּכּ֕וּ אֶת־הַֽכְּנַעֲנִ֖י וְאֶת־הַפְּרִזִּֽי׃
against-him   and-they-routed   ***   the-Canaanite   and   the-Perizzite

(6) וַיָּ֙נָס֙ אֲדֹנִ֣י בֶ֔זֶק וַֽיִּרְדְּפ֖וּ אַחֲרָ֑יו וַיֹּאחֲז֣וּ אֹת֔וֹ
and-he-fled   Adoni   Bezek   but-they-chased   after-him   and-they-caught   him

וַֽיְקַצְּצ֔וּ אֶת־בְּהֹנ֥וֹת* יָדָ֖יו וְרַגְלָֽיו׃
and-they-cut-off   ***   *thumbs/big-toes-of   hands-of-him   and-feet-of-him

(7) וַיֹּ֣אמֶר אֲדֹֽנִי־בֶ֗זֶק שִׁבְעִ֣ים ׀ מְלָכִ֡ים בְּהֹנוֹת* יְדֵיהֶ֣ם
then-he-said   Adoni   Bezek   seventy   kings   *thumbs/big-toes-of   hands-of-them

וְרַגְלֵיהֶ֞ם מְקֻצָּצִ֗ים הָי֤וּ מְלַקְּטִים֙ תַּ֣חַת
and-feet-of-them   ones-being-cut-off   they-are   ones-picking-up-scraps   under

שֻׁלְחָנִ֔י כַּאֲשֶׁ֣ר עָשִׂ֔יתִי כֵּ֖ן שִׁלַּם־לִ֣י אֱלֹהִ֑ים וַיְבִיאֻ֥הוּ
table-of-me   just-as   I-did   same   he-paid-back   to-me   God   and-they-brought-him

יְרוּשָׁלַ֖͏ִם וַיָּ֥מָת שָֽׁם׃ (8) וַיִּלָּחֲמ֤וּ בְנֵֽי־יְהוּדָה֙
Jerusalem   and-he-died   there   and-they-attacked   men-of   Judah

בִּיר֣וּשָׁלַ֔͏ִם וַיִּלְכְּד֣וּ אוֹתָ֔הּ וַיַּכּ֖וּהָ לְפִי־חָ֑רֶב וְאֶת־
against-Jerusalem   and-they-took   her   and-they-put-her   to-edge-of   sword   and

הָעִ֖יר שִׁלְּח֥וּ בָאֵֽשׁ׃ (9) וְאַחַ֗ר יָֽרְדוּ֙ בְּנֵ֣י יְהוּדָ֔ה
the-city   they-set   on-fire   then-after   they-went-down   men-of   Judah

לְהִלָּחֵ֖ם בַּֽכְּנַעֲנִ֑י יוֹשֵׁ֣ב הָהָ֔ר וְהַנֶּ֖גֶב
to-fight   against-the-Canaanite   living-of   the-hill-country   and-the-Negev

## Israel Fights the Remaining Canaanites

**1** After the death of Joshua, the Israelites asked the Lord, "Who will be the first to go up and fight for us against the Canaanites?"

[2]The Lord answered, "Judah is to go; I have given the land into their hands."

[3]Then the men of Judah said to the Simeonites their brothers, "Come up with us into the territory allotted to us, to fight against the Canaanites. We in turn will go with you into yours." So the Simeonites went with them.

[4]When Judah attacked, the Lord gave the Canaanites and Perizzites into their hands and they struck down ten thousand men at Bezek. [5]It was there that they found Adoni-Bezek and fought against him, putting to rout the Canaanites and Perizzites. [6]Adoni-Bezek fled, but they chased him and caught him, and cut off his thumbs and big toes.

[7]Then Adoni-Bezek said, "Seventy kings with their thumbs and big toes cut off have picked up scraps under my table. Now God has paid me back for what I did to them." They brought him to Jerusalem, and he died there.

[8]The men of Judah attacked Jerusalem also and took it. They put the city to the sword and set it on fire.

[9]After that, the men of Judah went down to fight against the Canaanites living in the hill country, the Negev and the

*6,7 This Hebrew word means both *thumb* and *big toe* as it is in construct to both *hands* and *feet*.

וְהַשְּׁפֵלָֽה:    וַיֵּ֣לֶךְ    יְהוּדָ֔ה    אֶל־    הַכְּנַעֲנִ֖י
and-the-foothill    (10)    so-he-advanced    Judah    against    the-Canaanite

הַיּוֹשֵׁ֣ב    בְּחֶבְר֑וֹן    וְשֵׁם־    חֶבְר֥וֹן    לְפָנִ֖ים    קִרְיַ֣ת אַרְבַּ֑ע
the-one-living    in-Hebron    now-name-of    Hebron    formerly    Kiriath Arba

וַיַּכּ֗וּ    אֶת־    שֵׁשַׁ֛י    וְאֶת־    אֲחִימַ֖ן    וְאֶת־    תַּלְמָֽי:    וַיֵּ֣לֶךְ
and-they-defeated    ***    Sheshai    and    Ahiman    and    Talmai    (11) and-he-advanced

מִשָּׁ֔ם    אֶל־    יוֹשְׁבֵ֖י    דְּבִ֑יר    וְשֵׁם־    דְּבִ֥יר    לְפָנִ֖ים    קִרְיַת־
from-there    against    ones-living-of    Debir    now-name-of    Debir    formerly    Kiriath

סֵֽפֶר:    וַיֹּ֣אמֶר    כָּלֵ֔ב    אֲשֶׁר־    יַכֶּ֥ה    אֶת־    קִרְיַת־    סֵ֖פֶר
Sepher    (12) and-he-said    Caleb    whoever    he-attacks    ***    Kiriath    Sepher

וּלְכָדָ֑הּ    וְנָתַ֥תִּי    ל֛וֹ    אֶת־    עַכְסָ֥ה    בִתִּ֖י    לְאִשָּֽׁה:
and-he-captures-her    then-I-will-give    to-him    ***    Acsah    daughter-of-me    as-wife

וַֽיִּלְכְּדָהּ֙    עָתְנִיאֵ֣ל    בֶּן־    קְנַ֔ז    אֲחִ֥י    כָלֵ֖ב    הַקָּטֹ֣ן
and-he-took-her    (13) Othniel    son-of    Kenaz    brother-of    Caleb    the-younger

מִמֶּ֑נּוּ    וַיִּתֶּן־    ל֛וֹ    אֶת־    עַכְסָ֥ה    בִתּ֖וֹ    לְאִשָּֽׁה:    וַיְהִ֣י
than-him    so-he-gave    to-him    ***    Acsah    daughter-of-him    as-wife    (14) and-he-was

בְּבוֹאָ֗הּ    וַתְּסִיתֵ֙הוּ֙    לִשְׁא֤וֹל    מֵֽאֵת־    אָבִ֙יהָ֙    הַשָּׂדֶ֔ה
when-to-come-her    then-she-urged-him    to-ask    from    father-of-her    the-field

וַתִּצְנַ֖ח    מֵעַ֣ל    הַחֲמ֑וֹר    וַיֹּֽאמֶר־    לָ֥הּ    כָּלֵ֖ב    מַה־    לָּֽךְ:
when-she-got-off    from-on    the-donkey    then-he-asked    to-her    Caleb    what?    for-you

וַתֹּ֨אמֶר    ל֜וֹ    הָֽבָה־    לִּ֣י    בְרָכָ֗ה    כִּ֣י    אֶ֤רֶץ    הַנֶּ֙גֶב֙
(15) and-she-replied    to-him    do!    for-me    favor    since    land-of    the-Negev

נְתַתָּ֔נִי    וְנָתַתָּ֥ה    לִ֖י    גֻּלֹּ֣ת    מָ֑יִם    וַיִּתֶּן־    לָ֣הּ    כָּלֵ֗ב
you-gave-me    then-you-give    to-me    springs-of    waters    then-he-gave    to-her    Caleb

אֵ֚ת    גֻּלֹּ֣ת    עִלִּ֔ית    וְאֵ֖ת    גֻּלֹּ֥ת    תַּחְתִּֽית:    וּבְנֵ֣י    קֵינִ֣י
***    springs-of    upper    and    springs-of    lower    (16) and-descendants-of    Kenite

חֹתֵ֣ן    מֹשֶׁ֗ה    עָל֞וּ    מֵעִ֤יר    הַתְּמָרִים֙    אֶת־    בְּנֵ֣י    יְהוּדָ֔ה
father-in-law-of    Moses    they-went-up    from-City-of    the-Palms    with    men-of    Judah

מִדְבַּ֣ר    יְהוּדָ֔ה    אֲשֶׁ֖ר    בְּנֶ֣גֶב    עֲרָ֑ד    וַיֵּ֖לֶךְ    וַיֵּ֥שֶׁב    אֶת־
Desert-of    Judah    that    in-Negev-of    Arad    and-he-went    and-he-lived    among

הָעָֽם:    וַיֵּ֤לֶךְ    יְהוּדָה֙    אֶת־    שִׁמְע֣וֹן    אָחִ֔יו    וַיַּכּ֕וּ
the-people    (17) then-he-went    Judah    with    Simeon    brother-of-him    and-they-attacked

אֶת־    הַכְּנַעֲנִ֖י    יוֹשֵׁ֣ב    צְפַ֑ת    וַיַּחֲרִ֣ימוּ    אוֹתָ֔הּ    וַיִּקְרָ֥א    אֶת־
***    the-Canaanite    living-of    Zephath    and-they-destoyed    her    and-he-called    ***

שֵׁם־    הָעִ֖יר    חָרְמָֽה:    וַיִּלְכֹּ֤ד    יְהוּדָה֙    אֶת־עַזָּ֣ה    וְאֶת־    גְּבוּלָ֔הּ
name-of    the-city    Hormah    (18) and-he-took    Judah    *** Gaza    and    territory-of-her

וְאֶת־    אַשְׁקְל֖וֹן    וְאֶת־    גְּבוּלָ֑הּ    וְאֶת־    עֶקְר֖וֹן    וְאֶת־    גְּבוּלָֽהּ:
and    Ashkelon    and    territory-of-her    and    Ekron    and    territory-of-her

---

western foothills. [10]They advanced against the Canaanites living in Hebron (formerly called Kiriath Arba) and defeated Sheshai, Ahiman and Talmai.

[11]From there they advanced against the people living in Debir (formerly called Kiriath Sepher). [12]And Caleb said, "I will give my daughter Acsah in marriage to the man who attacks and captures Kiriath Sepher." [13]Othniel son of Kenaz, Caleb's younger brother, took it; so Caleb gave him his daughter Acsah to him in marriage. [14]One day when she came to Othniel, she urged him[a] to ask her father for a field. When she got off her donkey, Caleb asked her, "What can I do for you?"

[15]She replied, "Do me a special favor. Since you have given me land in the Negev, give me also springs of water." Then Caleb gave her the upper and lower springs.

[16]The descendants of Moses' father-in-law, the Kenite, went up from the City of Palms[b] with the men of Judah to live among the people of the Desert of Judah in the Negev near Arad.

[17]Then the men of Judah went with the Simeonites their brothers and attacked the Canaanites living in Zephath, and they totally destroyed[c] the city. Therefore it was called Hormah.[d] [18]The men of Judah also took[e] Gaza, Ashkelon and Ekron—each city with its territory.

[a]14 Hebrew; Septuagint and Vulgate *Othniel, he urged her*
[b]16 That is, Jericho
[c]17 The Hebrew term refers to the irrevocable giving over of things or persons to the Lord, often by totally destroying them.
[d]17 *Hormah* means destruction.
[e]18 Hebrew; Septuagint *Judah did not take*

וַיְהִי יְהוָה אֶת־יְהוּדָה וַיֹּרֶשׁ אֶת־הָהָר כִּי
but the-hill-country *** and-he-possessed Judah with Yahweh and-he-was (19)

לֹא לְהוֹרִישׁ אֶת־יֹשְׁבֵי הָעֵמֶק כִּי־רֶכֶב בַּרְזֶל לָהֶם׃
to-them iron chariot-of for the-plain ones-living-of *** to-drive-out not

וַיִּתְּנוּ לְכָלֵב אֶת־חֶבְרוֹן כַּאֲשֶׁר דִּבֶּר מֹשֶׁה וַיּוֹרֶשׁ
and-he-drove Moses he-promised just-as Hebron *** to-Caleb and-they-gave (20)

מִשָּׁם אֶת־שְׁלֹשָׁה בְּנֵי הָעֲנָק׃ וְאֶת־הַיְבוּסִי יֹשֵׁב
living-of the-Jebusite but (21) the-Anak sons-of three *** from-there

יְרוּשָׁלִַם לֹא הוֹרִישׁוּ בְּנֵי בִנְיָמִן וַיֵּשֶׁב הַיְבוּסִי אֶת־
with the-Jebusite and-he-lives Benjamin sons-of they-dislodged not Jerusalem

בְּנֵי בִנְיָמִן בִּירוּשָׁלִַם עַד הַיּוֹם הַזֶּה׃ וַיַּעֲלוּ
now-they-attacked (22) the-this the-day to in-Jerusalem Benjamin sons-of

בֵית־יוֹסֵף גַּם־הֵם בֵּית־אֵל וַיהוָה עִמָּם׃
with-them and-Yahweh El Beth they indeed Joseph house-of

וַיָּתִירוּ בֵית־יוֹסֵף בְּבֵית־אֵל וְשֵׁם־הָעִיר
the-city now-name-of El to-Beth Joseph house-of and-they-sent-spies (23)

לְפָנִים לוּז׃ וַיִּרְאוּ הַשֹּׁמְרִים אִישׁ יוֹצֵא מִן־הָעִיר
the-city from coming-out man the-ones-spying and-they-saw (24) Luz formerly

וַיֹּאמְרוּ לוֹ הַרְאֵנוּ נָא אֶת־מְבוֹא הָעִיר וְעָשִׂינוּ
and-we-will-treat the-city entrance-of *** now! show-us! to-him and-they-said

עִמְּךָ חָסֶד׃ וַיַּרְאֵם אֶת־מְבוֹא הָעִיר וַיַּכּוּ
and-they-put the-city entrance-of *** so-he-showed-them (25) well with-you

אֶת־הָעִיר לְפִי־חָרֶב וְאֶת־הָאִישׁ וְאֶת־כָּל־מִשְׁפַּחְתּוֹ
family-of-him whole-of and the-man but sword to-edge-of the-city ***

שִׁלֵּחוּ׃ וַיֵּלֶךְ הָאִישׁ אֶרֶץ הַחִתִּים וַיִּבֶן עִיר
city and-he-built the-Hittites land-of the-man then-he-went (26) they-spared

וַיִּקְרָא שְׁמָהּ לוּז הוּא שְׁמָהּ עַד הַיּוֹם הַזֶּה׃
the-this the-day to name-of-her which Luz name-of-her and-he-called

וְלֹא־הוֹרִישׁ מְנַשֶּׁה אֶת־בֵּית־שְׁאָן וְאֶת־בְּנוֹתֶיהָ וְאֶת־
or settlements-of-her and Shan Beth *** Manasseh he-drove-out but-not (27)

תַּעְנַךְ וְאֶת־בְּנֹתֶיהָ וְאֶת־יוֹשְׁבֵי דוֹר וְאֶת־בְּנוֹתֶיהָ
settlements-of-her and Dor ones-living-of or settlements-of-her and Taanach

וְאֶת־יוֹשְׁבֵי יִבְלְעָם וְאֶת־בְּנֹתֶיהָ וְאֶת־יוֹשְׁבֵי מְגִדּוֹ
Meggido ones-living-of or settlements-of-her and Ibleam ones-living-of or

וְאֶת־בְּנוֹתֶיהָ וַיּוֹאֶל הַכְּנַעֲנִי לָשֶׁבֶת בָּאָרֶץ
in-the-land to-live the-Canaanite for-he-was-determined settlements-of-her and

הַזֹּאת׃ וַיְהִי כִּי־חָזַק יִשְׂרָאֵל וַיָּשֶׂם אֶת־
*** then-he-pressed Israel he-became-strong when and-he-was (28) the-that

[19]The LORD was with the
men of Judah. They took
possession of the hill country,
but they were unable to drive
the people from the plains, because they had iron chariots.
[20]As Moses had promised, Hebron was given to Caleb, who
drove from it the three sons of
Anak. [21]The Benjamites, however, failed to dislodge the Jebusites, who were living in
Jerusalem; to this day the Jebusites live there with the Benjamites.
[22]Now the house of Joseph
attacked Bethel, and the LORD
was with them. [23]When they
sent men to spy out Bethel
(formerly called Luz), [24]the
spies saw a man coming out of
the city and they said to him,
"Show us how to get into the
city and we will see that you
are treated well." [25]So he
showed them, and they put
the city to the sword but
spared the man and his whole
family. [26]He then went to the
land of the Hittites, where he
built a city and called it Luz,
which is its name to this day.
[27]But Manasseh did not
drive out the people of Beth
Shan or Taanach or Dor or
Ibleam or Megiddo and their
surrounding settlements, for
the Canaanites were determined to live in that land.
[28]When Israel became strong,
they pressed the Canaanites

°27 ק ישבי

הַכְּנַעֲנִי֙ לָמַ֔ס וְהוֹרֵ֖שׁ לֹ֥א הוֹרִישֽׁוֹ׃
the-Canaanite — into-forced-labor — but-to-drive-out — not — he-drove-out-him

(29) וְאֶפְרַ֗יִם לֹ֤א הוֹרִ֨ישׁ֙ אֶת־הַֽכְּנַעֲנִ֔י הַיּוֹשֵׁ֖ב בְּגָ֑זֶר
and-Ephraim — not — he-drove-out — *** the-Canaanite — the-one-living — in-Gezer

וַיֵּ֧שֶׁב הַֽכְּנַעֲנִ֛י בְּקִרְבּ֖וֹ בְּגָֽזֶר׃ (30) זְבוּלֻ֗ן לֹ֤א
but-he-lives — the-Canaanite — in-among-him — in-Gezer — Zebulun — not

הוֹרִישׁ֙ אֶת־יוֹשְׁבֵ֣י קִטְר֔וֹן וְאֶת־יֹשְׁבֵ֖י נַהֲלֹ֑ל וַיֵּ֨שֶׁב֙
he-drove-out — *** ones-living-of — Kitron — or ones-living-of — Nahalol — but-he-remained

הַֽכְּנַעֲנִ֣י בְּקִרְבּ֔וֹ וַיִּֽהְי֖וּ לָמַֽס׃ (31) אָשֵׁ֗ר לֹ֤א
the-Canaanite — in-among-him — but-they-became — at-forced-labor — Asher — not

הוֹרִישׁ֙ אֶת־יֹשְׁבֵ֣י עַכּ֔וֹ וְאֶת־ יוֹשְׁבֵ֖י צִיד֑וֹן וְאֶת־אַחְלָ֣ב וְאֶת־
he-drove-out — *** ones-living-of — Acco — or ones-living-of — Sidon — or Ahlab — or

אַכְזִ֗יב וְאֶת־ חֶלְבָּ֛ה וְאֶת־אֲפִ֖יק וְאֶת־רְחֹֽב׃ (32) וַיֵּ֙שֶׁב֙ הָאָ֣שֵׁרִ֔י בְּקֶ֥רֶב
Aczib — or Helbah — or Aphek — or Rehob — so-he-lived — the-Asherite — in-among

הַֽכְּנַעֲנִ֖י יֹשְׁבֵ֣י הָאָ֑רֶץ כִּ֖י לֹ֥א הוֹרִישֽׁוֹ׃
the-Canaanite — ones-inhabiting-of — the-land — for — not — he-drove-out-him

(33) נַפְתָּלִ֗י לֹֽא־הוֹרִ֞ישׁ אֶת־ יֹשְׁבֵ֤י בֵֽית־שֶׁ֙מֶשׁ֙ וְאֶת־ יֹשְׁבֵ֣י
Naphtali — not he-drove-out — *** ones-living-of — Beth Shemesh — or ones-living-of

בֵֽית־עֲנָ֔ת וַיֵּ֕שֶׁב בְּקֶ֥רֶב הַֽכְּנַעֲנִ֖י יֹשְׁבֵ֣י הָאָ֑רֶץ
Anath Beth — but-he-lived — in-among — the-Canaanite — ones-inhabiting-of — the-land

וְיֹשְׁבֵ֤י בֵֽית־שֶׁ֙מֶשׁ֙ וּבֵ֣ית עֲנָ֔ת הָי֥וּ לָהֶ֖ם
and-ones-living-of — Beth Shemesh — and-Beth Anath — they-became — for-them

לָמַֽס׃ (34) וַיִּלְחֲצ֧וּ הָאֱמֹרִ֛י אֶת־ בְּנֵי־ דָ֖ן
at-forced-labor — and-they-confined — the-Amorite — *** sons-of — Dan

הָהָ֑רָה כִּֽי־ לֹ֥א נְתָנ֖וֹ לָרֶ֥דֶת לָעֵֽמֶק׃
to-the-hill-country — and not — he-allowed-him — to-come-down — into-the-plain

(35) וַיּ֤וֹאֶל הָֽאֱמֹרִי֙ לָשֶׁ֣בֶת בְּהַר־ חֶ֑רֶס
and-he-was-determined — the-Amorite — to-hold-out — in-Mount-of — Heres

בְּאַיָּל֖וֹן וּבְשַֽׁעַלְבִ֑ים וַתִּכְבַּד֙ יַ֣ד בֵּית־ יוֹסֵ֔ף
in-Aijalon — and-in-Shaalbim — when-she-increased — power-of — house-of — Joseph

וַיִּהְי֖וּ לָמַֽס׃ (36) וּגְבוּל֙ הָאֱמֹרִ֔י מִֽמַּעֲלֵ֖ה
then-they-became — at-forced-labor — now-boundary-of — the-Amorite — from-Pass-of

עַקְרַבִּ֑ים מֵהַסֶּ֖לַע וָמָֽעְלָה׃ (2:1) וַיַּ֧עַל מַלְאַךְ־ יְהוָ֛ה מִן־
Scorpions — to-the-Sela — and-beyond — and-he-went-up — angel-of — Yahweh — from

הַגִּלְגָּ֖ל אֶל־ הַבֹּכִ֑ים וַיֹּ֗אמֶר אַעֲלֶ֤ה אֶתְכֶם֙ מִמִּצְרַ֔יִם וָאָבִ֤יא
the-Gilgal — to — the-Bokim — and-he-said — I-brought-up — you — from-Egypt — and-I-led

אֶתְכֶם֙ אֶל־הָאָ֔רֶץ אֲשֶׁ֥ר נִשְׁבַּ֖עְתִּי לַאֲבֹֽתֵיכֶ֑ם וָאֹמַ֕ר לֹֽא־ אָפֵ֧ר
you — into the-land — that — I-swore — to-fathers-of-you — and-I-said — not — I-will-break

into forced labor but never drove them out completely. 29Nor did Ephraim drive out the Canaanites living in Gezer, but the Canaanites continued to live there among them. 30Neither did Zebulun drive out the Canaanites living in Kitron or Nahalol, who remained among them; but they did subject them to forced labor. 31Nor did Asher drive out those living in Acco or Sidon or Ahlab or Aczib or Helbah or Aphek or Rehob, 32and because of this the people of Asher lived among the Canaanite inhabitants of the land. 33Neither did Naphtali drive out those living in Beth Shemesh or Beth Anath; but the Naphtalites too lived among the Canaanite inhabitants of the land, and those living in Beth Shemesh and Beth Anath became forced laborers for them. 34The Amorites confined the Danites to the hill country, not allowing them to come down into the plain. 35And the Amorites were determined also to hold out in Mount Heres, Aijalon and Shaalbim, but when the power of the house of Joseph increased, they too were pressed into forced labor. 36The boundary of the Amorites was from Scorpion*f* Pass to Sela and beyond.

*The Angel of the LORD at Bokim*

2 The angel of the LORD went up from Gilgal to Bokim and said, "I brought you up out of Egypt and led you into the land that I swore to give to your forefathers. I said, 'I will never break my

*f36 Hebrew Akrabbim*

בְּרִיתִי אִתְּכֶם לְעוֹלָם׃ וְאַתֶּם לֹא־ תִכְרְתוּ בְרִית

covenant you-shall-make not and-you (2) for-ever with-you covenant-of-me

לְיוֹשְׁבֵי הָאָרֶץ הַזֹּאת מִזְבְּחוֹתֵיהֶם תִּתֹּצוּן

you-shall-break-down altars-of-them the-this the-land with-ones-living-of

וְלֹא־ שְׁמַעְתֶּם בְּקֹלִי מַה־ זֹּאת עֲשִׂיתֶם׃ וְגַם אָמַרְתִּי לֹא־

not I-tell so-now (3) you-did this why? to-voice-of-me you-obeyed yet-not

אֲגָרֵשׁ אוֹתָם מִפְּנֵיכֶם וְהָיוּ לָכֶם לְצִדִּים

in-sides to-you and-they-will-be from-before-you them I-will-drive-out

וֵאלֹהֵיהֶם יִהְיוּ לָכֶם לְמוֹקֵשׁ׃ וַיְהִי כְּדַבֵּר

when-to-speak and-he-was (4) as-snare to-you they-will-be and-gods-of-them

מַלְאַךְ יְהוָה אֶת־ הַדְּבָרִים הָאֵלֶּה אֶל־ כָּל־ בְּנֵי יִשְׂרָאֵל

Israel sons-of all-of to the-these the-things *** Yahweh angel-of

וַיִּשְׂאוּ הָעָם אֶת־ קוֹלָם וַיִּבְכּוּ׃ וַיִּקְרְאוּ

and-they-called (5) and-they-wept voice-of-them *** the-people then-they-lifted

שֵׁם־ הַמָּקוֹם הַהוּא בֹּכִים וַיִּזְבְּחוּ־ שָׁם לַיהוָה׃

to-Yahweh there and-they-sacrificed Bokim the-that the-place name-of

וַיְשַׁלַּח יְהוֹשֻׁעַ אֶת־ הָעָם וַיֵּלְכוּ בְנֵי־ יִשְׂרָאֵל אִישׁ

each Israel sons-of and-they-went the-people *** Joshua then-he-dismissed (6)

לְנַחֲלָתוֹ לָרֶשֶׁת אֶת־ הָאָרֶץ׃ וַיַּעַבְדוּ הָעָם

the-people and-they-served (7) the-land *** to-possess to-inheritance-of-him

אֶת־ יְהוָה כֹּל יְמֵי יְהוֹשֻׁעַ וְכֹל יְמֵי הַזְּקֵנִים אֲשֶׁר

who the-elders days-of and-all-of Joshua days-of all-of Yahweh ***

הֶאֱרִיכוּ יָמִים אַחֲרֵי יְהוֹשׁוּעַ אֲשֶׁר רָאוּ אֵת כָּל־ מַעֲשֵׂה יְהוָה

Yahweh thing-of every-of *** they-saw who Joshua after days they-outlived

הַגָּדוֹל אֲשֶׁר עָשָׂה לְיִשְׂרָאֵל׃ וַיָּמָת יְהוֹשֻׁעַ בִּן־ נוּן עֶבֶד

servant-of Nun son-of Joshua and-he-died (8) for-Israel he-did that the-great

יְהוָה בֶּן־ מֵאָה וָעֶשֶׂר שָׁנִים׃ וַיִּקְבְּרוּ אוֹתוֹ בִּגְבוּל

in-land-of him and-they-buried (9) years and-ten hundred son-of Yahweh

נַחֲלָתוֹ בְּתִמְנַת־ חֶרֶס בְּהַר אֶפְרָיִם מִצְּפוֹן

to-north Ephraim in-hill-country-of Heres at-Timnath inheritance-of-him

לְהַר־ גָּעַשׁ׃ וְגַם כָּל־ הַדּוֹר הַהוּא

the-that the-generation whole-of and-also (10) Gaash of-Mount-of

נֶאֶסְפוּ אֶל־ אֲבוֹתָיו וַיָּקָם דּוֹר אַחֵר

another generation then-he-grew-up fathers-of-him to they-were-gathered

אַחֲרֵיהֶם אֲשֶׁר לֹא־ יָדְעוּ אֶת־ יְהוָה וְגַם אֶת־הַמַּעֲשֶׂה אֲשֶׁר עָשָׂה

he-did that the-deed *** nor-either Yahweh *** they-knew not who after-them

לְיִשְׂרָאֵל׃ וַיַּעֲשׂוּ בְנֵי־ יִשְׂרָאֵל אֶת־ הָרַע בְּעֵינֵי יְהוָה

Yahweh in-eyes-of the-evil *** Israel sons-of then-they-did (11) for-Israel

covenant with you, [2]and you shall not make a covenant with the people of this land, but you shall break down their altars.' Yet you have disobeyed me. Why have you done this? [3]Now therefore I tell you that I will not drive them out before you; they will be ⌊thorns⌋ in your sides and their gods will be a snare to you."

[4]When the angel of the LORD had spoken these things to all the Israelites, the people wept aloud, [5]and they called that place Bokim.[g] There they offered sacrifices to the LORD.

*Disobedience and Defeat*

[6]After Joshua had dismissed the Israelites, they went to take possession of the land, each to his own inheritance. [7]The people served the LORD throughout the lifetime of Joshua and of the elders who outlived him and who had seen all the great things the LORD had done for Israel.

[8]Joshua son of Nun, the servant of the LORD, died at the age of a hundred and ten. [9]And they buried him in the land of his inheritance, at Timnath Heres[h] in the hill country of Ephraim, north of Mount Gaash.

[10]After that whole generation had been gathered to their fathers, another generation grew up, who knew neither the LORD nor what he had done for Israel. [11]Then the Israelites did evil in the eyes of

g5 *Bokim* means *weepers.*

h9 Also known as *Timnath Serah* (see Joshua 19:50 and 24:30)

וַיַּעַבְדוּ אֶת־הַבְּעָלִים׃ וַיַּעַזְבוּ אֶת־יְהוָה ׀ אֱלֹהֵי
God-of Yahweh *** and-they-forsook (12) the-Baals *** and-they-served

אֲבוֹתָם הַמּוֹצִיא אוֹתָם מֵאֶרֶץ מִצְרַיִם וַיֵּלְכוּ
and-they-followed Egypt from-land-of them the-one-bringing fathers-of-them

אַחֲרֵי ׀ אֱלֹהִים אֲחֵרִים מֵאֱלֹהֵי הָעַמִּים אֲשֶׁר סְבִיבוֹתֵיהֶם
ones-around-them who the-peoples from-gods-of other-ones gods after

וַיִּשְׁתַּחֲווּ לָהֶם וַיַּכְעִסוּ אֶת־יְהוָה׃ וַיַּעַזְבוּ
for-they-forsook (13) Yahweh *** and-they-angered to-them and-they-worshiped

אֶת־יְהוָה וַיַּעַבְדוּ לַבַּעַל וְלָעַשְׁתָּרוֹת׃ וַיִּחַר־
and-he-burned (14) and-to-the-Ashtoreths to-the-Baal and-they-served Yahweh ***

אַף יְהוָה בְּיִשְׂרָאֵל וַיִּתְּנֵם בְּיַד־שֹׁסִים
ones-raiding into-hand-of and-he-gave-them against-Israel Yahweh anger-of

וַיָּשֹׁסּוּ אוֹתָם וַיִּמְכְּרֵם בְּיַד אוֹיְבֵיהֶם
being-enemies-of-them into-hand-of and-he-sold-them them and-they-plundered

מִסָּבִיב וְלֹא־יָכְלוּ עוֹד לַעֲמֹד לִפְנֵי אוֹיְבֵיהֶם׃
being-enemies-of-them against to-resist longer they-were-able and-not at-around

בְּכֹל ׀ אֲשֶׁר יָצְאוּ יַד־יְהוָה הָיְתָה־בָּם
against-them she-was Yahweh hand-of they-went-out when in-every (15)

לְרָעָה כַּאֲשֶׁר דִּבֶּר יְהוָה וְכַאֲשֶׁר נִשְׁבַּע יְהוָה לָהֶם
to-them Yahweh he-swore and-just-as Yahweh he-said just-as for-defeat

וַיֵּצֶר לָהֶם מְאֹד׃ וַיָּקֶם יְהוָה שֹׁפְטִים
ones-judging Yahweh then-he-raised-up (16) greatly to-them and-he-distressed

וַיּוֹשִׁיעוּם מִיַּד שֹׁסֵיהֶם׃ וְגַם אֶל־
to and-yet (17) ones-raiding-them from-hand-of and-they-saved-them

שֹׁפְטֵיהֶם לֹא שָׁמֵעוּ כִּי זָנוּ אַחֲרֵי אֱלֹהִים אֲחֵרִים
other-ones gods to they-prostituted but they-listened not ones-judging-them

וַיִּשְׁתַּחֲווּ לָהֶם סָרוּ מַהֵר מִן־הַדֶּרֶךְ אֲשֶׁר
which the-way from to-be-quick they-turned to-them and-they-worshiped

הָלְכוּ אֲבוֹתָם לִשְׁמֹעַ מִצְוֺת־יְהוָה לֹא־עָשׂוּ כֵן׃
this they-did not Yahweh commands-of to-obey fathers-of-them they-walked

וְכִי־הֵקִים יְהוָה ׀ לָהֶם שֹׁפְטִים וְהָיָה יְהוָה
Yahweh then-he-was ones-judging for-them Yahweh he-raised-up and-when (18)

עִם־הַשֹּׁפֵט וְהוֹשִׁיעָם מִיַּד אֹיְבֵיהֶם
being-enemies-of-them from-hand-of and-he-saved-them the-one-judging with

כֹּל יְמֵי הַשּׁוֹפֵט כִּי־יִנָּחֵם יְהוָה מִנַּאֲקָתָם
on-groan-of-them Yahweh he-had-compassion for the-one-judging days-of all-of

מִפְּנֵי לֹחֲצֵיהֶם וְדֹחֲקֵיהֶם׃ וְהָיָה ׀
but-he-was (19) and-ones-afflicting-them ones-oppressing-them from-under

the LORD and served the Baals.
12They forsook the LORD, the
God of their fathers, who had
brought them out of Egypt.
They followed and worshiped
various gods of the peoples
around them. They provoked
the LORD to anger 13because
they forsook him and served
Baal and the Ashtoreths. 14In
his anger against Israel the
LORD handed them over to
raiders who plundered them.
He sold them to their enemies
all around, whom they were
no longer able to resist.
15Whenever Israel went out to
fight, the hand of the LORD
was against them to defeat
them, just as he had sworn to
them. They were in great distress.
16Then the LORD raised up
judges,[i] who saved them out
of the hands of these raiders.
17Yet they would not listen to
their judges but prostituted
themselves to other gods and
worshiped them. Unlike their
fathers, they quickly turned
from the way in which their
fathers had walked, the way of
obedience to the LORD's commands. 18Whenever the LORD
raised up a judge for them, he
was with the judge and saved
them out of the hands of their
enemies as long as the judge
lived; for the LORD had compassion on them as they
groaned under those who oppressed and afflicted them.

[i]16 Or *leaders;* similarly in verses 17-19

בְּמוֹת הַשּׁוֹפֵט יָשֻׁבוּ וְהִשְׁחִיתוּ
and-they-were-corrupt they-returned the-one-judging when-to-die

מֵאֲבוֹתָם לָלֶכֶת אַחֲרֵי אֱלֹהִים אֲחֵרִים לְעָבְדָם
to-serve-them other-ones gods after to-follow more-than-fathers-of-them

וּלְהִשְׁתַּחֲוֹת לָהֶם לֹא הִפִּילוּ מִמַּעַלְלֵיהֶם
from-practices-of-them they-gave-up not to-them and-to-worship

וּמִדַּרְכָּם הַקָּשָׁה׃ וַיִּחַר־ אַף יְהוָה בְּיִשְׂרָאֵל
with-Israel Yahweh anger-of and-he-burned (20) the-stubborn and-from-way-them

וַיֹּאמֶר יַעַן אֲשֶׁר עָבְרוּ הַגּוֹי הַזֶּה אֶת־ בְּרִיתִי
covenant-of-me *** the-this the-nation they-violated that because and-he-said

אֲשֶׁר צִוִּיתִי אֶת־ אֲבוֹתָם וְלֹא שָׁמְעוּ לְקוֹלִי׃
to-voice-of-me they-listened and-not fathers-of-them for I-laid-down that

גַּם־ אֲנִי לֹא אוֹסִיף לְהוֹרִישׁ אִישׁ מִפְּנֵיהֶם מִן־
from from-before-them any to-drive-out I-will-continue not I indeed (21)

הַגּוֹיִם אֲשֶׁר־ עָזַב יְהוֹשֻׁעַ וַיָּמֹת׃ לְמַעַן נַסּוֹת בָּם
with-them to-test so-that (22) when-he-died Joshua he-left that the-nations

אֶת־יִשְׂרָאֵל הֲשֹׁמְרִים הֵם אֶת־ דֶּרֶךְ יְהוָה לָלֶכֶת בָּם
in-them to-walk Yahweh way-of *** they whether-ones-keeping Israel ***

כַּאֲשֶׁר שָׁמְרוּ אֲבוֹתָם אִם־לֹא׃ וַיַּנַּח יְהוָה אֶת־
*** Yahweh and-he-let-remain (23) not or fathers-of-them they-did just-as

הַגּוֹיִם הָאֵלֶּה לְבִלְתִּי הוֹרִישָׁם מַהֵר וְלֹא נְתָנָם
he-gave-them and-not to-be-quick to-drive-out-them not the-those the-nations

בְּיַד־ יְהוֹשֻׁעַ׃ וְאֵלֶּה הַגּוֹיִם אֲשֶׁר הִנִּיחַ יְהוָה לְנַסּוֹת
to-test Yahweh he-left that the-nations and-these (3:1) Joshua into-hand-of

בָּם אֶת־ יִשְׂרָאֵל אֵת כָּל־אֲשֶׁר לֹא־ יָדְעוּ אֵת כָּל־מִלְחֲמוֹת
wars-of any-of *** they-experienced not who all *** Israel *** with-them

כְּנָעַן׃ רַק לְמַעַן דַּעַת דֹּרוֹת בְּנֵי־ יִשְׂרָאֵל
Israel sons-of generations-of to-experience so-that only (2) Canaan

לְלַמְּדָם מִלְחָמָה רַק אֲשֶׁר־ לְפָנִים לֹא יְדָעוּם׃
they-experienced-them not previously who only warfare to-teach-them

חֲמֵשֶׁת׀ סַרְנֵי פְלִשְׁתִּים וְכָל־ הַכְּנַעֲנִי וְהַצִּידֹנִי
and-the-Sidonian the-Canaanite and-all-of Philistines rulers-of five-of (3)

וְהַחִוִּי יֹשֵׁב הַר הַלְּבָנוֹן מֵהַר בַּעַל חֶרְמוֹן
Hermon Baal from-Mount-of the-Lebanon mountain-of living-of and-the-Hivite

עַד לְבוֹא חֲמָת׃ וַיִּהְיוּ לְנַסּוֹת בָּם אֶת־יִשְׂרָאֵל לָדַעַת
to-see Israel *** with-them to-test and-they-were (4) Hamath Lebo to

הֲיִשְׁמְעוּ אֶת־ מִצְוֹת יְהוָה אֲשֶׁר־ צִוָּה אֶת־ אֲבוֹתָם
fathers-of-them *** he-gave which Yahweh commands-of *** whether-they-would-obey

[19]But when the judge died, the
people returned to ways even
more corrupt than those of
their fathers, following other
gods and serving and wor-
shiping them. They refused to
give up their evil practices and
stubborn ways.
[20]Therefore the LORD was
very angry with Israel and
said, "Because this nation has
violated the covenant that I
laid down for their forefathers
and has not listened to me, [21]I
will no longer drive out before
them any of the nations
Joshua left when he died. [22]I
will use them to test Israel and
see whether they will keep the
way of the LORD and walk in it
as their forefathers did." [23]The
LORD had allowed those nations to remain; he did not
drive them out at once by giving them into the hands of
Joshua.
3 These are the nations the
LORD left to test all those
Israelites who had not experienced any of the wars in Canaan [2](he did this only to
teach warfare to the descendants of the Israelites who had
not had previous battle experience): [3]the five rulers of the
Philistines, all the Canaanites,
the Sidonians, and the Hivites
living in the Lebanon mountains from Mount Baal Hermon to Lebo[j] Hamath. [4]They
were left to test the Israelites to
see whether they would obey
the LORD's commands, which
he had given their forefathers

[j]3 *Or to the entrance to*

בְּיַד־ מֹשֶׁה׃ וּבְנֵי יִשְׂרָאֵל יָשְׁבוּ בְּקֶרֶב הַכְּנַעֲנִי

the-Canaanite in-among they-lived Israel and-sons-of (5) Moses by-hand-of

הַחִתִּי וְהָאֱמֹרִי וְהַפְּרִזִּי וְהַחִוִּי וְהַיְבוּסִי׃

and-the-Jebusite and-the-Hivite and-the-Perizzite and-the-Amorite the-Hittite

וַיִּקְחוּ אֶת־ בְּנוֹתֵיהֶם לָהֶם לְנָשִׁים וְאֶת־ בְּנוֹתֵיהֶם

daughters-of-them and as-wives for-them daughters-of-them *** and-they-took (6)

נָתְנוּ לִבְנֵיהֶם וַיַּעַבְדוּ אֶת־ אֱלֹהֵיהֶם׃ וַיַּעֲשׂוּ

and-they-did (7) gods-of-them *** and-they-served to-sons-of-them they-gave

בְנֵי־ יִשְׂרָאֵל אֶת־ הָרַע בְּעֵינֵי יְהוָה וַיִּשְׁכְּחוּ אֶת־ יְהוָה

Yahweh *** and-they-forgot Yahweh in-eyes-of the-evil *** Israel sons-of

אֱלֹהֵיהֶם וַיַּעַבְדוּ אֶת־הַבְּעָלִים וְאֶת־הָאֲשֵׁרוֹת׃ וַיִּחַר־

and-he-burned (8) the-Asherahs and the-Baals *** and-they-served God-of-them

אַף יְהוָה בְּיִשְׂרָאֵל וַיִּמְכְּרֵם בְּיַד כּוּשַׁן רִשְׁעָתַיִם

Rishathaim Cushan into-hand-of so-he-sold-them against-Israel Yahweh anger-of

מֶלֶךְ אֲרַם נַהֲרָיִם וַיַּעַבְדוּ בְנֵי־ יִשְׂרָאֵל אֶת־ כּוּשַׁן רִשְׁעָתַיִם

Rishathaim Cushan *** Israel sons-of and-they-served Naharaim Aram king-of

שְׁמֹנֶה שָׁנִים׃ וַיִּזְעֲקוּ בְנֵי־ יִשְׂרָאֵל אֶל־ יְהוָה וַיָּקֶם

so-he-raised-up Yahweh to Israel sons-of but-they-cried (9) years eight

יְהוָה מוֹשִׁיעַ לִבְנֵי יִשְׂרָאֵל וַיּוֹשִׁיעֵם אֵת עָתְנִיאֵל בֶּן־

son-of Othniel *** and-he-saved-them Israel for-sons-of one-delivering Yahweh

קְנַז אֲחִי כָלֵב הַקָּטֹן מִמֶּנּוּ׃ וַתְּהִי עָלָיו רוּחַ־

Spirit-of upon-him and-she-came (10) than-him the-younger Caleb brother-of Kenaz

יְהוָה וַיִּשְׁפֹּט אֶת־ יִשְׂרָאֵל וַיֵּצֵא לַמִּלְחָמָה וַיִּתֵּן יְהוָה

Yahweh and-he-gave to-the-war and-he-went Israel *** and-he-judged Yahweh

בְּיָדוֹ אֶת־ כּוּשַׁן רִשְׁעָתַיִם מֶלֶךְ אֲרָם וַתָּעָז

and-she-overpowered Aram king-of Rishathaim Cushan *** into-hand-of-him

יָדוֹ עַל כּוּשַׁן רִשְׁעָתָיִם׃ וַתִּשְׁקֹט הָאָרֶץ אַרְבָּעִים

forty the-land so-she-had-peace (11) Rishathaim Cushan over hand-of-him

שָׁנָה וַיָּמָת עָתְנִיאֵל בֶּן־ קְנַז׃ וַיֹּסִפוּ בְּנֵי יִשְׂרָאֵל

Israel sons-of and-they-did-again (12) Kenaz son-of Othniel and-he-died year

לַעֲשׂוֹת הָרַע בְּעֵינֵי יְהוָה וַיְחַזֵּק יְהוָה אֶת־ עֶגְלוֹן מֶלֶךְ־

king-of Eglon *** Yahweh and-he-gave-power Yahweh in-eyes-of the-evil to-do

מוֹאָב עַל־יִשְׂרָאֵל עַל כִּי־ עָשׂוּ אֶת־ הָרַע בְּעֵינֵי יְהוָה׃

Yahweh in-eyes-of the-evil *** they-did that because Israel over Moab

וַיֶּאֱסֹף אֵלָיו אֶת־ בְּנֵי עַמּוֹן וַעֲמָלֵק וַיֵּלֶךְ

and-he-came and-Amalek Ammon sons-of *** with-him and-he-joined (13)

וַיַּךְ אֶת־ יִשְׂרָאֵל וַיִּירְשׁוּ אֶת־ עִיר הַתְּמָרִים׃

the-Palms City-of *** and-they-possessed Israel *** and-he-attacked

through Moses.

[5]The Israelites lived among the Canaanites, Hittites, Amorites, Perizzites, Hivites and Jebusites. [6]They took their daughters in marriage and gave their own daughters to their sons, and served their gods.

*Othniel*

[7]The Israelites did evil in the eyes of the LORD; they forgot the LORD their God and served the Baals and the Asherahs. [8]The anger of the LORD burned against Israel so that he sold them into the hands of Cushan-Rishathaim king of Aram Naharaim,[k] to whom the Israelites were subject for eight years. [9]But when they cried out to the LORD, he raised up for them a deliverer, Othniel son of Kenaz, Caleb's younger brother, who saved them. [10]The Spirit of the LORD came upon him, so that he became Israel's judge[l] and went to war. The LORD gave Cushan-Rishathaim king of Aram into the hands of Othniel, who overpowered him. [11]So the land had peace for forty years, until Othniel son of Kenaz died.

*Ehud*

[12]Once again the Israelites did evil in the eyes of the LORD, and because they did this evil the LORD gave Eglon king of Moab power over Israel. [13]Getting the Ammonites and Amalekites to join him, Eglon came and attacked Israel, and they took possession of

[k]8 That is, Northwest Mesopotamia
[l]10 Or *leader*

וַיַּעַבְדוּ בְּנֵי־ יִשְׂרָאֵל אֶת־עֶגְלוֹן מֶלֶךְ־מוֹאָב שְׁמוֹנֶה עֶשְׂרֵה שָׁנָה׃
year ten eight Moab king-of Eglon *** Israel sons-of and-they-served (14)

וַיִּזְעֲקוּ בְנֵי־ יִשְׂרָאֵל אֶל־ יְהוָה וַיָּקֶם יְהוָה לָהֶם
to-them Yahweh and-he-gave Yahweh to Israel sons-of and-they-cried (15)

מוֹשִׁיעַ אֶת־ אֵהוּד בֶּן־ גֵּרָא בֶּן־הַיְמִינִי אִישׁ אִטֵּר יַד־
hand-of bound-of man the-Benjamite Gera son-of Ehud *** one-delivering

יְמִינוֹ וַיִּשְׁלְחוּ בְנֵי־ יִשְׂרָאֵל בְּיָדוֹ מִנְחָה לְעֶגְלוֹן
to-Eglon tribute in-hand-of-him Israel sons-of and-they-sent right-of-him

מֶלֶךְ מוֹאָב׃ וַיַּעַשׂ לוֹ אֵהוּד חֶרֶב וְלָהּ שְׁנֵי פֵיוֹת
edges two-of and-on-her sword Ehud for-him now-he-made (16) Moab king-of

גֹּמֶד אָרְכָּהּ וַיַּחְגֹּר אוֹתָהּ מִתַּחַת לְמַדָּיו עַל
to to-clothes-of-him at-under her and-he-strapped length-of-her cubit

יֶרֶךְ יְמִינוֹ׃ וַיַּקְרֵב אֶת־ הַמִּנְחָה לְעֶגְלוֹן מֶלֶךְ
king-of to-Eglon the-tribute *** and-he-presented (17) right-of-him thigh-of

מוֹאָב וְעֶגְלוֹן אִישׁ בָּרִיא מְאֹד׃ וַיְהִי כַּאֲשֶׁר כִּלָּה לְהַקְרִיב אֶת־
*** to-present he-finished just-as and-he-was (18) very fat man now-Eglon Moab

הַמִּנְחָה וַיְשַׁלַּח אֶת־ הָעָם נֹשְׂאֵי הַמִּנְחָה׃
the-tribute ones-carrying-of the-people *** then-he-sent-away the-tribute

וְהוּא שָׁב מִן־הַפְּסִילִים אֲשֶׁר אֶת־ הַגִּלְגָּל וַיֹּאמֶר
and-he-said the-Gilgal near that the-idols at he-turned-back but-he (19)

דְּבַר־ סֵתֶר לִי אֵלֶיךָ הַמֶּלֶךְ וַיֹּאמֶר הָס וַיֵּצְאוּ
and-they-left quiet! and-he-said the-king for-you to-me secret message-of

מֵעָלָיו כָּל־ הָעֹמְדִים עָלָיו׃ וְאֵהוּד ׀ בָּא
he-approached then-Ehud (20) to-him the-ones-attending all-of from-with-him

אֵלָיו וְהוּא־ יֹשֵׁב בַּעֲלִיַּת הַמְּקֵרָה אֲשֶׁר־ לוֹ
to-him that the-summer-palace in-upper-room-of sitting while-he to-him

לְבַדּוֹ וַיֹּאמֶר אֵהוּד דְּבַר־ אֱלֹהִים לִי אֵלֶיךָ וַיָּקָם מֵעַל
from-on and-he-rose for-you to-me God message-of Ehud and-he-said by-himself

הַכִּסֵּא׃ וַיִּשְׁלַח אֵהוּד אֶת־ יַד שְׂמֹאלוֹ וַיִּקַּח אֶת־
and-he-drew left-of-him hand-of *** Ehud and-he-reached (21) the-seat

הַחֶרֶב מֵעַל יֶרֶךְ יְמִינוֹ וַיִּתְקָעֶהָ בְּבִטְנוֹ׃
into-belly-of-him and-he-plunged-her right-of-him thigh-of from-on the-sword

וַיָּבֹא גַם־ הַנִּצָּב אַחַר הַלַּהַב וַיִּסְגֹּר הַחֵלֶב בְּעַד
over the-fat and-he-closed the-blade after the-handle even and-he-sank-in (22)

הַלַּהַב כִּי לֹא שָׁלַף הַחֶרֶב מִבִּטְנוֹ וַיֵּצֵא
and-he-came-out from-belly-of-him the-sword he-pulled-out not for the-blade

הַפַּרְשְׁדֹנָה׃ וַיֵּצֵא אֵהוּד הַמִּסְדְּרוֹנָה וַיִּסְגֹּר דַּלְתוֹת
doors-of and-he-shut to-the-porch Ehud then-he-went-out (23) of-the-back

the City of Palms.[m] 14The Isra-
elites were subject to Eglon king of Moab for eighteen years.

15Again the Israelites cried
out to the LORD, and he gave them a deliverer—Ehud, a left-handed man, the son of Gera the Benjamite. The Israelites sent him with tribute to Eglon
king of Moab. 16Now Ehud
had made a double-edged sword about a foot and a half[n] long, which he strapped to his right thigh under his clothing.
17He presented the tribute to
Eglon king of Moab, who was a very fat man. 18After Ehud
had presented the tribute, he sent on their way the men who had carried it. 19At the
idols[o] near Gilgal he himself turned back and said, "I have a secret message for you, O king."

The king said, "Quiet!" And all his attendants left him.

20Ehud then approached
him while he was sitting alone in the upper room of his summer palace[p] and said, "I have a message from God for you." As the king rose from his seat,
21Ehud reached with his left
hand, drew the sword from his right thigh and plunged it into the king's belly. 22Even
the handle sank in after the blade, which came out his back. Ehud did not pull the sword out, and the fat closed in over it. 23Then Ehud went
out to the porch[q]; he shut the

[m] 13 That is, Jericho
[n] 16 Hebrew *a cubit* (about 0.5 meter)
[o] 19 Or *the stone quarries*; also in verse 26
[p] 20 The meaning of the Hebrew for this phrase is uncertain.
[q] 23 The meaning of the Hebrew for this word is uncertain.

הָעֲלִיָּה* בַּעֲדוֹ וְנָעָל׃ וְהוּא יָצָא וַעֲבָדָיו
and-servants-of-him he-went now-he (24) and-he-locked behind-him the-upper-room

בָּאוּ וַיִּרְאוּ וְהִנֵּה דַּלְתוֹת הָעֲלִיָּה נְעֻלוֹת
ones-being-locked the-upper-room doors-of and-see! and-they-looked they-came

וַיֹּאמְרוּ אַךְ מֵסִיךְ הוּא אֶת־ רַגְלָיו בַּחֲדַר הַמְּקֵרָה׃
the-house in-inner-room-of feet-of-him *** he covering indeed and-they-said

וַיָּחִילוּ עַד־ בּוֹשׁ וְהִנֵּה אֵינֶנּוּ פֹּתֵחַ דַּלְתוֹת
doors-of opening not-he but-see! to-be-embarrassed until and-they-waited (25)

הָעֲלִיָּה וַיִּקְחוּ אֶת־ הַמַּפְתֵּחַ וַיִּפְתָּחוּ וְהִנֵּה אֲדֹנֵיהֶם
lords-of-them and-see! and-they-unlocked the-key *** so-they-took the-upper-room

נֹפֵל אַרְצָה מֵת׃ וְאֵהוּד נִמְלַט עַד הִתְמַהְמְהָם
to-wait-them while he-got-away and-Ehud (26) being-dead on-floor one-falling

וְהוּא עָבַר אֶת־ הַפְּסִילִים וַיִּמָּלֵט הַשְּׂעִירָתָה׃ וַיְהִי
and-he-was (27) to-the-Seirah and-he-escaped the-idols *** he-passed-by and-he

בְּבוֹאוֹ וַיִּתְקַע בַּשּׁוֹפָר בְּהַר אֶפְרָיִם
Ephraim in-hill-country-of on-the-trumpet then-he-blew when-to-arrive-him

וַיֵּרְדוּ עִמּוֹ בְנֵי־ יִשְׂרָאֵל מִן־ הָהָר וְהוּא לִפְנֵיהֶם׃
before-them and-he the-hill from Israel sons-of with-him and-they-went-down

וַיֹּאמֶר אֲלֵהֶם רִדְפוּ אַחֲרַי כִּי־ נָתַן יְהוָה אֶת־
*** Yahweh he-gave for after-me follow! to-them and-he-ordered (28)

אֹיְבֵיכֶם אֶת־ מוֹאָב בְּיֶדְכֶם וַיֵּרְדוּ אַחֲרָיו
after-him so-they-followed into-hand-of-you Moab *** being-enemies-of-you

וַיִּלְכְּדוּ אֶת־ מַעְבְּרוֹת הַיַּרְדֵּן לְמוֹאָב וְלֹא־ נָתְנוּ
they-allowed and-not to-Moab the-Jordan fords-of *** and-they-possessed

אִישׁ לַעֲבֹר׃ וַיַּכּוּ אֶת־ מוֹאָב בָּעֵת הַהִיא
the-that at-the-time Moab *** and-he-struck-down (29) to-cross-over anyone

כַּעֲשֶׂרֶת אֲלָפִים אִישׁ כָּל־ שָׁמֵן וְכָל־ אִישׁ חָיִל וְלֹא
and-not strong man-of and-all-of vigorous all-of man thousands about-ten-of

נִמְלַט אִישׁ׃ וַתִּכָּנַע מוֹאָב בַּיּוֹם הַהוּא תַּחַת
under the-that on-the-day Moab and-she-was-made-subject (30) man he-escaped

יַד יִשְׂרָאֵל וַתִּשְׁקֹט הָאָרֶץ שְׁמוֹנִים שָׁנָה׃ וְאַחֲרָיו
and-after-him (31) year eighty the-land and-she-had-peace Israel hand-of

הָיָה שַׁמְגַּר בֶּן־ עֲנָת וַיַּךְ אֶת־ פְּלִשְׁתִּים שֵׁשׁ־ מֵאוֹת
hundreds six Philistines *** and-he-struck-down Anath son-of Shamgar he-came

אִישׁ בְּמַלְמַד הַבָּקָר וַיּוֹשַׁע גַּם־ הוּא אֶת־יִשְׂרָאֵל׃ וַיֹּסִפוּ
and-they-repeated (4:1) Israel *** he also and-he-saved the-ox with-goad-of man

בְּנֵי יִשְׂרָאֵל לַעֲשׂוֹת הָרַע בְּעֵינֵי יְהוָה וְאֵהוּד מֵת׃
he-died now-Ehud Yahweh in-eyes-of the-evil to-do Israel sons-of

doors of the upper room behind him and locked them.
24 After he had gone, the servants came and found the doors of the upper room locked. They said, "He must be relieving himself in the inner room of the house."
25 They waited to the point of embarrassment, but when he did not open the doors of the room, they took a key and unlocked them. There they saw their lord fallen to the floor, dead.
26 While they waited, Ehud got away. He passed by the idols and escaped to Seirah.
27 When he arrived there, he blew a trumpet in the hill country of Ephraim, and the Israelites went down with him from the hills, with him leading them.
28 "Follow me," he ordered, "for the LORD has given Moab, your enemy, into your hands." So they followed him down and, taking possession of the fords of the Jordan that led to Moab, they allowed no one to cross over.
29 At that time they struck down about ten thousand Moabites, all vigorous and strong; not a man escaped.
30 That day Moab was made subject to Israel, and the land had peace for eighty years.

*Shamgar*

31 After Ehud came Shamgar son of Anath, who struck down six hundred Philistines with an oxgoad. He too saved Israel.

*Deborah*

4 After Ehud died, the Israelites once again did evil in the eyes of the LORD.
2 So the

***23 Most mss have *hateph pathah* under the *ayin* (הָעֲ).**

וַיִּמְכְּרֵם יְהוָה בְּיַד יָבִין מֶלֶךְ־ כְּנַעַן אֲשֶׁר מָלַךְ
he-reigned who Canaan king-of Jabin into-hand-of Yahweh so-he-sold-them (2)

בְּחָצוֹר וְשַׂר־ צְבָאוֹ סִיסְרָא וְהוּא יוֹשֵׁב בַּחֲרֹשֶׁת
in-Harosheth living and-he Sisera army-of-him and-commander-of in-Hazor

הַגּוֹיִם׃ וַיִּצְעֲקוּ בְנֵי־ יִשְׂרָאֵל אֶל־ יְהוָה כִּי תְּשַׁע מֵאוֹת
hundreds nine-of for Yahweh to Israel sons-of and-they-cried (3) Haggoyim

רֶכֶב־ בַּרְזֶל לוֹ וְהוּא לָחַץ אֶת־ בְּנֵי יִשְׂרָאֵל בְּחָזְקָה
with-cruelty Israel sons-of *** he-oppressed and-he to-him iron chariot-of

עֶשְׂרִים שָׁנָה׃ וּדְבוֹרָה אִשָּׁה נְבִיאָה אֵשֶׁת לַפִּידוֹת הִיא שֹׁפְטָה
leading she Lappidoth wife-of prophetess woman now-Deborah (4) year twenty

אֶת־ יִשְׂרָאֵל בָּעֵת הַהִיא׃ וְהִיא יוֹשֶׁבֶת תַּחַת־ תֹּמֶר
Palm-of under holding-court and-she (5) the-that at-the-time Israel ***

דְּבוֹרָה בֵּין הָרָמָה וּבֵין בֵּית־ אֵל בְּהַר אֶפְרָיִם
Ephraim in-hill-country-of El Beth and-between the-Ramah between Deborah

וַיַּעֲלוּ אֵלֶיהָ בְּנֵי יִשְׂרָאֵל לַמִּשְׁפָּט׃ וַתִּשְׁלַח
and-she-sent (6) for-the-decision Israel sons-of to-her and-they-came

וַתִּקְרָא לְבָרָק בֶּן־ אֲבִינֹעַם מִקֶּדֶשׁ נַפְתָּלִי וַתֹּאמֶר
and-she-said Naphtali from-Kedesh-of Abinoam son-of for-Barak and-she-called

אֵלָיו הֲלֹא צִוָּה׀ יְהוָה אֱלֹהֵי־ יִשְׂרָאֵל לֵךְ וּמָשַׁכְתָּ בְּהַר
to-Mount-of and-you-lead-way go! Israel God-of Yahweh he-commands not? to-him

תָּבוֹר וְלָקַחְתָּ עִמְּךָ עֲשֶׂרֶת אֲלָפִים אִישׁ מִבְּנֵי נַפְתָּלִי
Naphtali from-sons-of man thousands ten-of with-you and-you-take Tabor

וּמִבְּנֵי זְבֻלוּן׃ וּמָשַׁכְתִּי אֵלֶיךָ אֶל־ נַחַל קִישׁוֹן אֶת־
*** Kishon River-of to to-you and-I-will-lure (7) Zebulun and-from-sons-of

סִיסְרָא שַׂר־ צְבָא יָבִין וְאֶת־ רִכְבּוֹ וְאֶת־ הֲמוֹנוֹ
troop-of-him and-with chariot-of-him with Jabin army-of commander-of Sisera

וּנְתַתִּיהוּ בְּיָדֶךָ׃ וַיֹּאמֶר אֵלֶיהָ בָּרָק אִם־ תֵּלְכִי
you-go if Barak to-her and-he-said (8) into-hand-of-you and-I-will-give-him

עִמִּי וְהָלָכְתִּי וְאִם־ לֹא תֵלְכִי עִמִּי לֹא אֵלֵךְ׃ וַתֹּאמֶר
and-she-said (9) I-will-go not with-me you-go not but-if then-I-will-go with-me

הָלֹךְ אֵלֵךְ עִמָּךְ אֶפֶס כִּי לֹא תִהְיֶה תִּפְאַרְתְּךָ עַל־
because-of honor-of-you she-will-be not indeed but with-you I-will-go to-go

הַדֶּרֶךְ אֲשֶׁר אַתָּה הוֹלֵךְ כִּי בְיַד־ אִשָּׁה יִמְכֹּר יְהוָה אֶת־
*** Yahweh he-will-give woman into-hand-of rather going you that the-way

סִיסְרָא וַתָּקָם דְּבוֹרָה וַתֵּלֶךְ עִם־ בָּרָק קֶדְשָׁה׃
to-Kedesh Barak with and-she-went Deborah so-she-got-up Sisera

וַיַּזְעֵק בָּרָק אֶת־ זְבוּלֻן וְאֶת־ נַפְתָּלִי קֶדְשָׁה וַיַּעַל
and-he-followed at-Kedesh Naphtali and Zebulun *** Barak and-he-summoned (10)

LORD sold them into the hands
of Jabin, a king of Canaan,
who reigned in Hazor. The
commander of his army was
Sisera, who lived in
Harosheth Haggoyim. 3Be-
cause he had nine hundred
iron chariots and had cruelly
oppressed the Israelites for
twenty years, they cried to the
LORD for help.

4Deborah, a prophetess, the
wife of Lappidoth, was leading[r] Israel at that time. 5She
held court under the Palm of
Deborah between Ramah and
Bethel in the hill country of
Ephraim, and the Israelites
came to her to have their disputes decided. 6She sent for
Barak son of Abinoam from
Kedesh in Naphtali and said
to him, "The LORD, the God of
Israel, commands you: 'Go,
take with you ten thousand
men of Naphtali and Zebulun
and lead the way to Mount Tabor. 7I will lure Sisera, the
commander of Jabin's army,
with his chariots and his
troops to the Kishon River
and give him into your
hands.'"

8Barak said to her, "If you go
with me, I will go; but if you
don't go with me, I won't go."

9"Very well," Deborah said,
"I will go with you. But because of the way you are going
about this,[s] the honor will not
be yours, for the LORD will
hand Sisera over to a woman."
So Deborah went with Barak
to Kedesh, 10where he summoned Zebulun and Naphtali.

[r]4 Traditionally *judging*
[s]9 Or *But on the expedition you are undertaking*

בְּרַגְלָיו עֲשֶׂרֶת אַלְפֵי אִישׁ וַתַּעַל עִמּוֹ דְּבוֹרָה׃
Deborah with-him and-she-went man thousands-of ten-of on-feet-of-him

וְחֶבֶר הַקֵּינִי נִפְרָד מִקַּיִן מִבְּנֵי חֹבָב חֹתֵן
father-in-law-of Hobab from-sons-of from-Ken leaving the-Kenite now-Heber (11)

מֹשֶׁה וַיֵּט אָהֳלוֹ עַד־ אֵלוֹן בְּצַעֲנַנִּים אֲשֶׁר אֶת־ קֶדֶשׁ׃
Kedesh near that in-Zaanannim great-tree by tent-of-him and-he-pitched Moses

וַיַּגִּדוּ לְסִיסְרָא כִּי עָלָה בָּרָק בֶּן־ אֲבִינֹעַם הַר־
Mount-of Abinoam son-of Barak he-went-up that to-Sisera when-they-told (12)

תָּבוֹר׃ וַיַּזְעֵק סִיסְרָא אֶת־ כָּל־ רִכְבּוֹ תְּשַׁע מֵאוֹת
hundreds nine-of chariot-of-him all-of *** Sisera then-he-gathered (13) Tabor

רֶכֶב בַּרְזֶל וְאֶת־כָּל־ הָעָם אֲשֶׁר אִתּוֹ מֵחֲרֹשֶׁת הַגּוֹיִם
Haggoyim from-Harosheth with-him who the-people all-of and iron chariot-of

אֶל־ נַחַל קִישׁוֹן׃ וַתֹּאמֶר דְּבֹרָה אֶל־בָּרָק קוּם כִּי זֶה הַיּוֹם
the-day this for go! Barak to Deborah then-she-said (14) Kishon River-of to

אֲשֶׁר נָתַן יְהוָה אֶת־ סִיסְרָא בְּיָדֶךָ הֲלֹא יְהוָה יָצָא
he-went Yahweh not? into-hand-of-you Sisera *** Yahweh he-gave that

לְפָנֶיךָ וַיֵּרֶד בָּרָק מֵהַר תָּבוֹר וַעֲשֶׂרֶת אֲלָפִים
thousands and-ten-of Tabor from-Mount-of Barak so-he-went-down ahead-of-you

אִישׁ אַחֲרָיו׃ וַיָּהָם יְהוָה אֶת־סִיסְרָא וְאֶת־כָּל־ הָרֶכֶב
the-chariot all-of and Sisera *** Yahweh and-he-routed (15) after-him man

וְאֶת־ כָּל־ הַמַּחֲנֶה לְפִי־ חֶרֶב לִפְנֵי בָרָק וַיֵּרֶד סִיסְרָא
Sisera and-he-abandoned Barak before sword by-edge-of the-army all-of and

מֵעַל הַמֶּרְכָּבָה וַיָּנָס בְּרַגְלָיו׃ וּבָרָק רָדַף
he-pursued but-Barak (16) on-feet-of-him and-he-fled the-chariot from-on

אַחֲרֵי הָרֶכֶב וְאַחֲרֵי הַמַּחֲנֶה עַד חֲרֹשֶׁת הַגּוֹיִם וַיִּפֹּל
and-he-fell Haggoyim Harosheth as-far-as the-army and-after the-chariot after

כָּל־ מַחֲנֵה סִיסְרָא לְפִי־ חֶרֶב לֹא נִשְׁאַר עַד־אֶחָד׃
one even he-was-left not sword by-edge-of Sisera troop-of all-of

וְסִיסְרָא נָס בְּרַגְלָיו אֶל־ אֹהֶל יָעֵל אֵשֶׁת חֶבֶר
Heber wife-of Jael tent-of to on-feet-of-him he-fled but-Sisera (17)

הַקֵּינִי כִּי שָׁלוֹם בֵּין יָבִין מֶלֶךְ־ חָצוֹר וּבֵין
and-between Hazor king-of Jabin between friendly-relation for the-Kenite

בֵּית חֶבֶר הַקֵּינִי׃ וַתֵּצֵא יָעֵל לִקְרַאת סִיסְרָא
Sisera to-meet Jael and-she-went-out (18) the-Kenite Heber clan-of

וַתֹּאמֶר אֵלָיו סוּרָה אֲדֹנִי סוּרָה אֵלַי אַל־ תִּירָא
you-be-afraid not with-me come-in! lord-of-me come! to-him and-she-said

וַיָּסַר אֵלֶיהָ הָאֹהֱלָה וַתְּכַסֵּהוּ בַּשְּׂמִיכָה׃
with-the-covering and-she-covered-him into-the-tent with-her so-he-entered

Ten thousand men followed him, and Deborah also went with him.

[11]Now Heber the Kenite had left the other Kenites, the descendants of Hobab, Moses' brother-in-law,[t] and pitched his tent by the great tree in Zaanannim near Kedesh.

[12]When they told Sisera that Barak son of Abinoam had gone up to Mount Tabor, [13]Sisera gathered together his nine hundred iron chariots and all the men with him, from Harosheth Haggoyim to the Kishon River.

[14]Then Deborah said to Barak, "Go! This is the day the LORD has given Sisera into your hands. Has not the LORD gone ahead of you?" So Barak went down Mount Tabor, followed by ten thousand men. [15]At Barak's advance, the LORD routed Sisera and all his chariots and army by the sword, and Sisera abandoned his chariot and fled on foot. [16]But Barak pursued the chariots and army as far as Harosheth Haggoyim. All the troops of Sisera fell by the sword; not a man was left.

[17]Sisera, however, fled on foot to the tent of Jael, the wife of Heber the Kenite, because there were friendly relations between Jabin king of Hazor and the clan of Heber the Kenite.

[18]Jael went out to meet Sisera and said to him, "Come, my lord, come right in. Don't be afraid." So he entered her tent, and she put a covering over him.

[t]*11 Or father-in-law*

°*11* ק בצעננים

וַיֹּאמֶר אֵלֶיהָ הַשְׁקִינִי־נָא מְעַט־מַיִם כִּי צָמֵאתִי
I-am-thirsty for waters little-of now! give-me! to-her and-he-said (19)

וַתִּפְתַּח אֶת־נֹאוד* הֶחָלָב וַתַּשְׁקֵהוּ וַתְּכַסֵּהוּ׃
and-she-covered-him and-she-gave-drink-him the-milk skin-of *** and-she-opened

וַיֹּאמֶר אֵלֶיהָ עֲמֹד פֶּתַח הָאֹהֶל וְהָיָה אִם־אִישׁ
someone if and-he-will-be the-tent doorway-of stand! to-her and-he-told (20)

יָבוֹא וּשְׁאֵלֵךְ וְאָמַר הֲיֵשׁ־פֹּה אִישׁ וְאָמַרְתְּ
then-you-say anyone here is-there? and-he-says and-he-asks-you he-comes-by

אָיִן׃ וַתִּקַּח יָעֵל אֵשֶׁת־חֶבֶר אֶת־יְתַד הָאֹהֶל וַתָּשֶׂם
and-she-took the-tent peg-of *** Heber wife-of Jael but-she-picked-up (21) no

אֶת־הַמַּקֶּבֶת בְּיָדָהּ וַתָּבוֹא אֵלָיו בַּלָּאט† וַתִּתְקַע
and-she-drove in-the-quiet to-him and-she-went in-hand-of-her the-hammer ***

אֶת־הַיָּתֵד בְּרַקָּתוֹ וַתִּצְנַח בָּאָרֶץ וְהוּא־
while-he in-the-ground and-she-stuck through-temple-of-him the-peg ***

נִרְדָּם וַיָּעַף וַיָּמֹת׃ וְהִנֵּה בָרָק רֹדֵף אֶת־
*** pursuing Barak and-see! (22) and-he-died for-he-was-exhausted sleeping

סִיסְרָא וַתֵּצֵא יָעֵל לִקְרָאתוֹ וַתֹּאמֶר לוֹ לֵךְ
come! to-him and-she-said to-meet-him Jael and-she-went-out Sisera

וְאַרְאֶךָּ אֶת־הָאִישׁ אֲשֶׁר־אַתָּה מְבַקֵּשׁ וַיָּבֹא אֵלֶיהָ
with-her so-he-went-in looking-for you whom the-man *** and-I-will-show-you

וְהִנֵּה סִיסְרָא נֹפֵל מֵת וְהַיָּתֵד בְּרַקָּתוֹ׃
through-temple-of-him and-the-tent-peg being-dead lying Sisera and-see!

וַיַּכְנַע אֱלֹהִים בַּיּוֹם הַהוּא אֵת יָבִין מֶלֶךְ־כְּנָעַן לִפְנֵי
before Canaan king-of Jabin *** the-that on-the-day God so-he-subdued (23)

בְּנֵי יִשְׂרָאֵל׃ וַתֵּלֶךְ יַד בְּנֵי־יִשְׂרָאֵל הָלוֹךְ וְקָשָׁה
also-strong to-grow Israel sons-of hand-of and-she-grew (24) Israel sons-of

עַל יָבִין מֶלֶךְ־כְּנָעַן עַד אֲשֶׁר הִכְרִיתוּ אֵת יָבִין מֶלֶךְ־
king-of Jabin *** they-destroyed when until Canaan king-of Jabin against

כְּנָעַן׃ וַתָּשַׁר דְּבוֹרָה וּבָרָק בֶּן־אֲבִינֹעַם בַּיּוֹם
on-the-day Abinoam son-of and-Barak Deborah and-she-sang (5:1) Canaan

הַהוּא לֵאמֹר׃ בִּפְרֹעַ פְּרָעוֹת בְּיִשְׂרָאֵל בְּהִתְנַדֵּב
when-to-offer-themselves in-Israel princes when-to-take-lead (2) to-say the-that

עָם בָּרְכוּ יְהוָה׃ שִׁמְעוּ מְלָכִים הַאֲזִינוּ רֹזְנִים אָנֹכִי לַיהוָה אָנֹכִי
I to-Yahweh I rulers listen! kings hear! (3) Yahweh praise! people

אָשִׁירָה אֲזַמֵּר לַיהוָה אֱלֹהֵי יִשְׂרָאֵל׃ יְהוָה
Yahweh (4) Israel God-of to-Yahweh I-will-make-music I-will-sing

בְּצֵאתְךָ מִשֵּׂעִיר בְּצַעְדְּךָ מִשְּׂדֵה אֱדוֹם אֶרֶץ
earth Edom from-land-of when-to-march-you from-Seir when-to-go-out-you

19 "I'm thirsty," he said. "Please give me some water." She opened a skin of milk, gave him a drink, and covered him up.

20 "Stand in the doorway of the tent," he told her. "If someone comes by and asks you, 'Is anyone here?' say 'No.' "

21 But Jael, Heber's wife, picked up a tent peg and a hammer and went quietly to him while he lay fast asleep, exhausted. She drove the peg through his temple into the ground, and he died.

22 Barak came by in pursuit of Sisera, and Jael went out to meet him. "Come," she said, "I will show you the man you're looking for." So he went in with her, and there lay Sisera with the tent peg through his temple—dead.

23 On that day God subdued Jabin, the Canaanite king, before the Israelites. 24 And the hand of the Israelites grew stronger and stronger against Jabin, the Canaanite king, until they destroyed him.

*The Song of Deborah*

5 On that day Deborah and Barak son of Abinoam sang this song:

2 "When the princes in Israel
take the lead,
when the people
willingly offer
themselves—
praise the LORD!

3 "Hear this, you kings!
Listen, you rulers!
I will sing to the LORD, I
will sing;
I will make music to the
LORD, the God of
Israel.

4 "O LORD, when you went
out from Seir,
when you marched from
the land of Edom,
the earth shook, the
heavens poured,
the clouds poured down
water.

*19 Many mss omit the *vav* or have (נאד) as a *Qere* form.

†21 Many mss omit the *aleph* or have (בַּלָּט) as a *Qere* form.

רָעֲשָׁה גַּם־שָׁמַיִם נָטָפוּ גַּם־עָבִים נָטְפוּ מָיִם׃
waters they-poured-down clouds also they-poured heavens also she-shook

(5) הָרִים נָזְלוּ מִפְּנֵי יְהוָה זֶה סִינַי מִפְּנֵי יְהוָה
Yahweh at-before Sinai One-of Yahweh at-before they-quaked mountains (5)

אֱלֹהֵי יִשְׂרָאֵל׃ (6) בִּימֵי שַׁמְגַּר בֶּן־עֲנָת בִּימֵי יָעֵל
Jael in-days-of Anath son-of Shamgar in-days-of (6) Israel God-of

חָדְלוּ אֳרָחוֹת וְהֹלְכֵי נְתִיבוֹת יֵלְכוּ אֳרָחוֹת
roads they-took paths and-ones-travelling-of roads they-were-abandoned

עֲקַלְקַלּוֹת׃ (7) חָדְלוּ פְרָזוֹן בְּיִשְׂרָאֵל חָדֵלּוּ עַד
until they-ceased in-Israel village-life they-ceased (7) winding-ones

שַׁקַּמְתִּי דְּבוֹרָה שַׁקַּמְתִּי אֵם בְּיִשְׂרָאֵל׃ (8) יִבְחַר אֱלֹהִים חֲדָשִׁים אָז
then new-ones gods they-chose (8) in-Israel mother I-arose Deborah I-arose

לָחֶם שְׁעָרִים מָגֵן אִם־יֵרָאֶה וָרֹמַח בְּאַרְבָּעִים אֶלֶף
thousand among-forty or-spear he-was-seen not shield city-gates war-of

בְּיִשְׂרָאֵל׃ (9) לִבִּי לְחוֹקְקֵי יִשְׂרָאֵל הַמִּתְנַדְּבִים
the-ones-volunteering Israel with-ones-ruling-of heart-of-me (9) in-Israel

בָּעָם בָּרְכוּ יְהוָה׃ (10) רֹכְבֵי אֲתֹנוֹת צְחֹרוֹת
white-ones donkeys ones-riding-of (10) Yahweh praise! among-the-people

יֹשְׁבֵי עַל־מִדִּין וְהֹלְכֵי עַל־דֶּרֶךְ שִׂיחוּ׃
consider! road on and-ones-walking-of saddle-blanket on ones-sitting-of

(11) מִקּוֹל מְחַצְצִים בֵּין מַשְׁאַבִּים שָׁם יְתַנּוּ
they-recite there watering-places at ones-singing to-voice-of (11)

צִדְקוֹת יְהוָה צִדְקֹת פִּרְזֹנוֹ בְּיִשְׂרָאֵל אָז
then in-Israel warrior-of-him righteous-acts-of Yahweh righteous-acts-of

יָרְדוּ לַשְּׁעָרִים עַם־יְהוָה׃ (12) עוּרִי עוּרִי
wake-up! wake-up! (12) Yahweh people-of to-the-city-gates they-went-down

דְּבוֹרָה עוּרִי עוּרִי דַּבְּרִי־שִׁיר קוּם בָּרָק וּשֲׁבֵה
and-capture! Barak arise! song break-out! wake-up! wake-up! Deborah

שֶׁבְיְךָ בֶּן־אֲבִינֹעַם׃ (13) אָז יְרַד שָׂרִיד לְאַדִּירִים
to-nobles one-left he-came-down then (13) Abinoam son-of captive-of-you

עָם יְהוָה יְרַד־לִי בַּגִּבּוֹרִים׃ (14) מִנִּי אֶפְרַיִם
Ephraim from (14) with-the-mighty-ones to-me he-came Yahweh people-of

שָׁרְשָׁם בַּעֲמָלֵק אַחֲרֶיךָ בִנְיָמִין בַּעֲמָמֶיךָ מִנִּי מָכִיר
Makir from with-people-of-you Benjamin following-you in-Amelek root-of-them

יָרְדוּ מְחֹקְקִים וּמִזְּבוּלֻן מֹשְׁכִים בְּשֵׁבֶט
of-staff-of ones-bearing and-from-Zebulun ones-commanding they-came-down

סֹפֵר׃ (15) וְשָׂרַי בְּיִשָּׂשכָר עִם־דְּבֹרָה וְיִשָּׂשכָר
and-Issachar Deborah with in-Issachar and-princes-of-me (15) one-commanding

5 The mountains quaked
before the LORD, the
One of Sinai,
before the LORD, the God
of Israel.

6 "In the days of Shamgar
son of Anath,
in the days of Jael, the
roads were abandoned;
travelers took to winding
paths.
7 Village life[u] in Israel
ceased,
ceased until I,[v] Deborah,
arose,
arose a mother in Israel.
8 When they chose new
gods,
war came to the city
gates,
and not a shield or spear
was seen
among forty thousand in
Israel.
9 My heart is with Israel's
princes,
with the willing
volunteers among the
people.
Praise the LORD!

10 "You who ride on white
donkeys,
sitting on your saddle
blankets,
and you who walk along
the road,
consider
11 the voice of the
singers[w] at the
watering places.
They recite the righteous
acts of the LORD,
the righteous acts of his
warriors[x] in Israel.
Then the people of the
LORD
went down to the city
gates.

12 "Wake up, wake up,
Deborah!
Wake up, wake up, break
out in song!
Arise, O Barak!
Take captive your
captives, O son of
Abinoam.

13 "Then the men who were
left
came down to the nobles;
the people of the LORD
came to me with the
mighty.
14 Some came from Ephraim,
whose roots were in
Amalek;
Benjamin was with the
people who followed
you.
From Makir captains came
down,
from Zebulun those who
bear a commander's
staff.

[u]7 Or *Warriors* [v]7 Or *you*
[w]11 Or *archers;* the meaning of the Hebrew for this word is uncertain. [x]11 Or *villagers*

כֵּן בָּרָק בָּעֵמֶק שֻׁלַּח בְּרַגְלָיו בִּפְלַגּוֹת רְאוּבֵן
Reuben in-districts-of on-feet-of-him he-rushed into-the-valley Barak same

גְּדֹלִים חִקְקֵי־ לֵב׃ (16) לָמָּה יָשַׁבְתָּ בֵּין הַמִּשְׁפְּתַיִם לִשְׁמֹעַ
to-hear the-campfires among you-stayed why? (16) heart searchings-of many

שְׁרִקוֹת עֲדָרִים לִפְלַגּוֹת רְאוּבֵן גְּדוֹלִים חִקְרֵי־ לֵב׃
heart searchings-of many Reuben in-districts-of flocks whistlings-of

(17) גִּלְעָד בְּעֵבֶר הַיַּרְדֵּן שָׁכֵן וְדָן לָמָּה יָגוּר אֳנִיּוֹת
ships he-lingered why? and-Dan he-stayed the-Jordan at-beyond Gilead (17)

אָשֵׁר יָשַׁב לְחוֹף יַמִּים וְעַל מִפְרָצָיו יִשְׁכּוֹן׃
he-stayed coves-of-him and-in seas on-coast-of he-remained Asher

(18) זְבֻלוּן עַם חֵרֵף נַפְשׁוֹ לָמוּת וְנַפְתָּלִי עַל מְרוֹמֵי
heights-of on and-Naphtali to-die life-of-him he-risked people Zebulun (18)

שָׂדֶה׃ (19) בָּאוּ מְלָכִים נִלְחָמוּ אָז נִלְחֲמוּ מַלְכֵי כְנַעַן
Canaan kings-of they-fought then they-fought kings they-came (19) field

בְּתַעְנַךְ עַל־ מֵי מְגִדּוֹ בֶּצַע כֶּסֶף לֹא לָקָחוּ׃
they-carried-off not silver plunder Megiddo waters-of by at-Taanach

(20) מִן־ שָׁמַיִם נִלְחָמוּ הַכּוֹכָבִים מִמְּסִלּוֹתָם נִלְחֲמוּ עִם־
against they-fought from-courses-them the-stars they-fought heavens from (20)

סִיסְרָא׃ (21) נַחַל קִישׁוֹן גְּרָפָם נַחַל קְדוּמִים נַחַל
River-of old-ages river-of he-swept-away-them Kishon River-of (21) Sisera

קִישׁוֹן תִּדְרְכִי נַפְשִׁי עֹז׃ (22) אָז הָלְמוּ עִקְּבֵי־
hoofs-of they-thundered then (22) strong soul-of-me you-march-on Kishon

סוּס מִדַּהֲרוֹת דַּהֲרוֹת אַבִּירָיו׃ (23) אוֹרוּ מֵרוֹז
Meroz curse! (23) mighty-ones-of-him gallopings-of from-gallopings-of horse

אָמַר מַלְאַךְ יְהוָה אֹרוּ אָרוֹר יֹשְׁבֶיהָ כִּי לֹא־ בָאוּ
they-came not for ones-populating-her to-curse curse! Yahweh angel-of he-said

לְעֶזְרַת יְהוָה לְעֶזְרַת יְהוָה בַּגִּבּוֹרִים׃ (24) תְּבֹרַךְ
you-are-blessed (24) against-mighty-ones Yahweh to-help-of Yahweh to-help-of

מִנָּשִׁים יָעֵל אֵשֶׁת חֶבֶר הַקֵּינִי מִנָּשִׁים בָּאֹהֶל
in-the-tent most-of-women the-Kenite Heber wife-of Jael most-of-women

תְּבֹרָךְ׃ (25) מַיִם שָׁאַל חָלָב נָתָנָה בְּסֵפֶל אַדִּירִים
nobles in-bowl-of she-gave milk he-asked waters (25) you-are-blessed

הִקְרִיבָה חֶמְאָה׃ (26) יָדָהּ לַיָּתֵד תִּשְׁלַחְנָה
they-reached for-the-tent-peg hand-of-her (26) curdled-milk she-brought

וִימִינָהּ לְהַלְמוּת עֲמֵלִים וְהָלְמָה סִיסְרָא מָחֲקָה
she-crushed Sisera and-she-struck workmen for-hammer-of and-right-of-her

רֹאשׁוֹ וּמָחֲצָה וְחָלְפָה רַקָּתוֹ׃ (27) בֵּין
at (27) temple-of-him and-she-pierced and-she-shattered head-of-him

15The princes of Issachar
were with Deborah;
yes, Issachar was with
Barak,
rushing after him into
the valley.
In the districts of Reuben
there was much
searching of heart.
16Why did you stay among
the campfires
to hear the whistling for
the flocks?
In the districts of Reuben
there was much
searching of heart.
17Gilead stayed beyond the
Jordan.
And Dan, why did he
linger by the ships?
Asher remained on the
seacoast
and stayed in his coves.
18The people of Zebulun
risked their very lives;
so did Naphtali on the
heights of the field.
19"Kings came, they fought;
the kings of Canaan
fought
at Taanach by the waters
of Megiddo,
but they carried off no
silver, no plunder.
20From the heavens the stars
fought,
from their courses they
fought against Sisera.
21The river Kishon swept
them away,
the age-old river, the
river Kishon.
March on, my soul; be
strong!
22Then thundered the horses'
hoofs—
galloping, galloping go
his mighty steeds.
23'Curse Meroz,' said the
angel of the LORD.
'Curse its people bitterly,
because they did not come
to help the LORD,
to help the LORD against
the mighty.'

24"Most blessed of women be
Jael,
the wife of Heber the
Kenite,
most blessed of
tent-dwelling women.
25He asked for water, and
she gave him milk;
in a bowl fit for nobles
she brought him
curdled milk.
26Her hand reached for the
tent peg,
her right hand for the
workman's hammer.
She struck Sisera, she
crushed his head,
she shattered and pierced
his temple.

רַגְלֶיהָ כָּרַע נָפַל שָׁכָב בֵּין רַגְלֶיהָ כָּרַע נָפַל בַּאֲשֶׁר

at-where he-fell he-sank feet-of-her at he-lay he-fell he-sank feet-of-her

כָּרַע שָׁם נָפַל שָׁדוּד׃ בְּעַד הַחַלּוֹן נִשְׁקְפָה

she-peered the-window through (28) being-dead he-fell there he-sank

וַתְּיַבֵּב אֵם סִיסְרָא בְּעַד הָאֶשְׁנָב מַדּוּעַ בֹּשֵׁשׁ

taking-long why? the-lattice behind Sisera mother-of and-she-cried-out

רִכְבּוֹ לָבוֹא מַדּוּעַ אֶחֱרוּ פַּעֲמֵי מַרְכְּבוֹתָיו׃

chariots-of-him clatters-of they-delay why? to-come chariot-of-him

חַכְמוֹת שָׂרוֹתֶיהָ תַּעֲנֶינָּה אַף־ הִיא תָּשִׁיב

she-repeats she indeed they-answer-her ladies-of-her wisest-ones-of (29)

אֲמָרֶיהָ לָהּ׃ הֲלֹא יִמְצְאוּ יְחַלְּקוּ שָׁלָל רַחַם רַחֲמָתַיִם

two-girls girl spoil they-divide they-find not? (30) to-her words-of-her

לְרֹאשׁ גֶּבֶר שְׁלַל צְבָעִים לְסִיסְרָא שְׁלַל

plunder-of for-Sisera colorful-garments plunder-of man for-each-of

צְבָעִים רִקְמָה צֶבַע רִקְמָתַיִם לְצַוְּארֵי

for-necks-of ones-embroidered garment-of embroidered colorful-garments

שָׁלָל׃ כֵּן יֹאבְדוּ כָל־ אוֹיְבֶיךָ יְהוָה

Yahweh being-enemies-of-you all-of may-they-perish so (31) plunder

וְאֹהֲבָיו כְּצֵאת הַשֶּׁמֶשׁ בִּגְבֻרָתוֹ וַתִּשְׁקֹט

then-she-had-peace in-strength-of-him the-sun like-to-rise but-ones-loving-him

הָאָרֶץ אַרְבָּעִים שָׁנָה׃ וַיַּעֲשׂוּ בְנֵי־ יִשְׂרָאֵל הָרַע בְּעֵינֵי

in-eyes-of the-evil Israel sons-of and-they-did (6:1) year forty the-land

יְהוָה וַיִּתְּנֵם יְהוָה בְּיַד־ מִדְיָן שֶׁבַע שָׁנִים׃

years seven Midian into-hand-of Yahweh and-he-gave-them Yahweh

וַתָּעָז יַד־ מִדְיָן עַל־ יִשְׂרָאֵל מִפְּנֵי מִדְיָן

Midian because-of Israel over Midian hand-of and-she-was-oppressive (2)

עָשׂוּ* לָהֶם ׀ בְּנֵי יִשְׂרָאֵל אֶת־ הַמִּנְהָרוֹת אֲשֶׁר בֶּהָרִים

in-the-mountains that the-shelters *** Israel sons-of for-them they-prepared

וְאֶת־ הַמְּעָרוֹת וְאֶת־ הַמְּצָדוֹת׃ וְהָיָה אִם־ זָרַע יִשְׂרָאֵל

Israel he-planted when and-he-was (3) the-strongholds and the-caves and

וְעָלָה מִדְיָן וַעֲמָלֵק וּבְנֵי־ קֶדֶם וְעָלוּ

and-they-invaded east and-people-of and-Amalek Midian then-he-invaded

עָלָיו׃ וַיַּחֲנוּ עֲלֵיהֶם וַיַּשְׁחִיתוּ אֶת־ יְבוּל

crop-of *** and-they-ruined against-them and-they-camped (4) against-him

הָאָרֶץ עַד־ בּוֹאֲךָ עַזָּה וְלֹא־ יַשְׁאִירוּ מִחְיָה בְּיִשְׂרָאֵל

for-Israel from-living-thing they-spared and-not Gaza to-go-you as the-land

וְשֶׂה וָשׁוֹר וַחֲמוֹר׃ כִּי הֵם וּמִקְנֵיהֶם יַעֲלוּ

they-came-up and-stock-of-them they for (5) nor-donkey nor-cattle neither-sheep

27 At her feet he sank,
he fell; there he lay.
At her feet he sank, he fell;
where he sank, there he
fell—dead.

28 "Through the window
peered Sisera's mother;
behind the lattice she
cried out,
'Why is his chariot so long
in coming?
Why is the clatter of his
chariots delayed?'
29 The wisest of her ladies
answer her;
indeed, she keeps saying
to herself,
30 'Are they not finding and
dividing the spoils:
a girl or two for each
man,
colorful garments as
plunder for Sisera,
colorful garments
embroidered,
highly embroidered
garments for my
neck—
all this as plunder?'

31 "So may all your enemies
perish, O LORD!
But may they who love
you be like the sun
when it rises in its
strength."

Then the land had peace forty years.

*Gideon*

6 Again the Israelites did
evil in the eyes of the
LORD, and for seven years he
gave them into the hands of
the Midianites. 2 Because the
power of Midian was so oppressive, the Israelites prepared shelters for themselves
in mountain clefts, caves and
strongholds. 3 Whenever the
Israelites planted their crops,
the Midianites, Amalekites
and other eastern peoples invaded the country. 4 They
camped on the land and
ruined the crops all the way to
Gaza and did not spare a living thing for Israel, neither
sheep nor cattle nor donkeys.
5 They came up with their livestock and their tents like

*2 Most mss have *maqqeph* binding this word to the following (עשׂו־).

וְאָהֳלֵיהֶם יָבֹאוּ° כְדֵי־ אַרְבֶּה לָרֹב וְלָהֶם
and-to-them in-number locust like-swarm-of and-they-came and-tents-of-them

וְלִגְמַלֵּיהֶם אֵין מִסְפָּר וַיָּבֹאוּ בָאָרֶץ לְשַׁחֲתָהּ׃
to-ravish-her on-the-land and-they-invaded number not and-to-camels-of-them

וַיִּדַּל יִשְׂרָאֵל מְאֹד מִפְּנֵי מִדְיָן וַיִּזְעֲקוּ
so-they-cried Midian because-of very Israel and-he-was-impoverished (6)

בְנֵי־ יִשְׂרָאֵל אֶל־ יְהוָה׃ וַיְהִי כִּי־ זָעֲקוּ בְנֵי־יִשְׂרָאֵל אֶל־
to Israel sons-of they-cried when and-he-was (7) Yahweh to Israel sons-of

יְהוָה עַל אֹדוֹת מִדְיָן׃ וַיִּשְׁלַח יְהוָה אִישׁ נָבִיא אֶל־ בְּנֵי
sons-of to prophet man Yahweh then-he-sent (8) Midian reasons-of for Yahweh

יִשְׂרָאֵל וַיֹּאמֶר לָהֶם כֹּה־ אָמַר יְהוָה ׀ אֱלֹהֵי יִשְׂרָאֵל אָנֹכִי הֶעֱלֵיתִי
I-brought-up I Israel God-of Yahweh he-says this to-them and-he-said Israel

אֶתְכֶם מִמִּצְרַיִם וָאֹצִיא אֶתְכֶם מִבֵּית עֲבָדִים׃ וָאַצִּל
and-I-snatched (9) slaveries from-house-of you and-I-brought from-Egypt you

אֶתְכֶם מִיַּד מִצְרַיִם וּמִיַּד כָּל־ לֹחֲצֵיכֶם וָאֲגָרֵשׁ
and-I-drove ones-oppressing-you all-of and-from-hand-of Egypt from-hand-of you

אוֹתָם מִפְּנֵיכֶם וָאֶתְּנָה לָכֶם אֶת־ אַרְצָם׃ וָאֹמְרָה
and-I-said (10) land-of-them *** to-you and-I-gave from-before-you them

לָכֶם אֲנִי יְהוָה אֱלֹהֵיכֶם לֹא תִירְאוּ אֶת־ אֱלֹהֵי הָאֱמֹרִי אֲשֶׁר
who the-Amorite gods-of *** you-worship not God-of-you Yahweh I to-you

אַתֶּם יוֹשְׁבִים בְּאַרְצָם וְלֹא שְׁמַעְתֶּם בְּקוֹלִי׃
to-voice-of-me you-listened but-not in-land-of-them ones-living you

וַיָּבֹא מַלְאַךְ יְהוָה וַיֵּשֶׁב תַּחַת הָאֵלָה אֲשֶׁר בְּעָפְרָה
in-Ophrah that the-oak under and-he-sat Yahweh angel-of and-he-came (11)

אֲשֶׁר לְיוֹאָשׁ אֲבִי הָעֶזְרִי וְגִדְעוֹן בְּנוֹ חֹבֵט חִטִּים
wheats threshing son-of-him and-Gideon the-Abiezrite to-Joash that

בַּגַּת לְהָנִיס מִפְּנֵי מִדְיָן׃ וַיֵּרָא אֵלָיו
to-him when-he-appeared (12) Midian from-before to-keep in-the-winepress

מַלְאַךְ יְהוָה וַיֹּאמֶר אֵלָיו יְהוָה עִמְּךָ גִּבּוֹר הֶחָיִל׃
the-mighty warrior-of with-you Yahweh to-him then-he-said Yahweh angel-of

וַיֹּאמֶר אֵלָיו גִּדְעוֹן בִּי אֲדֹנִי וְיֵשׁ יְהוָה עִמָּנוּ
with-us Yahweh if-he-is sir-of-me but Gideon to-him and-he-replied (13)

וְלָמָּה מְצָאַתְנוּ כָּל־ זֹאת וְאַיֵּה כָל־ נִפְלְאֹתָיו
being-wonders-of-him all-of and-where? this all-of she-happened-to-us then-why?

אֲשֶׁר סִפְּרוּ־ לָנוּ אֲבוֹתֵינוּ לֵאמֹר הֲלֹא מִמִּצְרַיִם הֶעֱלָנוּ
he-brought-us from-Egypt not? to-say fathers-of-us to-us they-told that

יְהוָה וְעַתָּה נְטָשָׁנוּ יְהוָה וַיִּתְּנֵנוּ בְּכַף־ מִדְיָן׃
Midian into-hand-of and-he-put-us Yahweh he-abandoned-us but-now Yahweh

swarms of locusts. It was impossible to count the men and their camels; they invaded the land to ravage it. [6]Midian so impoverished the Israelites that they cried out to the LORD for help.

[7]When the Israelites cried to the LORD because of Midian, [8]he sent them a prophet, who said, "This is what the LORD, the God of Israel, says: I brought you up out of Egypt, out of the land of slavery. [9]I snatched you from the power of Egypt and from the hand of all your oppressors. I drove them from before you and gave you their land. [10]I said to you, 'I am the LORD your God; do not worship the gods of the Amorites, in whose land you live.' But you have not listened to me."

[11]The angel of the LORD came and sat down under the oak in Ophrah that belonged to Joash the Abiezrite, where his son Gideon was threshing wheat in a winepress to keep it from the Midianites. [12]When the angel of the LORD appeared to Gideon, he said, "The LORD is with you, mighty warrior."

[13]"But sir," Gideon replied, "if the LORD is with us, why has all this happened to us? Where are all his wonders that our fathers told us about when they said, 'Did not the LORD bring us up out of Egypt?' But now the LORD has abandoned us and put us into the hand of Midian."

°5 ק ובאו

וַיִּפֶן אֵלָיו יְהוָה וַיֹּאמֶר לֵךְ בְּכֹחֲךָ זֶה
this in-strength-of-you go! and-he-said Yahweh to-him and-he-turned (14)

וְהוֹשַׁעְתָּ אֶת־יִשְׂרָאֵל מִכַּף מִדְיָן הֲלֹא שְׁלַחְתִּיךָ׃ וַיֹּאמֶר
and-he-asked (15) I-send-you not? Midian from-hand-of Israel *** and-you-save

אֵלָיו בִּי אֲדֹנָי בַּמָּה אוֹשִׁיעַ אֶת־יִשְׂרָאֵל הִנֵּה אַלְפִּי הַדַּל
the-weakest clan-of-me see! Israel *** I-save by-the-how? Lord but to-him

בִּמְנַשֶּׁה וְאָנֹכִי הַצָּעִיר בְּבֵית אָבִי׃ וַיֹּאמֶר
and-he-answered (16) father-of-me in-house-of the-least and-I in-Manasseh

אֵלָיו יְהוָה כִּי אֶהְיֶה עִמָּךְ וְהִכִּיתָ אֶת־מִדְיָן
Midian *** and-you-will-strike-down with-you I-will-be indeed Yahweh to-him

כְּאִישׁ אֶחָד׃ וַיֹּאמֶר אֵלָיו אִם־נָא מָצָאתִי חֵן בְּעֵינֶיךָ
in-eyes-of-you favor I-found now! if to-him and-he-replied (17) one as-man

וְעָשִׂיתָ לִּי אוֹת שָׁאַתָּה מְדַבֵּר עִמִּי׃ אַל־נָא תָמֻשׁ
you-go-away now! not (18) to-me talking that-you sign to-me then-you-give

מִזֶּה עַד־בֹּאִי אֵלֶיךָ וְהֹצֵאתִי אֶת־מִנְחָתִי וְהִנַּחְתִּי
and-I-set offering-of-me *** and-I-bring to-you to-come-back-me until from-here

לְפָנֶיךָ וַיֹּאמַר אָנֹכִי אֵשֵׁב עַד שׁוּבֶךָ׃ וְגִדְעוֹן
and-Gideon (19) to-return-you until I-will-wait I and-he-said before-you

בָּא וַיַּעַשׂ גְּדִי־עִזִּים וְאֵיפַת־קֶמַח
flour and-ephah-of goats young-one-of and-he-prepared he-went-in

מַצּוֹת הַבָּשָׂר שָׂם בַּסַּל וְהַמָּרַק שָׂם
he-put and-the-broth in-the-basket he-put the-meat breads-without-yeast

בַּפָּרוּר וַיּוֹצֵא אֵלָיו אֶל־תַּחַת הָאֵלָה וַיַּגַּשׁ׃
and-he-offered the-oak under at to-him and-he-brought-out in-the-pot

וַיֹּאמֶר אֵלָיו מַלְאַךְ הָאֱלֹהִים קַח אֶת־הַבָּשָׂר וְאֶת־
and the-meat *** take! the-God angel-of to-him and-he-said (20)

הַמַּצּוֹת וְהַנַּח אֶל־הַסֶּלַע הַלָּז וְאֶת־הַמָּרַק שְׁפוֹךְ
pour-out! the-broth and the-this the-rock on and-place! the-unleavened-breads

וַיַּעַשׂ כֵּן׃ וַיִּשְׁלַח מַלְאַךְ יְהוָה אֶת־קְצֵה הַמִּשְׁעֶנֶת
the-staff tip-of *** Yahweh angel-of and-he-reached-out (21) so and-he-did

אֲשֶׁר בְּיָדוֹ וַיִּגַּע בַּבָּשָׂר וּבַמַּצּוֹת
and-on-the-unleavened-breads on-the-meat and-he-touched in-hand-of-him that

וַתַּעַל הָאֵשׁ מִן־הַצּוּר וַתֹּאכַל אֶת־הַבָּשָׂר וְאֶת־
and the-meat *** and-she-consumed the-rock from the-fire and-she-flared

הַמַּצּוֹת וּמַלְאַךְ יְהוָה הָלַךְ מֵעֵינָיו׃
from-eyes-of-him he-went-away Yahweh and-angel-of the-unleavened-breads

וַיַּרְא גִּדְעוֹן כִּי־מַלְאַךְ יְהוָה הוּא וַיֹּאמֶר גִּדְעוֹן
Gideon then-he-exclaimed he Yahweh angel-of that Gideon when-he-realized (22)

14 The LORD turned to him and said, "Go in the strength you have and save Israel out of Midian's hand. Am I not sending you?"

15 "But Lord,[y]" Gideon asked, "how can I save Israel? My clan is the weakest in Manasseh, and I am the least in my family."

16 The LORD answered, "I will be with you, and you will strike down the Midianites as if they were but one man."

17 Gideon replied, "If now I have found favor in your eyes, give me a sign that it is really you talking to me. 18 Please do not go away until I come back and bring my offering and set it before you."

And the LORD said, "I will wait until you return."

19 Gideon went in, prepared a young goat, and from an ephah[z] of flour he made bread without yeast. Putting the meat in a basket and its broth in a pot, he brought them out and offered them to him under the oak.

20 The angel of God said to him, "Take the meat and the unleavened bread, place them on this rock, and pour out the broth." And Gideon did so. 21 With the tip of the staff that was in his hand, the angel of the LORD touched the meat and the unleavened bread. Fire flared from the rock, consuming the meat and the bread. And the angel of the LORD disappeared. 22 When Gideon realized that it was the angel of the LORD, he exclaimed, "Ah, Sovereign LORD!

y15 Or *sir*

z19 That is, probably about 1/2 bushel (about 22 liters)

אֲהָהּ אֲדֹנָי יְהוִה כִּי־ עַל־ כֵּן רָאִיתִי מַלְאַךְ יְהוָה פָּנִים אֶל־פָּנִים׃
faces to faces Yahweh angel-of I-saw that because for Yahweh Lord ah!

וַיֹּאמֶר לוֹ יְהוָה שָׁלוֹם לְךָ אַל־ תִּירָא לֹא תָּמוּת׃
you-will-die not you-be-afraid not to-you peace Yahweh to-him but-he-said (23)

וַיִּבֶן שָׁם גִּדְעוֹן מִזְבֵּחַ לַיהוָה וַיִּקְרָא־ לוֹ יְהוָה
Yahweh to-him and-he-called to-Yahweh altar Gideon there so-he-built (24)

שָׁלוֹם עַד הַיּוֹם הַזֶּה עוֹדֶנּוּ בְּעָפְרַת אֲבִי הָעֶזְרִי׃ וַיְהִי
and-he-was (25) the-Abiezite in-Ophrah-of still-he the-this the-day to Peace

בַּלַּיְלָה הַהוּא וַיֹּאמֶר לוֹ יְהוָה קַח אֶת־ פַּר־ הַשּׁוֹר
the-herd bull-of *** take! Yahweh to-him that-he-said the-that in-the-night

אֲשֶׁר לְאָבִיךָ וּפַר הַשֵּׁנִי שֶׁבַע שָׁנִים וְהָרַסְתָּ
and-you-tear-down years seven the-second even-bull-of to-father-of-you that

אֶת־ מִזְבַּח הַבַּעַל אֲשֶׁר לְאָבִיךָ וְאֶת־ הָאֲשֵׁרָה אֲשֶׁר־
that the-Asherah-pole and to-father-of-you that the-Baal altar-of ***

עָלָיו תִּכְרֹת׃ וּבָנִיתָ מִזְבֵּחַ לַיהוָה אֱלֹהֶיךָ עַל
on God-of-you to-Yahweh altar then-you-build (26) you-cut-down beside-him

רֹאשׁ הַמָּעוֹז הַזֶּה בַּמַּעֲרָכָה וְלָקַחְתָּ אֶת־ הַפָּר הַשֵּׁנִי
the-second the-bull *** then-you-take by-the-layer the-this the-bluff top-of

וְהַעֲלִיתָ עוֹלָה בַּעֲצֵי הָאֲשֵׁרָה אֲשֶׁר תִּכְרֹת׃
you-cut-down that the-Asherah-pole with-woods-of burnt-offering and-you-offer

וַיִּקַּח גִּדְעוֹן עֲשָׂרָה אֲנָשִׁים מֵעֲבָדָיו וַיַּעַשׂ כַּאֲשֶׁר
just-as and-he-did from-servants-of-him men ten Gideon so-he-took (27)

דִּבֶּר אֵלָיו יְהוָה וַיְהִי כַּאֲשֶׁר יָרֵא אֶת־ בֵּית
house-of *** he-was-afraid because but-he-was Yahweh to-him he-told

אָבִיו וְאֶת־ אַנְשֵׁי הָעִיר מֵעֲשׂוֹת יוֹמָם וַיַּעַשׂ לָיְלָה׃
night so-he-did by-day from-to-do the-town men-of and father-of-him

וַיַּשְׁכִּימוּ אַנְשֵׁי הָעִיר בַּבֹּקֶר וְהִנֵּה נֻתַּץ
he-was-demolished then-see! in-the-morning the-town men-of when-they-got-up (28)

מִזְבַּח הַבַּעַל וְהָאֲשֵׁרָה אֲשֶׁר־ עָלָיו כֹּרָתָה וְאֵת
and being-cut-down beside-him that and-the-Asherah-pole the-Baal altar-of

הַפָּר הַשֵּׁנִי הֹעֲלָה עַל־ הַמִּזְבֵּחַ הַבָּנוּי׃
the-one-being-built the-altar on he-was-sacrificed the-second the-bull

וַיֹּאמְרוּ אִישׁ אֶל־ רֵעֵהוּ מִי עָשָׂה הַדָּבָר הַזֶּה
the-this the-thing he-did who? other-of-him to each and-they-asked (29)

וַיִּדְרְשׁוּ וַיְבַקְשׁוּ וַיֹּאמְרוּ גִּדְעוֹן בֶּן־ יוֹאָשׁ
Joash son-of Gideon then-they-said and-they-searched when-they-investigated

עָשָׂה הַדָּבָר הַזֶּה׃ וַיֹּאמְרוּ אַנְשֵׁי הָעִיר אֶל־ יוֹאָשׁ
Joash to the-town men-of and-they-demanded (30) the-this the-thing he-did

I have seen the angel of the
LORD face to face!"
23But the LORD said to him,
"Peace! Do not be afraid. You
are not going to die."
24So Gideon built an altar to
the LORD there and called it
"The LORD is Peace." To this
day it stands in Ophrah of the
Abiezrites.
25That same night the LORD
said to him, "Take the second
bull from your father's herd,
the one seven years old.[a] Tear
down your father's altar to
Baal and cut down the
Asherah pole[b] beside it.
26Then build a proper kind of[c]
altar to the LORD your God on
the top of this bluff. Using the
wood of the Asherah pole that
you cut down, offer the second[d] bull as a burnt offering."
27So Gideon took ten of his
servants and did as the LORD
told him. But because he was
afraid of his family and the
men of the town, he did it at
night rather than in the daytime.
28In the morning when the
men of the town got up, there
was Baal's altar, demolished,
with the Asherah pole beside
it cut down and the second
bull sacrificed on the newly
built altar!
29They asked each other,
"Who did this?"
When they carefully investi-
gated, they were told, "Gideon
son of Joash did it."
30The men of the town de-
manded of Joash, "Bring out

[a]25 Or *Take a full-grown, mature bull from your father's herd*
[b]25 That is, a symbol of the goddess Asherah; here and elsewhere in Judges
[c]26 Or *build with layers of stone an*
[d]26 Or *full-grown;* also in verse 28

*24 Most mss have *pathah* under the *resh* ( תַ ).

הוֹצֵא אֶת־ בִּנְךָ וְיָמֹת כִּי נָתַץ אֶת־ מִזְבַּח
altar-of *** he-broke-down because for-he-must-die son-of-you *** bring-out!

הַבַּעַל וְכִי כָרַת הָאֲשֵׁרָה אֲשֶׁר־ עָלָיו׃
beside-him that the-Asherah-pole he-cut-down and-because the-Baal

(31) וַיֹּאמֶר יוֹאָשׁ לְכֹל אֲשֶׁר־ עָמְדוּ עָלָיו הַאַתֶּם ׀ תְּרִיבוּן
will-you-plead you? around-him they-stood who to-all Joash but-he-replied (31)

לַבַּעַל אִם־אַתֶּם תּוֹשִׁיעוּן אוֹתוֹ אֲשֶׁר יָרִיב לוֹ יוּמַת
he-will-die for-him he-fights whoever him will-you-save you or for-the-Baal

עַד־ הַבֹּקֶר אִם־אֱלֹהִים הוּא יָרֶב לוֹ כִּי נָתַץ אֶת־
*** he-breaks-down when for-him he-can-defend he god if the-morning by

מִזְבְּחוֹ׃ (32) וַיִּקְרָא־ לוֹ בַיּוֹם־ הַהוּא יְרֻבַּעַל לֵאמֹר
to-say Jerub-Baal the-that on-the-day to-him so-he-called (32) altar-of-him

יָרֶב בּוֹ הַבַּעַל כִּי נָתַץ אֶת־ מִזְבְּחוֹ׃
altar-of-him *** he-broke-down for the-Baal with-him let-him-contend

(33) וְכָל־ מִדְיָן וַעֲמָלֵק וּבְנֵי־ קֶדֶם נֶאֶסְפוּ יַחְדָּו
together they-joined east and-peoples-of and-Amalek Midian now-all-of (33)

וַיַּעַבְרוּ וַיַּחֲנוּ בְּעֵמֶק יִזְרְעֶאל׃ (34) וְרוּחַ
then-Spirit-of (34) Jezreel in-Valley-of and-they-camped and-they-crossed

יְהוָה לָבְשָׁה אֶת־ גִּדְעוֹן וַיִּתְקַע בַּשּׁוֹפָר וַיִּזָּעֵק
and-he-summoned on-the-trumpet and-he-blew Gideon *** she-came-upon Yahweh

אֲבִיעֶזֶר אַחֲרָיו׃ (35) וּמַלְאָכִים שָׁלַח בְּכָל־ מְנַשֶּׁה
Manasseh through-all-of he-sent and-messengers (35) after-him Abiezer

וַיִּזָּעֵק גַּם־ הוּא אַחֲרָיו וּמַלְאָכִים שָׁלַח בְּאָשֵׁר
into-Asher he-sent and-messengers after-him he also and-he-called

וּבִזְבֻלוּן וּבְנַפְתָּלִי וַיַּעֲלוּ לִקְרָאתָם׃ (36) וַיֹּאמֶר
and-he-said (36) to-meet-them so-they-went-up and-into-Naphtali and-into-Zebulun

גִּדְעוֹן אֶל־הָאֱלֹהִים אִם־ יֶשְׁךָ מוֹשִׁיעַ בְּיָדִי אֶת־יִשְׂרָאֵל כַּאֲשֶׁר
just-as Israel *** by-hand-of-me one-saving it-is-you if the-God to Gideon

דִּבַּרְתָּ׃ (37) הִנֵּה אָנֹכִי מַצִּיג אֶת־ גִּזַּת הַצֶּמֶר בַּגֹּרֶן
on-the-threshing-floor the-wool fleece-of *** placing I look! (37) you-promised

אִם טַל יִהְיֶה עַל־ הַגִּזָּה לְבַדָּהּ וְעַל־ כָּל־ הָאָרֶץ חֹרֶב
dryness the-ground all-of and-on by-herself the-fleece on he-is dew if

וְיָדַעְתִּי כִּי־ תוֹשִׁיעַ בְּיָדִי אֶת־יִשְׂרָאֵל כַּאֲשֶׁר
you-said just-as Israel *** by-hand-of-me you-will-save that then-I-will-know

(38) וַיְהִי־ כֵן וַיַּשְׁכֵּם מִמָּחֳרָת וַיָּזַר אֶת־
*** then-he-squeezed on-next-day when-he-rose so and-he-happened (38)

הַגִּזָּה וַיִּמֶץ טַל מִן־ הַגִּזָּה מְלוֹא הַסֵּפֶל מָיִם׃
waters the-bowl fullness-of the-fleece from dew and-he-wrung-out the-fleece

your son. He must die, because he has broken down Baal's altar and cut down the Asherah pole beside it."

31But Joash replied to the hostile crowd around him, "Are you going to plead Baal's cause? Are you trying to save him? Whoever fights for him shall be put to death by morning! If Baal really is a god, he can defend himself when someone breaks down his altar." 32So that day they called Gideon "Jerub-Baal,[e]" saying, "Let Baal contend with him," because he broke down Baal's altar.

33Now all the Midianites, Amalekites and other eastern peoples joined forces and crossed over the Jordan and camped in the Valley of Jezreel. 34Then the Spirit of the LORD came upon Gideon, and he blew a trumpet, summoning the Abiezrites to follow him. 35He sent messengers throughout Manasseh, calling them to arms, and also into Asher, Zebulun and Naphtali, so that they too went up to meet them.

36Gideon said to God, "If you will save Israel by my hand as you have promised—look, 37I will place a wool fleece on the threshing floor. If there is dew only on the fleece and all the ground is dry, then I will know that you will save Israel by my hand, as you said." 38And that is what happened. Gideon rose early the next day; he squeezed the fleece and wrung out the dew—a bowlful of water.

[e]32 *Jerub-Baal* means *let Baal contend.*

וַיֹּאמֶר גִּדְעוֹן אֶל־הָאֱלֹהִים אַל־יִחַר אַפְּךָ בִּי
against-me anger-of-you let-him-burn not the-God to Gideon then-he-said (39)

וַאֲדַבְּרָה אַךְ הַפָּעַם אֲנַסֶּה נָּא־רַק־הַפַּעַם
the-once only now! let-me-test the-once again but-let-me-request

בַגִּזָּה יְהִי־נָא חֹרֶב אֶל־הַגִּזָּה לְבַדָּהּ וְעַל־כָּל־
all-of and-on by-herself the-fleece on dryness now! may-he-be with-the-fleece

הָאָרֶץ יִהְיֶה־טָּל׃ וַיַּעַשׂ אֱלֹהִים כֵּן בַּלַּיְלָה הַהוּא
the-that on-the-night so God and-he-did (40) dew may-he-be the-ground

וַיְהִי־חֹרֶב אֶל־הַגִּזָּה לְבַדָּהּ וְעַל־כָּל־הָאָרֶץ הָיָה
he-was the-ground all-of and-on by-herself the-fleece on dryness and-he-was

טָל׃ וַיַּשְׁכֵּם יְרֻבַּעַל הוּא גִדְעוֹן וְכָל־הָעָם אֲשֶׁר
who the-people and-all-of Gideon that Jerub-Baal and-he-rose (7:1) dew

אִתּוֹ וַיַּחֲנוּ עַל־עֵין חֲרֹד וּמַחֲנֵה מִדְיָן הָיָה־לּוֹ
by-him he-was Midian now-camp-of Harod spring-of at and-they-camped with-him

מִצְּפוֹן מִגִּבְעַת הַמּוֹרֶה בָּעֵמֶק׃ וַיֹּאמֶר יְהוָה אֶל־
to Yahweh and-he-said (2) in-the-valley the-Moreh near-hill-of to-north

גִּדְעוֹן רַב הָעָם אֲשֶׁר אִתָּךְ מִתִּתִּי אֶת־מִדְיָן
Midian *** for-to-deliver-me with-you who the-people too-many Gideon

בְּיָדָם פֶּן־יִתְפָּאֵר עָלַי יִשְׂרָאֵל לֵאמֹר יָדִי
hand-of-me to-say Israel against-me he-may-boast so-not into-hand-of-them

הוֹשִׁיעָה לִּי׃ וְעַתָּה קְרָא נָא בְּאָזְנֵי הָעָם לֵאמֹר מִי־
whoever to-say the-people in-ears-of now! announce! so-now (3) to-me she-saved

יָרֵא וְחָרֵד יָשֹׁב וְיִצְפֹּר מֵהַר
from-Mount-of and-he-may-leave he-may-turn-back and-trembling fearful

הַגִּלְעָד וַיָּשָׁב מִן־הָעָם עֶשְׂרִים וּשְׁנַיִם אֶלֶף וַעֲשֶׂרֶת
and-ten-of thousand and-two twenty the-people from so-he-left the-Gilead

אֲלָפִים נִשְׁאָרוּ׃ וַיֹּאמֶר יְהוָה אֶל־גִּדְעוֹן עוֹד הָעָם
the-people still Gideon to Yahweh but-he-said (4) they-remained thousands

רָב הוֹרֵד אוֹתָם אֶל־הַמַּיִם וְאֶצְרְפֶנּוּ לְךָ שָׁם
there for-you and-I-will-sift-him the-waters to them take-down! too-many

וְהָיָה אֲשֶׁר אֹמַר אֵלֶיךָ זֶה יֵלֵךְ אִתָּךְ הוּא יֵלֵךְ
he-shall-go he with-you he-shall-go this to-you I-say whom and-he-will-be

אִתָּךְ וְכֹל אֲשֶׁר־אֹמַר אֵלֶיךָ זֶה לֹא־יֵלֵךְ עִמָּךְ הוּא לֹא
not he with-you he-shall-go not this to-you I-say whom but-all with-you

יֵלֵךְ׃ וַיּוֹרֶד אֶת־הָעָם אֶל־הַמָּיִם וַיֹּאמֶר
and-he-told the-waters to the-people *** so-he-took-down (5) he-shall-go

יְהוָה אֶל־גִּדְעוֹן כֹּל אֲשֶׁר־יָלֹק בִּלְשׁוֹנוֹ מִן־הַמַּיִם כַּאֲשֶׁר
just-as the-waters from with-tongue-of-him he-laps who all Gideon to Yahweh

39 Then Gideon said to God,
"Do not be angry with me. Let
me make just one more re-
quest. Allow me one more test
with the fleece. This time
make the fleece dry and the
ground covered with dew."
40 That night God did so. Only
the fleece was dry; all the
ground was covered with dew.

*Gideon Defeats the Midianites*

7 Early in the morning,
Jerub-Baal (that is, Gideon) and all his men camped at
the spring of Harod. The camp
of Midian was north of them
in the valley near the hill of
Moreh. 2 The LORD said to
Gideon, "You have too many
men for me to deliver Midian
into their hands. In order that
Israel may not boast against
me that her own strength has
saved her, 3 announce now to
the people, 'Anyone who
trembles with fear may turn
back and leave Mount Gil-
ead.'" So twenty-two thousand men left, while ten thousand remained.
4 But the LORD said to Gideon, "There are still too many
men. Take them down to the
water, and I will sift them for
you there. If I say, 'This one
shall go with you,' he shall go;
but if I say, 'This one shall not
go with you,' he shall not go."
5 So Gideon took the men
down to the water. There the
LORD told him, "Separate
those who lap the water with

יָלֹק הַכֶּלֶב תַּצִּיג אוֹתוֹ לְבָד וְכֹל אֲשֶׁר־יִכְרַע עַל־בִּרְכָּיו
knees-of-him on he-kneels who and-all by-self him you-separate the-dog he-laps

לִשְׁתּוֹת׃ וַיְהִי מִסְפַּר הַמְלַקְקִים בְּיָדָם אֶל־
to with-hand-of-them the-ones-lapping number-of and-he-was (6) to-drink

פִּיהֶם שְׁלֹשׁ מֵאוֹת אִישׁ וְכֹל יֶתֶר הָעָם כָּרְעוּ
they-kneeled the-people rest-of and-all-of man hundreds three-of mouth-of-them

עַל־בִּרְכֵיהֶם לִשְׁתּוֹת מָיִם׃ וַיֹּאמֶר יְהוָה אֶל־גִּדְעוֹן
Gideon to Yahweh then-he-said (7) waters to-drink knees-of-them on

בִּשְׁלֹשׁ מֵאוֹת הָאִישׁ הַמְלַקְקִים אוֹשִׁיעַ אֶתְכֶם וְנָתַתִּי
and-I-will-give you I-will-save the-ones-lapping the-man hundreds with-three-of

אֶת־מִדְיָן בְּיָדֶךָ וְכָל־הָעָם יֵלְכוּ אִישׁ לִמְקֹמוֹ׃
to-place-of-him each let-them-go the-people and-all-of into-hand-you Midian ***

וַיִּקְחוּ אֶת־צֵדָה הָעָם בְּיָדָם וְאֵת
and in-hand-of-them the-people provision *** so-they-took-over (8)

שׁוֹפְרֹתֵיהֶם וְאֵת כָּל־אִישׁ יִשְׂרָאֵל שִׁלַּח אִישׁ לְאֹהָלָיו
to-tents-of-him each he-sent Israel man-of rest-of and trumpets-of-them

וּבִשְׁלֹשׁ־מֵאוֹת הָאִישׁ הֶחֱזִיק וּמַחֲנֵה מִדְיָן הָיָה לוֹ
by-him he-was Midian now-camp-of he-kept the-man hundreds but-to-three-of

מִתַּחַת בָּעֵמֶק׃ וַיְהִי בַּלַּיְלָה הַהוּא וַיֹּאמֶר
then-he-said the-that in-the-night and-he-was (9) in-the-valley at-below

אֵלָיו יְהוָה קוּם רֵד בַּמַּחֲנֶה כִּי נְתַתִּיו בְּיָדֶךָ׃
into-hand-of-you I-gave-him for against-the-camp go-down! get-up! Yahweh to-him

וְאִם־יָרֵא אַתָּה לָרֶדֶת רֵד אַתָּה וּפֻרָה נַעַרְךָ אֶל־
to servant-of-you and-Purah you go-down! to-attack you afraid but-if (10)

הַמַּחֲנֶה׃ וְשָׁמַעְתָּ מַה־יְדַבֵּרוּ וְאַחַר תֶּחֱזַקְנָה
they-will-be-encouraged and-after they-say what and-you-listen (11) the-camp

יָדֶיךָ וְיָרַדְתָּ בַּמַּחֲנֶה וַיֵּרֶד הוּא
he so-he-went-down against-the-camp and-you-will-attack hands-of-you

וּפֻרָה נַעֲרוֹ אֶל־קְצֵה הַחֲמֻשִׁים אֲשֶׁר בַּמַּחֲנֶה׃
around-the-camp who the-ones-being-posted end-of to servant-of-him and-Purah

וּמִדְיָן וַעֲמָלֵק וְכָל־בְּנֵי־קֶדֶם נֹפְלִים
ones-being-settled east peoples-of and-all-of and-Amalek now-Midian (12)

בָּעֵמֶק כָּאַרְבֶּה לָרֹב וְלִגְמַלֵּיהֶם אֵין מִסְפָּר
count not and-to-camels-of-them in-number as-the-locust in-the-valley

כַּחוֹל שֶׁעַל־שְׂפַת הַיָּם לָרֹב׃ וַיָּבֹא גִדְעוֹן
Gideon and-he-arrived (13) in-number the-sea shore-of that-on as-the-sand

וְהִנֵּה־אִישׁ מְסַפֵּר לְרֵעֵהוּ חֲלוֹם וַיֹּאמֶר הִנֵּה חֲלוֹם חָלַמְתִּי
I-dreamed dream see! and-he-said dream to-friend-of-him telling man and-see!

their tongues like a dog from
those who kneel down to
drink." 6Three hundred men
lapped with their hands to
their mouths. All the rest got
down on their knees to drink.
7The LORD said to Gideon,
"With the three hundred men
that lapped I will save you and
give the Midianites into your
hands. Let all the other men
go, each to his own place." 8So
Gideon sent the rest of the Israelites to their tents but kept
the three hundred, who took
over the provisions and trumpets of the others.
Now the camp of Midian lay
below him in the valley. 9Dur-
ing that night the LORD said to
Gideon, "Get up, go down
against the camp, because I
am going to give it into your
hands. 10If you are afraid to attack, go down to the camp
with your servant Purah 11and
listen to what they are saying.
Afterward, you will be encouraged to attack the camp."
So he and Purah his servant
went down to the outposts of
the camp. 12The Midianites,
the Amalekites and all the other eastern peoples had settled
in the valley, thick as locusts.
Their camels could no more be
counted than the sand on the
seashore.
13Gideon arrived just as a
man was telling a friend his
dream. "I had a dream," he

וְהִנֵּה צְלוֹל לֶחֶם שְׂעֹרִים מִתְהַפֵּךְ בְּמַחֲנֵה מִדְיָן וַיָּבֹא
and-he-came Midian into-camp-of tumbling barleys bread-of round-loaf and-see!

עַד־ הָאֹהֶל וַיַּכֵּהוּ וַיִּפֹּל וַיַּהַפְכֵהוּ לְמַעְלָה
to-on-top and-he-overturned-him so-he-fell and-he-struck-him the-tent to

וְנָפַל הָאֹהֶל׃ וַיַּעַן רֵעֵהוּ וַיֹּאמֶר אֵין
not and-he-said friend-of-him and-he-responded (14) the-tent and-he-collapsed

זֹאת בִּלְתִּי אִם־ חֶרֶב גִּדְעוֹן בֶּן־ יוֹאָשׁ אִישׁ יִשְׂרָאֵל נָתַן הָאֱלֹהִים
the-God he-gave Israel man-of Joash son-of Gideon sword-of but nothing this

בְּיָדוֹ אֶת־ מִדְיָן וְאֶת־ כָּל־ הַמַּחֲנֶה׃ וַיְהִי כִשְׁמֹעַ
when-to-hear and-he-was (15) the-camp whole-of and Midian *** into-hand-of-him

גִּדְעוֹן אֶת־ מִסְפַּר הַחֲלוֹם וְאֶת־ שִׁבְרוֹ וַיִּשְׁתָּחוּ
then-he-worshiped interpretation-of-him and the-dream account-of *** Gideon

וַיָּשָׁב אֶל־ מַחֲנֵה יִשְׂרָאֵל וַיֹּאמֶר קוּמוּ כִּי־ נָתַן
he-gave for get-up! and-he-called-out Israel camp-of to and-he-returned

יְהוָה בְּיֶדְכֶם אֶת־ מַחֲנֵה מִדְיָן׃ וַיַּחַץ אֶת־ שְׁלֹשׁ־
three-of *** and-he-divided (16) Midian camp-of *** into-hand-of-you Yahweh

מֵאוֹת הָאִישׁ שְׁלֹשָׁה רָאשִׁים וַיִּתֵּן שׁוֹפָרוֹת בְּיַד־ כֻּלָּם
all-of-them in-hand-of trumpets and-he-placed companies three the-man hundreds

וְכַדִּים רֵקִים וְלַפִּדִים בְּתוֹךְ הַכַּדִּים׃ וַיֹּאמֶר אֲלֵיהֶם
to-them and-he-told (17) the-jars inside-of and-torches empty-ones and-jars

מִמֶּנִּי תִרְאוּ וְכֵן תַּעֲשׂוּ וְהִנֵּה אָנֹכִי בָא בִּקְצֵה הַמַּחֲנֶה
the-camp to-edge-of going I now-see! you-do and-same you-watch to-me

וְהָיָה כַאֲשֶׁר־אֶעֱשֶׂה כֵּן תַּעֲשׂוּן׃ וְתָקַעְתִּי בַּשּׁוֹפָר אָנֹכִי
I on-the-trumpet when-I-blow (18) you-do same I-do just-as and-he-will-be

וְכָל־ אֲשֶׁר אִתִּי וּתְקַעְתֶּם בַּשּׁוֹפָרוֹת גַּם־ אַתֶּם סְבִיבוֹת כָּל־
all-of ones-around you also on-the-trumpets then-you-blow with-me who and-all

הַמַּחֲנֶה וַאֲמַרְתֶּם לַיהוָה וּלְגִדְעוֹן׃ וַיָּבֹא גִדְעוֹן
Gideon and-he-reached (19) and-for-Gideon for-Yahweh and-you-shout the-camp

וּמֵאָה־ אִישׁ אֲשֶׁר־ אִתּוֹ בִּקְצֵה הַמַּחֲנֶה רֹאשׁ הָאַשְׁמֹרֶת
the-watch beginning-of the-camp to-edge-of with-him who man and-hundred

הַתִּיכוֹנָה אַךְ הָקֵם הֵקִימוּ אֶת־ הַשֹּׁמְרִים וַיִּתְקְעוּ
and-they-blew the-ones-guarding *** they-changed to-change after the-middle

בַּשּׁוֹפָרוֹת וְנָפוֹץ הַכַּדִּים אֲשֶׁר בְּיָדָם׃ וַיִּתְקְעוּ
and-they-blew (20) in-hand-of-them that the-jars and-to-break on-the-trumpets

שְׁלֹשֶׁת הָרָאשִׁים בַּשּׁוֹפָרוֹת וַיִּשְׁבְּרוּ הַכַּדִּים
the-jars and-they-smashed on-the-trumpets the-companies three-of

וַיַּחֲזִיקוּ בְיַד־ שְׂמֹאולָם בַּלַּפִּדִים וּבְיַד־
and-in-hand-of on-the-torches left-of-them in-hand-of and-they-grasped

was saying. "A round loaf of barley bread came tumbling into the Midianite camp. It struck the tent with such force that the tent overturned and collapsed."

14 His friend responded, "This can be nothing other than the sword of Gideon son of Joash, the Israelite. God has given the Midianites and the whole camp into his hands."

15 When Gideon heard the dream and its interpretation, he worshiped God. He returned to the camp of Israel and called out, "Get up! The LORD has given the Midianite camp into your hands." 16 Dividing the three hundred men into three companies, he placed trumpets and empty jars in the hands of all of them, with torches inside.

17 "Watch me," he told them. "Follow my lead. When I get to the edge of the camp, do exactly as I do. 18 When I and all who are with me blow our trumpets, then from all around the camp blow yours and shout, 'For the LORD and for Gideon.'"

19 Gideon and the hundred men with him reached the edge of the camp at the beginning of the middle watch, just after they had changed the guard. They blew their trumpets and broke the jars that were in their hands. 20 The three companies blew the trumpets and smashed the jars. Grasping the torches in their left hands and holding in

°13 ק צליל

יְמִינָם הַשּׁוֹפָרוֹת לִתְקוֹעַ וַיִּקְרְאוּ חֶרֶב לַיהוָה
for-Yahweh sword and-they-shouted to-blow the-trumpets right-of-them

וּלְגִדְעוֹן׃ וַיַּעַמְדוּ אִישׁ תַּחְתָּיו סָבִיב לַמַּחֲנֶה
to-the-camp around position-of-him each and-they-held (21) and-for-Gideon

וַיָּרָץ כָּל־ הַמַּחֲנֶה וַיָּרִיעוּ וַיָּנִיסוּ׃ וַיִּתְקְעוּ
when-they-sounded (22) and-they-fled and-they-cried-out the-camp all-of and-he-ran

שְׁלֹשׁ־ מֵאוֹת הַשּׁוֹפָרוֹת וַיָּשֶׂם יְהוָה אֵת חֶרֶב אִישׁ
each sword-of *** Yahweh then-he-caused the-trumpets hundreds three-of

בְּרֵעֵהוּ וּבְכָל־ הַמַּחֲנֶה וַיָּנָס הַמַּחֲנֶה עַד־
to the-army and-he-fled the-camp even-through-all-of against-other-of-him

בֵּית הַשִּׁטָּה צְרֵרָתָה עַד שְׂפַת־ אָבֵל מְחוֹלָה עַל־ טַבָּת׃
Tabbath near Meholah Abel border-of as-far-as toward-Zererah the-Shittah Beth

וַיִּצָּעֵק אִישׁ־ יִשְׂרָאֵל מִנַּפְתָּלִי וּמִן־ אָשֵׁר
Asher and-from from-Naphtali Israel man-of and-he-was-called-out (23)

וּמִן־ כָּל־ מְנַשֶּׁה וַיִּרְדְּפוּ אַחֲרֵי מִדְיָן׃ וּמַלְאָכִים
and-messengers (24) Midian after and-they-pursued Manasseh all-of and-from

שָׁלַח גִּדְעוֹן בְּכָל־ הַר אֶפְרַיִם לֵאמֹר רְדוּ
come-down! to-say Ephraim hill-country-of through-all-of Gideon he-sent

לִקְרַאת מִדְיָן וְלִכְדוּ לָהֶם אֶת־ הַמַּיִם עַד בֵּית
Beth as-far-as the-waters *** ahead-of-them and-sieze! Midian to-encounter

בָּרָה וְאֶת־ הַיַּרְדֵּן וַיִּצָּעֵק כָּל־ אִישׁ אֶפְרַיִם וַיִּלְכְּדוּ
and-they-took Ephraim man-of all-of so-he-was-called-out the-Jordan even Barah

אֶת־ הַמַּיִם עַד בֵּית בָּרָה וְאֶת־ הַיַּרְדֵּן׃ וַיִּלְכְּדוּ
and-they-captured (25) the-Jordan even Barah Beth as-far-as the-waters ***

שְׁנֵי־ שָׂרֵי מִדְיָן אֶת־ עֹרֵב וְאֶת־ זְאֵב וַיַּהַרְגוּ אֶת־ עוֹרֵב
Oreb *** and-they-killed Zeeb and Oreb *** Midian leaders-of two-of

בְּצוּר־ עוֹרֵב וְאֶת־ זְאֵב הָרְגוּ בְיֶקֶב־ זְאֵב וַיִּרְדְּפוּ
and-they-pursued Zeeb at-winepress-of they-killed Zeeb and Oreb at-rock-of

אֶל־ מִדְיָן וְרֹאשׁ־ עֹרֵב וּזְאֵב הֵבִיאוּ אֶל־ גִּדְעוֹן מֵעֵבֶר
by-side Gideon to they-brought and-Zeeb Oreb and-head-of Midian after

לַיַּרְדֵּן׃ וַיֹּאמְרוּ אֵלָיו אִישׁ אֶפְרַיִם מָה־ הַדָּבָר
the-thing what? Ephraim man-of to-him now-they-asked (8:1) of-the-Jordan

הַזֶּה עָשִׂיתָ לָּנוּ לְבִלְתִּי קְרֹאות לָנוּ כִּי הָלַכְתָּ לְהִלָּחֵם
to-fight you-went when to-us to-call not to-us you-treated the-this

בְּמִדְיָן וַיְרִיבוּן אִתּוֹ בְּחָזְקָה׃ וַיֹּאמֶר
but-he-answered (2) with-sharpness at-him and-they-criticized against-Midian

אֲלֵיהֶם מֶה־ עָשִׂיתִי עַתָּה כָּכֶם הֲלוֹא טוֹב עֹלְלוֹת
gleanings-of better not? compared-to-you now I-accomplished what? to-them

their right hands the trumpets they were to blow, they shouted, "A sword for the LORD and for Gideon!" 21While each man held his position around the camp, all the Midianites ran, crying out as they fled.

22When the three hundred trumpets sounded, the LORD caused the men throughout the camp to turn on each other with their swords. The army fled to Beth Shittah toward Zererah as far as the border of Abel Meholah near Tabbath. 23Israelites from Naphtali, Asher and all Manasseh were called out, and they pursued the Midianites. 24Gideon sent messengers throughout the hill country of Ephraim, saying, "Come down against the Midianites and seize the waters of the Jordan ahead of them as far as Beth Barah."

So all the men of Ephraim were called out and they took the waters of the Jordan as far as Beth Barah. 25They also captured two of the Midianite leaders, Oreb and Zeeb. They killed Oreb at the rock of Oreb, and Zeeb at the winepress of Zeeb. They pursued the Midianites and brought the heads of Oreb and Zeeb to Gideon, who was by the Jordan.

*Zebah and Zalmunna*

8 Now the Ephraimites asked Gideon, "Why have you treated us like this? Why didn't you call us when you went to fight Midian?" And they criticized him sharply.

2But he answered them, "What have I accomplished compared to you? Aren't the gleanings of Ephraim's grapes

°21 ק וינוסו

אֶפְרַיִם מִבְצִיר אֲבִיעֶזֶר׃ בְּיֶדְכֶם נָתַן אֱלֹהִים
God he-gave into-hand-of-you (3) Abiezer than-grape-harvest-of Ephraim

אֶת־ שָׂרֵי מִדְיָן אֶת־ עֹרֵב וְאֶת־ זְאֵב וּמַה־ יָּכֹלְתִּי עֲשׂוֹת
to-do was-I-able and-what? Zeeb and Oreb *** Midian leaders-of ***

כָּכֶם אָז רָפְתָה רוּחָם מֵעָלָיו
from-against-him resentment-of-them she-subsided then compared-to-you

בְּדַבְּרוֹ הַדָּבָר הַזֶּה׃ וַיָּבֹא גִדְעוֹן הַיַּרְדֵּנָה
to-the-Jordan Gideon and-he-came (4) the-this the-thing when-to-say-him

עֹבֵר הוּא וּשְׁלֹשׁ־ מֵאוֹת הָאִישׁ אֲשֶׁר אִתּוֹ עֲיֵפִים
ones-exhausted with-him who the-man hundreds and-three-of he crossing

וְרֹדְפִים׃ וַיֹּאמֶר לְאַנְשֵׁי סֻכּוֹת תְּנוּ־ נָא כִּכְּרוֹת לֶחֶם
bread cakes-of now! give! Succoth to-men-of and-he-said (5) yet-ones-pursuing

לָעָם אֲשֶׁר בְּרַגְלָי כִּי־ עֲיֵפִים הֵם וְאָנֹכִי רֹדֵף אַחֲרֵי
after pursuing and-I they ones-worn-out for at-feet-of-me who to-the-troop

זֶבַח וְצַלְמֻנָּע מַלְכֵי מִדְיָן׃ וַיֹּאמֶר שָׂרֵי סֻכּוֹת
Succoth officials-of but-he-said (6) Midian kings-of and-Zalmunna Zebah

הֲכַף זֶבַח וְצַלְמֻנָּע עַתָּה בְּיָדֶךָ כִּי־ נִתֵּן
we-should-give that in-hand-of-you already and-Zalmunna Zebah hand-of?

לִצְבָאֲךָ לָחֶם׃ וַיֹּאמֶר גִּדְעוֹן לָכֵן בְּתֵת יְהוָה
Yahweh when-to-give for-that Gideon then-he-replied (7) bread to-troop-of-you

אֶת־ זֶבַח וְאֶת־ צַלְמֻנָּע בְּיָדִי וְדַשְׁתִּי אֶת־ בְּשַׂרְכֶם
flesh-of-you *** then-I-will-tear into-hand-of-me Zalmunna and Zebah ***

אֶת־ קוֹצֵי הַמִּדְבָּר וְאֶת־ הַבַּרְקֳנִים׃ וַיַּעַל מִשָּׁם
from-there and-he-went-up (8) the-briers and-with the-desert thorns-of with

פְּנוּאֵל וַיְדַבֵּר אֲלֵיהֶם כָּזֹאת וַיַּעֲנוּ אוֹתוֹ אַנְשֵׁי פְנוּאֵל
Penuel men-of him but-they-answered as-that of-them and-he-requested Penuel

כַּאֲשֶׁר עָנוּ אַנְשֵׁי סֻכּוֹת׃ וַיֹּאמֶר גַּם־ לְאַנְשֵׁי פְנוּאֵל
Penuel to-men-of also so-he-said (9) Succoth men-of they-answered just-as

לֵאמֹר בְּשׁוּבִי בְשָׁלוֹם אֶתֹּץ אֶת־ הַמִּגְדָּל הַזֶּה׃
the-this the-tower *** I-will-tear-down in-triumph when-to-return-me to-say

וְזֶבַח וְצַלְמֻנָּע בַּקַּרְקֹר וּמַחֲנֵיהֶם עִמָּם
with-them and-forces-of-them in-the-Karkor and-Zalmunna now-Zebah (10)

כַּחֲמֵשֶׁת עָשָׂר אֶלֶף כֹּל הַנּוֹתָרִים מִכֹּל מַחֲנֵה
army-of from-all-of the-ones-being-left all-of thousand ten about-five-of

בְנֵי־ קֶדֶם וְהַנֹּפְלִים מֵאָה וְעֶשְׂרִים אֶלֶף אִישׁ
man thousand and-twenty hundred and-the-ones-having-fallen east peoples-of

שֹׁלֵף חָרֶב׃ וַיַּעַל גִּדְעוֹן דֶּרֶךְ הַשְּׁכוּנֵי
the-ones-dwelling-of way-of Gideon and-he-went-up (11) sword bearing-of

better than the full grape harvest of Abiezer? [3]God gave
Oreb and Zeeb, the Midianite leaders, into your hands. What was I able to do compared to you?" At this, their resentment against him subsided.

[4]Gideon and his three hundred men, exhausted yet keeping up the pursuit, came to the Jordan and crossed it.
[5]He said to the men of Succoth, "Give my troops some bread; they are worn out, and I am still pursuing Zebah and Zalmunna, the kings of Midian."

[6]But the officials of Succoth said, "Do you already have the hands of Zebah and Zalmunna in your possession? Why should we give bread to your troops?"

[7]Then Gideon replied, "Just for that, when the LORD has given Zebah and Zalmunna into my hand, I will tear your flesh with desert thorns and briers."

[8]From there he went up to Peniel[f] and made the same request of them, but they answered as the men of Succoth had.
[9]So he said to the men of Peniel, "When I return in triumph, I will tear down this tower."

[10]Now Zebah and Zalmunna were in Karkor with a force of about fifteen thousand men, all that were left of the armies of the eastern peoples; a hundred and twenty thousand swordsmen had fallen.
[11]Gideon went up by the route of the

[f]8 Hebrew *Penuel*, a variant of *Peniel;* also in verses 9 and 17

בָּאֳהָלִים מִקֶּדֶם לְנֹבַח וְיָגְבֳּהָה* וַיַּךְ אֶת־הַמַּחֲנֶה

the-army *** and-he-fell-upon and-Jogbehah of-Nobah to-east in-tents

וְהַמַּחֲנֶה הָיָה בֶטַח׃ וַיָּנוּסוּ† זֶבַח וְצַלְמֻנָּע

and-Zalmunna Zebah and-they-fled (12) unsuspecting he-was and-the-army

וַיִּרְדֹּף אַחֲרֵיהֶם וַיִּלְכֹּד אֶת־שְׁנֵי ׀ מַלְכֵי מִדְיָן אֶת־

*** Midian kings-of two-of *** and-he-captured after-them but-he-pursued

זֶבַח וְאֶת־צַלְמֻנָּע וְכָל־הַמַּחֲנֶה הֶחֱרִיד׃ וַיָּשָׁב

then-he-returned (13) he-routed the-army and-entire-of Zalmunna and Zebah

גִּדְעוֹן בֶּן־יוֹאָשׁ מִן־הַמִּלְחָמָה מִלְמַעֲלֵה הֶחָרֶס׃ וַיִּלְכָּד־

and-he-caught (14) the-Heres by-Pass-of the-battle from Joash son-of Gideon

נַעַר מֵאַנְשֵׁי סֻכּוֹת וַיִּשְׁאָלֵהוּ וַיִּכְתֹּב אֵלָיו אֶת־

*** for-him and-he-wrote and-he-questioned-him Succoth from-men-of young-man

שָׂרֵי סֻכּוֹת וְאֶת־זְקֵנֶיהָ שִׁבְעִים וְשִׁבְעָה אִישׁ׃ וַיָּבֹא

then-he-came (15) man and-seven seventy elders-of-her even Succoth officials-of

אֶל־אַנְשֵׁי סֻכּוֹת וַיֹּאמֶר הִנֵּה זֶבַח וְצַלְמֻנָּע אֲשֶׁר חֵרַפְתֶּם אוֹתִי

me you-taunted whom and-Zalmunna Zebah here! and-he-said Succoth men-of to

לֵאמֹר הֲכַף זֶבַח וְצַלְמֻנָּע עַתָּה בְּיָדֶךָ כִּי נִתֵּן

we-should-give that in-hand-of-you already and-Zalmunna Zebah hand-of? to-say

לַאֲנָשֶׁיךָ הַיְּעֵפִים לָחֶם׃ וַיִּקַּח אֶת־זִקְנֵי הָעִיר

the-town elders-of *** and-he-took (16) bread the-exhausted-ones to-men-of-you

וְאֶת־קוֹצֵי הַמִּדְבָּר וְאֶת־הַבַּרְקֳנִים וַיֹּדַע בָּהֶם אֵת

*** with-them and-he-taught-lesson the-briers and the-desert thorns-of and

אַנְשֵׁי סֻכּוֹת׃ וְאֶת־מִגְדַּל פְּנוּאֵל נָתָץ וַיַּהֲרֹג אֶת־

*** and-he-killed he-pulled-down Penuel tower-of also (17) Succoth men-of

אַנְשֵׁי הָעִיר׃ וַיֹּאמֶר אֶל־זֶבַח וְאֶל־צַלְמֻנָּע אֵיפֹה

what-kind? Zalmunna and-to Zebah to then-he-asked (18) the-town men-of

הָאֲנָשִׁים אֲשֶׁר הֲרַגְתֶּם בְּתָבוֹר וַיֹּאמְרוּ כָּמוֹךָ כְמוֹהֶם אֶחָד

each so-they like-you and-they-answered at-Tabor you-killed whom the-men

כְּתֹאַר בְּנֵי הַמֶּלֶךְ׃ וַיֹּאמַר אַחַי בְּנֵי־

sons-of brothers-of-me and-he-replied (19) the-king sons-of like-bearing-of

אִמִּי הֵם חַי־יְהוָה לוּ הַחֲיִתֶם אוֹתָם לֹא הָרַגְתִּי אֶתְכֶם׃

you I-would-kill not them you-spared if Yahweh life-of they mother-of-me

וַיֹּאמֶר לְיֶתֶר בְּכוֹרוֹ קוּם הֲרֹג אוֹתָם וְלֹא־שָׁלַף

he-drew but-not them kill! rise! oldest-son-of-him to-Jether and-he-said (20)

הַנַּעַר חַרְבּוֹ כִּי יָרֵא כִּי עוֹדֶנּוּ נָעַר׃ וַיֹּאמֶר זֶבַח

Zebah and-he-said (21) boy only-he for he-was-afraid for sword-of-him the-boy

וְצַלְמֻנָּע קוּם אַתָּה וּפְגַע־בָּנוּ כִּי כָאִישׁ גְּבוּרָתוֹ

strength-of-him as-the-man for against-us and-strike! you come! and-Zalmunna

nomads east of Nobah and Jogbehah and fell upon the unsuspecting army. [12]Zebah and Zalmunna, the two kings of Midian, fled, but he pursued them and captured them, routing their entire army.

[13]Gideon son of Joash then returned from the battle by the Pass of Heres. [14]He caught a young man of Succoth and questioned him, and the young man wrote down for him the names of the seventy-seven officials of Succoth, the elders of the town. [15]Then Gideon came and said to the men of Succoth, "Here are Zebah and Zalmunna, about whom you taunted me by saying, 'Do you already have the hands of Zebah and Zalmunna in your possession? Why should we give bread to your exhausted men?' " [16]He took the elders of the town and taught the men of Succoth a lesson by punishing them with desert thorns and briers. [17]He also pulled down the tower of Peniel and killed the men of the town.

[18]Then he asked Zebah and Zalmunna, "What kind of men did you kill at Tabor?"

"Men like you," they answered, "each one with the bearing of a prince."

[19]Gideon replied, "Those were my brothers, the sons of my own mother. As surely as the LORD lives, if you had spared their lives, I would not kill you." [20]Turning to Jether, his oldest son, he said, "Kill them!" But Jether did not draw his sword, because he was only a boy and was afraid.

[21]Zebah and Zalmunna said, "Come, do it yourself. 'As is the man, so is his strength.' "

**11* Most mss have no *dagesh* in and have simple *sheva* under the *beth* (׳בְ–).

†*12* Most mss have *qibbuts* instead of *shureq* ( וַיָּנֻסוּ ).

וַיָּקָם גִּדְעוֹן וַיַּהֲרֹג אֶת־ זֶבַח וְאֶת־ צַלְמֻנָּע וַיִּקַּח

and-he-took Zalmunna and Zebah *** and-he-killed Gideon so-he-stepped-forward

אֶת־ הַשַּׂהֲרֹנִים אֲשֶׁר בְּצַוְּארֵי גְמַלֵּיהֶם׃ וַיֹּאמְרוּ אִישׁ־

man-of and-they-said (22) camels-of-them on-necks-of that the-ornaments ***

יִשְׂרָאֵל אֶל־ גִּדְעוֹן מְשָׁל־ בָּנוּ גַּם־ אַתָּה גַּם־ בִּנְךָ גַּם בֶּן־

son-of also son-of-you also you indeed over-us rule! Gideon to Israel

בְּנֶךָ כִּי הוֹשַׁעְתָּנוּ מִיַּד מִדְיָן׃ וַיֹּאמֶר אֲלֵהֶם

to-them but-he-told (23) Midian from-hand-of you-saved-us for son-of-you

גִּדְעוֹן לֹא־ אֶמְשֹׁל אֲנִי בָּכֶם וְלֹא־ יִמְשֹׁל בְּנִי בָּכֶם

over-you son-of-me he-will-rule and-not over-you I I-will-rule not Gideon

יְהוָה יִמְשֹׁל בָּכֶם׃ וַיֹּאמֶר אֲלֵהֶם גִּדְעוֹן אֶשְׁאֲלָה

I-will-request Gideon to-them and-he-said (24) over-you he-will-rule Yahweh

מִכֶּם שְׁאֵלָה וּתְנוּ־ לִי אִישׁ נֶזֶם שְׁלָלוֹ כִּי־

for plunder-of-him earring-of each to-me that-give! request from-you

נִזְמֵי זָהָב לָהֶם כִּי יִשְׁמְעֵאלִים הֵם׃ וַיֹּאמְרוּ נָתוֹן

to-give and-they-answered (25) they Ishmaelites for to-them gold earrings-of

נִתֵּן וַיִּפְרְשׂוּ אֶת־ הַשִּׂמְלָה וַיַּשְׁלִיכוּ שָׁמָּה

onto-there and-they-threw the-garment *** so-they-spread-out we-will-give

אִישׁ נֶזֶם שְׁלָלוֹ׃ וַיְהִי מִשְׁקַל נִזְמֵי הַזָּהָב

the-gold earrings-of weight-of and-he-was (26) plunder-of-him earring-of each

אֲשֶׁר שָׁאָל אֶלֶף וּשְׁבַע־ מֵאוֹת זָהָב לְבַד מִן־ הַשַּׂהֲרֹנִים

the-ornaments from apart gold hundreds and-seven-of thousand he-asked-for that

וְהַנְּטִפוֹת וּבִגְדֵי הָאַרְגָּמָן שֶׁעַל מַלְכֵי מִדְיָן וּלְבַד

and-apart Midian kings-of that-on the-purple and-garments-of and-the-pendants

מִן־ הָעֲנָקוֹת אֲשֶׁר בְּצַוְּארֵי גְמַלֵּיהֶם׃ וַיַּעַשׂ אוֹתוֹ גִּדְעוֹן

Gideon him and-he-made (27) camels-of-them on-necks-of that the-chains from

לְאֵפוֹד וַיַּצֵּג אוֹתוֹ בְעִירוֹ בְּעָפְרָה וַיִּזְנוּ

and-they-prostituted in-Ophrah in-town-of-him him and-he-placed into-ephod

כָל־ יִשְׂרָאֵל אַחֲרָיו שָׁם וַיְהִי לְגִדְעוֹן וּלְבֵיתוֹ

and-to-family-of-him to-Gideon and-he-became there after-him Israel all-of

לְמוֹקֵשׁ׃ וַיִּכָּנַע מִדְיָן לִפְנֵי בְּנֵי יִשְׂרָאֵל וְלֹא

and-not Israel sons-of before Midian thus-he-was-subdued (28) as-snare

יָסְפוּ לָשֵׂאת רֹאשָׁם וַתִּשְׁקֹט הָאָרֶץ אַרְבָּעִים שָׁנָה

year forty the-land and-she-had-peace head-of-them to-raise they-repeated

בִּימֵי גִדְעוֹן׃ וַיֵּלֶךְ יְרֻבַּעַל בֶּן־ יוֹאָשׁ וַיֵּשֶׁב

and-he-lived Joash son-of Jerub-Baal and-he-went-back (29) Gideon in-days-of

בְּבֵיתוֹ׃ וּלְגִדְעוֹן הָיוּ שִׁבְעִים בָּנִים יֹצְאֵי

ones-coming-out-of sons seventy they-were and-to-Gideon (30) in-home-of-him

So Gideon stepped forward and killed them, and took the ornaments off their camels' necks.

*Gideon's Ephod*

22The Israelites said to Gideon, "Rule over us—you, your son and your grandson—because you have saved us out of the hand of Midian."

23But Gideon told them, "I will not rule over you, nor will my son rule over you. The LORD will rule over you."
24And he said, "I do have one request, that each of you give me an earring from your share of the plunder." (It was the custom of the Ishmaelites to wear gold earrings.)

25They answered, "We'll be glad to give them." So they spread out a garment, and each man threw a ring from his plunder onto it.
26The weight of the gold rings he asked for came to seventeen hundred shekels,[g] not counting the ornaments, the pendants and the purple garments worn by the kings of Midian or the chains that were on their camels' necks.
27Gideon made the gold into an ephod, which he placed in Ophrah, his town. All Israel prostituted themselves by worshiping it there, and it became a snare to Gideon and his family.

*Gideon's Death*

28Thus Midian was subdued before the Israelites and did not raise its head again. During Gideon's lifetime, the land enjoyed peace forty years.

29Jerub-Baal son of Joash went back home to live.
30He had seventy sons of his own,

*826* That is, about 43 pounds (about 19.5 kilograms)

יְרֵכוֹ כִּי־ נָשִׁים רַבּוֹת הָיוּ לוֹ׃ וּפִילַגְשׁוֹ אֲשֶׁר

who and-concubine-of-him (31) to-him they-were many wives for body-of-him

בִּשְׁכֶם יָלְדָה־ לּוֹ גַם־ הִיא בֵּן וַיָּשֶׂם אֶת־ שְׁמוֹ אֲבִימֶלֶךְ׃

Abimelech name-of-him *** and-he-gave son she also to-him she-bore in-Shechem

וַיָּמָת גִּדְעוֹן בֶּן־ יוֹאָשׁ בְּשֵׂיבָה טוֹבָה וַיִּקָּבֵר

and-he-was-buried good at-old-age Joash son-of Gideon and-he-died (32)

בְּקֶבֶר יוֹאָשׁ אָבִיו בְּעָפְרָה אֲבִי הָעֶזְרִי׃ וַיְהִי

and-he-was (33) the-Abiezrite in-Ophrah father-of-him Joash in-tomb-of

כַּאֲשֶׁר מֵת גִּדְעוֹן וַיָּשׁוּבוּ בְּנֵי יִשְׂרָאֵל וַיִּזְנוּ

and-they-prostituted Israel sons-of then-they-turned Gideon he-died just-as

אַחֲרֵי הַבְּעָלִים וַיָּשִׂימוּ לָהֶם בַּעַל בְּרִית לֵאלֹהִים׃ וְלֹא

and-not (34) as-god Berith Baal for-them and-they-set-up the-Baals to

זָכְרוּ בְּנֵי יִשְׂרָאֵל אֶת־ יְהוָה אֱלֹהֵיהֶם הַמַּצִּיל אוֹתָם

them the-one-rescuing God-of-them Yahweh *** Israel sons-of they-remembered

מִיַּד כָּל־ אֹיְבֵיהֶם מִסָּבִיב׃ וְלֹא־

and-not (35) on-every-side being-enemies-of-them all-of from-hand-of

עָשׂוּ חֶסֶד עִם־ בֵּית יְרֻבַּעַל גִּדְעוֹן כְּכָל־ הַטּוֹבָה

the-good for-all-of Gideon Jerub-Baal family-of to gratitude they-showed

אֲשֶׁר עָשָׂה עִם־ יִשְׂרָאֵל׃ וַיֵּלֶךְ אֲבִימֶלֶךְ בֶּן־ יְרֻבַּעַל

Jerub-Baal son-of Abimelech and-he-went (9:1) Israel for he-did that

שְׁכֶמָה אֶל־ אֲחֵי אִמּוֹ וַיְדַבֵּר אֲלֵיהֶם וְאֶל־ כָּל־

all-of and-to to-them and-he-spoke mother-of-him brothers-of to to-Shechem

מִשְׁפַּחַת בֵּית־ אֲבִי אִמּוֹ לֵאמֹר׃ דַּבְּרוּ־ נָא בְּאָזְנֵי

in-ears-of now! ask! (2) to-say mother-of-him father-of house-of clan-of

כָל־ בַּעֲלֵי שְׁכֶם מַה־ טּוֹב לָכֶם הַמְשֹׁל בָּכֶם שִׁבְעִים

seventy over-you to-rule? for-you better which? Shechem citizens-of all-of

אִישׁ כֹּל בְּנֵי יְרֻבַּעַל אִם־ מְשֹׁל בָּכֶם אִישׁ אֶחָד וּזְכַרְתֶּם

and-you-remember one man over-you to-rule or Jerub-Baal sons-of all-of man

כִּי־ עַצְמְכֶם וּבְשַׂרְכֶם אָנִי׃ וַיְדַבְּרוּ אֲחֵי־

brothers-of and-they-spoke (3) I and-flesh-of-you bone-of-you that

אִמּוֹ עָלָיו בְּאָזְנֵי כָּל־ בַּעֲלֵי שְׁכֶם אֵת כָּל־

all-of *** Shechem citizens-of all-of in-ears-of for-him mother-of-him

הַדְּבָרִים הָאֵלֶּה וַיֵּט לִבָּם אַחֲרֵי אֲבִימֶלֶךְ כִּי

for Abimelech after heart-of-them and-he-inclined the-these the-things

אָמְרוּ אָחִינוּ הוּא׃ וַיִּתְּנוּ־ לוֹ שִׁבְעִים כֶּסֶף

silver seventy to-him and-they-gave (4) he brother-of-us they-said

מִבֵּית בַּעַל בְּרִית וַיִּשְׂכֹּר בָּהֶם אֲבִימֶלֶךְ אֲנָשִׁים רֵיקִים

reckless-ones men Abimelech with-them and-he-hired Berith Baal from-temple-of

for he had many wives. [31]His
concubine, who lived in Shechem, also bore him a son,
whom he named Abimelech.
[32]Gideon son of Joash died at a
good old age and was buried
in the tomb of his father Joash
in Ophrah of the Abiezrites.
[33]No sooner had Gideon
died than the Israelites again
prostituted themselves to the
Baals. They set up Baal-Berith
as their god and [34]did not
remember the LORD their God,
who had rescued them from
the hands of all their enemies
on every side. [35]They also
failed to show gratitude to the
family of Jerub-Baal (that is,
Gideon) for all the good things
he had done for them.

*Abimelech*

9 Abimelech son of Jerub-
Baal went to his mother's
brothers in Shechem and said
to them and to all his mother's
clan, [2]"Ask all the citizens of
Shechem, 'Which is better for
you: to have all seventy of
Jerub-Baal's sons rule over
you, or just one man?'
Remember, I am your flesh
and blood."
[3]When the brothers repeated
all this to the citizens of Shechem, they were inclined to
follow Abimelech, for they
said, "He is our brother."
[4]They gave him seventy silver
shekels[h] from the temple of
Baal-Berith, and Abimelech
used them to hire reckless adventurers, who became his

[h]4 That is, about 1 3/4 pounds (about 0.8 kilogram)

*2 Most mss have *sheva* under the first *mem* (מְ).

וּפֹחֲזִים וַיֵּלְכוּ אַחֲרָיו׃ וַיָּבֹא בֵית־
home-of and-he-went (5) after-him and-they-followed and-ones-adventuring

אָבִיו עָפְרָתָה וַיַּהֲרֹג אֶת־ אֶחָיו בְנֵי־ יְרֻבַּעַל
Jerub-Baal sons-of brothers-of-him *** and-he-murdered in-Ophrah father-of-him

שִׁבְעִים אִישׁ עַל־אֶבֶן אֶחָת וַיִּוָּתֵר יוֹתָם בֶּן־ יְרֻבַּעַל הַקָּטֹן
the-young Jerub-Baal son-of Jotham but-he-escaped one stone on man seventy

כִּי נֶחְבָּא׃ וַיֵּאָסְפוּ כָּל־ בַּעֲלֵי שְׁכֶם וְכָל־ בֵּית
Beth and-all-of Shechem citizens-of all-of then-they-gathered (6) he-hid for

מִלּוֹא וַיֵּלְכוּ וַיַּמְלִיכוּ אֶת־ אֲבִימֶלֶךְ לְמֶלֶךְ עִם־ אֵלוֹן
great-tree beside as-king Abimelech *** and-they-crowned and-they-went Millo

מֻצָּב אֲשֶׁר בִּשְׁכֶם׃ וַיַּגִּדוּ לְיוֹתָם וַיֵּלֶךְ
then-he-climbed to-Jotham when-they-told (7) in-Shechem that *standing

וַיַּעֲמֹד בְּרֹאשׁ הַר־ גְּרִזִּים וַיִּשָּׂא קוֹלוֹ
voice-of-him and-he-raised Gerizim Mount-of on-top-of and-he-stood

וַיִּקְרָא וַיֹּאמֶר לָהֶם שִׁמְעוּ אֵלַי בַּעֲלֵי שְׁכֶם
Shechem citizens-of to-me listen! to-them and-he-said and-he-shouted

וְיִשְׁמַע אֲלֵיכֶם אֱלֹהִים׃ הָלוֹךְ הָלְכוּ הָעֵצִים לִמְשֹׁחַ
to-anoint the-trees they-went-out to-go-out (8) God to-you so-he-may-listen

עֲלֵיהֶם מֶלֶךְ וַיֹּאמְרוּ לַזַּיִת מָלוֹכָה עָלֵינוּ׃ וַיֹּאמֶר
but-he-said (9) over-us be-king! to-the-olive-tree and-they-said king for-them

לָהֶם הַזַּיִת הֶחֳדַלְתִּי אֶת־ דִּשְׁנִי אֲשֶׁר־ בִּי יְכַבְּדוּ
they-honor by-me which oil-of-me *** should-I-give-up? the-olive-tree to-them

אֱלֹהִים וַאֲנָשִׁים וְהָלַכְתִּי לָנוּעַ עַל־ הָעֵצִים׃ וַיֹּאמְרוּ הָעֵצִים
the-trees then-they-said (10) the-trees over to-wave and-I-go and-men gods

לַתְּאֵנָה לְכִי־ אַתְּ מָלְכִי עָלֵינוּ׃ וַתֹּאמֶר לָהֶם
to-them but-she-replied (11) over-us be-king! you come! to-the-fig-tree

הַתְּאֵנָה הֶחֳדַלְתִּי אֶת־ מָתְקִי וְאֶת־ תְּנוּבָתִי הַטּוֹבָה
the-good fruit-of-me and sweetness-of-me *** should-I-give-up! the-fig-tree

וְהָלַכְתִּי לָנוּעַ עַל־ הָעֵצִים׃ וַיֹּאמְרוּ הָעֵצִים לַגֶּפֶן
to-the-vine the-trees then-they-said (12) the-trees over to-wave and-I-go

לְכִי־אַתְּ מָלוֹכִי עָלֵינוּ׃ וַתֹּאמֶר לָהֶם הַגֶּפֶן הֶחֳדַלְתִּי
should-I-give-up? the-vine to-them but-she-said (13) over-us be-king! you come!

אֶת־ תִּירוֹשִׁי הַמְשַׂמֵּחַ אֱלֹהִים וַאֲנָשִׁים וְהָלַכְתִּי לָנוּעַ עַל־ הָעֵצִים׃
the-trees over to-wave and-I-go and-men gods the-one-cheering wine-of-me ***

וַיֹּאמְרוּ כָל־ הָעֵצִים אֶל־ הָאָטָד לֵךְ אַתָּה מְלָךְ־
be-king! you come! the-thornbush to the-trees all-of then-they-said (14)

עָלֵינוּ׃ וַיֹּאמֶר הָאָטָד אֶל־ הָעֵצִים אִם בֶּאֱמֶת אַתֶּם
you in-reality if the-trees to the-thornbush and-he-said (15) over-us

followers. [5]He went to his father's home in Ophrah and on one stone murdered his seventy brothers, the sons of Jerub-Baal. But Jotham, the youngest son of Jerub-Baal, escaped by hiding. [6]Then all the citizens of Shechem and Beth Millo gathered beside the great tree at the pillar in Shechem to crown Abimelech king.

[7]When Jotham was told about this, he climbed up on the top of Mount Gerizim and shouted to them, "Listen to me, citizens of Shechem, so that God may listen to you. [8]One day the trees went out to anoint a king for themselves. They said to the olive tree, 'Be our king.'

[9]"But the olive tree answered, 'Should I give up my oil, by which both gods and men are honored, to go waving over the trees?'

[10]"Next, the trees said to the fig tree, 'Come and be our king.'

[11]"But the fig tree replied, 'Should I give up my fruit, so good and sweet, to go waving over the trees?'

[12]"Then the trees said to the vine, 'Come and be our king.'

[13]"But the vine answered, 'Should I give up my wine, which cheers both gods and men, to go waving over the trees?'

[14]"Finally all the trees said to the thornbush, 'Come and be our king.'

[15]"The thornbush said to the trees, 'If you really want to

*6 On the basis of the Septuagint, the NIV adds the definite article and repoints this word as הַנִּמְצָא , *the-pillar*.

°8 ק מלכה

°12 ק מלכי

מֹשְׁחִים אֹתִי לְמֶלֶךְ עֲלֵיכֶם בֹּאוּ חֲסוּ בְצִלִּי וְאִם־
but-if in-shade-of-me take-refuge! come! over-you as-king me ones-anointing

אַיִן תֵּצֵא אֵשׁ מִן־ הָאָטָד וְתֹאכַל אֶת־ אַרְזֵי
cedars-of *** and-let-her-consume the-thornbush from fire let-her-come-out not

הַלְּבָנוֹן׃ וְעַתָּה אִם־ בֶּאֱמֶת וּבְתָמִים עֲשִׂיתֶם
you-acted and-in-good-faith in-honor if and-now (16) the-Lebanon

וַתַּמְלִיכוּ אֶת־ אֲבִימֶלֶךְ וְאִם־ טוֹבָה עֲשִׂיתֶם עִם־ יְרֻבַּעַל וְעִם־
and-to Jerub-Baal to you-were fair and-if Abimelech *** when-you-made-king

בֵּיתוֹ וְאִם־ כִּגְמוּל יָדָיו עֲשִׂיתֶם לוֹ׃ אֲשֶׁר־
for (17) to-him you-did hands-of-him as-deserving-of and-if family-of-him

נִלְחַם אָבִי עֲלֵיכֶם וַיַּשְׁלֵךְ אֶת־ נַפְשׁוֹ מִנֶּגֶד
in-front life-of-him *** and-he-risked for-you father-of-me he-fought

וַיַּצֵּל אֶתְכֶם מִיַּד מִדְיָן׃ וְאַתֶּם קַמְתֶּם עַל־
against you-revolted but-you (18) Midian from-hand-of you when-he-rescued

בֵּית אָבִי הַיּוֹם וַתַּהַרְגוּ אֶת־ בָּנָיו שִׁבְעִים אִישׁ
man seventy sons-of-him *** and-you-murdered the-day father-of-me family-of

עַל־ אֶבֶן אֶחָת וַתַּמְלִיכוּ אֶת־ אֲבִימֶלֶךְ בֶּן־ אֲמָתוֹ
slave-girl-of-him son-of Abimelech *** and-you-made-king single stone on

עַל־ בַּעֲלֵי שְׁכֶם כִּי אֲחִיכֶם הוּא׃ וְאִם־ בֶּאֱמֶת
in-honor then-if (19) he brother-of-you because Shechem citizens-of over

וּבְתָמִים עֲשִׂיתֶם עִם־ יְרֻבַּעַל וְעִם־ בֵּיתוֹ
family-of-him and-toward Jerub-Baal toward you-acted and-in-good-faith

הַיּוֹם הַזֶּה שִׂמְחוּ בַּאֲבִימֶלֶךְ וְיִשְׂמַח גַּם־ הוּא בָּכֶם׃
in-you he also and-may-he-have-joy in-Abimelech have-joy! the-this the-day

וְאִם־ אַיִן תֵּצֵא אֵשׁ מֵאֲבִימֶלֶךְ וְתֹאכַל אֶת־
*** and-let-her-consume from-Abimelech fire let-her-come-out not but-if (20)

בַּעֲלֵי שְׁכֶם וְאֶת־ בֵּית מִלּוֹא וְתֵצֵא אֵשׁ מִבַּעֲלֵי
from-citizens-of fire and-let-her-come-out Millo Beth and Shechem citizens-of

שְׁכֶם וּמִבֵּית מִלּוֹא וְתֹאכַל אֶת־ אֲבִימֶלֶךְ׃ וַיָּנָס
then-he-fled (21) Abimelech *** and-let-her-consume Millo and-from-Beth Shechem

יוֹתָם וַיִּבְרַח וַיֵּלֶךְ בְּאֵרָה וַיֵּשֶׁב שָׁם מִפְּנֵי
because-of there and-he-lived to-Beer and-he-went and-he-escaped Jotham

אֲבִימֶלֶךְ אָחִיו׃ וַיָּשַׂר אֲבִימֶלֶךְ עַל־ יִשְׂרָאֵל שָׁלֹשׁ
three Israel over Abimelech and-he-governed (22) brother-of-him Abimelech

שָׁנִים׃ וַיִּשְׁלַח אֱלֹהִים רוּחַ רָעָה בֵּין אֲבִימֶלֶךְ וּבֵין
and-between Abimelech between evil spirit God and-he-sent (23) years

בַּעֲלֵי שְׁכֶם וַיִּבְגְּדוּ בַעֲלֵי־ שְׁכֶם
Shechem citizens-of and-they-acted-treacherously Shechem citizens-of

anoint me king over you, come and take refuge in my shade; but if not, then let fire come out of the thornbush and consume the cedars of Lebanon!'

16 "Now if you have acted honorably and in good faith when you made Abimelech king, and if you have been fair to Jerub-Baal and his family, and if you have treated him as he deserves—
17 and to think that my father fought for you, risked his life to rescue you from the hand of Midian
18 (but today you have revolted against my father's family, murdered his seventy sons on a single stone, and made Abimelech, the son of his slave girl, king over the citizens of Shechem because he is your brother)—
19 if then you have acted honorably and in good faith toward Jerub-Baal and his family today, may Abimelech be your joy, and may you be his, too!
20 But if you have not, let fire come out from Abimelech and consume you, citizens of Shechem and Beth Millo, and let fire come out from you, citizens of Shechem and Beth Millo, and consume Abimelech!"

21 Then Jotham fled, escaping to Beer, and he lived there because he was afraid of his brother Abimelech.

22 After Abimelech had governed Israel three years,
23 God sent an evil spirit between Abimelech and the citizens of Shechem, who acted treacherously against Abimelech.

בַּאֲבִימֶלֶךְ׃ לָבוֹא חֲמַס שִׁבְעִים בְּנֵי־ יְרֻבָּעַל
Jerub-Baal sons-of seventy crime-of to-bring (24) against-Abimelech

וְדָמָם לָשׂוּם עַל־ אֲבִימֶלֶךְ אֲחִיהֶם אֲשֶׁר הָרַג אוֹתָם
them he-murdered who brother-of-them Abimelech on to-avenge and-blood-of-them

וְעַל בַּעֲלֵי שְׁכֶם אֲשֶׁר־ חִזְּקוּ אֶת־ יָדָיו לַהֲרֹג אֶת־
*** to-murder hands-of-him *** they-helped who Shechem citizens-of and-on

אֶחָיו׃ וַיָּשִׂימוּ לוֹ בַּעֲלֵי שְׁכֶם
Shechem citizens-of against-him and-they-set (25) brothers-of-him

מְאָרְבִים עַל רָאשֵׁי הֶהָרִים וַיִּגְזְלוּ אֵת כָּל־ אֲשֶׁר־ יַעֲבֹר
he-passed who everyone *** and-they-robbed the-hills tops-of on ones-ambushing

עֲלֵיהֶם בַּדָּרֶךְ וַיֻּגַּד לַאֲבִימֶלֶךְ׃ וַיָּבֹא גַּעַל
Gaal now-he-came (26) to-Abimelech and-he-was-reported on-the-road by-them

בֶּן־ עֶבֶד וְאֶחָיו וַיַּעַבְרוּ בִּשְׁכֶם וַיִּבְטְחוּ־
and-they-confided into-Shechem and-they-moved and-brothers-of-him Ebed son-of

בוֹ בַּעֲלֵי שְׁכֶם׃ וַיֵּצְאוּ הַשָּׂדֶה וַיִּבְצְרוּ
and-they-gathered the-field and-they-went-out (27) Shechem citizens-of in-him

אֶת־ כַּרְמֵיהֶם וַיִּדְרְכוּ וַיַּעֲשׂוּ הִלּוּלִים וַיָּבֹאוּ
and-they-entered festivals and-they-held and-they-trod grapes-of-them ***

בֵּית אֱלֹהֵיהֶם וַיֹּאכְלוּ וַיִּשְׁתּוּ וַיְקַלְלוּ אֶת־
*** and-they-cursed and-they-drank and-they-ate god-of-them temple-of

אֲבִימֶלֶךְ׃ וַיֹּאמֶר ׀ גַּעַל בֶּן־ עֶבֶד מִי־ אֲבִימֶלֶךְ וּמִי־ שְׁכֶם
Shechem and-who? Abimelech who? Ebed son-of Gaal then-he-said (28) Abimelech

כִּי נַעַבְדֶנּוּ הֲלֹא בֶן־ יְרֻבַּעַל וּזְבֻל פְּקִידוֹ
deputy-of-him and-Zebul Jerub-Baal son-of not? we-should-serve-him that

עִבְדוּ אֶת־ אַנְשֵׁי חֲמוֹר אֲבִי שְׁכֶם וּמַדּוּעַ נַעַבְדֶנּוּ אֲנָחְנוּ׃
we should-we-serve-him now-why? Shechem father-of Hamor men-of *** serve!

וּמִי יִתֵּן אֶת־ הָעָם הַזֶּה בְּיָדִי
under-command-of-me the-this the-people *** he-could-put now-who? (29)

וְאָסִירָה אֶת־ אֲבִימֶלֶךְ וַיֹּאמֶר לַאֲבִימֶלֶךְ רַבֶּה
gather! to-Abimelech and-I-would-say Abimelech *** then-I-would-get-rid

צְבָאֲךָ וָצֵאָה׃ וַיִּשְׁמַע זְבֻל שַׂר־ הָעִיר אֶת־
*** the-city governor-of Zebul when-he-heard (30) and-come-out! army-of-you

דִּבְרֵי גַּעַל בֶּן־ עֶבֶד וַיִּחַר אַפּוֹ׃ וַיִּשְׁלַח
and-he-sent (31) anger-of-him then-he-burned Ebed son-of Gaal words-of

מַלְאָכִים אֶל־ אֲבִימֶלֶךְ בְּתָרְמָה לֵאמֹר הִנֵּה גַעַל בֶּן־ עֶבֶד
Ebed son-of Gaal see! to-say under-cover Abimelech to messengers

וְאֶחָיו בָּאִים שְׁכֶמָה וְהִנָּם צָרִים אֶת־
*** ones-stirring-up and-see-they! to-Shechem ones-coming and-brothers-of-him

24 God did this in order that the crime against Jerub-Baal's seventy sons, the shedding of their blood, might be avenged on their brother Abimelech and on the citizens of Shechem, who had helped him murder his brothers. 25 In opposition to him these citizens of Shechem set men on the hilltops to ambush and rob everyone who passed by, and this was reported to Abimelech.

26 Now Gaal son of Ebed moved with his brothers into Shechem, and its citizens put their confidence in him. 27 After they had gone out into the fields and gathered the grapes and trodden them, they held a festival in the temple of their god. While they were eating and drinking, they cursed Abimelech. 28 Then Gaal son of Ebed said, "Who is Abimelech, and who is Shechem, that we should be subject to him? Isn't he Jerub-Baal's son, and isn't Zebul his deputy? Serve the men of Hamor, Shechem's father! Why should we serve Abimelech? 29 If only this people were under my command! Then I would get rid of him. I would say to Abimelech, 'Call out your whole army!' "[i]

30 When Zebul the governor of the city heard what Gaal son of Ebed said, he was very angry. 31 Under cover he sent messengers to Abimelech, saying, "Gaal son of Ebed and his brothers have come to Shechem and are stirring up the

[i] 29 Septuagint; Hebrew *him." Then he said to Abimelech, "Call out your whole army!"*

הָעִיר עָלֶיךָ׃ וְעַתָּה קוּם לַיְלָה אַתָּה וְהָעָם אֲשֶׁר־אִתָּךְ
with-you who and-the-people you night come! and-now (32) against-you the-city

וֶאֱרֹב בַּשָּׂדֶה׃ וְהָיָה בַבֹּקֶר כִּזְרֹחַ
as-to-rise in-the-morning and-he-will-be (33) in-the-field and-lie-in-wait!

הַשֶּׁמֶשׁ תַּשְׁכִּים וּפָשַׁטְתָּ עַל־הָעִיר וְהִנֵּה־הוּא וְהָעָם
and-the-people he and-see! the-city against and-you-advance you-get-up the-sun

אֲשֶׁר־אִתּוֹ יֹצְאִים אֵלֶיךָ וְעָשִׂיתָ לּוֹ כַּאֲשֶׁר תִּמְצָא
she-finds just-as to-him then-you-do against-you ones-coming-out with-him who

יָדֶךָ׃ וַיָּקָם אֲבִימֶלֶךְ וְכָל־הָעָם אֲשֶׁר־עִמּוֹ
with-him that the-troop and-all-of Abimelech so-he-set-out (34) hand-of-you

לַיְלָה וַיֶּאֶרְבוּ עַל־שְׁכֶם אַרְבָּעָה רָאשִׁים׃ וַיֵּצֵא גַּעַל
Gaal now-he-went-out (35) companies four Shechem near and-they-hid night

בֶּן־עֶבֶד וַיַּעֲמֹד פֶּתַח שַׁעַר הָעִיר וַיָּקָם
and-he-came-out the-city gate-of entrace-of and-he-stood Ebed son-of

אֲבִימֶלֶךְ וְהָעָם אֲשֶׁר־אִתּוֹ מִן־הַמַּאְרָב׃ וַיַּרְא־
when-he-saw (36) the-hiding-place from with-him who and-the-troop Abimelech

גַעַל אֶת־הָעָם וַיֹּאמֶר אֶל־זְבֻל הִנֵּה־עָם יוֹרֵד
coming-down people look! Zebul to then-he-said the-people *** Gaal

מֵרָאשֵׁי הֶהָרִים וַיֹּאמֶר אֵלָיו זְבֻל אֵת צֵל
shadow-of *** Zebul to-him and-he-replied the-mountains from-tops-of

הֶהָרִים אַתָּה רֹאֶה כַּאֲנָשִׁים׃* וַיֹּסֶף עוֹד גַּעַל לְדַבֵּר
to-speak Gaal again but-he-repeated (37) as-men seeing you the-mountains

וַיֹּאמֶר הִנֵּה־עָם יוֹרְדִים מֵעִם טַבּוּר הָאָרֶץ
the-land center-of from-in ones-coming-down people look! and-he-said

וְרֹאשׁ־אֶחָד בָּא מִדֶּרֶךְ אֵלוֹן מְעוֹנְנִים׃ וַיֹּאמֶר
then-he-said (38) ones-soothsaying oak-of from-direction-of coming one and-company

אֵלָיו זְבֻל אַיֵּה אֵפוֹא פִיךָ אֲשֶׁר תֹּאמַר מִי אֲבִימֶלֶךְ כִּי
that Abimelech who? you-said when talk-of-you now where? Zebul to-him

נַעַבְדֶנּוּ הֲלֹא זֶה הָעָם אֲשֶׁר מָאַסְתָּה בּוֹ צֵא־
go! against-him you-ridiculed whom the-people this not? we-should-serve-him

נָא עַתָּה וְהִלָּחֶם בּוֹ׃ וַיֵּצֵא גַעַל לִפְנֵי בַּעֲלֵי
citizens-of before Gaal so-he-went-out (39) against-him and-fight! now now!

שְׁכֶם וַיִּלָּחֶם בַּאֲבִימֶלֶךְ׃ וַיִּרְדְּפֵהוּ אֲבִימֶלֶךְ
Abimelech and-he-chased-him (40) against-Abimelech and-he-fought Shechem

וַיָּנָס מִפָּנָיו וַיִּפְּלוּ חֲלָלִים רַבִּים עַד־פֶּתַח
entrance-of to many ones-wounded and-they-fell from-before-him and-he-fled

הַשָּׁעַר׃ וַיֵּשֶׁב אֲבִימֶלֶךְ בָּארוּמָה וַיְגָרֶשׁ זְבֻל אֶת־גַּעַל
Gaal *** Zebul and-he-drove in-Arumah Abimelech and-he-stayed (41) the-gate

city against you. [32]Now then,
during the night you and your
men should come and lie in
wait in the fields. [33]In the
morning at sunrise, advance
against the city. When Gaal
and his men come out against
you, do whatever your hand
finds to do."
[34]So Abimelech and all his
troops set out by night and
took up concealed positions
near Shechem in four companies. [35]Now Gaal son of Ebed
had gone out and was standing at the entrance to the city
gate just as Abimelech and his
soldiers came out from their
hiding place.
[36]When Gaal saw them, he
said to Zebul, "Look, people
are coming down from the
tops of the mountains!"
Zebul replied, "You mistake
the shadows of the mountains
for men."
[37]But Gaal spoke up again:
"Look, people are coming
down from the center of the
land, and a company is coming from the direction of the
soothsayers' tree."
[38]Then Zebul said to him,
"Where is your big talk now,
you who said, 'Who is Abimelech that we should be subject
to him?' Aren't these the men
you ridiculed? Go out and
fight them!"
[39]So Gaal led out[i] the citizens of Shechem and fought
Abimelech. [40]Abimelech
chased him, and many fell
wounded in the flight—all the
way to the entrance to the
gate. [41]Abimelech stayed in
Arumah, and Zebul drove

i39 Or *Gaal went out in the sight of*

*36 Most mss have *pathah* under the *kaph* (כַּ).

וְאֶת־ אֶחָיו מִשֶּׁבֶת בִּשְׁכֶם׃ וַיְהִי מִמָּחֳרָת
on-next-day and-he-was (42) in-Shechem from-to-live brothers-of-him and

וַיֵּצֵא הָעָם הַשָּׂדֶה וַיַּגִּדוּ לַאֲבִימֶלֶךְ׃
to-Abimelech and-they-reported the-field the-people that-he-went-out

וַיִּקַּח אֶת־ הָעָם וַיֶּחֱצֵם לִשְׁלֹשָׁה רָאשִׁים
companies into-three and-he-divided-them the-people *** so-he-took (43)

וַיֶּאֱרֹב בַּשָּׂדֶה וַיַּרְא וְהִנֵּה הָעָם יֹצֵא מִן־
from coming the-people and-see! and-he-saw in-the-field and-he-set-ambush

הָעִיר וַיָּקָם עֲלֵיהֶם וַיַּכֵּם׃ וַאֲבִימֶלֶךְ
and-Abimelech (44) and-he-attacked-them against-them then-he-rose the-city

וְהָרָאשִׁים אֲשֶׁר עִמּוֹ פָּשְׁטוּ וַיַּעַמְדוּ
and-they-took-position they-rushed-forward with-him who and-the-companies

פֶּתַח שַׁעַר הָעִיר וּשְׁנֵי הָרָאשִׁים פָּשְׁטוּ עַל־ כָּל־
all upon they-rushed the-companies then-two-of the-city gate-of entrance-of

אֲשֶׁר בַּשָּׂדֶה וַיַּכּוּם׃ וַאֲבִימֶלֶךְ נִלְחָם
he-attacked and-Abimelech (45) and-they-struck-down-them in-the-field who

בָּעִיר כֹּל הַיּוֹם הַהוּא וַיִּלְכֹּד אֶת־ הָעִיר וְאֶת־
and the-city *** and-he-captured the-that the-day all-of against-the-city

הָעָם אֲשֶׁר־ בָּהּ הָרָג וַיִּתֹּץ אֶת־ הָעִיר
the-city *** then-he-destroyed he-killed in-her who the-people

וַיִּזְרָעֶהָ מֶלַח׃ וַיִּשְׁמְעוּ כָּל־ בַּעֲלֵי
citizens-of all-of when-they-heard (46) salt and-he-scattered-over-her

מִגְדַּל־ שְׁכֶם וַיָּבֹאוּ אֶל־ צְרִיחַ בֵּית אֵל בְּרִית׃
Berith El temple-of stronghold-of into then-they-went Shechem tower-of

וַיֻּגַּד לַאֲבִימֶלֶךְ כִּי הִתְקַבְּצוּ כָּל־ בַּעֲלֵי
citizens-of all-of they-assembled that to-Abimelech when-he-was-told (47)

מִגְדַּל־ שְׁכֶם׃ וַיַּעַל אֲבִימֶלֶךְ הַר־ צַלְמוֹן הוּא וְכָל־
and-all-of he Zalmon Mount-of Abimelech then-he-went-up (48) Shechem tower-of

הָעָם אֲשֶׁר־ אִתּוֹ וַיִּקַּח אֲבִימֶלֶךְ אֶת־הַקַּרְדֻּמּוֹת בְּיָדוֹ
in-hand-of-him the-axes *** Abimelech and-he-took with-him who the-people

וַיִּכְרֹת שׂוֹכַת עֵצִים וַיִּשָּׂאֶהָ וַיָּשֶׂם עַל־ שִׁכְמוֹ
shoulder-of-him on and-he-put and-he-lifted-her trees branch-of and-he-cut-off

וַיֹּאמֶר אֶל־ הָעָם אֲשֶׁר־ עִמּוֹ מָה רְאִיתֶם עָשִׂיתִי מַהֲרוּ
be-quick! I-did you-saw what with-him who the-people to and-he-ordered

עֲשׂוּ כָמוֹנִי׃ וַיִּכְרְתוּ גַם־ כָּל־ הָעָם אִישׁ שׂוֹכֹה
branch-of-him each the-people all-of also so-they-cut (49) like-me do!

וַיֵּלְכוּ אַחֲרֵי אֲבִימֶלֶךְ וַיָּשִׂימוּ עַל־ הַצְּרִיחַ
the-stronghold against and-they-piled Abimelech after and-they-followed

Gaal and his brothers out of
Shechem.
42 The next day the people of
Shechem went out to the
fields, and this was reported to
Abimelech. 43 So he took his
men, divided them into three
companies and set an ambush
in the fields. When he saw the
people coming out of the city,
he rose to attack them.
44 Abimelech and the companies with him rushed forward
to a position at the entrance to
the city gate. Then two companies rushed upon those in the
fields and struck them down.
45 All that day Abimelech
pressed his attack against the
city until he had captured it
and killed its people. Then he
destroyed the city and scattered salt over it.
46 On hearing this, the citizens in the tower of Shechem
went into the stronghold of
the temple of El-Berith.
47 When Abimelech heard that
they had assembled there, 48 he
and all his men went up
Mount Zalmon. He took an ax
and cut off some branches,
which he lifted to his shoulders. He ordered the men with
him, "Quick! Do what you
have seen me do!" 49 So all the
men cut branches and fol-
lowed Abimelech. They piled
them against the stronghold

וַיַּצִּיתוּ עֲלֵיהֶם אֶת־ הַצְּרִיחַ בָּאֵשׁ וַיָּמֻתוּ
and-they-died with-the-fire the-stronghold *** over-them and-they-set-fire

גַּם כָּל־ אַנְשֵׁי מִגְדַּל־ שְׁכֶם כְּאֶלֶף אִישׁ וְאִשָּׁה׃
and-woman man about-thousand Shechem tower-of people-of all-of also

(50) וַיֵּלֶךְ אֲבִימֶלֶךְ אֶל־ תֵּבֵץ וַיִּחַן בְּתֵבֵץ
against-Thebez and-he-besieged Thebez to Abimelech and-he-went (50)

וַיִּלְכְּדָהּ׃ (51) וּמִגְדַּל־ עֹז הָיָה בְתוֹךְ־ הָעִיר
the-city inside-of he-was strong now-tower-of (51) and-he-captured-her

וַיָּנֻסוּ שָׁמָּה כָּל־ הָאֲנָשִׁים וְהַנָּשִׁים וְכֹל בַּעֲלֵי
people-of and-all-of and-the-women the-men all-of to-there and-they-fled

הָעִיר וַיִּסְגְּרוּ בַּעֲדָם וַיַּעֲלוּ עַל־ גַּג הַמִּגְדָּל׃
the-tower roof-of on and-they-climbed-up after-them and-they-locked the-city

(52) וַיָּבֹא אֲבִימֶלֶךְ עַד־ הַמִּגְדָּל וַיִּלָּחֶם בּוֹ
against-him and-he-stormed the-tower to Abimelech and-he-went (52)

וַיִּגַּשׁ עַד־ פֶּתַח הַמִּגְדָּל לְשָׂרְפוֹ בָאֵשׁ׃
with-the-fire to-burn-him the-tower entrance-of to and-he-approached

(53) וַתַּשְׁלֵךְ אִשָּׁה אַחַת פֶּלַח רֶכֶב עַל־ רֹאשׁ אֲבִימֶלֶךְ
Abimelech head-of on upper millstone one woman but-she-dropped (53)

וַתָּרִץ אֶת־ גֻּלְגָּלְתּוֹ׃ (54) וַיִּקְרָא מְהֵרָה אֶל־ הַנַּעַר ׀
the-servant to hurriedly and-he-called (54) skull-of-him *** and-she-cracked

נֹשֵׂא כֵלָיו וַיֹּאמֶר לוֹ שְׁלֹף חַרְבְּךָ וּמוֹתְתֵנִי
and-kill-me! sword-of-you draw! to-him and-he-said armors-of-him bearing

פֶּן־ יֹאמְרוּ לִי אִשָּׁה הֲרָגָתְהוּ וַיִּדְקְרֵהוּ
so-he-ran-through-him she-killed-him woman about-me they-can-say so-not

נַעֲרוֹ וַיָּמֹת׃ (55) וַיִּרְאוּ אִישׁ־ יִשְׂרָאֵל כִּי מֵת
he-was-dead that Israel man-of when-they-saw (55) and-he-died servant-of-him

אֲבִימֶלֶךְ וַיֵּלְכוּ אִישׁ לִמְקֹמוֹ׃ (56) וַיָּשֶׁב אֱלֹהִים אֵת
*** God so-he-repaid (56) to-home-of-him each then-they-went Abimelech

רָעַת אֲבִימֶלֶךְ אֲשֶׁר עָשָׂה לְאָבִיו לַהֲרֹג אֶת־ שִׁבְעִים
seventy *** to-murder to-father-of-him he-did that Abimelech wickedness-of

אֶחָיו׃ (57) וְאֵת כָּל־ רָעַת אַנְשֵׁי שְׁכֶם הֵשִׁיב
he-brought Shechem men-of wickedness-of all-of and (57) brothers-of-him

אֱלֹהִים בְּרֹאשָׁם וַתָּבֹא אֲלֵיהֶם קִלְלַת יוֹתָם בֶּן־ יְרֻבָּעַל׃
Jerub-Baal son-of Jotham curse-of on-them and-she-came on-head-of-them God

(10:1) וַיָּקָם אַחֲרֵי אֲבִימֶלֶךְ לְהוֹשִׁיעַ אֶת־ יִשְׂרָאֵל תּוֹלָע בֶּן־ פּוּאָה
Puah son-of Tola Israel *** to-save Abimelech after and-he-rose (10:1)

בֶּן־ דּוֹדוֹ אִישׁ יִשָּׂשכָר וְהוּא־ יֹשֵׁב בְּשָׁמִיר בְּהַר אֶפְרָיִם׃
Ephraim in-hill-country-of in-Shamir living and-he Issachar man-of Dodo son-of

and set it on fire over the people inside. So all the people in the tower of Shechem, about a thousand men and women, also died.

50Next Abimelech went to Thebez and besieged it and captured it. 51Inside the city, however, was a strong tower, to which all the men and women—all the people of the city—fled. They locked themselves in and climbed up on the tower roof. 52Abimelech went to the tower and stormed it. But as he approached the entrance to the tower to set it on fire, 53a woman dropped an upper millstone on his head and cracked his skull.

54Hurriedly he called to his armor-bearer, "Draw your sword and kill me, so that they can't say, 'A woman killed him.'" So his servant ran him through, and he died. 55When the Israelites saw that Abimelech was dead, they went home.

56Thus God repaid the wickedness that Abimelech had done to his father by murdering his seventy brothers. 57God also made the men of Shechem pay for all their wickedness. The curse of Jotham son of Jerub-Baal came on them.

*Tola*

10 After the time of Abimelech a man of Issachar, Tola son of Puah, the son of Dodo, rose to save Israel. He lived in Shamir, in the hill country of Ephraim. 2He

וַיִּשְׁפֹּט אֶת־יִשְׂרָאֵל עֶשְׂרִים וְשָׁלֹשׁ שָׁנָה וַיָּמָת וַיִּקָּבֵר
and-he-was-buried then-he-died year and-three twenty Israel *** and-he-led (2)

בְּשָׁמִיר׃ וַיָּקָם אַחֲרָיו יָאִיר הַגִּלְעָדִי וַיִּשְׁפֹּט אֶת־יִשְׂרָאֵל
Israel *** and-he-led the-Gileadite Jair after-him and-he-rose (3) in-Shamir

עֶשְׂרִים וּשְׁתַּיִם שָׁנָה׃ וַיְהִי־ לוֹ שְׁלֹשִׁים בָּנִים רֹכְבִים עַל־שְׁלֹשִׁים
thirty on ones-riding sons thirty to-him and-he-was (4) year and-two twenty

עֲיָרִים וּשְׁלֹשִׁים עֲיָרִים* לָהֶם לָהֶם יִקְרְאוּ ׀ חַוֺּת יָאִיר עַד
to Jair Havvoth they-called to-them to-them *donkeys and-thirty donkeys

הַיּוֹם הַזֶּה אֲשֶׁר בְּאֶרֶץ הַגִּלְעָד׃ וַיָּמָת יָאִיר
Jair when-he-died (5) the-Gilead in-land-of that the-this the-day

וַיִּקָּבֵר בְּקָמוֹן׃ וַיֹּסִפוּ ׀ בְּנֵי יִשְׂרָאֵל לַעֲשׂוֹת
to-do Israel sons-of and-they-continued (6) in-Kamon then-he-was-buried

הָרַע בְּעֵינֵי יְהוָה וַיַּעַבְדוּ אֶת־ הַבְּעָלִים וְאֶת־ הָעַשְׁתָּרוֹת
the-Ashtoreths and the-Baals *** and-they-served Yahweh in-eyes-of the-evil

וְאֶת־אֱלֹהֵי אֲרָם וְאֶת־אֱלֹהֵי צִידוֹן וְאֵת ׀ אֱלֹהֵי מוֹאָב וְאֵת אֱלֹהֵי בְנֵי־
sons-of gods-of and Moab gods-of and Sidon gods-of and Aram gods-of and

עַמּוֹן וְאֵת אֱלֹהֵי פְלִשְׁתִּים וַיַּעַזְבוּ אֶת־ יְהוָה וְלֹא
and-not Yahweh *** and-they-forsook Philistines gods-of and Ammon

עֲבָדוּהוּ׃ וַיִּחַר־ אַף יְהוָה בְּיִשְׂרָאֵל
against-Israel Yahweh anger-of and-he-burned (7) they-served-him

וַיִּמְכְּרֵם בְּיַד־ פְּלִשְׁתִּים וּבְיַד בְּנֵי עַמּוֹן׃
Ammon sons-of and-into-hand-of Philistines into-hand-of and-he-sold-them

וַיִּרְעֲצוּ וַיְרֹצְצוּ אֶת־ בְּנֵי יִשְׂרָאֵל בַּשָּׁנָה הַהִיא
the-that in-the-year Israel sons-of *** and-they-crushed and-they-shattered (8)

שְׁמֹנֶה עֶשְׂרֵה שָׁנָה אֶת־כָּל־ בְּנֵי יִשְׂרָאֵל אֲשֶׁר בְּעֵבֶר הַיַּרְדֵּן
the-Jordan on-east-side-of who Israel sons-of all-of *** year ten eight

בְּאֶרֶץ הָאֱמֹרִי אֲשֶׁר בַּגִּלְעָד׃ וַיַּעַבְרוּ בְנֵי־
sons-of and-they-crossed (9) in-the-Gilead that the-Amorite in-land-of

עַמּוֹן אֶת־ הַיַּרְדֵּן לְהִלָּחֵם גַּם־ בִּיהוּדָה וּבְבִנְיָמִין
and-against-Benjamin against-Judah also to-fight the-Jordan *** Ammon

וּבְבֵית אֶפְרָיִם וַתֵּצֶר לְיִשְׂרָאֵל מְאֹד׃
greatly to-Israel and-she-was-distressing Ephraim and-against-house-of

וַיִּזְעֲקוּ בְּנֵי יִשְׂרָאֵל אֶל־יְהוָה לֵאמֹר חָטָאנוּ לָךְ
against-you we-sinned to-say Yahweh to Israel sons-of then-they-cried-out (10)

וְכִי עָזַבְנוּ אֶת־ אֱלֹהֵינוּ וַנַּעֲבֹד אֶת־הַבְּעָלִים׃ וַיֹּאמֶר
and-he-said (11) the-Baals *** and-we-served God-of-us *** we-forsook and-indeed

יְהוָה אֶל־ בְּנֵי יִשְׂרָאֵל הֲלֹא מִמִּצְרַיִם וּמִן־ הָאֱמֹרִי וּמִן־
and-when the-Amorite and-when when-Egypt not? Israel sons-of to Yahweh

led[k] Israel twenty-three years; then he died, and was buried in Shamir.

*Jair*

[3]He was followed by Jair of Gilead, who led Israel twenty-two years. [4]He had thirty sons, who rode thirty donkeys. They controlled thirty towns in Gilead, which to this day are called Havvoth Jair.[l]
[5]When Jair died, he was buried in Kamon.

*Jephthah*

[6]Again the Israelites did evil in the eyes of the LORD. They served the Baals and the Ashtoreths, and the gods of Aram, the gods of Sidon, the gods of Moab, the gods of the Ammonites and the gods of the Philistines. And because the Israelites forsook the LORD and no longer served him, [7]he became angry with them. He sold them into the hands of the Philistines and the Ammonites, [8]who that year shattered and crushed them. For eighteen years they oppressed all the Israelites on the east side of the Jordan in Gilead, the land of the Amorites. [9]The Ammonites also crossed the Jordan to fight against Judah, Benjamin and the house of Ephraim; and Israel was in great distress. [10]Then the Israelites cried out to the LORD, "We have sinned against you, forsaking our God and serving the Baals."
[11]The LORD replied, "When the Egyptians, the Amorites,

k2 Traditionally *judged;* also in verse 3
l4 Or *called the settlements of Jair*

*4 This word should probably be repointed with the ancient versions as עָרִים, *towns.*

בְּנֵ֣י עַמּ֔וֹן וּמִן־ פְּלִשְׁתִּֽים׃ וְצִידוֹנִ֗ים וַעֲמָלֵק֙ וּמָע֔וֹן
and-Maon and-Amalek and-Sidonians (12) Philistines and-when Ammon sons-of

לָחֲצ֖וּ אֶתְכֶ֑ם וַתִּצְעֲק֣וּ אֵלַ֔י וָאוֹשִׁ֥יעָה אֶתְכֶ֖ם מִיָּדָֽם׃
from-hand-of-them you then-I-saved to-me and-you-cried you they-oppressed

וְאַתֶּם֙ עֲזַבְתֶּ֣ם אוֹתִ֔י וַתַּעַבְד֖וּ אֱלֹהִ֣ים אֲחֵרִ֑ים לָכֵ֥ן לֹא־
not so other-ones gods and-you-served me you-forsook but-you (13)

אוֹסִ֖יף לְהוֹשִׁ֥יעַ אֶתְכֶֽם׃ לְכ֗וּ וְזַֽעֲקוּ֙ אֶל־הָ֣אֱלֹהִ֔ים אֲשֶׁ֖ר בְּחַרְתֶּ֣ם
you-chose whom the-gods to and-cry-out! go! (14) you to-save I-will-continue

בָּ֑ם הֵ֛מָּה יוֹשִׁ֥יעוּ לָכֶ֖ם בְּעֵ֥ת צָֽרַתְכֶֽם׃ וַיֹּאמְר֨וּ
but-they-said (15) trouble-of-you in-time-of to-you let-them-save they to-them

בְנֵֽי־ יִשְׂרָאֵ֤ל אֶל־ יְהוָה֙ חָטָ֔אנוּ עֲשֵׂה־אַתָּ֣ה לָ֔נוּ כְּכָל־ הַטּ֖וֹב
the-good as-all-of to-us you do! we-sinned Yahweh to Israel sons-of

בְּעֵינֶ֑יךָ אַ֛ךְ הַצִּילֵ֥נוּ נָ֖א הַיּ֥וֹם הַזֶּֽה׃ וַיָּסִ֜ירוּ
then-they-got-rid (16) the-this the-day now! rescue-us! but in-eyes-of-you

אֶת־ אֱלֹהֵ֤י הַנֵּכָר֙ מִקִּרְבָּ֔ם וַיַּעַבְד֖וּ אֶת־ יְהוָ֑ה
Yahweh *** and-they-served from-among-them the-foreign gods-of ***

וַתִּקְצַ֥ר נַפְשׁ֖וֹ בַּעֲמַ֥ל יִשְׂרָאֵֽל׃ וַיִּצָּעֲקוּ֙
and-they-gathered (17) Israel with-misery-of soul-of-him and-she-could-not-bear

בְּנֵ֣י עַמּ֔וֹן וַֽיַּחֲנ֖וּ בַּגִּלְעָ֑ד וַיֵּאָֽסְפוּ֙ בְּנֵ֣י
sons-of and-they-assembled in-the-Gilead and-they-camped Ammon sons-of

יִשְׂרָאֵ֔ל וַֽיַּחֲנ֖וּ בַּמִּצְפָּֽה׃ וַיֹּאמְר֨וּ הָעָ֜ם שָׂרֵ֤י
leaders-of the-people and-they-said (18) at-the-Mizpah and-they-camped Israel

גִלְעָד֙ אִ֣ישׁ אֶל־ רֵעֵ֔הוּ מִ֣י הָאִ֔ישׁ אֲשֶׁ֣ר יָחֵ֔ל לְהִלָּחֵ֖ם
to-attack he-launches who the-man whoever other-of-him to each Gilead

בִּבְנֵ֣י עַמּ֑וֹן יִֽהְיֶ֣ה לְרֹ֔אשׁ לְכֹ֖ל יֹשְׁבֵ֥י גִלְעָֽד׃
Gilead ones-living-of of-all-of as-head he-will-be Ammon against-sons-of

וְיִפְתָּ֣ח הַגִּלְעָדִ֗י הָיָה֙ גִּבּ֣וֹר חַ֔יִל וְה֖וּא בֶּן־ אִשָּׁ֣ה
woman son-of and-he mighty warrior-of he-was the-Gileadite now-Jephthah (11:1)

זוֹנָ֑ה וַיּ֥וֹלֶד גִּלְעָ֖ד אֶת־ יִפְתָּֽח׃ וַתֵּ֧לֶד אֵֽשֶׁת־
wife-of and-she-bore (2) Jephthah *** Gilead and-he-fathered being-prostitute

גִּלְעָ֛ד ל֖וֹ בָּנִ֑ים וַיִּגְדְּל֨וּ בְנֵֽי־ הָאִשָּׁ֜ה וַיְגָרְשׁ֣וּ
then-they-drove-away the-woman sons-of when-they-grew-up sons to-him Gilead

אֶת־ יִפְתָּ֗ח וַיֹּ֤אמְרוּ לוֹ֙ לֹֽא־ תִנְחַ֣ל בְּבֵית־
in-family-of you-will-inherit not to-him and-they-said Jephthah ***

אָבִ֔ינוּ כִּ֛י בֶּן־ אִשָּׁ֥ה אַחֶ֖רֶת אָֽתָּה׃ וַיִּבְרַ֤ח יִפְתָּח֙ מִפְּנֵ֣י
from-before Jephthah so-he-fled (3) you another woman son-of for father-of-us

אֶחָ֔יו וַיֵּ֖שֶׁב בְּאֶ֣רֶץ ט֑וֹב וַיִּֽתְלַקְּט֤וּ אֶל־
around and-they-gathered Tob in-land-of and-he-settled brothers-of-him

the Ammonites, the Philistines,
12the Sidonians, the
Amalekites and the Maonites[m]
oppressed you and you cried
to me for help, did I not save
you from their hands?
13But
you have forsaken me and
served other gods, so I will no
longer save you.
14Go and cry
out to the gods you have chosen. Let them save you when
you are in trouble!"

15But the Israelites said to the
LORD, "We have sinned. Do
with us whatever you think
best, but please rescue us
now."
16Then they got rid of
the foreign gods among them
and served the LORD. And he
could bear Israel's misery no
longer.

17When the Ammonites
were called to arms and
camped in Gilead, the Israelites assembled and camped at
Mizpah.
18The leaders of the
people of Gilead said to each
other, "Whoever will launch
the attack against the Ammonites will be the head of all
those living in Gilead."

11 Jephthah the Gileadite
was a mighty warrior.
His father was Gilead; his
mother was a prostitute.
2Gilead's wife also bore him sons,
and when they were grown
up, they drove Jephthah away.
"You are not going to get any
inheritance in our family,"
they said, "because you are
the son of another woman."
3So Jephthah fled from his
brothers and settled in the
land of Tob, where a group of
adventurers gathered around

m12 Hebrew; some Septuagint manuscripts *Midianites*

יִפְתָּח אֲנָשִׁים רֵיקִים וַיֵּצְאוּ עִמּוֹ׃ וַיְהִי מִיָּמִים
after-days and-he-was (4) after-him and-they-followed adventurers men Jephthah

וַיִּלָּחֲמוּ בְנֵי־ עַמּוֹן עִם־ יִשְׂרָאֵל׃ וַיְהִי כַּאֲשֶׁר־ נִלְחֲמוּ
they-made-war just-as and-he-was (5) Israel on Ammon sons-of then-they-made-war

בְנֵי־ עַמּוֹן עִם־ יִשְׂרָאֵל וַיֵּלְכוּ זִקְנֵי גִלְעָד לָקַחַת אֶת־ יִפְתָּח
Jephthah *** to-get Gilead elders-of then-they-went Israel on Ammon sons-of

מֵאֶרֶץ טוֹב׃ וַיֹּאמְרוּ לְיִפְתָּח לְכָה וְהָיִיתָה לָּנוּ
to-us and-you-be come! to-Jephthah and-they-said (6) Tob from-land-of

לְקָצִין וְנִלָּחֲמָה בִּבְנֵי עַמּוֹן׃ וַיֹּאמֶר יִפְתָּח
Jephthah and-he-said (7) Ammon against-sons-of so-we-can-fight as-commander

לְזִקְנֵי גִלְעָד הֲלֹא אַתֶּם שְׂנֵאתֶם אוֹתִי וַתְּגָרְשׁוּנִי מִבֵּית
from-house-of and-you-drove-me me you-hated you not? Gilead to-elders-of

אָבִי וּמַדּוּעַ בָּאתֶם אֵלַי עַתָּה כַּאֲשֶׁר צַר לָכֶם׃
to-you trouble just-when now to-me you-come so-why? father-of-me

וַיֹּאמְרוּ זִקְנֵי גִלְעָד אֶל־ יִפְתָּח לָכֵן עַתָּה שַׁבְנוּ
we-turn now nevertheless Jephthah to Gilead elders-of and-they-said (8)

אֵלֶיךָ וְהָלַכְתָּ עִמָּנוּ וְנִלְחַמְתָּ בִּבְנֵי עַמּוֹן וְהָיִיתָ
and-you-will-be Ammon against-sons-of and-you-fight with-us so-you-come to-you

לָּנוּ לְרֹאשׁ לְכֹל יֹשְׁבֵי גִלְעָד׃ וַיֹּאמֶר יִפְתָּח אֶל־
to Jephthah and-he-said (9) Gilead ones-living-of over-all-of as-head to-us

זִקְנֵי גִלְעָד אִם־ מְשִׁיבִים אַתֶּם אוֹתִי לְהִלָּחֵם בִּבְנֵי
against-sons-of to-fight me you ones-taking-back suppose Gilead elders-of

עַמּוֹן וְנָתַן יְהוָה אוֹתָם לְפָנָי אָנֹכִי אֶהְיֶה לָכֶם לְרֹאשׁ׃
as-head to-you will-I-be I to-me them Yahweh and-he-gives Ammon

וַיֹּאמְרוּ זִקְנֵי־ גִלְעָד אֶל־ יִפְתָּח יְהוָה יִהְיֶה שֹׁמֵעַ
witnessing he-is Yahweh Jephthah to Gilead elders-of and-they-replied (10)

בֵּינוֹתֵינוּ אִם־ לֹא כִדְבָרְךָ כֵּן נַעֲשֶׂה׃ וַיֵּלֶךְ יִפְתָּח
Jephthah so-he-went (11) we-will-do so as-word-of-you not if against-us

עִם־ זִקְנֵי גִלְעָד וַיָּשִׂימוּ הָעָם אוֹתוֹ עֲלֵיהֶם לְרֹאשׁ
as-head over-them him the-people and-they-made Gilead elders-of with

וּלְקָצִין וַיְדַבֵּר יִפְתָּח אֶת־ כָּל־ דְּבָרָיו לִפְנֵי
before words-of-him all-of *** Jephthah and-he-repeated and-as-commander

יְהוָה בַּמִּצְפָּה׃ וַיִּשְׁלַח יִפְתָּח מַלְאָכִים אֶל־ מֶלֶךְ בְּנֵי־
sons-of king-of to messengers Jephthah then-he-sent (12) in-the-Mizpah Yahweh

עַמּוֹן לֵאמֹר מַה־ לִּי וָלָךְ כִּי־ בָאתָ אֵלַי לְהִלָּחֵם
to-attack to-me you-came that and-to-you to-me what? to-say Ammon

בְּאַרְצִי׃ וַיֹּאמֶר מֶלֶךְ בְּנֵי־ עַמּוֹן אֶל־
to Ammon sons-of king-of and-he-answered (13) against-country-of-me

him and followed him.

4 Some time later, when the Ammonites made war on Israel, 5 the elders of Gilead went to get Jephthah from the land of Tob. 6 "Come," they said, "be our commander, so we can fight the Ammonites."

7 Jephthah said to them, "Didn't you hate me and drive me from my father's house? Why do you come to me now, when you're in trouble?"

8 The elders of Gilead said to him, "Nevertheless, we are turning to you now; come with us to fight the Ammonites, and you will be our head over all who live in Gilead."

9 Jephthah answered, "Suppose you take me back to fight the Ammonites and the LORD gives them to me—will I really be your head?"

10 The elders of Gilead replied, "The LORD is our witness; we will certainly do as you say." 11 So Jephthah went with the elders of Gilead, and the people made him head and commander over them. And he repeated all his words before the LORD in Mizpah.

12 Then Jephthah sent messengers to the Ammonite king with the question: "What do you have against us that you have attacked our country?"

13 The king of the Ammonites answered Jephthah's messengers, "When Israel came

מַלְאֲכֵי יִפְתָּח כִּי־לָקַח יִשְׂרָאֵל אֶת־אַרְצִי בַּעֲלוֹתוֹ
when-to-come-him land-of-me *** Israel he-took because Jephthah messengers-of

מִמִּצְרַיִם מֵאַרְנוֹן וְעַד־הַיַּבֹּק וְעַד־הַיַּרְדֵּן וְעַתָּה
and-now the-Jordan even-to the-Jabbok even-to from-Arnon from-Egypt

הָשִׁיבָה אֶתְהֶן בְּשָׁלוֹם׃ וַיּוֹסֶף עוֹד יִפְתָּח וַיִּשְׁלַח
and-he-sent Jephthah again and-he-repeated (14) in-peace them give-back!

מַלְאָכִים אֶל־מֶלֶךְ בְּנֵי עַמּוֹן׃ וַיֹּאמֶר לוֹ כֹּה אָמַר
he-says this to-him and-he-said (15) Ammon sons-of king-of to messengers

יִפְתָּח לֹא־לָקַח יִשְׂרָאֵל אֶת־אֶרֶץ מוֹאָב וְאֶת־אֶרֶץ בְּנֵי עַמּוֹן׃
Ammon sons-of land-of or Moab land-of *** Israel he-took not Jephthah

כִּי בַּעֲלוֹתָם מִמִּצְרָיִם וַיֵּלֶךְ יִשְׂרָאֵל בַּמִּדְבָּר
through-the-desert Israel then-he-went from-Egypt when-to-come-up-them but (16)

עַד־יַם־סוּף וַיָּבֹא קָדֵשָׁה׃ וַיִּשְׁלַח יִשְׂרָאֵל מַלְאָכִים ׀
messengers Israel then-he-sent (17) to-Kadesh and-he-went-on Reed Sea-of to

אֶל־מֶלֶךְ אֱדוֹם ׀ לֵאמֹר אֶעְבְּרָה־נָּא בְאַרְצֶךָ וְלֹא
but-not through-country-of-you now! let-me-go to-say Edom king-of to

שָׁמַע מֶלֶךְ אֱדוֹם וְגַם אֶל־מֶלֶךְ מוֹאָב שָׁלַח וְלֹא אָבָה
he-allowed but-not he-sent Moab king-of to and-also Edom king-of he-listened

וַיֵּשֶׁב יִשְׂרָאֵל בְּקָדֵשׁ׃ וַיֵּלֶךְ בַּמִּדְבָּר
through-the-desert so-he-travelled (18) at-Kadesh Israel so-he-stayed

וַיָּסָב אֶת־אֶרֶץ אֱדוֹם וְאֶת־אֶרֶץ מוֹאָב וַיָּבֹא מִמִּזְרַח־
along-rise-of and-he-passed Moab land-of and Edom land-of *** and-he-skirted

שֶׁמֶשׁ לְאֶרֶץ מוֹאָב וַיַּחֲנוּן בְּעֵבֶר אַרְנוֹן וְלֹא־
but-not Arnon on-other-side-of and-they-camped Moab of-country-of sun

בָאוּ בִּגְבוּל מוֹאָב כִּי אַרְנוֹן גְּבוּל מוֹאָב׃ וַיִּשְׁלַח
then-he-sent (19) Moab border-of Arnon for Moab into-territory-of they-entered

יִשְׂרָאֵל מַלְאָכִים אֶל־סִיחוֹן מֶלֶךְ־הָאֱמֹרִי מֶלֶךְ חֶשְׁבּוֹן וַיֹּאמֶר
and-he-said Heshbon king-of the-Amorite king-of Sihon to messengers Israel

לוֹ יִשְׂרָאֵל נַעְבְּרָה־נָּא בְאַרְצְךָ עַד־מְקוֹמִי׃
place-of-me to through-country-of-you now! let-us-pass Israel to-him

וְלֹא־הֶאֱמִין סִיחוֹן אֶת־יִשְׂרָאֵל עֲבֹר בִּגְבֻלוֹ
through-territory-of-him to-pass Israel *** Sihon he-trusted but-not (20)

וַיֶּאֱסֹף סִיחוֹן אֶת־כָּל־עַמּוֹ וַיַּחֲנוּ בְּיָהְצָה
at-Jahaz and-they-camped people-of-him all-of *** Sihon and-he-mustered

וַיִּלָּחֶם עִם־יִשְׂרָאֵל׃ וַיִּתֵּן יְהוָה אֱלֹהֵי־יִשְׂרָאֵל אֶת־סִיחוֹן
Sihon *** Israeh God-of Yahweh then-he-gave (21) Israel with and-he-fought

וְאֶת־כָּל־עַמּוֹ בְּיַד יִשְׂרָאֵל וַיַּכּוּם
and-they-defeated-them Israel into-hand-of people-of-him all-of and

up out of Egypt, they took away my land from the Arnon to the Jabbok, all the way to the Jordan. Now give it back peaceably."

[14]Jephthah sent back messengers to the Ammonite king, [15]saying:

"This is what Jephthah says: Israel did not take the land of Moab or the land of the Ammonites. [16]But when they came up out of Egypt, Israel went through the desert to the Red Sea[n] and on to Kadesh. [17]Then Israel sent messengers to the king of Edom, saying, 'Give us permission to go through your country,' but the king of Edom would not listen. They sent also to the king of Moab, and he refused. So Israel stayed at Kadesh.

[18]"Next they traveled through the desert, skirted the lands of Edom and Moab, passed along the eastern side of the country of Moab, and camped on the other side of the Arnon. They did not enter the territory of Moab, for the Arnon was its border.

[19]"Then Israel sent messengers to Sihon king of the Amorites, who ruled in Heshbon, and said to him, 'Let us pass through your country to our own place.' [20]Sihon, however, did not trust Israel[o] to pass through his territory. He mustered all his men and encamped at Jahaz and fought with Israel.

[21]"Then the LORD, the God of Israel, gave Sihon and all his men into Israel's hands, and they defeated

[n]16 Hebrew *Yam Suph;* that is, Sea of Reeds
[o]20 Or *however, would not make an agreement for Israel*

וַיִּירַשׁ יִשְׂרָאֵל אֵת כָּל־ אֶרֶץ הָאֱמֹרִי יוֹשֵׁב הָאָרֶץ
the-country living-of the-Amorite land-of all-of *** Israel and-he-took-over

הַהִיא׃ וַיִּירְשׁוּ אֵת כָּל־ גְּבוּל הָאֱמֹרִי מֵאַרְנוֹן
from-Arnon the-Amorite territory-of all-of *** and-they-captured (22) the-that

וְעַד־ הַיַּבֹּק וּמִן־ הַמִּדְבָּר וְעַד־ הַיַּרְדֵּן׃ וְעַתָּה
and-now (23) the-Jordan even-to the-desert and-from the-Jabbok even-to

יְהוָה׀ אֱלֹהֵי יִשְׂרָאֵל הוֹרִישׁ אֶת־ הָאֱמֹרִי מִפְּנֵי עַמּוֹ
people-of-him from-before the-Amorite *** he-drove-out Israel God-of Yahweh

יִשְׂרָאֵל וְאַתָּה תִּירָשֶׁנּוּ׃ הֲלֹא אֵת אֲשֶׁר יוֹרִישְׁךָ כְּמוֹשׁ
Chemosh he-gives-you what *** not? (24) will-you-take-over-him so-you Israel

אֱלֹהֶיךָ אוֹתוֹ תִירָשׁ וְאֵת כָּל־ אֲשֶׁר הוֹרִישׁ יְהוָה אֱלֹהֵינוּ
God-of-us Yahweh he-gave that all likewise you-will-take him god-of-you

מִפָּנֵינוּ אוֹתוֹ נִירָשׁ׃ וְעַתָּה הֲטוֹב טוֹב אַתָּה
you to-be-better to-be-better? and-indeed (25) we-will-possess him to-us

מִבָּלָק בֶּן־ צִפּוֹר מֶלֶךְ מוֹאָב הֲרוֹב רָב עִם־יִשְׂרָאֵל
Israel with he-quarrelled to-quarrel? Moab king-of Zippor son-of than-Balak

אִם־ נִלְחֹם נִלְחַם בָּם׃ בְּשֶׁבֶת יִשְׂרָאֵל בְּחֶשְׁבּוֹן
in-Heshbon Israel while-to-occupy (26) with-them he-fought to-fight or

וּבִבְנוֹתֶיהָ וּבְעַרְעוֹר וּבִבְנוֹתֶיהָ וּבְכָל־
and-in-all-of and-in-settlements-of-her and-in-Aroer and-in-settlements-of-her

הֶעָרִים אֲשֶׁר עַל־ יְדֵי אַרְנוֹן שְׁלֹשׁ מֵאוֹת שָׁנָה וּמַדּוּעַ לֹא־
not then-why? year hundreds three-of Arnon banks-of along that the-towns

הִצַּלְתֶּם בָּעֵת הַהִיא׃ וְאָנֹכִי לֹא־ חָטָאתִי לָךְ
against-you I-wronged not now-I (27) the-that during-the-time you-retook

וְאַתָּה עֹשֶׂה אִתִּי רָעָה לְהִלָּחֶם בִּי יִשְׁפֹּט יְהוָה
Yahweh let-him-decide against-me to-wage-war wrong to-me doing but-you

הַשֹּׁפֵט הַיּוֹם בֵּין בְּנֵי יִשְׂרָאֵל וּבֵין בְּנֵי עַמּוֹן׃
Ammon sons-of and-between Israel sons-of between the-day the-One-Judging

וְלֹא שָׁמַע מֶלֶךְ בְּנֵי עַמּוֹן אֶל־ דִּבְרֵי יִפְתָּח אֲשֶׁר
that Jephthah messages-of to Ammon sons-of king-of he-attended but-not (28)

שָׁלַח אֵלָיו׃ וַתְּהִי עַל־ יִפְתָּח רוּחַ יְהוָה וַיַּעֲבֹר
and-he-crossed Yahweh Spirit-of Jephthah upon then-she-came (29) to-him he-sent

אֶת־ הַגִּלְעָד וְאֶת־ מְנַשֶּׁה וַיַּעֲבֹר אֶת־ מִצְפֵּה גִלְעָד
Gilead Mizpah-of *** and-he-passed-through Manasseh and the-Gilead ***

וּמִמִּצְפֵּה גִלְעָד עָבַר בְּנֵי עַמּוֹן׃ וַיִּדַּר
and-he-vowed (30) Ammon sons-of he-advanced Gilead and-from-Mizpah-of

יִפְתָּח נֶדֶר לַיהוָה וַיֹּאמַר אִם־ נָתוֹן תִּתֵּן אֶת־ בְּנֵי עַמּוֹן
Ammon sons-of *** you-give to-give if and-he-said to-Yahweh vow Jephthah

them. Israel took over all the land of the Amorites who lived in that country, [22]capturing all of it from the Arnon to the Jabbok and from the desert to the Jordan.

[23]"Now since the LORD, the God of Israel, has driven the Amorites out before his people Israel, what right have you to take it over? [24]Will you not take what your god Chemosh gives you? Likewise, whatever the LORD our God has given us, we will possess. [25]Are you better than Balak son of Zippor, king of Moab? Did he ever quarrel with Israel or fight with them? [26]For three hundred years Israel occupied Heshbon, Aroer, the surrounding settlements and all the towns along the Arnon. Why didn't you retake them during that time? [27]I have not wronged you, but you are doing me wrong by waging war against me. Let the LORD, the Judge, decide the dispute this day between the Israelites and the Ammonites."

[28]The king of Ammon, however, paid no attention to the message Jephthah sent him.

[29]Then the Spirit of the LORD came upon Jephthah. He crossed Gilead and Manasseh, passed through Mizpah of Gilead, and from there he advanced against the Ammonites. [30]And Jephthah made a vow to the LORD: "If you give the Ammonites into my

בְּיָדִי׃ וְהָיָה הַיּוֹצֵא אֲשֶׁר יֵצֵא
he-comes-out that the-one-coming-out then-he-will-be (31) into-hand-of-me

מִדַּלְתֵי בֵיתִי לִקְרָאתִי בְּשׁוּבִי בְשָׁלוֹם מִבְּנֵי
from-sons-of in-triumph when-to-return-me to-meet-me house-of-me from-doors-of

עַמּוֹן וְהָיָה לַיהוָה וְהַעֲלִיתִהוּ עוֹלָה׃
burnt-offering and-I-will-sacrifice-him for-Yahweh then-he-will-be Ammon

וַיַּעֲבֹר יִפְתָּח אֶל־ בְּנֵי עַמּוֹן לְהִלָּחֶם בָּם
against-them to-fight Ammon sons-of to Jephthah then-he-went-over (32)

וַיִּתְּנֵם יְהוָה בְּיָדוֹ׃ וַיַּכֵּם מֵעֲרוֹעֵר
from-Aroer and-he-devastated-them (33) into-hand-of-him Yahweh and-he-gave-them

וְעַד־ בּוֹאֲךָ מִנִּית עֶשְׂרִים עִיר וְעַד אָבֵל כְּרָמִים מַכָּה
devastation Keramim Abel and-as-far-as town twenty Minnith to-go-you even-to

גְּדוֹלָה מְאֹד וַיִּכָּנְעוּ בְּנֵי עַמּוֹן מִפְּנֵי בְּנֵי יִשְׂרָאֵל׃
Israel sons-of from-before Ammon sons-of thus-they-were-subdued very great

וַיָּבֹא יִפְתָּח הַמִּצְפָּה אֶל־ בֵּיתוֹ וְהִנֵּה
then-see! home-of-him to the-Mizpah Jephthah when-he-returned (34)

בִתּוֹ יֹצֵאת לִקְרָאתוֹ בְּתֻפִּים* וּבִמְחֹלוֹת
and-with-dances with-tambourines to-meet-him coming-out daughter-of-him

וְרַק הִיא יְחִידָה אֵין־ לוֹ מִמֶּנּוּ† בֵּן אוֹ־ בַת׃ וַיְהִי
and-he-was (35) daughter or son from-him to-him not along she and-only

כִרְאוֹתוֹ אוֹתָהּ וַיִּקְרַע אֶת־ בְּגָדָיו וַיֹּאמֶר אֲהָהּ
oh! and-he-cried clothes-of-him *** then-he-tore her when-see-him

בִּתִּי הַכְרֵעַ הִכְרַעְתִּנִי וְאַתְּ הָיִיתְ††
you-are and-you you-made-wretched-me to-make-wretched daughter-of-me

בְּעֹכְרָי וְאָנֹכִי פָּצִיתִי־ פִי אֶל־ יְהוָה וְלֹא אוּכַל
I-can and-not Yahweh to mouth-of-me I-opened for-I being-miseries-of-me

לָשׁוּב׃ וַתֹּאמֶר אֵלָיו אָבִי פָּצִיתָה אֶת־ פִּיךָ
mouth-of-you *** you-opened father-of-me to-him and-she-said (36) to-break

אֶל־ יְהוָה עֲשֵׂה לִי כַּאֲשֶׁר יָצָא מִפִּיךָ אַחֲרֵי אֲשֶׁר עָשָׂה
he-gave that now from-mouth-of-you he-came-out just-as to-me do! Yahweh to

לְךָ יְהוָה נְקָמוֹת מֵאֹיְבֶיךָ מִבְּנֵי עַמּוֹן׃
Ammon on-sons-of on-being-enemies-of-you vengeances Yahweh to-you

וַתֹּאמֶר אֶל־ אָבִיהָ יֵעָשֶׂה לִּי הַדָּבָר הַזֶּה
the-this the-request to-me let-him-be-granted father-of-her to and-she-said (37)

הַרְפֵּה מִמֶּנִּי שְׁנַיִם חֳדָשִׁים וְאֵלְכָה וְיָרַדְתִּי עַל־ הֶהָרִים
the-hills on and-I-will-wander and-I-will-roam months two from-me let-alone!

וְאֶבְכֶּה עַל־ בְּתוּלַי אָנֹכִי וְרֵעֹיָתָי° ׃ וַיֹּאמֶר
and-he-said (38) and-friends-of-me I virginities-of-me over and-I-will-weep

hands, [31]whatever comes out
of the door of my house to
meet me when I return in triumph from the Ammonites
will be the LORD's, and I will
sacrifice it as a burnt offering."
[32]Then Jephthah went over
to fight the Ammonites, and
the LORD gave them into his
hands. [33]He devastated twenty
towns from Aroer to the
vicinity of Minnith, as far as
Abel Keramim. Thus Israel
subdued Ammon.
[34]When Jephthah returned
to his home in Mizpah, who
should come out to meet him
but his daughter, dancing to
the sound of tambourines! She
was an only child. Except for
her he had neither son nor
daughter. [35]When he saw her,
he tore his clothes and cried,
"Oh! My daughter! You have
made me miserable and
wretched, because I have
made a vow to the LORD that I
cannot break."
[36]"My father," she replied,
"you have given your word to
the LORD. Do to me just as you
promised, now that the LORD
has avenged you of your enemies, the Ammonites. [37]But
grant me this one request,"
she said. "Give me two
months to roam the hills and
weep with my friends, be-
cause I will never marry."

*34 Most mss have *dagesh* in the *beth* (בְּ').

†34 The NIV, with the ancient versions, replaces the masculine suffix with the feminine (מִמֶּנָּה), *except-her.*

††35 Most mss have no *sheva* under the *tav* (ת–).

°37 ק ורעותי

לֵכִי וַיִּשְׁלַח אוֹתָהּ שְׁנֵי חֳדָשִׁים וַתֵּלֶךְ הִיא וְרֵעוֹתֶיהָ
and-girl-friends-of-her she and-she-went months two-of her and-he-let-go go!

וַתֵּבְךְּ עַל־ בְּתוּלֶיהָ עַל־ הֶהָרִים׃ (39) וַיְהִי מִקֵּץ ׀
at-end-of and-he-was (39) the-hills into virginities-of-her over and-she-wept

שְׁנַיִם חֳדָשִׁים וַתָּשָׁב אֶל־ אָבִיהָ וַיַּעַשׂ לָהּ אֶת־
*** to-her and-he-did father-of-her to then-she-returned months two

נִדְרוֹ אֲשֶׁר נָדָר וְהִיא לֹא־ יָדְעָה אִישׁ וַתְּהִי־ חֹק
custom and-she-became man she-knew not and-she he-vowed that vow-of-him

בְּיִשְׂרָאֵל׃ (40) מִיָּמִים ׀ יָמִימָה תֵּלַכְנָה בְּנוֹת יִשְׂרָאֵל
Israel young-women-of they-go-out at-days from-days (40) in-Israel

לְתַנּוֹת לְבַת־ יִפְתָּח הַגִּלְעָדִי אַרְבַּעַת יָמִים בַּשָּׁנָה׃
in-the-year days four-of the-Gileadite Jephthah for-daughter-of to-commemorate

(12:1) וַיִּצָּעֵק אִישׁ אֶפְרַיִם וַיַּעֲבֹר צָפוֹנָה
to-Zaphon and-he-crossed-over Ephraim man-of and-he-was-called-out (12:1)

וַיֹּאמְרוּ לְיִפְתָּח מַדּוּעַ ׀ עָבַרְתָּ ׀ לְהִלָּחֵם בִּבְנֵי־ עַמּוֹן
Ammon against-sons-of to-fight you-went why? to-Jephthah and-they-said

וְלָנוּ לֹא קָרָאתָ לָלֶכֶת עִמָּךְ בֵּיתְךָ נִשְׂרֹף
we-will-burn-down house-of-you with-you to-go you-called not and-to-us

עָלֶיךָ בָּאֵשׁ׃ (2) וַיֹּאמֶר יִפְתָּח אֲלֵיהֶם אִישׁ רִיב
struggle man-of to-them Jephthah and-he-answered (2) with-the-fire over-you

הָיִיתִי אֲנִי וְעַמִּי וּבְנֵי־ עַמּוֹן מְאֹד וָאֶזְעַק אֶתְכֶם
to-you and-I-called great Ammon with-sons-of and-people-of-me I I-was

וְלֹא־ הוֹשַׁעְתֶּם אוֹתִי מִיָּדָם׃ (3) וָאֶרְאֶה כִּי־ אֵינְךָ מוֹשִׁיעַ
helping not-you that when-I-saw (3) from-hand-of-them me you-saved but-not

וָאָשִׂימָה נַפְשִׁי בְכַפִּי וָאֶעְבְּרָה אֶל־ בְּנֵי עַמּוֹן
Ammon sons-of to and-I-crossed-over in-hand-of-me life-of-me then-I-took

וַיִּתְּנֵם יְהוָה בְּיָדִי וְלָמָּה עֲלִיתֶם אֵלַי הַיּוֹם
the-day to-me you-came-up now-why? into-hand-of-me Yahweh and-he-gave-them

הַזֶּה לְהִלָּחֶם בִּי׃ (4) וַיִּקְבֹּץ יִפְתָּח אֶת־ כָּל־ אַנְשֵׁי
men-of all-of *** Jephthah then-he-called (4) against-me to-fight the-this

גִלְעָד וַיִּלָּחֶם אֶת־ אֶפְרָיִם וַיַּכּוּ אַנְשֵׁי גִלְעָד אֶת־
*** Gilead men-of and-they-struck-down Ephraim *** and-he-fought Gilead

אֶפְרַיִם כִּי אָמְרוּ פְּלִיטֵי אֶפְרַיִם אַתֶּם גִּלְעָד בְּתוֹךְ אֶפְרַיִם
Ephraim in-among Gilead you Ephraim renegades-of they-said because Ephraim

בְּתוֹךְ מְנַשֶּׁה׃ (5) וַיִּלְכֹּד גִּלְעָד אֶת־ מַעְבְּרוֹת הַיַּרְדֵּן
the-Jordan fords-of *** Gilead and-he-captured (5) Manasseh in-among

לְאֶפְרָיִם וְהָיָה כִּי יֹאמְרוּ פְּלִיטֵי אֶפְרַיִם אֶעֱבֹרָה
let-me-cross-over Ephraim survivors-of they-said when and-he-was to-Ephraim

38 "You may go," he said.
And he let her go for two
months. She and the girls
went into the hills and wept
because she would never marry. 39 After the two months, she
returned to her father and he
did to her as he had vowed.
And she was a virgin.
From this comes the Israelite
custom 40 that each year the
young women of Israel go out
for four days to commemorate
the daughter of Jephthah the
Gileadite.

*Jephthah and Ephraim*

12 The men of Ephraim
called out their forces,
crossed over to Zaphon and
said to Jephthah, "Why did
you go to fight the Ammonites
without calling us to go with
you? We're going to burn
down your house over your
head."
2 Jephthah answered, "I and
my people were engaged in a
great struggle with the Ammonites, and although I
called, you didn't save me out
of their hands. 3 When I saw
that you wouldn't help, I took
my life in my hands and
crossed over to fight the Ammonites, and the LORD gave
me the victory over them.
Now why have you come up
today to fight me?"
4 Jephthah then called together the men of Gilead and
fought against Ephraim. The
Gileadites struck them down
because the Ephraimites had
said, "You Gileadites are rene-
gades from Ephraim and
Manasseh." 5 The Gileadites
captured the fords of the Jordan leading to Ephraim, and
whenever a survivor of
Ephraim said, "Let me cross

וַיֹּאמְרוּ לוֹ אַנְשֵׁי־ גִלְעָד הַאֶפְרָתִי אַתָּה וַיֹּאמֶר ׀ לֹא׃
no and-he-replied you Ephramite? Gilead men-of to-him then-they-asked

וַיֹּאמְרוּ לוֹ אֱמָר־ נָא שִׁבֹּלֶת וַיֹּאמֶר סִבֹּלֶת וְלֹא
for-not sibboleth and-he-said shibboleth now! say! to-him then-they-said (6)

יָכִין לְדַבֵּר כֵּן וַיֹּאחֲזוּ אוֹתוֹ וַיִּשְׁחָטוּהוּ אֶל־
at and-they-killed-him him then-they-seized correctly to-pronounce he-could

מַעְבְּרוֹת הַיַּרְדֵּן וַיִּפֹּל בָּעֵת הַהִיא מֵאֶפְרַיִם אַרְבָּעִים
forty from-Ephraim the-that at-the-time and-he-fell the-Jordan fords-of

וּשְׁנַיִם אָלֶף׃ וַיִּשְׁפֹּט יִפְתָּח אֶת־יִשְׂרָאֵל שֵׁשׁ שָׁנִים וַיָּמָת
then-he-died years six Israel *** Jephthah and-he-led (7) thousand and-two

יִפְתָּח הַגִּלְעָדִי וַיִּקָּבֵר בְּעָרֵי גִלְעָד׃ וַיִּשְׁפֹּט
and-he-led (8) Gilead in-towns-of and-he-was-buried the-Gileadite Jephthah

אַחֲרָיו אֶת־יִשְׂרָאֵל אִבְצָן מִבֵּית לָחֶם׃ וַיְהִי־ לוֹ שְׁלֹשִׁים בָּנִים
sons thirty to-him and-he-was (9) Lehem of-Beth Ibzan Israel *** after-him

וּשְׁלֹשִׁים בָּנוֹת שִׁלַּח הַחוּצָה וּשְׁלֹשִׁים בָּנוֹת
young-women and-thirty to-the-outside he-gave-away daughters and-thirty

הֵבִיא לְבָנָיו מִן־ הַחוּץ וַיִּשְׁפֹּט אֶת־יִשְׂרָאֵל שֶׁבַע
seven Israel *** and-he-led the-outside from for-sons-of-him he-brought-in

שָׁנִים׃ וַיָּמָת אִבְצָן וַיִּקָּבֵר בְּבֵית לָחֶם׃ וַיִּשְׁפֹּט
and-he-led (11) Lehem in-Beth and-he-was-buried Ibzan then-he-died (10) years

אַחֲרָיו אֶת־יִשְׂרָאֵל אֵילוֹן הַזְּבוּלֹנִי וַיִּשְׁפֹּט אֶת־יִשְׂרָאֵל עֶשֶׂר שָׁנִים׃
years ten Israel *** and-he-led the-Zebulunite Elon Israel *** after-him

וַיָּמָת אֵלוֹן* הַזְּבוּלֹנִי וַיִּקָּבֵר בְּאַיָּלוֹן בְּאֶרֶץ
in-land-of in-Aijalon and-he-was-buried the-Zebulunite Elon then-he-died (12)

זְבוּלֻן׃ וַיִּשְׁפֹּט אַחֲרָיו אֶת־ יִשְׂרָאֵל עַבְדּוֹן בֶּן־ הִלֵּל
Hillel son-of Abdon Israel *** after-him and-he-led (13) Zebulun

הַפִּרְעָתוֹנִי׃ וַיְהִי־ לוֹ אַרְבָּעִים בָּנִים וּשְׁלֹשִׁים בְּנֵי בָנִים
sons sons-of and-thirty sons forty to-him and-he-was (14) the-Pirathonite

רֹכְבִים עַל־ שִׁבְעִים עֲיָרִם וַיִּשְׁפֹּט אֶת־ יִשְׂרָאֵל שְׁמֹנֶה שָׁנִים׃
years eight Israel *** and-he-led donkeys seventy on ones-riding

וַיָּמָת עַבְדּוֹן בֶּן־ הִלֵּל הַפִּרְעָתוֹנִי וַיִּקָּבֵר
and-he-was-buried the-Pirathonite Hillel son-of Abdon then-he-died (15)

בְּפִרְעָתוֹן בְּאֶרֶץ אֶפְרַיִם בְּהַר הָעֲמָלֵקִי׃
the-Amalekite in-hill-country-of Ephraim in-land-of at-Pirathon

וַיֹּסִפוּ בְּנֵי יִשְׂרָאֵל לַעֲשׂוֹת הָרַע בְּעֵינֵי יְהוָה
Yahweh in-eyes-of the-evil to-do Israel sons-of and-they-repeated (13:1)

וַיִּתְּנֵם יְהוָה בְּיַד־ פְּלִשְׁתִּים אַרְבָּעִים שָׁנָה׃ וַיְהִי
and-he-was (2) year forty Philistines into-hand-of Yahweh so-he-delivered-them

over," the men of Gilead asked him, "Are you an Ephraimite?" If he replied, "No," [6]they said, "All right, say 'Shibboleth.'" If he said, "Sibboleth," because he could not pronounce the word correctly, they seized him and killed him at the fords of the Jordan. Forty-two thousand Ephraimites were killed at that time.

[7]Jephthah led[p] Israel six years. Then Jephthah the Gileadite died, and was buried in a town in Gilead.

*Ibzan, Elon and Abdon*

[8]After him, Ibzan of Bethlehem led Israel. [9]He had thirty sons and thirty daughters. He gave his daughters away in marriage to those outside his clan, and for his sons he brought in thirty young women as wives from outside his clan. Ibzan led Israel seven years. [10]Then Ibzan died, and was buried in Bethlehem.

[11]After him, Elon the Zebulunite led Israel ten years. [12]Then Elon died, and was buried in Aijalon in the land of Zebulun.

[13]After him, Abdon son of Hillel, from Pirathon, led Israel. [14]He had forty sons and thirty grandsons, who rode on seventy donkeys. He led Israel eight years. [15]Then Abdon son of Hillel died, and was buried at Pirathon in Ephraim, in the hill country of the Amalekites.

*The Birth of Samson*

13 Again the Israelites did evil in the eyes of the LORD, so the LORD delivered them into the hands of the Philistines for forty years.

p7 Traditionally *judged;* also in verses 8-14

*12 Most mss have *yod* after the *aleph* (אילון), as in verse 11.

אִישׁ אֶחָד מִצָּרְעָה מִמִּשְׁפַּחַת הַדָּנִי וּשְׁמוֹ מָנוֹחַ
Manoah and-name-of-him the-Danite from-clan-of of-Zorah certain man

וְאִשְׁתּוֹ עֲקָרָה וְלֹא יָלָדָה׃ וַיֵּרָא מַלְאַךְ־
angel-of and-he-appeared (3) she-bore-child and-not sterile and-wife-of-him

יְהוָה אֶל־ הָאִשָּׁה וַיֹּאמֶר אֵלֶיהָ הִנֵּה־ נָא אַתְּ־ עֲקָרָה וְלֹא
and-not sterile you now! see! to-her and-he-said the-woman to Yahweh

יָלַדְתְּ וְהָרִית וְיָלַדְתְּ בֵּן׃ וְעַתָּה
and-now (4) son and-you-will-bear but-you-will-conceive you-bore-child

הִשָּׁמְרִי נָא וְאַל־ תִּשְׁתִּי יַיִן וְשֵׁכָר וְאַל־ תֹּאכְלִי
you-eat and-not or-fermented-drink wine you-drink that-not now! see!

כָּל־ טָמֵא׃ כִּי הִנָּךְ הָרָה וְיֹלַדְתְּ בֵּן
son and-you-will-bear conceiving see-you! because (5) unclean-thing any-of

וּמוֹרָה לֹא־ יַעֲלֶה עַל־ רֹאשׁוֹ כִּי־ נְזִיר אֱלֹהִים יִהְיֶה הַנַּעַר
the-boy he-will-be God Nazirite-of for head-of-him on he-may-go not and-razor

מִן־ הַבֶּטֶן וְהוּא יָחֵל לְהוֹשִׁיעַ אֶת־ יִשְׂרָאֵל מִיַּד
from-hand-of Israel *** to-deliver he-will-begin and-he the-womb from

פְּלִשְׁתִּים׃ וַתָּבֹא הָאִשָּׁה וַתֹּאמֶר לְאִישָׁהּ לֵאמֹר
to-say to-husband-of-her and-she-told the-woman then-she-went (6) Philistines

אִישׁ הָאֱלֹהִים בָּא אֵלַי וּמַרְאֵהוּ כְּמַרְאֵה מַלְאַךְ
angel-of like-appearance-of and-appearance-of-him to-me he-came the-God man-of

הָאֱלֹהִים נוֹרָא מְאֹד וְלֹא שְׁאִלְתִּיהוּ אֵי־ מִזֶּה הוּא וְאֶת־
and he from-there where? I-asked-him and-not very being-awesome the-God

שְׁמוֹ לֹא־ הִגִּיד לִי׃ וַיֹּאמֶר לִי הִנָּךְ הָרָה
conceiving see-you! to-me but-he-said (7) to-me he-told not name-of-him

וְיֹלַדְתְּ בֵּן וְעַתָּה אַל־ תִּשְׁתִּי ׀ יַיִן וְשֵׁכָר וְאַל־
and-not or-fermented-drink wine you-drink not now-then son and-you-will-bear

תֹּאכְלִי כָּל־ טֻמְאָה כִּי־ נְזִיר אֱלֹהִים יִהְיֶה הַנַּעַר מִן־
from the-boy he-will-be God Nazirite-of for unclean-thing any-of you-eat

הַבֶּטֶן עַד יוֹם מוֹתוֹ׃ וַיֶּעְתַּר מָנוֹחַ אֶל־ יְהוָה
Yahweh to Manoah then-he-prayed (8) death-of-him day-of until the-womb

וַיֹּאמַר בִּי אֲדוֹנָי אִישׁ הָאֱלֹהִים אֲשֶׁר שָׁלַחְתָּ יָבוֹא־ נָא עוֹד
again now! let-him-come you-sent whom the-God man-of Lord O! and-he-said

אֵלֵינוּ וְיוֹרֵנוּ מַה־ נַּעֲשֶׂה לַנַּעַר הַיּוּלָּד׃
the-one-being-born with-the-boy we-must-do what so-he-may-teach-us to-us

וַיִּשְׁמַע הָאֱלֹהִים בְּקוֹל מָנוֹחַ וַיָּבֹא מַלְאַךְ הָאֱלֹהִים
the-God angel-of and-he-came Manoah to-voice-of the-God and-he-heard (9)

עוֹד אֶל־ הָאִשָּׁה וְהִיא יוֹשֶׁבֶת בַּשָּׂדֶה וּמָנוֹחַ אִישָׁהּ אֵין
not husband-of-her but-Manoah in-the-field being and-she the-woman to again

[2]A certain man of Zorah, named Manoah, from the clan of the Danites, had a wife who was sterile and remained childless. [3]The angel of the LORD appeared to her and said, "You are sterile and childless, but you are going to conceive and have a son. [4]Now see to it that you drink no wine or other fermented drink and that you do not eat anything unclean, [5]because you will conceive and give birth to a son. No razor may be used on his head, because the boy is to be a Nazirite, set apart to God from birth, and he will begin the deliverance of Israel from the hands of the Philistines."

[6]Then the woman went to her husband and told him, "A man of God came to me. He looked like an angel of God, very awesome. I didn't ask him where he came from, and he didn't tell me his name. [7]But he said to me, 'You will conceive and give birth to a son. Now then, drink no wine or other fermented drink and do not eat anything unclean, because the boy will be a Nazirite of God from birth until the day of his death.'"

[8]Then Manoah prayed to the LORD: "O Lord, I beg you, let the man of God you sent to us come again to teach us how to bring up the boy who is to be born."

[9]God heard Manoah, and the angel of God came again to the woman while she was out in the field; but her husband Manoah was not with her. [10]The

עִמָּהּ׃ וַתְּמַהֵר הָאִשָּׁה וַתָּרָץ וַתַּגֵּד
and-she-told and-she-ran the-woman and-she-hurried (10) with-her

לְאִישָׁהּ וַתֹּאמֶר אֵלָיו הִנֵּה נִרְאָה אֵלַי הָאִישׁ אֲשֶׁר־
who the-man to-me he-appeared see! to-him and-she-said to-husband-of-her

בָּא בַיּוֹם אֵלָי׃ וַיָּקָם וַיֵּלֶךְ מָנוֹחַ אַחֲרֵי
after Manoah and-he-followed and-he-got-up (11) to-me on-the-day he-came

אִשְׁתּוֹ וַיָּבֹא אֶל־הָאִישׁ וַיֹּאמֶר לוֹ הַאַתָּה הָאִישׁ אֲשֶׁר־
who the-man you? to-him then-he-said the-man to when-he-came wife-of-him

דִּבַּרְתָּ אֶל־הָאִשָּׁה וַיֹּאמֶר אָנִי׃ וַיֹּאמֶר מָנוֹחַ עַתָּה
when Manoah so-he-asked (12) I and-he-said the-wife to you-talked

יָבֹא דְבָרֶיךָ מַה־יִּהְיֶה מִשְׁפַּט־הַנַּעַר וּמַעֲשֵׂהוּ׃
and-work-of-him the-boy rule-of he-will-be what? words-of-you he-fulfills

וַיֹּאמֶר מַלְאַךְ יְהוָה אֶל־מָנוֹחַ מִכֹּל אֲשֶׁר־אָמַרְתִּי אֶל־
to I-told that from-all Manoah to Yahweh angel-of and-he-answered (13)

הָאִשָּׁה תִּשָּׁמֵר׃ מִכֹּל אֲשֶׁר־יֵצֵא מִגֶּפֶן הַיַּיִן
the-grape from-vine-of he-comes that from-anything (14) she-must-do the-wife

לֹא תֹאכַל וְיַיִן וְשֵׁכָר אַל־תֵּשְׁתְּ וְכָל־
and-any-of she-must-drink not or-fermented-drink and-wine she-must-eat not

טֻמְאָה אַל־תֹּאכַל כֹּל אֲשֶׁר־צִוִּיתִיהָ תִּשְׁמֹר׃
she-must-do I-commanded-her that everything she-must-eat not unclean-thing

וַיֹּאמֶר מָנוֹחַ אֶל־מַלְאַךְ יְהוָה נַעְצְרָה־נָּא אוֹתָךְ
you now! let-us-detain Yahweh angel-of to Manoah then-he-said (15)

וְנַעֲשֶׂה לְפָנֶיךָ גְּדִי עִזִּים׃ וַיֹּאמֶר מַלְאַךְ
angel-of and-he-replied (16) goats young-goat-of for-you so-we-may-prepare

יְהוָה אֶל־מָנוֹחַ אִם־תַּעְצְרֵנִי לֹא־אֹכַל בְּלַחְמֶךָ וְאִם־
but-if from-food-of-you I-will-eat not you-detain-me though Manoah to Yahweh

תַּעֲשֶׂה עֹלָה לַיהוָה תַּעֲלֶנָּה כִּי לֹא־יָדַע מָנוֹחַ
Manoah he-realized not now you-offer-her to-Yahweh burnt-offering you-prepare

כִּי־מַלְאַךְ יְהוָה הוּא׃ וַיֹּאמֶר מָנוֹחַ אֶל־מַלְאַךְ יְהוָה
Yahweh angel-of of Manoah then-he-inquired (17) he Yahweh angel-of that

מִי שְׁמֶךָ כִּי־יָבֹא דְבָרְיךָ° וְכִבַּדְנוּךָ׃
then-we-may-honor-you word-of-you he-comes-true when name-of-you what?

וַיֹּאמֶר לוֹ מַלְאַךְ יְהוָה לָמָּה זֶּה תִּשְׁאַל לִשְׁמִי
about-name-of-me you-ask this why? Yahweh angel-of to-him and-he-replied (18)

וְהוּא־פֶלְאִי*׃ וַיִּקַּח מָנוֹחַ אֶת־גְּדִי הָעִזִּים וְאֶת־
and the-goats young-goat-of *** Manoah then-he-took (19) wonderful now-he

הַמִּנְחָה וַיַּעַל עַל־הַצּוּר לַיהוָה וּמַפְלִא
and-amazing-thing to-Yahweh the-rock on and-he-sacrificed the-grain-offering

woman hurried to tell her husband, "He's here! The man who appeared to me the other day!"

11 Manoah got up and followed his wife. When he came to the man, he said, "Are you the one who talked to my wife?"

"I am," he said.

12 So Manoah asked him, "When your words are fulfilled, what is to be the rule for the boy's life and work?"

13 The angel of the LORD answered, "Your wife must do all that I have told her. 14 She must not eat anything that comes from the grapevine, nor drink any wine or other fermented drink nor eat anything unclean. She must do everything I have commanded her."

15 Manoah said to the angel of the LORD, "We would like you to stay until we prepare a young goat for you."

16 The angel of the LORD replied, "Even though you detain me, I will not eat any of your food. But if you prepare a burnt offering, offer it to the LORD." (Manoah did not realize that it was the angel of the LORD.)

17 Then Manoah inquired of the angel of the LORD, "What is your name, so that we may honor you when your word comes true?"

18 He replied, "Why do you ask my name? It is beyond understanding.[q]" 19 Then Manoah took a young goat, together with the grain offering, and sacrificed it on a rock to

[q] 18 Or *is wonderful*

*18 Most mss point the textual form פֶּלְאִי and offer a *Qere* form (א)פְּלִי.

°17 ק דברך

לַעֲשׂוֹת וּמָנוֹחַ וְאִשְׁתּוֹ רֹאִים׃ וַיְהִי בַעֲלוֹת
as-to-blaze-up and-he-was (20) ones-watching and-wife-of-him and-Manoah to-do

הַלַּהַב מֵעַל הַמִּזְבֵּחַ הַשָּׁמַיְמָה וַיַּעַל מַלְאַךְ־
angel-of then-he-ascended toward-the-heavens the-altar from-on the-flame

יְהוָה בְּלַהַב הַמִּזְבֵּחַ וּמָנוֹחַ וְאִשְׁתּוֹ רֹאִים
ones-seeing and-wife-of-him and-Manoah the-altar in-flame-of Yahweh

וַיִּפְּלוּ עַל־ פְּנֵיהֶם אָרְצָה׃ וְלֹא־ יָסַף עוֹד
again he-repeated when-not (21) to-ground faces-of-them on then-they-fell

מַלְאַךְ יְהוָה לְהֵרָאֹה אֶל־ מָנוֹחַ וְאֶל־ אִשְׁתּוֹ אָז יָדַע
he-realized then wife-of-him and-to Manoah to to-show-himself Yahweh angel-of

מָנוֹחַ כִּי־ מַלְאַךְ יְהוָה הוּא׃ וַיֹּאמֶר מָנוֹחַ אֶל־ אִשְׁתּוֹ מוֹת
to-die wife-of-him to Manoah and-he-said (22) he Yahweh angel-of that Manoah

נָמוּת כִּי אֱלֹהִים רָאִינוּ׃ וַתֹּאמֶר לוֹ אִשְׁתּוֹ לוּ
if wife-of-him to-him but-she-answered (23) we-saw God for we-will-die

חָפֵץ יְהוָה לַהֲמִיתֵנוּ לֹא־ לָקַח מִיָּדֵנוּ עֹלָה
burnt-offering from-hand-of-us he-would-accept not to-kill-us Yahweh he-meant

וּמִנְחָה וְלֹא הֶרְאָנוּ אֶת־ כָּל־ אֵלֶּה וְכָעֵת
or-at-the-time these all-of *** he-would-show-us and-not and-grain-offering

לֹא הִשְׁמִיעָנוּ כָּזֹאת׃ וַתֵּלֶד הָאִשָּׁה בֵּן וַתִּקְרָא
and-she-called son the-woman and-she-bore (24) as-this he-would-tell-us not

אֶת־ שְׁמוֹ שִׁמְשׁוֹן וַיִּגְדַּל הַנַּעַר וַיְבָרְכֵהוּ יְהוָה׃
Yahweh and-he-blessed-him the-boy and-he-grew Samson name-of-him ***

וַתָּחֶל רוּחַ יְהוָה לְפַעֲמוֹ בְּמַחֲנֵה־ דָן בֵּין צָרְעָה
Zorah between Dan in-Mahaneh to-stir-him Yahweh Spirit-of and-she-began (25)

וּבֵין אֶשְׁתָּאֹל׃ וַיֵּרֶד שִׁמְשׁוֹן תִּמְנָתָה וַיַּרְא
and-he-saw to-Timnah Samson and-he-went-down (14:1) Eshtaol and-between

אִשָּׁה בְּתִמְנָתָה מִבְּנוֹת פְּלִשְׁתִּים׃ וַיַּעַל
when-he-returned (2) Philistines from-young-women-of in-Timnah woman

וַיַּגֵּד לְאָבִיו וּלְאִמּוֹ וַיֹּאמֶר אִשָּׁה רָאִיתִי
I-saw woman and-he-said and-to-mother-of-him to-father-of-him then-he-told

בְתִמְנָתָה מִבְּנוֹת פְּלִשְׁתִּים וְעַתָּה קְחוּ־ אוֹתָהּ לִי לְאִשָּׁה׃
as-wife for-me her get! and-now Philistines from-young-women-of in-Timnah

וַיֹּאמֶר לוֹ אָבִיו וְאִמּוֹ הַאֵין בִּבְנוֹת
among-women-of not? and-mother-of-him father-of-him to-him and-he-said (3)

אַחֶיךָ וּבְכָל־ עַמִּי אִשָּׁה כִּי־ אַתָּה הוֹלֵךְ לָקַחַת אִשָּׁה
wife to-get going you that woman people-of-me or-among-all-of relatives-of-you

מִפְּלִשְׁתִּים הָעֲרֵלִים וַיֹּאמֶר שִׁמְשׁוֹן אֶל־ אָבִיו
father-of-him to Samson but-he-said the-uncircumcised-ones from-Philistines

the LORD. And the LORD did an amazing thing while Manoah and his wife watched:
[20]As the flame blazed up from the altar toward heaven, the angel of the LORD ascended in the flame. Seeing this, Manoah and his wife fell with their faces to the ground.
[21]When the angel of the LORD did not show himself again to Manoah and his wife, Manoah realized that it was the angel of the LORD.
[22]"We are doomed to die!" he said to his wife. "We have seen God!"
[23]But his wife answered, "If the LORD had meant to kill us, he would not have accepted a burnt offering and grain offering from our hands, nor shown us all these things or now told us this."
[24]The woman gave birth to a boy and named him Samson. He grew and the LORD blessed him,
[25]and the Spirit of the LORD began to stir him while he was in Mahaneh Dan, between Zorah and Eshtaol.

*Samson's Marriage*

**14** Samson went down to Timnah and saw there a young Philistine woman.
[2]When he returned, he said to his father and mother, "I have seen a Philistine woman in Timnah; now get her for me as my wife."
[3]His father and mother replied, "Isn't there an acceptable woman among your relatives or among all our people? Must you go to the uncircumcised Philistines to get a wife?"
But Samson said to his father, "Get her for me. She's the

אוֹתָהּ קַח־ לִי כִּי־ הִיא יָשְׁרָה בְעֵינָי׃ וְאָבִיו
now-father-of-him (4) in-eyes-of-me she-is-right she for for-me get! her

וְאִמּוֹ לֹא יָדְעוּ כִּי מֵיְהוָה הִיא כִּי־ תֹאֲנָה הוּא־
he occasion for this from-Yahweh that they-knew not and-mother-of-him

מְבַקֵּשׁ מִפְּלִשְׁתִּים וּבָעֵת הַהִיא פְּלִשְׁתִּים מֹשְׁלִים
ones-ruling Philistines the-that for-at-the-time from-Philistines seeking

בְּיִשְׂרָאֵל׃ וַיֵּרֶד שִׁמְשׁוֹן וְאָבִיו וְאִמּוֹ
and-mother-of-him and-father-of-him Samson and-he-went-down (5) over-Israel

תִּמְנָתָה וַיָּבֹאוּ עַד־ כַּרְמֵי תִמְנָתָה וְהִנֵּה כְּפִיר
young-lion-of and-see! Timnah vineyards-of to and-they-approached to-Timnah

אֲרָיוֹת שֹׁאֵג לִקְרָאתוֹ׃ וַתִּצְלַח עָלָיו רוּחַ יְהוָה
Yahweh Spirit-of upon-him then-she-came (6) to-attack-him roaring lions

וַיְשַׁסְּעֵהוּ כְּשַׁסַּע הַגְּדִי וּמְאוּמָה אֵין בְּיָדוֹ
in-hand-of-him not but-anything the-young-goat as-to-tear and-he-tore-apart-him

וְלֹא הִגִּיד לְאָבִיו וּלְאִמּוֹ אֵת אֲשֶׁר עָשָׂה׃
he-did what *** or-to-mother-of-him to-father-of-him he-told but-not

וַיֵּרֶד וַיְדַבֵּר לָאִשָּׁה וַתִּישַׁר בְּעֵינֵי
in-eyes-of and-she-was-right with-the-woman and-he-talked then-he-went-down (7)

שִׁמְשׁוֹן׃ וַיָּשָׁב מִיָּמִים לְקַחְתָּהּ וַיָּסַר
then-he-turned-aside to-marry-her after-days when-he-went-back (8) Samson

לִרְאוֹת אֵת מַפֶּלֶת הָאַרְיֵה וְהִנֵּה עֲדַת דְּבוֹרִים בִּגְוִיַּת הָאַרְיֵה
the-lion in-body-of bees swarm-of and-see! the-lion carcass-of *** to-look

וּדְבָשׁ׃ וַיִּרְדֵּהוּ אֶל־ כַּפָּיו וַיֵּלֶךְ הָלוֹךְ
to-walk and-he-went hands-of-him with and-he-scooped-out-him (9) and-honey

וְאָכֹל וַיֵּלֶךְ אֶל־ אָבִיו וְאֶל־ אִמּוֹ וַיִּתֵּן
then-he-gave mother-of-him and-to father-of-him to when-he-came and-to-eat

לָהֶם וַיֹּאכֵלוּ וְלֹא־ הִגִּיד לָהֶם כִּי מִגְּוִיַּת הָאַרְיֵה
the-lion from-carcass-of that to-them he-told but-not and-they-ate to-them

רָדָה הַדְּבָשׁ׃ וַיֵּרֶד אָבִיהוּ אֶל־ הָאִשָּׁה וַיַּעַשׂ
and-he-made the-woman to father-of-him now-he-went-down (10) the-honey he-took

שָׁם שִׁמְשׁוֹן מִשְׁתֶּה כִּי כֵּן יַעֲשׂוּ הַבַּחוּרִים׃ וַיְהִי
and-he-was (11) the-bridegrooms they-did customary as feast Samson there

כִּרְאוֹתָם אוֹתוֹ וַיִּקְחוּ שְׁלֹשִׁים מֵרֵעִים וַיִּהְיוּ אִתּוֹ׃
with-him and-they-were companions thirty then-they-gave him when-to-see-them

וַיֹּאמֶר לָהֶם שִׁמְשׁוֹן אָחוּדָה־ נָּא לָכֶם חִידָה אִם־ הַגֵּד
to-tell if riddle to-you now! let-me-tell Samson to-them and-he-said (12)

תַּגִּידוּ אוֹתָהּ לִי שִׁבְעַת יְמֵי הַמִּשְׁתֶּה וּמְצָאתֶם
and-you-find-answer the-feast days-of seven-of to-me her you-tell

right one for me." 4(His parents did not know that this
was from the LORD, who was
seeking an occasion to confront the Philistines; for at that
time they were ruling over Israel.) 5Samson went down to
Timnah together with his father and mother. As they approached the vineyards of
Timnah, suddenly a young
lion came roaring toward him.
6The Spirit of the LORD came
upon him in power so that he
tore the lion apart with his
bare hands as he might have
torn a young goat. But he told
neither his father nor his
mother what he had done.
7Then he went down and
talked with the woman, and
he liked her.

8Some time later, when he
went back to marry her, he
turned aside to look at the
lion's carcass. In it was a
swarm of bees and some
honey, 9which he scooped out
with his hands and ate as he
went along. When he rejoined
his parents, he gave them
some, and they too ate it. But
he did not tell them that he
had taken the honey from the
lion's carcass.

10Now his father went down
to see the woman. And Samson made a feast there, as was
customary for bridegrooms.
11When he appeared, he was
given thirty companions.

12"Let me tell you a riddle,"
Samson said to them. "If you
can give me the answer within the seven days of the feast,

וְנָתַתִּי לָכֶם שְׁלֹשִׁים סְדִינִים וּשְׁלֹשִׁים חֲלִפֹת בְּגָדִים׃
clothes sets-of and-thirty linen-garments thirty to-you then-I-will-give

וְאִם־ לֹא תוּכְלוּ לְהַגִּיד לִי וּנְתַתֶּם אַתֶּם לִי שְׁלֹשִׁים
thirty to-me you then-you-must-give to-me to-answer you-can not but-if (13)

סְדִינִים וּשְׁלֹשִׁים חֲלִיפוֹת בְּגָדִים וַיֹּאמְרוּ לוֹ חוּדָה
tell! to-him and-they-said clothes sets-of and-thirty linen-garments

חִידָתְךָ וְנִשְׁמָעֶנָּה׃ וַיֹּאמֶר לָהֶם מֵהָאֹכֵל
from-the-one-eating to-them and-he-replied (14) and-let-us-hear-her riddle-of-you

יָצָא מַאֲכָל וּמֵעַז יָצָא מָתוֹק וְלֹא יָכְלוּ
they-could and-not sweet-thing he-came and-from-strong edible-thing he-came

לְהַגִּיד הַחִידָה שְׁלֹשֶׁת יָמִים׃ וַיְהִי | בַּיּוֹם הַשְּׁבִיעִי*
*the-seventh on-the-day and-he-was (15) days three-of the-riddle to-answer

וַיֹּאמְרוּ לְאֵשֶׁת־ שִׁמְשׁוֹן פַּתִּי אֶת־ אִישֵׁךְ וְיַגֶּד־ לָנוּ
for-us so-he-explains husband-of-you *** coax! Samson to-wife-of then-they-said

אֶת־הַחִידָה פֶּן־ נִשְׂרֹף אוֹתָךְ וְאֶת־ בֵּית אָבִיךְ בָּאֵשׁ
with-the-fire father-of-you household-of and you we-will-burn or the-riddle ***

הַלְיָרְשֵׁנוּ קְרָאתֶם לָנוּ הֲלֹא׃ וַתֵּבְךְּ אֵשֶׁת שִׁמְשׁוֹן
Samson wife-of then-she-sobbed (16) or-not to-us you-invited to-rob-us?

עָלָיו וַתֹּאמֶר רַק־ שְׂנֵאתַנִי וְלֹא אֲהַבְתָּנִי הַחִידָה
the-riddle you-love-me and-not you-hate-me indeed and-she-said on-him

חַדְתָּ לִבְנֵי עַמִּי וְלִי לֹא הִגַּדְתָּה וַיֹּאמֶר
and-he-replied you-told-answer not but-to-me people-of-me to-men-of you-gave

לָהּ הִנֵּה לְאָבִי וּלְאִמִּי לֹא הִגַּדְתִּי וְלָךְ
so-to-you I-explained not and-to-mother-of-me to-father-of-me see! to-her

אַגִּיד׃ וַתֵּבְךְּ עָלָיו שִׁבְעַת הַיָּמִים אֲשֶׁר־ הָיָה
he-was that the-days seven-of on-him and-she-cried (17) should-I-explain

לָהֶם הַמִּשְׁתֶּה וַיְהִי | בַּיּוֹם הַשְּׁבִיעִי וַיַּגֶּד־ לָהּ כִּי
for to-her then-he-told the-seventh on-the-day so-he-was the-feast to-them

הֱצִיקַתְהוּ וַתַּגֵּד הַחִידָה לִבְנֵי עַמָּהּ׃
people-of-her to-men-of the-riddle then-she-explained she-pressed-him

וַיֹּאמְרוּ לוֹ אַנְשֵׁי הָעִיר בַּיּוֹם הַשְּׁבִיעִי בְּטֶרֶם
at-before the-seventh on-the-day the-town men-of to-him and-they-said (18)

יָבֹא הַחַרְסָה מַה־ מָּתוֹק מִדְּבַשׁ וּמֶה עַז מֵאֲרִי
than-lion stronger and-what? than-honey sweeter what? the-sun he-set

וַיֹּאמֶר לָהֶם לוּלֵא חֲרַשְׁתֶּם בְּעֶגְלָתִי לֹא מְצָאתֶם
you-would-solve not with-heifer-of-me you-plowed if-not to-them and-he-said

חִידָתִי׃ וַתִּצְלַח עָלָיו רוּחַ יְהוָה וַיֵּרֶד
and-he-went-down Yahweh Spirit-of upon-him then-she-came (19) riddle-of-me

*15 The NIV, with some ancient versions, reads *resh* instead of *shin* הָרְבִיעִי, *the-fourth.*

I will give you thirty linen garments and thirty sets of clothes. [13]If you can't tell me the answer, you must give me thirty linen garments and thirty sets of clothes."

"Tell us your riddle," they said. "Let's hear it."

[14]He replied,

"Out of the eater,
something to eat;
out of the strong,
something sweet."

For three days they could not give the answer.

[15]On the fourth[r] day, they said to Samson's wife, "Coax your husband into explaining the riddle for us, or we will burn you and your father's household to death. Did you invite us here to rob us?"

[16]Then Samson's wife threw herself on him, sobbing, "You hate me! You don't really love me. You've given my people a riddle, but you haven't told me the answer."

"I haven't even explained it to my father or mother," he replied, "so why should I explain it to you?" [17]She cried the whole seven days of the feast. So on the seventh day he finally told her, because she continued to press him. She in turn explained the riddle to her people.

[18]Before sunset on the seventh day the men of the town said to him,

"What is sweeter than honey?
What is stronger than a lion?"

Samson said to them,

"If you had not plowed with my heifer,
you would not have solved my riddle."

[19]Then the Spirit of the LORD came upon him in power. He went down to Ashkelon,

r15 Some Septuagint manuscripts and Syriac; Hebrew *seventh*

אַשְׁקְלוֹן וַיַּךְ מֵהֶם ׀ שְׁלֹשִׁים אִישׁ וַיִּקַּח אֶת־
*** and-he-stripped man thirty from-them and-he-struck-down Ashkelon

חֲלִיצוֹתָם וַיִּתֵּן הַחֲלִיפוֹת לְמַגִּידֵי הַחִידָה
the-riddle to-ones-answering-of the-clothes and-he-gave belongings-of-them

וַיִּחַר אַפּוֹ וַיַּעַל בֵּית אָבִיהוּ׃
father-of-him house-of and-he-went-up anger-of-him and-he-burned

וַתְּהִי אֵשֶׁת שִׁמְשׁוֹן לְמֵרֵעֵהוּ אֲשֶׁר רֵעָה לוֹ׃
to-him he-attended who to-friend-of-him Samson wife-of and-she-became (20)

וַיְהִי מִיָּמִים בִּימֵי קְצִיר־ חִטִּים וַיִּפְקֹד
then-he-visited wheats harvest-of in-days-of after-days and-he-was (15:1)

שִׁמְשׁוֹן אֶת־ אִשְׁתּוֹ בִּגְדִי עִזִּים וַיֹּאמֶר אָבֹאָה אֶל־
into I-will-go and-he-said goats with-young-goat-of wife-of-him *** Samson

אִשְׁתִּי הֶחָדְרָה וְלֹא־ נְתָנוֹ אָבִיהָ לָבוֹא׃
to-go-in father-of-her he-let-him but-not into-the-room wife-of-me

וַיֹּאמֶר אָבִיהָ אָמֹר אָמַרְתִּי כִּי־ שָׂנֹא שְׂנֵאתָהּ
you-hated-her to-hate that I-say to-say father-of-her and-he-said (2)

וָאֶתְּנֶנָּה לְמֵרֵעֶךָ הֲלֹא אֲחֹתָהּ הַקְּטַנָּה טוֹבָה
attractive the-young sister-of-her not? to-friend-of-you so-I-gave-her

מִמֶּנָּה תְּהִי־ נָא לְךָ תַּחְתֶּיהָ׃ וַיֹּאמֶר לָהֶם
to-them and-he-said (3) instead-of-her for-you now! let-her-be more-than-her

שִׁמְשׁוֹן נִקֵּיתִי הַפַּעַם מִפְּלִשְׁתִּים כִּי־ עֹשֶׂה אֲנִי עִמָּם רָעָה׃
harm to-them I doing now from-Philistines the-time I-am-innocent Samson

וַיֵּלֶךְ שִׁמְשׁוֹן וַיִּלְכֹּד שְׁלֹשׁ־ מֵאוֹת שׁוּעָלִים וַיִּקַּח
and-he-got foxes hundreds three-of and-he-caught Samson so-he-went-out (4)

לַפִּדִים וַיֶּפֶן זָנָב אֶל־ זָנָב וַיָּשֶׂם לַפִּיד אֶחָד בֵּין־ שְׁנֵי
pair-of between one torch then-he-fastened tail to tail and-he-tied torches

הַזְּנָבוֹת בַּתָּוֶךְ׃ וַיַּבְעֶר־ אֵשׁ בַּלַּפִּידִים וַיְשַׁלַּח
and-he-let-loose on-the-torches fire and-he-lit (5) in-the-middle the-tails

בְּקָמוֹת פְּלִשְׁתִּים וַיַּבְעֵר מִגָּדִישׁ וְעַד־
even-to from-shock and-he-burned-up Philistines in-standing-grain-of

קָמָה וְעַד־ כֶּרֶם זָיִת׃ וַיֹּאמְרוּ פְלִשְׁתִּים מִי
who? Philistines when-they-asked (6) olive-grove vineyard even-to standing-grain

עָשָׂה זֹאת וַיֹּאמְרוּ שִׁמְשׁוֹן חֲתַן הַתִּמְנִי כִּי לָקַח
he-took because the-Timnite son-in-law-of Samson then-they-said this he-did

אֶת־ אִשְׁתּוֹ וַיִּתְּנָהּ לְמֵרֵעֵהוּ וַיַּעֲלוּ פְלִשְׁתִּים
Philistines so-they-went-up to-friend-of-him and-he-gave-her wife-of-him ***

וַיִּשְׂרְפוּ אוֹתָהּ וְאֶת־ אָבִיהָ בָּאֵשׁ׃ וַיֹּאמֶר לָהֶם
to-them and-he-said (7) with-the-fire father-of-her and her and-they-burned

struck down thirty of their men, stripped them of their belongings and gave their clothes to those who had explained the riddle. Burning with anger, he went up to his father's house. [20]And Samson's wife was given to the friend who had attended him at his wedding.

*Samson's Vengeance on the Philistines*

15 Later on, at the time of wheat harvest, Samson took a young goat and went to visit his wife. He said, "I'm going to my wife's room." But her father would not let him go in.

[2]"I was so sure you thoroughly hated her," he said, "that I gave her to your friend. Isn't her younger sister more attractive? Take her instead."

[3]Samson said to them, "This time I have a right to get even with the Philistines; I will really harm them." [4]So he went out and caught three hundred foxes and tied them tail to tail in pairs. He then fastened a torch to every pair of tails, [5]lit the torches and let the foxes loose in the standing grain of the Philistines. He burned up the shocks and standing grain, together with the vineyards and olive groves.

[6]When the Philistines asked, "Who did this?" they were told, "Samson, the Timnite's son-in-law, because his wife was given to his friend."

So the Philistines went up and burned her and her father to death. [7]Samson said to

שִׁמְשׁוֹן אִם־ תַּעֲשׂוּן כָּזֹאת כִּי אִם־ נִקַּמְתִּי בָכֶם

on-you I-will-get-revenge indeed then like-this you-acted since Samson

וְאַחַר אֶחְדָּל׃ וַיַּךְ אוֹתָם שׁוֹק עַל־ יָרֵךְ מַכָּה גְדוֹלָה

great slaughter thigh on leg them and-he-attacked (8) I-will-stop and-after

וַיֵּרֶד וַיֵּשֶׁב בִּסְעִיף סֶלַע עֵיטָם׃ וַיַּעֲלוּ

and-they-went-up (9) Etam rock-of in-cave-of and-he-stayed then-he-went-down

פְלִשְׁתִּים וַיַּחֲנוּ בִּיהוּדָה וַיִּנָּטְשׁוּ בַּלֶּחִי׃

near-the-Lehi and-they-spread-out in-Judah and-they-camped Philistines

וַיֹּאמְרוּ אִישׁ יְהוּדָה לָמָה עֲלִיתֶם עָלֵינוּ וַיֹּאמְרוּ

and-they-answered against-us you-came-up why? Judah man-of and-they-asked (10)

לֶאֱסוֹר אֶת־ שִׁמְשׁוֹן עָלִינוּ לַעֲשׂוֹת לוֹ כַּאֲשֶׁר עָשָׂה לָנוּ׃

to-us he-did just-as to-him to-do we-came Samson *** to-take-prisoner

וַיֵּרְדוּ שְׁלֹשֶׁת אֲלָפִים אִישׁ מִיהוּדָה אֶל־ סְעִיף סֶלַע

rock-of cave-of to from-Judah man thousands three-of then-they-went-down (11)

עֵיטָם וַיֹּאמְרוּ לְשִׁמְשׁוֹן הֲלֹא יָדַעְתָּ כִּי־ מֹשְׁלִים בָּנוּ

over-us ones-ruling that you-realize not? to-Samon and-they-said Etam

פְּלִשְׁתִּים וּמַה־ זֹּאת עָשִׂיתָ לָּנוּ וַיֹּאמֶר לָהֶם כַּאֲשֶׁר

just-as to-them and-he-answered to-us you-did this now-what? Philistines

עָשׂוּ לִי כֵּן עָשִׂיתִי לָהֶם׃ וַיֹּאמְרוּ לוֹ לֶאֱסָרְךָ

to-tie-up-you to-him and-they-said (12) to-them I-did same to-me they-did

יָרַדְנוּ לְתִתְּךָ בְּיַד־ פְּלִשְׁתִּים וַיֹּאמֶר לָהֶם שִׁמְשׁוֹן

Samson to-them and-he-said Philistines into-hand-of to-give-you we-came

הִשָּׁבְעוּ לִי פֶּן־ תִּפְגְּעוּן בִּי אַתֶּם׃ וַיֹּאמְרוּ

and-they-answered (13) yourselves to-me you-will-kill not to-me swear!

לוֹ לֵאמֹר לֹא כִּי־ אָסֹר נֶאֱסָרְךָ וּנְתַנּוּךָ

and-we-will-give-you we-will-tie-up-you to-tie-up only agreed to-say to-him

בְיָדָם וְהָמֵת לֹא נְמִיתֶךָ וַיַּאַסְרֻהוּ בִּשְׁנַיִם

with-two so-they-bound-him we-will-kill-you not but-to-kill into-hand-of-them

עֲבֹתִים חֲדָשִׁים וַיַּעֲלוּהוּ מִן־ הַסָּלַע׃ הוּא־ בָא עַד־

to he-approached he (14) the-rock from and-they-led-him new-ones ropes

לֶחִי וּפְלִשְׁתִּים הֵרִיעוּ לִקְרָאתוֹ וַתִּצְלַח עָלָיו

upon-him and-she-came to-come-to-him they-shouted and-Philistines Lehi

רוּחַ יְהוָה וַתִּהְיֶינָה הָעֲבֹתִים אֲשֶׁר עַל־ זְרוֹעוֹתָיו כַּפִּשְׁתִּים

like-the-flax arms-of-him on that the-ropes and-they-became Yahweh Spirit-of

אֲשֶׁר בָּעֲרוּ בָאֵשׁ וַיִּמַּסּוּ אֱסוּרָיו מֵעַל

from-on ones-binding-him and-they-dropped with-fire they-burned that

יָדָיו׃ וַיִּמְצָא לְחִי־ חֲמוֹר טְרִיָּה וַיִּשְׁלַח

and-he-reached fresh donkey jawbone-of and-he-found (15) hands-of-him

them, "Since you've acted like this, I won't stop until I get my revenge on you." [8]He attacked them viciously and slaughtered many of them. Then he went down and stayed in a cave in the rock of Etam.

[9]The Philistines went up and camped in Judah, spreading out near Lehi. [10]The men of Judah asked, "Why have you come to fight us?"

"We have come to take Samson prisoner," they answered, "to do to him as he did to us."

[11]Then three thousand men from Judah went down to the cave in the rock of Etam and said to Samson, "Don't you realize that the Philistines are rulers over us? What have you done to us?"

He answered, "I merely did to them what they did to me."

[12]They said to him, "We've come to tie you up and hand you over to the Philistines."

Samson said, "Swear to me that you won't kill me yourselves."

[13]"Agreed," they answered. "We will only tie you up and hand you over to them. We will not kill you." So they bound him with two new ropes and led him up from the rock. [14]As he approached Lehi, the Philistines came toward him shouting. The Spirit of the LORD came upon him in power. The ropes on his arms became like charred flax, and the bindings dropped from his hands. [15]Finding a fresh jawbone of a donkey, he grabbed

יָדוֹ וַיִּקָּחֶהָ וַיַּךְ־ בָּהּ אֶלֶף אִישׁ׃
man thousand with-her and-he-struck-down and-he-grabbed-her hand-of-him

(16) וַיֹּאמֶר שִׁמְשׁוֹן בִּלְחִי הַחֲמוֹר חֲמוֹר חֲמֹרָתָיִם
two-heaps heap the-donkey with-jawbone-of Samson then-he-said (16)

בִּלְחִי הַחֲמוֹר הִכֵּיתִי אֶלֶף אִישׁ׃ (17) וַיְהִי
and-he-was (17) man thousand I-killed the-donkey with-jawbone-of

כְּכַלֹּתוֹ לְדַבֵּר וַיַּשְׁלֵךְ הַלְּחִי מִיָּדוֹ
from-hand-of-him the-jawbone then-he-threw-away to-speak when-to-finish-him

וַיִּקְרָא לַמָּקוֹם הַהוּא רָמַת לֶחִי׃ (18) וַיִּצְמָא מְאֹד
very and-he-was-thirsty (18) Lehi Ramath the-that to-the-place and-he-called

וַיִּקְרָא אֶל־ יְהוָה וַיֹּאמַר אַתָּה נָתַתָּ בְיַד־ עַבְדְּךָ
servant-of-you into-hand-of you-gave you and-he-said Yahweh to and-he-cried

אֶת־ הַתְּשׁוּעָה הַגְּדֹלָה הַזֹּאת וְעַתָּה אָמוּת בַּצָּמָא
of-the-thirst must-I-die and-now the-this the-great the-victory ***

וְנָפַלְתִּי בְּיַד הָעֲרֵלִים׃ (19) וַיִּבְקַע אֱלֹהִים
God then-he-opened (19) the-uncircumcised-ones into-hand-of and-must-I-fall

אֶת־ הַמַּכְתֵּשׁ אֲשֶׁר־ בַּלֶּחִי וַיֵּצְאוּ מִמֶּנּוּ מַיִם
waters from-him and-they-came-out in-the-Lehi that the-hollow-place ***

וַיֵּשְׁתְּ וַתָּשָׁב רוּחוֹ וַיֶּחִי עַל־ כֵּן ׀
this for and-he-revived strength-of-him then-she-returned when-he-drank

קָרָא שְׁמָהּ עֵין הַקּוֹרֵא אֲשֶׁר בַּלֶּחִי עַד הַיּוֹם הַזֶּה׃
the-this the-day to in-the-Lehi that Hakkore En name-of-her he-called

(20) וַיִּשְׁפֹּט אֶת־ יִשְׂרָאֵל בִּימֵי פְלִשְׁתִּים עֶשְׂרִים שָׁנָה׃ (16:1) וַיֵּלֶךְ
and-he-went (16:1) year twenty Philistines in-days-of Israel *** and-he-led (20)

שִׁמְשׁוֹן עַזָּתָה וַיַּרְא־ שָׁם אִשָּׁה זוֹנָה וַיָּבֹא אֵלֶיהָ׃
into-her and-he-went being-prostitute woman there and-he-saw to-Gaza Samson

(2) לַעַזָּתִים ׀ לֵאמֹר בָּא שִׁמְשׁוֹן הֵנָּה וַיָּסֹבּוּ
so-they-surrounded to-here Samson he-came to-say to-the-Gazathites (2)

וַיֶּאֶרְבוּ־ לוֹ כָל־ הַלַּיְלָה בְּשַׁעַר הָעִיר
the-city at-gate-of the-night all-of for-him and-they-lay-in-wait

וַיִּתְחָרְשׁוּ כָל־ הַלַּיְלָה לֵאמֹר עַד־ אוֹר הַבֹּקֶר
the-morning dawn-of at to-say the-night all-of and-they-were-still

וַהֲרְגְנֻהוּ*׃ (3) וַיִּשְׁכַּב שִׁמְשׁוֹן עַד־ חֲצִי הַלַּיְלָה
the-night middle-of until Samson but-he-lay (3) then-we-will-kill-him

וַיָּקָם ׀ בַּחֲצִי הַלַּיְלָה וַיֶּאֱחֹז בְּדַלְתוֹת שַׁעַר־
gate-of of-doors-of and-he-took-hold the-night in-middle-of then-he-got-up

הָעִיר וּבִשְׁתֵּי הַמְּזוּזוֹת וַיִּסָּעֵם עִם־ הַבְּרִיחַ
the-bar with and-he-tore-loose-them the-posts and-of-two-of the-city

it and struck down a thousand men.

[16]Then Samson said,

"With a donkey's jawbone
I have made donkeys of them.[s]
With a donkey's jawbone
I have killed a thousand men."

[17]When he finished speaking, he threw away the jawbone; and the place was called Ramath Lehi.[t]

[18]Because he was very thirsty, he cried out to the LORD, "You have given your servant this great victory. Must I now die of thirst and fall into the hands of the uncircumcised?" [19]Then God opened up the hollow place in Lehi, and water came out of it. When Samson drank, his strength returned and he revived. So the spring was called En Hakkore,[u] and it is still there in Lehi.

[20]Samson led[v] Israel for twenty years in the days of the Philistines.

### *Samson and Delilah*

**16** One day Samson went to Gaza, where he saw a prostitute. He went in to spend the night with her. [2]The people of Gaza were told, "Samson is here!" So they surrounded the place and lay in wait for him all night at the city gate. They made no move during the night, saying, "At dawn we'll kill him."

[3]But Samson lay there only until the middle of the night. Then he got up and took hold of the doors of the city gate, together with the two posts, and tore them loose, bar and

[s]16 Or *made a heap or two;* the Hebrew for *donkey* sounds like the Hebrew for *heap.*
[t]17 *Ramath Lehi* means *jawbone hill.*
[u]19 *En Hakkore* means *caller's spring.*
[v]20 Traditionally *judged*

*2 Most mss have *pathah* under the *resh* (וַהֲרַגְ׳).

וַיָּשֶׂם עַל־ כְּתֵפָיו וַיַּעֲלֵם אֶל־רֹאשׁ הָהָר אֲשֶׁר
that the-hill top-of to and-he-carried-them shoulders-of-him to and-he-lifted

עַל־ פְּנֵי חֶבְרוֹן׃ וַיְהִי אַחֲרֵי־ כֵן וַיֶּאֱהַב אִשָּׁה
woman then-he-fell-in-love this after and-he-was (4) Hebron faces-of to

בְּנַחַל שֹׂרֵק וּשְׁמָהּ דְּלִילָה׃ וַיַּעֲלוּ אֵלֶיהָ סַרְנֵי
rulers-of to-her and-they-went (5) Delilah and-name-of-her Sorek in-Valley-of

פְלִשְׁתִּים וַיֹּאמְרוּ לָהּ פַּתִּי אוֹתוֹ וּרְאִי בַּמֶּה כֹּחוֹ
strength-of-him in-the-what and-see! him lure! to-her and-they-said Philistines

גָדוֹל וּבַמֶּה נוּכַל לוֹ וַאֲסַרְנֻהוּ
so-we-may-tie-up-him over-him we-can-overpower and-with-the-what great

לְעַנֹּתוֹ וַאֲנַחְנוּ נִתַּן־ לָךְ אִישׁ אֶלֶף וּמֵאָה כָּסֶף׃
silver and-hundred thousand each to-you we-will-give and-we to-subdue-him

וַתֹּאמֶר דְּלִילָה אֶל־שִׁמְשׁוֹן הַגִּידָה־נָּא לִי בַּמֶּה כֹּחֲךָ
strength-of-you in-the-what to-me now! tell! Samson to Delilah so-she-said (6)

גָדוֹל וּבַמֶּה תֵאָסֵר לְעַנּוֹתֶךָ׃ וַיֹּאמֶר
and-he-answered (7) to-subdue-you you-can-be-tied-up and-with-the-what great

אֵלֶיהָ שִׁמְשׁוֹן אִם־ יַאַסְרֻנִי בְּשִׁבְעָה יְתָרִים לַחִים אֲשֶׁר לֹא־
not that fresh-ones thongs with-seven they-tie-me if Samson to-her

חֹרָבוּ וְחָלִיתִי וְהָיִיתִי כְּאַחַד הָאָדָם׃
the-man as-any-of and-I-will-be then-I-will-become-weak they-were-dried

וַיַּעֲלוּ־ לָהּ סַרְנֵי פְלִשְׁתִּים שִׁבְעָה יְתָרִים לַחִים
fresh-ones thongs seven Philistines rulers-of to-her then-they-brought (8)

אֲשֶׁר לֹא־ חֹרָבוּ וַתַּאַסְרֵהוּ בָּהֶם׃ וְהָאֹרֵב
and-the-one-hiding (9) with-them and-she-tied-him they-were-dried not that

יֹשֵׁב לָהּ בַּחֶדֶר וַתֹּאמֶר אֵלָיו פְּלִשְׁתִּים עָלֶיךָ
upon-you Philistines to-him then-she-called in-the-room with-her staying

שִׁמְשׁוֹן וַיְנַתֵּק אֶת־ הַיְתָרִים כַּאֲשֶׁר יִנָּתֵק פְּתִיל־ הַנְּעֹרֶת
the-string piece-of he-snaps just-as the-thongs *** but-he-snapped Samson

בַּהֲרִיחוֹ אֵשׁ וְלֹא נוֹדַע כֹּחוֹ׃
strength-of-him he-was-discovered so-not flame when-to-come-close-him

וַתֹּאמֶר דְּלִילָה אֶל־שִׁמְשׁוֹן הִנֵּה הֵתַלְתָּ בִּי וַתְּדַבֵּר
and-you-told of-me you-made-fool see! Samson to Delilah then-she-said (10)

אֵלַי כְּזָבִים עַתָּה הַגִּידָה־נָּא לִי בַּמֶּה תֵּאָסֵר׃ וַיֹּאמֶר
and-he-said (11) you-can-be-tied with-the-what to-me now! tell! now lies to-me

אֵלֶיהָ אִם־ אָסוֹר יַאַסְרוּנִי בַּעֲבֹתִים חֲדָשִׁים אֲשֶׁר לֹא־ נַעֲשָׂה
he-was-done not that new-ones with-ropes they-tie-me to-tie if to-her

בָהֶם מְלָאכָה וְחָלִיתִי וְהָיִיתִי כְּאַחַד הָאָדָם׃
the-man as-any-of and-I-will-be then-I-will-become-weak work with-them

all. He lifted them to his shoulders and carried them to the top of the hill that faces Hebron.

4 Some time later, he fell in love with a woman in the Valley of Sorek whose name was Delilah. 5 The rulers of the Philistines went to her and said, "See if you can lure him into showing you the secret of his great strength and how we can overpower him so we may tie him up and subdue him. Each one of us will give you eleven hundred shekels[w] of silver."

6 So Delilah said to Samson, "Tell me the secret of your great strength and how you can be tied up and subdued."

7 Samson answered her, "If anyone ties me with seven fresh thongs[x] that have not been dried, I'll become as weak as any other man."

8 Then the rulers of the Philistines brought her seven fresh thongs that had not been dried, and she tied him with them. 9 With men hidden in the room, she called to him, "Samson, the Philistines are upon you!" But he snapped the thongs as easily as a piece of string snaps when it comes close to a flame. So the secret of his strength was not discovered.

10 Then Delilah said to Samson, "You have made a fool of me; you lied to me. Come now, tell me how you can be tied."

11 He said, "If anyone ties me securely with new ropes that have never been used, I'll become as weak as any other man."

[w]5 That is, about 28 pounds (about 13 kilograms)
[x]7 Or *bowstrings;* also in verses 8 and 9

וַתִּקַּח דְּלִילָה עֲבֹתִים חֲדָשִׁים וַתַּאַסְרֵהוּ בָהֶם
with-them and-she-tied-him new-ones ropes Delilah so-she-took (12)

וַתֹּאמֶר אֵלָיו פְּלִשְׁתִּים עָלֶיךָ שִׁמְשׁוֹן וְהָאֹרֵב יֹשֵׁב
staying and-the-one-hiding Samson upon-you Philistines to-him and-she-called

בֶּחָדֶר וַיְנַתְּקֵם מֵעַל זְרֹעֹתָיו כְּחוּט׃
as-the-thread arms-of-him from-on but-he-snapped-them in-the-room

וַתֹּאמֶר דְּלִילָה אֶל־ שִׁמְשׁוֹן עַד־ הֵנָּה הֵתַלְתָּ בִּי
of-me you-made-fool to-now until Samson to Delilah then-she-said (13)

וַתְּדַבֵּר אֵלַי כְּזָבִים הַגִּידָה לִּי בַּמֶּה תֵּאָסֵר וַיֹּאמֶר
and-he-said you-can-be-tied with-the-what to-me tell! lies to-me and-you-told

אֵלֶיהָ אִם־ תַּאַרְגִי אֶת־ שֶׁבַע מַחְלְפוֹת רֹאשִׁי עִם־ הַמַּסָּכֶת׃
the-fabric into head-of-me braids-of seven *** you-weave if to-her

*[וְתָקַעַתְּ בַּיָּתֵד וְחָלִיתִי וְהָיִיתִי כְּאַחַד הָאָדָם
the-man as-any-of and-I-will-be then-I-will-become-weak with-pin and-you-tighten]*

וַתְּיַשְּׁנֵהוּ וַתַּאֲרֹג אֶת־ שֶׁבַע מַחְלְפוֹת רֹאשׁוֹ עִם־ הַמַּסֶּכֶת]*
*[the-fabric into head-of-him braids-of seven *** and-she-wove so-she-put-to-sleep-him

וַתִּתְקַע בַּיָּתֵד וַתֹּאמֶר אֵלָיו פְּלִשְׁתִּים עָלֶיךָ
upon-you Philistines to-him and-she-called with-the-pin and-she-tightened (14)

שִׁמְשׁוֹן וַיִּיקַץ מִשְּׁנָתוֹ וַיִּסַּע אֶת־ הַיְתַד הָאֶרֶג
the-loom the-pin *** and-he-pulled-up from-sleep-of-him and-he-awoke Samson

וְאֶת־ הַמַּסָּכֶת׃ וַתֹּאמֶר אֵלָיו אֵיךְ תֹּאמַר אֲהַבְתִּיךְ
I-love-you can-you-say how? to-him then-she-said (15) the-fabric with

וְלִבְּךָ אֵין אִתִּי זֶה שָׁלֹשׁ פְּעָמִים הֵתַלְתָּ בִּי וְלֹא־
and-not of-me you-made-fool times three this with-me not when-heart-of-you

הִגַּדְתָּ לִּי בַּמֶּה כֹּחֲךָ גָדוֹל׃ וַיְהִי כִּי־
that and-he-was (16) great strength-of-you in-the-what to-me you-told

הֵצִיקָה לּוֹ בִדְבָרֶיהָ כָּל־ הַיָּמִים וַתְּאַלֲצֵהוּ
and-she-prodded-him the-days all-of with-words-of-her to-him she-nagged

וַתִּקְצַר נַפְשׁוֹ לָמוּת׃ וַיַּגֶּד־ לָהּ אֶת־ כָּל־
all-of *** to-her so-he-told (17) to-die life-of-him so-she-was-tired

לִבּוֹ וַיֹּאמֶר לָהּ מוֹרָה לֹא־ עָלָה עַל־ רֹאשִׁי כִּי־
for head-of-me on he-went not razor to-her and-he-said heart-of-him

נְזִיר אֱלֹהִים אֲנִי מִבֶּטֶן אִמִּי אִם־ גֻּלַּחְתִּי וְסָר
then-he-would-leave I-was-shaved if mother-of-me from-womb-of I God Nazirite-of

מִמֶּנִּי כֹחִי וְחָלִיתִי וְהָיִיתִי כְּכָל־
as-any-of and-I-would-be and-I-would-become-weak strength-of-me from-me

הָאָדָם׃ וַתֵּרֶא דְלִילָה כִּי־ הִגִּיד לָהּ אֶת־ כָּל־ לִבּוֹ
heart-of-him all-of *** to-her he-told that Delilah when-she-saw (18) the-man

12So Delilah took new ropes and tied him with them. Then, with men hidden in the room, she called to him, "Samson, the Philistines are upon you!" But he snapped the ropes off his arms as if they were threads.

13Delilah then said to Samson, "Until now, you have been making a fool of me and lying to me. Tell me how you can be tied."

He replied, "If you weave the seven braids of my head into the fabric ⌊on the loom⌋ and tighten it with the pin, I'll become as weak as any other man." So while he was sleeping, Delilah took the seven braids of his head, wove them into the fabric 14and[y] tightened it with the pin.

Again she called to him, "Samson, the Philistines are upon you!" He awoke from his sleep and pulled up the pin and the loom, with the fabric.

15Then she said to him, "How can you say, 'I love you,' when you won't confide in me? This is the third time you have made a fool of me and haven't told me the secret of your great strength." 16With such nagging she prodded him day after day until he was tired to death.

17So he told her everything. "No razor has ever been used on my head," he said, "because I have been a Nazirite set apart to God since birth. If my head were shaved, my strength would leave me, and I would become as weak as any other man."

18When Delilah saw that he had told her everything, she

[y]*13,14* Some Septuagint manuscripts; Hebrew *"⌊I can⌋ if you weave the seven braids of my head into the fabric ⌊on the loom⌋."* [14]*So she*

**13* The Hebrew text in brackets is conjectured on the basis of the Septuagint mss the NIV translates. See the introduction, page xiii.

ותשלח ותקרא לסרני פלשתים לאמר עלו
come-back! to-say Philistines to-rulers-of and-she-called then-she-sent

הפעם כי הגיד לה את כל לבו ועלו אליה
to-her so-they-returned heart-of-him all-of *** to-me he-told for the-once

סרני פלשתים ויעלו הכסף בידם:
in-hand-of-them the-silver and-they-brought Philistines rulers-of

(19) ותישנהו על ברכיה ותקרא לאיש
to-the-man and-she-called knees-of-her on and-she-put-to-sleep-him (19)

ותגלח את שבע מחלפות ראשו ותחל לענותו
to-subdue-him and-she-began head-of-him braids-of seven *** and-she-shaved

ויסר כחו מעליו: (20) ותאמר פלשתים
Philistines then-she-called (20) from-on-him strength-of-him and-he-left

עליך שמשון ויקץ משנתו ויאמר אצא
I-will-go-out and-he-thought from-sleep-of-him and-he-awoke Samson upon-you

כפעם בפעם ואנער והוא לא ידע כי יהוה
Yahweh that he-knew not but-he and-I-will-shake-myself-free in-time as-time

סר מעליו: (21) ויאחזוהו פלשתים וינקרו
and-they-gouged-out Philistines then-they-seized-him (21) from-on-him he-left

את עיניו ויורידו אותו עזתה ויאסרוהו
and-they-bound-him to-Gaza him and-they-took-down eyes-of-him ***

בנחשתים ויהי טוחן בבית האסירים:
the-prisons in-house-of one-grinding and-he-was with-the-bronze-shackles

(22) ויחל שער ראשו לצמח כאשר גלח:
he-was-shaved just-as to-grow head-of-him hair-of but-he-began (22)

(23) וסרני פלשתים נאספו לזבח זבח גדול
great sacrifice to-offer they-assembled Philistines now-rulers-of (23)

לדגון אלהיהם ולשמחה ויאמרו נתן אלהינו
god-of-us he-delivered and-they-said and-for-celebration god-of-them to-Dagon

בידנו את שמשון אויבינו: (24) ויראו אתו
him when-they-saw (24) being-enemies-of-us Samson *** into-hand-of-us

העם ויהללו את אלהיהם כי אמרו נתן
he-delivered they-said for god-of-them *** then-they-praised the-people

אלהינו בידנו את אויבנו ואת מחריב
one-laying-waste and being-enemy-of-us *** into-hand-of-us god-of-us

ארצנו ואשר הרבה את חללינו: (25) ויהי כי*
when and-he-was (25) ones-slain-of-us *** he-multiplied and-who land-of-us

טוב לבם ויאמרו קראו לשמשון
to-Samson call-out! and-they-shouted spirit-of-them to-be-high

sent word to the rulers of the Philistines, "Come back once more; he has told me everything." So the rulers of the Philistines returned with the silver in their hands. 19Having put him to sleep on her lap, she called a man to shave off the seven braids of his hair, and so began to subdue him.[z] And his strength left him.

20Then she called, "Samson, the Philistines are upon you!"

He awoke from his sleep and thought, "I'll go out as before and shake myself free." But he did not know that the LORD had left him.

21Then the Philistines seized him, gouged out his eyes and took him down to Gaza. Binding him with bronze shackles, they set him to grinding in the prison. 22But the hair on his head began to grow again after it had been shaved.

### *The Death of Samson*

23Now the rulers of the Philistines assembled to offer a great sacrifice to Dagon their god and to celebrate, saying, "Our god has delivered Samson, our enemy, into our hands."

24When the people saw him, they praised their god, saying,

"Our god has delivered our enemy
into our hands,
the one who laid waste our land
and multiplied our slain."

25While they were in high spirits, they shouted, "Bring out Samson to entertain us."

z19 Hebrew; some Septuagint manuscripts *and he began to weaken*

*25 Most mss have *hirek* under the *kaph* and *maqqeph* after the *yodh* (כי־טוב). L here supplies the pointing for the *Qere*.

°18 ק לי
°21 ק האסורים
°25 ק כטוב

וִישַׂחֶק־ לָנוּ וַיִּקְרְאוּ לְשִׁמְשׁוֹן מִבֵּית
from-house-of to-Samson so-they-called-out for-us so-he-may-entertain

הָאֲסִירִים° וַיְצַחֵק לִפְנֵיהֶם וַיַּעֲמִידוּ אוֹתוֹ בֵּין הָעַמּוּדִים׃
the-pillars among him and-they-stood before-them and-he-performed the-prisons

וַיֹּאמֶר שִׁמְשׁוֹן אֶל־ הַנַּעַר הַמַּחֲזִיק בְּיָדוֹ הַנִּיחָה
put! on-hand-of-him the-one-holding the-servant to Samson and-he-said (26)

אוֹתִי וְהֵימִשֵׁנִי° אֶת־ הָעַמֻּדִים אֲשֶׁר הַבַּיִת נָכוֹן עֲלֵיהֶם
by-them he-is-supported the-temple that the-pillars *** and-make-feel-me! me

וְאֶשָּׁעֵן עֲלֵיהֶם׃ וְהַבַּיִת מָלֵא הָאֲנָשִׁים
the-men he-was-crowded now-the-temple (27) against-them so-I-may-lean

וְהַנָּשִׁים וְשָׁמָּה כֹּל סַרְנֵי פְלִשְׁתִּים וְעַל־ הַגָּג
the-roof and-on Philistines rulers-of all-of and-at-there and-the-women

כִּשְׁלֹשֶׁת אֲלָפִים אִישׁ וְאִשָּׁה הָרֹאִים בִּשְׂחוֹק
at-performance-of the-ones-watching and-woman man thousands about-three-of

שִׁמְשׁוֹן׃ וַיִּקְרָא שִׁמְשׁוֹן אֶל־ יְהוָה וַיֹּאמַר אֲדֹנָי יֱהוִה
Yahweh Lord and-he-said Yahweh to Samson then-he-prayed (28) Samson

זָכְרֵנִי נָא וְחַזְּקֵנִי נָא אַךְ הַפַּעַם הַזֶּה הָאֱלֹהִים
the-God the-this the-once just now! and-strengthen-me! now! remember-me!

וְאִנָּקְמָה נְקַם־ אַחַת מִשְּׁתֵי עֵינַי מִפְּלִשְׁתִּים׃
on-Philistines eyes-of-me for-two-of one vengeance-of and-let-me-get-revenge

וַיִּלְפֹּת שִׁמְשׁוֹן אֶת־ שְׁנֵי ׀ עַמּוּדֵי הַתָּוֶךְ אֲשֶׁר הַבַּיִת
the-temple which the-center pillars-of two-of *** Samson then-he-reached (29)

נָכוֹן עֲלֵיהֶם וַיִּסָּמֵךְ עֲלֵיהֶם אֶחָד בִּימִינוֹ
on-right-of-him one against-them and-he-braced-himself on-them he-stood

וְאֶחָד בִּשְׂמֹאלוֹ׃ וַיֹּאמֶר שִׁמְשׁוֹן תָּמוֹת נַפְשִׁי עִם־
with life-of-me let-her-die Samson and-he-said (30) on-left-of-him and-one

פְּלִשְׁתִּים וַיֵּט בְּכֹחַ וַיִּפֹּל הַבַּיִת עַל־
on the-temple and-he-came-down with-might then-he-pushed Philistines

הַסְּרָנִים וְעַל־ כָּל־ הָעָם אֲשֶׁר־ בּוֹ וַיִּהְיוּ הַמֵּתִים
the-dead-ones and-they-were in-him who the-people all-of and-on the-rulers

אֲשֶׁר הֵמִית בְּמוֹתוֹ רַבִּים מֵאֲשֶׁר הֵמִית בְּחַיָּיו׃
in-lives-of-him he-killed more-than many in-death-of-him he-killed whom

וַיֵּרְדוּ אֶחָיו וְכָל־ בֵּית אָבִיהוּ
father-of-him family-of and-whole-of brothers-of-him then-they-went-down (31)

וַיִּשְׂאוּ אֹתוֹ וַיַּעֲלוּ ׀ וַיִּקְבְּרוּ אוֹתוֹ בֵּין צָרְעָה
Zorah between him and-they-buried and-they-brought-back him and-they-got

וּבֵין אֶשְׁתָּאֹל בְּקֶבֶר מָנוֹחַ אָבִיו וְהוּא שָׁפַט אֶת־יִשְׂרָאֵל
Israel *** he-led now-he father-of-him Manoah in-tomb-of Eshtaol and-between

°25 ק האסורים
°26 ק והמשני

So they called Samson out of the prison, and he performed for them.

When they stood him among the pillars, [26]Samson said to the servant who held his hand, "Put me where I can feel the pillars that support the temple, so that I may lean against them." [27]Now the temple was crowded with men and women; all the rulers of the Philistines were there, and on the roof were about three thousand men and women watching Samson perform. [28]Then Samson prayed to the LORD, "O Sovereign LORD, remember me. O God, please strengthen me just once more, and let me with one blow get revenge on the Philistines for my two eyes." [29]Then Samson reached toward the two central pillars on which the temple stood. Bracing himself against them, his right hand on the one and his left hand on the other, [30]Samson said, "Let me die with the Philistines!" Then he pushed with all his might, and down came the temple on the rulers and all the people in it. Thus he killed many more when he died than while he lived.

[31]Then his brothers and his father's whole family went down to get him. They brought him back and buried him between Zorah and Eshtaol in the tomb of Manoah his father. He led[a] Israel

[a]31 Traditionally *judged*

עֶשְׂרִים שָׁנָה׃ וַיְהִי־ אִישׁ מֵהַר־ אֶפְרָיִם וּשְׁמוֹ
and-name-of-him Ephraim from-hill-country-of man now-he-was (17:1) year twenty

מִיכָיְהוּ׃ וַיֹּאמֶר לְאִמּוֹ אֶלֶף וּמֵאָה הַכֶּסֶף
the-silver and-hundred thousand to-mother-of-him and-he-said (2) Micah

אֲשֶׁר לֻקַּח־ לָךְ וְאַתְּי אָלִית וְגַם אָמַרְתְּ
you-spoke and-also you-uttered-curse and-you from-you he-was-taken that

בְּאָזְנַי הִנֵּה־ הַכֶּסֶף אִתִּי אֲנִי לְקַחְתִּיו וַתֹּאמֶר אִמּוֹ
mother-of-him then-she-said I-took-him I with-me the-silver see! in-ears-of-me

בָּרוּךְ בְּנִי לַיהוָה׃ וַיָּשֶׁב אֶת־ אֶלֶף־
thousand *** when-he-returned (3) by-Yahweh son-of-me being-blessed

וּמֵאָה הַכֶּסֶף לְאִמּוֹ וַתֹּאמֶר אִמּוֹ
mother-of-him then-she-said to-mother-of-him the-silver and-hundred

הַקְדֵּשׁ הִקְדַּשְׁתִּי אֶת־ הַכֶּסֶף לַיהוָה מִיָּדִי
from-hand-of-me to-Yahweh the-silver *** I-consecrate to-consecrate

לִבְנִי לַעֲשׂוֹת פֶּסֶל וּמַסֵּכָה וְעַתָּה אֲשִׁיבֶנּוּ
I-will-give-back-him and-now and-cast-idol carved-image to-make for-son-of-me

לָךְ׃ וַיָּשֶׁב אֶת־ הַכֶּסֶף לְאִמּוֹ וַתִּקַּח
and-she-took to-mother-of-him the-silver *** so-he-returned (4) to-you

אִמּוֹ מָאתַיִם כֶּסֶף וַתִּתְּנֵהוּ לַצּוֹרֵף
to-the-one-being-silversmith and-she-gave-him silver two-hundreds mother-of-him

וַיַּעֲשֵׂהוּ פֶּסֶל וּמַסֵּכָה וַיְהִי בְּבֵית מִיכָיְהוּ׃ וְהָאִישׁ
now-the-man (5) Micah in-house-of and-he-was and-idol image and-he-made-him

מִיכָה לוֹ בֵּית אֱלֹהִים וַיַּעַשׂ אֵפוֹד וּתְרָפִים וַיְמַלֵּא אֶת־
*** and-he-installed and-idols ephod and-he-made gods shrine-of to-him Micah

יַד אַחַד מִבָּנָיו וַיְהִי־ לוֹ לְכֹהֵן׃ בַּיָּמִים
in-the-days (6) as-priest for-him and-he-was from-sons-of-him one hand-of

הָהֵם אֵין מֶלֶךְ בְּיִשְׂרָאֵל אִישׁ הַיָּשָׁר בְּעֵינָיו יַעֲשֶׂה׃
he-did in-eyes-of-him the-thing-fit everyone in-Israel king not the-those

וַיְהִי־ נַעַר מִבֵּית לֶחֶם יְהוּדָה מִמִּשְׁפַּחַת יְהוּדָה וְהוּא
and-he Judah from-clan-of Judah Lehem-of from-Beth young-man and-he-was (7)

לֵוִי וְהוּא גָר־ שָׁם׃ וַיֵּלֶךְ הָאִישׁ מֵהָעִיר מִבֵּית
from-Beth from-the-town the-man and-he-left (8) there he-lived but-he Levite

לֶחֶם יְהוּדָה לָגוּר בַּאֲשֶׁר יִמְצָא וַיָּבֹא הַר־
hill-country-of and-he-came he-would-find in-where to-stay Judah Lehem-of

אֶפְרַיִם עַד־ בֵּית מִיכָה לַעֲשׂוֹת דַּרְכּוֹ׃ וַיֹּאמֶר־ לוֹ
to-him and-he-asked (9) way-of-him to-carry-on Micah house-of to Ephraim

מִיכָה מֵאַיִן תָּבוֹא וַיֹּאמֶר אֵלָיו לֵוִי אָנֹכִי מִבֵּית לֶחֶם
Lehem-of from-Beth I Levite to-him and-he-said you-come from-where? Micah

°2 ק ואת

twenty years.

*Micah's Idols*

17 Now a man named Micah from the hill country of Ephraim [2]said to his mother, "The eleven hundred shekels[b] of silver that were taken from you and about which I heard you utter a curse—I have that silver with me; I took it."

Then his mother said, "The LORD bless you, my son!"

[3]When he returned the eleven hundred shekels of silver to his mother, she said, "I solemnly consecrate my silver to the LORD for my son to make a carved image and a cast idol. I will give it back to you."

[4]So he returned the silver to his mother, and she took two hundred shekels[c] of silver and gave them to a silversmith, who made them into the image and the idol. And they were put in Micah's house.

[5]Now this man Micah had a shrine, and he made an ephod and some idols and installed one of his sons as his priest. [6]In those days Israel had no king; everyone did as he saw fit.

[7]A young Levite from Bethlehem in Judah, who had been living within the clan of Judah, [8]left that town in search of some other place to stay. On his way[d] he came to Micah's house in the hill country of Ephraim.

[9]Micah asked him, "Where are you from?"

"I'm a Levite from Bethlehem in Judah," he said,

[b]2 That is, about 28 pounds (about 13 kilograms)
[c]4 That is, about 5 pounds (about 2.3 kilograms)
[d]8 Or *To carry on his profession*

יְהוּדָה וְאָנֹכִי הֹלֵךְ לָגוּר בַּאֲשֶׁר אֶמְצָא׃ וַיֹּאמֶר לוֹ מִיכָה
Micah to-him then-he-said (10) I-find at-where to-stay going and-I Judah

שְׁבָה עִמָּדִי וֶהְיֵה־ לִי לְאָב וּלְכֹהֵן וְאָנֹכִי אֶתֶּן־
I-will-give and-I and-as-priest as-father for-me and-be! with-me live!

לְךָ עֲשֶׂרֶת כֶּסֶף לַיָּמִים וְעֵרֶךְ בְּגָדִים וּמִחְיָתֶךָ
and-food-of-you clothes and-set-of for-the-days silver ten-of to-you

וַיֵּלֶךְ הַלֵּוִי׃ וַיּוֹאֶל הַלֵּוִי לָשֶׁבֶת אֶת־ הָאִישׁ
the-man with to-live the-Levite so-he-agreed (11) the-Levite and-he-came

וַיְהִי הַנַּעַר לוֹ כְּאַחַד מִבָּנָיו׃ וַיְמַלֵּא
then-he-installed (12) of-sons-of-him like-one to-him the-young-man and-he-was

מִיכָה אֶת־ יַד הַלֵּוִי וַיְהִי־ לוֹ הַנַּעַר לְכֹהֵן
as-priest the-young-man for-him and-he-became the-Levite hand-of *** Micah

וַיְהִי בְּבֵית מִיכָה׃ וַיֹּאמֶר מִיכָה עַתָּה יָדַעְתִּי כִּי־
that I-know now Micah and-he-said (13) Micah in-house-of and-he-lived

יֵיטִיב יְהוָה לִי כִּי הָיָה־ לִי הַלֵּוִי לְכֹהֵן׃
as-priest the-Levite for-me he-became since to-me Yahweh he-will-be-good

בַּיָּמִים הָהֵם אֵין מֶלֶךְ בְּיִשְׂרָאֵל וּבַיָּמִים הָהֵם
the-those and-in-the-days in-Israel king not the-those in-the-days (18:1)

שֵׁבֶט הַדָּנִי מְבַקֶּשׁ־ לוֹ נַחֲלָה לָשֶׁבֶת כִּי לֹא־ נָפְלָה
she-came not because to-settle place for-him seeking the-Danite tribe-of

לּוֹ עַד־ הַיּוֹם הַהוּא בְּתוֹךְ־ שִׁבְטֵי יִשְׂרָאֵל בְּנַחֲלָה׃
for-inheritance Israel tribes-of in-among the-that the-day to for-him

וַיִּשְׁלְחוּ בְנֵי־ דָן ׀ מִמִּשְׁפַּחְתָּם חֲמִשָּׁה אֲנָשִׁים מִקְצוֹתָם
from-all-of-them men five from-clan-of-them Dan sons-of so-they-sent (2)

אֲנָשִׁים בְּנֵי־ חַיִל מִצָּרְעָה וּמֵאֶשְׁתָּאֹל לְרַגֵּל אֶת־ הָאָרֶץ
the-land *** to-spy-out and-from-Eshtaol from-Zorah war men-of men

וּלְחָקְרָהּ וַיֹּאמְרוּ אֲלֵהֶם לְכוּ חִקְרוּ אֶת־ הָאָרֶץ
the-land *** explore! go! to-them and-they-told and-to-explore-her

וַיָּבֹאוּ הַר־ אֶפְרַיִם עַד־ בֵּית מִיכָה וַיָּלִינוּ
and-they-spent-night Micah house-of to Ephraim hill-country-of and-they-entered

שָׁם׃ הֵמָּה עִם־ בֵּית מִיכָה וְהֵמָּה הִכִּירוּ אֶת־ קוֹל
voice-of *** they-recognized and-they Micah house-of near they (3) there

הַנַּעַר הַלֵּוִי וַיָּסוּרוּ שָׁם וַיֹּאמְרוּ לוֹ מִי־
who? to-him and-they-asked there so-they-turned-in the-Levite the-young-man

הֱבִיאֲךָ הֲלֹם וּמָה־ אַתָּה עֹשֶׂה בָּזֶה וּמַה־ לְּךָ פֹה׃
here to-you and-why? in-this doing you and-what? here he-brought-you

וַיֹּאמֶר אֲלֵהֶם כָּזֹה וְכָזֶה עָשָׂה לִי מִיכָה
Micah for-me he-did and-as-that as-this to-them and-he-told (4)

"and I'm looking for a place to
stay."
10Then Micah said to him,
"Live with me and be my father and priest, and I'll give
you ten shekels[c] of silver a
year, your clothes and your
food." 11So the Levite agreed to
live with him, and the young
man was to him like one of his
sons. 12Then Micah installed
the Levite, and the young man
became his priest and lived in
his house. 13And Micah said,
"Now I know that the LORD
will be good to me, since this
Levite has become my priest."

*Danites Settle in Laish*

18 In those days Israel
had no king.
And in those days the tribe
of the Danites was seeking a
place of their own where they
might settle, because they had
not yet come into an inheritance among the tribes of Israel. 2So the Danites sent five
warriors from Zorah and Eshtaol to spy out the land and
explore it. These men represented all their clans. They
told them, "Go, explore the
land."
The men entered the hill
country of Ephraim and came
to the house of Micah, where
they spent the night. 3When
they were near Micah's house,
they recognized the voice of
the young Levite; so they
turned in there and asked
him, "Who brought you here?
What are you doing in this
place? Why are you here?"
4He told them what Micah
had done for him, and said,

[c]*10* That is, about 4 ounces (about 110 grams)

וַיִּשְׂכְּרֵנִי וָאֱהִי־ לוֹ לְכֹהֵן׃ וַיֹּאמְרוּ לוֹ שְׁאַל־
inquire! to-him then-they-said (5) as-priest for-him and-I-am and-he-hired-me

נָא בֵאלֹהִים וְנֵדְעָה הֲתַצְלִיחַ דַּרְכֵּנוּ אֲשֶׁר אֲנַחְנוּ
we that journey-of-us whether-she-will-succeed so-we-may-learn of-God now!

הֹלְכִים עָלֶיהָ׃ וַיֹּאמֶר לָהֶם הַכֹּהֵן לְכוּ לְשָׁלוֹם נֹכַח
approved-of in-peace go! the-priest to-them and-he-answered (6) on-her ones-going

יְהוָה דַּרְכְּכֶם אֲשֶׁר תֵּלְכוּ־ בָהּ׃ וַיֵּלְכוּ חֲמֵשֶׁת הָאֲנָשִׁים
the-men five-of so-they-left (7) on-her you-go that journey-of-you Yahweh

וַיָּבֹאוּ לָיְשָׁה וַיִּרְאוּ אֶת־ הָעָם אֲשֶׁר־ בְּקִרְבָּהּ
in-midst-of-her who the-people *** and-they-saw to-Laish and-they-came

יוֹשֶׁבֶת־ לָבֶטַח כְּמִשְׁפַּט צִדֹנִים שֹׁקֵט ׀ וּבֹטֵחַ
and-being-secure unsuspecting Sidonians like-custom-of in-safety living

וְאֵין־ מַכְלִים דָּבָר בָּאָרֶץ יוֹרֵשׁ עֶצֶר וּרְחֹקִים
and-ones-distant prosperity possessing in-the-land thing lacking since-not

הֵמָּה מִצִּדֹנִים וְדָבָר אֵין־ לָהֶם עִם־ אָדָם׃ וַיָּבֹאוּ
and-they-returned (8) anyone with to-them not and-relationship from-Sidonians they

אֶל־ אֲחֵיהֶם צָרְעָה וְאֶשְׁתָּאֹל וַיֹּאמְרוּ לָהֶם אֲחֵיהֶם
brothers-of-them to-them and-they-asked and-Eshtaol Zorah brothers-of-them to

מָה אַתֶּם׃ וַיֹּאמְרוּ קוּמָה וְנַעֲלֶה עֲלֵיהֶם כִּי רָאִינוּ
we-saw for against-them and-let-us-attack come! and-they-answered (9) you how?

אֶת־ הָאָרֶץ וְהִנֵּה טוֹבָה מְאֹד וְאַתֶּם מַחְשִׁים אַל־ תֵּעָצְלוּ
you-hesitate not ones-doing-nothing but-you very good and-see! the-land ***

לָלֶכֶת לָבֹא לָרֶשֶׁת אֶת־ הָאָרֶץ׃ כְּבֹאֲכֶם תָּבֹאוּ
you-will-come when-to-arrive-you (10) the-land *** to-take-over to-enter to-go

אֶל־ עַם בֹּטֵחַ וְהָאָרֶץ רַחֲבַת יָדַיִם כִּי־ נְתָנָהּ
he-put-her that measures spacious-of and-the-land unsuspecting people to

אֱלֹהִים בְּיֶדְכֶם מָקוֹם אֲשֶׁר אֵין־ שָׁם מַחְסוֹר כָּל־ דָּבָר אֲשֶׁר בָּאָרֶץ׃
in-the-land that thing any-of lack there not that place into-hand-of-you God

וַיִּסְעוּ מִשָּׁם מִמִּשְׁפַּחַת הַדָּנִי מִצָּרְעָה
from-Zorah the-Danite from-clan-of from-there then-they-set-out (11)

וּמֵאֶשְׁתָּאֹל שֵׁשׁ־ מֵאוֹת אִישׁ חָגוּר כְּלֵי מִלְחָמָה׃
battle things-of being-armed man hundreds six and-from-Eshtaol

וַיַּעֲלוּ וַיַּחֲנוּ בְּקִרְיַת יְעָרִים בִּיהוּדָה עַל־ כֵּן
this for in-Judah Jearim near-Kiriath and-they-camped and-they-went (12)

קָרְאוּ לַמָּקוֹם הַהוּא מַחֲנֵה־ דָן עַד הַיּוֹם הַזֶּה הִנֵּה
see! the-this the-day to Dan Mahaneh the-that to-the-place they-called

אַחֲרֵי קִרְיַת יְעָרִים׃ וַיַּעַבְרוּ מִשָּׁם הַר־ אֶפְרָיִם
Ephraim hill-country-of from-there and-they-went (13) Jearim Kiriath west-of

"He has hired me and I am his priest."

5 Then they said to him, "Please inquire of God to learn whether our journey will be successful."

6 The priest answered them, "Go in peace. Your journey has the LORD's approval."

7 So the five men left and came to Laish, where they saw that the people were living in safety, like the Sidonians, unsuspecting and secure. And since their land lacked nothing, they were prosperous.[f] Also, they lived a long way from the Sidonians and had no relationship with anyone else.[g]

8 When they returned to Zorah and Eshtaol, their brothers asked them, "How did you find things?"

9 They answered, "Come on, let's attack them! We have seen that the land is very good. Aren't you going to do something? Don't hesitate to go there and take it over. 10 When you get there, you will find an unsuspecting people and a spacious land that God has put into your hands, a land that lacks nothing whatever."

11 Then six hundred men from the clan of the Danites, armed for battle, set out from Zorah and Eshtaol. 12 On their way they set up camp near Kiriath Jearim in Judah. This is why the place west of Kiriath Jearim is called Mahaneh Dan[h] to this day. 13 From there they went on to the hill country of Ephraim and came

f7 The meaning of the Hebrew for this clause is uncertain.
g7 Hebrew; some Septuagint manuscripts *with the Arameans*
h12 *Mahaneh Dan* means *Dan's camp.*

וַיָּבֹאוּ עַד־ בֵּית מִיכָה׃ וַיַּעֲנוּ חֲמֵשֶׁת הָאֲנָשִׁים
the-men five-of then-they-said (14) Micah house-of to and-they-came

הַהֹלְכִים לְרַגֵּל אֶת־ הָאָרֶץ לַיִשׁ וַיֹּאמְרוּ אֶל־ אֲחֵיהֶם
brothers-of-them to and-they-said Laish the-land *** to-spy-out the-ones-going

הֲיְדַעְתֶּם כִּי יֵשׁ בַּבָּתִּים הָאֵלֶּה אֵפוֹד וּתְרָפִים
and-idols ephod the-these in-the-houses there-is that you-know?

וּפֶסֶל וּמַסֵּכָה וְעַתָּה דְּעוּ מַה־ תַּעֲשׂוּ׃
you-must-do what you-know and-now and-cast-idol and-carved-image

וַיָּסוּרוּ שָׁמָּה וַיָּבֹאוּ אֶל־ בֵּית־ הַנַּעַר
the-young-man house-of to and-they-went to-there so-they-turned-in (15)

הַלֵּוִי בֵּית מִיכָה וַיִּשְׁאֲלוּ־ לוֹ לְשָׁלוֹם׃ וְשֵׁשׁ־
and-six (16) for-peace to-him and-they-greeted Micah place-of the-Levite

מֵאוֹת אִישׁ חֲגוּרִים כְּלֵי מִלְחַמְתָּם נִצָּבִים
ones-standing battle-of-them things-of ones-being-armed man hundreds

פֶּתַח הַשָּׁעַר אֲשֶׁר מִבְּנֵי־ דָן׃ וַיַּעֲלוּ חֲמֵשֶׁת הָאֲנָשִׁים
the-men five-of and-they-went (17) Dan from-sons-of who the-gate entrance-of

הַהֹלְכִים לְרַגֵּל אֶת־ הָאָרֶץ בָּאוּ שָׁמָּה לָקְחוּ
they-took into-there they-entered the-land *** to-spy-out the-ones-going

אֶת־ הַפֶּסֶל וְאֶת־ הָאֵפוֹד וְאֶת־ הַתְּרָפִים וְאֶת־ הַמַּסֵּכָה
the-cast-idol and the-household-gods and the-ephod and the-carved-image ***

וְהַכֹּהֵן נִצָּב פֶּתַח הַשַּׁעַר וְשֵׁשׁ־ מֵאוֹת הָאִישׁ
the-man hundreds and-six the-gate entrance-of standing and-the-priest

הֶחָגוּר כְּלֵי הַמִּלְחָמָה׃ וְאֵלֶּה בָּאוּ בֵּית
house-of they-entered when-these (18) the-battle things-of the-one-being-armed

מִיכָה וַיִּקְחוּ אֶת־ פֶּסֶל הָאֵפוֹד וְאֶת־ הַתְּרָפִים
the-household-gods and the-ephod carved-image *** then-they-took Micah

וְאֶת־ הַמַּסֵּכָה וַיֹּאמֶר אֲלֵיהֶם הַכֹּהֵן מָה אַתֶּם עֹשִׂים׃
ones-doing you what? the-priest to-them and-he-said the-cast-idol and

וַיֹּאמְרוּ לוֹ הַחֲרֵשׁ שִׂים־ יָדְךָ עַל־ פִּיךָ
mouth-of-you over hand-of-you put! be-quiet! to-him and-they-answered (19)

וְלֵךְ עִמָּנוּ וֶהְיֵה־ לָנוּ לְאָב וּלְכֹהֵן הֲטוֹב ׀ הֱיוֹתְךָ
to-be-you better? and-as-priest as-father for-us and-be! with-us and-come!

כֹהֵן לְבֵית אִישׁ אֶחָד אוֹ הֱיוֹתְךָ כֹהֵן לְשֵׁבֶט וּלְמִשְׁפָּחָה
and-for-clan for-tribe priest to-be-you or one man for-household-of priest

בְּיִשְׂרָאֵל׃ וַיִּיטַב לֵב הַכֹּהֵן וַיִּקַּח אֶת־ הָאֵפוֹד
the-ephod *** and-he-took the-priest heart-of then-he-was-glad (20) in-Israel

וְאֶת־ הַתְּרָפִים הַפֶּסֶל וַיָּבֹא בְּקֶרֶב הָעָם׃ וַיִּפְנוּ
the-people in-among and-he-went the-carved-image and the-household-gods and

to Micah's house.
14Then the five men who had spied out the land of Laish said to their brothers, "Do you know that one of these houses has an ephod, other household gods, a carved image and a cast idol? Now you know what to do." 15So they turned in there and went to the house of the young Levite at Micah's place and greeted him. 16The six hundred Danites, armed for battle, stood at the entrance to the gate. 17The five men who had spied out the land went inside and took the carved image, the ephod, the other household gods and the cast idol while the priest and the six hundred armed men stood at the entrance to the gate.
18When these men went into Micah's house and took the carved image, the ephod, the other household gods and the cast idol, the priest said to them, "What are you doing?"
19They answered him, "Be quiet! Don't say a word. Come with us, and be our father and priest. Isn't it better that you serve a tribe and clan in Israel as priest rather than just one man's household?" 20Then the priest was glad. He took the ephod, the other household gods and the carved image and went along with the

וַיֵּלְכוּ וַיָּשִׂימוּ אֶת־ וְאֶת־ הַטַּף וְאֶת־

and the-little-child *** and-they-put and-they-left and-they-turned (21)

הַמִּקְנֶה וְאֶת־ הַכְּבוּדָּה לִפְנֵיהֶם׃ הֵמָּה הִרְחִיקוּ

they-went-distance they (22) in-front-of-them the-possession and the-livestock

מִבֵּית מִיכָה וְהָאֲנָשִׁים אֲשֶׁר בַּבָּתִּים אֲשֶׁר עִם־ בֵּית מִיכָה

Micah house-of near that in-the-houses who and-the-men Micah from-house-of

נִזְעֲקוּ וַיַּדְבִּיקוּ אֶת־ בְּנֵי־ דָן׃ וַיִּקְרְאוּ

and-they-shouted (23) Dan sons-of *** and-they-overtook they-were-called-together

אֶל־ בְּנֵי־ דָן וַיַּסֵּבּוּ פְּנֵיהֶם וַיֹּאמְרוּ לְמִיכָה מַה־

what? to-Micah and-they-said faces-of-them and-they-turned Dan sons-of after

לְּךָ כִּי נִזְעָקְתָּ׃ וַיֹּאמֶר אֶת־ אֱלֹהַי אֲשֶׁר־ עָשִׂיתִי

I-made that gods-of-me *** and-he-replied (24) you-called-out that to-you

לְקַחְתֶּם וְאֶת־ הַכֹּהֵן וַתֵּלֵכוּ וּמַה־ לִּי עוֹד וּמַה־ זֶּה

this now-how? else to-me so-what? and-you-went-away the-priest and you-took

תֹּאמְרוּ אֵלַי מַה־ לָּךְ׃ וַיֹּאמְרוּ אֵלָיו בְּנֵי־ דָן אַל־

not Dan sons-of to-him and-they-answered (25) to-you what? of-me you-ask

תַּשְׁמַע קוֹלְךָ עִמָּנוּ פֶּן־ יִפְגְּעוּ בָכֶם אֲנָשִׁים

men against-you they-will-attack or with-us voice-of-you you-make-heard

מָרֵי נֶפֶשׁ וְאָסַפְתָּה נַפְשְׁךָ וְנֶפֶשׁ בֵּיתֶךָ׃

family-of-you and-life-of life-of-you and-you-will-lose temper ones-hot-of

וַיֵּלְכוּ בְנֵי־ דָן לְדַרְכָּם וַיַּרְא מִיכָה כִּי־

that Micah and-he-saw on-way-of-them Dan sons-of so-they-went (26)

חֲזָקִים הֵמָּה מִמֶּנּוּ וַיִּפֶן וַיָּשָׁב אֶל־ בֵּיתוֹ׃

home-of-him to and-he-went-back so-he-turned than-him they stronger-ones

וְהֵמָּה לָקְחוּ אֵת אֲשֶׁר־ עָשָׂה מִיכָה וְאֶת־ הַכֹּהֵן אֲשֶׁר הָיָה־

he-was who the-priest and Micah he-made what *** they-took then-they (27)

לוֹ וַיָּבֹאוּ עַל־ לַיִשׁ עַל־ עַם שֹׁקֵט וּבֹטֵחַ

and-unsuspecting being-peaceful people against Laish to and-they-went for-him

וַיַּכּוּ אוֹתָם לְפִי־ חָרֶב וְאֶת־ הָעִיר שָׂרְפוּ בָאֵשׁ׃

with-fire they-burned the-city and sword with-edge-of them and-they-attacked

וְאֵין מַצִּיל כִּי רְחוֹקָה־ הִיא מִצִּידוֹן וְדָבָר אֵין־

not and-relationship from-Sidon she long-way for one-rescuing and-not (28)

לָהֶם עִם־ אָדָם וְהִיא בָּעֵמֶק אֲשֶׁר לְבֵית־ רְחוֹב וַיִּבְנוּ

and-they-rebuilt Rehob near-Beth that in-the-valley now-she anyone with to-them

אֶת־ הָעִיר וַיֵּשְׁבוּ בָהּ׃ וַיִּקְרְאוּ שֵׁם־ הָעִיר

the-city name-of and-they-called (29) in-her and-they-settled the-city ***

דָּן בְּשֵׁם דָּן אֲבִיהֶם אֲשֶׁר יוּלַּד לְיִשְׂרָאֵל וְאוּלָם

even-though to-Israel he-was-born who forefather-of-them Dan after-name-of Dan

people. 21 Putting their little children, their livestock and their possessions in front of them, they turned away and left.

22 When they had gone some distance from Micah's house, the men who lived near Micah were called together and overtook the Danites. 23 As they shouted after them, the Danites turned and said to Micah, "What's the matter with you that you called out your men to fight?"

24 He replied, "You took the gods I made, and my priest, and went away. What else do I have? How can you ask, 'What's the matter with you?' "

25 The Danites answered, "Don't argue with us, or some hot-tempered men will attack you, and you and your family will lose your lives." 26 So the Danites went their way, and Micah, seeing that they were too strong for him, turned around and went back home.

27 Then they took what Micah had made, and his priest, and went on to Laish, against a peaceful and unsuspecting people. They attacked them with the sword and burned down their city. 28 There was no one to rescue them because they lived a long way from Sidon and had no relationship with anyone else. The city was in a valley near Beth Rehob.

The Danites rebuilt the city and settled there. 29 They named it Dan after their forefather Dan, who was born

לַיִשׁ שֵׁם־ הָעִיר לָרִאשֹׁנָה׃ וַיָּקִימוּ לָהֶם בְּנֵי־
sons-of for-them and-they-set-up (30) before the-city name-of Laish

דָן אֶת־ הַפֶּסֶל וִיהוֹנָתָן בֶּן־ גֵּרְשֹׁם בֶּן־ מְנַשֶּׁה* הוּא וּבָנָיו
and-sons-of-him he *Moses son-of Gershom son-of and-Jonathan the-idol *** Dan

הָיוּ כֹּהֲנִים לְשֵׁבֶט הַדָּנִי עַד־ יוֹם גְּלוֹת הָאָרֶץ׃
the-land to-be-captured day to the-Danite for-tribe-of priests they-were

וַיָּשִׂימוּ לָהֶם אֶת־ פֶּסֶל מִיכָה אֲשֶׁר עָשָׂה כָּל־ יְמֵי
days-of all-of he-made that Micah idol-of *** for-them and-they-set-up (31)

הֱיוֹת בֵּית־ הָאֱלֹהִים בְּשִׁלֹה׃ וַיְהִי בַּיָּמִים הָהֵם
the-those in-the-days and-he-was (19:1) in-Shiloh the-God house-of to-be

וּמֶלֶךְ אֵין בְּיִשְׂרָאֵל וַיְהִי ׀ אִישׁ לֵוִי גָּר בְּיַרְכְּתֵי
in-remote-areas-of living Levite man now-he-was in-Israel he-was-not that-king

הַר־ אֶפְרַיִם וַיִּקַּח־ לוֹ אִשָּׁה פִּילֶגֶשׁ מִבֵּית
from-Beth concubine woman for-him and-he-took Ephraim hill-country-of

לֶחֶם יְהוּדָה׃ וַתִּזְנֶה עָלָיו פִּילַגְשׁוֹ וַתֵּלֶךְ
and-she-left concubine-of-him to-him but-she-was-unfaithful (2) Judah Lehem-of

מֵאִתּוֹ אֶל־ בֵּית אָבִיהָ אֶל־ בֵּית לֶחֶם יְהוּדָה וַתְּהִי־
and-she-was Judah Lehem-of Beth to father-of-her house-of to from-with-him

שָׁם יָמִים אַרְבָּעָה חֳדָשִׁים׃ וַיָּקָם אִישָׁהּ וַיֵּלֶךְ אַחֲרֶיהָ
after-her and-he-went husband-of-her then-he-rose (3) months four days there

לְדַבֵּר עַל־ לִבָּהּ לַהֲשִׁיבוֹ° וְנַעֲרוֹ עִמּוֹ וְצֶמֶד
and-two-of with-him and-servant-of-him to-return-her heart-of-her to to-speak

חֲמֹרִים וַתְּבִיאֵהוּ בֵּית אָבִיהָ וַיִּרְאֵהוּ אֲבִי
father-of when-he-saw-him father-of-her house-of and-she-took-him donkeys

הַנַּעֲרָה וַיִּשְׂמַח לִקְרָאתוֹ׃ וַיֶּחֱזַק־† בּוֹ
upon-him and-he-prevailed (4) to-welcome-him then-he-was-glad the-girl

חֹתְנוֹ אֲבִי הַנַּעֲרָה וַיֵּשֶׁב אִתּוֹ שְׁלֹשֶׁת
three-of with-him so-he-remained the-girl father-of father-in-law-of-him

יָמִים וַיֹּאכְלוּ וַיִּשְׁתּוּ וַיָּלִינוּ שָׁם׃ וַיְהִי
and-he-was (5) there and-they-slept and-they-drank and-they-ate days

בַּיּוֹם הָרְבִיעִי וַיַּשְׁכִּימוּ בַבֹּקֶר וַיָּקָם לָלֶכֶת
to-leave and-he-prepared in-the-morning that-they-got-up the-fourth on-the-day

וַיֹּאמֶר אֲבִי הַנַּעֲרָה אֶל־ חֲתָנוֹ סְעָד לִבְּךָ
heart-of-you refresh! son-in-law-of-him to the-girl father-of but-he-said

פַּת־ לֶחֶם וְאַחַר תֵּלֵכוּ׃ וַיֵּשְׁבוּ וַיֹּאכְלוּ שְׁנֵיהֶם
two-of-them and-they-ate so-they-sat (6) you-can-go and-then food piece-of

יַחְדָּו וַיִּשְׁתּוּ וַיֹּאמֶר אֲבִי הַנַּעֲרָה אֶל־ הָאִישׁ הוֹאֶל־
be-pleased! the-man to the-girl father-of then-he-said and-they-drank together

to Israel—though the city used to be called Laish. 30There the Danites set up for themselves the idols, and Jonathan son of Gershom, the son of Moses,[i] and his sons were priests for the tribe of Dan until the time of the captivity of the land. 31They continued to use the idols Micah had made, all the time the house of God was in Shiloh.

*A Levite and His Concubine*

19 In those days Israel had no king.

Now a Levite who lived in a remote area in the hill country of Ephraim took a concubine from Bethlehem in Judah. 2But she was unfaithful to him. She left him and went back to her father's house in Bethlehem, Judah. After she had been there four months, 3her husband went to her to persuade her to return. He had with him his servant and two donkeys. She took him into her father's house, and when her father saw him, he gladly welcomed him. 4His father-in-law, the girl's father, prevailed upon him to stay; so he remained with him three days, eating and drinking, and sleeping there.

5On the fourth day they got up early and he prepared to leave, but the girl's father said to his son-in-law, "Refresh yourself with something to eat; then you can go." 6So the two of them sat down to eat and drink together. Afterward the girl's father said, "Please

[i]*30* An ancient scribal tradition, some Septuagint manuscripts and Vulgate; Masoretic Text *Manasseh*

**30* The "suspended nun" appears to have been an ancient scribal insertion to alter the name *Moses* to *Manasseh* (see Ginsburg, pp. 335ff).

†*4* Most mss point this verb as a *Hiphil* ( וַיַּחֲזֵק ) rather than a *Qal.*

°*3* ק להשיבה

נָא וְלִין וְיִטַב לִבֶּךָ׃ וַיָּקָם הָאִישׁ
the-man when-he-got-up (7) heart-of-you and-let-him-enjoy and-stay! now!

לָלֶכֶת וַיִּפְצַר־ בּוֹ חֹתְנוֹ וַיָּשָׁב
so-he-stayed father-in-law-of-him over-him then-he-persuaded to-go

וַיָּלֶן שָׁם׃ וַיַּשְׁכֵּם בַּבֹּקֶר בַּיּוֹם הַחֲמִישִׁי
the-fifth of-the-day on-the-morning when-he-rose (8) there and-he-spent-night

לָלֶכֶת וַיֹּאמֶר | אֲבִי הַנַּעֲרָה סְעָד־ נָא לְבָבְךָ וְהִתְמַהְמְהוּ
and-wait! heart-of-you now! refresh! the-girl father-of then-he-said to-go

עַד־ נְטוֹת הַיּוֹם וַיֹּאכְלוּ שְׁנֵיהֶם׃ וַיָּקָם
when-he-got-up (9) two-of-them so-they-ate the-day to-stretch-out till

הָאִישׁ לָלֶכֶת הוּא וּפִילַגְשׁוֹ וְנַעֲרוֹ וַיֹּאמֶר לוֹ
to-him then-he-said and-servant-of-him and-concubine-of-him he to-go the-man

חֹתְנוֹ אֲבִי הַנַּעֲרָה הִנֵּה נָא רָפָה הַיּוֹם
the-day he-is-gone now! see! the-girl father-of father-in-law-of-him

לַעֲרֹב לִינוּ־ נָא הִנֵּה חֲנוֹת הַיּוֹם לִין פֹּה
here stay! the-day to-be-over see! now! spend-night! to-be-evening

וְיִיטַב לְבָבֶךָ וְהִשְׁכַּמְתֶּם מָחָר לְדַרְכְּכֶם
on-way-of-you tomorrow then-you-get-up heart-of-you and-let-him-enjoy

וְהָלַכְתָּ לְאֹהָלֶךָ׃ וְלֹא־ אָבָה הָאִישׁ לָלוּן
to-stay the-man he-was-willing but-not (10) to-tent-of-you and-you-can-go

וַיָּקָם וַיֵּלֶךְ וַיָּבֹא עַד־ נֹכַח יְבוּס הִיא יְרוּשָׁלִָם
Jerusalem that Jebus direction-of toward and-he-went and-he-left so-he-got-up

וְעִמּוֹ צֶמֶד חֲמוֹרִים חֲבוּשִׁים וּפִילַגְשׁוֹ עִמּוֹ׃
with-him and-concubine-of-him ones-being-saddled donkeys two-of and-with-him

הֵם עִם־ יְבוּס וְהַיּוֹם רַד מְאֹד וַיֹּאמֶר הַנַּעַר
the-servant and-he-said almost he-was-gone and-the-day Jebus near they (11)

אֶל־ אֲדֹנָיו לְכָה־ נָּא וְנָסוּרָה אֶל־ עִיר־ הַיְבוּסִי
the-Jebusite city-of into and-let-us-go now! come! masters-of-him to

הַזֹּאת וְנָלִין בָּהּ׃ וַיֹּאמֶר אֵלָיו אֲדֹנָיו
masters-of-him to-him and-he-replied (12) in-her and-let-us-spend-night the-this

לֹא נָסוּר אֶל־ עִיר נָכְרִי אֲשֶׁר לֹא־ מִבְּנֵי יִשְׂרָאֵל הֵנָּה
they Israel from-sons-of not who alien city into we-will-go not

וְעָבַרְנוּ עַד־ גִּבְעָה׃ וַיֹּאמֶר לְנַעֲרוֹ לְךָ°
come! to-servant-of-him and-he-said (13) Gibeah to so-we-will-go-on

וְנִקְרְבָה בְּאַחַד הַמְּקֹמוֹת וְלַנּוּ בַגִּבְעָה
in-the-Gibeah and-let-us-spend-night the-places to-one-of and-let-us-reach

אוֹ בָרָמָה׃ וַיַּעַבְרוּ וַיֵּלֵכוּ וַתָּבֹא לָהֶם
before-them and-she-set and-they-walked so-they-went (14) in-the-Ramah or

stay tonight and enjoy yourself." 7And when the man got
up to go, his father-in-law persuaded him, so he stayed there
that night. 8On the morning of
the fifth day, when he rose to
go, the girl's father said, "Refresh yourself. Wait till after-
noon!" So the two of them ate
together.
9Then when the man, with
his concubine and his servant,
got up to leave, his father-in-
law, the girl's father, said,
"Now look, it's almost evening. Spend the night here;
the day is nearly over. Stay
and enjoy yourself. Early tomorrow morning you can get
up and be on your way
home." 10But, unwilling to
stay another night, the man
left and went toward Jebus
(that is, Jerusalem), with his
two saddled donkeys and his
concubine.
11When they were near
Jebus and the day was almost
gone, the servant said to his
master, "Come, let's stop at
this city of the Jebusites and
spend the night."
12His master replied, "No.
We won't go into an alien city,
whose people are not Israelites. We will go on to Gibeah."
13He added, "Come, let's try to
reach Gibeah or Ramah and
spend the night in one of
those places." 14So they went

°13 ק לכה

הַשֶּׁמֶשׁ אֵצֶל הַגִּבְעָה אֲשֶׁר לְבִנְיָמִן׃ וַיָּסֻרוּ שָׁם לָבוֹא
to-go there so-they-stopped (15) in-Benjamin that the-Gibeah near the-sun

לָלוּן בַּגִּבְעָה וַיָּבֹא וַיֵּשֶׁב בִּרְחוֹב הָעִיר
the-city in-square-of and-he-sat and-he-went in-the-Gibeah to-spend-night

וְאֵין אִישׁ מְאַסֵּף־אוֹתָם הַבַּיְתָה לָלוּן׃ וְהִנֵּה ׀ אִישׁ זָקֵן
old man then-see! (16) to-spend-night into-the-home them taking man but-no

בָּא מִן־ מַעֲשֵׂהוּ מִן־ הַשָּׂדֶה בָּעֶרֶב וְהָאִישׁ
now-the-man in-the-evening the-field from work-of-him from coming-in

מֵהַר אֶפְרַיִם וְהוּא־ גָר בַּגִּבְעָה וְאַנְשֵׁי הַמָּקוֹם
the-place now-men-of in-the-Gibeah he-lived and-he Ephraim from-hill-country-of

בְּנֵי יְמִינִי׃ וַיִּשָּׂא עֵינָיו וַיַּרְא אֶת־ הָאִישׁ
the-man *** and-he-saw eyes-of-him when-he-lifted (17) Benjamites

הָאֹרֵחַ בִּרְחֹב הָעִיר וַיֹּאמֶר הָאִישׁ הַזָּקֵן אָנָה תֵלֵךְ
you-go where? the-old the-man then-he-asked the-city in-square-of the-traveling

וּמֵאַיִן תָּבוֹא׃ וַיֹּאמֶר אֵלָיו עֹבְרִים אֲנַחְנוּ מִבֵּית־
from-Beth we ones-going to-him and-he-answered (18) you-come and-from-where?

לֶחֶם יְהוּדָה עַד־ יַרְכְּתֵי הַר־ אֶפְרַיִם מִשָּׁם אָנֹכִי
I from-there Ephraim hill-country-of remote-areas-of to Judah Lehem-of

וָאֵלֵךְ עַד־ בֵּית לֶחֶם יְהוּדָה וְאֶת־ בֵּית יְהוָה אֲנִי הֹלֵךְ וְאֵין
but-no going I Yahweh house-of and Judah Lehem-of Beth to and-I-went

אִישׁ מְאַסֵּף אוֹתִי הַבָּיְתָה׃ וְגַם־ תֶּבֶן גַּם־ מִסְפּוֹא יֵשׁ
there-is fodder also straw now-both (19) into-the-house me taking man

לַחֲמוֹרֵינוּ וְגַם לֶחֶם וָיַיִן יֶשׁ־ לִי וְלַאֲמָתֶךָ
and-for-maid-of-you for-me there-is and-wine bread and-also for-donkeys-of-us

וְלַנַּעַר עִם־ עֲבָדֶיךָ אֵין מַחְסוֹר כָּל־ דָּבָר׃
thing any-of need there-is-no servants-of-you with and-for-the-young-man

וַיֹּאמֶר הָאִישׁ הַזָּקֵן שָׁלוֹם לָךְ רַק כָּל־ מַחְסוֹרְךָ
need-of-you all-of only to-you welcome the-old the-man and-he-said (20)

עָלָי רַק בָּרְחוֹב אַל־ תָּלַן׃ וַיְבִיאֵהוּ
so-he-took-him (21) you-spend-night not in-the-square only with-me

לְבֵיתוֹ וַיָּבָול° לַחֲמוֹרִים וַיִּרְחֲצוּ רַגְלֵיהֶם
feet-of-them and-they-washed for-donkeys and-he-fed into-house-of-him

וַיֹּאכְלוּ וַיִּשְׁתּוּ׃ הֵמָּה מֵיטִיבִים אֶת־ לִבָּם
heart-of-them *** ones-making-enjoy they (22) and-they-drank and-they-ate

וְהִנֵּה אַנְשֵׁי הָעִיר אַנְשֵׁי בְנֵי־ בְלִיַּעַל נָסַבּוּ אֶת־ הַבַּיִת
the-house *** they-surrounded wickedness sons-of men-of the-city men-of then-see!

מִתְדַּפְּקִים עַל־ הַדֶּלֶת וַיֹּאמְרוּ אֶל־ הָאִישׁ בַּעַל הַבַּיִת
the-house owner-of the-man to and-they-shouted the-door on ones-pounding

on, and the sun set as they
neared Gibeah in Benjamin.
15 There they stopped to spend
the night. They went and sat
in the city square, but no one
took them into his home for
the night.
16 That evening an old man
from the hill country of
Ephraim, who was living in
Gibeah (the men of the place
were Benjamites), came in
from his work in the fields.
17 When he looked and saw the
traveler in the city square, the
old man asked, "Where are
you going? Where did you
come from?"
18 He answered, "We are on
our way from Bethlehem in
Judah to a remote area in the
hill country of Ephraim where
I live. I have been to Bethlehem in Judah and now I am
going to the house of the LORD.
No one has taken me into his
house. 19 We have both straw
and fodder for our donkeys
and bread and wine for ourselves your servants—me,
your maidservant, and the
young man with us. We don't
need anything."
20 "You are welcome at my
house," the old man said. "Let
me supply whatever you need.
Only don't spend the night in
the square." 21 So he took him
into his house and fed his
donkeys. After they had
washed their feet, they had
something to eat and drink.
22 While they were enjoying
themselves, some of the
wicked men of the city surrounded the house. Pounding
on the door, they shouted to
the old man who owned the

°21 ק ויבל

הַזָּקֵן לֵאמֹר הוֹצֵא אֶת־ הָאִישׁ אֲשֶׁר־ בָּא אֶל־ בֵּיתְךָ
house-of-you to he-came who the-man *** bring-out! to-say the-old

וְנֵדָעֶנּוּ׃ (23) וַיֵּצֵא אֲלֵיהֶם הָאִישׁ בַּעַל
owner-of the-man to-them and-he-went-out (23) so-we-can-have-sex-with-him

הַבַּיִת וַיֹּאמֶר אֲלֵהֶם אַל־ אַחַי אַל־ תָּרֵעוּ נָא אַחֲרֵי
since now! you-be-vile not friends-of-me no to-them and-he-said the-house

אֲשֶׁר־ בָּא הָאִישׁ הַזֶּה אֶל־* בֵּיתִי אַל־ תַּעֲשׂוּ אֶת־ הַנְּבָלָה
the-disgrace *** you-do not house-of-me into the-this the-man he-came that

הַזֹּאת׃ (24) הִנֵּה בִתִּי הַבְּתוּלָה וּפִילַגְשֵׁהוּ
and-concubine-of-him the-virgin daughter-of-me look! (24) the-this

אוֹצִיאָה־ נָּא אוֹתָם וְעַנּוּ אוֹתָם וַעֲשׂוּ לָהֶם הַטּוֹב
the-good to-them and-do! them and-use! them now! I-will-bring-out

בְּעֵינֵיכֶם וְלָאִישׁ הַזֶּה לֹא תַעֲשׂוּ דְּבַר הַנְּבָלָה
the-disgrace thing-of you-do not the-this but-to-the-man in-eyes-of-you

הַזֹּאת׃ (25) וְלֹא־ אָבוּ הָאֲנָשִׁים לִשְׁמֹעַ לוֹ וַיַּחֲזֵק הָאִישׁ
the-man so-he-took to-him to-listen the-men they-wanted but-not (25) the-this

בְּפִילַגְשׁוֹ וַיֹּצֵא אֲלֵיהֶם הַחוּץ וַיֵּדְעוּ אוֹתָהּ
her and-they-raped the-outside to-them and-he-sent to-concubine-of-him

וַיִּתְעַלְּלוּ־ בָהּ כָּל־ הַלַּיְלָה עַד־ הַבֹּקֶר וַיְשַׁלְּחוּהָ
and-they-let-go-her the-morning to the-night all-of against-her and-they-abused

בַּעֲלוֹת° הַשָּׁחַר׃ (26) וַתָּבֹא הָאִשָּׁה לִפְנוֹת הַבֹּקֶר
the-day to-break the-woman and-she-went-back (26) the-dawn when-to-come

וַתִּפֹּל פֶּתַח בֵּית־ הָאִישׁ אֲשֶׁר־ אֲדוֹנֶיהָ שָּׁם עַד־
until there masters-of-her where the-man house-of door-of and-she-fell

הָאוֹר׃ (27) וַיָּקָם אֲדֹנֶיהָ בַּבֹּקֶר וַיִּפְתַּח
then-he-opened in-the-morning masters-of-her when-he-got-up (27) the-daylight

דַּלְתוֹת הַבַּיִת וַיֵּצֵא לָלֶכֶת לְדַרְכּוֹ וְהִנֵּה
and-see! on-way-of-him to-continue and-he-stepped-out the-house doors-of

הָאִשָּׁה פִילַגְשׁוֹ נֹפֶלֶת פֶּתַח הַבַּיִת וְיָדֶיהָ
and-hands-of-her the-house doorway-of having-fallen concubine-of-him the-woman

עַל־ הַסַּף׃ (28) וַיֹּאמֶר אֵלֶיהָ קוּמִי וְנֵלֵכָה וְאֵין
but-not and-let-us-go get-up! to-her and-he-said (28) the-threshold on

עֹנֶה וַיִּקָּחֶהָ עַל־ הַחֲמוֹר וַיָּקָם הָאִישׁ וַיֵּלֶךְ
and-he-went the-man and-he-set-out the-donkey on then-he-put-her answering

לִמְקֹמוֹ׃ (29) וַיָּבֹא אֶל־ בֵּיתוֹ וַיִּקַּח אֶת־ הַמַּאֲכֶלֶת
the-knife *** then-he-took home-of-him to when-he-reached (29) to-home-of-him

וַיַּחֲזֵק בְּפִילַגְשׁוֹ וַיְנַתְּחֶהָ לַעֲצָמֶיהָ לִשְׁנֵים
into-two by-limbs-of-her and-he-cut-up-her onto-concubine-of-him and-he-held

house, "Bring out the man
who came to your house so we
can have sex with him."
23 The owner of the house
went outside and said to them,
"No, my friends, don't be so
vile. Since this man is my
guest, don't do this disgraceful
thing. 24 Look, here is my virgin daughter, and his concubine. I will bring them out to
you now, and you can use
them and do to them whatever
you wish. But to this man,
don't do such a disgraceful
thing."
25 But the men would not listen to him. So the man took
his concubine and sent her
outside to them, and they
raped her and abused her
throughout the night, and at
dawn they let her go. 26 At daybreak the woman went back to
the house where her master
was staying, fell down at the
door and lay there until daylight.
27 When her master got up in
the morning and opened the
door of the house and stepped
out to continue on his way,
there lay his concubine, fallen
in the doorway of the house,
with her hands on the threshold. 28 He said to her, "Get up;
let's go." But there was no answer. Then the man put her on
his donkey and set out for
home.
29 When he reached home, he
took a knife and cut up his
concubine, limb by limb, into

*23 Most mss have *segol* under the *aleph* (אֶל).

°25 ק כעלות

עֲשָׂר נְתָחִים וַיְשַׁלְּחֶהָ בְּכֹל גְּבוּל יִשְׂרָאֵל׃ וְהָיָה
and-he-was (30) Israel area-of into-every-of and-he-sent-her parts ten

כָל־ הָרֹאֶה וְאָמַר לֹא־ נִהְיְתָה וְלֹא־ נִרְאֲתָה
she-was-seen and-not she-was not then-he-said the-one-seeing every-of

כָּזֹאת לְמִיּוֹם עֲלוֹת בְּנֵי־ יִשְׂרָאֵל מֵאֶרֶץ מִצְרַיִם עַד
to Egypt from-land-of Israel sons-of to-come-up on-since-day such-as-this

הַיּוֹם הַזֶּה שִׂימוּ־ לָכֶם עָלֶיהָ עֻצוּ וְדַבֵּרוּ׃
and-tell! consider! about-her for-you think! the-this the-day

וַיֵּצְאוּ כָּל־ בְּנֵי יִשְׂרָאֵל וַתִּקָּהֵל הָעֵדָה
the-assembly and-she-assembled Israel sons-of all-of then-they-came-out (20:1)

כְּאִישׁ אֶחָד לְמִדָּן וְעַד־ בְּאֵר שֶׁבַע וְאֶרֶץ הַגִּלְעָד אֶל־
before the-Gilead and-land-of Sheba Beer even-to at-from-Dan one as-man

יְהוָה הַמִּצְפָּה׃ וַיִּתְיַצְּבוּ פִּנּוֹת כָּל־ הָעָם כֹּל
all-of the-people all-of leaders-of and-they-took-places (2) the-Mizpah Yahweh

שִׁבְטֵי יִשְׂרָאֵל בִּקְהַל עַם הָאֱלֹהִים אַרְבַּע מֵאוֹת אֶלֶף
thousand hundreds four the-God people-of in-assembly-of Israel tribes-of

אִישׁ רַגְלִי שֹׁלֵף חָרֶב׃ וַיִּשְׁמְעוּ בְּנֵי בִנְיָמִן כִּי־
that Benjamin sons-of and-they-heard (3) sword being-armed soldier man

עָלוּ בְנֵי־ יִשְׂרָאֵל הַמִּצְפָּה וַיֹּאמְרוּ בְּנֵי יִשְׂרָאֵל דַּבְּרוּ
tell! Israel sons-of then-they-said the-Mizpah Israel sons-of they-went-up

אֵיכָה נִהְיְתָה הָרָעָה הַזֹּאת׃ וַיַּעַן הָאִישׁ הַלֵּוִי
the-Levite the-man so-he-said (4) the-this the-awful-thing she-happened how?

אִישׁ הָאִשָּׁה הַנִּרְצָחָה וַיֹּאמַר הַגִּבְעָתָה אֲשֶׁר
that to-the-Gibeah and-he-said the-being-murdered the-woman husband-of

לְבִנְיָמִן בָּאתִי אֲנִי וּפִילַגְשִׁי לָלוּן׃ וַיָּקֻמוּ
and-they-came (5) to-spend-night and-concubine-of-me I I-came in-Benjamin

עָלַי בַּעֲלֵי הַגִּבְעָה וַיָּסֹבּוּ עָלַי אֶת־ הַבַּיִת
the-house *** against-me and-they-surrounded the-Gibeah men-of after-me

לַיְלָה אוֹתִי דִּמּוּ לַהֲרֹג וְאֶת־ פִּילַגְשִׁי עִנּוּ וַתָּמֹת׃
and-she-died they-raped concubine-of-me and to-kill they-intended me night

וָאֹחֵז בְּפִילַגְשִׁי וָאֲנַתְּחֶהָ וָאֲשַׁלְּחֶהָ בְּכָל־
to-each-of and-I-sent-her and-I-cut-up-her to-concubine-of-me so-I-took (6)

שְׂדֵה נַחֲלַת יִשְׂרָאֵל כִּי עָשׂוּ זִמָּה וּנְבָלָה
and-disgrace lewd-act they-committed for Israel inheritance-of region-of

בְּיִשְׂרָאֵל׃ הִנֵּה כֻלְּכֶם בְּנֵי יִשְׂרָאֵל הָבוּ לָכֶם דָּבָר וְעֵצָה
and-verdict word for-you give! Israel sons-of all-of-you now! (7) in-Israel

הֲלֹם׃ וַיָּקָם כָּל־ הָעָם כְּאִישׁ אֶחָד לֵאמֹר לֹא נֵלֵךְ אִישׁ
man he-will-go not to-say one as-man the-people all-of and-he-rose (8) here

twelve parts and sent them
into all the areas of Israel.
30 Everyone who saw it said,
"Such a thing has never been
seen or done, not since the day
the Israelites came up out of
Egypt. Think about it! Consider it! Tell us what to do!"

*Israelites Fight the Benjamites*

20 Then all the Israelites
from Dan to Beersheba
and from the land of Gilead
came out as one man and assembled before the LORD in
Mizpah. 2 The leaders of all the
people of the tribes of Israel
took their places in the assembly of the people of God, four
hundred thousand soldiers
armed with swords. 3 (The
Benjamites heard that the Israelites had gone up to Mizpah.) Then the Israelites said,
"Tell us how this awful thing
happened."
4 So the Levite, the husband
of the murdered woman, said,
"I and my concubine came to
Gibeah in Benjamin to spend
the night. 5 During the night
the men of Gibeah came after
me and surrounded the house,
intending to kill me. They
raped my concubine, and she
died. 6 I took my concubine,
cut her into pieces and sent
one piece to each region of Israel's inheritance, because
they committed this lewd and
disgraceful act in Israel. 7 Now,
all you Israelites, speak up and
give your verdict."
8 All the people rose as one
man, saying, "None of us will

לְאָהֳלוֹ וְלֹא נָסוּר אִישׁ לְבֵיתוֹ׃ וְעַתָּה זֶה

this but-now (9) to-house-of-him man he-will-return and-not to-home-of-him

הַדָּבָר אֲשֶׁר נַעֲשֶׂה לַגִּבְעָה עָלֶיהָ בְּגוֹרָל׃ וְלָקַחְנוּ

now-we-will-take (10) by-lot against-her to-the-Gibeah we-will-do that the-thing

עֲשָׂרָה אֲנָשִׁים לַמֵּאָה לְכֹל ׀ שִׁבְטֵי יִשְׂרָאֵל וּמֵאָה

and-hundred Israel tribes-of from-all-of from-the-hundred men ten

לָאֶלֶף וְאֶלֶף לָרְבָבָה לָקַחַת צֵדָה

provision to-get from-the-ten-thousand and-thousand from-the-thousand

לָעָם לַעֲשׂוֹת לְבוֹאָם לְגֶבַע בִּנְיָמִן כְּכָל־ הַנְּבָלָה

the-vileness as-all-of Benjamin to-Gibeah-of to-arrive-them to-give for-the-army

אֲשֶׁר עָשָׂה בְּיִשְׂרָאֵל׃ וַיֵּאָסֵף כָּל־ אִישׁ יִשְׂרָאֵל אֶל־

against Israel man-of every-of so-he-got-together (11) in-Israel he-did that

הָעִיר כְּאִישׁ אֶחָד חֲבֵרִים׃ וַיִּשְׁלְחוּ שִׁבְטֵי יִשְׂרָאֵל אֲנָשִׁים

men Israel tribes-of and-they-sent (12) ones-united one as-man the-city

בְּכָל־ שִׁבְטֵי בִנְיָמִן לֵאמֹר מָה הָרָעָה הַזֹּאת אֲשֶׁר

that the-this the-awful-crime what? to-say Benjamin tribes-of through-all-of

נִהְיְתָה בָּכֶם׃ וְעַתָּה תְּנוּ אֶת־ הָאֲנָשִׁים בְּנֵי־

sons-of the-men *** surrender! and-now (13) among-you she-was-committed

בְלִיַּעַל אֲשֶׁר בַּגִּבְעָה וּנְמִיתֵם וּנְבַעֲרָה רָעָה מִיִּשְׂרָאֵל

from-Israel evil and-we-may-purge so-we-may-kill-them of-the-Gibeah who wickedness

וְלֹא אָבוּ * בִּנְיָמִן לִשְׁמֹעַ בְּקוֹל אֲחֵיהֶם

fellows-of-them to-voice-of to-listen Benjamin *sons-of they-wanted but-not

בְּנֵי־ יִשְׂרָאֵל׃ וַיֵּאָסְפוּ בְנֵי־ בִנְיָמִן מִן־ הֶעָרִים

the-towns from Benjamin sons-of and-they-came-together (14) Israel sons-of

הַגִּבְעָתָה לָצֵאת לַמִּלְחָמָה עִם־ בְּנֵי יִשְׂרָאֵל׃

Israel sons-of against to-the-fight to-go-out at-the-Gibeah

וַיִּתְפָּקְדוּ בְנֵי בִנְיָמִן בַּיּוֹם הַהוּא מֵהֶעָרִים

from-the-towns the-that on-the-day Benjamin sons-of and-they-mobilized (15)

עֶשְׂרִים וְשִׁשָּׁה אֶלֶף אִישׁ שֹׁלֵף חָרֶב לְבַד מִיֹּשְׁבֵי

from-ones-living-of aside sword carrying man thousand and-six twenty

הַגִּבְעָה הִתְפָּקְדוּ שְׁבַע מֵאוֹת אִישׁ בָּחוּר׃ מִכֹּל ׀

among-all-of (16) being-chosen man hundreds seven-of they-mobilized the-Gibeah

הָעָם הַזֶּה שְׁבַע מֵאוֹת אִישׁ בָּחוּר אִטֵּר יַד־

hand-of bound-of being-chosen man hundreds seven-of the-this the-people

יְמִינוֹ כָּל־ זֶה קֹלֵעַ בָּאֶבֶן אֶל־ הַשַּׂעֲרָה וְלֹא

and-not the-hair at with-the-stone slinging this each-of right-of-him

יַחֲטִא׃ וְאִישׁ יִשְׂרָאֵל הִתְפָּקְדוּ לְבַד מִבִּנְיָמִן אַרְבַּע

four from-Benjamin apart they-mustered Israel and-man-of (17) he-would-miss

go home. No, not one of us will return to his house. [9]But now this is what we'll do to Gibeah: We'll go up against it as the lot directs. [10]We'll take ten men out of every hundred from all the tribes of Israel, and a hundred from a thousand, and a thousand from ten thousand, to get provisions for the army. Then, when the army arrives at Gibeah in Benjamin, it can give them what they deserve for all this vileness done in Israel." [11]So all the men of Israel got together and united as one man against the city.

[12]The tribes of Israel sent men throughout the tribe of Benjamin, saying, "What about this awful crime that was committed among you? [13]Now surrender those wicked men of Gibeah so that we may put them to death and purge the evil from Israel."

But the Benjamites would not listen to their fellow Israelites. [14]From their towns they came together at Gibeah to fight against the Israelites. [15]At once the Benjamites mobilized twenty-six thousand swordsmen from their towns, in addition to seven hundred chosen men from those living in Gibeah. [16]Among all these soldiers there were seven hundred chosen men who were left-handed, each of whom could sling a stone at a hair and not miss.

[17]Israel, apart from Benjamin, mustered four hundred

*13 Most mss have the *Qere* בְּנֵי without a *Kethib* form.

מֵאוֹת אֶלֶף אִישׁ שֹׁלֵף חֶרֶב כָּל־ זֶה אִישׁ מִלְחָמָה׃
fight man-of this every-of sword carrying man thousand hundreds

וַיָּקֻמוּ וַיַּעֲלוּ בֵית־ אֵל וַיִּשְׁאֲלוּ בֵאלֹהִים
of-God and-they-inquired El Beth and-they-went-up and-they-rose (18)

וַיֹּאמְרוּ בְּנֵי יִשְׂרָאֵל מִי יַעֲלֶה־ לָּנוּ בַתְּחִלָּה לַמִּלְחָמָה
to-the-fight as-the-first of-us he-shall-go who? Israel sons-of and-they-said

עִם־ בְּנֵי בִנְיָמִן וַיֹּאמֶר יְהוָה יְהוּדָה בַתְּחִלָּה׃
as-the-first Judah Yahweh and-he-replied Benjamin sons-of against

וַיָּקוּמוּ בְנֵי־ יִשְׂרָאֵל בַּבֹּקֶר וַיַּחֲנוּ עַל־
near and-they-pitched-camp in-the-morning Israel sons-of and-they-got-up (19)

הַגִּבְעָה׃ וַיֵּצֵא אִישׁ יִשְׂרָאֵל לַמִּלְחָמָה עִם־ בִּנְיָמִן
Benjamin against to-the-fight Israel man-of and-he-went-out (20) the-Gibeah

וַיַּעַרְכוּ אִתָּם אִישׁ־ יִשְׂרָאֵל מִלְחָמָה אֶל־ הַגִּבְעָה׃
the-Gibeah at battle Israel man-of against-them and-they-took-positions

וַיֵּצְאוּ בְנֵי־ בִנְיָמִן מִן־ הַגִּבְעָה וַיַּשְׁחִיתוּ
and-they-cut-down the-Gibeah from Benjamin sons-of and-they-came-out (21)

בְיִשְׂרָאֵל בַּיּוֹם הַהוּא שְׁנַיִם וְעֶשְׂרִים אֶלֶף אִישׁ אָרְצָה׃
on-battlefield man thousand and-twenty two the-that on-the-day from-Israel

וַיִּתְחַזֵּק הָעָם אִישׁ יִשְׂרָאֵל וַיֹּסִפוּ
and-they-repeated Israel man-of the-people but-he-encouraged (22)

לַעֲרֹךְ מִלְחָמָה בַּמָּקוֹם אֲשֶׁר־ עָרְכוּ שָׁם בַּיּוֹם
on-the-day there they-stationed where in-the-place battle to-take-position

הָרִאשׁוֹן׃ וַיַּעֲלוּ בְנֵי־ יִשְׂרָאֵל וַיִּבְכּוּ לִפְנֵי־ יְהוָה
Yahweh before and-they-wept Israel sons-of and-they-went-up (23) the-first

עַד־ הָעֶרֶב וַיִּשְׁאֲלוּ בַּיהוָה לֵאמֹר הַאוֹסִיף לָגֶשֶׁת
to-go-up shall-I-repeat? to-say of-Yahweh and-they-inquired the-evening until

לַמִּלְחָמָה עִם־ בְּנֵי בִנְיָמִן אָחִי וַיֹּאמֶר יְהוָה
Yahweh and-he-answered brother-of-me Benjamin sons-of against to-the-battle

עֲלוּ אֵלָיו׃ וַיִּקְרְבוּ בְנֵי־ יִשְׂרָאֵל אֶל־ בְּנֵי בִנְיָמִן
Benjamin sons-of to Israel sons-of then-they-drew-near (24) against-him go-up!

בַּיּוֹם הַשֵּׁנִי׃ וַיֵּצֵא בִנְיָמִן ׀ לִקְרָאתָם ׀ מִן־
from to-oppose-them Benjamin when-he-came-out (25) the-second on-the-day

הַגִּבְעָה בַּיּוֹם הַשֵּׁנִי וַיַּשְׁחִיתוּ בִבְנֵי יִשְׂרָאֵל
Israel from-sons-of then-they-cut-down the-second on-the-day the-Gibeah

עוֹד שְׁמֹנַת עָשָׂר אֶלֶף אִישׁ אַרְצָה כָּל־ אֵלֶּה שֹׁלְפֵי
ones-bearing-of these all-of on-battlefield man thousand ten eight-of another

חָרֶב׃ וַיַּעֲלוּ כָל־ בְּנֵי יִשְׂרָאֵל וְכָל־ הָעָם
the-people and-all-of Israel sons-of all-of then-they-went-up (26) sword

thousand swordsmen, all of them fighting men.

[18]The Israelites went up to Bethel[j] and inquired of God. They said, "Who of us shall go first to fight against the Benjamites?"

The LORD replied, "Judah shall go first."

[19]The next morning the Israelites got up and pitched camp near Gibeah. [20]The men of Israel went out to fight the Benjamites and took up battle positions against them at Gibeah. [21]The Benjamites came out of Gibeah and cut down twenty-two thousand Israelites on the battlefield that day. [22]But the men of Israel encouraged one another and again took up their positions where they had stationed themselves the first day. [23]The Israelites went up and wept before the LORD until evening, and they inquired of the LORD. They said, "Shall we go up again to battle against the Benjamites, our brothers?"

The LORD answered, "Go up against them."

[24]Then the Israelites drew near to Benjamin the second day. [25]This time, when the Benjamites came out from Gibeah to oppose them, they cut down another eighteen thousand Israelites, all of them armed with swords.

[26]Then the Israelites, all the people, went up to Bethel, and

j18 Or *to the house of God*; also in verse 26

וַיָּבֹאוּ בֵית־אֵל וַיִּבְכּוּ וַיֵּשְׁבוּ שָׁם לִפְנֵי יְהוָה
Yahweh before there and-they-sat and-they-wept El Beth and-they-came

וַיָּצוּמוּ בַיּוֹם־הַהוּא עַד־הָעָרֶב וַיַּעֲלוּ
and-they-presented the-evening until the-that on-the-day and-they-fasted

עֹלוֹת וּשְׁלָמִים לִפְנֵי יְהוָה׃ וַיִּשְׁאֲלוּ
and-they-inquired (27) Yahweh before and-fellowship-offerings burnt-offerings

בְנֵי־יִשְׂרָאֵל בַּיהוָה וְשָׁם אֲרוֹן בְּרִית הָאֱלֹהִים בַּיָּמִים
in-the-days the-God covenant-of ark-of now-there of-Yahweh Israel sons-of

הָהֵם׃ וּפִינְחָס בֶּן־אֶלְעָזָר בֶּן־אַהֲרֹן עֹמֵד ׀
ministering Aaron son-of Eleazar son-of and-Phinehas (28) the-those

לְפָנָיו בַּיָּמִים הָהֵם לֵאמֹר הַאוֹסִף עוֹד לָצֵאת
to-go-up again shall-I-repeat? to-ask the-those in-the-days before-him

לַמִּלְחָמָה עִם־בְּנֵי־בִנְיָמִן אָחִי אִם־אֶחְדָּל
shall-I-not-go or brother-of-me Benjamin sons-of with to-the-battle

וַיֹּאמֶר יְהוָה עֲלוּ כִּי מָחָר אֶתְּנֶנּוּ בְיָדֶךָ׃
into-hand-of-you I-will-give-him tomorrow for go! Yahweh and-he-responded

וַיָּשֶׂם יִשְׂרָאֵל אֹרְבִים אֶל־הַגִּבְעָה סָבִיב׃
around the-Gibeah against ones-ambushing Israel then-he-set (29)

וַיַּעֲלוּ בְנֵי־יִשְׂרָאֵל אֶל־בְּנֵי בִנְיָמִן בַּיּוֹם
on-the-day Benjamin sons-of against Israel sons-of and-they-went-up (30)

הַשְּׁלִישִׁי וַיַּעַרְכוּ אֶל־הַגִּבְעָה כְּפַעַם בְּפָעַם׃
on-time as-time the-Gibeah against and-they-took-positions the-third

וַיֵּצְאוּ בְנֵי־בִנְיָמִן לִקְרַאת הָעָם הָנְתְּקוּ
they-were-drawn-away the-people to-meet Benjamin sons-of and-they-came-out (31)

מִן־הָעִיר וַיָּחֵלּוּ לְהַכּוֹת מֵהָעָם חֲלָלִים כְּפַעַם ׀
as-time casualties on-the-people to-inflict and-they-began the-city from

בְּפַעַם בַּמְסִלּוֹת אֲשֶׁר אַחַת עֹלָה בֵית־אֵל וְאַחַת גִּבְעָתָה
to-Gibeah and-one-of El Beth leading one-of that on-the-roads on-time

בַּשָּׂדֶה כִּשְׁלֹשִׁים אִישׁ בְּיִשְׂרָאֵל׃ וַיֹּאמְרוּ בְּנֵי בִנְיָמִן
Benjamin sons-of and-they-said (32) from-Israel man about-thirty in-the-field

נִגָּפִים הֵם לְפָנֵינוּ כְּבָרִאשֹׁנָה וּבְנֵי יִשְׂרָאֵל
Israel and-sons-of as-at-the-first before-us they ones-being-defeated

אָמְרוּ נָנוּסָה וּנְתַקְּנֻהוּ מִן־הָעִיר אֶל־הַמְסִלּוֹת׃
the-roads to the-city from and-let-us-draw-away-him let-us-retreat they-said

וְכֹל ׀ אִישׁ יִשְׂרָאֵל קָמוּ מִמְּקוֹמוֹ וַיַּעַרְכוּ
and-they-positioned from-place-of-him they-moved Israel man-of and-every-of (33)

בְּבַעַל תָּמָר וְאֹרֵב יִשְׂרָאֵל מֵגִיחַ מִמְּקֹמוֹ
from-place-of-him charging Israel and-one-ambushing-of Tamar at-Baal

there they sat weeping before the LORD. They fasted that day until evening and presented burnt offerings and fellowship offerings[k] to the LORD.
[27]And the Israelites inquired of the LORD. (In those days the ark of the covenant of God was there,
[28]with Phinehas son of Eleazar, the son of Aaron, ministering before it.) They asked, "Shall we go up again to battle with Benjamin our brother, or not?"

The LORD responded, "Go, for tomorrow I will give them into your hands."

[29]Then Israel set an ambush around Gibeah.
[30]They went up against the Benjamites on the third day and took up positions against Gibeah as they had done before.
[31]The Benjamites came out to meet them and were drawn away from the city. They began to inflict casualties on the Israelites as before, so that about thirty men fell in the open field and on the roads—the one leading to Bethel and the other to Gibeah.

[32]While the Benjamites were saying, "We are defeating them as before," the Israelites were saying, "Let's retreat and draw them away from the city to the roads."

[33]All the men of Israel moved from their places and took up positions at Baal Tamar, and the Israelite ambush charged out of its place on the

[k]26 Traditionally *peace offerings*

מִמַּעֲרֵה־ גָבַע׃ וַיָּבֹאוּ מִנֶּגֶד לְגִבְעָה עֲשֶׂרֶת
ten-of of-the-Gibeah against-front and-they-went (34) Gibeah *from-plain-of

אֲלָפִים אִישׁ בָּחוּר מִכָּל־ יִשְׂרָאֵל וְהַמִּלְחָמָה כָּבֵדָה
she-was-heavy and-the-fight Israel from-all-of being-chosen man thousands

וְהֵם לֹא יָדְעוּ כִּי־ נֹגַעַת עֲלֵיהֶם הָרָעָה׃
the-disaster to-them being-near that they-realized not and-they

וַיִּגֹּף יְהוָה׀ אֶת־ בִּנְיָמִן לִפְנֵי יִשְׂרָאֵל וַיַּשְׁחִיתוּ
and-they-struck-down Israel before Benjamin *** Yahweh and-he-defeated (35)

בְנֵי יִשְׂרָאֵל בְּבִנְיָמִן בַּיּוֹם הַהוּא עֶשְׂרִים וַחֲמִשָּׁה אֶלֶף
thousand and-five twenty the-that on-the-day from-Benjamin Israel sons-of

וּמֵאָה אִישׁ כָּל־ אֵלֶּה שֹׁלֵף חָרֶב׃ וַיִּרְאוּ בְנֵי־ בִנְיָמִן
Benjamin sons-of then-they-saw (36) sword bearing these all-of man and-hundred

כִּי נִגָּפוּ וַיִּתְּנוּ אִישׁ־ יִשְׂרָאֵל מָקוֹם לְבִנְיָמִן כִּי
for before-Benjamin way Israel man-of now-they-gave they-were-beaten that

בָטְחוּ אֶל־ הָאֹרֵב אֲשֶׁר† שָׂמוּ אֶל־ הַגִּבְעָה׃
the-Gibeah near they-set that the-one-ambushing on they-relied

וְהָאֹרֵב הֵחִישׁוּ וַיִּפְשְׁטוּ אֶל־ הַגִּבְעָה
the-Gibeah into and-they-dashed they-moved-suddenly and-the-one-ambushing (37)

וַיִּמְשֹׁךְ הָאֹרֵב וַיַּךְ אֶת־ כָּל־ הָעִיר
the-city whole-of *** and-he-put the-one-ambushing and-he-spread-out

לְפִי־ חָרֶב׃ וְהַמּוֹעֵד הָיָה לְאִישׁ יִשְׂרָאֵל עִם־
with Israel for-man-of he-was and-the-arrangement (38) sword to-edge-of

הָאֹרֵב הֶרֶב לְהַעֲלוֹתָם מַשְׂאַת הֶעָשָׁן מִן־
from the-smoke cloud-of to-send-up-them make-great! the-one-ambushing

הָעִיר׃ וַיַּהֲפֹךְ אִישׁ־ יִשְׂרָאֵל בַּמִּלְחָמָה וּבִנְיָמִן
now-Benjamin in-the-battle Israel man-of then-he-would-turn (39) the-city

הֵחֵל לְהַכּוֹת חֲלָלִים בְּאִישׁ־ יִשְׂרָאֵל כִּשְׁלֹשִׁים אִישׁ כִּי אָמְרוּ
they-said and man about-thirty Israel on-man-of casualties to-inflict he-began

אַךְ נָגוֹף נִגָּף הוּא לְפָנֵינוּ כַּמִּלְחָמָה הָרִאשֹׁנָה׃
the-first as-the-battle before-us he being-defeated to-be-defeated indeed

וְהַמַּשְׂאֵת הֵחֵלָּה לַעֲלוֹת מִן־ הָעִיר עַמּוּד עָשָׁן
smoke column-of the-city from to-rise she-began but-the-cloud (40)

וַיִּפֶן בִּנְיָמִן אַחֲרָיו וְהִנֵּה עָלָה כְלִיל־ הָעִיר
the-city whole-of he-went-up and-see! behind-him Benjamin and-he-turned

הַשָּׁמָיְמָה׃ וְאִישׁ יִשְׂרָאֵל הָפַךְ וַיִּבָּהֵל אִישׁ
man-of and-he-was-terrified he-turned Israel then-men-of (41) into-the-skies

בִּנְיָמִן כִּי רָאָה כִּי־ נָגְעָה עָלָיו הָרָעָה׃ וַיִּפְנוּ
so-they-fled (42) the-disaster upon-him she-came that he-realized for Benjamin

west[l] of Gibeah. [34]Then ten thousand of Israel's finest men made a frontal attack on Gibeah. The fighting was so heavy that the Benjamites did not realize how near disaster was. [35]The LORD defeated Benjamin before Israel, and on that day the Israelites struck down 25,100 Benjamites, all armed with swords. [36]Then the Benjamites saw that they were beaten.

Now the men of Israel had given way before Benjamin, because they relied on the ambush they had set near Gibeah. [37]The men who had been in ambush made a sudden dash into Gibeah, spread out and put the whole city to the sword. [38]The men of Israel had arranged with the ambush that they should send up a great cloud of smoke from the city, [39]and then the men of Israel would turn in the battle.

The Benjamites had begun to inflict casualties on the men of Israel (about thirty), and they said, "We are defeating them as in the first battle." [40]But when the column of smoke began to rise from the city, the Benjamites turned and saw the smoke of the whole city going up into the sky. [41]Then the men of Israel turned on them, and the men of Benjamin were terrified, because they realized that disaster had come upon them. [42]So

l33 Some Septuagint manuscripts and Vulgate; the meaning of the Hebrew for this word is uncertain.

*33 The NIV, with the versions listed above in footnote *1*, reads *beth* for *he* (־רֵב־), *on-west-of*.

†36 Most mss include the accent *mereka* (אֲשֶׁר).

לִפְנֵי אִישׁ יִשְׂרָאֵל אֶל־ דֶּרֶךְ הַמִּדְבָּר וְהַמִּלְחָמָה הִדְבִּיקָתְהוּ

she-pursued-him but-the-battle the-desert direction-of in Israel man-of before

וַאֲשֶׁר מֵהֶעָרִים מַשְׁחִיתִים אוֹתוֹ בְּתוֹכוֹ׃ כִּתְּרוּ

they-surrounded (43) among-him him ones-cutting-down from-the-towns and-whoever

אֶת־ בִּנְיָמִן הִרְדִיפֻהוּ מְנוּחָה הִדְרִיכֻהוּ עַד נֹכַח הַגִּבְעָה

the-Gibeah vicinity-of in they-overran-him *easily they-chased-him Benjamin ***

מִמִּזְרַח־ שָׁמֶשׁ׃ וַיִּפְּלוּ מִבִּנְיָמִן שְׁמֹנָה־ עָשָׂר אֶלֶף אִישׁ

man thousand ten eight from-Benjamin and-they-fell (44) sun toward-rise-of

אֶת־ כָּל־ אֵלֶּה אַנְשֵׁי־ חָיִל׃ וַיִּפְנוּ וַיָּנֻסוּ הַמִּדְבָּרָה

to-the-desert and-they-fled and-they-turned (45) valor men-of these all-of ***

אֶל־ סֶלַע הָרִמּוֹן וַיְעֹלְלֻהוּ בַּמְסִלּוֹת חֲמֵשֶׁת אֲלָפִים

thousands five-of along-the-roads and-they-cut-down-him the-Rimmon Rock-of to

אִישׁ וַיַּדְבִּיקוּ אַחֲרָיו עַד־ גִּדְעֹם וַיַּכּוּ מִמֶּנּוּ

from-him and-they-struck-down Gidom as-far-as after-him and-they-pressed man

אַלְפַּיִם אִישׁ׃ וַיְהִי כָל־ הַנֹּפְלִים מִבִּנְיָמִן

from-Benjamin the-ones-falling all-of and-he-was (46) man two-thousands

עֶשְׂרִים וַחֲמִשָּׁה אֶלֶף אִישׁ שֹׁלֵף חֶרֶב בַּיּוֹם הַהוּא אֶת־ כָּל־

all-of *** the-that on-the-day sword bearing man thousand and-five twenty

אֵלֶּה אַנְשֵׁי־ חָיִל׃ וַיִּפְנוּ וַיָּנֻסוּ הַמִּדְבָּרָה אֶל־

to into-the-desert and-they-fled but-they-turned (47) valor men-of these

סֶלַע הָרִמּוֹן שֵׁשׁ מֵאוֹת אִישׁ וַיֵּשְׁבוּ בְּסֶלַע רִמּוֹן אַרְבָּעָה

four Rimmon at-Rock-of and-they-stayed man hundreds six the-Rimmon Rock-of

חֳדָשִׁים׃ וְאִישׁ יִשְׂרָאֵל שָׁבוּ אֶל־ בְּנֵי בִנְיָמִן

Benjamin sons-of to they-went-back Israel and-man-of (48) months

וַיַּכּוּם לְפִי־ חֶרֶב מֵעִיר מְתֹם עַד־ בְּהֵמָה עַד

even animal including everything from-town sword to-edge-of and-they-put-them

כָּל־ הַנִּמְצָא גַּם כָּל־ הֶעָרִים הַנִּמְצָאוֹת

the-ones-being-found the-towns all-of also the-one-being-found every-of

שִׁלְּחוּ בָּאֵשׁ׃ וְאִישׁ יִשְׂרָאֵל נִשְׁבַּע בַּמִּצְפָּה

at-the-Mizpah he-took-oath Israel and-man-of (21:1) with-fire they-burned

לֵאמֹר אִישׁ מִמֶּנּוּ לֹא־ יִתֵּן בִּתּוֹ לְבִנְיָמִן לְאִשָּׁה׃

as-wife to-Benjamin daughter-of-him he-will-give not of-us one to-say

וַיָּבֹא הָעָם בֵּית־ אֵל וַיֵּשְׁבוּ שָׁם עַד־ הָעֶרֶב

the-evening until there and-they-sat El Beth the-people and-he-went (2)

לִפְנֵי הָאֱלֹהִים וַיִּשְׂאוּ קוֹלָם וַיִּבְכּוּ בְּכִי גָדוֹל׃

great weeping and-they-wept voice-of-them and-they-raised the-God before

וַיֹּאמְרוּ לָמָה יְהוָה אֱלֹהֵי יִשְׂרָאֵל הָיְתָה זֹּאת בְּיִשְׂרָאֵל

to-Israel this she-happened Israel God-of Yahweh why? and-they-cried (3)

they fled before the Israelites
in the direction of the desert,
but they could not escape the
battle. And the men of Israel
who came out of the towns cut
them down there. 43They surrounded the Benjamites,
chased them and easily[m] over-
ran them in the vicinity of
Gibeah on the east. 44Eighteen
thousand Benjamites fell, all of
them valiant fighters. 45As
they turned and fled toward
the desert to the rock of Rimmon, the Israelites cut down
five thousand men along the
roads. They kept pressing after
the Benjamites as far as Gidom
and struck down two thou-
sand more.

46On that day twenty-five
thousand Benjamite swordsmen fell, all of them valiant
fighters. 47But six hundred
men turned and fled into the
desert to the rock of Rimmon,
where they stayed four
months. 48The men of Israel
went back to Benjamin and
put all the towns to the sword,
including the animals and
everything else they found.
All the towns they came across
they set on fire.

*Wives for the Benjamites*

21 The men of Israel had taken an oath at Mizpah: "Not one of us will give his daughter in marriage to a Benjamite."

2The people went to Bethel,[n]
where they sat before God until evening, raising their
voices and weeping bitterly.
3"O LORD, the God of Israel,"
they cried, "why has this happened to Israel? Why should

[m]43 The meaning of the Hebrew for this word is uncertain.
[n]2 Or *to the house of God*

*43 Perhaps a place name, *from-Nubah* or *-Nobah*, as in the Septuagint, Codex B.

לְהִפָּקֵד הַיּוֹם מִיִּשְׂרָאֵל שֵׁבֶט אֶחָד׃ וַיְהִי מִמָּחֳרָת
on-next-day and-he-was (4) one tribe from-Israel the-day to-be-missing

וַיַּשְׁכִּימוּ הָעָם וַיִּבְנוּ־ שָׁם מִזְבֵּחַ וַיַּעֲלוּ
and-they-presented altar there and-they-built the-people that-they-got-up

עֹלוֹת וּשְׁלָמִים׃ וַיֹּאמְרוּ בְּנֵי יִשְׂרָאֵל
Israel sons-of then-they-asked (5) and-fellowship-offerings burnt-offerings

מִי אֲשֶׁר לֹא־ עָלָה בַקָּהָל מִכָּל־ שִׁבְטֵי יִשְׂרָאֵל אֶל־
before Israel tribes-of from-all-of to-the-assembly he-came-up not that who?

יְהוָה כִּי הַשְּׁבוּעָה הַגְּדוֹלָה הָיְתָה לַאֲשֶׁר לֹא־ עָלָה אֶל־
before he-came-up not that-whoever she-was the-solemn the-oath for Yahweh

יְהוָה הַמִּצְפָּה לֵאמֹר מוֹת יוּמָת׃ וַיִּנָּחֲמוּ בְּנֵי
sons-of now-they-grieved (6) he-must-die to-die to-say the-Mizpah Yahweh

יִשְׂרָאֵל אֶל־ בִּנְיָמִן אָחִיו וַיֹּאמְרוּ נִגְדַּע הַיּוֹם שֵׁבֶט
tribe the-day he-is-cut-off and-they-said brother-of-him Benjamin for Israel

אֶחָד מִיִּשְׂרָאֵל׃ מַה־ נַּעֲשֶׂה לָהֶם לַנּוֹתָרִים
for-the-ones-being-left for-them can-we-provide how? (7) from-Israel one

לְנָשִׁים וַאֲנַחְנוּ נִשְׁבַּעְנוּ בַיהוָה לְבִלְתִּי תֵת־ לָהֶם
to-them to-give not by-Yahweh we-took-oath since-we as-wives

מִבְּנוֹתֵינוּ לְנָשִׁים׃ וַיֹּאמְרוּ מִי אֶחָד מִשִּׁבְטֵי
of-tribes-of one which? then-they-asked (8) as-wives from-daughters-of-us

יִשְׂרָאֵל אֲשֶׁר לֹא־ עָלָה אֶל־ יְהוָה הַמִּצְפָּה וְהִנֵּה לֹא בָא־
he-came not and-see! the-Mizpah Yahweh before he-came-up not that Israel

אִישׁ אֶל־ הַמַּחֲנֶה מִיָּבֵישׁ גִּלְעָד אֶל־ הַקָּהָל׃ וַיִּתְפָּקֵד
for-they-counted (9) the-assembly for Gilead from-Jabesh the-camp to man

הָעָם וְהִנֵּה אֵין־ שָׁם אִישׁ מִיּוֹשְׁבֵי יָבֵשׁ גִּלְעָד׃
Gilead Jabesh from-ones-living-of person there not and-see! the-people

וַיִּשְׁלְחוּ־ שָׁם הָעֵדָה שְׁנֵים־עָשָׂר אֶלֶף אִישׁ מִבְּנֵי הֶחָיִל
the-fight from-men-of man thousand ten two the-assembly there so-they-sent (10)

וַיְצַוּוּ אוֹתָם לֵאמֹר לְכוּ וְהִכִּיתֶם אֶת־ יוֹשְׁבֵי יָבֵשׁ
Jabesh ones-living-of *** and-you-put go! to-say them and-they-instructed

גִּלְעָד לְפִי־ חֶרֶב וְהַנָּשִׁים וְהַטָּף׃ וְזֶה הַדָּבָר
the-thing and-this (11) and-the-child and-the-women sword to-edge-of Gilead

אֲשֶׁר תַּעֲשׂוּ כָּל־ זָכָר וְכָל־ אִשָּׁה יֹדַעַת מִשְׁכַּב־ זָכָר
male relation-of experiencing woman and-every-of male every-of you-do that

תַּחֲרִימוּ׃ וַיִּמְצְאוּ מִיּוֹשְׁבֵי ׀ יָבֵישׁ גִּלְעָד אַרְבַּע מֵאוֹת
hundreds four Gilead Jabesh among-ones-living-of and-they-found (12) you-kill

נַעֲרָה בְתוּלָה אֲשֶׁר לֹא־ יָדְעָה אִישׁ לְמִשְׁכַּב זָכָר
male for-relation-of man she-experienced not who virgin young-woman

one tribe be missing from Israel today?"

4Early the next day the people built an altar and presented burnt offerings and fellowship offerings.[o]

5Then the Israelites asked, "Who from all the tribes of Israel has failed to assemble before the LORD?" For they had taken a solemn oath that anyone who failed to assemble before the LORD at Mizpah should certainly be put to death.

6Now the Israelites grieved for their brothers, the Benjamites. "Today one tribe is cut off from Israel," they said. 7"How can we provide wives for those who are left, since we have taken an oath by the LORD not to give them any of our daughters in marriage?" 8Then they asked, "Which one of the tribes of Israel failed to assemble before the LORD at Mizpah?" They discovered that no one from Jabesh Gilead had come to the camp for the assembly. 9For when they counted the people, they found that none of the people of Jabesh Gilead were there.

10So the assembly sent twelve thousand fighting men with instructions to go to Jabesh Gilead and put to the sword those living there, including the women and children. 11"This is what you are to do," they said. "Kill every male and every woman who is not a virgin." 12They found among the people living in Jabesh Gilead four hundred young women who had never slept with a man, and they

[o]4 Traditionally *peace offerings*

וַיָּבִיאוּ אוֹתָם אֶל־הַמַּחֲנֶה שִׁלֹה אֲשֶׁר בְּאֶרֶץ כְּנָעַן׃
Canaan in-land-of that Shiloh the-camp to them and-they-took

וַיִּשְׁלְחוּ כָּל־הָעֵדָה וַיְדַבְּרוּ אֶל־בְּנֵי בִנְיָמִן
Benjamin sons-of to and-they-spoke the-assembly whole-of then-they-sent (13)

אֲשֶׁר בְּסֶלַע רִמּוֹן וַיִּקְרְאוּ לָהֶם שָׁלוֹם׃ וַיָּשָׁב
so-he-returned (14) peace to-them and-they-offered Rimmon at-Rock-of who

בִּנְיָמִן בָּעֵת הַהִיא וַיִּתְּנוּ לָהֶם הַנָּשִׁים אֲשֶׁר
whom the-women to-them and-they-gave the-that at-the-time Benjamin

חִיּוּ מִנְּשֵׁי יָבֵשׁ גִּלְעָד וְלֹא־מָצְאוּ לָהֶם כֵּן׃
enough for-them they-found but-not Gilead Jabesh from-women-of they-spared

וְהָעָם נִחָם לְבִנְיָמִן כִּי־עָשָׂה יְהוָה פֶּרֶץ
gap Yahweh he-made because for-Benjamin he-grieved and-the-people (15)

בְּשִׁבְטֵי יִשְׂרָאֵל׃ וַיֹּאמְרוּ זִקְנֵי הָעֵדָה מַה־
how? the-assembly elders-of and-they-said (16) Israel in-tribes-of

נַּעֲשֶׂה לַנּוֹתָרִים לְנָשִׁים כִּי־נִשְׁמְדָה
she-is-destroyed since as-wives for-the-ones-being-left shall-we-provide

מִבִּנְיָמִן אִשָּׁה׃ וַיֹּאמְרוּ יְרֻשַּׁת פְּלֵיטָה לְבִנְיָמִן וְלֹא־
so-not for-Benjmain survivor heir-of and-they-said (17) woman from-Benjamin

יִמָּחֶה שֵׁבֶט מִיִּשְׂרָאֵל׃ וַאֲנַחְנוּ לֹא נוּכַל לָתֵת־
to-give we-can not and-we (18) from-Israel tribe he-will-be-wiped-out

לָהֶם נָשִׁים מִבְּנוֹתֵינוּ כִּי־נִשְׁבְּעוּ בְנֵי־יִשְׂרָאֵל
Israel sons-of they-took-oath since from-daughters-of-us wives to-them

לֵאמֹר אָרוּר נֹתֵן אִשָּׁה לְבִנְיָמִן׃ וַיֹּאמְרוּ הִנֵּה
look! but-they-said (19) to-Benjamin wife one-giving being-cursed to-say

חַג־יְהוָה בְּשִׁלוֹ מִיָּמִים ׀ יָמִימָה אֲשֶׁר מִצְּפוֹנָה לְבֵית־אֵל
El of-Beth to-north that on-days from-days in-Shiloh Yahweh festival-of

מִזְרְחָה הַשֶּׁמֶשׁ לִמְסִלָּה הָעֹלָה מִבֵּית־אֵל שְׁכֶמָה וּמִנֶּגֶב
and-to-south to-Shechem El from-Beth the-one-going of-road the-sun rise-of

לִלְבוֹנָה׃ וַיְצַוּ° אֶת־בְּנֵי בִנְיָמִן לֵאמֹר לְכוּ
go! to-say Benjamin sons-of *** so-they-instructed (20) of-Lebonah

וַאֲרַבְתֶּם בַּכְּרָמִים׃ וּרְאִיתֶם וְהִנֵּה אִם־יֵצְאוּ
they-come-out when and-see! and-you-watch (21) in-the-vineyards and-you-hide

בְנוֹת־שִׁילוֹ לָחוּל בַּמְּחֹלוֹת וִיצָאתֶם מִן־הַכְּרָמִים
the-vineyards from then-you-rush-out in-the-dances to-join Shiloh girls-of

וַחֲטַפְתֶּם לָכֶם אִישׁ אִשְׁתּוֹ מִבְּנוֹת שִׁילוֹ וַהֲלַכְתֶּם
and-you-go Shiloh from-girls-of wife-of-him each for-you and-you-seize

אֶרֶץ בִּנְיָמִן׃ וְהָיָה כִּי־יָבֹאוּ אֲבוֹתָם אוֹ
or fathers-of-them they-come when and-he-will-be (22) Benjamin land-of

took them to the camp at Shiloh in Canaan.

[13]Then the assembly sent an offer of peace to the Benjamites at the rock of Rimmon. [14]So the Benjamites returned at that time and were given the women of Jabesh Gilead who had been spared. But there were not enough for all of them.

[15]The people grieved for Benjamin, because the LORD had made a gap in the tribes of Israel. [16]And the elders of the assembly said, "With the women of Benjamin destroyed, how shall we provide wives for the men who are left? [17]The Benjamite survivors must have heirs," they said, "so that a tribe of Israel will not be wiped out. [18]We can't give them our daughters as wives, since we Israelites have taken this oath: 'Cursed be anyone who gives a wife to a Benjamite.' [19]But look, there is the annual festival of the LORD in Shiloh, to the north of Bethel, and east of the road that goes from Bethel to Shechem, and to the south of Lebonah."

[20]So they instructed the Benjamites, saying, "Go and hide in the vineyards [21]and watch. When the girls of Shiloh come out to join in the dancing, then rush from the vineyards and each of you seize a wife from the girls of Shiloh and go to the land of Benjamin. [22]When their fathers or brothers complain to us, we will say

°20 ק ויצוו

אֲחֵיהֶם לָרֹוב ׀ אֵלֵינוּ וְאָמַרְנוּ אֲלֵיהֶם חָנּוּנוּ
do-kindness-to-us! to-them then-we-will-say to-us to-complain brothers-of-them

אוֹתָם כִּי לֹא לָקַחְנוּ אִישׁ אִשְׁתּוֹ בַּמִּלְחָמָה כִּי לֹא אַתֶּם
you not since during-the-war wife-of-him man we-got not because them

נְתַתֶּם לָהֶם כָּעֵת תֶּאְשָׁמוּ׃ וַיַּעֲשׂוּ־
so-they-did (23) you-would-have-been-guilty at-the-time to-them you-gave

כֵן בְּנֵי בִנְיָמִן וַיִּשְׂאוּ נָשִׁים לְמִסְפָּרָם מִן־
from by-number-of-them girls and-they-carried-off Benjamin sons-of that

הַמְחֹלְלוֹת אֲשֶׁר גָּזָלוּ וַיֵּלְכוּ וַיָּשׁוּבוּ אֶל־
to and-they-returned then-they-went they-caught whom the-ones-dancing

נַחֲלָתָם וַיִּבְנוּ אֶת־ הֶעָרִים וַיֵּשְׁבוּ בָּהֶם׃
in-them and-they-settled the-towns *** and-they-rebuilt inheritance-of-them

וַיִּתְהַלְּכוּ מִשָּׁם בְּנֵי־ יִשְׂרָאֵל בָּעֵת הַהִיא אִישׁ
each the-that at-the-time Israel sons-of from-there and-they-left (24)

לְשִׁבְטוֹ וּלְמִשְׁפַּחְתּוֹ וַיֵּצְאוּ מִשָּׁם אִישׁ
each from-there and-they-went and-to-clan-of-him to-tribe-of-him

לְנַחֲלָתוֹ׃ בַּיָּמִים הָהֵם אֵין מֶלֶךְ בְּיִשְׂרָאֵל
in-Israel king there-was-no the-those in-the-days (25) to-inheritance-of-him

אִישׁ הַיָּשָׁר בְּעֵינָיו יַעֲשֶׂה׃
he-did in-eyes-of-him the-thing-fit everyone

to them, 'Do us a kindness by helping them, because we did not get wives for them during the war, and you are innocent, since you did not give your daughters to them.' "

23 So that is what the Benjamites did. While the girls were dancing, each man caught one and carried her off to be his wife. Then they returned to their inheritance and rebuilt the towns and settled in them.

24 At that time the Israelites left that place and went home to their tribes and clans, each to his own inheritance.

25 In those days Israel had no king; everyone did as he saw fit.

°22 ק לריב

וַיְהִי בִּימֵי שְׁפֹט הַשֹּׁפְטִים וַיְהִי רָעָב
famine that-he-was the-ones-judging to-judge in-days-of and-he-was (1:1)

בָּאָרֶץ וַיֵּלֶךְ אִישׁ מִבֵּית לֶחֶם יְהוּדָה לָגוּר בִּשְׂדֵי
in-regions-of to-live Judah Lehem-of from-Beth man and-he-went in-the-land

מוֹאָב הוּא וְאִשְׁתּוֹ וּשְׁנֵי בָנָיו׃ וְשֵׁם הָאִישׁ
the-man now-name-of (2) sons-of-him and-two-of and-wife-of-him he Moab

אֱלִימֶלֶךְ וְשֵׁם אִשְׁתּוֹ נָעֳמִי וְשֵׁם שְׁנֵי־בָנָיו ׀
sons-of-him two-of and-name-of Naomi wife-of-him and-name-of Elimelech

מַחְלוֹן וְכִלְיוֹן אֶפְרָתִים מִבֵּית לֶחֶם יְהוּדָה וַיָּבֹאוּ
and-they-went Judah Lehem-of from-Beth Ephrathites and-Kilion Mahlon

שְׂדֵי־מוֹאָב וַיִּהְיוּ־שָׁם׃ וַיָּמָת אֱלִימֶלֶךְ אִישׁ
husband-of Elimelech now-he-died (3) there and-they-lived Moab regions-of

נָעֳמִי וַתִּשָּׁאֵר הִיא וּשְׁנֵי בָנֶיהָ׃ וַיִּשְׂאוּ
and-they-married (4) sons-of-her and-two-of she and-she-was-left Naomi

לָהֶם נָשִׁים מֹאֲבִיּוֹת שֵׁם הָאַחַת עָרְפָּה וְשֵׁם הַשֵּׁנִית רוּת
Ruth the-other and-name-of Orpah the-one name-of Moabites women for-them

וַיֵּשְׁבוּ שָׁם כְּעֶשֶׂר שָׁנִים׃ וַיָּמוּתוּ גַם־שְׁנֵיהֶם
both-of-them also and-they-died (5) years about-ten there and-they-lived

מַחְלוֹן וְכִלְיוֹן וַתִּשָּׁאֵר הָאִשָּׁה מִשְּׁנֵי יְלָדֶיהָ
sons-of-her without-two-of the-woman and-she-was-left and-Kilion Mahlon

וּמֵאִישָׁהּ׃ וַתָּקָם הִיא וְכַלֹּתֶיהָ
and-daughters-in-law-of-her she and-she-prepared (6) and-without-husband-of-her

וַתָּשָׁב מִשְּׂדֵי מוֹאָב כִּי שָׁמְעָה בִּשְׂדֵה מוֹאָב כִּי־
that Moab in-region-of she-heard when Moab from-regions-of and-she-returned

פָקַד יְהוָה אֶת־עַמּוֹ לָתֵת לָהֶם לָחֶם׃ וַתֵּצֵא
and-she-left (7) food for-them to-provide people-of-him *** Yahweh he-aided

מִן־הַמָּקוֹם אֲשֶׁר הָיְתָה־שָׁמָּה וּשְׁתֵּי כַלֹּתֶיהָ
daughters-in-law-of-her and-two-of at-there she-lived where the-place from

עִמָּהּ וַתֵּלַכְנָה בַדֶּרֶךְ לָשׁוּב אֶל־אֶרֶץ יְהוּדָה׃
Judah land-of to to-go-back on-the-road and-they-set-out with-her

וַתֹּאמֶר נָעֳמִי לִשְׁתֵּי כַלֹּתֶיהָ לֵכְנָה שֹּׁבְנָה אִשָּׁה
each go-back! go! daughters-in-law-of-her to-two-of Naomi then-she-said (8)

לְבֵית אִמָּהּ יַעֲשֶׂה יְהוָה עִמָּכֶם חֶסֶד כַּאֲשֶׁר
just-as kindness to-you Yahweh may-he-show mother-of-her to-home-of

עֲשִׂיתֶם עִם־הַמֵּתִים וְעִמָּדִי׃ יִתֵּן יְהוָה לָכֶם
to-you Yahweh may-he-grant (9) and-to-me the-dead-ones to you-showed

וּמְצֶאןָ מְנוּחָה אִשָּׁה בֵּית אִישָׁהּ וַתִּשַּׁק לָהֶן
on-them then-she-kissed husband-of-her home-of each rest and-find!

*Naomi and Ruth*

1 In the days when the judges ruled,[a] there was a
famine in the land, and a man
from Bethlehem in Judah, together with his wife and two
sons, went to live for a while
in the country of Moab.
2 The
man's name was Elimelech,
his wife's name Naomi, and
the names of his two sons
were Mahlon and Kilion.
They were Ephrathites from
Bethlehem, Judah. And they
went to Moab and lived there.
3 Now Elimelech, Naomi's
husband, died, and she was
left with her two sons.
4 They
married Moabite women, one
named Orpah and the other
Ruth. After they had lived
there about ten years,
5 both
Mahlon and Kilion also died,
and Naomi was left without
her two sons and her husband.
6 When she heard in Moab
that the LORD had come to the
aid of his people by providing
food for them, Naomi and her
daughters-in-law prepared to
return home from there.
7 With
her two daughters-in-law she
left the place where she had
been living and set out on the
road that would take them
back to the land of Judah.
8 Then Naomi said to her two
daughters-in-law, "Go back,
each of you, to your mother's
home. May the LORD show
kindness to you, as you have
shown to your dead and to me.
9 May the LORD grant that each
of you will find rest in the
home of another husband."
Then she kissed them and

[a] 1 Traditionally *judged*

°8 יעש ק

וַתִּשֶּׂאנָה קוֹלָן וַתִּבְכֶּינָה׃ וַתֹּאמַרְנָה־ לָּהּ כִּי־
indeed to-her and-they-said (10) and-they-wept voice-of-them and-they-raised

אִתָּךְ נָשׁוּב לְעַמֵּךְ׃ וַתֹּאמֶר נָעֳמִי שֹׁבְנָה
return! Naomi but-she-said (11) to-people-of-you we-will-go-back with-you

בְנֹתַי לָמָּה תֵלַכְנָה עִמִּי הַעוֹד־ לִי בָנִים
sons to-me any-more? with-me would-you-come why? daughters-of-me

בְּמֵעַי וְהָיוּ לָכֶם לַאֲנָשִׁים׃ שֹׁבְנָה
return! (12) as-husbands for-you that-they-could-become in-insides-of-me

בְנֹתַי לֵכְןָ כִּי זָקַנְתִּי מִהְיוֹת לְאִישׁ כִּי אָמַרְתִּי
I-thought if to-husband than-to-be I-am-too-old for go! daughters-of-me

יֶשׁ־ לִי תִקְוָה גַּם הָיִיתִי הַלַּיְלָה לְאִישׁ וְגַם יָלַדְתִּי בָנִים׃
sons I-bore and-then to-husband the-night I-was if hope for-me there-was

הֲלָהֵן ׀ תְּשַׂבֵּרְנָה עַד אֲשֶׁר יִגְדָּלוּ הֲלָהֵן תֵּעָגֵנָה
would-you-remain for-them? they-grew-up when until would-you-wait for-them? (13)

לְבִלְתִּי הֱיוֹת לְאִישׁ אַל בְּנֹתַי כִּי־ מַר־ לִי מְאֹד מִכֶּם
than-you more for-me bitter for daughters-of-me no to-husband to-become not

כִּי־ יָצְאָה בִי יַד־ יְהוָה׃ וַתִּשֶּׂנָה קוֹלָן
voice-of-them and-they-raised (14) Yahweh hand-of against-me she-went-out for

וַתִּבְכֶּינָה עוֹד וַתִּשַּׁק עָרְפָּה לַחֲמוֹתָהּ וְרוּת
but-Ruth on-mother-in-law-of-her Orpah then-she-kissed again and-they-wept

דָּבְקָה בָּהּ׃ וַתֹּאמֶר הִנֵּה שָׁבָה יְבִמְתֵּךְ
sister-in-law-of-you she-goes-back look! and-she-said (15) to-her she-clung

אֶל־ עַמָּהּ וְאֶל־ אֱלֹהֶיהָ שׁוּבִי אַחֲרֵי יְבִמְתֵּךְ׃
sister-in-law-of-you with go-back! gods-of-her and-to people-of-her to

וַתֹּאמֶר רוּת אַל־ תִּפְגְּעִי־ בִי לְעָזְבֵךְ לָשׁוּב
to-turn-back to-leave-you to-me you-urge not Ruth but-she-replied (16)

מֵאַחֲרָיִךְ כִּי אֶל־ אֲשֶׁר תֵּלְכִי אֵלֵךְ וּבַאֲשֶׁר תָּלִינִי אָלִין
I-will-stay you-stay and-at-where I-will-go you-go where to for from-after-you

עַמֵּךְ עַמִּי וֵאלֹהַיִךְ אֱלֹהָי׃ בַּאֲשֶׁר תָּמוּתִי
you-die at-where (17) God-of-me and-God-of-you people-of-me people-of-you

אָמוּת וְשָׁם אֶקָּבֵר כֹּה יַעֲשֶׂה יְהוָה לִי וְכֹה
and-so with-me Yahweh may-he-deal so I-will-be-buried and-there I-will-die

יֹסִיף כִּי הַמָּוֶת יַפְרִיד בֵּינִי וּבֵינֵךְ׃
and-between-you between-me he-separates the-death unless may-he-be-severe

וַתֵּרֶא כִּי־ מִתְאַמֶּצֶת הִיא לָלֶכֶת אִתָּהּ
with-her to-go she being-determined that when-she-realized (18)

וַתֶּחְדַּל לְדַבֵּר אֵלֶיהָ׃ וַתֵּלַכְנָה שְׁתֵּיהֶם עַד־
until two-of-them so-they-went-on (19) to-her to-urge then-she-stopped

they wept aloud [10]and said to
her, "We will go back with
you to your people."
[11]But Naomi said, "Return
home, my daughters. Why
would you come with me? Am
I going to have any more sons,
who could become your husbands? [12]Return home, my
daughters; I am too old to have
another husband. Even if I
thought there was still hope
for me—even if I had a husband tonight and then gave
birth to sons— [13]would you
wait until they grew up?
Would you remain unmarried
for them? No, my daughters. It
is more bitter for me than for
you, because the LORD's hand
has gone out against me!"
[14]At this they wept again.
Then Orpah kissed her
mother-in-law good-by, but
Ruth clung to her.
[15]"Look," said Naomi, "your
sister-in-law is going back to
her people and her gods. Go
back with her."
[16]But Ruth replied, "Don't
urge me to leave you or to turn
back from you. Where you go
I will go, and where you stay I
will stay. Your people will be
my people and your God my
God. [17]Where you die I will
die, and there I will be buried.
May the LORD deal with me, be
it ever so severely, if anything
but death separates you and
me." [18]When Naomi realized
that Ruth was determined to
go with her, she stopped urging her.
[19]So the two women went on

| | | | | | | |
|---|---|---|---|---|---|---|
| לֶחֶם | בֵּית | כְּבֹאָנָה | וַיְהִי | לָחֶם | בֵּית | בֹּאָנָה |
| Lehem | Beth | when-to-arrive-them | and-he-was | Lehem | Beth | to-come-them |

| | | | | |
|---|---|---|---|---|
| וַתֹּאמַרְנָה | עֲלֵיהֶן | הָעִיר | כָּל־ | וַתֵּהֹם |
| and-they-exclaimed | because-of-them | the-town | whole-of | then-she-was-stirred |

| | | | | | | | | | | |
|---|---|---|---|---|---|---|---|---|---|---|
| לִי | קְרֶאןָ | נָעֳמִי | לִי | תִּקְרֶאנָה | אַל־ | אֲלֵיהֶן | וַתֹּאמֶר | | נָעֳמִי׃ | הֲזֹאת |
| to-me | call! | Naomi | to-me | you-call | not | to-them | and-she-told | (20) | Naomi | this? |

| | | | | | | | | | |
|---|---|---|---|---|---|---|---|---|---|
| הָלַכְתִּי | מְלֵאָה | אֲנִי | | מְאֹד׃ | לִי | שַׁדַּי | הֵמַר | כִּי־ | מָרָא |
| I-went-away | full | I | (21) | very | for-me | Almighty | he-made-bitter | because | Mara |

| | | | | | | | |
|---|---|---|---|---|---|---|---|
| וַיהוָה | נָעֳמִי | לִי | תִקְרֶאנָה | לָמָּה | יְהוָה | הֱשִׁיבַנִי | וְרֵיקָם |
| now-Yahweh | Naomi | to-me | you-call | why? | Yahweh | he-brought-back-me | but-empty |

| | | | | |
|---|---|---|---|---|
| לִי׃ | הֵרַע | וְשַׁדַּי | בִי | עָנָה |
| upon-me | he-brought-misfortune | and-Almighty | to-me | he-afflicted |

| | | | | | |
|---|---|---|---|---|---|
| כַלָּתָהּ | הַמּוֹאֲבִיָּה | וְרוּת | נָעֳמִי | וַתָּשָׁב | |
| daughter-in-law-of-her | the-Moabitess | and-Ruth | Naomi | so-she-returned | (22) |

| | | | | | | |
|---|---|---|---|---|---|---|
| בֵּית | בָּאוּ | וְהֵמָּה | מוֹאָב | מִשְּׂדֵי | הַשָּׁבָה | עִמָּהּ |
| Beth | they-arrived | and-they | Moab | from-regions-of | who-she-returned | with-her |

| | | | | | | |
|---|---|---|---|---|---|---|
| מֹידַע° | וּלְנָעֳמִי | | שְׂעֹרִים׃ | קְצִיר | בִּתְחִלַּת | לֶחֶם |
| relative | now-to-Naomi | (2:1) | barleys | harvest-of | at-beginning-of | Lehem |

| | | | | | | |
|---|---|---|---|---|---|---|
| וּשְׁמוֹ | אֱלִימֶלֶךְ | מִמִּשְׁפַּחַת | חַיִל | גִּבּוֹר | אִישׁ | לְאִישָׁהּ |
| and-name-of-him | Elimelech | from-clan-of | standing | great-of | man | of-husband-of-her |

| | | | | | | | | | |
|---|---|---|---|---|---|---|---|---|---|
| הַשָּׂדֶה | נָּא | אֵלְכָה־ | נָעֳמִי | אֶל־ | הַמּוֹאֲבִיָּה | רוּת | וַתֹּאמֶר | | בֹעַז׃ |
| the-field | now! | let-me-go | Naomi | to | the-Moabitess | Ruth | and-she-said | (2) | Boaz |

| | | | | | | |
|---|---|---|---|---|---|---|
| בְּעֵינָיו | חֵן | אֶמְצָא־ | אֲשֶׁר | אַחַר | בַשִּׁבֳּלִים | וַאֲלַקֳטָה |
| in-eyes-of-him | favor | I-find | whom | behind | among-the-grains | and-let-me-pick-up |

| | | | | | | |
|---|---|---|---|---|---|---|
| וַתָּבוֹא | וַתֵּלֶךְ | | בִתִּי׃ | לְכִי | לָהּ | וַתֹּאמֶר |
| and-she-went | so-she-left | (3) | daughter-of-me | go! | to-her | and-she-said |

| | | | | |
|---|---|---|---|---|
| וַיִּקֶר | הַקֹּצְרִים | אַחֲרֵי | בַּשָּׂדֶה | וַתְּלַקֵּט |
| and-he-happened | the-ones-harvesting | behind | in-the-field | and-she-gleaned |

| | | | | | | |
|---|---|---|---|---|---|---|
| אֱלִימֶלֶךְ׃ | מִמִּשְׁפַּחַת | אֲשֶׁר | לְבֹעַז | הַשָּׂדֶה | חֶלְקַת | מִקְרֶהָ |
| Elimelech | from-clan-of | who | to-Boaz | the-field | section-of | happening-of-her |

| | | | | | | |
|---|---|---|---|---|---|---|
| וַיֹּאמֶר | לָחֶם | מִבֵּית | בָּא | בֹעַז | וְהִנֵּה־ | |
| and-he-greeted | Lehem | from-Beth | arriving | Boaz | then-see! | (4) |

| | | | | | |
|---|---|---|---|---|---|
| יְבָרֶכְךָ | לוֹ | וַיֹּאמְרוּ | עִמָּכֶם | יְהוָה | לַקּוֹצְרִים |
| may-he-bless-you | to-him | and-they-called | with-you | Yahweh | to-the-ones-harvesting |

| | | | | | | |
|---|---|---|---|---|---|---|
| עַל־ | הַנִּצָּב | לְנַעֲרוֹ | בֹּעַז | וַיֹּאמֶר | | יְהוָה׃ |
| over | the-one-being-foreman | to-servant-of-him | Boaz | and-he-asked | (5) | Yahweh |

| | | | | | | |
|---|---|---|---|---|---|---|
| הַנַּעַר | וַיַּעַן | | הַזֹּאת׃ | הַנַּעֲרָה | לְמִי | הַקּוֹצְרִים |
| the-servant | and-he-replied | (6) | the-that | the-woman | to-whom? | the-ones-harvesting |

until they came to Bethlehem.
When they arrived in Bethlehem, the whole town was
stirred because of them, and
the women exclaimed, "Can
this be Naomi?"
20"Don't call me Naomi,[b]"
she told them. "Call me Mara,[c]
because the Almighty[d] has
made my life very bitter. 21I
went away full, but the LORD
has brought me back empty.
Why call me Naomi? The LORD
has afflicted[e] me; the Almighty has brought misfortune upon me."
22So Naomi returned from
Moab accompanied by Ruth
the Moabitess, her daughter-
in-law, arriving in Bethlehem
as the barley harvest was beginning.

*Ruth Meets Boaz*

2 Now Naomi had a relative
on her husband's side,
from the clan of Elimelech, a
man of standing, whose name
was Boaz.
2And Ruth the Moabitess
said to Naomi, "Let me go to
the fields and pick up the left-
over grain behind anyone in
whose eyes I find favor."
Naomi said to her, "Go
ahead, my daughter." 3So she
went out and began to glean
in the fields behind the harvesters. As it turned out, she
found herself working in a
field belonging to Boaz, who
was from the clan of Elimelech.
4Just then Boaz arrived from
Bethlehem and greeted the
harvesters, "The LORD be with
you!"
"The LORD bless you!" they
called back.
5Boaz asked the foreman of
his harvesters, "Whose young
woman is that?"
6The foreman replied, "She

[b]20 *Naomi* means *pleasant;* also in verse 21.
[c]20 *Mara* means *bitter.*
[d]20 Hebrew *Shaddai;* also in verse 21
[e]21 Or *has testified against*

°1 ק מודע

הַנִּצָּב עַל־ הַקּוֹצְרִים וַיֹּאמַר נַעֲרָה
young-woman and-he-said the-ones-harvesting over the-one-being-foreman

מוֹאֲבִיָּה הִיא הַשָּׁבָה עִם־ נָעֳמִי מִשְּׂדֵה מוֹאָב׃ וַתֹּאמֶר
and-she-said (7) Moab from-region-of Naomi with who-she-came-back she Moabitess

אֲלַקֳטָה־ נָּא וְאָסַפְתִּי בָעֳמָרִים אַחֲרֵי הַקּוֹצְרִים
the-ones-harvesting behind among-the-sheaves and-let-me-gather now! let-me-glean

וַתָּבוֹא וַתַּעֲמוֹד מֵאָז הַבֹּקֶר וְעַד־ עַתָּה זֶה שִׁבְתָּהּ
to-rest-her except now even-till the-morning from-then and-she-worked so-she-went

הַבַּיִת מְעָט׃ וַיֹּאמֶר בֹּעַז אֶל־ רוּת הֲלוֹא שָׁמַעַתְּ בִּתִּי אַל־
not daughter-of-me you-heard not? Ruth to Boaz so-he-said (8) short the-shelter

תֵּלְכִי לִלְקֹט בְּשָׂדֶה אַחֵר וְגַם לֹא תַעֲבוּרִי מִזֶּה וְכֹה
but-here from-here you-go-away not and-also another in-field to-glean you-go

תִדְבָּקִין עִם־ נַעֲרֹתָי׃ עֵינַיִךְ בַּשָּׂדֶה אֲשֶׁר־
where in-the-field eyes-of-you (9) servant-girls-of-me with you-stay

יִקְצֹרוּן וְהָלַכְתְּ אַחֲרֵיהֶן הֲלוֹא צִוִּיתִי אֶת־הַנְּעָרִים לְבִלְתִּי
not the-men *** I-told not? after-them and-you-follow they-harvest

נָגְעֵךְ וְצָמִת וְהָלַכְתְּ אֶל־ הַכֵּלִים וְשָׁתִית
and-you-get-drink the-jars to then-you-go when-you-are-thirsty to-touch-you

מֵאֲשֶׁר יִשְׁאֲבוּן הַנְּעָרִים׃ וַתִּפֹּל עַל־ פָּנֶיהָ וַתִּשְׁתַּחוּ
and-she-bowed faces-of-her to and-she-fell (10) the-men they-filled from-what

אָרְצָה וַתֹּאמֶר אֵלָיו מַדּוּעַ מָצָאתִי חֵן בְּעֵינֶיךָ
in-eyes-of-you favor I-found why? to-him and-she-exclaimed to-ground

לְהַכִּירֵנִי וְאָנֹכִי נָכְרִיָּה׃ וַיַּעַן בֹּעַז וַיֹּאמֶר לָהּ
to-her and-he-said Boaz and-he-replied (11) foreigner yet-I to-notice-me

הֻגֵּד הֻגַּד לִי כֹּל אֲשֶׁר־ עָשִׂית אֶת־ חֲמוֹתֵךְ אַחֲרֵי
since mother-in-law-of-you for you-did that all to-me he-was-told to-be-told

מוֹת אִישֵׁךְ וַתַּעַזְבִי אָבִיךְ וְאִמֵּךְ
and-mother-of-you father-of-you that-you-left husband-of-you death-of

וְאֶרֶץ מוֹלַדְתֵּךְ וַתֵּלְכִי אֶל־ עַם אֲשֶׁר לֹא־ יָדַעַתְּ תְּמוֹל
yesterday you-knew not who people to and-you-came home-of-you and-land-of

שִׁלְשׁוֹם׃ יְשַׁלֵּם יְהוָה פָּעֳלֵךְ וּתְהִי מַשְׂכֻּרְתֵּךְ
reward-of-you and-may-she-be deed-of-you Yahweh may-he-repay (12) before

שְׁלֵמָה מֵעִם יְהוָה אֱלֹהֵי יִשְׂרָאֵל אֲשֶׁר־ בָּאת לַחֲסוֹת תַּחַת־
under to-take-refuge you-came whom Israel God-of Yahweh from-with rich

כְּנָפָיו׃ וַתֹּאמֶר אֶמְצָא־ חֵן בְּעֵינֶיךָ אֲדֹנִי
lord-of-me in-eyes-of-you favor may-I-find and-she-said (13) wings-of-him

כִּי נִחַמְתָּנִי וְכִי דִבַּרְתָּ עַל־ לֵב שִׁפְחָתֶךָ וְאָנֹכִי
though-I servant-of-you heart-of to you-spoke and-for you-comforted-me for

is the Moabitess who came back from Moab with Naomi.
7She said, 'Please let me glean and gather among the sheaves behind the harvesters.' She went into the field and has worked steadily from morning till now, except for a short rest in the shelter."

8So Boaz said to Ruth, "My daughter, listen to me. Don't go and glean in another field and don't go away from here. Stay here with my servant girls.
9Watch the field where the men are harvesting, and follow along after the girls. I have told the men not to touch you. And whenever you are thirsty, go and get a drink from the water jars the men have filled."

10At this, she bowed down with her face to the ground. She exclaimed, "Why have I found such favor in your eyes that you notice me—a foreigner?"

11Boaz replied, "I've been told all about what you have done for your mother-in-law since the death of your husband—how you left your father and mother and your homeland and came to live with a people you did not know before.
12May the LORD repay you for what you have done. May you be richly rewarded by the LORD, the God of Israel, under whose wings you have come to take refuge."

13"May I continue to find favor in your eyes, my lord," she said. "You have given me comfort and have spoken kindly to your servant—

לֹא אֶהְיֶה כְּאַחַת שִׁפְחֹתֶיךָ׃ וַיֹּאמֶר לָה בֹעַז
Boaz to-her and-he-said (14) servant-girls-of-you as-one-of I-am not

לְעֵת הָאֹכֶל גֹּשִׁי הֲלֹם וְאָכַלְתְּ מִן־ הַלֶּחֶם וְטָבַלְתְּ
and-you-dip the-bread from and-you-eat here come! the-meal at-time-of

פִּתֵּךְ בַּחֹמֶץ וַתֵּשֶׁב מִצַּד הַקֹּצְרִים
the-ones-harvesting at-side-of when-she-sat in-the-wine-vinegar piece-of-you

וַיִּצְבָּט־ לָהּ קָלִי וַתֹּאכַל וַתִּשְׂבַּע
and-she-was-filled and-she-ate roasted-grain to-her and-he-offered

וַתֹּתַר׃ וַתָּקָם לְלַקֵּט וַיְצַו בֹּעַז אֶת־
*** Boaz then-he-ordered to-glean as-she-got-up (15) and-she-had-left-over

נְעָרָיו לֵאמֹר גַּם בֵּין הָעֳמָרִים תְּלַקֵּט וְלֹא
then-not she-gathers the-sheaves among even-if to-say men-of-him

תַכְלִימוּהָ׃ וְגַם שֹׁל־ תָּשֹׁלּוּ לָהּ מִן־
from for-her you-pull-out to-pull-out but-rather (16) you-embarrass-her

הַצְּבָתִים וַעֲזַבְתֶּם וְלִקְּטָה וְלֹא תִגְעֲרוּ־ בָהּ׃
to-her you-rebuke and-not so-she-can-pick-up and-you-leave the-bundles

וַתְּלַקֵּט בַּשָּׂדֶה עַד־ הָעָרֶב וַתַּחְבֹּט אֵת
*** then-she-threshed the-evening until in-the-field so-she-gleaned (17)

אֲשֶׁר־ לִקֵּטָה וַיְהִי כְּאֵיפָה שְׂעֹרִים׃ וַתִּשָּׂא
and-she-carried (18) barleys about-ephah and-he-was she-gathered what

וַתָּבוֹא הָעִיר וַתֵּרֶא חֲמוֹתָהּ אֵת אֲשֶׁר־ לִקֵּטָה
she-gathered what *** mother-in-law-of-her and-she-saw the-town and-she-took

וַתּוֹצֵא וַתִּתֶּן־ לָהּ אֵת אֲשֶׁר־ הוֹתִרָה
she-had-left-over what *** to-her and-she-gave and-she-brought-out

מִשָּׂבְעָהּ׃ וַתֹּאמֶר לָהּ חֲמוֹתָהּ אֵיפֹה
where? mother-in-law-of-her to-her and-she-asked (19) from-to-be-filled-her

לִקַּטְתְּ הַיּוֹם וְאָנָה עָשִׂית יְהִי מַכִּירֵךְ
one-noticing-you may-he-be you-worked and-at-where? the-day you-gleaned

בָּרוּךְ וַתַּגֵּד לַחֲמוֹתָהּ אֵת אֲשֶׁר־ עָשְׂתָה
she-worked whom *** to-mother-in-law-of-her then-she-told being-blessed

עִמּוֹ וַתֹּאמֶר שֵׁם הָאִישׁ אֲשֶׁר עָשִׂיתִי עִמּוֹ הַיּוֹם בֹּעַז׃
Boaz the-day with-him I-worked whom the-man name-of and-she-said with-him

וַתֹּאמֶר נָעֳמִי לְכַלָּתָהּ בָּרוּךְ הוּא לַיהוָה
by-Yahweh he being-blessed to-daughter-in-law-of-her Naomi and-she-said (20)

אֲשֶׁר לֹא־ עָזַב חַסְדּוֹ אֶת־ הַחַיִּים וְאֶת־ הַמֵּתִים
the-dead-ones and-with the-living-ones with kindness-of-him he-stopped not who

וַתֹּאמֶר לָהּ נָעֳמִי קָרוֹב לָנוּ הָאִישׁ מִגֹּאֲלֵנוּ הוּא׃
he of-one-redeeming-us the-man to-us close Naomi to-her then-she-said

though I do not have the standing of one of your servant girls."

[14]At mealtime Boaz said to her, "Come over here. Have some bread and dip it in the wine vinegar."

When she sat down with the harvesters, he offered her some roasted grain. She ate all she wanted and had some left over. [15]As she got up to glean, Boaz gave orders to his men, "Even if she gathers among the sheaves, don't embarrass her. [16]Rather, pull out some stalks for her from the bundles and leave them for her to pick up, and don't rebuke her."

[17]So Ruth gleaned in the field until evening. Then she threshed the barley she had gathered, and it amounted to about an ephah.[f] [18]She carried it back to town, and her mother-in-law saw how much she had gathered. Ruth also brought out and gave her what she had left over after she had eaten enough.

[19]Her mother-in-law asked her, "Where did you glean today? Where did you work? Blessed be the man who took notice of you!"

Then Ruth told her mother-in-law about the one at whose place she had been working. "The name of the man I worked with today is Boaz," she said.

[20]"The LORD bless him!" Naomi said to her daughter-in-law. "The LORD has not stopped showing his kindness to the living and the dead." She added, "That man is our close relative; he is one of our kinsman-redeemers."

[f]17 That is, probably about 1/2 bushel (about 22 liters)

וַתֹּאמֶר רוּת הַמּוֹאֲבִיָּה גַּם ׀ כִּי־ אָמַר אֵלַי עִם־ הַנְּעָרִים
the-workers with to-me he-said even also the-Moabitess Ruth then-she-said (21)

אֲשֶׁר־ לִי תִּדְבָּקִין עַד אִם־ כִּלּוּ אֵת כָּל־ הַקָּצִיר אֲשֶׁר־ לִי׃
to-me that the-harvest all-of *** they-finish when until you-stay to-me who

וַתֹּאמֶר נָעֳמִי אֶל־ רוּת כַּלָּתָהּ טוֹב בִּתִּי
daughter-of-me good daughter-in-law-of-her Ruth to Naomi and-she-said (22)

כִּי תֵצְאִי עִם־ נַעֲרוֹתָיו וְלֹא יִפְגְּעוּ־ בָךְ בְּשָׂדֶה אַחֵר׃
another in-field to-you they-will-harm for-not girls-of-him with you-go that

וַתִּדְבַּק בְּנַעֲרוֹת בֹּעַז לְלַקֵּט עַד־ כְּלוֹת
to-be-finished until to-glean Boaz to-servant-girls-of so-she-stayed-close (23)

קְצִיר־ הַשְּׂעֹרִים וּקְצִיר הַחִטִּים וַתֵּשֶׁב אֶת־
with and-she-lived the-wheats and-harvest-of the-barleys harvest-of

חֲמוֹתָהּ׃ וַתֹּאמֶר לָהּ נָעֳמִי חֲמוֹתָהּ
mother-in-law-of-her Naomi to-her now-she-said (3:1) mother-in-law-of-her

בִּתִּי הֲלֹא אֲבַקֶּשׁ־ לָךְ מָנוֹחַ אֲשֶׁר יִיטַב־ לָךְ׃
for-you he-will-be-good where rest for-you I-should-seek not? daughter-of-me

וְעַתָּה הֲלֹא בֹעַז מֹדַעְתָּנוּ אֲשֶׁר הָיִית אֶת־ נַעֲרוֹתָיו
servant-girls-of-him with you-are whom kinsman-of-us Boaz not? and-now (2)

הִנֵּה־ הוּא זֹרֶה אֶת־ גֹּרֶן הַשְּׂעֹרִים הַלָּיְלָה׃ וְרָחַצְתְּ ׀
so-you-wash (3) the-night the-barleys threshing-floor-of *** winnowing he see!

וָסַכְתְּ וְשַׂמְתְּ שִׂמְלֹתֵךְ עָלַיִךְ וְיָרַדְתִּי
then-you-go-down on-you clothes-of-you and-you-put-on and-you-perfume

הַגֹּרֶן אַל־ תִּוָּדְעִי לָאִישׁ עַד כַּלֹּתוֹ
to-finish-him until to-the-man you-make-yourself-known not the-threshing-floor

לֶאֱכֹל וְלִשְׁתּוֹת׃ וִיהִי בְשָׁכְבוֹ וְיָדַעַתְּ
then-you-note when-to-lie-down-him and-he-will-be (4) and-to-drink to-eat

אֶת־ הַמָּקוֹם אֲשֶׁר יִשְׁכַּב־ שָׁם וּבָאת וְגִלִּית מַרְגְּלֹתָיו
feet-of-him and-you-uncover then-you-go there he-lies where the-place ***

וְשָׁכָבְתִּי וְהוּא יַגִּיד לָךְ אֵת אֲשֶׁר תַּעֲשִׂין׃
you-must-do what *** to-you he-will-tell then-he and-you-lie-down

וַתֹּאמֶר אֵלֶיהָ כֹּל אֲשֶׁר־תֹּאמְרִי ... * אֶעֱשֶׂה׃ וַתֵּרֶד
so-she-went-down (6) I-will-do *to-me you-say that all to-her and-she-answered (5)

הַגֹּרֶן וַתַּעַשׂ כְּכֹל אֲשֶׁר־ צִוַּתָּה חֲמוֹתָהּ׃
mother-in-law-of-her she-said that as-all and-she-did the-threshing-floor

וַיֹּאכַל בֹּעַז וַיֵּשְׁתְּ וַיִּיטַב לִבּוֹ וַיָּבֹא
then-he-went spirit-of-him and-he-was-good and-he-drank Boaz when-he-ate (7)

לִשְׁכַּב בִּקְצֵה הָעֲרֵמָה וַתָּבֹא בַלָּט
quietly and-she-approached the-grain-pile at-far-end-of to-lie-down

[21]Then Ruth the Moabitess said, "He even said to me, 'Stay with my workers until they finish harvesting all my grain.'"

[22]Naomi said to Ruth her daughter-in-law, "It will be good for you, my daughter, to go with his girls, because in someone else's field you might be harmed."

[23]So Ruth stayed close to the servant girls of Boaz to glean until the barley and wheat harvests were finished. And she lived with her mother-in-law.

*Ruth and Boaz at the Threshing Floor*

3 One day Naomi her mother-in-law said to her, "My daughter, should I not try to find a home[g] for you, where you will be well provided for? [2]Is not Boaz, with whose servant girls you have been, a kinsman of ours? Tonight he will be winnowing barley on the threshing floor. [3]Wash and perfume yourself, and put on your best clothes. Then go down to the threshing floor, but don't let him know you are there until he has finished eating and drinking. [4]When he lies down, note the place where he is lying. Then go and uncover his feet and lie down. He will tell you what to do."

[5]"I will do whatever you say," Ruth answered. [6]So she went down to the threshing floor and did everything her mother-in-law told her to do.

[7]When Boaz had finished eating and drinking and was in good spirits, he went over to lie down at the far end of the grain pile. Ruth approached quietly, uncovered

*g1* Hebrew *find rest* (see Ruth 1:9)

*5 Most mss include the *Qere* אֵלַי *to-me*, with no *Ketbib* form.

°*3a* ק שמלתיך
°*3b* ק וירדת
°*4* ק ושכבת

וַתְּגַל מַרְגְּלֹתָיו וַתִּשְׁכָּב׃ וַיְהִי בַּחֲצִי
in-middle-of and-he-was (8) and-she-lay-down feet-of-him and-she-uncovered

הַלַּיְלָה וַיֶּחֱרַד הָאִישׁ וַיִּלָּפֵת וְהִנֵּה אִשָּׁה שֹׁכֶבֶת
lying woman and-see! and-he-turned the-man that-he-was-startled the-night

מַרְגְּלֹתָיו׃ וַיֹּאמֶר מִי־ אָתְּ וַתֹּאמֶר אָנֹכִי רוּת אֲמָתֶךָ
servant-of-you Ruth I and-she-said you who? and-he-asked (9) feet-of-him

וּפָרַשְׂתָּ כְנָפֶךָ עַל־ אֲמָתְךָ כִּי גֹאֵל
one-redeeming since servant-of-you over garment-corner-of-you now-you-spread

אָתָּה׃ וַיֹּאמֶר בְּרוּכָה אַתְּ לַיהוָה בִּתִּי
daughter-of-me by-Yahweh you being-blessed and-he-replied (10) you

הֵיטַבְתְּ חַסְדֵּךְ הָאַחֲרוֹן מִן־ הָרִאשׁוֹן לְבִלְתִּי־לֶכֶת
to-run not the-earlier greater-than the-latter kindness-of-you you-showed

אַחֲרֵי הַבַּחוּרִים אִם־ דַּל וְאִם־ עָשִׁיר׃ וְעַתָּה בִּתִּי
daughter-of-me and-now (11) rich or-whether poor whether the-young-men after

אַל־ תִּירְאִי כֹּל אֲשֶׁר־ תֹּאמְרִי אֶעֱשֶׂה־ לָּךְ כִּי יוֹדֵעַ כָּל־
whole-of knowing for for-you I-will-do you-ask that all you-be-afraid not

שַׁעַר עַמִּי כִּי אֵשֶׁת חַיִל אָתְּ׃ וְעַתָּה כִּי אָמְנָם
true although and-now (12) you noble woman-of that people-of-me gate-of

כִּי אִם גֹאֵל אָנֹכִי וְגַם יֵשׁ גֹּאֵל קָרוֹב מִמֶּנִּי׃
than-I nearer one-redeeming there-is and-also I one-redeeming †indeed that

לִינִי הַלַּיְלָה וְהָיָה בַבֹּקֶר אִם־ יִגְאָלֵךְ טוֹב
good he-redeems-you if in-the-morning and-he-will-be the-night stay! (13)

יִגְאָל וְאִם־ לֹא יַחְפֹּץ לְגָאֳלֵךְ וּגְאַלְתִּיךְ
then-I-will-redeem-you to-redeem-you he-is-willing not but-if let-him-redeem

אָנֹכִי חַי־ יְהוָה שִׁכְבִי עַד־ הַבֹּקֶר׃ וַתִּשְׁכַּב מַרְגְּלֹתָו עַד־
until feet-of-him so-she-lay (14) the-morning until lie! Yahweh life-of I

הַבֹּקֶר וַתָּקָם בְּטֶרֶם יַכִּיר אִישׁ אֶת־ רֵעֵהוּ
neighbor-of-him *** man he-could-recognize at-before but-she-got-up the-morning

וַיֹּאמֶר אַל־ יִוָּדַע כִּי־ בָאָה הָאִשָּׁה הַגֹּרֶן׃
the-threshing-floor the-woman she-came that he-must-be-known not and-he-said

וַיֹּאמֶר הָבִי הַמִּטְפַּחַת אֲשֶׁר־עָלַיִךְ וְאֶחֳזִי־ בָהּ וַתֹּאחֶז
when-she-held onto-her and-hold! on-you that the-shawl bring! and-he-said (15)

בָּהּ וַיָּמָד שֵׁשׁ־ שְׂעֹרִים וַיָּשֶׁת עָלֶיהָ וַיָּבֹא
then-he-went-back on-her and-he-put barleys six-of then-he-poured onto-her

הָעִיר׃ וַתָּבוֹא אֶל־ חֲמוֹתָהּ וַתֹּאמֶר מִי־ אַתְּ
you who? then-she-asked mother-in-law-of-her to when-she-came (16) the-town

בִּתִּי וַתַּגֶּד־ לָהּ אֵת כָּל־ אֲשֶׁר עָשָׂה־ לָהּ הָאִישׁ׃
the-man for-her he-did that all *** to-her then-she-told daughter-of-me

his feet and lay down. 8In the
middle of the night something
startled the man, and he
turned and discovered a
woman lying at his feet.
9"Who are you?" he asked.
"I am your servant Ruth,"
she said. "Spread the corner of
your garment over me, since
you are a kinsman-redeemer."
10"The LORD bless you, my
daughter," he replied. "This
kindness is greater than that
which you showed earlier:
You have not run after the
younger men, whether rich or
poor. 11And now, my daughter, don't be afraid. I will do
for you all you ask. All my fellow townsmen know that you
are a woman of noble character. 12Although it is true that
I am near of kin, there is a
kinsman-redeemer nearer
than I. 13Stay here for the
night, and in the morning if
he wants to redeem, good; let
him redeem. But if he is not
willing, I vow that, as surely as
the LORD lives, I will do it. Lie
here until morning."
14So she lay at his feet until
morning, but got up before
anyone could be recognized;
and he said, "Don't let it be
known that a woman came to
the threshing floor."
15He also said, "Bring me the
shawl you are wearing and
hold it out." When she did so,
he poured into it six measures
of barley and put it on her.
Then he[h] went back to town.
16When Ruth came to her
mother-in-law, Naomi asked,
"How did it go, my daugh-
ter?"
Then she told her every-
thing Boaz had done for her

[h]15 Most Hebrew manuscripts; many Hebrew manuscripts, Vulgate and Syriac *she*

*9 Most mss have *sheva* under the *tav* ( אַתְּ ).

†12 Most mss have no vowel or *Qere* reading, indicating the Masoretes felt the word to be unnecessary and not to be read.

°14a ק מרגלתיו

°14b ק בטרם

וַתֹּאמֶר שֵׁשׁ־ הַשְּׂעֹרִים הָאֵלֶּה נָתַן לִי כִּי אָמַר

he-said for to-me he-gave the-these the-barleys six-of and-she-said (17)

*. . אַל־ תָּבוֹאִי רֵיקָם אֶל־ חֲמוֹתֵךְ׃ וַתֹּאמֶר

then-she-said (18) mother-in-law-of-you to empty-handed you-go-back not *to-me

שְׁבִי בִתִּי עַד אֲשֶׁר תֵּדְעִין אֵיךְ יִפֹּל דָּבָר כִּי

for matter he-happens what you-find-out when until daughter-of-me wait!

לֹא יִשְׁקֹט הָאִישׁ כִּי־ אִם־ כִּלָּה הַדָּבָר הַיּוֹם׃

the-day the-matter he-settles when until the-man he-will-rest not

וּבֹעַז עָלָה הַשַּׁעַר וַיֵּשֶׁב שָׁם וְהִנֵּה הַגֹּאֵל

the-one-redeeming and-see! there and-he-sat the-gate he-went-up now-Boaz (4:1)

עֹבֵר אֲשֶׁר דִּבֶּר־ בֹּעַז וַיֹּאמֶר סוּרָה שְׁבָה־ פֹּה

here sit-down! come-over! and-he-said Boaz he-mentioned whom coming-along

פְּלֹנִי אַלְמֹנִי וַיָּסַר וַיֵּשֵׁב׃ וַיִּקַּח עֲשָׂרָה אֲנָשִׁים

men ten and-he-took (2) and-he-sat-down so-he-went-over †friend-of-me

מִזִּקְנֵי הָעִיר וַיֹּאמֶר שְׁבוּ־ פֹה וַיֵּשֵׁבוּ׃ וַיֹּאמֶר

then-he-said (3) and-they-sat here sit! and-he-said the-town from-elders-of

לַגֹּאֵל חֶלְקַת הַשָּׂדֶה אֲשֶׁר לְאָחִינוּ לֶאֱלִימֶלֶךְ

to-Elimelech to-brother-of-us that the-land piece-of to-the-one-redeeming

מָכְרָה נָעֳמִי הַשָּׁבָה מִשְּׂדֵה מוֹאָב׃ וַאֲנִי אָמַרְתִּי

I-thought now-I (4) Moab from-region-of who-she-came-back Naomi she-sells

אֶגְלֶה אָזְנְךָ לֵאמֹר קְנֵה נֶגֶד הַיֹּשְׁבִים וְנֶגֶד

and-before the-ones-sitting before buy! to-suggest ear-of-you I-should-inform

זִקְנֵי עַמִּי אִם־ תִּגְאַל גְּאָל וְאִם־ לֹא יִגְאַל

he-will-redeem not but-if redeem! you-will-redeem if people-of-me elders-of

הַגִּידָה לִּי וְאֵדְעָ כִּי אֵין זוּלָתְךָ לִגְאוֹל וְאָנֹכִי אַחֲרֶיךָ

after-you and-I to-redeem except-you no-one for so-I-will-know to-me tell!

וַיֹּאמֶר אָנֹכִי אֶגְאָל׃ וַיֹּאמֶר בֹּעַז בְּיוֹם־ קְנוֹתְךָ הַשָּׂדֶה

the-land to-buy-you on-day Boaz then-he-said (5) I-will-redeem I and-he-said

מִיַּד נָעֳמִי וּמֵאֵת רוּת הַמּוֹאֲבִיָּה אֵשֶׁת־ הַמֵּת

the-dead-man widow-of the-Moabitess Ruth and-from Naomi from-hand-of

קָנִיתִי לְהָקִים שֵׁם־ הַמֵּת עַל־ נַחֲלָתוֹ׃

property-of-him with the-dead-man name-of to-maintain you-acquire

וַיֹּאמֶר הַגֹּאֵל לֹא אוּכַל לִגְאָול־ לִי פֶּן

because for-me to-redeem I-can not the-one-redeeming then-he-said (6)

אַשְׁחִית אֶת־ נַחֲלָתִי גְּאַל־ לְךָ אַתָּה אֶת־ גְּאֻלָּתִי

redemption-of-me *** you for-you redeem! estate-of-me *** I-might-endanger

כִּי לֹא־ אוּכַל לִגְאֹל׃ וְזֹאת לְפָנִים בְּיִשְׂרָאֵל עַל־

for in-Israel in-earlier-times now-this (7) to-redeem I-can not for

[17]and added, "He gave me these six measures of barley, saying, 'Don't go back to your mother-in-law empty-handed.' "

[18]Then Naomi said, "Wait, my daughter, until you find out what happens. For the man will not rest until the matter is settled today."

### *Boaz Marries Ruth*

**4** Meanwhile Boaz went up to the town gate and sat there. When the kinsman-redeemer he had mentioned came along, Boaz said, "Come over here, my friend, and sit down." So he went over and sat down.

[2]Boaz took ten of the elders of the town and said, "Sit here," and they did so. [3]Then he said to the kinsman-redeemer, "Naomi, who has come back from Moab, is selling the piece of land that belonged to our brother Elimelech. [4]I thought I should bring the matter to your attention and suggest that you buy it in the presence of these seated here and in the presence of the elders of my people. If you will redeem it, do so. But if you[i] will not, tell me, so I will know. For no one has the right to do it except you, and I am next in line."

"I will redeem it," he said.

[5]Then Boaz said, "On the day you buy the land from Naomi and from Ruth the Moabitess, you acquire[j] the dead man's widow, in order to maintain the name of the dead with his property."

[6]At this, the kinsman-redeemer said, "Then I cannot redeem it because I might endanger my own estate. You redeem it yourself. I cannot do it."

[i]4 Many Hebrew manuscripts, Septuagint, Vulgate and Syriac; most Hebrew manuscripts *he*

[j]5 Hebrew; Vulgate and Syriac *Naomi, you acquire Ruth the Moabitess,*

**17* Most mss include the Qere אֵלַי, *to-me*, with no *Kethib* form.

†*1* The meaning of this phrase is uncertain, perhaps used in place of a proper name, as the English idiom "so-and-so."

°4 ק ואדעה

°5 ק קניתה

°6 ק לגאל

הַגְּאוּלָּה וְעַל־ הַתְּמוּרָה לְקַיֵּם כָּל־ דָּבָר שָׁלַף
he-took-off matter any-of to-finalize the-transfer and-for the-redemption

אִישׁ נַעֲלוֹ וְנָתַן לְרֵעֵהוּ וְזֹאת הַתְּעוּדָה
the-legalizing-method now-this to-other-of-him and-he-gave sandal-of-him man

בְּיִשְׂרָאֵל׃ וַיֹּאמֶר הַגֹּאֵל לְבֹעַז קְנֵה־ לָךְ וַיִּשְׁלֹף
and-he-removed for-you buy! to-Boaz the-one-redeeming so-he-said (8) in-Israel

נַעֲלוֹ׃ וַיֹּאמֶר בֹּעַז לַזְּקֵנִים וְכָל־ הָעָם
the-people and-all-of to-the-elders Boaz then-he-announced (9) sandal-of-him

עֵדִים אַתֶּם הַיּוֹם כִּי קָנִיתִי אֶת־ כָּל־ אֲשֶׁר לֶאֱלִימֶלֶךְ וְאֵת כָּל־ אֲשֶׁר
that all and to-Elimelech that all *** I-bought that the-day you witnesses

לְכִלְיוֹן וּמַחְלוֹן מִיַּד נָעֳמִי׃ וְגַם אֶת־ רוּת הַמֹּאֲבִיָּה
the-Moabitess Ruth *** and-also (10) Naomi from-hand-of and-Mahlon to-Kilion

אֵשֶׁת מַחְלוֹן קָנִיתִי לִי לְאִשָּׁה לְהָקִים שֵׁם־ הַמֵּת עַל־
with the-dead name-of to-maintain as-wife for-me I-acquired Mahlon widow-of

נַחֲלָתוֹ וְלֹא־ יִכָּרֵת שֵׁם־ הַמֵּת מֵעִם
from-among the-dead name-of he-will-disappear so-not property-of-him

אֶחָיו וּמִשַּׁעַר מְקוֹמוֹ עֵדִים אַתֶּם הַיּוֹם׃
the-day you witnesses town-of-him or-from-gate-of brothers-of-him

וַיֹּאמְרוּ כָּל־ הָעָם אֲשֶׁר־ בַּשַּׁעַר וְהַזְּקֵנִים עֵדִים
witnesses and-the-elders at-the-gate who the-people all-of then-they-said (11)

יִתֵּן יְהוָה אֶת־ הָאִשָּׁה הַבָּאָה אֶל־ בֵּיתֶךָ כְּרָחֵל ׀
like-Rachel home-of-you into the-one-coming the-woman *** Yahweh may-he-make

וּכְלֵאָה אֲשֶׁר בָּנוּ שְׁתֵּיהֶם אֶת־ בֵּית יִשְׂרָאֵל וַעֲשֵׂה־
and-have! Israel house-of *** two-of-them they-built-up who and-like-Leah

חַיִל בְּאֶפְרָתָה וּקְרָא־ שֵׁם בְּבֵית לָחֶם׃ וִיהִי
and-may-he-be (12) Lehem in-Beth name and-call! in-Ephratah standing

בֵיתְךָ כְּבֵית פֶּרֶץ אֲשֶׁר־ יָלְדָה תָמָר לִיהוּדָה מִן־
through to-Judah Tamar she-bore whom Perez like-family-of family-of-you

הַזֶּרַע אֲשֶׁר יִתֵּן יְהוָה לְךָ מִן־ הַנַּעֲרָה הַזֹּאת׃
the-this the-young-woman by to-you Yahweh he-gives that the-offspring

וַיִּקַּח בֹּעַז אֶת־ רוּת וַתְּהִי־ לוֹ לְאִשָּׁה וַיָּבֹא
and-he-went for-wife to-him and-she-became Ruth *** Boaz so-he-took (13)

אֵלֶיהָ וַיִּתֵּן יְהוָה לָהּ הֵרָיוֹן וַתֵּלֶד בֵּן׃
son and-she-bore conception to-her Yahweh and-he-gave into-her

וַתֹּאמַרְנָה הַנָּשִׁים אֶל־ נָעֳמִי בָּרוּךְ יְהוָה אֲשֶׁר לֹא
not who Yahweh being-praised Naomi to the-women and-they-said (14)

הִשְׁבִּית לָךְ גֹּאֵל הַיּוֹם וְיִקָּרֵא שְׁמוֹ
name-of-him now-may-he-be-called the-day one-redeeming for-you he-let-cease

7(Now in earlier times in Israel, for the redemption and transfer of property to become final, one party took off his sandal and gave it to the other. This was the method of legalizing transactions in Israel.)
8So the kinsman-redeemer said to Boaz, "Buy it yourself." And he removed his sandal.
9Then Boaz announced to the elders and all the people, "Today you are witnesses that I have bought from Naomi all the property of Elimelech, Kilion and Mahlon.
10I have also acquired Ruth the Moabitess, Mahlon's widow, as my wife, in order to maintain the name of the dead with his property, so that his name will not disappear from among his family or from the town records. Today you are witnesses!"
11Then the elders and all those at the gate said, "We are witnesses. May the LORD make the woman who is coming into your home like Rachel and Leah, who together built up the house of Israel. May you have standing in Ephratah and be famous in Bethlehem.
12Through the offspring the LORD gives you by this young woman, may your family be like that of Perez, whom Tamar bore to Judah."

*The Genealogy of David*

13So Boaz took Ruth and she became his wife. And the LORD enabled her to conceive, and she gave birth to a son.
14The women said to Naomi: "Praise be to the LORD, who this day has not left you without a kinsman-redeemer. May he become famous throughout

בְּיִשְׂרָאֵל׃ וְהָיָה לָךְ לְמֵשִׁיב נֶפֶשׁ
life as-one-renewing for-you and-he-will-be (15) throughout-Israel

וּלְכַלְכֵּל אֶת־ שֵׂיבָתֵךְ כִּי כַלָּתֵךְ אֲשֶׁר־ אֲהֵבַתֶךְ
she-loves-you who daughter-in-law-of-you for old-age-of-you *** and-to-sustain

יְלָדַתּוּ אֲשֶׁר־ הִיא טוֹבָה לָךְ מִשִּׁבְעָה בָּנִים׃ וַתִּקַּח
then-she-took (16) sons than-seven to-you better she who she-bore-him

נָעֳמִי אֶת־ הַיֶּלֶד וַתְּשִׁתֵהוּ בְחֵיקָהּ וַתְּהִי־ לוֹ
for-him and-she-was in-lap-of-her and-she-laid-him the-child *** Naomi

לְאֹמֶנֶת׃ וַתִּקְרֶאנָה לוֹ הַשְּׁכֵנוֹת שֵׁם לֵאמֹר
to-say name the-women-living to-him and-they-called (17) as-one-caring

יֻלַּד־ בֵּן לְנָעֳמִי וַתִּקְרֶאנָה שְׁמוֹ עוֹבֵד הוּא אֲבִי־
father-of he Obed name-of-him and-they-called to-Naomi son he-was-born

יִשַׁי אֲבִי דָוִד׃ וְאֵלֶּה תּוֹלְדוֹת פָּרֶץ פֶּרֶץ הוֹלִיד
he-fathered Perez Perez family-lines-of so-these (18) David father-of Jesse

אֶת־ חֶצְרוֹן׃ וְחֶצְרוֹן הוֹלִיד אֶת־ רָם וְרָם הוֹלִיד אֶת־
*** he-fathered and-Ram Ram *** he-fathered and-Hezron (19) Hezron ***

עַמִּינָדָב׃ וְעַמִּינָדָב הוֹלִיד אֶת־ נַחְשׁוֹן וְנַחְשׁוֹן הוֹלִיד
he-fathered and-Nahshon Nahshon *** he-fathered and-Amminadab (20) Amminadab

אֶת־ שַׂלְמָה׃ וְשַׂלְמוֹן הוֹלִיד אֶת־ בֹּעַז וּבֹעַז הוֹלִיד אֶת־
*** he-fathered and-Boaz Boaz *** he-fathered and-Salmon (21) Salma ***

עוֹבֵד׃ וְעֹבֵד הוֹלִיד אֶת־ יִשָׁי וְיִשַׁי הוֹלִיד אֶת־ דָּוִד׃
David *** he-fathered and-Jesse Jesse *** he-fathered and-Obed (22) Obed

Israel! [15]He will renew your life and sustain you in your old age. For your daughter-in-law, who loves you and who is better to you than seven sons, has given him birth."

[16]Then Naomi took the child, laid him in her lap and cared for him. [17]The women living there said, "Naomi has a son." And they named him Obed. He was the father of Jesse, the father of David.

[18]This, then, is the family line of Perez:

Perez was the father of Hezron,
[19]Hezron the father of Ram
Ram the father of Amminadab,
[20]Amminadab the father of Nahshon,
Nahshon the father of Salmon,[k]
[21]Salmon the father of Boaz,
Boaz the father of Obed,
[22]Obed the father of Jesse,
and Jesse the father of David.

[k]20 A few Hebrew manuscripts, some Septuagint manuscripts and Vulgate (see also verse 21 and Septuagint of 1 Chron. 2:11); most Hebrew manuscripts *Salma*

וַיְהִי אִישׁ אֶחָד מִן־ הָרָמָתַיִם צוֹפִים מֵהַר
from-hill-country-of Zuphites the-Ramathaim from certain man now-he-was (1:1)

אֶפְרָיִם וּשְׁמוֹ אֶלְקָנָה בֶּן־ יְרֹחָם בֶּן־ אֱלִיהוּא בֶּן־ תֹּחוּ
Tohu son-of Elihu son-of Jeroham son-of Elkanah and-name-of-him Ephraim

בֶּן־ צוּף אֶפְרָתִי׃ וְלוֹ שְׁתֵּי נָשִׁים שֵׁם אַחַת חַנָּה
Hannah one name-of wives two-of now-to-him (2) Ephramite Zuph son-of

וְשֵׁם הַשֵּׁנִית פְּנִנָּה וַיְהִי לִפְנִנָּה יְלָדִים וּלְחַנָּה
but-to-Hannah children to-Peninnah and-he-was Peninnah the-other and-name-of

אֵין יְלָדִים׃ וְעָלָה הָאִישׁ הַהוּא מֵעִירוֹ מִיָּמִים
from-days from-town-of-him the-this the-man and-he-went-up (3) children no

יָמִימָה לְהִשְׁתַּחֲוֹת וְלִזְבֹּחַ לַיהוָה צְבָאוֹת בְּשִׁלֹה וְשָׁם
and-there at-Shiloh Hosts to-Yahweh-of and-to-sacrifice to-worship at-days

שְׁנֵי בְנֵי־ עֵלִי חָפְנִי וּפִנְחָס כֹּהֲנִים לַיהוָה׃ וַיְהִי
when-he-came (4) of-Yahweh priests and-Phinehas Hophni Eli sons-of two-of

הַיּוֹם וַיִּזְבַּח אֶלְקָנָה וְנָתַן לִפְנִנָּה אִשְׁתּוֹ
wife-of-him to-Peninnah then-he-gave Elkanah and-he-sacrificed the-day

וּלְכָל־ בָּנֶיהָ וּבְנוֹתֶיהָ מָנוֹת׃ וּלְחַנָּה
but-to-Hannah (5) portions and-daughters-of-her sons-of-her and-to-all-of

יִתֵּן מָנָה אַחַת אַפָּיִם כִּי אֶת־ חַנָּה אָהֵב וַיהוָה סָגַר
he-closed and-Yahweh he-loved Hannah *** because double one portion he-gave

רַחְמָהּ׃ וְכִעֲסַתָּה צָרָתָהּ גַּם־ כַּעַס בַּעֲבוּר
in-order provocation indeed rival-of-her and-she-provoked-her (6) womb-of-her

הַרְּעִמָהּ כִּי־ סָגַר יְהוָה בְּעַד רַחְמָהּ׃ וְכֵן
and-this (7) womb-of-her completely Yahweh he-closed because to-irritate-her

יַעֲשֶׂה שָׁנָה בְשָׁנָה מִדֵּי עֲלֹתָהּ בְּבֵית יְהוָה כֵּן
then Yahweh to-house-of to-go-up-her whenever after-year year he-went-on

תַּכְעִסֶנָּה וַתִּבְכֶּה וְלֹא תֹאכַל׃ וַיֹּאמֶר לָהּ אֶלְקָנָה
Elkanah to-her and-he-said (8) she-ate and-not so-she-wept she-provoked-her

אִישָׁהּ חַנָּה לָמֶה תִבְכִּי וְלָמֶה לֹא תֹאכְלִי וְלָמֶה יֵרַע
he-is-sad and-why? you-eat not and-why? you-weep why? Hannah husband-of-her

לְבָבֵךְ הֲלוֹא אָנֹכִי טוֹב לָךְ מֵעֲשָׂרָה בָּנִים׃ וַתָּקָם חַנָּה
Hannah now-she-stood-up (9) sons than-ten to-you better I not? heart-of-you

אַחֲרֵי אָכְלָה בְשִׁלֹה וְאַחֲרֵי שָׁתֹה וְעֵלִי הַכֹּהֵן יֹשֵׁב עַל־
on sitting the-priest now-Eli to-drink and-after in-Shiloh to-eat-her after

הַכִּסֵּא עַל־ מְזוּזַת הֵיכַל יְהוָה׃ וְהִיא מָרַת נָפֶשׁ
soul bitter-of and-she (10) Yahweh temple-of doorpost-of by the-chair

וַתִּתְפַּלֵּל עַל־ יְהוָה וּבָכֹה תִבְכֶּה׃ וַתִּדֹּר נֶדֶר
vow and-she-vowed (11) she-wept and-to-weep Yahweh to and-she-prayed

### *The Birth of Samuel*

1 There was a certain man
from Ramathaim, a Zuph-
ite[a] from the hill country of
Ephraim, whose name was Elkanah son of Jeroham, the son
of Elihu, the son of Tohu, the
son of Zuph, an Ephraimite.
2 He had two wives; one was
called Hannah and the other
Peninnah. Peninnah had children, but Hannah had none.
3 Year after year this man
went up from his town to worship and sacrifice to the LORD
Almighty at Shiloh, where
Hophni and Phinehas, the
two sons of Eli, were priests of
the LORD. 4 Whenever the day
came for Elkanah to sacrifice,
he would give portions of the
meat to his wife Peninnah and
to all her sons and daughters.
5 But to Hannah he gave a double portion because he loved
her, and the LORD had closed
her womb. 6 And because the
LORD had closed her womb,
her rival kept provoking her in
order to irritate her. 7 This
went on year after year.
Whenever Hannah went up to
the house of the LORD, her rival provoked her till she wept
and would not eat. 8 Elkanah
her husband would say to her,
"Hannah, why are you weeping? Why don't you eat? Why
are you downhearted? Don't I
mean more to you than ten
sons?"
9 Once when they had
finished eating and drinking
in Shiloh, Hannah stood up.
Now Eli the priest was sitting
on a chair by the doorpost of
the LORD's temple.[b] 10 In bitterness of soul Hannah wept
much and prayed to the LORD.
11 And she made a vow, saying,

[a] 1 Or *from Ramathaim Zuphim*
[b] 9 That is, tabernacle

וַתֹּאמַר יְהוָה צְבָאוֹת אִם־רָאֹה תִרְאֶה ׀ בָּעֳנִי

upon-misery-of you-will-look to-look if Hosts Yahweh-of and-she-said

אֲמָתֶךָ וּזְכַרְתַּנִי וְלֹא־תִשְׁכַּח אֶת־

*** you-will-forget and-not and-you-will-remember-me servant-of-you

אֲמָתֶךָ וְנָתַתָּה לַאֲמָתְךָ זֶרַע אֲנָשִׁים

men offspring-of to-servant-of-you but-you-will-give servant-of-you

וּנְתַתִּיו לַיהוָה כָּל־יְמֵי חַיָּיו וּמוֹרָה לֹא־

not and-razor lives-of-him days-of all-of to-Yahweh then-I-will-give-him

יַעֲלֶה עַל־רֹאשׁוֹ׃ (12) וְהָיָה כִּי הִרְבְּתָה לְהִתְפַּלֵּל לִפְנֵי

to to-pray she-kept-on as and-he-was (12) head-of-him on he-will-use

יְהוָה וְעֵלִי שֹׁמֵר אֶת־פִּיהָ׃ (13) וְחַנָּה הִיא מְדַבֶּרֶת עַל־

in praying she now-Hannah (13) mouth-of-her *** observing then-Eli Yahweh

לִבָּהּ רַק שְׂפָתֶיהָ נָּעוֹת וְקוֹלָהּ לֹא יִשָּׁמֵעַ

he-was-heard not but-voice-of-her ones-moving lips-of-her only heart-of-her

וַיַּחְשְׁבֶהָ עֵלִי לְשִׁכֹּרָה׃ (14) וַיֹּאמֶר אֵלֶיהָ עֵלִי עַד־מָתַי

when? until Eli to-her and-he-said (14) to-be-drunk Eli and-he-thought-her

תִּשְׁתַּכָּרִין הָסִירִי אֶת־יֵינֵךְ מֵעָלָיִךְ׃ (15) וַתַּעַן

and-she-replied (15) from-with-you wine-of-you *** get-rid! will-you-be-drunk

חַנָּה וַתֹּאמֶר לֹא אֲדֹנִי אִשָּׁה קְשַׁת־רוּחַ אָנֹכִי וְיַיִן

and-wine I spirit troubled-of woman lord-of-me not-so and-she-said Hannah

וְשֵׁכָר לֹא שָׁתִיתִי וָאֶשְׁפֹּךְ אֶת־נַפְשִׁי לִפְנֵי יְהוָה׃ (16) אַל־

not (16) Yahweh to soul-of-me *** but-I-poured-out I-drank not or-beer

תִּתֵּן אֶת־אֲמָתְךָ לִפְנֵי בַּת־בְּלִיָּעַל כִּי־מֵרֹב

in-greatness-of for wickedness daughter-of for servant-of-you *** you-take

שִׂיחִי וְכַעְסִי דִּבַּרְתִּי עַד־הֵנָּה׃ (17) וַיַּעַן עֵלִי

Eli and-he-answered (17) at-here at I-prayed and-grief-of-me anguish-of-me

וַיֹּאמֶר לְכִי לְשָׁלוֹם וֵאלֹהֵי יִשְׂרָאֵל יִתֵּן אֶת־שֵׁלָתֵךְ

request-of-you *** may-he-grant Israel and-God-of in-peace go! and-he-said

אֲשֶׁר שָׁאַלְתְּ מֵעִמּוֹ׃ (18) וַתֹּאמֶר תִּמְצָא שִׁפְחָתְךָ

servant-of-you may-she-find and-she-said (18) from-with-him you-asked that

חֵן בְּעֵינֶיךָ וַתֵּלֶךְ הָאִשָּׁה לְדַרְכָּהּ וַתֹּאכַל

and-she-ate on-way-of-her the-woman then-she-went in-eyes-of-you favor

וּפָנֶיהָ לֹא־הָיוּ־לָהּ עוֹד׃ (19) וַיַּשְׁכִּמוּ

and-they-arose (19) longer to-her they-were not and-faces-of-her

בַבֹּקֶר וַיִּשְׁתַּחֲווּ לִפְנֵי יְהוָה וַיָּשֻׁבוּ

then-they-returned Yahweh before and-they-worshiped in-the-morning

וַיָּבֹאוּ אֶל־בֵּיתָם הָרָמָתָה וַיֵּדַע אֶלְקָנָה אֶת־

*** Elkanah and-he-lay-with at-the-Ramah home-of-them to and-they-went-back

"O Lord Almighty, if you will
only look upon your servant's
misery and remember me, and
not forget your servant but
give her a son, then I will give
him to the Lord for all the days
of his life, and no razor will
ever be used on his head."
[12]As she kept on praying to
the Lord, Eli observed her
mouth. [13]Hannah was praying
in her heart, and her lips were
moving but her voice was not
heard. Eli thought she was
drunk [14]and said to her, "How
long will you keep on getting
drunk? Get rid of your wine."
[15]"Not so, my lord," Hannah
replied, "I am a woman who is
deeply troubled. I have not
been drinking wine or beer; I
was pouring out my soul to the
Lord. [16]Do not take your servant for a wicked woman; I
have been praying here out of
my great anguish and grief."
[17]Eli answered, "Go in
peace, and may the God of Israel grant you what you have
asked of him."
[18]She said, "May your servant find favor in your eyes."
Then she went her way and
ate something, and her face
was no longer downcast.
[19]Early the next morning
they arose and worshiped before the Lord and then went
back to their home at Ramah.
Elkanah lay with Hannah his

חַנָּה אִשְׁתּוֹ וַיִּזְכְּרֶהָ יְהוָה׃ וַיְהִי לִתְקֻפוֹת
in-courses-of so-he-was (20) Yahweh and-he-remembered-her wife-of-him Hannah

הַיָּמִים וַתַּהַר חַנָּה וַתֵּלֶד בֵּן וַתִּקְרָא אֶת־
*** and-she-called son and-she-bore Hannah then-she-conceived the-days

שְׁמוֹ שְׁמוּאֵל כִּי מֵיְהוָה שְׁאִלְתִּיו׃ וַיַּעַל
when-he-went-up (21) I-asked-for-him from-Yahweh because Samuel name-of-him

הָאִישׁ אֶלְקָנָה וְכָל־ בֵּיתוֹ לִזְבֹּחַ לַיהוָה אֶת־ זֶבַח
sacrifice-of *** to-Yahweh to-offer family-of-him and-all-of Elkanah the-man

הַיָּמִים וְאֶת־ נִדְרוֹ׃ וְחַנָּה לֹא עָלָתָה כִּי־ אָמְרָה
she-said for she-went not but-Hannah (22) vow-of-him and the-days

לְאִישָׁהּ עַד יִגָּמֵל הַנַּעַר וַהֲבִאֹתִיו
then-I-will-take-him the-boy he-is-weaned after to-husband-of-her

וְנִרְאָה אֶת־ פְּנֵי יְהוָה וְיָשַׁב שָׁם עַד־עוֹלָם׃
always for there and-he-will-live Yahweh before *** and-he-will-be-presented

וַיֹּאמֶר לָהּ אֶלְקָנָה אִישָׁהּ עֲשִׂי הַטּוֹב בְּעֵינַיִךְ
in-eyes-of-you the-good do! husband-of-her Elkanah to-her and-he-told (23)

שְׁבִי עַד־ גָּמְלֵךְ אֹתוֹ אַךְ יָקֵם יְהוָה אֶת־ דְּבָרוֹ
word-of-him *** Yahweh may-he-make-good only him to-wean-you until stay!

וַתֵּשֶׁב הָאִשָּׁה וַתֵּינֶק אֶת־ בְּנָהּ עַד־ גָמְלָהּ אֹתוֹ׃
him to-wean-her until son-of-her *** and-she-nursed the-woman so-she-stayed

וַתַּעֲלֵהוּ עִמָּהּ כַּאֲשֶׁר גְּמָלַתּוּ *בְּפָרִים שְׁלֹשָׁה*
*three with-bulls* she-weaned-him just-as with-her and-she-took-him (24)

וְאֵיפָה אַחַת קֶמַח וְנֵבֶל יַיִן וַתְּבִאֵהוּ בֵית־ יְהוָה
Yahweh house-of and-she-brought-him wine and-skin-of flour one and-ephah

שִׁלוֹ וְהַנַּעַר נָעַר׃ וַיִּשְׁחֲטוּ אֶת־ הַפָּר
the-bull *** when-they-slaughtered (25) young now-the-boy Shiloh

וַיָּבִאוּ אֶת־ הַנַּעַר אֶל־ עֵלִי׃ וַתֹּאמֶר בִּי אֲדֹנִי חֵי
life-of lord-of-me oh! and-she-said (26) Eli to the-boy *** then-they-brought

נַפְשְׁךָ אֲדֹנִי אֲנִי הָאִשָּׁה הַנִּצֶּבֶת עִמְּכָה בָּזֶה
at-here beside-you the-one-standing the-woman I lord-of-me soul-of-you

לְהִתְפַּלֵּל אֶל־ יְהוָה׃ אֶל־ הַנַּעַר הַזֶּה הִתְפַּלָּלְתִּי וַיִּתֵּן יְהוָה
Yahweh and-he-granted I-prayed the-this the-child for (27) Yahweh to to-pray

לִי אֶת־ שְׁאֵלָתִי אֲשֶׁר שָׁאַלְתִּי מֵעִמּוֹ׃ וְגַם אָנֹכִי הִשְׁאִלְתִּהוּ
I-give-him I so-now (28) from-with-him´ I-asked that request-of-me *** to-me

לַיהוָה כָּל־ הַיָּמִים אֲשֶׁר הָיָה הוּא שָׁאוּל לַיהוָה
to-Yahweh being-given he he-lives that the-days all-of to-Yahweh

וַיִּשְׁתַּחוּ שָׁם לַיהוָה׃ וַתִּתְפַּלֵּל חַנָּה וַתֹּאמַר
and-she-said Hannah then-she-prayed (2:1) to-Yahweh there and-he-worshiped

wife, and the LORD remembered her. [20]So in the course of time Hannah conceived and gave birth to a son. She named him Samuel,[e] saying, "Because I asked the LORD for him."

*Hannah Dedicates Samuel*

[21]When the man Elkanah went up with all his family to offer the annual sacrifice to the LORD and to fulfill his vow, [22]Hannah did not go. She said to her husband, "After the boy is weaned, I will take him and present him before the LORD, and he will live there always."

[23]"Do what seems best to you," Elkanah her husband told her. "Stay here until you have weaned him; only may the LORD make good his[f] word." So the woman stayed at home and nursed her son until she had weaned him.

[24]After he was weaned, she took the boy with her, young as he was, along with a three-year-old bull,[g] an ephah[h] of flour and a skin of wine, and brought him to the house of the LORD at Shiloh. [25]When they had slaughtered the bull, they brought the boy to Eli, [26]and she said to him, "As surely as you live, my lord, I am the woman who stood here beside you praying to the LORD. [27]I prayed for this child, and the LORD has granted me what I asked of him. [28]So now I give him to the LORD. For his whole life he will be given over to the LORD." And he worshiped the LORD there.

*Hannah's Prayer*

2 Then Hannah prayed and said:

[e]20 *Samuel* sounds like the Hebrew for *heard of God.*
[f]23 Masoretic Text; Dead Sea Scrolls, Septuagint and Syriac *your*
[g]24 Dead Sea Scrolls, Septuagint and Syriac; Masoretic Text *with three bulls*
[h]24 That is, probably about 1/2 bushel (about 22 liters)

*24 The Dead Sea Scrolls read
בקר משלש ולחם
*and-bread being-three-years-old bull* as do the ancient versions listed above in footnote *g*, (cf. verse 25).

עָלַץ לִבִּי בַּיהוָה רָמָה קַרְנִי בַּיהוָה
in-Yahweh horn-of-me she-is-lifted-high in-Yahweh heart-of-me he-rejoices

רָחַב פִּי עַל־ אוֹיְבַי כִּי שָׂמַחְתִּי
I-delight for being-enemies-of-me over mouth-of-me he-boasts

בִּישׁוּעָתֶךָ׃ (2) אֵין־ קָדוֹשׁ כַּיהוָה כִּי
indeed like-Yahweh holy there-is-no-one (2) in-deliverance-of-you

אֵין בִּלְתֶּךָ וְאֵין צוּר כֵּאלֹהֵינוּ׃ (3) אַל־
not (3) like-God-of-us Rock and-there-is-no besides-you there-is-no-one

תַּרְבּוּ תְדַבְּרוּ גְּבֹהָה גְבֹהָה יֵצֵא עָתָק מִפִּיכֶם
from-mouth-of-you arrogance he-comes proudly proudly you-talk you-keep-on

כִּי אֵל דֵּעוֹת יְהוָה וְלֹא נִתְכְּנוּ עֲלִלוֹת׃ (4) קֶשֶׁת
bow-of (4) deeds they-are-weighed and-by-him Yahweh knowings God-of for

גִּבֹּרִים חַתִּים וְנִכְשָׁלִים אָזְרוּ חָיִל׃
strength they-are-armed but-ones-stumbling ones-broken warriors

(5) שְׂבֵעִים בַּלֶּחֶם נִשְׂכָּרוּ וּרְעֵבִים חָדֵלּוּ
they-stop but-hungry-ones they-hire-themselves-out for-the-food full-ones (5)

עַד־ עֲקָרָה יָלְדָה שִׁבְעָה וְרַבַּת בָּנִים אֻמְלָלָה׃ (6) יְהוָה
Yahweh (6) pining-away sons but-many-of seven she-bore barren even

מֵמִית וּמְחַיֶּה מוֹרִיד שְׁאוֹל וַיָּעַל׃
and-he-raises-up Sheol bringing-down and-making-alive bringing-death

(7) יְהוָה מוֹרִישׁ וּמַעֲשִׁיר מַשְׁפִּיל אַף־ מְרוֹמֵם׃
exalting and humbling and-sending-wealth sending-poverty Yahweh (7)

(8) מֵקִים מֵעָפָר דָּל מֵאַשְׁפֹּת יָרִים אֶבְיוֹן לְהוֹשִׁיב עִם־
with to-seat needy he-lifts from-ash-heaps poor from-dust raising (8)

נְדִיבִים וְכִסֵּא כָבוֹד יַנְחִלֵם כִּי לַיהוָה מְצֻקֵי
foundations-of to-Yahweh for he-has-inherit-them honor and-throne-of princes

אֶרֶץ וַיָּשֶׁת עֲלֵיהֶם תֵּבֵל׃ (9) רַגְלֵי חֲסִידָו יִשְׁמֹר
he-will-guard saints-of-him feet-of (9) world upon-them and-he-set earth

וּרְשָׁעִים בַּחֹשֶׁךְ יִדָּמּוּ כִּי־ לֹא בְכֹחַ
by-strength not for they-will-be-silenced in-the-darkness but-wicked-ones

יִגְבַּר־ אִישׁ׃ (10) יְהוָה יֵחַתּוּ מְרִיבָו עָלָו
against-him ones-opposing-him he-shatters Yahweh (10) one he-prevails

בַּשָּׁמַיִם יַרְעֵם יְהוָה יָדִין אַפְסֵי־ אָרֶץ וְיִתֶּן־
he-will-give earth ends-of he-will-judge Yahweh he-thunders from-the-heavens

עֹז לְמַלְכּוֹ וְיָרֵם קֶרֶן מְשִׁיחוֹ׃
anointed-of-him horn-of he-will-exalt to-king-of-him strength

(11) וַיֵּלֶךְ אֶלְקָנָה הָרָמָתָה עַל־ בֵּיתוֹ וְהַנַּעַר הָיָה
he-was but-the-boy home-of-him to to-the-Ramah Elkanah then-he-went (11)

"My heart rejoices in the LORD;
in the LORD my horn[i] is lifted high.
My mouth boasts over my enemies,
for I delight in your deliverance.

2 "There is no one holy[j] like the LORD;
there is no one besides you;
there is no Rock like our God.

3 "Do not keep talking so proudly
or let your mouth speak such arrogance,
for the LORD is a God who knows,
and by him deeds are weighed.

4 "The bows of the warriors are broken,
but those who stumbled are armed with strength.
5 Those who were full hire themselves out for food,
but those who were hungry hunger no more.
She who was barren has borne seven children,
but she who has had many sons pines away.

6 "The LORD brings death and makes alive;
he brings down to the grave[k] and raises up.
7 The LORD sends poverty and wealth;
he humbles and he exalts.
8 He raises the poor from the dust
and lifts the needy from the ash heap;
he seats them with princes
and has them inherit a throne of honor.

"For the foundations of the earth are the LORD's;
upon them he has set the world.
9 He will guard the feet of his saints,
but the wicked will be silenced in darkness.

"It is not by strength that one prevails;
10 those who oppose the LORD will be shattered.
He will thunder against them from heaven;

[i] 1 *Horn* here symbolizes strength; also in verse 10.
[j] 2 Or *no Holy One*
[k] 6 Hebrew *Sheol*

°3 ק ולו ,°9 ק חסידיו
°10a ק מריביו ,°10b ק עליו

מְשָׁרֵת אֶת־ יְהוָה אֶת־ פְּנֵי עֵלִי הַכֹּהֵן׃ וּבְנֵי עֵלִי
Eli now-sons-of (12) the-priest Eli faces-of before Yahweh before ministering

בְּנֵי בְלִיָּעַל לֹא יָדְעוּ אֶת־ יְהוָה׃ וּמִשְׁפַּט הַכֹּהֲנִים
the-priests now-practice-of (13) Yahweh *** they-regarded not wickedness sons-of

אֶת־ הָעָם כָּל־ אִישׁ זֹבֵחַ זֶבַח וּבָא נַעַר
servant-of then-he-came sacrifice offering one any-of the-people with

הַכֹּהֵן כְּבַשֵּׁל הַבָּשָׂר וְהַמַּזְלֵג שְׁלֹשׁ־ הַשִּׁנַּיִם
the-prongs three-of and-the-fork the-meat while-to-boil the-priest

בְּיָדוֹ׃ וְהִכָּה בַכִּיּוֹר אוֹ בַדּוּד אוֹ
or into-the-kettle or into-the-pan and-he-plunged (14) in-hand-of-him

בַקַּלַּחַת אוֹ בַפָּרוּר כֹּל אֲשֶׁר יַעֲלֶה הַמַּזְלֵג יִקַּח
he-took the-fork he-brought-up that all into-the-pot or into-the-caldron

הַכֹּהֵן בּוֹ כָּכָה יַעֲשׂוּ לְכָל־ יִשְׂרָאֵל הַבָּאִים שָׁם
there the-ones-coming Israel to-all-of they-treated so for-him the-priest

בְּשִׁלֹה׃ גַּם בְּטֶרֶם יַקְטִרוּן אֶת־ הַחֵלֶב וּבָא נַעַר
servant-of then-he-came the-fat *** they-burned even-before but (15) to-Shiloh

הַכֹּהֵן וְאָמַר לָאִישׁ הַזֹּבֵחַ תְּנָה בָשָׂר לִצְלוֹת
to-roast meat give! the-one-sacrificing to-the-man and-he-said the-priest

לַכֹּהֵן וְלֹא־ יִקַּח מִמְּךָ בָּשָׂר מְבֻשָּׁל כִּי אִם־ חָי׃
raw only but being-boiled meat from-you he-will-accept for-not to-the-priest

וַיֹּאמֶר אֵלָיו הָאִישׁ קַטֵּר יַקְטִירוּן כַּיּוֹם הַחֵלֶב
the-fat as-the-day let-them-burn to-burn the-man to-him if-he-said (16)

וְקַח־ לְךָ כַּאֲשֶׁר תְּאַוֶּה נַפְשֶׁךָ וְאָמַר | לוֹ כִּי
but no then-he-answered self-of-you she-wants just-as for-you then-take!

עַתָּה תִתֵּן וְאִם־ לֹא לָקַחְתִּי בְחָזְקָה׃ וַתְּהִי חַטַּאת
sin-of and-she-was (17) by-force I-will-take not and-if you-hand-over now

הַנְּעָרִים גְּדוֹלָה מְאֹד אֶת־ פְּנֵי יְהוָה כִּי נִאֲצוּ
they-treated-with-contempt for Yahweh faces-of before very great the-young-men

הָאֲנָשִׁים אֵת מִנְחַת יְהוָה׃ וּשְׁמוּאֵל מְשָׁרֵת אֶת־ פְּנֵי
faces-of before ministering but-Samuel (18) Yahweh offering-of *** the-men

יְהוָה נַעַר חָגוּר אֵפוֹד בָּד׃ וּמְעִיל קָטֹן תַּעֲשֶׂה־ לּוֹ
for-him she-made little and-robe (19) linen ephod wearing boy Yahweh

אִמּוֹ וְהַעַלְתָה לוֹ מִיָּמִים | יָמִימָה בַּעֲלוֹתָהּ אֶת־
with when-to-go-up-her at-days on-days to-him and-she-took mother-of-him

אִישָׁהּ לִזְבֹּחַ אֶת־ זֶבַח הַיָּמִים׃ וּבֵרַךְ עֵלִי
Eli and-he-blessed (20) the-days sacrifice-of *** to-offer husband-of-her

אֶת־ אֶלְקָנָה וְאֶת־ אִשְׁתּוֹ וְאָמַר יָשֵׂם יְהוָה לְךָ זֶרַע מִן־
by child to-you Yahweh may-he-give and-he-said wife-of-him and Elkanah ***

°16 ק לא

the LORD will judge the
ends of the earth.
"He will give strength to
his king
and exalt the horn of his
anointed."

11 Then Elkanah went home to Ramah, but the boy ministered before the LORD under Eli the priest.

*Eli's Wicked Sons*

12 Eli's sons were wicked men; they had no regard for the LORD.
13 Now it was the practice of the priests with the people that whenever anyone offered a sacrifice and while the meat was being boiled, the servant of the priest would come with a three-pronged fork in his hand.
14 He would plunge it into the pan or kettle or caldron or pot, and the priest would take for himself whatever the fork brought up. This is how they treated all the Israelites who came to Shiloh.
15 But even before the fat was burned, the servant of the priest would come and say to the man who was sacrificing, "Give the priest some meat to roast; he won't accept boiled meat from you, but only raw."
16 If the man said to him, "Let the fat be burned up first, and then take whatever you want," the servant would then answer, "No, hand it over now; if you don't, I'll take it by force."
17 This sin of the young men was very great in the LORD's sight, for they[l] were treating the LORD's offering with contempt.
18 But Samuel was ministering before the LORD—a boy wearing a linen ephod.
19 Each year his mother made him a little robe and took it to him when she went up with her husband to offer the annual sacrifice.
20 Eli would bless Elkanah and his wife, saying, "May the LORD give you children by this woman to take

[l]17 Or *men*

הָאִשָּׁה הַזֹּאת תַּחַת הַשְּׁאֵלָה אֲשֶׁר שָׁאַל לַיהוָה

of-Yahweh he-asked that the-request in-place-of the-this the-woman

וְהָלְכוּ לִמְקֹמוֹ׃ כִּי־ פָקַד יְהוָה אֶת־ חַנָּה

Hannah to Yahweh he-was-gracious and (21) to-home-of-him then-they-went

וַתַּהַר וַתֵּלֶד שְׁלֹשָׁה־ בָנִים וּשְׁתֵּי בָנוֹת וַיִּגְדַּל

and-he-grew-up daughters and-two-of sons three and-she-bore and-she-conceived

הַנַּעַר שְׁמוּאֵל עִם־ יְהוָה׃ וְעֵלִי זָקֵן מְאֹד וְשָׁמַע אֵת כָּל־

all *** and-he-heard very he-was-old now-Eli (22) Yahweh with Samuel the-boy

אֲשֶׁר יַעֲשׂוּן בָּנָיו לְכָל־ יִשְׂרָאֵל וְאֵת אֲשֶׁר־ יִשְׁכְּבוּן אֶת־ הַנָּשִׁים

the-women with they-slept how and Israel to-all-of sons-of-him they-did that

הַצֹּבְאוֹת פֶּתַח אֹהֶל מוֹעֵד׃ וַיֹּאמֶר לָהֶם לָמָּה

why? to-them so-he-said (23) Meeting Tent-of entrance-of the-ones-serving

תַעֲשׂוּן כַּדְּבָרִים הָאֵלֶּה אֲשֶׁר אָנֹכִי שֹׁמֵעַ אֶת־ דִּבְרֵיכֶם רָעִים

wicked-ones deeds-of-you *** hearing I that the-these as-the-things you-do

מֵאֵת כָּל־ הָעָם אֵלֶּה׃ אַל בָּנָי כִּי לוֹא־ טוֹבָה הַשְּׁמֻעָה אֲשֶׁר

that the-report good not for sons-of-me no (24) these the-people all-of from

אָנֹכִי שֹׁמֵעַ מַעֲבִרִים עַם־ יְהוָה׃ אִם־ יֶחֱטָא אִישׁ לְאִישׁ

against-man man he-sins if (25) Yahweh people-of ones-spreading hearing I

וּפִלְלוֹ אֱלֹהִים וְאִם לַיהוָה יֶחֱטָא־ אִישׁ מִי

who? man he-sins against-Yahweh but-if God then-he-may-mediate-for-him

יִתְפַּלֶּל־ לוֹ וְלֹא יִשְׁמְעוּ לְקוֹל אֲבִיהֶם

father-of-them to-rebuke-of they-listened but-not for-him he-will-intercede

כִּי־ חָפֵץ יְהוָה לַהֲמִיתָם׃ וְהַנַּעַר שְׁמוּאֵל הֹלֵךְ

growing Samuel and-the-boy (26) to-kill-them Yahweh he-willed for

וְגָדֵל וָטוֹב גַּם עִם־ יְהוָה וְגַם עִם־ אֲנָשִׁים׃ וַיָּבֹא

now-he-came (27) men with and-also Yahweh with both and-favor both-stature

אִישׁ־ אֱלֹהִים אֶל־עֵלִי וַיֹּאמֶר אֵלָיו כֹּה אָמַר יְהוָה הֲנִגְלֹה

to-reveal-myself? Yahweh he-says this to-him and-he-said Eli to God man-of

נִגְלֵיתִי אֶל־ בֵּית אָבִיךָ בִּהְיוֹתָם בְּמִצְרַיִם

in-Egypt when-to-be-them father-of-you house-of to I-revealed-myself

לְבֵית פַּרְעֹה׃ וּבָחֹר אֹתוֹ מִכָּל־ שִׁבְטֵי יִשְׂרָאֵל

Israel tribes-of from-all-of him and-to-choose (28) Pharaoh under-house-of

לִי לְכֹהֵן לַעֲלוֹת עַל־ מִזְבְּחִי לְהַקְטִיר קְטֹרֶת לָשֵׂאת אֵפוֹד

ephod to-wear incense to-burn altar-of-me to to-go-up as-priest for-me

לְפָנַי וָאֶתְּנָה לְבֵית אָבִיךָ אֶת־ כָּל־

all-of *** father-of-you to-house-of and-I-gave in-presences-of-me

אִשֵּׁי בְּנֵי יִשְׂרָאֵל׃ לָמָּה תִבְעֲטוּ בְּזִבְחִי

at-sacrifice-of-me you-scorn why? (29) Israel sons-of fire-offerings-of

the place of the one she prayed
for and gave to the LORD."
Then they would go home.
[21]And the LORD was gracious
to Hannah; she conceived and
gave birth to three sons and
two daughters. Meanwhile,
the boy Samuel grew up in the
presence of the LORD.
[22]Now Eli, who was very old,
heard about everything his
sons were doing to all Israel
and how they slept with the
women who served at the entrance to the Tent of Meeting.
[23]So he said to them, "Why do
you do such things? I hear
from all the people about these
wicked deeds of yours. [24]No,
my sons; it is not a good report
that I hear spreading among
the LORD's people. [25]If a man
sins against another man,
God[m] may mediate for him;
but if a man sins against the
LORD, who will intercede for
him?" His sons, however, did
not listen to their father's
rebuke, for it was the LORD's
will to put them to death.
[26]And the boy Samuel continued to grow in stature and
in favor with the LORD and
with men.

*Prophecy Against the House of Eli*

[27]Now a man of God came to
Eli and said to him, "This is
what the LORD says: 'Did I not
clearly reveal myself to your
father's house when they were
in Egypt under Pharaoh? [28]I
chose your father out of all the
tribes of Israel to be my priest,
to go up to my altar, to burn
incense, and to wear an ephod
in my presence. I also gave
your father's house all the
offerings made with fire by
the Israelites. [29]Why do you[n]
scorn my sacrifice and

[m]25 Or *the judges*
[n]29 The Hebrew is plural.

וּבְמִנְחָתִי אֲשֶׁר צִוִּיתִי מָעוֹן וַתְּכַבֵּד אֶת־ בָּנֶיךָ
sons-of-you *** and-you-honor dwelling I-prescribed that and-at-offering-of-me

מִמֶּנִּי לְהַבְרִיאֲכֶם מֵרֵאשִׁית כָּל־ מִנְחַת יִשְׂרָאֵל
Israel offering-of every-of on-choice-part-of to-make-fat-you more-than-me

לְעַמִּי׃ (30) לָכֵן נְאֻם־ יְהוָה אֱלֹהֵי יִשְׂרָאֵל אָמוֹר
to-promise Israel God-of Yahweh declaration-of therefore (30) of-people-of-me

אָמַרְתִּי בֵּיתְךָ וּבֵית אָבִיךָ יִתְהַלְּכוּ
they-would-minister father-of-you and-house-of house-of-you I-promised

לְפָנַי עַד־ עוֹלָם וְעַתָּה נְאֻם־ יְהוָה חָלִילָה לִּי כִּי־
for from-me far-be-it! Yahweh declaration-of but-now forever for before-me

מְכַבְּדַי אֲכַבֵּד וּבֹזַי יֵקָלּוּ׃
they-will-be-disdained but-ones-despising-me I-will-honor ones-honoring-me

(31) הִנֵּה יָמִים בָּאִים וְגָדַעְתִּי אֶת־ זְרֹעֲךָ וְאֶת־
and strength-of-you *** when-I-will-cut-short ones-coming days see! (31)

זְרֹעַ בֵּית אָבִיךָ מִהְיוֹת זָקֵן בְּבֵיתֶךָ׃
in-family-of-you old-man not-to-be father-of-you house-of strength-of

(32) וְהִבַּטְתָּ צַר מָעוֹן בְּכֹל אֲשֶׁר־ יֵיטִיב
he-will-do-good that though-all dwelling distress-of and-you-will-see (32)

אֶת־ יִשְׂרָאֵל וְלֹא־ יִהְיֶה זָקֵן בְּבֵיתְךָ כָּל־ הַיָּמִים׃
the-days all-of in-family-of-you old-man he-will-be yet-not Israel ***

(33) וְאִישׁ לֹא־ אַכְרִית לְךָ מֵעִם מִזְבְּחִי לְכַלּוֹת אֶת־
*** to-blind altar-of-me from-at of-you I-cut-off not and-everyone (33)

עֵינֶיךָ וְלַאֲדִיב אֶת־ נַפְשֶׁךָ וְכָל־ מַרְבִּית
many-descendant-of and-all-of heart-of-you *** and-to-grieve eyes-of-you

בֵּיתְךָ יָמוּתוּ אֲנָשִׁים׃ (34) וְזֶה־ לְּךָ הָאוֹת אֲשֶׁר יָבֹא
he-happens that the-sign to-you and-this (34) men they-will-die family-of-you

אֶל־ שְׁנֵי בָנֶיךָ אֶל־ חָפְנִי וּפִינְחָס בְּיוֹם אֶחָד יָמוּתוּ
they-will-die same on-day and-Phinehas Hophni to sons-of-you two-of to

שְׁנֵיהֶם׃ (35) וַהֲקִימֹתִי לִי כֹּהֵן נֶאֱמָן כַּאֲשֶׁר
as-what being-faithful priest for-me and-I-will-raise-up (35) both-of-them

בִּלְבָבִי וּבְנַפְשִׁי יַעֲשֶׂה וּבָנִיתִי לוֹ
for-him and-I-will-establish he-will-do and-in-mind-of-me in-heart-of-me

בַּיִת נֶאֱמָן וְהִתְהַלֵּךְ לִפְנֵי־ מְשִׁיחִי כָּל־ הַיָּמִים׃
the-days all-of anointed-of-me before and-he-will-minister being-firm house

(36) וְהָיָה כָּל־ הַנּוֹתָר בְּבֵיתְךָ יָבוֹא
he-will-come in-family-of-you the-one-being-left every-of then-he-will-be (36)

לְהִשְׁתַּחֲוֹת לוֹ לַאֲגוֹרַת כֶּסֶף וְכִכַּר־ לֶחֶם וְאָמַר
and-he-will-plead bread and-crust-of silver for-piece-of before-him to-bow

offering that I prescribed for my dwelling? Why do you honor your sons more than me by fattening yourselves on the choice parts of every offering made by my people Israel?'

30"Therefore the LORD, the God of Israel, declares: 'I promised that your house and your father's house would minister before me forever.' But now the LORD declares: 'Far be it from me! Those who honor me I will honor, but those who despise me will be disdained. 31The time is coming when I will cut short your strength and the strength of your father's house, so that there will not be an old man in your family line 32and you will see distress in my dwelling. Although good will be done to Israel, in your family line there will never be an old man. 33Every one of you that I do not cut off from my altar will be spared only to blind your eyes with tears and to grieve your heart, and all your descendants will die in the prime of life.

34" 'And what happens to your two sons, Hophni and Phinehas, will be a sign to you—they will both die on the same day. 35I will raise up for myself a faithful priest, who will do according to what is in my heart and mind. I will firmly establish his house, and he will minister before my anointed one always. 36Then everyone left in your family line will come and bow down before him for a piece of silver and a crust of bread and plead,

*35 Most mss have *hireq* under the *he* (וְהִתְ).

סְפָחֵנִי נָא אֶל־ אַחַת הַכְּהֻנּוֹת לֶאֱכֹל פַּת־ לָחֶם׃
food bit-of to-eat the-priestly-offices one-of to now! appoint-me!

וְהַנַּעַר שְׁמוּאֵל מְשָׁרֵת אֶת־ יְהוָה לִפְנֵי עֵלִי וּדְבַר־
and-word-of Eli under Yahweh before ministering Samuel now-the-boy (3:1)

יְהוָה הָיָה יָקָר בַּיָּמִים הָהֵם אֵין חָזוֹן נִפְרָץ׃
being-many vision there-was-not the-those in-the-days rare he-was Yahweh

וַיְהִי בַּיּוֹם הַהוּא וְעֵלִי שֹׁכֵב בִּמְקֹמוֹ
in-place-of-him lying-down that-Eli the-that on-the-day and-he-was (2)

וְעֵינָו הֵחֵלּוּ כֵהוֹת לֹא יוּכַל לִרְאוֹת׃ וְנֵר
and-lamp-of (3) to-see he-could not weak-ones they-became now-eyes-of-him

אֱלֹהִים טֶרֶם יִכְבֶּה וּשְׁמוּאֵל שֹׁכֵב בְּהֵיכַל יְהוָה אֲשֶׁר־
where Yahweh in-temple-of lying-down and-Samuel he-went-out not-yet God

שָׁם אֲרוֹן אֱלֹהִים׃ וַיִּקְרָא יְהוָה אֶל־שְׁמוּאֵל וַיֹּאמֶר הִנֵּנִי׃
here-I! and-he-answered Samuel to Yahweh then-he-called (4) God ark-of there

וַיָּרָץ אֶל־ עֵלִי וַיֹּאמֶר הִנְנִי כִּי־ קָרָאתָ לִּי וַיֹּאמֶר
but-he-said to-me you-called for here-I! and-he-said Eli to and-he-ran (5)

לֹא־קָרָאתִי שׁוּב שְׁכָב וַיֵּלֶךְ וַיִּשְׁכָּב׃ וַיֹּסֶף
and-he-repeated (6) and-he-lay-down so-he-went lie-down! go-back! I-called not

יְהוָה קְרֹא עוֹד שְׁמוּאֵל וַיָּקָם שְׁמוּאֵל וַיֵּלֶךְ אֶל־עֵלִי
Eli to and-he-went Samuel and-he-got-up Samuel again to-call Yahweh

וַיֹּאמֶר הִנְנִי כִּי קָרָאתָ לִי וַיֹּאמֶר לֹא־ קָרָאתִי בְנִי
son-of-me I-called not but-he-said to-me you-called for here-I! and-he-said

שׁוּב שְׁכָב׃ וּשְׁמוּאֵל טֶרֶם יָדַע אֶת־ יְהוָה וְטֶרֶם
and-not-yet Yahweh *** he-knew not-yet now-Samuel (7) lie-down! go-back!

יִגָּלֶה אֵלָיו דְּבַר־ יְהוָה׃ וַיֹּסֶף יְהוָה קְרֹא־
to-call Yahweh and-he-repeated (8) Yahweh word-of to-him he-was-revealed

שְׁמוּאֵל בַּשְּׁלִשִׁית וַיָּקָם וַיֵּלֶךְ אֶל־ עֵלִי וַיֹּאמֶר הִנְנִי
here-I! and-he-said Eli to and-he-went and-he-got-up on-the-third Samuel

כִּי קָרָאתָ לִי וַיָּבֶן עֵלִי כִּי יְהוָה קֹרֵא לַנָּעַר׃
to-the-boy calling Yahweh that Eli then-he-realized to-me you-called for

וַיֹּאמֶר עֵלִי לִשְׁמוּאֵל לֵךְ שְׁכָב וְהָיָה אִם־ יִקְרָא אֵלֶיךָ
to-you he-calls if and-he-will-be lie-down! go! to-Samuel Eli so-he-told (9)

וְאָמַרְתָּ דַּבֵּר יְהוָה כִּי שֹׁמֵעַ עַבְדֶּךָ וַיֵּלֶךְ שְׁמוּאֵל
Samuel so-he-went servant-of-you listening for Yahweh speak! they-you-say

וַיִּשְׁכַּב בִּמְקוֹמוֹ׃ וַיָּבֹא יְהוָה וַיִּתְיַצַּב
and-he-stood Yahweh and-he-came (10) in-place-of-him and-he-lay-down

וַיִּקְרָא כְפַעַם־ בְּפַעַם שְׁמוּאֵל ׀ שְׁמוּאֵל וַיֹּאמֶר שְׁמוּאֵל דַּבֵּר כִּי
for speak! Samuel then-he-said Samuel Samuel at-time as-time and-he-called

"Appoint me to some priestly office so I can have food to eat." ' "

*The Lord Calls Samuel*

3 The boy Samuel minis-
tered before the LORD un-
der Eli. In those days the word
of the LORD was rare; there
were not many visions.
[2]One night Eli, whose eyes
were becoming so weak that
he could barely see, was lying
down in his usual place. [3]The
lamp of God had not yet gone
out, and Samuel was lying
down in the temple° of the
LORD, where the ark of God
was. [4]Then the LORD called
Samuel.
Samuel answered, "Here I
am." [5]And he ran to Eli and
said, "Here I am; you called
me."
But Eli said, "I did not call;
go back and lie down." So he
went and lay down.
[6]Again the LORD called,
"Samuel!" And Samuel got up
and went to Eli and said,
"Here I am; you called me."
"My son," Eli said, "I did
not call; go back and lie
down."
[7]Now Samuel did not yet
know the LORD: The word of
the LORD had not yet been revealed to him.
[8]The LORD called Samuel a
third time, and Samuel got up
and went to Eli and said,
"Here I am; you called me."
Then Eli realized that the
LORD was calling the boy. [9]So
Eli told Samuel, "Go and lie
down, and if he calls you, say,
'Speak, LORD, for your servant
is listening.' " So Samuel went
and lay down in his place.
[10]The LORD came and stood
there, calling as at the other
times, "Samuel! Samuel!"
Then Samuel said, "Speak,

°3 That is, tabernacle

°2 ק ועיניו

שֹׁמֵעַ עַבְדֶּךָ׃ וַיֹּאמֶר יְהוָה אֶל־שְׁמוּאֵל הִנֵּה אָנֹכִי עֹשֶׂה
doing I see! Samuel to Yahweh and-he-said (11) servant-of-you listening

דָּבָר בְּיִשְׂרָאֵל אֲשֶׁר כָּל־ שֹׁמְעוֹ תְּצִלֶּינָה שְׁתֵּי
both-of they-will-tingle one-hearing-him every-of that in-Israel something

אָזְנָיו׃ בַּיּוֹם הַהוּא אָקִים אֶל־ עֵלִי אֵת כָּל־
all *** Eli against I-will-carry-out the-that on-the-day (12) ears-of-him

אֲשֶׁר דִּבַּרְתִּי אֶל־ בֵּיתוֹ הָחֵל וְכַלֵּה׃ וְהִגַּדְתִּי
for-I-told (13) and-to-end to-begin family-of-him against I-spoke that

לוֹ כִּי־ שֹׁפֵט אֲנִי אֶת־ בֵּיתוֹ עַד־ עוֹלָם בַּעֲוֹן אֲשֶׁר־ יָדַע
he-knew that for-sin forever for family-of-him *** I judging that to-him

כִּי־ מְקַלְלִים לָהֶם בָּנָיו וְלֹא כִהָה
he-restrained and-not sons-of-him to-them ones-bringing-contempt for

בָּם׃ וְלָכֵן נִשְׁבַּעְתִּי לְבֵית עֵלִי אִם־ יִתְכַּפֵּר
he-will-be-atoned not Eli to-house-of I-swore so-therefore (14) against-them

עֲוֹן בֵּית־ עֵלִי בְּזֶבַח וּבְמִנְחָה עַד־ עוֹלָם׃ וַיִּשְׁכַּב
and-he-lay (15) forever for or-by-offering by-sacrifice Eli house-of guilt-of

שְׁמוּאֵל עַד־ הַבֹּקֶר וַיִּפְתַּח אֶת־ דַּלְתוֹת בֵּית־ יְהוָה
Yahweh house-of doors-of *** then-he-opened the-morning until Samuel

וּשְׁמוּאֵל יָרֵא מֵהַגִּיד אֶת־ הַמַּרְאָה אֶל־עֵלִי׃ וַיִּקְרָא
but-he-called (16) Eli to the-vision *** from-to-tell he-was-afraid now-Samuel

עֵלִי אֶת־ שְׁמוּאֵל וַיֹּאמֶר שְׁמוּאֵל בְּנִי וַיֹּאמֶר הִנֵּנִי׃
here-I! and-he-answered son-of-me Samuel and-he-said Samuel *** Eli

וַיֹּאמֶר מָה הַדָּבָר אֲשֶׁר דִּבֶּר אֵלֶיךָ אַל־ נָא תְכַחֵד
you-hide now! not to-you he-said that the-message what? and-he-asked (17)

מִמֶּנִּי כֹּה יַעֲשֶׂה־ לְּךָ אֱלֹהִים וְכֹה יוֹסִיף אִם־ תְּכַחֵד
you-hide if may-he-be-severe and-so God with-you may-he-deal so from-me

מִמֶּנִּי דָּבָר מִכָּל־ הַדָּבָר אֲשֶׁר־ דִּבֶּר אֵלֶיךָ׃ וַיַּגֶּד־
so-he-told (18) to-you he-told that the-message from-any-of anything from-me

לוֹ שְׁמוּאֵל אֶת־ כָּל־ הַדְּבָרִים וְלֹא כִחֵד מִמֶּנּוּ וַיֹּאמַר
and-he-said from-him he-hid and-not the-things all-of *** Samuel to-him

יְהוָה הוּא הַטּוֹב בְּעֵינָו יַעֲשֶׂה׃ וַיִּגְדַּל שְׁמוּאֵל
Samuel and-he-grew (19) let-him-do in-eyes-of-him the-good he Yahweh

וַיהוָה הָיָה עִמּוֹ וְלֹא־ הִפִּיל מִכָּל־ דְּבָרָיו
words-of-him from-any-of he-let-fall and-not with-him he-was and-Yahweh

אָרְצָה׃ וַיֵּדַע כָּל־ יִשְׂרָאֵל מִדָּן וְעַד־ בְּאֵר שָׁבַע
Sheba Beer even-to from-Dan Israel all-of and-he-recognized (20) to-ground

כִּי נֶאֱמָן שְׁמוּאֵל לְנָבִיא לַיהוָה׃ וַיֹּסֶף יְהוָה
Yahweh and-he-continued (21) of-Yahweh as-prophet Samuel being-attested that

°18 ק בעיניו

for your servant is listening."
11 And the LORD said to Samuel: "See, I am about to do something in Israel that will make the ears of everyone who hears of it tingle. 12 At that time I will carry out against Eli everything I spoke against his family—from beginning to end. 13 For I told him that I would judge his family forever because of the sin he knew about; his sons made themselves contemptible,[p] and he failed to restrain them. 14 Therefore, I swore to the house of Eli, 'The guilt of Eli's house will never be atoned for by sacrifice or offering.'"
15 Samuel lay down until morning and then opened the doors of the house of the LORD. He was afraid to tell Eli the vision, 16 but Eli called him and said, "Samuel, my son."
Samuel answered, "Here I am."
17 "What was it he said to you?" Eli asked. "Do not hide it from me. May God deal with you, be it ever so severely, if you hide from me anything he told you." 18 So Samuel told him everything, hiding nothing from him. Then Eli said, "He is the LORD; let him do what is good in his eyes."
19 The LORD was with Samuel as he grew up, and he let none of his words fall to the ground. 20 And all Israel from Dan to Beersheba recognized that Samuel was attested as a prophet of the LORD. 21 The LORD continued to appear at

[p]13 Masoretic Text; an ancient Hebrew scribal tradition and Septuagint *sons blasphemed God*

לְהֵרָאֹה בְּשִׁלֹה כִּֽי־ נִגְלָה יְהוָה אֶל־ שְׁמוּאֵל בְּשִׁלוֹ
at-Shiloh Samuel to Yahweh he-revealed-himself for at-Shiloh to-appear

בִּדְבַר יְהוָה׃ וַיְהִי דְבַר־ שְׁמוּאֵל לְכָל־ יִשְׂרָאֵל
Israel to-all-of Samuel word-of and-he-came (4:1) Yahweh through-word-of

וַיֵּצֵא יִשְׂרָאֵל לִקְרַאת פְּלִשְׁתִּים לַמִּלְחָמָה וַיַּחֲנוּ עַל־
at and-they-camped in-the-fight Philistines to-meet Israel now-he-went-out

הָאֶבֶן הָעֶזֶר וּפְלִשְׁתִּים חָנוּ בַאֲפֵק׃ וַיַּעַרְכוּ
and-they-deployed (2) at-Aphek they-camped and-Philistines the-Ezer the-Eben

פְלִשְׁתִּים לִקְרַאת יִשְׂרָאֵל וַתִּטֹּשׁ הַמִּלְחָמָה וַיִּנָּגֶף
and-he-was-defeated the-battle and-she-spread Israel to-meet Philistines

יִשְׂרָאֵל לִפְנֵי פְלִשְׁתִּים וַיַּכּוּ בַמַּעֲרָכָה בַּשָּׂדֶה
in-the-field on-the-battleground and-they-killed Philistines before Israel

כְּאַרְבַּעַת אֲלָפִים אִישׁ׃ וַיָּבֹא הָעָם אֶל־ הַמַּחֲנֶה
the-camp to the-people when-he-returned (3) man thousands about-four-of

וַיֹּאמְרוּ זִקְנֵי יִשְׂרָאֵל לָמָּה נְגָפָנוּ יְהוָה הַיּוֹם לִפְנֵי
before the-day Yahweh he-defeated-us why? Israel elders-of then-they-asked

פְלִשְׁתִּים נִקְחָה אֵלֵינוּ מִשִּׁלֹה אֶת־ אֲרוֹן בְּרִית יְהוָה
Yahweh covenant-of ark-of *** from-Shiloh to-us let-us-bring Philistines

וְיָבֹא בְקִרְבֵּנוּ וְיֹשִׁעֵנוּ מִכַּף אֹיְבֵינוּ׃
being-enemies-of-us from-hand-of and-he-may-save-us in-among-us so-he-may-go

וַיִּשְׁלַח הָעָם שִׁלֹה וַיִּשְׂאוּ מִשָּׁם אֵת אֲרוֹן
ark-of *** from-there and-they-brought Shiloh the-people so-he-sent (4)

בְּרִית־ יְהוָה צְבָאוֹת יֹשֵׁב הַכְּרֻבִים וְשָׁם שְׁנֵי
two-of and-there the-cherubim being-enthroned-of Hosts Yahweh-of covenant-of

בְּנֵֽי־ עֵלִי עִם־ אֲרוֹן בְּרִית הָאֱלֹהִים חָפְנִי וּפִינְחָס׃ וַיְהִי
and-he-was (5) and-Phinehas Hophni the-God covenant-of ark-of with Eli sons-of

כְּבוֹא אֲרוֹן בְּרִית־ יְהוָה אֶל־ הַמַּחֲנֶה וַיָּרִעוּ כָל־
all-of and-they-shouted the-camp into Yahweh covenant-of ark-of when-to-come

יִשְׂרָאֵל תְּרוּעָה גְדוֹלָה וַתֵּהֹם הָאָרֶץ׃ וַיִּשְׁמְעוּ פְלִשְׁתִּים
Philistines when-they-heard (6) the-ground so-she-shook great shout Israel

אֶת־ קוֹל הַתְּרוּעָה וַיֹּאמְרוּ מֶה קוֹל הַתְּרוּעָה הַגְּדוֹלָה
the-great the-shout sound-of what? then-they-asked the-uproar sound-of ***

הַזֹּאת בְּמַחֲנֵה הָעִבְרִים וַיֵּדְעוּ כִּי אֲרוֹן יְהוָה בָּא
he-came Yahweh ark-of that when-they-learned the-Hebrews in-camp-of the-this

אֶל־ הַמַּחֲנֶה׃ וַיִּרְאוּ הַפְּלִשְׁתִּים כִּי אָמְרוּ בָּא
he-came they-said for the-Philistines then-they-were-afraid (7) the-camp into

אֱלֹהִים אֶל־הַמַּחֲנֶה וַיֹּאמְרוּ אוֹי לָנוּ כִּי לֹא הָיְתָה כָּזֹאת
like-this she-happened not for to-us woe! and-they-said the-camp into god

Shiloh, and there he revealed himself to Samuel through his word.

**4** And Samuel's word came to all Israel.

### *The Philistines Capture the Ark*

Now the Israelites went out to fight against the Philistines. The Israelites camped at Ebenezer, and the Philistines at Aphek. [2]The Philistines deployed their forces to meet Israel, and as the battle spread, Israel was defeated by the Philistines, who killed about four thousand of them on the battlefield. [3]When the soldiers returned to camp, the elders of Israel asked, "Why did the LORD bring defeat upon us today before the Philistines? Let us bring the ark of the LORD's covenant from Shiloh, so that it[q] may go with us and save us from the hand of our enemies."

[4]So the people sent men to Shiloh, and they brought back the ark of the covenant of the LORD Almighty, who is enthroned between the cherubim. And Eli's two sons, Hophni and Phinehas, were there with the ark of the covenant of God.

[5]When the ark of the LORD's covenant came into the camp, all Israel raised such a great shout that the ground shook. [6]Hearing the uproar, the Philistines asked, "What's all this shouting in the Hebrew camp?"

When they learned that the ark of the LORD had come into the camp, [7]the Philistines were afraid. "A god has come into the camp," they said. "We're in trouble! Nothing like this has happened before.

[q]3 Or *he*

אתמול שלשם׃ אוי לנו מי יצילנו מיד האלהים
the-gods from-hand-of he-will-deliver-us who? to-us woe! (8) before yesterday

האדירים האלה אלה הם האלהים המכים את־ מצרים
Egyptians *** the-ones-striking the-gods they these the-these the-mighty-ones

בכל־ מכה במדבר׃ התחזקו והיו לאנשים פלשתים
Philistines like-men and-be! be-strong! (9) in-the-desert plague with-every-of

פן תעבדו לעברים כאשר עבדו לכם
to-you they-are-subject just-as to-the-Hebrews you-will-be-subject or

והייתם לאנשים ונלחמתם׃ וילחמו פלשתים
Philistines so-they-fought (10) and-you-fight like-men so-you-be

וינגף ישראל וינסו איש לאהליו ותהי
and-she-was to-tents-of-him each and-they-fled Israel and-he-was-defeated

המכה גדולה מאד ויפל מישראל שלשים אלף רגלי׃
foot-soldier thousand thirty from-Israel and-he-fell very great the-slaughter

וארון אלהים נלקח ושני בני־ עלי מתו חפני
Hophni they-died Eli sons-of and-two-of he-was-captured God and-ark-of (11)

ופינחס׃ וירץ איש־ בנימן מהמערכה ויבא
and-he-went from-the-battle-line Benjamin man-of and-he-ran (12) and-Phinehas

שלה ביום ההוא ומדיו קרעים ואדמה על־
on and-dust ones-being-torn and-clothes-of-him the-that on-the-day Shiloh

ראשו׃ ויבוא והנה עלי ישב על־ הכסא יך
side-of the-chair on sitting Eli then-see! when-he-arrived (13) head-of-him

דרך מצפה כי־ היה לבו חרד על ארון האלהים והאיש
when-the-man the-God ark-of for afraid heart-of-him he-was for watching road

בא להגיד בעיר ותזעק כל־ העיר׃
the-town whole-of then-she-cried in-the-town to-tell he-entered

וישמע עלי את־ קול הצעקה ויאמר מה קול
sound-of what? and-he-asked the-outcry sound-of *** Eli and-he-heard (14)

ההמון הזה והאיש מהר ויבא ויגד לעלי׃
to-Eli and-he-told and-he-went he-hurried and-the-man the-this the-uproar

ועלי בן־ תשעים ושמנה שנה ועיניו קמה ולא
so-not being-set and-eyes-of-him year and-eight ninety son-of now-Eli (15)

יכול לראות׃ ויאמר האיש אל־ עלי אנכי הבא מן־
from the-one-coming I Eli to the-man and-he-told (16) to-see he-could

המערכה ואני מן־ המערכה נסתי היום ויאמר מה־
what? and-he-asked the-day I-fled the-battle-line from and-I the-battle-line

היה הדבר בני׃ ויען המבשר
the-one-bringing-news and-he-replied (17) son-of-me the-thing he-happened

8 Woe to us! Who will deliver us
from the hand of these mighty
gods? They are the gods who
struck the Egyptians with all
kinds of plagues in the desert.
9 Be strong, Philistines! Be
men, or you will be subject to
the Hebrews, as they have
been to you. Be men, and
fight!"
10 So the Philistines fought,
and the Israelites were defeated and every man fled to
his tent. The slaughter was
very great; Israel lost thirty
thousand foot soldiers. 11 The
ark of God was captured, and
Eli's two sons, Hophni and
Phinehas, died.

*Death of Eli*

12 That same day a Benjamite
ran from the battle line and
went to Shiloh, his clothes
torn and dust on his head.
13 When he arrived, there was
Eli sitting on his chair by the
side of the road, watching, because his heart feared for the
ark of God. When the man entered the town and told what
had happened, the whole
town sent up a cry.
14 Eli heard the outcry and
asked, "What is the meaning
of this uproar?"
The man hurried over to Eli,
15 who was ninety-eight years
old and whose eyes were set so
that he could not see. 16 He told
Eli, "I have just come from the
battle line; I fled from it this
very day."
Eli asked, "What happened,
my son?"
17 The man who brought the

°13 ק יד

וַיֹּאמֶר נָס יִשְׂרָאֵל לִפְנֵי פְלִשְׁתִּים וְגַם מַגֵּפָה גְדוֹלָה הָיְתָה
she-was heavy loss and-also Philistines before Israel he-fled and-he-said

בָעָם וְגַם־ שְׁנֵי בָנֶיךָ מֵתוּ חָפְנִי וּפִינְחָס
and-Phinehas Hophni they-died sons-of-you two-of and-also among-the-people

וַאֲרוֹן הָאֱלֹהִים נִלְקָחָה׃ וַיְהִי כְּהַזְכִּירוֹ | אֶת־
*** when-to-mention-him and-he-was (18) she-was-captured the-God and-ark-of

אֲרוֹן הָאֱלֹהִים וַיִּפֹּל מֵעַל־ הַכִּסֵּא אֲחֹרַנִּית בְּעַד | יַד הַשַּׁעַר
the-gate side-of by backward the-chair from-on and-he-fell the-God ark-of

וַתִּשָּׁבֵר מַפְרַקְתּוֹ וַיָּמֹת כִּי־ זָקֵן הָאִישׁ וְכָבֵד
and-heavy the-man he-was-old for and-he-died neck-of-him and-she-was-broken

וְהוּא שָׁפַט אֶת־ יִשְׂרָאֵל אַרְבָּעִים שָׁנָה׃ וְכַלָּתוֹ אֵשֶׁת־
wife-of now-daughter-in-law-of-him (19) year forty Israel *** he-led and-he

פִּינְחָס הָרָה לָלַת וַתִּשְׁמַע אֶת־ הַשְּׁמֻעָה אֶל־ הִלָּקַח
to-be-captured that the-news *** when-she-heard to-deliver pregnant Phinehas

אֲרוֹן הָאֱלֹהִים וּמֵת חָמִיהָ וְאִישָׁהּ
and-husband-of-her father-in-law-of-her and-he-died the-God ark-of

וַתִּכְרַע וַתֵּלֶד כִּי־ נֶהֶפְכוּ עָלֶיהָ
over-her they-overcame but and-she-gave-birth then-she-went-into-labor

צִרֶיהָ׃ וּכְעֵת מוּתָהּ וַתְּדַבֵּרְנָה
then-they-said to-die-her and-at-time-of (20) labor-pains-of-her

הַנִּצָּבוֹת עָלֶיהָ אַל־ תִּירְאִי כִּי בֵן יָלָדְתְּ וְלֹא
but-not you-bore son for you-despair not to-her the-ones-attending

עָנְתָה וְלֹא־ שָׁתָה לִבָּהּ׃ וַתִּקְרָא לַנַּעַר
to-the-boy and-she-named (21) heart-of-her she-attended and-not she-responded

אִי־כָבוֹד לֵאמֹר גָּלָה כָבוֹד מִיִּשְׂרָאֵל אֶל־ הִלָּקַח אֲרוֹן
ark-of to-be-captured because from-Israel glory he-departed to-say Ichabod

הָאֱלֹהִים וְאֶל־ חָמִיהָ וְאִישָׁהּ׃
and-husband-of-her father-in-law-of-her and-because-of the-God

וַתֹּאמֶר גָּלָה כָבוֹד מִיִּשְׂרָאֵל כִּי נִלְקַח אֲרוֹן
ark-of he-was-captured for from-Israel glory he-departed and-she-said (22)

הָאֱלֹהִים׃ וּפְלִשְׁתִּים לָקְחוּ אֵת אֲרוֹן הָאֱלֹהִים וַיְבִאֻהוּ
and-they-took-him the-God ark-of *** they-captured now-Philistines (5:1) the-God

מֵאֶבֶן הָעֶזֶר אַשְׁדּוֹדָה׃ וַיִּקְחוּ פְלִשְׁתִּים אֶת־ אֲרוֹן
ark-of *** Philistines then-they-carried (2) to-Ashdod the-Ezer from-Eben

הָאֱלֹהִים וַיָּבִיאוּ אֹתוֹ בֵּית דָּגוֹן וַיַּצִּיגוּ אֹתוֹ אֵצֶל דָּגוֹן׃
Dagon beside him and-they-set Dagon temple-of him and-they-took the-God

וַיַּשְׁכִּמוּ אַשְׁדּוֹדִים מִמָּחֳרָת וְהִנֵּה דָגוֹן נֹפֵל
having-fallen Dagon then-see! on-next-day Ashdodites when-they-rose (3)

news replied, "Israel fled before the Philistines, and the army has suffered heavy losses. Also your two sons, Hophni and Phinehas, are dead, and the ark of God has been captured."

18 When he mentioned the ark of God, Eli fell backward off his chair by the side of the gate. His neck was broken and he died, for he was an old man and heavy. He had led[r] Israel forty years.

19 His daughter-in-law, the wife of Phinehas, was pregnant and near the time of delivery. When she heard the news that the ark of God had been captured and that her father-in-law and her husband were dead, she went into labor and gave birth, but was overcome by her labor pains. 20 As she was dying, the women attending her said, "Don't despair; you have given birth to a son." But she did not respond or pay any attention.

21 She named the boy Ichabod,[s] saying, "The glory has departed from Israel"—because of the capture of the ark of God and the deaths of her father-in-law and her husband. 22 She said, "The glory has departed from Israel, for the ark of God has been captured."

### *The Ark in Ashdod and Ekron*

5 After the Philistines had captured the ark of God, they took it from Ebenezer to Ashdod. 2 Then they carried the ark into Dagon's temple and set it beside Dagon. 3 When the people of Ashdod rose early the next day, there was Dagon, fallen on his face

[r] 18 Traditionally *judged*
[s] 21 *Ichabod* means *no glory*.

לְפָנָיו אַרְצָה לִפְנֵי אֲרוֹן יְהוָה וַיִּקְחוּ אֶת־ דָּגוֹן
Dagon *** and-they-took Yahweh ark-of before on-ground on-faces-of-him

וַיָּשִׁבוּ אֹתוֹ לִמְקוֹמוֹ׃ וַיַּשְׁכִּמוּ בַבֹּקֶר
in-the-morning but-they-rose (4) in-place-of-him him and-they-put-back

מִמָּחֳרָת וְהִנֵּה דָגוֹן נֹפֵל לְפָנָיו אַרְצָה לִפְנֵי
before on-ground on-faces-of-him having-fallen Dagon and-see! on-next-day

אֲרוֹן יְהוָה וְרֹאשׁ דָּגוֹן וּשְׁתֵּי | כַּפּוֹת יָדָיו
hands-of-him palms-of and-two-of Dagon and-head-of Yahweh ark-of

כְּרֻתוֹת אֶל־ הַמִּפְתָּן רַק דָּגוֹן נִשְׁאַר עָלָיו׃ עַל־
for (5) on-him he-remained Dagon only the-threshold on ones-being-broken-off

כֵּן לֹא־ יִדְרְכוּ כֹהֲנֵי דָגוֹן וְכָל־ הַבָּאִים בֵּית־
temple-of the-ones-entering or-any-of Dagon priests-of they-step not this

דָּגוֹן עַל־ מִפְתַּן דָּגוֹן בְּאַשְׁדּוֹד עַד הַיּוֹם הַזֶּה׃ וַתִּכְבַּד
and-she-was-heavy (6) the-this the-day to at-Ashdod Dagon threshold-of on Dagon

יַד־ יְהוָה אֶל־ הָאַשְׁדּוֹדִים וַיְשִׁמֵּם וַיַּךְ
and-he-afflicted and-he-brought-desolation the-Ashdodites upon Yahweh hand-of

אֹתָם בַּעְפֹלִים* אֶת־אַשְׁדּוֹד וְאֶת־ גְּבוּלֶיהָ׃ וַיִּרְאוּ אַנְשֵׁי־
men-of when-they-saw (7) vicinities-of-her and Ashdod *** *with-the-tumors them

אַשְׁדּוֹד כִּי־ כֵן וְאָמְרוּ לֹא־ יֵשֵׁב אֲרוֹן אֱלֹהֵי יִשְׂרָאֵל עִמָּנוּ
with-us Israel god-of ark-of he-must-stay not then-they-said so that Ashdod

כִּי־ קָשְׁתָה יָדוֹ עָלֵינוּ וְעַל דָּגוֹן אֱלֹהֵינוּ׃ וַיִּשְׁלְחוּ
so-they-sent (8) god-of-us Dagon and-upon upon-us hand-of-him she-is-heavy for

וַיַּאַסְפוּ אֶת־ כָּל־ סַרְנֵי פְלִשְׁתִּים אֲלֵיהֶם וַיֹּאמְרוּ
and-they-asked to-them Philistines rulers-of all-of *** and-they-called-together

מַה־ נַּעֲשֶׂה לַאֲרוֹן אֱלֹהֵי יִשְׂרָאֵל וַיֹּאמְרוּ גַּת
Gath and-they-answered Israel god-of with-ark-of shall-we-do what?

יִסֹּב אֲרוֹן אֱלֹהֵי יִשְׂרָאֵל וַיַּסֵּבּוּ אֶת־ אֲרוֹן אֱלֹהֵי יִשְׂרָאֵל׃
Israel God-of ark-of *** so-they-moved Israel god-of ark-of let-him-move

וַיְהִי אַחֲרֵי | הֵסַבּוּ אֹתוֹ וַתְּהִי יַד־ יְהוָה |
Yahweh hand-of then-she-was him they-moved after but-he-was (9)

בָּעִיר מְהוּמָה גְּדוֹלָה מְאֹד וַיַּךְ אֶת־ אַנְשֵׁי הָעִיר
the-city people-of *** and-he-afflicted very great panic against-the-city

מִקָּטֹן וְעַד־ גָּדוֹל וַיִּשָּׂתְרוּ לָהֶם עְפָלִים*׃ וַיְשַׁלְּחוּ
so-they-sent (10) *tumors on-them so-they-broke-out old even-to from-young

אֶת־ אֲרוֹן הָאֱלֹהִים עֶקְרוֹן וַיְהִי כְּבוֹא אֲרוֹן הָאֱלֹהִים עֶקְרוֹן
Ekron the-God ark-of as-to-enter and-he-was Ekron the-God ark-of ***

וַיִּזְעֲקוּ הָעֶקְרֹנִים לֵאמֹר הֵסַבּוּ אֵלַי אֶת־ אֲרוֹן אֱלֹהֵי
god-of ark-of *** to-me they-brought to-say the-Ekronites then-they-cried

on the ground before the ark of the LORD! They took Dagon and put him back in his place. [4]But the following morning when they rose, there was Dagon, fallen on his face on the ground before the ark of the LORD! His head and hands had been broken off and were lying on the threshold; only his body remained. [5]That is why to this day neither the priests of Dagon nor any others who enter Dagon's temple at Ashdod step on the threshold.

[6]The LORD's hand was heavy upon the people of Ashdod and its vicinity; he brought devastation upon them and afflicted them with tumors.[t] [7]When the men of Ashdod saw what was happening, they said, "The ark of the god of Israel must not stay here with us, because his hand is heavy upon us and upon Dagon our god." [8]So they called together all the rulers of the Philistines and asked them, "What shall we do with the ark of the god of Israel?"

They answered, "Have the ark of the god of Israel moved to Gath." So they moved the ark of the God of Israel.

[9]But after they had moved it, the LORD's hand was against that city, throwing it into a great panic. He afflicted the people of the city, both young and old, with an outbreak of tumors.[u] [10]So they sent the ark of God to Ekron.

As the ark of God was entering Ekron, the people of Ekron cried out, "They have brought the ark of the god of Israel

[t]6 Hebrew; Septuagint and Vulgate *tumors. And rats appeared in their land, and death and destruction were throughout the city*
[u]9 Or *with tumors in the groin* (see Septuagint)

*6, 9 The *Qere* is a less graphic synonym of the *Kethib*, see footnote *u* above.

°6 ק בטחרים
°9 ק טחרים

יִשְׂרָאֵל לַהֲמִיתֵנִי וְאֶת־ עַמִּי׃ וַיִּשְׁלְחוּ וַיַּאַסְפוּ
and-they-called-together so-they-sent (11) people-of-me and to-kill-me Israel

אֶת־ כָּל־ סַרְנֵי פְלִשְׁתִּים וַיֹּאמְרוּ שַׁלְּחוּ אֶת־ אֲרוֹן אֱלֹהֵי
god-of ark-of *** send-away! and-they-said Philistines rulers-of all-of ***

יִשְׂרָאֵל וְיָשֹׁב לִמְקֹמוֹ וְלֹא־ יָמִית אֹתִי וְאֶת־
and me he-will-kill so-not to-place-of-him and-let-him-go-back Israel

עַמִּי כִּי־ הָיְתָה מְהוּמַת־ מָוֶת בְּכָל־ הָעִיר כָּבְדָה
she-was-heavy the-city in-all-of death panic-of she-was for people-of-me

מְאֹד יַד הָאֱלֹהִים שָׁם׃ וְהָאֲנָשִׁים אֲשֶׁר לֹא־ מֵתוּ
they-died not who and-the-people (12) there the-God hand-of very

הֻכּוּ בַּעְפֹלִים* וַתַּעַל שַׁוְעַת הָעִיר
the-city outcry-of and-she-went-up *with-the-tumors they-were-afflicted

הַשָּׁמָיִם׃ וַיְהִי אֲרוֹן־ יְהוָה בִּשְׂדֵה פְלִשְׁתִּים שִׁבְעָה
seven Philistines in-territory-of Yahweh ark-of when-he-was (6:1) the-heavens

חֳדָשִׁים׃ וַיִּקְרְאוּ פְלִשְׁתִּים לַכֹּהֲנִים וְלַקֹּסְמִים
and-for-the-ones-divining for-the-priests Philistines then-he-called (2) months

לֵאמֹר מַה־ נַּעֲשֶׂה לַאֲרוֹן יְהוָה הוֹדִעֻנוּ בַּמֶּה
by-the-how tell-us! Yahweh with-ark-of shall-we-do what? to-say

נְשַׁלְּחֶנּוּ לִמְקוֹמוֹ׃ וַיֹּאמְרוּ אִם־ מְשַׁלְּחִים
ones-returning if and-they-answered (3) to-place-of-him we-should-send-him

אֶת־ אֲרוֹן אֱלֹהֵי יִשְׂרָאֵל אַל־ תְּשַׁלְּחוּ אֹתוֹ רֵיקָם כִּי־ הָשֵׁב תָּשִׁיבוּ
you-send to-send but empty him you-send-away not Israel god-of ark-of ***

לוֹ אָשָׁם אָז תֵּרָפְאוּ וְנוֹדַע לָכֶם
to-you and-he-will-be-made-known you-will-be-healed then guilt-offering to-him

לָמָּה לֹא־ תָסוּר יָדוֹ מִכֶּם׃ וַיֹּאמְרוּ מָה
what? and-they-asked (4) from-you hand-of-him she-was-lifted not why

הָאָשָׁם אֲשֶׁר נָשִׁיב לוֹ וַיֹּאמְרוּ מִסְפַּר
by-number-of and-they-replied to-him we-should-send that the-guilt-offering

סַרְנֵי פְלִשְׁתִּים חֲמִשָּׁה עְפֹלֵי* זָהָב וַחֲמִשָּׁה עַכְבְּרֵי זָהָב כִּי־ מַגֵּפָה
plague for gold rats-of and-five gold *tumors-of five Philistines rulers-of

אַחַת לְכֻלָּם וּלְסַרְנֵיכֶם׃ וַעֲשִׂיתֶם צַלְמֵי
models-of so-you-make (5) and-to-rulers-of-you to-all-of-them same

עְפֹלֵיכֶם* וְצַלְמֵי עַכְבְּרֵיכֶם הַמַּשְׁחִיתִם אֶת־ הָאָרֶץ
the-country *** the-ones-destroying rats-of-you and-models-of *tumors-of-you

וּנְתַתֶּם לֵאלֹהֵי יִשְׂרָאֵל כָּבוֹד אוּלַי יָקֵל אֶת־ יָדוֹ
hand-of-him *** he-will-lift perhaps honor Israel to-god-of and-you-give

מֵעֲלֵיכֶם וּמֵעַל אֱלֹהֵיכֶם וּמֵעַל אַרְצְכֶם׃ וְלָמָּה
now-why? (6) land-of-you and-from-on gods-of-you and-from-on from-on-you

around to us to kill us and our
people." 11So they called together all the rulers of the Philistines and said, "Send the ark
of the god of Israel away; let it
go back to its own place, or it[v]
will kill us and our people."
For death had filled the city
with panic; God's hand was
very heavy upon it. 12Those
who did not die were afflicted
with tumors, and the outcry of
the city went up to heaven.

*The Ark Returned to Israel*

6 When the ark of the LORD had been in Philistine territory seven months, 2the Philistines called for the priests
and the diviners and said,
"What shall we do with the
ark of the LORD? Tell us how
we should send it back to its
place."
3They answered, "If you return the ark of the god of Israel, do not send it away empty,
but by all means send a guilt
offering to him. Then you will
be healed, and you will know
why his hand has not been
lifted from you."
4The Philistines asked,
"What guilt offering should
we send to him?"
They replied, "Five gold tumors and five gold rats, according to the number of the
Philistine rulers, because the
same plague has struck both
you and your rulers. 5Make
models of the tumors and of
the rats that are destroying the
country, and pay honor to Israel's god. Perhaps he will lift
his hand from you and your
gods and your land. 6Why do

[v]11 Or *he*

*12, 4, 5 The *Qere* is a less graphic synonym of the *Ketbib*.

°12 ק בטחרים
°4 ק טחרי
°5 ק טחריכם

תְכַבְּדוּ אֶת־לְבַבְכֶם כַּאֲשֶׁר כִּבְּדוּ מִצְרַיִם וּפַרְעֹה אֶת־
*** and-Pharoah Egyptians they-hardened just-as heart-of-you *** you-harden

לִבָּם הֲלוֹא כַּאֲשֶׁר הִתְעַלֵּל בָּהֶם וַיְשַׁלְּחוּם
then-they-sent-them against-them he-treated-harshly as-when not? heart-of-them

וַיֵּלֵכוּ׃ וְעַתָּה קְחוּ וַעֲשׂוּ עֲגָלָה חֲדָשָׁה אֶחָת
one new cart and-make-ready! get! now-then (7) so-they-could-go-away

וּשְׁתֵּי פָרוֹת עָלוֹת אֲשֶׁר לֹא־עָלָה עֲלֵיהֶם עֹל וַאֲסַרְתֶּם
and-you-hitch yoke on-them he-went not that ones-having-calved cows and-two-of

אֶת־הַפָּרוֹת בָּעֲגָלָה וַהֲשֵׁיבֹתֶם בְּנֵיהֶם מֵאַחֲרֵיהֶם
from-after-them calves-of-them but-you-take-away to-the-cart the-cows ***

הַבָּיְתָה׃ וּלְקַחְתֶּם אֶת־אֲרוֹן יְהוָה וּנְתַתֶּם אֹתוֹ אֶל־הָעֲגָלָה
the-cart on him and-you-put Yahweh ark-of *** and-you-take (8) in-the-pen

וְאֵת ׀ כְּלֵי הַזָּהָב אֲשֶׁר הֲשֵׁבֹתֶם לוֹ אָשָׁם תָּשִׂימוּ
you-put guilt-offering to-him you-send-back that the-gold objects-of and

בָאַרְגַּז מִצִּדּוֹ וְשִׁלַּחְתֶּם אֹתוֹ וְהָלָךְ׃ וּרְאִיתֶם
but-you-watch (9) and-he-will-go him and-you-send at-side-of-him in-the-chest

אִם־דֶּרֶךְ גְּבוּלוֹ יַעֲלֶה בֵּית שֶׁמֶשׁ הוּא עָשָׂה לָנוּ אֶת־
*** on-us he-brought he Shemesh Beth he-goes-up territory-of-him way-of if

הָרָעָה הַגְּדוֹלָה הַזֹּאת וְאִם־לֹא וְיָדַעְנוּ כִּי לֹא
not that then-we-will-know not but-if the-this the-great the-disaster

יָדוֹ נָגְעָה בָּנוּ מִקְרֶה הוּא הָיָה לָנוּ׃ וַיַּעֲשׂוּ
so-they-did (10) to-us he-happened he chance against-us she-struck hand-of-him

הָאֲנָשִׁים כֵּן וַיִּקְחוּ שְׁתֵּי פָרוֹת עָלוֹת וַיַּאַסְרוּם
and-they-hitched-them ones-having-calved cows two-of and-they-took this the-men

בָּעֲגָלָה וְאֶת־בְּנֵיהֶם כָּלוּ בַבָּיִת׃ וַיָּשִׂמוּ
and-they-placed (11) in-the-pen they-penned-up calves-of-them and to-the-cart

אֶת־אֲרוֹן יְהוָה אֶל־הָעֲגָלָה וְאֵת הָאַרְגַּז וְאֵת עַכְבְּרֵי הַזָּהָב וְאֵת
and the-gold rats-of and the-chest and the-cart on Yahweh ark-of ***

צַלְמֵי טְחֹרֵיהֶם׃ וַיִשַּׁרְנָה הַפָּרוֹת בַּדֶּרֶךְ
up-the-road the-cows and-they-went-straight (12) tumors-of-them models-of

עַל־דֶּרֶךְ בֵּית שֶׁמֶשׁ בִּמְסִלָּה אַחַת הָלְכוּ הָלֹךְ וְגָעוֹ וְלֹא־
and-not and-to-low to-go they-went one on-path Shemesh Beth road-of on

סָרוּ יָמִין וּשְׂמֹאול וְסַרְנֵי פְלִשְׁתִּים הֹלְכִים אַחֲרֵיהֶם
after-them ones-following Philistines and-rulers-of or-left right they-turned

עַד־גְּבוּל בֵּית שָׁמֶשׁ׃ וּבֵית שֶׁמֶשׁ קֹצְרִים
ones-harvesting Shemesh now-Beth (13) Shemesh Beth border-of as-far-as

קְצִיר־חִטִּים בָּעֵמֶק וַיִּשְׂאוּ אֶת־עֵינֵיהֶם וַיִּרְאוּ
and-they-saw eyes-of-them *** when-they-lifted in-the-valley wheats harvest-of

you harden your hearts as the Egyptians and Pharaoh did? When he[w] treated them harshly, did they not send the Israelites out so they could go on their way?

7 "Now then, get a new cart ready, with two cows that have calved and have never been yoked. Hitch the cows to the cart, but take their calves away and pen them up.
8 Take the ark of the LORD and put it on the cart, and in a chest beside it put the gold objects you are sending back to him as a guilt offering. Send it on its way,
9 but keep watching it. If it goes up to its own territory, toward Beth Shemesh, then the LORD has brought this great disaster on us. But if it does not, then we will know that it was not his hand that struck us and that it happened to us by chance."

10 So they did this. They took two such cows and hitched them to the cart and penned up their calves.
11 They placed the ark of the LORD on the cart and along with it the chest containing the gold rats and the models of the tumors.
12 Then the cows went straight up toward Beth Shemesh, keeping on the road and lowing all the way; they did not turn to the right or to the left. The rulers of the Philistines followed them as far as the border of Beth Shemesh.

13 Now the people of Beth Shemesh were harvesting their wheat in the valley, and when they looked up and saw

w6 That is, God

*12 Most mss have *dagesh* in the *yod* (וַיִּ).

אֶת־הָאָרוֹן וַיִּשְׂמְחוּ לִרְאוֹת׃ וְהָעֲגָלָה בָּאָה אֶל־שְׂדֵה
field-of to she-came and-the-cart (14) to-see then-they-rejoiced the-ark ***

יְהוֹשֻׁעַ בֵּית־הַשִּׁמְשִׁי וַתַּעֲמֹד שָׁם וְשָׁם אֶבֶן גְּדוֹלָה
large stone now-there there and-she-stopped the-Shemeshite Beth Joshua

וַיְבַקְּעוּ אֶת־עֲצֵי הָעֲגָלָה וְאֶת־הַפָּרוֹת הֶעֱלוּ
they-sacrificed the-cows and the-cart woods-of *** and-they-chopped-up

עֹלָה לַיהוָה׃ וְהַלְוִיִּם הוֹרִידוּ | אֶת־אֲרוֹן
ark-of *** they-took-down and-the-Levites (15) to-Yahweh burnt-offering

יְהוָה וְאֶת־הָאַרְגַּז אֲשֶׁר־אִתּוֹ אֲשֶׁר־בּוֹ כְלֵי־זָהָב וַיָּשִׂמוּ
and-they-placed gold objects-of in-him that with-him that the-chest and Yahweh

אֶל־הָאֶבֶן הַגְּדוֹלָה וְאַנְשֵׁי בֵית־שֶׁמֶשׁ הֶעֱלוּ עֹלוֹת
burnt-offerings they-offered Shemesh Beth people-of the-large the-rock on

וַיִּזְבְּחוּ זְבָחִים בַּיּוֹם הַהוּא לַיהוָה׃ וַחֲמִשָּׁה
now-five (16) to-Yahweh the-that on-the-day sacrifices and-they-sacrificed

סַרְנֵי־פְלִשְׁתִּים רָאוּ וַיָּשֻׁבוּ עֶקְרוֹן בַּיּוֹם הַהוּא׃
the-that on-the-day Ekron then-they-returned they-saw Philistines rulers-of

וְאֵלֶּה טְחֹרֵי הַזָּהָב אֲשֶׁר הֵשִׁיבוּ פְלִשְׁתִּים אָשָׁם
guilt-offering Philistines they-sent that the-gold tumors-of now-these (17)

לַיהוָה לְאַשְׁדּוֹד אֶחָד לְעַזָּה אֶחָד לְאַשְׁקְלוֹן אֶחָד לְגַת אֶחָד
one for-Gath one for-Ashkelon one for-Gaza one for-Ashdod to-Yahweh

לְעֶקְרוֹן אֶחָד׃ וְעַכְבְּרֵי הַזָּהָב מִסְפַּר כָּל־עָרֵי
towns-of all-of by-number-of the-gold and-rats-of (18) one for-Ekron

פְלִשְׁתִּים לַחֲמֵשֶׁת הַסְּרָנִים מֵעִיר מִבְצָר וְעַד כֹּפֶר
village-of even-to fortified from-city-of the-rulers to-five-of Philistines

הַפְּרָזִי וְעַד* אָבֵל† הַגְּדוֹלָה אֲשֶׁר הִנִּיחוּ עָלֶיהָ אֵת
*** by-her they-set where the-Greater †Abel *even-to the-country-dweller

אֲרוֹן יְהוָה עַד הַיּוֹם הַזֶּה בִּשְׂדֵה יְהוֹשֻׁעַ בֵּית־הַשִּׁמְשִׁי׃
the-Shemeshite Beth Joshua in-field-of the-this the-day to Yahweh ark-of

וַיַּךְ בְּאַנְשֵׁי בֵית־שֶׁמֶשׁ כִּי רָאוּ בַּאֲרוֹן
into-ark-of they-looked because Shemesh Beth from-men-of but-he-struck-down (19)

יְהוָה וַיַּךְ בָּעָם שִׁבְעִים אִישׁ חֲמִשִּׁים אֶלֶף אִישׁ
man thousand fifty man seventy from-the-people and-he-struck-down Yahweh

וַיִּתְאַבְּלוּ הָעָם כִּי־הִכָּה יְהוָה בָּעָם מַכָּה
blow against-the-people Yahweh he-struck because the-people and-they-mourned

גְדוֹלָה†† וַיֹּאמְרוּ אַנְשֵׁי בֵית־שֶׁמֶשׁ מִי יוּכַל לַעֲמֹד
to-stand he-can who? Shemesh Beth men-of and-they-asked (20) heavy

לִפְנֵי יְהוָה הָאֱלֹהִים הַקָּדוֹשׁ הַזֶּה וְאֶל־מִי יַעֲלֶה
he-will-go-up whom? and-to the-this the-holy the-God Yahweh in-presences-of

the ark, they rejoiced at the
sight. 14The cart came to the
field of Joshua of Beth Shemesh, and there it stopped beside a large rock. The people chopped up the wood of the cart and sacrificed the cows as a burnt offering to the LORD.
15The Levites took down the ark of the LORD, together with the chest containing the gold objects, and placed them on the large rock. On that day the people of Beth Shemesh offered burnt offerings and made sacrifices to the LORD.
16The five rulers of the Philistines saw all this and then returned that same day to Ekron.
17These are the gold tumors the Philistines sent as a guilt offering to the LORD—one each for Ashdod, Gaza, Ashkelon, Gath and Ekron.
18And the number of the gold rats was according to the number of Philistine towns belonging to the five rulers—the fortified towns with their country villages. The large rock, on which[x] they set the ark of the LORD, is a witness to this day in the field of Joshua of Beth Shemesh.
19But God struck down some of the men of Beth Shemesh, putting seventy[y] of them to death because they had looked into the ark of the LORD. The people mourned because of the heavy blow the LORD had dealt them,
20and the men of Beth Shemesh asked, "Who can stand in the presence of the LORD, this holy God? To whom will the ark go up from

x18 A few Hebrew manuscripts and Septuagint; most Hebrew manuscripts *villages as far as Greater Abel, where*
y19 A few Hebrew manuscripts; most Hebrew manuscripts and Septuagint *50,070*

*18a The NIV repoints the *ayin* with *tsere* and adds *qamets he* ending to read וְעֵדָה , *and-witness* (cf. Joshua 24:27).

*18b The NIV, based on the versions listed above in footnote *x*, translates אבן , *rock*.

††19 Most mss end the verse with *soph pasuq* ( ׃ ).

מֵעָלֵֽינוּ׃ וַיִּשְׁלְחוּ מַלְאָכִים אֶל־ יוֹשְׁבֵי קִרְיַת־ יְעָרִים
Jearim Kiriath ones-living-of to messengers then-they-sent (21) from-with-us

לֵאמֹר הֵשִׁבוּ פְלִשְׁתִּים אֶת־ אֲרוֹן יְהוָה רְדוּ הַעֲלוּ אֹתוֹ
him take-up! come-down! Yahweh ark-of *** Philistines they-returned to-say

אֲלֵיכֶם׃ וַיָּבֹאוּ אַנְשֵׁי | קִרְיַת יְעָרִים וַיַּעֲלוּ אֶת־ אֲרוֹן
ark-of *** and-they-took-up Jearim Kiriath men-of so-they-came (7:1) to-you

יְהוָה וַיָּבִאוּ אֹתוֹ אֶל־ בֵּית אֲבִינָדָב בַּגִּבְעָה וְאֶת־ אֶלְעָזָר
Eleazar and on-the-hill Abinadab house-of to him and-they-took Yahweh

בְּנוֹ קִדְּשׁוּ לִשְׁמֹר אֶת־ אֲרוֹן יְהוָה׃ וַיְהִי מִיּוֹם
from-day and-he-was (2) Yahweh ark-of *** to-guard they-consecrated son-of-him

שֶׁבֶת הָאָרוֹן בְּקִרְיַת יְעָרִים וַיִּרְבּוּ הַיָּמִים וַיִּהְיוּ
and-they-were the-days and-they-were-many Jearim at-Kiriath the-ark to-remain

עֶשְׂרִים שָׁנָה וַיִּנָּהוּ כָּל־ בֵּית יִשְׂרָאֵל אַחֲרֵי יְהוָה׃
Yahweh after Israel house-of all-of then-they-mourned year twenty

וַיֹּאמֶר שְׁמוּאֵל אֶל־ כָּל־ בֵּית יִשְׂרָאֵל לֵאמֹר אִם־ בְּכָל־
with-all-of if to-say Israel house-of whole-of to Samuel and-he-said (3)

לְבַבְכֶם אַתֶּם שָׁבִים אֶל־ יְהוָה הָסִירוּ אֶת־ אֱלֹהֵי הַנֵּכָר
the-foreign gods-of *** be-rid! Yahweh to ones-returning you heart-of-you

מִתּוֹכְכֶם וְהָעַשְׁתָּרוֹת וְהָכִינוּ לְבַבְכֶם אֶל־ יְהוָה
Yahweh to heart-of-you and-commit! and-the-Ashtoreths from-among-you

וְעִבְדֻהוּ לְבַדּוֹ וְיַצֵּל אֶתְכֶם מִיַּד פְּלִשְׁתִּים׃
Philistines from-hand-of you and-he-will-deliver only-him and-serve-him!

וַיָּסִירוּ בְּנֵי יִשְׂרָאֵל אֶת־ הַבְּעָלִים וְאֶת־ הָעַשְׁתָּרֹת
the-Ashtoreths and the-Baals *** Israel sons-of so-they-put-away (4)

וַיַּעַבְדוּ אֶת־ יְהוָה לְבַדּוֹ׃ וַיֹּאמֶר שְׁמוּאֵל קִבְצוּ אֶת־
*** assemble! Samuel then-he-said (5) only-him Yahweh *** and-they-served

כָּל־ יִשְׂרָאֵל הַמִּצְפָּתָה וְאֶתְפַּלֵּל בַּעַדְכֶם אֶל־ יְהוָה׃
Yahweh with for-you and-I-will-intercede at-the-Mizpah Israel all-of

וַיִּקָּבְצוּ הַמִּצְפָּתָה וַיִּשְׁאֲבוּ־ מַיִם וַיִּשְׁפְּכוּ |
and-they-poured-out waters then-they-drew at-the-Mizpah when-they-assembled (6)

לִפְנֵי יְהוָה וַיָּצוּמוּ בַּיּוֹם הַהוּא וַיֹּאמְרוּ שָׁם
there and-they-confessed the-that on-the-day and-they-fasted Yahweh before

חָטָאנוּ לַיהוָה וַיִּשְׁפֹּט שְׁמוּאֵל אֶת־ בְּנֵי יִשְׂרָאֵל בַּמִּצְפָּה׃
at-the-Mizpah Israel sons-of *** Samuel and-he-led against-Yahweh we-sinned

וַיִּשְׁמְעוּ פְלִשְׁתִּים כִּי־ הִתְקַבְּצוּ בְנֵי־ יִשְׂרָאֵל
Israel sons-of they-assembled that Philistines when-they-heard (7)

הַמִּצְפָּתָה וַיַּעֲלוּ סַרְנֵי־ פְלִשְׁתִּים אֶל־ יִשְׂרָאֵל
Israel against Philistines rulers-of then-they-came-up at-the-Mizpah

here?"

21Then they sent messengers to the people of Kiriath Jearim, saying, "The Philistines have returned the ark of the LORD. Come down and take it up to

7 your place." 1So the men of Kiriath Jearim came and took up the ark of the LORD. They took it to Abinadab's house on the hill and consecrated Eleazar his son to guard the ark of the LORD.

*The Philistines Subdued at Mizpah*

2It was a long time, twenty years in all, that the ark remained at Kiriath Jearim, and all the people of Israel mourned and sought after the LORD. 3And Samuel said to the whole house of Israel, "If you are returning to the LORD with all your hearts, then rid yourselves of the foreign gods and the Ashtoreths and commit yourselves to the LORD and serve him only, and he will deliver you out of the hand of the Philistines." 4So the Israelites put away their Baals and Ashtoreths, and served the LORD only.

5Then Samuel said, "Assemble all Israel at Mizpah and I will intercede with the LORD for you." 6When they had assembled at Mizpah, they drew water and poured it out before the LORD. On that day they fasted and there they confessed, "We have sinned against the LORD." And Samuel was leader[z] of Israel at Mizpah.

7When the Philistines heard that Israel had assembled at Mizpah, the rulers of the Philistines came up to attack them.

[z]6 Traditionally *judge*

וַיִּשְׁמְעוּ בְּנֵי יִשְׂרָאֵל וַיִּרְאוּ מִפְּנֵי פְּלִשְׁתִּים׃
Philistines because-of then-they-were-afraid Israel sons-of when-they-heard

וַיֹּאמְרוּ בְנֵי־יִשְׂרָאֵל אֶל־שְׁמוּאֵל אַל־תַּחֲרֵשׁ מִמֶּנּוּ מִזְּעֹק
from-to-cry for-us you-stop not Samuel to Israel sons-of and-they-said (8)

אֶל־יְהוָה אֱלֹהֵינוּ וְיֹשִׁעֵנוּ מִיַּד פְּלִשְׁתִּים׃
Philistines from-hand-of so-he-may-rescue-us God-of-us Yahweh to

וַיִּקַּח שְׁמוּאֵל טְלֵה חָלָב אֶחָד וַיַּעֲלֶהָ עוֹלָה
burnt-offering and-he-offered-him one suckling lamb-of Samuel then-he-took (9)

כָּלִיל לַיהוָה וַיִּזְעַק שְׁמוּאֵל אֶל־יְהוָה בְּעַד יִשְׂרָאֵל
Israel on-behalf-of Yahweh to Samuel and-he-cried-out to-Yahweh whole

וַיַּעֲנֵהוּ יְהוָה׃ וַיְהִי שְׁמוּאֵל מַעֲלֶה
sacrificing Samuel while-he-was (10) Yahweh and-he-answered-him

הָעוֹלָה וּפְלִשְׁתִּים נִגְּשׁוּ לַמִּלְחָמָה בְּיִשְׂרָאֵל
with-Israel to-the-battle they-drew-near then-Philistines the-burnt-offering

וַיַּרְעֵם יְהוָה ׀ בְּקוֹל־גָּדוֹל בַּיּוֹם הַהוּא עַל־
against the-that on-the-day loud with-thunder Yahweh but-he-thundered

פְּלִשְׁתִּים וַיְהֻמֵּם וַיִּנָּגְפוּ לִפְנֵי יִשְׂרָאֵל׃
Israel before so-they-were-routed and-he-made-panic-them Philistines

וַיֵּצְאוּ אַנְשֵׁי יִשְׂרָאֵל מִן־הַמִּצְפָּה וַיִּרְדְּפוּ אֶת־
*** and-they-pursued the-Mizpah from Israel men-of and-they-rushed-out (11)

פְּלִשְׁתִּים וַיַּכּוּם עַד־מִתַּחַת לְבֵית כָּר׃ וַיִּקַּח
then-he-took (12) Car to-Beth at-below to and-they-slaughtered-them Philistines

שְׁמוּאֵל אֶבֶן אַחַת וַיָּשֶׂם בֵּין־הַמִּצְפָּה וּבֵין הַשֵּׁן
the-Shen and-between the-Mizpah between and-he-set-up one stone Samuel

וַיִּקְרָא אֶת־שְׁמָהּ אֶבֶן הָעָזֶר וַיֹּאמַר עַד־הֵנָּה
at-here to and-he-said the-Ezer Eben name-of-her *** and-he-called

עֲזָרָנוּ יְהוָה׃ וַיִּכָּנְעוּ הַפְּלִשְׁתִּים וְלֹא־
and-not the-Philistines so-they-were-subdued (13) Yahweh he-helped-us

יָסְפוּ עוֹד לָבוֹא בִּגְבוּל יִשְׂרָאֵל וַתְּהִי יַד־
hand-of and-she-was Israel into-territory-of to-invade again they-repeated

יְהוָה בַּפְּלִשְׁתִּים כֹּל יְמֵי שְׁמוּאֵל׃ וַתָּשֹׁבְנָה
and-they-were-restored (14) Samuel days-of all-of against-the-Philistines Yahweh

הֶעָרִים אֲשֶׁר לָקְחוּ־פְלִשְׁתִּים מֵאֵת יִשְׂרָאֵל ׀ לְיִשְׂרָאֵל מֵעֶקְרוֹן
from-Ekron to-Israel Israel from Philistines they-captured that the-towns

וְעַד־גַּת וְאֶת־גְּבוּלָן הִצִּיל יִשְׂרָאֵל מִיַּד פְּלִשְׁתִּים
Philistines from-hand-of Israel he-delivered territory-of-them and Gath even-to

וַיְהִי שָׁלוֹם בֵּין יִשְׂרָאֵל וּבֵין הָאֱמֹרִי׃ וַיִּשְׁפֹּט
and-he-judged (15) the-Amorite and-between Israel between peace and-he-was

And when the Israelites heard of it, they were afraid because of the Philistines. [8]They said to Samuel, "Do not stop crying out to the LORD our God for us, that he may rescue us from the hand of the Philistines." [9]Then Samuel took a suckling lamb and offered it up as a whole burnt offering to the LORD. He cried out to the LORD on Israel's behalf, and the LORD answered him.

[10]While Samuel was sacrificing the burnt offering, the Philistines drew near to engage Israel in battle. But that day the LORD thundered with loud thunder against the Philistines and threw them into such a panic that they were routed before the Israelites. [11]The men of Israel rushed out of Mizpah and pursued the Philistines, slaughtering them along the way to a point below Beth Car.

[12]Then Samuel took a stone and set it up between Mizpah and Shen. He named it Ebenezer,[a] saying, "Thus far has the LORD helped us." [13]So the Philistines were subdued and did not invade Israelite territory again.

Throughout Samuel's lifetime, the hand of the LORD was against the Philistines. [14]The towns from Ekron to Gath that the Philistines had captured from Israel were restored to her, and Israel delivered the neighboring territory from the power of the Philistines. And there was peace between Israel and the Amorites.

[15]Samuel continued as judge

[a]12 *Ebenezer* means *stone of help*.

°9 ק ויעלהו

שְׁמוּאֵל אֶת־יִשְׂרָאֵל כֹּל יְמֵי חַיָּיו׃ וְהָלַךְ מִדֵּי
as-needs-of and-he-went (16) lives-of-him days-of all-of Israel *** Samuel

שָׁנָה בְּשָׁנָה וְסָבַב בֵּית־אֵל וְהַגִּלְגָּל וְהַמִּצְפָּה
and-the-Mizpah and-the-Gilgal El Beth and-he-went-on-circuit by-year year

וְשָׁפַט אֶת־יִשְׂרָאֵל אֵת כָּל־הַמְּקוֹמוֹת הָאֵלֶּה׃ וּתְשֻׁבָתוֹ
but-return-of-him (17) the-those the-places all-of *** Israel *** and-he-judged

הָרָמָתָה כִּי־שָׁם בֵּיתוֹ וְשָׁם שָׁפָט אֶת־יִשְׂרָאֵל וַיִּבֶן־
and-he-built Israel *** he-judged and-there home-of-him there for to-the-Ramah

שָׁם מִזְבֵּחַ לַיהוָה׃ וַיְהִי כַּאֲשֶׁר זָקֵן שְׁמוּאֵל
Samuel he-grew-old as-when and-he-was (8:1) to-Yahweh altar there

וַיָּשֶׂם אֶת־ בָּנָיו שֹׁפְטִים לְיִשְׂרָאֵל׃ וַיְהִי
now-he-was (2) for-Israel ones-judging sons-of-him *** then-he-appointed

שֶׁם־ בְּנוֹ הַבְּכוֹר יוֹאֵל וְשֵׁם מִשְׁנֵהוּ אֲבִיָּה
Abijah second-of-him and-name-of Joel the-firstborn son-of-him name-of

שֹׁפְטִים בִּבְאֵר שָׁבַע׃ וְלֹא־ הָלְכוּ בָנָיו בִּדְרָכָו
in-ways-of-him sons-of-him they-walked but-not (3) Sheba at-Beer ones-judging

וַיִּטּוּ אַחֲרֵי הַבָּצַע וַיִּקְחוּ־ שֹׁחַד
bribe and-they-accepted the-dishonest-gain after and-they-turned-aside

וַיַּטּוּ מִשְׁפָּט׃ וַיִּתְקַבְּצוּ כֹּל זִקְנֵי יִשְׂרָאֵל
Israel elders-of all-of so-they-gathered (4) justice and-they-perverted

וַיָּבֹאוּ אֶל־שְׁמוּאֵל הָרָמָתָה׃ וַיֹּאמְרוּ אֵלָיו הִנֵּה אַתָּה
you see! to-him and-they-said (5) at-the-Ramah Samuel to and-they-came

זָקַנְתָּ וּבָנֶיךָ לֹא הָלְכוּ בִּדְרָכֶיךָ עַתָּה שִׂימָה־ לָּנוּ
for-us appoint! now in-ways-of-you they-walk not and-sons-of-you you-are-old

מֶלֶךְ לְשָׁפְטֵנוּ כְּכָל־ הַגּוֹיִם׃ וַיֵּרַע הַדָּבָר
the-thing but-he-was-displeasing (6) the-nations as-all-of to-lead-us king

בְּעֵינֵי שְׁמוּאֵל כַּאֲשֶׁר אָמְרוּ תְּנָה־ לָּנוּ מֶלֶךְ לְשָׁפְטֵנוּ וַיִּתְפַּלֵּל
so-he-prayed to-lead-us king to-us give! they-said as-when Samuel in-eyes-of

שְׁמוּאֵל אֶל־ יְהוָה׃ וַיֹּאמֶר יְהוָה אֶל־שְׁמוּאֵל שְׁמַע בְּקוֹל
to-voice-of listen! Samuel to Yahweh and-he-told (7) Yahweh to Samuel

הָעָם לְכֹל אֲשֶׁר־ יֹאמְרוּ אֵלֶיךָ כִּי לֹא אֹתְךָ מָאָסוּ כִּי־אֹתִי
me but they-rejected you not for to-you they-say that to-all the-people

מָאֲסוּ מִמְּלֹךְ עֲלֵיהֶם׃ כְּכָל־ הַמַּעֲשִׂים אֲשֶׁר־ עָשׂוּ
they-did that the-deeds as-all-of (8) over-them from-to-be-king they-rejected

מִיּוֹם הַעֲלֹתִי אֹתָם מִמִּצְרַיִם וְעַד־ הַיּוֹם הַזֶּה
the-this the-day even-to from-Egypt them to-bring-up-me from-day

וַיַּעַזְבֻנִי וַיַּעַבְדוּ אֱלֹהִים אֲחֵרִים כֵּן הֵמָּה עֹשִׂים גַּם־
also ones-doing they so other-ones gods and-they-served then-they-forsook-me

over Israel all the days of his
life. 16From year to year he
went on a circuit from Bethel
to Gilgal to Mizpah, judging
Israel in all those places. 17But
he always went back to
Ramah, where his home was,
and there he also judged Israel. And he built an altar there
to the LORD.

*Israel Asks for a King*

8 When Samuel grew old,
he appointed his sons as
judges for Israel. 2The name of
his firstborn was Joel and the
name of his second was Abijah, and they served at Beersheba. 3But his sons did not
walk in his ways. They turned
aside after dishonest gain and
accepted bribes and perverted
justice.

4So all the elders of Israel
gathered together and came to
Samuel at Ramah. 5They said
to him, "You are old, and your
sons do not walk in your
ways; now appoint a king to
lead[c] us, such as all the other
nations have."

6But when they said, "Give
us a king to lead us," this displeased Samuel; so he prayed
to the LORD. 7And the LORD
told him: "Listen to all that the
people are saying to you; it is
not you they have rejected as
their king, but me. 8As they
have done from the day I
brought them up out of Egypt
until this day, forsaking me
and serving other gods, so

c5 Traditionally *judge*; also in verses 6 and 20

c3 ק בדרכיו

לָךְ׃ וְעַתָּה שְׁמַע בְּקוֹלָם אַךְ כִּי־ הָעֵד תָּעִיד
to-you (9) and-now listen! to-voice-of-them but indeed to-warn you-warn

בָּהֶם וְהִגַּדְתָּ לָהֶם מִשְׁפַּט הַמֶּלֶךְ אֲשֶׁר יִמְלֹךְ
to-them and-you-make-known to-them leadership-of the-king who he-will-reign

עֲלֵיהֶם׃ וַיֹּאמֶר שְׁמוּאֵל אֵת כָּל־ דִּבְרֵי יְהוָה אֶל־ הָעָם
over-them (10) so-he-told Samuel *** all-of words-of Yahweh to the-people

הַשֹּׁאֲלִים מֵאִתּוֹ מֶלֶךְ׃ וַיֹּאמֶר זֶה יִהְיֶה מִשְׁפַּט
the-ones-asking from-him king (11) and-he-said this he-will-be leadership-of

הַמֶּלֶךְ אֲשֶׁר יִמְלֹךְ עֲלֵיכֶם אֶת־ בְּנֵיכֶם יִקָּח
the-king who he-will-reign over-you *** sons-of-you he-will-take

וְשָׂם לוֹ בְּמֶרְכַּבְתּוֹ וּבְפָרָשָׁיו
and-he-will-place for-him with-chariot-of-him and-with-horses-of-him

וְרָצוּ לִפְנֵי מֶרְכַּבְתּוֹ׃ וְלָשׂוּם לוֹ
and-they-will-run in-front-of chariot-of-him (12) and-to-assign for-him

שָׂרֵי אֲלָפִים וְשָׂרֵי חֲמִשִּׁים וְלַחֲרֹשׁ חֲרִישׁוֹ
commanders-of thousands and-commanders-of fifties and-to-plow ground-of-him

וְלִקְצֹר קְצִירוֹ וְלַעֲשׂוֹת כְּלֵי־ מִלְחַמְתּוֹ וּכְלֵי
and-to-reap harvest-of-him and-to-make weapons-of war-of-him and-equipments-of

רִכְבּוֹ׃ וְאֶת־ בְּנוֹתֵיכֶם יִקָּח לְרַקָּחוֹת
chariot-of-him (13) and daughters-of-you he-will-take as-perfumers

וּלְטַבָּחוֹת וּלְאֹפוֹת׃ וְאֶת־ שְׂדוֹתֵיכֶם וְאֶת־ כַּרְמֵיכֶם
and-as-cooks and-as-ones-baking (14) and fields-of-you and vineyards-of-you

וְזֵיתֵיכֶם הַטּוֹבִים יִקָּח וְנָתַן
and-olive-groves-of-you the-best-ones he-will-take and-he-will-give

לַעֲבָדָיו׃ וְזַרְעֵיכֶם וְכַרְמֵיכֶם יַעְשֹׂר
to-attendants-of-him (15) and-grains-of-you and-vintages-of-you he-will-take-tenth

וְנָתַן לְסָרִיסָיו וְלַעֲבָדָיו׃ וְאֶת־
and-he-will-give to-officials-of-him and-to-servants-of-him (16) and

עַבְדֵיכֶם וְאֶת־ שִׁפְחוֹתֵיכֶם וְאֶת־ בַּחוּרֵיכֶם הַטּוֹבִים
menservants-of-you and maidservants-of-you and young-men-of-you the-best-ones

וְאֶת־ חֲמוֹרֵיכֶם יִקָּח וְעָשָׂה לִמְלַאכְתּוֹ׃
and donkeys-of-you he-will-take and-he-will-use for-kingdom-of-him

צֹאנְכֶם יַעְשֹׂר וְאַתֶּם תִּהְיוּ־ לוֹ לַעֲבָדִים׃
(17) flock-of-you he-will-take-tenth and-you you-will-become for-him as-slaves

וּזְעַקְתֶּם בַּיּוֹם הַהוּא מִלִּפְנֵי מַלְכְּכֶם אֲשֶׁר
(18) and-you-will-cry-out on-the-day the-that because-of king-of-you whom

בְּחַרְתֶּם לָכֶם וְלֹא־ יַעֲנֶה יְהוָה אֶתְכֶם בַּיּוֹם הַהוּא׃
you-chose for-you but-not he-will-answer Yahweh you on-the-day the-that

they are doing to you. [9]Now listen to them; but warn them solemnly and let them know what the king who will reign over them will do."

[10]Samuel told all the words of the LORD to the people who were asking him for a king. [11]He said, "This is what the king who will reign over you will do: He will take your sons and make them serve with his chariots and horses, and they will run in front of his chariots. [12]Some he will assign to be commanders of thousands and commanders of fifties, and others to plow his ground and reap his harvest, and still others to make weapons of war and equipment for his chariots. [13]He will take your daughters to be perfumers and cooks and bakers. [14]He will take the best of your fields and vineyards and olive groves and give them to his attendants. [15]He will take a tenth of your grain and of your vintage and give it to his officials and attendants. [16]Your menservants and maidservants and the best of your cattle[d] and donkeys he will take for his own use. [17]He will take a tenth of your flocks, and you yourselves will become his slaves. [18]When that day comes, you will cry out for relief from the king you have chosen, and the LORD will not answer you in that day."

[d]16 Septuagint; Hebrew *young men*

וַיְמָאֲנוּ הָעָם לִשְׁמֹעַ בְּקוֹל שְׁמוּאֵל וַיֹּאמְרוּ
and-they-said Samuel to-voice-of to-listen the-people but-they-refused (19)

לֹּא כִּי אִם־ מֶלֶךְ יִהְיֶה עָלֵינוּ׃ וְהָיִינוּ גַם־אֲנַחְנוּ כְּכָל־
like-all-of we also then-we-will-be (20) over-us he-must-be king indeed but no

הַגּוֹיִם וּשְׁפָטָנוּ מַלְכֵּנוּ וְיָצָא לְפָנֵינוּ
before-us and-he-will-go-out king-of-us and-he-will-lead-us the-nations

וְנִלְחַם אֶת־ מִלְחֲמֹתֵנוּ׃ וַיִּשְׁמַע שְׁמוּאֵל אֵת כָּל־
all-of *** Samuel when-he-heard (21) battles-of-us *** and-he-will-fight

דִּבְרֵי הָעָם וַיְדַבְּרֵם בְּאָזְנֵי יְהוָה׃ וַיֹּאמֶר
and-he-said (22) Yahweh in-ears-of then-he-repeated-them the-people words-of

יְהוָה אֶל־ שְׁמוּאֵל שְׁמַע בְּקוֹלָם וְהִמְלַכְתָּ לָהֶם מֶלֶךְ
king to-them and-you-give-king to-voice-of-them listen! Samuel to Yahweh

וַיֹּאמֶר שְׁמוּאֵל אֶל־ אַנְשֵׁי יִשְׂרָאֵל לְכוּ אִישׁ לְעִירוֹ׃
to-town-of-him everyone go-back! Israel men-of to Samuel then-he-said

וַיְהִי־ אִישׁ מִבִּן° יָמִין וּשְׁמוֹ קִישׁ בֶּן־ אֲבִיאֵל בֶּן־
son-of Abiel son-of Kish and-name-of-him Jamin from-Ben man now-he-was (9:1)

צְרוֹר בֶּן־ בְּכוֹרַת בֶּן־ אֲפִיחַ בֶּן־ אִישׁ יְמִינִי גִּבּוֹר חָיִל׃
standing man-of *Jamite man-of son-of Aphiah son-of Becorath son-of Zeror

וְלוֹ־ הָיָה בֵן וּשְׁמוֹ שָׁאוּל בָּחוּר וָטוֹב
and-impressive young-man Saul and-name-of-him son he-was and-to-him (2)

וְאֵין אִישׁ מִבְּנֵי יִשְׂרָאֵל טוֹב מִמֶּנּוּ מִשִּׁכְמוֹ וָמַעְלָה
and-above from-shoulder-of-him than-him better Israel from-sons-of man and-not

גָּבֹהַּ מִכָּל־ הָעָם׃ וַתֹּאבַדְנָה הָאֲתֹנוֹת לְקִישׁ
of-Kish the-donkeys now-they-were-lost (3) the-people than-any-of taller

אֲבִי שָׁאוּל וַיֹּאמֶר קִישׁ אֶל־שָׁאוּל בְּנוֹ קַח־ נָא אִתְּךָ אֶת־
*** with-you now! take! son-of-him Saul to Kish and-he-said Saul father-of

אַחַד מֵהַנְּעָרִים וְקוּם לֵךְ בַּקֵּשׁ אֶת־ הָאֲתֹנֹת׃ וַיַּעֲבֹר
so-he-passed (4) the-donkeys *** look-for! go! and-rise! from-the-servants one

בְּהַר־ אֶפְרַיִם וַיַּעֲבֹר בְּאֶרֶץ־ שָׁלִשָׁה וְלֹא
but-not Shalisha through-area-of and-he-passed Ephraim through-hill-country-of

מָצָאוּ וַיַּעַבְרוּ בְאֶרֶץ־ שַׁעֲלִים וָאַיִן וַיַּעֲבֹר
so-he-passed but-there-was-not Shaalim into-district-of so-they-went they-found

בְּאֶרֶץ־ יְמִינִי וְלֹא מָצָאוּ׃ הֵמָּה בָּאוּ
they-reached they (5) they-found but-not *Jamite through-territory-of

בְּאֶרֶץ צוּף וְשָׁאוּל אָמַר לְנַעֲרוֹ אֲשֶׁר־ עִמּוֹ לְכָה
come! with-him who to-servant-of-him he-said and-Saul Zuph to-district-of

וְנָשׁוּבָה פֶּן־ יֶחְדַּל אָבִי מִן־ הָאֲתֹנוֹת
the-donkeys about father-of-me he-will-stop-thinking or and-let-us-go-back

[19]But the people refused to listen to Samuel. "No!" they said. "We want a king over us. [20]Then we will be like all the other nations, with a king to lead us and to go out before us and fight our battles."

[21]When Samuel heard all that the people said, he repeated it before the LORD. [22]The LORD answered, "Listen to them and give them a king."

Then Samuel said to the men of Israel, "Everyone go back to his town."

*Samuel Anoints Saul*

**9** There was a Benjamite, a man of standing, whose name was Kish son of Abiel, the son of Zeror, the son of Becorath, the son of Aphiah of Benjamin. [2]He had a son named Saul, an impressive young man without equal among the Israelites—a head taller than any of the others.

[3]Now the donkeys belonging to Saul's father Kish were lost, and Kish said to his son Saul, "Take one of the servants with you and go and look for the donkeys." [4]So he passed through the hill country of Ephraim and through the area around Shalisha, but they did not find them. They went on into the district of Shaalim, but the donkeys were not there. Then he passed through the territory of Benjamin, but they did not find them.

[5]When they reached the district of Zuph, Saul said to the servant who was with him, "Come, let's go back, or my father will stop thinking about

*1,4 Or *Benjamite.*

°1 ק מבנימין

וְדָאַג לָנוּ׃ וַיֹּאמֶר לוֹ הִנֵּה־ נָא אִישׁ־ אֱלֹהִים
God man-of now! look! to-him but-he-replied (6) about-us and-he-will-worry

בָּעִיר הַזֹּאת וְהָאִישׁ נִכְבָּד כֹּל אֲשֶׁר־ יְדַבֵּר בּוֹא
to-come-true he-says that all being-respected and-the-man the-this in-the-town

יָבוֹא עַתָּה נֵלֲכָה שָּׁם אוּלַי יַגִּיד לָנוּ אֶת־ דַּרְכֵּנוּ
way-of-us *** to-us he-will-tell perhaps there let-us-go now he-comes-true

אֲשֶׁר־ הָלַכְנוּ עָלֶיהָ׃ וַיֹּאמֶר שָׁאוּל לְנַעֲרוֹ וְהִנֵּה
now-see! to-servant-of-him Saul and-he-said (7) on-her you-should-go that

נֵלֵךְ וּמַה־ נָּבִיא לָאִישׁ כִּי הַלֶּחֶם אָזַל מִכֵּלֵינוּ
from-sacks-of-us he-is-gone the-food for to-the-man can-we-give then-what? we-go

וּתְשׁוּרָה אֵין־ לְהָבִיא לְאִישׁ הָאֱלֹהִים מָה אִתָּנוּ׃ וַיֹּסֶף
and-he-repeated (8) to-us what? the-God to-man-of to-take not and-gift

הַנַּעַר לַעֲנוֹת אֶת־ שָׁאוּל וַיֹּאמֶר הִנֵּה נִמְצָא בְיָדִי
in-hand-of-me being-found look! and-he-said Saul *** to-answer the-servant

רֶבַע שֶׁקֶל כָּסֶף וְנָתַתִּי לְאִישׁ הָאֱלֹהִים וְהִגִּיד
so-he-will-tell the-God to-man-of now-I-will-give silver shekel-of quarter-of

לָנוּ אֶת־ דַּרְכֵּנוּ׃ לְפָנִים ׀ בְּיִשְׂרָאֵל כֹּה־ אָמַר הָאִישׁ בְּלֶכְתּוֹ
when-to-go-him the-man he-said this in-Israel formerly (9) way-of-us *** to-us

לִדְרוֹשׁ אֱלֹהִים לְכוּ וְנֵלְכָה עַד־ הָרֹאֶה כִּי לַנָּבִיא הַיּוֹם
the-day to-the-prophet for the-seer to and-we-will-go come! God to-inquire

יִקָּרֵא לְפָנִים הָרֹאֶה׃ וַיֹּאמֶר שָׁאוּל לְנַעֲרוֹ
to-servant-of-him Saul and-he-said (10) the-seer formerly he-was-called

טוֹב דְּבָרְךָ לְכָה ׀ נֵלֵכָה וַיֵּלְכוּ אֶל־ הָעִיר אֲשֶׁר־ שָׁם
there were the-town for so-they-set-out let-us-go come! word-of-you good

אִישׁ הָאֱלֹהִים׃ הֵמָּה עֹלִים בְּמַעֲלֵה הָעִיר וְהֵמָּה מָצְאוּ
they-met and-they the-town on-hill-of ones-going-up they (11) the-God man-of

נְעָרוֹת יֹצְאוֹת לִשְׁאֹב מָיִם וַיֹּאמְרוּ לָהֶן הֲיֵשׁ בָּזֶה
at-here is-he? to-them and-they-asked waters to-draw ones-coming-out girls

הָרֹאֶה׃ וַתַּעֲנֶינָה אוֹתָם וַתֹּאמַרְנָה יֵשׁ הִנֵּה לְפָנֶיךָ
ahead-of-you see! he-is and-they-said them and-they-answered (12) the-seer

מַהֵר ׀ עַתָּה כִּי הַיּוֹם בָּא לָעִיר כִּי זֶבַח הַיּוֹם
the-day sacrifice for to-the-town he-came the-day for now hurry!

לָעָם בַּבָּמָה׃ כְּבֹאֲכֶם הָעִיר כֵּן
so the-town as-to-enter-you (13) at-the-high-place for-the-people

תִּמְצְאוּן אֹתוֹ בְּטֶרֶם יַעֲלֶה הַבָּמָתָה לֶאֱכֹל כִּי לֹא־
not for to-eat to-the-high-place he-goes-up at-before him you-will-find

יֹאכַל הָעָם עַד־ בֹּאוֹ כִּי־ הוּא יְבָרֵךְ הַזֶּבַח
the-sacrifice he-must-bless he for to-come-him until the-people he-will-eat

the donkeys and start worrying about us."

6 But the servant replied, "Look, in this town there is a man of God; he is highly respected, and everything he says comes true. Let's go there now. Perhaps he will tell us what way to take."

7 Saul said to his servant, "If we go, what can we give the man? The food in our sacks is gone. We have no gift to take to the man of God. What do we have?"

8 The servant answered him again. "Look," he said, "I have a quarter of a shekel[e] of silver. I will give it to the man of God so that he will tell us what way to take." 9 (Formerly in Israel, if a man went to inquire of God, he would say, "Come, let us go to the seer," because the prophet of today used to be called a seer.)

10 "Good," Saul said to his servant. "Come, let's go." So they set out for the town where the man of God was.

11 As they were going up the hill to the town, they met some girls coming out to draw water, and they asked them, "Is the seer here?"

12 "He is," they answered. "He's ahead of you. Hurry now; he has just come to our town today, for the people have a sacrifice at the high place. 13 As soon as you enter the town, you will find him before he goes up to the high place to eat. The people will not begin eating until he comes, because he must bless

e8 That is, about 1/10 ounce (about 3 grams)

אַחֲרֵי־כֵן יֹאכְלוּ הַקְּרֻאִים וְעַתָּה עֲלוּ כִּי־ אֹתוֹ
him for go-up! so-now the-ones-being-invited they-will-eat that after

כְהַיּוֹם תִּמְצְאוּן אֹתוֹ׃ וַיַּעֲלוּ הָעִיר הֵמָּה בָּאִים
ones-coming they the-town so-they-went-up (14) him you-will-find about-the-day

בְּתוֹךְ הָעִיר וְהִנֵּה שְׁמוּאֵל יֹצֵא לִקְרָאתָם לַעֲלוֹת
to-go-up to-meet-them coming-out Samuel and-see! the-town into-midst-of

הַבָּמָה׃ וַיהוָה גָּלָה אֶת־ אֹזֶן שְׁמוּאֵל יוֹם אֶחָד לִפְנֵי
before one day Samuel ear-of *** he-revealed now-Yahweh (15) the-high-place

בוֹא־ שָׁאוּל לֵאמֹר׃ כָּעֵת מָחָר אֶשְׁלַח אֵלֶיךָ אִישׁ
man to-you I-will-send tomorrow about-the-time (16) to-say Saul to-come

מֵאֶרֶץ בִּנְיָמִן וּמְשַׁחְתּוֹ לְנָגִיד עַל־ עַמִּי יִשְׂרָאֵל
Israel people-of-me over as-leader and-you-anoint-him Benjamin from-land-of

וְהוֹשִׁיעַ אֶת־ עַמִּי מִיַּד פְּלִשְׁתִּים כִּי רָאִיתִי
I-looked indeed Philistines from-hand-of people-of-me *** and-he-will-deliver

אֶת־ עַמִּי כִּי בָּאָה צַעֲקָתוֹ אֵלָי׃ וּשְׁמוּאֵל רָאָה אֶת־
*** he-saw when-Samuel (17) to-me cry-of-him she-reached for people-of-me ***

שָׁאוּל וַיהוָה עָנָהוּ הִנֵּה הָאִישׁ אֲשֶׁר אָמַרְתִּי אֵלֶיךָ זֶה
this-one to-you I-spoke whom the-man see! he-told-to-him then-Yahweh Saul

יַעְצֹר בְּעַמִּי׃ וַיִּגַּשׁ שָׁאוּל אֶת־ שְׁמוּאֵל
Samuel *** Saul and-he-approached (18) over-people-of-me he-will-govern

בְּתוֹךְ הַשָּׁעַר וַיֹּאמֶר הַגִּידָה־ נָּא לִי אֵי־ זֶה בֵּית
house-of this where? to-me now! tell! and-he-asked the-gateway inside-of

הָרֹאֶה׃ וַיַּעַן שְׁמוּאֵל אֶת־שָׁאוּל וַיֹּאמֶר אָנֹכִי הָרֹאֶה עֲלֵה
go-up! the-seer I and-he-said Saul *** Samuel and-he-replied (19) the-seer

לְפָנַי הַבָּמָה וַאֲכַלְתֶּם עִמִּי הַיּוֹם וְשִׁלַּחְתִּיךָ
and-I-will-let-go-you the-day with-me for-you-must-eat the-high-place ahead-of-me

בַבֹּקֶר וְכֹל אֲשֶׁר בִּלְבָבְךָ אַגִּיד לָךְ׃
to-you I-will-tell in-heart-of-you that and-all in-the-morning

וְלָאֲתֹנוֹת הָאֹבְדוֹת לְךָ הַיּוֹם שְׁלֹשֶׁת
three-of the-day from-you the-ones-being-lost as-for-the-donkeys (20)

הַיָּמִים אַל־ תָּשֶׂם אֶת־ לִבְּךָ לָהֶם כִּי נִמְצָאוּ
they-were-found for about-them heart-of-you *** you-upset not the-days

וּלְמִי כָּל־ חֶמְדַּת יִשְׂרָאֵל הֲלוֹא לְךָ וּלְכֹל בֵּית
family-of and-to-all-of to-you not? Israel desire-of all-of and-to-whom?

אָבִיךָ׃ וַיַּעַן שָׁאוּל וַיֹּאמֶר הֲלוֹא בֶן־יְמִינִי אָנֹכִי
I Benjamite not? and-he-said Saul and-he-answered (21) father-of-you

מִקְּטַנֵּי שִׁבְטֵי יִשְׂרָאֵל וּמִשְׁפַּחְתִּי הַצְּעִרָה מִכָּל־
from-all-of the-least and-clan-of-me Israel tribes-of from-smallest-ones-of

the sacrifice; afterward, those who are invited will eat. Go up now; you should find him about this time."

14 They went up to the town, and as they were entering it, there was Samuel, coming toward them on his way up to the high place.

15 Now the day before Saul came, the LORD had revealed this to Samuel: 16 "About this time tomorrow I will send you a man from the land of Benjamin. Anoint him leader over my people Israel; he will deliver my people from the hand of the Philistines. I have looked upon my people, for their cry has reached me."

17 When Samuel caught sight of Saul, the LORD said to him, "This is the man I spoke to you about; he will govern my people."

18 Saul approached Samuel in the gateway and asked, "Would you please tell me where the seer's house is?"

19 "I am the seer," Samuel replied. "Go up ahead of me to the high place, for today you are to eat with me, and in the morning I will let you go and will tell you all that is in your heart. 20 As for the donkeys you lost three days ago, do not worry about them; they have been found. And to whom is all the desire of Israel turned, if not to you and all your father's family?"

21 Saul answered, "But am I not a Benjamite, from the smallest tribe of Israel, and is not my clan the least of all the

מִשְׁפְּחוֹת שִׁבְטֵי בִנְיָמִן וְלָמָּה דִּבַּרְתָּ אֵלַי כַּדָּבָר הַזֶּה׃
the-this as-the-thing to-me you-say now-why? Benjamin tribes-of clans-of

וַיִּקַּח שְׁמוּאֵל אֶת־שָׁאוּל וְאֶת־נַעֲרוֹ וַיְבִיאֵם
and-he-brought-them servant-of-him and Saul *** Samuel then-he-took (22)

לִשְׁכָּתָה וַיִּתֵּן לָהֶם מָקוֹם בְּרֹאשׁ הַקְּרוּאִים וְהֵמָּה
now-they the-ones-being-invited at-head-of seat to-them and-he-gave into-hall

כִּשְׁלֹשִׁים אִישׁ׃ וַיֹּאמֶר שְׁמוּאֵל לַטַּבָּח תְּנָה אֶת־הַמָּנָה
the-piece *** bring! to-the-cook Samuel and-he-said (23) person about-thirty

אֲשֶׁר נָתַתִּי לָךְ אֲשֶׁר אָמַרְתִּי אֵלֶיךָ שִׂים אֹתָהּ עִמָּךְ׃ וַיָּרֶם
so-he-took (24) with-you her set-aside! to-you I-told that to-you I-gave that

הַטַּבָּח אֶת־הַשּׁוֹק וְהֶעָלֶיהָ וַיָּשֶׂם לִפְנֵי שָׁאוּל וַיֹּאמֶר הִנֵּה
see! and-he-said Saul before and-he-set and-what-on-her the-leg *** the-cook

הַנִּשְׁאָר שִׂים־לְפָנֶיךָ אֱכֹל כִּי לַמּוֹעֵד שָׁמוּר־
being-kept for-the-occasion for eat! before-you to-set the-one-being-kept

לְךָ לֵאמֹר הָעָם קָרָאתִי וַיֹּאכַל שָׁאוּל עִם־שְׁמוּאֵל בַּיּוֹם
on-the-day Samuel with Saul and-he-dined I-invited the-people to-say for-you

הַהוּא׃ וַיֵּרְדוּ מֵהַבָּמָה הָעִיר וַיְדַבֵּר
then-he-talked the-city from-the-high-place after-they-came-down (25) the-that

עִם־שָׁאוּל עַל־הַגָּג׃ וַיַּשְׁכִּמוּ וַיְהִי כַּעֲלוֹת הַשַּׁחַר
the-daybreak about-to-come and-he-was and-they-rose (26) the-roof on Saul with

וַיִּקְרָא שְׁמוּאֵל אֶל־שָׁאוּל הַגָּג לֵאמֹר קוּמָה וַאֲשַׁלְּחֶךָ
and-I-will-send-you get-ready! to-say on-the-roof Saul to Samuel and-he-called

וַיָּקָם שָׁאוּל וַיֵּצְאוּ שְׁנֵיהֶם הוּא וּשְׁמוּאֵל
and-Samuel he two-of-them then-they-went-out Saul when-he-got-ready

הַחוּצָה׃ הֵמָּה יוֹרְדִים בִּקְצֵה הָעִיר וּשְׁמוּאֵל
and-Samuel the-town to-edge-of ones-going-down they (27) to-the-outside

אָמַר אֶל־שָׁאוּל אֱמֹר לַנַּעַר וְיַעֲבֹר לְפָנֵינוּ וַיַּעֲבֹר
and-he-went-on ahead-of-us so-he-goes to-the-servant tell! Saul to he-said

וְאַתָּה עֲמֹד כַּיּוֹם וְאַשְׁמִיעֲךָ אֶת־דְּבַר אֱלֹהִים׃ וַיִּקַּח
then-he-took (10:1) God message-of *** so-I-may-tell-you as-the-day stay! but-you

שְׁמוּאֵל אֶת־פַּךְ הַשֶּׁמֶן וַיִּצֹק עַל־רֹאשׁוֹ וַיִּשָּׁקֵהוּ
and-he-kissed-him head-of-him on and-he-poured the-oil flask-of *** Samuel

וַיֹּאמֶר הֲלוֹא כִּי־מְשָׁחֲךָ יְהוָה עַל־נַחֲלָתוֹ לְנָגִיד׃
as-leader inheritance-of-him over Yahweh he-anointed-you indeed not? and-he-said

בְּלֶכְתְּךָ הַיּוֹם מֵעִמָּדִי וּמָצָאתָ שְׁנֵי אֲנָשִׁים
men two-of then-you-will-meet from-with-me the-day when-to-leave-you (2)

עִם־קְבֻרַת רָחֵל בִּגְבוּל בִנְיָמִן בְּצֶלְצַח וְאָמְרוּ אֵלֶיךָ
to-you and-they-will-say at-Zelzah Benjamin on-border-of Rachel tomb-of near

clans of the tribe of Benjamin? Why do you say such a thing to me?"

22Then Samuel brought Saul and his servant into the hall and seated them at the head of those who were invited—about thirty in number. 23Samuel said to the cook, "Bring the piece of meat I gave you, the one I told you to lay aside."

24So the cook took up the leg with what was on it and set it in front of Saul. Samuel said, "Here is what has been kept for you. Eat, because it was set aside for you for this occasion, from the time I said, 'I have invited guests.'" And Saul dined with Samuel that day.

25After they came down from the high place to the town, Samuel talked with Saul on the roof of his house. 26They rose about daybreak and Samuel called to Saul on the roof, "Get ready, and I will send you on your way." When Saul got ready, he and Samuel went outside together. 27As they were going down to the edge of the town, Samuel said to Saul, "Tell the servant to go on ahead of us"—and the servant did so—"but you stay here awhile, so that I may give you a message from God."

**10** Then Samuel took a flask of oil and poured it on Saul's head and kissed him, saying, "Has not the LORD anointed you leader over his inheritance?[f] 2When you leave me today, you will meet two men near Rachel's tomb, at Zelzah on the border of Benjamin. They will say to you,

[f] 1 Hebrew; Septuagint and Vulgate *over his people Israel? You will reign over the LORD's people and save them from the power of their enemies round about. And this will be a sign to you that the LORD has anointed you leader over his inheritance:*

°26 ק הגגה

נִמְצְאוּ הָאֲתֹנוֹת אֲשֶׁר הָלַכְתָּ לְבַקֵּשׁ וְהִנֵּה נָטַשׁ
he-stopped and-see! to-look-for you-set-out that the-donkeys they-were-found

אָבִיךָ אֶת־ דִּבְרֵי הָאֲתֹנוֹת וְדָאַג לָכֶם לֵאמֹר מָה
what? to-say about-you and-he-worries the-donkeys thoughts-of *** father-of-you

אֶעֱשֶׂה לִבְנִי׃ (3) וְחָלַפְתָּ מִשָּׁם וָהָלְאָה
and-onward from-there then-you-will-go (3) about-son-of-me shall-I-do

וּבָאתָ עַד־ אֵלוֹן תָּבוֹר וּמְצָאוּךָ שָׁם שְׁלֹשָׁה
three there and-they-will-meet-you Tabor great-tree-of to and-you-will-come

אֲנָשִׁים עֹלִים אֶל־הָאֱלֹהִים בֵּית־אֵל אֶחָד נֹשֵׂא | שְׁלֹשָׁה גְדָיִים
young-goats three carrying one El Beth the-God to ones-going-up men

וְאֶחָד נֹשֵׂא שְׁלֹשֶׁת כִּכְּרוֹת לֶחֶם וְאֶחָד נֹשֵׂא נֵבֶל־
skin-of carrying and-another bread loaves-of three-of carrying and-another

יָיִן׃ (4) וְשָׁאֲלוּ לְךָ לְשָׁלוֹם וְנָתְנוּ לְךָ
to-you and-they-will-give for-peace to-you and-they-will-greet (4) wine

שְׁתֵּי־ לֶחֶם וְלָקַחְתָּ מִיָּדָם׃ (5) אַחַר כֵּן תָּבוֹא
you-will-go that after (5) from-hand-of-them and-you-will-accept bread two-of

גִּבְעַת הָאֱלֹהִים אֲשֶׁר־ שָׁם נְצִבֵי פְלִשְׁתִּים וִיהִי
and-he-will-be Philistines ones-being-posted-of there where the-God Gibeah-of

כְבֹאֲךָ שָׁם הָעִיר וּפָגַעְתָּ חֶבֶל נְבִיאִים
prophets procession-of then-you-will-meet the-town there as-to-approach-you

יֹרְדִים מֵהַבָּמָה וְלִפְנֵיהֶם נֵבֶל וְתֹף
and-tambourine lyre and-before-them from-the-high-place ones-coming-down

וְחָלִיל וְכִנּוֹר וְהֵמָּה מִתְנַבְּאִים׃ (6) וְצָלְחָה עָלֶיךָ
upon-you and-she-will-come (6) ones-prophesying and-they and-harp and-flute

רוּחַ יְהוָה וְהִתְנַבִּיתָ עִמָּם וְנֶהְפַּכְתָּ
and-you-will-be-changed with-them and-you-will-prophesy Yahweh Spirit-of

לְאִישׁ אַחֵר׃ (7) וְהָיָה כִּי תְבֹאֶינָה הָאֹתוֹת
the-signs they-are-fulfilled once and-he-will-be (7) different into-person

הָאֵלֶּה לָךְ עֲשֵׂה לְךָ אֲשֶׁר תִּמְצָא יָדֶךָ כִּי הָאֱלֹהִים
the-God for hand-of-you she-finds whatever for-you do! for-you the-these

עִמָּךְ׃ (8) וְיָרַדְתָּ לְפָנַי הַגִּלְגָּל וְהִנֵּה אָנֹכִי יֹרֵד
coming-down I and-see! the-Gilgal ahead-of-me now-you-go-down (8) with-you

אֵלֶיךָ לְהַעֲלוֹת עֹלוֹת לִזְבֹּחַ זִבְחֵי שְׁלָמִים שִׁבְעַת
seven-of fellowships offerings-of to-sacrifice burnt-offerings to-offer to-you

יָמִים תּוֹחֵל עַד־ בּוֹאִי אֵלֶיךָ וְהוֹדַעְתִּי לְךָ אֵת אֲשֶׁר
what *** to-you and-I-tell to-you to-come-me until you-must-wait days

תַּעֲשֶׂה׃ (9) וְהָיָה כְּהַפְנֹתוֹ שִׁכְמוֹ לָלֶכֶת מֵעִם
from-with to-leave shoulder-of-him as-to-turn-him and-he-was (9) you-must-do

°7 ק תבאנה

'The donkeys you set out to look for have been found. And now your father has stopped thinking about them and is worried about you. He is asking, "What shall I do about my son?"'

3"Then you will go on from there until you reach the great tree of Tabor. Three men going up to God at Bethel will meet you there. One will be carrying three young goats, another three loaves of bread, and another a skin of wine. 4They will greet you and offer you two loaves of bread, which you will accept from them.

5"After that you will go to Gibeah of God, where there is a Philistine outpost. As you approach the town, you will meet a procession of prophets coming down from the high place with lyres, tambourines, flutes and harps being played before them, and they will be prophesying. 6The Spirit of the LORD will come upon you in power, and you will prophesy with them; and you will be changed into a different person. 7Once these signs are fulfilled, do whatever your hand finds to do, for God is with you.

8"Go down ahead of me to Gilgal. I will surely come down to you to sacrifice burnt offerings and fellowship offerings,[8] but you must wait seven days until I come to you and tell you what you are to do."

*Saul Made King*

9As Saul turned to leave

88 Traditionally *peace offerings*

שְׁמוּאֵל וַיַּהֲפָךְ־ לוֹ אֱלֹהִים לֵב אַחֵר וַיָּבֹאוּ
and-they-were-fulfilled different heart God for-him then-he-changed Samuel

כָּל־ הָאֹתוֹת הָאֵלֶּה בַּיּוֹם הַהוּא׃ וַיָּבֹאוּ שָׁם
there when-they-arrived (10) the-that on-the-day the-these the-signs all-of

הַגִּבְעָתָה וְהִנֵּה חֶבֶל־ נְבִאִים לִקְרָאתוֹ וַתִּצְלַח
and-she-came to-meet-him prophets procession-of then-see! at-the-Gibeah

עָלָיו רוּחַ אֱלֹהִים וַיִּתְנַבֵּא בְּתוֹכָם׃ וַיְהִי
and-he-was (11) in-among-them and-he-prophesied God Spirit-of upon-him

כָּל־ יוֹדְעוֹ מֵאִתְּמוֹל שִׁלְשֹׁם וַיִּרְאוּ וְהִנֵּה עִם־
with and-see! when-they-saw before from-yesterday one-knowing-him every-of

נְבִאִים נִבָּא וַיֹּאמֶר הָעָם אִישׁ אֶל־ רֵעֵהוּ מַה־
what? other-of-him to each the-people then-they-asked prophesying prophets

זֶּה הָיָה לְבֶן־ קִישׁ הֲגַם שָׁאוּל בַּנְּבִיאִים׃ וַיַּעַן
and-he-replied (12) among-the-prophets Saul also? Kish to-son-of he-happened this

אִישׁ מִשָּׁם וַיֹּאמֶר וּמִי אֲבִיהֶם עַל־ כֵּן הָיְתָה
she-became this for father-of-them and-who? and-he-said from-there man

לְמָשָׁל הֲגַם שָׁאוּל בַּנְּבִאִים׃ וַיְכַל מֵהִתְנַבּוֹת
from-to-prophesy after-he-stopped (13) among-the-prophets Saul also? as-saying

וַיָּבֹא הַבָּמָה׃ וַיֹּאמֶר דּוֹד שָׁאוּל אֵלָיו וְאֶל־
and-to to-him Saul uncle-of now-he-asked (14) the-high-place then-he-went

נַעֲרוֹ אָן הֲלַכְתֶּם וַיֹּאמֶר לְבַקֵּשׁ אֶת־ הָאֲתֹנוֹת
the-donkeys *** to-look-for and-he-said you-were where? servant-of-him

וַנִּרְאֶה כִּי־ אַיִן וַנָּבוֹא אֶל־שְׁמוּאֵל׃ וַיֹּאמֶר
and-he-said (15) Samuel to then-we-went there-was-not that when-we-saw

דּוֹד שָׁאוּל הַגִּידָה־נָּא לִי מָה־ אָמַר לָכֶם שְׁמוּאֵל׃ וַיֹּאמֶר
and-he-replied (16) Samuel to-you he-said what to-me now! tell! Saul uncle-of

שָׁאוּל אֶל־ דּוֹדוֹ הַגֵּד הִגִּיד לָנוּ כִּי נִמְצְאוּ
they-were-found that to-us he-assured to-assure uncle-of-him to Saul

הָאֲתֹנוֹת וְאֶת־ דְּבַר הַמְּלוּכָה לֹא־ הִגִּיד לוֹ אֲשֶׁר אָמַר
he-said what to-him he-told not the-kingship matter-of but the-donkeys

שְׁמוּאֵל׃ וַיַּצְעֵק שְׁמוּאֵל אֶת־ הָעָם אֶל־ יְהוָה הַמִּצְפָּה׃
the-Mizpah Yahweh to the-people *** Samuel and-he-summoned (17) Samuel

וַיֹּאמֶר ׀ אֶל־ בְּנֵי יִשְׂרָאֵל כֹּה־ אָמַר יְהוָה אֱלֹהֵי יִשְׂרָאֵל אָנֹכִי
I Israel God-of Yahweh he-says this Israel sons-of to and-he-said (18)

הֶעֱלֵיתִי אֶת־ יִשְׂרָאֵל מִמִּצְרַיִם וָאַצִּיל אֶתְכֶם מִיַּד מִצְרַיִם
Egypt from-hand-of you and-I-delivered from-Egypt Israel *** I-brought-up

וּמִיַּד כָּל־ הַמַּמְלָכוֹת הַלֹּחֲצִים אֶתְכֶם׃ וְאַתֶּם
but-you (19) you the-ones-oppressing the-kingdoms all-of and-from-hand-of

Samuel, God changed Saul's heart, and all these signs were fulfilled that day. [10]When they arrived at Gibeah, a procession of prophets met him; the Spirit of God came upon him in power, and he joined in their prophesying. [11]When all those who had formerly known him saw him prophesying with the prophets, they asked each other, "What is this that has happened to the son of Kish? Is Saul also among the prophets?"

[12]A man who lived there answered, "And who is their father?" So it became a saying: "Is Saul also among the prophets?" [13]After Saul stopped prophesying, he went to the high place.

[14]Now Saul's uncle asked him and his servant, "Where have you been?"

"Looking for the donkeys," he said. "But when we saw they were not to be found, we went to Samuel."

[15]Saul's uncle said, "Tell me what Samuel said to you."

[16]Saul replied, "He assured us that the donkeys had been found." But he did not tell his uncle what Samuel had said about the kingship.

[17]Samuel summoned the people of Israel to the LORD at Mizpah [18]and said to them, "This is what the LORD, the God of Israel, says: 'I brought Israel up out of Egypt, and I delivered you from the power of Egypt and all the kingdoms that oppressed you.' [19]But you

הַיּוֹם מְאַסְתֶּם אֶת־ אֱלֹהֵיכֶם אֲשֶׁר־ הוּא מוֹשִׁיעַ לָכֶם מִכָּל־
from-all-of to-you saving he who God-of-you *** you-rejected the-day

רָעוֹתֵיכֶם וְצָרֹתֵיכֶם וַתֹּאמְרוּ לוֹ כִּי־ מֶלֶךְ
king indeed to-him and-you-said and-distresses-of-you calamities-of-you

תָּשִׂים עָלֵינוּ וְעַתָּה הִתְיַצְּבוּ לִפְנֵי יְהוָה לְשִׁבְטֵיכֶם
by-tribes-of-you Yahweh before you-present-yourselves so-now over-us you-set

וּלְאַלְפֵיכֶם׃ וַיַּקְרֵב שְׁמוּאֵל אֵת כָּל־ שִׁבְטֵי
tribes-of all-of *** Samuel when-he-brought-near (20) and-by-clans-of-you

יִשְׂרָאֵל וַיִּלָּכֵד שֵׁבֶט בִּנְיָמִן׃ וַיַּקְרֵב אֶת־
*** then-he-brought-forward (21) Benjamin tribe-of then-he-was-chosen Israel

שֵׁבֶט בִּנְיָמִן לְמִשְׁפְּחֹתָו וַתִּלָּכֵד מִשְׁפַּחַת הַמַּטְרִי
the-Matri clan-of and-she-was-chosen by-clans-of-him Benjamin tribe-of

וַיִּלָּכֵד שָׁאוּל בֶּן־ קִישׁ וַיְבַקְשֻׁהוּ וְלֹא
and-not but-they-looked-for-him Kish son-of Saul then-he-was-chosen

נִמְצָא׃ וַיִּשְׁאֲלוּ־ עוֹד בַּיהוָה הֲבָא עוֹד הֲלֹם
here yet has-he-come? of-Yahweh further so-they-inquired (22) he-was-found

אִישׁ וַיֹּאמֶר יְהוָה הִנֵּה־ הוּא נֶחְבָּא אֶל־ הַכֵּלִים׃
the-baggages among he-hid-himself he see! Yahweh and-he-said man

וַיָּרֻצוּ וַיִּקָּחֻהוּ מִשָּׁם וַיִּתְיַצֵּב בְּתוֹךְ
in-among and-he-stood from-there and-they-brought-out-him and-they-ran (23)

הָעָם וַיִּגְבַּהּ מִכָּל־ הָעָם מִשִּׁכְמוֹ
from-shoulder-of-him the-people than-all-of and-he-was-taller the-people

וָמָעְלָה׃ וַיֹּאמֶר שְׁמוּאֵל אֶל־ כָּל־ הָעָם הַרְּאִיתֶם אֲשֶׁר
whom you-see? the-people all-of to Samuel and-he-said (24) and-upward

בָּחַר־ בּוֹ יְהוָה כִּי אֵין כָּמֹהוּ בְּכָל־ הָעָם
the-people among-all-of like-him there-is-not indeed Yahweh to-him he-chose

וַיָּרִעוּ כָל־ הָעָם וַיֹּאמְרוּ יְחִי הַמֶּלֶךְ׃
the-king may-he-live and-they-said the-people all-of then-they-shouted

וַיְדַבֵּר שְׁמוּאֵל אֶל־ הָעָם אֵת מִשְׁפַּט הַמְּלֻכָה
the-kingship regulation-of *** the-people to Samuel then-he-explained (25)

וַיִּכְתֹּב בַּסֵּפֶר וַיַּנַּח לִפְנֵי יְהוָה וַיְשַׁלַּח
then-he-dismissed Yahweh before and-he-deposited on-the-scroll and-he-wrote

שְׁמוּאֵל אֶת־כָּל־ הָעָם אִישׁ לְבֵיתוֹ׃ וְגַם־ שָׁאוּל הָלַךְ
he-went Saul and-also (26) to-home-of-him each the-people all-of *** Samuel

לְבֵיתוֹ גִּבְעָתָה וַיֵּלְכוּ עִמּוֹ הַחַיִל אֲשֶׁר־
whom the-valiant-man with-him and-they-went in-Gibeah to-home-of-him

נָגַע אֱלֹהִים בְּלִבָּם׃ וּבְנֵי בְלִיַּעַל אָמְרוּ מַה־
how? they-said trouble but-sons-of (27) on-heart-of-them God he-touched

have now rejected your God, who saves you out of all your calamities and distresses. And you have said, 'No, set a king over us.' So now present yourselves before the LORD by your tribes and clans."

[20]When Samuel brought all the tribes of Israel near, the tribe of Benjamin was chosen. [21]Then he brought forward the tribe of Benjamin, clan by clan, and Matri's clan was chosen. Finally Saul son of Kish was chosen. But when they looked for him, he was not to be found. [22]So they inquired further of the LORD, "Has the man come here yet?"

And the LORD said, "Yes, he has hidden himself among the baggage."

[23]They ran and brought him out, and as he stood among the people he was a head taller than any of the others. [24]Samuel said to all the people, "Do you see the man the LORD has chosen? There is no one like him among all the people."

Then the people shouted, "Long live the king!"

[25]Samuel explained to the people the regulations of the kingship. He wrote them down on a scroll and deposited it before the LORD. Then Samuel dismissed the people, each to his own home.

[26]Saul also went to his home in Gibeah, accompanied by valiant men whose hearts God had touched. [27]But some troublemakers said, "How can this

°21 ק למשפחתיו

יֹשִׁעֵנוּ זֶה וַיִּבְזֻהוּ וְלֹא־ הֵבִיאוּ לוֹ מִנְחָה

gift to-him they-brought and-not and-they-despised-him this can-he-save-us

וַיְהִי כְּמַחֲרִישׁ׃ וַיַּעַל נָחָשׁ הָעַמּוֹנִי

the-Ammonite Nahash and-he-went-up (11:1) as-one-being-silent but-he-was

וַיִּחַן עַל־ יָבֵשׁ גִּלְעָד וַיֹּאמְרוּ כָּל־ אַנְשֵׁי יָבֵישׁ אֶל־

to Jabesh men-of all-of and-they-said Gilead Jabesh against and-he-besieged

נָחָשׁ כְּרָת־ לָנוּ בְרִית וְנַעַבְדֶךָּ׃ וַיֹּאמֶר אֲלֵיהֶם

to-them but-he-replied (2) and-we-will-serve-you treaty with-us make! Nahash

נָחָשׁ הָעַמּוֹנִי בְּזֹאת אֶכְרֹת לָכֶם בִּנְקוֹר לָכֶם

of-you that-to-gouge-out with-you I-will-make-treaty on-this the-Ammonite Nahash

כָּל־ עֵין יָמִין וְשַׂמְתִּיהָ חֶרְפָּה עַל־ כָּל־ יִשְׂרָאֵל׃ וַיֹּאמְרוּ

and-they-said (3) Israel all-of on disgrace so-I-bring-her right eye every-of

אֵלָיו זִקְנֵי יָבֵישׁ הֶרֶף לָנוּ שִׁבְעַת יָמִים וְנִשְׁלְחָה מַלְאָכִים

messengers so-we-can-send days seven-of to-us give! Jabesh elders-of to-him

בְּכֹל גְּבוּל יִשְׂרָאֵל וְאִם־ אֵין מוֹשִׁיעַ אֹתָנוּ

us rescuing no-one and-if Israel territory-of through-all-of

וְיָצָאנוּ אֵלֶיךָ׃ וַיָּבֹאוּ הַמַּלְאָכִים גִּבְעַת שָׁאוּל

Saul Gibeah-of the-messengers when-they-came (4) to-you then-we-will-surrender

וַיְדַבְּרוּ הַדְּבָרִים בְּאָזְנֵי הָעָם וַיִּשְׂאוּ כָל־

all-of then-they-raised the-people in-ears-of the-terms and-they-reported

הָעָם אֶת־ קוֹלָם וַיִּבְכּוּ׃ וְהִנֵּה שָׁאוּל בָּא

returning Saul then-see! (5) and-they-wept voice-of-them *** the-people

אַחֲרֵי הַבָּקָר מִן־ הַשָּׂדֶה וַיֹּאמֶר שָׁאוּל מַה־ לָּעָם כִּי

that with-the-people what? Saul and-he-asked the-field from the-ox behind

יִבְכּוּ וַיְסַפְּרוּ־ לוֹ אֶת־ דִּבְרֵי אַנְשֵׁי יָבֵישׁ׃

Jabesh men-of words-of *** to-him then-they-repeated they-weep

וַתִּצְלַח רוּחַ־ אֱלֹהִים עַל־ שָׁאוּל בְּשָׁמְעוֹ אֶת־ הַדְּבָרִים

the-words *** when-to-hear-him Saul upon God Spirit-of and-she-came (6)

הָאֵלֶּה וַיִּחַר אַפּוֹ מְאֹד׃ וַיִּקַּח צֶמֶד בָּקָר

ox pair-of and-he-took (7) greatly anger-of-him and-he-burned the-these

וַיְנַתְּחֵהוּ וַיְשַׁלַּח בְּכָל־ גְּבוּל יִשְׂרָאֵל בְּיַד

by-hand-of Israel area-of to-every-of and-he-sent and-he-cut-up-him

הַמַּלְאָכִים ׀ לֵאמֹר אֲשֶׁר אֵינֶנּוּ יֹצֵא אַחֲרֵי שָׁאוּל וְאַחַר שְׁמוּאֵל כֹּה

this Samuel and-after Saul after following not-he who to-say the-messengers

יֵעָשֶׂה לִבְקָרוֹ וַיִּפֹּל פַּחַד־ יְהוָה עַל־ הָעָם

the-people on Yahweh terror-of then-he-fell to-ox-of-him he-will-be-done

וַיֵּצְאוּ כְּאִישׁ אֶחָד׃ וַיִּפְקְדֵם בְּבָזֶק

at-Bezek when-he-mustered-them (8) one as-man and-they-turned-out

fellow save us?" They despised him and brought him no gifts. But Saul kept silent.

*Saul Rescues the City of Jabesh*

**11** Nahash the Ammonite went up and besieged Jabesh Gilead. And all the men of Jabesh said to him, "Make a treaty with us, and we will be subject to you."

2But Nahash the Ammonite replied, "I will make a treaty with you only on the condition that I gouge out the right eye of every one of you and so bring disgrace on all Israel."

3The elders of Jabesh said to him, "Give us seven days so we can send messengers throughout Israel; if no one comes to rescue us, we will surrender to you."

4When the messengers came to Gibeah of Saul and reported these terms to the people, they all wept aloud. 5Just then Saul was returning from the fields, behind his oxen, and he asked, "What is wrong with the people? Why are they weeping?" Then they repeated to him what the men of Jabesh had said.

6When Saul heard their words, the Spirit of God came upon him in power, and he burned with anger. 7He took a pair of oxen, cut them into pieces, and sent the pieces by messengers throughout Israel, proclaiming, "This is what will be done to the oxen of anyone who does not follow Saul and Samuel." Then the terror of the LORD fell on the people, and they turned out as one man. 8When Saul mustered them at Bezek, the men

°6 ק כשמעו

וַיִּהְיוּ בְנֵי־ יִשְׂרָאֵל שְׁלֹשׁ מֵאוֹת אֶלֶף וְאִישׁ יְהוּדָה
Judah and-man-of thousand hundreds three-of Israel sons-of then-they-were

שְׁלֹשִׁים אָלֶף׃ וַיֹּאמְרוּ לַמַּלְאָכִים הַבָּאִים כֹּה
this the-ones-coming to-the-messengers and-they-told (9) thousand thirty

תֹאמְרוּן לְאִישׁ יָבֵישׁ גִּלְעָד מָחָר תִּהְיֶה־ לָכֶם תְּשׁוּעָה
deliverance to-you she-will-come tomorrow Gilead Jabesh to-man-of you-say

בְּחֹם הַשֶּׁמֶשׁ וַיָּבֹאוּ הַמַּלְאָכִים וַיַּגִּידוּ
and-they-reported the-messengers then-they-went the-sun when-to-be-hot

לְאַנְשֵׁי יָבֵישׁ וַיִּשְׂמָחוּ׃ וַיֹּאמְרוּ אַנְשֵׁי יָבֵישׁ
Jabesh men-of and-they-said (10) then-they-were-elated Jabesh to-men-of

מָחָר נֵצֵא אֲלֵיכֶם וַעֲשִׂיתֶם לָּנוּ כְּכָל־ הַטּוֹב
the-good as-all-of to-us and-you-can-do to-you we-will-surrender tomorrow

בְּעֵינֵיכֶם׃ וַיְהִי מִמָּחֳרָת וַיָּשֶׂם שָׁאוּל אֶת־
*** Saul that-he-separated on-next-day and-he-was (11) in-eyes-of-you

הָעָם שְׁלֹשָׁה רָאשִׁים וַיָּבֹאוּ בְתוֹךְ־ הַמַּחֲנֶה בְּאַשְׁמֹרֶת
in-watch-of the-camp into-midst-of and-they-broke divisions three the-people

הַבֹּקֶר וַיַּכּוּ אֶת־ עַמּוֹן עַד־ חֹם הַיּוֹם וַיְהִי
and-he-was the-day heat-of until Ammon *** and-they-slaughtered the-morning

הַנִּשְׁאָרִים וַיָּפֻצוּ וְלֹא נִשְׁאֲרוּ־ בָם שְׁנַיִם
two of-them they-were-left so-not that-they-were-scattered the-ones-surviving

יָחַד׃ וַיֹּאמֶר הָעָם אֶל־ שְׁמוּאֵל מִי הָאֹמֵר שָׁאוּל
Saul the-one-asking who? Samuel to the-people then-he-said (12) together

יִמְלֹךְ עָלֵינוּ תְּנוּ הָאֲנָשִׁים וּנְמִיתֵם׃ וַיֹּאמֶר
but-he-said (13) and-we-will-kill-them the-men bring! over-us shall-he-reign

שָׁאוּל לֹא־ יוּמַת אִישׁ בַּיּוֹם הַזֶּה כִּי הַיּוֹם עָשָׂה־
bringing the-day for the-this on-the-day man he-shall-be-killed not Saul

יְהוָה תְּשׁוּעָה בְּיִשְׂרָאֵל׃ וַיֹּאמֶר שְׁמוּאֵל אֶל־ הָעָם לְכוּ
come! the-people to Samuel then-he-said (14) to-Israel rescue Yahweh

וְנֵלְכָה הַגִּלְגָּל וּנְחַדֵּשׁ שָׁם הַמְּלוּכָה׃
the-kingship there and-we-will-reaffirm the-Gilgal and-let-us-go

וַיֵּלְכוּ כָל־ הָעָם הַגִּלְגָּל וַיַּמְלִכוּ
and-they-confirmed-as-king the-Gilgal the-people all-of so-they-went (15)

שָׁם אֶת־ שָׁאוּל לִפְנֵי יְהוָה בַּגִּלְגָּל וַיִּזְבְּחוּ־ שָׁם
there and-they-sacrificed at-the-Gilgal Yahweh in-presences-of Saul *** there

זְבָחִים שְׁלָמִים לִפְנֵי יְהוָה וַיִּשְׂמַח שָׁם שָׁאוּל וְכָל־
and-all-of Saul there and-he-celebrated Yahweh before fellowship-ones offerings

אַנְשֵׁי יִשְׂרָאֵל עַד־ מְאֹד׃ וַיֹּאמֶר שְׁמוּאֵל אֶל־ כָּל־ יִשְׂרָאֵל הִנֵּה
see! Israel all-of to Samuel and-he-said (12:1) greatly to Israel men-of

°9 ק כחם

of Israel numbered three hundred thousand and the men of Judah thirty thousand.

9They told the messengers who had come, "Say to the men of Jabesh Gilead, 'By the time the sun is hot tomorrow, you will be delivered.'" When the messengers went and reported this to the men of Jabesh, they were elated. 10They said to the Ammonites, "Tomorrow we will surrender to you, and you can do to us whatever seems good to you."

11The next day Saul separated his men into three divisions; during the last watch of the night they broke into the camp of the Ammonites and slaughtered them until the heat of the day. Those who survived were scattered, so that no two of them were left together.

### *Saul Confirmed as King*

12The people then said to Samuel, "Who was it that asked, 'Shall Saul reign over us?' Bring these men to us and we will put them to death."

13But Saul said, "No one shall be put to death today, for this day the LORD has rescued Israel."

14Then Samuel said to the people, "Come, let us go to Gilgal and there reaffirm the kingship." 15So all the people went to Gilgal and confirmed Saul as king in the presence of the LORD. There they sacrificed fellowship offerings[h] before the LORD, and Saul and all the Israelites held a great celebration.

### *Samuel's Farewell Speech*

12 Samuel said to all Israel, "I have listened to

[h]15 Traditionally *peace offerings*

שמעתי בקלכם לכל אשר־אמרתם לי ואמליך עליכם
over-you and-I-set-king to-me you-said that to-all to-voice-of-you I-listened

מלך׃ ועתה הנה המלך מתהלך לפניכם ואני זקנתי ושבתי
and-I-am-gray I-am-old and-I before-you going the-king see! and-now (2) king

ובני הנם אתכם ואני התהלכתי לפניכם מנערי
from-youths-of-me before-you I-went and-I with-you here-they! and-sons-of-me

עד־היום הזה׃ הנני ענו בי נגד יהוה
Yahweh before against-me testify! here-I! (3) the-this the-day until

ונגד משיחו את־שור | מי לקחתי וחמור מי לקחתי ואת־
and I-took whose? and-donkey I-took whose? ox *** anointed-of-him and-before

מי עשקתי את־מי רצותי ומיד־מי לקחתי
I-accepted whom? and-from-hand-of I-oppressed whom? *** I-cheated whom?

כפר ואעלים עיני בו ואשיב לכם׃
to-you and-I-will-make-right against-him eyes-of-me so-I-shut bribe

ויאמרו לא עשקתנו ולא רצותנו ולא־
and-not you-oppressed-us and-not you-cheated-us not and-they-replied (4)

לקחת מיד־איש מאומה׃ ויאמר אליהם עד יהוה
Yahweh witness to-them and-he-said (5) anything anyone from-hand-of you-took

בכם ועד משיחו היום הזה כי לא מצאתם
you-found not that the-this the-day anointed-of-him and-witness against-you

בידי מאומה ויאמרו עד׃ ויאמר שמואל אל־
to Samuel then-he-said (6) witness and-they-said anything in-hand-of-me

העם יהוה אשר עשה את־משה ואת־אהרן ואשר העלה
he-brought-out and-who Aaron and Moses *** he-appointed who Yahweh the-people

את־אבתיכם מארץ מצרים׃ ועתה התיצבו ואשפטה
for-I-will-give-evidence stand! then-now (7) Egypt from-land-of fathers-of-you ***

אתכם לפני יהוה את כל־צדקות יהוה אשר־עשה
he-performed that Yahweh righteous-acts-of all-of *** Yahweh before to-you

אתכם ואת־אבותיכם׃ כאשר־בא יעקב מצרים
Egypt Jacob he-entered after-when (8) fathers-of-you and-for for-you

ויזעקו אבותיכם אל־יהוה וישלח יהוה את־משה ואת־
and Moses *** Yahweh and-he-sent Yahweh to fathers-of-you then-they-cried

אהרן ויוציאו את־אבתיכם ממצרים וישבום
and-they-settled-them from-Egypt fathers-of-you *** and-they-brought Aaron

במקום הזה׃ וישכחו את־יהוה אלהיהם וימכר
so-he-sold God-of-them Yahweh *** but-they-forgot (9) the-this in-the-place

אתם ביד סיסרא שר־צבא חצור וביד־פלשתים
Philistines and-into-hand-of Hazor army-of commander-of Sisera into-hand-of them

everything you said to me and
have set a king over you. 2Now
you have a king as your leader.
As for me, I am old and gray,
and my sons are here with
you. I have been your leader
from my youth until this day.
3Here I stand. Testify against
me in the presence of the LORD
and his anointed. Whose ox
have I taken? Whose donkey
have I taken? Whom have I
cheated? Whom have I oppressed? From whose hand
have I accepted a bribe to
make me shut my eyes? If I
have done any of these, I will
make it right."
4"You have not cheated or
oppressed us," they replied.
"You have not taken anything
from anyone's hand."
5Samuel said to them, "The
LORD is witness against you,
and also his anointed is witness this day, that you have
not found anything in my
hand."
"He is witness," they said.
6Then Samuel said to the
people, "It is the LORD who appointed Moses and Aaron and
brought your forefathers up
out of Egypt. 7Now then, stand
here, because I am going to
confront you with evidence
before the LORD as to all the
righteous acts performed by
the LORD for you and your fathers.
8"After Jacob entered Egypt,
they cried to the LORD for help,
and the LORD sent Moses and
Aaron, who brought your
forefathers out of Egypt and
settled them in this place.
9"But they forgot the LORD
their God; so he sold them into
the hand of Sisera, the commander of the army of Hazor,

וּבְיַד מֶלֶךְ מוֹאָב וַיִּלָּחֲמוּ בָּם׃ וַיִּזְעֲקוּ
and-they-cried (10) against-them and-they-fought Moab king-of and-into-hand-of

אֶל־יְהוָה וַיֹּאמְר° חָטָאנוּ כִּי עָזַבְנוּ אֶת־יְהוָה וַנַּעֲבֹד
and-we-served Yahweh *** we-forsook for we-sinned and-they-said Yahweh to

אֶת־הַבְּעָלִים וְאֶת־הָעַשְׁתָּרוֹת וְעַתָּה הַצִּילֵנוּ מִיַּד
from-hand-of deliver-us! but-now the-Ashtoreths and the-Baals ***

אֹיְבֵינוּ וְנַעַבְדֶךָּ׃ וַיִּשְׁלַח יְהוָה אֶת־
*** Yahweh then-he-sent (11) and-we-will-serve-you being-enemies-of-us

יְרֻבַּעַל וְאֶת־בְּדָן וְאֶת־יִפְתָּח וְאֶת־שְׁמוּאֵל וַיַּצֵּל אֶתְכֶם מִיַּד
from-hand-of you and-he-delivered Samuel and Jephthah and Bedan and Jerub Baal

אֹיְבֵיכֶם מִסָּבִיב וַתֵּשְׁבוּ בֶּטַח׃ וַתִּרְאוּ
when-you-saw (12) securely so-you-lived on-every-side being-enemies-of-you

כִּי־נָחָשׁ מֶלֶךְ בְּנֵי־עַמּוֹן בָּא עֲלֵיכֶם וַתֹּאמְרוּ לִי
to-me then-you-said against-you moving Ammon sons-of king-of Nahash that

לֹּא כִּי־מֶלֶךְ יִמְלֹךְ עָלֵינוּ וַיהוָה אֱלֹהֵיכֶם מַלְכְּכֶם׃
king-of-you God-of-you though-Yahweh over-us let-him-rule king indeed no

וְעַתָּה הִנֵּה הַמֶּלֶךְ אֲשֶׁר בְּחַרְתֶּם אֲשֶׁר שְׁאֶלְתֶּם וְהִנֵּה נָתַן
he-set and-see! you-asked-for whom you-chose whom the-king here! so-now (13)

יְהוָה עֲלֵיכֶם מֶלֶךְ׃ אִם־תִּירְאוּ אֶת־יְהוָה וַעֲבַדְתֶּם אֹתוֹ
him and-you-serve Yahweh *** you-fear if (14) king over-you Yahweh

וּשְׁמַעְתֶּם בְּקֹלוֹ וְלֹא תַמְרוּ אֶת־פִּי יְהוָה
Yahweh command-of against you-rebel and-not to-voice-of-him and-you-obey

וִהְיִתֶם גַּם־אַתֶּם וְגַם־הַמֶּלֶךְ אֲשֶׁר מָלַךְ עֲלֵיכֶם אַחַר יְהוָה
Yahweh after over-you he-reigns who the-king and-also you both and-you-are

אֱלֹהֵיכֶם׃ וְאִם־לֹא תִשְׁמְעוּ בְּקוֹל יְהוָה וּמְרִיתֶם אֶת־
against and-you-rebel Yahweh to-voice-of you-obey not but-if (15) God-of-you

פִּי יְהוָה וְהָיְתָה יַד־יְהוָה בָּכֶם
against-you Yahweh hand-of then-she-will-be Yahweh command-of

וּבַאֲבֹתֵיכֶם׃ גַּם־עַתָּה הִתְיַצְּבוּ וּרְאוּ אֶת־הַדָּבָר
the-thing *** and-see! stand-still! now then (16) as-against-fathers-of-you

הַגָּדוֹל הַזֶּה אֲשֶׁר יְהוָה עֹשֶׂה לְעֵינֵיכֶם׃ הֲלוֹא קְצִיר־
harvest-of not? (17) before-eyes-of-you doing Yahweh that the-this the-great

חִטִּים הַיּוֹם אֶקְרָא אֶל־יְהוָה וְיִתֵּן קֹלוֹת וּמָטָר
and-rain thunders so-he-sends Yahweh upon I-will-call the-day wheats

וּדְעוּ וּרְאוּ כִּי־רָעַתְכֶם רַבָּה אֲשֶׁר עֲשִׂיתֶם בְּעֵינֵי יְהוָה
Yahweh in-eyes-of you-did that great evil-of-you that and-see! and-realize!

לִשְׁאוֹל לָכֶם מֶלֶךְ׃ וַיִּקְרָא שְׁמוּאֵל אֶל־יְהוָה וַיִּתֵּן יְהוָה
Yahweh and-he-sent Yahweh upon Samuel then-he-called (18) king for-you to-ask

°10 ק ויאמרו

and into the hands of the Philistines and the king of Moab, who fought against them.
[10]They cried out to the LORD
and said, 'We have sinned; we have forsaken the LORD and served the Baals and the Ashtoreths. But now deliver us from the hands of our enemies, and we will serve you.'
[11]Then the LORD sent Jerub-Baal,[i] Barak,[j] Jephthah and Samuel,[k] and he delivered you from the hands of your enemies on every side, so that you lived securely.
[12]"But when you saw that Nahash king of the Ammonites was moving against you, you said to me, 'No, we want a king to rule over us'—even though the LORD your God was
your king. [13]Now here is the
king you have chosen, the one you asked for; see, the LORD
has set a king over you. [14]If
you fear the LORD and serve and obey him and do not rebel against his commands, and if both you and the king who reigns over you follow the LORD your God—good! [15]But if
you do not obey the LORD, and if you rebel against his commands, his hand will be against you, as it was against your fathers.
[16]"Now then, stand still and see this great thing the LORD is about to do before your eyes!
[17]Is it not wheat harvest now? I will call upon the LORD to send thunder and rain. And you will realize what an evil thing you did in the eyes of the LORD when you asked for a king."
[18]Then Samuel called upon the LORD, and that same day the LORD sent thunder and

[i] *11* Also called *Gideon*
[j] *11* Some Septuagint manuscripts and Syriac; Hebrew *Bedan*
[k] *11* Hebrew; some Septuagint manuscripts and Syriac *Samson*

קֹלֹת וּמָטָר בַּיּוֹם הַהוּא וַיִּירָא כָל־ הָעָם
the-people all-of so-he-stood-in-awe the-that on-the-day and-rain thunders

מְאֹד אֶת־ יְהוָה וְאֶת־ שְׁמוּאֵל׃ וַיֹּאמְרוּ כָל־ הָעָם אֶל־ שְׁמוּאֵל
Samuel to the-people all-of and-they-said (19) Samuel and Yahweh *** greatly

הִתְפַּלֵּל בְּעַד־ עֲבָדֶיךָ אֶל־ יְהוָה אֱלֹהֶיךָ וְאַל־ נָמוּת כִּי־
for we-will-die so-not God-of-you Yahweh to servants-of-you for pray!

יָסַפְנוּ עַל־ כָּל־ חַטֹּאתֵינוּ רָעָה לִשְׁאֹל לָנוּ מֶלֶךְ׃ וַיֹּאמֶר
and-he-replied (20) king for-us to-ask evil sins-of-us all-of to we-added

שְׁמוּאֵל אֶל־ הָעָם אַל־ תִּירָאוּ אַתֶּם עֲשִׂיתֶם אֵת כָּל־ הָרָעָה
the-evil all-of *** you-did you you-be-afraid not the-people to Samuel

הַזֹּאת אַךְ אַל־ תָּסוּרוּ מֵאַחֲרֵי יְהוָה וַעֲבַדְתֶּם אֶת־ יְהוָה
Yahweh *** but-you-serve Yahweh from-after you-turn not yet the-this

בְּכָל־ לְבַבְכֶם׃ וְלֹא תָּסוּרוּ כִּי ׀ אַחֲרֵי הַתֹּהוּ
the-useless-idol after indeed you-turn and-not (21) heart-of-you with-all-of

אֲשֶׁר לֹא־ יוֹעִילוּ וְלֹא יַצִּילוּ כִּי־ תֹהוּ הֵמָּה׃ כִּי לֹא־
not for (22) they useless for they-rescue and-not they-do-good not that

יִטֹּשׁ יְהוָה אֶת־ עַמּוֹ בַּעֲבוּר שְׁמוֹ הַגָּדוֹל
the-great name-of-him for-sake-of people-of-him *** Yahweh he-will-reject

כִּי הוֹאִיל יְהוָה לַעֲשׂוֹת אֶתְכֶם לוֹ לְעָם׃ גַּם אָנֹכִי חָלִילָה
far-be-it! I now (23) as-people for-him you to-make Yahweh he-was-pleased for

לִּי מֵחֲטֹא לַיהוָה מֵחֲדֹל לְהִתְפַּלֵּל בַּעַדְכֶם וְהוֹרֵיתִי
and-I-will-teach for-you to-pray by-to-fail against-Yahweh from-to-sin from-me

אֶתְכֶם בְּדֶרֶךְ הַטּוֹבָה וְהַיְשָׁרָה׃ אַךְ ׀ יְראוּ אֶת־ יְהוָה וַעֲבַדְתֶּם
and-you-serve Yahweh *** fear! but (24) and-the-right the-good on-way-of you

אֹתוֹ בֶּאֱמֶת בְּכָל־ לְבַבְכֶם כִּי רְאוּ אֵת אֲשֶׁר־ הִגְדִּל
he-did-great-thing how *** consider! indeed heart-of-you with-all-of in-faith him

עִמָּכֶם׃ וְאִם־ הָרֵעַ תָּרֵעוּ גַּם־ אַתֶּם גַּם־ מַלְכְּכֶם
king-of-you and you both you-do-evil to-do-evil yet-if (25) for-you

תִּסָּפוּ׃ בֶּן־ שָׁנָה שָׁאוּל בְּמָלְכוֹ וּשְׁתֵּי
and-two-of when-to-become-king-him Saul year son-of (13:1) you-will-be-swept-away

שָׁנִים מָלַךְ עַל־ יִשְׂרָאֵל׃ וַיִּבְחַר־ לוֹ שָׁאוּל שְׁלֹשֶׁת
three-of Saul for-him and-he-chose (2) Israel over he-reigned years

אֲלָפִים מִיִּשְׂרָאֵל וַיִּהְיוּ עִם־ שָׁאוּל אַלְפַּיִם בְּמִכְמָשׂ
at-Micmash two-thousands Saul with and-they-were from-Israel thousands

וּבְהַר בֵּית־ אֵל וְאֶלֶף הָיוּ עִם־ יוֹנָתָן
Jonathan with they-were and-thousand El Beth and-in-hill-country-of

בְּגִבְעַת בִּנְיָמִין וְיֶתֶר הָעָם שִׁלַּח אִישׁ לְאֹהָלָיו׃
to-homes-of-him each he-sent-back the-people and-rest-of Benjamin at-Gibeah-of

rain. So all the people stood in awe of the LORD and of Samuel.

[19]The people all said to Samuel, "Pray to the LORD your God for your servants so that we will not die, for we have added to all our other sins the evil of asking for a king."

[20]"Do not be afraid," Samuel replied. "You have done all this evil; yet do not turn away from the LORD, but serve the LORD with all your heart. [21]Do not turn away after useless idols. They can do you no good, nor can they rescue you, because they are useless. [22]For the sake of his great name the LORD will not reject his people, because the LORD was pleased to make you his own. [23]As for me, far be it from me that I should sin against the LORD by failing to pray for you. And I will teach you the way that is good and right. [24]But be sure to fear the LORD and serve him faithfully with all your heart; consider what great things he has done for you. [25]Yet if you persist in doing evil, both you and your king will be swept away."

### *Samuel Rebukes Saul*

**13** Saul was ⌊thirty⌋[l] years old when he became king, and he reigned over Israel ⌊forty-⌋[m] two years.

[2]Saul[n] chose three thousand men from Israel; two thousand were with him at Micmash and in the hill country of Bethel, and a thousand were with Jonathan at Gibeah of Benjamin. The rest of the men he sent back to their homes.

[l]1 A few late manuscripts of the Septuagint; Hebrew does not have *thirty*.
[m]1 See the round number in Acts 13:21; Hebrew does not have *forty-*.
[n]1,2 Or *and when he had reigned over Israel two years, [2]he*

וַיַּךְ יוֹנָתָן אֵת נְצִיב פְּלִשְׁתִּים אֲשֶׁר בְּגֶבַע
at-Geba that Philistines outpost-of *** Jonathan and-he-attacked (3)

וַיִּשְׁמְעוּ פְּלִשְׁתִּים וְשָׁאוּל תָּקַע בַּשּׁוֹפָר בְּכָל־
through-all-of on-the-trumpet he-blew then-Saul Philistines and-they-heard

הָאָרֶץ לֵאמֹר יִשְׁמְעוּ הָעִבְרִים׃ וְכָל־ יִשְׂרָאֵל שָׁמְעוּ
they-heard Israel so-all-of (4) the-Hebrews let-them-hear to-say the-land

לֵאמֹר הִכָּה שָׁאוּל אֶת־ נְצִיב פְּלִשְׁתִּים וְגַם־ נִבְאַשׁ*
he-became-stench and-now Philistines outpost-of *** Saul he-attacked to-say

יִשְׂרָאֵל בַּפְּלִשְׁתִּים וַיִּצָּעֲקוּ הָעָם אַחֲרֵי שָׁאוּל
Saul after the-people and-they-were-summoned to-the-Philistines Israel

הַגִּלְגָּל׃ וּפְלִשְׁתִּים נֶאֶסְפוּ ׀ לְהִלָּחֵם עִם־יִשְׂרָאֵל שְׁלֹשִׁים
thirty Israel against to-fight they-assembled and-Philistines (5) the-Gilgal

אֶלֶף רֶכֶב וְשֵׁשֶׁת אֲלָפִים פָּרָשִׁים וְעָם כַּחוֹל אֲשֶׁר
that as-the-sand and-soldier charioteers thousands and-six-of chariot thousand

עַל־ שְׂפַת־ הַיָּם לָרֹב וַיַּעֲלוּ וַיַּחֲנוּ בְמִכְמָשׂ
at-Micmash and-they-camped and-they-went-up in-number the-sea shore-of on

קִדְמַת בֵּית אָוֶן׃ וְאִישׁ יִשְׂרָאֵל רָאוּ כִּי צַר־
he-was-critical that they-saw Israel when-man-of (6) Aven Beth east-of

לוֹ כִּי נִגַּשׂ הָעָם וַיִּתְחַבְּאוּ הָעָם בַּמְּעָרוֹת
in-the-caves the-army then-they-hid the-army he-was-hard-pressed for to-him

וּבַחֲוָחִים וּבַסְּלָעִים וּבַצְּרִחִים וּבַבֹּרוֹת׃
and-in-the-cisterns and-in-the-pits and-among-the-rocks and-in-the-thickets

וְעִבְרִים עָבְרוּ אֶת־ הַיַּרְדֵּן אֶרֶץ גָּד וְגִלְעָד וְשָׁאוּל
and-Saul and-Gilead Gad land-of the-Jordan *** they-crossed and-Hebrews (7)

עוֹדֶנּוּ בַגִּלְגָּל וְכָל־ הָעָם חָרְדוּ אַחֲרָיו׃
with-him they-quaked-with-fear the-troop and-all-of at-the-Gilgal still-he

וַיִּיחֶל ׀ שִׁבְעַת יָמִים לַמּוֹעֵד אֲשֶׁר שְׁמוּאֵל וְלֹא־ בָא
he-came but-not Samuel that as-the-set-time days seven-of and-he-waited (8)

שְׁמוּאֵל הַגִּלְגָּל וַיָּפֶץ הָעָם מֵעָלָיו׃ וַיֹּאמֶר
so-he-said (9) from-with-him the-people and-he-scattered the-Gilgal Samuel

שָׁאוּל הַגִּשׁוּ אֵלַי הָעֹלָה וְהַשְּׁלָמִים וַיַּעַל
and-he-offered and-the-fellowship-offerings the-burnt-offering to-me bring! Saul

הָעֹלָה׃ וַיְהִי כְּכַלֹּתוֹ לְהַעֲלוֹת הָעֹלָה
the-burnt-offering to-offer as-to-finish-him and-he-was (10) the-burnt-offering

וְהִנֵּה שְׁמוּאֵל בָּא וַיֵּצֵא שָׁאוּל לִקְרָאתוֹ לְבָרְכוֹ׃
to-greet-him to-meet-him Saul and-he-went-out arriving Samuel then-see!

וַיֹּאמֶר שְׁמוּאֵל מֶה עָשִׂיתָ וַיֹּאמֶר שָׁאוּל כִּי־ רָאִיתִי כִּי־
that I-saw when Saul and-he-replied you-did what? Samuel and-he-asked (11)

[3]Jonathan attacked the Philistine outpost at Geba, and the Philistines heard about it. Then Saul had the trumpet blown throughout the land and said, "Let the Hebrews hear!" [4]So all Israel heard the news: "Saul has attacked the Philistine outpost, and now Israel has become a stench to the Philistines." And the people were summoned to join Saul at Gilgal.

[5]The Philistines assembled to fight Israel, with three thousand[o] chariots, six thousand charioteers, and soldiers as numerous as the sand on the seashore. They went up and camped at Micmash, east of Beth Aven. [6]When the men of Israel saw that their situation was critical and that their army was hard pressed, they hid in caves and thickets, among the rocks, and in pits and cisterns. [7]Some Hebrews even crossed the Jordan to the land of Gad and Gilead.

Saul remained at Gilgal, and all the troops with him were quaking with fear. [8]He waited seven days, the time set by Samuel; but Samuel did not come to Gilgal, and Saul's men began to scatter. [9]So he said, "Bring me the burnt offering and the fellowship offerings.[p]" And Saul offered up the burnt offering. [10]Just as he finished making the offering, Samuel arrived, and Saul went out to greet him.

[11]"What have you done?" asked Samuel.

Saul replied, "When I saw

[o]5 Some Septuagint manuscripts and Syriac; Hebrew *thirty thousand*
[p]9 Traditionally *peace offerings*

*4 Most mss have the accent *mereka* under the *aleph* (אַ֥שׁ–).

°8 ק ויוחל

נָפַץ הָעָם מֵעָלַי וְאַתָּה לֹא־ בָאתָ לְמוֹעֵד

at-set-time-of you-came not and-you from-with-me the-people he-scattered

הַיָּמִים וּפְלִשְׁתִּים נֶאֱסָפִים מִכְמָשׂ׃ וָאֹמַר עַתָּה

now and-I-thought (12) Micmash ones-assembling and-Philistines the-days

יֵרְדוּ פְלִשְׁתִּים אֵלַי הַגִּלְגָּל וּפְנֵי יְהוָה

Yahweh and-faces-of the-Gilgal against-me Philistines they-will-come-down

לֹא חִלִּיתִי וָאֶתְאַפַּק וָאַעֲלֶה הָעֹלָה׃

the-burnt-offering and-I-offered so-I-felt-compelled I-sought not

וַיֹּאמֶר שְׁמוּאֵל אֶל־שָׁאוּל נִסְכָּלְתָּ לֹא שָׁמַרְתָּ אֶת־ מִצְוַת

command-of *** you-kept not you-were-foolish Saul to Samuel and-he-said (13)

יְהוָה אֱלֹהֶיךָ אֲשֶׁר צִוָּךְ כִּי עַתָּה הֵכִין יְהוָה אֶת־

*** Yahweh he-would-establish now or he-gave-you that God-of-you Yahweh

מַמְלַכְתְּךָ אֶל־ יִשְׂרָאֵל עַד־ עוֹלָם׃ וְעַתָּה מַמְלַכְתְּךָ לֹא־

not kingdom-of-you but-now (14) all-time for Israel over kingdom-of-you

תָקוּם בִּקֵּשׁ יְהוָה לוֹ אִישׁ כִּלְבָבוֹ

after-heart-of-him man for-him Yahweh he-sought she-will-endure

וַיְצַוֵּהוּ יְהוָה לְנָגִיד עַל־ עַמּוֹ כִּי לֹא שָׁמַרְתָּ

you-kept not for people-of-him over as-leader Yahweh and-he-appointed-him

אֵת אֲשֶׁר־ צִוְּךָ יְהוָה׃ וַיָּקָם שְׁמוּאֵל וַיַּעַל

and-he-went-up Samuel then-he-left (15) Yahweh he-commanded-you what ***

מִן־ הַגִּלְגָּל גִּבְעַת בִּנְיָמִן וַיִּפְקֹד שָׁאוּל אֶת־ הָעָם

the-people *** Saul and-he-counted Benjamin Gibeah-of the-Gilgal from

הַנִּמְצְאִים עִמּוֹ כְּשֵׁשׁ מֵאוֹת אִישׁ׃ וְשָׁאוּל

now-Saul (16) man hundreds about-six with-him the-ones-being-found

וְיוֹנָתָן בְּנוֹ וְהָעָם הַנִּמְצָא עִמָּם

with-them the-ones-being-found and-the-people son-of-him and-Jonathan

יֹשְׁבִים בְּגֶבַע בִּנְיָמִן וּפְלִשְׁתִּים חָנוּ בְמִכְמָשׂ׃

at-Micmash they-camped and-Philistines Benjamin in-Geba-of ones-staying

וַיֵּצֵא הַמַּשְׁחִית מִמַּחֲנֵה פְלִשְׁתִּים שְׁלֹשָׁה

three Philistines from-camp-of the-one-raiding and-he-went-out (17)

רָאשִׁים הָרֹאשׁ אֶחָד יִפְנֶה אֶל־ דֶּרֶךְ עָפְרָה אֶל־ אֶרֶץ

vicinity-of in Ophrah way-of toward he-turned one the-detachment detachments

שׁוּעָל׃ וְהָרֹאשׁ אֶחָד יִפְנֶה דֶּרֶךְ בֵּית חֹרוֹן

Horon Beth way-of he-turned another and-the-detachment (18) Shual

וְהָרֹאשׁ אֶחָד יִפְנֶה דֶּרֶךְ הַגְּבוּל הַנִּשְׁקָף

the-overlooking the-borderland way-of he-turned another and-the-detachment

עַל־ גֵּי הַצְּבֹעִים הַמִּדְבָּרָה׃ וְחָרָשׁ לֹא יִמָּצֵא

he-was-found not and-blacksmith (19) to-the-desert the-Zeboim Valley-of over

that the men were scattering, and that you did not come at the set time, and that the Philistines were assembling at Micmash, [12]I thought, 'Now the Philistines will come down against me at Gilgal, and I have not sought the LORD's favor.' So I felt compelled to offer the burnt offering."

[13]"You acted foolishly," Samuel said. "You have not kept the command the LORD your God gave you; if you had, he would have established your kingdom over Israel for all time. [14]But now your kingdom will not endure; the LORD has sought out a man after his own heart and appointed him leader of his people, because you have not kept the LORD's command."

[15]Then Samuel left Gilgal[s] and went up to Gibeah of Benjamin, and Saul counted the men who were with him. They numbered about six hundred.

*Israel Without Weapons*

[16]Saul and his son Jonathan and the men with them were staying in Geba of Benjamin, while the Philistines camped at Micmash. [17]Raiding parties went out from the Philistine camp in three detachments. One turned toward Ophrah in the vicinity of Shual, [18]another toward Beth Horon, and the third toward the borderland overlooking the Valley of Zeboim facing the desert.

[19]Not a blacksmith could be

[s]15 Hebrew; Septuagint *Gilgal and went his way; the rest of the people went after Saul to meet the army, and they went out of Gilgal*

בְּכֹל אֶרֶץ יִשְׂרָאֵל כִּי־ אָמְר° פְלִשְׁתִּים פֶּן יַעֲשׂוּ
they-will-make otherwise Philistines they-said for Israel land-of in-whole-of

הָעִבְרִים חֶרֶב אוֹ חֲנִית׃ וַיֵּרְדוּ כָל־ יִשְׂרָאֵל
Israel all-of so-they-went-down (20) spear or sword the-Hebrews

הַפְּלִשְׁתִּים לִלְטוֹשׁ אִישׁ אֶת־ מַחֲרַשְׁתּוֹ וְאֶת־ אֵתוֹ וְאֶת־
and mattock-of-him and plowshare-of-him *** each to-sharpen the-Philistines

קַרְדֻּמּוֹ וְאֵת מַחֲרֵשָׁתוֹ׃ וְהָיְתָה הַפְּצִירָה פִים*
*pim the-sharpening and-she-was (21) plowshare-of-him and ax-of-him

לַמַּחֲרֵשֹׁת וְלָאֵתִּים וְלִשְׁלֹשׁ קִלְּשׁוֹן וּלְהַקַּרְדֻּמִּים
and-for-the-axes fork and-for-third and-for-the-mattocks for-the-plowshares

וּלְהַצִּיב הַדָּרְבָן׃ וְהָיָה בְּיוֹם מִלְחֶמֶת וְלֹא נִמְצָא
he-was-found that-not battle on-day-of so-he-was (22) the-goad and-to-repoint

חֶרֶב וַחֲנִית בְּיַד כָּל־ הָעָם אֲשֶׁר אֶת־ שָׁאוּל וְאֶת־ יוֹנָתָן
Jonathan and-with Saul with who the-soldier any-of in-hand-of or-spear sword

וַתִּמָּצֵא לְשָׁאוּל וּלְיוֹנָתָן בְּנוֹ׃ וַיֵּצֵא
now-he-went-out (23) son-of-him and-with-Jonathan with-Saul but-she-was-found

מַצַּב פְּלִשְׁתִּים אֶל־ מַעֲבַר מִכְמָשׂ׃ וַיְהִי הַיּוֹם
the-day and-he-was (14:1) Micmash pass-of to Philistines detachment-of

וַיֹּאמֶר יוֹנָתָן בֶּן־ שָׁאוּל אֶל־ הַנַּעַר נֹשֵׂא כֵלָיו
armors-of-him bearing the-young-man to Saul son-of Jonathan that-he-said

לְכָה וְנַעְבְּרָה אֶל־ מַצַּב פְּלִשְׁתִּים אֲשֶׁר מֵעֵבֶר
on-other-side that Philistines outpost-of to and-let-us-go-over come!

הַלָּז וּלְאָבִיו לֹא הִגִּיד׃ וְשָׁאוּל יוֹשֵׁב בִּקְצֵה
at-outskirt-of staying now-Saul (2) he-told not but-to-father-of-him the-this

הַגִּבְעָה תַּחַת הָרִמּוֹן אֲשֶׁר בְּמִגְרוֹן וְהָעָם אֲשֶׁר
who and-the-people in-Migron that the-pomegranate-tree under the-Gibeah

עִמּוֹ כְּשֵׁשׁ מֵאוֹת אִישׁ׃ וַאֲחִיָּה בֶן־ אֲחִטוּב אֲחִי
brother-of Ahitub son-of and-Ahijah (3) man hundreds about-six-of with-him

אִיכָבוֹד ׀ בֶּן־ פִּינְחָס בֶּן־ עֵלִי כֹּהֵן ׀ יְהוָה בְּשִׁלוֹ נֹשֵׂא אֵפוֹד
ephod wearing in-Shiloh Yahweh priest-of Eli son-of Phinehas son-of Ichabod

וְהָעָם לֹא יָדַע כִּי הָלַךְ יוֹנָתָן׃ וּבֵין
now-between (4) Jonathan he-left that he-was-aware not now-the-people

הַמַּעְבְּרוֹת אֲשֶׁר בִּקֵּשׁ יוֹנָתָן לַעֲבֹר עַל־ מַצַּב פְּלִשְׁתִּים
Philistines outpost-of to to-cross Jonathan he-intended that the-passes

שֵׁן־ הַסֶּלַע מֵהָעֵבֶר מִזֶּה וְשֵׁן־ הַסֶּלַע מֵהָעֵבֶר
on-the-pass the-rock and-cliff-of on-one-side on-the-pass the-rock cliff-of

מִזֶּה וְשֵׁם הָאֶחָד בּוֹצֵץ וְשֵׁם הָאֶחָד סֶנֶּה׃
Seneh the-other and-name-of Bozez the-one and-name-of on-other-side

found in the whole land of Israel, because the Philistines
had said, "Otherwise the Hebrews will make swords or
spears!" [20]So all Israel went
down to the Philistines to
have their plowshares, mattocks, axes and sickles[t]
sharpened. [21]The price was
two thirds of a shekel[u] for
sharpening plowshares and
mattocks, and a third of a
shekel[v] for sharpening forks
and axes and for repointing
goads.
[22]So on the day of the battle
not a soldier with Saul and
Jonathan had a sword or spear
in his hand; only Saul and his
son Jonathan had them.

*Jonathan Attacks the Philistines*

**14** [23]Now a detachment of
Philistines had gone
out to the pass at Micmash.
[1]One day Jonathan son of Saul
said to the young man bearing
his armor, "Come, let's go
over to the Philistine outpost
on the other side." But he did
not tell his father.
[2]Saul was staying on the outskirts of Gibeah under a
pomegranate tree in Migron.
With him were about six hundred men, [3]among whom was
Ahijah, who was wearing an
ephod. He was a son of Ichabod's brother Ahitub son of
Phinehas, the son of Eli, the
LORD's priest in Shiloh. No
one was aware that Jonathan
had left.
[4]On each side of the pass
that Jonathan intended to
cross to reach the Philistine
outpost was a cliff; one was
called Bozez, and the other

[t] *20* Septuagint; Hebrew *plowshares*
[u] *21* Hebrew *pim*, that is, about 1/4 ounce (about 8 grams)
[v] *21* That is, about 1/8 ounce (about 4 grams)

**21* **This word occurs only here in the Hebrew Scriptures. Its weight is given in footnote *u*.**

°*19* ק אמרו

הַשֵּׁן הָאֶחָד מָצוּק מִצָּפוֹן מוּל מִכְמָשׂ וְהָאֶחָד מִנֶּגֶב
to-south and-the-other Micmash toward to-north pillar the-one the-cliff (5)

מוּל גָּבַע׃ וַיֹּאמֶר יְהוֹנָתָן אֶל־הַנַּעַר ׀ נֹשֵׂא כֵלָיו
armors-of-him bearing the-young-man to Jonathan and-he-said (6) Geba toward

לְכָה וְנַעְבְּרָה אֶל־מַצַּב הָעֲרֵלִים הָאֵלֶּה
the-those the-uncircumcised-ones outpost-of to and-let-us-go-over come!

אוּלַי יַעֲשֶׂה יְהוָה לָנוּ כִּי אֵין לַיהוָה מַעְצוֹר לְהוֹשִׁיעַ
to-save hindrance to-Yahweh nothing for for-us Yahweh he-will-act perhaps

בְּרַב אוֹ בִמְעָט׃ וַיֹּאמֶר לוֹ נֹשֵׂא כֵלָיו עֲשֵׂה כָּל־
all do! armors-of-him one-bearing to-him and-he-said (7) by-few or by-many

אֲשֶׁר בִּלְבָבֶךָ נְטֵה לָךְ הִנְנִי עִמְּךָ כִּלְבָבֶךָ׃
after-heart-of-you with-you see-I! for-you go-ahead! in-mind-of-you that

וַיֹּאמֶר יְהוֹנָתָן הִנֵּה אֲנַחְנוּ עֹבְרִים אֶל־הָאֲנָשִׁים וְנִגְלִינוּ
and-we-will-show the-men toward ones-crossing we see! Jonathan and-he-said (8)

אֲלֵיהֶם׃ אִם־כֹּה יֹאמְרוּ אֵלֵינוּ דֹּמּוּ עַד־הַגִּיעֵנוּ אֲלֵיכֶם וְעָמַדְנוּ
then-we-stay to-you to-come-us until wait! to-us they-say this if (9) to-them

תַחְתֵּינוּ וְלֹא נַעֲלֶה אֲלֵיהֶם׃ וְאִם־כֹּה יֹאמְרוּ עֲלוּ
come-up! they-say this but-if (10) to-them we-will-go-up and-not place-of-us

עָלֵינוּ וְעָלִינוּ כִּי־נְתָנָם יְהוָה בְּיָדֵנוּ וְזֶה־
and-this into-hand-of-us Yahweh he-gave-them for then-we-will-climb-up to-us

לָּנוּ הָאוֹת׃ וַיִּגָּלוּ שְׁנֵיהֶם אֶל־מַצַּב
outpost-of to both-of-them so-they-showed-themselves (11) the-sign to-us

פְּלִשְׁתִּים וַיֹּאמְרוּ פְלִשְׁתִּים הִנֵּה עִבְרִים יֹצְאִים מִן־
from ones-crawling-out Hebrews look! Philistines and-they-said Philistines

הַחֹרִים אֲשֶׁר הִתְחַבְּאוּ־שָׁם׃ וַיַּעֲנוּ אַנְשֵׁי הַמַּצָּבָה אֶת־
*** the-outpost men-of and-they-shouted (12) there they-hid that the-holes

יוֹנָתָן ׀ וְאֶת־נֹשֵׂא כֵלָיו וַיֹּאמְרוּ עֲלוּ אֵלֵינוּ
to-us come-up! and-they-said armors-of-him one-bearing and Jonathan

וְנוֹדִיעָה אֶתְכֶם דָּבָר וַיֹּאמֶר יוֹנָתָן אֶל־נֹשֵׂא כֵלָיו
armors-of-him one-bearing to Jonathan so-he-said lesson you and-we-will-teach

עֲלֵה אַחֲרַי כִּי־נְתָנָם יְהוָה בְּיַד יִשְׂרָאֵל׃
Israel into-hand-of Yahweh he-gave-them for after-me climb-up!

וַיַּעַל יוֹנָתָן עַל־יָדָיו וְעַל־רַגְלָיו
feet-of-him and-on hands-of-him on Jonathan and-he-climbed-up (13)

וְנֹשֵׂא כֵלָיו אַחֲרָיו וַיִּפְּלוּ לִפְנֵי יוֹנָתָן
Jonathan before and-they-fell after-him armors-of-him and-one-bearing

וְנֹשֵׂא כֵלָיו מְמוֹתֵת אַחֲרָיו׃ וַתְּהִי הַמַּכָּה
the-attack and-she-was (14) behind-him killing armors-of-him and-one-bearing

Seneh. [5]One cliff stood to the north toward Micmash, the other to the south toward Geba.

[6]Jonathan said to his young armor-bearer, "Come, let's go over to the outpost of those uncircumcised fellows. Perhaps the LORD will act in our behalf. Nothing can hinder the LORD from saving, whether by many or by few."

[7]"Do all that you have in mind," his armor-bearer said. "Go ahead; I am with you heart and soul."

[8]Jonathan said, "Come, then; we will cross over toward the men and let them see us. [9]If they say to us, 'Wait there until we come to you,' we will stay where we are and not go up to them. [10]But if they say, 'Come up to us,' we will climb up, because that will be our sign that the LORD has given them into our hands."

[11]So both of them showed themselves to the Philistine outpost. "Look!" said the Philistines. "The Hebrews are crawling out of the holes they were hiding in." [12]The men of the outpost shouted to Jonathan and his armor-bearer, "Come up to us and we'll teach you a lesson."

So Jonathan said to his armor-bearer, "Climb up after me; the LORD has given them into the hand of Israel."

[13]Jonathan climbed up, using his hands and feet, with his armor-bearer right behind him. The Philistines fell before Jonathan, and his armor-bearer followed and killed behind

הָרִאשֹׁנָה אֲשֶׁר הִכָּה יוֹנָתָן וְנֹשֵׂא כֵלָיו כְּעֶשְׂרִים
about-twenty armors-of-him and-one-bearing Jonathan he-killed that the-first

אִישׁ כְּבַחֲצִי מַעֲנָה צֶמֶד שָׂדֶה׃ וַתְּהִי חֲרָדָה
panic then-she-struck (15) field yoke work-area in-about-half-of man

בַמַּחֲנֶה בַשָּׂדֶה וּבְכָל־ הָעָם הַמַּצָּב וְהַמַּשְׁחִית
and-the-raiding the-outpost the-army and-in-whole-of in-the-field in-the-camp

חָרְדוּ גַּם־ הֵמָּה וַתִּרְגַּז הָאָרֶץ וַתְּהִי לְחֶרְדַּת אֱלֹהִים׃
God as-panic-of and-she-was the-ground and-she-shook they also they-panicked

וַיִּרְאוּ הַצֹּפִים לְשָׁאוּל בְּגִבְעַת בִּנְיָמִן וְהִנֵּה
and-see! Benjamin at-Gibeah-of of-Saul the-ones-looking-out and-they-saw (16)

הֶהָמוֹן נָמוֹג וַיֵּלֶךְ וַהֲלֹם׃ וַיֹּאמֶר שָׁאוּל
Saul then-he-said (17) indeed-everywhere and-he-went melting-away the-army

לָעָם אֲשֶׁר אִתּוֹ פִּקְדוּ־ נָא וּרְאוּ מִי הָלַךְ
he-left who and-see! now! muster-forces! with-him who to-the-people

מֵעִמָּנוּ וַיִּפְקְדוּ וְהִנֵּה אֵין יוֹנָתָן
Jonathan there-was-not then-see! when-they-mustered from-with-us

וְנֹשֵׂא כֵלָיו׃ וַיֹּאמֶר שָׁאוּל לַאֲחִיָּה הַגִּישָׁה אֲרוֹן
ark-of bring! to-Ahijah Saul and-he-said (18) armors-of-him and-one-bearing

הָאֱלֹהִים כִּי־ הָיָה אֲרוֹן הָאֱלֹהִים בַּיּוֹם הַהוּא וּבְנֵי יִשְׂרָאֵל׃
Israel with-sons-of the-that on-the-day the-God ark-of he-was for the-God

וַיְהִי עַד דִּבֶּר שָׁאוּל אֶל־ הַכֹּהֵן וְהֶהָמוֹן אֲשֶׁר
that that-the-tumult the-priest to Saul he-talked while and-he-was (19)

בְּמַחֲנֵה פְלִשְׁתִּים וַיֵּלֶךְ הָלוֹךְ וָרָב וַיֹּאמֶר שָׁאוּל אֶל־
to Saul so-he-said even-more to-go and-he-increased Philistines in-camp-of

הַכֹּהֵן אֱסֹף יָדֶךָ׃ וַיִּזָּעֵק שָׁאוּל וְכָל־
and-all-of Saul then-he-assembled (20) hand-of-you withdraw! the-priest

הָעָם אֲשֶׁר אִתּוֹ וַיָּבֹאוּ עַד־הַמִּלְחָמָה וְהִנֵּה הָיְתָה חֶרֶב
sword-of she-was and-see! the-battle to and-they-went with-him who the-people

אִישׁ בְּרֵעֵהוּ מְהוּמָה גְּדוֹלָה מְאֹד׃ וְהָעִבְרִים הָיוּ
they-were and-the-Hebrews (21) very great confusion against-fellow-of-him man

לַפְּלִשְׁתִּים כְּאֶתְמוֹל שִׁלְשׁוֹם אֲשֶׁר עָלוּ עִמָּם
with-them they-went-up who before as-yesterday with-the-Philistines

בַּמַּחֲנֶה סָבִיב וְגַם־ הֵמָּה לִהְיוֹת עִם־יִשְׂרָאֵל אֲשֶׁר עִם־שָׁאוּל וְיוֹנָתָן׃
and-Jonathan Saul with who Israel with to-be they and-also around to-the-camp

וְכֹל אִישׁ יִשְׂרָאֵל הַמִּתְחַבְּאִים בְּהַר־ אֶפְרַיִם
Ephraim in-hill-country-of the-ones-hiding Israel man-of when-all-of (22)

שָׁמְעוּ כִּי־ נָסוּ פְּלִשְׁתִּים וַיַּדְבְּקוּ גַם־ הֵמָּה אַחֲרֵיהֶם
after-them they also then-they-joined Philistines they-ran that they-heard

him. 14In that first attack Jonathan and his armor-bearer killed some twenty men in an area of about half an acre.[w]

*Israel Routs the Philistines*

15Then panic struck the whole army—those in the camp and field, and those in the outposts and raiding parties—and the ground shook. It was a panic sent by God.[x]

16Saul's lookouts at Gibeah of Benjamin saw the army melting away in all directions. 17Then Saul said to the men who were with him, "Muster the forces and see who has left us." When they did, it was Jonathan and his armor-bearer who were not there.

18Saul said to Ahijah, "Bring the ark of God." (At that time it was with the Israelites.)[y] 19While Saul was talking to the priest, the tumult in the Philistine camp increased more and more. So Saul said to the priest, "Withdraw your hand."

20Then Saul and all his men assembled and went to the battle. They found the Philistines in total confusion, striking each other with their swords. 21Those Hebrews who had previously been with the Philistines and had gone up with them to their camp went over to the Israelites who were with Saul and Jonathan. 22When all the Israelites who had hidden in the hill country of Ephraim heard that the Philistines were on the run, they joined the battle in hot

w14 Hebrew *half a yoke;* a "yoke" was the land plowed by a yoke of oxen in one day.
x15 Or *a terrible panic*
y18 Hebrew; some Septuagint manuscripts *"Bring the ephod." (At that time he wore the ephod before the Israelites.)*

בַּמִּלְחָמָה׃ (23) וַיּוֹשַׁע יְהוָה בַּיּוֹם הַהוּא אֶת־יִשְׂרָאֵל
Israel *** the-that on-the-day Yahweh so-he-rescued (23) in-the-battle

וְהַמִּלְחָמָה עָבְרָה אֶת־בֵּית אָוֶן׃ (24) וְאִישׁ־יִשְׂרָאֵל
Israel now-man-of (24) Aven Beth *** she-moved-on and-the-battle

נִגַּשׂ בַּיּוֹם הַהוּא וַיֹּאֶל שָׁאוּל אֶת־הָעָם
the-people *** Saul for-he-bound-oath the-that on-the-day he-was-distressed

לֵאמֹר אָרוּר הָאִישׁ אֲשֶׁר־יֹאכַל לֶחֶם עַד־הָעֶרֶב וְנִקַּמְתִּי
and-I-am-avenged the-evening before food he-eats who the-man being-cursed to-say

מֵאֹיְבַי וְלֹא טָעַם* כָּל־הָעָם לָחֶם׃ (25) וְכָל־
and-all-of (25) food the-troop any-of he-tasted so-not on-being-enemies-of-me

הָאָרֶץ בָּאוּ בַיָּעַר וַיְהִי דְבַשׁ עַל־פְּנֵי הַשָּׂדֶה׃
the-ground surface-of on honey and-he-was into-the-wood they-entered the-land

(26) וַיָּבֹא הָעָם אֶל־הַיַּעַר וְהִנֵּה הֵלֶךְ דְּבָשׁ וְאֵין־
yet-not honey oozing-of then-see! the-wood into the-army when-he-went (26)

מַשִּׂיג יָדוֹ אֶל־פִּיו כִּי־יָרֵא הָעָם אֶת־הַשְּׁבֻעָה׃
the-oath *** the-people he-feared for mouth-of-him to hand-of-him one-putting

(27) וְיוֹנָתָן לֹא־שָׁמַע בְּהַשְׁבִּיעַ אָבִיו אֶת־הָעָם
the-people *** father-of-him that-to-bind-oath he-heard not but-Jonathan (27)

וַיִּשְׁלַח אֶת־קְצֵה הַמַּטֶּה אֲשֶׁר בְּיָדוֹ וַיִּטְבֹּל אוֹתָהּ
her and-he-dipped in-hand-of-him that the-staff end-of *** so-he-reached

בְּיַעְרַת הַדְּבָשׁ וַיָּשֶׁב יָדוֹ אֶל־פִּיו
mouth-of-him to hand-of-him then-he-raised the-honey into-honeycomb-of

וַתָּרֹאנָה° עֵינָיו׃ (28) וַיַּעַן אִישׁ מֵהָעָם
from-the-soldier man then-he-told (28) eyes-of-him and-they-brightened

וַיֹּאמֶר הַשְׁבֵּעַ הִשְׁבִּיעַ אָבִיךָ אֶת־הָעָם לֵאמֹר
to-say the-army *** father-of-you he-bound-oath to-bind-oath and-he-said

אָרוּר הָאִישׁ אֲשֶׁר־יֹאכַל לֶחֶם הַיּוֹם וַיָּעַף הָעָם׃
the-people so-he-is-faint the-day food he-eats who the-man being-cursed

(29) וַיֹּאמֶר יוֹנָתָן עָכַר אָבִי אֶת־הָאָרֶץ רְאוּ־
see! the-country for father-of-me he-made-trouble Jonathan and-he-said (29)

נָא כִּי־אֹרוּ עֵינַי כִּי טָעַמְתִּי מְעַט דְּבַשׁ הַזֶּה׃
the-this honey little-of I-tasted when eyes-of-me they-brightened how now!

(30) אַף כִּי לוּא אָכֹל אָכַל הַיּוֹם הָעָם מִשְּׁלַל
from-plunder-of the-people the-day he-ate to-eat if how-much indeed (30)

אֹיְבָיו אֲשֶׁר מָצָא כִּי עַתָּה לֹא־רָבְתָה מַכָּה
slaughter she-would-be-greater not now for they-took that being-enemies-of-him

בַּפְּלִשְׁתִּים׃ (31) וַיַּכּוּ בַּיּוֹם הַהוּא
the-that on-the-day and-they-struck-down (31) of-the-Philistines

pursuit. 23So the LORD rescued Israel that day, and the battle moved on beyond Beth Aven.

*Jonathan Eats Honey*

24Now the men of Israel were in distress that day, because Saul had bound the people under an oath, saying, "Cursed be any man who eats food before evening comes, before I have avenged myself on my enemies!" So none of the troops tasted food.

25The entire army[a] entered the woods, and there was honey on the ground. 26When they went into the woods, they saw the honey oozing out, yet no one put his hand to his mouth, because they feared the oath. 27But Jonathan had not heard that his father had bound the people with the oath, so he reached out the end of the staff that was in his hand and dipped it into the honeycomb. He raised his hand to his mouth, and his eyes brightened.[b] 28Then one of the soldiers told him, "Your father bound the army under a strict oath, saying, 'Cursed be any man who eats food today!' That is why the men are faint."

29Jonathan said, "My father has made trouble for the country. See how my eyes brightened[c] when I tasted a little of this honey. 30How much better it would have been if the men had eaten today some of the plunder they took from their enemies. Would not the slaughter of the Philistines have been even greater?"

[a]25 Or *Now all the people of the land*
[b]27 Or *his strength was renewed*
[c]29 Or *my strength was renewed*

*24 Most mss bind these two words with *maqqeph* (ולא־טעם).

°27 ק ותארנה

בַּפְּלִשְׁתִּים מִמִּכְמָשׁ אַיָּלֹנָה וַיָּעַף הָעָם מְאֹד׃
very the-people and-he-was-exhausted to-Aijalon from-Micmash of-the-Philistines

וַיַּעַשׂ הָעָם אֶל־ שָׁלָל וַיִּקְחוּ צֹאן וּבָקָר
and-cattle sheep and-they-took the-plunder on the-people and-he-pounced (32)

וּבְנֵי בָקָר וַיִּשְׁחֲטוּ־ אָרְצָה וַיֹּאכַל הָעָם עַל־
with the-people and-he-ate on-ground and-they-butchered cattle and-calves-of

הַדָּם׃ וַיַּגִּידוּ לְשָׁאוּל לֵאמֹר הִנֵּה הָעָם חֹטְאִים
ones-sinning the-people look! to-say to-Saul and-he-told (33) the-blood

לַיהוָה לֶאֱכֹל עַל־ הַדָּם וַיֹּאמֶר בְּגַדְתֶּם גֹּלּוּ־
roll! you-broke-faith and-he-said the-blood with to-eat against-Yahweh

אֵלַי הַיּוֹם אֶבֶן גְּדוֹלָה׃ וַיֹּאמֶר שָׁאוּל פֻּצוּ בָעָם
among-the-people go-out! Saul then-he-said (34) large stone the-day to-me

וַאֲמַרְתֶּם לָהֶם הַגִּישׁוּ אֵלַי אִישׁ שׁוֹרוֹ וְאִישׁ שֵׂיֵהוּ
sheep-of-him and-each cattle-of-him each to-me bring! to-them and-you-tell

וּשְׁחַטְתֶּם בָּזֶה וַאֲכַלְתֶּם וְלֹא־ תֶחֶטְאוּ לַיהוָה לֶאֱכֹל
to-eat against-Yahweh you-sin and-not and-you-eat at-here and-you-slaughter

אֶל־ הַדָּם וַיַּגִּשׁוּ כָל־ הָעָם אִישׁ שׁוֹרוֹ בְיָדוֹ
in-hand-of-him ox-of-him each the-people all-of so-they-brought the-blood with

הַלַּיְלָה וַיִּשְׁחֲטוּ־ שָׁם׃ וַיִּבֶן שָׁאוּל מִזְבֵּחַ לַיהוָה
to-Yahweh altar Saul and-he-built (35) there and-they-slaughtered the-night

אֹתוֹ הֵחֵל לִבְנוֹת מִזְבֵּחַ לַיהוָה׃ וַיֹּאמֶר שָׁאוּל נֵרְדָה
let-us-go-down Saul and-he-said (36) to-Yahweh altar to-build he-was-first him

אַחֲרֵי פְלִשְׁתִּים ׀ לַיְלָה וְנָבֹזָה בָהֶם ׀ עַד־ אוֹר הַבֹּקֶר
the-morning dawn-of till from-them and-let-us-plunder night Philistines after

וְלֹא־ נַשְׁאֵר בָּהֶם אִישׁ וַיֹּאמְרוּ כָּל־ הַטּוֹב
the-good all-of and-they-replied one of-them let-us-leave and-not

בְּעֵינֶיךָ עֲשֵׂה וַיֹּאמֶר הַכֹּהֵן נִקְרְבָה הֲלֹם אֶל־הָאֱלֹהִים׃
the-God of here let-us-inquire the-priest but-he-said do! in-eyes-of-you

וַיִּשְׁאַל שָׁאוּל בֵּאלֹהִים הַאֵרֵד אַחֲרֵי פְלִשְׁתִּים
Philistines after shall-I-go-down? of-God Saul so-he-asked (37)

הֲתִתְּנֵם בְּיַד יִשְׂרָאֵל וְלֹא עָנָהוּ בַּיּוֹם
on-the-day he-answered-him but-not Israel into-hand-of will-you-give-them?

הַהוּא׃ וַיֹּאמֶר שָׁאוּל גֹּשׁוּ הֲלֹם כֹּל פִּנּוֹת הָעָם
the-army leaders-of all-of here come! Saul so-he-said (38) the-that

וּדְעוּ וּרְאוּ בַּמָּה הָיְתָה הַחַטָּאת הַזֹּאת הַיּוֹם׃
the-day the-this the-sin she-was-committed as-the-what and-see! and-know!

כִּי חַי־ יְהוָה הַמּוֹשִׁיעַ אֶת־יִשְׂרָאֵל כִּי אִם־ יֶשְׁנוֹ
it-is-him if even Israel *** the-one-rescuing Yahweh life-of for (39)

31 That day, after the Israelites had struck down the Philistines from Micmash to Aijalon, they were exhausted. 32 They pounced on the plunder and, taking sheep, cattle and calves, they butchered them on the ground and ate them, together with the blood. 33 Then someone said to Saul, "Look, the men are sinning against the LORD by eating meat that has blood in it."

"You have broken faith," he said. "Roll a large stone over here at once." 34 Then he said, "Go out among the men and tell them, 'Each of you bring me your cattle and sheep, and slaughter them here and eat them. Do not sin against the LORD by eating meat with blood still in it.' "

So everyone brought his ox that night and slaughtered it there. 35 Then Saul built an altar to the LORD; it was the first time he had done this.

36 Saul said, "Let us go down after the Philistines by night and plunder them till dawn, and let us not leave one of them alive."

"Do whatever seems best to you," they replied.

But the priest said, "Let us inquire of God here."

37 So Saul asked God, "Shall I go down after the Philistines? Will you give them into Israel's hand?" But God did not answer him that day.

38 Saul therefore said, "Come here, all you who are leaders of the army, and let us find out what sin has been committed today. 39 As surely as the LORD who rescues Israel lives, even

[d]41 Hebrew; Septuagint *"Why have you not answered your servant today? If the fault is in me or my son Jonathan, respond with Urim, but if the men of Israel are at fault, respond with Thummim."*

°32a ק ויעט
°32b ק השלל

בְּיוֹנָתָן בְּנִי כִּי מוֹת יָמוּת וְאֵין עֹנֵהוּ
answering-him but-not he-must-die to-die indeed son-of-me with-Jonathan

מִכָּל־ הָעָם׃ וַיֹּאמֶר אֶל־ כָּל־ יִשְׂרָאֵל אַתֶּם תִּהְיוּ
you-stand you Israel all-of to then-he-said (40) the-people from-any-of

לְעֵבֶר אֶחָד וַאֲנִי וְיוֹנָתָן בְּנִי נִהְיֶה לְעֵבֶר
at-over-here we-will-stand son-of-me and-Jonathan and-I one at-over-there

אֶחָד וַיֹּאמְרוּ הָעָם אֶל־ שָׁאוּל הַטּוֹב בְּעֵינֶיךָ עֲשֵׂה׃
do! in-eyes-of-you the-good Saul to the-people and-they-replied one

וַיֹּאמֶר שָׁאוּל אֶל־ יְהוָה אֱלֹהֵי יִשְׂרָאֵל הָבָה תָמִים
right-answer give! Israel God-of Yahweh to Saul then-he-prayed (41)

וַיִּלָּכֵד יוֹנָתָן וְשָׁאוּל וְהָעָם יָצָאוּ׃
they-went-away and-the-people and-Saul Jonathan and-he-was-taken

וַיֹּאמֶר שָׁאוּל הַפִּילוּ בֵּינִי וּבֵין יוֹנָתָן בְּנִי
son-of-me Jonathan and-between between-me cast-lot! Saul and-he-said (42)

וַיִּלָּכֵד יוֹנָתָן׃ וַיֹּאמֶר שָׁאוּל אֶל־ יוֹנָתָן הַגִּידָה לִּי מֶה
what to-me tell! Jonathan to Saul then-he-said (43) Jonathan and-he-was-taken

עָשִׂיתָה וַיַּגֶּד־ לוֹ יוֹנָתָן וַיֹּאמֶר טָעֹם טָעַמְתִּי בִּקְצֵה
with-end-of I-tasted to-taste and-he-said Jonathan to-him and-he-told you-did

הַמַּטֶּה אֲשֶׁר־ בְּיָדִי מְעַט דְּבַשׁ הִנְנִי אָמוּת׃ וַיֹּאמֶר
and-he-said (44) must-I-die now-I! honey little-of in-hand-of-me that the-staff

שָׁאוּל כֹּה־ יַעֲשֶׂה אֱלֹהִים וְכֹה יוֹסִף כִּי־ מוֹת תָּמוּת יוֹנָתָן׃
Jonathan you-die to-die if-not may-he-be-severe and-so God may-he-deal so Saul

וַיֹּאמֶר הָעָם אֶל־ שָׁאוּל הֲיוֹנָתָן ׀ יָמוּת אֲשֶׁר עָשָׂה
he-brought who should-he-die Jonathan? Saul to the-people but-he-said (45)

הַיְשׁוּעָה הַגְּדוֹלָה הַזֹּאת בְּיִשְׂרָאֵל חָלִילָה חַי־ יְהוָה אִם־
not Yahweh life-of never! in-Israel the-this the-great the-deliverance

יִפֹּל מִשַּׂעֲרַת רֹאשׁוֹ אַרְצָה כִּי־ עִם־ אֱלֹהִים עָשָׂה
he-did God with for to-ground head-of-him from-hair-of he-shall-fall

הַיּוֹם הַזֶּה וַיִּפְדּוּ הָעָם אֶת־ יוֹנָתָן וְלֹא־ מֵת׃
he-died and-not Jonathan *** the-people so-they-rescued the-this the-day

וַיַּעַל שָׁאוּל מֵאַחֲרֵי פְּלִשְׁתִּים וּפְלִשְׁתִּים הָלְכוּ
they-withdrew and-Philistines Philistines from-after Saul then-he-stopped (46)

לִמְקוֹמָם׃ וְשָׁאוּל לָכַד הַמְּלוּכָה עַל־ יִשְׂרָאֵל וַיִּלָּחֶם
and-he-fought Israel over the-rule he-assumed and-Saul (47) to-land-of-them

סָבִיב ׀ בְּכָל־ אֹיְבָיו בְּמוֹאָב ׀ וּבִבְנֵי־
and-against-sons-of against-Moab being-enemies-of-him against-all-of every-side

עַמּוֹן וּבֶאֱדוֹם וּבְמַלְכֵי צוֹבָה וּבַפְּלִשְׁתִּים
and-against-the-Philistines Zobah and-against-kings-of and-against-Edom Ammon

if it lies with my son Jonathan, he must die." But not one of the men said a word.

40 Saul then said to all the Israelites, "You stand over there; I and Jonathan my son will stand over here."

"Do what seems best to you," the men replied.

41 Then Saul prayed to the LORD, the God of Israel, "Give me the right answer."[d] And Jonathan and Saul were taken by lot, and the men were cleared. 42 Saul said, "Cast the lot between me and Jonathan my son." And Jonathan was taken.

43 Then Saul said to Jonathan, "Tell me what you have done."

So Jonathan told him, "I merely tasted a little honey with the end of my staff. And now must I die?"

44 Saul said, "May God deal with me, be it ever so severely, if you do not die, Jonathan."

45 But the men said to Saul, "Should Jonathan die—he who has brought about this great deliverance in Israel? Never! As surely as the LORD lives, not a hair of his head will fall to the ground, for he did this today with God's help." So the men rescued Jonathan, and he was not put to death.

46 Then Saul stopped pursuing the Philistines, and they withdrew to their own land.

47 After Saul had assumed rule over Israel, he fought against their enemies on every side: Moab, the Ammonites, Edom, the kings of Zobah, and the Philistines.

וּבְכֹל אֲשֶׁר־יִפְנֶה יַרְשִׁיעַ׃ וַיַּעַשׂ
and-he-fought (48) he-inflicted-punishment he-turned where and-at-every

חַיִל וַיַּךְ אֶת־עֲמָלֵק וַיַּצֵּל אֶת־יִשְׂרָאֵל מִיַּד
from-hand-of Israel *** and-he-delivered Amalek *** and-he-defeated valiantly

שֹׁסֵהוּ׃ וַיִּהְיוּ בְּנֵי שָׁאוּל יוֹנָתָן וְיִשְׁוִי
and-Ishvi Jonathan Saul sons-of now-they-were (49) one-plundering-him

וּמַלְכִּי־שׁוּעַ וְשֵׁם שְׁתֵּי בְנֹתָיו שֵׁם הַבְּכִירָה
the-older-daughter name-of daughters-of-him two-of and-name-of Shua and-Malki

מֵרַב וְשֵׁם הַקְּטַנָּה מִיכַל׃ וְשֵׁם אֵשֶׁת שָׁאוּל אֲחִינֹעַם
Ahinoam Saul wife-of and-name-of (50) Michal the-younger and-name-of Merab

בַּת־אֲחִימָעַץ וְשֵׁם שַׂר־צְבָאוֹ אֲבִינֵר בֶּן־נֵר
Ner son-of Abner army-of-him commander-of and-name-of Ahimaaz daughter-of

דּוֹד שָׁאוּל׃ וְקִישׁ אֲבִי־שָׁאוּל וְנֵר אֲבִי־אַבְנֵר בֶּן־
son-of Abner father-of and-Ner Saul father-of and-Kish (51) Saul uncle-of

אֲבִיאֵל׃ וַתְּהִי הַמִּלְחָמָה חֲזָקָה עַל־פְּלִשְׁתִּים כֹּל יְמֵי שָׁאוּל
Saul days-of all-of Philistines with bitter the-war and-she-was (52) Abiel

וְרָאָה שָׁאוּל כָּל־אִישׁ גִּבּוֹר וְכָל־בֶּן־חַיִל וַיַּאַסְפֵהוּ
then-he-added-him bravery son-of or-any-of mighty man any-of Saul when-he-saw

אֵלָיו׃ וַיֹּאמֶר שְׁמוּאֵל אֶל־שָׁאוּל אֹתִי שָׁלַח יְהוָה לִמְשָׁחֲךָ
to-anoint-you Yahweh he-sent me Saul to Samuel and-he-said (15:1) to-him

לְמֶלֶךְ עַל־עַמּוֹ עַל־יִשְׂרָאֵל וְעַתָּה שְׁמַע לְקוֹל דִּבְרֵי
words-of to-message-of listen! so-now Israel over people-of-him over as-king

יְהוָה׃ כֹּה אָמַר יְהוָה צְבָאוֹת פָּקַדְתִּי אֵת אֲשֶׁר־עָשָׂה עֲמָלֵק
Amalek he-did what *** I-will-punish Hosts Yahweh-of he-says this (2) Yahweh

לְיִשְׂרָאֵל אֲשֶׁר־שָׂם לוֹ בַּדֶּרֶךְ בַּעֲלֹתוֹ מִמִּצְרָיִם׃
from-Egypt as-to-come-up-them on-the-way to-him he-waylaid when to-Israel

עַתָּה לֵךְ וְהִכִּיתָה אֶת־עֲמָלֵק וְהַחֲרַמְתֶּם אֶת־כָּל־אֲשֶׁר־לוֹ
to-him that all *** and-you-destroy Amalek *** and-you-attack go! now (3)

וְלֹא תַחְמֹל עָלָיו וְהֵמַתָּה מֵאִישׁ עַד־אִשָּׁה מֵעֹלֵל
from-child woman to from-man but-you-kill from-them you-spare and-not

וְעַד־יוֹנֵק מִשּׁוֹר וְעַד־שֶׂה מִגָּמָל וְעַד־חֲמוֹר׃
donkey even-to from-camel sheep even-to from-cattle one-nursing even-to

וַיְשַׁמַּע שָׁאוּל אֶת־הָעָם וַיִּפְקְדֵם בַּטְּלָאִים
at-the-Telaim and-he-mustered-them the-people *** Saul so-he-summoned (4)

מָאתַיִם אֶלֶף רַגְלִי וַעֲשֶׂרֶת אֲלָפִים אֶת־אִישׁ יְהוּדָה׃
Judah man-of *** thousands and-ten-of foot-soldier thousand two-hundreds

וַיָּבֹא שָׁאוּל עַד־עִיר עֲמָלֵק וַיָּרֶב בַּנָּחַל׃
in-the-ravine and-he-set-ambush Amalek city-of to Saul and-he-went (5)

Wherever he turned, he inflicted punishment on them.[e] 48He fought valiantly and defeated the Amalekites, delivering Israel from the hands of those who had plundered them.

*Saul's Family*

49Saul's sons were Jonathan, Ishvi[f] and Malki-Shua. The name of his older daughter was Merab, and that of the younger was Michal. 50His wife's name was Ahinoam daughter of Ahimaaz. The name of the commander of Saul's army was Abner son of Ner, and Ner was Saul's uncle. 51Saul's father Kish and Abner's father Ner were sons of Abiel.

52All the days of Saul there was bitter war with the Philistines, and whenever Saul saw a mighty or brave man, he took him into his service.

*The Lord Rejects Saul as King*

15 Samuel said to Saul, "I am the one the LORD sent to anoint you king over his people Israel; so listen now to the message from the LORD. 2This is what the LORD Almighty says: 'I will punish the Amalekites for what they did to Israel when they waylaid them as they came up from Egypt. 3Now go, attack the Amalekites and totally destroy[g] everything that belongs to them. Do not spare them; put to death men and women, children and infants, cattle and sheep, camels and donkeys.' "

4So Saul summoned the men and mustered them at Telaim—two hundred thousand foot soldiers and ten thousand men from Judah. 5Saul went to the city of Amalek and set an ambush in the ravine. 6Then

[e]47 Hebrew; Septuagint *he was victorious*
[f]49 Also known as *Ish-Bosheth* and *Esh-Baal*

וַיֹּאמֶר שָׁאוּל אֶל־הַקֵּינִי לְכוּ סֻּרוּ רְדוּ מִתּוֹךְ עֲמָלֵקִי
Amalekite from-among go-away! leave! go! the-Kenite to Saul then-he-said (6)

פֶּן־אֹסִפְךָ עִמּוֹ וְאַתָּה עָשִׂיתָה חֶסֶד עִם־כָּל־בְּנֵי
sons-of all-of to kindness you-showed for-you with-him I-destroy-you so-not

יִשְׂרָאֵל בַּעֲלוֹתָם מִמִּצְרָיִם וַיָּסַר קֵינִי מִתּוֹךְ
from-among Kenite so-he-moved-away from-Egypt when-to-come-up-them Israel

עֲמָלֵק׃ וַיַּךְ שָׁאוּל אֶת־עֲמָלֵק מֵחֲוִילָה בּוֹאֲךָ שׁוּר אֲשֶׁר
that Shur to-go-you from-Havilah Amalek *** Saul then-he-attacked (7) Amalek

עַל־פְּנֵי מִצְרָיִם׃ וַיִּתְפֹּשׂ אֶת־אֲגַג מֶלֶךְ־עֲמָלֵק חָי וְאֶת־כָּל־
all-of and alive Amalek king-of Agag *** and-he-took (8) Egypt east-of to

הָעָם הֶחֱרִים לְפִי־חָרֶב׃ וַיַּחְמֹל שָׁאוּל וְהָעָם
and-the-army Saul but-he-spared (9) sword with-edge-of he-destroyed the-people

עַל־אֲגָג וְעַל־מֵיטַב הַצֹּאן וְהַבָּקָר וְהַמִּשְׁנִים וְעַל־
and-to and-the-fat-calves and-the-cattle the-sheep best-of and-to Agag to

הַכָּרִים וְעַל־כָּל־הַטּוֹב וְלֹא אָבוּ הַחֲרִימָם
to-destroy-them they-were-willing and-not the-good all-of and-to the-lambs

וְכָל־הַמְּלָאכָה נְמִבְזָה* וְנָמֵס אֹתָהּ הֶחֱרִימוּ׃
they-destroyed her and-being-weak *being-despised the-thing but-every-of

וַיְהִי דְּבַר־יְהוָה אֶל־שְׁמוּאֵל לֵאמֹר׃ נִחַמְתִּי כִּי־
that I-am-grieved (11) to-say Samuel to Yahweh word-of then-he-came (10)

הִמְלַכְתִּי אֶת־שָׁאוּל לְמֶלֶךְ כִּי־שָׁב מֵאַחֲרַי וְאֶת־דְּבָרַי
instructions-of-me and from-after-me he-turned for as-king Saul *** I-made-king

לֹא הֵקִים וַיִּחַר לִשְׁמוּאֵל וַיִּזְעַק אֶל־יְהוָה כָּל־
all-of Yahweh to and-he-cried-out to-Samuel and-he-troubled he-carried-out not

הַלָּיְלָה׃ וַיַּשְׁכֵּם שְׁמוּאֵל לִקְרַאת שָׁאוּל בַּבֹּקֶר וַיֻּגַּד
but-he-was-told in-the-morning Saul to-meet Samuel and-he-got-up (12) the-night

לִשְׁמוּאֵל לֵאמֹר בָּא־שָׁאוּל הַכַּרְמֶלָה וְהִנֵּה מַצִּיב לוֹ
to-him setting-up and-see! to-the-Carmel Saul he-went to-say to-Samuel

יָד וַיִּסֹּב וַיַּעֲבֹר וַיֵּרֶד הַגִּלְגָּל׃
the-Gilgal and-he-went-down and-he-left and-he-turned monument

וַיָּבֹא שְׁמוּאֵל אֶל־שָׁאוּל וַיֹּאמֶר לוֹ שָׁאוּל בָּרוּךְ
being-blessed Saul to-him then-he-said Saul to Samuel when-he-reached (13)

אַתָּה לַיהוָה הֲקִימֹתִי אֶת־דְּבַר יְהוָה׃ וַיֹּאמֶר שְׁמוּאֵל
Samuel but-he-said (14) Yahweh instruction-of *** I-carried-out by-Yahweh you

וּמֶה קוֹל־הַצֹּאן הַזֶּה בְּאָזְנָי וְקוֹל
and-lowing-of in-ears-of-me the-this the-sheep bleating-of then-what?

הַבָּקָר אֲשֶׁר אָנֹכִי שֹׁמֵעַ׃ וַיֹּאמֶר שָׁאוּל מֵעֲמָלֵקִי
from-Amalekite Saul and-he-answered (15) hearing I that the-cattle

he said to the Kenites, "Go away, leave the Amalekites so that I do not destroy you along with them; for you showed kindness to all the Israelites when they came up out of Egypt." So the Kenites moved away from the Amalekites.

[7]Then Saul attacked the Amalekites all the way from Havilah to Shur, to the east of Egypt. [8]He took Agag king of the Amalekites alive, and all his people he totally destroyed with the sword. [9]But Saul and the army spared Agag and the best of the sheep and cattle, the fat calves[h] and lambs—everything that was good. These they were unwilling to destroy completely, but everything that was despised and weak they totally destroyed.

[10]Then the word of the LORD came to Samuel: [11]"I am grieved that I have made Saul king, because he has turned away from me and has not carried out my instructions." Samuel was troubled, and he cried out to the LORD all that night.

[12]Early in the morning Samuel got up and went to meet Saul, but he was told, "Saul has gone to Carmel. There he has set up a monument in his own honor and has turned and gone on down to Gilgal."

[13]When Samuel reached him, Saul said, "The LORD bless you! I have carried out the LORD's instructions."

[14]But Samuel said, "What then is this bleating of sheep in my ears? What is this lowing of cattle that I hear?"

[15]Saul answered, "The soldiers brought them from the

[g]3 The Hebrew term refers to the irrevocable giving over of things or persons to the LORD, often by totally destroying them; also in verses 8, 9, 15, 18, 20 and 21.
[h]9 Or *the grown bulls;* the meaning of the Hebrew for this phrase is uncertain.

*9 Without the *mem*, this word would read as a normal Niphal participle. Most lexicons suggest this letter resulted from a scribal error.

הֱבִיאוּם אֲשֶׁר חָמַל הָעָם עַל־מֵיטַב הַצֹּאן
the-sheep best-of from the-soldier he-spared which they-brought-them

וְהַבָּקָר לְמַעַן זְבֹחַ לַיהוָה אֱלֹהֶיךָ וְאֶת־הַיּוֹתֵר
the-remaining but God-of-you to-Yahweh to-sacrifice in-order-to and-the-cattle

הֶחֱרַמְנוּ׃ וַיֹּאמֶר שְׁמוּאֵל אֶל־שָׁאוּל הֶרֶף וְאַגִּידָה לְּךָ
to-you and-let-me-tell stop! Saul to Samuel and-he-said (16) we-destroyed

אֵת אֲשֶׁר דִּבֶּר יְהוָה אֵלַי הַלָּיְלָה וַיֹּאמְרוּ° לוֹ דַּבֵּר׃
tell! to-him and-he-replied the-night to-me Yahweh he-said what ***

וַיֹּאמֶר שְׁמוּאֵל הֲלוֹא אִם־קָטֹן אַתָּה בְּעֵינֶיךָ רֹאשׁ
head-of in-eyes-of-you you small although not? Samuel and-he-said (17)

שִׁבְטֵי יִשְׂרָאֵל אָתָּה וַיִּמְשָׁחֲךָ יְהוָה לְמֶלֶךְ עַל־יִשְׂרָאֵל׃
Israel over as-king Yahweh and-he-anointed-you you Israel tribes-of

וַיִּשְׁלָחֲךָ יְהוָה בְּדָרֶךְ וַיֹּאמֶר לֵךְ וְהַחֲרַמְתָּה אֶת־
*** and-you-destroy go! and-he-said on-mission Yahweh and-he-sent-you (18)

הַחַטָּאִים אֶת־עֲמָלֵק וְנִלְחַמְתָּ בוֹ עַד כַּלּוֹתָם
to-wipe-out-them until on-him and-you-make-war Amalek *** the-wicked-ones

אֹתָם׃ וְלָמָּה לֹא־שָׁמַעְתָּ בְּקוֹל יְהוָה וַתַּעַט אֶל־
on and-you-pounced Yahweh to-voice-of you-obeyed not so-why? (19) them

הַשָּׁלָל וַתַּעַשׂ הָרַע בְּעֵינֵי יְהוָה׃ וַיֹּאמֶר שָׁאוּל אֶל־
to Saul and-he-said (20) Yahweh in-eyes-of the-evil and-you-did the-plunder

שְׁמוּאֵל אֲשֶׁר שָׁמַעְתִּי בְּקוֹל יְהוָה וָאֵלֵךְ בַּדֶּרֶךְ אֲשֶׁר־
that on-the-mission and-I-went Yahweh to-voice-of I-obeyed that Samuel

שְׁלָחַנִי יְהוָה וָאָבִיא אֶת־אֲגַג מֶלֶךְ עֲמָלֵק וְאֶת־עֲמָלֵק
Amalek and Amalek king-of Agag *** and-I-brought-back Yahweh he-assigned-me

הֶחֱרַמְתִּי׃ וַיִּקַּח הָעָם מֵהַשָּׁלָל צֹאן וּבָקָר
and-cattle sheep from-the-plunder the-soldier and-he-took (21) I-destroyed

רֵאשִׁית הַחֵרֶם לִזְבֹּחַ לַיהוָה אֱלֹהֶיךָ בַּגִּלְגָּל׃
at-the-Gilgal God-of-you to-Yahweh to-sacrifice the-devoted-thing best-of

וַיֹּאמֶר שְׁמוּאֵל הַחֵפֶץ לַיהוָה בְּעֹלוֹת וּזְבָחִים
and-sacrifices in-burnt-offerings to-Yahweh delight? Samuel but-he-replied (22)

כִּשְׁמֹעַ בְּקוֹל יְהוָה הִנֵּה שְׁמֹעַ מִזֶּבַח טוֹב לְהַקְשִׁיב
to-heed better than-sacrifice to-obey see! Yahweh to-voice-of as-to-obey

מֵחֵלֶב אֵילִים׃ כִּי חַטַּאת־קֶסֶם מֶרִי וְאָוֶן וּתְרָפִים
and-idolatries and-evil rebellion divination sin-of for (23) rams than-fat-of

הַפְצַר יַעַן מָאַסְתָּ אֶת־דְּבַר יְהוָה וַיִּמְאָסְךָ
so-he-rejected-you Yahweh word-of *** you-rejected because to-be-arrogant

מִמֶּלֶךְ׃ וַיֹּאמֶר שָׁאוּל אֶל־שְׁמוּאֵל חָטָאתִי כִּי־עָבַרְתִּי אֶת־
*** I-violated indeed I-sinned Samuel to Saul then-he-said (24) as-king

°16 ק ויאמר

Amalekites; they spared the best of the sheep and cattle to sacrifice to the LORD your God, but we totally destroyed the rest."

16"Stop!" Samuel said to Saul. "Let me tell you what the LORD said to me last night."

"Tell me," Saul replied.

17Samuel said, "Although you were once small in your own eyes, did you not become the head of the tribes of Israel? The LORD anointed you king over Israel. 18And he sent you on a mission, saying, 'Go and completely destroy those wicked people, the Amalekites; make war on them until you have wiped them out.' 19Why did you not obey the LORD? Why did you pounce on the plunder and do evil in the eyes of the LORD?"

20"But I did obey the LORD," Saul said. "I went on the mission the LORD assigned me. I completely destroyed the Amalekites and brought back Agag their king. 21The soldiers took sheep and cattle from the plunder, the best of what was devoted to God, in order to sacrifice them to the LORD your God at Gilgal."

22But Samuel replied:

"Does the LORD delight in
burnt offerings and
sacrifices
as much as in obeying
the voice of the LORD?
To obey is better than
sacrifice,
and to heed is better
than the fat of rams.
23For rebellion is like the sin
of divination,
and arrogance like the
evil of idolatry.
Because you have rejected
the word of the LORD,
he has rejected you as
king."

24Then Saul said to Samuel, "I have sinned. I violated the

פִּי־ יְהוָה וְאֶת־ דְּבָרֶיךָ כִּי יָרֵאתִי אֶת־ הָעָם
the-people *** I-was-afraid for instructions-of-you and Yahweh command-of

וָאֶשְׁמַע בְּקוֹלָם׃ וְעַתָּה שָׂא נָא אֶת־ חַטָּאתִי
sin-of-me *** now! forgive! and-now (25) to-voice-of-them so-I-gave-in

וְשׁוּב עִמִּי וְאֶשְׁתַּחֲוֶה לַיהוָה׃ וַיֹּאמֶר שְׁמוּאֵל
Samuel but-he-said (26) to-Yahweh so-I-may-worship with-me and-come-back!

אֶל־שָׁאוּל לֹא אָשׁוּב עִמָּךְ כִּי מָאַסְתָּה אֶת־ דְּבַר יְהוָה
Yahweh word-of *** you-rejected for with-you I-will-go-back not Saul to

וַיִּמְאָסְךָ יְהוָה מִהְיוֹת מֶלֶךְ עַל־ יִשְׂרָאֵל׃ וַיִּסֹּב
as-he-turned (27) Israel over king from-to-be Yahweh and-he-rejected-you

שְׁמוּאֵל לָלֶכֶת וַיַּחֲזֵק בִּכְנַף־ מְעִילוֹ וַיִּקָּרַע׃
and-he-tore robe-of-him of-edge-of then-he-caught-hold to-leave Samuel

וַיֹּאמֶר אֵלָיו שְׁמוּאֵל קָרַע יְהוָה אֶת־ מַמְלְכוּת יִשְׂרָאֵל
Israel kingdom-of *** Yahweh he-tore Samuel to-him and-he-said (28)

מֵעָלֶיךָ הַיּוֹם וּנְתָנָהּ לְרֵעֲךָ הַטּוֹב מִמֶּךָּ׃
than-you the-better to-neighbor-of-you and-he-gave-her the-day from-with-you

וְגַם נֵצַח יִשְׂרָאֵל לֹא יְשַׁקֵּר וְלֹא יִנָּחֵם כִּי לֹא
not for he-changes-mind and-not he-lies not Israel Glory-of and-also (29)

אָדָם הוּא לְהִנָּחֵם׃ וַיֹּאמֶר חָטָאתִי עַתָּה כַּבְּדֵנִי נָא נֶגֶד
before now! honor-me! but I-sinned and-he-replied (30) to-change-mind he man

זִקְנֵי־ עַמִּי וְנֶגֶד יִשְׂרָאֵל וְשׁוּב עִמִּי וְהִשְׁתַּחֲוֵיתִי
so-I-may-worship with-me and-come-back! Israel and-before people-of-me elders-of

לַיהוָה אֱלֹהֶיךָ׃ וַיָּשָׁב שְׁמוּאֵל אַחֲרֵי שָׁאוּל וַיִּשְׁתַּחוּ
and-he-worshipped Saul with Samuel so-he-went-back (31) God-of-you to-Yahweh

שָׁאוּל לַיהוָה׃ וַיֹּאמֶר שְׁמוּאֵל הַגִּישׁוּ אֵלַי אֶת־ אֲגַג מֶלֶךְ עֲמָלֵק
Amalek king-of Agag *** to-me bring! Samuel then-he-said (32) to-Yahweh Saul

וַיֵּלֶךְ אֵלָיו אֲגַג מַעֲדַנֹּת וַיֹּאמֶר אֲגַג אָכֵן סָר
he-is-past surely Agag and-he-thought confidently Agag to-him and-he-came

מַר־ הַמָּוֶת׃ וַיֹּאמֶר שְׁמוּאֵל כַּאֲשֶׁר שִׁכְּלָה
she-made-childless just-as Samuel but-he-said (33) the-death bitterness-of

נָשִׁים חַרְבֶּךָ כֵּן־ תִּשְׁכַּל מִנָּשִׁים אִמֶּךָ
mother-of-you among-women she-will-be-childless so sword-of-you women

וַיְשַׁסֵּף שְׁמוּאֵל אֶת־ אֲגָג לִפְנֵי יְהוָה בַּגִּלְגָּל׃ וַיֵּלֶךְ
then-he-left (34) at-the-Gilgal Yahweh before Agag *** Samuel and-he-killed

שְׁמוּאֵל הָרָמָתָה וְשָׁאוּל עָלָה אֶל־ בֵּיתוֹ גִּבְעַת שָׁאוּל׃
Saul Gibeah-of home-of-him to he-went-up but-Saul for-the-Ramah Samuel

וְלֹא־ יָסַף שְׁמוּאֵל לִרְאוֹת אֶת־שָׁאוּל עַד־ יוֹם מוֹתוֹ
death-of-him day-of until Saul *** to-see Samuel he-went-again and-not (35)

LORD's command and your instructions. I was afraid of the people and so I gave in to
them. [25]Now I beg you, forgive my sin and come back with me, so that I may worship the LORD."
[26]But Samuel said to him, "I will not go back with you. You have rejected the word of the LORD, and the LORD has rejected you as king over Israel!"
[27]As Samuel turned to leave, Saul caught hold of the edge of
his robe, and it tore. [28]Samuel said to him, "The LORD has torn the kingdom of Israel from you today and has given it to one of your neighbors—to
one better than you. [29]He who is the Glory of Israel does not lie or change his mind; for he is not a man, that he should change his mind."
[30]Saul replied, "I have sinned. But please honor me before the elders of my people and before Israel; come back with me, so that I may worship the LORD your God." [31]So Samuel went back with Saul, and Saul worshiped the LORD.
[32]Then Samuel said, "Bring me Agag king of the Amalekites."

Agag came to him confidently,[i] thinking, "Surely the bitterness of death is past."
[33]But Samuel said,

"As your sword has made
women childless,
so will your mother be
childless among
women."

And Samuel put Agag to death before the LORD at Gilgal.
[34]Then Samuel left for Ramah, but Saul went up to his home in Gibeah of Saul.
[35]Until the day Samuel died, he did not go to see Saul again,

[i]32 Or *him trembling, yet*

כִּי־ הִתְאַבֵּל שְׁמוּאֵל אֶל־שָׁאוּל וַיהוָה נִחָם כִּי־ הִמְלִיךְ
he-made-king that he-was-grieved and-Yahweh Saul for Samuel he-mourned though

אֶת־שָׁאוּל עַל־יִשְׂרָאֵל׃ וַיֹּאמֶר יְהוָה אֶל־שְׁמוּאֵל עַד־ מָתַי אַתָּה
you when? until Samuel to Yahweh and-he-said (16:1) Israel over Saul ***

מִתְאַבֵּל אֶל־ שָׁאוּל וַאֲנִי מְאַסְתִּיו מִמְּלֹךְ עַל־יִשְׂרָאֵל מַלֵּא קַרְנְךָ
horn-of-you fill! Israel over as-king I-rejected-him since-I Saul for mourning

שֶׁמֶן וְלֵךְ אֶשְׁלָחֲךָ אֶל־ יִשַׁי בֵּית־הַלַּחְמִי כִּי־ רָאִיתִי בְּבָנָיו
of-sons-of-him I-chose for the-Bethlehemite Jesse to I-send-you and-go! oil

לִי מֶלֶךְ׃ וַיֹּאמֶר שְׁמוּאֵל אֵיךְ אֵלֵךְ וְשָׁמַע שָׁאוּל
Saul for-he-will-hear can-I-go how? Samuel but-he-said (2) king for-me

וַהֲרָגָנִי וַיֹּאמֶר יְהוָה עֶגְלַת בָּקָר תִּקַּח בְּיָדֶךָ
in-hand-of-you you-take herd heifer-of Yahweh and-he-said and-he-will-kill-me

וְאָמַרְתָּ לִזְבֹּחַ לַיהוָה בָּאתִי׃ וְקָרָאתָ לְיִשַׁי
to-Jesse and-you-invite (3) I-came to-Yahweh to-sacrifice and-you-say

בַּזָּבַח וְאָנֹכִי אוֹדִיעֲךָ אֵת אֲשֶׁר־ תַּעֲשֶׂה וּמָשַׁחְתָּ
and-you-anoint you-must-do what *** I-will-show-you and-I to-the-sacrifice

לִי אֵת אֲשֶׁר־ אֹמַר אֵלֶיךָ׃ וַיַּעַשׂ שְׁמוּאֵל אֵת אֲשֶׁר דִּבֶּר
he-said what *** Samuel and-he-did (4) to-you I-indicate whom *** for-me

יְהוָה וַיָּבֹא בֵּית לָחֶם וַיֶּחֶרְדוּ זִקְנֵי הָעִיר
the-town elders-of then-they-trembled Lehem Beth when-he-arrived Yahweh

לִקְרָאתוֹ וַיֹּאמֶר שָׁלֹם בּוֹאֶךָ׃ וַיֹּאמֶר ׀ שָׁלוֹם
peacefully and-he-replied (5) to-come-you peacefully and-they-asked to-meet-him

לִזְבֹּחַ לַיהוָה בָּאתִי הִתְקַדְּשׁוּ וּבָאתֶם אִתִּי
with-me and-you-come consecrate-yourselves! I-came to-Yahweh to-sacrifice

בַּזָּבַח וַיְקַדֵּשׁ אֶת־ יִשַׁי וְאֶת־ בָּנָיו וַיִּקְרָא
and-he-invited sons-of-him and Jesse *** then-he-consecrated to-the-sacrifice

לָהֶם לַזָּבַח׃ וַיְהִי בְּבוֹאָם וַיַּרְא אֶת־
*** then-he-saw when-to-arrive-them and-he-was (6) to-the-sacrifice to-them

אֱלִיאָב וַיֹּאמֶר אַךְ נֶגֶד יְהוָה מְשִׁיחוֹ׃ וַיֹּאמֶר
but-he-said (7) anointed-of-him Yahweh before surely and-he-thought Eliab

יְהוָה אֶל־ שְׁמוּאֵל אַל־ תַּבֵּט אֶל־ מַרְאֵהוּ וְאֶל־ גְּבֹהַּ
height-of or-to appearance-of-him to you-consider not Samuel to Yahweh

קוֹמָתוֹ כִּי מְאַסְתִּיהוּ כִּי ׀ לֹא אֲשֶׁר יִרְאֶה הָאָדָם כִּי הָאָדָם
the-man for the-man he-looks-at what not for I-rejected-him for height-of-him

יִרְאֶה לַעֵינַיִם וַיהוָה יִרְאֶה לַלֵּבָב׃ וַיִּקְרָא
then-he-called (8) at-the-heart he-looks but-Yahweh at-the-eyes he-looks

יִשַׁי אֶל־אֲבִינָדָב וַיַּעֲבִרֵהוּ לִפְנֵי שְׁמוּאֵל וַיֹּאמֶר גַּם־
also but-he-said Samuel in-front-of and-he-had-pass-him Abinadab to Jesse

though Samuel mourned for him. And the LORD was grieved that he had made Saul king over Israel.

*Samuel Anoints David*

16 The LORD said to Samuel, "How long will you mourn for Saul, since I have rejected him as king over Israel? Fill your horn with oil and be on your way; I am sending you to Jesse of Bethlehem. I have chosen one of his sons to be king."

2 But Samuel said, "How can I go? Saul will hear about it and kill me."

The LORD said, "Take a heifer with you and say, 'I have come to sacrifice to the LORD.'
3 Invite Jesse to the sacrifice, and I will show you what to do. You are to anoint for me the one I indicate."

4 Samuel did what the LORD said. When he arrived at Bethlehem, the elders of the town trembled when they met him. They asked, "Do you come in peace?"

5 Samuel replied, "Yes, in peace; I have come to sacrifice to the LORD. Consecrate yourselves and come to the sacrifice with me." Then he consecrated Jesse and his sons and invited them to the sacrifice.

6 When they arrived, Samuel saw Eliab and thought, "Surely the LORD's anointed stands here before the LORD."

7 But the LORD said to Samuel, "Do not consider his appearance or his height, for I have rejected him. The LORD does not look at the things man looks at. Man looks at the outward appearance, but the LORD looks at the heart."

8 Then Jesse called Abinadab and had him pass in front of Samuel. But Samuel said, "The

בָּזֶה לֹא־ בָחַר יְהוָה׃ (9) וַיַּעֲבֵר יִשַׁי שַׁמָּה וַיֹּאמֶר
but-he-said Shammah Jesse then-he-had-pass (9) Yahweh he-chose not to-this

גַּם־ בָּזֶה לֹא־ בָחַר יְהוָה׃ (10) וַיַּעֲבֵר יִשַׁי שִׁבְעַת
seven-of Jesse and-he-had-pass (10) Yahweh he-chose not to-this also

בָּנָיו לִפְנֵי שְׁמוּאֵל וַיֹּאמֶר שְׁמוּאֵל אֶל־יִשַׁי לֹא־ בָחַר יְהוָה
Yahweh he-chose not Jesse to Samuel but-he-said Samuel before sons-of-him

בָּאֵלֶּה׃ (11) וַיֹּאמֶר שְׁמוּאֵל אֶל־יִשַׁי הֲתַמּוּ הַנְּעָרִים וַיֹּאמֶר
and-he-said the-sons are-they-all? Jesse to Samuel so-he-asked (11) to-these

עוֹד שָׁאַר הַקָּטָן וְהִנֵּה רֹעֶה בַּצֹּאן וַיֹּאמֶר שְׁמוּאֵל
Samuel and-he-said to-the-sheep tending but-see! the-young he-remains still

אֶל־יִשַׁי שִׁלְחָה וְקָחֶנּוּ כִּי לֹא־ נָסֹב עַד־ בֹּאוֹ פֹה׃
here to-arrive-him until we-will-gather not for and-get-him! send! Jesse to

(12) וַיִּשְׁלַח וַיְבִיאֵהוּ וְהוּא אַדְמוֹנִי עִם־ יְפֵה עֵינַיִם
eyes fineness-of with ruddy now-he and-he-had-brought-him so-he-sent (12)

וְטוֹב רֹאִי וַיֹּאמֶר יְהוָה קוּם מְשָׁחֵהוּ כִּי־ זֶה הוּא׃
he this for anoint-him! rise! Yahweh then-he-said feature and-handsome-of

(13) וַיִּקַּח שְׁמוּאֵל אֶת־ קֶרֶן הַשֶּׁמֶן וַיִּמְשַׁח אֹתוֹ בְּקֶרֶב
in-presence-of him and-he-anointed the-oil horn-of *** Samuel so-he-took (13)

אֶחָיו וַתִּצְלַח רוּחַ־ יְהוָה אֶל־ דָּוִד מֵהַיּוֹם הַהוּא
the-that from-the-day David upon Yahweh Spirit-of and-she-came brothers-of-him

וָמָעְלָה וַיָּקָם שְׁמוּאֵל וַיֵּלֶךְ הָרָמָתָה׃ (14) וְרוּחַ
now-Spirit-of (14) to-the-Ramah and-he-went Samuel then-he-rose and-onward

יְהוָה סָרָה מֵעִם שָׁאוּל וּבִעֲתַתּוּ רוּחַ־ רָעָה מֵאֵת
from evil spirit and-she-tormented-him Saul from-with she-departed Yahweh

יְהוָה׃ (15) וַיֹּאמְרוּ עַבְדֵי־ שָׁאוּל אֵלָיו הִנֵּה־ נָא רוּחַ־ אֱלֹהִים
God spirit-of now! see! to-him Saul attendants-of and-they-said (15) Yahweh

רָעָה מְבַעִתֶּךָ׃ (16) יֹאמַר־ נָא אֲדֹנֵנוּ עֲבָדֶיךָ
servants-of-you lord-of-us now! let-him-command (16) tormenting-you evil

לְפָנֶיךָ יְבַקְשׁוּ אִישׁ יֹדֵעַ מְנַגֵּן בַּכִּנּוֹר וְהָיָה
and-he-will-be on-the-harp playing knowing someone let-them-seek before-you

בִּהְיוֹת עָלֶיךָ רוּחַ־ אֱלֹהִים רָעָה וְנִגֵּן בְּיָדוֹ
with-hand-of-him then-he-will-play evil God spirit-of upon-you when-to-come

וְטוֹב לָךְ׃ (17) וַיֹּאמֶר שָׁאוּל אֶל־ עֲבָדָיו רְאוּ־ נָא
now! find! attendants-of-him to Saul so-he-said (17) for-you and-better

לִי אִישׁ מֵיטִיב לְנַגֵּן וַהֲבִיאוֹתֶם אֵלָי׃ (18) וַיַּעַן
and-he-answered (18) to-me and-you-bring to-play doing-well someone for-me

אֶחָד מֵהַנְּעָרִים וַיֹּאמֶר הִנֵּה רָאִיתִי בֵּן לְיִשַׁי בֵּית הַלַּחְמִי
the-Bethlehemite of-Jesse son I-saw see! and-he-said of-the-servants one

LORD has not chosen this one
either." 9Jesse then had Shammah pass by, but Samuel said,
"Nor has the LORD chosen this
one." 10Jesse had seven of his
sons pass before Samuel, but
Samuel said to him, "The LORD
has not chosen these." 11So he
asked Jesse, "Are these all the
sons you have?"

"There is still the youngest," Jesse answered, "but he is tending the sheep."

Samuel said, "Send for him; we will not sit down[j] until he arrives."

12So he sent and had him
brought in. He was ruddy, with a fine appearance and handsome features.

Then the LORD said, "Rise and anoint him; he is the one."

13So Samuel took the horn of
oil and anointed him in the presence of his brothers, and from that day on the Spirit of the LORD came upon David in power. Samuel then went to Ramah.

*David in Saul's Service*

14Now the Spirit of the LORD
had departed from Saul, and an evil[k] spirit from the LORD tormented him.

15Saul's attendants said to
him, "See, an evil spirit from God is tormenting you.
16Let
our lord command his servants here to search for someone who can play the harp. He will play when the evil spirit from God comes upon you, and you will feel better."

17So Saul said to his atten-
dants, "Find someone who plays well and bring him to me."

18One of the servants an-
swered, "I have seen a son of Jesse of Bethlehem who

j11 Some Septuagint manuscripts; Hebrew *not gather around*
k14 Or *injurious;* also in verses 15, 16 and 23

יֹדֵעַ נַגֵּן וְגִבּוֹר חַיִל וְאִישׁ מִלְחָמָה וּנְבוֹן דָּבָר
speech and-being-wise-of war and-man-of valor and-brave-of to-play knowing

וְאִישׁ תֹּאַר וַיהוָה עִמּוֹ׃ וַיִּשְׁלַח שָׁאוּל מַלְאָכִים
messengers Saul then-he-sent (19) with-him and-Yahweh fine-looking and-man

אֶל־יִשָׁי וַיֹּאמֶר שִׁלְחָה אֵלַי אֶת־דָּוִד בִּנְךָ אֲשֶׁר בַּצֹּאן׃
with-the-sheep who son-of-you David *** to-me send! and-he-said Jesse to

וַיִּקַּח יִשַׁי חֲמוֹר לֶחֶם וְנֹאד יַיִן וּגְדִי
and-young-goat-of wine and-skin-of bread donkey-of Jesse so-he-took (20)

עִזִּים אֶחָד וַיִּשְׁלַח בְּיַד־ דָּוִד בְּנוֹ אֶל־שָׁאוּל׃ וַיָּבֹא
and-he-came (21) Saul to son-of-him David in-hand-of and-he-sent one goats

דָוִד אֶל־ שָׁאוּל וַיַּעֲמֹד לְפָנָיו וַיֶּאֱהָבֵהוּ מְאֹד
very-much and-he-liked-him before-him and-he-served Saul to David

וַיְהִי־ לוֹ נֹשֵׂא כֵלִים׃ וַיִּשְׁלַח שָׁאוּל אֶל־יִשַׁי
Jesse to Saul then-he-sent (22) armors one-bearing for-him and-he-became

לֵאמֹר יַעֲמָד־ נָא דָוִד לְפָנַי כִּי־ מָצָא חֵן בְּעֵינָי׃
in-eyes-of-me favor he-found for before-me David now! let-him-serve to-say

וְהָיָה בִּהְיוֹת רוּחַ־ אֱלֹהִים אֶל־שָׁאוּל וְלָקַח דָּוִד אֶת־
*** David then-he-took Saul to God spirit-of when-to-come and-he-was (23)

הַכִּנּוֹר וְנִגֵּן בְּיָדוֹ וְרָוַח לְשָׁאוּל וְטוֹב
and-better to-Saul and-he-was-relief with-hand-of-him and-he-played the-harp

לוֹ וְסָרָה מֵעָלָיו רוּחַ הָרָעָה׃ וַיַּאַסְפוּ
now-they-gathered (17:1) the-evil spirit-of from-upon-him and-she-left for-him

פְלִשְׁתִּים אֶת־ מַחֲנֵיהֶם לַמִּלְחָמָה וַיֵּאָסְפוּ שֹׂכֹה אֲשֶׁר
that Socoh and-they-assembled for-the-war forces-of-them *** Philistines

לִיהוּדָה וַיַּחֲנוּ בֵּין־ שׂוֹכֹה וּבֵין־ עֲזֵקָה בְּאֶפֶס דַּמִּים׃
Dammim at-Ephes Azekah and-between Socoh between and-they-camped in-Judah

וְשָׁאוּל וְאִישׁ־ יִשְׂרָאֵל נֶאֶסְפוּ וַיַּחֲנוּ בְּעֵמֶק
in-Valley-of and-they-camped they-assembled Israel and-man-of and-Saul (2)

הָאֵלָה וַיַּעַרְכוּ מִלְחָמָה לִקְרַאת פְּלִשְׁתִּים׃ וּפְלִשְׁתִּים
and-Philistines (3) Philistines to-meet battle-line and-they-drew-up the-Elah

עֹמְדִים אֶל־ הָהָר מִזֶּה וְיִשְׂרָאֵל עֹמְדִים אֶל־ הָהָר
the-hill on ones-occupying and-Israel on-this-side the-hill on ones-occupying

מִזֶּה וְהַגַּיְא בֵּינֵיהֶם׃ וַיֵּצֵא אִישׁ־
man-of now-he-came-out (4) between-them and-the-valley on-other-side

הַבֵּנַיִם מִמַּחֲנוֹת פְּלִשְׁתִּים גָּלְיָת שְׁמוֹ מִגַּת
from-Gath name-of-him Goliath Philistines from-camps-of the-spaces-between

גָּבְהוֹ שֵׁשׁ אַמּוֹת וָזָרֶת׃ וְכוֹבַע נְחֹשֶׁת עַל־ רֹאשׁוֹ
head-of-him on bronze and-helmet-of (5) and-span cubits six height-of-him

knows how to play the harp. He is a brave man and a warrior. He speaks well and is a fine-looking man. And the LORD is with him."

[19]Then Saul sent messengers to Jesse and said, "Send me your son David, who is with the sheep." [20]So Jesse took a donkey loaded with bread, a skin of wine and a young goat and sent them with his son David to Saul.

[21]David came to Saul and entered his service. Saul liked him very much, and David became one of his armor-bearers. [22]Then Saul sent word to Jesse, saying, "Allow David to remain in my service, for I am pleased with him."

[23]Whenever the spirit from God came upon Saul, David would take his harp and play. Then relief would come to Saul; he would feel better, and the evil spirit would leave him.

*David and Goliath*

**17** Now the Philistines gathered their forces for war and assembled at Socoh in Judah. They pitched camp at Ephes Dammim, between Socoh and Azekah. [2]Saul and the Israelites assembled and camped in the Valley of Elah and drew up their battle line to meet the Philistines. [3]The Philistines occupied one hill and the Israelites another, with the valley between them.

[4]A champion named Goliath, who was from Gath, came out of the Philistine camp. He was over nine feet[l] tall. [5]He had a bronze helmet

[l]4 Hebrew *was six cubits and a span* (about 3 meters)

וְשִׁרְיוֹן קַשְׂקַשִּׂים הוּא לָבוּשׁ וּמִשְׁקַל הַשִּׁרְיוֹן חֲמֵשֶׁת־אֲלָפִים
thousands five-of the-coat and-weight-of wearing he scale-armors and-coat-of

שְׁקָלִים נְחֹשֶׁת׃ וּמִצְחַת נְחֹשֶׁת עַל־רַגְלָיו וְכִידוֹן נְחֹשֶׁת
bronze and-javelin-of legs-of-him on bronze and-greave-of (6) bronze shekels

בֵּין כְּתֵפָיו׃ וְחֵץ חֲנִיתוֹ כִּמְנוֹר אֹרְגִים
ones-weaving like-rod-of spear-of-him and-shaft-of (7) shoulders-of-him between

וְלַהֶבֶת חֲנִיתוֹ שֵׁשׁ־מֵאוֹת שְׁקָלִים בַּרְזֶל וְנֹשֵׂא הַצִּנָּה
the-shield and-one-bearing iron shekels hundreds six spear-of-him and-point-of

הֹלֵךְ לְפָנָיו׃ וַיַּעֲמֹד וַיִּקְרָא אֶל־מַעַרְכֹת יִשְׂרָאֵל
Israel ranks-of to and-he-shouted and-he-stood (8) ahead-of-him going

וַיֹּאמֶר לָהֶם לָמָּה תֵצְאוּ לַעֲרֹךְ מִלְחָמָה הֲלוֹא אָנֹכִי הַפְּלִשְׁתִּי
the-Philistine I not? battle to-line-up you-come-out why? to-them and-he-said

וְאַתֶּם עֲבָדִים לְשָׁאוּל בְּרוּ־לָכֶם אִישׁ וְיֵרֵד אֵלָי׃
to-me and-have-him-come-down man for-you choose! of-Saul servants and-you

אִם־יוּכַל לְהִלָּחֵם אִתִּי וְהִכָּנִי וְהָיִינוּ לָכֶם
to-you then-we-will-become and-he-kills-me with-me to-fight he-is-able if (9)

לַעֲבָדִים וְאִם־אֲנִי אוּכַל־לוֹ וְהִכִּיתִיו וִהְיִיתֶם
then-you-will-become and-I-kill-him over-him I-overcome I but-if as-subjects

לָנוּ לַעֲבָדִים וַעֲבַדְתֶּם אֹתָנוּ׃ וַיֹּאמֶר הַפְּלִשְׁתִּי אֲנִי
I the-Philistine then-he-said (10) us and-you-will-serve as-subjects to-us

חֵרַפְתִּי אֶת־מַעַרְכוֹת יִשְׂרָאֵל הַיּוֹם הַזֶּה תְּנוּ־לִי אִישׁ וְנִלָּחֲמָה
and-let-us-fight man to-me! give! the-this the-day Israel ranks-of *** I-defy

יָחַד׃ וַיִּשְׁמַע שָׁאוּל וְכָל־יִשְׂרָאֵל אֶת־דִּבְרֵי
words-of *** Israel and-all-of Saul when-he-heard (11) each-other

הַפְּלִשְׁתִּי הָאֵלֶּה וַיֵּחַתּוּ וַיִּרְאוּ מְאֹד׃
very and-they-were-terrified then-they-were-dismayed the-these the-Philistine

וְדָוִד בֶּן־אִישׁ אֶפְרָתִי הַזֶּה מִבֵּית לֶחֶם יְהוּדָה
Judah Lehem-of from-Beth the-this Ephrathite man son-of now-David (12)

וּשְׁמוֹ יִשַׁי וְלוֹ שְׁמֹנָה בָנִים וְהָאִישׁ בִּימֵי שָׁאוּל
Saul in-days-of and-the-man sons eight and-to-him Jesse and-name-of-him

זָקֵן בָּא בַאֲנָשִׁים׃ וַיֵּלְכוּ שְׁלֹשֶׁת בְּנֵי־
sons-of three-of and-they-followed (13) among-men he-was-advanced he-was-old

יִשַׁי הַגְּדֹלִים הָלְכוּ אַחֲרֵי־שָׁאוּל לַמִּלְחָמָה וְשֵׁם ׀ שְׁלֹשֶׁת
three-of and-name-of to-the-war Saul after they-went the-old-ones Jesse

בָּנָיו אֲשֶׁר הָלְכוּ בַּמִּלְחָמָה אֱלִיאָב הַבְּכוֹר וּמִשְׁנֵהוּ
and-second-of-him the-firstborn Eliab to-the-war they-went who sons-of-him

אֲבִינָדָב וְהַשְּׁלִשִׁי שַׁמָּה׃ וְדָוִד הוּא הַקָּטָן וּשְׁלֹשָׁה
and-three the-youngest he now-David (14) Shammah and-the-third Abinadab

on his head and wore a coat of scale armor of bronze weighing five thousand shekels[m]; 6on his legs he wore bronze greaves, and a bronze javelin was slung on his back. 7His spear shaft was like a weaver's rod, and its iron point weighed six hundred shekels.[o] His shield bearer went ahead of him.

8Goliath stood and shouted to the ranks of Israel, "Why do you come out and line up for battle? Am I not a Philistine, and are you not the servants of Saul? Choose a man and have him come down to me. 9If he is able to fight and kill me, we will become your subjects; but if I overcome him and kill him, you will become our subjects and serve us." 10Then the Philistine said, "This day I defy the ranks of Israel! Give me a man and let us fight each other." 11On hearing the Philistine's words, Saul and all the Israelites were dismayed and terrified.

12Now David was the son of an Ephrathite named Jesse, who was from Bethlehem in Judah. Jesse had eight sons, and in Saul's time he was old and well advanced in years. 13Jesse's three oldest sons had followed Saul to the war: The firstborn was Eliab; the second, Abinadab; and the third, Shammah. 14David was the

m5 That is, about 125 pounds (about 57 kilograms)
o7 That is, about 15 pounds (about 7 kilograms)
p17 That is, probably about 1/2 bushel (about 22 liters)

°7 ק ועץ

הַגְּדֹלִים הָלְכוּ אַחֲרֵי שָׁאוּל׃ וְדָוִד הֹלֵךְ וָשָׁב
and-returning going but-David (15) Saul after they-followed the-old-ones

מֵעַל שָׁאוּל לִרְעוֹת אֶת־ צֹאן אָבִיו בֵּית־ לָחֶם׃
Lehem Beth father-of-him sheep-of *** to-tend Saul from-with

וַיִּגַּשׁ הַפְּלִשְׁתִּי הַשְׁכֵּם וְהַעֲרֵב
and-to-be-evening to-be-morning the-Philistine and-he-came-forward (16)

וַיִּתְיַצֵּב אַרְבָּעִים יוֹם׃ וַיֹּאמֶר יִשַׁי לְדָוִד בְּנוֹ קַח־
take! son-of-him to-David Jesse now-he-said (17) day forty and-he-took-stand

נָא לְאַחֶיךָ אֵיפַת הַקָּלִיא הַזֶּה וַעֲשָׂרָה לֶחֶם
bread and-ten the-this the-roasted-grain ephah-of to-brothers-of-you now!

הַזֶּה וְהָרֵץ הַמַּחֲנֶה לְאַחֶיךָ׃ וְאֵת עֲשֶׂרֶת חֲרִצֵי
pieces-of ten and (18) to-brothers-of-you the-camp and-hurry! the-this

הֶחָלָב הָאֵלֶּה תָּבִיא לְשַׂר־ הָאָלֶף וְאֶת־ אַחֶיךָ
brothers-of-you and the-unit to-commander-of you-take the-these the-cheese

תִּפְקֹד לְשָׁלוֹם וְאֶת־ עֲרֻבָּתָם תִּקָּח׃ וְשָׁאוּל
now-Saul (19) you-bring-back assurance-of-them and about-welfare you-see

וְהֵמָּה וְכָל־ אִישׁ יִשְׂרָאֵל בְּעֵמֶק הָאֵלָה נִלְחָמִים עִם־
against ones-fighting the-Elah in-Valley-of Israel man-of and-all-of and-they

פְּלִשְׁתִּים׃ וַיַּשְׁכֵּם דָּוִד בַּבֹּקֶר וַיִּטֹּשׁ אֶת־ הַצֹּאן
the-flock *** and-he-left in-the-morning David so-he-rose (20) Philistines

עַל־ שֹׁמֵר וַיִּשָּׂא וַיֵּלֶךְ כַּאֲשֶׁר צִוָּהוּ
he-directed-him just-as and-he-set-out and-he-loaded-up one-shepherding with

יִשָׁי וַיָּבֹא הַמַּעְגָּלָה וְהַחַיִל הַיֹּצֵא אֶל־ הַמַּעֲרָכָה
the-position to the-one-going-out and-the-army the-camp and-he-reached Jesse

וְהֵרֵעוּ בַּמִּלְחָמָה׃ וַתַּעֲרֹךְ יִשְׂרָאֵל וּפְלִשְׁתִּים
and-Philistines Israel and-he-drew-up (21) for-the-battle and-they-shouted

מַעֲרָכָה לִקְרַאת מַעֲרָכָה׃ וַיִּטֹּשׁ דָּוִד אֶת־ הַכֵּלִים מֵעָלָיו עַל־
with from-with-him the-things *** David and-he-left (22) line to-face line

יַד שׁוֹמֵר הַכֵּלִים וַיָּרָץ הַמַּעֲרָכָה וַיָּבֹא
and-he-came the-battle-line and-he-ran the-supplies one-keeping hand-of

וַיִּשְׁאַל לְאֶחָיו לְשָׁלוֹם׃ וְהוּא ׀ מְדַבֵּר עִמָּם
with-them talking and-he (23) for-peace to-brothers-of-him and-he-greeted

וְהִנֵּה אִישׁ הַבֵּנַיִם עוֹלֶה גָּלְיָת הַפְּלִשְׁתִּי
the-Philistine Goliath stepping-out the-spaces-between man-of and-see!

שְׁמוֹ מִגַּת מִמַּעַרְוֹת פְּלִשְׁתִּים וַיְדַבֵּר כַּדְּבָרִים
as-the-words and-he-shouted Philistines from-lines-of from-Gath name-of-him

הָאֵלֶּה וַיִּשְׁמַע דָּוִד׃ וְכֹל אִישׁ יִשְׂרָאֵל בִּרְאוֹתָם
when-to-see-them Israel man-of and-every-of (24) David and-he-heard the-these

youngest. The three oldest followed Saul, [15]but David went back and forth from Saul to tend his father's sheep at Bethlehem.

[16]For forty days the Philistine came forward every morning and evening and took his stand.

[17]Now Jesse said to his son David, "Take this ephah[p] of roasted grain and these ten loaves of bread for your brothers and hurry to their camp. [18]Take along these ten cheeses to the commander of their unit.[q] See how your brothers are and bring back some assurance[r] from them. [19]They are with Saul and all the men of Israel in the Valley of Elah, fighting against the Philistines."

[20]Early in the morning David left the flock with a shepherd, loaded up and set out, as Jesse had directed. He reached the camp as the army was going out to its battle positions, shouting the war cry. [21]Israel and the Philistines were drawing up their lines facing each other. [22]David left his things with the keeper of supplies, ran to the battle lines and greeted his brothers. [23]As he was talking with them, Goliath, the Philistine champion from Gath, stepped out from his lines and shouted his usual defiance, and David heard it. [24]When the Israelites

[q]18 Hebrew *thousand*
[r]18 Or *some token;* or *some pledge of spoils*

°23 ק ממערכות

אֶת־ הָאִישׁ וַיָּנֻסוּ מִפָּנָיו וַיִּֽירְאוּ מְאֹד׃
greatly and-they-feared from-before-him then-they-ran the-man ***

וַיֹּאמֶר ׀ אִישׁ יִשְׂרָאֵל הַרְּאִיתֶם הָאִישׁ הָעֹלֶה הַזֶּה
the-this the-one-coming-out the-man you-see? Israel man-of now-he-said (25)

כִּי לְחָרֵף אֶת־ יִשְׂרָאֵל עֹלֶה וְהָיָה הָאִישׁ אֲשֶׁר־ יַכֶּנּוּ
he-kills-him who the-man and-he-will-be coming-out Israel *** to-defy that

יַעְשְׁרֶנּוּ הַמֶּלֶךְ ׀ עֹשֶׁר גָּדוֹל וְאֶת־ בִּתּוֹ יִתֶּן־ לוֹ
to-him he-will-give daughter-of-him and great wealth the-king he-will-give-him

וְאֵת בֵּית אָבִיו יַעֲשֶׂה חָפְשִׁי בְּיִשְׂרָאֵל׃ וַיֹּאמֶר
and-he-asked (26) in-Israel tax-exempt he-will-make father-of-him family-of and

דָּוִד אֶל־ הָאֲנָשִׁים הָעֹמְדִים עִמּוֹ לֵאמֹר מַה־ יֵּעָשֶׂה
he-will-be-done what? to-say near-him the-ones-standing the-men to David

לָאִישׁ אֲשֶׁר יַכֶּה אֶת־ הַפְּלִשְׁתִּי הַלָּז וְהֵסִיר חֶרְפָּה
disgrace and-he-removes the-this the-Philistine *** he-kills who for-the-man

מֵעַל יִשְׂרָאֵל כִּי מִי הַפְּלִשְׁתִּי הֶעָרֵל הַזֶּה כִּי
that the-this the-uncircumcised the-Philistine who for Israel from-on

חֵרֵף מַעַרְכוֹת אֱלֹהִים חַיִּים׃ וַיֹּאמֶר לוֹ הָעָם
the-people to-him and-he-told (27) ones-living God armies-of he-defies

כַּדָּבָר הַזֶּה לֵאמֹר כֹּה יֵעָשֶׂה לָאִישׁ אֲשֶׁר יַכֶּנּוּ׃
he-kills-him who for-the-man he-will-be-done this to-say the-this as-the-saying

וַיִּשְׁמַע אֱלִיאָב אָחִיו הַגָּדוֹל בְּדַבְּרוֹ אֶל־הָאֲנָשִׁים
the-men to when-to-speak-him the-old brother-of-him Eliab when-he-heard (28)

וַיִּחַר־ אַף אֱלִיאָב בְּדָוִד וַיֹּאמֶר ׀ לָמָּה־ זֶּה יָרַדְתָּ
you-came-down this why? and-he-asked at-David Eliab anger-of then-he-burned

וְעַל־ מִי נָטַשְׁתָּ מְעַט הַצֹּאן הָהֵנָּה בַּמִּדְבָּר אֲנִי יָדַעְתִּי
I-know I in-the-desert the-those the-sheep few-of you-left whom? and-with

אֶת־ זְדֹנְךָ וְאֵת רֹעַ לְבָבֶךָ כִּי לְמַעַן רְאוֹת
to-watch in-order-to only heart-of-you wickedness-of and conceit-of-you ***

הַמִּלְחָמָה יָרָדְתָּ׃ וַיֹּאמֶר דָּוִד מֶה עָשִׂיתִי עָתָּה הֲלוֹא דָּבָר
word not? now I-did what? David and-he-said (29) you-came-down the-battle

הוּא׃ וַיִּסֹּב מֵאֶצְלוֹ אֶל־ מוּל אַחֵר וַיֹּאמֶר
and-he-asked another face-of to from-with-him then-he-turned (30) he

כַּדָּבָר הַזֶּה וַיְשִׁבֻהוּ הָעָם דָּבָר כַּדָּבָר
as-the-answer answer the-people and-they-answered-him the-same as-the-matter

הָרִאשׁוֹן׃ וַיִּשָּׁמְעוּ הַדְּבָרִים אֲשֶׁר דִּבֶּר דָּוִד
David he-said that the-words and-they-were-overheard (31) the-previous

וַיַּגִּדוּ לִפְנֵי־ שָׁאוּל וַיִּקָּחֵהוּ׃ וַיֹּאמֶר דָּוִד
David and-he-said (32) and-he-sent-for-him Saul to-before and-they-reported

saw the man, they all ran from him in great fear.

25 Now the Israelites had been saying, "Do you see how this man keeps coming out? He comes out to defy Israel. The king will give great wealth to the man who kills him. He will also give him his daughter in marriage and will exempt his father's family from taxes in Israel."

26 David asked the men standing near him, "What will be done for the man who kills this Philistine and removes this disgrace from Israel? Who is this uncircumcised Philistine that he should defy the armies of the living God?"

27 They repeated to him what they had been saying and told him, "This is what will be done for the man who kills him."

28 When Eliab, David's oldest brother, heard him speaking with the men, he burned with anger at him and asked, "Why have you come down here? And with whom did you leave those few sheep in the desert? I know how conceited you are and how wicked your heart is; you came down only to watch the battle."

29 "Now what have I done?" said David. "Can't I even speak?"
30 He then turned away to someone else and brought up the same matter, and the men answered him as before.
31 What David said was overheard and reported to Saul, and Saul sent for him.

32 David said to Saul, "Let no

*31 Most mss have *hireq* under the *yod* ( וַיִּ ).

אֶל־שָׁאוּל אַל־יִפֹּל לֵב־אָדָם עָלָיו עַבְדְּךָ
servant-of-you on-account-of-him anyone heart-of let-him-lose not Saul to

יֵלֵךְ וְנִלְחַם עִם־הַפְּלִשְׁתִּי הַזֶּה׃ וַיֹּאמֶר
and-he-replied (33) the-this the-Philistine with and-he-will-fight he-will-go

שָׁאוּל אֶל־דָּוִד לֹא תוּכַל לָלֶכֶת אֶל־הַפְּלִשְׁתִּי הַזֶּה
the-this the-Philistine against to-go-out you-are-able not David to Saul

לְהִלָּחֵם עִמּוֹ כִּי־נַעַר אַתָּה וְהוּא אִישׁ מִלְחָמָה מִנְּעֻרָיו׃
from-youths-of-him fighting man-of and-he you boy for with-him to-fight

וַיֹּאמֶר דָּוִד אֶל־שָׁאוּל רֹעֶה הָיָה עַבְדְּךָ
servant-of-you he-is one-keeping Saul to David but-he-said (34)

לְאָבִיו בַּצֹּאן וּבָא הָאֲרִי וְאֶת־הַדּוֹב
the-bear or the-lion when-he-came over-the-sheep for-father-of-him

וְנָשָׂא שֶׂה מֵהָעֵדֶר׃ וְיָצָאתִי אַחֲרָיו
after-him then-I-went (35) from-the-flock sheep and-he-carried-off

וְהִכִּתִיו וְהִצַּלְתִּי מִפִּיו וַיָּקָם עָלַי
on-me when-he-turned from-mouth-of-him and-I-rescued and-I-struck-him

וְהֶחֱזַקְתִּי בִּזְקָנוֹ וְהִכִּתִיו וַהֲמִיתִּיו׃ גַּם אֶת־
*** both (36) and-I-killed-him and-I-struck-him by-hair-of-him then-I-seized

הָאֲרִי גַּם־הַדּוֹב הִכָּה עַבְדֶּךָ וְהָיָה הַפְּלִשְׁתִּי
the-Philistine and-he-will-be servant-of-you he-killed the-bear and the-lion

הֶעָרֵל הַזֶּה כְּאַחַד מֵהֶם כִּי חֵרֵף מַעַרְכֹת אֱלֹהִים
God armies-of he-defied for of-them like-one the-this the-uncircumcised

חַיִּים׃ וַיֹּאמֶר דָּוִד יְהוָה אֲשֶׁר הִצִּלַנִי מִיַּד
from-paw-of he-delivered-me who Yahweh David and-he-said (37) ones-living

הָאֲרִי וּמִיַּד הַדֹּב הוּא יַצִּילֵנִי מִיַּד
from-hand-of he-will-deliver-me he the-bear and-from-paw-of the-lion

הַפְּלִשְׁתִּי הַזֶּה וַיֹּאמֶר שָׁאוּל אֶל־דָּוִד לֵךְ וַיהוָה יִהְיֶה
may-he-be and-Yahweh go! David to Saul and-he-said the-this the-Philistine

עִמָּךְ׃ וַיַּלְבֵּשׁ שָׁאוּל אֶת־דָּוִד מַדָּיו וְנָתַן
and-he-put tunics-of-him David *** Saul then-he-dressed (38) with-you

קוֹבַע נְחֹשֶׁת עַל־רֹאשׁוֹ וַיַּלְבֵּשׁ אֹתוֹ שִׁרְיוֹן׃
coat-of-armor him and-he-dressed head-of-him on bronze helmet-of

וַיַּחְגֹּר דָּוִד אֶת־חַרְבּוֹ מֵעַל לְמַדָּיו
to-tunics-of-him on-over sword-of-him *** David and-he-fastened (39)

וַיֹּאֶל לָלֶכֶת כִּי לֹא־נִסָּה וַיֹּאמֶר דָּוִד אֶל־שָׁאוּל לֹא אוּכַל
I-can not Saul to David and-he-said he-tested not for to-walk and-he-tried

לָלֶכֶת בָּאֵלֶּה כִּי לֹא נִסִּיתִי וַיְסִרֵם דָּוִד מֵעָלָיו׃
from-on-him David so-he-took-off-them I-tested not for in-the-these to-go

one lose heart on account of this Philistine; your servant will go and fight him."

[33]Saul replied, "You are not able to go out against this Philistine and fight him; you are only a boy, and he has been a fighting man from his youth."

[34]But David said to Saul, "Your servant has been keeping his father's sheep. When a lion or a bear came and carried off a sheep from the flock, [35]I went after it, struck it and rescued the sheep from its mouth. When it turned on me, I seized it by its hair, struck it and killed it. [36]Your servant has killed both the lion and the bear; this uncircumcised Philistine will be like one of them, because he has defied the armies of the living God. [37]The LORD who delivered me from the paw of the lion and the paw of the bear will deliver me from the hand of this Philistine."

Saul said to David, "Go, and the LORD be with you."

[38]Then Saul dressed David in his own tunic. He put a coat of armor on him and a bronze helmet on his head. [39]David fastened on his sword over the tunic and tried walking around, because he was not used to them.

"I cannot go in these," he said to Saul, "because I am not used to them." So he took

וַיִּקַּח מַקְלוֹ בְּיָדוֹ וַיִּבְחַר־ לוֹ חֲמִשָּׁה
five for-him and-he-chose in-hand-of-him staff-of-him then-he-took (40)

חַלֻּקֵי־ אֲבָנִים ׀ מִן־ הַנַּחַל וַיָּשֶׂם אֹתָם בִּכְלִי הָרֹעִים
ones-herding in-bag-of them and-he-put the-stream from stones smooth-ones-of

אֲשֶׁר־ לוֹ וּבַיַּלְקוּט וְקַלְעוֹ בְיָדוֹ וַיִּגַּשׁ
and-he-approached in-hand-of-him and-sling-of-him even-in-the-pouch to-him that

אֶל־ הַפְּלִשְׁתִּי׃ וַיֵּלֶךְ הַפְּלִשְׁתִּי הֹלֵךְ וְקָרֵב אֶל־ דָּוִד
David to and-closer coming the-Philistine and-he-came (41) the-Philistine to

וְהָאִישׁ נֹשֵׂא הַצִּנָּה לְפָנָיו׃ וַיַּבֵּט
and-he-looked-over (42) in-front-of-him the-shield bearing and-the-man

הַפְּלִשְׁתִּי וַיִּרְאֶה אֶת־ דָּוִד וַיִּבְזֵהוּ כִּי־ הָיָה נַעַר
boy he-was for and-he-despised-him David *** and-he-saw the-Philistine

וְאַדְמֹנִי עִם־ יְפֵה מַרְאֶה׃ וַיֹּאמֶר הַפְּלִשְׁתִּי אֶל־ דָּוִד
David to the-Philistine and-he-said (43) feature handsome-of with and-ruddy

הֲכֶלֶב אָנֹכִי כִּי־אַתָּה בָא־ אֵלַי בַּמַּקְלוֹת וַיְקַלֵּל הַפְּלִשְׁתִּי
the-Philistine and-he-cursed with-the-sticks at-me coming you that I dog?

אֶת־ דָּוִד בֵּאלֹהָיו׃ וַיֹּאמֶר הַפְּלִשְׁתִּי אֶל־ דָּוִד לְכָה
come! David to the-Philistine and-he-said (44) by-gods-of-him David ***

אֵלַי וְאֶתְּנָה אֶת־ בְּשָׂרְךָ לְעוֹף הַשָּׁמַיִם וּלְבֶהֱמַת
and-to-beast-of the-airs to-bird-of flesh-of-you *** and-I-will-give to-me

הַשָּׂדֶה׃ וַיֹּאמֶר דָּוִד אֶל־ הַפְּלִשְׁתִּי אַתָּה בָּא אֵלַי
against-me coming you the-Philistine to David and-he-said (45) the-field

בְּחֶרֶב וּבַחֲנִית וּבְכִידוֹן וְאָנֹכִי בָא־ אֵלֶיךָ בְּשֵׁם
in-name-of against-you coming but-I and-with-javelin and-with-spear with-sword

יְהוָה צְבָאוֹת אֱלֹהֵי מַעַרְכוֹת יִשְׂרָאֵל אֲשֶׁר חֵרַפְתָּ׃ הַיּוֹם
the-day (46) you-defied whom Israel armies-of God-of Hosts Yahweh-of

הַזֶּה יְסַגֶּרְךָ יְהוָה בְּיָדִי וְהִכִּיתִךָ
and-I-will-strike-down-you to-hand-of-me Yahweh he-will-hand-over-you the-this

וַהֲסִרֹתִי אֶת־ רֹאשְׁךָ מֵעָלֶיךָ וְנָתַתִּי פֶּגֶר
carcass-of and-I-will-give from-on-you head-of-you *** and-I-will-cut-off

מַחֲנֵה פְלִשְׁתִּים הַיּוֹם הַזֶּה לְעוֹף הַשָּׁמַיִם וּלְחַיַּת
and-to-beast-of the-airs to-bird-of the-this the-day Philistines army-of

הָאָרֶץ וְיֵדְעוּ כָּל־ הָאָרֶץ כִּי יֵשׁ אֱלֹהִים לְיִשְׂרָאֵל׃
in-Israel God there-is that the-world whole-of and-they-will-know the-earth

וְיֵדְעוּ כָּל־ הַקָּהָל הַזֶּה כִּי־ לֹא בְּחֶרֶב
by-sword not that the-this the-gathering all-of and-they-will-know (47)

וּבַחֲנִית יְהוֹשִׁיעַ יְהוָה כִּי לַיהוָה הַמִּלְחָמָה וְנָתַן אֶתְכֶם
you and-he-will-give the-battle to-Yahweh for Yahweh he-saves or-by-spear

them off. 40Then he took his
staff in his hand, chose five
smooth stones from the
stream, put them in the pouch
of his shepherd's bag and,
with his sling in his hand, approached the Philistine.
41Meanwhile, the Philistine,
with his shield bearer in front
of him, kept coming closer to
David. 42He looked David over
and saw that he was only a
boy, ruddy and handsome,
and he despised him. 43He said
to David, "Am I a dog, that
you come at me with sticks?"
And the Philistine cursed David by his gods. 44"Come
here," he said, "and I'll give
your flesh to the birds of the
air and the beasts of the field!"
45David said to the Philistine, "You come against me
with sword and spear and
javelin, but I come against you
in the name of the LORD Almighty, the God of the armies
of Israel, whom you have
defied. 46This day the LORD
will hand you over to me, and
I'll strike you down and cut off
your head. Today I will give
the carcasses of the Philistine
army to the birds of the air
and the beasts of the earth,
and the whole world will
know that there is a God in
Israel. 47All those gathered
here will know that it is not by
sword or spear that the LORD
saves; for the battle is the
LORD's, and he will give all of

בְּיָדֵנוּ׃ וְהָיָה כִּי־ קָם הַפְּלִשְׁתִּי וַיֵּלֶךְ
and-he-moved the-Philistine he-rose as and-he-was (48) into-hand-of-us

וַיִּקְרַב לִקְרַאת דָּוִד וַיְמַהֵר דָּוִד וַיָּרָץ
and-he-ran David then-he-was-quick David to-attack and-he-came-closer

הַמַּעֲרָכָה לִקְרַאת הַפְּלִשְׁתִּי׃ וַיִּשְׁלַח דָּוִד אֶת־
*** David and-he-reached (49) the-Philistine to-meet the-battle-line

יָדוֹ אֶל־ הַכֶּלִי וַיִּקַּח מִשָּׁם אֶבֶן וַיְקַלַּע
and-he-slung stone from-there and-he-took the-bag into hand-of-him

וַיַּךְ אֶת־ הַפְּלִשְׁתִּי אֶל־ מִצְחוֹ וַתִּטְבַּע הָאֶבֶן
the-stone and-she-sank forehead-of-him on the-Philistine *** and-he-struck

בְּמִצְחוֹ וַיִּפֹּל עַל־ פָּנָיו אָרְצָה׃ וַיֶּחֱזַק
so-he-triumphed (50) on-ground faces-of-him on and-he-fell into-forehead-of-him

דָּוִד מִן־ הַפְּלִשְׁתִּי בַּקֶּלַע וּבָאֶבֶן וַיַּךְ
and-he-struck-down and-with-the-stone with-the-sling the-Philistine over David

אֶת־ הַפְּלִשְׁתִּי וַיְמִיתֵהוּ וְחֶרֶב אֵין בְּיַד־ דָּוִד׃
David in-hand-of not and-sword and-he-killed-him the-Philistine ***

וַיָּרָץ דָּוִד וַיַּעֲמֹד אֶל־ הַפְּלִשְׁתִּי וַיִּקַּח אֶת־
*** and-he-took-hold the-Philistine over and-he-stood David and-he-ran (51)

חַרְבּוֹ וַיִּשְׁלְפָהּ מִתַּעְרָהּ וַיְמֹתְתֵהוּ
and-he-killed-him from-scabbard-of-her and-he-drew-her sword-of-him

וַיִּכְרָת־ בָּהּ אֶת־ רֹאשׁוֹ וַיִּרְאוּ הַפְּלִשְׁתִּים כִּי־
that the-Philistines when-they-saw head-of-him *** with-her and-he-cut-off

מֵת גִּבּוֹרָם וַיָּנֻסוּ׃ וַיָּקֻמוּ אַנְשֵׁי
men-of then-they-surged-forward (52) then-they-ran hero-of-them he-was-dead

יִשְׂרָאֵל וִיהוּדָה וַיָּרִעוּ וַיִּרְדְּפוּ אֶת־ הַפְּלִשְׁתִּים עַד־
to the-Philistines *** and-they-pursued and-they-shouted and-Judah Israel

בּוֹאֲךָ גַיְא וְעַד שַׁעֲרֵי עֶקְרוֹן וַיִּפְּלוּ חַלְלֵי
ones-dead-of and-they-were-strewn Ekron gates-of and-to valley to-enter-you

פְלִשְׁתִּים בְּדֶרֶךְ שַׁעֲרַיִם וְעַד־ גַּת וְעַד־ עֶקְרוֹן*
*Ekron and-to Gath even-to Shaaraim along-road-of Philistines

וַיָּשֻׁבוּ בְּנֵי יִשְׂרָאֵל מִדְּלֹק אַחֲרֵי פְלִשְׁתִּים
Philistines after from-to-chase Israel sons-of when-they-returned (53)

וַיָּשֹׁסּוּ אֶת־ מַחֲנֵיהֶם׃ וַיִּקַּח דָּוִד אֶת־ רֹאשׁ
head-of *** David and-he-took (54) camps-of-them *** then-they-plundered

הַפְּלִשְׁתִּי וַיְבִאֵהוּ יְרוּשָׁלִָם וְאֶת־ כֵּלָיו שָׂם
he-put weapons-of-him and Jerusalem and-he-brought-him the-Philistine

בְּאָהֳלוֹ׃ וְכִרְאוֹת שָׁאוּל אֶת־ דָּוִד יֹצֵא לִקְרַאת
to-meet going-out David *** Saul and-as-to-watch (55) in-tent-of-him

*52 Most mss end verse 52 with *soph pasuq* ( : ).

you into our hands."
[48]As the Philistine moved
closer to attack him, David ran
quickly toward the battle line
to meet him. [49]Reaching into
his bag and taking out a stone,
he slung it and struck the Philistine on the forehead. The
stone sank into his forehead,
and he fell facedown on the
ground.
[50]So David triumphed over
the Philistine with a sling and
a stone; without a sword in his
hand he struck down the Philistine and killed him.
[51]David ran and stood over
him. He took hold of the Philistine's sword and drew it
from the scabbard. After he
killed him, he cut off his head
with the sword.
When the Philistines saw
that their hero was dead, they
turned and ran. [52]Then the
men of Israel and Judah
surged forward with a shout
and pursued the Philistines to
the entrance of Gath[s] and to
the gates of Ekron. Their dead
were strewn along the Shaaraim road to Gath and Ekron.
[53]When the Israelites returned
from chasing the Philistines,
they plundered their camp.
[54]David took the Philistine's
head and brought it to Jerusalem, and he put the Philistine's weapons in his own
tent.
[55]As Saul watched David going out to meet the Philistine,

[s]52 Some Septuagint manuscripts; Hebrew *a valley*

הַפְּלִשְׁתִּי אָמַר אֶל־ אַבְנֵר שַׂר הַצָּבָא בֶּן־ מִי־ זֶה
that whom? son-of the-army commander-of Abner to he-said the-Philistine

הַנַּעַר אַבְנֵר וַיֹּאמֶר אַבְנֵר חֵי־ נַפְשְׁךָ הַמֶּלֶךְ אִם־
not the-king soul-of-you life-of Abner and-he-replied Abner the-young-man

יָדַעְתִּי׃ וַיֹּאמֶר הַמֶּלֶךְ שְׁאַל אַתָּה בֶּן־ מִי־ זֶה הָעָלֶם׃
the-young-man this whom? son-of you find-out! the-king and-he-said (56) I-know

וּכְשׁוּב דָּוִד מֵהַכּוֹת אֶת־ הַפְּלִשְׁתִּי וַיִּקַּח אֹתוֹ
him then-he-took the-Philistine *** from-to-kill David and-as-to-return (57)

אַבְנֵר וַיְבִאֵהוּ לִפְנֵי שָׁאוּל וְרֹאשׁ הַפְּלִשְׁתִּי בְּיָדוֹ׃
in-hand-of-him the-Philistine and-head-of Saul before and-he-brought-him Abner

וַיֹּאמֶר אֵלָיו שָׁאוּל בֶּן־ מִי אַתָּה הַנָּעַר וַיֹּאמֶר
and-he-said the-young-man you whom? son-of Saul to-him and-he-asked (58)

דָּוִד בֶּן־ עַבְדְּךָ יִשַׁי בֵּית הַלַּחְמִי׃ וַיְהִי
and-he-was (18:1) the-Bethlehemite Jesse servant-of-you son-of David

כְּכַלֹּתוֹ לְדַבֵּר אֶל־ שָׁאוּל וְנֶפֶשׁ יְהוֹנָתָן נִקְשְׁרָה
she-became-one Jonathan then-spirit-of Saul with to-talk after-to-finish-him

בְּנֶפֶשׁ דָּוִד וַיֶּאֱהָבוֹ° יְהוֹנָתָן כְּנַפְשׁוֹ׃
as-self-of-him Jonathan and-he-loved-him David with-spirit-of

וַיִּקָּחֵהוּ שָׁאוּל בַּיּוֹם הַהוּא וְלֹא נְתָנוֹ לָשׁוּב
to-return he-let-him and-not the-that from-the-day Saul and-he-kept-him (2)

בֵּית אָבִיו׃ וַיִּכְרֹת יְהוֹנָתָן וְדָוִד בְּרִית
covenant with-David Jonathan and-he-made (3) father-of-him house-of

בְּאַהֲבָתוֹ אֹתוֹ כְּנַפְשׁוֹ׃ וַיִּתְפַּשֵּׁט יְהוֹנָתָן אֶת־
*** Jonathan and-he-took-off (4) as-self-of-him him because-to-love-him

הַמְּעִיל אֲשֶׁר עָלָיו וַיִּתְּנֵהוּ לְדָוִד וּמַדָּיו וְעַד־
and-even and-tunics-of-him to-David and-he-gave-him on-him that the-robe

חַרְבּוֹ וְעַד־ קַשְׁתּוֹ וְעַד־ חֲגֹרוֹ׃ וַיֵּצֵא
when-he-went-out (5) belt-of-him and-even bow-of-him and-even sword-of-him

דָּוִד בְּכֹל° אֲשֶׁר יִשְׁלָחֶנּוּ שָׁאוּל יַשְׂכִּיל וַיְשִׂמֵהוּ
and-he-set-him he-did-successfully Saul he-sent-him that in-anything David

שָׁאוּל עַל אַנְשֵׁי הַמִּלְחָמָה וַיִּיטַב בְּעֵינֵי כָל־ הָעָם
the-people all-of in-eyes-of and-he-was-pleasing the-army men-of over Saul

וְגַם בְּעֵינֵי עַבְדֵי שָׁאוּל׃ וַיְהִי בְּבוֹאָם
when-to-return-them and-he-was (6) Saul officers-of in-eyes-of and-also

בְּשׁוּב דָּוִד מֵהַכּוֹת אֶת־ הַפְּלִשְׁתִּי וַתֵּצֶאנָה
then-they-came-out the-Philistine *** from-to-kill David after-to-come-back

הַנָּשִׁים מִכָּל־ עָרֵי יִשְׂרָאֵל לָשׁוּר° וְהַמְּחֹלוֹת לִקְרַאת שָׁאוּל
Saul to-meet and-the-dances to-sing Israel towns-of from-all-of the-women

he said to Abner, commander of the army, "Abner, whose son is that young man?"

Abner replied, "As surely as you live, O king, I don't know."

56 The king said, "Find out whose son this young man is."

57 As soon as David returned from killing the Philistine, Abner took him and brought him before Saul, with David still holding the Philistine's head.

58 "Whose son are you, young man?" Saul asked him.

David said, "I am the son of your servant Jesse of Bethlehem."

*Saul's Jealousy of David*

18 After David had finished talking with Saul, Jonathan became one in spirit with David, and he loved him as himself. 2 From that day Saul kept David with him and did not let him return to his father's house. 3 And Jonathan made a covenant with David because he loved him as himself. 4 Jonathan took off the robe he was wearing and gave it to David, along with his tunic, and even his sword, his bow and his belt.

5 Whatever Saul sent him to do, David did it so successfully[t] that Saul gave him a high rank in the army. This pleased all the people, and Saul's officers as well.

6 When the men were returning home after David had killed the Philistine, the women came out from all the towns of Israel to meet King

[t]5 Or *wisely*

°1 ק ויאהבהו
°6 ק לשיר

הַמֶּלֶךְ בְּתֻפִּים בְּשִׂמְחָה וּבְשָׁלִשִׁים׃ וַתַּעֲנֶינָה

and-they-sang (7) and-with-lutes with-joyful-song with-tamboures the-king

הַנָּשִׁים הַמְשַׂחֲקוֹת וַתֹּאמַרְןָ הִכָּה שָׁאוּל בַּאֲלָפָו

to-thousands-of-him Saul he-has-slain and-they-said the-ones-dancing the-women

וְדָוִד בְּרִבְבֹתָיו׃ וַיִּחַר לְשָׁאוּל מְאֹד

very to-Saul and-he-was-angry (8) to-tens-of-thousands-of-him and-David

וַיֵּרַע בְּעֵינָיו הַדָּבָר הַזֶּה וַיֹּאמֶר

and-he-thought the-this the-refrain in-eyes-of-him and-he-was-galling

נָתְנוּ לְדָוִד רְבָבוֹת וְלִי נָתְנוּ הָאֲלָפִים

the-thousands they-credited but-to-me tens-of-thousands to-David they-credited

וְעוֹד לוֹ אַךְ הַמְּלוּכָה׃ וַיְהִי שָׁאוּל עֹוֵן אֶת־

*** jealously-eyeing Saul and-he-was (9) the-kingdom but to-him and-more

דָּוִד מֵהַיּוֹם הַהוּא וָהָלְאָה׃ וַיְהִי מִמָּחֳרָת וַתִּצְלַח

then-she-came on-next-day and-he-was (10) and-on the-that from-the-day David

רוּחַ אֱלֹהִים ׀ רָעָה ׀ אֶל־שָׁאוּל וַיִּתְנַבֵּא בְתוֹךְ־ הַבַּיִת וְדָוִד

and-David the-house inside-of and-he-prophesied Saul upon evil God spirit-of

מְנַגֵּן בְּיָדוֹ כְּיוֹם ׀ בְּיוֹם וְהַחֲנִית בְּיַד־ שָׁאוּל׃

Saul in-hand-of and-the-spear on-day as-day with-hand-of-him playing

וַיָּטֶל שָׁאוּל אֶת־ הַחֲנִית וַיֹּאמֶר אַכֶּה בְדָוִד

through-David I-will-pin and-he-said the-spear *** Saul and-he-hurled (11)

וּבַקִּיר וַיִּסֹּב דָּוִד מִפָּנָיו פַּעֲמָיִם׃ וַיִּרָא

and-he-feared (12) twice from-before-him David but-he-eluded and-to-the-wall

שָׁאוּל מִלִּפְנֵי דָוִד כִּי־ הָיָה יְהוָה עִמּוֹ וּמֵעִם שָׁאוּל סָר׃

he-left Saul but-from-with with-him Yahweh he-was for David because-of Saul

וַיְסִרֵהוּ שָׁאוּל מֵעִמּוֹ וַיְשִׂמֵהוּ לוֹ שַׂר־

commander-of for-him and-he-made-him from-with-him Saul so-he-sent-him (13)

אֶלֶף וַיֵּצֵא וַיָּבֹא לִפְנֵי הָעָם׃ וַיְהִי דָוִד

David and-he-was (14) the-troop before and-he-led so-he-went-out thousand

לְכָל־ דְּרָכָו מַשְׂכִּיל וַיהוָה עִמּוֹ׃ וַיַּרְא שָׁאוּל

Saul when-he-saw (15) with-him for-Yahweh succeeding ways-of-him in-all-of

אֲשֶׁר־הוּא מַשְׂכִּיל מְאֹד וַיָּגָר מִפָּנָיו׃ וְכָל־

but-all-of (16) because-of-him then-he-was-afraid greatly succeeding he that

יִשְׂרָאֵל וִיהוּדָה אֹהֵב אֶת־ דָּוִד כִּי־ הוּא יוֹצֵא וָבָא לִפְנֵיהֶם׃

before-them and-leading going-out he for David *** loving and-Judah Israel

וַיֹּאמֶר שָׁאוּל אֶל־ דָּוִד הִנֵּה בִּתִּי הַגְּדוֹלָה מֵרַב אֹתָהּ

her Merab the-old daughter-of-me see! David to Saul and-he-said (17)

אֶתֶּן־ לְךָ לְאִשָּׁה אַךְ הֱיֵה־ לִּי לְבֶן־ חַיִל וְהִלָּחֵם

and-fight! bravery as-man-of to-me be! only as-wife to-you I-will-give

Saul with singing and dancing, with joyful songs and with tambourines and lutes.
7As they danced, they sang:

"Saul has slain his thousands,
and David his tens of thousands."

8Saul was very angry; this refrain galled him. "They have credited David with tens of thousands," he thought, "but me with only thousands. What more can he get but the kingdom?"
9And from that time on Saul kept a jealous eye on David.

10The next day an evil[u] spirit from God came forcefully upon Saul. He was prophesying in his house, while David was playing the harp, as he usually did. Saul had a spear in his hand
11and he hurled it, saying to himself, "I'll pin David to the wall." But David eluded him twice.

12Saul was afraid of David, because the LORD was with David but had left Saul.
13So he sent David away from him and gave him command over a thousand men, and David led the troops in their campaigns.
14In everything he did he had great success,[v] because the LORD was with him.
15When Saul saw how successful[w] he was, he was afraid of him.
16But all Israel and Judah loved David, because he led them in their campaigns.

17Saul said to David, "Here is my older daughter Merab. I will give her to you in marriage; only serve me bravely

[u] 10 Or *injurious* [v] 14 Or *he was very wise* [w] 15 Or *wise*

°7 ק באלפיו
°9 ק עוין
°14 ק דרכיו

מִלְחֲמ֣וֹת יְהוָ֑ה וְשָׁא֣וּל אָמַ֗ר אַל־ תְּהִ֤י יָדִי֙ בּ֔וֹ
against-him hand-of-me she-will-be not he-said for-Saul Yahweh battles-of

וּתְהִי־ ב֖וֹ יַד־ פְּלִשְׁתִּֽים׃ וַיֹּ֨אמֶר דָּוִ֜ד אֶל־
to David but-he-said (18) Philistines hand-of against-him but-let-her-be

שָׁא֗וּל מִ֤י אָנֹכִי֙ וּמִ֣י חַיַּ֔י מִשְׁפַּ֥חַת אָבִ֖י בְּיִשְׂרָאֵ֑ל כִּֽי־
that in-Israel father-of-me clan-of families-of-me and-what? I who? Saul

אֶהְיֶ֥ה חָתָ֖ן לַמֶּֽלֶךְ׃ וַיְהִ֗י בְּעֵ֛ת תֵּ֥ת אֶת־ מֵרַ֥ב
Merab *** to-give at-time-of so-he-was (19) of-the-king son-in-law I-become

בַּת־ שָׁא֖וּל לְדָוִ֑ד וְהִ֥יא נִתְּנָ֛ה לְעַדְרִיאֵ֥ל הַֽמְּחֹלָתִ֖י
the-Meholathite to-Adriel she-was-given then-she to-David Saul daughter-of

לְאִשָּֽׁה׃ וַתֶּאֱהַ֛ב מִיכַ֥ל בַּת־ שָׁא֖וּל אֶת־דָּוִ֑ד וַיַּגִּ֣דוּ
when-they-told David *** Saul daughter-of Michal now-she-loved (20) as-wife

לְשָׁא֔וּל וַיִּשַׁ֥ר הַדָּבָ֖ר בְּעֵינָֽיו׃ וַיֹּ֨אמֶר
and-he-thought (21) in-eyes-of-him the-thing then-he-was-pleasing to-Saul

שָׁא֜וּל אֶתְּנֶ֤נָּה לּוֹ֙ וּתְהִי־ ל֣וֹ לְמוֹקֵ֔שׁ וּתְהִי־
so-she-may-be as-snare to-him so-she-may-be to-him I-will-give-her Saul

ב֖וֹ יַד־ פְּלִשְׁתִּ֑ים וַיֹּ֤אמֶר שָׁאוּל֙ אֶל־ דָּוִ֔ד בִּשְׁתַּ֛יִם
for-second-time David to Saul so-he-said Philistines hand-of against-him

תִּתְחַתֵּ֥ן בִּ֖י הַיּֽוֹם׃ וַיְצַ֨ו שָׁא֜וּל אֶת־
*** Saul then-he-ordered (22) the-day of-me you-may-become-son-in-law

עֲבָדָ֗ו דַּבְּר֨וּ אֶל־ דָּוִ֤ד בַּלָּט֙ לֵאמֹ֔ר הִנֵּ֨ה חָפֵ֤ץ
he-is-pleased see! to-say in-the-private David to speak! attendants-of-him

בְּךָ֙ הַמֶּ֔לֶךְ וְכָל־ עֲבָדָ֖יו אֲהֵב֑וּךָ וְעַתָּ֖ה
so-now they-like-you attendants-of-him and-all-of the-king with-you

הִתְחַתֵּ֥ן בַּמֶּֽלֶךְ׃ וַֽיְדַבְּר֞וּ עַבְדֵ֤י שָׁאוּל֙
Saul attendants-of so-they-spoke (23) of-the-king become-son-in-law!

בְּאָזְנֵ֣י דָוִ֔ד אֶת־ הַדְּבָרִ֖ים הָאֵ֑לֶּה וַיֹּ֣אמֶר דָּוִ֗ד הֲנְקַלָּ֤ה
being-small? David but-he-said the-these the-words *** David in-ears-of

בְעֵינֵיכֶם֙ הִתְחַתֵּ֣ן בַּמֶּ֔לֶךְ וְאָנֹכִ֖י אִישׁ־ רָ֥שׁ
being-poor man now-I of-the-king to-become-son-in-law in-eyes-of-you

וְנִקְלֶֽה׃ וַיַּגִּ֜דוּ עַבְדֵ֥י שָׁא֛וּל ל֖וֹ לֵאמֹ֑ר
to-say to-him Saul servants-of when-they-told (24) and-being-little-known

כַּדְּבָרִ֣ים הָאֵ֔לֶּה דִּבֶּ֖ר דָּוִֽד׃ וַיֹּ֨אמֶר שָׁא֜וּל כֹּֽה־ תֹאמְר֣וּ
you-say this Saul and-he-replied (25) David he-says the-these as-the-words

לְדָוִ֗ד אֵֽין־ חֵ֤פֶץ לַמֶּ֙לֶךְ֙ בְּמֹ֔הַר כִּ֗י בְּמֵאָה֙
for-hundred other-than for-bride-price to-the-king desire not to-David

עָרְל֣וֹת פְּלִשְׁתִּ֔ים לְהִנָּקֵ֖ם בְּאֹיְבֵ֣י הַמֶּ֑לֶךְ וְשָׁא֣וּל
now-Saul the-king on-being-enemies-of to-take-revenge Philistines foreskins-of

and fight the battles of the LORD." For Saul said to himself, "I will not raise a hand against him. Let the Philistines do that!"
[18]But David said to Saul, "Who am I, and what is my family or my father's clan in Israel, that I should become the king's son-in-law?" [19]So[x] when the time came for Merab, Saul's daughter, to be given to David, she was given in marriage to Adriel of Meholah.
[20]Now Saul's daughter Michal was in love with David, and when they told Saul about it, he was pleased. [21]"I will give her to him," he thought, "so that she may be a snare to him and so that the hand of the Philistines may be against him." So Saul said to David, "Now you have a second opportunity to become my son-in-law."
[22]Then Saul ordered his attendants: "Speak to David privately and say, 'Look, the king is pleased with you, and his attendants all like you; now become his son-in-law.' "
[23]They repeated these words to David. But David said, "Do you think it is a small matter to become the king's son-in-law? I'm only a poor man and little known."
[24]When Saul's servants told him what David had said, [25]Saul replied, "Say to David, 'The king wants no other price for the bride than a hundred Philistine foreskins, to take revenge on his enemies.' "

x19 Or *However,*

°22 ק עבדיו

חָשַׁב לְהַפִּיל אֶת־ דָּוִד בְּיַד־ פְּלִשְׁתִּים׃ וַיַּגִּדוּ

when-they-told (26) Philistines by-hand-of David *** to-have-fall he-planned

עֲבָדָיו לְדָוִד אֶת־ הַדְּבָרִים הָאֵלֶּה וַיִּשַׁר

then-he-was-pleasing the-these the-things *** to-David attendants-of-him

הַדָּבָר בְּעֵינֵי דָוִד לְהִתְחַתֵּן בַּמֶּלֶךְ וְלֹא

and-not of-the-king to-become-son-in-law David in-eyes-of the-thing

מָלְאוּ הַיָּמִים׃ וַיָּקָם דָּוִד וַיֵּלֶךְ ׀ הוּא וַאֲנָשָׁיו

and-men-of-him he and-he-went-out David and-he-rose (27) the-days they-elapsed

וַיַּךְ בַּפְּלִשְׁתִּים מָאתַיִם אִישׁ וַיָּבֵא דָוִד אֶת־

*** David and-he-brought man two-hundreds of-the-Philistines and-he-killed

עָרְלֹתֵיהֶם וַיְמַלְאוּם לַמֶּלֶךְ לְהִתְחַתֵּן

to-be-son-in-law to-the-king and-they-gave-fullness-of-them foreskins-of-them

בַּמֶּלֶךְ וַיִּתֶּן־ לוֹ שָׁאוּל אֶת־ מִיכַל בִּתּוֹ לְאִשָּׁה׃

as-wife daughter-of-him Michal *** Saul to-him then-he-gave of-the-king

וַיַּרְא שָׁאוּל וַיֵּדַע כִּי יְהוָה עִם־ דָּוִד וּמִיכַל

and-Michal David with Yahweh that and-he-knew Saul when-he-realized (28)

בַּת־ שָׁאוּל אֲהֵבַתְהוּ׃ וַיֹּאסֶף שָׁאוּל לֵרֹא מִפְּנֵי

because-of to-fear Saul then-he-increased (29) she-loved-him Saul daughter-of

דָוִד עוֹד וַיְהִי שָׁאוּל אֹיֵב אֶת־ דָּוִד כָּל־ הַיָּמִים׃

the-days all-of David *** being-enemy Saul and-he-remained more David

וַיֵּצְאוּ שָׂרֵי פְלִשְׁתִּים וַיְהִי ׀ מִדֵּי

as-often-of and-he-was Philistines commanders-of and-they-went-out (30)

צֵאתָם שָׂכַל דָּוִד מִכֹּל עַבְדֵי שָׁאוּל

Saul officers-of over-all-of David he-succeeded to-go-out-them

וַיִּיקַר שְׁמוֹ מְאֹד׃ וַיְדַבֵּר שָׁאוּל אֶל־ יוֹנָתָן

Jonathan to Saul and-he-told (19:1) well name-of-him and-he-became-known

בְּנוֹ וְאֶל־ כָּל־ עֲבָדָיו לְהָמִית אֶת־ דָּוִד וִיהוֹנָתָן

but-Jonathan David *** to-kill attendants-of-him all-of and-to son-of-him

בֶּן־ שָׁאוּל חָפֵץ בְּדָוִד מְאֹד׃ וַיַּגֵּד יְהוֹנָתָן לְדָוִד

to-David Jonathan and-he-warned (2) very of-David he-was-fond Saul son-of

לֵאמֹר מְבַקֵּשׁ שָׁאוּל אָבִי לַהֲמִיתֶךָ וְעַתָּה הִשָּׁמֶר־ נָא

now! be-on-guard! so-now to-kill-you father-of-me Saul looking to-say

בַבֹּקֶר וְיָשַׁבְתָּ בַסֵּתֶר וְנַחְבֵּאתָ׃ וַאֲנִי אֵצֵא

I-will-go-out and-I (3) and-you-stay into-the-hiding and-you-go in-the-morning

וְעָמַדְתִּי לְיַד־ אָבִי בַּשָּׂדֶה אֲשֶׁר אַתָּה שָׁם וַאֲנִי

and-I there you where in-the-field father-of-me by-hand-of and-I-will-stand

אֲדַבֵּר בְּךָ אֶל־ אָבִי וְרָאִיתִי מָה וְהִגַּדְתִּי

and-I-will-tell what and-I-will-find-out father-of-me to about-you I-will-speak

Saul's plan was to have David fall by the hands of the Philistines.

[26]When the attendants told David these things, he was pleased to become the king's son-in-law. So before the allotted time elapsed, [27]David and his men went out and killed two hundred Philistines. He brought their foreskins and presented the full number to the king so that he might become the king's son-in-law. Then Saul gave him his daughter Michal in marriage.

[28]When Saul realized that the LORD was with David and that his daughter Michal loved David, [29]Saul became still more afraid of him, and he remained his enemy the rest of his days.

[30]The Philistine commanders continued to go out to battle, and as often as they did, David met with more success[y] than the rest of Saul's officers, and his name became well known.

*Saul Tries to Kill David*

19 Saul told his son Jonathan and all the attendants to kill David. But Jonathan was very fond of David [2]and warned him, "My father Saul is looking for a chance to kill you. Be on your guard tomorrow morning; go into hiding and stay there. [3]I will go out and stand with my father in the field where you are. I'll speak to him about you and will tell you what I find out."

[y]30 Or *David acted more wisely*

לָךְ׃ (4) וַיְדַבֵּר יְהוֹנָתָן בְּדָוִד טוֹב אֶל־שָׁאוּל אָבִיו

father-of-him Saul to well of-David Jonathan and-he-spoke (4) to-you

וַיֹּאמֶר אֵלָיו אַל־יֶחֱטָא הַמֶּלֶךְ בְּעַבְדּוֹ בְדָוִד

to-David to-servant-of-him the-king let-him-do-wrong not to-him and-he-said

כִּי לוֹא חָטָא לָךְ וְכִי מַעֲשָׂיו טוֹב־לְךָ מְאֹד׃

greatly to-you beneficial deeds-of-him and-for to-you he-wronged not for

(5) וַיָּשֶׂם אֶת־נַפְשׁוֹ בְכַפּוֹ וַיַּךְ אֶת־

*** when-he-killed in-hand-of-him life-of-him *** and-he-took (5)

הַפְּלִשְׁתִּי וַיַּעַשׂ יְהוָה תְּשׁוּעָה גְדוֹלָה לְכָל־יִשְׂרָאֵל רָאִיתָ

you-saw Israel for-all-of great victory Yahweh and-he-won the-Philistine

וַתִּשְׂמָח וְלָמָּה תֶחֱטָא בְּדָם נָקִי לְהָמִית

to-kill innocent to-blood you-would-do-wrong then-why? and-you-were-glad

אֶת־דָּוִד חִנָּם׃ (6) וַיִּשְׁמַע שָׁאוּל בְּקוֹל יְהוֹנָתָן

Jonathan to-voice-of Saul and-he-listened (6) without-reason David ***

וַיִּשָּׁבַע שָׁאוּל חַי־יְהוָה אִם־יוּמָת׃ (7) וַיִּקְרָא

so-he-called (7) he-will-be-killed not Yahweh life-of Saul and-he-took-oath

יְהוֹנָתָן לְדָוִד וַיַּגֶּד־לוֹ יְהוֹנָתָן אֵת כָּל־הַדְּבָרִים

the-conversations all-of *** Jonathan to-him and-he-told to-David Jonathan

הָאֵלֶּה וַיָּבֵא יְהוֹנָתָן אֶת־דָּוִד אֶל־שָׁאוּל וַיְהִי לְפָנָיו

before-him and-he-was Saul to David *** Jonathan and-he-brought the-these

כְּאֶתְמוֹל שִׁלְשׁוֹם׃ (8) וַתּוֹסֶף הַמִּלְחָמָה לִהְיוֹת וַיֵּצֵא

and-he-went-out to-break-out the-war and-she-repeated (8) before as-yesterday

דָוִד וַיִּלָּחֶם בַּפְּלִשְׁתִּים וַיַּךְ בָּהֶם מַכָּה

force against-them and-he-struck with-the-Philistines and-he-fought David

גְדוֹלָה וַיָּנֻסוּ מִפָּנָיו׃ (9) וַתְּהִי רוּחַ יְהוָה ׀ רָעָה

evil Yahweh spirit-of but-she-came (9) from-before-him and-they-fled great

אֶל־שָׁאוּל וְהוּא בְּבֵיתוֹ יוֹשֵׁב וַחֲנִיתוֹ בְּיָדוֹ

in-hand-of-him and-spear-of-him sitting in-house-of-him as-he Saul upon

וְדָוִד מְנַגֵּן בְּיָד׃ (10) וַיְבַקֵּשׁ שָׁאוּל לְהַכּוֹת בַּחֲנִית

with-spear to-pin Saul and-he-tried (10) with-hand playing and-David

בְּדָוִד וּבַקִּיר וַיִּפְטַר מִפְּנֵי שָׁאוּל וַיַּךְ

and-he-drove Saul from-before but-he-eluded and-to-the-wall through-David

אֶת־הַחֲנִית בַּקִּיר וְדָוִד נָס וַיִּמָּלֵט בַּלַּיְלָה

in-the-night and-he-escaped he-fled and-David into-the-wall the-spear ***

הוּא׃ (11) וַיִּשְׁלַח שָׁאוּל מַלְאָכִים אֶל־בֵּית דָּוִד לְשָׁמְרוֹ

to-watch-him David house-of to men Saul and-he-sent (11) the-that

וְלַהֲמִיתוֹ בַּבֹּקֶר וַתַּגֵּד לְדָוִד מִיכַל אִשְׁתּוֹ

wife-of-him Michal to-David but-she-warned in-the-morning and-to-kill-him

4Jonathan spoke well of David to Saul his father and said to him, "Let not the king do wrong to his servant David; he has not wronged you, and what he has done has benefited you greatly. 5He took his life in his hands when he killed the Philistine. The LORD won a great victory for all Israel, and you saw it and were glad. Why then would you do wrong to an innocent man like David by killing him for no reason?"

6Saul listened to Jonathan and took this oath: "As surely as the LORD lives, David will not be put to death."

7So Jonathan called David and told him the whole conversation. He brought him to Saul, and David was with Saul as before.

8Once more war broke out, and David went out and fought the Philistines. He struck them with such force that they fled before him.

9But an evil[z] spirit from the LORD came upon Saul as he was sitting in his house with his spear in his hand. While David was playing the harp, 10Saul tried to pin him to the wall with his spear, but David eluded him as Saul drove the spear into the wall. That night David made good his escape.

11Saul sent men to David's house to watch it and to kill him in the morning. But Michal, David's wife, warned

z9 Or *injurious*

לֵאמֹר אִם־ אֵינְךָ֩ מְמַלֵּ֨ט אֶת־ נַפְשְׁךָ֤ הַלַּ֙יְלָה֙ מָחָ֣ר אַתָּ֣ה מוּמָֽת׃
being-killed　you　tomorrow　the-night　life-of-you　for　running　not-you　if　to-say

וַתֹּ֧רֶד מִיכַ֛ל אֶת־ דָּוִ֖ד בְּעַ֣ד הַחַלּ֑וֹן וַיֵּ֥לֶךְ
and-he-went　the-window　through　David　***　Michal　so-she-let-down　(12)

וַיִּבְרַ֖ח וַיִּמָּלֵֽט׃ (13) וַתִּקַּ֣ח מִיכַ֗ל אֶת־ הַתְּרָפִים֒
the-idols　***　Michal　then-she-took　(13)　and-he-escaped　and-he-fled

וַתָּ֙שֶׂם֙ אֶל־ הַמִּטָּ֔ה וְאֵת֙ כְּבִ֣יר הָֽעִזִּ֔ים שָׂ֖מָה מְרַֽאֲשֹׁתָ֑יו
at-heads-of-him　she-put　the-goat-hairs　material-of　and　the-bed　on　and-she-laid

וַתְּכַ֖ס בַּבָּֽגֶד׃ (14) וַיִּשְׁלַ֤ח שָׁאוּל֙ מַלְאָכִ֔ים לָקַ֖חַת אֶת־
***　to-capture　men　Saul　when-he-sent　(14)　with-the-garment　and-she-covered

דָּוִ֑ד וַתֹּ֖אמֶר חֹלֶ֥ה הֽוּא׃ (15) וַיִּשְׁלַ֤ח שָׁאוּל֙ אֶת־ הַמַּלְאָכִ֔ים
the-men　***　Saul　but-he-sent-back　(15)　he　being-ill　then-she-said　David

לִרְא֥וֹת אֶת־ דָּוִ֖ד לֵאמֹ֑ר הַעֲל֨וּ אֹת֥וֹ בַמִּטָּ֛ה אֵלַ֖י לַהֲמִתֽוֹ׃
to-kill-him　to-me　in-the-bed　him　bring-up!　to-say　David　***　to-see

וַיָּבֹ֙אוּ֙ הַמַּלְאָכִ֔ים וְהִנֵּ֥ה הַתְּרָפִ֖ים אֶל־ הַמִּטָּ֑ה וּכְבִ֥יר
and-material-of　the-bed　in　the-idols　then-see!　the-men　when-they-entered　(16)

הָעִזִּ֖ים מְרַאֲשֹׁתָֽיו׃ (17) וַיֹּ֨אמֶר שָׁא֜וּל אֶל־ מִיכַ֗ל לָ֤מָּה כָּ֙כָה֙
like-this　why?　Michal　to　Saul　and-he-said　(17)　at-heads-of-him　the-goat-hairs

רִמִּיתִ֔נִי וַתְּשַׁלְּחִ֥י אֶת־ אֹיְבִ֖י וַיִּמָּלֵ֑ט
so-he-escaped　being-enemy-of-me　***　and-you-sent-away　you-deceived-me

וַתֹּ֤אמֶר מִיכַל֙ אֶל־ שָׁא֔וּל ה֥וּא אָמַ֛ר אֵלַ֖י שַׁלְּחִ֣נִי לָמָ֥ה
why?　let-get-away-me!　to-me　he-said　he　Saul　to　Michal　and-she-told

אֲמִיתֵֽךְ׃ (18) וְדָוִ֞ד בָּרַ֣ח וַיִּמָּלֵ֗ט וַיָּבֹ֤א אֶל־
to　then-he-went　and-he-escaped　he-fled　when-David　(18)　should-I-kill-you

שְׁמוּאֵל֙ הָרָמָ֔תָה וַיַּ֨גֶּד־ ל֔וֹ אֵ֛ת כָּל־ אֲשֶׁ֥ר עָֽשָׂה־ ל֖וֹ שָׁא֑וּל
Saul　to-him　he-did　that　all　***　to-him　and-he-told　at-the-Ramah　Samuel

וַיֵּ֤לֶךְ הוּא֙ וּשְׁמוּאֵ֔ל וַיֵּשְׁב֖וּ בְּנָיֽוֹת׃ (19) וַיֻּגַּ֥ד
and-he-was-told　(19)　in-Naioth　and-they-stayed　and-Samuel　he　then-he-went

לְשָׁא֖וּל לֵאמֹ֑ר הִנֵּ֣ה דָוִ֔ד בְּנָי֖וֹת בָּרָמָֽה׃ (20) וַיִּשְׁלַ֤ח שָׁאוּל֙ מַלְאָכִים֒
men　Saul　so-he-sent　(20)　at-the-Ramah　in-Naioth　David　see!　to-say　to-Saul

לָקַ֣חַת אֶת־ דָּוִ֒ד וַיַּ֞רְא אֶֽת־ לַהֲקַ֤ת הַנְּבִיאִים֙ נִבְּאִ֔ים
ones-prophesying　the-prophets　group-of　***　but-they-saw　David　***　to-capture

וּשְׁמוּאֵ֕ל עֹמֵ֥ד נִצָּ֖ב עֲלֵיהֶ֑ם וַתְּהִ֞י עַל־ מַלְאֲכֵ֤י שָׁאוּל֙
Saul　men-of　upon　and-she-came　over-them　leading　standing　and-Samuel

ר֣וּחַ אֱלֹהִ֔ים וַיִּֽתְנַבְּא֖וּ גַּם־ הֵֽמָּה׃ (21) וַיַּגִּ֣דוּ לְשָׁא֗וּל
to-Saul　and-they-told　(21)　they　also　and-they-prophesied　God　Spirit-of

וַיִּשְׁלַ֞ח מַלְאָכִ֤ים אֲחֵרִים֙ וַיִּֽתְנַבְּא֖וּ גַּם־ הֵ֑מָּה וַיֹּ֧סֶף שָׁא֣וּל
Saul　and-he-repeated　they　also　and-they-prophesied　more-ones　men　and-he-sent

him, "If you don't run for your life tonight, tomorrow you'll be killed." [12]So Michal let David down through a window, and he fled and escaped. [13]Then Michal took an idol[a] and laid it on the bed, covering it with a garment and putting some goats' hair at the head.

[14]When Saul sent the men to capture David, Michal said, "He is ill."

[15]Then Saul sent the men back to see David and told them, "Bring him up to me in his bed so that I may kill him." [16]But when the men entered, there was the idol in the bed, and at the head was some goats' hair.

[17]Saul said to Michal, "Why did you deceive me like this and send my enemy away so that he escaped?"

Michal told him, "He said to me, 'Let me get away. Why should I kill you?' "

[18]When David had fled and made his escape, he went to Samuel at Ramah and told him all that Saul had done to him. Then he and Samuel went to Naioth and stayed there. [19]Word came to Saul: "David is in Naioth at Ramah"; [20]so he sent men to capture him. But when they saw a group of prophets prophesying, with Samuel standing there as their leader, the Spirit of God came upon Saul's men and they also prophesied. [21]Saul was told about it, and he sent more men, and they prophesied too.

[a]13 Hebrew teraphim; also in verse 16

°18 ק בְּנָיֽוֹת
°19 ק בְּנָיֽוֹת

וַיִּשְׁלַח מַלְאָכִים שְׁלִשִׁים וַיִּתְנַבְּאוּ גַּם־הֵמָּה׃ וַיֵּלֶךְ
then-he-left (22) they also and-they-prophesied third-ones men and-he-sent

גַּם־הוּא הָרָמָתָה וַיָּבֹא עַד־בּוֹר הַגָּדוֹל אֲשֶׁר בַּשֶּׂכוּ
at-the-Secu that the-great cistern-of to and-he-went for-the-Ramah he also

וַיִּשְׁאַל וַיֹּאמֶר אֵיפֹה שְׁמוּאֵל וְדָוִד וַיֹּאמֶר הִנֵּה בְּנָוֹית
in-Naioth see! and-he-said and-David Samuel where? and-he-said and-he-asked

בָּרָמָה׃ וַיֵּלֶךְ שָׁם אֶל־נָוֹית בָּרָמָה וַתְּהִי
but-she-came at-the-Ramah Naioth to there so-he-went (23) at-the-Ramah

עָלָיו גַּם־הוּא רוּחַ אֱלֹהִים וַיֵּלֶךְ הָלוֹךְ וַיִּתְנַבֵּא עַד־
until and-he-prophesied to-walk and-he-walked God Spirit-of he also upon-him

בֹּאוֹ בְּנָוֹית בָּרָמָה׃ וַיִּפְשַׁט גַּם־הוּא
he also and-he-stripped-off (24) at-the-Ramah to-Naioth to-come-him

בְּגָדָיו וַיִּתְנַבֵּא גַם־הוּא לִפְנֵי שְׁמוּאֵל וַיִּפֹּל עָרֹם
naked and-he-lay Samuel in-presences-of he also and-he-prophesied robes-of-him

כָּל־הַיּוֹם הַהוּא וְכָל־הַלָּיְלָה עַל־כֵּן יֹאמְרוּ הֲגַם שָׁאוּל
Saul also? they-say this for the-night and-all-of the-that the-day all-of

בַּנְּבִיאִם׃ וַיִּבְרַח דָּוִד מִנָּוֹות בָּרָמָה
at-the-Ramah from-Naioth David then-he-fled (20:1) among-the-prophets

וַיָּבֹא וַיֹּאמֶר ׀ לִפְנֵי יְהוֹנָתָן מֶה עָשִׂיתִי מֶה־עֲוֹנִי וּמֶה־
and-how? crime-of-me what? I-did what? Jonathan to and-he-asked and-he-went

חַטָּאתִי לִפְנֵי אָבִיךָ כִּי מְבַקֵּשׁ אֶת־נַפְשִׁי׃ וַיֹּאמֶר
and-he-replied (2) life-of-me *** seeking that father-of-you to I-did-wrong

לוֹ חָלִילָה לֹא תָמוּת הִנֵּה לוֹ־עָשָׂה אָבִי דָּבָר גָּדוֹל
great anything father-of-me he-does not look! you-will-die not never! to-him

אוֹ דָּבָר קָטֹן וְלֹא יִגְלֶה אֶת־אָזְנִי וּמַדּוּעַ יַסְתִּיר
would-he-hide now-why? ear-of-me *** he-confides that-not small anything or

אָבִי מִמֶּנִּי אֶת־הַדָּבָר הַזֶּה אֵין זֹאת׃ וַיִּשָּׁבַע
but-he-took-oath (3) so not the-this the-thing *** from-me father-of-me

עוֹד דָּוִד וַיֹּאמֶר יָדֹעַ יָדַע אָבִיךָ כִּי־מָצָאתִי חֵן
favor I-found that father-of-you he-knows to-know and-he-said David again

בְּעֵינֶיךָ וַיֹּאמֶר אַל־יֵדַע־זֹאת יְהוֹנָתָן פֶּן־יֵעָצֵב
he-will-be-grieved or Jonathan this he-must-know not and-he-said in-eyes-of-you

וְאוּלָם חַי־יְהוָה וְחֵי נַפְשֶׁךָ כִּי כְפֶשַׂע בֵּינִי
between-me only-step indeed self-of-you and-life-of Yahweh life-of and-yet

וּבֵין הַמָּוֶת׃ וַיֹּאמֶר יְהוֹנָתָן אֶל־דָּוִד מַה־תֹּאמַר
she-asks whatever David to Jonathan and-he-said (4) the-death and-between

נַפְשְׁךָ וְאֶעֱשֶׂה־לָּךְ׃ וַיֹּאמֶר דָּוִד אֶל־יְהוֹנָתָן הִנֵּה־
look! Jonathan to David so-he-said (5) for-you then-I-will-do self-of-you

Saul sent men a third time,
and they also prophesied. 22Fi-
nally, he himself left for
Ramah and went to the great
cistern at Secu. And he asked,
"Where are Samuel and Da-
vid?"

"Over in Naioth at Ramah,"
they said.

23So Saul went to Naioth at
Ramah. But the Spirit of God
came even upon him, and he
walked along prophesying until he came to Naioth. 24He
stripped off his robes and also
prophesied in Samuel's presence. He lay that way all that
day and night. This is why
people say, "Is Saul also
among the prophets?"

*David and Jonathan*

20 Then David fled from
Naioth at Ramah and
went to Jonathan and asked,
"What have I done? What is
my crime? How have I
wronged your father, that he
is trying to take my life?"

2"Never!" Jonathan replied.
"You are not going to die!
Look, my father doesn't do
anything, great or small, without confiding in me. Why
would he hide this from me?
It's not so!"

3But David took an oath and
said, "Your father knows very
well that I have found favor in
your eyes, and he has said to
himself, 'Jonathan must not
know this or he will be
grieved.' Yet as surely as the
LORD lives and as you live,
there is only a step between
me and death."

4Jonathan said to David,
"Whatever you want me to do,
I'll do for you."

°22 ק בניות
°23a ק ניות
°23b ק בניות
°1 ק מניות
°2a ק לא
°2b ק יעשה

חֹדֶשׁ מָחָר וְאָנֹכִי יָשֹׁב־ אֵשֵׁב עִם־ הַמֶּלֶךְ לֶאֱכוֹל
to-dine the-king with I-should-sit to-sit and-I tomorrow New-Moon-festival

וְשִׁלַּחְתַּנִי וְנִסְתַּרְתִּי בַשָּׂדֶה עַד הָעֶרֶב הַשְּׁלִשִׁית׃
the-third the-evening until in-the-field and-I-will-hide but-you-let-go-me

(6) אִם־ פָּקֹד יִפְקְדֵנִי אָבִיךָ וְאָמַרְתָּ נִשְׁאֹל נִשְׁאַל
he-asked to-ask then-you-tell father-of-you he-misses-me to-miss if (6)

מִמֶּנִּי דָוִד לָרוּץ בֵּית־ לֶחֶם עִירוֹ כִּי זֶבַח הַיָּמִים
the-days sacrifice-of for town-of-him Lehem Beth to-hurry David from-me

שָׁם לְכָל־ הַמִּשְׁפָּחָה׃ (7) אִם־ כֹּה יֹאמַר טוֹב שָׁלוֹם
safe very-well he-says this if (7) the-clan for-whole-of there

לְעַבְדֶּךָ וְאִם־ חָרֹה יֶחֱרֶה לוֹ דַּע כִּי־
that be-sure! to-him he-is-angry to-be-angry but-if for-servant-of-you

כָלְתָה הָרָעָה מֵעִמּוֹ׃ (8) וְעָשִׂיתָ חֶסֶד עַל־
to kindness then-you-show (8) from-with-him the-harm she-is-determined

עַבְדֶּךָ כִּי בִּבְרִית יְהוָה הֵבֵאתָ אֶת־ עַבְדְּךָ
servant-of-you *** you-brought Yahweh into-covenant-of for servant-of-you

עִמָּךְ וְאִם־ יֶשׁ־ בִּי עָוֺן הֲמִיתֵנִי אַתָּה וְעַד־ אָבִיךָ לָמָּה־
why? father-of-you for-to you kill-me! guilt in-me there-is but-if with-you

זֶּה תְבִיאֵנִי׃ (9) וַיֹּאמֶר יְהוֹנָתָן חָלִילָה לָּךְ כִּי ׀ אִם־ יָדֹעַ
to-know if for to-you never! Jonathan and-he-said (9) you-hand-over-me this

אֵדַע כִּי־ כָלְתָה הָרָעָה מֵעִם אָבִי לָבוֹא
to-go father-of-me from-with the-harm she-was-determined that I-knew

עָלֶיךָ וְלֹא אֹתָהּ אַגִּיד לָךְ׃ (10) וַיֹּאמֶר דָּוִד אֶל־
to David and-he-asked (10) to-you I-would-tell her then-not against-you

יְהוֹנָתָן מִי יַגִּיד לִי אוֹ מַה־ יַּעַנְךָ אָבִיךָ
father-of-you he-answers-you something if to-me he-will-tell who? Jonathan

קָשָׁה׃ (11) וַיֹּאמֶר יְהוֹנָתָן אֶל־ דָּוִד לְכָה וְנֵצֵא הַשָּׂדֶה
the-field and-let-us-go-out come! David to Jonathan then-he-said (11) harsh

וַיֵּצְאוּ שְׁנֵיהֶם הַשָּׂדֶה׃ (12) וַיֹּאמֶר יְהוֹנָתָן אֶל־ דָּוִד
David to Jonathan then-he-said (12) the-field two-of-them so-they-went

יְהוָה אֱלֹהֵי יִשְׂרָאֵל כִּי־ אֶחְקֹר אֶת־ אָבִי כָּעֵת ׀
by-the-time father-of-me *** I-will-sound-out surely Israel God-of Yahweh

מָחָר הַשְּׁלִשִׁית וְהִנֵּה־ טוֹב אֶל־ דָּוִד וְלֹא־ אָז אֶשְׁלַח
I-will-send then then-not David to favorable and-if the-third tomorrow

אֵלֶיךָ וְגָלִיתִי אֶת־ אָזְנֶךָ׃ (13) כֹּה־ יַעֲשֶׂה יְהוָה
Yahweh may-he-deal so (13) ear-of-you *** and-I-will-let-know to-you

לִיהוֹנָתָן וְכֹה יֹסִיף כִּי־ יֵיטִב אֶל־ אָבִי אֶת־
*** father-of-me to he-pleases if may-he-be-severe and-so with-Jonathan

5So David said, "Look, tomorrow is the New Moon festival, and I am supposed to dine with the king; but let me go and hide in the field until the evening of the day after tomorrow.
6If your father misses me at all, tell him, 'David earnestly asked my permission to hurry to Bethlehem, his home town, because an annual sacrifice is being made there for his whole clan.'
7If he says, 'Very well,' then your servant is safe. But if he loses his temper, you can be sure that he is determined to harm me.
8As for you, show kindness to your servant, for you have brought him into a covenant with you before the LORD. If I am guilty, then kill me yourself! Why hand me over to your father?"

9"Never!" Jonathan said. "If I had the least inkling that my father was determined to harm you, wouldn't I tell you?"

10David asked, "Who will tell me if your father answers you harshly?"

11"Come," Jonathan said, "let's go out into the field." So they went there together.

12Then Jonathan said to David: "By the LORD, the God of Israel, I will surely sound out my father by this time the day after tomorrow! If he is favorably disposed toward you, will I not send you word and let you know?
13But if my father is inclined to harm you, may the LORD deal with me, be it ever

| וְהָלַכְתָּ | וְשִׁלַּחְתִּיךָ | אָזְנֶךָ | אֶת־ | וְגָלִיתִי | עָלֶיךָ | הָרָעָה |
|---|---|---|---|---|---|---|
| and-you-go | and-I-send-you | ear-of-you | *** | and-I-let-know | to-you | the-harm |

| אָבִי׃ | עִם־ | הָיָה | כַּאֲשֶׁר | עִמָּךְ | יְהוָה | וִיהִי | לְשָׁלוֹם |
|---|---|---|---|---|---|---|---|
| father-of-me | with | he-was | just-as | with-you | Yahweh | and-may-he-be | in-safety |

| יְהוָה | חֶסֶד | עִמָּדִי | תַעֲשֶׂה | וְלֹא־ | חָי | עוֹדֶנִּי | אִם־ | וְלֹא | |
|---|---|---|---|---|---|---|---|---|---|
| Yahweh | kindness-of | to-me | will-you-show | then-not | alive | still-I | if | and-not | (14) |

| מֵעִם | חַסְדְּךָ | אֶת־ | תַכְרִת | וְלֹא־ | | אָמוּת׃ | וְלֹא |
|---|---|---|---|---|---|---|---|
| from-with | kindness-of-you | *** | you-cut-off | and-not | (15) | I-die | so-not |

| אֹיְבֵי | אֶת־ | יְהוָה | בְּהַכְרִת | וְלֹא | עוֹלָם | עַד־ | בֵּיתִי |
|---|---|---|---|---|---|---|---|
| being-enemies-of | *** | Yahweh | when-to-cut-off | even-not | ever | for | family-of-me |

| עִם־ | יְהוֹנָתָן | וַיִּכְרֹת | | הָאֲדָמָה׃ | פְּנֵי | מֵעַל | אִישׁ | דָּוִד |
|---|---|---|---|---|---|---|---|---|
| with | Jonathan | so-he-made-covenant | (16) | the-earth | faces-of | from-on | each | David |

| אֹיְבֵי | מִיַּד | יְהוָה | וּבִקֵּשׁ | דָּוִד | בֵּית |
|---|---|---|---|---|---|
| being-enemies-of | from-hand-of | Yahweh | and-may-he-call-account | David | house-of |

| בְּאַהֲבָתוֹ | דָּוִד | אֶת־ | לְהַשְׁבִּיעַ | יְהוֹנָתָן | וַיּוֹסֶף | | דָוִד׃ |
|---|---|---|---|---|---|---|---|
| from-love-of-him | David | *** | to-make-swear | Jonathan | and-he-repeated | (17) | David |

| יְהוֹנָתָן | לוֹ | וַיֹּאמֶר־ | | אֲהֵבוֹ׃ | נַפְשׁוֹ | אַהֲבַת | כִּי־ | אֹתוֹ |
|---|---|---|---|---|---|---|---|---|
| Jonathan | to-him | then-he-said | (18) | he-loved-him | self-of-him | love-of | for | for-him |

| יִפָּקֵד | כִּי | וְנִפְקַדְתָּ | חֹדֶשׁ | מָחָר |
|---|---|---|---|---|
| he-will-be-empty | for | and-you-will-be-missed | New-Moon-festival | tomorrow |

| אֶל־ | וּבָאתָ | מְאֹד | תֵּרֵד | וְשִׁלַּשְׁתָּ | | מוֹשָׁבֶךָ׃ |
|---|---|---|---|---|---|---|
| to | and-you-go | quickly | you-go-down | and-you-act-on-third-day | (19) | seat-of-you |

| הָאֶבֶן | אֵצֶל | וְיָשַׁבְתָּ | הַמַּעֲשֶׂה | בְּיוֹם | שָּׁם | נִסְתַּרְתָּ | אֲשֶׁר־ | הַמָּקוֹם |
|---|---|---|---|---|---|---|---|---|
| the-stone | by | and-you-wait | the-deed | on-day-of | there | you-hid | where | the-place |

| לְשַׁלַּח־ | אוֹרֶה | צִדָּה | הַחִצִּים | שְׁלֹשֶׁת | וַאֲנִי | | הָאָזֶל׃ |
|---|---|---|---|---|---|---|---|
| to-shoot | I-will-shoot | side-of-her | the-arrows | three-of | and-I | (20) | the-Ezel |

| אֶת־ | מְצָא | לֵךְ | הַנַּעַר | אֶת־ | אֶשְׁלַח | וְהִנֵּה | | לַמַּטָּרָה׃ | לִי |
|---|---|---|---|---|---|---|---|---|---|
| *** | find! | go! | the-boy | *** | I-will-send | then-see! | (21) | at-target | for-me |

| וָהֵנָּה | מִמְּךָ | הַחִצִּים ׀ | הִנֵּה | לַנַּעַר | אֹמַר | אָמֹר | אִם־ | הַחִצִּים |
|---|---|---|---|---|---|---|---|---|
| and-beside | by-you | the-arrows | look! | to-the-boy | I-say | to-say | if | the-arrows |

| יְהוָה׃ | חַי־ | דָּבָר | וְאֵין | לְךָ | שָׁלוֹם | כִּי־ | וָבֹאָה | קָחֶנּוּ ׀ |
|---|---|---|---|---|---|---|---|---|
| Yahweh | life-of | danger | and-no | for-you | safe | for | then-come! | bring-him! |

| לֵךְ | וָהָלְאָה | מִמְּךָ | הַחִצִּים | הִנֵּה | לָעֶלֶם | אֹמַר | כֹּה | וְאִם־ | |
|---|---|---|---|---|---|---|---|---|---|
| go! | and-beyond | from-you | the-arrows | look! | to-the-boy | I-say | this | but-if | (22) |

| וָאָתָּה | אֲנִי | דִּבַּרְנוּ | אֲשֶׁר | וְהַדָּבָר | | יְהוָה׃ | שִׁלַּחֲךָ | כִּי |
|---|---|---|---|---|---|---|---|---|
| and-you | I | we-discussed | that | and-the-matter | (23) | Yahweh | he-sent-away-you | for |

| דָּוִד | וַיִּסָּתֵר | | עוֹלָם׃ | עַד־ | וּבֵינְךָ | בֵּינִי | יְהוָה | הִנֵּה |
|---|---|---|---|---|---|---|---|---|
| David | so-he-hid | (24) | forever | to | and-between-you | between-me | Yahweh | see! |

so severely, if I do not let you
know and send you away
safely. May the LORD be with
you as he has been with my
father. [14]But show me unfailing kindness like that of the
LORD as long as I live, so that I
may not be killed, [15]and do not
ever cut off your kindness
from my family—not even
when the LORD has cut off
every one of David's enemies
from the face of the earth."
[16]So Jonathan made a covenant with the house of David, saying, "May the LORD
call David's enemies to account." [17]And Jonathan had
David reaffirm his oath out of
love for him, because he loved
him as he loved himself.
[18]Then Jonathan said to David: "Tomorrow is the New
Moon festival. You will be
missed, because your seat will
be empty. [19]The day after tomorrow, toward evening, go
to the place where you hid
when this trouble began, and
wait by the stone Ezel. [20]I will
shoot three arrows to the side
of it, as though I were shooting at a target. [21]Then I will
send a boy and say, 'Go, find
the arrows.' If I say to him,
'Look, the arrows are on this
side of you; bring them here,'
then come, because, as surely
as the LORD lives, you are safe;
there is no danger. [22]But if I
say to the boy, 'Look, the arrows are beyond you,' then
you must go, because the LORD
has sent you away. [23]And
about the matter you and I discussed—remember, the LORD
is witness between you and
me forever."
[24]So David hid in the field,

בַּשָּׂדֶה וַיְהִי הַחֹדֶשׁ וַיֵּשֶׁב הַמֶּלֶךְ עַל־
at the-king then-he-sat-down the-New-Moon-festival when-he-came in-the-field

הַלֶּחֶם לֶאֱכוֹל׃ וַיֵּשֶׁב הַמֶּלֶךְ עַל־ מוֹשָׁבוֹ כְּפַעַם ׀ בְּפַעַם אֶל־
at at-time as-time place-of-him in the-king and-he-sat (25) to-eat the-meal

מוֹשַׁב הַקִּיר וַיָּקָם יְהוֹנָתָן וַיֵּשֶׁב אַבְנֵר מִצַּד שָׁאוּל
Saul at-side-of Abner and-he-sat Jonathan and-he-arose the-wall place-of

וַיִּפָּקֵד מְקוֹם דָּוִד׃ וְלֹא־ דִבֶּר שָׁאוּל מְאוּמָה בַּיּוֹם
on-the-day anything Saul he-said and-not (26) David place-of but-he-was-empty

הַהוּא כִּי אָמַר מִקְרֶה הוּא בִּלְתִּי טָהוֹר הוּא כִּי־ לֹא טָהוֹר׃
clean not surely he clean not he happening he-thought for the-that

וַיְהִי מִמָּחֳרַת הַחֹדֶשׁ הַשֵּׁנִי וַיִּפָּקֵד
then-he-was-empty the-second the-month on-next-day-of but-he-was (27)

מְקוֹם דָּוִד וַיֹּאמֶר שָׁאוּל אֶל־יְהוֹנָתָן בְּנוֹ מַדּוּעַ לֹא־ בָא
he-came not why? son-of-him Jonathan to Saul then-he-said David place-of

בֶן־ יִשַׁי גַּם־ תְּמוֹל גַּם־ הַיּוֹם אֶל־ הַלָּחֶם׃ וַיַּעַן
and-he-answered (28) the-meal to the-day or yesterday either Jesse son-of

יְהוֹנָתָן אֶת־ שָׁאוּל נִשְׁאֹל נִשְׁאַל דָּוִד מֵעִמָּדִי עַד־ בֵּית לָחֶם׃
Lehem Beth to from-with-me David he-asked to-ask Saul *** Jonathan

וַיֹּאמֶר שַׁלְּחֵנִי נָא כִּי זֶבַח מִשְׁפָּחָה לָנוּ בָּעִיר
in-the-town of-us family sacrifice-of for now! let-go-me! and-he-said (29)

וְהוּא צִוָּה־ לִי אָחִי וְעַתָּה אִם־מָצָאתִי חֵן בְּעֵינֶיךָ
in-eyes-of-you favor I-found if so-now brother-of-me to-me he-ordered and-he

אִמָּלְטָה נָּא וְאֶרְאֶה אֶת־ אֶחָי עַל־ כֵּן לֹא־ בָא
he-came not this for brothers-of-me *** and-let-me-see now! let-me-get-away

אֶל־ שֻׁלְחַן הַמֶּלֶךְ׃ וַיִּחַר־ אַף שָׁאוּל בִּיהוֹנָתָן
against-Jonathan Saul anger-of and-he-flared-up (30) the-king table-of to

וַיֹּאמֶר לוֹ בֶּן־ נַעֲוַת הַמַּרְדּוּת הֲלוֹא יָדַעְתִּי
I-know not? the-rebellion woman-being-perverse-of son-of to-him and-he-said

כִּי־ בֹחֵר אַתָּה לְבֶן־ יִשַׁי לְבָשְׁתְּךָ וּלְבֹשֶׁת עֶרְוַת
nakedness-of and-to-shame-of to-shame-of-you Jesse with-son-of you siding that

אִמֶּךָ׃ כִּי כָל־ הַיָּמִים אֲשֶׁר בֶּן־ יִשַׁי חַי עַל־הָאֲדָמָה
the-earth on alive Jesse son-of that the-days all-of for (31) mother-of-you

לֹא תִכּוֹן אַתָּה וּמַלְכוּתֶךָ וְעַתָּה שְׁלַח וְקַח
and-bring! send! and-now or-kingdom-of-you you you-will-be-established not

אֹתוֹ אֵלַי כִּי בֶן־ מָוֶת הוּא׃ וַיַּעַן יְהוֹנָתָן אֶת־שָׁאוּל
Saul *** Jonathan and-he-asked (32) he death son-of for to-me him

אָבִיו וַיֹּאמֶר אֵלָיו לָמָּה יוּמַת מֶה עָשָׂה׃
he-did what? should-he-die why? to-him and-he-said father-of-him

and when the New Moon festival came, the king sat down to eat. 25He sat in his customary place by the wall. Jonathan sat opposite him,[b] and Abner sat next to Saul, but David's place was empty. 26Saul said nothing that day, for he thought, "Something must have happened to David to make him ceremonially unclean—surely he is unclean." 27But the next day, the second day of the month, David's place was empty again. Then Saul said to his son Jonathan, "Why hasn't the son of Jesse come to the meal, either yesterday or today?"

28Jonathan answered, "David earnestly asked me for permission to go to Bethlehem. 29He said, 'Let me go, because our family is observing a sacrifice in the town and my brother has ordered me to be there. If I have found favor in your eyes, let me get away to see my brothers.' That is why he has not come to the king's table."

30Saul's anger flared up at Jonathan and he said to him, "You son of a perverse and rebellious woman! Don't I know that you have sided with the son of Jesse to your own shame and to the shame of the mother who bore you? 31As long as the son of Jesse lives on this earth, neither you nor your kingdom will be established. Now send and bring him to me, for he must die!"

32"Why should he be put to death? What has he done?" Jonathan asked his father.

[b]25 Septuagint; Hebrew *Jonathan arose*

°24 ק אל

וַיָּטֶל שָׁאוּל אֶת־הַחֲנִית עָלָיו לְהַכֹּתוֹ וַיֵּדַע
then-he-knew to-kill-him at-him the-spear *** Saul but-he-hurled (33)

יְהוֹנָתָן כִּי־כָלָה הִיא מֵעִם אָבִיו לְהָמִית אֶת־דָּוִד׃
David *** to-kill father-of-him from-with this he-intended that Jonathan

וַיָּקָם יְהוֹנָתָן מֵעִם הַשֻּׁלְחָן בָּחֳרִי־אָף וְלֹא־
and-not anger in-fierceness-of the-table from-at Jonathan so-he-got-up (34)

אָכַל בְּיוֹם־הַחֹדֶשׁ הַשֵּׁנִי לֶחֶם כִּי נֶעְצַב אֶל־דָּוִד כִּי
for David for he-was-grieved for food the-second the-month on-day-of he-ate

הִכְלִמוֹ אָבִיו׃ וַיְהִי בַבֹּקֶר וַיֵּצֵא
then-he-went-out in-the-morning and-he-was (35) father-of-him he-shamed-him

יְהוֹנָתָן הַשָּׂדֶה לְמוֹעֵד דָּוִד וְנַעַר קָטֹן עִמּוֹ׃ וַיֹּאמֶר
and-he-said (36) with-him small and-boy David for-meeting-of the-field Jonathan

לְנַעֲרוֹ רֻץ מְצָא נָא אֶת־הַחִצִּים אֲשֶׁר אָנֹכִי מוֹרֶה הַנַּעַר רָץ
he-ran the-boy shooting I that the-arrows *** now! find! run! to-boy-of-him

וְהוּא־יָרָה הַחֵצִי לְהַעֲבִרוֹ׃ וַיָּבֹא הַנַּעַר עַד־
to the-boy when-he-came (37) to-go-beyond-him the-arrow he-shot and-he

מְקוֹם הַחֵצִי אֲשֶׁר יָרָה יְהוֹנָתָן וַיִּקְרָא יְהוֹנָתָן אַחֲרֵי
after Jonathan then-he-called Jonathan he-shot where the-arrow place-of

הַנַּעַר וַיֹּאמֶר הֲלוֹא הַחֵצִי מִמְּךָ וָהָלְאָה׃ וַיִּקְרָא
then-he-shouted (38) and-beyond from-you the-arrow not? and-he-said the-boy

יְהוֹנָתָן אַחֲרֵי הַנַּעַר מְהֵרָה חוּשָׁה אַל־תַּעֲמֹד וַיְלַקֵּט נַעַר
boy-of and-he-picked-up you-stop not go-quickly! hurry the-boy after Jonathan

יְהוֹנָתָן אֶת־הַחִצִּי° וַיָּבֹא אֶל־אֲדֹנָיו׃ וְהַנַּעַר
now-the-boy (39) masters-of-him to and-he-returned the-arrows *** Jonathan

לֹא־יָדַע מְאוּמָה אַךְ יְהוֹנָתָן וְדָוִד יָדְעוּ אֶת־הַדָּבָר׃
the-matter *** they-knew and-David Jonathan only anything he-knew not

וַיִּתֵּן יְהוֹנָתָן אֶת־כֵּלָיו אֶל־הַנַּעַר אֲשֶׁר־לוֹ
with-him who the-boy to weapons-of-him *** Jonathan then-he-gave (40)

וַיֹּאמֶר לוֹ לֵךְ הָבֵיא הָעִיר׃ הַנַּעַר בָּא וְדָוִד
then-David he-went the-boy (41) the-town carry-back! go! to-him and-he-said

קָם מֵאֵצֶל הַנֶּגֶב וַיִּפֹּל לְאַפָּיו אַרְצָה
to-ground on-faces-of-him and-he-fell the-south from-side-of he-got-up

וַיִּשְׁתַּחוּ שָׁלֹשׁ פְּעָמִים וַיִּשְּׁקוּ | אִישׁ אֶת־רֵעֵהוּ וַיִּבְכּוּ
and-they-wept other-of-him *** each then-they-kissed times three and-he-bowed

אִישׁ אֶת־רֵעֵהוּ עַד־דָּוִד הִגְדִּיל׃ וַיֹּאמֶר יְהוֹנָתָן
Jonathan and-he-said (42) he-did-more David but other-of-him with each

לְדָוִד לֵךְ לְשָׁלוֹם אֲשֶׁר נִשְׁבַּעְנוּ שְׁנֵינוּ אֲנַחְנוּ בְּשֵׁם יְהוָה לֵאמֹר
to-say Yahweh in-name-of we both-of-us we-swore for in-peace go! to-David

33 But Saul hurled his spear at
him to kill him. Then Jonathan knew that his father intended to kill David.
34 Jonathan got up from the
table in fierce anger; on that
second day of the month he
did not eat, because he was
grieved at his father's shameful treatment of David.
35 In the morning Jonathan
went out to the field for his
meeting with David. He had a
small boy with him,
36 and he
said to the boy, "Run and find
the arrows I shoot." As the
boy ran, he shot an arrow
beyond him.
37 When the boy
came to the place where Jonathan's arrow had fallen, Jonathan called out after him,
"Isn't the arrow beyond you?"
38 Then he shouted, "Hurry! Go
quickly! Don't stop!" The boy
picked up the arrow and returned to his master.
39 (The
boy knew nothing of all this;
only Jonathan and David
knew.)
40 Then Jonathan gave
his weapons to the boy and
said, "Go, carry them back to
town."
41 After the boy had gone,
David got up from the south
side of the stone[c] and bowed
down before Jonathan three
times, with his face to the
ground. Then they kissed each
other and wept together—but
David wept the most.
42 Jonathan said to David,
"Go in peace, for we have
sworn friendship with each
other in the name of the LORD,

[c] 41 Septuagint; Hebrew does not have *of the stone*.

°38 ק החצים

יְהוָה יִהְיֶה ׀ בֵּינִי וּבֵינֶךָ וּבֵין זַרְעִי
descendant-of-me and-between and-between-you between-me he-is Yahweh

וּבֵין זַרְעֲךָ עַד־עוֹלָם׃ וַיָּקָם וַיֵּלַךְ
and-he-left then-he-got-up *(21:1) forever to descendant-of-you and-between

וִיהוֹנָתָן בָּא הָעִיר׃ וַיָּבֹא דָוִד נֹבֶה אֶל־אֲחִימֶלֶךְ
Ahimelech to to-Nob David and-he-went (2) the-town he-went-back and-Jonathan

הַכֹּהֵן וַיֶּחֱרַד אֲחִימֶלֶךְ לִקְרַאת דָּוִד וַיֹּאמֶר לוֹ מַדּוּעַ
why? to-him and-he-said David to-meet Ahimelech and-he-trembled the-priest

אַתָּה לְבַדֶּךָ וְאִישׁ אֵין אִתָּךְ׃ וַיֹּאמֶר דָּוִד
David and-he-answered (3) with-you not and-man by-self-of-you you

לַאֲחִימֶלֶךְ הַכֹּהֵן הַמֶּלֶךְ צִוַּנִי דָבָר וַיֹּאמֶר אֵלַי אִישׁ
man to-me and-he-said matter he-charged-me the-king the-priest to-Ahimelech

אַל־יֵדַע מְאוּמָה אֶת־הַדָּבָר אֲשֶׁר־אָנֹכִי שֹׁלֵחֲךָ וַאֲשֶׁר
and-that sending-you I that the-mission *** anything he-must-know not

צִוִּיתִךָ וְאֶת־הַנְּעָרִים יוֹדַעְתִּי אֶל־מְקוֹם פְּלֹנִי אַלְמוֹנִי׃ וְעַתָּה מַה־
what? then-now (4) some certain place at I-told the-men and I-instruct-you

יֵשׁ תַּחַת־יָדְךָ חֲמִשָּׁה־לֶחֶם תְּנָה בְיָדִי אוֹ
or into-hand-of-me give! bread five hand-of-you under there-is

הַנִּמְצָא׃ וַיַּעַן הַכֹּהֵן אֶת־דָּוִד וַיֹּאמֶר
and-he-said David *** the-priest but-he-answered (5) the-thing-being-found

אֵין־לֶחֶם חֹל אֶל־תַּחַת יָדִי כִּי־אִם־לֶחֶם קֹדֶשׁ יֵשׁ
there-is consecrated bread however but hand-of-me under at ordinary bread not

אִם־נִשְׁמְרוּ הַנְּעָרִים אַךְ מֵאִשָּׁה׃ וַיַּעַן דָּוִד אֶת־
*** David and-he-replied (6) from-woman only the-men they-kept-themselves if

הַכֹּהֵן וַיֹּאמֶר לוֹ כִּי אִם־אִשָּׁה עֲצֻרָה־לָנוּ
from-us being-kept woman indeed that to-him and-he-said the-priest

כִּתְמוֹל שִׁלְשֹׁם בְּצֵאתִי וַיִּהְיוּ כְלֵי־הַנְּעָרִים קֹדֶשׁ
holy the-men things-of and-they-are when-to-set-out-me before as-yesterday

וְהוּא דֶּרֶךְ חֹל וְאַף כִּי הַיּוֹם יִקְדַּשׁ בַּכֶּלִי׃
concerning-the-thing he-is-holy the-day more so-also not-holy mission when-he

וַיִּתֶּן־לוֹ הַכֹּהֵן קֹדֶשׁ כִּי לֹא־הָיָה שָׁם לֶחֶם
bread there he-was not since consecrated the-priest to-him so-he-gave (7)

כִּי־אִם־לֶחֶם הַפָּנִים הַמּוּסָרִים מִלִּפְנֵי יְהוָה
Yahweh from-before the-ones-being-removed the-Presences bread-of only except

לָשׂוּם לֶחֶם חֹם בְּיוֹם הִלָּקְחוֹ׃ וְשָׁם אִישׁ
man now-there (8) to-be-taken-him on-day hot bread to-be-replaced

מֵעַבְדֵי שָׁאוּל בַּיּוֹם הַהוּא נֶעְצָר לִפְנֵי יְהוָה
Yahweh before being-detained the-that on-the-day Saul from-servants-of

saying, 'The LORD is witness between you and me, and between your descendants and my descendants forever.' " Then David left, and Jonathan went back to the town.

*David at Nob*

21 David went to Nob, to Ahimelech the priest. Ahimelech trembled when he met him, and asked, "Why are you alone? Why is no one with you?"

2 David answered Ahimelech the priest, "The king charged me with a certain matter and said to me, 'No one is to know anything about your mission and your instructions.' As for my men, I have told them to meet me at a certain place.
3 Now then, what do you have on hand? Give me five loaves of bread, or whatever you can find."

4 But the priest answered David, "I don't have any ordinary bread on hand; however, there is some consecrated bread here—provided the men have kept themselves from women."

5 David replied, "Indeed women have been kept from us, as usual whenever[d] I set out. The men's things[e] are holy even on missions that are not holy. How much more so today!" 6 So the priest gave him the consecrated bread, since there was no bread there except the bread of the Presence that had been removed from before the LORD and replaced by hot bread on the day it was taken away.

7 Now one of Saul's servants was there that day, detained

[d] 5 Or *from us in the past few days since*
[e] 5 Or *bodies*

*1 The Hebrew enumeration of chapter 21 begins in the middle of verse 42 of chapter 20 in the English; thus there is a one-verse discrepancy throughout chapter 21.

וְשְׁמוֹ דֹּאֵג הָאֲדֹמִי אַבִּיר הָרֹעִים אֲשֶׁר לְשָׁאוּל׃
to-Saul who the-ones-shepherding head-of the-Edomite Doeg and-name-of-him

(9) וַיֹּאמֶר דָּוִד לַאֲחִימֶלֶךְ וְאִין יֶשׁ־ פֹּה תַחַת־ יָדְךָ
hand-of-you under here there-is now-not to-Ahimelech David and-he-asked (9)

חֲנִית אוֹ־ חֶרֶב כִּי גַם־ חַרְבִּי וְגַם־ כֵּלַי לֹא־ לָקַחְתִּי
I-brought not weapons-of-me or-even sword-of-me either for sword or spear

בְיָדִי כִּי־ הָיָה דְבַר־ הַמֶּלֶךְ נָחוּץ׃ (10) וַיֹּאמֶר
and-he-replied (10) being-urgent the-king business-of he-was for in-hand-of-me

הַכֹּהֵן חֶרֶב גָּלְיָת הַפְּלִשְׁתִּי אֲשֶׁר־ הִכִּיתָ ׀ בְּעֵמֶק
in-Valley-of you-killed whom the-Philistine Goliath sword-of the-priest

הָאֵלָה הִנֵּה־ הִיא לוּטָה בַשִּׂמְלָה אַחֲרֵי הָאֵפוֹד אִם־אֹתָהּ
her if the-ephod behind in-the-cloth being-wrapped she see! the-Elah

תִּקַּח־ לְךָ קָח כִּי אֵין אַחֶרֶת זוּלָתָהּ בָּזֶה וַיֹּאמֶר
and-he-said at-here except-her other not for take! for-you you-would-take

דָּוִד אֵין כָּמוֹהָ תְּנֶנָּה לִּי׃ (11) וַיָּקָם דָּוִד וַיִּבְרַח
and-he-fled David then-he-rose (11) to-me give-her! like-her not David

בַּיּוֹם־ הַהוּא מִפְּנֵי שָׁאוּל וַיָּבֹא אֶל־ אָכִישׁ מֶלֶךְ גַּת׃
Gath king-of Achish to and-he-went Saul from-before the-that on-the-day

(12) וַיֹּאמְרוּ עַבְדֵי אָכִישׁ אֵלָיו הֲלוֹא־ זֶה דָוִד מֶלֶךְ
king-of David this not? to-him Achish servants-of but-they-said (12)

הָאָרֶץ הֲלוֹא לָזֶה יַעֲנוּ בַמְּחֹלוֹת לֵאמֹר הִכָּה שָׁאוּל
Saul he-killed to-say in-the-dances they-sing about-this not? the-land

בַּאֲלָפָו וְדָוִד בְּרִבְבֹתָו׃ (13) וַיָּשֶׂם
and-he-took (13) to-ten-of-thousands-of-him and-David to-thousands-of-him

דָּוִד אֶת־ הַדְּבָרִים הָאֵלֶּה בִּלְבָבוֹ וַיִּרָא מְאֹד
very-much and-he-was-afraid to-heart-of-him the-these the-words *** David

מִפְּנֵי אָכִישׁ מֶלֶךְ־ גַּת׃ (14) וַיְשַׁנּוֹ אֶת־ טַעְמוֹ
insanity-of-him *** and-he-feigned-him (14) Gath king-of Achish from-before

בְּעֵינֵיהֶם וַיִּתְהֹלֵל בְּיָדָם וַיְתָו
and-he-marked in-hand-of-them and-he-acted-like-madman before-eyes-of-them

עַל־ דַּלְתוֹת הַשַּׁעַר וַיּוֹרֶד רִירוֹ אֶל־ זְקָנוֹ׃
beard-of-him into saliva-of-him and-he-let-run-down the-gate doors-of on

(15) וַיֹּאמֶר אָכִישׁ אֶל־ עֲבָדָיו הִנֵּה תִרְאוּ אִישׁ מִשְׁתַּגֵּעַ
being-insane man you-see look! servants-of-him to Achish and-he-said (15)

לָמָּה תָּבִיאוּ אֹתוֹ אֵלָי׃ (16) חֲסַר מְשֻׁגָּעִים אָנִי כִּי־ הֲבֵאתֶם
you-bring that I ones-being-mad short-of (16) to-me him you-bring why?

אֶת־ זֶה לְהִשְׁתַּגֵּעַ עָלָי הֲזֶה יָבוֹא אֶל־ בֵּיתִי׃
house-of-me into must-he-come this? in-front-of-me to-act-madly this ***

before the LORD; he was Doeg the Edomite, Saul's head shepherd.

8 David asked Ahimelech, "Don't you have a spear or a sword here? I haven't brought my sword or any other weapon, because the king's business was urgent."

9 The priest replied, "The sword of Goliath the Philistine, whom you killed in the Valley of Elah, is here; it is wrapped in a cloth behind the ephod. If you want it, take it; there is no sword here but that one."

David said, "There is none like it; give it to me."

*David at Gath*

10 That day David fled from Saul and went to Achish king of Gath. 11 But the servants of Achish said to him, "Isn't this David, the king of the land? Isn't he the one they sing about in their dances:

" 'Saul has slain his
thousands,
and David his tens of
thousands'?"

12 David took these words to heart and was very much afraid of Achish king of Gath. 13 So he feigned insanity in their presence; and while he was in their hands he acted like a madman, making marks on the doors of the gate and letting saliva run down his beard.

14 Achish said to his servants, "Look at the man! He is insane! Why bring him to me? 15 Am I so short of madmen that you have to bring this fellow here to carry on like this in front of me? Must this man come into my house?"

*See the note on page 220.

°12a ק באלפיו
°12b ק ברבבתיו
°14 ק ויתיו

וַיֵּ֤לֶךְ דָּוִד֙ מִשָּׁ֔ם וַיִּמָּלֵ֖ט אֶל־מְעָרַ֣ת עֲדֻלָּ֑ם
(22:1) and-he-left · David · from-there · and-he-escaped · to · cave-of · Adullam

וַיִּשְׁמְע֤וּ אֶחָיו֙ וְכָל־בֵּ֣ית אָבִ֔יו
when-they-heard · brothers-of-him · and-all-of · household-of · father-of-him

וַיֵּרְד֥וּ אֵלָ֖יו שָֽׁמָּה׃ (2) וַיִּתְקַבְּצ֣וּ אֵלָ֗יו כָּל־
then-they-went-down · to-him · at-there · (2) · and-they-gathered · around-him · every-of

אִ֤ישׁ מָצוֹק֙ וְכָל־אִ֣ישׁ אֲשֶׁר־ל֣וֹ נֹשֶׁ֔א וְכָל־
distressed · man · and-every-of · man · that · to-him · one-being-creditor · and-every-of

אִ֖ישׁ מַר־נֶ֑פֶשׁ וַיְהִ֥י עֲלֵיהֶ֖ם לְשָׂ֑ר וַיִּהְי֣וּ
man · discontent-of · spirit · and-he-became · to-them · as-leader · and-they-were

עִמּ֔וֹ כְּאַרְבַּ֥ע מֵא֖וֹת אִֽישׁ׃ (3) וַיֵּ֧לֶךְ דָּוִ֛ד מִשָּׁ֖ם מִצְפֵּ֣ה
with-him · about-four · hundreds · man · (3) · and-he-went · David · from-there · Mizpah-of

מוֹאָ֑ב וַיֹּ֣אמֶר ׀ אֶל־מֶ֣לֶךְ מוֹאָ֗ב יֵֽצֵא־נָ֞א אָבִ֤י
Moab · and-he-said · to · king-of · Moab · let-him-stay · now! · father-of-me

וְאִמִּי֙ אִתְּכֶ֔ם עַ֚ד אֲשֶׁ֣ר אֵדַ֔ע מַה־יַּֽעֲשֶׂה־לִּ֖י אֱלֹהִֽים׃
and-mother-of-me · with-you · until · when · I-learn · what · he-will-do · for-me · God

וַיַּנְחֵ֕ם אֶת־פְּנֵ֖י מֶ֣לֶךְ מוֹאָ֑ב וַיֵּשְׁב֣וּ עִמּ֔וֹ
(4) so-he-left-them · in · presences-of · king-of · Moab · and-they-stayed · with-him

כָּל־יְמֵ֥י הֱיוֹת־דָּוִ֖ד בַּמְּצוּדָֽה׃ (5) וַיֹּ֩אמֶר֩ גָּ֨ד הַנָּבִ֜יא
all-of · days-of · to-be · David · in-the-stronghold · (5) · but-he-said · Gad · the-prophet

אֶל־דָּוִ֗ד לֹ֤א תֵשֵׁב֙ בַּמְּצוּדָ֔ה לֵ֥ךְ וּבָֽאתָ־לְּךָ֖ אֶ֣רֶץ
to · David · not · you-stay · in-the-stronghold · go! · and-you-enter · for-you · land-of

יְהוּדָ֑ה וַיֵּ֣לֶךְ דָּוִ֔ד וַיָּבֹ֖א יַ֥עַר חָֽרֶת׃ (6) וַיִּשְׁמַ֣ע שָׁא֔וּל
Judah · so-he-left · David · and-he-went · forest-of · Hereth · (6) · now-he-heard · Saul

כִּ֚י נוֹדַ֣ע דָּוִ֔ד וַֽאֲנָשִׁ֖ים אֲשֶׁ֣ר אִתּ֑וֹ וְשָׁאוּל֩ יוֹשֵׁ֨ב
that · he-was-discovered · David · and-men · who · with-him · and-Saul · sitting

בַּגִּבְעָ֜ה תַּֽחַת־הָאֶ֤שֶׁל בָּֽרָמָה֙ וַחֲנִית֣וֹ בְיָד֔וֹ
in-the-Gibeah · under · the-tamarisk · on-the-hill · and-spear-of-him · in-hand-of-him

וְכָל־עֲבָדָ֖יו נִצָּבִ֥ים עָלָֽיו׃ (7) וַיֹּ֣אמֶר שָׁא֗וּל
and-all-of · officials-of-him · ones-standing · around-him · (7) · and-he-said · Saul

לַֽעֲבָדָיו֙ הַנִּצָּבִ֣ים עָלָ֔יו שִׁמְעוּ־נָ֖א בְּנֵ֣י יְמִינִ֑י
to-officials-of-him · the-ones-standing · around-him · listen! · now! · sons-of · Jamite†

גַּם־לְכֻלְּכֶ֗ם יִתֵּ֤ן בֶּן־יִשַׁי֙ שָׂד֣וֹת וּכְרָמִ֔ים
indeed · to-all-of-you · will-he-give · son-of · Jesse · fields · and-vineyards

לְכֻלְּכֶ֣ם יָשִׂ֔ים שָׂרֵ֥י אֲלָפִ֖ים וְשָׂרֵ֥י מֵאֽוֹת׃
to-all-of-you · will-he-make · commanders-of · thousands · and-commanders-of · hundreds

כִּ֤י קְשַׁרְתֶּם֙ כֻּלְּכֶ֣ם עָלַ֔י וְאֵין־גֹּלֶ֥ה אֶת־
(8) indeed · you-conspired · all-of-you · against-me · and-no-one · he-tells · ***

## David at Adullam and Mizpah

**22** David left Gath and escaped to the cave of Adullam. When his brothers and his father's household heard about it, they went down to him there. ²All those who were in distress or in debt or discontented gathered around him, and he became their leader. About four hundred men were with him.

³From there David went to Mizpah in Moab and said to the king of Moab, "Would you let my father and mother come and stay with you until I learn what God will do for me?" ⁴So he left them with the king of Moab, and they stayed with him as long as David was in the stronghold.

⁵But the prophet Gad said to David, "Do not stay in the stronghold. Go into the land of Judah." So David left and went to the forest of Hereth.

## Saul Kills the Priests of Nob

⁶Now Saul heard that David and his men had been discovered. And Saul, spear in hand, was seated under the tamarisk tree on the hill at Gibeah, with all his officials standing around him. ⁷Saul said to them, "Listen, men of Benjamin! Will the son of Jesse give all of you fields and vineyards? Will he make all of you commanders of thousands and commanders of hundreds? ⁸Is that why you have all conspired against me? No one tells me when my son

*6 Most mss have *tsere* under the *aleph* ( הָאָ ).

†7 That is, *Benjamites.*

אָזְנִי בִּכְרָת־ בְּנִי עִם־ בֶּן־ יִשַׁי וְאֵין־
and-no-one Jesse son-of with son-of-me when-to-make-covenant ear-of-me

חֹלֶה מִכֶּם עָלַי וְגֹלֶה אֶת־ אָזְנִי כִּי הֵקִים
he-incited that ear-of-me *** or-telling about-me from-you being-concerned

בְּנִי אֶת־ עַבְדִּי עָלַי לְאֹרֵב כַּיּוֹם הַזֶּה׃
the-this as-the-day to-lie-in-wait against-me servant-of-me *** son-of-me

וַיַּעַן דֹּאֵג הָאֲדֹמִי וְהוּא נִצָּב עַל־ עַבְדֵי־ שָׁאוּל
Saul officials-of with standing now-he the-Edomite Doeg but-he-said (9)

וַיֹּאמַר רָאִיתִי אֶת־ בֶּן־ יִשַׁי בָּא נֹבֶה אֶל־ אֲחִימֶלֶךְ בֶּן־אֲחִטוּב׃
Ahitub son-of Ahimelech to to-Nob coming Jesse son-of *** I-saw and-he-said

וַיִּשְׁאַל־ לוֹ בַּיהוָה וְצֵידָה נָתַן לוֹ וְאֵת
and to-him he-gave and-provision of-Yahweh for-him and-he-inquired (10)

חֶרֶב גָּלְיָת הַפְּלִשְׁתִּי נָתַן לוֹ׃ וַיִּשְׁלַח הַמֶּלֶךְ
the-king then-he-sent (11) to-him he-gave the-Philistine Goliath sword-of

לִקְרֹא אֶת־אֲחִימֶלֶךְ בֶּן־ אֲחִיטוּב הַכֹּהֵן וְאֵת כָּל־ בֵּית
family-of whole-of and the-priest Ahitub son-of Ahimelech *** to-call

אָבִיו הַכֹּהֲנִים אֲשֶׁר בְּנֹב וַיָּבֹאוּ כֻלָּם אֶל־הַמֶּלֶךְ׃
the-king to all-of-them and-they-came at-Nob who the-priests father-of-him

וַיֹּאמֶר שָׁאוּל שְׁמַע־ נָא בֶּן־ אֲחִיטוּב וַיֹּאמֶר הִנְנִי
here-I and-he-answered Ahitub son-of now! listen! Saul and-he-said (12)

אֲדֹנִי׃ וַיֹּאמֶר אֵלָו שָׁאוּל לָמָּה קְשַׁרְתֶּם עָלַי אַתָּה
you against-me you-conspired why? Saul to-him and-he-said (13) lord-of-me

וּבֶן־ יִשָׁי בְּתִתְּךָ לוֹ לֶחֶם וְחֶרֶב וְשָׁאוֹל
and-to-inquire and-sword bread to-him when-to-give-you Jesse and-son-of

לוֹ בֵּאלֹהִים לָקוּם אֵלַי לְאֹרֵב כַּיּוֹם הַזֶּה׃
the-this as-the-day to-lie-in-wait against-me to-rebel of-God for-him

וַיַּעַן אֲחִימֶלֶךְ אֶת־ הַמֶּלֶךְ וַיֹּאמַר וּמִי בְכָל־
of-all-of and-who? and-he-said the-king *** Ahimelech and-he-answered (14)

עֲבָדֶיךָ כְּדָוִד נֶאֱמָן וַחֲתַן הַמֶּלֶךְ וְסָר
and-captain the-king even-son-in-law-of being-loyal as-David servants-of-you

אֶל־ מִשְׁמַעְתֶּךָ וְנִכְבָּד בְּבֵיתֶךָ׃ הַיּוֹם
the-day (15) in-household-of-you and-being-respected bodyguard-of-you of

הַחִלֹּתִי לִשְׁאָול־ לוֹ בֵאלֹהִים חָלִילָה לִּי אַל־ יָשֵׂם הַמֶּלֶךְ
the-king let-him-bring not for-me no! of-God for-him to-inquire was-I-first

בְּעַבְדּוֹ דָבָר בְּכָל־ בֵּית אָבִי כִּי
for father-of-me family-of against-any-of accusation against-servant-of-him

לֹא־ יָדַע עַבְדְּךָ בְּכָל־ זֹאת דָּבָר קָטֹן אוֹ גָדוֹל׃
great or small affair this about-any-of servant-of-you he-knows not

makes a covenant with the son of Jesse. None of you is concerned about me or tells me that my son has incited my servant to lie in wait for me, as he does today."

9 But Doeg the Edomite, who was standing with Saul's officials, said, "I saw the son of Jesse come to Ahimelech son of Ahitub at Nob.
10 Ahimelech inquired of the LORD for him; he also gave him provisions and the sword of Goliath the Philistine."

11 Then the king sent for the priest Ahimelech son of Ahitub and his father's whole family, who were the priests at Nob, and they all came to the king.
12 Saul said, "Listen now, son of Ahitub."

"Yes, my lord," he answered.

13 Saul said to him, "Why have you conspired against me, you and the son of Jesse, giving him bread and a sword and inquiring of God for him, so that he has rebelled against me and lies in wait for me, as he does today?"

14 Ahimelech answered the king, "Who of all your servants is as loyal as David, the king's son-in-law, captain of your bodyguard and highly respected in your household?
15 Was that day the first time I inquired of God for him? Of course not! Let not the king accuse your servant or any of his father's family, for your servant knows nothing at all about this whole affair."

°13 ק אליו
°15 ק לשאל

וַיֹּאמֶר הַמֶּלֶךְ מוֹת תָּמוּת אֲחִימֶלֶךְ אַתָּה וְכָל־
and-whole-of you Ahimelech you-will-die to-die the-king but-he-said (16)

בֵּית אָבִיךָ׃ וַיֹּאמֶר הַמֶּלֶךְ לָרָצִים
to-the-ones-guarding the-king then-he-ordered (17) father-of-you family-of

הַנִּצָּבִים עָלָיו סֹבּוּ וְהָמִיתוּ׀ כֹּהֲנֵי יְהוָה כִּי גַם־
also for Yahweh priests-of and-kill! turn! by-him the-ones-standing

יָדָם עִם־ דָּוִד וְכִי יָדְעוּ כִּי־ בֹרֵחַ הוּא וְלֹא גָלוּ
they-told yet-not he fleeing that they-knew and-for David with hand-of-them

אֶת־ °אָזְנֹו וְלֹא־ אָבוּ עַבְדֵי הַמֶּלֶךְ לִשְׁלֹחַ אֶת־
*** to-raise the-king officials-of they-were-willing but-not ear-of-me ***

יָדָם לִפְגֹּעַ בְּכֹהֲנֵי יְהוָה׃ וַיֹּאמֶר
then-he-ordered (18) Yahweh against-priests-of to-strike hand-of-them

הַמֶּלֶךְ °לְדֹויֵג סֹב אַתָּה וּפְגַע בַּכֹּהֲנִים וַיִּסֹּב °דֹּויֵג
Doeg so-he-turned against-the-priests and-strike! you turn! to-Doeg the-king

הָאֲדֹמִי וַיִּפְגַּע־ הוּא בַּכֹּהֲנִים וַיָּמֶת׀ בַּיּוֹם
on-the-day and-he-killed against-the-priests he and-he-struck the-Edomite

הַהוּא שְׁמֹנִים וַחֲמִשָּׁה אִישׁ נֹשֵׂא אֵפוֹד בָּד׃ וְאֵת נֹב עִיר־
town-of Nob also (19) linen ephod wearing man and-five eighty the-that

הַכֹּהֲנִים הִכָּה לְפִי־ חֶרֶב מֵאִישׁ וְעַד־ אִשָּׁה מֵעוֹלֵל
from-child woman even-to from-man sword to-edge-of he-put the-priests

וְעַד־ יוֹנֵק וְשׁוֹר וַחֲמוֹר וָשֶׂה לְפִי־ חָרֶב׃
sword to-edge-of and-sheep and-donkey and-cattle one-nursing even-to

וַיִּמָּלֵט בֵּן־ אֶחָד לַאֲחִימֶלֶךְ בֶּן־ אֲחִטוּב וּשְׁמוֹ
and-name-of-him Ahitub son-of of-Ahimelech one son but-he-escaped (20)

אֶבְיָתָר וַיִּבְרַח אַחֲרֵי דָוִד׃ וַיַּגֵּד אֶבְיָתָר לְדָוִד כִּי
that to-David Abiathar and-he-told (21) David after and-he-fled Abiathar

הָרַג שָׁאוּל אֵת כֹּהֲנֵי יְהוָה׃ וַיֹּאמֶר דָּוִד לְאֶבְיָתָר
to-Abiathar David then-he-said (22) Yahweh priests-of *** Saul he-killed

יָדַעְתִּי בַּיּוֹם הַהוּא כִּי־ שָׁם °דֹּויֵג הָאֲדֹמִי כִּי־ הַגֵּד
to-tell that the-Edomite Doeg there when the-that on-the-day I-knew

יַגִּיד לְשָׁאוּל אָנֹכִי סַבֹּתִי בְּכָל־ נֶפֶשׁ בֵּית
family-of life-of for-every-of I-am-responsible I to-Saul he-would-tell

אָבִיךָ׃ שְׁבָה אִתִּי אַל־ תִּירָא כִּי אֲשֶׁר־ יְבַקֵּשׁ אֶת־
*** he-seeks who for you-be-afraid not with-me stay! (23) father-of-you

נַפְשִׁי יְבַקֵּשׁ אֶת־ נַפְשֶׁךָ כִּי־ מִשְׁמֶרֶת אַתָּה עִמָּדִי׃
with-me you safe indeed life-of-you *** he-seeks life-of-me

וַיַּגִּדוּ לְדָוִד לֵאמֹר הִנֵּה פְלִשְׁתִּים נִלְחָמִים
ones-fighting Philistines look! to-say to-David when-they-told (23:1)

16 But the king said, "You will surely die, Ahimelech, you and your father's whole family."

17 Then the king ordered the guards at his side: "Turn and kill the priests of the LORD, because they too have sided with David. They knew he was fleeing, yet they did not tell me."

But the king's officials were not willing to raise a hand to strike the priests of the LORD.

18 The king then ordered Doeg, "You turn and strike down the priests." So Doeg the Edomite turned and struck them down. That day he killed eighty-five men who wore the linen ephod. 19 He also put to the sword Nob, the town of the priests, with its men and women, its children and infants, and its cattle, donkeys and sheep.

20 But Abiathar, a son of Ahimelech son of Ahitub, escaped and fled to join David. 21 He told David that Saul had killed the priests of the LORD. 22 Then David said to Abiathar: "That day, when Doeg the Edomite was there, I knew he would be sure to tell Saul. I am responsible for the death of your father's whole family. 23 Stay with me; don't be afraid; the man who is seeking your life is seeking mine also. You will be safe with me."

*David Saves Keilah*

23 When David was told, "Look, the Philistines

°17 ק אזני
°18a ק לדואג
°18b ק דואג
°22 ק דואג

בִּקְעִילָה וְהֵמָּה שֹׁסִים אֶת־ הַגֳּרָנוֹת׃

the-threshing-floors *** ones-looting and-they against-Keilah

וַיִּשְׁאַל דָּוִד בַּיהוָה לֵאמֹר הַאֵלֵךְ וְהִכֵּיתִי

and-shall-I-attack shall-I-go? to-say of-Yahweh David and-he-inquired (2)

בַּפְּלִשְׁתִּים הָאֵלֶּה וַיֹּאמֶר יְהוָה אֶל־ דָּוִד לֵךְ

go! David to Yahweh and-he-answered the-these against-the-Philistines

וְהִכִּיתָ בַפְּלִשְׁתִּים וְהוֹשַׁעְתָּ אֶת־קְעִילָה׃ וַיֹּאמְרוּ

but-they-said (3) Keilah *** and-you-save against-the-Philistines and-you-attack

אַנְשֵׁי דָוִד אֵלָיו הִנֵּה אֲנַחְנוּ פֹה בִּיהוּדָה יְרֵאִים וְאַף כִּי־

if and-more ones-being-afraid in-Judah here we see! to-him David men-of

נֵלֵךְ קְעִלָה אֶל־ מַעַרְכוֹת פְּלִשְׁתִּים׃ וַיּוֹסֶף עוֹד דָּוִד

David again and-he-repeated (4) Philistines forces-of against Keilah we-go

לִשְׁאֹל בַּיהוָה וַיַּעֲנֵהוּ יְהוָה וַיֹּאמֶר קוּם רֵד

go-down! rise! and-he-said Yahweh and-he-answered-him of-Yahweh to-inquire

קְעִילָה כִּי־ אֲנִי נֹתֵן אֶת־ פְּלִשְׁתִּים בְּיָדֶךָ׃ וַיֵּלֶךְ דָּוִד

David so-he-went (5) into-hand-of-you Philistines *** giving I for Keilah

וַאֲנָשָׁו קְעִילָה וַיִּלָּחֶם בַּפְּלִשְׁתִּים וַיִּנְהַג

and-he-carried-off against-the-Philistines and-he-fought Keilah and-men-of-him

אֶת־ מִקְנֵיהֶם וַיַּךְ בָּהֶם מַכָּה גְדוֹלָה וַיֹּשַׁע

and-he-saved heavy loss on-them and-he-inflicted livestocks-of-them ***

דָּוִד אֵת יֹשְׁבֵי קְעִילָה׃ וַיְהִי בִּבְרֹחַ אֶבְיָתָר בֶּן־

son-of Abiathar when-to-flee now-he-was (6) Keilah ones-living-of *** David

אֲחִימֶלֶךְ אֶל־ דָּוִד קְעִילָה אֵפוֹד יָרַד בְּיָדוֹ׃

in-hand-of-him he-brought-down ephod Keilah David to Ahimelech

וַיֻּגַּד לְשָׁאוּל כִּי־ בָא דָוִד קְעִילָה וַיֹּאמֶר שָׁאוּל

Saul and-he-said Keilah David he-went that to-Saul and-he-was-told (7)

נִכַּר אֹתוֹ אֱלֹהִים בְּיָדִי כִּי נִסְגַּר לָבוֹא בְּעִיר

into-town to-enter he-imprisoned-himself for into-hand-of-me God him he-gave

דְּלָתַיִם וּבְרִיחַ׃ וַיְשַׁמַּע שָׁאוּל אֶת־ כָּל־ הָעָם לַמִּלְחָמָה

for-the-battle the-force all-of *** Saul and-he-called-up (8) and-bar gates

לָרֶדֶת קְעִילָה לָצוּר אֶל־ דָּוִד וְאֶל־ אֲנָשָׁיו׃

men-of-him and-against David against to-besiege Keilah to-go-down

וַיֵּדַע דָּוִד כִּי עָלָיו שָׁאוּל מַחֲרִישׁ הָרָעָה וַיֹּאמֶר

then-he-said the-harm plotting Saul against-him that David when-he-learned (9)

אֶל־אֶבְיָתָר הַכֹּהֵן הַגִּישָׁה הָאֵפוֹד׃ וַיֹּאמֶר דָּוִד יְהוָה אֱלֹהֵי

God-of Yahweh David and-he-said (10) the-ephod bring! the-priest Abiathar to

יִשְׂרָאֵל שָׁמֹעַ שָׁמַע עַבְדְּךָ כִּי־ מְבַקֵּשׁ שָׁאוּל לָבוֹא אֶל־קְעִילָה

Keilah to to-come Saul planning that servant-of-you he-heard to-hear Israel

are fighting against Keilah
and are looting the threshing
floors," [2]he inquired of the
LORD, saying, "Shall I go and
attack these Philistines?"
The LORD answered him,
"Go, attack the Philistines and
save Keilah."
[3]But David's men said to
him, "Here in Judah we are
afraid. How much more, then,
if we go to Keilah against the
Philistine forces!"
[4]Once again David inquired
of the LORD, and the LORD answered him, "Go down to Keilah, for I am going to give the
Philistines into your hand."
[5]So David and his men went
to Keilah, fought the Philistines and carried off their livestock. He inflicted heavy
losses on the Philistines and
saved the people of Keilah.
[6](Now Abiathar son of Ahimelech had brought the ephod
down with him when he fled
to David at Keilah.)

*Saul Pursues David*

[7]Saul was told that David
had gone to Keilah, and he
said, "God has handed him
over to me, for David has imprisoned himself by entering
a town with gates and bars."
[8]And Saul called up all his
forces for battle, to go down to
Keilah to besiege David and
his men.
[9]When David learned that
Saul was plotting against him,
he said to Abiathar the priest,
"Bring the ephod." [10]David
said, "O LORD, God of Israel,
your servant has heard
definitely that Saul plans to
come to Keilah and destroy

°5 ק ואנשיו

לְשַׁחֵת לָעִיר בַּעֲבוּרִי׃ הֲיַסְגִּרֻנִי בַעֲלֵי

citizens-of will-they-surrender-me? (11) on-account-of-me to-the-city to-destroy

קְעִילָה בְיָדוֹ הֲיֵרֵד שָׁאוּל כַּאֲשֶׁר שָׁמַע עַבְדֶּךָ

servant-of-you he-heard just-as Saul will-he-come-down? into-hand-of-him Keilah

יְהוָה אֱלֹהֵי יִשְׂרָאֵל הַגֶּד־ נָא לְעַבְדֶּךָ וַיֹּאמֶר יְהוָה

Yahweh and-he-said to-servant-of-you now! tell! Israel God-of Yahweh

יֵרֵד׃ וַיֹּאמֶר דָּוִד הֲיַסְגִּרוּ בַּעֲלֵי

citizens-of will-they-surrender? David and-he-asked (12) he-will-come-down

קְעִילָה אֹתִי וְאֶת־ אֲנָשַׁי בְּיַד־ שָׁאוּל וַיֹּאמֶר יְהוָה יַסְגִּירוּ׃

they-will-surrender Yahweh and-he-said Saul into-hand-of men-of-me and me Keilah

וַיָּקָם דָּוִד וַאֲנָשָׁיו כְּשֵׁשׁ־ מֵאוֹת אִישׁ וַיֵּצְאוּ

and-they-left man hundreds about-six and-men-of-him David so-he-rose (13)

מִקְּעִלָה וַיִּתְהַלְּכוּ בַּאֲשֶׁר יִתְהַלָּכוּ וּלְשָׁאוּל הֻגַּד כִּי־

that he-was-told when-to-Saul they-moved to-where and-they-moved from-Keilah

נִמְלַט דָּוִד מִקְּעִילָה וַיֶּחְדַּל לָצֵאת׃ וַיֵּשֶׁב דָּוִד

David and-he-stayed (14) to-go then-he-did-not from-Keilah David he-escaped

בַּמִּדְבָּר בַּמְּצָדוֹת וַיֵּשֶׁב בָּהָר בְּמִדְבַּר־ זִיף

Ziph in-Desert-of in-the-hill and-he-stayed in-the-strongholds in-the-desert

וַיְבַקְשֵׁהוּ שָׁאוּל כָּל־ הַיָּמִים וְלֹא־ נְתָנוֹ אֱלֹהִים

God he-gave-him but-not the-days all-of Saul and-he-searched-for-him

בְּיָדוֹ׃ וַיַּרְא דָּוִד* כִּי־ יָצָא שָׁאוּל לְבַקֵּשׁ

to-take Saul he-came-out that David and-he-learned (15) into-hand-of-him

אֶת־ נַפְשׁוֹ וְדָוִד בְּמִדְבַּר־ זִיף בַּחֹרְשָׁה׃ וַיָּקָם

and-he-rose (16) at-the-Horesh Ziph in-Desert-of while-David life-of-him ***

יְהוֹנָתָן בֶּן־ שָׁאוּל וַיֵּלֶךְ אֶל־ דָּוִד חֹרְשָׁה וַיְחַזֵּק אֶת־

*** and-he-strengthened at-Horesh David to and-he-went Saul son-of Jonathan

יָדוֹ בֵּאלֹהִים׃ וַיֹּאמֶר אֵלָיו אַל־ תִּירָא כִּי לֹא

not for you-be-afraid not to-him and-he-said (17) in-God hand-of-him

תִמְצָאֲךָ יַד שָׁאוּל אָבִי וְאַתָּה תִּמְלֹךְ עַל־

over you-will-be-king and-you father-of-me Saul hand-of she-will-find-you

יִשְׂרָאֵל וְאָנֹכִי אֶהְיֶה־ לְּךָ לְמִשְׁנֶה וְגַם־ שָׁאוּל אָבִי יֹדֵעַ

knowing father-of-me Saul and-even as-second to-you I-will-be and-I Israel

כֵּן׃ וַיִּכְרְתוּ שְׁנֵיהֶם בְּרִית לִפְנֵי יְהוָה וַיֵּשֶׁב

and-he-remained Yahweh before covenant two-of-them and-they-made (18) this

דָּוִד בַּחֹרְשָׁה וִיהוֹנָתָן הָלַךְ לְבֵיתוֹ׃ וַיַּעֲלוּ

and-they-went-up (19) to-home-of-him he-went but-Jonathan at-the-Horesh David

זִפִים אֶל־ שָׁאוּל הַגִּבְעָתָה לֵאמֹר הֲלוֹא דָוִד מִסְתַּתֵּר עִמָּנוּ

among-us hiding David not? to-say at-the-Gibeah Saul to Ziphites

the town on account of me.
[11]Will the citizens of Keilah surrender me to him? Will Saul come down, as your servant has heard? O LORD, God of Israel, tell your servant."

And the LORD said, "He will."

[12]Again David asked, "Will the citizens of Keilah surrender me and my men to Saul?"

And the LORD said, "They will."

[13]So David and his men, about six hundred in number, left Keilah and kept moving from place to place. When Saul was told that David had escaped from Keilah, he did not go there.

[14]David stayed in the desert strongholds and in the hills of the Desert of Ziph. Day after day Saul searched for him, but God did not give David into his hands.

[15]While David was at Horesh in the Desert of Ziph, he learned that Saul had come out to take his life. [16]And Saul's son Jonathan went to David at Horesh and helped him find strength in God. [17]"Don't be afraid," he said. "My father Saul will not lay a hand on you. You will be king over Israel, and I will be second to you. Even my father Saul knows this." [18]The two of them made a covenant before the LORD. Then Jonathan went home, but David remained at Horesh.

[19]The Ziphites went up to Saul at Gibeah and said, "Is not David hiding among us in

*15 Most mss have dagesh in the first *daleth* (ד׳).

בִּמְצָדוֹת בַּחֹרְשָׁה בְּגִבְעַת הַחֲכִילָה אֲשֶׁר מִימִין
to-south-of that the-Hakilah on-hill-of at-the-Horesh in-the-strongholds

הַיְשִׁימוֹן׃ וְעַתָּה לְכָל־ אַוַּת נַפְשְׁךָ הַמֶּלֶךְ
the-king self-of-you pleasure-of as-any-of and-now (20) the-Jeshimon

לָרֶדֶת רֵד וְלָנוּ הַסְגִּירוֹ בְּיַד הַמֶּלֶךְ׃
the-king into-hand-of to-turn-over-him and-to-us come-down! to-come-down

וַיֹּאמֶר שָׁאוּל בְּרוּכִים אַתֶּם לַיהוָה כִּי חֲמַלְתֶּם
you-are-concerned for by-Yahweh you ones-being-blessed Saul and-he-replied (21)

עָלָי׃ לְכוּ־ נָא הָכִינוּ עוֹד וּדְעוּ וּרְאוּ אֶת־ מְקוֹמוֹ
place-of-him *** and-see! and-find-out! further prepare! now! go! (22) for-me

אֲשֶׁר תִּהְיֶה רַגְלוֹ מִי רָאָהוּ שָׁם כִּי אָמַר אֵלַי
to-me he-said for there he-saw-him who foot-of-him she-goes where

עָרוֹם יַעְרִם הוּא׃ וּרְאוּ וּדְעוּ מִכֹּל
about-all-of and-find-out! and-see! (23) he he-is-crafty to-be-crafty

הַמַּחֲבֹאִים אֲשֶׁר יִתְחַבֵּא שָׁם וְשַׁבְתֶּם אֵלַי אֶל־
with to-me and-you-come-back there he-hides where the-hiding-places

נָכוֹן וְהָלַכְתִּי אִתְּכֶם וְהָיָה אִם־ יֶשְׁנוֹ
there-is-him if and-he-will-be with-you then-I-will-go being-definite

בָאָרֶץ וְחִפַּשְׂתִּי אֹתוֹ בְּכֹל אַלְפֵי יְהוּדָה׃
Judah clans-of among-all-of him then-I-will-track-down in-the-area

וַיָּקוּמוּ וַיֵּלְכוּ זִיפָה לִפְנֵי שָׁאוּל וְדָוִד
now-David Saul ahead-of to-Ziph and-they-went so-they-set-out (24)

וַאֲנָשָׁיו בְּמִדְבַּר מָעוֹן בָּעֲרָבָה אֶל יְמִין הַיְשִׁימוֹן׃
the-Jeshimon south-of to in-the-Arabah Maon in-Desert-of and-men-of-him

וַיֵּלֶךְ שָׁאוּל וַאֲנָשָׁיו לְבַקֵּשׁ וַיַּגִּדוּ לְדָוִד
to-David when-they-told to-search and-men-of-him Saul and-he-began (25)

וַיֵּרֶד הַסֶּלַע וַיֵּשֶׁב בְּמִדְבַּר מָעוֹן וַיִּשְׁמַע
when-he-heard Maon in-Desert-of and-he-stayed the-rock then-he-went-down

שָׁאוּל וַיִּרְדֹּף אַחֲרֵי־ דָוִד מִדְבַּר מָעוֹן׃ וַיֵּלֶךְ שָׁאוּל
Saul and-he-went (26) Maon into-Desert-of David after then-he-pursued Saul

מִצַּד הָהָר מִזֶּה וְדָוִד וַאֲנָשָׁיו מִצַּד
along-side-of and-men-of-him and-David on-one the-mountain along-side-of

הָהָר מִזֶּה וַיְהִי דָוִד נֶחְפָּז לָלֶכֶת מִפְּנֵי שָׁאוּל
Saul from-before to-go hurrying David and-he-was on-other the-mountain

וְשָׁאוּל וַאֲנָשָׁיו עֹטְרִים אֶל־ דָּוִד וְאֶל־ אֲנָשָׁיו
men-of-him and-on David on ones-closing-in and-men-of-him and-Saul

לְתָפְשָׂם׃ וּמַלְאָךְ בָּא אֶל־ שָׁאוּל לֵאמֹר מַהֲרָה וְלֵכָה
and-come! be-quick! to-say Saul to he-came and-messenger (27) to-capture-them

the strongholds at Horesh, on the hill of Hakilah, south of Jeshimon? [20]Now, O king, come down whenever it pleases you to do so, and we will be responsible for handing him over to the king."

[21]Saul replied, "The LORD bless you for your concern for me. [22]Go and make further preparation. Find out where David usually goes and who has seen him there. They tell me he is very crafty. [23]Find out about all the hiding places he uses and come back to me with definite information.[f] Then I will go with you; if he is in the area, I will track him down among all the clans of Judah."

[24]So they set out and went to Ziph ahead of Saul. Now David and his men were in the Desert of Maon, in the Arabah south of Jeshimon. [25]Saul and his men began the search, and when David was told about it, he went down to the rock and stayed in the Desert of Maon. When Saul heard this, he went into the Desert of Maon in pursuit of David.

[26]Saul was going along one side of the mountain, and David and his men were on the other side, hurrying to get away from Saul. As Saul and his forces were closing in on David and his men to capture them, [27]a messenger came to Saul, saying, "Come quickly!

[f]23 Or *me at Nacon*

כִּי־ פָשְׁטוּ פְלִשְׁתִּים עַל־ הָאָרֶץ׃ וַיָּשָׁב שָׁאוּל
Saul then-he-broke-off (28) the-land over Philistines they-raid for

מִרְדֹף אַחֲרֵי דָוִד וַיֵּלֶךְ לִקְרַאת פְּלִשְׁתִּים עַל־ כֵּן קָרְאוּ
they-call this for Philistines to-meet and-he-went David after from-to-pursue

לַמָּקוֹם הַהוּא סֶלַע הַמַּחְלְקוֹת׃ וַיַּעַל דָּוִד מִשָּׁם
from-there David and-he-went-up *(24:1) Hammahlekoth Sela the-this to-the-place

וַיֵּשֶׁב בִּמְצָדוֹת עֵין־ גֶּדִי׃ וַיְהִי כַּאֲשֶׁר שָׁב
he-returned just-as and-he-was (2) Gedi En in-strongholds-of and-he-lived

שָׁאוּל מֵאַחֲרֵי פְּלִשְׁתִּים וַיַּגִּדוּ לוֹ לֵאמֹר הִנֵּה דָוִד
David see! to-say to-him then-they-told Philistines from-after Saul

בְּמִדְבַּר עֵין גֶּדִי׃ וַיִּקַּח שָׁאוּל שְׁלֹשֶׁת אֲלָפִים אִישׁ בָּחוּר
being-chosen man thousands three-of Saul so-he-took (3) Gedi En in-Desert-of

מִכָּל־ יִשְׂרָאֵל וַיֵּלֶךְ לְבַקֵּשׁ אֶת־ דָּוִד וַאֲנָשָׁיו
and-men-of-him David *** to-look-for and-he-set-out Israel from-all-of

עַל־ פְּנֵי צוּרֵי הַיְּעֵלִים׃ וַיָּבֹא אֶל־ גִּדְרוֹת הַצֹּאן
the-sheep pens-of to and-he-came (4) the-Wild-Goats Crags-of faces-of near

עַל־ הַדֶּרֶךְ וְשָׁם מְעָרָה וַיָּבֹא שָׁאוּל לְהָסֵךְ אֶת־ רַגְלָיו
feet-of-him *** to-cover Saul and-he-went-in cave and-there the-way along

וְדָוִד וַאֲנָשָׁיו בְּיַרְכְּתֵי הַמְּעָרָה יֹשְׁבִים׃
ones-staying the-cave in-back-parts-of and-men-of-him and-David

וַיֹּאמְרוּ אַנְשֵׁי דָוִד אֵלָיו הִנֵּה הַיּוֹם אֲשֶׁר־ אָמַר יְהוָה
Yahweh he-said that the-day see! to-him David men-of and-they-said (5)

אֵלֶיךָ הִנֵּה אָנֹכִי נֹתֵן אֶת־ אֹיִבְךָ בְּיָדֶךָ וְעָשִׂיתָ
and-you-deal into-hand-of-you being-enemy-of-you *** giving I see! to-you

לּוֹ כַּאֲשֶׁר יִטַב בְּעֵינֶיךָ וַיָּקָם דָּוִד וַיִּכְרֹת
and-he-cut David then-he-crept-up in-eyes-of-you he-is-good just-as with-him

אֶת־ כְּנַף־ הַמְּעִיל אֲשֶׁר־לְשָׁאוּל בַּלָּט׃ וַיְהִי אַחֲרֵי־ כֵן
this after and-he-was (6) unnoticed to-Saul that the-robe corner-of ***

וַיַּךְ לֵב־ דָּוִד אֹתוֹ עַל אֲשֶׁר כָּרַת אֶת־ כָּנָף אֲשֶׁר
that corner *** he-cut-off when for him David conscience-of then-he-struck

לְשָׁאוּל׃ וַיֹּאמֶר לַאֲנָשָׁיו חָלִילָה לִּי מֵיְהוָה אִם־
that by-Yahweh from-me far-be-it! to-men-of-him and-he-said (7) to-Saul

אֶעֱשֶׂה אֶת־ הַדָּבָר הַזֶּה לַאדֹנִי לִמְשִׁיחַ יְהוָה
Yahweh to-anointed-of to-master-of-me the-this the-thing *** I-should-do

לִשְׁלֹחַ יָדִי בּוֹ כִּי־ מְשִׁיחַ יְהוָה הוּא׃ וַיְשַׁסַּע
and-he-rebuked (8) he Yahweh anointed-of for against-him hand-of-me to-lift

דָּוִד אֶת־ אֲנָשָׁיו בַּדְּבָרִים וְלֹא נְתָנָם לָקוּם אֶל־
against to-attack he-allowed-them and-not with-the-words men-of-him *** David

The Philistines are raiding the land." [28]Then Saul broke off his pursuit of David and went to meet the Philistines. That is why they call this place Sela Hammahlekoth.[g] [29]And David went up from there and lived in the strongholds of En Gedi.

*David Spares Saul's Life*

**24** After Saul returned from pursuing the Philistines, he was told, "David is in the Desert of En Gedi." [2]So Saul took three thousand chosen men from all Israel and set out to look for David and his men near the Crags of the Wild Goats.

[3]He came to the sheep pens along the way; a cave was there, and Saul went in to relieve himself. David and his men were far back in the cave. [4]The men said, "This is the very day the LORD spoke of when he said to you, 'I will give your enemy into your hands for you to deal with as you wish.' " Then David crept up unnoticed and cut off a corner of Saul's robe.

[5]Afterward, David was conscience-stricken for having cut off a corner of his robe. [6]He said to his men, "The LORD forbid that I should do such a thing to my master, the LORD's anointed, or lift my hand against him; for he is the anointed of the LORD." [7]With these words David rebuked his men and did not allow

*g28 Sela Hammahlekoth* means *rock of parting.*

***1* The Hebrew enumeration of chapter 24 begins with verse 29 of chapter 23 in the English; thus there is a one-verse discrepancy throughout chapter 24.**

ק איבך 5

שָׁא֑וּל וְשָׁא֞וּל קָ֥ם מֵהַמְּעָרָ֖ה וַיֵּ֥לֶךְ בַּדָּֽרֶךְ׃ וַיָּ֨קָם
then-he-rose (9) on-the-way and-he-went from-the-cave he-left and-Saul Saul

דָּוִ֜ד אַחֲרֵי־ כֵ֗ן וַיֵּצֵא֙ מִן־° הַמְּעָרָ֔ה וַיִּקְרָ֥א אַחֲרֵי־שָׁא֖וּל
Saul after and-he-called the-cave from and-he-went-out this after David

לֵאמֹ֑ר אֲדֹנִ֣י הַמֶּ֑לֶךְ וַיַּבֵּ֤ט שָׁאוּל֙ אַחֲרָ֔יו וַיִּקֹּ֨ד דָּוִ֥ד
David then-he-bowed behind-him Saul when-he-looked the-king lord-of-me to-say

אַפַּ֛יִם אַ֖רְצָה וַיִּשְׁתָּֽחוּ׃ וַיֹּ֤אמֶר דָּוִד֙ לְשָׁא֔וּל לָ֣מָּה
why? to-Saul David and-he-said (10) and-he-prostrated-himself to-ground faces

תִשְׁמַ֛ע אֶת־ דִּבְרֵ֥י אָדָ֖ם לֵאמֹ֑ר הִנֵּ֣ה דָוִ֔ד מְבַקֵּ֖שׁ רָעָתֶֽךָ׃ הִנֵּ֡ה
see! (11) harm-of-you seeking David see! to-say man words-of *** you-listen

הַיּ֨וֹם הַזֶּ֜ה רָא֣וּ עֵינֶ֗יךָ אֵ֣ת אֲשֶׁר־ נְתָֽנְךָ֩ יְהוָ֨ה ׀ הַיּ֤וֹם ׀
the-day Yahweh he-delivered-you how *** eyes-of-you they-saw the-this the-day

בְּיָדִי֙ בַּמְּעָרָ֔ה וְאָמַ֥ר לַהֲרָגְךָ֖ וַתָּ֣חָס עָלֶ֑יךָ
to-you †but-she-spared to-kill-you and-he-urged in-the-cave into-hand-of-me

וָאֹמַ֗ר לֹֽא־ אֶשְׁלַ֤ח יָדִי֙ בַּֽאדֹנִ֔י כִּֽי־ מְשִׁ֥יחַ
anointed-of for against-master-of-me hand-of-me I-will-lift not and-I-said

יְהוָ֖ה הֽוּא׃ וְאָבִ֣י רְאֵ֔ה גַּ֗ם רְאֵ֛ה אֶת־ כְּנַ֥ף מְעִֽילְךָ֖
robe-of-you piece-of *** look-at! indeed look-at! now-father-of-me (12) he Yahweh

בְּיָדִ֑י כִּ֡י בְּכָרְתִי֩ אֶת־ כְּנַ֨ף מְעִֽילְךָ֜ וְלֹ֣א הֲרַגְתִּ֗יךָ
I-killed-you but-not robe-of-you corner-of *** to-cut-off-me for in-hand-of-me

דַּ֣ע וּרְאֵ֡ה כִּי֩ אֵ֨ין בְּיָדִ֜י רָעָ֣ה וָפֶ֗שַׁע
or-rebellion wrong in-hand-of-me not that and-recognize! understand!

וְלֹא־ חָטָ֣אתִי לָ֔ךְ וְאַתָּ֛ה צֹדֶ֥ה אֶת־ נַפְשִׁ֖י לְקַחְתָּֽהּ׃
to-take-her life-of-me *** hunting but-you against-you I-wronged and-not

יִשְׁפֹּ֤ט יְהוָה֙ בֵּינִ֣י וּבֵינֶ֔ךָ וּנְקָמַ֥נִי
and-may-he-avenge-me and-between-you between-me Yahweh may-he-judge (13)

יְהוָ֖ה מִמֶּ֑ךָּ וְיָדִ֖י לֹ֥א תִֽהְיֶה־ בָּֽךְ׃ כַּאֲשֶׁ֣ר
just-as (14) against-you she-will-be not but-hand-of-me from-you Yahweh

יֹאמַ֗ר מְשַׁל֙ הַקַּדְמֹנִ֔י מֵרְשָׁעִ֖ים יֵ֣צֵא רֶ֑שַׁע וְיָדִ֖י
so-hand-of-me evil-deed he-comes from-evildoers the-old saying-of she-says

לֹ֥א תִֽהְיֶה־ בָּֽךְ׃ אַחֲרֵ֨י מִ֤י יָצָא֙ מֶ֣לֶךְ יִשְׂרָאֵ֔ל
Israel king-of he-came-out whom? against (15) against-you she-will-be not

אַחֲרֵ֥י מִ֖י אַתָּ֣ה רֹדֵ֑ף אַֽחֲרֵי֙ כֶּ֣לֶב מֵ֔ת אַחֲרֵ֖י פַּרְעֹ֥שׁ אֶחָֽד׃
one flea after being-dead dog after pursuing you whom? after

וְהָיָ֤ה יְהוָה֙ לְדַיָּ֔ן וְשָׁפַ֖ט בֵּינִ֣י וּבֵינֶ֑ךָ
and-between-you between-me and-may-he-decide as-judge Yahweh now-may-he-be (16)

וְיֵ֙רֶא֙ וְיָרֵ֣ב אֶת־ רִיבִ֔י וְיִשְׁפְּטֵ֖נִי
and-may-he-vindicate-me cause-of-me *** and-may-he-uphold and-may-he-consider

them to attack Saul. And Saul left the cave and went his way.

[8]Then David went out of the cave and called out to Saul, "My lord the king!" When Saul looked behind him, David bowed down and prostrated himself with his face to the ground. [9]He said to Saul, "Why do you listen when men say, 'David is bent on harming you'? [10]This day you have seen with your own eyes how the LORD delivered you into my hands in the cave. Some urged me to kill you, but I spared you; I said, 'I will not lift my hand against my master, because he is the LORD's anointed.' [11]See, my father, look at this piece of your robe in my hand! I cut off the corner of your robe but did not kill you. Now understand and recognize that I am not guilty of wrongdoing or rebellion. I have not wronged you, but you are hunting me down to take my life. [12]May the LORD judge between you and me. And may the LORD avenge the wrongs you have done to me, but my hand will not touch you. [13]As the old saying goes, 'From evildoers come evil deeds,' so my hand will not touch you.

[14]"Against whom has the king of Israel come out? Whom are you pursuing? A dead dog? A flea? [15]May the LORD be our judge and decide between us. May he consider my cause and uphold it; may he vindicate me by delivering

*See the note on page 228.

†*11* The major ancient versions read this as first person, *"but-I-spared"*.

°9 ק מהמערה

מִיָּדֶֽךָ׃ וַיְהִ֣י ׀ כְּכַלּ֣וֹת דָּוִ֗ד לְדַבֵּ֞ר אֶת־הַדְּבָרִ֤ים
the-words *** to-say David when-to-finish and-he-was (17) from-hand-of-you

הָאֵ֙לֶּה֙ אֶל־שָׁא֔וּל וַיֹּ֣אמֶר שָׁא֔וּל הֲקֹלְךָ֥ זֶ֖ה בְּנִ֣י דָוִ֑ד
David son-of-me that voice-of-you? Saul and-he-asked Saul to the-these

וַיִּשָּׂ֥א שָׁא֛וּל קֹל֖וֹ וַיֵּֽבְךְּ׃ וַיֹּ֙אמֶר֙ אֶל־דָּוִ֔ד
David to and-he-said (18) and-he-wept voice-of-him Saul and-he-raised

צַדִּ֥יק אַתָּ֖ה מִמֶּ֑נִּי כִּ֤י אַתָּה֙ גְּמַלְתַּ֣נִי הַטּוֹבָ֔ה וַאֲנִ֖י גְּמַלְתִּ֥יךָ
I-treated-you but-I the-good you-treated-me you for more-than-I you righteous

הָרָעָֽה׃ וְאַ֙תְּ֙ הִגַּ֣דְתָּ הַיּ֔וֹם אֵ֛ת אֲשֶׁר־עָשִׂ֥יתָה אִתִּ֖י טוֹבָ֑ה אֵת֩ אֲשֶׁ֨ר
that *** good to-me you-did that *** the-day you-told and-you (19) the-bad

סִגְּרַ֧נִי יְהוָ֛ה בְּיָדְךָ֖ וְלֹ֥א הֲרַגְתָּֽנִי׃ וְכִֽי־
now-when (20) you-killed-me but-not into-hand-of-you Yahweh he-delivered-me

יִמְצָ֥א אִישׁ֙ אֶת־אֹ֣יְב֔וֹ וְשִׁלְּח֖וֹ בְּדֶ֣רֶךְ טוֹבָ֑ה
unharmed on-way then-does-he-let-go-him being-enemy-of-him *** man he-finds

וַֽיהוָה֙ יְשַׁלֶּמְךָ֣ טוֹבָ֔ה תַּ֚חַת הַיּ֣וֹם הַזֶּ֔ה אֲשֶׁ֥ר עָשִׂ֖יתָה
you-treated how the-this the-day for well may-he-reward-you now-Yahweh

לִֽי׃ וְעַתָּה֙ הִנֵּ֣ה יָדַ֔עְתִּי כִּ֥י מָלֹ֖ךְ תִּמְל֑וֹךְ
you-will-be-king to-be-king that I-know see! and-now (21) to-me

וְקָ֙מָה֙ בְּיָ֣דְךָ֔ מַמְלֶ֖כֶת יִשְׂרָאֵֽל׃ וְעַתָּ֗ה
and-now (22) Israel kingdom-of in-hand-of-you and-she-will-be-established

הִשָּׁ֤בְעָה לִּי֙ בַּֽיהוָ֔ה אִם־תַּכְרִ֥ית אֶת־זַרְעִ֖י אַחֲרָ֑י
after-me descendant-of-me *** you-will-cut-off not by-Yahweh to-me swear!

וְאִם־תַּשְׁמִ֥יד אֶת־שְׁמִ֖י מִבֵּ֥ית אָבִֽי׃
father-of-me from-family-of name-of-me *** you-will-wipe-out and-not

וַיִּשָּׁבַ֥ע דָּוִ֖ד לְשָׁא֑וּל וַיֵּ֤לֶךְ שָׁאוּל֙ אֶל־בֵּית֔וֹ
home-of-him to Saul and-he-returned to-Saul David so-he-gave-oath (23)

וְדָוִד֙ וַאֲנָשָׁ֔יו עָל֖וּ עַל־הַמְּצוּדָֽה׃ וַיָּ֣מָת
now-he-died (25:1) the-stronghold to they-went-up and-men-of-him but-David

שְׁמוּאֵ֔ל וַיִּקָּבְצ֤וּ כָל־יִשְׂרָאֵל֙ וַיִּסְפְּדוּ־ל֔וֹ
for-him and-they-mourned Israel all-of and-they-assembled Samuel

וַיִּקְבְּרֻ֥הוּ בְּבֵית֖וֹ בָּרָמָ֑ה וַיָּ֣קָם דָּוִ֔ד
David then-he-rose in-the-Ramah at-home-of-him and-they-buried-him

וַיֵּ֖רֶד אֶל־מִדְבַּ֥ר פָּארָֽן׃ וְאִ֨ישׁ בְּמָע֜וֹן וּמַעֲשֵׂ֣הוּ
and-property-of-him in-Maon now-man (2) Paran Desert-of to and-he-moved-down

בַכַּרְמֶ֗ל וְהָאִישׁ֙ גָּד֣וֹל מְאֹ֔ד וְל֛וֹ צֹ֥אן שְׁלֹֽשֶׁת־אֲלָפִ֖ים
thousands three-of sheep and-to-him very wealthy and-the-man at-the-Carmel

וְאֶ֣לֶף עִזִּ֑ים וַיְהִ֛י בִּגְזֹ֥ז אֶת־צֹאנ֖וֹ בַּכַּרְמֶֽל׃
in-the-Carmel sheep-of-him *** when-to-shear and-he-was goats and-thousand

me from your hand."
16When David finished saying this, Saul asked, "Is that your voice, David my son?" And he wept aloud. 17"You are more righteous than I," he said. "You have treated me well, but I have treated you badly. 18You have just now told me of the good you did to me; the LORD delivered me into your hands, but you did not kill me. 19When a man finds his enemy, does he let him get away unharmed? May the LORD reward you well for the way you treated me today. 20I know that you will surely be king and that the kingdom of Israel will be established in your hands. 21Now swear to me by the LORD that you will not cut off my descendants or wipe out my name from my father's family."

22So David gave his oath to Saul. Then Saul returned home, but David and his men went up to the stronghold.

*David, Nabal and Abigail*

25 Now Samuel died, and all Israel assembled and mourned for him; and they buried him at his home in Ramah.

Then David moved down into the Desert of Maon.[h] 2A certain man in Maon, who had property there at Carmel, was very wealthy. He had a thousand goats and three thousand sheep, which he was shearing in Carmel. 3His

[h]1 Some Septuagint manuscripts; Hebrew *Paran*

*See the note on page 228.

°19 ק ואתה

וְשֵׁם הָאִישׁ נָבָל וְשֵׁם אִשְׁתּוֹ אֲבִגָיִל וְהָאִשָּׁה

and-the-woman Abigail wife-of-him and-name-of Nabal the-man and-name-of (3)

טֽוֹבַת־ שֶׂכֶל וִיפַת תֹּאַר וְהָאִישׁ קָשֶׁה וְרַע

and-mean-of surly but-the-husband form and-beautiful-of intelligence good-of

מַעֲלָלִים וְהוּא כָלִבּוֹ׃ וַיִּשְׁמַע דָּוִד בַּמִּדְבָּר כִּֽי־ גֹזֵז

shearing that in-the-desert David and-he-heard (4) Calebite and-he dealings

נָבָל אֶת־ צֹאנֽוֹ׃ וַיִּשְׁלַח דָּוִד עֲשָׂרָה נְעָרִים וַיֹּאמֶר דָּוִד

David and-he-said young-men ten David so-he-sent (5) sheep-of-him *** Nabal

לַנְּעָרִים עֲלוּ כַרְמֶלָה וּבָאתֶם אֶל־ נָבָל וּשְׁאֶלְתֶּם־ לוֹ

to-him and-you-greet Nabal to and-you-go to-Carmel go-up! to-the-men

בִשְׁמִי לְשָׁלֽוֹם׃ וַאֲמַרְתֶּם כֹּה לֶחָי וְאַתָּה שָׁלוֹם

health and-you to-life this and-you-say (6) for-peace in-name-of-me

וּבֵיתְךָ שָׁלוֹם וְכֹל אֲשֶׁר־ לְךָ שָׁלֽוֹם׃ וְעַתָּה שָׁמַעְתִּי

I-hear and-now (7) health to-you that and-all health and-household-of-you

כִּי גֹזְזִים לָךְ עַתָּה הָרֹעִים אֲשֶׁר־ לְךָ הָיוּ עִמָּנוּ

with-us they-were to-you who the-ones-herding when to-you ones-shearing that

לֹא הֶכְלַמְנוּם וְלֹא־ נִפְקַד לָהֶם מְאוּמָה כָּל־ יְמֵי

days-of all-of anything of-them he-was-missed and-not we-mistreated-them not

הֱיוֹתָם בַּכַּרְמֶֽל׃ שְׁאַל אֶת־ נְעָרֶיךָ וְיַגִּידוּ

and-they-will-tell servants-of-you *** ask! (8) at-the-Carmel to-be-them

לָךְ וְיִמְצְאוּ הַנְּעָרִים חֵן בְּעֵינֶיךָ כִּֽי־ עַל־ יוֹם

day on since in-eyes-of-you favor the-young-men now-may-they-find to-you

טוֹב בָּנוּ תְּנָה־ נָּא אֵת אֲשֶׁר תִּמְצָא יָדְךָ לַעֲבָדֶיךָ

to-servants-of-you hand-of-you she-finds what *** now! give! to-us festive

וּלְבִנְךָ לְדָוִֽד׃ וַיָּבֹאוּ נַעֲרֵי דָוִד וַיְדַבְּרוּ

then-they-spoke David men-of when-they-arrived (9) to-David and-to-son-of-you

אֶל־נָבָל כְּכָל־ הַדְּבָרִים הָאֵלֶּה בְּשֵׁם דָּוִד וַיָּנֽוּחוּ׃

and-they-waited David in-name-of the-these the-messages as-all-of Nabal to

וַיַּעַן נָבָל אֶת־ עַבְדֵי דָוִד וַיֹּאמֶר מִי דָוִד

David who? and-he-said David servants-of *** Nabal and-he-answered (10)

וּמִי בֶן־ יִשָׁי הַיּוֹם רַבּוּ עֲבָדִים הַמִּתְפָּרְצִים

the-ones-breaking-away servants they-are-many the-day Jesse son-of and-who?

אִישׁ מִפְּנֵי אֲדֹנָֽיו׃ וְלָקַחְתִּי אֶת־ לַחְמִי וְאֶת־

and bread-of-me *** now-should-I-take (11) masters-of-him from-before each

מֵימַי וְאֵת טִבְחָתִי אֲשֶׁר טָבַחְתִּי לְגֹזְזָי

for-ones-shearing-of-me I-slaughtered that meat-of-me and waters-of-me

וְנָתַתִּי לַאֲנָשִׁים אֲשֶׁר לֹא יָדַעְתִּי אֵי מִזֶּה הֵמָּה׃ וַיַּהַפְכוּ

so-they-turned (12) they from-there where I-know not whom to-men and-I-give

name was Nabal and his wife's name was Abigail. She was an intelligent and beautiful woman, but her husband, a Calebite, was surly and mean in his dealings.

[4]While David was in the desert, he heard that Nabal was shearing sheep. [5]So he sent ten young men and said to them, "Go up to Nabal at Carmel and greet him in my name. [6]Say to him: 'Long life to you! Good health to you and your household! And good health to all that is yours!

[7]"'Now I hear that it is sheep-shearing time. When your shepherds were with us, we did not mistreat them, and the whole time they were at Carmel nothing of theirs was missing. [8]Ask your own servants and they will tell you. Therefore be favorable toward my young men, since we come at a festive time. Please give your servants and your son David whatever you can find for them.'"

[9]When David's men arrived, they gave Nabal this message in David's name. Then they waited.

[10]Nabal answered David's servants, "Who is this David? Who is this son of Jesse? Many servants are breaking away from their masters these days. [11]Why should I take my bread and water, and the meat I have slaughtered for my shearers, and give it to men coming from who knows where?"

°3 ק כלבי

נַעֲרֵי־ דָוִד לְדַרְכָּם וַיָּשֻׁבוּ וַיָּבֹאוּ וַיַּגִּדוּ
then-they-told when-they-arrived and-they-went-back to-way-of-them David men-of

לוֹ כְּכֹל הַדְּבָרִים הָאֵלֶּה׃ וַיֹּאמֶר דָּוִד לַאֲנָשָׁיו
to-men-of-him David and-he-said (13) the-these the-words as-all-of to-him

חִגְרוּ ׀ אִישׁ אֶת־ חַרְבּוֹ וַיַּחְגְּרוּ אִישׁ אֶת־ חַרְבּוֹ
sword-of-him *** each so-they-put-on sword-of-him *** each put-on!

וַיַּחְגֹּר גַּם־ דָּוִד אֶת־ חַרְבּוֹ וַיַּעֲלוּ ׀ אַחֲרֵי דָוִד
David with and-they-went-up sword-of-him *** David also and-he-put-on

כְּאַרְבַּע מֵאוֹת אִישׁ וּמָאתַיִם יָשְׁבוּ עַל־ הַכֵּלִים׃
the-supplies with they-stayed and-two-hundreds man hundreds about-four

וְלַאֲבִיגַיִל אֵשֶׁת נָבָל הִגִּיד נַעַר־ אֶחָד מֵהַנְּעָרִים לֵאמֹר
to-say from-servants one servant he-told Nabal wife-of now-to-Abigail (14)

הִנֵּה שָׁלַח דָּוִד מַלְאָכִים ׀ מֵהַמִּדְבָּר לְבָרֵךְ אֶת־ אֲדֹנֵינוּ
masters-of-us *** to-greet from-the-desert messengers David he-sent see!

וַיָּעַט בָּהֶם׃ וְהָאֲנָשִׁים טֹבִים לָנוּ מְאֹד וְלֹא
and-not very to-us ones-good yet-the-men (15) at-them but-he-insulted

הָכְלַמְנוּ וְלֹא־ פָקַדְנוּ מְאוּמָה כָּל־ יְמֵי הִתְהַלַּכְנוּ
to-walk-us days-of all-of anything we-missed and-not they-mistreated-us

אִתָּם בִּהְיוֹתֵנוּ בַּשָּׂדֶה׃ חוֹמָה הָיוּ עָלֵינוּ גַּם־
both around-us they-were wall (16) in-the-field when-to-be-us near-them

לַיְלָה גַּם־ יוֹמָם כָּל־ יְמֵי הֱיוֹתֵנוּ עִמָּם רֹעִים הַצֹּאן׃
the-sheep ones-herding near-them to-be-us days-of all-of by-day and night

וְעַתָּה דְּעִי וּרְאִי מַה־ תַּעֲשִׂי כִּי־ כָלְתָה הָרָעָה
the-disaster she-hangs for you-can-do what and-see! think-over! and-now (17)

אֶל־ אֲדֹנֵינוּ וְעַל כָּל־ בֵּיתוֹ וְהוּא בֶּן־ בְּלִיַּעַל
wicked son-of now-he household-of-him whole-of and-over masters-of-us over

מִדַּבֵּר אֵלָיו׃ וַתְּמַהֵר אֲבוֹגַיִל וַתִּקַּח מָאתַיִם
two-hundreds and-she-took Abigail and-she-hurried (18) to-him from-to-talk

לֶחֶם וּשְׁנַיִם נִבְלֵי־ יַיִן וְחָמֵשׁ צֹאן עֲשׂוּוֹת וְחָמֵשׁ
and-five ones-being-dressed sheep and-five wine skins-of and-two bread

סְאִים קָלִי וּמֵאָה צִמֻּקִים וּמָאתַיִם דְּבֵלִים
pressed-figs and-two-hundreds raisin-cakes and-hundred roasted-grain seahs

וַתָּשֶׂם עַל־ הַחֲמֹרִים׃ וַתֹּאמֶר לִנְעָרֶיהָ עִבְרוּ
go-on! to-servants-of-her then-she-told (19) the-donkeys on and-she-loaded

לְפָנַי הִנְנִי אַחֲרֵיכֶם בָּאָה וּלְאִישָׁהּ נָבָל לֹא
not Nabal but-to-husband-of-her following after-you see-I! ahead-of-me

הִגִּידָה׃ וְהָיָה הִיא ׀ רֹכֶבֶת עַל־הַחֲמוֹר וְיֹרֶדֶת בְּסֵתֶר
into-ravine-of and-descending the-donkey on riding she and-he-was (20) she-told

°18a ק אביגיל
°18b ק עשויות

12 David's men turned
around and went back. When
they arrived, they reported
every word. 13 David said to his
men, "Put on your swords!" So
they put on their swords, and
David put on his. About four
hundred men went up with
David, while two hundred
stayed with the supplies.
14 One of the servants told
Nabal's wife Abigail: "David
sent messengers from the
desert to give our master his
greetings, but he hurled insults at them. 15 Yet these men
were very good to us. They did
not mistreat us, and the whole
time we were out in the fields
near them nothing was missing. 16 Night and day they were
a wall around us all the time
we were herding our sheep
near them. 17 Now think it over
and see what you can do, because disaster is hanging over
our master and his whole
household. He is such a
wicked man that no one can
talk to him."
18 Abigail lost no time. She
took two hundred loaves of
bread, two skins of wine, five
dressed sheep, five seahs[i] of
roasted grain, a hundred cakes
of raisins and two hundred
cakes of pressed figs, and loaded them on donkeys. 19 Then
she told her servants, "Go on
ahead; I'll follow you." But she
did not tell her husband Nabal.
20 As she came riding her

[i] *18 That is, probably about a bushel (about 37 liters)*

הָהָ֗ר וְהִנֵּ֤ה דָוִד֙ וַאֲנָשָׁ֔יו יֹרְדִ֖ים לִקְרָאתָ֑הּ
the-mountain  and-see!  David  and-men-of-him  ones-descending  to-encounter-her

וַתִּפְגֹּ֖שׁ אֹתָֽם: (21) וְדָוִ֣ד אָמַ֔ר אַ֤ךְ לַשֶּׁ֙קֶר֙ שָׁמַ֔רְתִּי
and-she-met  them  (21)  and-David  he-said  indeed  for-the-uselessness  I-watched

אֶֽת־כָּל־אֲשֶׁ֥ר לָזֶ֛ה בַּמִּדְבָּ֖ר וְלֹא־נִפְקַ֣ד מִכָּל־אֲשֶׁר־
***  that  all  to-this-one  in-the-desert  so-not  he-was-missed  that  from-all

ל֑וֹ מְא֑וּמָה וַיָּֽשֶׁב־לִ֥י רָעָ֖ה תַּ֥חַת טוֹבָֽה: (22) כֹּֽה־יַעֲשֶׂ֧ה
to-him  anything  now-he-paid-back  for-me  evil  so  good  (22)  may-he-deal

אֱלֹהִ֛ים לְאֹיְבֵ֥י דָוִ֖ד וְכֹ֣ה יֹסִ֑יף אִם־אַשְׁאִ֧יר
God  with-being-enemies-of  David  and-so  may-he-be-severe  if  I-leave-alive

מִכָּל־אֲשֶׁר־ל֛וֹ עַד־הַבֹּ֖קֶר מַשְׁתִּ֥ין בְּקִֽיר: (23) וַתֵּ֣רֶא
of-all  that  to-him  by  the-morning  one-urinating  against-wall  (23)  when-she-saw

אֲבִיגַ֣יִל אֶת־דָּוִ֔ד וַתְּמַהֵ֕ר וַתֵּ֖רֶד מֵעַ֣ל הַחֲמ֑וֹר
Abigail  ***  David  then-she-was-quick  and-she-got-off  from-on  the-donkey

וַתִּפֹּ֞ל לְאַפֵּ֤י דָוִד֙ עַל־פָּנֶ֔יהָ וַתִּשְׁתַּ֖חוּ אָֽרֶץ:
and-she-fell  before-faces-of  David  on  faces-of-her  and-she-bowed  ground

(24) וַתִּפֹּל֙ עַל־רַגְלָ֔יו וַתֹּ֕אמֶר בִּי־אֲנִ֥י אֲדֹנִ֖י הֶֽעָוֺ֑ן
(24)  and-she-fell  at  feet-of-him  and-she-said  upon-me  me  lord-of-me  the-blame

וּֽתְדַבֶּר־נָ֤א אֲמָֽתְךָ֙ בְּאָזְנֶ֔יךָ וּשְׁמַ֕ע אֵ֖ת דִּבְרֵ֥י
and-let-her-speak  now!  servant-of-you  into-ears-of-you  and-hear!  ***  words-of

אֲמָתֶֽךָ: (25) אַל־נָ֣א יָשִׂ֣ים אֲדֹנִ֣י ׀ אֶת־לִבּ֗וֹ אֶל־
servant-of-you  (25)  not  now!  may-he-attend  lord-of-me  ***  to-heart-of-him  to

אִ֣ישׁ הַבְּלִיַּ֤עַל הַזֶּה֙ עַל־נָבָ֔ל כִּ֥י כִשְׁמוֹ֙ כֶּן־ה֔וּא נָבָ֣ל
man-of  the-wickedness  the-this  to  Nabal  for  like-name-of-him  so  he  Fool

שְׁמ֔וֹ וּנְבָלָ֖ה עִמּ֑וֹ וַֽאֲנִי֙ אֲמָ֣תְךָ֔ לֹ֥א רָאִ֖יתִי אֶת־נַעֲרֵ֥י
name-of-him  and-folly  with-him  but-I  servant-of-you  not  I-saw  ***  men-of

אֲדֹנִ֖י אֲשֶׁ֥ר שָׁלָֽחְתָּ: (26) וְעַתָּ֣ה אֲדֹנִ֗י חַי־יְהוָ֤ה
master-of-me  whom  you-sent  (26)  and-now  master-of-me  life-of  Yahweh

וְחֵֽי־נַפְשְׁךָ֙ אֲשֶׁ֨ר מְנָעֲךָ֤ יְהוָה֙ מִבּ֣וֹא בְדָמִ֔ים
and-life-of  self-of-you  since  he-kept-you  Yahweh  from-to-come  to-bloodsheds

וְהוֹשֵׁ֥עַ יָדְךָ֖ לָ֑ךְ וְעַתָּ֗ה יִהְי֤וּ כְנָבָל֙
and-to-avenge  hand-of-you  for-you  and-now  may-they-be  like-Nabal

אֹיְבֶ֔יךָ וְהַֽמְבַקְשִׁ֥ים אֶל־אֲדֹנִ֖י רָעָֽה: (27) וְעַתָּה֙
being-enemies-of-you  and-the-ones-intending  to  master-of-me  harm  (27)  and-now

הַבְּרָכָ֣ה הַזֹּ֗את אֲשֶׁר־הֵבִ֥יא שִׁפְחָתְךָ֖ לַֽאדֹנִ֑י
the-gift  the-this  which  he-brought  servant-of-you  to-master-of-me

וְנִתְּנָה֙ לַנְּעָרִ֔ים הַמִּֽתְהַלְּכִ֖ים בְּרַגְלֵ֥י אֲדֹנִֽי:
and-let-her-be-given  to-the-men  the-ones-following  at-feet-of  master-of-me

donkey into a mountain ravine, there were David and his men descending toward her, and she met them. [21]David had just said, "It's been useless—all my watching over this fellow's property in the desert so that nothing of his was missing. He has paid me back evil for good. [22]May God deal with David,[i] be it ever so severely, if by morning I leave alive one male of all who belong to him!"

[23]When Abigail saw David, she quickly got off her donkey and bowed down before David with her face to the ground. [24]She fell at his feet and said: "My lord, let the blame be on me alone. Please let your servant speak to you; hear what your servant has to say. [25]May my lord pay no attention to that wicked man Nabal. He is just like his name—his name is Fool, and folly goes with him. But as for me, your servant, I did not see the men my master sent.

[26]"Now since the LORD has kept you, my master, from bloodshed and from avenging yourself with your own hands, as surely as the LORD lives and as you live, may your enemies and all who intend to harm my master be like Nabal. [27]And let this gift, which your servant has brought to my master, be given to the men

*i22 Some Septuagint manuscripts; Hebrew with David's enemies*

שָׂא נָא לְפֶשַׁע אֲמָתֶךָ כִּי עָשֹׂה־יַעֲשֶׂה
he-will-make to-make for servant-of-you to-offense-of now! forgive! (28)

יְהוָה לַאדֹנִי בַּיִת נֶאֱמָן כִּי־מִלְחֲמוֹת יְהוָה אֲדֹנִי
master-of-me Yahweh battles-of for lasting dynasty for-master-of-me Yahweh

נִלְחָם וְרָעָה לֹא־תִמָּצֵא בְךָ מִיָּמֶיךָ׃
during-days-of-you in-you let-her-be-found not and-wrongdoing fighting

וַיָּקָם אָדָם לִרְדָפְךָ וּלְבַקֵּשׁ אֶת־נַפְשֶׁךָ
life-of-you *** and-to-take to-pursue-you someone though-he-rises (29)

וְהָיְתָה נֶפֶשׁ אֲדֹנִי צְרוּרָה ׀ בִּצְרוֹר הַחַיִּים
the-ones-alive in-bundle-of being-bound master-of-me life-of then-she-will-be

אֵת יְהוָה אֱלֹהֶיךָ וְאֵת נֶפֶשׁ אֹיְבֶיךָ יְקַלְּעֶנָּה
he-will-hurl-away-her being-enemies-of-you life-of but God-of-you Yahweh by

בְּתוֹךְ כַּף הַקָּלַע׃ וְהָיָה כִּי־יַעֲשֶׂה יְהוָה
Yahweh he-does when and-he-will-be (30) the-sling pocket-of inside-of

לַאדֹנִי כְּכֹל אֲשֶׁר־דִּבֶּר אֶת־הַטּוֹבָה עָלֶיךָ
about-you the-good *** he-promised that as-all for-master-of-me

וְצִוְּךָ לְנָגִיד עַל־יִשְׂרָאֵל׃ וְלֹא תִהְיֶה זֹאת ׀
this she-will-be then-not (31) Israel over as-leader and-he-appoints-you

לְךָ לְפוּקָה וּלְמִכְשׁוֹל לֵב לַאדֹנִי וְלִשְׁפָּךְ־
that-to-shed of-master-of-me conscience or-for-stumbling-of for-staggering to-you

דָּם חִנָּם וּלְהוֹשִׁיעַ אֲדֹנִי לוֹ וְהֵיטִב
when-he-brings-success for-him master-of-me or-to-avenge needlessly blood

יְהוָה לַאדֹנִי וְזָכַרְתָּ אֶת־אֲמָתֶךָ׃ וַיֹּאמֶר
and-he-said (32) servant-of-you *** then-you-remember to-master-of-me Yahweh

דָּוִד לַאֲבִיגַל בָּרוּךְ יְהוָה אֱלֹהֵי יִשְׂרָאֵל אֲשֶׁר שְׁלָחֵךְ הַיּוֹם
the-day he-sent-you who Israel God-of Yahweh being-praised to-Abigail David

הַזֶּה לִקְרָאתִי׃ וּבָרוּךְ טַעְמֵךְ וּבְרוּכָה
and-being-blessed judgment-of-you and-being-blessed (33) to-meet-me the-this

אָתְּ אֲשֶׁר כְּלִתִנִי הַיּוֹם הַזֶּה מִבּוֹא בְדָמִים וְהֹשֵׁעַ
and-to-avenge to-bloodsheds from-to-come the-this the-day you-kept-me for you

יָדִי לִי׃ וְאוּלָם חַי־יְהוָה אֱלֹהֵי יִשְׂרָאֵל אֲשֶׁר
who Israel God-of Yahweh life-of for-otherwise (34) for-me hand-of-me

מְנָעַנִי מֵהָרַע אֹתָךְ כִּי ׀ לוּלֵי מִהַרְתְּ וַתָּבֹאתִי לִקְרָאתִי
to-meet-me and-you-came you-were-quick not if you from-to-harm he-kept-me

כִּי אִם־נוֹתַר לְנָבָל עַד־אוֹר הַבֹּקֶר מַשְׁתִּין
one-urinating the-morning light-of by to-Nabal he-would-be-left not indeed

בְּקִיר׃ וַיִּקַּח דָּוִד מִיָּדָהּ אֵת אֲשֶׁר־הֵבִיאָה
she-brought what *** from-hand-of-her David then-he-accepted (35) against-wall

who follow you. 28Please forgive your servant's offense, for
the LORD will certainly make a
lasting dynasty for my master,
because he fights the LORD's
battles. Let no wrongdoing be
found in you as long as you
live. 29Even though someone
is pursuing you to take your
life, the life of my master will
be bound securely in the bun-
dle of the living by the LORD
your God. But the lives of your
enemies he will hurl away as
from the pocket of a sling.
30When the LORD has done for
my master every good thing
he promised concerning him
and has appointed him leader
over Israel, 31my master will
not have on his conscience the
staggering burden of needless
bloodshed or of having
avenged himself. And when
the LORD has brought my master success, remember your
servant."
32David said to Abigail,
"Praise be to the LORD, the God
of Israel, who has sent you today to meet me. 33May you be
blessed for your good judgment and for keeping me from
bloodshed this day and from
avenging myself with my own
hands. 34Otherwise, as surely
as the LORD, the God of Israel,
lives, who has kept me from
harming you, if you had not
come quickly to meet me, not
one male belonging to Nabal
would have been left alive by
daybreak."
35Then David accepted from
her hand what she had

°34 ק ותבאת

לוֹ וְלָהּ אָמַר עֲלִי לְשָׁלוֹם לְבֵיתֵךְ רְאִי שָׁמַעְתִּי
I-heard see! to-home-of-you in-peace go! he-said and-to-her to-him

בְקוֹלֵךְ וָאֶשָּׂא פָּנָיִךְ׃ וַתָּבֹא אֲבִיגַיִל ׀
Abigail when-she-went (36) requests-of-you and-I-granted to-word-of-you

אֶל־ נָבָל וְהִנֵּה־ לוֹ מִשְׁתֶּה בְּבֵיתוֹ כְּמִשְׁתֵּה הַמֶּלֶךְ
the-king like-banquet-of in-house-of-him banquet to-him then-see! Nabal to

וְלֵב נָבָל טוֹב עָלָיו וְהוּא שִׁכֹּר עַד־ מְאֹד וְלֹא־ הִגִּידָה לּוֹ
to-him she-told so-not very-much to drunk and-he in-him good Nabal and-heart-of

דָּבָר קָטֹן וְגָדוֹל עַד־ אוֹר הַבֹּקֶר׃ וַיְהִי בַבֹּקֶר
in-the-morning then-he-was (37) the-morning light-of until or-great small thing

בְּצֵאת הַיַּיִן מִנָּבָל וַתַּגֶּד־ לוֹ אִשְׁתּוֹ אֶת־
*** wife-of-him to-him then-she-told from-Nabal the-wine when-to-leave

הַדְּבָרִים הָאֵלֶּה וַיָּמָת לִבּוֹ בְּקִרְבּוֹ וְהוּא הָיָה
he-became and-he in-midst-of-him heart-of-him and-he-failed the-these the-things

לְאָבֶן׃ וַיְהִי כַּעֲשֶׂרֶת הַיָּמִים וַיִּגֹּף יְהוָה אֶת־
*** Yahweh and-he-struck the-days about-ten-of and-he-was (38) like-stone

נָבָל וַיָּמֹת׃ וַיִּשְׁמַע דָּוִד כִּי מֵת נָבָל וַיֹּאמֶר
then-he-said Nabal he-died that David when-he-heard (39) and-he-died Nabal

בָּרוּךְ יְהוָה אֲשֶׁר רָב אֶת־ רִיב חֶרְפָּתִי מִיַּד
against-hand-of contempt-of-me cause-of *** he-upheld who Yahweh being-praised

נָבָל וְאֶת־ עַבְדּוֹ חָשַׂךְ מֵרָעָה וְאֵת רָעַת נָבָל
Nabal wrongdoing-of and from-wrongdoing he-kept servant-of-him and Nabal

הֵשִׁיב יְהוָה בְּרֹאשׁוֹ וַיִּשְׁלַח דָּוִד וַיְדַבֵּר בַּאֲבִיגַיִל
to-Abigail and-he-asked David then-he-sent on-head-of-him Yahweh he-brought

לְקַחְתָּהּ לוֹ לְאִשָּׁה׃ וַיָּבֹאוּ עַבְדֵי דָוִד אֶל־אֲבִיגָיִל
Abigail to David servants-of and-they-went (40) as-wife for-him to-take-her

הַכַּרְמֶלָה וַיְדַבְּרוּ אֵלֶיהָ לֵאמֹר דָּוִד שְׁלָחָנוּ אֵלַיִךְ לְקַחְתֵּךְ
to-take-you to-you he-sent-us David to-say to-her and-they-said at-the-Carmel

לוֹ לְאִשָּׁה׃ וַתָּקָם וַתִּשְׁתַּחוּ אַפַּיִם אָרְצָה וַתֹּאמֶר
and-she-said to-ground faces and-she-bowed and-she-rose (41) as-wife for-him

הִנֵּה אֲמָתְךָ לְשִׁפְחָה לִרְחֹץ רַגְלֵי עַבְדֵי אֲדֹנִי׃
master-of-me servants-of feet-of to-wash for-service maidservant-of-you see!

וַתְּמַהֵר וַתָּקָם אֲבִיגַיִל וַתִּרְכַּב עַל־ הַחֲמוֹר
the-donkey on and-she-got-on Abigail and-she-rose and-she-was-quick (42)

וְחָמֵשׁ נַעֲרֹתֶיהָ הַהֹלְכוֹת לְרַגְלָהּ וַתֵּלֶךְ אַחֲרֵי
with and-she-went at-foot-of-her the-ones-attending maids-of-her and-five

מַלְאֲכֵי דָוִד וַתְּהִי־ לוֹ לְאִשָּׁה׃ וְאֶת־אֲחִינֹעַם לָקַח
he-married Ahinoam and (43) as-wife to-him and-she-became David messengers-of

brought him and said, "Go home in peace. I have heard your words and granted your request."

[36]When Abigail went to Nabal, he was in the house holding a banquet like that of a king. He was in high spirits and very drunk. So she told him nothing until daybreak. [37]Then in the morning, when Nabal was sober, his wife told him all these things, and his heart failed him and he became like a stone. [38]About ten days later, the LORD struck Nabal and he died.

[39]When David heard that Nabal was dead, he said, "Praise be to the LORD, who has upheld my cause against Nabal for treating me with contempt. He has kept me from doing wrong and has brought Nabal's wrongdoing down on his own head."

Then David sent word to Abigail, asking her to become his wife. [40]His servants went to Carmel and said to Abigail, "David has sent us to you to take you to become his wife."

[41]She bowed down with her face to the ground and said, "Here is your maidservant, ready to serve you and wash the feet of my master's servants." [42]Abigail quickly got on a donkey and, attended by her five maids, went with David's messengers and became his wife. [43]David had also married Ahinoam of Jezreel, and

דָּוִד מִיִּזְרְעֶאל וַתִּהְיֶיןָ גַּם־ שְׁתֵּיהֶן לוֹ לְנָשִׁים׃
as-wives for-him both-of-them also and-they-were of-Jezreel David

וְשָׁאוּל נָתַן אֶת־ מִיכַל בִּתּוֹ אֵשֶׁת דָּוִד לְפַלְטִי
to-Palti David wife-of daughter-of-him Michal *** he-gave but-Saul (44)

בֶן־ לַיִשׁ אֲשֶׁר מִגַּלִּים׃ וַיָּבֹאוּ הַזִּפִים אֶל־שָׁאוּל
Saul to the-Ziphites and-they-went (26:1) from-Gallim who Laish son-of

הַגִּבְעָתָה לֵאמֹר הֲלוֹא דָוִד מִסְתַּתֵּר בְּגִבְעַת הַחֲכִילָה עַל פְּנֵי
faces-of to the-Hakilah on-hill-of hiding David not? to-say at-the-Gibeah

הַיְשִׁימֹן׃ וַיָּקָם שָׁאוּל וַיֵּרֶד אֶל־ מִדְבַּר־ זִיף
Ziph Desert-of to and-he-went-down Saul so-he-rose (2) the-Jeshimon

וְאִתּוֹ שְׁלֹשֶׁת־ אֲלָפִים אִישׁ בְּחוּרֵי יִשְׂרָאֵל לְבַקֵּשׁ
to-search Israel ones-being-chosen-of man thousands three-of and-with-him

אֶת־ דָּוִד בְּמִדְבַּר־ זִיף׃ וַיִּחַן שָׁאוּל בְּגִבְעַת הַחֲכִילָה
the-Hakilah on-hill-of Saul and-he-camped (3) Ziph in-Desert-of David ***

אֲשֶׁר עַל־ פְּנֵי הַיְשִׁימֹן עַל־ הַדָּרֶךְ וְדָוִד יֹשֵׁב בַּמִּדְבָּר
in-the-desert staying but-David the-road beside the-Jeshimon faces-of to that

וַיַּרְא כִּי בָא שָׁאוּל אַחֲרָיו הַמִּדְבָּרָה׃ וַיִּשְׁלַח
then-he-sent (4) to-the-desert after-him Saul he-followed that when-he-saw

דָּוִד מְרַגְּלִים וַיֵּדַע כִּי־ בָא שָׁאוּל אֶל־ נָכוֹן׃
to-be-definite to Saul he-arrived that and-he-learned ones-scouting David

וַיָּקָם דָּוִד וַיָּבֹא אֶל־ הַמָּקוֹם אֲשֶׁר חָנָה־ שָׁם
there he-camped where the-place to and-he-went David then-he-set-out (5)

שָׁאוּל וַיַּרְא דָּוִד אֶת־ הַמָּקוֹם אֲשֶׁר שָׁכַב־ שָׁם שָׁאוּל וְאַבְנֵר
and-Abner Saul there he-laid-down where the-place *** David and-he-saw Saul

בֶּן־ נֵר שַׂר־ צְבָאוֹ וְשָׁאוּל שֹׁכֵב בַּמַּעְגָּל
inside-the-camp lying now-Saul army-of-him commander-of Ner son-of

וְהָעָם חֹנִים סְבִיבֹתָו׃ וַיַּעַן דָּוִד וַיֹּאמֶר ׀ אֶל־
to and-he-said David then-he-asked (6) around-him ones-camping and-the-army

אֲחִימֶלֶךְ הַחִתִּי וְאֶל־ אֲבִישַׁי בֶּן־ צְרוּיָה אֲחִי יוֹאָב לֵאמֹר
to-say Joab brother-of Zeruiah son-of Abishai and-to the-Hittite Ahimelech

מִי־ יֵרֵד אִתִּי אֶל־שָׁאוּל אֶל־הַמַּחֲנֶה וַיֹּאמֶר אֲבִישַׁי אֲנִי
I Abishai and-he-said the-camp into Saul to with-me will-he-go-down who?

אֵרֵד עִמָּךְ׃ וַיָּבֹא דָוִד וַאֲבִישַׁי ׀ אֶל־ הָעָם לַיְלָה
night the-army to and-Abishai David so-he-went (7) with-you I-will-go

וְהִנֵּה שָׁאוּל שֹׁכֵב יָשֵׁן בַּמַּעְגָּל וַחֲנִיתוֹ מְעוּכָה־
being-stuck and-spear-of-him inside-the-camp asleep lying Saul and-see!

בָאָרֶץ מְרַאֲשֹׁתָו וְאַבְנֵר וְהָעָם שֹׁכְבִים
ones-lying and-the-soldier and-Abner near-heads-of-him in-the-ground

they both were his wives. [44]But Saul had given his daughter Michal, David's wife, to Paltiel[k] son of Laish, who was from Gallim.

*David Again Spares Saul's Life*

26 The Ziphites went to Saul at Gibeah and said, "Is not David hiding on the hill of Hakilah, which faces Jeshimon?"

[2]So Saul went down to the Desert of Ziph, with his three thousand chosen men of Israel, to search there for David. [3]Saul made his camp beside the road on the hill of Hakilah facing Jeshimon, but David stayed in the desert. When he saw that Saul had followed him there, [4]he sent out scouts and learned that Saul had definitely arrived.[l]

[5]Then David set out and went to the place where Saul had camped. He saw where Saul and Abner son of Ner, the commander of the army, had lain down. Saul was lying inside the camp, with the army encamped around him.

[6]David then asked Ahimelech the Hittite and Abishai son of Zeruiah, Joab's brother, "Who will go down into the camp with me to Saul?"

"I'll go with you," said Abishai.

[7]So David and Abishai went to the army by night, and there was Saul, lying asleep inside the camp with his spear stuck in the ground near his head. Abner and the soldiers were lying around him.

[k]44 Hebrew *Palti*, a variant of *Paltiel*
[l]4 Or *had come to Nacon*

°5 ק סביבתיו
°7 ק מראשתיו

סְבִיבֹתָו׃ וַיֹּאמֶר אֲבִישַׁי אֶל־דָּוִד סִגַּר אֱלֹהִים הַיּוֹם אֶת־
*** the-day God he-delivered David to Abishai and-he-said (8) around-him

אוֹיִבְךָ בְּיָדֶךָ וְעַתָּה אַכֶּנּוּ נָא בַּחֲנִית
with-the-spear now! let-me-pin-him and-now into-hand-of-you being-enemy-of-you

וּבָאָרֶץ פַּעַם אַחַת וְלֹא אֶשְׁנֶה לוֹ׃ וַיֹּאמֶר
but-he-said (9) to-him I-will-do-twice and-not one thrust and-into-the-ground

דָּוִד אֶל־אֲבִישַׁי אַל־תַּשְׁחִיתֵהוּ כִּי מִי שָׁלַח יָדוֹ
hand-of-him he-can-lay who? for you-destroy-him not Abishai to David

בִּמְשִׁיחַ יְהוָה וְנִקָּה׃ וַיֹּאמֶר דָּוִד חַי־
life-of David and-he-said (10) and-he-be-guiltless Yahweh on-anointed-of

יְהוָה כִּי אִם־יְהוָה יִגָּפֶנּוּ* אוֹ־יוֹמוֹ יָבוֹא
he-will-come day-of-him either he-will-strike-him Yahweh indeed that Yahweh

וָמֵת אוֹ בַמִּלְחָמָה יֵרֵד וְנִסְפָּה׃
and-he-will-perish he-will-go into-the-battle or and-he-will-die

חָלִילָה לִּי מֵיהוָה מִשְּׁלֹחַ יָדִי בִּמְשִׁיחַ
on-anointed-of hand-of-me from-to-lay by-Yahweh from-me far-be-it! (11)

יְהוָה וְעַתָּה קַח־נָא אֶת־הַחֲנִית אֲשֶׁר מְרַאֲשֹׁתָו וְאֶת־צַפַּחַת
jug-of and at-heads-of-him that the-spear *** now! get! and-now Yahweh

הַמַּיִם וְנֵלְכָה לָּנוּ׃ וַיִּקַּח דָּוִד אֶת־הַחֲנִית וְאֶת־
and the-spear *** David so-he-took (12) for-us and-let-us-go the-waters

צַפַּחַת הַמַּיִם מֵרַאֲשֹׁתֵי שָׁאוּל וַיֵּלְכוּ לָהֶם וְאֵין רֹאֶה
seeing and-no-one for-them and-they-left Saul near-head-of the-waters jug-of

וְאֵין יוֹדֵעַ וְאֵין מֵקִיץ כִּי כֻלָּם יְשֵׁנִים כִּי
for ones-sleeping all-of-them for waking and-no-one knowing and-no-one

תַּרְדֵּמַת יְהוָה נָפְלָה עֲלֵיהֶם׃ וַיַּעֲבֹר דָּוִד
David then-he-crossed-over (13) upon-them she-fell Yahweh deep-sleep-of

הָעֵבֶר וַיַּעֲמֹד עַל־רֹאשׁ־הָהָר מֵרָחֹק רַב הַמָּקוֹם
the-space wide at-distance the-hill top-of on and-he-stood the-other-side

בֵּינֵיהֶם׃ וַיִּקְרָא דָוִד אֶל־הָעָם וְאֶל־אַבְנֵר בֶּן־נֵר
Ner son-of Abner and-to the-army to David and-he-called (14) between-them

לֵאמֹר הֲלוֹא תַעֲנֶה אַבְנֵר וַיַּעַן אַבְנֵר וַיֹּאמֶר מִי אַתָּה
you who? and-he-said Abner and-he-replied Abner will-you-answer not? to-say

קָרָאתָ אֶל־הַמֶּלֶךְ׃ וַיֹּאמֶר דָּוִד אֶל־אַבְנֵר הֲלוֹא־אִישׁ אַתָּה וּמִי
and-who? you man not? Abner to David and-he-said (15) the-king to you-call

כָמוֹךָ בְּיִשְׂרָאֵל וְלָמָּה לֹא שָׁמַרְתָּ אֶל־אֲדֹנֶיךָ הַמֶּלֶךְ כִּי־
for the-king lords-of-you over you-guarded not and-why? in-Israel like-you

בָא אַחַד הָעָם לְהַשְׁחִית אֶת־הַמֶּלֶךְ אֲדֹנֶיךָ׃ לֹא־טוֹב
good not (16) lords-of-you the-king *** to-destroy the-people one-of he-came

[8]Abishai said to David, "Today God has delivered your
enemy into your hands. Now
let me pin him to the ground
with one thrust of my spear; I
won't strike him twice."
[9]But David said to Abishai,
"Don't destroy him! Who can
lay a hand on the LORD's
anointed and be guiltless? [10]As
surely as the LORD lives," he
said, "the LORD himself will
strike him; either his time will
come and he will die, or he
will go into battle and perish.
[11]But the LORD forbid that I
should lay a hand on the
LORD's anointed. Now get the
spear and water jug that are
near his head, and let's go."
[12]So David took the spear
and water jug near Saul's
head, and they left. No one
saw or knew about it, nor did
anyone wake up. They were
all sleeping, because the LORD
had put them into a deep
sleep.
[13]Then David crossed over to
the other side and stood on top
of the hill some distance away;
there was a wide space between them. [14]He called out to
the army and to Abner son of
Ner, "Aren't you going to answer me, Abner?"
Abner replied, "Who are
you who calls to the king?"
[15]David said, "You're a man,
aren't you? And who is like
you in Israel? Why didn't you
guard your lord the king?
Someone came to destroy your
lord the king. [16]What you have

*10 Most mss have *hateph qamets* under the *gimel* ( יְגָּ ).

°7 ק סביבתיו

°11 ק מראשתיו

הַדָּבָר הַזֶּה אֲשֶׁר עָשִׂיתָ חַי־ יְהוָה כִּי בְנֵי־ מָוֶת אַתֶּם אֲשֶׁר
who you death sons-of indeed Yahweh life-of you-did that the-this the-thing

לֹא־ שְׁמַרְתֶּם עַל־ אֲדֹנֵיכֶם עַל־ מְשִׁיחַ יְהוָה וְעַתָּה ׀ רְאֵה
look! and-now Yahweh anointed-of over masters-of-you over you-guarded not

אֵי־ חֲנִית הַמֶּלֶךְ וְאֶת־ צַפַּחַת הַמַּיִם אֲשֶׁר מְרַאֲשֹׁתָו׃
near-heads-of-him that the-waters jug-of and the-king spear-of where?

וַיַּכֵּר שָׁאוּל אֶת־ קוֹל דָּוִד וַיֹּאמֶר הֲקוֹלְךָ זֶה
that voice-of-you? and-he-said David voice-of *** Saul and-he-recognized (17)

בְּנִי דָוִד וַיֹּאמֶר דָּוִד קוֹלִי אֲדֹנִי הַמֶּלֶךְ׃
the-king lord-of-me voice-of-me David and-he-replied David son-of-me

וַיֹּאמֶר לָמָּה זֶּה אֲדֹנִי רֹדֵף אַחֲרֵי עַבְדּוֹ כִּי
for servant-of-him after pursuing lord-of-me this why? and-he-said (18)

מֶה עָשִׂיתִי וּמַה־ בְּיָדִי רָעָה׃ וְעַתָּה יִשְׁמַע־ נָא
now! let-him-listen and-now (19) wrong in-hand-of-me and-what? I-did what?

אֲדֹנִי הַמֶּלֶךְ אֵת דִּבְרֵי עַבְדּוֹ אִם־ יְהוָה הֱסִיתְךָ
he-incited-you Yahweh if servant-of-him words-of *** the-king lord-of-me

בִי יָרַח מִנְחָה וְאִם ׀ בְּנֵי הָאָדָם אֲרוּרִים
ones-being-cursed the-man sons-of but-if offering may-he-accept against-me

הֵם לִפְנֵי יְהוָה כִּי־ גֵרְשׁוּנִי הַיּוֹם מֵהִסְתַּפֵּחַ בְּנַחֲלַת
in-inheritance-of from-to-share the-day they-drove-me for Yahweh before they

יְהוָה לֵאמֹר לֵךְ עֲבֹד אֱלֹהִים אֲחֵרִים׃ וְעַתָּה אַל־ יִפֹּל
let-him-fall not and-now (20) other-ones gods serve! go! to-say Yahweh

דָּמִי אַרְצָה מִנֶּגֶד פְּנֵי יְהוָה כִּי־ יָצָא מֶלֶךְ
king-of he-came-out indeed Yahweh presences-of from-near to-ground blood-of-me

יִשְׂרָאֵל לְבַקֵּשׁ אֶת־פַּרְעֹשׁ אֶחָד כַּאֲשֶׁר יִרְדֹּף הַקֹּרֵא בֶּהָרִים׃
in-the-mountains the-partridge he-hunts just-as one flea *** to-look-for Israel

וַיֹּאמֶר שָׁאוּל חָטָאתִי שׁוּב בְּנִי־ דָוִד כִּי לֹא־ אָרַע
I-will-harm not for David son-of-me come-back! I-sinned Saul then-he-said (21)

לְךָ עוֹד תַּחַת אֲשֶׁר יָקְרָה נַפְשִׁי בְּעֵינֶיךָ הַיּוֹם
the-day in-eyes-of-you life-of-me she-was-precious that because again to-you

הַזֶּה הִנֵּה הִסְכַּלְתִּי וָאֶשְׁגֶּה הַרְבֵּה מְאֹד׃ וַיַּעַן
and-he-answered (22) very to-be-great and-I-erred I-was-foolish see! the-this

דָּוִד וַיֹּאמֶר הִנֵּה הַחֲנִית הַמֶּלֶךְ וְיַעֲבֹר אֶחָד
one now-let-him-come-over the-king spear-of see! and-he-said David

מֵהַנְּעָרִים וְיִקָּחֶהָ׃ וַיהוָה יָשִׁיב לָאִישׁ
to-the-man he-rewards now-Yahweh (23) and-let-him-get-her of-the-young-men

אֶת־ צִדְקָתוֹ וְאֶת־ אֱמֻנָתוֹ אֲשֶׁר נְתָנְךָ יְהוָה ׀
Yahweh he-delivered-you for faithfulness-of-him and righteousness-of-him ***

done is not good. As surely as the LORD lives, you and your men deserve to die, because you did not guard your master, the LORD's anointed. Look around you. Where are the king's spear and water jug that were near his head?"

17Saul recognized David's voice and said, "Is that your voice, David my son?"

David replied, "Yes it is, my lord the king." 18And he added, "Why is my lord pursuing his servant? What have I done, and what wrong am I guilty of? 19Now let my lord the king listen to his servant's words. If the LORD has incited you against me, then may he accept an offering. If, however, men have done it, may they be cursed before the LORD! They have now driven me from my share in the LORD's inheritance and have said, 'Go, serve other gods.' 20Now do not let my blood fall to the ground far from the presence of the LORD. The king of Israel has come out to look for a flea—as one hunts a partridge in the mountains."

21Then Saul said, "I have sinned. Come back, David my son. Because you considered my life precious today, I will not try to harm you again. Surely I have acted like a fool and have erred greatly."

22"Here is the king's spear," David answered. "Let one of your young men come over and get it. 23The LORD rewards every man for his righteousness and faithfulness. The LORD delivered you into my

°16 ק מראשתיו
°22 ק חנית

הַיּוֹם בְּיָד וְלֹא אָבִיתִי לִשְׁלֹחַ יָדִי בִּמְשִׁיחַ יְהוָה׃
Yahweh on-anointed-of hand-of-me to-lay I-would but-not into-hand the-day

וְהִנֵּה כַּאֲשֶׁר גָּדְלָה נַפְשְׁךָ הַיּוֹם הַזֶּה
the-this the-day life-of-you she-was-valued surely-as and-see! (24)

בְּעֵינָי כֵּן תִּגְדַּל נַפְשִׁי בְּעֵינֵי יְהוָה
Yahweh in-eyes-of life-of-me may-she-be-valued so in-eyes-of-me

וְיַצִּלֵנִי מִכָּל־ צָרָה׃ וַיֹּאמֶר שָׁאוּל אֶל־דָּוִד
David to Saul then-he-said (25) trouble from-all-of and-may-he-deliver-me

בָּרוּךְ אַתָּה בְּנִי דָוִד גַּם עָשֹׂה תַעֲשֶׂה וְגַם
and-indeed you-will-do to-do indeed David son-of-me you being-blessed

יָכֹל תּוּכָל וַיֵּלֶךְ דָּוִד לְדַרְכּוֹ וְשָׁאוּל
and-Saul on-way-of-him David so-he-went you-will-triumph to-triumph

שָׁב לִמְקוֹמוֹ׃ וַיֹּאמֶר דָּוִד אֶל־ לִבּוֹ עַתָּה
now heart-of-him in David but-he-thought (27:1) to-home-of-him he-returned

אֶסָּפֶה יוֹם־אֶחָד בְּיַד־ שָׁאוּל אֵין־ לִי טוֹב כִּי הִמָּלֵט
to-escape unless good to-me not Saul by-hand-of one day I-will-be-destroyed

אִמָּלֵט ׀ אֶל־ אֶרֶץ פְּלִשְׁתִּים וְנוֹאַשׁ מִמֶּנִּי שָׁאוּל
Saul from-me then-he-will-give-up Philistines land-of to I-escape

לְבַקְשֵׁנִי עוֹד בְּכָל־ גְּבוּל יִשְׂרָאֵל וְנִמְלַטְתִּי
and-I-will-slip-out Israel part-of in-any-of ever to-search-for-me

מִיָּדוֹ׃ וַיָּקָם דָּוִד וַיַּעֲבֹר הוּא וְשֵׁשׁ־ מֵאוֹת אִישׁ
man hundreds and-six he and-he-went-over David so-he-left (2) of-hand-of-him

אֲשֶׁר עִמּוֹ אֶל־אָכִישׁ בֶּן־ מָעוֹךְ מֶלֶךְ גַּת׃ וַיֵּשֶׁב דָּוִד
David and-he-settled (3) Gath king-of Maoch son-of Achish to with-him who

עִם־אָכִישׁ בְּגַת הוּא וַאֲנָשָׁיו אִישׁ וּבֵיתוֹ דָּוִד וּשְׁתֵּי
and-two-of David and-family-of-him man and-men-of-him he in-Gath Achish with

נָשָׁיו אֲחִינֹעַם הַיִּזְרְעֵאלִית וַאֲבִיגַיִל אֵשֶׁת־ נָבָל הַכַּרְמְלִית׃
the-Carmelite Nabal widow-of and-Abigail the-Jezreelite Ahinoam wives-of-him

וַיֻּגַּד לְשָׁאוּל כִּי־ בָרַח דָּוִד גַּת וְלֹא־ יוֹסֵף
he-continued then-not Gath David he-fled that to-Saul when-he-was-told (4)

עוֹד לְבַקְשׁוֹ׃ וַיֹּאמֶר דָּוִד אֶל־ אָכִישׁ אִם־ נָא מָצָאתִי
I-found now! if Achish to David then-he-said (5) to-search-for-him longer

חֵן בְּעֵינֶיךָ יִתְּנוּ־ לִי מָקוֹם בְּאַחַת עָרֵי
towns-of in-one-of place to-me let-them-assign in-eyes-of-you favor

הַשָּׂדֶה וְאֵשְׁבָה שָּׁם וְלָמָּה יֵשֵׁב עַבְדְּךָ
servants-of-you should-he-live for-why? there that-I-may-live the-country

בְּעִיר הַמַּמְלָכָה עִמָּךְ׃ וַיִּתֶּן־ לוֹ אָכִישׁ בַּיּוֹם
on-the-day Achish to-him so-he-gave (6) with-you the-royal in-city-of

°4 ק יסף

hands today, but I would not lay a hand on the LORD's anointed. [24]As surely as I valued your life today, so may the LORD value my life and deliver me from all trouble."

[25]Then Saul said to David, "May you be blessed, my son David; you will do great things and surely triumph."

So David went on his way, and Saul returned home.

*David Among the Philistines*

**27** But David thought to himself, "One of these days I will be destroyed by the hand of Saul. The best thing I can do is to escape to the land of the Philistines. Then Saul will give up searching for me anywhere in Israel, and I will slip out of his hand."

[2]So David and the six hundred men with him left and went over to Achish son of Maoch king of Gath. [3]David and his men settled in Gath with Achish. Each man had his family with him, and David had his two wives: Ahinoam of Jezreel and Abigail of Carmel, the widow of Nabal. [4]When Saul was told that David had fled to Gath, he no longer searched for him.

[5]Then David said to Achish, "If I have found favor in your eyes, let a place be assigned to me in one of the country towns, that I may live there. Why should your servant live in the royal city with you?"

[6]So on that day Achish gave

הַהוּא אֶת־צִקְלָג לָכֵן הָיְתָה צִקְלַג לְמַלְכֵי יְהוּדָה עַד הַיּוֹם
the-day to Judah to-kings-of Ziklag she-belongs thus Ziklag *** the-that

הַזֶּה׃ וַיְהִי מִסְפַּר הַיָּמִים אֲשֶׁר־יָשַׁב דָּוִד בִּשְׂדֵה
in-territory-of David he-lived that the-days number-of and-he-was (7) the-this

פְלִשְׁתִּים יָמִים וְאַרְבָּעָה חֳדָשִׁים׃ וַיַּעַל דָּוִד וַאֲנָשָׁיו
and-men-of-him David now-he-went-up (8) months and-four days Philistines

וַיִּפְשְׁטוּ אֶל־הַגְּשׁוּרִי וְהַגִּרְזִי וְהָעֲמָלֵקִי כִּי הֵנָּה
they now and-the-Amalekite *and-the-Girzite the-Geshurite on and-they-raided

יֹשְׁבוֹת הָאָרֶץ אֲשֶׁר מֵעוֹלָם בּוֹאֲךָ שׁוּרָה וְעַד־אֶרֶץ
land-of and-to to-Shur to-go-you from-ancient that the-land ones-living-of

מִצְרָיִם׃ וְהִכָּה דָוִד אֶת־הָאָרֶץ וְלֹא יְחַיֶּה אִישׁ
man he-left-alive then-not the-area *** David when-he-attacked (9) Egypt

וְאִשָּׁה וְלָקַח צֹאן וּבָקָר וַחֲמֹרִים וּגְמַלִּים וּבְגָדִים
and-clothes and-camels and-donkeys and-cattle sheep but-he-took or-woman

וַיָּשָׁב וַיָּבֹא אֶל־אָכִישׁ׃ וַיֹּאמֶר אָכִישׁ אַל־†
†not Achish when-he-asked (10) Achish to and-he-went then-he-returned

פְּשַׁטְתֶּם הַיּוֹם וַיֹּאמֶר דָּוִד עַל־נֶגֶב יְהוּדָה וְעַל־
or-against Judah Negev-of against David and-he-said the-day you-raided

נֶגֶב הַיִּרְחְמְאֵלִי†† וְאֶל־נֶגֶב הַקֵּינִי׃ וְאִישׁ וְאִשָּׁה
or-woman and-man (11) the-Kenite Negev-of or-against the-Jerahmeelite Negev-of

לֹא־יְחַיֶּה דָוִד לְהָבִיא גַת לֵאמֹר פֶּן־יַגִּדוּ עָלֵינוּ לֵאמֹר
to-say on-us they-inform lest to-say Gath to-bring David he-left-alive not

כֹּה־עָשָׂה דָוִד וְכֹה מִשְׁפָּטוֹ כָּל־הַיָּמִים אֲשֶׁר יָשַׁב
he-lived that the-days all-of practice-of-him and-such David he-did this

בִּשְׂדֵה פְלִשְׁתִּים׃ וַיַּאֲמֵן אָכִישׁ בְּדָוִד לֵאמֹר
to-say in-David Achish and-he-trusted (12) Philistines in-territory-of

הַבְאֵשׁ הִבְאִישׁ בְּעַמּוֹ בְיִשְׂרָאֵל וְהָיָה
so-he-will-be to-Israel to-people-of-him he-became-odious to-become-odious

לִי לְעֶבֶד עוֹלָם׃ וַיְהִי בַּיָּמִים הָהֵם
the-those in-the-days and-he-was (28:1) forever as-servant to-me

וַיִּקְבְּצוּ פְלִשְׁתִּים אֶת־מַחֲנֵיהֶם לַצָּבָא לְהִלָּחֵם
to-fight for-the-army forces-of-them *** Philistines then-they-gathered

בְּיִשְׂרָאֵל וַיֹּאמֶר אָכִישׁ אֶל־דָּוִד יָדֹעַ תֵּדַע
you-must-understand to-understand David to Achish and-he-said against-Israel

כִּי אִתִּי תֵּצֵא בַמַּחֲנֶה אַתָּה וַאֲנָשֶׁיךָ׃ וַיֹּאמֶר
and-he-said (2) and-men-of-you you in-the-army you-will-accompany with-me that

דָּוִד אֶל־אָכִישׁ לָכֵן אַתָּה תֵדַע אֵת אֲשֶׁר־יַעֲשֶׂה עַבְדֶּךָ
servant-of-you he-can-do what *** you-will-see you then Achish to David

him Ziklag, and it has belonged to the kings of Judah ever since. [7]David lived in Philistine territory a year and four months.

[8]Now David and his men went up and raided the Geshurites, the Girzites and the Amalekites. (From ancient times these peoples had lived in the land extending to Shur and Egypt.) [9]Whenever David attacked an area, he did not leave a man or woman alive, but took sheep and cattle, donkeys and camels, and clothes. Then he returned to Achish. [10]When Achish asked, "Where did you go raiding today?" David would say, "Against the Negev of Judah" or "Against the Negev of Jerahmeel" or "Against the Negev of the Kenites." [11]He did not leave a man or woman alive to be brought to Gath, for he thought, "They might inform on us and say, 'This is what David did.'" And such was his practice as long as he lived in Philistine territory. [12]Achish trusted David and said to himself, "He has become so odious to his people, the Israelites, that he will be my servant forever."

*Saul and the Witch of Endor*

**28** In those days the Philistines gathered their forces to fight against Israel. Achish said to David, "You must understand that you and your men will accompany me in the army."

[2]David said, "Then you will see for yourself what your servant can do."

*8 The NIV here translates the *Kethib* form; the *Qere* reads *and-the-Gizrite.*

†*10* Some mss and versions read אֵי, *where?*

††*10* Most mss have *sheva* under the *yod* and *pathah* under the *resh* (הַיְרַ).

°8 ק והגזרי

וַיֹּאמֶר אָכִישׁ אֶל־ דָּוִד לָכֵן שֹׁמֵר לְרֹאשִׁי
of-head-of-me being-guard very-well David to Achish and-he-replied

אֲשִׂימְךָ כָּל־ הַיָּמִים׃ וּשְׁמוּאֵל מֵת וַיִּסְפְּדוּ־
and-they-mourned he-was-dead now-Samuel (3) the-days all-of I-will-make-you

לוֹ כָּל־ יִשְׂרָאֵל וַיִּקְבְּרֻהוּ בָרָמָה וּבְעִירוֹ
even-in-town-of-him in-the-Ramah and-they-buried-him Israel all-of for-him

וְשָׁאוּל הֵסִיר הָאֹבוֹת וְאֶת־ הַיִּדְּעֹנִים מֵהָאָרֶץ׃
from-the-land the-spiritists and the-mediums he-expelled and-Saul

וַיִּקָּבְצוּ פְלִשְׁתִּים וַיָּבֹאוּ וַיַּחֲנוּ בְשׁוּנֵם
at-Shunem and-they-camped and-they-came Philistines and-they-assembled (4)

וַיִּקְבֹּץ שָׁאוּל אֶת־ כָּל־ יִשְׂרָאֵל וַיַּחֲנוּ בַּגִּלְבֹּעַ׃
at-the-Gilboa and-they-camped Israel all-of *** Saul and-he-gathered

וַיַּרְא שָׁאוּל אֶת־ מַחֲנֵה פְלִשְׁתִּים וַיִּרָא וַיֶּחֱרַד
and-he-was-terrified then-he-feared Philistines army-of *** Saul when-he-saw (5)

לִבּוֹ מְאֹד׃ וַיִּשְׁאַל שָׁאוּל בַּיהוָה וְלֹא עָנָהוּ
he-answered-him but-not of-Yahweh Saul and-he-inquired (6) greatly heart-of-him

יְהוָה גַּם בַּחֲלֹמוֹת גַּם בָּאוּרִים גַּם בַּנְּבִיאִם׃ וַיֹּאמֶר
then-he-said (7) by-the-prophets or by-the-Urim or by-dreams either Yahweh

שָׁאוּל לַעֲבָדָיו בַּקְּשׁוּ־ לִי אֵשֶׁת בַּעֲלַת־ אוֹב וְאֵלְכָה
so-I-may-go medium mistress-of woman-of for-me find! to-attendants-of-him Saul

אֵלֶיהָ וְאֶדְרְשָׁה־ בָּהּ וַיֹּאמְרוּ עֲבָדָיו אֵלָיו הִנֵּה
see! to-him attendants-of-him and-they-said of-her and-I-may-inquire to-her

אֵשֶׁת בַּעֲלַת־ אוֹב בְּעֵין דּוֹר׃ וַיִּתְחַפֵּשׂ שָׁאוּל
Saul so-he-disguised-himself (8) Dor in-En medium mistress-of woman-of

וַיִּלְבַּשׁ בְּגָדִים אֲחֵרִים וַיֵּלֶךְ הוּא וּשְׁנֵי אֲנָשִׁים עִמּוֹ
with-him men and-two-of he and-he-went other-ones clothes and-he-put-on

וַיָּבֹאוּ אֶל־ הָאִשָּׁה לָיְלָה וַיֹּאמֶר קָסוֹמִי־ נָא לִי
for-me now! consult! and-he-said night the-woman to and-they-came

בָּאוֹב וְהַעֲלִי לִי אֵת אֲשֶׁר־ אֹמַר אֵלָיִךְ׃ וַתֹּאמֶר
but-she-said (9) to-you I-name whom *** for-me and-bring-up! with-the-spirit

הָאִשָּׁה אֵלָיו הִנֵּה אַתָּה יָדַעְתָּ אֵת אֲשֶׁר־ עָשָׂה שָׁאוּל אֲשֶׁר הִכְרִית אֶת־
*** he-cut-off that Saul he-did what *** you-know you see! to-him the-woman

הָאֹבוֹת וְאֶת־ הַיִּדְּעֹנִי מִן־ הָאָרֶץ וְלָמָה אַתָּה מִתְנַקֵּשׁ
setting-trap you now-why? the-land from the-spiritist and the-mediums

בְּנַפְשִׁי לַהֲמִיתֵנִי׃ וַיִּשָּׁבַע לָהּ שָׁאוּל בַּיהוָה לֵאמֹר
to-say by-Yahweh Saul to-her and-he-swore (10) to-kill-me for-life-of-me

חַי־ יְהוָה אִם־ יִקְּרֵךְ עָוֹן בַּדָּבָר הַזֶּה׃
the-this for-the-thing punishment he-will-come-on-you not Yahweh life-of

Achish replied, "Very well, I will make you my bodyguard for life."

3Now Samuel was dead, and all Israel had mourned for him and buried him in his own town of Ramah. Saul had expelled the mediums and spiritists from the land.

4The Philistines assembled and came and set up camp at Shunem, while Saul gathered all the Israelites and set up camp at Gilboa. 5When Saul saw the Philistine army, he was afraid; terror filled his heart. 6He inquired of the LORD, but the LORD did not answer him by dreams or Urim or prophets. 7Saul then said to his attendants, "Find me a woman who is a medium, so I may go and inquire of her."

"There is one in Endor," they said.

8So Saul disguised himself, putting on other clothes, and at night he and two men went to the woman. "Consult a spirit for me," he said, "and bring up for me the one I name."

9But the woman said to him, "Surely you know what Saul has done. He has cut off the mediums and spiritists from the land. Why have you set a trap for my life to bring about my death?"

10Saul swore to her by the LORD, "As surely as the LORD lives, you will not be punished for this."

m13 Or *see spirits*; or *see gods*

°8 ק קסמי

וַתֹּאמֶר הָאִשָּׁה אֶת־ מִי אַעֲלֶה־ לָּךְ וַיֹּאמֶר

and-he-said for-you shall-I-bring-up whom? *** the-woman then-she-asked (11)

אֶת־שְׁמוּאֵל הַעֲלִי־ לִי׃ וַתֵּרֶא הָאִשָּׁה אֶת־ שְׁמוּאֵל

Samuel *** the-woman when-she-saw (12) for-me bring-up! Samuel ***

וַתִּזְעַק בְּקוֹל גָּדוֹל וַתֹּאמֶר הָאִשָּׁה אֶל־שָׁאוּל לֵאמֹר לָמָּה

why? to-say Saul to the-woman and-she-said loud with-voice then-she-cried-out

רִמִּיתָנִי וְאַתָּה שָׁאוּל׃ וַיֹּאמֶר לָהּ הַמֶּלֶךְ אַל־ תִּירְאִי

you-fear not the-king to-her and-he-said (13) Saul for-you you-deceived-me

כִּי מָה רָאִית וַתֹּאמֶר הָאִשָּׁה אֶל־שָׁאוּל אֱלֹהִים רָאִיתִי עֹלִים

ones-coming-up I-see spirits Saul to the-woman and-she-said you-see what? now

מִן־ הָאָרֶץ׃ וַיֹּאמֶר לָהּ מַה־ תָּאֳרוֹ וַתֹּאמֶר אִישׁ

man and-she-said look-of-him what? to-her and-he-asked (14) the-ground from

זָקֵן עֹלֶה וְהוּא עֹטֶה מְעִיל וַיֵּדַע שָׁאוּל כִּי־ שְׁמוּאֵל הוּא

he Samuel that Saul then-he-knew robe wearing and-he coming-up old

וַיִּקֹּד אַפַּיִם אַרְצָה וַיִּשְׁתָּחוּ׃ וַיֹּאמֶר שְׁמוּאֵל

Samuel and-he-said (15) and-he-prostrated-himself to-ground faces and-he-bowed

אֶל־שָׁאוּל לָמָּה הִרְגַּזְתַּנִי לְהַעֲלוֹת אֹתִי וַיֹּאמֶר שָׁאוּל צַר־

he-distresses Saul and-he-said me to-bring-up you-disturbed-me why? Saul to

לִי מְאֹד וּפְלִשְׁתִּים ׀ נִלְחָמִים בִּי וֵאלֹהִים סָר

he-turned-away and-God against-me ones-fighting and-Philistines greatly to-me

מֵעָלַי וְלֹא־ עָנָנִי עוֹד גַּם בְּיַד־ הַנְּבִאִים גַּם־

or the-prophets by-hand-of either longer he-answers-me and-not from-with-me

בַּחֲלֹמוֹת וָאֶקְרָאֶה לְךָ לְהוֹדִיעֵנִי מָה אֶעֱשֶׂה׃ וַיֹּאמֶר

and-he-said (16) I-should-do what to-tell-me on-you so-I-called by-dreams

שְׁמוּאֵל וְלָמָּה תִּשְׁאָלֵנִי וַיהוָה סָר מֵעָלֶיךָ וַיְהִי

and-he-became from-with-you he-turned for-Yahweh you-consult-me so-why? Samuel

עָרֶךָ׃ וַיַּעַשׂ יְהוָה לוֹ כַּאֲשֶׁר דִּבֶּר בְּיָדִי

by-hand-of-me he-predicted just-as for-him Yahweh and-he-did (17) enemy-of-you

וַיִּקְרַע יְהוָה אֶת־ הַמַּמְלָכָה מִיָּדֶךָ וַיִּתְּנָהּ

and-he-gave-her from-hand-of-you the-kingdom *** Yahweh and-he-tore

לְרֵעֲךָ לְדָוִד׃ כַּאֲשֶׁר לֹא־ שָׁמַעְתָּ בְּקוֹל יְהוָה

Yahweh to-voice-of you-obeyed not because (18) to-David to-neighbor-of-you

וְלֹא־ עָשִׂיתָ חֲרוֹן־ אַפּוֹ בַּעֲמָלֵק עַל־ כֵּן

this for against-Amalek wrath-of-him fierceness-of you-carried-out and-not

הַדָּבָר הַזֶּה עָשָׂה־ לְךָ יְהוָה הַיּוֹם הַזֶּה׃ וְיִתֵּן

and-he-will-give (19) the-this the-day Yahweh to-you he-did the-this the-thing

יְהוָה גַּם אֶת־ יִשְׂרָאֵל עִמְּךָ בְּיַד־ פְּלִשְׁתִּים וּמָחָר אַתָּה

you and-tomorrow Philistines into-hand-of with-you Israel *** both Yahweh

11Then the woman asked, "Whom shall I bring up for you?"

"Bring up Samuel," he said.

12When the woman saw Samuel, she cried out at the top of her voice and said to Saul, "Why have you deceived me? You are Saul!"

13The king said to her, "Don't be afraid. What do you see?"

The woman said, "I see a spirit[m] coming up out of the ground."

14"What does he look like?" he asked.

"An old man wearing a robe is coming up," she said.

Then Saul knew it was Samuel, and he bowed down and prostrated himself with his face to the ground.

15Samuel said to Saul, "Why have you disturbed me by bringing me up?"

"I am in great distress," Saul said. "The Philistines are fighting against me, and God has turned away from me. He no longer answers me, either by prophets or by dreams. So I have called on you to tell me what to do."

16Samuel said, "Why do you consult me, now that the LORD has turned away from you and become your enemy? 17The LORD has done what he predicted through me. The LORD has torn the kingdom out of your hands and given it to one of your neighbors—to David. 18Because you did not obey the LORD or carry out his fierce wrath against the Amalekites, the LORD has done this to you today. 19The LORD will hand over both Israel and you to the Philistines, and tomorrow you

וּבָנֶיךָ עִמִּי גַּם אֶת־ מַחֲנֵה יִשְׂרָאֵל יִתֵּן יְהוָה
Yahweh he-will-give Israel army-of *** also with-me and-sons-of-you

בְּיַד־ פְלִשְׁתִּים׃ וַיְמַהֵר שָׁאוּל וַיִּפֹּל מְלֹא־
full-of and-he-fell Saul and-he-was-quick (20) Philistines into-hand-of

קוֹמָתוֹ אַרְצָה וַיִּרָא מְאֹד מִדִּבְרֵי שְׁמוּאֵל גַּם־
also Samuel from-words-of greatly and-he-feared on-ground length-of-him

כֹּחַ לֹא־ הָיָה בוֹ כִּי לֹא אָכַל לֶחֶם כָּל־ הַיּוֹם וְכָל־
and-all-of the-day all-of food he-ate not for in-him he-was not strength

הַלָּיְלָה׃ וַתָּבוֹא הָאִשָּׁה אֶל־ שָׁאוּל וַתֵּרֶא כִּי־ נִבְהַל
being-shaken that and-she-saw Saul to the-woman when-she-came (21) the-night

מְאֹד וַתֹּאמֶר אֵלָיו הִנֵּה שָׁמְעָה שִׁפְחָתְךָ בְּקוֹלֶךָ
to-voice-of-you servant-of-you she-obeyed see! to-him then-she-said greatly

וָאָשִׂים נַפְשִׁי בְּכַפִּי וָאֶשְׁמַע אֶת־ דְּבָרֶיךָ אֲשֶׁר דִּבַּרְתָּ
you-told that words-of-you *** and-I-did in-hand-of-me life-of-me and-I-took

אֵלָי׃ וְעַתָּה שְׁמַע־ נָא גַם־ אַתָּה בְּקוֹל שִׁפְחָתֶךָ
servant-of-you to-voice-of you also now! listen! and-now (22) to-me

וְאָשִׂמָה לְפָנֶיךָ פַּת־ לֶחֶם וֶאֱכוֹל וִיהִי בְךָ כֹּחַ
strength in-you so-he-will-be and-eat! food some-of before-you and-let-me-set

כִּי תֵלֵךְ בַּדָּרֶךְ׃ וַיְמָאֵן וַיֹּאמֶר לֹא אֹכַל
I-will-eat not and-he-said and-he-refused (23) on-the-way you-can-go so

וַיִּפְרְצוּ־ בוֹ עֲבָדָיו וְגַם־ הָאִשָּׁה וַיִּשְׁמַע
and-he-listened the-woman and-also men-of-him with-him but-they-urged

לְקֹלָם וַיָּקָם מֵהָאָרֶץ וַיֵּשֶׁב אֶל־ הַמִּטָּה׃
the-couch on and-he-sat from-the-ground and-he-got-up to-voice-of-them

וְלָאִשָּׁה עֵגֶל־ מַרְבֵּק בַּבַּיִת וַתְּמַהֵר
and-she-hurried at-the-house fattened calf-of now-to-the-woman (24)

וַתִּזְבָּחֵהוּ וַתִּקַּח־ קֶמַח וַתָּלָשׁ וַתֹּפֵהוּ
and-she-baked-him and-she-kneaded flour and-she-took and-she-butchered-him

מַצּוֹת׃ וַתַּגֵּשׁ לִפְנֵי־ שָׁאוּל וְלִפְנֵי עֲבָדָיו
men-of-him and-before Saul before then-she-set (25) breads-without-yeast

וַיֹּאכֵלוּ וַיָּקֻמוּ וַיֵּלְכוּ בַּלַּיְלָה הַהוּא׃
the-that on-the-night and-they-left then-they-got-up and-they-ate

וַיִּקְבְּצוּ פְלִשְׁתִּים אֶת־ כָּל־ מַחֲנֵיהֶם אֲפֵקָה
at-Aphek forces-of-them all-of *** Philistines and-they-gathered (29:1)

וְיִשְׂרָאֵל חֹנִים בַּעַיִן אֲשֶׁר בְּיִזְרְעֶאל׃ וְסַרְנֵי
and-rulers-of (2) in-Jezreel that by-the-spring ones-camping and-Israel

פְלִשְׁתִּים עֹבְרִים לְמֵאוֹת וְלַאֲלָפִים וְדָוִד
and-David and-with-thousands with-hundreds ones-marching Philistines

and your sons will be with me. The LORD will also hand over the army of Israel to the Philistines."

[20]Immediately Saul fell full length on the ground, filled with fear because of Samuel's words. His strength was gone, for he had eaten nothing all that day and night.

[21]When the woman came to Saul and saw that he was greatly shaken, she said, "Look, your maidservant has obeyed you. I took my life in my hands and did what you told me to do. [22]Now please listen to your servant and let me give you some food so you may eat and have the strength to go on your way."

[23]He refused and said, "I will not eat."

But his men joined the woman in urging him, and he listened to them. He got up from the ground and sat on the couch.

[24]The woman had a fattened calf at the house, which she butchered at once. She took some flour, kneaded it and baked bread without yeast. [25]Then she set it before Saul and his men, and they ate. That same night they got up and left.

*Achish Sends David Back to Ziklag*

29 The Philistines gathered all their forces at Aphek, and Israel camped by the spring in Jezreel. [2]As the Philistine rulers marched with their units of hundreds and thousands, David and his men

וַאֲנָשָׁיו עֹבְרִים בָּאַחֲרֹנָה עִם־אָכִישׁ׃ וַיֹּאמְרוּ
and-they-asked (3) Achish with at-the-rear ones-marching and-men-of-him

שָׂרֵי פְלִשְׁתִּים מָה הָעִבְרִים הָאֵלֶּה וַיֹּאמֶר אָכִישׁ
Achish and-he-replied the-these the-Hebrews what? Philistines commanders-of

אֶל־שָׂרֵי פְלִשְׁתִּים הֲלוֹא־זֶה דָוִד עֶבֶד ׀ שָׁאוּל מֶלֶךְ־יִשְׂרָאֵל
Israel king-of Saul officer-of David this not? Philistines commanders-of to

אֲשֶׁר הָיָה אִתִּי זֶה יָמִים אוֹ־זֶה שָׁנִים וְלֹא־מָצָאתִי בוֹ מְאוּמָה
anything in-him I-found and-not years this or days this with-me he-was who

מִיּוֹם נָפְלוֹ עַד־הַיּוֹם הַזֶּה׃ וַיִּקְצְפוּ עָלָיו
with-him but-they-were-angry (4) the-this the-day to to-leave-him from-day

שָׂרֵי פְלִשְׁתִּים וַיֹּאמְרוּ לוֹ שָׂרֵי פְלִשְׁתִּים
Philistines commanders-of to-him and-they-said Philistines commanders-of

הָשֵׁב אֶת־הָאִישׁ וְיָשֹׁב אֶל־מְקוֹמוֹ אֲשֶׁר הִפְקַדְתּוֹ
you-assigned-him that place-of-him to that-he-may-return the-man *** send-back!

שָׁם וְלֹא־יֵרֵד עִמָּנוּ בַּמִּלְחָמָה וְלֹא־יִהְיֶה־
he-will-be so-not into-the-battle with-us he-must-go-down for-not there

לָּנוּ לְשָׂטָן בַּמִּלְחָמָה וּבַמֶּה יִתְרַצֶּה
could-he-regain-favor for-by-the-what? in-the-battle as-adversary against-us

זֶה אֶל־אֲדֹנָיו הֲלוֹא בְּרָאשֵׁי הָאֲנָשִׁים הָהֵם׃ הֲלוֹא־זֶה
this not? (5) the-these the-men with-heads-of not? masters-of-him with this

דָוִד אֲשֶׁר יַעֲנוּ־לוֹ בַּמְּחֹלוֹת לֵאמֹר הִכָּה שָׁאוּל
Saul he-has-slain to-say in-the-dances about-him they-sang whom David

בַּאֲלָפָיו וְדָוִד בְּרִבְבֹתָו׃° וַיִּקְרָא
so-he-called (6) to-tens-of-thousands-of-him and-David to-thousands-of-him

אָכִישׁ אֶל־דָּוִד וַיֹּאמֶר אֵלָיו חַי־יְהוָה כִּי־יָשָׁר אַתָּה
you reliable indeed Yahweh life-of to-him and-he-said David to Achish

וְטוֹב בְּעֵינַי צֵאתְךָ וּבֹאֲךָ אִתִּי בַּמַּחֲנֶה
in-the-army with-me and-to-serve-you to-go-out-you in-eyes-of-me and-pleasing

כִּי לֹא־מָצָאתִי בְךָ רָעָה מִיּוֹם בֹּאֲךָ אֵלַי עַד־הַיּוֹם
the-day until to-me to-come-you from-day fault in-you I-found not for

הַזֶּה וּבְעֵינֵי הַסְּרָנִים לֹא־טוֹב אָתָּה׃ וְעַתָּה שׁוּב
turn-back! so-now (7) you pleasing not the-rulers but-in-eyes-of the-this

וְלֵךְ בְּשָׁלוֹם וְלֹא־תַעֲשֶׂה רָע בְּעֵינֵי סַרְנֵי פְלִשְׁתִּים׃
Philistines rulers-of in-eyes-of displeasing you-do and-not in-peace and-go!

וַיֹּאמֶר דָּוִד אֶל־אָכִישׁ כִּי מֶה עָשִׂיתִי וּמַה־מָּצָאתָ
you-found and-what? I-did what? but Achish to David and-he-asked (8)

בְעַבְדְּךָ מִיּוֹם אֲשֶׁר הָיִיתִי לְפָנֶיךָ עַד הַיּוֹם הַזֶּה
the-this the-day until before-you I-came that from-day against-servant-of-you

were marching at the rear with Achish. [3]The commanders of the Philistines asked, "What about these Hebrews?"

Achish replied, "Is this not David, who was an officer of Saul king of Israel? He has already been with me for over a year, and from the day he left Saul until now, I have found no fault in him."

[4]But the Philistine commanders were angry with him and said, "Send the man back, that he may return to the place you assigned him. He must not go with us into battle, or he will turn against us during the fighting. How better could he regain his master's favor than by taking the heads of our own men? [5]Isn't this the David they sang about in their dances:

"'Saul has slain his
thousands,
and David his tens of
thousands'?"

[6]So Achish called David and said to him, "As surely as the LORD lives, you have been reliable, and I would be pleased to have you serve with me in the army. From the day you came to me until now, I have found no fault in you, but the rulers don't approve of you. [7]Turn back and go in peace; do nothing to displease the Philistine rulers."

[8]"But what have I done?" asked David. "What have you found against your servant from the day I came to you until now? Why can't I go and

°5 ק ברבבתיו

כִּי לֹא אָבוֹא וְנִלְחַמְתִּי בְּאֹיְבֵי אֲדֹנִי הַמֶּלֶךְ׃

the-king lord-of-me against-being-enemies-of and-I-can-fight I-can-go not that

וַיַּעַן אָכִישׁ וַיֹּאמֶר אֶל־דָּוִד יָדַעְתִּי כִּי טוֹב אַתָּה

you pleasing that I-know David to and-he-said Achish and-he-answered (9)

בְּעֵינַי כְּמַלְאַךְ אֱלֹהִים אַךְ שָׂרֵי פְלִשְׁתִּים אָמְרוּ

they-said Philistines commanders-of nevertheless God as-angel-of in-eyes-of-me

לֹא־יַעֲלֶה עִמָּנוּ בַּמִּלְחָמָה׃ וְעַתָּה הַשְׁכֵּם בַּבֹּקֶר

in-the-morning get-up! and-now (10) into-the-battle with-us he-must-go-up not

וְעַבְדֵי אֲדֹנֶיךָ אֲשֶׁר־בָּאוּ אִתָּךְ וְהִשְׁכַּמְתֶּם

and-you-get-up with-you they-came who masters-of-you and-servants-of

בַּבֹּקֶר וְאוֹר לָכֶם וָלֵכוּ׃ וַיַּשְׁכֵּם דָּוִד

David so-he-got-up (11) then-leave! to-you when-to-be-light in-the-morning

הוּא וַאֲנָשָׁיו לָלֶכֶת בַּבֹּקֶר לָשׁוּב אֶל־אֶרֶץ פְּלִשְׁתִּים

Philistines land-of to to-go-back in-the-morning to-leave and-men-of-him he

וּפְלִשְׁתִּים עָלוּ יִזְרְעֶאל׃ וַיְהִי בְּבֹא דָוִד

David when-to-reach and-he-was (30:1) Jezreel they-went-up and-Philistines

וַאֲנָשָׁיו צִקְלַג בַּיּוֹם הַשְּׁלִישִׁי וַעֲמָלֵקִי פָשְׁטוּ אֶל־נֶגֶב

Negev in they-raided now-Amalekite the-third on-the-day Ziklag and-men-of-him

וְאֶל־צִקְלַג וַיַּכּוּ אֶת־צִקְלַג וַיִּשְׂרְפוּ אֹתָהּ בָּאֵשׁ׃

with-fire her and-they-burned Ziklag *** and-they-attacked Ziklag and-in

וַיִּשְׁבּוּ אֶת־הַנָּשִׁים אֲשֶׁר־בָּהּ מִקָּטֹן וְעַד־גָּדוֹל לֹא

not old even-to from-young in-her who the-women *** and-they-captured (2)

הֵמִיתוּ אִישׁ וַיִּנְהֲגוּ וַיֵּלְכוּ לְדַרְכָּם׃

on-way-of-them and-they-went but-they-carried-off any they-killed

וַיָּבֹא דָוִד וַאֲנָשָׁיו אֶל־הָעִיר וְהִנֵּה שְׂרוּפָה

being-destroyed then-see! the-town to and-men-of-him David when-he-came (3)

בָּאֵשׁ וּנְשֵׁיהֶם וּבְנֵיהֶם וּבְנֹתֵיהֶם

and-daughters-of-them and-sons-of-them and-wives-of-them by-fire

נִשְׁבּוּ׃ וַיִּשָּׂא דָוִד וְהָעָם אֲשֶׁר־אִתּוֹ אֶת־

*** with-him who and-the-people David so-he-raised (4) they-were-captured

קוֹלָם וַיִּבְכּוּ עַד אֲשֶׁר אֵין־בָּהֶם כֹּחַ לִבְכּוֹת׃

to-weep strength in-them not when until and-they-wept voice-of-them

וּשְׁתֵּי נְשֵׁי־דָוִד נִשְׁבּוּ אֲחִינֹעַם הַיִּזְרְעֵלִית

the-Jezreelite Ahinoam they-were-captured David wives-of and-two-of (5)

וַאֲבִיגַיִל אֵשֶׁת נָבָל הַכַּרְמְלִי׃ וַתֵּצֶר לְדָוִד

to-David and-she-distressed (6) the-Carmelite Nabal widow-of and-Abigail

מְאֹד כִּי־אָמְרוּ הָעָם לְסָקְלוֹ כִּי־מָרָה נֶפֶשׁ

spirit-of she-was-bitter for to-stone-him the-people they-talked for greatly

fight against the enemies of my lord the king?"

9 Achish answered, "I know that you have been as pleasing in my eyes as an angel of God; nevertheless, the Philistine commanders have said, 'He must not go up with us into battle.' 10 Now get up early, along with your master's servants who have come with you, and leave in the morning as soon as it is light."

11 So David and his men got up early in the morning to go back to the land of the Philistines, and the Philistines went up to Jezreel.

*David Destroys the Amalekites*

30 David and his men reached Ziklag on the third day. Now the Amalekites had raided the Negev and Ziklag. They had attacked Ziklag and burned it, 2 and had taken captive the women and all who were in it, both young and old. They killed none of them, but carried them off as they went on their way.

3 When David and his men came to Ziklag, they found it destroyed by fire and their wives and sons and daughters taken captive. 4 So David and his men wept aloud until they had no strength left to weep. 5 David's two wives had been captured—Ahinoam of Jezreel and Abigail, the widow of Nabal of Carmel. 6 David was greatly distressed because the men were talking of stoning him; each one was bitter in

כָּל־הָעָם אִישׁ עַל־בָּנָו° וְעַל־בְּנֹתָיו
daughters-of-him and-because-of sons-of-him because-of each the-people all-of

וַיִּתְחַזֵּק דָּוִד בַּיהוָה אֱלֹהָיו׃ וַיֹּאמֶר דָּוִד אֶל־
to David then-he-said (7) God-of-him in-Yahweh David but-he-found-strength

אֶבְיָתָר הַכֹּהֵן בֶּן־אֲחִימֶלֶךְ הַגִּישָׁה־נָּא לִי הָאֵפֹד וַיַּגֵּשׁ
so-he-brought the-ephod to-me now! bring! Ahimelech son-of the-priest Abiathar

אֶבְיָתָר אֶת־הָאֵפֹד אֶל־דָּוִד׃ וַיִּשְׁאַל דָּוִד בַּיהוָה לֵאמֹר
to-say of-Yahweh David and-he-inquired (8) David to the-ephod *** Abiathar

אֶרְדֹּף אַחֲרֵי הַגְּדוּד־הַזֶּה הַאַשִּׂגֶנּוּ
will-I-overtake-him? the-this the-raiding-party after shall-I-pursue

וַיֹּאמֶר לוֹ רְדֹף כִּי־הַשֵּׂג תַּשִּׂיג וְהַצֵּל
and-to-rescue you-will-overtake to-overtake for pursue! to-him and-he-answered

תַּצִּיל׃ וַיֵּלֶךְ דָּוִד הוּא וְשֵׁשׁ־מֵאוֹת אִישׁ אֲשֶׁר אִתּוֹ
with-him who man hundreds and-six he David and-he-went (9) you-will-rescue

וַיָּבֹאוּ עַד־נַחַל הַבְּשׂוֹר וְהַנּוֹתָרִים עָמָדוּ׃
they-stayed and-the-ones-remaining the-Besor Ravine-of to and-they-came

וַיִּרְדֹּף דָּוִד הוּא וְאַרְבַּע־מֵאוֹת אִישׁ וַיַּעַמְדוּ מָאתַיִם
two-hundreds but-they-stayed man hundreds and-four he David and-he-pursued (10)

אִישׁ אֲשֶׁר פִּגְּרוּ מֵעֲבֹר אֶת־נַחַל הַבְּשׂוֹר׃
the-Besor Ravine-of *** from-to-cross they-were-exhausted who man

וַיִּמְצְאוּ אִישׁ־מִצְרִי בַּשָּׂדֶה וַיִּקְחוּ אֹתוֹ אֶל־דָּוִד
David to him and-they-brought in-the-field Egyptian man and-they-found (11)

וַיִּתְּנוּ־לוֹ לֶחֶם וַיֹּאכַל וַיַּשְׁקֻהוּ מָיִם׃
waters and-they-gave-to-drink-him and-he-ate food to-him and-they-gave

וַיִּתְּנוּ־לוֹ פֶלַח דְּבֵלָה וּשְׁנֵי צִמֻּקִים
raisin-cakes and-two-of pressed-fig-cake part-of to-him and-they-gave (12)

וַיֹּאכַל וַתָּשָׁב רוּחוֹ אֵלָיו כִּי לֹא־אָכַל לֶחֶם וְלֹא־
and-not food he-ate not for to-him spirit-of-him and-she-returned and-he-ate

שָׁתָה מַיִם שְׁלֹשָׁה יָמִים וּשְׁלֹשָׁה לֵילוֹת׃ וַיֹּאמֶר לוֹ דָוִד
David to-him and-he-asked (13) nights and-three days three waters he-drank

לְמִי־אַתָּה וְאֵי מִזֶּה אָתָּה וַיֹּאמֶר נַעַר מִצְרִי אָנֹכִי עֶבֶד
slave I Egyptian man and-he-said you from-there and-where? you to-whom?

לְאִישׁ עֲמָלֵקִי וַיַּעַזְבֵנִי אֲדֹנִי כִּי חָלִיתִי הַיּוֹם
the-day I-became-ill for master-of-me and-he-abandoned-me Amalekite of-man

שְׁלֹשָׁה׃ אֲנַחְנוּ פָּשַׁטְנוּ נֶגֶב הַכְּרֵתִי וְעַל־אֲשֶׁר לִיהוּדָה וְעַל־
and-in to-Judah what and-in the-Kerethite Negev-of we-raided we (14) three

נֶגֶב כָּלֵב וְאֶת־צִקְלַג שָׂרַפְנוּ בָאֵשׁ׃ וַיֹּאמֶר אֵלָיו דָּוִד
David to-him and-he-asked (15) with-fire we-burned Ziklag and Caleb Negev-of

spirit because of his sons and daughters. But David found strength in the LORD his God.

7Then David said to Abiathar the priest, the son of Ahimelech, "Bring me the ephod." Abiathar brought it to him, 8and David inquired of the LORD, "Shall I pursue this raiding party? Will I overtake them?"

"Pursue them," he answered. "You will certainly overtake them and succeed in the rescue."

9David and the six hundred men with him came to the Besor Ravine, where some stayed behind, 10for two hundred men were too exhausted to cross the ravine. But David and four hundred men continued the pursuit.

11They found an Egyptian in a field and brought him to David. They gave him water to drink and food to eat— 12part of a cake of pressed figs and two cakes of raisins. He ate and was revived, for he had not eaten any food or drunk any water for three days and three nights.

13David asked him, "To whom do you belong, and where do you come from?"

He said, "I am an Egyptian, the slave of an Amalekite. My master abandoned me when I became ill three days ago. 14We raided the Negev of the Kerethites and the territory belonging to Judah and the Negev of Caleb. And we burned Ziklag."

15David asked him, "Can

°6 ק בניו

הֲתוֹרִדֵנִי אֶל־ הַגְּדוּד הַזֶּה וַיֹּאמֶר הִשָּׁבְעָה לִּי

to-me swear! and-he-answered the-this the-raiding-party to can-you-lead-me?

בֵאלֹהִים אִם־ תְּמִיתֵנִי וְאִם־ תַּסְגִּרֵנִי בְּיַד־

to-hand-of you-will-turn-over-me and-not you-will-kill-me not before-God

אֲדֹנִי וְאוֹרִדְךָ אֶל־ הַגְּדוּד הַזֶּה׃

the-this the-raiding-party to and-I-will-take-you master-of-me

וַיֹּרִדֵהוּ וְהִנֵּה נְטֻשִׁים עַל־ פְּנֵי כָל־

all-of surfaces-of over ones-being-scattered and-see! so-he-led-down-him (16)

הָאָרֶץ אֹכְלִים וְשֹׁתִים וְחֹגְגִים בְּכֹל

over-all-of and-ones-reveling and-ones-drinking ones-eating the-country

הַשָּׁלָל הַגָּדוֹל אֲשֶׁר לָקְחוּ מֵאֶרֶץ פְּלִשְׁתִּים וּמֵאֶרֶץ

and-from-land-of Philistines from-land-of they-took that the-great the-plunder

יְהוּדָה׃ וַיַּכֵּם דָּוִד מֵהַנֶּשֶׁף וְעַד־ הָעֶרֶב

the-evening even-to from-the-dusk David and-he-fought-them (17) Judah

לְמָחֳרָתָם וְלֹא־ נִמְלַט מֵהֶם אִישׁ כִּי אִם־אַרְבַּע

four only except any from-them he-got-away and-not of-next-day-of-them

מֵאוֹת אִישׁ־ נַעַר אֲשֶׁר־ רָכְבוּ עַל־ הַגְּמַלִּים וַיָּנֻסוּ׃

and-they-fled the-camels on they-rode-off who young man hundreds

וַיַּצֵּל דָּוִד אֵת כָּל־אֲשֶׁר לָקְחוּ עֲמָלֵק וְאֶת־ שְׁתֵּי

two-of including Amalek they-took that all *** David so-he-recovered (18)

נָשָׁיו הִצִּיל דָּוִד׃ וְלֹא נֶעְדַּר־ לָהֶם מִן־

from from-them he-was-missing and-nothing (19) David he-recovered wives-of-him

הַקָּטֹן וְעַד־ הַגָּדוֹל וְעַד־ בָּנִים וּבָנוֹת וּמִשָּׁלָל וְעַד

even-to or-from-plunder and-girls boys and-to the-old even-to the-young

כָּל־ אֲשֶׁר לָקְחוּ לָהֶם הַכֹּל הֵשִׁיב דָּוִד׃

David he-brought-back the-whole for-them they-took that anything

וַיִּקַּח דָּוִד אֶת־ כָּל־ הַצֹּאן וְהַבָּקָר נָהֲגוּ לִפְנֵי

ahead-of they-drove and-the-herd the-flock all-of *** David and-he-took (20)

הַמִּקְנֶה הַהוּא וַיֹּאמְרוּ זֶה שְׁלַל דָּוִד׃ וַיָּבֹא

then-he-came (21) David plunder-of this and-they-said the-this the-stock

דָּוִד אֶל־ מָאתַיִם הָאֲנָשִׁים אֲשֶׁר־ פִּגְּרוּ ׀ מִלֶּכֶת ׀ אַחֲרֵי

after from-to-follow they-were-exhausted who the-men two-hundreds to David

דָּוִד וַיֹּשִׁבֻם בְּנַחַל הַבְּשׂוֹר וַיֵּצְאוּ לִקְרַאת

to-meet and-they-came-out the-Besor at-Ravine-of and-they-left-them David

דָּוִד וְלִקְרַאת הָעָם אֲשֶׁר־ אִתּוֹ וַיִּגַּשׁ דָּוִד אֶת־

*** David and-he-approached with-him who the-people and-to-meet David

הָעָם וַיִּשְׁאַל לָהֶם לְשָׁלוֹם׃ וַיַּעַן כָּל־ אִישׁ־

man every-of but-he-said (22) for-peace to-them and-he-greeted the-people

you lead me down to this raiding party?"

He answered, "Swear to me before God that you will not kill me or hand me over to my master, and I will take you down to them."

[16]He led David down, and there they were, scattered over the countryside, eating, drinking and reveling because of the great amount of plunder they had taken from the land of the Philistines and from Judah. [17]David fought them from dusk until the evening of the next day, and none of them got away, except four hundred young men who rode off on camels and fled. [18]David recovered everything the Amalekites had taken, including his two wives. [19]Nothing was missing: young or old, boy or girl, plunder or anything else they had taken. David brought everything back. [20]He took all the flocks and herds, and his men drove them ahead of the other livestock, saying, "This is David's plunder."

[21]Then David came to the two hundred men who had been too exhausted to follow him and who were left behind at the Besor Ravine. They came out to meet David and the people with him. As David and his men approached, he greeted them. [22]But all the evil

רָ֣ע וּבְלִיַּ֗עַל מֵהָאֲנָשִׁים֙ אֲשֶׁ֣ר הָלְכ֣וּ עִם־ דָּוִד֒ וַיֹּאמְר֗וּ
and-they-said David with they-followed who among-the-men and-troublemaker evil

יַ֚עַן אֲשֶׁ֣ר לֹֽא־ הָלְכ֣וּ עִמִּ֔י לֹֽא־ נִתֵּ֣ן לָהֶ֔ם
with-them he-will-be-shared not with-me they-went not that because

מֵהַשָּׁלָ֖ל אֲשֶׁ֣ר הִצַּ֑לְנוּ כִּֽי־ אִם־ אִ֤ישׁ אֶת־ אִשְׁתּוֹ֙ וְאֶת־
and wife-of-him *** each that except we-recovered that from-the-plunder

בָּנָ֔יו וְיִנְהֲג֖וּ וְיֵלֵֽכוּ׃ וַיֹּ֣אמֶר דָּוִ֔ד
David but-he-replied (23) and-they-may-go and-they-make-take children-of-him

לֹֽא־תַעֲשׂ֥וּ כֵ֖ן אֶחָ֑י אֵ֣ת אֲשֶׁר־ נָתַ֤ן יְהוָה֙ לָ֔נוּ וַיִּשְׁמֹ֣ר
for-he-protected to-us Yahweh he-gave what with brothers-of-me that you-do not

אֹתָ֔נוּ וַיִּתֵּ֗ן אֶֽת־ הַגְּד֛וּד הַבָּ֥א עָלֵ֖ינוּ בְּיָדֵֽנוּ׃
into-hand-of-us against-us the-one-coming the-force *** and-he-gave us

וּמִי֙ יִשְׁמַ֣ע לָכֶ֔ם לַדָּבָ֖ר הַזֶּ֑ה כִּ֡י כְּחֵ֣לֶק ׀
as-share-of for the-this to-the-word to-you he-will-listen now-who? (24)

הַיֹּרֵ֣ד בַּמִּלְחָמָ֗ה וּֽכְחֵ֛לֶק הַיֹּשֵׁ֥ב עַל־ הַכֵּלִ֖ים
the-supplies with the-one-staying so-as-share-of to-the-battle the-one-going-down

יַחְדָּ֥ו יַחֲלֹֽקוּ׃ וַֽיְהִ֔י מֵהַיּ֥וֹם הַה֖וּא וָמָ֑עְלָה
and-onward the-that from-the-day and-he-was (25) they-will-share alike

וַיְשִׂמֶ֜הָ לְחֹ֣ק וּלְמִשְׁפָּ֗ט לְיִשְׂרָאֵ֔ל עַ֖ד הַיּ֥וֹם הַזֶּֽה׃
the-this the-day to for-Israel and-as-ordinace as-statute that-he-made-her

וַיָּבֹ֤א דָוִד֙ אֶל־ צִ֣קְלַ֔ג וַיְשַׁלַּ֧ח מֵהַשָּׁלָ֛ל לְזִקְנֵ֥י
to-elders-of from-the-plunder then-he-sent Ziklag in David when-he-arrived (26)

יְהוּדָ֖ה לְרֵעֵ֣הוּ לֵאמֹ֑ר הִנֵּ֤ה לָכֶם֙ בְּרָכָ֔ה מִשְּׁלַ֖ל
from-plunder-of present for-you see! to-say to-friends-of-him Judah

אֹיְבֵ֥י יְהוָֽה׃ לַאֲשֶׁ֥ר בְּבֵֽית־ אֵ֖ל וְלַאֲשֶׁ֣ר בְּרָמֽוֹת־ נֶ֑גֶב
Negev in-Ramoth and-to-whom El in-Beth to-whom (27) Yahweh being-enemies-of

וְלַאֲשֶׁ֖ר בְּיַתִּֽר׃ וְלַאֲשֶׁ֤ר בַּעֲרֹעֵר֙ וְלַאֲשֶׁ֣ר בְּשִׂפְמ֔וֹת
in-Siphmoth and-to-whom in-Aroer and-to-whom (28) in-Jattir and-to-whom

וְלַאֲשֶׁ֖ר בְּאֶשְׁתְּמֹֽעַ׃ וְלַאֲשֶׁ֣ר בְּרָכָ֔ל וְלַאֲשֶׁר֙ בְּעָרֵ֣י
in-towns-of and-to-whom in-Racal and-to-whom (29) in-Eshtemoa and-to-whom

הַיְּרַחְמְאֵלִ֔י וְלַאֲשֶׁ֖ר בְּעָרֵ֥י הַקֵּינִֽי׃ וְלַאֲשֶׁ֧ר בְּחָרְמָ֛ה
in-Hormah and-to-whom (30) the-Kenite in-towns-of and-to-whom the-Jerahmeelite

וְלַאֲשֶׁ֥ר בְּבוֹר־ עָשָׁ֖ן וְלַאֲשֶׁ֥ר בַּעֲתָֽךְ׃ וְלַאֲשֶׁ֥ר בְּחֶבְר֖וֹן
in-Hebron and-to-whom (31) in-Athach and-to-whom Ashan in-Bor and-to-whom

וּֽלְכָל־ הַמְּקֹמ֛וֹת אֲשֶׁר־ הִתְהַלֶּךְ־ שָׁ֥ם דָּוִ֖ד ה֥וּא וַאֲנָשָֽׁיו׃
and-men-of-him he David there he-roamed where the-places and-to-all-of

וּפְלִשְׁתִּ֖ים נִלְחָמִ֣ים בְּיִשְׂרָאֵ֑ל וַיָּנֻ֜סוּ אַנְשֵׁ֣י יִשְׂרָאֵ֗ל
Israel men-of and-they-fled against-Israel ones-fighting now-Philistines (31:1)

men and troublemakers among David's followers said, "Because they did not go out with us, we will not share with them the plunder we recovered. However, each man may take his wife and children and go."

23David replied, "No, my brothers, you must not do that with what the LORD has given us. He has protected us and handed over to us the forces that came against us. 24Who will listen to what you say? The share of the man who stayed with the supplies is to be the same as that of him who went down to the battle. All will share alike." 25David made this a statute and ordinance for Israel from that day to this.

26When David arrived in Ziklag, he sent some of the plunder to the elders of Judah, who were his friends, saying, "Here is a present for you from the plunder of the LORD's enemies."

27He sent it to those who were in Bethel, Ramoth Negev and Jattir; 28to those in Aroer, Siphmoth, Eshtemoa 29and Racal; to those in the towns of the Jerahmeelites and the Kenites; 30to those in Hormah, Bor Ashan, Athach 31and Hebron; and to those in all the other places where David and his men had roamed.

*Saul Takes His Life*

31 Now the Philistines fought against Israel; the Israelites fled before them,

מִפְּנֵי פְלִשְׁתִּים וַיִּפְּלוּ חֲלָלִים בְּהַר הַגִּלְבֹּעַ׃

the-Gilboa on-Mount-of ones-slain and-they-fell Philistines from-before

וַיַּדְבְּקוּ פְלִשְׁתִּים אֶת־ שָׁאוּל וְאֶת־ בָּנָיו וַיַּכּוּ

and-they-killed sons-of-him and Saul *** Philistines and-they-pressed-after (2)

פְלִשְׁתִּים אֶת־ יְהוֹנָתָן וְאֶת־ אֲבִינָדָב וְאֶת־ מַלְכִּי־ שׁוּעַ בְּנֵי שָׁאוּל׃

Saul sons-of Shua Malki and Abinadab and Jonathan *** Philistines

וַתִּכְבַּד הַמִּלְחָמָה אֶל־ שָׁאוּל וַיִּמְצָאֻהוּ

and-they-overtook-him Saul around the-fighting and-she-grew-fierce (3)

הַמּוֹרִים אֲנָשִׁים בַּקָּשֶׁת וַיָּחֶל מְאֹד

critically and-he-was-wounded with-the-bow men the-ones-shooting

מֵהַמּוֹרִים׃ וַיֹּאמֶר שָׁאוּל לְנֹשֵׂא כֵלָיו שְׁלֹף

draw! armors-of-him to-one-bearing Saul and-he-said (4) by-the-ones-shooting

חַרְבְּךָ ׀ וְדָקְרֵנִי בָהּ פֶּן־ יָבוֹאוּ

they-will-come or with-her and-run-through-me! sword-of-you

הָעֲרֵלִים הָאֵלֶּה וּדְקָרֻנִי וְהִתְעַלְּלוּ־

and-they-will-abuse and-they-will-run-through-me the-these the-uncircumcised-ones

בִי וְלֹא אָבָה נֹשֵׂא כֵלָיו כִּי יָרֵא מְאֹד

very he-was-terrified for armors-of-him one-bearing he-would but-not at-me

וַיִּקַּח שָׁאוּל אֶת־ הַחֶרֶב וַיִּפֹּל עָלֶיהָ׃ וַיַּרְא נֹשֵׂא־

one-bearing when-he-saw (5) on-her and-he-fell the-sword *** Saul so-he-took

כֵלָיו כִּי מֵת שָׁאוּל וַיִּפֹּל גַּם־ הוּא עַל־ חַרְבּוֹ

sword-of-him on he also then-he-fell Saul he-was-dead that armors-of-him

וַיָּמָת עִמּוֹ׃ וַיָּמָת שָׁאוּל וּשְׁלֹשֶׁת בָּנָיו

sons-of-him and-three-of Saul so-he-died (6) with-him and-he-died

וְנֹשֵׂא כֵלָיו גַּם כָּל־ אֲנָשָׁיו בַּיּוֹם הַהוּא

the-that on-the-day men-of-him all-of and armors-of-him and-one-bearing

יַחְדָּו׃ וַיִּרְאוּ אַנְשֵׁי־ יִשְׂרָאֵל אֲשֶׁר־ בְּעֵבֶר הָעֵמֶק וַאֲשֶׁר ׀

and-who the-valley at-along who Israel men-of when-they-saw (7) together

בְּעֵבֶר הַיַּרְדֵּן כִּי־ נָסוּ אַנְשֵׁי יִשְׂרָאֵל וְכִי־ מֵתוּ

they-were-dead and-that Israel men-of they-fled that the-Jordan at-across

שָׁאוּל וּבָנָיו וַיַּעַזְבוּ אֶת־ הֶעָרִים וַיָּנֻסוּ

and-they-fled the-towns *** then-they-abandoned and-sons-of-him Saul

וַיָּבֹאוּ פְלִשְׁתִּים וַיֵּשְׁבוּ בָּהֶן׃ וַיְהִי

and-he-was (8) in-them and-they-occupied Philistines and-they-came

מִמָּחֳרָת וַיָּבֹאוּ פְלִשְׁתִּים לְפַשֵּׁט אֶת־ הַחֲלָלִים

the-ones-dead *** to-strip Philistines when-they-came on-next-day

וַיִּמְצְאוּ אֶת־ שָׁאוּל וְאֶת־ שְׁלֹשֶׁת בָּנָיו נֹפְלִים

ones-having-fallen sons-of-him three-of and Saul *** then-they-found

---

and many fell slain on Mount Gilboa. 2 The Philistines pressed hard after Saul and his sons, and they killed his sons Jonathan, Abinadab and Malki-Shua. 3 The fighting grew fierce around Saul, and when the archers overtook him, they wounded him critically.

4 Saul said to his armor-bearer, "Draw your sword and run me through, or these uncircumcised fellows will come and run me through and abuse me."

But his armor-bearer was terrified and would not do it; so Saul took his own sword and fell on it. 5 When the armor-bearer saw that Saul was dead, he too fell on his sword and died with him. 6 So Saul and three of his sons and his armor-bearer and all his men died together that same day.

7 When the Israelites along the valley and those across the Jordan saw that the Israelite army had fled and that Saul and his sons had died, they abandoned their towns and fled. And the Philistines came and occupied them.

8 The next day, when the Philistines came to strip the dead, they found Saul and his three sons fallen on Mount

בְּהַר הַגִּלְבֹּעַ׃ וַיִּכְרְתוּ אֶת־ רֹאשׁוֹ וַיַּפְשִׁטוּ

and-they-stripped head-of-him *** and-they-cut-off (9) the-Gilboa on-Mount-of

אֶת־ כֵּלָיו וַיְשַׁלְּחוּ בְאֶרֶץ־ פְּלִשְׁתִּים סָבִיב

around Philistines through-land-of and-they-sent armors-of-him ***

לְבַשֵּׂר בֵּית עֲצַבֵּיהֶם וְאֶת־ הָעָם׃ וַיָּשִׂמוּ אֶת־

*** and-they-put (10) the-people and idols-of-them temple-of to-proclaim

כֵּלָיו בֵּית עַשְׁתָּרוֹת וְאֶת־ גְּוִיָּתוֹ תָּקְעוּ בְּחוֹמַת

to-wall-of they-fastened body-of-him and Ashtoreths temple-of armors-of-him

בֵּית שָׁן׃ וַיִּשְׁמְעוּ אֵלָיו יֹשְׁבֵי יָבֵישׁ גִּלְעָד אֵת

*** Gilead Jabesh ones-living-of about-him when-they-heard (11) Shan Beth

אֲשֶׁר־ עָשׂוּ פְלִשְׁתִּים לְשָׁאוּל׃ וַיָּקוּמוּ כָּל־ אִישׁ חַיִל

valor man-of every-of then-they-rose (12) to-Saul Philistines they-did what

וַיֵּלְכוּ כָל־ הַלַּיְלָה וַיִּקְחוּ אֶת־ גְּוִיַּת שָׁאוּל וְאֵת

and Saul body-of *** and-they-took-down the-night all-of and-they-journeyed

גְּוִיֹּת בָּנָיו מֵחוֹמַת בֵּית שָׁן וַיָּבֹאוּ יָבֵשָׁה

to-Jabesh and-they-went Shan Beth from-wall-of sons-of-him bodies-of

וַיִּשְׂרְפוּ אֹתָם שָׁם׃ וַיִּקְחוּ אֶת־ עַצְמֹתֵיהֶם

bones-of-them *** then-they-took (13) there them and-they-burned

וַיִּקְבְּרוּ תַחַת־ הָאֶשֶׁל בְּיָבֵשָׁה וַיָּצֻמוּ שִׁבְעַת יָמִים׃

days seven-of and-they-fasted in-Jabesh the-tamarisk under and-they-buried

Gilboa. [9]They cut off his head and stripped off his armor, and they sent messengers throughout the land of the Philistines to proclaim the news in the temple of their idols and among their people. [10]They put his armor in the temple of the Ashtoreths and fastened his body to the wall of Beth Shan.

[11]When the people of Jabesh Gilead heard of what the Philistines had done to Saul, [12]all their valiant men journeyed through the night to Beth Shan. They took down the bodies of Saul and his sons from the wall of Beth Shan and went to Jabesh, where they burned them. [13]Then they took their bones and buried them under a tamarisk tree at Jabesh, and they fasted seven days.

וַיְהִי אַחֲרֵי מוֹת שָׁאוּל וְדָוִד שָׁב מֵהַכּוֹת
from-to-defeat he-returned then-David Saul death-of after and-he-was (1:1)

אֶת־ הָעֲמָלֵק וַיֵּשֶׁב דָּוִד בְּצִקְלָג יָמִים שְׁנָיִם׃ וַיְהִי ׀
and-he-was (2) two days in-Ziklag David and-he-stayed the-Amalek ***

בַּיּוֹם הַשְּׁלִישִׁי וְהִנֵּה אִישׁ בָּא מִן־ הַמַּחֲנֶה מֵעִם שָׁאוּל
Saul from-with the-camp from arriving man then-see! the-third on-the-day

וּבְגָדָיו קְרֻעִים וַאֲדָמָה עַל־ רֹאשׁוֹ וַיְהִי
and-he-was head-of-him on and-dust ones-being-torn and-clothes-of-him

בְּבֹאוֹ אֶל־ דָּוִד וַיִּפֹּל אַרְצָה וַיִּשְׁתָּחוּ׃
and-he-paid-honor to-ground then-he-fell David to when-to-come-him

וַיֹּאמֶר לוֹ דָּוִד אֵי מִזֶּה תָּבוֹא וַיֹּאמֶר
and-he-answered you-came from-there where? David to-him and-he-asked (3)

אֵלָיו מִמַּחֲנֵה יִשְׂרָאֵל נִמְלָטְתִּי׃ וַיֹּאמֶר אֵלָיו דָּוִד מֶה־
what? David to-him and-he-asked (4) I-escaped Israel from-camp-of to-him

הָיָה הַדָּבָר הַגֶּד־ נָא לִי וַיֹּאמֶר אֲשֶׁר־ נָס הָעָם
the-people he-fled that and-he-said to-me now! tell! the-thing he-happened

מִן־ הַמִּלְחָמָה וְגַם־ הַרְבֵּה נָפַל מִן־ הָעָם וַיָּמֻתוּ
and-they-died the-people from he-fell to-be-many and-also the-battle from

וְגַם שָׁאוּל וִיהוֹנָתָן בְּנוֹ מֵתוּ׃ וַיֹּאמֶר דָּוִד אֶל־
to David then-he-said (5) they-died son-of-him and-Jonathan Saul and-also

הַנַּעַר הַמַּגִּיד לוֹ אֵיךְ יָדַעְתָּ כִּי־ מֵת שָׁאוּל
Saul he-died that you-know how? to-him the-one-reporting the-young-man

וִיהוֹנָתָן בְּנוֹ׃ וַיֹּאמֶר הַנַּעַר ׀ הַמַּגִּיד
the-one-reporting the-young-man and-he-said (6) son-of-him and-Jonathan

לוֹ נִקְרֹא נִקְרֵיתִי בְּהַר הַגִּלְבֹּעַ וְהִנֵּה שָׁאוּל נִשְׁעָן עַל־
on leaning Saul and-see! the-Gilboa on-Mount-of I-happened to-happen to-him

חֲנִיתוֹ וְהִנֵּה הָרֶכֶב וּבַעֲלֵי הַפָּרָשִׁים הִדְבִּקֻהוּ׃
they-were-upon-him the-horsemen and-masters-of the-chariot and-see! spear-of-him

וַיִּפֶן אַחֲרָיו וַיִּרְאֵנִי וַיִּקְרָא אֵלַי וָאֹמַר
and-I-said to-me then-he-called and-he-saw-me after-me when-he-turned (7)

הִנֵּנִי׃ וַיֹּאמֶר לִי מִי־ אָתָּה וָיֹּאמַר אֵלָיו עֲמָלֵקִי אָנֹכִי׃
I Amalekite to-him and-I-answered you who? to-me and-he-asked (8) here-I!

וַיֹּאמֶר אֵלַי עֲמָד־ נָא עָלַי וּמֹתְתֵנִי כִּי אֲחָזַנִי
he-holds-me for and-kill-me! over-me now! stand! to-me then-he-said (9)

הַשָּׁבָץ כִּי־ כָל־ עוֹד נַפְשִׁי בִּי׃ וָאֶעֱמֹד עָלָיו
over-him so-I-stood (10) in-me life-of-me still all-of but the-death-throe

וַאֲמֹתְתֵהוּ כִּי יָדַעְתִּי כִּי לֹא יִחְיֶה אַחֲרֵי נִפְלוֹ
to-fall-him after he-could-survive not that I-knew for and-I-killed-him

°8 ק ואמר

*David Hears of Saul's Death*

1 After the death of Saul,
David returned from de-
feating the Amalekites and
stayed in Ziklag two days. 2On
the third day a man arrived
from Saul's camp, with his
clothes torn and with dust on
his head. When he came to
David, he fell to the ground to
pay him honor.
3"Where have you come
from?" David asked him.
He answered, "I have es-
caped from the Israelite
camp."
4"What happened?" David
asked. "Tell me."
He said, "The men fled from
the battle. Many of them fell
and died. And Saul and his
son Jonathan are dead."
5Then David said to the
young man who brought him
the report, "How do you know
that Saul and his son Jonathan
are dead?"
6"I happened to be on
Mount Gilboa," the young
man said, "and there was
Saul, leaning on his spear,
with the chariots and riders almost upon him. 7When he
turned around and saw me, he
called out to me, and I said,
'What can I do?'
8"He asked me, 'Who are
you?'
"'An Amalekite,' I an-
swered.
9"Then he said to me, 'Stand
over me and kill me! I am in
the throes of death, but I'm
still alive.'
10"So I stood over him and
killed him, because I knew
that after he had fallen he
could not survive. And I took

וָאֶקַּח הַנֵּזֶר ׀ אֲשֶׁר עַל־ רֹאשׁוֹ וְאֶצְעָדָה אֲשֶׁר עַל־ זְרֹעוֹ
arm-of-him on that and-band head-of-him on that the-crown and-I-took

וָאֲבִיאֵם אֶל־ אֲדֹנִי הֵנָּה׃ וַיַּחֲזֵק דָּוִד
David and-he-took-hold (11) to-here lord-of-me to and-I-brought-them

°בִּבְגָדָו וַיִּקְרָעֵם וְגַם כָּל־ הָאֲנָשִׁים אֲשֶׁר אִתּוֹ׃
with-him who the-men all-of and-also and-he-tore-them of-clothes-of-him

וַיִּסְפְּדוּ וַיִּבְכּוּ וַיָּצֻמוּ עַד־ הָעָרֶב עַל־
for the-evening till and-they-fasted and-they-wept and-they-mourned (12)

שָׁאוּל וְעַל־ יְהוֹנָתָן בְּנוֹ וְעַל־ עַם יְהוָה וְעַל־ בֵּית
house-of and-for Yahweh army-of and-for son-of-him Jonathan and-for Saul

יִשְׂרָאֵל כִּי נָפְלוּ בֶּחָרֶב׃ וַיֹּאמֶר דָּוִד אֶל־ הַנַּעַר
the-young-man to David and-he-said (13) by-the-sword they-fell for Israel

הַמַּגִּיד לוֹ אֵי מִזֶּה אָתָּה וַיֹּאמֶר בֶּן־ אִישׁ
man son-of and-he-answered you from-there where? to-him the-one-reporting

גֵּר עֲמָלֵקִי אָנֹכִי׃ וַיֹּאמֶר אֵלָיו דָּוִד אֵיךְ לֹא יָרֵאתָ
you-were-afraid not why? David to-him and-he-asked (14) I Amalekite alien

לִשְׁלֹחַ יָדְךָ לְשַׁחֵת אֶת־ מְשִׁיחַ יְהוָה׃ וַיִּקְרָא
then-he-called (15) Yahweh anointed-of *** to-destroy hand-of-you to-lift

דָוִד לְאַחַד מֵהַנְּעָרִים וַיֹּאמֶר גַּשׁ פְּגַע־ בּוֹ
against-him strike-down! go! and-he-said of-the-men to-one David

וַיַּכֵּהוּ וַיָּמֹת׃ וַיֹּאמֶר אֵלָיו דָּוִד °דָּמְיךָ עַל־
on blood-of-you David to-him for-he-said (16) and-he-died so-he-struck-him

רֹאשֶׁךָ כִּי פִיךָ עָנָה בְךָ לֵאמֹר אָנֹכִי מֹתַתִּי
I-killed I to-say against-you he-testified mouth-of-you for head-of-you

אֶת־ מְשִׁיחַ יְהוָה׃ וַיְקֹנֵן דָּוִד אֶת־ הַקִּינָה הַזֹּאת
the-this the-lament *** David and-he-lamented (17) Yahweh anointed-of ***

עַל־ שָׁאוּל וְעַל־ יְהוֹנָתָן בְּנוֹ׃ וַיֹּאמֶר
and-he-ordered (18) son-of-him Jonathan and-concerning Saul concerning

לְלַמֵּד בְּנֵי־ יְהוּדָה קָשֶׁת הִנֵּה כְתוּבָה עַל־ סֵפֶר הַיָּשָׁר׃
the-Jashar Book-of in being-written see! bow-lament Judah men-of to-teach

הַצְּבִי יִשְׂרָאֵל עַל־ בָּמוֹתֶיךָ חָלָל אֵיךְ נָפְלוּ גִבּוֹרִים׃
mighty-ones they-fell how! slain heights-of-you on Israel the-glory (19)

אַל־ תַּגִּידוּ בְגַת אַל־ תְּבַשְּׂרוּ בְּחוּצֹת אַשְׁקְלוֹן פֶּן־
lest Ashkelon in-streets-of you-proclaim not in-Gath you-tell not (20)

תִּשְׂמַחְנָה בְּנוֹת פְּלִשְׁתִּים פֶּן־ תַּעֲלֹזְנָה בְּנוֹת
daughters-of they-rejoice lest Philistines daughters-of they-be-glad

הָעֲרֵלִים׃ הָרֵי בַגִּלְבֹּעַ אַל־ טַל וְאַל־ מָטָר עֲלֵיכֶם
on-you rain and-no dew no of-the-Gilboa mountains-of (21) uncircumcised-ones

the crown that was on his head and the band on his arm and have brought them here to my lord."

11 Then David and all the men with him took hold of their clothes and tore them. 12 They mourned and wept and fasted till evening for Saul and his son Jonathan, and for the army of the LORD and the house of Israel, because they had fallen by the sword.

13 David said to the young man who brought him the report, "Where are you from?"

"I am the son of an alien, an Amalekite," he answered.

14 David asked him, "Why were you not afraid to lift your hand to destroy the LORD's anointed?"

15 Then David called one of his men and said, "Go, strike him down!" So he struck him down, and he died. 16 For David had said to him, "Your blood be on your own head. Your own mouth testified against you when you said, 'I killed the LORD's anointed.'"

*David's Lament for Saul and Jonathan*

17 David took up this lament concerning Saul and his son Jonathan, 18 and ordered that the men of Judah be taught this lament of the bow (it is written in the Book of Jashar):

19 "Your glory, O Israel, lies slain on your heights.
How the mighty have fallen!

20 "Tell it not in Gath,
proclaim it not in the streets of Ashkelon,
lest the daughters of the Philistines be glad,
lest the daughters of the uncircumcised rejoice.

21 "O mountains of Gilboa,
may you have neither dew nor rain,

°*11* ק בבגדיו
°*16* ק דמך

וְשְׂדֵי תְרוּמֹת כִּי שָׁם נִגְעַל מָגֵן גִּבּוֹרִים
mighty-ones shield-of he-was-defiled there for offerings nor-fields-of

מָגֵן שָׁאוּל בְּלִי מְשִׁיחַ בַּשָּׁמֶן׃ מִדַּם חֲלָלִים
ones-slain from-blood-of (22) with-the-oil rubbed no-longer Saul shield-of

מֵחֵלֶב גִּבּוֹרִים קֶשֶׁת יְהוֹנָתָן לֹא נָשׂוֹג אָחוֹר וְחֶרֶב
and-sword-of back he-turned not Jonathan bow-of mighty-ones from-flesh-of

שָׁאוּל לֹא תָשׁוּב רֵיקָם׃ שָׁאוּל וִיהוֹנָתָן הַנֶּאֱהָבִים
the-ones-being-loved and-Jonathan Saul (23) unsatisfied she-returned not Saul

וְהַנְּעִימִם בְּחַיֵּיהֶם וּבְמוֹתָם לֹא נִפְרָדוּ
they-were-parted not and-in-death-of-them in-lives-of-them and-the-gracious-ones

מִנְּשָׁרִים קַלּוּ מֵאֲרָיוֹת גָּבֵרוּ׃
they-were-strong more-than-lions they-were-swift more-than-eagles

בְּנוֹת יִשְׂרָאֵל אֶל־ שָׁאוּל בְּכֶינָה הַמַּלְבִּשְׁכֶם שָׁנִי עִם־
and scarlet the-one-clothing-you weep! Saul for Israel daughters-of (24)

עֲדָנִים הַמַּעֲלֶה עֲדִי זָהָב עַל לְבוּשְׁכֶן׃ אֵיךְ
how! (25) garment-of-you on gold ornament-of the-one-adorning fineries

נָפְלוּ גִבֹּרִים בְּתוֹךְ הַמִּלְחָמָה יְהוֹנָתָן עַל־ בָּמוֹתֶיךָ חָלָל׃
slain heights-of-you on Jonathan the-battle in-midst-of mighty-ones they-fell

צַר־ לִי עָלֶיךָ אָחִי יְהוֹנָתָן נָעַמְתָּ לִּי
to-me you-were-dear Jonathan brother-of-me for-you to-me he-grieves (26)

מְאֹד נִפְלְאַתָה אַהֲבָתְךָ לִי מֵאַהֲבַת נָשִׁים׃ אֵיךְ
how! (27) women more-than-love-of for-me love-of-you she-was-wonderful very

נָפְלוּ גִבּוֹרִים וַיֹּאבְדוּ כְּלֵי מִלְחָמָה׃ וַיְהִי
and-he-was (2:1) war weapons-of and-they-perished mighty-ones they-fell

אַחֲרֵי־ כֵן וַיִּשְׁאַל דָּוִד בַּיהוָה ׀ לֵאמֹר הַאֶעֱלֶה בְּאַחַת
to-one-of shall-I-go-up? to-say of-Yahweh David then-he-inquired this after

עָרֵי יְהוּדָה וַיֹּאמֶר יְהוָה אֵלָיו עֲלֵה וַיֹּאמֶר דָּוִד אָנָה
to-where? David and-he-asked go-up! to-him Yahweh and-he-said Judah towns-of

אֶעֱלֶה וַיֹּאמֶר חֶבְרֹנָה׃ וַיַּעַל שָׁם דָּוִד וְגַם
and-also David there so-he-went-up (2) to-Hebron and-he-answered shall-I-go

שְׁתֵּי נָשָׁיו אֲחִינֹעַם הַיִּזְרְעֵלִית וַאֲבִיגַיִל אֵשֶׁת נָבָל
Nabal widow-of and-Abigail the-Jezreelite Ahinoam wives-of-him two-of

הַכַּרְמְלִי׃ וַאֲנָשָׁיו אֲשֶׁר־ עִמּוֹ הֶעֱלָה דָוִד אִישׁ
each David he-took with-him who and-men-of-him (3) the-Carmelite

וּבֵיתוֹ וַיֵּשְׁבוּ בְּעָרֵי חֶבְרוֹן׃ וַיָּבֹאוּ
then-they-came (4) Hebron in-towns-of and-they-settled with-family-of-him

אַנְשֵׁי יְהוּדָה וַיִּמְשְׁחוּ־ שָׁם אֶת־ דָּוִד לְמֶלֶךְ עַל־ בֵּית יְהוּדָה
Judah house-of over as-king David *** there and-they-anointed Judah men-of

---

nor fields that yield
offerings ⌞of grain⌟.
For there the shield of the
mighty was defiled,
the shield of Saul—no
longer rubbed with oil.
22From the blood of the
slain,
from the flesh of the
mighty,
the bow of Jonathan did
not turn back,
the sword of Saul did not
return unsatisfied.

23"Saul and Jonathan—
in life they were loved
and gracious,
and in death they were
not parted.
They were swifter than
eagles,
they were stronger than
lions.

24"O daughters of Israel,
weep for Saul,
who clothed you in scarlet
and finery,
who adorned your
garments with
ornaments of gold.

25"How the mighty have
fallen in battle!
Jonathan lies slain on
your heights.
26I grieve for you, Jonathan
my brother;
you were very dear to
me.
Your love for me was
wonderful,
more wonderful than
that of women.

27"How the mighty have
fallen!
The weapons of war
have perished!"

### *David Anointed King Over Judah*

2 In the course of time, David inquired of the LORD. "Shall I go up to one of the towns of Judah?" he asked.
The LORD said, "Go up."
David asked, "Where shall I go?"
"To Hebron," the LORD answered.
2So David went up there with his two wives, Ahinoam of Jezreel and Abigail, the widow of Nabal of Carmel.
3David also took the men who were with him, each with his family, and they settled in Hebron and its towns.
4Then the men of Judah came to Hebron and there they anointed David king over the house of Judah.

וַיַּגִּדוּ לְדָוִד לֵאמֹר אַנְשֵׁי יָבֵישׁ גִּלְעָד אֲשֶׁר קָבְרוּ אֶת־שָׁאוּל׃
Saul *** they-buried who Gilead Jabesh men-of to-say to-David when-they-told

וַיִּשְׁלַח דָּוִד מַלְאָכִים אֶל־אַנְשֵׁי יָבֵישׁ גִּלְעָד וַיֹּאמֶר אֲלֵיהֶם
to-them and-he-said Gilead Jabesh men-of to messengers David then-he-sent (5)

בְּרֻכִים אַתֶּם לַיהוָה אֲשֶׁר עֲשִׂיתֶם הַחֶסֶד הַזֶּה עִם־
to the-this the-kindness you-showed who by-Yahweh you ones-being-blessed

אֲדֹנֵיכֶם עִם־שָׁאוּל וַתִּקְבְּרוּ אֹתוֹ׃ וְעַתָּה יַעַשׂ־יְהוָה
Yahweh may-he-show and-now (6) him when-you-buried Saul to masters-of-you

עִמָּכֶם חֶסֶד וֶאֱמֶת וְגַם אָנֹכִי אֶעֱשֶׂה אִתְּכֶם הַטּוֹבָה
the-favor to-you I-will-show I and-also and-faithfulness kindness to-you

הַזֹּאת אֲשֶׁר עֲשִׂיתֶם הַדָּבָר הַזֶּה׃ וְעַתָּה ׀ תֶּחֱזַקְנָה
may-they-be-strong then-now (7) the-this the-thing you-did for the-this

יְדֵיכֶם וִהְיוּ לִבְנֵי־חַיִל כִּי־מֵת אֲדֹנֵיכֶם שָׁאוּל וְגַם־
and-also Saul masters-of-you dead for bravery as-men-of and-be! hands-of-you

אֹתִי מָשְׁחוּ בֵית־יְהוּדָה לְמֶלֶךְ עֲלֵיהֶם׃ וְאַבְנֵר בֶּן־נֵר
Ner son-of now-Abner (8) over-them as-king Judah house-of they-anointed me

שַׂר־צָבָא אֲשֶׁר לְשָׁאוּל לָקַח אֶת־אִישׁ בֹּשֶׁת בֶּן־שָׁאוּל
Saul son-of Bosheth Ish *** he-took to-Saul that army commander-of

וַיַּעֲבִרֵהוּ מַחֲנָיִם׃ וַיַּמְלִכֵהוּ אֶל־הַגִּלְעָד
the-Gilead over and-he-made-king-him (9) Mahanaim and-he-brought-him

וְאֶל־הָאֲשׁוּרִי וְאֶל־יִזְרְעֶאל וְעַל־אֶפְרַיִם וְעַל־בִּנְיָמִן
Benjamin and-over Ephraim and-over Jezreel and-over the-Ashuri and-over

וְעַל־יִשְׂרָאֵל כֻּלֹּה׃ בֶּן־אַרְבָּעִים שָׁנָה אִישׁ־בֹּשֶׁת בֶּן־שָׁאוּל
Saul son-of Bosheth Ish year forty son-of (10) all-of-him Israel and-over

בְּמָלְכוֹ עַל־יִשְׂרָאֵל וּשְׁתַּיִם שָׁנִים מָלָךְ אַךְ בֵּית
house-of however he-reigned years and-two Israel over when-to-become-king-him

יְהוּדָה הָיוּ אַחֲרֵי דָוִד׃ וַיְהִי מִסְפַּר הַיָּמִים אֲשֶׁר הָיָה
he-was that the-days length-of and-he-was (11) David after they-went Judah

דָוִד מֶלֶךְ בְּחֶבְרוֹן עַל־בֵּית יְהוּדָה שֶׁבַע שָׁנִים וְשִׁשָּׁה חֳדָשִׁים׃
months and-six years seven Judah house-of over in-Hebron king David

וַיֵּצֵא אַבְנֵר בֶּן־נֵר וְעַבְדֵי אִישׁ־בֹּשֶׁת בֶּן־שָׁאוּל מִמַּחֲנַיִם
Mahanaim Saul son-of Bosheth Ish and-men-of Ner son-of Abner and-he-left (12)

גִּבְעוֹנָה׃ וְיוֹאָב בֶּן־צְרוּיָה וְעַבְדֵי דָוִד יָצְאוּ
they-went-out David and-men-of Zeruiah son-of and-Joab (13) to-Gibeon

וַיִּפְגְּשׁוּם עַל־בְּרֵכַת גִּבְעוֹן יַחְדָּו וַיֵּשְׁבוּ אֵלֶּה עַל־הַבְּרֵכָה
the-pool at these and-they-sat together Gibeon pool-of at and-they-met-them

מִזֶּה וְאֵלֶּה עַל־הַבְּרֵכָה מִזֶּה׃ וַיֹּאמֶר אַבְנֵר אֶל־
to Abner then-he-said (14) at-other-side the-pool at and-these at-one-side

When David was told that it was the men of Jabesh Gilead who had buried Saul, [5]he sent messengers to the men of Jabesh Gilead to say to them, "The LORD bless you for showing this kindness to Saul your master by burying him. [6]May the LORD now show you kindness and faithfulness, and I too will show you the same favor because you have done this. [7]Now then, be strong and brave, for Saul your master is dead, and the house of Judah has anointed me king over them."

### *War Between the Houses of David and Saul*

[8]Meanwhile, Abner son of Ner, the commander of Saul's army, had taken Ish-Bosheth son of Saul and brought him over to Mahanaim. [9]He made him king over Gilead, Ashuri[a] and Jezreel, and also over Ephraim, Benjamin and all Israel.

[10]Ish-Bosheth son of Saul was forty years old when he became king over Israel, and he reigned two years. The house of Judah, however, followed David. [11]The length of time David was king in Hebron over the house of Judah was seven years and six months.

[12]Abner son of Ner, together with the men of Ish-Bosheth son of Saul, left Mahanaim and went to Gibeon. [13]Joab son of Zeruiah and David's men went out and met them at the pool of Gibeon. One group sat down on one side of the pool and one group on the other side.

[14]Then Abner said to Joab,

[a]9 Or *Asher*

יוֹאָב יָקוּמוּ נָא הַנְּעָרִים וִישַׂחֲקוּ לְפָנֵינוּ

before-us and-let-them-fight the-young-men now! let-them-get-up Joab

וַיֹּאמֶר יוֹאָב יָקֻמוּ׃ וַיָּקֻמוּ וַיַּעַבְרוּ בְמִסְפָּר

by-number and-they-went so-they-stood-up (15) let-them-get-up Joab and-he-said

שְׁנֵים עָשָׂר לְבִנְיָמִן וּלְאִישׁ בֹּשֶׁת בֶּן־שָׁאוּל וּשְׁנֵים עָשָׂר מֵעַבְדֵי

from-men-of ten and-two Saul son-of Bosheth and-for-Ish for-Benjamin ten two

דָוִד׃ וַיַּחֲזִקוּ אִישׁ ׀ בְּרֹאשׁ רֵעֵהוּ וְחַרְבּוֹ

and-dagger-of-him opponent-of-him by-head each then-they-grabbed (16) David

בְּצַד רֵעֵהוּ וַיִּפְּלוּ יַחְדָּו וַיִּקְרָא לַמָּקוֹם

to-the-place so-he-called together and-they-fell opponent-of-him in-side-of

הַהוּא חֶלְקַת הַצֻּרִים אֲשֶׁר בְּגִבְעוֹן׃ וַתְּהִי הַמִּלְחָמָה קָשָׁה

fierce the-battle and-she-was (17) in-Gibeon that Hazzurim Helkath the-that

עַד־מְאֹד בַּיּוֹם הַהוּא וַיִּנָּגֶף אַבְנֵר וְאַנְשֵׁי יִשְׂרָאֵל

Israel and-men-of Abner and-he-was-defeated the-that on-the-day very-much to

לִפְנֵי עַבְדֵי דָוִד׃ וַיִּהְיוּ־שָׁם שְׁלֹשָׁה בְּנֵי צְרוּיָה יוֹאָב

Joab Zeruiah sons-of three there and-they-were (18) David men-of before

וַאֲבִישַׁי וַעֲשָׂהאֵל וַעֲשָׂהאֵל קַל בְּרַגְלָיו כְּאַחַד הַצְּבָיִם

the-gazelles as-one-of in-feet-of-him fleet now-Asahel and-Asahel and-Abishai

אֲשֶׁר בַּשָּׂדֶה׃ וַיִּרְדֹּף עֲשָׂהאֵל אַחֲרֵי אַבְנֵר וְלֹא־נָטָה

he-turned and-not Abner after Asahel and-he-chased (19) in-the-wild that

לָלֶכֶת עַל־הַיָּמִין וְעַל־הַשְּׂמֹאול מֵאַחֲרֵי אַבְנֵר׃ וַיִּפֶן אַבְנֵר

Abner and-he-looked (20) Abner from-after the-left or-to the-right to to-go

אַחֲרָיו וַיֹּאמֶר הַאַתָּה זֶה עֲשָׂהאֵל וַיֹּאמֶר אָנֹכִי׃ וַיֹּאמֶר

then-he-said (21) I and-he-answered Asahel that you? and-he-asked behind-him

לוֹ אַבְנֵר נְטֵה לְךָ עַל־יְמִינְךָ אוֹ עַל־שְׂמֹאלֶךָ וֶאֱחֹז

and-take-on! left-of-you to or right-of-you to for-you turn! Abner to-him

לְךָ אֶחָד מֵהַנְּעָרִים וְקַח־לְךָ אֶת־חֲלִצָתוֹ וְלֹא־

but-not weapon-of-him *** for-you and-strip! of-the-young-men one for-you

אָבָה עֲשָׂהאֵל לָסוּר מֵאַחֲרָיו׃ וַיֹּסֶף עוֹד אַבְנֵר

Abner again and-he-repeated (22) from-after-him to-turn Asahel he-would

לֵאמֹר אֶל־עֲשָׂהאֵל סוּר לְךָ מֵאַחֲרָי לָמָּה אַכֶּכָּה

should-I-strike-you why? from-after-me for-you turn! Asahel to to-warn

אַרְצָה וְאֵיךְ אֶשָּׂא פָנַי אֶל־יוֹאָב אָחִיךָ׃

brother-of-you Joab to faces-of-me could-I-lift and-how? to-ground

וַיְמָאֵן לָסוּר וַיַּכֵּהוּ אַבְנֵר בְּאַחֲרֵי הַחֲנִית

the-spear with-butt-of Abner so-he-struck-him to-turn but-he-refused (23)

אֶל־הַחֹמֶשׁ וַתֵּצֵא הַחֲנִית מֵאַחֲרָיו וַיִּפָּל־

and-he-fell through-back-of-him the-spear and-she-came-out the-stomach into

"Let's have some of the young men get up and fight hand to hand in front of us."

"All right, let them do it," Joab said.

15So they stood up and were counted off—twelve men for Benjamin and Ish-Bosheth son of Saul, and twelve for David. 16Then each man grabbed his opponent by the head and thrust his dagger into his opponent's side, and they fell down together. So that place in Gibeon was called Helkath Hazzurim.[b]

17The battle that day was very fierce, and Abner and the men of Israel were defeated by David's men.

18The three sons of Zeruiah were there: Joab, Abishai and Asahel. Now Asahel was as fleet-footed as a wild gazelle. 19He chased Abner, turning neither to the right nor to the left as he pursued him. 20Abner looked behind him and asked, "Is that you, Asahel?"

"It is," he answered.

21Then Abner said to him, "Turn aside to the right or to the left; take on one of the young men and strip him of his weapons." But Asahel would not stop chasing him.

22Again Abner warned Asahel, "Stop chasing me! Why should I strike you down? How could I look your brother Joab in the face?"

23But Asahel refused to give up the pursuit; so Abner thrust the butt of his spear into Asahel's stomach, and the spear came out through his back. He fell there and died on

b16 *Helkath Hazzurim* means *field of daggers* or *field of hostilities.*

שָׁם וַיָּ֫מָת תַּחְתָּו וַיְהִי כָּל־ הַבָּא אֶל־
to the-one-coming every-of and-he-was in-place-of-him and-he-died there

הַמָּקוֹם֒ אֲשֶׁר־ נָפַל שָׁם עֲשָׂהאֵל וַיָּמֹת וַיַּעֲמֹדוּ׃
then-they-stopped and-he-died Asahel there he-fell where the-place

וַיִּרְדְּפוּ יוֹאָב וַאֲבִישַׁי אַחֲרֵי אַבְנֵר וְהַשֶּׁמֶשׁ בָּאָה
she-set and-the-sun Abner after and-Abishai Joab but-they-pursued (24)

וְהֵמָּה בָּאוּ עַד־ גִּבְעַת אַמָּה אֲשֶׁר עַל־ פְּנֵי־ גִיחַ דֶּרֶךְ
way-of Giah faces-of near that Ammah hill-of to they-came and-they

מִדְבַּר גִּבְעוֹן׃ וַיִּתְקַבְּצוּ בְנֵי־ בִנְיָמִן אַחֲרֵי אַבְנֵר
Abner behind Benjamin men-of then-they-rallied (25) Gibeon wasteland-of

וַיִּהְיוּ לַאֲגֻדָּה אֶחָת וַיַּעַמְדוּ עַל רֹאשׁ־גִּבְעָה אֶחָת׃ וַיִּקְרָא
and-he-called (26) one hill top-of on and-they-stood one as-group and-they-were

אַבְנֵר אֶל־יוֹאָב וַיֹּאמֶר הֲלָנֶצַח תֹּאכַל חֶרֶב הֲלוֹא יָדַעְתָּה
you-realize not? sword must-she-devour for-ever? and-he-said Joab to Abner

כִּי־ מָרָה תִהְיֶה בָּאַחֲרוֹנָה וְעַד־ מָתַי לֹא־ תֹאמַר
you-will-order not when? and-until in-the-end she-will-be bitter that

לָעָם לָשׁוּב מֵאַחֲרֵי אֲחֵיהֶם׃ וַיֹּאמֶר יוֹאָב
Joab and-he-answered (27) brothers-of-them from-after to-turn to-the-people

חַי הָאֱלֹהִים כִּי לוּלֵא דִּבַּרְתָּ כִּי אָז מֵהַבֹּקֶר
until-the-morning then indeed you-spoke not if the-God life-of

נַעֲלָה הָעָם אִישׁ מֵאַחֲרֵי אָחִיו׃ וַיִּתְקַע
so-he-blew (28) brother-of-him from-after each the-people he-would-continue

יוֹאָב בַּשּׁוֹפָר וַיַּעַמְדוּ כָּל־ הָעָם וְלֹא־ יִרְדְּפוּ
they-pursued and-not the-people all-of and-they-halted on-the-trumpet Joab

עוֹד אַחֲרֵי יִשְׂרָאֵל וְלֹא־ יָסְפוּ עוֹד לְהִלָּחֵם׃ וְאַבְנֵר
and-Abner (29) to-fight-them again they-repeated and-not Israel after longer

וַאֲנָשָׁיו הָלְכוּ בָּעֲרָבָה כֹּל הַלַּיְלָה הַהוּא
the-that the-night all-of through-the-Arabah they-marched and-men-of-him

וַיַּעַבְרוּ אֶת־ הַיַּרְדֵּן וַיֵּלְכוּ כָּל־ הַבִּתְרוֹן
the-Bithron whole-of and-they-continued the-Jordan *** and-they-crossed

וַיָּבֹאוּ מַחֲנָיִם׃ וְיוֹאָב שָׁב מֵאַחֲרֵי אַבְנֵר
Abner from-after he-returned then-Joab (30) Mahanaim and-they-came

וַיִּקְבֹּץ אֶת־ כָּל־ הָעָם וַיִּפָּקְדוּ מֵעַבְדֵי דָוִד
David from-men-of and-they-were-missing the-people all-of *** and-he-assembled

תִּשְׁעָה־ עָשָׂר אִישׁ וַעֲשָׂהאֵל׃ וְעַבְדֵי דָוִד הִכּוּ מִבִּנְיָמִן
from-Benjamin they-killed David but-men-of (31) and-Asahel man ten nine

וּבְאַנְשֵׁי אַבְנֵר שְׁלֹשׁ־ מֵאוֹת וְשִׁשִּׁים אִישׁ מֵתוּ׃ וַיִּשְׂאוּ
and-they-took (32) they-died man and-sixty hundreds three-of Abner and-of-men-of

°23 ק תחתיו

the spot. And every man stopped when he came to the place where Asahel had fallen and died.
24But Joab and Abishai pursued Abner, and as the sun was setting, they came to the hill of Ammah, near Giah on the way to the wasteland of Gibeon.
25Then the men of Benjamin rallied behind Abner. They formed themselves into a group and took their stand on top of a hill.
26Abner called out to Joab, "Must the sword devour forever? Don't you realize that this will end in bitterness? How long before you order your men to stop pursuing their brothers?"
27Joab answered, "As surely as God lives, if you had not spoken, the men would have continued the pursuit of their brothers until morning.[c]"
28So Joab blew the trumpet, and all the men came to a halt; they no longer pursued Israel, nor did they fight anymore.
29All that night Abner and his men marched through the Arabah. They crossed the Jordan, continued through the whole Bithron[d] and came to Mahanaim.
30Then Joab returned from pursuing Abner and assembled all his men. Besides Asahel, nineteen of David's men were found missing.
31But David's men had killed three hundred and sixty Benjamites who were with Abner.

c27 Or *spoken this morning, the men would not have taken up the pursuit of their brothers;* or *spoken, the men would have given up the pursuit of their brothers by morning*

d29 Or *morning;* or *ravine;* the meaning of the Hebrew for this word is uncertain.

אֶת־עֲשָׂהאֵל וַיִּקְבְּרֻהוּ בְּקֶבֶר אָבִיו אֲשֶׁר בֵּית לָחֶם
Lehem Beth that father-of-him in-tomb-of and-they-buried-him Asahel ***

וַיֵּלְכוּ כָל־הַלַּיְלָה יוֹאָב וַאֲנָשָׁיו וַיֵּאֹר לָהֶם
to-them and-he-dawned and-men-of-him Joab the-night all-of then-they-marched

בְּחֶבְרוֹן׃ וַתְּהִי הַמִּלְחָמָה אֲרֻכָּה בֵּין בֵּית שָׁאוּל וּבֵין
and-between Saul house-of between long the-war and-she-was (3:1) at-Hebron

בֵּית דָּוִד וְדָוִד הֹלֵךְ וְחָזֵק וּבֵית שָׁאוּל
Saul while-house-of and-he-was-strong growing and-David David house-of

הֹלְכִים וְדַלִּים׃ וַיִּלָּדוּ° לְדָוִד בָנִים בְּחֶבְרוֹן
in-Hebron sons to-David and-they-were-born (2) and-ones-weak ones-growing

וַיְהִי בְכוֹרוֹ אַמְנוֹן לַאֲחִינֹעַם הַיִּזְרְעֵאלִת׃
the-Jezreelite of-Ahinoam Amnon firstborn-of-him and-he-was

וּמִשְׁנֵהוּ כִלְאָב לַאֲבִיגַל° אֵשֶׁת נָבָל הַכַּרְמְלִי
the-Carmelite Nabal widow-of of-Abigail Kileab and-second-of-him (3)

וְהַשְּׁלִשִׁי אַבְשָׁלוֹם בֶּן־מַעֲכָה בַת־תַּלְמַי מֶלֶךְ גְּשׁוּר׃
Geshur king-of Talmai daughter-of Maacah son-of Absalom and-the-third

וְהָרְבִיעִי אֲדֹנִיָּה בֶן־חַגִּית וְהַחֲמִישִׁי שְׁפַטְיָה בֶן־
son-of Shephatiah and-the-fifth Haggith son-of Adonijah and-the-fourth (4)

אֲבִיטָל׃ וְהַשִּׁשִּׁי יִתְרְעָם לְעֶגְלָה אֵשֶׁת דָּוִד אֵלֶּה יֻלְּדוּ
they-were-born these David wife-of of-Eglah Ithream and-the-sixth (5) Abital

לְדָוִד בְּחֶבְרוֹן׃ וַיְהִי בִּהְיוֹת הַמִּלְחָמָה בֵּין בֵּית שָׁאוּל
Saul house-of between the-war while-to-be and-he-was (6) in-Hebron to-David

וּבֵין בֵּית דָּוִד וְאַבְנֵר הָיָה מִתְחַזֵּק בְּבֵית
in-house-of strengthening-himself he-was now-Abner David house-of and-between

שָׁאוּל׃ וּלְשָׁאוּל פִּלֶגֶשׁ וּשְׁמָהּ רִצְפָּה בַת־אַיָּה
Aiah daughter-of Rizpah and-name-of-her concubine now-to-Saul (7) Saul

וַיֹּאמֶר אֶל־אַבְנֵר מַדּוּעַ בָּאתָה אֶל־פִּילֶגֶשׁ אָבִי׃
father-of-me concubine-of into you-went why? Abner to and-he-said

וַיִּחַר לְאַבְנֵר מְאֹד עַל־דִּבְרֵי אִישׁ־בֹּשֶׁת וַיֹּאמֶר
and-he-said Bosheth Ish words-of because-of very to-Abner and-he-angered (8)

הֲרֹאשׁ כֶּלֶב אָנֹכִי אֲשֶׁר לִיהוּדָה הַיּוֹם אֶעֱשֶׂה־חֶסֶד עִם־בֵּית ׀ שָׁאוּל
Saul house-of to loyalty I-show the-day to-Judah that I dog head-of?

אָבִיךָ אֶל־אֶחָיו וְאֶל־מֵרֵעֵהוּ וְלֹא הִמְצִיתִךָ
I-gave-you and-not friend-of-him and-to brothers-of-him to father-of-you

בְּיַד־דָּוִד וַתִּפְקֹד עָלַי עֲוֺן הָאִשָּׁה הַיּוֹם׃
the-day the-woman offense-of against-me but-you-accuse David into-hand-of

כֹּה־יַעֲשֶׂה אֱלֹהִים לְאַבְנֵר וְכֹה יֹסִיף לוֹ כִּי
if-not to-him may-he-be-severe and-so with-Abner God may-he-deal so (9)

32 They took Asahel and buried
him in his father's tomb at
Bethlehem. Then Joab and his
men marched all night and arrived at Hebron by daybreak.
3 The war between the
house of Saul and the
house of David lasted a long
time. David grew stronger and
stronger, while the house of
Saul grew weaker and weaker.
2 Sons were born to David in
Hebron:
His firstborn was Am-
non the son of Ahinoam
of Jezreel;
3 his second, Kileab the
son of Abigail the widow
of Nabal of Carmel;
the third, Absalom the
son of Maacah daughter
of Talmai king of Geshur;
4 the fourth, Adonijah the
son of Haggith;
the fifth, Shephatiah the
son of Abital;
5 and the sixth, Ithream
the son of David's wife
Eglah.
These were born to Da-
vid in Hebron.

*Abner Goes Over to David*

6 During the war between
the house of Saul and the
house of David, Abner had
been strengthening his own
position in the house of Saul.
7 Now Saul had had a concubine named Rizpah daughter
of Aiah. And Ish-Bosheth said
to Abner, "Why did you sleep
with my father's concubine?"
8 Abner was very angry because of what Ish-Bosheth
said and he answered, "Am I
a dog's head—on Judah's side?
This very day I am loyal to the
house of your father Saul and
to his family and friends. I
haven't handed you over to
David. Yet now you accuse me
of an offense involving this
woman! 9 May God deal with
Abner, be it ever so severely, if

°2 ק ויולדו
°3 ק לאביגיל

כַּאֲשֶׁר נִשְׁבַּע יְהוָה֙ לְדָוִד כִּֽי־ כֵן אֶֽעֱשֶׂה־ לּֽוֹ׃ לְהַעֲבִיר
to-transfer (10) for-him I-do so if-not to-David Yahweh he-swore just-as

הַמַּמְלָכָה מִבֵּית שָׁאוּל וּלְהָקִים אֶת־ כִּסֵּא דָוִד עַל־
over David throne-of *** and-to-establish Saul from-house-of the-kingdom

יִשְׂרָאֵל֙ וְעַל־ יְהוּדָה מִדָּן וְעַד־ בְּאֵר שָֽׁבַע׃ וְלֹֽא־ יָכֹל
he-dared and-not (11) Sheba Beer even-to from-Dan Judah and-over Israel

עוֹד לְהָשִׁיב אֶת־ אַבְנֵר דָּבָר מִיִּרְאָתוֹ אֹתֽוֹ׃ וַיִּשְׁלַח
then-he-sent (12) him because-to-fear-him word Abner *** to-return again

אַבְנֵר מַלְאָכִים ׀ אֶל־ דָּוִד תַּחְתָּו לֵאמֹר לְמִי־ אָרֶץ לֵאמֹר
to-say land to-whom? to-say on-behalf-of-him David to messengers Abner

כָּרְתָה בְרִֽיתְךָ֙ אִתִּי וְהִנֵּה֙ יָדִי עִמָּךְ לְהָסֵב
to-bring with-you hand-of-me and-see! with-me agreement-of-you you-make

אֵלֶיךָ אֶת־ כָּל־ יִשְׂרָאֵֽל׃ וַיֹּאמֶר טוֹב אֲנִי אֶכְרֹת אִתְּךָ
with-you I-will-make I good and-he-said (13) Israel all-of *** to-you

בְּרִית אַךְ דָּבָר אֶחָד אָנֹכִי֩ שֹׁאֵל מֵאִתְּךָ לֵאמֹר֙ לֹא־ תִרְאֶה
you-will-see not to-say from-with-you demanding I one thing but agreement

אֶת־ פָּנַי כִּי ׀ אִם־ לִפְנֵי הֲבִֽיאֲךָ אֵת מִיכַל בַּת־ שָׁאוּל
Saul daughter-of Michal *** to-bring-you before if unless faces-of-me ***

בְּבֹאֲךָ לִרְאוֹת אֶת־ פָּנָֽי׃ וַיִּשְׁלַח דָּוִד מַלְאָכִים
messengers David then-he-sent (14) faces-of-me *** to-see when-to-come-you

אֶל־אִֽישׁ־ בֹּשֶׁת בֶּן־ שָׁאוּל לֵאמֹר תְּנָה אֶת־ אִשְׁתִּי֙ אֶת־ מִיכַל אֲשֶׁר
whom Michal *** wife-of-me *** give! to-demand Saul son-of Bosheth Ish to

אֵרַשְׂתִּי לִי בְּמֵאָה עָרְלוֹת פְּלִשְׁתִּֽים׃ וַיִּשְׁלַח֙
so-he-gave-order (15) Philistines foreskins-of for-hundred to-me I-betrothed

אִישׁ בֹּשֶׁת וַיִּקָּחֶהָ מֵעִם אִישׁ מֵעִם פַּלְטִיאֵל בֶּן־
son-of Paltiel from-with husband from-with and-he-had-taken-her Bosheth Ish

לָֽוִשׁ׃ וַיֵּלֶךְ אִתָּהּ אִישָׁהּ הָלוֹךְ וּבָכֹה אַחֲרֶיהָ
behind-her and-to-weep to-go husband-of-her with-her but-he-went (16) Laish

עַד־ בַּֽחֻרִים וַיֹּאמֶר אֵלָיו אַבְנֵר לֵךְ שׁוּב וַיָּשֹֽׁב׃
so-he-went-back go-back! go! Abner to-him then-he-said Bahurim to

וּדְבַר־ אַבְנֵר הָיָה עִם־ זִקְנֵי יִשְׂרָאֵל לֵאמֹר גַּם־
indeed to-say Israel elders-of with he-was Abner then-conference-of (17)

תְּמוֹל֙ גַּם־ שִׁלְשֹׁם הֱיִיתֶם מְבַקְשִׁים אֶת־ דָּוִד לְמֶלֶךְ עֲלֵיכֶֽם׃
over-you as-king David *** ones-wanting you-were before and yesterday

וְעַתָּה עֲשׂוּ כִּי יְהוָה אָמַר אֶל־ דָּוִד֙ לֵאמֹר בְּיַד ׀ דָּוִד
David by-hand-of to-say David to he-promised Yahweh for do! so-now (18)

עַבְדִּי הוֹשִׁיעַ אֶת־ עַמִּי יִשְׂרָאֵל֙ מִיַּד פְלִשְׁתִּים
Philistines from-hand-of Israel people-of-me *** he-will-rescue servant-of-me

I do not do for David what the LORD promised him on oath [10]and transfer the kingdom from the house of Saul and establish David's throne over Israel and Judah from Dan to Beersheba." [11]Ish-Bosheth did not dare to say another word to Abner, because he was afraid of him.

[12]Then Abner sent messengers on his behalf to say to David, "Whose land is it? Make an agreement with me, and I will help you bring all Israel over to you."

[13]"Good," said David. "I will make an agreement with you. But I demand one thing of you: Do not come into my presence unless you bring Michal daughter of Saul when you come to see me." [14]Then David sent messengers to Ish-Bosheth son of Saul, demanding, "Give me my wife Michal, whom I betrothed to myself for the price of a hundred Philistine foreskins."

[15]So Ish-Bosheth gave orders and had her taken away from her husband Paltiel son of Laish. [16]Her husband, however, went with her, weeping behind her all the way to Bahurim. Then Abner said to him, "Go back home!" So he went back.

[17]Abner conferred with the elders of Israel and said, "For some time you have wanted to make David your king. [18]Now do it! For the LORD promised David, 'By my servant David I will rescue my people Israel

°12 ק תחתיו
°15 ק ליש

וּמִיַּד כָּל־ אֹיְבֵיהֶם׃ וַיְדַבֵּר גַּם־ אַבְנֵר
Abner also and-he-spoke (19) being-enemies-of-them all-of and-from-hand-of

בְּאָזְנֵי בִנְיָמִין וַיֵּלֶךְ גַּם־ אַבְנֵר לְדַבֵּר בְּאָזְנֵי דָוִד
David in-ears-of to-tell Abner also then-he-went Benjamin in-ears-of

בְּחֶבְרוֹן אֵת כָּל־ אֲשֶׁר־ טוֹב בְּעֵינֵי יִשְׂרָאֵל וּבְעֵינֵי כָּל־
whole-of and-in-eyes-of Israel in-eyes-of good that all *** at-Hebron

בֵּית בִּנְיָמִן׃ וַיָּבֹא אַבְנֵר אֶל־ דָּוִד חֶבְרוֹן וְאִתּוֹ
and-with-him Hebron David to Abner when-he-came (20) Benjamin house-of

עֶשְׂרִים אֲנָשִׁים וַיַּעַשׂ דָּוִד לְאַבְנֵר וְלַאֲנָשִׁים אֲשֶׁר־ אִתּוֹ מִשְׁתֶּה׃
feast with-him who and-for-the-men for-Abner David then-he-prepared men twenty

וַיֹּאמֶר אַבְנֵר אֶל־ דָּוִד אָקוּמָה ׀ וְאֵלֵכָה וְאֶקְבְּצָה
and-let-me-assemble and-let-me-go let-me-rise David to Abner then-he-said (21)

אֶל־ אֲדֹנִי הַמֶּלֶךְ אֶת־ כָּל־ יִשְׂרָאֵל וְיִכְרְתוּ אִתְּךָ בְּרִית
compact with-you so-they-may-make Israel all-of *** the-king lord-of-me for

וּמָלַכְתָּ בְּכֹל אֲשֶׁר־ תְּאַוֶּה נַפְשֶׁךָ וַיְשַׁלַּח* דָּוִד
David so-he-sent-away heart-of-you she-desires that over-all and-you-may-rule

אֶת־אַבְנֵר וַיֵּלֶךְ בְּשָׁלוֹם׃ וְהִנֵּה עַבְדֵי דָוִד וְיוֹאָב בָּא
returning and-Joab David men-of then-see! (22) in-peace and-he-went Abner ***

מֵהַגְּדוּד וְשָׁלָל רָב עִמָּם הֵבִיאוּ וְאַבְנֵר אֵינֶנּוּ
not-he but-Abner they-brought with-them great-deal and-plunder from-the-raid

עִם־ דָּוִד בְּחֶבְרוֹן כִּי שִׁלְּחוֹ וַיֵּלֶךְ בְּשָׁלוֹם׃ וְיוֹאָב
when-Joab (23) in-peace and-he-went he-sent-away-him for in-Hebron David with

וְכָל־ הַצָּבָא אֲשֶׁר־ אִתּוֹ בָּאוּ וַיַּגִּדוּ לְיוֹאָב לֵאמֹר
to-say to-Joab then-they-told they-arrived with-him who the-army and-all-of

בָּא־ אַבְנֵר בֶּן־ נֵר אֶל־ הַמֶּלֶךְ וַיְשַׁלְּחֵהוּ וַיֵּלֶךְ
and-he-went and-he-sent-away-him the-king to Ner son-of Abner he-came

בְּשָׁלוֹם׃ וַיָּבֹא יוֹאָב אֶל־ הַמֶּלֶךְ וַיֹּאמֶר מֶה עָשִׂיתָה הִנֵּה־
look! you-did what? and-he-said the-king to Joab so-he-went (24) in-peace

בָא אַבְנֵר אֵלֶיךָ לָמָּה־ זֶּה שִׁלַּחְתּוֹ וַיֵּלֶךְ הָלוֹךְ׃ יָדַעְתָּ
you-know (25) to-go and-he-went you-let-go-him this why? to-you Abner he-came

אֶת־אַבְנֵר בֶּן־ נֵר כִּי לְפַתֹּתְךָ בָּא וְלָדַעַת אֶת־
*** and-to-observe he-came to-deceive-you that Ner son-of Abner ***

מוֹצָאֲךָ וְאֶת־ מְבוֹאֶךָ° וְלָדַעַת אֵת כָּל־ אֲשֶׁר אַתָּה עֹשֶׂה׃
doing you that all *** and-to-find-out coming-of-you and going-of-you

וַיֵּצֵא יוֹאָב מֵעִם דָּוִד וַיִּשְׁלַח מַלְאָכִים אַחֲרֵי אַבְנֵר
Abner after messengers and-he-sent David from-with Joab then-he-left (26)

וַיָּשִׁבוּ אֹתוֹ מִבּוֹר הַסִּרָה וְדָוִד לֹא יָדָע׃
he-knew not but-David the-Sirah from-well-of him and-they-brought-back

from the hand of the Philistines and from the hand of all their enemies.' "

[19]Abner also spoke to the Benjamites in person. Then he went to Hebron to tell David everything that Israel and the whole house of Benjamin wanted to do. [20]When Abner, who had twenty men with him, came to David at Hebron, David prepared a feast for him and his men. [21]Then Abner said to David, "Let me go at once and assemble all Israel for my lord the king, so that they may make a compact with you, and that you may rule over all that your heart desires." So David sent Abner away, and he went in peace.

*Joab Murders Abner*

[22]Just then David's men and Joab returned from a raid and brought with them a great deal of plunder. But Abner was no longer with David in Hebron, because David had sent him away, and he had gone in peace. [23]When Joab and all the soldiers with him arrived, he was told that Abner son of Ner had come to the king and that the king had sent him away and that he had gone in peace.

[24]So Joab went to the king and said, "What have you done? Look, Abner came to you. Why did you let him go? Now he is gone! [25]You know Abner son of Ner; he came to deceive you and observe your movements and find out everything you are doing."

[26]Joab then left David and sent messengers after Abner, and they brought him back from the well of Sirah. But David did not know it. [27]Now

*21 Most mss have no *dagesh* in the *yod* (וַיְ).

°25 ק מובאך

וישב אבנר חברון ויטהו יואב אל־תוך
midst-of into Joab then-he-took-aside-him Hebron Abner when-he-returned (27)

השער לדבר אתו בשלי ויכהו שם
there and-he-stabbed-him in-the-private with-him to-speak the-gateway

החמש וימת בדם עשה־אל אחיו: וישמע
when-he-heard (28) brother-of-him Asahel for-blood-of and-he-died the-stomach

דוד מאחרי כן ויאמר נקי אנכי וממלכתי מעם
from-before and-kingdom-of-me I innocent then-he-said this from-after David

יהוה עד־עולם מדמי אבנר בן־נר: יחלו
may-they-fall (29) Ner son-of Abner concerning-bloods-of forever to Yahweh

על־ראש יואב ואל כל־בית אביו ואל־
and-not father-of-him house-of all-of and-upon Joab head-of upon

יכרת מבית יואב זב ומצרע
or-one-being-leprous running-sore Joab from-house-of may-he-be-cut-off

ומחזיק בפלך ונפל בחרב וחסר־לחם:
food or-lack-of by-the-sword or-one-falling on-the-crutch or-one-leaning

ויואב ואבישי אחיו הרגו לאבנר על אשר
that because to-Abner they-murdered brother-of-him and-Abishai now-Joab (30)

המית את־עשהאל אחיהם בגבעון במלחמה: ויאמר
then-he-said (31) in-the-battle at-Gibeon brother-of-them Asahel *** he-killed

דוד אל־יואב ואל־כל־העם אשר־אתו קרעו בגדיכם
clothes-of-you tear! with-him who the-people all-of and-to Joab to David

וחגרו שקים וספדו לפני אבנר והמלך דוד
David and-the-king Abner in-front-of and-mourn! sackcloths and-put-on!

הלך אחרי המטה: ויקברו את־אבנר בחברון וישא*
and-he-raised in-Hebron Abner *** and-they-buried (32) the-bier behind walking

המלך את־קולו ויבך אל־קבר אבנר ויבכו כל־
all-of and-they-wept Abner tomb-of at and-he-wept voice-of-him *** the-king

העם: ויקנן המלך אל־אבנר ויאמר הכמות
as-death-of? and-he-said Abner for the-king and-he-sang-lament (33) the-people

נבל ימות אבנר: ידך לא־אסרות ורגליך
and-feet-of-you ones-being-bound not hand-of-you Abner should-he-die lawless

לא־לנחשתים הגשו כנפול לפני בני־עולה נפלת
you-fell wickedness men-of before as-to-fall they-were-held in-fetters not

ויספו כל־העם לבכות עליו: ויבא כל־
all-of then-he-came (35) over-him to-weep the-people all-of and-they-repeated

העם להברות את־דוד לחם בעוד היום וישבע
but-he-took-oath the-day while-still food David *** to-urge-to-eat the-people

when Abner returned to Hebron, Joab took him aside into the gateway, as though to speak with him privately. And there, to avenge the blood of his brother Asahel, Joab stabbed him in the stomach, and he died.

28 Later, when David heard about this, he said, "I and my kingdom are forever innocent before the LORD concerning the blood of Abner son of Ner.
29 May his blood fall upon the head of Joab and upon all his father's house! May Joab's house never be without someone who has a running sore or leprosy[e] or who leans on a crutch or who falls by the sword or who lacks food."

30 (Joab and his brother Abishai murdered Abner because he had killed their brother Asahel in the battle at Gibeon.)

31 Then David said to Joab and all the people with him, "Tear your clothes and put on sackcloth and walk in mourning in front of Abner." King David himself walked behind the bier.
32 They buried Abner in Hebron, and the king wept aloud at Abner's tomb. All the people wept also.

33 The king sang this lament for Abner:

"Should Abner have died
as the lawless die?
34 Your hands were not
bound,
your feet were not
fettered.
You fell as one falls before
wicked men."

And all the people wept over him again.

35 Then they all came and urged David to eat something while it was still day; but David took an oath, saying,

[e]29 The Hebrew word was used for various diseases affecting the skin—not necessarily leprosy.

*32 Most mss have *dagesh* in the *yod* (י).

דָּוִד לֵאמֹר כֹּה יַעֲשֶׂה־ לִּי אֱלֹהִים וְכֹה יֹסִיף כִּי אִם־

indeed if may-he-be-severe and-so God with-me may-he-deal so to-say David

לִפְנֵי בוֹא־ הַשֶּׁמֶשׁ אֶטְעַם־ לֶחֶם אוֹ כָל־ מְאוּמָה׃ וְכָל־

and-all-of (36) thing any-of or bread I-taste the-sun to-set before

הָעָם הִכִּירוּ וַיִּיטַב בְּעֵינֵיהֶם כְּכֹל אֲשֶׁר

that as-all in-eyes-of-them and-he-was-pleasing they-took-note the-people

עָשָׂה הַמֶּלֶךְ בְּעֵינֵי כָל־ הָעָם טוֹב׃ וַיֵּדְעוּ

so-they-knew (37) pleasant the-people all-of in-eyes-of the-king he-did

כָל־ הָעָם וְכָל־ יִשְׂרָאֵל בַּיּוֹם הַהוּא כִּי לֹא הָיְתָה

she-was not that the-that on-the-day Israel and-all-of the-people all-of

מֵהַמֶּלֶךְ לְהָמִית אֶת־ אַבְנֵר בֶּן־ נֵר׃ וַיֹּאמֶר הַמֶּלֶךְ אֶל־

to the-king then-he-said (38) Ner son-of Abner *** to-murder from-the-king

עֲבָדָיו הֲלוֹא תֵדְעוּ כִּי־ שַׂר וְגָדוֹל נָפַל הַיּוֹם

the-day he-fell and-great-man prince that you-realize not? men-of-him

הַזֶּה בְּיִשְׂרָאֵל׃ וְאָנֹכִי הַיּוֹם רַךְ וּמָשׁוּחַ מֶלֶךְ

king though-being-anointed weak the-day and-I (39) in-Israel the-this

וְהָאֲנָשִׁים הָאֵלֶּה בְּנֵי צְרוּיָה קָשִׁים מִמֶּנִּי יְשַׁלֵּם

may-he-repay more-than-I ones-strong Zeruiah sons-of the-these and-the-men

יְהוָה לְעֹשֵׂה הָרָעָה כְּרָעָתוֹ׃ וַיִּשְׁמַע בֶּן־ שָׁאוּל

Saul son-of when-he-heard (4:1) as-evil-of-him the-evil to-one-doing Yahweh

כִּי מֵת אַבְנֵר בְּחֶבְרוֹן וַיִּרְפּוּ יָדָיו וְכָל־ יִשְׂרָאֵל

Israel and-all-of hands-of-him then-they-fell in-Hebron Abner he-died that

נִבְהָלוּ׃ וּשְׁנֵי אֲנָשִׁים שָׂרֵי־ גְדוּדִים הָיוּ

they-were raiding-bands leaders-of men now-two-of (2) they-became-alarmed

בֶן־ שָׁאוּל שֵׁם הָאֶחָד בַּעֲנָה וְשֵׁם הַשֵּׁנִי רֵכָב בְּנֵי רִמּוֹן

Rimmon sons-of Recab the-other and-name-of Baanah the-one name-of Saul son-of

הַבְּאֶרֹתִי* מִבְּנֵי בִנְיָמִן כִּי גַּם־ בְּאֵרוֹת תֵּחָשֵׁב עַל־

in she-is-considered Beeroth indeed now Benjamin from-sons-of the-Beerothite

בִּנְיָמִן׃ וַיִּבְרְחוּ הַבְּאֵרֹתִים גִּתָּיְמָה וַיִּהְיוּ־ שָׁם

there and-they-live to-Gittaim the-Beerothites for-they-fled (3) Benjamin

גָּרִים עַד הַיּוֹם הַזֶּה׃ וְלִיהוֹנָתָן בֶּן־ שָׁאוּל בֵּן

son Saul son-of now-to-Jonathan (4) the-this the-day to ones-being-aliens

נְכֵה רַגְלָיִם בֶּן־ חָמֵשׁ שָׁנִים הָיָה בְּבֹא שְׁמֻעַת שָׁאוּל

Saul news-of when-to-come he-was years five son-of both-feet lame-of

וִיהוֹנָתָן מִיִּזְרְעֶאל וַתִּשָּׂאֵהוּ אֹמַנְתּוֹ וַתָּנֹס

and-she-fled one-nursing-him and-she-picked-up-him from-Jezreel and-Jonathan

וַיְהִי בְּחָפְזָהּ לָנוּס וַיִּפֹּל וַיִּפָּסֵחַ

and-he-became-crippled then-he-fell to-leave as-to-hurry-her but-he-was

"May God deal with me, be it ever so severely, if I taste bread or anything else before the sun sets!"

36All the people took note and were pleased; indeed, everything the king did pleased them. 37So on that day all the people and all Israel knew that the king had no part in the murder of Abner son of Ner.

38Then the king said to his men, "Do you not realize that a prince and a great man has fallen in Israel this day? 39And today, though I am the anointed king, I am weak, and these sons of Zeruiah are too strong for me. May the LORD repay the evildoer according to his evil deeds!"

### *Ish-Bosheth Murdered*

4 When Ish-Bosheth son of Saul heard that Abner had died in Hebron, he lost courage, and all Israel became alarmed. 2Now Saul's son had two men who were leaders of raiding bands. One was named Baanah and the other Recab; they were sons of Rimmon the Beerothite from the tribe of Benjamin—Beeroth is considered part of Benjamin, 3because the people of Beeroth fled to Gittaim and have lived there as aliens to this day.

4(Jonathan son of Saul had a son who was lame in both feet. He was five years old when the news about Saul and Jonathan came from Jezreel. His nurse picked him up and fled, but as she hurried to

*2 Most mss have *tsere* under the *aleph* (הַבֵּאֹ׳).

וּשְׁמוֹ מְפִיבֹשֶׁת׃ וַיֵּלְכוּ בְּנֵֽי־ רִמּוֹן הַבְּאֵרֹתִי

the-Beerothite Rimmon sons-of now-they-set-out (5) Mephibosheth and-name-of-him

רֵכָב וּבַעֲנָה וַיָּבֹאוּ כְּחֹם הַיּוֹם אֶל־ בֵּית אִישׁ בֹּשֶׁת

Bosheth Ish house-of at the-day in-heat-of and-they-arrived and-Baanah Recab

וְהוּא שֹׁכֵב אֵת מִשְׁכַּב הַצָּהֳרָיִם׃ וְהֵנָּה בָּאוּ עַד־

into they-went and-to-there (6) the-noonday rest-of *** resting while-he

תּוֹךְ הַבַּיִת לֹקְחֵי חִטִּים וַיַּכֻּהוּ אֶל־

in and-they-stabbed-him wheats ones-getting-of the-house inner-part-of

הַחֹמֶשׁ וְרֵכָב וּבַעֲנָה אָחִיו נִמְלָטוּ׃

they-slipped-away brother-of-him and-Baanah then-Racab the-stomach

וַיָּבֹאוּ הַבַּיִת וְהוּא־ שֹׁכֵב עַל־ מִטָּתוֹ בַּחֲדַר

in-room-of bed-of-him on lying while-he the-house now-they-entered (7)

מִשְׁכָּבוֹ וַיַּכֻּהוּ וַיְמִתֻהוּ וַיָּסִירוּ אֶת־

*** and-they-cut-off and-they-killed-him and-they-stabbed-him bed-of-him

רֹאשׁוֹ וַיִּקְחוּ אֶת־ רֹאשׁוֹ וַיֵּלְכוּ דֶּרֶךְ הָעֲרָבָה

the-Arabah way-of and-they-traveled head-of-him *** and-they-took head-of-him

כָּל־ הַלָּיְלָה׃ וַיָּבִאוּ אֶת־ רֹאשׁ אִישׁ־ בֹּשֶׁת אֶל־ דָּוִד

David to Bosheth Ish head-of *** and-they-brought (8) the-night all-of

חֶבְרוֹן וַיֹּאמְרוּ אֶל־ הַמֶּלֶךְ הִנֵּה־ רֹאשׁ אִישׁ־ בֹּשֶׁת בֶּן־ שָׁאוּל

Saul son-of Bosheth Ish head-of see! the-king to and-they-said Hebron

אֹיִבְךָ אֲשֶׁר בִּקֵּשׁ אֶת־ נַפְשֶׁךָ וַיִּתֵּן יְהוָה

Yahweh now-he-gave life-of-you *** he-sought who being-enemy-of-you

לַאדֹנִי הַמֶּלֶךְ נְקָמוֹת הַיּוֹם הַזֶּה מִשָּׁאוּל

against-Saul the-this the-day vengeances the-king to-lord-of-me

וּמִזַּרְעוֹ׃ וַיַּעַן דָּוִד אֶת־ רֵכָב ׀ וְאֶת־ בַּעֲנָה

Baanah and Recab *** David and-he-answered (9) and-against-offspring-of-him

אָחִיו בְּנֵי רִמּוֹן הַבְּאֵרֹתִי וַיֹּאמֶר לָהֶם חַי־

life-of to-them and-he-said the-Beerothite Rimmon sons-of brother-of-him

יְהוָה אֲשֶׁר־ פָּדָה אֶת־ נַפְשִׁי מִכָּל־ צָרָה׃ כִּי

when (10) trouble from-all-of life-of-me *** he-delivered who Yahweh

הַמַּגִּיד לִי לֵאמֹר הִנֵּה־ מֵת שָׁאוּל וְהוּא־ הָיָה

he-was and-he Saul he-is-dead see! to-say to-me the-one-telling

כִמְבַשֵּׂר בְּעֵינָיו וָאֹחֲזָה בוֹ

onto-him then-I-seized in-eyes-of-him like-one-bringing-good-news

וָאֶהְרְגֵהוּ בְּצִקְלָג אֲשֶׁר לְתִתִּי־ לוֹ בְּשֹׂרָה׃ אַף

much-more (11) good-news to-him to-reward-me that in-Ziklag and-I-killed-him

כִּי־ אֲנָשִׁים רְשָׁעִים הָרְגוּ אֶת־ אִישׁ־ צַדִּיק בְּבֵיתוֹ עַל־

on in-house-of-him innocent man *** they-killed wicked-ones men when

leave, he fell and became crippled. His name was Mephibosheth.)

5Now Recab and Baanah, the sons of Rimmon the Beerothite, set out for the house of Ish-Bosheth, and they arrived there in the heat of the day while he was taking his noonday rest. 6They went into the inner part of the house as if to get some wheat, and they stabbed him in the stomach. Then Recab and his brother Baanah slipped away.

7They had gone into the house while he was lying on the bed in his bedroom. After they stabbed and killed him, they cut off his head. Taking it with them, they traveled all night by way of the Arabah. 8They brought the head of Ish-Bosheth to David at Hebron and said to the king, "Here is the head of Ish-Bosheth son of Saul, your enemy, who tried to take your life. This day the LORD has avenged my lord the king against Saul and his offspring."

9David answered Recab and his brother Baanah, the sons of Rimmon the Beerothite, "As surely as the LORD lives, who has delivered me out of all trouble, 10when a man told me, 'Saul is dead,' and thought he was bringing good news, I seized him and put him to death in Ziklag. That was the reward I gave him for his news! 11How much more—when wicked men have killed an innocent man in his own

מִשְׁכָּבוֹ וְעַתָּה הֲלוֹא אֲבַקֵּשׁ אֶת־ דָּמוֹ מִיֶּדְכֶם
from-hand-of-you blood-of-him *** I-should-demand not? then-now bed-of-him

וּבִעַרְתִּי אֶתְכֶם מִן־ הָאָרֶץ׃ וַיְצַו דָּוִד אֶת־הַנְּעָרִים
the-men *** David so-he-ordered (12) the-earth from you and-I-remove

וַיַּהַרְגוּם וַיְקַצְּצוּ אֶת־ יְדֵיהֶם וְאֶת־ רַגְלֵיהֶם
feet-of-them and hands-of-them *** and-they-cut-off and-they-killed-them

וַיִּתְלוּ עַל־הַבְּרֵכָה בְּחֶבְרוֹן וְאֵת רֹאשׁ אִישׁ־ בֹּשֶׁת לָקָחוּ
they-took Bosheth Ish head-of but in-Hebron the-pool by and-they-hung

וַיִּקְבְּרוּ בְקֶבֶר־ אַבְנֵר בְּחֶבְרוֹן׃ וַיָּבֹאוּ כָּל־
all-of and-they-came (5:1) at-Hegron Abner in-tomb-of and-they-buried

שִׁבְטֵי יִשְׂרָאֵל אֶל־דָּוִד חֶבְרוֹנָה וַיֹּאמְרוּ לֵאמֹר הִנְנוּ עַצְמְךָ
bone-of-you see-us! to-say and-they-said at-Hebron David to Israel tribes-of

וּבְשָׂרְךָ אֲנָחְנוּ׃ גַּם־ אֶתְמוֹל גַּם־ שִׁלְשׁוֹם בִּהְיוֹת שָׁאוּל מֶלֶךְ
king Saul while-to-be before and yesterday now (2) we and-flesh-of-you

עָלֵינוּ אַתָּה הָיִיתָה °מוֹצִיא וְהַמֵּבִי° אֶת־יִשְׂרָאֵל
Israel *** and-the-one-leading-in the-one-leading-out you-were you over-us

וַיֹּאמֶר יְהוָה לְךָ אַתָּה תִרְעֶה אֶת־ עַמִּי אֶת־יִשְׂרָאֵל
Israel *** people-of-me *** you-will-sheperd you to-you Yahweh and-he-said

וְאַתָּה תִּהְיֶה לְנָגִיד עַל־ יִשְׂרָאֵל׃ וַיָּבֹאוּ כָּל־
all-of when-they-came (3) Israel over as-ruler you-will-become and-you

זִקְנֵי יִשְׂרָאֵל אֶל־הַמֶּלֶךְ חֶבְרוֹנָה וַיִּכְרֹת לָהֶם הַמֶּלֶךְ דָּוִד
David the-king with-them then-he-made at-Hebron the-king to Israel elders-of

בְּרִית בְּחֶבְרוֹן לִפְנֵי יְהוָה וַיִּמְשְׁחוּ אֶת־ דָּוִד לְמֶלֶךְ עַל־
over as-king David *** and-they-anointed Yahweh before at-Hebron compact

יִשְׂרָאֵל׃ בֶּן־ שְׁלֹשִׁים שָׁנָה דָּוִד בְּמָלְכוֹ אַרְבָּעִים שָׁנָה
year forty when-to-become-king-him David year thirty son-of (4) Israel

מָלָךְ׃ בְּחֶבְרוֹן מָלַךְ עַל־ יְהוּדָה שֶׁבַע שָׁנִים וְשִׁשָּׁה חֳדָשִׁים
months and-six years seven Judah over he-reigned in-Hebron (5) he-reigned

וּבִירוּשָׁלַםִ מָלַךְ שְׁלֹשִׁים וְשָׁלֹשׁ שָׁנָה עַל כָּל־ יִשְׂרָאֵל
Israel all-of over year and-three thirty he-reigned and-in-Jerusalem

וִיהוּדָה׃ וַיֵּלֶךְ הַמֶּלֶךְ וַאֲנָשָׁיו יְרוּשָׁלַםִ אֶל־
against Jerusalem and-men-of-him the-king then-he-marched (6) and-Judah

הַיְבֻסִי יוֹשֵׁב הָאָרֶץ וַיֹּאמֶר לְדָוִד לֵאמֹר לֹא־ תָבוֹא
you-will-get-in not to-say to-David and-he-said the-land living-of the-Jebusite

הֵנָּה כִּי אִם־ הֱסִירְךָ הַעִוְרִים וְהַפִּסְחִים
and-the-lame-ones the-blind-ones he-can-ward-off-you even for to-here

לֵאמֹר לֹא־ יָבוֹא דָוִד הֵנָּה׃ וַיִּלְכֹּד דָּוִד אֵת
*** David but-he-captured (7) to-here David he-can-get-in not to-think

house and on his own bed—
should I not now demand his
blood from your hand and rid
the earth of you!"
12So David gave an order to
his men, and they killed them.
They cut off their hands and
feet and hung the bodies by
the pool in Hebron. But they
took the head of Ish-Bosheth
and buried it in Abner's tomb
at Hebron.

*David Becomes King Over Israel*

5 All the tribes of Israel
came to David at Hebron
and said, "We are your own
flesh and blood. 2In the past,
while Saul was king over us,
you were the one who led Israel on their military campaigns.
And the LORD said to you, 'You
will shepherd my people Israel, and you will become their
ruler.' "
3When all the elders of Israel
had come to King David at
Hebron, the king made a compact with them at Hebron before the LORD, and they
anointed David king over Israel.
4David was thirty years old
when he became king, and he
reigned forty years. 5In Hebron he reigned over Judah
seven years and six months,
and in Jerusalem he reigned
over all Israel and Judah
thirty-three years.

*David Conquers Jerusalem*

6The king and his men
marched to Jerusalem to attack
the Jebusites, who lived there.
The Jebusites said to David,
"You will not get in here; even
the blind and the lame can
ward you off." They thought,
"David cannot get in here."
7Nevertheless, David captured

°2a ק היית המוציא
°2b ק והמביא

מְצֻדַת צִיֹּן הִיא עִיר דָּוִד׃ וַיֹּאמֶר דָּוִד בַּיּוֹם הַהוּא

the-that on-the-day David and-he-said (8) David City-of that Zion fortress-of

כָּל־ מַכֵּה יְבֻסִי וְיִגַּע בַּצִּנּוֹר

through-the-water-shaft then-he-must-reach Jebusite one-conquering any-of

וְאֶת־ הַפִּסְחִים וְאֶת־ הַעִוְרִים שְׂנֻאֵו נֶפֶשׁ דָּוִד עַל־ כֵּן

this for David life-of being-enemies-of the-blind-ones and the-lame-ones both

יֹאמְרוּ עִוֵּר וּפִסֵּחַ לֹא יָבוֹא אֶל־ הַבָּיִת׃ וַיֵּשֶׁב

then-he-resided (9) the-palace into he-will-enter not and-lame blind they-say

דָּוִד בַּמְּצֻדָה וַיִּקְרָא־ לָהּ עִיר דָּוִד וַיִּבֶן דָּוִד

David and-he-built-up David City-of to-her and-he-called in-the-fortress David

סָבִיב מִן־ הַמִּלּוֹא וָבָיְתָה׃ וַיֵּלֶךְ דָּוִד הָלוֹךְ

to-increase David and-he-continued (10) and-inward the-terrace from around

וְגָדוֹל וַיהוָה אֱלֹהֵי צְבָאוֹת עִמּוֹ׃ וַיִּשְׁלַח חִירָם מֶלֶךְ־

king-of Hiram now-he-sent (11) with-him Hosts God-of for-Yahweh and-powerful

צֹר מַלְאָכִים אֶל־ דָּוִד וַעֲצֵי אֲרָזִים וְחָרָשֵׁי עֵץ וְחָרָשֵׁי

and-carvers-of wood and-carvers-of cedars and-logs-of David to messengers Tyre

אֶבֶן קִיר וַיִּבְנוּ־ בַיִת לְדָוִד׃ וַיֵּדַע דָּוִד כִּי־

that David and-he-knew (12) for-David palace and-they-built wall stone-of

הֱכִינוֹ יְהוָה לְמֶלֶךְ עַל־ יִשְׂרָאֵל וְכִי נִשֵּׂא

he-exalted and-that Israel over as-king Yahweh he-established-him

מַמְלַכְתּוֹ בַּעֲבוּר עַמּוֹ יִשְׂרָאֵל׃ וַיִּקַּח דָּוִד עוֹד

more David and-he-took (13) Israel people-of-him for-sake-of kingdom-of-him

פִּלַגְשִׁים וְנָשִׁים מִירוּשָׁלִַם אַחֲרֵי בֹּאוֹ מֵחֶבְרוֹן

from-Hebron to-leave-him after in-Jerusalem and-wives concubines

וַיִּוָּלְדוּ עוֹד לְדָוִד בָּנִים וּבָנוֹת׃ וְאֵלֶּה שְׁמוֹת

names-of and-these (14) and-daughters sons to-David more and-they-were-born

הַיִּלֹּדִים לוֹ בִּירוּשָׁלִָם שַׁמּוּעַ וְשׁוֹבָב וְנָתָן וּשְׁלֹמֹה׃

and-Solomon and-Nathan and-Shobab Shammua in-Jerusalem to-him the-ones-born

וְיִבְחָר וֶאֱלִישׁוּעַ וְנֶפֶג וְיָפִיעַ׃ וֶאֱלִישָׁמָע וְאֶלְיָדָע

and-Eliada and-Elishama (16) and-Japhia and-Nepheg and-Elishua and-Ibhar (15)

וֶאֱלִיפָלֶט׃ וַיִּשְׁמְעוּ פְלִשְׁתִּים כִּי־ מָשְׁחוּ אֶת־ דָּוִד

David *** they-anointed that Philistines when-they-heard (17) and-Eliphelet

לְמֶלֶךְ עַל־ יִשְׂרָאֵל וַיַּעֲלוּ כָל־ פְּלִשְׁתִּים לְבַקֵּשׁ אֶת־

*** to-search-for Philistines all-of then-they-went-up Israel over as-king

דָּוִד וַיִּשְׁמַע דָּוִד וַיֵּרֶד אֶל־ הַמְּצוּדָה׃ וּפְלִשְׁתִּים

now-Philistines (18) the-stronghold to and-he-went-down David but-he-heard David

בָּאוּ וַיִּנָּטְשׁוּ בְּעֵמֶק רְפָאִים׃ וַיִּשְׁאַל דָּוִד

David and-he-inquired (19) Rephaim in-Valley-of and-they-spread-out they-came

the fortress of Zion, the City of David.

8 On that day, David said, "Anyone who conquers the Jebusites will have to use the water shaft[f] to reach those 'lame and blind' who are David's enemies.[g]" That is why they say, "The 'blind and lame' will not enter the palace."

9 David then took up residence in the fortress and called it the City of David. He built up the area around it, from the supporting terraces[h] inward. 10 And he became more and more powerful, because the LORD God Almighty was with him.

11 Now Hiram king of Tyre sent messengers to David, along with cedar logs and carpenters and stonemasons, and they built a palace for David. 12 And David knew that the LORD had established him as king over Israel and had exalted his kingdom for the sake of his people Israel.

13 After he left Hebron, David took more concubines and wives in Jerusalem, and more sons and daughters were born to him. 14 These are the names of the children born to him there: Shammua, Shobab, Nathan, Solomon, 15 Ibhar, Elishua, Nepheg, Japhia, 16 Elishama, Eliada and Eliphelet.

*David Defeats the Philistines*

17 When the Philistines heard that David had been anointed king over Israel, they went up in full force to search for him, but David heard about it and went down to the stronghold. 18 Now the Philistines had come and spread out in the Valley of Rephaim; 19 so David

*f8 Or use scaling hooks*
*g8 Or are hated by David* *h9 Or the Millo*

°8 ק שנאי

בַּֽיהוָה֙ לֵאמֹ֔ר הַאֶֽעֱלֶה֙ אֶל־פְּלִשְׁתִּ֔ים הֲתִתְּנֵ֖ם
will-you-give-them? Philistines against shall-I-go? to-ask of-Yahweh

בְּיָדִ֑י וַיֹּ֨אמֶר יְהוָ֤ה אֶל־דָּוִד֙ עֲלֵ֔ה כִּֽי־נָתֹ֥ן אֶתֵּ֛ן
I-will-give to-give for go! David to Yahweh and-he-answered into-hand-of-me

אֶת־הַפְּלִשְׁתִּ֖ים בְּיָדֶֽךָ׃ וַיָּבֹ֨א דָוִ֜ד בְּבַ֣עַל־פְּרָצִים֮
Perazim to-Baal David so-he-went (20) into-hand-of-you the-Philistines ***

וַיַּכֵּ֣ם שָׁ֣ם דָּוִד֒ וַיֹּ֗אמֶר פָּרַ֨ץ יְהוָ֧ה אֶת־
against Yahweh he-broke-out and-he-said David there and-he-defeated-them

אֹיְבַ֛י לְפָנַ֖י כְּפֶ֣רֶץ מָ֑יִם עַל־כֵּ֗ן קָרָ֛א
he-called this for waters as-breaking-out-of before-me being-enemies-of-me

שֵֽׁם־הַמָּק֥וֹם הַה֖וּא בַּ֥עַל פְּרָצִֽים׃ וַיַּֽעַזְבוּ־שָׁ֖ם אֶת־
*** there and-they-abandoned (21) Perazim Baal the-that the-place name-of

עֲצַבֵּיהֶ֑ם וַיִּשָּׂאֵ֥ם דָּוִ֖ד וַאֲנָשָֽׁיו׃ וַיֹּסִ֥פוּ
and-they-repeated (22) and-men-of-him David and-he-carried-off-them idols-of-them

ע֥וֹד פְּלִשְׁתִּ֖ים לַעֲל֑וֹת וַיִּנָּטְשׁ֖וּ בְּעֵ֥מֶק רְפָאִֽים׃
Rephaim in-Valley-of and-they-spread-out to-come-up Philistines again

וַיִּשְׁאַ֤ל דָּוִד֙ בַּֽיהוָ֔ה וַיֹּ֖אמֶר לֹ֣א תַעֲלֶ֑ה הָסֵב֙
circle! you-go-up not and-he-answered of-Yahweh David so-he-inquired (23)

אֶל־אַ֣חֲרֵיהֶ֔ם וּבָ֥אתָ לָהֶ֖ם מִמּ֥וּל בְּכָאִֽים׃
balsam-trees in-front-of against-them and-you-attack behind-them to

וִיהִ֗י בְּשָׁמְעֲךָ֞° אֶת־ק֤וֹל צְעָדָה֙ בְּרָאשֵׁ֣י
in-tops-of marching sound-of *** as-to-hear-you and-he-will-be (24)

הַבְּכָאִ֔ים אָ֖ז תֶּחֱרָ֑ץ כִּ֣י אָ֞ז יָצָ֤א יְהוָה֙ לְפָנֶ֔יךָ
before-you Yahweh he-went-out then for you-move-quickly then the-balsam-trees

לְהַכּ֖וֹת בְּמַחֲנֵ֥ה פְלִשְׁתִּֽים׃ וַיַּ֤עַשׂ דָּוִד֙ כֵּ֔ן כַּאֲשֶׁ֖ר
just-as this David so-he-did (25) Philistines against-camp-of to-strike

צִוָּ֣הוּ יְהוָ֑ה וַיַּךְ֙ אֶת־פְּלִשְׁתִּ֔ים מִגֶּ֖בַע עַד־
to from-Geba Philitines *** and-he-struck Yahweh he-commanded-him

בֹּאֲךָ֥ גָֽזֶר׃ וַיֹּ֨סֶף ע֥וֹד דָּוִ֛ד אֶת־כָּל־
all-of *** David again and-he-brought-together (6:1) Gezer to-go-you

בָּח֥וּר בְּיִשְׂרָאֵ֖ל שְׁלֹשִׁ֥ים אָֽלֶף׃ וַיָּ֣קָם ׀ וַיֵּ֣לֶךְ דָּוִ֗ד
David and-he-set-out and-he-rose (2) thousand thirty from-Israel being-chosen

וְכָל־הָעָם֙ אֲשֶׁ֣ר אִתּ֔וֹ מִֽבַּעֲלֵ֖י יְהוּדָ֑ה לְהַעֲל֣וֹת מִשָּׁ֗ם
from-there to-bring-up Judah from-Baale-of with-him who the-people and-all-of

אֵ֚ת אֲר֣וֹן הָאֱלֹהִ֔ים אֲשֶׁר־נִקְרָ֣א שֵׁ֗ם שֵׁ֣ם יְהוָ֧ה צְבָא֛וֹת
Hosts Yahweh-of name-of Name he-is-called which the-God ark-of ***

יֹשֵׁ֥ב הַכְּרֻבִ֖ים עָלָֽיו׃ וַיַּרְכִּ֜בוּ אֶת־אֲר֤וֹן הָאֱלֹהִים֙
the-God ark-of *** and-they-set (3) on-him the-cherubim being-enthroned-of

inquired of the LORD, "Shall I go and attack the Philistines? Will you hand them over to me?"

The LORD answered him, "Go, for I will surely hand the Philistines over to you."

20So David went to Baal Perazim, and there he defeated them. He said, "As waters break out, the LORD has broken out against my enemies before me." So that place was called Baal Perazim.[i] 21The Philistines abandoned their idols there, and David and his men carried them off.

22Once more the Philistines came up and spread out in the Valley of Rephaim; 23so David inquired of the LORD, and he answered, "Do not go straight up, but circle around behind them and attack them in front of the balsam trees. 24As soon as you hear the sound of marching in the tops of the balsam trees, move quickly, because that will mean the LORD has gone out in front of you to strike the Philistine army." 25So David did as the LORD commanded him, and he struck down the Philistines all the way from Gibeon[j] to Gezer.

### *The Ark Brought to Jerusalem*

6 David again brought together out of Israel chosen men, thirty thousand in all. 2He and all his men set out from Baalah of Judah[k] to bring up from there the ark of God, which is called by the Name,[l] the name of the LORD Almighty, who is enthroned between the cherubim that are on the ark. 3They set the ark of

[i]20 *Baal Perazim* means *the lord who breaks out.*
[j]25 Septuagint (see also 1 Chron. 14:16); Hebrew *Geba*
[k]2 That is, Kiriath Jearim; Hebrew *Baale Judah*, a variant of *Baalah of Judah*
[l]2 Hebrew; Septuagint and Vulgate do not have *the Name.*

°24 כשמעך ק

אֶל־עֲגָלָה חֲדָשָׁה וַיִּשָּׂאֻהוּ מִבֵּית אֲבִינָדָב אֲשֶׁר בַּגִּבְעָה
on-the-hill which Abinadab from-house-of and-they-brought-him new cart on

וְעֻזָּא וְאַחְיוֹ בְּנֵי אֲבִינָדָב נֹהֲגִים אֶת־הָעֲגָלָה חֲדָשָׁה׃
new the-cart *** ones-guiding Abinadab sons-of and-Ahio and-Uzzah

וַיִּשָּׂאֻהוּ מִבֵּית אֲבִינָדָב אֲשֶׁר בַּגִּבְעָה עִם אֲרוֹן
ark-of with on-the-hill which Abinadab from-house-of and-they-brought-him (4)

הָאֱלֹהִים וְאַחְיוֹ הֹלֵךְ לִפְנֵי הָאָרוֹן׃ וְדָוִד | וְכָל־
and-whole-of now-David (5) the-ark in-front-of walking and-Ahio the-God

בֵּית יִשְׂרָאֵל מְשַׂחֲקִים לִפְנֵי יְהוָה בְּכֹל עֲצֵי
instruments-of with-all-of Yahweh before ones-celebrating Israel house-of

בְרוֹשִׁים וּבְכִנֹּרוֹת וּבִנְבָלִים וּבְתֻפִּים וּבִמְנַעַנְעִים
and-with-sistrums and-with-tambourines and-with-lyres and-with-harps pines

וּבְצֶלְצֶלִים׃ וַיָּבֹאוּ עַד־גֹּרֶן נָכוֹן וַיִּשְׁלַח
then-he-reached Nacon threshing-floor-of to when-they-came (6) and-with-cymbals

עֻזָּא אֶל־אֲרוֹן הָאֱלֹהִים וַיֹּאחֶז בּוֹ כִּי שָׁמְטוּ הַבָּקָר׃
the-ox they-stumbled for onto-him and-he-held the-God ark-of to Uzzah

וַיִּחַר־אַף יְהוָה בְּעֻזָּה וַיַּכֵּהוּ שָׁם
there and-he-struck-down-him against-Uzzah Yahweh anger-of and-he-burned (7)

הָאֱלֹהִים עַל־הַשַּׁל וַיָּמָת שָׁם עִם אֲרוֹן הָאֱלֹהִים׃
the-God ark-of beside there and-he-died the-irreverent-act because-of the-God

וַיִּחַר לְדָוִד עַל אֲשֶׁר פָּרַץ יְהוָה פֶּרֶץ
breaking-out Yahweh he-broke-out that because to-David and-he-angered (8)

בְּעֻזָּה וַיִּקְרָא לַמָּקוֹם הַהוּא פֶּרֶץ עֻזָּה עַד הַיּוֹם
the-day to Uzzah Perez the-that to-the-place so-he-called against-Uzzah

הַזֶּה׃ וַיִּרָא דָוִד אֶת־יְהוָה בַּיּוֹם הַהוּא וַיֹּאמֶר
and-he-said the-that on-the-day Yahweh *** David and-he-feared (9) the-this

אֵיךְ יָבוֹא אֵלַי אֲרוֹן יְהוָה׃ וְלֹא־אָבָה דָוִד
David he-was-willing and-not (10) Yahweh ark-of to-me can-he-come how?

לְהָסִיר אֵלָיו אֶת־אֲרוֹן יְהוָה עַל־עִיר דָּוִד וַיַּטֵּהוּ דָוִד
David so-he-took-him David City-of in Yahweh ark-of *** with-him to-take

בֵּית עֹבֵד־אֱדֹם הַגִּתִּי׃ וַיֵּשֶׁב אֲרוֹן יְהוָה בֵּית
house-of Yahweh ark-of and-he-remained (11) the-Gittite Edom Obed house-of

עֹבֵד אֱדֹם הַגִּתִּי שְׁלֹשָׁה חֳדָשִׁים וַיְבָרֶךְ יְהוָה אֶת־עֹבֵד אֱדֹם וְאֶת־
and Edom Obed *** Yahweh and-he-blessed months three the-Gittite Edom Obed

כָּל־בֵּיתוֹ׃ וַיֻּגַּד לַמֶּלֶךְ דָּוִד לֵאמֹר
to-say David to-the-king now-he-was-told (12) household-of-him entire-of

בֵּרַךְ יְהוָה אֶת־בֵּית עֹבֵד אֱדֹם וְאֶת־כָּל־אֲשֶׁר־לוֹ בַּעֲבוּר
because-of to-him that all and Edom Obed household-of *** Yahweh he-blessed

God on a new cart and
brought it from the house of
Abinadab, which was on the
hill. Uzzah and Ahio, sons of
Abinadab, were guiding the
new cart 4with the ark of God
on it,[m] and Ahio was walking
in front of it. 5David and the
whole house of Israel were
celebrating with all their
might before the LORD, with
songs[n] and with harps, lyres,
tambourines, sistrums and
cymbals.
6When they came to the
threshing floor of Nacon, Uzzah reached out and took hold
of the ark of God, because the
oxen stumbled. 7The LORD's
anger burned against Uzzah
because of his irreverent act;
therefore God struck him
down and he died there beside
the ark of God.
8Then David was angry be-
cause the LORD's wrath had
broken out against Uzzah, and
to this day that place is called
Perez Uzzah.[o]
9David was afraid of the
LORD that day and said, "How
can the ark of the LORD ever
come to me?" 10He was not
willing to take the ark of the
LORD to be with him in the
City of David. Instead, he took
it aside to the house of Obed-
Edom the Gittite. 11The ark of
the LORD remained in the
house of Obed-Edom the Gittite for three months, and the
LORD blessed him and his entire household.
12Now King David was told,
"The LORD has blessed the
household of Obed-Edom and
everything he has, because of

[m]3,4 Some Septuagint manuscripts; Hebrew *cart* 4*and they brought it with the ark of God from the house of Abinadab, which was on the hill*
[n]5 See Septuagint and 1 Chronicles 13:8; Hebrew *celebrating before the LORD with all kinds of instruments made of pine*
[o]8 *Perez Uzzah* means *outbreak against Uzzah.*

אֲרוֹן הָאֱלֹהִים וַיֵּלֶךְ דָּוִד וַיַּעַל אֶת־אֲרוֹן הָאֱלֹהִים
the-God ark-of *** and-he-brought-up David so-he-went-down the-God ark-of

מִבֵּית עֹבֵד אֱדֹם עִיר דָּוִד בְּשִׂמְחָה׃ וַיְהִי כִּי
when and-he-was (13) with-rejoicing David City-of Edom Obed from-house-of

צָעֲדוּ נֹשְׂאֵי אֲרוֹן־יְהוָה שִׁשָּׁה צְעָדִים וַיִּזְבַּח שׁוֹר
bull then-he-sacrificed steps six Yahweh ark-of ones-carrying-of they-walked

וּמְרִיא׃ וְדָוִד מְכַרְכֵּר בְּכָל־עֹז לִפְנֵי יְהוָה
Yahweh before might with-all-of dancing and-David (14) and-fattened-calf

וְדָוִד חָגוּר אֵפוֹד בָּד׃ וְדָוִד וְכָל־בֵּית יִשְׂרָאֵל
Israel house-of and-entire-of and-David (15) linen ephod wearing now-David

מַעֲלִים אֶת־אֲרוֹן יְהוָה בִּתְרוּעָה וּבְקוֹל שׁוֹפָר׃
trumpet and-with-sound-of with-shout Yaheh ark-of *** ones-bringing-up

וְהָיָה אֲרוֹן יְהוָה בָּא עִיר דָּוִד וּמִיכַל בַּת־
daughter-of and-Michal David City-of entering Yahweh ark-of and-he-was (16)

שָׁאוּל נִשְׁקְפָה׀ בְּעַד הַחַלּוֹן וַתֵּרֶא אֶת־הַמֶּלֶךְ דָּוִד מְפַזֵּז
leaping David the-king *** when-she-saw the-window from watching Saul

וּמְכַרְכֵּר לִפְנֵי יְהוָה וַתִּבֶז לוֹ בְּלִבָּהּ׃
in-heart-of-her at-him then-she-despised Yahweh before and-dancing

וַיָּבִאוּ אֶת־אֲרוֹן יְהוָה וַיַּצִּגוּ אֹתוֹ בִּמְקוֹמוֹ
in-place-of-him him and-they-set Yahweh ark-of *** and-they-brought (17)

בְּתוֹךְ הָאֹהֶל אֲשֶׁר נָטָה־לוֹ דָּוִד וַיַּעַל דָּוִד
David and-he-sacrificed David for-him he-pitched that the-tent inside-of

עֹלוֹת לִפְנֵי יְהוָה וּשְׁלָמִים׃ וַיְכַל
when-he-finished (18) and-fellowship-offerings Yahweh before burnt-offerings

דָּוִד מֵהַעֲלוֹת הָעוֹלָה וְהַשְּׁלָמִים
and-the-fellowship-offerings the-burnt-offering from-to-sacrifice David

וַיְבָרֶךְ אֶת־הָעָם בְּשֵׁם יְהוָה צְבָאוֹת׃ וַיְחַלֵּק
then-he-gave (19) Hosts Yahweh-of in-name-of the-people *** then-he-blessed

לְכָל־הָעָם לְכָל־הֲמוֹן יִשְׂרָאֵל לְמֵאִישׁ וְעַד־אִשָּׁה
woman even-to to-both-man Israel crowd-of in-whole-of the-people to-each-of

לְאִישׁ חַלַּת לֶחֶם אַחַת וְאֶשְׁפָּר אֶחָד וַאֲשִׁישָׁה אֶחָת וַיֵּלֶךְ
and-he-went one and-raisin-cake one and-date-cake one bread loaf-of to-each

כָּל־הָעָם אִישׁ לְבֵיתוֹ׃ וַיָּשָׁב דָּוִד לְבָרֵךְ
to-bless David when-he-returned (20) to-home-of-him each the-people all-of

אֶת־בֵּיתוֹ וַתֵּצֵא מִיכַל בַּת־שָׁאוּל לִקְרַאת דָּוִד
David to-meet Saul daughter-of Michal then-she-came-out household-of-him ***

וַתֹּאמֶר מַה־נִּכְבַּד הַיּוֹם מֶלֶךְ יִשְׂרָאֵל אֲשֶׁר
when Israel king-of the-day he-distinguished-himself how! and-she-said

the ark of God." So David went down and brought up the ark of God from the house of Obed-Edom to the City of David with rejoicing. 13When those who were carrying the ark of the LORD had taken six steps, he sacrificed a bull and a fattened calf. 14David, wearing a linen ephod, danced before the LORD with all his might, 15while he and the entire house of Israel brought up the ark of the LORD with shouts and the sound of trumpets.

16As the ark of the LORD was entering the City of David, Michal daughter of Saul watched from a window. And when she saw King David leaping and dancing before the LORD, she despised him in her heart.

17They brought the ark of the LORD and set it in its place inside the tent that David had pitched for it, and David sacrificed burnt offerings and fellowship offerings[p] before the LORD. 18After he had finished sacrificing the burnt offerings and fellowship offerings, he blessed the people in the name of the LORD Almighty. 19Then he gave a loaf of bread, a cake of dates and a cake of raisins to each person in the whole crowd of Israelites, both men and women. And all the people went to their homes.

20When David returned home to bless his household, Michal daughter of Saul came out to meet him and said, "How the king of Israel has distinguished himself today,

p17 Traditionally *peace offerings;* also in verse 18

נִגְלָה הַיּוֹם לְעֵינֵי אַמְהוֹת עֲבָדָיו כְּהִגָּלוֹת
as-to-disrobe servants-of-him slave-girls-of before-eyes-of the-day he-disrobed

נִגְלוֹת אַחַד הָרֵקִים׃ וַיֹּאמֶר דָּוִד אֶל־מִיכַל לִפְנֵי
before Michal to David and-he-said (21) the-vulgar-fellows one-of to-disrobe

יְהוָה אֲשֶׁר בָּחַר־ בִּי מֵאָבִיךְ וּמִכָּל־
or-rather-than-all-of rather-than-father-of-you to-me he-chose who Yahweh

בֵּיתוֹ לְצַוֺּת אֹתִי נָגִיד עַל־ עַם יְהוָה עַל־יִשְׂרָאֵל
Israel over Yahweh people-of over ruler me to-appoint house-of-him

וְשִׂחַקְתִּי לִפְנֵי יְהוָה׃ וּנְקַלֹּתִי עוֹד
more and-I-will-become-undignified (22) Yahweh before and-I-will-celebrate

מִזֹּאת וְהָיִיתִי שָׁפָל בְּעֵינָי וְעִם־ הָאֲמָהוֹת אֲשֶׁר
whom the-slave-girls but-by in-eyes-of-me humiliated and-I-will-be than-this

אָמַרְתְּ עִמָּם אִכָּבֵדָה׃ וּלְמִיכַל בַּת־ שָׁאוּל לֹא־
not Saul daughter-of and-to-Michal (23) I-will-be-honored by-them you-spoke

הָיָה לָהּ יָלֶד עַד יוֹם מוֹתָהּ׃ וַיְהִי כִּי־
after and-he-was (7:1) death-of-her day-of until child to-her he-was

יָשַׁב הַמֶּלֶךְ בְּבֵיתוֹ וַיהוָה הֵנִיחַ־ לוֹ מִסָּבִיב
at-around to-him he-gave-rest and-Yahweh in-palace-of-him the-king he-settled

מִכָּל־ אֹיְבָיו׃ וַיֹּאמֶר הַמֶּלֶךְ אֶל־ נָתָן
Nathan to the-king then-he-said (2) being-enemies-of-him from-all-of

הַנָּבִיא רְאֵה נָא אָנֹכִי יוֹשֵׁב בְּבֵית אֲרָזִים וַאֲרוֹן הָאֱלֹהִים
the-God while-ark-of cedars in-palace-of living I now! see! the-prophet

יֹשֵׁב בְּתוֹךְ הַיְרִיעָה׃ וַיֹּאמֶר נָתָן אֶל־ הַמֶּלֶךְ כֹּל אֲשֶׁר
that all the-king to Nathan and-he-replied (3) the-tent inside-of remaining

בִּלְבָבְךָ לֵךְ עֲשֵׂה כִּי יְהוָה עִמָּךְ׃ וַיְהִי בַּלַּיְלָה
in-the-night and-he-was (4) with-you Yahweh for do! go-ahead! in-heart-of-you

הַהוּא וַיְהִי דְּבַר־ יְהוָה אֶל־ נָתָן לֵאמֹר׃ לֵךְ וְאָמַרְתָּ
and-you-tell go! (5) to-say Nathan to Yahweh word-of then-he-came the-that

אֶל־ עַבְדִּי אֶל־ דָּוִד כֹּה אָמַר יְהוָה הַאַתָּה תִּבְנֶה־ לִּי
for-me will-you-build you? Yahweh he-says this David to servant-of-me to

בַיִת לְשִׁבְתִּי׃ כִּי לֹא יָשַׁבְתִּי בְּבַיִת לְמִיּוֹם הַעֲלֹתִי אֶת־
*** to-bring-me at-from-day in-house I-dwelt not for (6) to-dwell-me house

בְּנֵי יִשְׂרָאֵל מִמִּצְרַיִם וְעַד הַיּוֹם הַזֶּה וָאֶהְיֶה מִתְהַלֵּךְ בְּאֹהֶל
in-tent moving and-I-was the-this the-day even-to from-Egypt Israel sons-of

וּבְמִשְׁכָּן׃ בְּכֹל אֲשֶׁר־הִתְהַלַּכְתִּי בְּכָל־ בְּנֵי יִשְׂרָאֵל
Israel sons-of with-all-of I-moved that in-everywhere (7) and-in-dwelling

הֲדָבָר דִּבַּרְתִּי אֶת־אַחַד שִׁבְטֵי יִשְׂרָאֵל אֲשֶׁר צִוִּיתִי לִרְעוֹת אֶת־
*** to-shepherd I-commanded whom Israel rulers-of one-of *** I-said word?

disrobing in the sight of the slave girls of his servants as any vulgar fellow would!"

21 David said to Michal, "It was before the LORD, who chose me rather than your father or anyone from his house when he appointed me ruler over the LORD's people Israel—I will celebrate before the LORD.
22 I will become even more undignified than this, and I will be humiliated in my own eyes. But by these slave girls you spoke of, I will be held in honor."

23 And Michal daughter of Saul had no children to the day of her death.

*God's Promise to David*

7 After the king was settled in his palace and the LORD had given him rest from all his enemies around him,
2 he said to Nathan the prophet, "Here I am, living in a palace of cedar, while the ark of God remains in a tent."

3 Nathan replied to the king, "Whatever you have in mind, go ahead and do it, for the LORD is with you."

4 That night the word of the LORD came to Nathan, saying:

5 "Go and tell my servant David, 'This is what the LORD says: Are you the one to build me a house to dwell in?
6 I have not dwelt in a house from the day I brought the Israelites up out of Egypt to this day. I have been moving from place to place with a tent as my dwelling.
7 Wherever I have moved with all the Israelites, did I ever say to any of their rulers whom I commanded to shepherd

עַמִּי אֶת־ יִשְׂרָאֵל לֵאמֹר לָמָּה לֹא־ בְנִיתֶם לִי בֵּית אֲרָזִים׃
cedars house-of for-me you-built not why? to-say Israel *** people-of-me

וְעַתָּה כֹּה־ תֹאמַר לְעַבְדִּי לְדָוִד כֹּה אָמַר יְהוָה
Yahweh-of he-says this to-David to-servant-of-me you-tell this then-now (8)

צְבָאוֹת אֲנִי לְקַחְתִּיךָ מִן־ הַנָּוֶה מֵאַחַר הַצֹּאן לִהְיוֹת נָגִיד עַל־
over ruler to-be the-flock from-after the-pasture from I-took-you I Hosts

עַמִּי עַל־ יִשְׂרָאֵל׃ וָאֶהְיֶה עִמְּךָ בְּכֹל אֲשֶׁר הָלַכְתָּ
you-went that in-everywhere with-you and-I-was (9) Israel ,over people-of-me

וָאַכְרִתָה אֶת־ כָּל־ אֹיְבֶיךָ מִפָּנֶיךָ וְעָשִׂתִי
now-I-will-make from-before-you being-enemies-of-you all-of *** and-I-cut-off

לְךָ שֵׁם גָּדוֹל כְּשֵׁם הַגְּדֹלִים אֲשֶׁר בָּאָרֶץ׃
of-the-earth who the-great-ones like-name-of great name of-you

וְשַׂמְתִּי מָקוֹם לְעַמִּי לְיִשְׂרָאֵל וּנְטַעְתִּיו
and-I-will-plant-him for-Israel for-people-of-me place and-I-will-provide (10)

וְשָׁכַן תַּחְתָּיו וְלֹא יִרְגַּז עוֹד וְלֹא־
and-not longer he-will-be-disturbed and-not place-of-him so-he-can-stay

יֹסִיפוּ בְנֵי־ עַוְלָה לְעַנּוֹתוֹ כַּאֲשֶׁר בָּרִאשׁוֹנָה׃
at-the-beginning just-as to-oppress-him wickedness sons-of they-will-continue

וּלְמִן־ הַיּוֹם אֲשֶׁר צִוִּיתִי שֹׁפְטִים עַל־ עַמִּי
people-of-me over ones-leading I-appointed when the-day and-at-from (11)

יִשְׂרָאֵל וַהֲנִיחֹתִי לְךָ מִכָּל־ אֹיְבֶיךָ
being-enemies-of-you from-all-of to-you and-I-will-give-rest Israel

וְהִגִּיד לְךָ יְהוָה כִּי־ בַיִת יַעֲשֶׂה־ לְּךָ יְהוָה׃
Yahweh for-you he-will-establish house that Yahweh to-you and-he-declares

כִּי ׀ יִמְלְאוּ יָמֶיךָ וְשָׁכַבְתָּ אֶת־ אֲבֹתֶיךָ
fathers-of-you with and-you-rest days-of-you they-are-over when (12)

וַהֲקִימֹתִי אֶת־ זַרְעֲךָ אַחֲרֶיךָ אֲשֶׁר יֵצֵא
he-will-come who after-you offspring-of-you *** then-I-will-raise-up

מִמֵּעֶיךָ וַהֲכִינֹתִי אֶת־ מַמְלַכְתּוֹ׃ הוּא
he (13) kingdom-of-him *** and-I-will-establish from-bodies-of-you

יִבְנֶה־ בַּיִת לִשְׁמִי וְכֹנַנְתִּי אֶת־ כִּסֵּא
throne-of *** and-I-will-establish for-Name-of-me house he-will-build

מַמְלַכְתּוֹ עַד־ עוֹלָם׃ אֲנִי אֶהְיֶה־ לּוֹ לְאָב וְהוּא יִהְיֶה־
he-will-be and-he as-father to-him I-will-be I (14) forever to kingdom-of-him

לִּי לְבֵן אֲשֶׁר בְּהַעֲוֺתוֹ וְהֹכַחְתִּיו בְּשֵׁבֶט אֲנָשִׁים
men with-rod-of then-I-will-punish-him when-to-do-wrong-him when as-son to-me

וּבְנִגְעֵי בְּנֵי אָדָם׃ וְחַסְדִּי לֹא־ יָסוּר
he-will-be-taken not but-love-of-me (15) man sons-of and-with-floggings-of

my people Israel, "Why
have you not built me a
house of cedar?"'
8"Now then, tell my ser-
vant David, 'This is what
the LORD Almighty says: I
took you from the pasture
and from following the
flock to be ruler over my
people Israel. 9I have been
with you wherever you
have gone, and I have cut
off all your enemies from
before you. Now I will
make your name great, like
the names of the greatest
men of the earth. 10And I
will provide a place for my
people Israel and will plant
them so that they can have
a home of their own and no
longer be disturbed.
Wicked people will not oppress them anymore, as
they did at the beginning
11and have done ever since
the time I appointed leaders[q] over my people Israel. I
will also give you rest from
all your enemies.
"'The LORD declares to
you that the LORD himself
will establish a house for
you: 12When your days are
over and you rest with your
fathers, I will raise up your
offspring to succeed you,
who will come from your
own body, and I will establish his kingdom. 13He is
the one who will build a
house for my Name, and I
will establish the throne of
his kingdom forever. 14I
will be his father, and he
will be my son. When he
does wrong, I will punish
him with the rod of men,
with floggings inflicted by
men. 15But my love will

q11 Traditionally *judges*

מִמֶּנּוּ כַּאֲשֶׁר הֲסִרֹתִי מֵעִם שָׁאוּל אֲשֶׁר הֲסִרֹתִי מִלְּפָנֶיךָ׃
from-before-you I-removed whom Saul from-with I-took just-as from-him

וְנֶאְמַן בֵּיתְךָ[s] וּמַמְלַכְתְּךָ עַד־עוֹלָם לְפָנֶיךָ
before-you forever to and-kingdom-of-you house-of-you and-he-will-endure (16)

כִּסְאֲךָ יִהְיֶה נָכוֹן עַד־עוֹלָם׃ כְּכֹל
as-all-of (17) forever to being-established he-will-be throne-of-you

הַדְּבָרִים הָאֵלֶּה וּכְכֹל הַחִזָּיוֹן הַזֶּה כֵּן דִּבֶּר
he-reported so the-this the-revelation and-as-all-of the-these the-words

נָתָן אֶל־דָּוִד׃ וַיָּבֹא הַמֶּלֶךְ דָּוִד וַיֵּשֶׁב לִפְנֵי יְהוָה
Yahweh before and-he-sat David the-king then-he-went-in (18) David to Nathan

וַיֹּאמֶר מִי אָנֹכִי אֲדֹנָי יְהוִה וּמִי בֵיתִי כִּי הֲבִיאֹתַנִי
you-brought-me that family-of-me and-what? Yahweh Lord I who? and-he-said

עַד־הֲלֹם׃ וַתִּקְטַן עוֹד זֹאת בְּעֵינֶיךָ אֲדֹנָי יְהוִה
Yahweh Lord in-eyes-of-you this still if-she-was-small (19) this-far to

וַתְּדַבֵּר גַּם אֶל־בֵּית־עַבְדְּךָ לְמֵרָחוֹק וְזֹאת
now-this about-in-future servant-of-you house-of of also then-you-spoke

תּוֹרַת הָאָדָם אֲדֹנָי יְהוִה׃ וּמַה־יּוֹסִיף דָּוִד עוֹד
more David can-he-add now-what? (20) Yahweh Lord the-man usual-dealing-of

לְדַבֵּר אֵלֶיךָ וְאַתָּה יָדַעְתָּ אֶת־עַבְדְּךָ אֲדֹנָי יְהוִה׃ בַּעֲבוּר
for-sake-of (21) Yahweh Lord servant-of-you *** you-know for-you to-you to-say

דְּבָרְךָ וּכְלִבְּךָ עָשִׂיתָ אֵת כָּל־הַגְּדוּלָּה
the-great-thing all-of *** you-did and-according-to-will-of-you word-of-you

הַזֹּאת לְהוֹדִיעַ אֶת־עַבְדֶּךָ׃ עַל־כֵּן גָּדַלְתָּ אֲדֹנָי
Lord you-are-great this for (22) servant-of-you *** to-make-known the-this

יְהוָה כִּי־אֵין כָּמוֹךָ וְאֵין אֱלֹהִים זוּלָתֶךָ בְּכֹל אֲשֶׁר־שָׁמַעְנוּ
we-heard that as-all but-you God and-no like-you no-one for Yahweh

בְּאָזְנֵינוּ׃ וּמִי כְעַמְּךָ כְּיִשְׂרָאֵל גּוֹי אֶחָד
one nation like-Israel like-people-of-you and-who? (23) with-ears-of-us

בָּאָרֶץ אֲשֶׁר הָלְכוּ־אֱלֹהִים לִפְדּוֹת־לוֹ לְעָם[s] וְלָשׂוּם
and-to-make as-people for-him to-redeem God they-went-out that on-the-earth

לוֹ שֵׁם וְלַעֲשׂוֹת לָכֶם הַגְּדוּלָּה וְנֹרָאוֹת
and-things-being-wonders the-great-thing for-you and-to-perform name for-him

לְאַרְצֶךָ מִפְּנֵי עַמְּךָ אֲשֶׁר פָּדִיתָ לְּךָ
for-you you-redeemed whom people-of-you from-before for-land-of-you

מִמִּצְרַיִם גּוֹיִם וֵאלֹהָיו׃ וַתְּכוֹנֵן לְךָ אֶת־
*** for-you and-you-established (24) and-gods-of-him nations from-Egypt

עַמְּךָ יִשְׂרָאֵל ׀ לְךָ לְעָם עַד־עוֹלָם וְאַתָּה יְהוָה הָיִיתָ
you-became Yahweh and-you forever to as-people for-you Israel people-of-you

never be taken away from him, as I took it away from Saul, whom I removed from before you. [16]Your house and your kingdom will endure forever before me[r]; your throne will be established forever.' "

[17]Nathan reported to David all the words of this entire revelation.

*David's Prayer*

[18]Then King David went in and sat before the LORD, and he said:

"Who am I, O Sovereign LORD, and what is my family, that you have brought me this far? [19]And as if this were not enough in your sight, O Sovereign LORD, you have also spoken about the future of the house of your servant. Is this your usual way of dealing with man, O Sovereign LORD?

[20]"What more can David say to you? For you know your servant, O Sovereign LORD. [21]For the sake of your word and according to your will, you have done this great thing and made it known to your servant.

[22]"How great you are, O Sovereign LORD! There is no one like you, and there is no God but you, as we have heard with our own ears. [23]And who is like your people Israel—the one nation on earth that God went out to redeem as a people for himself, and to make a name for himself, and to perform great and awesome wonders by driving out nations and their gods from before your people, whom you redeemed from Egypt?[s] [24]You have established your people Israel as your very own forever, and you, O LORD, have become

[r]16 Some Hebrew manuscripts and Septuagint; most Hebrew manuscripts *you*
[s]23 See Septuagint and 1 Chronicles 17:21; Hebrew *wonders for your land and before your people, whom you redeemed from Egypt, from the nations and their gods*

לָהֶם לֵאלֹהִים׃ וְעַתָּה֙ יְהוָה אֱלֹהִים הַדָּבָר אֲשֶׁר דִּבַּרְתָּ עַל־
concerning you-made that the-promise God Yahweh and-now (25) as-God for-them

עַבְדְּךָ֙ וְעַל־ בֵּיתוֹ הָקֵם עַד־ עוֹלָם וַעֲשֵׂה כַּאֲשֶׁר
just-as and-do! forever to keep! house-of-him and-concerning servant-of-you

דִּבַּרְתָּ׃ וְיִגְדַּל שִׁמְךָ עַד־ עוֹלָם֙ לֵאמֹר יְהוָה
Yahweh-of to-say forever to name-of-you so-he-will-be-great (26) you-promised

צְבָאוֹת אֱלֹהִים עַל־ יִשְׂרָאֵל וּבֵית֙ עַבְדְּךָ דָוִד יִהְיֶה
he-will-be David servant-of-you and-house-of Israel over God Hosts

נָכוֹן לְפָנֶיךָ׃ כִּי־ אַתָּה֙ יְהוָה צְבָאוֹת אֱלֹהֵי יִשְׂרָאֵל
Israel God-of Hosts Yahweh-of you now (27) before-you being-established

גָּלִיתָה אֶת־ אֹזֶן עַבְדְּךָ֙ לֵאמֹר בַּיִת אֶבְנֶה־ לָּךְ
for-you I-will-build house to-say servant-of-you ear-of to you-revealed

עַל־ כֵּן מָצָא עַבְדְּךָ֙ אֶת־ לִבּוֹ לְהִתְפַּלֵּל אֵלֶיךָ אֶת־
*** to-you to-offer courage-of-him *** servant-of-you he-found this for

הַתְּפִלָּה הַזֹּאת׃ וְעַתָּה ׀ אֲדֹנָי יְהוִה אַתָּה־ הוּא הָאֱלֹהִים וּדְבָרֶיךָ
and-words-of-you the-God he you Yahweh Lord and-now (28) the-this the-prayer

יִהְיוּ אֱמֶת וַתְּדַבֵּר֙ אֶל־ עַבְדְּךָ אֶת־ הַטּוֹבָה הַזֹּאת׃
the-this the-good *** servant-of-you to and-you-promised trustworthy they-are

וְעַתָּה הוֹאֵל֙ וּבָרֵךְ֙ אֶת־ בֵּית עַבְדְּךָ לִהְיוֹת
to-continue servant-of-you house-of *** and-bless! be-pleased! and-now (29)

לְעוֹלָם לְפָנֶיךָ כִּי־ אַתָּה אֲדֹנָי יְהוִה֙ דִּבַּרְתָּ וּמִבִּרְכָתְךָ
and-with-blessing-of-you you-spoke Yahweh Lord you for before-you to-forever

יְבֹרַךְ בֵּית־ עַבְדְּךָ לְעוֹלָם׃ וַיְהִי֙ אַחֲרֵי־
after and-he-was (8:1) to-forever servant-of-you house-of he-will-be-blessed

כֵן וַיַּךְ דָּוִד אֶת־ פְּלִשְׁתִּים וַיַּכְנִיעֵם וַיִּקַּח
and-he-took and-he-subdued-them Philistines *** David then-he-defeated this

דָּוִד אֶת־ מֶתֶג הָאַמָּה מִיַּד פְּלִשְׁתִּים׃ וַיַּךְ אֶת־
*** and-he-defeated (2) Philistines from-hand-of the-Ammah Metheg-of *** David

מוֹאָב וַיְמַדְּדֵם בַּחֶבֶל֙ הַשְׁכֵּב אוֹתָם אַרְצָה
on-ground them to-make-lie-down with-the-cord and-he-measured-them Moab

וַיְמַדֵּד שְׁנֵי־ חֲבָלִים֙ לְהָמִית וּמְלֹא הַחֶבֶל לְהַחֲיוֹת
to-let-live the-length and-fullness-of to-kill lengths two-of and-he-measured

וַתְּהִי מוֹאָב֙ לְדָוִד לַעֲבָדִים נֹשְׂאֵי מִנְחָה׃
tribute ones-bringing-of as-subjects to-David Moab so-she-became

וַיַּךְ דָּוִד אֶת־ הֲדַדְעֶזֶר בֶּן־ רְחֹב מֶלֶךְ צוֹבָה בְּלֶכְתּוֹ
when-to-go-him Zobah king-of Rehob son-of Hadadezer *** David and-he-fought (3)

לְהָשִׁיב יָדוֹ בִּנְהַר־ ׃ וַיִּלְכֹּד דָּוִד
David and-he-captured (4) *Euphrates along-River-of control-of-him to-restore

their God.

[25]"And now, LORD God, keep forever the promise you have made concerning your servant and his house. Do as you promised, [26]so that your name will be great forever. Then men will say, 'The LORD Almighty is God over Israel!' And the house of your servant David will be established before you.

[27]"O LORD Almighty, God of Israel, you have revealed this to your servant, saying, 'I will build a house for you.' So your servant has found courage to offer you this prayer. [28]O Sovereign LORD, you are God! Your words are trustworthy, and you have given this good promise to your servant. [29]Now be pleased to bless the house of your servant, that it may continue forever in your sight; for you, O Sovereign LORD, have spoken, and with your blessing the house of your servant will be blessed forever."

*David's Victories*

**8** In the course of time, David defeated the Philistines and subdued them, and he took Metheg Ammah from the control of the Philistines.

[2]David also defeated the Moabites. He made them lie down on the ground and measured them off with a length of cord. Every two lengths of them were put to death, and the third length was allowed to live. So the Moabites became subject to David and brought tribute.

[3]Moreover, David fought Hadadezer son of Rehob, king of Zobah, when he went to restore his control along the Euphrates River. [4]David captured a thousand of his chariots, seven thousand

[a]4 Septuagint (see also 1 Chron. 18:4); Hebrew *captured seventeen hundred of his charioteers*

*3 Many mss include פרת, *Euphrates*, or include the reading as a marginal *Qere*.

מִמֶּנּוּ אֶלֶף וּשְׁבַע־ מֵאוֹת פָּרָשִׁים וְעֶשְׂרִים אֶלֶף אִישׁ
man thousand and-twenty charioteers hundreds and-seven-of thousand from-him

רַגְלִי וַיְעַקֵּר דָּוִד אֶת־ כָּל־ הָרֶכֶב וַיּוֹתֵר
but-he-left the-chariot-horse all-of *** David and-he-hamstrung foot-soldier

מִמֶּנּוּ מֵאָה רָכֶב׃ וַתָּבֹא אֲרַם דַּמֶּשֶׂק לַעְזֹר
to-help Damascus Aram-of when-she-came (5) chariot-horse hundred from-him

לַהֲדַדְעֶזֶר מֶלֶךְ צוֹבָה וַיַּךְ דָּוִד בַּאֲרָם עֶשְׂרִים־ וּשְׁנַיִם
and-two twenty of-Aram David then-he-struck-down Zobah king-of to-Hadadezer

אֶלֶף אִישׁ׃ וַיָּשֶׂם דָּוִד נְצִבִים בַּאֲרַם דַּמֶּשֶׂק וַתְּהִי
and-she-became Damascus in-Aram-of garrisons David and-he-put (6) man thousand

אֲרָם לְדָוִד לַעֲבָדִים נוֹשְׂאֵי מִנְחָה וַיֹּשַׁע יְהוָה
Yahweh and-he-gave-victory tribute ones-bringing-of as-subjects to-David Aram

אֶת־ דָּוִד בְּכֹל אֲשֶׁר הָלָךְ׃ וַיִּקַּח דָּוִד אֵת שִׁלְטֵי
shields-of *** David and-he-took (7) he-went that in-everywhere David to

הַזָּהָב אֲשֶׁר הָיוּ אֶל עַבְדֵי הֲדַדְעָזֶר וַיְבִיאֵם יְרוּשָׁלָםִ׃
Jerusalem and-he-brought-them Hadadezer officers-of to they-were that the-gold

וּמִבֶּטַח וּמִבֵּרֹתַי עָרֵי הֲדַדְעָזֶר לָקַח הַמֶּלֶךְ
the-king he-took Hadadezer towns-of and-from-Berothai and-from-Betah (8)

דָּוִד נְחֹשֶׁת הַרְבֵּה מְאֹד׃ וַיִּשְׁמַע תֹּעִי מֶלֶךְ חֲמָת כִּי
that Hamath king-of Toi when-he-heard (9) very to-be-great bronze David

הִכָּה דָוִד אֵת כָּל־ חֵיל הֲדַדְעָזֶר׃ וַיִּשְׁלַח תֹּעִי
Toi then-he-sent (10) Hadadezer army-of entire-of *** David he-defeated

אֶת־ יוֹרָם־ בְּנוֹ אֶל־ הַמֶּלֶךְ־ דָּוִד לִשְׁאָל־ לוֹ לְשָׁלוֹם
for-peace to-him to-greet David the-king to son-of-him Joram ***

וּלְבָרְכוֹ עַל אֲשֶׁר נִלְחַם בַּהֲדַדְעֶזֶר
against-Hadadezer he-fought that because and-to-congratulate-him

וַיַּכֵּהוּ כִּי־ אִישׁ מִלְחֲמוֹת תֹּעִי הָיָה הֲדַדְעָזֶר וּבְיָדוֹ
and-in-hand-of-him Hadadezer he-was Toi wars-of man-of for and-he-defeated-him

הָיוּ כְּלֵי־ כֶסֶף וּכְלֵי־ זָהָב וּכְלֵי נְחֹשֶׁת׃
bronze and-articles-of gold and-articles-of silver articles-of they-were

גַּם־ אֹתָם הִקְדִּישׁ הַמֶּלֶךְ דָּוִד לַיהוָה עִם־ הַכֶּסֶף
the-silver with to-Yahweh David the-king he-dedicated them also (11)

וְהַזָּהָב אֲשֶׁר הִקְדִּישׁ מִכָּל־ הַגּוֹיִם אֲשֶׁר כִּבֵּשׁ׃
he-subdued that the-nations from-all-of he-dedicated that and-the-gold

מֵאֲרָם וּמִמּוֹאָב וּמִבְּנֵי עַמּוֹן וּמִפְּלִשְׁתִּים
and-from-Philistines Ammon and-from-sons-of and-from-Moab from-Aram (12)

וּמֵעֲמָלֵק וּמִשְּׁלַל הֲדַדְעֶזֶר בֶּן־ רְחֹב מֶלֶךְ צוֹבָה׃
Zobah king-of Rehob son-of Hadadezer and-from-plunder-of and-from-Amalek

charioteers[t] and twenty thousand foot soldiers. He hamstrung all but a hundred of the chariot horses.

[5]When the Arameans of Damascus came to help Hadadezer king of Zobah, David struck down twenty-two thousand of them. [6]He put garrisons in the Aramean kingdom of Damascus, and the Arameans became subject to him and brought tribute. The LORD gave David victory everywhere he went.

[7]David took the gold shields that belonged to the officers of Hadadezer and brought them to Jerusalem. [8]From Tebah[u] and Berothai, towns that belonged to Hadadezer, King David took a great quantity of bronze.

[9]When Tou[v] king of Hamath heard that David had defeated the entire army of Hadadezer, [10]he sent his son Joram[w] to King David to greet him and congratulate him on his victory in battle over Hadadezer, who had been at war with Tou. Joram brought with him articles of silver and gold and bronze.

[11]King David dedicated these articles to the LORD, as he had done with the silver and gold from all the nations he had subdued: [12]Edom[x] and Moab, the Ammonites and the Philistines, and Amalek. He also dedicated the plunder taken from Hadadezer son of Rehob, king of Zobah.

[u]8 See some Septuagint manuscripts (see also 1 Chron. 18:8); Hebrew *Betah*
[v]9 Hebrew *Toi,* a variant of *Tou;* also in verse 10
[w]10 A variant of *Hadoram*
[x]12 Some Hebrew manuscripts, Septuagint and Syriac (see also 1 Chron. 18:11); most Hebrew manuscripts *Aram*

וַיַּעַשׂ דָּוִד֙ שֵׁם בְּשֻׁבוֹ מֵהַכּוֹתוֹ אֶת־

*** from-to-strike-down-him when-to-return-him name David and-he-made (13)

אֲרָם בְּגֵיא־ מֶלַח שְׁמוֹנָה עָשָׂר אָלֶף׃ וַיָּשֶׂם בֶּאֱדוֹם

throughout-Edom and-he-put (14) thousand ten eight Salt in-Valley-of Aram

נְצִבִים בְּכָל־ אֱדוֹם֙ שָׂם נְצִבִים וַיְהִי כָל־ אֱדוֹם עֲבָדִים

subjects Edom all-of and-he-became garrisons he-put Edom in-all-of garrisons

לְדָוִד וַיּוֹשַׁע יְהוָה֙ אֶת־ דָּוִד בְּכֹל אֲשֶׁר הָלָךְ׃

he-went that in-everywhere David to Yahweh and-he-gave-victory to-David

וַיִּמְלֹךְ דָּוִד עַל־ כָּל־ יִשְׂרָאֵל וַיְהִי דָוִד עֹשֶׂה מִשְׁפָּט

justice doing David and-he-was Israel all-of over David and-he-reigned (15)

וּצְדָקָה לְכָל־ עַמּוֹ׃ וְיוֹאָב בֶּן־ צְרוּיָה עַל־ הַצָּבָא

the-army over Zeruiah son-of and-Joab (16) people-of-him for-all-of and-right

וִיהוֹשָׁפָט בֶּן־ אֲחִילוּד מַזְכִּיר׃ וְצָדוֹק בֶּן־ אֲחִיטוּב

Ahitub son-of and-Zadok (17) one-recording Ahilud son-of and-Jehoshaphat

וַאֲחִימֶלֶךְ בֶּן־ אֶבְיָתָר כֹּהֲנִים וּשְׂרָיָה סוֹפֵר׃

one-being-secretary and-Seraiah priests Abiathar son-of and-Ahimelech

וּבְנָיָהוּ בֶּן־ יְהוֹיָדָע וְהַכְּרֵתִי וְהַפְּלֵתִי

and-the-Pelethites and-the-Kerethites Jehoiada son-of and-Benaiah (18)

וּבְנֵי דָוִד כֹּהֲנִים הָיוּ׃ וַיֹּאמֶר דָּוִד הֲכִי

indeed? David and-he-asked (9:1) they-were royal-advisers David and-sons-of

יֶשׁ־ עוֹד אֲשֶׁר נוֹתַר לְבֵית שָׁאוּל וְאֶעֱשֶׂה עִמּוֹ֙ חֶסֶד

kindness to-him that-I-can-show Saul of-house-of he-is-left who still is-he

בַּעֲבוּר יְהוֹנָתָן׃ וּלְבֵית שָׁאוּל עֶבֶד֙ וּשְׁמוֹ

and-name-of-him servant Saul now-of-household-of (2) Jonathan for-sake-of

צִיבָא וַיִּקְרְאוּ־ לוֹ אֶל־ דָּוִד וַיֹּאמֶר הַמֶּלֶךְ אֵלָיו הַאַתָּה צִיבָא

Ziba you? to-him the-king and-he-said David to to-him and-they-called Ziba

וַיֹּאמֶר עַבְדֶּךָ׃ וַיֹּאמֶר הַמֶּלֶךְ הַאֶפֶס עוֹד אִישׁ֙

one still not? the-king and-he-asked (3) servant-of-you and-he-replied

לְבֵית שָׁאוּל וְאֶעֱשֶׂה עִמּוֹ חֶסֶד אֱלֹהִים וַיֹּאמֶר צִיבָא֙

Ziba and-he-answered God kindness-of to-him that-I-can-show Saul of-house-of

אֶל־ הַמֶּלֶךְ עוֹד בֵּן לִיהוֹנָתָן נְכֵה רַגְלָיִם׃ וַיֹּאמֶר־

and-he-asked (4) both-feet crippled-of of-Jonathan son still the-king to

לוֹ הַמֶּלֶךְ אֵיפֹה הוּא וַיֹּאמֶר צִיבָא אֶל־הַמֶּלֶךְ הִנֵּה־הוּא בֵּית

house-of he see! the-king to Ziba and-he-answered he where? the-king to-him

מָכִיר בֶּן־ עַמִּיאֵל בְּלוֹ דְבָר׃ וַיִּשְׁלַח הַמֶּלֶךְ דָּוִד

David the-king so-he-sent (5) Debar in-Lo Ammiel son-of Makir

וַיִּקָּחֵהוּ מִבֵּית מָכִיר בֶּן־ עַמִּיאֵל מִלּוֹ דְבָר׃

Debar from-Lo Ammiel son-of Makir from-house-of and-he-had-brought-him

[13]And David became famous after he returned from striking down eighteen thousand Edomites[y] in the Valley of Salt.

[14]He put garrisons throughout Edom, and all the Edomites became subject to David. The LORD gave David victory everywhere he went.

*David's Officials*

[15]David reigned over all Israel, doing what was just and right for all his people. [16]Joab son of Zeruiah was over the army; Jehoshaphat son of Ahilud was recorder; [17]Zadok son of Ahitub and Ahimelech son of Abiathar were priests; Seraiah was secretary; [18]Benaiah son of Jehoiada was over the Kerethites and Pelethites; and David's sons were royal advisers.[z]

*David and Mephibosheth*

9 David asked, "Is there anyone still left of the house of Saul to whom I can show kindness for Jonathan's sake?"

[2]Now there was a servant of Saul's household named Ziba. They called him to appear before David, and the king said to him, "Are you Ziba?"

"Your servant," he replied.

[3]The king asked, "Is there no one still left of the house of Saul to whom I can show God's kindness?"

Ziba answered the king, "There is still a son of Jonathan; he is crippled in both feet."

[4]"Where is he?" the king asked.

Ziba answered, "He is at the house of Makir son of Ammiel in Lo Debar."

[5]So King David had him brought from Lo Debar, from the house of Makir son of Ammiel.

[y]13 A few Hebrew manuscripts, Septuagint and Syriac (see also 1 Chron. 18:12); most Hebrew manuscripts *Aram* (that is, Arameans)
[z]18 Or *were priests*

וַיָּבֹא מְפִיבֹשֶׁת בֶּן־ יְהוֹנָתָן בֶּן־ שָׁאוּל אֶל־ דָּוִד
David to Saul son-of Jonathan son-of Mephibosheth when-he-came (6)

וַיִּפֹּל עַל־ פָּנָיו וַיִּשְׁתָּחוּ וַיֹּאמֶר דָּוִד מְפִיבֹשֶׁת
Mephibosheth David and-he-said and-he-paid-honor faces-of-him on then-he-fell

וַיֹּאמֶר הִנֵּה עַבְדֶּךָ׃ וַיֹּאמֶר לוֹ דָוִד אַל־ תִּירָא
you-fear not David to-him and-he-said (7) servant-of-you see! and-he-replied

כִּי עָשֹׂה אֶעֱשֶׂה עִמְּךָ חֶסֶד בַּעֲבוּר יְהוֹנָתָן אָבִיךָ
father-of-you Jonathan for-sake-of kindness to-you I-will-show to-show for

וַהֲשִׁבֹתִי לְךָ אֶת־ כָּל־ שְׂדֵה שָׁאוּל אָבִיךָ וְאַתָּה
and-you father-of-you Saul land-of all-of *** to-you and-I-will-restore

תֹּאכַל לֶחֶם עַל־ שֻׁלְחָנִי תָּמִיד׃ וַיִּשְׁתַּחוּ וַיֹּאמֶר מֶה
what? and-he-said and-he-bowed (8) always table-of-me at food you-will-eat

עַבְדֶּךָ כִּי פָנִיתָ אֶל־ הַכֶּלֶב הַמֵּת אֲשֶׁר כָּמוֹנִי׃
like-me that the-dead the-dog to you-notice that servant-of-you

וַיִּקְרָא הַמֶּלֶךְ אֶל־ צִיבָא נַעַר שָׁאוּל וַיֹּאמֶר אֵלָיו
to-him and-he-said Saul servant-of Ziba to the-king then-he-summoned (9)

כֹּל אֲשֶׁר הָיָה לְשָׁאוּל וּלְכָל־ בֵּיתוֹ נָתַתִּי לְבֶן־
to-son-of I-gave family-of-him and-to-all-of to-Saul he-was that all

אֲדֹנֶיךָ׃ וְעָבַדְתָּ לּוֹ אֶת־הָאֲדָמָה אַתָּה וּבָנֶיךָ
and-sons-of-you you the-land *** for-him and-you-shall-farm (10) masters-of-you

וַעֲבָדֶיךָ וְהֵבֵאתָ וְהָיָה לְבֶן־ אֲדֹנֶיךָ
masters-of-you for-son-of so-he-may-be and-you-bring-in and-servants-of-you

לֶּחֶם וַאֲכָלוֹ וּמְפִיבֹשֶׁת בֶּן־ אֲדֹנֶיךָ
masters-of-you son-of and-Mephibosheth and-he-may-eat-him provision

יֹאכַל תָּמִיד לֶחֶם עַל־ שֻׁלְחָנִי וּלְצִיבָא חֲמִשָּׁה עָשָׂר בָּנִים וְעֶשְׂרִים
and-twenty sons ten five now-to-Ziba table-of-me at food always he-will-eat

עֲבָדִים׃ וַיֹּאמֶר צִיבָא אֶל־ הַמֶּלֶךְ כְּכֹל אֲשֶׁר יְצַוֶּה
he-commands that as-all the-king to Ziba then-he-said (11) servants

אֲדֹנִי הַמֶּלֶךְ אֶת־ עַבְדּוֹ כֵּן יַעֲשֶׂה עַבְדֶּךָ
servant-of-you he-will-do so servant-of-him *** the-king master-of-me

וּמְפִיבֹשֶׁת אֹכֵל עַל־ שֻׁלְחָנִי כְּאַחַד מִבְּנֵי הַמֶּלֶךְ׃
the-king of-sons-of like-one table-of-me at eating so-Mephibosheth

וְלִמְפִיבֹשֶׁת בֵּן־ קָטָן וּשְׁמוֹ מִיכָא וְכֹל
and-every-of Mica and-name-of-him young son now-to-Mephibosheth (12)

מוֹשַׁב בֵּית־ צִיבָא עֲבָדִים לִמְפִיבֹשֶׁת׃ וּמְפִיבֹשֶׁת
and-Mephibosheth (13) of-Mephibosheth servants Ziba household-of member-of

יֹשֵׁב בִּירוּשָׁלַםִ כִּי עַל־ שֻׁלְחַן הַמֶּלֶךְ תָּמִיד הוּא אֹכֵל וְהוּא
and-he eating he always the-king table-of at because in-Jerusalem living

6 When Mephibosheth son of
Jonathan, the son of Saul,
came to David, he bowed
down to pay him honor.
David said, "Me-
phibosheth!"
"Your servant," he replied.
7 "Don't be afraid," David
said to him, "for I will surely
show you kindness for the
sake of your father Jonathan. I
will restore to you all the land
that belonged to your grandfather Saul, and you will always eat at my table."
8 Mephibosheth bowed
down and said, "What is your
servant, that you should notice a dead dog like me?"
9 Then the king summoned
Ziba, Saul's servant, and said
to him, "I have given your
master's grandson everything
that belonged to Saul and his
family.
10 You and your sons
and your servants are to farm
the land for him and bring in
the crops, so that your master's grandson may be provided for. And Mephibosheth,
grandson of your master, will
always eat at my table." (Now
Ziba had fifteen sons and
twenty servants.)
11 Then Ziba said to the king,
"Your servant will do whatever my lord the king commands his servant to do." So
Mephibosheth ate at David's[a]
table like one of the king's
sons.
12 Mephibosheth had a
young son named Mica, and
all the members of Ziba's
household were servants of
Mephibosheth.
13 And Me-
phibosheth lived in Jerusalem,
because he always ate at the

[a] 11 Septuagint; Hebrew *my*

פִּסֵּחַ שְׁתֵּי רַגְלָיו׃ וַיְהִי אַחֲרֵי־ כֵן וַיָּמָת

then-he-died this after and-he-was (10:1) feet-of-him both-of crippled

מֶלֶךְ בְּנֵי עַמּוֹן וַיִּמְלֹךְ חָנוּן בְּנוֹ תַּחְתָּיו׃

in-place-of-him son-of-him Hanun and-he-became-king Ammon sons-of king-of

וַיֹּאמֶר דָּוִד אֶעֱשֶׂה־ חֶסֶד ׀ עִם־ חָנוּן בֶּן־ נָחָשׁ כַּאֲשֶׁר

just-as Nahash son-of Hanun to kindness I-will-show David and-he-thought (2)

עָשָׂה אָבִיו עִמָּדִי חֶסֶד וַיִּשְׁלַח דָּוִד לְנַחֲמוֹ

to-console-him David so-he-sent kindness to-me father-of-him he-showed

בְּיַד־ עֲבָדָיו אֶל־ אָבִיו וַיָּבֹאוּ עַבְדֵי

men-of when-they-came father-of-him concerning delegates-of-him by-hand-of

דָוִד אֶרֶץ בְּנֵי עַמּוֹן׃ וַיֹּאמְרוּ שָׂרֵי בְנֵי־ עַמּוֹן אֶל־

to Ammon sons-of nobles-of then-they-said (3) Ammon sons-of land-of David

חָנוּן אֲדֹנֵיהֶם הַמְכַבֵּד דָּוִד אֶת־ אָבִיךָ בְּעֵינֶיךָ כִּי־

because in-eyes-of-you father-of-you *** David honoring? lords-of-them Hanun

שָׁלַח לְךָ מְנַחֲמִים הֲלוֹא בַּעֲבוּר חֲקוֹר אֶת־ הָעִיר

the-city *** to-explore in-order not? ones-expressing-sympathy to-you he-sends

וּלְרַגְּלָהּ וּלְהָפְכָהּ שָׁלַח דָּוִד אֶת־ עֲבָדָיו אֵלֶיךָ׃

to-you men-of-him *** David he-sent and-to-overthrow-her and-to-spy-out-her

וַיִּקַּח חָנוּן אֶת־ עַבְדֵי דָוִד וַיְגַלַּח אֶת־ חֲצִי

half-of *** and-he-shaved-off David men-of *** Hanun so-he-seized (4)

זְקָנָם וַיִּכְרֹת אֶת־ מַדְוֵיהֶם בַּחֵצִי עַד שְׁתוֹתֵיהֶם

buttocks-of-them at in-middle garments-of-them *** and-he-cut-off beard-of-them

וַיְשַׁלְּחֵם׃ וַיַּגִּדוּ לְדָוִד וַיִּשְׁלַח לִקְרָאתָם

to-meet-them then-he-sent to-David when-they-told (5) and-he-sent-away-them

כִּי־ הָיוּ הָאֲנָשִׁים נִכְלָמִים מְאֹד וַיֹּאמֶר הַמֶּלֶךְ

the-king and-he-said greatly ones-being-humiliated the-men they-were for

שְׁבוּ בִירֵחוֹ עַד־ יְצַמַּח זְקַנְכֶם וְשַׁבְתֶּם׃

then-you-come-back beard-of-you he-grows till at-Jericho stay!

וַיִּרְאוּ בְּנֵי עַמּוֹן כִּי נִבְאֲשׁוּ בְּדָוִד

to-David they-became-stench that Ammon sons-of when-they-realized (6)

וַיִּשְׁלְחוּ בְנֵי־ עַמּוֹן וַיִּשְׂכְּרוּ אֶת־ אֲרַם בֵּית־ רְחוֹב וְאֶת־

and Rehob Beth Aram-of *** and-they-hired Ammon sons-of then-they-sent

אֲרַם צוֹבָא עֶשְׂרִים אֶלֶף רַגְלִי וְאֶת־ מֶלֶךְ מַעֲכָה אֶלֶף אִישׁ

man thousand Maacah king-of and foot-soldier thousand twenty Zobah Aram-of

וְאִישׁ טוֹב שְׁנֵים־עָשָׂר אֶלֶף אִישׁ׃ וַיִּשְׁמַע דָּוִד וַיִּשְׁלַח אֶת־

*** then-he-sent David when-he-heard (7) man thousand ten two Tob and-man-of

יוֹאָב וְאֵת כָּל־ הַצָּבָא הַגִּבֹּרִים׃ וַיֵּצְאוּ בְּנֵי

sons-of and-they-came-out (8) the-fighting-men the-army entire-of and Joab

king's table, and he was crippled in both feet.

*David Defeats the Ammonites*

10 In the course of time, the king of the Ammonites died, and his son Hanun succeeded him as king.
2 David thought, "I will show kindness to Hanun son of Nahash, just as his father showed kindness to me." So David sent a delegation to express his sympathy to Hanun concerning his father.

When David's men came to the land of the Ammonites,
3 the Ammonite nobles said to Hanun their lord, "Do you think David is honoring your father by sending men to you to express sympathy? Hasn't David sent them to you to explore the city and spy it out and overthrow it?"
4 So Hanun seized David's men, shaved off half of each man's beard, cut off their garments in the middle at the buttocks, and sent them away.
5 When David was told about this, he sent messengers to meet the men, for they were greatly humiliated. The king said, "Stay at Jericho till your beards have grown, and then come back."
6 When the Ammonites realized that they had become a stench in David's nostrils, they hired twenty thousand Aramean foot soldiers from Beth Rehob and Zobah, as well as the king of Maacah with a thousand men, and also twelve thousand men from Tob.
7 On hearing this, David sent Joab out with the entire army of fighting men.
8 The Ammonites came out and drew up

עַמּוֹן וַיַּעַרְכוּ מִלְחָמָה פֶּתַח הַשָּׁעַר וַאֲרַם
and-Aram-of the-gate entrance-of battle-formation and-they-drew-up Ammon

צוֹבָא וּרְחוֹב וְאִישׁ־ טוֹב וּמַעֲכָה לְבַדָּם בַּשָּׂדֶה׃
in-the-open-country by-themselves and-Maacah Tob and-man-of and-Rehob Zobah

(9) וַיַּרְא יוֹאָב כִּי־ הָיְתָה אֵלָיו פְּנֵי הַמִּלְחָמָה מִפָּנִים
in-front the-battle lines-of to-him she-was that Joab and-he-saw (9)

וּמֵאָחוֹר וַיִּבְחַר מִכֹּל בְּחוּרֵי בְיִשְׂרָאֵל
Israel ones-being-chosen-of from-all-of so-he-selected and-at-behind

וַיַּעֲרֹךְ לִקְרַאת אֲרָם׃ (10) וְאֵת יֶתֶר הָעָם נָתַן בְּיַד
under-hand-of he-put the-people rest-of and (10) Aram to-meet and-he-deployed

אַבְשַׁי אָחִיו וַיַּעֲרֹךְ לִקְרַאת בְּנֵי עַמּוֹן׃ (11) וַיֹּאמֶר
and-he-said (11) Ammon sons-of to-meet and-he-deployed brother-of-him Abishai

אִם־ תֶּחֱזַק אֲרָם מִמֶּנִּי וְהָיִתָה לִּי לִישׁוּעָה
for-rescue to-me then-you-must-come more-than-me Aram she-is-strong if

וְאִם־ בְּנֵי עַמּוֹן יֶחֶזְקוּ מִמְּךָ וְהָלַכְתִּי לְהוֹשִׁיעַ
to-rescue then-I-will-come more-than-you they-are-strong Ammon sons-of but-if

לָךְ׃ (12) חֲזַק וְנִתְחַזַּק בְּעַד־ עַמֵּנוּ וּבְעַד
and-for people-of-us for and-let-us-fight-bravely be-strong! (12) to-you

עָרֵי אֱלֹהֵינוּ וַיהוָה יַעֲשֶׂה הַטּוֹב בְּעֵינָיו׃
in-eyes-of-him the-good he-will-do and-Yahweh God-of-us cities-of

(13) וַיִּגַּשׁ יוֹאָב וְהָעָם אֲשֶׁר עִמּוֹ לַמִּלְחָמָה בַּאֲרָם
with-Aram to-the-fight with-him who and-the-troop Joab then-he-advanced (13)

וַיָּנֻסוּ מִפָּנָיו׃ (14) וּבְנֵי עַמּוֹן רָאוּ כִּי־ נָס
he-fled that they-saw Ammon when-sons-of (14) from-before-him and-they-fled

אֲרָם וַיָּנֻסוּ מִפְּנֵי אֲבִישַׁי וַיָּבֹאוּ הָעִיר
the-city and-they-went-inside Abishai from-before then-they-fled Aram

וַיָּשָׁב יוֹאָב מֵעַל בְּנֵי עַמּוֹן וַיָּבֹא יְרוּשָׁלִָם׃
Jerusalem and-he-came Ammon sons-of from-against Joab so-he-returned

(15) וַיַּרְא אֲרָם כִּי נִגַּף לִפְנֵי יִשְׂרָאֵל וַיֵּאָסְפוּ
then-they-regrouped Israel before he-was-routed that Aram after-he-saw (15)

יָחַד׃ (16) וַיִּשְׁלַח הֲדַדְעֶזֶר וַיֹּצֵא אֶת־ אֲרָם אֲשֶׁר מֵעֵבֶר
at-beyond who Aram *** and-he-had-brought Hadadezer and-he-sent (16) together

הַנָּהָר וַיָּבֹאוּ חֵילָם וְשׁוֹבַךְ שַׂר־ צְבָא הֲדַדְעֶזֶר
Hadadezer army-of commander-of and-Shobach Helam and-they-went the-River

לִפְנֵיהֶם׃ (17) וַיֻּגַּד לְדָוִד וַיֶּאֱסֹף אֶת־ כָּל־יִשְׂרָאֵל
Israel all-of *** then-he-gathered to-David when-he-was-told (17) before-them

וַיַּעֲבֹר אֶת־ הַיַּרְדֵּן וַיָּבֹא חֵלָאמָה וַיַּעַרְכוּ אֲרָם
Aram and-they-formed-line to-Helam and-he-went the-Jordan *** and-he-crossed

in battle formation at the entrance to their city gate, while
the Arameans of Zobah and
Rehob and the men of Tob
and Maacah were by them-
selves in the open country.
[9]Joab saw that there were
battle lines in front of him and
behind him; so he selected
some of the best troops in Israel and deployed them against
the Arameans. [10]He put the
rest of the men under the command of Abishai his brother
and deployed them against
the Ammonites. [11]Joab said,
"If the Arameans are too
strong for me, then you are to
come to my rescue; but if the
Ammonites are too strong for
you, then I will come to rescue
you. [12]Be strong and let us fight
bravely for our people and the
cities of our God. The LORD
will do what is good in his
sight."
[13]Then Joab and the troops
with him advanced to fight
the Arameans, and they fled
before him. [14]When the Ammonites saw that the Ara-
means were fleeing, they fled
before Abishai and went inside the city. So Joab returned
from fighting the Ammonites
and came to Jerusalem.
[15]After the Arameans saw
that they had been routed by
Israel, they regrouped. [16]Hada-
dezer had Arameans brought
from beyond the River[b]; they
went to Helam, with Shobach
the commander of Hadade-
zer's army leading them.
[17]When David was told of
this, he gathered all Israel,
crossed the Jordan and went to
Helam. The Arameans formed

[b]16 That is, the Euphrates

*11 Most mss have *segol* under the *beth* (יֶחֶ).

°9 ק ישראל

לִקְרַאת דָּוִד וַיִּלָּחֲמוּ עִמּוֹ׃ וַיָּנָס אֲרָם מִפְּנֵי
from-before Aram but-he-fled (18) against-him and-they-fought David to-meet

יִשְׂרָאֵל וַיַּהֲרֹג דָּוִד מֵאֲרָם שְׁבַע מֵאוֹת רֶכֶב וְאַרְבָּעִים
and-forty charioteer hundreds seven-of from-Aram David and-he-killed Israel

אֶלֶף פָּרָשִׁים וְאֵת שׁוֹבַךְ שַׂר־ צְבָאוֹ הִכָּה
he-struck-down army-of-him commander-of Shobach and horsemen thousand

וַיָּמָת שָׁם׃ וַיִּרְאוּ כָל־ הַמְּלָכִים עַבְדֵי הֲדַדְעֶזֶר
Hadadezer vassals-of the-kings all-of when-they-saw (19) there and-he-died

כִּי נִגְּפוּ לִפְנֵי יִשְׂרָאֵל וַיַּשְׁלִמוּ אֶת־ יִשְׂרָאֵל
Israel with then-they-made-peace Israel before they-were-defeated that

וַיַּעַבְדוּם וַיִּרְאוּ אֲרָם לְהוֹשִׁיעַ עוֹד אֶת־
*** anymore to-help Aram so-they-were-afraid and-they-became-subject-to-them

בְּנֵי עַמּוֹן׃ וַיְהִי לִתְשׁוּבַת הַשָּׁנָה לְעֵת ׀ צֵאת
to-go-off at-time-of the-year in-spring-of and-he-was (11:1) Ammon sons-of

הַמַּלְאכִים וַיִּשְׁלַח דָּוִד אֶת־ יוֹאָב וְאֶת־ עֲבָדָיו עִמּוֹ וְאֶת־ כָּל־
whole-of and with-him men-of-him and Joab *** David then-he-sent the-kings

יִשְׂרָאֵל וַיַּשְׁחִתוּ אֶת־ בְּנֵי עַמּוֹן וַיָּצֻרוּ עַל־ רַבָּה
Rabbah against and-they-besieged Ammon sons-of *** and-they-destroyed Israel

וְדָוִד יוֹשֵׁב בִּירוּשָׁלִָם׃ וַיְהִי ׀ לְעֵת הָעֶרֶב
the-evening at-time-of and-he-was (2) in-Jerusalem remaining but-David

וַיָּקָם דָּוִד מֵעַל מִשְׁכָּבוֹ וַיִּתְהַלֵּךְ עַל־ גַּג בֵּית־
palace-of roof-of on and-he-walked bed-of-him from-on David then-he-got-up

הַמֶּלֶךְ וַיַּרְא אִשָּׁה רֹחֶצֶת מֵעַל הַגָּג וְהָאִשָּׁה טוֹבַת
beautiful-of now-the-woman the-roof from-on bathing woman and-he-saw the-king

מַרְאֶה מְאֹד׃ וַיִּשְׁלַח דָּוִד וַיִּדְרֹשׁ לָאִשָּׁה
about-the-woman and-he-found-out David and-he-sent (3) very appearance

וַיֹּאמֶר הֲלוֹא־ זֹאת בַּת־ שֶׁבַע בַּת־ אֱלִיעָם אֵשֶׁת אוּרִיָּה הַחִתִּי׃
the-Hittite Uriah wife-of Eliam daughter-of Sheba Bath this not? and-he-said

וַיִּשְׁלַח דָּוִד מַלְאָכִים וַיִּקָּחֶהָ וַתָּבוֹא אֵלָיו
to-him and-she-came and-he-got-her messengers David then-he-sent (4)

וַיִּשְׁכַּב עִמָּהּ וְהִיא מִתְקַדֶּשֶׁת מִטֻּמְאָתָהּ
from-uncleanness-of-her purifying-herself now-she with-her and-he-slept

וַתָּשָׁב אֶל־ בֵּיתָהּ׃ וַתַּהַר הָאִשָּׁה וַתִּשְׁלַח
and-she-sent the-woman and-she-conceived (5) home-of-her to then-she-went-back

וַתַּגֵּד לְדָוִד וַתֹּאמֶר הָרָה אָנֹכִי׃ וַיִּשְׁלַח דָּוִד אֶל־יוֹאָב
Joab to David so-he-sent (6) I pregnant and-she-said to-David and-she-told

שְׁלַח אֵלַי אֶת־ אוּרִיָּה הַחִתִּי וַיִּשְׁלַח יוֹאָב אֶת־ אוּרִיָּה אֶל־ דָּוִד׃
David to Uriah *** Joab and-he-sent the-Hittite Uriah *** to-me send!

their battle lines to meet David and fought against him. [18]But they fled before Israel, and David killed seven hundred of their charioteers and forty thousand of their foot soldiers.[c] He also struck down Shobach the commander of their army, and he died there. [19]When all the kings who were vassals of Hadadezer saw that they had been defeated by Israel, they made peace with the Israelites and became subject to them.

So the Arameans were afraid to help the Ammonites anymore.

*David and Bathsheba*

11 In the spring, at the time when kings go off to war, David sent Joab out with the king's men and the whole Israelite army. They destroyed the Ammonites and besieged Rabbah. But David remained in Jerusalem.

[2]One evening David got up from his bed and walked around on the roof of the palace. From the roof he saw a woman bathing. The woman was very beautiful, [3]and David sent someone to find out about her. The man said, "Isn't this Bathsheba, the daughter of Eliam and the wife of Uriah the Hittite?" [4]Then David sent messengers to get her. She came to him, and he slept with her. (She had purified herself from her uncleanness.) Then[d] she went back home. [5]The woman conceived and sent word to David, saying, "I am pregnant."

[6]So David sent this word to Joab: "Send me Uriah the Hittite." And Joab sent him to

[c]18 Some Septuagint manuscripts (see also 1 Chron. 19:18); Hebrew *horsemen*
[d]4 Or *with her. When she purified herself from her uncleanness,*

*1 Some mss have *sheva* under the *mem* and *qamets* under the *lamed* (הַמְּלָא׳); some mss spell the form without *aleph* (לכים–); others have a note about the unnecessary *aleph*.

וַיָּבֹא אוּרִיָּה אֵלָיו וַיִּשְׁאַל דָּוִד לִשְׁלוֹם יוֹאָב
Joab about-welfare-of David then-he-asked to-him Uriah when-he-came (7)

וְלִשְׁלוֹם הָעָם וְלִשְׁלוֹם הַמִּלְחָמָה׃ וַיֹּאמֶר
then-he-said (8) the-war and-about-welfare-of the-people and-about-welfare-of

דָּוִד לְאוּרִיָּה רֵד לְבֵיתְךָ וּרְחַץ רַגְלֶיךָ וַיֵּצֵא
so-he-left feet-of-you and-wash! to-house-of-you go-down! to-Uriah David

אוּרִיָּה מִבֵּית הַמֶּלֶךְ וַתֵּצֵא אַחֲרָיו מַשְׂאַת הַמֶּלֶךְ׃
the-king gift-of after-him and-she-went the-king from-palace-of Uriah

וַיִּשְׁכַּב אוּרִיָּה פֶּתַח בֵּית הַמֶּלֶךְ אֵת כָּל־ עַבְדֵי
servants-of all-of with the-king palace-of entrance-of Uriah but-he-slept (9)

אֲדֹנָיו וְלֹא יָרַד אֶל־ בֵּיתוֹ׃ וַיַּגִּדוּ
when-they-told (10) house-of-him to he-went-down and-not masters-of-him

לְדָוִד לֵאמֹר לֹא־ יָרַד אוּרִיָּה אֶל־ בֵּיתוֹ וַיֹּאמֶר דָּוִד
David then-he-asked home-of-him to Uriah he-went-down not to-say to-David

אֶל־אוּרִיָּה הֲלוֹא מִדֶּרֶךְ אַתָּה בָא מַדּוּעַ לֹא־ יָרַדְתָּ אֶל־ בֵּיתֶךָ׃
home-of-you to you-went-down not why? coming you from-distance not? Uriah to

וַיֹּאמֶר אוּרִיָּה אֶל־ דָּוִד הָאָרוֹן וְיִשְׂרָאֵל וִיהוּדָה יֹשְׁבִים
ones-staying and-Judah and-Israel the-ark David to Uriah and-he-said (11)

בַּסֻּכּוֹת וַאדֹנִי יוֹאָב וְעַבְדֵי אֲדֹנִי עַל־ פְּנֵי
surfaces-of on lord-of-me and-men-of Joab and-master-of-me in-the-tents

הַשָּׂדֶה חֹנִים וַאֲנִי אָבוֹא אֶל־ בֵּיתִי לֶאֱכֹל וְלִשְׁתּוֹת
and-to-drink to-eat house-of-me to could-I-go now-I ones-camping the-field

וְלִשְׁכַּב עִם־ אִשְׁתִּי חַיֶּךָ וְחֵי נַפְשֶׁךָ אִם־ אֶעֱשֶׂה
I-will-do not self-of-you and-life-of life-of-you wife-of-me with and-to-lie

אֶת־ הַדָּבָר הַזֶּה׃ וַיֹּאמֶר דָּוִד אֶל־אוּרִיָּה שֵׁב בָּזֶה גַּם־
also at-here stay! Uriah to David then-he-said (12) the-this the-thing ***

הַיּוֹם וּמָחָר אֲשַׁלְּחֶךָּ וַיֵּשֶׁב אוּרִיָּה בִירוּשָׁלִַם
in-Jerusalem Uriah so-he-remained I-will-send-back-you and-tomorrow the-day

בַּיּוֹם הַהוּא וּמִמָּחֳרָת׃ וַיִּקְרָא־ לוֹ דָוִד
David to-him and-he-invited (13) and-on-next-day the-that on-the-day

וַיֹּאכַל לְפָנָיו וַיֵּשְׁתְּ וַיְשַׁכְּרֵהוּ וַיֵּצֵא
but-he-went-out and-he-made-drunk-him and-he-drank before-him and-he-ate

בָעֶרֶב לִשְׁכַּב בְּמִשְׁכָּבוֹ עִם־ עַבְדֵי אֲדֹנָיו וְאֶל־
and-to masters-of-him servants-of among on-mat-of-him to-sleep in-the-evening

בֵּיתוֹ לֹא יָרָד׃ וַיְהִי בַבֹּקֶר וַיִּכְתֹּב דָּוִד
David then-he-wrote in-the-morning and-he-was (14) he-went not home-of-him

סֵפֶר אֶל־יוֹאָב וַיִּשְׁלַח בְּיַד אוּרִיָּה׃ וַיִּכְתֹּב בַּסֵּפֶר
in-the-letter and-he-wrote (15) Uriah by-hand-of and-he-sent Joab to letter

David. 7When Uriah came to him, David asked him how Joab was, how the soldiers were and how the war was going. 8Then David said to Uriah, "Go down to your house and wash your feet." So Uriah left the palace, and a gift from the king was sent after him. 9But Uriah slept at the entrance to the palace with all his master's servants and did not go down to his house.

10When David was told, "Uriah did not go home," he asked him, "Haven't you just come from a distance? Why didn't you go home?"

11Uriah said to David, "The ark and Israel and Judah are staying in tents, and my master Joab and my lord's men are camped in the open fields. How could I go to my house to eat and drink and lie with my wife? As surely as you live, I will not do such a thing!"

12Then David said to him, "Stay here one more day, and tomorrow I will send you back." So Uriah remained in Jerusalem that day and the next. 13At David's invitation, he ate and drank with him, and David made him drunk. But in the evening Uriah went out to sleep on his mat among his master's servants; he did not go home.

14In the morning David wrote a letter to Joab and sent it with Uriah. 15In it he wrote,

e21 Also known as *Jerub-Baal* (that is, Gideon)

לֵאמֹר הָבוּ אֶת־אוּרִיָּה אֶל־מוּל פְּנֵי הַמִּלְחָמָה הַחֲזָקָה וְשַׁבְתֶּם
then-you-withdraw the-fierce the-battle faces-of front in Uriah *** put! to-say

מֵאַחֲרָיו וְנִכָּה וָמֵת׃ וַיְהִי
and-he-was (16) and-he-will-die so-he-will-be-struck-down from-behind-him

בִּשְׁמוֹר יוֹאָב אֶל־הָעִיר וַיִּתֵּן אֶת־אוּרִיָּה אֶל־הַמָּקוֹם
the-place at Uriah *** then-he-put the-city against Joab while-to-besiege

אֲשֶׁר יָדַע כִּי אַנְשֵׁי־חַיִל שָׁם׃ וַיֵּצְאוּ אַנְשֵׁי
men-of when-they-came-out (17) there strength defenders-of that he-knew where

הָעִיר וַיִּלָּחֲמוּ אֶת־יוֹאָב וַיִּפֹּל מִן־הָעָם מֵעַבְדֵי דָוִד
David from-men-of the-army from then-he-fell Joab *** and-they-fought the-city

וַיָּמָת גַּם אוּרִיָּה הַחִתִּי׃ וַיִּשְׁלַח יוֹאָב וַיַּגֵּד לְדָוִד
to-David and-he-told Joab and-he-sent (18) the-Hittite Uriah also and-he-died

אֶת־כָּל־דִּבְרֵי הַמִּלְחָמָה׃ וַיְצַו אֶת־הַמַּלְאָךְ
the-messenger *** and-he-instructed (19) the-battle accounts-of all-of ***

לֵאמֹר כְּכַלּוֹתְךָ אֵת כָּל־דִּבְרֵי הַמִּלְחָמָה לְדַבֵּר אֶל־
to to-tell the-battle accounts-of all-of *** when-to-finish-you to-say

הַמֶּלֶךְ׃ וְהָיָה אִם־תַּעֲלֶה חֲמַת הַמֶּלֶךְ וְאָמַר
and-he-says the-king anger-of she-flares-up if and-he-will-be (20) the-king

לְךָ מַדּוּעַ נִגַּשְׁתֶּם אֶל־הָעִיר לְהִלָּחֵם הֲלוֹא יְדַעְתֶּם אֵת אֲשֶׁר־
that *** you-know not? to-fight the-city to you-got-close why? to-you

יֹרוּ מֵעַל הַחוֹמָה׃ מִי־הִכָּה אֶת־אֲבִימֶלֶךְ בֶּן־
son-of Abimelech *** he-killed who? (21) the-wall from-on they-shoot

יְרֻבֶּשֶׁת הֲלוֹא־אִשָּׁה הִשְׁלִיכָה עָלָיו פֶּלַח רֶכֶב מֵעַל הַחוֹמָה
the-wall from-on millstone half-of on-him she-threw woman not? Jerub-Besheth

וַיָּמָת בְּתֵבֵץ לָמָּה נִגַּשְׁתֶּם אֶל־הַחוֹמָה וְאָמַרְתָּ גַּם
also then-you-say the-wall to you-got-close why? in-Thebez so-he-died

עַבְדְּךָ אוּרִיָּה הַחִתִּי מֵת׃ וַיֵּלֶךְ הַמַּלְאָךְ
the-messenger so-he-set-out (22) he-is-dead the-Hittite Uriah servant-of-you

וַיָּבֹא וַיַּגֵּד לְדָוִד אֵת כָּל־אֲשֶׁר שְׁלָחוֹ יוֹאָב׃
Joab he-sent-him that all *** to-David then-he-told when-he-arrived

וַיֹּאמֶר הַמַּלְאָךְ אֶל־דָּוִד כִּי־גָבְרוּ עָלֵינוּ
over-us they-overpowered indeed David to the-messenger and-he-said (23)

הָאֲנָשִׁים וַיֵּצְאוּ אֵלֵינוּ הַשָּׂדֶה וַנִּהְיֶה עֲלֵיהֶם עַד־
to upon-them but-we-were the-open against-us and-they-came-out the-men

פֶּתַח הַשָּׁעַר׃ וַיֹּרְאוּ° הַמּוֹרְאִים° אֶל־
at the-ones-being-archers then-they-shot (24) the-gate entrance-of

עֲבָדֶיךָ מֵעַל הַחוֹמָה וַיָּמוּתוּ מֵעַבְדֵי הַמֶּלֶךְ וְגַם
and-also the-king from-men-of and-they-died the-wall from-on servant-of-you

"Put Uriah in the front line where the fighting is fiercest. Then withdraw from him so he will be struck down and die."

16 So while Joab had the city under siege, he put Uriah at a place where he knew the strongest defenders were. 17 When the men of the city came out and fought against Joab, some of the men in David's army fell; moreover, Uriah the Hittite was dead.

18 Joab sent David a full account of the battle. 19 He instructed the messenger: "When you have finished giving the king this account of the battle, 20 the king's anger may flare up, and he may ask you, 'Why did you get so close to the city to fight? Didn't you know they would shoot arrows from the wall? 21 Who killed Abimelech son of Jerub-Besheth[c]? Didn't a woman throw an upper millstone on him from the wall, so that he died in Thebez? Why did you get so close to the wall?' If he asks you this, then say to him, 'Also, your servant Uriah the Hittite is dead.'"

22 The messenger set out, and when he arrived he told David everything Joab had sent him to say. 23 The messenger said to David, "The men overpowered us and came out against us in the open, but we drove them back to the entrance to the city gate. 24 Then the archers shot arrows at your servants from the wall, and some

°24a ק וירו
°24b ק המורים

עַבְדְּךָ אוּרִיָּה הַחִתִּי מֵת׃ וַיֹּאמֶר דָּוִד אֶל־
to David and-he-told (25) he-is-dead the-Hittite Uriah servant-of-you

הַמַּלְאָךְ כֹּה־ תֹאמַר אֶל־ יוֹאָב אַל־ יֵרַע בְּעֵינֶיךָ אֶת־
*** in-eyes-of-you let-him-be-evil not Joab to you-say this the-messenger

הַדָּבָר הַזֶּה כִּי־ כָזֹה וְכָזֶה תֹּאכַל הֶחָרֶב
the-sword she-devours so-as-that-one as-this-one for the-this the-thing

הַחֲזֵק מִלְחַמְתְּךָ אֶל־ הָעִיר וְהָרְסָהּ וְחַזְּקֵהוּ׃
so-encourage-him! and-destroy-her! the-city against attack-of-you press!

וַתִּשְׁמַע אֵשֶׁת אוּרִיָּה כִּי־ מֵת אוּרִיָּה אִישָׁהּ
husband-of-her Uriah he-was-dead that Uriah wife-of when-she-heard (26)

וַתִּסְפֹּד עַל־ בַּעְלָהּ׃ וַיַּעֲבֹר הָאֵבֶל
the-mourning-time when-he-was-over (27) husband-of-her for then-she-mourned

וַיִּשְׁלַח דָּוִד וַיַּאַסְפָהּ אֶל־ בֵּיתוֹ וַתְּהִי־
and-she-became house-of-him to and-he-had-brought-her David then-he-sent

לוֹ לְאִשָּׁה וַתֵּלֶד לוֹ בֵּן וַיֵּרַע הַדָּבָר אֲשֶׁר־
that the-thing but-he-was-displeasing son to-him and-she-bore as-wife to-him

עָשָׂה דָוִד בְּעֵינֵי יְהוָה׃ וַיִּשְׁלַח יְהוָה אֶת־ נָתָן אֶל־ דָּוִד
David to Nathan *** Yahweh and-he-sent (12:1) Yahweh in-eyes-of David he-did

וַיָּבֹא אֵלָיו וַיֹּאמֶר לוֹ שְׁנֵי אֲנָשִׁים הָיוּ בְּעִיר אֶחָת
certain in-town they-were men two-of to-him then-he-said to-him when-he-came

אֶחָד עָשִׁיר וְאֶחָד רָאשׁ׃ לְעָשִׁיר הָיָה צֹאן וּבָקָר הַרְבֵּה
to-be-many and-cattle sheep he-was to-rich (2) being-poor and-other rich one

מְאֹד׃ וְלָרָשׁ אֵין־ כֹּל כִּי אִם־ כִּבְשָׂה אַחַת קְטַנָּה
little one ewe-lamb except only anything not but-to-the-being-poor (3) very

אֲשֶׁר קָנָה וַיְחַיֶּהָ וַתִּגְדַּל עִמּוֹ וְעִם־
and-with with-him and-she-grew-up and-he-raised-her he-bought that

בָּנָיו יַחְדָּו מִפִּתּוֹ תֹאכַל וּמִכֹּסוֹ
and-from-cup-of-him she-ate from-food-of-him together children-of-him

תִשְׁתֶּה וּבְחֵיקוֹ תִשְׁכָּב וַתְּהִי־ לוֹ כְּבַת׃
like-daughter to-him and-she-was she-slept and-on-chest-of-him she-drank

וַיָּבֹא הֵלֶךְ לְאִישׁ הֶעָשִׁיר וַיַּחְמֹל לָקַחַת
to-take but-he-refrained the-rich to-man traveller now-he-came (4)

מִצֹּאנוֹ וּמִבְּקָרוֹ לַעֲשׂוֹת לָאֹרֵחַ
for-the-one-travelling to-prepare or-from-cattle-of-him from-sheep-of-him

הַבָּא־ לוֹ וַיִּקַּח אֶת־ כִּבְשַׂת הָאִישׁ הָרָאשׁ
the-one-being-poor the-man ewe-lamb-of *** so-he-took to-him the-one-coming

וַיַּעֲשֶׂהָ לָאִישׁ הַבָּא אֵלָיו׃ וַיִּחַר־
and-he-burned (5) to-him the-one-coming for-the-man and-he-prepared-her

of the king's men died. Moreover, your servant Uriah the Hittite is dead."

25David told the messenger, "Say this to Joab: 'Don't let this upset you; the sword devours one as well as another. Press the attack against the city and destroy it.' Say this to encourage Joab."

26When Uriah's wife heard that her husband was dead, she mourned for him. 27After the time of mourning was over, David had her brought to his house, and she became his wife and bore him a son. But the thing David had done displeased the LORD.

*Nathan Rebukes David*

12 The LORD sent Nathan to David. When he came to him, he said, "There were two men in a certain town, one rich and the other poor. 2The rich man had a very large number of sheep and cattle, 3but the poor man had nothing except one little ewe lamb he had bought. He raised it, and it grew up with him and his children. It shared his food, drank from his cup and even slept in his arms. It was like a daughter to him.

4"Now a traveler came to the rich man, but the rich man refrained from taking one of his own sheep or cattle to prepare a meal for the traveler who had come to him. Instead, he took the ewe lamb that belonged to the poor man and prepared it for the one who had come to him."

אַף דָּוִד בָּאִישׁ מְאֹד וַיֹּאמֶר אֶל־נָתָן חַי־יְהוָה

**Yahweh life-of Nathan to and-he-said very against-the-man David anger-of**

כִּי בֶן־מָוֶת הָאִישׁ הָעֹשֶׂה זֹאת׃ וְאֶת־הַכִּבְשָׂה יְשַׁלֵּם

**he-must-pay-for the-lamb and (6) this the-one-doing the-man death son-of indeed**

אַרְבַּעְתָּיִם עֵקֶב אֲשֶׁר עָשָׂה אֶת־הַדָּבָר הַזֶּה וְעַל אֲשֶׁר לֹא־

**not that and-because the-this the-thing *** he-did that because four-times**

חָמָל׃ וַיֹּאמֶר נָתָן אֶל־דָּוִד אַתָּה הָאִישׁ כֹּה־אָמַר יְהוָה

**Yahweh he-says this the-man you David to Nathan then-he-said (7) he-had-pity**

אֱלֹהֵי יִשְׂרָאֵל אָנֹכִי מְשַׁחְתִּיךָ לְמֶלֶךְ עַל־יִשְׂרָאֵל וְאָנֹכִי הִצַּלְתִּיךָ

**I-delivered-you and-I Israel over as-king I-anointed-you I Israel God-of**

מִיַּד שָׁאוּל׃ וָאֶתְּנָה לְךָ אֶת־בֵּית אֲדֹנֶיךָ וְאֶת־

**and masters-of-you house-of *** to-you and-I-gave (8) Saul from-hand-of**

נְשֵׁי אֲדֹנֶיךָ בְּחֵיקֶךָ וָאֶתְּנָה לְךָ אֶת־בֵּית יִשְׂרָאֵל

**Israel house-of *** to-you and-I-gave into-arm-of-you masters-of-you wives-of**

וִיהוּדָה וְאִם־מְעָט וְאֹסִפָה לְּךָ כָּהֵנָּה וְכָהֵנָּה׃

**and-as-those as-these to-you then-I-would-give too-little and-if and-Judah**

מַדּוּעַ בָּזִיתָ ׀ אֶת־דְּבַר יְהוָה לַעֲשׂוֹת הָרַע בְּעֵינָו אֵת

***** in-eyes-of-me the-evil to-do Yahweh word-of *** you-despised why? (9)**

אוּרִיָּה הַחִתִּי הִכִּיתָ בַחֶרֶב וְאֶת־אִשְׁתּוֹ לָקַחְתָּ

**you-took wife-of-him and with-the-sword you-struck-down the-Hittite Uriah**

לְּךָ לְאִשָּׁה וְאֹתוֹ הָרַגְתָּ בְּחֶרֶב בְּנֵי עַמּוֹן׃ וְעַתָּה

**so-now (10) Ammon sons-of with-sword-of you-killed and-him as-wife for-you**

לֹא־תָסוּר חֶרֶב מִבֵּיתְךָ עַד־עוֹלָם עֵקֶב כִּי

**that because forever to from-house-of-you sword she-will-depart not**

בְזִתָנִי וַתִּקַּח אֶת־אֵשֶׁת אוּרִיָּה הַחִתִּי לִהְיוֹת לְךָ

**for-you to-be the-Hittite Uriah wife-of *** and-you-took you-despised-me**

לְאִשָּׁה׃ כֹּה ׀ אָמַר יְהוָה הִנְנִי מֵקִים עָלֶיךָ רָעָה

**calamity on-you bringing see-I! Yahweh he-says this (11) as-wife**

מִבֵּיתֶךָ וְלָקַחְתִּי אֶת־נָשֶׁיךָ לְעֵינֶיךָ

**before-eyes-of-you wives-of-you *** and-I-will-take from-household-of-you**

וְנָתַתִּי לְרֵעֶיךָ וְשָׁכַב עִם־נָשֶׁיךָ

**wives-of-you with and-he-will-lie to-one-close-of-you and-I-will-give**

לְעֵינֵי הַשֶּׁמֶשׁ הַזֹּאת׃ כִּי אַתָּה עָשִׂיתָ בַסָּתֶר וַאֲנִי

**but-I in-the-secret you-did you indeed (12) the-this the-sun before-eyes-of**

אֶעֱשֶׂה אֶת־הַדָּבָר הַזֶּה נֶגֶד כָּל־יִשְׂרָאֵל וְנֶגֶד הַשָּׁמֶשׁ׃

**the-sun and-before Israel all-of before the-this the-thing *** I-will-do**

וַיֹּאמֶר דָּוִד אֶל־נָתָן חָטָאתִי לַיהוָה וַיֹּאמֶר

**and-he-replied against-Yahweh I-sinned Nathan to David then-he-said (13)**

5 David burned with anger against the man and said to Nathan, "As surely as the LORD lives, the man who did this deserves to die! 6 He must pay for that lamb four times over, because he did such a thing and had no pity."

7 Then Nathan said to David, "You are the man! This is what the LORD, the God of Israel, says: 'I anointed you king over Israel, and I delivered you from the hand of Saul. 8 I gave your master's house to you, and your master's wives into your arms. I gave you the house of Israel and Judah. And if all this had been too little, I would have given you even more. 9 Why did you despise the word of the LORD by doing what is evil in his eyes? You struck down Uriah the Hittite with the sword and took his wife to be your own. You killed him with the sword of the Ammonites. 10 Now, therefore, the sword will never depart from your house, because you despised me and took the wife of Uriah the Hittite to be your own.'

11 "This is what the LORD says: 'Out of your own household I am going to bring calamity upon you. Before your very eyes I will take your wives and give them to one who is close to you, and he will lie with your wives in broad daylight. 12 You did it in secret, but I will do this thing in broad daylight before all Israel.' "

13 Then David said to Nathan, "I have sinned against the LORD."

9 ק בעיני

נָתָן אֶל־דָּוִד גַּם־יְהוָה הֶעֱבִיר חַטָּאתְךָ לֹא תָמוּת׃ אֶפֶס

but (14) you-will-die not sin-of-you he-took-away Yahweh also David to Nathan

כִּי־נִאֵץ נִאַצְתָּ אֶת־אֹיְבֵי

being-enemies-of *** you-made-show-contempt to-make-show-contempt because

יְהוָה בַּדָּבָר הַזֶּה גַּם הַבֵּן הַיִּלּוֹד לְךָ מוֹת

to-die to-you the-one-born the-son indeed the-this by-the-thing Yahweh

יָמוּת׃ וַיֵּלֶךְ נָתָן אֶל־בֵּיתוֹ וַיִּגֹּף יְהוָה

Yahweh then-he-struck home-of-him to Nathan after-he-went (15) he-will-die

אֶת־הַיֶּלֶד אֲשֶׁר יָלְדָה אֵשֶׁת־אוּרִיָּה לְדָוִד וַיֵּאָנַשׁ׃

and-he-became-ill to-David Uriah wife-of she-bore whom the-child ***

וַיְבַקֵּשׁ דָּוִד אֶת־הָאֱלֹהִים בְּעַד הַנָּעַר וַיָּצָם דָּוִד

David and-he-fasted the-child for the-God with David and-he-pleaded (16)

צוֹם וּבָא וְלָן וְשָׁכַב אָרְצָה׃ וַיָּקֻמוּ

and-they-stood (17) on-ground and-he-lay and-he-spent-night and-he-went fast

זִקְנֵי בֵיתוֹ עָלָיו לַהֲקִימוֹ מִן־הָאָרֶץ וְלֹא

but-not the-ground from to-get-up-him beside-him household-of-him elders-of

אָבָה וְלֹא־בָרָא אִתָּם לָחֶם׃ וַיְהִי בַּיּוֹם הַשְּׁבִיעִי

the-seventh on-the-day and-he-was (18) food with-them he-ate and-not he-would

וַיָּמָת הַיָּלֶד וַיִּרְאוּ עַבְדֵי דָוִד לְהַגִּיד לוֹ ׀

to-him to-tell David servants-of and-they-were-afraid the-child then-he-died

כִּי־מֵת הַיֶּלֶד כִּי אָמְרוּ הִנֵּה בִהְיוֹת הַיֶּלֶד חַי

alive the-child while-to-be see! they-thought for the-child he-was-dead that

דִּבַּרְנוּ אֵלָיו וְלֹא־שָׁמַע בְּקוֹלֵנוּ וְאֵיךְ נֹאמַר

can-we-tell so-how? to-voice-of-us he-listened but-not to-him we-spoke

אֵלָיו מֵת הַיֶּלֶד וְעָשָׂה רָעָה׃ וַיַּרְא

and-he-noticed (19) desperate-thing for-he-may-do the-child he-is-dead to-him

דָּוִד כִּי עֲבָדָיו מִתְלַחֲשִׁים וַיָּבֶן דָּוִד כִּי

that David and-he-realized ones-whispering servants-of-him that David

מֵת הַיָּלֶד וַיֹּאמֶר דָּוִד אֶל־עֲבָדָיו הֲמֵת

is-he-dead? servants-of-him to David so-he-asked the-child he-was-dead

הַיֶּלֶד וַיֹּאמְרוּ מֵת׃ וַיָּקָם דָּוִד מֵהָאָרֶץ

from-the-ground David then-he-got-up (20) he-is-dead and-they-replied the-child

וַיִּרְחַץ וַיָּסֶךְ וַיְחַלֵּף שִׂמְלֹתָו וַיָּבֹא

and-he-went clothes-of-him and-he-changed and-he-put-on-lotion and-he-washed

בֵית־יְהוָה וַיִּשְׁתָּחוּ וַיָּבֹא אֶל־בֵּיתוֹ וַיִּשְׁאַל

and-he-requested house-of-him to then-he-went and-he-worshiped Yahweh house-of

וַיָּשִׂימוּ לוֹ לֶחֶם וַיֹּאכַל׃ וַיֹּאמְרוּ עֲבָדָיו

servants-of-him and-they-asked (21) and-he-ate food to-him and-they-served

Nathan replied, "The LORD has taken away your sin. You are not going to die. [14]But because by doing this you have made the enemies of the LORD show utter contempt,[f] the son born to you will die."

[15]After Nathan had gone home, the LORD struck the child that Uriah's wife had borne to David, and he became ill. [16]David pleaded with God for the child. He fasted and went into his house and spent the nights lying on the ground. [17]The elders of his household stood beside him to get him up from the ground, but he refused, and he would not eat any food with them.

[18]On the seventh day the child died. David's servants were afraid to tell him that the child was dead, for they thought, "While the child was still living, we spoke to David but he would not listen to us. How can we tell him the child is dead? He may do something desperate."

[19]David noticed that his servants were whispering among themselves and he realized the child was dead. "Is the child dead?" he asked.

"Yes," they replied, "he is dead."

[20]Then David got up from the ground. After he had washed, put on lotions and changed his clothes, he went into the house of the LORD and worshiped. Then he went to his own house, and at his request they served him food, and he ate.

[21]His servants asked him,

[f]14 Masoretic Text; an ancient Hebrew scribal tradition *this you have shown utter contempt for the LORD*

°20 ק שמלתיו

אֵלָ֔יו מֶה־ הַדָּבָ֥ר הַזֶּ֖ה אֲשֶׁ֣ר עָשִׂ֑יתָה בַּעֲב֞וּר הַיֶּ֤לֶד חַי֙
alive  the-child  for-sake-of  you-act  that  the-this  the-way  why?  to-him

צַ֔מְתָּ וַתֵּ֖בְךְּ וְכַאֲשֶׁר֙ מֵ֣ת הַיֶּ֔לֶד קַ֖מְתָּ וַתֹּ֥אכַל
and-you-eat  you-get-up  the-child  he-is-dead  but-just-as  and-you-wept  you-fasted

לָֽחֶם׃ (22) וַיֹּ֕אמֶר בְּעוֹד֙ הַיֶּ֣לֶד חַ֔י צַ֖מְתִּי וָֽאֶבְכֶּ֑ה כִּ֣י
for  and-I-wept  I-fasted  alive  the-child  while-still  and-he-answered  (22)  food

אָמַ֗רְתִּי מִ֤י יוֹדֵ֙עַ֙ יְחָנַּ֣נִי יְהוָ֔ה וְחַ֖י
and-he-may-live  Yahweh  now-he-may-be-gracious-to-me  knowing  who?  I-thought

הַיָּֽלֶד׃ (23) וְעַתָּ֣ה ׀ מֵ֗ת לָ֤מָּה זֶּה֙ אֲנִ֣י צָ֔ם הַאוּכַ֥ל לַהֲשִׁיב֖וֹ
to-bring-back-him  can-I?  fasting  I  then  why?  he-is-dead  but-now  (23)  the-child

ע֑וֹד אֲנִ֤י הֹלֵךְ֙ אֵלָ֔יו וְה֖וּא לֹֽא־ יָשׁ֥וּב אֵלָֽי׃ (24) וַיְנַחֵ֣ם
then-he-comforted  (24)  to-me  he-will-return  not  but-he  to-him  going  I  again

דָּוִ֗ד אֵ֚ת בַּת־ שֶׁ֣בַע אִשְׁתּ֔וֹ וַיָּבֹ֥א אֵלֶ֖יהָ וַיִּשְׁכַּ֣ב עִמָּ֑הּ
with-her  and-he-lay  to-her  and-he-went  wife-of-him  Sheba  Bath  ***  David

וַתֵּ֣לֶד בֵּ֗ן וַיִּקְרָ֤א אֶת־ שְׁמוֹ֙ שְׁלֹמֹ֔ה וַֽיהוָ֖ה
and-Yahweh  Solomon  name-of-him  ***  and-she-called  son  and-she-bore

אֲהֵבֽוֹ׃ (25) וַיִּשְׁלַ֗ח בְּיַד֙ נָתָ֣ן הַנָּבִ֔יא וַיִּקְרָ֥א אֶת־
***  and-he-called  the-prophet  Nathan  by-hand-of  so-he-sent  (25)  he-loved-him

שְׁמ֖וֹ יְדִ֣ידְיָ֑הּ בַּעֲב֖וּר יְהוָֽה׃ (26) וַיִּלָּ֣חֶם יוֹאָ֔ב בְּרַבַּ֖ת
against-Rabbah-of  Joab  now-he-fought  (26)  Yahweh  because-of  Jedidiah  name-of-him

בְּנֵ֣י עַמּ֑וֹן וַיִּלְכֹּ֖ד אֶת־ עִ֥יר הַמְּלוּכָֽה׃ (27) וַיִּשְׁלַ֥ח
then-he-sent  (27)  the-royal  citadel-of  ***  and-he-captured  Ammon  sons-of

יוֹאָ֛ב מַלְאָכִ֖ים אֶל־ דָּוִ֑ד וַיֹּ֙אמֶר֙ נִלְחַ֣מְתִּי בְרַבָּ֔ה גַּם־ לָכַ֖דְתִּי אֶת־
***  I-took  also  against-Rabbah  I-fought  and-he-said  David  to  messengers  Joab

עִ֥יר הַמָּֽיִם׃ (28) וְעַתָּ֗ה אֱסֹ֞ף אֶת־ יֶ֤תֶר הָעָם֙ וַחֲנֵ֣ה
and-besiege!  the-troop  rest-of  ***  muster!  and-now  (28)  the-waters  city-of

עַל־ הָעִ֔יר וְלָכְדָ֑הּ פֶּן־ אֶלְכֹּ֤ד אֲנִי֙ אֶת־ הָעִ֔יר
the-city  ***  I  I-will-take  otherwise  and-capture-her!  the-city  against

וְנִקְרָ֥א שְׁמִ֖י עָלֶֽיהָ׃ (29) וַיֶּאֱסֹ֥ף דָּוִ֛ד אֶת־ כָּל־
entire-of  ***  David  so-he-mustered  (29)  to-her  name-of-me  and-he-will-be-called

הָעָ֖ם וַיֵּ֣לֶךְ רַבָּ֑תָה וַיִּלָּ֥חֶם בָּ֖הּ וַֽיִּלְכְּדָֽהּ׃
and-he-captured-her  against-her  and-he-attacked  to-Rabbah  and-he-went  the-army

וַיִּקַּ֣ח אֶת־ עֲטֶֽרֶת־ מַלְכָּם֩ מֵעַ֨ל רֹאשׁ֜וֹ
head-of-him  from-on  king-of-them  crown-of  ***  and-he-took  (30)

וּמִשְׁקָלָ֨הּ כִּכַּ֤ר זָהָב֙ וְאֶ֣בֶן יְקָרָ֔ה וַתְּהִ֖י עַל־ רֹ֣אשׁ
head-of  on  and-she-was  precious  and-stone  gold  talent-of  and-weight-of-her

דָּוִ֑ד וּשְׁלַ֥ל הָעִ֛יר הוֹצִ֥יא הַרְבֵּ֖ה מְאֹֽד׃ (31) וְאֶת־ הָעָ֣ם
the-people  and  (31)  very  to-be-great  he-took  the-city  and-plunder-of  David

"Why are you acting this way? While the child was alive, you fasted and wept, but now that the child is dead, you get up and eat!" [22]He answered, "While the child was still alive, I fasted and wept. I thought, 'Who knows? The Lord may be gracious to me and let the child live.' [23]But now that he is dead, why should I fast? Can I bring him back again? I will go to him, but he will not return to me."

[24]Then David comforted his wife Bathsheba, and he went to her and lay with her. She gave birth to a son, and they named him Solomon. The Lord loved him; [25]and because the Lord loved him, he sent word through Nathan the prophet to name him Jedidiah.[g]

[26]Meanwhile Joab fought against Rabbah of the Ammonites and captured the royal citadel. [27]Joab then sent messengers to David, saying, "I have fought against Rabbah and taken its water supply. [28]Now muster the rest of the troops and besiege the city and capture it. Otherwise I will take the city, and it will be named after me."

[29]So David mustered the entire army and went to Rabbah, and attacked and captured it. [30]He took the crown from the head of their king[h]—its weight was a talent[i] of gold, and it was set with precious stones— and it was placed on David's head. He took a great quantity of plunder from the city [31]and

g25 Jedidiah means loved by the Lord.
h30 Or of Milcom (that is, Molech)
i30 That is, about 75 pounds (about 34 kilograms)

ק וחנני 22°
ק ותקרא 24°

אֲשֶׁר־בָּהּ הוֹצִיא וַיָּשֶׂם בַּמְּגֵרָה וּבַחֲרִצֵי
and-to-picks-of to-the-saw and-he-consigned he-brought-out in-her who

הַבַּרְזֶל וּבְמַגְזְרֹת הַבַּרְזֶל וְהֶעֱבִיר אוֹתָם בַּמַּלְכֵּן
at-the-brickmaking them and-he-made-work the-iron and-to-axes-of the-iron

וְכֵן יַעֲשֶׂה לְכֹל עָרֵי בְנֵי־עַמּוֹן וַיָּשָׁב דָּוִד
David then-he-returned Ammon sons-of towns-of to-all-of he-did and-this

וְכָל־הָעָם יְרוּשָׁלִָם׃ וַיְהִי אַחֲרֵי־כֵן וּלְאַבְשָׁלוֹם
that-to-Absalom this after and-he-was (13:1) Jerusalem the-army and-entire-of

בֶּן־דָּוִד אָחוֹת יָפָה וּשְׁמָהּ תָּמָר וַיֶּאֱהָבֶהָ אַמְנוֹן
Amnon and-he-loved-her Tamar and-name-of-her beautiful sister David son-of

בֶּן־דָּוִד׃ וַיֵּצֶר לְאַמְנוֹן לְהִתְחַלּוֹת בַּעֲבוּר
an-account-of to-be-ill to-Amnon and-he-became-frustrating (2) David son-of

תָּמָר אֲחֹתוֹ כִּי בְתוּלָה הִיא וַיִּפָּלֵא בְּעֵינֵי אַמְנוֹן
Amnon in-eyes-of and-he-was-impossible she virgin for sister-of-him Tamar

לַעֲשׂוֹת לָהּ מְאוּמָה׃ וּלְאַמְנוֹן רֵעַ וּשְׁמוֹ יוֹנָדָב בֶּן־
son-of Jonadab and-name-of-him friend now-to-Amnon (3) anything to-her to-do

שִׁמְעָה אֲחִי דָוִד וְיוֹנָדָב אִישׁ חָכָם מְאֹד׃ וַיֹּאמֶר לוֹ
to-him and-he-asked (4) very shrewd man now-Jonadab David brother-of Shimeah

מַדּוּעַ אַתָּה כָּכָה דַּל בֶּן־הַמֶּלֶךְ בַּבֹּקֶר בַּבֹּקֶר הֲלוֹא
not? in-the-morning in-the-morning the-king son-of haggard so you why?

תַּגִּיד לִי וַיֹּאמֶר לוֹ אַמְנוֹן אֶת־תָּמָר אֲחוֹת אַבְשָׁלֹם
Absalom sister-of Tamar *** Amnon to-him and-he-said to-me you-tell

אָחִי אֲנִי אֹהֵב׃ וַיֹּאמֶר לוֹ יְהוֹנָדָב שְׁכַב עַל־מִשְׁכָּבְךָ
bed-of-you in lie! Jonadab to-him and-he-said (5) loving I brother-of-me

וְהִתְחָל וּבָא אָבִיךָ לִרְאוֹתֶךָ וְאָמַרְתָּ אֵלָיו
to-him then-you-say to-see-you father-of-you when-he-comes and-act-ill!

תָּבֹא נָא תָמָר אֲחוֹתִי וְתַבְרֵנִי לֶחֶם
food and-let-her-feed-me sister-of-me Tamar now! let-her-come

וְעָשְׂתָה לְעֵינַי אֶת־הַבִּרְיָה לְמַעַן אֲשֶׁר אֶרְאֶה
I-may-watch *** so-that the-food *** before-eyes-of-me and-let-her-prepare

וְאָכַלְתִּי מִיָּדָהּ׃ וַיִּשְׁכַּב אַמְנוֹן וַיִּתְחָל
and-he-acted-ill Amnon so-he-lay-down (6) from-hand-of-her then-I-may-eat

וַיָּבֹא הַמֶּלֶךְ לִרְאֹתוֹ וַיֹּאמֶר אַמְנוֹן אֶל־הַמֶּלֶךְ תָּבוֹא־
let-her-come the-king to Amnon then-he-said to-see-him the-king when-he-came

נָא תָמָר אֲחֹתִי וּתְלַבֵּב לְעֵינַי שְׁתֵּי
two-of before-eyes-of-me and-let-her-make-bread sister-of-me Tamar now!

לְבִבוֹת וְאֶבְרֶה מִיָּדָהּ׃ וַיִּשְׁלַח דָּוִד אֶל־תָּמָר
Tamar to David so-he-sent (7) from-hand-of-her so-I-may-eat breads

°31 ק במלבן

brought out the people who were there, consigning them to labor with saws and with iron picks and axes, and he made them work at brickmaking.[k] He did this to all the Ammonite towns. Then David and his entire army returned to Jerusalem.

*Amnon and Tamar*

13 In the course of time, Amnon son of David fell in love with Tamar, the beautiful sister of Absalom son of David.

2Amnon became frustrated to the point of illness on account of his sister Tamar, for she was a virgin, and it seemed impossible for him to do anything to her.

3Now Amnon had a friend named Jonadab son of Shimeah, David's brother. Jonadab was a very shrewd man. 4He asked Amnon, "Why do you, the king's son, look so haggard morning after morning? Won't you tell me?"

Amnon said to him, "I'm in love with Tamar, my brother Absalom's sister."

5"Go to bed and pretend to be ill," Jonadab said. "When your father comes to see you, say to him, 'I would like my sister Tamar to come and give me something to eat. Let her prepare the food in my sight so I may watch her and then eat it from her hand.' "

6So Amnon lay down and pretended to be ill. When the king came to see him, Amnon said to him, "I would like my sister Tamar to come and make some special bread in my sight, so I may eat from her hand."

7David sent word to Tamar

[k]31 The meaning of the Hebrew for this clause is uncertain.

הַבַּיְתָה לֵאמֹר לְכִי נָא בֵּית אַמְנוֹן אָחִיךְ וַעֲשִׂי־
and-prepare! brother-of-you Amnon house-of now! go! to-say at-the-palace

לוֹ הַבִּרְיָה׃ וַתֵּלֶךְ תָּמָר בֵּית אַמְנוֹן אָחִיהָ וְהוּא
and-he brother-of-her Amnon house-of Tamar so-she-went (8) the-food for-him

שֹׁכֵב וַתִּקַּח אֶת־ הַבָּצֵק וַתָּלָושׁ וַתְּלַבֵּב
and-she-made-bread and-she-kneaded the-dough *** and-she-took lying-down

לְעֵינָיו וַתְּבַשֵּׁל אֶת־הַלְּבִבוֹת׃ וַתִּקַּח אֶת־ הַמַּשְׂרֵת
the-pan *** then-she-took (9) the-breads *** and-she-baked before-eyes-of-him

וַתִּצֹק לְפָנָיו וַיְמָאֵן לֶאֱכוֹל וַיֹּאמֶר אַמְנוֹן הוֹצִיאוּ
send-out! Amnon and-he-said to-eat but-he-refused before-him and-she-served

כָל־ אִישׁ מֵעָלַי וַיֵּצְאוּ כָל־ אִישׁ מֵעָלָיו׃
from-with-him person every-of so-they-left from-with-me person every-of

וַיֹּאמֶר אַמְנוֹן אֶל־ תָּמָר הָבִיאִי הַבִּרְיָה הַחֶדֶר וְאֶבְרֶה
so-I-may-eat the-bedroom the-food bring! Tamar to Amnon then-he-said (10)

מִיָּדֵךְ וַתִּקַּח תָּמָר אֶת־ הַלְּבִבוֹת אֲשֶׁר עָשָׂתָה
she-prepared that the-breads *** Tamar and-she-took from-hand-of-you

וַתָּבֵא לְאַמְנוֹן אָחִיהָ הֶחָדְרָה׃ וַתַּגֵּשׁ
when-she-took (11) in-the-bedroom brother-of-her to-Amnon and-she-brought

אֵלָיו לֶאֱכֹל וַיַּחֲזֶק־ בָּהּ וַיֹּאמֶר לָהּ בּוֹאִי שִׁכְבִי
come-to-bed! come! to-her and-he-said onto-her then-he-grabbed to-eat to-him

עִמִּי אֲחוֹתִי׃ וַתֹּאמֶר לוֹ אַל־ אָחִי אַל־
not brother-of-me no to-him and-she-said (12) sister-of-me with-me

תְּעַנֵּנִי כִּי לֹא־ יֵעָשֶׂה כֵן בְּיִשְׂרָאֵל אַל־תַּעֲשֵׂה אֶת־
*** you-do not in-Israel such he-should-be-done not for you-force-me

הַנְּבָלָה הַזֹּאת׃ וַאֲנִי אָנָה אוֹלִיךְ אֶת־ חֶרְפָּתִי
disgrace-of-me *** could-I-get-rid where? and-I (13) the-this the-wicked-thing

וְאַתָּה תִּהְיֶה כְּאַחַד הַנְּבָלִים בְּיִשְׂרָאֵל וְעַתָּה דַּבֶּר־
speak! so-now in-Israel the-wicked-fools like-one-of you-would-be and-you

נָא אֶל־הַמֶּלֶךְ כִּי לֹא יִמְנָעֵנִי מִמֶּךָּ׃ וְלֹא אָבָה
he-wanted but-not (14) from-you he-will-keep-me not for the-king to now!

לִשְׁמֹעַ בְּקוֹלָהּ וַיֶּחֱזַק מִמֶּנָּה וַיְעַנֶּהָ
and-he-raped-her than-her and-he-was-stronger to-voice-of-her to-listen

וַיִּשְׁכַּב אֹתָהּ׃ וַיִּשְׂנָאֶהָ אַמְנוֹן שִׂנְאָה גְּדוֹלָה מְאֹד כִּי
in-fact very intense hatred Amnon then-he-hated-her (15) her and-he-lay-with

גְדוֹלָה הַשִּׂנְאָה אֲשֶׁר שְׂנֵאָהּ מֵאַהֲבָה אֲשֶׁר אֲהֵבָהּ
he-loved-her which than-love he-hated-her which the-hatred greater

וַיֹּאמֶר־ לָהּ אַמְנוֹן קוּמִי לֵכִי׃ וַתֹּאמֶר לוֹ אַל־
no to-him and-she-said (16) get-out! get-up! Amnon to-her and-he-said

at the palace: "Go to the house of your brother Amnon and prepare some food for him." [8]So Tamar went to the house of her brother Amnon, who was lying down. She took some dough, kneaded it, made the bread in his sight and baked it. [9]Then she took the pan and served him the bread, but he refused to eat.

"Send everyone out of here," Amnon said. So everyone left him. [10]Then Amnon said to Tamar, "Bring the food here into my bedroom so I may eat from your hand." And Tamar took the bread she had prepared and brought it to her brother Amnon in his bedroom. [11]But when she took it to him to eat, he grabbed her and said, "Come to bed with me, my sister."

[12]"Don't, my brother!" she said to him. "Don't force me. Such a thing should not be done in Israel! Don't do this wicked thing. [13]What about me? Where could I get rid of my disgrace? And what about you? You would be like one of the wicked fools in Israel. Please speak to the king; he will not keep me from being married to you." [14]But he refused to listen to her, and since he was stronger than she, he raped her.

[15]Then Amnon hated her with intense hatred. In fact, he hated her more than he had loved her. Amnon said to her, "Get up and get out!"

[16]"No!" she said to him.

°8 ק ותלש

אֹד֗וֹת הָרָעָ֤ה הַגְּדוֹלָה֙ הַזֹּ֔את מֵאַחֶ֖רֶת אֲשֶׁר־עָשִׂ֣יתָ עִמִּ֑י
to-me you-did that more-than-other the-this the-great the-wrong causes-of

לְשַׁלְּחֵ֑נִי וְלֹ֥א אָבָ֖ה לִשְׁמֹ֥עַ לָֽהּ׃ וַיִּקְרָ֗א אֶת־
*** and-he-called (17) to-her to-listen he-wanted but-not to-send-away-me

נַעֲרוֹ֙ מְשָׁ֣רְת֔וֹ וַיֹּ֕אמֶר שִׁלְחוּ־נָ֥א אֶת־זֹ֛את
this-woman *** now! send-out! and-he-said one-attending-him servant-of-him

מֵעָלַ֖י הַח֑וּצָה וּנְעֹ֥ל הַדֶּ֖לֶת אַחֲרֶֽיהָ׃ וְעָלֶ֨יהָ֙
now-on-her (18) after-her the-door and-bolt! to-the-outside from-with-me

כְּתֹ֣נֶת פַּסִּ֔ים כִּ֣י כֵ֞ן תִּלְבַּ֧שְׁןָ בְנוֹת־הַמֶּ֛לֶךְ הַבְּתוּלֹ֖ת
the-virgins the-king daughters-of they-wore this for ornaments robe-of

מְעִילִ֑ים וַיֹּצֵ֨א אוֹתָ֜הּ מְשָׁ֣רְתוֹ֙ הַח֔וּץ וְנָעַ֥ל
and-he-bolted the-outside one-attending-him her and-he-put-out garments

הַדֶּ֖לֶת אַחֲרֶֽיהָ׃ וַתִּקַּ֨ח תָּמָ֥ר אֵ֨פֶר֙ עַל־רֹאשָׁ֔הּ וּכְתֹ֧נֶת
and-robe-of head-of-her on ash Tamar and-she-put (19) after-her the-door

הַפַּסִּ֛ים אֲשֶׁ֥ר עָלֶ֖יהָ קָרָ֑עָה וַתָּ֤שֶׂם יָדָהּ֙ עַל־רֹאשָׁ֔הּ
head-of-her on hand-of-her and-she-put she-tore on-her that the-ornaments

וַתֵּ֥לֶךְ הָל֖וֹךְ וְזָעָֽקָה׃ וַיֹּ֨אמֶר אֵלֶ֜יהָ אַבְשָׁל֣וֹם אָחִ֗יהָ
brother-of-her Absalom to-her and-he-said (20) and-she-wept to-go and-she-went

הַאֲמִינ֣וֹן אָחִיךְ֮ הָיָ֣ה עִמָּךְ֒ וְעַתָּ֤ה אֲחוֹתִי֙ הַחֲרִ֔ישִׁי
be-quiet! sister-of-me and-now with-you was-he brother-of-you Amnon?

אָחִ֣יךְ ה֑וּא אַל־תָּשִׁ֥יתִי אֶת־לִבֵּ֖ךְ לַדָּבָ֣ר הַזֶּ֑ה
the-this to-the-thing heart-of-you *** you-take not he brother-of-you

וַתֵּ֤שֶׁב תָּמָר֙ וְשֹׁ֣מֵמָ֔ה בֵּ֖ית אַבְשָׁל֥וֹם אָחִֽיהָ׃
brother-of-her Absalom house-of and-being-desolate Tamar and-she-lived

וְהַמֶּ֣לֶךְ דָּוִ֔ד שָׁמַ֕ע אֵ֥ת כָּל־הַדְּבָרִ֖ים הָאֵ֑לֶּה
the-these the-things all-of *** he-heard David when-the-king (21)

וַיִּ֥חַר ל֖וֹ מְאֹֽד׃ וְלֹֽא־דִבֶּ֧ר אַבְשָׁל֛וֹם עִם־אַמְנ֖וֹן
Amnon to Absalom he-said-word and-not (22) very to-him then-he-was-furious

לְמֵרָ֣ע וְעַד־ט֑וֹב כִּֽי־שָׂנֵ֤א אַבְשָׁלוֹם֙ אֶת־אַמְנ֔וֹן עַל־דְּבַר֙ אֲשֶׁ֣ר
that reason-of for Amnon *** Absalom he-hated for good even-to to-from-bad

עִנָּ֔ה אֵ֖ת תָּמָ֥ר אֲחֹתֽוֹ׃ וַֽיְהִ֖י לִשְׁנָתַ֣יִם יָמִ֑ים
days after-two-years and-he-was (23) sister-of-him Tamar *** he-disgraced

וַיִּהְי֤וּ גֹֽזְזִים֙ לְאַבְשָׁל֔וֹם בְּבַ֥עַל חָצ֖וֹר אֲשֶׁ֣ר עִם־אֶפְרָ֑יִם
Ephraim near that Hazor at-Baal for-Absalom ones-sheepshearing when-they-were

וַיִּקְרָ֥א אַבְשָׁל֖וֹם לְכָל־בְּנֵ֥י הַמֶּֽלֶךְ׃ וַיָּבֹ֥א אַבְשָׁל֖וֹם
Absalom and-he-went (24) the-king sons-of to-all-of Absalom then-he-invited

אֶל־הַמֶּ֑לֶךְ וַיֹּ֕אמֶר הִנֵּה־נָ֥א גֹזְזִ֖ים לְעַבְדֶּ֑ךָ יֵֽלֶךְ־
will-he-come for-servant-of-you ones-shearing now! see! and-he-said the-king to

"Sending me away would be a greater wrong than what you have already done to me."

But he refused to listen to her. [17]He called his personal servant and said, "Get this woman out of here and bolt the door after her." [18]So his servant put her out and bolted the door after her. She was wearing a richly ornamented[l] robe, for this was the kind of garment the virgin daughters of the king wore. [19]Tamar put ashes on her head and tore the ornamented[m] robe she was wearing. She put her hand on her head and went away, weeping aloud as she went.

[20]Her brother Absalom said to her, "Has that Amnon, your brother, been with you? Be quiet now, my sister; he is your brother. Don't take this thing to heart." And Tamar lived in her brother Absalom's house, a desolate woman.

[21]When King David heard all this, he was furious. [22]Absalom never said a word to Amnon, either good or bad; he hated Amnon because he had disgraced his sister Tamar.

### Absalom Kills Amnon

[23]Two years later, when Absalom's sheepshearers were at Baal Hazor near the border of Ephraim, he invited all the king's sons to come there. [24]Absalom went to the king and said, "Your servant has had shearers come. Will the

[l]18 The meaning of the Hebrew for this phrase is uncertain.
[m]19 The meaning of the Hebrew for this word is uncertain.

נָא הַמֶּלֶךְ וַעֲבָדָיו עִם־ עַבְדֶּךָ׃ וַיֹּאמֶר
and-he-replied (25) servant-of-you with and-officials-of-him the-king now!

הַמֶּלֶךְ אֶל־אַבְשָׁלוֹם אַל־ בְּנִי אַל־ נָא נֵלֵךְ כֻּלָּנוּ וְלֹא
so-not all-of-us we-should-go now! not son-of-me no Absalom to the-king

נִכְבַּד עָלֶיךָ וַיִּפְרָץ־ בּוֹ וְלֹא־ אָבָה לָלֶכֶת
to-go he-wanted but-not to-him although-he-urged to-you we-would-be-burden

וַיְבָרְכֵהוּ׃ וַיֹּאמֶר אַבְשָׁלוֹם וָלֹא יֵלֶךְ־ נָא אִתָּנוּ
with-us now! let-him-come if-not Absalom then-he-said (26) but-he-blessed-him

אַמְנוֹן אָחִי וַיֹּאמֶר לוֹ הַמֶּלֶךְ לָמָּה יֵלֵךְ עִמָּךְ׃
with-you should-he-go why? the-king-to-him and-he-asked brother-of-me Amnon

וַיִּפְרָץ־ בּוֹ אַבְשָׁלוֹם וַיִּשְׁלַח אִתּוֹ אֶת־ אַמְנוֹן וְאֵת כָּל־
all-of and Amnon *** with-him so-he-sent Absalom to-him but-he-urged (27)

בְּנֵי הַמֶּלֶךְ׃ וַיְצַו אַבְשָׁלוֹם אֶת־ נְעָרָיו לֵאמֹר רְאוּ נָא
now! see! to-say men-of-him *** Absalom and-he-ordered (28) the-king sons-of

כְּטוֹב לֵב־ אַמְנוֹן בַּיַּיִן וְאָמַרְתִּי אֲלֵיכֶם הַכּוּ
strike-down! to-you and-I-say from-the-wine Amnon spirit-of when-to-be-high

אֶת־אַמְנוֹן וַהֲמִתֶּם אֹתוֹ אַל־ תִּירָאוּ הֲלוֹא כִּי אָנֹכִי צִוִּיתִי אֶתְכֶם
you I-ordered I indeed not? you-be-afraid not him then-you-kill Amnon ***

חִזְקוּ וִהְיוּ לִבְנֵי־ חָיִל׃ וַיַּעֲשׂוּ נַעֲרֵי אַבְשָׁלוֹם
Absalom men-of so-they-did (29) bravery as-sons-of and-be! be-strong!

לְאַמְנוֹן כַּאֲשֶׁר צִוָּה אַבְשָׁלוֹם וַיָּקֻמוּ ׀ כָּל־ בְּנֵי הַמֶּלֶךְ
the-king sons-of all-of then-they-got-up Absalom he-ordered just-as to-Amnon

וַיִּרְכְּבוּ אִישׁ עַל־ פִּרְדּוֹ וַיָּנֻסוּ׃ וַיְהִי הֵמָּה
they whle-he-was (30) and-they-fled mule-of-him on each and-they-mounted

בַדֶּרֶךְ וְהַשְּׁמֻעָה בָּאָה אֶל־ דָּוִד לֵאמֹר הִכָּה אַבְשָׁלוֹם
Absalom he-struck-down to-say David to she-came then-the-report on-the-way

אֶת־ כָּל־ בְּנֵי הַמֶּלֶךְ וְלֹא־ נוֹתַר מֵהֶם אֶחָד׃ וַיָּקָם
and-he-stood-up (31) one of-them he-is-left and-not the-king sons-of all-of ***

הַמֶּלֶךְ וַיִּקְרַע אֶת־ בְּגָדָיו וַיִּשְׁכַּב אָרְצָה וְכָל־
and-all-of on-ground and-he-lay clothes-of-him *** and-he-tore the-king

עֲבָדָיו נִצָּבִים קְרֻעֵי בְגָדִים׃ וַיַּעַן
but-he-said (32) clothes ones-being-torn-of ones-standing servants-of-him

יוֹנָדָב ׀ בֶּן־ שִׁמְעָה אֲחִי־ דָוִד וַיֹּאמֶר אַל־ יֹאמַר
he-should-think not and-he-said David brother-of Shimeah son-of Jonadab

אֲדֹנִי אֵת כָּל־ הַנְּעָרִים בְּנֵי־ הַמֶּלֶךְ הֵמִיתוּ כִּי־ אַמְנוֹן
Amnon only they-killed the-king sons-of the-princes all-of *** lord-of-me

לְבַדּוֹ מֵת כִּי־ עַל־ פִּי אַבְשָׁלוֹם הָיְתָה שׂוּמָה מִיּוֹם
from-day intention she-was Absalom mouth-of on for he-is-dead by-himself

king and his officials please
join me?"
25"No, my son," the king replied. "All of us should not go;
we would only be a burden to
you." Although Absalom
urged him, he still refused to
go, but gave him his blessing.
26Then Absalom said, "If
not, please let my brother Amnon come with us."
The king asked him, "Why
should he go with you?" 27But
Absalom urged him, so he sent
with him Amnon and the rest
of the king's sons.
28Absalom ordered his men,
"Listen! When Amnon is in
high spirits from drinking
wine and I say to you, 'Strike
Amnon down,' then kill him.
Don't be afraid. Have not I
given you this order? Be
strong and brave." 29So Absalom's men did to Amnon what
Absalom had ordered. Then all
the king's sons got up, mounted their mules and fled.
30While they were on their
way, the report came to David:
"Absalom has struck down all
the king's sons; not one of
them is left." 31The king stood
up, tore his clothes and lay
down on the ground; and all
his servants stood by with
their clothes torn.
32But Jonadab son of Shimeah, David's brother, said,
"My lord should not think
that they killed all the princes;
only Amnon is dead. This has
been Absalom's expressed intention ever since the day

*30 Most mss have *sheva* in the *kaph* ( ךְ ).

עִנֹּתוֹ אֵת תָּמָר אֲחֹתוֹ׃ (33) וְעַתָּה אַל־יָשֵׂם אֲדֹנִי

lord-of-me he-should-take not so-now (33) sister-of-him Tamar *** to-rape-him

הַמֶּלֶךְ אֶל־לִבּוֹ דָּבָר לֵאמֹר כָּל־בְּנֵי הַמֶּלֶךְ מֵתוּ

they-are-dead the-king sons-of all-of to-say report heart-of-him to the-king

כִּי־אִם־אַמְנוֹן לְבַדּוֹ מֵת׃ (34) וַיִּבְרַח אַבְשָׁלוֹם וַיִּשָּׂא

and-he-lifted Absalom and-he-fled (34) he-is-dead by-himself Amnon only for

הַנַּעַר הַצֹּפֶה אֶת־עֵינָו וַיַּרְא וְהִנֵּה עַם־

people and-see! and-he-looked eyes-of-him *** the-one-standing-watch the-man

רַב הֹלְכִים מִדֶּרֶךְ אַחֲרָיו מִצַּד הָהָר׃ (35) וַיֹּאמֶר

and-he-said (35) the-hill on-side-of west-of-him on-road ones-coming many

יוֹנָדָב אֶל־הַמֶּלֶךְ הִנֵּה בְנֵי־הַמֶּלֶךְ בָּאוּ כִּדְבַר עַבְדְּךָ

servant-of-you as-word-of they-come the-king sons-of see! the-king to Jonadab

כֵּן הָיָה׃ (36) וַיְהִי ׀ כְּכַלֹּתוֹ לְדַבֵּר וְהִנֵּה בְנֵי־

sons-of then-see! to-speak as-to-finish-him and-he-was (36) he-happened so

הַמֶּלֶךְ בָּאוּ וַיִּשְׂאוּ קוֹלָם וַיִּבְכּוּ וְגַם־

and-also and-they-wailed voice-of-them and-they-lifted they-came the-king

הַמֶּלֶךְ וְכָל־עֲבָדָיו בָּכוּ בְּכִי גָּדוֹל מְאֹד׃

very bitter weeping they-wept servants-of-him and-all-of the-king

(37) וְאַבְשָׁלוֹם בָּרַח וַיֵּלֶךְ אֶל־תַּלְמַי בֶּן־עַמִּיחוּר מֶלֶךְ גְּשׁוּר

Geshur king-of Ammihud son-of Talmai to and-he-went he-fled and-Absalom (37)

וַיִּתְאַבֵּל עַל־בְּנוֹ כָּל־הַיָּמִים׃ (38) וְאַבְשָׁלוֹם בָּרַח

he-fled and-Absalom (38) the-days all-of son-of-him for but-he-mourned

וַיֵּלֶךְ גְּשׁוּר וַיְהִי־שָׁם שָׁלֹשׁ שָׁנִים׃ (39) וַתְּכַל דָּוִד

David *and-she-longed (39) years three there and-he-stayed Geshur and-he-went

הַמֶּלֶךְ לָצֵאת אֶל־אַבְשָׁלוֹם כִּי־נִחַם עַל־אַמְנוֹן כִּי־מֵת׃

he-died that Amnon concerning he-was-consoled for Absalom to to-go the-king

(14:1) וַיֵּדַע יוֹאָב בֶּן־צְרֻיָה כִּי־לֵב הַמֶּלֶךְ עַל־אַבְשָׁלוֹם׃

Absalom for the-king heart-of that Zeruiah son-of Joab and-he-knew (14:1)

(2) וַיִּשְׁלַח יוֹאָב תְּקוֹעָה וַיִּקַּח מִשָּׁם אִשָּׁה חֲכָמָה

wise woman from-there and-he-had-brought to-Tekoa Joab so-he-sent (2)

וַיֹּאמֶר אֵלֶיהָ הִתְאַבְּלִי־נָא וְלִבְשִׁי־נָא בִגְדֵי־אֵבֶל

mourning clothes-of now! and-dress! now! pretend-to-mourn! to-her and-he-said

וְאַל־תָּסוּכִי שֶׁמֶן וְהָיִית כְּאִשָּׁה זֶה יָמִים רַבִּים מִתְאַבֶּלֶת עַל־

for grieving many days this like-woman and-you-act lotion you-use and-not

מֵת׃ (3) וּבָאת אֶל־הַמֶּלֶךְ וְדִבַּרְתְּ אֵלָיו כַּדָּבָר הַזֶּה

the-this as-the-word to-him and-you-speak the-king to then-you-go (3) dead

וַיָּשֶׂם יוֹאָב אֶת־הַדְּבָרִים בְּפִיהָ׃ (4) וַתֹּאמֶר הָאִשָּׁה

the-woman when-she-spoke (4) in-mouth-of-her the-words *** Joab and-he-put

---

Amnon raped his sister Tamar. 33 My lord the king should not be concerned about the report that all the king's sons are dead. Only Amnon is dead."

34 Meanwhile, Absalom had fled.

Now the man standing watch looked up and saw many people on the road west of him, coming down the side of the hill. The watchman went and told the king, "I see men in the direction of Horonaim, on the side of the hill."[n]

35 Jonadab said to the king, "See, the king's sons are here; it has happened just as your servant said."

36 As he finished speaking, the king's sons came in, wailing loudly. The king, too, and all his servants wept very bitterly.

37 Absalom fled and went to Talmai son of Ammihud, the king of Geshur. But King David mourned for his son every day.

38 After Absalom fled and went to Geshur, he stayed there three years. 39 And the spirit of the king[o] longed to go to Absalom, for he was consoled concerning Amnon's death.

*Absalom Returns to Jerusalem*

**14** Joab son of Zeruiah knew that the king's heart longed for Absalom. 2 So Joab sent someone to Tekoa and had a wise woman brought from there. He said to her, "Pretend you are in mourning. Dress in mourning clothes, and don't use any cosmetic lotions. Act like a woman who has spent many days grieving for the dead. 3 Then go to the king and speak these words to him." And Joab put the words in her mouth.

4 When the woman from

n34 Septuagint; Hebrew does not have this sentence.
o39 Some Septuagint manuscripts; Hebrew *But* ⌊*the spirit of*⌋ *David the king*

*39 Apparently the feminine subject, *spirit*, evident in some versions, has dropped out of text.

°34 ק עיניו
°37 ק עמיהוד

הַתְּקֹעִית אֶל־הַמֶּלֶךְ וַתִּפֹּל עַל־אַפֶּיהָ אַרְצָה וַתִּשְׁתָּחוּ
and-she-honored to-ground faces-of-her on then-she-fell the-king to the-Tekoaite

וַתֹּאמֶר הוֹשִׁעָה הַמֶּלֶךְ׃ וַיֹּאמֶר־לָהּ הַמֶּלֶךְ מַה־לָּךְ
to-you what? the-king to-her and-he-asked (5) the-king help! and-she-said

וַתֹּאמֶר אֲבָל אִשָּׁה־אַלְמָנָה אָנִי וַיָּמָת אִישִׁי׃
husband-of-me and-he-is-dead I widow woman indeed and-she-said

וּלְשִׁפְחָתְךָ שְׁנֵי בָנִים וַיִּנָּצוּ שְׁנֵיהֶם בַּשָּׂדֶה
in-the-field two-of-them and-they-fought sons two-of and-to-servant-of-you (6)

וְאֵין מַצִּיל בֵּינֵיהֶם וַיַּכּוּ הָאֶחָד אֶת־הָאֶחָד
the-other *** the-one and-he-struck-him between-them one-separating and-not

וַיָּמֶת אֹתוֹ׃ וְהִנֵּה קָמָה כָל־הַמִּשְׁפָּחָה עַל־
against the-clan whole-of she-rose-up now-see! (7) him and-he-killed

שִׁפְחָתֶךָ וַיֹּאמְרוּ תְּנִי ׀ אֶת־מַכֵּה אָחִיו
brother-of-him one-striking-down *** hand-over! and-they-say servant-of-you

וּנְמִתֵהוּ בְּנֶפֶשׁ אָחִיו אֲשֶׁר הָרָג וְנַשְׁמִידָה
and-we-will-get-rid he-killed whom brother-of-him for-life-of so-we-may-kill-him

גַּם אֶת־הַיּוֹרֵשׁ וְכִבּוּ אֶת־גַּחַלְתִּי אֲשֶׁר
that burning-coal-of-me *** and-they-will-put-out the-one-being-heir *** also

נִשְׁאָרָה לְבִלְתִּי שׂוֹם־לְאִישִׁי שֵׁם וּשְׁאֵרִית עַל־פְּנֵי
faces-of on or-descendant name to-husband-of-me to-leave not being-left

הָאֲדָמָה׃ וַיֹּאמֶר הַמֶּלֶךְ אֶל־הָאִשָּׁה לְכִי לְבֵיתֵךְ וַאֲנִי
and-I to-home-of-you go! the-woman to the-king and-he-said (8) the-earth

אֲצַוֶּה עָלָיִךְ׃ וַתֹּאמֶר הָאִשָּׁה הַתְּקוֹעִית אֶל־הַמֶּלֶךְ
the-king to the-Tekoaite the-woman but-she-said (9) for-you I-will-issue-order

עָלַי אֲדֹנִי הַמֶּלֶךְ הֶעָוֺן וְעַל־בֵּית אָבִי וְהַמֶּלֶךְ
and-the-king father-of-me family-of and-on the-blame the-king lord-of-me on-me

וְכִסְאוֹ נָקִי׃ וַיֹּאמֶר הַמֶּלֶךְ הַמְדַבֵּר
the-one-saying the-king and-he-replied (10) without-guilt and-throne-of-him

אֵלַיִךְ וַהֲבֵאתוֹ אֵלַי וְלֹא־יֹסִיף עוֹד לָגַעַת
to-bother again he-will-repeat and-not to-me then-bring-him! to-you

בָּךְ׃ וַתֹּאמֶר יִזְכָּר־נָא הַמֶּלֶךְ אֶת־יְהוָה
Yahweh *** the-king now! let-him-invoke and-she-said (11) against-you

אֱלֹהֶיךָ מֵהַרְבַּית גֹּאֵל הַדָּם לְשַׁחֵת וְלֹא
so-not to-destroy the-blood one-avenging-of from-to-add God-of-you

יַשְׁמִידוּ אֶת־בְּנִי וַיֹּאמֶר חַי־יְהוָה אִם־יִפֹּל
he-will-fall not Yahweh life-of and-he-said son-of-me *** they-will-destroy

מִשַּׂעֲרַת בִּנֵךְ אַרְצָה׃ וַתֹּאמֶר הָאִשָּׁה תְּדַבֶּר־
let-her-speak the-woman then-she-said (12) to-ground son-of-you from-hair-of

Tekoa went[p] to the king, she fell with her face to the ground to pay him honor, and she said, "Help me, O king!"

5 The king asked her, "What is troubling you?"

She said, "I am indeed a widow; my husband is dead. 6 I your servant had two sons. They got into a fight with each other in the field, and no one was there to separate them. One struck the other and killed him. 7 Now the whole clan has risen up against your servant; they say, 'Hand over the one who struck his brother down, so that we may put him to death for the life of his brother whom he killed; then we will get rid of the heir as well.' They would put out the only burning coal I have left, leaving my husband neither name nor descendant on the face of the earth."

8 The king said to the woman, "Go home, and I will issue an order in your behalf."

9 But the woman from Tekoa said to him, "My lord the king, let the blame rest on me and on my father's family, and let the king and his throne be without guilt."

10 The king replied, "If anyone says anything to you, bring him to me, and he will not bother you again."

11 She said, "Then let the king invoke the LORD his God to prevent the avenger of blood from adding to the destruction, so that my son will not be destroyed."

"As surely as the LORD lives," he said, "not one hair of your son's head will fall to the ground."

12 Then the woman said, "Let

p4 Many Hebrew manuscripts, Septuagint, Vulgate and Syriac; most Hebrew manuscripts *spoke*

°7 ק שים
°11 ק מהרבת

נָא שִׁפְחָתְךָ אֶל־ אֲדֹנִי הַמֶּלֶךְ דָּבָר וַיֹּאמֶר דַּבֵּרִי׃
speak! and-he-replied word the-king lord-of-me to servant-of-you now!

וַתֹּאמֶר הָאִשָּׁה וְלָמָּה חָשַׁבְתָּה כָּזֹאת עַל־ עַם
people-of against like-this you-devised then-why? the-woman and-she-said (13)

אֱלֹהִים וּמִדַּבֵּר הַמֶּלֶךְ הַדָּבָר הַזֶּה כְּאָשֵׁם לְבִלְתִּי
not as-conviction the-this the-thing the-king and-when-to-say God

הָשִׁיב הַמֶּלֶךְ אֶת־ נִדְּחוֹ׃ כִּי־ מוֹת
to-die for (14) one-being-banished-of-him *** the-king to-bring-back

נָמוּת וְכַמַּיִם הַנִּגָּרִים אַרְצָה אֲשֶׁר לֹא
not which on-ground the-ones-being-spilled and-like-the-waters we-must-die

יֵאָסֵפוּ וְלֹא־ יִשָּׂא אֱלֹהִים נֶפֶשׁ וְחָשַׁב מַחֲשָׁבוֹת
ways but-he-devises life God he-takes-away but-not they-can-be-recovered

לְבִלְתִּי יִדַּח מִמֶּנּוּ נִדָּח׃ וְעַתָּה אֲשֶׁר־
that and-now (15) one-being-banished from-him he-remains-estranged so-not

בָּאתִי לְדַבֵּר אֶל־ הַמֶּלֶךְ אֲדֹנִי אֶת־ הַדָּבָר הַזֶּה כִּי
for the-this the-word *** lord-of-me the-king to to-say I-came

יֵרְאֻנִי הָעָם וַתֹּאמֶר שִׁפְחָתְךָ אֲדַבְּרָה־
I-will-speak servant-of-you and-she-thought the-people they-make-afraid-me

נָּא אֶל־הַמֶּלֶךְ אוּלַי יַעֲשֶׂה הַמֶּלֶךְ אֶת־ דְּבַר אֲמָתוֹ׃
servant-of-him request-of *** the-king he-will-do perhaps the-king to now!

כִּי יִשְׁמַע הַמֶּלֶךְ לְהַצִּיל אֶת־ אֲמָתוֹ מִכַּף
from-hand-of servant-of-him *** to-deliver the-king he-will-agree perhaps (16)

הָאִישׁ לְהַשְׁמִיד אֹתִי וְאֶת־ בְּנִי יַחַד מִנַּחֲלַת אֱלֹהִים׃
God from-inheritance-of together son-of-me and me to-cut-off the-man

וַתֹּאמֶר שִׁפְחָתְךָ יִהְיֶה־ נָּא דְּבַר־ אֲדֹנִי הַמֶּלֶךְ
the-king lord-of-me word-of now! may-he-be servant-of-you now-she-says (17)

לִמְנוּחָה כִּי ׀ כְּמַלְאַךְ הָאֱלֹהִים כֵּן אֲדֹנִי הַמֶּלֶךְ לִשְׁמֹעַ הַטּוֹב
the-good to-discern the-king lord-of-me so the-God like-angel-of for as-rest

וְהָרָע וַיהוָה אֱלֹהֶיךָ יְהִי עִמָּךְ׃ וַיַּעַן
then-he-answered (18) with-you may-he-be God-of-you and-Yahweh and-the-evil

הַמֶּלֶךְ וַיֹּאמֶר אֶל־ הָאִשָּׁה אַל־ נָא תְכַחֲדִי מִמֶּנִּי דָּבָר אֲשֶׁר אָנֹכִי
I that answer from-me you-keep now! not the-woman and-he-said the-king

שֹׁאֵל אֹתָךְ וַתֹּאמֶר הָאִשָּׁה יְדַבֶּר־ נָא אֲדֹנִי הַמֶּלֶךְ׃
the-king lord-of-me now! let-him-speak the-woman and-she-said you asking

וַיֹּאמֶר הַמֶּלֶךְ הֲיַד יוֹאָב אִתָּךְ בְּכָל־ זֹאת
this in-all-of with-you Joab hand-of? the-king and-he-asked (19)

וַתַּעַן הָאִשָּׁה וַתֹּאמֶר חֵי־ נַפְשְׁךָ אֲדֹנִי
lord-of-me self-of-you life-of and-she-said the-woman and-she-answered

your servant speak a word to my lord the king."

"Speak," he replied.

[13]The woman said, "Why then have you devised a thing like this against the people of God? When the king says this, does he not convict himself, for the king has not brought back his banished son? [14]Like water spilled on the ground, which cannot be recovered, so we must die. But God does not take away life; instead, he devises ways so that a banished person may not remain estranged from him.

[15]"And now I have come to say this to my lord the king because the people have made me afraid. Your servant thought, 'I will speak to the king; perhaps he will do what his servant asks. [16]Perhaps the king will agree to deliver his servant from the hand of the man who is trying to cut off both me and my son from the inheritance God gave us.'

[17]"And now your servant says, 'May the word of my lord the king bring me rest, for my lord the king is like an angel of God in discerning good and evil. May the LORD your God be with you.' "

[18]Then the king said to the woman, "Do not keep from me the answer to what I am going to ask you."

"Let my lord the king speak," the woman said.

[19]The king asked, "Isn't the hand of Joab with you in all this?"

The woman answered, "As surely as you live, my lord the

הַמֶּ֣לֶךְ אִם־ אִ֣שׁ ׀ לְהֵמִ֣ין וּֽלְהַשְׂמִ֗יל מִכֹּ֛ל אֲשֶׁר־ דִּבֶּ֖ר
he-says that from-anything or-to-turn-left to-turn-right he-is not the-king

אֲדֹנִ֣י הַמֶּ֑לֶךְ כִּֽי־ עַבְדְּךָ֤ יוֹאָב֙ ה֣וּא צִוָּ֔נִי וְה֗וּא
and-he he-instructed-me he Joab servant-of-you indeed the-king lord-of-me

שָׂ֚ם בְּפִ֣י שִׁפְחָֽתְךָ֔ אֵ֥ת כָּל־ הַדְּבָרִ֖ים הָאֵֽלֶּה׃
the-these the-words all-of *** servant-of-you into-mouth-of he-put

(20) לְבַֽעֲב֗וּר סַבֵּב֙ אֶת־ פְּנֵ֣י הַדָּבָ֔ר עָשָׂ֛ה עַבְדְּךָ֥
servant-of-you he-did the-situation faces-of *** to-change in-order-to (20)

יוֹאָ֖ב אֶת־ הַדָּבָ֣ר הַזֶּ֑ה וַֽאדֹנִ֣י חָכָ֗ם כְּחָכְמַת֙ מַלְאַ֣ךְ
angel-of like-wisdom-of wise and-lord-of-me the-this the-thing *** Joab

הָֽאֱלֹהִ֔ים לָדַ֖עַת אֶת־ כָּל־ אֲשֶׁ֥ר בָּאָֽרֶץ׃ (21) וַיֹּ֨אמֶר הַמֶּ֜לֶךְ אֶל־
to the-king and-he-said (21) in-the-land that everything *** to-know the-God

יוֹאָ֗ב הִנֵּה־ נָ֛א עָשִׂ֖יתִי אֶת־ הַדָּבָ֣ר הַזֶּ֑ה וְלֵ֕ךְ הָשֵׁ֥ב אֶת־
*** bring-back! now-go! the-this the-thing *** I-will-do-now! see! Joab

הַנַּ֖עַר אֶת־ אַבְשָׁלֽוֹם׃ (22) וַיִּפֹּ֨ל° יוֹאָ֤ב אֶל־ פָּנָיו֙ אַ֔רְצָה
to-ground faces-of-him on Joab and-he-fell (22) Absalom *** the-young-man

וַיִּשְׁתַּ֖חוּ וַיְבָ֣רֶךְ אֶת־ הַמֶּ֑לֶךְ וַיֹּ֣אמֶר יוֹאָ֗ב הַיּוֹם֩
the-day Joab and-he-said the-king *** and-he-blessed and-he-paid-honor

יָדַ֨ע עַבְדְּךָ֜ כִּֽי־ מָצָ֨אתִי חֵ֤ן בְּעֵינֶ֙יךָ֙ אֲדֹנִ֣י
lord-of-me on-eyes-of-you favor I-found that servant-of-you he-knows

הַמֶּ֔לֶךְ אֲשֶׁר־ עָשָׂ֥ה הַמֶּ֖לֶךְ אֶת־ דְּבַ֥ר עַבְדֽוֹ׃
servant-of-you request-of *** the-king he-granted that the-king

(23) וַיָּ֥קָם יוֹאָ֖ב וַיֵּ֣לֶךְ גְּשׁ֑וּרָה וַיָּ֥בֵא אֶת־אַבְשָׁל֖וֹם
Absalom *** and-he-brought-back to-Geshur and-he-went Joab then-he-rose (23)

יְרוּשָׁלָֽםִ׃ (24) וַיֹּ֤אמֶר הַמֶּ֙לֶךְ֙ יִסֹּ֣ב אֶל־ בֵּית֔וֹ וּפָנַ֖י
and-faces-of-me house-of-him to he-must-go the-king but-he-said (24) Jerusalem

לֹ֣א יִרְאֶ֑ה וַיִּסֹּ֤ב אַבְשָׁלוֹם֙ אֶל־ בֵּית֔וֹ וּפְנֵ֥י הַמֶּ֖לֶךְ
the-king and-faces-of house-of-him to Absalom so-he-went he-must-see not

לֹ֥א רָאָֽה׃ (25) וּכְאַבְשָׁל֗וֹם לֹא־ הָיָ֧ה אִישׁ־ יָפֶ֛ה בְּכָל־יִשְׂרָאֵ֖ל
Israel in-all-of handsome man-of he-was not now-as-Absalom (25) he-saw not

לְהַלֵּ֣ל מְאֹ֑ד מִכַּ֤ף רַגְלוֹ֙ וְעַ֣ד קָדְקֳד֔וֹ לֹא־ הָ֥יָה
he-was not head-of-him even-to foot-of-him from-sole-of highly to-praise

ב֖וֹ מֽוּם׃ (26) וּֽבְגַלְּח֞וֹ אֶת־ רֹאשׁ֗וֹ וְ֠הָיָה מִקֵּ֨ץ
from-end-of and-he-was head-of-him *** and-when-to-cut-him (26) blemish on-him

יָמִ֤ים ׀ לַיָּמִים֙ אֲשֶׁ֣ר יְגַלֵּ֔חַ כִּֽי־ כָבֵ֥ד עָלָ֖יו וְגִלְּח֑וֹ
then-he-cut-him on-him heavy when he-would-cut that to-the-days days

וְשָׁקַל֙ אֶת־ שְׂעַ֣ר רֹאשׁ֔וֹ מָאתַ֥יִם שְׁקָלִ֖ים בְּאֶ֥בֶן
by-standard-of shekels two-hundreds head-of-him hair-of *** and-he-would-weigh

king, no one can turn to the right or to the left from anything my lord the king says. Yes, it was your servant Joab who instructed me to do this and who put all these words into the mouth of your servant. [20]Your servant Joab did this to change the present situation. My lord has wisdom like that of an angel of God—he knows everything that happens in the land."

[21]The king said to Joab, "Very well, I will do it. Go, bring back the young man Absalom."

[22]Joab fell with his face to the ground to pay him honor, and he blessed the king. Joab said, "Today your servant knows that he has found favor in your eyes, my lord the king, because the king has granted his servant's request."

[23]Then Joab went to Geshur and brought Absalom back to Jerusalem. [24]But the king said, "He must go to his own house; he must not see my face." So Absalom went to his own house and did not see the face of the king.

[25]In all Israel there was not a man so highly praised for his handsome appearance as Absalom. From the top of his head to the sole of his foot there was no blemish in him. [26]Whenever he cut the hair of his head—he used to cut his hair from time to time when it became too heavy for him—he would weigh it, and its weight was two hundred shekels[q] by the royal standard.

[q]26 That is, about 5 pounds (about 2.3 kilograms)

°22 ק עבדך

הַמֶּלֶךְ׃ וַיִּוָּלְדוּ לְאַבְשָׁלוֹם שְׁלוֹשָׁה בָנִים וּבַת אַחַת
one and-daughter sons three to-Absalom and-they-were-born (27) the-king

וּשְׁמָהּ תָּמָר הִיא הָיְתָה אִשָּׁה יְפַת מַרְאֶה׃
appearance beautiful-of woman she-became she Tamar and-name-of-her

וַיֵּשֶׁב אַבְשָׁלוֹם בִּירוּשָׁלִַם שְׁנָתַיִם יָמִים וּפְנֵי הַמֶּלֶךְ
the-king and-faces-of days two-years in-Jerusalem Absalom and-he-lived (28)

לֹא רָאָה׃ וַיִּשְׁלַח אַבְשָׁלוֹם אֶל־יוֹאָב לִשְׁלֹחַ אֹתוֹ אֶל־הַמֶּלֶךְ וְלֹא
but-not the-king to him to-send Joab for Absalom then-he-sent (29) he-saw not

אָבָה לָבוֹא אֵלָיו וַיִּשְׁלַח עוֹד שֵׁנִית וְלֹא אָבָה לָבוֹא׃
to-come he-wanted but-not second again so-he-sent to-him to-come he-wanted

וַיֹּאמֶר אֶל־עֲבָדָיו רְאוּ חֶלְקַת יוֹאָב אֶל־יָדִי
hand-of-me at Joab field-of look! servants-of-him to then-he-said (30)

וְלוֹ־שָׁם שְׂעֹרִים לְכוּ וְהוֹצִתִיהָ בָאֵשׁ וַיַּצִּתוּ
so-they-set-on-fire with-fire and-set-on-fire-her! go! barleys there and-to-him

עַבְדֵי אַבְשָׁלוֹם אֶת־הַחֶלְקָה בָּאֵשׁ׃ וַיָּקָם יוֹאָב וַיָּבֹא
and-he-went Joab then-he-rose (31) with-fire the-field *** Absalom servants-of

אֶל־אַבְשָׁלוֹם הַבָּיְתָה וַיֹּאמֶר אֵלָיו לָמָּה הִצִּיתוּ
they-set-on-fire why? to-him and-he-said at-the-house Absalom to

עֲבָדֶיךָ אֶת־הַחֶלְקָה אֲשֶׁר־לִי בָּאֵשׁ׃ וַיֹּאמֶר אַבְשָׁלוֹם
Absalom and-he-said (32) with-fire to-me that the-field *** servant-of-you

אֶל־יוֹאָב הִנֵּה שָׁלַחְתִּי אֵלֶיךָ ׀ לֵאמֹר בֹּא הֵנָּה וְאֶשְׁלְחָה אֹתְךָ אֶל־
to you so-I-can-send to-here come! to-say to-you I-sent see! Joab to

הַמֶּלֶךְ לֵאמֹר לָמָּה בָּאתִי מִגְּשׁוּר טוֹב לִי עֹד אֲנִי־שָׁם וְעַתָּה
and-now there I still for-me better from-Geshur I-came why? to-say the-king

אֶרְאֶה פְּנֵי הַמֶּלֶךְ וְאִם־יֶשׁ־בִּי עָוֺן וֶהֱמִתָנִי׃
then-let-him-kill-me guilt in-me there-is and-if the-king faces-of I-would-see

וַיָּבֹא יוֹאָב אֶל־הַמֶּלֶךְ וַיַּגֶּד־לוֹ וַיִּקְרָא אֶל־
to then-he-summoned to-him and-he-told the-king to Joab so-he-went (33)

אַבְשָׁלוֹם וַיָּבֹא אֶל־הַמֶּלֶךְ וַיִּשְׁתַּחוּ לוֹ עַל־אַפָּיו
faces-of-him on before-him and-he-bowed the-king to and-he-came Absalom

אַרְצָה לִפְנֵי הַמֶּלֶךְ וַיִּשַּׁק הַמֶּלֶךְ לְאַבְשָׁלוֹם׃ וַיְהִי
and-he-was (15:1) on-Absalom the-king and-he-kissed the-king before to-ground

מֵאַחֲרֵי כֵן וַיַּעַשׂ לוֹ אַבְשָׁלוֹם מֶרְכָּבָה וְסֻסִים וַחֲמִשִּׁים
and-fifty and-horses chariot Absalom for-him that-he-provided this at-after

אִישׁ רָצִים לְפָנָיו׃ וְהִשְׁכִּים אַבְשָׁלוֹם וְעָמַד עַל־
by and-he-stood Absalom and-he-got-up (2) ahead-of-him ones-running man

יַד דֶּרֶךְ הַשָּׁעַר וַיְהִי כָּל־הָאִישׁ אֲשֶׁר־יִהְיֶה־לּוֹ־
to-him he-was who the-person any-of and-he-was the-gate road-of side-of

[27]Three sons and a daughter were born to Absalom. The daughter's name was Tamar, and she became a beautiful woman.

[28]Absalom lived two years in Jerusalem without seeing the king's face. [29]Then Absalom sent for Joab in order to send him to the king, but Joab refused to come to him. So he sent a second time, but he refused to come. [30]Then he said to his servants, "Look, Joab's field is next to mine, and he has barley there. Go and set it on fire." So Absalom's servants set the field on fire.

[31]Then Joab did go to Absalom's house and he said to him, "Why have your servants set my field on fire?"

[32]Absalom said to Joab, "Look, I sent word to you and said, 'Come here so I can send you to the king to ask, "Why have I come from Geshur? It would be better for me if I were still there!" ' Now then, I want to see the king's face, and if I am guilty of anything, let him put me to death."

[33]So Joab went to the king and told him this. Then the king summoned Absalom, and he came in and bowed down with his face to the ground before the king. And the king kissed Absalom.

*Absalom's Conspiracy*

15 In the course of time, Absalom provided himself with a chariot and horses and with fifty men to run ahead of him. [2]He would get up early and stand by the side of the road leading to the city gate. Whenever anyone

°30 ק והציתוה

רִיב לָבוֹא אֶל־ הַמֶּלֶךְ לַמִּשְׁפָּט וַיִּקְרָא אַבְשָׁלוֹם

Absalom then-he-called for-the-decision the-king before to-place complaint

אֵלָיו וַיֹּאמֶר אֵי־ מִזֶּה עִיר אַתָּה וַיֹּאמֶר מֵאַחַד

from-one-of and-he-answered you town from-there where? and-he-said to-him

שִׁבְטֵי־ יִשְׂרָאֵל עַבְדֶּךָ׃ וַיֹּאמֶר אֵלָיו אַבְשָׁלוֹם רְאֵה

look! Absalom to-him then-he-said (3) servant-of-you Israel tribes-of

דְבָרֶךָ טוֹבִים וּנְכֹחִים וְשֹׁמֵעַ אֵין־ לְךָ מֵאֵת

from for-you not but-one-hearing and-proper-ones valid-ones claim-of-you

הַמֶּלֶךְ׃ וַיֹּאמֶר אַבְשָׁלוֹם מִי־ יְשִׂמֵנִי שֹׁפֵט

one-judging he-appointed-me if-only Absalom and-he-said (4) the-king

בָּאָרֶץ וְעָלַי יָבוֹא כָּל־ אִישׁ אֲשֶׁר־ יִהְיֶה־ לּוֹ־

to-him he-is who person every-of he-could-come then-to-me in-the-land

רִיב וּמִשְׁפָּט וְהִצְדַּקְתִּיו׃ וְהָיָה

and-he-was (5) then-I-would-bring-justice-to-him or-case complaint

בִּקְרָב־ אִישׁ לְהִשְׁתַּחֲוֹת לוֹ וְשָׁלַח אֶת־ יָדוֹ

hand-of-him *** then-he-reached-out before-him to-bow anyone when-to-approach

וְהֶחֱזִיק לוֹ וְנָשַׁק לוֹ׃ וַיַּעַשׂ אַבְשָׁלוֹם

Absalom and-he-behaved (6) on-him and-he-kissed of-him and-he-took-hold

כַּדָּבָר הַזֶּה לְכָל־ יִשְׂרָאֵל אֲשֶׁר־ יָבֹאוּ לַמִּשְׁפָּט אֶל־

to for-the-justice they-came who Israel to-all-of the-this in-the-way

הַמֶּלֶךְ וַיְגַנֵּב אַבְשָׁלוֹם אֶת־ לֵב אַנְשֵׁי יִשְׂרָאֵל׃ וַיְהִי

and-he-was (7) Israel men-of heart-of *** Absalom so-he-stole the-king

מִקֵּץ אַרְבָּעִים שָׁנָה וַיֹּאמֶר אַבְשָׁלוֹם אֶל־ הַמֶּלֶךְ אֵלְכָה נָּא

now! let-me-go the-king to Absalom then-he-said year forty at-end-of

וַאֲשַׁלֵּם* אֶת־ נִדְרִי אֲשֶׁר־ נָדַרְתִּי לַיהוָה בְּחֶבְרוֹן׃ כִּי־

for (8) to-Hebron to-Yahweh I-made that vow-of-me *** and-let-me-fulfill

נֵדֶר נָדַר עַבְדְּךָ בְּשִׁבְתִּי בִגְשׁוּר בַּאֲרָם לֵאמֹר אִם־

if to-say in-Aram at-Geshur while-to-live-me servant-of-you he-made vow

יָשׁוֹב° יְשִׁיבֵנִי יְהוָה יְרוּשָׁלַם וְעָבַדְתִּי אֶת־

*** then-I-will-worship Jerusalem Yahweh he-takes-back-me to-take-back

יְהוָה׃ וַיֹּאמֶר־ לוֹ הַמֶּלֶךְ לֵךְ בְּשָׁלוֹם וַיָּקָם וַיֵּלֶךְ

and-he-went so-he-rose in-peace go! the-king to-him and-he-said (9) Yahweh

חֶבְרוֹנָה׃ וַיִּשְׁלַח אַבְשָׁלוֹם מְרַגְּלִים בְּכָל־

through-all-of ones-bringing-message Absalom then-he-sent (10) to-Hebron

שִׁבְטֵי יִשְׂרָאֵל לֵאמֹר כְּשָׁמְעֲכֶם אֶת־ קוֹל הַשֹּׁפָר וַאֲמַרְתֶּם

then-you-say the-trumpet sound-of *** as-to-hear-you to-say Israel tribes-of

מָלַךְ אַבְשָׁלוֹם בְּחֶבְרוֹן׃ וְאֶת־ אַבְשָׁלוֹם הָלְכוּ

they-accompanied Absalom and-with (11) in-Hebron Absalom he-is-king

came with a complaint to be placed before the king for a decision, Absalom would call out to him, "What town are you from?" He would answer, "Your servant is from one of the tribes of Israel." 3Then Absalom would say to him, "Look, your claims are valid and proper, but there is no representative of the king to hear you." 4And Absalom would add, "If only I were appointed judge in the land! Then everyone who has a complaint or case could come to me and I would see that he gets justice."

5Also, whenever anyone approached him to bow down before him, Absalom would reach out his hand, take hold of him and kiss him. 6Absalom behaved in this way toward all the Israelites who came to the king asking for justice, and so he stole the hearts of the men of Israel.

7At the end of four[r] years, Absalom said to the king, "Let me go to Hebron and fulfill a vow I made to the LORD. 8While your servant was living at Geshur in Aram, I made this vow: 'If the LORD takes me back to Jerusalem, I will worship the LORD in Hebron.[s]' "

9The king said to him, "Go in peace." So he went to Hebron.

10Then Absalom sent secret messengers throughout the tribes of Israel to say, "As soon as you hear the sound of the trumpets, then say, 'Absalom is king in Hebron.' " 11Two hundred men from Jerusalem had accompanied Absalom.

r7 Some Septuagint manuscripts, Syriac and Josephus; Hebrew *forty*
s8 Some Septuagint manuscripts; Hebrew does not have *in Hebron*.

*7 Most mss have the accent *darga* ( וַאֲשַׁלֵּם ).

°8 ק ישוב

מָאתַיִם אִישׁ מִירוּשָׁלַ͏ִם קְרֻאִים וְהֹלְכִים
and-ones-going ones-being-invited from-Jerusalem man two-hundreds

לְתֻמָּם וְלֹא יָדְעוּ כָּל־ דָּבָר׃ (12) וַיִּשְׁלַח אַבְשָׁלוֹם
Absalom and-he-sent (12) matter any-of they-knew and-not in-innocence-of-them

אֶת־ אֲחִיתֹפֶל הַגִּילֹנִי יוֹעֵץ דָּוִד מֵעִירוֹ
from-town-of-him David one-counselling-of the-Gilonite Ahithophel ***

מִגִּלֹה בְּזָבְחוֹ אֶת־ הַזְּבָחִים וַיְהִי הַקֶּשֶׁר
the-conspiracy and-he-became the-sacrifices *** while-to-offer-him from-Giloh

אַמִּץ וְהָעָם הוֹלֵךְ וָרָב אֶת־ אַבְשָׁלוֹם׃ (13) וַיָּבֹא
and-he-came (13) Absalom with and-great increasing and-the-people strong

הַמַּגִּיד אֶל־ דָּוִד לֵאמֹר הָיָה לֶב־ אִישׁ יִשְׂרָאֵל אַחֲרֵי
with Israel man-of heart-of he-is to-say David to the-one-bringing-message

אַבְשָׁלוֹם׃ (14) וַיֹּאמֶר דָּוִד לְכָל־ עֲבָדָיו אֲשֶׁר־ אִתּוֹ
with-him who officials-of-him to-all-of David then-he-said (14) Absalom

בִירוּשָׁלַ͏ִם קוּמוּ וְנִבְרָחָה כִּי לֹא־ תִהְיֶה־ לָּנוּ פְלֵיטָה
escape for-us she-will-be not or now-we-must-flee come! in-Jerusalem

מִפְּנֵי אַבְשָׁלֹם מַהֲרוּ לָלֶכֶת פֶּן־ יְמַהֵר
he-will-move-quickly or to-leave be-immediate! Absalom from-before

וְהִשִּׂגֻנוּ וְהִדִּיחַ עָלֵינוּ אֶת־ הָרָעָה וְהִכָּה
and-he-will-put the-ruin *** on-us and-he-will-bring and-he-will-overtake-us

הָעִיר לְפִי־ חָרֶב׃ (15) וַיֹּאמְרוּ עַבְדֵי־ הַמֶּלֶךְ אֶל־
to the-king officials-of and-they-answered (15) sword to-edge-of the-city

הַמֶּלֶךְ כְּכֹל אֲשֶׁר־ יִבְחַר אֲדֹנִי הַמֶּלֶךְ הִנֵּה עֲבָדֶיךָ׃
servants-of-you see! the-king lord-of-me he-chooses that as-all the-king

(16) וַיֵּצֵא הַמֶּלֶךְ וְכָל־ בֵּיתוֹ בְּרַגְלָיו
at-feet-of-him household-of-him and-entire-of the-king and-he-set-out (16)

וַיַּעֲזֹב הַמֶּלֶךְ אֵת עֶשֶׂר נָשִׁים פִּלַגְשִׁים לִשְׁמֹר הַבָּיִת׃
the-palace to-take-care-of concubines women ten *** the-king but-he-left

(17) וַיֵּצֵא הַמֶּלֶךְ וְכָל־ הָעָם בְּרַגְלָיו
at-feet-of-him the-people and-all-of the-king so-he-set-out (17)

וַיַּעַמְדוּ בֵּית הַמֶּרְחָק׃ (18) וְכָל־ עֲבָדָיו עֹבְרִים
ones-passing men-of-him and-all-of (18) the-distance place-of and-they-halted

עַל־ יָדוֹ וְכָל־ הַכְּרֵתִי וְכָל־ הַפְּלֵתִי וְכָל־
and-all-of the-Pelethite and-all-of the-Kerethite and-all-of hand-of-him under

הַגִּתִּים שֵׁשׁ־ מֵאוֹת אִישׁ אֲשֶׁר־ בָּאוּ בְרַגְלוֹ מִגַּת
from-Gath at-feet-of-him they-came who man hundreds six the-Gittites

עֹבְרִים עַל־ פְּנֵי הַמֶּלֶךְ׃ (19) וַיֹּאמֶר הַמֶּלֶךְ אֶל־ אִתַּי
Ittai to the-king and-he-said (19) the-king faces-of before ones-marching

They had been invited as guests and went quite innocently, knowing nothing about the matter.
12 While Absalom was offering sacrifices, he also sent for Ahithophel the Gilonite, David's counselor, to come from Giloh, his home town. And so the conspiracy gained strength, and Absalom's following kept on increasing.

*David Flees*

13 A messenger came and told David, "The hearts of the men of Israel are with Absalom."
14 Then David said to all his officials who were with him in Jerusalem, "Come! We must flee, or none of us will escape from Absalom. We must leave immediately, or he will move quickly to overtake us and bring ruin upon us and put the city to the sword."
15 The king's officials answered him, "Your servants are ready to do whatever our lord the king chooses."
16 The king set out, with his entire household following him; but he left ten concubines to take care of the palace.
17 So the king set out, with all the people following him, and they halted at a place some distance away.
18 All his men marched past him, along with all the Kerethites and Pelethites; and all the six hundred Gittites who had accompanied him from Gath marched before the king.
19 The king said to Ittai the

הַגִּתִּי לָמָּה תֵלֵךְ גַּם־אַתָּה אִתָּנוּ שׁוּב וְשֵׁב עִם־הַמֶּלֶךְ
the-king with and-stay! go-back! with-us you indeed you-go why? the-Gittite

כִּי־נָכְרִי אַתָּה וְגַם־גֹּלֶה אַתָּה לִמְקוֹמֶךָ׃
from-homeland-of-you you one-being-exiled and-also you foreigner for

תְּמוֹל ׀ בּוֹאֶךָ וְהַיּוֹם אֲנִוֹעֲךָ עִמָּנוּ לָלֶכֶת
to-go with-us shall-I-make-wander-you and-the-day to-come-you yesterday (20)

וַאֲנִי הוֹלֵךְ עַל אֲשֶׁר־אֲנִי הוֹלֵךְ שׁוּב וְהָשֵׁב אֶת־אַחֶיךָ
countrymen-of-you *** and-take! go-back! going I where to going when-I

עִמָּךְ חֶסֶד וֶאֱמֶת׃ וַיַּעַן אִתַּי אֶת־הַמֶּלֶךְ
the-king *** Ittai but-he-replied (21) and-faithfulness kindness with-you

וַיֹּאמַר חַי־יְהוָה וְחֵי אֲדֹנִי הַמֶּלֶךְ כִּי אִם־
*whether indeed the-king lord-of-me and-life-of Yahweh life-of and-he-said

בִּמְקוֹם אֲשֶׁר יִהְיֶה־שָּׁם ׀ אֲדֹנִי הַמֶּלֶךְ אִם־לְמָוֶת אִם־
or for-death whether the-king lord-of-me there he-may-be where in-place-of

לְחַיִּים כִּי־שָׁם יִהְיֶה עַבְדֶּךָ׃ וַיֹּאמֶר דָּוִד אֶל־
to David and-he-said (22) servant-of-you he-will-be there indeed for-lives

אִתַּי לֵךְ וַעֲבֹר וַיַּעֲבֹר אִתַּי הַגִּתִּי וְכָל־
and-all-of the-Gittite Ittai so-he-marched-on and-march-on! go! Ittai

אֲנָשָׁיו וְכָל־הַטַּף אֲשֶׁר אִתּוֹ׃ וְכָל־הָאָרֶץ
the-country and-whole-of (23) with-him that the-family and-all-of men-of-him

בּוֹכִים קוֹל גָּדוֹל וְכָל־הָעָם עֹבְרִים וְהַמֶּלֶךְ
and-the-king ones-passing-by the-people as-all-of loud voice ones-weeping

עֹבֵר בְּנַחַל קִדְרוֹן וְכָל־הָעָם עֹבְרִים עַל־
toward ones-moving-on the-people and-all-of Kidron over-Valley-of crossing

פְּנֵי־דֶרֶךְ אֶת־הַמִּדְבָּר׃ וְהִנֵּה גַם־צָדוֹק וְכָל־הַלְוִיִּם
the-Levites and-all-of Zadok also and-see! (24) the-desert *** road surfaces-of

אִתּוֹ נֹשְׂאִים אֶת־אֲרוֹן בְּרִית הָאֱלֹהִים וַיַּצִּקוּ אֶת־
*** and-they-set-down the-God covenant-of ark-of *** ones-carrying with-him

אֲרוֹן הָאֱלֹהִים וַיַּעַל אֶבְיָתָר עַד־תֹּם כָּל־הָעָם
the-people all-of to-finish until Abiathar and-he-sacrificed the-God ark-of

לַעֲבוֹר מִן־הָעִיר׃ וַיֹּאמֶר הַמֶּלֶךְ לְצָדוֹק הָשֵׁב אֶת־
*** take-back! to-Zadok the-king then-he-said (25) the-city from to-leave

אֲרוֹן הָאֱלֹהִים הָעִיר אִם־אֶמְצָא חֵן בְּעֵינֵי יְהוָה וֶהֱשִׁבַנִי
then-he-will-return-me Yahweh in-eyes-of favor I-find if the-city the-God ark-of

וְהִרְאַנִי אֹתוֹ וְאֶת־נָוֵהוּ׃ וְאִם כֹּה יֹאמַר לֹא
not he-says this but-if (26) dwelling-of-him and him and-he-will-let-see-me

חָפַצְתִּי בָּךְ הִנְנִי יַעֲשֶׂה־לִּי כַּאֲשֶׁר טוֹב בְּעֵינָיו׃
in-eyes-of-him good just-as to-me let-him-do see-I! with-you I-am-pleased

Gittite, "Why should you
come along with us? Go back
and stay with King Absalom.
You are a foreigner, an exile
from your homeland. [20]You
came only yesterday. And today shall I make you wander
about with us, when I do not
know where I am going? Go
back, and take your countrymen. May kindness and faithfulness be with you."
[21]But Ittai replied to the king,
"As surely as the LORD lives,
and as my lord the king lives,
wherever my lord the king
may be, whether it means life
or death, there will your servant be."
[22]David said to Ittai, "Go
ahead, march on." So Ittai the
Gittite marched on with all his
men and the families that
were with him.
[23]The whole countryside
wept aloud as all the people
passed by. The king also
crossed the Kidron Valley, and
all the people moved on
toward the desert.
[24]Zadok was there, too, and
all the Levites who were with
him were carrying the ark of
the covenant of God. They set
down the ark of God, and
Abiathar offered sacrifices[t]
until all the people had
finished leaving the city.
[25]Then the king said to
Zadok, "Take the ark of God
back into the city. If I find favor in the LORD's eyes, he will
bring me back and let me see
it and his dwelling place
again. [26]But if he says, 'I am
not pleased with you,' then I
am ready; let him do to me
whatever seems good to him."

[t]24 Or *Abiathar went up*

***21 Most mss eliminate this word from the text in a *Qere* reading or omit it without a note.**

°20 ק אניעך

וַיֹּאמֶר הַמֶּלֶךְ אֶל־ צָדוֹק הַכֹּהֵן הֲרוֹאֶה אַתָּה שֻׁבָה הָעִיר
the-city go-back! you seer? the-priest Zadok to the-king and-he-said (27)

בְּשָׁלוֹם וַאֲחִימַעַץ בִּנְךָ וִיהוֹנָתָן בֶּן־ אֶבְיָתָר שְׁנֵי
two-of Abiathar son-of and-Jonathan son-of-you and-Ahimaaz in-peace

בְנֵיכֶם אִתְּכֶם׃ רְאוּ אָנֹכִי מִתְמַהְמֵהַּ בְּעַבְרוֹת הַמִּדְבָּר עַד בּוֹא
to-come until the-desert at-fords-of waiting I see! (28) with-you sons-of-you

דָבָר מֵעִמָּכֶם לְהַגִּיד לִי׃ וַיָּשֶׁב צָדוֹק וְאֶבְיָתָר
and-Abiathar Zadok so-he-took-back (29) to-me to-inform from-with-you word

אֶת־אֲרוֹן הָאֱלֹהִים יְרוּשָׁלָםִ וַיֵּשְׁבוּ שָׁם׃ וְדָוִד עֹלֶה
going-up but-David (30) there and-they-stayed Jerusalem the-God ark-of ***

בְמַעֲלֵה הַזֵּיתִים עֹלֶה ׀ וּבוֹכֶה וְרֹאשׁ לוֹ חָפוּי
being-covered on-him and-head and-weeping going the-Olives on-Mount-of

וְהוּא הֹלֵךְ יָחֵף וְכָל־ הָעָם אֲשֶׁר־ אִתּוֹ חָפוּ אִישׁ
each they-covered with-him who the-people and-all-of barefoot walking and-he

רֹאשׁוֹ וְעָלוּ עָלֹה וּבָכֹה׃ וְדָוִד הִגִּיד
he-told now-David (31) and-to-weep to-go-up and-they-went-up head-of-him

לֵאמֹר אֲחִיתֹפֶל בַּקֹּשְׁרִים עִם־ אַבְשָׁלוֹם וַיֹּאמֶר דָּוִד
David so-he-prayed Absalom with among-the-ones-conspiring Ahithophel to-say

סַכֶּל־ נָא אֶת־ עֲצַת אֲחִיתֹפֶל יְהוָה׃ וַיְהִי דָוִד
David when-he-was (32) Yahweh Ahithophel counsel-of *** now! turn-foolish!

בָּא עַד־ הָרֹאשׁ אֲשֶׁר־ יִשְׁתַּחֲוֶה שָׁם לֵאלֹהִים וְהִנֵּה לִקְרָאתוֹ
to-meet-him then-see! to-God there he-worshiped where the-summit at arriving

חוּשַׁי הָאַרְכִּי קָרוּעַ כֻּתָּנְתּוֹ וַאֲדָמָה עַל־ רֹאשׁוֹ׃
head-of-him on and-dust robe-of-him being-torn the-Arkite Hushai

וַיֹּאמֶר לוֹ דָּוִד אִם עָבַרְתָּ אִתִּי וְהָיִתָ עָלַי
to-me then-you-will-be with-me you-go if David to-him and-he-said (33)

לְמַשָּׂא׃ וְאִם־ הָעִיר תָּשׁוּב וְאָמַרְתָּ לְאַבְשָׁלוֹם
to-Absalom and-you-say you-return the-city but-if (34) as-burden

עַבְדְּךָ אֲנִי הַמֶּלֶךְ אֶהְיֶה עֶבֶד אָבִיךָ וַאֲנִי מֵאָז
in-past also-I father-of-you servant-of I-will-be the-king I servant-of-you

וְעַתָּה וַאֲנִי עַבְדֶּךָ וְהֵפַרְתָּה לִי אֵת עֲצַת
advice-of *** for-me then-you-can-frustrate servant-of-you also-I but-now

אֲחִיתֹפֶל׃ וַהֲלוֹא עִמְּךָ שָׁם צָדוֹק וְאֶבְיָתָר הַכֹּהֲנִים
the-priests and-Abiathar Zadok there with-you and-not? (35) Ahithophel

וְהָיָה כָּל־ הַדָּבָר אֲשֶׁר תִּשְׁמַע מִבֵּית הַמֶּלֶךְ תַּגִּיד
you-tell the-king in-palace-of you-hear that the-thing any-of and-he-will-be

לְצָדוֹק וּלְאֶבְיָתָר הַכֹּהֲנִים׃ הִנֵּה־ שָׁם עִמָּם שְׁנֵי
two-of with-them there see! (36) the-priests and-to-Abiathar to-Zadok

27 The king also said to Zadok the priest, "Aren't you a seer? Go back to the city in peace, with your son Ahimaaz and Jonathan son of Abiathar. You and Abiathar take your two sons with you. 28 I will wait at the fords in the desert until word comes from you to inform me." 29 So Zadok and Abiathar took the ark of God back to Jerusalem and stayed there.

30 But David continued up the Mount of Olives, weeping as he went; his head was covered and he was barefoot. All the people with him covered their heads too and were weeping as they went up. 31 Now David had been told, "Ahithophel is among the conspirators with Absalom." So David prayed, "O LORD, turn Ahithophel's counsel into foolishness."

32 When David arrived at the summit, where people used to worship God, Hushai the Arkite was there to meet him, his robe torn and dust on his head. 33 David said to him, "If you go with me, you will be a burden to me. 34 But if you return to the city and say to Absalom, 'I will be your servant, O king; I was your father's servant in the past, but now I will be your servant,' then you can help me by frustrating Ahithophel's advice. 35 Won't the priests Zadok and Abiathar be there with you? Tell them anything you hear in the king's

°28 ק בערבות

בְּנֵיהֶם אֲחִימַעַץ לְצָדוֹק וִיהוֹנָתָן לְאֶבְיָתָר וּשְׁלַחְתֶּם
and-you-send of-Abiathar and-Jonathan of-Zadok Ahimaaz sons-of-them

בְּיָדָם אֵלַי כָּל־ דָּבָר אֲשֶׁר תִּשְׁמָעוּ׃ וַיָּבֹא חוּשַׁי
Hushai so-he-arrived (37) you-hear that thing any-of to-me by-hand-of-them

רֵעֶה דָוִד הָעִיר וְאַבְשָׁלֹם יָבֹא יְרוּשָׁלִָם׃ וְדָוִד
when-David (16:1) Jerusalem he-entered and-Absalom the-city David friend-of

עָבַר מְעַט מֵהָרֹאשׁ וְהִנֵּה צִיבָא נַעַר מְפִי־ בֹשֶׁת
Bosheth Mephi steward-of Ziba then-see! from-the-summit little he-went-beyond

לִקְרָאתוֹ וְצֶמֶד חֲמֹרִים חֲבֻשִׁים וַעֲלֵיהֶם מָאתַיִם
two-hundreds and-on-them ones-being-saddled donkeys and-string-of to-meet-him

לֶחֶם וּמֵאָה צִמּוּקִים וּמֵאָה קַיִץ וְנֵבֶל יָיִן׃
wine and-skin-of fig-cake and-hundred raisin-cakes and-hundred bread

וַיֹּאמֶר הַמֶּלֶךְ אֶל־ צִיבָא מָה־ אֵלֶּה לָּךְ וַיֹּאמֶר צִיבָא
Ziba and-he-answered with-you these why? Ziba to the-king and-he-asked (2)

הַחֲמוֹרִים לְבֵית־ הַמֶּלֶךְ לִרְכֹּב וּלְהַלֶּחֶם וְהַקַּיִץ
and-the-fruit and-the-bread to-ride the-king for-household-of the-donkeys

לֶאֱכוֹל הַנְּעָרִים וְהַיַּיִן לִשְׁתּוֹת הַיָּעֵף בַּמִּדְבָּר׃
in-the-desert the-one-exhausted to-refresh and-the-wine the-men to-eat

וַיֹּאמֶר הַמֶּלֶךְ וְאַיֵּה בֶּן־ אֲדֹנֶיךָ וַיֹּאמֶר צִיבָא
Ziba and-he-said masters-of-you son-of and-where? the-king then-he-asked (3)

אֶל־הַמֶּלֶךְ הִנֵּה יוֹשֵׁב בִּירוּשָׁלִַם כִּי אָמַר הַיּוֹם יָשִׁיבוּ
they-will-give-back the-day he-thinks for in-Jerusalem staying see! the-king to

לִי בֵּית יִשְׂרָאֵל אֵת מַמְלְכוּת אָבִי׃ וַיֹּאמֶר הַמֶּלֶךְ
the-king then-he-said (4) father-of-me kingdom-of *** Israel house-of to-me

לְצִבָא הִנֵּה לְךָ כֹּל אֲשֶׁר לִמְפִי־ בֹשֶׁת וַיֹּאמֶר צִיבָא הִשְׁתַּחֲוֵיתִי
I-humbly-bow Ziba and-he-said Bosheth to-Mephi that all to-you see! to-Ziba

אֶמְצָא־ חֵן בְּעֵינֶיךָ אֲדֹנִי הַמֶּלֶךְ׃ וּבָא
as-he-approached (5) the-king lord-of-me in-eyes-of-you favor may-I-find

הַמֶּלֶךְ דָּוִד עַד־בַּחוּרִים וְהִנֵּה מִשָּׁם אִישׁ יוֹצֵא מִמִּשְׁפַּחַת
from-clan-of coming-out man from-there then-see! Bahurim to David the-king

בֵּית־ שָׁאוּל וּשְׁמוֹ שִׁמְעִי בֶן־ גֵּרָא יֹצֵא יָצוֹא
to-come-out coming-out Gera son-of Shimei and-name-of-him Saul house-of

וּמְקַלֵּל׃ וַיְסַקֵּל בָּאֲבָנִים אֶת־ דָּוִד וְאֶת־ כָּל־ עַבְדֵי
officials-of all-of and David *** with-the-stones and-he-pelted (6) and-cursing

הַמֶּלֶךְ דָּוִד וְכָל־ הָעָם וְכָל־ הַגִּבֹּרִים מִימִינוֹ
on-right-of-him the-guards and-all-of the-troop though-all-of David the-king

וּמִשְּׂמֹאלוֹ׃ וְכֹה־ אָמַר שִׁמְעִי בְּקַלְלוֹ צֵא
get-out! as-to-curse-him Shimei he-said and-this (7) and-on-left-of-him

palace. [36]Their two sons, Ahimaaz son of Zadok and Jonathan son of Abiathar, are there
with them. Send them to me
with anything you hear."
[37]So David's friend Hushai
arrived at Jerusalem as Absalom was entering the city.

*David and Ziba*

16 When David had gone
a short distance
beyond the summit, there was
Ziba, the steward of Me-
phibosheth, waiting to meet
him. He had a string of donkeys saddled and loaded with
two hundred loaves of bread, a
hundred cakes of raisins, a
hundred cakes of figs and a
skin of wine.
[2]The king asked Ziba, "Why
have you brought these?"
Ziba answered, "The don-
keys are for the king's
household to ride on, the
bread and fruit are for the men
to eat, and the wine is to refresh those who become exhausted in the desert."
[3]The king then asked,
"Where is your master's
grandson?"
Ziba said to him, "He is
staying in Jerusalem, because
he thinks, 'Today the house of
Israel will give me back my
grandfather's kingdom.'"
[4]Then the king said to Ziba,
"All that belonged to Me-
phibosheth is now yours."
"I humbly bow," Ziba said.
"May I find favor in your eyes,
my lord the king."

*Shimei Curses David*

[5]As King David approached
Bahurim, a man from the
same clan as Saul's family
came out from there. His
name was Shimei son of Gera,
and he cursed as he came out.
[6]He pelted David and all the
king's officials with stones,
though all the troops and the
special guard were on David's
right and left. [7]As he cursed,
Shimei said, "Get out, get out,

°2 ק והלחם

צֵא אִישׁ הַדָּמִים וְאִישׁ הַבְּלִיָּעַל׃ הֵשִׁיב עָלֶיךָ
to-you he-repaid (8) the-worthless and-man-of the-bloods man-of get-out!

יְהוָה כֹּל ׀ דְּמֵי בֵית־ שָׁאוּל אֲשֶׁר מָלַכְתָּ תַּחְתָּו
in-place-of-him you-reigned who Saul household-of bloods-of all-of Yahweh

וַיִּתֵּן יְהוָה אֶת־ הַמְּלוּכָה בְּיַד אַבְשָׁלוֹם בְּנֶךָ
son-of-you Absalom into-hand-of the-kingdom *** Yahweh and-he-handed

וְהִנְּךָ בְּרָעָתֶךָ כִּי אִישׁ דָּמִים אָתָּה׃ וַיֹּאמֶר אֲבִישַׁי
Abishai then-he-said (9) you bloods man-of for in-ruin-of-you and-see-you!

בֶן־ צְרוּיָה אֶל־ הַמֶּלֶךְ לָמָּה יְקַלֵּל הַכֶּלֶב הַמֵּת הַזֶּה
the-this the-dead the-dog should-he-curse why? the-king to Zeruiah son-of

אֶת־ אֲדֹנִי הַמֶּלֶךְ אֶעְבְּרָה־ נָּא וְאָסִירָה אֶת־ רֹאשׁוֹ׃
head-of-him *** and-let-me-cut-off now! let-me-go-over the-king lord-of-me ***

וַיֹּאמֶר הַמֶּלֶךְ מַה־ לִּי וְלָכֶם בְּנֵי צְרֻיָה כֹּי
so Zeruiah sons-of and-to-you to-me what? the-king but-he-said (10)

יְקַלֵּל וְכִּי יְהוָה אָמַר לוֹ קַלֵּל אֶת־ דָּוִד וּמִי יֹאמַר
he-can-ask and-who? David *** curse! to-him he-said Yahweh if he-may-curse

מַדּוּעַ עָשִׂיתָה כֵּן׃ וַיֹּאמֶר דָּוִד אֶל־ אֲבִישַׁי וְאֶל־ כָּל־
all-of and-to Abishai to David then-he-said (11) this you-do why?

עֲבָדָיו הִנֵּה בְנִי אֲשֶׁר־ יָצָא מִמֵּעַי מְבַקֵּשׁ אֶת־
*** seeking from-flesh-of-me he-came who son-of-me see! officials-of-him

נַפְשִׁי וְאַף כִּי־ עַתָּה בֶּן־הַיְמִינִי הַנִּחוּ לוֹ
to-him leave-alone! the-Benjamite now indeed and-more life-of-me

וִיקַלֵּל כִּי אָמַר־ לוֹ יְהוָה׃ אוּלַי יִרְאֶה יְהוָה
Yahweh he-will-see perhaps (12) Yahweh to-him he-told for and-let-him-curse

בְּעוֹנִי וְהֵשִׁיב יְהוָה לִי טוֹבָה תַּחַת קִלְלָתוֹ
curse-of-him for good to-me Yahweh and-he-will-repay to-distress-of-me

הַיּוֹם הַזֶּה׃ וַיֵּלֶךְ דָּוִד וַאֲנָשָׁיו בַּדָּרֶךְ
along-the-road and-men-of-him David so-he-went (13) the-this the-day

וְשִׁמְעִי הֹלֵךְ בְּצֵלַע הָהָר לְעֻמָּתוֹ הָלוֹךְ וַיְקַלֵּל
and-he-cursed to-go at-opposite-of-him the-hill along-side-of going and-Shimei

וַיְסַקֵּל בָּאֲבָנִים לְעֻמָּתוֹ וְעִפַּר בֶּעָפָר׃
with-the-dirt and-he-showered at-side-of-him with-the-stones and-he-pelted

וַיָּבֹא הַמֶּלֶךְ וְכָל־ הָעָם אֲשֶׁר־ אִתּוֹ עֲיֵפִים
ones-exhausted with-him who the-people and-all-of the-king and-he-arrived (14)

וַיִּנָּפֵשׁ שָׁם׃ וְאַבְשָׁלוֹם וְכָל־ הָעָם אִישׁ
man-of the-people and-all-of now-Absalom (15) there and-he-refreshed-himself

יִשְׂרָאֵל בָּאוּ יְרוּשָׁלִָם וַאֲחִיתֹפֶל אִתּוֹ׃ וַיְהִי כַּאֲשֶׁר־
just-then and-he-was (16) with-him and-Ahithophel Jerusalem they-came Israel

you man of blood, you scoundrel! [8]The LORD has repaid you for all the blood you shed in the household of Saul, in whose place you have reigned. The LORD has handed the kingdom over to your son Absalom. You have come to ruin because you are a man of blood!"

[9]Then Abishai son of Zeruiah said to the king, "Why should this dead dog curse my lord the king? Let me go over and cut off his head."

[10]But the king said, "What do you and I have in common, you sons of Zeruiah? If he is cursing because the LORD said to him, 'Curse David,' who can ask, 'Why do you do this?' "

[11]David then said to Abishai and all his officials, "My son, who is of my own flesh, is trying to take my life. How much more, then, this Benjamite! Leave him alone; let him curse, for the LORD has told him to. [12]It may be that the LORD will see my distress and repay me with good for the cursing I am receiving today."

[13]So David and his men continued along the road while Shimei was going along the hillside opposite him, cursing as he went and throwing stones at him and showering him with dirt. [14]The king and all the people with him arrived at their destination exhausted. And there he refreshed himself.

*The Advice of Hushai and Ahithophel*

[15]Meanwhile, Absalom and all the men of Israel came to Jerusalem, and Ahithophel was with him. [16]Then Hushai

°8 ק תחתיו
°10a ק כה
°10b ק כי
°12 ק בעיני

בָּא חוּשַׁי הָאַרְכִּי רֵעֶה דָוִד אֶל־אַבְשָׁלֹם וַיֹּאמֶר חוּשַׁי אֶל־
to Hushai and-he-said Absalom to David friend-of the-Arkite Hushai he-went

אַבְשָׁלֹם יְחִי הַמֶּלֶךְ יְחִי הַמֶּלֶךְ׃ וַיֹּאמֶר אַבְשָׁלוֹם
Absalom and-he-asked (17) the-king may-he-live the-king may-he-live Absalom

אֶל־חוּשַׁי זֶה חַסְדְּךָ אֶת־רֵעֶךָ לָמָּה לֹא־הָלַכְתָּ אֶת־
with you-went not why? friend-of-you for love-of-you this Hushai to

רֵעֶךָ׃ וַיֹּאמֶר חוּשַׁי אֶל־אַבְשָׁלֹם לֹא כִּי אֲשֶׁר בָּחַר יְהוָה
Yahweh he-chose whom for no Absalom to Hushai and-he-said (18) friend-of-you

וְהָעָם הַזֶּה וְכָל־אִישׁ יִשְׂרָאֵל לֹא אֶהְיֶה וְאִתּוֹ
and-with-him I-will-be to-him Israel man-of and-all-of the-this and-the-people

אֵשֵׁב׃ וְהַשֵּׁנִית לְמִי אֲנִי אֶעֱבֹד הֲלוֹא לִפְנֵי
before not? I-should-serve I to-whom? and-the-further (19) I-will-remain

בְנוֹ כַּאֲשֶׁר עָבַדְתִּי לִפְנֵי אָבִיךָ כֵּן אֶהְיֶה לְפָנֶיךָ׃
before-you I-will-be so father-of-you before I-served just-as son-of-him

וַיֹּאמֶר אַבְשָׁלֹום אֶל־אֲחִיתֹפֶל הָבוּ לָכֶם עֵצָה מַה־נַּעֲשֶׂה׃
should-we-do what? advice for-you give! Ahithophel to Absalom and-he-said (20)

וַיֹּאמֶר אֲחִיתֹפֶל אֶל־אַבְשָׁלֹם בּוֹא אֶל־פִּלַגְשֵׁי אָבִיךָ
father-of-you concubines-of into go! Absalom to Ahithophel and-he-answered (21)

אֲשֶׁר הִנִּיחַ לִשְׁמוֹר הַבָּיִת וְשָׁמַע כָּל־יִשְׂרָאֵל כִּי־
that Israel all-of then-he-will-hear the-palace to-care-for he-left whom

נִבְאַשְׁתָּ אֶת־אָבִיךָ וְחָזְקוּ
and-they-will-become-strong father-of-you *** you-made-yourself-stench

יְדֵי כָּל־אֲשֶׁר אִתָּךְ׃ וַיַּטּוּ לְאַבְשָׁלוֹם הָאֹהֶל עַל־
on the-tent for-Absalom so-they-pitched (22) with-you who all hands-of

הַגָּג וַיָּבֹא אַבְשָׁלוֹם אֶל־פִּלַגְשֵׁי אָבִיו לְעֵינֵי
before-eyes-of father-of-him concubines-of into Absalom and-he-went the-roof

כָּל־יִשְׂרָאֵל׃ וַעֲצַת אֲחִיתֹפֶל אֲשֶׁר יָעַץ בַּיָּמִים הָהֵם
the-those in-the-days he-gave that Ahithophel now-advice-of (23) Israel all-of

כַּאֲשֶׁר יִשְׁאַל־ * בִּדְבַר הָאֱלֹהִים כֵּן כָּל־עֲצַת אֲחִיתֹפֶל
Ahithophel advice-of all-of so the-God of-word-of * he-inquired like-that

גַּם־לְדָוִד גַּם לְאַבְשָׁלֹם׃ וַיֹּאמֶר אֲחִיתֹפֶל אֶל־אַבְשָׁלֹם
Absalom to Ahithophel and-he-said (17:1) to-Absalom and to-David both

אֶבְחֲרָה נָּא שְׁנֵים־עָשָׂר אֶלֶף אִישׁ וְאָקוּמָה וְאֶרְדְּפָה
and-let-me-pursue and-let-me-rise man thousand ten two now! let-me-choose

אַחֲרֵי־דָוִד הַלָּיְלָה׃ וְאָבוֹא עָלָיו וְהוּא יָגֵעַ
weary while-he against-him and-let-me-attack (2) the-night David after

וּרְפֵה יָדַיִם וְהַחֲרַדְתִּי אֹתוֹ וְנָס כָּל־הָעָם
the-people all-of and-he-will-flee him and-I-will-terrify hands and-weak-of

the Arkite, David's friend, went to Absalom and said to him, "Long live the king! Long live the king!"

17 Absalom asked Hushai, "Is this the love you show your friend? Why didn't you go with your friend?"

18 Hushai said to Absalom, "No, the one chosen by the LORD, by these people, and by all the men of Israel—his I will be, and I will remain with him. 19 Furthermore, whom should I serve? Should I not serve the son? Just as I served your father, so I will serve you."

20 Absalom said to Ahithophel, "Give us your advice. What should we do?"

21 Ahithophel answered, "Lie with your father's concubines whom he left to take care of the palace. Then all Israel will hear that you have made yourself a stench in your father's nostrils, and the hands of everyone with you will be strengthened." 22 So they pitched a tent for Absalom on the roof, and he lay with his father's concubines in the sight of all Israel.

23 Now in those days the advice Ahithophel gave was like that of one who inquires of God. That was how both David and Absalom regarded all of Ahithophel's advice.

# 17

Ahithophel said to Absalom, "I would[u] choose twelve thousand men and set out tonight in pursuit of David. 2 I would[v] attack him when he is weary and weak. I would[v] strike him with terror, and then all the people with him will flee. I would[v] strike

[u] 1 Or *Let me* [v] 2 Or *will*

*23 Many mss have אִישׁ, *one* (*man*), as a *Qere* reading.

°18 ק לו

אֲשֶׁר־ אִתּוֹ וְהִכֵּיתִי אֶת־ הַמֶּלֶךְ לְבַדּוֹ׃
by-himself the-king *** and-I-will-strike-down with-him who

וְאָשִׁיבָה כָל־ הָעָם אֵלֶיךָ כְּשׁוּב הַכֹּל
the-whole as-to-return to-you the-people all-of and-I-will-bring-back (3)

הָאִישׁ אֲשֶׁר אַתָּה מְבַקֵּשׁ כָּל־ הָעָם יִהְיֶה שָׁלוֹם׃
unharmed he-will-be the-people all-of seeking you whom the-man

וַיִּישַׁר הַדָּבָר בְּעֵינֵי אַבְשָׁלֹם וּבְעֵינֵי כָּל־
all-of and-in-eyes-of Absalom in-eyes-of the-plan and-he-was-good (4)

זִקְנֵי יִשְׂרָאֵל׃ וַיֹּאמֶר אַבְשָׁלוֹם קְרָא נָא גַּם לְחוּשַׁי
to-Hushai also now! summon! Absalom but-he-said (5) Israel elders-of

הָאַרְכִּי וְנִשְׁמְעָה מַה־ בְּפִיו גַּם־ הוּא׃ וַיָּבֹא
when-he-came (6) he also in-mouth-of-him what so-we-can-hear the-Arkite

חוּשַׁי אֶל־אַבְשָׁלוֹם וַיֹּאמֶר אַבְשָׁלוֹם אֵלָיו לֵאמֹר כַּדָּבָר הַזֶּה
the-this as-the-advice to-say to-him Absalom then-he-said Absalom to Hushai

דִּבֶּר אֲחִיתֹפֶל הֲנַעֲשֶׂה אֶת־ דְּבָרוֹ אִם־ אַיִן אַתָּה דַבֵּר׃
give-opinion! you not if saying-of-him *** should-we-do? Ahithophel he-spoke

וַיֹּאמֶר חוּשַׁי אֶל־אַבְשָׁלוֹם לֹא־טוֹבָה הָעֵצָה אֲשֶׁר־יָעַץ אֲחִיתֹפֶל
Ahithophel he-gave that the-advice good not Absalom to Hushai and-he-replied (7)

בַּפַּעַם הַזֹּאת׃ וַיֹּאמֶר חוּשַׁי אַתָּה יָדַעְתָּ אֶת־ אָבִיךָ
father-of-you *** you-know you Hushai and-he-said (8) the-this at-the-time

וְאֶת־ אֲנָשָׁיו כִּי גִבֹּרִים הֵמָּה וּמָרֵי נֶפֶשׁ הֵמָּה כְּדֹב
as-bear they spirit and-ones-fierce-of they fighters that men-of-him and

שַׁכּוּל בַּשָּׂדֶה וְאָבִיךָ אִישׁ מִלְחָמָה וְלֹא
and-not fight man-of and-father-of-you in-the-wild robbed-of-cubs

יָלִין אֶת־ הָעָם׃ הִנֵּה עַתָּה הוּא־ נֶחְבָּא בְּאַחַת
in-one-of hiding he now see! (9) the-troop with he-will-spend-night

הַפְּחָתִים אוֹ בְּאַחַד הַמְּקוֹמֹת וְהָיָה כִּנְפֹל בָּהֶם
of-them when-to-fall and-he-will-be the-places in-one-of or the-caves

בַּתְּחִלָּה וְשָׁמַע הַשֹּׁמֵעַ וְאָמַר הָיְתָה מַגֵּפָה
slaughter she-was then-he-will-say the-one-hearing when-he-hears at-the-first

בָּעָם אֲשֶׁר אַחֲרֵי אַבְשָׁלֹם׃ וְהוּא גַם־ בֶּן־ חַיִל אֲשֶׁר
who bravery son-of even then-he (10) Absalom after who among-the-troop

לִבּוֹ כְּלֵב הָאַרְיֵה הִמֵּס יִמָּס כִּי־ יֹדֵעַ כָּל־
all-of knowing for he-will-melt to-melt the-lion like-heart-of heart-of-him

יִשְׂרָאֵל כִּי־ גִבּוֹר אָבִיךָ וּבְנֵי־ חַיִל אֲשֶׁר אִתּוֹ׃ כִּי
so (11) with-him who bravery and-sons-of father-of-you fighter that Israel

יָעַצְתִּי הֵאָסֹף יֵאָסֵף עָלֶיךָ כָל־ יִשְׂרָאֵל מִדָּן
from-Dan Israel all-of to-you let-him-be-gathered to-be-gathered I-advise

down only the king [3]and bring
all the people back to you. The
death of the man you seek will
mean the return of all; all the
people will be unharmed."
[4]This plan seemed good to Absalom and to all the elders of
Israel.
[5]But Absalom said, "Summon also Hushai the Arkite,
so we can hear what he has to
say." [6]When Hushai came to
him, Absalom said, "Ahithophel has given this advice.
Should we do what he says? If
not, give us your opinion."
[7]Hushai replied to Absalom,
"The advice Ahithophel has
given is not good this time.
[8]You know your father and his
men; they are fighters, and as
fierce as a wild bear robbed of
her cubs. Besides, your father
is an experienced fighter; he
will not spend the night with
the troops. [9]Even now, he is
hidden in a cave or some other
place. If he should attack your
troops first,[w] whoever hears
about it will say, 'There has
been a slaughter among the
troops who follow Absalom.'
[10]Then even the bravest soldier, whose heart is like the
heart of a lion, will melt with
fear, for all Israel knows that
your father is a fighter and
that those with him are brave.
[11]"So I advise you: Let all Israel, from Dan to Beersheba—

[w]9 Or *When some of the men fall at the first attack*

וְעַד־ בְּאֵר שֶׁבַע כַּחוֹל אֲשֶׁר־עַל־ הַיָּם לָרֹב וּפָנֶיךָ
and-faces-of-you in-the-number the-sea by that as-the-sand Sheba Beer even-to

הֹלְכִים בַּקְרָב׃ וּבָאנוּ אֵלָיו בְּאַחַת°
at-one-of against-him then-we-will-go (12) into-the-battle ones-leading

הַמְּקוֹמֹת אֲשֶׁר נִמְצָא שָׁם וְנַחְנוּ עָלָיו כַּאֲשֶׁר יִפֹּל הַטַּל
the-dew he-settles just-as on-him and-we there he-is-found where the-places

עַל־הָאֲדָמָה וְלֹא־ נוֹתַר בּוֹ וּבְכָל־ הָאֲנָשִׁים אֲשֶׁר־
who the-men or-of-any-of of-him he-will-be-left-alive and-not the-ground on

אִתּוֹ גַּם־אֶחָד׃ וְאִם־אֶל־ עִיר יֵאָסֵף וְהִשִּׂיאוּ
then-they-will-bring he-withdraws city to and-if (13) one even with-him

כָל־ יִשְׂרָאֵל אֶל־ הָעִיר הַהִיא חֲבָלִים וְסָחַבְנוּ אֹתוֹ עַד־ הַנַּחַל
the-valley to him and-we-will-drag ropes the-that the-city to Israel all-of

עַד אֲשֶׁר־ לֹא־ נִמְצָא שָׁם גַּם־צְרוֹר׃ וַיֹּאמֶר אַבְשָׁלוֹם
Absalom and-he-said (14) piece even there he-can-be-found not when until

וְכָל־ אִישׁ יִשְׂרָאֵל טוֹבָה עֲצַת חוּשַׁי הָאַרְכִּי מֵעֲצַת
than-advice-of the-Arkite Hushai advice-of better Israel man-of and-all-of

אֲחִיתֹפֶל וַיהוָה צִוָּה לְהָפֵר אֶת־ עֲצַת אֲחִיתֹפֶל
Ahithophel advice-of *** to-frustrate he-determined for-Yahweh Ahithophel

הַטּוֹבָה לְבַעֲבוּר הָבִיא יְהוָה אֶל־ אַבְשָׁלוֹם אֶת־ הָרָעָה׃
the-disaster *** Absalom on Yahweh to-bring in-order-to the-good

וַיֹּאמֶר חוּשַׁי אֶל־ צָדוֹק וְאֶל־ אֶבְיָתָר הַכֹּהֲנִים כָּזֹאת
as-such the-priests Abiathar and-to Zadok to Hushai then-he-told (15)

וְכָזֹאת יָעַץ אֲחִיתֹפֶל אֶת־אַבְשָׁלֹם וְאֵת זִקְנֵי יִשְׂרָאֵל וְכָזֹאת
but-as-so Israel elders-of and Absalom *** Ahithophel he-advised and-as-such

וְכָזֹאת יָעַצְתִּי אָנִי׃ וְעַתָּה שִׁלְחוּ מְהֵרָה וְהַגִּידוּ לְדָוִד
to-David and-tell! immediately send! and-now (16) I I-advised and-as-so

לֵאמֹר אַל־ תָּלֶן הַלַּיְלָה בְּעַרְבוֹת הַמִּדְבָּר וְגַם
but-indeed the-desert at-fords-of the-night you-spend-night not to-say

עָבוֹר תַּעֲבוֹר פֶּן יְבֻלַּע לַמֶּלֶךְ
to-the-king he-will-be-swallowed-up or you-cross-over to-cross-over

וּלְכָל־ הָעָם אֲשֶׁר אִתּוֹ׃ וִיהוֹנָתָן וַאֲחִימַעַץ
and-Ahimaaz now-Jonathan (17) with-him who the-people and-to-all-of

עֹמְדִים בְּעֵין־ רֹגֵל וְהָלְכָה הַשִּׁפְחָה וְהִגִּידָה
and-she-informed the-servant-girl and-she-went Rogel at-En ones-staying

לָהֶם וְהֵם יֵלְכוּ וְהִגִּידוּ לַמֶּלֶךְ דָּוִד כִּי לֹא
not for David to-the-king and-they-would-tell they-would-go so-they to-them

יוּכְלוּ לְהֵרָאוֹת לָבוֹא הָעִירָה׃ וַיַּרְא אֹתָם נַעַר
young-man them but-he-saw (18) into-the-city to-enter to-be-seen they-could

as numerous as the sand on
the seashore—be gathered to
you, with you yourself leading
them into battle. 12Then we
will attack him wherever he
may be found, and we will fall
on him as dew settles on the
ground. Neither he nor any of
his men will be left alive. 13If
he withdraws into a city, then
all Israel will bring ropes to
that city, and we will drag it
down to the valley until not
even a piece of it can be
found."

14Absalom and all the men of
Israel said, "The advice of Hushai the Arkite is better than
that of Ahithophel." For the
LORD had determined to frustrate the good advice of Ahithophel in order to bring disaster on Absalom.

15Hushai told Zadok and
Abiathar, the priests, "Ahithophel has advised Absalom
and the elders of Israel to do
such and such, but I have advised them to do so and so.
16Now send a message
immediately and tell David,
'Do not spend the night at the
fords in the desert; cross over
without fail, or the king and
all the people with him will be
swallowed up.' "

17Jonathan and Ahimaaz
were staying at En Rogel. A
servant girl was to go and inform them, and they were to
go and tell King David, for
they could not risk being seen
entering the city. 18But a
young man saw them and told

°12 ק באחד

וַיַּגִּד לְאַבְשָׁלֹם וַיֵּלְכוּ שְׁנֵיהֶם מְהֵרָה וַיָּבֹאוּ | אֶל־
to and-they-went quickly two-of-them so-they-left to-Absalom and-he-told

בֵּית־ אִישׁ בְּבַחוּרִים וְלוֹ בְאֵר בַּחֲצֵרוֹ וַיֵּרְדוּ
and-they-went-down in-courtyard-of-him well and-to-him in-Bahurim man house-of

שָׁם׃ וַתִּקַּח הָאִשָּׁה וַתִּפְרֹשׂ אֶת־ הַמָּסָךְ עַל־
over the-covering *** and-she-spread the-wife and-she-took (19) there

פְּנֵי הַבְּאֵר וַתִּשְׁטַח עָלָיו הָרִפוֹת וְלֹא
and-not the-grains over-him and-she-scattered the-well openings-of

נוֹדַע דָּבָר׃ וַיָּבֹאוּ עַבְדֵי אַבְשָׁלוֹם אֶל־ הָאִשָּׁה
the-woman to Absalom men-of when-they-came (20) matter he-was-known

הַבַּיְתָה וַיֹּאמְרוּ אַיֵּה אֲחִימַעַץ וִיהוֹנָתָן וַתֹּאמֶר
and-she-answered and-Jonathan Ahimaaz where? then-they-asked at-the-house

לָהֶם הָאִשָּׁה עָבְרוּ מִיכַל הַמָּיִם וַיְבַקְשׁוּ
and-they-searched the-waters brook-of they-crossed-over the-woman to-them

וְלֹא מָצָאוּ וַיָּשֻׁבוּ יְרוּשָׁלִָם׃ וַיְהִי | אַחֲרֵי
after and-he-was (21) Jerusalem so-they-returned they-found but-not

לֶכְתָּם וַיַּעֲלוּ מֵהַבְּאֵר וַיֵּלְכוּ וַיַּגִּדוּ
and-they-informed and-they-went from-the-well then-they-climbed-up to-go-them

לַמֶּלֶךְ דָּוִד וַיֹּאמְרוּ אֶל־ דָּוִד קוּמוּ וְעִבְרוּ מְהֵרָה אֶת־
*** at-once and-cross! set-out! David to and-they-said David to-the-king

הַמַּיִם כִּי־ כָכָה יָעַץ עֲלֵיכֶם אֲחִיתֹפֶל׃ וַיָּקָם
so-he-set-out (22) Ahithophel against-you he-advised such for the-waters

דָּוִד וְכָל־ הָעָם אֲשֶׁר אִתּוֹ וַיַּעַבְרוּ אֶת־ הַיַּרְדֵּן
the-Jordan *** and-they-crossed with-him who the-people and-all-of David

עַד־ אוֹר הַבֹּקֶר עַד־ אַחַד לֹא נֶעְדַּר אֲשֶׁר לֹא־ עָבַר אֶת־
*** he-crossed not who he-was-left not one even the-morning light-of by

הַיַּרְדֵּן׃ וַאֲחִיתֹפֶל רָאָה כִּי לֹא נֶעֶשְׂתָה עֲצָתוֹ
advice-of-him she-was-followed not that he-saw when-Ahithophel (23) the-Jordan

וַיַּחֲבֹשׁ אֶת־ הַחֲמוֹר וַיָּקָם וַיֵּלֶךְ אֶל־ בֵּיתוֹ
house-of-him to and-he-went and-he-set-out the-donkey *** then-he-saddled

אֶל־ עִירוֹ וַיְצַו אֶל־ בֵּיתוֹ וַיֵּחָנַק
then-he-hanged-himself house-of-him to and-he-put-in-order town-of-him in

וַיָּמָת וַיִּקָּבֵר בְּקֶבֶר אָבִיו׃ וְדָוִד בָּא
he-went now-David (24) father-of-him in-tomb-of and-he-was-buried so-he-died

מַחֲנָיְמָה וְאַבְשָׁלֹם עָבַר אֶת־ הַיַּרְדֵּן הוּא וְכָל־ אִישׁ
man-of and-all-of he the-Jordan *** he-crossed and-Absalom to-Mahanaim

יִשְׂרָאֵל עִמּוֹ׃ וְאֶת־עֲמָשָׂא שָׂם אַבְשָׁלֹם תַּחַת יוֹאָב עַל־
over Joab in-place-of Absalom he-appointed Amasa and (25) with-him Israel

Absalom. So the two of them
left quickly and went to the
house of a man in Bahurim.
He had a well in his courtyard,
and they climbed down into
it. 19His wife took a covering
and spread it out over the
opening of the well and scattered grain over it. No one
knew anything about it.
20When Absalom's men
came to the woman at the
house, they asked, "Where are
Ahimaaz and Jonathan?"
The woman answered them,
"They crossed over the
brook."[x] The men searched
but found no one, so they returned to Jerusalem.
21After the men had gone,
the two climbed out of the well
and went to inform King David. They said to him, "Set out
and cross the river at once; A-
hithophel has advised such
and such against you." 22So
David and all the people with
him set out and crossed the
Jordan. By daybreak, no one
was left who had not crossed
the Jordan.
23When Ahithophel saw that
his advice had not been followed, he saddled his donkey
and set out for his house in his
home town. He put his house
in order and then hanged
himself. So he died and was
buried in his father's tomb.
24David went to Mahanaim,
and Absalom crossed the Jordan with all the men of Israel.
25Absalom had appointed
Amasa over the army in place

[x]20 Or *"They passed by the sheep pen toward the water."*

הַצָּבָא וַעֲמָשָׂא בֶן־ אִישׁ וּשְׁמוֹ יִתְרָא הַיִּשְׂרְאֵלִי אֲשֶׁר־

who the-Israelite Ithra and-name-of-him man son-of now-Amasa the-army

בָּא אֶל־ אֲבִיגַל בַּת־ נָחָשׁ אֲחוֹת צְרוּיָה אֵם יוֹאָב׃

Joab mother-of Zeruiah sister-of Nahash daughter-of Abigal into he-went

וַיִּחַן יִשְׂרָאֵל וְאַבְשָׁלֹם אֶרֶץ הַגִּלְעָד׃ וַיְהִי

and-he-was (27) the-Gilead land-of and-Absalom Israel and-he-camped (26)

כְּבוֹא דָוִד מַחֲנָיְמָה וְשֹׁבִי בֶן־ נָחָשׁ מֵרַבַּת בְּנֵי־

sons-of from-Rabbah-of Nahash son-of then-Shobi to-Mahanaim David when-to-come

עַמּוֹן וּמָכִיר בֶּן־ עַמִּיאֵל מִלֹּא דְבָר וּבַרְזִלַּי הַגִּלְעָדִי

the-Gileadite and-Barzillai Debar from-Lo Ammiel son-of and-Makir Ammon

מֵרֹגְלִים׃ מִשְׁכָּב וְסַפּוֹת וּכְלִי יוֹצֵר

one-making-pottery and-articles-of and-bowls bedding (28) from-Rogelim

וְחִטִּים וּשְׂעֹרִים וְקֶמַח וְקָלִי וּפוֹל וַעֲדָשִׁים

and-lentils and-bean and-roasted-grain and-flour and-barleys and-wheats

וְקָלִי׃ וּדְבַשׁ וְחֶמְאָה וְצֹאן וּשְׁפוֹת בָּקָר

cow and-cheese-of and-sheep and-curd and-honey (29) and-roasted-grain

הִגִּישׁוּ לְדָוִד וְלָעָם אֲשֶׁר־ אִתּוֹ לֶאֱכוֹל כִּי אָמְרוּ

they-said for to-eat with-him who and-for-the-people for-David they-brought

הָעָם רָעֵב וְעָיֵף וְצָמֵא בַּמִּדְבָּר׃ וַיִּפְקֹד

and-he-mustered (18:1) in-the-desert and-thirsty and-tired hungry the-people

דָּוִד אֵת־ הָעָם אֲשֶׁר אִתּוֹ וַיָּשֶׂם עֲלֵיהֶם שָׂרֵי

commanders-of over-them and-he-appointed with-him who the-people *** David

אֲלָפִים וְשָׂרֵי מֵאוֹת׃ וַיְשַׁלַּח דָּוִד אֶת־ הָעָם

the-troop *** David and-he-sent-out (2) hundreds and-commanders-of thousands

הַשְּׁלִשִׁית בְּיַד־ יוֹאָב וְהַשְּׁלִשִׁית בְּיַד אֲבִישַׁי בֶּן־

son-of Abishai under-hand-of and-the-third Joab under-hand-of the-third

צְרוּיָה אֲחִי יוֹאָב וְהַשְּׁלִשִׁת בְּיַד אִתַּי הַגִּתִּי

the-Gittite Ittai under-hand-of and-the-third Joab brother-of Zeruiah

וַיֹּאמֶר הַמֶּלֶךְ אֶל־ הָעָם יָצֹא אֵצֵא גַּם־ אֲנִי

I even I-will-march-out to-march-out the-troop to the-king and-he-told

עִמָּכֶם׃ וַיֹּאמֶר הָעָם לֹא תֵצֵא כִּי אִם־ נֹס

to-flee if for you-must-go-out not the-people but-he-said (3) with-you

נָנוּס לֹא־ יָשִׂימוּ אֵלֵינוּ לֵב וְאִם־ יָמֻתוּ חֶצְיֵנוּ לֹא־

not half-of-us they-die even-if heart to-us they-will-set not we-must-flee

יָשִׂימוּ אֵלֵינוּ לֵב כִּי־ עַתָּה כָמֹנוּ עֲשָׂרָה אֲלָפִים וְעַתָּה טוֹב כִּי־

that better so-now thousands ten like-us now for heart to-us they-will-set

תִּהְיֶה־ לָּנוּ מֵעִיר לַעְזִיר׃ וַיֹּאמֶר אֲלֵיהֶם הַמֶּלֶךְ

the-king to-them and-he-answered (4) to-give-help from-city for-us you-be

of Joab. Amasa was the son of a man named Jether,[y] an Israelite[z] who had married Abigail,[a] the daughter of Nahash and sister of Zeruiah the mother of Joab. 26 The Israelites and Absalom camped in the land of Gilead.

27 When David came to Mahanaim, Shobi son of Nahash from Rabbah of the Ammonites, and Makir son of Ammiel from Lo Debar, and Barzillai the Gileadite from Rogelim 28 brought bedding and bowls and articles of pottery. They also brought wheat and barley, flour and roasted grain, beans and lentils,[b] 29 honey and curds, sheep, and cheese from cows' milk for David and his people to eat. For they said, "The people have become hungry and tired and thirsty in the desert."

*Absalom's Death*

18 David mustered the men who were with him and appointed over them commanders of thousands and commanders of hundreds. 2 David sent the troops out—a third under the command of Joab, a third under Joab's brother Abishai son of Zeruiah, and a third under Ittai the Gittite. The king told the troops, "I myself will surely march out with you."

3 But the men said, "You must not go out; if we are forced to flee, they won't care about us. Even if half of us die, they won't care; but you are worth ten thousand of us.[c] It would be better now for you to give us support from the city."

4 The king answered, "I will

[y] 25 Hebrew *Ithra,* a variant of *Jether*
[z] 25 Hebrew and some Septuagint manuscripts; other Septuagint manuscripts (see also 1 Chron. 2:17) *Ishmaelite* or *Jezreelite*
[a] 25 Hebrew *Abigal,* a variant of *Abigail*
[b] 28 Most Septuagint manuscripts and Syriac; Hebrew *lentils, and roasted grain*
[c] 3 Two Hebrew manuscripts, some Septuagint manuscripts and Vulgate; most Hebrew manuscripts *care; for now there are ten thousand like us*

°3 ק לעזור

אֲשֶׁר־ יִיטַב בְּעֵינֵיכֶם אֶעֱשֶׂה וַיַּעֲמֹד הַמֶּלֶךְ אֶל־ יַד
side-of at the-king so-he-stood I-will-do in-eyes-of-you he-is-good what

הַשַּׁעַר וְכָל־ הָעָם יָצְאוּ לְמֵאוֹת וְלַאֲלָפִים׃
and-in-thousands in-hundreds they-marched-out the-people while-all-of the-gate

(5) וַיְצַו הַמֶּלֶךְ אֶת־ יוֹאָב וְאֶת־ אֲבִישַׁי וְאֶת־ אִתַּי לֵאמֹר
to-say Ittai and Abishai and Joab *** the-king and-he-commanded (5)

לְאַט־ לִי לַנַּעַר לְאַבְשָׁלוֹם וְכָל־ הָעָם
the-troop and-all-of with-Absalom with-the-young-man for-me for-gentleness

שָׁמְעוּ בְּצַוֺּת הַמֶּלֶךְ אֶת־ כָּל־ הַשָּׂרִים עַל־ דְּבַר
matter-of about the-commanders each-of *** the-king when-to-order they-heard

אַבְשָׁלוֹם׃ (6) וַיֵּצֵא הָעָם הַשָּׂדֶה לִקְרַאת יִשְׂרָאֵל
Israel to-fight the-field the-army and-he-marched-out (6) Absalom

וַתְּהִי הַמִּלְחָמָה בְּיַעַר אֶפְרָיִם׃ (7) וַיִּנָּגְפוּ שָׁם
there and-they-were-defeated (7) Ephraim in-forest-of the-battle and-she-was

עַם יִשְׂרָאֵל לִפְנֵי עַבְדֵי דָוִד וַתְּהִי־ שָׁם הַמַּגֵּפָה גְדוֹלָה
great the-casualty there and-she-was David men-of before Israel army-of

בַּיּוֹם הַהוּא עֶשְׂרִים אָלֶף׃ (8) וַתְּהִי־ שָׁם הַמִּלְחָמָה
the-battle there and-she-was (8) thousand twenty the-that on-the-day

נָפֹצֶית° עַל־ פְּנֵי כָל־ הָאָרֶץ וַיֶּרֶב
and-he-was-greater the-country whole-of surfaces-of over being-spread

הַיַּעַר לֶאֱכֹל בָּעָם מֵאֲשֶׁר אָכְלָה הַחֶרֶב
the-sword she-consumed than-what of-the-people to-consune the-forest

בַּיּוֹם הַהוּא׃ (9) וַיִּקָּרֵא אַבְשָׁלוֹם לִפְנֵי עַבְדֵי דָוִד וְאַבְשָׁלוֹם
now-Absalom David men-of by Absalom and-he-was-met (9) the-that on-the-day

רֹכֵב עַל־ הַפֶּרֶד וַיָּבֹא הַפֶּרֶד תַּחַת שׂוֹבֶךְ הָאֵלָה הַגְּדוֹלָה
the-large the-oak branch-of under the-mule and-he-went the-mule on riding

וַיֶּחֱזַק רֹאשׁוֹ בָאֵלָה וַיֻּתַּן בֵּין הַשָּׁמַיִם
the-skies between and-he-was-left in-the-oak head-of-him and-he-was-caught

וּבֵין הָאָרֶץ וְהַפֶּרֶד אֲשֶׁר־ תַּחְתָּיו עָבָר׃
he-went-on under-him that while-the-mule the-ground and-between

(10) וַיַּרְא אִישׁ אֶחָד וַיַּגֵּד לְיוֹאָב וַיֹּאמֶר הִנֵּה רָאִיתִי אֶת־
*** I-saw see! and-he-said to-Joab then-he-told one man when-he-saw (10)

אַבְשָׁלֹם תָּלוּי בָּאֵלָה׃ (11) וַיֹּאמֶר יוֹאָב לָאִישׁ הַמַּגִּיד
the-one-telling to-the-man Joab and-he-said (11) in-the-oak hanging Absalom

לוֹ וְהִנֵּה רָאִיתָ וּמַדּוּעַ לֹא־ הִכִּיתוֹ שָׁם אַרְצָה
to-ground there you-struck-down-him not so-why? you-saw now-what! to-him

וְעָלַי לָתֶת לְךָ עֲשָׂרָה כֶּסֶף וַחֲגֹרָה אֶחָת׃ (12) וַיֹּאמֶר
but-he-said (12) one and-belt-of-warrior silver ten to-you to-give then-upon-me

do whatever seems best to you."

So the king stood beside the gate while all the men marched out in units of hundreds and of thousands. [5]The king commanded Joab, Abishai and Ittai, "Be gentle with the young man Absalom for my sake." And all the troops heard the king giving orders concerning Absalom to each of the commanders.

[6]The army marched into the field to fight Israel, and the battle took place in the forest of Ephraim. [7]There the army of Israel was defeated by David's men, and the casualties that day were great—twenty thousand men. [8]The battle spread out over the whole countryside, and the forest claimed more lives that day than the sword.

[9]Now Absalom happened to meet David's men. He was riding his mule, and as the mule went under the thick branches of a large oak, Absalom's head got caught in the tree. He was left hanging in midair, while the mule he was riding kept on going.

[10]When one of the men saw this, he told Joab, "I just saw Absalom hanging in an oak tree."

[11]Joab said to the man who had told him this, "What! You saw him? Why didn't you strike him to the ground right there? Then I would have had to give you ten shekels[d] of silver and a warrior's belt."

[d]11 That is, about 4 ounces (about 115 grams)

°8 ק נפוצת

הָאִישׁ אֶל־יוֹאָב וְלֹא אָנֹכִי שֹׁקֵל עַל־ כַּפַּי אֶלֶף כֶּסֶף לֹא־
not silver thousand hands-of-me into weighing I even-if Joab to the-man

אֶשְׁלַח יָדִי אֶל־ בֶּן־ הַמֶּלֶךְ כִּי בְאָזְנֵינוּ צִוָּה
he-commanded in-ears-of-us for the-king son-of against hand-of-me I-would-lift

הַמֶּלֶךְ אֹתְךָ וְאֶת־ אֲבִישַׁי וְאֶת־אִתַּי לֵאמֹר שִׁמְרוּ־ מִי בַּנַּעַר
to-the-young-man whoever protect! to-say Ittai and Abishai and you the-king

בְּאַבְשָׁלוֹם׃ אוֹ־עָשִׂיתִי בְנַפְשׁוֹ שֶׁקֶר וְכָל־ דָּבָר
thing and-any-of treacherously against-life-of-me I-acted if (13) to-Absalom

לֹא־ יִכָּחֵד מִן־ הַמֶּלֶךְ וְאַתָּה תִּתְיַצֵּב מִנֶּגֶד׃
from-before you-would-keep-distance then-you the-king from he-is-hidden not

וַיֹּאמֶר יוֹאָב לֹא־ כֵן אֹחִילָה לְפָנֶיךָ וַיִּקַּח שְׁלֹשָׁה
three so-he-took before-you I-will-wait like-this not Joab and-he-said (14)

שְׁבָטִים בְּכַפּוֹ וַיִּתְקָעֵם בְּלֵב אַבְשָׁלוֹם עוֹדֶנּוּ
while-he Absalom into-heart-of and-he-plunged-them in-hand-of-him javelins

חַי בְּלֵב הָאֵלָה׃ וַיָּסֹבּוּ עֲשָׂרָה נְעָרִים נֹשְׂאֵי
ones-bearing-of men ten and-they-surrounded (15) the-oak in-heart-of alive

כְּלֵי יוֹאָב וַיַּכּוּ אֶת־ אַבְשָׁלוֹם וַיְמִיתֻהוּ׃
and-they-killed-him Absalom *** and-they-struck Joab armors-of

וַיִּתְקַע יוֹאָב בַּשֹּׁפָר וַיָּשָׁב הָעָם
the-troop and-he-stopped on-the-trumpet Joab then-he-sounded (16)

מִרְדֹף אַחֲרֵי יִשְׂרָאֵל כִּי־ חָשַׂךְ יוֹאָב אֶת־ הָעָם׃ וַיִּקְחוּ
and-they-took (17) the-troop *** Joab he-halted for Israel after from-to-pursue

אֶת־ אַבְשָׁלוֹם וַיַּשְׁלִיכוּ אֹתוֹ בַיַּעַר אֶל־ הַפַּחַת הַגָּדוֹל
the-big the-pit into in-the-forest him and-they-threw Absalom ***

וַיַּצִּבוּ עָלָיו גַּל־ אֲבָנִים גָּדוֹל מְאֹד וְכָל־ יִשְׂרָאֵל נָסוּ
they-fled Israel and-all-of very large rocks heap-of over-him and-they-piled

אִישׁ לְאֹהָלָו׃ וְאַבְשָׁלֹם לָקַח וַיַּצֶּב־ לוֹ
to-himself and-he-erected he-took now-Absalom (18) to-homes-of-him each

בְחַיָּו אֶת־ מַצֶּבֶת אֲשֶׁר בְּעֵמֶק־ הַמֶּלֶךְ כִּי אָמַר אֵין־
not he-thought for the-King in-Valley-of that pillar *** during-lives-of-him

לִי בֵן בַּעֲבוּר הַזְכִּיר שְׁמִי וַיִּקְרָא לַמַּצֶּבֶת
to-the-pillar so-he-named name-of-me to-carry-on-memory in-order-to son to-me

עַל־ שְׁמוֹ וַיִּקָּרֵא לָהּ יַד אַבְשָׁלֹם עַד הַיּוֹם
the-day to Absalom Monument-of to-her and-he-is-called name-of-him after

הַזֶּה׃ וַאֲחִימַעַץ בֶּן־ צָדוֹק אָמַר אָרוּצָה נָּא
now! let-me-run he-said Zadok son-of now-Ahimaaz (19) the-this

וַאֲבַשְּׂרָה אֶת־ הַמֶּלֶךְ כִּי־ שְׁפָטוֹ יְהוָה מִיַּד
from-hand-of Yahweh he-delivered-him that the-king *** and-let-me-take-news

12 But the man replied, "Even if a thousand shekels[f] were weighed out into my hands, I would not lift my hand against the king's son. In our hearing the king commanded you and Abishai and Ittai, 'Protect the young man Absalom for my sake.[g]' 13 And if I had put my life in jeopardy[h]—and nothing is hidden from the king—you would have kept your distance from me."

14 Joab said, "I'm not going to wait like this for you." So he took three javelins in his hand and plunged them into Absalom's heart while Absalom was still alive in the oak tree. 15 And ten of Joab's armor-bearers surrounded Absalom, struck him and killed him.

16 Then Joab sounded the trumpet, and the troops stopped pursuing Israel, for Joab halted them. 17 They took Absalom, threw him into a big pit in the forest and piled up a large heap of rocks over him. Meanwhile, all the Israelites fled to their homes.

18 During his lifetime Absalom had taken a pillar and erected it in the King's Valley as a monument to himself, for he thought, "I have no son to carry on the memory of my name." He named the pillar after himself, and it is called Absalom's Monument to this day.

*David Mourns*

19 Now Ahimaaz son of Zadok said, "Let me run and take the news to the king that the LORD has delivered him

[f] 12 That is, about 25 pounds (about 11 kilograms)
[g] 12 A few Hebrew manuscripts, Septuagint, Vulgate and Syriac; most Hebrew manuscripts may be translated *Absalom, whoever you may be.*
[h] 13 Or *Otherwise, if I had acted treacherously toward him*

°12 ק ולו
°13 ק בנפשי
°17 ק לאהליו

אֹיְבָיו׃ וַיֹּאמֶר לוֹ יוֹאָב לֹא אִישׁ בְּשֹׂרָה אַתָּה הַיּוֹם
the-day you news man-of not Joab to-him and-he-told (20) being-enemies-of-him

הַזֶּה וּבִשַּׂרְתָּ בְּיוֹם אַחֵר וְהַיּוֹם הַזֶּה לֹא
not the-this but-the-day another on-day now-you-may-take-news the-this

תְבַשֵּׂר כִּי־ עַל * בֶּן־ הַמֶּלֶךְ מֵת׃ וַיֹּאמֶר
then-he-said (21) he-is-dead the-king son-of * for because you-take-news

יוֹאָב לַכּוּשִׁי לֵךְ הַגֵּד לַמֶּלֶךְ אֲשֶׁר רָאִיתָה וַיִּשְׁתַּחוּ כוּשִׁי
Cushite and-he-bowed you-saw what to-the-king tell! go! to-the-Cushite Joab

לְיוֹאָב וַיָּרֹץ׃ וַיֹּסֶף עוֹד אֲחִימַעַץ בֶּן־ צָדוֹק
Zadok son-of Ahimaaz again and-he-repeated (22) and-he-ran-off before-Joab

וַיֹּאמֶר אֶל־יוֹאָב וִיהִי מָה אָרֻצָה־ נָּא גַם־אָנִי אַחֲרֵי
after I also now! let-me-run whatever now-may-he-be Joab to and-he-said

הַכּוּשִׁי וַיֹּאמֶר יוֹאָב לָמָּה־ זֶּה אַתָּה רָץ בְּנִי וּלְכָה
for-to-you son-of-me running you this why? Joab but-he-replied the-Cushite

אֵין־בְּשׂוֹרָה מֹצֵאת׃ וִיהִי־ מָה אָרוּץ וַיֹּאמֶר לוֹ
to-him so-he-said I-would-run whatever now-may-he-be (23) bringing news not

רוּץ וַיָּרָץ אֲחִימַעַץ דֶּרֶךְ הַכִּכָּר וַיַּעֲבֹר אֶת־ הַכּוּשִׁי׃
the-Cushite *** and-he-outran the-plain way-of Ahimaaz then-he-ran run!

וְדָוִד יוֹשֵׁב בֵּין־ שְׁנֵי הַשְּׁעָרִים וַיֵּלֶךְ
and-he-went-up the-gates two-of between sitting now-David (24)

הַצֹּפֶה אֶל־ גַּג הַשַּׁעַר אֶל־ הַחוֹמָה וַיִּשָּׂא אֶת־
*** and-he-raised the-wall by the-gateway roof-of to the-one-watching

עֵינָיו וַיַּרְא וְהִנֵּה־ אִישׁ רָץ לְבַדּוֹ׃ וַיִּקְרָא
and-he-called (25) by-himself running man and-see! and-he-looked eyes-of-him

הַצֹּפֶה וַיַּגֵּד לַמֶּלֶךְ וַיֹּאמֶר הַמֶּלֶךְ אִם־
if the-king and-he-said to-the-king and-he-reported the-one-watching

לְבַדּוֹ בְּשׂוֹרָה בְּפִיו וַיֵּלֶךְ הָלוֹךְ וְקָרֵב׃
even-close to-come and-he-came in-mouth-of-him good-news by-himself

וַיַּרְא הַצֹּפֶה אִישׁ־ אַחֵר רָץ וַיִּקְרָא
and-he-called running another man the-one-watching then-he-saw (26)

הַצֹּפֶה אֶל־ הַשֹּׁעֵר וַיֹּאמֶר הִנֵּה־ אִישׁ רָץ לְבַדּוֹ
by-himself running man look! and-he-said the-gatekeeper to the-one-watching

וַיֹּאמֶר הַמֶּלֶךְ גַּם־ זֶה מְבַשֵּׂר׃ וַיֹּאמֶר
and-he-said (27) one-bringing-good-news he also the-king and-he-said

הַצֹּפֶה אֲנִי רֹאֶה אֶת־ מְרוּצַת הָרִאשׁוֹן כִּמְרֻצַת אֲחִימַעַץ בֶּן־
son-of Ahimaaz running-of the-first running-of *** seeing I the-one-watching

צָדוֹק וַיֹּאמֶר הַמֶּלֶךְ אִישׁ־ טוֹב זֶה וְאֶל־ בְּשׂוֹרָה טוֹבָה יָבוֹא׃
he-comes good news and-with this good man the-king and-he-said Zadok

from the hand of his enemies."

[20]"You are not the one to take the news today," Joab told him. "You may take the news another time, but you must not do so today, because the king's son is dead."

[21]Then Joab said to a Cushite, "Go, tell the king what you have seen." The Cushite bowed down before Joab and ran off.

[22]Ahimaaz son of Zadok again said to Joab, "Come what may, please let me run behind the Cushite."

But Joab replied, "My son, why do you want to go? You don't have any news that will bring you a reward."

[23]He said, "Come what may, I want to run."

So Joab said, "Run!" Then Ahimaaz ran by way of the plain[i] and outran the Cushite.

[24]While David was sitting between the inner and outer gates, the watchman went up to the roof of the gateway by the wall. As he looked out, he saw a man running alone. [25]The watchman called out to the king and reported it.

The king said, "If he is alone, he must have good news." And the man came closer and closer.

[26]Then the watchman saw another man running, and he called down to the gatekeeper, "Look, another man running alone!"

The king said, "He must be bringing good news, too."

[27]The watchman said, "It seems to me that the first one runs like Ahimaaz son of Zadok."

"He's a good man," the king said. "He comes with good news."

[i]23 That is, the plain of the Jordan

*21 Many mss have כן, *this*, as a *Qere* to be read with the *tsere* under על.

וַיִּקְרָא אֲחִימַעַץ וַיֹּאמֶר אֶל־ הַמֶּלֶךְ שָׁלוֹם וַיִּשְׁתַּחוּ
and-he-bowed well the-king to and-he-said Ahimaaz then-he-called (28)

לַמֶּלֶךְ לְאַפָּיו אָרְצָה וַיֹּאמֶר בָּרוּךְ יְהוָה
Yahweh being-praised and-he-said to-ground on-faces-of-him before-the-king

אֱלֹהֶיךָ אֲשֶׁר סִגַּר אֶת־ הָאֲנָשִׁים אֲשֶׁר־ נָשְׂאוּ אֶת־ יָדָם
hand-of-them *** they-lifted who the-men *** he-delivered-up who God-of-you

בַּאדֹנִי הַמֶּלֶךְ׃ וַיֹּאמֶר הַמֶּלֶךְ שָׁלוֹם לַנַּעַר
to-the-young-man safe the-king and-he-asked (29) the-king against-lord-of-me

לְאַבְשָׁלוֹם וַיֹּאמֶר אֲחִימַעַץ רָאִיתִי הֶהָמוֹן הַגָּדוֹל לִשְׁלֹחַ
to-send the-great the-confusion I-saw Ahimaaz and-he-answered to-Absalom

אֶת־ עֶבֶד הַמֶּלֶךְ יוֹאָב וְאֶת־ עַבְדְּךָ וְלֹא יָדַעְתִּי מָה׃
what I-knew but-not servant-of-you and Joab the-king servant-of ***

וַיֹּאמֶר הַמֶּלֶךְ סֹב הִתְיַצֵּב כֹּה וַיִּסֹּב
so-he-stepped-aside here and-wait! stand-aside! the-king and-he-said (30)

וַיַּעֲמֹד׃ וְהִנֵּה הַכּוּשִׁי בָּא וַיֹּאמֶר הַכּוּשִׁי
the-Cushite and-he-said arriving the-Cushite then-see! (31) and-he-stood

יִתְבַּשֵּׂר אֲדֹנִי הַמֶּלֶךְ כִּי־ שְׁפָטְךָ יְהוָה הַיּוֹם
the-day Yahweh he-delivered-you for the-king lord-of-me may-he-hear-good-news

מִיַּד כָּל־ הַקָּמִים עָלֶיךָ׃ וַיֹּאמֶר הַמֶּלֶךְ
the-king and-he-asked (32) against-you the-ones-rising all-of from-hand-of

אֶל־ הַכּוּשִׁי הֲשָׁלוֹם לַנַּעַר לְאַבְשָׁלוֹם וַיֹּאמֶר הַכּוּשִׁי
the-Cushite and-he-replied to-Absalom to-the-young-man safe? the-Cushite to

יִהְיוּ כַנַּעַר אֹיְבֵי אֲדֹנִי הַמֶּלֶךְ
the-king lord-of-me being-enemies-of like-the-young-man may-they-be

וְכֹל אֲשֶׁר־ קָמוּ עָלֶיךָ לְרָעָה׃ וַיִּרְגַּז הַמֶּלֶךְ
the-king and-he-was-shaken *(19:1) to-harm against-you they-rise who and-all

וַיַּעַל עַל־ עֲלִיַּת הַשַּׁעַר וַיֵּבְךְּ וְכֹה אָמַר
he-said and-this and-he-wept the-gateway upper-room-of to and-he-went-up

בְּלֶכְתּוֹ בְּנִי אַבְשָׁלוֹם בְּנִי בְנִי אַבְשָׁלוֹם מִי־ יִתֵּן
he-would-grant who? Absalom son-of-me son-of-me Absalom son-of-me as-to-go-him

מוּתִי אֲנִי תַחְתֶּיךָ אַבְשָׁלוֹם בְּנִי בְנִי׃ וַיֻּגַּד
and-he-was-told (2) son-of-me son-of-me Absalom instead-of-you I to-die-me

לְיוֹאָב הִנֵּה הַמֶּלֶךְ בֹּכֶה וַיִּתְאַבֵּל עַל־ אַבְשָׁלֹם׃ וַתְּהִי
and-she-turned (3) Absalom for and-he-mourns weeping the-king see! to-Joab

הַתְּשֻׁעָה בַּיּוֹם הַהוּא לְאֵבֶל לְכָל־ הָעָם כִּי־
for the-army for-all-of into-mourning the-that on-the-day the-victory

שָׁמַע הָעָם בַּיּוֹם הַהוּא לֵאמֹר נֶעֱצַב הַמֶּלֶךְ עַל־
for the-king he-grieves to-say the-that on-the-day the-troop he-heard

28Then Ahimaaz called out to the king, "All is well!" He bowed down before the king with his face to the ground and said, "Praise be to the LORD your God! He has delivered up the men who lifted their hands against my lord the king."

29The king asked, "Is the young man Absalom safe?"

Ahimaaz answered, "I saw great confusion just as Joab was about to send the king's servant and me, your servant, but I don't know what it was."

30The king said, "Stand aside and wait here." So he stepped aside and stood there.

31Then the Cushite arrived and said, "My lord the king, hear the good news! The LORD has delivered you today from all who rose up against you."

32The king asked the Cushite, "Is the young man Absalom safe?"

The Cushite replied, "May the enemies of my lord the king and all who rise up to harm you be like that young man."

33The king was shaken. He went up to the room over the gateway and wept. As he went, he said: "O my son Absalom! My son, my son Absalom! If only I had died instead of you—O Absalom, my son, my son!"

**19** Joab was told, "The king is weeping and mourning for Absalom." 2And for the whole army the victory that day was turned into mourning, because on that day the troops heard it said, "The king is grieving for his

*1 The Hebrew numeration of chapter 19 begins with verse 33 of chapter 18 in English; thus, there is a one-verse discrepancy throughout chapter 18.

בְּנוֹ׃ (4) וַיִּתְגַּנֵּב הָעָם בַּיּוֹם הַהוּא לָבוֹא הָעִיר
the-city to-enter the-that on-the-day the-people and-he-stole-in (4) son-of-him

כַּאֲשֶׁר יִתְגַּנֵּב הָעָם הַנִּכְלָמִים בְּנוּסָם
when-to-flee-them the-ones-being-ashamed the-people he-steals-in just-as

בַּמִּלְחָמָה׃ (5) וְהַמֶּלֶךְ לָאַט אֶת־ פָּנָיו וַיִּזְעַק
and-he-cried faces-of-him *** he-covered and-the-king (5) from-the-battle

הַמֶּלֶךְ קוֹל גָּדוֹל בְּנִי אַבְשָׁלוֹם אַבְשָׁלוֹם בְּנִי בְנִי׃
son-of-me son-of-me Absalom Absalom son-of-me loud voice the-king

(6) וַיָּבֹא יוֹאָב אֶל־ הַמֶּלֶךְ הַבָּיִת וַיֹּאמֶר הֹבַשְׁתָּ
you-humiliated and-he-said the-house the-king into Joab then-he-went (6)

הַיּוֹם אֶת־ פְּנֵי כָל־ עֲבָדֶיךָ הַמְמַלְּטִים אֶת־ נַפְשְׁךָ
life-of-you *** the-ones-saving men-of-you all-of faces-of *** the-day

הַיּוֹם וְאֵת נֶפֶשׁ בָּנֶיךָ וּבְנֹתֶיךָ וְנֶפֶשׁ נָשֶׁיךָ
wives-of-you and-life-of and-daughters-of-you sons-of-you life-of and the-day

וְנֶפֶשׁ פִּלַגְשֶׁיךָ׃ (7) לְאַהֲבָה אֶת־ שֹׂנְאֶיךָ וְלִשְׂנֹא
and-to-hate ones-hating-you *** to-love (7) concubines-of-you and-life-of

אֶת־ אֹהֲבֶיךָ כִּי | הִגַּדְתָּ הַיּוֹם כִּי אֵין לְךָ שָׂרִים
commanders to-you nothing that the-day you-made-clear for ones-loving-you ***

וַעֲבָדִים כִּי | יָדַעְתִּי הַיּוֹם כִּי לֹא° אַבְשָׁלוֹם חַי וְכֻלָּנוּ הַיּוֹם
the-day and-all-of-us alive Absalom if that the-day I-see indeed and-men

מֵתִים כִּי־ אָז יָשָׁר בְּעֵינֶיךָ׃ (8) וְעַתָּה קוּם צֵא
go-out! rise! and-now (8) in-eyes-of-you pleasing then that ones-dead

וְדַבֵּר עַל־ לֵב עֲבָדֶיךָ כִּי בַיהוָה נִשְׁבַּעְתִּי כִּי־אֵינְךָ יוֹצֵא
going-out not-you if I-swear by-Yahweh for men-of-you heart-of to and-speak!

אִם־ יָלִין אִישׁ אִתְּךָ הַלַּיְלָה וְרָעָה לְךָ זֹאת מִכָּל־
than-all-of this for-you and-worse the-night with-you man he-will-remain not

הָרָעָה אֲשֶׁר־ בָּאָה עָלֶיךָ מִנְּעֻרֶיךָ עַד־ עָתָּה׃
now till from-youths-of-you upon-you she-came that the-calamity

(9) וַיָּקָם הַמֶּלֶךְ וַיֵּשֶׁב בַּשָּׁעַר וּלְכָל־ הָעָם
the-people and-to-all-of in-the-gateway and-he-sat the-king so-he-got-up (9)

הִגִּידוּ לֵאמֹר הִנֵּה הַמֶּלֶךְ יוֹשֵׁב בַּשַּׁעַר וַיָּבֹא כָל־
all-of and-he-came in-the-gateway sitting the-king see! to-say they-told

הָעָם לִפְנֵי הַמֶּלֶךְ וְיִשְׂרָאֵל נָס אִישׁ לְאֹהָלָיו׃
to-homes-of-him each he-fled now-Israel the-king before the-people

(10) וַיְהִי כָל־ הָעָם נָדוֹן בְּכָל־ שִׁבְטֵי יִשְׂרָאֵל
Israel tribes-of through-all-of arguing the-people all-of and-he-was (10)

לֵאמֹר הַמֶּלֶךְ הִצִּילָנוּ | מִכַּף אֹיְבֵינוּ וְהוּא
and-he being-enemies-of-us from-hand-of he-delivered-us the-king to-say

son." [3]The men stole into the city that day as men steal in who are ashamed when they flee from battle. [4]The king covered his face and cried aloud, "O my son Absalom! O Absalom, my son, my son!"

[5]Then Joab went into the house to the king and said, "Today you have humiliated all your men, who have just saved your life and the lives of your sons and daughters and the lives of your wives and concubines. [6]You love those who hate you and hate those who love you. You have made it clear today that the commanders and their men mean nothing to you. I see that you would be pleased if Absalom were alive today and all of us were dead. [7]Now go out and encourage your men. I swear by the LORD that if you don't go out, not a man will be left with you by nightfall. This will be worse for you than all the calamities that have come upon you from your youth till now."

[8]So the king got up and took his seat in the gateway. When the men were told, "The king is sitting in the gateway," they all came before him.

### *David Returns to Jerusalem*

Meanwhile, the Israelites had fled to their homes. [9]Throughout the tribes of Israel, the people were all arguing with each other, saying, "The king delivered us from the hand of our enemies; he is the

*See the note on page 307.

°7 ק לו

מִלְּטָנוּ מִכַּף פְּלִשְׁתִּים וְעַתָּה בָּרַח מִן־הָאָרֶץ
the-country from he-fled but-now Philistines from-hand-of he-rescued-us

מֵעַל אַבְשָׁלוֹם׃ וְאַבְשָׁלוֹם אֲשֶׁר מָשַׁחְנוּ עָלֵינוּ מֵת
he-died over-us we-anointed whom and-Absalom (11) Absalom because-of

בַּמִּלְחָמָה וְעַתָּה לָמָה אַתֶּם מַחֲרִשִׁים לְהָשִׁיב אֶת־הַמֶּלֶךְ׃
the-king *** to-bring-back ones-saying-nothing you why? so-now in-the-battle

וְהַמֶּלֶךְ דָּוִד שָׁלַח אֶל־צָדוֹק וְאֶל־אֶבְיָתָר הַכֹּהֲנִים לֵאמֹר
to-say the-priests Abiathar and-to Zadok to he-sent David now-the-king

דַּבְּרוּ אֶל־זִקְנֵי יְהוּדָה לֵאמֹר לָמָּה תִהְיוּ אַחֲרֹנִים לְהָשִׁיב
to-bring-back last-ones should-you-be why? to-say Judah elders-of to ask!

אֶת־הַמֶּלֶךְ אֶל־בֵּיתוֹ וּדְבַר כָּל־יִשְׂרָאֵל בָּא אֶל־
to he-reached Israel all-of since-word-of palace-of-him to the-king ***

הַמֶּלֶךְ אֶל־בֵּיתוֹ׃ אַחַי אַתֶּם עַצְמִי וּבְשָׂרִי
and-flesh-of-me bone-of-me you brothers-of-me (13) residence-of-him at the-king

אַתֶּם וְלָמָּה תִהְיוּ אַחֲרֹנִים לְהָשִׁיב אֶת־הַמֶּלֶךְ׃
the-king *** to-bring-back last-ones should-you-be so-why? you

וְלַעֲמָשָׂא תֹּמְרוּ הֲלוֹא עַצְמִי וּבְשָׂרִי אַתָּה כֹּה יַעֲשֶׂה־
may-he-deal so you and-flesh-of-me bone-of-me not? you-say and-to-Amasa (14)

לִּי אֱלֹהִים וְכֹה יוֹסִיף אִם־לֹא שַׂר־צָבָא תִּהְיֶה
you-are army commander-of not if may-he-be-severe and-so God with-me

לְפָנַי כָּל־הַיָּמִים תַּחַת יוֹאָב׃ וַיַּט אֶת־לְבַב
heart-of *** and-he-won-over (15) Joab in-place-of the-days all-of before-me

כָּל־אִישׁ־יְהוּדָה כְּאִישׁ אֶחָד וַיִּשְׁלְחוּ אֶל־הַמֶּלֶךְ שׁוּב אַתָּה
you return! the-king to and-they-sent one as-man Judah man-of all-of

וְכָל־עֲבָדֶיךָ׃ וַיָּשָׁב הַמֶּלֶךְ וַיָּבֹא עַד־
as-far-as and-he-went the-king then-he-returned (16) men-of-you and-all-of

הַיַּרְדֵּן וִיהוּדָה בָּא הַגִּלְגָּלָה לָלֶכֶת לִקְרַאת הַמֶּלֶךְ
the-king to-meet to-go-out to-the-Gilgal he-came now-Judah the-Jordan

לְהַעֲבִיר אֶת־הַמֶּלֶךְ אֶת־הַיַּרְדֵּן׃ וַיְמַהֵר שִׁמְעִי בֶן־
son-of Shimei and-he-hurried (17) the-Jordan *** the-king *** to-bring-across

גֵּרָא בֶּן־הַיְמִינִי אֲשֶׁר מִבַּחוּרִים וַיֵּרֶד עִם־אִישׁ יְהוּדָה
Judah man-of with and-he-went-down from-Bahurim who the-Benjamite Gera

לִקְרַאת הַמֶּלֶךְ דָּוִד׃ וְאֶלֶף אִישׁ עִמּוֹ מִבִּנְיָמִן וְצִיבָא
and-Ziba from-Benjamin with-him man and-thousand (18) David the-king to-meet

נַעַר בֵּית שָׁאוּל וַחֲמֵשֶׁת עָשָׂר בָּנָיו וְעֶשְׂרִים
and-twenty sons-of-him ten and-five-of Saul household-of steward-of

עֲבָדָיו אִתּוֹ וְצָלְחוּ הַיַּרְדֵּן לִפְנֵי הַמֶּלֶךְ׃
the-king before the-Jordan and-they-rushed with-him servants-of-him

one who rescued us from the
hand of the Philistines. But
now he has fled the country
because of Absalom; [10]and Absalom, whom we anointed to
rule over us, has died in battle.
So why do you say nothing
about bringing the king
back?"
[11]King David sent this message to Zadok and Abiathar,
the priests: "Ask the elders of
Judah, 'Why should you be the
last to bring the king back to
his palace, since what is being
said throughout Israel has
reached the king at his quarters? [12]You are my brothers,
my own flesh and blood. So
why should you be the last to
bring back the king?' [13]And
say to Amasa, 'Are you not my
own flesh and blood? May
God deal with me, be it ever so
severely, if from now on you
are not the commander of my
army in place of Joab.' "
[14]He won over the hearts of
all the men of Judah as though
they were one man. They sent
word to the king, "Return, you
and all your men." [15]Then the
king returned and went as far
as the Jordan.
Now the men of Judah had
come to Gilgal to go out and
meet the king and bring him
across the Jordan. [16]Shimei
son of Gera, the Benjamite
from Bahurim, hurried down
with the men of Judah to meet
King David. [17]With him were
a thousand Benjamites, along
with Ziba, the steward of
Saul's household, and his
fifteen sons and twenty servants. They rushed to the Jordan, where the king was.

*See the note on page 307.

ועברה העברה לעביר את־ בית המלך ולעשות
and-to-do the-king household-of *** to-take-over the-ford and-she-crossed (19)

הטוב בעינו ושמעי בן־ גרא נפל לפני המלך
the-king before he-fell Gera son-of and-Shimei in-eyes-of-him the-good

בעברו בירדן: ויאמר אל־ המלך אל־
not the-king to and-he-said (20) over-the-Jordan when-to-cross-him

יחשב־ לי אדני עון ואל־ תזכר את אשר
how *** you-remember and-not guilt lord-of-me against-me may-he-hold

העוה עבדך ביום אשר־ יצא אדני־ המלך
the-king lord-of-me he-left that on-the-day servant-of-you he-did-wrong

מירושלם לשום המלך אל־ לבו: כי ידע
he-knows for (21) heart-of-him to the-king to-take from-Jerusalem

עבדך כי אני חטאתי והנה־ באתי היום ראשון לכל־
of-whole-of first the-day I-came but-see! I-sinned I that servant-of-you

בית יוסף לרדת לקראת אדני המלך: ויען
then-he-replied (22) the-king lord-of-me to-meet to-come-down Joseph house-of

אבישי בן־ צרויה ויאמר התחת זאת לא יומת שמעי
Shimei he-should-be-killed not this for? and-he-said Zeruiah son-of Abishai

כי קלל את־ משיח יהוה: ויאמר דוד מה־ לי
to-me what? David and-he-replied (23) Yahweh anointed-of *** he-cursed for

ולכם בני צרויה כי־ תהיו־ לי היום לשטן היום
the-day as-adversary the-day to-me you-became for Zeruiah sons-of and-to-you

יומת איש בישראל כי הלוא ידעתי כי היום
the-day that I-know not? indeed in-Israel anyone should-he-be-killed

אני־ מלך על־ ישראל: ויאמר המלך אל־ שמעי לא תמות
you-shall-die not Shimei to the-king so-he-said (24) Israel over king I

וישבע לו המלך: ומפבשת בן־ שאול
Saul son-of and-Mephibosheth (25) the-king to-him and-he-promised-on-oath

ירד לקראת המלך ולא־ עשה רגליו ולא־
and-not feet-of-him he-took-care and-not the-king to-meet he-went-down

עשה שפמו ואת־ בגדיו לא כבס למן־ היום
the-day at-from washed not clothes-of-him and mustache-of-him he-trimmed

לכת המלך עד־ היום אשר־ בא בשלום: ויהי
and-he-was (26) in-safety he-returned that the-day until the-king to-leave

כי־ בא ירושלם לקראת המלך ויאמר לו המלך למה
why? the-king to-him and-he-asked the-king to-meet Jerusalem he-left when

לא־ הלכת עמי מפיבשת: ויאמר אדני המלך
the-king lord-of-me and-he-said (27) Mephibosheth with-me you-went not

[18]They crossed at the ford to
take the king's household over
and to do whatever he wished.
When Shimei son of Gera
crossed the Jordan, he fell
prostrate before the king [19]and
said to him, "May my lord not
hold me guilty. Do not remember
how your servant did
wrong on the day my lord the
king left Jerusalem. May the
king put it out of his mind.
[20]For I your servant know that
I have sinned, but today I
have come here as the first of
the whole house of Joseph to
come down and meet my lord
the king."
[21]Then Abishai son of Zeruiah
said, "Shouldn't Shimei be
put to death for this? He
cursed the LORD's anointed."
[22]David replied, "What do
you and I have in common,
you sons of Zeruiah? This day
you have become my adversaries!
Should anyone be put
to death in Israel today? Do I
not know that today I am king
over Israel?" [23]So the king said
to Shimei, "You shall not die."
And the king promised him
on oath.
[24]Mephibosheth, Saul's
grandson, also went down to
meet the king. He had not taken
care of his feet or trimmed
his mustache or washed his
clothes from the day the king
left until the day he returned
safely. [25]When he came from
Jerusalem to meet the king, the
king asked him, "Why didn't
you go with me, Mephibosheth?"
[26]He said, "My lord the king,

*See the note on page 307.

°19 ק בעיניו

עַבְדִּי רִמָּנִי כִּי־אָמַר עַבְדְּךָ אֶחְבְּשָׁה־

I-will-have-saddled servant-of-you he-said for he-betrayed-me servant-of-me

לִּי הַחֲמוֹר וְאֶרְכַּב עָלֶיהָ וְאֵלֵךְ אֶת־הַמֶּלֶךְ כִּי פִסֵּחַ

lame for the-king with so-I-can-go on-her and-I-will-ride the-donkey for-me

עַבְדֶּךָ׃ וַיְרַגֵּל בְּעַבְדְּךָ אֶל־אֲדֹנִי

lord-of-me to against-servant-of-you and-he-slandered (28) servant-of-you

הַמֶּלֶךְ וַאדֹנִי הַמֶּלֶךְ כְּמַלְאַךְ הָאֱלֹהִים וַעֲשֵׂה הַטּוֹב

the-good so-do! the-God like-angel-of the-king and-lord-of-me the-king

בְּעֵינֶיךָ׃ כִּי לֹא הָיָה כָּל־בֵּית אָבִי

father-of-me descendant-of any-of he-was not for (29) in-eyes-of-you

כִּי אִם־אַנְשֵׁי־מָוֶת לַאדֹנִי הַמֶּלֶךְ וַתָּשֶׁת אֶת־

*** but-you-gave-place the-king from-lord-of-me death men-of only except

עַבְדְּךָ בְּאֹכְלֵי שֻׁלְחָנֶךָ וּמַה־יֶּשׁ־לִי

to-me there-is so-what? table-of-you with-ones-eating-of servant-of-you

עוֹד צְדָקָה וְלִזְעֹק עוֹד אֶל־הַמֶּלֶךְ׃ וַיֹּאמֶר לוֹ

to-him and-he-said (30) the-king to any-more that-to-appeal right any-more

הַמֶּלֶךְ לָמָּה תְּדַבֵּר עוֹד דְּבָרֶיךָ אָמַרְתִּי אַתָּה וְצִיבָא תַּחְלְקוּ

you-divide and-Ziba you I-order words-of-you more you-speak why? the-king

אֶת־הַשָּׂדֶה׃ וַיֹּאמֶר מְפִיבֹשֶׁת אֶל־הַמֶּלֶךְ גַּם אֶת־הַכֹּל

the-whole *** indeed the-king to Mephibosheth and-he-said (31) the-field ***

יִקָּח אַחֲרֵי אֲשֶׁר־בָּא אֲדֹנִי הַמֶּלֶךְ† בְּשָׁלוֹם אֶל־

at in-safety the-king lord-of-me he-arrived when after let-him-take

בֵּיתוֹ׃ וּבַרְזִלַּי הַגִּלְעָדִי יָרַד מֵרֹגְלִים

from-Rogelim he-came-down the-Gileadite and-Barzillai (32) home-of-him

וַיַּעֲבֹר אֶת־הַמֶּלֶךְ הַיַּרְדֵּן לְשַׁלְּחוֹ אֶת־°בַּיַּרְדֵּן׃

the-Jordan *** to-send-him the-Jordan the-king with and-he-crossed

וּבַרְזִלַּי זָקֵן מְאֹד בֶּן־שְׁמֹנִים שָׁנָה וְהוּא־כִלְכַּל

he-provided and-he year eighty son-of very he-was-old now-Barzillai (33)

אֶת־הַמֶּלֶךְ בְּשִׁיבָתוֹ בְמַחֲנַיִם כִּי־אִישׁ גָּדוֹל הוּא מְאֹד׃

very he wealthy man for in-Mahanaim during-stay-of-him the-king ***

וַיֹּאמֶר הַמֶּלֶךְ אֶל־בַּרְזִלָּי אַתָּה עֲבֹר אִתִּי

with-me cross-over! you Barzillai to the-king and-he-said (34)

וְכִלְכַּלְתִּי אֹתְךָ עִמָּדִי בִּירוּשָׁלִָם׃ וַיֹּאמֶר בַּרְזִלַּי

Barzillai but-he-answered (35) in-Jerusalem with-me you and-I-will-provide

אֶל־הַמֶּלֶךְ כַּמָּה יְמֵי שְׁנֵי חַיַּי כִּי־אֶעֱלֶה

I-should-go-up that lives-of-me years-of days-of like-the-what? the-king to

אֶת־הַמֶּלֶךְ יְרוּשָׁלִָם׃ בֶּן־שְׁמֹנִים שָׁנָה אָנֹכִי הַיּוֹם הַאֵדַע ׀

can-I-tell? the-day I year eighty son-of (36) Jerusalem the-king with

since I your servant am lame, I said, 'I will have my donkey saddled and will ride on it, so I can go with the king.' But Ziba my servant betrayed me. [27]And he has slandered your servant to my lord the king. My lord the king is like an angel of God; so do whatever pleases you. [28]All my grandfather's descendants deserved nothing but death from my lord the king, but you gave your servant a place among those who sat at your table. So what right do I have to make any more appeals to the king?"

[29]The king said to him, "Why say more? I order you and Ziba to divide the fields."

[30]Mephibosheth said to the king, "Let him take everything, now that my lord the king has arrived home safely."

[31]Barzillai the Gileadite also came down from Rogelim to cross the Jordan with the king and to send him on his way from there. [32]Now Barzillai was a very old man, eighty years of age. He had provided for the king during his stay in Mahanaim, for he was a very wealthy man. [33]The king said to Barzillai, "Cross over with me and stay with me in Jerusalem, and I will provide for you."

[34]But Barzillai answered the king, "How many more years will I live, that I should go up to Jerusalem with the king? [35]I am now eighty years old. Can

*See the note on page 307.

†*31* Most mss have *sheva* in the *kaph* ( ךְ ).

°*32* ק הירדן

בֵּין־ טוֹב לְרָע אִם־ יִטְעַם עַבְדְּךָ אֶת־ אֲשֶׁר אֹכַל וְאֶת־
or I-eat what *** servant-of-you can-he-taste or from-bad good between

אֲשֶׁר אֶשְׁתֶּה אִם־ אֶשְׁמַע עוֹד בְּקוֹל שָׁרִים וְשָׁרוֹת
and-women-singing men-singing to-voice-of still can-I-hear or I-drink what

וְלָמָּה יִהְיֶה עַבְדְּךָ עוֹד לְמַשָּׂא אֶל־ אֲדֹנִי הַמֶּלֶךְ׃
the-king lord-of-me to as-burden more servant-of-you should-he-be so-why?

כִּמְעַט יַעֲבֹר עַבְדְּךָ אֶת־ הַיַּרְדֵּן אֶת־ הַמֶּלֶךְ
the-king with the-Jordan *** servant-of-you he-will-cross just-little (37)

וְלָמָּה יִגְמְלֵנִי הַמֶּלֶךְ הַגְּמוּלָה הַזֹּאת׃ יָשָׁב־
let-him-return (38) the-this the-reward the-king should-he-reward-me but-why?

נָא עַבְדְּךָ וְאָמֻת בְּעִירִי עִם קֶבֶר אָבִי
father-of-me tomb-of near in-town-of-me so-I-may-die servant-of-you now!

וְאִמִּי וְהִנֵּה ׀ עַבְדְּךָ כִמְהָם יַעֲבֹר עִם־
with let-him-cross-over Kimham servant-of-you but-see! and-mother-of-me

אֲדֹנִי הַמֶּלֶךְ וַעֲשֵׂה־ לוֹ אֵת אֲשֶׁר־ טוֹב בְּעֵינֶיךָ׃
in-eyes-of-you good what *** for-him and-do! the-king lord-of-me

וַיֹּאמֶר הַמֶּלֶךְ אִתִּי יַעֲבֹר כִּמְהָם וַאֲנִי אֶעֱשֶׂה־
I-will-do and-I Kimham he-shall-cross-over with-me the-king and-he-said (39)

לּוֹ אֶת־ הַטּוֹב בְּעֵינֶיךָ וְכֹל אֲשֶׁר־ תִּבְחַר עָלַי אֶעֱשֶׂה־
I-will-do from-me you-desire that and-all in-eyes-of-you the-good *** for-him

לָּךְ׃ וַיַּעֲבֹר כָּל־ הָעָם אֶת־ הַיַּרְדֵּן וְהַמֶּלֶךְ
then-the-king the-Jordan *** the-people all-of so-he-crossed (40) for-you

עָבָר וַיִּשַּׁק הַמֶּלֶךְ לְבַרְזִלַּי וַיְבָרְכֵהוּ
and-he-blessed-him to-Barzillai the-king and-he-kissed he-crossed-over

וַיָּשָׁב לִמְקֹמוֹ׃ וַיַּעֲבֹר הַמֶּלֶךְ הַגִּלְגָּלָה
to-the-Gilgal the-king when-he-crossed (41) to-home-of-him and-he-returned

וְכִמְהָן עָבַר עִמּוֹ וְכָל־ עַם יְהוּדָה וַיֶּעֶבְרוּ° אֶת־
*** they-took-over Judah troop-of and-all-of with-him he-crossed then-Kimham

הַמֶּלֶךְ וְגַם חֲצִי עַם יִשְׂרָאֵל׃ וְהִנֵּה כָּל־ אִישׁ
man-of all-of then-see! (42) Israel troop-of half-of and-also the-king

יִשְׂרָאֵל בָּאִים אֶל־ הַמֶּלֶךְ† וַיֹּאמְרוּ אֶל־ הַמֶּלֶךְ מַדּוּעַ גְּנָבוּךָ
they-stole-you why? the-king to and-they-said the-king to ones-coming Israel

אַחֵינוּ אִישׁ יְהוּדָה וַיַּעֲבִרוּ אֶת־ הַמֶּלֶךְ וְאֶת־
and the-king *** and-they-brought-across Judah man-of brothers-of-us

בֵּיתוֹ אֶת־ הַיַּרְדֵּן וְכָל־ אַנְשֵׁי דָוִד עִמּוֹ׃
with-him David men-of and-all-of the-Jordan *** household-of-him

וַיַּעַן כָּל־ אִישׁ יְהוּדָה עַל־ אִישׁ יִשְׂרָאֵל כִּי־ קָרוֹב
close because Israel man-of to Judah man-of all-of and-he-answered (43)

I tell the difference between what is good and what is not? Can your servant taste what he eats and drinks? Can I still hear the voices of men and women singers? Why should your servant be an added burden to my lord the king? [36]Your servant will cross over the Jordan with the king for a short distance, but why should the king reward me in this way? [37]Let your servant return, that I may die in my own town near the tomb of my father and mother. But here is your servant Kimham. Let him cross over with my lord the king. Do for him whatever pleases you."

[38]The king said, "Kimham shall cross over with me, and I will do for him whatever pleases you. And anything you desire from me I will do for you."

[39]So all the people crossed the Jordan, and then the king crossed over. The king kissed Barzillai and gave him his blessing, and Barzillai returned to his home.

[40]When the king crossed over to Gilgal, Kimham crossed with him. All the troops of Judah and half the troops of Israel had taken the king over.

[41]Soon all the men of Israel were coming to the king and saying to him, "Why did our brothers, the men of Judah, steal the king away and bring him and his household across the Jordan, together with all his men?"

[42]All the men of Judah answered the men of Israel, "We

*See the note on page 307.

†42 Most mss have *sheva* in the *kaph* ( ךְ־ ).

°41 ק העבירו

הַמֶּ֫לֶךְ אֵלַי וְלָ֫מָּה זֶּה חָרָה לְךָ עַל־ הַדָּבָר הַזֶּה
the-this the-thing about to-you he-angers this now-why? to-us the-king

הֶאָכוֹל אָכַ֫לְנוּ מִן־ הַמֶּ֫לֶךְ אִם־ נִשֵּׂאת נִשָּׂא לָנוּ׃ וַיַּ֫עַן
then-he-answered (44) for-us we-took anything or the-king from we-ate to-eat?

אִישׁ־ יִשְׂרָאֵל° אֶת־ אִישׁ יְהוּדָה וַיֹּ֫אמֶר עֶשֶׂר־ יָדוֹת לִי בַמֶּ֫לֶךְ
in-the-king to-me shares ten and-he-said Judah man-of *** Israel man-of

וְגַם־ בְּדָוִד֙ אֲנִי מִמְּךָ וּמַדּ֫וּעַ הֱקִלֹּתַ֫נִי†
you-treat-with-contempt-me so-why? more-than-you I to-David and-besides

וְלֹא־ הָיָה דְבָרִי רִאשׁוֹן לִי לְהָשִׁיב אֶת־ מַלְכִּי
king-of-me *** to-bring-back to-me first word-of-me he-was now-not

וַיִּ֫קֶשׁ דְּבַר־ אִישׁ יְהוּדָה מִדְּבַר אִישׁ יִשְׂרָאֵל׃
Israel man-of more-than-word-of Judah man-of response-of but-he-was-harsh

וְשָׁם נִקְרָא אִישׁ בְּלִיַּ֫עַל וּשְׁמוֹ שֶׁ֫בַע בֶּן־
son-of Sheba and-name-of-him troublemaker man-of he-happened now-there (20:1)

בִּכְרִי אִישׁ יְמִינִי וַיִּתְקַע בַּשֹּׁפָר וַיֹּ֫אמֶר אֵין־
not and-he-shouted on-the-trumpet and-he-sounded ††Jamite man-of Bicri

לָנוּ חֵ֫לֶק בְּדָוִד וְלֹא נַחֲלָה־לָנוּ בְּבֶן־ יִשַׁי אִישׁ לְאֹהָלָיו
to-tent-of-him each Jesse in-son-of to-us part and-not in-David share to-us

יִשְׂרָאֵל׃ וַיַּ֫עַל כָּל־ אִישׁ יִשְׂרָאֵל מֵאַחֲרֵי דָוִד אַחֲרֵי שֶׁ֫בַע
Sheba after David from-after Israel man-of all-of so-he-deserted (2) Israel

בֶּן־ בִּכְרִי וְאִישׁ יְהוּדָה דָּבְקוּ בְמַלְכָּם מִן־ הַיַּרְדֵּן
the-Jordan from by-king-of-them they-stayed Judah but-man-of Bicri son-of

וְעַד־ יְרוּשָׁלָ͏ִם׃ וַיָּבֹא דָוִד אֶל־ בֵּיתוֹ יְרוּשָׁלַ͏ִם
Jerusalem palace-of-him to David when-he-returned (3) Jerusalem even-to

וַיִּקַּח הַמֶּ֫לֶךְ אֵת עֶשֶׂר־נָשִׁים ׀ פִּלַגְשִׁים אֲשֶׁר הִנִּיחַ לִשְׁמֹר
to-take-care-of he-left whom concubines women ten *** the-king then-he-took

הַבַּ֫יִת וַיִּתְּנֵם בֵּית־ מִשְׁמֶ֫רֶת וַיְכַלְכְּלֵם וַאֲלֵיהֶם
but-into-them and-he-provided-for-them guard house-of and-he-put-them the-palace

לֹא־ בָא וַתִּהְיֶינָה צְרֻרוֹת עַד־ יוֹם מֻתָן
death-of-them day-of till ones-being-confined and-they-were he-went not

אַלְמְנוּת חַיּוּת׃ וַיֹּ֫אמֶר הַמֶּ֫לֶךְ אֶל־עֲמָשָׂא הַזְעֶק־ לִי אֶת־
*** to-me summon! Amasa to the-king then-he-said (4) living widowhood-of

אִישׁ־ יְהוּדָה שְׁלֹ֫שֶׁת יָמִים וְאַתָּה פֹּה עֲמֹד׃ וַיֵּ֫לֶךְ עֲמָשָׂא
Amasa when-he-went (5) be! here and-you days three-of Judah man-of

לְהַזְעִיק אֶת־יְהוּדָה וַיִּ֫יחַר° מִן־ הַמּוֹעֵד אֲשֶׁר יְעָדוֹ׃
he-set-for-him that the-time than then-he-took-longer Judah *** to-summon

וַיֹּ֫אמֶר דָּוִד אֶל־אֲבִישַׁי עַתָּה יֵרַע לָנוּ שֶׁ֫בַע בֶּן־ בִּכְרִי
Bicri son-of Sheba to-us he-will-harm now Abishai to David and-he-said (6)

did this because the king is closely related to us. Why are you angry about it? Have we eaten any of the king's provisions? Have we taken anything for ourselves?"

43 Then the men of Israel answered the men of Judah, "We have ten shares in the king; and besides, we have a greater claim on David than you have. So why do you treat us with contempt? Were we not the first to speak of bringing back our king?"

But the men of Judah responded even more harshly than the men of Israel.

*Sheba Rebels Against David*

20 Now a troublemaker named Sheba son of Bicri, a Benjamite, happened to be there. He sounded the trumpet and shouted,

"We have no share in
 David,
 no part in Jesse's son!
Every man to his tent, O
 Israel!"

2 So all the men of Israel deserted David to follow Sheba son of Bicri. But the men of Judah stayed by their king all the way from the Jordan to Jerusalem.

3 When David returned to his palace in Jerusalem, he took the ten concubines he had left to take care of the palace and put them in a house under guard. He provided for them, but did not lie with them. They were kept in confinement till the day of their death, living as widows.

4 Then the king said to Amasa, "Summon the men of Judah to come to me within three days, and be here yourself." 5 But when Amasa went to summon Judah, he took longer than the time the king had set for him.

6 David said to Abishai, "Now Sheba son of Bicri will

*See the note on page 307.

†44 Most mss have *hateph pathah* under the *he* (הֲ).

††1 That is, *Benjamite*.

°5 ק ויוחר

מִן־ אַבְשָׁלוֹם אַתָּה קַח אֶת־עַבְדֵי אֲדֹנֶיךָ וּרְדֹף אַחֲרָיו
after-him and-pursue! masters-of-you men-of *** take! you Absalom more-than

פֶּן־ מָצָא לוֹ עָרִים בְּצֻרוֹת וְהִצִּיל
and-he-will-escape ones-being-fortified cities for-him he-will-find or

עֵינֵנוּ׃ וַיֵּצְאוּ אַחֲרָיו אַנְשֵׁי יוֹאָב וְהַכְּרֵתִי
and-the-Kerethite Joab men-of after-him so-he-went-out (7) eye-of-us

וְהַפְּלֵתִי וְכָל־ הַגִּבֹּרִים וַיֵּצְאוּ מִירוּשָׁלִַם
from-Jerusalem and-they-marched-out the-warriors and-all-of and-the-Pelethite

לִרְדֹּף אַחֲרֵי שֶׁבַע בֶּן־ בִּכְרִי׃ הֵם עִם־ הָאֶבֶן הַגְּדוֹלָה אֲשֶׁר
that the-great the-rock at they (8) Bicri son-of Sheba after to-pursue

בְּגִבְעוֹן וַעֲמָשָׂא בָּא לִפְנֵיהֶם וְיוֹאָב חָגוּר ׀ מִדּוֹ
military-tunic-of-him wearing now-Joab before-them he-came and-Amasa in-Gibeon

לְבֻשׁוֹ וְעָלָו° חֲגוֹר חֶרֶב מְצֻמֶּדֶת עַל־ מָתְנָיו
waists-of-him at being-strapped dagger belt-of and-over-him clothing-of-him

בְּתַעְרָהּ וְהוּא יָצָא וַתִּפֹּל׃ וַיֹּאמֶר
and-he-said (9) then-she-dropped-out he-stepped-forward as-he in-sheath-of-her

יוֹאָב לַעֲמָשָׂא הֲשָׁלוֹם אַתָּה אָחִי וַתֹּחֶז יַד־ יְמִין
right-of hand-of then-she-grabbed brother-of-me you well? to-Amasa Joab

יוֹאָב בִּזְקַן עֲמָשָׂא לִנְשָׁק־ לוֹ׃ וַעֲמָשָׂא לֹא־ נִשְׁמַר
he-was-on-guard not and-Amasa (10) on-him to-kiss Amasa on-beard-of Joab

בַּחֶרֶב ׀ אֲשֶׁר בְּיַד־ יוֹאָב וַיַּכֵּהוּ בָהּ אֶל־
into with-her and-he-stabbed-him Joab in-hand-of that against-the-sword

הַחֹמֶשׁ וַיִּשְׁפֹּךְ מֵעָיו אַרְצָה וְלֹא־ שָׁנָה
he-did-again and-not on-ground intestines-of-him and-he-spilled-out the-belly

לוֹ וַיָּמֹת וְיוֹאָב וַאֲבִישַׁי אָחִיו רָדַף אַחֲרֵי
after he-pursued brother-of-him and-Abishai then-Joab and-he-died to-him

שֶׁבַע בֶּן־ בִּכְרִי׃ וְאִישׁ עָמַד עָלָיו מִנַּעֲרֵי יוֹאָב
Joab from-men-of beside-him he-stood and-man (11) Bicri son-of Sheba

וַיֹּאמֶר מִי אֲשֶׁר חָפֵץ בְּיוֹאָב וּמִי אֲשֶׁר־ לְדָוִד אַחֲרֵי יוֹאָב׃
Joab after for-David ever and-who to-Joab he-favors ever who and-he-said

וַעֲמָשָׂא מִתְגֹּלֵל בַּדָּם בְּתוֹךְ הַמְסִלָּה וַיַּרְא
and-he-saw the-road in-middle-of in-the-blood wallowing and-Amasa (12)

הָאִישׁ כִּי־ עָמַד כָּל־ הָעָם וַיַּסֵּב אֶת־ עֲמָשָׂא מִן־
from Amasa *** and-he-dragged the-troop all-of he-halted that the-man

הַמְסִלָּה הַשָּׂדֶה וַיַּשְׁלֵךְ עָלָיו בֶּגֶד כַּאֲשֶׁר רָאָה
he-realized as-soon-as garment over-him and-he-threw the-field the-road

כָּל־ הַבָּא עָלָיו וְעָמָד׃ כַּאֲשֶׁר הֹגָה
he-removed as-soon-as (13) then-he-stopped to-him the-one-coming every-of

do us more harm than Absalom did. Take your master's men and pursue him, or he will find fortified cities and escape from us." [7]So Joab's men and the Kerethites and Pelethites and all the mighty warriors went out under the command of Abishai. They marched out from Jerusalem to pursue Sheba son of Bicri.

[8]While they were at the great rock in Gibeon, Amasa came to meet them. Joab was wearing his military tunic, and strapped over it at his waist was a belt with a dagger in its sheath. As he stepped forward, it dropped out of its sheath.

[9]Joab said to Amasa, "How are you, my brother?" Then Joab took Amasa by the beard with his right hand to kiss him. [10]Amasa was not on his guard against the dagger in Joab's hand, and Joab plunged it into his belly, and his intestines spilled out on the ground. Without being stabbed again, Amasa died. Then Joab and his brother Abishai pursued Sheba son of Bicri.

[11]One of Joab's men stood beside Amasa and said, "Whoever favors Joab, and whoever is for David, let him follow Joab!" [12]Amasa lay wallowing in his blood in the middle of the road, and the man saw that all the troops came to a halt there. When he realized that everyone who came up to Amasa stopped, he dragged him from the road into a field and threw a garment over him. [13]After Amasa had been removed from the

°8 ק ועליו

מִן־הַמְסִלָּה עָבַר כָּל־ אִישׁ אַחֲרֵי יוֹאָב לִרְדֹּף אַחֲרֵי שֶׁבַע בֶּן־
son-of Sheba after to-pursue Joab with man every-of he-went-on the-road from

בִּכְרִי׃ וַיַּעֲבֹר בְּכָל־ שִׁבְטֵי יִשְׂרָאֵל אָבֵלָה וּבֵית
even-Beth to-Abel Israel tribes-of through-all-of and-he-passed (14) Bicri

מַעֲכָה וְכָל־ הַבֵּרִים וַיִּקָּלֲהוּ וַיָּבֹאוּ אַף־
also and-they-followed and-they-gathered the-Berites and-all-of Maacah

אַחֲרָיו׃ וַיָּבֹאוּ וַיָּצֻרוּ עָלָיו בְּאָבֵלָה בֵּית
Beth in-Abel against-him and-they-besieged and-they-came (15) after-him

הַמַּעֲכָה וַיִּשְׁפְּכוּ סֹלְלָה אֶל־ הָעִיר וַתַּעֲמֹד
and-she-stood the-city up-to siege-ramp and-they-built the-Maacah

בַּחֵל וְכָל־ הָעָם אֲשֶׁר אֶת־ יוֹאָב
Joab with that the-troop and-all-of against-the-outer-fortification

מַשְׁחִיתִם לְהַפִּיל הַחוֹמָה׃ וַתִּקְרָא אִשָּׁה חֲכָמָה מִן־
from wise woman and-she-called (16) the-wall to-bring-down ones-battering

הָעִיר שִׁמְעוּ שִׁמְעוּ אִמְרוּ־ נָא אֶל־יוֹאָב קְרַב עַד־הֵנָּה וַאֲדַבְּרָה
so-I-can-speak here to come! Joab to now! tell! listen! listen! the-city

אֵלֶיךָ׃ וַיִּקְרַב אֵלֶיהָ וַתֹּאמֶר הָאִשָּׁה הַאַתָּה יוֹאָב
Joab you? the-woman and-she-asked toward-her and-he-went (17) to-you

וַיֹּאמֶר אָנִי וַתֹּאמֶר לוֹ שְׁמַע דִּבְרֵי אֲמָתֶךָ
servant-of-you words-of listen! to-him and-she-said I and-he-answered

וַיֹּאמֶר שֹׁמֵעַ אָנֹכִי׃ וַתֹּאמֶר לֵאמֹר דַּבֵּר יְדַבְּרוּ
they-said to-say to-say and-she-spoke (18) I listening and-he-said

בָרִאשֹׁנָה לֵאמֹר שָׁאֹל יְשָׁאֲלוּ בְּאָבֵל וְכֵן הֵתַמּוּ׃[a]
they-settled and-so at-Abel they-get-answer to-get-answer to-say in-the-past

אָנֹכִי שְׁלֻמֵי אֱמוּנֵי יִשְׂרָאֵל אַתָּה מְבַקֵּשׁ
trying you Israel ones-being-faithful-of ones-being-peaceful-of I (19)

לְהָמִית עִיר וְאֵם בְּיִשְׂרָאֵל לָמָּה תְבַלַּע נַחֲלַת
inheritance-of would-you-swallow why? in-Israel and-mother city to-destroy

יְהוָה׃ וַיַּעַן יוֹאָב וַיֹּאמַר חָלִילָה חָלִילָה לִי אִם־
if from-me far-be-it! far-be-it! and-he-said Joab and-he-replied (20) Yahweh

אֲבַלַּע וְאִם־ אַשְׁחִית׃ לֹא־כֵן הַדָּבָר כִּי אִישׁ מֵהַר
from-hill-country-of man but the-case this not (21) I-destroy or-if I-swallow-up

אֶפְרַיִם שֶׁבַע בֶּן־ בִּכְרִי שְׁמוֹ נָשָׂא יָדוֹ בַּמֶּלֶךְ
against-the-king hand-of-him he-lifted name-of-him Bicri son-of Sheba Ephraim

בְּדָוִד תְּנוּ־ אֹתוֹ לְבַדּוֹ וְאֵלְכָה מֵעַל
from-against and-I-will-withdraw by-himself him hand-over! against-David

הָעִיר וַתֹּאמֶר הָאִשָּׁה אֶל־יוֹאָב הִנֵּה רֹאשׁוֹ מֻשְׁלָךְ אֵלֶיךָ
to-you being-thrown head-of-him see! Joab to the-woman and-she-said the-city

road, all the men went on with Joab to pursue Sheba son of Bicri.

[14]Sheba passed through all the tribes of Israel to Abel Beth Maacah[j] and through the entire region of the Berites, who gathered together and followed him. [15]All the troops with Joab came and besieged Sheba in Abel Beth Maacah. They built a siege ramp up to the city, and it stood against the outer fortifications. While they were battering the wall to bring it down, [16]a wise woman called from the city, "Listen! Listen! Tell Joab to come here so I can speak to him." [17]He went toward her, and she asked, "Are you Joab?"

"I am," he answered.

She said, "Listen to what your servant has to say."

"I'm listening," he said.

[18]She continued, "Long ago they used to say, 'Get your answer at Abel,' and that settled it. [19]We are the peaceful and faithful in Israel. You are trying to destroy a city that is a mother in Israel. Why do you want to swallow up the LORD's inheritance?"

[20]"Far be it from me!" Joab replied, "Far be it from me to swallow up or destroy! [21]That is not the case. A man named Sheba son of Bicri, from the hill country of Ephraim, has lifted up his hand against the king, against David. Hand over this one man, and I'll withdraw from the city."

The woman said to Joab,

j14 Or *Abel, even Beth Maacah;* also in verse 15

°14 ק ויקהלו

בְּעַד הַחוֹמָה׃ וַתָּבוֹא הָאִשָּׁה אֶל־ כָּל־ הָעָם
the-people all-of to the-woman then-she-went (22) the-wall from

בְּחָכְמָתָהּ וַיִּכְרְתוּ אֶת־ רֹאשׁ שֶׁבַע בֶּן־ בִּכְרִי
Bicri son-of Sheba head-of *** and-they-cut-off with-wise-advice-of-her

וַיַּשְׁלִכוּ אֶל־ יוֹאָב וַיִּתְקַע בַּשּׁוֹפָר וַיָּפֻצוּ
and-they-dispersed on-the-trumpet so-he-sounded Joab to and-they-threw

מֵעַל־ הָעִיר אִישׁ לְאֹהָלָיו וְיוֹאָב שָׁב יְרוּשָׁלַםִ
Jerusalem he-went-back and-Joab to-homes-of-him each the-city from-against

אֶל־הַמֶּלֶךְ׃ וְיוֹאָב אֶל כָּל־ הַצָּבָא יִשְׂרָאֵל וּבְנָיָה בֶּן־
son-of and-Benaiah Israel the-army entire-of over now-Joab (23) the-king to

יְהוֹיָדָע עַל־ הַכְּרֵי וְעַל־ הַפְּלֵתִי׃ וַאֲדֹרָם עַל־
over and-Adoram (24) the-Pelethite and-over the-Kerethite over Jehoiada

הַמַּס וִיהוֹשָׁפָט בֶּן־ אֲחִילוּד הַמַּזְכִּיר׃
the-one-recording Ahilud son-of and-Jehoshaphat the-forced-labor

וּשְׁיָא סֹפֵר וְצָדוֹק וְאֶבְיָתָר כֹּהֲנִים׃ וְגַם עִירָא
Ira and-also (26) priests and-Abiathar and-Zadok secretary and-Sheva (25)

הַיָּאִרִי הָיָה כֹהֵן לְדָוִד׃ וַיְהִי רָעָב בִּימֵי דָוִד
David in-days-of famine and-he-was (21:1) to-David priest he-was the-Jairite

שָׁלֹשׁ שָׁנִים שָׁנָה אַחֲרֵי שָׁנָה וַיְבַקֵּשׁ דָּוִד אֶת־ פְּנֵי יְהוָה
Yahweh faces-of *** David so-he-sought year after year years three

וַיֹּאמֶר יְהוָה אֶל־ שָׁאוּל וְאֶל־ בֵּית הַדָּמִים
the-bloods house-of and-on-account-of Saul on-account-of Yahweh and-he-said

עַל־ אֲשֶׁר־ הֵמִית אֶת־ הַגִּבְעֹנִים׃ וַיִּקְרָא הַמֶּלֶךְ
the-king and-he-summoned (2) the-Gibeonites *** he-killed that because

לַגִּבְעֹנִים וַיֹּאמֶר אֲלֵיהֶם וְהַגִּבְעֹנִים לֹא מִבְּנֵי
from-sons-of not now-the-Gibeonites to-them and-he-spoke to-the-Gibeonites

יִשְׂרָאֵל הֵמָּה כִּי אִם־ מִיֶּתֶר הָאֱמֹרִי וּבְנֵי יִשְׂרָאֵל
Israel and-sons-of the-Amorite from-survivor-of rather but they Israel

נִשְׁבְּעוּ לָהֶם וַיְבַקֵּשׁ שָׁאוּל לְהַכֹּתָם בְּקַנֹּאתוֹ
in-zeal-of-him to-annihilate-them Saul but-he-tried to-them they-swore

לִבְנֵי־ יִשְׂרָאֵל וִיהוּדָה׃ וַיֹּאמֶר דָּוִד אֶל־ הַגִּבְעֹנִים מָה
what? the-Gibeonites to David and-he-asked (3) and-Judah Israel for-sons-of

אֶעֱשֶׂה לָכֶם וּבַמָּה אֲכַפֵּר וּבָרְכוּ אֶת־
*** so-bless! shall-I-make-amends and-by-the-how? for-you shall-I-do

נַחֲלַת יְהוָה׃ וַיֹּאמְרוּ לוֹ הַגִּבְעֹנִים אֵין־ לִי
to-us not the-Gibeonites to-him and-they-answered (4) Yahweh inheritance-of

כֶּסֶף וְזָהָב עִם־ שָׁאוּל וְעִם־ בֵּיתוֹ וְאֵין־ לָנוּ אִישׁ לְהָמִית
to-kill anyone to-us and-not family-of-him or-from Saul from or-gold silver

"His head will be thrown to you from the wall."

22Then the woman went to all the people with her wise advice, and they cut off the head of Sheba son of Bicri and threw it to Joab. So he sounded the trumpet, and his men dispersed from the city, each returning to his home. And Joab went back to the king in Jerusalem.

23Joab was over Israel's entire army; Benaiah son of Jehoiada was over the Kerethites and Pelethites; 24Adoniram[k] was in charge of forced labor; Jehoshaphat son of Ahilud was recorder; 25Sheva was secretary; Zadok and Abiathar were priests; 26and Ira the Jairite was David's priest.

*The Gibeonites Avenged*

21 During the reign of David, there was a famine for three successive years; so David sought the face of the LORD. The LORD said, "It is on account of Saul and his blood-stained house; it is because he put the Gibeonites to death."

2The king summoned the Gibeonites and spoke to them. (Now the Gibeonites were not a part of Israel but were survivors of the Amorites; the Israelites had sworn to ⌊spare⌋ them, but Saul in his zeal for Israel and Judah had tried to annihilate them.) 3David asked the Gibeonites, "What shall I do for you? How shall I make amends so that you will bless the LORD's inheritance?"

4The Gibeonites answered him, "We have no right to demand silver or gold from Saul or his family, nor do we have the right to put anyone in Israel to death."

[k]24 Septuagint (see also 1 Kings 4:6 and 5:14); Hebrew *Adoram*

°23 ק הכרתי
°25 ק ושוא
°4 ק לנו

בְּיִשְׂרָאֵל וַיֹּאמֶר מָה־ אַתֶּם אֹמְרִים אֶעֱשֶׂה לָכֶם׃
for-you I-should-do ones-asking you what? and-he-asked in-Israel

וַיֹּאמְרוּ אֶל־ הַמֶּלֶךְ הָאִישׁ אֲשֶׁר כִּלָּנוּ וַאֲשֶׁר
and-who he-destroyed-us who the-man the-king to and-they-answered (5)

דִּמָּה־ לָנוּ נִשְׁמַדְנוּ מֵהִתְיַצֵּב בְּכָל־ גְּבֻל
place-of in-any-of from-to-have-place he-decimated-us against-us he-plotted

יִשְׂרָאֵל׃ °יֻנְתַּן־ לָנוּ שִׁבְעָה אֲנָשִׁים מִבָּנָיו
from-sons-of-him men seven to-us let-him-be-given (6) Israel

וְהוֹקַעֲנוּם לַיהוָה בְּגִבְעַת שָׁאוּל בְּחִיר יְהוָה
Yahweh chosen-of Saul at-Gibeah-of before-Yahweh and-let-them-expose-them

וַיֹּאמֶר הַמֶּלֶךְ אֲנִי אֶתֵּן׃ וַיַּחְמֹל הַמֶּלֶךְ עַל־ מְפִיבֹשֶׁת
Mephibosheth to the-king and-he-spared (7) I-will-give I the-king so-he-said

בֶּן־ יְהוֹנָתָן בֶּן־ שָׁאוּל עַל־ שְׁבֻעַת יְהוָה אֲשֶׁר בֵּינֹתָם
between-them that Yahweh oath-of because-of Saul son-of Jonathan son-of

בֵּין דָּוִד וּבֵין יְהוֹנָתָן בֶּן־ שָׁאוּל׃ וַיִּקַּח הַמֶּלֶךְ אֶת־
*** the-king but-he-took (8) Saul son-of Jonathan and-between David between

שְׁנֵי בְּנֵי רִצְפָּה בַת־ אַיָּה אֲשֶׁר יָלְדָה לְשָׁאוּל אֶת־ אַרְמֹנִי
Armoni *** to-Saul she-bore whom Aiah daughter-of Rizpah sons-of two-of

וְאֶת־ מְפִבֹשֶׁת וְאֶת־ חֲמֵשֶׁת בְּנֵי מִיכַל בַּת־ שָׁאוּל אֲשֶׁר יָלְדָה
she-bore whom Saul daughter-of Michal sons-of five-of and Mephibosheth and

לְעַדְרִיאֵל בֶּן־ בַּרְזִלַּי הַמְּחֹלָתִי׃ וַיִּתְּנֵם בְּיַד
into-hand-of and-he-gave-them (9) the-Meholathite Barzillai son-of to-Adriel

הַגִּבְעֹנִים וַיֹּקִיעֻם בָּהָר לִפְנֵי יְהוָה וַיִּפְּלוּ
and-they-fell Yahweh before on-the-hill and-they-exposed-them the-Gibeonites

°שִׁבְעָתִים יָחַד °וְהֵם הֻמְתוּ בִּימֵי קָצִיר
harvest in-days-of they-were-killed now-they together seven-of-them

בָּרִאשֹׁנִים °תְּחִלַּת קְצִיר שְׂעֹרִים׃ וַתִּקַּח
and-she-took (10) barleys harvest-of at-beginning-of during-the-first-ones

רִצְפָּה בַת־ אַיָּה אֶת־ הַשַּׂק וַתַּטֵּהוּ לָהּ אֶל־
on for-her and-she-spread-out-him the-sackcloth *** Aiah daughter-of Rizpah

הַצּוּר מִתְּחִלַּת קָצִיר עַד נִתַּךְ־ מַיִם עֲלֵיהֶם מִן־
from on-them rains he-poured-down till harvest from-beginning-of the-rock

הַשָּׁמָיִם וְלֹא־ נָתְנָה עוֹף הַשָּׁמַיִם לָנוּחַ עֲלֵיהֶם יוֹמָם וְאֶת־
or by-day on-them to-touch the-skies bird-of she-let and-not the-heavens

חַיַּת הַשָּׂדֶה לָיְלָה׃ וַיֻּגַּד לְדָוִד אֵת אֲשֶׁר־ עָשְׂתָה
she-did what *** to-David when-he-was-told (11) night the-field animal-of

רִצְפָּה בַת־ אַיָּה פִּלֶגֶשׁ שָׁאוּל׃ וַיֵּלֶךְ דָּוִד וַיִּקַּח
and-he-took David then-he-went (12) Saul concubine-of Aiah daughter-of Rizpah

"What do you want me to do for you?" David asked.

[5]They answered the king, "As for the man who destroyed us and plotted against us so that we have been decimated and have no place anywhere in Israel, [6]let seven of his male descendants be given to us to be killed and exposed before the LORD at Gibeah of Saul—the Lord's chosen one."

So the king said, "I will give them to you."

[7]The king spared Mephibosheth son of Jonathan, the son of Saul, because of the oath before the LORD between David and Jonathan son of Saul. [8]But the king took Armoni and Mephibosheth, the two sons of Aiah's daughter Rizpah, whom she had borne to Saul, together with the five sons of Saul's daughter Merab,[l] whom she had borne to Adriel son of Barzillai the Meholathite. [9]He handed them over to the Gibeonites, who killed and exposed them on a hill before the LORD. All seven of them fell together; they were put to death during the first days of the harvest, just as the barley harvest was beginning.

[10]Rizpah daughter of Aiah took sackcloth and spread it out for herself on a rock. From the beginning of the harvest till the rain poured down from the heavens on the bodies, she did not let the birds of the air touch them by day or the wild animals by night. [11]When David was told what Aiah's daughter Rizpah, Saul's concubine, had done, [12]he went

[l]8 Two Hebrew manuscripts, some Septuagint manuscripts and Syriac (see also 1 Samuel 18:19); most Hebrew and Septuagint manuscripts *Michal*

°6 ק יתן
°9a ק שבעתם
°9b ק והמה
°9c ק בתחלת

אֶת־עַצְמוֹת שָׁאוּל וְאֶת־עַצְמוֹת יְהוֹנָתָן בְּנוֹ מֵאֵת בַּעֲלֵי יָבֵישׁ

Jabesh citizens-of from son-of-him Jonathan bones-of and Saul bones-of ***

גִּלְעָד אֲשֶׁר גָּנְבוּ אֹתָם מֵרְחֹב בֵּית־שַׁן אֲשֶׁר

where Shan Beth from-square-of them they-secretly-took who Gilead

תְּלָוּם שָׁם הַפְּלִשְׁתִּים בְּיוֹם הַכּוֹת פְּלִשְׁתִּים אֶת־שָׁאוּל

Saul *** Philistines to-strike on-day Philistines at-there they-hung-them

בַּגִּלְבֹּעַ׃ וַיַּעַל מִשָּׁם אֶת־עַצְמוֹת שָׁאוּל וְאֶת־עַצְמוֹת

bones-of and Saul bones-of *** from-there and-he-brought-up (13) on-the-Gilboa

יְהוֹנָתָן בְּנוֹ וַיַּאַסְפוּ אֶת־עַצְמוֹת הַמּוּקָעִים׃

the-ones-being-exposed bones-of *** and-they-gathered son-of-him Jonathan

וַיִּקְבְּרוּ אֶת־עַצְמוֹת־שָׁאוּל וִיהוֹנָתָן־בְּנוֹ בְּאֶרֶץ

in-land-of son-of-him and-Jonathan Saul bones-of *** and-they-buried (14)

בִּנְיָמִן בְּצֵלָע בְּקֶבֶר קִישׁ אָבִיו וַיַּעֲשׂוּ כֹּל אֲשֶׁר־

that all and-they-did father-of-him Kish in-tomb-of at-Zela Benjamin

צִוָּה הַמֶּלֶךְ וַיֵּעָתֵר אֱלֹהִים לָאָרֶץ אַחֲרֵי־כֵן׃

that after for-the-land God and-he-answered-prayer the-king he-commanded

וַתְּהִי־עוֹד מִלְחָמָה לַפְּלִשְׁתִּים אֶת־יִשְׂרָאֵל

Israel against with-the-Philistines battle again and-she-was (15)

וַיֵּרֶד דָּוִד וַעֲבָדָיו עִמּוֹ וַיִּלָּחֲמוּ אֶת־

against and-they-fought with-him and-men-of-him David and-he-went-down

פְּלִשְׁתִּים וַיָּעַף דָּוִד׃ וְיִשְׁבּוֹ בְּנֹב אֲשֶׁר ׀

who Benob and-Ishbi (16) David and-he-became-exhausted Philistines

בִּילִידֵי הָרָפָה וּמִשְׁקַל קֵינוֹ שְׁלֹשׁ מֵאוֹת

hundreds three-of spearhead-of-him and-weight-of the-Rapha of-descendants-of

מִשְׁקַל נְחֹשֶׁת וְהוּא חָגוּר חֲדָשָׁה וַיֹּאמֶר לְהַכּוֹת אֶת־דָּוִד׃

David *** to-kill and-he-said new being-armed and-he bronze weight-of

וַיַּעֲזָר־לוֹ אֲבִישַׁי בֶּן־צְרוּיָה וַיַּךְ אֶת־

*** and-he-struck-down Zeruiah son-of Abishai to-him but-he-rescued (17)

הַפְּלִשְׁתִּי וַיְמִיתֵהוּ אָז נִשְׁבְּעוּ אַנְשֵׁי־דָוִד לוֹ לֵאמֹר

to-say to-him David men-of they-swore then and-he-killed-him the-Philistine

לֹא־תֵצֵא עוֹד אִתָּנוּ לַמִּלְחָמָה וְלֹא תְכַבֶּה אֶת־

*** you-extinguish so-not to-the-battle with-us again you-will-go-out not

נֵר יִשְׂרָאֵל׃ וַיְהִי אַחֲרֵי־כֵן וַתְּהִי־עוֹד הַמִּלְחָמָה

the-battle again then-she-was this after and-he-was (18) Israel lamp-of

בְּגוֹב עִם־פְּלִשְׁתִּים אָז הִכָּה סִבְּכַי הַחֻשָׁתִי אֶת־סַף

Saph *** the-Hushathite Sibbecai he-killed then Philistines with at-Gob

אֲשֶׁר בִּילִדֵי הָרָפָה׃ וַתְּהִי־עוֹד הַמִּלְחָמָה בְּגוֹב

at-Gob the-battle again and-she-was (19) the-Rapha of-descendants-of who

and took the bones of Saul and his son Jonathan from the citizens of Jabesh Gilead. (They had taken them secretly from the public square at Beth Shan, where the Philistines had hung them after they struck Saul down on Gilboa.) [13]David brought the bones of Saul and his son Jonathan from there, and the bones of those who had been killed and exposed were gathered up.

[14]They buried the bones of Saul and his son Jonathan in the tomb of Saul's father Kish, at Zela in Benjamin, and did everything the king commanded. After that, God answered prayer in behalf of the land.

*Wars Against the Philistines*

[15]Once again there was a battle between the Philistines and Israel. David went down with his men to fight against the Philistines, and he became exhausted. [16]And Ishbi-Benob, one of the descendants of Rapha, whose bronze spearhead weighed three hundred shekels[m] and who was armed with a new ⌞sword⌟, said he would kill David. [17]But Abishai son of Zeruiah came to David's rescue; he struck the Philistine down and killed him. Then David's men swore to him, saying, "Never again will you go out with us to battle, so that the lamp of Israel will not be extinguished."

[18]In the course of time, there was another battle with the Philistines, at Gob. At that

[m]*16* That is, about 7 1/2 pounds (about 3.5 kilograms)

°*12a* ק תלאום
°*12b* ק שמה פלשתים
°*16* ק וישבי

עִם־ פְּלִשְׁתִּים וַיַּךְ אֶלְחָנָן בֶּן־ יַעְרֵי אֹרְגִים בֵּית הַלַּחְמִי
the-Bethlehemite Oregim Jaare son-of Elhanan and-he-killed Philistines with

אֵת גָּלְיָת הַגִּתִּי וְעֵץ חֲנִיתוֹ כִּמְנוֹר אֹרְגִים׃
ones-weaving like-rod-of spear-of-him and-shaft-of the-Gittite Goliath ***

וַתְּהִי־ עוֹד מִלְחָמָה בְּגַת וַיְהִי ׀ אִישׁ מָדִין° וְאֶצְבְּעֹת
and-fingers-of huge man and-he-was at-Gath battle again and-she-was (20)

יָדָיו וְאֶצְבְּעוֹת רַגְלָיו שֵׁשׁ וָשֵׁשׁ עֶשְׂרִים וְאַרְבַּע מִסְפָּר
total and-four twenty and-six six feet-of-him and-toes-of hands-of-him

וְגַם־ הוּא יֻלַּד לְהָרָפָה׃ וַיְחָרֵף אֶת־יִשְׂרָאֵל
Israel *** when-he-taunted (21) from-the-Rapha he-was-descended he and-also

וַיַּכֵּהוּ יְהוֹנָתָן בֶּן־ שִׁמְעֵי° אֲחִי דָוִד׃ אֶת־אַרְבַּעַת
four-of *** (22) David brother-of Shimeah son-of Jonathan then-he-killed-him

אֵלֶּה יֻלְּדוּ לְהָרָפָה בְּגַת וַיִּפְּלוּ בְיַד־
at-hand-of and-they-fell in-Gath from-the-Rapha they-were-descended these

דָוִד וּבְיַד עֲבָדָיו׃ וַיְדַבֵּר דָּוִד לַיהוָה אֶת־
*** to-Yahweh David and-he-sang (22:1) men-of-him and-at-hand-of David

דִּבְרֵי הַשִּׁירָה הַזֹּאת בְּיוֹם הִצִּיל יְהוָה אֹתוֹ מִכַּף כָּל־
all-of from-hand-of him Yahweh he-delivered on-day the-this the-song words-of

אֹיְבָיו וּמִכַּף שָׁאוּל׃ וַיֹּאמַר יְהוָה סַלְעִי
rock-of-me Yahweh and-he-said (2) Saul and-from-hand-of being-enemies-of-him

וּמְצֻדָתִי וּמְפַלְטִי־ לִי׃ אֱלֹהֵי צוּרִי
rock-of-me God-of (3) for-me and-one-delivering-me and-fortress-of-me

אֶחֱסֶה־ בּוֹ מָגִנִּי וְקֶרֶן יִשְׁעִי מִשְׂגַּבִּי
stronghold-of-me salvation-of-me and-horn-of shield-of-me in-him I-take-refuge

וּמְנוּסִי מֹשִׁעִי מֵחָמָס תֹּשִׁעֵנִי׃ מְהֻלָּל
being-praised (4) you-save-me from-violence one-saving-me and-refuge-of-me

אֶקְרָא יְהוָה וּמֵאֹיְבַי אִוָּשֵׁעַ׃ כִּי
indeed (5) I-am-saved and-from-being-enemies-of-me Yahweh I-call

אֲפָפֻנִי מִשְׁבְּרֵי־ מָוֶת נַחֲלֵי בְלִיַּעַל
destruction torrents-of death waves-of they-swirled-around-me

יְבַעֲתֻנִי׃ חֶבְלֵי שְׁאוֹל סַבֻּנִי
they-coiled-around-me Sheol cords-of (6) they-overwhelmed-me

קִדְּמֻנִי מֹקְשֵׁי־ מָוֶת׃ בַּצַּר־ לִי אֶקְרָא יְהוָה
Yahweh I-called of-me in-the-distress (7) death snares-of they-confronted-me

וְאֶל־ אֱלֹהַי אֶקְרָא וַיִּשְׁמַע מֵהֵיכָלוֹ קוֹלִי
voice-of-me from-temple-of-him and-he-heard I-called-out God-of-me and-to

וְשַׁוְעָתִי בְּאָזְנָיו׃ וַתִּגְעַשׁ° וַתִּרְעַשׁ הָאָרֶץ
the-earth and-she-quaked and-she-trembled (8) in-ears-of-him and-cry-of-me

time Sibbecai the Hushathite killed Saph, one of the descendants of Rapha.

19 In another battle with the Philistines at Gob, Elhanan son of Jaare-Oregim[n] the Bethlehemite killed Goliath[o] the Gittite, who had a spear with a shaft like a weaver's rod.

20 In still another battle, which took place at Gath, there was a huge man with six fingers on each hand and six toes on each foot—twenty-four in all. He also was descended from Rapha. 21 When he taunted Israel, Jonathan son of Shimeah, David's brother, killed him.

22 These four were descendants of Rapha in Gath, and they fell at the hands of David and his men.

*David's Song of Praise*

22 David sang to the LORD the words of this song when the LORD delivered him from the hand of all his enemies and from the hand of Saul. 2 He said:

"The LORD is my rock, my
fortress and my
deliverer;
3 my God is my rock, in
whom I take refuge,
my shield and the horn[p]
of my salvation.
He is my stronghold, my
refuge and my savior—
from violent men you
save me.
4 I call to the LORD, who is
worthy of praise,
and I am saved from my
enemies.

5 "The waves of death
swirled about me;
the torrents of
destruction
overwhelmed me.
6 The cords of the grave[q]
coiled around me;
the snares of death
confronted me.
7 In my distress I called to
the LORD;
I called out to my God.
From his temple he heard
my voice;
my cry came to his ears.

8 "The earth trembled and
quaked,

[n] 19 Or *son of Jair the weaver*
[o] 19 Hebrew and Septuagint; 1 Chronicles 20:5 *son of Jair killed Lahmi the brother of Goliath*
[p] 3 *Horn* here symbolizes strength.
[q] 6 Hebrew *Sheol*

°20 ק מדון
°21 ק שמעה
°8 ק ויתגעש

מוֹסְדוֹת הַשָּׁמַיִם יִרְגָּזוּ וַיִּתְגָּעֲשׁוּ כִּי־ חָרָה
he-angered because and-they-trembled they-shook the-heavens foundations-of

לוֹ׃ (9) עָלָה עָשָׁן בְּאַפּוֹ וְאֵשׁ מִפִּיו
from-mouth-of-him and-fire from-nostril-of-him smoke he-rose (9) to-him

תֹּאכֵל גֶּחָלִים בָּעֲרוּ מִמֶּנּוּ׃ (10) וַיֵּט שָׁמַיִם
heavens and-he-parted (10) from-him they-burned coals she-consumed

וַיֵּרַד וַעֲרָפֶל תַּחַת רַגְלָיו׃ (11) וַיִּרְכַּב עַל־
on and-he-mounted (11) feet-of-him under and-dark-cloud and-he-came-down

כְּרוּב וַיָּעֹף וַיֵּרָא עַל־ כַּנְפֵי־ רוּחַ׃ (12) וַיָּשֶׁת
and-he-made (12) wind wings-of on and-he-appeared and-he-flew cherub

חֹשֶׁךְ סְבִיבֹתָיו סֻכּוֹת חַשְׁרַת־ מַיִם עָבֵי שְׁחָקִים׃
dark-clouds clouds-of waters mass-of canopies around-him darkness

(13) מִנֹּגַהּ נֶגְדּוֹ בָּעֲרוּ גַּחֲלֵי־ אֵשׁ׃
lightning bolts-of they-blazed presence-of-him from-brightness-of (13)

(14) יַרְעֵם מִן־ שָׁמַיִם יְהוָה וְעֶלְיוֹן יִתֵּן
he-resounded and-Most-High Yahweh heavens from he-thundered (14)

קוֹלוֹ׃ (15) וַיִּשְׁלַח חִצִּים וַיְפִיצֵם בָּרָק
lightning-bolt and-he-scattered-them arrows and-he-shot (15) voice-of-him

°וַיָּהְמֹם׃ (16) וַיֵּרָאוּ אֲפִקֵי יָם יִגָּלוּ
they-were-laid-bare sea valleys-of and-they-were-exposed (16) and-he-routed

מֹסְדוֹת תֵּבֵל בְּגַעֲרַת יְהוָה מִנִּשְׁמַת רוּחַ אַפּוֹ׃
nostril-of-him breath-of at-blast-of Yahweh at-rebuke-of earth foundations-of

(17) יִשְׁלַח מִמָּרוֹם יִקָּחֵנִי יַמְשֵׁנִי מִמַּיִם
from-waters he-drew-out-me he-took-hold-of-me from-on-high he-reached (17)

רַבִּים׃ (18) יַצִּילֵנִי מֵאֹיְבִי עָז
powerful from-being-enemy-of-me he-rescued-me (18) deep-ones

מִשֹּׂנְאַי כִּי אָמְצוּ מִמֶּנִּי׃ (19) יְקַדְּמֻנִי
they-confronted-me (19) for-me they-were-too-strong for from-ones-hating-me

בְּיוֹם אֵידִי וַיְהִי יְהוָה מִשְׁעָן לִי׃
to-me support Yahweh but-he-was disaster-of-me in-day-of

(20) וַיֹּצֵא לַמֶּרְחָב אֹתִי יְחַלְּצֵנִי כִּי־
because he-rescued-me me to-the-spacious-place and-he-brought-out (20)

חָפֵץ בִּי׃ (21) יִגְמְלֵנִי יְהוָה כְּצִדְקָתִי
as-righteousness-of-me Yahweh he-dealt-with-me (21) in-me he-delighted

כְּבֹר יָדַי יָשִׁיב לִי׃ (22) כִּי שָׁמַרְתִּי דַּרְכֵי
ways-of I-kept for (22) to-me he-rewarded hands-of-me as-cleanness-of

יְהוָה וְלֹא רָשַׁעְתִּי מֵאֱלֹהָי׃ (23) כִּי כָל־ °מִשְׁפָּטָו
laws-of-him all-of indeed (23) from-God-of-me I-did-evil and-not Yahweh

the foundations of the
heavens[r] shook;
they trembled because he
was angry.
9 Smoke rose from his
nostrils;
consuming fire came
from his mouth,
burning coals blazed out
of it.
10 He parted the heavens and
came down;
dark clouds were under
his feet.
11 He mounted the cherubim
and flew;
he soared[s] on the wings
of the wind.
12 He made darkness his
canopy around him—
the dark[t] rain clouds of
the sky.
13 Out of the brightness of
his presence
bolts of lightning blazed
forth.
14 The LORD thundered from
heaven;
the voice of the Most
High resounded.
15 He shot arrows and
scattered ⌊the enemies⌋,
bolts of lightning and
routed them.
16 The valleys of the sea were
exposed
and the foundations of
the earth laid bare
at the rebuke of the LORD,
at the blast of breath
from his nostrils.

17 "He reached down from on
high and took hold of
me;
he drew me out of deep
waters.
18 He rescued me from my
powerful enemy,
from my foes, who were
too strong for me.
19 They confronted me in the
day of my disaster,
but the LORD was my
support.
20 He brought me out into a
spacious place;
he rescued me because
he delighted in me.

21 "The LORD has dealt with
me according to my
righteousness;
according to the
cleanness of my hands
he has rewarded me.
22 For I have kept the ways of
the LORD;
I have not done evil by
turning from my God.

r8 Hebrew; Vulgate and Syriac (see also Psalm 18:7) *mountains*
s11 Many Hebrew manuscripts (see also Psalm 18:10); most Hebrew manuscripts *appeared*
t12 Septuagint and Vulgate (see also Psalm 18:11); Hebrew *massed*

°15 ק ויהם °23 ק משפטיו

לְנֶגְדִּי וְחֻקֹּתָיו לֹא־אָסוּר מִמֶּנָּה׃ וָאֶהְיֶה

and-I-was (24) from-her I-turned-away not and-decrees-of-him at-before-me

תָמִים לוֹ וָאֶשְׁתַּמְּרָה מֵעֲוֺנִי׃ וַיָּשֶׁב

and-he-rewarded (25) from-sin-of-me and-I-kept-myself before-him blameless

יְהוָה לִי כְּצִדְקָתִי כְּבֹרִי לְנֶגֶד עֵינָיו׃

eyes-of-him at-before as-cleanness-of-me as-righteousness-of-me to-me Yahweh

עִם־חָסִיד תִּתְחַסָּד עִם־גְּבוֹר תָּמִים

blameless man-of to you-show-yourself-faithful faithful to (26)

תִּתַּמָּם׃ עִם־נָבָר תִּתָּבָר

you-show-yourself-pure one-being-pure to (27) you-show-yourself-blameless

וְעִם־עִקֵּשׁ תִּתַּפָּל׃ וְאֶת־עַם עָנִי תּוֹשִׁיעַ

you-save humble people-of and (28) you-show-yourself-shrewd crooked but-to

וְעֵינֶיךָ עַל־רָמִים תַּשְׁפִּיל׃ כִּי־אַתָּה

you indeed (29) you-bring-low ones-being-haughty on but-eyes-of-you

נֵירִי יְהוָה וַיהוָה יַגִּיהַּ חָשְׁכִּי׃ כִּי

indeed (30) darkness-of-me he-makes-light and-Yahweh Yahweh lamp-of-me

בְכָה אָרוּץ גְּדוּד בֵּאלֹהַי אֲדַלֶּג־שׁוּר׃ הָאֵל

the-God (31) wall I-can-scale with-God-of-me troop I-can-advance with-you

תָּמִים דַּרְכּוֹ אִמְרַת יְהוָה צְרוּפָה מָגֵן הוּא לְכֹל

to-all-of he shield being-flawless Yahweh word-of way-of-him perfect

הַחֹסִים בּוֹ׃ כִּי מִי־אֵל מִבַּלְעֲדֵי יְהוָה וּמִי צוּר

Rock and-who? Yahweh besides God who? for (32) in-him the-ones-taking-refuge

מִבַּלְעֲדֵי אֱלֹהֵינוּ׃ הָאֵל מָעוּזִּי חָיִל וַיַּתֵּר תָּמִים

perfect and-he-makes strong refuge-of-me the-God (33) God-of-us besides

דַּרְכּוֹ׃ מְשַׁוֶּה רַגְלָיו כָּאַיָּלוֹת וְעַל־בָּמוֹתַי

heights-of-me and-on like-the-deer feet-of-me one-making (34) way-of-me

יַעֲמִידֵנִי׃ מְלַמֵּד יָדַי לַמִּלְחָמָה

for-the-battle hands-of-me one-training (35) he-makes-stand-me

וְנִחַת קֶשֶׁת־נְחוּשָׁה זְרֹעֹתָי׃ וַתִּתֶּן־לִי מָגֵן

shield-of to-me and-you-give (36) arms-of-me bronze bow-of and-he-can-bend

יִשְׁעֶךָ וַעֲנֹתְךָ תַּרְבֵּנִי׃ תַּרְחִיב

you-broaden (37) you-make-great-me and-to-stoop-down-you victory-of-you

צַעֲדִי תַּחְתֵּנִי וְלֹא מָעֲדוּ קַרְסֻלָּי׃ אֶרְדְּפָה

I-pursued (38) ankles-of-me they-turn so-not beneath-me path-of-me

אֹיְבַי וָאַשְׁמִידֵם וְלֹא אָשׁוּב עַד־

till I-turned-back and-not and-I-crushed-them being-enemies-of-me

כַּלּוֹתָם׃ וָאֲכַלֵּם וָאֶמְחָצֵם וְלֹא

so-not and-I-crushed-them and-I-destroyed-them (39) to-destroy-them

23 All his laws are before me;
I have not turned away from his decrees.
24 I have been blameless before him
and have kept myself from sin.
25 The LORD has rewarded me according to my righteousness,
according to my cleanness[u] in his sight.

26 "To the faithful you show yourself faithful,
to the blameless you show yourself blameless,
27 to the pure you show yourself pure,
but to the crooked you show yourself shrewd.
28 You save the humble,
but your eyes are on the haughty to bring them low.
29 You are my lamp, O LORD;
the LORD turns my darkness into light.
30 With your help I can advance against a troop[v];
with my God I can scale a wall.

31 "As for God, his way is perfect;
the word of the LORD is flawless.
He is a shield
for all who take refuge in him.
32 For who is God besides the LORD?
And who is the Rock except our God?
33 It is God who arms me with strength[w]
and makes my way perfect.
34 He makes my feet like the feet of a deer;
he enables me to stand on the heights.
35 He trains my hands for battle;
my arms can bend a bow of bronze.
36 You give me your shield of victory;
you stoop down to make me great.
37 You broaden the path beneath me,
so that my ankles do not turn.

38 "I pursued my enemies and crushed them;
I did not turn back till they were destroyed.

[u] 25 Hebrew; Septuagint and Vulgate (see also Psalm 18:24) *to the cleanness of my hands*
[v] 30 Or *can run through a barricade*
[w] 33 Dead Sea Scrolls, some Septuagint manuscripts, Vulgate and Syriac (see also Psalm 18:32); Masoretic Text *who is my strong refuge*

°33 ק דרכי °34 ק רגלי

יְקוּמוּן וַיִּפְּלוּ תַּחַת רַגְלָי׃ וַתַּזְרֵנִי
and-you-armed-me (40) feet-of-me beneath and-they-fell they-could-rise

חַיִל לַמִּלְחָמָה תַּכְרִיעַ קָמַי תַּחְתֵּנִי׃
beneath-me adversaries-of-me you-made-bow for-the-battle strength

וְאֹיְבַי תַּתָּה לִּי עֹרֶף מְשַׂנְאַי
ones-hating-me back to-me you-made-turn and-being-enemies-of-me (41)

וָאַצְמִיתֵם׃ יִשְׁעוּ וְאֵין מֹשִׁיעַ אֶל־ יְהוָה
Yahweh to saving but-no-one they-cried-for-help (42) also-I-destroyed-them

וְלֹא עָנָם׃ וְאֶשְׁחָקֵם כַּעֲפַר־ אָרֶץ
earth like-dust-of and-I-beat-them (43) he-answered-them but-not

כְּטִיט־ חוּצוֹת אֲדִקֵּם אֶרְקָעֵם׃ וַתְּפַלְּטֵנִי
and-you-delivered-me (44) I-trampled-them I-pounded-them streets like-mud-of

מֵרִיבֵי עַמִּי תִּשְׁמְרֵנִי לְרֹאשׁ גּוֹיִם עַם לֹא־
not people nations as-head-of you-preserved-me people-of-me from-attacks-of

יָדַעְתִּי יַעַבְדֻנִי׃ בְּנֵי נֵכָר יִתְכַּחֲשׁוּ־
they-come-cringing foreigner sons-of (45) they-are-subject-to-me I-know

לִי לִשְׁמוֹעַ אֹזֶן יִשָּׁמְעוּ לִי׃ בְּנֵי נֵכָר יִבֹּלוּ
they-lose-heart foreigner sons-of (46) to-me they-obey ear to-hear to-me

וְיַחְגְּרוּ מִמִּסְגְּרוֹתָם׃ חַי־ יְהוָה
Yahweh life-of (47) from-strongholds-of-them and-they-arm-themselves

וּבָרוּךְ צוּרִי וְיָרֻם אֱלֹהֵי צוּר
Rock-of God-of and-may-he-be-exalted Rock-of-me and-being-praised

יִשְׁעִי׃ הָאֵל הַנֹּתֵן נְקָמֹת לִי וּמוֹרִיד
and-one-putting to-me vengeances the-one-giving the-God (48) Savior-of-me

עַמִּים תַּחְתֵּנִי׃ וּמוֹצִיאִי מֵאֹיְבָי
from-being-enemies-of-me and-one-setting-free-me (49) under-me nations

וּמִקָּמַי תְּרוֹמְמֵנִי מֵאִישׁ חֲמָסִים תַּצִּילֵנִי׃
you-rescued-me violences from-man-of you-exalted-me and-above-foes-of-me

עַל־ כֵּן אוֹדְךָ יְהוָה בַּגּוֹיִם וּלְשִׁמְךָ
and-to-name-of-you among-the-nations Yahweh I-will-praise-you this for (50)

אֲזַמֵּר׃ מִגְדּוֹל יְשׁוּעוֹת מַלְכּוֹ וְעֹשֶׂה־
and-showing king-of-him victories-of greatness-of (51) I-will-sing-praise

חֶסֶד לִמְשִׁיחוֹ לְדָוִד וּלְזַרְעוֹ
and-to-descendant-of-him to-David to-anointed-of-him unfailing-kindness

עַד־ עוֹלָם׃ וְאֵלֶּה דִּבְרֵי דָוִד הָאַחֲרֹנִים נְאֻם דָּוִד
David oracle-of the-last-ones David words-of and-these (23:1) forever to

בֶּן־ יִשַׁי וּנְאֻם הַגֶּבֶר הֻקַם עָל מְשִׁיחַ אֱלֹהֵי
God-of anointed-of above he-was-exalted the-man and-oracle-of Jesse son-of

39 I crushed them completely,
and they could not
rise;
they fell beneath my feet.
40 You armed me with
strength for battle;
you made my adversaries
bow at my feet.
41 You made my enemies turn
their backs in flight,
and I destroyed my foes.
42 They cried for help, but
there was no one to
save them—
to the LORD, but he did
not answer.
43 I beat them as fine as the
dust of the earth;
I pounded and trampled
them like mud in the
streets.

44 "You have delivered me
from the attacks of my
people;
you have preserved me
as the head of nations.
People I did not know are
subject to me,
45 and foreigners come
cringing to me;
as soon as they hear me,
they obey me.
46 They all lose heart;
they come trembling[x]
from their strongholds.

47 "The LORD lives! Praise be
to my Rock!
Exalted be God, the Rock,
my Savior!
48 He is the God who avenges
me,
who puts the nations
under me,
49 who sets me free from
my enemies.
You exalted me above my
foes;
from violent men you
rescued me.
50 Therefore I will praise you,
O LORD, among the
nations;
I will sing praises to your
name.
51 He gives his king great
victories;
he shows unfailing
kindness to his
anointed,
to David and his
descendants forever."

### *The Last Words of David*

23 These are the last words of David:

"The oracle of David son of
Jesse,
the oracle of the man
exalted by the Most
High,
the man anointed by the
God of Jacob,
Israel's singer of songs[y]:

[x]46 See Septuagint, Vulgate and Psalm 18:45; Masoretic Text *they arm themselves*
[y]1 Or *Israel's beloved singer*

יַעֲקֹב וּנְעִים זְמִרוֹת יִשְׂרָאֵל׃ רוּחַ יְהוָה דִּבֶּר־ בִּי

through-me he-spoke Yahweh Spirit-of (2) Israel songs-of and-singer-of Jacob

וּמִלָּתוֹ עַל־ לְשׁוֹנִי׃ אָמַר אֱלֹהֵי יִשְׂרָאֵל לִי דִבֶּר

he-said to-me Israel God-of he-spoke (3) tongue-of-me on and-word-of-him

צוּר יִשְׂרָאֵל מוֹשֵׁל בָּאָדָם צַדִּיק מוֹשֵׁל יִרְאַת

fear-of one-ruling righteousness over-the-man one-ruling Israel Rock-of

אֱלֹהִים׃ וּכְאוֹר בֹּקֶר יִזְרַח־ שָׁמֶשׁ בֹּקֶר לֹא עָבוֹת

clouds without morning sun he-rises morning and-as-light-of (4) God

מִנֹּגַהּ מִמָּטָר דֶּשֶׁא מֵאָרֶץ׃ כִּי־ לֹא־ כֵן

right not indeed (5) from-earth grass after-rain like-brightness

בֵּיתִי עִם־ אֵל כִּי בְרִית עוֹלָם שָׂם לִי

with-me he-made everlasting covenant-of indeed God with house-of-me

עֲרוּכָה בַכֹּל וּשְׁמֻרָה כִּי־ כָל־ יִשְׁעִי

salvation-of-me all-of indeed and-being-secured in-the-whole being-arranged

וְכָל־ חֵפֶץ כִּי־ לֹא יַצְמִיחַ׃ וּבְלִיַּעַל

but-evil (6) he-will-bring-to-fruition not indeed desire and-every-of

כְּקוֹץ מֻנָד כֻּלָּהַם כִּי־ לֹא בְיָד יִקָּחוּ׃

they-are-gathered with-hand not that all-of-them being-cast-aside like-thorn

וְאִישׁ יִגַּע בָּהֶם יִמָּלֵא בַרְזֶל וְעֵץ חֲנִית

spear or-shaft-of iron he-is-used on-them he-touches and-whoever (7)

וּבָאֵשׁ שָׂרוֹף יִשָּׂרְפוּ בַּשָּׁבֶת׃ אֵלֶּה שְׁמוֹת

names-of these (8) in-the-place they-are-burned to-burn and-with-fire

הַגִּבֹּרִים אֲשֶׁר לְדָוִד יֹשֵׁב בַּשֶּׁבֶת תַּחְכְּמֹנִי | רֹאשׁ הַשָּׁלִשִׁי

the-three chief-of Tahkemonite Basshebeth Josheb of-David who the-mighty-men

הוּא עֲדִינוֹ הָעֶצְנוֹ עַל־ שְׁמֹנֶה מֵאוֹת חָלָל בְּפַעַם אֶחָד׃

one in-encounter killed hundreds eight against the-Eznite Adino he

וְאַחֲרוֹ אֶלְעָזָר בֶּן־ דֹּדִי* בֶּן־ אֲחֹחִי בִּשְׁלֹשָׁה

of-three Ahohi son-of *Dodai son-of Eleazar and-next-to-him (9)

גִּבֹּרִים עִם־ דָּוִד בְּחָרְפָם בַּפְּלִשְׁתִּים

against-the-Philistines when-to-taunt-them David with the-mighty-men

נֶאֶסְפוּ־ שָׁם לַמִּלְחָמָה וַיַּעֲלוּ אִישׁ יִשְׂרָאֵל׃

Israel man-of then-they-retreated for-the-battle there they-gathered

הוּא קָם וַיַּךְ בַּפְּלִשְׁתִּים עַד | כִּי־

when until against-the-Philistines and-he-struck he-stood he (10)

יָגְעָה יָדוֹ וַתִּדְבַּק יָדוֹ אֶל־ הַחֶרֶב

the-sword to hand-of-him and-she-froze hand-of-him she-grew-tired

וַיַּעַשׂ יְהוָה תְּשׁוּעָה גְדוֹלָה בַּיּוֹם הַהוּא וְהָעָם

and-the-troop the-that on-the-day great victory Yahweh and-he-brought

2 "The Spirit of the LORD
spoke through me;
his word was on my
tongue.
3 The God of Israel spoke,
the Rock of Israel said to
me:
'When one rules over men
in righteousness,
when he rules in the fear
of God,
4 he is like the light of
morning at sunrise
on a cloudless morning,
like the brightness after
rain
that brings the grass
from the earth.'

5 "Is not my house right
with God?
Has he not made with
me an everlasting
covenant,
arranged and secured in
every part?
Will he not bring to
fruition my salvation
and grant me my every
desire?
6 But evil men are all to be
cast aside like thorns,
which are not gathered
with the hand.
7 Whoever touches thorns
uses a tool of iron or the
shaft of a spear;
they are burned up
where they lie."

*David's Mighty Men*

8 These are the names of David's mighty men:
Josheb-Basshebeth,[z] a Tahkemonite,[a] was chief of the Three; he raised his spear against eight hundred men, whom he killed[b] in one encounter.
9 Next to him was Eleazar son of Dodai the Ahohite. As one of the three mighty men, he was with David when they taunted the Philistines gathered ⌊at Pas Dammim⌋[c] for battle. Then the men of Israel retreated, 10 but he stood his ground and struck down the Philistines till his hand grew tired and froze to the sword. The LORD brought about a

[z] 8 Hebrew; Septuagint suggests *Ish-Bosheth,* that is, *Esh-Baal* (see also 1 Chron. 11:11 *Jashobeam*).
[a] 8 Probably a variant of Hacmonite
[b] 8 Some Septuagint manuscripts (see also 1 Chron. 11:11); Hebrew and other Septuagint manuscripts *Three; it was Adino the Eznite who killed eight hundred men*
[c] 9 See 1 Chronicles 11:13; Hebrew *gathered there.*

*9 The NIV transliterates the *Kethib* form; the *Qere* reads *Dodo* or *uncle-of-him.*

°8a ק העצני °8b ק אחת
°9a ק ואחריו °9b ק דדו
°9c ק הגברים

יָשֻׁבוּ אַחֲרָיו אַךְ־לְפַשֵּׁט׃ וְאַחֲרָיו שַׁמָּא בֶן־אָגֵא
Agee son-of Shammah and-next-to-him (11) to-strip only to-him they-returned

הָרָרִי וַיֵּאָסְפוּ פְלִשְׁתִּים לַחַיָּה וַתְּהִי־שָׁם
there and-she-was as-the-group Philistines when-they-banded-together Hararite

חֶלְקַת הַשָּׂדֶה מְלֵאָה עֲדָשִׁים וְהָעָם נָס מִפְּנֵי
from-before he-fled and-the-troop lentils full the-field portion-of

פְלִשְׁתִּים׃ וַיִּתְיַצֵּב בְּתוֹךְ־הַחֶלְקָה וַיַּצִּילֶהָ
and-he-defended-her the-field in-middle-of but-he-took-stand (12) Philistines

וַיַּךְ אֶת־פְּלִשְׁתִּים וַיַּעַשׂ יְהוָה תְּשׁוּעָה גְדוֹלָה׃
great victory Yahweh and-he-brought Philistines *** and-he-struck-down

וַיֵּרְדוּ שְׁלֹשִׁים° מֵהַשְּׁלֹשִׁים רֹאשׁ וַיָּבֹאוּ אֶל־
during and-they-went chief of-the-thirty three and-they-came-down (13)

קָצִיר אֶל־דָּוִד אֶל־מְעָרַת עֲדֻלָּם וְחַיַּת פְּלִשְׁתִּים חֹנָה
camping Philistines and-band-of Adullam cave-of at David to harvest

בְּעֵמֶק רְפָאִים׃ וְדָוִד אָז בַּמְּצוּדָה וּמַצַּב
and-garrison-of in-the-stronghold then and-David (14) Rephaim in-Valley-of

פְּלִשְׁתִּים אָז בֵּית לָחֶם׃ וַיִּתְאַוֶּה דָוִד וַיֹּאמַר מִי
who? and-he-said David and-he-longed (15) Lehem Beth then Philistines

יַשְׁקֵנִי מַיִם מִבֹּאר בֵּית־לֶחֶם אֲשֶׁר בַּשָּׁעַר׃
near-the-gate that Lehem Beth from-well-of waters he-will-get-drink-for-me

וַיִּבְקְעוּ שְׁלֹשֶׁת הַגִּבֹּרִים בְּמַחֲנֵה פְלִשְׁתִּים
Philistines through-line-of the-mighty-men three-of so-they-broke (16)

וַיִּשְׁאֲבוּ־מַיִם מִבֹּאר בֵּית־לֶחֶם אֲשֶׁר בַּשַּׁעַר
near-the-gate that Lehem Beth from-well-of waters and-they-drew

וַיִּשְׂאוּ וַיָּבִאוּ אֶל־דָּוִד וְלֹא אָבָה לִשְׁתּוֹתָם
to-drink-them he-would but-not David to and-they-brought and-they-carried

וַיַּסֵּךְ אֹתָם לַיהוָה׃ וַיֹּאמֶר חָלִילָה לִּי
from-me far-be-it! and-he-said (17) before-Yahweh them but-he-poured-out

יְהוָה מֵעֲשֹׂתִי זֹאת הֲדַם הָאֲנָשִׁים הַהֹלְכִים בְּנַפְשׁוֹתָם
at-lives-of-them the-ones-going the-men blood-of? this from-to-do-me Yahweh

וְלֹא אָבָה לִשְׁתּוֹתָם אֵלֶּה עָשׂוּ שְׁלֹשֶׁת הַגִּבֹּרִים׃
the-mighty-men three-of they-did these to-drink-them he-would and-not

וַאֲבִישַׁי אֲחִי ׀ יוֹאָב בֶּן־צְרוּיָה הוּא רֹאשׁ הַשְּׁלֹשִׁי° וְהוּא
and-he the-Three chief-of he Zeruiah son-of Joab brother-of and-Abishai (18)

עוֹרֵר אֶת־חֲנִיתוֹ עַל־שְׁלֹשׁ מֵאוֹת חָלָל וְלוֹ־
so-to-him killed hundreds three-of against spear-of-him *** one-raising

שֵׁם בַּשְּׁלֹשָׁה׃ מִן־הַשְּׁלֹשָׁה הֲכִי נִכְבָּד
being-honored indeed? the-Three more-than (19) among-the-Three name

°13 ק שלשה
°18 ק השלשה

great victory that day. The troops returned to Eleazar, but only to strip the dead.

11Next to him was Shammah son of Agee the Hararite. When the Philistines banded together at a place where there was a field full of lentils, Israel's troops fled from them. 12But Shammah took his stand in the middle of the field. He defended it and struck the Philistines down, and the LORD brought about a great victory.

13During harvest time, three of the thirty chief men came down to David at the cave of Adullam, while a band of Philistines was encamped in the Valley of Rephaim. 14At that time David was in the stronghold, and the Philistine garrison was at Bethlehem. 15David longed for water and said, "Oh, that someone would get me a drink of water from the well near the gate of Bethlehem!" 16So the three mighty men broke through the Philistine lines, drew water from the well near the gate of Bethlehem and carried it back to David. But he refused to drink it; instead, he poured it out before the LORD. 17"Far be it from me, O LORD, to do this!" he said. "Is it not the blood of men who went at the risk of their lives?" And David would not drink it.

Such were the exploits of the three mighty men.

18Abishai the brother of Joab son of Zeruiah was chief of the Three.[d] He raised his spear against three hundred men, whom he killed, and so he became as famous as the Three. 19Was he not held in greater honor than the Three?

[d] *18* Most Hebrew manuscripts (see also 1 Chron. 11:20); two Hebrew manuscripts and Syriac *Thirty*

וַיְהִי לָהֶם לְשָׂר וְעַד־ הַשְּׁלֹשָׁה לֹא־ בָא׃

he-came not the-Three though-among as-commander to-them and-he-became

וּבְנָיָהוּ בֶן־ יְהוֹיָדָע בֶּן־ אִישׁ־ חַי° רַב־ פְּעָלִים

exploits great-of valor man-of son-of Jehoiada son-of and-Benaiah (20)

מִקַּבְצְאֵל הוּא הִכָּה אֵת שְׁנֵי אֲרִאֵל מוֹאָב וְהוּא

and-he Moab best-man-of two-of *** he-struck-down he from-Kabzeel

יָרַד וְהִכָּה אֶת־ הָאֲרִיָּה° בְּתוֹךְ הַבֹּאר בְּיוֹם הַשָּׁלֶג׃

the-snow on-day-of the-pit inside-of the-lion *** and-he-killed he-went-down

וְהוּא־ הִכָּה אֶת־ אִישׁ מִצְרִי אֲשֶׁר° מַרְאֶה וּבְיַד

though-in-hand-of huge man-of Egyptian man *** he-struck-down and-he (21)

הַמִּצְרִי חֲנִית וַיֵּרֶד אֵלָיו בַּשָּׁבֶט וַיִּגְזֹל אֶת־

*** and-he-snatched with-the-club against-him and-he-went spear the-Egyptian

הַחֲנִית מִיַּד הַמִּצְרִי וַיַּהַרְגֵהוּ בַּחֲנִיתוֹ׃

with-spear-of-him and-he-killed-him the-Egyptian from-hand-of the-spear

אֵלֶּה עָשָׂה בְּנָיָהוּ בֶּן־ יְהוֹיָדָע וְלוֹ־ שֵׁם בִּשְׁלֹשָׁה

among-three name and-to-him Jehoiada son-of Benaiah he-did these (22)

הַגִּבֹּרִים׃ מִן־ הַשְּׁלֹשִׁים נִכְבָּד וְאֶל־ הַשְּׁלֹשָׁה

the-Three though-among being-honored the-Thirty more-than (23) the-mighty-men

לֹא־ בָא וַיְשִׂמֵהוּ דָוִד אֶל־ מִשְׁמַעְתּוֹ׃

bodyguard-of-him over David and-he-put-in-charge-him he-came not

עֲשָׂה־ אֵל אֲחִי־ יוֹאָב בַּשְּׁלֹשִׁים אֶלְחָנָן בֶּן־ דֹּדוֹ בֵּית לָחֶם׃

Lehem Beth Dodo son-of Elhanan among-the-Thirty Joab brother-of El Asah (24)

שַׁמָּה הַחֲרֹדִי אֱלִיקָא הַחֲרֹדִי׃ חֶלֶץ הַפַּלְטִי עִירָא

Ira the-Paltite Helez (26) the-Harodite Elika the-Harodite Shammah (25)

בֶן־ עִקֵּשׁ הַתְּקוֹעִי׃ אֲבִיעֶזֶר הָעַנְּתֹתִי מְבֻנַּי

Mebunnai the-Anathothite Abiezer (27) the-Tekoaite Ikkesh son-of

הַחֻשָׁתִי׃ צַלְמוֹן הָאֲחֹחִי מַהְרַי הַנְּטֹפָתִי׃ חֵלֶב

Heleb (29) the-Netophathite Maharai the-Ahohite Zalmon (28) the-Hushathite

בֶּן־ בַּעֲנָה הַנְּטֹפָתִי אִתַּי בֶּן־ רִיבַי מִגִּבְעַת בְּנֵי

sons-of from-Gibeah-of Ribai son-of Ithai the-Netophathite Baanah son-of

בִנְיָמִן׃ בְּנָיָהוּ פִּרְעָתֹנִי הִדַּי מִנַּחֲלֵי גָעַשׁ׃ אֲבִי־עַלְבוֹן

Albon Abi (31) Gaash from-ravines-of Hiddai Pirathonite Benaiah (30) Benjamin

הָעַרְבָתִי עַזְמָוֶת הַבַּרְחֻמִי׃ אֶלְיַחְבָּא הַשַּׁעַלְבֹנִי בְּנֵי

sons-of the-Shaalbonite Eliahba (32) the-Barhumite Azmaveth the-Arbathite

יָשֵׁן יְהוֹנָתָן׃ שַׁמָּה הַהֲרָרִי אֲחִיאָם בֶּן־ שָׁרָר הָאֲרָרִי׃

Hararite Sharar son-of Ahiam the-Hararite Shammah (33) Jonathan Jashen

אֱלִיפֶלֶט בֶּן־ אֲחַסְבַּי בֶּן־ הַמַּעֲכָתִי אֱלִיעָם בֶּן־ אֲחִיתֹפֶל

Ahithophel son-of Eliam the-Maacathite son-of Ahasbai son-of Eliphelet (34)

He became their commander, even though he was not included among them.

20Benaiah son of Jehoiada was a valiant fighter from Kabzeel, who performed great exploits. He struck down two of Moab's best men. He also went down into a pit on a snowy day and killed a lion.
21And he struck down a huge Egyptian. Although the Egyptian had a spear in his hand, Benaiah went against him with a club. He snatched the spear from the Egyptian's hand and killed him with his own spear.
22Such were the exploits of Benaiah son of Jehoiada; he too was as famous as the three mighty men.
23He was held in greater honor than any of the Thirty, but he was not included among the Three. And David put him in charge of his bodyguard.

24Among the Thirty were:
Asahel the brother of Joab,
Elhanan son of Dodo from Bethlehem,
25Shammah the Harodite,
Elika the Harodite,
26Helez the Paltite,
Ira son of Ikkesh from Tekoa,
27Abiezer from Anathoth,
Mebunnai[e] the Hushathite,
28Zalmon the Ahohite,
Maharai the Netophathite,
29Heled[f] son of Baanah the Netophathite,
Ithai son of Ribai from Gibeah of Benjamin,
30Benaiah the Pirathonite,
Hiddai[g] from the ravines of Gaash,
31Abi-Albon the Arbathite,
Azmaveth the Barhumite,
32Eliahba the Shaalbonite,
the sons of Jashen,
Jonathan 33son of[h] Shammah the Hararite,
Ahiam son of Sharar[i] the Hararite,
34Eliphelet son of Ahasbai the Maacathite,

[e] 27 Hebrew; some Septuagint manuscripts (see also 1 Chron. 11:29) *Sibbecai*
[f] 29 Some Hebrew manuscripts and Vulgate (see also 1 Chron. 11:30); most Hebrew manuscripts *Heleb*
[g] 30 Hebrew; some Septuagint manuscripts (see also 1 Chron. 11:32) *Hurai*
[h] 33 Some Septuagint manuscripts (see also 1 Chron. 11:34); Hebrew does not have *son of*.
[i] 33 Hebrew; some Septuagint manuscripts (see also 1 Chron. 11:35) *Sacar*

°*20a* ק חיל °*20b* ק הארי
°*21* ק איש

הַגִּלֹנִי׃ חֶצְרוֹ הַכַּרְמְלִי פַּעֲרַי הָאַרְבִּי׃ יִגְאָל בֶּן־
son-of Igal (36) the-Arbite Paarai the-Carmelite *Hezro (35) the-Gilonite

נָתָן מִצֹּבָה בָּנִי הַגָּדִי׃ צֶלֶק הָעַמֹּנִי נַחְרַי
Naharai the-Ammonite Zelek (37) †Haggadi son-of† from-Zobah Nathan

הַבְּאֵרֹתִי נֹשֵׂא כְּלֵי יוֹאָב בֶּן־ צְרֻיָה׃ עִירָא הַיִּתְרִי
the-Ithrite Ira (38) Zeruiah son-of Joab armors-of one-bearing the-Beerothite

גָּרֵב הַיִּתְרִי׃ אוּרִיָּה הַחִתִּי כֹּל שְׁלֹשִׁים וְשִׁבְעָה׃
and-seven thirty total-of the-Hittite Uriah (39) the-Ithrite Gareb

וַיֹּסֶף אַף־ יְהוָה לַחֲרוֹת בְּיִשְׂרָאֵל וַיָּסֶת
and-he-incited against-Israel to-burn Yahweh anger-of and-he-repeated (24:1)

אֶת־ דָּוִד בָּהֶם לֵאמֹר לֵךְ מְנֵה אֶת־ יִשְׂרָאֵל וְאֶת־ יְהוּדָה׃ וַיֹּאמֶר
so-he-said (2) Judah and Israel *** count! go! to-say against-them David ***

הַמֶּלֶךְ אֶל־ יוֹאָב ׀ שַׂר־ הַחַיִל אֲשֶׁר־ אִתּוֹ שׁוּט־ נָא בְּכָל־
through-all-of now! go! with-him who the-army commander-of Joab to the-king

שִׁבְטֵי יִשְׂרָאֵל מִדָּן וְעַד־ בְּאֵר שֶׁבַע וּפִקְדוּ אֶת־ הָעָם
the-people *** and-enroll! Sheba Beer even-to from-Dan Israel tribes-of

וְיָדַעְתִּי אֵת מִסְפַּר הָעָם׃ וַיֹּאמֶר יוֹאָב אֶל־ הַמֶּלֶךְ
the-king to Joab but-he-replied (3) the-people number-of *** so-I-may-know

וְיוֹסֵף יְהוָה אֱלֹהֶיךָ אֶל־ הָעָם כָּהֵם ׀ וְכָהֵם
and-as-they as-they the-troop to God-of-you Yahweh now-may-he-multiply

מֵאָה פְעָמִים וְעֵינֵי אֲדֹנִי־ הַמֶּלֶךְ רֹאוֹת וַאדֹנִי
but-lord-of-me ones-seeing the-king lord-of-me and-eyes-of times hundred

הַמֶּלֶךְ לָמָּה חָפֵץ בַּדָּבָר הַזֶּה׃ וַיֶּחֱזַק דְּבַר־
word-of but-he-overruled (4) the-this for-the-thing he-wants why? the-king

הַמֶּלֶךְ אֶל־ יוֹאָב וְעַל שָׂרֵי הֶחָיִל וַיֵּצֵא יוֹאָב
Joab so-he-left the-army commanders-of and-over Joab over the-king

וְשָׂרֵי הַחַיִל לִפְנֵי הַמֶּלֶךְ לִפְקֹד אֶת־ הָעָם
the-people *** to-enroll the-king presences-of the-army and-commanders-of

אֶת־ יִשְׂרָאֵל׃ וַיַּעַבְרוּ אֶת־ הַיַּרְדֵּן וַיַּחֲנוּ בַעֲרוֹעֵר
near-Aroer and-they-camped the-Jordan *** and-they-crossed (5) Israel ***

יְמִין הָעִיר אֲשֶׁר בְּתוֹךְ־ הַנַּחַל הַגָּד וְאֶל־ יַעְזֵר׃
Jazer and-to the-Gad the-gorge in-midst-of that the-town south-of

וַיָּבֹאוּ הַגִּלְעָדָה וְאֶל־ אֶרֶץ תַּחְתִּים חָדְשִׁי וַיָּבֹאוּ
and-they-went Hodshi Tahtim region-of and-to to-the-Gilead and-they-went (6)

דָּנָה יַּעַן וְסָבִיב אֶל־ צִידוֹן׃ וַיָּבֹאוּ מִבְצַר־ צֹר
Tyre fortress-of then-they-went (7) Sidon toward and-around Jaan to-Dan

וְכָל־ עָרֵי הַחִוִּי וְהַכְּנַעֲנִי וַיֵּצְאוּ אֶל־ נֶגֶב
Negev-of to and-they-went and-the-Canaanite the-Hivite towns-of and-all-of

Eliam son of Ahithophel the Gilonite,
35 Hezro the Carmelite,
Paarai the Arbite,
36 Igal son of Nathan from Zobah,
the son of Hagri,[j]
37 Zelek the Ammonite,
Naharai the Beerothite,
the armor-bearer of Joab son of Zeruiah,
38 Ira the Ithrite,
Gareb the Ithrite
39 and Uriah the Hittite.
There were thirty-seven in all.

### *David Counts the Fighting Men*

24 Again the anger of the LORD burned against Israel, and he incited David against them, saying, "Go and count Israel and Judah."
2 So the king said to Joab and the army commanders[k] with him, "Go throughout the tribes of Israel from Dan to Beersheba and enroll the fighting men, so that I may know how many there are."
3 But Joab replied to the king, "May the LORD your God multiply the troops a hundred times over, and may the eyes of my lord the king see it. But why does my lord the king want to do such a thing?"
4 The king's word, however, overruled Joab and the army commanders; so they left the presence of the king to enroll the fighting men of Israel.
5 After crossing the Jordan, they camped near Aroer, south of the town in the gorge, and then went through Gad and on to Jazer.
6 They went to Gilead and the region of Tahtim Hodshi, and on to Dan Jaan and around toward Sidon.
7 Then they went toward the fortress of Tyre and all the towns of the Hivites and Canaanites. Finally, they went on to Beersheba in the Negev of Judah.

[j] 36 Some Septuagint manuscripts (see also 1 Chron. 11:38); Hebrew *Haggadi*
[k] 2 Septuagint (see also verse 4 and 1 Chron. 21:2); Hebrew *Joab the army commander*

*35 The NIV transliterates the *Kethib* Form; the *Qere* reads *Hezrai*.

†36 The NIV translates here in harmony with 1 Chronicles 11:38; the forms as written are the proper name *Bani the-Gadite*.

°35 ק חצרי
°37 ק נשא

יְהוּדָה בְּאֵר שָׁבַע׃ וַיָּשֻׁטוּ בְּכָל־ הָאָרֶץ וַיָּבֹאוּ
then-they-came the-land through-entire-of and-they-went (8) Sheba Beer Judah

מִקְצֵה תִשְׁעָה חֳדָשִׁים וְעֶשְׂרִים יוֹם יְרוּשָׁלִָם׃ וַיִּתֵּן יוֹאָב אֶת־
*** Joab and-he-reported (9) Jerusalem day and-twenty months nine at-end-of

מִסְפַּר מִפְקַד־ הָעָם אֶל־ הַמֶּלֶךְ וַתְּהִי יִשְׂרָאֵל שְׁמֹנֶה מֵאוֹת
hundreds eight Israel and-she-was the-king to the-people list-of number-of

אֶלֶף אִישׁ־ חַיִל שֹׁלֵף חֶרֶב וְאִישׁ יְהוּדָה חֲמֵשׁ־ מֵאוֹת
hundreds five-of Judah and-man-of sword handling ability man-of thousand

אֶלֶף אִישׁ׃ וַיַּךְ לֵב־ דָּוִד אֹתוֹ אַחֲרֵי־ כֵן סָפַר
he-counted this after him David conscience-of and-he-struck (10) man thousand

אֶת־ הָעָם וַיֹּאמֶר דָּוִד אֶל־ יְהוָה חָטָאתִי מְאֹד אֲשֶׁר עָשִׂיתִי
I-did what greatly I-sinned Yahweh to David and-he-said the-people ***

וְעַתָּה יְהוָה הַעֲבֶר־ נָא אֶת־ עֲוֺן עַבְדְּךָ כִּי נִסְכַּלְתִּי
I-was-foolish for servant-of-you guilt-of *** now! take-away! Yahweh and-now

מְאֹד׃ וַיָּקָם דָּוִד בַּבֹּקֶר וּדְבַר־ יְהוָה הָיָה אֶל־
to he-came Yahweh and-word-of in-the-morning David and-he-got-up (11) very

גָּד הַנָּבִיא חֹזֵה דָוִד לֵאמֹר׃ הָלוֹךְ וְדִבַּרְתָּ אֶל־ דָּוִד כֹּה
this David to and-you-tell to-go (12) to-say David seer-of the-prophet Gad

אָמַר יְהוָה שָׁלֹשׁ אָנֹכִי נוֹטֵל עָלֶיךָ בְּחַר־ לְךָ אַחַת־ מֵהֶם
of-them one for-you choose! to-you giving I three Yahweh he-says

וְאֶעֱשֶׂה־ לָּךְ׃ וַיָּבֹא־ גָד אֶל־ דָּוִד וַיַּגֶּד־ לוֹ
to-him and-he-told David to Gad so-he-went (13) to-you and-I-will-do

וַיֹּאמֶר לוֹ הֲתָבוֹא לְךָ שֶׁבַע שָׁנִים ׀ רָעָב ׀ בְּאַרְצֶךָ
in-land-of-you famine years seven upon-you shall-she-come? to-him and-he-said

אִם־ שְׁלֹשָׁה חֳדָשִׁים נֻסְךָ לִפְנֵי־ צָרֶיךָ וְהוּא רֹדְפֶךָ
pursuing-you while-he enemies-of-you before to-flee-you months three or

וְאִם־ הֱיוֹת שְׁלֹשֶׁת יָמִים דֶּבֶר בְּאַרְצֶךָ עַתָּה דַּע וּרְאֵה מָה־
how? and-decide! think! now in-land-of-you plague days three-of to-be or-if

אָשִׁיב שֹׁלְחִי דָּבָר׃ וַיֹּאמֶר דָּוִד אֶל־ גָּד צַר־
distress Gad to David and-he-said (14) answer one-sending-me should-I-bring

לִי מְאֹד נִפְּלָה־ נָּא בְיַד־ יְהוָה כִּי־ רַבִּים רַחֲמָו°
mercies-of-him great-ones for Yahweh into-hand-of now! let-us-fall deep to-me

וּבְיַד־ אָדָם אַל־ אֶפֹּלָה׃ וַיִּתֵּן יְהוָה דֶּבֶר בְּיִשְׂרָאֵל
on-Israel plague Yahweh so-he-sent (15) let-me-fall not man but-into-hand-of

מֵהַבֹּקֶר וְעַד־ עֵת מוֹעֵד וַיָּמָת מִן־ הָעָם
the-people from and-he-died designated time-of even-to from-the-morning

מִדָּן וְעַד־ בְּאֵר שֶׁבַע שִׁבְעִים אֶלֶף אִישׁ׃ וַיִּשְׁלַח
when-he-stretched (16) man thousand seventy Sheba Beer even-to from-Dan

8After they had gone
through the entire land, they
came back to Jerusalem at the
end of nine months and
twenty days.
9Joab reported the number of
the fighting men to the king:
In Israel there were eight hundred thousand able-bodied
men who could handle a
sword, and in Judah five hundred thousand.
10David was conscience-
stricken after he had counted
the fighting men, and he said
to the LORD, "I have sinned
greatly in what I have done.
Now, O LORD, I beg you, take
away the guilt of your servant.
I have done a very foolish
thing."
11Before David got up the
next morning, the word of the
LORD had come to Gad the
prophet, David's seer: 12"Go
and tell David, 'This is what
the LORD says: I am giving you
three options. Choose one of
them for me to carry out
against you.'"
13So Gad went to David and
said to him, "Shall there come
upon you three[l] years of famine in your land? Or three
months of fleeing from your
enemies while they pursue
you? Or three days of plague
in your land? Now then, think
it over and decide how I
should answer the one who
sent me."
14David said to Gad, "I am in
deep distress. Let us fall into
the hands of the LORD, for his
mercy is great; but do not let
me fall into the hands of
men."
15So the LORD sent a plague
on Israel from that morning
until the end of the time designated, and seventy thousand
of the people from Dan to
Beersheba died. 16When the

[l] *13* Some Septuagint manuscripts (see also 1 Chron. 21:12); Hebrew *seven*

°*14* ק רחמיו

יָדוֹ | הַמַּלְאָךְ | יְרוּשָׁלִַם לְשַׁחֲתָהּ וַיִּנָּחֶם יְהוָה
Yahweh then-he-was-grieved to-destroy-her Jerusalem the-angel hand-of-him

אֶל־ הָרָעָה וַיֹּאמֶר לַמַּלְאָךְ הַמַּשְׁחִית
the-one-afflicting to-the-angel and-he-said the-calamity because-of

בָּעָם רַב עַתָּה הֶרֶף יָדֶךָ וּמַלְאַךְ יְהוָה
Yahweh now-angel-of hand-of-you withdraw! now enough against-the-people

הָיָה עִם־ גֹּרֶן הָאֲוַרְנָה הַיְבֻסִי׃ וַיֹּאמֶר דָּוִד
David and-he-said (17) the-Jebusite the-Araunah threshing-floor-of at he-was

אֶל־ יְהוָה בִּרְאֹתוֹ | אֶת־ הַמַּלְאָךְ | הַמַּכֶּה בָעָם
against-the-people the-one-striking the-angel *** when-to-see-him Yahweh to

וַיֹּאמֶר הִנֵּה אָנֹכִי חָטָאתִי וְאָנֹכִי הֶעֱוֵיתִי וְאֵלֶּה הַצֹּאן מֶה
what? the-sheep and-these I-did-wrong and-I I-sinned I see! and-he-said

עָשׂוּ תְּהִי נָא יָדְךָ בִּי וּבְבֵית אָבִי׃
father-of-me and-upon-house-of upon-me hand-of-you now! let-her-fall they-did

וַיָּבֹא־ גָד אֶל־ דָּוִד בַּיּוֹם הַהוּא וַיֹּאמֶר לוֹ עֲלֵה
go-up! to-him and-he-said the-that on-the-day David to Gad and-he-went (18)

הָקֵם לַיהוָה מִזְבֵּחַ בְּגֹרֶן אֲרַנְיָה הַיְבֻסִי׃
the-Jebusite Araunah on-threshing-floor-of altar to-Yahweh build!

וַיַּעַל דָּוִד כִּדְבַר־ גָּד כַּאֲשֶׁר צִוָּה יְהוָה׃
Yahweh he-commanded just-as Gad as-word-of David so-he-went-up (19)

וַיַּשְׁקֵף אֲרַוְנָה וַיַּרְא אֶת־ הַמֶּלֶךְ וְאֶת־ עֲבָדָיו
men-of-him and the-king *** and-he-saw Araunah when-he-looked (20)

עֹבְרִים עָלָיו וַיֵּצֵא אֲרַוְנָה וַיִּשְׁתַּחוּ לַמֶּלֶךְ
before-the-king and-he-bowed Araunah then-he-went-out toward-him ones-coming

אַפָּיו אָרְצָה׃ וַיֹּאמֶר אֲרַוְנָה מַדּוּעַ בָּא אֲדֹנִי־
lord-of-me he-comes why? Araunah and-he-said (21) to-ground faces-of-him

הַמֶּלֶךְ אֶל־ עַבְדּוֹ וַיֹּאמֶר דָּוִד לִקְנוֹת מֵעִמְּךָ אֶת־
*** from-with-you to-buy David and-he-answered servant-of-him to the-king

הַגֹּרֶן לִבְנוֹת מִזְבֵּחַ לַיהוָה וְתֵעָצַר הַמַּגֵּפָה
the-plague so-she-may-be-stopped to-Yahweh altar to-build the-threshing-floor

מֵעַל הָעָם׃ וַיֹּאמֶר אֲרַוְנָה אֶל־ דָּוִד יִקַּח
let-him-take David to Araunah and-he-said (22) the-people from-on

וְיַעַל אֲדֹנִי הַמֶּלֶךְ הַטּוֹב בְּעֵינָו רְאֵה הַבָּקָר
the-ox see! in-eyes-of-him the-good the-king lord-of-me and-let-him-offer

לָעֹלָה וְהַמֹּרִגִּים וּכְלֵי הַבָּקָר
the-ox and-yokes-of and-the-threshing-sledges for-the-burnt-offering

לָעֵצִים׃ הַכֹּל נָתַן אֲרַוְנָה הַמֶּלֶךְ לַמֶּלֶךְ
to-the-king the-king Araunah he-gives the-whole (23) for-the-woods

angel stretched out his hand to destroy Jerusalem, the LORD was grieved because of the calamity and said to the angel who was afflicting the people, "Enough! Withdraw your hand." The angel of the LORD was then at the threshing floor of Araunah the Jebusite.

17 When David saw the angel who was striking down the people, he said to the LORD, "I am the one who has sinned and done wrong. These are but sheep. What have they done? Let your hand fall upon me and my family."

*David Builds an Altar*

18 On that day Gad went to David and said to him, "Go up and build an altar to the LORD on the threshing floor of Araunah the Jebusite."
19 So David went up, as the LORD had commanded through Gad.
20 When Araunah looked and saw the king and his men coming toward him, he went out and bowed down before the king with his face to the ground.

21 Araunah said, "Why has my lord the king come to his servant?"

"To buy your threshing floor," David answered, "so I can build an altar to the LORD, that the plague on the people may be stopped."

22 Araunah said to David, "Let my lord the king take whatever pleases him and offer it up. Here are oxen for the burnt offering, and here are threshing sledges and ox yokes for the wood.
23 O king, Araunah gives all this to the

°16 ק הארונה
°18 ק ארונה
°22 ק בעיניו

וַיֹּאמֶר אֲרַוְנָה אֶל־ הַמֶּלֶךְ יְהוָה אֱלֹהֶיךָ יִרְצֶךָ׃
may-he-accept-you God-of-you Yahweh the-king to Araunah and-he-said

וַיֹּאמֶר הַמֶּלֶךְ אֶל־ אֲרַוְנָה לֹא כִּי־ קָנוֹ אֶקְנֶה
I-will-buy to-buy indeed no Araunah to the-king but-he-replied (24)

מֵאוֹתְךָ בִּמְחִיר וְלֹא אַעֲלֶה לַיהוָה אֱלֹהַי
God-of-me to-Yahweh I-will-sacrifice for-not for-price from-you

עֹלוֹת חִנָּם וַיִּקֶן דָּוִד אֶת־ הַגֹּרֶן
the-threshing-floor *** David so-he-bought without-cost burnt-offerings

וְאֶת־ הַבָּקָר בְּכֶסֶף שְׁקָלִים חֲמִשִּׁים׃ וַיִּבֶן שָׁם דָּוִד מִזְבֵּחַ
altar David there and-he-built (25) fifty shekels with-silver the-ox and

לַיהוָה וַיַּעַל עֹלוֹת וּשְׁלָמִים
and-fellowship-offerings burnt-offerings and-he-sacrificed to-Yahweh

וַיֵּעָתֵר יְהוָה לָאָרֶץ וַתֵּעָצַר
and-she-was-stopped in-behalf-of-the-land Yahweh and-he-answered-prayer

הַמַּגֵּפָה מֵעַל יִשְׂרָאֵל׃
Israel from-on the-plague

king." Araunah also said to him, "May the LORD your God accept you."

24But the king replied to Araunah, "No, I insist on paying you for it. I will not sacrifice to the LORD my God burnt offerings that cost me nothing."

So David bought the threshing floor and the oxen and paid fifty shekels[m] of silver for them. 25David built an altar to the LORD there and sacrificed burnt offerings and fellowship offerings.[n] Then the LORD answered prayer in behalf of the land, and the plague on Israel was stopped.

[m]24 That is, about 1 1/4 pounds (about 0.6 kilogram)
[n]25 Traditionally *peace offerings*

וְהַמֶּלֶךְ דָּוִד זָקֵן בָּא בַּיָּמִים

in-the-days he-was-advanced he-was-old David now-the-king (1)

וַיְכַסֻּהוּ בַּבְּגָדִים וְלֹא יִחַם לוֹ׃

for-him he-was-warm but-not with-the-garments and-they-covered-him

וַיֹּאמְרוּ לוֹ עֲבָדָיו יְבַקְשׁוּ לַאדֹנִי

for-lord-of-me let-them-look-for servants-of-him to-him so-they-said (2)

הַמֶּלֶךְ נַעֲרָה בְתוּלָה וְעָמְדָה לִפְנֵי הַמֶּלֶךְ וּתְהִי־

and-she-may-be the-king before so-she-may-attend virgin young-woman the-king

לוֹ סֹכֶנֶת וְשָׁכְבָה בְחֵיקֶךָ וְחַם

so-he-may-be-warm at-side-of-you and-she-can-lie one-caring for-him

לַאדֹנִי הַמֶּלֶךְ׃ וַיְבַקְשׁוּ נַעֲרָה יָפָה בְּכֹל

through-all-of beautiful girl then-they-searched (3) the-king for-lord-of-me

גְּבוּל יִשְׂרָאֵל וַיִּמְצְאוּ אֶת־ אֲבִישַׁג הַשּׁוּנַמִּית וַיָּבִאוּ

and-they-brought the-Shunammite Abishag *** and-they-found Israel territory-of

אֹתָהּ לַמֶּלֶךְ׃ וְהַנַּעֲרָה יָפָה עַד־ מְאֹד וַתְּהִי

and-she-was very-much to beautiful and-the-girl (4) to-the-king her

לַמֶּלֶךְ סֹכֶנֶת וַתְּשָׁרְתֵהוּ וְהַמֶּלֶךְ לֹא יְדָעָהּ׃

he-knew-her not but-the-king and-she-waited-on-him one-caring for-the-king

וַאֲדֹנִיָּה בֶן־ חַגִּית מִתְנַשֵּׂא לֵאמֹר אֲנִי אֶמְלֹךְ

I-will-be-king I to-say putting-himself-forward Haggith son-of now-Adonijah (5)

וַיַּעַשׂ לוֹ רֶכֶב וּפָרָשִׁים וַחֲמִשִּׁים אִישׁ רָצִים

ones-running man and-fifty and-horses chariot for-him and-he-got-ready

לְפָנָיו׃ וְלֹא־ עֲצָבוֹ אָבִיו מִיָּמָיו

in-days-of-him father-of-him he-interfered-with-him and-not (6) ahead-of-him

לֵאמֹר מַדּוּעַ כָּכָה עָשִׂיתָ וְגַם־ הוּא טוֹב־ תֹּאַר מְאֹד וְאֹתוֹ יָלְדָה

she-bore and-him very form handsome-of he now-also you-behave so why? to-ask

אַחֲרֵי אַבְשָׁלוֹם׃ וַיִּהְיוּ דְבָרָיו עִם יוֹאָב בֶּן־ צְרוּיָה

Zeruiah son-of Joab with words-of-him and-they-were (7) Absalom after

וְעִם אֶבְיָתָר הַכֹּהֵן וַיַּעְזְרוּ אַחֲרֵי אֲדֹנִיָּה׃ וְצָדוֹק

but-Zadok (8) Adonijah to and-they-gave-support the-priest Abiathar and-with

הַכֹּהֵן וּבְנָיָהוּ בֶן־ יְהוֹיָדָע וְנָתָן הַנָּבִיא וְשִׁמְעִי

and-Shimei the-prophet and-Nathan Jehoiada son-of and-Benaiah the-priest

וְרֵעִי וְהַגִּבּוֹרִים אֲשֶׁר לְדָוִד לֹא הָיוּ עִם־ אֲדֹנִיָּהוּ׃

Adonijah with they-were not to-David that and-the-special-guards and-Rei

וַיִּזְבַּח אֲדֹנִיָּהוּ צֹאן וּבָקָר וּמְרִיא עִם אֶבֶן

Stone-of at and-fattened-calf and-cattle sheep Adonijah then-he-sacrificed (9)

הַזֹּחֶלֶת אֲשֶׁר־ אֵצֶל עֵין רֹגֵל וַיִּקְרָא אֶת־ כָּל־ אֶחָיו

brothers-of-him all-of *** and-he-invited Rogel En near that the-Zoheleth

### *Adonijah Sets Himself Up as King*

1 When King David was old
and well advanced in
years, he could not keep warm
even when they put covers
over him. 2So his servants said
to him, "Let us look for a
young virgin to attend the
king and take care of him. She
can lie beside him so that our
lord the king may keep
warm."
3Then they searched
throughout Israel for a beautiful girl and found Abishag, a
Shunammite, and brought her
to the king. 4The girl was very
beautiful; she took care of the
king and waited on him, but
the king had no intimate relations with her.
5Now Adonijah, whose
mother was Haggith, put himself forward and said, "I will
be king." So he got chariots
and horses[a] ready, with fifty
men to run ahead of him. 6(His
father had never interfered
with him by asking, "Why do
you behave as you do?" He
was also very handsome and
was born next after Absalom.)
7Adonijah conferred with
Joab son of Zeruiah and with
Abiathar the priest, and they
gave him their support. 8But
Zadok the priest, Benaiah son
of Jehoiada, Nathan the
prophet, Shimei and Rei[b] and
David's special guard did not
join Adonijah.
9Adonijah then sacrificed
sheep, cattle and fattened
calves at the Stone of Zoheleth
near En Rogel. He invited all
his brothers, the king's sons,

[a]5 Or *charioteers* [b]8 Or *and his friends*

בְּנֵי הַמֶּלֶךְ וּלְכָל־ אַנְשֵׁי יְהוּדָה עַבְדֵי הַמֶּלֶךְ׃ וְאֶת־
but (10) the-king officials-of Judah men-of and-to-all-of the-king sons-of

נָתָן הַנָּבִיא וּבְנָיָהוּ וְאֶת־ הַגִּבּוֹרִים וְאֶת־ שְׁלֹמֹה אָחִיו
brother-of-him Solomon or the-special-guards or or-Benaiah the-prophet Nathan

לֹא קָרָא׃ וַיֹּאמֶר נָתָן אֶל־ בַּת־ שֶׁבַע אֵם־ שְׁלֹמֹה
Solomon mother-of Sheba Bath to Nathan then-he-asked (11) he-invited not

לֵאמֹר הֲלוֹא שָׁמַעַתְּ כִּי מָלַךְ אֲדֹנִיָּהוּ בֶן־ חַגִּית
Haggith son-of Adonijah he-became-king that you-heard not? to-say

וַאֲדֹנֵינוּ דָוִד לֹא יָדָע׃ וְעַתָּה לְכִי אִיעָצֵךְ נָא
now! let-me-advise-you come! so-now (12) he-knows not David and-lords-of-us

עֵצָה וּמַלְּטִי אֶת־ נַפְשֵׁךְ וְאֶת־ נֶפֶשׁ בְּנֵךְ שְׁלֹמֹה׃ לְכִי
come! (13) Solomon son-of-you life-of and life-of-you *** and-save! advice

וּבֹאִי ׀ אֶל־ הַמֶּלֶךְ דָּוִד וְאָמַרְתְּ אֵלָיו הֲלֹא־אַתָּה אֲדֹנִי הַמֶּלֶךְ
the-king lord-of-me you not? to-him and-you-say David the-king to and-go!

נִשְׁבַּעְתָּ לַאֲמָתְךָ לֵאמֹר כִּי־ שְׁלֹמֹה בְנֵךְ יִמְלֹךְ
he-shall-be-king son-of-you Solomon surely to-say to-servant-of-you you-swore

אַחֲרַי וְהוּא יֵשֵׁב עַל־ כִּסְאִי וּמַדּוּעַ מָלַךְ אֲדֹנִיָהוּ*׃
Adonijah he-became-king then-why? throne-of-me on he-will-sit and-he after-me

הִנֵּה עוֹדָךְ מְדַבֶּרֶת שָׁם עִם־ הַמֶּלֶךְ וַאֲנִי אָבוֹא אַחֲרַיִךְ
after-you I-will-come-in then-I the-king to there talking still-you see! (14)

וּמִלֵּאתִי אֶת־ דְּבָרָיִךְ׃ וַתָּבֹא בַת־ שֶׁבַע† אֶל־הַמֶּלֶךְ
the-king to Sheba Bath so-she-went (15) words-of-you *** and-I-will-confirm

הַחַדְרָה וְהַמֶּלֶךְ זָקֵן מְאֹד וַאֲבִישַׁג הַשּׁוּנַמִּית מְשָׁרַת
attending the-Shunammite and-Abishag very he-was-old and-the-king in-the-room

אֶת־הַמֶּלֶךְ׃ וַתִּקֹּד בַּת־ שֶׁבַע וַתִּשְׁתַּחוּ לַמֶּלֶךְ
before-the-king and-she-knelt Sheba Bath and-she-bowed (16) the-king to

וַיֹּאמֶר הַמֶּלֶךְ מַה־ לָּךְ׃ וַתֹּאמֶר לוֹ אֲדֹנִי
lord-of-me to-him and-she-said (17) to-you what? the-king and-he-asked

אַתָּה נִשְׁבַּעְתָּ בַּיהוָה אֱלֹהֶיךָ לַאֲמָתֶךָ כִּי־ שְׁלֹמֹה
Solomon surely to-servant-of-you God-of-you by-Yahweh you-swore you

בְנֵךְ יִמְלֹךְ אַחֲרָי וְהוּא יֵשֵׁב עַל־ כִּסְאִי׃
throne-of-me on he-will-sit and-he after-me he-shall-be-king son-of-you

וְעַתָּה הִנֵּה אֲדֹנִיָּה מָלָךְ וְעַתָּה אֲדֹנִי הַמֶּלֶךְ לֹא
not the-king lord-of-me and-now he-became-king Adonijah see! but-now (18)

יָדָעְתָּ׃ וַיִּזְבַּח שׁוֹר וּמְרִיא־ וְצֹאן
and-sheep and-fattened-calf cattle and-he-sacrificed (19) you-know

לָרֹב וַיִּקְרָא לְכָל־ בְּנֵי הַמֶּלֶךְ וּלְאֶבְיָתָר
and-to-Abiathar the-king sons-of to-all-of and-he-invited to-great-number

and all the men of Judah who
were royal officials, [10]but he
did not invite Nathan the
prophet or Benaiah or the
special guard or his brother
Solomon.
[11]Then Nathan asked Bathsheba, Solomon's mother,
"Have you not heard that
Adonijah, the son of Haggith,
has become king without our
lord David's knowing it?
[12]Now then, let me advise you
how you can save your own
life and the life of your son
Solomon. [13]Go in to King David and say to him, 'My lord
the king, did you not swear to
me your servant: "Surely Solomon your son shall be king after me, and he will sit on my
throne"? Why then has
Adonijah become king?'
[14]While you are still there talking to the king, I will come in
and confirm what you have
said."
[15]So Bathsheba went to see
the aged king in his room,
where Abishag the Shunam-
mite was attending him.
[16]Bathsheba bowed low and
knelt before the king.
"What is it you want?" the
king asked.
[17]She said to him, "My lord,
you yourself swore to me your
servant by the LORD your God:
'Solomon your son shall be
king after me, and he will sit
on my throne.' [18]But now
Adonijah has become king,
and you, my lord the king, do
not know about it. [19]He has
sacrificed great numbers of
cattle, fattened calves, and
sheep, and has invited all the
king's sons, Abiathar the

*13 Most mss have *dagesh* in the *yod* (יָּהוּ־).

†15 Most mss have *pathah* under the *beth* (שַׁבַע).

הַכֹּהֵן וּלְיֹאָב שַׂר הַצָּבָא וְלִשְׁלֹמֹה עַבְדְּךָ
servant-of-you but-to-Solomon the-army commander-of and-to-Joab the-priest

לֹא קָרָא׃ (20) וְאַתָּה אֲדֹנִי הַמֶּלֶךְ עֵינֵי כָל־יִשְׂרָאֵל עָלֶיךָ
on-you Israel all-of eyes-of the-king lord-of-me and-you (20) he-invited not

לְהַגִּיד לָהֶם מִי יֵשֵׁב עַל־ כִּסֵּא אֲדֹנִי־ הַמֶּלֶךְ אַחֲרָיו׃
after-him the-king lord-of-me throne-of on he-will-sit who to-them to-tell

(21) וְהָיָה כִּשְׁכַב אֲדֹנִי־ הַמֶּלֶךְ עִם־ אֲבֹתָיו
fathers-of-him with the-king lord-of-me when-to-lie or-he-will-be (21)

וְהָיִיתִי אֲנִי וּבְנִי שְׁלֹמֹה חַטָּאִים׃ (22) וְהִנֵּה עוֹדֶנָּה
still-she and-see! (22) criminals Solomon and-son-of-me I then-I-will-be

מְדַבֶּרֶת עִם־ הַמֶּלֶךְ וְנָתָן הַנָּבִיא בָּא׃ (23) וַיַּגִּידוּ
and-they-told (23) he-arrived the-prophet then-Nathan the-king with speaking

לַמֶּלֶךְ לֵאמֹר הִנֵּה נָתָן הַנָּבִיא וַיָּבֹא לִפְנֵי הַמֶּלֶךְ
the-king before so-he-went the-prophet Nathan see! to-say to-the-king

וַיִּשְׁתַּחוּ לַמֶּלֶךְ עַל־ אַפָּיו אָרְצָה׃ (24) וַיֹּאמֶר
and-he-said (24) to-ground faces-of-him on before-the-king and-he-bowed

נָתָן אֲדֹנִי הַמֶּלֶךְ אַתָּה אָמַרְתָּ אֲדֹנִיָּהוּ יִמְלֹךְ
he-shall-be-king Adonijah you-declared you the-king lord-of-me Nathan

אַחֲרָי וְהוּא יֵשֵׁב עַל־ כִּסְאִי׃ (25) כִּי ׀ יָרַד הַיּוֹם
the-day he-went-down for (25) throne-of-me on he-will-sit and-he after-me

וַיִּזְבַּח שׁוֹר וּמְרִיא־ וְצֹאן לָרֹב
to-great-number and-sheep and-fattened-calf cattle and-he-sacrificed

וַיִּקְרָא לְכָל־ בְּנֵי הַמֶּלֶךְ וּלְשָׂרֵי הַצָּבָא
the-army and-to-commanders-of the-king sons-of to-all-of and-he-invited

וּלְאֶבְיָתָר הַכֹּהֵן וְהִנָּם אֹכְלִים וְשֹׁתִים
and-ones-drinking ones-eating and-see-they! the-priest and-to-Abiathar

לְפָנָיו וַיֹּאמְרוּ יְחִי הַמֶּלֶךְ אֲדֹנִיָּהוּ׃ (26) וְלִי אֲנִי־
I but-to-me (26) Adonijah the-king may-he-live and-they-say with-him

עַבְדֶּךָ וּלְצָדֹק הַכֹּהֵן וְלִבְנָיָהוּ בֶן־ יְהוֹיָדָע
Jehoiada son-of and-to-Benaiah the-priest and-to-Zadok servant-of-you

וְלִשְׁלֹמֹה עַבְדְּךָ לֹא קָרָא׃ (27) אִם מֵאֵת אֲדֹנִי
lord-of-me from indeed? (27) he-invited not servant-of-you and-to-Solomon

הַמֶּלֶךְ נִהְיָה הַדָּבָר הַזֶּה וְלֹא הוֹדַעְתָּ אֶת־
*** you-let-know and-not the-this the-thing he-was-done the-king

עַבְדֶּיךָ מִי יֵשֵׁב עַל־ כִּסֵּא אֲדֹנִי־ הַמֶּלֶךְ אַחֲרָיו׃
after-him the-king lord-of-me throne-of on he-would-sit who servant-of-you

(28) וַיַּעַן הַמֶּלֶךְ דָּוִד וַיֹּאמֶר קִרְאוּ־ לִי לְבַת־ שֶׁבַע
Sheba to-Bath to-me call! and-he-said David the-king then-he-answered (28)

priest and Joab the commander of the army, but he has not invited Solomon your servant.
20My lord the king, the eyes of all Israel are on you, to learn from you who will sit on the throne of my lord the king after him.
21Otherwise, as soon as my lord the king is laid to rest with his fathers, I and my son Solomon will be treated as criminals."

22While she was still speaking with the king, Nathan the prophet arrived.
23And they told the king, "Nathan the prophet is here." So he went before the king and bowed with his face to the ground.

24Nathan said, "Have you, my lord the king, declared that Adonijah shall be king after you, and that he will sit on your throne?
25Today he has gone down and sacrificed great numbers of cattle, fattened calves, and sheep. He has invited all the king's sons, the commanders of the army and Abiathar the priest. Right now they are eating and drinking with him and saying, 'Long live King Adonijah!'
26But me your servant, and Zadok the priest, and Benaiah son of Jehoiada, and your servant Solomon he did not invite.
27Is this something my lord the king has done without letting his servants know who should sit on the throne of my lord the king after him?"

*David Makes Solomon King*

28Then King David said, "Call in Bathsheba." So she

°27 ק עבדך

וַתָּבֹא לִפְנֵי הַמֶּלֶךְ וַתַּעֲמֹד לִפְנֵי הַמֶּלֶךְ׃
the-king before and-she-stood the-king into-presences-of so-she-came

וַיִּשָּׁבַע הַמֶּלֶךְ וַיֹּאמַר חַי־ יְהוָה אֲשֶׁר־ פָּדָה
he-delivered who Yahweh life-of and-he-said the-king and-he-took-oath (29)

אֶת־ נַפְשִׁי מִכָּל־ צָרָה׃ כִּי כַּאֲשֶׁר נִשְׁבַּעְתִּי לְךָ
to-you I-swore just-as surely (30) trouble from-every-of life-of-me ***

בַּיהוָה אֱלֹהֵי יִשְׂרָאֵל לֵאמֹר כִּי־ שְׁלֹמֹה בְנֵךְ יִמְלֹךְ
he-shall-be-king son-of-you Solomon surely to-say Israel God-of by-Yahweh

אַחֲרַי וְהוּא יֵשֵׁב עַל־ כִּסְאִי תַּחְתָּי כִּי כֵּן
this surely in-place-of-me throne-of-me on he-will-sit and-he after-me

אֶעֱשֶׂה הַיּוֹם הַזֶּה׃ וַתִּקֹּד בַּת־ שֶׁבַע אַפַּיִם
faces Sheba Bath then-she-bowed (31) the-this the-day I-will-carry-out

אֶרֶץ וַתִּשְׁתַּחוּ לַמֶּלֶךְ וַתֹּאמֶר יְחִי אֲדֹנִי
lord-of-me may-he-live and-she-said before-the-king and-she-knelt ground

הַמֶּלֶךְ דָּוִד לְעֹלָם׃ וַיֹּאמֶר ׀ הַמֶּלֶךְ דָּוִד קִרְאוּ־ לִי
to-me call! David the-king and-he-said (32) to-forever David the-king

לְצָדוֹק הַכֹּהֵן וּלְנָתָן הַנָּבִיא וְלִבְנָיָהוּ בֶּן־ יְהוֹיָדָע
Jehoiada son-of and-to-Benaiah the-prophet and-to-Nathan the-priest to-Zadok

וַיָּבֹאוּ לִפְנֵי הַמֶּלֶךְ׃ וַיֹּאמֶר הַמֶּלֶךְ לָהֶם קְחוּ
take! to-them the-king and-he-said (33) the-king before and-they-came

עִמָּכֶם אֶת־ עַבְדֵי אֲדֹנֵיכֶם וְהִרְכַּבְתֶּם אֶת־ שְׁלֹמֹה בְנִי עַל־
on son-of-me Solomon *** and-you-set lords-of-you servants-of *** with-you

הַפִּרְדָּה אֲשֶׁר־ לִי וְהוֹרַדְתֶּם אֹתוֹ אֶל־ גִּחוֹן׃ וּמָשַׁח
and-he-will-anoint (34) Gihon to him and-you-take-down to-me that the-mule

אֹתוֹ שָׁם צָדוֹק הַכֹּהֵן וְנָתָן הַנָּבִיא לְמֶלֶךְ עַל־ יִשְׂרָאֵל
Israel over as-king the-prophet and-Nathan the-priest Zadok there him

וּתְקַעְתֶּם בַּשּׁוֹפָר וַאֲמַרְתֶּם יְחִי הַמֶּלֶךְ שְׁלֹמֹה׃
Solomon the-king may-he-live and-you-shout on-the-trumpet and-you-blow

וַעֲלִיתֶם אַחֲרָיו וּבָא וְיָשַׁב עַל־
on and-he-shall-sit and-he-shall-come with-him then-you-go-up (35)

כִּסְאִי וְהוּא יִמְלֹךְ תַּחְתָּי וְאֹתוֹ צִוִּיתִי לִהְיוֹת
to-be I-appointed now-him in-place-of-me he-shall-reign and-he throne-of-me

נָגִיד עַל־ יִשְׂרָאֵל וְעַל־ יְהוּדָה׃ וַיַּעַן בְּנָיָהוּ בֶן־ יְהוֹיָדָע
Jehoiada son-of Benaiah and-he-answered (36) Judah and-over Israel over ruler

אֶת־ הַמֶּלֶךְ וַיֹּאמֶר ׀ אָמֵן כֵּן יֹאמַר יְהוָה אֱלֹהֵי אֲדֹנִי
lord-of-me God-of Yahweh may-he-declare so amen! and-he-said the-king ***

הַמֶּלֶךְ׃ כַּאֲשֶׁר הָיָה יְהוָה עִם־ אֲדֹנִי הַמֶּלֶךְ כֵּן יְהִי°
may-he-be so the-king lord-of-me with Yahweh he-was just-as (37) the-king

came into the king's presence
and stood before him.
29The king then took an
oath: "As surely as the LORD
lives, who has delivered me
out of every trouble, 30I will
surely carry out today what I
swore to you by the LORD, the
God of Israel: Solomon your
son shall be king after me, and
he will sit on my throne in my
place."
31Then Bathsheba bowed
low with her face to the
ground and, kneeling before
the king, said, "May my lord
King David live forever!"
32King David said, "Call in
Zadok the priest, Nathan the
prophet and Benaiah son of
Jehoiada." When they came
before the king, 33he said to
them: "Take your lord's servants with you and set Solomon my son on my own mule
and take him down to Gihon.
34There have Zadok the priest
and Nathan the prophet
anoint him king over Israel.
Blow the trumpet and shout,
'Long live King Solomon!'
35Then you are to go up with
him, and he is to come and sit
on my throne and reign in my
place. I have appointed him
ruler over Israel and Judah."
36Benaiah son of Jehoiada
answered the king, "Amen!
May the LORD, the God of my
lord the king, so declare it. 37As
the LORD was with my lord the

°37 ק יהיה

עִם־ שְׁלֹמֹה וִיגַדֵּל אֶת־ כִּסְאוֹ מִכִּסֵּא
more-than-throne-of throne-of-him *** and-may-he-make-great Solomon with

אֲדֹנִי הַמֶּלֶךְ דָּוִד׃ וַיֵּרֶד צָדוֹק הַכֹּהֵן וְנָתָן
and-Nathan the-priest Zadok so-he-went-down (38) David the-king lord-of-me

הַנָּבִיא וּבְנָיָהוּ בֶן־ יְהוֹיָדָע וְהַכְּרֵתִי וְהַפְּלֵתִי
and-the-Pelethite and-the-Kerethite Jehoiada son-of and-Benaiah the-prophet

וַיַּרְכִּבוּ אֶת־ שְׁלֹמֹה עַל־ פִּרְדַּת הַמֶּלֶךְ דָּוִד וַיֹּלִכוּ אֹתוֹ
him and-they-escorted David the-king donkey-of on Solomon *** and-they-put

עַל־ גִּחוֹן׃ וַיִּקַּח צָדוֹק הַכֹּהֵן אֶת־ קֶרֶן הַשֶּׁמֶן מִן־ הָאֹהֶל
the-tent from the-oil horn-of *** the-priest Zadok and-he-took (39) Gihon to

וַיִּמְשַׁח אֶת־ שְׁלֹמֹה וַיִּתְקְעוּ בַּשּׁוֹפָר וַיֹּאמְרוּ
and-they-shouted on-the-trumpet then-they-sounded Solomon *** and-he-anointed

כָּל־ הָעָם יְחִי הַמֶּלֶךְ שְׁלֹמֹה׃ וַיַּעֲלוּ כָל־
all-of and-they-went-up (40) Solomon the-king may-he-live the-people all-of

הָעָם אַחֲרָיו וְהָעָם מְחַלְּלִים בַּחֲלִלִים וּשְׂמֵחִים
and-ones-joyful on-flutes ones-playing and-the-people after-him the-people

שִׂמְחָה גְדוֹלָה וַתִּבָּקַע הָאָרֶץ בְּקוֹלָם׃ וַיִּשְׁמַע
and-he-heard (41) with-sound-of-them the-ground so-she-shook great joy

אֲדֹנִיָּהוּ וְכָל־ הַקְּרֻאִים אֲשֶׁר אִתּוֹ וְהֵם כִּלּוּ
they-finished and-they with-him who the-ones-being-invited and-all-of Adonijah

לֶאֱכֹל וַיִּשְׁמַע יוֹאָב אֶת־ קוֹל הַשּׁוֹפָר וַיֹּאמֶר מַדּוּעַ
what? then-he-asked the-trumpet sound-of *** Joab when-he-heard to-feast

קוֹל־ הַקִּרְיָה הוֹמָה׃ עוֹדֶנּוּ מְדַבֵּר וְהִנֵּה יוֹנָתָן בֶּן־
son-of Jonathan and-see! speaking still-he (42) noise the-city sound-of

אֶבְיָתָר הַכֹּהֵן בָּא וַיֹּאמֶר אֲדֹנִיָּהוּ בֹּא כִּי אִישׁ חַיִל
worthy man-of for come! Adonijah and-he-said he-arrived the-priest Abiathar

אַתָּה וְטוֹב תְּבַשֵּׂר׃ וַיַּעַן יוֹנָתָן וַיֹּאמֶר
and-he-said Jonathan and-he-answered (43) you-bring-news and-good you

לַאֲדֹנִיָּהוּ אֲבָל אֲדֹנֵינוּ הַמֶּלֶךְ־ דָּוִד הִמְלִיךְ אֶת־ שְׁלֹמֹה׃
Solomon *** he-made-king David the-king lord-of-us no! to-Adonijah

וַיִּשְׁלַח אִתּוֹ־ הַמֶּלֶךְ אֶת־ צָדוֹק הַכֹּהֵן וְאֶת־ נָתָן
Nathan and the-priest Zadok *** the-king with-him and-he-sent (44)

הַנָּבִיא וּבְנָיָהוּ בֶּן־ יְהוֹיָדָע וְהַכְּרֵתִי וְהַפְּלֵתִי
and-the-Pelethite and-the-Kerethite Jehoiada son-of and-Benaiah the-prophet

וַיַּרְכִּבוּ אֹתוֹ עַל פִּרְדַּת הַמֶּלֶךְ׃ וַיִּמְשְׁחוּ אֹתוֹ צָדוֹק
Zadok him and-they-anointed (45) the-king mule-of on him and-they-put

הַכֹּהֵן וְנָתָן הַנָּבִיא לְמֶלֶךְ בְּגִחוֹן וַיַּעֲלוּ מִשָּׁם
from-there and-they-went-up at-Gihon as-king the-prophet and-Nathan the-priest

king, so may he be with Solomon to make his throne even greater than the throne of my lord King David!"
38So Zadok the priest, Nathan the prophet, Benaiah son of Jehoiada, the Kerethites and the Pelethites went down and put Solomon on King David's mule and escorted him to Gihon.
39Zadok the priest took the horn of oil from the sacred tent and anointed Solomon. Then they sounded the trumpet and all the people shouted, "Long live King Solomon!"
40And all the people went up after him, playing flutes and rejoicing greatly, so that the ground shook with the sound.
41Adonijah and all the guests who were with him heard it as they were finishing their feast. On hearing the sound of the trumpet, Joab asked, "What's the meaning of all the noise in the city?"
42Even as he was speaking, Jonathan son of Abiathar the priest arrived. Adonijah said, "Come in. A worthy man like you must be bringing good news."
43"Not at all!" Jonathan answered. "Our lord King David has made Solomon king.
44The king has sent with him Zadok the priest, Nathan the prophet, Benaiah son of Jehoiada, the Kerethites and the Pelethites, and they have put him on the king's mule,
45and Zadok the priest and Nathan the prophet have anointed him king at Gihon. From there they have gone up cheering,

שְׂמֵחִים וַתֵּהֹם הַקִּרְיָה הוּא הַקּוֹל אֲשֶׁר שְׁמַעְתֶּם׃
you-hear that the-noise that the-city and-she-resounds ones-cheerful

וְגַם יָשַׁב שְׁלֹמֹה עַל כִּסֵּא הַמְּלוּכָה׃ וְגַם־ בָּאוּ
they-came and-also (47) the-royal throne-of on Solomon he-sat and-more (46)

עַבְדֵי הַמֶּלֶךְ לְבָרֵךְ אֶת־ אֲדֹנֵינוּ הַמֶּלֶךְ דָּוִד לֵאמֹר
to-say David the-king lords-of-us *** to-congratulate the-king officials-of

יֵיטֵב אֱלֹהֶיךָ אֶת־ שֵׁם שְׁלֹמֹה מִשְּׁמֶךָ
more-than-name-of-you Solomon name-of *** God may-he-make-famous

וִיגַדֵּל אֶת־ כִּסְאוֹ מִכִּסְאֶךָ וַיִּשְׁתַּחוּ
and-he-bowed more-than-throne-of-you throne-of-him *** and-may-he-make-great

הַמֶּלֶךְ עַל־הַמִּשְׁכָּב׃ וְגַם־ כָּכָה אָמַר הַמֶּלֶךְ בָּרוּךְ יְהוָה
Yahweh being-praised the-king he-said this and-also (48) the-bed in the-king

אֱלֹהֵי יִשְׂרָאֵל אֲשֶׁר נָתַן הַיּוֹם יֹשֵׁב עַל־ כִּסְאִי וְעֵינַי
and-eyes-of-me throne-of-me on one-sitting the-day he-gave who Israel God-of

רֹאוֹת׃ וַיֶּחֶרְדוּ וַיָּקֻמוּ כָּל־
all-of and-they-rose and-they-were-alarmed (49) ones-seeing

הַקְּרֻאִים אֲשֶׁר לַאֲדֹנִיָּהוּ וַיֵּלְכוּ אִישׁ לְדַרְכּוֹ׃
on-way-of-him each and-they-dispersed with-Adonijah who the-ones-being-invited

וַאֲדֹנִיָּהוּ יָרֵא מִפְּנֵי שְׁלֹמֹה וַיָּקָם וַיֵּלֶךְ
and-he-went and-he-rose Solomon from-before he-feared but-Adonijah (50)

וַיַּחֲזֵק בְּקַרְנוֹת הַמִּזְבֵּחַ׃ וַיֻּגַּד לִשְׁלֹמֹה
to-Solomon then-he-was-told (51) the-altar of-horns-of and-he-took-hold

לֵאמֹר הִנֵּה אֲדֹנִיָּהוּ יָרֵא אֶת־ הַמֶּלֶךְ שְׁלֹמֹה וְהִנֵּה אָחַז
he-clings and-see! Solomon the-king *** he-fears Adonijah see! to-say

בְּקַרְנוֹת הַמִּזְבֵּחַ לֵאמֹר יִשָּׁבַע־ לִי כַיּוֹם הַמֶּלֶךְ שְׁלֹמֹה
Solomon the-king as-the-day to-me let-him-swear to-say the-altar to-horns-of

אִם־ יָמִית אֶת־ עַבְדּוֹ בֶּחָרֶב׃ וַיֹּאמֶר
and-he-replied (52) with-the-sword servant-of-him *** he-will-kill not

שְׁלֹמֹה אִם יִהְיֶה לְבֶן־ חַיִל לֹא־ יִפֹּל מִשַּׂעֲרָתוֹ
from-hair-of-him he-will-fall not worthiness as-son-of he-is if Solomon

אַרְצָה וְאִם־ רָעָה תִמָּצֵא־ בוֹ וָמֵת׃ וַיִּשְׁלַח
then-he-sent (53) then-he-will-die in-him she-is-found evil but-if to-ground

הַמֶּלֶךְ שְׁלֹמֹה וַיֹּרִדֻהוּ מֵעַל הַמִּזְבֵּחַ וַיָּבֹא
and-he-came the-altar from-on and-they-brought-down-him Solomon the-king

וַיִּשְׁתַּחוּ לַמֶּלֶךְ שְׁלֹמֹה וַיֹּאמֶר־ לוֹ שְׁלֹמֹה לֵךְ
go! Solomon to-him and-he-said Solomon before-the-king and-he-bowed

לְבֵיתֶךָ׃ וַיִּקְרְבוּ יְמֵי־ דָוִד לָמוּת וַיְצַו
then-he-charged to-die David days-of when-they-drew-near (2:1) to-home-of-you

°47 ק אלהים

and the city resounds with it.
That's the noise you hear.
[46]Moreover, Solomon has taken his seat on the royal throne.
[47]Also, the royal officials have come to congratulate our lord King David, saying, 'May your God make Solomon's name more famous than yours and his throne greater than yours!' And the king bowed in worship on his bed
[48]and said, 'Praise be to the LORD, the God of Israel, who has allowed my eyes to see a successor on my throne today.' "
[49]At this, all Adonijah's guests rose in alarm and dispersed.
[50]But Adonijah, in fear of Solomon, went and took hold of the horns of the altar.
[51]Then Solomon was told, "Adonijah is afraid of King Solomon and is clinging to the horns of the altar. He says, 'Let King Solomon swear to me today that he will not put his servant to death with the sword.' "
[52]Solomon replied, "If he shows himself to be a worthy man, not a hair of his head will fall to the ground; but if evil is found in him, he will die."
[53]Then King Solomon sent men, and they brought him down from the altar. And Adonijah came and bowed down to King Solomon, and Solomon said, "Go to your home."

*David's Charge to Solomon*

2 When the time drew near for David to die, he gave a

[c]6 Hebrew *Sheol*; also in verse 9

אֶת־ שְׁלֹמֹה בְנוֹ לֵאמֹר׃ אָנֹכִי הֹלֵךְ בְּדֶרֶךְ כָּל־ הָאָרֶץ
the-earth all-of on-way-of going I (2) to-say son-of-him Solomon ***

וְחָזַקְתָּ וְהָיִיתָ לְאִישׁ׃ וְשָׁמַרְתָּ אֶת־ מִשְׁמֶרֶת ׀
requirement-of *** and-you-observe (3) as-man and-you-be so-you-be-strong

יְהוָה אֱלֹהֶיךָ לָלֶכֶת בִּדְרָכָיו לִשְׁמֹר חֻקֹּתָיו
decrees-of-him to-keep in-ways-of-him to-walk God-of-you Yahweh

מִצְוֹתָיו וּמִשְׁפָּטָיו וְעֵדְוֹתָיו כַּכָּתוּב
as-the-being-written and-requirements-of-him and-laws-of-him commands-of-him

בְּתוֹרַת מֹשֶׁה לְמַעַן תַּשְׂכִּיל אֵת כָּל־אֲשֶׁר תַּעֲשֶׂה וְאֵת כָּל־
everywhere and you-do that all *** you-may-prosper so-that Moses in-Law-of

אֲשֶׁר תִּפְנֶה שָׁם׃ לְמַעַן יָקִים יְהוָה אֶת־ דְּבָרוֹ אֲשֶׁר
that promise-of-him *** Yahweh he-may-keep so-that (4) there you-go that

דִּבֶּר עָלַי לֵאמֹר אִם־ יִשְׁמְרוּ בָנֶיךָ אֶת־ דַּרְכָּם
way-of-them *** descendants-of-you they-watch if to-say to-me he-promised

לָלֶכֶת לְפָנַי בֶּאֱמֶת בְּכָל־ לְבָבָם וּבְכָל־
and-with-all-of heart-of-them with-all-of in-faith before-me to-walk

נַפְשָׁם לֵאמֹר לֹא־ יִכָּרֵת לְךָ אִישׁ מֵעַל כִּסֵּא
throne-of from-on man of-you he-will-be-cut-off not to-say soul-of-them

יִשְׂרָאֵל׃ וְגַם אַתָּה יָדַעְתָּ אֵת אֲשֶׁר־ עָשָׂה לִי יוֹאָב בֶּן־ צְרוּיָה
Zeruiah son-of Joab to-me he-did what *** you-know you now-also (5) Israel

אֲשֶׁר עָשָׂה לִשְׁנֵי־ שָׂרֵי צִבְאוֹת יִשְׂרָאֵל לְאַבְנֵר בֶּן־ נֵר
Ner son-of to-Abner Israel armies-of commanders-of to-two-of he-did what

וְלַעֲמָשָׂא בֶן־ יֶתֶר וַיַּהַרְגֵם וַיָּשֶׂם דְּמֵי־ מִלְחָמָה
battle bloods-of and-he-shed that-he-killed-them Jether son-of and-to-Amasa

בְּשָׁלֹם וַיִּתֵּן דְּמֵי מִלְחָמָה בַּחֲגֹרָתוֹ אֲשֶׁר
that on-belts-of-him battle bloods-of and-he-put in-peacetime

בְּמָתְנָיו וּבְנַעֲלוֹ אֲשֶׁר בְּרַגְלָיו׃ וְעָשִׂיתָ
so-you-deal (6) on-feet-of-him that and-on-sandal-of-him around-waists-of-him

כְּחָכְמָתֶךָ וְלֹא־ תוֹרֵד שֵׂיבָתוֹ בְּשָׁלֹם שְׁאֹל׃
Sheol in-peace gray-head-of-him you-let-go-down but-not as-wisdom-of-you

וְלִבְנֵי בַרְזִלַּי הַגִּלְעָדִי תַּעֲשֶׂה־ חֶסֶד וְהָיוּ
and-let-them-be kindness you-show the-Gileadite Barzillai but-to-sons-of (7)

בְּאֹכְלֵי שֻׁלְחָנֶךָ כִּי־ כֵן קָרְבוּ אֵלַי
by-me they-stood-by indeed for table-of-you among-ones-eating-of

בְּבָרְחִי מִפְּנֵי אַבְשָׁלוֹם אָחִיךָ׃ וְהִנֵּה עִמְּךָ
with-you and-see! (8) brother-of-you Absalom from-before when-to-flee-me

שִׁמְעִי בֶן־ גֵּרָא בֶן־הַיְמִינִי מִבַּחֻרִים וְהוּא קִלְלַנִי קְלָלָה
curse he-cursed-me and-he from-Bahurim the-Benjamite Gera son-of Shimei

charge to Solomon his son.
2"I am about to go the way of all the earth," he said. "So be strong, show yourself a man, 3and observe what the LORD your God requires: Walk in his ways, and keep his decrees and commands, his laws and requirements, as written in the Law of Moses, so that you may prosper in all you do and wherever you go, 4and that the LORD may keep his promise to me: 'If your descendants watch how they live, and if they walk faithfully before me with all their heart and soul, you will never fail to have a man on the throne of Israel.'
5"Now you yourself know what Joab son of Zeruiah did to me—what he did to the two commanders of Israel's armies, Abner son of Ner and Amasa son of Jether. He killed them, shedding their blood in peacetime as if in battle, and with that blood stained the belt around his waist and the sandals on his feet. 6Deal with him according to your wisdom, but do not let his gray head go down to the grave[c] in peace.
7"But show kindness to the sons of Barzillai of Gilead and let them be among those who eat at your table. They stood by me when I fled from your brother Absalom.
8"And remember, you have with you Shimei son of Gera, the Benjamite from Bahurim, who called down bitter curses

נִמְרֶצֶת בְּיוֹם לֶכְתִּי מַחֲנָיִם וְהוּא־ יָרַד לִקְרָאתִי
to-meet-me he-came-down when-he Mahanaim to-go-me on-day being-bitter

הַיַּרְדֵּן וָאֶשָּׁבַע לוֹ בַיהוָה לֵאמֹר אִם־ אֲמִיתְךָ
I-will-kill-you not to-say by-Yahweh to-him then-I-swore the-Jordan

בֶּחָרֶב׃ וְעַתָּה אַל־ תְּנַקֵּהוּ כִּי אִישׁ חָכָם אָתָּה
you wise man for you-consider-innocent-him not but-now (9) with-the-sword

וְיָדַעְתָּ אֵת אֲשֶׁר תַּעֲשֶׂה־ לּוֹ וְהוֹרַדְתָּ אֶת־
*** and-you-bring-down to-him you-must-do what *** and-you-will-know

שֵׂיבָתוֹ בְּדָם שְׁאוֹל׃ וַיִּשְׁכַּב דָּוִד עִם־ אֲבֹתָיו
fathers-of-him with David then-he-rested (10) Sheol in-blood gray-head-of-him

וַיִּקָּבֵר בְּעִיר דָּוִד׃ וְהַיָּמִים אֲשֶׁר מָלַךְ דָּוִד
David he-reigned that and-the-days (11) David in-City-of and-he-was-buried

עַל־יִשְׂרָאֵל אַרְבָּעִים שָׁנָה בְּחֶבְרוֹן מָלַךְ שֶׁבַע שָׁנִים וּבִירוּשָׁלַםִ
and-in-Jerusalem years seven he-reigned in-Hebron year forty Israel over

מָלַךְ שְׁלֹשִׁים וְשָׁלֹשׁ שָׁנִים׃ וּשְׁלֹמֹה יָשַׁב עַל־ כִּסֵּא דָּוִד
David throne-of on he-sat so-Solomon (12) years and-three thirty he-reigned

אָבִיו וַתִּכֹּן מַלְכֻתוֹ מְאֹד׃ וַיָּבֹא
now-he-went (13) firmly kingdom-of-him and-she-was-established father-of-him

אֲדֹנִיָּהוּ בֶן־ חַגִּית* אֶל־ בַּת־ שֶׁבַע אֵם־ שְׁלֹמֹה וַתֹּאמֶר
and-she-asked Solomon mother-of Sheba Bath to Hagith son-of Adonijah

הֲשָׁלוֹם בֹּאֶךָ וַיֹּאמֶר שָׁלוֹם׃ וַיֹּאמֶר דָּבָר
word then-he-said (14) peacefully and-he-answered to-come-you peacefully?

לִי אֵלָיִךְ וַתֹּאמֶר דַּבֵּר׃ וַיֹּאמֶר אַתְּ יָדַעַתְּ כִּי־ לִי
to-me that you-know you and-he-said (15) speak! and-she-replied to-you of-me

הָיְתָה הַמְּלוּכָה וְעָלַי שָׂמוּ כָל־ יִשְׂרָאֵל פְּנֵיהֶם
faces-of-them Israel all-of they-turned and-to-me the-kingdom she-was

לִמְלֹךְ וַתִּסֹּב הַמְּלוּכָה וַתְּהִי לְאָחִי כִּי
for to-brother-of-me and-she-went the-kingdom but-she-changed to-be-king

מֵיְהוָה הָיְתָה לּוֹ׃ וְעַתָּה שְׁאֵלָה אַחַת אָנֹכִי שֹׁאֵל מֵאִתָּךְ
from-with-you asking I one request and-now (16) to-him she-came from-Yahweh

אַל־ תָּשִׁבִי אֶת־ פָּנָי וַתֹּאמֶר אֵלָיו דַּבֵּר׃ וַיֹּאמֶר
so-he-said (17) speak! to-him and-she-said faces-of-me *** you-refuse not

אִמְרִי־ נָא לִשְׁלֹמֹה הַמֶּלֶךְ כִּי לֹא־ יָשִׁיב אֶת־ פָּנָיִךְ
faces-of-you *** he-will-refuse not for the-king to-Solomon now! ask!

וְיִתֶּן־ לִי אֶת־ אֲבִישַׁג הַשּׁוּנַמִּית לְאִשָּׁה׃ וַתֹּאמֶר
and-she-replied (18) as-wife the-Shunammite Abishag *** to-me so-he-gives

בַּת־ שֶׁבַע טוֹב אָנֹכִי אֲדַבֵּר עָלֶיךָ אֶל־ הַמֶּלֶךְ׃ וַתָּבֹא
when-she-went (19) the-king to for-you I-will-speak I very-well Sheba Bath

on me the day I went to Mahanaim. When he came down to meet me at the Jordan, I swore to him by the LORD: 'I will not put you to death by the sword.' 9But now, do not consider him innocent. You are a man of wisdom; you will know what to do to him. Bring his gray head down to the grave in blood."

10Then David rested with his fathers and was buried in the City of David. 11He had reigned forty years over Israel—seven years in Hebron and thirty-three in Jerusalem. 12So Solomon sat on the throne of his father David, and his rule was firmly established.

*Solomon's Throne Established*

13Now Adonijah, the son of Haggith, went to Bathsheba, Solomon's mother. Bathsheba asked him, "Do you come peacefully?"

He answered, "Yes, peacefully." 14Then he added, "I have something to say to you."

"You may say it," she replied.

15"As you know," he said, "the kingdom was mine. All Israel looked to me as their king. But things changed, and the kingdom has gone to my brother; for it has come to him from the LORD. 16Now I have one request to make of you. Do not refuse me."

"You may make it," she said.

17So he continued, "Please ask King Solomon—he will not refuse you—to give me Abishag the Shunammite as my wife."

18"Very well," Bathsheba replied, "I will speak to the king for you."

19When Bathsheba went to

*13 Most mss have *bireq* under the *gimel* (חַגִּית).

בַּת־ שֶׁ֫בַע אֶל־הַמֶּ֫לֶךְ שְׁלֹמֹה לְדַבֶּר־ לוֹ עַל־ אֲדֹנִיָּ֫הוּ וַיָּקָם
and-he-stood-up Adonijah for to-him to-speak Solomon the-king to Sheba Bath

הַמֶּ֫לֶךְ לִקְרָאתָהּ וַיִּשְׁתַּחוּ לָהּ וַיֵּשֶׁב עַל־ כִּסְאוֹ
throne-of-him on and-he-sat to-her and-he-bowed to-meet-her the-king

וַיָּשֶׂם כִּסֵּא לְאֵם הַמֶּ֫לֶךְ וַתֵּשֶׁב לִימִינוֹ׃
at-right-of-him and-she-sat the-king for-mother-of throne and-he-had-brought

וַתֹּאמֶר שְׁאֵלָה אַחַת קְטַנָּה אָנֹכִי שֹׁאֶלֶת מֵאִתָּךְ אַל־ תָּשֶׁב
you-refuse not from-with-you asking I small one request and-she-said (20)

אֶת־ פָּנָי וַיֹּאמֶר־ לָהּ הַמֶּ֫לֶךְ שַׁאֲלִי אִמִּי כִּי לֹא־
not for mother-of-me ask! the-king to-her and-he-replied faces-of-me ***

אָשִׁיב אֶת־ פָּנָיִךְ׃ וַתֹּאמֶר יֻתַּן אֶת־ אֲבִישַׁג
Abishag *** let-him-be-given so-she-said (21) faces-of-you *** I-will-refuse

הַשֻּׁנַמִּית לַאֲדֹנִיָּהוּ אָחִיךָ לְאִשָּׁה׃ וַיַּעַן
and-he-answered (22) as-wife brother-of-you to-Adonijah the-Shunammite

הַמֶּ֫לֶךְ שְׁלֹמֹה וַיֹּאמֶר לְאִמּוֹ וְלָמָה אַתְּ שֹׁאֶלֶת אֶת־
*** requesting you now-why? to-mother-of-him and-he-said Solomon the-king

אֲבִישַׁג הַשֻּׁנַמִּית לַאֲדֹנִיָּהוּ וְשַׁאֲלִי־ לוֹ אֶת־ הַמְּלוּכָה כִּי
for the-kingdom *** for-him now-request! for-Adonijah the-Shunammite Abishag

הוּא אָחִי הַגָּדוֹל מִמֶּנִּי וְלוֹ וּלְאֶבְיָתָר הַכֹּהֵן
the-priest and-for-Abiathar and-for-him than-me the-older brother-of-me he

וּלְיוֹאָב בֶּן־ צְרוּיָה׃ וַיִּשָּׁבַע הַמֶּ֫לֶךְ שְׁלֹמֹה בַּיהוָה
by-Yahweh Solomon the-king then-he-swore (23) Zeruiah son-of and-for-Joab

לֵאמֹר כֹּה יַעֲשֶׂה־ לִּי אֱלֹהִים וְכֹה יוֹסִיף כִּי
if-not may-he-be-severe and-so God with-me may-he-deal so to-say

בְנַפְשׁוֹ דִּבֶּר אֲדֹנִיָּהוּ אֶת־ הַדָּבָר הַזֶּה׃ וְעַתָּה
and-now (24) the-this the-request *** Adonijah he-pays with-life-of-him

חַי־ יְהוָה אֲשֶׁר הֱכִינַנִי וַיּוֹשִׁיבִינִי° עַל־ כִּסֵּא דָּוִד
David throne-of on and-he-made-sit-me he-established-me who Yahweh life-of

אָבִי וַאֲשֶׁר עָשָׂה־ לִי בַּיִת כַּאֲשֶׁר דִּבֵּר כִּי
indeed he-promised just-as dynasty for-me he-founded and-who father-of-me

הַיּוֹם יוּמַת אֲדֹנִיָּהוּ׃ וַיִּשְׁלַח הַמֶּ֫לֶךְ שְׁלֹמֹה
Solomon the-king so-he-gave-order (25) Adonijah he-shall-die the-day

בְּיַד בְּנָיָהוּ בֶן־ יְהוֹיָדָע וַיִּפְגַּע־ בּוֹ וַיָּמֹת׃
and-he-died against-him and-he-struck Jehoiada son-of Benaiah to-hand-of

וּלְאֶבְיָתָר הַכֹּהֵן אָמַר הַמֶּ֫לֶךְ עֲנָתֹת לֵךְ עַל־
to go-back! Anathoth the-king he-said the-priest and-to-Abiathar (26)

שָׂדֶיךָ כִּי אִישׁ מָוֶת אָתָּה וּבַיּוֹם הַזֶּה לֹא
not the-this but-on-the-day you death man-of indeed fields-of-you

King Solomon to speak to him for Adonijah, the king stood up to meet her, bowed down to her and sat down on his throne. He had a throne brought for the king's mother, and she sat down at his right hand.

[20]"I have one small request to make of you," she said. "Do not refuse me."

The king replied, "Make it, my mother; I will not refuse you."

[21]So she said, "Let Abishag the Shunammite be given in marriage to your brother Adonijah."

[22]King Solomon answered his mother, "Why do you request Abishag the Shunammite for Adonijah? You might as well request the kingdom for him—after all, he is my older brother—yes, for him and for Abiathar the priest and Joab son of Zeruiah!"

[23]Then King Solomon swore by the LORD: "May God deal with me, be it ever so severely, if Adonijah does not pay with his life for this request!
[24]And now, as surely as the LORD lives—he who has established me securely on the throne of my father David and has founded a dynasty for me as he promised—Adonijah shall be put to death today!"
[25]So King Solomon gave orders to Benaiah son of Jehoiada, and he struck down Adonijah and he died.

[26]To Abiathar the priest the king said, "Go back to your fields in Anathoth. You deserve to die, but I will not put you to death now, because you

*24 Most mss have *tsere* under the *beth* and no *yod* after the *beth* (בֵּנִי—).

°24 ק וישיבני

אֲמִיתֶךָ כִּי־ נָשָׂאתָ אֶת־ אֲרוֹן אֲדֹנָי יְהוִה לִפְנֵי דָּוִד
David before Yahweh Lord ark-of *** you-carried for I-will-kill-you

אָבִי וְכִי הִתְעַנִּיתָ בְּכֹל אֲשֶׁר־ הִתְעַנָּה
he-had-hardship that in-all you-shared-hardship and-for father-of-me

אָבִי׃ וַיְגָרֶשׁ שְׁלֹמֹה אֶת־ אֶבְיָתָר מִהְיוֹת כֹּהֵן
priest from-to-be Abiathar *** Solomon so-he-removed (27) father-of-me

לַיהוָה לְמַלֵּא אֶת־ דְּבַר יְהוָה אֲשֶׁר דִּבֶּר עַל־ בֵּית עֵלִי
Eli house-of about he-spoke that Yahweh word-of *** to-fulfill of-Yahweh

בְּשִׁלֹה׃ וְהַשְּׁמֻעָה בָּאָה עַד־יוֹאָב כִּי יוֹאָב נָטָה אַחֲרֵי
with he-conspired Joab now Joab to she-reached when-the-news (28) at-Shiloh

אֲדֹנִיָּה וְאַחֲרֵי אַבְשָׁלוֹם לֹא נָטָה וַיָּנָס יוֹאָב אֶל־ אֹהֶל
tent-of to Joab then-he-fled he-conspired not Absalom but-with Adonijah

יְהוָה וַיַּחֲזֵק בְּקַרְנוֹת הַמִּזְבֵּחַ׃ וַיֻּגַּד
when-he-was-told (29) the-altar of-horns-of and-he-took-hold Yahweh

לַמֶּלֶךְ שְׁלֹמֹה כִּי נָס יוֹאָב אֶל־ אֹהֶל יְהוָה וְהִנֵּה אֵצֶל
beside and-see! Yahweh tent-of to Joab he-fled that Solomon to-the-king

הַמִּזְבֵּחַ וַיִּשְׁלַח שְׁלֹמֹה אֶת־ בְּנָיָהוּ בֶן־ יְהוֹיָדָע לֵאמֹר לֵךְ
go! to-say Jehoiada son-of Benaiah *** Solomon then-he-ordered the-altar

פְּגַע־ בּוֹ׃ וַיָּבֹא בְנָיָהוּ אֶל־ אֹהֶל יְהוָה
Yahweh tent-of into Benaiah so-he-entered (30) against-him strike!

וַיֹּאמֶר אֵלָיו כֹּה־ אָמַר הַמֶּלֶךְ צֵא וַיֹּאמֶר ׀ לֹא כִּי
for no but-he-answered come-out! the-king he-says this to-him and-he-said

פֹה אָמוּת וַיָּשֶׁב בְּנָיָהוּ אֶת־ הַמֶּלֶךְ דָּבָר לֵאמֹר כֹּה־ דִבֶּר
he-said this to-say report the-king *** Benaiah and-he-sent I-will-die here

יוֹאָב וְכֹה עָנָנִי׃ וַיֹּאמֶר לוֹ הַמֶּלֶךְ עֲשֵׂה
do! the-king to-him then-he-commanded (31) he-answered-me and-this Joab

כַּאֲשֶׁר דִּבֶּר וּפְגַע־ בּוֹ וּקְבַרְתּוֹ וַהֲסִירֹתָ ׀
so-you-clear and-you-bury-him against-him and-strike! he-says just-as

דְּמֵי חִנָּם אֲשֶׁר שָׁפַךְ יוֹאָב מֵעָלַי וּמֵעַל
and-from-against from-against-me Joab he-shed that innocent bloods-of

בֵּית אָבִי׃ וְהֵשִׁיב יְהוָה אֶת־ דָּמוֹ עַל־
on blood-of-him *** Yahweh and-he-will-repay (32) father-of-me house-of

רֹאשׁוֹ אֲשֶׁר פָּגַע בִּשְׁנֵי־ אֲנָשִׁים צַדִּקִים וְטֹבִים
and-ones-good ones-upright men against-two-of he-attacked because head-of-him

מִמֶּנּוּ וַיַּהַרְגֵם בַּחֶרֶב וְאָבִי דָוִד לֹא
not David and-father-of-me with-the-sword and-he-killed-them more-than-him

יָדָע אֶת־אַבְנֵר בֶּן־ נֵר שַׂר־ צְבָא יִשְׂרָאֵל וְאֶת־עֲמָשָׂא בֶן־
son-of Amasa and Israel army-of commander-of Ner son-of Abner *** he-knew

carried the ark of the Sovereign LORD before my father
David and shared all my father's hardships." 27So Solomon removed Abiathar from
the priesthood of the LORD,
fulfilling the word the LORD
had spoken at Shiloh about
the house of Eli.
28When the news reached
Joab, who had conspired with
Adonijah though not with
Absalom, he fled to the tent of
the LORD and took hold of the
horns of the altar. 29King Solomon was told that Joab had
fled to the tent of the LORD and
was beside the altar. Then
Solomon ordered Benaiah son
of Jehoiada, "Go, strike him
down!"
30So Benaiah entered the
tent of the LORD and said to
Joab, "The king says, 'Come
out!' "
But he answered, "No, I will
die here."
Benaiah reported to the
king, "This is how Joab answered me."
31Then the king commanded
Benaiah, "Do as he says.
Strike him down and bury
him, and so clear me and my
father's house of the guilt of
the innocent blood that Joab
shed. 32The LORD will repay
him for the blood he shed, because without the knowledge
of my father David he attacked
two men and killed them with
the sword. Both of them—
Abner son of Ner, commander
of Israel's army, and Amasa
son of Jether, commander of
Judah's army—were better
men and more upright than

יֶתֶר שַׂר־ צְבָא יְהוּדָה׃ (33) וְשָׁבוּ דְמֵיהֶם
bloods-of-them and-may-they-rest (33) Judah army-of commander-of Jether

בְּרֹאשׁ יוֹאָב וּבְרֹאשׁ זַרְעוֹ לְעֹלָם וּלְדָוִד
but-on-David to-forever descendant-of-him and-on-head-of Joab on-head-of

וּלְזַרְעוֹ וּלְבֵיתוֹ וּלְכִסְאוֹ יִהְיֶה
may-he-be and-on-throne-of-him and-on-house-of-him and-on-descendant-of-him

שָׁלוֹם עַד־ עוֹלָם מֵעִם יְהוָה׃ (34) וַיַּעַל בְּנָיָהוּ בֶּן־ יְהוֹיָדָע
Jehoiada son-of Benaiah so-he-went-up (34) Yahweh from-with forever to peace

וַיִּפְגַּע־ בּוֹ וַיְמִתֵהוּ וַיִּקָּבֵר בְּבֵיתוֹ
in-tomb-of-him and-he-was-buried and-he-killed-him against-him and-he-struck

בַּמִּדְבָּר׃ (35) וַיִּתֵּן הַמֶּלֶךְ אֶת־ בְּנָיָהוּ בֶן־ יְהוֹיָדָע
Jehoiada son-of Benaiah *** the-king and-he-put (35) in-the-desert

תַּחְתָּיו עַל־ הַצָּבָא וְאֶת־ צָדוֹק הַכֹּהֵן נָתַן הַמֶּלֶךְ
the-king he-put the-priest Zadok and the-army over in-place-of-him

תַּחַת אֶבְיָתָר׃ (36) וַיִּשְׁלַח הַמֶּלֶךְ וַיִּקְרָא לְשִׁמְעִי
for-Shimei and-he-called the-king then-he-sent (36) Abiathar in-place-of

וַיֹּאמֶר לוֹ בְּנֵה־ לְךָ בַיִת בִּירוּשָׁלַםִ וְיָשַׁבְתָּ שָׁם
there and-you-live in-Jerusalem house for-you build! to-him and-he-said

וְלֹא־ תֵצֵא מִשָּׁם אָנֶה וָאָנָה׃ (37) וְהָיָה׀ בְּיוֹם
on-day for-he-will-be (37) or-to-there to-here from-there you-go but-not

צֵאתְךָ וְעָבַרְתָּ אֶת־ נַחַל קִדְרוֹן יָדֹעַ תֵּדַע
you-can-be-sure to-be-sure Kidron Valley-of *** and-you-cross to-leave-you

כִּי מוֹת תָּמוּת דָּמְךָ יִהְיֶה בְרֹאשֶׁךָ׃
on-head-of-you he-will-be blood-of-you you-will-die to-die that

(38) וַיֹּאמֶר שִׁמְעִי לַמֶּלֶךְ טוֹב הַדָּבָר כַּאֲשֶׁר דִּבֶּר
he-said just-as the-word good to-the-king Shimei and-he-answered (38)

אֲדֹנִי הַמֶּלֶךְ כֵּן יַעֲשֶׂה עַבְדֶּךָ וַיֵּשֶׁב שִׁמְעִי
Shimei and-he-stayed servant-of-you he-will-do so the-king lord-of-me

בִּירוּשָׁלַםִ יָמִים רַבִּים׃ (39) וַיְהִי מִקֵּץ שָׁלֹשׁ שָׁנִים וַיִּבְרְחוּ
then-they-ran-off days three at-end-of but-he-was (39) many days in-Jerusalem

שְׁנֵי־ עֲבָדִים לְשִׁמְעִי אֶל־ אָכִישׁ בֶּן־ מַעֲכָה מֶלֶךְ גַּת וַיַּגִּידוּ
and-they-told Gath king-of Maacah son-of Achish to of-Shimei slaves two-of

לְשִׁמְעִי לֵאמֹר הִנֵּה עֲבָדֶיךָ בְּגַת׃ (40) וַיָּקָם שִׁמְעִי
Shimei so-he-rose (40) in-Gath slaves-of-you see! to-say to-Shimei

וַיַּחֲבֹשׁ אֶת־ חֲמֹרוֹ וַיֵּלֶךְ גַּתָה אֶל־ אָכִישׁ לְבַקֵּשׁ
to-search-for Achish to to-Gath and-he-went donkey-of-him *** and-he-saddled

אֶת־ עֲבָדָיו וַיֵּלֶךְ שִׁמְעִי וַיָּבֵא אֶת־ עֲבָדָיו
slaves-of-him *** and-he-brought-back Shimei so-he-went slaves-of-him ***

he. 33May the guilt of their
blood rest on the head of Joab
and his descendants forever.
But on David and his descendants, his house and his throne,
may there be the LORD's peace
forever."
34So Benaiah son of Jehoiada
went up and struck down Joab
and killed him, and he was
buried on his own land[d] in the
desert. 35The king put Benaiah
son of Jehoiada over the army
in Joab's position and replaced Abiathar with Zadok
the priest.
36Then the king sent for
Shimei and said to him,
"Build yourself a house in
Jerusalem and live there, but
do not go anywhere else. 37The
day you leave and cross the
Kidron Valley, you can be sure
you will die; your blood will
be on your own head."
38Shimei answered the king,
"What you say is good. Your
servant will do as my lord the
king has said." And Shimei
stayed in Jerusalem for a long
time.
39But three years later, two of
Shimei's slaves ran off to Achish son of Maacah, king of
Gath, and Shimei was told,
"Your slaves are in Gath." 40At
this, he saddled his donkey
and went to Achish at Gath in
search of his slaves. So Shimei
went away and brought the
slaves back from Gath.

[d]34 Or *buried in his tomb*

מִגַּת׃ וַיֻּגַּד לִשְׁלֹמֹה כִּי־ הָלַךְ שִׁמְעִי מִירוּשָׁלַםִ

from-Jerusalem Shimei he-went that to-Solomon when-he-was-told (41) from-Gath

גַּת וַיָּשֹׁב׃ וַיִּשְׁלַח הַמֶּלֶךְ וַיִּקְרָא לְשִׁמְעִי

to-Shimei and-he-called the-king then-he-summoned (42) and-he-returned Gath

וַיֹּאמֶר אֵלָיו הֲלוֹא הִשְׁבַּעְתִּיךָ בַיהוָה וָאָעִד בְּךָ

to-you and-I-warned by-Yahweh I-made-swear-you not? to-him and-he-said

לֵאמֹר בְּיוֹם צֵאתְךָ וְהָלַכְתָּ אָנֶה וָאָנָה יָדֹעַ

to-be-sure or-to-there to-here and-you-go to-leave-you on-day to-say

תֵּדַע כִּי מוֹת תָּמוּת וַתֹּאמֶר אֵלַי טוֹב הַדָּבָר

the-word good to-me and-you-said you-will-die to-die that you-can-be-sure

שָׁמָעְתִּי׃ וּמַדּוּעַ לֹא שָׁמַרְתָּ אֵת שְׁבֻעַת יְהוָה וְאֶת־ הַמִּצְוָה

the-command and Yahweh oath-of *** you-kept not then-why? (43) I-will-obey

אֲשֶׁר־צִוִּיתִי עָלֶיךָ׃ וַיֹּאמֶר הַמֶּלֶךְ אֶל־שִׁמְעִי אַתָּה יָדַעְתָּ אֵת

*** you-know you Shimei to the-king and-he-said (44) to-you I-gave that

כָּל־ הָרָעָה אֲשֶׁר יָדַע לְבָבְךָ אֲשֶׁר עָשִׂיתָ לְדָוִד אָבִי

father-of-me to-David you-did that heart-of-you he-knows that the-wrong all-of

וְהֵשִׁיב יְהוָה אֶת־ רָעָתְךָ בְּרֹאשֶׁךָ׃ וְהַמֶּלֶךְ

but-the-king (45) on-head-of-you wrongdoing-of-you *** Yahweh now-he-will-repay

שְׁלֹמֹה בָּרוּךְ וְכִסֵּא דָוִד יִהְיֶה נָכוֹן לִפְנֵי

before being-secure he-will-remain David and-throne-of being-blessed Solomon

יְהוָה עַד־ עוֹלָם׃ וַיְצַו הַמֶּלֶךְ אֶת־ בְּנָיָהוּ בֶּן־ יְהוֹיָדָע

Jehoiada son-of Benaiah *** the-king then-he-ordered (46) forever to Yahweh

וַיֵּצֵא וַיִּפְגַּע־ בּוֹ וַיָּמֹת וְהַמַּמְלָכָה

and-the-kingdom and-he-died against-him and-he-struck and-he-went-out

נָכוֹנָה בְּיַד־ שְׁלֹמֹה׃ וַיִּתְחַתֵּן שְׁלֹמֹה אֶת־

with Solomon and-he-made-alliance (3:1) Solomon in-hand-of being-established

פַּרְעֹה מֶלֶךְ מִצְרָיִם וַיִּקַּח אֶת־ בַּת־ פַּרְעֹה וַיְבִיאֶהָ

and-he-brought-her Pharaoh daughter-of *** and-he-married Egypt king-of Pharaoh

אֶל־ עִיר דָּוִד עַד כַּלֹּתוֹ לִבְנוֹת אֶת־ בֵּיתוֹ וְאֶת־ בֵּית

temple-of and palace-of-him *** to-build to-finish-him until David City-of to

יְהוָה וְאֶת־חוֹמַת יְרוּשָׁלַםִ סָבִיב׃ רַק הָעָם מְזַבְּחִים

ones-sacrificing the-people however (2) around Jerusalem wall-of and Yahweh

בַּבָּמוֹת כִּי לֹא־ נִבְנָה בַיִת לְשֵׁם יְהוָה עַד

at Yahweh for-Name-of temple he-was-built not for at-the-high-places

הַיָּמִים הָהֵם׃ וַיֶּאֱהַב שְׁלֹמֹה אֶת־ יְהוָה לָלֶכֶת

to-walk Yahweh *** Solomon and-he-showed-love (3) the-those the-days

בְּחֻקּוֹת דָּוִד אָבִיו רַק בַּבָּמוֹת הוּא מְזַבֵּחַ

sacrificing he at-the-high-places except father-of-him David in-statutes-of

41 When Solomon was told that Shimei had gone from Jerusalem to Gath and had returned, 42 the king summoned Shimei and said to him, "Did I not make you swear by the LORD and warn you, 'On the day you leave to go anywhere else, you can be sure you will die'? At that time you said to me, 'What you say is good. I will obey.' 43 Why then did you not keep your oath to the LORD and obey the command I gave you?"

44 The king also said to Shimei, "You know in your heart all the wrong you did to my father David. Now the LORD will repay you for your wrongdoing. 45 But King Solomon will be blessed, and David's throne will remain secure before the LORD forever."

46 Then the king gave the order to Benaiah son of Jehoiada, and he went out and struck Shimei down and killed him.

The kingdom was now firmly established in Solomon's hands.

*Solomon Asks for Wisdom*

3 Solomon made an alliance with Pharaoh king of Egypt and married his daughter. He brought her to the City of David until he finished building his palace and the temple of the LORD, and the wall around Jerusalem. 2 The people, however, were still sacrificing at the high places,

וַיֵּ֣לֶךְ הַמֶּ֧לֶךְ גִּבְעֹ֛נָה לִזְבֹּ֥חַ שָׁ֖ם כִּ֥י וּמַקְטִֽיר׃
and-he-went the-king to-Gibeon to-sacrifice there for (4) and-burning-incense

הִ֖יא הַבָּמָ֣ה הַגְּדוֹלָ֑ה אֶ֤לֶף עֹלוֹת֙ יַעֲלֶ֣ה שְׁלֹמֹ֔ה
that the-high-place the-important thousand burnt-offerings he-offered Solomon

עַ֖ל הַמִּזְבֵּ֥חַ הַהֽוּא׃ בְּגִבְע֛וֹן נִרְאָ֧ה יְהוָ֛ה אֶל־שְׁלֹמֹ֖ה בַּחֲל֣וֹם
on the-altar the-that at-Gibeon he-appeared Yahweh to Solomon in-dream-of

הַלָּ֑יְלָה וַיֹּ֣אמֶר אֱלֹהִ֔ים שְׁאַ֖ל מָ֥ה אֶתֶּן־לָֽךְ׃ וַיֹּ֣אמֶר
the-night and-he-said God ask! whatever I-should-give to-you (6) and-he-said

שְׁלֹמֹ֗ה אַתָּ֨ה עָשִׂ֜יתָ עִם־עַבְדְּךָ֩ דָוִ֨ד אָבִ֜י חֶ֣סֶד גָּדוֹל֒
Solomon you you-showed to servant-of-you David father-of-me kindness great

כַּאֲשֶׁר֩ הָלַ֨ךְ לְפָנֶ֜יךָ בֶּאֱמֶ֧ת וּבִצְדָקָ֛ה
because-that he-walked before-you in-faithfulness and-in-righteousness

וּבְיִשְׁרַ֤ת לֵבָב֙ עִמָּ֔ךְ וַתִּשְׁמָר־ל֗וֹ אֶת־הַחֶ֤סֶד
and-in-uprightness-of heart with-you and-you-continued to-him *** the-kindness

הַגָּדוֹל֙ הַזֶּ֔ה וַתִּתֶּן־ל֥וֹ בֵ֛ן יֹשֵׁ֥ב עַל־כִּסְא֖וֹ
the-great the-this and-you-gave to-him son sitting on throne-of-him

כַּיּ֥וֹם הַזֶּֽה׃ וְעַתָּה֙ יְהוָ֣ה אֱלֹהָ֔י אַתָּה֙ הִמְלַ֣כְתָּ אֶת־
as-the-day the-this (7) and-now Yahweh God-of-me you you-made-king ***

עַבְדְּךָ֔ תַּ֖חַת דָּוִ֣ד אָבִ֑י וְאָֽנֹכִי֙ נַ֣עַר קָטֹ֔ן לֹ֥א אֵדַ֖ע
servant-of-you in-place-of David father-of-me but-I child little not I-know

צֵ֥את וָבֹֽא׃ וְעַ֨בְדְּךָ֔ בְּת֥וֹךְ עַמְּךָ֖ אֲשֶׁ֣ר בָּחָ֑רְתָּ
to-go or-to-come (8) and-servant-of-you among people-of-you whom you-chose

עַם־רָ֕ב אֲשֶׁ֧ר לֹֽא־יִמָּנֶ֛ה וְלֹ֥א יִסָּפֵ֖ר מֵרֹֽב׃
people great who not he-can-be-counted and-not he-can-be-numbered for-number

וְנָתַתָּ֨ לְעַבְדְּךָ֜ לֵ֤ב שֹׁמֵ֙עַ֙ לִשְׁפֹּ֣ט אֶת־עַמְּךָ֔
so-you-give (9) to-servant-of-you heart discerning to-govern *** people-of-you

לְהָבִ֖ין בֵּֽין־ט֣וֹב לְרָ֑ע כִּ֣י מִ֤י יוּכַל֙ לִשְׁפֹּ֔ט אֶת־
to-distinguish between right from-wrong for who? he-is-able to-govern ***

עַמְּךָ֥ הַכָּבֵ֖ד הַזֶּֽה׃ וַיִּיטַ֥ב הַדָּבָ֖ר
people-of-you the-great the-this (10) and-he-was-pleasing the-thing

בְּעֵינֵ֣י אֲדֹנָ֑י כִּ֚י שָׁאַ֣ל שְׁלֹמֹ֔ה אֶת־הַדָּבָ֖ר הַזֶּֽה׃ וַיֹּ֨אמֶר
in-eyes-of Lord that he-asked Solomon *** the-thing the-this (11) so-he-said

אֱלֹהִ֜ים אֵלָ֗יו יַ֚עַן אֲשֶׁ֤ר שָׁאַ֙לְתָּ֙ אֶת־הַדָּבָ֣ר הַזֶּ֔ה וְלֹֽא־שָׁאַ֣לְתָּ
God to-him since that you-asked *** the-thing the-this and-not you-asked

לְּךָ֩ יָמִ֨ים רַבִּ֜ים וְלֹֽא־שָׁאַ֧לְתָּ לְּךָ֣ עֹ֗שֶׁר וְלֹ֥א שָׁאַ֖לְתָּ נֶ֣פֶשׁ
for-you days many and-not you-asked for-you wealth and-not you-asked life-of

אֹיְבֶ֑יךָ וְשָׁאַ֧לְתָּ לְּךָ֛ הָבִ֖ין לִשְׁמֹ֥עַ מִשְׁפָּֽט׃
being-enemies-of-you but-you-asked for-you to-discern to-administer justice

because a temple had not yet been built for the Name of the Lord. ³Solomon showed his love for the Lord by walking according to the statutes of his father David, except that he offered sacrifices and burned incense on the high places.

⁴The king went to Gibeon to offer sacrifices, for that was the most important high place, and Solomon offered a thousand burnt offerings on that altar. ⁵At Gibeon the Lord appeared to Solomon during the night in a dream, and God said, "Ask for whatever you want me to give you."

⁶Solomon answered, "You have shown great kindness to your servant, my father David, because he was faithful to you and righteous and upright in heart. You have continued this great kindness to him and have given him a son to sit on his throne this very day.

⁷"Now, O Lord my God, you have made your servant king in place of my father David. But I am only a little child and do not know how to carry out my duties. ⁸Your servant is here among the people you have chosen, a great people, too numerous to count or number. ⁹So give your servant a discerning heart to govern your people and to distinguish between right and wrong. For who is able to govern this great people of yours?"

¹⁰The Lord was pleased that Solomon had asked for this. ¹¹So God said to him, "Since you have asked for this and not for long life or wealth for yourself, nor have asked for the death of your enemies but for discernment in administering justice, ¹²I will do what

(12) הִנֵּה עָשִׂיתִי כִּדְבָרֶיךָ הִנֵּה | נָתַתִּי לְךָ לֵב חָכָם
wise heart to-you I-will-give see! as-requests-of-you I-will-do see! (12)

וְנָבוֹן אֲשֶׁר כָּמוֹךָ לֹא־ הָיָה לְפָנֶיךָ וְאַחֲרֶיךָ לֹא־
not or-after-you before-you he-was not like-you that and-discerning

יָקוּם כָּמוֹךָ׃ (13) וְגַם אֲשֶׁר לֹא־ שָׁאַלְתָּ נָתַתִּי לָךְ
to-you I-will-give you-asked not what and-more (13) like-you he-will-rise

גַּם־ עֹשֶׁר גַּם־ כָּבוֹד אֲשֶׁר לֹא־ הָיָה כָמוֹךָ אִישׁ בַּמְּלָכִים
among-the-kings anyone like-you he-will-be not that honor and wealth both

כָּל־ יָמֶיךָ׃ (14) וְאִם | תֵּלֵךְ בִּדְרָכַי לִשְׁמֹר חֻקַּי
statutes-of-me to-obey in-ways-of-me you-walk and-if (14) days-of-you all-of

וּמִצְוֺתַי כַּאֲשֶׁר הָלַךְ דָּוִיד אָבִיךָ וְהַאַרַכְתִּי
then-I-will-make-long father-of-you David he-walked just-as and-commands-of-me

אֶת־ יָמֶיךָ׃ (15) וַיִּקַץ שְׁלֹמֹה וְהִנֵּה חֲלוֹם וַיָּבוֹא
and-he-returned dream and-see! Solomon then-he-awoke (15) days-of-you ***

יְרוּשָׁלַםִ וַיַּעֲמֹד | לִפְנֵי | אֲרוֹן בְּרִית־ אֲדֹנָי וַיַּעַל
and-he-sacrificed Lord covenant-of ark-of before and-he-stood Jerusalem

עֹלוֹת וַיַּעַשׂ שְׁלָמִים וַיַּעַשׂ מִשְׁתֶּה
feast then-he-gave fellowship-offerings and-he-offered burnt-offerings

לְכָל־ עֲבָדָיו׃ (16) אָז תָּבֹאנָה שְׁתַּיִם נָשִׁים זֹנוֹת
being-prostitutes women two they-came now (16) courtiers-of-him for-all-of

אֶל־ הַמֶּלֶךְ וַתַּעֲמֹדְנָה לְפָנָיו׃ (17) וַתֹּאמֶר הָאִשָּׁה הָאַחַת
the-one the-woman and-she-said (17) before-him and-they-stood the-king to

בִּי אֲדֹנִי אֲנִי וְהָאִשָּׁה הַזֹּאת יֹשְׁבֹת בְּבַיִת אֶחָד
same in-house ones-living the-this and-the-woman I lord-of-me oh!

וָאֵלֵד עִמָּהּ בַּבָּיִת׃ (18) וַיְהִי בַּיּוֹם הַשְּׁלִישִׁי
the-third on-the-day and-he-was (18) in-the-house with-her and-I-had-baby

לְלִדְתִּי וַתֵּלֶד גַּם־ הָאִשָּׁה הַזֹּאת וַאֲנַחְנוּ יַחְדָּו
alone and-we the-this the-woman also then-she-had-baby to-give-birth-me

אֵין־ זָר אִתָּנוּ בַּבַּיִת זוּלָתִי שְׁתַּיִם־אֲנַחְנוּ בַּבָּיִת׃
in-the-house we two but in-the-house with-us one-being-stranger not

(19) וַיָּמָת בֶּן־ הָאִשָּׁה הַזֹּאת לָיְלָה אֲשֶׁר שָׁכְבָה עָלָיו׃
on-him she-lay because night the-this the-woman son-of and-he-died (19)

(20) וַתָּקָם בְּתוֹךְ הַלַּיְלָה וַתִּקַּח אֶת־ בְּנִי
son-of-me *** and-she-took the-night in-middle-of so-she-got-up (20)

מֵאֶצְלִי וַאֲמָתְךָ יְשֵׁנָה וַתַּשְׁכִּיבֵהוּ
and-she-put-him she-was-asleep while-servant-of-you from-beside-me

בְּחֵיקָהּ וְאֶת־ בְּנָהּ הַמֵּת הִשְׁכִּיבָה בְחֵיקִי׃
by-breast-of-me she-put the-dead son-of-her and by-breast-of-her

you have asked. I will give you a wise and discerning heart, so that there will never have been anyone like you, nor will there ever be. [13]Moreover, I will give you what you have not asked for—both riches and honor—so that in your lifetime you will have no equal among kings. [14]And if you walk in my ways and obey my statutes and commands as David your father did, I will give you a long life." [15]Then Solomon awoke—and he realized it had been a dream.

He returned to Jerusalem, stood before the ark of the Lord's covenant and sacrificed burnt offerings and fellowship offerings.[e] Then he gave a feast for all his court.

### *A Wise Ruling*

[16]Now two prostitutes came to the king and stood before him. [17]One of them said, "My lord, this woman and I live in the same house. I had a baby while she was there with me. [18]The third day after my child was born, this woman also had a baby. We were alone; there was no one in the house but the two of us.

[19]"During the night this woman's son died because she lay on him. [20]So she got up in the middle of the night and took my son from my side while I your servant was asleep. She put him by her breast and put her dead son by

[e]15 Traditionally *peace offerings*

וָאָקֻם בַּבֹּקֶר לְהֵינִיק אֶת־ בְּנִי וְהִנֵּה־ מֵת
dead and-see! son-of-me *** to-nurse in-the-morning and-I-got-up (21)

וָאֶתְבּוֹנֵן אֵלָיו בַּבֹּקֶר וְהִנֵּה לֹא־ הָיָה בְנִי
son-of-me he-was not then-see! in-the-morning at-him when-I-looked-closely

אֲשֶׁר יָלָדְתִּי׃ וַתֹּאמֶר הָאִשָּׁה הָאַחֶרֶת לֹא כִי בְּנִי הַחַי
the-living son-of-me so not the-other the-woman and-she-said (22) I-bore whom

וּבְנֵךְ הַמֵּת וְזֹאת אֹמֶרֶת לֹא כִי בְּנֵךְ הַמֵּת
the-dead son-of-you so not insisting but-this-one the-dead and-son-of-you

וּבְנִי הֶחָי וַתְּדַבֵּרְנָה לִפְנֵי הַמֶּלֶךְ׃ וַיֹּאמֶר
and-he-said (23) the-king before so-they-argued the-living and-son-of-me

הַמֶּלֶךְ זֹאת אֹמֶרֶת זֶה־ בְּנִי הַחַי וּבְנֵךְ הַמֵּת
the-dead and-son-of-you the-living son-of-me this saying this-one the-king

וְזֹאת אֹמֶרֶת לֹא כִי בְּנֵךְ הַמֵּת וּבְנִי הֶחָי׃
the-living and-son-of-me the-dead son-of-you so not saying while-that-one

וַיֹּאמֶר הַמֶּלֶךְ קְחוּ לִי־ חָרֶב וַיָּבִאוּ הַחֶרֶב
the-sword so-they-brought sword to-me bring! the-king then-he-said (24)

לִפְנֵי הַמֶּלֶךְ׃ וַיֹּאמֶר הַמֶּלֶךְ גִּזְרוּ אֶת־ הַיֶּלֶד הַחַי
the-living the-child *** cut! the-king then-he-ordered (25) the-king before

לִשְׁנָיִם וּתְנוּ אֶת־ הַחֲצִי לְאַחַת וְאֶת־ הַחֲצִי לְאֶחָת׃ וַתֹּאמֶר
and-she-said (26) to-other the-half and to-one the-half *** and-give! in-two

הָאִשָּׁה אֲשֶׁר־ בְּנָהּ הַחַי אֶל־ הַמֶּלֶךְ כִּי־ נִכְמְרוּ
they-were-warmed for the-king to the-living son-of-her who the-woman

רַחֲמֶיהָ עַל־ בְּנָהּ וַתֹּאמֶר ׀ בִּי אֲדֹנִי תְּנוּ־
give! lord-of-me please! and-she-said son-of-her for compassions-of-her

לָהּ אֶת־ הַיָּלוּד הַחַי וְהָמֵת אַל־ תְּמִיתֻהוּ
you-kill-him not but-to-kill the-living the-one-being-born *** to-her

וְזֹאת אֹמֶרֶת גַּם־ לִי גַם־ לָךְ לֹא יִהְיֶה גְּזֹרוּ׃
cut-in-two! he-shall-be not to-you also to-me also saying but-that-one

וַיַּעַן הַמֶּלֶךְ וַיֹּאמֶר תְּנוּ־ לָהּ אֶת־ הַיָּלוּד
the-one-being-born *** to-her give! and-he-said the-king then-he-ruled (27)

הַחַי וְהָמֵת לֹא תְמִיתֻהוּ הִיא אִמּוֹ׃ וַיִּשְׁמְעוּ
when-they-heard (28) mother-of-him she you-kill-him not and-to-kill the-living

כָל־ יִשְׂרָאֵל אֶת־ הַמִּשְׁפָּט אֲשֶׁר שָׁפַט הַמֶּלֶךְ וַיִּרְאוּ
then-they-were-in-awe the-king he-gave that the-verdict *** Israel all-of

מִפְּנֵי הַמֶּלֶךְ כִּי רָאוּ כִּי־ חָכְמַת אֱלֹהִים בְּקִרְבּוֹ
in-inside-of-him God wisdom-of that they-saw because the-king from-before

לַעֲשׂוֹת מִשְׁפָּט׃ וַיְהִי הַמֶּלֶךְ שְׁלֹמֹה מֶלֶךְ עַל־ כָּל־
all-of over ruler Solomon the-king so-he-was (4:1) justice to-administer

my breast. 21 The next morning, I got up to nurse my son—
and he was dead! But when I
looked at him closely in the
morning light, I saw that it
wasn't the son I had borne."
22 The other woman said,
"No! The living one is my son;
the dead one is yours."
But the first one insisted,
"No! The dead one is yours;
the living one is mine." And
so they argued before the king.
23 The king said, "This one
says, 'My son is alive and your
son is dead,' while that one
says, 'No! Your son is dead
and mine is alive.' "
24 Then the king said, "Bring
me a sword." So they brought
a sword for the king. 25 He then
gave an order: "Cut the living
child in two and give half to
one and half to the other."
26 The woman whose son
was alive was filled with compassion for her son and said to
the king, "Please, my lord,
give her the living baby! Don't
kill him!"
But the other said, "Neither
I nor you shall have him. Cut
him in two!"
27 Then the king gave his ruling: "Give the living baby to
the first woman. Do not kill
him; she is his mother."
28 When all Israel heard the
verdict the king had given,
they held the king in awe, because they saw that he had
wisdom from God to administer justice.

### *Solomon's Officials and Governors*

4 So King Solomon ruled
over all Israel. 2 And these

יִשְׂרָאֵל׃ וְאֵלֶּה הַשָּׂרִים אֲשֶׁר־ לוֹ עֲזַרְיָהוּ בֶן־ צָדוֹק
Zadok son-of Azariah to-him who the-chief-officials and-these (2) Israel

הַכֹּהֵן׃ אֱלִיחֹרֶף וַאֲחִיָּה בְּנֵי שִׁישָׁא סֹפְרִים יְהוֹשָׁפָט
Jehoshaphat secretaries Shisha sons-of and-Ahijah Elihoreph (3) the-priest

בֶּן־ אֲחִילוּד הַמַּזְכִּיר׃ וּבְנָיָהוּ בֶּן־ יְהוֹיָדָע עַל־
over Jehoiada son-of and-Benaiah (4) the-one-recording Ahilud son-of

הַצָּבָא וְצָדוֹק וְאֶבְיָתָר כֹּהֲנִים׃ וַעֲזַרְיָהוּ בֶן־ נָתָן עַל־
over Nathan son-of and-Azariah (5) priests and-Abiathar and-Zadok the-army

הַנִּצָּבִים וְזָבוּד בֶּן־ נָתָן כֹּהֵן רֵעֶה
personal-adviser-of priest Nathan son-of and-Zabud the-ones-being-officers

הַמֶּלֶךְ׃ וַאֲחִישָׁר עַל־ הַבָּיִת וַאֲדֹנִירָם בֶּן־ עַבְדָּא עַל־
over Abda son-of and-Adoniram the-palace over and-Abishar (6) the-king

הַמַּס׃ וְלִשְׁלֹמֹה שְׁנֵים־ עָשָׂר נִצָּבִים עַל־ כָּל־
all-of over ones-governing ten two and-to-Solomon (7) the-forced-labor

יִשְׂרָאֵל וְכִלְכְּלוּ אֶת־ הַמֶּלֶךְ וְאֶת־ בֵּיתוֹ חֹדֶשׁ
month house-of-him and the-king *** and-they-supplied-provision Israel

בַּשָּׁנָה יִהְיֶה עַל־ אֶחָד לְכַלְכֵּל׃ וְאֵלֶּה שְׁמוֹתָם
names-of-them and-these (8) to-provide the-each for he-was in-the-year

בֶּן־ חוּר בְּהַר אֶפְרָיִם׃ בֶּן־ דֶּקֶר בְּמָקַץ וּבְשַׁעַלְבִים
and-in-Shaalbim in-Makaz Deker Ben (9) Ephraim in-hill-country-of Hur Ben

וּבֵית שָׁמֶשׁ וְאֵילוֹן בֵּית חָנָן׃ בֶּן־ חֶסֶד בָּאֲרֻבּוֹת לוֹ
to-him in-the-Arubboth Hesed Ben (10) Hanan Beth and-Elon Shemesh and-Beth

שֹׂכֹה וְכָל־ אֶרֶץ חֵפֶר׃ בֶּן־ אֲבִינָדָב כָּל־ נָפַת דֹּאר טָפַת
Taphath Dor Naphoth all-of Abinadab Ben (11) Hepher land-of and-all-of Socoh

בַּת־ שְׁלֹמֹה הָיְתָה לּוֹ לְאִשָּׁה׃ בַּעֲנָא בֶּן־ אֲחִילוּד תַּעְנַךְ
Taanach Ahilud son-of Baana (12) as-wife to-him she-was Solomon daughter-of

וּמְגִדּוֹ וְכָל־ בֵּית שְׁאָן אֲשֶׁר אֵצֶל צָרְתַנָה מִתַּחַת לְיִזְרְעֶאל
to-Jezreel at-below to-Zarethan next that Shan Beth and-all-of and-Megiddo

מִבֵּית שְׁאָן עַד אָבֵל מְחוֹלָה עַד מֵעֵבֶר לְיָקְמְעָם׃ בֶּן־ גֶּבֶר
Geber Ben (13) to-Jokmeam at-across to Meholath Abel to Shan from-Beth

בְּרָמֹת גִּלְעָד לוֹ חַוֹּת יָאִיר בֶּן־ מְנַשֶּׁה אֲשֶׁר בַּגִּלְעָד
in-the-Gilead that Manasseh son-of Jair settlements-of to-him Gilead in-Ramoth

לוֹ חֶבֶל אַרְגֹּב אֲשֶׁר בַּבָּשָׁן שִׁשִּׁים עָרִים גְּדֹלוֹת חוֹמָה
wall large-ones cities sixty in-the-Bashan that Argob district-of to-him

וּבְרִיחַ נְחֹשֶׁת׃ אֲחִינָדָב בֶּן־ עִדֹּא מַחֲנָיְמָה׃ אֲחִימַעַץ
Ahimaaz (15) in-Mahanaim Iddo son-of Ahinadab (14) bronze and-gate-bar-of

בְּנַפְתָּלִי גַּם־ הוּא לָקַח אֶת־ בָּשְׂמַת בַּת־ שְׁלֹמֹה לְאִשָּׁה׃
as-wife Solomon daughter-of Basemath *** he-took he also in-Naphtali

were his chief officials:

Azariah son of Zadok—the priest;
3 Elihoreph and Ahijah, sons of Shisha—secretaries;
Jehoshaphat son of Ahilud—recorder;
4 Benaiah son of Jehoiada—commander in chief;
Zadok and Abiathar—priests;
5 Azariah son of Nathan—in charge of the district officers;
Zabud son of Nathan—a priest and personal adviser to the king;
6 Ahishar—in charge of the palace;
Adoniram son of Abda—in charge of forced labor.

7 Solomon also had twelve district governors over all Israel, who supplied provisions for the king and the royal household. Each one had to provide supplies for one month in the year. 8 These are their names:

Ben-Hur—in the hill country of Ephraim;
9 Ben-Deker—in Makaz, Shaalbim, Beth Shemesh and Elon Bethhanan;
10 Ben-Hesed—in Arubboth (Socoh and all the land of Hepher were his);
11 Ben-Abinadab—in Naphoth Dor[f] (he was married to Taphath daughter of Solomon);
12 Baana son of Ahilud—in Taanach and Megiddo, and in all of Beth Shan next to Zarethan below Jezreel, from Beth Shan to Abel Meholah across to Jokmeam;
13 Ben-Geber—in Ramoth Gilead (the settlements of Jair son of Manasseh in Gilead were his, as well as the district of Argob in Bashan and its sixty large walled cities with bronze gate bars);
14 Ahinadab son of Iddo—in Mahanaim;
15 Ahimaaz—in Naphtali (he had married Basemath daughter of Solomon);

f11 Or *in the heights of Dor*

°7 ק האחד

בַּעֲנָא בֶּן־ חוּשַׁי בְּאָשֵׁר וּבְעָלוֹת׃ יְהוֹשָׁפָט בֶּן־
son-of Jehoshaphat (17) and-in-Aloth in-Asher Hushai son-of Baana (16)

פָּרוּחַ בְּיִשָּׂשכָר׃† שִׁמְעִי בֶן־ אֵלָא בְּבִנְיָמִן׃ גֶּבֶר בֶּן־ אֻרִי
Uri son-of Geber (19) in-Benjamin Ela son-of Shimei (18) in-Issachar Paruah

בְּאֶרֶץ גִּלְעָד אֶרֶץ סִיחוֹן ׀ מֶלֶךְ הָאֱמֹרִי וְעוֹג מֶלֶךְ
king-of and-Og the-Amorite king-of Sihon country-of Gilead in-land-of

הַבָּשָׁן וּנְצִיב אֶחָד אֲשֶׁר בָּאָרֶץ׃ יְהוּדָה וְיִשְׂרָאֵל
and-Israel Judah (20) over-the-district that only and-governor the-Bashan

רַבִּים כַּחוֹל אֲשֶׁר־ עַל־ הַיָּם לָרֹב אֹכְלִים
ones-eating in-number the-sea by that as-the-sand ones-numerous

וְשֹׁתִים וּשְׂמֵחִים׃ וּשְׁלֹמֹה הָיָה מוֹשֵׁל
ruling he-was and-Solomon *(5:1[21]) and-ones-happy and-ones-drinking

בְּכָל־ הַמַּמְלָכוֹת מִן־ הַנָּהָר אֶרֶץ פְּלִשְׁתִּים וְעַד
and-as-far-as Philistines land-of the-River from the-kingdoms over-all-of

גְּבוּל מִצְרַיִם מַגִּשִׁים מִנְחָה וְעֹבְדִים אֶת־ שְׁלֹמֹה כָּל־
all-of Solomon *** and-ones-serving tribute ones-bringing Egypt border-of

יְמֵי חַיָּיו׃ וַיְהִי לֶחֶם־ שְׁלֹמֹה לְיוֹם אֶחָד
one for-day Solomon provision-of and-he-was (2[22]) lives-of-him days-of

שְׁלֹשִׁים כֹּר סֹלֶת וְשִׁשִּׁים כֹּר קָמַח׃ עֲשָׂרָה בָקָר בְּרִאִים
ones-stall-fed cattle ten (3[23]) meal cor and-sixty fine-flour cor thirty

וְעֶשְׂרִים בָּקָר רְעִי וּמֵאָה צֹאן לְבַד מֵאַיָּל
from-deer apart-from sheep and-hundred pasture-fed cattle and-twenty

וּצְבִי וְיַחְמוּר וּבַרְבֻּרִים אֲבוּסִים׃ כִּי־ הוּא רֹדֶה ׀
ruling he for (4[24]) ones-being-choice and-fowls and-roebuck and-gazelle

בְּכָל־ עֵבֶר הַנָּהָר מִתִּפְסַח וְעַד־ עַזָּה בְּכָל־
over-all-of Gaza even-to from-Tiphsah the-River west-of over-all-of

מַלְכֵי עֵבֶר הַנָּהָר וְשָׁלוֹם הָיָה לוֹ מִכָּל־ עֲבָרָיו
sides-of-him on-all-of to-him he-was and-peace the-River west-of kingdoms-of

מִסָּבִיב׃ וַיֵּשֶׁב יְהוּדָה וְיִשְׂרָאֵל לָבֶטַח אִישׁ תַּחַת
under each in-safety and-Israel Judah and-he-lived (5[25]) at-around

גַּפְנוֹ וְתַחַת תְּאֵנָתוֹ מִדָּן וְעַד־ בְּאֵר שָׁבַע כֹּל יְמֵי
days-of all-of Sheba Beer even-to from-Dan fig-of-him and-under vine-of-him

שְׁלֹמֹה׃ וַיְהִי לִשְׁלֹמֹה אַרְבָּעִים אֶלֶף אֻרְוֹת סוּסִים
horses stalls-of thousand forty to-Solomon and-he-was (6[26]) Solomon

לְמֶרְכָּבוֹ וּשְׁנֵים־ עָשָׂר אֶלֶף פָּרָשִׁים׃ וְכִלְכְּלוּ
and-they-provided (7[27]) horses thousand ten and-two for-chariot-of-him

הַנִּצָּבִים הָאֵלֶּה אֶת־ הַמֶּלֶךְ שְׁלֹמֹה וְאֵת כָּל־
all-of and Solomon the-king *** the-these the-ones-being-officers

[16]Baana son of Hushai—in Asher and in Aloth;
[17]Jehoshaphat son of Paruah—in Issachar;
[18]Shimei son of Ela—in Benjamin;
[19]Geber son of Uri—in Gilead (the country of Sihon king of the Amorites and the country of Og king of Bashan). He was the only governor over the district.

*Solomon's Daily Provisions*

[20]The people of Judah and Israel were as numerous as the sand on the seashore; they ate, they drank and they were happy. [21]And Solomon ruled over all the kingdoms from the River[g] to the land of the Philistines, as far as the border of Egypt. These countries brought tribute and were Solomon's subjects all his life.

[22]Solomon's daily provisions were thirty cors[h] of fine flour and sixty cors[i] of meal, [23]ten head of stall-fed cattle, twenty of pasture-fed cattle and a hundred sheep and goats, as well as deer, gazelles, roebucks and choice fowl. [24]For he ruled over all the kingdoms west of the River, from Tiphsah to Gaza, and had peace on all sides. [25]During Solomon's lifetime Judah and Israel, from Dan to Beersheba, lived in safety, each man under his own vine and fig tree.

[26]Solomon had four[j] thousand stalls for chariot horses, and twelve thousand horses.[k]

[27]The district officers, each in his month, supplied provisions for King Solomon and

g21 That is, the Euphrates; also in verse 24
h22 That is, probably about 185 bushels (about 6.6 kiloliters)
i22 That is, probably about 375 bushels (about 13.2 kiloliters)
j26 Some Septuagint manuscripts (see also 2 Chron. 9:25); Hebrew *forty*
k26 Or *charioteers*

*The Hebrew numeration of chapter 5 begins with verse 21 of chapter 4 in English. The number in brackets indicates the English numeration.

†17 Most mss have *dagesh* in the *sin* (בְּיִשּׂ).

הַקָּרֵב אֶל־ שֻׁלְחַן הַמֶּלֶךְ־ שְׁלֹמֹה אִישׁ חָדְשׁוֹ לֹא יְעַדְּרוּ
they-lacked not month-of-him each Solomon the-king table-of to the-one-near

דָּבָר׃ (8[28]) וְהַשְּׂעֹרִים וְהַתֶּבֶן לַסּוּסִים
for-the-horses and-the-straw and-the-barleys (8[28]) thing

וְלָרֶכֶשׁ יָבִאוּ אֶל־ הַמָּקוֹם אֲשֶׁר יִהְיֶה־ שָּׁם אִישׁ
each there he-was where the-place to they-brought and-for-the-chariot-horse

כְּמִשְׁפָּטוֹ׃ (9[29]) וַיִּתֵּן אֱלֹהִים חָכְמָה לִשְׁלֹמֹה וּתְבוּנָה
and-insight to-Solomon wisdom God and-he-gave (9[29]) as-quota-of-him

הַרְבֵּה מְאֹד וְרֹחַב לֵב כַּחוֹל אֲשֶׁר עַל־ שְׂפַת
shore-of on that as-the-sand understanding and-breadth-of very to-be-great

הַיָּם׃ (10[30]) וַתֵּרֶב חָכְמַת שְׁלֹמֹה מֵחָכְמַת
more-than-wisdom-of Solomon wisdom-of and-she-was-great (10[30]) the-sea

כָּל־ בְּנֵי־ קֶדֶם וּמִכֹּל חָכְמַת מִצְרָיִם׃ (11[31]) וַיֶּחְכַּם
and-he-was-wise (11[31]) Egypt wisdom-of and-more-than-all-of East men-of all-of

מִכָּל־ הָאָדָם מֵאֵיתָן הָאֶזְרָחִי וְהֵימָן וְכַלְכֹּל
and-Calcol and-Heman the-Ezrahite more-than-Ethan the-man more-than-any-of

וְדַרְדַּע בְּנֵי מָחוֹל וַיְהִי־ שְׁמוֹ בְכָל־ הַגּוֹיִם סָבִיב׃
around the-nations to-all-of name-of-him and-he-was Mahol sons-of and-Darda

(12[32]) וַיְדַבֵּר שְׁלֹשֶׁת אֲלָפִים מָשָׁל וַיְהִי שִׁירוֹ חֲמִשָּׁה
five song-of-him and-he-was proverb thousands three-of and-he-spoke (12[32])

וָאָלֶף׃ (13[33]) וַיְדַבֵּר עַל־ הָעֵצִים מִן־ הָאֶרֶז אֲשֶׁר
that the-cedar from the-plants about and-he-described (13[33]) and-thousand

בַּלְּבָנוֹן וְעַד הָאֵזוֹב אֲשֶׁר יֹצֵא בַּקִּיר וַיְדַבֵּר
and-he-taught from-the-wall growing that the-hyssop even-to of-the-Lebanon

עַל־ הַבְּהֵמָה וְעַל־ הָעוֹף וְעַל־ הָרֶמֶשׂ וְעַל־ הַדָּגִים׃
the-fishes and-about the-reptile and-about the-bird and-about the-animal about

(14[34]) וַיָּבֹאוּ מִכָּל־ הָעַמִּים לִשְׁמֹעַ אֵת חָכְמַת
wisdom-of *** to-listen the-nations from-all-of and-they-came (14[34])

שְׁלֹמֹה מֵאֵת כָּל־ מַלְכֵי הָאָרֶץ אֲשֶׁר שָׁמְעוּ אֶת־ חָכְמָתוֹ׃
wisdom-of-him *** they-heard who the-world kings-of all-of from Solomon

(15[1]) וַיִּשְׁלַח חִירָם מֶלֶךְ־ צוֹר אֶת־ עֲבָדָיו אֶל־ שְׁלֹמֹה כִּי
when Solomon to envoys-of-him *** Tyre king-of Hiram and-he-sent (15[1])

שָׁמַע כִּי אֹתוֹ מָשְׁחוּ לְמֶלֶךְ תַּחַת אָבִיהוּ כִּי
for father-of-him in-place-of as-king they-anointed him that he-heard

אֹהֵב הָיָה חִירָם לְדָוִד כָּל־ הַיָּמִים׃ (16[2]) וַיִּשְׁלַח
and-he-sent (16[2]) the-days all-of with-David Hiram he-was being-friendly

שְׁלֹמֹה אֶל־חִירָם לֵאמֹר׃ (17[3]) אַתָּה יָדַעְתָּ אֶת־ דָּוִד אָבִי כִּי
that father-of-me David *** you-know you (17[3]) to-say Hiram to Solomon

all who came to the king's table. They saw to it that nothing was lacking. [28]They also brought to the proper place their quotas of barley and straw for the chariot horses and the other horses.

*Solomon's Wisdom*

[29]God gave Solomon wisdom and very great insight, and a breadth of understanding as measureless as the sand on the seashore. [30]Solomon's wisdom was greater than the wisdom of all the men of the East, and greater than all the wisdom of Egypt. [31]He was wiser than any other man, including Ethan the Ezrahite—wiser than Heman, Calcol and Darda, the sons of Mahol. And his fame spread to all the surrounding nations. [32]He spoke three thousand proverbs and his songs numbered a thousand and five. [33]He described plant life, from the cedar of Lebanon to the hyssop that grows out of walls. He also taught about animals and birds, reptiles and fish. [34]Men of all nations came to listen to Solomon's wisdom, sent by all the kings of the world, who had heard of his wisdom.

*Preparations for Building the Temple*

5 When Hiram king of Tyre heard that Solomon had been anointed king to succeed his father David, he sent his envoys to Solomon, because he had always been on friendly terms with David. [2]Solomon sent back this message to Hiram:

[3]"You know that because

*See the note on page 346.

לֹא יָכֹל לִבְנוֹת בַּיִת לְשֵׁם יְהוָה אֱלֹהָיו מִפְּנֵי הַמִּלְחָמָה
the-war because-of God-of-him Yahweh for-Name-of temple to-build he-could not

אֲשֶׁר סְבָבֻהוּ עַד תֵּת־ יְהוָה אֹתָם תַּחַת כַּפּוֹת רַגְלָו׃
feet-of-him soles-of under them Yahweh to-put until they-surrounded-him that

(18[4]) וְעַתָּה הֵנִיחַ יְהוָה אֱלֹהַי לִי מִסָּבִיב אֵין שָׂטָן
adversary no at-around to-me God-of-me Yahweh he-gave-peace but-now (18[4])

וְאֵין פֶּגַע רָע׃ (19[5]) וְהִנְנִי אֹמֵר לִבְנוֹת בַּיִת
temple to-build intending so-see-I! (19[5]) disaster incident-of and-no

לְשֵׁם יְהוָה אֱלֹהָי כַּאֲשֶׁר ׀ דִּבֶּר יְהוָה אֶל־ דָּוִד אָבִי
father-of-me David to Yahweh he-told just-as God-of-me Yahweh for-Name-of

לֵאמֹר בִּנְךָ אֲשֶׁר אֶתֵּן תַּחְתֶּיךָ עַל־ כִּסְאֶךָ הוּא־
he throne-of-you on in-place-of-you I-will-put whom son-of-you to-say

יִבְנֶה הַבַּיִת לִשְׁמִי׃ (20[6]) וְעַתָּה צַוֵּה
give-order! so-now (20[6]) for-Name-of-me the-temple he-will-build

וְיִכְרְתוּ־ לִי אֲרָזִים מִן־ הַלְּבָנוֹן וַעֲבָדַי יִהְיוּ עִם־
with they-will-be and-men-of-me the-Lebanon from cedars for-me so-they-cut

עֲבָדֶיךָ וּשְׂכַר עֲבָדֶיךָ אֶתֵּן לְךָ כְּכֹל אֲשֶׁר תֹּאמֵר
you-say that as-all to-you I-will-pay men-of-you and-wage-of men-of-you

כִּי ׀ אַתָּה יָדַעְתָּ כִּי אֵין בָּנוּ אִישׁ יֹדֵעַ לִכְרָת־ עֵצִים
timbers to-fell being-skilled man among-us not that you-know you for

כַּצִּדֹנִים׃ (21[7]) וַיְהִי כִּשְׁמֹעַ חִירָם אֶת־ דִּבְרֵי שְׁלֹמֹה
Solomon words-of *** Hiram when-to-hear and-he-was (21[7]) as-the-Sidonians

וַיִּשְׂמַח מְאֹד וַיֹּאמֶר בָּרוּךְ יְהוָה הַיּוֹם אֲשֶׁר
who the-day Yahweh being-praised and-he-said greatly then-he-was-pleased

נָתַן לְדָוִד בֵּן חָכָם עַל־ הָעָם הָרָב הַזֶּה׃ (22[8]) וַיִּשְׁלַח
so-he-sent (22[8]) the-this the-great the-nation over wise son to-David he-gave

חִירָם אֶל־שְׁלֹמֹה לֵאמֹר שָׁמַעְתִּי אֵת אֲשֶׁר־שָׁלַחְתָּ אֵלָי אֲנִי אֶעֱשֶׂה אֶת־
*** I-will-do I to-me you-sent what *** I-received to-say Solomon to Hiram

כָּל־ חֶפְצְךָ בַּעֲצֵי אֲרָזִים וּבַעֲצֵי בְרוֹשִׁים׃ (23[9]) עֲבָדַי
men-of-me (23[9]) pines and-in-logs-of cedars in-logs-of desire-of-you all-of

יֹרִדוּ מִן־ הַלְּבָנוֹן יָמָּה וַאֲנִי אֲשִׂימֵם דֹּבְרוֹת
rafts I-will-float-them and-I to-sea the-Lebanon from they-will-haul-down

בַּיָּם עַד־ הַמָּקוֹם אֲשֶׁר־ תִּשְׁלַח אֵלַי וְנִפַּצְתִּים שָׁם
there and-I-will-separate-them to-me you-specify that the-place to by-the-sea

וְאַתָּה תִּשָּׂא וְאַתָּה תַּעֲשֶׂה אֶת־ חֶפְצִי לָתֵת לֶחֶם
food-of to-provide wish-of-me *** you-grant and-you you-take-away and-you

בֵּיתִי׃ (24[10]) וַיְהִי חִירוֹם נֹתֵן לִשְׁלֹמֹה עֲצֵי אֲרָזִים
cedars logs-of to-Solomon supplying Hiram so-he-was (24[10]) household-of-me

of the wars waged against my father David from all sides, he could not build a temple for the Name of the LORD his God until the LORD put his enemies under his feet. [4]But now the LORD my God has given me peace on every side, and there is no adversary or disaster. [5]I intend, therefore, to build a temple for the Name of the LORD my God, as the LORD told my father David, when he said, 'Your son whom I will put on the throne in your place will build the temple for my Name.'

[6]"So give orders that cedars of Lebanon be cut for me. My men will work with yours, and I will pay you for your men whatever wages you set. You know that we have no one so skilled in felling timber as the Sidonians."

[7]When Hiram heard Solomon's message, he was greatly pleased and said, "Praise be to the LORD today, for he has given David a wise son to rule over this great nation."

[8]So Hiram sent word to Solomon:

"I have received the message you sent me and will do all you want in providing the cedar and pine logs. [9]My men will haul them down from Lebanon to the sea, and I will float them in rafts by sea to the place you specify. There I will separate them and you can take them away. And you are to grant my wish by providing food for my royal household."

[10]In this way Hiram kept Solomon supplied with all the

*See the note on page 346.

°17 ק רגלי

וַעֲצֵי בְרוֹשִׁים כָּל־חֶפְצוֹ׃ וּשְׁלֹמֹה נָתַן לְחִירָם
to-Hiram he-gave and-Solomon (25[11]) desire-of-him all-of pines and-logs-of

עֶשְׂרִים אֶלֶף כֹּר חִטִּים מַכֹּלֶת לְבֵיתוֹ וְעֶשְׂרִים כֹּר שֶׁמֶן
olive-oil cor and-twenty for-household-of-him food wheats cor thousand twenty

כָּתִית כֹּה־יִתֵּן שְׁלֹמֹה לְחִירָם שָׁנָה בְשָׁנָה׃ וַיהוָה
and-Yahweh (26[12]) after-year year for-Hiram Solomon he-did so pressed

נָתַן חָכְמָה לִשְׁלֹמֹה כַּאֲשֶׁר דִּבֶּר־לוֹ וַיְהִי שָׁלֹם
peace and-he-was to-him he-promised just-as to-Solomon wisdom he-gave

בֵּין חִירָם וּבֵין שְׁלֹמֹה וַיִּכְרְתוּ בְרִית שְׁנֵיהֶם׃
two-of-them treaty and-they-made Solomon and-between Hiram between

וַיַּעַל הַמֶּלֶךְ שְׁלֹמֹה מַס מִכָּל־יִשְׂרָאֵל
Israel from-all-of laborer Solomon the-king and-he-conscripted (27[13])

וַיְהִי הַמַּס שְׁלֹשִׁים אֶלֶף אִישׁ׃ וַיִּשְׁלָחֵם
and-he-sent-off-them (28[14]) man thousand thirty the-laborer and-he-was

לְבָנוֹנָה עֲשֶׂרֶת אֲלָפִים בַּחֹדֶשׁ חֲלִיפוֹת חֹדֶשׁ יִהְיוּ בַלְּבָנוֹן
in-the-Lebanon they-were month shifts in-the-month thousands ten-of to-Lebanon

שְׁנַיִם חֳדָשִׁים בְּבֵיתוֹ וַאֲדֹנִירָם עַל־הַמַּס׃ וַיְהִי
and-he-was (29[15]) the-forced-labor over and-Adoniram at-home-of-him months two

לִשְׁלֹמֹה שִׁבְעִים אֶלֶף נֹשֵׂא סַבָּל וּשְׁמֹנִים אֶלֶף חֹצֵב
stone-cutting thousand and-eighty burden carrying thousand seventy to-Solomon

בָּהָר׃ לְבַד מִשָּׂרֵי הַנִּצָּבִים
the-ones-being-appointed from-foremen-of apart-from (30[16]) in-the-hill

לִשְׁלֹמֹה אֲשֶׁר עַל־הַמְּלָאכָה שְׁלֹשֶׁת אֲלָפִים וּשְׁלֹשׁ מֵאוֹת
hundreds and-three-of thousands three-of the-project over who to-Solomon

הָרֹדִים בָּעָם הָעֹשִׂים בַּמְּלָאכָה׃
on-the-project the-ones-working over-the-people the-ones-supervising

וַיְצַו הַמֶּלֶךְ וַיַּסִּעוּ אֲבָנִים גְּדֹלוֹת אֲבָנִים
stones large-ones stones and-they-removed the-king and-he-commanded (31[17])

יְקָרוֹת לְיַסֵּד הַבָּיִת אַבְנֵי גָזִית׃
dressed stones-of the-temple to-provide-foundation quality-ones

וַיִּפְסְלוּ בֹּנֵי שְׁלֹמֹה וּבֹנֵי
and-ones-being-craftsmen-of Solomon ones-being-craftsmen-of and-they-cut (32[18])

חִירוֹם וְהַגִּבְלִים וַיָּכִינוּ הָעֵצִים וְהָאֲבָנִים לִבְנוֹת
to-build and-the-stones the-timbers and-they-prepared and-the-Gebalites Hiram

הַבָּיִת׃ וַיְהִי בִשְׁמוֹנִים שָׁנָה וְאַרְבַּע מֵאוֹת שָׁנָה לְצֵאת
to-come-out year hundreds and-four year in-eighty and-he-was (6:1) the-temple

בְּנֵי־יִשְׂרָאֵל מֵאֶרֶץ־מִצְרַיִם בַּשָּׁנָה הָרְבִיעִית בְּחֹדֶשׁ זִו
Ziv in-month-of the-fourth in-the-year Egypt from-land-of Israel sons-of

cedar and pine logs he wanted, [11]and Solomon gave Hiram twenty thousand cors[l] of wheat as food for his household, in addition to twenty thousand baths[m] [n] of pressed olive oil. Solomon continued to do this for Hiram year after year. [12]The LORD gave Solomon wisdom, just as he had promised him. There were peaceful relations between Hiram and Solomon, and the two of them made a treaty.

[13]King Solomon conscripted laborers from all Israel—thirty thousand men. [14]He sent them off to Lebanon in shifts of ten thousand a month, so that they spent one month in Lebanon and two months at home. Adoniram was in charge of the forced labor. [15]Solomon had seventy thousand carriers and eighty thousand stonecutters in the hills, [16]as well as thirty-three hundred[o] foremen who supervised the project and directed the workmen. [17]At the king's command they removed from the quarry large blocks of quality stone to provide a foundation of dressed stone for the temple. [18]The craftsmen of Solomon and Hiram and the men of Gebal[p] cut and prepared the timber and stone for the building of the temple.

### *Solomon Builds the Temple*

6 In the four hundred and eightieth[q] year after the Israelites had come out of Egypt, in the fourth year of

[l]11 That is, probably about 125,000 bushels (about 4,400 kiloliters)
[m]11 Septuagint (see also 2 Chron. 2:10); Hebrew *twenty cors*
[n]11 That is, about 115,000 gallons (about 440 kiloliters)
[o]16 Hebrew; some Septuagint manuscripts (see also 2 Chron. 2:2, 18) *thirty-six hundred*
[p]18 That is, Byblos
[q]1 Hebrew; Septuagint *four hundred and fortieth*

*See the note on page 346.

הוּא הַחֹדֶשׁ הַשֵּׁנִי לִמְלֹךְ שְׁלֹמֹה עַל־יִשְׂרָאֵל וַיִּבֶן
then-he-built Israel over Solomon to-reign the-second the-month this

הַבַּיִת לַיהוָה׃ וְהַבַּיִת אֲשֶׁר בָּנָה הַמֶּלֶךְ שְׁלֹמֹה
Solomon the-king he-built that and-the-temple (2) of-Yahweh the-temple

לַיהוָה שִׁשִּׁים־אַמָּה אָרְכּוֹ וְעֶשְׂרִים רָחְבּוֹ וּשְׁלֹשִׁים
and-thirty width-of-him and-twenty length-of-him cubit sixty for-Yahweh

אַמָּה קוֹמָתוֹ׃ וְהָאוּלָם עַל־פְּנֵי הֵיכַל הַבַּיִת
the-temple main-hall-of front-of at and-the-portico (3) height-of-him cubit

עֶשְׂרִים אַמָּה אָרְכּוֹ עַל־פְּנֵי רֹחַב הַבָּיִת עֶשֶׂר בָּאַמָּה
by-the-cubit ten the-temple width-of front-of at length-of-him cubit twenty

רָחְבּוֹ עַל־פְּנֵי הַבָּיִת׃ וַיַּעַשׂ לַבָּיִת
in-the-temple and-he-made (4) the-temple front-of at projection-of-him

חַלּוֹנֵי שְׁקֻפִים אֲטֻמִים׃ וַיִּבֶן עַל־קִיר
wall-of against and-he-built (5) ones-being-narrow clerestories windows-of

הַבַּיִת יָצוֹעַ° סָבִיב אֶת־קִירוֹת הַבַּיִת סָבִיב לַהֵיכָל
of-the-main-hall around the-building walls-of *** around side-room the-building

וְלַדְּבִיר וַיַּעַשׂ צְלָעוֹת סָבִיב׃ הַיָּצוֹעַ°
the-floor (6) around structures and-he-made and-of-the-inner-sanctuary

הַתַּחְתֹּנָה חָמֵשׁ בָּאַמָּה רָחְבָּהּ וְהַתִּיכֹנָה שֵׁשׁ בָּאַמָּה
by-the-cubit six and-the-middle width-of-her by-the-cubit five the-lowest

רָחְבָּהּ וְהַשְּׁלִישִׁית שֶׁבַע בָּאַמָּה רָחְבָּהּ כִּי
indeed width-of-her by-the-cubit seven and-the-third width-of-her

מִגְרָעוֹת נָתַן לַבַּיִת סָבִיב חוּצָה לְבִלְתִּי אֲחֹז
to-insert not at-outside around on-the-temple he-made offset-ledges

בְּקִירוֹת־הַבָּיִת׃ וְהַבַּיִת בְּהִבָּנֹתוֹ אֶבֶן־שְׁלֵמָה
dressed block when-to-be-built-him and-the-temple (7) the-temple in-walls-of

מַסָּע נִבְנָה וּמַקָּבוֹת וְהַגַּרְזֶן כָּל־כְּלִי בַרְזֶל לֹא־
not iron tool-of any-of and-the-chisel and-hammers being-used quarry

נִשְׁמַע בַּבַּיִת בְּהִבָּנֹתוֹ׃ פֶּתַח הַצֵּלָע
the-floor entrance-of (8) when-to-be-built-him at-the-temple he-was-heard

הַתִּיכֹנָה אֶל־כֶּתֶף הַבַּיִת הַיְמָנִית וּבְלוּלִּים יַעֲלוּ עַל־
to they-went-up and-on-stairs the-south the-temple side-of on the-middle

הַתִּיכֹנָה וּמִן־הַתִּיכֹנָה אֶל־הַשְּׁלִשִׁים׃ וַיִּבֶן אֶת־
*** so-he-built (9) the-third-ones to the-middle and-from the-middle

הַבַּיִת וַיְכַלֵּהוּ וַיִּסְפֹּן אֶת־הַבַּיִת גֵּבִים וּשְׂדֵרֹת
and-planks beams the-temple *** and-he-roofed and-he-completed-him the-temple

בָּאֲרָזִים׃ וַיִּבֶן אֶת־הַיָּצוֹעַ° עַל־כָּל־הַבַּיִת
the-temple all-of along the-side-room *** and-he-built (10) of-the-cedars

Solomon's reign over Israel, in the month of Ziv, the second month, he began to build the temple of the LORD.

2The temple that King Solomon built for the LORD was sixty cubits long, twenty wide and thirty high.[r] 3The portico at the front of the main hall of the temple extended the width of the temple, that is twenty cubits,[s] and projected ten cubits[t] from the front of the temple. 4He made narrow clerestory windows in the temple. 5Against the walls of the main hall and inner sanctuary he built a structure around the building, in which there were side rooms. 6The lowest floor was five cubits[u] wide, the middle floor six cubits[v] and the third floor seven.[w] He made offset ledges around the outside of the temple so that nothing would be inserted into the temple walls.

7In building the temple, only blocks dressed at the quarry were used, and no hammer, chisel or any other iron tool was heard at the temple site while it was being built.

8The entrance to the lowest[x] floor was on the south side of the temple; a stairway led up to the middle level and from there to the third. 9So he built the temple and completed it, roofing it with beams and cedar planks. 10And he built the

r2 That is, about 90 feet (about 27 meters) long and 30 feet (about 9 meters) wide and 45 feet (about 13.5 meters) high
s3 That is, about 30 feet (about 9 meters)
t3 That is, about 15 feet (about 4.5 meters)
u6 That is, about 7 1/2 feet (about 2.3 meters)
v6 That is, about 9 feet (about 2.7 meters)
w6 That is, about 10 1/2 feet (about 3.1 meters)
x8 Septuagint; Hebrew *middle*

°5 ק יציע
°6 ק היציע
°10 ק היציע

חָמֵשׁ אַמּוֹת קוֹמָתוֹ וַיֶּאֱחֹז אֶת־ הַבַּיִת בַּעֲצֵי אֲרָזִים׃
cedars by-beams-of the-temple *** and-he-attached height-of-him cubits five

וַיְהִי דְּבַר־ יְהוָה אֶל־ שְׁלֹמֹה לֵאמֹר׃ הַבַּיִת הַזֶּה
the-this the-temple (12) to-say Solomon to Yahweh word-of and-he-came (11)

אֲשֶׁר־אַתָּה בֹנֶה אִם־ תֵּלֵךְ בְּחֻקֹּתַי וְאֶת־ מִשְׁפָּטַי
regulations-of-me and in-decrees-of-me you-follow if building you that

תַּעֲשֶׂה וְשָׁמַרְתָּ אֶת־ כָּל־ מִצְוֹתַי לָלֶכֶת בָּהֶם
to-them to-obey commands-of-me all-of *** and-you-keep you-carry-out

וַהֲקִמֹתִי אֶת־ דְּבָרִי אִתָּךְ אֲשֶׁר דִּבַּרְתִּי אֶל־ דָּוִד
David to I-gave that through-you promise-of-me *** then-I-will-fulfill

אָבִיךָ׃ וְשָׁכַנְתִּי בְּתוֹךְ בְּנֵי יִשְׂרָאֵל וְלֹא אֶעֱזֹב
I-will-abandon and-not Israel sons-of among and-I-will-live (13) father-of-you

אֶת־ עַמִּי יִשְׂרָאֵל׃ וַיִּבֶן שְׁלֹמֹה אֶת־ הַבַּיִת
the-temple *** Solomon so-he-built (14) Israel people-of-me ***

וַיְכַלֵּהוּ׃ וַיִּבֶן אֶת־ קִירוֹת הַבַּיִת מִבַּיְתָה
at-interior the-temple walls-of *** and-he-lined (15) and-he-completed-him

בְּצַלְעוֹת אֲרָזִים מִקַּרְקַע הַבַּיִת עַד־ קִירוֹת הַסִּפֻּן
the-ceiling rafters-of to the-temple from-floor-of cedars with-boards-of

צִפָּה עֵץ מִבָּיִת וַיְצַף אֶת־ קַרְקַע הַבָּיִת
the-temple floor-of *** and-he-covered at-interior wood he-paneled

בְּצַלְעוֹת בְּרוֹשִׁים׃ וַיִּבֶן אֶת־ עֶשְׂרִים אַמָּה מִֽיַּרְכְּתֵי°
at-rear-parts-of cubit twenty *** and-he-partitioned (16) pines with-planks-of

הַבַּיִת בְּצַלְעוֹת אֲרָזִים מִן־ הַקַּרְקַע עַד־ הַקִּירוֹת וַיִּבֶן
and-he-formed the-ceilings to the-floor from cedars with-boards-of the-temple

לוֹ מִבַּיִת לִדְבִיר לְקֹדֶשׁ הַקֳּדָשִׁים׃
the-Holy-Places for-Holy-of for-inner-sanctuary within-temple for-him

וְאַרְבָּעִים בָּאַמָּה הָיָה הַבָּיִת הוּא הַהֵיכָל
the-main-hall this the-room he-was by-the-cubit and-forty (17)

לִפְנָֽי׃ וְאֶרֶז אֶל־ הַבַּיִת פְּנִימָה מִקְלַעַת פְּקָעִים
gourds carved-of at-inside the-temple in and-cedar (18) *in-front-of-me

וּפְטוּרֵי צִצִּים הַכֹּל אֶרֶז אֵין אֶבֶן נִרְאָה׃
he-was-seen stone no cedar the-whole flowers and-ones-being-opened-of

וּדְבִיר בְּתוֹךְ־ הַבַּיִת מִפְּנִימָה הֵכִין לְתִתֵּן
†to-set he-prepared at-inside the-temple within and-inner-sanctuary (19)

שָׁם אֶת־ אֲרוֹן בְּרִית יְהוָה׃ וְלִפְנֵי הַדְּבִיר
the-inner-sanctuary and-front-of (20) Yahweh covenant-of ark-of *** there

עֶשְׂרִים אַמָּה אֹרֶךְ וְעֶשְׂרִים אַמָּה רֹחַב וְעֶשְׂרִים אַמָּה קוֹמָתוֹ
height-of-him cubit and-twenty width cubit and-twenty length cubit twenty

side rooms all along the temple. The height of each was five cubits,[y] and they were attached to the temple by beams of cedar.

[11]The word of the LORD came to Solomon: [12]"As for this temple you are building, if you follow my decrees, carry out my regulations and keep all my commands and obey them, I will fulfill through you the promise I gave to David your father. [13]And I will live among the Israelites and will not abandon my people Israel."

[14]So Solomon built the temple and completed it. [15]He lined its interior walls with cedar boards, paneling them from the floor of the temple to the ceiling, and covered the floor of the temple with planks of pine. [16]He partitioned off twenty cubits[z] at the rear of the temple with cedar boards from floor to ceiling to form within the temple an inner sanctuary, the Most Holy Place. [17]The main hall in front of this room was forty cubits[a] long. [18]The inside of the temple was cedar, carved with gourds and open flowers. Everything was cedar; no stone was to be seen.

[19]He prepared the inner sanctuary within the temple to set the ark of the covenant of the LORD there. [20]The inner sanctuary was twenty cubits long, twenty wide and twenty

[y] *10* That is, about 7 1/2 feet (about 2.3 meters); also in verse 24
[z] *16* That is, about 30 feet (about 9 meters)
[a] *17* That is, about 60 feet (about 18 meters)

**17* Pointed with *tsere* instead of *qamets* (לִפְנֵי), this would read simply *in-front*.

†*19* This form should probably be read (לָתֵת), as in the *Ketbib-Qere* of 17:14.

°*16* ק מירכתי

וַיְצַפֵּהוּ זָהָב סָגוּר וַיְצַף מִזְבֵּחַ אֶרֶז׃ וַיְצַף
and-he-covered (21) cedar altar and-he-overlaid pure gold and-he-overlaid-him

שְׁלֹמֹה אֶת־ הַבַּיִת מִפְּנִימָה זָהָב סָגוּר וַיְעַבֵּר בְּרַתִּיקוֹת°
with-chains-of and-he-extended pure gold at-inside the-temple *** Solomon

זָהָב לִפְנֵי הַדְּבִיר וַיְצַפֵּהוּ זָהָב׃ וְאֶת־ כָּל־
whole-of so (22) gold and-he-overlaid-him the-inner-sanctuary front-of gold

הַבַּיִת צִפָּה זָהָב עַד־ תֹּם כָּל־ הַבָּיִת
the-interior whole-of to-be-finished until gold he-overlaid the-interior

וְכָל־ הַמִּזְבֵּחַ אֲשֶׁר־ לַדְּבִיר צִפָּה זָהָב׃ וַיַּעַשׂ
and-he-made (23) gold he-overlaid to-the-sanctuary that the-altar and-whole-of

בַּדְּבִיר שְׁנֵי כְרוּבִים עֲצֵי־ שָׁמֶן עֶשֶׂר אַמּוֹת קוֹמָתוֹ׃
height-of-him cubits ten olive woods-of cherubim pair-of in-the-inner-sanctuary

וְחָמֵשׁ אַמּוֹת כְּנַף הַכְּרוּב הָאֶחָת וְחָמֵשׁ אַמּוֹת כְּנַף
wing-of cubits and-five the-first the-cherub wing-of cubits and-five (24)

הַכְּרוּב הַשֵּׁנִית עֶשֶׂר אַמּוֹת מִקְצוֹת כְּנָפָיו וְעַד־ קְצוֹת
tips-of even-to wings-of-him from-tips cubits ten the-other the-cherub

כְּנָפָיו׃ וְעֶשֶׂר בָּאַמָּה הַכְּרוּב הַשֵּׁנִי מִדָּה אַחַת
identical size the-second the-cherub by-the-cubit and-ten (25) wings-of-him

וְקֶצֶב אֶחָד לִשְׁנֵי הַכְּרֻבִים׃ קוֹמַת הַכְּרוּב
the-cherub height-of (26) the-cherubim for-two-of identical and-shape

הָאֶחָד עֶשֶׂר בָּאַמָּה וְכֵן הַכְּרוּב הַשֵּׁנִי׃ וַיִּתֵּן
and-he-placed (27) the-second the-cherub and-same by-the-cubit ten the-first

אֶת־ הַכְּרוּבִים בְּתוֹךְ ׀ הַבַּיִת הַפְּנִימִי וַיִּפְרְשׂוּ אֶת־
*** and-they-spread-out the-innermost the-temple inside-of the-cherubim ***

כַּנְפֵי הַכְּרֻבִים וַתִּגַּע כְּנַף־ הָאֶחָד בַּקִּיר וּכְנַף
and-wing-of on-the-wall the-one wing-of and-she-touched the-cherubim wings-of

הַכְּרוּב הַשֵּׁנִי נֹגַעַת בַּקִּיר הַשֵּׁנִי וְכַנְפֵיהֶם אֶל־
in and-wings-of-them the-other on-the-wall touching the-other the-cherub

תּוֹךְ הַבַּיִת נֹגְעֹת כָּנָף אֶל־ כָּנָף׃ וַיְצַף אֶת־
*** and-he-overlaid (28) wing to wing ones-touching the-room middle-of

הַכְּרוּבִים זָהָב׃ וְאֵת כָּל־ קִירוֹת הַבַּיִת מֵסַב ׀ קָלַע
he-carved around the-temple walls-of all-of and (29) gold the-cherubim

פִּתּוּחֵי מִקְלְעוֹת כְּרוּבִים וְתִמֹרֹת וּפְטוּרֵי
and-ones-being-open-of and-palm-trees cherubim carvings-of engravings-of

צִצִּים מִלִּפְנִים וְלַחִיצוֹן׃ וְאֶת־ קַרְקַע הַבַּיִת צִפָּה
he-covered the-temple floor-of and (30) and-on-the-outside on-inside flowers

זָהָב לִפְנִימָה וְלַחִיצוֹן׃ וְאֵת פֶּתַח הַדְּבִיר
the-inner-sanctuary entrance-of and (31) and-on-the-outside on-inside gold

°21 ק ברתוקות

high.[b] He overlaid the inside
with pure gold, and he also
overlaid the altar of cedar.
21Solomon covered the inside
of the temple with pure gold,
and he extended gold chains
across the front of the inner
sanctuary, which was overlaid
with gold. 22So he overlaid the
whole interior with gold. He
also overlaid with gold the altar that belonged to the inner
sanctuary.
23In the inner sanctuary he
made a pair of cherubim of olive wood, each ten cubits[c]
high. 24One wing of the first
cherub was five cubits long,
and the other wing five cubits—ten cubits from wing tip
to wing tip. 25The second
cherub also measured ten cubits, for the two cherubim
were identical in size and
shape. 26The height of each
cherub was ten cubits. 27He
placed the cherubim inside
the innermost room of the
temple, with their wings
spread out. The wing of one
cherub touched one wall,
while the wing of the other
touched the other wall, and
their wings touched each other in the middle of the room.
28He overlaid the cherubim
with gold.
29On the walls all around the
temple, in both the inner and
outer rooms, he carved cherubim, palm trees and open
flowers. 30He also covered the
floors of both the inner and
outer rooms of the temple with
gold.
31For the entrance of the inner sanctuary he made doors

[b]20 That is, about 30 feet (about 9 meters) long, wide and high
[c]23 That is, about 15 feet (about 4.5 meters)

עָשָׂה דַּלְתוֹת עֲצֵי־שָׁמֶן הָאַיִל מְזוּזוֹת חֲמִשִׁית׃ (32) וּשְׁתֵּי
and-two-of (32) five-sided jambs the-lintel olive woods-of doors-of he-made

דַּלְתוֹת עֲצֵי־שֶׁמֶן וְקָלַע עֲלֵיהֶם מִקְלְעוֹת כְּרוּבִים
cherubim carvings-of on-them and-he-carved olive woods-of doors-of

וְתִמֹרוֹת וּפְטוּרֵי צִצִּים וְצִפָּה זָהָב
gold and-he-overlaid flowers and-ones-being-open-of and-palm-trees

וַיָּרֶד עַל־הַכְּרוּבִים וְעַל־הַתִּמֹרוֹת אֶת־הַזָּהָב׃
the-gold *** the-palm-trees and-over the-cherubim over and-he-beat

(33) וְכֵן עָשָׂה לְפֶתַח הַהֵיכָל מְזוּזוֹת עֲצֵי־שָׁמֶן
olive woods-of jambs-of the-main-hall for-entrance-of he-made and-same (33)

מֵאֵת רְבִעִית׃ (34) וּשְׁתֵּי דַלְתוֹת עֲצֵי בְרוֹשִׁים שְׁנֵי צְלָעִים
leaves two-of pines woods-of doors-of and-two-of (34) four-sided from

הַדֶּלֶת הָאַחַת גְּלִילִים וּשְׁנֵי קְלָעִים הַדֶּלֶת
the-door leaves and-two-of ones-turning-in-sockets the-one the-door

הַשֵּׁנִית גְּלִילִים׃ (35) וְקָלַע כְּרוּבִים וְתִמֹרוֹת
and-palm-trees cherubim and-he-carved (35) ones-turning-in-sockets the-other

וּפְטֻרֵי צִצִּים וְצִפָּה זָהָב מְיֻשָּׁר עַל־
over being-even gold and-he-overlaid flowers and-ones-being-open-of

הַמְּחֻקֶּה׃ (36) וַיִּבֶן אֶת־הֶחָצֵר הַפְּנִימִית שְׁלֹשָׁה טוּרֵי
courses-of three the-inner the-courtyard *** and-he-built (36) the-carving

גָזִית וְטוּר כְּרֻתֹת אֲרָזִים׃ (37) בַּשָּׁנָה
in-the-year (37) cedars ones-being-trimmed-of and-course-of dressed-stone

הָרְבִיעִית יֻסַּד בֵּית יְהוָה בְּיֶרַח זִו׃ (38) וּבַשָּׁנָה
and-in-the-year (38) Ziv in-month-of Yahweh temple-of he-was-founded the-fourth

הָאַחַת עֶשְׂרֵה בְּיֶרַח בּוּל הוּא הַחֹדֶשׁ הַשְּׁמִינִי כָּלָה הַבַּיִת
the-temple he-finished the-eighth the-month this Bul in-month-of ten the-one

לְכָל־דְּבָרָיו וּלְכָל־מִשְׁפָּטָו° וַיִּבְנֵהוּ
and-he-built-him specifications-of-him and-in-all-of details-of-him in-all-of

שֶׁבַע שָׁנִים׃ (7:1) וְאֶת־בֵּיתוֹ בָּנָה שְׁלֹמֹה שְׁלֹשׁ עֶשְׂרֵה שָׁנָה
year ten three-of Solomon he-built palace-of-him but (7:1) years seven

וַיְכַל אֶת־כָּל־בֵּיתוֹ׃ (2) וַיִּבֶן אֶת־בֵּית
Palace-of *** and-he-built (2) palace-of-him all-of *** then-he-completed

יַעַר הַלְּבָנוֹן מֵאָה אַמָּה אָרְכּוֹ וַחֲמִשִּׁים אַמָּה רָחְבּוֹ
width-of-him cubit and-fifty length-of-him cubit hundred the-Lebanon Forest-of

וּשְׁלֹשִׁים אַמָּה קוֹמָתוֹ עַל אַרְבָּעָה טוּרֵי עַמּוּדֵי אֲרָזִים
cedars columns-of rows-of four with height-of-him cubit and-thirty

וּכְרֻתוֹת אֲרָזִים עַל־הָעַמּוּדִים׃ (3) וְסָפֻן
and-being-roofed (3) the-columns on cedars and-ones-being-trimmed-of

of olive wood with five-sided jambs. [32]And on the two olive wood doors he carved cherubim, palm trees and open flowers, and overlaid the cherubim and palm trees with beaten gold. [33]In the same way he made four-sided jambs of olive wood for the entrance to the main hall. [34]He also made two pine doors, each having two leaves that turned in sockets. [35]He carved cherubim, palm trees and open flowers on them and overlaid them with gold hammered evenly over the carvings.

[36]And he built the inner courtyard of three courses of dressed stone and one course of trimmed cedar beams.

[37]The foundation of the temple of the LORD was laid in the fourth year, in the month of Ziv. [38]In the eleventh year in the month of Bul, the eighth month, the temple was finished in all its details according to its specifications. He had spent seven years building it.

*Solomon Builds His Palace*

7 It took Solomon thirteen years, however, to complete the construction of his palace. [2]He built the Palace of the Forest of Lebanon a hundred cubits long, fifty wide and thirty high,[d] with four rows of cedar columns supporting trimmed cedar beams. [3]It was roofed with cedar

[d]2 That is, about 150 feet (about 46 meters) long, 75 feet (about 23 meters) wide and 45 feet (about 13.5 meters) high

°38 ק משפטיו

בָּאֶ֫רֶז מִמַּ֫עַל עַל־ הַצְּלָעֹת֙ אֲשֶׁ֣ר עַל־ הָעַמּוּדִ֔ים אַרְבָּעִ֖ים וַחֲמִשָּׁ֑ה
and-five forty the-columns on that the-beams over at-above with-the-cedar

חֲמִשָּׁ֥ה עָשָׂ֖ר הַטּֽוּר׃ וּשְׁקֻפִ֖ים שְׁלֹשָׁ֣ה טוּרִ֑ים וּמֶחֱזָ֥ה אֶל־מֶחֱזָ֖ה שָׁלֹ֥שׁ פְּעָמִֽים׃
times three face to and-face sets three and-windows (4) the-row ten five

וְכָל־ הַפְּתָחִ֥ים וְהַמְּזוּזֹ֖ת רְבֻעִ֣ים שָׁ֑קֶף וּמ֗וּל
and-front frame ones-rectangular and-the-jambs the-doorways and-all-of (5)

מֶחֱזָ֥ה אֶל־מֶחֱזָ֖ה שָׁלֹ֥שׁ פְּעָמִֽים׃ וְאֵ֨ת אוּלָ֤ם הָֽעַמּוּדִים֙ עָשָׂ֔ה חֲמִשִּׁ֤ים
fifty he-made the-pillars colonnade-of and (6) times three face to face

אַמָּה֙ אָרְכּ֔וֹ וּשְׁלֹשִׁ֥ים אַמָּ֖ה רָחְבּ֑וֹ וְאוּלָם֙ עַל־ פְּנֵיהֶ֔ם
front-of-them at and-portico width-of-him cubit and-thirty length-of-him cubit

וְעַמֻּדִ֥ים וְעָ֖ב עַל־ פְּנֵיהֶֽם׃ וְאוּלָ֤ם הַכִּסֵּא֙
the-throne and-hall-of (7) front-of-them at and-overhanging-roof and-pillars

אֲשֶׁ֣ר יִשְׁפָּט־ שָׁ֔ם אֻלָ֥ם הַמִּשְׁפָּ֖ט עָשָׂ֑ה וְסָפ֣וּן
and-being-covered he-built the-Justice Hall-of there he-judged where

בָּאֶ֔רֶז מֵהַקַּרְקַ֖ע עַד־ הַקַּרְקָֽע׃ וּבֵיתוֹ֩ אֲשֶׁר־
where and-palace-of-him (8) the-floor to from-the-floor with-the-cedar

יֵ֨שֶׁב שָׁ֜ם חָצֵ֣ר הָאַחֶ֗רֶת מִבֵּית֙ לָֽאוּלָ֔ם
of-the-hall from-building-of the-one-back courtyard there he-lived

כַּֽמַּעֲשֶׂ֥ה הַזֶּ֖ה הָיָ֑ה וּבַ֜יִת יַעֲשֶׂ֤ה לְבַת־ פַּרְעֹה֙
Pharaoh for-daughter-of he-made and-palace he-was the-this like-the-design

אֲשֶׁ֣ר לָקַ֣ח שְׁלֹמֹ֔ה כָּאוּלָ֖ם הַזֶּֽה׃ כָּל־ אֵ֗לֶּה אֲבָנִ֤ים
stones these all-of (9) the-this like-the-hall Solomon he-married whom

יְקָרֹת֙ כְּמִדֹּ֣ת גָּזִ֔ית מְגֹרָר֥וֹת בַּמְּגֵרָ֖ה מִבַּ֣יִת
inside with-the-saw ones-being-trimmed cutting as-sizes-of high-grade-ones

וּמִח֑וּץ וּמִמַּסָּד֙ עַד־ הַטְּפָח֔וֹת וּמִח֖וּץ עַד־ הֶחָצֵ֥ר
the-courtyard to and-outside the-eaves to and-from-foundation and-outside

הַגְּדוֹלָֽה׃ וּמְיֻסָּ֕ד אֲבָנִ֥ים יְקָר֖וֹת אֲבָנִ֣ים גְּדֹל֑וֹת
large-ones stones quality-ones stones and-being-founded (10) the-great

אַבְנֵי֙ עֶ֣שֶׂר אַמּ֔וֹת וְאַבְנֵ֖י שְׁמֹנֶ֥ה אַמּֽוֹת׃ וּמִלְמַ֕עְלָה אֲבָנִ֥ים
stones and-at-above (11) cubits eight and-stones-of cubits ten stones-of

יְקָר֛וֹת כְּמִדּ֥וֹת גָּזִ֖ית וָאָֽרֶז׃ וְחָצֵ֨ר הַגְּדוֹלָ֜ה
the-great and-courtyard (12) and-cedar cutting as-sizes-of high-grade-ones

סָבִ֗יב שְׁלֹשָׁ֤ה טוּרִים֙ גָּזִ֔ית וְט֖וּר כְּרֻתֹ֣ת אֲרָזִ֑ים
cedars ones-being-trimmed-of and-course dressed-stone courses three surrounded

וְלַחֲצַ֧ר בֵּית־ יְהוָ֛ה הַפְּנִימִ֖ית וּלְאֻלָ֥ם הַבָּֽיִת׃
the-temple and-to-portico-of the-inner Yahweh temple-of also-to-courtyard-of

וַיִּשְׁלַח֙ הַמֶּ֣לֶךְ שְׁלֹמֹ֔ה וַיִּקַּ֥ח אֶת־ חִירָ֖ם מִצֹּֽר׃
from-Tyre Hiram *** and-he-brought Solomon the-king and-he-sent (13)

above the beams that rested on the columns—forty-five beams, fifteen to a row. [4]Its windows were placed high in sets of three, facing each other. [5]All the doorways had rectangular frames; they were in the front part in sets of three, facing each other.[e]

[6]He made a colonnade fifty cubits long and thirty wide.[f] In front of it was a portico, and in front of that were pillars and an overhanging roof. [7]He built the throne hall, the Hall of Justice, where he was to judge, and he covered it with cedar from floor to ceiling.[g] [8]And the palace in which he was to live, set farther back, was similar in design. Solomon also made a palace like this hall for Pharaoh's daughter, whom he had married.

[9]All these structures, from the outside to the great courtyard and from foundation to eaves, were made of blocks of high-grade stone cut to size and trimmed with a saw on their inner and outer faces. [10]The foundations were laid with large stones of good quality, some measuring ten cubits[h] and some eight.[i] [11]Above were high-grade stones, cut to size, and cedar beams. [12]The great courtyard was surrounded by a wall of three courses of dressed stone and one course of trimmed cedar beams, as was the inner courtyard of the temple of the LORD with its portico.

*The Temple's Furnishings*

[13]King Solomon sent to Tyre and brought Huram,[j] [14]whose

[e]5 The meaning of the Hebrew for this verse is uncertain.
[f]6 That is, about 75 feet (about 23 meters) long and 45 feet (about 13.5 meters) wide
[g]7 Vulgate and Syriac; Hebrew *floor*
[h]10 That is, about 15 feet (about 4.5 meters)
[i]10 That is, about 12 feet (about 3.6 meters)
[j]13 Hebrew *Hiram*, a variant of *Huram*; also in verses 40 and 45

בֶּן־ אִשָּׁה אַלְמָנָה הוּא מִמַּטֵּה נַפְתָּלִי וְאָבִיו אִישׁ־
man and-father-of-him Naphtali from-tribe-of he widow woman son-of (14)

צֹרִי חֹרֵשׁ נְחֹשֶׁת וַיִּמָּלֵא אֶת־ הַחָכְמָה וְאֶת־ הַתְּבוּנָה
the-experience and the-skill *** and-he-was-filled bronze one-crafting Tyrian

וְאֶת־ הַדַּעַת לַעֲשׂוֹת כָּל־מְלָאכָה בַּנְּחֹשֶׁת וַיָּבוֹא אֶל־ הַמֶּלֶךְ
the-king to and-he-came with-the-bronze work all-of to-do the-knowledge and

שְׁלֹמֹה וַיַּעַשׂ אֶת־ כָּל־ מְלַאכְתּוֹ׃ וַיָּצַר אֶת־ שְׁנֵי
two-of *** and-he-cast (15) work-of-him all-of *** and-he-did Solomon

הָעַמּוּדִים נְחֹשֶׁת שְׁמֹנֶה עֶשְׂרֵה אַמָּה קוֹמַת הָעַמּוּד הָאֶחָד וְחוּט
and-line the-each the-pillar height-of cubit ten eight bronze the-pillars

שְׁתֵּים־עֶשְׂרֵה אַמָּה יָסֹב אֶת־ הָעַמּוּד הַשֵּׁנִי׃ וּשְׁתֵּי
and-two-of (16) the-second the-pillar *** he-went-around cubit ten two

כֹתָרֹת עָשָׂה לָתֵת עַל־ רָאשֵׁי הָעַמּוּדִים מֻצַק נְחֹשֶׁת חָמֵשׁ
five bronze being-cast-of the-pillars tops-of on to-set he-made capitals

אַמּוֹת קוֹמַת הַכֹּתֶרֶת הָאֶחָת וְחָמֵשׁ אַמּוֹת קוֹמַת הַכֹּתֶרֶת
the-capital height-of cubits and-five the-one the-capital height-of cubits

הַשֵּׁנִית׃ שְׂבָכִים מַעֲשֵׂה שְׂבָכָה גְּדִלִים מַעֲשֵׂה שַׁרְשְׁרוֹת לַכֹּתָרֹת
on-the-capitals chains work-of festoons net work-of networks (17) the-second

אֲשֶׁר עַל־ רֹאשׁ הָעַמּוּדִים שִׁבְעָה לַכֹּתֶרֶת הָאֶחָת וְשִׁבְעָה
and-seven the-one for-the-capital seven the-pillars top-of on that

לַכֹּתֶרֶת הַשֵּׁנִית׃ וַיַּעַשׂ אֶת־ הָעַמּוּדִים וּשְׁנֵי טוּרִים
rows and-two-of the-pillars *** and-he-made (18) the-second for-the-capital

סָבִיב עַל־ הַשְּׂבָכָה הָאֶחָת לְכַסּוֹת אֶת־ הַכֹּתָרֹת אֲשֶׁר עַל־
on that the-capitals *** to-decorate the-each the-network on encircling

רֹאשׁ הָרִמֹּנִים וְכֵן עָשָׂה לַכֹּתֶרֶת הַשֵּׁנִית׃
the-second for-the-capital he-did and-same the-pomegranates top-of

וְכֹתָרֹת אֲשֶׁר עַל־ רֹאשׁ הָעַמּוּדִים מַעֲשֵׂה שׁוּשַׁן בָּאוּלָם
in-the-portico lily shape-of the-pillars top-of on that and-capitals (19)

אַרְבַּע אַמּוֹת׃ וְכֹתָרֹת עַל־ שְׁנֵי הָעַמּוּדִים גַּם־ מִמַּעַל
at-above indeed the-pillars both-of on and-capitals (20) cubits four

מִלְּעֻמַּת הַבֶּטֶן אֲשֶׁר לְעֵבֶר °שְׂבָכָה וְהָרִמּוֹנִים
and-the-pomegranates the-network at-next-to that the-bowl-shape at-close-of

מָאתַיִם טֻרִים סָבִיב עַל הַכֹּתֶרֶת הַשֵּׁנִית׃ וַיָּקֶם אֶת־
*** and-he-erected (21) the-second the-capital on around rows two-hundreds

הָעַמֻּדִים לְאֻלָם הַהֵיכָל וַיָּקֶם אֶת־ הָעַמּוּד הַיְמָנִי
the-south the-pillar *** and-he-erected the-temple at-portico-of the-pillars

וַיִּקְרָא אֶת־ שְׁמוֹ יָכִין וַיָּקֶם אֶת־ הָעַמּוּד הַשְּׂמָאלִי
the-north the-pillar *** and-he-erected Jakin name-of-him *** and-he-called

mother was a widow from the tribe of Naphtali and whose father was a man of Tyre and a craftsman in bronze. Huram was highly skilled and experienced in all kinds of bronze work. He came to King Solomon and did all the work assigned to him.

15 He cast two bronze pillars, each eighteen cubits high and twelve cubits around,[m] by line. 16 He also made two capitals of cast bronze to set on the tops of the pillars; each capital was five cubits[n] high. 17 A network of interwoven chains festooned the capitals on top of the pillars, seven for each capital. 18 He made pomegranates in two rows[o] encircling each network to decorate the capitals on top of the pillars.[p] He did the same for each capital. 19 The capitals on top of the pillars in the portico were in the shape of lilies, four cubits[r] high. 20 On the capitals of both pillars, above the bowl-shaped part next to the network, were the two hundred pomegranates in rows all around. 21 He erected the pillars at the portico of the temple. The pillar to the south he named Jakin[s] and

m15 That is, about 27 feet (about 8.1 meters) high and 18 feet (about 5.4 meters) around

n16 That is, about 7 1/2 feet (about 2.3 meters); also in verse 23

o18 Two Hebrew manuscripts and Septuagint; most Hebrew manuscripts *made the pillars, and there were two rows*

p18 Many Hebrew manuscripts and Syriac; most Hebrew manuscripts *pomegranates*

r19 That is, about 6 feet (about 1.8 meters); also in verse 38

s21 *Jakin* probably means *he establishes.*

°20 ק השבכה

וַיִּקְרָא אֶת־ שְׁמוֹ בֹּעַז׃ וְעַל רֹאשׁ הָעַמּוּדִים מַעֲשֵׂה
shape-of the-pillars top-of and-on (22) Boaz name-of-him *** and-he-called

שׁוֹשָׁן וַתִּתֹּם מְלֶאכֶת הָעַמּוּדִים׃ וַיַּעַשׂ אֶת־ הַיָּם
the-Sea *** and-he-made (23) the-pillars work-of so-she-was-completed lily

מוּצָק עֶשֶׂר בָּאַמָּה מִשְּׂפָתוֹ עַד־ שְׂפָתוֹ עָגֹל ׀ סָבִיב
around circular rim-of-him to from-rim-of-him by-the-cubit ten being-cast

וְחָמֵשׁ בָּאַמָּה קוֹמָתוֹ וְקָוֹה שְׁלֹשִׁים בָּאַמָּה
by-the-cubit thirty and-line height-of-him by-the-cubit and-five

יָסֹב אֹתוֹ סָבִיב׃ וּפְקָעִים מִתַּחַת לִשְׂפָתוֹ ׀ סָבִיב
around to-rim-of-him at-below and-gourds (24) around him he-measured-around

סֹבְבִים אֹתוֹ עֶשֶׂר בָּאַמָּה מַקִּפִים אֶת־ הַיָּם סָבִיב
around the-Sea *** ones-encircling to-the-cubit ten him ones-encircling

שְׁנֵי טוּרִים הַפְּקָעִים יְצֻקִים בִּיצֻקָתוֹ׃ עֹמֵד עַל־ שְׁנֵי
two-of on standing (25) with-casting-of-him ones-cast the-gourds rows two-of

עָשָׂר בָּקָר שְׁלֹשָׁה פֹנִים ׀ צָפוֹנָה וּשְׁלֹשָׁה פֹנִים ׀ יָמָּה וּשְׁלֹשָׁה ׀
and-three to-west ones-facing and-three to-north ones-facing three bull ten

פֹּנִים נֶגְבָּה וּשְׁלֹשָׁה פֹּנִים מִזְרָחָה וְהַיָּם עֲלֵיהֶם
on-them and-the-Sea to-east ones-facing and-three to-south ones-facing

מִלְמָעְלָה וְכָל־ אֲחֹרֵיהֶם בָּיְתָה׃ וְעָבְיוֹ
and-thickness-of-him (26) toward-center hindquarters-of-them and-all-of at-on-top

טֶפַח וּשְׂפָתוֹ כְּמַעֲשֵׂה שְׂפַת־ כּוֹס פֶּרַח שׁוֹשָׁן
lily blossom-of cup rim-of like-shape-of and-rim-of-him handbreadth

אַלְפַּיִם בַּת יָכִיל׃ וַיַּעַשׂ אֶת־ הַמְּכֹנוֹת עֶשֶׂר
ten the-movable-stands *** and-he-made (27) he-held bath two-thousands

נְחֹשֶׁת אַרְבַּע בָּאַמָּה אֹרֶךְ הַמְּכוֹנָה הָאֶחָת וְאַרְבַּע בָּאַמָּה
by-the-cubit and-four the-each the-stand length-of by-the-cubit four bronze

רָחְבָּהּ וְשָׁלֹשׁ בָּאַמָּה קוֹמָתָהּ׃ וְזֶה מַעֲשֵׂה
make-up-of and-this (28) height-of-her by-the-cubit and-three width-of-her

הַמְּכוֹנָה מִסְגְּרֹת לָהֶם וּמִסְגְּרֹת בֵּין הַשְׁלַבִּים׃ וְעַל־
and-on (29) the-uprights between and-side-panels to-them side-panels the-stand

הַמִּסְגְּרוֹת אֲשֶׁר ׀ בֵּין הַשְׁלַבִּים אֲרָיוֹת ׀ בָּקָר וּכְרוּבִים וְעַל־
and-on and-cherubim bull lions the-uprights between that the-side-panels

הַשְׁלַבִּים כֵּן מִמָּעַל וּמִתַּחַת לַאֲרָיוֹת וְלַבָּקָר לֹיוֹת
wreaths and-to-the-bull to-the-lions and-at-below at-above same the-uprights

מַעֲשֵׂה מוֹרָד׃ וְאַרְבָּעָה אוֹפַנֵּי נְחֹשֶׁת לַמְּכוֹנָה הָאַחַת
the-each for-the-stand bronze wheels-of and-four (30) hammer work-of

וְסַרְנֵי נְחֹשֶׁת וְאַרְבָּעָה פַעֲמֹתָיו כְּתֵפֹת לָהֶם מִתַּחַת לַכִּיֹּר
to-the-basin at-below to-them supports feet-of-him and-four bronze and-axles-of

the one to the north Boaz.[t] 22The capitals on top were in the shape of lilies. And so the work on the pillars was completed.

23He made the Sea of cast metal, circular in shape, measuring ten cubits[u] from rim to rim and five cubits high. It took a line of thirty cubits[v] to measure around it. 24Below the rim, gourds encircled it—ten to a cubit. The gourds were cast in two rows in one piece with the Sea.

25The Sea stood on twelve bulls, three facing north, three facing west, three facing south and three facing east. The Sea rested on top of them, and their hindquarters were toward the center. 26It was a handbreadth in thickness, and its rim was like the rim of a cup, like a lily blossom. It held two thousand baths.[w]

27He also made ten movable stands of bronze; each was four cubits long, four wide and three high.[x] 28This is how the stands were made: They had side panels attached to uprights. 29On the panels between the uprights were lions, bulls and cherubim—and on the uprights as well. Above and below the lions and bulls were wreaths of hammered work. 30Each stand had four bronze wheels with bronze axles, and each had a basin resting on four supports, cast with

[t]21 *Boaz* probably means *in him is strength.*
[u]23 That is, about 15 feet (about 4.5 meters)
[v]23 That is, about 45 feet (about 13.5 meters)
[w]26 That is, probably about 11,500 gallons (about 44 kiloliters); the Septuagint does not have this sentence.
[x]27 That is, about 6 feet (about 1.8 meters) long and wide and about 4 1/2 feet (about 1.3 meters) high

°23 ק וקו

הַכְּתֵפֹת יְצֻקוֹת מֵעֵבֶר אִישׁ לֹיוֹת׃ וּפִיהוּ
and-opening-of-him (31) wreaths each on-side-of ones-cast the-supports

מִבֵּית לַכֹּתֶרֶת וָמַעְלָה בָּאַמָּה וּפִיהָ עָגֹל
round and-opening-of-her at-the-cubit and-above of-the-stand on-inside-of

מַעֲשֵׂה־כֵן אַמָּה וַחֲצִי הָאַמָּה וְגַם־עַל־פִּיהָ
opening-of-her around and-also the-cubit and-half-of cubit base work-of

מִקְלָעוֹת וּמִסְגְּרֹתֵיהֶם מְרֻבָּעוֹת לֹא עֲגֻלּוֹת׃ וְאַרְבַּעַת
and-four-of (32) ones-round not ones-being-square and-panels-of-them engravings

הָאוֹפַנִּים לְמִתַּחַת לַמִּסְגְּרוֹת וִידוֹת הָאוֹפַנִּים בַּמְּכֹנָה
on-the-stand the-wheels and-axles-of to-the-panels at-under the-wheels

וְקוֹמַת הָאוֹפַן הָאֶחָד אַמָּה וַחֲצִי הָאַמָּה׃
the-cubit and-half-of cubit the-each the-wheel and-diameter-of

וּמַעֲשֵׂה הָאוֹפַנִּים כְּמַעֲשֵׂה אוֹפַן הַמֶּרְכָּבָה יְדוֹתָם
axles-of-them the-chariot wheel-of like-make-of the-wheels and-make-of (33)

וְגַבֵּיהֶם וְחִשֻּׁקֵיהֶם וְחִשֻּׁרֵיהֶם הַכֹּל מוּצָק׃
being-cast the-whole and-hubs-of-them and-spokes-of-them and-rims-of-them

וְאַרְבַּע כְּתֵפוֹת אֶל אַרְבַּע פִּנּוֹת הַמְּכֹנָה הָאֶחָת מִן־הַמְּכֹנָה
the-stand from the-each the-stand corners four on handles and-four (34)

כְּתֵפֶיהָ׃ וּבְרֹאשׁ הַמְּכוֹנָה חֲצִי הָאַמָּה קוֹמָה
height the-cubit half-of the-stand and-at-top-of (35) projections-of-her

עָגֹל ׀ סָבִיב וְעַל רֹאשׁ הַמְּכֹנָה יְדֹתֶיהָ וּמִסְגְּרֹתֶיהָ
and-panels-of-her supports-of-her the-stand top-of and-on around circle

מִמֶּנָּה׃ וַיְפַתַּח עַל־הַלֻּחֹת יְדֹתֶיהָ וְעַל
and-on supports-of-her the-surfaces on and-he-engraved (36) from-her

וּמִסְגְּרֹתֶיהָ כְּרוּבִים אֲרָיוֹת וְתִמֹרֹת כְּמַעַר־אִישׁ וְלֹיוֹת
and-wreaths each as-space-of and-palm-trees lions cherubim panels-of-her

סָבִיב׃ כָּזֹאת עָשָׂה אֵת עֶשֶׂר הַמְּכֹנוֹת מוּצָק אֶחָד מִדָּה אַחַת
identical size same mold the-stands ten *** he-made as-this (37) around

קֶצֶב אֶחָד לְכֻלָּהְנָה׃ וַיַּעַשׂ עֲשָׂרָה כִיֹּרוֹת נְחֹשֶׁת
bronze basins-of ten then-he-made (38) for-all-of-them identical shape

אַרְבָּעִים בַּת יָכִיל ׀ הַכִּיּוֹר הָאֶחָד אַרְבַּע בָּאַמָּה הַכִּיּוֹר הָאֶחָד
the-each the-basin by-the-cubit four the-each the-basin he-held bath forty

כִּיּוֹר אֶחָד עַל־הַמְּכוֹנָה הָאַחַת לְעֶשֶׂר הַמְּכֹנוֹת׃ וַיִּתֵּן אֶת־
*** and-he-placed (39) the-stands for-ten the-each the-stand on one basin

הַמְּכֹנוֹת חָמֵשׁ עַל־כֶּתֶף הַבַּיִת מִיָּמִין וְחָמֵשׁ עַל־כֶּתֶף הַבַּיִת
the-temple side-of at and-five at-south the-temple side-of on five the-stands

מִשְּׂמֹאלוֹ וְאֶת־הַיָּם נָתַן מִכֶּתֶף הַבַּיִת הַיְמָנִית
the-south the-temple on-side-of he-placed the-Sea and at-north-of-him

wreaths on each side. 31On the inside of the stand there was an opening that had a circular frame one cubit[y] deep. This opening was round, and with its basework it measured a cubit and a half.[z] Around its opening there was engraving. The panels of the stands were square, not round. 32The four wheels were under the panels, and the axles of the wheels were attached to the stand. The diameter of each wheel was a cubit and a half. 33The wheels were made like chariot wheels; the axles, rims, spokes and hubs were all of cast metal.

34Each stand had four handles, one on each corner, projecting from the stand. 35At the top of the stand there was a circular band half a cubit[a] deep. The supports and panels were attached to the top of the stand. 36He engraved cherubim, lions and palm trees on the surfaces of the supports and on the panels, in every available space, with wreaths all around. 37This is the way he made the ten stands. They were all cast in the same molds and were identical in size and shape.

38He then made ten bronze basins, each holding forty baths[b] and measuring four cubits across, one basin to go on each of the ten stands. 39He placed five of the stands on the south side of the temple and five on the north. He placed the Sea on the south side, at

[y] *31* That is, about 1 1/2 feet (about 0.5 meter)
[z] *31* That is, about 2 1/4 feet (about 0.7 meter); also in verse 32
[a] *35* That is, about 3/4 foot (about 0.2 meter)
[b] *38* That is, about 230 gallons (about 880 liters)

°36 ק מסגרתיה

קֵדְמָה מִמּוּל נֶגֶב׃ וַיַּעַשׂ חִירוֹם אֶת־הַכִּיֹּרוֹת וְאֶת־
and the-basins *** Hiram and-he-made (40) south at-corner-of at-east

הַיָּעִים וְאֶת־הַמִּזְרָקוֹת וַיְכַל חִירָם לַעֲשׂוֹת אֶת־כָּל־
all-of *** to-do Hiram so-he-finished the-sprinkling-bowls and the-shovels

הַמְּלָאכָה אֲשֶׁר עָשָׂה לַמֶּלֶךְ שְׁלֹמֹה בֵּית יְהוָה׃
Yahweh temple-of Solomon for-the-king he-undertook that the-work

עַמֻּדִים שְׁנַיִם וְגֻלֹּת הַכֹּתָרֹת אֲשֶׁר־עַל־רֹאשׁ הָעַמֻּדִים שְׁתָּיִם
two the-pillars top-of on that the-capitals and-bowls-of two pillars (41)

וְהַשְּׂבָכוֹת שְׁתַּיִם לְכַסּוֹת אֶת־שְׁתֵּי גֻּלֹּת הַכֹּתָרֹת אֲשֶׁר עַל־
on that the-capitals bowls-of two-of *** to-decorate two and-the-networks

רֹאשׁ הָעַמּוּדִים׃ וְאֶת־הָרִמֹּנִים אַרְבַּע מֵאוֹת לִשְׁתֵּי
for-two-of hundreds four the-pomegranates and (42) the-pillars top-of

הַשְּׂבָכוֹת שְׁנֵי־טוּרִים רִמֹּנִים לַשְּׂבָכָה הָאֶחָת לְכַסּוֹת
to-decorate the-each for-the-network pomegranates rows two-of the-networks

אֶת־שְׁתֵּי גֻּלֹּת הַכֹּתָרֹת אֲשֶׁר עַל־פְּנֵי הָעַמּוּדִים׃ וְאֶת־
and (43) the-pillars tops-of on that the-capitals bowls-of two-of ***

הַמְּכֹנוֹת עֶשֶׂר וְאֶת־הַכִּיֹּרֹת עֲשָׂרָה עַל־הַמְּכֹנוֹת׃ וְאֶת־הַיָּם הָאֶחָד
the-one the-Sea and (44) the-stands on ten the-basins and ten the-stands

וְאֶת־הַבָּקָר שְׁנֵים־עָשָׂר תַּחַת הַיָּם׃ וְאֶת־הַסִּירוֹת וְאֶת־הַיָּעִים
the-shovels and the-pots and (45) the-Sea under ten two the-bull and

וְאֶת־הַמִּזְרָקוֹת וְאֵת כָּל־הַכֵּלִים °הָאֹהֶל אֲשֶׁר עָשָׂה חִירָם
Hiram he-made that the-these the-objects all-of and the-sprinkling-bowls and

לַמֶּלֶךְ שְׁלֹמֹה בֵּית יְהוָה נְחֹשֶׁת מְמֹרָט׃ בְּכִכַּר
in-plain-of (46) being-burnished bronze Yahweh temple-of Solomon for-the-king

הַיַּרְדֵּן יְצָקָם הַמֶּלֶךְ בְּמַעֲבֵה הָאֲדָמָה בֵּין סֻכּוֹת
Succoth between the-ground in-clay-of the-king he-cast-them the-Jordan

וּבֵין צָרְתָן׃ וַיַּנַּח שְׁלֹמֹה אֶת־כָּל־הַכֵּלִים
the-things all-of *** Solomon and-he-left (47) Zarethan and-between

מֵרֹב מְאֹד מְאֹד לֹא נֶחְקַר מִשְׁקַל הַנְּחֹשֶׁת׃
the-bronze weight-of he-was-determined not many many for-number

וַיַּעַשׂ שְׁלֹמֹה אֵת כָּל־הַכֵּלִים אֲשֶׁר בֵּית יְהוָה
Yahweh temple-of that the-furnishings all-of *** Solomon and-he-made (48)

אֵת מִזְבַּח הַזָּהָב וְאֶת־הַשֻּׁלְחָן אֲשֶׁר עָלָיו לֶחֶם הַפָּנִים
the-Presences bread-of on-him that the-table and the-gold altar-of ***

זָהָב׃ וְאֶת־הַמְּנֹרוֹת חָמֵשׁ מִיָּמִין וְחָמֵשׁ מִשְּׂמֹאול לִפְנֵי
in-front-of on-left and-five on-right five the-lampstands and (49) gold

הַדְּבִיר זָהָב סָגוּר וְהַפֶּרַח וְהַנֵּרֹת וְהַמֶּלְקַחַיִם*
and-the-tongs and-the-lamps and-the-floral-work pure gold the-inner-sanctuary

the southeast corner of the temple. [40]He also made the basins and shovels and sprinkling bowls.

So Huram finished all the work he had undertaken for King Solomon in the temple of the LORD:

[41]the two pillars;
the two bowl-shaped capitals on top of the pillars;
the two sets of network decorating the two bowl-shaped capitals on top of the pillars;
[42]the four hundred pomegranates for the two sets of network (two rows of pomegranates for each network, decorating the bowl-shaped capitals on top of the pillars);
[43]the ten stands with their ten basins;
[44]the Sea and the twelve bulls under it;
[45]the pots, shovels and sprinkling bowls.

All these objects that Huram made for King Solomon for the temple of the LORD were of burnished bronze. [46]The king had them cast in clay molds in the plain of the Jordan between Succoth and Zarethan. [47]Solomon left all these things unweighed, because there were so many; the weight of the bronze was not determined.

[48]Solomon also made all the furnishings that were in the LORD's temple:

the golden altar;
the golden table on which was the bread of the Presence;
[49]the lampstands of pure gold (five on the right and five on the left, in front of the inner sanctuary);
the gold floral work and lamps and tongs;

*49 Most mss have *qamets* under the *qoph* (ʹקָ—).

°45 ק האלה

זָהָב׃ (50) וְהַסִּפּוֹת וְהַמְזַמְּרוֹת וְהַמִּזְרָקוֹת
and-the-sprinkling-bowls and-the-wick-trimmers and-the-dishes (50) gold

וְהַכַּפּוֹת וְהַמַּחְתּוֹת זָהָב סָגוּר וְהַפֹּתוֹת לְדַלְתוֹת
for-doors-of and-the-sockets pure gold and-the-censers and-the-ladles

הַבַּיִת הַפְּנִימִי לְקֹדֶשׁ הַקֳּדָשִׁים לְדַלְתֵי הַבַּיִת
the-temple for-doors-of the-Holy-Places for-Holy-of the-innermost the-room

לְהֵיכָל זָהָב׃ (51) וַתִּשְׁלַם כָּל־ הַמְּלָאכָה אֲשֶׁר
that the-work all-of when-she-was-finished (51) gold for-the-main-hall

עָשָׂה הַמֶּלֶךְ שְׁלֹמֹה בֵּית יְהוָה וַיָּבֵא שְׁלֹמֹה אֶת־
*** Solomon then-he-brought-in Yahweh temple-of Solomon the-king he-did

קָדְשֵׁי ׀ דָּוִד אָבִיו אֶת־ הַכֶּסֶף וְאֶת־ הַזָּהָב וְאֶת־
and the-gold and the-silver *** father-of-him David dedicated-things-of

הַכֵּלִים נָתַן בְּאֹצְרוֹת בֵּית יְהוָה׃ (8:1) אָז
then (8:1) Yahweh temple-of in-treasuries-of he-placed the-furnishings

יַקְהֵל שְׁלֹמֹה אֶת־ זִקְנֵי יִשְׂרָאֵל אֶת־ כָּל־ רָאשֵׁי הַמַּטּוֹת
the-tribes heads-of all-of *** Israel elders-of *** Solomon he-summoned

נְשִׂיאֵי הָאָבוֹת לִבְנֵי יִשְׂרָאֵל אֶל־ הַמֶּלֶךְ שְׁלֹמֹה יְרוּשָׁלִָם
Jerusalem Solomon the-king to Israel of-sons-of the-families chiefs-of

לְהַעֲלוֹת אֶת־ אֲרוֹן בְּרִית־ יְהוָה מֵעִיר דָּוִד הִיא צִיּוֹן׃
Zion this David from-City-of Yahweh covenant-of ark-of *** to-bring-up

(2) וַיִּקָּהֲלוּ אֶל־ הַמֶּלֶךְ שְׁלֹמֹה כָּל־ אִישׁ יִשְׂרָאֵל בְּיֶרַח
in-month-of Israel man-of all-of Solomon the-king to and-they-came-together (2)

הָאֵתָנִים בֶּחָג הוּא הַחֹדֶשׁ הַשְּׁבִיעִי׃ (3) וַיָּבֹאוּ
when-they-arrived (3) the-seventh the-month this in-the-festival the-Ethanim

כֹּל זִקְנֵי יִשְׂרָאֵל וַיִּשְׂאוּ הַכֹּהֲנִים אֶת־ הָאָרוֹן׃
the-ark *** the-priests then-they-took-up Israel elders-of all-of

(4) וַיַּעֲלוּ אֶת־ אֲרוֹן יְהוָה וְאֶת־ אֹהֶל מוֹעֵד וְאֶת־ כָּל־
all-of and Meeting Tent-of and Yahweh ark-of *** and-they-brought-up (4)

כְּלֵי הַקֹּדֶשׁ אֲשֶׁר בָּאֹהֶל וַיַּעֲלוּ אֹתָם
them and-they-carried-up in-the-Tent that the-sacred furnishings-of

הַכֹּהֲנִים וְהַלְוִיִּם׃ (5) וְהַמֶּלֶךְ שְׁלֹמֹה וְכָל־ עֲדַת
assembly-of and-entire-of Solomon and-the-king (5) the-Levites the-priests

יִשְׂרָאֵל הַנּוֹעָדִים עָלָיו אִתּוֹ לִפְנֵי הָאָרוֹן מְזַבְּחִים
ones-sacrificing the-ark before with-him about-him the-ones-gathering Israel

צֹאן וּבָקָר אֲשֶׁר לֹא־ יִסָּפְרוּ וְלֹא יִמָּנוּ
they-could-be-counted and-not they-could-be-recorded not that and-cattle sheep

מֵרֹב׃ (6) וַיָּבִאוּ הַכֹּהֲנִים אֶת־ אֲרוֹן בְּרִית־ יְהוָה
Yahweh covenant-of ark-of *** the-priests then-they-brought (6) for-number

[50]the pure gold dishes, wick trimmers, sprinkling bowls, ladles and censers;
and the gold sockets for the doors of the innermost room, the Most Holy Place, and also for the doors of the main hall of the temple.

[51]When all the work King Solomon had done for the temple of the LORD was finished, he brought in the things his father David had dedicated—the silver and gold and the furnishings—and he placed them in the treasuries of the LORD's temple.

### *The Ark Brought to the Temple*

8 Then King Solomon summoned into his presence at Jerusalem the elders of Israel, all the heads of the tribes and the chiefs of the Israelite families, to bring up the ark of the LORD's covenant from
Zion, the City of David. [2]All
the men of Israel came together to King Solomon at the time of the festival in the month of Ethanim, the seventh month.
[3]When all the elders of Israel had arrived, the priests took
up the ark, [4]and they brought up the ark of the LORD and the Tent of Meeting and all the sacred furnishings in it. The priests and Levites carried
them up, [5]and King Solomon and, with him, the entire assembly of Israel that had gathered about him were before the ark, sacrificing so many sheep and cattle that they could not be recorded or counted.
[6]The priests then brought the ark of the LORD's covenant

אֶל־מְקוֹמוֹ אֶל־דְּבִיר הַבַּיִת אֶל־קֹדֶשׁ הַקֳּדָשִׁים
the-Holy-Places Holy-of to the-temple inner-sanctuary-of in place-of-him to

אֶל־תַּחַת כַּנְפֵי הַכְּרוּבִים׃ כִּי הַכְּרוּבִים פֹּרְשִׂים כְּנָפַיִם
wings ones-spreading the-cherubim for (7) the-cherubim wings-of beneath at

אֶל־מְקוֹם הָאָרוֹן וַיָּסֹכּוּ הַכְּרֻבִים עַל־הָאָרוֹן וְעַל־
and-over the-ark over the-cherubim and-they-overshadow the-ark place-of over

בַּדָּיו מִלְמָעְלָה׃ וַיַּאֲרִכוּ הַבַּדִּים וַיֵּרָאוּ
so-they-could-be-seen the-poles and-they-were-long (8) at-above poles-of-him

רָאשֵׁי הַבַּדִּים מִן־הַקֹּדֶשׁ עַל־פְּנֵי הַדְּבִיר וְלֹא
but-not the-inner-sanctuary front-of at the-Holy-Place from the-poles ends-of

יֵרָאוּ הַחוּצָה וַיִּהְיוּ שָׁם עַד הַיּוֹם הַזֶּה׃
the-this the-day to there and-they-are from-the-outside they-could-be-seen

אֵין בָּאָרוֹן רַק שְׁנֵי לֻחוֹת הָאֲבָנִים אֲשֶׁר הִנִּחַ
he-placed that the-stones tablets-of two-of except in-the-ark nothing (9)

שָׁם מֹשֶׁה בְּחֹרֵב אֲשֶׁר כָּרַת יְהוָה עִם־בְּנֵי יִשְׂרָאֵל
Israel sons-of with Yahweh he-made-covenant where at-Horeb Moses there

בְּצֵאתָם מֵאֶרֶץ מִצְרָיִם׃ וַיְהִי בְּצֵאת
when-to-withdraw and-he-was (10) Egypt from-land-of after-to-come-out-them

הַכֹּהֲנִים מִן־הַקֹּדֶשׁ וְהֶעָנָן מָלֵא אֶת־בֵּית
temple-of *** he-filled then-the-cloud the-Holy-Place from the-priests

יְהוָה׃ וְלֹא־יָכְלוּ הַכֹּהֲנִים לַעֲמֹד לְשָׁרֵת מִפְּנֵי
because-of to-serve to-stand the-priests they-could and-not (11) Yahweh

הֶעָנָן כִּי־מָלֵא כְבוֹד־יְהוָה אֶת־בֵּית יְהוָה׃ אָז
then (12) Yahweh temple-of *** Yahweh glory-of he-filled for the-cloud

אָמַר שְׁלֹמֹה יְהוָה אָמַר לִשְׁכֹּן בָּעֲרָפֶל׃ בָּנֹה
to-build (13) in-the-dark-cloud to-dwell he-said Yahweh Solomon he-said

בָנִיתִי בֵּית זְבֻל לָךְ מָכוֹן לְשִׁבְתְּךָ עוֹלָמִים׃
forevers to-dwell-you place for-you magnificence temple-of I-built

וַיַּסֵּב הַמֶּלֶךְ אֶת־פָּנָיו וַיְבָרֶךְ אֵת כָּל־
whole-of *** and-he-blessed faces-of-him *** the-king and-he-turned (14)

קְהַל יִשְׂרָאֵל וְכָל־קְהַל יִשְׂרָאֵל עֹמֵד׃ וַיֹּאמֶר
then-he-said (15) standing Israel assembly-of while-all-of Israel assembly-of

בָּרוּךְ יְהוָה אֱלֹהֵי יִשְׂרָאֵל אֲשֶׁר דִּבֶּר בְּפִיו אֵת
*** with-mouth-of-him he-promised who Israel God-of Yahweh being-praised

דָּוִד אָבִי וּבְיָדוֹ מִלֵּא לֵאמֹר׃ מִן־הַיּוֹם
the-day since (16) to-say he-fulfilled and-with-hand-of-him father-of-me David

אֲשֶׁר הוֹצֵאתִי אֶת־עַמִּי אֶת־יִשְׂרָאֵל מִמִּצְרַיִם לֹא־בָחַרְתִּי בְעִיר
to-city I-chose not from-Egypt Israel *** people-of-me *** I-brought that

to its place in the inner sanctuary of the temple, the Most
Holy Place, and put it beneath
the wings of the cherubim.
7The cherubim spread their
wings over the place of the ark
and overshadowed the ark
and its carrying poles. 8These
poles were so long that their
ends could be seen from the
Holy Place in front of the inner sanctuary, but not from
outside the Holy Place; and
they are still there today.
9There was nothing in the ark
except the two stone tablets
that Moses had placed in it at
Horeb, where the LORD made a
covenant with the Israelites
after they came out of Egypt.
10When the priests with-
drew from the Holy Place, the
cloud filled the temple of the
LORD. 11And the priests could
not perform their service because of the cloud, for the glory of the LORD filled his temple.
12Then Solomon said, "The
LORD has said that he would
dwell in a dark cloud; 13I have
indeed built a magnificent
temple for you, a place for you
to dwell forever."
14While the whole assembly
of Israel was standing there,
the king turned around and
blessed them. 15Then he said:

"Praise be to the LORD,
the God of Israel, who with
his own hand has fulfilled
what he promised with his
own mouth to my father
David. For he said, 16'Since
the day I brought my
people Israel out of Egypt, I
have not chosen a city in

מִכֹּל֙ שִׁבְטֵ֣י יִשְׂרָאֵ֔ל לִבְנ֣וֹת בַּ֔יִת לִהְי֥וֹת שְׁמִ֖י שָׁ֑ם וָאֶבְחַ֣ר
but-I-chose there Name-of-me to-be temple to-build Israel tribes-of in-any-of

בְּדָוִ֔ד לִהְי֖וֹת עַל־ עַמִּ֥י יִשְׂרָאֵֽל׃ וַיְהִ֕י עִם־ לְבַ֖ב דָּוִ֣ד
David heart-of in and-he-was (17) Israel people-of-me over to-be to-David

אָבִ֑י לִבְנ֣וֹת בַּ֔יִת לְשֵׁ֕ם יְהוָ֖ה אֱלֹהֵ֥י יִשְׂרָאֵֽל׃ וַיֹּ֤אמֶר
but-he-said (18) Israel God-of Yahweh for-Name-of temple to-build father-of-me

יְהוָה֙ אֶל־ דָּוִ֣ד אָבִ֔י יַ֚עַן אֲשֶׁ֣ר הָיָה֙ עִם־ לְבָ֣בְךָ֔ לִבְנ֥וֹת
to-build heart-of-you in he-was that because father-of-me David to Yahweh

בַּ֖יִת לִשְׁמִ֑י הֱטִיבֹ֔תָ כִּ֥י הָיָ֖ה עִם־ לְבָבֶֽךָ׃ רַ֚ק
nevertheless (19) heart-of-you in he-was for you-did-well for-Name-of-me temple

אַתָּ֔ה לֹ֥א תִבְנֶ֖ה הַבָּ֑יִת כִּ֤י אִם־ בִּנְךָ֙ הַיֹּצֵ֣א
the-one-coming son-of-you rather but the-temple you-will-build not you

מֵחֲלָצֶ֔יךָ הֽוּא־ יִבְנֶ֥ה הַבַּ֖יִת לִשְׁמִֽי׃ וַיָּ֣קֶם
and-he-kept (20) for-Name-of-me the-temple he-will-build he from-loins-of-you

יְהוָ֔ה אֶת־ דְּבָר֖וֹ אֲשֶׁ֣ר דִּבֵּ֑ר וָאָקֻ֡ם תַּחַת֩ דָּוִ֨ד
David after and-I-succeeded he-made that promise-of-him *** Yahweh

אָבִ֜י וָאֵשֵׁ֣ב עַל־ כִּסֵּ֣א יִשְׂרָאֵ֗ל כַּאֲשֶׁר֙ דִּבֶּ֣ר יְהוָ֔ה
Yahweh he-promised just-as Israel throne-of on and-I-sit father-of-me

וָאֶבְנֶ֣ה הַבַּ֔יִת לְשֵׁ֥ם יְהוָ֖ה אֱלֹהֵ֥י יִשְׂרָאֵֽל׃ וָאָשִׂ֨ם
and-I-provided (21) Israel God-of Yahweh for-Name-of the-temple and-I-built

שָׁ֤ם מָקוֹם֙ לָֽאָר֔וֹן אֲשֶׁר־ שָׁ֖ם בְּרִ֣ית יְהוָ֑ה אֲשֶׁ֤ר כָּרַת֙ עִם־
with he-made that Yahweh covenant-of there where for-the-ark place there

אֲבֹתֵ֔ינוּ בְּהוֹצִיא֥וֹ אֹתָ֖ם מֵאֶ֥רֶץ מִצְרָֽיִם׃ וַיַּעֲמֹ֣ד
then-he-stood (22) Egypt from-land-of them when-to-bring-out-him fathers-of-us

שְׁלֹמֹ֗ה לִפְנֵי֙ מִזְבַּ֣ח יְהוָ֔ה נֶ֖גֶד כָּל־ קְהַ֣ל יִשְׂרָאֵ֑ל
Israel assembly-of whole-of in-front-of Yahweh altar-of before Solomon

וַיִּפְרֹ֥שׂ כַּפָּ֖יו הַשָּׁמָֽיִם׃ וַיֹּאמַ֗ר יְהוָ֞ה אֱלֹהֵ֤י
God-of Yahweh and-he-said (23) the-heavens hands-of-him and-he-spread-out

יִשְׂרָאֵל֙ אֵין־כָּמ֣וֹךָ אֱלֹהִ֔ים בַּשָּׁמַ֣יִם מִמַּ֔עַל וְעַל־ הָאָ֖רֶץ מִתָּ֑חַת
at-below the-earth or-on at-above in-the-heavens God like-you not Israel

שֹׁמֵ֤ר הַבְּרִית֙ וְהַחֶ֔סֶד לַעֲבָדֶ֕יךָ הַהֹלְכִ֥ים
the-ones-walking with-servants-of-you and-the-love the-covenant keeping

לְפָנֶ֖יךָ בְּכָל־ לִבָּֽם׃ אֲשֶׁ֣ר שָׁמַ֗רְתָּ לְעַבְדְּךָ֙
to-servant-of-you you-kept who (24) heart-of-them with-whole-of before-you

דָּוִ֣ד אָבִ֔י אֵ֥ת אֲשֶׁר־ דִּבַּ֖רְתָּ ל֑וֹ וַתְּדַבֵּ֥ר
and-you-promised to-him you-promised what *** father-of-me David

בְּפִ֛יךָ וּבְיָדְךָ֥ מִלֵּ֖אתָ כַּיּ֥וֹם הַזֶּֽה׃
the-this as-the-day you-fulfilled and-with-hand-of-you with-mouth-of-you

any tribe of Israel to have a temple built for my Name to be there, but I have chosen David to rule my people Israel.'

17"My father David had it in his heart to build a temple for the Name of the LORD, the God of Israel. 18But the LORD said to my father David, 'Because it was in your heart to build a temple for my Name, you did well to have this in your heart. 19Nevertheless, you are not the one to build the temple, but your son, who is your own flesh and blood—he is the one who will build the temple for my Name.'

20"The LORD has kept the promise he made: I have succeeded David my father and now I sit on the throne of Israel, just as the LORD promised, and I have built the temple for the Name of the LORD, the God of Israel. 21I have provided a place there for the ark, in which is the covenant of the LORD that he made with our fathers when he brought them out of Egypt."

*Solomon's Prayer of Dedication*

22Then Solomon stood before the altar of the LORD in front of the whole assembly of Israel, spread out his hands toward heaven 23and said:

"O LORD, God of Israel, there is no God like you in heaven above or on earth below—you who keep your covenant of love with your servants who continue wholeheartedly in your way. 24You have kept your promise to your servant David my father; with your mouth you have promised and with your hand you have fulfilled it—as it is today.

וְעַתָּה יְהוָה ׀ אֱלֹהֵי יִשְׂרָאֵל שְׁמֹר לְעַבְדְּךָ דָוִד אָבִי
father-of-me David for-servant-of-you keep! Israel God-of Yahweh and-now (25)

אֵת אֲשֶׁר דִּבַּרְתָּ לּוֹ לֵאמֹר לֹא־ יִכָּרֵת לְךָ אִישׁ
man of-you he-shall-be-cut-off not to-say to-him you-promised what ***

מִלְּפָנַי יֹשֵׁב עַל־ כִּסֵּא יִשְׂרָאֵל רַק אִם־ יִשְׁמְרוּ
they-are-careful if only Israel throne-of on sitting from-before-me

בָנֶיךָ אֶת־ דַּרְכָּם לָלֶכֶת לְפָנַי כַּאֲשֶׁר הָלַכְתָּ לְפָנָי׃
before-me you-walked just-as before-me to-walk way-of-them *** sons-of-you

וְעַתָּה אֱלֹהֵי יִשְׂרָאֵל יֵאָמֶן נָא דְּבָרְיךָ אֲשֶׁר
that word-of-you now! let-him-come-true Israel God-of and-now (26)

דִּבַּרְתָּ לְעַבְדְּךָ דָּוִד אָבִי׃ כִּי הַאֻמְנָם
really? but (27) father-of-me David to-servant-of-you you-promised

יֵשֵׁב אֱלֹהִים עַל־הָאָרֶץ הִנֵּה הַשָּׁמַיִם וּשְׁמֵי הַשָּׁמַיִם
the-heavens and-heavens-of the-heavens see! the-earth on God will-he-dwell

לֹא יְכַלְכְּלוּךָ אַף כִּי־ הַבַּיִת הַזֶּה אֲשֶׁר
that the-this the-temple indeed how-much-less they-can-contain-you not

בָּנִיתִי׃ וּפָנִיתָ אֶל־ תְּפִלַּת עַבְדְּךָ וְאֶל־
and-to servant-of-you prayer-of to yet-you-give-attention (28) I-built

תְּחִנָּתוֹ יְהוָה אֱלֹהָי לִשְׁמֹעַ אֶל־ הָרִנָּה וְאֶל־ הַתְּפִלָּה
the-prayer and-to the-cry to to-hear God-of-me Yahweh mercy-plea-of-him

אֲשֶׁר עַבְדְּךָ מִתְפַּלֵּל לְפָנֶיךָ הַיּוֹם׃ לִהְיוֹת
to-be (29) the-day in-presences-of-you praying servant-of-you that

עֵינֶךָ פְתֻחוֹת אֶל־ הַבַּיִת הַזֶּה לַיְלָה וָיוֹם אֶל־
toward and-day night the-this the-temple toward ones-being-open eye-of-you

הַמָּקוֹם אֲשֶׁר אָמַרְתָּ יִהְיֶה שְׁמִי שָׁם לִשְׁמֹעַ אֶל־ הַתְּפִלָּה
the-prayer to to-hear there Name-of-me he-shall-be you-said which the-place

אֲשֶׁר יִתְפַּלֵּל עַבְדְּךָ אֶל־ הַמָּקוֹם הַזֶּה׃ וְשָׁמַעְתָּ אֶל־
to and-you-hear (30) the-this the-place toward servant-of-you he-prays that

תְּחִנַּת עַבְדְּךָ וְעַמְּךָ יִשְׂרָאֵל אֲשֶׁר יִתְפַּלְלוּ אֶל־
toward they-pray when Israel and-people-of-you servant-of-you prayer-of

הַמָּקוֹם הַזֶּה וְאַתָּה תִּשְׁמַע אֶל־ מְקוֹם שִׁבְתְּךָ אֶל־
from to-dwell-you place-of from you-hear and-you the-this the-place

הַשָּׁמַיִם וְשָׁמַעְתָּ וְסָלָחְתָּ׃ אֵת אֲשֶׁר יֶחֱטָא אִישׁ
man he-wrongs when *** (31) then-you-forgive when-you-hear the-heavens

לְרֵעֵהוּ וְנָשָׁא־ בוֹ אָלָה לְהַאֲלֹתוֹ וּבָא
and-he-comes to-take-oath-him oath on-him and-he-takes to-neighbor-of-him

אָלָה לִפְנֵי מִזְבַּחֲךָ בַּבַּיִת הַזֶּה׃ וְאַתָּה ׀
then-you (32) the-this in-the-temple altar-of-you before he-swears-oath

°26 ק דברך

25 "Now LORD, God of Israel, keep for your servant David my father the promises you made to him when you said, 'You shall never fail to have a man to sit before me on the throne of Israel, if only your sons are careful in all they do to walk before me as you have done.' 26 And now, O God of Israel, let your word that you promised your servant David my father come true.

27 "But will God really dwell on earth? The heavens, even the highest heaven, cannot contain you. How much less this temple I have built! 28 Yet give attention to your servant's prayer and his plea for mercy, O LORD my God. Hear the cry and the prayer that your servant is praying in your presence this day. 29 May your eyes be open toward this temple night and day, this place of which you said, 'My Name shall be there,' so that you will hear the prayer your servant prays toward this place. 30 Hear the supplication of your servant and of your people Israel when they pray toward this place. Hear from heaven, your dwelling place, and when you hear, forgive.

31 "When a man wrongs his neighbor and is required to take an oath and he comes and swears the oath before your altar in this temple, 32 then hear

תִּשְׁמַע הַשָּׁמַיִם וְעָשִׂיתָ וְשָׁפַטְתָּ אֶת־ עֲבָדֶיךָ לְהַרְשִׁיעַ
to-condemn servants-of-you *** and-you-judge and-you-act the-heavens you-hear

רָשָׁע לָתֵת דַּרְכּוֹ בְּרֹאשׁוֹ וּלְהַצְדִּיק צַדִּיק
innocent and-to-declare-innocent on-head-of-him way-of-him to-bring guilty

לָתֶת לוֹ כְּצִדְקָתוֹ׃ בְּהִנָּגֵף עַמְּךָ
people-of-you when-to-be-defeated (33) as-innocence-of-him for-him to-establish

יִשְׂרָאֵל לִפְנֵי אוֹיֵב אֲשֶׁר יֶחֶטְאוּ־ לָךְ וְשָׁבוּ
when-they-turn-back against-you they-sinned because being-enemy before Israel

אֵלֶיךָ וְהוֹדוּ אֶת־ שְׁמֶךָ וְהִתְפַּלְלוּ וְהִתְחַנְּנוּ
and-they-make-supplication and-they-pray name-of-you *** and-they-confess to-you

אֵלֶיךָ בַּבַּיִת הַזֶּה׃ וְאַתָּה תִּשְׁמַע הַשָּׁמַיִם
the-heavens you-hear then-you (34) the-this in-the-temple to-you

וְסָלַחְתָּ לְחַטַּאת עַמְּךָ יִשְׂרָאֵל וַהֲשֵׁבֹתָם אֶל־
to and-you-bring-back-them Israel people-of-you to-sin-of and-you-forgive

הָאֲדָמָה אֲשֶׁר נָתַתָּ לַאֲבוֹתָם׃ בְּהֵעָצֵר שָׁמַיִם
heavens when-to-be-shut-up (35) to-fathers-of-them you-gave that the-land

וְלֹא־ יִהְיֶה מָטָר כִּי יֶחֶטְאוּ־ לָךְ וְהִתְפַּלְלוּ אֶל־
toward when-they-pray against-you they-sinned because rain he-is and-not

הַמָּקוֹם הַזֶּה וְהוֹדוּ אֶת־ שְׁמֶךָ וּמֵחַטָּאתָם
and-from-sin-of-them name-of-you *** and-they-confess the-this the-place

יְשׁוּבוּן כִּי תַעֲנֵם׃ וְאַתָּה ׀ תִּשְׁמַע הַשָּׁמַיִם
the-heavens you-hear then-you (36) you-afflicted-them because they-turn

וְסָלַחְתָּ לְחַטַּאת עֲבָדֶיךָ וְעַמְּךָ יִשְׂרָאֵל כִּי
indeed Israel and-people-of-you servants-of-you to-sin-of and-you-forgive

תוֹרֵם אֶת־ הַדֶּרֶךְ הַטּוֹבָה אֲשֶׁר יֵלְכוּ־ בָהּ
in-her they-should-walk that the-right the-way *** you-teach-them

וְנָתַתָּה מָטָר עַל־ אַרְצְךָ אֲשֶׁר־ נָתַתָּה לְעַמְּךָ
to-people-of-you you-gave that land-of-you on rain and-you-send

לְנַחֲלָה׃ רָעָב כִּי־ יִהְיֶה בָאָרֶץ דֶּבֶר כִּי־ יִהְיֶה
he-comes when plague on-the-land he-comes when famine (37) for-inheritance

שִׁדָּפוֹן יֵרָקוֹן אַרְבֶּה חָסִיל כִּי יִהְיֶה כִּי יָצַר־ לוֹ
against-him he-besieges when he-comes when grasshopper locust mildew blight

אֹיְבוֹ בְּאֶרֶץ שְׁעָרָיו כָּל־ נֶגַע כָּל־ מַחֲלָה׃
disease any-of disaster any-of gates-of-him in-land-of being-enemy-of-him

כָּל־ תְּפִלָּה כָל־ תְּחִנָּה אֲשֶׁר תִהְיֶה לְכָל־ הָאָדָם
the-person from-any-of she-comes that plea any-of prayer any-of (38)

לְכֹל עַמְּךָ יִשְׂרָאֵל אֲשֶׁר יֵדְעוּן אִישׁ נֶגַע
affliction-of each they-are-aware who Israel people-of-you from-any-of

from heaven and act. Judge between your servants, condemning the guilty and bringing down on his own head what he has done. Declare the innocent not guilty, and so establish his innocence.

33 "When your people Israel have been defeated by an enemy because they have sinned against you, and when they turn back to you and confess your name, praying and making supplication to you in this temple, 34 then hear from heaven and forgive the sin of your people Israel and bring them back to the land you gave to their fathers.

35 "When the heavens are shut up and there is no rain because your people have sinned against you, and when they pray toward this place and confess your name and turn from their sin because you have afflicted them, 36 then hear from heaven and forgive the sin of your servants, your people Israel. Teach them the right way to live, and send rain on the land you gave your people for an inheritance.

37 "When famine or plague comes to the land, or blight or mildew, locusts or grasshoppers, or when an enemy besieges them in any of their cities, whatever disaster or disease may come, 38 and when a prayer or plea is made by any of your people Israel—each one aware of the

לְבָבוֹ וּפָרַשׂ כַּפָּיו אֶל־ הַבַּיִת הַזֶּה׃
the-this the-temple toward hands-of-him and-he-spreads-out heart-of-him

וְאַתָּה תִּשְׁמַע הַשָּׁמַיִם מְכוֹן שִׁבְתֶּךָ וְסָלַחְתָּ
and-you-forgive to-dwell-you place-of the-heavens you-hear then-you (39)

וְעָשִׂיתָ וְנָתַתָּ לָאִישׁ כְּכָל־ דְּרָכָיו אֲשֶׁר תֵּדַע
you-know since ways-of-him as-all-of with-the-each and-you-deal and-you-act

אֶת־ לְבָבוֹ כִּי־ אַתָּה יָדַעְתָּ לְבַדְּךָ אֶת־ לְבַב כָּל־ בְּנֵי
sons-of all-of heart-of *** by-yourself you-know you for heart-of-him ***

הָאָדָם׃ לְמַעַן יִרָאוּךָ כָּל־ הַיָּמִים אֲשֶׁר־ הֵם חַיִּים
ones-alive they that the-days all-of they-will-fear-you so-that (40) the-man

עַל־ פְּנֵי הָאֲדָמָה אֲשֶׁר נָתַתָּה לַאֲבֹתֵינוּ׃ וְגַם אֶל־
for and-also (41) to-fathers-of-us you-gave that the-land faces-of on

הַנָּכְרִי אֲשֶׁר לֹא־ מֵעַמְּךָ יִשְׂרָאֵל הוּא וּבָא מֵאֶרֶץ
from-land but-he-came he Israel from-people-of-you not who the-foreigner

רְחוֹקָה לְמַעַן שְׁמֶךָ׃ כִּי יִשְׁמְעוּן אֶת־ שִׁמְךָ
name-of-you *** they-will-hear for (42) name-of-you because-of distant

הַגָּדוֹל וְאֶת־ יָדְךָ הַחֲזָקָה וּזְרֹעֲךָ הַנְּטוּיָה
the-being-outstretched and-arm-of-you the-mighty hand-of-you and the-great

וּבָא וְהִתְפַּלֵּל אֶל־ הַבַּיִת הַזֶּה׃ אַתָּה תִּשְׁמַע
you-hear you (43) the-this the-temple toward and-he-prays when-he-comes

הַשָּׁמַיִם מְכוֹן שִׁבְתֶּךָ וְעָשִׂיתָ כְּכֹל אֲשֶׁר־ יִקְרָא אֵלֶיךָ
of-you he-asks that as-all and-you-do to-dwell-you place-of the-heavens

הַנָּכְרִי לְמַעַן יֵדְעוּן כָּל־ עַמֵּי הָאָרֶץ אֶת־
*** the-earth peoples-of all-of they-may-know so-that the-foreigner

שְׁמֶךָ לְיִרְאָה אֹתְךָ כְּעַמְּךָ יִשְׂרָאֵל וְלָדַעַת כִּי־ שִׁמְךָ
Name-of-you that and-to-know Israel as-people-of-you you to-fear name-of-you

נִקְרָא עַל־ הַבַּיִת הַזֶּה אֲשֶׁר בָּנִיתִי׃ כִּי־ יֵצֵא
he-goes-out when (44) I-built that the-this the-house on he-is-called

עַמְּךָ לַמִּלְחָמָה עַל־ אֹיְבוֹ בַּדֶּרֶךְ אֲשֶׁר
that in-the-way being-enemy-of-him against to-the-war people-of-you

תִּשְׁלָחֵם וְהִתְפַּלְלוּ אֶל־ יְהוָה דֶּרֶךְ הָעִיר אֲשֶׁר בָּחַרְתָּ
you-chose that the-city direction-of Yahweh to and-they-pray you-send-them

בָּהּ וְהַבַּיִת אֲשֶׁר־ בָּנִתִי לִשְׁמֶךָ׃ וְשָׁמַעְתָּ
then-you-hear (45) for-Name-of-you I-built that and-the-temple to-her

הַשָּׁמַיִם אֶת־ תְּפִלָּתָם וְאֶת־ תְּחִנָּתָם וְעָשִׂיתָ מִשְׁפָּטָם׃
cause-of-them and-you-uphold plea-of-them and prayer-of-them *** the-heavens

כִּי יֶחֶטְאוּ־ לָךְ כִּי אֵין אָדָם אֲשֶׁר לֹא־ יֶחֱטָא וְאָנַפְתָּ
and-you-are-angry he-sins not who person no for against-you they-sin when (46)

afflictions of his own heart, and spreading out his hands toward this temple—
[39]then hear from heaven, your dwelling place. Forgive and act; deal with each man according to all he does, since you know his heart (for you alone know the hearts of all men), [40]so that they will fear you all the time they live in the land you gave our fathers.

[41]"As for the foreigner who does not belong to your people Israel but has come from a distant land because of your name—[42]for men will hear of your great name and your mighty hand and your outstretched arm—when he comes and prays toward this temple, [43]then hear from heaven, your dwelling place, and do whatever the foreigner asks of you, so that all the peoples of the earth may know your name and fear you, as do your own people Israel, and may know that this house I have built bears your Name.

[44]"When your people go to war against their enemies, wherever you send them, and when they pray to the LORD toward the city you have chosen and the temple I have built for your Name, [45]then hear from heaven their prayer and their plea, and uphold their cause.

[46]"When they sin against you—for there is no one who does not sin—and you become angry with them

בָּם וּנְתַתָּם לִפְנֵי אוֹיֵב וְשָׁבוּם
and-they-take-captive-them being-enemy over-to and-you-give-them with-them

שֹׁבֵיהֶם אֶל־ אֶרֶץ הָאוֹיֵב רְחוֹקָה אוֹ קְרוֹבָה׃
near or far-away the-one-being-enemy land-of to ones-being-captive-of-them

(47) וְהֵשִׁיבוּ אֶל־ לִבָּם בָּאָרֶץ אֲשֶׁר נִשְׁבּוּ־
they-are-held-captive where in-the-land heart-of-them in and-they-change (47)

שָׁם וְשָׁבוּ׀ וְהִתְחַנְּנוּ אֵלֶיךָ בְּאֶרֶץ שֹׁבֵיהֶם
ones-conquering-them in-land-of with-you and-they-plead and-they-repent there

לֵאמֹר חָטָאנוּ וְהֶעֱוִינוּ רָשָׁעְנוּ׃ (48) וְשָׁבוּ
and-they-turn (48) and-we-acted-wickedly and-we-did-wrong we-sinned to-say

אֵלֶיךָ בְּכָל־ לְבָבָם וּבְכָל־ נַפְשָׁם בְּאֶרֶץ
in-land-of soul-of-them and-with-all-of heart-of-them with-all-of to-you

אֹיְבֵיהֶם אֲשֶׁר־ שָׁבוּ אֹתָם וְהִתְפַּלְלוּ אֵלֶיךָ
to-you and-they-pray them they-captured who ones-being-enemies-of-them

דֶּרֶךְ אַרְצָם אֲשֶׁר נָתַתָּה לַאֲבוֹתָם הָעִיר אֲשֶׁר
that the-city to-fathers-of-them you-gave that land-of-them direction-of

בָּחַרְתָּ וְהַבַּיִת אֲשֶׁר־ בָּנִית לִשְׁמֶךָ׃ (49) וְשָׁמַעְתָּ
then-you-hear (49) for-Name-of-you I-built that and-the-temple you-chose

הַשָּׁמַיִם מְכוֹן שִׁבְתְּךָ אֶת־ תְּפִלָּתָם וְאֶת־ תְּחִנָּתָם
plea-of-them and prayer-of-them *** to-dwell-you place-of the-heavens

וְעָשִׂיתָ מִשְׁפָּטָם׃ (50) וְסָלַחְתָּ לְעַמְּךָ אֲשֶׁר
who to-people-of-you and-you-forgive (50) cause-of-them and-you-uphold

חָטְאוּ־ לָךְ וּלְכָל־ פִּשְׁעֵיהֶם אֲשֶׁר פָּשְׁעוּ־
they-committed that offenses-of-them and-to-all-of against-you they-sinned

בָךְ וּנְתַתָּם לְרַחֲמִים לִפְנֵי שֹׁבֵיהֶם
ones-conquering-them before into-mercies and-you-give-them against-you

וְרִחֲמוּם׃ (51) כִּי־ עַמְּךָ וְנַחֲלָתְךָ הֵם
they and-inheritance-of-you people-of-you for (51) so-they-show-mercy-to-them

אֲשֶׁר הוֹצֵאתָ מִמִּצְרַיִם מִתּוֹךְ כּוּר הַבַּרְזֶל׃ (52) לִהְיוֹת
to-be (52) the-iron furnace-of from-midst-of from-Egypt you-brought whom

עֵינֶיךָ פְתֻחוֹת אֶל־ תְּחִנַּת עַבְדְּךָ וְאֶל־ תְּחִנַּת
plea-of and-to servant-of-you plea-of to ones-being-open eyes-of-you

עַמְּךָ יִשְׂרָאֵל לִשְׁמֹעַ אֲלֵיהֶם בְּכֹל קָרְאָם אֵלֶיךָ׃ (53) כִּי־
for (53) to-you to-cry-them in-all to-them to-listen Israel people-of-you

אַתָּה הִבְדַּלְתָּם לְךָ לְנַחֲלָה מִכֹּל עַמֵּי
nations-of from-all-of as-inheritance for-you you-singled-out-them you

הָאָרֶץ כַּאֲשֶׁר דִּבַּרְתָּ בְּיַד׀ מֹשֶׁה עַבְדֶּךָ
servant-of-you Moses by-hand-of you-declared just-as the-earth

and give them over to the enemy, who takes them captive to his own land, far away or near;
47 and if they have a change of heart in the land where they are held captive, and repent and plead with you in the land of their conquerors and say, 'We have sinned, we have done wrong, we have acted wickedly';
48 and if they turn back to you with all their heart and soul in the land of their enemies who took them captive, and pray to you toward the land you gave their fathers, toward the city you have chosen and the temple I have built for your Name;
49 then from heaven, your dwelling place, hear their prayer and their plea, and uphold their cause.
50 And forgive your people, who have sinned against you; forgive all the offenses they have committed against you, and cause their conquerors to show them mercy;
51 for they are your people and your inheritance, whom you brought out of Egypt, out of that iron-smelting furnace.

52 "May your eyes be open to your servant's plea and to the plea of your people Israel, and may you listen to them whenever they cry out to you.
53 For you singled them out from all the nations of the world to be your own inheritance, just as you declared through your servant Moses when

°48 ק בניתי

בְּהוֹצִיאֲךָ אֶת־ אֲבֹתֵינוּ מִמִּצְרַיִם אֲדֹנָי יְהוִה׃ וַיְהִי ׀
and-he-was (54) Yahweh Lord from-Egypt fathers-of-us *** when-to-bring-you

כְּכַלּוֹת שְׁלֹמֹה לְהִתְפַּלֵּל אֶל־ יְהוָה אֵת כָּל־ הַתְּפִלָּה
the-prayer all-of *** Yahweh to to-pray Solomon when-to-finish

וְהַתְּחִנָּה הַזֹּאת קָם מִלִּפְנֵי מִזְבַּח יְהוָה
Yahweh altar-of from-before he-rose the-this and-the-supplication

מִכְּרֹעַ עַל־ בִּרְכָּיו וְכַפָּיו פְּרֻשׂוֹת
ones-being-spread-out and-hands-of-him knees-of-him on from-to-kneel

הַשָּׁמָיִם׃ וַיַּעֲמֹד וַיְבָרֶךְ אֵת כָּל־ קְהַל יִשְׂרָאֵל
Israel assembly-of whole-of *** and-he-blessed and-he-stood (55) the-heavens

קוֹל גָּדוֹל לֵאמֹר׃ בָּרוּךְ יְהוָה אֲשֶׁר נָתַן מְנוּחָה לְעַמּוֹ
to-people-of-him rest he-gave who Yahweh being-praised (56) to-say loud voice

יִשְׂרָאֵל כְּכֹל אֲשֶׁר דִּבֵּר לֹא־ נָפַל דָּבָר אֶחָד מִכֹּל דְּבָרוֹ
promise-of-him of-all-of one word he-failed not he-promised that as-all Israel

הַטּוֹב אֲשֶׁר דִּבֶּר בְּיַד מֹשֶׁה עַבְדּוֹ׃ יְהִי
may-he-be (57) servant-of-him Moses by-hand-of he-promised that the-good

יְהוָה אֱלֹהֵינוּ עִמָּנוּ כַּאֲשֶׁר הָיָה עִם־ אֲבֹתֵינוּ אַל־
not fathers-of-us with he-was just-as with-us God-of-us Yahweh

יַעַזְבֵנוּ וְאַל־ יִטְּשֵׁנוּ׃ לְהַטּוֹת לְבָבֵנוּ אֵלָיו
to-him heart-of-us to-turn (58) may-he-forsake-us and-not may-he-leave-us

לָלֶכֶת בְּכָל־ דְּרָכָיו וְלִשְׁמֹר מִצְוֹתָיו וְחֻקָּיו
and-decrees-of-him commands-of-him to-keep ways-of-him in-all-of to-walk

וּמִשְׁפָּטָיו אֲשֶׁר צִוָּה אֶת־ אֲבֹתֵינוּ׃ וְיִהְיוּ
and-may-they-be (59) fathers-of-us *** he-gave that and-regulations-of-him

דְבָרַי אֵלֶּה אֲשֶׁר הִתְחַנַּנְתִּי לִפְנֵי יְהוָה קְרֹבִים אֶל־ יְהוָה אֱלֹהֵינוּ
God-of-us Yahweh to ones-near Yahweh before I-prayed which these words-of-me

יוֹמָם וָלָיְלָה לַעֲשׂוֹת ׀ מִשְׁפַּט עַבְדּוֹ וּמִשְׁפַּט עַמּוֹ
people-of-him and-cause-of servant-of-him cause-of to-uphold and-night by-day

יִשְׂרָאֵל דְּבַר־ יוֹם בְּיוֹמוֹ׃ לְמַעַן דַּעַת כָּל־ עַמֵּי
peoples-of all-of to-know so-that (60) in-day-of-him day need-of Israel

הָאָרֶץ כִּי יְהוָה הוּא הָאֱלֹהִים אֵין עוֹד׃ וְהָיָה לְבַבְכֶם
heart-of-you but-he-must-be (61) other no the-God he Yahweh that the-earth

שָׁלֵם עִם יְהוָה אֱלֹהֵינוּ לָלֶכֶת בְּחֻקָּיו וְלִשְׁמֹר
and-to-obey by-decrees-of-him to-live God-of-us Yahweh to fully-committed

מִצְוֹתָיו כַּיּוֹם הַזֶּה׃ וְהַמֶּלֶךְ וְכָל־ יִשְׂרָאֵל
Israel and-all-of then-the-king (62) the-this as-the-day commands-of-him

עִמּוֹ זֹבְחִים זֶבַח לִפְנֵי יְהוָה׃ וַיִּזְבַּח שְׁלֹמֹה
Solomon and-he-offered (63) Yahweh before sacrifice ones-offering with-him

you, O Sovereign LORD, brought our fathers out of Egypt."

54When Solomon had finished all these prayers and supplications to the LORD, he rose from before the altar of the LORD, where he had been kneeling with his hands spread out toward heaven. 55He stood and blessed the whole assembly of Israel in a loud voice, saying:

56"Praise be to the LORD, who has given rest to his people Israel just as he promised. Not one word has failed of all the good promises he gave through his servant Moses. 57May the LORD our God be with us as he was with our fathers; may he never leave or forsake us. 58May he turn our hearts to him, to walk in all his ways and to keep the commands, decrees and regulations he gave our fathers. 59And may these words of mine, which I have prayed before the LORD, be near to the LORD our God day and night, that he may uphold the cause of his servant and the cause of his people Israel according to each day's need, 60so that all the peoples of the earth may know that the LORD is God and that there is no other. 61But your hearts must be fully committed to the LORD our God, to live by his decrees and obey his commands, as at this time."

*The Dedication of the Temple*

62Then the king and all Israel with him offered sacrifices before the LORD. 63Solomon

אֵת זֶבַח הַשְּׁלָמִים אֲשֶׁר זָבַח לַיהוָה בָּקָר
cattle to-Yahweh he-offered which the-fellowship-offerings sacrifice-of ***

עֶשְׂרִים וּשְׁנַיִם אֶלֶף וְצֹאן מֵאָה וְעֶשְׂרִים אֶלֶף וַיַּחְנְכוּ
so-they-dedicated thousand and-twenty hundred and-sheep thousand and-two twenty

אֶת־ בֵּית יְהוָה הַמֶּלֶךְ וְכָל־ בְּנֵי יִשְׂרָאֵל׃ בַּיּוֹם
on-the-day (64) Israel sons-of and-all-of the-king Yahweh temple-of ***

הַהוּא קִדַּשׁ הַמֶּלֶךְ אֶת־ תּוֹךְ הֶחָצֵר אֲשֶׁר לִפְנֵי
in-front-of that the-courtyard middle-of *** the-king he-consecrated the-same

בֵית־ יְהוָה כִּי־ עָשָׂה שָׁם אֶת־ הָעֹלָה וְאֶת־
and the-burnt-offering *** there he-offered for Yahweh temple-of

הַמִּנְחָה וְאֵת חֶלְבֵי הַשְּׁלָמִים כִּי־ מִזְבַּח
altar-of for the-fellowship-offerings fat-parts-of and the-grain-offering

הַנְּחֹשֶׁת אֲשֶׁר לִפְנֵי יְהוָה קָטֹן מֵהָכִיל אֶת־ הָעֹלָה וְאֶת־
and the-burnt-offering *** than-to-hold smaller Yahweh before that the-bronze

הַמִּנְחָה וְאֵת חֶלְבֵי הַשְּׁלָמִים׃ וַיַּעַשׂ
so-he-observed (65) the-fellowship-offerings fat-parts-of and the-grain-offering

שְׁלֹמֹה בָעֵת־ הַהִיא ׀ אֶת־ הֶחָג וְכָל־ יִשְׂרָאֵל עִמּוֹ
with-him Israel and-all-of the-festival *** the-that at-the-time Solomon

קָהָל גָּדוֹל מִלְּבוֹא חֲמָת ׀ עַד־ נַחַל מִצְרַיִם לִפְנֵי יְהוָה אֱלֹהֵינוּ
God-of-us Yahweh before Egypt Wadi-of to Hamath from-Lebo vast assembly

שִׁבְעַת יָמִים וְשִׁבְעַת יָמִים אַרְבָּעָה עָשָׂר יוֹם׃ בַּיּוֹם הַשְּׁמִינִי
the-eighth on-the-day (66) day ten four days and-seven-of days seven-of

שִׁלַּח אֶת־ הָעָם וַיְבָרְכוּ אֶת־ הַמֶּלֶךְ וַיֵּלְכוּ
then-they-went the-king *** and-they-blessed the-people *** he-sent-away

לְאָהֳלֵיהֶם שְׂמֵחִים וְטוֹבֵי לֵב עַל כָּל־ הַטּוֹבָה
the-good all-of for heart and-ones-glad-of ones-joyful to-homes-of-them

אֲשֶׁר עָשָׂה יְהוָה לְדָוִד עַבְדּוֹ וּלְיִשְׂרָאֵל עַמּוֹ׃
people-of-him and-for-Israel servant-of-him for-David Yahweh he-did that

וַיְהִי כְּכַלּוֹת שְׁלֹמֹה לִבְנוֹת אֶת־ בֵּית־ יְהוָה וְאֶת־
and Yahweh temple-of *** to-build Solomon when-to-finish and-he-was (9:1)

בֵּית הַמֶּלֶךְ וְאֵת כָּל־ חֵשֶׁק שְׁלֹמֹה אֲשֶׁר חָפֵץ לַעֲשׂוֹת׃
to-do he-desired that Solomon desire-of all-of and the-king palace-of

וַיֵּרָא יְהוָה אֶל־ שְׁלֹמֹה שֵׁנִית כַּאֲשֶׁר נִרְאָה
he-appeared just-as second-time Solomon to Yahweh then-he-appeared (2)

אֵלָיו בְּגִבְעוֹן׃ וַיֹּאמֶר יְהוָה אֵלָיו שָׁמַעְתִּי אֶת־ תְּפִלָּתְךָ
prayer-of-you *** I-heard to-him Yahweh and-he-said (3) at-Gibeon to-him

וְאֶת־ תְּחִנָּתְךָ אֲשֶׁר הִתְחַנַּנְתָּה לְפָנַי הִקְדַּשְׁתִּי אֶת־ הַבַּיִת
the-temple *** I-consecrated before-me you-prayed that plea-of-you and

offered a sacrifice of fellowship offerings[c] to the LORD: twenty-two thousand cattle and a hundred and twenty thousand sheep and goats. So the king and all the Israelites dedicated the temple of the LORD.

64On that same day the king consecrated the middle part of the courtyard in front of the temple of the LORD, and there he offered burnt offerings, grain offerings and the fat of the fellowship offerings, because the bronze altar before the LORD was too small to hold the burnt offerings, the grain offerings and the fat of the fellowship offerings.

65So Solomon observed the festival at that time, and all Israel with him—a vast assembly, people from Lebo[d] Hamath to the Wadi of Egypt. They celebrated it before the LORD our God for seven days and seven days more, fourteen days in all. 66On the following day he sent the people away. They blessed the king and then went home, joyful and glad in heart for all the good the LORD had done for his servant David and his people Israel.

*The LORD Appears to Solomon*

9 When Solomon had finished building the temple of the LORD and the royal palace, and had achieved all he had desired to do, 2the LORD appeared to him a second time, as he had appeared to him at Gibeon. 3The LORD said to him:

"I have heard the prayer and plea you have made before me; I have consecrated this temple, which

[c]63 Traditionally *peace offerings;* also in verse 64
[d]65 Or *from the entrance to*

הַזֶּה אֲשֶׁר בָּנִתָה לָשׂוּם־ שְׁמִי שָׁם עַד־ עוֹלָם וְהָיוּ
and-they-will-be forever to there Name-of-me to-put you-built which the-this

עֵינַי וְלִבִּי שָׁם כָּל־ הַיָּמִים׃ (4) וְאַתָּה אִם־ תֵּלֵךְ
you-walk if and-you (4) the-days all-of there and-heart-of-me eyes-of-me

לְפָנַי כַּאֲשֶׁר הָלַךְ דָּוִד אָבִיךָ בְּתָם־ לֵבָב
heart in-integrity-of father-of-you David he-walked just-as before-me

וּבְיֹשֶׁר לַעֲשׂוֹת כְּכֹל אֲשֶׁר צִוִּיתִיךָ חֻקַּי
decrees-of-me I-command-you that as-all to-do and-in-uprightness

וּמִשְׁפָּטַי תִּשְׁמֹר׃ (5) וַהֲקִמֹתִי אֶת־ כִּסֵּא
throne-of *** then-I-will-establish (5) you-observe and-judgments-of-me

מַמְלַכְתְּךָ עַל־ יִשְׂרָאֵל לְעֹלָם כַּאֲשֶׁר דִּבַּרְתִּי עַל־ דָּוִד
David to I-promised just-as to-forever Israel over kingdom-of-you

אָבִיךָ לֵאמֹר לֹא־ יִכָּרֵת לְךָ אִישׁ מֵעַל כִּסֵּא
throne-of from-on man of-you he-shall-be-cut-off not to-say father-of-you

יִשְׂרָאֵל׃ (6) אִם־ שׁוֹב תְּשֻׁבוּן אַתֶּם וּבְנֵיכֶם מֵאַחֲרַי וְלֹא
and-not from-after-me or-sons-of-you you you-turn to-turn if (6) Israel

תִשְׁמְרוּ מִצְוֹתַי חֻקֹּתַי אֲשֶׁר נָתַתִּי לִפְנֵיכֶם וַהֲלַכְתֶּם
and-you-go before-you I-gave that decrees-of-me commands-of-me you-observe

וַעֲבַדְתֶּם אֱלֹהִים אֲחֵרִים וְהִשְׁתַּחֲוִיתֶם לָהֶם׃ (7) וְהִכְרַתִּי
then-I-will-cut-off (7) to-them and-you-worship other-ones gods and-you-serve

אֶת־יִשְׂרָאֵל מֵעַל פְּנֵי הָאֲדָמָה אֲשֶׁר נָתַתִּי לָהֶם וְאֶת־ הַבַּיִת
the-temple and to-them I-gave that the-land surfaces-of from-on Israel ***

אֲשֶׁר הִקְדַּשְׁתִּי לִשְׁמִי אֲשַׁלַּח מֵעַל פָּנָי
faces-of-me from-before I-will-reject for-Name-of-me I-consecrated that

וְהָיָה יִשְׂרָאֵל לְמָשָׁל וְלִשְׁנִינָה בְּכָל־
among-all-of and-as-object-of-ridicule as-byword Israel then-he-will-become

הָעַמִּים׃ (8) וְהַבַּיִת הַזֶּה יִהְיֶה עֶלְיוֹן כָּל־ עֹבֵר
passing every-of imposing he-is the-this though-the-temple (8) the-peoples

עָלָיו יִשֹּׁם וְשָׁרַק וְאָמְרוּ עַל־ מֶה
why? for and-they-will-say and-he-will-scoff he-will-be-appalled by-him

עָשָׂה יְהוָה כָּכָה לָאָרֶץ הַזֹּאת וְלַבַּיִת הַזֶּה׃
the-this and-to-the-temple the-this to-the-land such Yahweh he-did

(9) וְאָמְרוּ עַל אֲשֶׁר עָזְבוּ אֶת־ יְהוָה אֱלֹהֵיהֶם
God-of-them Yahweh *** they-forsook that because and-they-will-answer (9)

אֲשֶׁר הוֹצִיא אֶת־ אֲבֹתָם מֵאֶרֶץ מִצְרַיִם וַיַּחֲזִקוּ
and-they-embraced Egypt from-land-of fathers-of-them *** he-brought who

בֵּאלֹהִים אֲחֵרִים וַיִּשְׁתַּחֲוֻ לָהֶם וַיַּעַבְדֻם עַל־ כֵּן
this for and-they-served-them to-them and-they-worshiped other-ones on-gods

you have built, by putting my Name there forever. My eyes and my heart will always be there.

4"As for you, if you walk before me in integrity of heart and uprightness, as David your father did, and do all I command and observe my decrees and laws, 5I will establish your royal throne over Israel forever, as I promised David your father when I said, 'You shall never fail to have a man on the throne of Israel.'

6"But if you[e] or your sons turn away from me and do not observe the commands and decrees I have given you[e] and go off to serve other gods and worship them, 7then I will cut off Israel from the land I have given them and will reject this temple I have consecrated for my Name. Israel will then become a byword and an object of ridicule among all peoples. 8And though this temple is now imposing, all who pass by will be appalled and will scoff and say, 'Why has the LORD done such a thing to this land and to this temple?' 9People will answer, 'Because they have forsaken the LORD their God, who brought their fathers out of Egypt, and have embraced other gods, worshiping and serving them—that is why

[e]6 The Hebrew is plural.

°9 ק וישתחוו

הֵבִיא יְהוָה עֲלֵיהֶם אֶת כָּל־ הָרָעָה הַזֹּאת׃ וַיְהִי
and-he-was (10) the-this the-disaster all-of *** God-of-them Yahweh he-brought

מִקְצֵה עֶשְׂרִים שָׁנָה אֲשֶׁר־ בָּנָה שְׁלֹמֹה אֶת־ שְׁנֵי הַבָּתִּים אֶת־
*** the-buildings two-of *** Solomon he-built when year twenty at-end-of

בֵּית יְהוָה וְאֶת־ בֵּית הַמֶּלֶךְ׃ חִירָם מֶלֶךְ־ צֹר נִשָּׂא
he-supplied Tyre king-of Hiram (11) the-king palace-of and Yahweh temple-of

אֶת־ שְׁלֹמֹה בַּעֲצֵי אֲרָזִים וּבַעֲצֵי בְרוֹשִׁים וּבַזָּהָב
and-with-the-gold pines and-with-woods-of cedars with-woods-of Solomon ***

לְכָל־ חֶפְצוֹ אָז יִתֵּן הַמֶּלֶךְ שְׁלֹמֹה לְחִירָם עֶשְׂרִים עִיר
town twenty to-Hiram Solomon the-king he-gave then want-of-him as-all-of

בְּאֶרֶץ הַגָּלִיל׃ וַיֵּצֵא חִירָם מִצֹּר לִרְאוֹת אֶת־ הֶעָרִים
the-towns *** to-see from-Tyre Hiram but-he-went (12) the-Galilee in-land-of

אֲשֶׁר נָתַן־ לוֹ שְׁלֹמֹה וְלֹא יָשְׁרוּ בְּעֵינָיו׃
in-eyes-of-him they-were-pleasant but-not Solomon to-him he-gave that

וַיֹּאמֶר מָה הֶעָרִים הָאֵלֶּה אֲשֶׁר־ נָתַתָּה לִּי אָחִי
brother-of-me to-me you-gave that the-these the-towns what? and-he-asked (13)

וַיִּקְרָא לָהֶם אֶרֶץ כָּבוּל עַד הַיּוֹם הַזֶּה׃ וַיִּשְׁלַח
now-he-sent (14) the-this the-day to Cabul Land-of to-them and-he-called

חִירָם לַמֶּלֶךְ מֵאָה וְעֶשְׂרִים כִּכַּר זָהָב׃ וְזֶה דְּבַר־
account-of now-this (15) gold talent-of and-twenty hundred to-the-king Hiram

הַמַּס אֲשֶׁר־ הֶעֱלָה ׀ הַמֶּלֶךְ שְׁלֹמֹה לִבְנוֹת אֶת־ בֵּית
temple-of *** to-build Solomon the-king he-conscripted that the-forced-labor

יְהוָה וְאֶת־ בֵּיתוֹ וְאֶת־ הַמִּלּוֹא וְאֵת חוֹמַת יְרוּשָׁלִָם
Jerusalem wall-of and the-supporting-terrace and palace-of-him and Yahweh

וְאֶת־ חָצֹר וְאֶת־ מְגִדּוֹ וְאֶת־ גָּזֶר׃ פַּרְעֹה מֶלֶךְ־ מִצְרַיִם עָלָה
he-attacked Egypt king-of Pharaoh (16) Gezer and Megiddo and Hazor and

וַיִּלְכֹּד אֶת־ גֶּזֶר וַיִּשְׂרְפָהּ בָּאֵשׁ וְאֶת־ הַכְּנַעֲנִי
the-Canaanite and with-fire and-he-burned-her Gezer *** and-he-captured

הַיֹּשֵׁב בָּעִיר הָרָג וַיִּתְּנָהּ שִׁלֻּחִים
wedding-gifts then-he-gave-her he-killed in-the-city the-one-inhabiting

לְבִתּוֹ אֵשֶׁת שְׁלֹמֹה׃ וַיִּבֶן שְׁלֹמֹה אֶת־ גֶּזֶר וְאֶת־
and Gezer *** Solomon and-he-rebuilt (17) Solomon wife-of to-daughter-of-him

בֵּית חֹרֹן תַּחְתּוֹן׃ וְאֶת־ בַּעֲלָת וְאֶת־ תַּמֹר בַּמִּדְבָּר בָּאָרֶץ׃
within-the-land in-the-desert Tadmor and Baalath and (18) Lower Horon Beth

וְאֵת כָּל־ עָרֵי הַמִּסְכְּנוֹת אֲשֶׁר הָיוּ לִשְׁלֹמֹה וְאֵת עָרֵי
towns-of and to-Solomon they-were that the-stores cities-of all-of and (19)

הָרֶכֶב וְאֵת עָרֵי הַפָּרָשִׁים וְאֵת ׀ חֵשֶׁק שְׁלֹמֹה אֲשֶׁר חָשַׁק
he-desired that Solomon desire-of and the-horses towns-of and the-chariot

°18 ק תדמר

the LORD brought all this disaster on them.' "

*Solomon's Other Activities*

10 At the end of twenty years, during which Solomon built these two buildings—the temple of the LORD and the royal palace—
11 King Solomon gave twenty towns in Galilee to Hiram king of Tyre, because Hiram had supplied him with all the cedar and pine and gold he wanted.
12 But when Hiram went from Tyre to see the towns that Solomon had given him, he was not pleased with them.
13 "What kind of towns are these you have given me, my brother?" he asked. And he called them the Land of Cabul,[f] a name they have to this day.
14 Now Hiram had sent to the king 120 talents[g] of gold.

15 Here is the account of the forced labor King Solomon conscripted to build the LORD's temple, his own palace, the supporting terraces,[h] the wall of Jerusalem, and Hazor, Megiddo and Gezer.
16 (Pharaoh king of Egypt had attacked and captured Gezer. He had set it on fire. He killed its Canaanite inhabitants and then gave it as a wedding gift to his daughter, Solomon's wife.
17 And Solomon rebuilt Gezer.) He built up Lower Beth Horon,
18 Baalath, and Tadmor[i] in the desert, within his land,
19 as well as all his store cities and the towns for his chariots and for his horses[j]—whatever he desired

[f]13 *Cabul* sounds like the Hebrew for *good-for-nothing.*
[g]14 That is, about 4 1/2 tons (about 4 metric tons)
[h]15 Or *the Millo;* also in verse 24
[i]18 The Hebrew may also be read *Tamar.*
[j]19 Or *charioteers*

לִבְנוֹת בִּירוּשָׁלַ͏ִם וּבַלְּבָנוֹן וּבְכֹל אֶרֶץ
territory-of and-through-all-of and-in-the-Lebanon in-Jerusalem to-build

מֶמְשַׁלְתּוֹ׃ (20) כָּל־ הָעָם הַנּוֹתָר מִן־ הָאֱמֹרִי
the-Amorite from the-one-being-left the-people all-of (20) rule-of-him

הַחִתִּי הַפְּרִזִּי הַחִוִּי וְהַיְבוּסִי אֲשֶׁר לֹא־ מִבְּנֵי
from-sons-of not who and-the-Jebusite the-Hivite the-Perizzite the-Hittite

יִשְׂרָאֵל הֵמָּה׃ (21) בְּנֵיהֶם אֲשֶׁר נֹתְרוּ אַחֲרֵיהֶם בָּאָרֶץ
in-the-land after-them they-remained who descendants-of-them (21) they Israel

אֲשֶׁר לֹא־ יָכְלוּ בְּנֵי יִשְׂרָאֵל לְהַחֲרִימָם וַיַּעֲלֵם
now-he-conscripted-them to-exterminate-them Israel sons-of they-could not who

שְׁלֹמֹה לְמַס־ עֹבֵד עַד הַיּוֹם הַזֶּה׃ (22) וּמִבְּנֵי
but-from-sons-of (22) the-this the-day to being-slave to-forced-labor-of Solomon

יִשְׂרָאֵל לֹא־ נָתַן שְׁלֹמֹה עָבֶד כִּי־ הֵם אַנְשֵׁי הַמִּלְחָמָה וַעֲבָדָיו
and-officials-of-him the-fight men-of they for slave Solomon he-made not Israel

וְשָׂרָיו וְשָׁלִשָׁיו וְשָׂרֵי רִכְבּוֹ
chariot-of-him and-commanders-of and-captains-of-him and-officers-of-him

וּפָרָשָׁיו׃ (23) אֵלֶּה ׀ שָׂרֵי הַנִּצָּבִים אֲשֶׁר עַל־
over who the-ones-being-officials chiefs-of these (23) and-charioteers-of-him

הַמְּלָאכָה לִשְׁלֹמֹה חֲמִשִּׁים וַחֲמֵשׁ מֵאוֹת הָרֹדִים
the-ones-supervising hundreds and-five-of fifty of-Solomon the-project

בָּעָם הָעֹשִׂים בַּמְּלָאכָה׃ (24) אַךְ בַּת־ פַּרְעֹה
Pharaoh daughter-of also (24) in-the-work the-ones-doing over-the-people

עָלְתָה מֵעִיר דָּוִד אֶל־ בֵּיתָהּ אֲשֶׁר בָּנָה־ לָהּ אָז
then for-her he-built that palace-of-her to David from-City-of she-came-up

בָּנָה אֶת־ הַמִּלּוֹא׃ (25) וְהֶעֱלָה שְׁלֹמֹה שָׁלֹשׁ
three Solomon and-he-sacrificed (25) the-supporting-terrace *** he-built

פְּעָמִים בַּשָּׁנָה עֹלוֹת וּשְׁלָמִים עַל־ הַמִּזְבֵּחַ אֲשֶׁר
that the-altar on and-fellowship-offerings burnt-offerings in-the-year times

בָּנָה לַיהוָה וְהַקְטֵיר אִתּוֹ אֲשֶׁר לִפְנֵי יְהוָה
Yahweh before that with-him and-he-burned-incense for-Yahweh he-built

וְשִׁלַּם אֶת־ הַבָּיִת׃ (26) וָאֳנִי עָשָׂה הַמֶּלֶךְ שְׁלֹמֹה
Solomon the-king he-built and-ship (26) the-temple *** so-he-fulfilled

בְּעֶצְיוֹן־ גֶּבֶר אֲשֶׁר אֶת־ אֵלוֹת עַל־ שְׂפַת יַם־ סוּף בְּאֶרֶץ אֱדוֹם׃
Edom in-land-of Reed Sea-of shore-of on Elath near that Geber at-Ezion

וַיִּשְׁלַח חִירָם בָּאֳנִי אֶת־ עֲבָדָיו אַנְשֵׁי אֳנִיּוֹת יֹדְעֵי
ones-knowing-of ships men-of men-of-him *** to-fleet Hiram and-he-sent (27)

הַיָּם עִם עַבְדֵי שְׁלֹמֹה׃ (28) וַיָּבֹאוּ אוֹפִירָה וַיִּקְחוּ
and-they-brought to-Ophir and-they-sailed (28) Solomon men-of with the-sea

to build in Jerusalem, in Lebanon and throughout all the territory he ruled.

20 All the people left from the Amorites, Hittites, Perizzites, Hivites and Jebusites (these peoples were not Israelites),
21 that is, their descendants remaining in the land, whom the Israelites could not exterminate[k]—these Solomon conscripted for his slave labor force, as it is to this day. 22 But Solomon did not make slaves of any of the Israelites; they were his fighting men, his government officials, his officers, his captains, and the commanders of his chariots and charioteers. 23 They were also the chief officials in charge of Solomon's projects—550 officials supervising the men who did the work.

24 After Pharaoh's daughter had come up from the City of David to the palace Solomon had built for her, he constructed the supporting terraces.

25 Three times a year Solomon sacrificed burnt offerings and fellowship offerings[l] on the altar he had built for the LORD, burning incense before the LORD along with them, and so fulfilled the temple obligations.

26 King Solomon also built ships at Ezion Geber, which is near Elath in Edom, on the shore of the Red Sea.[m] 27 And Hiram sent his men—sailors who knew the sea—to serve in the fleet with Solomon's men.
28 They sailed to Ophir and

[k] *21* The Hebrew term refers to the irrevocable giving over of things or persons to the LORD, often by totally destroying them.
[l] *25* Traditionally *peace offerings*
[m] *26* Hebrew *Yam Suph;* that is, Sea of Reeds

משם זהב ארבע־מאות ועשרים ככר ויבאו אל־המלך
the-king to and-they-delivered talent and-twenty hundreds four gold from-there

שלמה׃ ומלכת־ שבא שמעת את־ שמע שלמה לשם
to-name-of Solomon fame-of *** hearing Sheba when-queen-of (10:1) Solomon

יהוה ותבא לנסתו בחידות׃ ותבא
and-she-arrived (2) with-hard-questions to-test-him then-she-came Yahweh

ירושלמה בחיל כבד מאד גמלים נשאים בשמים וזהב
and-gold spices ones-carrying camels very great with-caravan at-Jerusalem

רב־ מאד ואבן יקרה ותבא אל־ שלמה ותדבר אליו
with-him and-she-talked Solomon to and-she-came precious and-stone very much

את כל־אשר היה עם־ לבבה׃ ויגד־ לה שלמה את־
*** Solomon to-her and-he-answered (3) mind-of-her on he-was that all ***

כל־ דבריה לא־ היה דבר נעלם מן־ המלך אשר
that the-king for being-too-hard question he-was not questions-of-her all-of

לא הגיד לה׃ ותרא מלכת־ שבא את כל־ חכמת
wisdom-of all-of *** Sheba queen-of when-she-saw (4) to-her he-explained not

שלמה והבית אשר בנה׃ ומאכל שלחנו
table-of-him and-food-of (5) he-built that and-the-palace Solomon

ומושב עבדיו ומעמד משרתו°
ones-attending-him and-station-of officials-of-him and-seating-of

ומלבשיהם ומשקיו ועלתו אשר
that and-burnt-offering-of-him and-cupbearers-of-him and-robes-of-them

יעלה בית יהוה ולא־ היה בה עוד רוח׃
breath longer in-her he-was then-not Yahweh temple-of he-offered

ותאמר אל־ המלך אמת היה הדבר אשר שמעתי
I-heard that the-report he-was true the-king to and-she-said (6)

בארצי על־ דבריך ועל־ חכמתך׃
wisdom-of-you and-about achievements-of-you about in-country-of-me

ולא־ האמנתי לדברים עד אשר־ באתי ותראינה
and-they-saw I-came when until in-the-things I-believed but-not (7)

עיני והנה לא־ הגד־ לי החצי הוספת חכמה
wisdom you-exceeded the-half to-me he-was-told not and-see! eyes-of-me

וטוב אל־ השמועה אשר שמעתי׃ אשרי אנשיך
men-of-you happinesses-of (8) I-heard that the-report beyond and-wealth

אשרי עבדיך אלה העמדים לפניך תמיד
continually before-you the-ones-standing these officials-of-you happinesses-of

השמעים את־ חכמתך׃ יהי יהוה אלהיך
God-of-you Yahweh may-he-be (9) wisdom-of-you *** the-ones-hearing

brought back 420 talents[n] of
gold, which they delivered to
King Solomon.

### *The Queen of Sheba Visits Solomon*

**10** When the queen of
Sheba heard about the
fame of Solomon and his relation to the name of the LORD,
she came to test him with hard
questions. 2 Arriving at Jerusalem with a very great caravan—with camels carrying
spices, large quantities of gold,
and precious stones—she
came to Solomon and talked
with him about all that she
had on her mind. 3 Solomon
answered all her questions;
nothing was too hard for the
king to explain to her. 4 When
the queen of Sheba saw all the
wisdom of Solomon and the
palace he had built, 5 the food
on his table, the seating of his
officials, the attending servants in their robes, his cup-
bearers, and the burnt
offerings he made at[o] the temple of the LORD, she was overwhelmed.

6 She said to the king, "The
report I heard in my own
country about your achievements and your wisdom is
true. 7 But I did not believe
these things until I came and
saw with my own eyes. In-
deed, not even half was told
me; in wisdom and wealth
you have far exceeded the report I heard. 8 How happy your
men must be! How happy
your officials, who continually
stand before you and hear
your wisdom! 9 Praise be to the

[n]28 That is, about 16 tons (about 14.5 metric tons)
[o]5 Or *the ascent by which he went up to*

°5 ק משרתיו

בָּרוּךְ אֲשֶׁר חָפֵץ בְּךָ לְתִתְּךָ עַל־ כִּסֵּא יִשְׂרָאֵל
Israel throne-of on to-place-you in-you he-delighted who being-praised

בְּאַהֲבַת יְהוָה אֶת־ יִשְׂרָאֵל לְעֹלָם וַיְשִׂימְךָ לְמֶלֶךְ
as-king and-he-made-you to-forever Israel *** Yahweh because-to-love

לַעֲשׂוֹת מִשְׁפָּט וּצְדָקָה׃ וַתִּתֵּן לַמֶּלֶךְ מֵאָה
hundred to-the-king and-she-gave (10) and-righteousness justice to-maintain

וְעֶשְׂרִים ׀ כִּכַּר זָהָב וּבְשָׂמִים הַרְבֵּה מְאֹד וְאֶבֶן יְקָרָה
precious and-stone very to-be-many and-spices gold talent-of and-twenty

לֹא־ בָא כַבֹּשֶׂם הַהוּא עוֹד לָרֹב אֲשֶׁר־ נָתְנָה
she-gave that in-quantity again the-this like-the-spice he-came never

מַלְכַּת־ שְׁבָא לַמֶּלֶךְ שְׁלֹמֹה׃ וְגַם אֳנִי חִירָם אֲשֶׁר־
that Hiram ship-of and-also (11) Solomon to-the-king Sheba queen-of

נָשָׂא זָהָב מֵאוֹפִיר הֵבִיא מֵאֹפִיר עֲצֵי אַלְמֻגִּים הַרְבֵּה
to-be-great almugs woods-of from-Ophir he-brought from-Ophir gold he-brought

מְאֹד וְאֶבֶן יְקָרָה׃ וַיַּעַשׂ הַמֶּלֶךְ אֶת־ עֲצֵי הָאַלְמֻגִּים
the-almugs woods-of *** the-king and-he-made (12) precious and-stone very

מִסְעָד לְבֵית־ יְהוָה וּלְבֵית הַמֶּלֶךְ וְכִנֹּרוֹת וּנְבָלִים
and-lyres and-harps the-king and-for-palace-of Yahweh for-temple-of support

לַשָּׁרִים לֹא בָא־ כֵן עֲצֵי אַלְמֻגִּים וְלֹא
and-never almugs woods-of so-much he-came never for-the-ones-making-music

נִרְאָה עַד הַיּוֹם הַזֶּה׃ וְהַמֶּלֶךְ שְׁלֹמֹה נָתַן לְמַלְכַּת־
to-queen-of he-gave Solomon and-the-king (13) the-this the-day to he-was-seen

שְׁבָא אֶת־ כָּל־ חֶפְצָהּ אֲשֶׁר שָׁאָלָה מִלְּבַד אֲשֶׁר נָתַן־
he-gave what besides she-asked-for that desire-of-her all-of *** Sheba

לָהּ כְּיַד הַמֶּלֶךְ שְׁלֹמֹה וַתֵּפֶן וַתֵּלֶךְ
and-she-returned then-she-left Solomon the-king as-hand-of to-her

לְאַרְצָהּ הִיא וַעֲבָדֶיהָ׃ וַיְהִי מִשְׁקַל הַזָּהָב
the-gold weight-of and-he-was (14) and-servants-of-her she to-country-of-her

אֲשֶׁר־ בָּא לִשְׁלֹמֹה בְּשָׁנָה אֶחָת שֵׁשׁ מֵאוֹת שִׁשִּׁים וָשֵׁשׁ כִּכַּר
talent-of and-six sixty hundreds six each in-year to-Solomon he-came that

זָהָב׃ לְבַד מֵאַנְשֵׁי הַתָּרִים וּמִסְחַר
and-revenue-of the-ones-being-merchants from-men-of besides (15) gold

הָרֹכְלִים וְכָל־ מַלְכֵי הָעֶרֶב וּפַחוֹת הָאָרֶץ׃
the-land and-governors-of the-Arab kings-of and-all-of the-ones-trading

וַיַּעַשׂ הַמֶּלֶךְ שְׁלֹמֹה מָאתַיִם צִנָּה זָהָב שָׁחוּט
being-hammered gold shield two-hundreds Solomon the-king and-he-made (16)

שֵׁשׁ־ מֵאוֹת זָהָב יַעֲלֶה עַל־ הַצִּנָּה הָאֶחָת׃ וּשְׁלֹשׁ־ מֵאוֹת
hundreds and-three-of (17) the-each the-shield into he-went gold hundreds six

LORD your God, who has delighted in you and placed you on the throne of Israel. Because of the LORD's eternal love for Israel, he has made you king, to maintain justice and righteousness."

[10]And she gave the king 120 talents[p] of gold, large quantities of spices, and precious stones. Never again were so many spices brought in as those the queen of Sheba gave to King Solomon.

[11](Hiram's ships brought gold from Ophir; and from there they brought great cargoes of almugwood[r] and precious stones. [12]The king used the almugwood to make supports for the temple of the LORD and for the royal palace, and to make harps and lyres for the musicians. So much almugwood has never been imported or seen since that day.)

[13]King Solomon gave the queen of Sheba all she desired and asked for, besides what he had given her out of his royal bounty. Then she left and returned with her retinue to her own country.

*Solomon's Splendor*

[14]The weight of the gold that Solomon received yearly was 666 talents,[s] [15]not including the revenues from merchants and traders and from all the Arabian kings and the governors of the land.

[16]King Solomon made two hundred large shields of hammered gold; six hundred bekas[t] of gold went into each shield. [17]He also made three

[p] *10* That is, about 4 1/2 tons (about 4 metric tons)
[r] *11* Probably a variant of *algumwood;* also in verse 12
[s] *14* That is, about 25 tons (about 23 metric tons)
[t] *16* That is, about 7 1/2 pounds (about 3.5 kilograms)

מָגִנִּים֙ זָהָב֙ שָׁח֔וּט שְׁלֹ֣שֶׁת מָנִ֔ים זָהָ֖ב יַעֲלֶ֣ה עַל־הַמָּגֵ֑ן
small-shields gold being-hammered three-of minas gold he-went into the-shield

הָאֶחָ֑ת וַֽיִּתְּנֵ֣ם הַמֶּ֔לֶךְ בֵּ֖ית יַ֥עַר הַלְּבָנֽוֹן׃
the-each and-he-put-them the-king Palace-of Forest-of the-Lebanon

וַיַּ֧עַשׂ הַמֶּ֛לֶךְ כִּסֵּא־שֵׁ֖ן גָּד֑וֹל וַיְצַפֵּ֖הוּ זָהָֽב
(18) then-he-made the-king throne-of ivory great and-he-overlaid-them gold

מוּפָֽז׃ שֵׁ֧שׁ מַעֲל֣וֹת לַכִּסֵּ֗ה וְרֹאשׁ־עָגֹ֤ל עָנֵל֙ לַכִּסֵּ֔ה
being-fine (19) six-of steps to-the-throne and-top rounded rounded on-the-throne

מֵאַחֲרָ֑יו וְיָדֹ֣ת מִזֶּ֤ה וּמִזֶּה֙ אֶל־מְק֣וֹם
on-backs-of-him and-armrests on-this-side and-on-that-side at place-of

הַשָּׁ֔בֶת וּשְׁנַ֣יִם אֲרָי֔וֹת עֹמְדִ֖ים אֵ֣צֶל הַיָּדֽוֹת׃ וּשְׁנֵ֥ים עָשָׂ֛ר
the-seat and-two lions ones-standing beside the-armrests (20) and-two ten

אֲרָיִ֗ם עֹמְדִ֥ים שָׁ֛ם עַל־שֵׁ֥שׁ הַֽמַּעֲל֖וֹת מִזֶּ֣ה וּמִזֶּ֑ה לֹֽא־
lions ones-standing there on six-of the-steps on-this-end and-on-that-end not

נַעֲשָׂ֥ה כֵ֛ן לְכׇל־מַמְלָכֽוֹת׃ וְכֹ֗ל כְּלֵ֨י מַשְׁקֵ֜ה
he-was-made like for-any-of kingdoms (21) and-all-of goblets-of drinking-of

הַמֶּ֤לֶךְ שְׁלֹמֹה֙ זָהָ֔ב וְכֹ֗ל כְּלֵ֛י בֵּית־יַ֥עַר הַלְּבָנ֖וֹן
the-king Solomon gold and-all-of articles-of Palace-of Forest-of the-Lebanon

זָהָ֣ב סָג֑וּר אֵ֣ין כֶּ֗סֶף לֹ֤א נֶחְשָׁב֙ בִּימֵ֣י שְׁלֹמֹ֔ה
pure gold nothing-of silver not being-considered in-days-of Solomon

לִמְאֽוּמָה׃ כִּי֩ אֳנִ֨י תַרְשִׁ֤ישׁ לַמֶּ֙לֶךְ֙ בַּיָּ֔ם עִ֖ם אֳנִ֣י
as-anything (22) indeed ship-of Tarshish to-the-king at-the-sea with ship-of

חִירָ֑ם אַחַ֗ת לְשָׁלֹ֤שׁ שָׁנִים֙ תָּב֣וֹא ׀ אֳנִ֣י תַרְשִׁ֔ישׁ נֹֽשְׂאֹת֙ זָהָ֣ב
Hiram once in-three years she-returned ship-of Tarshish carrying gold

וָכֶ֔סֶף שֶׁנְהַבִּ֥ים וְקֹפִ֖ים וְתֻכִּיִּֽים׃ וַיִּגְדַּל֙ הַמֶּ֣לֶךְ
and-silver ivories and-apes and-baboons (23) and-he-was-great the-king

שְׁלֹמֹ֔ה מִכֹּ֖ל מַלְכֵ֣י הָאָ֑רֶץ לְעֹ֖שֶׁר וּלְחׇכְמָֽה׃
Solomon more-than-all-of kings-of the-earth in-wealth and-in-wisdom

וְכׇ֨ל־הָאָ֔רֶץ מְבַקְשִׁ֖ים אֶת־פְּנֵ֣י שְׁלֹמֹ֑ה לִשְׁמֹ֙עַ֙ אֶת־
(24) and-all-of the-earth ones-seeking *** faces-of Solomon to-hear ***

חׇכְמָת֔וֹ אֲשֶׁר־נָתַ֥ן אֱלֹהִ֖ים בְּלִבּֽוֹ׃ וְהֵ֣מָּה מְבִאִ֡ים
wisdom-of-him that he-put God in-heart-of-him (25) and-they ones-bringing

אִ֣ישׁ מִנְחָת֡וֹ כְּלֵ֣י כֶ֩סֶף֩ וּכְלֵ֨י זָהָ֤ב וּשְׂלָמוֹת֙ וְנֵ֣שֶׁק
each gift-of-him articles-of silver and-articles-of gold and-robes and-weapon

וּבְשָׂמִ֔ים סוּסִ֖ים וּפְרָדִ֑ים דְּבַר־שָׁנָ֖ה בְּשָׁנָֽה׃ וַיֶּאֱסֹ֣ף
and-spices horses and-mules event-of year after-year (26) and-he-accumulated

שְׁלֹמֹה֮ רֶ֣כֶב וּפָרָשִׁים֒ וַיְהִי־ל֗וֹ אֶ֤לֶף וְאַרְבַּע־מֵאוֹת֙
Solomon chariot and-horses and-he-was to-him thousand and-four hundreds

hundred small shields of hammered gold, with three minas[u] of gold in each shield. The king put them in the Palace of the Forest of Lebanon. [18]Then the king made a great throne inlaid with ivory and overlaid with fine gold. [19]The throne had six steps, and its back had a rounded top. On both sides of the seat were armrests, with a lion standing beside each of them. [20]Twelve lions stood on the six steps, one at either end of each step. Nothing like it had ever been made for any other kingdom. [21]All King Solomon's goblets were gold, and all the household articles in the Palace of the Forest of Lebanon were pure gold. Nothing was made of silver, because silver was considered of little value in Solomon's days. [22]The king had a fleet of trading ships[v] at sea along with the ships of Hiram. Once every three years it returned carrying gold, silver and ivory, and apes and baboons.

[23]King Solomon was greater in riches and wisdom than all the other kings of the earth. [24]The whole world sought audience with Solomon to hear the wisdom God had put in his heart. [25]Year after year, everyone who came brought a gift—articles of silver and gold, robes, weapons and spices, and horses and mules.

[26]Solomon accumulated chariots and horses; he had fourteen hundred chariots and

[u]17 That is, about 3 3/4 pounds (about 1.7 kilograms)
[v]22 Hebrew of ships of Tarshish

רֶ֫כֶב וּשְׁנֵים־ עָשָׂר אֶ֫לֶף פָּרָשִׁים וַיַּנְחֵם בְּעָרֵי הָרֶ֫כֶב
the-chariot in-cities-of and-he-kept-them horses thousand ten and-two chariot

וְעִם־ הַמֶּ֫לֶךְ בִּירוּשָׁלִָם׃ וַיִּתֵּן הַמֶּ֫לֶךְ אֶת־ הַכֶּ֫סֶף
the-silver *** the-king and-he-made (27) in-Jerusalem the-king and-with

בִּירוּשָׁלִַם כָּאֲבָנִים וְאֵת הָאֲרָזִים נָתַן כַּשִּׁקְמִים
as-the-sycamore-fig-trees he-made the-cedars and as-the-stones in-Jerusalem

אֲשֶׁר־ בַּשְּׁפֵלָה לָרֹב׃ וּמוֹצָא הַסּוּסִים אֲשֶׁר
that the-horses and-importing-of (28) in-number in-the-foothill that

לִשְׁלֹמֹה מִמִּצְרָיִם וּמִקְוֵה סֹחֲרֵי הַמֶּלֶךְ
the-king ones-being-merchants-of and-from-Kue from-Egypt to-Solomon

יִקְחוּ מִקְוֵה בִּמְחִיר׃ וַתַּעֲלֶה וַתֵּצֵא
and-she-came-out and-she-came-up (29) for-price from-Kue they-purchased

מֶרְכָּבָה מִמִּצְרַיִם בְּשֵׁשׁ מֵאוֹת כֶּסֶף וְסוּס בַּחֲמִשִּׁים וּמֵאָה
and-hundred for-fifty and-horse silver hundreds for-six from-Egypt chariot

וְכֵן לְכָל־ מַלְכֵי הַחִתִּים וּלְמַלְכֵי אֲרָם בְּיָדָם
to-hand-of-them Aram and-to-kings-of the-Hittites kings-of to-all-of and-so

יֹצִאוּ׃ וְהַמֶּלֶךְ שְׁלֹמֹה אָהַב נָשִׁים נָכְרִיּוֹת רַבּוֹת
many foreign-ones women he-loved Solomon but-the-king (11:1) they-exported

וְאֶת־ בַּת־ פַּרְעֹה מוֹאֲבִיּוֹת עַמֳּנִיּוֹת אֲדֹמִיֹּת צֵדְנִיֹּת חִתִּיֹּת׃
Hittites Sidonians Edomites Ammonites Moabites Pharaoh daughter-of besides

מִן־ הַגּוֹיִם אֲשֶׁר אָמַר־ יְהוָה אֶל־ בְּנֵי יִשְׂרָאֵל לֹא־ תָבֹאוּ
you-must-go not Israel sons-of to Yahweh he-told which the-nations from (2)

בָהֶם וְהֵם לֹא־ יָבֹאוּ בָכֶם אָכֵן יַטּוּ אֶת־
*** they-will-turn because into-you they-must-come not and-they into-them

לְבַבְכֶם אַחֲרֵי אֱלֹהֵיהֶם בָּהֶם דָּבַק שְׁלֹמֹה לְאַהֲבָה׃
in-love Solomon he-held-fast to-them gods-of-them after heart-of-you

וַיְהִי־ לוֹ נָשִׁים שָׂרוֹת שְׁבַע מֵאוֹת וּפִלַגְשִׁים
and-concubines hundreds seven-of royal-ones wives to-him and-he-was (3)

שְׁלֹשׁ מֵאוֹת וַיַּטּוּ נָשָׁיו אֶת־ לִבּוֹ׃
heart-of-him *** wives-of-him and-they-led-astray hundreds three-of

וַיְהִי לְעֵת זִקְנַת שְׁלֹמֹה נָשָׁיו הִטּוּ אֶת־
*** they-turned wives-of-him Solomon old-age-of at-time-of and-he-was (4)

לְבָבוֹ אַחֲרֵיאֱלֹהִים אֲחֵרִים וְלֹא־ הָיָה לְבָבוֹ שָׁלֵם
fully-devoted heart-of-him he-was and-not other-ones gods after heart-of-him

עִם־ יְהוָה אֱלֹהָיו כִּלְבַב דָּוִיד אָבִיו׃ וַיֵּלֶךְ
and-he-followed (5) father-of-him David as-heart-of God-of-him Yahweh to

שְׁלֹמֹה אַחֲרֵי עַשְׁתֹּרֶת אֱלֹהֵי צִדֹנִים וְאַחֲרֵי מִלְכֹּם שִׁקֻּץ
detestable-one-of Milcom and-after Sidonians gods-of Ashtoreth after Solomon

twelve thousand horses,[w]
which he kept in the chariot
cities and also with him in
Jerusalem. 27The king made
silver as common in Jerusalem
as stones, and cedar as plentiful as sycamore-fig trees in the
foothills. 28Solomon's horses
were imported from Egypt[x]
and from Kue[y]—the royal merchants purchased them from
Kue. 29They imported a chariot
from Egypt for six hundred
shekels[z] of silver, and a horse
for a hundred and fifty.[a] They
also exported them to all the
kings of the Hittites and of the
Arameans.

*Solomon's Wives*

11 King Solomon, how-
ever, loved many for-
eign women besides Phar-
aoh's daughter—Moabites,
Ammonites, Edomites,
Sidonians and Hittites. 2They
were from nations about
which the LORD had told the
Israelites, "You must not intermarry with them, because
they will surely turn your
hearts after their gods."
Nevertheless, Solomon held
fast to them in love. 3He had
seven hundred wives of royal
birth and three hundred concubines, and his wives led
him astray. 4As Solomon grew
old, his wives turned his heart
after other gods, and his heart
was not fully devoted to the
LORD his God, as the heart of
David his father had been. 5He
followed Ashtoreth the goddess of the Sidonians, and
Molech[b] the detestable god of

[w]26 Or *charioteers*
[x]28 Or possibly *Muzur*, a region in Cilicia; also in verse 29
[y]28 Probably *Cilicia*
[z]29 That is, about 15 pounds (about 7 kilograms)
[a]29 That is, about 3 3/4 pounds (about 1.7 kilograms)
[b]5 Hebrew *Milcom*; also in verse 33

עַמֹּנִים׃ וַיַּעַשׂ שְׁלֹמֹה הָרַע בְּעֵינֵי יְהוָה וְלֹא

and-not Yahweh in-eyes-of the-evil Solomon so-he-did (6) Ammonites

מִלֵּא אַחֲרֵי יְהוָה כְּדָוִד אָבִיו׃ אָז יִבְנֶה

he-built then (7) father-of-him as-David Yahweh after he-was-complete

שְׁלֹמֹה בָּמָה לִכְמוֹשׁ שִׁקֻּץ מוֹאָב בָּהָר אֲשֶׁר עַל־

to that on-the-hill Moab detestable-one-of for-Chemosh high-place Solomon

פְּנֵי יְרוּשָׁלָםִ וּלְמֹלֶךְ שִׁקֻּץ בְּנֵי עַמּוֹן׃

Ammon sons-of detestable-one-of and-for-Molech Jerusalem east-of

וְכֵן עָשָׂה לְכָל־ נָשָׁיו הַנָּכְרִיּוֹת מַקְטִירוֹת

ones-burning-incense the-foreign-ones wives-of-him for-all-of he-did and-same (8)

וּמְזַבְּחוֹת לֵאלֹהֵיהֶן׃ וַיִּתְאַנַּף יְהוָה

Yahweh and-he-became-angry (9) to-gods-of-them and-ones-offering-sacrifices

בִּשְׁלֹמֹה כִּי־ נָטָה לְבָבוֹ מֵעִם יְהוָה אֱלֹהֵי

God-of Yahweh from-with heart-of-him he-turned-away because with-Solomon

יִשְׂרָאֵל הַנִּרְאָה אֵלָיו פַּעֲמָיִם׃ וְצִוָּה אֵלָיו עַל־

about to-him though-he-commanded (10) twice to-him who-he-appeared Israel

הַדָּבָר הַזֶּה לְבִלְתִּי־ לֶכֶת אַחֲרֵי אֱלֹהִים אֲחֵרִים וְלֹא שָׁמַר אֵת

*** he-kept but-not other-ones gods after to-follow not the-this the-thing

אֲשֶׁר־ צִוָּה יְהוָה׃ וַיֹּאמֶר יְהוָה לִשְׁלֹמֹה יַעַן אֲשֶׁר

that since to-Solomon Yahweh so-he-said (11) Yahweh he-commanded what

הָיְתָה־ זֹּאת עִמָּךְ וְלֹא שָׁמַרְתָּ בְּרִיתִי וְחֻקֹּתַי

and-decrees-of-me covenant-of-me you-kept and-not with-you this she-was

אֲשֶׁר צִוִּיתִי עָלֶיךָ קָרֹעַ אֶקְרַע אֶת־ הַמַּמְלָכָה

the-kingdom *** I-will-tear-away to-tear-away to-you I-commanded which

מֵעָלֶיךָ וּנְתַתִּיהָ לְעַבְדֶּךָ׃ אַךְ־

nevertheless (12) to-subordinate-of-you and-I-will-give-her from-on-you

בְּיָמֶיךָ לֹא אֶעֱשֶׂנָּה לְמַעַן דָּוִד אָבִיךָ מִיַּד

from-hand-of father-of-you David for-sake-of I-will-do-her not in-days-of-you

בִּנְךָ אֶקְרָעֶנָּה׃ רַק אֶת־ כָּל־ הַמַּמְלָכָה לֹא

not the-kingdom whole-of *** yet (13) I-will-tear-her son-of-you

אֶקְרָע שֵׁבֶט אֶחָד אֶתֵּן לִבְנֶךָ לְמַעַן דָּוִד

David for-sake-of to-son-of-you I-will-give one tribe I-will-tear-away

עַבְדִּי וּלְמַעַן יְרוּשָׁלַםִ אֲשֶׁר בָּחָרְתִּי׃ וַיָּקֶם

then-he-raised-up (14) I-chose which Jerusalem and-for-sake-of servant-of-me

יְהוָה שָׂטָן לִשְׁלֹמֹה אֵת הֲדַד הָאֲדֹמִי מִזֶּרַע הַמֶּלֶךְ

the-king from-line-of the-Edomite Hadad *** against-Solomon adversary Yahweh

הוּא בֶּאֱדוֹם׃ וַיְהִי בִּהְיוֹת דָּוִד אֶת־ אֱדוֹם בַּעֲלוֹת יוֹאָב

Joab when-to-go-up Edom against David when-to-be and-he-was (15) in-Edom he

the Ammonites. [6]So Solomon did evil in the eyes of the LORD; he did not follow the LORD completely, as David his father had done.

[7]On a hill east of Jerusalem, Solomon built a high place for Chemosh the detestable god of Moab, and for Molech the detestable god of the Ammonites. [8]He did the same for all his foreign wives, who burned incense and offered sacrifices to their gods.

[9]The LORD became angry with Solomon because his heart had turned away from the LORD, the God of Israel, who had appeared to him twice. [10]Although he had forbidden Solomon to follow other gods, Solomon did not keep the LORD's command. [11]So the LORD said to Solomon, "Since this is your attitude and you have not kept my covenant and my decrees, which I commanded you, I will most certainly tear the kingdom away from you and give it to one of your subordinates. [12]Nevertheless, for the sake of David your father, I will not do it during your lifetime. I will tear it out of the hand of your son. [13]Yet I will not tear the whole kingdom from him, but will give him one tribe for the sake of David my servant and for the sake of Jerusalem, which I have chosen."

*Solomon's Adversaries*

[14]Then the LORD raised up against Solomon an adversary, Hadad the Edomite, from the royal line of Edom. [15]Earlier when David was fighting with Edom, Joab the

שַׂר הַצָּבָא לְקַבֵּר אֶת־ הַחֲלָלִים וַיַּךְ כָּל־
all-of then-he-struck-down the-dead-ones *** to-bury the-army commander-of

זָכָר בֶּאֱדוֹם׃ כִּי שֵׁשֶׁת חֳדָשִׁים יָשַׁב־ שָׁם יוֹאָב וְכָל־ יִשְׂרָאֵל
Israel and-all-of Joab there he-stayed months six-of for (16) in-Edom man

עַד־ הִכְרִית כָּל־ זָכָר בֶּאֱדוֹם׃ וַיִּבְרַח אֲדַד הוּא וַאֲנָשִׁים
and-men he Hadad but-he-fled (17) in-Edom man all-of he-destroyed until

אֲדֹמִיִּים מֵעַבְדֵי אָבִיו אִתּוֹ לָבוֹא מִצְרָיִם וַהֲדַד נַעַר
boy now-Hadad Egypt to-go with-him father-of-him from-officials-of Edomites

קָטָן׃ וַיָּקֻמוּ מִמִּדְיָן וַיָּבֹאוּ פָּארָן וַיִּקְחוּ
then-they-took Paran and-they-went from-Midian and-they-set-out (18) small

אֲנָשִׁים עִמָּם מִפָּארָן וַיָּבֹאוּ מִצְרַיִם אֶל־פַּרְעֹה מֶלֶךְ־מִצְרַיִם
Egypt king-of Pharaoh to Egypt and-they-went from-Paran with-them men

וַיִּתֶּן־ לוֹ בַיִת וְלֶחֶם אָמַר לוֹ וְאֶרֶץ נָתַן
he-gave and-land from-him he-provided and-food house to-him and-he-gave

לוֹ׃ וַיִּמְצָא הֲדַד חֵן בְּעֵינֵי פַרְעֹה מְאֹד וַיִּתֶּן־
so-he-gave great Pharaoh in-eyes-of favor Hadad and-he-found (19) to-him

לוֹ אִשָּׁה אֶת־ אֲחוֹת אִשְׁתּוֹ אֲחוֹת תַּחְפְּנֵיס הַגְּבִירָה׃
the-queen Tahpenes sister-of wife-of-him sister-of *** wife to-him

וַתֵּלֶד לוֹ אֲחוֹת תַּחְפְּנֵיס אֵת גְּנֻבַת בְּנוֹ
son-of-him Genubath *** Tahpenes sister-of to-him and-she-bore (20)

וַתִּגְמְלֵהוּ תַחְפְּנֵס בְּתוֹךְ בֵּית פַּרְעֹה וַיְהִי
and-he-was Pharaoh palace-of inside-of Tahpenes and-she-brought-up-him

גְנֻבַת בֵּית פַּרְעֹה בְּתוֹךְ בְּנֵי פַרְעֹה׃ וַהֲדַד
and-Hadad (21) Pharaoh children-of in-among Pharaoh palace-of Genubath

שָׁמַע בְּמִצְרַיִם כִּי־ שָׁכַב דָּוִד עִם־ אֲבֹתָיו וְכִי־
and-that fathers-of-him with David he-rested that in-Egypt he-heard

מֵת יוֹאָב שַׂר־ הַצָּבָא וַיֹּאמֶר הֲדַד אֶל־ פַּרְעֹה
Pharaoh to Hadad then-he-said the-army commander-of Joab he-was-dead

שַׁלְּחֵנִי וְאֵלֵךְ אֶל־ אַרְצִי׃ וַיֹּאמֶר לוֹ פַרְעֹה
Pharaoh to-him and-he-asked (22) country-of-me to so-I-may-return let-go-me!

כִּי מָה־ אַתָּה חָסֵר עִמִּי וְהִנְּךָ מְבַקֵּשׁ לָלֶכֶת אֶל־
to to-go-back wanting so-see-you! with-me lacking you what? indeed

אַרְצֶךָ וַיֹּאמֶר ׀ לֹא כִּי שַׁלֵּחַ תְּשַׁלְּחֵנִי׃
you-let-go-me to-let-go but nothing and-he-replied country-of-you

וַיָּקֶם אֱלֹהִים לוֹ שָׂטָן אֶת־ רְזוֹן בֶּן־ אֶלְיָדָע אֲשֶׁר
who Eliada son-of Rezon *** adversary against-him God and-he-raised-up (23)

בָּרַח מֵאֵת הֲדַדְעֶזֶר מֶלֶךְ־ צוֹבָה אֲדֹנָיו׃ וַיִּקְבֹּץ
and-he-gathered (24) masters-of-him Zobah king-of Hadadezer from he-fled

commander of the army, who had gone up to bury the dead, had struck down all the men in Edom.
[16]Joab and all the Israelites stayed there for six months, until they had destroyed all the men in Edom.
[17]But Hadad, still only a boy, fled to Egypt with some Edomite officials who had served his father.
[18]They set out from Midian and went to Paran. Then taking men from Paran with them, they went to Egypt, to Pharaoh king of Egypt, who gave Hadad a house and land and provided him with food.

[19]Pharaoh was so pleased with Hadad that he gave him a sister of his own wife, Queen Tahpenes, in marriage.
[20]The sister of Tahpenes bore him a son named Genubath, whom Tahpenes brought up in the royal palace. There Genubath lived with Pharaoh's own children.

[21]While he was in Egypt, Hadad heard that David rested with his fathers and that Joab the commander of the army was also dead. Then Hadad said to Pharaoh, "Let me go, that I may return to my own country."

[22]"What have you lacked here that you want to go back to your own country?" Pharaoh asked.

"Nothing," Hadad replied, "but do let me go!"

[23]And God raised up against Solomon another adversary, Rezon son of Eliada, who had fled from his master, Hadadezer king of Zobah.
[24]He gathered men around him and

עָלָיו אֲנָשִׁים וַיְהִי שַׂר־ גְּדוּד בַּהֲרֹג דָּוִד
David when-to-destroy rebel-band leader-of and-he-became men around-him

אֹתָם וַיֵּלְכוּ דַמֶּשֶׂק וַיֵּשְׁבוּ בָהּ וַיִּמְלְכוּ
and-they-took-control in-her and-they-settled Damascus and-they-went them

בְּדַמָּשֶׂק׃ וַיְהִי שָׂטָן לְיִשְׂרָאֵל כָּל־ יְמֵי שְׁלֹמֹה
Solomon days-of all-of to-Israel adversary and-he-was (25) over-Damascus

וְאֶת־ הָרָעָה אֲשֶׁר הֲדָד וַיָּקָץ בְּיִשְׂרָאֵל וַיִּמְלֹךְ
and-he-ruled toward-Israel and-he-was-hostile Hadad that the-trouble plus

עַל־אֲרָם׃ וְיָרָבְעָם בֶּן־ נְבָט אֶפְרָתִי מִן־ הַצְּרֵדָה
the-Zeredah from Ephraimite Nebat son-of and-Jeroboam (26) Aram in

וְשֵׁם אִמּוֹ צְרוּעָה אִשָּׁה אַלְמָנָה עֶבֶד לִשְׁלֹמֹה
of-Solomon official widow woman Zeruah mother-of-him and-name-of

וַיָּרֶם יָד בַּמֶּלֶךְ׃ וְזֶה הַדָּבָר אֲשֶׁר־ הֵרִים
he-raised how the-account and-this (27) against-the-king hand and-he-raised

יָד בַּמֶּלֶךְ שְׁלֹמֹה בָּנָה אֶת־ הַמִּלּוֹא סָגַר
he-filled the-supporting-terrace *** he-built Solomon against-the-king hand

אֶת־פֶּרֶץ עִיר דָּוִד אָבִיו׃ וְהָאִישׁ יָרָבְעָם גִּבּוֹר חָיִל
standing man-of Jeroboam now-the-man (28) father-of-him David city-of gap ***

וַיַּרְא שְׁלֹמֹה אֶת־ הַנַּעַר כִּי־ עֹשֵׂה מְלָאכָה הוּא וַיַּפְקֵד
then-he-put-in-charge he work doing that the-young-man *** Solomon when-he-saw

אֹתוֹ לְכָל־ סֵבֶל בֵּית יוֹסֵף׃ וַיְהִי בָּעֵת
about-the-time and-he-was (29) Joseph house-of labor-force of-whole-of him

הַהִיא וְיָרָבְעָם יָצָא מִירוּשָׁלִַם וַיִּמְצָא אֹתוֹ אֲחִיָּה
Ahijah him and-he-met from-Jerusalem he-went-out now-Jeroboam the-this

הַשִּׁילֹנִי הַנָּבִיא בַּדֶּרֶךְ וְהוּא מִתְכַּסֶּה בְּשַׂלְמָה חֲדָשָׁה
new with-cloak being-clothed and-he on-the-way the-prophet the-Shilonite

וּשְׁנֵיהֶם לְבַדָּם בַּשָּׂדֶה׃ וַיִּתְפֹּשׂ אֲחִיָּה
Ahijah and-he-took-hold (30) in-the-country by-themselves and-two-of-them

בַּשַּׂלְמָה הַחֲדָשָׁה אֲשֶׁר עָלָיו וַיִּקְרָעֶהָ שְׁנֵים עָשָׂר קְרָעִים׃
pieces ten two and-he-tore-her on-him that the-new on-the-cloak

וַיֹּאמֶר לְיָרָבְעָם קַח־ לְךָ עֲשָׂרָה קְרָעִים כִּי כֹה אָמַר
he-says this for pieces ten for-you take! to-Jeroboam then-he-said (31)

יְהוָה אֱלֹהֵי יִשְׂרָאֵל הִנְנִי קֹרֵעַ אֶת־ הַמַּמְלָכָה מִיַּד שְׁלֹמֹה
Solomon from-hand-of the-kingdom *** tearing see-I! Israel God-of Yahweh

וְנָתַתִּי לְךָ אֵת עֲשָׂרָה הַשְּׁבָטִים׃ וְהַשֵּׁבֶט הָאֶחָד
the-one but-the-tribe (32) the-tribes ten *** to-you and-I-will-give

יִהְיֶה־ לּוֹ לְמַעַן עַבְדִּי דָוִד וּלְמַעַן יְרוּשָׁלִַם
Jerusalem and-for-sake-of David servant-of-me for-sake-of for-him he-will-be

became the leader of a band of rebels when David destroyed the forces[d] ⌞of Zobah⌟; the rebels went to Damascus, where they settled and took control.
25Rezon was Israel's adversary as long as Solomon lived, adding to the trouble caused by Hadad. So Rezon ruled in Aram and was hostile toward Israel.

### *Jeroboam Rebels Against Solomon*

26Also, Jeroboam son of Nebat rebelled against the king. He was one of Solomon's officials, an Ephraimite from Zeredah, and his mother was a widow named Zeruah.

27Here is the account of how he rebelled against the king: Solomon had built the supporting terraces[e] and had filled in the gap in the wall of the city of David his father.
28Now Jeroboam was a man of standing, and when Solomon saw how well the young man did his work, he put him in charge of the whole labor force of the house of Joseph.

29About that time Jeroboam was going out of Jerusalem, and Ahijah the prophet of Shiloh met him on the way, wearing a new cloak. The two of them were alone out in the country, 30and Ahijah took hold of the new cloak he was wearing and tore it into twelve pieces. 31Then he said to Jeroboam, "Take ten pieces for yourself, for this is what the LORD, the God of Israel, says: 'See, I am going to tear the kingdom out of Solomon's hand and give you ten tribes.
32But for the sake of my servant David and the city of

[d]24 Hebrew *destroyed them*
[e]27 Or *the Millo*

הָעִיר אֲשֶׁר בָּחַרְתִּי בָּהּ מִכֹּל שִׁבְטֵי יִשְׂרָאֵל׃ יַעַן אֲשֶׁר
that because (33) Israel tribes-of from-all-of to-her I-choose which the-city

עֲזָבוּנִי וַיִּשְׁתַּחֲווּ לְעַשְׁתֹּרֶת אֱלֹהֵי צִדֹנִין לִכְמוֹשׁ
to-Chemosh Sidonian gods-of to-Ashtoreth and-they-worshiped they-forsook-me

אֱלֹהֵי מוֹאָב וּלְמִלְכֹּם אֱלֹהֵי בְנֵי־עַמּוֹן וְלֹא־הָלְכוּ
they-walked and-not Ammon sons-of gods-of and-to-Milcom Moab gods-of

בִדְרָכַי לַעֲשׂוֹת הַיָּשָׁר בְּעֵינַי וְחֻקֹּתַי וּמִשְׁפָּטַי
or-laws-of-me or-statutes-of-me in-eyes-of-me the-right to-do in-ways-of-me

כְּדָוִד אָבִיו׃ וְלֹא־אֶקַּח אֶת־כָּל־הַמַּמְלָכָה
the-kingdom whole-of *** I-will-take but-not (34) father-of-him as-David

מִיָּדוֹ כִּי נָשִׂיא אֲשִׁתֶנּוּ כֹּל יְמֵי חַיָּיו
lives-of-him days-of all-of I-made-him ruler because from-hand-of-him

לְמַעַן דָּוִד עַבְדִּי אֲשֶׁר בָּחַרְתִּי אֹתוֹ אֲשֶׁר שָׁמַר
he-observed who him I-chose whom servant-of-me David for-sake-of

מִצְוֺתַי וְחֻקֹּתָי׃ וְלָקַחְתִּי הַמְּלוּכָה
the-kingdom so-I-will-take (35) and-statutes-of-me commands-of-me

מִיַּד בְּנוֹ וּנְתַתִּיהָ לְּךָ אֵת עֲשֶׂרֶת הַשְּׁבָטִים׃
the-tribes ten-of *** to-you and-I-will-give-her son-of-him from-hand-of

וְלִבְנוֹ אֶתֵּן שֵׁבֶט־אֶחָד לְמַעַן הֱיוֹת־נִיר לְדָוִיד־
for-David lamp to-be so-that one tribe I-will-give and-to-son-of-him (36)

עַבְדִּי כָּל־הַיָּמִים לְפָנַי בִּירוּשָׁלִַם הָעִיר אֲשֶׁר בָּחַרְתִּי
I-chose which the-city in-Jerusalem before-me the-days all-of servant-of-me

לִי לָשׂוּם שְׁמִי שָׁם׃ וְאֹתְךָ אֶקַּח וּמָלַכְתָּ
and-you-will-rule I-will-take but-you (37) there Name-of-me to-put for-me

בְּכֹל אֲשֶׁר־תְּאַוֶּה נַפְשֶׁךָ וְהָיִיתָ מֶּלֶךְ עַל־יִשְׂרָאֵל׃
Israel over king and-you-will-be heart-of-you she-desires that over-all

וְהָיָה אִם־תִּשְׁמַע אֶת־כָּל־אֲשֶׁר אֲצַוֶּךָ וְהָלַכְתָּ
and-you-walk I-command-you that all *** you-do if and-he-will-be (38)

בִדְרָכַי וְעָשִׂיתָ הַיָּשָׁר בְּעֵינַי לִשְׁמוֹר חֻקּוֹתַי
statutes-of-me to-keep in-eyes-of-me the-right and-you-do in-ways-of-me

וּמִצְוֺתַי כַּאֲשֶׁר עָשָׂה דָּוִד עַבְדִּי וְהָיִיתִי עִמָּךְ
with-you and-I-will-be servant-of-me David he-did just-as and-commands-of-me

וּבָנִיתִי לְךָ בַיִת־נֶאֱמָן כַּאֲשֶׁר בָּנִיתִי לְדָוִד
for-David I-built just-as enduring dynasty for-you and-I-will-build

וְנָתַתִּי לְךָ אֶת־יִשְׂרָאֵל׃ וַאְעַנֶּה* אֶת־זֶרַע
descendant-of *** and-I-will-humble (39) Israel *** to-you and-I-will-give

דָּוִד לְמַעַן זֹאת אַךְ לֹא כָל־הַיָּמִים׃ וַיְבַקֵּשׁ שְׁלֹמֹה
Solomon and-he-tried (40) the-days all-of not but this because-of David

Jerusalem, which I have chosen out of all the tribes of Israel, he will have one tribe. 33I
will do this because they have[g]
forsaken me and worshiped
Ashtoreth the goddess of the
Sidonians, Chemosh the god
of the Moabites, and Molech[h]
the god of the Ammonites,
and have not walked in my
ways, nor done what is right
in my eyes, nor kept my statutes and laws as David, Solomon's father, did.
34" 'But I will not take the
whole kingdom out of Solomon's hand; I have made him
ruler all the days of his life for
the sake of David my servant,
whom I chose and who ob-
served my commands and
statutes. 35I will take the kingdom from his son's hands and
give you ten tribes. 36I will
give one tribe to his son so
that David my servant may always have a lamp before me
in Jerusalem, the city where I
chose to put my Name. 37How-
ever, as for you, I will take
you, and you will rule over all
that your heart desires; you
will be king over Israel. 38If
you do whatever I command
you and walk in my ways and
do what is right in my eyes by
keeping my statutes and commands, as David my servant
did, I will be with you. I will
build you a dynasty as enduring as the one I built for David
and will give Israel to you. 39I
will humble David's descendants because of this, but not
forever.' "

g33 Hebrew; Septuagint, Vulgate and Syriac *because he has*
h33 Hebrew *Milcom*

*39 Most mss have the Qere form ( ועֲנֶּה ), though the *ketbib* form should probably remain, with *bateph pathah* under the *aleph* (וַאֲעַנֶּה).

לְהָמִית אֶת־יָרָבְעָם וַיָּקָם יָרָבְעָם וַיִּבְרַח מִצְרַיִם אֶל־שִׁישַׁק

Shishak to Egypt and-he-fled Jeroboam but-he-got-up Jeroboam *** to-kill

מֶלֶךְ־מִצְרַיִם וַיְהִי בְמִצְרַיִם עַד־מוֹת שְׁלֹמֹה׃ וְיֶתֶר

and-rest-of (41) Solomon death-of until in-Egypt and-he-stayed Egypt king-of

דִּבְרֵי שְׁלֹמֹה וְכָל־אֲשֶׁר עָשָׂה וְחָכְמָתוֹ הֲלוֹא־הֵם

they not? and-wisdom-of-him he-did that and-all Solomon events-of

כְּתֻבִים עַל־סֵפֶר דִּבְרֵי שְׁלֹמֹה׃ וְהַיָּמִים אֲשֶׁר

that and-the-days (42) Solomon annals-of book-of in ones-being-written

מָלַךְ שְׁלֹמֹה בִירוּשָׁלִַם עַל־כָּל־יִשְׂרָאֵל אַרְבָּעִים שָׁנָה׃

year forty Israel all-of over in-Jerusalem Solomon he-reigned

וַיִּשְׁכַּב שְׁלֹמֹה עִם־אֲבֹתָיו וַיִּקָּבֵר בְּעִיר

in-city-of and-he-was-buried fathers-of-him with Solomon then-he-rested (43)

דָּוִד אָבִיו וַיִּמְלֹךְ רְחַבְעָם בְּנוֹ תַּחְתָּיו׃

in-place-of-him son-of-him Rehoboam and-he-became-king father-of-him David

וַיֵּלֶךְ רְחַבְעָם שְׁכֶם כִּי שְׁכֶם בָּא כָל־יִשְׂרָאֵל

Israel all-of he-went Shechem for Shechem Rehoboam and-he-went (12:1)

לְהַמְלִיךְ אֹתוֹ׃ וַיְהִי כִּשְׁמֹעַ ׀ יָרָבְעָם בֶּן־נְבָט וְהוּא

now-he Nebat son-of Jeroboam when-to-hear and-he-was (2) him to-make-king

עוֹדֶנּוּ בְמִצְרַיִם אֲשֶׁר בָּרַח מִפְּנֵי הַמֶּלֶךְ שְׁלֹמֹה וַיֵּשֶׁב

and-he-remained Solomon the-king from-before he-fled where in-Egypt still-he

יָרָבְעָם בְּמִצְרָיִם׃ וַיִּשְׁלְחוּ וַיִּקְרְאוּ־לוֹ וַיָּבֹאו

and-he-went for-him and-they-called so-they-sent (3) in-Egypt Jeroboam

יָרָבְעָם וְכָל־קְהַל יִשְׂרָאֵל וַיְדַבְּרוּ אֶל־רְחַבְעָם לֵאמֹר׃

to-say Rehoboam to and-they-said Israel assembly-of and-whole-of Jeroboam

אָבִיךָ הִקְשָׁה אֶת־עֻלֵּנוּ וְאַתָּה עַתָּה הָקֵל

lighten! now but-you yoke-of-us *** he-made-heavy father-of-you (4)

מֵעֲבֹדַת אָבִיךָ הַקָּשָׁה וּמֵעֻלּוֹ הַכָּבֵד אֲשֶׁר־

that the-heavy and-from-yoke-of-him the-harsh father-of-you from-labor-of

נָתַן עָלֵינוּ וְנַעַבְדֶךָּ׃ וַיֹּאמֶר אֲלֵיהֶם לְכוּ עֹד

for go-away! to-them and-he-answered (5) and-we-will-serve-you on-us he-put

שְׁלֹשָׁה יָמִים וְשׁוּבוּ אֵלָי וַיֵּלְכוּ הָעָם׃

the-people so-they-went-away to-me then-come-back! days three

וַיִּוָּעַץ הַמֶּלֶךְ רְחַבְעָם אֶת־הַזְּקֵנִים אֲשֶׁר־הָיוּ

they-were who the-elders with Rehoboam the-king then-he-consulted (6)

עֹמְדִים אֶת־פְּנֵי שְׁלֹמֹה אָבִיו בִּהְיֹתוֹ חַי לֵאמֹר

to-say alive while-to-be-him father-of-him Solomon before *** ones-serving

אֵיךְ אַתֶּם נוֹעָצִים לְהָשִׁיב אֶת־הָעָם־הַזֶּה דָּבָר׃

answer the-this the-people *** to-return ones-advising you how?

°3 ק ויבא

40 Solomon tried to kill Jeroboam, but Jeroboam fled to Egypt, to Shishak the king, and stayed there until Solomon's death.

*Solomon's Death*

41 As for the other events of Solomon's reign—all he did and the wisdom he displayed—are they not written in the book of the annals of Solomon? 42 Solomon reigned in Jerusalem over all Israel forty years. 43 Then he rested with his fathers and was buried in the city of David his father. And Rehoboam his son succeeded him as king.

*Israel Rebels Against Rehoboam*

12 Rehoboam went to Shechem, for all the Israelites had gone there to make him king. 2 When Jeroboam son of Nebat heard this (he was still in Egypt, where he had fled from King Solomon), he returned from[i] Egypt. 3 So they sent for Jeroboam, and he and the whole assembly of Israel went to Rehoboam and said to him: 4 "Your father put a heavy yoke on us, but now lighten the harsh labor and the heavy yoke he put on us, and we will serve you."

5 Rehoboam answered, "Go away for three days and then come back to me." So the people went away.

6 Then King Rehoboam consulted the elders who had served his father Solomon during his lifetime. "How would you advise me to answer these people?" he asked.

[i]2 Or *he remained in*

(7) וַיְדַבְּרוּ אֵלָיו לֵאמֹר אִם־הַיּוֹם תִּהְיֶה־ עֶבֶד לָעָם
to-the-people servant you-will-be the-day if to-say to-him and-they-replied (7)

הַזֶּה וַעֲבַדְתָּם וַעֲנִיתָם וְדִבַּרְתָּ אֲלֵיהֶם
to-them and-you-speak and-you-answer-them and-you-serve-them the-this

דְּבָרִים טוֹבִים וְהָיוּ לְךָ עֲבָדִים כָּל־ הַיָּמִים׃
the-days all-of servants to-you then-they-will-be favorable-ones answers

(8) וַיַּעֲזֹב אֶת־ עֲצַת הַזְּקֵנִים אֲשֶׁר יְעָצֻהוּ וַיִּוָּעַץ
and-he-consulted they-gave-him that the-elders advice-of *** but-he-rejected (8)

אֶת־ הַיְלָדִים אֲשֶׁר גָּדְלוּ אִתּוֹ אֲשֶׁר הָעֹמְדִים
the-ones-serving who with-him they-grew-up who the-young-men ***

לְפָנָיו׃ (9) וַיֹּאמֶר אֲלֵיהֶם מָה אַתֶּם נוֹעָצִים וְנָשִׁיב
that-we-should-give ones-advising you what? to-them and-he-asked (9) before-him

דָּבָר אֶת־ הָעָם הַזֶּה אֲשֶׁר דִּבְּרוּ אֵלַי לֵאמֹר הָקֵל מִן־
from lighten! to-say to-me they-say who the-this the-people *** answer

הָעֹל אֲשֶׁר־ נָתַן אָבִיךָ עָלֵינוּ׃ (10) וַיְדַבְּרוּ אֵלָיו
to-him and-they-replied (10) on-us father-of-you he-put that the-yoke

הַיְלָדִים אֲשֶׁר גָּדְלוּ אִתּוֹ לֵאמֹר כֹּה־ תֹאמַר לָעָם
to-the-people you-tell this to-say with-him they-grew-up who the-young-men

הַזֶּה אֲשֶׁר דִּבְּרוּ אֵלֶיךָ לֵאמֹר אָבִיךָ הִכְבִּיד אֶת־
*** he-made-heavy father-of-you to-say to-you they-said who the-this

עֻלֵּנוּ וְאַתָּה הָקֵל מֵעָלֵינוּ כֹּה תְדַבֵּר אֲלֵיהֶם
to-them you-tell this from-yoke-of-us you-make-light but-you yoke-of-us

קָטָנִּי עָבָה מִמָּתְנֵי אָבִי׃ (11) וְעַתָּה
and-now (11) father-of-me more-than-waists-of he-is-thick little-one-of-me

אָבִי הֶעְמִיס עֲלֵיכֶם עֹל כָּבֵד וַאֲנִי אוֹסִיף עַל־ עֻלְּכֶם
yoke-of-you to I-will-add but-I heavy yoke on-you he-laid father-of-me

אָבִי יִסַּר אֶתְכֶם בַּשּׁוֹטִים וַאֲנִי אֲיַסֵּר אֶתְכֶם
you I-will-scourge but-I with-the-whips you he-scourged father-of-me

בָּעַקְרַבִּים׃ (12) וַיָּבוֹ יָרָבְעָם וְכָל־ הָעָם אֶל־
to the-people and-all-of Jeroboam and-he-returned (12) with-the-scorpions

רְחַבְעָם בַּיּוֹם הַשְּׁלִישִׁי כַּאֲשֶׁר דִּבֶּר הַמֶּלֶךְ לֵאמֹר שׁוּבוּ
come-back! to-say the-king he-said just-as the-third on-the-day Rehoboam

אֵלַי בַּיּוֹם הַשְּׁלִישִׁי׃ (13) וַיַּעַן הַמֶּלֶךְ אֶת־ הָעָם
the-people *** the-king and-he-answered (13) the-third on-the-day to-me

קָשָׁה וַיַּעֲזֹב אֶת־ עֲצַת הַזְּקֵנִים אֲשֶׁר יְעָצֻהוּ׃
they-gave-him that the-elders advice-of *** and-he-rejected harshly

(14) וַיְדַבֵּר אֲלֵיהֶם כַּעֲצַת הַיְלָדִים לֵאמֹר אָבִי
father-of-me to-say the-young-men as-advice-of to-them and-he-spoke (14)

7They replied, "If today you
will be a servant to these
people and serve them and
give them a favorable answer,
they will always be your servants."
8But Rehoboam rejected the
advice the elders gave him
and consulted the young men
who had grown up with him
and were serving him. 9He
asked them, "What is your advice? How should we answer
these people who say to me,
'Lighten the yoke your father
put on us'?"
10The young men who had
grown up with him replied,
"Tell these people who have
said to you, 'Your father put a
heavy yoke on us, but make
our yoke lighter'—tell them,
'My little finger is thicker than
my father's waist. 11My father
laid on you a heavy yoke; I
will make it even heavier. My
father scourged you with
whips; I will scourge you with
scorpions.' "
12Three days later Jeroboam
and all the people returned to
Rehoboam, as the king had
said, "Come back to me in
three days." 13The king answered the people harshly. Rejecting the advice given him
by the elders, 14he followed the
advice of the young men and
said, "My father made your

°7 ק וידברו
°12 ק ויבוא

הִכְבִּיד אֶת־ עֻלְּכֶם וַאֲנִי אֹסִיף עַל־ עֻלְּכֶם אָבִי
father-of-me yoke-of-you to I-will-add but-I yoke-of-you *** he-made-heavy

יִסַּר אֶתְכֶם בַּשּׁוֹטִים וַאֲנִי אֲיַסֵּר אֶתְכֶם בָּעַקְרַבִּים׃
with-the-scorpions you I-will-scourge but-I with-the-whips you he-scourged

וְלֹא־ שָׁמַע הַמֶּלֶךְ אֶל־ הָעָם כִּי־ הָיְתָה סִבָּה
turn-of-events she-was for the-people to the-king he-listened so-not (15)

מֵעִם יְהוָה לְמַעַן הָקִים אֶת־ דְּבָרוֹ אֲשֶׁר דִּבֶּר יְהוָה
Yahweh he-spoke that word-of-him *** to-fulfill in-order-to Yahweh from-with

בְּיַד אֲחִיָּה הַשִּׁילֹנִי אֶל־ יָרָבְעָם בֶּן־ נְבָט׃ וַיַּרְא
when-he-saw (16) Nebat son-of Jeroboam to the-Shilonite Ahijah by-hand-of

כָּל־ יִשְׂרָאֵל כִּי לֹא־ שָׁמַע הַמֶּלֶךְ אֲלֵיהֶם וַיָּשִׁבוּ הָעָם
the-people then-they-gave to-them the-king he-listened not that Israel all-of

אֶת־הַמֶּלֶךְ דָּבָר ׀ לֵאמֹר מַה־ לָּנוּ חֵלֶק בְּדָוִד וְלֹא־ נַחֲלָה בְּבֶן־
in-son-of part and-not in-David share to-us what? to-say answer the-king ***

יִשַׁי לְאֹהָלֶיךָ יִשְׂרָאֵל עַתָּה רְאֵה בֵיתְךָ דָּוִד וַיֵּלֶךְ
so-he-went David house-of-you look-after! now Israel to-tents-of-you Jesse

יִשְׂרָאֵל לְאֹהָלָיו׃ וּבְנֵי יִשְׂרָאֵל הַיֹּשְׁבִים בְּעָרֵי
in-towns-of the-ones-living Israel but-sons-of (17) to-homes-of-him Israel

יְהוּדָה וַיִּמְלֹךְ עֲלֵיהֶם רְחַבְעָם׃ וַיִּשְׁלַח הַמֶּלֶךְ רְחַבְעָם
Rehoboam the-king and-he-sent-out (18) Rehoboam over-them and-he-ruled Judah

אֶת־אֲדֹרָם אֲשֶׁר עַל־ הַמַּס וַיִּרְגְּמוּ כָל־ יִשְׂרָאֵל בּוֹ
on-him Israel all-of but-they-stoned the-forced-labor over who Adoram ***

אֶבֶן וַיָּמֹת וְהַמֶּלֶךְ רְחַבְעָם הִתְאַמֵּץ לַעֲלוֹת בַּמֶּרְכָּבָה
into-the-chariot to-get-up he-managed Rehoboam but-the-king and-he-died stone

לָנוּס יְרוּשָׁלִָם׃ וַיִּפְשְׁעוּ יִשְׂרָאֵל בְּבֵית דָּוִד עַד
to David against-house-of Israel so-they-rebelled (19) Jerusalem to-escape

הַיּוֹם הַזֶּה׃ וַיְהִי כִּשְׁמֹעַ כָּל־ יִשְׂרָאֵל כִּי־ שָׁב
he-returned that Israel all-of when-to-hear and-he-was (20) the-this the-day

יָרָבְעָם וַיִּשְׁלְחוּ וַיִּקְרְאוּ אֹתוֹ אֶל־ הָעֵדָה וַיַּמְלִיכוּ
and-they-made-king the-assembly to him and-they-called then-they-sent Jeroboam

אֹתוֹ עַל־ כָּל־ יִשְׂרָאֵל לֹא הָיָה אַחֲרֵי בֵית־ דָּוִד זוּלָתִי שֵׁבֶט־
tribe-of except David house-of after he-was not Israel all-of over him

יְהוּדָה לְבַדּוֹ׃ וַיָּבֹאוּ רְחַבְעָם יְרוּשָׁלִַם וַיַּקְהֵל° אֶת־
*** then-he-mustered Jerusalem Rehoboam when-he-arrived (21) by-himself Judah

כָּל־ בֵּית יְהוּדָה וְאֶת־ שֵׁבֶט בִּנְיָמִן מֵאָה וּשְׁמֹנִים אֶלֶף
thousand and-eighty hundred Benjamin tribe-of and Judah house-of whole-of

בָּחוּר עֹשֵׂה מִלְחָמָה לְהִלָּחֵם עִם־ בֵּית יִשְׂרָאֵל לְהָשִׁיב אֶת־
*** to-regain Israel house-of against to-make-war fight doing being-chosen

yoke heavy; I will make it even heavier. My father scourged you with whips; I will scourge you with scorpions."
15 So the king did not listen to the people, for this turn of events was from the LORD, to fulfill the word the LORD had spoken to Jeroboam son of Nebat through Ahijah the Shilonite.

16 When all Israel saw that the king refused to listen to them, they answered the king:

> "What share do we have in David,
> what part in Jesse's son?
> To your tents, O Israel!
> Look after your own house, O David!"

So the Israelites went home.
17 But as for the Israelites who were living in the towns of Judah, Rehoboam still ruled over them.

18 King Rehoboam sent out Adoniram,[j] who was in charge of forced labor, but all Israel stoned him to death. King Rehoboam, however, managed to get into his chariot and escape to Jerusalem.
19 So Israel has been in rebellion against the house of David to this day.

20 When all the Israelites heard that Jeroboam had returned, they sent and called him to the assembly and made him king over all Israel. Only the tribe of Judah remained loyal to the house of David.

21 When Rehoboam arrived in Jerusalem, he mustered the whole house of Judah and the tribe of Benjamin—a hundred and eighty thousand fighting men—to make war against the house of Israel and to regain

*j18* Some Septuagint manuscripts and Syriac (see also 1 Kings 4:6 and 5:14); Hebrew *Adoram*

°*21* ק ויבא

הַמְּלוּכָה לִרְחַבְעָם בֶּן־ שְׁלֹמֹה׃ וַיְהִי דְּבַר הָאֱלֹהִים
the-God word-of but-he-came (22) Solomon son-of for-Rehoboam the-kingdom

אֶל־שְׁמַעְיָה אִישׁ־הָאֱלֹהִים לֵאמֹר׃ אֱמֹר אֶל־רְחַבְעָם בֶּן־ שְׁלֹמֹה
Solomon son-of Rehoboam to say! (23) to-say the-God man-of Shemaiah to

מֶלֶךְ יְהוּדָה וְאֶל־ כָּל־ בֵּית יְהוּדָה וּבִנְיָמִין וְיֶתֶר
and-rest-of and-Benjamin Judah house-of whole-of and-to Judah king-of

הָעָם לֵאמֹר׃ כֹּה אָמַר יְהוָה לֹא־ תַעֲלוּ וְלֹא־ תִלָּחֲמוּן
you-fight and-not you-go-up not Yahweh he-says this (24) to-say the-people

עִם־ אֲחֵיכֶם בְּנֵי־ יִשְׂרָאֵל שׁוּבוּ אִישׁ לְבֵיתוֹ כִּי
for to-home-of-him each go-back! Israel sons-of brothers-of-you against

מֵאִתִּי נִהְיָה הַדָּבָר הַזֶּה וַיִּשְׁמְעוּ אֶת־ דְּבַר יְהוָה
Yahweh word-of *** so-they-obeyed the-this the-thing he-is-done from-with-me

וַיָּשֻׁבוּ לָלֶכֶת כִּדְבַר יְהוָה׃ וַיִּבֶן יָרׇבְעָם
Jeroboam then-he-fortified (25) Yahweh as-order-of to-go and-they-returned

אֶת־ שְׁכֶם בְּהַר אֶפְרַיִם וַיֵּשֶׁב בָּהּ וַיֵּצֵא
and-he-went-out in-her and-he-lived Ephraim in-hill-country-of Shechem ***

מִשָּׁם וַיִּבֶן אֶת־ פְּנוּאֵל׃ וַיֹּאמֶר יָרׇבְעָם
Jeroboam and-he-thought (26) Penuel *** and-he-built-up from-there

בְּלִבּוֹ עַתָּה תָּשׁוּב הַמַּמְלָכָה לְבֵית דָּוִד׃ אִם־
if (27) David to-house-of the-kingdom she-will-revert now in-heart-of-him

יַעֲלֶה ׀ הָעָם הַזֶּה לַעֲשׂוֹת זְבָחִים בְּבֵית־ יְהוָה
Yahweh at-temple-of sacrifices to-offer the-this the-people he-goes-up

בִּירוּשָׁלַםִ וְשָׁב לֵב הָעָם הַזֶּה אֶל־ אֲדֹנֵיהֶם
lords-of-them to the-this the-people heart-of then-he-will-return in-Jerusalem

אֶל־ רְחַבְעָם מֶלֶךְ יְהוּדָה וַהֲרָגֻנִי וְשָׁבוּ אֶל־
to and-they-will-return and-they-will-kill-me Judah king-of Rehoboam to

רְחַבְעָם מֶלֶךְ־ יְהוּדָה׃ וַיִּוָּעַץ הַמֶּלֶךְ וַיַּעַשׂ שְׁנֵי
two-of and-he-made the-king and-he-sought-advice (28) Judah king-of Rehoboam

עֶגְלֵי זָהָב וַיֹּאמֶר אֲלֵהֶם רַב־ לָכֶם מֵעֲלוֹת יְרוּשָׁלַםִ
Jerusalem from-to-go-up for-you too-much to-them and-he-said gold calves-of

הִנֵּה אֱלֹהֶיךָ יִשְׂרָאֵל אֲשֶׁר הֶעֱלוּךָ מֵאֶרֶץ מִצְרָיִם׃
Egypt from-land-of they-brought-up-you who Israel gods-of-you here!

וַיָּשֶׂם אֶת־ הָאֶחָד בְּבֵית־ אֵל וְאֶת־ הָאֶחָד נָתַן בְּדָן׃
in-Dan he-set-up the-other and El in-Beth the-one *** and-he-set-up (29)

וַיְהִי הַדָּבָר הַזֶּה לְחַטָּאת וַיֵּלְכוּ הָעָם לִפְנֵי
before the-people and-they-went as-sin the-this the-thing and-he-became (30)

הָאֶחָד עַד־ דָּן׃ וַיַּעַשׂ אֶת־ בֵּית בָּמוֹת
high-places shrine-of *** and-he-built (31) Dan as-far-as the-one

the kingdom for Rehoboam son of Solomon.

22But this word of God came to Shemaiah the man of God: 23"Say to Rehoboam son of Solomon king of Judah, to the whole house of Judah and Benjamin, and to the rest of the people, 24'This is what the LORD says: Do not go up to fight against your brothers, the Israelites. Go home, every one of you, for this is my doing.'" So they obeyed the word of the LORD and went home again, as the LORD had ordered.

*Golden Calves at Bethel and Dan*

25Then Jeroboam fortified Shechem in the hill country of Ephraim and lived there. From there he went out and built up Peniel.[k]

26Jeroboam thought to himself, "The kingdom will now likely revert to the house of David. 27If these people go up to offer sacrifices at the temple of the LORD in Jerusalem, they will again give their allegiance to their lord, Rehoboam king of Judah. They will kill me and return to King Rehoboam."

28After seeking advice, the king made two golden calves. He said to the people, "It is too much for you to go up to Jerusalem. Here are your gods, O Israel, who brought you up out of Egypt." 29One he set up in Bethel, and the other in Dan. 30And this thing became a sin; the people went even as far as Dan to worship the one there.

31Jeroboam built shrines on high places and appointed

[k]25 Hebrew *Penuel,* a variant of *Peniel*

וַיַּעַשׂ כֹּהֲנִים מִקְצוֹת הָעָם אֲשֶׁר לֹא־הָיוּ
they-were not who the-people from-ends-of priests and-he-appointed

מִבְּנֵי לֵוִי׃ וַיַּעַשׂ יָרָבְעָם ׀ חָג בַּחֹדֶשׁ
in-the-month festival Jeroboam and-he-instituted (32) Levi from-sons-of

הַשְּׁמִינִי בַּחֲמִשָּׁה־עָשָׂר יוֹם ׀ לַחֹדֶשׁ כֶּחָג ׀ אֲשֶׁר בִּיהוּדָה
in-Judah that like-festival of-the-month day ten on-five the-eighth

וַיַּעַל עַל־הַמִּזְבֵּחַ כֵּן עָשָׂה בְּבֵית־אֵל לְזַבֵּחַ לָעֲגָלִים
to-the-calves to-sacrifice El in-Beth he-did this the-altar on and-he-offered

אֲשֶׁר־עָשָׂה וְהֶעֱמִיד בְּבֵית אֵל אֶת־כֹּהֲנֵי הַבָּמוֹת אֲשֶׁר
that the-high-places priests-of *** El at-Beth and-he-installed he-made that

עָשָׂה׃ וַיַּעַל עַל־הַמִּזְבֵּחַ ׀ אֲשֶׁר־עָשָׂה בְּבֵית־אֵל בַּחֲמִשָּׁה
on-five El at-Beth he-made that the-altar on and-he-offered (33) he-made

עָשָׂר יוֹם בַּחֹדֶשׁ הַשְּׁמִינִי בַּחֹדֶשׁ אֲשֶׁר־בָּדָא מִלְּבַד
by-himself he-chose that in-the-month the-eighth of-the-month day ten

וַיַּעַשׂ חָג לִבְנֵי יִשְׂרָאֵל וַיַּעַל עַל־הַמִּזְבֵּחַ
the-altar to and-he-went-up Israel for-sons-of festival so-he-instituted

לְהַקְטִיר׃ וְהִנֵּה ׀ אִישׁ אֱלֹהִים בָּא מִיהוּדָה בִּדְבַר
by-word-of from-Judah coming God man-of then-see! (13:1) to-make-offering

יְהוָה אֶל־בֵּית־אֵל וְיָרָבְעָם עֹמֵד עַל־הַמִּזְבֵּחַ לְהַקְטִיר׃
to-make-offering the-altar by standing and-Jeroboam El Beth to Yahweh

וַיִּקְרָא עַל־הַמִּזְבֵּחַ בִּדְבַר יְהוָה וַיֹּאמֶר מִזְבֵּחַ
altar and-he-said Yahweh by-word-of the-altar against and-he-cried-out (2)

מִזְבֵּחַ כֹּה אָמַר יְהוָה הִנֵּה־בֵן נוֹלָד לְבֵית־דָּוִד יֹאשִׁיָּהוּ
Josiah David to-house-of being-born son see! Yahweh he-says this altar

שְׁמוֹ וְזָבַח עָלֶיךָ אֶת־כֹּהֲנֵי הַבָּמוֹת
the-high-places priests-of *** on-you and-he-will-sacrifice name-of-him

הַמַּקְטִרִים עָלֶיךָ וְעַצְמוֹת אָדָם יִשְׂרְפוּ עָלֶיךָ׃
on-you they-will-burn human and-bones-of on-you the-ones-making-offerings

וְנָתַן בַּיּוֹם הַהוּא מוֹפֵת לֵאמֹר זֶה הַמּוֹפֵת אֲשֶׁר
that the-sign this to-say sign the-that on-the-day and-he-gave (3)

דִּבֶּר יְהוָה הִנֵּה הַמִּזְבֵּחַ נִקְרָע וְנִשְׁפַּךְ
and-he-will-be-poured-out being-split-apart the-altar see! Yahweh he-declared

הַדֶּשֶׁן אֲשֶׁר־עָלָיו׃ וַיְהִי כִשְׁמֹעַ הַמֶּלֶךְ אֶת־דְּבַר אִישׁ־
man-of word-of *** the-king when-to-hear and-he-was (4) on-him that the-ash

הָאֱלֹהִים אֲשֶׁר קָרָא עַל־הַמִּזְבֵּחַ בְּבֵית־אֵל וַיִּשְׁלַח
and-he-stretched-out El at-Beth the-altar against he-cried-out that the-God

יָרָבְעָם אֶת־יָדוֹ מֵעַל הַמִּזְבֵּחַ לֵאמֹר ׀ תִּפְשֻׂהוּ וַתִּיבַשׁ
but-she-shriveled seize-him! to-say the-altar from-on hand-of-him *** Jeroboam

priests from all sorts of people, even though they were not Levites. 32 He instituted a festival on the fifteenth day of the eighth month, like the festival held in Judah, and offered sacrifices on the altar. This he did in Bethel, sacrificing to the calves he had made. And at Bethel he also installed priests at the high places he had made. 33 On the fifteenth day of the eighth month, a month of his own choosing, he offered sacrifices on the altar he had built at Bethel. So he instituted the festival for the Israelites and went up to the altar to make offerings.

*The Man of God From Judah*

13 By the word of the LORD a man of God came from Judah to Bethel, as Jeroboam was standing by the altar to make an offering. 2 He cried out against the altar by the word of the LORD: "O altar, altar! This is what the LORD says: 'A son named Josiah will be born to the house of David. On you he will sacrifice the priests of the high places who now make offerings here, and human bones will be burned on you.' " 3 That same day the man of God gave a sign: "This is the sign the LORD has declared: The altar will be split apart and the ashes on it will be poured out."

4 When King Jeroboam heard what the man of God cried out against the altar at Bethel, he stretched out his hand from the altar and said, "Seize him!" But the hand he

°33 ק מלבו

יָדוֹ אֲשֶׁר שָׁלַח עָלָיו וְלֹא יָכֹל לַהֲשִׁיבָהּ
to-pull-back-her he-could so-not toward-him he-stretched that hand-of-him

אֵלָיו׃ וְהַמִּזְבֵּחַ נִקְרָע וַיִּשָּׁפֵךְ הַדֶּשֶׁן
the-ash and-he-was-poured-out he-was-split-apart and-the-altar (5) to-him

מִן־ הַמִּזְבֵּחַ כַּמּוֹפֵת אֲשֶׁר נָתַן אִישׁ הָאֱלֹהִים בִּדְבַר יְהוָה׃
Yahweh by-word-of the-God man-of he-gave that as-the-sign the-altar from

וַיַּעַן הַמֶּלֶךְ וַיֹּאמֶר ׀ אֶל־ אִישׁ הָאֱלֹהִים חַל־ נָא
now! intercede! the-God man-of to and-he-said the-king then-he-replied (6)

אֶת־ פְּנֵי יְהוָה אֱלֹהֶיךָ וְהִתְפַּלֵּל בַּעֲדִי וְתָשֹׁב
so-she-may-be-restored on-behalf-of-me and-pray! God-of-you Yahweh before ***

יָדִי אֵלָי וַיְחַל אִישׁ־ הָאֱלֹהִים אֶת־ פְּנֵי יְהוָה
Yahweh before *** the-God man-of so-he-interceded to-me hand-of-me

וַתָּשָׁב יַד־ הַמֶּלֶךְ אֵלָיו וַתְּהִי כְּבָרִאשֹׁנָה׃
as-before and-she-became to-him the-king hand-of and-she-was-restored

וַיְדַבֵּר הַמֶּלֶךְ אֶל־ אִישׁ הָאֱלֹהִים בֹּאָה־ אִתִּי הַבַּיְתָה
to-the-home with-me come! the-God man-of to the-king and-he-said (7)

וּסְעָדָה וְאֶתְּנָה לְךָ מַתָּת׃ וַיֹּאמֶר אִישׁ־ הָאֱלֹהִים
the-God man-of but-he-answered (8) gift to-you and-I-will-give and-eat!

אֶל־הַמֶּלֶךְ אִם־ תִּתֶּן־ לִי אֶת־ חֲצִי בֵיתֶךָ לֹא אָבֹא
I-would-go not house-of-you half-of *** to-me you-gave if the-king to

עִמָּךְ וְלֹא־ אֹכַל לֶחֶם וְלֹא אֶשְׁתֶּה־ מַּיִם בַּמָּקוֹם
at-the-place waters I-would-drink and-not bread I-would-eat and-not with-you

הַזֶּה׃ כִּי־ כֵן ׀ צִוָּה אֹתִי בִּדְבַר יְהוָה לֵאמֹר לֹא־
not to-say Yahweh by-word-of me he-commanded thus for (9) the-this

תֹאכַל לֶחֶם וְלֹא תִשְׁתֶּה־ מָּיִם וְלֹא תָשׁוּב
you-must-return and-not waters you-must-drink and-not bread you-must-eat

בַּדֶּרֶךְ אֲשֶׁר הָלָכְתָּ׃ וַיֵּלֶךְ בְּדֶרֶךְ אַחֵר וְלֹא־ שָׁב
he-returned and-not another by-road so-he-went (10) you-came that by-the-way

בַּדֶּרֶךְ אֲשֶׁר בָּא בָהּ אֶל־בֵּית־ אֵל׃ וְנָבִיא אֶחָד זָקֵן
old certain now-prophet (11) El Beth to on-her he-came that by-the-way

יֹשֵׁב בְּבֵית־ אֵל וַיָּבוֹא בְנוֹ וַיְסַפֶּר־ לוֹ אֶת־ כָּל־
all-of *** to-him and-he-told son-of-him and-he-came El in-Beth living

הַמַּעֲשֶׂה אֲשֶׁר־עָשָׂה אִישׁ־הָאֱלֹהִים ׀ הַיּוֹם בְּבֵית־אֵל אֶת־הַדְּבָרִים אֲשֶׁר
that the-things *** El in-Beth the-day the-God man-of he-did that the-deed

דִּבֶּר אֶל־ הַמֶּלֶךְ וַיְסַפְּרוּם לַאֲבִיהֶם׃ וַיְדַבֵּר
and-he-asked (12) to-father-of-them and-they-told-them the-king to he-said

אֲלֵהֶם אֲבִיהֶם אֵי־ זֶה הַדֶּרֶךְ הָלָךְ וַיִּרְאוּ
and-they-showed he-went the-way this where? father-of-them to-them

stretched out toward the man
shriveled up, so that he could
not pull it back. 5Also, the altar
was split apart and its ashes
poured out according to the
sign given by the man of God
by the word of the LORD.
6Then the king said to the
man of God, "Intercede with
the LORD your God and pray
for me that my hand may be
restored." So the man of God
interceded with the LORD, and
the king's hand was restored
and became as it was before.
7The king said to the man of
God, "Come home with me
and have something to eat,
and I will give you a gift."
8But the man of God an-
swered the king, "Even if you
were to give me half your
possessions, I would not go
with you, nor would I eat
bread or drink water here. 9For
I was commanded by the
word of the LORD: 'You must
not eat bread or drink water or
return by the way you came.' "
10So he took another road and
did not return by the way he
had come to Bethel.
11Now there was a certain
old prophet living in Bethel,
whose sons came and told him
all that the man of God had
done there that day. They also
told their father what he had
said to the king. 12Their father
asked them, "Which way did
he go?" And his sons showed

בָּנָיו אֶת־הַדֶּרֶךְ אֲשֶׁר הָלַךְ אִישׁ הָאֱלֹהִים אֲשֶׁר־בָּא מִיהוּדָה׃
from-Judah he-came who the-God man-of he-went that the-road *** sons-of-him

וַיֹּאמֶר אֶל־בָּנָיו חִבְשׁוּ־לִי הַחֲמוֹר וַיַּחְבְּשׁוּ־
and-they-saddled the-donkey for-me saddle! sons-of-him to so-he-said (13)

לוֹ הַחֲמוֹר וַיִּרְכַּב עָלָיו׃ וַיֵּלֶךְ אַחֲרֵי אִישׁ
man-of after and-he-rode (14) on-him and-he-mounted the-donkey for-him

הָאֱלֹהִים וַיִּמְצָאֵהוּ יֹשֵׁב תַּחַת הָאֵלָה וַיֹּאמֶר אֵלָיו
to-him and-he-asked the-oak-tree under sitting and-he-found-him the-God

הַאַתָּה אִישׁ־הָאֱלֹהִים אֲשֶׁר־בָּאתָ מִיהוּדָה וַיֹּאמֶר אָנִי׃ וַיֹּאמֶר
so-he-said (15) I and-he-replied from-Judah you-came who the-God man-of you?

אֵלָיו לֵךְ אִתִּי הַבַּיְתָה וֶאֱכֹל לָחֶם׃ וַיֹּאמֶר לֹא אוּכַל
I-can not and-he-said (16) bread and-eat! to-the-home with-me come! to-him

לָשׁוּב אִתָּךְ וְלָבוֹא אִתָּךְ וְלֹא־אֹכַל לֶחֶם וְלֹא־
and-not bread I-can-eat and-not with-you and-to-go with-you to-turn-back

אֶשְׁתֶּה אִתְּךָ מַיִם בַּמָּקוֹם הַזֶּה׃ כִּי־דָבָר אֵלַי
to-me he-told for (17) the-this in-the-place waters with-you I-can-drink

בִּדְבַר יְהוָה לֹא־תֹאכַל לֶחֶם וְלֹא־תִשְׁתֶּה שָׁם מָיִם
waters there you-must-drink and-not bread you-must-eat not Yahweh by-word-of

לֹא־תָשׁוּב לָלֶכֶת בַּדֶּרֶךְ אֲשֶׁר־הָלַכְתָּ בָּהּ׃ וַיֹּאמֶר
and-he-answered (18) on-her you-came that by-the-way to-go you-must-return not

לוֹ גַּם־אֲנִי נָבִיא כָּמוֹךָ וּמַלְאָךְ דִּבֶּר אֵלַי בִּדְבַר יְהוָה
Yahweh by-word-of to-me he-said and-angel as-you prophet I also to-him

לֵאמֹר הֲשִׁבֵהוּ אִתְּךָ אֶל־בֵּיתֶךָ וְיֹאכַל לֶחֶם
bread so-may-he-eat house-of-you to with-you bring-back-him! to-say

וְיֵשְׁתְּ מָיִם כִּחֵשׁ לוֹ׃ וַיָּשָׁב אִתּוֹ
with-him so-he-returned (19) to-him he-lied waters and-he-may-drink

וַיֹּאכַל לֶחֶם בְּבֵיתוֹ וַיֵּשְׁתְּ מָיִם׃ וַיְהִי הֵם
they and-he-was (20) waters and-he-drank in-house-of-him bread and-he-ate

יֹשְׁבִים אֶל־הַשֻּׁלְחָן וַיְהִי דְּבַר־יְהוָה אֶל־הַנָּבִיא אֲשֶׁר
who the-prophet to Yahweh word-of and-he-came the-table at ones-sitting

הֱשִׁיבוֹ׃ וַיִּקְרָא אֶל־אִישׁ הָאֱלֹהִים אֲשֶׁר־בָּא
he-came who the-God man-of to and-he-cried-out (21) he-brought-back-him

מִיהוּדָה לֵאמֹר כֹּה אָמַר יְהוָה יַעַן כִּי מָרִיתָ פִּי יְהוָה
Yahweh word-of you-defied that because Yahweh he-says this to-say from-Judah

וְלֹא שָׁמַרְתָּ אֶת־הַמִּצְוָה אֲשֶׁר צִוְּךָ יְהוָה אֱלֹהֶיךָ׃
God-of-you Yahweh he-commanded-you that the-command *** you-kept and-not

וַתָּשָׁב וַתֹּאכַל לֶחֶם וַתֵּשְׁתְּ מַיִם בַּמָּקוֹם
in-the-place waters and-you-drank bread and-you-ate and-you-came-back (22)

him which road the man of
God from Judah had taken.
13So he said to his sons, "Saddle the donkey for me." And
when they had saddled the
donkey for him, he mounted it
14and rode after the man of
God. He found him sitting under an oak tree and asked,
"Are you the man of God who
came from Judah?"
"I am," he replied.
15So the prophet said to him,
"Come home with me and
eat."
16The man of God said, "I
cannot turn back and go with
you, nor can I eat bread or
drink water with you in this
place. 17I have been told by the
word of the LORD: 'You must
not eat bread or drink water
there or return by the way you
came.' "
18The old prophet answered,
"I too am a prophet, as you
are. And an angel said to me
by the word of the LORD:
'Bring him back with you to
your house so that he may eat
bread and drink water.' " (But
he was lying to him.) 19So the
man of God returned with
him and ate and drank in his
house.
20While they were sitting at
the table, the word of the LORD
came to the old prophet who
had brought him back. 21He
cried out to the man of God
who had come from Judah,
"This is what the LORD says:
'You have defied the word of
the LORD and have not kept
the command the LORD your
God gave you. 22You came
back and ate bread and drank
water in the place where he

אֲשֶׁ֨ר דִּבֶּ֥ר אֵלֶ֛יךָ אַל־ תֹּ֥אכַל לֶ֖חֶם וְאַל־ תֵּ֣שְׁתְּ מָ֑יִם לֹֽא־
where  he-told  to-you  not  you-eat  bread  and-not  you-drink  waters  not

תָב֤וֹא נִבְלָֽתְךָ֙ אֶל־ קֶ֣בֶר אֲבֹתֶֽיךָ׃ (23) וַיְהִ֣י אַחֲרֵ֣י
she-will-go  body-of-you  into  tomb-of  fathers-of-you  and-he-was  after

אָכְל֤וֹ לֶ֙חֶם֙ וְאַחֲרֵ֣י שְׁתוֹת֔וֹ וַיַּחֲבָשׁ־ ל֖וֹ הַחֲמ֑וֹר
to-eat-him  bread  and-after  to-drink-him  then-he-saddled  for-him  the-donkey

לַנָּבִ֖יא אֲשֶׁ֥ר הֱשִׁיב֑וֹ (24) וַיֵּ֕לֶךְ וַיִּמְצָאֵ֣הוּ
by-the-prophet  who  he-brought-back-him  and-he-went  and-he-met-him

אַרְיֵ֤ה בַּדֶּ֙רֶךְ֙ וַיְמִיתֵ֔הוּ וַתְּהִ֥י נִבְלָתוֹ֙ מֻשְׁלֶ֣כֶת
lion  on-the-road  and-he-killed-him  and-she-was  body-of-him  being-thrown-down

בַּדֶּ֔רֶךְ וְהַחֲמוֹר֙ עֹמֵ֣ד אֶצְלָ֔הּ וְהָ֣אַרְיֵ֔ה עֹמֵ֖ד אֵ֣צֶל
on-the-road  and-the-donkey  standing  beside-her  and-the-lion  standing  beside

הַנְּבֵלָֽה׃ (25) וְהִנֵּ֧ה אֲנָשִׁ֣ים עֹבְרִ֗ים וַיִּרְא֤וּ אֶת־ הַנְּבֵלָה֙
the-body  then-see!  people  ones-passing-by  and-they-saw  ***  the-body

מֻשְׁלֶ֙כֶת֙ בַּדֶּ֔רֶךְ וְאֶת־ הָ֣אַרְיֵ֔ה עֹמֵ֖ד אֵ֣צֶל הַנְּבֵלָ֑ה
being-thrown-down  on-the-road  and  the-lion  standing  beside  the-body

וַיָּבֹ֙אוּ֙ וַיְדַבְּר֣וּ בָעִ֔יר אֲשֶׁ֛ר הַנָּבִ֥יא הַזָּקֵ֖ן יֹשֵׁ֥ב
and-they-went  and-they-reported  in-the-city  where  the-prophet  the-old  living

בָּֽהּ׃ (26) וַיִּשְׁמַ֣ע הַנָּבִיא֮ אֲשֶׁ֣ר הֱשִׁיב֮וֹ מִן־
in-her  when-he-heard  the-prophet  who  he-brought-back-him  from

הַדֶּרֶךְ֒ וַיֹּ֙אמֶר֙ אִ֤ישׁ הָאֱלֹהִים֙ ה֔וּא אֲשֶׁ֥ר מָרָ֖ה אֶת־ פִּ֣י יְהוָ֑ה
the-journey  then-he-said  man-of  the-God  he  who  he-defied  ***  word-of  Yahweh

וַיִּתְּנֵ֤הוּ יְהוָה֙ לָֽאַרְיֵ֔ה וַֽיִּשְׁבְּרֵ֖הוּ וַיְמִתֵ֑הוּ
and-he-gave-him  Yahweh  to-the-lion  and-he-mauled-him  and-he-killed-him

כִּדְבַ֣ר יְהוָ֔ה אֲשֶׁ֖ר דִּבֶּר־ לֽוֹ׃ (27) וַיְדַבֵּ֤ר אֶל־ בָּנָיו֙
as-word-of  Yahweh  that  he-warned  to-him  and-he-said  to  sons-of-him

לֵאמֹ֔ר חִבְשׁוּ־ לִ֖י אֶת־ הַחֲמ֑וֹר וַֽיַּחֲבֹֽשׁוּ׃ (28) וַיֵּ֗לֶךְ
to-say  saddle!  for-me  ***  the-donkey  so-they-saddled  then-he-went-out

וַיִּמְצָ֤א אֶת־ נִבְלָתוֹ֙ מֻשְׁלֶ֣כֶת בַּדֶּ֔רֶךְ וַחֲמוֹר֙
and-he-found  ***  body-of-him  being-thrown-down  on-the-road  and-donkey

וְהָ֣אַרְיֵ֔ה עֹמְדִ֖ים אֵ֣צֶל הַנְּבֵלָ֑ה לֹֽא־ אָכַ֤ל הָֽאַרְיֵה֙ אֶת־ הַנְּבֵלָ֔ה
and-the-lion  ones-standing  beside  the-body  not  he-ate  the-lion  ***  the-body

וְלֹ֥א שָׁבַ֖ר אֶת־ הַחֲמֽוֹר׃ (29) וַיִּשָּׂ֨א הַנָּבִ֜יא אֶת־
and-not  he-mauled  ***  the-donkey  so-he-picked-up  the-prophet  ***

נִבְלַ֣ת אִישׁ־ הָאֱלֹהִ֗ים וַיַּנִּחֵ֙הוּ֙ אֶל־ הַחֲמ֔וֹר וַיְשִׁיבֵ֑הוּ
body-of  man-of  the-God  and-he-laid-him  on  the-donkey  and-he-brought-back-him

וַיָּבֹ֗א אֶל־ עִ֛יר הַזָּקֵ֖ן הַנָּבִ֥יא לִסְפֹּ֥ד וּלְקָבְרֽוֹ׃
and-he-brought  to  city-of  the-old  the-prophet  to-mourn  and-to-bury-him

told you not to eat or drink. Therefore your body will not be buried in the tomb of your fathers.' "

[23]When the man of God had finished eating and drinking, the prophet who had brought him back saddled his donkey for him. [24]As he went on his way, a lion met him on the road and killed him, and his body was thrown down on the road, with both the donkey and the lion standing beside it. [25]Some people who passed by saw the body thrown down there, with the lion standing beside the body, and they went and reported it in the city where the old prophet lived.

[26]When the prophet who had brought him back from his journey heard of it, he said, "It is the man of God who defied the word of the LORD. The LORD has given him over to the lion, which has mauled him and killed him, as the word of the LORD had warned him."

[27]The prophet said to his sons, "Saddle the donkey for me," and they did so. [28]Then he went out and found the body thrown down on the road, with the donkey and the lion standing beside it. The lion had neither eaten the body nor mauled the donkey. [29]So the prophet picked up the body of the man of God, laid it on the donkey, and brought it back to his own city to mourn for him and bury him. [30]Then

(30) וַיַּנַּח אֶת־ נִבְלָתוֹ בְּקִבְרוֹ וַיִּסְפְּדוּ עָלָיו
over-him and-they-mourned in-tomb-of-him body-of-him *** then-he-laid (30)

הוֹי אָחִי׃ (31) וַיְהִי אַחֲרֵי קָבְרוֹ אֹתוֹ וַיֹּאמֶר אֶל־
to then-he-said him to-bury-him after and-he-was (31) brother-of-me oh!

בָּנָיו לֵאמֹר בְּמוֹתִי וּקְבַרְתֶּם אֹתִי בַּקֶּבֶר אֲשֶׁר
where in-the-grave me then-you-bury when-to-die-me to-say sons-of-him

אִישׁ הָאֱלֹהִים קָבוּר בּוֹ אֵצֶל עַצְמֹתָיו הַנִּיחוּ אֶת־ עַצְמֹתָי׃
bones-of-me *** lay! bones-of-him beside in-him being-buried the-God man-of

(32) כִּי הָיֹה יִהְיֶה הַדָּבָר אֲשֶׁר קָרָא בִּדְבַר
by-word-of he-declared that the-message he-will-come-true to-come-true for (32)

יְהוָה עַל־ הַמִּזְבֵּחַ אֲשֶׁר בְּבֵית־ אֵל וְעַל כָּל־ בָּתֵּי
shrines-of all-of and-against El in-Beth that the-altar against Yahweh

הַבָּמוֹת אֲשֶׁר בְּעָרֵי שֹׁמְרוֹן׃ (33) אַחַר הַדָּבָר הַזֶּה לֹא־
not the-this the-event after (33) Samaria in-towns-of that the-high-places

שָׁב יָרָבְעָם מִדַּרְכּוֹ הָרָעָה וַיָּשָׁב וַיַּעַשׂ
and-he-appointed but-he-returned the-evil from-way-of-him Jeroboam he-changed

מִקְצוֹת הָעָם כֹּהֲנֵי בָמוֹת הֶחָפֵץ יְמַלֵּא
he-consecrated the-one-wanting high-places priests-of the-people from-ends-of

אֶת־ יָדוֹ וִיהִי כֹּהֲנֵי בָמוֹת׃ (34) וַיְהִי
and-he-became (34) high-places priests-of so-he-became hand-of-him ***

בַּדָּבָר הַזֶּה לְחַטַּאת בֵּית יָרָבְעָם וּלְהַכְחִיד
and-to-bring-down Jeroboam house-of as-sin-of the-this in-the-thing

וּלְהַשְׁמִיד מֵעַל פְּנֵי הָאֲדָמָה׃ (14:1) בָּעֵת הַהִיא
the-that at-the-time (14:1) the-earth faces-of from-on and-to-destroy

חָלָה אֲבִיָּה בֶן־ יָרָבְעָם׃ (2) וַיֹּאמֶר יָרָבְעָם לְאִשְׁתּוֹ
to-wife-of-him Jeroboam and-he-said (2) Jeroboam son-of Abijah he-becme-ill

קוּמִי נָא וְהִשְׁתַּנִּית וְלֹא יֵדְעוּ כִּי־ אַתִּי אֵשֶׁת
wife-of you that they-will-recognize so-not and-disguise-yourself! now! go!

יָרָבְעָם וְהָלַכְתְּ שִׁלֹה הִנֵּה־ שָׁם אֲחִיָּה הַנָּבִיא הוּא־ דִבֶּר עָלַי
to-me he-told he the-prophet Ahijah there see! Shiloh then-you-go Jeroboam

לְמֶלֶךְ עַל־ הָעָם הַזֶּה׃ (3) וְלָקַחַתְּ בְּיָדֵךְ עֲשָׂרָה לֶחֶם
bread ten in-hand-of-you and-you-take (3) the-this the-people over as-king

וְנִקֻּדִים וּבַקְבֻּק דְּבַשׁ וּבָאת אֵלָיו הוּא יַגִּיד לָךְ מַה־
what to-you he-will-tell he to-him and-you-go honey and-jar-of and-cakes

יִהְיֶה לַנָּעַר׃ (4) וַתַּעַשׂ כֵּן אֵשֶׁת יָרָבְעָם וַתָּקָם
and-she-got-up Jeroboam wife-of so and-she-did (4) to-the-boy he-will-happen

וַתֵּלֶךְ שִׁלֹה וַתָּבֹא בֵּית אֲחִיָּה וַאֲחִיָּהוּ לֹא־ יָכֹל
he-could not now-Ahijah Ahijah house-of and-she-came Shiloh and-she-went

°2 ק את

he laid the body in his own
tomb, and they mourned over
him and said, "Oh, my brother!"
31After burying him, he said
to his sons, "When I die, bury
me in the grave where the
man of God is buried; lay my
bones beside his bones. 32For
the message he declared by the
word of the LORD against the
altar in Bethel and against all
the shrines on the high places
in the towns of Samaria will
certainly come true."
33Even after this, Jeroboam
did not change his evil ways,
but once more appointed
priests for the high places
from all sorts of people. Anyone who wanted to become a
priest he consecrated for the
high places. 34This was the sin
of the house of Jeroboam that
led to its downfall and to its
destruction from the face of
the earth.

### *Ahijah's Prophecy Against Jeroboam*

14 At that time Abijah son
of Jeroboam became ill,
2and Jeroboam said to his
wife, "Go, disguise yourself,
so you won't be recognized as
the wife of Jeroboam. Then go
to Shiloh. Ahijah the prophet
is there—the one who told me
I would be king over this
people. 3Take ten loaves of
bread with you, some cakes
and a jar of honey, and go to
him. He will tell you what will
happen to the boy." 4So Jeroboam's wife did what he said
and went to Ahijah's house in
Shiloh.
Now Ahijah could not see;

לִרְא֔וֹת כִּ֥י קָ֖מוּ עֵינָ֥יו מִשֵּׂיבֽוֹ׃ וַיהוָ֞ה
but-Yahweh (5) because-of-age-of-him eyes-of-him they-were-gone for to-see

אָמַ֣ר אֶל־אֲחִיָּ֗הוּ הִנֵּה֩ אֵ֨שֶׁת יָרָבְעָ֜ם בָּאָ֡ה לִדְרֹשׁ֩ דָּבָ֨ר מֵעִמְּךָ֜
from-with-you word to-ask coming Jeroboam wife-of see! Ahijah to he-told

אֶל־בְּנָ֗הּ כִּי־חֹלֶ֥ה ה֙וּא כָּזֹ֥ה וְכָזֶ֖ה תְּדַבֵּ֣ר אֵלֶ֑יהָ
to-her you-answer and-as-such as-such he being-ill for son-of-her about

וִיהִ֣י כְבֹאָ֔הּ וְהִ֖יא מִֽתְנַכֵּרָֽה׃ וַיְהִי֩
and-he-was (6) being-someone-else then-she when-to-arrive-her and-he-will-be

כִשְׁמֹ֨עַ אֲחִיָּ֜הוּ אֶת־ק֤וֹל רַגְלֶ֙יהָ֙ בָּאָ֣ה בַפֶּ֔תַח וַיֹּ֕אמֶר
and-he-said to-the-door coming feet-of-her sound-of *** Ahijah when-to-hear

בֹּ֖אִי אֵ֣שֶׁת יָרָבְעָ֑ם לָ֤מָּה זֶּה֙ אַ֣תְּ מִֽתְנַכֵּרָ֔ה וְאָנֹכִ֛י שָׁל֥וּחַ אֵלַ֖יִךְ
to-you being-sent now-I pretending you this why? Jeroboam wife-of come-in!

קָשָֽׁה׃ לְכִ֞י אִמְרִ֣י לְיָרָבְעָ֗ם כֹּֽה־אָמַ֤ר יְהוָה֙ אֱלֹהֵ֣י יִשְׂרָאֵ֔ל יַ֚עַן
because Israel God-of Yahweh he-says this to-Jeroboam tell! go! (7) bad-news

אֲשֶׁ֣ר הֲרִימֹתִ֔יךָ מִתּ֖וֹךְ הָעָ֑ם וָאֶתֶּנְךָ֣ נָגִ֔יד עַ֖ל
over leader and-I-made-you the-people from-among I-raised-up-you that

עַמִּ֥י יִשְׂרָאֵֽל׃ וָאֶקְרַ֤ע אֶת־הַמַּמְלָכָה֙ מִבֵּ֣ית דָּוִ֔ד
David from-house-of the-kingdom *** and-I-tore (8) Israel people-of-me

וָאֶתְּנֶ֖הָ לָ֑ךְ וְלֹֽא־הָיִ֜יתָ כְּעַבְדִּ֣י דָוִ֗ד אֲשֶׁר֩ שָׁמַ֨ר
he-kept who David like-servant-of-me you-were but-not to-you and-I-gave-her

מִצְוֺתַ֜י וַאֲשֶׁר־הָלַ֤ךְ אַחֲרַי֙ בְּכָל־לְבָב֔וֹ לַעֲשׂ֕וֹת
to-do heart-of-him with-all-of after-me he-followed and-who commands-of-me

רַ֖ק הַיָּשָׁ֥ר בְּעֵינָֽי׃ וַתָּ֣רַע לַעֲשׂ֔וֹת מִכֹּ֖ל אֲשֶׁר־
who more-than-all to-do and-you-did-evil (9) in-eyes-of-me the-right only

הָי֣וּ לְפָנֶ֑יךָ וַתֵּ֡לֶךְ וַתַּֽעֲשֶׂה־לְּךָ֩ אֱלֹהִ֨ים אֲחֵרִ֤ים
other-ones gods for-you and-you-made and-you-went before-you they-lived

וּמַסֵּכוֹת֙ לְהַכְעִיסֵ֔נִי וְאֹתִ֥י הִשְׁלַ֖כְתָּ אַחֲרֵ֥י גַוֶּֽךָ׃
back-of-you behind you-thrust and-me to-make-angry-me and-metal-idols

לָכֵ֗ן הִנְנִ֨י מֵבִ֤יא רָעָה֙ אֶל־בֵּ֣ית יָרָבְעָ֔ם וְהִכְרַתִּ֤י
and-I-will-cut-off Jeroboam house-of on disaster bringing see-I! therefore (10)

לְיָֽרָבְעָם֙ מַשְׁתִּ֣ין בְּקִ֔יר עָצ֥וּר וְעָז֖וּב בְּיִשְׂרָאֵ֑ל
in-Israel or-being-free being-slave against-wall one-urinating from-Jeroboam

וּבִעַרְתִּ֤י אַחֲרֵי֙ בֵית־יָרָבְעָ֔ם כַּאֲשֶׁ֥ר יְבַעֵ֛ר הַגָּלָ֖ל עַד־
until the-dung he-burns just-as Jeroboam house-of after and-I-will-burn

תֻּמּֽוֹ׃ הַמֵּ֤ת לְיָרָבְעָם֙ בָּעִ֔יר יֹאכְל֖וּ הַכְּלָבִ֑ים
the-dogs they-will-eat in-the-city of-Jeroboam the-dead (11) to-be-gone-him

וְהַמֵּת֙ בַּשָּׂדֶ֔ה יֹאכְל֖וּ ע֣וֹף הַשָּׁמָ֑יִם כִּ֥י יְהוָ֖ה
Yahweh for the-airs bird-of they-will-eat in-the-country and-the-dead

his sight was gone because of his age. [5]But the LORD had told Ahijah, "Jeroboam's wife is coming to ask you about her son, for he is ill, and you are to give her such and such an answer. When she arrives, she will pretend to be someone else."

[6]So when Ahijah heard the sound of her footsteps at the door, he said, "Come in, wife of Jeroboam. Why this pretense? I have been sent to you with bad news. [7]Go, tell Jeroboam that this is what the LORD, the God of Israel, says: 'I raised you up from among the people and made you a leader over my people Israel. [8]I tore the kingdom away from the house of David and gave it to you, but you have not been like my servant David, who kept my commands and followed me with all his heart, doing only what was right in my eyes. [9]You have done more evil than all who lived before you. You have made for yourself other gods, idols made of metal; you have provoked me to anger and thrust me behind your back.

[10]" 'Because of this, I am going to bring disaster on the house of Jeroboam. I will cut off from Jeroboam every last male in Israel—slave or free. I will burn up the house of Jeroboam as one burns dung, until it is all gone. [11]Dogs will eat those belonging to Jeroboam who die in the city, and the birds of the air will feed on those who die in the country. The LORD has spoken!'

[l] *14* The meaning of the Hebrew for this sentence is uncertain.
[m] *15* That is, the Euphrates
[n] *15* That is, symbols of the goddess Asherah; here and elsewhere in 1 Kings

דִּבֵּר׃ וְאַתְּ קוּמִי לְכִי לְבֵיתֵךְ בְּבֹאָה
when-to-enter to-home-of-you go-back! get-up! now-you (12) he-spoke

רַגְלַיִךְ הָעִירָה וּמֵת הַיָּלֶד׃ וְסָפְדוּ־
and-they-will-mourn (13) the-boy then-he-will-die into-the-city feet-of-you

לוֹ כָל־ יִשְׂרָאֵל וְקָבְרוּ אֹתוֹ כִּי־ זֶה לְבַדּוֹ
by-himself this-one indeed him and-they-will-bury Israel all-of for-him

יָבֹא לְיָרָבְעָם אֶל־ קָבֶר יַעַן נִמְצָא־ בוֹ דָּבָר טוֹב אֶל־
to good thing in-him he-was-found because tomb into of-Jeroboam he-will-go

יְהוָה אֱלֹהֵי יִשְׂרָאֵל בְּבֵית יָרָבְעָם׃ וְהֵקִים יְהוָה
Yahweh and-he-will-raise-up (14) Jeroboam in-house-of Israel God-of Yahweh

לוֹ מֶלֶךְ עַל־ יִשְׂרָאֵל אֲשֶׁר יַכְרִית אֶת־ בֵּית יָרָבְעָם זֶה
this Jeroboam house-of *** he-will-cut-off who Israel over king for-him

הַיּוֹם וּמֶה גַּם־ עָתָּה׃ וְהִכָּה יְהוָה אֶת־ יִשְׂרָאֵל
Israel *** Yahweh and-he-will-strike (15) now indeed now-what? the-day

כַּאֲשֶׁר יָנוּד הַקָּנֶה בַּמַּיִם וְנָתַשׁ אֶת־ יִשְׂרָאֵל
Israel *** and-he-will-uproot in-the-waters the-reed he-sways just-as

מֵעַל הָאֲדָמָה הַטּוֹבָה הַזֹּאת אֲשֶׁר נָתַן לַאֲבוֹתֵיהֶם
to-fathers-of-them he-gave that the-this the-good the-land from-on

וְזֵרָם מֵעֵבֶר לַנָּהָר יַעַן אֲשֶׁר עָשׂוּ אֶת־
*** they-made that because to-the-River at-beyond and-he-will-scatter-them

אֲשֵׁרֵיהֶם מַכְעִיסִים אֶת־ יְהוָה׃ וְיִתֵּן
and-he-will-give-up (16) Yahweh *** ones-making-angry Asherah-poles-of-them

אֶת־ יִשְׂרָאֵל בִּגְלַל חַטֹּאות יָרָבְעָם אֲשֶׁר חָטָא וַאֲשֶׁר
and-that he-committed that Jeroboam sins-of on-account-of Israel ***

הֶחֱטִיא אֶת־ יִשְׂרָאֵל׃ וַתָּקָם אֵשֶׁת יָרָבְעָם
Jeroboam wife-of then-she-got-up (17) Israel *** he-caused-to-commit

וַתֵּלֶךְ וַתָּבֹא תִרְצָתָה הִיא בָּאָה בְסַף־ הַבַּיִת
the-house over-threshold-of stepping she to-Tirzah and-she-went and-she-left

וְהַנַּעַר מֵת׃ וַיִּקְבְּרוּ אֹתוֹ וַיִּסְפְּדוּ־ לוֹ כָּל־
all-of for-him and-they-mourned him and-they-buried (18) he-died and-the-boy

יִשְׂרָאֵל כִּדְבַר יְהוָה אֲשֶׁר דִּבֶּר בְּיַד־ עַבְדּוֹ אֲחִיָּהוּ
Ahijah servant-of-him by-hand-of he-said that Yahweh as-word-of Israel

הַנָּבִיא׃ וְיֶתֶר דִּבְרֵי יָרָבְעָם אֲשֶׁר נִלְחַם וַאֲשֶׁר
and-how he-warred how Jeroboam events-of and-rest-of (19) the-prophet

מָלָךְ הִנָּם כְּתוּבִים עַל־ סֵפֶר דִּבְרֵי הַיָּמִים
the-days annals-of book-of in ones-being-written see-they! he-ruled

לְמַלְכֵי יִשְׂרָאֵל׃ וְהַיָּמִים אֲשֶׁר מָלַךְ יָרָבְעָם עֶשְׂרִים וּשְׁתַּיִם
and-two twenty Jeroboam he-reigned that and-the-days (20) Israel of-kings-of

12"As for you, go back home.
When you set foot in your city,
the boy will die. 13All Israel
will mourn for him and bury
him. He is the only one belonging to Jeroboam who will
be buried, because he is the
only one in the house of Jeroboam in whom the LORD, the
God of Israel, has found anything good.
14"The LORD will raise up for
himself a king over Israel who
will cut off the family of Jeroboam. This is the day! What?
Yes, even now.[l] 15And the
LORD will strike Israel, so that
it will be like a reed swaying
in the water. He will uproot
Israel from this good land that
he gave to their forefathers
and scatter them beyond the
River,[m] because they provoked
the LORD to anger by making
Asherah poles.[n] 16And he will
give Israel up because of the
sins Jeroboam has committed
and has caused Israel to commit."
17Then Jeroboam's wife got
up and left and went to Tirzah.
As soon as she stepped over
the threshold of the house, the
boy died. 18They buried him,
and all Israel mourned for him
as the LORD had said through
his servant the prophet Ahijah.
19The other events of Jeroboam's reign, his wars and
how he ruled, are written in
the book of the annals of the
kings of Israel. 20He reigned
for twenty-two years and then

שָׁנָה וַיִּשְׁכַּב עִם־ אֲבֹתָיו וַיִּמְלֹךְ נָדָב בְּנוֹ
son-of-him Nadab and-he-became-king fathers-of-him with then-he-rested year

תַּחְתָּיו׃ וּרְחַבְעָם בֶּן־ שְׁלֹמֹה מָלַךְ בִּיהוּדָה בֶּן־
son-of in-Judah he-was-king Solomon son-of and-Rehoboam (21) on-place-of-him

אַרְבָּעִים וְאַחַת שָׁנָה רְחַבְעָם בְּמָלְכוֹ וּשְׁבַע עֶשְׂרֵה
ten and-seven-of when-to-become-king-him Rehoboam year and-one forty

שָׁנָה ׀ מָלַךְ בִּירוּשָׁלַםִ הָעִיר אֲשֶׁר־ בָּחַר יְהוָה לָשׂוּם אֶת־
*** to-put Yahweh he-chose which the-city in-Jerusalem he-reigned year

שְׁמוֹ שָׁם מִכֹּל שִׁבְטֵי יִשְׂרָאֵל וְשֵׁם אִמּוֹ
mother-of-him and-name-of Israel tribes-of from-all-of there Name-of-him

נַעֲמָה הָעַמֹּנִית׃ וַיַּעַשׂ יְהוּדָה הָרַע בְּעֵינֵי יְהוָה
Yahweh in-eyes-of the-evil Judah and-he-did (22) the-Ammonite Naamah

וַיְקַנְאוּ אֹתוֹ מִכֹּל אֲשֶׁר עָשׂוּ אֲבֹתָם
fathers-of-them they-did that more-than-all him and-they-made-jealous

בְּחַטֹּאתָם אֲשֶׁר חָטָאוּ׃ וַיִּבְנוּ גַם־ הֵמָּה לָהֶם
for-them they indeed and-they-set-up (23) they-committed that by-sin-of-them

בָּמוֹת וּמַצֵּבוֹת וַאֲשֵׁרִים עַל כָּל־ גִּבְעָה גְבֹהָה
high hill every-of on and-Asherah-poles and-sacred-stones high-places

וְתַחַת כָּל־ עֵץ רַעֲנָן׃ וְגַם־ קָדֵשׁ הָיָה
he-was male-prostitute and-even (24) spreading tree every-of and-under

בָּאָרֶץ עָשׂוּ כְּכֹל הַתּוֹעֲבֹת הַגּוֹיִם אֲשֶׁר
that the-nations the-detestable-practices-of as-all-of they-did in-the-land

הוֹרִישׁ יְהוָה מִפְּנֵי בְּנֵי יִשְׂרָאֵל׃ וַיְהִי בַּשָּׁנָה
in-the-year and-he-was (25) Israel sons-of from-before Yahweh he-drove-out

הַחֲמִישִׁית לַמֶּלֶךְ רְחַבְעָם עָלָה שׁוֹשַׁק מֶלֶךְ־ מִצְרַיִם עַל־
against Egypt king-of Shishak he-attacked Rehoboam of-the-king the-fifth

יְרוּשָׁלָםִ׃ וַיִּקַּח אֶת־ אֹצְרוֹת בֵּית־ יְהוָה וְאֶת־
and Yahweh temple-of treasures-of *** and-he-carried-off (26) Jerusalem

אוֹצְרוֹת בֵּית הַמֶּלֶךְ וְאֶת־ הַכֹּל לָקָח וַיִּקַּח אֶת־ כָּל־
all-of *** and-he-took he-took the-whole and the-king palace-of treasures-of

מָגִנֵּי הַזָּהָב אֲשֶׁר עָשָׂה שְׁלֹמֹה׃ וַיַּעַשׂ הַמֶּלֶךְ רְחַבְעָם
Rehoboam the-king so-he-made (27) Solomon he-made that the-gold shields-of

תַּחְתָּם מָגִנֵּי נְחֹשֶׁת וְהִפְקִיד עַל־ יַד שָׂרֵי
commanders-of hand-of under and-he-assigned bronze shields-of in-place-of-them

הָרָצִים הַשֹּׁמְרִים פֶּתַח בֵּית הַמֶּלֶךְ׃
the-king palace-of entrance-of the-ones-being-on-duty the-ones-guarding

וַיְהִי מִדֵּי־ בֹא הַמֶּלֶךְ בֵּית יְהוָה יִשָּׂאוּם
they-bore-them Yahweh temple-of the-king to-come as-often-as and-he-was (28)

rested with his fathers. And
Nadab his son succeeded him
as king.

*Rehoboam King of Judah*

21Rehoboam son of Solomon
was king in Judah. He was
forty-one years old when he
became king, and he reigned
seventeen years in Jerusalem,
the city the LORD had chosen
out of all the tribes of Israel in
which to put his Name. His
mother's name was Naamah;
she was an Ammonite.
22Judah did evil in the eyes
of the LORD. By the sins they
committed they stirred up his
jealous anger more than their
fathers had done. 23They also
set up for themselves high
places, sacred stones and
Asherah poles on every high
hill and under every spreading tree. 24There were even
male shrine prostitutes in the
land; the people engaged in all
the detestable practices of the
nations the LORD had driven
out before the Israelites.
25In the fifth year of King
Rehoboam, Shishak king of
Egypt attacked Jerusalem. 26He
carried off the treasures of the
temple of the LORD and the
treasures of the royal palace.
He took everything, including
all the gold shields Solomon
had made. 27So King Reho-
boam made bronze shields to
replace them and assigned
these to the commanders of
the guard on duty at the entrance to the royal palace.
28Whenever the king went to
the LORD's temple, the guards

°25 ק שישק

הָרָצִים וֶהֱשִׁיבוּם אֶל־ תָּא הָרָצִים׃
the-ones-guarding room-of to then-they-returned-them the-ones-guarding

(29) וְיֶתֶר דִּבְרֵי רְחַבְעָם וְכָל־ אֲשֶׁר עָשָׂה הֲלֹא־הֵמָּה
they not? he-did that and-all Rehoboam events-of and-rest-of (29)

כְּתוּבִים עַל־ סֵפֶר דִּבְרֵי הַיָּמִים לְמַלְכֵי יְהוּדָה׃
Judah of-kings-of the-days annals-of book-of in ones-being-written

(30) וּמִלְחָמָה הָיְתָה בֵין־ רְחַבְעָם וּבֵין יָרָבְעָם כָּל־הַיָּמִים׃
the-days all-of Jeroboam and-between Rehoboam between she-was and-warfare (30)

(31) וַיִּשְׁכַּב רְחַבְעָם עִם־ אֲבֹתָיו וַיִּקָּבֵר עִם־
with and-he-was-buried fathers-of-him with Rehoboam and-he-rested (31)

אֲבֹתָיו בְּעִיר דָּוִד וְשֵׁם אִמּוֹ נַעֲמָה הָעַמֹּנִית
the-Ammonite Naamah mother-of-him and-name-of David in-City-of fathers-of-him

וַיִּמְלֹךְ אֲבִיָּם בְּנוֹ תַּחְתָּיו׃ (15:1) וּבִשְׁנַת
and-in-years-of (15:1) in-place-of-him son-of-him Abijam and-he-became-king

שְׁמֹנֶה עֶשְׂרֵה לַמֶּלֶךְ יָרָבְעָם בֶּן־ נְבָט מָלַךְ אֲבִיָּם עַל־יְהוּדָה׃
Judah over Abijam he-became-king Nebat son-of Jeroboam of-the-king ten eight

(2) שָׁלֹשׁ שָׁנִים מָלַךְ בִּירוּשָׁלִָם וְשֵׁם אִמּוֹ מַעֲכָה
Maacah mother-of-him and-name-of in-Jerusalem he-reigned years three (2)

בַּת־ אֲבִישָׁלוֹם׃ (3) וַיֵּלֶךְ בְּכָל־ חַטֹּאות אָבִיו
father-of-him sins-of in-all-of and-he-walked (3) Abishalom daughter-of

אֲשֶׁר־עָשָׂה לְפָנָיו וְלֹא־ הָיָה לְבָבוֹ שָׁלֵם עִם־ יְהוָה
Yahweh to fully-devoted heart-of-him he-was and-not before-him he-did that

אֱלֹהָיו כִּלְבַב דָּוִד אָבִיו׃ (4) כִּי לְמַעַן
for-sake-of nevertheless (4) forefather-of-him David as-heart-of God-of-him

דָּוִד נָתַן יְהוָה אֱלֹהָיו לוֹ נִיר בִּירוּשָׁלִָם לְהָקִים אֶת־
*** to-raise-up in-Jerusalem lamp to-him God-of-him Yahweh he-gave David

בְּנוֹ אַחֲרָיו וּלְהַעֲמִיד אֶת־ יְרוּשָׁלִָם׃ (5) אֲשֶׁר עָשָׂה דָוִד
Dvaid he-did for (5) Jerusalem *** and-to-make-strong after-him son-of-him

אֶת־ הַיָּשָׁר בְּעֵינֵי יְהוָה וְלֹא־ סָר מִכֹּל אֲשֶׁר־
that from-anything he-turned and-not Yahweh in-eyes-of the-right ***

צִוָּהוּ כֹּל יְמֵי חַיָּיו רַק בִּדְבַר אוּרִיָּה
Uriah in-case-of except lives-of-him days-of all-of he-commanded-him

הַחִתִּי׃ (6) וּמִלְחָמָה הָיְתָה בֵין־ רְחַבְעָם וּבֵין יָרָבְעָם כָּל־
all-of Jeroboam and-between Rehoboam between she-was and-war (6) the-Hittite

יְמֵי חַיָּיו׃ (7) וְיֶתֶר דִּבְרֵי אֲבִיָּם וְכָל־ אֲשֶׁר עָשָׂה
he-did that and-all Abijam events-of and-rest-of (7) lives-of-him days-of

הֲלוֹא־הֵם כְּתוּבִים עַל־ סֵפֶר דִּבְרֵי הַיָּמִים לְמַלְכֵי יְהוּדָה
Judah of-kings-of the-days annals-of book-of in ones-being-written they not?

bore the shields, and afterward they returned them to the guardroom.

29 As for the other events of Rehoboam's reign, and all he did, are they not written in the book of the annals of the kings of Judah? 30 There was continual warfare between Rehoboam and Jeroboam. 31 And Rehoboam rested with his fathers and was buried with them in the City of David. His mother's name was Naamah; she was an Ammonite. And Abijah[n] his son succeeded him as king.

*Abijah King of Judah*

15 In the eighteenth year of the reign of Jeroboam son of Nebat, Abijah[o] became king of Judah, 2 and he reigned in Jerusalem three years. His mother's name was Maacah daughter of Abishalom.[p]

3 He committed all the sins his father had done before him; his heart was not fully devoted to the LORD his God, as the heart of David his forefather had been. 4 Nevertheless, for David's sake the LORD his God gave him a lamp in Jerusalem by raising up a son to succeed him and by making Jerusalem strong. 5 For David had done what was right in the eyes of the LORD and had not failed to keep any of the LORD's commands all the days of his life—except in the case of Uriah the Hittite.

6 There was war between Rehoboam[q] and Jeroboam throughout ⌞Abijah's⌟ lifetime. 7 As for the other events of Abijah's reign, and all he did, are they not written in the book of the annals of the kings

[n] *31* Some Hebrew manuscripts and Septuagint (see also 2 Chron 12:16); most Hebrew manuscripts *Abijam*
[o] *1* Some Hebrew manuscripts and Septuagint (see also 2 Chron 12:16); most Hebrew manuscripts *Abijam;* also in verse 7 and 8
[p] *2* A variant of *Absalom;* also in verse 10
[q] *6* Most Hebrew manuscripts; some Hebrew manuscripts and Syriac *Abijam* (that is, Abijah)

וּמִלְחָמָה הָיְתָה בֵּין אֲבִיָּם וּבֵין יָרָבְעָם׃ וַיִּשְׁכַּב אֲבִיָּם
Abijam and-he-rested (8) Jeroboam and-between Abijam between she-was and-war

עִם־ אֲבֹתָיו וַיִּקְבְּרוּ אֹתוֹ בְּעִיר דָּוִד וַיִּמְלֹךְ
and-he-became-king David in-City-of him and-they-buried fathers-of-him with

אָסָא בְנוֹ תַּחְתָּיו׃ וּבִשְׁנַת עֶשְׂרִים לְיָרָבְעָם מֶלֶךְ
king-of of-Jeroboam twenty and-in-year-of (9) in-place-of-him son-of-him Asa

יִשְׂרָאֵל מָלַךְ אָסָא מֶלֶךְ יְהוּדָה׃ וְאַרְבָּעִים וְאַחַת שָׁנָה
year and-one and-forty (10) Judah king-of Asa he-became-king Israel

מָלַךְ בִּירוּשָׁלָ͏ִם וְשֵׁם אִמּוֹ מַעֲכָה בַּת־
daughter-of Maacah mother-of-him and-name-of in-Jerusalem he-reigned

אֲבִישָׁלוֹם׃ וַיַּעַשׂ אָסָא הַיָּשָׁר בְּעֵינֵי יְהוָה כְּדָוִד
as-David Yahweh in-eyes-of the-right Asa and-he-did (11) Abishalom

אָבִיו׃ וַיַּעֲבֵר הַקְּדֵשִׁים מִן־ הָאָרֶץ
the-land from the-male-prostitutes and-he-expelled (12) father-of-him

וַיָּסַר אֶת־ כָּל־ הַגִּלֻּלִים אֲשֶׁר עָשׂוּ אֲבֹתָיו׃
fathers-of-him they-made that the-idols all-of *** and-he-got-rid

וְגַם ׀ אֶת־ מַעֲכָה אִמּוֹ וַיְסִרֶהָ מִגְּבִירָה
from-queen-mother also-he-deposed-her mother-of-him Maacah *** and-even (13)

אֲשֶׁר־ עָשְׂתָה מִפְלֶצֶת לָאֲשֵׁרָה וַיִּכְרֹת אָסָא אֶת־
*** Asa and-he-cut-down to-the-Asherah repulsive-pole she-made because

מִפְלַצְתָּהּ וַיִּשְׂרֹף בְּנַחַל קִדְרוֹן׃ וְהַבָּמוֹת
but-the-high-places (14) Kidron in-Valley-of and-he-burned repulsive-pole-of-her

לֹא־ סָרוּ רַק לְבַב־ אָסָא הָיָה שָׁלֵם עִם־ יְהוָה
Yahweh to fully-committed he-was Asa heart-of however they-removed not

כָּל־ יָמָיו׃ וַיָּבֵא אֶת־ קָדְשֵׁי אָבִיו
father-of-him dedicated-things-of *** and-he-brought (15) days-of-him all-of

וְקָדְשָׁו בֵּית יְהוָה כֶּסֶף וְזָהָב וְכֵלִים׃
and-articles and-gold silver Yahweh temple-of *and-dedicated-things-of-him

וּמִלְחָמָה הָיְתָה בֵּין אָסָא וּבֵין בַּעְשָׁא מֶלֶךְ־ יִשְׂרָאֵל כָּל־
all-of Israel king-of Baasha and-between Asa between she-was and-war (16)

יְמֵיהֶם׃ וַיַּעַל בַּעְשָׁא מֶלֶךְ־ יִשְׂרָאֵל עַל־ יְהוּדָה
Judah against Israel king-of Baasha and-he-went-up (17) days-of-them

וַיִּבֶן אֶת־ הָרָמָה לְבִלְתִּי תֵּת יֹצֵא וָבָא
or-one-entering one-leaving to-allow not the-Ramah *** and-he-fortified

לְאָסָא מֶלֶךְ יְהוּדָה׃ וַיִּקַּח אָסָא אֶת־ כָּל־ הַכֶּסֶף וְהַזָּהָב
and-the-gold the-silver all-of *** Asa then-he-took (18) Judah king-of to-Asa

הַנּוֹתָרִים ׀ בְּאוֹצְרוֹת בֵּית־ יְהוָה וְאֶת־ אוֹצְרוֹת
treasuries-of and Yahweh temple-of in-treasuries-of the-ones-being-left

of Judah? There was war between Abijah and Jeroboam. [8]And Abijah rested with his fathers and was buried in the City of David. And Asa his son succeeded him as king.

*Asa King of Judah*

[9]In the twentieth year of Jeroboam king of Israel, Asa became king of Judah, [10]and he reigned in Jerusalem forty-one years. His grandmother's name was Maacah daughter of Abishalom.

[11]Asa did what was right in the eyes of the LORD, as his father David had done. [12]He expelled the male shrine prostitutes from the land and got rid of all the idols his fathers had made. [13]He even deposed his grandmother Maacah from her position as queen mother, because she had made a repulsive Asherah pole. Asa cut the pole down and burned it in the Kidron Valley. [14]Although he did not remove the high places, Asa's heart was fully committed to the LORD all his life. [15]He brought into the temple of the LORD the silver and gold and the articles that he and his father had dedicated.

[16]There was war between Asa and Baasha king of Israel throughout their reigns. [17]Baasha king of Israel went up against Judah and fortified Ramah to prevent anyone from leaving or entering the territory of Asa king of Judah.

[18]Asa then took all the silver and gold that was left in the treasuries of the LORD's temple

*15 This translation follows the NIV in rendering the *Ketib* form rather than the *Qere, and-dedicated-things-of*.

°15 ק וקדשי

בֵּית־מֶלֶךְ וַיִּתְּנֵם בְּיַד־ עֲבָדָיו
officials-of-him into-hand-of and-he-entrusted-them the-king palace-of

וַיִּשְׁלָחֵם הַמֶּלֶךְ אָסָא אֶל־בֶּן־ הֲדַד בֶּן־ טַבְרִמֹּן בֶּן־ חֶזְיוֹן
Hezion son-of Tabrimmon son-of Hadad Ben to Asa the-king and-he-sent-them

מֶלֶךְ אֲרָם הַיֹּשֵׁב בְּדַמֶּשֶׂק לֵאמֹר׃ בְּרִית בֵּינִי
between-me treaty (19) to-say in-Damascus the-one-ruling Aram king-of

וּבֵינֶךָ בֵּין אָבִי וּבֵין אָבִיךָ הִנֵּה שָׁלַחְתִּי
I-send see! father-of-you and-between father-of-me between and-between-you

לְךָ שֹׁחַד כֶּסֶף וְזָהָב לֵךְ הָפֵרָה אֶת־ בְּרִיתְךָ אֶת־ בַּעְשָׁא
Baasha with treaty-of-you *** break! come! and-gold silver gift-of to-you

מֶלֶךְ־ יִשְׂרָאֵל וְיַעֲלֶה מֵעָלָי׃ וַיִּשְׁמַע בֶּן־
Ben and-he-agreed (20) from-against-me so-he-will-withdraw Israel king-of

הֲדַד אֶל־ הַמֶּלֶךְ אָסָא וַיִּשְׁלַח אֶת־ שָׂרֵי הַחֲיָלִים אֲשֶׁר־ לוֹ
to-him that the-forces commanders-of *** and-he-sent Asa the-king with Hadad

עַל־ עָרֵי יִשְׂרָאֵל וַיַּךְ אֶת־עִיּוֹן וְאֶת־דָּן וְאֵת אָבֵל בֵּית־מַעֲכָה
Maacah Beth Abel and Dan and Ijon *** and-he-conquered Israel towns-of against

וְאֵת כָּל־ כִּנְרוֹת עַל כָּל־ אֶרֶץ נַפְתָּלִי׃ וַיְהִי כִּשְׁמֹעַ
when-to-hear and-he-was (21) Naphtali land-of all-of with Kinnereth all-of and

בַּעְשָׁא וַיֶּחְדַּל מִבְּנוֹת אֶת־ הָרָמָה וַיֵּשֶׁב בְּתִרְצָה׃
to-Tirzah and-he-withdrew the-Ramah *** from-to-build then-he-stopped Baasha

וְהַמֶּלֶךְ אָסָא הִשְׁמִיעַ אֶת־ כָּל־ יְהוּדָה אֵין נָקִי
exempt no-one Judah all-of *** he-issued-order Asa then-the-king (22)

וַיִּשְׂאוּ אֶת־ אַבְנֵי הָרָמָה וְאֶת־ עֵצֶיהָ אֲשֶׁר
that timbers-of-her and the-Ramah stones-of *** and-they-carried-away

בָּנָה בַּעְשָׁא וַיִּבֶן בָּם הַמֶּלֶךְ אָסָא אֶת־ גֶּבַע בִּנְיָמִן
Benjamin Geba-of *** Asa the-king with-them and-he-built-up Baasha he-used

וְאֶת־ הַמִּצְפָּה׃ וְיֶתֶר כָּל־ דִּבְרֵי־ אָסָא וְכָל־
and-all-of Asa events-of all-of and-rest-of (23) the-Mizpah and

גְּבוּרָתוֹ וְכָל־ אֲשֶׁר עָשָׂה וְהֶעָרִים אֲשֶׁר בָּנָה הֲלֹא־
not? he-built that and-the-cities he-did that and-all achievement-of-him

הֵמָּה כְתוּבִים עַל־ סֵפֶר דִּבְרֵי הַיָּמִים לְמַלְכֵי יְהוּדָה
Judah of-kings-of the-days annals-of book-of in ones-being-written they

רַק לְעֵת זִקְנָתוֹ חָלָה אֶת־ רַגְלָיו׃
feet-of-him *** he-became-diseased old-age-of-him at-time-of however

וַיִּשְׁכַּב אָסָא עִם־ אֲבֹתָיו וַיִּקָּבֵר עִם־
with and-he-was-buried fathers-of-him with Asa then-he-rested (24)

אֲבֹתָיו בְּעִיר דָּוִד אָבִיו וַיִּמְלֹךְ יְהוֹשָׁפָט
Jehoshaphat and-he-became-king father-of-him David in-City-of fathers-of-him

and of his own palace. He entrusted it to his officials and
sent them to Ben-Hadad son
of Tabrimmon, the son of Hezion, the king of Aram, who
was ruling in Damascus.
19 "Let there be a treaty between me and you," he said,
"as there was between my father and your father. See, I am
sending you a gift of silver
and gold. Now break your
treaty with Baasha king of Israel so he will withdraw from
me."
20 Ben-Hadad agreed with
King Asa and sent the commanders of his forces against
the towns of Israel. He conquered Ijon, Dan, Abel Beth-
maacah and all Kinnereth in
addition to Naphtali. 21 When
Baasha heard this, he stopped
building Ramah and with-
drew to Tirzah. 22 Then King
Asa issued an order to all
Judah—no one was exempt—
and they carried away from
Ramah the stones and timber
Baasha had been using there.
With them King Asa built up
Geba in Benjamin, and also
Mizpah.
23 As for all the other events
of Asa's reign, all his achievements, all he did and the cities
he built, are they not written
in the book of the annals of
the kings of Judah? In his old
age, however, his feet became
diseased. 24 Then Asa rested
with his fathers and was buried with them in the city of his
father David. And Jehoshaphat his son succeeded him as
king.

°18 ק המלך

בְּנוֹ תַּחְתָּיו׃ וְנָדָב בֶּן־ יָרָבְעָם מָלַךְ עַל־
over he-became-king Jeroboam son-of and-Nadab (25) in-place-of-him son-of-him

יִשְׂרָאֵל בִּשְׁנַת שְׁתַּיִם לְאָסָא מֶלֶךְ יְהוּדָה וַיִּמְלֹךְ עַל־יִשְׂרָאֵל
Israel over and-he-reigned Judah king-of of-Asa two in-year-of Israel

שְׁנָתָיִם׃ וַיַּעַשׂ הָרַע בְּעֵינֵי יְהוָה וַיֵּלֶךְ בְּדֶרֶךְ
in-way-of and-he-walked Yahweh in-eyes-of the-evil and-he-did (26) two-years

אָבִיו וּבְחַטָּאתוֹ אֲשֶׁר הֶחֱטִיא אֶת־יִשְׂרָאֵל׃
Israel *** he-caused-to-commit which and-in-sin-of-him father-of-him

וַיִּקְשֹׁר עָלָיו בַּעְשָׁא בֶן־ אֲחִיָּה לְבֵית יִשָּׂשכָר
Issachar of-house-of Ahijah son-of Baasha against-him and-he-plotted (27)

וַיַּכֵּהוּ בַעְשָׁא בְּגִבְּתוֹן אֲשֶׁר לַפְּלִשְׁתִּים וְנָדָב
and-Nadab of-the-Philistines that at-Gibbethon Baasha and-he-struck-down-him

וְכָל־ יִשְׂרָאֵל צָרִים עַל־ גִּבְּתוֹן׃ וַיְמִתֵהוּ
and-he-killed-him (28) Gibbethon against ones-besieging Israel and-all-of

בַעְשָׁא בִּשְׁנַת שָׁלֹשׁ לְאָסָא מֶלֶךְ יְהוּדָה וַיִּמְלֹךְ
and-he-became-king Judah king-of of-Asa three in-year-of Baasha

תַּחְתָּיו׃ וַיְהִי כְמָלְכוֹ הִכָּה אֶת־ כָּל־
whole-of *** he-killed as-to-reign-him and-he-was (29) in-place-of-him

בֵּית יָרָבְעָם לֹא־הִשְׁאִיר כָּל־ נְשָׁמָה לְיָרָבְעָם עַד־ הִשְׁמִדוֹ
he-destroyed-him but to-Jeroboam breath any-of he-left not Jeroboam family-of

כִּדְבַר יְהוָה אֲשֶׁר דִּבֶּר בְּיַד־ עַבְדּוֹ אֲחִיָּה הַשִּׁילֹנִי׃
the-Shilonite Ahijah servant-of-him by-hand-of he-gave that Yahweh as-word-of

עַל־ חַטֹּאות יָרָבְעָם אֲשֶׁר חָטָא וַאֲשֶׁר הֶחֱטִיא
he-caused-to-commit and-that he-committed that Jeroboam sins-of because-of (30)

אֶת־יִשְׂרָאֵל בְּכַעְסוֹ אֲשֶׁר הִכְעִיס אֶת־ יְהוָה אֱלֹהֵי
God-of Yahweh *** he-provoked-to-anger for in-provocation-of-him Israel ***

יִשְׂרָאֵל׃ וְיֶתֶר דִּבְרֵי נָדָב וְכָל־ אֲשֶׁר עָשָׂה הֲלֹא־ הֵם
they not? he-did that and-all Nadab events-of and-rest-of (31) Israel

כְּתוּבִים עַל־ סֵפֶר דִּבְרֵי הַיָּמִים לְמַלְכֵי יִשְׂרָאֵל׃
Israel of-kings-of the-days annals-of book-of in ones-being-written

וּמִלְחָמָה הָיְתָה בֵּין אָסָא וּבֵין בַּעְשָׁא מֶלֶךְ־ יִשְׂרָאֵל כָּל־
all-of Israel king-of Baasha and-between Asa between she-was and-war (32)

יְמֵיהֶם׃ בִּשְׁנַת שָׁלֹשׁ לְאָסָא מֶלֶךְ יְהוּדָה מָלַךְ
he-became-king Judah king-of of-Asa three in-year-of (33) days-of-them

בַּעְשָׁא בֶן־ אֲחִיָּה עַל־ כָּל־יִשְׂרָאֵל בְּתִרְצָה עֶשְׂרִים וְאַרְבַּע שָׁנָה׃
year and-four twenty in-Tirzah Israel all-of over Ahijah son-of Baasha

וַיַּעַשׂ הָרַע בְּעֵינֵי יְהוָה וַיֵּלֶךְ בְּדֶרֶךְ יָרָבְעָם
Jeroboam in-way-of and-he-walked Yahweh in-eyes-of the-evil and-he-did (34)

*Nadab King of Israel*

25 Nadab son of Jeroboam
became king of Israel in the
second year of Asa king of
Judah, and he reigned over Israel two years. 26 He did evil in
the eyes of the LORD, walking
in the ways of his father and
in his sin, which he had
caused Israel to commit.
27 Baasha son of Ahijah of the
house of Issachar plotted
against him, and he struck
him down at Gibbethon, a
Philistine town, while Nadab
and all Israel were besieging
it. 28 Baasha killed Nadab in the
third year of Asa king of Judah
and succeeded him as king.
29 As soon as he began to
reign, he killed Jeroboam's
whole family. He did not leave
Jeroboam anyone that
breathed, but destroyed them
all, according to the word of
the LORD given through his
servant Ahijah the Shilonite—
30 because of the sins Jeroboam
had committed and had
caused Israel to commit, and
because he provoked the LORD,
the God of Israel, to anger.
31 As for the other events of
Nadab's reign, and all he did,
are they not written in the
book of the annals of the kings
of Israel? 32 There was war between Asa and Baasha king of
Israel throughout their reigns.

*Baasha King of Israel*

33 In the third year of Asa
king of Judah, Baasha son of
Ahijah became king of all Israel in Tirzah, and he reigned
twenty-four years. 34 He did
evil in the eyes of the LORD,
walking in the ways of Jeroboam and in his sin, which he

וּבְחַטָּאתוֹ אֲשֶׁר הֶחֱטִיא אֶת־יִשְׂרָאֵל׃ וַיְהִי
then-he-came (16:1) Israel *** he-caused-to-commit which and-in-sin-of-him

דְבַר־יְהוָה אֶל־יֵהוּא בֶן־חֲנָנִי עַל־בַּעְשָׁא לֵאמֹר׃ יַעַן אֲשֶׁר
that because (2) to-say Baasha against Hanani son-of Jehu to Yahweh word-of

הֲרִימֹתִיךָ מִן־הֶעָפָר וָאֶתֶּנְךָ נָגִיד עַל עַמִּי יִשְׂרָאֵל
Israel people-of-me over leader and-I-made-you the-dust from I-lifted-up-you

וַתֵּלֶךְ ׀ בְּדֶרֶךְ יָרָבְעָם וַתַּחֲטִא אֶת־עַמִּי
people-of-me *** and-you-caused-to-sin Jeroboam in-way-of but-you-walked

יִשְׂרָאֵל לְהַכְעִיסֵנִי בְּחַטֹּאתָם׃ הִנְנִי מַבְעִיר אַחֲרֵי
after consuming see-I! (3) by-sins-of-them to-provoke-to-anger-me Israel

בַעְשָׁא וְאַחֲרֵי בֵיתוֹ וְנָתַתִּי אֶת־בֵּיתְךָ כְּבֵית
like-house-of house-of-you *** and-I-will-make house-of-him and-after Baasha

יָרָבְעָם בֶּן־נְבָט׃ הַמֵּת לְבַעְשָׁא בָּעִיר יֹאכְלוּ
they-will-eat in-the-city of-Baasha the-dead (4) Nebat son-of Jeroboam

הַכְּלָבִים וְהַמֵּת לוֹ בַּשָּׂדֶה יֹאכְלוּ עוֹף הַשָּׁמָיִם׃
the-airs bird-of they-will-eat in-the-field of-him and-the-dead the-dogs

וְיֶתֶר דִּבְרֵי בַעְשָׁא וַאֲשֶׁר עָשָׂה וּגְבוּרָתוֹ הֲלֹא־
not? and-achievement-of-him he-did and-what Baasha events-of and-rest-of (5)

הֵם כְּתוּבִים עַל־סֵפֶר דִּבְרֵי הַיָּמִים לְמַלְכֵי יִשְׂרָאֵל׃
Israel of-kings-of the-days annals-of book-of in ones-being-written they

וַיִּשְׁכַּב בַּעְשָׁא עִם־אֲבֹתָיו וַיִּקָּבֵר בְּתִרְצָה
in-Tirzah and-he-was-buried fathers-of-him with Baasha then-he-rested (6)

וַיִּמְלֹךְ אֵלָה בְנוֹ תַּחְתָּיו׃ וְגַם בְּיַד־
by-hand-of and-also (7) in-place-of-him son-of-him Elah and-he-became-king

יֵהוּא בֶן־חֲנָנִי הַנָּבִיא דְּבַר־יְהוָה הָיָה אֶל־בַּעְשָׁא וְאֶל־
and-to Baasha to he-came Yahweh word-of the-prophet Hanani son-of Jehu

בֵּיתוֹ וְעַל כָּל־הָרָעָה ׀ אֲשֶׁר־עָשָׂה ׀ בְּעֵינֵי יְהוָה
Yahweh in-eyes-of he-did that the-evil all-of and-because-of house-of-him

לְהַכְעִיסוֹ בְּמַעֲשֵׂה יָדָיו לִהְיוֹת כְּבֵית
like-house-of to-become hands-of-him by-deed-of to-provoke-to-anger-him

יָרָבְעָם וְעַל אֲשֶׁר־הִכָּה אֹתוֹ׃ בִּשְׁנַת עֶשְׂרִים וָשֵׁשׁ
and-six twenty in-year-of (8) him he-destroyed that and-because Jeroboam

שָׁנָה לְאָסָא מֶלֶךְ יְהוּדָה מָלַךְ אֵלָה בֶן־בַּעְשָׁא עַל־יִשְׂרָאֵל
Israel over Baasha son-of Elah he-became-king Judah king-of of-Asa year

בְּתִרְצָה שְׁנָתָיִם׃ וַיִּקְשֹׁר עָלָיו עַבְדּוֹ זִמְרִי
Zimri official-of-him against-him and-he-plotted (9) two-years in-Tirzah

שַׂר מַחֲצִית הָרֶכֶב וְהוּא בְתִרְצָה שֹׁתֶה שִׁכּוֹר בֵּית
home-of drunk drinking in-Tirzah now-he the-chariot half-of commander-of

had caused Israel to commit.
16 Then the word of the
LORD came to Jehu son
of Hanani against Baasha: 2"I
lifted you up from the dust
and made you leader of my
people Israel, but you walked
in the ways of Jeroboam and
caused my people Israel to sin
and to provoke me to anger by
their sins. 3So I am about to
consume Baasha and his
house, and I will make your
house like that of Jeroboam
son of Nebat. 4Dogs will eat
those belonging to Baasha
who die in the city, and the
birds of the air will feed on
those who die in the country."
5As for the other events of
Baasha's reign, what he did
and his achievements, are
they not written in the book of
the annals of the kings of Israel? 6Baasha rested with his fathers and was buried in Tirzah. And Elah his son succeeded him as king.
7Moreover, the word of the
LORD came through the
prophet Jehu son of Hanani to
Baasha and his house, because
of all the evil he had done in
the eyes of the LORD, provoking him to anger by the things
he did, and becoming like the
house of Jeroboam—and also
because he destroyed it.

*Elah King of Israel*

8In the twenty-sixth year of
Asa king of Judah, Elah son of
Baasha became king of Israel,
and he reigned in Tirzah two
years.
9Zimri, one of his officials,
who had command of half his
chariots, plotted against him.
Elah was in Tirzah at the time,
getting drunk in the home of

אַרְצָא אֲשֶׁר עַל־הַבַּיִת בְּתִרְצָה׃ וַיָּבֹא זִמְרִי וַיַּכֵּהוּ
and-he-struck-him Zimri and-he-came-in (10) at-Tirzah the-palace over who Arza

וַיְמִיתֵהוּ בִּשְׁנַת עֶשְׂרִים וָשֶׁבַע לְאָסָא מֶלֶךְ יְהוּדָה
Judah king-of of-Asa and-seven twenty in-year-of and-he-killed-him

וַיִּמְלֹךְ תַּחְתָּיו׃ וַיְהִי בְמָלְכוֹ
when-to-reign-him and-he-was (11) in-place-of-him and-he-became-king

כְּשִׁבְתּוֹ עַל־ כִּסְאוֹ הִכָּה אֶת־ כָּל־ בֵּית בַּעְשָׁא לֹא־
not Baasha family-of entire-of *** he-killed throne-of-him on as-to-sit-him

הִשְׁאִיר לוֹ מַשְׁתִּין בְּקִיר וְגֹאֲלָיו
or-ones-being-relatives-of-him against-wall one-urinating of-him he-spared

וְרֵעֵהוּ׃ וַיַּשְׁמֵד זִמְרִי אֵת כָּל־ בֵּית בַּעְשָׁא
Baasha family-of whole-of *** Zimri so-he-destroyed (12) of-friend-of-him

כִּדְבַר יְהוָה אֲשֶׁר דִּבֶּר אֶל־ בַּעְשָׁא בְּיַד יֵהוּא הַנָּבִיא׃
the-prophet Jehu by-hand-of Baasha against he-spoke that Yahweh as-word-of

אֶל כָּל־ חַטֹּאות בַּעְשָׁא וְחַטֹּאות אֵלָה בְנוֹ אֲשֶׁר
that son-of-him Elah and-sins-of Baasha sins-of all-of because-of (13)

חָטְאוּ וַאֲשֶׁר הֶחֱטִיאוּ אֶת־ יִשְׂרָאֵל לְהַכְעִיס
to-provoke-to-anger Israel *** they-caused-to-commit and-that they-committed

אֶת־ יְהוָה אֱלֹהֵי יִשְׂרָאֵל בְּהַבְלֵיהֶם׃ וְיֶתֶר דִּבְרֵי
events-of and-rest-of (14) by-worthless-ones-them Israel God-of Yahweh ***

אֵלָה וְכָל־ אֲשֶׁר עָשָׂה הֲלוֹא־הֵם כְּתוּבִים עַל־ סֵפֶר דִּבְרֵי
annals-of book-of in ones-being-written they not? he-did that and-all Elah

הַיָּמִים לְמַלְכֵי יִשְׂרָאֵל׃ בִּשְׁנַת עֶשְׂרִים וָשֶׁבַע שָׁנָה לְאָסָא
of-Asa year and-seven twenty in-year-of (15) Israel of-kings-of the-days

מֶלֶךְ יְהוּדָה מָלַךְ זִמְרִי שִׁבְעַת יָמִים בְּתִרְצָה וְהָעָם
and-the-army in-Tirzah days seven-of Zimri he-reigned Judah king-of

חֹנִים עַל־ גִּבְּתוֹן אֲשֶׁר לַפְּלִשְׁתִּים׃ וַיִּשְׁמַע
when-he-heard (16) of-the-Philistines that Gibbethon near ones-camping

הָעָם הַחֹנִים לֵאמֹר קָשַׁר זִמְרִי וְגַם הִכָּה אֶת־
*** he-murdered and-also Zimri he-plotted to-say the-ones-camping the-army

הַמֶּלֶךְ וַיַּמְלִכוּ כָל־ יִשְׂרָאֵל אֶת־עָמְרִי שַׂר־ צָבָא עַל־
over army commander-of Omri *** Israel all-of then-they-made-king the-king

יִשְׂרָאֵל בַּיּוֹם הַהוּא בַּמַּחֲנֶה׃ וַיַּעֲלֶה עָמְרִי וְכָל־
and-all-of Omri then-he-withdrew (17) in-the-camp the-that on-the-day Israel

יִשְׂרָאֵל עִמּוֹ מִגִּבְּתוֹן וַיָּצֻרוּ עַל־ תִּרְצָה׃ וַיְהִי
and-he-was (18) Tirzah to and-they-laid-siege from-Gibbethon with-him Israel

כִּרְאוֹת זִמְרִי כִּי־ נִלְכְּדָה הָעִיר וַיָּבֹא אֶל־ אַרְמוֹן
citadel-of into then-he-went the-city she-was-taken that Zimri when-to-see

Arza, the man in charge of the palace at Tirzah. [10]Zimri came in, struck him down and killed him in the twenty-seventh year of Asa king of Judah. Then he succeeded him as king.

[11]As soon as he began to reign and was seated on the throne, he killed off Baasha's whole family. He did not spare a single male, whether relative or friend. [12]So Zimri destroyed the whole family of Baasha, in accordance with the word of the LORD spoken against Baasha through the prophet Jehu— [13]because of all the sins Baasha and his son Elah had committed and had caused Israel to commit, so that they provoked the LORD, the God of Israel to anger by their worthless idols.

[14]As for the other events of Elah's reign, and all he did, are they not written in the book of the annals of the kings of Israel?

*Zimri King of Israel*

[15]In the twenty-seventh year of Asa king of Judah, Zimri reigned in Tirzah seven days. The army was encamped near Gibbethon, a Philistine town. [16]When the Israelites in the camp heard that Zimri had plotted against the king and murdered him, they proclaimed Omri, the commander of the army, king over Israel that very day there in the camp. [17]Then Omri and all the Israelites with him withdrew from Gibbethon and laid siege to Tirzah. [18]When Zimri saw that the city was taken, he went into the citadel of the

בֵּית־ הַמֶּ֫לֶךְ וַיִּשְׂרֹף עָלָ֖יו אֶת־ בֵּית־ מֶ֫לֶךְ בָּאֵשׁ
palace-of the-king and-he-set-fire around-him *** palace-of king with-fire

וַיָּ֫מֹת: (19) עַל־ חַטֹּאתָיו֙ אֲשֶׁר חָטָ֔א לַעֲשׂ֥וֹת הָרַ֖ע
so-he-died (19) because-of sins-of-him that he-committed to-do the-evil

בְּעֵינֵ֣י יְהוָ֔ה לָלֶ֙כֶת֙ בְּדֶ֣רֶךְ יָרָבְעָ֔ם וּבְחַטָּאתוֹ֙ אֲשֶׁ֣ר
in-eyes-of Yahweh to-walk in-way-of Jeroboam and-in-sin-of-him that

עָשָׂ֔ה לְהַחֲטִ֖יא אֶת־ יִשְׂרָאֵֽל: (20) וְיֶ֛תֶר דִּבְרֵ֥י זִמְרִ֖י
he-committed to-cause-to-commit *** Israel (20) and-rest-of events-of Zimri

וְקִשְׁר֣וֹ אֲשֶׁ֣ר קָשָׁ֑ר הֲלֹא־ הֵ֣ם כְּתוּבִ֗ים עַל־
and-rebellion-of-him that he-rebelled not? they ones-being-written in

סֵ֛פֶר דִּבְרֵ֥י הַיָּמִ֖ים לְמַלְכֵ֥י יִשְׂרָאֵֽל: (21) אָ֣ז יֵחָלֵ֞ק הָעָ֤ם
book-of annals-of the-days of-kings-of Israel (21) then he-was-split the-people

יִשְׂרָאֵל֙ לַחֵ֔צִי חֲצִ֤י הָעָם֙ הָיָ֗ה אַחֲרֵ֞י תִבְנִ֤י בֶן־ גִּינַת֙
Israel in-two half-of the-people he-was after Tibni son-of Ginath

לְהַמְלִיכ֔וֹ וְהַחֲצִ֖י אַחֲרֵ֣י עָמְרִֽי: (22) וַיֶּחֱזַ֣ק הָעָ֗ם
to-make-king-him and-the-half after Omri (22) but-he-was-stronger the-people

אֲשֶׁ֤ר אַחֲרֵ֣י עָמְרִי֙ אֶת־ הָעָ֔ם אֲשֶׁ֣ר אַחֲרֵ֕י תִּבְנִ֥י בֶן־ גִּינַ֖ת וַיָּ֥מָת
who after Omri *** the-people who after Tibni son-of Ginath so-he-died

תִּבְנִ֖י וַיִּמְלֹ֥ךְ עָמְרִֽי: (23) בִּשְׁנַת֩ שְׁלֹשִׁ֨ים וְאַחַ֜ת שָׁנָ֗ה לְאָסָא֙
Tibni and-he-became-king Omri (23) in-year-of thirty and-one year of-Asa

מֶ֣לֶךְ יְהוּדָ֔ה מָלַ֤ךְ עָמְרִי֙ עַל־יִשְׂרָאֵ֔ל שְׁתֵּ֥ים עֶשְׂרֵ֖ה שָׁנָ֑ה בְּתִרְצָ֖ה
king-of Judah he-became-king Omri over-Israel two ten year in-Tirzah

מָלַ֣ךְ שֵׁ֥שׁ שָׁנִֽים: (24) וַיִּ֜קֶן אֶת־ הָהָ֤ר שֹׁמְרוֹן֙ מֵאֵ֣ת שֶׁ֔מֶר
he-reigned six years (24) and-he-bought *** the-hill Samaria from Shemer

בְּכִכְּרַ֣יִם כָּ֑סֶף וַיִּ֙בֶן֙ אֶת־ הָהָ֔ר וַיִּקְרָ֗א אֶת־ שֵׁ֤ם
for-two-talents silver and-he-built *** the-hill and-he-called *** name-of

הָעִיר֙ אֲשֶׁ֣ר בָּנָ֔ה עַ֣ל שֶׁם־ שֶׁ֔מֶר אֲדֹנֵ֥י הָהָ֖ר שֹׁמְרֽוֹן:
the-city that he-built after name-of Shemer owners-of the-hill Samaria

(25) וַיַּעֲשֶׂ֥ה עָמְרִ֛י הָרַ֖ע בְּעֵינֵ֣י יְהוָ֑ה וַיָּ֕רַע מִכֹּ֖ל
(25) but-he-did Omri the-evil in-eyes-of Yahweh and-he-sinned more-than-all

אֲשֶׁ֥ר לְפָנָֽיו: (26) וַיֵּ֗לֶךְ בְּכָל־ דֶּ֙רֶךְ֙ יָרָבְעָ֣ם בֶּן־ נְבָ֔ט
who before-him (26) and-he-walked in-all-of way-of Jeroboam son-of Nebat

וּֽבְחַטֹּאותָ֗יו אֲשֶׁ֤ר הֶחֱטִיא֙ אֶת־ יִשְׂרָאֵ֔ל לְהַכְעִ֗יס
and-in-sin-of-him which he-caused-to-commit *** Israel to-provoke-to-anger

אֶת־ יְהוָ֛ה אֱלֹהֵ֥י יִשְׂרָאֵ֖ל בְּהַבְלֵיהֶֽם: (27) וְיֶ֙תֶר֙ דִּבְרֵ֣י
*** Yahweh God-of Israel by-worthless-ones-of-them (27) and-rest-of events-of

עָמְרִ֔י אֲשֶׁ֥ר עָשָׂ֖ה וּגְבוּרָת֣וֹ אֲשֶׁ֣ר עָשָׂ֑ה הֲלֹא־ הֵ֣ם
Omri what he-did and-achievement-of-him that he-did not? they

royal palace and set the palace
on fire around him. So he
died, [19]because of the sins he
had committed, doing evil in
the eyes of the LORD and walking in the ways of Jeroboam
and in the sin he had committed and had caused Israel to
commit.

[20]As for the other events of
Zimri's reign, and the rebellion he carried out, are they
not written in the book of the
annals of the kings of Israel?

*Omri King of Israel*

[21]Then the people of Israel
were split into two factions;
half supported Tibni son of
Ginath for king, and the other
half supported Omri. [22]But
Omri's followers proved
stronger than those of Tibni
son of Ginath. So Tibni died
and Omri became king.

[23]In the thirty-first year of
Asa king of Judah, Omri
became king of Israel, and he
reigned twelve years, six of
them in Tirzah. [24]He bought
the hill of Samaria from Shemer for two talents' of silver
and built a city on the hill,
calling it Samaria, after Shemer, the name of the former
owner of the hill.

[25]But Omri did evil in the
eyes of the LORD and sinned
more than all those before
him. [26]He walked in all the
ways of Jeroboam son of
Nebat and in his sin, which
he had caused Israel to commit, so that they provoked the
LORD, the God of Israel, to anger by their worthless idols.
[27]As for the other events of
Omri's reign, what he did and
the things he achieved, are

'24 That is, about 150 pounds (about 70
kilograms)

*26 Most mss end this verse with *soph
pasuq* ( : ).

ק חטאתיו 19°

ק ובחטאתו 26°

כְּתוּבִים עַל־ סֵפֶר דִּבְרֵי הַיָּמִים לְמַלְכֵי יִשְׂרָאֵל׃
Israel of-kings-of the-days annals-of book-of in ones-being-written

וַיִּשְׁכַּב עָמְרִי עִם־ אֲבֹתָיו וַיִּקָּבֵר בְּשֹׁמְרוֹן
in-Samaria and-he-was-buried fathers-of-him with Omri and-he-rested (28)

וַיִּמְלֹךְ אַחְאָב בְּנוֹ תַּחְתָּיו׃ וְאַחְאָב בֶּן־ עָמְרִי
Omri son-of and-Ahab (29) in-place-of-him son-of-him Ahab and-he-became-king

מָלַךְ עַל־יִשְׂרָאֵל בִּשְׁנַת שְׁלֹשִׁים וּשְׁמֹנֶה שָׁנָה לְאָסָא מֶלֶךְ
king-of of-Asa year and-eight thirty in-year-of Israel over he-became-king

יְהוּדָה וַיִּמְלֹךְ אַחְאָב בֶּן־ עָמְרִי עַל־יִשְׂרָאֵל בְּשֹׁמְרוֹן עֶשְׂרִים וּשְׁתַּיִם
and-two twenty in-Samaria Israel over Omri son-of Ahab and-he-reigned Judah

שָׁנָה׃ וַיַּעַשׂ אַחְאָב בֶּן־ עָמְרִי הָרַע בְּעֵינֵי יְהוָה מִכֹּל
more-than-all Yahweh in-eyes-of the-evil Omri son-of Ahab and-he-did (30) year

אֲשֶׁר לְפָנָיו׃ וַיְהִי הֲנָקֵל לֶכְתּוֹ בְּחַטֹּאות יָרָבְעָם
Jeroboam in-sins-of to-walk-him being-trivial? and-he-was (31) before-him who

בֶּן־ נְבָט וַיִּקַּח אִשָּׁה אֶת־ אִיזֶבֶל בַּת־ אֶתְבַּעַל מֶלֶךְ
king-of Ethbaal daughter-of Jezebel *** wife but-he-took Nebat son-of

צִידֹנִים וַיֵּלֶךְ וַיַּעֲבֹד אֶת־ הַבַּעַל וַיִּשְׁתַּחוּ לוֹ׃
to-him and-he-worshiped the-Baal *** and-he-served and-he-went Sidonians

וַיָּקֶם מִזְבֵּחַ לַבָּעַל בֵּית הַבַּעַל אֲשֶׁר בָּנָה
he-built that the-Baal temple-of to-the-Baal altar and-he-set-up (32)

בְּשֹׁמְרוֹן׃ וַיַּעַשׂ אַחְאָב אֶת־ הָאֲשֵׁרָה וַיּוֹסֶף אַחְאָב
Ahab and-he-added the-Asherah-pole *** Ahab and-he-made (33) in-Samaria

לַעֲשׂוֹת לְהַכְעִיס אֶת־ יְהוָה אֱלֹהֵי יִשְׂרָאֵל מִכֹּל מַלְכֵי
kings-of more-than-all-of Israel God-of Yahweh *** to-provoke-to-anger to-do

יִשְׂרָאֵל אֲשֶׁר הָיוּ לְפָנָיו׃ בְּיָמָיו בָּנָה חִיאֵל
Hiel he-rebuilt in-days-of-him (34) before-him they-were who Israel

בֵּית הָאֱלִי אֶת־ יְרִיחֹה בַּאֲבִירָם בְּכֹרוֹ יִסְּדָהּ
he-founded-her firstborn-of-him with-Abiram Jericho *** the-Bethelite

וּבִשְׂגִיב° צְעִירוֹ הִצִּיב דְּלָתֶיהָ כִּדְבַר יְהוָה אֲשֶׁר
that Yahweh as-word-of gates-of-her he-set-up youngest-of-him and-with-Segub

דִּבֶּר בְּיַד יְהוֹשֻׁעַ בִּן־ נוּן׃ וַיֹּאמֶר אֵלִיָּהוּ הַתִּשְׁבִּי
the-Tishbite Elijah now-he-said (17:1) Nun son-of Joshua by-hand-of he-spoke

מִתֹּשָׁבֵי גִלְעָד אֶל־אַחְאָב חַי־ יְהוָה אֱלֹהֵי יִשְׂרָאֵל אֲשֶׁר עָמַדְתִּי
I-serve whom Israel God-of Yahweh life-of Ahab to Gilead from-Tishbe-of

לְפָנָיו אִם־ יִהְיֶה הַשָּׁנִים הָאֵלֶּה טַל וּמָטָר כִּי אִם־
if except or-rain dew the-these the-years he-will-be not before-him

לְפִי דְבָרִי׃ וַיְהִי דְבַר־ יְהוָה אֵלָיו לֵאמֹר׃
to-say to-him Yahweh word-of then-he-came (2) word-of-me at-mouth-of

they not written in the book of
the annals of the kings of Israel? [28]Omri rested with his fathers and was buried in Samaria. And Ahab his son succeeded him as king.

*Ahab Becomes King of Israel*

[29]In the thirty-eighth year of
Asa king of Judah, Ahab son
of Omri became king of Israel,
and he reigned in Samaria
over Israel twenty-two years.
[30]Ahab son of Omri did more
evil in the eyes of the LORD
than any of those before him.
[31]He not only considered it
trivial to commit the sins of
Jeroboam son of Nebat, but he
also married Jezebel daughter
of Ethbaal king of the Sidonians, and began to serve Baal
and worship him. [32]He set up
an altar for Baal in the temple
of Baal that he built in Samaria. [33]Ahab also made an
Asherah pole and did more to
provoke the LORD, the God of
Israel, to anger than did all the
kings of Israel before him.
[34]In Ahab's time, Hiel of
Bethel rebuilt Jericho. He laid
its foundations at the cost of
his firstborn son Abiram, and
he set up its gates at the cost of
his youngest son Segub, in accordance with the word of the
LORD spoken by Joshua son of
Nun.

*Elijah Fed by Ravens*

17 Now Elijah the Tish-
bite, from Tishbe[s] in
Gilead, said to Ahab, "As the
LORD, the God of Israel, lives,
whom I serve, there will be
neither dew nor rain in the
next few years except at my
word."
[2]Then the word of the LORD

[s]1 Or *Tishbite, of the settlers*

°*34* ק ובשגוב

לֵךְ מִזֶּה וּפָנִיתָ לְּךָ קֵדְמָה וְנִסְתַּרְתָּ בְּנַחַל
in-Ravine-of and-you-hide to-east to-you and-you-turn from-here leave! (3)

כְּרִית אֲשֶׁר עַל־ פְּנֵי הַיַּרְדֵּן׃ וְהָיָה מֵהַנַּחַל
from-the-brook and-he-will-be (4) the-Jordan east-of to that Kerith

תִּשְׁתֶּה וְאֶת־ הָעֹרְבִים צִוִּיתִי לְכַלְכֶּלְךָ שָׁם׃ וַיֵּלֶךְ
so-he-went (5) there to-feed-you I-ordered the-ravens and you-will-drink

וַיַּעַשׂ כִּדְבַר יְהוָה וַיֵּלֶךְ וַיֵּשֶׁב בְּנַחַל כְּרִית
Kerith at-Ravine-of and-he-stayed and-he-went Yahweh as-word-of and-he-did

אֲשֶׁר עַל־ פְּנֵי הַיַּרְדֵּן׃ וְהָעֹרְבִים מְבִיאִים לוֹ לֶחֶם
bread to-him ones-bringing and-the-ravens (6) the-Jordan east-of at that

וּבָשָׂר בַּבֹּקֶר וְלֶחֶם וּבָשָׂר בָּעָרֶב וּמִן־ הַנַּחַל
the-brook and-from in-the-evening and-meat and-bread in-the-morning and-meat

יִשְׁתֶּה׃ וַיְהִי מִקֵּץ יָמִים וַיִּיבַשׁ הַנָּחַל כִּי
because the-brook then-he-dried-up days at-end-of and-he-was (7) he-drank

לֹא־ הָיָה גֶשֶׁם בָּאָרֶץ׃ וַיְהִי דְבַר־ יְהוָה אֵלָיו לֵאמֹר׃
to-say to-him Yahweh word-of then-he-came (8) on-the-land rain he-was not

קוּם לֵךְ צָרְפַתָה אֲשֶׁר לְצִידוֹן וְיָשַׁבְתָּ שָׁם הִנֵּה צִוִּיתִי
I-commanded see! there and-you-stay of-Sidon that to-Zarephath go! rise! (9)

שָׁם אִשָּׁה אַלְמָנָה לְכַלְכְּלֶךָ׃ וַיָּקָם ׀ וַיֵּלֶךְ צָרְפַתָה
to-Zarephath and-he-went so-he-rose (10) to-supply-you widow woman there

וַיָּבֹא אֶל־ פֶּתַח הָעִיר וְהִנֵּה־ שָׁם אִשָּׁה אַלְמָנָה מְקֹשֶׁשֶׁת
gathering widow woman there then-see! the-town gate-of to when-he-came

עֵצִים וַיִּקְרָא אֵלֶיהָ וַיֹּאמַר קְחִי־ נָא לִי מְעַט־ מַיִם
waters little-of to-me now! bring! and-he-said to-her and-he-called sticks

בַּכְּלִי וְאֶשְׁתֶּה׃ וַתֵּלֶךְ לָקַחַת וַיִּקְרָא אֵלֶיהָ
to-her and-he-called to-get and-she-went (11) so-I-may-drink in-the-jar

וַיֹּאמַר לִקְחִי־ נָא לִי פַּת־ לֶחֶם בְּיָדֵךְ׃ וַתֹּאמֶר
and-she-said (12) in-hand-of-you bread piece-of to-me now! bring! and-he-said

חַי־ יְהוָה אֱלֹהֶיךָ אִם־ יֶשׁ־ לִי מָעוֹג כִּי אִם־ מְלֹא
fullness-of only but bread to-me there-is not God-of-you Yahweh life-of

כַף־ קֶמַח בַּכַּד וּמְעַט־ שֶׁמֶן בַּצַּפָּחַת וְהִנְנִי מְקֹשֶׁשֶׁת
gathering and-see-I! in-the-jug oil and-little-of in-the-jar flour hand-of

שְׁנַיִם עֵצִים וּבָאתִי וַעֲשִׂיתִיהוּ לִי וְלִבְנִי
and-for-son-of-me for-me and-I-will-make-him then-I-will-go sticks two

וַאֲכַלְנֻהוּ וָמָתְנוּ׃ וַיֹּאמֶר אֵלֶיהָ אֵלִיָּהוּ אַל־ תִּירְאִי
you-fear not Elijah to-her and-he-said (13) and-we-may-die so-we-may-eat-him

בֹּאִי עֲשִׂי כִדְבָרֵךְ אַךְ עֲשִׂי־ לִי מִשָּׁם עֻגָה קְטַנָּה בָרִאשֹׁנָה
at-the-first small cake from-there for-me make! but as-word-of-you do! go!

came to Elijah: 3"Leave here, turn eastward and hide in the Kerith Ravine, east of the Jordan. 4You will drink from the brook, and I have ordered the ravens to feed you there."
5So he did what the LORD had told him. He went to the Kerith Ravine, east of the Jordan, and stayed there. 6The ravens brought him bread and meat in the morning and bread and meat in the evening, and he drank from the brook.

*The Widow at Zarephath*

7Some time later the brook dried up because there had been no rain in the land.
8Then the word of the LORD came to him: 9"Go at once to Zarephath of Sidon and stay there. I have commanded a widow in that place to supply you with food." 10So he went to Zarephath. When he came to the town gate, a widow was there gathering sticks. He called to her and asked, "Would you bring me a little water in a jar so I may have a drink?" 11As she was going to get it, he called, "And bring me, please, a piece of bread."
12"As surely as the LORD your God lives," she replied, "I don't have any bread—only a handful of flour in a jar and a little oil in a jug. I am gathering a few sticks to take home and make a meal for myself and my son, that we may eat it—and die."
13Elijah said to her, "Don't be afraid. Go home and do as you have said. But first make a small cake of bread for me from what you have and bring

וְהוֹצֵאתְ* לִי וְלָךְ וְלִבְנֵךְ תַּעֲשִׂי בָּאַחֲרֹנָה׃
at-the-afterward you-make and-for-son-of-you then-for-you to-me and-you-bring

כִּי כֹה° אָמַר יְהוָה אֱלֹהֵי יִשְׂרָאֵל כַּד הַקֶּמַח לֹא
not the-flour jar-of Israel God-of Yahweh he-says this for (14)

תִּכְלָה וְצַפַּחַת הַשֶּׁמֶן לֹא תֶחְסָר עַד יוֹם תֵּתֶן־
to-give day until she-will-run-dry not the-oil and-jug-of she-will-be-used-up

יְהוָה גֶּשֶׁם עַל־ פְּנֵי הָאֲדָמָה׃ וַתֵּלֶךְ וַתַּעֲשֶׂה כִּדְבַר
as-word-of and-she-did so-she-went (15) the-land surfaces-of on rain Yahweh

אֵלִיָּהוּ וַתֹּאכַל הִוא־° וָהִיא° וּבֵיתָהּ יָמִים׃ כַּד הַקֶּמַח
the-flour jar-of (16) days and-family-of-her and-he she and-she-ate Elijah

לֹא כָלָתָה וְצַפַּחַת הַשֶּׁמֶן לֹא חָסֵר כִּדְבַר יְהוָה
Yahweh as-word-of he-ran-dry not the-oil and-jug-of she-was-used-up not

אֲשֶׁר דִּבֶּר בְּיַד אֵלִיָּהוּ׃ וַיְהִי אַחַר הַדְּבָרִים הָאֵלֶּה
the-these the-things after and-he-was (17) Elijah by-hand-of he-spoke that

חָלָה בֶּן־ הָאִשָּׁה בַּעֲלַת הַבָּיִת וַיְהִי חָלְיוֹ
illness-of-him and-he-became the-house owner-of the-woman son-of he-became-ill

חָזָק מְאֹד עַד אֲשֶׁר לֹא־ נוֹתְרָה־ בּוֹ נְשָׁמָה׃ וַתֹּאמֶר אֶל־
to and-she-said (18) breath in-him she-remained not when until very worse

אֵלִיָּהוּ מַה־ לִּי וָלָךְ אִישׁ הָאֱלֹהִים בָּאתָ אֵלַי לְהַזְכִּיר אֶת־
*** to-remind to-me you-came the-God man-of and-to-you to-me what? Elijah

עֲוֹנִי וּלְהָמִית אֶת־ בְּנִי׃ וַיֹּאמֶר אֵלֶיהָ תְּנִי־ לִי
to-me give! to-her and-he-replied (19) son-of-me *** and-to-kill sin-of-me

אֶת־ בְּנֵךְ וַיִּקָּחֵהוּ מֵחֵיקָהּ וַיַּעֲלֵהוּ אֶל־
to and-he-carried-him from-bosom-of-her and-he-took-him son-of-you ***

הָעֲלִיָּה אֲשֶׁר־ הוּא יֹשֵׁב שָׁם וַיַּשְׁכִּבֵהוּ עַל־ מִטָּתוֹ׃
bed-of-him on and-he-laid-him there staying he where the-upper-room

וַיִּקְרָא אֶל־ יְהוָה וַיֹּאמַר יְהוָה אֱלֹהָי הֲגַם עַל־
upon also? God-of-me Yahweh and-he-said Yahweh to then-he-cried-out (20)

הָאַלְמָנָה אֲשֶׁר־אֲנִי מִתְגּוֹרֵר עִמָּהּ הֲרֵעוֹתָ לְהָמִית אֶת־ בְּנָהּ׃
son-of-her *** to-kill you-brought-evil with-her staying I whom the-widow

וַיִּתְמֹדֵד עַל־ הַיֶּלֶד שָׁלֹשׁ פְּעָמִים וַיִּקְרָא אֶל־ יְהוָה
Yahweh to and-he-cried times three the-boy on then-he-stretched-out (21)

וַיֹּאמַר יְהוָה אֱלֹהָי תָּשָׁב נָא נֶפֶשׁ־ הַיֶּלֶד הַזֶּה
the-this the-boy life-of now! let-her-return God-of-me Yahweh and-he-said

עַל־ קִרְבּוֹ׃ וַיִּשְׁמַע יְהוָה בְּקוֹל אֵלִיָּהוּ וַתָּשָׁב
and-she-returned Elijah to-cry-of Yahweh and-he-heard (22) body-of-him to

נֶפֶשׁ־ הַיֶּלֶד עַל־ קִרְבּוֹ וַיֶּחִי׃ וַיִּקַּח אֵלִיָּהוּ
Elijah then-he-picked-up (23) and-he-lived body-of-him to the-boy life-of

it to me, and then make something for yourself and your
son. 14For this is what the
LORD, the God of Israel, says:
'The jar of flour will not be
used up and the jug of oil will
not run dry until the day the
LORD gives rain on the land.' "
15She went away and did as
Elijah had told her. So there
was food every day for Elijah
and for the woman and her
family. 16For the jar of flour
was not used up and the jug of
oil did not run dry, in keeping
with the word of the LORD
spoken by Elijah.
17Some time later the son of
the woman who owned the
house became ill. He grew
worse and worse, and finally
stopped breathing. 18She said
to Elijah, "What do you have
against me, man of God? Did
you come to remind me of my
sin and kill my son?"
19"Give me your son," Elijah
replied. He took him from her
arms, carried him to the upper
room where he was staying,
and laid him on his bed.
20Then he cried out to the
LORD, "O LORD my God, have
you brought tragedy also upon
this widow I am staying with,
by causing her son to die?"
21Then he stretched himself
out on the boy three times and
cried to the LORD, "O LORD my
God, let this boy's life return
to him!"
22The LORD heard Elijah's
cry, and the boy's life returned
to him, and he lived. 23Elijah

*13 Most mss have no *sheva* under the *tav* (תְ–).

°14 ק תת
°15a ק היא
°15b ק והוא

אֶת־הַיֶּלֶד וַיֹּרִדֵהוּ מִן־הָעֲלִיָּה הַבַּיְתָה
into-the-house the-upper-room from and-he-carried-down-him the-child ***

וַיִּתְּנֵהוּ לְאִמּוֹ וַיֹּאמֶר אֵלִיָּהוּ רְאִי חַי בְּנֵךְ׃
son-of-you alive look! Elijah and-he-said to-mother-of-him and-he-gave-him

וַתֹּאמֶר הָאִשָּׁה אֶל־אֵלִיָּהוּ עַתָּה זֶה יָדַעְתִּי כִּי אִישׁ אֱלֹהִים
God man-of that I-know this now Elijah to the-woman then-she-said (24)

אַתָּה וּדְבַר־יְהוָה בְּפִיךָ אֱמֶת׃ וַיְהִי יָמִים רַבִּים
many days and-he-was (18:1) truth from-mouth-of-you Yahweh and-word-of you

וּדְבַר־יְהוָה הָיָה אֶל־אֵלִיָּהוּ בַּשָּׁנָה הַשְּׁלִישִׁית לֵאמֹר לֵךְ
go! to-say the-third in-the-year Elijah to he-came Yahweh and-word-of

הֵרָאֵה אֶל־אַחְאָב וְאֶתְּנָה מָטָר עַל־פְּנֵי הָאֲדָמָה׃
the-land surfaces-of on rain and-I-will-send Ahab to present-yourself!

וַיֵּלֶךְ אֵלִיָּהוּ לְהֵרָאוֹת אֶל־אַחְאָב וְהָרָעָב חָזָק
severe now-the-famine Ahab to to-present-himself Elijah so-he-went (2)

בְּשֹׁמְרוֹן׃ וַיִּקְרָא אַחְאָב אֶל־עֹבַדְיָהוּ אֲשֶׁר עַל־הַבָּיִת
the-palace over who Obadiah to Ahab and-he-summoned (3) in-Samaria

וְעֹבַדְיָהוּ הָיָה יָרֵא אֶת־יְהוָה מְאֹד׃ וַיְהִי בְּהַכְרִית
while-to-kill and-he-was (4) devoutly Yahweh *** fearing he-was now-Obadiah

אִיזֶבֶל אֵת נְבִיאֵי יְהוָה וַיִּקַּח עֹבַדְיָהוּ מֵאָה נְבִאִים
prophets hundred Obadiah then-he-took Yahweh prophets-of *** Jezebel

וַיַּחְבִּיאֵם חֲמִשִּׁים אִישׁ בַּמְּעָרָה וְכִלְכְּלָם לֶחֶם וָמָיִם׃
and-waters food and-he-supplied-them in-the-cave each fifty and-he-hid-them

וַיֹּאמֶר אַחְאָב אֶל־עֹבַדְיָהוּ לֵךְ בָּאָרֶץ אֶל־כָּל־מַעְיְנֵי
springs-of all-of to through-the-land go! Obadiah to Ahab and-he-said (5)

הַמַּיִם וְאֶל כָּל־הַנְּחָלִים אוּלַי ׀ נִמְצָא חָצִיר
grass we-can-find perhaps the-valleys all-of and-to the-waters

וּנְחַיֶּה סוּס וָפֶרֶד וְלוֹא נַכְרִית מֵהַבְּהֵמָה׃
from-the-animal we-must-kill so-not and-mule horse and-we-can-keep-alive

וַיְחַלְּקוּ לָהֶם אֶת־הָאָרֶץ לַעֲבָר־בָּהּ אַחְאָב
Ahab through-her to-cover the-land *** between-them so-they-divided (6)

הָלַךְ בְּדֶרֶךְ אֶחָד לְבַדּוֹ וְעֹבַדְיָהוּ הָלַךְ בְּדֶרֶךְ־אֶחָד
another in-direction he-went and-Obadiah by-himself one in-direction he-went

לְבַדּוֹ׃ וַיְהִי עֹבַדְיָהוּ בַּדֶּרֶךְ וְהִנֵּה אֵלִיָּהוּ לִקְרָאתוֹ
to-meet-him Elijah and-see! on-the-way Obadiah and-he-was (7) by-himself

וַיַּכִּרֵהוּ וַיִּפֹּל עַל־פָּנָיו וַיֹּאמֶר הַאַתָּה זֶה
this you? and-he-said faces-of-him on and-he-bowed and-he-recognized-him

אֲדֹנִי אֵלִיָּהוּ׃ וַיֹּאמֶר לוֹ אָנִי לֵךְ אֱמֹר לַאדֹנֶיךָ
to-masters-of-you tell! go! I to-him and-he-replied (8) Elijah lord-of-me

picked up the child and carried him down from the room into the house. He gave him to his mother and said, "Look, your son is alive!"

[24]Then the woman said to Elijah, "Now I know that you are a man of God and that the word of the LORD from your mouth is the truth."

*Elijah and Obadiah*

18 After a long time, in the third year, the word of the LORD came to Elijah: "Go and present yourself to Ahab, and I will send rain on the land." [2]So Elijah went to present himself to Ahab.

Now the famine was severe in Samaria, [3]and Ahab had summoned Obadiah, who was in charge of his palace. (Obadiah was a devout believer in the LORD. [4]While Jezebel was killing off the LORD's prophets, Obadiah had taken a hundred prophets and hidden them in two caves, fifty in each, and had supplied them with food and water.) [5]Ahab had said to Obadiah, "Go through the land to all the springs and valleys. Maybe we can find some grass to keep the horses and mules alive so we will not have to kill any of our animals." [6]So they divided the land they were to cover, Ahab going in one direction and Obadiah in another.

[7]As Obadiah was walking along, Elijah met him. Obadiah recognized him, bowed down to the ground, and said, "Is it really you, my lord Elijah?"

[8]"Yes," he replied. "Go tell

הִנֵּה אֵלִיָּהוּ׃ וַיֹּאמֶר מֶה חָטָאתִי כִּֽי־ אַתָּה נֹתֵן אֶת־
*** handing you that I-did-wrong what? and-he-said (9) Elijah see!

עַבְדְּךָ בְּיַד־ אַחְאָב לַהֲמִיתֵֽנִי׃ חַי ׀ יְהוָה אֱלֹהֶיךָ
God-of-you Yahweh life-of (10) to-kill-me Ahab into-hand-of servant-of-you

אִם־ יֶשׁ־ גּוֹי וּמַמְלָכָה אֲשֶׁר לֹֽא־ שָׁלַח אֲדֹנִי שָׁם
there master-of-me he-sent not where or-kingdom nation there-is not

לְבַקֶּשְׁךָ וְאָמְרוּ אָיִן וְהִשְׁבִּיעַ אֶת־ הַמַּמְלָכָה
the-kingdom *** and-he-made-swear he-is-not and-they-said to-look-for-you

וְאֶת־ הַגּוֹי כִּי לֹא יִמְצָאֶֽכָּה׃ וְעַתָּה אַתָּה אֹמֵר לֵךְ
go! telling you but-now (11) he-could-find-you not that the-nation and

אֱמֹר לַאדֹנֶיךָ הִנֵּה אֵלִיָּהוּ׃ וְהָיָה אֲנִי ׀ אֵלֵךְ
I-will-leave I and-he-will-be (12) Elijah see! to-masters-of-you say!

מֵאִתָּךְ וְרוּחַ יְהוָה ׀ יִשָּׂאֲךָ עַל אֲשֶׁר לֹֽא־ אֵדָע
I-know not where to he-may-carry-you Yahweh and-Spirit-of from-with-you

וּבָאתִי לְהַגִּיד לְאַחְאָב וְלֹא יִמְצָאֲךָ וַהֲרָגָנִי
then-he-will-kill-me he-finds-you and-not to-Ahab to-tell if-I-go

וְעַבְדְּךָ יָרֵא אֶת־ יְהוָה מִנְּעֻרָֽי׃ הֲלֹֽא־
not? (13) from-youths-of-me Yahweh *** worshiping yet-servant-of-you

הֻגַּד לַאדֹנִי אֵת אֲשֶׁר־ עָשִׂיתִי בַּהֲרֹג אִיזֶבֶל אֵת
*** Jezebel while-to-kill I-did what *** to-lord-of-me he-was-told

נְבִיאֵי יְהוָה וָאַחְבִּא מִנְּבִיאֵי יְהוָה מֵאָה אִישׁ חֲמִשִּׁים
fifty man hundred Yahweh from-prophets-of and-I-hid Yahweh prophets-of

חֲמִשִּׁים אִישׁ בַּמְּעָרָה וָאֲכַלְכְּלֵם לֶחֶם וָמָֽיִם׃ וְעַתָּה
but-now (14) and-waters food and-I-supplied-them in-the-cave each fifty

אַתָּה אֹמֵר לֵךְ אֱמֹר לַאדֹנֶיךָ הִנֵּה אֵלִיָּהוּ וַהֲרָגָֽנִי׃
and-he-will-kill-me Elijah see! to-masters-of-you say! go! telling you

וַיֹּאמֶר אֵלִיָּהוּ חַי יְהוָה צְבָאוֹת אֲשֶׁר עָמַדְתִּי לְפָנָיו
before-him I-serve whom Hosts Yahweh-of life-of Elijah and-he-said (15)

כִּי הַיּוֹם אֵרָאֶה אֵלָֽיו׃ וַיֵּלֶךְ עֹבַדְיָהוּ לִקְרַאת
to-meet Obadiah so-he-went (16) to-him I-will-present-myself the-day surely

אַחְאָב וַיַּגֶּד־ לוֹ וַיֵּלֶךְ אַחְאָב לִקְרַאת אֵלִיָּֽהוּ׃ וַיְהִי
and-he-was (17) Elijah to-meet Ahab and-he-went to-him and-he-told Ahab

כִּרְאוֹת אַחְאָב אֶת־אֵלִיָּהוּ וַיֹּאמֶר אַחְאָב אֵלָיו הַאַתָּה זֶה עֹכֵר
one-troubling that you? to-him Ahab then-he-said Elijah *** Ahab when-to-see

יִשְׂרָאֵֽל׃ וַיֹּאמֶר לֹא עָכַרְתִּי אֶת־ יִשְׂרָאֵל כִּי אִם־ אַתָּה
you rather but Israel *** I-troubled not and-he-said (18) Israel

וּבֵית אָבִיךָ בַּעֲזָבְכֶם אֶת־ מִצְוֺת יְהוָה
Yahweh commands-of *** when-to-abandon-you father-of-you and-family-of

your master, 'Elijah is here.' "
9"What have I done wrong,"
asked Obadiah, "that you are
handing your servant over to
Ahab to be put to death? 10As
surely as the LORD your God
lives, there is not a nation or
kingdom where my master
has not sent someone to look
for you. And whenever a nation or kingdom claimed you
were not there, he made them
swear they could not find you.
11But now you tell me to go to
my master and say, 'Elijah is
here.' 12I don't know where
the Spirit of the LORD may carry you when I leave you. If I go
and tell Ahab and he doesn't
find you, he will kill me. Yet I
your servant have worshiped
the LORD since my youth.
13Haven't you heard, my lord,
what I did while Jezebel was
killing the prophets of the
LORD? I hid a hundred of the
LORD's prophets in two caves,
fifty in each, and supplied
them with food and water.
14And now you tell me to go to
my master and say, 'Elijah is
here.' He will kill me!"
15Elijah said, "As the LORD
Almighty lives, whom I serve,
I will surely present myself to
Ahab today."

*Elijah on Mount Carmel*

16So Obadiah went to meet
Ahab and told him, and Ahab
went to meet Elijah. 17When
he saw Elijah, he said to him,
"Is that you, you troubler of
Israel?"
18"I have not made trouble
for Israel," Elijah replied. "But
you and your father's family
have. You have abandoned
the LORD's commands and

וַתֵּלֶךְ אַחֲרֵי הַבְּעָלִים׃ וְעַתָּה שְׁלַח קְבֹץ אֵלַי אֶת־
*** to-me gather! summon! and-now (19) the-Baals after and-you-followed

כָּל־יִשְׂרָאֵל אֶל־הַר הַכַּרְמֶל וְאֶת־נְבִיאֵי הַבַּעַל אַרְבַּע מֵאוֹת
hundreds four the-Baal prophets-of and the-Carmel Mount-of on Israel all-of

וַחֲמִשִּׁים וּנְבִיאֵי הָאֲשֵׁרָה אַרְבַּע מֵאוֹת אֹכְלֵי שֻׁלְחַן
table-of ones-eating-of hundreds four the-Asherah and-prophets-of and-fifty

אִיזָבֶל׃ וַיִּשְׁלַח אַחְאָב בְּכָל־בְּנֵי יִשְׂרָאֵל וַיִּקְבֹּץ
and-he-assembled Israel sons-of through-all-of Ahab so-he-sent (20) Jezebel

אֶת־הַנְּבִיאִים אֶל־הַר הַכַּרְמֶל׃ וַיִּגַּשׁ אֵלִיָּהוּ אֶל־
before Elijah and-he-went (21) the-Carmel Mount-of on the-prophets ***

כָּל־הָעָם וַיֹּאמֶר עַד־מָתַי אַתֶּם פֹּסְחִים עַל־שְׁתֵּי
two-of between ones-wavering you when? until and-he-said the-people all-of

הַסְּעִפִּים אִם־יְהוָה הָאֱלֹהִים לְכוּ אַחֲרָיו וְאִם־הַבַּעַל לְכוּ
follow! the-Baal but-if after-him follow! the-God Yahweh if the-opinions

אַחֲרָיו וְלֹא־עָנוּ הָעָם אֹתוֹ דָּבָר׃ וַיֹּאמֶר אֵלִיָּהוּ
Elijah then-he-said (22) anything him the-people they-said but-not after-him

אֶל־הָעָם אֲנִי נוֹתַרְתִּי נָבִיא לַיהוָה לְבַדִּי וּנְבִיאֵי
but-prophets-of by-myself of-Yahweh prophet I-am-left I the-people to

הַבַּעַל אַרְבַּע־מֵאוֹת וַחֲמִשִּׁים אִישׁ׃ וְיִתְּנוּ־לָנוּ שְׁנַיִם פָּרִים
bulls two for-us now-you-get (23) man and-fifty hundreds four the-Baal

וְיִבְחֲרוּ לָהֶם הַפָּר הָאֶחָד וִינַתְּחֻהוּ
and-let-them-cut-up-him the-one the-bull for-them and-let-them-choose

וְיָשִׂימוּ עַל־הָעֵצִים וְאֵשׁ לֹא יָשִׂימוּ וַאֲנִי אֶעֱשֶׂה ׀
I-will-prepare and-I let-them-set not but-fire the-woods on and-let-them-put

אֶת־הַפָּר הָאֶחָד וְנָתַתִּי עַל־הָעֵצִים וְאֵשׁ לֹא אָשִׂים׃
I-will-set not but-fire the-woods on and-I-will-put the-other the-bull ***

וּקְרָאתֶם בְּשֵׁם אֱלֹהֵיכֶם וַאֲנִי אֶקְרָא בְשֵׁם־
on-name-of I-will-call and-I gods-of-you on-name-of then-you-call (24)

יְהוָה וְהָיָה הָאֱלֹהִים אֲשֶׁר־יַעֲנֶה בָאֵשׁ הוּא הָאֱלֹהִים
the-God he by-fire he-answers who the-God and-he-will-be Yahweh

וַיַּעַן כָּל־הָעָם וַיֹּאמְרוּ טוֹב הַדָּבָר׃
the-word good and-they-said the-people all-of and-they-replied

וַיֹּאמֶר אֵלִיָּהוּ לִנְבִיאֵי הַבַּעַל בַּחֲרוּ לָכֶם הַפָּר
the-bull for-you choose! the-Baal to-prophets-of Elijah then-he-said (25)

הָאֶחָד וַעֲשׂוּ רִאשֹׁנָה כִּי אַתֶּם הָרַבִּים וְקִרְאוּ בְּשֵׁם אֱלֹהֵיכֶם
gods-of-you on-name-of and-call! the-many you since first and-prepare! the-one

וְאֵשׁ לֹא תָשִׂימוּ׃ וַיִּקְחוּ אֶת־הַפָּר אֲשֶׁר־נָתַן לָהֶם
to-them he-gave that the-bull *** so-they-took (26) you-set not but-fire

have followed the Baals. [19]Now summon the people from all over Israel to meet me on Mount Carmel. And bring the four hundred and fifty prophets of Baal and the four hundred prophets of Asherah, who eat at Jezebel's table."

[20]So Ahab sent word throughout all Israel and assembled the prophets on Mount Carmel. [21]Elijah went before the people and said, "How long will you waver between two opinions? If the LORD is God, follow him; but if Baal is God, follow him."

But the people said nothing.

[22]Then Elijah said to them, "I am the only one of the LORD's prophets left, but Baal has four hundred and fifty prophets. [23]Get two bulls for us. Let them choose one for themselves, and let them cut it into pieces and put it on the wood but not set fire to it. I will prepare the other bull and put it on the wood but not set fire to it. [24]Then you call on the name of your god, and I will call on the name of the LORD. The god who answers by fire—he is God."

Then all the people said, "What you say is good."

[25]Elijah said to the prophets of Baal, "Choose one of the bulls and prepare it first, since there are so many of you. Call on the name of your god, but do not light the fire." [26]So they took the bull given them and

וַיַּעֲשׂוּ וַיִּקְרְאוּ בְשֵׁם־ הַבַּעַל מֵהַבֹּקֶר

from-the-morning the-Baal on-name-of and-they-called and-they-prepared

וְעַד־ הַצָּהֳרַיִם לֵאמֹר הַבַּעַל עֲנֵנוּ וְאֵין קוֹל וְאֵין עֹנֶה

answering and-no response but-no answer-us! the-Baal to-say the-noon and-till

וַיְפַסְּחוּ עַל־ הַמִּזְבֵּחַ אֲשֶׁר עָשָׂה׃ וַיְהִי בַצָּהֳרַיִם

at-the-noon and-he-was (27) he-made that the-altar around and-they-danced

וַיְהַתֵּל בָּהֶם אֵלִיָּהוּ וַיֹּאמֶר קִרְאוּ בְקוֹל־ גָּדוֹל כִּי־

surely loud with-voice shout! and-he-said Elijah against-them then-he-taunted

אֱלֹהִים הוּא כִּי שִׂיחַ וְכִי־ שִׂיג לוֹ וְכִי־ דֶרֶךְ לוֹ

to-him travel or-perhaps to-him busy or-perhaps thoughtful perhaps he God

אוּלַי יָשֵׁן הוּא וְיִקָץ׃ וַיִּקְרְאוּ בְּקוֹל גָּדוֹל

loud with-voice so-they-shouted (28) and-he-must-awaken he sleeping maybe

וַיִּתְגֹּדְדוּ כְּמִשְׁפָּטָם בַּחֲרָבוֹת וּבָרְמָחִים

and-with-the-spears with-the-swords as-custom-of-them and-they-slashed-themselves

עַד־ שְׁפָךְ־ דָּם עֲלֵיהֶם׃ וַיְהִי כַּעֲבֹר הַצָּהֳרַיִם

the-midday as-to-pass and-he-was (29) on-them blood to-flow until

וַיִּתְנַבְּאוּ עַד לַעֲלוֹת הַמִּנְחָה וְאֵין־ קוֹל

response but-no the-evening-sacrifice to-offer until and-they-prophesied

וְאֵין־ עֹנֶה וְאֵין קָשֶׁב׃ וַיֹּאמֶר אֵלִיָּהוּ לְכָל־

to-all-of Elijah then-he-said (30) attention and-no answering and-no

הָעָם גְּשׁוּ אֵלַי וַיִּגְּשׁוּ כָל־ הָעָם אֵלָיו וַיְרַפֵּא

and-he-repaired to-him the-people all-of then-they-came to-me come! the-people

אֶת־ מִזְבַּח יְהוָה הֶהָרוּס׃ וַיִּקַּח אֵלִיָּהוּ שְׁתֵּים

two Elijah then-he-took (31) the-one-being-in-ruins Yahweh altar-of ***

עֶשְׂרֵה אֲבָנִים כְּמִסְפַּר שִׁבְטֵי בְנֵי־ יַעֲקֹב אֲשֶׁר הָיָה דְבַר־

word-of he-came whom Jacob sons-of tribes-of as-number-of stones ten

יְהוָה אֵלָיו לֵאמֹר יִשְׂרָאֵל יִהְיֶה שְׁמֶךָ׃ וַיִּבְנֶה אֶת־

*** and-he-built (32) name-of-you he-shall-be Israel to-say to-him Yahweh

הָאֲבָנִים מִזְבֵּחַ בְּשֵׁם יְהוָה וַיַּעַשׂ תְּעָלָה כְּבֵית

as-container-of trench and-he-dug Yahweh in-name-of altar the-stones

סָאתַיִם זֶרַע סָבִיב לַמִּזְבֵּחַ׃ וַיַּעֲרֹךְ אֶת־ הָעֵצִים

the-woods *** and-he-arranged (33) to-the-altar around seed two-seahs

וַיְנַתַּח אֶת־ הַפָּר וַיָּשֶׂם עַל־ הָעֵצִים׃ וַיֹּאמֶר

then-he-said *(34) the-woods on and-he-laid the-bull *** and-he-cut-up

מִלְאוּ אַרְבָּעָה כַדִּים מַיִם וְיִצְקוּ עַל־ הָעֹלָה וְעַל־ הָעֵצִים

the-woods and-on the-offering on and-pour! waters jars four fill!

וַיֹּאמֶר שְׁנוּ וַיִּשְׁנוּ וַיֹּאמֶר שַׁלֵּשׁוּ

do-third-time! and-he-ordered and-they-did-again do-again! and-he-said

prepared it.
Then they called on the
name of Baal from morning
till noon. "O Baal, answer us!"
they shouted. But there was no
response; no one answered.
And they danced around the
altar they had made.
[27]At noon Elijah began to
taunt them. "Shout louder!"
he said. "Surely he is a god!
Perhaps he is deep in thought,
or busy, or traveling. Maybe
he is sleeping and must be
awakened." [28]So they shouted
louder and slashed themselves
with swords and spears, as
was their custom, until their
blood flowed. [29]Midday
passed, and they continued
their frantic prophesying until
the time for the evening sacrifice. But there was no response, no one answered, no
one paid attention.
[30]Then Elijah said to all the
people, "Come here to me."
They came to him, and he repaired the altar of the LORD,
which was in ruins. [31]Elijah
took twelve stones, one for
each of the tribes descended
from Jacob, to whom the word
of the LORD had come, saying,
"Your name shall be Israel."
[32]With the stones he built an
altar in the name of the LORD,
and he dug a trench around it
large enough to hold two
seahs[t] of seed. [33]He arranged
the wood, cut the bull into
pieces and laid it on the wood.
Then he said to them, "Fill
four large jars with water and
pour it on the offering and on
the wood."
[34]"Do it again," he said, and
they did it again.
"Do it a third time," he ordered, and they did it the third

[t]32 That is, probably about 13 quarts (about 15 liters)

***34 Verse 34 in Hebrew begins in the middle of verse 33 in English.**

וַיְשַׁלֵּשׁוּ׃ וַיֵּלְכוּ הַמַּיִם סָבִיב לַמִּזְבֵּחַ
to-the-altar around the-waters and-they-ran (35) and-they-did-third-time

וְגַם אֶת־ הַתְּעָלָה מִלֵּא־ מָיִם׃ וַיְהִי ׀ בַּעֲלוֹת
when-to-offer and-he-was (36) waters he-filled the-trench *** and-even

הַמִּנְחָה וַיִּגַּשׁ אֵלִיָּהוּ הַנָּבִיא וַיֹּאמַר
and-he-prayed the-prophet Elijah then-he-stepped-forward the-sacrifice

יְהוָה אֱלֹהֵי אַבְרָהָם יִצְחָק וְיִשְׂרָאֵל הַיּוֹם יִוָּדַע כִּי־אַתָּה
you that let-him-be-known the-day and-Israel Isaac Abraham God-of Yahweh

אֱלֹהִים בְּיִשְׂרָאֵל וַאֲנִי עַבְדֶּךָ וּבִדְבָרְיךָ עָשִׂיתִי אֵת כָּל־
all-of *** I-did and-at-command-of-you servant-of-you and-I in-Israel God

הַדְּבָרִים הָאֵלֶּה׃ עֲנֵנִי יְהוָה עֲנֵנִי וְיֵדְעוּ
so-they-will-know answer-me! Yahweh answer-me! (37) the-these the-things

הָעָם הַזֶּה כִּי־ אַתָּה יְהוָה הָאֱלֹהִים וְאַתָּה הֲסִבֹּתָ אֶת־
*** you-will-turn and-you the-God Yahweh you that the-this the-people

לִבָּם אֲחֹרַנִּית׃ וַתִּפֹּל אֵשׁ־ יְהוָה וַתֹּאכַל אֶת־
*** and-she-burned-up Yahweh fire-of then-she-fell (38) back heart-of-them

הָעֹלָה וְאֶת־ הָעֵצִים וְאֶת־ הָאֲבָנִים וְאֶת־ הֶעָפָר וְאֶת־ הַמַּיִם אֲשֶׁר־
that the-waters and the-soil and the-stones and the-woods and the-sacrifice

בַּתְּעָלָה לִחֵכָה׃ וַיַּרְא כָּל־ הָעָם וַיִּפְּלוּ
then-they-fell the-people all-of when-he-saw (39) she-licked-up in-the-trench

עַל־ פְּנֵיהֶם וַיֹּאמְרוּ יְהוָה הוּא הָאֱלֹהִים יְהוָה הוּא הָאֱלֹהִים׃
the-God he Yahweh the-God he Yahweh and-they-said faces-of-them on

וַיֹּאמֶר אֵלִיָּהוּ לָהֶם תִּפְשׂוּ ׀ אֶת־ נְבִיאֵי הַבַּעַל אִישׁ
anyone the-Baal prophets-of *** seize! to-them Elijah then-he-commanded (40)

אַל־ יִמָּלֵט מֵהֶם וַיִּתְפְּשׂוּם וַיּוֹרִדֵם
and-he-brought-down-them and-they-seized-them from-them let-him-get-away not

אֵלִיָּהוּ אֶל־ נַחַל קִישׁוֹן וַיִּשְׁחָטֵם שָׁם׃ וַיֹּאמֶר
and-he-said (41) there and-he-slaughtered-them Kishon Valley-of to Elijah

אֵלִיָּהוּ לְאַחְאָב עֲלֵה אֱכֹל וּשְׁתֵה כִּי־ קוֹל הֲמוֹן הַגָּשֶׁם׃
the-rain heaviness-of sound-of for and-drink! eat! go! to-Ahab Elijah

וַיַּעֲלֶה אַחְאָב לֶאֱכֹל וְלִשְׁתּוֹת וְאֵלִיָּהוּ עָלָה אֶל־
to he-climbed but-Elijah and-to-drink to-eat Ahab so-he-went-off (42)

רֹאשׁ הַכַּרְמֶל וַיִּגְהַר אַרְצָה וַיָּשֶׂם פָּנָיו בֵּין
between faces-of-him and-he-put to-ground and-he-bent-down the-Carmel top-of

בִּרְכָּו׃ וַיֹּאמֶר אֶל־ נַעֲרוֹ עֲלֵה־ נָא הַבֵּט דֶּרֶךְ־
direction-of look! now! go! servant-of-him to and-he-told (43) knees-of-him

יָם וַיַּעַל וַיַּבֵּט וַיֹּאמֶר אֵין מְאוּמָה
anything there-is-not and-he-said and-he-looked and-he-went-up sea

time. 35The water ran down around the altar and even filled the trench.

36At the time of sacrifice, the prophet Elijah stepped forward and prayed: "O LORD, God of Abraham, Isaac and Israel, let it be known today that you are God in Israel and that I am your servant and have done all these things at your command. 37Answer me, O LORD, answer me, so these people will know that you, O LORD, are God, and that you are turning their hearts back again."

38Then the fire of the LORD fell and burned up the sacrifice, the wood, the stones and the soil, and also licked up the water in the trench.

39When all the people saw this, they fell prostrate and cried, "The LORD, he is God! The LORD—he is God!"

40Then Elijah commanded them, "Seize the prophets of Baal. Don't let anyone get away!" They seized them, and Elijah had them brought down to the Kishon Valley and slaughtered there.

41And Elijah said to Ahab, "Go, eat and drink, for there is the sound of a heavy rain." 42So Ahab went off to eat and drink, but Elijah climbed to the top of Carmel, bent down to the ground and put his face between his knees.

43"Go and look toward the sea," he told his servant. And he went up and looked.

"There is nothing there," he said.

°36 ק ובדברך
°42 ק ברכיו

וַיֹּאמֶר שֻׁב שֶׁבַע פְּעָמִים׃ וַיְהִי בַּשְּׁבִעִית וַיֹּאמֶר
then-he-said on-the-seventh and-he-was (44) times seven go-back! and-he-said

הִנֵּה־עָב קְטַנָּה כְּכַף־אִישׁ עֹלָה מִיָּם וַיֹּאמֶר עֲלֵה אֱמֹר אֶל־
to tell! go! so-he-said from-sea rising man as-hand-of small cloud see!

אַחְאָב אֱסֹר וָרֵד וְלֹא יַעַצָרְכָה* הַגָּשֶׁם׃ וַיְהִי ׀
and-he-was (45) the-rain he-stops-you so-not and-go-down! hitch-up! Ahab

עַד־כֹּה וְעַד־כֹּה וְהַשָּׁמַיִם הִתְקַדְּרוּ עָבִים וְרוּחַ
and-wind clouds they-grew-black then-the-skies that and-while this while

וַיְהִי גֶּשֶׁם גָּדוֹל וַיִּרְכַּב אַחְאָב וַיֵּלֶךְ יִזְרְעֶאלָה׃
to-Jezreel and-he-went Ahab and-he-rode heavy rain and-he-came

וְיַד־יְהוָה הָיְתָה אֶל־אֵלִיָּהוּ וַיְשַׁנֵּס
and-he-tucked-in-cloak Elijah upon she-came Yahweh and-hand-of (46)

מָתְנָיו וַיָּרָץ לִפְנֵי אַחְאָב עַד־בֹּאֲכָה יִזְרְעֶאלָה׃
to-Jezreel to-go-you to Ahab ahead-of and-he-ran loins-of-him

וַיַּגֵּד אַחְאָב לְאִיזֶבֶל אֵת כָּל־אֲשֶׁר עָשָׂה אֵלִיָּהוּ וְאֵת כָּל־אֲשֶׁר
how all and Elijah he-did that all *** to-Jezebel Ahab now-he-told (19:1)

הָרַג אֶת־כָּל־הַנְּבִיאִים בֶּחָרֶב׃ וַתִּשְׁלַח אִיזֶבֶל
Jezebel so-she-sent (2) with-the-sword the-prophets all-of *** he-killed

מַלְאָךְ אֶל־אֵלִיָּהוּ לֵאמֹר כֹּה־יַעֲשׂוּן אֱלֹהִים וְכֹה יוֹסִפוּן
may-they-be-severe and-so gods may-they-deal so to-say Elijah to messenger

כִּי־כָעֵת מָחָר אָשִׂים אֶת־נַפְשְׁךָ כְּנֶפֶשׁ אַחַד מֵהֶם׃
of-them one as-life-of life-of-you *** I-make tomorrow by-the-time if-not

וַיַּרְא וַיָּקָם וַיֵּלֶךְ אֶל־נַפְשׁוֹ וַיָּבֹא
when-he-came life-of-him for and-he-ran and-he-got-up and-he-was-afraid (3)

בְּאֵר שֶׁבַע אֲשֶׁר לִיהוּדָה וַיַּנַּח אֶת־נַעֲרוֹ שָׁם׃ וְהוּא־
while-he (4) there servant-of-him *** then-he-left in-Judah that Sheba Beer

הָלַךְ בַּמִּדְבָּר דֶּרֶךְ יוֹם וַיָּבֹא וַיֵּשֶׁב תַּחַת
under and-he-sat and-he-came day journey-of into-the-desert he-went

רֹתֶם אֶחָת וַיִּשְׁאַל אֶת־נַפְשׁוֹ לָמוּת וַיֹּאמֶר ׀ רַב עַתָּה
now enough and-he-said to-die life-of-him *** and-he-prayed one broom-tree

יְהוָה קַח נַפְשִׁי כִּי־לֹא־טוֹב אָנֹכִי מֵאֲבֹתָי׃ וַיִּשְׁכַּב
then-he-lay (5) than-ancestors-of-me I better not for life-of-me take! Yahweh

וַיִּישַׁן תַּחַת רֹתֶם אֶחָד וְהִנֵּה־זֶה מַלְאָךְ נֹגֵעַ בּוֹ
on-him touching angel there and-see! one broom-tree under and-he-fell-asleep

וַיֹּאמֶר לוֹ קוּם אֱכוֹל׃ וַיַּבֵּט וְהִנֵּה מְרַאֲשֹׁתָיו
by-heads-of-him and-see! and-he-looked (6) eat! get-up! to-him and-he-said

עֻגַת רְצָפִים וְצַפַּחַת מָיִם וַיֹּאכַל וַיֵּשְׁתְּ וַיָּשָׁב
and-he-returned and-he-drank and-he-ate waters and-jar-of coals-baked cake-of

Seven times Elijah said, "Go back."
44The seventh time the servant reported, "A cloud as small as a man's hand is rising from the sea."
So Elijah said, "Go and tell Ahab, 'Hitch up your chariot and go down before the rain stops you.' "
45Meanwhile, the sky grew black with clouds, the wind rose, a heavy rain came on and Ahab rode off to Jezreel.
46The power of the LORD came upon Elijah and, tucking his cloak into his belt, he ran ahead of Ahab all the way to Jezreel.

*Elijah Flees to Horeb*

19 Now Ahab told Jezebel everything Elijah had done and how he had killed all the prophets with the sword.
2So Jezebel sent a messenger to Elijah to say, "May the gods deal with me, be it ever so severely, if by this time tomorrow I do not make your life like that of one of them."
3Elijah was afraid[u] and ran for his life. When he came to Beersheba in Judah, he left his servant there,
4while he himself went a day's journey into the desert. He came to a broom tree, sat down under it and prayed that he might die. "I have had enough, LORD," he said. "Take my life; I am no better than my ancestors."
5Then he lay down under the tree and fell asleep.
All at once an angel touched him and said, "Get up and eat."
6He looked around, and there by his head was a cake of bread baked over hot coals, and a jar of water. He ate and drank and then lay down again.

u3 Or *Elijah saw*

*44 Most mss have *bateph pathah* under the *ayin* (יַעַצָ).

°4 ק אחד

וַיִּשְׁכָּב׃ (7) וַיָּשָׁב מַלְאַךְ יְהוָה ׀ שֵׁנִית וַיִּגַּע־
and-he-touched second Yahweh angel-of and-he-came-back (7) and-he-lay-down

בּוֹ וַיֹּאמֶר קוּם אֱכֹל כִּי רַב מִמְּךָ הַדָּרֶךְ׃
the-journey for-you too-much for eat! get-up! and-he-said on-him

(8) וַיָּקָם וַיֹּאכַל וַיִּשְׁתֶּה וַיֵּלֶךְ בְּכֹחַ ׀
in-strength-of and-he-traveled and-he-drank and-he-ate so-he-got-up (8)

הָאֲכִילָה הַהִיא אַרְבָּעִים יוֹם וְאַרְבָּעִים לַיְלָה עַד הַר הָאֱלֹהִים חֹרֵב׃
Horeb the-God mountain-of until night and-forty day forty the-that the-food

(9) וַיָּבֹא־ שָׁם אֶל־ הַמְּעָרָה וַיָּלֶן שָׁם וְהִנֵּה
and-see! there and-he-spent-night the-cave into there and-he-went (9)

דְבַר־ יְהוָה אֵלָיו וַיֹּאמֶר לוֹ מַה־ לְּךָ פֹה אֵלִיָּהוּ׃
Elijah here to-you what? to-him and-he-said to-him Yahweh word-of

(10) וַיֹּאמֶר קַנֹּא קִנֵּאתִי לַיהוָה ׀ אֱלֹהֵי צְבָאוֹת כִּי־
for Hosts God-of for-Yahweh I-was-zealous to-be-zealous and-he-replied (10)

עָזְבוּ בְרִיתְךָ בְּנֵי יִשְׂרָאֵל אֶת־ מִזְבְּחֹתֶיךָ הָרָסוּ
they-broke-down altars-of-you *** Israel sons-of covenant-of-you they-rejected

וְאֶת־ נְבִיאֶיךָ הָרְגוּ בֶחָרֶב וָאִוָּתֵר אֲנִי לְבַדִּי
by-myself I and-I-am-left with-the-sword they-killed prophets-of-you and

וַיְבַקְשׁוּ אֶת־ נַפְשִׁי לְקַחְתָּהּ׃ (11) וַיֹּאמֶר צֵא וְעָמַדְתָּ
and-you-stand go! and-he-said (11) to-take-her life-of-me *** and-they-seek

בָהָר לִפְנֵי יְהוָה וְהִנֵּה יְהוָה עֹבֵר וְרוּחַ
then-wind passing-by Yahweh for-see! Yahweh in-presences-of on-the-mountain

גְּדוֹלָה וְחָזָק מְפָרֵק הָרִים וּמְשַׁבֵּר סְלָעִים לִפְנֵי יְהוָה
Yahweh before rocks and-shattering mountains tearing-apart and-powerful great

לֹא בָרוּחַ יְהוָה וְאַחַר הָרוּחַ רַעַשׁ לֹא בָרַעַשׁ
in-the-earthquake not earthquake the-wind and-after Yahweh in-the-wind not

יְהוָה׃ (12) וְאַחַר הָרַעַשׁ אֵשׁ לֹא בָאֵשׁ יְהוָה וְאַחַר
and-after Yahweh in-the-fire not fire the-earthquake and-after (12) Yahweh

הָאֵשׁ קוֹל דְּמָמָה דַקָּה׃ (13) וַיְהִי ׀ כִּשְׁמֹעַ אֵלִיָּהוּ
Elijah when-to-hear and-he-was (13) gentle whisper voice the-fire

וַיָּלֶט פָּנָיו בְּאַדַּרְתּוֹ וַיֵּצֵא וַיַּעֲמֹד
and-he-stood and-he-went-out with-cloak-of-him faces-of-him then-he-covered

פֶּתַח הַמְּעָרָה וְהִנֵּה אֵלָיו קוֹל וַיֹּאמֶר מַה־ לְּךָ פֹה
here to-you what? and-he-said voice to-him then-see! the-cave mouth-of

אֵלִיָּהוּ׃ (14) וַיֹּאמֶר קַנֹּא קִנֵּאתִי לַיהוָה ׀ אֱלֹהֵי
God-of for-Yahweh I-was-zealous to-be-zealous and-he-replied (14) Elijah

צְבָאוֹת כִּי־ עָזְבוּ בְרִיתְךָ בְּנֵי יִשְׂרָאֵל אֶת־ מִזְבְּחֹתֶיךָ
altars-of-you *** Israel sons-of covenant-of-you they-rejected for Hosts

7The angel of the LORD came
back a second time and
touched him and said, "Get up
and eat, for the journey is too
much for you." 8So he got up
and ate and drank.
Strengthened by that food, he
traveled forty days and forty
nights until he reached Horeb,
the mountain of God. 9There
he went into a cave and spent
the night.

*The LORD Appears to Elijah*

And the word of the LORD
came to him: "What are you
doing here, Elijah?"

10He replied, "I have been
very zealous for the LORD God
Almighty. The Israelites have
rejected your covenant, broken down your altars, and put
your prophets to death with
the sword. I am the only one
left, and now they are trying
to kill me too."

11The LORD said, "Go out and
stand on the mountain in the
presence of the LORD, for the
LORD is about to pass by."

Then a great and powerful
wind tore the mountains apart
and shattered the rocks before
the LORD, but the LORD was not
in the wind. After the wind
there was an earthquake, but
the LORD was not in the earthquake.
12After the earthquake
came a fire, but the LORD was
not in the fire. And after the
fire came a gentle whisper.
13When Elijah heard it, he
pulled his cloak over his face
and went out and stood at the
mouth of the cave.

Then a voice said to him,
"What are you doing here, Elijah?"

14He replied, "I have been
very zealous for the LORD God
Almighty. The Israelites have
rejected your covenant, broken down your altars, and put

הָרְסוּ וְאֶת־ נְבִיאֶיךָ הָרְגוּ בֶחָרֶב וָאִוָּתֵר
and-I-am-left with-the-sword they-killed prophets-of-you and they-broke-down

אֲנִי לְבַדִּי וַיְבַקְשׁוּ אֶת־ נַפְשִׁי לְקַחְתָּהּ׃ (15) וַיֹּאמֶר יְהוָה
Yahweh and-he-said (15) to-take-her life-of-me *** and-they-seek by-myself I

אֵלָיו לֵךְ שׁוּב לְדַרְכְּךָ מִדְבַּרָה דַמָּשֶׂק וּבָאתָ
when-you-arrive Damascus to-Desert-of on-way-of-you go-back! go! to-him

וּמָשַׁחְתָּ אֶת־ חֲזָאֵל לְמֶלֶךְ עַל־ אֲרָם׃ (16) וְאֵת יֵהוּא בֶן־ נִמְשִׁי
Nimshi son-of Jehu and (16) Aram over as-king Hazael *** then-you-anoint

תִּמְשַׁח לְמֶלֶךְ עַל־ יִשְׂרָאֵל וְאֶת־ אֱלִישָׁע בֶּן־ שָׁפָט מֵאָבֵל מְחוֹלָה
Meholah from-Abel Shaphat son-of Elisha and Israel over as-king you-anoint

תִּמְשַׁח לְנָבִיא תַּחְתֶּיךָ׃ (17) וְהָיָה הַנִּמְלָט
the-one-escaping and-he-will-be (17) in-place-of-you as-prophet you-anoint

מֵחֶרֶב חֲזָאֵל יָמִית יֵהוּא וְהַנִּמְלָט מֵחֶרֶב
from-sword-of and-the-one-escaping Jehu he-will-kill Hazael from-sword-of

יֵהוּא יָמִית אֱלִישָׁע׃ (18) וְהִשְׁאַרְתִּי בְיִשְׂרָאֵל שִׁבְעַת אֲלָפִים
thousands seven-of in-Israel yet-I-reserve (18) Elisha he-will-kill Jehu

כָּל־ הַבִּרְכַּיִם אֲשֶׁר לֹא־ כָרְעוּ לַבַּעַל וְכָל־ הַפֶּה אֲשֶׁר
that the-mouth and-all-of to-the-Baal they-bowed not that the-knees all-of

לֹא־ נָשַׁק לוֹ׃ (19) וַיֵּלֶךְ מִשָּׁם וַיִּמְצָא אֶת־ אֱלִישָׁע
Elisha *** and-he-found from-there so-he-went (19) on-him he-kissed not

בֶּן־ שָׁפָט וְהוּא חֹרֵשׁ שְׁנֵים־ עָשָׂר צְמָדִים לְפָנָיו וְהוּא בִּשְׁנֵים
with-two and-he before-him yokes ten two plowing now-he Shaphat son-of

הֶעָשָׂר וַיַּעֲבֹר אֵלִיָּהוּ אֵלָיו וַיַּשְׁלֵךְ אַדַּרְתּוֹ אֵלָיו׃
around-him cloak-of-him and-he-threw to-him Elijah and-he-went-up the-ten

(20) וַיַּעֲזֹב אֶת־ הַבָּקָר וַיָּרָץ אַחֲרֵי אֵלִיָּהוּ וַיֹּאמֶר אֶשְּׁקָה־
let-me-kiss and-he-said Elijah after and-he-ran the-ox *** then-he-left (20)

נָּא לְאָבִי וּלְאִמִּי וְאֵלְכָה אַחֲרֶיךָ
after-you then-I-will-come and-on-mother-of-me on-father-of-me now!

וַיֹּאמֶר לוֹ לֵךְ שׁוּב כִּי מֶה־ עָשִׂיתִי לָךְ׃ (21) וַיָּשָׁב
so-he-went-back (21) to-you I-did what? for go-back! go! to-him and-he-replied

מֵאַחֲרָיו וַיִּקַּח אֶת־ צֶמֶד הַבָּקָר וַיִּזְבָּחֵהוּ
and-he-slaughtered-him the-ox yoke-of *** and-he-took from-after-him

וּבִכְלִי הַבָּקָר בִּשְּׁלָם הַבָּשָׂר וַיִּתֵּן לָעָם
to-the-people and-he-gave the-meat he-cooked-them the-ox and-with-equipment-of

וַיֹּאכֵלוּ וַיָּקָם וַיֵּלֶךְ אַחֲרֵי אֵלִיָּהוּ וַיְשָׁרְתֵהוּ׃
and-he-attended-him Elijah after and-he-followed then-he-set-out and-they-ate

(20:1) וּבֶן־ הֲדַד מֶלֶךְ־ אֲרָם קָבַץ אֶת־ כָּל־ חֵילוֹ
army-of-him entire-of *** he-mustered Aram king-of Hadad now-Ben (20:1)

your prophets to death with
the sword. I am the only one
left, and now they are trying
to kill me too."
15 The LORD said to him, "Go
back the way you came, and
go to the Desert of Damascus.
When you get there, anoint
Hazael king over Aram. 16 Also,
anoint Jehu son of Nimshi
king over Israel, and anoint
Elisha son of Shaphat from
Abel Meholah to succeed you
as prophet. 17 Jehu will put to
death any who escape the
sword of Hazael, and Elisha
will put to death any who escape the sword of Jehu. 18 Yet I
reserve seven thousand in Israel—all whose knees have not
bowed down to Baal and all
whose mouths have not kissed
him."

*The Call of Elisha*

19 So Elijah went from there
and found Elisha son of Shaphat. He was plowing with
twelve yoke of oxen, and he
himself was driving the
twelfth pair. Elijah went up to
him and threw his cloak
around him. 20 Elisha then left
his oxen and ran after Elijah.
"Let me kiss my father and
mother good-by," he said,
"and then I will come with
you."
"Go back," Elijah replied.
"What have I done to you?"
21 So Elisha left him and
went back. He took his yoke of
oxen and slaughtered them.
He burned the plowing equipment to cook the meat and
gave it to the people, and they
ate. Then he set out to follow
Elijah and became his attendant.

*Ben-Hadad Attacks Samaria*

20 Now Ben-Hadad king
of Aram mustered his
entire army. Accompanied by

וּשְׁלֹשִׁים וּשְׁנַיִם מֶלֶךְ אִתּוֹ וְסוּס וָרֶכֶב וַיַּעַל
and-he-went-up and-chariot and-horse with-him king and-two and-thirty

וַיָּצַר עַל־ שֹׁמְרוֹן וַיִּלָּחֶם בָּהּ׃ וַיִּשְׁלַח
and-he-sent (2) against-her and-he-attacked Samaria against and-he-besieged

מַלְאָכִים אֶל־אַחְאָב מֶלֶךְ־יִשְׂרָאֵל הָעִירָה׃ וַיֹּאמֶר לוֹ כֹּה
this to-him and-he-said *(3) into-the-city Israel king-of Ahab to messengers

אָמַר בֶּן־ הֲדַד כַּסְפְּךָ וּזְהָבְךָ לִי־ הוּא וְנָשֶׁיךָ
and-wives-of-you he to-me and-gold-of-you silver-of-you Hadad Ben he-says

וּבָנֶיךָ הַטּוֹבִים לִי־ הֵם׃ וַיַּעַן מֶלֶךְ־יִשְׂרָאֵל
Israel king-of and-he-answered (4) they to-me the-best-ones and-sons-of-you

וַיֹּאמֶר כִּדְבָרְךָ אֲדֹנִי הַמֶּלֶךְ לְךָ אֲנִי וְכָל־ אֲשֶׁר־ לִי׃
to-me that and-all I to-you the-king lord-of-me as-word-of-you and-he-said

וַיָּשֻׁבוּ הַמַּלְאָכִים וַיֹּאמְרוּ כֹּה־ אָמַר בֶּן־ הֲדַד
Hadad Ben he-says this and-they-said the-messengers and-they-came-again (5)

לֵאמֹר כִּי־ שָׁלַחְתִּי אֵלֶיךָ לֵאמֹר כַּסְפְּךָ וּזְהָבְךָ
and-gold-of-you silver-of-you to-demand to-you I-sent indeed to-say

וְנָשֶׁיךָ וּבָנֶיךָ לִי תִתֵּן׃ כִּי | אִם־ כָּעֵת
at-the-time rather but (6) you-give to-me and-sons-of-you and-wives-of-you

מָחָר אֶשְׁלַח אֶת־ עֲבָדַי אֵלֶיךָ וְחִפְּשׂוּ אֶת־
*** and-they-will-search to-you officials-of-me *** I-will-send tomorrow

בֵּיתְךָ וְאֵת בָּתֵּי עֲבָדֶיךָ וְהָיָה כָּל־ מַחְמַד
value-of any-of and-he-will-be officials-of-you houses-of and palace-of-you

עֵינֶיךָ יָשִׂימוּ בְיָדָם וְלָקָחוּ׃
and-they-will-take in-hand-of-them they-will-seize eyes-of-you

וַיִּקְרָא מֶלֶךְ־יִשְׂרָאֵל לְכָל־ זִקְנֵי הָאָרֶץ וַיֹּאמֶר
and-he-said the-land elders-of to-all-of Israel king-of and-he-summoned (7)

דְּעוּ־ נָא וּרְאוּ כִּי רָעָה זֶה מְבַקֵּשׁ כִּי־ שָׁלַח אֵלַי
to-me he-sent when looking-for this-man trouble that and-see! now! know!

לְנָשַׁי וּלְבָנַי וּלְכַסְפִּי וְלִזְהָבִי
and-for-gold-of-me and-for-silver-of-me and-for-sons-of-me for-wives-of-me

וְלֹא מָנַעְתִּי מִמֶּנּוּ׃ וַיֹּאמְרוּ אֵלָיו כָּל־ הַזְּקֵנִים
the-elders all-of to-him and-they-answered (8) from-him I-refused then-not

וְכָל־ הָעָם אַל־ תִּשְׁמַע וְלוֹא תֹאבֶה׃ וַיֹּאמֶר
so-he-replied (9) you-agree and-not you-listen not the-people and-all-of

לְמַלְאֲכֵי בֶן־ הֲדַד אִמְרוּ לַאדֹנִי הַמֶּלֶךְ כֹּל אֲשֶׁר־שָׁלַחְתָּ
you-sent that all the-king to-lord-of-me tell! Hadad Ben to-messengers-of

אֶל־ עַבְדְּךָ בָרִאשֹׁנָה אֶעֱשֶׂה וְהַדָּבָר הַזֶּה לֹא אוּכַל
I-can not the-this but-the-demand I-will-do at-the-first servant-of-you to

thirty-two kings with their
horses and chariots, he went
up and besieged Samaria and
attacked it. [2]He sent messengers into the city to Ahab king
of Israel, saying, "This is what
Ben-Hadad says: [3]'Your silver
and gold are mine, and the
best of your wives and children are mine.' "
[4]The king of Israel an-
swered, "Just as you say, my
lord the king. I and all I have
are yours."
[5]The messengers came again
and said, "This is what Ben-
Hadad says: 'I sent to demand
your silver and gold, your
wives and your children. [6]But
about this time tomorrow I am
going to send my officials to
search your palace and the
houses of your officials. They
will seize everything you value and carry it away.' "
[7]The king of Israel summoned all the elders of the
land and said to them, "See
how this man is looking for
trouble! When he sent for my
wives and my children, my
silver and my gold, I did not
refuse him."
[8]The elders and the people
all answered, "Don't listen to
him or agree to his demands."
[9]So he replied to Ben-
Hadad's messengers, "Tell my
lord the king, 'Your servant
will do all you demanded the
first time, but this demand I

*3 Verse 3 in Hebrew begins in the middle of verse 2 in English.

לַעֲשׂוֹת וַיֵּלְכוּ הַמַּלְאָכִים וַיְשִׁבֻהוּ דָּבָר׃
answer and-they-took-back-him the-messengers and-they-left to-meet

וַיִּשְׁלַח אֵלָיו בֶּן־ הֲדַד וַיֹּאמֶר כֹּה־ יַעֲשׂוּן לִי
with-me may-they-deal so and-he-said Hadad Ben to-him then-he-sent (10)

אֱלֹהִים וְכֹה יוֹסִפוּ אִם־ יִשְׂפֹּק עֲפַר שֹׁמְרוֹן לִשְׁעָלִים
for-handfuls Samaria dust-of he-is-enough if may-they-be-severe and-so gods

לְכָל־ הָעָם אֲשֶׁר בְּרַגְלָי׃ וַיַּעַן מֶלֶךְ־יִשְׂרָאֵל
Israel king-of and-he-answered (11) at-feet-of-me who the-people for-all-of

וַיֹּאמֶר דַּבְּרוּ אַל־ יִתְהַלֵּל חֹגֵר כִּמְפַתֵּחַ׃
like-one-taking-off one-putting-on-armor he-should-boast not tell! and-he-said

וַיְהִי כִּשְׁמֹעַ אֶת־ הַדָּבָר הַזֶּה וְהוּא שֹׁתֶה
drinking then-he the-this the-message *** when-to-hear and-he-was (12)

הוּא וְהַמְּלָכִים בַּסֻּכּוֹת וַיֹּאמֶר אֶל־ עֲבָדָיו שִׂימוּ
prepare! men-of-him to and-he-ordered in-the-tents and-the-kings he

וַיָּשִׂימוּ עַל־ הָעִיר׃ וְהִנֵּה׀ נָבִיא אֶחָד נִגַּשׁ אֶל־
to he-came one prophet then-see! (13) the-city against so-they-prepared

אַחְאָב מֶלֶךְ־יִשְׂרָאֵל וַיֹּאמֶר כֹּה אָמַר יְהוָה הֲרָאִיתָ אֵת כָּל־
all-of *** you-see? Yahweh he-says this and-he-announced Israel king-of Ahab

הֶהָמוֹן הַגָּדוֹל הַזֶּה הִנְנִי נֹתְנוֹ בְיָדְךָ הַיּוֹם
the-day into-hand-of-you giving-him see-I! the-this the-vast the-army

וְיָדַעְתָּ כִּי־ אֲנִי יְהוָה׃ וַיֹּאמֶר אַחְאָב בְּמִי
by-whom? Ahab and-he-asked (14) Yahweh I that then-you-will-know

וַיֹּאמֶר כֹּה־ אָמַר יְהוָה בְּנַעֲרֵי שָׂרֵי הַמְּדִינוֹת
the-provinces commanders-of by-young-men-of Yahweh he-says this and-he-replied

וַיֹּאמֶר מִי־ יֶאְסֹר הַמִּלְחָמָה וַיֹּאמֶר אָתָּה׃
you and-he-answered the-battle he-will-start who? and-he-asked

וַיִּפְקֹד אֶת־ נַעֲרֵי שָׂרֵי הַמְּדִינוֹת
the-provinces commanders-of young-men-of *** so-he-summoned (15)

וַיִּהְיוּ מָאתַיִם שְׁנַיִם וּשְׁלֹשִׁים וְאַחֲרֵיהֶם פָּקַד אֶת־
*** he-assembled and-after-them and-thirty two two-hundreds and-they-were

כָּל־ הָעָם כָּל־ בְּנֵי יִשְׂרָאֵל שִׁבְעַת אֲלָפִים׃ וַיֵּצְאוּ
and-they-set-out (16) thousands seven-of Israel sons-of all-of the-people all-of

בַּצָּהֳרָיִם וּבֶן־ הֲדַד שֹׁתֶה שִׁכּוֹר בַּסֻּכּוֹת הוּא וְהַמְּלָכִים
and-the-kings he in-the-tents drunken drinking Hadad while-Ben at-the-noon

שְׁלֹשִׁים־וּשְׁנַיִם מֶלֶךְ עֹזֵר אֹתוֹ׃ וַיֵּצְאוּ נַעֲרֵי
young-men-of and-they-went-out (17) with-him allying king and-two thirty

שָׂרֵי הַמְּדִינוֹת בָּרִאשֹׁנָה וַיִּשְׁלַח בֶּן־ הֲדַד
Hadad Ben and-he-dispatched at-the-first the-provinces commanders-of

cannot meet.' " They left and took the answer back to Ben-Hadad.

10 Then Ben-Hadad sent another message to Ahab: "May the gods deal with me, be it ever so severely, if enough dust remains in Samaria to give each of my men a handful."

11 The king of Israel answered, "Tell him: 'One who puts on his armor should not boast like one who takes it off.' "

12 Ben-Hadad heard this message while he and the kings were drinking in their tents,[v] and he ordered his men: "Prepare to attack." So they prepared to attack the city.

*Ahab Defeats Ben-Hadad*

13 Meanwhile a prophet came to Ahab king of Israel and announced, "This is what the LORD says: 'Do you see this vast army? I will give it into your hand today, and then you will know that I am the LORD.' "

14 "But who will do this?" asked Ahab.

The prophet replied, "This is what the LORD says: 'The young officers of the provincial commanders will do it.' "

"And who will start the battle?" he asked.

The prophet answered, "You will."

15 So Ahab summoned the young officers of the provincial commanders, 232 men. Then he assembled the rest of the Israelites, 7,000 in all. 16 They set out at noon while Ben-Hadad and the 32 kings allied with him were in their tents getting drunk. 17 The young officers of the provincial commanders went out first.

[v] 12 Or *in Succoth*; also in verse 16

וַיַּגִּידוּ לוֹ לֵאמֹר אֲנָשִׁים יָצְאוּ מִשֹּׁמְרוֹן׃ וַיֹּאמֶר
and-he-said (18) from-Samaria they-advance men to-say to-him and-they-reported

אִם־לְשָׁלוֹם יָצָאוּ תִּפְשׂוּם חַיִּים וְאִם לְמִלְחָמָה
for-war and-if ones-alive you-take-them they-come-out for-peace if

יָצָאוּ חַיִּים תִּפְשׂוּם׃ וְאֵלֶּה יָצְאוּ מִן־
from they-marched-out and-these (19) you-take-them ones-alive they-come-out

הָעִיר נַעֲרֵי שָׂרֵי הַמְּדִינוֹת וְהַחַיִל אֲשֶׁר אַחֲרֵיהֶם׃
behind-them who and-the-army the-provinces commanders-of young-men-of the-city

וַיַּכּוּ אִישׁ אִישׁוֹ וַיָּנֻסוּ אֲרָם
Aram and-they-fled opponent-of-him each and-they-struck-down (20)

וַיִּרְדְּפֵם יִשְׂרָאֵל וַיִּמָּלֵט בֶּן־הֲדַד מֶלֶךְ אֲרָם עַל־סוּס
horse on Aram king-of Hadad Ben but-he-escaped Israel and-he-pursued-them

וּפָרָשִׁים׃ וַיֵּצֵא מֶלֶךְ יִשְׂרָאֵל וַיַּךְ אֶת־
*** and-he-overpowered Israel king-of and-he-advanced (21) with-horsemen

הַסּוּס וְאֶת־הָרָכֶב וְהִכָּה בַאֲרָם מַכָּה גְדוֹלָה׃
heavy loss on-Aram and-he-inflicted-loss the-chariot and the-horse

וַיִּגַּשׁ הַנָּבִיא אֶל־מֶלֶךְ יִשְׂרָאֵל וַיֹּאמֶר לוֹ לֵךְ
go! to-him and-he-said Israel king-of to the-prophet and-he-came (22)

הִתְחַזַּק וְדַע וּרְאֵה אֵת אֲשֶׁר־תַּעֲשֶׂה כִּי לִתְשׁוּבַת
at-return-of for you-must-do what *** and-see! and-know! strengthen-yourself!

הַשָּׁנָה מֶלֶךְ אֲרָם עֹלֶה עָלֶיךָ׃ וְעַבְדֵי מֶלֶךְ־
king-of and-officials-of (23) against-you attacking Aram king-of the-year

אֲרָם אָמְרוּ אֵלָיו אֱלֹהֵי הָרִים אֱלֹהֵיהֶם עַל־כֵּן חָזְקוּ
they-are-strong this for gods-of-them hills gods-of to-him they-advised Aram

מִמֶּנּוּ וְאוּלָם נִלָּחֵם אִתָּם בַּמִּישׁוֹר אִם־לֹא
surely then on-the-plain with-them we-fight but-if more-than-us

נֶחֱזַק מֵהֶם׃ וְאֶת־הַדָּבָר הַזֶּה עֲשֵׂה הָסֵר
remove! do! the-this the-thing and (24) more-than-they we-will-be-strong

הַמְּלָכִים אִישׁ מִמְּקֹמוֹ וְשִׂים פַּחוֹת תַּחְתֵּיהֶם׃
in-place-of-them officers and-put from-command-of-him each the-kings

וְאַתָּה תִמְנֶה ־ לְךָ ׀ חַיִל כַּחַיִל הַנֹּפֵל
the-one-being-lost like-the-army army for-you you-must-raise and-you (25)

מֵאוֹתָךְ וְסוּס כַּסּוּס ׀ וְרֶכֶב כָּרֶכֶב וְנִלָּחֲמָה
so-we-can-fight like-the-chariot and-chariot like-the-horse and-horse from-you

אוֹתָם בַּמִּישׁוֹר אִם־לֹא נֶחֱזַק מֵהֶם וַיִּשְׁמַע
and-he-listened more-than-they we-will-be-strong surely then on-the-plain them

לְקֹלָם וַיַּעַשׂ כֵּן׃ וַיְהִי לִתְשׁוּבַת
at-return-of and-he-was (26) accordingly and-he-acted to-voice-of-them

Now Ben-Hadad had dispatched scouts, who reported, "Men are advancing from Samaria."

[18]He said, "If they have come out for peace, take them alive; if they have come out for war, take them alive."

[19]The young officers of the provincial commanders marched out of the city with the army behind them [20]and each one struck down his opponent. At that, the Arameans fled, with the Israelites in pursuit. But Ben-Hadad king of Aram escaped on horseback with some of his horsemen. [21]The king of Israel advanced and overpowered the horses and chariots and inflicted heavy losses on the Arameans.

[22]Afterward, the prophet came to the king of Israel and said, "Strengthen your position and see what must be done, because next spring the king of Aram will attack you again."

[23]Meanwhile, the officials of the king of Aram advised him, "Their gods are gods of the hills. That is why they were too strong for us. But if we fight them on the plains, surely we will be stronger than they. [24]Do this: Remove all the kings from their commands and replace them with other officers. [25]You must also raise an army like the one you lost—horse for horse and chariot for chariot—so we can fight Israel on the plains. Then surely we will be stronger than they." He agreed with them and acted accordingly.

הַשָּׁנָה וַיִּפְקֹד בֶּן־ הֲדַד אֶת־ אֲרָם וַיַּעַל אֲפֵקָה
to-Aphek and-he-went-up Aram *** Hadad Ben then-he-mustered the-year

לַמִּלְחָמָה עִם־ יִשְׂרָאֵל׃ וּבְנֵי יִשְׂרָאֵל הָתְפָּקְדוּ
they-were-mustered Israel and-sons-of (27) Israel against to-the-fight

וְכָלְכְּלוּ וַיֵּלְכוּ לִקְרָאתָם וַיַּחֲנוּ
and-they-camped to-meet-them and-they-marched-out and-they-were-provided

בְנֵי־ יִשְׂרָאֵל נֶגְדָּם כִּשְׁנֵי חֲשִׂפֵי עִזִּים וַאֲרָם
while-Aram goats small-flocks-of like-two-of opposite-them Israel sons-of

מִלְאוּ אֶת־ הָאָרֶץ׃ וַיִּגַּשׁ אִישׁ הָאֱלֹהִים
the-God man-of and-he-came-up (28) the-countryside *** they-covered

וַיֹּאמֶר אֶל־ מֶלֶךְ יִשְׂרָאֵל וַיֹּאמֶר כֹּה־ אָמַר יְהוָה יַעַן אֲשֶׁר
that because Yahweh he-says this and-he-said Israel king-of to and-he-told

אָמְרוּ אֲרָם אֱלֹהֵי הָרִים יְהוָה וְלֹא־ אֱלֹהֵי עֲמָקִים הוּא וְנָתַתִּי
then-I-will-give he valleys God-of and-not Yahweh hills God-of Aram they-think

אֶת־ כָּל־ הֶהָמוֹן הַגָּדוֹל הַזֶּה בְּיָדֶךָ וִידַעְתֶּם
and-you-will-know into-hand-of-you the-this the-vast the-army all-of ***

כִּי־ אֲנִי יְהוָה׃ וַיַּחֲנוּ אֵלֶּה נֹכַח אֵלֶּה שִׁבְעַת יָמִים
days seven-of those opposite these and-they-camped (29) Yahweh I that

וַיְהִי | בַּיּוֹם הַשְּׁבִיעִי וַתִּקְרַב הַמִּלְחָמָה
the-battle then-she-was-joined the-seventh on-the-day and-he-was

וַיַּכּוּ בְנֵי־ יִשְׂרָאֵל אֶת־ אֲרָם מֵאָה־ אֶלֶף
thousand hundred Aram *** Israel sons-of and-they-inflicted-casualties

רַגְלִי בְּיוֹם אֶחָד׃ וַיָּנֻסוּ הַנּוֹתָרִים | אֲפֵקָה
to-Aphek the-ones-remaining and-they-escaped (30) one on-day foot-soldier

אֶל־הָעִיר וַתִּפֹּל הַחוֹמָה עַל־ עֶשְׂרִים וְשִׁבְעָה אֶלֶף אִישׁ
man thousand and-seven twenty on the-wall and-she-collapsed the-city to

הַנּוֹתָרִים וּבֶן־ הֲדַד נָס וַיָּבֹא אֶל־ הָעִיר חֶדֶר
room the-city into and-he-went he-fled Hadad and-Ben the-ones-remaining

בְּחָדֶר׃ וַיֹּאמְרוּ אֵלָיו עֲבָדָיו הִנֵּה־ נָא שָׁמַעְנוּ כִּי
that we-heard now! look! officials-of-him to-him and-they-said (31) in-room

מַלְכֵי בֵּית יִשְׂרָאֵל כִּי־ מַלְכֵי חֶסֶד הֵם נָשִׂימָה נָּא שַׂקִּים
sackcloths now! let-us-put they mercy kings-of that Israel house-of kings-of

בְּמָתְנֵינוּ וַחֲבָלִים בְּרֹאשֵׁנוּ וְנֵצֵא אֶל־ מֶלֶךְ
king-of to and-let-us-go around-head-of-us and-ropes around-waists-of-us

יִשְׂרָאֵל אוּלַי יְחַיֶּה אֶת־ נַפְשֶׁךָ׃ וַיַּחְגְּרוּ שַׂקִּים
sackcloths so-they-wore (32) life-of-you *** he-will-spare perhaps Israel

בְּמָתְנֵיהֶם וַחֲבָלִים בְּרָאשֵׁיהֶם וַיָּבֹאוּ אֶל־ מֶלֶךְ
king-of to and-they-went around-heads-of-them and-ropes around-waists-of-them

26 The next spring Ben-Hadad mustered the Arameans and went up to Aphek to fight against Israel. 27 When the Israelites were also mustered and given provisions, they marched out to meet them. The Israelites camped opposite them like two small flocks of goats, while the Arameans covered the countryside.

28 The man of God came up and told the king of Israel, "This is what the LORD says: 'Because the Arameans think the LORD is a god of the hills and not a god of the valleys, I will deliver this vast army into your hands, and you will know that I am the LORD.' "

29 For seven days they camped opposite each other, and on the seventh day the battle was joined. The Israelites inflicted a hundred thousand casualties on the Aramean foot soldiers in one day. 30 The rest of them escaped to the city of Aphek, where the wall collapsed on twenty-seven thousand of them. And Ben-Hadad fled to the city and hid in an inner room.

31 His officials said to him, "Look, we have heard that the kings of the house of Israel are merciful. Let us go to the king of Israel with sackcloth around our waists and ropes around our heads. Perhaps he will spare your life."

32 Wearing sackcloth around their waists and ropes around their heads, they went to the

יִשְׂרָאֵל וַיֹּאמְרוּ עַבְדְּךָ בֶן־ הֲדַד אָמַר תְּחִי־ נָא

now! let-her-live he-says Hadad Ben servant-of-you and-they-said Israel

נַפְשִׁי וַיֹּאמֶר הַעוֹדֶנּוּ חַי אָחִי הוּא׃ וְהָאֲנָשִׁים

and-the-men (33) he brother-of-me alive still-he? and-he-answered life-of-me

יְנַחֲשׁוּ וַיְמַהֲרוּ ˚וַיַּחְלְטוּ הֲמִמֶּנּוּ˚

*whether-from-him and-they-picked-up* and-they-were-quick they-took-as-good-sign

וַיֹּאמְרוּ אָחִיךָ בֶן־ הֲדַד וַיֹּאמֶר בֹּאוּ קָחֻהוּ וַיֵּצֵא

when-he-came get-him! go! and-he-said Hadad Ben brother-of-you and-they-said

אֵלָיו בֶּן־ הֲדַד וַיַּעֲלֵהוּ עַל־ הַמֶּרְכָּבָה׃ וַיֹּאמֶר

and-he-said (34) the-chariot into then-he-brought-up-him Hadad Ben to-him

אֵלָיו הֶעָרִים אֲשֶׁר־ לָקַח־ אָבִי מֵאֵת אָבִיךָ אָשִׁיב

I-will-return father-of-you from father-of-me he-took that the-cities to-him

וְחוּצוֹת תָּשִׂים לְךָ בְדַמֶּשֶׂק כַּאֲשֶׁר־ שָׂם

he-set-up just-as in-Damascus for-you you-may-set-up and-market-areas

אָבִי בְּשֹׁמְרוֹן וַאֲנִי בַּבְּרִית אֲשַׁלְּחֶךָּ וַיִּכְרָת־

so-he-made I-will-set-free-you in-the-treaty and-I in-Samaria father-of-me

לוֹ בְרִית וַיְשַׁלְּחֵהוּ׃ וְאִישׁ אֶחָד מִבְּנֵי הַנְּבִיאִים

the-prophets of-sons-of one and-man (35) and-he-let-go-him treaty with-him

אָמַר אֶל־ רֵעֵהוּ בִּדְבַר יְהוָה הַכֵּינִי נָא וַיְמָאֵן

but-he-refused now! strike-me! Yahweh by-word-of companion-of-him to he-said

הָאִישׁ לְהַכֹּתוֹ׃ וַיֹּאמֶר לוֹ יַעַן אֲשֶׁר לֹא־ שָׁמַעְתָּ

you-obeyed not that because to-him so-he-said (36) to-strike-him the-man

בְּקוֹל יְהוָה הִנְּךָ הוֹלֵךְ מֵאִתִּי וְהִכְּךָ

and-he-will-kill-you from-with-me leaving see-you! Yahweh to-voice-of

הָאַרְיֵה וַיֵּלֶךְ מֵאֶצְלוֹ וַיִּמְצָאֵהוּ הָאַרְיֵה וַיַּכֵּהוּ׃

and-he-killed-him the-lion and-he-found-him from-with-him and-he-went the-lion

וַיִּמְצָא אִישׁ אַחֵר וַיֹּאמֶר הַכֵּינִי נָא וַיַּכֵּהוּ

so-he-struck-him now! strike-me! and-he-said another man and-he-found (37)

הָאִישׁ הַכֵּה וּפָצֹעַ׃ וַיֵּלֶךְ הַנָּבִיא וַיַּעֲמֹד

and-he-stood the-prophet then-he-went (38) and-to-wound to-strike the-man

לַמֶּלֶךְ עַל־ הַדָּרֶךְ וַיִּתְחַפֵּשׂ בָּאֲפֵר עַל־

over with-the-headband and-he-disguised-himself the-road by for-the-king

עֵינָיו׃ וַיְהִי הַמֶּלֶךְ עֹבֵר וְהוּא צָעַק אֶל־

to he-called-out and-he passing-by the-king and-he-was (39) eyes-of-him

הַמֶּלֶךְ וַיֹּאמֶר עַבְדְּךָ | יָצָא בְקֶרֶב־ הַמִּלְחָמָה וְהִנֵּה־

and-see! the-battle into-thick-of he-went servant-of-you and-he-said the-king

אִישׁ סָר וַיָּבֵא אֵלַי אִישׁ וַיֹּאמֶר שְׁמֹר אֶת־ הָאִישׁ הַזֶּה

the-this the-man *** guard! and-he-said man to-me and-he-brought coming man

king of Israel and said, "Your servant Ben-Hadad says: 'Please let me live.' "

The king answered, "Is he still alive? He is my brother."

33The men took this as a good sign and were quick to pick up his word. "Yes, your brother Ben-Hadad!" they said.

"Go and get him," the king said. When Ben-Hadad came out, Ahab had him come up into his chariot.

34"I will return the cities my father took from your father," Ben-Hadad offered. "You may set up your own market areas in Damascus, as my father did in Samaria."

⌞Ahab said,⌟ "On the basis of a treaty I will set you free." So he made a treaty with him, and let him go.

### *A Prophet Condemns Ahab*

35By the word of the LORD one of the sons of the prophets said to his companion, "Strike me with your weapon," but the man refused.

36So the prophet said, "Because you have not obeyed the LORD, as soon as you leave me a lion will kill you." And after the man went away, a lion found him and killed him.

37The prophet found another man and said, "Strike me, please." So the man struck him and wounded him. 38Then the prophet went and stood by the road waiting for the king. He disguised himself with his headband down over his eyes. 39As the king passed by, the prophet called out to him, "Your servant went into the thick of the battle, and someone came to me with a captive and said, 'Guard this

***33 Many Western mss emend this *Ketbib* form with the *Qere* ( הֲ מִ׳ —וּהָ ), *and-they-picked-up-her from-him*, which is the *Ketbib* in some Eastern mss.**

אִם־ הִפָּקֵד֙ יִפָּקֵ֔ד וְהָיְתָ֤ה נַפְשְׁךָ֙ תַּ֣חַת נַפְשׁ֔וֹ
if  to-be-missing  he-is-missing  then-she-will-be  for  life-of-you  for  life-of-him

א֥וֹ כִכַּר־ כֶּ֖סֶף תִּשְׁק֑וֹל: וַיְהִי֙ עַבְדְּךָ֜ עֹשֶׂ֥ה
or  talent-of  silver  you-must-pay  (40)  and-he-was  servant-of-you  being-busy

הֵ֣נָּה וָהֵ֔נָּה וְה֖וּא אֵינֶ֑נּוּ וַיֹּ֧אמֶר אֵלָ֛יו מֶֽלֶךְ־ יִשְׂרָאֵ֖ל כֵּ֥ן
at-here  and-at-there  and-he  not-he  and-he-said  to-him  king-of  Israel  that

מִשְׁפָּטֶ֖ךָ אַתָּ֥ה חָרָֽצְתָּ: וַיְמַהֵ֕ר וַיָּ֕סַר אֶת־
sentence-of-you  you  you-pronounced  (41)  then-he-was-quick  and-he-removed  ***

הָֽאֲפֵ֖ר מֵעַ֣ל עֵינָ֑יו וַיַּכֵּ֤ר אֹתוֹ֙ מֶ֣לֶךְ יִשְׂרָאֵ֔ל כִּ֥י
the-headband  from-over  eyes-of-him  and-he-recognized  him  king-of  Israel  that

מֵהַנְּבִיאִ֖ים ה֑וּא וַיֹּ֣אמֶר אֵלָ֗יו כֹּ֚ה אָמַ֣ר יְהוָ֔ה יַ֗עַן
from-the-prophets  he  (42)  and-he-said  to-him  this  he-says  Yahweh  because

שִׁלַּ֛חְתָּ אֶת־ אִישׁ־ חֶרְמִ֖י מִיָּ֑ד וְהָיְתָ֤ה נַפְשְׁךָ֙
you-set-free  ***  man  determined-to-die  from-hand  then-she-shall-be  life-of-you

תַּ֣חַת נַפְשׁ֔וֹ וְעַמְּךָ֖ תַּ֥חַת עַמּֽוֹ: וַיֵּ֧לֶךְ מֶֽלֶךְ־
for  life-of-him  and-people-of-you  for  people-of-him  (43)  and-he-went  king-of

יִשְׂרָאֵ֛ל עַל־ בֵּית֖וֹ סַ֣ר וְזָעֵ֑ף וַיָּבֹ֖א שֹׁמְרֽוֹנָה:
Israel  to  palace-of-him  sullen  and-angry  and-he-went  to-Samaria

וַיְהִ֗י אַחַר֙ הַדְּבָרִ֣ים הָאֵ֔לֶּה כֶּ֧רֶם הָיָ֛ה לְנָב֖וֹת
(21:1)  and-he-was  after  the-things  the-these  vineyard  he-was  to-Naboth

הַיִּזְרְעֵאלִ֑י אֲשֶׁ֣ר בְּיִזְרְעֶ֗אל אֵ֚צֶל הֵיכַ֣ל אַחְאָ֔ב מֶ֖לֶךְ שֹׁמְרֽוֹן:
the-Jezreelite  that  in-Jezreel  close-to  palace-of  Ahab  king-of  Samaria

וַיְדַבֵּ֣ר אַחְאָ֣ב אֶל־ נָב֣וֹת | לֵאמֹר֩ תְּנָה־ לִּ֨י אֶת־ כַּרְמְךָ֜
(2)  and-he-said  to  Ahab  to-say  Naboth  give!  to-me  ***  vineyard-of-you

וִֽיהִי־ לִ֣י לְגַן־ יָרָ֗ק כִּ֣י ה֤וּא קָרוֹב֙ אֵ֣צֶל
and-let-him-be  for-me  as-garden-of  vegetable  since  he  close  next-to

בֵּיתִ֔י וְאֶתְּנָ֤ה לְךָ֙ תַּחְתָּ֔יו כֶּ֖רֶם ט֣וֹב
palace-of-me  and-I-will-give  to-you  in-exchange-for-him  vineyard  better

מִמֶּ֑נּוּ אִ֚ם ט֣וֹב בְּעֵינֶ֔יךָ אֶתְּנָה־ לְךָ֥ כֶ֖סֶף מְחִ֥יר זֶֽה:
than-he  or  good  in-eyes-of-you  I-will-give  to-you  silver  value-of  this

וַיֹּ֥אמֶר נָב֖וֹת אֶל־ אַחְאָ֑ב חָלִ֤ילָה לִּי֙ מֵֽיהוָ֔ה
(3)  but-he-replied  Naboth  to  Ahab  far-be-it!  from-me  from-Yahweh

מִתִּתִּ֛י אֶת־ נַחֲלַ֥ת אֲבֹתַ֖י לָֽךְ: וַיָּבֹ֩א אַחְאָ֨ב
from-to-give-me  ***  inheritance-of  fathers-of-me  to-you  (4)  so-he-went  Ahab

אֶל־ בֵּית֜וֹ סַ֣ר וְזָעֵ֗ף עַל־ הַדָּבָר֙ אֲשֶׁר־ דִּבֶּ֣ר אֵלָ֜יו
to  home-of-him  sullen  and-angry  because-of  the-word  that  he-said  to-him

נָבוֹת֙ הַיִּזְרְעֵאלִ֔י וַיֹּ֕אמֶר לֹֽא־ אֶתֵּ֥ן לְךָ֖ אֶת־ נַחֲלַ֣ת
Naboth  the-Jezreelite  and-he-said  not  I-will-give  to-you  ***  inheritance-of

man. If he is missing, it will be your life for his life, or you must pay a talent[w] of silver.' [40]While your servant was busy here and there, the man disappeared."

"That is your sentence," the king of Israel said. "You have pronounced it yourself." [41]Then the prophet quickly removed the headband from his eyes, and the king of Israel recognized him as one of the prophets. [42]He said to the king, "This is what the LORD says: 'You have set free a man I had determined should die.[x] Therefore it is your life for his life, your people for his people.' " [43]Sullen and angry, the king of Israel went to his palace in Samaria.

### Naboth's Vineyard

**21** Some time later there was an incident involving a vineyard belonging to Naboth the Jezreelite. The vineyard was in Jezreel, close to the palace of Ahab king of Samaria. [2]Ahab said to Naboth, "Let me have your vineyard to use for a vegetable garden, since it is close to my palace. In exchange I will give you a better vineyard or, if you prefer, I will pay you whatever it is worth."

[3]But Naboth replied, "The LORD forbid that I should give you the inheritance of my fathers."

[w]39 That is, about 75 pounds (about 34 kilograms)
[x]42 The Hebrew term refers to the irrevocable giving over of things or persons to the LORD, often by totally destroying them.

°41 ק מעלי

אֲבֹתָ֑י וַיִּשְׁכַּב֙ עַל־ מִטָּת֔וֹ וַיַּסֵּ֥ב אֶת־ פָּנָ֖יו וְלֹא־
and-not faces-of-him *** and-he-turned bed-of-him on and-he-lay fathers-of-me

אָ֥כַל לָֽחֶם׃ וַתָּבֹ֥א אֵלָ֖יו אִיזֶ֣בֶל אִשְׁתּ֑וֹ וַתְּדַבֵּ֣ר אֵלָ֔יו
to-him and-she-asked wife-of-him Jezebel to-him and-she-came (5) food he-ate

מַה־ זֶּה֙ רוּחֲךָ֣ סָרָ֔ה וְאֵינְךָ֖ אֹכֵ֥ל לָֽחֶם׃ וַיְדַבֵּ֣ר
and-he-answered (6) food eating and-not-you sullen spirit-of-you this what?

אֵלֶ֗יהָ כִּֽי־ אֲדַבֵּ֞ר אֶל־ נָב֣וֹת הַיִּזְרְעֵאלִ֗י וָאֹ֤מַר לוֹ֙ תְּנָה־ לִּ֤י
to-me sell! to-him and-I-said the-Jezreelite Naboth to I-spoke because to-her

אֶת־ כַּרְמְךָ֙ בְּכֶ֔סֶף א֚וֹ אִם־ חָפֵ֣ץ אַתָּ֔ה אֶתְּנָה־ לְךָ֥
to-you I-will-give you he-pleases if or for-silver vineyard-of-you ***

כֶ֖רֶם תַּחְתָּ֑יו וַיֹּ֕אמֶר לֹֽא־ אֶתֵּ֥ן לְךָ֖ אֶת־ כַּרְמִֽי׃
vineyard-of-me *** to-you I-will-give not but-he-said in-place-of-him vineyard

וַתֹּ֤אמֶר אֵלָיו֙ אִיזֶ֣בֶל אִשְׁתּ֔וֹ אַתָּ֕ה עַתָּ֛ה תַּעֲשֶׂ֥ה מְלוּכָ֖ה עַל־יִשְׂרָאֵ֑ל
Israel over king you-act now you wife-of-him Jezebel to-him and-she-said (7)

ק֤וּם אֱכָל־ לֶ֙חֶם֙ וְיִטַ֣ב לִבֶּ֔ךָ אֲנִי֙ אֶתֵּ֣ן לְךָ֔
for-you I-will-get I heart-of-you and-let-him-cheer-up food eat! get-up!

אֶת־ כֶּ֖רֶם נָב֥וֹת הַיִּזְרְעֵאלִֽי׃ וַתִּכְתֹּ֤ב סְפָרִים֙ בְּשֵׁ֣ם
in-name-of letters so-she-wrote (8) the-Jezreelite Naboth vineyard-of ***

אַחְאָ֔ב וַתַּחְתֹּ֖ם בְּחֹתָמ֑וֹ וַתִּשְׁלַ֤ח הַסְּפָרִים֙ אֶל־ הַזְּקֵנִ֣ים*
the-elders to letters and-she-sent with-seal-of-him and-she-sealed Ahab

וְאֶל־ הַֽחֹרִים֙ אֲשֶׁ֣ר בְּעִיר֔וֹ הַיֹּשְׁבִ֖ים אֶת־ נָבֽוֹת׃
Naboth with the-ones-living in-city-of-him who the-nobles and-to

וַתִּכְתֹּ֥ב בַּסְּפָרִ֖ים לֵאמֹ֑ר קִרְאוּ־ צ֔וֹם וְהוֹשִׁ֥יבוּ אֶת־ נָב֖וֹת
Naboth *** and-seat! fast proclaim! to-say in-the-letters and-she-wrote (9)

בְּרֹ֥אשׁ הָעָֽם׃ וְ֠הוֹשִׁיבוּ שְׁנַ֨יִם אֲנָשִׁ֥ים בְּנֵֽי־ בְלִיַּ֮עַל֮ נֶגְדּוֹ֒
opposite-him scoundrel sons-of men two but-seat! (10) the-people at-head-of

וִיעִדֻ֣הוּ לֵאמֹ֔ר בֵּרַ֥כְתָּ אֱלֹהִ֖ים וָמֶ֑לֶךְ
and-king God you-cursed to-say and-they-shall-testify-against-him

וְהוֹצִיאֻ֥הוּ וְסִקְלֻ֖הוּ וְיָמֹֽת׃ וַיַּעֲשׂ֣וּ אַנְשֵׁ֣י
men-of and-they-did (11) so-he-dies and-stone-him! then-take-out-him!

עִיר֡וֹ הַזְּקֵנִים֩ וְהַחֹרִ֨ים אֲשֶׁ֤ר הַיֹּשְׁבִים֙ בְּעִיר֔וֹ
in-city-of-him the-ones-living who and-the-nobles the-elders city-of-him

כַּאֲשֶׁ֛ר שָׁלְחָ֥ה אֲלֵיהֶ֖ם אִיזָ֑בֶל כַּאֲשֶׁר֙ כָּת֔וּב בַּסְּפָרִ֖ים
in-the-letters being-written just-as Jezebel to-them she-directed just-as

אֲשֶׁ֥ר שָׁלְחָ֖ה אֲלֵיהֶֽם׃ קָרְא֖וּ צ֑וֹם וְהֹשִׁ֥יבוּ אֶת־ נָב֖וֹת
Naboth *** and-they-seated fast they-proclaimed (12) to-them she-sent that

בְּרֹ֥אשׁ הָעָֽם׃ וַ֠יָּבֹאוּ שְׁנֵ֨י הָאֲנָשִׁ֤ים בְּנֵֽי־ בְלִיַּ֙עַל֙
scoundrel sons-of the-men two-of then-they-came (13) the-people at-head-of

4So Ahab went home, sullen
and angry because Naboth the
Jezreelite had said, "I will not
give you the inheritance of my
fathers." He lay on his bed
sulking and refused to eat.
5His wife Jezebel came in
and asked him, "Why are you
so sullen? Why won't you
eat?"
6He answered her, "Because
I said to Naboth the Jezreelite,
'Sell me your vineyard; or if
you prefer, I will give you another vineyard in its place.'
But he said, 'I will not give you
my vineyard.' "
7Jezebel his wife said, "Is
this how you act as king over
Israel? Get up and eat! Cheer
up. I'll get you the vineyard of
Naboth the Jezreelite."
8So she wrote letters in
Ahab's name, placed his seal
on them, and sent them to the
elders and nobles who lived in
Naboth's city with him. 9In
those letters she wrote:

> "Proclaim a day of fasting and seat Naboth in a prominent place among the people. 10But seat two scoundrels opposite him and have them testify that he has cursed both God and the king. Then take him out and stone him to death."

11So the elders and nobles
who lived in Naboth's city did
as Jezebel directed in the letters she had written to them.
12They proclaimed a fast and
seated Naboth in a prominent
place among the people.
13Then two scoundrels came

*8 Most mss have *dagesh* in the *zayin* (הַזְּ).

°8 ק ספרים

וַיֵּשְׁבוּ נֶגְדּוֹ וַיְעִדֻהוּ אַנְשֵׁי הַבְּלִיַּעַל
the-scoundrel men-of and-they-testified-against-him opposite-him and-they-sat

אֶת־ נָבוֹת נֶגֶד הָעָם לֵאמֹר בֵּרַךְ נָבוֹת אֱלֹהִים וָמֶלֶךְ
and-king God Naboth he-cursed to-say the-people before Naboth ***

וַיֹּצִאֻהוּ מִחוּץ לָעִיר וַיִּסְקְלֻהוּ בָאֲבָנִים
with-the-stones and-they-stoned-him of-the-city outside and-they-took-him

וַיָּמֹת׃ וַיִּשְׁלְחוּ אֶל־ אִיזֶבֶל לֵאמֹר סֻקַּל נָבוֹת
Naboth he-was-stoned to-say Jezebel to and-they-sent (14) so-he-died

וַיָּמֹת׃ וַיְהִי כִּשְׁמֹעַ אִיזֶבֶל כִּי־ סֻקַּל
he-was-stoned that Jezebel when-to-hear and-he-was (15) and-he-is-dead

נָבוֹת וַיָּמֹת וַתֹּאמֶר אִיזֶבֶל אֶל־אַחְאָב קוּם רֵשׁ אֶת־
*** possess! get-up! Ahab to Jezebel then-she-said and-he-died Naboth

כֶּרֶם ׀ נָבוֹת הַיִּזְרְעֵאלִי אֲשֶׁר מֵאֵן לָתֶת־ לְךָ בְכֶסֶף
for-silver to-you to-sell he-refused that the-Jezreelite Naboth vineyard-of

כִּי אֵין נָבוֹת חַי כִּי־ מֵת׃ וַיְהִי כִשְׁמֹעַ אַחְאָב כִּי
that Ahab when-to-hear and-he-was (16) dead but alive Naboth not for

מֵת נָבוֹת וַיָּקָם אַחְאָב לָרֶדֶת אֶל־ כֶּרֶם נָבוֹת
Naboth vineyard-of to to-go-down Ahab then-he-got-up Naboth he-was-dead

הַיִּזְרְעֵאלִי לְרִשְׁתּוֹ׃ וַיְהִי דְּבַר־ יְהוָה אֶל־אֵלִיָּהוּ
Elijah to Yahweh word-of then-he-came (17) to-possess-him the-Jezreelite

הַתִּשְׁבִּי לֵאמֹר׃ קוּם רֵד לִקְרַאת אַחְאָב מֶלֶךְ־יִשְׂרָאֵל
Israel king-of Ahab to-meet go-down! get-up! (18) to-say the-Tishbite

אֲשֶׁר בְּשֹׁמְרוֹן הִנֵּה בְּכֶרֶם נָבוֹת אֲשֶׁר־ יָרַד שָׁם לְרִשְׁתּוֹ׃
to-possess-him there he-went where Naboth in-vineyard-of see! in-Samaria who

וְדִבַּרְתָּ אֵלָיו לֵאמֹר כֹּה אָמַר יְהוָה הֲרָצַחְתָּ וְגַם־
and-also you-murdered? Yahweh he-says this to-say to-him and-you-say (19)

יָרָשְׁתָּ וְדִבַּרְתָּ אֵלָיו לֵאמֹר כֹּה אָמַר יְהוָה
Yahweh he-says this to-say to-him then-you-say you-seized-property

בִּמְקוֹם אֲשֶׁר לָקְקוּ הַכְּלָבִים אֶת־ דַּם נָבוֹת יָלֹקּוּ
they-will-lick-up Naboth blood-of *** the-dogs they-licked-up where in-place

הַכְּלָבִים אֶת־ דָּמְךָ גַּם־ אָתָּה׃ וַיֹּאמֶר אַחְאָב אֶל־אֵלִיָּהוּ
Elijah to Ahab and-he-said (20) you also blood-of-you *** the-dogs

הַמְצָאתַנִי אֹיְבִי וַיֹּאמֶר מָצָאתִי יַעַן הִתְמַכֶּרְךָ
to-sell-you because I-found and-he-answered being-enemy-of-me you-found-me?

לַעֲשׂוֹת הָרַע בְּעֵינֵי יְהוָה׃ הִנְנִי מֵבִי אֵלֶיךָ רָעָה
disaster on-you bringing see-I! (21) Yahweh in-eyes-of the-evil to-do

וּבִעַרְתִּי אַחֲרֶיךָ וְהִכְרַתִּי לְאַחְאָב מַשְׁתִּין
one-urinating from-Ahab and-I-will-cut-off after-you and-I-will-consume

and sat opposite him and
brought charges against
Naboth before the people, saying, "Naboth has cursed both
God and the king." So they
took him outside the city and
stoned him to death. [14]Then
they sent word to Jezebel:
"Naboth has been stoned and
is dead."
[15]As soon as Jezebel heard
that Naboth had been stoned
to death, she said to Ahab,
"Get up and take possession of
the vineyard of Naboth the
Jezreelite that he refused to sell
you. He is no longer alive, but
dead." [16]When Ahab heard
that Naboth was dead, he got
up and went down to take
possession of Naboth's vineyard.
[17]Then the word of the LORD
came to Elijah the Tishbite:
[18]"Go down to meet Ahab king
of Israel, who rules in Samaria. He is now in Naboth's
vineyard, where he has gone
to take possession of it. [19]Say
to him, 'This is what the LORD
says: Have you not murdered
a man and seized his property?' Then say to him, 'This is
what the LORD says: In the
place where dogs licked up
Naboth's blood, dogs will lick
up your blood—yes, yours!' "
[20]Ahab said to Elijah, "So
you have found me, my enemy!"
"I have found you," he answered, "because you have
sold yourself to do evil in the
eyes of the LORD. [21]'I am going
to bring disaster on you. I will
consume your descendants
and cut off from Ahab every

°21 ק מביא

בְּקִיר וְעָצוּר וְעָזוּב בְּיִשְׂרָאֵל׃ וְנָתַתִּי
and-I-will-make (22) in-Israel or-being-free and-being-slave against-wall

אֶת־ בֵּיתְךָ כְּבֵית יָרָבְעָם בֶּן־ נְבָט וּכְבֵית בַּעְשָׁא
Baasha and-like-house-of Nebat son-of Jeroboam like-house-of house-of-you ***

בֶן־ אֲחִיָּה אֶל־ הַכַּעַס אֲשֶׁר הִכְעַסְתָּ וַתַּחֲטִא
and-you-caused-to-sin you-provoked-anger that the-anger for Ahijah son-of

אֶת־יִשְׂרָאֵל׃ וְגַם־ לְאִיזֶבֶל דִּבֶּר יְהוָה לֵאמֹר הַכְּלָבִים
the-dogs to-say Yahweh he-speaks about-Jezebel and-also (23) Israel ***

יֹאכְלוּ אֶת־ אִיזֶבֶל בְּחֵל יִזְרְעֶאל׃ הַמֵּת לְאַחְאָב
of-Ahab the-dead (24) Jezreel by-wall-of Jezebel *** they-will-devour

בָּעִיר יֹאכְלוּ הַכְּלָבִים וְהַמֵּת בַּשָּׂדֶה יֹאכְלוּ
they-will-eat in-the-country and-the-dead the-dogs they-will-eat in-the-city

עוֹף הַשָּׁמָיִם׃ רַק לֹא־ הָיָה כְאַחְאָב אֲשֶׁר הִתְמַכֵּר לַעֲשׂוֹת
to-do he-sold-himself who like-Ahab he-was not indeed (25) the-airs bird-of

הָרַע בְּעֵינֵי יְהוָה אֲשֶׁר־ הֵסַתָּה אֹתוֹ אִיזֶבֶל אִשְׁתּוֹ׃
wife-of-him Jezebel him she-urged-on whom Yahweh in-eyes-of the-evil

וַיַּתְעֵב מְאֹד לָלֶכֶת אַחֲרֵי הַגִּלֻּלִים כְּכֹל אֲשֶׁר עָשׂוּ
they-did that like-all the-idols after to-go very and-he-behaved-vilely (26)

הָאֱמֹרִי אֲשֶׁר הוֹרִישׁ יְהוָה מִפְּנֵי בְּנֵי יִשְׂרָאֵל׃
Israel sons-of from-before Yahweh he-drove-out whom the-Amorite

וַיְהִי כִשְׁמֹעַ אַחְאָב אֶת־ הַדְּבָרִים הָאֵלֶּה וַיִּקְרַע
then-he-tore the-these the-words *** Ahab when-to-hear and-he-was (27)

בְּגָדָיו וַיָּשֶׂם־ שַׂק עַל־ בְּשָׂרוֹ וַיָּצוֹם וַיִּשְׁכַּב
and-he-lay and-he-fasted body-of-him on sackcloth and-he-put clothes-of-him

בַּשָּׂק וַיְהַלֵּךְ אַט׃ וַיְהִי דְּבַר־ יְהוָה אֶל־
to Yahweh word-of then-he-came (28) meekly and-he-walked in-the-sackcloth

אֵלִיָּהוּ הַתִּשְׁבִּי לֵאמֹר׃ הֲרָאִיתָ כִּי־ נִכְנַע אַחְאָב
Ahab he-humbled-himself how you-noticed? (29) to-say the-Tishbite Elijah

מִלְּפָנָי יַעַן כִּי־ נִכְנַע מִפָּנַי לֹא־ אָבִי°
I-will-bring not from-before-me he-humbled-himself that because from-before-me

הָרָעָה בְּיָמָיו בִּימֵי בְנוֹ אָבִיא הָרָעָה
the-disaster I-will-bring son-of-him in-days-of in-days-of-him the-disaster

עַל־ בֵּיתוֹ׃ וַיֵּשְׁבוּ שָׁלֹשׁ שָׁנִים אֵין מִלְחָמָה בֵּין
between war there-was-no years three and-they-remained (22:1) house-of-him on

אֲרָם וּבֵין יִשְׂרָאֵל׃ וַיְהִי בַּשָּׁנָה הַשְּׁלִישִׁית וַיֵּרֶד
he-went-down the-third in-the-year but-he-was (2) Israel and-between Aram

יְהוֹשָׁפָט מֶלֶךְ־ יְהוּדָה אֶל־ מֶלֶךְ יִשְׂרָאֵל׃ וַיֹּאמֶר מֶלֶךְ־יִשְׂרָאֵל
Israel king-of and-he-said (3) Israel king-of to Judah king-of Jehoshaphat

last male in Israel—slave or free. [22]I will make your house like that of Jeroboam son of Nebat and that of Baasha son of Ahijah, because you have provoked me to anger and have caused Israel to sin.'

[23]"And also concerning Jezebel the LORD says: 'Dogs will devour Jezebel by the wall of[y] Jezreel.'

[24]"Dogs will eat those belonging to Ahab who die in the city, and the birds of the air will feed on those who die in the country."

[25](There was never a man like Ahab, who sold himself to do evil in the eyes of the LORD, urged on by Jezebel his wife. [26]He behaved in the vilest manner by going after idols, like the Amorites the LORD drove out before Israel.)

[27]When Ahab heard these words, he tore his clothes, put on sackcloth and fasted. He lay in sackcloth and went around meekly.

[28]Then the word of the LORD came to Elijah the Tishbite: [29]"Have you noticed how Ahab has humbled himself before me? Because he has humbled himself, I will not bring this disaster in his day, but I will bring it on his house in the days of his son."

### *Micaiah Prophesies Against Ahab*

**22** For three years there was no war between Aram and Israel. [2]But in the third year Jehoshaphat king of Judah went down to see the king of Israel. [3]The king of Israel had said to his officials,

[y]23 Most Hebrew manuscripts; a few Hebrew manuscripts, Vulgate and Syriac (see also 2 Kings 9:26) *the plot of ground at*

°29 ק אביא

אֶל־ עֲבָדָיו הַיְדַעְתֶּם כִּי־ לָנוּ רָמֹת גִּלְעָד וַאֲנַחְנוּ
yet-we Gilead Ramoth to-us that you-know? officials-of-him to

מַחְשִׁים מִקַּחַת אֹתָהּ מִיַּד מֶלֶךְ אֲרָם׃
Aram king-of from-hand-of her from-to-retake ones-doing-nothing

וַיֹּאמֶר אֶל־ יְהוֹשָׁפָט הֲתֵלֵךְ אִתִּי לַמִּלְחָמָה רָמֹת גִּלְעָד
Gilead Ramoth to-the-fight with-me will-you-go? Jehoshaphat to so-he-asked (4)

וַיֹּאמֶר יְהוֹשָׁפָט אֶל־ מֶלֶךְ יִשְׂרָאֵל כָּמוֹנִי כָמוֹךָ כְּעַמִּי
so-people-of-me as-you so-me Israel king-of to Jehoshaphat and-he-replied

כְעַמֶּךָ כְּסוּסַי כְּסוּסֶיךָ׃ וַיֹּאמֶר יְהוֹשָׁפָט
Jehoshaphat but-he-said (5) as-horses-of-you so-horses-of-me as-people-of-you

אֶל־ מֶלֶךְ יִשְׂרָאֵל דְּרָשׁ־ נָא כַיּוֹם אֶת־ דְּבַר יְהוָה׃
Yahweh counsel-of *** as-the-day now! seek! Israel king-of to

וַיִּקְבֹּץ מֶלֶךְ־ יִשְׂרָאֵל אֶת־ הַנְּבִיאִים כְּאַרְבַּע מֵאוֹת אִישׁ
man hundreds about-four the-prophets *** Israel king-of so-he-gathered (6)

וַיֹּאמֶר אֲלֵהֶם הַאֵלֵךְ עַל־ רָמֹת גִּלְעָד לַמִּלְחָמָה אִם־
or to-the-war Gilead Ramoth against shall-I-go? to-them and-he-asked

אֶחְדָּל וַיֹּאמְרוּ עֲלֵה וְיִתֵּן אֲדֹנָי בְּיַד
into-hand-of Lord for-he-will-give go! and-they-answered shall-I-refrain

הַמֶּלֶךְ׃ וַיֹּאמֶר יְהוֹשָׁפָט הַאֵין פֹּה נָבִיא לַיהוָה עוֹד
still of-Yahweh prophet here not? Jehoshaphat but-he-asked (7) the-king

וְנִדְרְשָׁה מֵאוֹתוֹ׃ וַיֹּאמֶר מֶלֶךְ־יִשְׂרָאֵל ׀ אֶל־יְהוֹשָׁפָט
Jehoshaphat to Israel king-of and-he-answered (8) of-him that-we-can-inquire

עוֹד אִישׁ־אֶחָד לִדְרֹשׁ אֶת־ יְהוָה מֵאֹתוֹ וַאֲנִי שְׂנֵאתִיו כִּי
because I-hate-him but-I through-him Yahweh *** to-inquire one man still

לֹא־ יִתְנַבֵּא עָלַי טוֹב כִּי אִם־ רָע מִיכָיְהוּ בֶּן־ יִמְלָה
Imlah son-of Micaiah bad rather but good about-me he-prophesies not

וַיֹּאמֶר יְהוֹשָׁפָט אַל־ יֹאמַר הַמֶּלֶךְ כֵּן׃ וַיִּקְרָא
so-he-called (9) that the-king he-should-say not Jehoshaphat and-he-replied

מֶלֶךְ יִשְׂרָאֵל אֶל־ סָרִיס אֶחָד וַיֹּאמֶר מַהֲרָה מִיכָיְהוּ בֶן־
son-of Micaiah bring-at-once! and-he-said one official *** Israel king-of

יִמְלָה׃ וּמֶלֶךְ יִשְׂרָאֵל וִיהוֹשָׁפָט מֶלֶךְ־ יְהוּדָה יֹשְׁבִים
ones-sitting Judah king-of and-Jehoshaphat Israel and-king-of (10) Imlah

אִישׁ עַל־ כִּסְאוֹ מְלֻבָּשִׁים בְּגָדִים בְּגֹרֶן פֶּתַח
entrance-of at-threshing-floor robes ones-being-dressed throne-of-him on each

שַׁעַר שֹׁמְרוֹן וְכָל־ הַנְּבִיאִים מִתְנַבְּאִים לִפְנֵיהֶם׃
before-them ones-prophesying the-prophets and-all-of Samaria gate-of

וַיַּעַשׂ לוֹ צִדְקִיָּה בֶן־ כְּנַעֲנָה קַרְנֵי בַרְזֶל וַיֹּאמֶר
and-he-said iron horns-of Kenaanah son-of Zedekiah for-him now-he-made (11)

"Don't you know that Ramoth Gilead belongs to us and yet we are doing nothing to retake it from the king of Aram?"
4So he asked Jehoshaphat, "Will you go with me to fight against Ramoth Gilead?"
Jehoshaphat replied to the king of Israel, "I am as you are, my people as your people, my horses as your horses."
5But Jehoshaphat also said to the king of Israel, "First seek the counsel of the LORD."
6So the king of Israel brought together the prophets—about four hundred men—and asked them, "Shall I go to war against Ramoth Gilead, or shall I refrain?"
"Go," they answered, "for the Lord will give it into the king's hand."
7But Jehoshaphat asked, "Is there not a prophet of the LORD here whom we can inquire of?"
8The king of Israel answered Jehoshaphat, "There is still one man through whom we can inquire of the LORD, but I hate him because he never prophesies anything good about me, but always bad. He is Micaiah son of Imlah."
"The king should not say that," Jehoshaphat replied.
9So the king of Israel called one of his officials and said, "Bring Micaiah son of Imlah at once."
10Dressed in their royal robes, the king of Israel and Jehoshaphat king of Judah were sitting on their thrones at the threshing floor by the entrance of the gate of Samaria, with all the prophets prophesying before them.
11Now Zedekiah son of Kenaanah had made iron horns and

כֹּה־ אָמַר יְהוָה בְּאֵלֶּה תְּנַגַּח אֶת־ אֲרָם עַד־ כַּלֹּתָם׃
to-destroy-them until Aram *** you-will-gore with-these Yahweh he-says this

וְכָל־ הַנְּבִאִים נִבְּאִים כֵּן לֵאמֹר עֲלֵה רָמֹת
Ramoth attack! to-say same ones-prophesying the-prophets and-all-of (12)

גִּלְעָד וְהַצְלַח וְנָתַן יְהוָה בְּיַד הַמֶּלֶךְ׃
the-king into-hand-of Yahweh for-he-will-give and-be-victorious! Gilead

וְהַמַּלְאָךְ אֲשֶׁר־ הָלַךְ ׀ לִקְרֹא מִיכָיְהוּ דִּבֶּר אֵלָיו לֵאמֹר
to-say to-him he-said Micaiah to-summon he-went who and-the-messenger (13)

הִנֵּה־ נָא דִּבְרֵי הַנְּבִיאִים פֶּה־ אֶחָד טוֹב אֶל־ הַמֶּלֶךְ
the-king for success one mouth the-prophets words-of now! look!

יְהִי־ נָא דְבָרְיךָ° כִּדְבַר אַחַד מֵהֶם וְדִבַּרְתָּ טּוֹב׃
favorably and-you-speak with-them one as-word word-of-you now! let-him-be

וַיֹּאמֶר מִיכָיְהוּ חַי־ יְהוָה כִּי אֶת־ אֲשֶׁר יֹאמַר יְהוָה אֵלַי
to-me Yahweh he-tells what *** only Yahweh life-of Micaiah but-he-said (14)

אֹתוֹ אֲדַבֵּר׃ וַיָּבוֹא אֶל־ הַמֶּלֶךְ וַיֹּאמֶר הַמֶּלֶךְ
the-king then-he-asked the-king at when-he-arrived (15) I-can-tell him

אֵלָיו מִיכָיְהוּ הֲנֵלֵךְ אֶל־ רָמֹת גִּלְעָד לַמִּלְחָמָה אִם־
or to-the-war Gilead Ramoth against shall-we-go? Micaiah to-him

נֶחְדָּל וַיֹּאמֶר אֵלָיו עֲלֵה וְהַצְלַח
and-be-victorious! attack! to-him and-he-answered shall-we-refrain

וְנָתַן יְהוָה בְּיַד הַמֶּלֶךְ׃ וַיֹּאמֶר אֵלָיו
to-him but-he-said (16) the-king into-hand-of Yahweh for-he-will-give

הַמֶּלֶךְ עַד־ כַּמֶּה פְעָמִים אֲנִי מַשְׁבִּעֶךָ אֲשֶׁר לֹא־ תְדַבֵּר
you-tell not that making-swear-you I times as-the-how-many? to the-king

אֵלַי רַק־ אֱמֶת בְּשֵׁם יְהוָה׃ וַיֹּאמֶר רָאִיתִי אֶת־ כָּל־
all-of *** I-saw then-he-answered (17) Yahweh in-name-of truth only to-me

יִשְׂרָאֵל נְפֹצִים אֶל - הֶהָרִים כַּצֹּאן אֲשֶׁר אֵין־ לָהֶם
to-them not that like-the-sheep the-hills on ones-being-scattered Israel

רֹעֶה וַיֹּאמֶר יְהוָה לֹא־ אֲדֹנִים לָאֵלֶּה יָשׁוּבוּ אִישׁ־
each let-them-go to-these masters not Yahweh and-he-said one-shepherding

לְבֵיתוֹ בְּשָׁלוֹם׃ וַיֹּאמֶר מֶלֶךְ־ יִשְׂרָאֵל אֶל־ יְהוֹשָׁפָט הֲלוֹא
not? Jehoshaphat to Israel king-of and-he-said (18) in-peace to-home-of-him

אָמַרְתִּי אֵלֶיךָ לוֹא־ יִתְנַבֵּא עָלַי טוֹב כִּי אִם־ רָע׃ וַיֹּאמֶר
and-he-said (19) bad only but good about-me he-prophesies not to-you I-told

לָכֵן שְׁמַע דְּבַר־ יְהוָה רָאִיתִי אֶת־ יְהוָה יֹשֵׁב עַל־ כִּסְאוֹ
throne-of-him on sitting Yahweh *** I-saw Yahweh word-of hear! therefore

וְכָל־ צְבָא הַשָּׁמַיִם עֹמֵד עָלָיו מִימִינוֹ
on-right-of-him around-him standing the-heavens host-of and-all-of

he declared, "This is what the
LORD says: 'With these you
will gore the Arameans until
they are destroyed.' "
12 All the other prophets were
prophesying the same thing.
"Attack Ramoth Gilead and be
victorious," they said, "for the
LORD will give it into the
king's hand."
13 The messenger who had
gone to summon Micaiah said
to him, "Look, as one man the
other prophets are predicting
success for the king. Let your
word agree with theirs, and
speak favorably."
14 But Micaiah said, "As surely as the LORD lives, I can tell
him only what the LORD tells
me."
15 When he arrived, the king
asked him, "Micaiah, shall we
go to war against Ramoth Gilead, or shall I refrain?"
"Attack and be victorious,"
he answered, "for the LORD
will give it into the king's
hand."
16 The king said to him,
"How many times must I
make you swear to tell me
nothing but the truth in the
name of the LORD?"
17 Then Micaiah answered,
"I saw all Israel scattered on
the hills like sheep without a
shepherd, and the LORD said,
'These people have no master.
Let each one go home in
peace.' "
18 The king of Israel said to
Jehoshaphat, "Didn't I tell you
that he never prophesies anything good about me, but only
bad?"
19 Micaiah continued,
"Therefore hear the word of
the LORD: I saw the LORD sitting on his throne with all the
host of heaven standing
around him on his right and

°13 ק דברך

וּמִשְּׂמֹאלוֹ׃ וַיֹּאמֶר יְהוָה מִי יְפַתֶּה אֶת־אַחְאָב
Ahab *** he-will-lure who? Yahweh and-he-said (20) and-on-left-of-him

וְיַעַל וְיִפֹּל בְּרָמֹת גִּלְעָד וַיֹּאמֶר זֶה בְּכֹה
as-such this and-he-suggested Gilead at-Ramoth and-he-falls so-he-attacks

וְזֶה אֹמֵר בְּכֹה׃ וַיֵּצֵא הָרוּחַ וַיַּעֲמֹד
and-he-stood the-spirit and-he-came-forward (21) as-such suggesting and-that

לִפְנֵי יְהוָה וַיֹּאמֶר אֲנִי אֲפַתֶּנּוּ וַיֹּאמֶר יְהוָה אֵלָיו
to-him Yahweh and-he-asked I-will-lure-him I and-he-said Yahweh before

בַּמָּה׃ וַיֹּאמֶר אֵצֵא וְהָיִיתִי רוּחַ שֶׁקֶר
lying spirit and-I-will-be I-will-go-out and-he-said (22) by-the-how?

בְּפִי כָּל־ נְבִיאָיו וַיֹּאמֶר תְּפַתֶּה וְגַם־
and-also you-will-lure and-he-said prophets-of-him all-of in-mouth-of

תּוּכָל צֵא וַעֲשֵׂה־ כֵן׃ וְעַתָּה הִנֵּה נָתַן יְהוָה רוּחַ
spirit Yahweh he-put see! so-now (23) this and-do! go! you-will-succeed

שֶׁקֶר בְּפִי כָּל־ נְבִיאֶיךָ אֵלֶּה וַיהוָה דִּבֶּר
he-decreed and-Yahweh these prophets-of-you all-of in-mouth-of lying

עָלֶיךָ רָעָה׃ וַיִּגַּשׁ צִדְקִיָּהוּ בֶן־ כְּנַעֲנָה וַיַּכֶּה
and-he-slapped Kenaanah son-of Zedekiah then-he-went-up (24) disaster for-you

אֶת־מִיכָיְהוּ עַל־ הַלֶּחִי וַיֹּאמֶר אֵי־ זֶה עָבַר רוּחַ־ יְהוָה
Yahweh spirit-of he-went this where? and-he-asked the-cheek on Micaiah ***

מֵאִתִּי לְדַבֵּר אוֹתָךְ׃ וַיֹּאמֶר מִיכָיְהוּ הִנְּךָ
see-you! Micaiah and-he-replied (25) to-you to-speak from-with-me

רֹאֶה בַּיּוֹם הַהוּא אֲשֶׁר תָּבֹא חֶדֶר בְּחֶדֶר לְהֵחָבֵה׃
to-hide in-room room you-go when the-that on-the-day finding-out

וַיֹּאמֶר מֶלֶךְ יִשְׂרָאֵל קַח אֶת־ מִיכָיְהוּ וַהֲשִׁיבֵהוּ אֶל־
to and-send-back-him! Micaiah *** take! Israel king-of then-he-ordered (26)

אָמֹן שַׂר־ הָעִיר וְאֶל־ יוֹאָשׁ בֶּן־ הַמֶּלֶךְ׃ וְאָמַרְתָּ כֹּה
this and-you-say (27) the-king son-of Joash and-to the-city ruler-of Amon

אָמַר הַמֶּלֶךְ שִׂימוּ אֶת־ זֶה בֵּית הַכֶּלֶא וְהַאֲכִילֻהוּ
and-give-to-eat-him! the-prison house-of this-one *** put! the-king he-says

לֶחֶם לַחַץ וּמַיִם לַחַץ עַד בֹּאִי בְשָׁלוֹם׃ וַיֹּאמֶר
and-he-said (28) in-safety to-return-me until scanty and-waters scanty bread

מִיכָיְהוּ אִם־ שׁוֹב תָּשׁוּב בְּשָׁלוֹם לֹא־ דִבֶּר יְהוָה בִּי
through-me Yahweh he-spoke not in-safety you-return to-return if Micaiah

וַיֹּאמֶר שִׁמְעוּ עַמִּים כֻּלָּם׃ וַיַּעַל מֶלֶךְ־
king-of so-he-went-up (29) all-of-them peoples mark-words! then-he-said

יִשְׂרָאֵל וִיהוֹשָׁפָט* מֶלֶךְ־ יְהוּדָה רָמֹת גִּלְעָד׃ וַיֹּאמֶר מֶלֶךְ
king-of and-he-said (30) Gilead Ramoth Judah king-of and-Jehoshaphat Israel

on his left. [20]And the LORD
said, 'Who will lure Ahab into
attacking Ramoth Gilead and
going to his death there?'
"One suggested this, and
another that. [21]Finally, a spirit
came forward, stood before
the LORD and said, 'I will lure
him.'
[22]" 'By what means?' the
LORD asked.
" 'I will go out and be a lying
spirit in the mouths of all his
prophets,' he said.
" 'You will succeed in luring
him,' said the LORD. 'Go and
do it.'
[23]"So now the LORD has put a
lying spirit in the mouths of
all these prophets of yours.
The LORD has decreed disaster
for you."
[24]Then Zedekiah son of
Kenaanah went up and
slapped Micaiah in the face.
"Which way did the spirit
from[z] the LORD go when he
went from me to speak to
you?" he asked.
[25]Micaiah replied, "You will
find out on the day you go to
hide in an inner room."
[26]The king of Israel then ordered, "Take Micaiah and
send him back to Amon the
ruler of the city and to Joash
the king's son [27]and say, 'This
is what the king says: Put this
fellow in prison and give him
nothing but bread and water
until I return safely.' "
[28]Micaiah declared, "If you
ever return safely, the LORD
has not spoken through me."
Then he added, "Mark my
words, all you people!"

### *Ahab Killed at Ramoth Gilead*

[29]So the king of Israel and Jehoshaphat king of Judah went
up to Ramoth Gilead. [30]The

z24 Or *Spirit of*

*29 Most mss have *hireq* under the *vav* (וִיהוֹ).

יִשְׂרָאֵל אֶל־יְהוֹשָׁפָט הִתְחַפֵּשׂ וָבֹא בַמִּלְחָמָה
into-the-battle and-he-will-enter he-will-disguise-himself Jehoshaphat to Israel

וְאַתָּה לְבַשׁ בְּגָדֶיךָ וַיִּתְחַפֵּשׂ מֶלֶךְ יִשְׂרָאֵל וַיָּבוֹא
and-he-went Israel king-of so-he-disguised-himself robes-of-you wear! but-you

בַּמִּלְחָמָה׃ וּמֶלֶךְ אֲרָם צִוָּה אֶת־שָׂרֵי
commanders-of *** he-ordered Aram now-king-of (31) into-the-battle

הָרֶכֶב אֲשֶׁר־לוֹ שְׁלֹשִׁים וּשְׁנַיִם לֵאמֹר לֹא תִּלָּחֲמוּ אֶת־קָטֹן וְאֶת־
or small *** you-fight not to-say and-two thirty to-him that the-chariot

גָּדוֹל כִּי אִם־אֶת־מֶלֶךְ יִשְׂרָאֵל לְבַדּוֹ׃ וַיְהִי כִּרְאוֹת
when-to-see and-he-was (32) by-himself Israel king-of *** only except great

שָׂרֵי הָרֶכֶב אֶת־יְהוֹשָׁפָט וְהֵמָּה אָמְרוּ אַךְ
surely they-thought then-they Jehoshaphat *** the-chariot commanders-of

מֶלֶךְ־יִשְׂרָאֵל הוּא וַיָּסֻרוּ עָלָיו לְהִלָּחֵם וַיִּזְעַק
but-he-cried-out to-attack against-him so-they-turned this Israel king-of

יְהוֹשָׁפָט׃ וַיְהִי כִּרְאוֹת שָׂרֵי הָרֶכֶב כִּי־לֹא־
not that the-chariot commanders-of when-to-see then-he-was (33) Jehoshaphat

מֶלֶךְ יִשְׂרָאֵל הוּא וַיָּשׁוּבוּ מֵאַחֲרָיו׃ וְאִישׁ מָשַׁךְ
he-drew but-someone (34) from-after-him then-they-turned he Israel king-of

בַּקֶּשֶׁת לְתֻמּוֹ וַיַּכֶּה אֶת־מֶלֶךְ יִשְׂרָאֵל בֵּין
between Israel king-of *** and-he-hit at-random-of-him on-the-bow

הַדְּבָקִים וּבֵין הַשִּׁרְיָן וַיֹּאמֶר לְרַכָּבוֹ
to-chariot-driver-of-him and-he-told the-armor and-between the-sections

הֲפֹךְ יָדְךָ וְהוֹצִיאֵנִי מִן־הַמַּחֲנֶה כִּי הָחֳלֵיתִי׃
I-am-wounded for the-fight from and-get-out-me! hand-of-you turn-around!

וַתַּעֲלֶה הַמִּלְחָמָה בַּיּוֹם הַהוּא וְהַמֶּלֶךְ הָיָה
he-was and-the-king the-that through-the-day the-battle and-she-raged (35)

מָעֳמָד בַּמֶּרְכָּבָה נֹכַח אֲרָם וַיָּמָת בָּעֶרֶב
in-the-evening and-he-died Aram facing in-the-chariot being-propped-up

וַיִּצֶק דַּם־הַמַּכָּה אֶל־חֵיק הָרָכֶב׃ וַיַּעֲבֹר
and-he-spread (36) the-chariot floor-of onto the-wound blood-of and-he-ran

הָרִנָּה בַּמַּחֲנֶה כְּבֹא הַשֶּׁמֶשׁ לֵאמֹר אִישׁ אֶל־עִירוֹ
town-of-him to each to-say the-sun as-to-set through-the-army the-cry

וְאִישׁ אֶל־אַרְצוֹ׃ וַיָּמָת הַמֶּלֶךְ וַיָּבוֹא שֹׁמְרוֹן
Samaria and-he-went the-king so-he-died (37) land-of-him to and-each

וַיִּקְבְּרוּ אֶת־הַמֶּלֶךְ בְּשֹׁמְרוֹן׃ וַיִּשְׁטֹף אֶת־הָרֶכֶב
the-chariot *** and-he-washed (38) in-Samaria the-king *** and-they-buried

עַל ׀ בְּרֵכַת שֹׁמְרוֹן וַיָּלֹקּוּ הַכְּלָבִים אֶת־דָּמוֹ
blood-of-him *** the-dogs and-they-licked-up Samaria pool-of in

king of Israel said to Jehoshaphat, "I will enter the battle in disguise, but you wear your royal robes." So the king of Israel disguised himself and went into battle.

31 Now the king of Aram had ordered his thirty-two chariot commanders, "Do not fight with anyone, small or great, except the king of Israel."
32 When the chariot commanders saw Jehoshaphat, they thought, "Surely this is the king of Israel." So they turned to attack him, but when Jehoshaphat cried out,
33 the chariot commanders saw that he was not the king of Israel and stopped pursuing him.

34 But someone drew his bow at random and hit the king of Israel between the sections of his armor. The king told his chariot driver, "Wheel around and get me out of the fighting. I've been wounded."
35 All day long the battle raged, and the king was propped up in his chariot facing the Arameans. The blood from his wound ran onto the floor of the chariot, and that evening he died.
36 As the sun was setting, a cry spread through the army: "Every man to his town; everyone to his land!"

37 So the king died and was brought to Samaria, and they buried him there.
38 They washed the chariot at a pool in Samaria (where the prostitutes bathed)[a] and the dogs licked up his blood, as the word of

[a]38 Or *Samaria and cleaned the weapons*

וְהַזֹּנוֹת רָחָצוּ כִּדְבַר יְהוָה אֲשֶׁר
that Yahweh as-word-of they-bathed and-the-ones-being-prostitutes

דִּבֵּר׃ וְיֶתֶר דִּבְרֵי אַחְאָב וְכָל־ אֲשֶׁר עָשָׂה וּבֵית
and-palace-of he-did that and-all Ahab events-of and-rest-of (39) he-declared

הַשֵּׁן אֲשֶׁר בָּנָה וְכָל־ הֶעָרִים אֲשֶׁר בָּנָה הֲלוֹא־
not? he-fortified that the-cities and-all-of he-built that the-ivory

הֵם כְּתוּבִים עַל־ סֵפֶר דִּבְרֵי הַיָּמִים לְמַלְכֵי יִשְׂרָאֵל׃
Israel of-kings-of the-days annals-of book-of in ones-being-written they

וַיִּשְׁכַּב אַחְאָב עִם־ אֲבֹתָיו וַיִּמְלֹךְ אֲחַזְיָהוּ
Ahaziah and-he-became-king fathers-of-him with Ahab and-he-rested (40)

בְנוֹ תַּחְתָּיו׃ וִיהוֹשָׁפָט בֶּן־ אָסָא מָלַךְ
he-became-king Asa son-of now-Jehoshaphat (41) in-place-of-him son-of-him

עַל־ יְהוּדָה בִּשְׁנַת אַרְבַּע לְאַחְאָב מֶלֶךְ יִשְׂרָאֵל׃ יְהוֹשָׁפָט בֶּן־
son-of Jehoshaphat (42) Israel king-of of-Ahab four in-year-of Judah over

שְׁלֹשִׁים וְחָמֵשׁ שָׁנָה בְּמָלְכוֹ וְעֶשְׂרִים וְחָמֵשׁ שָׁנָה
year and-five and-twenty when-to-become-king-him year and-five thirty

מָלַךְ בִּירוּשָׁלָ͏ִם וְשֵׁם אִמּוֹ עֲזוּבָה בַּת־
daughter-of Azubah mother-of-him and-name-of in-Jerusalem he-reigned

שִׁלְחִי׃ וַיֵּלֶךְ בְּכָל־ דֶּרֶךְ אָסָא אָבִיו לֹא־ סָר
he-strayed not father-of-him Asa way-of in-all-of and-he-walked (43) Shilhi

מִמֶּנּוּ לַעֲשׂוֹת הַיָּשָׁר בְּעֵינֵי יְהוָה׃ אַךְ הַבָּמוֹת
the-high-places however *(44) Yahweh in-eyes-of the-right to-do from-him

לֹא־ סָרוּ עוֹד הָעָם מְזַבְּחִים
and-ones-offering-sacrifices the-people still they-were-removed not

וּמְקַטְּרִים בַּבָּמוֹת׃ וַיַּשְׁלֵם
and-he-was-at-peace (45) at-the-high-places and-ones-burning-incense

יְהוֹשָׁפָט עִם־ מֶלֶךְ יִשְׂרָאֵל׃ וְיֶתֶר דִּבְרֵי יְהוֹשָׁפָט
Jehoshaphat events-of and-rest-of (46) Israel king-of with Jehoshaphat

וּגְבוּרָתוֹ אֲשֶׁר־ עָשָׂה וַאֲשֶׁר נִלְחָם הֲלֹא־ הֵם
they not? he-fought and-how he-did that and-achievement-of-him

כְּתוּבִים עַל־ סֵפֶר דִּבְרֵי הַיָּמִים לְמַלְכֵי יְהוּדָה׃
Judah of-kings-of the-days annals-of book-of in ones-being-written

וְיֶתֶר הַקָּדֵשׁ אֲשֶׁר נִשְׁאַר בִּימֵי אָסָא
Asa from-days-of he-remained who the-male-prostitute and-rest-of (47)

אָבִיו בִּעֵר מִן־ הָאָרֶץ׃ וּמֶלֶךְ אֵין בֶּאֱדוֹם
in-Edom there-was-not and-king (48) the-land from he-rid father-of-him

נִצָּב מֶלֶךְ׃ יְהוֹשָׁפָט עָשַׂר אֳנִיּוֹת תַּרְשִׁישׁ לָלֶכֶת
to-go Tarshish ships-of he-built Jehoshaphat (49) ruler one-being-appointed

the LORD had declared.
39As for the other events of
Ahab's reign, including all he
did, the palace he built and inlaid with ivory, and the cities
he fortified, are they not written in the book of the annals
of the kings of Israel? 40Ahab
rested with his fathers. And
Ahaziah his son succeeded
him as king.

*Jehoshaphat King of Judah*

41Jehoshaphat son of Asa
became king of Judah in the
fourth year of Ahab king of Israel. 42Jehoshaphat was thirty-
five years old when he became
king, and he reigned in
Jerusalem twenty-five years.
His mother's name was Azubah daughter of Shilhi. 43In
everything he walked in the
ways of his father Asa and did
not stray from them; he did
what was right in the eyes of
the LORD. The high places,
however, were not removed,
and the people continued to
offer sacrifices and burn incense there. 44Jehoshaphat was
also at peace with the king of
Israel.
45As for the other events of
Jehoshaphat's reign, the
things he achieved and his
military exploits, are they not
written in the book of the annals of the kings of Judah?
46He rid the land of the rest of
the male shrine prostitutes
who remained there even after the reign of his father Asa.
47There was then no king in
Edom; a deputy ruled.
48Now Jehoshaphat built a
fleet of trading ships[b] to go to

[b]48 Hebrew *of ships of Tarshish*

*44 Verse 44 in Hebrew begins in the middle of verse 43 in English and creates a one-verse discrepancy through the rest of the chapter.

°49 ק עשה

אוֹפִירָה לַזָּהָב וְלֹא הָלָךְ כִּי־ נִשְׁבְּרָה אֳנִיּוֹת
ships they-were-wrecked for he-sailed but-not for-the-gold to-Ophir

בְּעֶצְיוֹן גָּבֶר׃ אָז אָמַר אֲחַזְיָהוּ בֶן־ אַחְאָב אֶל־ יְהוֹשָׁפָט
Jehoshaphat to Ahab son-of Ahaziah he-said then (50) Geber at-Ezion

יֵלְכוּ עֲבָדַי עִם־ עֲבָדֶיךָ בָּאֳנִיּוֹת וְלֹא אָבָה
he-allowed but-not in-the-ships men-of-you with men-of-me let-them-sail

יְהוֹשָׁפָט׃ וַיִּשְׁכַּב יְהוֹשָׁפָט עִם־ אֲבֹתָיו
fathers-of-him with Jehoshaphat then-he-rested (51) Jehoshaphat

וַיִּקָּבֵר עִם־ אֲבֹתָיו בְּעִיר דָּוִד אָבִיו
father-of-him David in-City-of fathers-of-him with and-he-was-buried

וַיִּמְלֹךְ יְהוֹרָם בְּנוֹ תַּחְתָּיו׃ אֲחַזְיָהוּ בֶן־
son-of Ahaziah (52) in-place-of-him son-of-him Jehoram and-he-became-king

אַחְאָב מָלַךְ עַל־ יִשְׂרָאֵל בְּשֹׁמְרוֹן בִּשְׁנַת שְׁבַע עֶשְׂרֵה
ten seven-of in-year-of in-Samaria Israel over he-became-king Ahab

לִיהוֹשָׁפָט מֶלֶךְ יְהוּדָה וַיִּמְלֹךְ עַל־ יִשְׂרָאֵל שְׁנָתָיִם׃
two-years Israel over and-he-reigned Judah king-of of-Jehoshaphat

וַיַּעַשׂ הָרַע בְּעֵינֵי יְהוָה וַיֵּלֶךְ בְּדֶרֶךְ
in-way-of and-he-walked Yahweh in-eyes-of the-evil and-he-did (53)

אָבִיו וּבְדֶרֶךְ אִמּוֹ וּבְדֶרֶךְ יָרָבְעָם בֶּן־
son-of Jeroboam and-in-way-of mother-of-him and-in-way-of father-of-him

נְבָט אֲשֶׁר הֶחֱטִיא אֶת־יִשְׂרָאֵל׃ וַיַּעֲבֹד אֶת־ הַבַּעַל
the-Baal *** and-he-served (54) Israel *** he-caused-to-sin who Nebat

וַיִּשְׁתַּחֲוֶה לוֹ וַיַּכְעֵס אֶת־ יְהוָה אֱלֹהֵי יִשְׂרָאֵל
Israel God-of Yahweh *** and-he-provoked-to-anger to-him and-he-worshiped

כְּכֹל אֲשֶׁר־ עָשָׂה אָבִיו׃
father-of-him he-did that as-all

Ophir for gold, but they never
set sail—they were wrecked at
Ezion Geber. 49 At that time
Ahaziah son of Ahab said to
Jehoshaphat, "Let my men sail
with your men," but Jehoshaphat refused.

50 Then Jehoshaphat rested
with his fathers and was buried with them in the city of
David his father. And Jehoram
his son succeeded him.

*Ahaziah King of Israel*

51 Ahaziah son of Ahab
became king of Israel in Samaria in the seventeenth year
of Jehoshaphat king of Judah,
and he reigned over Israel two
years. 52 He did evil in the eyes
of the LORD, because he
walked in the ways of his father and mother and in the
ways of Jeroboam son of
Nebat, who caused Israel to
sin. 53 He served and worshiped Baal and provoked the
LORD, the God of Israel, to anger, just as his father had
done.

*See the note on page 422.

°49 ק נשברו

וַיִּפְשַׁע מוֹאָב בְּיִשְׂרָאֵל אַחֲרֵי מוֹת אַחְאָב׃ וַיִּפֹּל
now-he-fell (2) Ahab death-of after against-Israel Moab and-he-rebelled (1)

אֲחַזְיָה בְּעַד הַשְּׂבָכָה בַּעֲלִיָּתוֹ אֲשֶׁר בְּשֹׁמְרוֹן
in-Samaria that of-upper-room-of-him the-lattice-work through Ahaziah

וַיִּחַל וַיִּשְׁלַח מַלְאָכִים וַיֹּאמֶר אֲלֵהֶם לְכוּ דִרְשׁוּ
consult! go! to-them and-he-said messengers so-he-sent and-he-was-injured

בְּבַעַל זְבוּב אֱלֹהֵי עֶקְרוֹן אִם־ אֶחְיֶה מֵחֳלִי זֶה׃
this from-injury I-will-recover whether Ekron gods-of Zebub with-Baal

וּמַלְאַךְ יְהוָה דִּבֶּר אֶל־אֵלִיָּה הַתִּשְׁבִּי קוּם עֲלֵה לִקְרַאת
to-meet go-up! rise! the-Tishbite Elijah to he-said Yahweh but-angel-of (3)

מַלְאֲכֵי מֶלֶךְ־ שֹׁמְרוֹן וְדַבֵּר אֲלֵהֶם הַמִבְּלִי אֵין־
there-is-no because-not? of-them and-ask! Samaria king-of messengers-of

אֱלֹהִים בְּיִשְׂרָאֵל אַתֶּם הֹלְכִים לִדְרֹשׁ בְּבַעַל זְבוּב אֱלֹהֵי עֶקְרוֹן׃
Ekron gods-of Zebub with-Baal to-consult ones-going you in-Israel God

וְלָכֵן כֹּה־ אָמַר יְהוָה הַמִּטָּה אֲשֶׁר־ עָלִיתָ שָּׁם לֹא־
not there you-lie that the-bed Yahweh he-says this now-therefore (4)

תֵרֵד מִמֶּנָּה כִּי מוֹת תָּמוּת וַיֵּלֶךְ אֵלִיָּה׃
Elijah so-he-went you-will-die to-die for from-her you-will-leave

וַיָּשׁוּבוּ הַמַּלְאָכִים אֵלָיו וַיֹּאמֶר אֲלֵיהֶם מַה־ זֶּה
this why? to-them then-he-asked to-him the-messengers when-they-returned (5)

שַׁבְתֶּם׃ וַיֹּאמְרוּ אֵלָיו אִישׁ ׀ עָלָה לִקְרָאתֵנוּ וַיֹּאמֶר
and-he-said to-meet-us he-came man to-him and-they-replied (6) you-came-back

אֵלֵינוּ לְכוּ שׁוּבוּ אֶל־ הַמֶּלֶךְ אֲשֶׁר־ שָׁלַח אֶתְכֶם וְדִבַּרְתֶּם אֵלָיו כֹּה
this to-him and-you-tell you he-sent who the-king to go-back! go! to-us

אָמַר יְהוָה הַמִבְּלִי אֵין־ אֱלֹהִים בְּיִשְׂרָאֵל אַתָּה שֹׁלֵחַ לִדְרֹשׁ
to-consult sending you in-Israel God there-is-no because-not? Yahweh he-says

בְּבַעַל זְבוּב אֱלֹהֵי עֶקְרוֹן לָכֵן הַמִּטָּה אֲשֶׁר־ עָלִיתָ שָּׁם לֹא־
not there you-lie that the-bed therefore Ekron gods-of Zebub with-Baal

תֵרֵד מִמֶּנָּה כִּי־ מוֹת תָּמוּת׃ וַיְדַבֵּר אֲלֵהֶם
to-them and-he-asked (7) you-will-die to-die for from-her you-will-leave

מֶה מִשְׁפַּט הָאִישׁ אֲשֶׁר עָלָה לִקְרַאתְכֶם וַיְדַבֵּר אֲלֵיכֶם אֶת־
*** to-you and-he-told to-meet-you he-came who the-man kind-of what?

הַדְּבָרִים הָאֵלֶּה׃ וַיֹּאמְרוּ אֵלָיו אִישׁ בַּעַל שֵׂעָר
hair-garment owner-of man-of to-him and-they-replied (8) the-these the-things

וְאֵזוֹר עוֹר אָזוּר בְּמָתְנָיו וַיֹּאמַר אֵלִיָּה
Elijah and-he-said around-waists-of-him being-tied leather and-belt-of

הַתִּשְׁבִּי הוּא׃ וַיִּשְׁלַח אֵלָיו שַׂר־ חֲמִשִּׁים וַחֲמִשָּׁיו
with-fifty-of-him fifty captain-of to-him then-he-sent (9) that the-Tishbite

*The LORD's Judgment on Ahaziah*

1 After Ahab's death, Moab rebelled against Israel. [2]Now Ahaziah had fallen through the lattice of his upper room in Samaria and injured himself. So he sent messengers, saying to them, "Go and consult Baal-Zebub, the god of Ekron, to see if I will recover from this injury."

[3]But the angel of the LORD said to Elijah the Tishbite, "Go up and meet the messengers of the king of Samaria and ask them, 'Is it because there is no God in Israel that you are going off to consult Baal-Zebub, the god of Ekron?' [4]Therefore this is what the LORD says: 'You will not leave the bed you are lying on. You will certainly die!' " So Elijah went.

[5]When the messengers returned to the king, he asked them, "Why have you come back?"

[6]"A man came to meet us," they replied. "And he said to us, 'Go back to the king who sent you and tell him, "This is what the LORD says: Is it because there is no God in Israel that you are sending men to consult Baal-Zebub, the god of Ekron? Therefore you will not leave the bed you are lying on. You will certainly die!" ' "

[7]The king asked them, "What kind of man was it who came to meet you and told you this?"

[8]They replied, "He was a man with a garment of hair and a leather belt around his waist."

The king said, "That was Elijah the Tishbite."

[9]Then he sent to Elijah a captain with his company of fifty

וַיַּעַל אֵלָיו וְהִנֵּה יֹשֵׁב עַל־רֹאשׁ הָהָר וַיְדַבֵּר אֵלָיו
to-him and-he-said the-hill top-of on sitting and-see! to-him and-he-went-up

אִישׁ הָאֱלֹהִים הַמֶּלֶךְ דִּבֶּר רֵדָה׃ וַיַּעֲנֶה אֵלִיָּהוּ
Elijah and-he-answered (10) come-down! he-says the-king the-God man-of

וַיְדַבֵּר אֶל־שַׂר הַחֲמִשִּׁים וְאִם־אִישׁ אֱלֹהִים אָנִי תֵּרֶד
may-she-come-down I God man-of now-if the-fifty captain-of to and-he-said

אֵשׁ מִן־הַשָּׁמַיִם וְתֹאכַל אֹתְךָ וְאֶת־חֲמִשֶּׁיךָ וַתֵּרֶד
then-she-fell fifty-of-you and you and-may-she-consume the-heavens from fire

אֵשׁ מִן־הַשָּׁמַיִם וַתֹּאכַל אֹתוֹ וְאֶת־חֲמִשָּׁיו׃ וַיָּשָׁב
and-he-returned (11) fifty-of-him and him and-she-consumed the-heavens from fire

וַיִּשְׁלַח אֵלָיו שַׂר־חֲמִשִּׁים אַחֵר וַחֲמִשָּׁיו וַיַּעַן
and-he-answered with-fifty-of-him another fifty captain-of to-him and-he-sent

וַיְדַבֵּר אֵלָיו אִישׁ הָאֱלֹהִים כֹּה־אָמַר הַמֶּלֶךְ מְהֵרָה רֵדָה׃
come-down! hurry! the-king he-says this the-God man-of to-him and-he-said

וַיַּעַן אֵלִיָּה וַיְדַבֵּר אֲלֵיהֶם אִם־אִישׁ הָאֱלֹהִים אָנִי
I the-God man-of if to-them and-he-said Elijah and-he-replied (12)

תֵּרֶד אֵשׁ מִן־הַשָּׁמַיִם וְתֹאכַל אֹתְךָ וְאֶת־
and you and-may-she-consume the-heavens from fire may-she-come-down

חֲמִשֶּׁיךָ וַתֵּרֶד אֵשׁ־אֱלֹהִים מִן־הַשָּׁמַיִם וַתֹּאכַל אֹתוֹ
him and-she-consumed the-heavens from God fire-of then-she-fell fifty-of-you

וְאֶת־חֲמִשָּׁיו׃ וַיָּשָׁב וַיִּשְׁלַח שַׂר־חֲמִשִּׁים שְׁלִשִׁים
third-ones fifty captain-of and-he-sent so-he-returned (13) fifty-of-him and

וַחֲמִשָּׁיו וַיַּעַל וַיָּבֹא שַׂר־הַחֲמִשִּׁים הַשְּׁלִישִׁי
the-third the-fifty captain-of and-he-came and-he-went-up with-fifty-of-him

וַיִּכְרַע עַל־בִּרְכָּיו ׀ לְנֶגֶד אֵלִיָּהוּ וַיִּתְחַנֵּן אֵלָיו
to-him and-he-begged Elijah at-before knees-of-him on and-he-knelt

וַיְדַבֵּר אֵלָיו אִישׁ הָאֱלֹהִים תִּיקַר־נָא נַפְשִׁי
life-of-me now! let-her-be-respected the-God man-of to-him and-he-said

וְנֶפֶשׁ עֲבָדֶיךָ אֵלֶּה חֲמִשִּׁים בְּעֵינֶיךָ׃ הִנֵּה יָרְדָה
she-fell see! (14) in-eyes-of-you fifty these servants-of-you and-life-of

אֵשׁ מִן־הַשָּׁמַיִם וַתֹּאכַל אֶת־שְׁנֵי שָׂרֵי הַחֲמִשִּׁים
the-fifty captains-of two-of *** and-she-consumed the-heavens from fire

הָרִאשֹׁנִים וְאֶת־חֲמִשֵּׁיהֶם וְעַתָּה תִּיקַר נַפְשִׁי
life-of-me let-her-be-respected but-now fifty-of-them and the-first-ones

בְּעֵינֶיךָ׃ וַיְדַבֵּר מַלְאַךְ יְהוָה אֶל־אֵלִיָּהוּ רֵד אוֹתוֹ
with-him go-down! Elijah to Yahweh angel-of and-he-said (15) in-eyes-of-you

אַל־תִּירָא מִפָּנָיו וַיָּקָם וַיֵּרֶד אוֹתוֹ אֶל־
to with-him and-he-went-down so-he-got-up because-of-him you-be-afraid not

men. The captain went up to Elijah, who was sitting on the top of a hill, and said to him, "Man of God, the king says, 'Come down!' "

10 Elijah answered the captain, "If I am a man of God, may fire come down from heaven and consume you and your fifty men!" Then fire fell from heaven and consumed the captain and his men.

11 At this the king sent to Elijah another captain with his fifty men. The captain said to him, "Man of God, this is what the king says, 'Come down at once!' "

12 "If I am a man of God," Elijah replied, "may fire come down from heaven and consume you and your fifty men!" Then the fire of God fell from heaven and consumed him and his fifty men.

13 So the king sent a third captain with his fifty men. This third captain went up and fell on his knees before Elijah. "Man of God," he begged, "please have respect for my life and the lives of these fifty men, your servants!
14 See, fire has fallen from heaven and consumed the first two captains and all their men. But now have respect for my life!"

15 The angel of the LORD said to Elijah, "Go down with him; do not be afraid of him." So Elijah got up and went down with him to the king.

הַמֶּֽלֶךְ׃ וַיְדַבֵּ֣ר אֵלָ֗יו כֹּֽה־ אָמַ֤ר יְהוָ֔ה יַ֗עַן אֲשֶׁר־ שָׁלַ֣חְתָּ
the-king   and-he-told   to-him   this   he-says   Yahweh   because   that   you-sent

מַלְאָכִים֮ לִדְרֹ֣שׁ בְּבַ֣עַל זְב֗וּב אֱלֹהֵ֣י עֶקְר֔וֹן הַֽמִבְּלִ֥י אֵ֛ין
messengers   to-consult   with-Baal   Zebub   gods-of   Ekron   because-not   there-is-no

אֱלֹהִים֙ בְּיִשְׂרָאֵ֔ל לִדְרֹ֖שׁ בִּדְבָר֑וֹ לָכֵ֗ן הַמִּטָּ֞ה אֲשֶׁר־ עָלִ֤יתָ
God   in-Israel   to-consult   with-word-of-him   therefore   the-bed   that   you-lie

שָּׁם֙ לֹֽא־ תֵרֵ֣ד מִמֶּ֔נָּה כִּֽי־ מ֥וֹת תָּמֽוּת׃ וַיָּ֕מָת
there   not   you-will-leave   from-her   for   to-die   you-will-die   (17)   so-he-died

כִּדְבַ֥ר יְהוָ֖ה׀ אֲשֶׁר־ דִּבֶּ֣ר אֵלִיָּ֑הוּ וַיִּמְלֹ֤ךְ יְהוֹרָם֙
as-word-of   Yahweh   that   he-spoke   Elijah   and-he-became-king   Jehoram

תַּחְתָּ֔יו בִּשְׁנַ֣ת שְׁתַּ֔יִם לִיהוֹרָ֖ם בֶּן־ יְהוֹשָׁפָ֑ט מֶ֖לֶךְ יְהוּדָ֑ה
in-place-of-him   in-year-of   two   of-Jehoram   son-of   Jehoshaphat   king-of   Judah

כִּ֥י לֹֽא־ הָ֥יָה ל֖וֹ בֵּֽן׃ וְיֶ֛תֶר דִּבְרֵ֥י אֲחַזְיָ֖הוּ אֲשֶׁ֣ר עָשָׂ֑ה
because   not   he-was   to-him   son   (18)   and-rest-of   events-of   Ahaziah   what   he-did

הֲלֹֽא־ הֵ֣מָּה כְתוּבִ֗ים עַל־ סֵ֛פֶר דִּבְרֵ֥י הַיָּמִ֖ים לְמַלְכֵ֥י יִשְׂרָאֵֽל׃
they-not?   in   ones-being-written   book-of   annals-of   the-days   of-kings-of   Israel

וַיְהִ֗י בְּהַעֲל֤וֹת יְהוָה֙ אֶת־אֵ֣לִיָּ֔הוּ בַּֽסְּעָרָ֖ה הַשָּׁמָֽיִם
and-he-was   (2:1)   when-to-take   Yahweh   ***   Elijah   in-the-whirlwind   the-heavens

וַיֵּ֧לֶךְ אֵלִיָּ֛הוּ וֶאֱלִישָׁ֖ע מִן־ הַגִּלְגָּֽל׃ וַיֹּ֩אמֶר֩ אֵלִיָּ֨הוּ אֶל־
then-he-went   Elijah   and-Elisha   from   the-Gilgal   (2)   and-he-said   Elijah   to

אֱלִישָׁ֜ע שֵֽׁב־ נָ֣א פֹ֗ה כִּ֤י יְהוָה֙ שְׁלָחַ֣נִי עַד־ בֵּֽית־אֵ֔ל וַיֹּ֣אמֶר אֱלִישָׁ֗ע
Elisha   stay!   now!   here   for   Yahweh   he-sent-me   to   Beth   El   but-he-said   Elisha

חַי־ יְהוָ֤ה וְחֵֽי־ נַפְשְׁךָ֙ אִם־ אֶעֶזְבֶ֔ךָּ וַיֵּרְד֖וּ
life-of   Yahweh   and-life-of   soul-of-you   not   I-will-leave-you   so-they-went-down

בֵּֽית־אֵֽל׃ וַיֵּצְא֨וּ בְנֵֽי־ הַנְּבִיאִ֤ים אֲשֶׁר־ בֵּֽית־אֵל֙ אֶל־ אֱלִישָׁ֔ע
El   Beth   (3)   and-they-came-out   sons-of   the-prophets   who   Beth   El   to   Elisha

וַיֹּאמְר֣וּ אֵלָ֗יו הֲיָדַ֨עְתָּ֙ כִּ֣י הַיּ֔וֹם יְהוָ֛ה לֹקֵ֥חַ אֶת־
and-they-asked   to-him   do-you-know?   that   the-day   Yahweh   taking   ***

אֲדֹנֶ֖יךָ מֵעַ֣ל רֹאשֶׁ֑ךָ וַיֹּ֛אמֶר גַּם־ אֲנִ֥י יָדַ֖עְתִּי
masters-of-you   from-over   head-of-you   and-he-replied   indeed   I   I-know

הֶחֱשֽׁוּ׃ וַיֹּאמֶר֩ ל֨וֹ אֵלִיָּ֜הוּ אֱלִישָׁ֣ע׀ שֵֽׁב־ נָ֣א פֹ֗ה כִּ֤י
do-not-speak!   (4)   then-he-said   to-him   Elijah   Elisha   stay!   now!   here   for

יְהוָה֙ שְׁלָחַ֣נִי יְרִיח֔וֹ וַיֹּ֕אמֶר חַי־ יְהוָ֖ה וְחֵֽי־
Yahweh   he-sent-me   Jericho   and-he-replied   life-of   Yahweh   and-life-of

נַפְשְׁךָ֛ אִם־ אֶעֶזְבֶ֖ךָּ וַיָּבֹ֥אוּ יְרִיחֽוֹ׃ וַיִּגְּשׁ֨וּ
soul-of-you   not   I-will-leave-you   so-they-went   Jericho   (5)   and-they-went-up

בְנֵֽי־ הַנְּבִיאִ֤ים אֲשֶׁר־ בִּֽירִיחוֹ֙ אֶל־ אֱלִישָׁ֔ע וַיֹּאמְר֣וּ אֵלָ֔יו
sons-of   the-prophets   who   in-Jericho   to   Elisha   and-they-asked   to-him

[16]He told the king, "This is what the LORD says: Is it because there is no God in Israel for you to consult that you have sent messengers to consult Baal-Zebub, the god of Ekron? Because you have done this, you will never leave the bed you are lying on. You will certainly die!" [17]So he died, according to the word of the LORD that Elijah had spoken.

Because Ahaziah had no son, Joram[a] succeeded him as king in the second year of Jehoram son of Jehoshaphat king of Judah. [18]As for all the other events of Ahaziah's reign, and what he did, are they not written in the book of the annals of the kings of Israel?

*Elijah Taken Up to Heaven*

**2** When the LORD was about to take Elijah up to heaven in a whirlwind, Elijah and Elisha were on their way from Gilgal. [2]Elijah said to Elisha, "Stay here; the LORD has sent me to Bethel."

But Elisha said, "As surely as the LORD lives and as you live, I will not leave you." So they went down to Bethel.

[3]The company of the prophets at Bethel came out to Elisha and asked, "Do you know that the LORD is going to take your master from you today?"

"Yes, I know," Elisha replied, "but do not speak of it."

[4]Then Elijah said to him, "Stay here, Elisha; the LORD has sent me to Jericho."

And he replied, "As surely as the LORD lives and as you live, I will not leave you." So they went to Jericho.

[5]The company of the prophets at Jericho went up to Elisha

*a17* Hebrew *Jehoram*, a variant of *Joram*

הֲיָדַעְתָּ כִּי הַיּוֹם יְהוָה לֹקֵחַ אֶת־ אֲדֹנֶיךָ מֵעַל
from-over masters-of-you *** taking Yahweh the-day that do-you-know?

רֹאשֶׁךָ וַיֹּאמֶר גַּם־ אֲנִי יָדַעְתִּי הֶחֱשׁוּ׃ (6) וַיֹּאמֶר
then-he-said (6) do-not-speak! I-know I indeed and-he-replied head-of-you

לוֹ אֵלִיָּהוּ שֵׁב־ נָא פֹה כִּי יְהוָה שְׁלָחַנִי הַיַּרְדֵּנָה
to-the-Jordan he-sent-me Yahweh for here now! stay! Elijah to-him

וַיֹּאמֶר חַי־ יְהוָה וְחֵי־ נַפְשְׁךָ אִם־ אֶעֶזְבֶךָּ
I-will-leave-you not soul-of-you and-life-of Yahweh life-of and-he-replied

וַיֵּלְכוּ שְׁנֵיהֶם׃ (7) וַחֲמִשִּׁים אִישׁ מִבְּנֵי הַנְּבִיאִים
the-prophets of-sons-of man and-fifty (7) two-of-them so-they-walked-on

הָלְכוּ וַיַּעַמְדוּ מִנֶּגֶד מֵרָחוֹק וּשְׁנֵיהֶם עָמְדוּ
they-stopped and-two-of-them at-distance at-facing and-they-stood they-went

עַל־ הַיַּרְדֵּן׃ (8) וַיִּקַּח אֵלִיָּהוּ אֶת־ אַדַּרְתּוֹ וַיִּגְלֹם
and-he-rolled-up cloak-of-him *** Elijah and-he-took (8) the-Jordan at

וַיַּכֶּה אֶת־ הַמַּיִם וַיֵּחָצוּ הֵנָּה וָהֵנָּה
and-to-there to-here and-they-divided the-waters *** and-he-struck

וַיַּעַבְרוּ שְׁנֵיהֶם בֶּחָרָבָה׃ (9) וַיְהִי
and-he-was (9) on-the-dry-ground two-of-them and-they-crossed-over

כְעָבְרָם וְאֵלִיָּהוּ אָמַר אֶל־אֱלִישָׁע שְׁאַל מָה אֶעֱשֶׂה־
can-I-do what? tell! Elisha to he-said then-Elijah when-to-cross-over-them

לָּךְ בְּטֶרֶם אֶלָּקַח מֵעִמָּךְ וַיֹּאמֶר אֱלִישָׁע
Elisha and-he-replied from-with-you I-am-taken at-before for-you

וִיהִי־ נָא פִּי־ שְׁנַיִם בְּרוּחֲךָ אֵלָי׃ (10) וַיֹּאמֶר
and-he-said (10) for-me of-spirit-of-you double portion-of now! now-let-him-be

הִקְשִׁיתָ לִשְׁאוֹל אִם־תִּרְאֶה אֹתִי לֻקָּח מֵאִתָּךְ יְהִי־
he-will-be from-with-you he-is-taken me you-see if to-ask you-made-difficult

לְךָ כֵן וְאִם־ אַיִן לֹא יִהְיֶה׃ (11) וַיְהִי הֵמָּה הֹלְכִים
ones-walking they and-he-was (11) he-will-be not not but-if this for-you

הָלוֹךְ וְדַבֵּר וְהִנֵּה רֶכֶב־ אֵשׁ וְסוּסֵי אֵשׁ
fire and-horses-of fire chariot-of and-see! and-to-talk to-walk

וַיַּפְרִדוּ בֵּין שְׁנֵיהֶם וַיַּעַל אֵלִיָּהוּ בַּסְּעָרָה
in-the-whirlwind Elijah and-he-went-up two-of-them between and-they-separated

הַשָּׁמָיִם׃ (12) וֶאֱלִישָׁע רֹאֶה וְהוּא מְצַעֵק אָבִי ׀ אָבִי
father-of-me father-of-me crying-out and-he seeing and-Elisha (12) the-heavens

רֶכֶב יִשְׂרָאֵל וּפָרָשָׁיו וְלֹא רָאָהוּ עוֹד
any-more he-saw-him and-not and-horses-of-him Israel chariot-of

וַיַּחֲזֵק בִּבְגָדָיו וַיִּקְרָעֵם לִשְׁנַיִם קְרָעִים׃
pieces into-two and-he-tore-them of-clothes-of-him then-he-took-hold

and asked him, "Do you know
that the LORD is going to take
your master from you today?"
"Yes, I know," he replied,
"but do not speak of it."
6Then Elijah said to him,
"Stay here; the LORD has sent
me to the Jordan."
And he replied, "As surely
as the LORD lives and as you
live, I will not leave you." So
the two of them walked on.
7Fifty men of the company
of the prophets went and
stood at a distance, facing the
place where Elijah and Elisha
had stopped at the Jordan.
8Elijah took his cloak, rolled it
up and struck the water with
it. The water divided to the
right and to the left, and the
two of them crossed over on
dry ground.
9When they had crossed, Elijah said to Elisha, "Tell me,
what can I do for you before I
am taken from you?"
"Let me inherit a double
portion of your spirit," Elisha
replied.
10"You have asked a difficult
thing," Elijah said, "yet if you
see me when I am taken from
you, it will be yours—otherwise not."
11As they were walking
along and talking together,
suddenly a chariot of fire and
horses of fire appeared and
separated the two of them,
and Elijah went up to heaven
in a whirlwind. 12Elisha saw
this and cried out, "My father!
My father! The chariots and
horsemen of Israel!" And Elisha saw him no more. Then he
took hold of his own clothes
and tore them apart.

וַיָּרֶם אֶת־ אַדֶּרֶת אֵלִיָּהוּ אֲשֶׁר נָפְלָה מֵעָלָיו
from-on-him she-fell that Elijah cloak-of *** and-he-picked-up (13)

וַיָּשָׁב וַיַּעֲמֹד עַל־ שְׂפַת הַיַּרְדֵּן׃ וַיִּקַּח אֶת־
*** then-he-took (14) the-Jordan bank-of on and-he-stood and-he-went-back

אַדֶּרֶת אֵלִיָּהוּ אֲשֶׁר־ נָפְלָה מֵעָלָיו וַיַּכֶּה אֶת־ הַמַּיִם
the-waters *** and-he-struck from-on-him she-fell that Elijah cloak-of

וַיֹּאמַר אַיֵּה יְהוָה אֱלֹהֵי אֵלִיָּהוּ אַף־הוּא | וַיַּכֶּה אֶת־ הַמַּיִם
the-waters *** when-he-struck he also Elijah God-of Yahweh where? and-he-said

וַיֵּחָצוּ הֵנָּה וָהֵנָּה וַיַּעֲבֹר אֱלִישָׁע׃
Elisha and-he-crossed-over and-to-there to-here then-they-divided

וַיִּרְאֻהוּ בְנֵי־ הַנְּבִיאִים אֲשֶׁר־ בִּירִיחוֹ מִנֶּגֶד
at-facing from-Jericho who the-prophets sons-of and-they-watched-him (15)

וַיֹּאמְרוּ נָחָה רוּחַ אֵלִיָּהוּ עַל־אֱלִישָׁע וַיָּבֹאוּ לִקְרָאתוֹ
to-meet-him and-they-went Elisha on Elijah spirit-of she-rests and-they-said

וַיִּשְׁתַּחֲווּ־ לוֹ אָרְצָה׃ וַיֹּאמְרוּ אֵלָיו הִנֵּה־ נָא
now! look! to-him and-they-said (16) to-ground before-him and-they-bowed

יֵשׁ־ אֶת־ עֲבָדֶיךָ חֲמִשִּׁים אֲנָשִׁים בְּנֵי־ חַיִל יֵלְכוּ נָא
now! let-them-go ability sons-of men fifty servants-of-you with there-is

וִיבַקְשׁוּ אֶת־ אֲדֹנֶיךָ פֶּן־ נְשָׂאוֹ רוּחַ
Spirit-of he-picked-up-him perhaps masters-of-you *** and-let-them-look-for

יְהוָה וַיַּשְׁלִכֵהוּ בְּאַחַד הֶהָרִים אוֹ בְּאַחַת הַגֵּיאָוֹת
the-valleys in-one-of or the-mountains on-one-of and-he-set-down-him Yahweh

וַיֹּאמֶר לֹא תִשְׁלָחוּ׃ וַיִּפְצְרוּ־ בוֹ עַד־
until with-him but-they-persisted (17) you-send not but-he-replied

בֹּשׁ וַיֹּאמֶר שְׁלָחוּ וַיִּשְׁלְחוּ חֲמִשִּׁים אִישׁ וַיְבַקְשׁוּ
and-they-searched man fifty and-they-sent send! so-he-said to-be-ashamed

שְׁלֹשָׁה־יָמִים וְלֹא מְצָאֻהוּ׃ וַיָּשֻׁבוּ אֵלָיו וְהוּא
now-he to-him when-they-returned (18) they-found-him but-not days three

יֹשֵׁב בִּירִיחוֹ וַיֹּאמֶר אֲלֵהֶם הֲלוֹא־אָמַרְתִּי אֲלֵיכֶם אַל־ תֵּלֵכוּ׃
you-go not to-you I-told not? to-them then-he-said in-Jericho staying

וַיֹּאמְרוּ אַנְשֵׁי הָעִיר אֶל־אֱלִישָׁע הִנֵּה־ נָא מוֹשַׁב הָעִיר
the-city situation-of now! look! Elisha to the-city men-of and-they-said (19)

טוֹב כַּאֲשֶׁר אֲדֹנִי רֹאֶה וְהַמַּיִם רָעִים וְהָאָרֶץ
and-the-land bad-ones but-the-waters seeing lord-of-me just-as good

מְשַׁכָּלֶת׃ וַיֹּאמֶר קְחוּ־ לִי צְלֹחִית חֲדָשָׁה וְשִׂימוּ שָׁם
there and-put! new bowl to-me bring! and-he-said (20) being-unproductive

מֶלַח וַיִּקְחוּ אֵלָיו׃ וַיֵּצֵא אֶל־ מוֹצָא הַמַּיִם
the-waters spring-of to then-he-went-out (21) to-him so-they-brought salt

[13]He picked up the cloak that
had fallen from Elijah and
went back and stood on the
bank of the Jordan. [14]Then he
took the cloak that had fallen
from him and struck the water
with it. "Where now is the
LORD, the God of Elijah?" he
asked. When he struck the
water, it divided to the right
and to the left, and he crossed
over.
[15]The company of the prophets from Jericho, who were
watching, said, "The spirit of
Elijah is resting on Elisha."
And they went to meet him
and bowed to the ground before him. [16]"Look," they said,
"we your servants have fifty
able men. Let them go and
look for your master. Perhaps
the Spirit of the LORD has
picked him up and set him
down on some mountain or in
some valley."
"No," Elisha replied, "do
not send them."
[17]But they persisted until he
was too ashamed to refuse. So
he said, "Send them." And
they sent fifty men, who
searched for three days but did
not find him. [18]When they returned to Elisha, who was
staying in Jericho, he said to
them, "Didn't I tell you not to
go?"

*Healing of the Water*

[19]The men of the city said to
Elisha, "Look, our lord, this
town is well situated, as you
can see, but the water is bad
and the land is unproductive."
[20]"Bring me a new bowl," he
said, "and put salt in it." So
they brought it to him.
[21]Then he went out to the

°*16* ק הגאיות

וַיַּשְׁלֶךְ־ שָׁם מֶלַח וַיֹּאמֶר כֹּה־ אָמַר יְהוָה רִפִּאתִי
I-healed Yahweh he-says this and-he-said salt there and-he-threw

לַמַּיִם הָאֵלֶּה לֹא־ יִהְיֶה מִשָּׁם עוֹד מָוֶת
death again from-there he-will-be not the-these to-the-waters

וּמְשַׁכָּלֶת׃ וַיֵּרָפוּ הַמַּיִם עַד הַיּוֹם
the-day to the-waters and-they-are-wholesome (22) or-being-unproductive

הַזֶּה כִּדְבַר אֱלִישָׁע אֲשֶׁר דִּבֵּר׃ וַיַּעַל מִשָּׁם
from-there and-he-went-up (23) he-spoke that Elisha as-word-of the-this

בֵּית־ אֵל וְהוּא | עֹלֶה בַדֶּרֶךְ וּנְעָרִים קְטַנִּים יָצְאוּ
they-came-out young-ones and-youths along-the-road walking and-he El Beth

מִן־ הָעִיר וַיִּתְקַלְּסוּ־ בוֹ וַיֹּאמְרוּ לוֹ עֲלֵה קֵרֵחַ
baldhead go-up! to-him and-they-said at-him and-they-jeered the-town from

עֲלֵה קֵרֵחַ׃ וַיִּפֶן אַחֲרָיו וַיִּרְאֵם
and-he-looked-at-them behind-him and-he-turned (24) baldhead go-up!

וַיְקַלְלֵם בְּשֵׁם יְהוָה וַתֵּצֶאנָה שְׁתַּיִם דֻּבִּים מִן־
from bears two then-they-came-out Yahweh in-name-of and-he-cursed-them

הַיַּעַר וַתְּבַקַּעְנָה מֵהֶם אַרְבָּעִים וּשְׁנֵי יְלָדִים׃ וַיֵּלֶךְ
and-he-went-on (25) youths and-two-of forty of-them and-they-mauled the-wood

מִשָּׁם אֶל־ הַר הַכַּרְמֶל וּמִשָּׁם שָׁב שֹׁמְרוֹן׃
Samaria he-returned and-from-there the-Carmel Mount-of to from-there

וִיהוֹרָם בֶּן־ אַחְאָב מָלַךְ עַל־יִשְׂרָאֵל בְּשֹׁמְרוֹן בִּשְׁנַת
in-year-of in-Samaria Israel over he-became-king Ahab son-of now-Jehoram (3:1)

שְׁמֹנֶה עֶשְׂרֵה לִיהוֹשָׁפָט מֶלֶךְ יְהוּדָה וַיִּמְלֹךְ שְׁתֵּים־עֶשְׂרֵה שָׁנָה׃
year ten two and-he-reigned Judah king-of of-Jehoshaphat ten eight

וַיַּעֲשֶׂה הָרַע בְּעֵינֵי יְהוָה רַק לֹא כְּאָבִיו
as-father-of-him not but Yahweh in-eyes-of the-evil and-he-did (2)

וּכְאִמּוֹ וַיָּסַר אֶת־ מַצְּבַת הַבַּעַל אֲשֶׁר עָשָׂה
he-made that the-Baal sacred-stone-of *** and-he-got-rid and-as-mother-of-him

אָבִיו׃ רַק בְּחַטֹּאות יָרָבְעָם בֶּן־ נְבָט אֲשֶׁר־
which Nebat son-of Jeroboam to-sins-of nevertheless (3) father-of-him

הֶחֱטִיא אֶת־יִשְׂרָאֵל דָּבֵק לֹא־ סָר מִמֶּנָּה׃ וּמֵישַׁע
now-Mesha (4) from-her he-turned not he-clung Israel *** he-caused-to-sin

מֶלֶךְ־ מוֹאָב הָיָה נֹקֵד וְהֵשִׁיב לְמֶלֶךְ־ יִשְׂרָאֵל מֵאָה־
hundred Israel to-king-of and-he-supplied sheep-raiser he-was Moab king-of

אֶלֶף כָּרִים וּמֵאָה אֶלֶף אֵילִים צָמֶר׃ וַיְהִי כְּמוֹת
when-to-die but-he-was (5) wool rams thousand and-hundred lambs thousand

אַחְאָב וַיִּפְשַׁע מֶלֶךְ־ מוֹאָב בְּמֶלֶךְ יִשְׂרָאֵל׃ וַיֵּצֵא
so-he-set-out (6) Israel against-king-of Moab king-of then-he-rebelled Ahab

spring and threw the salt into it, saying, "This is what the LORD says: 'I have healed this water. Never again will it cause death or make the land unproductive.'" [22]And the water has remained wholesome to this day, according to the word Elisha had spoken.

### *Elisha Is Jeered*

[23]From there Elisha went up to Bethel. As he was walking along the road, some youths came out of the town and jeered at him. "Go on up, you baldhead!" they said. "Go on up, you baldhead!" [24]He turned around, looked at them and called down a curse on them in the name of the LORD. Then two bears came out of the woods and mauled forty-two of the youths. [25]And he went on to Mount Carmel and from there returned to Samaria.

### *Moab Revolts*

3 Joram[b] son of Ahab became king of Israel in Samaria in the eighteenth year of Jehoshaphat king of Judah, and he reigned twelve years. [2]He did evil in the eyes of the LORD, but not as his father and mother had done. He got rid of the sacred stone of Baal that his father had made. [3]Nevertheless he clung to the sins of Jeroboam son of Nebat, which he had caused Israel to commit; he did not turn away from them.

[4]Now Mesha king of Moab raised sheep, and he had to supply the king of Israel with a hundred thousand lambs and with the wool of a hundred thousand rams. [5]But after Ahab died, the king of Moab rebelled against the king of Israel. [6]So at that time King

[b]1 Hebrew *Jehoram*, a variant of *Joram*; also in verse 6

הַמֶּלֶךְ יְהוֹרָם בַּיּוֹם הַהוּא מִשֹּׁמְרוֹן וַיִּפְקֹד אֶת־כָּל־
all-of *** and-he-mobilized from-Samaria the-that on-the-day Jehoram the-king

יִשְׂרָאֵל׃ וַיֵּלֶךְ וַיִּשְׁלַח אֶל־יְהוֹשָׁפָט מֶלֶךְ־יְהוּדָה לֵאמֹר
to-say Judah king-of Jehoshaphat to and-he-sent and-he-went (7) Israel

מֶלֶךְ מוֹאָב פָּשַׁע בִּי הֲתֵלֵךְ אִתִּי אֶל־מוֹאָב
Moab against with-me will-you-go? against-me he-rebelled Moab king-of

לַמִּלְחָמָה וַיֹּאמֶר אֶעֱלֶה כָּמוֹנִי כָמוֹךָ כְּעַמִּי
so-people-of-me as-you so-me I-will-go and-he-replied to-the-fight

כְּעַמֶּךָ כְּסוּסַי כְּסוּסֶיךָ׃ וַיֹּאמֶר אֵי־
where? and-he-asked (8) as-horses-of-you so-horses-of-me as-people-of-you

זֶה הַדֶּרֶךְ נַעֲלֶה וַיֹּאמֶר דֶּרֶךְ מִדְבַּר אֱדוֹם׃
Edom Desert-of route-of and-he-answered we-shall-attack the-route this

וַיֵּלֶךְ מֶלֶךְ יִשְׂרָאֵל וּמֶלֶךְ־יְהוּדָה וּמֶלֶךְ אֱדוֹם
Edom and-king-of Judah and-king-of Israel king-of so-he-set-out (9)

וַיָּסֹבּוּ דֶּרֶךְ שִׁבְעַת יָמִים וְלֹא־הָיָה מַיִם
waters he-was and-not days seven-of journey-of and-they-marched-around

לַמַּחֲנֶה וְלַבְּהֵמָה אֲשֶׁר בְּרַגְלֵיהֶם׃ וַיֹּאמֶר
and-he-exclaimed (10) at-feet-of-them that or-for-the-animal for-the-army

מֶלֶךְ יִשְׂרָאֵל אֲהָהּ כִּי־קָרָא יְהוָה לִשְׁלֹשֶׁת הַמְּלָכִים הָאֵלֶּה
the-these the-kings to-three-of Yahweh he-called indeed what! Israel king-of

לָתֵת אוֹתָם בְּיַד־מוֹאָב׃ וַיֹּאמֶר יְהוֹשָׁפָט הַאֵין
is-there-not? Jehoshaphat but-he-asked (11) Moab into-hand-of them to-give

פֹּה נָבִיא לַיהוָה וְנִדְרְשָׁה אֶת־יְהוָה מֵאוֹתוֹ
through-him Yahweh *** that-we-may-inquire of-Yahweh prophet here

וַיַּעַן אֶחָד מֵעַבְדֵי מֶלֶךְ־יִשְׂרָאֵל וַיֹּאמֶר פֹּה אֱלִישָׁע
Elisha here and-he-said Israel king-of of-officers-of one and-he-answered

בֶּן־שָׁפָט אֲשֶׁר־יָצַק מַיִם עַל־יְדֵי אֵלִיָּהוּ׃ וַיֹּאמֶר
then-he-said (12) Elijah hands-of on waters he-poured who Shaphat son-of

יְהוֹשָׁפָט יֵשׁ אוֹתוֹ דְּבַר־יְהוָה וַיֵּרְדוּ אֵלָיו מֶלֶךְ
king-of to-him so-they-went-down Yahweh word-of with-him there-is Jehoshaphat

יִשְׂרָאֵל וִיהוֹשָׁפָט וּמֶלֶךְ אֱדוֹם׃ וַיֹּאמֶר אֱלִישָׁע אֶל־מֶלֶךְ
king-of to Elisha and-he-said (13) Edom and-king-of and-Jehoshaphat Israel

יִשְׂרָאֵל מַה־לִּי וָלָךְ לֵךְ אֶל־נְבִיאֵי אָבִיךָ וְאֶל־
and-to father-of-you prophets-of to go! and-to-you to-me what? Israel

נְבִיאֵי אִמֶּךָ וַיֹּאמֶר לוֹ מֶלֶךְ יִשְׂרָאֵל אַל כִּי־
for no Israel king-of to-him and-he-answered mother-of-you prophets-of

קָרָא יְהוָה לִשְׁלֹשֶׁת הַמְּלָכִים הָאֵלֶּה לָתֵת אוֹתָם בְּיַד־
into-hand-of them to-give the-these the-kings to-three-of Yahweh he-called

Joram set out from Samaria
and mobilized all Israel. 7He
also sent this message to Jehoshaphat king of Judah: "The
king of Moab has rebelled
against me. Will you go with
me to fight against Moab?"
"I will go with you," he replied. "I am as you are, my
people as your people, my
horses as your horses."
8"By what route shall we attack?" he asked.
"Through the Desert of
Edom," he answered.
9So the king of Israel set out
with the king of Judah and the
king of Edom. After a round-
about march of seven days,
the army had no more water
for themselves or for the animals with them.
10"What!" exclaimed the
king of Israel. "Has the LORD
called us three kings together
only to hand us over to
Moab?"
11But Jehoshaphat asked, "Is
there no prophet of the LORD
here, that we may inquire of
the LORD through him?"
An officer of the king of Israel answered, "Elisha son of
Shaphat is here. He used to
pour water on the hands of
Elijah.[c]"
12Jehoshaphat said, "The
word of the LORD is with him."
So the king of Israel and Jehoshaphat and the king of
Edom went down to him.
13Elisha said to the king of
Israel, "What do we have to do
with each other? Go to the
prophets of your father and
the prophets of your mother."
"No," the king of Israel answered, "because it was the
LORD who called us three kings
together to hand us over to

[c]*11* That is, he was Elijah's personal servant.

*9 Most mss have *sheva* in the *kaph* (ךְ—).

מוֹאָב׃ וַיֹּאמֶר אֱלִישָׁע חַי־ יְהוָה צְבָאוֹת אֲשֶׁר עָמַדְתִּי לְפָנָיו
before-him I-serve whom Hosts Yahweh-of life-of Elisha and-he-said (14) Moab

כִּי לוּלֵי פְּנֵי יְהוֹשָׁפָט מֶלֶךְ־ יְהוּדָה אֲנִי נֹשֵׂא אִם־
not respecting I Judah king-of Jehoshaphat presences-of if-not indeed

אַבִּיט אֵלֶיךָ וְאִם־ אֶרְאֶךָּ׃ וְעַתָּה קְחוּ־ לִי
to-me bring! but-now (15) I-would-notice-you and-not at-you I-would-look

מְנַגֵּן וְהָיָה כְּנַגֵּן הַמְנַגֵּן וַתְּהִי
then-she-came the-one-playing-harp while-to-play and-he-was one-playing-harp

עָלָיו יַד־ יְהוָה׃ וַיֹּאמֶר כֹּה אָמַר יְהוָה עָשֹׂה
to-make Yahweh he-says this and-he-said (16) Yahweh hand-of upon-him

הַנַּחַל הַזֶּה גֵּבִים ׀ גֵּבִים׃ כִּי־ כֹה ׀ אָמַר יְהוָה לֹא־
not Yahweh he-says this for (17) ditches ditches the-this the-valley

תִרְאוּ רוּחַ וְלֹא־ תִרְאוּ גֶשֶׁם וְהַנַּחַל הַהוּא
the-this yet-the-valley rain you-will-see and-not wind you-will-see

יִמָּלֵא מָיִם וּשְׁתִיתֶם אַתֶּם וּמִקְנֵיכֶם
and-cattle-of-you you and-you-will-drink waters he-will-be-filled

וּבְהֶמְתְּכֶם׃ וְנָקַל זֹאת בְּעֵינֵי יְהוָה וְנָתַן
and-he-will-give Yahweh in-eyes-of this and-he-is-easy (18) and-animal-of-you

אֶת־ מוֹאָב בְּיֶדְכֶם׃ וְהִכִּיתֶם כָּל־ עִיר
city-of every-of and-you-will-overthrow (19) into-hand-of-you Moab ***

מִבְצָר וְכָל־ עִיר מִבְחוֹר וְכָל־ עֵץ טוֹב
good tree and-every-of major town-of and-every-of fortification

תַּפִּילוּ וְכָל־ מַעְיְנֵי־ מַיִם תִּסְתֹּמוּ וְכֹל
and-every-of you-will-stop-up waters springs-of and-all-of you-will-cut-down

הַחֶלְקָה הַטּוֹבָה תַּכְאִבוּ בָּאֲבָנִים׃ וַיְהִי
and-he-was (20) with-the-stones you-will-ruin the-good the-field

בַבֹּקֶר כַּעֲלוֹת הַמִּנְחָה וְהִנֵּה־ מַיִם בָּאִים
ones-flowing waters then-see! the-sacrifice when-to-offer in-the-morning

מִדֶּרֶךְ אֱדוֹם וַתִּמָּלֵא הָאָרֶץ אֶת־ הַמָּיִם׃ וְכָל־
now-all-of (21) waters *** the-land and-she-was-filled Edom from-direction-of

מוֹאָב שָׁמְעוּ כִּי־ עָלוּ הַמְּלָכִים לְהִלָּחֶם בָּם וַיִּצָּעֲקוּ
and-they-called against-them to-fight the-kings they-came that they-heard Moab

מִכֹּל חֹגֵר חֲגֹרָה וָמָעְלָה וַיַּעַמְדוּ עַל־ הַגְּבוּל׃
the-border on and-they-stationed and-upward arm bearing from-every-of

וַיַּשְׁכִּימוּ בַבֹּקֶר וְהַשֶּׁמֶשׁ זָרְחָה עַל־ הַמָּיִם
the-waters on she-shined then-the-sun in-the-morning when-they-got-up (22)

וַיִּרְאוּ מוֹאָב מִנֶּגֶד אֶת־ הַמַּיִם אֲדֻמִּים כַּדָּם׃
like-the-blood ones-red the-waters *** at-across Moab and-they-saw

Moab."

14 Elisha said, "As surely as the LORD Almighty lives, whom I serve, if I did not have respect for the presence of Jehoshaphat king of Judah, I would not look at you or even notice you. 15 But now bring me a harpist."

While the harpist was playing, the hand of the LORD came upon Elisha 16 and he said, "This is what the LORD says: Make this valley full of ditches. 17 For this is what the LORD says: You will see neither wind nor rain, yet this valley will be filled with water, and you, your cattle and your other animals will drink. 18 This is an easy thing in the eyes of the LORD; he will also hand Moab over to you. 19 You will overthrow every fortified city and every major town. You will cut down every good tree, stop up all the springs, and ruin every good field with stones."

20 The next morning, about the time for offering the sacrifice, there it was—water flowing from the direction of Edom! And the land was filled with water.

21 Now all the Moabites had heard that the kings had come to fight against them; so every man, young and old, who could bear arms was called up and stationed on the border. 22 When they got up early in the morning, the sun was shining on the water. To the Moabites across the way, the water looked red—like blood.

וַיֹּאמְרוּ דָּם זֶה הָחֳרֵב נֶחֶרְבוּ הַמְּלָכִים
the-kings they-fought to-fight that blood and-they-said (23)

וַיַּכּוּ אִישׁ אֶת־ רֵעֵהוּ וְעַתָּה לַשָּׁלָל מוֹאָב׃
Moab to-the-plunder and-now fellow-of-him *** each and-they-slaughtered

וַיָּבֹאוּ אֶל־ מַחֲנֵה יִשְׂרָאֵל וַיָּקֻמוּ יִשְׂרָאֵל וַיַּכּוּ
and-they-fought Israel then-they-rose-up Israel camp-of to when-they-came (24)

אֶת־ מוֹאָב וַיָּנֻסוּ מִפְּנֵיהֶם וַיָּבוּ־° בָהּ
into-her and-they-invaded from-before-them so-they-fled Moab ***

וְהַכּוֹת אֶת־ מוֹאָב׃ וְהֶעָרִים יַהֲרֹסוּ וְכָל־
and-every-of they-destroyed and-the-towns (25) Moab *** and-to-slaughter

חֶלְקָה טוֹבָה יַשְׁלִיכוּ אִישׁ־ אַבְנוֹ וּמִלְאוּהָ וְכָל־
and-every-of so-they-covered-her stone-of-him man they-threw good field

מַעְיַן־ מַיִם יִסְתְּמוּ וְכָל־ עֵץ־ טוֹב יַפִּילוּ עַד־
until they-cut-down good tree and-every-of they-stopped-up waters spring-of

הִשְׁאִיר אֲבָנֶיהָ בַּקִּיר חֲרָשֶׂת* וַיָּסֹבּוּ הַקַּלָּעִים
the-slingers but-they-surrounded Hareseth in-the-Kir stones-of-her he-left

וַיַּכּוּהָ׃ וַיַּרְא מֶלֶךְ מוֹאָב כִּי־ חָזַק
he-prevailed that Moab king-of when-he-saw (26) and-they-attacked-her

מִמֶּנּוּ הַמִּלְחָמָה וַיִּקַּח אוֹתוֹ שְׁבַע־ מֵאוֹת אִישׁ שֹׁלֵף
drawing man hundreds seven-of with-him then-he-took the-battle against-him

חֶרֶב לְהַבְקִיעַ אֶל־ מֶלֶךְ אֱדוֹם וְלֹא יָכֹלוּ׃ וַיִּקַּח
then-he-took (27) they-could but-not Edom king-of to to-break-through sword

אֶת־ בְּנוֹ הַבְּכוֹר אֲשֶׁר־ יִמְלֹךְ תַּחְתָּיו
in-place-of-him he-would-become-king who the-firstborn son-of-him ***

וַיַּעֲלֵהוּ עֹלָה עַל־ הַחֹמָה וַיְהִי קֶצֶף־ גָּדוֹל עַל־
against great fury and-he-was the-wall on sacrifice and-he-offered-him

יִשְׂרָאֵל וַיִּסְעוּ מֵעָלָיו וַיָּשֻׁבוּ לָאָרֶץ׃
to-the-land and-they-returned from-against-him so-they-withdrew Israel

וְאִשָּׁה אַחַת מִנְּשֵׁי בְנֵי־ הַנְּבִיאִים צָעֲקָה אֶל־
to she-cried-out the-prophets sons-of from-wives-of one now-woman (4:1)

אֱלִישָׁע לֵאמֹר עַבְדְּךָ אִישִׁי מֵת וְאַתָּה יָדַעְתָּ כִּי
that you-know and-you he-is-dead husband-of-me servant-of-you to-say Elisha

עַבְדְּךָ הָיָה יָרֵא אֶת־ יְהוָה וְהַנֹּשֶׁה בָּא
coming but-the-one-being-creditor Yahweh *** revering he-was servant-of-you

לָקַחַת אֶת־ שְׁנֵי יְלָדַי לוֹ לַעֲבָדִים׃ וַיֹּאמֶר אֵלֶיהָ
to-her and-he-replied (2) as-slaves to-him boys-of-me two-of *** to-take

אֱלִישָׁע מָה אֶעֱשֶׂה־ לָּךְ הַגִּידִי לִי מַה־ יֶּשׁ־ לָכִי° בַּבָּיִת
in-the-house to-you is-there what? to-me tell! for-you can-I-do what? Elisha

23"That's blood!" they said.
"Those kings must have
fought and slaughtered each
other. Now to the plunder,
Moab!"
24But when the Moabites
came to the camp of Israel, the
Israelites rose up and fought
them until they fled. And the
Israelites invaded the land
and slaughtered the Moabites.
25They destroyed the towns,
and each man threw a stone
on every good field until it was
covered. They stopped up all
the springs and cut down
every good tree. Only Kir
Hareseth was left with its
stones in place, but men
armed with slings surrounded
it and attacked it as well.
26When the king of Moab
saw that the battle had gone
against him, he took with him
seven hundred swordsmen to
break through to the king of
Edom, but they failed. 27Then
he took his firstborn son, who
was to succeed him as king,
and offered him as a sacrifice
on the city wall. The fury
against Israel was great; they
withdrew and returned to
their own land.

*The Widow's Oil*

4 The wife of a man from
the company of the
prophets cried out to Elisha,
"Your servant my husband is
dead, and you know that he
revered the LORD. But now his
creditor is coming to take my
two boys as his slaves."
2Elisha replied to her, "How
can I help you? Tell me, what
do you have in your house?"

*25 Some mss have *shin* for *sin* (שֶׁת).

°24 ק ויכו

°2 ק לך

וַתֹּאמֶר אֵין לְשִׁפְחָתְךָ כֹל בַּבַּיִת כִּי אִם־
only except in-the-house all-of to-servant-of-you nothing and-she-said

אָסוּךְ שָׁמֶן׃ וַיֹּאמֶר לְכִי שַׁאֲלִי־ לָךְ כֵּלִים מִן־ הַחוּץ מֵאֵת
from the-area from jars for-you ask! go! and-he-said (3) oil flask-of

כָּל־ שְׁכֵנָכִי כֵּלִים רֵקִים אַל־ תַּמְעִיטִי׃ וּבָאת
then-you-go (4) you-get-few not empty-ones jars neighbors-of-you all-of

וְסָגַרְתְּ הַדֶּלֶת בַּעֲדֵךְ וּבְעַד־ בָּנַיִךְ וְיָצַקְתְּ עַל
in and-you-pour sons-of-you and-behind behind-you the-door and-you-shut

כָּל־ הַכֵּלִים הָאֵלֶּה וְהַמָּלֵא תַּסִּיעִי׃ וַתֵּלֶךְ
so-she-left (5) you-put-aside and-the-one-filled the-these the-jars all-of

מֵאִתּוֹ וַתִּסְגֹּר הַדֶּלֶת בַּעֲדָהּ וּבְעַד בָּנֶיהָ הֵם
they sons-of-her and-behind behind-her the-door and-she-shut from-with-him

מַגִּשִׁים אֵלֶיהָ וְהִיא מֹיצָקֶת׃ וַיְהִי כִּמְלֹאת הַכֵּלִים
the-jars when-to-be-full and-he-was (6) pouring and-she to-her ones-bringing

וַתֹּאמֶר אֶל־ בְּנָהּ הַגִּישָׁה אֵלַי עוֹד כֶּלִי וַיֹּאמֶר אֵלֶיהָ
to-her but-he-replied jar another to-me bring! son-of-her to then-she-said

אֵין עוֹד כֶּלִי וַיַּעֲמֹד הַשָּׁמֶן׃ וַתָּבֹא וַתַּגֵּד
and-she-told then-she-went (7) the-oil then-he-stopped jar another not

לְאִישׁ הָאֱלֹהִים וַיֹּאמֶר לְכִי מִכְרִי אֶת־ הַשֶּׁמֶן וְשַׁלְּמִי אֶת־ נִשְׁיֵכִי
debts-of-you *** and-pay! the-oil *** sell! go! and-he-said the-God to-man-of

וְאַתְּ בָּנַיִכִי תִּחְיִי בַּנּוֹתָר׃ וַיְהִי
and-he-was (8) on-the-being-left you-can-live and-sons-of-you and-you

הַיּוֹם וַיַּעֲבֹר אֱלִישָׁע אֶל־ שׁוּנֵם וְשָׁם אִשָּׁה גְדוֹלָה וַתַּחֲזֶק־
and-she-urged well-to-do woman and-there Shunem to Elisha then-he-went the-day

בּוֹ לֶאֱכָל־לָחֶם וַיְהִי מִדֵּי עָבְרוֹ יָסֻר שָׁמָּה
at-there he-stopped to-come-by-him at-times-of so-he-was meal to-eat with-him

לֶאֱכָל־לָחֶם׃ וַתֹּאמֶר אֶל־ אִישָׁהּ הִנֵּה־ נָא יָדַעְתִּי כִּי אִישׁ
man-of that I-know now! see! husband-of-her to and-she-said (9) meal to-eat

אֱלֹהִים קָדוֹשׁ הוּא עֹבֵר עָלֵינוּ תָּמִיד׃ נַעֲשֶׂה־ נָּא עֲלִיַּת־ קִיר
roof upper-room-of now! let-us-make (10) often to-us coming he holy God

קְטַנָּה וְנָשִׂים לוֹ שָׁם מִטָּה וְשֻׁלְחָן וְכִסֵּא וּמְנוֹרָה
and-lamp and-chair and-table bed there for-him and-let-us-put small

וְהָיָה בְּבֹאוֹ אֵלֵינוּ יָסוּר שָׁמָּה׃ וַיְהִי
and-he-was (11) at-there he-can-stay to-us when-to-come-him and-he-will-be

הַיּוֹם וַיָּבֹא שָׁמָּה וַיָּסַר אֶל־ הָעֲלִיָּה וַיִּשְׁכַּב־ שָׁמָּה׃
at-there and-he-lay the-room to and-he-went to-there then-he-came the-day

וַיֹּאמֶר אֶל־ גֵּיחֲזִי נַעֲרוֹ קְרָא לַשּׁוּנַמִּית הַזֹּאת
the-this to-the-Shunnamite call! servant-of-him Gehazi to and-he-said (12)

"Your servant has nothing there at all," she said, "except a little oil."

[3]Elisha said, "Go around and ask all your neighbors for empty jars. Don't ask for just a few. [4]Then go inside and shut the door behind you and your sons. Pour oil into all the jars, and as each is filled, put it to one side."

[5]She left him and afterward shut the door behind her and her sons. They brought the jars to her and she kept pouring. [6]When all the jars were full, she said to her son, "Bring me another one."

But he replied, "There is not a jar left." Then the oil stopped flowing.

[7]She went and told the man of God, and he said, "Go, sell the oil and pay your debts. You and your sons can live on what is left."

*The Shunammite's Son Restored to Life*

[8]One day Elisha went to Shunem. And a well-to-do woman was there, who urged him to stay for a meal. So whenever he came by, he stopped there to eat. [9]She said to her husband, "I know that this man who often comes our way is a holy man of God. [10]Let's make a small room on the roof and put in it a bed and a table, a chair and a lamp for him. Then he can stay there whenever he comes to us."

[11]One day when Elisha came, he went up to his room and lay down there. [12]He said to his servant Gehazi, "Call

°3 ק שכניך
°5 ק מוצקת
°7a ק נשיך
°7b ק ובניך

וַיִּקְרָא־ לָהּ וַתַּעֲמֹד לְפָנָיו׃ וַיֹּאמֶר לוֹ אֱמָר־
tell! to-him and-he-said (13) before-him and-she-stood to-her so-he-called

נָא אֵלֶיהָ הִנֵּה חָרַדְתְּ ׀ אֵלֵינוּ אֶת־ כָּל־ הַחֲרָדָה הַזֹּאת
the-this the-care all-of *** for-us you-went-to-trouble see! to-her! now!

מֶה לַעֲשׂוֹת לָךְ הֲיֵשׁ לְדַבֶּר־ לָךְ אֶל־ הַמֶּלֶךְ אוֹ אֶל־ שַׂר
commander-of to or the-king to for-you to-speak is-there? for-you to-do what?

הַצָּבָא וַתֹּאמֶר בְּתוֹךְ עַמִּי אָנֹכִי יֹשָׁבֶת׃ וַיֹּאמֶר
and-he-asked (14) having-home I people-of-me among and-she-replied the-army

וּמֶה לַעֲשׂוֹת לָהּ וַיֹּאמֶר גֵּיחֲזִי אֲבָל בֵּן אֵין־ לָהּ
to-her there-is-not son well Gehazi and-he-said for-her to-do now-what?

וְאִישָׁהּ זָקֵן׃ וַיֹּאמֶר קְרָא־ לָהּ וַיִּקְרָא־
so-he-called to-her call! then-he-said (15) he-is-old and-husband-of-her

לָהּ וַתַּעֲמֹד בַּפָּתַח׃ וַיֹּאמֶר לַמּוֹעֵד הַזֶּה
the-this at-the-season and-he-said (16) in-the-doorway and-she-stood to-her

כָּעֵת חַיָּה אַתְּי חֹבֶקֶת בֵּן וַתֹּאמֶר אַל־ אֲדֹנִי אִישׁ הָאֱלֹהִים
the-God man-of lord-of-me no but-she-said son holding you spring at-time-of

אַל־ תְּכַזֵּב בְּשִׁפְחָתֶךָ׃ וַתַּהַר הָאִשָּׁה
the-woman but-she-became-pregnant (17) to-servant-of-you you-mislead not

וַתֵּלֶד בֵּן לַמּוֹעֵד הַזֶּה כָּעֵת חַיָּה אֲשֶׁר־ דִּבֶּר
he-told as the-spring at-time-of the-that at-the-season son and-she-bore

אֵלֶיהָ אֱלִישָׁע׃ וַיִּגְדַּל הַיָּלֶד וַיְהִי הַיּוֹם וַיֵּצֵא
then-he-went-out the-day and-he-was the-child and-he-grew (18) Elisha to-her

אֶל־ אָבִיו אֶל־ הַקֹּצְרִים׃ וַיֹּאמֶר אֶל־ אָבִיו
father-of-him to and-he-said (19) the-ones-reaping to father-of-him to

רֹאשִׁי ׀ רֹאשִׁי וַיֹּאמֶר אֶל־ הַנַּעַר שָׂאֵהוּ אֶל־ אִמּוֹ׃
mother-of-him to carry-him! the-servant to and-he-told head-of-me head-of-me

וַיִּשָּׂאֵהוּ וַיְבִיאֵהוּ אֶל־ אִמּוֹ וַיֵּשֶׁב עַל־
on and-he-sat mother-of-him to and-he-carried-him so-he-lifted-him (20)

בִּרְכֶּיהָ עַד־ הַצָּהֳרַיִם וַיָּמֹת׃ וַתַּעַל וַתַּשְׁכִּבֵהוּ
and-she-laid-him then-she-went-up (21) then-he-died the-noon until knees-of-her

עַל־ מִטַּת אִישׁ הָאֱלֹהִים וַתִּסְגֹּר בַּעֲדוֹ וַתֵּצֵא׃
and-she-went-out behind-him then-she-shut the-God man-of bed-of on

וַתִּקְרָא אֶל־ אִישָׁהּ וַתֹּאמֶר שִׁלְחָה נָא לִי אֶחָד
one to-me now! send! and-she-said husband-of-her to and-she-called (22)

מִן־ הַנְּעָרִים וְאַחַת הָאֲתֹנוֹת וְאָרוּצָה עַד־ אִישׁ
man-of to so-I-can-go-quickly the-donkeys and-one-of the-servants from

הָאֱלֹהִים וְאָשׁוּבָה׃ וַיֹּאמֶר מַדּוּעַ אַתְּי הֹלֶכְתִּי אֵלָיו הַיּוֹם
the-day to-him going you why? and-he-asked (23) and-I-can-return the-God

the Shunammite." So he called her, and she stood before him. [13]Elisha said to him, "Tell her, 'You have gone to all this trouble for us. Now what can be done for you? Can we speak on your behalf to the king or the commander of the army?' "

She replied, "I have a home among my own people."

[14]"What can be done for her?" Elisha asked.

Gehazi said, "Well, she has no son and her husband is old."

[15]Then Elisha said, "Call her." So he called her, and she stood in the doorway. [16]"About this time next year," Elisha said, "you will hold a son in your arms."

"No, my lord," she objected. "Don't mislead your servant, O man of God!"

[17]But the woman became pregnant, and the next year about that same time she gave birth to a son, just as Elisha had told her.

[18]The child grew, and one day he went out to his father, who was with the reapers. [19]"My head! My head!" he said to his father.

His father told a servant, "Carry him to his mother." [20]After the servant had lifted him up and carried him to his mother, the boy sat on her lap until noon, and then he died. [21]She went up and laid him on the bed of the man of God, then shut the door and went out.

[22]She called her husband and said, "Please send me one of the servants and a donkey so I can go to the man of God quickly and return."

[23]"Why go to him today?" he

°16 ק את
°23a ק את
°23b ק הלכת

לֹא־ חֹדֶשׁ וְלֹא שַׁבָּת וַתֹּאמֶר שָׁלוֹם׃ וַתַּחֲבֹשׁ
and-she-saddled (24) all-right and-she-said Sabbath and-not New-Moon not

הָאָתוֹן וַתֹּאמֶר אֶל־ נַעֲרָהּ נְהַג וָלֵךְ אַל־ תַּעֲצָר־
you-slow-down not and-go! lead-on! servant-of-her to and-she-said the-donkey

לִי לִרְכֹּב כִּי אִם־אָמַרְתִּי לָךְ׃ וַתֵּלֶךְ וַתָּבוֹא אֶל־
to and-she-came so-she-set-out (25) to-you I-tell if except to-ride for-me

אִישׁ הָאֱלֹהִים אֶל־ הַר הַכַּרְמֶל וַיְהִי כִּרְאוֹת אִישׁ־הָאֱלֹהִים
the-God man-of when-to-see and-he-was the-Carmel Mount-of at the-God man-of

אֹתָהּ מִנֶּגֶד וַיֹּאמֶר אֶל־ גֵּיחֲזִי נַעֲרוֹ הִנֵּה הַשּׁוּנַמִּית
the-Shunnamite look! servant-of-him Gehazi to then-he-said in-distance her

הַלָּז׃ עַתָּה רוּץ־ נָא לִקְרָאתָהּ וֶאֱמָר־ לָהּ הֲשָׁלוֹם לָךְ
with-you all-right? of-her and-ask! to-meet-her now! run! now (26) the-that

הֲשָׁלוֹם לְאִישֵׁךְ הֲשָׁלוֹם לַיָּלֶד וַתֹּאמֶר
and-she-said with-the-child all-right? with-husband-of-you all-right?

שָׁלוֹם׃ וַתָּבֹא אֶל־ אִישׁ הָאֱלֹהִים אֶל־ הָהָר
the-mountain at the-God man-of to when-she-reached (27) all-right

וַתַּחֲזֵק בְּרַגְלָיו וַיִּגַּשׁ גֵּיחֲזִי לְהָדְפָהּ
to-push-away-her Gehazi and-he-came-over of-feet-of-him then-she-took-hold

וַיֹּאמֶר אִישׁ הָאֱלֹהִים הַרְפֵּה־ לָהּ כִּי־ נַפְשָׁהּ מָרָה־
she-is-bitter spirit-of-her for to-her leave-alone! the-God man-of but-he-said

לָהּ וַיהוָה הֶעְלִים מִמֶּנִּי וְלֹא הִגִּיד לִי׃ וַתֹּאמֶר
and-she-said (28) to-me he-told and-not from-me he-hid but-Yahweh to-her

הֲשָׁאַלְתִּי בֵן מֵאֵת אֲדֹנִי הֲלֹא אָמַרְתִּי לֹא תַשְׁלֶה אֹתִי׃
me you-raise-hope not I-told not? lord-of-me from son did-I-ask?

וַיֹּאמֶר לְגֵיחֲזִי חֲגֹר מָתְנֶיךָ וְקַח מִשְׁעַנְתִּי
staff-of-me and-take! waists-of-you tuck-cloak! to-Gehazi and-he-said (29)

בְּיָדְךָ וָלֵךְ כִּי־ תִמְצָא אִישׁ לֹא תְבָרְכֶנּוּ וְכִי־
and-if you-greet-him not anyone you-meet if and-run! in-hand-of-you

יְבָרֶכְךָ אִישׁ לֹא תַעֲנֶנּוּ וְשַׂמְתָּ מִשְׁעַנְתִּי עַל־ פְּנֵי
faces-of on staff-of-me then-you-lay you-answer-him not anyone he-greets-you

הַנָּעַר׃ וַתֹּאמֶר אֵם הַנַּעַר חַי־ יְהוָה וְחֵי־
and-life-of Yahweh life-of the-child mother-of but-she-said (30) the-boy

נַפְשְׁךָ אִם־ אֶעֶזְבֶךָּ וַיָּקָם וַיֵּלֶךְ אַחֲרֶיהָ׃
after-her and-he-followed so-he-got-up I-will-leave-you not soul-of-you

וְגֵחֲזִי עָבַר לִפְנֵיהֶם וַיָּשֶׂם אֶת־ הַמִּשְׁעֶנֶת עַל־
on the-staff *** and-he-laid ahead-of-them he-went-on and-Gehazi (31)

פְּנֵי הַנַּעַר וְאֵין קוֹל וְאֵין קָשֶׁב
response and-there-was-no sound but-there-was-no the-boy faces-of

asked. "It's not the New Moon
or the Sabbath."
"It's all right," she said.
[24]She saddled the donkey
and said to her servant, "Lead
on; don't slow down for me
unless I tell you." [25]So she set
out and came to the man of
God at Mount Carmel.
When he saw her in the distance, the man of God said to
his servant Gehazi, "Look!
There's the Shunammite!
[26]Run to meet her and ask her,
'Are you all right? Is your husband all right? Is your child all
right?' "
"Everything is all right,"
she said.
[27]When she reached the man
of God at the mountain, she
took hold of his feet. Gehazi
came over to push her away,
but the man of God said,
"Leave her alone! She is in bitter distress, but the LORD has
hidden it from me and has not
told me why."
[28]"Did I ask you for a son,
my lord?" she said. "Didn't I
tell you, 'Don't raise my
hopes'?"
[29]Elisha said to Gehazi,
"Tuck your cloak into your
belt, take my staff in your
hand and run. If you meet
anyone, do not greet him, and
if anyone greets you, do not
answer. Lay my staff on the
boy's face."
[30]But the child's mother said,
"As surely as the LORD lives
and as you live, I will not leave
you." So he got up and followed her.
[31]Gehazi went on ahead and
laid the staff on the boy's face,
but there was no sound or response. So Gehazi went back

וַיָּשָׁב לִקְרָאתוֹ וַיַּגֶּד־לוֹ לֵאמֹר לֹא הֵקִיץ הַנָּעַר׃
the-boy he-awoke not to-say to-him and-he-told to-meet-him so-he-went-back

(32) וַיָּבֹא אֱלִישָׁע הַבַּיְתָה וְהִנֵּה הַנַּעַר מֵת מֻשְׁכָּב
lying he-was-dead the-boy then-see! to-the-house Elisha when-he-reached (32)

עַל־מִטָּתוֹ׃ (33) וַיָּבֹא וַיִּסְגֹּר הַדֶּלֶת בְּעַד שְׁנֵיהֶם
two-of-them behind the-door and-he-shut and-he-went-in (33) couch-of-him on

וַיִּתְפַּלֵּל אֶל־יְהוָה׃ (34) וַיַּעַל וַיִּשְׁכַּב עַל־הַיֶּלֶד
the-boy upon and-he-lay then-he-got-on (34) Yahweh to and-he-prayed

וַיָּשֶׂם פִּיו עַל־פִּיו וְעֵינָיו עַל־עֵינָיו
eyes-of-him to and-eyes-of-him mouth-of-him to mouth-of-him and-he-put

וְכַפָּיו עַל־כַּפָּו° וַיִּגְהַר עָלָיו וַיָּחָם
and-he-grew-warm upon-him and-he-stretched-out hands-of-him to and-hands-of-him

בְּשַׂר הַיָּלֶד׃ (35) וַיָּשָׁב וַיֵּלֶךְ בַּבַּיִת אַחַת
once in-the-room and-he-walked and-he-turned-away (35) the-boy body-of

הֵנָּה וְאַחַת הֵנָּה וַיַּעַל וַיִּגְהַר עָלָיו
upon-him and-he-stretched-out then-he-got-on to-there and-once to-here

וַיְזוֹרֵר הַנַּעַר עַד־שֶׁבַע פְּעָמִים וַיִּפְקַח הַנַּעַר אֶת־עֵינָיו׃
eyes-of-him *** the-boy and-he-opened times seven to the-boy and-he-sneezed

(36) וַיִּקְרָא אֶל־גֵּיחֲזִי וַיֹּאמֶר קְרָא אֶל־הַשֻּׁנַמִּית הַזֹּאת
the-this the-Shunnamite to call! and-he-said Gehazi to and-he-summoned (36)

וַיִּקְרָאֶהָ וַתָּבוֹא אֵלָיו וַיֹּאמֶר שְׂאִי בְנֵךְ׃
son-of-you take! and-he-said to-him and-she-came and-he-called-her

(37) וַתָּבֹא וַתִּפֹּל עַל־רַגְלָיו וַתִּשְׁתַּחוּ אָרְצָה
to-ground and-she-bowed feet-of-him at and-she-fell and-she-came-in (37)

וַתִּשָּׂא אֶת־בְּנָהּ וַתֵּצֵא׃ (38) וֶאֱלִישָׁע שָׁב
he-returned and-Elisha (38) and-she-went-out son-of-her *** then-she-took

הַגִּלְגָּלָה וְהָרָעָב בָּאָרֶץ וּבְנֵי הַנְּבִיאִים
the-prophets and-sons-of in-the-region and-the-famine to-the-Gilgal

יֹשְׁבִים לְפָנָיו וַיֹּאמֶר לְנַעֲרוֹ שְׁפֹת הַסִּיר
the-pot put-on! to-servant-of-him and-he-said before-him ones-sitting

הַגְּדוֹלָה וּבַשֵּׁל נָזִיד לִבְנֵי הַנְּבִיאִים׃ (39) וַיֵּצֵא אֶחָד
one and-he-went-out (39) the-prophets for-sons-of stew and-cook! the-large

אֶל־הַשָּׂדֶה לְלַקֵּט אֹרֹת וַיִּמְצָא גֶּפֶן שָׂדֶה וַיְלַקֵּט
and-he-gathered field vine-of and-he-found herbs to-gather the-field into

מִמֶּנּוּ פַּקֻּעֹת שָׂדֶה מְלֹא בִגְדוֹ וַיָּבֹא
when-he-returned cloak-of-him fullness-of field gourds-of from-him

וַיְפַלַּח אֶל־סִיר הַנָּזִיד כִּי־לֹא יָדָעוּ׃ (40) וַיִּצְקוּ
and-they-poured (40) they-knew not though the-stew pot-of into then-he-cut-up

°34 ק כפיו

to meet Elisha and told him,
"The boy has not awakened."
32 When Elisha reached the
house, there was the boy lying
dead on his couch. 33 He went
in, shut the door on the two of
them and prayed to the LORD.
34 Then he got on the bed and
lay upon the boy, mouth to
mouth, eyes to eyes, hands to
hands. As he stretched himself
out upon him, the boy's body
grew warm. 35 Elisha turned
away and walked back and
forth in the room and then got
on the bed and stretched out
upon him once more. The boy
sneezed seven times and
opened his eyes.
36 Elisha summoned Gehazi
and said, "Call the Shunammite." And he did. When she
came, he said, "Take your
son." 37 She came in, fell at his
feet and bowed to the ground.
Then she took her son and
went out.

*Death in the Pot*

38 Elisha returned to Gilgal
and there was a famine in that
region. While the company of
the prophets was meeting
with him, he said to his servant, "Put on the large pot and
cook some stew for these
men."
39 One of them went out into
the fields to gather herbs and
found a wild vine. He gathered some of its gourds and
filled the fold of his cloak.
When he returned, he cut
them up into the pot of stew,
though no one knew what

לָאֲנָשִׁים לֶאֱכוֹל וַיְהִי כְּאָכְלָם מֵהַנָּזִיד וְהֵמָּה
then-they from-the-stew as-to-eat-them but-he-was to-eat for-the-men

צָעָקוּ וַיֹּאמְרוּ מָוֶת בַּסִּיר אִישׁ הָאֱלֹהִים וְלֹא
and-not the-God man-of in-the-pot death and-they-said they-cried-out

יָכְלוּ לֶאֱכֹל׃ (41) וַיֹּאמֶר וּקְחוּ־קֶמַח וַיַּשְׁלֵךְ אֶל־הַסִּיר
the-pot into and-he-put flour now-get! and-he-said (41) to-eat they-could

וַיֹּאמֶר צַק לָעָם וְיֹאכֵלוּ וְלֹא הָיָה דָּבָר רָע
harmful anything he-was and-not so-they-eat to-the-people serve! and-he-said

בַּסִּיר׃ (42) וְאִישׁ בָּא מִבַּעַל שָׁלִשָׁה וַיָּבֵא לְאִישׁ
to-man-of and-he-brought Shalishah from-Baal he-came now-man (42) in-the-pot

הָאֱלֹהִים לֶחֶם בִּכּוּרִים עֶשְׂרִים־לֶחֶם שְׂעֹרִים וְכַרְמֶל
and-new-grain barleys loaf-of twenty first-fruits bread-of the-God

בְּצִקְלֹנוֹ וַיֹּאמֶר תֵּן לָעָם וְיֹאכֵלוּ׃ (43) וַיֹּאמֶר
and-he-asked (43) so-they-eat to-the-people give! and-he-said in-bag-of-him

מְשָׁרְתוֹ מָה אֶתֵּן זֶה לִפְנֵי מֵאָה אִישׁ וַיֹּאמֶר תֵּן
give! but-he-answered man hundred before this can-I-set how? one-serving-him

לָעָם וְיֹאכֵלוּ כִּי כֹה אָמַר יְהוָה אָכֹל וְהוֹתֵר׃
and-to-be-left-over to-eat Yahweh he-says this for so-they-eat to-the-people

(44) וַיִּתֵּן לִפְנֵיהֶם וַיֹּאכְלוּ וַיּוֹתִרוּ כִּדְבַר
as-word-of and-they-had-left-over and-they-ate before-them then-he-set (44)

יְהוָה׃ (5:1) וְנַעֲמָן שַׂר־צְבָא מֶלֶךְ־אֲרָם הָיָה אִישׁ גָּדוֹל
great man he-was Aram king-of army-of commander-of now-Naaman (5:1) Yahweh

לִפְנֵי אֲדֹנָיו וּנְשֻׂא פָנִים כִּי־בוֹ
through-him because faces and-being-regarded-of masters-of-him before

נָתַן־יְהוָה תְּשׁוּעָה לַאֲרָם וְהָאִישׁ הָיָה גִּבּוֹר חַיִל
valiant soldier he-was and-the-man to-Aram victory Yahweh he-gave

מְצֹרָע׃ (2) וַאֲרָם יָצְאוּ גְדוּדִים וַיִּשְׁבּוּ
and-they-took-captive bands they-went-out and-Aram (2) having-leprosy

מֵאֶרֶץ יִשְׂרָאֵל נַעֲרָה קְטַנָּה וַתְּהִי לִפְנֵי אֵשֶׁת נַעֲמָן׃
Naaman wife-of before and-she-was young girl Israel from-land-of

(3) וַתֹּאמֶר אֶל־גְּבִרְתָּהּ אַחֲלֵי אֲדֹנִי לִפְנֵי הַנָּבִיא
the-prophet before master-of-me if-only mistress-of-her to and-she-said (3)

אֲשֶׁר בְּשֹׁמְרוֹן אָז יֶאֱסֹף אֹתוֹ מִצָּרַעְתּוֹ׃ (4) וַיָּבֹא
and-he-went (4) of-leprosy-of-him him he-would-cure then in-Samaria who

וַיַּגֵּד לַאדֹנָיו לֵאמֹר כָּזֹאת וְכָזֹאת דִּבְּרָה הַנַּעֲרָה
the-girl she-said and-as-that as-this to-say to-masters-of-him and-he-told

אֲשֶׁר מֵאֶרֶץ יִשְׂרָאֵל׃ (5) וַיֹּאמֶר מֶלֶךְ־אֲרָם לֶךְ־בֹּא
go! leave! Aram king-of and-he-replied (5) Israel from-land-of who

they were. 40The stew was poured out for the men, but as they began to eat it, they cried out, "O man of God, there is death in the pot!" And they could not eat it.

41Elisha said, "Get some flour." He put it into the pot and said, "Serve it to the people to eat." And there was nothing harmful in the pot.

*Feeding of a Hundred*

42A man came from Baal Shalishah, bringing the man of God twenty loaves of barley bread baked from the first ripe grain, along with some heads of new grain. "Give it to the people to eat," Elisha said.

43"How can I set this before a hundred men?" his servant asked.

But Elisha answered, "Give it to the people to eat. For this is what the LORD says: 'They will eat and have some left over.' " 44Then he set it before them, and they ate and had some left over, according to the word of the LORD.

*Naaman Healed of Leprosy*

5 Now Naaman was commander of the army of the king of Aram. He was a great man in the sight of his master and highly regarded, because through him the LORD had given victory to Aram. He was a valiant soldier, but he had leprosy.[d]

2Now bands from Aram had gone out and had taken captive a young girl from Israel, and she served Naaman's wife. 3She said to her mistress, "If only my master would see the prophet who is in Samaria! He would cure him of his leprosy."

4Naaman went to his master and told him what the girl from Israel had said. 5"By all means, go," the king of Aram

[d]1 The Hebrew word was used for various diseases affecting the skin—not necessarily leprosy.

וְאֶשְׁלְחָה סֵפֶר אֶל־ מֶלֶךְ יִשְׂרָאֵל וַיֵּלֶךְ וַיִּקַּח בְּיָדוֹ
in-hand-of-him and-he-took so-he-left Israel king-of to letter and-I-will-send

עֶשֶׂר כִּכְּרֵי־ כֶסֶף וְשֵׁשֶׁת אֲלָפִים זָהָב וְעֶשֶׂר חֲלִיפוֹת בְּגָדִים׃
clothings sets-of and-ten gold thousands and-six-of silver talents-of ten

(6) וַיָּבֵא הַסֵּפֶר אֶל־ מֶלֶךְ יִשְׂרָאֵל לֵאמֹר וְעַתָּה כְּבוֹא
as-to-come and-now to-say Israel king-of to the-letter and-he-took (6)

הַסֵּפֶר הַזֶּה אֵלֶיךָ הִנֵּה שָׁלַחְתִּי אֵלֶיךָ אֶת־ נַעֲמָן עַבְדִּי
servant-of-me Naaman *** to-you I-send see! to-you the-this the-letter

וַאֲסַפְתּוֹ מִצָּרַעְתּוֹ׃ (7) וַיְהִי כִּקְרֹא מֶלֶךְ־
king-of as-to-read and-he-was (7) of-leprosy-of-him so-you-may-cure-him

יִשְׂרָאֵל אֶת־ הַסֵּפֶר וַיִּקְרַע בְּגָדָיו וַיֹּאמֶר הַאֱלֹהִים אָנִי
I God? and-he-said robes-of-him then-he-tore the-letter *** Israel

לְהָמִית וּלְהַחֲיוֹת כִּי־ זֶה שֹׁלֵחַ אֵלַי לֶאֱסֹף אִישׁ
someone to-cure to-me sending this-one that and-to-bring-to-life to-kill

מִצָּרַעְתּוֹ כִּי אַךְ־ דְּעוּ־ נָא וּרְאוּ כִּי־ מִתְאַנֶּה הוּא
he picking-quarrel that and-see! now! know! indeed so of-leprosy-of-him

לִי׃ (8) וַיְהִי כִּשְׁמֹעַ ׀ אֱלִישָׁע אִישׁ־ הָאֱלֹהִים כִּי־ קָרַע
he-tore that the-God man-of Elisha when-to-hear and-he-was (8) with-me

מֶלֶךְ־ יִשְׂרָאֵל אֶת־ בְּגָדָיו וַיִּשְׁלַח אֶל־ הַמֶּלֶךְ לֵאמֹר לָמָּה
why? to-say the-king to then-he-sent robes-of-him *** Israel king-of

קָרַעְתָּ בְּגָדֶיךָ יָבֹא־ נָא אֵלַי וְיֵדַע כִּי
that and-he-will-know to-me now! have-him-come robes-of-you you-tore

יֵשׁ נָבִיא בְּיִשְׂרָאֵל׃ (9) וַיָּבֹא נַעֲמָן בְּסוּסָו°
with-horses-of-him Naaman so-he-went (9) in-Israel prophet there-is

וּבְרִכְבּוֹ וַיַּעֲמֹד פֶּתַח־ הַבַּיִת לֶאֱלִישָׁע׃
of-Elisha the-house door-of and-he-stopped and-with-chariot-of-him

(10) וַיִּשְׁלַח אֵלָיו אֱלִישָׁע מַלְאָךְ לֵאמֹר הָלוֹךְ וְרָחַצְתָּ שֶׁבַע־
seven and-you-wash to-go to-say messenger Elisha to-him and-he-sent (10)

פְּעָמִים בַּיַּרְדֵּן וְיָשֹׁב בְּשָׂרְךָ לְךָ וּטְהָר׃
and-be-clean! to-you flesh-of-you and-he-will-be-restored in-the-Jordan times

(11) וַיִּקְצֹף נַעֲמָן וַיֵּלַךְ וַיֹּאמֶר הִנֵּה אָמַרְתִּי
I-thought see! and-he-said and-he-went-away Naaman but-he-became-angry (11)

אֵלַי ׀ יֵצֵא יָצוֹא וְעָמַד וְקָרָא
and-he-would-call and-he-would-stand to-come-out he-would-come-out to-me

בְּשֵׁם־ יְהוָה אֱלֹהָיו וְהֵנִיף יָדוֹ אֶל־ הַמָּקוֹם
the-spot over hand-of-him and-he-would-wave God-of-him Yahweh on-name-of

וְאָסַף הַמְּצֹרָע׃ (12) הֲלֹא טוֹב אֲבָנָה° וּפַרְפַּר
and-Pharpar Abana better not? (12) the-part-being-leprous and-he-would-cure

replied. "I will send a letter to the king of Israel." So Naaman left, taking with him ten talents[e] of silver, six thousand shekels[f] of gold and ten sets of clothing. [6]The letter that he took to the king of Israel read: "With this letter I am sending my servant Naaman to you so that you may cure him of his leprosy."

[7]As soon as the king of Israel read the letter, he tore his robes and said, "Am I God? Can I kill and bring back to life? Why does this fellow send someone to me to be cured of his leprosy? See how he is trying to pick a quarrel with me!"

[8]When Elisha the man of God heard that the king of Israel had torn his robes, he sent him this message: "Why have you torn your robes? Have the man come to me and he will know that there is a prophet in Israel." [9]So Naaman went with his horses and chariots and stopped at the door of Elisha's house. [10]Elisha sent a messenger to say to him, "Go, wash yourself seven times in the Jordan, and your flesh will be restored and you will be cleansed."

[11]But Naaman went away angry and said, "I thought that he would surely come out to me and stand and call on the name of the LORD his God, wave his hand over the spot and cure me of my leprosy. [12]Are not Abana and Pharpar,

[e]5 That is, about 750 pounds (about 340 kilograms)
[f]5 That is, about 150 pounds (about 70 kilograms)

°9 ק בסוסיו
°12 ק אמנה

נַהֲרוֹת דַּמֶּשֶׂק מִכֹּל מֵימֵי יִשְׂרָאֵל הֲלֹא־ אֶרְחַץ בָּהֶם
in-them I-could-wash not? Israel waters-of than-all-of Damascus rivers-of

וְטָהָרְתִּי וַיִּפֶן וַיֵּלֶךְ בְּחֵמָה׃ וַיִּגְּשׁוּ
and-they-went (13) in-rage and-he-went-off so-he-turned and-I-would-be-cleansed

עֲבָדָיו וַיְדַבְּרוּ אֵלָיו וַיֹּאמְרוּ אָבִי דָּבָר גָּדוֹל
great thing father-of-me and-they-said to-him and-they-spoke servants-of-him

הַנָּבִיא דִּבֶּר אֵלֶיךָ הֲלוֹא תַעֲשֶׂה וְאַף כִּי־ אָמַר
he-tells when then-how-much-more you-would-do not? to-you he-told the-prophet

אֵלֶיךָ רְחַץ וּטְהָר׃ וַיֵּרֶד וַיִּטְבֹּל בַּיַּרְדֵּן
in-the-Jordan and-he-dipped so-he-went-down (14) and-be-cleansed! wash! to-you

שֶׁבַע פְּעָמִים כִּדְבַר אִישׁ הָאֱלֹהִים וַיָּשָׁב בְּשָׂרוֹ
flesh-of-him and-he-was-restored the-God man-of as-word-of times seven

כִּבְשַׂר נַעַר קָטֹן וַיִּטְהָר׃ וַיָּשָׁב אֶל־ אִישׁ
man-of to then-he-went-back (15) and-he-became-clean young boy as-flesh-of

הָאֱלֹהִים הוּא וְכָל־ מַחֲנֵהוּ וַיָּבֹא וַיַּעֲמֹד לְפָנָיו
before-him and-he-stood and-he-went attendant-of-him and-all-of he the-God

וַיֹּאמֶר הִנֵּה־ נָא יָדַעְתִּי כִּי אֵין אֱלֹהִים בְּכָל־ הָאָרֶץ כִּי
except the-world in-all-of God there-is-no that I-know now! see! and-he-said

אִם־ בְּיִשְׂרָאֵל וְעַתָּה קַח־ נָא בְרָכָה מֵאֵת עַבְדֶּךָ׃ וַיֹּאמֶר
but-he-said (16) servant-of-you from gift now! accept! and-now in-Israel only

חַי־ יְהוָה אֲשֶׁר־ עָמַדְתִּי לְפָנָיו אִם־ אֶקָּח וַיִּפְצַר־
and-he-urged I-will-accept not before-him I-serve whom Yahweh life-of

בּוֹ לָקַחַת וַיְמָאֵן׃ וַיֹּאמֶר נַעֲמָן וָלֹא
if-not Naaman and-he-said (17) but-he-refused to-accept with-him

יֻתַּן־ נָא לְעַבְדְּךָ מַשָּׂא צֶמֶד־ פְּרָדִים אֲדָמָה כִּי לוֹא־
not for earth mules pair-of load-of servant-of-you now! let-him-be-given

יַעֲשֶׂה עוֹד עַבְדְּךָ עֹלָה וָזֶבַח לֵאלֹהִים
to-gods or-sacrifice burnt-offering servant-of-you again he-will-make

אֲחֵרִים כִּי אִם־ לַיהוָה׃ לַדָּבָר הַזֶּה יִסְלַח
may-he-forgive the-this to-the-thing (18) to-Yahweh only except other-ones

יְהוָה לְעַבְדֶּךָ בְּבוֹא אֲדֹנִי בֵית־ רִמּוֹן
Rimmon temple-of master-of-me when-to-enter to-servant-of-you Yahweh

לְהִשְׁתַּחֲוֹת שָׁמָּה וְהוּא | נִשְׁעָן עַל־ יָדִי וְהִשְׁתַּחֲוֵיתִי בֵּית
temple-of and-I-bow arm-of-me on leaning and-he at-there to-bow-down

רִמֹּן בְּהִשְׁתַּחֲוָיָתִי בֵּית רִמֹּן יִסְלַח־ נא* יְהוָה
Yahweh now! may-he-forgive Rimmon temple-of when-to-bow-down-me Rimmon

לְעַבְדְּךָ בַּדָּבָר הַזֶּה׃ וַיֹּאמֶר לוֹ לֵךְ לְשָׁלוֹם
in-peace go! to-him and-he-said (19) the-this for-the-thing to-servant-of-you

the rivers of Damascus, better than any of the waters of Israel? Couldn't I wash in them and be cleansed?" So he turned and went off in a rage.

[13]Naaman's servants went to him and said, "My father, if the prophet had told you to do some great thing, would you not have done it? How much more, then, when he tells you, 'Wash and be cleansed'!" [14]So he went down and dipped himself in the Jordan seven times, as the man of God had told him, and his flesh was restored and became clean like that of a young boy.

[15]Then Naaman and all his attendants went back to the man of God. He stood before him and said, "Now I know that there is no God in all the world except in Israel. Please accept now a gift from your servant."

[16]The prophet answered, "As surely as the LORD lives, whom I serve, I will not accept a thing." And even though Naaman urged him, he refused.

[17]"If you will not," said Naaman, "please let me, your servant, be given as much earth as a pair of mules can carry, for your servant will never again make burnt offerings and sacrifices to any other god but the LORD. [18]But may the LORD forgive your servant for this one thing: When my master enters the temple of Rimmon to bow down and he is leaning on my arm and I bow there also—when I bow down in the temple of Rimmon, may the LORD forgive your servant for this."

[19]"Go in peace," Elisha said.

*18 Many mss omit this word or indicate in the *Qere* that it is not to be read.

וַיֵּלֶךְ מֵאִתּוֹ כִּבְרַת־ אָרֶץ׃ וַיֹּאמֶר גֵּיחֲזִי נַעַר

servant-of Gehazi and-he-said (20) land distance-of from-with-him so-he-went

אֱלִישָׁע אִישׁ־ הָאֱלֹהִים הִנֵּה ׀ חָשַׂךְ אֲדֹנִי אֶת־ נַעֲמָן הָאֲרַמִּי

the-Aramean Naaman *** master-of-me he-was-easy see! the-God man-of Elisha

הַזֶּה מִקַּחַת מִיָּדוֹ אֵת אֲשֶׁר־ הֵבִיא חַי־ יְהוָה

Yahweh life-of he-brought what *** from-hand-of-him from-to-accept the-this

כִּי־ אִם־ רַצְתִּי אַחֲרָיו וְלָקַחְתִּי מֵאִתּוֹ מְאוּמָה׃

something from-with-him and-I-will-get after-him I-will-run indeed that

וַיִּרְדֹּף גֵּיחֲזִי אַחֲרֵי נַעֲמָן וַיִּרְאֶה נַעֲמָן רָץ אַחֲרָיו

after-him running Naaman when-he-saw Naaman after Gehazi so-he-pursued (21)

וַיִּפֹּל מֵעַל הַמֶּרְכָּבָה לִקְרָאתוֹ וַיֹּאמֶר הֲשָׁלוֹם׃

all-right? and-he-asked to-meet-him the-chariot from-on then-he-got-down

וַיֹּאמֶר ׀ שָׁלוֹם אֲדֹנִי שְׁלָחַנִי לֵאמֹר הִנֵּה עַתָּה זֶה

here now see! to-say he-sent-me master-of-me all-right and-he-answered (22)

בָּאוּ אֵלַי שְׁנֵי־ נְעָרִים מֵהַר אֶפְרַיִם מִבְּנֵי

from-sons-of Ephraim from-hill-country-of young-men two-of to-me they-came

הַנְּבִיאִים תְּנָה־ נָּא לָהֶם כִּכַּר־ כֶּסֶף וּשְׁתֵּי חֲלִפוֹת בְּגָדִים׃

clothes sets-of and-two-of silver talent-of to-them now! give! the-prophets

וַיֹּאמֶר נַעֲמָן הוֹאֵל קַח כִּכָּרָיִם וַיִּפְרָץ־ בּוֹ

with-him and-he-urged two-talents take! be-willing! Naaman and-he-said (23)

וַיָּצַר כִּכְּרַיִם כֶּסֶף בִּשְׁנֵי חֲרִטִים וּשְׁתֵּי חֲלִפוֹת בְּגָדִים

clothes sets-of and-two-of bags in-two-of silver two-talents then-he-tied-up

וַיִּתֵּן אֶל־ שְׁנֵי נְעָרָיו וַיִּשְׂאוּ לְפָנָיו׃

ahead-of-him and-they-carried servants-of-him two-of to and-he-gave

וַיָּבֹא אֶל־ הָעֹפֶל וַיִּקַּח מִיָּדָם וַיִּפְקֹד

and-he-put-away from-hand-of-them then-he-took the-hill to when-he-came (24)

בַּבָּיִת וַיְשַׁלַּח אֶת־ הָאֲנָשִׁים וַיֵּלֵכוּ׃ וְהוּא־

then-he (25) and-they-left the-men *** then-he-sent-away in-the-house

בָא וַיַּעֲמֹד אֶל־ אֲדֹנָיו וַיֹּאמֶר אֵלָיו אֱלִישָׁע

Elisha to-him and-he-asked masters-of-him before and-he-stood he-went-in

°מֵאָן גֵּחֲזִי וַיֹּאמֶר לֹא־ הָלַךְ עַבְדְּךָ אָנֶה

to-here servant-of-you he-went not and-he-answered Gehazi from-where?

וָאָנָה׃ וַיֹּאמֶר אֵלָיו לֹא־ לִבִּי הָלַךְ כַּאֲשֶׁר

as-when he-went spirit-of-me not to-him but-he-said (26) or-to-there

הָפַךְ־ אִישׁ מֵעַל מֶרְכַּבְתּוֹ לִקְרָאתֶךָ הַעֵת לָקַחַת אֶת־

*** to-take time? to-meet-you chariot-of-him from-on man he-got-down

הַכֶּסֶף וְלָקַחַת בְּגָדִים וְזֵיתִים וּכְרָמִים וְצֹאן וּבָקָר

or-herd or-flock or-vineyards or-olive-groves clothes or-to-accept the-silver

°25 ק מאין

After Naaman had traveled some distance, [20]Gehazi, the servant of Elisha the man of God, said to himself, "My master was too easy on Naaman, this Aramean, by not accepting from him what he brought. As surely as the LORD lives, I will run after him and get something from him."

[21]So Gehazi hurried after Naaman. When Naaman saw him running toward him, he got down from the chariot to meet him. "Is everything all right?" he asked.

[22]"Everything is all right," Gehazi answered. "My master sent me to say, 'Two young men from the company of the prophets have just come to me from the hill country of Ephraim. Please give them a talent[g] of silver and two sets of clothing.'"

[23]"By all means, take two talents," said Naaman. He urged Gehazi to accept them, and then tied up the two talents of silver in two bags, with two sets of clothing. He gave them to two of his servants, and they carried them ahead of Gehazi. [24]When Gehazi came to the hill, he took the things from the servants and put them away in the house. He sent the men away and they left. [25]Then he went in and stood before his master Elisha.

"Where have you been, Gehazi?" Elisha asked.

"Your servant didn't go anywhere," Gehazi answered.

[26]But Elisha said to him, "Was not my spirit with you when the man got down from his chariot to meet you? Is this the time to take money, or to accept clothes, olive groves, vineyards, flocks, herds, or

g22 That is, about 75 pounds (about 34 kilograms)

וַעֲבָדִים וּשְׁפָחוֹת׃ וְצָרַעַת נַעֲמָן תִּדְבַּק־
she-will-cling Naaman now-leprosy-of (27) or-maidservants or-menservants

בְּךָ וּבְזַרְעֲךָ* לְעוֹלָם וַיֵּצֵא מִלְּפָנָיו
from-presences-of-him then-he-went to-forever and-to-descendant-of-you to-you

מְצֹרָע כַּשָּׁלֶג׃ וַיֹּאמְרוּ בְנֵי־ הַנְּבִיאִים אֶל־אֱלִישָׁע
Elisha to the-prophets sons-of and-they-said (6:1) as-the-snow being-leprous

הִנֵּה־ נָא הַמָּקוֹם אֲשֶׁר אֲנַחְנוּ יֹשְׁבִים שָׁם לְפָנֶיךָ צַר מִמֶּנּוּ׃
for-us too-small before-you there ones-sitting we where the-place now! look!

נֵלְכָה־ נָּא עַד־ הַיַּרְדֵּן וְנִקְחָה מִשָּׁם אִישׁ קוֹרָה אֶחָת
one pole each from-there and-let-us-get the-Jordan to now! let-us-go (2)

וְנַעֲשֶׂה־ לָּנוּ שָׁם מָקוֹם לָשֶׁבֶת שָׁם וַיֹּאמֶר לֵכוּ׃
go! and-he-said there to-live place there for-us and-let-us-build

וַיֹּאמֶר הָאֶחָד הוֹאֶל נָא וְלֵךְ אֶת־ עֲבָדֶיךָ
servants-of-you with and-come! now! be-willing! the-one then-he-said (3)

וַיֹּאמֶר אֲנִי אֵלֵךְ׃ וַיֵּלֶךְ אִתָּם וַיָּבֹאוּ
and-they-went with-them and-he-went (4) I-will-go I and-he-replied

הַיַּרְדֵּנָה וַיִּגְזְרוּ הָעֵצִים׃ וַיְהִי הָאֶחָד מַפִּיל
cutting-down the-one and-he-was (5) the-trees and-they-cut-down to-the-Jordan

הַקּוֹרָה וְאֶת־ הַבַּרְזֶל נָפַל אֶל־ הַמָּיִם וַיִּצְעַק וַיֹּאמֶר
and-he-said and-he-cried-out the-waters into he-fell the-iron and the-tree

אֲהָהּ אֲדֹנִי וְהוּא שָׁאוּל׃ וַיֹּאמֶר אִישׁ־ הָאֱלֹהִים
the-God man-of and-he-asked (6) being-borrowed now-he lord-of-me oh!

אָנָה נָפָל וַיַּרְאֵהוּ אֶת־ הַמָּקוֹם וַיִּקְצָב־ עֵץ
stick then-he-cut the-place *** when-he-showed-him he-fell at-where?

וַיַּשְׁלֶךְ־ שָׁמָּה וַיָּצֶף הַבַּרְזֶל׃ וַיֹּאמֶר הָרֶם
lift-out! and-he-said (7) the-iron and-he-made-float at-there and-he-threw

לָךְ וַיִּשְׁלַח יָדוֹ וַיִּקָּחֵהוּ׃ וּמֶלֶךְ אֲרָם
Aram now-king-of (8) and-he-took-him hand-of-him then-he-reached-out to-you

הָיָה נִלְחָם בְּיִשְׂרָאֵל וַיִּוָּעַץ אֶל־ עֲבָדָיו לֵאמֹר אֶל־
in to-say officers-of-him with and-he-conferred with-Israel warring he-was

מְקוֹם פְּלֹנִי אַלְמֹנִי תַּחֲנֹתִי׃ וַיִּשְׁלַח אִישׁ הָאֱלֹהִים אֶל־ מֶלֶךְ
king-of to the-God man-of and-he-sent (9) camp-of-me such such place-of

יִשְׂרָאֵל לֵאמֹר הִשָּׁמֶר מֵעֲבֹר הַמָּקוֹם הַזֶּה כִּי־ שָׁם אֲרָם
Aram there for the-that the-place of-to-pass beware! to-say Israel

נְחִתִּים׃ וַיִּשְׁלַח מֶלֶךְ יִשְׂרָאֵל אֶל־ הַמָּקוֹם אֲשֶׁר אָמַר־
he-told that the-place to Israel king-of and-he-sent (10) ones-going-down

לוֹ אִישׁ־ הָאֱלֹהִים וְהִזְהִירֹה° וְנִשְׁמַר שָׁם לֹא אַחַת
once not there so-he-was-on-guard and-he-warned-him the-God man-of to-him

menservants and maidservants? [27]Naaman's leprosy will cling to you and to your descendants forever." Then Gehazi went from Elisha's presence and he was leprous, as white as snow.

*An Axhead Floats*

6 The company of the prophets said to Elisha, "Look, the place where we meet with you is too small for us. [2]Let us go to the Jordan, where each of us can get a pole; and let us build a place there for us to live."

And he said, "Go."

[3]Then one of them said, "Won't you please come with your servants?"

"I will," Elisha replied. [4]And he went with them.

They went to the Jordan and began to cut down trees. [5]As one of them was cutting down a tree, the iron axhead fell into the water. "Oh, my lord," he cried out, "it was borrowed!"

[6]The man of God asked, "Where did it fall?" When he showed him the place, Elisha cut a stick and threw it there, and made the iron float. [7]"Lift it out," he said. Then the man reached out his hand and took it.

*Elisha Traps Blinded Arameans*

[8]Now the king of Aram was at war with Israel. After conferring with his officers, he said, "I will set up my camp in such and such a place."

[9]The man of God sent word to the king of Israel: "Beware of passing that place, because the Arameans are going down there." [10]So the king of Israel checked on the place indicated by the man of God. Time and again Elisha warned the king, so that he was on his guard in such places.

*27 Most mss have the accent *tipbha* ( ךָ־ ).

°*10* ק והזהירו

וְלֹא שְׁתָּיִם׃ וַיִּסָּעֵר לֵב מֶלֶךְ־אֲרָם עַל־הַדָּבָר
the-thing over Aram king-of heart-of and-he-was-enraged (11) twice and-not

הַזֶּה וַיִּקְרָא אֶל־ עֲבָדָיו וַיֹּאמֶר אֲלֵיהֶם הֲלוֹא תַּגִּידוּ
you-tell not? to-them and-he-said officers-of-him to and-he-summoned the-this

לִי מִי מִשֶּׁלָּנוּ אֶל־ מֶלֶךְ יִשְׂרָאֵל׃ וַיֹּאמֶר אַחַד
one and-he-said (12) Israel king-of with from-who-of-us who? to-me

מֵעֲבָדָיו לוֹא אֲדֹנִי הַמֶּלֶךְ כִּי־ אֱלִישָׁע הַנָּבִיא אֲשֶׁר
who the-prophet Elisha but the-king lord-of-me none from-officers-of-him

בְּיִשְׂרָאֵל יַגִּיד לְמֶלֶךְ יִשְׂרָאֵל אֶת־הַדְּבָרִים אֲשֶׁר תְּדַבֵּר בַּחֲדַר
in-room-of-you you-speak that the-words *** Israel to-king-of he-tells in-Israel

מִשְׁכָּבֶךָ׃ וַיֹּאמֶר לְכוּ וּרְאוּ אֵיכֹה הוּא וְאֶשְׁלַח
so-I-can-send he where and-find-out! go! and-he-ordered (13) sleep-of-you

וְאֶקָּחֵהוּ וַיֻּגַּד־ לוֹ לֵאמֹר הִנֵּה בְדֹתָן׃
in-Dothan see! to-say to-him and-he-was-reported and-I-can-capture-him

וַיִּשְׁלַח־ שָׁמָּה סוּסִים וְרֶכֶב וְחַיִל כָּבֵד וַיָּבֹאוּ
and-they-went strong and-force and-chariot horses to-there then-he-sent (14)

לַיְלָה וַיַּקִּפוּ עַל־ הָעִיר׃ וַיַּשְׁכֵּם מְשָׁרֵת
one-serving when-he-got-up (15) the-city around and-they-surrounded night

אִישׁ הָאֱלֹהִים לָקוּם וַיֵּצֵא וְהִנֵּה־ חַיִל סוֹבֵב אֶת־
*** surrounding army then-see! and-he-went-out to-rise the-God man-of

הָעִיר וְסוּס וָרָכֶב וַיֹּאמֶר נַעֲרוֹ אֵלָיו אֲהָהּ
oh! to-him servant-of-him and-he-asked and-chariot and-horse the-city

אֲדֹנִי אֵיכָה נַעֲשֶׂה׃ וַיֹּאמֶר אַל־ תִּירָא כִּי
for you-be-afraid not and-he-answered (16) shall-we-do what? lord-of-me

רַבִּים אֲשֶׁר אִתָּנוּ מֵאֲשֶׁר אוֹתָם׃ וַיִּתְפַּלֵּל אֱלִישָׁע
Elisha and-he-prayed (17) with-them more-than-who with-us who ones-many

וַיֹּאמַר יְהוָה פְּקַח־ נָא אֶת־ עֵינָיו וְיִרְאֶה וַיִּפְקַח
then-he-opened so-may-he-see eyes-of-him *** now! open! Yahweh and-he-said

יְהוָה אֶת־ עֵינֵי הַנַּעַר וַיַּרְא וְהִנֵּה הָהָר מָלֵא
being-full the-hill and-see! and-he-looked the-servant eyes-of *** Yahweh

סוּסִים וְרֶכֶב אֵשׁ סְבִיבֹת אֱלִישָׁע׃ וַיֵּרְדוּ
and-they-came-down (18) Elisha ones-around fire and-chariot-of horses

אֵלָיו וַיִּתְפַּלֵּל אֱלִישָׁע אֶל־ יְהוָה וַיֹּאמַר הַךְ־ נָא אֶת־
*** now! strike! and-he-said Yahweh to Elisha and-he-prayed toward-him

הַגּוֹי־ הַזֶּה בַּסַּנְוֵרִים וַיַּכֵּם בַּסַּנְוֵרִים
with-the-blindnesses so-he-struck-them with-the-blindnesses the-this the-people

כִּדְבַר אֱלִישָׁע׃ וַיֹּאמֶר אֲלֵהֶם אֱלִישָׁע לֹא זֶה הַדֶּרֶךְ
the-road this not Elisha to-them and-he-told (19) Elisha as-request-of

[11]This enraged the king of
Aram. He summoned his
officers and demanded of
them, "Will you not tell me
which of us is on the side of
the king of Israel?"
[12]"None of us, my lord the
king," said one of his officers,
"but Elisha, the prophet who
is in Israel, tells the king of Israel the very words you speak
in your bedroom."
[13]"Go, find out where he is,"
the king ordered, "so I can
send men and capture him."
The report came back: "He is
in Dothan." [14]Then he sent
horses and chariots and a
strong force there. They went
by night and surrounded the
city.
[15]When the servant of the
man of God got up and went
out early the next morning, an
army with horses and chariots
had surrounded the city. "Oh,
my lord, what shall we do?"
the servant asked.
[16]"Don't be afraid," the
prophet answered. "Those
who are with us are more than
those who are with them."
[17]And Elisha prayed, "O
LORD, open his eyes so he may
see." Then the LORD opened
the servant's eyes, and he
looked and saw the hills full of
horses and chariots of fire all
around Elisha.
[18]As the enemy came down
toward him, Elisha prayed to
the LORD, "Strike these people
with blindness." So he struck
them with blindness, as Elisha
had asked.
[19]Elisha told them, "This is
not the road and this is not the

וְלֹא זֶה הָעִיר לְכוּ אַחֲרַי וְאוֹלִיכָה אֶתְכֶם אֶל־ הָאִישׁ
the-man to you and-I-will-lead after-me follow! the-city this and-not

אֲשֶׁר תְּבַקֵּשׁוּן וַיֹּלֶךְ אוֹתָם שֹׁמְרוֹנָה׃ וַיְהִי כְּבֹאָם
as-to-enter-them and-he-was (20) to-Samaria them and-he-led you-look-for whom

שֹׁמְרוֹן וַיֹּאמֶר אֱלִישָׁע יְהוָה פְּקַח אֶת־ עֵינֵי־ אֵלֶּה וְיִרְאוּ
so-they-can-see these eyes-of *** open! Yahweh Elisha then-he-said Samaria

וַיִּפְקַח יְהוָה אֶת־ עֵינֵיהֶם וַיִּרְאוּ וְהִנֵּה בְּתוֹךְ
inside-of and-see! and-they-looked eyes-of-them *** Yahweh then-he-opened

שֹׁמְרוֹן׃ וַיֹּאמֶר מֶלֶךְ־ יִשְׂרָאֵל אֶל־אֱלִישָׁע כִּרְאֹתוֹ אוֹתָם
them when-to-see-him Elisha to Israel king-of and-he-asked (21) Samaria

הַאַכֶּה אַכֶּה אָבִי׃ וַיֹּאמֶר לֹא תַכֶּה
you-kill not and-he-answered (22) father-of-me shall-I-kill shall-I-kill?

הַאֲשֶׁר שָׁבִיתָ בְּחַרְבְּךָ וּבְקַשְׁתְּךָ אַתָּה מַכֶּה
killing you and-with-bow-of-you with-sword-of-you you-captured whom?

שִׂים לֶחֶם וָמַיִם לִפְנֵיהֶם וְיֹאכְלוּ וְיִשְׁתּוּ
and-they-may-drink so-they-may-eat before-them and-waters food set!

וְיֵלְכוּ אֶל־ אֲדֹנֵיהֶם׃ וַיִּכְרֶה לָהֶם
for-them then-he-gave-feast (23) masters-of-them to then-they-may-go-back

כֵּרָה גְדוֹלָה וַיֹּאכְלוּ וַיִּשְׁתּוּ וַיְשַׁלְּחֵם וַיֵּלְכוּ
and-they-returned and-he-sent-away-them and-they-drank and-they-ate great feast

אֶל־ אֲדֹנֵיהֶם וְלֹא־ יָסְפוּ עוֹד גְּדוּדֵי אֲרָם לָבוֹא
to-raid Aram bands-of again they-repeated and-not masters-of-them to

בְּאֶרֶץ יִשְׂרָאֵל׃ וַיְהִי אַחֲרֵי־ כֵן וַיִּקְבֹּץ בֶּן־ הֲדַד
Hadad Ben then-he-mobilized this after and-he-was (24) Israel in-territory-of

מֶלֶךְ־ אֲרָם אֶת־ כָּל־ מַחֲנֵהוּ וַיַּעַל וַיָּצַר
and-he-laid-siege and-he-marched-up army-of-him entire-of *** Aram king-of

עַל־שֹׁמְרוֹן׃ וַיְהִי רָעָב גָּדוֹל בְּשֹׁמְרוֹן וְהִנֵּה צָרִים
ones-laying-siege and-see! in-Samaria great famine and-he-was (25) Samaria to

עָלֶיהָ עַד הֱיוֹת רֹאשׁ־ חֲמוֹר בִּשְׁמֹנִים כֶּסֶף וְרֹבַע הַקַּב
the-cab and-fourth-of silver for-eighty donkey head-of to-be until to-them

חריוֹנים בַּחֲמִשָּׁה־ כָסֶף׃ וַיְהִי מֶלֶךְ יִשְׂרָאֵל עֹבֵר עַל־
on passing-by Israel king-of and-he-was (26) silver for-five dung-of-doves

הַחֹמָה וְאִשָּׁה צָעֲקָה אֵלָיו לֵאמֹר הוֹשִׁיעָה אֲדֹנִי הַמֶּלֶךְ׃
the-king lord-of-me help! to-say to-him she-cried and-woman the-wall

וַיֹּאמֶר אַל־ יוֹשִׁעֵךְ יְהוָה מֵאַיִן אוֹשִׁיעֵךְ
I-can-help-you from-where? Yahweh he-helps-you not and-he-replied (27)

הֲמִן־ הַגֹּרֶן אוֹ מִן־ הַיָּקֶב׃ וַיֹּאמֶר־ לָהּ
to-her then-he-asked (28) the-winepress from or the-threshing-floor from?

city. Follow me, and I will lead
you to the man you are looking for." And he led them to
Samaria.
20After they entered the city,
Elisha said, "LORD, open the
eyes of these men so they can
see." Then the LORD opened
their eyes and they looked,
and there they were, inside
Samaria.
21When the king of Israel
saw them, he asked Elisha,
"Shall I kill them, my father?
Shall I kill them?"
22"Do not kill them," he answered. "Would you kill men
you have captured with your
own sword or bow? Set food
and water before them so that
they may eat and drink and
then go back to their master."
23So he prepared a great feast
for them, and after they had
finished eating and drinking,
he sent them away, and they
returned to their master. So
the bands from Aram stopped
raiding Israel's territory.

*Famine in Besieged Samaria*

24Some time later, Ben-
Hadad king of Aram mobi-
lized his entire army and
marched up and laid siege to
Samaria. 25There was a great
famine in the city; the siege
lasted so long that a donkey's
head sold for eighty shekels[h]
of silver, and a fourth of a cab[i]
of seed pods[j] for five shekels.[k]
26As the king of Israel was
passing by on the wall, a
woman cried to him, "Help
me, my lord the king!"
27The king replied, "If the
LORD does not help you, where
can I get help for you? From
the threshing floor? From the
winepress?" 28Then he asked

[h]25 That is, about 2 pounds (about 1 kilogram)
[i]25 That is, probably about 1/2 pint (about 0.3 liter)
[j]25 Or *of dove's dung*
[k]25 That is, about 2 ounces (about 55 grams)

°25 ק דביונים

הַמֶּלֶךְ מַה־ לָּךְ וַתֹּאמֶר הָאִשָּׁה הַזֹּאת אָמְרָה אֵלַי
to-me she-said the-this the-woman and-she-answered to-you what? the-king

תְּנִי אֶת־ בְּנֵךְ וְנֹאכְלֶנּוּ הַיּוֹם וְאֶת־ בְּנִי נֹאכַל
we-will-eat son-of-me and the-day so-we-may-eat-him son-of-you *** give-up!

מָחָר׃ (29) וַנְּבַשֵּׁל אֶת־ בְּנִי וַנֹּאכְלֵהוּ וָאֹמַר אֵלֶיהָ
to-her and-I-said and-we-ate-him son-of-me *** so-we-cooked (29) tomorrow

בַּיּוֹם הָאַחֵר תְּנִי אֶת־ בְּנֵךְ וְנֹאכְלֶנּוּ וַתַּחְבִּא
but-she-hid so-we-may-eat-him son-of-you *** give-up! the-next on-the-day

אֶת־ בְּנָהּ׃ (30) וַיְהִי כִשְׁמֹעַ הַמֶּלֶךְ אֶת־ דִּבְרֵי הָאִשָּׁה
the-woman words-of *** the-king when-to-hear and-he-was (30) son-of-her ***

וַיִּקְרַע אֶת־ בְּגָדָיו וְהוּא עֹבֵר עַל־ הַחֹמָה וַיַּרְא
and-he-looked the-wall on going-along and-he robes-of-him *** then-he-tore

הָעָם וְהִנֵּה הַשַּׂק עַל־ בְּשָׂרוֹ מִבָּיִת׃ (31) וַיֹּאמֶר
and-he-said (31) underneath body-of-him on the-sackcloth and-see! the-people

כֹּה־ יַעֲשֶׂה־ לִּי אֱלֹהִים וְכֹה יוֹסִף אִם־ יַעֲמֹד רֹאשׁ
head-of he-remains if may-he-be-severe and-so God with-me may-he-deal so

אֱלִישָׁע בֶּן־ שָׁפָט עָלָיו הַיּוֹם׃ (32) וֶאֱלִישָׁע יֹשֵׁב בְּבֵיתוֹ
in-house-of-him sitting now-Elisha (32) the-day on-him Shaphat son-of Elisha

וְהַזְּקֵנִים יֹשְׁבִים אִתּוֹ וַיִּשְׁלַח אִישׁ מִלְּפָנָיו
at-ahead-of-him man and-he-sent with-him ones-sitting and-the-elders

בְּטֶרֶם יָבֹא הַמַּלְאָךְ אֵלָיו וְהוּא | אָמַר אֶל־ הַזְּקֵנִים
the-elders to he-said then-he to-him the-messenger he-arrived but-before

הַרְּאִיתֶם כִּי־ שָׁלַח בֶּן־ הַמְרַצֵּחַ הַזֶּה לְהָסִיר אֶת־
*** to-cut-off the-this the-one-murdering son-of he-sends how you-see?

רֹאשִׁי רְאוּ | כְּבֹא הַמַּלְאָךְ סִגְרוּ הַדֶּלֶת וּלְחַצְתֶּם
and-you-hold-shut the-door shut! the-messenger when-to-come look! head-of-me

אֹתוֹ בַּדֶּלֶת הֲלוֹא קוֹל רַגְלֵי אֲדֹנָיו אַחֲרָיו׃
behind-him masters-of-him feet-of sound-of not? with-the-door him

(33) עוֹדֶנּוּ מְדַבֵּר עִמָּם וְהִנֵּה הַמַּלְאָךְ יֹרֵד אֵלָיו
to-him coming-down the-messenger then-see! to-them talking while-he (33)

וַיֹּאמֶר הִנֵּה־ זֹאת הָרָעָה מֵאֵת יְהוָה מָה־ אוֹחִיל לַיהוָה
for-Yahweh should-I-wait why? Yahweh from the-disaster this see! and-he-said

עוֹד׃ (7:1) וַיֹּאמֶר אֱלִישָׁע שִׁמְעוּ דְּבַר־ יְהוָה כֹּה | אָמַר יְהוָה
Yahweh he-says this Yahweh word-of hear! Elisha and-he-said (7:1) longer

כָּעֵת | מָחָר סְאָה־ סֹלֶת בְּשֶׁקֶל וְסָאתַיִם שְׂעֹרִים
barleys and-two-seahs for-shekel flour seah tomorrow about-the-time

בְּשֶׁקֶל בְּשַׁעַר שֹׁמְרוֹן׃ (2) וַיַּעַן הַשָּׁלִישׁ אֲשֶׁר־ לַמֶּלֶךְ
by-the-king who the-officer and-he-answered (2) Samaria at-gate-of for-shekel

her, "What's the matter?"
She answered, "This woman said to me, 'Give up your son so we may eat him today, and tomorrow we'll eat my son.'
29 So we cooked my son and ate him. The next day I said to her, 'Give up your son so we may eat him,' but she had hidden him."
30 When the king heard the woman's words, he tore his robes. As he went along the wall, the people looked, and there, underneath, he had sackcloth on his body.
31 He said, "May God deal with me, be it ever so severely, if the head of Elisha son of Shaphat remains on his shoulders today!"
32 Now Elisha was sitting in his house, and the elders were sitting with him. The king sent a messenger ahead, but before he arrived, Elisha said to the elders, "Don't you see how this murderer is sending someone to cut off my head? Look, when the messenger comes, shut the door and hold it shut against him. Is not the sound of his master's footsteps behind him?"
33 While he was still talking to them, the messenger came down to him. And ⌞the king⌟ said, "This disaster is from the LORD. Why should I wait for the LORD any longer?"

7 Elisha said, "Hear the word of the LORD. This is what the LORD says: About this time tomorrow, a seah[l] of flour will sell for a shekel[m] and two seahs[n] of barley for a shekel at the gate of Samaria."
2 The officer on whose arm

[l] 1 That is, probably about 7 quarts (about 7.3 liters); also in verses 16 and 18

[m] 1 That is, about 2/5 ounce (about 11 grams); also in verses 16 and 18

[n] 1 That is, probably about 13 quarts (about 15 liters); also in verses 16 and 18

נִשְׁעָן עַל־ יָדוֹ אֶת־ אִישׁ הָאֱלֹהִים וַיֹּאמַר הִנֵּה יְהוָה עֹשֶׂה
opening Yahweh look! and-he-said the-God man-of *** arm-of-him on leaning

אֲרֻבּוֹת בַּשָּׁמַיִם הֲיִהְיֶה הַדָּבָר הַזֶּה וַיֹּאמֶר
and-he-answered the-this the-thing could-he-happen? of-the-heavens floodgates

הִנְּכָה רֹאֶה בְּעֵינֶיךָ וּמִשָּׁם לֹא תֹאכֵל׃ וְאַרְבָּעָה
now-four (3) you-will-eat not but-from-there with-eyes-of-you seeing see-you!

אֲנָשִׁים הָיוּ מְצֹרָעִים פֶּתַח הַשָּׁעַר וַיֹּאמְרוּ אִישׁ
each and-they-said the-gate entrance-of ones-being-leprous they-were men

אֶל־ רֵעֵהוּ מָה אֲנַחְנוּ יֹשְׁבִים פֹּה עַד־ מָתְנוּ׃ אִם־אָמַרְנוּ
we-say if (4) we-die until here ones-staying we why? fellow-of-him to

נָבוֹא הָעִיר וְהָרָעָב בָּעִיר וָמַתְנוּ שָׁם
there and-we-will-die in-the-city then-the-famine the-city we-will-go-into

וְאִם־ יָשַׁבְנוּ פֹה וָמָתְנוּ וְעַתָּה לְכוּ וְנִפְּלָה אֶל־
at and-let-us-surrender go! so-now then-we-will-die here we-stay and-if

מַחֲנֵה אֲרָם אִם־ יְחַיֻּנוּ נִחְיֶה וְאִם־ יְמִיתֻנוּ וָמָתְנוּ׃
then-we-will-die they-kill-us and-if we-will-live they-spare-us if Aram camp-of

וַיָּקֻמוּ בַנֶּשֶׁף לָבוֹא אֶל־ מַחֲנֵה אֲרָם וַיָּבֹאוּ עַד־
to when-they-reached Aram camp-of to to-go at-the-dusk and-they-got-up (5)

קְצֵה מַחֲנֵה אֲרָם וְהִנֵּה אֵין־ שָׁם אִישׁ׃ וַאדֹנָי
for-Lord (6) man there there-was-not then-see! Aram camp-of edge-of

הִשְׁמִיעַ אֶת־ מַחֲנֵה אֲרָם קוֹל רֶכֶב קוֹל סוּס קוֹל
sound-of horse sound-of chariot sound-of Aram camp-of *** he-caused-to-hear

חַיִל גָּדוֹל וַיֹּאמְרוּ אִישׁ אֶל־ אָחִיו הִנֵּה שָׂכַר־ עָלֵינוּ
against-us he-hired look! fellow-of-him to each so-they-said great army

מֶלֶךְ יִשְׂרָאֵל אֶת־ מַלְכֵי הַחִתִּים וְאֶת־ מַלְכֵי מִצְרַיִם לָבוֹא
to-attack Egypt kings-of and the-Hittites kings-of *** Israel king-of

עָלֵינוּ׃ וַיָּקוּמוּ וַיָּנוּסוּ בַנֶּשֶׁף וַיַּעַזְבוּ
and-they-abandoned into-the-dusk and-they-fled so-they-got-up (7) against-us

אֶת־ אָהֳלֵיהֶם וְאֶת־ סוּסֵיהֶם וְאֶת־ חֲמֹרֵיהֶם הַמַּחֲנֶה כַּאֲשֶׁר־
just-as the-camp donkeys-of-them and horses-of-them and tents-of-them ***

הִיא וַיָּנֻסוּ אֶל־ נַפְשָׁם׃ וַיָּבֹאוּ הַמְצֹרָעִים
the-ones-having-leprosy and-they-reached (8) life-of-them for and-they-ran she

הָאֵלֶּה עַד־ קְצֵה הַמַּחֲנֶה וַיָּבֹאוּ אֶל־ אֹהֶל אֶחָד וַיֹּאכְלוּ
and-they-ate one tent into and-they-went the-camp edge-of to the-these

וַיִּשְׁתּוּ וַיִּשְׂאוּ מִשָּׁם כֶּסֶף וְזָהָב וּבְגָדִים
and-clothes and-gold silver from-there and-they-carried and-they-drank

וַיֵּלְכוּ וַיַּטְמִנוּ וַיָּשֻׁבוּ וַיָּבֹאוּ אֶל־ אֹהֶל
tent into and-they-went and-they-returned and-they-hid and-they-went-off

the king was leaning said to the man of God, "Look, even if the LORD should open the floodgates of the heavens, could this happen?"

"You will see it with your own eyes," answered Elisha, "but you will not eat any of it!"

*The Siege Lifted*

[3]Now there were four men with leprosy° at the entrance of the city gate. They said to each other, "Why stay here until we die? [4]If we say, 'We'll go into the city'—the famine is there, and we will die. And if we stay here, we will die. So let's go over to the camp of the Arameans and surrender. If they spare us, we live; if they kill us, then we die."

[5]At dusk they got up and went to the camp of the Arameans. When they reached the edge of the camp, not a man was there, [6]for the Lord had caused the Arameans to hear the sound of chariots and horses and a great army, so that they said to one another, "Look, the king of Israel has hired the Hittite and Egyptian kings to attack us!" [7]So they got up and fled in the dusk and abandoned their tents and their horses and donkeys. They left the camp as it was and ran for their lives.

[8]The men who had leprosy reached the edge of the camp and entered one of the tents. They ate and drank, and carried away silver, gold and clothes, and went off and hid them. They returned and entered another tent and took

°3 The Hebrew word is used for various diseases affecting the skin—not necessarily leprosy; also in verse 8.

אַחֵר וַיִּשְׂאוּ מִשָּׁם וַיֵּלְכוּ וַיַּטְמִנוּ׃ וַיֹּאמְרוּ
then-they-said (9) and-they-hid and-they-went from-there and-they-took another

אִישׁ אֶל־ רֵעֵהוּ לֹא־ כֵן ׀ אֲנַחְנוּ עֹשִׂים הַיּוֹם הַזֶּה יוֹם־
day-of the-this the-day ones-doing we right not fellow-of-him to each

בְּשֹׂרָה הוּא וַאֲנַחְנוּ מַחְשִׁים וְחִכִּינוּ עַד־ אוֹר
light-of until if-we-wait ones-keeping-silent and-we he good-news

הַבֹּקֶר וּמְצָאָנוּ עָווֹן וְעַתָּה לְכוּ וְנָבֹאָה
and-let-us-go go! so-now punishment then-he-will-overtake-us the-morning

וְנַגִּידָה בֵּית הַמֶּלֶךְ׃ וַיָּבֹאוּ וַיִּקְרְאוּ אֶל־
to and-they-called so-they-went (10) the-king palace-of and-let-us-report

שֹׁעֵר הָעִיר וַיַּגִּידוּ לָהֶם לֵאמֹר בָּאנוּ אֶל־ מַחֲנֵה
camp-of into we-went to-say to-them and-they-told the-city gatekeeper-of

אֲרָם וְהִנֵּה אֵין־ שָׁם אִישׁ וְקוֹל אָדָם כִּי אִם־
only except anyone or-sound-of man there there-was-not and-see! Aram

הַסּוּס אָסוּר וְהַחֲמוֹר אָסוּר וְאֹהָלִים כַּאֲשֶׁר־
just-as and-tents being-tethered and-the-donkey being-tethered the-horse

הֵמָּה׃ וַיִּקְרָא הַשֹּׁעֲרִים וַיַּגִּידוּ בֵּית הַמֶּלֶךְ
the-king palace-of and-they-reported the-gatekeepers and-he-shouted (11) they

פְּנִימָה׃ וַיָּקָם הַמֶּלֶךְ לַיְלָה וַיֹּאמֶר אֶל־ עֲבָדָיו
officers-of-him to and-he-said night the-king and-he-got-up (12) at-inside

אַגִּידָה־ נָּא לָכֶם אֵת אֲשֶׁר־ עָשׂוּ לָנוּ אֲרָם יָדְעוּ כִּי־
that they-know Aram to-us they-did what *** to-you now! I-will-tell

רְעֵבִים אֲנַחְנוּ וַיֵּצְאוּ מִן־ הַמַּחֲנֶה לְהֵחָבֵה בַהשָּׂדֶה לֵאמֹר
to-think in-the-field to-hide the-camp from so-they-left we ones-starving

כִּי־ יֵצְאוּ מִן־ הָעִיר וְנִתְפְּשֵׂם חַיִּים
ones-alive then-we-will-take-them the-city from they-will-come-out surely

וְאֶל־ הָעִיר נָבֹא׃ וַיַּעַן אֶחָד מֵעֲבָדָיו
of-officers-of-him one and-he-answered (13) we-will-go the-city and-into

וַיֹּאמֶר וְיִקְחוּ־ נָא חֲמִשָּׁה מִן־ הַסּוּסִים הַנִּשְׁאָרִים
the-ones-being-left the-horses from five now! now-let-them-take and-he-said

אֲשֶׁר נִשְׁאֲרוּ־ בָהּ הִנָּם כְּכָל־ הֶהָמוֹן יִשְׂרָאֵל אֲשֶׁר נִשְׁאֲרוּ־
they-are-left who Israel rest-of as-all-of see-they! in-her they-are-left that

בָהּ הִנָּם כְּכָל־ הֲמוֹן יִשְׂרָאֵל אֲשֶׁר־ תָּמּוּ וְנִשְׁלְחָה
now-let-us-send they-are-doomed who Israel rest-of as-all-of see-they! in-her

וְנִרְאֶה׃ וַיִּקְחוּ שְׁנֵי רֶכֶב סוּסִים וַיִּשְׁלַח
and-he-sent horses chariot-of two-of so-they-selected (14) and-let-us-find-out

הַמֶּלֶךְ אַחֲרֵי מַחֲנֵה־ אֲרָם לֵאמֹר לְכוּ וּרְאוּ׃ וַיֵּלְכוּ
and-they-followed (15) and-find-out! go! to-say Aram army-of after the-king

some things from it and hid them also.

9 Then they said to each other, "We're not doing right. This is a day of good news and we are keeping it to ourselves. If we wait until daylight, punishment will overtake us. Let's go at once and report this to the royal palace."

10 So they went and called out to the city gatekeepers and told them, "We went into the Aramean camp and not a man was there—not a sound of anyone—only tethered horses and donkeys, and the tents left just as they were." 11 The gatekeepers shouted the news, and it was reported within the palace.

12 The king got up in the night and said to his officers, "I will tell you what the Arameans have done to us. They know we are starving; so they have left the camp to hide in the countryside, thinking, 'They will surely come out, and then we will take them alive and get into the city.'"

13 One of his officers answered, "Have some men take five of the horses that are left in the city. Their plight will be like that of all the Israelites left here—yes, they will only be like all these Israelites who are doomed. So let us send them to find out what happened."

14 So they selected two chariots with their horses, and the king sent them after the Aramean army. He commanded the drivers, "Go and find out what has happened." 15 They

°12 ק בשדה
°13 ק המון

אַחֲרֵיהֶם עַד־ הַיַּרְדֵּן וְהִנֵּה כָל־ הַדֶּרֶךְ מְלֵאָה בְגָדִים
clothes full the-road whole-of and-see! the-Jordan as-far-as after-them

וְכֵלִים אֲשֶׁר־ הִשְׁלִיכוּ אֲרָם בְּהֶחָפְזָם וַיָּשֻׁבוּ
so-they-returned when-to-flee-them Aram they-threw-down that and-equipments

הַמַּלְאָכִים וַיַּגִּדוּ לַמֶּלֶךְ׃ וַיֵּצֵא הָעָם
the-people then-he-went-out (16) to-the-king and-they-reported the-messengers

וַיָּבֹזּוּ אֵת מַחֲנֵה אֲרָם וַיְהִי סְאָה־ סֹלֶת בְּשֶׁקֶל
for-shekel flour seah so-he-was Aram camp-of *** and-they-plundered

וְסָאתַיִם שְׂעֹרִים בְּשֶׁקֶל כִּדְבַר יְהוָה׃ וְהַמֶּלֶךְ
now-the-king (17) Yahweh as-word-of for-shekel barleys and-two-seahs

הִפְקִיד אֶת־ הַשָּׁלִישׁ אֲשֶׁר־ נִשְׁעָן עַל־ יָדוֹ עַל־ הַשַּׁעַר
the-gate over arm-of-him on leaning whom the-officer *** he-put-in-charge

וַיִּרְמְסֻהוּ הָעָם בַּשַּׁעַר וַיָּמֹת כַּאֲשֶׁר
just-as and-he-died in-the-gateway the-people and-they-trampled-him

דִּבֶּר אִישׁ הָאֱלֹהִים אֲשֶׁר דִּבֶּר בְּרֶדֶת הַמֶּלֶךְ אֵלָיו׃
to-him the-king when-to-come-down he-foretold who the-God man-of he-foretold

וַיְהִי כְּדַבֵּר אִישׁ הָאֱלֹהִים אֶל־ הַמֶּלֶךְ לֵאמֹר סָאתַיִם
two-seahs to-say the-king to the-God man-of as-to-say and-he-happened (18)

שְׂעֹרִים בְּשֶׁקֶל וּסְאָה־ סֹלֶת בְּשֶׁקֶל יִהְיֶה כָּעֵת
about-the-time he-will-be for-shekel flour and-seah for-shekel barleys

מָחָר בְּשַׁעַר שֹׁמְרוֹן׃ וַיַּעַן הַשָּׁלִישׁ אֶת־ אִישׁ
man-of *** the-officer and-he-answered (19) Samaria at-gate-of tomorrow

הָאֱלֹהִים וַיֹּאמַר וְהִנֵּה יְהוָה עֹשֶׂה אֲרֻבּוֹת בַּשָּׁמַיִם
of-the-heavens floodgates opening Yahweh now-look! and-he-said the-God

הֲיִהְיֶה כַּדָּבָר הַזֶּה וַיֹּאמֶר הִנְּךָ רֹאֶה
seeing see-you! and-he-replied the-this as-the-thing could-he-happen?

בְּעֵינֶיךָ וּמִשָּׁם לֹא תֹאכֵל׃ וַיְהִי־ לוֹ
to-him and-he-happened (20) you-will-eat not but-from-there with-eyes-of-you

כֵּן וַיִּרְמְסוּ אֹתוֹ הָעָם בַּשַּׁעַר וַיָּמֹת׃
so-he-died in-the-gateway the-people him for-they-trampled exactly

וֶאֱלִישָׁע דִּבֶּר אֶל־ הָאִשָּׁה אֲשֶׁר־ הֶחֱיָה אֶת־ בְּנָהּ
son-of-her *** he-restored-to-life whom the-woman to he-said now-Elisha (8:1)

לֵאמֹר קוּמִי וּלְכִי אַתְּי וּבֵיתֵךְ וְגוּרִי בַּאֲשֶׁר
at-where and-stay! and-family-of-you you and-go-away! get-up! to-say

תָּגוּרִי כִּי־ קָרָא יְהוָה לָרָעָב וְגַם־ בָּא
he-will-come and-also for-the-famine Yahweh he-decreed for you-can-stay

אֶל־ הָאָרֶץ שֶׁבַע שָׁנִים׃ וַתָּקָם הָאִשָּׁה וַתַּעַשׂ כִּדְבַר
as-word-of and-she-did the-woman so-she-got-up (2) years seven the-land onto

followed them as far as the Jordan, and they found the whole
road strewn with the clothing
and equipment the Arameans
had thrown away in their
headlong flight. So the messengers returned and reported
to the king. [16]Then the people
went out and plundered the
camp of the Arameans. So a
seah of flour sold for a shekel,
and two seahs of barley sold
for a shekel, as the LORD had
said.

[17]Now the king had put the
officer on whose arm he
leaned in charge of the gate,
and the people trampled him
in the gateway, and he died,
just as the man of God had
foretold when the king came
down to his house. [18]It happened as the man of God had
said to the king: "About this
time tomorrow, a seah of flour
will sell for a shekel and two
seahs of barley for a shekel at
the gate of Samaria."

[19]The officer had said to the
man of God, "Look, even if the
LORD should open the floodgates of the heavens, could
this happen?" The man of God
had replied, "You will see it
with your own eyes, but you
will not eat any of it!" [20]And
that is exactly what happened
to him, for the people trampled him in the gateway, and
he died.

*The Shunammite's Land Restored*

8 Now Elisha had said to
the woman whose son he
had restored to life, "Go away
with your family and stay for
a while wherever you can, because the LORD has decreed a
famine in the land that will
last seven years." [2]The woman
proceeded to do as the man of

°15 ק בחפזם
°1 ק את

אִישׁ הָאֱלֹהִים וַתֵּלֶךְ הִיא וּבֵיתָהּ וַתָּגָר
and-she-stayed and-family-of-her she and-she-went-away the-God man-of

בְּאֶרֶץ־ פְּלִשְׁתִּים שֶׁבַע שָׁנִים׃ וַיְהִי מִקְצֵה שֶׁבַע שָׁנִים
years seven at-end-of and-he-was (3) years seven Philistines in-land-of

וַתָּשָׁב הָאִשָּׁה מֵאֶרֶץ פְּלִשְׁתִּים וַתֵּצֵא לִצְעֹק
to-beg and-she-went Philistines from-land-of the-woman then-she-came-back

אֶל־ הַמֶּלֶךְ אֶל־ בֵּיתָהּ וְאֶל־ שָׂדָהּ׃ וְהַמֶּלֶךְ מְדַבֵּר
talking and-the-king (4) land-of-her and-for house-of-her for the-king to

אֶל־ גֵּחֲזִי נַעַר אִישׁ־ הָאֱלֹהִים לֵאמֹר סַפְּרָה־ נָּא לִי אֵת כָּל־
all-of *** to-me now! tell! to-say the-God man-of servant-of Gehazi to

הַגְּדֹלוֹת אֲשֶׁר־ עָשָׂה אֱלִישָׁע׃ וַיְהִי הוּא מְסַפֵּר לַמֶּלֶךְ
to-the-king telling he and-he-was (5) Elisha he-did that the-great-things

אֵת אֲשֶׁר־ הֶחֱיָה אֶת־ הַמֵּת וְהִנֵּה הָאִשָּׁה אֲשֶׁר־
whom the-woman then-see! the-dead *** he-restored-to-life how ***

הֶחֱיָה אֶת־ בְּנָהּ צֹעֶקֶת אֶל־ הַמֶּלֶךְ עַל־ בֵּיתָהּ
house-of-her for the-king to begging son-of-her *** he-restored-to-life

וְעַל־ שָׂדָהּ וַיֹּאמֶר גֵּחֲזִי אֲדֹנִי הַמֶּלֶךְ זֹאת הָאִשָּׁה
the-woman this the-king lord-of-me Gehazi and-he-said land-of-her and-for

וְזֶה־ בְּנָהּ אֲשֶׁר־ הֶחֱיָה אֱלִישָׁע׃ וַיִּשְׁאַל הַמֶּלֶךְ
the-king and-he-asked (6) Elisha he-restored-to-life whom son-of-her and-this

לָאִשָּׁה וַתְּסַפֶּר־ לוֹ וַיִּתֶּן־ לָהּ הַמֶּלֶךְ סָרִיס
official the-king to-her then-he-assigned to-him and-she-told to-the-woman

אֶחָד לֵאמֹר הָשֵׁיב אֶת־ כָּל־ אֲשֶׁר־ לָהּ וְאֵת כָּל־ תְּבוּאֹת הַשָּׂדֶה
the-land income-of all-of and to-her that all *** give-back! to-say one

מִיּוֹם עָזְבָה אֶת־ הָאָרֶץ וְעַד־ עָתָּה׃ וַיָּבֹא אֱלִישָׁע דַּמֶּשֶׂק
Damascus Elisha now-he-went (7) now and-to the-land *** she-left from-day

וּבֶן־ הֲדַד מֶלֶךְ־ אֲרָם חֹלֶה וַיֻּגַּד־ לוֹ לֵאמֹר בָּא
he-came to-say to-him when-he-was-told being-ill Aram king-of Hadad and-Ben

אִישׁ הָאֱלֹהִים עַד־ הֵנָּה׃ וַיֹּאמֶר הַמֶּלֶךְ אֶל־ חֲזָהאֵל קַח
take! Hazael to the-king and-he-said (8) to-here to the-God man-of

בְּיָדְךָ מִנְחָה וְלֵךְ לִקְרַאת אִישׁ הָאֱלֹהִים וְדָרַשְׁתָּ אֶת־
*** and-you-consult the-God man-of to-meet and-go! gift in-hand-of-you

יְהוָה מֵאוֹתוֹ לֵאמֹר הַאֶחְיֶה מֵחֳלִי זֶה׃ וַיֵּלֶךְ
so-he-went (9) this from-illness will-I-recover? to-ask through-him Yahweh

חֲזָאֵל לִקְרָאתוֹ וַיִּקַּח מִנְחָה בְיָדוֹ וְכָל־ טוּב
finery-of and-all-of in-hand-of-him gift and-he-took to-meet-him Hazael

דַּמֶּשֶׂק מַשָּׂא אַרְבָּעִים גָּמָל וַיָּבֹא וַיַּעֲמֹד לְפָנָיו וַיֹּאמֶר
and-he-said before-him and-he-stood and-he-went camel forty load-of Damascus

God said. She and her family went away and stayed in the land of the Philistines seven years.

[3]At the end of the seven years she came back from the land of the Philistines and went to the king to beg for her house and land.
[4]The king was talking to Gehazi, the servant of the man of God, and had said, "Tell me about all the great things Elisha has done."
[5]Just as Gehazi was telling the king how Elisha had restored the dead to life, the woman whose son Elisha had brought back to life came to beg the king for her house and land.

Gehazi said, "This is the woman, my lord the king, and this is her son whom Elisha restored to life."
[6]The king asked the woman about it, and she told him.

Then he assigned an official to her case and said to him, "Give back everything that belonged to her, including all the income from her land from the day she left the country until now."

*Hazael Murders Ben-Hadad*

[7]Elisha went to Damascus, and Ben-Hadad king of Aram was ill. When the king was told, "The man of God has come all the way up here,"
[8]he said to Hazael, "Take a gift with you and go to meet the man of God. Consult the LORD through him; ask him, 'Will I recover from this illness?' "

[9]Hazael went to meet Elisha, taking with him as a gift forty camel-loads of all the finest wares of Damascus. He went in and stood before him, and

בִּנְךָ֩ בֶן־הֲדַ֨ד מֶֽלֶךְ־אֲרָ֜ם שְׁלָחַ֤נִי אֵלֶ֙יךָ֙ לֵאמֹ֔ר הַאֶחְיֶ֖ה
will-I-recover? to-ask to-you he-sent-me Aram king-of Hadad Ben son-of-you

מֵחֳלִ֥י זֶֽה׃ (10) וַיֹּ֤אמֶר אֵלָיו֙ אֱלִישָׁ֔ע לֵ֥ךְ אֱמָר־ *לֹ֖א
*to-him say! go! Elisha to-him and-he-answered (10) this from-illness

חָיֹ֣ה תִֽחְיֶ֑ה וְהִרְאַ֥נִי יְהוָ֖ה כִּֽי־ מ֥וֹת
to-die that Yahweh but-he-revealed-to-me you-will-recover to-recover

יָמֽוּת׃ (11) וַיַּעֲמֵ֥ד אֶת־ פָּנָ֖יו וַיָּ֣שֶׂם עַד־
until and-he-stared faces-of-him *** and-he-set (11) he-will-die

בֹּ֑שׁ וַיֵּ֖בְךְּ אִ֥ישׁ הָאֱלֹהִֽים׃ (12) וַיֹּ֣אמֶר חֲזָאֵ֔ל מַדּ֖וּעַ
why? Hazael then-he-asked (12) the-God man-of then-he-wept to-be-ashamed

אֲדֹנִ֣י בֹכֶ֑ה וַיֹּ֡אמֶר כִּֽי־ יָדַ֡עְתִּי אֵת֩ אֲשֶׁר־ תַּעֲשֶׂ֨ה
you-will-do that *** I-know because and-he-answered weeping lord-of-me

לִבְנֵ֣י יִשְׂרָאֵל֮ רָעָה֒ מִבְצְרֵיהֶ֞ם תְּשַׁלַּ֣ח בָּאֵ֗שׁ
with-fire you-will-set fortified-places-of-them harm Israel to-sons-of

וּבַחֻרֵיהֶם֙ בַּחֶ֣רֶב תַּהֲרֹ֔ג וְעֹלְלֵיהֶ֣ם
and-children-of-them you-will-kill with-the-sword and-young-men-of-them

תְּרַטֵּ֔שׁ וְהָרֹתֵיהֶ֖ם תְּבַקֵּֽעַ׃
you-will-rip-open and-pregnant-women-of-them you-will-dash-to-ground

(13) וַיֹּ֣אמֶר חֲזָהאֵ֔ל כִּ֣י מָ֤ה עַבְדְּךָ֙ הַכֶּ֔לֶב כִּ֣י יַעֲשֶׂ֔ה
he-could-do indeed the-dog servant-of-you how? indeed Hazael and-he-said (13)

הַדָּבָ֥ר הַגָּד֖וֹל הַזֶּ֑ה וַיֹּ֣אמֶר אֱלִישָׁ֔ע הִרְאַ֧נִי יְהוָ֛ה אֹתְךָ֖
you Yahweh he-showed-me Elisha and-he-answered the-this the-great the-feat

מֶ֥לֶךְ עַל־ אֲרָֽם׃ (14) וַיֵּלֶךְ֙ ׀ מֵאֵ֣ת אֱלִישָׁ֔ע וַיָּבֹא֙ אֶל־ אֲדֹנָ֔יו
masters-of-him to and-he-returned Elisha from then-he-left (14) Aram over king

וַיֹּ֣אמֶר ל֔וֹ מָֽה־ אָמַ֥ר לְךָ֖ אֱלִישָׁ֑ע וַיֹּ֕אמֶר אָ֥מַר
he-told and-he-replied Elisha to-you he-said what? to-him when-he-asked

לִ֖י חָיֹ֥ה תִֽחְיֶֽה׃ (15) וַיְהִ֣י מִֽמָּחֳרָ֗ת וַיִּקַּ֤ח
then-he-took on-next-day but-he-was (15) you-will-recover to-recover to-me

הַמַּכְבֵּר֙ וַיִּטְבֹּ֣ל בַּמַּ֔יִם וַיִּפְרֹ֥שׂ עַל־ פָּנָ֖יו
faces-of-him over and-he-spread in-the-waters and-he-soaked the-cloth

וַיָּמֹ֑ת וַיִּמְלֹ֥ךְ חֲזָהאֵ֖ל תַּחְתָּֽיו׃ (16) וּבִשְׁנַ֣ת חָמֵ֗שׁ
five in-year-of (16) in-place-of-him Hazael and-he-became-king and-he-died

לְיוֹרָ֤ם בֶּן־ אַחְאָב֙ מֶ֣לֶךְ יִשְׂרָאֵ֔ל וִיהוֹשָׁפָ֖ט מֶ֣לֶךְ יְהוּדָ֑ה
Judah king-of when-Jehoshaphat Israel king-of Ahab son-of of-Joram

מָלַ֛ךְ יְהוֹרָ֥ם בֶּן־ יְהוֹשָׁפָ֖ט מֶ֥לֶךְ יְהוּדָֽה׃ (17) בֶּן־ שְׁלֹשִׁ֨ים
thirty son-of (17) Judah king-of Jehoshaphat son-of Jehoram he-became-king

וּשְׁתַּ֤יִם שָׁנָה֙ הָיָ֣ה בְמָלְכ֔וֹ וּשְׁמֹנֶ֣ה שָׁנָ֔ה מָלַ֖ךְ
he-reigned years and-eight when-to-become-king-him he-was year and-two

said, "Your son Ben-Hadad king of Aram has sent me to ask, 'Will I recover from this illness?' "

10 Elisha answered, "Go and say to him, 'You will certainly recover'; but[p] the LORD has revealed to me that he will in fact die." 11 He stared at him with a fixed gaze until Hazael felt ashamed. Then the man of God began to weep.

12 "Why is my lord weeping?" asked Hazael.

"Because I know the harm you will do to the Israelites," he answered. "You will set fire to their fortified places, kill their young men with the sword, dash their little children to the ground, and rip open their pregnant women."

13 Hazael said, "How could your servant, a mere dog, accomplish such a feat?"

"The LORD has shown me that you will become king of Aram," answered Elisha.

14 Then Hazael left Elisha and returned to his master. When Ben-Hadad asked, "What did Elisha say to you?" Hazael replied, "He told me that you would certainly recover." 15 But the next day he took a thick cloth, soaked it in water and spread it over the king's face, so that he died. Then Hazael succeeded him as king.

*Jehoram King of Judah*

16 In the fifth year of Joram son of Ahab king of Israel, when Jehoshaphat was king of Judah, Jehoram son of Jehoshaphat began his reign as king of Judah. 17 He was thirty-two years old when he became king, and he reigned in

p10 *The Hebrew may also be read Go and say, 'You will certainly not recover,' for.*

*10 The *Kethib* form reads *not;* the *Qere* reads *to-him.*

°10 ק לו

°17 ק שנים

בִּירוּשָׁלִָם׃ וַיֵּלֶךְ בְּדֶרֶךְ מַלְכֵי יִשְׂרָאֵל כַּאֲשֶׁר עָשׂוּ
they-did just-as Israel kings-of in-way-of and-he-walked (18) in-Jerusalem

בֵּית אַחְאָב כִּי בַת־אַחְאָב הָיְתָה־לּוֹ לְאִשָּׁה וַיַּעַשׂ
and-he-did as-wife to-him she-was Ahab daughter-of for Ahab house-of

הָרַע בְּעֵינֵי יְהוָה׃ וְלֹא־אָבָה יְהוָה לְהַשְׁחִית
to-destroy Yahweh he-was-willing but-not (19) Yahweh in-eyes-of the-evil

אֶת־יְהוּדָה לְמַעַן דָּוִד עַבְדּוֹ כַּאֲשֶׁר אָמַר־לוֹ
to-him he-promised just-as servant-of-him David for-sake-of Judah ***

לָתֵת לוֹ נִיר לְבָנָיו כָּל־הַיָּמִים׃
the-days all-of for-descendants-of-him lamp for-him to-maintain

בְּיָמָיו פָּשַׁע אֱדוֹם מִתַּחַת יַד־יְהוּדָה וַיַּמְלִכוּ
and-they-set-king Judah hand-of from-under Edom he-rebelled in-days-of-him (20)

עֲלֵיהֶם מֶלֶךְ׃ וַיַּעֲבֹר יוֹרָם צָעִירָה וְכָל־הָרֶכֶב עִמּוֹ
with-him the-chariot and-all-of to-Zair Joram so-he-went (21) king over-them

וַיְהִי־הוּא קָם לַיְלָה וַיַּכֶּה אֶת־אֱדוֹם הַסֹּבֵיב
the-one-surrounding Edom *** and-he-broke-through night he-rose he and-he-was

אֵלָיו וְאֵת שָׂרֵי הָרֶכֶב וַיָּנָס הָעָם לְאֹהָלָיו׃
to-homes-of-him the-army but-he-fled the-chariot commanders-of and around-him

וַיִּפְשַׁע אֱדוֹם מִתַּחַת יַד־יְהוּדָה עַד הַיּוֹם הַזֶּה אָז
then the-this the-day to Judah hand-of from-under Edom and-he-rebels (22)

תִּפְשַׁע לִבְנָה בָּעֵת הַהִיא׃ וְיֶתֶר דִּבְרֵי יוֹרָם
Joram events-of and-rest-of (23) the-same at-the-time Libnah she-revolted

וְכָל־אֲשֶׁר עָשָׂה הֲלוֹא־הֵם כְּתוּבִים עַל־סֵפֶר דִּבְרֵי
annals-of book-of in ones-being-written they not? he-did that and-all

הַיָּמִים לְמַלְכֵי יְהוּדָה׃ וַיִּשְׁכַּב יוֹרָם עִם־אֲבֹתָיו
fathers-of-him with Joram and-he-rested (24) Judah of-kings-of the-days

וַיִּקָּבֵר עִם־אֲבֹתָיו בְּעִיר דָּוִד וַיִּמְלֹךְ
and-he-became-king David in-City-of fathers-of-him with and-he-was-buried

אֲחַזְיָהוּ בְנוֹ תַּחְתָּיו׃ בִּשְׁנַת שְׁתֵּים־עֶשְׂרֵה שָׁנָה לְיוֹרָם
of-Joram year ten two in-year-of (25) in-place-of-him son-of-him Ahaziah

בֶּן־אַחְאָב מֶלֶךְ יִשְׂרָאֵל מָלַךְ אֲחַזְיָהוּ בֶן־יְהוֹרָם מֶלֶךְ
king-of Jehoram son-of Ahaziah he-became-king Israel king-of Ahab son-of

יְהוּדָה׃ בֶּן־עֶשְׂרִים וּשְׁתַּיִם שָׁנָה אֲחַזְיָהוּ בְמָלְכוֹ
when-to-become-king-him Ahaziah year and-two twenty son-of (26) Judah

וְשָׁנָה אַחַת מָלַךְ בִּירוּשָׁלִָם וְשֵׁם אִמּוֹ עֲתַלְיָהוּ
Athaliah mother-of-him and-name-of in-Jerusalem he-reigned one and-year

בַּת־עָמְרִי מֶלֶךְ יִשְׂרָאֵל׃ וַיֵּלֶךְ בְּדֶרֶךְ בֵּית אַחְאָב
Ahab house-of in-way-of and-he-walked (27) Israel king-of Omri daughter-of

Jerusalem eight years. 18He
walked in the ways of the
kings of Israel, as the house of
Ahab had done, for he married a daughter of Ahab. He
did evil in the eyes of the
LORD. 19Nevertheless, for the
sake of his servant David, the
LORD was not willing to destroy Judah. He had promised
to maintain a lamp for David
and his descendants forever.
20In the time of Jehoram,
Edom rebelled against Judah
and set up its own king. 21So
Jehoram[q] went to Zair with all
his chariots. The Edomites
surrounded him and his chariot commanders, but he rose
up and broke through by
night; his army, however, fled
back home. 22To this day
Edom has been in rebellion
against Judah. Libnah revolted at the same time.
23As for the other events of
Jehoram's reign, and all he
did, are they not written in the
book of the annals of the kings
of Judah? 24Jehoram rested
with his fathers and was buried with them in the City of
David. And Ahaziah his son
succeeded him as king.

*Ahaziah King of Judah*

25In the twelfth year of
Joram son of Ahab king of Israel, Ahaziah son of Jehoram
king of Judah began to reign.
26Ahaziah was twenty-two
years old when he became
king, and he reigned in
Jerusalem one year. His
mother's name was Athaliah,
a granddaughter of Omri king
of Israel. 27He walked in the
ways of the house of Ahab and

q21 Hebrew *Joram*, a variant of *Jehoram*; also in verses 23 and 24

וַיַּעַשׂ הָרַע בְּעֵינֵי יְהוָה כְּבֵית אַחְאָב כִּי חֲתַן
son-in-law-of for Ahab as-house-of Yahweh in-eyes-of the-evil and-he-did

בֵּית־אַחְאָב הוּא׃ וַיֵּלֶךְ אֶת־ יוֹרָם בֶּן־ אַחְאָב לַמִּלְחָמָה עִם־
against to-the-war Ahab son-of Joram with and-he-went (28) he Ahab house-of

חֲזָהאֵל מֶלֶךְ־ אֲרָם בְּרָמֹת גִּלְעָד וַיַּכּוּ אֲרַמִּים אֶת־יוֹרָם׃
Joram *** Arameans and-they-wounded Gilead at-Ramoth Aram king-of Hazael

וַיָּשָׁב יוֹרָם הַמֶּלֶךְ לְהִתְרַפֵּא בְיִזְרְעֶאל מִן־ הַמַּכִּים
the-wounds from in-Jezreel to-recover the-king Joram so-he-returned (29)

אֲשֶׁר יַכֻּהוּ אֲרַמִּים בָּרָמָה בְּהִלָּחֲמוֹ אֶת־
*** when-to-fight-him at-the-Ramah Arameans they-inflicted-on-him that

חֲזָהאֵל מֶלֶךְ אֲרָם וַאֲחַזְיָהוּ בֶן־ יְהוֹרָם מֶלֶךְ יְהוּדָה יָרַד
he-went-down Judah king-of Jehoram son-of then-Ahaziah Aram king-of Hazael

לִרְאוֹת אֶת־יוֹרָם בֶּן־ אַחְאָב בְּיִזְרְעֶאל כִּי־ חֹלֶה הוּא׃ וֶאֱלִישָׁע
now-Elisha (9:1) he being-wounded for to-Jezreel Ahab son-of Joram *** to-see

הַנָּבִיא קָרָא לְאַחַד מִבְּנֵי הַנְּבִיאִים וַיֹּאמֶר לוֹ
to-him and-he-said the-prophets from-sons-of to-one he-summoned the-prophet

חֲגֹר מָתְנֶיךָ וְקַח פַּךְ הַשֶּׁמֶן הַזֶּה בְּיָדֶךָ
in-hand-of-you the-this the-oil flask-of and-take! belts-of-you tuck-in-cloak!

וְלֵךְ רָמֹת גִּלְעָד׃ וּבָאתָ שָׁמָּה וּרְאֵה־ שָׁם יֵהוּא בֶן־
son-of Jehu there then-look! to-there when-you-get (2) Gilead Ramoth and-go!

יְהוֹשָׁפָט בֶּן־ נִמְשִׁי וּבָאתָ וַהֲקֵמֹתוֹ מִתּוֹךְ*
from-among and-you-get-away-him and-you-go Nimshi son-of Jehoshaphat

אֶחָיו וְהֵבֵיאתָ אֹתוֹ חֶדֶר בְּחָדֶר׃ וְלָקַחְתָּ פַךְ־
flask-of then-you-take (3) in-room room him and-you-take companions-of-him

הַשֶּׁמֶן וְיָצַקְתָּ עַל־ רֹאשׁוֹ וְאָמַרְתָּ כֹּה־ אָמַר יְהוָה
Yahweh he-says this and-you-declare head-of-him on and-you-pour the-oil

מְשַׁחְתִּיךָ לְמֶלֶךְ אֶל־יִשְׂרָאֵל וּפָתַחְתָּ הַדֶּלֶת וְנַסְתָּה וְלֹא
and-not and-you-run the-door then-you-open Israel over as-king I-anoint-you

תְחַכֶּה׃ וַיֵּלֶךְ הַנַּעַר הַנַּעַר הַנָּבִיא רָמֹת
Ramoth the-prophet the-young-man the-young-man so-he-went (4) you-delay

גִּלְעָד׃ וַיָּבֹא וְהִנֵּה שָׂרֵי הַחַיִל יֹשְׁבִים
ones-sitting the-army officers-of then-see! when-he-arrived (5) Gilead

וַיֹּאמֶר דָּבָר לִי אֵלֶיךָ הַשָּׂר וַיֹּאמֶר יֵהוּא אֶל־
for Jehu and-he-asked the-commander for-you with-me message and-he-said

מִי מִכֻּלָּנוּ וַיֹּאמֶר אֵלֶיךָ הַשָּׂר׃ וַיָּקָם
and-he-got-up (6) the-commander for-you and-he-replied of-all-of-us whom?

וַיָּבֹא הַבַּיְתָה וַיִּצֹק הַשֶּׁמֶן אֶל־ רֹאשׁוֹ
head-of-him on the-oil then-he-poured into-the-house and-he-went

did evil in the eyes of the LORD, as the house of Ahab had done, for he was related by marriage to Ahab's family.

28 Ahaziah went with Joram son of Ahab to war against Hazael king of Aram at Ramoth Gilead. The Arameans wounded Joram; 29 so King Joram returned to Jezreel to recover from the wounds the Arameans had inflicted on him at Ramoth[r] in his battle with Hazael king of Aram.

Then Ahaziah son of Jehoram king of Judah went down to Jezreel to see Joram son of Ahab, because he had been wounded.

### *Jehu Anointed King of Israel*

9 The prophet Elisha summoned a man from the company of the prophets and said to him, "Tuck your cloak into your belt, take this flask of oil with you and go to Ramoth Gilead. 2 When you get there, look for Jehu son of Jehoshaphat, the son of Nimshi. Go to him, get him away from his companions and take him into an inner room. 3 Then take the flask and pour the oil on his head and declare, 'This is what the LORD says: I anoint you king over Israel.' Then open the door and run; don't delay!"

4 So the young man, the prophet, went to Ramoth Gilead. 5 When he arrived, he found the army officers sitting together. "I have a message for you, commander," he said.

"For which of us?" asked Jehu.

"For you, commander," he replied.

6 Jehu got up and went into the house. Then the prophet poured the oil on Jehu's head

[r]29 Hebrew *Ramah*, a variant of *Ramoth*

*2 Most mss have *sheva* in the *kaph* (ךְ).

וַיֹּאמֶר לוֹ כֹּה־ אָמַר יְהוָה אֱלֹהֵי יִשְׂרָאֵל מְשַׁחְתִּיךָ
I-anoint-you Israel God-of Yahweh he-says this to-him and-he-declared

לְמֶלֶךְ אֶל ־עַם יְהוָה אֶל ־יִשְׂרָאֵל׃ (7) וְהִכִּיתָה אֶת־
*** and-you-must-destroy (7) Israel over Yahweh people-of over as-king

בֵּית אַחְאָב אֲדֹנֶיךָ וְנִקַּמְתִּי דְּמֵי ׀ עֲבָדַי
servants-of-me bloods-of and-I-will-avenge masters-of-you Ahab house-of

הַנְּבִיאִים וּדְמֵי כָּל־ עַבְדֵי יְהוָה מִיַּד אִיזָבֶל׃
Jezebel by-hand-of Yahweh servants-of all-of and-bloods-of the-prophets

(8) וְאָבַד כָּל־ בֵּית אַחְאָב וְהִכְרַתִּי לְאַחְאָב
from-Ahab and-I-will-cut-off Ahab house-of whole-of and-he-will-perish (8)

מַשְׁתִּין בְּקִיר וְעָצוּר וְעָזוּב בְּיִשְׂרָאֵל׃
in-Israel or-being-free and-being-slave against-wall one-urinating

(9) וְנָתַתִּי אֶת־ בֵּית אַחְאָב כְּבֵית יָרָבְעָם בֶּן־ נְבָט
Nebat son-of Jeroboam like-house-of Ahab house-of *** and-I-will-make (9)

וּכְבֵית בַּעְשָׁא בֶן־ אֲחִיָּה׃ (10) וְאֶת־ אִיזֶבֶל יֹאכְלוּ
they-will-devour Jezebel and (10) Ahijah son-of Baasha and-like-house-of

הַכְּלָבִים בְּחֵלֶק יִזְרְעֶאל וְאֵין קֹבֵר וַיִּפְתַּח
then-he-opened burying and-no-one Jezreel on-plot-of-ground-of the-dogs

הַדֶּלֶת וַיָּנֹס׃ (11) וְיֵהוּא יָצָא אֶל־ עַבְדֵי אֲדֹנָיו
masters-of-him officers-of to he-went-out when-Jehu (11) and-he-ran the-door

וַיֹּאמֶר לוֹ הֲשָׁלוֹם מַדּוּעַ בָּא־ הַמְשֻׁגָּע הַזֶּה
the-this the-one-being-mad he-came why? all-right? to-him then-they-asked

אֵלֶיךָ וַיֹּאמֶר אֲלֵיהֶם אַתֶּם יְדַעְתֶּם אֶת־ הָאִישׁ וְאֶת־ שִׂיחוֹ׃
saying-of-him and the-man *** you-know you to-them and-he-replied to-you

(12) וַיֹּאמְרוּ שֶׁקֶר הַגֶּד־ נָא לָנוּ וַיֹּאמֶר כָּזֹאת וְכָזֹאת
and-as-that as-this and-he-said to-us now! tell! not-true and-they-said (12)

אָמַר אֵלַי לֵאמֹר כֹּה אָמַר יְהוָה מְשַׁחְתִּיךָ לְמֶלֶךְ אֶל־יִשְׂרָאֵל׃
Israel over as-king I-anoint-you Yahweh he-says this to-say to-me he-told

(13) וַיְמַהֲרוּ וַיִּקְחוּ אִישׁ בִּגְדוֹ וַיָּשִׂימוּ
and-they-spread cloak-of-him each and-they-took and-they-hurried (13)

תַחְתָּיו אֶל־ גֶּרֶם הַמַּעֲלוֹת וַיִּתְקְעוּ בַּשּׁוֹפָר וַיֹּאמְרוּ
and-they-said on-the-trumpet then-they-blew the-steps bare-part-of on under-him

מָלַךְ יֵהוּא׃ (14) וַיִּתְקַשֵּׁר יֵהוּא בֶּן־ יְהוֹשָׁפָט בֶּן־ נִמְשִׁי
Nimshi son-of Jehoshaphat son-of Jehu so-he-conspired (14) Jehu he-is-king

אֶל ־יוֹרָם וְיוֹרָם הָיָה שֹׁמֵר בְּרָמֹת גִּלְעָד הוּא וְכָל־
and-all-of he Gilead at-Ramoth defending he-was now-Joram Joram against

יִשְׂרָאֵל מִפְּנֵי חֲזָאֵל מֶלֶךְ־ אֲרָם׃ (15) וַיָּשָׁב יְהוֹרָם הַמֶּלֶךְ
the-king Jehoram but-he-returned (15) Aram king-of Hazael from-before Israel

and declared, "This is what the LORD, the God of Israel, says: 'I anoint you king over the LORD's people Israel. [7]You are to destroy the house of Ahab your master, and I will avenge the blood of my servants the prophets and the blood of all the LORD's servants shed by Jezebel. [8]The whole house of Ahab will perish. I will cut off from Ahab every last male in Israel—slave or free. [9]I will make the house of Ahab like the house of Jeroboam son of Nebat and like the house of Baasha son of Ahijah. [10]As for Jezebel, dogs will devour her on the plot of ground at Jezreel, and no one will bury her.' " Then he opened the door and ran.

[11]When Jehu went out to his fellow officers, one of them asked him, "Is everything all right? Why did this madman come to you?"

"You know the man and the sort of things he says," Jehu replied.

[12]"That's not true!" they said. "Tell us."

Jehu said, "Here is what he told me: 'This is what the LORD says: I anoint you king over Israel.' "

[13]They hurried and took their cloaks and spread them under him on the bare steps. Then they blew the trumpet and shouted, "Jehu is king!"

*Jehu Kills Joram and Ahaziah*

[14]So Jehu son of Jehoshaphat, the son of Nimshi, conspired against Joram. (Now Joram and all Israel had been defending Ramoth Gilead against Hazael king of Aram, [15]but King Joram[s] had returned to Jezreel to recover

[s]15 Hebrew *Jehoram,* a variant of *Joram;* also in verses 17 and 21-24

לְהִתְרַפֵּא בְּיִזְרְעֶאל* מִן־ הַמַּכִּים אֲשֶׁר יַכֻּהוּ אֲרַמִּים
Arameans they-inflicted-on-him that the-wounds from in-Jezreel to-recover

בְּהִלָּחֲמוֹ אֶת־ חֲזָאֵל מֶלֶךְ אֲרָם וַיֹּאמֶר יֵהוּא אִם־ יֵשׁ
this-is if Jehu and-he-said Aram king-of Hazael *** when-to-fight-him

נַפְשְׁכֶם אַל־ יֵצֵא פָלִיט מִן־ הָעִיר לָלֶכֶת לְגִּיד°
to-tell-news to-go the-city from escapee let-him-slip-out not feeling-of-you

בְּיִזְרְעֶאל׃ וַיִּרְכַּב יֵהוּא וַיֵּלֶךְ יִזְרְעֶאלָה כִּי
because to-Jezreel and-he-went Jehu then-he-got-into-chariot (16) in-Jezreel

יוֹרָם שֹׁכֵב שָׁמָּה וַאֲחַזְיָה מֶלֶךְ יְהוּדָה יָרַד לִרְאוֹת
to-see he-went-down Judah king-of and-Ahaziah at-there resting Joram

אֶת־ יוֹרָם׃ וְהַצֹּפֶה עֹמֵד עַל־ הַמִּגְדָּל בְּיִזְרְעֶאל
in-Jezreel the-tower on standing and-the-one-looking-out (17) Joram ***

וַיַּרְא אֶת־ שִׁפְעַת יֵהוּא בְּבֹאוֹ וַיֹּאמֶר
then-he-called-out when-to-approach-him Jehu troop-of *** when-he-saw

שִׁפְעַת אֲנִי רֹאֶה וַיֹּאמֶר יְהוֹרָם קַח רַכָּב וּשְׁלַח לִקְרָאתָם
to-meet-them and-send! horseman get! Jehoram and-he-ordered seeing I troop-of

וְיֹאמַר הֲשָׁלוֹם׃ וַיֵּלֶךְ רֹכֵב הַסּוּס לִקְרָאתוֹ
to-meet-him the-horse one-riding so-he-went (18) peace? and-he-shall-ask

וַיֹּאמֶר כֹּה־ אָמַר הַמֶּלֶךְ הֲשָׁלוֹם וַיֹּאמֶר יֵהוּא מַה־ לְּךָ
to-you what? Jehu and-he-replied peace? the-king he-says this and-he-said

וּלְשָׁלוֹם סֹב אֶל־ אַחֲרָי וַיַּגֵּד הַצֹּפֶה
the-one-looking-out and-he-reported behind-me at fall-in! and-to-peace

לֵאמֹר בָּא־ הַמַּלְאָךְ עַד־ הֵם וְלֹא־ שָׁב׃ וַיִּשְׁלַח
so-he-sent (19) he-came-back but-not them to the-messenger he-reached to-say

רֹכֵב סוּס שֵׁנִי וַיָּבֹא אֲלֵהֶם וַיֹּאמֶר כֹּה־ אָמַר
he-says this then-he-said to-them when-he-came second horse one-riding

הַמֶּלֶךְ שָׁלוֹם וַיֹּאמֶר יֵהוּא מַה־ לְּךָ וּלְשָׁלוֹם סֹב אֶל־
at fall-in! and-to-peace to-you what? Jehu and-he-replied peace the-king

אַחֲרָי׃ וַיַּגֵּד הַצֹּפֶה לֵאמֹר בָּא עַד־
to he-reached to-say the-one-looking-out and-he-reported (20) behind-me

אֲלֵיהֶם וְלֹא־ שָׁב וְהַמִּנְהָג כְּמִנְהַג יֵהוּא בֶן־
son-of Jehu like-driving-of and-the-driving he-came-back but-not with-them

נִמְשִׁי כִּי בְשִׁגָּעוֹן יִנְהָג׃ וַיֹּאמֶר יְהוֹרָם אֱסֹר
hitch-up! Jehoram and-he-ordered (21) he-drives like-madman for Nimshi

וַיֶּאְסֹר רִכְבּוֹ וַיֵּצֵא יְהוֹרָם מֶלֶךְ־ יִשְׂרָאֵל
Israel king-of Jehoram then-he-rode-out chariot-of-him when-he-hitched-up

וַאֲחַזְיָהוּ מֶלֶךְ־ יְהוּדָה אִישׁ בְּרִכְבּוֹ וַיֵּצְאוּ לִקְרַאת
to-meet and-they-rode-out in-chariot-of-him each Judah king-of and-Ahaziah

from the wounds the Arameans had inflicted on him in the battle with Hazael king of Aram.) Jehu said, "If this is the way you feel, don't let anyone slip out of the city to go and tell the news in Jezreel."
16Then he got into his chariot and rode to Jezreel, because Joram was resting there and Ahaziah king of Judah had gone down to see him.
17When the lookout standing on the tower in Jezreel saw Jehu's troops approaching, he called out, "I see some troops coming."

"Get a horseman," Joram ordered. "Send him to meet them and ask, 'Do you come in peace?' "
18The horseman rode off to meet Jehu and said, "This is what the king says: 'Do you come in peace?' "

"What do you have to do with peace?" Jehu replied. "Fall in behind me."

The lookout reported, "The messenger has reached them, but he isn't coming back."
19So the king sent out a second horseman. When he came to them he said, "This is what the king says: 'Do you come in peace?' "

Jehu replied, "What do you have to do with peace? Fall in behind me."
20The lookout reported, "He has reached them, but he isn't coming back either. The driving is like that of Jehu son of Nimshi—he drives like a madman."
21"Hitch up my chariot," Joram ordered. And when it was hitched up, Joram king of Israel and Ahaziah king of Judah rode out, each in his own chariot, to meet Jehu.

*15 Most mss have *sheva* under the *beth* and *hireq* under the *yod* ( בְּיִזְ ).

°15 ק להגיד

יֵהוּא וַיִּמְצָאֻהוּ בְּחֶלְקַת נָבוֹת הַיִּזְרְעֵאלִי׃
the-Jezreelite Naboth at-plot-of-ground-of and-they-met-him Jehu

(22) וַיְהִי כִּרְאוֹת יְהוֹרָם אֶת־יֵהוּא וַיֹּאמֶר הֲשָׁלוֹם יֵהוּא
Jehu peace? then-he-asked Jehu *** Jehoram when-to-see and-he-was (22)

וַיֹּאמֶר מָה הַשָּׁלוֹם עַד־זְנוּנֵי אִיזֶבֶל אִמְּךָ
mother-of-you Jezebel idolatries-of as-long-as the-peace how? and-he-replied

וּכְשָׁפֶיהָ הָרַבִּים׃ (23) וַיַּהֲפֹךְ יְהוֹרָם
Jehoram and-he-turned-about (23) the-many-ones and-witchcrafts-of-her

יָדָיו וַיָּנָס וַיֹּאמֶר אֶל־אֲחַזְיָהוּ מִרְמָה אֲחַזְיָה׃
Ahaziah treachery Ahaziah to and-he-called-out and-he-fled hands-of-him

(24) וְיֵהוּא מִלֵּא יָדוֹ בַקֶּשֶׁת וַיַּךְ אֶת־יְהוֹרָם
Jehoram *** and-he-shot on-the-bow hand-of-him he-drew then-Jehu (24)

בֵּין זְרֹעָיו וַיֵּצֵא הַחֵצִי מִלִּבּוֹ
from-heart-of-him the-arrow and-he-came-out shoulders-of-him between

וַיִּכְרַע בְּרִכְבּוֹ׃ (25) וַיֹּאמֶר אֶל־בִּדְקַר שָׁלִשֹׁה°
officer-of-him Bidkar to and-he-said (25) in-chariot-of-him and-he-slumped

שָׂא הַשְׁלִכֵהוּ בְּחֶלְקַת שְׂדֵה נָבוֹת הַיִּזְרְעֵאלִי כִּי־
for the-Jezreelite Naboth field-of in-portion-of throw-him! pick-up!

זְכֹר אֲנִי וָאַתָּה אֵת רֹכְבִים צְמָדִים אַחֲרֵי אַחְאָב אָבִיו
father-of-him Ahab behind ones-together ones-riding with and-you I remember!

וַיהוָה נָשָׂא עָלָיו אֶת־הַמַּשָּׂא הַזֶּה׃ (26) אִם־
surely (26) the-this the-prophecy *** about-him he-prophesied when-Yahweh

לֹא אֶת־דְּמֵי נָבוֹת וְאֶת־דְּמֵי בָנָיו רָאִיתִי אֶמֶשׁ
yesterday I-saw sons-of-him bloods-of and Naboth bloods-of *** indeed

נְאֻם־יְהוָה וְשִׁלַּמְתִּי לְךָ בַּחֶלְקָה
for-the-plot-of-ground to-you and-I-will-make-pay Yahweh declaration-of

הַזֹּאת נְאֻם־יְהוָה וְעַתָּה שָׂא הַשְׁלִכֵהוּ בַּחֶלְקָה
on-the-plot throw-him! pick-up! so-now Yahweh declaration-of the-this

כִּדְבַר יְהוָה׃ (27) וַאֲחַזְיָה מֶלֶךְ־יְהוּדָה רָאָה וַיָּנָס
then-he-fled he-saw Judah king-of when-Ahaziah (27) Yahweh as-word-of

דֶּרֶךְ בֵּית הַגָּן וַיִּרְדֹּף אַחֲרָיו יֵהוּא וַיֹּאמֶר גַּם־אֹתוֹ
him also and-he-shouted Jehu after-him and-he-chased Haggan Beth road-of

הַכֻּהוּ אֶל־הַמֶּרְכָּבָה בְּמַעֲלֵה־גוּר אֲשֶׁר אֶת־יִבְלְעָם וַיָּנָס
but-he-escaped Ibleam near that Gur on-way-up-of the-chariot in kill-him!

מְגִדּוֹ וַיָּמָת שָׁם׃ (28) וַיַּרְכִּבוּ אֹתוֹ עֲבָדָיו
servants-of-him him and-they-took-by-chariot (28) there and-he-died Megiddo

יְרוּשָׁלְָמָה וַיִּקְבְּרוּ אֹתוֹ בִקְבֻרָתוֹ עִם־אֲבֹתָיו
fathers-of-him with in-tomb-of-him him and-they-buried to-Jerusalem

°25 ק שלשו

They met him at the plot of ground that had belonged to Naboth the Jezreelite. [22]When Joram saw Jehu he asked, "Have you come in peace, Jehu?"

"How can there be peace," Jehu replied, "as long as all the idolatry and witchcraft of your mother Jezebel abound?"

[23]Joram turned about and fled, calling out to Ahaziah, "Treachery, Ahaziah!"

[24]Then Jehu drew his bow and shot Joram between the shoulders. The arrow pierced his heart and he slumped down in his chariot. [25]Jehu said to Bidkar, his chariot officer, "Pick him up and throw him on the field that belonged to Naboth the Jezreelite. Remember how you and I were riding together in chariots behind Ahab his father when the LORD made this prophecy about him: [26]'Yesterday I saw the blood of Naboth and the blood of his sons, declares the LORD, and I will surely make you pay for it on this plot of ground, declares the LORD.'[t] Now then, pick him up and throw him on that plot, in accordance with the word of the LORD."

[27]When Ahaziah king of Judah saw what had happened, he fled up the road to Beth Haggan.[u] Jehu chased him, shouting, "Kill him too!" They wounded him in his chariot on the way up to Gur near Ibleam, but he escaped to Megiddo and died there. [28]His servants took him by chariot to Jerusalem and buried him with his fathers in his tomb in

t26 See 1 Kings 21:19.
u27 Or *fled by way of the garden house*

בְּעִיר דָּוִד׃ וּבִשְׁנַת אַחַת עֶשְׂרֵה שָׁנָה לְיוֹרָם בֶּן־
son-of of-Joram year ten-of one-of now-in-year-of (29) David in-City-of

אַחְאָב מָלַךְ אֲחַזְיָה עַל־ יְהוּדָה׃ וַיָּבוֹא יֵהוּא יִזְרְעֶאלָה
to-Jezreel Jehu then-he-went (30) Judah over Ahaziah he-became-king Ahab

וְאִיזֶבֶל שָׁמְעָה וַתָּשֶׂם בַּפּוּךְ עֵינֶיהָ
eyes-of-her with-the-paint then-she-prepared she-heard when-Jezebel

וַתֵּיטֶב אֶת־ רֹאשָׁהּ וַתַּשְׁקֵף בְּעַד הַחַלּוֹן׃
the-window out-of and-she-looked hair-of-her *** and-she-made-good

וְיֵהוּא בָּא בַשָּׁעַר וַתֹּאמֶר הֲשָׁלוֹם זִמְרִי
Zimri peace? and-she-asked through-the-gate he-entered and-Jehu (31)

הֹרֵג אֲדֹנָיו׃ וַיִּשָּׂא פָנָיו אֶל־ הַחַלּוֹן
the-window to faces-of-him and-he-lifted (32) masters-of-him one-murdering

וַיֹּאמֶר מִי אִתִּי מִי וַיַּשְׁקִיפוּ אֵלָיו שְׁנַיִם שְׁלֹשָׁה
three two at-him and-they-looked-down who? with-me who? and-he-called-out

סָרִיסִים׃ וַיֹּאמֶר שִׁמְטֻהוּ וַיִּשְׁמְטוּהָ°
so-they-threw-down-her throw-down-her! and-he-said (33) eunuchs

וַיִּז מִדָּמָהּ אֶל־ הַקִּיר וְאֶל־ הַסּוּסִים
the-horses and-on the-wall on from-blood-of-her and-he-spattered

וַיִּרְמְסֶנָּה׃ וַיָּבֹא וַיֹּאכַל וַיֵּשְׁתְּ וַיֹּאמֶר
and-he-said and-he-drank and-he-ate then-he-went-in (34) and-he-trampled-her

פִּקְדוּ־ נָא אֶת־ הָאֲרוּרָה הַזֹּאת וְקִבְרוּהָ כִּי
for and-bury-her! the-that the-woman-being-cursed *** now! take-care!

בַת־ מֶלֶךְ הִיא׃ וַיֵּלְכוּ לְקָבְרָהּ וְלֹא־ מָצְאוּ
they-found then-nothing to-bury-her when-they-went (35) she king daughter-of

בָהּ כִּי אִם־ הַגֻּלְגֹּלֶת וְהָרַגְלַיִם וְכַפּוֹת הַיָּדָיִם׃
the-hands and-palms-of and-the-feet the-skull only except of-her

וַיָּשֻׁבוּ וַיַּגִּידוּ לוֹ וַיֹּאמֶר דְּבַר־ יְהוָה
Yahweh word-of and-she-said to-him and-they-told and-they-went-back (36)

הוּא אֲשֶׁר דִּבֶּר בְּיַד־ עַבְדּוֹ אֵלִיָּהוּ הַתִּשְׁבִּי לֵאמֹר
to-say the-Tishbite Elijah servant-of-him by-hand-of he-spoke that this

בְּחֵלֶק יִזְרְעֶאל יֹאכְלוּ הַכְּלָבִים אֶת־ בְּשַׂר אִיזָבֶל׃
Jezebel flesh-of *** the-dogs they-will-devour Jezreel on-plot-of-ground-of

וְהָיְתָ° נִבְלַת אִיזֶבֶל כְּדֹמֶן עַל־ פְּנֵי הַשָּׂדֶה
the-ground surfaces-of on like-refuse Jezebel body-of and-she-will-be (37)

בְּחֵלֶק יִזְרְעֶאל אֲשֶׁר לֹא־ יֹאמְרוּ זֹאת אִיזָבֶל׃ וּלְאַחְאָב
now-to-Ahab (10:1) Jezebel this they-will-say not that Jezreel at-plot-of

שִׁבְעִים בָּנִים בְּשֹׁמְרוֹן וַיִּכְתֹּב יֵהוּא סְפָרִים וַיִּשְׁלַח שֹׁמְרוֹן אֶל־
to Samaria and-he-sent letters Jehu so-he-wrote in-Samaria sons seventy

the City of David. [29](In the eleventh year of Joram son of Ahab, Ahaziah had become king of Judah.)

*Jezebel Killed*

[30]Then Jehu went to Jezreel. When Jezebel heard about it, she painted her eyes, arranged her hair and looked out of a window. [31]As Jehu entered the gate, she asked, "Have you come in peace, Zimri, you murderer of your master?"[v]

[32]He looked up at the window and called out, "Who is on my side? Who?" Two or three eunuchs looked down at him. [33]"Throw her down!" Jehu said. So they threw her down, and some of her blood spattered the wall and the horses as they trampled her underfoot.

[34]Jehu went in and ate and drank. "Take care of that cursed woman," he said, "and bury her, for she was a king's daughter." [35]But when they went out to bury her, they found nothing except her skull, her feet and her hands. [36]They went back and told Jehu, who said, "This is the word of the LORD that he spoke through his servant Elijah the Tishbite: On the plot of ground at Jezreel dogs will devour Jezebel's flesh.[w] [37]Jezebel's body will be like refuse on the ground in the plot at Jezreel, so that no one will be able to say, 'This is Jezebel.' "

*Ahab's Family Killed*

**10** Now there were in Samaria seventy sons of the house of Ahab. So Jehu wrote letters and sent them to

[v]31 Or *"Did Zimri have peace, who murdered his master?"*
[w]36 See 1 Kings 21:23.

°33 ק שמטוה
°37 ק והיתה

שָׂרֵי יִזְרְעֶאל הַזְּקֵנִים וְאֶל־ הָאֹמְנִים אַחְאָב לֵאמֹר׃
to-say Ahab the-ones-guarding and-to the-elders Jezreel officials-of

(2) וְעַתָּה כְּבֹא הַסֵּפֶר הַזֶּה אֲלֵיכֶם וְאִתְּכֶם בְּנֵי
sons-of since-with-you to-you the-this the-letter as-to-reach and-now (2)

אֲדֹנֵיכֶם וְאִתְּכֶם הָרֶכֶב וְהַסּוּסִים וְעִיר מִבְצָר
fortified and-city and-the-horses the-chariot and-with-you masters-of-you

וְהַנָּשֶׁק׃ (3) וּרְאִיתֶם הַטּוֹב וְהַיָּשָׁר מִבְּנֵי
from-sons-of and-the-worthy the-good now-you-choose (3) and-the-weapon

אֲדֹנֵיכֶם וְשַׂמְתֶּם עַל־ כִּסֵּא אָבִיו וְהִלָּחֲמוּ עַל־
for then-fight! father-of-him throne-of on and-you-set masters-of-you

בֵּית אֲדֹנֵיכֶם׃ (4) וַיִּרְאוּ מְאֹד מְאֹד וַיֹּאמְרוּ
and-they-said very very but-they-were-terrified (4) masters-of-you house-of

הִנֵּה שְׁנֵי הַמְּלָכִים לֹא עָמְדוּ לְפָנָיו וְאֵיךְ נַעֲמֹד
can-we-resist so-how? before-him they-could-resist not the-kings two-of see!

אֲנָחְנוּ׃ (5) וַיִּשְׁלַח אֲשֶׁר־ עַל־ הַבַּיִת וַאֲשֶׁר עַל־ הָעִיר וְהַזְּקֵנִים
and-the-elders the-city over and-who the-palace over who so-he-sent (5) we

וְהָאֹמְנִים אֶל־ יֵהוּא ׀ לֵאמֹר עֲבָדֶיךָ אֲנַחְנוּ וְכֹל אֲשֶׁר־
that and-all we servants-of-you to-say Jehu to and-the-ones-guarding

תֹּאמַר אֵלֵינוּ נַעֲשֶׂה לֹא־ נַמְלִיךְ אִישׁ הַטּוֹב
the-good anyone we-will-appoint-as-king not we-will-do to-us you-say

בְּעֵינֶיךָ עֲשֵׂה׃ (6) וַיִּכְתֹּב אֲלֵיהֶם סֵפֶר ׀ שֵׁנִית לֵאמֹר אִם־ לִי
to-me if to-say second letter to-them then-he-wrote (6) do! in-eyes-of-you

אַתֶּם וּלְקֹלִי ׀ אַתֶּם שֹׁמְעִים קְחוּ אֶת־ רָאשֵׁי אַנְשֵׁי בְנֵי־
sons-of men-of heads-of *** take! ones-obeying you and-to-voice-of-me you

אֲדֹנֵיכֶם וּבֹאוּ אֵלַי כָּעֵת מָחָר יִזְרְעֶאלָה וּבְנֵי
now-sons-of in-Jezreel tomorrow by-the-time to-me and-come! masters-of-you

הַמֶּלֶךְ שִׁבְעִים אִישׁ אֶת־ גְּדֹלֵי הָעִיר מְגַדְּלִים אוֹתָם׃
them ones-rearing the-city leading-men-of with man seventy the-king

(7) וַיְהִי כְּבֹא הַסֵּפֶר אֲלֵיהֶם וַיִּקְחוּ אֶת־ בְּנֵי
sons-of *** then-they-took to-them the-letter when-to-arrive and-he-was (7)

הַמֶּלֶךְ וַיִּשְׁחֲטוּ שִׁבְעִים אִישׁ וַיָּשִׂימוּ אֶת־ רָאשֵׁיהֶם
heads-of-them *** and-they-put man seventy and-they-slaughtered the-king

בַּדּוּדִים וַיִּשְׁלְחוּ אֵלָיו יִזְרְעֶאלָה׃ (8) וַיָּבֹא
when-he-arrived (8) in-Jezreel to-him and-they-sent in-the-baskets

הַמַּלְאָךְ וַיַּגֶּד־ לוֹ לֵאמֹר הֵבִיאוּ רָאשֵׁי בְנֵי־
sons-of heads-of they-brought to-say to-him then-he-told the-messenger

הַמֶּלֶךְ וַיֹּאמֶר שִׂימוּ אֹתָם שְׁנֵי צִבֻּרִים פֶּתַח הַשַּׁעַר
the-city-gate entrance-of piles two-of them put! then-he-ordered the-king

Samaria: to the officials of Jezreel,[x] to the elders and to the
guardians of Ahab's children.
He said, 2"As soon as this letter reaches you, since your
master's sons are with you
and you have chariots and
horses, a fortified city and
weapons, 3choose the best and
most worthy of your master's
sons and set him on his father's throne. Then fight for
your master's house."
4But they were terrified and
said, "If two kings could not
resist him, how can we?"
5So the palace administrator,
the city governor, the elders
and the guardians sent this
message to Jehu: "We are your
servants and we will do anything you say. We will not appoint anyone as king; you do
whatever you think best."
6Then Jehu wrote them a
second letter, saying, "If you
are on my side and will obey
me, take the heads of your
master's sons and come to me
in Jezreel by this time tomorrow."
Now the royal princes, seventy of them, were with the
leading men of the city, who
were rearing them. 7When the
letter arrived, these men took
the princes and slaughtered all
seventy of them. They put
their heads in baskets and
sent them to Jehu in Jezreel.
8When the messenger arrived,
he told Jehu, "They have
brought the heads of the
princes."
Then Jehu ordered, "Put
them in two piles at the entrance of the city gate until

[x]1 Hebrew; some Septuagint manuscripts and Vulgate *of the city*

עַד־הַבֹּקֶר׃ וַיְהִי בַבֹּקֶר וַיֵּצֵא וַיַּעֲמֹד
and-he-stood then-he-went-out in-the-morning and-he-was (9) the-morning until

וַיֹּאמֶר אֶל־כָּל־הָעָם צַדִּקִים אַתֶּם הִנֵּה אֲנִי קָשַׁרְתִּי
I-conspired I see! you ones-innocent the-people all-of to and-he-said

עַל־אֲדֹנִי וָאֶהֶרְגֵהוּ וּמִי הִכָּה אֶת־כָּל־אֵלֶּה׃
these all-of *** he-killed but-who? and-I-killed-him master-of-me against

דְּעוּ אֵפוֹא כִּי לֹא יִפֹּל מִדְּבַר יְהוָה אַרְצָה אֲשֶׁר־
that to-ground Yahweh from-word-of he-will-fall not that then know! (10)

דִּבֶּר יְהוָה עַל־בֵּית אַחְאָב וַיהוָה עָשָׂה אֵת אֲשֶׁר
what *** he-did for-Yahweh Ahab house-of against Yahweh he-spoke

דִּבֶּר בְּיַד עַבְדּוֹ אֵלִיָּהוּ׃ וַיַּךְ יֵהוּא אֵת
*** Jehu so-he-killed (11) Elijah servant-of-him by-hand-of he-promised

כָּל־הַנִּשְׁאָרִים לְבֵית־אַחְאָב בְּיִזְרְעֶאל וְכָל־
and-all-of in-Jezreel Ahab of-house-of the-ones-remaining all-of

גְּדֹלָיו וּמְיֻדָּעָיו וְכֹהֲנָיו עַד־בִּלְתִּי הִשְׁאִיר־
he-left not until and-priests-of-him and-ones-knowing-him chief-men-of-him

לוֹ שָׂרִיד׃ וַיָּקָם וַיָּבֹא וַיֵּלֶךְ שֹׁמְרוֹן הוּא
he Samaria and-he-went and-he-set-out then-he-got-up (12) survivor to-him

בֵּית־עֵקֶד הָרֹעִים בַּדָּרֶךְ׃ וְיֵהוּא מָצָא אֶת־
*** he-met and-Jehu (13) on-the-way the-Ones-Shepherding Eked-of Beth

אֲחֵי אֲחַזְיָהוּ מֶלֶךְ־יְהוּדָה וַיֹּאמֶר מִי אַתֶּם וַיֹּאמְרוּ
and-they-said you who? and-he-asked Judah king-of Ahaziah relatives-of

אֲחֵי אֲחַזְיָהוּ אֲנַחְנוּ וַנֵּרֶד לִשְׁלוֹם בְּנֵי־הַמֶּלֶךְ
the-king families-of for-greeting-of and-we-came-down we Ahaziah relatives-of

וּבְנֵי הַגְּבִירָה׃ וַיֹּאמֶר תִּפְשׂוּם חַיִּים
ones-alive take-them! and-he-ordered (14) the-queen-mother and-families-of

וַיִּתְפְּשׂוּם חַיִּים וַיִּשְׁחָטוּם אֶל־בּוֹר בֵּית־עֵקֶד
Eked Beth well-of by and-they-slaughtered-them ones-alive so-they-took-them

אַרְבָּעִים וּשְׁנַיִם אִישׁ וְלֹא־הִשְׁאִיר אִישׁ מֵהֶם׃ וַיֵּלֶךְ
and-he-left (15) of-them anyone he-left-survivor and-not man and-two forty

מִשָּׁם וַיִּמְצָא אֶת־יְהוֹנָדָב בֶּן־רֵכָב לִקְרָאתוֹ
to-meet-him Recab son-of Jehonadab *** and-he-came-upon from-there

וַיְבָרְכֵהוּ וַיֹּאמֶר אֵלָיו הֲיֵשׁ אֶת־לְבָבְךָ יָשָׁר
in-accord heart-of-you *** is-there? to-him and-he-said and-he-greeted-him

כַּאֲשֶׁר לְבָבִי עִם־לְבָבֶךָ וַיֹּאמֶר יְהוֹנָדָב יֵשׁ
there-is Jehonadab and-he-said heart-of-you with heart-of-me just-as

וָיֵשׁ תְּנָה אֶת־יָדֶךָ וַיִּתֵּן יָדוֹ וַיַּעֲלֵהוּ
and-he-helped-up-him hand-of-him so-he-gave hand-of-you *** give! if-there-is

morning."
[9]The next morning Jehu
went out. He stood before all
the people and said, "You are
innocent. It was I who conspired against my master and
killed him, but who killed all
these? [10]Know then, that not a
word the LORD has spoken
against the house of Ahab will
fail. The LORD has done what
he promised through his servant Elijah." [11]So Jehu killed
everyone in Jezreel who remained of the house of Ahab,
as well as all his chief men, his
close friends and his priests,
leaving him no survivor.
[12]Jehu then set out and went
toward Samaria. At Beth Eked
of the Shepherds, [13]he met
some relatives of Ahaziah
king of Judah and asked,
"Who are you?"
They said, "We are relatives
of Ahaziah, and we have come
down to greet the families of
the king and of the queen
mother."
[14]"Take them alive!" he ordered. So they took them alive
and slaughtered them by the
well of Beth Eked—forty-two
men. He left no survivor.
[15]After he left there, he came
upon Jehonadab son of Recab,
who was on his way to meet
him. Jehu greeted him and
said, "Are you in accord with
me, as I am with you?"
"I am," Jehonadab an-
swered.
"If so," said Jehu, "give me
your hand." So he did, and
Jehu helped him up into the

אֵלָיו אֶל־ הַמֶּרְכָּבָה׃ וַיֹּאמֶר לְכָה אִתִּי וּרְאֵה
and-see! with-me come! and-he-said (16) the-chariot into to-him

בְּקִנְאָתִי לַיהוָה וַיַּרְכִּבוּ אֹתוֹ בְּרִכְבּוֹ׃
in-chariot-of-him him then-he-had-ride for-Yahweh to-zeal-of-me

וַיָּבֹא שֹׁמְרוֹן וַיַּךְ אֶת־ כָּל־ הַנִּשְׁאָרִים
the-ones-being-left all-of *** then-he-killed Samaria when-he-came (17)

לְאַחְאָב בְּשֹׁמְרוֹן עַד־ הִשְׁמִידוֹ כִּדְבַר יְהוָה אֲשֶׁר דִּבֶּר
he-spoke that Yahweh as-word-of he-destroyed-him until in-Samaria of-Ahab

אֶל־ אֵלִיָּהוּ׃ וַיִּקְבֹּץ יֵהוּא אֶת־ כָּל־ הָעָם
the-people all-of *** Jehu then-he-brought-together (18) Elijah to

וַיֹּאמֶר אֲלֵהֶם אַחְאָב עָבַד אֶת־ הַבַּעַל מְעָט יֵהוּא יַעַבְדֶנּוּ
he-will-serve-him Jehu little the-Baal *** he-served Ahab to-them and-he-said

הַרְבֵּה׃ וְעַתָּה כָל־ נְבִיאֵי הַבַּעַל כָּל־ עֹבְדָיו
ones-ministering-him all-of the-Baal prophets-of all-of so-now (19) to-be-much

וְכָל־ כֹּהֲנָיו קִרְאוּ אֵלַי אִישׁ אַל־ יִפָּקֵד כִּי
because let-him-be-missing not anyone to-me summon! priests-of-him and-all-of

זֶבַח גָּדוֹל לִי לַבַּעַל כֹּל אֲשֶׁר־ יִפָּקֵד לֹא יִחְיֶה
he-will-live not he-is-missing who anyone for-the-Baal by-me great sacrifice

וְיֵהוּא עָשָׂה בְעָקְבָּה לְמַעַן הַאֲבִיד אֶת־ עֹבְדֵי
ones-ministering-of *** to-destroy in-order on-deception he-acted but-Jehu

הַבָּעַל׃ וַיֹּאמֶר יֵהוּא קַדְּשׁוּ עֲצָרָה לַבַּעַל
for-the-Baal assembly set-apart! Jehu and-he-said (20) the-Baal

וַיִּקְרָאוּ׃ וַיִּשְׁלַח יֵהוּא בְּכָל־ יִשְׂרָאֵל וַיָּבֹאוּ
and-they-came Israel through-all-of Jehu then-he-sent (21) so-they-proclaimed

כָּל־ עֹבְדֵי הַבַּעַל וְלֹא־ נִשְׁאַר אִישׁ אֲשֶׁר לֹא־ בָא
he-came not who one he-was-left and-not the-Baal ones-ministering-of all-of

וַיָּבֹאוּ בֵּית הַבַּעַל וַיִּמָּלֵא בֵית־ הַבַּעַל פֶּה
end the-Baal temple-of so-he-was-full the-Baal temple-of and-they-entered

לָפֶה׃ וַיֹּאמֶר לַאֲשֶׁר עַל־ הַמֶּלְתָּחָה הוֹצֵא לְבוּשׁ לְכֹל
for-all-of robe bring! the-wardrobe over to-whom and-he-said (22) to-end

עֹבְדֵי הַבַּעַל וַיֹּצֵא לָהֶם הַמַּלְבּוּשׁ׃
the-robe for-them so-he-brought-out the-Baal ones-ministering-of

וַיָּבֹא יֵהוּא וִיהוֹנָדָב בֶּן־ רֵכָב בֵּית הַבָּעַל
the-Baal temple-of Recab son-of and-Jehonadab Jehu then-he-went (23)

וַיֹּאמֶר לְעֹבְדֵי הַבַּעַל חַפְּשׂוּ וּרְאוּ פֶּן־
not and-see! look-around! the-Baal to-ones-ministering-of and-he-said

יֶשׁ־ פֹּה עִמָּכֶם מֵעַבְדֵי יְהוָה כִּי אִם־ עֹבְדֵי
ones-ministering-of only but Yahweh from-servants-of with-you here there-is

chariot. 16 Jehu said, "Come
with me and see my zeal for
the LORD." Then he had him
ride along in his chariot.
17 When Jehu came to Samaria,
he killed all who were
left there of Ahab's family; he
destroyed them, according to
the word of the LORD spoken
to Elijah.

*Ministers of Baal Killed*

18 Then Jehu brought all the
people together and said to
them, "Ahab served Baal a little;
Jehu will serve him much.
19 Now summon all the prophets
of Baal, all his ministers
and all his priests. See that no
one is missing, because I am
going to hold a great sacrifice
for Baal. Anyone who fails to
come will no longer live." But
Jehu was acting deceptively in
order to destroy the ministers
of Baal.
20 Jehu said, "Call an assembly
in honor of Baal." So they
proclaimed it.
21 Then he sent
word throughout Israel, and
all the ministers of Baal came;
not one stayed away. They
crowded into the temple of
Baal until it was full from one
end to the other.
22 And Jehu
said to the keeper of the wardrobe,
"Bring robes for all the
ministers of Baal." So he
brought out robes for them.
23 Then Jehu and Jehonadab
son of Recab went into the
temple of Baal. Jehu said to the
ministers of Baal, "Look
around and see that no servants
of the LORD are here
with you—only ministers of

הַבַּעַל לְבַדָּם׃ (24) וַיָּבֹאוּ לַעֲשׂוֹת זְבָחִים
sacrifices to-make so-they-went-in (24) by-themselves the-Baal

וְעֹלוֹת וְיֵהוּא שָׂם־ לוֹ בַחוּץ שְׁמֹנִים אִישׁ
man eighty at-the-outside for-him he-posted now-Jehu and-burnt-offerings

וַיֹּאמֶר הָאִישׁ אֲשֶׁר־ יִמָּלֵט מִן־ הָאֲנָשִׁים אֲשֶׁר אֲנִי מֵבִיא עַל־
in placing I whom the-men from he-lets-escape who the-one and-he-said

יְדֵיכֶם נַפְשׁוֹ תַּחַת נַפְשׁוֹ׃ (25) וַיְהִי כְּכַלֹּתוֹ ׀
as-to-finish-him and-he-was (25) life-of-him for life-of-him hands-of-you

לַעֲשׂוֹת הָעֹלָה וַיֹּאמֶר יֵהוּא לָרָצִים
to-the-ones-guarding Jehu then-he-ordered the-burnt-offering to-make

וְלַשָּׁלִשִׁים בֹּאוּ הַכּוּם אִישׁ אַל־ יֵצֵא
he-must-escape not anyone kill-them! go-in! and-to-the-officers

וַיַּכּוּם לְפִי־ חָרֶב וַיַּשְׁלִכוּ הָרָצִים
the-ones-guarding and-they-threw-out sword with-edge-of so-they-cut-down-them

וְהַשָּׁלִשִׁים וַיֵּלְכוּ עַד־ עִיר בֵּית־ הַבָּעַל׃
the-Baal temple-of inner-shrine-of into then-they-went and-the-officers

(26) וַיֹּצִאוּ אֶת־ מַצְּבוֹת בֵּית־ הַבַּעַל
the-Baal temple-of sacred-stones-of *** and-they-brought-out (26)

וַיִּשְׂרְפוּהָ׃ (27) וַיִּתְּצוּ אֵת מַצְּבַת הַבָּעַל
the-Baal sacred-stone-of *** and-they-demolished (27) and-they-burned-her

וַיִּתְּצוּ אֶת־ בֵּית הַבַּעַל וַיְשִׂמֻהוּ לְמַחֲרָאוֹת*
*as-latrines and-they-used-him the-Baal temple-of *** and-they-tore-down

עַד־הַיּוֹם׃ (28) וַיַּשְׁמֵד יֵהוּא אֶת־ הַבַּעַל מִיִּשְׂרָאֵל׃ (29) רַק
however (29) from-Israel the-Baal *** Jehu so-he-destroyed (28) the-day to

חֲטָאֵי יָרָבְעָם בֶּן־ נְבָט אֲשֶׁר הֶחֱטִיא אֶת־יִשְׂרָאֵל לֹא־
not Israel *** he-caused-to-commit which Nebat son-of Jeroboam sins-of

סָר יֵהוּא מֵאַחֲרֵיהֶם עֶגְלֵי הַזָּהָב אֲשֶׁר בֵּית־אֵל
El Beth that the-gold calves-of from-after-them Jehu he-turned-away

וַאֲשֶׁר בְּדָן׃ (30) וַיֹּאמֶר יְהוָה אֶל־יֵהוּא יַעַן אֲשֶׁר־ הֱטִיבֹתָ
you-did-well that because Jehu to Yahweh and-he-said (30) at-Dan and-that

לַעֲשׂוֹת הַיָּשָׁר בְּעֵינַי כְּכֹל אֲשֶׁר בִּלְבָבִי עָשִׂיתָ
you-did in-mind-of-me that as-all in-eyes-of-me the-right to-accomplish

לְבֵית אַחְאָב בְּנֵי רְבִעִים יֵשְׁבוּ לְךָ עַל־ כִּסֵּא
throne-of on of-you they-will-sit fourth-ones sons-of Ahab to-house-of

יִשְׂרָאֵל׃ (31) וְיֵהוּא לֹא שָׁמַר לָלֶכֶת בְּתוֹרַת־ יְהוָה אֱלֹהֵי־
God-of Yahweh to-law-of to-keep he-was-careful not yet-Jehu (31) Israel

יִשְׂרָאֵל בְּכָל־ לְבָבוֹ לֹא סָר מֵעַל חַטֹּאות יָרָבְעָם
Jeroboam sins-of away-from he-turned not heart-of-him with-all-of Israel

Baal." 24So they went in to
make sacrifices and burnt
offerings. Now Jehu had posted eighty men outside with
this warning: "If one of you
lets any of the men I am placing in your hands escape, it
will be your life for his life."
25As soon as Jehu had
finished making the burnt
offering, he ordered the
guards and officers: "Go in
and kill them; let no one escape." So they cut them down
with the sword. The guards
and officers threw the bodies
out and then entered the inner
shrine of the temple of Baal.
26They brought the sacred
stone out of the temple of Baal
and burned it. 27They demolished the sacred stone of Baal
and tore down the temple of
Baal, and people have used it
for a latrine to this day.
28So Jehu destroyed Baal
worship in Israel. 29However,
he did not turn away from the
sins of Jeroboam son of Nebat,
which he had caused Israel to
commit—the worship of the
golden calves at Bethel and
Dan.
30The LORD said to Jehu, "Because you have done well in
accomplishing what is right in
my eyes and have done to the
house of Ahab all I had in
mind to do, your descendants
will sit on the throne of Israel
to the fourth generation."
31Yet Jehu was not careful to
keep the law of the LORD, the
God of Israel, with all his
heart. He did not turn away
from the sins of Jeroboam,

*27 The *Qere for-going-out,* is a less graphic word than the *Ketbib.*

°27 ק למוצאות

אֲשֶׁר הֶחֱטִיא אֶת־ יִשְׂרָאֵל׃ בַּיָּמִים הָהֵם הֵחֵל
he-began the-those in-the-days (32) Israel *** he-caused-to-commit which

יְהוָה לְקַצּוֹת בְּיִשְׂרָאֵל וַיַּכֵּם חֲזָאֵל בְּכָל־
through-all-of Hazael and-he-overpowered-them of-Israel to-reduce-size Yahweh

גְּבוּל יִשְׂרָאֵל׃ מִן־ הַיַּרְדֵּן מִזְרַח הַשֶּׁמֶשׁ אֵת כָּל־ אֶרֶץ
land-of all-of *** the-sun rise-of the-Jordan from (33) Israel territory-of

הַגִּלְעָד הַגָּדִי וְהָרְאוּבֵנִי* וְהַמְנַשִּׁי מֵעֲרֹעֵר אֲשֶׁר
that from-Aroer and-the-Manassite and-the-Reubenite the-Gadite the-Gilead

עַל־ נַחַל אַרְנֹן וְהַגִּלְעָד וְהַבָּשָׁן׃ וְיֶתֶר דִּבְרֵי
events-of and-rest-of (34) and-the-Bashan and-the-Gilead Arnon Gorge-of by

יֵהוּא וְכָל־ אֲשֶׁר עָשָׂה וְכָל־ גְּבוּרָתוֹ הֲלוֹא־ הֵם
they not? achievement-of-him and-all-of he-did that and-all Jehu

כְּתוּבִים עַל־ סֵפֶר דִּבְרֵי הַיָּמִים לְמַלְכֵי יִשְׂרָאֵל׃
Israel of-kings-of the-days annals-of book-of in ones-being-written

וַיִּשְׁכַּב יֵהוּא עִם־ אֲבֹתָיו וַיִּקְבְּרוּ אֹתוֹ בְּשֹׁמְרוֹן
in-Samaria him and-they-buried fathers-of-him with Jehu and-he-rested (35)

וַיִּמְלֹךְ יְהוֹאָחָז בְּנוֹ תַּחְתָּיו׃ וְהַיָּמִים
and-the-days (36) in-place-of-him son-of-him Jehoahaz and-he-became-king

אֲשֶׁר מָלַךְ יֵהוּא עַל־ יִשְׂרָאֵל עֶשְׂרִים וּשְׁמֹנֶה־ שָׁנָה בְּשֹׁמְרוֹן׃
in-Samaria year and-eight twenty Israel over Jehu he-reigned that

וַעֲתַלְיָה אֵם אֲחַזְיָהוּ וּרָאֲתָה כִּי מֵת בְּנָהּ
son-of-her he-was-dead that she-saw Ahaziah mother-of when-Athaliah (11:1)

וַתָּקָם וַתְּאַבֵּד אֵת כָּל־ זֶרַע הַמַּמְלָכָה׃
the-royal family-of whole-of *** and-she-destroyed then-she-proceeded

וַתִּקַּח יְהוֹשֶׁבַע בַּת־ הַמֶּלֶךְ־ יוֹרָם אֲחוֹת אֲחַזְיָהוּ אֶת־
*** Ahaziah sister-of Joram the-king daughter-of Jehosheba but-she-took (2)

יוֹאָשׁ בֶּן־ אֲחַזְיָה וַתִּגְנֹב אֹתוֹ מִתּוֹךְ בְּנֵי־ הַמֶּלֶךְ
the-king sons-of from-among him and-she-stole-away Ahaziah son-of Joash

הַמְּמוֹתָתִים אֹתוֹ וְאֶת־ מֵינִקְתּוֹ בַּחֲדַר הַמִּטּוֹת
the-beds in-room-of one-nursing-him and him the-ones-being-murdered

וַיַּסְתִּרוּ אֹתוֹ מִפְּנֵי עֲתַלְיָהוּ וְלֹא הוּמָת׃ וַיְהִי
and-he-was (3) he-was-killed so-not Athaliah from-before him and-they-hid

אִתָּהּ בֵּית יְהוָה מִתְחַבֵּא שֵׁשׁ שָׁנִים וַעֲתַלְיָה מֹלֶכֶת עַל־
over ruling while-Athaliah years six hiding Yahweh temple-of with-her

הָאָרֶץ׃ וּבַשָּׁנָה הַשְּׁבִיעִית שָׁלַח יְהוֹיָדָע וַיִּקַּח אֶת־
*** and-he-got Jehoiada he-sent the-seventh and-in-the-year (4) the-land

שָׂרֵי הַמֵּאיוֹת לַכָּרִי וְלָרָצִים
and-for-the-ones-guarding for-the-Carite the-hundreds commanders-of

which he had caused Israel to
commit.
32In those days the LORD began to reduce the size of Israel.
Hazael overpowered the Israelites throughout their territory 33east of the Jordan in all
the land of Gilead (the region
of Gad, Reuben and Manas-
seh), from Aroer by the Arnon
Gorge through Gilead to Bashan.
34As for the other events of
Jehu's reign, all he did, and all
his achievements, are they not
written in the book of the annals of the kings of Israel?
35Jehu rested with his fathers
and was buried in Samaria.
And Jehoahaz his son suc-
ceeded him as king. 36The time
that Jehu reigned over Israel
in Samaria was twenty-eight
years.

*Athaliah and Joash*

11 When Athaliah the
mother of Ahaziah saw
that her son was dead, she
proceeded to destroy the
whole royal family. 2But Jehosheba, the daughter of King
Jehoram[y] and sister of Ahaziah, took Joash son of Ahaziah and stole him away from
among the royal princes who
were about to be murdered.
She put him and his nurse in
a bedroom to hide him from
Athaliah; so he was not killed.
3He remained hidden with his
nurse at the temple of the LORD
for six years while Athaliah
ruled the land.
4In the seventh year Jehoiada sent for the commanders
of units of a hundred, the Carites and the guards and had

[y]2 Hebrew *Joram*, a variant of *Jehoram*

*33 Most mss have *dagesh* in the *vav* and no *qibbuts* under the *resh* (ראו־).

°1 ק ראתה
°2 ק המומתים
°4 ק המאות

וַיָּבֵ֨א אֹתָ֤ם אֵלָיו֙ בֵּ֣ית יְהוָ֔ה וַיִּכְרֹ֨ת לָהֶ֜ם בְּרִ֗ית
covenant with-them and-he-made Yahweh temple-of to-him them and-he-brought

וַיַּשְׁבַּ֤ע אֹתָם֙ בְּבֵ֣ית יְהוָ֔ה וַיַּ֥רְא אֹתָ֖ם אֶת־
*** them then-he-showed Yahweh at-temple-of them and-he-put-under-oath

בֶּן־הַמֶּֽלֶךְ׃ (5) וַיְצַוֵּ֣ם לֵאמֹ֔ר זֶ֥ה הַדָּבָ֖ר אֲשֶׁ֣ר
that the-thing this to-say and-he-commanded-them (5) the-king son-of

תַּעֲשׂ֑וּן הַשְּׁלִשִׁ֣ית מִכֶּם֙ בָּאֵ֣י הַשַּׁבָּ֔ת
the-Sabbath ones-going-on-duty-of of-you the-third you-must-do

וְשֹׁמְרֵ֖י מִשְׁמֶ֥רֶת בֵּ֥ית הַמֶּֽלֶךְ׃ (6) וְהַשְּׁלִשִׁית֙
and-the-third (6) the-king palace-of guard-of and-ones-guarding-of

בְּשַׁ֣עַר ס֔וּר וְהַשְּׁלִשִׁ֥ית בַּשַּׁ֖עַר אַחַ֣ר הָרָצִ֑ים
the-ones-guarding behind at-the-gate and-the-third Sur at-Gate-of

וּשְׁמַרְתֶּ֛ם אֶת־מִשְׁמֶ֥רֶת הַבַּ֖יִת מַסָּֽח׃ (7) וּשְׁתֵּ֤י הַיָּדוֹת֙
the-companies and-two-of (7) in-turn the-temple guard-of *** and-you-guard

בָּכֶ֔ם כֹּ֖ל יֹצְאֵ֣י הַשַּׁבָּ֑ת וְשָׁמְר֛וּ אֶת־
*** then-they-must-guard the-Sabbath ones-going-off-duty-of all-of of-you

מִשְׁמֶ֥רֶת בֵּית־יְהוָ֖ה אֶל־הַמֶּֽלֶךְ׃ (8) וְהִקַּפְתֶּ֞ם עַל־
by and-you-station-yourselves (8) the-king for Yahweh temple-of guard-of

הַמֶּ֤לֶךְ סָבִיב֙ אִ֣ישׁ וְכֵלָ֣יו בְּיָד֔וֹ וְהַבָּ֥א
and-the-one-approaching in-hand-of-him with-weapons-of-him each around the-king

אֶל־הַשְּׂדֵר֖וֹת יוּמָ֑ת וִהְי֥וּ אֶת־הַמֶּ֖לֶךְ בְּצֵאת֥וֹ
when-to-go-him the-king with and-stay! he-must-be-killed the-ranks to

וּבְבֹאֽוֹ׃ (9) וַֽיַּעֲשׂ֞וּ שָׂרֵ֣י הַמֵּאיוֹת֮ כְּכֹ֣ל אֲשֶׁר־
that as-all the-hundreds commanders-of and-they-did (9) and-when-to-come-him

צִוָּה֮ יְהוֹיָדָ֣ע הַכֹּהֵן֒ וַיִּקְחוּ֙ אִ֣ישׁ אֶת־אֲנָשָׁ֔יו
men-of-him *** each and-they-took the-priest Jehoiada he-ordered

בָּאֵ֣י הַשַּׁבָּ֔ת עִ֖ם יֹצְאֵ֣י הַשַּׁבָּ֑ת
the-Sabbath ones-going-off-duty-of with the-Sabbath ones-going-on-duty-of

וַיָּבֹ֖אוּ אֶל־יְהוֹיָדָ֥ע הַכֹּהֵֽן׃ (10) וַיִּתֵּ֨ן הַכֹּהֵ֜ן
the-priest then-he-gave (10) the-priest Jehoiada to and-they-came

לְשָׂרֵ֤י הַמֵּאיוֹת֙ אֶֽת־הַחֲנִית֙ וְאֶת־הַשְּׁלָטִ֔ים אֲשֶׁ֖ר לַמֶּ֣לֶךְ
to-the-king that the-shields and the-spear *** the-hundreds to-commanders-of

דָּוִ֑ד אֲשֶׁ֖ר בְּבֵ֥ית יְהוָֽה׃ (11) וַיַּעַמְד֨וּ הָרָצִ֜ים
the-ones-guarding and-they-stationed (11) Yahweh in-temple-of that David

אִ֣ישׁ ׀ וְכֵלָ֣יו בְּיָד֗וֹ מִכֶּ֨תֶף הַבַּ֤יִת הַיְמָנִית֙
the-south the-temple from-side-of in-hand-of-him with-weapons-of-him each

עַד־כֶּ֤תֶף הַבַּ֙יִת֙ הַשְּׂמָאלִ֔ית לַמִּזְבֵּ֖חַ וְלַבָּ֑יִת עַל־
by and-near-the-temple near-the-altar the-north the-temple side-of to

°9 ק המאות
°10 ק המאות

them brought to him at the temple of the LORD. He made a covenant with them and put them under oath at the temple of the LORD. Then he showed them the king's son.
5 He commanded them, saying, "This is what you are to do: You who are in the three companies that are going on duty on the Sabbath—a third of you guarding the royal palace,
6 a third at the Sur Gate, and a third at the gate behind the guard, who take turns guarding the temple—
7 and you who are in the other two companies that normally go off Sabbath duty are all to guard the temple for the king.
8 Station yourselves around the king, each man with his weapon in his hand. Anyone who approaches your ranks[z] must be put to death. Stay close to the king wherever he goes."
9 The commanders of units of a hundred did just as Jehoiada the priest ordered. Each one took his men—those who were going on duty on the Sabbath and those who were going off duty—and came to Jehoiada the priest.
10 Then he gave the commanders the spears and shields that had belonged to King David and that were in the temple of the LORD.
11 The guards, each with his weapon in his hand, stationed themselves around the king—near the altar and the temple, from the south side to the north side of the temple.

z8 Or *approaches the precincts*

הַמֶּלֶךְ סָבִיב׃ וַיּוֹצִא אֶת־ בֶּן־ הַמֶּלֶךְ וַיִּתֵּן
and-he-put the-king son-of *** and-he-brought-out (12) around the-king

עָלָיו אֶת־ הַנֵּזֶר וְאֶת־ הָעֵדוּת וַיַּמְלִכוּ אֹתוֹ
him and-they-proclaimed-king the-covenant and the-crown *** on-him

וַיִּמְשָׁחֻהוּ וַיַּכּוּ־ כָף וַיֹּאמְרוּ יְחִי
may-he-live and-they-shouted hand and-they-clapped and-they-anointed-him

הַמֶּלֶךְ׃ וַתִּשְׁמַע עֲתַלְיָה אֶת־ קוֹל הָרָצִין
the-ones-guarding noise-of *** Athaliah when-she-heard (13) the-king

הָעָם וַתָּבֹא אֶל־ הָעָם בֵּית יְהוָה׃ וַתֵּרֶא
and-she-looked (14) Yahweh temple-of the-people to then-she-went the-people

וְהִנֵּה הַמֶּלֶךְ עֹמֵד עַל־ הָעַמּוּד כַּמִּשְׁפָּט וְהַשָּׂרִים
and-the-officers as-the-custom the-pillar by standing the-king and-see!

וְהַחֲצֹצְרוֹת אֶל־ הַמֶּלֶךְ וְכָל־ עַם הָאָרֶץ שָׂמֵחַ
rejoicing the-land people-of and-all-of the-king beside and-the-trumpeters

וְתֹקֵעַ בַּחֲצֹצְרוֹת וַתִּקְרַע עֲתַלְיָה אֶת־ בְּגָדֶיהָ
robes-of-her *** Athaliah then-she-tore on-the-trumpets and-blowing

וַתִּקְרָא קֶשֶׁר קָשֶׁר׃ וַיְצַו יְהוֹיָדָע הַכֹּהֵן
the-priest Jehoiada then-he-ordered (15) treason treason and-she-called-out

אֶת־ שָׂרֵי הַמֵּאיוֹת° פְּקֻדֵי הַחַיִל וַיֹּאמֶר
and-he-said the-troop ones-being-in-charge-of the-hundreds commanders-of ***

אֲלֵיהֶם הוֹצִיאוּ אֹתָהּ אֶל־ מִבֵּית לַשְּׂדֵרֹת וְהַבָּא
and-the-one-following of-the-ranks outside-of to her bring-out! to-them

אַחֲרֶיהָ הָמֵת בֶּחָרֶב כִּי אָמַר הַכֹּהֵן אַל־ תּוּמַת
she-must-be-killed not the-priest he-said for with-the-sword to-kill after-her

בֵּית יְהוָה׃ וַיָּשִׂמוּ לָהּ יָדַיִם וַתָּבוֹא דֶּרֶךְ־
place-of as-she-reached hands on-her so-they-laid (16) Yahweh temple-of

מְבוֹא הַסּוּסִים בֵּית הַמֶּלֶךְ וַתּוּמַת שָׁם׃
there and-she-was-killed the-king palace-of the-horses entrance-of

וַיִּכְרֹת יְהוֹיָדָע אֶת־ הַבְּרִית בֵּין יְהוָה וּבֵין
and-between Yahweh between the-covenant *** Jehoiada then-he-made (17)

הַמֶּלֶךְ וּבֵין הָעָם לִהְיוֹת לְעָם לַיהוָה וּבֵין
and-between of-Yahweh as-people to-be the-people and-between the-king

הַמֶּלֶךְ וּבֵין הָעָם׃ וַיָּבֹאוּ כָל־ עַם הָאָרֶץ
the-land people-of all-of and-they-went (18) the-people and-between the-king

בֵּית־ הַבַּעַל וַיִּתְּצֻהוּ אֶת־ מִזְבְּחֹתָו° וְאֶת־ צְלָמָיו
idols-of-him and altars-of-him *** and-they-tore-down-him the-Baal temple-of

שִׁבְּרוּ הֵיטֵב וְאֵת מַתָּן כֹּהֵן הַבַּעַל הָרְגוּ לִפְנֵי
in-front-of they-killed the-Baal priest-of Mattan and to-do-well they-smashed

[12]Jehoiada brought out the king's son and put the crown on him; he presented him with a copy of the covenant and proclaimed him king. They anointed him, and the people clapped their hands and shouted, "Long live the king!"

[13]When Athaliah heard the noise made by the guards and the people, she went to the people at the temple of the LORD. [14]She looked and there was the king, standing by the pillar, as the custom was. The officers and the trumpeters were beside the king, and all the people of the land were rejoicing and blowing trumpets. Then Athaliah tore her robes and called out, "Treason! Treason!"

[15]Jehoiada the priest ordered the commanders of units of a hundred, who were in charge of the troops: "Bring her out between the ranks[a] and put to the sword anyone who follows her." For the priest had said, "She must not be put to death in the temple of the LORD." [16]So they seized her as she reached the place where the horses enter the palace grounds, and there she was put to death.

[17]Jehoiada then made a covenant between the LORD and the king and people that they would be the LORD's people. He also made a covenant between the king and the people. [18]All the people of the land went to the temple of Baal and tore it down. They smashed the altars and idols to pieces and killed Mattan the priest of Baal in front of the altars.

[a]15 Or *out from the precincts*

°15 ק המאות

°18 ק מזבחתיו

הַמִּזְבְּחֹת וַיָּשֶׂם הַכֹּהֵן פְּקֻדּוֹת עַל־ בֵּית יְהוָה׃
the-altars then-he-posted the-priest guards at temple-of Yahweh

(19) וַיִּקַּח אֶת־ שָׂרֵי הַמֵּאוֹת וְאֶת־ הַכָּרִי וְאֶת־
(19) and-he-took *** commanders-of the-hundreds and the-Carite and

הָרָצִים וְאֵת ׀ כָּל־ עַם הָאָרֶץ וַיֹּרִידוּ אֶת־
the-ones-guarding and all-of people-of the-land and-they-brought-down ***

הַמֶּלֶךְ מִבֵּית יְהוָה וַיָּבוֹאוּ דֶּרֶךְ־ שַׁעַר הָרָצִים
the-king from-temple-of Yahweh and-they-went way-of gate-of the-ones-guarding

בֵּית הַמֶּלֶךְ וַיֵּשֶׁב עַל־ כִּסֵּא הַמְּלָכִים׃
palace-of the-king then-he-took-place on throne-of the-kings

(20) וַיִּשְׂמַח כָּל־ עַם־ הָאָרֶץ וְהָעִיר שָׁקָטָה
(20) and-he-rejoiced all-of people-of the-land and-the-city she-was-quiet

וְאֶת־ עֲתַלְיָהוּ הֵמִיתוּ בַחֶרֶב בֵּית °מֶלֶךְ׃ *(12:1) בֶּן־
and Athaliah they-killed with-the-sword palace-of the-king *(12:1) son-of

שֶׁבַע שָׁנִים יְהוֹאָשׁ בְּמָלְכוֹ׃ (2) בִּשְׁנַת־ שֶׁבַע לְיֵהוּא
seven years Jehoash when-to-reign-him (2) in-year-of seven of-Jehu

מָלַךְ יְהוֹאָשׁ וְאַרְבָּעִים שָׁנָה מָלַךְ בִּירוּשָׁלָםִ וְשֵׁם
he-became-king Jehoash and-forty year he-reigned in-Jerusalem and-name-of

אִמּוֹ צִבְיָה מִבְּאֵר שָׁבַע׃ (3) וַיַּעַשׂ יְהוֹאָשׁ הַיָּשָׁר
mother-of-him Zibiah from-Beer Sheba (3) and-he-did Jehoash the-right

בְּעֵינֵי יְהוָה כָּל־ יָמָיו אֲשֶׁר הוֹרָהוּ יְהוֹיָדָע
in-eyes-of Yahweh all-of days-of-him that he-instructed-him Jehoiada

הַכֹּהֵן׃ (4) רַק הַבָּמוֹת לֹא־ סָרוּ עוֹד הָעָם
the-priest (4) however the-high-places not they-removed still the-people

מְזַבְּחִים וּמְקַטְּרִים בַּבָּמוֹת׃
ones-offering-sacrifices and-ones-burning-incense at-the-high-places

(5) וַיֹּאמֶר יְהוֹאָשׁ אֶל־ הַכֹּהֲנִים כֹּל† כֶּסֶף הַקֳּדָשִׁים
(5) and-he-said Jehoash to the-priests all-of money-of the-sacred-offerings

אֲשֶׁר־ יוּבָא בֵית־ יְהוָה כֶּסֶף עוֹבֵר אִישׁ כֶּסֶף
that he-is-brought temple-of Yahweh money-of passing-by-of man money-of

נַפְשׁוֹת עֶרְכּוֹ כָּל־ כֶּסֶף אֲשֶׁר יַעֲלֶה עַל לֶב־ אִישׁ
persons-of value-of-him all-of money that he-comes from heart-of man

לְהָבִיא בֵּית יְהוָה׃ (6) יִקְחוּ לָהֶם הַכֹּהֲנִים אִישׁ
to-bring temple-of Yahweh (6) let-them-receive for-them the-priests each

מֵאֵת מַכָּרוֹ וְהֵם יְחַזְּקוּ אֶת־ בֶּדֶק הַבַּיִת
from treasurer-of-him and-they let-them-repair *** damage-of the-temple

לְכֹל אֲשֶׁר־ יִמָּצֵא שָׁם בָּדֶק׃ (7) וַיְהִי בִּשְׁנַת עֶשְׂרִים
for-all that he-is-found there damage (7) but-he-was by-year-of twenty

Then Jehoiada the priest posted guards at the temple of the LORD. 19He took with him the commanders of hundreds, the Carites, the guards and all the people of the land, and together they brought the king down from the temple of the LORD and went into the palace, entering by way of the gate of the guards. The king then took his place on the royal throne, 20and all the people of the land rejoiced. And the city was quiet, because Athaliah had been slain with the sword at the palace.

21Joash[b] was seven years old when he began to reign.

*Joash Repairs the Temple*

12 In the seventh year of Jehu, Joash[c] became king, and he reigned in Jerusalem forty years. His mother's name was Zibiah; she was from Beersheba. 2Joash did what was right in the eyes of the LORD all the years Jehoiada the priest instructed him. 3The high places, however, were not removed; the people continued to offer sacrifices and burn incense there.

4Joash said to the priests, "Collect all the money that is brought as sacred offerings to the temple of the LORD—the money collected in the census, the money received from personal vows and the money brought voluntarily to the temple. 5Let every priest receive the money from one of the treasurers, and let it be used to repair whatever damage is found in the temple."

6But by the twenty-third

[b]21 Hebrew *Jehoash*, a variant of *Joash*
[c]1 Hebrew *Jehoash*, a variant of *Joash*; also in verses 2, 4, 6, 7 and 18

*The Hebrew numeration of chapter 12 begins with verse 21 of chapter 11 in English; thus, there is a one-verse discrepancy throughout chapter 12.

†19 Most mss have *sheva* in the *kaph* (כְּ–).

°20 ק המלך

וְשָׁלֹשׁ שָׁנָה לַמֶּלֶךְ יְהוֹאָשׁ לֹא־ חִזְּקוּ הַכֹּהֲנִים אֶת־
*** the-priests they-repaired not Jehoash of-the-king year and-three

בֶּדֶק הַבָּיִת׃ וַיִּקְרָא הַמֶּלֶךְ יְהוֹאָשׁ לִיהוֹיָדָע
for-Jehoiada Jehoash the-king so-he-summoned (8) the-temple damage-of

הַכֹּהֵן וְלַכֹּהֲנִים וַיֹּאמֶר אֲלֵהֶם מַדּוּעַ אֵינְכֶם
not-you why? to-them and-he-asked and-for-the-priests the-priest

מְחַזְּקִים אֶת־ בֶּדֶק הַבָּיִת וְעַתָּה אַל־ תִּקְחוּ־ כֶסֶף מֵאֵת
from money you-take not and-now the-temple damage-of *** ones-repairing

מַכָּרֵיכֶם כִּי־ לְבֶדֶק הַבַּיִת תִּתְּנֻהוּ׃
you-hand-over-him the-temple for-damage-of but treasuries-of-you

וַיֵּאֹתוּ הַכֹּהֲנִים לְבִלְתִּי קְחַת־ כֶּסֶף מֵאֵת הָעָם וּלְבִלְתִּי
and-not the-people from money to-collect not the-priests and-they-agreed (9)

חַזֵּק אֶת־ בֶּדֶק הַבָּיִת׃ וַיִּקַּח יְהוֹיָדָע הַכֹּהֵן
the-priest Jehoiada and-he-took (10) the-temple damage-of *** to-repair

אֲרוֹן אֶחָד וַיִּקֹּב חֹר בְּדַלְתּוֹ וַיִּתֵּן אֹתוֹ אֵצֶל הַמִּזְבֵּחַ
the-altar next-to him and-he-placed in-lid-of-him hole and-he-bored one chest

בַּיָּמִין° בְּבוֹא־ אִישׁ בֵּית יְהוָה וְנָתְנוּ־ שָׁמָּה הַכֹּהֲנִים
the-priests at-there and-they-put Yahweh temple-of one as-to-enter on-right

שֹׁמְרֵי הַסַּף אֶת־ כָּל־ הַכֶּסֶף הַמּוּבָא
the-one-being-brought the-money all-of *** the-entrance ones-guarding-of

בֵית־ יְהוָה׃ וַיְהִי כִּרְאוֹתָם כִּי־ רַב הַכֶּסֶף
the-money large-amount that when-to-see-them and-he-was (11) Yahweh temple-of

בָּאָרוֹן וַיַּעַל סֹפֵר הַמֶּלֶךְ וְהַכֹּהֵן הַגָּדוֹל
the-high and-the-priest the-king secretary-of then-he-came in-the-chest

וַיָּצֻרוּ וַיִּמְנוּ אֶת־ הַכֶּסֶף הַנִּמְצָא
the-one-being-brought the-money *** and-they-counted and-they-bagged

בֵית־ יְהוָה׃ וְנָתְנוּ אֶת־ הַכֶּסֶף הַמְתֻכָּן
the-one-being-determined the-money *** and-they-gave (12) Yahweh temple-of

עַל־ יָדוֹ° עֹשֵׂי הַמְּלָאכָה הַפְּקֻדִים° בֵּית
temple-of the-ones-being-appointed the-work ones-supervising-of hands-of into

יְהוָה וַיּוֹצִיאֻהוּ לְחָרָשֵׁי הָעֵץ וְלַבֹּנִים
and-to-the-ones-building the-wood to-ones-cutting-of and-they-paid-him Yahweh

הָעֹשִׂים בֵּית יְהוָה׃ וְלַגֹּדְרִים
and-to-the-ones-being-masons (13) Yahweh temple-of the-ones-working

וּלְחֹצְבֵי הָאֶבֶן וְלִקְנוֹת עֵצִים וְאַבְנֵי
and-stones-of timbers and-to-purchase the-stone and-to-ones-cutting-of

מַחְצֵב לְחַזֵּק אֶת־ בֶּדֶק בֵּית־ יְהוָה וּלְכֹל אֲשֶׁר־ יֵצֵא
he-paid that and-for-all Yahweh temple-of damage-of *** to-repair dressed

year of King Joash the priests still had not repaired the temple. [7]Therefore King Joash summoned Jehoiada the priest and the other priests and asked them, "Why aren't you repairing the damage done to the temple? Take no more money from your treasurers, but hand it over for repairing the temple." [8]The priests agreed that they would not collect any more money from the people and that they would not repair the temple themselves.

[9]Jehoiada the priest took a chest and bored a hole in its lid. He placed it beside the altar, on the right side as one enters the temple of the LORD. The priests who guarded the entrance put into the chest all the money that was brought to the temple of the LORD. [10]Whenever they saw that there was a large amount of money in the chest, the royal secretary and the high priest came, counted the money that had been brought into the temple of the LORD and put it into bags. [11]When the amount had been determined, they gave the money to the men appointed to supervise the work on the temple. With it they paid those who worked on the temple of the LORD—the carpenters and builders, [12]the masons and stonecutters. They purchased timber and dressed stone for the repair of the temple of the LORD, and met all the

*See the note on page 463.

°10 ק מימין
°12a ק ידי
°12b ק המפקדים

עַל־ הַבַּיִת לְחָזְקָה׃ אַךְ לֹא יֵעָשֶׂה בֵּית יְהוָה
Yahweh temple-of he-was-made not however (14) to-repair the-temple for

סִפּוֹת כֶּסֶף מְזַמְּרוֹת מִזְרָקוֹת חֲצֹצְרוֹת כָּל־ כְּלִי
article-of any-of trumpets sprinkling-bowls wick-trimmers silver basins-of

זָהָב וּכְלִי־ כָסֶף מִן־ הַכֶּסֶף הַמּוּבָא בֵית־
temple-of the-one-being-brought the-money from silver or-article-of gold

יְהוָה׃ כִּי־ לְעֹשֵׂי הַמְּלָאכָה יִתְּנֻהוּ וְחִזְּקוּ־
and-they-repaired they-paid-him the-work to-ones-doing-of for (15) Yahweh

בוֹ אֶת־ בֵּית יְהוָה׃ וְלֹא יְחַשְּׁבוּ אֶת־
*** they-required-to-account and-not (16) Yahweh temple-of *** with-him

הָאֲנָשִׁים אֲשֶׁר יִתְּנוּ אֶת־ הַכֶּסֶף עַל־ יָדָם לָתֵת לְעֹשֵׂי
to-ones-doing-of to-pay hand-of-them into the-money *** they-gave whom the-men

הַמְּלָאכָה כִּי בֶאֱמֻנָה הֵם עֹשִׂים׃ כֶּסֶף אָשָׁם
guilt-offering money-of (17) ones-acting they in-honesty because the-work

וְכֶסֶף חַטָּאוֹת לֹא יוּבָא בֵּית יְהוָה לַכֹּהֲנִים
for-the-priests Yahweh temple-of he-was-brought not sin-offerings and-money-of

יִהְיוּ׃ אָז יַעֲלֶה חֲזָאֵל מֶלֶךְ אֲרָם וַיִּלָּחֶם עַל־
against and-he-attacked Aram king-of Hazael he-went-up then (18) they-were

גַּת וַיִּלְכְּדָהּ וַיָּשֶׂם חֲזָאֵל פָּנָיו לַעֲלוֹת עַל־
against to-attack faces-of-him Hazael then-he-turned and-he-captured-her Gath

יְרוּשָׁלִָם׃ וַיִּקַּח יְהוֹאָשׁ מֶלֶךְ־ יְהוּדָה אֵת כָּל־ הַקֳּדָשִׁים
the-sacred-objects all-of *** Judah king-of Jehoash but-he-took (19) Jerusalem

אֲשֶׁר־ הִקְדִּישׁוּ יְהוֹשָׁפָט וִיהוֹרָם וַאֲחַזְיָהוּ אֲבֹתָיו
fathers-of-him and-Ahaziah and-Jehoram Jehoshaphat they-dedicated that

מַלְכֵי יְהוּדָה וְאֶת־ קֳדָשָׁיו וְאֵת כָּל־ הַזָּהָב הַנִּמְצָא
the-being-found the-gold all-of and dedicated-gifts-of-him and Judah kings-of

בְּאֹצְרוֹת בֵּית־ יְהוָה וּבֵית הַמֶּלֶךְ וַיִּשְׁלַח
and-he-sent the-king and-palace-of Yahweh temple-of in-treasuries-of

לַחֲזָאֵל מֶלֶךְ אֲרָם וַיַּעַל מֵעַל יְרוּשָׁלִָם׃ וְיֶתֶר
and-rest-of (20) Jerusalem from-against and-he-withdrew Aram king-of to-Hazael

דִּבְרֵי יוֹאָשׁ וְכָל־ אֲשֶׁר עָשָׂה הֲלוֹא־ הֵם כְּתוּבִים עַל־ סֵפֶר
book-of in ones-being-written they not? he-did that and-all Joash events-of

דִּבְרֵי הַיָּמִים לְמַלְכֵי יְהוּדָה׃ וַיָּקֻמוּ עֲבָדָיו
officials-of-him and-they-rose (21) Judah of-kings-of the-days annals-of

וַיִּקְשְׁרוּ־ קָשֶׁר וַיַּכּוּ אֶת־ יוֹאָשׁ בֵּית מִלֹּא
Millo Beth Joash *** and-they-assassinated conspiracy and-they-conspired

הַיֹּרֵד סִלָּא׃ וְיוֹזָבָד בֶּן־ שִׁמְעָת וִיהוֹזָבָד
and-Jehozabad Shimeath son-of and-Jozabad (22) Silla the-one-going-down

other expenses of restoring the temple.
[13]The money brought into the temple was not spent for making silver basins, wick trimmers, sprinkling bowls, trumpets or any other articles of gold or silver for the temple of the LORD; [14]it was paid to the workmen, who used it to repair the temple. [15]They did not require an accounting from those to whom they gave the money to pay the workers, because they acted with complete honesty. [16]The money from the guilt offerings and sin offerings was not brought into the temple of the LORD; it belonged to the priests.
[17]About this time Hazael king of Aram went up and attacked Gath and captured it. Then he turned to attack Jerusalem. [18]But Joash king of Judah took all the sacred objects dedicated by his fathers—Jehoshaphat, Jehoram and Ahaziah, the kings of Judah—and the gifts he himself had dedicated and all the gold found in the treasuries of the temple of the LORD and of the royal palace, and he sent them to Hazael king of Aram, who then withdrew from Jerusalem.
[19]As for the other events of the reign of Joash, and all he did, are they not written in the book of the annals of the kings of Judah? [20]His officials conspired against him and assassinated him at Beth Millo, on the road down to Silla. [21]The officials who murdered him were Jozabad son of Shimeath

*See the note on page 463.

בֶּן־ שֹׁמֵר | עֲבָדָיו הִכֻּהוּ וַיָּמֹת וַיִּקְבְּרוּ
and-they-buried and-he-died they-murdered-him officials-of-him Shomer son-of

אֹתוֹ עִם־ אֲבֹתָיו בְּעִיר דָּוִד וַיִּמְלֹךְ אֲמַצְיָה
Amaziah and-he-became-king David in-City-of fathers-of-him with him

בְּנוֹ תַּחְתָּיו׃ בִּשְׁנַת עֶשְׂרִים וְשָׁלֹשׁ שָׁנָה לְיוֹאָשׁ
of-Joash year and-three twenty in-year-of (13:1) in-place-of-him son-of-him

בֶּן־ אֲחַזְיָהוּ מֶלֶךְ יְהוּדָה מָלַךְ יְהוֹאָחָז בֶּן־ יֵהוּא עַל־יִשְׂרָאֵל
Israel over Jehu son-of Jehoahaz he-became-king Judah king-of Ahaziah son-of

בְּשֹׁמְרוֹן שְׁבַע עֶשְׂרֵה שָׁנָה׃ וַיַּעַשׂ הָרַע בְּעֵינֵי יְהוָה
Yahweh in-eyes-of the-evil and-he-did (2) year ten seven-of in-Samaria

וַיֵּלֶךְ אַחַר חַטֹּאת יָרָבְעָם בֶּן־ נְבָט אֲשֶׁר־ הֶחֱטִיא
he-caused-to-commit which Nebat son-of Jeroboam sins-of after and-he-followed

אֶת־יִשְׂרָאֵל לֹא־ סָר מִמֶּנָּה׃ וַיִּחַר־ אַף יְהוָה
Yahweh anger-of so-he-burned (3) from-her he-turned-away not Israel ***

בְּיִשְׂרָאֵל וַיִּתְּנֵם בְּיַד | חֲזָאֵל מֶלֶךְ־ אֲרָם
Aram king-of Hazael under-power-of and-he-kept-them against-Israel

וּבְיַד בֶּן־ הֲדַד בֶּן־ חֲזָאֵל כָּל־ הַיָּמִים׃ וַיְחַל
then-he-sought (4) the-days all-of Hazael son-of Hadad Ben and-under-power-of

יְהוֹאָחָז אֶת־ פְּנֵי יְהוָה וַיִּשְׁמַע אֵלָיו יְהוָה כִּי רָאָה אֶת־
*** he-saw for Yahweh to-him and-he-listened Yahweh faces-of *** Jehoahaz

לַחַץ יִשְׂרָאֵל כִּי־ לָחַץ אֹתָם מֶלֶךְ אֲרָם׃ וַיִּתֵּן
and-he-provided (5) Aram king-of them he-oppressed that Israel oppression-of

יְהוָה לְיִשְׂרָאֵל מוֹשִׁיעַ וַיֵּצְאוּ מִתַּחַת יַד־ אֲרָם
Aram power-of from-under and-they-escaped one-delivering for-Israel Yahweh

וַיֵּשְׁבוּ בְנֵי־ יִשְׂרָאֵל בְּאָהֳלֵיהֶם כִּתְמוֹל שִׁלְשׁוֹם׃ אַךְ
but (6) before as-yesterday in-homes-of-them Israel sons-of so-they-lived

לֹא־ סָרוּ מֵחַטֹּאות בֵּית־ יָרָבְעָם אֲשֶׁר־ הֶחֱטִי
he-caused-to-commit which Jeroboam house-of from-sins-of they-turned-away not

אֶת־יִשְׂרָאֵל בָּהּ הָלָךְ וְגַם הָאֲשֵׁרָה עָמְדָה בְּשֹׁמְרוֹן׃
in-Samaria she-stood the-Asherah-pole and-also he-continued in-her Israel ***

כִּי לֹא הִשְׁאִיר לִיהוֹאָחָז עָם כִּי אִם־ חֲמִשִּׁים פָּרָשִׁים וַעֲשָׂרָה
and-ten horsemen fifty only except army to-Jehoahaz he-left not for (7)

רֶכֶב וַעֲשֶׂרֶת אֲלָפִים רַגְלִי כִּי אִבְּדָם מֶלֶךְ אֲרָם
Aram king-of he-destroyed-them for foot-soldier thousands and-ten-of chariot

וַיְשִׂמֵם כֶּעָפָר לָדֻשׁ׃ וְיֶתֶר דִּבְרֵי יְהוֹאָחָז
Jehoahaz events-of and-rest-of (8) to-thresh like-the-dust and-he-made-them

וְכָל־ אֲשֶׁר עָשָׂה וּגְבוּרָתוֹ הֲלוֹא־ הֵם כְּתוּבִים עַל־
in ones-being-written they not? and-achievement-of-him he-did that and-all

and Jehozabad son of Shomer.
He died and was buried with
his fathers in the City of David. And Amaziah his son succeeded him as king.

*Jehoahaz King of Israel*

13 In the twenty-third
year of Joash son of
Ahaziah king of Judah, Jehoahaz son of Jehu became king
of Israel in Samaria, and he
reigned seventeen years. 2He
did evil in the eyes of the LORD
by following the sins of Jeroboam son of Nebat, which he
had caused Israel to commit,
and he did not turn away from
them. 3So the LORD's anger
burned against Israel, and for
a long time he kept them under the power of Hazael king
of Aram and Ben-Hadad his
son.
4Then Jehoahaz sought the
LORD's favor, and the LORD listened to him, for he saw how
severely the king of Aram was
oppressing Israel. 5The LORD
provided a deliverer for Israel,
and they escaped from the
power of Aram. So the Israelites lived in their own homes
as they had before. 6But they
did not turn away from the
sins of the house of Jeroboam,
which he had caused Israel to
commit; they continued in
them. Also, the Asherah pole[d]
remained standing in Sa-
maria.
7Nothing had been left of
the army of Jehoahaz except
fifty horsemen, ten chariots
and ten thousand foot soldiers, for the king of Aram had
destroyed the rest and made
them like the dust at threshing
time.
8As for the other events of
the reign of Jehoahaz, all he
did and his achievements, are
they not written in the book of

[d]6 That is, a symbol of the goddess Asherah; here and elsewhere in 2 Kings

*See the note on page 463.

°6 ק החטיא

סֵפֶר דִּבְרֵי הַיָּמִים לְמַלְכֵי יִשְׂרָאֵל׃ וַיִּשְׁכַּב יְהוֹאָחָז
Jehoahaz and-he-rested (9) Israel of-kings-of the-days annals-of book-of

עִם־ אֲבֹתָיו וַיִּקְבְּרֻהוּ בְּשֹׁמְרוֹן וַיִּמְלֹךְ יוֹאָשׁ
Joash and-he-became-king in-Samaria and-they-buried-him fathers-of-him with

בְּנוֹ תַּחְתָּיו׃ בִּשְׁנַת שְׁלֹשִׁים וָשֶׁבַע שָׁנָה לְיוֹאָשׁ
of-Joash year and-seven thirty in-year-of (10) in-place-of-him son-of-him

מֶלֶךְ יְהוּדָה מָלַךְ יְהוֹאָשׁ בֶּן־ יְהוֹאָחָז עַל־ יִשְׂרָאֵל בְּשֹׁמְרוֹן
in-Samaria Israel over Jehoahaz son-of Jehoash he-became-king Judah king-of

שֵׁשׁ עֶשְׂרֵה שָׁנָה׃ וַיַּעֲשֶׂה הָרַע בְּעֵינֵי יְהוָה לֹא סָר
he-turned-away not Yahweh in-eyes-of the-evil and-he-did (11) year ten six-of

מִכָּל־ חַטֹּאות יָרָבְעָם בֶּן־ נְבָט אֲשֶׁר־ הֶחֱטִיא אֶת־ יִשְׂרָאֵל
Israel *** he-caused-to-sin which Nebat son-of Jeroboam sins-of from-any-of

בָּהּ הָלָךְ׃ וְיֶתֶר דִּבְרֵי יוֹאָשׁ וְכָל־ אֲשֶׁר עָשָׂה
he-did that and-all Joash events-of and-rest-of (12) he-continued in-her

וּגְבוּרָתוֹ אֲשֶׁר נִלְחַם עִם אֲמַצְיָה מֶלֶךְ־ יְהוּדָה הֲלוֹא־
not? Judah king-of Amaziah against he-warred when and-achievement-of-him

הֵם כְּתוּבִים עַל־ סֵפֶר דִּבְרֵי הַיָּמִים לְמַלְכֵי יִשְׂרָאֵל׃
Israel of-kings-of the-days annals-of book-of in ones-being-written they

וַיִּשְׁכַּב יוֹאָשׁ עִם־ אֲבֹתָיו וְיָרָבְעָם יָשַׁב עַל־
on he-sat and-Jeroboam fathers-of-him with Joash and-he-rested (13)

כִּסְאוֹ וַיִּקָּבֵר יוֹאָשׁ בְּשֹׁמְרוֹן עִם מַלְכֵי יִשְׂרָאֵל׃
Israel kings-of with in-Samaria Joash and-he-was-buried throne-of-him

וֶאֱלִישָׁע חָלָה אֶת־ חָלְיוֹ אֲשֶׁר יָמוּת בּוֹ
from-him he-would-die which illness-of-him *** he-suffered now-Elisha (14)

וַיֵּרֶד אֵלָיו יוֹאָשׁ מֶלֶךְ־ יִשְׂרָאֵל וַיֵּבְךְּ עַל־ פָּנָיו
faces-of-him over and-he-wept Israel king-of Joash to-him and-he-went-down

וַיֹּאמַר אָבִי ׀ אָבִי רֶכֶב יִשְׂרָאֵל וּפָרָשָׁיו׃
and-horsemen-of-him Israel chariot-of father-of-me father-of-me and-he-cried

וַיֹּאמֶר לוֹ אֱלִישָׁע קַח קֶשֶׁת וְחִצִּים וַיִּקַּח אֵלָיו קֶשֶׁת
bow for-him so-he-got and-arrows bow get! Elisha to-him and-he-said (15)

וְחִצִּים׃ וַיֹּאמֶר ׀ לְמֶלֶךְ יִשְׂרָאֵל הַרְכֵּב יָדְךָ עַל־ הַקֶּשֶׁת
the-bow on hand-of-you place! Israel to-king-of and-he-said (16) and-arrows

וַיַּרְכֵּב יָדוֹ וַיָּשֶׂם אֱלִישָׁע יָדָיו עַל־ יְדֵי
hands-of on hands-of-him Elisha then-he-put hand-of-him when-he-placed

הַמֶּלֶךְ׃ וַיֹּאמֶר פְּתַח הַחַלּוֹן קֵדְמָה וַיִּפְתָּח וַיֹּאמֶר
and-he-said and-he-opened to-east the-window open! and-he-said (17) the-king

אֱלִישָׁע יְרֵה וַיּוֹר וַיֹּאמֶר חֵץ־ תְּשׁוּעָה לַיהוָה
of-Yahweh victory arrow-of and-he-declared and-he-shot shoot! Elisha

the annals of the kings of Israel? 9 Jehoahaz rested with his
fathers and was buried in Samaria. And Jehoash[e] his son
succeeded him as king.

*Jehoash King of Israel*

10 In the thirty-seventh year
of Joash king of Judah, Jehoash son of Jehoahaz became
king of Israel in Samaria, and
he reigned sixteen years. 11 He
did evil in the eyes of the LORD
and did not turn away from
any of the sins of Jeroboam
son of Nebat, which he had
caused Israel to commit; he
continued in them.
12 As for the other events of
the reign of Jehoash, all he did
and his achievements, including his war against Amaziah
king of Judah, are they not
written in the book of the annals of the kings of Israel? 13 Jehoash rested with his fathers,
and Jeroboam succeeded him
on the throne. Jehoash was
buried in Samaria with the
kings of Israel.
14 Now Elisha was suffering
from the illness from which he
died. Jehoash king of Israel
went down to see him and
wept over him. "My father!
My father!" he cried. "The
chariots and horsemen of Israel!"
15 Elisha said, "Get a bow
and some arrows," and he did
so. 16 "Take the bow in your
hands," he said to the king of
Israel. When he had taken it,
Elisha put his hands on the
king's hands.
17 "Open the east window,"
he said, and he opened it.
"Shoot!" Elisha said, and he
shot. "The LORD's arrow of victory, the arrow of victory over

[e]9 Hebrew *Joash*, a variant of *Jehoash*; also in verses 12-14 and 25

וְחֵץ תְּשׁוּעָה בַאֲרָם וְהִכִּיתָ אֶת־אֲרָם בַּאֲפֵק עַד־
to at-Aphek Aram *** now-you-will-destroy over-Aram victory and-arrow-of

כַּלֵּה׃ (18) וַיֹּאמֶר קַח הַחִצִּים וַיִּקָּח וַיֹּאמֶר
and-he-told and-he-took the-arrows take! then-he-said (18) to-be-complete

לְמֶלֶךְ־יִשְׂרָאֵל הַךְ־אַרְצָה וַיַּךְ שָׁלֹשׁ־פְּעָמִים וַיַּעֲמֹד׃
and-he-stopped times three and-he-struck on-ground strike! Israel to-king-of

(19) וַיִּקְצֹף עָלָיו אִישׁ הָאֱלֹהִים וַיֹּאמֶר לְהַכּוֹת חָמֵשׁ
five to-strike and-he-said the-God man-of with-him and-he-was-angry (19)

אוֹ־שֵׁשׁ פְּעָמִים אָז הִכִּיתָ אֶת־אֲרָם עַד־כַּלֵּה
to-completely-destroy to Aram *** you-would-defeat then times six or

וְעַתָּה שָׁלֹשׁ פְּעָמִים תַּכֶּה אֶת־אֲרָם׃ (20) וַיָּמָת אֱלִישָׁע
Elisha and-he-died (20) Aram *** you-will-defeat times three but-now

וַיִּקְבְּרֻהוּ וּגְדוּדֵי מוֹאָב יָבֹאוּ בָאָרֶץ
into-the-country they-entered Moab now-raiders-of and-they-buried-him

בָּא שָׁנָה׃ (21) וַיְהִי הֵם ׀ קֹבְרִים אִישׁ וְהִנֵּה רָאוּ אֶת־
*** they-saw and-see! man ones-burying they and-he-was (21) year coming-of

הַגְּדוּד וַיַּשְׁלִיכוּ אֶת־הָאִישׁ בְּקֶבֶר אֱלִישָׁע וַיֵּלֶךְ
when-he-went Elisha into-tomb-of the-man *** so-they-threw the-band

וַיִּגַּע הָאִישׁ בְּעַצְמוֹת אֱלִישָׁע וַיְחִי וַיָּקָם
and-he-stood-up then-he-came-to-life Elisha on-bones-of the-man and-he-touched

עַל־רַגְלָיו׃ (22) וַחֲזָאֵל מֶלֶךְ אֲרָם לָחַץ אֶת־יִשְׂרָאֵל
Israel *** he-oppressed Aram king-of and-Hazael (22) feet-of-him on

כֹּל יְמֵי יְהוֹאָחָז׃ (23) וַיָּחָן יְהוָה אֹתָם
to-them Yahweh but-he-was-gracious (23) Jehoahaz days-of all-of

וַיְרַחֲמֵם וַיִּפֶן אֲלֵיהֶם לְמַעַן
because-of for-them and-he-showed-concern and-he-had-compassion-for-them

בְּרִיתוֹ אֶת־אַבְרָהָם יִצְחָק וְיַעֲקֹב וְלֹא אָבָה
he-was-willing and-not and-Jacob Isaac Abraham with covenant-of-him

הַשְׁחִיתָם וְלֹא־הִשְׁלִיכָם מֵעַל־פָּנָיו עַד־
to presences-of-him from-before he-banished-them and-not to-destroy-them

עַתָּה׃ (24) וַיָּמָת חֲזָאֵל מֶלֶךְ־אֲרָם וַיִּמְלֹךְ בֶּן־הֲדַד
Hadad Ben and-he-became-king Aram king-of Hazael and-he-died (24) now

בְּנוֹ תַּחְתָּיו׃ (25) וַיָּשָׁב יְהוֹאָשׁ בֶּן־יְהוֹאָחָז
Jehoahaz son-of Jehoash then-he-returned (25) in-place-of-him son-of-him

וַיִּקַּח אֶת־הֶעָרִים מִיַּד בֶּן־הֲדַד בֶּן־חֲזָאֵל אֲשֶׁר
that Hazael son-of Hadad Ben from-hand-of the-towns *** and-he-recaptured

לָקַח מִיַּד יְהוֹאָחָז אָבִיו בַּמִּלְחָמָה שָׁלֹשׁ פְּעָמִים
times three in-the-battle father-of-him Jehoahaz from-hand-of he-took

Aram!" Elisha declared. "You will completely destroy the Arameans at Aphek."

[18]Then he said, "Take the arrows," and the king took them. Elisha told him, "Strike the ground." He struck it three times and stopped. [19]The man of God was angry with him and said, "You should have struck the ground five or six times; then you would have defeated Aram and completely destroyed it. But now you will defeat it only three times."

[20]Elisha died and was buried.

Now Moabite raiders used to enter the country every spring. [21]Once while some Israelites were burying a man, suddenly they saw a band of raiders; so they threw the man's body into Elisha's tomb. When the body touched Elisha's bones, the man came to life and stood up on his feet.

[22]Hazael king of Aram oppressed Israel throughout the reign of Jehoahaz. [23]But the LORD was gracious to them and had compassion and showed concern for them because of his covenant with Abraham, Isaac and Jacob. To this day he has been unwilling to destroy them or banish them from his presence.

[24]Hazael king of Aram died, and Ben-Hadad his son succeeded him as king. [25]Then Jehoash son of Jehoahaz recaptured from Ben-Hadad son of Hazael the towns he had taken

הִכָּהוּ יוֹאָשׁ וַיָּשֶׁב אֶת־ עָרֵי יִשְׂרָאֵל׃ בִּשְׁנַת
in-year-of (14:1) Israel towns-of *** so-he-recovered Joash he-defeated-him

שְׁתַּיִם לְיוֹאָשׁ בֶּן־ יוֹאָחָז מֶלֶךְ יִשְׂרָאֵל מָלַךְ אֲמַצְיָהוּ בֶן־
son-of Amaziah he-became-king Israel king-of Jehoahaz son-of of-Joash two

יוֹאָשׁ מֶלֶךְ יְהוּדָה׃ בֶּן־ עֶשְׂרִים וְחָמֵשׁ שָׁנָה הָיָה
he-was year and-five twenty son-of (2) Judah king-of Joash

בְמָלְכוֹ וְעֶשְׂרִים וָתֵשַׁע שָׁנָה מָלַךְ בִּירוּשָׁלָ͏ִם
in-Jerusalem he-reigned year and-nine and-twenty when-to-become-king-him

וְשֵׁם אִמּוֹ יְהוֹעַדִּין מִן־ יְרוּשָׁלָ͏ִם׃ וַיַּעַשׂ הַיָּשָׁר
the-right and-he-did (3) Jerusalem from Jehoaddin mother-of-him and-name-of

בְּעֵינֵי יְהוָה רַק לֹא כְּדָוִד אָבִיו כְּכֹל אֲשֶׁר־ עָשָׂה יוֹאָשׁ
Joash he-did that as-all father-of-him as-David not but Yahweh in-eyes-of

אָבִיו עָשָׂה׃ רַק הַבָּמוֹת לֹא־ סָרוּ עוֹד
still they-removed not the-high-places however (4) he-followed father-of-him

הָעָם מְזַבְּחִים וּמְקַטְּרִים בַּבָּמוֹת׃
at-the-high-places and-ones-burning-incense ones-offering-sacrifices the-people

וַיְהִי כַּאֲשֶׁר חָזְקָה הַמַּמְלָכָה בְּיָדוֹ וַיַּךְ
then-he-executed in-hand-of-him the-kingdom she-was-firm just-as and-he-was (5)

אֶת־ עֲבָדָיו הַמַּכִּים אֶת־ הַמֶּלֶךְ אָבִיו׃ וְאֶת־
yet (6) father-of-him the-king *** the-ones-murdering officials-of-him ***

בְּנֵי הַמַּכִּים לֹא הֵמִית כַּכָּתוּב
as-the-thing-being-written he-killed not the-ones-assassinating sons-of

בְּסֵפֶר תּוֹרַת־מֹשֶׁה אֲשֶׁר־ צִוָּה יְהוָה לֵאמֹר לֹא־ יוּמְתוּ
they-shall-be-killed not to-say Yahweh he-commanded where Moses Law-of in-Book-of

אָבוֹת עַל־ בָּנִים וּבָנִים לֹא־ יוּמְתוּ עַל־ אָבוֹת כִּי
for fathers for they-shall-be-killed not and-children children for fathers

אִם־ אִישׁ בְּחֶטְאוֹ יָמוּת׃ הוּא־ הִכָּה אֶת־אֱדוֹם
Edom *** he-defeated he (7) he-shall-be-killed for-sin-of-him each only

בְּגֵיא־ הַמֶּלַח עֲשֶׂרֶת אֲלָפִים וְתָפַשׂ אֶת־ הַסֶּלַע בַּמִּלְחָמָה
in-the-battle the-Sela *** and-he-captured thousands ten-of Salt in-Valley-of

וַיִּקְרָא אֶת־ שְׁמָהּ יָקְתְאֵל עַד הַיּוֹם הַזֶּה׃ אָז שָׁלַח
he-sent then (8) the-this the-day to Joktheel name-of-her *** and-he-called

אֲמַצְיָה מַלְאָכִים אֶל־יְהוֹאָשׁ בֶּן־ יְהוֹאָחָז בֶּן־ יֵהוּא מֶלֶךְ יִשְׂרָאֵל
Israel king-of Jehu son-of Jehoahaz son-of Jehoash to messengers Amaziah

לֵאמֹר לְכָה נִתְרָאֶה פָנִים׃ וַיִּשְׁלַח יְהוֹאָשׁ מֶלֶךְ־ יִשְׂרָאֵל אֶל־
to Israel king-of Jehoash but-he-replied (9) faces let-us-meet come! to-say

אֲמַצְיָהוּ מֶלֶךְ־ יְהוּדָה לֵאמֹר הַחוֹחַ אֲשֶׁר בַּלְּבָנוֹן שָׁלַח אֶל־
to he-sent in-the-Lebanon that the-thistle to-say Judah king-of Amaziah

°2 ק יהועדן
°6 ק יומת
°7 ק מלח

in battle from his father Jehoahaz. Three times Jehoash defeated him, and so he recovered the Israelite towns.

*Amaziah King of Judah*

**14** In the second year of Jehoash[f] son of Jehoahaz king of Israel, Amaziah son of Joash king of Judah began to reign. 2He was twenty-five years old when he became king, and he reigned in Jerusalem twenty-nine years. His mother's name was Jehoaddin; she was from Jerusalem. 3He did what was right in the eyes of the LORD, but not as his father David had done. In everything he followed the example of his father Joash. 4The high places, however, were not removed; the people continued to offer sacrifices and burn incense there.

5After the kingdom was firmly in his grasp, he executed the officials who had murdered his father the king. 6Yet he did not put the sons of the assassins to death, in accordance with what is written in the Book of the Law of Moses where the LORD commanded: "Fathers shall not be put to death for their children, nor children put to death for their fathers; each is to die for his own sins."[g]

7He was the one who defeated ten thousand Edomites in the Valley of Salt and captured Sela in battle, calling it Joktheel, the name it has to this day.

8Then Amaziah sent messengers to Jehoash son of Jehoahaz, the son of Jehu, king of Israel, with the challenge: "Come, meet me face to face."

9But Jehoash king of Israel replied to Amaziah king of Judah: "A thistle in Lebanon

f1 Hebrew *Joash*, a variant of *Jehoash*; also in verses 13, 23 and 27
g6 Deut. 24:16

הָאֶרֶז אֲשֶׁר בַּלְּבָנוֹן לֵאמֹר תְּנָה־ אֶת־ בִּתְּךָ לִבְנִי
to-son-of-me daughter-of-you *** give! to-say in-the-Lebanon that the-cedar

לְאִשָּׁה וַתַּעֲבֹר חַיַּת הַשָּׂדֶה אֲשֶׁר בַּלְּבָנוֹן
in-the-Lebanon that the-field beast-of then-she-came-along as-wife

וַתִּרְמֹס אֶת־ הַחוֹחַ׃ הַכֵּה הִכִּיתָ אֶת־ אֱדוֹם
Edom *** you-defeated to-defeat (10) the-thistle *** and-she-trampled

וּנְשָׂאֲךָ לִבֶּךָ הִכָּבֵד וְשֵׁב בְּבֵיתֶךָ וְלָמָּה
now-why? at-home-of-you but-stay! glory! heart-of-you and-he-lifted-you

תִתְגָּרֶה בְּרָעָה וְנָפַלְתָּה אַתָּה וִיהוּדָה עִמָּךְ׃ וְלֹא־
but-not (11) with-you and-Judah you so-you-fall for-trouble you-ask

שָׁמַע אֲמַצְיָהוּ וַיַּעַל יְהוֹאָשׁ מֶלֶךְ־ יִשְׂרָאֵל וַיִּתְרָאוּ פָנִים
faces and-they-met Israel king-of Jehoash so-he-attacked Amaziah he-listened

הוּא וַאֲמַצְיָהוּ מֶלֶךְ־ יְהוּדָה בְּבֵית שֶׁמֶשׁ אֲשֶׁר לִיהוּדָה׃
in-Judah that Shemesh at-Beth Judah king-of and-Amaziah he

וַיִּנָּגֶף יְהוּדָה לִפְנֵי יִשְׂרָאֵל וַיָּנֻסוּ אִישׁ לְאֹהָלָו׃°
to-homes-of-him each and-they-fled Israel before Judah and-he-was-routed (12)

וְאֵת אֲמַצְיָהוּ מֶלֶךְ־ יְהוּדָה בֶּן־ יְהוֹאָשׁ בֶּן־אֲחַזְיָהוּ תָּפַשׂ
he-captured Ahaziah son-of Jehoash son-of Judah king-of Amaziah and (13)

יְהוֹאָשׁ מֶלֶךְ־ יִשְׂרָאֵל בְּבֵית שֶׁמֶשׁ וַיָּבֹאוּ° יְרוּשָׁלַםִ וַיִּפְרֹץ
and-he-broke Jerusalem then-he-went Shemesh at-Beth Israel king-of Jehoash

בְּחוֹמַת יְרוּשָׁלַםִ בְּשַׁעַר אֶפְרַיִם עַד־ שַׁעַר הַפִּנָּה אַרְבַּע
four the-Corner Gate-of to Ephraim from-Gate-of Jerusalem through-wall-of

מֵאוֹת אַמָּה׃ וְלָקַח אֶת־ כָּל־ הַזָּהָב־ וְהַכֶּסֶף וְאֵת
and and-the-silver the-gold all-of *** and-he-took (14) cubit hundreds

כָּל־ הַכֵּלִים הַנִּמְצְאִים בֵּית־ יְהוָה וּבְאֹצְרוֹת
and-in-treasuries-of Yahweh temple-of the-ones-being-found the-articles all-of

בֵּית הַמֶּלֶךְ וְאֵת בְּנֵי הַתַּעֲרֻבוֹת וַיָּשָׁב שֹׁמְרוֹנָה׃
to-Samaria and-he-returned the-hostages sons-of and the-king palace-of

וְיֶתֶר דִּבְרֵי יְהוֹאָשׁ אֲשֶׁר עָשָׂה וּגְבוּרָתוֹ וַאֲשֶׁר
and-how and-achievement-of-him he-did what Jehoash events-of and-rest-of (15)

נִלְחַם עִם אֲמַצְיָהוּ מֶלֶךְ־ יְהוּדָה הֲלֹא־ הֵם כְּתוּבִים עַל־
in ones-being-written they not? Judah king-of Amaziah against he-warred

סֵפֶר דִּבְרֵי הַיָּמִים לְמַלְכֵי יִשְׂרָאֵל׃ וַיִּשְׁכַּב יְהוֹאָשׁ
Jehoash and-he-rested (16) Israel of-kings-of the-days annals-of book-of

עִם־ אֲבֹתָיו וַיִּקָּבֵר בְּשֹׁמְרוֹן עִם מַלְכֵי יִשְׂרָאֵל
Israel kings-of with in-Samaria and-he-was-buried fathers-of-him with

וַיִּמְלֹךְ יָרָבְעָם בְּנוֹ תַּחְתָּיו׃ וַיְחִי
and-he-lived (17) in-place-of-him son-of-him Jeroboam and-he-became-king

sent a message to a cedar in Lebanon, 'Give your daughter to my son in marriage.' Then a wild beast in Lebanon came along and trampled the thistle underfoot. [10]You have indeed defeated Edom and now you are arrogant. Glory in your victory, but stay at home! Why ask for trouble and cause your own downfall and that of Judah also?"

[11]Amaziah, however, would not listen, so Jehoash king of Israel attacked. He and Amaziah king of Judah faced each other at Beth Shemesh in Judah. [12]Judah was routed by Israel, and every man fled to his home. [13]Jehoash king of Israel captured Amaziah king of Judah, the son of Joash, the son of Ahaziah, at Beth Shemesh. Then Jehoash went to Jerusalem and broke down the wall of Jerusalem from the Ephraim Gate to the Corner Gate—a section about six hundred feet long.[h] [14]He took all the gold and silver and all the articles found in the temple of the LORD and in the treasuries of the royal palace. He also took hostages and returned to Samaria.

[15]As for the other events of the reign of Jehoash, what he did and his achievements, including his war against Amaziah king of Judah, are they not written in the book of the annals of the kings of Israel? [16]Jehoash rested with his fathers and was buried in Samaria with the kings of Israel. And Jeroboam his son succeeded him as king.

[h]13 Hebrew *four hundred cubits* (about 180 meters)

°*12* ק לאהליו
°*13* ק ויבא

אֲמַצְיָהוּ בֶּן־ יוֹאָשׁ מֶלֶךְ יְהוּדָה אַחֲרֵי מוֹת יְהוֹאָשׁ בֶּן־ יְהוֹאָחָז
Jehoahaz son-of Jehoash death-of after Judah king-of Joash son-of Amaziah

מֶלֶךְ יִשְׂרָאֵל חֲמֵשׁ עֶשְׂרֵה שָׁנָה׃ וְיֶתֶר דִּבְרֵי אֲמַצְיָהוּ הֲלֹא־
not? Amaziah events-of and-rest-of (18) year ten five-of Israel king-of

הֵם כְּתוּבִים עַל־ סֵפֶר דִּבְרֵי הַיָּמִים לְמַלְכֵי יְהוּדָה׃
Judah of-kings-of the-days annals-of book-of in ones-being-written they

וַיִּקְשְׁרוּ עָלָיו קֶשֶׁר בִּירוּשָׁלַם וַיָּנָס
and-he-fled in-Jerusalem conspiracy against-him and-they-conspired (19)

לָכִישָׁה וַיִּשְׁלְחוּ אַחֲרָיו לָכִישָׁה וַיְמִתֻהוּ שָׁם׃
there and-they-killed-him to-Lachish after-him but-they-sent to-Lachish

וַיִּשְׂאוּ אֹתוֹ עַל־ הַסּוּסִים וַיִּקָּבֵר בִּירוּשָׁלַם
in-Jerusalem and-he-was-buried the-horses on him and-they-brought-back (20)

עִם־ אֲבֹתָיו בְּעִיר דָּוִד׃ וַיִּקְחוּ כָּל־ עַם
people-of all-of then-they-took (21) David in-City-of fathers-of-him with

יְהוּדָה אֶת־ עֲזַרְיָה וְהוּא בֶּן־ שֵׁשׁ עֶשְׂרֵה שָׁנָה וַיַּמְלִכוּ אֹתוֹ
him and-they-made-king year ten six-of son-of now-he Azariah *** Judah

תַּחַת אָבִיו אֲמַצְיָהוּ׃ הוּא בָּנָה אֶת־ אֵילַת
Elath *** he-rebuilt he (22) Amaziah father-of-him in-place-of

וַיְשִׁבֶהָ לִיהוּדָה אַחֲרֵי שְׁכַב־ הַמֶּלֶךְ עִם־ אֲבֹתָיו׃
fathers-of-him with the-king to-rest after to-Judah and-he-restored-her

בִּשְׁנַת חֲמֵשׁ־עֶשְׂרֵה שָׁנָה לַאֲמַצְיָהוּ בֶן־ יוֹאָשׁ מֶלֶךְ יְהוּדָה
Judah king-of Joash son-of of-Amaziah year ten five-of in-year-of (23)

מָלַךְ יָרָבְעָם בֶּן־ יוֹאָשׁ מֶלֶךְ־ יִשְׂרָאֵל בְּשֹׁמְרוֹן אַרְבָּעִים
forty in-Samaria Israel king-of Joash son-of Jeroboam he-became-king

וְאַחַת שָׁנָה׃ וַיַּעַשׂ הָרַע בְּעֵינֵי יְהוָה לֹא סָר
he-turned-away not Yahweh in-eyes-of the-evil and-he-did (24) year and-one

מִכָּל־ חַטֹּאות יָרָבְעָם בֶּן־ נְבָט אֲשֶׁר הֶחֱטִיא אֶת־
*** he-caused-to-commit which Nebat son-of Jeroboam sins-of from-any-of

יִשְׂרָאֵל׃ הוּא הֵשִׁיב אֶת־ גְּבוּל יִשְׂרָאֵל מִלְּבוֹא חֲמָת עַד־
to Hamath from-Lebo Israel boundary-of *** he-restored he (25) Israel

יָם הָעֲרָבָה כִּדְבַר יְהוָה אֱלֹהֵי יִשְׂרָאֵל אֲשֶׁר דִּבֶּר בְּיַד־
by-hand-of he-spoke that Israel God-of Yahweh as-word-of the-Arabah Sea-of

עַבְדּוֹ יוֹנָה בֶן־ אֲמִתַּי הַנָּבִיא אֲשֶׁר מִגַּת הַחֵפֶר׃
the-Hepher from-Gath-of who the-prophet Amittai son-of Jonah servant-of-him

כִּי־ רָאָה יְהוָה אֶת־ עֳנִי יִשְׂרָאֵל מֹרֶה מְאֹד וְאֶפֶס
and-whether very being-bitter Israel suffering-of *** Yahweh he-saw for (26)

עָצוּר וְאֶפֶס עָזוּב וְאֵין עֹזֵר לְיִשְׂרָאֵל׃ וְלֹא־
and-not (27) to-Israel helping and-no-one being-free or-whether being-slave

17Amaziah son of Joash king
of Judah lived for fifteen years
after the death of Jehoash son
of Jehoahaz king of Israel. 18As
for the other events of Amaziah's reign, are they not written in the book of the annals
of the kings of Judah?

19They conspired against him in Jerusalem, and he fled to Lachish, but they sent men after him to Lachish and killed him there. 20He was brought back by horse and was buried in Jerusalem with his fathers, in the City of David.

21Then all the people of Judah took Azariah,[i] who was sixteen years old, and made him king in place of his father Amaziah. 22He was the one who rebuilt Elath and restored it to Judah after Amaziah rested with his fathers.

*Jeroboam II King of Israel*

23In the fifteenth year of Amaziah son of Joash king of Judah, Jeroboam son of Jehoash king of Israel became king in Samaria, and he reigned forty-one years. 24He did evil in the eyes of the LORD and did not turn away from any of the sins of Jeroboam son of Nebat, which he had caused Israel to commit. 25He was the one who restored the boundaries of Israel from Lebo[j] Hamath to the Sea of the Arabah,[k] in accordance with the word of the LORD, the God of Israel, spoken through his servant Jonah son of Amittai, the prophet from Gath Hepher.

26The LORD had seen how bitterly everyone in Israel, whether slave or free, was suffering; there was no one to help them. 27And since the

[i]21 Also called *Uzziah*
[j]25 Or *from the entrance to*
[k]25 That is, the Dead Sea

דִּבֶּר יְהוָה לִמְחוֹת אֶת־ שֵׁם יִשְׂרָאֵל מִתַּחַת הַשָּׁמָיִם
the-heavens from-under Israel name-of *** to-blot-out Yahweh he-said

וַיּוֹשִׁיעֵם בְּיַד יָרָבְעָם בֶּן־ יוֹאָשׁ׃ וְיֶתֶר דִּבְרֵי
events-of and-rest-of (28) Joash son-of Jeroboam by-hand-of so-he-saved-them

יָרָבְעָם וְכָל־ אֲשֶׁר עָשָׂה וּגְבוּרָתוֹ אֲשֶׁר־ נִלְחָם וַאֲשֶׁר
and-how he-fought that and-achievement-of-him he-did that and-all Jeroboam

הֵשִׁיב אֶת־ דַּמֶּשֶׂק וְאֶת־ חֲמָת לִיהוּדָה בְּיִשְׂרָאֵל הֲלֹא־ הֵם
they not? for-Israel of-Judah Hamath and Damascus *** he-recovered

כְּתוּבִים עַל־ סֵפֶר דִּבְרֵי הַיָּמִים לְמַלְכֵי יִשְׂרָאֵל׃
Israel of-kings-of the-days annals-of book-of in ones-being-written

וַיִּשְׁכַּב יָרָבְעָם עִם־ אֲבֹתָיו עִם מַלְכֵי יִשְׂרָאֵל
Israel kings-of with fathers-of-him with Jeroboam and-he-rested (29)

וַיִּמְלֹךְ זְכַרְיָה בְנוֹ תַּחְתָּיו׃ בִּשְׁנַת
in-year-of (15:1) in-place-of-him son-of-him Zechariah and-he-became-king

עֶשְׂרִים וָשֶׁבַע שָׁנָה לְיָרָבְעָם מֶלֶךְ יִשְׂרָאֵל מָלַךְ עֲזַרְיָה
Azariah he-became-king Israel king-of of-Jeroboam year and-seven twenty

בֶן־ אֲמַצְיָה מֶלֶךְ יְהוּדָה׃ בֶּן־ שֵׁשׁ עֶשְׂרֵה שָׁנָה הָיָה
he-was year ten six-of son-of (2) Judah king-of Amaziah son-of

בְמָלְכוֹ וַחֲמִשִּׁים וּשְׁתַּיִם שָׁנָה מָלַךְ בִּירוּשָׁלָם
in-Jerusalem he-reigned year and-two and-fifty when-to-become-king-him

וְשֵׁם אִמּוֹ יְכָלְיָהוּ מִירוּשָׁלָם׃ וַיַּעַשׂ הַיָּשָׁר
the-right and-he-did (3) from-Jerusalem Jecoliah mother-of-him and-name-of

בְּעֵינֵי יְהוָה כְּכֹל אֲשֶׁר־ עָשָׂה אֲמַצְיָהוּ אָבִיו׃ רַק
however (4) father-of-him Amaziah he-did that as-all Yahweh in-eyes-of

הַבָּמוֹת לֹא־ סָרוּ עוֹד הָעָם מְזַבְּחִים
ones-offering-sacrifices the-people still they-removed not the-high-places

וּמְקַטְּרִים בַּבָּמוֹת׃ וַיְנַגַּע יְהוָה אֶת־
*** Yahweh and-he-afflicted (5) at-the-high-places and-ones-burning-incense

הַמֶּלֶךְ וַיְהִי מְצֹרָע עַד־ יוֹם מֹתוֹ וַיֵּשֶׁב
and-he-lived death-of-him day-of until being-leprous and-he-was the-king

בְּבֵית הַחָפְשִׁית וְיוֹתָם בֶּן־ הַמֶּלֶךְ עַל־ הַבַּיִת שֹׁפֵט
governing the-palace over the-king son-of and-Jotham the-separate in-house-of

אֶת־ עַם הָאָרֶץ׃ וְיֶתֶר דִּבְרֵי עֲזַרְיָהוּ וְכָל־ אֲשֶׁר עָשָׂה
he-did that and-all Azariah events-of and-rest-of (6) the-land people-of ***

הֲלֹא־ הֵם כְּתוּבִים עַל־ סֵפֶר דִּבְרֵי הַיָּמִים לְמַלְכֵי יְהוּדָה׃
Judah of-kings-of the-days annals-of book-of in ones-being-written they not?

וַיִּשְׁכַּב עֲזַרְיָה עִם־ אֲבֹתָיו וַיִּקְבְּרוּ אֹתוֹ עִם־
with him and-they-buried fathers-of-him with Azariah and-he-rested (7)

LORD had not said he would blot out the name of Israel from under heaven, he saved them by the hand of Jeroboam son of Jehoash.
28 As for the other events of Jeroboam's reign, all he did, and his military achievements, including how he recovered for Israel both Damascus and Hamath, which had belonged to Yaudi,[l] are they not written in the book of the annals of the kings of Israel? 29 Jeroboam rested with his fathers, the kings of Israel. And Zechariah his son succeeded him as king.

*Azariah King of Judah*

15 In the twenty-seventh year of Jeroboam king of Israel, Azariah son of Amaziah king of Judah began to reign. 2 He was sixteen years old when he became king, and he reigned in Jerusalem fifty-two years. His mother's name was Jecoliah; she was from Jerusalem. 3 He did what was right in the eyes of the LORD, just as his father Amaziah had done. 4 The high places, however, were not removed; the people continued to offer sacrifices and burn incense there.
5 The LORD afflicted the king with leprosy[m] until the day he died, and he lived in a separate house.[n] Jotham the king's son had charge of the palace and governed the people of the land.
6 As for the other events of Azariah's reign, and all he did, are they not written in the book of the annals of the kings of Judah? 7 Azariah rested with his fathers and was buried

[l] 28 Or *Judah*
[m] 5 The Hebrew word was used for various diseases affecting the skin—not necessarily leprosy.
[n] 5 Or *in a house where he was relieved of responsibility*

אֲבֹתָיו בְּעִיר דָּוִד וַיִּמְלֹךְ יוֹתָם בְּנוֹ
son-of-him Jotham and-he-became-king David in-City-of fathers-of-him

תַּחְתָּיו׃ (8) בִּשְׁנַת שְׁלֹשִׁים וּשְׁמֹנֶה שָׁנָה לַעֲזַרְיָהוּ מֶלֶךְ
king-of of-Azariah year and-eight thirty in-year-of (8) in-place-of-him

יְהוּדָה מָלַךְ זְכַרְיָהוּ בֶן־ יָרָבְעָם עַל־ יִשְׂרָאֵל בְּשֹׁמְרוֹן שִׁשָּׁה
six in-Samaria Israel over Jeroboam son-of Zechariah he-became-king Judah

חֳדָשִׁים׃ וַיַּעַשׂ הָרַע בְּעֵינֵי יְהוָה כַּאֲשֶׁר עָשׂוּ
they-did just-as Yahweh in-eyes-of the-evil and-he-did (9) months

אֲבֹתָיו לֹא סָר מֵחַטֹּאות יָרָבְעָם בֶּן־ נְבָט אֲשֶׁר
which Nebat son-of Jeroboam from-sins-of he-turned-away not fathers-of-him

הֶחֱטִיא אֶת־ יִשְׂרָאֵל׃ וַיִּקְשֹׁר עָלָיו שַׁלֻּם
Shallum against-him and-he-conspired (10) Israel *** he-caused-to-commit

בֶּן־ יָבֵשׁ וַיַּכֵּהוּ קָבָל־ עָם וַיְמִיתֵהוּ
and-he-assassinated-him people in-front-of and-he-attacked-him Jabesh son-of

וַיִּמְלֹךְ תַּחְתָּיו׃ וְיֶתֶר דִּבְרֵי זְכַרְיָה
Zechariah events-of and-rest-of (11) in-place-of-him and-he-became-king

הִנָּם כְּתוּבִים עַל־ סֵפֶר דִּבְרֵי הַיָּמִים לְמַלְכֵי יִשְׂרָאֵל׃
Israel of-kings-of the-days annals-of book-of in ones-being-written see-they!

הוּא דְבַר־ יְהוָה אֲשֶׁר דִּבֶּר אֶל־ יֵהוּא לֵאמֹר בְּנֵי רְבִיעִים
fourth-ones sons-of to-say Jehu to he-spoke that Yahweh word-of this (12)

יֵשְׁבוּ לְךָ עַל־ כִּסֵּא יִשְׂרָאֵל וַיְהִי־ כֵן׃ שַׁלּוּם בֶּן־
son-of Shallum (13) so and-he-was Israel throne-of on of-you they-will-sit

יָבֵישׁ מָלַךְ בִּשְׁנַת שְׁלֹשִׁים וָתֵשַׁע שָׁנָה לְעֻזִּיָּה* מֶלֶךְ
king-of of-Uzziah year and-nine thirty in-year-of he-became-king Jabesh

יְהוּדָה וַיִּמְלֹךְ יֶרַח־ יָמִים בְּשֹׁמְרוֹן׃ וַיַּעַל מְנַחֵם
Menahem then-he-went-up (14) in-Samaria days month-of and-he-reigned Judah

בֶּן־ גָּדִי מִתִּרְצָה וַיָּבֹא שֹׁמְרוֹן וַיַּךְ אֶת־ שַׁלּוּם
Shallum *** and-he-attacked Samaria and-he-went from-Tirzah Gadi son-of

בֶּן־ יָבֵישׁ בְּשֹׁמְרוֹן וַיְמִיתֵהוּ וַיִּמְלֹךְ
and-he-became-king and-he-assassinated-him in-Samaria Jabesh son-of

תַּחְתָּיו׃ וְיֶתֶר דִּבְרֵי שַׁלּוּם וְקִשְׁרוֹ
and-conspiracy-of-him Shallum events-of and-rest-of (15) in-place-of-him

אֲשֶׁר קָשָׁר הִנָּם כְּתֻבִים עַל־ סֵפֶר דִּבְרֵי
annals-of book-of in ones-being-written see-they! he-conspired that

הַיָּמִים לְמַלְכֵי יִשְׂרָאֵל׃ אָז יַכֶּה־ מְנַחֵם אֶת־ תִּפְסַח וְאֶת־
and Tiphsah *** Menahem he-attacked then (16) Israel of-kings-of the-days

כָּל־ אֲשֶׁר־ בָּהּ וְאֶת־ גְּבוּלֶיהָ מִתִּרְצָה כִּי לֹא פָתַח
he-opened not for from-Tirzah vicinity-of-her and in-her who all

near them in the City of David. And Jotham his son succeeded him as king.

*Zechariah King of Israel*

8In the thirty-eighth year of Azariah king of Judah, Zechariah son of Jeroboam became king of Israel in Samaria, and he reigned six months. 9He did evil in the eyes of the LORD, as his fathers had done. He did not turn away from the sins of Jeroboam son of Nebat, which he had caused Israel to commit.

10Shallum son of Jabesh conspired against Zechariah. He attacked him in front of the people,[o] assassinated him and succeeded him as king. 11The other events of Zechariah's reign are written in the book of the annals of the kings of Israel. 12So the word of the LORD spoken to Jehu was fulfilled: "Your descendants will sit on the throne of Israel to the fourth generation."[p]

*Shallum King of Israel*

13Shallum son of Jabesh became king in the thirty-ninth year of Uzziah king of Judah, and he reigned in Samaria one month. 14Then Menahem son of Gadi went from Tirzah up to Samaria. He attacked Shallum son of Jabesh in Samaria, assassinated him and succeeded him as king.

15The other events of Shallum's reign, and the conspiracy he led, are written in the book of the annals of the kings of Israel.

16At that time Menahem, starting out from Tirzah, attacked Tiphsah and everyone in the city and its vicinity, because they refused to open

[o]10 Hebrew; some Septuagint manuscripts *in Ibleam*
[p]12 2 Kings 10:30

*13 Most mss have *dagesh* in the *zayin* ( זּ ).

וַיַּךְ אֶת כָּל־ הֶהָרוֹתֶיהָ בִּקֵּעַ׃
he-ripped-open the-pregnant-women-of-her all-of *** and-he-sacked

בִּשְׁנַת שְׁלֹשִׁים וָתֵשַׁע שָׁנָה לַעֲזַרְיָה מֶלֶךְ יְהוּדָה מָלַךְ
he-became-king Judah king-of of-Azariah year and-nine thirty in-year-of (17)

מְנַחֵם בֶּן־ גָּדִי עַל־ יִשְׂרָאֵל עֶשֶׂר שָׁנִים בְּשֹׁמְרוֹן׃ וַיַּעַשׂ הָרַע
the-evil and-he-did (18) in-Samaria years ten Israel over Gadi son-of Menahem

בְּעֵינֵי יְהוָה לֹא סָר מֵעַל חַטֹּאות יָרָבְעָם בֶּן־ נְבָט
Nebat son-of Jeroboam sins-of away-from he-turned-away not Yahweh in-eyes-of

אֲשֶׁר־ הֶחֱטִיא אֶת־ יִשְׂרָאֵל כָּל־ יָמָיו׃ בָּא פוּל
Pul he-invaded (19) days-of-him all-of Israel *** he-caused-to-commit which

מֶלֶךְ־ אַשּׁוּר עַל־ הָאָרֶץ וַיִּתֵּן מְנַחֵם לְפוּל אֶלֶף כִּכַּר־
talent-of thousand to-Pul Menaham and-he-gave the-land into Assyria king-of

כָּסֶף לִהְיוֹת יָדָיו אִתּוֹ לְהַחֲזִיק הַמַּמְלָכָה בְּיָדוֹ׃
in-hand-of-him the-kingdom to-strengthen with-him hands-of-him to-be silver

וַיֹּצֵא מְנַחֵם אֶת־ הַכֶּסֶף עַל־ יִשְׂרָאֵל עַל כָּל־ גִּבּוֹרֵי
men-of all-of from Israel from the-money *** Menahem and-he-exacted (20)

הַחַיִל לָתֵת לְמֶלֶךְ אַשּׁוּר חֲמִשִּׁים שְׁקָלִים כֶּסֶף לְאִישׁ
from-man silver shekels fifty Assyria to-king-of to-contribute the-wealth

אֶחָד וַיָּשָׁב מֶלֶךְ אַשּׁוּר וְלֹא־ עָמַד שָׁם בָּאָרֶץ׃
in-the-land there he-stayed and-not Assyria king-of so-he-withdrew each

וְיֶתֶר דִּבְרֵי מְנַחֵם וְכָל־ אֲשֶׁר עָשָׂה הֲלוֹא־ הֵם
they not? he-did that and-all Menahem events-of and-rest-of (21)

כְּתוּבִים עַל־ סֵפֶר דִּבְרֵי הַיָּמִים לְמַלְכֵי יִשְׂרָאֵל׃
Israel of-kings-of the-days annals-of book-of in ones-being-written

וַיִּשְׁכַּב מְנַחֵם עִם־ אֲבֹתָיו וַיִּמְלֹךְ פְּקַחְיָה
Pekahiah and-he-became-king fathers-of-him with Menahem and-he-rested (22)

בְנוֹ תַּחְתָּיו׃ בִּשְׁנַת חֲמִשִּׁים שָׁנָה לַעֲזַרְיָה מֶלֶךְ
king-of of-Azariah year fifty in-year-of (23) in-place-of-him son-of-him

יְהוּדָה מָלַךְ פְּקַחְיָה בֶן־ מְנַחֵם עַל־ יִשְׂרָאֵל בְּשֹׁמְרוֹן שְׁנָתָיִם׃
two-years in-Samaria Israel over Menahem son-of Pekahiah he-became-king Judah

וַיַּעַשׂ הָרַע בְּעֵינֵי יְהוָה לֹא סָר מֵחַטֹּאות
from-sins-of he-turned-away not Yahweh in-eyes-of the-evil and-he-did (24)

יָרָבְעָם בֶּן־ נְבָט אֲשֶׁר הֶחֱטִיא אֶת־ יִשְׂרָאֵל׃ וַיִּקְשֹׁר
and-he-conspired (25) Israel *** he-caused-to-commit which Nebat son-of Jeroboam

עָלָיו פֶּקַח בֶּן־ רְמַלְיָהוּ שָׁלִישׁוֹ וַיַּכֻּהוּ
and-he-assassinated-him chief-officer-of-him Remaliah son-of Pekah against-him

בְשֹׁמְרוֹן בְּאַרְמוֹן בֵּית־ מֶלֶךְ אֶת־ אַרְגֹּב וְאֶת־ הָאַרְיֵה
the-Arieh and-with Argob with the-king palace-of in-citadel-of in-Samaria

their gates. He sacked Tiphsah and ripped open all the pregnant women.

*Menahem King of Israel*

17In the thirty-ninth year of Azariah king of Judah, Menahem son of Gadi became king of Israel, and he reigned in Samaria ten years. 18He did evil in the eyes of the LORD. During his entire reign he did not turn away from the sins of Jeroboam son of Nebat, which he had caused Israel to commit.

19Then Pul[q] king of Assyria invaded the land, and Menahem gave him a thousand talents[r] of silver to gain his support and strengthen his own hold on the kingdom. 20Menahem exacted this money from Israel. Every wealthy man had to contribute fifty shekels[s] of silver to be given to the king of Assyria. So the king of Assyria withdrew and stayed in the land no longer.

21As for the other events of Menahem's reign, and all he did, are they not written in the book of the annals of the kings of Israel? 22Menahem rested with his fathers. And Pekahiah his son succeeded him as king.

*Pekahiah King of Israel*

23In the fiftieth year of Azariah king of Judah, Pekahiah son of Menahem became king of Israel in Samaria, and he reigned two years. 24Pekahiah did evil in the eyes of the LORD. He did not turn away from the sins of Jeroboam son of Nebat, which he had caused Israel to commit. 25One of his chief officers, Pekah son of Remaliah, conspired against

q19 Also called *Tiglath-Pileser*
r19 That is, about 37 tons (about 34 metric tons)
s20 That is, about 1 1/4 pounds (about 0.6 kilogram)

°25 ק המלך

וְעִמּוֹ חֲמִשִּׁים אִישׁ מִבְּנֵי גִלְעָדִים וַיְמִתֵהוּ

so-he-killed-him Gileadites from-men-of man fifty and-with-him

וַיִּמְלֹךְ תַּחְתָּיו׃ וְיֶתֶר דִּבְרֵי פְקַחְיָה

Pekahiah events-of and-rest-of (26) in-place-of-him and-he-became-king

וְכָל־ אֲשֶׁר עָשָׂה הִנָּם כְּתוּבִים עַל־ סֵפֶר דִּבְרֵי

annals-of book-of in ones-being-written see-they! he-did that and-all

הַיָּמִים לְמַלְכֵי יִשְׂרָאֵל׃ בִּשְׁנַת חֲמִשִּׁים וּשְׁתַּיִם שָׁנָה לַעֲזַרְיָה

of-Azariah year and-two fifty in-year-of (27) Israel of-kings-of the-days

מֶלֶךְ יְהוּדָה מָלַךְ פֶּקַח בֶּן־ רְמַלְיָהוּ עַל־ יִשְׂרָאֵל בְּשֹׁמְרוֹן

in-Samaria Israel over Remaliah son-of Pekah he-became-king Judah king-of

עֶשְׂרִים שָׁנָה׃ וַיַּעַשׂ הָרַע בְּעֵינֵי יְהוָה לֹא סָר

he-turned-away not Yahweh in-eyes-of the-evil and-he-did (28) year twenty

מִן־ חַטֹּאות יָרָבְעָם בֶּן־ נְבָט אֲשֶׁר הֶחֱטִיא אֶת־ יִשְׂרָאֵל׃

Israel *** he-caused-to-commit which Nebat son-of Jeroboam sins-of from

בִּימֵי פֶּקַח מֶלֶךְ־ יִשְׂרָאֵל בָּא תִּגְלַת פִּלְאֶסֶר מֶלֶךְ אַשּׁוּר

Assyria king-of Pileser Tiglath he-came Israel king-of Pekah in-days-of (29)

וַיִּקַּח אֶת־ עִיּוֹן וְאֶת־אָבֵל בֵּית־מַעֲכָה וְאֶת־יָנוֹחַ וְאֶת־ קֶדֶשׁ וְאֶת־ חָצוֹר

Hazor and Kedesh and Janoah and Maacah Beth Abel and Ijon *** and-he-took

וְאֶת־ הַגִּלְעָד וְאֶת־ הַגָּלִילָה כֹּל אֶרֶץ נַפְתָּלִי וַיַּגְלֵם

and-he-deported-them Naphtali land-of all-of to-the-Galilee and the-Gilead and

אַשּׁוּרָה׃ וַיִּקְשָׁר־ קֶשֶׁר הוֹשֵׁעַ בֶּן־ אֵלָה עַל־

against Elah son-of Hoshea conspiracy then-he-conspired (30) to-Assyria

פֶּקַח בֶּן־ רְמַלְיָהוּ וַיַּכֵּהוּ וַיְמִיתֵהוּ

and-he-assassinated-him and-he-attacked-him Remaliah son-of Pekah

וַיִּמְלֹךְ תַּחְתָּיו בִּשְׁנַת עֶשְׂרִים לְיוֹתָם בֶּן־ עֻזִיָּה*׃

Uzziah son-of of-Jotham twenty in-year-of in-place-of-him and-he-became-king

וְיֶתֶר דִּבְרֵי־ פֶקַח וְכָל־ אֲשֶׁר עָשָׂה הִנָּם

see-they! he-did that and-all Pekah events-of and-rest-of (31)

כְּתוּבִים עַל־ סֵפֶר דִּבְרֵי הַיָּמִים לְמַלְכֵי יִשְׂרָאֵל׃

Israel of-kings-of the-days annals-of book-of in ones-being-written

בִּשְׁנַת שְׁתַּיִם לְפֶקַח בֶּן־ רְמַלְיָהוּ מֶלֶךְ יִשְׂרָאֵל מָלַךְ

he-became-king Israel king-of Remaliah son-of of-Pekah two in-year-of (32)

יוֹתָם בֶּן־ עֻזִיָּהוּ* מֶלֶךְ יְהוּדָה׃ בֶּן־ עֶשְׂרִים וְחָמֵשׁ שָׁנָה הָיָה

he-was year and-five twenty son-of (33) Judah king-of Uzziah son-of Jotham

בְמָלְכוֹ וְשֵׁשׁ־ עֶשְׂרֵה שָׁנָה מָלַךְ בִּירוּשָׁלָ͏ִם וְשֵׁם

and-name-of in-Jerusalem he-reigned year ten and-six-of when-to-become-king-him

אִמּוֹ יְרוּשָׁא בַּת־ צָדוֹק׃ וַיַּעַשׂ הַיָּשָׁר בְּעֵינֵי

in-eyes-of the-right and-he-did (34) Zadok daughter-of Jerusha mother-of-him

him. Taking fifty men of Gilead with him, he assassinated Pekahiah, along with Argob and Arieh, in the citadel of the royal palace at Samaria. So Pekah killed Pekahiah and succeeded him as king.

[26]The other events of Pekahiah's reign, and all he did, are written in the book of the annals of the kings of Israel.

*Pekah King of Israel*

[27]In the fifty-second year of Azariah king of Judah, Pekah son of Remaliah became king of Israel in Samaria, and he reigned twenty years. [28]He did evil in the eyes of the LORD. He did not turn away from the sins of Jeroboam son of Nebat, which he had caused Israel to commit.

[29]In the time of Pekah king of Israel, Tiglath-Pileser king of Assyria came and took Ijon, Abel Beth Maacah, Janoah, Kedesh and Hazor. He took Gilead and Galilee—all the land of Naphtali—and deported the people to Assyria. [30]Then Hoshea son of Elah conspired against Pekah son of Remaliah. He attacked and assassinated him, and then succeeded him as king in the twentieth year of Jotham son of Uzziah.

[31]As for the other events of Pekah's reign, and all he did, are they not written in the book of the annals of the kings of Israel?

*Jotham King of Judah*

[32]In the second year of Pekah son of Remaliah king of Israel, Jotham son of Uzziah king of Judah began to reign. [33]He was twenty-five years old when he became king, and he reigned in Jerusalem sixteen years. His mother's name was Jerusha daughter of Zadok. [34]He did what was right in the eyes of

*30,32 Most mss have *dagesh* in the *zayin* ( זִּ־ ).

יְהוָה כְּכֹל אֲשֶׁר־ עָשָׂה עֻזִיָּהוּ* אָבִיו עָשָׂה׃ רַק
however (35) he-did father-of-him Uzziah he-did that as-all Yahweh

הַבָּמוֹת לֹא סָרוּ עוֹד הָעָם מְזַבְּחִים
ones-offering-sacrifices the-people still they-removed not the-high-places

וּמְקַטְּרִים בַּבָּמוֹת הוּא בָּנָה אֶת־ שַׁעַר
Gate-of *** he-rebuilt he at-the-high-places and-ones-burning-incense

בֵּית־ יְהוָה הָעֶלְיוֹן׃ וְיֶתֶר דִּבְרֵי יוֹתָם אֲשֶׁר עָשָׂה
he-did what Jotham events-of and-rest-of (36) the-Upper Yahweh temple-of

הֲלֹא־ הֵם כְּתוּבִים עַל־ סֵפֶר דִּבְרֵי הַיָּמִים לְמַלְכֵי יְהוּדָה׃
Judah of-kings-of the-days annals-of book-of in ones-being-written they not?

בַּיָּמִים הָהֵם הֵחֵל יְהוָה לְהַשְׁלִיחַ בִּיהוּדָה רְצִין
Rezin against-Judah to-send Yahweh he-began the-those in-the-days (37)

מֶלֶךְ אֲרָם וְאֵת פֶּקַח בֶּן־ רְמַלְיָהוּ׃ וַיִּשְׁכַּב יוֹתָם עִם־
with Jotham and-he-rested (38) Remaliah son-of Pekah and Aram king-of

אֲבֹתָיו וַיִּקָּבֵר עִם־ אֲבֹתָיו בְּעִיר דָּוִד
David in-City-of fathers-of-him with and-he-was-buried fathers-of-him

אָבִיו וַיִּמְלֹךְ אָחָז בְּנוֹ תַּחְתָּיו׃
in-place-of-him son-of-him Ahaz and-he-became-king father-of-him

בִּשְׁנַת שְׁבַע־ עֶשְׂרֵה שָׁנָה לְפֶקַח בֶּן־ רְמַלְיָהוּ מָלַךְ
he-became-king Remaliah son-of of-Pekah year ten seven-of in-year-of (16:1)

אָחָז בֶּן־ יוֹתָם מֶלֶךְ יְהוּדָה׃ בֶּן־ עֶשְׂרִים שָׁנָה אָחָז
Ahaz year twenty son-of (2) Judah king-of Jotham son-of Ahaz

בְּמָלְכוֹ וְשֵׁשׁ־ עֶשְׂרֵה שָׁנָה מָלַךְ בִּירוּשָׁלִָם וְלֹא־
but-not in-Jerusalem he-reigned year ten and-six-of when-to-become-king-him

עָשָׂה הַיָּשָׁר בְּעֵינֵי יְהוָה אֱלֹהָיו כְּדָוִד אָבִיו׃
father-of-him like-David God-of-him Yahweh in-eyes-of the-right he-did

וַיֵּלֶךְ בְּדֶרֶךְ מַלְכֵי יִשְׂרָאֵל וְגַם אֶת־ בְּנוֹ
son-of-him *** and-even Israel kings-of in-way-of and-he-walked (3)

הֶעֱבִיר בָּאֵשׁ כְּתֹעֲבוֹת הַגּוֹיִם אֲשֶׁר
that the-nations as-detestable-ways-of through-the-fire he-made-pass

הוֹרִישׁ יְהוָה אֹתָם מִפְּנֵי בְּנֵי יִשְׂרָאֵל׃ וַיְזַבֵּחַ
and-he-sacrificed (4) Israel sons-of from-before them Yahweh he-drove-out

וַיְקַטֵּר בַּבָּמוֹת וְעַל־ הַגְּבָעוֹת וְתַחַת
and-under the-hilltops and-on at-the-high-places and-he-burned-incense

כָּל־ עֵץ רַעֲנָן׃ אָז יַעֲלֶה רְצִין מֶלֶךְ־ אֲרָם
Aram king-of Rezin he-marched-up then (5) spreading tree-of every-of

וּפֶקַח בֶּן־ רְמַלְיָהוּ מֶלֶךְ־ יִשְׂרָאֵל יְרוּשָׁלִַם לַמִּלְחָמָה
to-the-fight Jerusalem Israel king-of Remaliah son-of and-Pekah

the LORD, just as his father Uzziah had done. [35]The high places, however, were not removed; the people continued to offer sacrifices and burn incense there. Jotham rebuilt the Upper Gate of the temple of the LORD.

[36]As for the other events of Jotham's reign, and what he did, are they not written in the book of the annals of the kings of Judah? [37](In those days the LORD began to send Rezin king of Aram and Pekah son of Remaliah against Judah.) [38]Jotham rested with his fathers and was buried with them in the City of David, the city of his father. And Ahaz his son succeeded him as king.

*Ahaz King of Judah*

16 In the seventeenth year of Pekah son of Remaliah, Ahaz son of Jotham king of Judah began to reign. [2]Ahaz was twenty years old when he became king, and he reigned in Jerusalem sixteen years. Unlike David his father, he did not do what was right in the eyes of the LORD his God. [3]He walked in the ways of the kings of Israel and even sacrificed his son in[t] the fire, following the detestable ways of the nations the LORD had driven out before the Israelites. [4]He offered sacrifices and burned incense at the high places, on the hilltops and under every spreading tree.

[5]Then Rezin king of Aram and Pekah son of Remaliah king of Israel marched up to fight against Jerusalem and

[t]3 Or *even made his son pass through*

*34 Most mss have *dagesh* in the *zayin* ( ־זִּ ).

וַיָּצֻרוּ עַל־ אָחָז וְלֹא יָכְלוּ לְהִלָּחֵם׃
to-overpower they-could but-not Ahaz against and-they-besieged

בָּעֵת הַהִיא הֵשִׁיב רְצִין מֶלֶךְ־ אֲרָם אֶת־אֵילַת לַאֲרָם
for-Aram Elath *** Aram king-of Rezin he-recovered the-that at-the-time (6)

וַיְנַשֵּׁל אֶת־ הַיְּהוּדִים מֵאֵילוֹת וַאֲרַמִּים בָּאוּ
they-moved-into and-Edomites from-Elath the-Judahites *** and-he-drove-out

אֵילַת וַיֵּשְׁבוּ שָׁם עַד הַיּוֹם הַזֶּה׃ וַיִּשְׁלַח אָחָז
Ahaz and-he-sent (7) the-this the-day to there and-they-lived Elath

מַלְאָכִים אֶל־ תְּגְלַת פְּלֶסֶר מֶלֶךְ־ אַשּׁוּר לֵאמֹר עַבְדְּךָ
servant-of-you to-say Assyria king-of Pileser Tiglath to messengers

וּבִנְךָ אָנִי עֲלֵה וְהוֹשִׁעֵנִי מִכַּף מֶלֶךְ־ אֲרָם
Aram king-of from-hand-of and-save-me! come-up! I and-vassal-of-you

וּמִכַּף מֶלֶךְ יִשְׂרָאֵל הַקּוֹמִים עָלָי׃ וַיִּקַּח
and-he-took (8) against-me the-ones-attacking Israel king-of and-from-hand-of

אָחָז אֶת־ הַכֶּסֶף וְאֶת־ הַזָּהָב הַנִּמְצָא בֵּית יְהוָה
Yahweh temple-of the-one-being-found the-gold and the-silver *** Ahaz

וּבְאֹצְרוֹת בֵּית הַמֶּלֶךְ וַיִּשְׁלַח לְמֶלֶךְ־ אַשּׁוּר שֹׁחַד׃
gift Assyria to-king-of and-he-sent the-king palace-of and-in-treasuries-of

וַיִּשְׁמַע אֵלָיו מֶלֶךְ אַשּׁוּר וַיַּעַל מֶלֶךְ אַשּׁוּר
Assyria king-of and-he-attacked Assyria king-of to-him and-he-listened (9)

אֶל־ דַּמֶּשֶׂק וַיִּתְפְּשֶׂהָ וַיַּגְלֶהָ קִירָה וְאֶת־ רְצִין
Rezin and to-Kir and-he-deported-her and-he-captured-her Damascus against

הֵמִית׃ וַיֵּלֶךְ הַמֶּלֶךְ אָחָז לִקְרַאת תִּגְלַת פִּלְאֶסֶר מֶלֶךְ־
king-of Pileser Tiglath to-meet Ahaz the-king then-he-went (10) he-killed

אַשּׁוּר דּוּמֶּשֶׂק וַיַּרְא אֶת־ הַמִּזְבֵּחַ אֲשֶׁר בְּדַמָּשֶׂק וַיִּשְׁלַח
and-he-sent in-Damascus that the-altar *** and-he-saw Damascus Assyria

הַמֶּלֶךְ אָחָז אֶל־אוּרִיָּה הַכֹּהֵן אֶת־ דְּמוּת הַמִּזְבֵּחַ וְאֶת־ תַּבְנִיתוֹ
plan-of-him and the-altar sketch-of *** the-priest Uriah to Ahaz the-king

לְכָל־ מַעֲשֵׂהוּ׃ וַיִּבֶן אוּרִיָּה הַכֹּהֵן אֶת־
*** the-priest Uriah so-he-built (11) construction-of-him for-all-of

הַמִּזְבֵּחַ כְּכֹל אֲשֶׁר־ שָׁלַח הַמֶּלֶךְ אָחָז מִדַּמֶּשֶׂק כֵּן עָשָׂה
he-finished so from-Damascus Ahaz the-king he-sent that as-all the-altar

אוּרִיָּה הַכֹּהֵן עַד־ בּוֹא הַמֶּלֶךְ־ אָחָז מִדַּמָּשֶׂק׃ וַיָּבֹא
when-he-came (12) from-Damascus Ahaz the-king to-return before the-priest Uriah

הַמֶּלֶךְ מִדַּמֶּשֶׂק וַיַּרְא הַמֶּלֶךְ אֶת־ הַמִּזְבֵּחַ וַיִּקְרַב
then-he-approached the-altar *** the-king and-he-saw from-Damascus the-king

הַמֶּלֶךְ עַל־ הַמִּזְבֵּחַ וַיַּעַל עָלָיו׃ וַיַּקְטֵר
and-he-offered (13) on-him and-he-presented-offering the-altar to the-king

°6 ק ואדמים

besieged Ahaz, but they could
not overpower him. [6]At that
time, Rezin king of Aram
recovered Elath for Aram by
driving out the men of Judah.
Edomites then moved into
Elath and have lived there to
this day.
[7]Ahaz sent messengers to
say to Tiglath-Pileser king of
Assyria, "I am your servant
and vassal. Come up and save
me out of the hand of the king
of Aram and of the king of Israel, who are attacking me."
[8]And Ahaz took the silver and
gold found in the temple of the
Lord and in the treasuries of
the royal palace and sent it as
a gift to the king of Assyria.
[9]The king of Assyria complied
by attacking Damascus and
capturing it. He deported its
inhabitants to Kir and put Rezin to death.
[10]Then King Ahaz went to
Damascus to meet Tiglath-
Pileser king of Assyria. He saw
an altar in Damascus and sent
to Uriah the priest a sketch of
the altar, with detailed plans
for its construction. [11]So Uriah
the priest built an altar in accordance with all the plans
that King Ahaz had sent from
Damascus and finished it before King Ahaz returned.
[12]When the king came back
from Damascus and saw the
altar, he approached it and
presented offerings[u] on it. [13]He

[u]12 *Or and went up*

אֶת־ עֹלָתוֹ וְאֶת־ מִנְחָתוֹ וַיַּסֵּךְ אֶת־
*** and-he-poured-out grain-offering-of-him and burnt-offering-of-him ***

נִסְכּוֹ וַיִּזְרֹק אֶת־ דַּם־ הַשְּׁלָמִים
the-fellowship-offerings blood-of *** and-he-sprinkled drink-offering-of-him

אֲשֶׁר־ לוֹ עַל־ הַמִּזְבֵּחַ׃ וְאֵת הַמִּזְבַּח הַנְּחֹשֶׁת אֲשֶׁר לִפְנֵי יְהוָה
Yahweh before that the-bronze the-altar and (14) the-altar on to-him that

וַיַּקְרֵב מֵאֵת פְּנֵי הַבַּיִת מִבֵּין הַמִּזְבֵּחַ
the-altar from-between the-temple front-of from now-he-brought

וּמִבֵּין בֵּית יְהוָה וַיִּתֵּן אֹתוֹ עַל־ יֶרֶךְ הַמִּזְבֵּחַ
the-altar side-of on him and-he-put Yahweh temple-of and-from-between

צָפוֹנָה׃ וַיְצַוֵּהוּ הַמֶּלֶךְ־ אָחָז אֶת־ אוּרִיָּה הַכֹּהֵן לֵאמֹר עַל
on to-say the-priest Uriah *** Ahaz the-king then-he-ordered (15) to-north

הַמִּזְבֵּחַ הַגָּדוֹל הַקְטֵר אֶת־ עֹלַת־ הַבֹּקֶר וְאֶת־
and the-morning burnt-offering-of *** offer! the-large the-altar

מִנְחַת הָעֶרֶב וְאֶת־ עֹלַת הַמֶּלֶךְ וְאֶת־
and the-king burnt-offering-of and the-evening grain-offering-of

מִנְחָתוֹ וְאֵת עֹלַת כָּל־ עַם הָאָרֶץ
the-land people-of all-of burnt-offering-of and grain-offering-of-him

וּמִנְחָתָם וְנִסְכֵּיהֶם וְכָל־ דַּם
blood-of and-all-of and-drink-offerings-of-them and-grain-offering-of-them

עֹלָה וְכָל־ דַּם־ זֶבַח עָלָיו תִּזְרֹק וּמִזְבַּח
but-altar-of you-sprinkle on-him sacrifice blood-of and-all-of burnt-offering

הַנְּחֹשֶׁת יִהְיֶה־ לִּי לְבַקֵּר׃ וַיַּעַשׂ אוּרִיָּה
Uriah and-he-did (16) to-seek-guidance for-me he-will-be the-bronze

הַכֹּהֵן כְּכֹל אֲשֶׁר־ צִוָּה הַמֶּלֶךְ אָחָז׃ וַיְקַצֵּץ
and-he-took-away (17) Ahaz the-king he-ordered that as-all the-priest

הַמֶּלֶךְ אָחָז אֶת־ הַמִּסְגְּרוֹת הַמְּכֹנוֹת וַיָּסַר
and-he-removed the-movable-stands the-side-panels *** Ahaz the-king

מֵעֲלֵיהֶם וְאֶת־ הַכִּיֹּר וְאֶת־ הַיָּם הוֹרִד מֵעַל הַבָּקָר הַנְּחֹשֶׁת
the-bronze the-bull from-on he-removed the-Sea and the-basin *** from-on-them

אֲשֶׁר תַּחְתֶּיהָ וַיִּתֵּן אֹתוֹ עַל מַרְצֶפֶת אֲבָנִים׃ וְאֶת־ מֵיסַךְ
canopy-of and (18) stones base-of on him and-he-set under-her that

הַשַּׁבָּת אֲשֶׁר־ בָּנוּ בַבַּיִת וְאֶת־ מְבוֹא הַמֶּלֶךְ
the-king entryway-of and at-the-temple they-built that the-Sabbath

הַחִיצוֹנָה הֵסֵב בֵּית יְהוָה מִפְּנֵי מֶלֶךְ אַשּׁוּר׃
Assyria king-of because-of Yahweh temple-of he-removed at-the-outside

וְיֶתֶר דִּבְרֵי אָחָז אֲשֶׁר עָשָׂה הֲלֹא־ הֵם כְּתוּבִים עַל־
in ones-being-written they not? he-did what Ahaz events-of and-rest-of (19)

°15 ק ויצוה
°17 ק את
°18 ק מוסך

offered up his burnt offering
and grain offering, poured out
his drink offering, and sprinkled the blood of his fellowship offerings[v] on the altar.
14 The bronze altar that stood
before the LORD he brought
from the front of the temple—
from between the new altar
and the temple of the LORD—
and put it on the north side of
the new altar.
15 King Ahaz then gave these
orders to Uriah the priest: "On
the large new altar, offer the
morning burnt offering and
the evening grain offering, the
king's burnt offering and his
grain offering, and the burnt
offering of all the people of the
land, and their grain offering
and their drink offering.
Sprinkle on the altar all the
blood of the burnt offerings
and sacrifices. But I will use
the bronze altar for seeking
guidance." 16 And Uriah the
priest did just as King Ahaz
had ordered.
17 King Ahaz took away the
side panels and removed the
basins from the movable
stands. He removed the Sea
from the bronze bulls that supported it and set it on a stone
base. 18 He took away the Sabbath canopy[w] that had been
built at the temple and
removed the royal entryway
outside the temple of the LORD,
in deference to the king of Assyria.
19 As for the other events of
the reign of Ahaz, and what
he did, are they not written in

v13 Traditionally *peace offerings*
w18 Or *the dais of his throne* (see Septuagint)

סֵפֶר דִּבְרֵי הַיָּמִים לְמַלְכֵי יְהוּדָה׃ וַיִּשְׁכַּב אָחָז עִם־
with Ahaz and-he-rested (20) Judah of-kings-of the-days annals-of book-of

אֲבֹתָיו וַיִּקָּבֵר עִם־ אֲבֹתָיו בְּעִיר דָּוִד
David in-City-of fathers-of-him with and-he-was-buried fathers-of-him

וַיִּמְלֹךְ חִזְקִיָּהוּ בְנוֹ תַּחְתָּיו׃ בִּשְׁנַת
in-year-of (17:1) in-place-of-him son-of-him Hezekiah and-he-became-king

שְׁתֵּים עֶשְׂרֵה לְאָחָז מֶלֶךְ יְהוּדָה מָלַךְ הוֹשֵׁעַ בֶּן־ אֵלָה בְשֹׁמְרוֹן
in-Samaria Elah son-of Hoshea he-became-king Judah king-of of-Ahaz ten two

עַל־יִשְׂרָאֵל תֵּשַׁע שָׁנִים׃ וַיַּעַשׂ הָרַע בְּעֵינֵי יְהוָה רַק לֹא
not but Yahweh in-eyes-of the-evil and-he-did (2) years nine Israel over

כְּמַלְכֵי יִשְׂרָאֵל אֲשֶׁר הָיוּ לְפָנָיו׃ עָלָיו עָלָה
he-came-up against-him (3) before-him they-were who Israel like-kings-of

שַׁלְמַנְאֶסֶר מֶלֶךְ אַשּׁוּר וַיְהִי־ לוֹ הוֹשֵׁעַ עֶבֶד וַיָּשֶׁב
and-he-paid vassal Hoshea to-him now-he-was Assyria king-of Shalmaneser

לוֹ מִנְחָה׃ וַיִּמְצָא מֶלֶךְ־ אַשּׁוּר בְּהוֹשֵׁעַ קֶשֶׁר
traitor about-Hoshea Assyria king-of but-he-discovered (4) tribute to-him

אֲשֶׁר שָׁלַח מַלְאָכִים אֶל־סוֹא מֶלֶךְ־מִצְרַיִם וְלֹא־ הֶעֱלָה מִנְחָה לְמֶלֶךְ
to-king-of tribute he-paid and-not Egypt king-of So to envoys he-sent for

אַשּׁוּר כְּשָׁנָה בְשָׁנָה וַיַּעַצְרֵהוּ מֶלֶךְ אַשּׁוּר וַיַּאַסְרֵהוּ
and-he-imprisoned-him Assyria king-of so-he-seized-him by-year as-year Assyria

בֵּית כֶּלֶא׃ וַיַּעַל מֶלֶךְ־ אַשּׁוּר בְּכָל־ הָאָרֶץ
the-land through-entire-of Assyria king-of and-he-invaded (5) prison house-of

וַיַּעַל שֹׁמְרוֹן וַיָּצַר עָלֶיהָ שָׁלֹשׁ שָׁנִים׃ בִּשְׁנַת
in-year-of (6) years three to-her and-he-laid-siege Samaria and-he-marched

הַתְּשִׁיעִית לְהוֹשֵׁעַ לָכַד מֶלֶךְ־ אַשּׁוּר אֶת־ שֹׁמְרוֹן וַיֶּגֶל
and-he-deported Samaria *** Assyria king-of he-captured of-Hoshea the-ninth

אֶת־ יִשְׂרָאֵל אַשּׁוּרָה וַיֹּשֶׁב אֹתָם בַּחְלַח וּבְחָבוֹר נְהַר
River-of and-on-Habor in-Halah them and-he-settled to-Assyria Israel ***

גּוֹזָן וְעָרֵי מָדָי׃ וַיְהִי כִּי־ חָטְאוּ בְנֵי־
sons-of they-sinned because and-he-took-place (7) Medes and-towns-of Gozan

יִשְׂרָאֵל לַיהוָה אֱלֹהֵיהֶם הַמַּעֲלֶה אֹתָם מֵאֶרֶץ מִצְרַיִם
Egypt from-land-of them the-one-bringing-up God-of-them against-Yahweh Israel

מִתַּחַת יַד פַּרְעֹה מֶלֶךְ־ מִצְרָיִם וַיִּירְאוּ אֱלֹהִים אֲחֵרִים׃
other-ones gods and-they-worshiped Egypt king-of Pharaoh power-of from-under

וַיֵּלְכוּ בְּחֻקּוֹת הַגּוֹיִם אֲשֶׁר הוֹרִישׁ יְהוָה
Yahweh he-drove-out that the-nations after-practices-of and-they-followed (8)

מִפְּנֵי בְּנֵי יִשְׂרָאֵל וּמַלְכֵי יִשְׂרָאֵל אֲשֶׁר עָשׂוּ׃
they-introduced which Israel and-kings-of Israel sons-of from-before

the book of the annals of the
kings of Judah? [20]Ahaz rested
with his fathers and was buried with them in the City of
David. And Hezekiah his son
succeeded him as king.

*Hoshea Last King of Israel*

17 In the twelfth year of
Ahaz king of Judah,
Hoshea son of Elah became
king of Israel in Samaria, and
he reigned nine years. [2]He did
evil in the eyes of the LORD,
but not like the kings of Israel
who preceded him.
[3]Shalmaneser king of Assyria came up to attack Hoshea, who had been Shal-
maneser's vassal and had paid
him tribute. [4]But the king of
Assyria discovered that Hoshea was a traitor, for he had
sent envoys to So[x] king of
Egypt, and he no longer paid
tribute to the king of Assyria,
as he had done year by year.
Therefore Shalmaneser seized
him and put him in prison.
[5]The king of Assyria invaded
the entire land, marched
against Samaria and laid siege
to it for three years. [6]In the
ninth year of Hoshea, the king
of Assyria captured Samaria
and deported the Israelites to
Assyria. He settled them in
Halah, in Gozan on the Habor
River and in the towns of the
Medes.

*Israel Exiled Because of Sin*

[7]All this took place because
the Israelites had sinned
against the LORD their God,
who had brought them up out
of Egypt from under the
power of Pharaoh king of
Egypt. They worshiped other
gods [8]and followed the practices of the nations the LORD
had driven out before them, as
well as the practices which the
kings of Israel had introduced.

[x]4 Or *to Sais, to the; So* is possibly an abbreviation for *Osorkon.*

וַיְחַפְּאוּ בְנֵֽי־ יִשְׂרָאֵל דְּבָרִים אֲשֶׁר לֹא־ כֵן עַל־ יְהוָה
Yahweh against right not that things Israel sons-of and-they-did-secretly (9)

אֱלֹהֵיהֶם וַיִּבְנוּ לָהֶם בָּמוֹת בְּכָל־ עָרֵיהֶם
towns-of-them in-all-of high-places for-them and-they-built God-of-them

מִמִּגְדַּל נוֹצְרִים עַד־ עִיר מִבְצָר׃ וַיַּצִּבוּ
and-they-set-up (10) fortified city-of to ones-watching from-tower-of

לָהֶם מַצֵּבוֹת וַאֲשֵׁרִים עַל כָּל־ גִּבְעָה גְבֹהָה וְתַחַת
and-under high hill every-of on and-Asherah-poles sacred-stones for-them

כָּל־ עֵץ רַעֲנָן׃ וַיְקַטְּרוּ־ שָׁם בְּכָל־
at-all-of there and-they-burned-incense (11) spreading tree-of every-of

בָּמוֹת כַּגּוֹיִם אֲשֶׁר־ הֶגְלָה יְהוָה מִפְּנֵיהֶם
from-before-them Yahweh he-drove-out whom as-the-nations high-places

וַיַּעֲשׂוּ דְּבָרִים רָעִים לְהַכְעִיס אֶת־ יְהוָה׃
Yahweh *** to-provoke-to-anger wicked-ones things and-they-did

וַיַּעַבְדוּ הַגִּלֻּלִים אֲשֶׁר אָמַר יְהוָה לָהֶם לֹא תַעֲשׂוּ
you-shall-do not to-them Yahweh he-said that the-idols and-they-worshiped (12)

אֶת־ הַדָּבָר הַזֶּה׃ וַיָּעַד יְהוָה בְּיִשְׂרָאֵל וּבִיהוּדָה
and-to-Judah to-Israel Yahweh and-he-warned (13) the-this the-thing ***

בְּיַד כָּל־ נְבִיאוֹ כָל־ חֹזֶה לֵאמֹר שֻׁבוּ מִדַּרְכֵיכֶם
from-ways-of-you turn! to-say seer all-of prophets-of all-of by-hand-of

הָרָעִים וְשִׁמְרוּ מִצְוֹתַי חֻקּוֹתַי כְּכָל־ הַתּוֹרָה
the-Law as-entire-of decrees-of-me commands-of-me and-observe! the-evil-ones

אֲשֶׁר צִוִּיתִי אֶת־ אֲבֹתֵיכֶם וַאֲשֶׁר שָׁלַחְתִּי אֲלֵיכֶם בְּיַד
by-hand-of to-you I-delivered and-that fathers-of-you *** I-commanded that

עֲבָדַי הַנְּבִיאִים׃ וְלֹא שָׁמֵעוּ וַיַּקְשׁוּ
and-they-made-stiff they-listened but-not (14) the-prophets servants-of-me

אֶת־ עָרְפָּם כְּעֹרֶף אֲבוֹתָם אֲשֶׁר לֹא הֶאֱמִינוּ בַּיהוָה
in-Yahweh they-trusted not who fathers-of-them as-neck-of neck-of-them ***

אֱלֹהֵיהֶם׃ וַיִּמְאֲסוּ אֶת־ חֻקָּיו וְאֶת־ בְּרִיתוֹ
covenant-of-him and decrees-of-him *** and-they-rejected (15) God-of-them

אֲשֶׁר כָּרַת אֶת־ אֲבוֹתָם וְאֵת עֵדְוֹתָיו אֲשֶׁר הֵעִיד בָּם
to-them he-warned that warnings-of-him and fathers-of-them with he-made that

וַיֵּלְכוּ אַחֲרֵי הַהֶבֶל וַיֶּהְבָּלוּ
and-they-became-worthless the-worthless-thing after and-they-followed

וְאַחֲרֵי הַגּוֹיִם אֲשֶׁר סְבִיבֹתָם אֲשֶׁר צִוָּה יְהוָה אֹתָם לְבִלְתִּי
not them Yahweh he-ordered whom ones-around-them who the-nations and-after

עֲשׂוֹת כָּהֶם׃ וַיַּעַזְבוּ אֶת־ כָּל־ מִצְוֹת יְהוָה אֱלֹהֵיהֶם
God-of-them Yahweh commands-of all-of *** and-they-forsook (16) as-they to-do

9The Israelites secretly did
things against the LORD their
God that were not right. From
watchtower to fortified city
they built themselves high
places in all their towns.
10They set up sacred stones
and Asherah poles on every
high hill and under every
spreading tree. 11At every high
place they burned incense, as
the nations whom the LORD
had driven out before them
had done. They did wicked
things that provoked the LORD
to anger. 12They worshiped
idols, though the LORD had
said, "You shall not do this."[y]
13The LORD warned Israel and
Judah through all his prophets
and seers: "Turn from your
evil ways. Observe my commands and decrees, in accordance with the entire Law that
I commanded your fathers to
obey and that I delivered to
you through my servants the
prophets."

14But they would not listen
and were as stiff-necked as
their fathers, who did not trust
in the LORD their God. 15They
rejected his decrees and the
covenant he had made with
their fathers and the warnings
he had given them. They followed worthless idols and
themselves became worthless.
They imitated the nations
around them although the
LORD had ordered them, "Do
not do as they do," and they
did the things the LORD had
forbidden them to do.

16They forsook all the commands of the LORD their God

y12 Exodus 20:4, 5

°13 ק נביאי

וַיַּעֲשׂוּ לָהֶם מַסֵּכָה שְׁנֵים עֲגָלִים וַיַּעֲשׂוּ אֲשֵׁרָה
Asherah-pole and-they-made calves two-of cast-idol for-them and-they-made

וַיִּשְׁתַּחֲווּ לְכָל־ צְבָא הַשָּׁמַיִם וַיַּעַבְדוּ אֶת־
*** and-they-worshiped the-heavens host-of to-all-of and-they-bowed-down

הַבָּעַל׃ (17) וַיַּעֲבִירוּ אֶת־ בְּנֵיהֶם וְאֶת־ בְּנוֹתֵיהֶם
daughters-of-them and sons-of-them *** and-they-made-pass (17) the-Baal

בָּאֵשׁ וַיִּקְסְמוּ קְסָמִים וַיְנַחֵשׁוּ
and-they-practiced-sorcery divinations and-they-practiced through-the-fire

וַיִּתְמַכְּרוּ לַעֲשׂוֹת הָרַע בְּעֵינֵי יְהוָה לְהַכְעִיסוֹ׃
to-make-angry-him Yahweh in-eyes-of the-evil to-do and-they-sold-themselves

(18) וַיִּתְאַנַּף יְהוָה מְאֹד בְּיִשְׂרָאֵל וַיְסִרֵם מֵעַל
from-before and-he-removed-them with-Israel very Yahweh so-he-was-angry (18)

פָּנָיו לֹא נִשְׁאַר רַק שֵׁבֶט יְהוּדָה לְבַדּוֹ׃ (19) גַּם־ יְהוּדָה
Judah even (19) by-himself Judah tribe-of only he-was-left not faces-of-him

לֹא שָׁמַר אֶת־ מִצְוֺת יְהוָה אֱלֹהֵיהֶם וַיֵּלְכוּ
and-they-followed God-of-them Yahweh commands-of *** he-kept not

בְּחֻקּוֹת יִשְׂרָאֵל אֲשֶׁר עָשׂוּ׃ (20) וַיִּמְאַס יְהוָה
Yahweh so-he-rejected (20) they-introduced that Israel after-practices-of

בְּכָל־ זֶרַע יִשְׂרָאֵל וַיְעַנֵּם וַיִּתְּנֵם בְּיַד־
into-hand-of and-he-gave-them and-he-afflicted-them Israel people-of to-all-of

שֹׁסִים עַד אֲשֶׁר הִשְׁלִיכָם מִפָּנָיו׃ (21) כִּי־
when (21) from-presences-of-him he-thrust-them when until ones-plundering

קָרַע יִשְׂרָאֵל מֵעַל בֵּית דָּוִד וַיַּמְלִיכוּ אֶת־ יָרָבְעָם
Jeroboam *** then-they-made-king David house-of from-with Israel he-tore

בֶּן־ נְבָט וַיַּדַּא יָרָבְעָם אֶת־ יִשְׂרָאֵל מֵאַחֲרֵי יְהוָה
Yahweh from-after Israel *** Jeroboam and-he-enticed Nebat son-of

וְהֶחֱטִיאָם* חֲטָאָה גְדוֹלָה׃ (22) וַיֵּלְכוּ בְּנֵי יִשְׂרָאֵל
Israel sons-of and-they-persisted (22) great sin and-he-caused-to-sin-them

בְּכָל־ חַטֹּאות יָרָבְעָם אֲשֶׁר עָשָׂה לֹא־ סָרוּ מִמֶּנָּה׃
from-her they-turned-away not he-did that Jeroboam sins-of in-all-of

(23) עַד אֲשֶׁר־ הֵסִיר יְהוָה אֶת־ יִשְׂרָאֵל מֵעַל פָּנָיו
presences-of-him from-before Israel *** Yahweh he-removed when until (23)

כַּאֲשֶׁר דִּבֶּר בְּיַד כָּל־ עֲבָדָיו הַנְּבִיאִים
the-prophets servants-of-him all-of by-hand-of he-warned just-as

וַיִּגֶל יִשְׂרָאֵל מֵעַל אַדְמָתוֹ אַשּׁוּרָה עַד הַיּוֹם
the-day to to-Assyria homeland-of-him from-on Israel so-he-went-into-exile

הַזֶּה׃ (24) וַיָּבֵא מֶלֶךְ־ אַשּׁוּר מִבָּבֶל וּמִכּוּתָה
and-from-Cuthah from-Babylon Assyria king-of and-he-brought (24) the-this

and made for themselves two idols cast in the shape of calves, and an Asherah pole. They bowed down to all the starry hosts, and they worshiped Baal. [17]They sacrificed their sons and daughters in[z] the fire. They practiced divination and sorcery and sold themselves to do evil in the eyes of the LORD, provoking him to anger.

[18]So the LORD was very angry with Israel and removed them from his presence. Only the tribe of Judah was left, [19]and even Judah did not keep the commands of the LORD their God. They followed the practices Israel had introduced. [20]Therefore the LORD rejected all the people of Israel; he afflicted them and gave them into the hands of plunderers, until he thrust them from his presence.

[21]When he tore Israel away from the house of David, they made Jeroboam son of Nebat their king. Jeroboam enticed Israel away from following the LORD and caused them to commit a great sin. [22]The Israelites persisted in all the sins of Jeroboam and did not turn away from them [23]until the LORD removed them from his presence, as he had warned through all his servants the prophets. So the people of Israel were taken from their homeland into exile in Assyria, and they are still there.

*Samaria Resettled*

[24]The king of Assyria brought people from Babylon,

[z]17 Or *They made their sons and daughters pass through*

*21 Most mss have *bireq* under the *teth* (טִי–).

°*16* ק שני

°*21* ק וידה

וּמֵעַוָּא וּמֵחֲמָת וּסְפַרְוַיִם וַיֹּשֶׁב בְּעָרֵי
in-towns-of and-he-settled and-Sepharvaim and-from-Hamath and-from-Avva

שֹׁמְרוֹן תַּחַת בְּנֵי יִשְׂרָאֵל וַיִּרְשׁוּ אֶת־ שֹׁמְרוֹן
Samaria *** and-they-took-over Israel sons-of in-place-of Samaria

וַיֵּשְׁבוּ בְּעָרֶיהָ׃ (25) וַיְהִי בִּתְחִלַּת שִׁבְתָּם
to-live-them when-to-begin and-he-was (25) in-towns-of-her and-they-lived

שָׁם לֹא יָרְאוּ אֶת־ יְהוָה וַיְשַׁלַּח יְהוָה בָּהֶם אֶת־ הָאֲרָיוֹת
the-lions *** among-them Yahweh so-he-sent Yahweh *** they-worshiped not there

וַיִּהְיוּ הֹרְגִים בָּהֶם׃ (26) וַיֹּאמְרוּ לְמֶלֶךְ אַשּׁוּר
Assyria to-king-of and-they-reported (26) of-them ones-killing and-they-were

לֵאמֹר הַגּוֹיִם אֲשֶׁר הִגְלִיתָ וַתּוֹשֶׁב בְּעָרֵי שֹׁמְרוֹן
Samaria in-towns-of and-you-resettled you-deported whom the-peoples to-say

לֹא יָדְעוּ אֶת־ מִשְׁפַּט אֱלֹהֵי הָאָרֶץ וַיְשַׁלַּח־ בָּם
among-them and-he-sent the-country gods-of requirement-of *** they-know not

אֶת־ הָאֲרָיוֹת וְהִנָּם מְמִיתִים אוֹתָם כַּאֲשֶׁר אֵינָם יֹדְעִים
ones-knowing not-they because them ones-killing and-see-they! the-lions ***

אֶת־ מִשְׁפַּט אֱלֹהֵי הָאָרֶץ׃ (27) וַיְצַו מֶלֶךְ־ אַשּׁוּר
Assyria king-of then-he-ordered (27) the-country gods-of requirement-of ***

לֵאמֹר הֹלִיכוּ שָׁמָּה אֶחָד מֵהַכֹּהֲנִים אֲשֶׁר הִגְלִיתֶם
you-took-captive whom of-the-priests one to-there send-back! to-say

מִשָּׁם וְיֵלְכוּ וְיֵשְׁבוּ שָׁם וְיֹרֵם
and-let-him-teach-them there and-let-them-live and-let-them-go-back from-there

אֶת־ מִשְׁפַּט אֱלֹהֵי הָאָרֶץ׃ (28) וַיָּבֹא אֶחָד מֵהַכֹּהֲנִים אֲשֶׁר
who of-the-priests one so-he-came (28) the-land gods-of requirement-of ***

הִגְלוּ מִשֹּׁמְרוֹן וַיֵּשֶׁב בְּבֵית־ אֵל וַיְהִי מוֹרֶה אֹתָם
them teaching and-he-was El in-Beth and-he-lived from-Samaria they-exiled

אֵיךְ יִירְאוּ אֶת־ יְהוָה׃ (29) וַיִּהְיוּ עֹשִׂים גּוֹי
nation ones-making but-they-were (29) Yahweh *** they-should-worship how

גּוֹי אֱלֹהָיו וַיַּנִּיחוּ | בְּבֵית הַבָּמוֹת אֲשֶׁר עָשׂוּ
they-made that the-high-places in-shrine-of and-they-set-up gods-of-him nation

הַשֹּׁמְרֹנִים גּוֹי גּוֹי בְּעָרֵיהֶם אֲשֶׁר הֵם יֹשְׁבִים שָׁם׃
there ones-settling they where in-towns-of-them nation nation the-Samaritans

(30) וְאַנְשֵׁי בָבֶל עָשׂוּ אֶת־ סֻכּוֹת בְּנוֹת וְאַנְשֵׁי־ כוּת
Cuthah and-men-of Benoth Succoth *** they-made Babylon and-men-of (30)

עָשׂוּ אֶת־ נֵרְגַל וְאַנְשֵׁי חֲמָת עָשׂוּ אֶת־ אֲשִׁימָא׃
Ashima *** they-made Hamath and-men-of Nergal *** they-made

(31) וְהָעַוִּים עָשׂוּ נִבְחַז וְאֶת־ תַּרְתָּק וְהַסְפַרְוִים
and-the-Sepharvites Tartak and Nibhaz they-made and-the-Avvites (31)

Cuthah, Avva, Hamath and Sepharvaim and settled them in the towns of Samaria to replace the Israelites. They took over Samaria and lived in its towns. [25]When they first lived there, they did not worship the LORD; so he sent lions among them and they killed some of the people. [26]It was reported to the king of Assyria: "The people you deported and resettled in the towns of Samaria do not know what the god of that country requires. He has sent lions among them, which are killing them off, because the people do not know what he requires."

[27]Then the king of Assyria gave this order: "Have one of the priests you took captive from Samaria go back to live there and teach the people what the god of the land requires." [28]So one of the priests who had been exiled from Samaria came to live in Bethel and taught them how to worship the LORD.

[29]Nevertheless, each national group made its own gods in the several towns where they settled, and set them up in the shrines the people of Samaria had made at the high places. [30]The men from Babylon made Succoth Benoth, the men from Cuthah made Nergal, and the men from Hamath made Ashima; [31]the Avvites made Nibhaz

שֹׂרְפִים אֶת־ בְּנֵיהֶם בָּאֵשׁ לְאַדְרַמֶּלֶךְ וַעֲנַמֶּלֶךְ
and-Anammelech to-Adrammelech in-the-fire children-of-them *** ones-burning

אֱלֹהֵ° סְפַרְוָיִם°׃ (32) וַיִּהְיוּ יְרֵאִים אֶת־ יְהוָה
Yahweh *** ones-worshiping and-they-were (32) Sepharvaim gods-of

וַיַּעֲשׂוּ לָהֶם מִקְצוֹתָם כֹּהֲנֵי בָמוֹת
high-places priests-of from-ends-of-them for-them but-they-appointed

וַיִּהְיוּ עֹשִׂים לָהֶם בְּבֵית הַבָּמוֹת׃
the-high-places in-shrine-of for-them ones-officiating and-they-were

(33) אֶת־ יְהוָה הָיוּ יְרֵאִים וְאֶת־ אֱלֹהֵיהֶם הָיוּ
they-were gods-of-them but ones-worshiping they-were Yahweh *** (33)

עֹבְדִים כְּמִשְׁפַּט הַגּוֹיִם אֲשֶׁר־ הִגְלוּ אֹתָם מִשָּׁם׃
from-there them they-brought which the-nations as-custom-of ones-serving

(34) עַד הַיּוֹם הַזֶּה הֵם עֹשִׂים כַּמִּשְׁפָּטִים הָרִאשֹׁנִים
the-former-ones in-the-practices ones-persisting they the-this the-day to (34)

אֵינָם יְרֵאִים אֶת־ יְהוָה וְאֵינָם עֹשִׂים
ones-adhering and-not-they Yahweh *** ones-worshiping not-they

כְּחֻקֹּתָם וּכְמִשְׁפָּטָם וְכַתּוֹרָה וְכַמִּצְוָה
or-to-the-command or-to-the-law or-to-ordinance-of-them to-decrees-of-them

אֲשֶׁר צִוָּה יְהוָה אֶת־ בְּנֵי יַעֲקֹב אֲשֶׁר־ שָׂם שְׁמוֹ יִשְׂרָאֵל׃
Israel name-of-him he-gave whom Jacob sons-of *** Yahweh he-gave that

(35) וַיִּכְרֹת יְהוָה אִתָּם בְּרִית וַיְצַוֵּם לֵאמֹר
to-say then-he-commanded-them covenant with-them Yahweh when-he-made (35)

לֹא תִירְאוּ אֱלֹהִים אֲחֵרִים וְלֹא־ תִשְׁתַּחֲווּ לָהֶם וְלֹא
and-not to-them you-bow-down and-not other-ones gods you-worship not

תַעַבְדוּם וְלֹא תִזְבְּחוּ לָהֶם׃ (36) כִּי אִם־ אֶת־ יְהוָה אֲשֶׁר
who Yahweh *** only but (36) to-them you-sacrifice and-not you-serve-them

הֶעֱלָה אֶתְכֶם מֵאֶרֶץ מִצְרַיִם בְּכֹחַ גָּדוֹל וּבִזְרוֹעַ
and-with-arm mighty with-power Egypt from-land-of you he-brought-up

נְטוּיָה אֹתוֹ תִירָאוּ וְלוֹ תִשְׁתַּחֲווּ וְלוֹ
and-to-him you-shall-bow and-to-him you-must-worship him being-outstretched

תִזְבָּחוּ׃ (37) וְאֶת־ הַחֻקִּים וְאֶת־ הַמִּשְׁפָּטִים וְהַתּוֹרָה
and-the-law the-ordinances and the-decrees and (37) you-shall-sacrifice

וְהַמִּצְוָה אֲשֶׁר כָּתַב לָכֶם תִּשְׁמְרוּן לַעֲשׂוֹת כָּל־
all-of to-keep you-must-be-careful for-you he-wrote that and-the-command

הַיָּמִים וְלֹא תִירְאוּ אֱלֹהִים אֲחֵרִים׃ (38) וְהַבְּרִית אֲשֶׁר־
that and-the-covenant (38) other-ones gods you-worship and-not the-days

כָּרַתִּי אִתְּכֶם לֹא תִשְׁכָּחוּ וְלֹא תִירְאוּ אֱלֹהִים אֲחֵרִים׃
other-ones gods you-worship and-not you-forget not with-you I-made

and Tartak, and the Sepharvites burned their children in the fire as sacrifices to Adrammelech and Anammelech, the gods of Sepharvaim. [32]They worshiped the LORD, but they also appointed all sorts of their own people to officiate for them as priests in the shrines at the high places. [33]They worshiped the LORD, but they also served their own gods in accordance with the customs of the nations from which they had been brought.

[34]To this day they persist in their former practices. They neither worship the LORD nor adhere to the decrees and ordinances, the laws and commands that the LORD gave the descendants of Jacob, whom he named Israel. [35]When the LORD made a covenant with the Israelites, he commanded them: "Do not worship any other gods or bow down to them, serve them or sacrifice to them. [36]But the LORD, who brought you up out of Egypt with mighty power and outstretched arm, is the one you must worship. To him you shall bow down and to him offer sacrifices. [37]You must always be careful to keep the decrees and ordinances, the laws and commands he wrote for you. Do not worship other gods. [38]Do not forget the covenant I have made with you, and do not worship other

°*31a* ק אלהי
°*31b* ק ספרוים

כִּי אִם־ אֶת־ יְהוָה אֱלֹהֵיכֶם תִּירָאוּ וְהוּא יַצִּיל

he-will-deliver and-he you-worship God-of-you Yahweh *** only rather (39)

אֶתְכֶם מִיַּד כָּל־ אֹיְבֵיכֶם׃ וְלֹא שָׁמֵעוּ כִּי

but they-listened but-not (40) being-enemies-of-you all-of from-hand-of you

אִם־ כְּמִשְׁפָּטָם הָרִאשׁוֹן הֵם עֹשִׂים׃ וַיִּהְיוּ ׀

so-they-were (41) ones-persisting they the-former as-practice-of-them rather

הַגּוֹיִם הָאֵלֶּה יְרֵאִים אֶת־ יְהוָה וְאֶת־ פְּסִילֵיהֶם הָיוּ

they-were idols-of-them and Yawheh *** ones-worshiping the-these the-nations

עֹבְדִים גַּם־ בְּנֵיהֶם ׀ וּבְנֵי בְנֵיהֶם כַּאֲשֶׁר

just-as children-of-them and-children-of children-of-them and ones-serving

עָשׂוּ אֲבֹתָם הֵם עֹשִׂים עַד הַיּוֹם הַזֶּה׃ וַיְהִי

and-he-was (18:1) the-this the-day to ones-doing they fathers-of-them they-did

בִּשְׁנַת שָׁלֹשׁ לְהוֹשֵׁעַ בֶּן־ אֵלָה מֶלֶךְ יִשְׂרָאֵל מָלַךְ חִזְקִיָּה

Hezekiah he-became-king Israel king-of Elah son-of of-Hoshea three in-year-of

בֶּן־ אָחָז מֶלֶךְ יְהוּדָה׃ בֶּן־ עֶשְׂרִים וְחָמֵשׁ שָׁנָה הָיָה

he-was year and-five twenty son-of (2) Judah king-of Ahaz son-of

בְמָלְכוֹ וְעֶשְׂרִים וָתֵשַׁע שָׁנָה מָלַךְ בִּירוּשָׁלִָם

in-Jerusalem he-reigned year and-nine and-twenty when-to-become-king-him

וְשֵׁם אִמּוֹ אֲבִי בַּת־ זְכַרְיָה׃ וַיַּעַשׂ הַיָּשָׁר

the-right and-he-did (3) Zechariah daughter-of Abi mother-of-him and-name-of

בְּעֵינֵי יְהוָה כְּכֹל אֲשֶׁר־ עָשָׂה דָּוִד אָבִיו׃ הוּא ׀ הֵסִיר

he-removed he (4) father-of-him David he-did that as-all Yahweh in-eyes-of

אֶת־ הַבָּמוֹת וְשִׁבַּר אֶת־ הַמַּצֵּבֹת וְכָרַת

and-he-cut-down the-sacred-stones *** and-he-smashed the-high-places ***

אֶת־ הָאֲשֵׁרָה וְכִתַּת נְחַשׁ הַנְּחֹשֶׁת אֲשֶׁר־ עָשָׂה מֹשֶׁה

Moses he-made that the-bronze snake-of and-he-broke-up the-Asherah-pole ***

כִּי עַד־ הַיָּמִים הָהֵמָּה הָיוּ בְנֵי־ יִשְׂרָאֵל מְקַטְּרִים

ones-burning-incense Israel sons-of they-were the-those the-days up-to for

לוֹ וַיִּקְרָא־ לוֹ נְחֻשְׁתָּן׃ בַּיהוָה אֱלֹהֵי־ יִשְׂרָאֵל בָּטָח

he-trusted Israel God-of in-Yahweh (5) Nehushtan to-him now-he-called to-him

וְאַחֲרָיו לֹא־ הָיָה כָמֹהוּ בְּכֹל מַלְכֵי יְהוּדָה וַאֲשֶׁר הָיוּ

he-was or-who Judah kings-of among-all-of like-him he-was not and-after-him

לְפָנָיו׃ וַיִּדְבַּק בַּיהוָה לֹא־ סָר מֵאַחֲרָיו

from-after-him he-turned-away not to-Yahweh and-he-held-fast (6) before-him

וַיִּשְׁמֹר מִצְוֹתָיו אֲשֶׁר־ צִוָּה יְהוָה אֶת־ מֹשֶׁה׃ וְהָיָה

and-he-was (7) Moses *** Yahweh he-gave that commands-of-him and-he-kept

יְהוָה עִמּוֹ בְּכֹל אֲשֶׁר־ יֵצֵא יַשְׂכִּיל וַיִּמְרֹד

and-he-rebelled he-was-successful he-undertook that in-all with-him Yahweh

gods. 39Rather, worship the
LORD your God; it is he who
will deliver you from the hand
of all your enemies."

40They would not listen,
however, but persisted in
their former practices. 41Even
while these people were worshiping the LORD, they were
serving their idols. To this day
their children and grandchildren continue to do as their
fathers did.

*Hezekiah King of Judah*

18 In the third year of Hoshea son of Elah king
of Israel, Hezekiah son of
Ahaz king of Judah began to
reign. 2He was twenty-five
years old when he became
king, and he reigned in
Jerusalem twenty-nine years.
His mother's name was Abijah[a] daughter of Zechariah.
3He did what was right in the
eyes of the LORD, just as his
father David had done. 4He
removed the high places,
smashed the sacred stones and
cut down the Asherah poles.
He broke into pieces the
bronze snake Moses had
made, for up to that time the
Israelites had been burning
incense to it. (It was called[b]
Nehushtan.[c])

5Hezekiah trusted in the
LORD, the God of Israel. There
was no one like him among all
the kings of Judah, either before him or after him. 6He held
fast to the LORD and did not
cease to follow him; he kept
the commands the LORD had
given Moses. 7And the LORD
was with him; he was successful in whatever he undertook.
He rebelled against the king of

[a]2 Hebrew *Abi*, a variant of *Abijah*
[b]4 Or *He called it*
[c]4 *Nehushtan* sounds like the Hebrew for *bronze* and *snake* and *unclean thing*.

בְּמֶלֶךְ־ אַשּׁוּר וְלֹא עֲבָדוֹ׃ הוּא־ הִכָּה אֶת־
*** he-defeated he (8) he-served-him and-not Assyria against-king-of

פְּלִשְׁתִּים עַד־ עַזָּה וְאֶת־ גְּבוּלֶיהָ מִמִּגְדַּל נוֹצְרִים
ones-watching from-tower-of territories-of-her and Gaza as-far-as Philistines

עַד־ עִיר מִבְצָר׃ וַיְהִי בַּשָּׁנָה הָרְבִיעִית לַמֶּלֶךְ
of-the-king the-fourth in-the-year and-he-was (9) fortified city-of to

חִזְקִיָּהוּ הִיא הַשָּׁנָה הַשְּׁבִיעִית לְהוֹשֵׁעַ בֶּן־ אֵלָה מֶלֶךְ יִשְׂרָאֵל
Israel king-of Elah son-of of-Hoshea the-seventh the-year this Hezekiah

עָלָה שַׁלְמַנְאֶסֶר מֶלֶךְ־ אַשּׁוּר עַל־ שֹׁמְרוֹן וַיָּצַר
and-he-laid-siege Samaria against Assyria king-of Shalmaneser he-marched

עָלֶיהָ׃ וַיִּלְכְּדֻהָ מִקְצֵה שָׁלֹשׁ שָׁנִים בִּשְׁנַת־ שֵׁשׁ
six in-year-of years three at-end-of and-they-took-her (10) to-her

לְחִזְקִיָּה הִיא שְׁנַת־ תֵּשַׁע לְהוֹשֵׁעַ מֶלֶךְ יִשְׂרָאֵל נִלְכְּדָה
she-was-captured Israel king-of of-Hoshea nine year-of this of-Hezekiah

שֹׁמְרוֹן׃ וַיֶּגֶל מֶלֶךְ־ אַשּׁוּר אֶת־ יִשְׂרָאֵל אַשּׁוּרָה
to-Assyria Israel *** Assyria king-of and-he-deported (11) Samaria

וַיַּנְחֵם בַּחְלַח וּבְחָבוֹר נְהַר גּוֹזָן וְעָרֵי
and-in-towns-of Gozan River-of and-on-Habor in-Halah and-he-settled-them

מָדָי׃ עַל ׀ אֲשֶׁר לֹא־ שָׁמְעוּ בְּקוֹל יְהוָה אֱלֹהֵיהֶם
God-of-them Yahweh to-voice-of they-obeyed not because for (12) Medes

וַיַּעַבְרוּ אֶת־ בְּרִיתוֹ אֵת כָּל־ אֲשֶׁר צִוָּה מֹשֶׁה
Moses he-commanded that all *** covenant-of-him *** but-they-violated

עֶבֶד יְהוָה וְלֹא שָׁמְעוּ וְלֹא עָשׂוּ׃
they-carried-out and-not they-listened and-not Yahweh servant-of

וּבְאַרְבַּע עֶשְׂרֵה שָׁנָה לַמֶּלֶךְ חִזְקִיָּה עָלָה סַנְחֵרִיב
Sennacherib he-attacked Hezekiah of-the-king year ten in-four-of (13)

מֶלֶךְ־ אַשּׁוּר עַל כָּל־ עָרֵי יְהוּדָה הַבְּצֻרוֹת
the-ones-being-fortified Judah cities-of all-of against Assyria king-of

וַיִּתְפְּשֵׂם׃ וַיִּשְׁלַח חִזְקִיָּה מֶלֶךְ־ יְהוּדָה אֶל־ מֶלֶךְ־
king-of to Judah king-of Hezekiah so-he-sent (14) and-he-captured-them

אַשּׁוּר ׀ לָכִישָׁה ׀ לֵאמֹר ׀ חָטָאתִי שׁוּב מֵעָלַי אֵת אֲשֶׁר־
what *** from-against-me withdraw! I-did-wrong to-say at-Lachish Assyria

תִּתֵּן עָלַי אֶשָּׂא וַיָּשֶׂם מֶלֶךְ־ אַשּׁוּר עַל־ חִזְקִיָּה
Hezekiah from Assyria king-of and-he-exacted I-will-pay of-me you-demand

מֶלֶךְ־ יְהוּדָה שְׁלֹשׁ מֵאוֹת כִּכַּר־ כֶּסֶף וּשְׁלֹשִׁים כִּכַּר זָהָב׃
gold talent-of and-thirty silver talent-of hundreds three-of Judah king-of

וַיִּתֵּן חִזְקִיָּה אֶת־ כָּל־ הַכֶּסֶף הַנִּמְצָא בֵית־
temple-of the-one-being-found the-silver all-of *** Hezekiah so-he-gave (15)

Assyria and did not serve him.
[8]From watchtower to fortified
city, he defeated the Philistines, as far as Gaza and its territory.
[9]In King Hezekiah's fourth
year, which was the seventh
year of Hoshea son of Elah
king of Israel, Shalmaneser
king of Assyria marched
against Samaria and laid siege
to it. [10]At the end of three years
the Assyrians took it. So Samaria was captured in Hezekiah's sixth year, which was
the ninth year of Hoshea king
of Israel. [11]The king of Assyria
deported Israel to Assyria and
settled them in Halah, in Gozan on the Habor River and in
towns of the Medes. [12]This
happened because they had
not obeyed the LORD their
God, but had violated his
covenant—all that Moses the
servant of the LORD com-
manded. They neither lis-
tened to the commands nor
carried them out.
[13]In the fourteenth year of
King Hezekiah's reign, Sennacherib king of Assyria attacked all the fortified cities of
Judah and captured them. [14]So
Hezekiah king of Judah sent
this message to the king of Assyria at Lachish: "I have done
wrong. Withdraw from me,
and I will pay whatever you
demand of me." The king of
Assyria exacted from Hezekiah king of Judah three hundred talents[d] of silver and
thirty talents[e] of gold. [15]So
Hezekiah gave him all the silver that was found in the temple of the LORD and in the

[d]14 That is, about 11 tons (about 10 metric tons)
[e]14 That is, about 1 ton (about 1 metric ton)

יְהוָה וּבְאֹצְרוֹת בֵּית הַמֶּלֶךְ׃ בָּעֵת הַהִיא
the-this at-the-time (16) the-king palace-of and-in-treasuries-of Yahweh

קִצַּץ חִזְקִיָּה אֶת־ דַּלְתוֹת הֵיכַל יְהוָה וְאֶת־ הָאֹמְנוֹת
the-posts-supporting and Yahweh temple-of doors-of *** Hezekiah he-stripped

אֲשֶׁר צִפָּה חִזְקִיָּה מֶלֶךְ יְהוּדָה וַיִּתְּנֵם לְמֶלֶךְ אַשּׁוּר׃
Assyria to-king-of and-he-gave-them Judah king-of Hezekiah he-covered which

וַיִּשְׁלַח מֶלֶךְ־ אַשּׁוּר אֶת־ תַּרְתָּן וְאֶת־ רַב־ סָרִיס ׀
officer chief-of and supreme-commander *** Assyria king-of and-he-sent (17)

וְאֶת־ רַב־ שָׁקֵה מִן־ לָכִישׁ אֶל־ הַמֶּלֶךְ חִזְקִיָּהוּ בְּחֵיל
with-army Hezekiah the-king to Lachish from field-commander chief-of and

כָּבֵד יְרוּשָׁלִָם וַיַּעֲלוּ וַיָּבֹאוּ יְרוּשָׁלִַם וַיַּעֲלוּ
and-they-went-up Jerusalem and-they-came and-they-went-up Jerusalem large

וַיָּבֹאוּ וַיַּעַמְדוּ בִּתְעָלַת הַבְּרֵכָה הָעֶלְיוֹנָה אֲשֶׁר
that the-Upper the-Pool at-aqueduct-of and-they-stopped and-they-came

בִּמְסִלַּת שְׂדֵה כוֹבֵס׃ וַיִּקְרְאוּ אֶל־ הַמֶּלֶךְ
the-king for and-they-called (18) One-Washing Field-of on-road-of

וַיֵּצֵא אֲלֵהֶם אֶלְיָקִים בֶּן־ חִלְקִיָּהוּ אֲשֶׁר עַל־ הַבָּיִת וְשֶׁבְנָה
and-Shebna the-palace over who Hilkiah son-of Eliakim to-them and-he-went-out

הַסֹּפֵר וְיוֹאָח בֶּן־ אָסָף הַמַּזְכִּיר׃ וַיֹּאמֶר
and-he-said (19) the-one-recording Asaph son-of and-Joah the-secretary

אֲלֵהֶם רַב־ שָׁקֵה אִמְרוּ־ נָא אֶל־ חִזְקִיָּהוּ כֹּה־ אָמַר
he-says this Hezekiah to now! tell! field-commander chief-of to-them

הַמֶּלֶךְ הַגָּדוֹל מֶלֶךְ אַשּׁוּר מָה הַבִּטָּחוֹן הַזֶּה אֲשֶׁר
that the-this the-confidence what? Assyria king-of the-great the-king

בָּטָחְתָּ׃ אָמַרְתָּ אַךְ־ דְּבַר־ שְׂפָתַיִם עֵצָה וּגְבוּרָה
and-strength strategy lips word-of only you-speak (20) you-confiding

לַמִּלְחָמָה עַתָּה עַל־ מִי בָטַחְתָּ כִּי מָרַדְתָּ בִּי׃ עַתָּה
now (21) against-me you-rebel that you-depend whom? on now of-the-military

הִנֵּה בָטַחְתָּ לְּךָ עַל־ מִשְׁעֶנֶת הַקָּנֶה הָרָצוּץ
the-one-being-splintered the-reed staff-of on for-you you-depend look!

הַזֶּה עַל־מִצְרַיִם אֲשֶׁר יִסָּמֵךְ אִישׁ עָלָיו וּבָא בְכַפּוֹ
through-hand-of-him and-he-pierces on-him man he-leans which Egypt on the-this

וּנְקָבָהּ כֵּן פַּרְעֹה מֶלֶךְ־ מִצְרַיִם לְכָל־ הַבֹּטְחִים
the-ones-depending to-all-of Egypt king-of Pharaoh such and-he-wounds-her

עָלָיו׃ וְכִי־ תֹאמְרוּן אֵלַי אֶל־יְהוָה אֱלֹהֵינוּ בָּטָחְנוּ הֲלוֹא־הוּא
he not? we-depend God-of-us Yahweh on to-me you-say and-if (22) on-him

אֲשֶׁר הֵסִיר חִזְקִיָּהוּ אֶת־ בָּמֹתָיו וְאֶת־ מִזְבְּחֹתָיו וַיֹּאמֶר
and-he-said altars-of-him and high-places-of-him *** Hezekiah he-removed who

treasuries of the royal palace.
16 At this time Hezekiah king
of Judah stripped off the gold
with which he had covered
the doors and doorposts of the
temple of the LORD, and gave it
to the king of Assyria.

*Sennacherib Threatens Jerusalem*

17 The king of Assyria sent
his supreme commander, his
chief officer and his field commander with a large army,
from Lachish to King Hezekiah at Jerusalem. They came
up to Jerusalem and stopped at
the aqueduct of the Upper
Pool, on the road to the Washerman's Field. 18 They called
for the king; and Eliakim son
of Hilkiah the palace administrator, Shebna the secretary,
and Joah son of Asaph the
recorder went out to them.
19 The field commander said
to them, "Tell Hezekiah:

" 'This is what the great
king, the king of Assyria,
says: On what are you basing this confidence of
yours? 20 You say you have
strategy and military
strength—but you speak
only empty words. On
whom are you depending,
that you rebel against me?
21 Look now, you are de-
pending on Egypt, that
splintered reed of a staff,
which pierces a man's
hand and wounds him if he
leans on it! Such is Pharaoh
king of Egypt to all who depend on him. 22 And if you
say to me, "We are depending on the LORD our
God"—isn't he the one
whose high places and al-
tars Hezekiah removed,

לִֽיהוּדָה֙ וְלִיר֣וּשָׁלַ֔ם לִפְנֵי֙ הַמִּזְבֵּ֣חַ הַזֶּ֔ה תִּֽשְׁתַּחֲו֖וּ

you-must-worship the-this the-altar before and-to-Jerusalem to-Judah

בִּירוּשָׁלִָֽם׃ וְעַתָּה֙ הִתְעָ֣רֶב נָ֔א אֶת־ אֲדֹנִ֖י אֶת־ מֶ֣לֶךְ

king-of with master-of-me with now! make-bargain! and-now (23) in-Jerusalem

אַשּׁ֑וּר וְאֶתְּנָ֤ה לְךָ֙ אַלְפַּ֣יִם סוּסִ֔ים אִם־ תּוּכַ֕ל לָ֥תֶת

to-put you-can if horses two-thousands to-you and-I-will-give Assyria

לְךָ֖ רֹכְבִ֥ים עֲלֵיהֶֽם׃ וְאֵ֣יךְ תָּשִׁ֗יב אֵ֣ת פְּנֵ֨י

faces-of *** can-you-repulse now-how? (24) on-them ones-riding of-you

פַחַ֥ת אַחַ֛ד עַבְדֵ֥י אֲדֹנִ֖י הַקְּטַנִּ֑ים וַתִּבְטַ֤ח

though-you-depend the-least-ones master-of-me officials-of one-of officer-of

לְךָ֙ עַל־ מִצְרַ֔יִם לְרֶ֖כֶב וּלְפָרָשִֽׁים׃ עַתָּה֙ הֲמִבַּלְעֲדֵ֣י יְהוָ֔ה

Yahweh apart-from? now (25) and-for-horsemen for-chariot Egypt on for-you

עָלִ֛יתִי עַל־ הַמָּק֥וֹם הַזֶּ֖ה לְהַשְׁחִת֑וֹ יְהוָה֙ אָמַ֣ר אֵלַ֔י

to-me he-told Yahweh to-destroy-him the-this the-place against I-came

עֲלֵ֛ה עַל־ הָאָ֥רֶץ הַזֹּ֖את וְהַשְׁחִיתָֽהּ׃ וַיֹּ֣אמֶר

then-he-said (26) and-destroy-her! the-this the-country against march!

אֶלְיָקִ֣ים בֶּן־ חִ֠לְקִיָּהוּ וְשֶׁבְנָ֨ה וְיוֹאָ֜ח אֶל־ רַב־ שָׁקֵ֗ה

field-commander chief-of to and-Joah and-Shebna Hilkiah son-of Eliakim

דַּבֶּר־ נָ֤א אֶל־ עֲבָדֶ֙יךָ֙ אֲרָמִ֔ית כִּ֥י שֹׁמְעִ֖ים אֲנָ֑חְנוּ וְאַל־

but-not we ones-understanding since Aramaic servants-of-you to now! speak!

תְּדַבֵּ֤ר עִמָּ֙נוּ֙ יְהוּדִ֔ית בְּאָזְנֵ֣י הָעָ֔ם אֲשֶׁ֖ר עַל־הַחֹמָֽה׃ וַיֹּ֨אמֶר

but-he-said (27) the-wall on who the-people in-ears-of Hebrew to-us you-speak

אֲלֵיהֶ֜ם רַב־ שָׁקֵ֗ה הַ֠עַל אֲדֹנֶ֨יךָ וְאֵלֶ֜יךָ שְׁלָחַ֤נִי

he-sent-me and-to-you masters-of-you to? field-commander chief-of to-them

אֲדֹנִי֙ לְדַבֵּ֔ר אֶת־הַדְּבָרִ֖ים הָאֵ֑לֶּה הֲלֹ֣א עַל־הָאֲנָשִׁ֗ים הַיֹּֽשְׁבִים֙

the-ones-sitting the-men to not? the-these the-things *** to-say master-of-me

עַל־ הַחֹמָ֔ה לֶאֱכֹ֣ל אֶת־ חֲרֵיהֶם֙* וְלִשְׁתּ֛וֹת אֶת־ שֵׁינֵיהֶ֖ם†

†urines-of-them *** and-to-drink *filth-of-them *** to-eat the-wall on

עִמָּכֶֽם׃ וַיַּעֲמֹד֙ רַב־ שָׁקֵ֔ה וַיִּקְרָ֥א בְקוֹל־

with-voice and-he-called field-commander chief-of then-he-stood (28) like-you

גָּד֖וֹל יְהוּדִ֑ית וַיְדַבֵּ֣ר וַיֹּ֗אמֶר שִׁמְע֛וּ דְּבַר־ הַמֶּ֥לֶךְ הַגָּד֖וֹל מֶ֥לֶךְ

king-of the-great the-king word-of hear! and-he-said and-he-spoke Hebrew loud

אַשּֽׁוּר׃ כֹּ֚ה אָמַ֣ר הַמֶּ֔לֶךְ אַל־ יַשִּׁ֥א לָכֶ֖ם חִזְקִיָּ֑הוּ כִּי־

for Hezekiah to-you let-him-deceive not the-king he-says this (29) Assyria

לֹ֣א יוּכַ֔ל לְהַצִּ֥יל אֶתְכֶ֖ם מִיָּדֽוֹ׃ וְאַל־ יַבְטַ֨ח

let-him-cause-to-trust and-not (30) from-hand-of-him you to-deliver he-can not

אֶתְכֶ֤ם חִזְקִיָּ֙הוּ֙ אֶל־יְהוָ֣ה לֵאמֹ֔ר הַצֵּ֥ל יַצִּילֵ֖נוּ יְהוָ֑ה וְלֹ֤א

and-not Yahweh he-will-deliver-us to-deliver to-say Yahweh in Hezekiah you

saying to Judah and Jerusalem, "You must worship before this altar in Jerusalem"?

23 "'Come now, make a bargain with my master, the king of Assyria: I will give you two thousand horses, if you can put riders on them. 24 How can you repulse one officer of the least of my master's officials, even though you are depending on Egypt for chariots and horsemen[f]? 25 Furthermore, have I come to attack and destroy this place without word from the LORD? The LORD himself told me to march against this country and destroy it.'"

26 Then Eliakim son of Hilkiah, and Shebna and Joah said to the field commander, "Please speak to your servants in Aramaic, since we understand it. Don't speak to us in Hebrew in the hearing of the people on the wall."

27 But the commander replied, "Was it only to your master and you that my master sent me to say these things, and not to the men sitting on the wall—who, like you, will have to eat their own filth and drink their own urine?"

28 Then the commander stood and called out in Hebrew: "Hear the word of the great king, the king of Assyria! 29 This is what the king says: Do not let Hezekiah deceive you. He cannot deliver you from my hand. 30 Do not let Hezekiah persuade you to trust in the LORD when he says, 'The LORD will surely deliver us; this city will not be

f24 Or *charioteers*

*27a The *Qere, outgoing-of-them,* is a less graphic word than the *Ketbib.*

†27b The *Qere, waters-of feet-of-them,* is a less graphic word than the *Ketbib.*

°27a ק צואתם

°27b ק מימי רגליהם

תִּנָּתֵן אֶת־ הָעִיר הַזֹּאת בְּיַד מֶלֶךְ אַשּׁוּר׃
Assyria king-of into-hand-of the-this the-city *** she-will-be-given

אַל־ תִּשְׁמְעוּ אֶל־חִזְקִיָּהוּ כִּי כֹה אָמַר מֶלֶךְ אַשּׁוּר עֲשׂוּ־
make! Assyria king-of he-says this for Hezekiah to you-listen not (31)

אִתִּי בְרָכָה וּצְאוּ אֵלַי וְאִכְלוּ אִישׁ־ גַּפְנוֹ וְאִישׁ
and-each vine-of-him each then-eat! to-me and-come-out! peace with-me

תְּאֵנָתוֹ וּשְׁתוּ אִישׁ מֵי־ בוֹרוֹ׃ עַד־ בֹּאִי
to-come-me until (32) cistern-of-him waters-of each and-drink! fig-tree-of-him

וְלָקַחְתִּי אֶתְכֶם אֶל־ אֶרֶץ כְּאַרְצְכֶם אֶרֶץ דָּגָן וְתִירוֹשׁ אֶרֶץ
land-of and-new-wine grain land-of like-land-of-you land to you and-I-take

לֶחֶם וּכְרָמִים אֶרֶץ זֵית יִצְהָר וּדְבַשׁ וִחְיוּ וְלֹא
and-not now-live! and-honey oil olive-tree-of land-of and-vineyards bread

תָמֻתוּ וְאַל־ תִּשְׁמְעוּ אֶל־חִזְקִיָּהוּ כִּי ־יַסִּית אֶתְכֶם לֵאמֹר יְהוָה
Yahweh to-say you he-misleads for Hezekiah to you-listen and-not you-die

יַצִּילֵנוּ׃ הַהַצֵּל הִצִּילוּ אֱלֹהֵי הַגּוֹיִם אִישׁ
any the-nations gods-of they-delivered to-deliver? (33) he-will-deliver-us

אֶת־ אַרְצוֹ מִיַּד מֶלֶךְ אַשּׁוּר׃ אַיֵּה אֱלֹהֵי חֲמָת
Hamath gods-of where? (34) Assyria king-of from-hand-of land-of-him ***

וְאַרְפָּד אַיֵּה אֱלֹהֵי סְפַרְוַיִם הֵנַע וְעִוָּה כִּי־ הִצִּילוּ אֶת־
*** they-rescued indeed and-Ivvah Hena Sepharvaim gods-of where? and-Arpad

שֹׁמְרוֹן מִיָּדִי׃ מִי בְּכָל־ אֱלֹהֵי הָאֲרָצוֹת אֲשֶׁר־
who the-countries gods-of of-all-of who? (35) from-hand-of-me Samaria

הִצִּילוּ אֶת־ אַרְצָם מִיָּדִי כִּי־ יַצִּיל יְהוָה אֶת־
*** Yahweh can-he-deliver indeed from-hand-of-me land-of-them *** they-saved

יְרוּשָׁלַםִ מִיָּדִי׃ וְהֶחֱרִישׁוּ הָעָם וְלֹא־
and-not the-people but-they-remained-silent (36) from-hand-of-me Jerusalem

עָנוּ אֹתוֹ דָּבָר כִּי־ מִצְוַת הַמֶּלֶךְ הִיא לֵאמֹר לֹא תַעֲנֻהוּ׃
you-answer-him not to-say this the-king command-of for word him they-replied

וַיָּבֹא אֶלְיָקִים בֶּן־ חִלְקִיָּה אֲשֶׁר־עַל־ הַבַּיִת וְשֶׁבְנָא
and-Shebna the-palace over who Hilkiah son-of Eliakim then-he-went (37)

הַסֹּפֵר וְיוֹאָח בֶּן־ אָסָף הַמַּזְכִּיר אֶל־ חִזְקִיָּהוּ
Hezekiah to the-one-recording Asaph son-of and-Joah the-secretary

קְרוּעֵי בְגָדִים וַיַּגִּדוּ לוֹ דִּבְרֵי רַב־
chief-of words-of to-him and-they-told clothes ones-being-torn-of

שָׁקֵה׃ וַיְהִי כִּשְׁמֹעַ הַמֶּלֶךְ חִזְקִיָּהוּ וַיִּקְרַע
then-he-tore Hezekiah the-king when-to-hear and-he-was (19:1) field-commander

אֶת־ בְּגָדָיו וַיִּתְכַּס בַּשָּׂק וַיָּבֹא
and-he-went-into with-the-sackcloth and-he-covered-himself clothes-of-him ***

given into the hand of the king of Assyria.'

31"Do not listen to Hezekiah. This is what the king of Assyria says: Make peace with me and come out to me. Then every one of you will eat from his own vine and fig tree and drink water from his own cistern, 32until I come and take you to a land like your own, a land of grain and new wine, a land of bread and vineyards, a land of olive trees and honey. Choose life and not death!

"Do not listen to Hezekiah, for he is misleading you when he says, 'The LORD will deliver us.' 33Has the god of any nation ever delivered his land from the hand of the king of Assyria? 34Where are the gods of Hamath and Arpad? Where are the gods of Sepharvaim, Hena and Ivvah? Have they rescued Samaria from my hand? 35Who of all the gods of these countries has been able to save his land from me? How then can the LORD deliver Jerusalem from my hand?"

36But the people remained silent and said nothing in reply, because the king had commanded, "Do not answer him."

37Then Eliakim son of Hilkiah the palace administrator, Shebna the secretary and Joah son of Asaph the recorder went to Hezekiah, with their clothes torn, and told him what the field commander had said.

*Jerusalem's Deliverance Foretold*

19 When King Hezekiah heard this, he tore his clothes and put on sackcloth

בֵּית יְהוָה׃ (2) וַיִּשְׁלַח אֶת־אֶלְיָקִים אֲשֶׁר־עַל־הַבַּיִת וְשֶׁבְנָא
and-Shebna the-palace over who Eliakim *** and-he-sent (2) Yahweh temple-of

הַסֹּפֵר וְאֵת זִקְנֵי הַכֹּהֲנִים מִתְכַּסִּים בַּשַּׂקִּים
in-the-sackcloths ones-being-clothed the-priests elders-of and the-secretary

אֶל־יְשַׁעְיָהוּ הַנָּבִיא בֶּן־אָמוֹץ׃ (3) וַיֹּאמְרוּ אֵלָיו כֹּה אָמַר
he-says this to-him and-they-told (3) Amoz son-of the-prophet Isaiah to

חִזְקִיָּהוּ יוֹם־צָרָה וְתוֹכֵחָה וּנְאָצָה הַיּוֹם הַזֶּה כִּי
as-when the-this the-day and-disgrace and-rebuke distress day-of Hezekiah

בָאוּ בָנִים עַד־מַשְׁבֵּר וְכֹחַ אַיִן לְלֵדָה׃ (4) אוּלַי
perhaps (4) to-deliver there-is-no and-strength birth to children they-come

יִשְׁמַע יְהוָה אֱלֹהֶיךָ אֵת כָּל־דִּבְרֵי רַב־שָׁקֵה
field-commander chief-of words-of all-of *** God-of-you Yahweh he-will-hear

אֲשֶׁר שְׁלָחוֹ מֶלֶךְ־אַשּׁוּר אֲדֹנָיו לְחָרֵף אֱלֹהִים חַי
living God to-ridicule masters-of-him Assyria king-of he-sent-him whom

וְהוֹכִיחַ בַּדְּבָרִים אֲשֶׁר שָׁמַע יְהוָה אֱלֹהֶיךָ וְנָשָׂאתָ
so-you-lift God-of-you Yahweh he-heard that for-the-words and-he-will-rebuke

תְפִלָּה בְּעַד הַשְּׁאֵרִית הַנִּמְצָאָה׃ (5) וַיָּבֹאוּ עַבְדֵי
officials-of when-they-came (5) the-one-surviving the-remnant for prayer

הַמֶּלֶךְ חִזְקִיָּהוּ אֶל־יְשַׁעְיָהוּ׃* (6) וַיֹּאמֶר לָהֶם יְשַׁעְיָהוּ כֹּה תֹאמְרוּן
you-tell this Isaiah to-them then-he-said (6) Isaiah to Hezekiah the-king

אֶל־אֲדֹנֵיכֶם כֹּה אָמַר יְהוָה אַל־תִּירָא מִפְּנֵי הַדְּבָרִים
the-words from-before you-be-afraid not Yahweh he-says this masters-of-you to

אֲשֶׁר שָׁמַעְתָּ אֲשֶׁר גִּדְּפוּ נַעֲרֵי מֶלֶךְ־אַשּׁוּר אֹתִי׃
me Assyria king-of underlings-of they-blasphemed which you-heard that

(7) הִנְנִי נֹתֵן בּוֹ רוּחַ וְשָׁמַע שְׁמוּעָה וְשָׁב
then-he-will-return report when-he-hears spirit in-him putting see-I! (7)

לְאַרְצוֹ וְהִפַּלְתִּיו בַּחֶרֶב בְּאַרְצוֹ׃
in-country-of-him with-the-sword and-I-will-have-cut-down-him to-country-of-him

(8) וַיָּשָׁב רַב־שָׁקֵה וַיִּמְצָא אֶת־מֶלֶךְ
king-of *** and-he-found field-commander chief-of and-he-withdrew (8)

אַשּׁוּר נִלְחָם עַל־לִבְנָה כִּי שָׁמַע כִּי נָסַע מִלָּכִישׁ׃
from-Lachish he-left that he-heard when Libnah against fighting Assyria

(9) וַיִּשְׁמַע אֶל־תִּרְהָקָה מֶלֶךְ־†כּוּשׁ לֵאמֹר הִנֵּה יָצָא
he-marched-out see! to-say Cush king-of Tirhakah about now-he-heard (9)

לְהִלָּחֵם אִתָּךְ וַיָּשָׁב וַיִּשְׁלַח מַלְאָכִים אֶל־חִזְקִיָּהוּ
Hezekiah to messengers and-he-sent so-he-repeated against-you to-fight

לֵאמֹר׃ (10) כֹּה תֹאמְרוּן אֶל־חִזְקִיָּהוּ מֶלֶךְ־יְהוּדָה לֵאמֹר אַל־
not to-say Judah king-of Hezekiah to you-say this (10) to-say

and went into the temple of the LORD. [2]He sent Eliakim the palace administrator, Shebna the secretary and the leading priests, all wearing sackcloth, to the prophet Isaiah son of Amoz. [3]They told him, "This is what Hezekiah says: This day is a day of distress and rebuke and disgrace, as when children come to the point of birth and there is no strength to deliver them. [4]It may be that the LORD your God will hear all the words of the field commander, whom his master, the king of Assyria, has sent to ridicule the living God, and that he will rebuke him for the words the LORD your God has heard. Therefore pray for the remnant that still survives."

[5]When King Hezekiah's officials came to Isaiah, [6]Isaiah said to them, "Tell your master, 'This is what the LORD says: Do not be afraid of what you have heard—those words with which the underlings of the king of Assyria have blasphemed me. [7]Listen! I am going to put such a spirit in him that when he hears a certain report, he will return to his own country, and there I will have him cut down with the sword.' "

[8]When the field commander heard that the king of Assyria had left Lachish, he withdrew and found the king fighting against Libnah.

[9]Now Sennacherib received a report that Tirhakah, the Cushite[g] king ⌊of Egypt⌋, was marching out to fight against him. So he again sent messengers to Hezekiah with this word: [10]"Say to Hezekiah king of Judah: Do not let the god

g9 That is, from the upper Nile region

*5 Most mss have *sheva* under the *ayin* (עְ־).

†9 Most mss have *sheva* under the *kaph* (ךְ־).

יַשִּׁאֲךָ אֱלֹהֶיךָ אֲשֶׁר אַתָּה בֹּטֵחַ בּוֹ לֵאמֹר לֹא
not to-say on-him depending you whom God-of-you let-him-deceive-you

תִּנָּתֵן יְרוּשָׁלַםִ בְּיַד מֶלֶךְ אַשּׁוּר׃ הִנֵּה ׀ אַתָּה שָׁמַעְתָּ
you-heard you see! (11) Assyria king-of into-hand-of Jerusalem she-will-given

אֵת אֲשֶׁר עָשׂוּ מַלְכֵי אַשּׁוּר לְכָל־ הָאֲרָצוֹת לְהַחֲרִימָם
to-destroy-them the-countries to-all-of Assyria kings-of they-did what ***

וְאַתָּה תִּנָּצֵל׃ הַהִצִּילוּ אֹתָם אֱלֹהֵי הַגּוֹיִם
the-nations gods-of them did-they-deliver? (12) will-you-be-delivered and-you

אֲשֶׁר שִׁחֲתוּ אֲבוֹתַי אֶת־ גּוֹזָן וְאֶת־ חָרָן וְרֶצֶף וּבְנֵי־
and-sons-of and-Rezeph Haran and Gozan *** fathers-of-me they-destroyed that

עֶדֶן אֲשֶׁר בִּתְלַאשָּׂר׃ אַיּוֹ מֶלֶךְ־ חֲמָת וּמֶלֶךְ אַרְפָּד
Arpad and-king-of Hamath king-of where-he? (13) in-Tel-Assar who Eden

וּמֶלֶךְ לָעִיר סְפַרְוָיִם הֵנַע וְעִוָּה׃ וַיִּקַּח חִזְקִיָּהוּ
Hezekiah and-he-received (14) or-Avvah Hena Sepharvaim of-city-of and-king

אֶת־ הַסְּפָרִים מִיַּד הַמַּלְאָכִים וַיִּקְרָאֵם וַיַּעַל
then-he-went-up and-he-read-them the-messengers from-hand-of the-letters ***

בֵּית יְהוָה וַיִּפְרְשֵׂהוּ חִזְקִיָּהוּ לִפְנֵי יְהוָה׃
Yahweh before Hezekiah and-he-spread-out-him Yahweh temple-of

וַיִּתְפַּלֵּל חִזְקִיָּהוּ לִפְנֵי יְהוָה וַיֹּאמַר יְהוָה אֱלֹהֵי יִשְׂרָאֵל
Israel God-of Yahweh and-he-said Yahweh to Hezekiah and-he-prayed (15)

יֹשֵׁב הַכְּרֻבִים אַתָּה־ הוּא הָאֱלֹהִים לְבַדְּךָ לְכֹל
over-all-of by-yourself the-God he you the-cherubim being-enthroned-of

מַמְלְכוֹת הָאָרֶץ אַתָּה עָשִׂיתָ אֶת־ הַשָּׁמַיִם וְאֶת־ הָאָרֶץ׃ הַטֵּה
give! (16) the-earth and the-heavens *** you-made you the-earth kingdoms-of

יְהוָה ׀ אָזְנְךָ וּשְׁמָע פְּקַח יְהוָה עֵינֶיךָ וּרְאֵה וּשְׁמַע
and-listen! and-see! eyes-of-you Yahweh open! and-hear! ear-of-you Yahweh

אֵת דִּבְרֵי סַנְחֵרִיב אֲשֶׁר שְׁלָחוֹ לְחָרֵף אֱלֹהִים חָי׃ אָמְנָם
truly (17) living God to-insult he-sent-him that Sennacherib words-of ***

יְהוָה הֶחֱרִיבוּ מַלְכֵי אַשּׁוּר אֶת־ הַגּוֹיִם וְאֶת־ אַרְצָם׃
land-of-them and the-nations *** Assyria kings-of they-laid-waste Yahweh

וְנָתְנוּ אֶת־ אֱלֹהֵיהֶם בָּאֵשׁ כִּי לֹא אֱלֹהִים הֵמָּה כִּי
but they gods not for into-the-fire gods-of-them *** and-they-threw (18)

אִם־ מַעֲשֵׂה יְדֵי־ אָדָם עֵץ וָאֶבֶן וַיְאַבְּדוּם׃ וְעַתָּה
so-now (19) and-they-destroyed-them and-stone wood man hands-of work-of only

יְהוָה אֱלֹהֵינוּ הוֹשִׁיעֵנוּ נָא מִיָּדוֹ וְיֵדְעוּ כָּל־
all-of so-they-may-know from-hand-of-him now! deliver-us! God-of-us Yahweh

מַמְלְכוֹת הָאָרֶץ כִּי אַתָּה יְהוָה אֱלֹהִים לְבַדֶּךָ׃ וַיִּשְׁלַח
then-he-sent (20) by-yourself God Yahweh you that the-earth kingdoms-of

you depend on deceive you when he says, 'Jerusalem will not be handed over to the king of Assyria.' 11Surely you have heard what the kings of Assyria have done to all the countries, destroying them completely. And will you be delivered? 12Did the gods of the nations that were destroyed by my forefathers deliver them: the gods of Gozan, Haran, Rezeph and the people of Eden who were in Tel Assar? 13Where is the king of Hamath, the king of Arpad, the king of the city of Sepharvaim, or of Hena or Ivvah?"

*Hezekiah's Prayer*

14Hezekiah received the letter from the messengers and read it. Then he went up to the temple of the LORD and spread it out before the LORD. 15And Hezekiah prayed to the LORD: "O LORD, God of Israel, enthroned between the cherubim, you alone are God over all the kingdoms of the earth. You have made heaven and earth. 16Give ear, O LORD, and hear; open your eyes, O LORD, and see; listen to the words Sennacherib has sent to insult the living God.

17"It is true, O LORD, that the Assyrian kings have laid waste these nations and their lands. 18They have thrown their gods into the fire and destroyed them, for they were not gods but only wood and stone, fashioned by men's hands. 19Now, O LORD our God, deliver us from his hand, so that all kingdoms on earth may know that you alone, O LORD, are God."

יְשַׁעְיָהוּ בֶן־אָמוֹץ אֶל־חִזְקִיָּהוּ לֵאמֹר כֹּה־אָמַר יְהוָה אֱלֹהֵי יִשְׂרָאֵל
Israel God-of Yahweh he-says this to-say Hezekiah to Amoz son-of Isaiah

אֲשֶׁר הִתְפַּלַּלְתָּ אֵלַי אֶל־סַנְחֵרִב מֶלֶךְ־אַשּׁוּר שָׁמָעְתִּי׃ זֶה
this (21) I-heard Assyria king-of Sennacherib about to-me you-prayed what

הַדָּבָר אֲשֶׁר־דִּבֶּר יְהוָה עָלָיו בָּזָה לְךָ לָעֲגָה
she-mocks against-you she-despises against-him Yahweh he-spoke that the-word

לְךָ בְּתוּלַת בַּת־צִיּוֹן אַחֲרֶיךָ רֹאשׁ הֵנִיעָה בַּת
Daughter-of she-tosses head after-you Zion Daughter-of Virgin-of at-you

יְרוּשָׁלִָם׃ אֶת־מִי חֵרַפְתָּ וְגִדַּפְתָּ וְעַל־מִי
whom? and-against and-you-blasphemed you-insulted who? *** (22) Jerusalem

הֲרִימוֹתָ קּוֹל וַתִּשָּׂא מָרוֹם עֵינֶיךָ עַל־קְדוֹשׁ יִשְׂרָאֵל׃
Israel Holy-One-of against eyes-of-you pride and-you-lifted voice you-raised

בְּיַד מַלְאָכֶיךָ חֵרַפְתָּ ׀ אֲדֹנָי וַתֹּאמֶר בְּרֹכֶב
with-many-of and-you-said Lord you-insulted messengers-of-you by-hand-of (23)

רִכְבִּי אֲנִי עָלִיתִי מְרוֹם הָרִים יַרְכְּתֵי לְבָנוֹן
Lebanon utmost-heights-of mountains height-of I-ascended I chariot-of-me

וְאֶכְרֹת קוֹמַת אֲרָזָיו מִבְחוֹר בְּרֹשָׁיו
pines-of-him choice-of cedars-of-him tall-one-of and-I-cut-down

וְאָבוֹאָה מְלוֹן קִצֹּה יַעַר כַּרְמִלּוֹ׃
garden-of-him forest-of remote-part-of-him shelter-of and-I-reached

אֲנִי קַרְתִּי וְשָׁתִיתִי מַיִם זָרִים וְאַחְרִב
and-I-dried-up ones-being-foreign waters and-I-drank I-dug-well I (24)

בְּכַף־פְּעָמַי כֹּל יְאֹרֵי מָצוֹר׃ הֲלֹא־שָׁמַעְתָּ
you-heard not? (25) Egypt streams-of all-of feet-of-me with-sole-of

לְמֵרָחוֹק אֹתָהּ עָשִׂיתִי לְמִימֵי קֶדֶם וִיצַרְתִּיהָ
then-I-planned-her old at-from-days-of I-ordained her at-from-long-ago

עַתָּה הֲבֵיאתִיהָ וּתְהִי לְהַשְׁוֹת גַּלִּים נִצִּים
ones-being-ruins piles-of-stones to-turn so-you-were I-brought-to-pass-her now

עָרִים בְּצֻרוֹת׃ וְיֹשְׁבֵיהֶן קִצְרֵי־
ones-drained-of and-ones-living-of-them (26) ones-being-fortified cities

יָד חַתּוּ וַיֵּבֹשׁוּ הָיוּ עֵשֶׂב שָׂדֶה
field plant-of they-are and-they-are-put-to-shame they-are-dismayed power

וִירַק דֶּשֶׁא חֲצִיר גַּגּוֹת וּשְׁדֵפָה לִפְנֵי קָמָה׃
growing-up before and-scorched housetops grass-of grass and-tender-shoot-of

וְשִׁבְתְּךָ וְצֵאתְךָ וּבֹאֲךָ יָדָעְתִּי וְאֵת הִתְרַגֶּזְךָ
to-rage-you and I-know and-to-come-you and-to-go-you but-to-stay-you (27)

אֵלָי׃ יַעַן הִתְרַגֶּזְךָ אֵלַי וְשַׁאֲנַנְךָ
and-insolence-of-you against-me to-rage-you because (28) against-me

### *Isaiah Prophesies Sennacherib's Fall*

[20]Then Isaiah son of Amoz sent a message to Hezekiah: "This is what the LORD, the God of Israel, says: I have heard your prayer concerning Sennacherib king of Assyria. [21]This is the word that the LORD has spoken against him:

" 'The Virgin Daughter of Zion
despises you and mocks you.
The Daughter of Jerusalem
tosses her head as you flee.
[22]Who is it you have insulted and blasphemed?
Against whom have you raised your voice
and lifted your eyes in pride?
Against the Holy One of Israel!
[23]By your messengers
you have heaped insults on the Lord.
And you have said,
"With my many chariots
I have ascended the heights of the mountains,
the utmost heights of Lebanon.
I have cut down its tallest cedars,
the choicest of its pines.
I have reached its remotest parts,
the finest of its forests.
[24]I have dug wells in foreign lands
and drunk the water there.
With the soles of my feet
I have dried up all the streams of Egypt."
[25]" 'Have you not heard?
Long ago I ordained it.
In days of old I planned it;
now I have brought it to pass,
that you have turned fortified cities
into piles of stone.
[26]Their people, drained of power,
are dismayed and put to shame.
They are like plants in the field,
like tender green shoots,
like grass sprouting on the housetops,
scorched before it grows up.
[27]" 'But I know where you stay
and when you come and go

°23a ק ברב
°23b ק קצו

עָלָה בְאָזְנָי וְשַׂמְתִּי חַחִי בְּאַפֶּךָ
he-reached to-ears-of-me and-I-will-put hook-of-me in-nose-of-you

וּמִתְגִּי בִּשְׂפָתֶיךָ וַהֲשִׁבֹתִיךָ בַּדֶּרֶךְ אֲשֶׁר־
and-bit-of-me in-lips-of-you and-I-will-make-return-you by-the-way that

בָּאתָ בָּהּ׃ (29) וְזֶה־ לְּךָ הָאוֹת אָכוֹל הַשָּׁנָה סָפִיחַ
you-came on-her (29) and-this for-you the-sign to-eat the-year growth

וּבַשָּׁנָה הַשֵּׁנִית סָחִישׁ וּבַשָּׁנָה הַשְּׁלִישִׁית זִרְעוּ
and-in-the-year the-second aftergrowth but-in-the-year the-third sow!

וְקִצְרוּ וְנִטְעוּ כְרָמִים וְאִכְלוּ פִרְיָם׃ (30) וְיָסְפָה
and-reap! and-plant! vineyards and-eat! fruit-of-them (30) for-she-will-repeat

פְּלֵיטַת בֵּית־ יְהוּדָה הַנִּשְׁאָרָה שֹׁרֶשׁ לְמָטָּה וְעָשָׂה
remnant-of house-of Judah the-one-remaining root at-below and-he-will-bear

פְרִי לְמָעְלָה׃ (31) כִּי מִירוּשָׁלַםִ תֵּצֵא שְׁאֵרִית וּפְלֵיטָה
fruit at-above (31) for from-Jerusalem she-will-come remnant and-survivor

מֵהַר צִיּוֹן קִנְאַת יְהוָה * תַּעֲשֶׂה־ זֹּאת׃ (32) לָכֵן
from-Mount-of Zion zeal-of Yahweh * she-will-accomplish this (32) therefore

כֹּה־ אָמַר יְהוָה אֶל־ מֶלֶךְ אַשּׁוּר לֹא יָבֹא אֶל־ הָעִיר
this he-says Yahweh to king-of Assyria not he-will-enter into the-city

הַזֹּאת וְלֹא־ יוֹרֶה שָׁם חֵץ וְלֹא־ יְקַדְּמֶנָּה
the-this and-not he-will-shoot here arrow and-not he-will-come-before-her

מָגֵן וְלֹא־ יִשְׁפֹּךְ עָלֶיהָ סֹלְלָה׃ (33) בַּדֶּרֶךְ אֲשֶׁר־
shield and-not he-will-build against-her siege-ramp (33) by-the-way that

יָבֹא בָהּ יָשׁוּב וְאֶל־ הָעִיר הַזֹּאת לֹא יָבֹא
he-came on-her he-will-return and-into the-city the-this not he-will-enter

נְאֻם־ יְהוָה׃ (34) וְגַנּוֹתִי אֶל־ הָעִיר הַזֹּאת
declaration-of Yahweh (34) and-I-will-defend to the-city the-this

לְהוֹשִׁיעָהּ לְמַעֲנִי וּלְמַעַן דָּוִד עַבְדִּי׃ (35) וַיְהִי
to-save-her for-sake-of-me and-sake-of David servant-of-me (35) and-he-was

בַּלַּיְלָה הַהוּא וַיֵּצֵא ׀ מַלְאַךְ יְהוָה וַיַּךְ
on-the-night the-that then-he-went-out angel-of Yahweh and-he-killed

בְּמַחֲנֵה אַשּׁוּר מֵאָה שְׁמוֹנִים וַחֲמִשָּׁה אָלֶף וַיַּשְׁכִּימוּ
in-camp-of Assyria hundred eighty and-five thousand when-they-got-up

בַבֹּקֶר וְהִנֵּה כֻלָּם פְּגָרִים מֵתִים׃
in-the-morning then-see! all-of-them bodies ones-being-dead

(36) וַיִּסַּע וַיֵּלֶךְ וַיָּשָׁב סַנְחֵרִיב מֶלֶךְ־
(36) so-he-broke-camp and-he-withdrew and-he-returned Sennacherib king-of

אַשּׁוּר וַיֵּשֶׁב בְּנִינְוֵה׃ (37) וַיְהִי הוּא מִשְׁתַּחֲוֶה בֵּית ׀
Assyria and-he-stayed in-Nineveh (37) and-he-was he worshiping temple-of

and how you rage
against me.
28 Because you rage against
me
and your insolence has
reached my ears,
I will put my hook in your
nose
and my bit in your
mouth,
and I will make you return
by the way you came.'
29 "This will be the sign for
you, O Hezekiah:

This year you will eat what
grows by itself,
and the second year
what springs from
that.
But in the third year sow
and reap,
plant vineyards and eat
their fruit.
30 Once more a remnant of
the house of Judah
will take root below and
bear fruit above.
31 For out of Jerusalem will
come a remnant,
and out of Mount Zion a
band of survivors.

The zeal of the LORD Almighty
will accomplish this.

32 "Therefore this is what the
LORD says concerning the king
of Assyria:

"He will not enter this city
or shoot an arrow here.
He will not come before it
with shield
or build a siege ramp
against it.
33 By the way that he came
he will return;
he will not enter this
city,
declares the LORD.
34 I will defend this city and
save it,
for my sake and for the
sake of David my
servant."

35 That night the angel of the
LORD went out and put to
death a hundred and eighty-
five thousand men in the Assyrian camp. When the people
got up the next morning—
there were all the dead bodies!
36 So Sennacherib king of Assyria broke camp and withdrew. He returned to Nineveh
and stayed there.
37 One day, while he was
worshiping in the temple of

*31 Many mss have the *Qere* ( צבאות ), *Hosts*, from the parallel passage in Isaiah 37:32.

נִסְרֹךְ אֱלֹהָיו וְאַדְרַמֶּלֶךְ וְשַׂרְאֶצֶר * הִכֻּהוּ
they-cut-down-him * and-Sharezer and-Adrammelech gods-of-him Nisroch

בַחֶרֶב וְהֵמָּה נִמְלְטוּ אֶרֶץ אֲרָרָט וַיִּמְלֹךְ
and-he-became-king Ararat land-of they-escaped and-they with-the-sword

אֵסַר־ חַדֹּן בְּנוֹ תַּחְתָּיו׃ בַּיָּמִים הָהֵם
the-those in-the-days (20:1) in-place-of-him son-of-him Haddon Esar

חָלָה חִזְקִיָּהוּ לָמוּת וַיָּבֹא אֵלָיו יְשַׁעְיָהוּ בֶן־ אָמוֹץ
Amoz son-of Isaiah to-him and-he-went to-die Hezekiah he-became-ill

הַנָּבִיא וַיֹּאמֶר אֵלָיו כֹּה־ אָמַר יְהוָה צַו
put-in-order! Yahweh he-says this to-him and-he-said the-prophet

לְבֵיתֶךָ כִּי מֵת אַתָּה וְלֹא תִחְיֶה׃ וַיַּסֵּב
and-he-turned (2) you-will-recover and-not you dying for to-house-of-you

אֶת־ פָּנָיו אֶל־ הַקִּיר וַיִּתְפַּלֵּל אֶל־ יְהוָה לֵאמֹר׃ אָנָּה יְהוָה
Yahweh O! (3) to-say Yahweh to and-he-prayed the-wall to faces-of-him ***

זְכָר־ נָא אֵת אֲשֶׁר הִתְהַלַּכְתִּי לְפָנֶיךָ בֶּאֱמֶת וּבְלֵבָב שָׁלֵם
whole and-with-heart in-faith before-you I-walked how *** now! remember!

וְהַטּוֹב בְּעֵינֶיךָ עָשִׂיתִי וַיֵּבְךְּ חִזְקִיָּהוּ בְּכִי גָדוֹל׃
bitter weeping Hezekiah and-he-wept I-did in-eyes-of-you and-the-good

וַיְהִי יְשַׁעְיָהוּ לֹא יָצָא הָעִיר° הַתִּיכֹנָה וּדְבַר־ יְהוָה
Yahweh and-word-of the-middle court he-left not Isaiah and-he-was (4)

הָיָה אֵלָיו לֵאמֹר׃ שׁוּב וְאָמַרְתָּ אֶל־ חִזְקִיָּהוּ נְגִיד־
leader-of Hezekiah to and-you-tell go-back! (5) to-say to-him he-came

עַמִּי כֹּה־ אָמַר יְהוָה אֱלֹהֵי דָּוִד אָבִיךָ שָׁמַעְתִּי אֶת־
*** I-heard father-of-you David God-of Yahweh he-says this people-of-me

תְּפִלָּתֶךָ רָאִיתִי אֶת־ דִּמְעָתֶךָ הִנְנִי רֹפֵא לָךְ בַּיּוֹם
on-the-day to-you healing see-I! tear-of-you *** I-saw prayer-of-you

הַשְּׁלִישִׁי תַּעֲלֶה בֵּית יְהוָה׃ וְהֹסַפְתִּי עַל־ יָמֶיךָ
days-of-you to and-I-will-add (6) Yahweh temple-of you-will-go-up the-third

חֲמֵשׁ עֶשְׂרֵה שָׁנָה וּמִכַּף מֶלֶךְ־ אַשּׁוּר אַצִּילְךָ וְאֵת
and I-will-deliver-you Assyria king-of and-from-hand-of year ten five-of

הָעִיר הַזֹּאת וְגַנּוֹתִי עַל־ הָעִיר הַזֹּאת לְמַעֲנִי
for-sake-of-me the-this the-city to and-I-will-defend the-this the-city

וּלְמַעַן דָּוִד עַבְדִּי׃ וַיֹּאמֶר יְשַׁעְיָהוּ קְחוּ
prepare! Isaiah then-he-said (7) servant-of-me David and-for-sake-of

דְּבֶלֶת תְּאֵנִים וַיִּקְחוּ וַיָּשִׂימוּ עַל־ הַשְּׁחִין
the-boil to and-they-applied so-they-prepared figs poultice-of

וַיֶּחִי׃ וַיֹּאמֶר חִזְקִיָּהוּ אֶל־ יְשַׁעְיָהוּ מָה אוֹת כִּי־
that sign what? Isaiah to Hezekiah now-he-asked (8) and-he-recovered

his god Nisroch, his sons Adrammelech and Sharezer cut him down with the sword, and they escaped to the land of Ararat. And Esarhaddon his son succeeded him as king.

*Hezekiah's Illness*

20 In those days Hezekiah became ill and was at the point of death. The prophet Isaiah son of Amoz went to him and said, "This is what the LORD says: Put your house in order, because you will die; you will not recover."
2Hezekiah turned his face to the wall and prayed to the LORD, 3"Remember, O LORD, how I have walked before you faithfully and with wholehearted devotion and have done what is good in your eyes." And Hezekiah wept bitterly.
4Before Isaiah had left the middle court, the word of the LORD came to him: 5"Go back and tell Hezekiah, the leader of my people, 'This is what the LORD, the God of your father David, says: I have heard your prayer and seen your tears; I will heal you. On the third day from now you will go up to the temple of the LORD. 6I will add fifteen years to your life. And I will deliver you and this city from the hand of the king of Assyria. I will defend this city for my sake and for the sake of my servant David.' "
7Then Isaiah said, "Prepare a poultice of figs." They did so and applied it to the boil, and he recovered.
8Hezekiah had asked Isaiah, "What will be the sign that the

*37 Many mss have the *Qere* ( בניו ), *sons-of-him*, from the parallel passage in Isaiah 37:38.

°4 ק חצר

יִרְפָּא יְהוָה לִי וְעָלִיתִי בַּיּוֹם הַשְּׁלִישִׁי בֵּית
temple-of the-third on-the-day and-I-will-go-up to-me Yahweh he-will-heal

יְהוָה׃ וַיֹּאמֶר יְשַׁעְיָהוּ זֶה־ לְּךָ הָאוֹת מֵאֵת יְהוָה כִּי
that Yahweh from the-sign to-you this Isaiah and-he-answered (9) Yahweh

יַעֲשֶׂה יְהוָה אֶת־ הַדָּבָר אֲשֶׁר דִּבֵּר הָלַךְ
shall-he-go-forward he-promised that the-thing *** Yahweh he-will-do

הַצֵּל עֶשֶׂר מַעֲלוֹת אִם־ יָשׁוּב עֶשֶׂר מַעֲלוֹת׃ וַיֹּאמֶר יְחִזְקִיָּהוּ
Hezekiah and-he-said (10) steps ten shall-he-go-back or steps ten the-shadow

נָקֵל לַצֵּל לִנְטוֹת עֶשֶׂר מַעֲלוֹת לֹא כִּי יָשׁוּב
let-him-go-back so not steps ten to-go-forward for-the-shadow he-is-simple

הַצֵּל אֲחֹרַנִּית עֶשֶׂר מַעֲלוֹת׃ וַיִּקְרָא יְשַׁעְיָהוּ הַנָּבִיא אֶל־
upon the-prophet Isaiah then-he-called (11) steps ten backward the-shadow

יְהוָה וַיָּשֶׁב אֶת־ הַצֵּל בַּמַּעֲלוֹת אֲשֶׁר יָרְדָה
she-went-down that on-the-steps the-shadow *** and-he-made-go-back Yahweh

בְּמַעֲלוֹת אָחָז אֲחֹרַנִּית עֶשֶׂר מַעֲלוֹת׃ בָּעֵת הַהִיא שָׁלַח
he-sent the-that at-the-time (12) steps ten backward Ahaz on-steps-of

בְּרֹאדַךְ בַּלְאֲדָן בֶּן־ בַּלְאֲדָן מֶלֶךְ־ בָּבֶל סְפָרִים וּמִנְחָה אֶל־ חִזְקִיָּהוּ
Hezekiah to and-gift letters Babylon king-of Baladan son-of Baladan Merodach

כִּי שָׁמַע כִּי חָלָה חִזְקִיָּהוּ׃ וַיִּשְׁמַע עֲלֵיהֶם
to-them and-he-received (13) Hezekiah he-was-ill that he-heard because

חִזְקִיָּהוּ וַיַּרְאֵם אֶת־ כָּל־ בֵּית °נְכֹתֹה אֶת־ הַכֶּסֶף
the-silver *** store-of-him house-of all-of *** and-he-showed-them Hezekiah

וְאֶת־ הַזָּהָב וְאֶת־ הַבְּשָׂמִים וְאֵת ׀ שֶׁמֶן הַטּוֹב וְאֵת בֵּית כֵּלָיו
arms-of-him house-of and the-fine oil-of and the-spices and the-gold and

וְאֵת כָּל־ אֲשֶׁר נִמְצָא בְּאוֹצְרֹתָיו לֹא־ הָיָה דָבָר אֲשֶׁר לֹא־
not that thing he-was not among-treasures-of-him he-was-found that all and

הֶרְאָם חִזְקִיָּהוּ בְּבֵיתוֹ וּבְכָל־ מֶמְשַׁלְתּוֹ׃
kingdom-of-him or-in-all-of in-palace-of-him Hezekiah he-showed-them

וַיָּבֹא יְשַׁעְיָהוּ הַנָּבִיא אֶל־ הַמֶּלֶךְ חִזְקִיָּהוּ וַיֹּאמֶר
and-he-asked Hezekiah the-king to the-prophet Isaiah then-he-went (14)

אֵלָיו מָה אָמְרוּ ׀ הָאֲנָשִׁים הָאֵלֶּה וּמֵאַיִן יָבֹאוּ אֵלֶיךָ
to-you they-came and-from-where? the-those the-men they-said what? to-him

וַיֹּאמֶר חִזְקִיָּהוּ מֵאֶרֶץ רְחוֹקָה בָּאוּ מִבָּבֶל׃
from-Babylon they-came distant from-land Hezekiah and-he-replied

וַיֹּאמֶר מָה רָאוּ בְּבֵיתֶךָ וַיֹּאמֶר חִזְקִיָּהוּ אֵת
*** Hezekiah and-he-said in-palace-of-you they-saw what? and-he-said (15)

כָּל־ אֲשֶׁר בְּבֵיתִי רָאוּ לֹא־ הָיָה דָבָר אֲשֶׁר לֹא־ הִרְאִיתִם
I-showed-them not that thing he-was not they-saw in-palace-of-me that all

LORD will heal me and that I will go up to the temple of the LORD on the third day from now?"

9 Isaiah answered, "This is the LORD's sign to you that the LORD will do what he has promised: Shall the shadow go forward ten steps, or shall it go back ten steps?"

10 "It is a simple matter for the shadow to go forward ten steps," said Hezekiah. "Rather, have it go back ten steps."

11 Then the prophet Isaiah called upon the LORD, and the LORD made the shadow go back the ten steps it had gone down on the stairway of Ahaz.

*Envoys From Babylon*

12 At that time Merodach-Baladan son of Baladan king of Babylon sent Hezekiah letters and a gift, because he had heard of Hezekiah's illness. 13 Hezekiah received the messengers and showed them all that was in his storehouses—the silver, the gold, the spices and the fine oil—his armory and everything found among his treasures. There was nothing in his palace or in all his kingdom that Hezekiah did not show them.

14 Then Isaiah the prophet went to King Hezekiah and asked, "What did those men say, and where did they come from?"

"From a distant land," Hezekiah replied. "They came from Babylon."

15 The prophet asked, "What did they see in your palace?"

"They saw everything in my palace," Hezekiah said. "There is nothing among my treasures that I did not show them."

°*13* ק נכתו

בְּאֹצְרֹתָֽי׃     (16)     וַיֹּ֙אמֶר֙     יְשַֽׁעְיָ֔הוּ     אֶל־     חִזְקִיָּ֑הוּ     שְׁמַ֖ע     דְּבַר־
among-treasures-of-me     (16)     then-he-said     Isaiah     to     Hezekiah     hear!     word-of

יְהוָֽה׃     (17)     הִנֵּה֮     יָמִ֣ים     בָּאִ֒ים     וְנִשָּׂ֣א ׀     כָּל־     אֲשֶׁ֣ר
Yahweh     (17)     see!     days     ones-coming     and-he-will-be-carried-off     all     that

בְּבֵיתֶ֗ךָ     וַאֲשֶׁ֨ר     אָצְר֧וּ     אֲבֹתֶ֛יךָ     עַד־     הַיּ֥וֹם     הַזֶּ֖ה
in-palace-of-you     and-that     they-stored     fathers-of-you     until     the-day     the-this

בָּבֶ֑לָה     לֹֽא־     יִוָּתֵ֥ר     דָּבָ֖ר     אָמַ֥ר     יְהוָֽה׃     (18)     וּמִבָּנֶ֜יךָ
to-Babylon     not     he-will-be-left     thing     he-says     Yahweh     (18)     and-from-sons-of-you

אֲשֶׁ֧ר     יֵצְא֛וּ     מִמְּךָ֖     אֲשֶׁ֣ר     תּוֹלִ֑יד     יִקָּ֑ח
who     they-will-come     from-you     that     you-will-father     they-will-be-taken-away

וְהָיוּ֙     סָֽרִיסִ֔ים     בְּהֵיכַ֖ל     מֶ֥לֶךְ     בָּבֶֽל׃     (19)     וַיֹּ֤אמֶר
and-they-will-become     eunuchs     in-palace-of     king-of     Babylon     (19)     and-he-replied

חִזְקִיָּ֙הוּ֙     אֶל־יְשַֽׁעְיָ֔הוּ     ט֥וֹב     דְּבַר־     יְהוָ֖ה     אֲשֶׁ֣ר     דִּבַּ֑רְתָּ     וַיֹּ֕אמֶר     הֲל֛וֹא
Hezekiah     to Isaiah     good     word-of     Yahweh     that     you-spoke     for-he-thought     not?

אִם־     שָׁל֧וֹם     וֶאֱמֶ֛ת     יִהְיֶ֖ה     בְיָמָֽי׃     (20)     וְיֶ֨תֶר     דִּבְרֵ֤י
indeed     peace     and-security     he-will-be     in-days-of-me     (20)     and-rest-of     events-of

חִזְקִיָּ֙הוּ֙     וְכָל־     גְּב֣וּרָת֔וֹ     וַאֲשֶׁ֣ר     עָשָׂ֗ה     אֶת־     הַבְּרֵכָה֙     וְאֶת־
Hezekiah     and-all-of     achievement-of-him     and-how     he-made     ***     the-pool     and

הַתְּעָלָ֔ה     וַיָּבֵ֥א     אֶת־     הַמַּ֖יִם     הָעִ֑ירָה     הֲלֹא־     הֵ֣ם
the-tunnel     and-he-brought     ***     the-waters     into-the-city     not?     they

כְּתוּבִ֗ים     עַל־     סֵ֛פֶר     דִּבְרֵ֥י     הַיָּמִ֖ים     לְמַלְכֵ֥י     יְהוּדָֽה׃
ones-being-written     in     book-of     annals-of     the-days     of-kings-of     Judah

(21)     וַיִּשְׁכַּ֤ב     חִזְקִיָּ֙הוּ֙     עִם־     אֲבֹתָ֔יו     וַיִּמְלֹ֛ךְ     מְנַשֶּׁ֥ה
(21)     and-he-rested     Hezekiah     with     fathers-of-him     and-became-king     Manasseh

בְנ֖וֹ     תַּחְתָּֽיו׃     (21:1)     בֶּן־     שְׁתֵּ֙ים     עֶשְׂרֵ֤ה     שָׁנָה֙     מְנַשֶּׁ֣ה
son-of-him     in-place-of-him     (21:1)     son-of     two     ten     year     Manasseh

בְמָלְכ֔וֹ     וַחֲמִשִּׁ֤ים     וְחָמֵשׁ֙     שָׁנָ֔ה     מָלַ֖ךְ     בִּירוּשָׁלָ֑͏ִם
when-to-become-king-him     and-fifty     and-five     year     he-reigned     in-Jerusalem

וְשֵׁ֥ם     אִמּ֖וֹ     חֶפְצִי־     בָֽהּ׃     (2)     וַיַּ֥עַשׂ     הָרַ֖ע     בְּעֵינֵ֣י
and-name-of     mother-of-him     Hephzi     Bah     (2)     and-he-did     the-evil     in-eyes-of

יְהוָ֑ה     כְּתֽוֹעֲבֹת֙     הַגּוֹיִ֔ם     אֲשֶׁר֙     הוֹרִ֣ישׁ     יְהוָ֔ה
Yahweh     as-detestable-practices-of     the-nations     that     he-drove-out     Yahweh

מִפְּנֵ֖י     בְּנֵ֣י     יִשְׂרָאֵֽל׃     (3)     וַיָּ֗שָׁב     וַיִּ֙בֶן֙     אֶת־
from-before     sons-of     Israel     (3)     and-he-returned     and-he-rebuilt     ***

הַבָּמ֔וֹת     אֲשֶׁ֥ר     אִבַּ֖ד     חִזְקִיָּ֣הוּ     אָבִ֑יו     וַיָּ֙קֶם֙
the-high-places     that     he-destroyed     Hezekiah     father-of-him     and-he-erected

מִזְבְּחֹ֣ת     לַבַּ֗עַל     וַיַּ֤עַשׂ     אֲשֵׁרָה֙     כַּאֲשֶׁ֤ר     עָשָׂה֙     אַחְאָ֣ב     מֶ֣לֶךְ
altars     to-the-Baal     and-he-made     Asherah-pole     just-as     he-did     Ahab     king-of

[18] ק יקחו

[16]Then Isaiah said to Hezekiah, "Hear the word of the Lord: [17]The time will surely come when everything in your palace, and all that your fathers have stored up until this day, will be carried off to Babylon. Nothing will be left, says the Lord. [18]And some of your descendants, your own flesh and blood, that will be born to you, will be taken away, and they will become eunuchs in the palace of the king of Babylon."

[19]"The word of the Lord you have spoken is good," Hezekiah replied. For he thought, "Will there not be peace and security in my lifetime?"

[20]As for the other events of Hezekiah's reign, all his achievements and how he made the pool and the tunnel by which he brought water into the city, are they not written in the book of the annals of the kings of Judah? [21]Hezekiah rested with his fathers. And Manasseh his son succeeded him as king.

## Manasseh King of Judah

**21** Manasseh was twelve years old when he became king, and he reigned in Jerusalem fifty-five years. His mother's name was Hephzibah. [2]He did evil in the eyes of the Lord, following the detestable practices of the nations the Lord had driven out before the Israelites. [3]He rebuilt the high places his father Hezekiah had destroyed; he also erected altars to Baal and made an Asherah pole, as

יִשְׂרָאֵל וַיִּשְׁתַּחוּ לְכָל־ צְבָא הַשָּׁמַיִם וַיַּעֲבֹד אֹתָם׃

them and-he-worshiped the-heavens host-of to-all-of and-he-bowed Israel

וּבָנָה מִזְבְּחֹת בְּבֵית יְהוָה אֲשֶׁר אָמַר יְהוָה בִּירוּשָׁלִַם

in-Jerusalem Yahweh he-said which Yahweh in-temple-of altars and-he-built (4)

אָשִׂים אֶת־ שְׁמִי׃ וַיִּבֶן מִזְבְּחוֹת לְכָל־ צְבָא

host-of to-all-of altars and-he-built (5) Name-of-me *** I-will-put

הַשָּׁמַיִם בִּשְׁתֵּי חַצְרוֹת בֵּית־ יְהוָה׃ וְהֶעֱבִיר אֶת־

*** and-he-made-pass (6) Yahweh temple-of courts-of in-both-of the-heavens

בְּנוֹ בָּאֵשׁ וְעוֹנֵן וְנִחֵשׁ

and-he-practiced-divination and-he-practiced-sorcery through-the-fire son-of-him

וְעָשָׂה אוֹב וְיִדְּעֹנִים הִרְבָּה לַעֲשׂוֹת הָרַע בְּעֵינֵי

in-eyes-of the-evil to-do he-did-much and-spiritists medium and-he-consulted

יְהוָה לְהַכְעִיס׃ וַיָּשֶׂם אֶת־ פֶּסֶל הָאֲשֵׁרָה

the-Asherah carved-pole-of *** and-he-put (7) to-provoke-to-anger Yahweh

אֲשֶׁר עָשָׂה בַּבַּיִת אֲשֶׁר אָמַר יְהוָה אֶל־ דָּוִד וְאֶל־ שְׁלֹמֹה

Solomon and-to David to Yahweh he-said which in-the-temple he-made that

בְנוֹ בַּבַּיִת הַזֶּה וּבִירוּשָׁלִַם אֲשֶׁר בָּחַרְתִּי מִכֹּל

from-all-of I-chose which and-in-Jerusalem the-this in-the-temple son-of-him

שִׁבְטֵי יִשְׂרָאֵל אָשִׂים אֶת־ שְׁמִי לְעוֹלָם׃ וְלֹא

and-not (8) to-forever Name-of-me *** I-will-put Israel tribes-of

אֹסִיף לְהָנִיד רֶגֶל יִשְׂרָאֵל מִן־ הָאֲדָמָה אֲשֶׁר נָתַתִּי

I-gave that the-land from Israel foot-of to-make-wander I-will-repeat

לַאֲבוֹתָם רַק ׀ אִם־ יִשְׁמְרוּ לַעֲשׂוֹת כְּכֹל אֲשֶׁר צִוִּיתִים

I-commanded-them that as-all to-do they-are-careful if only to-fathers-of-them

וּלְכָל־ הַתּוֹרָה אֲשֶׁר־ צִוָּה אֹתָם עַבְדִּי מֹשֶׁה׃ וְלֹא

but-not (9) Moses servant-of-me them he-gave that the-Law and-to-whole-of

שָׁמֵעוּ וַיַּתְעֵם מְנַשֶּׁה לַעֲשׂוֹת אֶת־ הָרָע מִן־

more-than the-evil *** to-do Manasseh and-he-led-astray-them they-listened

הַגּוֹיִם אֲשֶׁר הִשְׁמִיד יְהוָה מִפְּנֵי בְּנֵי יִשְׂרָאֵל׃

Israel sons-of from-before Yahweh he-destroyed that the-nations

וַיְדַבֵּר יְהוָה בְּיַד־ עֲבָדָיו הַנְּבִיאִים לֵאמֹר׃

to-say the-prophets servants-of-him by-hand-of Yahweh and-he-spoke (10)

יַעַן אֲשֶׁר עָשָׂה מְנַשֶּׁה מֶלֶךְ־ יְהוּדָה הַתֹּעֵבוֹת

the-detestable-sins Judah king-of Manasseh he-did that because (11)

הָאֵלֶּה הֵרַע מִכֹּל אֲשֶׁר־ עָשׂוּ הָאֱמֹרִי אֲשֶׁר לְפָנָיו

before-him who the-Amorite they-did that more-than-all he-did-evil the-these

וַיַּחֲטִא גַם־ אֶת־ יְהוּדָה בְּגִלּוּלָיו׃ לָכֵן כֹּה־

this therefore (12) with-idols-of-him Judah *** also and-he-led-to-sin

Ahab king of Israel had done. He bowed down to all the starry hosts and worshiped them.
4He built altars in the temple of the LORD, of which the LORD had said, "In Jerusalem I will put my Name."
5In both courts of the temple of the LORD, he built altars to all the starry hosts.
6He sacrificed his own son in[h] the fire, practiced sorcery and divination, and consulted mediums and spiritists. He did much evil in the eyes of the LORD, provoking him to anger.

7He took the carved Asherah pole he had made and put it in the temple, of which the LORD had said to David and to his son Solomon, "In this temple and in Jerusalem, which I have chosen out of all the tribes of Israel, I will put my Name forever.
8I will not again make the feet of the Israelites wander from the land I gave their forefathers, if only they will be careful to do everything I commanded them and will keep the whole Law that my servant Moses gave them."
9But the people did not listen. Manasseh led them astray, so that they did more evil than the nations the LORD had destroyed before the Israelites.

10The LORD said through his servants the prophets:
11"Manasseh king of Judah has committed these detestable sins. He has done more evil than the Amorites who preceded him and has led Judah into sin with his idols.
12Therefore this is what the

[h]6 Or *He made his own son pass through*

אָמַר יְהוָה אֱלֹהֵי יִשְׂרָאֵל הִנְנִי מֵבִיא רָעָה עַל־יְרוּשָׁלִַם וִיהוּדָה
and-Judah Jersualem on disaster bringing see-I! Israel God-of Yahweh he-says

אֲשֶׁר כָּל־ שֹׁמְעָיו תִּצַּלְנָה שְׁתֵּי אָזְנָיו׃
ears-of-him both-of they-will-tingle one-hearing-her every-of that

וְנָטִיתִי עַל־ יְרוּשָׁלִַם אֵת קָו שֹׁמְרוֹן וְאֶת־
and Samaria measuring-line-of *** Jerusalem over and-I-will-stretch (13)

מִשְׁקֹלֶת בֵּית אַחְאָב וּמָחִיתִי אֶת־ יְרוּשָׁלִַם כַּאֲשֶׁר־
just-as Jerusalem *** and-I-will-wipe-out Ahab house-of plumb-line-of

יִמְחֶה אֶת־ הַצַּלַּחַת מָחָה וְהָפַךְ עַל־ פָּנֶיהָ׃
faces-of-her on and-he-overturns he-wipes the-dish *** he-wipes

וְנָטַשְׁתִּי אֵת שְׁאֵרִית נַחֲלָתִי וּנְתַתִּים
and-I-will-give-them inheritance-of-me remnant-of *** and-I-will-forsake (14)

בְּיַד אֹיְבֵיהֶם וְהָיוּ לְבַז
for-loot and-they-will-be ones-being-enemies-of-them into-hand-of

וְלִמְשִׁסָּה לְכָל־ אֹיְבֵיהֶם׃ יַעַן אֲשֶׁר עָשׂוּ
they-did that because (15) ones-being-foes-of-them by-all-of and-for-plunder

אֶת־ הָרַע בְּעֵינַי וַיִּהְיוּ מַכְעִסִים אֹתִי מִן־ הַיּוֹם
the-day from me ones-making-angry and-they-were in-eyes-of-me the-evil ***

אֲשֶׁר יָצְאוּ אֲבוֹתָם מִמִּצְרַיִם וְעַד הַיּוֹם הַזֶּה׃
the-this the-day even-to from-Egypt fathers-of-them they-came-out that

וְגַם דָּם נָקִי שָׁפַךְ מְנַשֶּׁה הַרְבֵּה מְאֹד עַד אֲשֶׁר־
when until very to-be-much Manasseh he-shed innocent blood and-also (16)

מִלֵּא אֶת־ יְרוּשָׁלִַם פֶּה לָפֶה לְבַד מֵחַטָּאתוֹ אֲשֶׁר הֶחֱטִיא
he-made-sin that from-sin-of-him apart to-end end Jerusalem *** he-filled

אֶת־יְהוּדָה לַעֲשׂוֹת הָרַע בְּעֵינֵי יְהוָה׃ וְיֶתֶר דִּבְרֵי
events-of and-rest-of (17) Yahweh in-eyes-of the-evil to-do Judah ***

מְנַשֶּׁה וְכָל־ אֲשֶׁר עָשָׂה וְחַטָּאתוֹ אֲשֶׁר חָטָא הֲלֹא־ הֵם
they not? he-did that and-sin-of-him he-did that and-all Manasseh

כְּתוּבִים עַל־ סֵפֶר דִּבְרֵי הַיָּמִים לְמַלְכֵי יְהוּדָה׃
Judah of-kings-of the-days annals-of book-of in ones-being-written

וַיִּשְׁכַּב מְנַשֶּׁה עִם־ אֲבֹתָיו וַיִּקָּבֵר בְּגַן־
in-garden-of and-he-was-buried fathers-of-him with Manasseh and-he-rested (18)

בֵּיתוֹ בְּגַן־ עֻזָּא וַיִּמְלֹךְ אָמוֹן בְּנוֹ
son-of-him Amon and-he-became-king Uzza in-garden-of palace-of-him

תַּחְתָּיו׃ בֶּן־ עֶשְׂרִים וּשְׁתַּיִם שָׁנָה אָמוֹן בְּמָלְכוֹ
when-to-become-king-him Amon year and-two twenty son-of (19) in-place-of-him

וּשְׁתַּיִם שָׁנִים מָלַךְ בִּירוּשָׁלִָם וְשֵׁם אִמּוֹ מְשֻׁלֶּמֶת
Meshullemeth mother-of-him and-name-of in-Jerusalem he-reigned years and-two

LORD, the God of Israel, says: I
am going to bring such disaster on Jerusalem and Judah
that the ears of everyone who
hears of it will tingle. [13]I will
stretch out over Jerusalem the
measuring line used against
Samaria and the plumb line
used against the house of
Ahab. I will wipe out Jerusalem as one wipes a dish, wip-
ing it and turning it upside
down. [14]I will forsake the remnant of my inheritance and
hand them over to their enemies. They will be looted and
plundered by all their foes,
[15]because they have done evil
in my eyes and have provoked
me to anger from the day their
forefathers came out of Egypt
until this day."
[16]Moreover, Manasseh also
shed so much innocent blood
that he filled Jerusalem from
end to end—besides the sin
that he had caused Judah to
commit, so that they did evil
in the eyes of the LORD.
[17]As for the other events of
Manasseh's reign, and all he
did, including the sin he committed, are they not written in
the book of the annals of the
kings of Judah? [18]Manasseh
rested with his fathers and
was buried in his palace garden, the garden of Uzza. And
Amon his son succeeded him
as king.

*Amon King of Judah*

[19]Amon was twenty-two
years old when he became
king, and he reigned in
Jerusalem two years. His
mother's name was Meshul-
lemeth daughter of Haruz; she

°12 ק שמעה

בַּת־ חָרוּץ מִן־ יָטְבָה׃ (20) וַיַּעַשׂ הָרַע בְּעֵינֵי יְהוָה
Yahweh in-eyes-of the-evil and-he-did (20) Jotbah from Haruz daughter-of

כַּאֲשֶׁר עָשָׂה מְנַשֶּׁה אָבִיו׃ (21) וַיֵּלֶךְ בְּכָל־ הַדֶּרֶךְ
the-way in-all-of and-he-walked (21) father-of-him Manasseh he-did just-as

אֲשֶׁר־ הָלַךְ אָבִיו וַיַּעֲבֹד אֶת־ הַגִּלֻּלִים אֲשֶׁר עָבַד
he-worshiped that the-idols *** and-he-worshiped father-of-him he-walked that

אָבִיו וַיִּשְׁתַּחוּ לָהֶם׃ (22) וַיַּעֲזֹב אֶת־ יְהוָה אֱלֹהֵי
God-of Yahweh *** and-he-forsook (22) to-them and-he-bowed father-of-him

אֲבֹתָיו וְלֹא הָלַךְ בְּדֶרֶךְ יְהוָה׃ (23) וַיִּקְשְׁרוּ
and-he-conspired (23) Yahweh in-way-of he-walked and-not fathers-of-him

עַבְדֵי־ אָמוֹן עָלָיו וַיָּמִיתוּ אֶת־ הַמֶּלֶךְ
the-king *** and-they-assassinated against-him Amon officials-of

בְּבֵיתוֹ׃ (24) וַיַּךְ עַם־ הָאָרֶץ אֵת כָּל־
all-of *** the-land people-of and-he-killed (24) in-palace-of-him

הַקֹּשְׁרִים עַל־ הַמֶּלֶךְ אָמוֹן וַיַּמְלִיכוּ עַם־
people-of and-they-make-king Amon the-king against the-ones-conspiring

הָאָרֶץ אֶת־ יֹאשִׁיָּהוּ בְנוֹ תַּחְתָּיו׃ (25) וְיֶתֶר דִּבְרֵי
events-of and-rest-of (25) in-place-of-him son-of-him Josiah *** the-land

אָמוֹן אֲשֶׁר עָשָׂה הֲלֹא־ הֵם כְּתוּבִים עַל־ סֵפֶר דִּבְרֵי הַיָּמִים
the-days annals-of book-of in ones-being-written they not? he-did what Amon

לְמַלְכֵי יְהוּדָה׃ (26) וַיִּקְבֹּר* אֹתוֹ בִּקְבֻרָתוֹ בְּגַן־ עֻזָּא
Uzza in-garden-of in-grave-of-him him and-he-buried (26) Judah of-kings-of

וַיִּמְלֹךְ יֹאשִׁיָּהוּ בְנוֹ תַּחְתָּיו׃ (22:1) בֶּן־ שְׁמֹנֶה
eight son-of (22:1) in-place-of-him son-of-him Josiah and-he-became-king

שָׁנָה יֹאשִׁיָּהוּ בְמָלְכוֹ וּשְׁלֹשִׁים וְאַחַת שָׁנָה מָלַךְ
he-reigned year and-one and-thirty when-to-become-king-him Josiah year

בִּירוּשָׁלִָם וְשֵׁם אִמּוֹ יְדִידָה בַת־ עֲדָיָה† מִבָּצְקַת׃
from-Bozkath Adaiah daughter-of Jedidah mother-of-him and-name-of in-Jerusalem

(2) וַיַּעַשׂ הַיָּשָׁר בְּעֵינֵי יְהוָה וַיֵּלֶךְ בְּכָל־ דֶּרֶךְ
way-of in-all-of and-he-walked Yahweh in-eyes-of the-right and-he-did (2)

דָּוִד אָבִיו וְלֹא־ סָר יָמִין וּשְׂמֹאול׃ (3) וַיְהִי בִּשְׁמֹנֶה
in-eight and-he-was (3) or-left right he-turned and-not father-of-him David

עֶשְׂרֵה שָׁנָה לַמֶּלֶךְ יֹאשִׁיָּהוּ שָׁלַח הַמֶּלֶךְ אֶת־ שָׁפָן בֶּן־ אֲצַלְיָהוּ
Azaliah son-of Shaphan *** the-king he-sent Josiah of-the-king year ten

בֶן־ מְשֻׁלָּם הַסֹּפֵר בֵּית יְהוָה לֵאמֹר׃ (4) עֲלֵה אֶל־ חִלְקִיָּהוּ
Hilkiah to go-up! (4) to-say Yahweh temple-of the-secretary Meshullam son-of

הַכֹּהֵן הַגָּדוֹל וְיַתֵּם אֶת־ הַכֶּסֶף הַמּוּבָא
the-being-brought the-money *** and-let-him-get-ready the-high the-priest

was from Jotbah. [20]He did evil
in the eyes of the LORD, as his
father Manasseh had done.
[21]He walked in all the ways of
his father; he worshiped the
idols his father had wor-
shiped, and bowed down to
them. [22]He forsook the LORD,
the God of his fathers, and did
not walk in the way of the
LORD.

[23]Amon's officials conspired
against him and assassinated
the king in his palace. [24]Then
the people of the land killed all
who had plotted against King
Amon, and they made Josiah
his son king in his place.

[25]As for the other events of
Amon's reign, and what he
did, are they not written in the
book of the annals of the kings
of Judah? [26]He was buried in
his grave in the garden of
Uzza. And Josiah his son succeeded him as king.

*The Book of the Law Found*

22 Josiah was eight years
old when he became
king, and he reigned in
Jerusalem thirty-one years.
His mother's name was Jedidah daughter of Adaiah; she
was from Bozkath. [2]He did
what was right in the eyes of
the LORD and walked in all the
ways of his father David, not
turning aside to the right or to
the left.

[3]In the eighteenth year of
his reign, King Josiah sent the
secretary, Shaphan son of
Azaliah, the son of Meshullam, to the temple of the LORD.
He said: [4]"Go up to Hilkiah
the high priest and have him
get ready the money that has

*26 Some mss have no *sheva* under the *beth* (בֹּר־); others have no *holem* and end with *shureq* (רוּ־), *and-they-buried.*

†1 Most mss have the accent on the final syllable (עֲדָיָה).

בֵּית יְהוָה אֲשֶׁר אָסְפוּ שֹׁמְרֵי הַסַּף מֵאֵת הָעָם׃
the-people / from / the-door / ones-keeping-of / they-collected / which / Yahweh / temple-of

וְיִתְּנֹה עַל־ יַד עֹשֵׂי הַמְּלָאכָה
the-work / ones-supervising-of / hand-of / into / and-let-them-entrust-him / (5)

הַמֻּפְקָדִים בְּבֵית יְהוָה וְיִתְּנוּ אֹתוֹ
him / and-let-them-pay / Yahweh / temple-of / the-ones-being-appointed

לְעֹשֵׂי הַמְּלָאכָה אֲשֶׁר בְּבֵית יְהוָה לְחַזֵּק בֶּדֶק
damage-of / to-repair / Yahweh / on-temple-of / that / the-work / to-ones-doing-of

הַבָּיִת׃ לֶחָרָשִׁים וְלַבֹּנִים
and-to-the-ones-building / to-the-carpenters / (6) / the-temple

וְלַגֹּדְרִים וְלִקְנוֹת עֵצִים וְאַבְנֵי מַחְצֵב
dressed / and-stones-of / timbers / and-to-purchase / and-to-the-ones-being-masons

לְחַזֵּק אֶת־ הַבָּיִת׃ אַךְ לֹא יֵחָשֵׁב אִתָּם הַכֶּסֶף
the-money / with-them / he-must-be-accounted / not / but / (7) / the-temple / *** / to-repair

הַנִּתָּן עַל־ יָדָם כִּי בֶאֱמוּנָה הֵם עֹשִׂים׃
ones-acting / they / in-faith / because / hand-of-them / into / the-one-being-entrusted

וַיֹּאמֶר חִלְקִיָּהוּ הַכֹּהֵן הַגָּדוֹל עַל־ שָׁפָן הַסֹּפֵר סֵפֶר
Book-of / the-secretary / Shaphan / to / the-high / the-priest / Hilkiah / and-he-said / (8)

הַתּוֹרָה מָצָאתִי בְּבֵית יְהוָה וַיִּתֵּן חִלְקִיָּה אֶת־ הַסֵּפֶר אֶל־
to / the-book / *** / Hilkiah / and-he-gave / Yahweh / in-temple-of / I-found / the-Law

שָׁפָן וַיִּקְרָאֵהוּ׃ וַיָּבֹא שָׁפָן הַסֹּפֵר אֶל־ הַמֶּלֶךְ
the-king / to / the-secretary / Shaphan / then-he-went / (9) / and-he-read-him / Shaphan

וַיָּשֶׁב אֶת־ הַמֶּלֶךְ דָּבָר וַיֹּאמֶר הִתִּיכוּ עֲבָדֶיךָ
officials-of-you / they-paid-out / and-he-said / report / the-king / *** / and-he-gave

אֶת־ הַכֶּסֶף הַנִּמְצָא בַבָּיִת וַיִּתְּנֻהוּ עַל־
into / and-they-entrusted-him / in-the-temple / the-one-being-found / the-money / ***

יַד עֹשֵׂי הַמְּלָאכָה הַמֻּפְקָדִים בֵּית יְהוָה׃
Yahweh / temple-of / the-ones-supervising / the-work / ones-doing-of / hand-of

וַיַּגֵּד שָׁפָן הַסֹּפֵר לַמֶּלֶךְ לֵאמֹר סֵפֶר נָתַן
he-gave / book / to-say / to-the-king / the-secretary / Shaphan / then-he-informed / (10)

לִי חִלְקִיָּה הַכֹּהֵן וַיִּקְרָאֵהוּ שָׁפָן לִפְנֵי הַמֶּלֶךְ׃
the-king / in-presences-of / Shaphan / and-he-read-him / the-priest / Hilkiah / to-me

וַיְהִי כִּשְׁמֹעַ הַמֶּלֶךְ אֶת־ דִּבְרֵי סֵפֶר הַתּוֹרָה
the-Law / Book-of / words-of / *** / the-king / when-to-hear / and-he-was / (11)

וַיִּקְרַע אֶת־ בְּגָדָיו׃ וַיְצַו הַמֶּלֶךְ אֶת־ חִלְקִיָּה
Hilkiah / *** / the-king / and-he-ordered / (12) / robes-of-him / *** / then-he-tore

הַכֹּהֵן וְאֶת־ אֲחִיקָם בֶּן־ שָׁפָן וְאֶת־עַכְבּוֹר בֶּן־ מִיכָיָה וְאֶת׀ שָׁפָן
Shaphan / and / Micaiah / son-of / Acbor / and / Shaphat / son-of / Ahikam / and / the-priest

been brought into the temple of the LORD, which the door-keepers have collected from the people. ⁵Have them entrust it to the men appointed to supervise the work on the temple. And have these men pay the workers who repair the temple of the LORD— ⁶the carpenters, the builders and the masons. Also have them purchase timber and dressed stone to repair the temple. ⁷But they need not account for the money entrusted to them, because they are acting faithfully."

⁸Hilkiah the high priest said to Shaphan the secretary, "I have found the Book of the Law in the temple of the LORD." He gave it to Shaphan, who read it. ⁹Then Shaphan the secretary went to the king and reported to him: "Your officials have paid out the money that was in the temple of the LORD and have entrusted it to the workers and supervisors at the temple." ¹⁰Then Shaphan the secretary informed the king, "Hilkiah the priest has given me a book." And Shaphan read from it in the presence of the king.

¹¹When the king heard the words of the Book of the Law, he tore his robes. ¹²He gave these orders to Hilkiah the priest, Ahikam son of Shaphan, Acbor son of Micaiah,

ק וִיתְּנֻהוּ 5a°
ק בֵּית 5b°

הַסֹּפֵר וְאֵת עֲשָׂיָה עֶבֶד־ הַמֶּלֶךְ לֵאמֹר׃ לְכוּ דִרְשׁוּ אֶת־
*** inquire! go! (13) to-say the-king attendant-of Asaiah and the-secretary

יְהוָה בַּעֲדִי וּבְעַד־ הָעָם וּבְעַד כָּל־ יְהוּדָה עַל־ דִּבְרֵי
words-of about Judah all-of and-for the-people and-for for-me Yahweh

הַסֵּפֶר הַנִּמְצָא הַזֶּה כִּי־ גְדוֹלָה חֲמַת יְהוָה אֲשֶׁר־הִיא
she that Yahweh anger-of great for the-this the-one-being-found the-book

נִצְּתָה בָנוּ עַל אֲשֶׁר לֹא־ שָׁמְעוּ אֲבֹתֵינוּ עַל־ דִּבְרֵי
words-of to fathers-of-us they-obeyed not that because against-us she-burns

הַסֵּפֶר הַזֶּה לַעֲשׂוֹת כְּכָל־ הַכָּתוּב עָלֵינוּ׃
about-us the-thing-being-written as-all-of to-do the-this the-book

וַיֵּלֶךְ חִלְקִיָּהוּ הַכֹּהֵן וַאֲחִיקָם וְעַכְבּוֹר וְשָׁפָן
and-Shaphan and-Acbor and-Ahikam the-priest Hilkiah and-he-went (14)

וַעֲשָׂיָה אֶל־ חֻלְדָּה הַנְּבִיאָה אֵשֶׁת ׀ שַׁלֻּם בֶּן־ תִּקְוָה בֶּן־
son-of Tikvah son-of Shallum wife-of the-prophetess Huldah to and-Asaiah

חַרְחַס שֹׁמֵר הַבְּגָדִים וְהִיא יֹשֶׁבֶת בִּירוּשָׁלִַם
in-Jerusalem living now-she the-clothes one-keeping-of Harhas

בַּמִּשְׁנֶה וַיְדַבְּרוּ אֵלֶיהָ׃ וַתֹּאמֶר אֲלֵיהֶם כֹּה־
this to-them and-she-said (15) to-her and-they-spoke in-the-Second-District

אָמַר יְהוָה אֱלֹהֵי יִשְׂרָאֵל אִמְרוּ לָאִישׁ אֲשֶׁר־ שָׁלַח אֶתְכֶם אֵלָי׃
to-me you he-sent who to-the-man tell! Israel God-of Yahweh he-says

כֹּה אָמַר יְהוָה הִנְנִי מֵבִיא רָעָה אֶל־הַמָּקוֹם הַזֶּה
the-this the-place on disaster bringing see-I! Yahweh he-says this (16)

וְעַל־ יֹשְׁבָיו אֵת כָּל־ דִּבְרֵי הַסֵּפֶר אֲשֶׁר קָרָא מֶלֶךְ
king-of he-read that the-book words-of all-of *** ones-living-of-him and-on

יְהוּדָה׃ תַּחַת ׀ אֲשֶׁר עֲזָבוּנִי וַיְקַטְּרוּ לֵאלֹהִים
to-gods and-they-burned-incense they-forsook-me that because (17) Judah

אֲחֵרִים לְמַעַן הַכְעִיסֵנִי בְּכֹל מַעֲשֵׂה יְדֵיהֶם
hands-of-them work-of by-all-of to-anger-me in-order-to other-ones

וְנִצְּתָה חֲמָתִי בַּמָּקוֹם הַזֶּה וְלֹא
and-not the-this against-the-place anger-of-me and-she-will-burn

תִכְבֶּה׃ וְאֶל־ מֶלֶךְ יְהוּדָה הַשֹּׁלֵחַ אֶתְכֶם לִדְרֹשׁ
to-inquire you the-one-sending Judah king-of and-to (18) she-will-be-quenched

אֶת־ יְהוָה כֹּה תֹאמְרוּ אֵלָיו כֹּה־ אָמַר יְהוָה אֱלֹהֵי יִשְׂרָאֵל הַדְּבָרִים
the-words Israel God-of Yahweh he-says this to-him you-tell this Yahweh ***

אֲשֶׁר שָׁמָעְתָּ׃ יַעַן רַךְ־ לְבָבְךָ וַתִּכָּנַע ׀
and-you-humbled-self heart-of-you he-was-responsive because (19) you-heard that

מִפְּנֵי יְהוָה בְּשָׁמְעֲךָ אֲשֶׁר דִּבַּרְתִּי עַל־ הַמָּקוֹם הַזֶּה
the-this the-place against I-spoke what when-to-hear-you Yahweh from-before

Shaphan the secretary and Asaiah the king's attendant:
13"Go and inquire of the LORD for me and for the people and for all Judah about what is written in this book that has been found. Great is the LORD's anger that burns against us because our fathers have not obeyed the words of this book; they have not acted in accordance with all that is written there concerning us."

14Hilkiah the priest, Ahikam, Acbor, Shaphan and Asaiah went to speak to the prophetess Huldah, who was the wife of Shallum son of Tikvah, the son of Harhas, keeper of the wardrobe. She lived in Jerusalem, in the Second District.

15She said to them, "This is what the LORD, the God of Israel, says: Tell the man who
sent you to me, 16'This is what the LORD says: I am going to bring disaster on this place and its people, according to everything written in the book the king of Judah has
read. 17Because they have forsaken me and burned incense to other gods and provoked me to anger by all the idols their hands have made,[i] my anger will burn against this place and will not be
quenched.' 18Tell the king of Judah, who sent you to inquire of the LORD, 'This is what the LORD, the God of Israel, says concerning the
words you heard: 19Because your heart was responsive and you humbled yourself before the LORD when you heard what I have spoken against

[i]17 Or *by everything they have done*

וְעַל־ יֹשְׁבָיו לִהְיוֹת לְשַׁמָּה וְלִקְלָלָה וַתִּקְרַע
and-against ones-living-of-him to-become as-waste and-as-curse and-you-tore

אֶת־ בְּגָדֶיךָ וַתִּבְכֶּה לְפָנָי וְגַם אָנֹכִי שָׁמַעְתִּי נְאֻם־
*** robes-of-you and-you-wept before-me now-indeed I I-heard declaration-of

יְהוָה׃ (20) לָכֵן הִנְנִי אֹסִפְךָ עַל־ אֲבֹתֶיךָ
Yahweh (20) therefore see-I I-will-gather-you to fathers-of-you

וְנֶאֱסַפְתָּ אֶל־ קִבְרֹתֶיךָ בְּשָׁלוֹם וְלֹא־ תִרְאֶינָה
and-you-will-be-buried in tombs-of-you in-peace and-not they-will-see

עֵינֶיךָ בְּכֹל הָרָעָה אֲשֶׁר־אֲנִי מֵבִיא עַל־ הַמָּקוֹם הַזֶּה
eyes-of-you to-all-of the-disaster that I bringing on the-place the-this

וַיָּשִׁיבוּ אֶת־ הַמֶּלֶךְ דָּבָר׃ (23:1) וַיִּשְׁלַח הַמֶּלֶךְ
so-they-took-back *** the-king answer (23:1) then-he-called the-king

וַיַּאַסְפוּ אֵלָיו כָּל־ זִקְנֵי יְהוּדָה וִירוּשָׁלִָם׃
and-they-came-together to-him all-of elders-of Judah and-Jerusalem

(2) וַיַּעַל הַמֶּלֶךְ בֵּית־ יְהוָה וְכָל־ אִישׁ יְהוּדָה
(2) and-he-went-up the-king temple-of Yahweh and-all-of man-of Judah

וְכָל־ יֹשְׁבֵי יְרוּשָׁלִַם אִתּוֹ וְהַכֹּהֲנִים וְהַנְּבִיאִים
and-all-of ones-living-of Jerusalem with-him and-the-priests and-the-prophets

וְכָל־ הָעָם לְמִקָּטֹן וְעַד־ גָּדוֹל וַיִּקְרָא
and-all-of the-people to-from-least even-to greatest and-he-read

בְאָזְנֵיהֶם אֶת־ כָּל־ דִּבְרֵי סֵפֶר הַבְּרִית הַנִּמְצָא
in-ears-of-them *** all-of words-of Book-of the-Covenant the-one-being-found

בְּבֵית יְהוָה׃ (3) וַיַּעֲמֹד הַמֶּלֶךְ עַל־ הָעַמּוּד וַיִּכְרֹת
in-temple-of Yahweh (3) and-he-stood the-king by the-pillar and-he-renewed

אֶת־ הַבְּרִית ׀ לִפְנֵי יְהוָה לָלֶכֶת אַחַר יְהוָה וְלִשְׁמֹר
*** the-covenant in-presences-of Yahweh to-follow after Yahweh and-to-keep

מִצְוֹתָיו וְאֶת־ עֵדְוֹתָיו וְאֶת־ חֻקֹּתָיו בְּכָל־ לֵב
commands-of-him and regulations-of-him and decrees-of-him with-all-of heart

וּבְכָל־ נֶפֶשׁ לְהָקִים אֶת־ דִּבְרֵי הַבְּרִית הַזֹּאת
and-with-all-of soul to-confirm *** words-of the-covenant the-this

הַכְּתֻבִים עַל־ הַסֵּפֶר הַזֶּה וַיַּעֲמֹד כָּל־ הָעָם
the-ones-being-written in the-book the-this then-he-pledged all-of the-people

בַּבְּרִית׃ (4) וַיְצַו הַמֶּלֶךְ אֶת־חִלְקִיָּהוּ הַכֹּהֵן הַגָּדוֹל
to-the-covenant (4) then-he-ordered the-king *** Hilkiah the-priest the-high

וְאֶת־ כֹּהֲנֵי הַמִּשְׁנֶה וְאֶת־ שֹׁמְרֵי הַסַּף לְהוֹצִיא
and priests-of the-second and ones-keeping-of the-door to-remove

מֵהֵיכַל יְהוָה אֵת כָּל־ הַכֵּלִים הָעֲשׂוּיִם
from-temple-of Yahweh *** all-of the-articles the-ones-being-made

this place and its people, that
they would become accursed
and laid waste, and because
you tore your robes and wept
in my presence, I have heard
you, declares the LORD.
20 Therefore I will gather you to
your fathers, and you will be
buried in peace. Your eyes will
not see all the disaster I am going to bring on this place.' "
So they took her answer
back to the king.

*Josiah Renews the Covenant*

23 Then the king called together all the elders of
Judah and Jerusalem. 2 He
went up to the temple of the
LORD with the men of Judah,
the people of Jerusalem, the
priests and the prophets—all
the people from the least to the
greatest. He read in their hearing all the words of the Book of
the Covenant, which had
been found in the temple of
the LORD. 3 The king stood by
the pillar and renewed the
covenant in the presence of
the LORD—to follow the LORD
and keep his commands, regulations and decrees with all his
heart and all his soul, thus
confirming the words of the
covenant written in this book.
Then all the people pledged
themselves to the covenant.
4 The king ordered Hilkiah
the high priest, the priests
next in rank and the doorkeepers to remove from the
temple of the LORD all the articles made for Baal and

לַבַּעַל וְלָאֲשֵׁרָה וּלְכֹל צְבָא הַשָּׁמָיִם
the-heavens host-of and-for-all-of and-for-the-Asherah for-the-Baal

וַיִּשְׂרְפֵם מִחוּץ לִירוּשָׁלִַם בְּשַׁדְמוֹת קִדְרוֹן וְנָשָׂא
and-he-took Kidron in-fields-of of-Jerusalem at-outside and-he-burned-them

אֶת־ עֲפָרָם בֵּית־ אֵל׃ וְהִשְׁבִּית אֶת־ הַכְּמָרִים אֲשֶׁר
whom the-pagan-priests *** and-he-did-away (5) El Beth ash-of-them ***

נָתְנוּ מַלְכֵי יְהוּדָה וַיְקַטֵּר בַּבָּמוֹת
at-the-high-places and-he-burned-incense Judah kings-of they-appointed

בְּעָרֵי יְהוּדָה וּמְסִבֵּי יְרוּשָׁלָ͏ִם וְאֶת־ הַמְקַטְּרִים
the-ones-burning-incense and Jerusalem and-ones-around-of Judah of-towns-of

לַבַּעַל לַשֶּׁמֶשׁ וְלַיָּרֵחַ וְלַמַּזָּלוֹת וּלְכֹל
and-of-all-of and-to-the-constellations and-to-the-moon to-the-sun to-the-Baal

צְבָא הַשָּׁמָיִם׃ וַיֹּצֵא אֶת־ הָאֲשֵׁרָה מִבֵּית
from-temple-of the-Asherah-pole *** and-he-took-out (6) the-heavens host-of

יְהוָה מִחוּץ לִירוּשָׁלִַם אֶל־ נַחַל קִדְרוֹן וַיִּשְׂרֹף אֹתָהּ
her and-he-burned Kidron Valley-of to of-Jerusalem at-outside Yahweh

בְּנַחַל קִדְרוֹן וַיָּדֶק לְעָפָר וַיַּשְׁלֵךְ אֶת־ עֲפָרָהּ
dust-of-her *** and-he-scattered to-powder and-he-ground Kidron in-Valley-of

עַל־ קֶבֶר בְּנֵי הָעָם׃ וַיִּתֹּץ אֶת־ בָּתֵּי
quarters-of *** and-he-tore-down (7) the-people sons-of grave-of over

הַקְּדֵשִׁים אֲשֶׁר בְּבֵית יְהוָה אֲשֶׁר הַנָּשִׁים אֹרְגוֹת
ones-weaving the-women where Yahweh in-temple-of which the-shrine-prostitutes

שָׁם בָּתִּים לָאֲשֵׁרָה׃ וַיָּבֵא אֶת־ כָּל־ הַכֹּהֲנִים
the-priests all-of *** and-he-brought (8) for-Asherah garments there

מֵעָרֵי יְהוּדָה וַיְטַמֵּא אֶת־ הַבָּמוֹת אֲשֶׁר
where the-high-places *** and-he-desecrated Judah from-towns-of

קִטְּרוּ־ שָׁמָּה הַכֹּהֲנִים מִגֶּבַע עַד־ בְּאֵר שָׁבַע
Sheba Beer to from-Geba the-priests at-there they-burned-incense

וְנָתַץ אֶת־ בָּמוֹת הַשְּׁעָרִים אֲשֶׁר־ פֶּתַח שַׁעַר יְהוֹשֻׁעַ
Joshua Gate-of entrance-of that the-gates shrines *** and-he-broke-down

שַׂר־ הָעִיר אֲשֶׁר־עַל־שְׂמֹאול אִישׁ בְּשַׁעַר הָעִיר׃ אַךְ לֹא
not although (9) the-city at-gate-of each left on which the-city governor-of

יַעֲלוּ כֹּהֲנֵי הַבָּמוֹת אֶל־ מִזְבַּח יְהוָה בִּירוּשָׁלִָם כִּי
yet in-Jerusalem Yahweh altar-of at the-high-places priests-of they-served

אִם־ אָכְלוּ מַצּוֹת בְּתוֹךְ אֲחֵיהֶם׃
brothers-of-them in-among unleavened-breads they-ate indeed

וְטִמֵּא אֶת־ הַתֹּפֶת אֲשֶׁר בְּגֵי בְנֵי־ הִנֹּם לְבִלְתִּי
so-not Hinnom Ben in-Valley-of which the-Topheth *** and-he-desecrated (10)

°10 ק בן

Asherah and all the starry hosts. He burned them outside Jerusalem in the fields of the Kidron Valley and took the ashes to Bethel. [5]He did away with the pagan priests appointed by the kings of Judah to burn incense on the high places of the towns of Judah and on those around Jerusalem—those who burned incense to Baal, to the sun and moon, to the constellations and to all the starry hosts. [6]He took the Asherah pole from the temple of the LORD to the Kidron Valley outside Jerusalem and burned it there. He ground it to powder and scattered the dust over the graves of the common people. [7]He also tore down the quarters of the male shrine prostitutes, which were in the temple of the LORD and where women did weaving for Asherah.

[8]Josiah brought all the priests from the towns of Judah and desecrated the high places, from Geba to Beersheba, where the priests had burned incense. He broke down the shrines[i] at the gates—at the entrance to the Gate of Joshua, the city governor, which is on the left of the city gate. [9]Although the priests of the high places did not serve at the altar of the LORD in Jerusalem, they ate unleavened bread with their fellow priests.

[10]He desecrated Topheth, which was in the Valley of Ben Hinnom, so no one could

i8 Or *high places*

לְהַעֲבִיר אִישׁ אֶת־ בְּנוֹ וְאֶת־ בִּתּוֹ בָּאֵשׁ

through-the-fire daughter-of-him or son-of-him *** one to-make-pass-through

לַמֹּלֶךְ׃ (11) וַיַּשְׁבֵּת אֶת־ הַסּוּסִים אֲשֶׁר נָתְנוּ

they-dedicated that the-horses *** and-he-removed (11) to-the-Molech

מַלְכֵי יְהוּדָה לַשֶּׁמֶשׁ מִבֹּא בֵית־ יְהוָה אֶל־ לִשְׁכַּת

room-of near Yahweh temple-of from-to-enter to-the-sun Judah kings-of

נְתַן־ מֶלֶךְ הַסָּרִיס אֲשֶׁר בַּפַּרְוָרִים וְאֶת־ מַרְכְּבוֹת הַשֶּׁמֶשׁ

the-sun chariots-of and among-the-colonades that the-official Melech Nathan

שָׂרַף בָּאֵשׁ׃ (12) וְאֶת־הַמִּזְבְּחוֹת אֲשֶׁר עַל־ הַגָּג עֲלִיַּת אָחָז

Ahaz upper-room-of the-roof on that the-altars and (12) in-fire he-burned

אֲשֶׁר־ עָשׂוּ ׀ מַלְכֵי יְהוּדָה וְאֶת־ הַמִּזְבְּחוֹת אֲשֶׁר־ עָשָׂה מְנַשֶּׁה

Manasseh he-built that the-altars and Judah kings-of they-erected that

בִּשְׁתֵּי חַצְרוֹת בֵּית־ יְהוָה נָתַץ הַמֶּלֶךְ וַיָּרָץ

and-he-removed the-king he-pulled-down Yahweh temple-of courts-of in-two-of

מִשָּׁם וְהִשְׁלִיךְ אֶת־ עֲפָרָם אֶל־ נַחַל קִדְרוֹן׃ (13) וְאֶת־

and (13) Kidron Valley-of into rubble-of-them *** and-he-threw from-there

הַבָּמוֹת אֲשֶׁר ׀ עַל־ פְּנֵי יְרוּשָׁלִַם אֲשֶׁר מִימִין לְהַר־

of-Hill-of on-south that Jerusalem east-of to that the-high-places

הַמַּשְׁחִית אֲשֶׁר בָּנָה שְׁלֹמֹה מֶלֶךְ־ יִשְׂרָאֵל לְעַשְׁתֹּרֶת ׀

for-Ashtoreth Israel king-of Solomon he-built that the-Corruption

שִׁקֻּץ צִידֹנִים וְלִכְמוֹשׁ שִׁקֻּץ מוֹאָב וּלְמִלְכֹּם

and-for-Milcom Moab vile-thing-of and-for-Chemosh Sidonians vile-thing-of

תּוֹעֲבַת בְּנֵי־ עַמּוֹן טִמֵּא הַמֶּלֶךְ׃ (14) וְשִׁבַּר

and-he-smashed (14) the-king he-desecrated Ammon sons-of detestable-one-of

אֶת־ הַמַּצֵּבוֹת וַיִּכְרֹת אֶת־ הָאֲשֵׁרִים וַיְמַלֵּא

and-he-covered the-Asherah-poles *** and-he-cut-down the-sacred-stones ***

אֶת־ מְקוֹמָם עַצְמוֹת אָדָם׃ (15) וְגַם אֶת־ הַמִּזְבֵּחַ אֲשֶׁר בְּבֵית־ אֵל

El at-Beth that the-altar *** and-even (15) human bones-of site-of-them ***

הַבָּמָה אֲשֶׁר עָשָׂה יָרָבְעָם בֶּן־ נְבָט אֲשֶׁר הֶחֱטִיא אֶת־

*** he-caused-to-sin who Nebat son-of Jeroboam he-made that the-high-place

יִשְׂרָאֵל גַּם אֶת־ הַמִּזְבֵּחַ הַהוּא וְאֶת־ הַבָּמָה נָתָץ

he-demolished the-high-place and the-that the-altar *** even Israel

וַיִּשְׂרֹף אֶת־ הַבָּמָה הֵדַק לְעָפָר וְשָׂרַף

and-he-burned to-powder he-ground the-high-place *** and-he-burned

אֲשֵׁרָה׃ (16) וַיִּפֶן יֹאשִׁיָּהוּ וַיַּרְא אֶת־ הַקְּבָרִים

the-tombs *** and-he-saw Josiah then-he-looked-around (16) Asherah-pole

אֲשֶׁר־ שָׁם בָּהָר וַיִּשְׁלַח וַיִּקַּח אֶת־ הָעֲצָמוֹת מִן־

from the-bones *** and-he-removed and-he-sent on-the-hillside there that

use it to sacrifice his son or daughter in[k] the fire to Molech. [11]He removed from the entrance to the temple of the LORD the horses that the kings of Judah had dedicated to the sun. They were in the court near the room of an official named Nathan-Melech. Josiah then burned the chariots dedicated to the sun.

[12]He pulled down the altars the kings of Judah had erected on the roof near the upper room of Ahaz, and the altars Manasseh had built in the two courts of the temple of the LORD. He removed them from there, smashed them to pieces and threw the rubble into the Kidron Valley. [13]The king also desecrated the high places that were east of Jerusalem on the south of the Hill of Corruption—the ones Solomon king of Israel had built for Ashtoreth the vile goddess of the Sidonians, for Chemosh the vile god of Moab, and for Molech[l] the detestable god of the people of Ammon. [14]Josiah smashed the sacred stones and cut down the Asherah poles and covered the sites with human bones.

[15]Even the altar at Bethel, the high place made by Jeroboam son of Nebat, who had caused Israel to sin—even that altar and high place he demolished. He burned the high place and ground it to powder, and burned the Asherah pole also. [16]Then Josiah looked around, and when he saw the tombs that were there on the hillside, he had the bones removed

[k]10 *Or to make his son or daughter pass through*

[l]13 Hebrew *Milcom*

הַקְּבָרִים וַיִּשְׂרֹף עַל־ הַמִּזְבֵּחַ וַֽיְטַמְּאֵהוּ כִּדְבַר יְהוָה

Yahweh as-word-of and-he-defiled-him the-altar on and-he-burned the-tombs

אֲשֶׁר קָרָא אִישׁ הָאֱלֹהִים אֲשֶׁר קָרָא אֶת־ הַדְּבָרִים הָאֵלֶּה׃

the-these the-things *** he-foretold who the-God man-of he-proclaimed that

וַיֹּאמֶר מָה הַצִּיּוּן הַלָּז אֲשֶׁר אֲנִי רֹאֶה וַיֹּאמְרוּ

and-they-said seeing I that the-this the-tombstone what? and-he-asked (17)

אֵלָיו אַנְשֵׁי הָעִיר הַקֶּבֶר אִישׁ־ הָאֱלֹהִים אֲשֶׁר־ בָּא מִיהוּדָה

from-Judah he-came who the-God man-of the-tomb the-city men-of to-him

וַיִּקְרָא אֶת־הַדְּבָרִים הָאֵלֶּה אֲשֶׁר עָשִׂיתָ עַל הַמִּזְבַּח בֵּית־אֵל׃

El Beth the-altar to you-did that the-these the-things *** and-he-pronounced

וַיֹּאמֶר הַנִּיחוּ לוֹ אִישׁ אַל־ יָנַע עַצְמֹתָיו

bones-of-him let-him-disturb not anyone to-him leave-alone! and-he-said (18)

וַיְמַלְּטוּ עַצְמֹתָיו אֵת עַצְמוֹת הַנָּבִיא אֲשֶׁר־ בָּא מִשֹּׁמְרוֹן׃

from-Samaria he-came who the-prophet bones-of *** bones-of-him so-they-spared

וְגַם אֶת־ כָּל־ בָּתֵּי הַבָּמוֹת אֲשֶׁר׀ בְּעָרֵי שֹׁמְרוֹן

Samaria in-towns-of that the-high-places shrines-of all-of *** and-also (19)

אֲשֶׁר עָשׂוּ מַלְכֵי יִשְׂרָאֵל לְהַכְעִיס הֵסִיר יֹאשִׁיָּהוּ וַיַּעַשׂ

and-he-did Josiah he-removed to-make-angry Israel kings-of they-built that

לָהֶם כְּכָל־ הַמַּעֲשִׂים אֲשֶׁר עָשָׂה בְּבֵית־ אֵל׃ וַיִּזְבַּח

and-he-slaughtered (20) El at-Beth he-did that the-actions as-all-of to-them

אֶת־ כָּל־ כֹּהֲנֵי הַבָּמוֹת אֲשֶׁר־ שָׁם עַל־הַמִּזְבְּחוֹת וַיִּשְׂרֹף

and-he-burned the-altars on there who the-high-places priests-of all-of ***

אֶת־עַצְמוֹת אָדָם עֲלֵיהֶם וַיָּשָׁב יְרוּשָׁלָ‍ִם׃ וַיְצַו

then-he-ordered (21) Jerusalem then-he-went-back on-them human bones-of ***

הַמֶּלֶךְ אֶת־ כָּל־ הָעָם לֵאמֹר עֲשׂוּ פֶסַח לַיהוָה

to-Yahweh Passover celebrate! to-say the-people all-of *** the-king

אֱלֹהֵיכֶם כַּכָּתוּב עַל סֵפֶר הַבְּרִית הַזֶּה׃

the-this the-Covenant Book-of in as-the-thing-being-written God-of-you

כִּי לֹא נַעֲשָׂה כַּפֶּסַח הַזֶּה מִימֵי

from-days-of the-this like-the-Passover he-was-observed not indeed (22)

הַשֹּׁפְטִים אֲשֶׁר שָׁפְטוּ אֶת־יִשְׂרָאֵל וְכֹל יְמֵי מַלְכֵי יִשְׂרָאֵל

Israel kings-of days-of nor-all-of Israel *** they-led who the-ones-judging

וּמַלְכֵי יְהוּדָה׃ כִּי אִם־ בִּשְׁמֹנֶה עֶשְׂרֵה שָׁנָה לַמֶּלֶךְ יֹאשִׁיָּהוּ

Josiah of-the-king year ten in-eight indeed but (23) Judah and-kings-of

נַעֲשָׂה הַפֶּסַח הַזֶּה לַיהוָה בִּירוּשָׁלָ‍ִם׃ וְגַם

and-also (24) in-Jerusalem to-Yahweh the-this the-Passover he-was-celebrated

אֶת־ הָאֹבוֹת וְאֶת־ הַיִּדְּעֹנִים וְאֶת־ הַתְּרָפִים וְאֶת־ הַגִּלֻּלִים

the-idols and the-household-gods and the-spiritists and the-mediums ***

from them and burned on the altar to defile it, in accordance with the word of the LORD proclaimed by the man of God who foretold these things.

17The king asked, "What is that tombstone I see?"

The men of the city said, "It marks the tomb of the man of God who came from Judah and pronounced against the altar of Bethel the very things you have done to it."

18"Leave it alone," he said. "Don't let anyone disturb his bones." So they spared his bones and those of the prophet who had come from Samaria.

19Just as he had done at Bethel, Josiah removed and defiled all the shrines at the high places that the kings of Israel had built in the towns of Samaria that had provoked the LORD to anger. 20Josiah slaughtered all the priests of those high places on the altars and burned human bones on them. Then he went back to Jerusalem.

21The king gave this order to all the people: "Celebrate the Passover to the LORD your God, as it is written in this Book of the Covenant." 22Not since the days of the judges who led Israel, nor throughout the days of the kings of Israel and the kings of Judah, had any such Passover been observed. 23But in the eighteenth year of King Josiah, this Passover was celebrated to the LORD in Jerusalem.

24Furthermore, Josiah got rid of the mediums and spiritists, the household gods, the idols

וְאֵת כָּל־ הַשִּׁקֻּצִים אֲשֶׁר נִרְאוּ בְּאֶרֶץ יְהוּדָה
Judah in-land-of they-were-seen that the-detestable-things all-of and

וּבִירוּשָׁלִַם בִּעֵר יֹאשִׁיָּהוּ לְמַעַן הָקִים אֶת־ דִּבְרֵי
requirements-of *** to-fulfill in-order-to Josiah he-got-rid and-in-Jerusalem

הַתּוֹרָה הַכְּתֻבִים עַל־ הַסֵּפֶר אֲשֶׁר מָצָא חִלְקִיָּהוּ
Hilkiah he-discovered that the-book in the-ones-being-written the-law

הַכֹּהֵן בֵּית יְהוָה׃ וְכָמֹהוּ לֹא־ הָיָה לְפָנָיו מֶלֶךְ
king before-him he-was not and-like-him (25) Yahweh temple-of the-priest

אֲשֶׁר־ שָׁב אֶל־ יְהוָה בְּכָל־ לְבָבוֹ וּבְכָל־ נַפְשׁוֹ
soul-of-him and-with-all-of heart-of-him with-all-of Yahweh to he-turned who

וּבְכָל־ מְאֹדוֹ כְּכֹל תּוֹרַת מֹשֶׁה וְאַחֲרָיו לֹא־
not and-after-him Moses Law-of as-all-of strength-of-him and-with-all-of

קָם כָּמֹהוּ׃ אַךְ ׀ לֹא־ שָׁב יְהוָה מֵחֲרוֹן
from-heat-of Yahweh he-turned-away not nevertheless (26) like-him he-rose

אַפּוֹ הַגָּדוֹל אֲשֶׁר־ חָרָה אַפּוֹ בִּיהוּדָה עַל
because-of against-Judah anger-of-him he-burned which the-fierce anger-of-him

כָּל־ הַכְּעָסִים אֲשֶׁר הִכְעִיסוֹ מְנַשֶּׁה׃ וַיֹּאמֶר
so-he-said (27) Manasseh he-provoked-to-anger-him that the-provokings all-of

יְהוָה גַּם אֶת־יְהוּדָה אָסִיר מֵעַל פָּנַי כַּאֲשֶׁר
just-as presences-of-me from-before I-will-remove Judah *** also Yahweh

הֲסִרֹתִי אֶת־יִשְׂרָאֵל וּמָאַסְתִּי אֶת־ הָעִיר הַזֹּאת אֲשֶׁר־בָּחַרְתִּי
I-chose that the-this the-city *** and-I-will-reject Israel *** I-removed

אֶת־ יְרוּשָׁלִַם וְאֶת־ הַבַּיִת אֲשֶׁר אָמַרְתִּי יִהְיֶה שְׁמִי שָׁם׃
there Name-of-me he-shall-be I-said which the-temple and Jerusalem ***

וְיֶתֶר דִּבְרֵי יֹאשִׁיָּהוּ וְכָל־ אֲשֶׁר עָשָׂה הֲלֹא־ הֵם
they not? he-did that and-all Josiah events-of and-rest-of (28)

כְּתוּבִים עַל־ סֵפֶר דִּבְרֵי הַיָּמִים לְמַלְכֵי יְהוּדָה׃
Judah of-kings-of the-days annals-of book-of in ones-being-written

בְּיָמָיו עָלָה פַרְעֹה נְכֹה מֶלֶךְ־מִצְרַיִם עַל־ מֶלֶךְ
king-of to Egypt king-of Neco Pharaoh he-went-up in-days-of-him (29)

אַשּׁוּר עַל־ נְהַר־ פְּרָת וַיֵּלֶךְ הַמֶּלֶךְ יֹאשִׁיָּהוּ לִקְרָאתוֹ
to-meet-him Josiah the-king and-he-marched-out Euphrates River-of to Assyria

וַיְמִיתֵהוּ בִּמְגִדּוֹ כִּרְאֹתוֹ אֹתוֹ׃ וַיַּרְכִּבֻהוּ
and-they-drove-him (30) him when-to-face-him at-Megiddo but-he-killed-him

עֲבָדָיו מֵת מִמְּגִדּוֹ וַיְבִאֻהוּ יְרוּשָׁלִַם
Jerusalem and-they-brought-him from-Megiddo being-dead servants-of-him

וַיִּקְבְּרֻהוּ בִּקְבֻרָתוֹ וַיִּקַּח עַם־ הָאָרֶץ אֶת־
*** the-land people-of and-he-took in-tomb-of-him and-they-buried-him

and all the other detestable things seen in Judah and Jerusalem. This he did to fulfill the requirements of the law written in the book that Hilkiah the priest had discovered in the temple of the LORD. [25]Neither before nor after Josiah was there a king like him who turned to the LORD as he did—with all his heart and with all his soul and with all his strength, in accordance with all the Law of Moses.

[26]Nevertheless, the LORD did not turn away from the heat of his fierce anger, which burned against Judah because of all that Manasseh had done to provoke him to anger. [27]So the LORD said, "I will remove Judah also from my presence as I removed Israel, and I will reject Jerusalem, the city I chose, and this temple, about which I said, 'There shall my Name be.'[m]"

[28]As for the other events of Josiah's reign, and all he did, are they not written in the book of the annals of the kings of Judah?

[29]While Josiah was king, Pharaoh Neco king of Egypt went up to the Euphrates River to help the king of Assyria. King Josiah marched out to meet him in battle, but Neco faced him and killed him at Megiddo. [30]Josiah's servants brought his body in a chariot from Megiddo to Jerusalem and buried him in his own tomb. And the people of the

m27 1 Kings 8:29

יְהוֹאָחָז בֶּן־ יֹאשִׁיָּהוּ וַיִּמְשְׁחוּ אֹתוֹ וַיַּמְלִיכוּ אֹתוֹ
him and-they-made-king him and-they-anointed Josiah son-of Jehoahaz

תַּחַת אָבִיו׃ בֶּן־ עֶשְׂרִים וְשָׁלֹשׁ שָׁנָה יְהוֹאָחָז
Jehoahaz year and-three twenty son-of (31) father-of-him in-place-of

בְּמָלְכוֹ וּשְׁלֹשָׁה חֳדָשִׁים מָלַךְ בִּירוּשָׁלָ͏ִם וְשֵׁם
and-name-of in-Jerusalem he-reigned months and-three when-to-become-king-him

אִמּוֹ חֲמוּטַל בַּת־ יִרְמְיָהוּ מִלִּבְנָה׃ וַיַּעַשׂ
and-he-did (32) from-Libnah Jeremiah daughter-of Hamutal mother-of-him

הָרַע בְּעֵינֵי יְהוָה כְּכֹל אֲשֶׁר־ עָשׂוּ אֲבֹתָיו׃
fathers-of-him they-did that as-all Yahweh in-eyes-of the-evil

וַיַּאַסְרֵהוּ פַרְעֹה נְכֹה בְרִבְלָה בְּאֶרֶץ חֲמָת בִּמְלֹךְ
from-to-reign Hamath in-land-of at-Riblah Neco Pharaoh and-he-chained-him (33)

בִּירוּשָׁלָ͏ִם וַיִּתֶּן־ עֹנֶשׁ עַל־ הָאָרֶץ מֵאָה כִכַּר־ כֶּסֶף
silver talent-of hundred the-land on levy and-he-imposed in-Jerusalem

וְכִכַּר זָהָב׃ וַיַּמְלֵךְ פַּרְעֹה נְכֹה אֶת־ אֶלְיָקִים בֶּן־
son-of Eliakim *** Neco Pharaoh and-he-made-king (34) gold and-talent-of

יֹאשִׁיָּהוּ תַּחַת יֹאשִׁיָּהוּ אָבִיו וַיַּסֵּב אֶת־ שְׁמוֹ
name-of-him *** and-he-changed father-of-him Josiah in-place-of Josiah

יְהוֹיָקִים וְאֶת־ יְהוֹאָחָז לָקָח וַיָּבֹא מִצְרַיִם וַיָּמָת שָׁם׃
there and-he-died Egypt and-he-carried-off he-took Jehoahaz but Jehoiakim

וְהַכֶּסֶף וְהַזָּהָב נָתַן יְהוֹיָקִים לְפַרְעֹה אַךְ הֶעֱרִיךְ
he-taxed but to-Pharaoh Jehoiakim he-paid and-the-gold and-the-silver (35)

אֶת־ הָאָרֶץ לָתֵת אֶת־ הַכֶּסֶף עַל־ פִּי פַרְעֹה אִישׁ
each Pharaoh demand-of at the-silver *** to-pay the-land ***

כְּעֶרְכּוֹ נָגַשׂ אֶת־ הַכֶּסֶף וְאֶת־ הַזָּהָב אֶת־ עַם
people-of *** the-gold and the-silver *** he-exacted as-assessment-of-him

הָאָרֶץ לָתֵת לְפַרְעֹה נְכֹה׃ בֶּן־ עֶשְׂרִים וְחָמֵשׁ שָׁנָה יְהוֹיָקִים
Jehoiakim year and-five twenty son-of (36) Neco to-Pharaoh to-pay the-land

בְּמָלְכוֹ וְאַחַת עֶשְׂרֵה שָׁנָה מָלַךְ בִּירוּשָׁלָ͏ִם
in-Jerusalem he-reigned year ten and-one-of when-to-become-king-him

וְשֵׁם אִמּוֹ זְבִידָּה בַת־ פְּדָיָה מִן־ רוּמָה׃
Rumah from Pedaiah daughter-of Zebidah mother-of-him and-name-of

וַיַּעַשׂ הָרַע בְּעֵינֵי יְהוָה כְּכֹל אֲשֶׁר־ עָשׂוּ אֲבֹתָיו׃
fathers-of-him they-did that as-all Yahweh in-eyes-of the-evil and-he-did (37)

בְּיָמָיו עָלָה נְבֻכַדְנֶאצַּר מֶלֶךְ בָּבֶל וַיְהִי־
and-he-was Babylon king-of Nebuchadnezzar he-invaded in-days-of-him (24:1)

לוֹ יְהוֹיָקִים עֶבֶד שָׁלֹשׁ שָׁנִים וַיָּשָׁב וַיִּמְרָד־
and-he-rebelled but-he-changed-mind years three vassal Jehoiakim to-him

land took Jehoahaz son of Josiah and anointed him and made him king in place of his father.

*Jehoahaz King of Judah*

31Jehoahaz was twenty-three years old when he became king, and he reigned in Jerusalem three months. His mother's name was Hamutal daughter of Jeremiah; she was from Libnah. 32He did evil in the eyes of the LORD, just as his fathers had done. 33Pharaoh Neco put him in chains at Riblah in the land of Hamath[n] so that he might not reign in Jerusalem, and he imposed on Judah a levy of a hundred talents[o] of silver and a talent[p] of gold. 34Pharaoh Neco made Eliakim son of Josiah king in place of his father Josiah and changed Eliakim's name to Jehoiakim. But he took Jehoahaz and carried him off to Egypt, and there he died. 35Jehoiakim paid Pharaoh Neco the silver and gold he demanded. In order to do so, he taxed the land and exacted the silver and gold from the people of the land according to their assessments.

*Jehoiakim King of Judah*

36Jehoiakim was twenty-five years old when he became king, and he reigned in Jerusalem eleven years. His mother's name was Zebidah daughter of Pedaiah; she was from Rumah. 37And he did evil in the eyes of the LORD, just as his fathers had done.

24 During Jehoiakim's reign, Nebuchadnezzar king of Babylon invaded the land, and Jehoiakim became his vassal for three years. But then he changed his mind and rebelled against

[n]33 Hebrew; Septuagint (see also 2 Chron. 36:3) *Neco at Riblah in Hamath removed him*
[o]33 That is, about 3 3/4 tons (about 3.4 metric tons)
[p]33 That is, about 75 pounds (about 34 kilograms)

°33 ק ממלך
°36 ק זבודה

בּוֹ׃ (2) וַיְשַׁלַּח יְהוָה ׀ בּוֹ אֶת־ גְּדוּדֵי כַשְׂדִּים וְאֶת־
and Chaldeans raiders-of *** against-him Yahweh and-he-sent (2) against-him

גְּדוּדֵי אֲרָם וְאֵת ׀ גְּדוּדֵי מוֹאָב וְאֵת גְּדוּדֵי בְנֵי־ עַמּוֹן
Ammon sons-of raiders-of and Moab raiders-of and Aram raiders-of

וַיְשַׁלְּחֵם בִּיהוּדָה לְהַאֲבִידוֹ כִּדְבַר יְהוָה אֲשֶׁר דִּבֶּר
he-proclaimed that Yahweh as-word-of to-destroy-him to-Judah and-he-sent-them

בְּיַד עֲבָדָיו הַנְּבִיאִים׃ (3) אַךְ ׀ עַל־ פִּי יְהוָה
Yahweh command-of at surely (3) the-prophets servants-of-him by-hand-of

הָיְתָה בִּיהוּדָה לְהָסִיר מֵעַל פָּנָיו בְּחַטֹּאת
for-sins-of presences-of-him from-before to-remove to-Judah she-happened

מְנַשֶּׁה כְּכֹל אֲשֶׁר עָשָׂה׃ (4) וְגַם דַּם־ הַנָּקִי אֲשֶׁר שָׁפָךְ
he-shed that the-innocent blood-of and-also (4) he-did that as-all Manasseh

וַיְמַלֵּא אֶת־ יְרוּשָׁלִַם דָּם נָקִי וְלֹא־ אָבָה יְהוָה
Yahweh he-was-willing and-not innocent blood Jerusalem *** for-he-filled

לִסְלֹחַ׃ (5) וְיֶתֶר דִּבְרֵי יְהוֹיָקִים וְכָל־ אֲשֶׁר עָשָׂה הֲלֹא־
not? he-did that and-all Jehoiakim events-of and-rest-of (5) to-forgive

הֵם כְּתוּבִים עַל־ סֵפֶר דִּבְרֵי הַיָּמִים לְמַלְכֵי יְהוּדָה׃
Judah of-kings-of the-days annals-of book-of in ones-being-written they

(6) וַיִּשְׁכַּב יְהוֹיָקִים עִם־ אֲבֹתָיו וַיִּמְלֹךְ יְהוֹיָכִין
Jehoiachin and-he-became-king fathers-of-him with Jehoiakim and-he-rested (6)

בְּנוֹ תַּחְתָּיו׃ (7) וְלֹא־ הֹסִיף עוֹד מֶלֶךְ מִצְרַיִם
Egypt king-of again he-repeated and-not (7) in-place-of-him son-of-him

לָצֵאת מֵאַרְצוֹ כִּי־ לָקַח מֶלֶךְ בָּבֶל מִנַּחַל
from-Wadi-of Babylon king-of he-took for from-country-of-him to-march-out

מִצְרַיִם עַד־ נְהַר־ פְּרָת כֹּל אֲשֶׁר הָיְתָה לְמֶלֶךְ מִצְרָיִם׃ (8) בֶּן־
son-of (8) Egypt to-king-of she-was that all Euphrates River-of to Egypt

שְׁמֹנֶה עֶשְׂרֵה שָׁנָה יְהוֹיָכִין בְּמָלְכוֹ וּשְׁלֹשָׁה חֳדָשִׁים
months and-three when-to-become-king-him Jehoiachin year ten eight

מָלַךְ בִּירוּשָׁלִָם וְשֵׁם אִמּוֹ נְחֻשְׁתָּא בַת־
daughter-of Nehushta mother-of-him and-name-of in-Jerusalem he-reigned

אֶלְנָתָן מִירוּשָׁלִָם׃ (9) וַיַּעַשׂ הָרַע בְּעֵינֵי יְהוָה כְּכֹל
as-all Yahweh in-eyes-of the-evil and-he-did (9) from-Jerusalem Elnathan

אֲשֶׁר־ עָשָׂה אָבִיו׃ (10) בָּעֵת הַהִיא עָלָה
they-advanced the-that at-the-time (10) father-of-him he-did that

עַבְדֵי נְבֻכַדְנֶאצַּר מֶלֶךְ־ בָּבֶל יְרוּשָׁלִָם וַתָּבֹא הָעִיר
the-city and-she-lay Jerusalem Babylon king-of Nebuchadnezzar officers-of

בַּמָּצוֹר׃ (11) וַיָּבֹא נְבוּכַדְנֶאצַּר מֶלֶךְ־ בָּבֶל עַל־ הָעִיר
the-city to Babylon king-of Nebuchadnezzar and-he-came (11) under-the-siege

Nebuchadnezzar. [2]The LORD sent Babylonian,[q] Aramean, Moabite and Ammonite raiders against him. He sent them to destroy Judah, in accordance with the word of the LORD proclaimed by his servants the prophets. [3]Surely these things happened to Judah according to the LORD's command, in order to remove them from his presence because of the sins of Manasseh and all he had done, [4]including the shedding of innocent blood. For he had filled Jerusalem with innocent blood, and the LORD was not willing to forgive.

[5]As for the other events of Jehoiakim's reign, and all he did, are they not written in the book of the annals of the kings of Judah? [6]Jehoiakim rested with his fathers. And Jehoiachin his son succeeded him as king.

[7]The king of Egypt did not march out from his own country again, because the king of Babylon had taken all his territory, from the Wadi of Egypt to the Euphrates River.

*Jehoiachin King of Judah*

[8]Jehoiachin was eighteen years old when he became king, and he reigned in Jerusalem three months. His mother's name was Nehushta daughter of Elnathan; she was from Jerusalem. [9]He did evil in the eyes of the LORD, just as his father had done.

[10]At that time the officers of Nebuchadnezzar king of Babylon advanced on Jerusalem and laid siege to it, [11]and Nebuchadnezzar himself came up to the city while his

q2 Or *Chaldean*

°10 ק עלו

וַעֲבָדָיו צָרִים עָלֶיהָ׃ וַיֵּצֵא

and-he-surrendered (12) against-her ones-besieging and-officers-of-him

יְהוֹיָכִין מֶלֶךְ־יְהוּדָה עַל־מֶלֶךְ בָּבֶל הוּא וְאִמּוֹ

and-mother-of-him he Babylon king-of to Judah king-of Jehoiachin

וַעֲבָדָיו וְשָׂרָיו וְסָרִיסָיו וַיִּקַּח אֹתוֹ

him and-he-took and-officials-of-him and-nobles-of-him and-attendants-of-him

מֶלֶךְ בָּבֶל בִּשְׁנַת שְׁמֹנֶה לְמָלְכוֹ׃ וַיּוֹצֵא מִשָּׁם

from-there and-he-removed (13) to-reign-him eight in-year-of Babylon king-of

אֶת־כָּל־אוֹצְרוֹת בֵּית יְהוָה וְאוֹצְרוֹת בֵּית הַמֶּלֶךְ

the-king palace-of and-treasures-of Yahweh temple-of treasures-of all-of ***

וַיְקַצֵּץ אֶת־כָּל־כְּלֵי הַזָּהָב אֲשֶׁר עָשָׂה שְׁלֹמֹה מֶלֶךְ־

king-of Solomon he-made that the-gold articles-of all-of *** and-he-took-away

יִשְׂרָאֵל בְּהֵיכַל יְהוָה כַּאֲשֶׁר דִּבֶּר יְהוָה׃ וְהִגְלָה

and-he-exiled (14) Yahweh he-declared just-as Yahweh for-temple-of Israel

אֶת־כָּל־יְרוּשָׁלַםִ וְאֶת־כָּל־הַשָּׂרִים וְאֵת ׀ כָּל־גִּבּוֹרֵי הַחַיִל

the-fight men-of all-of and the-officers all-of and Jerusalem all-of ***

עֲשָׂרָה אֲלָפִים גּוֹלֶה וְכָל־הֶחָרָשׁ וְהַמַּסְגֵּר לֹא

not and-the-artisan the-craftsman and-all-of being-exiled thousands ten-of

נִשְׁאַר זוּלַת דַּלַּת עַם־הָאָרֶץ׃ וַיֶּגֶל אֶת־

*** and-he-took-captive (15) the-land people-of poor-of except he-was-left

יְהוֹיָכִין בָּבֶלָה וְאֶת־אֵם הַמֶּלֶךְ וְאֶת־נְשֵׁי הַמֶּלֶךְ וְאֶת־

and the-king wives-of and the-king mother-of and to-Babylon Jehoiachin

סָרִיסָיו וְאֵת אוּלֵי הָאָרֶץ הוֹלִיךְ גּוֹלָה מִירוּשָׁלַםִ

from-Jerusalem exile he-took the-land leaders-of and officials-of-him

בָּבֶלָה׃ וְאֵת כָּל־אַנְשֵׁי הַחַיִל שִׁבְעַת אֲלָפִים

thousands seven-of the-fight men-of all-of and (16) to-Babylon

וְהֶחָרָשׁ וְהַמַּסְגֵּר אֶלֶף הַכֹּל גִּבּוֹרִים

ones-strong the-whole thousand and-the-artisan and-the-craftsman

עֹשֵׂי מִלְחָמָה וַיְבִיאֵם מֶלֶךְ־בָּבֶל גּוֹלָה בָּבֶלָה׃

to-Babylon exile Babylon king-of and-he-took-them war ones-making-of

וַיַּמְלֵךְ מֶלֶךְ־בָּבֶל אֶת־מַתַּנְיָה דֹּדוֹ

uncle-of-him Mattaniah *** Babylon king-of and-he-made-king (17)

תַּחְתָּיו וַיַּסֵּב אֶת־שְׁמוֹ צִדְקִיָּהוּ׃ בֶּן־עֶשְׂרִים

twenty son-of (18) Zedekiah name-of-him *** and-he-changed in-place-of-him

וְאַחַת שָׁנָה צִדְקִיָּהוּ בְמָלְכוֹ וְאַחַת עֶשְׂרֵה שָׁנָה מָלַךְ

he-reigned year ten and-one-of when-to-become-king-him Zedekiah year and-one

בִּירוּשָׁלָםִ וְשֵׁם אִמּוֹ חֲמִיטַל בַּת־יִרְמְיָהוּ

Jeremiah daughter-of Hamutal mother-of-him and-name-of in-Jerusalem

officers were besieging it. [12]Jehoiachin king of Judah, his mother, his attendants, his nobles and his officials all surrendered to him.

In the eighth year of the reign of the king of Babylon, he took Jehoiachin prisoner. [13]As the LORD had declared, Nebuchadnezzar removed all the treasures from the temple of the LORD and from the royal palace, and took away all the gold articles that Solomon king of Israel had made for the temple of the LORD. [14]He carried into exile all Jerusalem: all the officers and fighting men, and all the craftsmen and artisans—a total of ten thousand. Only the poorest people of the land were left.

[15]Nebuchadnezzar took Jehoiachin captive to Babylon. He also took from Jerusalem to Babylon the king's mother, his wives, his officials and the leading men of the land. [16]The king of Babylon also deported to Babylon the entire force of seven thousand fighting men, strong and fit for war, and a thousand craftsmen and artisans. [17]He made Mattaniah, Jehoiachin's uncle, king in his place and changed his name to Zedekiah.

*Zedekiah King of Judah*

[18]Zedekiah was twenty-one years old when he became king, and he reigned in Jerusalem eleven years. His mother's name was Hamutal daughter of Jeremiah; she was

°14 ק עשרת
°15 ק אילי
°18 ק חמוטל

מִלִּבְנָה׃ וַיַּעַשׂ הָרַע בְּעֵינֵי יְהוָה כְּכֹל אֲשֶׁר־ עָשָׂה
he-did that as-all Yahweh in-eyes-of the-evil and-he-did (19) from-Libnah

יְהוֹיָקִים׃ כִּי ׀ עַל־ אַף יְהוָה הָיְתָה בִּירוּשָׁלַםִ
to-Jerusalem she-happened Yahweh anger-of because-of for (20) Jehoiachin

וּבִיהוּדָה עַד־ הִשְׁלִכוֹ אֹתָם מֵעַל פָּנָיו
presences-of-him from-before them he-thrust-him until and-to-Judah

וַיִּמְרֹד צִדְקִיָּהוּ בְּמֶלֶךְ בָּבֶל׃ וַיְהִי
so-he-was (25:1) Babylon against-king-of Zedekiah now-he-rebelled

בִּשְׁנַת הַתְּשִׁיעִית לְמָלְכוֹ בַּחֹדֶשׁ הָעֲשִׂירִי בֶּעָשׂוֹר
on-the-ten the-tenth in-the-month to-reign-him the-ninth in-year-of

לַחֹדֶשׁ בָּא נְבֻכַדְנֶאצַּר מֶלֶךְ־ בָּבֶל הוּא וְכָל־
and-whole-of he Babylon king-of Nebuchadnezzar he-marched of-the-month

חֵילוֹ עַל־ יְרוּשָׁלַםִ וַיִּחַן עָלֶיהָ וַיִּבְנוּ
and-they-built against-her and-he-encamped Jerusalem against army-of-him

עָלֶיהָ דָּיֵק סָבִיב׃ וַתָּבֹא הָעִיר בַּמָּצוֹר
under-the-siege the-city and-she-went (2) around siege-work against-her

עַד עַשְׁתֵּי עֶשְׂרֵה שָׁנָה לַמֶּלֶךְ צִדְקִיָּהוּ׃ בְּתִשְׁעָה לַחֹדֶשׁ
of-the-month on-nine (3) Zedekiah of-the-king year ten one-of until

וַיֶּחֱזַק הָרָעָב בָּעִיר וְלֹא־ הָיָה לֶחֶם לְעַם
for-people-of food he-was so-not in-the-city the-famine then-he-was-severe

הָאָרֶץ׃ וַתִּבָּקַע הָעִיר וְכָל־ אַנְשֵׁי
men-of and-all-of the-city then-she-was-broken-through (4) the-land

הַמִּלְחָמָה ׀ הַלַּיְלָה דֶּרֶךְ שַׁעַר ׀ בֵּין הַחֹמֹתַיִם אֲשֶׁר עַל־ גַּן
garden-of near that the-two-walls between gate way-of the-night the-war

הַמֶּלֶךְ וְכַשְׂדִּים עַל־ הָעִיר סָבִיב וַיֵּלֶךְ דֶּרֶךְ הָעֲרָבָה׃
the-Arabah way-of and-he-fled around the-city at but-Chaldeans the-king

וַיִּרְדְּפוּ חֵיל־ כַּשְׂדִּים אַחַר הַמֶּלֶךְ וַיַּשִּׂגוּ אֹתוֹ
him and-they-overtook the-king after Chaldeans army-of but-they-pursued (5)

בְּעַרְבוֹת יְרֵחוֹ וְכָל־ חֵילוֹ נָפֹצוּ מֵעָלָיו׃
from-him they-were-separated army-of-him and-all-of Jericho in-plains-of

וַיִּתְפְּשׂוּ אֶת־ הַמֶּלֶךְ וַיַּעֲלוּ אֹתוֹ אֶל־ מֶלֶךְ בָּבֶל
Babylon king-of to him and-they-took the-king *** and-they-captured (6)

רִבְלָתָה וַיְדַבְּרוּ אִתּוֹ מִשְׁפָּט׃ וְאֶת־ בְּנֵי צִדְקִיָּהוּ
Zedekiah sons-of and (7) sentence on-him and-they-pronounced at-Riblah

שָׁחֲטוּ לְעֵינָיו וְאֶת־ עֵינֵי צִדְקִיָּהוּ עִוֵּר
he-put-out Zedekiah eyes-of then before-eyes-of-him they-killed

וַיַּאַסְרֵהוּ בַּנְחֻשְׁתַּיִם וַיְבִאֵהוּ בָּבֶל׃
Babylon and-he-took-him with-the-bronze-shackles and-he-bound-him

from Libnah. 19He did evil in the eyes of the LORD, just as Jehoiakim had done. 20It was because of the LORD's anger that all this happened to Jerusalem and Judah, and in the end he thrust them from his presence.

*The Fall of Jerusalem*

Now Zedekiah rebelled against the king of Babylon.

25 So in the ninth year of Zedekiah's reign, on the tenth day of the tenth month, Nebuchadnezzar king of Babylon marched against Jerusalem with his whole army. He encamped outside the city and built siege works all around it. 2The city was kept under siege until the eleventh year of King Zedekiah. 3By the ninth day of the ⌊fourth⌋[s] month the famine in the city had become so severe that there was no food for the people to eat. 4Then the city wall was broken through, and the whole army fled at night through the gate between the two walls near the king's garden, though the Babylonians[t] were surrounding the city. They fled toward the Arabah,[u] 5but the Babylonian[v] army pursued the king and overtook him in the plains of Jericho. All his soldiers were separated from him and scattered, 6and he was captured. He was taken to the king of Babylon at Riblah, where sentence was pronounced on him. 7They killed the sons of Zedekiah before his eyes. Then they put out his eyes, bound him with bronze shackles and took him to Babylon.

s3 See Jeremiah 52:6.
t4 Or *Chaldeans;* also in verses 13, 25 and 26
u4 Or *the Jordan Valley*
v5 Or *Chaldean;* also in verses 10 and 24

| וּבַחֹ֙דֶשׁ֙ | הַחֲמִישִׁי֙ | בְּשִׁבְעָ֣ה | לַחֹ֔דֶשׁ | הִ֕יא | שְׁנַ֣ת | תְּשַֽׁע־ |
|---|---|---|---|---|---|---|
| and-in-the-month | the-fifth | on-seven | of-the-month | this | year-of | nine-of | (8) |

| עֶשְׂרֵ֣ה שָׁנָ֔ה | לַמֶּ֖לֶךְ | נְבֻכַדְנֶאצַּ֑ר | מֶֽלֶךְ־ | בָּבֶ֑ל | בָּ֗א | נְבוּזַרְאֲדָן֙ |
|---|---|---|---|---|---|---|
| ten year | of-the-king | Nebuchadnezzar | king-of | Babylon | he-came | Nebuzaradan |

| רַב־ | טַבָּחִ֛ים | עֶ֥בֶד | מֶֽלֶךְ־ | בָּבֶ֖ל | יְרוּשָׁלָֽ͏ִם׃ |
|---|---|---|---|---|---|
| commander-of | imperial-guards | official-of | king-of | Babylon | Jerusalem |

| וַיִּשְׂרֹ֥ף | אֶת־ | בֵּית־ | יְהוָ֖ה | וְאֶת־ | בֵּ֣ית | הַמֶּ֑לֶךְ | וְאֵ֖ת כָּל־ |
|---|---|---|---|---|---|---|---|
| and-he-set-fire | *** | temple-of | Yahweh | and | palace-of | the-king | and all-of | (9) |

| בָּתֵּ֧י | יְרוּשָׁלַ֛͏ִם | וְאֶת־ | כָּל־ | בֵּ֥ית | גָּד֖וֹל | שָׂרַ֥ף | בָּאֵֽשׁ׃ |
|---|---|---|---|---|---|---|---|
| houses-of | Jerusalem | and | every-of | building-of | importance | he-burned | with-fire |

| וְאֶת־ | חוֹמֹ֥ת | יְרוּשָׁלַ֖͏ִם | סָבִ֑יב | נָֽתְצוּ֙ | כָּל־ | חֵ֣יל |
|---|---|---|---|---|---|---|
| and | walls-of | Jerusalem | around | they-broke-down | whole-of | army-of | (10) |

| כַּשְׂדִּ֔ים | אֲשֶׁ֖ר | רַב־ | טַבָּחִֽים׃ | וְאֵת֩ | יֶ֨תֶר | הָעָ֜ם |
|---|---|---|---|---|---|---|
| Chaldeans | that | commander-of | imperial-guards | (11) and | rest-of | the-people |

| הַנִּשְׁאָרִ֣ים | בָּעִ֗יר | וְאֶת־ | הַנֹּֽפְלִים֙ | אֲשֶׁ֤ר | נָֽפְלוּ֙ |
|---|---|---|---|---|---|
| the-ones-remaining | in-the-city | and | the-ones-going-over | who | they-went-over |

| עַל־ | הַמֶּ֣לֶךְ | בָּבֶ֔ל | וְאֵ֖ת | יֶ֣תֶר | הֶהָמ֑וֹן | הֶגְלָ֕ה | נְבוּזַרְאֲדָ֖ן |
|---|---|---|---|---|---|---|---|
| to | the-king-of | Babylon | and | rest-of | the-populace | he-exiled | Nebuzaradan |

| רַב־ | טַבָּחִֽים׃ | וּמִדַּלַּ֣ת | הָאָ֔רֶץ | הִשְׁאִ֖יר |
|---|---|---|---|---|
| commander-of | imperial-guards | (12) but-from-poor-of | the-land | he-left-behind |

| רַב־ | טַבָּחִ֑ים | לְכֹרְמִ֖ים | וּלְיֹגְבִֽים׃ |
|---|---|---|---|
| commander-of | imperial-guards | as-ones-working-vineyards | and-as-ones-working-fields |

| וְאֶת־ | עַמּוּדֵ֣י | הַנְּחֹ֗שֶׁת | אֲשֶׁ֤ר | בֵּית־ | יְהוָ֔ה | וְאֶת־ | הַמְּכֹנ֞וֹת |
|---|---|---|---|---|---|---|---|
| and | pillars-of | the-bronze | that | temple-of | Yahweh | and | the-movable-stands | (13) |

| וְאֶת־ | יָ֣ם | הַנְּחֹ֗שֶׁת | אֲשֶׁ֣ר | בְּבֵית־ | יְהוָ֔ה | שִׁבְּר֖וּ | כַשְׂדִּ֑ים |
|---|---|---|---|---|---|---|---|
| and | Sea-of | the-bronze | that | in-temple-of | Yahweh | they-broke-up | Chaldeans |

| וַיִּשְׂא֥וּ | אֶת־ | נְחֻשְׁתָּ֖ם | בָּבֶֽלָה׃ | וְאֶת־ | הַסִּירֹ֨ת | וְאֶת־ |
|---|---|---|---|---|---|---|
| and-they-carried | *** | bronze-of-them | to-Babylon | (14) and | the-pots | and |

| הַיָּעִ֜ים | וְאֶת־ | הַֽמְזַמְּר֣וֹת | וְאֶת־ | הַכַּפּ֗וֹת | וְאֵ֤ת כָּל־ | כְּלֵ֥י |
|---|---|---|---|---|---|---|
| the-shovels | and | the-wick-trimmers | and | the-ladles | and all-of | articles-of |

| הַנְּחֹ֛שֶׁת | אֲשֶׁ֥ר | יְשָׁרְתוּ־ | בָ֖ם | לָקָֽחוּ׃ | וְאֶת־ | הַמַּחְתּוֹת֙ וְאֶת־ |
|---|---|---|---|---|---|---|
| the-bronze | that | they-served | with-them | they-took | (15) and | the-censers and |

| הַמִּזְרָק֗וֹת | אֲשֶׁ֤ר | זָהָ֣ב | זָהָ֔ב | וַאֲשֶׁר־ | כֶּ֥סֶף | כֶּ֖סֶף | לָקַ֑ח |
|---|---|---|---|---|---|---|---|
| the-sprinkling-bowls | that | gold | gold | or-that | silver | silver | he-took-away |

| רַב־ | טַבָּחִֽים׃ | הָעַמּוּדִ֣ים ׀ | שְׁנַ֗יִם | הַיָּ֤ם | הָֽאֶחָד֙ |
|---|---|---|---|---|---|
| commander-of | imperial-guards | (16) the-pillars | two | the-Sea | the-one |

| וְהַמְּכֹנ֔וֹת | אֲשֶׁר־ | עָשָׂ֥ה | שְׁלֹמֹ֖ה | לְבֵ֣ית | יְהוָ֑ה | לֹ֣א | הָיָ֥ה |
|---|---|---|---|---|---|---|---|
| and-the-movable-stands | which | he-made | Solomon | for-temple-of | Yahweh | not | he-was |

[8]On the seventh day of the fifth month, in the nineteenth year of Nebuchadnezzar king of Babylon, Nebuzaradan commander of the imperial guard, an official of the king of Babylon, came to Jerusalem. [9]He set fire to the temple of the Lord, the royal palace and all the houses of Jerusalem. Every important building he burned down. [10]The whole Babylonian army, under the commander of the imperial guard, broke down the walls around Jerusalem. [11]Nebuzaradan the commander of the guard carried into exile the people who remained in the city, along with the rest of the populace and those who had gone over to the king of Babylon. [12]But the commander left behind some of the poorest people of the land to work the vineyards and fields.

[13]The Babylonians broke up the bronze pillars, the movable stands and the bronze Sea that were at the temple of the Lord and they carried the bronze to Babylon. [14]They also took away the pots, shovels, wick trimmers, ladles and all the bronze articles used in the temple service. [15]The commander of the imperial guard took away the censers and sprinkling bowls—all that were made of gold or silver.

[16]The bronze from the two pillars, the Sea and the movable stands, which Solomon had made for the temple of the Lord, was more than could be

מִשְׁקָל לִנְחֹשֶׁת כָּל־ הַכֵּלִים הָאֵלֶּה׃ שְׁמֹנֶה עֶשְׂרֵה אַמָּה
cubit ten eight (17) the-these the-articles all-of of-bronze-of weight

קוֹמַת׀ הָעַמּוּד הָאֶחָד וְכֹתֶרֶת עָלָיו׀ נְחֹשֶׁת וְקוֹמַת
and-height-of bronze on-him and-capital the-each the-pillar height-of

הַכֹּתֶרֶת שָׁלֹשׁ אַמָּה וּשְׂבָכָה וְרִמֹּנִים עַל־ הַכֹּתֶרֶת סָבִיב
around the-capital on and-pomegranates and-network cubits three the-capital

הַכֹּל נְחֹשֶׁת וְכָאֵלֶּה לַעַמּוּד הַשֵּׁנִי עַל־ הַשְּׂבָכָה׃
the-network with the-second on-the-pillar and-like-these bronze the-whole

וַיִּקַּח רַב־ טַבָּחִים אֶת־ שְׂרָיָה כֹּהֵן הָרֹאשׁ וְאֶת־
and the-chief priest-of Seraiah *** guards commander-of and-he-took (18)

צְפַנְיָהוּ כֹּהֵן מִשְׁנֶה וְאֶת־ שְׁלֹשֶׁת שֹׁמְרֵי הַסַּף׃
the-door ones-keeping-of three-of and second priest-of Zephaniah

וּמִן־ הָעִיר לָקַח סָרִיס אֶחָד אֲשֶׁר־הוּא פָקִיד׀ עַל־ אַנְשֵׁי
men-of over leader he who one officer he-took the-city and-from (19)

הַמִּלְחָמָה וַחֲמִשָּׁה אֲנָשִׁים מֵרֹאֵי פְנֵי־ הַמֶּלֶךְ אֲשֶׁר נִמְצְאוּ
they-were-found who the-king faces-of of-ones-seeing-of men and-five the-fight

בָעִיר וְאֵת הַסֹּפֵר שַׂר הַצָּבָא הַמַּצְבִּא אֶת־
*** the-one-conscripting the-host chief-of the-secretary and in-the-city

עַם הָאָרֶץ וְשִׁשִּׁים אִישׁ מֵעַם הָאָרֶץ הַנִּמְצְאִים
the-ones-being-found the-land from-people-of man and-sixty the-land people-of

בָּעִיר׃ וַיִּקַּח אֹתָם נְבוּזַרְאֲדָן רַב־ טַבָּחִים
guards commander-of Nebuzaradan them and-he-took (20) in-the-city

וַיֹּלֶךְ אֹתָם עַל־ מֶלֶךְ בָּבֶל רִבְלָתָה׃ וַיַּךְ
and-he-executed (21) at-Riblah Babylon king-of to them and-he-brought

אֹתָם מֶלֶךְ בָּבֶל וַיְמִיתֵם בְּרִבְלָה בְּאֶרֶץ חֲמָת
Hamath in-land-of at-Riblah and-he-killed-them Babylon king-of them

וַיִּגֶל יְהוּדָה מֵעַל אַדְמָתוֹ׃ וְהָעָם
and-the-people (22) land-of-him from-on Judah so-he-went-to-captivity

הַנִּשְׁאָר בְּאֶרֶץ יְהוּדָה אֲשֶׁר הִשְׁאִיר נְבוּכַדְנֶאצַּר
Nebuchadnezzar he-left-behind that Judah in-land-of the-one-being-left

מֶלֶךְ בָּבֶל וַיַּפְקֵד עֲלֵיהֶם אֶת־ גְּדַלְיָהוּ בֶּן־ אֲחִיקָם בֶּן־
son-of Ahikam son-of Gedeliah *** over-them then-he-appointed Babylon king-of

שָׁפָן׃ וַיִּשְׁמְעוּ כָל־ שָׂרֵי הַחֲיָלִים הֵמָּה וְהָאֲנָשִׁים
and-the-men they the-armies officers-of all-of when-they-heard (23) Shaphan

כִּי־ הִפְקִיד מֶלֶךְ־ בָּבֶל אֶת־ גְּדַלְיָהוּ וַיָּבֹאוּ אֶל־ גְּדַלְיָהוּ
Gedeliah to then-they-came Gedeliah *** Babylon king-of he-appointed that

הַמִּצְפָּה וְיִשְׁמָעֵאל בֶּן־ נְתַנְיָה וְיוֹחָנָן בֶּן־ קָרֵחַ וּשְׂרָיָה
and-Seraiah Kareah son-of and-Johanan Nethaniah son-of and-Ishmael the-Mizpah

°17 ק אמות

---

weighed. [17]Each pillar was
twenty-seven feet[w] high. The
bronze capital on top of one
pillar was four and a half feet[x]
high and was decorated with a
network and pomegranates of
bronze all around. The other
pillar, with its network, was
similar.
[18]The commander of the
guard took as prisoners Seraiah
the chief priest, Zephaniah
the priest next in rank
and the three doorkeepers.
[19]Of those still in the city, he
took the officer in charge of
the fighting men and five royal
advisers. He also took the
secretary who was chief officer
in charge of conscripting the
people of the land and sixty of
his men who were found in
the city. [20]Nebuzaradan the
commander took them all and
brought them to the king of
Babylon at Riblah. [21]There at
Riblah, in the land of Hamath,
the king had them executed.
So Judah went into captivity,
away from her land.
[22]Nebuchadnezzar king of
Babylon appointed Gedaliah
son of Ahikam, the son of Shaphan,
to be over the people he
had left behind in Judah.
[23]When all the army officers
and their men heard that the
king of Babylon had appointed
Gedaliah as governor, they
came to Gedaliah at Mizpah—
Ishmael son of Nethaniah,
Johanan son of Kareah, Seraiah
son of Tanhumeth the

[w]17 Hebrew *eighteen cubits* (about 8.1 meters)
[x]17 Hebrew *three cubits* (about 1.3 meters)

בֶּן־ תַּנְחֻמֶת הַנְּטֹפָתִי וְיַאֲזַנְיָהוּ בֶּן־ הַמַּעֲכָתִי הֵמָּה
they the-Maacathite son-of and-Jaazaniah the-Netophathite Tanhumeth son-of

וְאַנְשֵׁיהֶם׃ (24) וַיִּשָּׁבַע לָהֶם גְּדַלְיָהוּ וּלְאַנְשֵׁיהֶם
and-for-men-of-them Gedeliah for-them and-he-took-oath (24) and-men-of-them

וַיֹּאמֶר לָהֶם אַל־ תִּירְאוּ מֵעַבְדֵי הַכַּשְׂדִּים שְׁבוּ
settle! the-Chaldeans of-officials-of you-be-afraid not to-them and-he-said

בָאָרֶץ וְעִבְדוּ אֶת־ מֶלֶךְ בָּבֶל וְיִטַב לָכֶם׃
with-you and-he-will-go-well Babylon king-of *** and-serve! in-the-land

(25) וַיְהִי ׀ בַּחֹדֶשׁ הַשְּׁבִיעִי בָּא יִשְׁמָעֵאל בֶּן־ נְתַנְיָה
Nethaniah son-of Ishmael he-came the-seventh in-the-month but-he-was (25)

בֶּן־ אֱלִישָׁמָע מִזֶּרַע הַמְּלוּכָה וַעֲשָׂרָה אֲנָשִׁים אִתּוֹ
with-him men and-ten the-royalty from-descendant-of Elishama son-of

וַיַּכּוּ אֶת־ גְּדַלְיָהוּ וַיָּמֹת וְאֶת־ הַיְּהוּדִים וְאֶת־
and the-Judahites and so-he-died Gedeliah *** and-they-assassinated

הַכַּשְׂדִּים אֲשֶׁר־ הָיוּ אִתּוֹ בַּמִּצְפָּה׃ (26) וַיָּקֻמוּ כָל־
all-of and-they-rose (26) at-the-Mizpah with-him they-were who the-Chaldeans

הָעָם מִקָּטֹן וְעַד־ גָּדוֹל וְשָׂרֵי הַחֲיָלִים וַיָּבֹאוּ
and-they-fled the-armies and-officers-of great even-to from-least the-people

מִצְרָיִם כִּי יָרְאוּ מִפְּנֵי כַשְׂדִּים׃ (27) וַיְהִי בִשְׁלֹשִׁים
in-thirty and-he-was (27) Chaldeans because-of they-feared for Egypt

וָשֶׁבַע שָׁנָה לְגָלוּת יְהוֹיָכִין מֶלֶךְ־ יְהוּדָה בִּשְׁנֵים עָשָׂר חֹדֶשׁ
month ten in-two Judah king-of Jehoiachin of-being-exiled year and-seven

בְּעֶשְׂרִים וְשִׁבְעָה לַחֹדֶשׁ נָשָׂא אֱוִיל מְרֹדַךְ מֶלֶךְ בָּבֶל
Babylon king-of Merodach Evil he-released of-the-month and-seven on-twenty

בִּשְׁנַת מָלְכוֹ אֶת־ רֹאשׁ יְהוֹיָכִין מֶלֶךְ־ יְהוּדָה
Judah king-of Jehoiachin head-of *** to-become-king-him in-year-of

מִבֵּית כֶּלֶא׃ (28) וַיְדַבֵּר אִתּוֹ טֹבוֹת וַיִּתֵּן אֶת־
*** and-he-gave kind-things to-him and-he-spoke (28) prison from-house-of

כִּסְאוֹ מֵעַל כִּסֵּא הַמְּלָכִים אֲשֶׁר אִתּוֹ בְּבָבֶל׃
in-Babylon with-him who the-kings seat-of higher-than seat-of-him

(29) וְשִׁנָּא אֵת בִּגְדֵי כִלְאוֹ וְאָכַל לֶחֶם תָּמִיד
regularly food and-he-ate prison-of-him clothes-of *** so-he-put-aside (29)

לְפָנָיו כָּל־ יְמֵי חַיָּיו׃ (30) וַאֲרֻחָתוֹ
and-allowance-of-him (30) lives-of-him days-of all-of before-him

אֲרֻחַת תָּמִיד נִתְּנָה־ לּוֹ מֵאֵת הַמֶּלֶךְ דְּבַר־ יוֹם
day matter-of the-king from to-him she-was-given regular allowance-of

בְּיוֹמוֹ כֹּל יְמֵי חַיָּו׃
life-of-him days-of all-of by-day-of-him

Netophathite, Jaazaniah the son of the Maacathite, and their men. 24Gedaliah took an oath to reassure them and their men. "Do not be afraid of the Babylonian officials," he said. "Settle down in the land and serve the king of Babylon, and it will go well with you."

25In the seventh month, however, Ishmael son of Nethaniah, the son of Elishama, who was of royal blood, came with ten men and assassinated Gedaliah and also the men of Judah and the Babylonians who were with him at Mizpah. 26At this, all the people from the least to the greatest, together with the army officers, fled to Egypt for fear of the Babylonians.

*Jehoiachin Released*

27In the thirty-seventh year of the exile of Jehoiachin king of Judah, in the year Evil-Merodach[y] became king of Babylon, he released Jehoiachin from prison on the twenty-seventh day of the twelfth month. 28He spoke kindly to him and gave him a seat of honor higher than those of the other kings who were with him in Babylon. 29So Jehoiachin put aside his prison clothes and for the rest of his life ate regularly at the king's table. 30Day by day the king gave Jehoiachin a regular allowance as long as he lived.

[y]27 Also called *Amel-Marduk*

The NIV

# Interlinear Hebrew-English Old Testament

## Volume Three
## 1 Chronicles–Song of Songs

אָדָם שֵׁת אֱנוֹשׁ׃ קֵינָן מַהֲלַלְאֵל יָרֶד׃ חֲנוֹךְ מְתוּשֶׁלַח
Methuselah Enoch (3) Jared Mahalalel Kenan (2) Enosh Seth Adam (1:1)

לָמֶךְ׃ נֹחַ שֵׁם חָם וָיָפֶת׃ בְּנֵי יֶפֶת גֹּמֶר וּמָגוֹג
and-Magog Gomer Japheth sons-of (5) and-Japheth Ham Shem Noah (4) Lamech

וּמָדַי וְיָוָן וְתֻבָל וּמֶשֶׁךְ וְתִירָס׃ וּבְנֵי
and-sons-of (6) and-Tiras and-Meshech and-Tubal and-Javan and-Madai

גֹּמֶר אַשְׁכְּנַז* וְדִיפַת וְתוֹגַרְמָה׃ וּבְנֵי יָוָן אֱלִישָׁה
Elishah Javan and-sons-of (7) and-Togarmah and-Diphath Ashkenaz Gomer

וְתַרְשִׁישָׁה כִּתִּים וְרוֹדָנִים׃ בְּנֵי חָם כּוּשׁ וּמִצְרַיִם פּוּט
Put and-Mizraim Cush Ham sons-of (8) and-Rodanim Kittim and-Tarshish

וּכְנָעַן׃ וּבְנֵי כוּשׁ סְבָא וַחֲוִילָה וְסַבְתָּא וְרַעְמָא
and-Raamah and-Sabta and-Havilah Seba Cush and-sons-of (9) and-Canaan

וְסַבְתְּכָא וּבְנֵי רַעְמָא שְׁבָא וּדְדָן׃ וְכוּשׁ יָלַד
he-fathered and-Cush (10) and-Dedan Sheba Raamah and-sons-of and-Sabteca

אֶת־ נִמְרוֹד הוּא הֵחֵל לִהְיוֹת גִּבּוֹר בָּאָרֶץ׃ וּמִצְרַיִם
and-Mizraim (11) on-the-earth mighty-warrior to-be he-grew he Nimrod ***

יָלַד אֶת־ לוּדִיִּים° וְאֶת־ עֲנָמִים וְאֶת־ לְהָבִים וְאֶת־ נַפְתֻּחִים׃
Naphtuhites and Lehabites and Anamites and Ludites *** he-fathered

וְאֶת־ פַּתְרֻסִים וְאֶת־ כַּסְלֻחִים אֲשֶׁר יָצְאוּ מִשָּׁם
from-there they-came who Casluhites and Pathrusites and (12)

פְּלִשְׁתִּים וְאֶת־ כַּפְתֹּרִים׃ וּכְנַעַן יָלַד אֶת־ צִידוֹן
Sidon *** he-fathered and-Canaan (13) Caphtorites and Philistines

בְּכֹרוֹ וְאֶת־ חֵת׃ וְאֶת־ הַיְבוּסִי וְאֶת־ הָאֱמֹרִי
the-Amorite and the-Jebusite and (14) Heth and firstborn-of-him

וְאֵת הַגִּרְגָּשִׁי׃ וְאֶת־ הַחִוִּי וְאֶת־ הַעַרְקִי וְאֶת־ הַסִּינִי׃
the-Sinite and the-Arkite and the-Hivite and (15) the-Girgashite and

וְאֶת־ הָאַרְוָדִי וְאֶת־ הַצְּמָרִי וְאֶת־ הַחֲמָתִי׃ בְּנֵי
sons-of (17) the-Hamathite and the-Zemarite and the-Arvadite and (16)

שֵׁם עֵילָם וְאַשּׁוּר וְאַרְפַּכְשַׁד וְלוּד וַאֲרָם וְעוּץ
and-Uz and-Aram and-Lud and-Arphaxad and-Asshur Elam Shem

וְחוּל וְגֶתֶר וָמֶשֶׁךְ׃ וְאַרְפַּכְשַׁד יָלַד אֶת־
*** he-fathered and-Arphaxad (18) and-Meshech and-Gether and-Hul

שָׁלַח וְשֶׁלַח יָלַד אֶת־ עֵבֶר׃ וּלְעֵבֶר יֻלַּד
he-was-born and-to-Eber (19) Eber *** he-fathered and-Shelah Shelah

שְׁנֵי בָנִים שֵׁם הָאֶחָד פֶּלֶג כִּי בְיָמָיו
in-days-of-him because Peleg the-one name-of sons two-of

נִפְלְגָה הָאָרֶץ וְשֵׁם אָחִיו יָקְטָן׃
Joktan brother-of-him and-name-of the-earth she-was-divided

## *Historical Records From Adam to Abraham*

### *To Noah's Sons*

1 Adam, Seth, Enosh, 2Kenan, Mahalalel, Jared, 3Enoch, Methuselah, Lamech, Noah.

4The sons of Noah:[a]
Shem, Ham and Japheth.

### *The Japhethites*

5The sons[b] of Japheth:
Gomer, Magog, Madai, Javan, Tubal, Meshech and Tiras.
6The sons of Gomer:
Ashkenaz, Riphath and Togarmah.
7The sons of Javan:
Elishah, Tarshish, the Kittim and the Rodanim.

### *The Hamites*

8The sons of Ham:
Cush, Mizraim,[c] Put and Canaan.
9The sons of Cush:
Seba, Havilah, Sabta, Raamah and Sabteca.
The sons of Raamah:
Sheba and Dedan.
10Cush was the father[d] of
Nimrod, who grew to be a mighty warrior on earth.
11Mizraim was the father of
the Ludites, Anamites, Lehabites, Naphtuhites, 12Pathrusites, Casluhites (from whom the Philistines came) and Caphtorites.
13Canaan was the father of
Sidon his firstborn,[e] and of the Hittites, 14Jebusites, Amorites, Girgashites, 15Hivites, Arkites, Sinites, 16Arvadites, Zemarites and Hamathites.

### *The Semites*

17The sons of Shem:
Elam, Asshur, Arphaxad, Lud and Aram.
The sons of Aram[f]:
Uz, Hul, Gether and Meshech.
18Arphaxad was the father of
Shelah,
and Shelah the father of
Eber.
19Two sons were born to

[a]4 Septuagint; Hebrew does not have *The sons of Noah:*
[b]5 *Sons* may mean *descendants* or *successors* or *nations;* also in verses 6-10, 17 and 20.
[c]8 That is, Egypt; also in verse 11
[d]10 *Father* may mean *ancestor* or *predecessor* or *founder;* also in verses 11, 13, 18 and 20.
[e]13 Or *of the Sidonians, the foremost*
[f]17 One Hebrew manuscript and some Septuagint manuscripts (see also Gen. 10:23); most Hebrew manuscripts do not have this line.

*6 Most mss have *sheva* under the *kaph* (כְּ־).

°11 ק לודים

וְיָקְטָן יָלַד אֶת־אַלְמוֹדָד וְאֶת־שָׁלֶף וְאֶת־חֲצַרְמָוֶת
Hazarmaveth and Sheleph and Almodad *** he-fathered and-Joktan (20)

וְאֶת־יָרַח׃ וְאֶת־הֲדוֹרָם וְאֶת־אוּזָל וְאֶת־דִּקְלָה׃ וְאֶת־עֵיבָל וְאֶת־
and Ebal and (22) Diklah and Uzal and Hadoram and (21) Jerah and

אֲבִימָאֵל וְאֶת־שְׁבָא׃ וְאֶת־אוֹפִיר וְאֶת־חֲוִילָה וְאֶת־יוֹבָב כָּל־אֵלֶּה
these all-of Jobab and Havilah and Ophir and (23) Sheba and Abimael

בְּנֵי יָקְטָן׃ שֵׁם ׀ אַרְפַּכְשַׁד שָׁלַח׃ עֵבֶר פֶּלֶג רְעוּ׃
Reu Peleg Eber (25) Shelah Arphaxad Shem (24) Joktan sons-of

שְׂרוּג נָחוֹר תָּרַח׃ אַבְרָם הוּא אַבְרָהָם׃ בְּנֵי אַבְרָהָם
Abraham sons-of (28) Abraham he Abram (27) Terah Nahor Serug (26)

יִצְחָק וְיִשְׁמָעֵאל׃ אֵלֶּה תֹּלְדוֹתָם בְּכוֹר יִשְׁמָעֵאל
Ishmael firstborn-of descendants-of-them these (29) and-Ishmael Isaac

נְבָיוֹת וְקֵדָר וְאַדְבְּאֵל וּמִבְשָׂם׃ מִשְׁמָע וְדוּמָה
and-Dumah Mishma (30) and-Mibsam and-Adbeel and-Kedar Nebaioth

מַשָּׂא חֲדַד וְתֵימָא׃ יְטוּר נָפִישׁ וָקֵדְמָה אֵלֶּה הֵם
they these and-Kedemah Naphish Jetur (31) and-Tema Hadad Massa

בְּנֵי יִשְׁמָעֵאל׃ וּבְנֵי קְטוּרָה פִּילֶגֶשׁ אַבְרָהָם
Abraham concubine-of Keturah and-sons-of (32) Ishmael sons-of

יָלְדָה אֶת־זִמְרָן וְיָקְשָׁן וּמְדָן וּמִדְיָן וְיִשְׁבָּק
and-Ishbak and-Midian and-Medan and-Jokshan Zimran *** she-bore

וְשׁוּחַ וּבְנֵי יָקְשָׁן שְׁבָא וּדְדָן׃ וּבְנֵי מִדְיָן
Midian and-sons-of (33) and-Dedan Sheba Jokshan and-sons-of and-Shua

עֵיפָה וָעֵפֶר וַחֲנוֹךְ וַאֲבִידָע וְאֶלְדָּעָה כָּל־אֵלֶּה
these all-of and-Eldaah and-Abida and-Hanoch and-Epher Ephah

בְּנֵי קְטוּרָה׃ וַיּוֹלֶד אַבְרָהָם אֶת־יִצְחָק
Isaac *** Abraham and-he-fathered (34) Keturah descendants-of

בְּנֵי יִצְחָק עֵשָׂו וְיִשְׂרָאֵל׃ בְּנֵי עֵשָׂו אֱלִיפַז רְעוּאֵל וִיעוּשׁ
and-Jeush Reuel Eliphaz Esau sons-of (35) and-Israel Esau Isaac sons-of

וְיַעְלָם וְקֹרַח׃ בְּנֵי אֱלִיפַז תֵּימָן וְאוֹמָר צְפִי
Zephi and-Omar Teman Eliphaz sons-of (36) and-Korah and-Jalam

וְגַעְתָּם קְנַז וְתִמְנָע וַעֲמָלֵק׃ בְּנֵי רְעוּאֵל נַחַת
Nahath Reuel sons-of (37) and-Amalek and-Timna Kenaz and-Gatam

זֶרַח שַׁמָּה וּמִזָּה׃ וּבְנֵי שֵׂעִיר לוֹטָן וְשׁוֹבָל
and-Shobal Lotan Seir and-sons-of (38) and-Mizzah Shammah Zerah

וְצִבְעוֹן וַעֲנָה וְדִישׁוֹן וְאֵצֶר וְדִישָׁן׃ וּבְנֵי
and-sons-of (39) and-Dishan and-Ezer and-Dishon and-Anah and-Zibeon

לוֹטָן חֹרִי וְהוֹמָם וַאֲחוֹת לוֹטָן תִּמְנָע׃
Timna Lotan and-sister-of and-Homam Hori Lotan

Eber:
One was named Peleg,[g] because in his time the earth was divided; his brother was named Joktan.
20Joktan was the father of Almodad, Sheleph, Hazarmaveth, Jerah,
21Hadoram, Uzal, Diklah,
22Obal,[h] Abimael, Sheba,
23Ophir, Havilah and Jobab. All these were sons of Joktan.

24Shem, Arphaxad,[i] Shelah,
25Eber, Peleg, Reu,
26Serug, Nahor, Terah
27and Abram (that is, Abraham).

*The Family of Abraham*

28The sons of Abraham: Isaac and Ishmael.

*Descendants of Hagar*

29These were their descendants:
Nebaioth the firstborn of Ishmael, Kedar, Adbeel, Mibsam, 30Mishma, Dumah, Massa, Hadad, Tema, 31Jetur, Naphish and Kedemah. These were the sons of Ishmael.

*Descendants of Keturah*

32The sons born to Keturah, Abraham's concubine:
Zimran, Jokshan, Medan, Midian, Ishbak and Shuah.
The sons of Jokshan:
Sheba and Dedan.
33The sons of Midian:
Ephah, Epher, Hanoch, Abida and Eldaah.
All these were descendants of Keturah.

*Descendants of Sarah*

34Abraham was the father of Isaac.
The sons of Isaac:
Esau and Israel.
35The sons of Esau:
Eliphaz, Reuel, Jeush, Jalam and Korah.
36The sons of Eliphaz:
Teman, Omar, Zepho,[j] Gatam and Kenaz;
by Timna: Amalek.[k]
37The sons of Reuel:
Nahath, Zerah, Shammah and Mizzah.

[g]19 *Peleg* means *division.*
[h]22 Some Hebrew manuscripts and Syriac (see also Gen. 10:28); most Hebrew manuscripts *Ebal*
[i]24 Hebrew; some Septuagint manuscripts *Arphaxad, Cainan* (see also note at Gen. 11:10)
[j]36 Many Hebrew manuscripts, some Septuagint manuscripts and Syriac (see also Gen. 36:11); most Hebrew manuscripts *Zephi*
[k]36 Some Septuagint manuscripts (see also Gen. 36:12); Hebrew *Gatam, Kenaz, Timna and Amalek*

בְּנֵי שׁוֹבָל עַלְיָן וּמָנַחַת וְעֵיבָל שְׁפִי וְאוֹנָם
and-Onam Shephi and-Ebal and-Manahath Alian Shobal sons-of (40)

וּבְנֵי צִבְעוֹן אַיָּה וַעֲנָה׃ בְּנֵי עֲנָה דִּישׁוֹן
Dishon Anah sons-of (41) and-Anah Aiah Zibeon and-sons-of

וּבְנֵי דִישׁוֹן חַמְרָן וְאֶשְׁבָּן וְיִתְרָן וּכְרָן׃
and-Keran and-Ithran and-Eshban Hamran Dishon and-sons-of

בְּנֵי־אֵצֶר בִּלְהָן וְזַעֲוָן יַעֲקָן בְּנֵי דִישׁוֹן עוּץ
Uz Dishon sons-of Jaakan and-Zaavan Bilhan Ezer sons-of (42)

וַאֲרָן׃ וְאֵלֶּה הַמְּלָכִים אֲשֶׁר מָלְכוּ בְּאֶרֶץ אֱדוֹם
Edom in-land-of they-reigned who the-kings and-these (43) and-Aran

לִפְנֵי מְלָךְ־מֶלֶךְ לִבְנֵי יִשְׂרָאֵל בֶּלַע בֶּן־בְּעוֹר וְשֵׁם
and-name-of Beor son-of Bela Israel of-sons-of king to-reign before

עִירוֹ דִּנְהָבָה׃ וַיָּמָת בָּלַע וַיִּמְלֹךְ
then-he-became-king Bela when-he-died (44) Dinhabah city-of-him

תַּחְתָּיו יוֹבָב בֶּן־זֶרַח מִבָּצְרָה׃ וַיָּמָת
when-he-died (45) from-Bozrah Zerah son-of Jobab in-place-of-him

יוֹבָב וַיִּמְלֹךְ תַּחְתָּיו חוּשָׁם מֵאֶרֶץ
from-land-of Husham in-place-of-him then-he-became-king Jobab

הַתֵּימָנִי׃ וַיָּמָת חוּשָׁם וַיִּמְלֹךְ
then-he-became-king Husham when-he-died (46) the-Temanite

תַּחְתָּיו הֲדַד בֶּן־בְּדַד הַמַּכֶּה אֶת־מִדְיָן
Midian *** the-one-defeating Bedad son-of Hadad in-place-of-him

בִּשְׂדֵה מוֹאָב וְשֵׁם עִירוֹ עֲיוֹת׃ וַיָּמָת
when-he-died (47) Avith city-of-him and-name-of Moab in-country-of

הֲדָד וַיִּמְלֹךְ תַּחְתָּיו שַׂמְלָה מִמַּשְׂרֵקָה׃
from-Masrekah Samlah in-place-of-him then-he-became-king Hadad

וַיָּמָת שַׂמְלָה וַיִּמְלֹךְ תַּחְתָּיו שָׁאוּל
Shaul in-place-of-him then-he-became-king Samlah when-he-died (48)

מֵרְחֹבוֹת הַנָּהָר׃ וַיָּמָת שָׁאוּל וַיִּמְלֹךְ
then-he-became-king Shaul when-he-died (49) the-river from-Rehoboth-of

תַּחְתָּיו בַּעַל חָנָן בֶּן־עַכְבּוֹר׃ וַיָּמָת בַּעַל חָנָן
Hanan Baal when-he-died (50) Acbor son-of Hanan Baal in-place-of-him

וַיִּמְלֹךְ תַּחְתָּיו הֲדַד וְשֵׁם עִירוֹ
city-of-him and-name-of Hadad in-place-of-him then-he-became-king

פָּעִי וְשֵׁם אִשְׁתּוֹ מְהֵיטַבְאֵל בַּת־מַטְרֵד
Matred daughter-of Mehetabel wife-of-him and-name-of Pai

בַּת מֵי זָהָב׃ וַיָּמָת הֲדַד וַיִּהְיוּ אַלּוּפֵי
chiefs-of and-they-were Hadad and-he-died (51) Zahab Me daughter-of

*The Edomites*

*The People of Seir*

38The sons of Seir:
Lotan, Shobal, Zibeon, Anah, Dishon, Ezer and Dishan.
39The sons of Lotan:
Hori and Homam. Timna was Lotan's sister.
40The sons of Shobal:
Alvan,[l] Manahath, Ebal, Shepho and Onam.
The sons of Zibeon:
Aiah and Anah.
41The son of Anah:
Dishon.
The sons of Dishon:
Hemdan,[m] Eshban, Ithran and Keran.
42The sons of Ezer:
Bilhan, Zaavan and Akan.[n]
The sons of Dishan[o]:
Uz and Aran.

*The Rulers of Edom*

43These were the kings who reigned in Edom before any Israelite king reigned[p]:
Bela son of Beor, whose city was named Dinhabah.
44When Bela died, Jobab son of Zerah from Bozrah succeeded him as king.
45When Jobab died, Husham from the land of the Temanites succeeded him as king.
46When Husham died, Hadad son of Bedad, who defeated Midian in the country of Moab, succeeded him as king. His city was named Avith.
47When Hadad died, Samlah from Masrekah succeeded him as king.
48When Samlah died, Shaul from Rehoboth on the river[q] succeeded him as king.
49When Shaul died, Baal-Hanan son of Acbor succeeded him as king.
50When Baal-Hanan died, Hadad succeeded him as king. His city was named Pau,[r] and his wife's name was Mehetabel daughter of Matred, the

[l] *40* Many Hebrew manuscripts and some Septuagint manuscripts (see also Gen. 36:23); most Hebrew manuscripts *Alian*
[m] *41* Many Hebrew manuscripts and some Septuagint manuscripts (see also Gen. 36:26); most Hebrew manuscripts *Hamran*
[n] *42* Many Hebrew and Septuagint manuscripts (see also Gen. 36:27); most Hebrew manuscripts *Zaavan, Jaakan*
[o] *42* Hebrew *Dishon,* a variant of *Dishan*
[p] *43* Or *before an Israelite king reigned over them*
[q] *48* Or *River*
[r] *50* Many Hebrew manuscripts, some Septuagint manuscripts, Vulgate and Syriac (see also Gen. 36:39); most Hebrew manuscripts *Pai*

°46 ק עוית

אֱדוֹם אַלּוּף תִּמְנָע אַלּוּף עַלְיָה° אַלּוּף יְתֵת׃ אַלּוּף אָהֳלִיבָמָה
Oholibamah Chief (52) Jetheth Chief Alvah Chief Timna Chief Edom

אַלּוּף אֵלָה אַלּוּף פִּינֹן׃ אַלּוּף קְנַז אַלּוּף תֵּימָן אַלּוּף מִבְצָר׃
Mibzar Chief Teman Chief Kenaz Chief (53) Pinon Chief Elah Chief

אַלּוּף מַגְדִּיאֵל אַלּוּף עִירָם אֵלֶּה אַלּוּפֵי אֱדוֹם׃ אֵלֶּה
these (2:1) Edom chiefs-of these Iram Chief Magdiel Chief (54)

בְּנֵי יִשְׂרָאֵל רְאוּבֵן שִׁמְעוֹן לֵוִי וִיהוּדָה יִשָּׂשכָר* וּזְבֻלוּן׃
and-Zebulun Issachar and-Judah Levi Simeon Reuben Israel sons-of

דָּן יוֹסֵף וּבִנְיָמִן נַפְתָּלִי גָּד וְאָשֵׁר׃ בְּנֵי
sons-of (3) and-Asher Gad Naphtali and-Benjamin Joseph Dan (2)

יְהוּדָה עֵר וְאוֹנָן וְשֵׁלָה שְׁלוֹשָׁה נוֹלַד לוֹ מִבַּת־שׁוּעַ
Shua by-Bath to-him he-was-born three and-Shelah and-Onan Er Judah

הַכְּנַעֲנִית וַיְהִי עֵר ׀ בְּכוֹר יְהוּדָה רַע בְּעֵינֵי
in-eyes-of wicked Judah firstborn-of Er and-he-was the-Canaanite-woman

יְהוָה וַיְמִיתֵהוּ׃ וְתָמָר כַּלָּתוֹ יָלְדָה
she-bore daughter-in-law-of-him and-Tamar (4) so-he-put-to-death-him Yahweh

לוֹ אֶת־פֶּרֶץ וְאֶת־זָרַח כָּל־בְּנֵי יְהוּדָה חֲמִשָּׁה׃ בְּנֵי־פֶרֶץ
Perez sons-of (5) five Judah sons-of all-of Zerah and Perez *** to-him

חֶצְרוֹן וְחָמוּל׃ וּבְנֵי זֶרַח זִמְרִי וְאֵיתָן וְהֵימָן
and-Heman and-Ethan Zimri Zerah and-sons-of (6) and-Hamul Hezron

וְכַלְכֹּל וָדָרַע כֻּלָּם חֲמִשָּׁה׃ וּבְנֵי כַּרְמִי עָכָר
Achar Carmi and-sons-of (7) five all-of-them and-Dara and-Calcol

עוֹכֵר יִשְׂרָאֵל אֲשֶׁר מָעַל בַּחֵרֶם׃
against-the-devoted-thing he-violated who Israel one-bringing-disaster-of

וּבְנֵי אֵיתָן עֲזַרְיָה׃ וּבְנֵי חֶצְרוֹן אֲשֶׁר נוֹלַד־
he-was-born who Hezron and-sons-of (9) Azariah Ethan and-sons-of (8)

לוֹ אֶת־יְרַחְמְאֵל וְאֶת־רָם וְאֶת־כְּלוּבָי׃ וְרָם הוֹלִיד אֶת־
*** he-fathered and-Ram (10) Kelubai and Ram and Jerahmeel *** to-him

עַמִּינָדָב וְעַמִּינָדָב הוֹלִיד אֶת־נַחְשׁוֹן נְשִׂיא בְּנֵי יְהוּדָה׃
Judah people-of leader-of Nahshon *** he-fathered and-Amminadab Amminadab

וְנַחְשׁוֹן הוֹלִיד אֶת־שַׂלְמָא וְשַׂלְמָא הוֹלִיד אֶת־בֹּעַז׃
Boaz *** he-fathered and-Salma Salma *** he-fathered and-Nahshon (11)

וּבֹעַז הוֹלִיד אֶת־עוֹבֵד וְעוֹבֵד הוֹלִיד אֶת־יִשָׁי׃
Jesse *** he-fathered and-Obed Obed *** he-fathered and-Boaz (12)

וְאִישַׁי הוֹלִיד אֶת־בְּכֹרוֹ אֶת־אֱלִיאָב וַאֲבִינָדָב
and-Abinadab Eliab *** firstborn-of-him *** he-fathered and-Jesse (13)

הַשֵּׁנִי וְשִׁמְעָא הַשְּׁלִישִׁי׃ נְתַנְאֵל הָרְבִיעִי רַדַּי הַחֲמִישִׁי׃
the-fifth Raddai the-fourth Nethanel (14) the-third and-Shimea the-second

daughter of Me-Zahab.
51 Hadad also died.

The chiefs of Edom were:
Timna, Alvah, Jetheth,
52 Oholibamah, Elah, Pinon,
53 Kenaz, Teman,
Mibzar, 54 Magdiel and
Iram. These were the
chiefs of Edom.

*Israel's Sons*

**2** These were the sons of Israel:
Reuben, Simeon, Levi,
Judah, Issachar, Zebulun,
2 Dan, Joseph, Benjamin,
Naphtali, Gad and Asher.

*Judah*

*To Hezron's Sons*

3 The sons of Judah:
Er, Onan and Shelah.
These three were born to
him by Bathshua,[t] a Canaanite woman. Er,
Judah's firstborn, was
wicked in the LORD's
sight; so the LORD put
him to death.
4 Tamar,
Judah's daughter-in-law,
bore him Perez and
Zerah. Judah had five
sons in all.

5 The sons of Perez:
Hezron and Hamul.
6 The sons of Zerah:
Zimri, Ethan, Heman,
Calcol and Darda[u]—five
in all.
7 The son of Carmi:
Achar,[v] who brought
disaster on Israel by violating the ban on taking
devoted things.[w]
8 The son of Ethan:
Azariah.
9 The sons born to Hezron
were:
Jerahmeel, Ram and
Caleb.[x]

*From Ram Son of Hezron*

10 Ram was the father of
Amminadab, and Amminadab the father of
Nahshon, the leader of
the people of Judah.
11 Nahshon was the father
of Salmon,[y] Salmon the
father of Boaz,
12 Boaz the
father of Obed and Obed
the father of Jesse.

[t] 3 Or *by the daughter of Shua*
[u] 6 Many Hebrew manuscripts, some Septuagint manuscripts and Syriac (see also 1 Kings 4:31); most Hebrew manuscripts *Dara*
[v] 7 *Achar* means *disaster; Achar* is called *Achan* in Joshua.
[w] 7 The Hebrew term refers to the irrevocable giving over of things or persons to the LORD, often by totally destroying them.
[x] 9 Hebrew *Kelubai*, a variant of *Caleb*
[y] 11 Septuagint (see also Ruth 4:21); Hebrew *Salma*

*1 Most mss have *dagesh* in the first *sin* (יִשָּׂ).

°51 ק עלוה

אצם הששי דויד השבעי׃ ואחיתיהם°
(15) Ozem the-sixth David the-seventh (16) and-sisters-of-them

צרויה ואביגיל ובני צרויה אבשי ויואב ועשה־אל
Zeruiah and-Abigail and-sons-of Zeruiah Abishai and-Joab and-Asah El

שלשה׃ ואביגיל ילדה את־עמשא ואבי עמשא יתר
three (17) and-Abigail she-bore *** Amasa now-father-of Amasa Jether

הישמעאלי׃ וכלב בן־חצרון הוליד את־עזובה אשה
the-Ishmaelite (18) and-Caleb son-of Hezron he-fathered by Azubah wife

ואת־יריעות ואלה בניה ישר ושובב וארדון׃
and-by Jerioth and-these sons-of-her Jesher and-Shobab and-Ardon

ותמת עזובה ויקח־לו כלב את־אפרת
(19) when-she-died Azubah and-he-married to-him Caleb *** Ephrath

ותלד לו את־חור׃ וחור הוליד את־אורי ואורי
and-she-bore to-him *** Hur (20) and-Hur he-fathered *** Uri and-Uri

הוליד את־בצלאל׃ ואחר בא חצרון אל־בת־
he-fathered *** Bezalel (21) and-later he-went Hezron into daughter-of

מכיר אבי גלעד והוא לקחה והוא בן־ששים
Makir father-of Gilead and-he he-married-her when-he son-of sixty

שנה ותלד לו את־שגוב׃ ושגוב הוליד את־יאיר
year and-she-bore to-him *** Segub (22) and-Segub he-fathered *** Jair

ויהי־לו עשרים ושלוש ערים בארץ הגלעד׃
and-he-was to-him twenty and-three towns in-land-of the-Gilead

ויקח גשור־וארם את־חות יאיר מאתם
(23) but-he-captured Geshur and-Aram *** Havvoth Jair from-among-them

את־קנת ואת־בנתיה ששים עיר כל־אלה בני
*** Kenath and settlements-of-her sixty town all-of these descendants-of

מכיר אבי־גלעד׃ ואחר מות־חצרון בכלב אפרתה
Makir father-of Gilead (24) and-after death-of Hezron in-Caleb Ephrathah

ואשת חצרון אביה ותלד לו את־אשחור אבי
now-wife-of Hezron Abijah and-she-bore to-him *** Ashhur father-of

תקוע׃ ויהיו בני־ירחמאל בכור חצרון הבכור |
Tekoa (25) and-they-were sons-of Jerahmeel firstborn-of Hezron the-firstborn

רם ובונה וארן ואצם אחיה׃ ותהי אשה אחרת
Ram and-Bunah and-Oren and-Ozem and-Ahijah (26) and-she-was wife another

לירחמאל ושמה עטרה היא אם אונם׃ ויהיו
to-Jerahmeel and-name-of-her Atarah she mother-of Onam (27) and-they-were

בני־רם בכור ירחמאל מעץ וימין ועקר׃
sons-of Ram firstborn-of Jerahmeel Maaz and-Jamin and-Eker

[13]Jesse was the father of Eliab his firstborn; the second son was Abinadab, the third Shimea, [14]the fourth Nethanel, the fifth Raddai, [15]the sixth Ozem and the seventh David. [16]Their sisters were Zeruiah and Abigail. Zeruiah's three sons were Abishai, Joab and Asahel. [17]Abigail was the mother of Amasa, whose father was Jether the Ishmaelite.

*Caleb Son of Hezron*

[18]Caleb son of Hezron had children by his wife Azubah (and by Jerioth). These were her sons: Jesher, Shobab and Ardon. [19]When Azubah died, Caleb married Ephrath, who bore him Hur. [20]Hur was the father of Uri, and Uri the father of Bezalel.

[21]Later, Hezron lay with the daughter of Makir the father of Gilead (he had married her when he was sixty years old), and she bore him Segub. [22]Segub was the father of Jair, who controlled twenty-three towns in Gilead. [23](But Geshur and Aram captured Havvoth Jair,[a] as well as Kenath with its surrounding settlements—sixty towns.) All these were descendants of Makir the father of Gilead.

[24]After Hezron died in Caleb Ephrathah, Abijah the wife of Hezron bore him Ashhur the father[b] of Tekoa.

*Jerahmeel Son of Hezron*

[25]The sons of Jerahmeel the firstborn of Hezron:
Ram his firstborn, Bunah, Oren, Ozem and[c] Ahijah. [26]Jerahmeel had another wife, whose name was Atarah; she was the mother of Onam.

[27]The sons of Ram the firstborn of Jerahmeel:
Maaz, Jamin and Eker.

[a]23 Or *captured the settlements of Jair*
[b]24 *Father* may mean *civic leader* or *military leader;* also in verses 42, 45, 49-52 and possibly elsewhere.
[c]25 Or *Oren and Ozem, by*

°16 ק ואחיותיהם

וַיִּהְיוּ בְנֵי־ אוֹנָם שַׁמַּי וְיָדָע וּבְנֵי שַׁמַּי
Shammai and-sons-of and-Jada Shammai Onam sons-of and-they-were (28)

נָדָב וַאֲבִישׁוּר׃ וְשֵׁם אֵשֶׁת אֲבִישׁוּר אֲבִיהָיִל וַתֵּלֶד
and-she-bore Abihail Abishur wife-of and-name-of (29) and-Abishur Nadab

לוֹ אֶת־ אַחְבָּן וְאֶת־ מוֹלִיד׃ וּבְנֵי נָדָב סֶלֶד וְאַפָּיִם
and-Appaim Seled Nadab and-sons-of (30) Molid and Ahban *** to-him

וַיָּמָת סֶלֶד לֹא בָנִים׃ וּבְנֵי אַפַּיִם יִשְׁעִי וּבְנֵי
and-sons-of Ishi Appaim and-sons-of (31) children no Seled and-he-died

יִשְׁעִי שֵׁשָׁן וּבְנֵי שֵׁשָׁן אַחְלָי׃ וּבְנֵי יָדָע אֲחִי
brother-of Jada and-sons-of (32) Ahlai Sheshan and-sons-of Sheshan Ishi

שַׁמַּי יֶתֶר וְיוֹנָתָן וַיָּמָת יֶתֶר לֹא בָנִים׃
children no Jether and-he-died and-Jonathan Jether Shammai

וּבְנֵי יוֹנָתָן פֶּלֶת וְזָזָא אֵלֶּה הָיוּ בְּנֵי
descendants-of they-were these and-Zaza Peleth Jonathan and-sons-of (33)

יְרַחְמְאֵל׃ וְלֹא־ הָיָה לְשֵׁשָׁן בָּנִים כִּי אִם־ בָּנוֹת
daughters only but sons to-Sheshan he-was and-not (34) Jerahmeel

וּלְשֵׁשָׁן עֶבֶד מִצְרִי וּשְׁמוֹ יַרְחָע׃ וַיִּתֵּן
and-he-gave (35) Jarha and-name-of-him Egyptian servant and-to-Sheshan

שֵׁשָׁן אֶת־ בִּתּוֹ לְיַרְחָע עַבְדּוֹ לְאִשָּׁה וַתֵּלֶד
and-she-bore as-wife servant-of-him to-Jarha daughter-of-him *** Sheshan

לוֹ אֶת־ עַתָּי׃ וְעַתַּי הֹלִיד אֶת־ נָתָן וְנָתָן
and-Nathan Nathan *** he-fathered and-Attai (36) Attai *** to-him

הוֹלִיד אֶת־ זָבָד׃ וְזָבָד הוֹלִיד אֶת־ אֶפְלָל וְאֶפְלָל
and-Ephlal Ephlal *** he-fathered and-Zabad (37) Zabad *** he-fathered

הוֹלִיד אֶת־ עוֹבֵד׃ וְעוֹבֵד הוֹלִיד אֶת־ יֵהוּא וְיֵהוּא
and-Jehu Jehu *** he-fathered and-Obed (38) Obed *** he-fathered

הוֹלִיד אֶת־ עֲזַרְיָה׃ וַעֲזַרְיָה הֹלִיד אֶת־ חָלֶץ וְחֶלֶץ
and-Helez Helez *** he-fathered and-Azariah (39) Azariah *** he-fathered

הֹלִיד אֶת־ אֶלְעָשָׂה׃ וְאֶלְעָשָׂה הֹלִיד אֶת־ סִסְמָי וְסִסְמַי
and-Sismai Sismai *** he-fathered and-Eleasah (40) Eleasah *** he-fathered

הֹלִיד אֶת־ שַׁלּוּם׃ וְשַׁלּוּם הוֹלִיד אֶת־ יְקַמְיָה
Jekamiah *** he-fathered and-Shallum (41) Shallum *** he-fathered

וִיקַמְיָה הֹלִיד אֶת־ אֱלִישָׁמָע׃ וּבְנֵי כָלֵב אֲחִי
brother-of Caleb and-sons-of (42) Elishama *** he-fathered and-Jekamiah

יְרַחְמְאֵל מֵישָׁע בְּכֹרוֹ הוּא אֲבִי־ זִיף וּבְנֵי מָרֵשָׁה
Mareshah and-sons-of Ziph father-of he firstborn-of-him Mesha Jerahmeel

אֲבִי חֶבְרוֹן׃ וּבְנֵי חֶבְרוֹן קֹרַח וְתַפֻּחַ וְרֶקֶם
and-Rekem and-Tappuah Korah Hebron and-sons-of (43) Hebron father-of

28 The sons of Onam:
Shammai and Jada.
The sons of Shammai:
Nadab and Abishur.
29 Abishur's wife was named Abihail, who bore him Ahban and Molid.
30 The sons of Nadab:
Seled and Appaim. Seled died without children.
31 The son of Appaim:
Ishi, who was the father of Sheshan.
Sheshan was the father of Ahlai.
32 The sons of Jada, Shammai's brother:
Jether and Jonathan. Jether died without children.
33 The sons of Jonathan:
Peleth and Zaza.
These were the descendants of Jerahmeel.
34 Sheshan had no sons—only daughters.
He had an Egyptian servant named Jarha.
35 Sheshan gave his daughter in marriage to his servant Jarha, and she bore him Attai.
36 Attai was the father of Nathan,
Nathan the father of Zabad,
37 Zabad the father of Ephlal,
Ephlal the father of Obed,
38 Obed the father of Jehu,
Jehu the father of Azariah,
39 Azariah the father of Helez,
Helez the father of Eleasah,
40 Eleasah the father of Sismai,
Sismai the father of Shallum,
41 Shallum the father of Jekamiah,
and Jekamiah the father of Elishama.

*The Clans of Caleb*

42 The sons of Caleb the brother of Jerahmeel:
Mesha his firstborn, who was the father of Ziph, and his son Mareshah,[d] who was the father of Hebron.
43 The sons of Hebron:
Korah, Tappuah, Rekem

[d] 42 The meaning of the Hebrew for this phrase is uncertain.

וָשָׁמַע׃ (44) וְשֶׁמַע הוֹלִיד אֶת־רַחַם אֲבִי יָרְקְעָם וְרֶקֶם
and-Rekem Jorkeam father-of Raham *** he-fathered and-Shema (44) and-Shema

הוֹלִיד אֶת־שַׁמָּי׃ (45) וּבֶן־שַׁמַּי מָעוֹן וּמָעוֹן אֲבִי
father-of and-Maon Maon Shammai and-son-of (45) Shammai *** he-fathered

בֵית־צוּר׃ (46) וְעֵיפָה פִּילֶגֶשׁ כָּלֵב יָלְדָה אֶת־חָרָן וְאֶת־מוֹצָא
Moza and Haran *** she-bore Caleb concubine-of and-Ephah (46) Zur Beth

וְאֶת־גָּזֵז וְחָרָן הֹלִיד אֶת־גָּזֵז׃ (47) וּבְנֵי יָהְדָּי
Jahdai and-sons-of (47) Gazez *** he-fathered and-Haran Gazez and

רֶגֶם וְיוֹתָם וְגֵישָׁן וָפֶלֶט וְעֵיפָה וָשָׁעַף׃
and-Shaaph and-Ephah and-Pelet and-Geshan and-Jotham Regem

(48) פִּלֶגֶשׁ כָּלֵב מַעֲכָה יָלַד שֶׁבֶר וְאֶת־תִּרְחֲנָה׃
Tirhanah and Sheber he-bore Maacah Caleb concubine-of (48)

(49) וַתֵּלֶד שַׁעַף אֲבִי מַדְמַנָּה אֶת־שְׁוָא אֲבִי מַכְבֵּנָה
Macbenah father-of Sheva *** Madmannah father-of Shaaph and-she-bore (49)

וַאֲבִי גִבְעָא וּבַת־כָּלֵב עַכְסָה׃ (50) אֵלֶּה הָיוּ
they-were these (50) Acsah Caleb and-daughter-of Gibea and-father-of

בְּנֵי כָלֵב בֶּן־חוּר בְּכוֹר אֶפְרָתָה שׁוֹבָל אֲבִי
father-of Shobal Ephrathah firstborn-of Hur son-of Caleb descendants-of

קִרְיַת יְעָרִים׃ (51) שַׂלְמָא אֲבִי בֵית־לָחֶם חָרֵף אֲבִי בֵית־גָּדֵר׃
Gader Beth father-of Hareph Lehem Beth father-of Salma (51) Jearim Kiriath

(52) וַיִּהְיוּ בָנִים לְשׁוֹבָל אֲבִי קִרְיַת יְעָרִים הָרֹאֶה
Haroeh Jearim Kiriath father-of of-Shobal descendants and-they-were (52)

חֲצִי הַמְּנֻחוֹת׃ (53) וּמִשְׁפְּחוֹת קִרְיַת יְעָרִים הַיִּתְרִי
the-Ithrite Jearim Kiriath and-clans-of (53) the-Manahathites half-of

וְהַפּוּתִי וְהַשֻּׁמָתִי וְהַמִּשְׁרָעִי מֵאֵלֶּה
from-these and-the-Mishraite and-the-Shumathite and-the-Puthite

יָצְאוּ הַצָּרְעָתִי וְהָאֶשְׁתָּאֻלִי׃ (54) בְּנֵי שַׂלְמָא
Salma descendants-of (54) and-the-Eshtaolite the-Zorathite they-descended

בֵּית לֶחֶם וּנְטוֹפָתִי עַטְרוֹת בֵּית יוֹאָב וַחֲצִי הַמָּנַחְתִּי
the-Manahathite and-half-of Joab Beth Atroth and-Netophathite Lehem Beth

הַצָּרְעִי׃ (55) וּמִשְׁפְּחוֹת סֹפְרִים °יֹשְׁבֵו יַעְבֵּץ
Jabez ones-living-of ones-being-scribes and-clans-of (55) the-Zorite

תִּרְעָתִים שִׁמְעָתִים שׂוּכָתִים הֵמָּה הַקִּינִים הַבָּאִים
the-ones-coming the-Kenites these Sucathites Shimeathites Tirathites

מֵחַמַּת אֲבִי בֵית־רֵכָב׃ (3:1) וְאֵלֶּה הָיוּ בְּנֵי
sons-of they-were and-these (3:1) Recab house-of father-of from-Hammath

דָּוִיד* אֲשֶׁר נוֹלַד־לוֹ בְּחֶבְרוֹן הַבְּכוֹר ׀ אַמְנֹן לַאֲחִינֹעַם
of-Ahinoam Amnon the-firstborn in-Hebron to-him he-was-born who David

and Shema. 44 Shema was
the father of Raham, and
Raham the father of Jorkeam. Rekem was the father of Shammai. 45 The
son of Shammai was
Maon, and Maon was the
father of Beth Zur.
46 Caleb's concubine Ephah
was the mother of Haran,
Moza and Gazez. Haran
was the father of Gazez.
47 The sons of Jahdai:
Regem, Jotham, Geshan,
Pelet, Ephah and Shaaph.
48 Caleb's concubine Maacah
was the mother of Sheber
and Tirhanah. 49 She also
gave birth to Shaaph the
father of Madmannah
and to Sheva the father of
Macbenah and Gibea.
Caleb's daughter was Acsah.

50 These were the descendants of Caleb:
The sons of Hur the
firstborn of Ephrathah:
Shobal the father of
Kiriath Jearim, 51 Salma
the father of Bethlehem,
and Hareph the father of
Beth Gader.
52 The descendants of Shobal
the father of Kiriath Jearim were:
Haroeh, half the Manahathites, 53 and the clans
of Kiriath Jearim: the Ithrites, Puthites, Shumathites and Mishraites.
From these descended
the Zorathites and Eshtaolites.
54 The descendants of Salma:
Bethlehem, the Netophathites, Atroth Beth Joab,
half the Manahathites,
the Zorites, 55 and the
clans of scribes[e] who
lived at Jabez: the Tirathites, Shimeathites and
Sucathites. These are the
Kenites who came from
Hammath, the father of
the house of Recab.[f]

*The Sons of David*

3 These were the sons of
David born to him in Hebron:
The firstborn was Amnon the son of Ahinoam
of Jezreel;

e55 Or *of the Sopherites*
f55 Or *father of Beth Recab*

*1 Most mss have the *hireq* under and the *zaqeph* over the *vav* (דָּוִיד).

°55 ק ישבי

הַיִּזְרְעֵאלִית שֵׁנִי דָּנִיֵּאל לַאֲבִיגַיִל הַכַּרְמְלִית׃ (2) הַשְּׁלִשִׁי
the-third (2) the-Carmelite of-Abigail Daniel second the-Jezreelite

לְאַבְשָׁלוֹם בֶּן־מַעֲכָה בַּת־תַּלְמַי מֶלֶךְ גְּשׁוּר הָרְבִיעִי
the-fourth Geshur king-of Talmai daughter-of Maacah son-of of-Absalom

אֲדֹנִיָּה בֶן־חַגִּית׃ (3) הַחֲמִישִׁי שְׁפַטְיָה לַאֲבִיטָל הַשִּׁשִּׁי
the-sixth of-Abital Shephatiah the-fifth (3) Haggith son-of Adonijah

יִתְרְעָם לְעֶגְלָה אִשְׁתּוֹ׃ (4) שִׁשָּׁה נוֹלַד־לוֹ בְחֶבְרוֹן
in-Hebron to-him he-was-born six (4) wife-of-him of-Eglah Ithream

וַיִּמְלָךְ־שָׁם שֶׁבַע שָׁנִים וְשִׁשָּׁה חֳדָשִׁים וּשְׁלֹשִׁים וְשָׁלוֹשׁ שָׁנָה
year and-three and-thirty months and-six years seven there and-he-reigned

מָלַךְ בִּירוּשָׁלָםִ׃ (5) וְאֵלֶּה נוּלְּדוּ־לוֹ בִּירוּשָׁלָיִם
in-Jerusalem to-him they-were-born and-these (5) in-Jerusalem he-reigned

שִׁמְעָא וְשׁוֹבָב וְנָתָן וּשְׁלֹמֹה אַרְבָּעָה לְבַת־שׁוּעַ בַּת־
daughter-of Shua by-Bath four and-Solomon and-Nathan and-Shobab Shimea

עַמִּיאֵל׃ (6) וְיִבְחָר וֶאֱלִישָׁמָע וֶאֱלִיפָלֶט׃ (7) וְנֹגַהּ וְנֶפֶג
and-Nepheg and-Nogah (7) and-Eliphelet and-Elishama and-Ibhar (6) Ammiel

וְיָפִיעַ׃ (8) וֶאֱלִישָׁמָע וְאֶלְיָדָע וֶאֱלִיפֶלֶט תִּשְׁעָה׃ (9) כֹּל
all (9) nine and-Eliphelet and-Eliada and-Elishama (8) and-Japhia

בְּנֵי דָוִיד מִלְּבַד בְּנֵי־פִילַגְשִׁים וְתָמָר אֲחוֹתָם׃
sister-of-them and-Tamar concubines sons-of besides David sons-of

(10) וּבֶן־שְׁלֹמֹה רְחַבְעָם אֲבִיָּה בְנוֹ אָסָא בְנוֹ
son-of-him Asa son-of-him Abijah Rehoboam Solomon and-son-of (10)

יְהוֹשָׁפָט בְּנוֹ׃ (11) יוֹרָם בְּנוֹ אֲחַזְיָהוּ בְנוֹ יוֹאָשׁ
Joash son-of-him Ahaziah son-of-him Joram (11) son-of-him Jehoshaphat

בְּנוֹ׃ (12) אֲמַצְיָהוּ בְנוֹ עֲזַרְיָה בְנוֹ יוֹתָם בְּנוֹ׃
son-of-him Jotham son-of-him Azariah son-of-him Amaziah (12) son-of-him

(13) אָחָז בְּנוֹ חִזְקִיָּהוּ בְנוֹ מְנַשֶּׁה בְנוֹ׃ (14) אָמוֹן
Amon (14) son-of-him Manasseh son-of-him Hezekiah son-of-him Ahaz (13)

בְּנוֹ יֹאשִׁיָּהוּ בְנוֹ׃ (15) וּבְנֵי יֹאשִׁיָּהוּ הַבְּכוֹר יוֹחָנָן
Johanan the-firstborn Josiah and-sons-of (15) son-of-him Josiah son-of-him

הַשֵּׁנִי יְהוֹיָקִים הַשְּׁלִשִׁי צִדְקִיָּהוּ הָרְבִיעִי שַׁלּוּם׃
Shallum the-fourth Zedekiah the-third Jehoiakim the-second

(16) וּבְנֵי יְהוֹיָקִים יְכָנְיָה בְנוֹ צִדְקִיָּה בְנוֹ׃
son-of-him Zedekiah son-of-him Jeconiah Jehoiakim and-successors-of (16)

(17) וּבְנֵי יְכָנְיָה אַסִּר שְׁאַלְתִּיאֵל בְּנוֹ׃
son-of-him Shealtiel captive Jeconiah and-descendants-of (17)

(18) וּמַלְכִּירָם וּפְדָיָה וְשֶׁנְאַצַּר יְקַמְיָה הוֹשָׁמָע וּנְדַבְיָה׃
and-Nedabiah Hoshama Jekamiah and-Shenazzar and-Pedaiah and-Malkiram (18)

the second, Daniel the son of Abigail of Carmel;
2 the third, Absalom the son of Maacah daughter of Talmai king of Geshur;
the fourth, Adonijah the son of Haggith;
3 the fifth, Shephatiah the son of Abital;
and the sixth, Ithream, by his wife Eglah.
4 These six were born to David in Hebron, where he reigned seven years and six months.
David reigned in Jerusalem thirty-three years,
5 and these were the children born to him there:
Shammua,[g] Shobab, Nathan and Solomon. These four were by Bathsheba[h] daughter of Ammiel.
6 There were also Ibhar, Elishua,[i] Eliphelet,
7 Nogah, Nepheg, Japhia,
8 Elishama, Eliada and Eliphelet—nine in all.
9 All these were the sons of David, besides his sons by his concubines. And Tamar was their sister.

*The Kings of Judah*

10 Solomon's son was Rehoboam,
Abijah his son,
Asa his son,
Jehoshaphat his son,
11 Jehoram[j] his son,
Ahaziah his son,
Joash his son,
12 Amaziah his son,
Azariah his son,
Jotham his son,
13 Ahaz his son,
Hezekiah his son,
Manasseh his son,
14 Amon his son,
Josiah his son.
15 The sons of Josiah:
Johanan the firstborn,
Jehoiakim the second son,
Zedekiah the third,
Shallum the fourth.
16 The successors of Jehoiakim:
Jehoiachin[k] his son,
and Zedekiah.

*The Royal Line After the Exile*

17 The descendants of Jehoiachin the captive:
Shealtiel his son,
18 Malkiram, Pedaiah, Shenazzar, Jekamiah, Hoshama

[g] 5 Hebrew *Shimea*, a variant of *Shammua*
[h] 5 One Hebrew manuscript, Septuagint and Vulgate (see also 2 Samuel 11:3 and elsewhere); most Hebrew manuscripts *Bathshua*
[i] 6 Two Hebrew manuscripts and some Septuagint manuscripts (see also 2 Samuel 5:15 and 1 Chron. 14:5); most Hebrew manuscripts *Elishama*
[j] 11 Hebrew *Joram*, a variant of *Jehoram*
[k] 16 Hebrew *Jeconiah*, a variant of *Jehoiachin*; also in verse 17

וּבְנֵי פְדָיָה זְרֻבָּבֶל וְשִׁמְעִי וּבֶן־ זְרֻבָּבֶל
Zerubbabel and-son-of and-Shimei Zerubbabel Pedaiah and-sons-of (19)

מְשֻׁלָּם וַחֲנַנְיָה וּשְׁלֹמִית אֲחוֹתָם׃ וַחֲשֻׁבָה
and-Hashubah (20) sister-of-them and-Shelomith and-Hananiah Meshullam

וָאֹהֶל וּבֶרֶכְיָה וַחֲסַדְיָה יוּשַׁב חֶסֶד חָמֵשׁ׃ וּבֶן־
and-descendant-of (21) five Hesed Jushab and-Hasadiah and-Berekiah and-Ohel

חֲנַנְיָה פְּלַטְיָה וִישַׁעְיָה בְּנֵי רְפָיָה בְּנֵי אַרְנָן בְּנֵי
sons-of Arnan sons-of Rephaiah sons-of and-Jeshaiah Pelatiah Hananiah

עֹבַדְיָה בְּנֵי שְׁכַנְיָה׃ וּבְנֵי שְׁכַנְיָה שְׁמַעְיָה
Shemaiah Shecaniah and-descendants-of (22) Shecaniah sons-of Obadiah

וּבְנֵי שְׁמַעְיָה חַטּוּשׁ וְיִגְאָל וּבָרִיחַ וּנְעַרְיָה וְשָׁפָט
and-Shaphat and-Neariah and-Bariah and-Igal Hattush Shemaiah and-sons-of

שִׁשָּׁה׃ וּבֶן־ נְעַרְיָה אֶלְיוֹעֵינַי וְחִזְקִיָּה וְעַזְרִיקָם שְׁלֹשָׁה׃
three and-Azrikam and-Hizkiah Elioenai Neariah and-son-of (23) six

וּבְנֵי אֶלְיוֹעֵינַי הֹדַיְוָהוּ וְאֶלְיָשִׁיב וּפְלָיָה וְעַקּוּב
and-Akkub and-Pelaiah and-Eliashib Hodaviah Elioenai and-sons-of (24)

וְיוֹחָנָן וּדְלָיָה וַעֲנָנִי שִׁבְעָה׃ בְּנֵי יְהוּדָה
Judah descendants-of (4:1) seven and-Anani and-Delaiah and-Johanan

פֶּרֶץ חֶצְרוֹן וְכַרְמִי וְחוּר וְשׁוֹבָל׃ וּרְאָיָה בֶן־ שׁוֹבָל
Shobal son-of and-Reaiah (2) and-Shobal and-Hur and-Carmi Hezron Perez

הוֹלִיד אֶת־ יַחַת וְיַחַת הוֹלִיד אֶת־ אֲחוּמַי וְאֶת־ לָהַד אֵלֶּה
these Lahad and Ahumai *** he-fathered and-Jahath Jahath *** he-fathered

מִשְׁפְּחוֹת הַצָּרְעָתִי׃ וְאֵלֶּה אֲבִי עֵיטָם יִזְרְעֶאל וְיִשְׁמָא
and-Ishma Jezreel Etam father-of and-these (3) the-Zorathite clans-of

וְיִדְבָּשׁ וְשֵׁם אֲחוֹתָם הַצְלֶלְפּוֹנִי׃ וּפְנוּאֵל אֲבִי
father-of and-Penuel (4) Hazzelelponi sister-of-them and-name-of and-Idbash

גְדֹר וְעֵזֶר אֲבִי חוּשָׁה אֵלֶּה בְנֵי־ חוּר בְּכוֹר
firstborn-of Hur descendants-of these Hushah father-of and-Ezer Gedor

אֶפְרָתָה אֲבִי בֵּית לָחֶם׃ וּלְאַשְׁחוּר אֲבִי תְקוֹעַ הָיוּ
they-were Tekoa father-of and-to-Ashhur (5) Lehem Beth father-of Ephrathah

שְׁתֵּי נָשִׁים חֶלְאָה וְנַעֲרָה׃ וַתֵּלֶד לוֹ נַעֲרָה אֶת־ אֲחֻזָּם
Ahuzzam *** Naarah to-him and-she-bore (6) and-Naarah Helah wives two-of

וְאֶת־ חֵפֶר וְאֶת־ תֵּימְנִי וְאֶת־ הָאֲחַשְׁתָּרִי אֵלֶּה בְּנֵי נַעֲרָה׃
Naarah descendants-of these Haahashtari and Temeni and Hepher and

וּבְנֵי חֶלְאָה צֶרֶת יִצְחָר וְאֶתְנָן׃ וְקוֹץ הוֹלִיד
he-fathered and-Koz (8) and-Ethnan and-Zohar Zereth Helah and-sons-of (7)

אֶת־ עָנוּב וְאֶת־ הַצֹּבֵבָה וּמִשְׁפְּחוֹת אֲחַרְחֵל בֶּן־ הָרוּם׃
Harum son-of Aharhel and-clans-of Hazzobebah and Anub ***

and Nedabiah.
19 The sons of Pedaiah:
Zerubbabel and Shimei.
The sons of Zerubbabel:
Meshullam and Hananiah.
Shelomith was their sister.
20 There were also five others:
Hashubah, Ohel, Berekiah, Hasadiah and Jushab-Hesed.
21 The descendants of Hananiah:
Pelatiah and Jeshaiah, and the sons of Rephaiah, of Arnan, of Obadiah and of Shecaniah.
22 The descendants of Shecaniah:
Shemaiah and his sons: Hattush, Igal, Bariah, Neariah and Shaphat—six in all.
23 The sons of Neariah:
Elioenai, Hizkiah and Azrikam—three in all.
24 The sons of Elioenai:
Hodaviah, Eliashib, Pelaiah, Akkub, Johanan, Delaiah and Anani—seven in all.

*Other Clans of Judah*

4 The descendants of Judah:
Perez, Hezron, Carmi, Hur and Shobal.
2 Reaiah son of Shobal was the father of Jahath, and Jahath the father of Ahumai and Lahad. These were the clans of the Zorathites.
3 These were the sons[l] of Etam:
Jezreel, Ishma and Idbash. Their sister was named Hazzelelponi.
4 Penuel was the father of Gedor, and Ezer the father of Hushah.
These were the descendants of Hur, the firstborn of Ephrathah and father[m] of Bethlehem.
5 Ashhur the father of Tekoa had two wives, Helah and Naarah.
6 Naarah bore him Ahuzzam, Hepher, Temeni and Haahashtari. These were the descendants of Naarah.
7 The sons of Helah:
Zereth, Zohar, Ethnan,
8 and Koz, who was the father of Anub and Hazzobebah and of the clans of Aharhel son of Harum.

l3 Some Septuagint manuscripts (see also Vulgate); Hebrew *father*
m4 *Father* may mean *civic leader* or *military leader;* also in verses 12, 14, 17, 18 and possibly elsewhere.

°7 ק וצחר °24 ק הודויהו

וַיְהִי יַעְבֵּץ נִכְבָּד מֵאֶחָיו
more-than-brothers-of-him being-honorable Jabez and-he-was (9)

וְאִמּוֹ קָרְאָה שְׁמוֹ יַעְבֵּץ לֵאמֹר כִּי יָלַדְתִּי
I-gave-birth because to-say Jabez name-of-him she-called and-mother-of-him

בְּעֹצֶב׃ וַיִּקְרָא יַעְבֵּץ לֵאלֹהֵי יִשְׂרָאֵל לֵאמֹר אִם־ בָּרֵךְ
to-bless if to-say Israel to-God-of Jabez and-he-cried-out (10) in-pain

תְּבָרְכֵנִי וְהִרְבִּיתָ אֶת־ גְּבוּלִי וְהָיְתָה
now-let-her-be territory-of-me *** and-you-would-enlarge you-would-bless-me

יָדְךָ עִמִּי וְעָשִׂיתָ מֵּרָעָה* לְבִלְתִּי עָצְבִּי
to-have-pain-me not from-harm and-you-keep with-me hand-of-you

וַיָּבֵא אֱלֹהִים אֵת אֲשֶׁר־ שָׁאָל׃ וּכְלוּב אֲחִי־ שׁוּחָה
Shuhah brother-of and-Kelub (11) he-requested what *** God and-he-granted

הוֹלִיד אֶת־ מְחִיר הוּא אֲבִי אֶשְׁתּוֹן׃ וְאֶשְׁתּוֹן הוֹלִיד אֶת־
*** he-fathered and-Eshton (12) Eshton father-of he Mehir *** he-fathered

בֵּית רָפָא וְאֶת־ פָּסֵחַ וְאֶת־ תְּחִנָּה אֲבִי עִיר נָחָשׁ אֵלֶּה אַנְשֵׁי רֵכָה׃
Recah men-of these Nahash Ir father-of Tehinnah and Paseah and Rapha Beth

וּבְנֵי קְנַז עָתְנִיאֵל וּשְׂרָיָה וּבְנֵי עָתְנִיאֵל חֲתַת׃
Hathath Othniel and-sons-of and-Seraiah Othniel Kenaz and-sons-of (13)

וּמְעוֹנֹתַי הוֹלִיד אֶת־ עָפְרָה וּשְׂרָיָה הוֹלִיד אֶת־
*** he-fathered and-Seraiah Ophrah *** he-fathered and-Meonothai (14)

יוֹאָב אֲבִי גֵּיא חֲרָשִׁים כִּי חֲרָשִׁים הָיוּ׃ וּבְנֵי
and-sons-of (15) they-were craftsmen because Harashim Ge father-of Joab

כָּלֵב בֶּן־ יְפֻנֶּה עִירוּ אֵלָה וָנָעַם וּבְנֵי אֵלָה וּקְנַז׃
and-Kenaz Elah and-sons-of and-Naam Elah Iru Jephunneh son-of Caleb

וּבְנֵי יְהַלֶּלְאֵל זִיף וְזִיפָה תִּירְיָא וַאֲשַׂרְאֵל׃
and-Asarel Tiria and-Ziphah Ziph Jehallelel and-sons-of (16)

וּבֶן־ עֶזְרָה יֶתֶר וּמֶרֶד וְעֵפֶר וְיָלוֹן וַתַּהַר
and-she-bore and-Jalon and-Epher and-Mered Jether Ezrah and-son-of (17)

אֶת־ מִרְיָם וְאֶת־ שַׁמַּי וְאֶת־ יִשְׁבָּח אֲבִי אֶשְׁתְּמֹעַ׃
Eshtemoa father-of Ishbah and Shammai and Miriam ***

וְאִשְׁתּוֹ הַיְהֻדִיָּה יָלְדָה אֶת־ יֶרֶד אֲבִי גְדוֹר וְאֶת־
and Gedor father-of Jered *** she-bore the-Judean and-wife-of-him (18)

חֶבֶר אֲבִי שׂוֹכוֹ וְאֶת־ יְקוּתִיאֵל אֲבִי זָנוֹחַ וְאֵלֶּה בְּנֵי
children-of and-these Zanoah father-of Jekuthiel and Soco father-of Heber

בִּתְיָה בַת־ פַּרְעֹה אֲשֶׁר לָקַח מָרֶד׃ וּבְנֵי
and-sons-of (19) Mered he-married whom Pharaoh daughter-of Bithiah

אֵשֶׁת הוֹדִיָּה אֲחוֹת נַחַם אֲבִי קְעִילָה הַגַּרְמִי וְאֶשְׁתְּמֹעַ
and-Eshtemoa the-Garmite Keilah father-of Naham sister-of Hodiah wife-of

9 Jabez was more honorable
than his brothers. His mother
had named him Jabez,[n] saying, "I gave birth to him in
pain." 10 Jabez cried out to
the God of Israel, "Oh,
that you would bless me and
enlarge my territory! Let your
hand be with me, and keep me
from harm so that I will be free
from pain." And God granted
his request.

11 Kelub, Shuhah's brother,
was the father of Mehir,
who was the father of
Eshton. 12 Eshton was the
father of Beth Rapha, Pa-
seah and Tehinnah the
father of Ir Nahash.[o]
These were the men of
Recah.

13 The sons of Kenaz:
Othniel and Seraiah.
The sons of Othniel:
Hathath and Meono-
thai.[p] 14 Meonothai was
the father of Ophrah.
Seraiah was the father of
Joab,
the father of Ge Hara-
shim.[q] It was called this
because its people were
craftsmen.
15 The sons of Caleb son of Jephunneh:
Iru, Elah and Naam.
The son of Elah:
Kenaz.
16 The sons of Jehallelel:
Ziph, Ziphah, Tiria and
Asarel.
17 The sons of Ezrah:
Jether, Mered, Epher and
Jalon. One of Mered's
wives gave birth to Mir-
iam, Shammai and Ish-
bah the father of Esh-
temoa. 18 (His Judean wife
gave birth to Jered the father of Gedor, Heber the
father of Soco, and Jeku-
thiel the father of Za-
noah.) These were the
children of Pharaoh's
daughter Bithiah, whom
Mered had married.
19 The sons of Hodiah's wife,
the sister of Naham:
the father of Keilah the
Garmite, and Eshtemoa
the Maacathite.

[n] 9 *Jabez* sounds like the Hebrew for *pain.*
[o] 12 Or *of the city of Nahash*
[p] 13 Some Septuagint manuscripts and Vulgate; Hebrew does not have *and Meonothai.*
[q] 14 *Ge Harashim* means *valley of craftsmen.*

*10 Most mss have no *dagesh* in the *mem* ( מֵ ).

הַמַּעֲכָתִי׃ וּבְנֵי שִׁימוֹן אַמְנוֹן וְרִנָּה בֶּן־חָנָן וְתוּלוֹן
the-Maacathite (20) and-sons-of Shimon Amnon and-Rinnah Ben Hanan and-Tilon

וּבְנֵי יִשְׁעִי זוֹחֵת וּבֶן־זוֹחֵת׃ בְּנֵי שֵׁלָה בֶן־
and-descendants-of Ishi Zoheth and-Ben Zoheth (21) sons-of Shelah son-of

יְהוּדָה עֵר אֲבִי לֵכָה וְלַעְדָּה אֲבִי מָרֵשָׁה וּמִשְׁפְּחוֹת
Judah Er father-of Lecah and-Laadah father-of Mareshah and-clans-of

בֵּית־עֲבֹדַת הַבֻּץ לְבֵית אַשְׁבֵּעַ׃ וְיוֹקִים וְאַנְשֵׁי
house-of worker-of the-linen at-Beth Ashbea (22) and-Jokim and-men-of

כֹזֵבָא וְיוֹאָשׁ וְשָׂרָף אֲשֶׁר־בָּעֲלוּ לְמוֹאָב וְיָשֻׁבִי לָחֶם
Cozeba and-Joash and-Saraph who they-ruled in-Moab and-Jashubi Lehem

וְהַדְּבָרִים עַתִּיקִים׃ הֵמָּה הַיּוֹצְרִים וְיֹשְׁבֵי נְטָעִים
and-the-records ancient-ones (23) they the-potters and-ones-living-of Netaim

וּגְדֵרָה עִם־הַמֶּלֶךְ בִּמְלַאכְתּוֹ יָשְׁבוּ שָׁם׃ בְּנֵי
and-Gederah with the-king in-work-of-him they-stayed there (24) descendants-of

שִׁמְעוֹן נְמוּאֵל וְיָמִין יָרִיב זֶרַח שָׁאוּל׃ שַׁלֻּם בְּנוֹ מִבְשָׂם
Simeon Nemuel and-Jamin Jarib Zerah Shaul (25) Shallum son-of-him Mibsam

בְּנוֹ מִשְׁמָע בְּנוֹ׃ וּבְנֵי מִשְׁמָע חַמּוּאֵל
son-of-him Mishma son-of-him (26) and-descendants-of Mishma Hammuel

בְּנוֹ זַכּוּר בְּנוֹ שִׁמְעִי בְּנוֹ׃ וּלְשִׁמְעִי בָּנִים
son-of-him Zaccur son-of-him Shimei son-of-him (27) and-to-Shimei sons

שִׁשָּׁה עָשָׂר וּבָנוֹת שֵׁשׁ וּלְאֶחָיו אֵין בָּנִים רַבִּים
six ten and-daughters six but-to-brothers-of-him not children many

וְכֹל מִשְׁפַּחְתָּם לֹא הִרְבּוּ עַד־בְּנֵי יְהוּדָה׃
so-entire-of clan-of-them not they-became-numerous as people-of Judah

וַיֵּשְׁבוּ בִּבְאֵר־שֶׁבַע וּמוֹלָדָה וַחֲצַר שׁוּעָל׃
(28) and-they-lived in-Beer Sheba and-Moladah and-Hazar Shual

וּבְבִלְהָה וּבְעֶצֶם וּבְתוֹלָד׃ וּבִבְתוּאֵל וּבְחָרְמָה
(29) and-in-Bilhah and-in-Ezem and-in-Tolad (30) and-in-Bethuel and-in-Hormah

וּבְצִיקְלָג׃ וּבְבֵית מַרְכָּבוֹת וּבַחֲצַר סוּסִים וּבְבֵית
and-in-Ziklag (31) and-in-Beth Marcaboth and-in-Hazar Susim and-in-Beth

בִּרְאִי וּבְשַׁעֲרָיִם אֵלֶּה עָרֵיהֶם עַד־מְלֹךְ דָּוִיד׃
Biri and-in-Shaaraim these towns-of-them until to-reign David

וְחַצְרֵיהֶם עֵיטָם וָעַיִן רִמּוֹן וְתֹכֶן וְעָשָׁן
(32) and-villages-of-them Etam and-Ain Rimmon and-Token and-Ashan

עָרִים חָמֵשׁ׃ וְכָל־חַצְרֵיהֶם אֲשֶׁר סְבִיבוֹת הֶעָרִים
towns five (33) and-all-of villages-of-them that ones-around the-towns

הָאֵלֶּה עַד־בָּעַל זֹאת מוֹשְׁבֹתָם וְהִתְיַחְשָׂם
the-these as-far-as Baal this settlements-of-them and-to-keep-record-them

[20]The sons of Shimon:
Amnon, Rinnah, Ben-Hanan and Tilon.
The descendants of Ishi:
Zoheth and Ben-Zoheth.
[21]The sons of Shelah son of Judah:
Er the father of Lecah, Laadah the father of Mareshah and the clans of the linen workers at Beth Ashbea, [22]Jokim, the men of Cozeba, and Joash and Saraph, who ruled in Moab and Jashubi Lehem. (These records are from ancient times.) [23]They were the potters who lived at Netaim and Gederah; they stayed there and worked for the king.

*Simeon*

[24]The descendants of Simeon:
Nemuel, Jamin, Jarib, Zerah and Shaul;
[25]Shallum was Shaul's son, Mibsam his son and Mishma his son.
[26]The descendants of Mishma:
Hammuel his son, Zaccur his son and Shimei his son.

[27]Shimei had sixteen sons and six daughters, but his brothers did not have many children; so their entire clan did not become as numerous as the people of Judah. [28]They lived in Beersheba, Moladah, Hazar Shual, [29]Bilhah, Ezem, Tolad, [30]Bethuel, Hormah, Ziklag, [31]Beth Marcaboth, Hazar Susim, Beth Biri and Shaaraim. These were their towns until the reign of David. [32]Their surrounding villages were Etam, Ain, Rimmon, Token and Ashan—five towns—[33]and all the villages around these towns as far as Baalath.[r] These were their settlements. And they kept a genealogical record.

[r]33 Some Septuagint manuscripts (see also Joshua 19:8); Hebrew *Baal*

°20 ק ותילון

לָהֶֽם׃ וּמְשׁוֹבָב וְיַמְלֵךְ וְיוֹשָׁה בֶּן־אֲמַצְיָֽה׃
Amaziah son-of and-Joshah and-Jamlech and-Meshobab (34) for-them

וְיוֹאֵל וְיֵהוּא בֶּן־יוֹשִׁבְיָה בֶּן־שְׂרָיָה בֶּן־עֲשִׂיאֵֽל׃
Asiel son-of Seraiah son-of Joshibiah son-of and-Jehu and-Joel (35)

וְאֶלְיוֹעֵינַי וְיַעֲקֹבָה וִישׁוֹחָיָה וַעֲשָׂיָה וַעֲדִיאֵל
and-Adiel and-Asaiah and-Jeshohaiah and-Jaakobah also-Elioenai (36)

וִישִׂימִאֵל וּבְנָיָֽה׃ וְזִיזָא בֶּן־שִׁפְעִי בֶן־אַלּוֹן בֶּן־
son-of Allon son-of Shiphi son-of and-Ziza (37) and-Benaiah and-Jesimiel

יְדָיָה בֶּן־שִׁמְרִי בֶּן־שְׁמַעְיָֽה׃ אֵלֶּה הַבָּאִים
the-ones-being-listed these (38) Shemaiah son-of Shimri son-of Jedaiah

בְּשֵׁמוֹת נְשִׂיאִים בְּמִשְׁפְּחוֹתָם וּבֵית אֲבוֹתֵיהֶם
fathers-of-them and-family-of of-clans-of-them leaders by-names

פָּרְצוּ לָרֽוֹב׃ וַיֵּלְכוּ לִמְבוֹא גְדֹר עַד
at Gedor to-outskirt-of and-they-went (39) to-greatness they-increased

לְמִזְרַח הַגָּיְא לְבַקֵּשׁ מִרְעֶה לְצֹאנָֽם׃ וַיִּמְצְאוּ
and-they-found (40) for-flock-of-them pasture to-search the-valley to-east-of

מִרְעֶה שָׁמֵן וָטוֹב וְהָאָרֶץ רַחֲבַת יָדַיִם וְשֹׁקֶטֶת
and-being-peaceful measures spacious-of and-the-land and-good rich pasture

וּשְׁלֵוָה כִּי מִן־חָם הַיֹּשְׁבִים שָׁם לְפָנִֽים׃ וַיָּבֹאוּ
and-they-came (41) formerly there the-ones-living Ham from now and-quiet

אֵלֶּה הַכְּתוּבִים בְּשֵׁמוֹת בִּימֵי ׀ יְחִזְקִיָּהוּ מֶֽלֶךְ־יְהוּדָה
Judah king-of Hezekiah in-days-of by-names the-ones-being-listed these

וַיַּכּוּ אֶת־אָהֳלֵיהֶם וְאֶת־הַמְּעִינִים אֲשֶׁר נִמְצְאוּ־
they-were-found who the-Meunites and dwellings-of-them *** and-they-attacked

שָׁמָּה וַיַּחֲרִימֻם עַד־הַיּוֹם הַזֶּה וַיֵּשְׁבוּ
then-they-settled the-this the-day to and-they-destroyed-them at-there

תַּחְתֵּיהֶם כִּֽי־מִרְעֶה לְצֹאנָם שָֽׁם׃ וּמֵהֶם ׀
and-from-them (42) there for-flock-of-them pasture because in-place-of-them

מִן־בְּנֵי שִׁמְעוֹן הָלְכוּ לְהַר שֵׂעִיר אֲנָשִׁים חֲמֵשׁ
five-of men Seir into-hill-country-of they-invaded Simeon sons-of from

מֵאוֹת וּפְלַטְיָה וּנְעַרְיָה וּרְפָיָה וְעֻזִּיאֵל בְּנֵי יִשְׁעִי
Ishi sons-of and-Uzziel and-Rephaiah and-Neariah and-Pelatiah hundreds

בְּרֹאשָֽׁם׃ וַיַּכּוּ אֶת־שְׁאֵרִית הַפְּלֵטָה לַעֲמָלֵק
of-Amalek the-escapee remainder-of *** and-they-killed (43) at-head-of-them

וַיֵּשְׁבוּ שָׁם עַד הַיּוֹם הַזֶּֽה׃ וּבְנֵי רְאוּבֵן
Reuben and-sons-of (5:1) the-this the-day to there and-they-lived

בְּכוֹר־יִשְׂרָאֵל כִּי הוּא הַבְּכוֹר וּבְחַלְּלוֹ יְצוּעֵי
beds-of but-when-to-defile-him the-firstborn he now Israel firstborn-of

[34]Meshobab, Jamlech, Joshah son of Amaziah, [35]Joel, Jehu son of Joshibiah, the son of Seraiah, the son of Asiel, [36]also Elioenai, Jaakobah, Jeshohaiah, Asaiah, Adiel, Jesimiel, Benaiah, [37]and Ziza son of Shiphi, the son of Allon, the son of Jedaiah, the son of Shimri, the son of Shemaiah.

[38]The men listed above by name were leaders of their clans. Their families increased greatly, [39]and they went to the outskirts of Gedor to the east of the valley in search of pasture for their flocks. [40]They found rich, good pasture, and the land was spacious, peaceful and quiet. Some Hamites had lived there formerly.

[41]The men whose names were listed came in the days of Hezekiah king of Judah. They attacked the Hamites in their dwellings and also the Meunites who were there and completely destroyed[t] them, as is evident to this day. Then they settled in their place, because there was pasture for their flocks. [42]And five hundred of these Simeonites, led by Pelatiah, Neariah, Rephaiah and Uzziel, the sons of Ishi, invaded the hill country of Seir. [43]They killed the remaining Amalekites who had escaped, and they have lived there to this day.

*Reuben*

5 The sons of Reuben the firstborn of Israel (he was the firstborn, but when he defiled his father's marriage

[t]*41* The Hebrew term refers to the irrevocable giving over of things or persons to the LORD, often by totally destroying them.

°*41* ק המעונים

אָבִיו נִתְּנָה בְּכֹרָתוֹ לִבְנֵי יוֹסֵף בֶּן־
son-of Joseph to-sons-of firstborn-right-of-him she-was-given father-of-him

יִשְׂרָאֵל וְלֹא לְהִתְיַחֵשׂ לַבְּכֹרָה׃ (2) כִּי יְהוּדָה
Judah though (2) according-to-the-birthright to-be-listed so-not Israel

גָּבַר בְּאֶחָיו וּלְנָגִיד מִמֶּנּוּ
from-him and-though-ruler among-brothers-of-him he-was-strong

וְהַבְּכֹרָה לְיוֹסֵף׃ (3) בְּנֵי רְאוּבֵן בְּכוֹר יִשְׂרָאֵל
Israel firstborn-of Reuben sons-of (3) to-Joseph but-the-firstborn-right

חֲנוֹךְ וּפַלּוּא חֶצְרוֹן וְכַרְמִי׃ (4) בְּנֵי יוֹאֵל שְׁמַעְיָה
Shemaiah Joel descendants-of (4) and-Carmi Hezron and-Pallu Hanoch

בְנוֹ גּוֹג בְּנוֹ שִׁמְעִי בְנוֹ׃ (5) מִיכָה בְנוֹ רְאָיָה
Reaiah son-of-him Micah (5) son-of-him Shimei son-of-him Gog son-of-him

בְנוֹ בַּעַל בְּנוֹ׃ (6) בְּאֵרָה בְנוֹ אֲשֶׁר הֶגְלָה תִּלְּגַת
Tiglath he-exiled whom son-of-him Beerah (6) son-of-him Baal son-of-him

פִּלְנְאֶסֶר מֶלֶךְ אַשֻּׁר הוּא נָשִׂיא לָראוּבֵנִי׃ (7) וְאֶחָיו
and-relatives-of-him (7) of-the-Reubenite leader he Assyria king-of Pileser

לְמִשְׁפְּחֹתָיו בְּהִתְיַחֵשׂ לְתֹלְדוֹתָם הָרֹאשׁ יְעִיאֵל
Jeiel the-chief by-records-of-them when-to-be-listed by-clans-of-him

וּזְכַרְיָהוּ׃ (8) וּבֶלַע בֶּן־ עָזָז בֶּן־ שֶׁמַע בֶּן־ יוֹאֵל הוּא
he Joel son-of Shema son-of Azaz son-of and-Bela (8) and-Zechariah

יוֹשֵׁב בַּעֲרֹעֵר וְעַד־ נְבוֹ וּבַעַל מְעוֹן׃ (9) וְלַמִּזְרָח
and-to-the-east (9) Meon and-Baal Nebo and-to in-Aroer one-settling

יָשַׁב עַד־ לְבוֹא מִדְבָּרָה לְמִן־ הַנָּהָר פְּרָת כִּי
because Euphrates the-River to-from into-desert to-enter to he-occupied

מִקְנֵיהֶם רָבוּ בְּאֶרֶץ גִּלְעָד׃ (10) וּבִימֵי שָׁאוּל
Saul and-in-days-of (10) Gilead in-land-of they-increased livestocks-of-them

עָשׂוּ מִלְחָמָה עִם־ הַהַגְרִאִים וַיִּפְּלוּ בְּיָדָם
at-hand-of-them and-they-were-defeated the-Hagrites against war they-waged

וַיֵּשְׁבוּ בְּאָהֳלֵיהֶם עַל־ כָּל־ פְּנֵי מִזְרָח
east regions-of entire-of through in-dwellings-of-them and-they-occupied

לַגִּלְעָד׃ (11) וּבְנֵי־ גָד לְנֶגְדָּם יָשְׁבוּ בְּאֶרֶץ
in-land-of they-lived at-next-to-them Gad and-sons-of (11) of-the-Gilead

הַבָּשָׁן עַד־ סַלְכָה׃ (12) יוֹאֵל הָרֹאשׁ וְשָׁפָם הַמִּשְׁנֶה
the-second and-Shapham the-chief Joel (12) Salecah as-far-as the-Bashan

וְיַעְנַי וְשָׁפָט בַּבָּשָׁן׃ (13) וַאֲחֵיהֶם לְבֵית
by-family-of and-relatives-of-them (13) in-the-Bashan and-Shaphat then-Janai

אֲבוֹתֵיהֶם מִיכָאֵל וּמְשֻׁלָּם וְשֶׁבַע וְיוֹרַי וְיַעְכָּן וְזִיעַ
and-Zia and-Jacan and-Jorai and-Sheba and-Meshullam Michael fathers-of-them

bed, his rights as firstborn
were given to the sons of Joseph son of Israel; so he could
not be listed in the genealogical record in accordance with
his birthright, [2]and though
Judah was the strongest of his
brothers and a ruler came from
him, the rights of the firstborn
belonged to Joseph)– [3]the
sons of Reuben the firstborn
of Israel:
Hanoch, Pallu, Hezron and
Carmi.
[4]The descendants of Joel:
Shemaiah his son, Gog
his son,
Shimei his son, [5]Micah
his son,
Reaiah his son, Baal his
son,
[6]and Beerah his son,
whom Tiglath-Pileser[u]
king of Assyria took into
exile. Beerah was a leader
of the Reubenites.
[7]Their relatives by clans,
listed according to their
genealogical records:
Jeiel the chief, Zechariah,
[8]and Bela son of Azaz, the
son of Shema, the son of
Joel. They settled in the
area from Aroer to Nebo
and Baal Meon. [9]To the
east they occupied the
land up to the edge of the
desert that extends to the
Euphrates River, because
their livestock had in-
creased in Gilead.
[10]During Saul's reign
they waged war against
the Hagrites, who were defeated at their hands; they
occupied the dwellings of
the Hagrites throughout
the entire region east of
Gilead.

*Gad*

[11]The Gadites lived next to
them in Bashan, as far as
Salecah:
[12]Joel was the chief, Sha-
pham the second, then
Janai and Shaphat, in Ba-
shan.
[13]Their relatives, by families,
were:
Michael, Meshullam,
Sheba, Jorai, Jacan, Zia

[u]6 Hebrew *Tilgath-Pilneser*, a variant of *Tiglath-Pileser*; also in verse 26

וָעֵבֶר שִׁבְעָה׃ אֵלֶּה ׀ בְּנֵי אֲבִיחַיִל בֶּן־ חוּרִי בֶּן־ יָרוֹחַ בֶּן־
son-of Jaroah son-of Huri son-of Abihail sons-of these (14) seven and-Eber

גִּלְעָד בֶּן־ מִיכָאֵל בֶּן־ יְשִׁישַׁי בֶּן־ יַחְדּוֹ בֶּן־ בּוּז׃ אֲחִי
Ahi (15) Buz son-of Jahdo son-of Jeshishai son-of Michael son-of Gilead

בֶּן־עַבְדִּיאֵל בֶּן־ גּוּנִי רֹאשׁ לְבֵית אֲבוֹתָם׃ וַיֵּשְׁבוּ
and-they-lived (16) fathers-of-them of-family-of head Guni son-of Abdiel son-of

בַּגִּלְעָד בַּבָּשָׁן וּבִבְנֹתֶיהָ וּבְכָל־ מִגְרְשֵׁי
pastures-of and-on-all-of and-in-villages-of-her in-the-Bashan in-the-Gilead

שָׁרוֹן עַל־ תּוֹצְאוֹתָם׃ כֻּלָּם הִתְיַחְשׂוּ
they-were-recorded all-of-them (17) extensions-of-them as-far-as Sharon

בִּימֵי יוֹתָם מֶלֶךְ־ יְהוּדָה וּבִימֵי יָרָבְעָם מֶלֶךְ־יִשְׂרָאֵל׃
Israel king-of Jeroboam and-in-days-of Judah king-of Jotham in-days-of

בְּנֵי־ רְאוּבֵן וְגָדִי וַחֲצִי שֵׁבֶט־ מְנַשֶּׁה מִן־ בְּנֵי־
men-of from Manasseh tribe-of and-half-of and-Gadite Reuben sons-of (18)

חַיִל אֲנָשִׁים נֹשְׂאֵי מָגֵן וְחֶרֶב וְדֹרְכֵי קֶשֶׁת
bow and-ones-using-of and-sword shield ones-handling-of men ability

וּלְמוּדֵי מִלְחָמָה אַרְבָּעִים וְאַרְבָּעָה אֶלֶף וּשְׁבַע־
and-seven-of thousand and-four forty battle and-ones-being-trained-of

מֵאוֹת וְשִׁשִּׁים יֹצְאֵי צָבָא׃ וַיַּעֲשׂוּ מִלְחָמָה
war and-they-waged (19) military ones-being-ready-of and-sixty hundreds

עִם־ הַהַגְרִיאִים וִיטוּר וְנָפִישׁ וְנוֹדָב׃ וַיֵּעָזְרוּ
and-they-were-helped (20) and-Nodab and-Naphish and-Jetur the-Hagrites against

עֲלֵיהֶם וַיִּנָּתְנוּ בְיָדָם הַהַגְרִיאִים וְכֹל
and-all-of the-Hagrites into-hand-of-them and-they-were-given against-them

שֶׁעִמָּהֶם כִּי לֵאלֹהִים זָעֲקוּ בַּמִּלְחָמָה
during-the-battle they-cried-out to-God because who-with-them

וְנַעְתּוֹר לָהֶם כִּי־ בָטְחוּ בוֹ׃ וַיִּשְׁבּוּ
and-they-seized (21) in-him they-trusted because for-them and-to-answer-prayer

מִקְנֵיהֶם גְּמַלֵּיהֶם חֲמִשִּׁים אֶלֶף וְצֹאן מָאתַיִם
two-hundreds and-sheep thousand fifty camels-of-them livestocks-of-them

וַחֲמִשִּׁים אֶלֶף וַחֲמוֹרִים אַלְפַּיִם וְנֶפֶשׁ אָדָם מֵאָה
hundred human and-living-of two-thousands and-donkeys thousand and-fifty

אָלֶף׃ כִּי־ חֲלָלִים רַבִּים נָפָלוּ כִּי מֵהָאֱלֹהִים
from-the-God because they-fell many ones-slain indeed (22) thousand

הַמִּלְחָמָה וַיֵּשְׁבוּ תַחְתֵּיהֶם עַד־ הַגֹּלָה׃
the-exile until in-place-of-them and-they-occupied the-battle

וּבְנֵי חֲצִי שֵׁבֶט מְנַשֶּׁה יָשְׁבוּ בָּאָרֶץ
in-the-land they-settled Manasseh tribe-of half-of and-people-of (23)

and Eber—seven in all.
14 These were the sons of
Abihail son of Huri, the
son of Jaroah, the son of
Gilead, the son of Mi-
chael, the son of Jeshi-
shai, the son of Jahdo,
the son of Buz.
15 Ahi son of Abdiel, the
son of Guni, was head of
their family.
16 The Gadites lived in Gilead,
in Bashan and its outly-
ing villages, and on all
the pasturelands of Shar-
on as far as they ex-
tended.
17 All these were entered in
the genealogical records during the reigns of Jotham king
of Judah and Jeroboam king of
Israel.

18 The Reubenites, the Gadites and the half-tribe of
Manasseh had 44,760 men
ready for military service—
able-bodied men who could
handle shield and sword, who
could use a bow, and who
were trained for battle.
19 They
waged war against the Ha-
grites, Jetur, Naphish and
Nodab.
20 They were helped in
fighting them, and God handed the Hagrites and all their
allies over to them, because
they cried out to him during
the battle. He answered their
prayers, because they trusted
in him.
21 They seized the live-
stock of the Hagrites—fifty
thousand camels, two hun-
dred fifty thousand sheep and
two thousand donkeys. They
also took one hundred thousand people captive,
22 and
many others fell slain, because
the battle was God's. And they
occupied the land until the exile.

*The Half-Tribe of Manasseh*

23 The people of the half-tribe
of Manasseh were numerous;
they settled in the land from

מִבָּשָׁן עַד־בַּעַל חֶרְמוֹן וּשְׂנִיר וְהַר־ חֶרְמוֹן הֵמָּה
they Hermon indeed-Mount-of indeed-Senir Hermon Baal to from-Bashan

רָבוּ׃ (24) וְאֵלֶּה רָאשֵׁי בֵית־ אֲבוֹתָם
fathers-of-them family-of heads-of and-these (24) they-were-numerous

וְעֵפֶר וְיִשְׁעִי וֶאֱלִיאֵל וְעַזְרִיאֵל וְיִרְמְיָה וְהוֹדַוְיָה
and-Hodaviah and-Jeremiah and-Azriel and-Elial and-Ishi and-Epher

וְיַחְדִּיאֵל אֲנָשִׁים גִּבּוֹרֵי חַיִל אַנְשֵׁי שֵׁמוֹת רָאשִׁים לְבֵית
of-family-of heads names men-of bravery warriors-of men and-Jahdiel

אֲבוֹתָם׃ (25) וַיִּמְעֲלוּ בֵּאלֹהֵי אֲבוֹתֵיהֶם
fathers-of-them to-God-of but-they-were-unfaithful (25) fathers-of-them

וַיִּזְנוּ אַחֲרֵי אֱלֹהֵי עַמֵּי־ הָאָרֶץ אֲשֶׁר־ הִשְׁמִיד אֱלֹהִים
God he-destroyed whom the-land peoples-of gods-of to and-they-prostituted

מִפְּנֵיהֶם׃ (26) וַיָּעַר אֱלֹהֵי יִשְׂרָאֵל אֶת־ רוּחַ ׀ פּוּל
Pul spirit-of *** Israel God-of so-he-stirred-up (26) from-before-them

מֶלֶךְ־ אַשּׁוּר וְאֶת־ רוּחַ תִּלְגַת פִּלְנֶסֶר מֶלֶךְ אַשּׁוּר
Assyria king-of Pileser Tiglath spirit-of indeed Assyria king-of

וַיַּגְלֵם לָראוּבֵנִי וְלַגָּדִי וְלַחֲצִי
and-of-half-of and-of-the-Gadite of-the-Reubenite and-he-exiled-them

שֵׁבֶט מְנַשֶּׁה וַיְבִיאֵם לַחְלַח וְחָבוֹר וְהָרָא וּנְהַר
and-river-of and-Hara and-Habor to-Halah and-he-took-them Manasseh tribe-of

גּוֹזָן עַד הַיּוֹם הַזֶּה׃ *(27[1]) בְּנֵי לֵוִי גֵּרְשׁוֹן קְהָת וּמְרָרִי׃
and-Merari Kohath Gershon Levi sons-of *(27[1]) the-this the-day to Gozan

(28[2]) וּבְנֵי קְהָת עַמְרָם יִצְהָר וְחֶבְרוֹן וְעֻזִּיאֵל׃
and-Uzziel and-Hebron Izhar Amram Kohath and-sons-of (28[2])

(29[3]) וּבְנֵי עַמְרָם אַהֲרֹן וּמֹשֶׁה וּמִרְיָם וּבְנֵי אַהֲרֹן
Aaron and-sons-of and-Miriam and-Moses Aaron Amram and-children-of (29[3])

נָדָב וַאֲבִיהוּא אֶלְעָזָר וְאִיתָמָר׃ (30[4]) אֶלְעָזָר הוֹלִיד אֶת־
*** he-fathered Eleazar (30[4]) and-Ithamar Eleazar and-Abihu Nadab

פִּינְחָס פִּינְחָס הֹלִיד אֶת־ אֲבִישׁוּעַ׃ (31[5]) וַאֲבִישׁוּעַ הוֹלִיד
he-fathered and-Abishua (31[5]) Abishua *** he-fathered Phinehas Phinehas

אֶת־ בֻּקִּי וּבֻקִּי הוֹלִיד אֶת־ עֻזִּי׃ (32[6]) וְעֻזִּי הוֹלִיד אֶת־
*** he-fathered and-Uzzi (32[6]) Uzzi *** he-fathered and-Bukki Bukki ***

זְרַחְיָה וּזְרַחְיָה הוֹלִיד אֶת־ מְרָיוֹת׃ (33[7]) מְרָיוֹת הוֹלִיד
he-fathered Meraioth (33[7]) Meraioth *** he-fathered and-Zerahiah Zerahiah

אֶת־ אֲמַרְיָה וַאֲמַרְיָה הוֹלִיד אֶת־ אֲחִיטוּב׃ (34[8]) וַאֲחִיטוּב
and-Ahitub (34[8]) Ahitub *** he-fathered and-Amariah Amariah ***

הוֹלִיד אֶת־ צָדוֹק וְצָדוֹק הוֹלִיד אֶת־ אֲחִימָעַץ׃ (35[9]) וַאֲחִימַעַץ
and-Ahimaaz (35[9]) Ahimaaz *** he-fathered and-Zadok Zadok *** he-fathered

Bashan to Baal Hermon, that is, to Senir (Mount Hermon).
[24]These were the heads of their families: Epher, Ishi, Eliel, Azriel, Jeremiah, Hodaviah and Jahdiel. They were brave warriors, famous men, and heads of their families.
[25]But they were unfaithful to the God of their fathers and prostituted themselves to the gods of the peoples of the land, whom God had destroyed before them.
[26]So the God of Israel stirred up the spirit of Pul king of Assyria (that is, Tiglath-Pileser king of Assyria), who took the Reubenites, the Gadites and the half-tribe of Manasseh into exile. He took them to Halah, Habor, Hara and the river of Gozan, where they are to this day.

*Levi*

6 The sons of Levi:
Gershon, Kohath and Merari.
[2]The sons of Kohath:
Amram, Izhar, Hebron and Uzziel.
[3]The children of Amram:
Aaron, Moses and Miriam.
The sons of Aaron:
Nadab, Abihu, Eleazar and Ithamar.
[4]Eleazar was the father of Phinehas,
Phinehas the father of Abishua,
[5]Abishua the father of Bukki,
Bukki the father of Uzzi,
[6]Uzzi the father of Zerahiah,
Zerahiah the father of Meraioth,
[7]Meraioth the father of Amariah,
Amariah the father of Ahitub,
[8]Ahitub the father of Zadok,
Zadok the father of Ahimaaz,
[9]Ahimaaz the father of

*27 The Hebrew numeration of chapter 6 begins with verse 16 in English. The number in brackets indicates the English numeration.

הוֹלִיד אֶת־ עֲזַרְיָה וַעֲזַרְיָה הוֹלִיד אֶת־ יוֹחָנָן׃ וְיוֹחָנָן
and-Johanan (36[10]) Johanan *** he-fathered and-Azariah Azariah *** he-fathered

הוֹלִיד אֶת־ עֲזַרְיָה הוּא אֲשֶׁר כִּהֵן בַּבַּיִת אֲשֶׁר־
that in-the-temple he-served-as-priest who he Azariah *** he-fathered

בָּנָה שְׁלֹמֹה בִּירוּשָׁלִָם׃ וַיּוֹלֶד עֲזַרְיָה אֶת־ אֲמַרְיָה
Amariah *** Azariah and-he-fathered (37[11]) in-Jerusalem Solomon he-built

וַאֲמַרְיָה הוֹלִיד אֶת־ אֲחִיטוּב׃ וַאֲחִיטוּב הוֹלִיד אֶת־
*** he-fathered and-Ahitub (38[12]) Ahitub *** he-fathered and-Amariah

צָדוֹק וְצָדוֹק הוֹלִיד אֶת־ שַׁלּוּם׃ וְשַׁלּוּם הוֹלִיד
he-fathered and-Shallum (39[13]) Shallum *** he-fathered and-Zadok Zadok

אֶת־ חִלְקִיָּה וְחִלְקִיָּה הוֹלִיד אֶת־ עֲזַרְיָה׃ וַעֲזַרְיָה
and-Azariah (40[14]) Azariah *** he-fathered and-Hilkiah Hilkiah ***

הוֹלִיד אֶת־ שְׂרָיָה וּשְׂרָיָה הוֹלִיד אֶת־ יְהוֹצָדָק׃
Jehozadak *** he-fathered and-Seraiah Seraiah *** he-fathered

וִיהוֹצָדָק הָלַךְ בְּהַגְלוֹת יְהוָה אֶת־ יְהוּדָה וִירוּשָׁלִָם
and-Jerusalem Judah *** Yahweh when-to-exile he-left and-Jehozadak (41[15])

בְּיַד נְבֻכַדְנֶאצַּר׃ בְּנֵי לֵוִי גֵּרְשֹׁם קְהָת וּמְרָרִי׃
and-Merari Kohath Gershom Levi sons-of (1[16]) Nebuchadnezzar by-hand-of

וְאֵלֶּה שְׁמוֹת בְּנֵי־ גֵרְשׁוֹם לִבְנִי וְשִׁמְעִי׃
and-Shimei Libni Gershom sons-of names-of and-these (2[17])

וּבְנֵי קְהָת עַמְרָם וְיִצְהָר וְחֶבְרוֹן וְעֻזִּיאֵל׃
and-Uzziel and-Hebron and-Izhar Amram Kohath and-sons-of (3[18])

בְּנֵי מְרָרִי מַחְלִי וּמֻשִׁי וְאֵלֶּה מִשְׁפְּחוֹת הַלֵּוִי
the-Levite clans-of and-these and-Mushi Mahli Merari sons-of (4[19])

לַאֲבוֹתֵיהֶם׃ לְגֵרְשׁוֹם לִבְנִי בְנוֹ יַחַת בְּנוֹ
son-of-him Jehath son-of-him Libni of-Gershom (5[20]) by-fathers-of-them

זִמָּה בְנוֹ׃ יוֹאָח בְּנוֹ עִדּוֹ בְנוֹ זֶרַח בְּנוֹ
son-of-him Zerah son-of-him Iddo son-of-him Joah (6[21]) son-of-him Zimmah

יְאָתְרַי בְּנוֹ׃ בְּנֵי קְהָת עַמִּינָדָב בְּנוֹ
son-of-him Amminadab Kohath descendants-of (7[22]) son-of-him Jeatherai

קֹרַח בְּנוֹ אַסִּיר בְּנוֹ׃ אֶלְקָנָה בְנוֹ וְאֶבְיָסָף
and-Ebiasaph son-of-him Elkanah (8[23]) son-of-him Assir son-of-him Korah

בְּנוֹ וְאַסִּיר בְּנוֹ׃ תַּחַת בְּנוֹ אוּרִיאֵל בְּנוֹ
son-of-him Uriel son-of-him Tahath (9[24]) son-of-him and-Assir son-of-him

עֻזִּיָּה בְנוֹ וְשָׁאוּל בְּנוֹ׃ וּבְנֵי אֶלְקָנָה
Elkanah and-descendants-of (10[25]) son-of-him and-Shaul son-of-him Uzziah

עֲמָשַׂי וַאֲחִימוֹת׃ אֶלְקָנָה °בְּנֵי אֶלְקָנָה צוֹפַי בְּנוֹ
son-of-him Zophai Elkanah sons-of Elkanah (11[26]) and-Ahimoth Amasai

---

Azariah,
Azariah the father of Johanan,
10 Johanan the father of Azariah (it was he who served as priest in the temple Solomon built in Jerusalem),
11 Azariah the father of Amariah,
Amariah the father of Ahitub,
12 Ahitub the father of Zadok,
Zadok the father of Shallum,
13 Shallum the father of Hilkiah,
Hilkiah the father of Azariah,
14 Azariah the father of Seraiah,
and Seraiah the father of Jehozadak.
15 Jehozadak was deported when the LORD sent Judah and Jerusalem into exile by the hand of Nebuchadnezzar.

16 The sons of Levi:
Gershon,[v] Kohath and Merari.
17 These are the names of the sons of Gershon:
Libni and Shimei.
18 The sons of Kohath:
Amram, Izhar, Hebron and Uzziel.
19 The sons of Merari:
Mahli and Mushi.
These are the clans of the Levites listed according to their fathers:
20 Of Gershon:
Libni his son, Jehath his son,
Zimmah his son, 21 Joah his son,
Iddo his son, Zerah his son
and Jeatherai his son.
22 The descendants of Kohath:
Amminadab his son,
Korah his son,
Assir his son, 23 Elkanah his son,
Ebiasaph his son, Assir his son,
24 Tahath his son, Uriel his son,
Uzziah his son and Shaul his son.
25 The descendants of Elkanah:
Amasai, Ahimoth,
26 Elkanah his son,[w] Zophai his son,

[v]16 Hebrew *Gershom*, a variant of *Gershon*; also in verses 17, 20, 43, 62 and 71
[w]26 Some Hebrew manuscripts, Septuagint and Syriac; most Hebrew manuscripts *Ahimoth* [26]*and Elkanah. The sons of Elkanah:*

*See the note on page 15.

°11 ק בני

וְנַ֥חַת בְּנ֖וֹ׃ אֱלִיאָ֥ב בְּנ֛וֹ יְרֹחָ֥ם בְּנ֖וֹ אֶלְקָנָ֥ה
Elkanah son-of-him Jeroham son-of-him Eliab (12[27]) son-of-him and-Nahath

בְּנֽוֹ׃ וּבְנֵ֖י שְׁמוּאֵ֑ל הַבְּכֹ֥ר וַשְׁנִ֖י וַאֲבִיָּֽה׃
and-Abijah and-second the-firstborn Samuel and-sons-of (13[28]) son-of-him

בְּנֵ֥י מְרָרִ֖י מַחְלִ֑י לִבְנִ֥י בְנ֛וֹ שִׁמְעִ֥י בְנ֖וֹ
son-of-him Shimei son-of-him Libni Mahli Merari descendants-of (14[29])

עֻזָּ֥ה בְנֽוֹ׃ שִׁמְעָ֥א בְנ֛וֹ חַגִּיָּ֥ה בְנ֖וֹ עֲשָׂיָ֥ה
Asaiah son-of-him Haggiah son-of-him Shimea (15[30]) son-of-him Uzzah

בְנֽוֹ׃ וְאֵ֕לֶּה אֲשֶׁ֥ר הֶעֱמִ֛יד דָּוִ֖יד עַל־ יְדֵי־
ones-over-of at David he-put-in-charge whom and-these (16[31]) son-of-him

שִׁ֑יר בֵּ֣ית יְהוָ֑ה מִמְּנ֖וֹחַ הָאָרֽוֹן׃ וַיִּהְי֨וּ
and-they-were (17[32]) the-ark after-resting-of Yahweh house-of music-of

מְשָׁרְתִ֞ים לִפְנֵ֨י מִשְׁכַּ֤ן אֹֽהֶל־ מוֹעֵד֙ בַּשִּׁ֔יר עַד־
until with-the-music Meeting Tent-of tabernacle before ones-ministering

בְּנ֧וֹת שְׁלֹמֹ֛ה אֶת־ בֵּ֥ית יְהוָ֖ה בִּירוּשָׁלִָ֑ם וַיַּעַמְד֥וּ
and-they-performed in-Jerusalem Yahweh temple-of *** Solomon to-build

כְּמִשְׁפָּטָ֖ם עַל־ עֲבוֹדָתָֽם׃ וְאֵ֥לֶּה
and-these (18[33]) duty-of-them for according-to-regulation-of-them

הָעֹמְדִ֖ים וּבְנֵיהֶ֑ם מִבְּנֵי֙ הַקְּהָתִ֔י הֵימָן֙
Heman the-Kohathite from-sons-of and-sons-of-them the-ones-serving

הַמְשׁוֹרֵ֔ר בֶּן־ יוֹאֵ֖ל בֶּן־ שְׁמוּאֵֽל׃ בֶּן־ אֶלְקָנָה֙
Elkanah son-of (19[34]) Samuel son-of Joel son-of the-one-making-music

בֶּן־ יְרֹחָ֔ם בֶּן־ אֱלִיאֵ֖ל בֶּן־ תּֽוֹחַ׃ בֶּן־ °צִיף֙ בֶּן־ אֶלְקָנָ֔ה
Elkanah son-of Zuph son-of (20[35]) Toah son-of Eliel son-of Jeroham son-of

בֶּן־ מַ֥חַת בֶּן־ עֲמָשָֽׁי׃ בֶּן־ אֶלְקָנָ֔ה בֶּן־ יוֹאֵ֖ל בֶּן־
son-of Joel son-of Elkanah son-of (21[36]) Amasai son-of Mahath son-of

עֲזַרְיָ֖ה בֶּן־ צְפַנְיָֽה׃ בֶּן־ תַּ֙חַת֙ בֶּן־ אַסִּ֔יר בֶּן־ אֶבְיָסָ֖ף
Ebiasaph son-of Assir son-of Tahath son-of (22[37]) Zephaniah son-of Azariah

בֶּן־ קֹֽרַח׃ בֶּן־ יִצְהָ֥ר בֶּן־ קְהָ֖ת בֶּן־ לֵוִ֥י בֶּן־ יִשְׂרָאֵֽל׃
Israel son-of Levi son-of Kohath son-of Izhar son-of (23[38]) Korah son-of

וְאָחִ֣יו אָסָ֔ף הָעֹמֵ֖ד עַל־ יְמִינ֑וֹ
right-hand-of-him at the-one-serving Asaph and-associate-of-him (24[39])

אָסָ֣ף בֶּן־ בֶּרֶכְיָ֔הוּ בֶּן־ שִׁמְעָֽא׃ בֶּן־ מִיכָאֵ֥ל בֶּן־ בַּעֲשֵׂיָ֖ה
Baaseiah son-of Michael son-of (25[40]) Shimea son-of Berekiah son-of Asaph

בֶּן־ מַלְכִּיָּֽה׃ בֶּן־ אֶתְנִ֥י בֶן־ זֶ֖רַח בֶּן־ עֲדָיָֽה׃
Adaiah son-of Zerah son-of Ethni son-of (26[41]) Malkijah son-of

בֶּן־ אֵיתָ֥ן בֶּן־ זִמָּ֖ה בֶּן־ שִׁמְעִֽי׃ בֶּן־ יַ֥חַת
Jahath son-of (28[43]) Shimei son-of Zimmah son-of Ethan son-of (27[42])

Nahath his son, [27]Eliab
his son,
Jeroham his son, Elkanah
his son
and Samuel his son.[x]
[28]The sons of Samuel:
Joel[y] the firstborn
and Abijah the second
son.
[29]The descendants of Merari:
Mahli, Libni his son,
Shimei his son, Uzzah
his son,
[30]Shimea his son, Haggiah
his son
and Asaiah his son.

*The Temple Musicians*

[31]These are the men David
put in charge of the music in
the house of the LORD after the
ark came to rest there. [32]They
ministered with music before
the tabernacle—the Tent of
Meeting—until Solomon built
the temple of the LORD in
Jerusalem. They performed
their duties according to the
regulations laid down for
them.
[33]Here are the men who
served, together with their
sons:
From the Kohathites:
Heman, the musician,
the son of Joel, the son of
Samuel,
[34]the son of Elkanah, the
son of Jeroham,
the son of Eliel, the son of
Toah,
[35]the son of Zuph, the son
of Elkanah,
the son of Mahath, the
son of Amasai,
[36]the son of Elkanah, the
son of Joel,
the son of Azariah, the
son of Zephaniah,
[37]the son of Tahath, the
son of Assir,
the son of Ebiasaph, the
son of Korah,
[38]the son of Izhar, the son
of Kohath,
the son of Levi, the son of
Israel;
[39]and Heman's associate
Asaph, who served at his
right hand:
Asaph son of Berekiah,
the son of Shimea,
[40]the son of Michael, the
son of Baaseiah,[z]
the son of Malkijah, [41]the
son of Ethni,
the son of Zerah, the son

[x]27 Some Septuagint manuscripts (see also 1 Samuel 1:19,20 and 1 Chron. 6:33,34); Hebrew does not have *and Samuel his son.*
[y]28 Some Septuagint manuscripts and Syriac (see also 1 Samuel 8:2 and 1 Chron. 6:33); Hebrew does not have *Joel.*
[z]40 Most Hebrew manuscripts; some Hebrew manuscripts, one Septuagint manuscript and Syriac *Maaseiah*

*See the note on page 15.

°20 ק צוף

בֶּן־ גֵּרְשֹׁם בֶּן־ לֵוִי׃ וּבְנֵי מְרָרִי אֲחֵיהֶם
associates-of-them Merari and-sons-of (29[44]) Levi son-of Gershom son-of

עַל־ הַשְּׂמֹאול אֵיתָן בֶּן־ קִישִׁי בֶּן־ עַבְדִּי בֶּן־ מַלּוּךְ׃
Malluch son-of Abdi son-of Kishi son-of Ethan the-left-hand at

בֶּן־ חֲשַׁבְיָה בֶּן־ אֲמַצְיָה בֶּן־ חִלְקִיָּה׃ בֶּן־
son-of (31[46]) Hilkiah son-of Amaziah son-of Hashabiah son-of (30[45])

אַמְצִי בֶּן־ בָּנִי בֶּן־ שָׁמֶר׃ בֶּן־ מַחְלִי בֶּן־ מוּשִׁי בֶּן־
son-of Mushi son-of Mahli son-of (32[47]) Shemer son-of Bani son-of Amzi

מְרָרִי בֶּן־ לֵוִי׃ וַאֲחֵיהֶם הַלְוִיִּם
the-Levites and-fellows-of-them (33[48]) Levi son-of Merari

נְתוּנִים לְכָל־ עֲבוֹדַת מִשְׁכַּן בֵּית הָאֱלֹהִים׃
the-God house-of tabernacle duty-of to-all-of ones-being-assigned

וְאַהֲרֹן וּבָנָיו מַקְטִירִים עַל־ מִזְבַּח
altar-of on ones-offering and-descendants-of-him but-Aaron (34[49])

הָעוֹלָה וְעַל־ מִזְבַּח הַקְּטֹרֶת לְכֹל מְלֶאכֶת
work-of for-all-of the-incense altar-of and-on the-burnt-offering

קֹדֶשׁ הַקֳּדָשִׁים וּלְכַפֵּר עַל־ יִשְׂרָאֵל כְּכֹל אֲשֶׁר
that as-all Israel for and-to-atone the-Holy-Places Most-Holy-of

צִוָּה מֹשֶׁה עֶבֶד הָאֱלֹהִים׃ וְאֵלֶּה בְּנֵי
descendants-of and-these (35[50]) the-God servant-of Moses he-commanded

אַהֲרֹן אֶלְעָזָר בְּנוֹ פִּינְחָס בְּנוֹ אֲבִישׁוּעַ בְּנוֹ׃
son-of-him Abishua son-of-him Phinehas son-of-him Eleazar Aaron

בֻּקִּי בְנוֹ עֻזִּי בְנוֹ זְרַחְיָה בְנוֹ׃
son-of-him Zerahiah son-of-him Uzzi son-of-him Bukki (36[51])

מְרָיוֹת בְּנוֹ אֲמַרְיָה בְנוֹ אֲחִיטוּב בְּנוֹ׃
son-of-him Ahitub son-of-him Amariah son-of-him Meraioth (37[52])

צָדוֹק בְּנוֹ אֲחִימַעַץ בְּנוֹ׃ וְאֵלֶּה
and-these (39[54]) son-of-him Ahimaaz son-of-him Zadok (38[53])

מוֹשְׁבוֹתָם לְטִירוֹתָם בִּגְבוּלָם לִבְנֵי
to-descendants-of in-territory-of-them by-locations-of-them settlements-of-them

אַהֲרֹן לְמִשְׁפַּחַת† הַקְּהָתִי כִּי לָהֶם הָיָה הַגּוֹרָל׃
the-lot he-was for-them because the-Kohathite of-clan-of Aaron

וַיִּתְּנוּ לָהֶם אֶת־ חֶבְרוֹן בְּאֶרֶץ יְהוּדָה וְאֶת־
with Judah in-land-of Hebron *** to-them and-they-gave (40[55])

מִגְרָשֶׁיהָ סְבִיבֹתֶיהָ׃ וְאֶת־ שְׂדֵה הָעִיר וְאֶת־
and the-city field-of but (41[56]) ones-around-her pasturelands-of-her

חֲצֵרֶיהָ נָתְנוּ לְכָלֵב בֶּן־ יְפֻנֶּה׃ וְלִבְנֵי
so-to-sons-of (42[57]) Jephunneh son-of to-Caleb they-gave villages-of-her

of Adaiah,
42the son of Ethan, the son
of Zimmah,
the son of Shimei, 43the
son of Jahath,
the son of Gershon, the
son of Levi;
44and from their associates,
the Merarites, at his left
hand:
Ethan son of Kishi, the
son of Abdi,
the son of Malluch, 45the
son of Hashabiah,
the son of Amaziah, the
son of Hilkiah,
46the son of Amzi, the son
of Bani,
the son of Shemer, 47the
son of Mahli,
the son of Mushi, the son
of Merari,
the son of Levi.

48Their fellow Levites were
assigned to all the other duties
of the tabernacle, the house of
God. 49But Aaron and his descendants were the ones who
presented offerings on the altar of burnt offering and on
the altar of incense in connection with all that was done in
the Most Holy Place, making
atonement for Israel, in accordance with all that Moses
the servant of God had commanded.

50These were the descend-
ants of Aaron:
Eleazar his son, Phinehas
his son,
Abishua his son, 51Bukki
his son,
Uzzi his son, Zerahiah
his son,
52Meraioth his son, Ama-
riah his son,
Ahitub his son, 53Zadok
his son
and Ahimaaz his son.

54These were the locations of
their settlements allotted as
their territory (they were assigned to the descendants of
Aaron who were from the Kohathite clan, because the first
lot was for them):
55They were given He-
bron in Judah with its surrounding pasturelands.
56But the fields and villages
around the city were given
to Caleb son of Jephunneh.
57So the descendants of

*See the note on page 15.

†39 Most mss have the accent under the *pe* (-פַּ֫חַת).

אַהֲרֹן נָתְנוּ אֶת־ עָרֵי הַמִּקְלָט אֶת־ חֶבְרוֹן וְאֶת־ לִבְנָה וְאֶת־
and Libnah and Hebron *** the-refuge cities-of *** they-gave Aaron

מִגְרָשֶׁיהָ וְאֶת־ יַתִּר וְאֶת־ אֶשְׁתְּמֹעַ וְאֶת־ מִגְרָשֶׁיהָ׃ וְאֶת־
and (43[58]) pastures-of-her and Eshtemoa and Jattir and pastures-of-her

חִילֵז וְאֶת־ מִגְרָשֶׁיהָ אֶת־ דְּבִיר וְאֶת־ מִגְרָשֶׁיהָ׃ וְאֶת־
and (44[59]) pastures-of-her and Debir *** pastures-of-her and Hilen

עָשָׁן וְאֶת־ מִגְרָשֶׁיהָ וְאֶת־ בֵּית שֶׁמֶשׁ וְאֶת־ מִגְרָשֶׁיהָ׃
pastures-of-her and Shemesh Beth and pastures-of-her and Ashan

וּמִמַּטֵּה בִנְיָמִן אֶת־ גֶּבַע וְאֶת־ מִגְרָשֶׁיהָ וְאֶת־ עָלֶמֶת
Alemeth and pastures-of-her and Geba *** Benjamin and-from-tribe-of (45[60])

וְאֶת־ מִגְרָשֶׁיהָ וְאֶת־ עֲנָתוֹת וְאֶת־ מִגְרָשֶׁיהָ כָּל־ עָרֵיהֶם
towns-of-them all-of pastures-of-her and Anathoth and pastures-of-her and

שְׁלֹשׁ־ עֶשְׂרֵה עִיר בְּמִשְׁפְּחוֹתֵיהֶם׃ וְלִבְנֵי קְהָת
Kohath and-to-descendants-of (46[61]) among-clans-of-them town ten three-of

הַנּוֹתָרִים מִמִּשְׁפַּחַת הַמַּטֶּה מִמַּחֲצִית מַטֵּה חֲצִי
half-of tribe-of from-half-of the-tribe from-clan-of the-ones-being-left

מְנַשֶּׁה בַּגּוֹרָל עָרִים עֶשֶׂר׃ וְלִבְנֵי גֵּרְשׁוֹם
Gershom and-to-descendants-of (47[62]) ten towns by-the-lot Manasseh

לְמִשְׁפְּחוֹתָם מִמַּטֵּה יִשָּׂשכָר וּמִמַּטֵּה אָשֵׁר
Asher and-from-tribe-of Issachar from-tribe-of by-clans-of-them

וּמִמַּטֵּה נַפְתָּלִי וּמִמַּטֵּה מְנַשֶּׁה בַּבָּשָׁן עָרִים
towns in-the-Bashan Manasseh and-from-tribe-of Naphtali and-from-tribe-of

שְׁלֹשׁ עֶשְׂרֵה׃ לִבְנֵי מְרָרִי לְמִשְׁפְּחוֹתָם מִמַּטֵּה
from-tribe-of by-clans-of-them Merari to-descendants-of (48[63]) ten three-of

רְאוּבֵן וּמִמַּטֵּה־ גָד וּמִמַּטֵּה זְבוּלֻן בַּגּוֹרָל עָרִים
towns by-the-lot Zebulun and-from-tribe-of Gad and-from-tribe-of Reuben

שְׁתֵּים עֶשְׂרֵה׃ וַיִּתְּנוּ בְנֵי־ יִשְׂרָאֵל לַלְוִיִּם אֶת־ הֶעָרִים
the-towns *** to-the-Levites Israel sons-of so-they-gave (49[64]) ten two

וְאֶת־ מִגְרְשֵׁיהֶם׃ וַיִּתְּנוּ בַגּוֹרָל מִמַּטֵּה בְּנֵי־
sons-of from-tribe-of by-the-lot and-they-gave (50[65]) pastures-of-them and

יְהוּדָה וּמִמַּטֵּה בְנֵי־ שִׁמְעוֹן וּמִמַּטֵּה בְּנֵי בִנְיָמִן
Benjamin sons-of and-from-tribe-of Simeon sons-of and-from-tribe-of Judah

אֵת הֶעָרִים הָאֵלֶּה אֲשֶׁר־ יִקְרְאוּ אֶתְהֶם בְּשֵׁמוֹת׃
by-names them they-called which the-these the-towns ***

וּמִמִּשְׁפְּחוֹת בְּנֵי קְהָת וַיְהִי עָרֵי גְּבוּלָם
territory-of-them towns-of and-he-was Kohath sons-of and-from-clans-of (51[66])

מִמַּטֵּה אֶפְרָיִם׃ וַיִּתְּנוּ לָהֶם אֶת־ עָרֵי הַמִּקְלָט
the-refuge cities-of *** to-them and-they-gave (52[67]) Ephraim from-tribe-of

Aaron were given Hebron (a city of refuge), and Libnah,[a] Jattir, Eshtemoa, [58]Hilen, Debir, [59]Ashan, Juttah[b] and Beth Shemesh, together with their pasturelands. [60]And from the tribe of Benjamin they were given Gibeon,[c] Geba, Alemeth and Anathoth, together with their pasturelands.

These towns, which were distributed among the Kohathite clans, were thirteen in all.

[61]The rest of Kohath's descendants were allotted ten towns from the clans of half the tribe of Manasseh.

[62]The descendants of Gershon, clan by clan, were allotted thirteen towns from the tribes of Issachar, Asher and Naphtali, and from the part of the tribe of Manasseh that is in Bashan.

[63]The descendants of Merari, clan by clan, were allotted twelve towns from the tribes of Reuben, Gad and Zebulun.

[64]So the Israelites gave the Levites these towns and their pasturelands. [65]From the tribes of Judah, Simeon and Benjamin they allotted the previously named towns.

[66]Some of the Kohathite clans were given as their territory towns from the tribe of Ephraim.

[67]In the hill country of Ephraim they were given Shechem (a city of refuge),

[a]57 See Joshua 21:13; Hebrew *given the cities of refuge: Hebron, Libnah.*
[b]59 Syriac (see also Septuagint and Joshua 21:16); Hebrew does not have *Juttah.*
[c]60 See Joshua 21:17; Hebrew does not have *Gibeon.*

*See the note on page 15.

אֶת־ שְׁכֶם וְאֶת־ מִגְרָשֶׁיהָ בְּהַר אֶפְרָיִם וְאֶת־ גֶּזֶר וְאֶת־
and Gezer and Ephraim in-hill-country-of pastures-of-her and Shechem ***

מִגְרָשֶׁיהָ׃ וְאֶת־ יָקְמְעָם וְאֶת־ מִגְרָשֶׁיהָ וְאֶת־ בֵּית חוֹרוֹן
Horon Beth and pastures-of-her and Jokmeam and (53[68]) pastures-of-her

וְאֶת־ מִגְרָשֶׁיהָ׃ וְאֶת־אַיָּלוֹן וְאֶת־ מִגְרָשֶׁיהָ וְאֶת־ גַּת־ רִמּוֹן
Rimmon Gath and pastures-of-her and Aijalon and (54[69]) pastures-of-her and

וְאֶת־ מִגְרָשֶׁיהָ׃ וּמִמַּחֲצִית מַטֵּה מְנַשֶּׁה אֶת־ עָנֵר
Aner *** Manasseh tribe-of and-from-half-of (55[70]) pastures-of-her and

וְאֶת־ מִגְרָשֶׁיהָ וְאֶת־ בִּלְעָם וְאֶת־ מִגְרָשֶׁיהָ לְמִשְׁפַּחַת לִבְנֵי־
of-sons-of to-clan pastures-of-her and Bileam and pastures-of-her and

קְהָת הַנּוֹתָרִים׃ לִבְנֵי גֵּרְשׁוֹם מִמִּשְׁפַּחַת חֲצִי
half-of from-clan-of Gershom to-sons-of (56[71]) the-ones-being-left Kohath

מַטֵּה מְנַשֶּׁה אֶת־ גּוֹלָן בַּבָּשָׁן וְאֶת־ מִגְרָשֶׁיהָ וְאֶת־עַשְׁתָּרוֹת
Ashtaroth and pastures-of-her and in-the-Bashan Golan *** Manasseh tribe-of

וְאֶת־ מִגְרָשֶׁיהָ׃ וּמִמַּטֵּה יִשָּׂשכָר אֶת־ קֶדֶשׁ וְאֶת־
and Kedesh *** Issachar and-from-tribe-of (57[72]) pastures-of-her and

מִגְרָשֶׁיהָ אֶת־ דָּבְרַת וְאֶת־ מִגְרָשֶׁיהָ׃ וְאֶת־ רָאמוֹת וְאֶת־
and Ramoth and (58[73]) pastures-of-her and Daberath *** pastures-of-her

מִגְרָשֶׁיהָ וְאֶת־ עָנֵם וְאֶת־ מִגְרָשֶׁיהָ׃ וּמִמַּטֵּה
and-from-tribe-of (59[74]) pastures-of-her and Anem and pastures-of-her

אָשֵׁר אֶת־ מָשָׁל וְאֶת־ מִגְרָשֶׁיהָ וְאֶת־ עַבְדּוֹן וְאֶת־ מִגְרָשֶׁיהָ׃
pastures-of-her and Abdon and pastures-of-her and Mashal *** Asher

וְאֶת־ חוּקֹק וְאֶת־ מִגְרָשֶׁיהָ וְאֶת־ רְחֹב וְאֶת־ מִגְרָשֶׁיהָ׃
pastures-of-her and Rehob and pastures-of-her and Hukok and (60[75])

וּמִמַּטֵּה נַפְתָּלִי אֶת־ קֶדֶשׁ בַּגָּלִיל וְאֶת־
and in-the-Galilee Kedesh *** Naphtali and-from-tribe-of (61[76])

מִגְרָשֶׁיהָ וְאֶת־ חַמּוֹן וְאֶת־ מִגְרָשֶׁיהָ וְאֶת־ קִרְיָתַיִם וְאֶת־
and Kiriathaim and pastures-of-her and Hammon and pastures-of-her

מִגְרָשֶׁיהָ׃ לִבְנֵי מְרָרִי הַנּוֹתָרִים מִמַּטֵּה
from-tribe-of the-ones-being-left Merari to-sons-of (62[77]) pastures-of-her

זְבוּלֻן אֶת־ רִמּוֹנוֹ וְאֶת־ מִגְרָשֶׁיהָ אֶת־ תָּבוֹר וְאֶת־ מִגְרָשֶׁיהָ׃
pastures-of-her and Tabor *** pastures-of-her and Rimmono *** Zebulun

וּמֵעֵבֶר לְיַרְדֵּן יְרֵחוֹ לְמִזְרַח הַיַּרְדֵּן
the-Jordan at-east-of Jericho of-Jordan and-from-across (63[78])

מִמַּטֵּה רְאוּבֵן אֶת־ בֶּצֶר בַּמִּדְבָּר וְאֶת־ מִגְרָשֶׁיהָ וְאֶת־ יַהְצָה
Jahzah and pastures-of-her and in-the-desert Bezer *** Reuben from-tribe-of

וְאֶת־ מִגְרָשֶׁיהָ׃ וְאֶת־ קְדֵמוֹת וְאֶת־ מִגְרָשֶׁיהָ וְאֶת־ מֵיפַעַת
Mephaath and pastures-of-her and Kedemoth and (64[79]) pastures-of-her and

and Gezer,[d] 68Jokmeam, Beth Horon, 69Aijalon and Gath Rimmon, together with their pasturelands.

70And from half the tribe of Manasseh the Israelites gave Aner and Bileam, together with their pasturelands, to the rest of the Kohathite clans.

71The Gershonites received the following:
From the clan of the half-tribe of Manasseh
they received Golan in Bashan and also Ashtaroth, together with their pasturelands;
72from the tribe of Issachar
they received Kedesh, Daberath, 73Ramoth and Anem, together with their pasturelands;
74from the tribe of Asher
they received Mashal, Abdon, 75Hukok and Rehob, together with their pasturelands;
76and from the tribe of Naphtali
they received Kedesh in Galilee, Hammon and Kiriathaim, together with their pasturelands.

77The Merarites (the rest of the Levites) received the following:
From the tribe of Zebulun
they received Jokneam, Kartah,[e] Rimmono and Tabor, together with their pasturelands;
78from the tribe of Reuben across the Jordan east of Jericho
they received Bezer in the desert, Jahzah, 79Kedemoth and Mephaath, together with their pasturelands;

[d]67 See Joshua 21:21; Hebrew *given the cities of refuge: Shechem, Gezer.*
[e]77 See Septuagint and Joshua 21:34; Hebrew does not have *Jokneam, Kartah.*

*See the note on page 15.

וְאֶת־ מִגְרָשֶׁהָ׃ וּמִמַּטֵּה־ גָד אֶת־ רָאמוֹת בַּגִּלְעָד
in-the-Gilead Ramoth *** Gad and-from-tribe-of (65[80]) pastures-of-her and

וְאֶת־ מִגְרָשֶׁהָ וְאֶת־ מַחֲנַיִם וְאֶת־ מִגְרָשֶׁהָ׃ וְאֶת־ חֶשְׁבּוֹן
Heshbon and (66[81]) pastures-of-her and Mahanaim and pastures-of-her and

וְאֶת־ מִגְרָשֶׁהָ וְאֶת־ יַעְזֵיר וְאֶת־ מִגְרָשֶׁהָ׃ וְלִבְנֵי
and-to-sons-of (7:1) pastures-of-her and Jazer and pastures-of-her and

יִשָּׂשכָר תּוֹלָע וּפוּאָה °יָשִׁיב וְשִׁמְרוֹן אַרְבָּעָה׃ וּבְנֵי תוֹלָע עֻזִּי
Uzzi Tola and-sons-of (2) four and-Shimron Jashub and-Puah Tola Issachar

וּרְפָיָה וִירִיאֵל וְיַחְמַי וְיִבְשָׂם וּשְׁמוּאֵל רָאשִׁים לְבֵית־
of-family-of heads and-Samuel and-Ibsam and-Jahmai and-Jeriel and-Rephaiah

אֲבוֹתָם לְתוֹלָע גִּבּוֹרֵי חַיִל לְתֹלְדוֹתָם מִסְפָּרָם
number-of-them in-genealogies-of-them fight men-of of-Tola fathers-of-them

בִּימֵי דָוִיד עֶשְׂרִים־ וּשְׁנַיִם אֶלֶף וְשֵׁשׁ מֵאוֹת׃ וּבְנֵי
and-sons-of (3) hundreds and-six thousand and-two twenty David in-days-of

עֻזִּי יִזְרַחְיָה וּבְנֵי יִזְרַחְיָה מִיכָאֵל וְעֹבַדְיָה וְיוֹאֵל יִשִּׁיָּה
Isshiah and-Joel and-Obadiah Michael Izrahiah and-sons-of Izrahiah Uzzi

חֲמִשָּׁה רָאשִׁים כֻּלָּם׃ וַעֲלֵיהֶם לְתֹלְדוֹתָם לְבֵית
by-family-of by-genealogies-of-them and-with-them (4) all-of-them chiefs five

אֲבוֹתָם גְּדוּדֵי צְבָא מִלְחָמָה שְׁלֹשִׁים וְשִׁשָּׁה אָלֶף כִּי־
for thousand and-six thirty battle army-of men-of fathers-of-them

הִרְבּוּ נָשִׁים וּבָנִים׃ וַאֲחֵיהֶם לְכֹל
of-all-of and-relatives-of-them (5) and-children wives they-had-many

מִשְׁפְּחוֹת יִשָּׂשכָר גִּבּוֹרֵי חֲיָלִים שְׁמוֹנִים וְשִׁבְעָה אֶלֶף הִתְיַחְשָׂם
to-be-listed-them thousand and-seven eighty fights men-of Issachar clans-of

לַכֹּל׃ בִּנְיָמִן בֶּלַע וָבֶכֶר וִידִיעֲאֵל שְׁלֹשָׁה׃ וּבְנֵי
and-sons-of (7) three and-Jediael and-Beker Bela Benjamin (6) as-the-total

בֶלַע אֶצְבּוֹן וְעֻזִּי וְעֻזִּיאֵל וִירִימוֹת וְעִירִי חֲמִשָּׁה רָאשֵׁי
heads-of five and-Iri and-Jerimoth and-Uzziel and-Uzzi Ezbon Bela

בֵּית אָבוֹת גִּבּוֹרֵי חֲיָלִים וְהִתְיַחְשָׂם עֶשְׂרִים וּשְׁנַיִם
and-two twenty and-to-be-listed-them fights men-of fathers family-of

אֶלֶף וּשְׁלֹשִׁים וְאַרְבָּעָה׃ וּבְנֵי בֶכֶר זְמִירָה וְיוֹעָשׁ
and-Joash Zemirah Beker and-sons-of (8) and-four and-thirty thousand

וֶאֱלִיעֶזֶר וְאֶלְיוֹעֵינַי וְעָמְרִי וִירֵמוֹת וַאֲבִיָּה וַעֲנָתוֹת
and-Anathoth and-Abijah and-Jeremoth and-Omri and-Elioenai and-Eliezer

וְעָלָמֶת כָּל־ אֵלֶּה בְּנֵי־ בָכֶר׃ וְהִתְיַחְשָׂם
and-to-be-listed-them (9) Beker sons-of these all-of and-Alemeth

לְתֹלְדוֹתָם רָאשֵׁי בֵּית אֲבוֹתָם גִּבּוֹרֵי חָיִל
fight men-of fathers-of-them family-of heads-of in-genealogies-of-them

[80]and from the tribe of Gad
they received Ramoth in
Gilead, Mahanaim,
[81]Heshbon and Jazer, together with their pasturelands.

*Issachar*

7 The sons of Issachar:
Tola, Puah, Jashub and
Shimron—four in all.
[2]The sons of Tola:
Uzzi, Rephaiah, Jeriel, Jahmai, Ibsam and Samuel—heads of their families. During the reign of David, the descendants of Tola listed as fighting men in their genealogy numbered 22,600.
[3]The son of Uzzi:
Izrahiah.
The sons of Izrahiah:
Michael, Obadiah, Joel and Isshiah. All five of
them were chiefs. [4]According to their family genealogy, they had 36,000 men ready for battle, for they had many wives and children.
[5]The relatives who were fighting men belonging to all the clans of Issachar, as listed in their genealogy, were 87,000 in all.

*Benjamin*

[6]Three sons of Benjamin:
Bela, Beker and Jediael.
[7]The sons of Bela:
Ezbon, Uzzi, Uzziel, Jerimoth and Iri, heads of families—five in all. Their genealogical record listed 22,034 fighting men.
[8]The sons of Beker:
Zemirah, Joash, Eliezer, Elioenai, Omri, Jeremoth, Abijah, Anathoth and Alemeth. All these were the sons of Beker.
[9]Their genealogical record listed the heads of families and 20,200 fighting men.

*See the note on page 15.

°1 ק ישוב

עֶשְׂרִים אֶלֶף וּמָאתָיִם׃ וּבְנֵי יְדִיעֲאֵל בִּלְהָן וּבְנֵי
and-sons-of Bilhan Jediael and-sons-of (10) and-two-hundreds thousand twenty

בִלְהָן יְעִישׁ וּבִנְיָמִן וְאֵהוּד וּכְנַעֲנָה וְזֵיתָן וְתַרְשִׁישׁ
and-Tarshish and-Zethan and-Kenaanah and-Ehud and-Benjamin Jeush Bilhan

וַאֲחִישָׁחַר׃ כָּל־ אֵלֶּה בְּנֵי יְדִיעֲאֵל לְרָאשֵׁי הָאָבוֹת
the-fathers of-heads-of Jediael sons-of these all-of (11) and-Ahishahar

גִּבּוֹרֵי חֲיָלִים שִׁבְעָה־עָשָׂר אֶלֶף וּמָאתַיִם יֹצְאֵי צָבָא
army ones-going-out-of and-two-hundreds thousand ten seven fights men-of

לַמִּלְחָמָה׃ וְשֻׁפִּם וְחֻפִּם בְּנֵי עִיר חֻשִׁם
Hushites Ir descendants-of and-Huppites and-Shuppites (12) to-the-war

בְּנֵי אַחֵר׃ בְּנֵי נַפְתָּלִי יַחֲצִיאֵל וְגוּנִי וְיֵצֶר
and-Jezer and-Guni Jahziel Naphtali sons-of (13) Aher descendants-of

וְשַׁלּוּם בְּנֵי בִלְהָה׃ בְּנֵי מְנַשֶּׁה אַשְׂרִיאֵל אֲשֶׁר יָלָדָה
she-bore whom Asriel Manasseh descendants-of (14) Bilhah sons-of and-Shallum

פִּילַגְשׁוֹ הָאֲרַמִּיָּה יָלְדָה אֶת־ מָכִיר אֲבִי גִלְעָד׃
Gilead father-of Makir *** she-bore the-Aramean concubine-of-him

וּמָכִיר לָקַח אִשָּׁה לְחֻפִּים וּלְשֻׁפִּים וְשֵׁם
and-name-of and-from-Shuppites from-Huppites wife he-took and-Makir (15)

אֲחֹתוֹ מַעֲכָה וְשֵׁם הַשֵּׁנִי צְלָפְחָד וַתִּהְיֶנָה
and-they-were Zelophehad the-second and-name-of Maacah sister-of-him

לִצְלָפְחָד בָּנוֹת׃ וַתֵּלֶד מַעֲכָה אֵשֶׁת־ מָכִיר בֵּן
son Makir wife-of Maacah and-she-bore (16) daughters to-Zelophehad

וַתִּקְרָא שְׁמוֹ פֶּרֶשׁ וְשֵׁם אָחִיו שָׁרֶשׁ
Sheresh brother-of-him and-name-of Peresh name-of-him and-she-called

וּבָנָיו אוּלָם וָרָקֶם׃ וּבְנֵי אוּלָם בְּדָן אֵלֶּה בְּנֵי
sons-of these Bedan Ulam and-sons-of (17) and-Rakem Ulam and-sons-of-him

גִלְעָד בֶּן־ מָכִיר בֶּן־ מְנַשֶּׁה׃ וַאֲחֹתוֹ הַמֹּלֶכֶת
Hammoleketh and-sister-of-him (18) Manasseh son-of Makir son-of Gilead

יָלְדָה אֶת־ אִישְׁהוֹד וְאֶת־ אֲבִיעֶזֶר וְאֶת־ מַחְלָה׃ וַיִּהְיוּ בְּנֵי
sons-of and-they-were (19) Mahlah and Abiezer and Ishhod *** she-bore

שְׁמִידָע אַחְיָן וָשֶׁכֶם וְלִקְחִי וַאֲנִיעָם׃ וּבְנֵי
and-descendants-of (20) and-Aniam and-Likhi and-Shechem Ahian Shemida

אֶפְרַיִם שׁוּתָלַח וּבֶרֶד בְּנוֹ וְתַחַת בְּנוֹ וְאֶלְעָדָה
and-Eleadah son-of-him and-Tahath son-of-him and-Bered Shuthelah Ephraim

בְנוֹ וְתַחַת בְּנוֹ׃ וְזָבָד בְּנוֹ וְשׁוּתֶלַח
and-Shuthelah son-of-him and-Zabad (21) son-of-him and-Tahath son-of-him

בְּנוֹ וְעֵזֶר וְאֶלְעָד וַהֲרָגוּם אַנְשֵׁי־ גַת
Gath men-of now-they-killed-them and-Elead now-Ezer son-of-him

10 The son of Jediael:
Bilhan.
The sons of Bilhan:
Jeush, Benjamin, Ehud,
Kenaanah, Zethan, Tarshish and Ahishahar.
11 All these sons of Jediael were heads of families. There were 17,200 fighting men ready to go out to war.
12 The Shuppites and Huppites were the descendants of Ir, and the Hushites the descendants of Aher.

*Naphtali*

13 The sons of Naphtali:
Jahziel, Guni, Jezer and Shillem[f]—his sons by Bilhah.

*Manasseh*

14 The descendants of Manasseh:
Asriel was his descendant through his Aramean concubine. She gave birth to Makir the father of Gilead. 15 Makir took a wife from among the Huppites and Shuppites. His sister's name was Maacah.
Another descendant was named Zelophehad, who had only daughters.
16 Makir's wife Maacah gave birth to a son and named him Peresh. His brother was named Sheresh, and his sons were Ulam and Rakem.
17 The son of Ulam:
Bedan.
These were the sons of Gilead son of Makir, the son of Manasseh. 18 His sister Hammoleketh gave birth to Ishhod, Abiezer and Mahlah.
19 The sons of Shemida were:
Ahian, Shechem, Likhi and Aniam.

*Ephraim*

20 The descendants of Ephraim:
Shuthelah, Bered his son,
Tahath his son, Eleadah his son,
Tahath his son, 21 Zabad his son
and Shuthelah his son.
Ezer and Elead were killed by the native-born men of Gath, when they

[f] 13 Some Hebrew and Septuagint manuscripts (see also Gen. 46:24 and Num. 26:49); most Hebrew manuscripts *Shallum*

°10 ק יעוש

הַנּוֹלָדִים בָּאָרֶץ כִּי יָרְדוּ לָקַחַת אֶת־
*** to-seize they-went-down when in-the-land the-ones-being-born

מִקְנֵיהֶם׃ וַיִּתְאַבֵּל אֶפְרַיִם אֲבִיהֶם יָמִים רַבִּים
many days father-of-them Ephraim and-he-mourned (22) livestocks-of-them

וַיָּבֹאוּ אֶחָיו לְנַחֲמוֹ׃ וַיָּבֹא אֶל־
into then-he-went (23) to-comfort-him relatives-of-him and-they-came

אִשְׁתּוֹ וַתַּהַר וַתֵּלֶד בֵּן וַיִּקְרָא אֶת־
*** and-he-called son and-she-bore and-she-became-pregnant wife-of-him

שְׁמוֹ בְּרִיעָה כִּי בְרָעָה הָיְתָה בְּבֵיתוֹ׃
in-family-of-him she-was in-misfortune because Beriah name-of-him

וּבִתּוֹ שֶׁאֱרָה וַתִּבֶן אֶת־ בֵּית־ חוֹרוֹן הַתַּחְתּוֹן
the-Lower Horon Beth *** and-she-built Sheerah and-daughter-of-him (24)

וְאֶת־ הָעֶלְיוֹן וְאֵת אֻזֵּן שֶׁאֱרָה׃ וְרֶפַח בְּנוֹ וְרֶשֶׁף
and-Resheph son-of-him and-Rephah (25) Sheerah Uzzen and the-Upper and

וְתֶלַח בְּנוֹ וְתַחַן בְּנוֹ׃ לַעְדָּן בְּנוֹ עַמִּיהוּד
Ammihud son-of-him Ladan (26) son-of-him and-Tahan son-of-him and-Telah

בְּנוֹ אֱלִישָׁמָע בְּנוֹ׃ נוֹן בְּנוֹ יְהוֹשֻׁעַ בְּנוֹ׃
son-of-him Joshua son-of-him Nun (27) son-of-him Elishama son-of-him

וַאֲחֻזָּתָם וּמֹשְׁבוֹתָם בֵּית־ אֵל וּבְנֹתֶיהָ
and-villages-of-her El Beth and-settlements-of-them and-land-of-them (28)

וְלַמִּזְרָח נַעֲרָן וְלַמַּעֲרָב גֶּזֶר וּבְנֹתֶיהָ וּשְׁכֶם
and-Shechem and-villages-of-her Gezer and-to-the-west Naaran and-to-the-east

וּבְנֹתֶיהָ עַד־ עַיָּה וּבְנֹתֶיהָ׃ וְעַל־ יְדֵי
borders-of and-along (29) and-villages-of-her Ayyah to and-villages-of-her

בְנֵי־ מְנַשֶּׁה בֵּית־ שְׁאָן וּבְנֹתֶיהָ תַּעְנַךְ וּבְנֹתֶיהָ
and-villages-of-her Taanach and-villages-of-her Shan Beth Manasseh sons-of

מְגִדּוֹ וּבְנוֹתֶיהָ דּוֹר וּבְנוֹתֶיהָ בְּאֵלֶּה יָשְׁבוּ
they-lived in-these and-villages-of-her Dor and-villages-of-her Megiddo

בְּנֵי יוֹסֵף בֶּן־ יִשְׂרָאֵל׃ בְּנֵי אָשֵׁר יִמְנָה וְיִשְׁוָה
and-Ishvah Imnah Asher sons-of (30) Israel son-of Joseph descendants-of

וְיִשְׁוִי וּבְרִיעָה וְשֶׂרַח אֲחוֹתָם׃ וּבְנֵי בְרִיעָה
Beriah and-sons-of (31) sister-of-them and-Serah and-Beriah and-Ishvi

חֶבֶר וּמַלְכִּיאֵל הוּא אֲבִי בִרְזָוִת׃ וְחֶבֶר הוֹלִיד אֶת־
*** he-fathered and-Heber (32) Birzaith father-of he and-Malkiel Heber

יַפְלֵט וְאֶת־ שׁוֹמֵר וְאֶת־ חוֹתָם וְאֵת שׁוּעָא אֲחוֹתָם׃ וּבְנֵי
and-sons-of (33) sister-of-them Shua and Hotham and Shomer and Japhlet

יַפְלֵט פָּסַךְ וּבִמְהָל וְעַשְׁוָת אֵלֶּה בְּנֵי יַפְלֵט׃
Japhlet sons-of these and-Ashvath and-Bimhal Pasach Japhlet

went down to seize their livestock. 22 Their father Ephraim mourned for them many days, and his relatives came to comfort him. 23 Then he lay with his wife again, and she became pregnant and gave birth to a son. He named him Beriah,[g] because there had been misfortune in his family. 24 His daughter was Sheerah, who built Lower and Upper Beth Horon as well as Uzzen Sheerah.

25 Rephah was his son, Resheph his son,
Telah his son, Tahan his son,
26 Ladan his son, Ammihud his son,
Elishama his son, 27 Nun his son
and Joshua his son.

28 Their lands and settlements included Bethel and its surrounding villages, Naaran to the east, Gezer and its villages to the west, and Shechem and its villages all the way to Ayyah and its villages. 29 Along the borders of Manasseh were Beth Shan, Taanach, Megiddo and Dor, together with their villages. The descendants of Joseph son of Israel lived in these towns.

*Asher*

30 The sons of Asher:
Imnah, Ishvah, Ishvi and Beriah. Their sister was Serah.
31 The sons of Beriah:
Heber and Malkiel, who was the father of Birzaith.
32 Heber was the father of Japhlet, Shomer and Hotham and of their sister Shua.
33 The sons of Japhlet:
Pasach, Bimhal and Ashvath.
These were Japhlet's sons.

g23 *Beriah* sounds like the Hebrew for *misfortune*.

°31 ק ברזית

ובני שמר אחי ורוהגה יחבה וארם: ובן־
and-son-of (35) and-Aram and-Hubbah and-Rohgah Ahi Shomer and-sons-of (34)

הלם אחיו צופח וימנע ושלש ועמל: בני
sons-of (36) and-Amal and-Shelesh and-Imna Zophah brother-of-him Helem

צופח סוח וחרנפר ושועל ובירי וימרה: בצר והוד
and-Hod Bezer (37) and-Imrah and-Beri and-Shual and-Harnepher Suah Zophah

ושמא ושלשה ויתרן ובארא: ובני יתר
Jether and-sons-of (38) and-Beera and-Ithran and-Shilshah and-Shamma

יפנה ופספה וארא: ובני עלא ארח וחניאל
and-Hanniel Arah Ulla and-sons-of (39) and-Ara and-Pispah Jephunneh

ורציא: כל־ אלה בני־ אשר ראשי בית־
family-of heads-of Asher descendants-of these all-of (40) and-Rizia

האבות ברורים גבורי חילים ראשי
outstanding-ones-of brave-ones warriors-of ones-being-choice the-fathers

הנשיאים והתיחשם בצבא במלחמה מספרם
number-of-them for-the-battle in-the-army and-to-be-listed-them the-leaders

אנשים עשרים וששה אלף: ובנימן הוליד את־בלע
Bela *** he-fathered and-Benjamin (8:1) thousand and-six twenty men

בכרו אשבל השני ואחרח השלישי: נוחה הרביעי
the-fourth Nohah (2) the-third and-Aharah the-second Ashbel firstborn-of-him

ורפא החמישי: ויהיו בנים לבלע אדר וגרא ואביהוד:
and-Abihud and-Gera Addar of-Bela sons and-they-were (3) the-fifth and-Rapha

ואבישוע ונעמן ואחוח: וגרא ושפופן וחורם:
and-Huram and-Shephuphan and-Gera (5) and-Ahoah and-Naaman and-Abishua (4)

ואלה בני אחוד אלה הם ראשי אבות
fathers heads-of they these Ehud descendants-of and-these (6)

ליושבי גבע ויגלום אל־ מנחת: ונעמן
and-Naaman (7) Manahath to and-they-deported-them Geba of-ones-living-of

ואחיה וגרא הוא הגלם והוליד את־עזא ואת־אחיחד:
Ahihud and Uzza *** and-he-fathered he-deported-them he and-Gera and-Ahijah

ושחרים הוליד בשדה מואב מן־ שלחו אתם
them to-divorce-him after Moab in-country-of he-fathered and-Shaharaim (8)

חושים ואת־בערא נשיו: ויולד מן־ חדש אשתו
wife-of-him Hodesh by and-he-fathered (9) wives-of-him Baara and Hushim

את־יובב ואת־צביא ואת־מישא ואת־מלכם: ואת־יעוץ ואת־שכיה ואת־
and Sakia and Jeuz and (10) Malcam and Mesha and Zibia and Jobab ***

מרמה אלה בניו ראשי אבות: ומחשים הוליד
he-fathered and-by-Hushim (11) fathers heads-of sons-of-him these Mirmah

34The sons of Shomer:
Ahi, Rohgah,[h] Hubbah and Aram.
35The sons of his brother Helem:
Zophah, Imna, Shelesh and Amal.
36The sons of Zophah:
Suah, Harnepher, Shual, Beri, Imrah, 37Bezer, Hod, Shamma, Shilshah, Ithran[i] and Beera.
38The sons of Jether:
Jephunneh, Pispah and Ara.
39The sons of Ulla:
Arah, Hanniel and Rizia.
40All these were descendants of Asher—heads of families, choice men, brave warriors and outstanding leaders. The number of men ready for battle, as listed in their genealogy, was 26,000.

*The Genealogy of Saul the Benjamite*

8 Benjamin was the father of Bela his firstborn,
Ashbel the second son,
Aharah the third,
2Nohah the fourth and Rapha the fifth.
3The sons of Bela were:
Addar, Gera, Abihud,[j]
4Abishua, Naaman, Ahoah, 5Gera, Shephuphan and Huram.
6These were the descendants of Ehud, who were heads of families of those living in Geba and were deported to Manahath:
7Naaman, Ahijah, and Gera, who deported them and who was the father of Uzza and Ahihud.
8Sons were born to Shaharaim in Moab after he had divorced his wives Hushim and Baara. 9By his wife Hodesh he had Jobab, Zibia, Mesha, Malcam, 10Jeuz, Sakia and Mirmah. These were his sons, heads of families.

h34 Or *of his brother Shomer: Rohgah*
i37 Possibly a variant of *Jether*
j3 Or *Gera the father of Ehud*

°34a ק ורהגה
°34b ק וחבה

אֶת־אֲבִיטוּב וְאֶת־אֶלְפָּעַל׃ וּבְנֵי אֶלְפַּעַל עֵבֶר וּמִשְׁעָם וָשָׁמֶד
and-Shemed and-Misham Eber Elpaal and-sons-of (12) Elpaal and Abitub ***

הוּא בָּנָה אֶת־אוֹנוֹ וְאֶת־לֹד וּבְנֹתֶיהָ׃ וּבְרִעָה וָשֶׁמַע
and-Shema and-Beriah (13) and-villages-of-her Lod and Ono *** he-built he

הֵמָּה רָאשֵׁי הָאָבוֹת לְיוֹשְׁבֵי אַיָּלוֹן הֵמָּה הִבְרִיחוּ אֶת־
*** they-drove-out they Aijalon of-ones-living-of the-fathers heads-of they

יוֹשְׁבֵי גַת׃ וְאַחְיוֹ שָׁשָׁק וִירֵמוֹת׃ וּזְבַדְיָה
and-Zebadiah (15) and-Jeremoth Shashak and-Ahio (14) Gath ones-inhabiting-of

וַעֲרָד וָעֶדֶר׃ וּמִיכָאֵל וְיִשְׁפָּה וְיוֹחָא בְּנֵי בְרִיעָה׃
Beriah sons-of and-Joha and-Ishpah and-Michael (16) and-Eder and-Arad

וּזְבַדְיָה וּמְשֻׁלָּם וְחִזְקִי וָחָבֶר׃ וְיִשְׁמְרַי
and-Ishmerai (18) and-Heber and-Hizki and-Meshullam and-Zebadiah (17)

וְיִזְלִיאָה וְיוֹבָב בְּנֵי אֶלְפָּעַל׃ וְיָקִים וְזִכְרִי וְזַבְדִּי׃
and-Zabdi and-Zicri and-Jakim (19) Elpaal sons-of and-Jobab and-Izliah

וֶאֱלִיעֵינַי וְצִלְּתָי וֶאֱלִיאֵל׃ וַעֲדָיָה וּבְרָאיָה
and-Beraiah and-Adaiah (21) and-Eliel and-Zillethai and-Elienai (20)

וְשִׁמְרָת בְּנֵי שִׁמְעִי׃ וְיִשְׁפָּן וָעֵבֶר וֶאֱלִיאֵל׃
and-Eliel and-Eber and-Ishpan (22) Shimei sons-of and-Shimrath

וְעַבְדּוֹן וְזִכְרִי וְחָנָן׃ וַחֲנַנְיָה וְעֵילָם וְעַנְתֹתִיָּה׃
and-Anthothijah and-Elam and-Hananiah (24) and-Hanan and-Zicri and-Abdon (23)

וְיִפְדְיָה וּפְנִיאֵל° בְּנֵי שָׁשָׁק׃ וְשַׁמְשְׁרַי
and-Shamsherai (26) Shashak sons-of and-Penuel and-Iphdeiah (25)

וּשְׁחַרְיָה וַעֲתַלְיָה׃ וְיַעֲרֶשְׁיָה וְאֵלִיָּה וְזִכְרִי בְּנֵי
sons-of and-Zicri and-Elijah and-Jaareshiah (27) and-Athaliah and-Sheharaiah

יְרֹחָם׃ אֵלֶּה רָאשֵׁי אָבוֹת לְתֹלְדוֹתָם רָאשִׁים אֵלֶּה
these chiefs in-genealogies-of-them fathers heads-of these (28) Jeroham

יָשְׁבוּ בִּירוּשָׁלָם׃ וּבְגִבְעוֹן יָשְׁבוּ אֲבִי גִבְעוֹן
Gibeon father-of they-lived and-in-Gibeon (29) in-Jerusalem they-lived

וְשֵׁם אִשְׁתּוֹ מַעֲכָה׃ וּבְנוֹ הַבְּכוֹר עַבְדּוֹן
Abdon the-firstborn and-son-of-him (30) Maacah wife-of-him and-name-of

וְצוּר וְקִישׁ וּבַעַל וְנָדָב׃ וּגְדוֹר וְאַחְיוֹ וָזָכֶר׃
and-Zeker and-Ahio and-Gedor (31) and-Nadab and-Baal and-Kish and-Zur

וּמִקְלוֹת הוֹלִיד אֶת־שִׁמְאָה וְאַף־הֵמָּה נֶגֶד אֲחֵיהֶם
relatives-of-them near they and-also Shimeah *** he-fathered and-Mikloth (32)

יָשְׁבוּ בִּירוּשָׁלַם עִם־אֲחֵיהֶם׃ וְנֵר הוֹלִיד אֶת־
*** he-fathered and-Ner (33) relatives-of-them with in-Jerusalem they-lived

קִישׁ וְקִישׁ הוֹלִיד אֶת־שָׁאוּל וְשָׁאוּל הוֹלִיד אֶת־יְהוֹנָתָן וְאֶת־
and Jonathan *** he-fathered and-Saul Saul *** he-fathered and-Kish Kish

[11]By Hushim he had Abitub and Elpaal.
[12]The sons of Elpaal:
Eber, Misham, Shemed (who built Ono and Lod with its surrounding villages), [13]and Beriah and Shema, who were heads of families of those living in Aijalon and who drove out the inhabitants of Gath.
[14]Ahio, Shashak, Jeremoth, [15]Zebadiah, Arad, Eder, [16]Michael, Ishpah and Joha were the sons of Beriah.
[17]Zebadiah, Meshullam, Hizki, Heber, [18]Ishmerai, Izliah and Jobab were the sons of Elpaal.
[19]Jakim, Zicri, Zabdi, [20]Elienai, Zillethai, Eliel, [21]Adaiah, Beraiah and Shimrath were the sons of Shimei.
[22]Ishpan, Eber, Eliel, [23]Abdon, Zicri, Hanan, [24]Hananiah, Elam, Anthothijah, [25]Iphdeiah and Penuel were the sons of Shashak.
[26]Shamsherai, Shehariah, Athaliah, [27]Jaareshiah, Elijah and Zicri were the sons of Jeroham.
[28]All these were heads of families, chiefs as listed in their genealogy, and they lived in Jerusalem.

[29]Jeiel[k] the father[l] of Gibeon lived in Gibeon.
His wife's name was Maacah, [30]and his firstborn son was Abdon, followed by Zur, Kish, Baal, Ner,[m] Nadab, [31]Gedor, Ahio, Zeker [32]and Mikloth, who was the father of Shimeah. They too lived near their relatives in Jerusalem.
[33]Ner was the father of Kish, Kish the father of Saul, and Saul the father of Jonathan, Malki-Shua,

[k]29 Some Septuagint manuscripts (see also 1 Chron. 9:35); Hebrew does not have *Jeiel*.
[l]29 *Father* may mean *civic leader* or *military leader*.
[m]30 Some Septuagint manuscripts (see also 1 Chron. 9:36); Hebrew does not have *Ner*.

°25 ק ופנואל

מַלְכִּי־שׁוּעַ וְאֶת־אֲבִינָדָב וְאֶת־אֶשְׁבָּעַל׃ וּבֶן־יְהוֹנָתָן מְרִיב בָּעַל
Baal Merib Jonathan and-son-of (34) Esh-Baal and Abinadab and Shua Malki

וּמְרִיב בַּעַל הוֹלִיד אֶת־מִיכָה׃ וּבְנֵי מִיכָה פִּיתוֹן וָמֶלֶךְ
and-Melech Pithon Micah and-sons-of (35) Micah *** he-fathered Baal and-Merib

וְתַאְרֵעַ וְאָחָז׃ וְאָחָז הוֹלִיד אֶת־יְהוֹעַדָּה וִיהוֹעַדָּה
and-Jehoaddah Jehoaddah *** he-fathered and-Ahaz (36) and-Ahaz and-Tarea

הוֹלִיד אֶת־עָלֶמֶת וְאֶת־עַזְמָוֶת וְאֶת־זִמְרִי וְזִמְרִי הוֹלִיד אֶת־
*** he-fathered and-Zimri Zimri and Azmaveth and Alemeth *** he-fathered

מוֹצָא׃ וּמוֹצָא הוֹלִיד אֶת־בִּנְעָא רָפָה בְנוֹ אֶלְעָשָׂה
Eleasah son-of-him Raphah Binea *** he-fathered and-Moza (37) Moza

בְנוֹ אָצֵל בְּנוֹ׃ וּלְאָצֵל שִׁשָּׁה בָנִים וְאֵלֶּה שְׁמוֹתָם
names-of-them and-these sons six and-to-Azel (38) son-of-him Azel son-of-him

עַזְרִיקָם ׀ בֹּכְרוּ וְיִשְׁמָעֵאל וּשְׁעַרְיָה וְעֹבַדְיָה וְחָנָן כָּל־אֵלֶּה
these all-of and-Hanan and-Obadiah and-Sheariah and-Ishmael Bokeru Azrikam

בְּנֵי אָצֵל׃ וּבְנֵי עֵשֶׁק אָחִיו אוּלָם בְּכֹרוֹ
firstborn-of-him Ulam brother-of-him Eshek and-sons-of (39) Azel sons-of

יְעוּשׁ הַשֵּׁנִי וֶאֱלִיפֶלֶט הַשְּׁלִשִׁי׃ וַיִּהְיוּ בְנֵי־אוּלָם
Ulam sons-of and-they-were (40) the-third and-Eliphelet the-second Jeush

אֲנָשִׁים גִּבֹּרֵי־חַיִל דֹּרְכֵי קֶשֶׁת וּמַרְבִּים בָּנִים
sons and-ones-having-many bow ones-handling-of bravery warriors-of men

וּבְנֵי בָנִים מֵאָה וַחֲמִשִּׁים כָּל־אֵלֶּה מִבְּנֵי בִנְיָמִן׃
Benjamin from-descendants-of these all-of and-fifty hundred sons and-sons-of

וְכָל־יִשְׂרָאֵל הִתְיַחְשׂוּ וְהִנָּם כְּתוּבִים
ones-being-recorded and-see-they! they-were-listed Israel and-all-of (9:1)

עַל־סֵפֶר מַלְכֵי יִשְׂרָאֵל וִיהוּדָה הָגְלוּ לְבָבֶל
to-Babylon they-were-taken-captive and-Judah Israel kings-of book-of in

בְּמַעֲלָם׃ וְהַיּוֹשְׁבִים הָרִאשֹׁנִים אֲשֶׁר
who the-first-ones now-the-ones-resettling (2) for-unfaithfulness-of-them

בַּאֲחֻזָּתָם בְּעָרֵיהֶם יִשְׂרָאֵל הַכֹּהֲנִים הַלְוִיִּם
the-Levites the-priests Israel in-towns-of-them on-property-of-them

וְהַנְּתִינִים׃ וּבִירוּשָׁלִַם יָשְׁבוּ מִן־בְּנֵי יְהוּדָה
Judah sons-of from they-lived and-in-Jerusalem (3) and-the-temple-servants

וּמִן־בְּנֵי בִנְיָמִן וּמִן־בְּנֵי אֶפְרַיִם וּמְנַשֶּׁה׃ עוּתַי
Uthai (4) and-Manasseh Ephraim sons-of and-from Benjamin sons-of and-from

בֶּן־עַמִּיהוּד בֶּן־עָמְרִי בֶּן־אִמְרִי בֶן־בָּנִימִן־ בְּנֵי־
descendants-of from Bani son-of Imri son-of Omri son-of Ammihud son-of

פֶרֶץ בֶּן־יְהוּדָה׃ וּמִן־הַשִּׁילוֹנִי עֲשָׂיָה הַבְּכוֹר
the-firstborn Asaiah the-Shilonite and-from (5) Judah son-of Perez

Abinadab and Esh-Baal.[o]
34The son of Jonathan:
Merib-Baal,[p] who was the father of Micah.
35The sons of Micah:
Pithon, Melech, Tarea and Ahaz.
36Ahaz was the father of Jehoaddah, Jehoaddah was the father of Alemeth, Azmaveth and Zimri, and Zimri was the father of Moza. 37Moza was the father of Binea; Raphah was his son, Eleasah his son and Azel his son.
38Azel had six sons, and these were their names:
Azrikam, Bokeru, Ishmael, Sheariah, Obadiah and Hanan. All these were the sons of Azel.
39The sons of his brother Eshek:
Ulam his firstborn, Jeush the second son and Eliphelet the third. 40The sons of Ulam were brave warriors who could handle the bow. They had many sons and grandsons—150 in all.
All these were the descendants of Benjamin.

9 All Israel was listed in the genealogies recorded in the book of the kings of Israel.

*The People in Jerusalem*

The people of Judah were taken captive to Babylon because of their unfaithfulness.
2Now the first to resettle on their own property in their own towns were some Israelites, priests, Levites and temple servants.
3Those from Judah, from Benjamin, and from Ephraim and Manasseh who lived in Jerusalem were:
4Uthai son of Ammihud, the son of Omri, the son of Imri, the son of Bani, a descendant of Perez son of Judah.
5Of the Shilonites:
Asaiah the firstborn and

o33 Also known as *Ish-Bosheth*
p34 Also known as *Mephibosheth*

°4 ק בני מן־

וּבָנָיו׃ (6) וּמִן־ בְּנֵי־ זֶרַח יְעוּאֵל וַאֲחֵיהֶם
and-brothers-of-them Jeuel Zerah sons-of and-from (6) and-sons-of-him

שֵׁשׁ־ מֵאוֹת וְתִשְׁעִים׃ (7) וּמִן־ בְּנֵי בִּנְיָמִן סַלּוּא בֶּן־ מְשֻׁלָּם
Meshullam son-of Sallu Benjamin sons-of and-from (7) and-ninety hundreds six

בֶּן־ הוֹדַוְיָה בֶּן־ הַסְּנֻאָה׃ (8) וְיִבְנְיָה בֶּן־ יְרֹחָם וְאֵלָה
and-Elah Jeroham son-of and-Ibneiah (8) Hassenuah son-of Hodaviah son-of

בֶּן־ עֻזִּי בֶּן־ מִכְרִי וּמְשֻׁלָּם בֶּן־ שְׁפַטְיָה בֶּן־ רְעוּאֵל
Reuel son-of Shephatiah son-of and-Meshullam Micri son-of Uzzi son-of

בֶּן־ יִבְנִיָּה׃ (9) וַאֲחֵיהֶם לְתֹלְדוֹתָם תְּשַׁע
nine-of in-genealogies-of-them and-brothers-of-them (9) Ibnijah son-of

מֵאוֹת וַחֲמִשִּׁים וְשִׁשָּׁה כָּל־ אֵלֶּה אֲנָשִׁים רָאשֵׁי אָבוֹת לְבֵית
of-family-of fathers heads-of men these all-of and-six and-fifty hundreds

אֲבֹתֵיהֶם׃ (10) וּמִן־ הַכֹּהֲנִים יְדַעְיָה וִיהוֹיָרִיב וְיָכִין׃
and-Jakin and-Jehoiarib Jedaiah the-priests and-from (10) fathers-of-them

(11) וַעֲזַרְיָה בֶּן־ חִלְקִיָּה בֶּן־ מְשֻׁלָּם בֶּן־ צָדוֹק בֶּן־
son-of Zadok son-of Meshullam son-of Hilkiah son-of and-Azariah (11)

מְרָיוֹת בֶּן־ אֲחִיטוּב נְגִיד בֵּית הָאֱלֹהִים׃ (12) וַעֲדָיָה בֶּן־
son-of and-Adaiah (12) the-God house-of official-of Ahitub son-of Meraioth

יְרֹחָם בֶּן־ פַּשְׁחוּר בֶּן־ מַלְכִּיָּה וּמַעְשַׂי בֶּן־ עֲדִיאֵל בֶּן־
son-of Adiel son-of and-Maasai Malkijah son-of Pashhur son-of Jeroham

יַחְזֵרָה בֶּן־ מְשֻׁלָּם בֶּן־ מְשִׁלֵּמִית בֶּן־ אִמֵּר׃
Immer son-of Meshillemith son-of Meshullam son-of Jahzerah

(13) וַאֲחֵיהֶם רָאשִׁים לְבֵית אֲבוֹתָם אֶלֶף
thousand fathers-of-them of-family-of heads and-brothers-of-them (13)

וּשְׁבַע מֵאוֹת וְשִׁשִּׁים גִּבּוֹרֵי חֵיל מְלֶאכֶת עֲבוֹדַת
ministry-of responsible-of ability men-of and-sixty hundreds and-seven-of

בֵּית־ הָאֱלֹהִים׃ (14) וּמִן־ הַלְוִיִּם שְׁמַעְיָה בֶן־ חַשּׁוּב בֶּן־
son-of Hasshub son-of Shemaiah the-Levites and-from (14) the-God house-of

עַזְרִיקָם בֶּן־ חֲשַׁבְיָה מִן־ בְּנֵי מְרָרִי׃ (15) וּבַקְבַּקַּר חֶרֶשׁ
Heresh and-Bakbakkar (15) Merari sons-of from Hashabiah son-of Azrikam

וְגָלָל וּמַתַּנְיָה בֶּן־ מִיכָא בֶּן־ זִכְרִי בֶּן־ אָסָף׃
Asaph son-of Zicri son-of Mica son-of and-Mattaniah and-Galal

(16) וְעֹבַדְיָה בֶּן־ שְׁמַעְיָה בֶּן־ גָּלָל בֶּן־ יְדוּתוּן וּבֶרֶכְיָה
and-Berekiah Jeduthun son-of Galal son-of Shemaiah son-of and-Obadiah (16)

בֶן־ אָסָא בֶּן־ אֶלְקָנָה הַיּוֹשֵׁב בְּחַצְרֵי נְטוֹפָתִי׃
Netophathite in-villages-of the-one-living Elkanah son-of Asa son-of

(17) וְהַשֹּׁעֲרִים שַׁלּוּם וְעַקּוּב וְטַלְמֹן וַאֲחִימָן
and-Ahiman and-Talmon and-Akkub Shallum and-the-gatekeepers (17)

his sons.

6 Of the Zerahites:
Jeuel.
The people from Judah numbered 690.

7 Of the Benjamites:
Sallu son of Meshullam, the son of Hodaviah, the son of Hassenuah;
8 Ibneiah son of Jeroham; Elah son of Uzzi, the son of Micri; and Meshullam son of Shephatiah, the son of Reuel, the son of Ibnijah.
9 The people from Benjamin, as listed in their genealogy, numbered 956. All these men were heads of their families.

10 Of the priests:
Jedaiah; Jehoiarib; Jakin;
11 Azariah son of Hilkiah, the son of Meshullam, the son of Zadok, the son of Meraioth, the son of Ahitub, the official in charge of the house of God;
12 Adaiah son of Jeroham, the son of Pashhur, the son of Malkijah; and Maasai son of Adiel, the son of Jahzerah, the son of Meshullam, the son of Meshillemith, the son of Immer.
13 The priests, who were heads of families, numbered 1,760. They were able men, responsible for ministering in the house of God.

14 Of the Levites:
Shemaiah son of Hasshub, the son of Azrikam, the son of Hashabiah, a Merarite; 15 Bakbakkar, Heresh, Galal and Mattaniah son of Mica, the son of Zicri, the son of Asaph; 16 Obadiah son of Shemaiah, the son of Galal, the son of Jeduthun; and Berekiah son of Asa, the son of Elkanah, who lived in the villages of the Netophathites.

17 The gatekeepers:
Shallum, Akkub, Talmon, Ahiman and their

וַאֲחִיהֶם שַׁלּוּם הָרֹאשׁ׃ וְעַד־ הֵנָּה בְּשַׁעַר הַמֶּלֶךְ
the-King at-Gate-of now and-to (18) the-chief Shallum and-brother-of-them

מִזְרָחָה הֵמָּה הַשֹּׁעֲרִים לְמַחֲנוֹת בְּנֵי לֵוִי׃ וְשַׁלּוּם
and-Shallum (19) Levi sons-of of-camps-of the-gatekeepers they on-east

בֶּן־ קוֹרֵא בֶּן־ אֶבְיָסָף בֶּן־ קֹרַח וְאֶחָיו לְבֵית־
from-family-of and-fellows-of-him Korah son-of Ebiasaph son-of Kore son-of

אָבִיו הַקָּרְחִים עַל מְלֶאכֶת הָעֲבוֹדָה שֹׁמְרֵי
ones-guarding-of the-service responsibility-of over the-Korahites father-of-him

הַסִּפִּים לָאֹהֶל וַאֲבֹתֵיהֶם עַל־ מַחֲנֵה יְהוָה
Yahweh dwelling-of over and-fathers-of-them of-the-tent the-thresholds

שֹׁמְרֵי הַמָּבוֹא׃ וּפִינְחָס בֶּן־ אֶלְעָזָר נָגִיד
leader Eleazar son-of and-Phinehas (20) the-entrance ones-guarding-of

הָיָה עֲלֵיהֶם לְפָנִים יְהוָה ׀ עִמּוֹ׃ זְכַרְיָה בֶּן מְשֶׁלֶמְיָה
Meshelemiah son-of Zechariah (21) with-him Yahweh earlier over-them he-was

שֹׁעֵר פֶּתַח לְאֹהֶל מוֹעֵד׃ כֻּלָּם
all-of-them (22) Meeting of-Tent-of entrance gatekeeper-of

הַבְּרוּרִים לְשֹׁעֲרִים בַּסִּפִּים מָאתַיִם וּשְׁנֵים
and-two two-hundreds at-the-thresholds as-gatekeepers the-ones-being-chosen

עָשָׂר הֵמָּה בְחַצְרֵיהֶם הִתְיַחְשָׂם הֵמָּה יִסַּד דָּוִיד
David he-assigned them to-be-registered-them in-villages-of-them they ten

וּשְׁמוּאֵל הָרֹאֶה בֶּאֱמוּנָתָם׃ וְהֵם וּבְנֵיהֶם
and-descendants-of-them and-they (23) to-trust-of-them the-seer and-Samuel

עַל־ הַשְּׁעָרִים לְבֵית־ יְהוָה לְבֵית־ הָאֹהֶל לְמִשְׁמָרוֹת׃
as-guards the-Tent of-house-of Yahweh of-house-of the-gates over

לְאַרְבַּע רוּחוֹת יִהְיוּ הַשֹּׁעֲרִים מִזְרָח יָמָּה צָפוֹנָה
at-north at-west east the-gatekeepers they-were sides at-four-of (24)

וָנֶגְבָּה׃ וַאֲחֵיהֶם בְּחַצְרֵיהֶם לָבוֹא
to-come in-villages-of-them and-brothers-of-them (25) and-at-south

לְשִׁבְעַת הַיָּמִים מֵעֵת אֶל־ עֵת עִם־ אֵלֶּה׃ כִּי בֶאֱמוּנָה הֵמָּה
they in-trust but (26) these with time to from-time the-days for-seven-of

אַרְבַּעַת גִּבֹּרֵי הַשֹּׁעֲרִים הֵם הַלְוִיִּם וְהָיוּ עַל־
over and-they-were the-Levites they the-gatekeepers principal-ones-of four-of

הַלְּשָׁכוֹת וְעַל הָאֹצְרוֹת בֵּית הָאֱלֹהִים׃ וּסְבִיבוֹת
and-ones-around-of (27) the-God house-of the-treasuries and-over the-rooms

בֵּית־ הָאֱלֹהִים יָלִינוּ כִּי־ עֲלֵיהֶם מִשְׁמֶרֶת וְהֵם
and-they guard-duty upon-them because they-spent-night the-God house-of

עַל־ הַמַּפְתֵּחַ וְלַבֹּקֶר לַבֹּקֶר׃ וּמֵהֶם עַל־
over and-from-them (28) for-the-morning also-for-the-morning the-key over

brothers, Shallum their chief [18]being stationed at the King's Gate on the east, up to the present time. These were the gatekeepers belonging to the camp of the Levites. [19]Shallum son of Kore, the son of Ebiasaph, the son of Korah, and his fellow gatekeepers from his family (the Korahites) were responsible for guarding the thresholds of the tent[q] just as their fathers had been responsible for guarding the entrance to the dwelling of the LORD. [20]In earlier times Phinehas son of Eleazar was in charge of the gatekeepers, and the LORD was with him. [21]Zechariah son of Meshelemiah was the gatekeeper at the entrance to the Tent of Meeting.

[22]Altogether, those chosen to be gatekeepers at the thresholds numbered 212. They were registered by genealogy in their villages. The gatekeepers had been assigned to their positions of trust by David and Samuel the seer. [23]They and their descendants were in charge of guarding the gates of the house of the LORD—the house called the Tent. [24]The gatekeepers were on the four sides: east, west, north and south. [25]Their brothers in their villages had to come from time to time and share their duties for seven-day periods. [26]But the four principal gatekeepers, who were Levites, were entrusted with the responsibility for the rooms and treasuries in the house of God. [27]They would spend the night stationed around the house of God, because they had to guard it; and they had charge of the key for opening it each morning.

[28]Some of them were in

q19 That is, the temple; also in verse 21

כְּלֵי הָעֲבוֹדָה כִּֽי־ בְמִסְפָּר יְבִיאוּם
they-brought-in-them according-to-count indeed the-service articles-of

וּבְמִסְפָּר יוֹצִיאוּם׃ וּמֵהֶם מְמֻנִּים
ones-being-assigned and-from-them (29) they-took-out-them and-according-to-count

עַל־ הַכֵּלִים וְעַל כָּל־ כְּלֵי הַקֹּדֶשׁ וְעַל־
and-over the-sanctuary articles-of all-of and-over the-furnishings over

הַסֹּלֶת וְהַיַּיִן וְהַשֶּׁמֶן וְהַלְּבוֹנָה וְהַבְּשָׂמִים׃
and-the-spices and-the-incense and-the-oil and-the-wine the-flour

וּמִן־ בְּנֵי הַכֹּהֲנִים רֹקְחֵי הַמִּרְקַחַת לַבְּשָׂמִים׃
of-the-spices the-mixture ones-mixing-of the-priests sons-of but-from (30)

וּמַתִּתְיָה מִן־ הַלְוִיִּם הוּא הַבְּכוֹר לְשַׁלֻּם הַקָּרְחִי
the-Korahite of-Shallum the-firstborn he the-Levites from and-Mattithiah (31)

בֶּאֱמוּנָה עַל מַעֲשֵׂה הַחֲבִתִּים׃ וּמִן־ בְּנֵי
sons-of and-from (32) the-offering-bread baking-of over with-trust

הַקְּהָתִי מִן־ אֲחֵיהֶם עַל־ לֶחֶם הַמַּעֲרָכֶת לְהָכִין
to-prepare the-setting-out bread-of over brothers-of-them from the-Kohathite

שַׁבַּת שַׁבָּת׃ וְאֵלֶּה הַמְשֹׁרְרִים רָאשֵׁי אָבוֹת
fathers heads-of the-ones-making-music and-those (33) Sabbath Sabbath-of

לַלְוִיִּם בַּלְּשָׁכֹת פְּטוּרִים כִּי־ יוֹמָם וָלַיְלָה
and-night by-day because ones-being-exempt in-the-rooms of-the-Levites

עֲלֵיהֶם בַּמְּלָאכָה׃ אֵלֶּה רָאשֵׁי הָאָבוֹת לַלְוִיִּם
of-the-Levites the-fathers heads-of these (34) for-the-work upon-them

לְתֹלְדוֹתָם רָאשִׁים אֵלֶּה יָשְׁבוּ בִירוּשָׁלָ͏ִם׃ וּבְגִבְעוֹן
and-in-Gibeon (35) in-Jerusalem they-lived these chiefs by-genealogies-of-them

יָשְׁבוּ אֲבִי־ גִבְעוֹן יְעוּאֵל וְשֵׁם אִשְׁתּוֹ מַעֲכָה׃
Maacah wife-of-him and-name-of Jeiel Gibeon father-of they-lived

וּבְנוֹ הַבְּכוֹר עַבְדּוֹן וְצוּר וְקִישׁ וּבַעַל וְנֵר
and-Ner and-Baal and-Kish and-Zur Abdon the-firstborn and-son-of-him (36)

וְנָדָב׃ וּגְדוֹר וְאַחְיוֹ וּזְכַרְיָה וּמִקְלוֹת׃ וּמִקְלוֹת
and-Mikloth (38) and-Mikloth and-Zechariah and-Ahio and-Gedor (37) and-Nadab

הוֹלִיד אֶת־ שִׁמְאָם וְאַף־ הֵם נֶגֶד אֲחֵיהֶם יָשְׁבוּ
they-lived relatives-of-them near they and-also Shimeam *** he-fathered

בִירוּשָׁלַ͏ִם עִם־ אֲחֵיהֶם׃ וְנֵר הוֹלִיד אֶת־ קִישׁ
Kish *** he-fathered and-Ner (39) relatives-of-them with in-Jerusalem

וְקִישׁ הוֹלִיד אֶת־ שָׁאוּל וְשָׁאוּל הוֹלִיד אֶת־ יְהוֹנָתָן וְאֶת־
and Jonathan *** he-fathered and-Saul Saul *** he-fathered and-Kish

מַלְכִּי־שׁוּעַ וְאֶת־אֲבִינָדָב וְאֶת־אֶשְׁבָּעַל׃ וּבֶן־ יְהוֹנָתָן מְרִיב בָּעַל
Baal Merib Jonathan and-son-of (40) Esh-Baal and Abinadab and Shua Malki

charge of the articles used in the temple service; they counted them when they were brought in and when they were taken out. [29]Others were assigned to take care of the furnishings and all the other articles of the sanctuary, as well as the flour and wine, and the oil, incense and spices. [30]But some of the priests took care of mixing the spices. [31]A Levite named Mattithiah, the firstborn son of Shallum the Korahite, was entrusted with the responsibility for baking the offering bread. [32]Some of their Kohathite brothers were in charge of preparing for every Sabbath the bread set out on the table.

[33]Those who were musicians, heads of Levite families, stayed in the rooms of the temple and were exempt from other duties because they were responsible for the work day and night.

[34]All these were heads of Levite families, chiefs as listed in their genealogy, and they lived in Jerusalem.

*The Genealogy of Saul*

[35]Jeiel the father[r] of Gibeon
lived in Gibeon.
His wife's name was
Maacah, [36]and his
firstborn son was Abdon,
followed by Zur, Kish,
Baal, Ner, Nadab, [37]Gedor, Ahio, Zechariah and
Mikloth. [38]Mikloth was
the father of Shimeam.
They too lived near their
relatives in Jerusalem.
[39]Ner was the father of Kish,
Kish the father of Saul,
and Saul the father of
Jonathan, Malki-Shua,
Abinadab and Esh-Baal.[s]
[40]The son of Jonathan:
Merib-Baal,[t] who was

[r]35 *Father* may mean *civic leader* or *military leader*.
[s]39 Also known as *Ish-Bosheth*
[t]40 Also known as *Mephibosheth*

°33 ק פטורים
°35 ק יעיאל

וּמְרִי־ בַעַל הוֹלִיד אֶת־ מִיכָה׃ וּבְנֵי מִיכָה פִּיתֹן
Pithon Micah and-sons-of (41) Micah *** he-fathered Baal and-Merib

וָמֶלֶךְ וְתַחְרֵעַ׃ וְאָחָז הוֹלִיד אֶת־ יַעְרָה וְיַעְרָה
and-Jarah Jarah *** he-fathered and-Ahaz (42) and-Tahrea and-Melech

הוֹלִיד אֶת־ עָלֶמֶת וְאֶת־ עַזְמָוֶת וְאֶת־ זִמְרִי וְזִמְרִי הוֹלִיד אֶת־
*** he-fathered and-Zimri Zimri and Azmaveth and Alemeth *** he-fathered

מוֹצָא׃ וּמוֹצָא הוֹלִיד אֶת־ בִּנְעָא וּרְפָיָה בְנוֹ אֶלְעָשָׂה
Eleasah son-of-him and-Rephaiah Binea *** he-fathered and-Moza (43) Moza

בְנוֹ אָצֵל בְּנוֹ׃ וּלְאָצֵל שִׁשָּׁה בָנִים וְאֵלֶּה שְׁמוֹתָם
names-of-them and-these sons six and-to-Azel (44) son-of-him Azel son-of-him

עַזְרִיקָם ׀ בֹּכְרוּ וְיִשְׁמָעֵאל וּשְׁעַרְיָה וְעֹבַדְיָה וְחָנָן אֵלֶּה בְּנֵי
sons-of these and-Hanan and-Obadiah and-Sheariah and-Ishmael Bokeru Azrikam

אָצֵל׃ וּפְלִשְׁתִּים נִלְחֲמוּ בְיִשְׂרָאֵל וַיָּנָס אִישׁ־
man-of and-he-fled against-Israel they-fought now-Philistines (10:1) Azel

יִשְׂרָאֵל מִפְּנֵי פְלִשְׁתִּים וַיִּפְּלוּ חֲלָלִים בְּהַר גִּלְבֹּעַ׃
Gilboa on-Mount-of ones-slain and-they-fell Philistines from-before Israel

וַיַּדְבְּקוּ פְלִשְׁתִּים אַחֲרֵי שָׁאוּל וְאַחֲרֵי בָנָיו
sons-of-him and-after Saul after Philistines and-they-pressed-hard (2)

וַיַּכּוּ פְלִשְׁתִּים אֶת־ יוֹנָתָן וְאֶת־ אֲבִינָדָב וְאֶת־ מַלְכִּי־ שׁוּעַ
Shua Malki and Abinadab and Jonathan *** Philistines and-they-killed

בְּנֵי שָׁאוּל׃ וַתִּכְבַּד הַמִּלְחָמָה עַל־ שָׁאוּל
Saul around the-fighting and-she-grew-fierce (3) Saul sons-of

וַיִּמְצָאֻהוּ הַמּוֹרִים בַּקָּשֶׁת וַיָּחֶל
and-he-was-wounded with-the-bow the-ones-shooting and-they-overtook-him

מִן־ הַיּוֹרִים׃ וַיֹּאמֶר שָׁאוּל אֶל־ נֹשֵׂא כֵלָיו
armors-of-him one-bearing-of to Saul and-he-said (4) the-ones-shooting by

שְׁלֹף חַרְבְּךָ ׀ וְדָקְרֵנִי בָהּ פֶּן־ יָבֹאוּ
they-will-come or with-her and-run-through-me! sword-of-you draw!

הָעֲרֵלִים הָאֵלֶּה וְהִתְעַלְּלוּ־ בִי וְלֹא
but-not against-me and-they-will-abuse the-these the-uncircumcised-ones

אָבָה נֹשֵׂא כֵלָיו כִּי יָרֵא מְאֹד וַיִּקַּח
so-he-took very he-was-terrified for armors-of-him one-bearing-of he-would

שָׁאוּל אֶת־ הַחֶרֶב וַיִּפֹּל עָלֶיהָ׃ וַיַּרְא נֹשֵׂא־
one-bearing-of when-he-saw (5) on-her and-he-fell the-sword *** Saul

כֵלָיו כִּי מֵת שָׁאוּל וַיִּפֹּל גַּם־ הוּא עַל־ הַחֶרֶב
the-sword on he also then-he-fell Saul he-was-dead that armors-of-him

וַיָּמֹת׃ וַיָּמָת שָׁאוּל וּשְׁלֹשֶׁת בָּנָיו וְכָל־
and-all-of sons-of-him and-three-of Saul so-he-died (6) and-he-died

the father of Micah.
41 The sons of Micah:
Pithon, Melech, Tahrea
and Ahaz.[u]
42 Ahaz was the father of
Jadah, Jadah[v] was the father of Alemeth, Az-
maveth and Zimri, and
Zimri was the father of
Moza. 43 Moza was the fa-
ther of Binea; Rephaiah
was his son, Eleasah his
son and Azel his son.
44 Azel had six sons, and these
were their names:
Azrikam, Bokeru, Ishma-
el, Sheariah, Obadiah
and Hanan. These were
the sons of Azel.

*Saul Takes His Life*

10 Now the Philistines
fought against Israel;
the Israelites fled before them,
and many fell slain on Mount
Gilboa. 2 The Philistines
pressed hard after Saul and his
sons, and they killed his sons
Jonathan, Abinadab and
Malki-Shua. 3 The fighting
grew fierce around Saul, and
when the archers overtook
him, they wounded him.
4 Saul said to his armor-bearer, "Draw your sword and run
me through, or these uncircumcised fellows will come
and abuse me."
But his armor-bearer was
terrified and would not do it;
so Saul took his own sword
and fell on it. 5 When the armor-bearer saw that Saul was
dead, he too fell on his sword
and died. 6 So Saul and three of
his sons died, and all his

[u] *41* Vulgate and Syriac (see also Septuagint and 1 Chron. 8:35); Hebrew does not have *and Ahaz.*
[v] *42* Some Hebrew manuscripts and Septuagint (see also 1 Chron. 8:36); most Hebrew manuscripts *Jarah, Jarah*

בֵּיתוֹ יַחְדָּו מֵתוּ׃ וַיִּרְאוּ כָּל־ אִישׁ יִשְׂרָאֵל אֲשֶׁר־
who Israel man-of all-of when-they-saw (7) they-died together house-of-him

בָּעֵמֶק כִּי נָסוּ וְכִי־ מֵתוּ שָׁאוּל וּבָנָיו
and-sons-of-him Saul they-were-dead and-that they-fled that in-the-valley

וַיַּעַזְבוּ עָרֵיהֶם וַיָּנֻסוּ וַיָּבֹאוּ פְלִשְׁתִּים
Philistines and-they-came and-they-fled towns-of-them then-they-abandoned

וַיֵּשְׁבוּ בָּהֶם׃ וַיְהִי מִמָּחֳרָת וַיָּבֹאוּ
when-they-came on-next-day and-he-was (8) in-them and-they-occupied

פְלִשְׁתִּים לְפַשֵּׁט אֶת־ הַחֲלָלִים וַיִּמְצְאוּ אֶת־ שָׁאוּל וְאֶת־
and Saul *** then-they-found the-dead-ones *** to-strip Philistines

בָּנָיו נֹפְלִים בְּהַר גִּלְבֹּעַ׃ וַיַּפְשִׁיטֻהוּ
and-they-stripped-him (9) Gilboa on-Mount-of ones-having-fallen sons-of-him

וַיִּשְׂאוּ אֶת־ רֹאשׁוֹ וְאֶת־ כֵּלָיו וַיְשַׁלְּחוּ בְאֶרֶץ־
through-land-of and-they-sent armors-of-him and head-of-him *** and-they-took

פְלִשְׁתִּים* סָבִיב לְבַשֵּׂר אֶת־ עֲצַבֵּיהֶם וְאֶת־ הָעָם׃
the-people and-among idols-of-them among to-proclaim-news around Philistines

וַיָּשִׂימוּ אֶת־ כֵּלָיו בֵּית אֱלֹהֵיהֶם וְאֶת־ גֻּלְגָּלְתּוֹ
head-of-him and gods-of-them temple-of armors-of-him *** and-they-put (10)

תָּקְעוּ בֵּית דָּגוֹן׃ וַיִּשְׁמְעוּ כֹּל יָבֵישׁ גִּלְעָד אֵת
*** Gilead Jabesh all-of when-they-heard (11) Dagon temple-of they-hung-up

כָּל־ אֲשֶׁר־ עָשׂוּ פְלִשְׁתִּים לְשָׁאוּל׃ וַיָּקוּמוּ כָּל־ אִישׁ
man-of every-of then-they-went (12) to-Saul Philistines they-did that all

חַיִל וַיִּשְׂאוּ אֶת־ גּוּפַת שָׁאוּל וְאֵת גּוּפֹת בָּנָיו
sons-of-him bodies-of and Saul body-of *** and-they-took valor

וַיְבִיאוּם יָבֵישָׁה וַיִּקְבְּרוּ אֶת־ עַצְמוֹתֵיהֶם תַּחַת
under bones-of-them *** then-they-buried to-Jabesh and-they-brought-them

הָאֵלָה בְּיָבֵשׁ וַיָּצוּמוּ שִׁבְעַת יָמִים׃ וַיָּמָת שָׁאוּל
Saul and-he-died (13) days seven-of and-they-fasted in-Jabesh the-great-tree

בְּמַעֲלוֹ אֲשֶׁר מָעַל בַּיהוָה עַל־ דְּבַר
word-of against to-Yahweh he-was-unfaithful when for-unfaithfulness-of-him

יְהוָה אֲשֶׁר לֹא־ שָׁמָר וְגַם־ לִשְׁאוֹל בָּאוֹב לִדְרוֹשׁ׃
to-seek-guidance with-medium to-consult and-even he-kept not which Yahweh

וְלֹא־ דָרַשׁ בַּיהוָה וַיְמִיתֵהוּ וַיַּסֵּב אֶת־
*** and-he-turned-over so-he-killed-him of-Yahweh he-inquired and-not (14)

הַמְּלוּכָה לְדָוִיד בֶּן־ יִשָׁי׃ וַיִּקָּבְצוּ כָל־
all-of and-they-came-together (11:1) Jesse son-of to-David the-kingdom

יִשְׂרָאֵל אֶל־ דָּוִיד חֶבְרוֹנָה לֵאמֹר הִנֵּה עַצְמְךָ וּבְשָׂרְךָ אֲנָחְנוּ׃
we and-flesh-of-you bone-of-you see! to-say at-Hebron David to Israel

house died together.
7When all the Israelites in
the valley saw that the army
had fled and that Saul and his
sons had died, they aban-
doned their towns and fled.
And the Philistines came and
occupied them.
8The next day, when the
Philistines came to strip the
dead, they found Saul and his
sons fallen on Mount Gilboa.
9They stripped him and took
his head and his armor, and
sent messengers throughout
the land of the Philistines to
proclaim the news among
their idols and their people.
10They put his armor in the
temple of their gods and hung
up his head in the temple of
Dagon.
11When all the inhabitants
of Jabesh Gilead heard of
everything the Philistines had
done to Saul, 12all their valiant
men went and took the bodies
of Saul and his sons and
brought them to Jabesh. Then
they buried their bones under
the great tree in Jabesh, and
they fasted seven days.
13Saul died because he was
unfaithful to the LORD; he did
not keep the word of the LORD
and even consulted a medium
for guidance, 14and did not inquire of the LORD. So the LORD
put him to death and turned
the kingdom over to David
son of Jesse.

### *David Becomes King Over Israel*

11 All Israel came together
to David at Hebron
and said, "We are your own
flesh and blood. 2In the past,

*9 Most mss have *dagesh* in the *pe* ( פּ ).

גַּם־ תְּמוֹל גַּם־ שִׁלְשׁוֹם גַּם בִּהְיוֹת שָׁאוּל מֶלֶךְ אַתָּה
you king Saul while-to-be even before even yesterday even (2)

הַמּוֹצִיא וְהַמֵּבִיא אֶת־ יִשְׂרָאֵל וַיֹּאמֶר יְהוָה
Yahweh and-he-said Israel *** and-the-one-leading-in the-one-leading-out

אֱלֹהֶיךָ לְךָ אַתָּה תִרְעֶה אֶת־ עַמִּי אֶת־ יִשְׂרָאֵל וְאַתָּה
and-you Israel *** people-of-me *** you-will-shepherd you to-you God-of-you

תִּהְיֶה נָגִיד עַל עַמִּי יִשְׂרָאֵל׃ וַיָּבֹאוּ כָּל־
all-of when-they-came (3) Israel people-of-me over ruler you-will-become

זִקְנֵי יִשְׂרָאֵל אֶל־ הַמֶּלֶךְ חֶבְרוֹנָה וַיִּכְרֹת לָהֶם דָּוִיד בְּרִית
compact David with-them then-he-made at-Hebron the-king to Israel elders-of

בְּחֶבְרוֹן לִפְנֵי יְהוָה וַיִּמְשְׁחוּ אֶת־ דָּוִיד לְמֶלֶךְ עַל־ יִשְׂרָאֵל
Israel over as-king David *** and-they-anointed Yahweh before at-Hebron

כִּדְבַר יְהוָה בְּיַד־ שְׁמוּאֵל׃ וַיֵּלֶךְ דָּוִיד וְכָל־
and-all-of David then-he-marched (4) Samuel by-hand-of Yahweh as-promise-of

יִשְׂרָאֵל יְרוּשָׁלִַם הִיא יְבוּס וְשָׁם הַיְבוּסִי יֹשְׁבֵי הָאָרֶץ׃
the-land ones-living-of the-Jebusite and-there Jebus that Jerusalem Israel

וַיֹּאמְרוּ יֹשְׁבֵי יְבוּס לְדָוִיד לֹא תָבוֹא הֵנָּה
to-here you-will-get-in not to-David Jebus ones-living-of and-they-said (5)

וַיִּלְכֹּד דָּוִיד אֶת־ מְצֻדַת צִיּוֹן הִיא עִיר דָּוִיד׃ וַיֹּאמֶר
and-he-said (6) David City-of that Zion fortress-of *** David but-he-captured

דָּוִיד כָּל־ מַכֵּה יְבוּסִי בָּרִאשֹׁנָה יִהְיֶה לְרֹאשׁ
as-commander he-will-become at-the-first Jebusite one-attacking any-of David

וּלְשָׂר וַיַּעַל בָּרִאשׁוֹנָה יוֹאָב בֶּן־ צְרוּיָה וַיְהִי
so-he-became Zeruiah son-of Joab at-the-first and-he-went-up and-as-chief

לְרֹאשׁ׃ וַיֵּשֶׁב דָּוִיד בַּמְּצָד עַל־ כֵּן קָרְאוּ־
they-called this for in-the-fortress David then-he-resided (7) as-commander

לוֹ עִיר דָּוִיד׃ וַיִּבֶן הָעִיר מִסָּבִיב מִן־ הַמִּלּוֹא
the-terrace from at-around the-city and-he-built-up (8) David City-of to-him

וְעַד־ הַסָּבִיב וְיוֹאָב יְחַיֶּה אֶת־ שְׁאָר הָעִיר
the-city rest-of *** he-restored while-Joab the-one-surrounding and-to

וַיֵּלֶךְ דָּוִיד הָלוֹךְ וְגָדוֹל וַיהוָה
and-Yahweh-of and-to-become-powerful to-continue David and-he-continued (9)

צְבָאוֹת עִמּוֹ׃ וְאֵלֶּה רָאשֵׁי הַגִּבּוֹרִים אֲשֶׁר לְדָוִיד
of-David who the-mighty-men chiefs-of and-these (10) with-him Hosts

הַמִּתְחַזְּקִים עִמּוֹ בְמַלְכוּתוֹ עִם - כָּל־ יִשְׂרָאֵל
Israel all-of with in-kingship-of-him to-him the-ones-giving-support

לְהַמְלִיכוֹ כִּדְבַר יְהוָה עַל־ יִשְׂרָאֵל׃ וְאֵלֶּה מִסְפַּר
list-of and-these (11) Israel over Yahweh as-promise-of to-make-king-him

even while Saul was king, you were the one who led Israel on their military campaigns. And the LORD your God said to you, 'You will shepherd my people Israel, and you will become their ruler.' "
3When all the elders of Israel had come to King David at Hebron, he made a compact with them at Hebron before the LORD, and they anointed David king over Israel, as the LORD had promised through Samuel.

*David Conquers Jerusalem*

4David and all the Israelites marched to Jerusalem, that is, Jebus. The Jebusites who lived
there 5said to David, "You will not get in here." Nevertheless, David captured the fortress of Zion, the City of David.
6David had said, "Whoever leads the attack on the Jebusites will become commander-in-chief." Joab son of Zeruiah went up first, and so he received the command.
7David then took up residence in the fortress, and so it was called the City of David.
8He built up the city around it, from the supporting terraces[w] to the surrounding wall, while Joab restored the rest of the
city. 9And David became more and more powerful, because the LORD Almighty was with him.

*David's Mighty Men*

10These were the chiefs of David's mighty men—they, together with all Israel, gave his kingship strong support to extend it over the whole land, as the LORD had promised—

[w]8 Or *the Millo*

הַגִּבֹּרִים אֲשֶׁר לְדָוִיד יָשָׁבְעָם בֶּן־ חַכְמוֹנִי רֹאשׁ הַשָּׁלוֹשִׁים°
the-Thirty chief-of Hacmoni son-of Jashobeam of-David who the-mighty-men

הוּא־ עוֹרֵר אֶת־ חֲנִיתוֹ עַל־ שְׁלֹשׁ־ מֵאוֹת חָלָל
killed hundreds three-of against spear-of-him *** one-raising he

בְּפַעַם אֶחָת׃ וְאַחֲרָיו אֶלְעָזָר בֶּן־ דּוֹדוֹ הָאֲחוֹחִי הוּא
he the-Ahohite Dodai son-of Eleazar and-next-to-him (12) one in-encounter

בִּשְׁלוֹשָׁה הַגִּבֹּרִים׃ הוּא־ הָיָה עִם־ דָּוִיד בַּפַּס דַּמִּים
Dammim at-the-Pas David with he-was he (13) the-mighty-men of-three

וְהַפְּלִשְׁתִּים נֶאֶסְפוּ־ שָׁם לַמִּלְחָמָה וַתְּהִי
and-she-was for-the-battle there they-gathered when-the-Philistines

חֶלְקַת הַשָּׂדֶה מְלֵאָה שְׂעוֹרִים וְהָעָם נָסוּ מִפְּנֵי
from-before they-fled and-the-troop barleys full the-field place-of

פְלִשְׁתִּים׃ וַיִּתְיַצְּבוּ בְתוֹךְ־ הַחֶלְקָה
the-field in-middle-of but-they-took-stand (14) Philistines

וַיַּצִּילוּהָ וַיַּכּוּ אֶת־ פְּלִשְׁתִּים
Philistines *** and-they-struck-down and-they-defended-her

וַיּוֹשַׁע יְהוָה תְּשׁוּעָה גְדוֹלָה׃ וַיֵּרְדוּ שְׁלוֹשָׁה
three and-they-came-down (15) great victory Yahweh and-he-brought-victory

מִן־ הַשְּׁלוֹשִׁים רֹאשׁ עַל־ הַצֻּר אֶל־ דָּוִיד אֶל־ מְעָרַת עֲדֻלָּם וּמַחֲנֵה
and-band-of Adullam cave-of at David to the-rock to chief the-thirty from

פְלִשְׁתִּים חֹנָה בְּעֵמֶק רְפָאִים׃ וְדָוִיד אָז בַּמְּצוּדָה
in-the-stronghold then and-David (16) Rephaim in-Valley-of camping Philistines

וּנְצִיב פְּלִשְׁתִּים אָז בְּבֵית לָחֶם׃ וַיִּתְאָו° דָּוִיד
David and-he-longed (17) Lehem at-Beth then Philistines and-garrison-of

וַיֹּאמַר מִי יַשְׁקֵנִי מַיִם מִבּוֹר בֵּית־ לֶחֶם אֲשֶׁר
that Lehem Beth from-well-of waters he-will-draw-for-me who? and-he-said

בַּשָּׁעַר׃ וַיִּבְקְעוּ הַשְּׁלֹשָׁה בְּמַחֲנֵה פְלִשְׁתִּים
Philistines through-line-of the-Three and-they-broke (18) near-the-gate

וַיִּשְׁאֲבוּ־ מַיִם מִבּוֹר בֵּית־ לֶחֶם אֲשֶׁר בַּשַּׁעַר
near-the-gate that Lehem Beth from-well-of waters and-they-drew

וַיִּשְׂאוּ וַיָּבִאוּ אֶל־ דָּוִיד וְלֹא־ אָבָה דָוִיד
David he-would but-not David to and-they-brought and-they-carried

לִשְׁתּוֹתָם וַיְנַסֵּךְ אֹתָם לַיהוָה׃ וַיֹּאמֶר
and-he-said (19) before-Yahweh them and-he-poured-out to-drink-them

חָלִילָה לִּי מֵאֱלֹהַי מֵעֲשׂוֹת זֹאת הֲדַם הָאֲנָשִׁים
the-men blood-of? this from-to-do from-God-of-me from-me far-be-it!

הָאֵלֶּה אֶשְׁתֶּה בְנַפְשׁוֹתָם כִּי בְנַפְשׁוֹתָם
at-lives-of-them because at-lives-of-them should-I-drink the-these

11 this is the list of David's mighty men:
Jashobeam,[x] a Hacmonite, was chief of the officers[y]; he raised his spear against three hundred men, whom he killed in one encounter.
12 Next to him was Eleazar son of Dodai the Ahohite, one of the three mighty men.
13 He was with David at Pas Dammim when the Philistines gathered there for battle. At a place where there was a field full of barley, the troops fled from the Philistines.
14 But they took their stand in the middle of the field. They defended it and struck the Philistines down, and the LORD brought about a great victory.
15 Three of the thirty chiefs came down to David to the rock at the cave of Adullam, while a band of Philistines was encamped in the Valley of Rephaim.
16 At that time David was in the stronghold, and the Philistine garrison was at Bethlehem.
17 David longed for water and said, "Oh, that someone would get me a drink of water from the well near the gate of Bethlehem!"
18 So the Three broke through the Philistine lines, drew water from the well near the gate of Bethlehem and carried it back to David. But he refused to drink it; instead, he poured it out before the LORD.
19 "God forbid that I should do this!" he said. "Should I drink the blood of these men who went at the risk of their lives?" Because they risked their lives to bring

[x] 11 Possibly a variant of *Jashob-Baal*
[y] 11 Or *Thirty;* some Septuagint manuscripts *Three* (see also 2 Samuel 23:8)

°11 ק השלישים
°17 ק ויתאיו

הֱבִיאוּם וְלֹא אָבָה לִשְׁתּוֹתָם אֵלֶּה עָשׂוּ שְׁלֹשֶׁת
three-of they-did these to-drink-them he-would then-not they-brought-them

הַגִּבּוֹרִים׃ (20) וְאַבְשַׁי אֲחִי־יוֹאָב הוּא הָיָה רֹאשׁ הַשְּׁלוֹשָׁה
the-Three chief-of he-was he Joab brother-of and-Abishai (20) the-mighty-men

וְהוּא עוֹרֵר אֶת־חֲנִיתוֹ עַל־שְׁלֹשׁ מֵאוֹת חָלָל
one-killed hundreds three-of against spear-of-him *** one-raising and-he

וְלֹא־שֵׁם בַּשְּׁלוֹשָׁה׃ (21) מִן־הַשְּׁלוֹשָׁה בַשְּׁנַיִם
by-the-two-times the-Three above (21) among-the-Three name so-to-him

נִכְבָּד וַיְהִי לָהֶם לְשָׂר וְעַד־הַשְּׁלוֹשָׁה לֹא־
not the-Three though-among as-commander to-them and-he-became being-honored

בָא׃ (22) בְּנָיָה בֶן־יְהוֹיָדָע בֶּן־אִישׁ־חַיִל רַב־
great-of valor man-of son-of Jehoiada son-of Benaiah (22) he-entered

פְּעָלִים מִן־קַבְצְאֵל הוּא הִכָּה אֵת שְׁנֵי אֲרִיאֵל מוֹאָב וְהוּא
and-he Moab best-man-of two-of *** he-struck-down he Kabzeel from exploits

יָרַד וְהִכָּה אֶת־הָאֲרִי בְּתוֹךְ הַבּוֹר בְּיוֹם הַשָּׁלֶג׃
the-snow on-day-of the-pit inside-of the-lion *** and-he-killed he-went-down

(23) וְהוּא־הִכָּה אֶת־הָאִישׁ הַמִּצְרִי אִישׁ מִדָּה ׀ חָמֵשׁ
five size man-of the-Egyptian the-man *** he-struck-down and-he (23)

בָּאַמָּה וּבְיַד הַמִּצְרִי חֲנִית כִּמְנוֹר אֹרְגִים
ones-weaving like-rod-of spear the-Egyptian though-in-hand-of by-the-cubit

וַיֵּרֶד אֵלָיו בַּשָּׁבֶט וַיִּגְזֹל אֶת־הַחֲנִית
the-spear *** and-he-snatched with-the-club against-him and-he-went

מִיַּד הַמִּצְרִי וַיַּהַרְגֵהוּ בַּחֲנִיתוֹ׃ (24) אֵלֶּה
these (24) with-spear-of-him and-he-killed-him the-Egyptian from-hand-of

עָשָׂה בְּנָיָהוּ בֶּן־יְהוֹיָדָע וְלוֹ־שֵׁם בִּשְׁלוֹשָׁה הַגִּבֹּרִים׃
the-mighty-men among-three name and-to-him Jehoiada son-of Benaiah he-did

(25) מִן־הַשְּׁלוֹשִׁים הִנּוֹ נִכְבָּד הוּא וְאֶל־הַשְּׁלוֹשָׁה לֹא־
not the-Three but-among he being-honored see-he! the-Thirty more-than (25)

בָא וַיְשִׂימֵהוּ דָוִיד עַל־מִשְׁמַעְתּוֹ׃
bodyguard-of-him over David and-he-put-in-charge-him he-entered

(26) וְגִבּוֹרֵי הַחֲיָלִים עֲשָׂה־אֵל אֲחִי יוֹאָב אֶלְחָנָן
Elhanan Joab brother-of El Asah the-valiant-ones and-mighty-men-of (26)

בֶּן־דּוֹדוֹ מִבֵּית לָחֶם׃ (27) שַׁמּוֹת הַהֲרוֹרִי חֶלֶץ הַפְּלוֹנִי׃
the-Pelonite Helez the-Harorite Shammoth (27) Lehem from-Beth Dodo son-of

(28) עִירָא בֶן־עִקֵּשׁ הַתְּקוֹעִי אֲבִיעֶזֶר הָעַנְּתוֹתִי׃ (29) סִבְּכַי
Sibbecai (29) the-Anathothite Abiezer the-Tekoaite Ikkesh son-of Ira (28)

הַחֻשָׁתִי עִילַי הָאֲחוֹחִי׃ (30) מַהְרַי הַנְּטֹפָתִי חֵלֶד בֶּן־
son-of Heled the-Netophathite Maharai (30) the-Ahohite Ilai the-Hushathite

°20 ק ולו

it back, David would not drink it.

Such were the exploits of the three mighty men.

[20]Abishai the brother of Joab was chief of the Three. He raised his spear against three hundred men, whom he killed, and so he became as famous as the Three. [21]He was doubly honored above the Three and became their commander, even though he was not included among them.

[22]Benaiah son of Jehoiada was a valiant fighter from Kabzeel, who performed great exploits. He struck down two of Moab's best men. He also went down into a pit on a snowy day and killed a lion. [23]And he struck down an Egyptian who was seven and a half feet[z] tall. Although the Egyptian had a spear like a weaver's rod in his hand, Benaiah went against him with a club. He snatched the spear from the Egyptian's hand and killed him with his own spear. [24]Such were the exploits of Benaiah son of Jehoiada; he too was as famous as the three mighty men. [25]He was held in greater honor than any of the Thirty, but he was not included among the Three. And David put him in charge of his bodyguard.

[26]The mighty men were:
Asahel the brother of Joab,
Elhanan son of Dodo from Bethlehem,
[27]Shammoth the Harorite,
Helez the Pelonite,
[28]Ira son of Ikkesh from Tekoa,
Abiezer from Anathoth,
[29]Sibbecai the Hushathite,
Ilai the Ahohite,
[30]Maharai the Netophathite,
Heled son of Baanah the

[z]23 Hebrew *five cubits* (about 2.3 meters)

בענה הנטופתי: איתי בן־ ריבי מגבעת בני
sons-of from-Gibeah-of Ribai son-of Ithai (31) the-Netophathite Baanah

בנימן בניה הפרעתני: חורי מנחלי געש אביאל
Abiel Gaash from-ravines-of Hurai (32) the-Pirathonite Benaiah Benjamin

הערבתי: עזמות הבחרומי אליחבא השעלבני:
the-Shaalbonite Eliahba the-Baharumite Azmaveth (33) the-Arbathite

בני השם הגזוני יונתן בן־ שגה ההררי:
the-Hararite Shagee son-of Jonathan the-Gizonite Hashem sons-of (34)

אחיאם בן־ שכר ההררי אליפל בן־ אור: חפר
Hepher (36) Ur son-of Eliphal the-Hararite Sacar son-of Ahiam (35)

המכרתי אחיה הפלני: חצרו הכרמלי נערי בן־
son-of Naarai the-Carmelite Hezro (37) the-Pelonite Ahijah the-Mekerathite

אזבי: יואל אחי נתן מבחר בן־ הגרי: צלק
Zelek (39) Hagri son-of Mibhar Nathan brother-of Joel (38) Ezbai

העמוני נחרי הברתי נשא כלי יואב בן־
son-of Joab armors-of one-bearing-of the-Berothite Naharai the-Ammonite

צרויה: עירא היתרי גרב היתרי: אוריה החתי
the-Hittite Uriah (41) the-Ithrite Gareb the-Ithrite Ira (40) Zeruiah

זבד בן־ אחלי: עדינא בן־ שיזא הראובני ראש
chief the-Reubenite Shiza son-of Adina (42) Ahlai son-of Zabad

לראובני ועליו שלושים: חנן בן־ מעכה ויושפט
and-Joshaphat Maacah son-of Hanan (43) thirty and-with-him of-the-Reubenite

המתני: עזיא העשתרתי שמע ויעואל° בני חותם
Hotham sons-of and-Jeiel Shama the-Ashterathite Uzzia (44) the-Mithnite

הערערי: ידיעאל בן־ שמרי ויחא אחיו התיצי:
the-Tizite brother-of-him and-Joha Shimri son-of Jediael (45) the-Aroerite

אליאל המחוים ויריבי ויושויה בני אלנעם ויתמה
and-Ithmah Elnaam sons-of and-Joshaviah and-Jeribai the-Mahavite Eliel (46)

המואבי: אליאל ועובד ויעשיאל המצביה: ואלה
and-these (12:1) the-Mezobaite and-Jaasiel and-Obed Eliel (47) the-Moabite

הבאים אל־ דויד לציקלג עוד עצור מפני
from-presences-of being-banished while at-Ziklag David to the-ones-coming

שאול בן־ קיש והמה בגבורים עזרי המלחמה:
the-battle ones-helping-of among-the-warriors and-they Kish son-of Saul

נשקי קשת מימינים ומשמאלים
and-ones-using-left-hand ones-using-right-hand bow ones-being-armed-of (2)

באבנים ובחצים בקשת מאחי שאול
Saul from-kinsmen-of with-the-bow and-with-the-arrows with-the-stones

Netophathite,
31 Ithai son of Ribai from
Gibeah of Benjamin,
Benaiah the Pirathonite,
32 Hurai from the ravines of
Gaash,
Abiel the Arbathite,
33 Azmaveth the Baharu-
mite,
Eliahba the Shaalbonite,
34 the sons of Hashem the
Gizonite,
Jonathan son of Shagee
the Hararite,
35 Ahiam son of Sacar the
Hararite,
Eliphal son of Ur,
36 Hepher the Mekerathite,
Ahijah the Pelonite,
37 Hezro the Carmelite,
Naarai son of Ezbai,
38 Joel the brother of Nathan,
Mibhar son of Hagri,
39 Zelek the Ammonite,
Naharai the Berothite,
the armor-bearer of Joab
son of Zeruiah,
40 Ira the Ithrite,
Gareb the Ithrite,
41 Uriah the Hittite,
Zabad son of Ahlai,
42 Adina son of Shiza the
Reubenite, who was
chief of the Reubenites,
and the thirty with him,
43 Hanan son of Maacah,
Joshaphat the Mithnite,
44 Uzzia the Ashterathite,
Shama and Jeiel the sons
of Hotham the Aroerite,
45 Jediael son of Shimri,
his brother Joha the Ti-
zite,
46 Eliel the Mahavite,
Jeribai and Joshaviah the
sons of Elnaam,
Ithmah the Moabite,
47 Eliel, Obed and Jaasiel
the Mezobaite.

*Warriors Join David*

12 These were the men
who came to David at
Ziklag, while he was banished
from the presence of Saul son
of Kish (they were among the
warriors who helped him in
battle; 2 they were armed with
bows and were able to shoot
arrows or to sling stones right-
handed or left-handed; they
were kinsmen of Saul from the

°44 ק ויעיאל

מִבִּנְיָמִן׃ (3) הָרֹאשׁ אֲחִיעֶזֶר וְיוֹאָשׁ בְּנֵי הַשְּׁמָעָה
from-Benjamin (3) the-chief Ahiezer and-Joash sons-of the-Shemaah

הַגִּבְעָתִי וִיזוֹאֵל וָפֶלֶט בְּנֵי עַזְמָוֶת וּבְרָכָה וְיֵהוּא
the-Gibeathite and-Jeziel and-Pelet sons-of Azmaveth and-Beracah and-Jehu

הָעַנְּתֹתִי׃ (4) וְיִשְׁמַעְיָה הַגִּבְעוֹנִי גִּבּוֹר בַּשְּׁלֹשִׁים
the-Anathothite (4) and-Ishmaiah the-Gibeonite mighty-man among-the-Thirty

וְעַל־ הַשְּׁלֹשִׁים׃ *(5) וְיִרְמְיָה וְיַחֲזִיאֵל וְיוֹחָנָן וְיוֹזָבָד
and-over the-Thirty *(5) and-Jeremiah and-Jahaziel and-Johanan and-Jozabad

הַגְּדֵרָתִי׃ (6) אֶלְעוּזַי וִירִימוֹת וּבְעַלְיָה וּשְׁמַרְיָהוּ
the-Gederathite (6) Eluzai and-Jerimoth and-Bealiah and-Shemariah

וּשְׁפַטְיָהוּ הַחֲרִיפִי׃ (7) אֶלְקָנָה וְיִשִּׁיָּהוּ וַעֲזַרְאֵל וְיוֹעֶזֶר
and-Shephatiah the-Haruphite (7) Elkanah and-Isshiah and-Azarel and-Joezer

וְיָשָׁבְעָם הַקָּרְחִים׃ (8) וְיוֹעֵאלָה וּזְבַדְיָה בְּנֵי יְרֹחָם
and-Jashobeam the-Korahites (8) and-Joelah and-Zebadiah sons-of Jeroham

מִן־ הַגְּדוֹר׃ (9) וּמִן־ הַגָּדִי נִבְדְּלוּ אֶל־ דָּוִיד
from the-Gedor (9) and-from the-Gadite they-defected to David

לַמְצַד מִדְבָּרָה גִּבֹּרֵי הַחַיִל אַנְשֵׁי צָבָא
at-the-stronghold in-desert warriors-of the-bravery men-of army

לַמִּלְחָמָה עֹרְכֵי צִנָּה וָרֹמַח וּפְנֵי אַרְיֵה
for-the-battle ones-handling-of shield and-spear and-faces-of lion

פְּנֵיהֶם וְכִצְבָאיִם עַל־ הֶהָרִים לְמַהֵר׃ (10) עֵזֶר
faces-of-them and-as-gazelles in the-mountains to-be-swift (10) Ezer

הָרֹאשׁ עֹבַדְיָה הַשֵּׁנִי אֱלִיאָב הַשְּׁלִשִׁי׃ (11) מִשְׁמַנָּה הָרְבִיעִי
the-chief Obadiah the-second Eliab the-third (11) Mishmannah the-fourth

יִרְמְיָה הַחֲמִשִׁי׃ (12) עַתַּי הַשִּׁשִּׁי אֱלִיאֵל הַשְּׁבִעִי׃ (13) יוֹחָנָן
Jeremiah the-fifth (12) Attai the-sixth Eliel the-seventh (13) Johanan

הַשְּׁמִינִי אֶלְזָבָד הַתְּשִׁיעִי׃ (14) יִרְמְיָהוּ הָעֲשִׂירִי מַכְבַּנַּי עַשְׁתֵּי עָשָׂר׃
the-eighth Elzabad the-ninth (14) Jeremiah the-tenth Macbannai one-of ten

(15) אֵלֶּה מִבְּנֵי־ גָד רָאשֵׁי הַצָּבָא אֶחָד לְמֵאָה הַקָּטָן
(15) these from-sons-of Gad commanders-of the-army one for-hundred the-least

וְהַגָּדוֹל לְאָלֶף׃ (16) אֵלֶּה הֵם אֲשֶׁר עָבְרוּ אֶת־
and-the-greatest for-thousand (16) these they who they-crossed ***

הַיַּרְדֵּן בַּחֹדֶשׁ הָרִאשׁוֹן וְהוּא מְמַלֵּא עַל־ כָּל־
the-Jordan in-the-month the-first when-he overflowing over all-of

גִּדְיֹתָיו וַיַּבְרִיחוּ אֶת־ כָּל־ הָעֲמָקִים לַמִּזְרָח
banks-of-him and-they-put-to-flight *** all-of the-valleys to-the-east

וְלַמַּעֲרָב׃ (17) וַיָּבֹאוּ מִן־ בְּנֵי בִנְיָמִן וִיהוּדָה עַד־
and-to-the-west (17) and-they-came from sons-of Benjamin and-Judah to

tribe of Benjamin):
3Ahiezer their chief and
Joash the sons of Shemaah
the Gibeathite; Jeziel and
Pelet the sons of Azmaveth;
Beracah, Jehu the Ana-
thothite, 4and Ishmaiah the
Gibeonite, a mighty man
among the Thirty, who was
a leader of the Thirty; Jeremiah, Jahaziel, Johanan,
Jozabad the Gederathite,
5Eluzai, Jerimoth, Bealiah,
Shemariah and Shephatiah
the Haruphite; 6Elkanah,
Isshiah, Azarel, Joezer and
Jashobeam the Korahites;
7and Joelah and Zebadiah
the sons of Jeroham from
Gedor.

8Some Gadites defected to
David at his stronghold in the
desert. They were brave warriors, ready for battle and able to
handle the shield and spear.
Their faces were the faces of
lions, and they were as swift
as gazelles in the mountains.
9Ezer was the chief,
Obadiah the second in
command, Eliab the
third,
10Mishmannah the fourth,
Jeremiah the fifth,
11Attai the sixth, Eliel the
seventh,
12Johanan the eighth, El-
zabad the ninth,
13Jeremiah the tenth and
Macbannai the eleventh.
14These Gadites were army
commanders; the least was a
match for a hundred, and the
greatest for a thousand. 15It
was they who crossed the Jordan in the first month when it
was overflowing all its banks,
and they put to flight everyone living in the valleys, to the
east and to the west.
16Other Benjamites and
some men from Judah also

*5 Verse 5 in Hebrew is equivalent to the second half of verse 4 in English; thus, there is a one-verse discrepancy through the rest of the chapter.

°3 ק ויזיאל
°6 ק החרופי
°16 ק גדותיו

לַמְּצַד לְדָוִיד׃ וַיֵּצֵא דָוִיד לִפְנֵיהֶם

before-them David and-he-went-out (18) to-David to-the-stronghold

וַיַּעַן וַיֹּאמֶר לָהֶם אִם־לְשָׁלוֹם בָּאתֶם אֵלַי לְעָזְרֵנִי

to-help-me to-me you-came in-peace if to-them and-he-said and-he-replied

יִהְיֶה־לִּי עֲלֵיכֶם לֵבָב לְיָחַד וְאִם־לְרַמּוֹתַנִי לְצָרַי

to-enemies-of-me to-betray-me but-if as-one heart with-you of-me he-will-be

בְּלֹא חָמָס בְּכַפַּי יֵרֶא אֱלֹהֵי אֲבוֹתֵינוּ

fathers-of-us God-of may-he-see in-hands-of-me violence when-not

וְיוֹכַח׃ וְרוּחַ לָבְשָׁה אֶת־עֲמָשַׂי רֹאשׁ

chief-of Amasai *** she-came-upon then-Spirit (19) and-may-he-judge

°הַשְּׁלוֹשִׁים לְךָ דָוִיד וְעִמְּךָ בֶן־יִשַׁי שָׁלוֹם ׀ שָׁלוֹם לְךָ

to-you success success Jesse son-of and-with-you David to-you the-Thirty

וְשָׁלוֹם לְעֹזְרֶךָ כִּי עֲזָרְךָ אֱלֹהֶיךָ

God-of-you he-will-help-you for to-one-helping-you and-success

וַיְקַבְּלֵם דָּוִיד וַיִּתְּנֵם בְּרָאשֵׁי הַגְּדוּד׃

the-raiding-band as-leaders-of and-he-made-them David so-he-received-them

וּמִמְּנַשֶּׁה נָפְלוּ עַל־דָּוִיד בְּבֹאוֹ עִם־

with when-to-go-him David to they-defected and-from-Manasseh (20)

פְּלִשְׁתִּים עַל־שָׁאוּל לַמִּלְחָמָה וְלֹא עֲזָרֻם כִּי

because they-helped-them but-not to-the-fight Saul against Philistines

בְעֵצָה שִׁלְּחֻהוּ סַרְנֵי פְלִשְׁתִּים לֵאמֹר

to-say Philistines rulers-of they-sent-away-him after-consultation

בְּרָאשֵׁינוּ יִפּוֹל אֶל־אֲדֹנָיו שָׁאוּל׃ בְּלֶכְתּוֹ אֶל־

to when-to-go-him (21) Saul masters-of-him to if-he-deserts at-heads-of-us

צִיקְלַג נָפְלוּ עָלָיו ׀ מִמְּנַשֶּׁה עַדְנַח וְיוֹזָבָד וִידִיעֲאֵל

and-Jediael and-Jozabad Adnah from-Manasseh to-him they-defected Ziklag

וּמִיכָאֵל וְיוֹזָבָד וֶאֱלִיהוּא וְצִלְּתָי רָאשֵׁי הָאֲלָפִים

the-thousands leaders-of and-Zillethai and-Elihu and-Jozabad and-Michael

אֲשֶׁר לִמְנַשֶּׁה׃ וְהֵמָּה עָזְרוּ עִם־דָּוִיד עַל־הַגְּדוּד

the-raiding-band against David to they-helped and-they (22) in-Manasseh who

כִּי־גִבּוֹרֵי חַיִל כֻּלָּם וַיִּהְיוּ שָׂרִים בַּצָּבָא׃

in-the-army commanders and-they-were all-of-them bravery warriors-of for

כִּי לְעֶת־יוֹם בְּיוֹם יָבֹאוּ עַל־דָּוִיד לְעָזְרוֹ עַד־

until to-help-him David to they-came after-day day at-time-of indeed (23)

לְמַחֲנֶה גָדוֹל כְּמַחֲנֵה אֱלֹהִים׃ וְאֵלֶּה מִסְפְּרֵי רָאשֵׁי

heads-of numbers-of and-these (24) mighty-ones like-army-of great to-army

הֶחָלוּץ לַצָּבָא בָּאוּ עַל־דָּוִיד חֶבְרוֹנָה לְהָסֵב

to-turn-over at-Hebron David to they-came for-the-battle the-one-being-armed

came to David in his stronghold. [17]David went out to meet
them and said to them, "If you
have come to me in peace, to
help me, I am ready to have
you unite with me. But if you
have come to betray me to my
enemies when my hands are
free from violence, may the
God of our fathers see it and
judge you."

[18]Then the Spirit came upon
Amasai, chief of the Thirty,
and he said:

"We are yours, O David!
We are with you, O son
of Jesse!
Success, success to you,
and success to those who
help you,
for your God will help
you."

So David received them and
made them leaders of his raiding bands.

[19]Some of the men of Manasseh defected to David when he
went with the Philistines to
fight against Saul. (He and his
men did not help the Philistines because, after consulta-
tion, their rulers sent him
away. They said, "It will cost
us our heads if he deserts to
his master Saul.") [20]When David went to Ziklag, these were
the men of Manasseh who defected to him: Adnah, Jozabad,
Jediael, Michael, Jozabad,
Elihu and Zillethai, leaders of
units of a thousand in Manasseh. [21]They helped David
against raiding bands, for all
of them were brave warriors,
and they were commanders in
his army. [22]Day after day men
came to help David, until he
had a great and mighty army.

*Others Join David at Hebron*

[23]These are the numbers of
the men armed for battle who
came to David at Hebron to

*See the note on page 36.

°19 ק השלישים

מַלְכוּת שָׁאוּל אֵלָיו כְּפִי יְהוָה׃ בְּנֵי יְהוּדָה נֹשְׂאֵי
ones-carrying-of Judah men-of (25) Yahweh as-saying-of to-him Saul kingdom-of

צִנָּה וָרֹמַח שֵׁשֶׁת אֲלָפִים וּשְׁמוֹנֶה מֵאוֹת חֲלוּצֵי
ones-being-armed-of hundreds and-eight thousands six-of and-spear shield

צָבָא׃ מִן־ בְּנֵי שִׁמְעוֹן גִּבּוֹרֵי חַיִל לַצָּבָא שִׁבְעַת
seven-of for-the-battle bravery warriors-of Simeon men-of from (26) battle

אֲלָפִים וּמֵאָה׃ מִן־ בְּנֵי הַלֵּוִי אַרְבַּעַת אֲלָפִים וְשֵׁשׁ
and-six thousands four-of the-Levite men-of from (27) and-hundred thousands

מֵאוֹת׃ וִיהוֹיָדָע הַנָּגִיד לְאַהֲרֹן וְעִמּוֹ שְׁלֹשֶׁת
three-of and-with-him of-Aaron the-leader and-Jehoiada (28) hundreds

אֲלָפִים וּשְׁבַע מֵאוֹת׃ וְצָדוֹק נַעַר גִּבּוֹר חָיִל
bravery warrior-of young and-Zadok (29) hundreds and-seven-of thousands

וּבֵית־ אָבִיו שָׂרִים עֶשְׂרִים וּשְׁנָיִם׃ וּמִן־ בְּנֵי
men-of and-from (30) and-two twenty officers father-of-him and-family-of

בִּנְיָמִן אֲחֵי שָׁאוּל שְׁלֹשֶׁת אֲלָפִים וְעַד־ הֵנָּה מַרְבִּיתָם
most-of-them to-then and-until thousands three-of Saul kinsmen-of Benjamin

שֹׁמְרִים מִשְׁמֶרֶת בֵּית שָׁאוּל׃ וּמִן־ בְּנֵי אֶפְרַיִם
Ephraim men-of and-from (31) Saul house-of loyalty-of ones-being-loyal

עֶשְׂרִים אֶלֶף וּשְׁמוֹנֶה מֵאוֹת גִּבּוֹרֵי חַיִל אַנְשֵׁי שֵׁמוֹת
names men-of bravery warriors-of hundreds and-eight thousand twenty

לְבֵית אֲבוֹתָם׃ וּמֵחֲצִי מַטֵּה מְנַשֶּׁה שְׁמוֹנָה
eight Manasseh tribe-of and-from-half-of (32) fathers-of-them in-family-of

עָשָׂר אֶלֶף אֲשֶׁר נִקְּבוּ בְּשֵׁמוֹת לָבוֹא לְהַמְלִיךְ אֶת־
*** and-to-make-king to-come by-names they-were-designated who thousand ten

דָּוִיד׃ וּמִבְּנֵי יִשָּׂשכָר יוֹדְעֵי בִינָה לַעִתִּים
of-the-times understanding ones-knowing-of Issachar and-from-men-of (33) David

לָדַעַת מַה־ יַּעֲשֶׂה יִשְׂרָאֵל רָאשֵׁיהֶם מָאתַיִם וְכָל־
and-all-of two-hundreds chiefs-of-them Israel he-should-do what to-know

אֲחֵיהֶם עַל־ פִּיהֶם׃ מִזְּבֻלוּן יוֹצְאֵי
ones-going-out-of from-Zebulun (34) command-of-them under relatives-of-them

צָבָא עֹרְכֵי מִלְחָמָה בְּכָל־ כְּלֵי מִלְחָמָה חֲמִשִּׁים
fifty battle weapons-of with-all-of battle ones-being-prepared-of army

אֶלֶף וְלַעֲדֹר בְּלֹא־ לֵב וָלֵב׃ וּמִנַּפְתָּלִי שָׂרִים
officers and-from-Naphtali (35) and-heart heart with-not and-to-help thousand

אֶלֶף וְעִמָּהֶם בְּצִנָּה וַחֲנִית שְׁלֹשִׁים וְשִׁבְעָה אָלֶף׃
thousand and-seven thirty and-spear with-shield and-with-them thousand

וּמִן־ הַדָּנִי עֹרְכֵי מִלְחָמָה עֶשְׂרִים־ וּשְׁמוֹנָה אֶלֶף
thousand and-eight twenty battle ones-being-ready-of the-Danite and-from (36)

turn Saul's kingdom over to him, as the LORD had said:
24 men of Judah, carrying shield and spear—6,800 armed for battle;
25 men of Simeon, warriors ready for battle—7,100;
26 men of Levi—4,600,
27 including Jehoiada, leader of the family of Aaron, with 3,700 men,
28 and Zadok, a brave young warrior, with 22 officers from his family;
29 men of Benjamin, Saul's kinsmen—3,000, most of whom had remained loyal to Saul's house until then;
30 men of Ephraim, brave warriors, famous in their own clans—20,800;
31 men of half the tribe of Manasseh, designated by name to come and make David king—18,000;
32 men of Issachar, who understood the times and knew what Israel should do—200 chiefs, with all their relatives under their command;
33 men of Zebulun, experienced soldiers prepared for battle with every type of weapon, to help David with undivided loyalty—50,000;
34 men of Naphtali—1,000 officers, together with 37,000 men carrying shields and spears;
35 men of Dan, ready for battle—28,600;

*See the note on page 36.

וְשֵׁשׁ מֵאוֹת׃ וּמֵאָשֵׁר יוֹצְאֵי צָבָא לַעֲרֹךְ
to-be-prepared army ones-going-out-of and-from-Asher (37) hundreds and-six

מִלְחָמָה אַרְבָּעִים אָלֶף׃ וּמֵעֵבֶר לַיַּרְדֵּן מִן־הָרְאוּבֵנִי
the-Reubenite from of-the-Jordan and-from-east (38) thousand forty battle

וְהַגָּדִי וַחֲצִי ׀ שֵׁבֶט מְנַשֶּׁה בְּכֹל כְּלֵי צְבָא
army-of weapons-of with-all-of Manasseh tribe-of and-half-of and-the-Gadite

מִלְחָמָה מֵאָה וְעֶשְׂרִים אָלֶף׃ כָּל־אֵלֶּה אַנְשֵׁי מִלְחָמָה
fight men-of these all-of (39) thousand and-twenty hundred war

עֹדְרֵי מַעֲרָכָה בְּלֵבָב שָׁלֵם בָּאוּ חֶבְרוֹנָה לְהַמְלִיךְ אֶת־
*** to-make-king to-Hebron they-came whole with-heart rank ones-serving-of

דָּוִיד עַל־כָּל־יִשְׂרָאֵל וְגַם כָּל־שֵׁרִית יִשְׂרָאֵל לֵב אֶחָד
one mind Israel rest-of all-of and-also Israel all-of over David

לְהַמְלִיךְ אֶת־דָּוִיד׃ וַיִּהְיוּ־שָׁם עִם־דָּוִיד יָמִים שְׁלוֹשָׁה
three days David with there and-they-were (40) David *** to-make-king

אֹכְלִים וְשׁוֹתִים כִּי־הֵכִינוּ לָהֶם אֲחֵיהֶם׃
families-of-them for-them they-supplied for and-ones-drinking ones-eating

וְגַם הַקְּרוֹבִים־אֲלֵיהֶם עַד־יִשָּׂשכָר וּזְבֻלוּן
and-Zebulun Issachar as-far-as to-them the-neighbors and-also (41)

וְנַפְתָּלִי מְבִיאִים לֶחֶם בַּחֲמוֹרִים וּבַגְּמַלִּים
and-on-the-camels on-the-donkeys food ones-bringing and-Naphtali

וּבַפְּרָדִים ׀ וּבַבָּקָר מַאֲכָל קֶמַח דְּבֵלִים וְצִמּוּקִים
and-raisin-cakes fig-cakes flour supply and-on-the-ox and-on-the-mules

וְיַיִן־וְשֶׁמֶן וּבָקָר וְצֹאן לָרֹב כִּי שִׂמְחָה בְּיִשְׂרָאֵל׃
in-Israel joy for to-plenty and-sheep and-cattle and-oil and-wine

וַיִּוָּעַץ דָּוִיד עִם־שָׂרֵי הָאֲלָפִים
the-thousands commanders-of with David and-he-conferred (13:1)

וְהַמֵּאוֹת לְכָל־נָגִיד׃ וַיֹּאמֶר דָּוִיד לְכֹל ׀
to-whole-of David then-he-said (2) officer with-each-of and-the-hundreds

קְהַל יִשְׂרָאֵל אִם־עֲלֵיכֶם טוֹב וּמִן־יְהוָה אֱלֹהֵינוּ נִפְרְצָה
let-us-spread-out God-of-us Yahweh and-from good to-you if Israel assembly-of

נִשְׁלְחָה עַל־אַחֵינוּ הַנִּשְׁאָרִים בְּכֹל
through-all-of the-ones-being-left brothers-of-us to let-us-send

אַרְצוֹת יִשְׂרָאֵל וְעִמָּהֶם הַכֹּהֲנִים וְהַלְוִיִּם בְּעָרֵי
in-towns-of and-the-Levites the-priests and-with-them Israel territories-of

מִגְרְשֵׁיהֶם וְיִקָּבְצוּ אֵלֵינוּ׃ וְנָסֵבָּה אֶת־
*** and-let-us-bring-back (3) with-us and-let-them-join pastures-of-them

אֲרוֹן אֱלֹהֵינוּ אֵלֵינוּ כִּי־לֹא דְרַשְׁנֻהוּ בִּימֵי שָׁאוּל׃
Saul in-days-of we-inquired-of-him not for to-us God-of-us ark-of

36men of Asher, experienced soldiers prepared for battle—40,000;

37and from east of the Jordan, men of Reuben, Gad and the half-tribe of Manasseh, armed with every type of weapon—120,000.

38All these were fighting
men who volunteered to serve
in the ranks. They came to Hebron fully determined to make
David king over all Israel. All
the rest of the Israelites were
also of one mind to make David king. 39The men spent
three days there with David,
eating and drinking, for their
families had supplied provisions for them. 40Also, their
neighbors from as far away as
Issachar, Zebulun and Naphtali came bringing food on
donkeys, camels, mules and
oxen. There were plentiful
supplies of flour, fig cakes, raisin cakes, wine, oil, cattle and
sheep, for there was joy in Israel.

*Bringing Back the Ark*

13 David conferred with
each of his officers, the
commanders of thousands
and commanders of hundreds.
2He then said to the whole assembly of Israel, "If it seems
good to you and if it is the will
of the LORD our God, let us
send word far and wide to the
rest of our brothers throughout the territories of Israel,
and also to the priests and Levites who are with them in
their towns and pasturelands,
to come and join us. 3Let us
bring the ark of our God back
to us, for we did not inquire
of[a] it[b] during the reign of

[a]3 Or *we neglected* [b]3 Or *him*

*See the note on page 36.

וַיֹּאמְרוּ כָל־ הַקָּהָל לַעֲשׂוֹת כֵּן כִּי־ יָשַׁר
he-was-right because this to-do the-assembly whole-of and-they-said (4)

הַדָּבָר בְּעֵינֵי כָל־ הָעָם׃ וַיַּקְהֵל דָּוִיד אֶת־ כָּל־
all-of *** David so-he-assembled (5) the-people all-of in-eyes-of the-thing

יִשְׂרָאֵל מִן־ שִׁיחוֹר מִצְרַיִם וְעַד־ לְבוֹא חֲמָת לְהָבִיא אֶת־ אֲרוֹן
ark-of *** to-bring Hamath Lebo and-to Egypt Shihor-of from Israel

הָאֱלֹהִים מִקִּרְיַת יְעָרִים׃ וַיַּעַל דָּוִיד וְכָל־ יִשְׂרָאֵל
Israel and-all-of David and-he-went (6) Jearim from-Kiriath the-God

בַּעֲלָתָה אֶל־ קִרְיַת יְעָרִים אֲשֶׁר לִיהוּדָה לְהַעֲלוֹת מִשָּׁם אֵת אֲרוֹן
ark-of *** from-there to-bring-up in-Judah that Jearim Kiriath to to-Baalah

הָאֱלֹהִים׀ יְהוָה יוֹשֵׁב הַכְּרוּבִים אֲשֶׁר־ נִקְרָא שֵׁם׃
Name he-is-called that the-cherubim being-enthroned-of Yahweh the-God

וַיַּרְכִּיבוּ אֶת־אֲרוֹן הָאֱלֹהִים עַל־עֲגָלָה חֲדָשָׁה מִבֵּית אֲבִינָדָב
Abinadab from-house-of new cart on the-God ark-of *** and-they-moved (7)

וְעֻזָּא וְאַחְיוֹ נֹהֲגִים בָּעֲגָלָה׃ וְדָוִיד וְכָל־ יִשְׂרָאֵל
Israel and-all-of and-David (8) to-the-cart ones-guiding and-Ahio and-Uzzah

מְשַׂחֲקִים לִפְנֵי הָאֱלֹהִים בְּכָל־ עֹז וּבְשִׁירִים
and-with-songs might with-all-of the-God before ones-celebrating

וּבְכִנֹּרוֹת וּבִנְבָלִים וּבְתֻפִּים וּבִמְצִלְתַּיִם
and-with-cymbals and-with-tambourines and-with-lyres and-with-harps

וּבַחֲצֹצְרוֹת׃ וַיָּבֹאוּ עַד־ גֹּרֶן כִּידֹן
Kidon threshing-floor-of to when-they-came (9) and-with-trumpets

וַיִּשְׁלַח עֻזָּא אֶת־ יָדוֹ לֶאֱחֹז אֶת־ הָאָרוֹן כִּי
because the-ark *** to-steady hand-of-him *** Uzzah then-he-reached

שָׁמְטוּ הַבָּקָר׃ וַיִּחַר־ אַף יְהוָה בְּעֻזָּא
against-Uzzah Yahweh anger-of and-he-burned (10) the-ox they-stumbled

וַיַּכֵּהוּ עַל אֲשֶׁר־ שָׁלַח יָדוֹ עַל־ הָאָרוֹן וַיָּמָת
so-he-died the-ark on hand-of-him he-put that because and-he-struck-down-him

שָׁם לִפְנֵי אֱלֹהִים׃ וַיִּחַר לְדָוִיד כִּי־ פָרַץ יְהוָה
Yahweh he-broke-out because to-David then-he-angered (11) God before there

פֶּרֶץ בְּעֻזָּא וַיִּקְרָא לַמָּקוֹם הַהוּא פֶּרֶץ עֻזָּא
Uzzah Perez the-that to-the-place and-he-called against-Uzzah breaking-out

עַד הַיּוֹם הַזֶּה׃ וַיִּירָא דָוִיד אֶת־הָאֱלֹהִים בַּיּוֹם
on-the-day the-God *** David and-he-was-afraid (12) the-this the-day to

הַהוּא לֵאמֹר הֵיךְ אָבִיא אֵלַי אֵת אֲרוֹן הָאֱלֹהִים׃ וְלֹא־
and-not (13) the-God ark-of *** to-me can-I-bring how? to-ask the-that

הֵסִיר דָּוִיד אֶת־ הָאָרוֹן אֵלָיו אֶל־ עִיר דָּוִיד וַיַּטֵּהוּ
but-he-took-aside-him David City-of to with-him the-ark *** David he-took

Saul." 4The whole assembly
agreed to do this, because it
seemed right to all the people.
5So David assembled all the
Israelites, from the Shihor
River in Egypt to Lebo[c]
Hamath, to bring the ark of
God from Kiriath Jearim. 6Da-
vid and all the Israelites with
him went to Baalah of Judah
(Kiriath Jearim) to bring up
from there the ark of God the
LORD, who is enthroned between the cherubim—the ark
that is called by the Name.
7They moved the ark of God
from Abinadab's house on a
new cart, with Uzzah and
Ahio guiding it. 8David and all
the Israelites were celebrating
with all their might before
God, with songs and with
harps, lyres, tambourines,
cymbals and trumpets.
9When they came to the
threshing floor of Kidon, Uzzah reached out his hand to
steady the ark, because the
oxen stumbled. 10The LORD's
anger burned against Uzzah,
and he struck him down because he had put his hand on
the ark. So he died there before God.
11Then David was angry because the LORD's wrath had
broken out against Uzzah, and
to this day that place is called
Perez Uzzah.[d]
12David was afraid of God
that day and asked, "How can
I ever bring the ark of God to
me?" 13He did not take the ark
to be with him in the City of
David. Instead, he took it

[c]5 Or *to the entrance to*
[d]11 *Perez Uzzah* means *outbreak against Uzzah.*

אֶל־ בֵּית עֹבֵד־ אֱדֹם הַגִּתִּי׃ וַיֵּשֶׁב אֲרוֹן הָאֱלֹהִים עִם־
with the-God ark-of and-he-remained (14) the-Gittite Edom Obed house-of to

בֵּית עֹבֵד אֱדֹם בְּבֵיתוֹ שְׁלֹשָׁה חֳדָשִׁים וַיְבָרֶךְ יְהוָה אֶת־
*** Yahweh and-he-blessed months three in-house-of-him Edom Obed family-of

בֵּית עֹבֵד־אֱדֹם וְאֶת־כָּל־אֲשֶׁר־לוֹ׃ וַיִּשְׁלַח חִירָם° מֶלֶךְ־
king-of Hiram now-he-sent (14:1) to-him that all and Edom Obed household-of

צֹר מַלְאָכִים אֶל־ דָּוִיד וַעֲצֵי אֲרָזִים וְחָרָשֵׁי קִיר
wall and-stonemasons-of cedars and-logs-of David to messengers Tyre

וְחָרָשֵׁי עֵצִים לִבְנוֹת לוֹ בָּיִת׃ וַיֵּדַע דָּוִיד כִּי־
that David and-he-knew (2) palace for-him to-build woods and-craftsmen-of

הֱכִינוֹ יְהוָה לְמֶלֶךְ עַל־ יִשְׂרָאֵל כִּי־ נִשֵּׂאת לְמַעְלָה
to-above being-exalted that Israel over as-king Yahweh he-established-him

מַלְכוּתוֹ בַּעֲבוּר עַמּוֹ יִשְׂרָאֵל׃ וַיִּקַּח דָּוִיד עוֹד
more David and-he-took (3) Israel people-of-him for-sake-of kingdom-of-him

נָשִׁים בִּירוּשָׁלִָם וַיּוֹלֶד דָּוִיד עוֹד בָּנִים וּבָנוֹת׃
and-daughters sons more David and-he-fathered in-Jerusalem wives

וְאֵלֶּה שְׁמוֹת הַיְלוּדִים אֲשֶׁר הָיוּ־ לוֹ בִּירוּשָׁלִָם
in-Jerusalem to-him they-were who the-ones-being-born names-of and-these (4)

שַׁמּוּעַ וְשׁוֹבָב נָתָן וּשְׁלֹמֹה׃ וְיִבְחָר וֶאֱלִישׁוּעַ וְאֶלְפָּלֶט׃
and-Elpelet and-Elishua and-Ibhar (5) and-Solomon Nathan and-Shobab Shammua

וְנֹגַהּ וְנֶפֶג וְיָפִיעַ׃ וֶאֱלִישָׁמָע וּבְעֶלְיָדָע
and-Beeliada and-Elishama (7) and-Japhia and-Nepheg and-Nogah (6)

וֶאֱלִיפָלֶט׃ וַיִּשְׁמְעוּ פְלִשְׁתִּים כִּי־ נִמְשַׁח דָּוִיד
David he-was-anointed that Philistines when-they-heard (8) and-Eliphelet

לְמֶלֶךְ עַל־ כָּל־ יִשְׂרָאֵל וַיַּעֲלוּ כָל־ פְּלִשְׁתִּים לְבַקֵּשׁ
to-search Philistines all-of then-they-went-up Israel all-of over as-king

אֶת־ דָּוִיד וַיִּשְׁמַע דָּוִיד וַיֵּצֵא לִפְנֵיהֶם׃ וּפְלִשְׁתִּים
now-Philistines (9) against-them and-he-went-out David but-he-heard David ***

בָּאוּ וַיִּפְשְׁטוּ בְּעֵמֶק רְפָאִים׃ וַיִּשְׁאַל דָּוִיד
David so-he-inquired (10) Rephaim in-Valley-of and-they-raided they-came

בֵּאלֹהִים לֵאמֹר הַאֶעֱלֶה עַל־ פְּלִשְׁתִּיִּים° וּנְתַתָּם
and-will-you-give-them Philistines against shall-I-go? to-say of-God

בְּיָדִי וַיֹּאמֶר לוֹ יְהוָה עֲלֵה וּנְתַתִּים
and-I-will-give-them go! Yahweh to-him and-he-answered into-hand-of-me

בְּיָדֶךָ׃ וַיַּעֲלוּ בְּבַעַל־ פְּרָצִים וַיַּכֵּם
and-he-defeated-them Perazim to-Baal so-they-went-up (11) into-hand-of-you

שָׁם דָּוִיד וַיֹּאמֶר דָּוִיד פָּרַץ הָאֱלֹהִים אֶת־ אוֹיְבַי
being-enemies-of-me against the-God he-broke-out David and-he-said David there

aside to the house of Obed-
Edom the Gittite. 14The ark of
God remained with the family
of Obed-Edom in his house
for three months, and the
LORD blessed his household
and everything he had.

*David's House and Family*

14 Now Hiram king of
Tyre sent messengers
to David, along with cedar
logs, stonemasons and carpenters to build a palace for
him. 2And David knew that
the LORD had established him
as king over Israel and that his
kingdom had been highly exalted for the sake of his people
Israel.
3In Jerusalem David took
more wives and became the
father of more sons and
daughters. 4These are the
names of the children born to
him there: Shammua, Shobab,
Nathan, Solomon, 5Ibhar, Elishua, Elpelet, 6Nogah, Nepheg, Japhia, 7Elishama,
Beeliada[e] and Eliphelet.

*David Defeats the Philistines*

8When the Philistines heard
that David had been anointed
king over all Israel, they went
up in full force to search for
him, but David heard about it
and went out to meet them.
9Now the Philistines had come
and raided the Valley of Rephaim; 10so David inquired of
God: "Shall I go and attack the
Philistines? Will you hand
them over to me?"
The LORD answered him,
"Go, I will hand them over to
you."
11So David and his men
went up to Baal Perazim, and
there he defeated them. He
said, "As waters break out,
God has broken out against
my enemies by my hand." So

[e]7 A variant of *Eliada*

°1 ק חורם
°10 ק פלשתים

בְּיָדִי כְּפֶרֶץ מָיִם עַל־ כֵּן קָרְאוּ שֵׁם־
name-of they-called this for waters as-breaking-out-of by-hand-of-me

הַמָּקוֹם הַהוּא בַּעַל פְּרָצִים׃ וַיַּעַזְבוּ־ שָׁם אֶת־ אֱלֹהֵיהֶם
gods-of-them *** there and-they-abandoned (12) Perazim Baal the-that the-place

וַיֹּאמֶר דָּוִיד וַיִּשָּׂרְפוּ בָּאֵשׁ׃ וַיֹּסִיפוּ
and-they-repeated (13) in-the-fire and-they-were-burned David and-he-ordered

עוֹד פְּלִשְׁתִּים וַיִּפְשְׁטוּ בָּעֵמֶק׃ וַיִּשְׁאַל עוֹד
again so-he-inquired (14) in-the-valley and-they-raided Philistines again

דָּוִיד בֵּאלֹהִים וַיֹּאמֶר לוֹ הָאֱלֹהִים לֹא תַעֲלֶה אַחֲרֵיהֶם
after-them you-go-up not the-God to-him and-he-answered of-God David

הָסֵב מֵעֲלֵיהֶם וּבָאתָ לָהֶם מִמּוּל הַבְּכָאִים׃
the-balsams at-front-of to-them and-you-attack from-upon-them circle-around!

וִיהִי כְּשָׁמְעֲךָ אֶת־ קוֹל הַצְּעָדָה בְּרָאשֵׁי
in-tops-of the-marching sound-of *** as-to-hear-you and-he-will-be (15)

הַבְּכָאִים אָז תֵּצֵא בַמִּלְחָמָה כִּי־ יָצָא הָאֱלֹהִים
the-God he-went-out because to-the-battle you-move-out then the-balsams

לְפָנֶיךָ לְהַכּוֹת אֶת־ מַחֲנֵה פְלִשְׁתִּים׃ וַיַּעַשׂ דָּוִיד כַּאֲשֶׁר
just-as David so-he-did (16) Philistines army-of *** to-strike before-you

צִוָּהוּ הָאֱלֹהִים וַיַּכּוּ אֶת־ מַחֲנֵה פְלִשְׁתִּים
Philistines army-of *** and-they-struck-down the-God he-commanded-him

מִגִּבְעוֹן וְעַד־ גָּזְרָה׃ וַיֵּצֵא שֵׁם־ דָּוִיד
David name-of so-he-spread-out (17) to-Gezer even-to from-Gibeon

בְּכָל־ הָאֲרָצוֹת וַיהוָה נָתַן אֶת־ פַּחְדּוֹ עַל־ כָּל־
all-of on fear-of-him *** he-put and-Yahweh the-lands through-all-of

הַגּוֹיִם׃ וַיַּעַשׂ־ לוֹ בָתִּים בְּעִיר דָּוִיד
David in-City-of buildings for-him and-he-constructed (15:1) the-nations

וַיָּכֶן מָקוֹם לַאֲרוֹן הָאֱלֹהִים וַיֶּט־ לוֹ אֹהֶל׃
tent for-him and-he-pitched the-God for-ark-of place and-he-prepared

אָז אָמַר דָּוִיד לֹא לָשֵׂאת אֶת־ אֲרוֹן הָאֱלֹהִים כִּי אִם־
only except the-God ark-of *** to-carry not David he-said then (2)

הַלְוִיִּם כִּי־ בָם׀ בָּחַר יְהוָה לָשֵׂאת אֶת־ אֲרוֹן יְהוָה
Yahweh ark-of *** to-carry Yahweh he-chose to-them because the-Levites

וּלְשָׁרְתוֹ עַד־ עוֹלָם׃ וַיַּקְהֵל דָּוִיד אֶת־ כָּל־
all-of *** David and-he-assembled (3) forever to and-to-minister-to-him

יִשְׂרָאֵל אֶל־יְרוּשָׁלִָם לְהַעֲלוֹת אֶת־ אֲרוֹן יְהוָה אֶל־ מְקוֹמוֹ אֲשֶׁר־
that place-of-him to Yahweh ark-of *** to-bring-up Jerusalem to Israel

הֵכִין לוֹ׃ וַיֶּאֱסֹף דָּוִיד אֶת־ בְּנֵי
descendants-of *** David and-he-called-together (4) for-him he-prepared

that place was called Baal Perazim.[f] 12The Philistines had abandoned their gods there, and David gave orders to burn them in the fire.

13Once more the Philistines raided the valley; 14so David inquired of God again, and God answered him, "Do not go straight up, but circle around them and attack them in front of the balsam trees. 15As soon as you hear the sound of marching in the tops of the balsam trees, move out to battle, because that will mean God has gone out in front of you to strike the Philistine army." 16So David did as God commanded him, and they struck down the Philistine army, all the way from Gibeon to Gezer.

17So David's fame spread throughout every land, and the LORD made all the nations fear him.

### *The Ark Brought to Jerusalem*

15 After David had constructed buildings for himself in the City of David, he prepared a place for the ark of God and pitched a tent for it. 2Then David said, "No one but the Levites may carry the ark of God, because the LORD chose them to carry the ark of the LORD and to minister before him forever."

3David assembled all Israel in Jerusalem to bring up the ark of the LORD to the place he had prepared for it. 4He called together the descendants of

[f]11 *Baal Perazim* means *the lord who breaks out.*

אַהֲרֹן וְאֶת־ הַלְוִיִּם׃ לִבְנֵי קְהָת אוּרִיאֵל הַשָּׂר
the-leader Uriel Kohath from-descendants-of (5) the-Levites and Aaron

וְאֶחָיו מֵאָה וְעֶשְׂרִים׃ לִבְנֵי מְרָרִי
Merari from-descendants-of (6) and-twenty hundred and-relatives-of-him

עֲשָׂיָה הַשָּׂר וְאֶחָיו מָאתַיִם וְעֶשְׂרִים׃
and-twenty two-hundreds and-relatives-of-him the-leader Asaiah

לִבְנֵי גֵרְשׁוֹם יוֹאֵל הַשָּׂר וְאֶחָיו מֵאָה
hundred and-relatives-of-him the-leader Joel Gershom from-descendants-of (7)

וּשְׁלֹשִׁים׃ לִבְנֵי אֱלִיצָפָן שְׁמַעְיָה הַשָּׂר
the-leader Shemaiah Elizaphan from-descendants-of (8) and-thirty

וְאֶחָיו מָאתָיִם׃ לִבְנֵי חֶבְרוֹן אֱלִיאֵל
Eliel Hebron from-descendants-of (9) two-hundreds and-relatives-of-him

הַשָּׂר וְאֶחָיו שְׁמוֹנִים׃ לִבְנֵי עֻזִּיאֵל
Uzziel from-descendants-of (10) eighty and-relatives-of-him the-leader

עַמִּינָדָב הַשָּׂר וְאֶחָיו מֵאָה וּשְׁנַיִם עָשָׂר׃
ten and-two hundred and-relatives-of-him the-leader Amminadab

וַיִּקְרָא דָוִיד לְצָדוֹק וּלְאֶבְיָתָר הַכֹּהֲנִים
the-priests and-to-Abiathar to-Zadok David then-he-summoned (11)

וְלַלְוִיִּם לְאוּרִיאֵל עֲשָׂיָה וְיוֹאֵל שְׁמַעְיָה וֶאֱלִיאֵל
and-Eliel Shemaiah and-Joel Asaiah and-to-Uriel and-to-the-Levites

וְעַמִּינָדָב׃ וַיֹּאמֶר לָהֶם אַתֶּם רָאשֵׁי הָאָבוֹת
the-fathers heads-of you to-them and-he-said (12) and-Amminadab

לַלְוִיִּם הִתְקַדְּשׁוּ אַתֶּם וַאֲחֵיכֶם וְהַעֲלִיתֶם
and-you-bring-up and-fellows-of-you you consecrate-yourselves! of-the-Levites

אֵת אֲרוֹן יְהוָה אֱלֹהֵי יִשְׂרָאֵל אֶל־ הֲכִינוֹתִי לוֹ׃ כִּי
because (13) for-him I-prepared to Israel God-of Yahweh ark-of ***

לְמַבָּרִאשׁוֹנָה לֹא אַתֶּם פָּרַץ יְהוָה אֱלֹהֵינוּ בָּנוּ כִּי־ לֹא
not for against-us God-of-us Yahweh he-broke-out you not for-what-the-first

דְרַשְׁנֻהוּ כַּמִּשְׁפָּט׃ וַיִּתְקַדְּשׁוּ
so-they-consecrated-themselves (14) in-the-prescribed-way we-inquired-of-him

הַכֹּהֲנִים וְהַלְוִיִּם לְהַעֲלוֹת אֶת־ אֲרוֹן יְהוָה אֱלֹהֵי יִשְׂרָאֵל׃
Israel God-of Yahweh ark-of *** to-bring-up and-the-Levites the-priests

וַיִּשְׂאוּ בְנֵי־ הַלְוִיִּם אֵת אֲרוֹן הָאֱלֹהִים כַּאֲשֶׁר
just-as the-God ark-of *** the-Levites sons-of and-they-carried (15)

צִוָּה מֹשֶׁה כִּדְבַר יְהוָה בִּכְתֵפָם בַּמֹּטוֹת
with-the-poles on-shoulder-of-them Yahweh as-word-of Moses he-commanded

עֲלֵיהֶם׃ וַיֹּאמֶר דָּוִיד לְשָׂרֵי הַלְוִיִּם לְהַעֲמִיד אֶת־
*** to-appoint the-Levites to-leaders-of David and-he-told (16) on-them

Aaron and the Levites:
5 From the descendants of
Kohath,
Uriel the leader and 120
relatives;
6 from the descendants of
Merari,
Asaiah the leader and
220 relatives;
7 from the descendants of
Gershon,[g]
Joel the leader and 130
relatives;
8 from the descendants of Elizaphan,
Shemaiah the leader and
200 relatives;
9 from the descendants of
Hebron,
Eliel the leader and 80
relatives;
10 from the descendants of
Uzziel,
Amminadab the leader
and 112 relatives.
11 Then David summoned
Zadok and Abiathar the
priests, and Uriel, Asaiah, Joel,
Shemaiah, Eliel and Am-
minadab the Levites. 12 He said
to them, "You are the heads of
the Levitical families; you and
your fellow Levites are to
consecrate yourselves and
bring up the ark of the LORD,
the God of Israel, to the place
I have prepared for it. 13 It was
because you, the Levites, did
not bring it up the first time
that the LORD our God broke
out in anger against us. We
did not inquire of him about
how to do it in the prescribed
way." 14 So the priests and Levites consecrated themselves
in order to bring up the ark of
the LORD, the God of Israel.
15 And the Levites carried the
ark of God with the poles on
their shoulders, as Moses had
commanded in accordance
with the word of the LORD.
16 David told the leaders of
the Levites to appoint their

g7 Hebrew *Gershom,* a variant of *Gershon*

אֲחֵיהֶם֙ הַמְשֹׁרְרִ֔ים בִּכְלֵי־ שִׁ֖יר נְבָלִ֣ים וְכִנֹּר֑וֹת
and-harps lyres music with-instruments-of the-ones-singing brothers-of-them

וּמְצִלְתָּ֑יִם מַשְׁמִיעִ֖ים לְהָרִֽים־ בְּק֖וֹל לְשִׂמְחָֽה׃
of-joy with-sound to-raise-high ones-making-sound and-cymbals

וַיַּעֲמִ֣ידוּ הַלְוִיִּ֗ם אֵ֣ת הֵימָן֮ בֶּן־ יוֹאֵל֒ וּמִן־
and-from Joel son-of Heman *** the-Levites so-they-appointed (17)

אֶחָ֔יו אָסָ֖ף בֶּן־ בֶּֽרֶכְיָ֑הוּ וּמִן־ בְּנֵ֤י מְרָרִי֙ אֲחֵיהֶ֔ם
brothers-of-them Merari sons-of and-from Berekiah son-of Asaph brothers-of-him

אֵיתָ֖ן בֶּן־ קֽוּשָׁיָֽהוּ׃ וְעִמָּהֶ֖ם אֲחֵיהֶ֣ם הַמִּשְׁנִ֑ים
the-next-ones brothers-of-them and-with-them (18) Kushaiah son-of Ethan

זְכַרְיָ֙הוּ֙ בֵּ֜ן וְיַעֲזִיאֵ֗ל וּשְׁמִירָמ֡וֹת וִֽיחִיאֵל ׀ וְעֻנִּ֨י אֱלִיאָ֜ב
Eliab and-Unni and-Jehiel and-Shemiramoth and-Jaaziel son Zechariah

וּבְנָיָ֗הוּ וּמַעֲשֵׂיָ֡הוּ וּמַתִּתְיָ֡הוּ וֶאֱלִֽיפְלֵ֡הוּ וּמִקְנֵיָ֡הוּ
and-Mikneiah and-Eliphelehu and-Mattithiah and-Maaseiah and-Benaiah

וְעֹבֵ֥ד אֱדֹ֛ם וִֽיעִיאֵ֖ל הַשֹּׁעֲרִֽים׃ וְהַמְשֹׁ֣רְרִ֔ים
and-the-ones-making-music (19) the-gatekeepers and-Jeiel Edom and-Obed

הֵימָ֥ן אָסָ֖ף וְאֵיתָ֑ן בִּמְצִלְתַּ֥יִם נְחֹ֖שֶׁת לְהַשְׁמִֽיעַ׃ וּזְכַרְיָ֡ה
and-Zechariah (20) to-make-sound bronze with-cymbals and-Ethan Asaph Heman

וַעֲזִיאֵ֡ל וּשְׁמִֽירָמ֡וֹת וִֽיחִיאֵל֩ וְעֻנִּ֨י וֶאֱלִיאָ֜ב וּמַעֲשֵׂיָ֙הוּ֙
and-Maaseiah and-Eliab and-Unni and-Jehiel and-Shemiramoth and-Aziel

וּבְנָיָ֔הוּ בִּנְבָלִ֖ים עַל־ עֲלָמֽוֹת׃ וּמַתִּתְיָ֡הוּ
and-Mattithiah (21) alamoth according-to with-lyres and-Benaiah

וֶאֱלִֽיפְלֵ֡הוּ וּמִקְנֵיָ֡הוּ וְעֹבֵ֥ד אֱדֹ֛ם וִֽיעִיאֵ֖ל וַעֲזַזְיָ֑הוּ בְּכִנֹּר֥וֹת
with-harps and-Azaziah and-Jeiel Edom and-Obed and-Mikneiah and-Eliphelehu

עַל־ הַשְּׁמִינִ֖ית לְנַצֵּֽחַ׃ וּכְנַנְיָ֥הוּ שַֽׂר־ הַלְוִיִּ֖ם
the-Levites head-of and-Kenaniah (22) to-direct the-sheminith according-to

בְּמַשָּׂ֑א יָסֹר֙ בַּמַּשָּׂ֔א כִּ֥י מֵבִ֖ין הֽוּא׃
he being-skillful because of-the-singing to-be-in-charge of-singing

וּבֶרֶכְיָה֙ וְאֶלְקָנָ֔ה שֹׁעֲרִ֖ים לָאָרֽוֹן׃ וּשְׁבַנְיָ֡הוּ
and-Shebaniah (24) for-the-ark doorkeepers and-Elkanah and-Berekiah (23)

וְיוֹשָׁפָ֡ט וּנְתַנְאֵ֡ל וַעֲמָשַׂ֡י וּזְכַרְיָ֡הוּ וּבְנָיָ֙הוּ֙ וֶֽאֱלִיעֶ֔זֶר
and-Eliezer and-Benaiah and-Zechariah and-Amasai and-Nethanel and-Joshaphat

הַכֹּ֣הֲנִ֔ים מַחְצְצִרִים֙ בַּחֲצֹ֣צְר֔וֹת לִפְנֵ֖י אֲר֣וֹן הָאֱלֹהִ֑ים וְעֹבֵ֣ד אֱדֹ֔ם
Edom and-Obed the-God ark-of before on-the-trumpets ones-blowing the-priests

וִֽיחִיָּ֔ה שֹׁעֲרִ֖ים לָאָרֽוֹן׃ וַיְהִ֥י דָוִ֛יד וְזִקְנֵ֥י יִשְׂרָאֵ֖ל
Israel and-elders-of David so-he-was (25) for-the-ark doorkeepers and-Jehiah

וְשָׂרֵ֣י הָאֲלָפִ֑ים הַהֹלְכִ֗ים לְהַעֲל֞וֹת אֶת־ אֲר֧וֹן
ark-of *** to-bring-up the-ones-going the-thousands and-commanders-of

brothers as singers to sing joyful songs, accompanied by musical instruments: lyres, harps and cymbals.
17So the Levites appointed Heman son of Joel; from his brothers, Asaph son of Berekiah; and from their brothers the Merarites, Ethan son of Kushaiah;
18and with them their brothers next in rank: Zechariah,[h] Jaaziel, Shemiramoth, Jehiel, Unni, Eliab, Benaiah, Maaseiah, Mattithiah, Eliphelehu, Mikneiah, Obed-Edom and Jeiel,[i] the gatekeepers.
19The musicians Heman, Asaph and Ethan were to sound the bronze cymbals;
20Zechariah, Aziel, Shemiramoth, Jehiel, Unni, Eliab, Maaseiah and Benaiah were to play the lyres according to *alamoth*,[j]
21and Mattithiah, Eliphelehu, Mikneiah, Obed-Edom, Jeiel and Azaziah were to play the harps, directing according to *sheminith*.[j]
22Kenaniah the head Levite was in charge of the singing; that was his responsibility because he was skillful at it.
23Berekiah and Elkanah were to be doorkeepers for the ark.
24Shebaniah, Joshaphat, Nethanel, Amasai, Zechariah, Benaiah and Eliezer the priests were to blow trumpets before the ark of God. Obed-Edom and Jehiah were also to be doorkeepers for the ark.
25So David and the elders of Israel and the commanders of units of a thousand went to

[h] *18* Three Hebrew manuscripts and Septuagint (see also verse 20 and 1 Chron. 16:5); most Hebrew manuscripts *Zechariah son and* or *Zechariah, Ben and*
[i] *18* Hebrew; Septuagint (see also verse 21) *Jeiel and Azaziah*
[j] *20,21* Probably a musical term

°*24* ק מחצרים

בְּרִית־ יְהוָה מִן־ בֵּית עֹבֵד־ אֱדֹם בְּשִׂמְחָה׃ וַיְהִי
and-he-was (26) with-rejoicing Edom Obed house-of from Yahweh covenant-of

בֶּעְזֹר הָאֱלֹהִים אֶת־ הַלְוִיִּם נֹשְׂאֵי אֲרוֹן בְּרִית־
covenant-of ark-of ones-carrying-of the-Levites *** the-God because-to-help

יְהוָה וַיִּזְבְּחוּ שִׁבְעָה־ פָרִים וְשִׁבְעָה אֵילִים׃ וְדָוִיד
now-David (27) rams and-seven bulls seven then-they-sacrificed Yahweh

מְכֻרְבָּל ׀ בִּמְעִיל בּוּץ וְכָל־ הַלְוִיִּם הַנֹּשְׂאִים
the-ones-carrying the-Levites and-all-of fine-linen in-robe-of being-clothed

אֶת־ הָאָרוֹן וְהַמְשֹׁרְרִים וּכְנַנְיָה הַשַּׂר הַמַּשָּׂא
the-song the-leader and-Kenaniah and-the-ones-singing the-ark ***

הַמְשֹׁרְרִים וְעַל־ דָּוִיד אֵפוֹד בָּד׃ וְכָל־ יִשְׂרָאֵל
Israel so-all-of (28) linen ephod-of David and-on the-ones-singing

מַעֲלִים אֶת־ אֲרוֹן בְּרִית־ יְהוָה בִּתְרוּעָה וּבְקוֹל
and-with-sound-of with-shout Yahweh covenant-of ark-of *** ones-bringing-up

שׁוֹפָר וּבַחֲצֹצְרוֹת וּבִמְצִלְתָּיִם מַשְׁמִעִים בִּנְבָלִים
on-lyres ones-making-sound and-with-cymbals and-with-trumpets horn-of-ram

וְכִנֹּרוֹת׃ וַיְהִי אֲרוֹן בְּרִית יְהוָה בָּא עַד־ עִיר
City-of into entering Yahweh covenant-of ark-of and-he-was (29) and-harps

דָּוִיד וּמִיכַל בַּת־ שָׁאוּל נִשְׁקְפָה ׀ בְּעַד הַחַלּוֹן וַתֵּרֶא
when-she-saw the-window from she-watched Saul daughter-of and-Michal David

אֶת־ הַמֶּלֶךְ דָּוִיד מְרַקֵּד וּמְשַׂחֵק וַתִּבֶז לוֹ
against-him then-she-despised and-celebrating dancing David the-king ***

בְּלִבָּהּ׃ וַיָּבִיאוּ אֶת־ אֲרוֹן הָאֱלֹהִים וַיַּצִּיגוּ
and-they-set the-God ark-of *** and-they-brought (16:1) in-heart-of-her

אֹתוֹ בְּתוֹךְ הָאֹהֶל אֲשֶׁר נָטָה־ לוֹ דָּוִיד וַיַּקְרִיבוּ
and-they-presented David for-him he-pitched that the-tent inside-of him

עֹלוֹת וּשְׁלָמִים לִפְנֵי הָאֱלֹהִים׃ וַיְכַל
when-he-finished (2) the-God before and-fellowship-offerings burnt-offerings

דָּוִיד מֵהַעֲלוֹת הָעֹלָה וְהַשְּׁלָמִים
and-the-fellowship-offerings the-burnt-offerings from-to-sacrifice David

וַיְבָרֶךְ אֶת־ הָעָם בְּשֵׁם יְהוָה׃ וַיְחַלֵּק לְכָל־
to-each-of then-he-gave (3) Yahweh in-name-of the-people *** then-he-blessed

אִישׁ יִשְׂרָאֵל מֵאִישׁ וְעַד־ אִשָּׁה לְאִישׁ כִּכַּר־ לֶחֶם וְאֶשְׁפָּר
and-date-cake bread loaf-of to-each woman even-to from-man Israel person-of

וַאֲשִׁישָׁה׃ וַיִּתֵּן לִפְנֵי אֲרוֹן יְהוָה מִן־ הַלְוִיִּם
the-Levites from Yahweh ark-of before and-he-appointed (4) and-raisin-cake

מְשָׁרְתִים וּלְהַזְכִּיר וּלְהוֹדוֹת וּלְהַלֵּל לַיהוָה
to-Yahweh and-to-praise and-to-give-thanks and-to-petition ones-ministering

bring up the ark of the covenant of the LORD from the
house of Obed-Edom, with rejoicing.
26Because God had
helped the Levites who were
carrying the ark of the covenant of the LORD, seven bulls
and seven rams were sac-
rificed.
27Now David was
clothed in a robe of fine linen,
as were all the Levites who
were carrying the ark, and as
were the singers, and Kenaniah, who was in charge of the
singing of the choirs. David
also wore a linen ephod.
28So
all Israel brought up the ark of
the covenant of the LORD with
shouts, with the sounding of
rams' horns and trumpets,
and of cymbals, and the playing of lyres and harps.

29As the ark of the covenant
of the LORD was entering the
City of David, Michal daughter of Saul watched from a
window. And when she saw
King David dancing and celebrating, she despised him in
her heart.

16 They brought the ark of
God and set it inside
the tent that David had
pitched for it, and they
presented burnt offerings and
fellowship offerings[k] before
God.
2After David had
finished sacrificing the burnt
offerings and fellowship
offerings, he blessed the
people in the name of the
LORD.
3Then he gave a loaf of
bread, a cake of dates and a
cake of raisins to each Israelite
man and woman.

4He appointed some of the
Levites to minister before the
ark of the LORD, to make petition, to give thanks, and to

k1 Traditionally *peace offerings;* also in verse 2

אֱלֹהֵי יִשְׂרָאֵל׃ אָסָף הָרֹאשׁ וּמִשְׁנֵהוּ זְכַרְיָה יְעִיאֵל
Jeiel Zechariah and-second-of-him the-chief Asaph (5) Israel God-of

וּשְׁמִירָמוֹת וִיחִיאֵל וּמַתִּתְיָה וֶאֱלִיאָב וּבְנָיָהוּ וְעֹבֵד אֱדֹם
Edom and-Obed and-Benaiah and-Eliab and-Mattithiah and-Jehiel and-Shemiramoth

וִיעִיאֵל בִּכְלֵי נְבָלִים וּבְכִנֹּרוֹת וְאָסָף בַּמְצִלְתַּיִם
with-the-cymbals and-Asaph and-with-harps lyres with-instruments-of and-Jeiel

מַשְׁמִיעַ׃ וּבְנָיָהוּ וְיַחֲזִיאֵל הַכֹּהֲנִים בַּחֲצֹצְרוֹת
with-trumpets the-priests and-Jahaziel and-Benaiah (6) ones-making-sound

תָּמִיד לִפְנֵי אֲרוֹן בְּרִית־הָאֱלֹהִים׃ בַּיּוֹם הַהוּא אָז
then the-that on-the-day (7) the-God covenant-of ark-of before regularly

נָתַן דָּוִיד בָּרֹאשׁ לְהֹדוֹת לַיהוָה בְּיַד־אָסָף
Asaph into-hand-of to-Yahweh to-give-thanks at-the-first David he-committed

וְאֶחָיו׃ הוֹדוּ לַיהוָה קִרְאוּ בִשְׁמוֹ
on-name-of-him call! to-Yahweh give-thanks! (8) and-associates-of-him

הוֹדִיעוּ בָעַמִּים עֲלִילֹתָיו׃ שִׁירוּ לוֹ זַמְּרוּ־
sing-praise! to-him sing! (9) deeds-of-him among-the-nations make-known!

לוֹ שִׂיחוּ בְּכָל־נִפְלְאֹתָיו׃ הִתְהַלְלוּ בְּשֵׁם
in-name-of glory! (10) acts-being-wonders-of-him of-all-of tell! to-him

קָדְשׁוֹ יִשְׂמַח לֵב מְבַקְשֵׁי יְהוָה׃ דִּרְשׁוּ
look-to! (11) Yahweh ones-seeking-of heart-of let-him-rejoice holiness-of-him

יְהוָה וְעֻזּוֹ בַּקְּשׁוּ פָנָיו תָּמִיד׃ זִכְרוּ
remember! (12) always faces-of-him seek! and-strength-of-him Yahweh

נִפְלְאֹתָיו אֲשֶׁר עָשָׂה מֹפְתָיו וּמִשְׁפְּטֵי־
and-judgments-of miracles-of-him he-did that acts-being-wonders-of-him

פִיהוּ׃ זֶרַע יִשְׂרָאֵל עַבְדּוֹ בְּנֵי יַעֲקֹב
Jacob sons-of servant-of-him Israel descendant-of (13) mouth-of-him

בְּחִירָיו׃ הוּא יְהוָה אֱלֹהֵינוּ בְּכָל־הָאָרֶץ
the-earth in-all-of God-of-us Yahweh he (14) chosen-ones-of-him

מִשְׁפָּטָיו׃ זִכְרוּ לְעוֹלָם בְּרִיתוֹ דָּבָר צִוָּה
he-commanded word covenant-of-him to-forever remember! (15) judgments-of-him

לְאֶלֶף דּוֹר׃ אֲשֶׁר כָּרַת אֶת־אַבְרָהָם וּשְׁבוּעָתוֹ
and-oath-of-him Abraham with he-made which (16) generation for-thousand-of

לְיִצְחָק׃ וַיַּעֲמִידֶהָ לְיַעֲקֹב לְחֹק לְיִשְׂרָאֵל בְּרִית
covenant-of to-Israel as-decree to-Jacob and-he-confirmed-her (17) to-Isaac

עוֹלָם׃ לֵאמֹר לְךָ אֶתֵּן אֶרֶץ־כְּנָעַן חֶבֶל
portion-of Canaan land-of I-will-give to-you to-say (18) everlasting

נַחֲלַתְכֶם׃ בִּהְיוֹתְכֶם מְתֵי מִסְפָּר כִּמְעַט
as-few number people-of when-to-be-you (19) inheritance-of-you

praise the LORD, the God of Israel: [5]Asaph was the chief, Zechariah second, then Jeiel, Shemiramoth, Jehiel, Mattithiah, Eliab, Benaiah, Obed-Edom and Jeiel. They were to play the lyres and harps, Asaph was to sound the cymbals, [6]and Benaiah and Jahaziel the priests were to blow the trumpets regularly before the ark of the covenant of God.

*David's Psalm of Thanks*

[7]That day David first committed to Asaph and his associates this psalm of thanks to the LORD:

[8]Give thanks to the LORD, call on his name;
make known among the nations what he has done.
[9]Sing to him, sing praise to him;
tell of all his wonderful acts.
[10]Glory in his holy name;
let the hearts of those who seek the LORD rejoice.
[11]Look to the LORD and his strength;
seek his face always.
[12]Remember the wonders he has done,
his miracles, and the judgments he pronounced,
[13]O descendants of Israel his servant,
O sons of Jacob, his chosen ones.

[14]He is the LORD our God;
his judgments are in all the earth.
[15]He remembers[l] his covenant forever,
the word he commanded, for a thousand generations,
[16]the covenant he made with Abraham,
the oath he swore to Isaac.
[17]He confirmed it to Jacob as a decree,
to Israel as an everlasting covenant:
[18]"To you I will give the land of Canaan
as the portion you will inherit."

[19]When they were but few in number,

[l]15 Some Septuagint manuscripts (see also Psalm 105:8); Hebrew *Remember*

וְגָרִ֥ים בָּֽהּ׃ וַיִּֽתְהַלְּכוּ֙ מִגּ֣וֹי אֶל־גּ֔וֹי
nation to from-nation and-they-wandered (20) in-her and-ones-being-strangers

וּמִמַּמְלָכָ֖ה אֶל־עַ֥ם אַחֵֽר׃ לֹֽא־הִנִּ֤יחַ לְאִישׁ֙
to-man he-allowed not (21) another people to and-from-kingdom

לְעָשְׁקָ֔ם וַיּ֥וֹכַח עֲלֵיהֶ֖ם מְלָכִֽים׃ אַֽל־תִּגְּעוּ֙
you-touch not (22) kings for-them and-he-rebuked to-oppress-them

בִּמְשִׁיחָ֔י וּבִנְבִיאַ֖י אַל־תָּרֵֽעוּ׃ שִׁ֤ירוּ
sing! (23) you-do-harm not and-to-prophets-of-me on-anointed-ones-of-me

לַֽיהוָה֙ כָּל־הָאָ֔רֶץ בַּשְּׂר֥וּ מִיּֽוֹם־אֶל־י֖וֹם יְשׁוּעָתֽוֹ׃
salvation-of-him day to from-day proclaim! the-earth all-of to-Yahweh

סַפְּר֤וּ בַגּוֹיִם֙ אֶת־כְּבוֹד֔וֹ בְּכָל־הָֽעַמִּ֖ים
the-peoples among-all-of glory-of-him *** among-the-nations declare! (24)

נִפְלְאֹתָֽיו׃ כִּי֩ גָד֨וֹל יְהוָ֤ה וּמְהֻלָּל֙ מְאֹ֔ד
greatly and-being-praised Yahweh great for (25) deeds-being-marvelous-of-him

וְנוֹרָ֥א ה֖וּא עַל־כָּל־אֱלֹהִֽים׃ כִּ֞י כָּל־אֱלֹהֵ֤י הָֽעַמִּים֙
the-nations gods-of all-of for (26) gods all-of above he and-being-feared

אֱלִילִ֔ים וַֽיהוָ֖ה שָׁמַ֥יִם עָשָֽׂה׃ ה֤וֹד וְהָדָר֙ לְפָנָ֔יו
before-him and-majesty splendor (27) he-made heavens but-Yahweh idols

עֹ֥ז וְחֶדְוָ֖ה בִּמְקֹמֽוֹ׃ הָב֤וּ לַֽיהוָה֙ מִשְׁפְּח֣וֹת
families-of to-Yahweh ascribe! (28) in-dwelling-of-him and-joy strength

עַמִּ֔ים הָב֥וּ לַֽיהוָ֖ה כָּב֥וֹד וָעֹֽז׃ הָב֥וּ לַֽיהוָ֖ה
to-Yahweh ascribe! (29) and-strength glory to-Yahweh ascribe! nations

כְּב֣וֹד שְׁמ֑וֹ שְׂא֤וּ מִנְחָה֙ וּבֹ֣אוּ לְפָנָ֔יו הִשְׁתַּחֲו֥וּ לַֽיהוָ֖ה
to-Yahweh worship! before-him and-come! offering bring! name-of-him glory-of

בְּהַדְרַת־קֹֽדֶשׁ׃ חִ֤ילוּ מִלְּפָנָיו֙ כָּל־הָאָ֔רֶץ
the-earth all-of at-before-him tremble! (30) holiness in-splendor-of

אַף־תִּכּ֥וֹן תֵּבֵ֖ל בַּל־תִּמּֽוֹט׃ יִשְׂמְח֤וּ
let-them-rejoice (31) she-can-be-moved not world she-is-established indeed

הַשָּׁמַ֙יִם֙ וְתָגֵ֣ל הָאָ֔רֶץ וְיֹאמְר֥וּ בַגּוֹיִ֖ם
among-the-nations and-let-them-say the-earth and-let-her-be-glad the-heavens

יְהוָ֥ה מָלָֽךְ׃ יִרְעַ֤ם הַיָּם֙ וּמְלוֹא֔וֹ
and-fullness-of-him the-sea let-him-resound (32) he-reigns Yahweh

יַעֲלֹ֥ץ הַשָּׂדֶ֖ה וְכָל־אֲשֶׁר־בּֽוֹ׃ אָ֥ז יְרַנְּנ֖וּ
they-will-sing then (33) in-him that and-all the-field let-him-be-jubilant

עֲצֵ֣י הַיָּ֑עַר מִלִּפְנֵ֣י יְהוָ֔ה כִּי־בָ֖א לִשְׁפּ֥וֹט אֶת־הָאָֽרֶץ׃
the-earth *** to-judge he-comes for Yahweh at-before the-forest trees-of

הוֹד֤וּ לַֽיהוָה֙ כִּ֣י ט֔וֹב כִּ֥י לְעוֹלָ֖ם חַסְדּֽוֹ׃
love-of-him to-forever for good for to-Yahweh give-thanks! (34)

few indeed, and
strangers in it,
[20]they[m] wandered from
nation to nation,
from one kingdom to
another.
[21]He allowed no man to
oppress them;
for their sake he rebuked
kings:
[22]"Do not touch my anointed
ones;
do my prophets no
harm."

[23]Sing to the LORD, all the
earth;
proclaim his salvation
day after day.
[24]Declare his glory among
the nations,
his marvelous deeds
among all peoples.
[25]For great is the LORD and
most worthy of praise;
he is to be feared above
all gods.
[26]For all the gods of the
nations are idols,
but the LORD made the
heavens.
[27]Splendor and majesty are
before him;
strength and joy in his
dwelling place.
[28]Ascribe to the LORD, O
families of nations,
ascribe to the LORD glory
and strength,
[29] ascribe to the LORD the
glory due his name.
Bring an offering and come
before him;
worship the LORD in the
splendor of his[n]
holiness.
[30]Tremble before him, all the
earth!
The world is firmly
established; it cannot
be moved.
[31]Let the heavens rejoice, let
the earth be glad;
let them say among the
nations, "The LORD
reigns!"
[32]Let the sea resound, and all
that is in it;
let the fields be jubilant,
and everything in
them!
[33]Then the trees of the forest
will sing,
they will sing for joy
before the LORD,
for he comes to judge the
earth.

[34]Give thanks to the LORD,
for he is good;
his love endures forever.

[m]18-20 One Hebrew manuscript, Septuagint and Vulgate (see also Psalm 105:12); most Hebrew manuscripts *inherit, / [19]though you are but few in number, / few indeed, and strangers in it." / [20]They*
[n]29 Or *LORD with the splendor of*

וְאִמְרוּ הוֹשִׁיעֵנוּ אֱלֹהֵי יִשְׁעֵנוּ וְקַבְּצֵנוּ
and-gather-us! salvation-of-us God-of save-us! and-cry-out! (35)

וְהַצִּילֵנוּ מִן־ הַגּוֹיִם לְהֹדוֹת לְשֵׁם קָדְשֶׁךָ
holiness-of-you to-name-of to-give-thanks the-nations from and-deliver-us!

לְהִשְׁתַּבֵּחַ בִּתְהִלָּתֶךָ׃ בָּרוּךְ יְהוָה אֱלֹהֵי יִשְׂרָאֵל מִן־
from Israel God-of Yahweh being-praised (36) in-praise-of-you to-glory

הָעוֹלָם וְעַד הָעֹלָם וַיֹּאמְרוּ כָל־ הָעָם אָמֵן
amen the-people all-of and-they-said the-everlasting and-to the-everlasting

וְהַלֵּל לַיהוָה׃ וַיַּעֲזָב־ שָׁם לִפְנֵי אֲרוֹן בְּרִית־
covenant-of ark-of before there and-he-left (37) to-Yahweh and-praise!

יְהוָה לְאָסָף וּלְאֶחָיו לְשָׁרֵת לִפְנֵי הָאָרוֹן תָּמִיד
regularly the-ark before to-minister and-to-associates-of-him to-Asaph Yahweh

לִדְבַר־ יוֹם בְּיוֹמוֹ׃ וְעֹבֵד אֱדֹם וַאֲחֵיהֶם
and-associates-of-them Edom and-Obed (38) in-day-of-him day as-requirement-of

שִׁשִּׁים וּשְׁמוֹנָה וְעֹבֵד אֱדֹם בֶּן־ יְדִיתוּן וְחֹסָה לְשֹׁעֲרִים׃
as-gatekeepers and-Hosah Jeduthun son-of Edom and-Obed and-eight sixty

וְאֵת | צָדוֹק הַכֹּהֵן וְאֶחָיו הַכֹּהֲנִים לִפְנֵי מִשְׁכַּן
tabernacle-of before the-priests and-fellows-of-him the-priest Zadok and (39)

יְהוָה בַּבָּמָה אֲשֶׁר בְּגִבְעוֹן׃ לְהַעֲלוֹת עֹלוֹת
burnt-offerings to-present (40) in-Gibeon that at-the-high-place Yahweh

לַיהוָה עַל־ מִזְבַּח הָעֹלָה תָּמִיד לַבֹּקֶר
in-the-morning regularly the-burnt-offering altar-of on to-Yahweh

וְלָעֶרֶב וּלְכָל־ הַכָּתוּב בְּתוֹרַת יְהוָה
Yahweh in-Law-of the-thing-being-written and-as-all-of and-in-the-evening

אֲשֶׁר צִוָּה עַל־יִשְׂרָאֵל׃ וְעִמָּהֶם הֵימָן וִידוּתוּן וּשְׁאָר
and-rest-of and-Jeduthun Heman and-with-them (41) Israel to he-gave which

הַבְּרוּרִים אֲשֶׁר נִקְּבוּ בְּשֵׁמוֹת לְהֹדוֹת
to-give-thanks by-names they-were-designated who the-ones-being-chosen

לַיהוָה כִּי לְעוֹלָם חַסְדּוֹ׃ וְעִמָּהֶם הֵימָן וִידוּתוּן
and-Jeduthun Heman and-with-them (42) love-of-him to-forever for to-Yahweh

הַחֲצֹצְרוֹת וּמְצִלְתַּיִם לְמַשְׁמִיעִים וּכְלֵי שִׁיר
song-of and-instruments-of for-ones-making-sound and-cymbals trumpets

הָאֱלֹהִים וּבְנֵי יְדוּתוּן לַשָּׁעַר׃ וַיֵּלְכוּ כָל־
all-of then-they-left (43) at-the-gate Jeduthun and-sons-of the-God

הָעָם אִישׁ לְבֵיתוֹ וַיִּסֹּב דָּוִיד לְבָרֵךְ אֶת־
*** to-bless David and-he-returned for-house-of-him each the-people

בֵּיתוֹ׃ וַיְהִי כַּאֲשֶׁר יָשַׁב דָּוִיד בְּבֵיתוֹ
in-palace-of-him David he-settled just-as and-he-was (17:1) family-of-him

35 Cry out, "Save us, O God our Savior;
gather us and deliver us from the nations,
that we may give thanks to your holy name,
that we may glory in your praise."
36 Praise be to the LORD, the God of Israel,
from everlasting to everlasting.

Then all the people said "Amen" and "Praise the LORD."

37 David left Asaph and his associates before the ark of the covenant of the LORD to minister there regularly, according to each day's requirements.
38 He also left Obed-Edom and his sixty-eight associates to minister with them. Obed-Edom son of Jeduthun, and also Hosah, were gatekeepers.
39 David left Zadok the priest and his fellow priests before the tabernacle of the LORD at the high place in Gibeon
40 to present burnt offerings to the LORD on the altar of burnt offering regularly, morning and evening, in accordance with everything written in the Law of the LORD, which he had given Israel.
41 With them were Heman and Jeduthun and the rest of those chosen and designated by name to give thanks to the LORD, "for his love endures forever."
42 Heman and Jeduthun were responsible for the sounding of the trumpets and cymbals and for the playing of the other instruments for sacred song. The sons of Jeduthun were stationed at the gate.
43 Then all the people left, each for his own home, and David returned home to bless his family.

*God's Promise to David*

17 After David was settled in his palace, he said to

וַיֹּאמֶר דָּוִיד אֶל־ נָתָן הַנָּבִיא הִנֵּה אָנֹכִי יוֹשֵׁב בְּבֵית

in-palace-of living I see! the-prophet Nathan to David then-he-said

הָאֲרָזִים וַאֲרוֹן בְּרִית־ יְהוָה תַּחַת יְרִיעוֹת׃

tent-curtains under Yahweh covenant-of while-ark-of the-cedars

וַיֹּאמֶר נָתָן אֶל־ דָּוִיד כֹּל אֲשֶׁר בִּלְבָבְךָ עֲשֵׂה כִּי

for do! in-mind-of-you that all David to Nathan and-he-replied (2)

הָאֱלֹהִים עִמָּךְ׃ וַיְהִי בַּלַּיְלָה הַהוּא וַיְהִי דְּבַר־

word-of and-he-came the-that in-the-night and-he-was (3) with-you the-God

אֱלֹהִים אֶל־נָתָן לֵאמֹר׃ לֵךְ וְאָמַרְתָּ אֶל־ דָּוִיד עַבְדִּי כֹּה

this servant-of-me David to and-you-tell go! (4) to-say Nathan to God

אָמַר יְהוָה לֹא אַתָּה תִּבְנֶה־ לִּי הַבַּיִת לָשָׁבֶת׃ כִּי לֹא

not for (5) to-dwell the-house for-me you-will-build you not Yahweh he-says

יָשַׁבְתִּי בְּבַיִת מִן־ הַיּוֹם אֲשֶׁר הֶעֱלֵיתִי אֶת־ יִשְׂרָאֵל עַד הַיּוֹם

the-day to Israel *** I-brought-up when the-day from in-house I-dwelt

הַזֶּה וָאֶהְיֶה מֵאֹהֶל אֶל־ אֹהֶל וּמִמִּשְׁכָּן׃ בְּכֹל אֲשֶׁר־

where in-all (6) and-from-dwelling tent to from-tent but-I-moved the-this

הִתְהַלַּכְתִּי בְּכָל־ יִשְׂרָאֵל הֲדָבָר דִּבַּרְתִּי אֶת־ אַחַד שֹׁפְטֵי

ones-leading-of one-of to I-said statement? Israel with-all-of I-moved

יִשְׂרָאֵל אֲשֶׁר צִוִּיתִי לִרְעוֹת אֶת־ עַמִּי לֵאמֹר לָמָּה לֹא־

not why? to-say people-of-me *** to-shepherd I-commanded whom Israel

בְנִיתֶם לִי בֵּית אֲרָזִים׃ וְעַתָּה כֹּה־ תֹאמַר לְעַבְדִּי

to-servant-of-me you-tell this then-now (7) cedars house-of for-me you-built

לְדָוִיד כֹּה אָמַר יְהוָה צְבָאוֹת אֲנִי לְקַחְתִּיךָ מִן־ הַנָּוֶה מִן־

from the-pasture from I-took-you I Hosts Yahweh-of he-says this to-David

אַחֲרֵי הַצֹּאן לִהְיוֹת נָגִיד עַל עַמִּי יִשְׂרָאֵל׃ וָאֶהְיֶה עִמְּךָ

with-you and-I-was (8) Israel people-of-me over ruler to-be the-flock after

בְּכֹל אֲשֶׁר הָלַכְתָּ וָאַכְרִית אֶת־ כָּל־ אוֹיְבֶיךָ

ones-being-enemies-of-you all-of *** and-I-cut-off you-went where in-all

מִפָּנֶיךָ וְעָשִׂיתִי לְךָ שֵׁם כְּשֵׁם הַגְּדוֹלִים

the-great-men like-name-of name for-you and-I-will-make from-before-you

אֲשֶׁר בָּאָרֶץ׃ וְשַׂמְתִּי מָקוֹם לְעַמִּי יִשְׂרָאֵל

Israel for-people-of-me place and-I-will-provide (9) of-the-earth who

וּנְטַעְתִּיהוּ וְשָׁכַן תַּחְתָּיו וְלֹא יִרְגַּז

he-will-be-disturbed and-not in-him so-he-can-make-home and-I-will-plant-him

עוֹד וְלֹא־ יוֹסִיפוּ בְנֵי־ עַוְלָה לְבַלֹּתוֹ כַּאֲשֶׁר

just-as to-oppress-him wickedness sons-of they-will-repeat and-not again

בָּרִאשׁוֹנָה׃ וּלְמִיָּמִים אֲשֶׁר צִוִּיתִי שֹׁפְטִים עַל־

over ones-leading I-appointed when and-at-from-days (10) at-the-beginning

Nathan the prophet, "Here I am, living in a palace of cedar, while the ark of the covenant of the LORD is under a tent."
2Nathan replied to David, "Whatever you have in mind, do it, for God is with you."
3That night the word of God came to Nathan, saying:

4"Go and tell my servant David, 'This is what the LORD says: You are not the one to build me a house to dwell in.
5I have not dwelt in a house from the day I brought Israel up out of Egypt to this day. I have moved from one tent site to another, from one dwelling place to another.
6Wherever I have moved with all the Israelites, did I ever say to any of their leaders[o] whom I commanded to shepherd my people, "Why have you not built me a house of cedar?"'

7"Now then, tell my servant David, 'This is what the LORD Almighty says: I took you from the pasture and from following the flock, to be ruler over my people Israel.
8I have been with you wherever you have gone, and I have cut off all your enemies from before you. Now I will make your name like the names of the greatest men of the earth.
9And I will provide a place for my people Israel and will plant them so that they can have a home of their own and no longer be disturbed. Wicked people will not oppress them anymore, as they did at the beginning
10and have done ever since the time I appointed leaders over my people Israel. I

[o]6 Traditionally *judges;* also in verse 10

עַמִּי יִשְׂרָאֵל וְהִכְנַעְתִּי אֶת־ כָּל־ אוֹיְבֶיךָ
ones-being-enemies-of-you all-of *** and-I-will-subdue Israel people-of-me

וָאַגִּד לָךְ וּבַיִת יִבְנֶה־ לְּךָ יְהוָה׃
Yahweh for-you he-will-build also-house to-you now-I-declare

(11) וְהָיָה כִּי־ מָלְאוּ יָמֶיךָ לָלֶכֶת עִם־ אֲבֹתֶיךָ
fathers-of-you with to-go days-of-you they-are-over when and-he-will-be (11)

וַהֲקִימוֹתִי אֶת־ זַרְעֲךָ אַחֲרֶיךָ אֲשֶׁר יִהְיֶה
he-will-be who after-you offspring-of-you *** then-I-will-raise-up

מִבָּנֶיךָ וַהֲכִינוֹתִי אֶת־ מַלְכוּתוֹ׃ (12) הוּא יִבְנֶה־
he-will-build he (12) kingdom-of-him *** and-I-will-establish from-sons-of-you

לִּי בָּיִת וְכֹנַנְתִּי אֶת־ כִּסְאוֹ עַד־ עוֹלָם׃ (13) אֲנִי
I (13) forever to throne-of-him *** and-I-will-establish house for-me

אֶהְיֶה־ לּוֹ לְאָב וְהוּא יִהְיֶה־ לִּי לְבֵן וְחַסְדִּי
and-love-of-me as-son to-me he-will-be and-he as-father to-him I-will-be

לֹא־ אָסִיר מֵעִמּוֹ כַּאֲשֶׁר הֲסִירוֹתִי מֵאֲשֶׁר הָיָה לְפָנֶיךָ׃
before-you he-was from-whom I-took just-as from-with-him I-will-take never

(14) וְהַעֲמַדְתִּיהוּ בְּבֵיתִי וּבְמַלְכוּתִי עַד־
to and-over-kingdom-of-me over-house-of-me and-I-will-set-him (14)

הָעוֹלָם וְכִסְאוֹ יִהְיֶה נָכוֹן עַד־ עוֹלָם׃
forever to being-established he-will-be and-throne-of-him the-forever

(15) כְּכֹל הַדְּבָרִים הָאֵלֶּה וּכְכֹל הֶחָזוֹן הַזֶּה
the-this the-revelation and-as-all-of the-these the-words as-all-of (15)

כֵּן דִּבֶּר נָתָן אֶל־ דָּוִיד׃ (16) וַיָּבֹא הַמֶּלֶךְ דָּוִיד וַיֵּשֶׁב
and-he-sat David the-king then-he-went (16) David to Nathan he-reported so

לִפְנֵי יְהוָה וַיֹּאמֶר מִי־ אֲנִי יְהוָה אֱלֹהִים וּמִי בֵיתִי כִּי
that family-of-me and-what? God Yahweh I who? and-he-said Yahweh before

הֲבִיאֹתַנִי עַד־ הֲלֹם׃ (17) וַתִּקְטַן זֹאת בְּעֵינֶיךָ אֱלֹהִים
God in-eyes-of-you this and-she-is-not-enough (17) here to you-brought-me

וַתְּדַבֵּר עַל־ בֵּית־ עַבְדְּךָ לְמֵרָחוֹק וּרְאִיתַנִי
and-you-saw-me about-at-future servant-of-you house-of about and-you-spoke

כְּתוֹר הָאָדָם הַמַּעֲלָה יְהוָה אֱלֹהִים׃ (18) מַה־ יּוֹסִיף עוֹד דָּוִיד
David more can-he-add what? (18) God Yahweh the-exalted the-man as-rank-of

אֵלֶיךָ לְכָבוֹד אֶת־ עַבְדֶּךָ וְאַתָּה אֶת־ עַבְדְּךָ יָדָעְתָּ׃
you-know servant-of-you *** for-you servant-of-you *** for-honor to-you

(19) יְהוָה בַּעֲבוּר עַבְדְּךָ וּכְלִבְּךָ עָשִׂיתָ אֵת
*** you-did and-as-will-of-you servant-of-you for-sake-of Yahweh (19)

כָּל־ הַגְּדוּלָּה הַזֹּאת לְהֹדִיעַ אֶת־ כָּל־ הַגְּדֻלּוֹת׃
the-great-things all-of *** to-make-known the-this the-greatness all-of

will also subdue all your
enemies.
" 'I declare to you that the
LORD will build a house for
you: [11]When your days are
over and you go to be with
your fathers, I will raise up
your offspring to succeed
you, one of your own sons,
and I will establish his
kingdom. [12]He is the one
who will build a house for
me, and I will establish his
throne forever. [13]I will be
his father, and he will be
my son. I will never take
my love away from him, as
I took it away from your
predecessor. [14]I will set him
over my house and my
kingdom forever; his
throne will be established
forever.' "

[15]Nathan reported to David
all the words of this entire
revelation.

*David's Prayer*

[16]Then King David went in
and sat before the LORD, and
he said:

"Who am I, O LORD God,
and what is my family, that
you have brought me this
far? [17]And as if this were
not enough in your sight, O
God, you have spoken
about the future of the
house of your servant. You
have looked on me as
though I were the most exalted of men, O LORD God.
[18]"What more can David
say to you for honoring
your servant? For you
know your servant, [19]O
LORD. For the sake of your
servant and according to
your will, you have done
this great thing and made
known all these great
promises.

יְהוָה֙ אֵ֣ין כָּמ֔וֹךָ וְאֵ֥ין אֱלֹהִ֖ים זוּלָתֶ֑ךָ בְּכֹ֖ל אֲשֶׁר־
(20) Yahweh there-is-none like-you and-there-is-no God but-you as-all that

שָׁמַ֥עְנוּ בְּאָזְנֵֽינוּ: (21) וּמִ֚י כְּעַמְּךָ֣ יִשְׂרָאֵ֔ל גּ֖וֹי אֶחָ֑ד
we-heard with-ears-of-us and-who? like-people-of-you Israel nation one

בָּאָ֑רֶץ אֲשֶׁ֨ר הָלַ֧ךְ הָאֱלֹהִ֛ים לִפְדּ֥וֹת ל֖וֹ עָ֑ם לָשׂ֣וּם
on-the-earth who he-went-out the-God to-redeem for-him people to-make

לְךָ֥ שֵׁ֖ם גְּדֻלּ֣וֹת וְנֹרָא֑וֹת לְגָרֵ֖שׁ מִפְּנֵ֥י
for-you name great-things and-wonders-being-awesome to-drive-out from-before

עַמְּךָ֗ אֲשֶׁ֨ר פָּדִ֧יתָ מִמִּצְרַ֛יִם גּוֹיִֽם: (22) וַתִּתֵּ֣ן אֶת־
people-of-you whom you-redeemed from-Egypt nations and-you-made ***

עַמְּךָ֣ יִשְׂרָאֵ֣ל ׀ לְךָ֗ לְעָ֛ם עַד־עוֹלָ֖ם וְאַתָּ֣ה יְהוָ֔ה הָיִ֥יתָ
people-of-you Israel for-you as-people to forever and-you Yahweh you-became

לָהֶ֖ם לֵאלֹהִֽים: (23) וְעַתָּ֣ה יְהוָ֔ה הַדָּבָ֗ר אֲשֶׁ֨ר דִּבַּ֤רְתָּ עַל־
for-them as-God and-now Yahweh the-promise that you-promised concerning

עַבְדְּךָ֙ וְעַל־בֵּית֔וֹ יֵאָמֵ֖ן עַד־עוֹלָ֑ם
servant-of-you and-concerning house-of-him let-him-be-established to forever

וַעֲשֵׂ֖ה כַּאֲשֶׁ֥ר דִּבַּֽרְתָּ: (24) וְיֵאָמֵ֞ן
and-do! just-as you-promised so-he-will-be-established

וְיִגְדַּ֣ל שִׁמְךָ֣ עַד־עוֹלָ֗ם לֵאמֹ֚ר יְהוָ֣ה צְבָא֔וֹת אֱלֹהֵ֥י
and-he-will-be-great name-of-you to forever to-say Yahweh-of Hosts God-of

יִשְׂרָאֵ֖ל אֱלֹהִ֣ים לְיִשְׂרָאֵ֑ל וּבֵית־דָּוִ֥יד עַבְדְּךָ֖ נָכ֥וֹן
Israel God of-Israel and-house-of David servant-of-you being-established

לְפָנֶֽיךָ: (25) כִּ֣י ׀ אַתָּ֣ה אֱלֹהַ֗י גָּלִ֙יתָ֙ אֶת־אֹ֣זֶן עַבְדְּךָ֔
before-you indeed you God-of-me you-uncovered *** ear-of servant-of-you

לִבְנ֣וֹת ל֖וֹ בָּ֑יִת עַל־כֵּ֗ן מָצָ֤א עַבְדְּךָ֙ לְהִתְפַּלֵּ֣ל לְפָנֶֽיךָ:
to-build for-him house for this he-found servant-of-you to-pray before-you

(26) וְעַתָּ֣ה יְהוָ֔ה אַתָּה־ה֖וּא הָאֱלֹהִ֑ים וַתְּדַבֵּר֙ עַל־עַבְדְּךָ֔
and-now Yahweh you he the-God and-you-promised to servant-of-you

הַטּוֹבָ֖ה הַזֹּֽאת: (27) וְעַתָּ֗ה הוֹאַ֙לְתָּ֙ לְבָרֵךְ֙ אֶת־בֵּ֣ית
the-good the-this and-now you-are-pleased to-bless *** house-of

עַבְדְּךָ֔ לִהְי֥וֹת לְעוֹלָ֖ם לְפָנֶ֑יךָ כִּֽי־אַתָּ֤ה יְהוָה֙ בֵּרַ֔כְתָּ
servant-of-you to-be to-forever before-you for you Yahweh you-blessed

וּמְבֹרָ֖ךְ לְעוֹלָֽם: (18:1) וַיְהִי֙ אַחֲרֵי־כֵ֔ן וַיַּ֥ךְ
and-being-blessed to-forever and-he-was after this then-he-defeated

דָּוִ֛יד אֶת־פְּלִשְׁתִּ֖ים וַיַּכְנִיעֵ֑ם וַיִּקַּ֛ח אֶת־גַּ֥ת
David *** Philistines and-he-subdued-them and-he-took *** Gath

וּבְנֹתֶ֖יהָ מִיַּ֥ד פְּלִשְׁתִּֽים: (2) וַיַּ֖ךְ אֶת־מוֹאָ֑ב
and-villages-of-her from-control-of Philistines also-he-defeated *** Moab

[20]"There is no one like you, O LORD, and there is no God but you, as we have heard with our own ears. [21]And who is like your people Israel—the one nation on earth whose God went out to redeem a people for himself, and to make a name for yourself, and to perform great and awesome wonders by driving out nations from before your people, whom you redeemed from Egypt? [22]You made your people Israel your very own forever, and you, O LORD, have become their God.

[23]"And now, LORD, let the promise you have made concerning your servant and his house be established forever. Do as you promised, [24]so that it will be established and that your name will be great forever. Then men will say, 'The LORD Almighty, the God over Israel, is Israel's God!' And the house of your servant David will be established before you.

[25]"You, my God, have revealed to your servant that you will build a house for him. So your servant has found courage to pray to you. [26]O LORD, you are God! You have given this good promise to your servant. [27]Now you have been pleased to bless the house of your servant, that it may continue forever in your sight; for you, O LORD, have blessed it, and it will be blessed forever."

## David's Victories

**18** In the course of time, David defeated the Philistines and subdued them, and he took Gath and its surrounding villages from the control of the Philistines.

וַיִּהְיוּ מוֹאָב עֲבָדִים לְדָוִיד נֹשְׂאֵי מִנְחָה׃
tribute ones-bringing-of to-David subjects Moab and-they-became

וַיַּךְ דָּוִיד אֶת־הֲדַדְעֶזֶר מֶלֶךְ־צוֹבָה חֲמָתָה בְּלֶכְתּוֹ
when-to-go-him to-Hamath Zobah king-of Hadadezer *** David and-he-fought (3)

לְהַצִּיב יָדוֹ בִּנְהַר־פְּרָת׃ וַיִּלְכֹּד
and-he-captured (4) Euphrates along-River-of control-of-him to-establish

דָּוִיד מִמֶּנּוּ אֶלֶף רֶכֶב וְשִׁבְעַת אֲלָפִים פָּרָשִׁים
charioteers thousands and-seven-of chariot thousand from-him David

וְעֶשְׂרִים אֶלֶף אִישׁ רַגְלִי וַיְעַקֵּר דָּוִיד אֶת־כָּל־
all-of *** David and-he-hamstrung foot-soldier man thousand and-twenty

הָרֶכֶב וַיּוֹתֵר מִמֶּנּוּ מֵאָה רָכֶב׃ וַיָּבֹא
when-he-came (5) chariot-horse hundred from-him but-he-left the-chariot-horse

אֲרַם דַּרְמֶשֶׂק לַעְזוֹר לַהֲדַדְעֶזֶר מֶלֶךְ צוֹבָה וַיַּךְ
then-he-struck-down Zobah king-of to-Hadadezer to-help Damascus Aram-of

דָּוִיד בַּאֲרָם עֶשְׂרִים־וּשְׁנַיִם אֶלֶף אִישׁ׃ וַיָּשֶׂם דָּוִיד
David and-he-put-garrison (6) man thousand and-two twenty of-Aram David

בַּאֲרַם דַּרְמֶשֶׂק וַיְהִי אֲרָם לְדָוִיד עֲבָדִים נֹשְׂאֵי
ones-bearing-of subjects to-David Aram and-he-became Damascus in-Aram-of

מִנְחָה וַיּוֹשַׁע יְהוָה לְדָוִיד בְּכֹל אֲשֶׁר הָלָךְ׃
he-went where in-all to-David Yahweh and-he-gave-victory tribute

וַיִּקַּח דָּוִיד אֵת שִׁלְטֵי הַזָּהָב אֲשֶׁר הָיוּ עַל עַבְדֵי
officers-of on they-were that the-gold shields-of *** David and-he-took (7)

הֲדַדְעָזֶר וַיְבִיאֵם יְרוּשָׁלִָם׃ וּמִטִּבְחַת וּמִכּוּן
and-from-Cun and-from-Tibhath (8) Jerusalem and-he-brought-them Hadadezer

עָרֵי הֲדַדְעֶזֶר לָקַח דָּוִיד נְחֹשֶׁת רַבָּה מְאֹד בָּהּ׀ עָשָׂה שְׁלֹמֹה
Solomon he-made with-her very much bronze David he-took Hadadezer towns-of

אֶת־יָם הַנְּחֹשֶׁת וְאֶת־הָעַמּוּדִים וְאֵת כְּלֵי הַנְּחֹשֶׁת׃
the-bronze articles-of and the-pillars and the-bronze Sea-of ***

וַיִּשְׁמַע תֹּעוּ מֶלֶךְ חֲמָת כִּי הִכָּה דָוִיד אֶת־כָּל־
entire-of *** David he-defeated that Hamath king-of Tou when-he-heard (9)

חֵיל הֲדַדְעֶזֶר מֶלֶךְ־צוֹבָה׃ וַיִּשְׁלַח אֶת־הֲדוֹרָם־בְּנוֹ אֶל־
to son-of-him Hadoram *** then-he-sent (10) Zobah king-of Hadadezer army-of

הַמֶּלֶךְ־דָּוִיד לִשְׁאוֹל־°לוֹ לְשָׁלוֹם וּלְבָרֲכוֹ עַל אֲשֶׁר
when on and-to-congratulate-him about-peace to-him to-greet David the-king

נִלְחַם בַּהֲדַדְעֶזֶר וַיַּכֵּהוּ כִּי־אִישׁ מִלְחֲמוֹת תֹּעוּ
Tou wars-of man-of for and-he-defeated-him against-Hadadezer he-fought

הָיָה הֲדַדְעֶזֶר וְכֹל כְּלֵי זָהָב וָכֶסֶף וּנְחֹשֶׁת׃
and-bronze and-silver gold articles-of and-all-of Hadadezer he-was

2David also defeated the Moabites, and they became subject to him and brought tribute.
3Moreover, David fought
Hadadezer king of Zobah, as
far as Hamath, when he went
to establish his control along
the Euphrates River. 4David
captured a thousand of his
chariots, seven thousand
charioteers and twenty thousand foot soldiers. He hamstrung all but a hundred of the
chariot horses.
5When the Arameans of
Damascus came to help Hadadezer king of Zobah, David
struck down twenty-two
thousand of them. 6He put garrisons in the Aramean kingdom of Damascus, and the
Arameans became subject to
him and brought tribute. The
LORD gave David victory
everywhere he went.
7David took the gold shields
carried by the officers of Hadadezer and brought them to
Jerusalem. 8From Tebah[p] and
Cun, towns that belonged to
Hadadezer, David took a great
quantity of bronze, which
Solomon used to make the
bronze Sea, the pillars and
various bronze articles.
9When Tou king of Hamath
heard that David had defeated
the entire army of Hadadezer
king of Zobah, 10he sent his
son Hadoram to King David to
greet him and congratulate
him on his victory in battle
over Hadadezer, who had
been at war with Tou. Ha-
doram brought all kinds of articles of gold and silver and
bronze.

p8 Hebrew *Tibhath*, a variant of *Tebah*

°10 ק לשאל

גַּם־ אֹתָם הִקְדִּישׁ הַמֶּלֶךְ דָּוִיד לַיהוָה עִם־ הַכֶּסֶף
the-silver with to-Yahweh David the-king he-dedicated them also (11)

וְהַזָּהָב אֲשֶׁר נָשָׂא מִכָּל־ הַגּוֹיִם מֵאֱדוֹם וּמִמּוֹאָב
and-from-Moab from-Edom the-nations from-all-of he-took that and-the-gold

וּמִבְּנֵי עַמּוֹן וּמִפְּלִשְׁתִּים וּמֵעֲמָלֵק׃ וְאַבְשַׁי
and-Abishai (12) and-from-Amalek and-from-Philistines Ammon and-from-sons-of

בֶן־ צְרוּיָה הִכָּה אֶת־ אֱדוֹם בְּגֵיא הַמֶּלַח שְׁמוֹנָה עָשָׂר
ten eight the-Salt in-Valley-of Edom *** he-struck-down Zeruiah son-of

אָלֶף׃ וַיָּשֶׂם בֶּאֱדוֹם נְצִיבִים וַיִּהְיוּ כָל־ אֱדוֹם
Edom all-of and-they-became garrisons in-Edom and-he-put (13) thousand

עֲבָדִים לְדָוִיד וַיּוֹשַׁע יְהוָה אֶת־ דָּוִיד בְּכֹל אֲשֶׁר הָלָךְ׃
he-went where in-all David *** Yahweh and-he-gave-victory to-David subjects

וַיִּמְלֹךְ דָּוִיד עַל־ כָּל־ יִשְׂרָאֵל וַיְהִי עֹשֶׂה מִשְׁפָּט
justice doing and-he-was Israel all-of over David and-he-reigned (14)

וּצְדָקָה לְכָל־ עַמּוֹ׃ וְיוֹאָב בֶּן־ צְרוּיָה עַל־
over Zeruiah son-of and-Joab (15) people-of-him for-all-of and-righteousness

הַצָּבָא וִיהוֹשָׁפָט בֶּן־ אֲחִילוּד מַזְכִּיר׃ וְצָדוֹק בֶּן־
son-of and-Zadok (16) one-recording Ahilud son-of and-Jehoshaphat the-army

אֲחִיטוּב וַאֲבִימֶלֶךְ בֶּן־ אֶבְיָתָר כֹּהֲנִים וְשַׁוְשָׁא סוֹפֵר׃
secretary and-Shavsha priests Abiathar son-of and-Abimelech Ahitub

וּבְנָיָהוּ בֶּן־ יְהוֹיָדָע עַל־ הַכְּרֵתִי וְהַפְּלֵתִי
and-the-Pelethite the-Kerethite over Jehoiada son-of and-Benaiah (17)

וּבְנֵי־ דָוִיד הָרִאשֹׁנִים לְיַד הַמֶּלֶךְ׃ וַיְהִי
and-he-was (19:1) the-king at-side-of the-chief-officials David and-sons-of

אַחֲרֵי־ כֵן וַיָּמָת נָחָשׁ מֶלֶךְ בְּנֵי־ עַמּוֹן וַיִּמְלֹךְ
and-he-became-king Ammon sons-of king-of Nahash then-he-died this after

בְּנוֹ תַּחְתָּיו׃ וַיֹּאמֶר דָּוִיד אֶעֱשֶׂה־ חֶסֶד ׀
kindness I-will-show David and-he-thought (2) in-place-of-him son-of-him

עִם־ חָנוּן בֶּן־ נָחָשׁ כִּי־ עָשָׂה אָבִיו עִמִּי חֶסֶד
kindness to-me father-of-him he-showed because Nahash son-of Hanun to

וַיִּשְׁלַח דָּוִיד מַלְאָכִים לְנַחֲמוֹ עַל־ אָבִיו
father-of-him about to-express-sympathy-to-him delegates David so-he-sent

וַיָּבֹאוּ עַבְדֵי דָוִיד אֶל־ אֶרֶץ בְּנֵי־ עַמּוֹן אֶל־ חָנוּן
Hanun to Ammon sons-of land-of to David men-of when-they-came

לְנַחֲמוֹ׃ וַיֹּאמְרוּ שָׂרֵי בְנֵי־ עַמּוֹן
Ammon sons-of nobles-of and-they-said (3) to-express-sympathy-to-him

לְחָנוּן הַמְכַבֵּד דָּוִיד אֶת־ אָבִיךָ בְּעֵינֶיךָ כִּי־ שָׁלַח
he-sent because in-eyes-of-you father-of-you *** David honoring? to-Hanun

11King David dedicated these articles to the LORD, as he had done with the silver and gold he had taken from all these nations: Edom and Moab, the Ammonites and the Philistines, and Amalek.

12Abishai son of Zeruiah struck down eighteen thousand Edomites in the Valley of Salt. 13He put garrisons in Edom, and all the Edomites became subject to David. The LORD gave David victory everywhere he went.

*David's Officials*

14David reigned over all Israel, doing what was just and right for all his people. 15Joab son of Zeruiah was over the army; Jehoshaphat son of Ahilud was recorder; 16Zadok son of Ahitub and Ahimelech[b] son of Abiathar were priests; Shavsha was secretary; 17Benaiah son of Jehoiada was over the Kerethites and Pelethites; and David's sons were chief officials at the king's side.

*The Battle Against the Ammonites*

19 In the course of time, Nahash king of the Ammonites died, and his son succeeded him as king. 2David thought, "I will show kindness to Hanun son of Nahash, because his father showed kindness to me." So David sent a delegation to express his sympathy to Hanun concerning his father.

When David's men came to Hanun in the land of the Ammonites to express sympathy to him, 3the Ammonite nobles said to Hanun, "Do you think David is honoring your father

[b]16 Some Hebrew manuscripts, Vulgate and Syriac (see also 2 Samuel 8:17); most Hebrew manuscripts *Abimelech*

לְךָ מְנַחֲמִים הֲלֹא בַּעֲבוּר לַחְקֹר וְלַהֲפֹךְ
and-to-overthrow to-explore in-order-to not? ones-sympathizing to-you

וּלְרַגֵּל הָאָרֶץ בָּאוּ עֲבָדָיו אֵלֶיךָ׃ וַיִּקַּח חָנוּן
Hanun so-he-seized (4) to-you men-of-him they-came the-country and-to-spy-out

אֶת־ עַבְדֵי דָוִיד וַיְגַלְּחֵם וַיִּכְרֹת אֶת־ מַדְוֵיהֶם
garments-of-them *** and-he-cut-off and-he-shaved-them David men-of ***

בַּחֵצִי עַד־ הַמִּפְשָׂעָה וַיְשַׁלְּחֵם׃ וַיֵּלְכוּ
when-they-came (5) and-he-sent-away-them the-buttocks at in-the-middle

וַיַּגִּידוּ לְדָוִיד עַל־ הָאֲנָשִׁים וַיִּשְׁלַח לִקְרָאתָם כִּי־ הָיוּ
they-were for to-meet-them then-he-sent the-men about to-David and-they-told

הָאֲנָשִׁים נִכְלָמִים מְאֹד וַיֹּאמֶר הַמֶּלֶךְ שְׁבוּ בִירֵחוֹ
at-Jericho stay! the-king and-he-said greatly ones-being-humiliated the-men

עַד אֲשֶׁר־ יְצַמַּח זְקַנְכֶם וְשַׁבְתֶּם׃ וַיִּרְאוּ
when-they-realized (6) then-you-come-back beard-of-you he-grows when till

בְּנֵי עַמּוֹן כִּי הִתְבָּאֲשׁוּ עִם־ דָּוִיד וַיִּשְׁלַח חָנוּן
Hanun then-he-sent David to they-became-stench that Ammon sons-of

וּבְנֵי עַמּוֹן אֶלֶף כִּכַּר־ כֶּסֶף לִשְׂכֹּר לָהֶם מִן־ אֲרַם
Aram-of from for-them to-hire silver talent-of thousand Ammon and-sons-of

נַהֲרַיִם וּמִן־ אֲרַם מַעֲכָה וּמִצּוֹבָה רֶכֶב וּפָרָשִׁים׃
and-charioteers chariot and-from-Zobah Maacah Aram-of and-from Naharaim

וַיִּשְׂכְּרוּ לָהֶם שְׁנַיִם וּשְׁלֹשִׁים אֶלֶף רֶכֶב וְאֶת־ מֶלֶךְ
king-of and chariot thousand and-thirty two for-them and-they-hired (7)

מַעֲכָה וְאֶת־ עַמּוֹ וַיָּבֹאוּ וַיַּחֲנוּ לִפְנֵי מֵידְבָא וּבְנֵי
and-sons-of Medeba near and-they-camped and-they-came troop-of-him and Maacah

עַמּוֹן נֶאֶסְפוּ מֵעָרֵיהֶם וַיָּבֹאוּ לַמִּלְחָמָה׃
for-the-battle and-they-moved-out from-towns-of-them they-were-mustered Ammon

וַיִּשְׁמַע דָּוִיד וַיִּשְׁלַח אֶת־ יוֹאָב וְאֵת כָּל־ צָבָא
army entire-of and Joab *** then-he-sent-out David when-he-heard (8)

הַגִּבּוֹרִים׃ וַיֵּצְאוּ בְּנֵי עַמּוֹן וַיַּעַרְכוּ
and-they-drew-up Ammon sons-of and-they-came-out (9) the-fighting-men

מִלְחָמָה פֶּתַח הָעִיר וְהַמְּלָכִים אֲשֶׁר־ בָּאוּ לְבַדָּם
by-themselves they-came who and-the-kings the-city entrance-of battle

בַּשָּׂדֶה׃ וַיַּרְא יוֹאָב כִּי־ הָיְתָה פְנֵי־ הַמִּלְחָמָה
the-battle lines-of she-was that Joab and-he-saw (10) in-the-open-country

אֵלָיו פָּנִים וְאָחוֹר וַיִּבְחַר מִכָּל־ בָּחוּר בְּיִשְׂרָאֵל
in-Israel being-best from-all-of so-he-selected and-behind fronts to-him

וַיַּעֲרֹךְ לִקְרַאת אֲרָם׃ וְאֵת יֶתֶר הָעָם נָתַן בְּיַד
under-hand-of he-put the-people rest-of and (11) Aram to-meet and-he-deployed

by sending men to you to express sympathy? Haven't his men come to you to explore and spy out the country and overthrow it?" 
4So Hanun seized David's men, shaved them, cut off their garments in the middle at the buttocks, and sent them away.
5When someone came and told David about the men, he sent messengers to meet them, for they were greatly humiliated. The king said, "Stay at Jericho till your beards have grown, and then come back."
6When the Ammonites realized that they had become a stench in David's nostrils, Hanun and the Ammonites sent a thousand talents[r] of silver to hire chariots and charioteers from Aram Naharaim,[s] Aram Maacah and Zobah.
7They hired thirty-two thousand chariots and charioteers, as well as the king of Maacah with his troops, who came and camped near Medeba, while the Ammonites were mustered from their towns and moved out for battle.
8On hearing this, David sent Joab out with the entire army of fighting men.
9The Ammonites came out and drew up in battle formation at the entrance to their city, while the kings who had come were by themselves in the open country.
10Joab saw that there were battle lines in front of him and behind him; so he selected some of the best troops in Israel and deployed them against the Arameans.
11He put the rest of the men under the command of Abishai his brother,

r6 That is, about 37 tons (about 34 metric tons)
s6 That is, Northwest Mesopotamia

אַבְשַׁי אָחִיו וַיַּעַרְכוּ לִקְרַאת בְּנֵי עַמּוֹן׃
Ammon sons-of to-meet and-they-deployed brother-of-him Abishai

וַיֹּאמֶר אִם־ תֶּחֱזַק מִמֶּנִּי אֲרָם וְהָיִיתָ לִּי
to-me then-you-be Aram more-than-me she-is-strong if and-he-said (12)

לִתְשׁוּעָה וְאִם־ בְּנֵי עַמּוֹן יֶחֶזְקוּ מִמְּךָ
more-than-you they-are-strong Ammon sons-of but-if for-rescue

וְהוֹשַׁעְתִּיךָ׃ חֲזַק וְנִתְחַזְּקָה בְּעַד־
for and-let-us-fight-bravely! be-strong! (13) then-I-will-rescue-you

עַמֵּנוּ וּבְעַד עָרֵי אֱלֹהֵינוּ וַיהוָה הַטּוֹב בְּעֵינָיו
in-eyes-of-him the-good and-Yahweh God-of-us cities-of and-for people-of-us

יַעֲשֶׂה׃ וַיִּגַּשׁ יוֹאָב וְהָעָם אֲשֶׁר־ עִמּוֹ לִפְנֵי
against with-him who and-the-troop Joab then-he-advanced (14) he-will-do

אֲרָם לַמִּלְחָמָה וַיָּנוּסוּ מִפָּנָיו׃ וּבְנֵי עַמּוֹן
Ammon when-sons-of (15) from-before-him and-they-fled to-the-fight Aram

רָאוּ כִּי־ נָס אֲרָם וַיָּנוּסוּ גַם־ הֵם מִפְּנֵי אַבְשַׁי
Abishai from-before they also then-they-fled Aram fleeing that they-saw

אָחִיו וַיָּבֹאוּ הָעִירָה וַיָּבֹא יוֹאָב יְרוּשָׁלִָם׃
Jerusalem Joab so-he-went-back into-the-city and-they-went brother-of-him

וַיַּרְא אֲרָם כִּי נִגְּפוּ לִפְנֵי יִשְׂרָאֵל וַיִּשְׁלְחוּ
then-they-sent Israel before they-were-routed that Aram after-he-saw (16)

מַלְאָכִים וַיּוֹצִיאוּ אֶת־ אֲרָם אֲשֶׁר מֵעֵבֶר הַנָּהָר וְשׁוֹפַךְ
and-Shophach the-River from-beyond who Aram *** and-they-brought messengers

שַׂר־ צְבָא הֲדַדְעֶזֶר לִפְנֵיהֶם׃ וַיֻּגַּד לְדָוִיד
to-David when-he-was-told (17) before-them Hadadezer army-of commander-of

וַיֶּאֱסֹף אֶת־ כָּל־ יִשְׂרָאֵל וַיַּעֲבֹר הַיַּרְדֵּן וַיָּבֹא
and-he-advanced the-Jordan and-he-crossed Israel all-of *** then-he-gathered

אֲלֵהֶם וַיַּעֲרֹךְ אֲלֵהֶם וַיַּעֲרֹךְ דָּוִיד לִקְרַאת אֲרָם
Aram to-meet David and-he-formed opposite-them and-he-formed against-them

מִלְחָמָה וַיִּלָּחֲמוּ עִמּוֹ׃ וַיָּנָס אֲרָם מִלִּפְנֵי יִשְׂרָאֵל
Israel from-before Aram but-he-fled (18) against-him and-they-fought battle

וַיַּהֲרֹג דָּוִיד מֵאֲרָם שִׁבְעַת אֲלָפִים רֶכֶב וְאַרְבָּעִים
and-forty charioteer thousands seven-of from-Aram David and-he-killed

אֶלֶף אִישׁ רַגְלִי וְאֵת שׁוֹפַךְ שַׂר־ הַצָּבָא הֵמִית׃
he-killed the-army commander-of Shophach and foot-soldier man thousand

וַיִּרְאוּ עַבְדֵי הֲדַדְעֶזֶר כִּי נִגְּפוּ לִפְנֵי
before they-were-defeated that Hadadezer vassals-of when-they-saw (19)

יִשְׂרָאֵל וַיַּשְׁלִימוּ עִם־ דָּוִיד וַיַּעַבְדֻהוּ
and-they-became-subject-to-him David with then-they-made-peace Israel

and they were deployed against the Ammonites. [12]Joab said, "If the Arameans are too strong for me, then you are to rescue me; but if the Ammonites are too strong for you, then I will rescue you. [13]Be strong and let us fight bravely for our people and the cities of our God. The LORD will do what is good in his sight."

[14]Then Joab and the troops with him advanced to fight the Arameans, and they fled before him. [15]When the Ammonites saw that the Arameans were fleeing, they too fled before his brother Abishai and went inside the city. So Joab went back to Jerusalem.

[16]After the Arameans saw that they had been routed by Israel, they sent messengers and had Arameans brought from beyond the River,[t] with Shophach the commander of Hadadezer's army leading them.

[17]When David was told of this, he gathered all Israel and crossed the Jordan; he advanced against them and formed his battle lines opposite them. David formed his lines to meet the Arameans in battle, and they fought against him. [18]But they fled before Israel, and David killed seven thousand of their charioteers and forty thousand of their foot soldiers. He also killed Shophach the commander of their army.

[19]When the vassals of Hadadezer saw that they had been defeated by Israel, they made peace with David and became subject to him.

[t]16 That is, the Euphrates

וְלֹא־ אָבָה אֲרָם לְהוֹשִׁיעַ אֶת־ בְּנֵי־ עַמּוֹן עוֹד׃ וַיְהִי
and-he-was (20:1) again Ammon sons-of *** to-help Aram he-was-willing so-not

לְעֵת תְּשׁוּבַת הַשָּׁנָה לְעֵת ׀ צֵאת הַמְּלָכִים וַיִּנְהַג
then-he-led-out the-kings to-go-off at-time-of the-year return-of at-time-of

יוֹאָב אֶת־ חֵיל הַצָּבָא וַיַּשְׁחֵת ׀ אֶת־ אֶרֶץ בְּנֵי־ עַמּוֹן
Ammon sons-of land-of *** and-he-laid-waste the-army force-of *** Joab

וַיָּבֹא וַיָּצַר אֶת־ רַבָּה וְדָוִיד יֹשֵׁב בִּירוּשָׁלִָם
in-Jerusalem remaining but-David Rabbah *** and-he-besieged and-he-went

וַיַּךְ יוֹאָב אֶת־ רַבָּה וַיֶּהֶרְסֶהָ׃ וַיִּקַּח דָּוִיד אֶת־
*** David and-he-took (2) and-he-ruined-her Rabbah *** Joab and-he-attacked

עֲטֶרֶת־ מַלְכָּם מֵעַל רֹאשׁוֹ וַיִּמְצָאָהּ ׀ מִשְׁקַל
weight-of and-he-found-her head-of-him from-upon king-of-them crown-of

כִּכַּר־ זָהָב וּבָהּ אֶבֶן יְקָרָה וַתְּהִי עַל־ רֹאשׁ דָּוִיד
David head-of on and-she-was precious stone and-in-her gold talent-of

וּשְׁלַל הָעִיר הוֹצִיא הַרְבֵּה מְאֹד׃ וְאֶת־ הָעָם אֲשֶׁר־
who the-people and (3) very to-be-great he-took the-city and-plunder-of

בָּהּ הוֹצִיא וַיָּשַׂר בַּמְּגֵרָה וּבַחֲרִיצֵי הַבַּרְזֶל
the-iron and-to-picks-of to-the-saw and-he-consigned he-brought-out in-her

וּבַמְּגֵרוֹת וְכֵן יַעֲשֶׂה דָוִיד לְכֹל עָרֵי בְנֵי־ עַמּוֹן
Ammon sons-of towns-of to-all-of David he-did and-this and-to-the-axes

וַיָּשָׁב דָּוִיד וְכָל־ הָעָם יְרוּשָׁלִָם׃ וַיְהִי
and-he-was (4) Jerusalem the-army and-entire-of David then-he-returned

אַחֲרֵיכֵן וַתַּעֲמֹד מִלְחָמָה בְּגֶזֶר עִם־ פְּלִשְׁתִּים אָז הִכָּה
he-killed then Philistines with at-Gezer war then-she-broke-out after-this

סִבְּכַי הַחֻשָׁתִי אֶת־ סִפַּי מִילִדֵי הָרְפָאִים
the-Rephaites from-descendants-of Sippai *** the-Hushathite Sibbecai

וַיִּכָּנֵעוּ׃ וַתְּהִי־ עוֹד מִלְחָמָה אֶת־ פְּלִשְׁתִּים
Philistines with battle another and-she-was (5) and-they-were-subjugated

וַיַּךְ אֶלְחָנָן בֶּן־ יָעוֹר אֶת־ לַחְמִי אֲחִי גָּלְיָת הַגִּתִּי
the-Gittite Goliath brother-of Lahmi *** Jair son-of Elhanan and-he-killed

וְעֵץ חֲנִיתוֹ כִּמְנוֹר אֹרְגִים׃ וַתְּהִי־ עוֹד
another and-she-was (6) ones-weaving like-rod-of spear-of-him and-shaft-of

מִלְחָמָה בְּגַת וַיְהִי ׀ אִישׁ מִדָּה וְאֶצְבְּעֹתָיו שֵׁשׁ־ וָשֵׁשׁ
and-six six and-fingers-of-him size man-of and-he-was at-Gath battle

עֶשְׂרִים וְאַרְבַּע וְגַם־ הוּא נוֹלַד לְהָרָפָא׃
from-the-Rapha he-was-descended he and-also and-four twenty

וַיְחָרֵף אֶת־יִשְׂרָאֵל וַיַּכֵּהוּ יְהוֹנָתָן בֶּן־ שִׁמְעָא
Shimea son-of Jonathan then-he-killed-him Israel *** when-he-taunted (7)

°5 יעיר ק

So the Arameans were not willing to help the Ammonites anymore.

*The Capture of Rabbah*

20 In the spring, at the time when kings go off to war, Joab led out the armed forces. He laid waste the land of the Ammonites and went to Rabbah and besieged it, but David remained in Jerusalem. Joab attacked Rabbah and left it in ruins.
2 David took the crown from the head of their king[u]—its weight was found to be a talent[v] of gold, and it was set with precious stones—and it was placed on David's head. He took a great quantity of plunder from the city
3 and brought out the people who were there, consigning them to labor with saws and with iron picks and axes. David did this to all the Ammonite towns. Then David and his entire army returned to Jerusalem.

*War With the Philistines*

4 In the course of time, war broke out with the Philistines, at Gezer. At that time Sibbecai the Hushathite killed Sippai, one of the descendants of the Rephaites, and the Philistines were subjugated.
5 In another battle with the Philistines, Elhanan son of Jair killed Lahmi the brother of Goliath the Gittite, who had a spear with a shaft like a weaver's rod.
6 In still another battle, which took place at Gath, there was a huge man with six fingers on each hand and six toes on each foot—twenty-four in all. He also was descended from Rapha.
7 When he taunted Israel, Jonathan

[u]2 Or *of Milcom,* that is, Molech
[v]2 That is, about 75 pounds (about 34 kilograms)

אֲחִי דָוִיד׃ אֵל נוּלְּדוּ לְהָרָפָא בְּגַת

in-Gath from-the-Rapha they-were-descended these (8) David brother-of

וַיִּפְּלוּ בְיַד־ דָּוִיד וּבְיַד־ עֲבָדָיו׃ וַיַּעֲמֹד

and-he-rose (21:1) men-of-him and-at-hand-of David at-hand-of and-they-fell

שָׂטָן עַל־ יִשְׂרָאֵל וַיָּסֶת אֶת־ דָּוִיד לִמְנוֹת אֶת־ יִשְׂרָאֵל׃

Israel *** to-take-census David *** and-he-incited Israel against Satan

וַיֹּאמֶר דָּוִיד אֶל־יוֹאָב וְאֶל־ שָׂרֵי הָעָם לְכוּ סִפְרוּ

and-count! go! the-troop commanders-of and-to Joab to David so-he-said (2)

אֶת־ יִשְׂרָאֵל מִבְּאֵר שֶׁבַע וְעַד־ דָּן וְהָבִיאוּ אֵלַי וְאֵדְעָה

so-I-may-know to-me and-report-back! Dan even-to Sheba from-Beer Israel ***

אֶת־ מִסְפָּרָם׃ וַיֹּאמֶר יוֹאָב יוֹסֵף יְהוָה עַל־

to Yahweh may-he-multiply Joab but-he-replied (3) number-of-them ***

עַמּוֹ | כָּהֵם מֵאָה פְּעָמִים הֲלֹא אֲדֹנִי הַמֶּלֶךְ כֻּלָּם

all-of-them the-king lord-of-me not? times hundred as-they troop-of-him

לַאדֹנִי לַעֲבָדִים לָמָּה יְבַקֵּשׁ זֹאת אֲדֹנִי לָמָּה יִהְיֶה

should-he-be why? lord-of-me this he-wants why? as-subjects to-lord-of-me

לְאַשְׁמָה לְיִשְׂרָאֵל׃ וּדְבַר־ הַמֶּלֶךְ חָזַק עַל־ יוֹאָב וַיֵּצֵא

so-he-left Joab over he-prevailed the-king but-word-of (4) on-Israel for-guilt

יוֹאָב וַיִּתְהַלֵּךְ בְּכָל־ יִשְׂרָאֵל וַיָּבֹא יְרוּשָׁלִָם׃

Jerusalem then-he-came-back Israel through-all-of and-he-went Joab

וַיִּתֵּן יוֹאָב אֶת־ מִסְפַּר מִפְקַד־ הָעָם אֶל־ דָּוִיד

David to the-people group-of number-of *** Joab and-he-reported (5)

וַיְהִי כָל־ יִשְׂרָאֵל אֶלֶף אֲלָפִים וּמֵאָה אֶלֶף אִישׁ

man thousand and-hundred thousands thousand-of Israel all-of and-he-was

שֹׁלֵף חֶרֶב וִיהוּדָה אַרְבַּע מֵאוֹת וְשִׁבְעִים אֶלֶף אִישׁ

man thousand and-seventy hundreds four-of and-Judah sword handling-of

שֹׁלֵף חָרֶב׃ וְלֵוִי וּבִנְיָמִן לֹא פָקַד בְּתוֹכָם

in-among-them he-included not and-Benjamin but-Levi (6) sword handling-of

כִּי־ נִתְעַב דְּבַר־ הַמֶּלֶךְ אֶת־יוֹאָב׃ וַיֵּרַע

and-he-was-evil (7) Joab *** the-king command-of he-was-repulsive because

בְּעֵינֵי הָאֱלֹהִים עַל־ הַדָּבָר הַזֶּה וַיַּךְ אֶת־יִשְׂרָאֵל׃

Israel *** so-he-punished the-this the-command concerning the-God in-eyes-of

וַיֹּאמֶר דָּוִיד אֶל־הָאֱלֹהִים חָטָאתִי מְאֹד אֲשֶׁר עָשִׂיתִי אֶת־ הַדָּבָר

the-thing *** I-did that greatly I-sinned the-God to David then-he-said (8)

הַזֶּה וְעַתָּה הַעֲבֶר־ נָא אֶת־ עֲווֹן עַבְדְּךָ כִּי

for servant-of-you guilt-of *** now! take-away! and-now the-this

נִסְכַּלְתִּי מְאֹד׃ וַיְדַבֵּר יְהוָה אֶל־ גָּד חֹזֵה דָוִיד לֵאמֹר׃

to-say David seer-of Gad to Yahweh and-he-said (9) very I-acted-foolishly

son of Shimea, David's brother, killed him.

8 These were descendants of Rapha in Gath, and they fell at the hands of David and his men.

*David Numbers the Fighting Men*

**21** Satan rose up against Israel and incited David to take a census of Israel.
2 So David said to Joab and the commanders of the troops, "Go and count the Israelites from Beersheba to Dan. Then report back to me so that I may know how many there are."
3 But Joab replied, "May the LORD multiply his troops a hundred times over. My lord the king, are they not all my lord's subjects? Why does my lord want to do this? Why should he bring guilt on Israel?"
4 The king's word, however, overruled Joab; so Joab left and went throughout Israel and then came back to Jerusalem.
5 Joab reported the number of the fighting men to David: In all Israel there were one million one hundred thousand men who could handle a sword, including four hundred and seventy thousand in Judah.
6 But Joab did not include Levi and Benjamin in the numbering, because the king's command was repulsive to him.
7 This command was also evil in the sight of God; so he punished Israel.
8 Then David said to God, "I have sinned greatly by doing this. Now, I beg you, take away the guilt of your servant. I have done a very foolish thing."

לֵךְ וְדִבַּרְתָּ אֶל־דָּוִיד לֵאמֹר כֹּה אָמַר יְהוָה שָׁלוֹשׁ אֲנִי נֹטֶה
giving I three Yahweh he-says this to-say David to and-you-tell go! (10)

עָלֶיךָ בְּחַר־ לְךָ אַחַת מֵהֵנָּה וְאֶעֱשֶׂה־ לָּךְ׃
against-you and-I-will-carry-out of-them one for-you choose! to-you

וַיָּבֹא גָד אֶל־דָּוִיד וַיֹּאמֶר לוֹ כֹּה־ אָמַר יְהוָה קַבֶּל־
choose! Yahweh he-says this to-him and-he-said David to Gad so-he-went (11)

לָךְ׃ אִם־ שָׁלוֹשׁ שָׁנִים רָעָב וְאִם־ שְׁלֹשָׁה חֳדָשִׁים
months three or-whether famine years three whether (12) for-you

נִסְפֶּה מִפְּנֵי־ צָרֶיךָ וְחֶרֶב אוֹיְבֶיךָ ׀
being-enemies-of-you and-sword-of enemies-of-you from-before being-swept-away

לְמַשֶּׂגֶת וְאִם־ שְׁלֹשֶׁת יָמִים חֶרֶב יְהוָה וְדֶבֶר בָּאָרֶץ
in-the-land and-plague Yahweh sword-of days three-of or-whether as-overtaking

וּמַלְאַךְ יְהוָה מַשְׁחִית בְּכָל־ גְּבוּל יִשְׂרָאֵל וְעַתָּה רְאֵה
decide! then-now Israel part-of in-every-of ravaging Yahweh and-angel-of

מָה־ אָשִׁיב אֶת־ שֹׁלְחִי דָּבָר׃ וַיֹּאמֶר דָּוִיד אֶל־ גָּד
Gad to David and-he-said (13) answer one-sending-me *** I-should-give how

צַר־ לִי מְאֹד אֶפְּלָה־ נָּא בְיַד־ יְהוָה כִּי־ רַבִּים
great-ones for Yahweh into-hand-of now! let-me-fall deeply to-me distress

רַחֲמָיו מְאֹד וּבְיַד־ אָדָם אַל־ אֶפֹּל׃ וַיִּתֵּן
so-he-sent (14) let-me-fall not man but-into-hand-of very mercies-of-him

יְהוָה דֶּבֶר בְּיִשְׂרָאֵל וַיִּפֹּל מִיִּשְׂרָאֵל שִׁבְעִים אֶלֶף אִישׁ׃
man thousand seventy of-Israel and-he-fell on-Israel plague Yahweh

וַיִּשְׁלַח הָאֱלֹהִים ׀ מַלְאָךְ ׀ לִירוּשָׁלַםִ לְהַשְׁחִיתָהּ וּכְהַשְׁחִית
but-as-to-destroy to-destroy-her to-Jerusalem angel the-God and-he-sent (15)

רָאָה יְהוָה וַיִּנָּחֶם עַל־ הָרָעָה וַיֹּאמֶר
and-he-said the-calamity because-of and-he-was-grieved Yahweh he-saw

לַמַּלְאָךְ הַמַּשְׁחִית רַב עַתָּה הֶרֶף יָדֶךָ וּמַלְאַךְ
now-angel-of hand-of-you withdraw! now enough the-one-destroying to-the-angel

יְהוָה עֹמֵד עִם־ גֹּרֶן אָרְנָן הַיְבוּסִי׃ וַיִּשָּׂא
and-he-raised (16) the-Jebusite Ornan threshing-floor-of at standing Yahweh

דָוִיד אֶת־ עֵינָיו וַיַּרְא אֶת־ מַלְאַךְ יְהוָה עֹמֵד בֵּין
between standing Yahweh angel-of *** and-he-saw eyes-of-him *** David

הָאָרֶץ וּבֵין הַשָּׁמַיִם וְחַרְבּוֹ שְׁלוּפָה בְּיָדוֹ
in-hand-of-him being-drawn and-sword-of-him the-heavens and-between the-earth

נְטוּיָה עַל־ יְרוּשָׁלָםִ וַיִּפֹּל דָּוִיד וְהַזְּקֵנִים
and-the-elders David then-he-fell Jerusalem over being-extended

מְכֻסִּים בַּשַּׂקִּים עַל־ פְּנֵיהֶם׃ וַיֹּאמֶר דָּוִיד
David and-he-said (17) faces-of-them on in-the-sackcloths ones-being-clothed

9The LORD said to Gad, David's seer, 10"Go and tell David, 'This is what the LORD
says: I am giving you three options. Choose one of them for
me to carry out against you.' "
11So Gad went to David and
said to him, "This is what the
LORD says: 'Take your choice:
12three years of famine, three
months of being swept away[w]
before your enemies, with
their swords overtaking you,
or three days of the sword of
the LORD—days of plague in
the land, with the angel of the
LORD ravaging every part of Israel.' Now then, decide how I
should answer the one who
sent me."
13David said to Gad, "I am in
deep distress. Let me fall into
the hands of the LORD, for his
mercy is very great; but do not
let me fall into the hands of
men."
14So the LORD sent a plague
on Israel, and seventy thousand men of Israel fell dead.
15And God sent an angel to destroy Jerusalem. But as the angel was doing so, the LORD saw
it and was grieved because of
the calamity and said to the
angel who was destroying the
people, "Enough! Withdraw
your hand." The angel of the
LORD was then standing at the
threshing floor of Araunah[x]
the Jebusite.
16David looked up and saw
the angel of the LORD standing
between heaven and earth,
with a drawn sword in his
hand extended over Jerusalem. Then David and the elders, clothed in sackcloth, fell
facedown.
17David said to God, "Was it

[w]12 Hebrew; Septuagint and Vulgate (see also 2 Samuel 24:13) *of fleeing*

[x]15 Hebrew *Ornan,* a variant of *Araunah;* also in verses 18-28

אֶל־הָאֱלֹהִים הֲלֹא אֲנִי אָמַרְתִּי לִמְנוֹת בָּעָם וַאֲנִי־הוּא אֲשֶׁר־חָטָאתִי
I-sinned who he and-I of-the-people to-count I-ordered I not? the-God to

וְהָרֵעַ הֲרֵעוֹתִי וְאֵלֶּה הַצֹּאן מֶה עָשׂוּ יְהוָה אֱלֹהַי
God-of-me Yahweh they-did what? the-sheep and-these I-did-wrong and-to-do-wrong

תְּהִי נָא יָדְךָ בִּי וּבְבֵית אָבִי
father-of-me and-upon-family-of upon-me hand-of-you now! let-her-fall

וּבְעַמְּךָ לֹא לְמַגֵּפָה׃ וּמַלְאַךְ יְהוָה אָמַר
he-ordered Yahweh then-angel-of (18) with-plague not but-on-people-of-you

אֶל־גָּד לֵאמֹר לְדָוִיד כִּי ׀ יַעֲלֶה דָוִיד לְהָקִים מִזְבֵּחַ לַיהוָה
to-Yahweh altar to-build David he-go-up that to-David to-tell Gad to

בְּגֹרֶן אָרְנָן הַיְבֻסִי׃ וַיַּעַל דָּוִיד בִּדְבַר־
at-word-of David so-he-went-up (19) the-Jebusite Ornan on-threshing-floor-of

גָּד אֲשֶׁר דִּבֶּר בְּשֵׁם יְהוָה׃ וַיָּשָׁב אָרְנָן וַיַּרְא אֶת־
*** and-he-saw Ornan and-he-turned (20) Yahweh in-name-of he-spoke that Gad

הַמַּלְאָךְ וְאַרְבַּעַת בָּנָיו עִמּוֹ מִתְחַבְּאִים וְאָרְנָן דָּשׁ
threshing now-Ornan ones-hiding with-him sons-of-him and-four-of the-angel

חִטִּים׃ וַיָּבֹא דָוִיד עַד־אָרְנָן וַיַּבֵּט אָרְנָן וַיַּרְא
and-he-saw Ornan when-he-looked Ornan to David then-he-approached (21) wheats

אֶת־דָּוִיד וַיֵּצֵא מִן־הַגֹּרֶן וַיִּשְׁתַּחוּ לְדָוִיד
before-David and-he-bowed the-threshing-floor from then-he-left David ***

אַפַּיִם אָרְצָה׃ וַיֹּאמֶר דָּוִיד אֶל־אָרְנָן תְּנָה־לִּי מְקוֹם
site-of to-me sell! Ornan to David and-he-said (22) to-ground faces

הַגֹּרֶן וְאֶבְנֶה־בּוֹ מִזְבֵּחַ לַיהוָה בְּכֶסֶף מָלֵא
full at-price to-Yahweh altar on-him so-I-can-build the-threshing-floor

תְּנֵהוּ לִי וְתֵעָצַר הַמַּגֵּפָה מֵעַל הָעָם׃
the-people from-on the-plague so-she-may-be-stopped to-me sell-him!

וַיֹּאמֶר אָרְנָן אֶל־דָּוִיד קַח־לָךְ וְיַעַשׂ אֲדֹנִי
lord-of-me and-let-him-do for-you take! David to Ornan and-he-said (23)

הַמֶּלֶךְ הַטּוֹב בְּעֵינָיו רְאֵה נָתַתִּי הַבָּקָר לָעֹלוֹת
for-the-offerings the-ox I-will-give look! in-eyes-of-him the-good the-king

וְהַמּוֹרִגִּים לָעֵצִים וְהַחִטִּים לַמִּנְחָה
for-the-grain-offering and-the-wheats for-the-woods and-the-threshing-sledges

הַכֹּל נָתָתִּי׃ וַיֹּאמֶר הַמֶּלֶךְ דָּוִיד לְאָרְנָן לֹא כִּי־
for no to-Ornan David the-king but-he-replied (24) I-will-give the-whole

קָנֹה אֶקְנֶה בְּכֶסֶף מָלֵא כִּי לֹא־אֶשָּׂא אֲשֶׁר־לְךָ לַיהוָה
for-Yahweh to-you what I-will-take not for full at-price I-will-pay to-pay

וְהַעֲלוֹת עוֹלָה חִנָּם׃ וַיִּתֵּן דָּוִיד לְאָרְנָן
to-Ornan David so-he-paid (25) without-cost burnt-offering or-to-sacrifice

not I who ordered the fighting men to be counted? I am the one who has sinned and done wrong. These are but sheep. What have they done? O LORD my God, let your hand fall upon me and my family, but do not let this plague remain on your people."

[18]Then the angel of the LORD ordered Gad to tell David to go up and build an altar to the LORD on the threshing floor of Araunah the Jebusite. [19]So David went up in obedience to the word that Gad had spoken in the name of the LORD.

[20]While Araunah was threshing wheat, he turned and saw the angel; his four sons who were with him hid themselves. [21]Then David approached, and when Araunah looked and saw him, he left the threshing floor and bowed down before David with his face to the ground.

[22]David said to him, "Let me have the site of your threshing floor so I can build an altar to the LORD, that the plague on the people may be stopped. Sell it to me at the full price."

[23]Araunah said to David, "Take it! Let my lord the king do whatever pleases him. Look, I will give the oxen for the burnt offerings, the threshing sledges for the wood, and the wheat for the grain offering. I will give all this."

[24]But King David replied to Araunah, "No, I insist on paying the full price. I will not take for the LORD what is yours, or sacrifice a burnt offering that costs me nothing."

[25]So David paid Araunah six

בַּמָּקוֹם שִׁקְלֵי זָהָב מִשְׁקַל שֵׁשׁ מֵאוֹת׃ וַיִּבֶן
and-he-built (26) hundreds six-of weight gold shekels-of for-the-site

שָׁם דָּוִיד מִזְבֵּחַ לַיהוָה וַיַּעַל עֹלוֹת
burnt-offerings and-he-sacrificed to-Yahweh altar David there

וּשְׁלָמִים וַיִּקְרָא אֶל־ יְהוָה וַיַּעֲנֵהוּ
and-he-answerered-him Yahweh on and-he-called and-fellowship-offerings

בָאֵשׁ מִן־ הַשָּׁמַיִם עַל מִזְבַּח הָעֹלָה׃ וַיֹּאמֶר
then-he-spoke (27) the-burnt-offering altar-of on the-heavens from with-fire

יְהוָה לַמַּלְאָךְ וַיָּשֶׁב חַרְבּוֹ אֶל־ נְדָנָהּ׃
sheath-of-her into sword-of-him and-he-put-back to-the-angel Yahweh

בָּעֵת הַהִיא בִּרְאוֹת דָּוִיד כִּי־ עָנָהוּ יְהוָה
Yahweh he-answered-him that David when-to-see the-that at-the-time (28)

בְּגֹרֶן אָרְנָן הַיְבוּסִי וַיִּזְבַּח שָׁם׃
there then-he-sacrificed the-Jebusite Ornan on-threshing-floor-of

וּמִשְׁכַּן יְהוָה אֲשֶׁר־ עָשָׂה מֹשֶׁה בַמִּדְבָּר וּמִזְבַּח
and-altar-of in-the-desert Moses he-made which Yahweh now-tabernacle-of (29)

הָעוֹלָה בָּעֵת הַהִיא בַּבָּמָה בְּגִבְעוֹן׃
at-Gibeon on-the-high-place the-that at-the-time the-burnt-offering

וְלֹא־ יָכֹל דָּוִיד לָלֶכֶת לְפָנָיו לִדְרֹשׁ אֱלֹהִים כִּי
because God to-inquire before-him to-go David he-could but-not (30)

נִבְעַת מִפְּנֵי חֶרֶב מַלְאַךְ יְהוָה׃ וַיֹּאמֶר דָּוִיד
David then-he-said (22:1) Yahweh angel-of sword-of because-of he-was-afraid

זֶה הוּא בֵּית יְהוָה הָאֱלֹהִים וְזֶה־ מִּזְבֵּחַ לְעֹלָה לְיִשְׂרָאֵל׃
for-Israel of-burnt-offering altar and-here the-God Yahweh house-of he here

וַיֹּאמֶר דָּוִיד לִכְנוֹס אֶת־ הַגֵּרִים אֲשֶׁר בְּאֶרֶץ יִשְׂרָאֵל
Israel in-land-of who the-aliens *** to-assemble David so-he-ordered (2)

וַיַּעֲמֵד חֹצְבִים לַחְצוֹב אַבְנֵי גָזִית לִבְנוֹת בֵּית
house-of to-build dressed stones-of to-prepare ones-cutting and-he-appointed

הָאֱלֹהִים׃ וּבַרְזֶל ׀ לָרֹב לַמִּסְמְרִים לְדַלְתוֹת הַשְּׁעָרִים
the-gateways for-doors-of for-the-nails for-much and-iron (3) the-God

וְלַמְחַבְּרוֹת הֵכִין דָּוִיד וּנְחֹשֶׁת לָרֹב אֵין
there-was-no for-much and-bronze David he-provided and-for-the-fittings

מִשְׁקָל׃ וַעֲצֵי אֲרָזִים לְאֵין מִסְפָּר כִּי הֵבִיאוּ
they-brought for count as-there-was-no cedars and-logs-of (4) weight

הַצִּידֹנִים וְהַצֹּרִים עֲצֵי אֲרָזִים לָרֹב לְדָוִיד׃ וַיֹּאמֶר
and-he-said (5) to-David for-much cedars logs-of and-the-Tyrians the-Sidonians

דָּוִיד שְׁלֹמֹה בְנִי נַעַר וָרָךְ וְהַבַּיִת לִבְנוֹת
to-build and-the-house and-inexperienced young son-of-me Solomon David

---

hundred shekels[y] of gold for the site. 26 David built an altar to the LORD there and sacrificed burnt offerings and fellowship offerings.[z] He called on the LORD, and the LORD answered him with fire from heaven on the altar of burnt offering.

27 Then the LORD spoke to the angel, and he put his sword back into its sheath. 28 At that time, when David saw that the LORD had answered him on the threshing floor of Araunah the Jebusite, he offered sacrifices there. 29 The tabernacle of the LORD, which Moses had made in the desert, and the altar of burnt offering were at that time on the high place at Gibeon. 30 But David could not go before it to inquire of God, because he was afraid of the sword of the angel of the LORD.

22 Then David said, "The house of the LORD God is to be here, and also the altar of burnt offering for Israel."

*Preparations for the Temple*

2 So David gave orders to assemble the aliens living in Israel, and from among them he appointed stonecutters to prepare dressed stone for building the house of God. 3 He provided a large amount of iron to make nails for the doors of the gateways and for the fittings, and more bronze than could be weighed. 4 He also provided more cedar logs than could be counted, for the Sidonians and Tyrians had brought large numbers of them to David.

5 David said, "My son Solomon is young and inexperienced, and the house to be

y25 That is, about 15 pounds (about 7 kilograms)
z26 Traditionally *peace offerings*

לַיהוָה לְהַגְדִּיל | לְמַעְלָה לְשֵׁם וּלְתִפְאֶרֶת לְכָל־
before-all-of and-of-splendor of-name of-magnificence to-make-great for-Yahweh

הָאֲרָצוֹת אָכִינָה נָּא לוֹ וַיָּכֶן דָּוִיד לָרֹב לִפְנֵי
before for-much David so-he-prepared for-him now! I-will-prepare the-nations

מוֹתוֹ׃ וַיִּקְרָא לִשְׁלֹמֹה בְנוֹ וַיְצַוֵּהוּ
and-he-charged-him son-of-him for-Solomon then-he-called (6) death-of-him

לִבְנוֹת בַּיִת לַיהוָה אֱלֹהֵי יִשְׂרָאֵל׃ וַיֹּאמֶר דָּוִיד לִשְׁלֹמֹה
to-Solomon David and-he-said (7) Israel God-of for-Yahweh house to-build

בְּנוֹ° אֲנִי הָיָה עִם־ לְבָבִי לִבְנוֹת בַּיִת לְשֵׁם יְהוָה
Yahweh for-Name-of house to-build heart-of-me in he-was I son-of-me

אֱלֹהָי׃ וַיְהִי עָלַי דְּבַר־ יְהוָה לֵאמֹר דָּם לָרֹב
for-much blood to-say Yahweh word-of to-me but-he-came (8) God-of-me

שָׁפַכְתָּ וּמִלְחָמוֹת גְּדֹלוֹת עָשִׂיתָ לֹא־ תִבְנֶה בַיִת
house you-shall-build not you-fought many-ones and-wars you-shed

לִשְׁמִי כִּי דָּמִים רַבִּים שָׁפַכְתָּ אַרְצָה לְפָנָי׃
before-faces-of-me on-earth you-shed many-ones bloods because for-Name-of-me

הִנֵּה־ בֵן נוֹלָד לָךְ הוּא יִהְיֶה אִישׁ מְנוּחָה וַהֲנִחוֹתִי
and-I-will-give-rest rest man-of he-will-be he to-you being-born son see! (9)

לוֹ מִכָּל־ אוֹיְבָיו מִסָּבִיב כִּי שְׁלֹמֹה יִהְיֶה
he-will-be Solomon indeed at-around being-enemies-of-him from-all-of to-him

שְׁמוֹ וְשָׁלוֹם וָשֶׁקֶט אֶתֵּן עַל־ יִשְׂרָאֵל בְּיָמָיו׃
during-days-of-him Israel to I-will-grant and-quiet and-peace name-of-him

הוּא־ יִבְנֶה בַיִת לִשְׁמִי וְהוּא יִהְיֶה־ לִּי לְבֵן
as-son to-me he-will-be and-he for-Name-of-me house he-will-build he (10)

וַאֲנִי־ לוֹ לְאָב וַהֲכִינוֹתִי כִּסֵּא מַלְכוּתוֹ עַל־
over kingdom-of-him throne-of and-I-will-establish as-father to-him and-I

יִשְׂרָאֵל עַד־ עוֹלָם׃ עַתָּה בְנִי יְהִי יְהוָה עִמָּךְ
with-you Yahweh may-he-be son-of-me now (11) forever to Israel

וְהִצְלַחְתָּ וּבָנִיתָ בֵּית יְהוָה אֱלֹהֶיךָ כַּאֲשֶׁר
just-as God-of-you Yahweh house-of and-may-you-build and-may-you-succeed

דִּבֶּר עָלֶיךָ׃ אַךְ יִתֶּן־ לְךָ יְהוָה שֶׂכֶל
discretion Yahweh to-you may-he-give also (12) about-you he-said

וּבִינָה וִיצַוְּךָ עַל־ יִשְׂרָאֵל וְלִשְׁמוֹר אֶת־
*** and-to-keep Israel over when-he-puts-in-command-you and-understanding

תּוֹרַת יְהוָה אֱלֹהֶיךָ׃ אָז תַּצְלִיחַ אִם־ תִּשְׁמוֹר
you-are-careful if you-will-succeed then (13) God-of-you Yahweh law-of

לַעֲשׂוֹת אֶת־הַחֻקִּים וְאֶת־ הַמִּשְׁפָּטִים אֲשֶׁר צִוָּה יְהוָה אֶת־מֹשֶׁה עַל־
for Moses *** Yahweh he-gave that the-laws and the-decrees *** to-observe

built for the LORD should be of
great magnificence and fame
and splendor in the sight of all
the nations. Therefore I will
make preparations for it." So
David made extensive preparations before his death.
[6]Then he called for his son
Solomon and charged him to
build a house for the LORD, the
God of Israel. [7]David said to
Solomon: "My son, I had it in
my heart to build a house for
the Name of the LORD my God.
[8]But this word of the LORD
came to me: 'You have shed
much blood and have fought
many wars. You are not to
build a house for my Name,
because you have shed much
blood on the earth in my sight.
[9]But you will have a son who
will be a man of peace and
rest, and I will give him rest
from all his enemies on every
side. His name will be Solomon,[a] and I will grant Israel
peace and quiet during his
reign. [10]He is the one who will
build a house for my Name.
He will be my son, and I will
be his father. And I will establish the throne of his kingdom
over Israel forever.'
[11]"Now, my son, the LORD be
with you, and may you have
success and build the house of
the LORD your God, as he said
you would. [12]May the LORD
give you discretion and
understanding when he puts
you in command over Israel,
so that you may keep the law
of the LORD your God. [13]Then
you will have success if you
are careful to observe the decrees and laws that the LORD
gave Moses for Israel. Be

[a]9 *Solomon* sounds like and may be derived from the Hebrew for *peace*.

°7 ק בני

| וְאַל־ | תִּירָא | אַל־ | וֶאֱמָץ | חֲזַק | יִשְׂרָאֵל |
|---|---|---|---|---|---|
| and-not | you-be-afraid | not | and-be-courageous! | be-strong! | Israel |

| לְבֵית־ | הֲכִינוֹתִי | בְעָנְיִי | וְהִנֵּה | | תֵּחָת׃ |
|---|---|---|---|---|---|
| for-temple-of | I-provided | in-pain-of-me | now-see! | (14) | you-be-discouraged |

| אֲלָפִים | אֶלֶף | וְכֶסֶף | אֶלֶף | מֵאָה־ | כִּכָּרִים | זָהָב | יְהוָה |
|---|---|---|---|---|---|---|---|
| thousands | thousand-of | and-silver | thousand | hundred | talents | gold | Yahweh |

| לָרֹב | כִּי | מִשְׁקָל | אֵין | וְלַבַּרְזֶל | וְלַנְּחֹשֶׁת | כִּכָּרִים |
|---|---|---|---|---|---|---|
| as-much | for | weight | there-is-no | and-of-the-iron | and-of-the-bronze | talents |

| תּוֹסִיף׃ | וַעֲלֵיהֶם | הֲכִינוֹתִי | וַאֲבָנִים | וְעֵצִים | הָיָה |
|---|---|---|---|---|---|
| you-may-add | and-to-them | I-provided | and-stones | and-woods | he-is |

| וְחָרָשֵׁי | חֹצְבִים | מְלָאכָה | עֹשֵׂי | לָרֹב | וְעִמְּךָ | |
|---|---|---|---|---|---|---|
| and-carvers-of | ones-cutting | work | ones-doing-of | as-many | now-with-you | (15) |

| לַזָּהָב | | מְלָאכָה׃ | בְּכָל־ | חָכָם | וְכָל־ | וָעֵץ | אֶבֶן |
|---|---|---|---|---|---|---|---|
| in-the-gold | (16) | work | in-every-of | one-skilled | and-every-of | and-wood | stone |

| קוּם | מִסְפָּר | אֵין | וְלַבַּרְזֶל | וְלַנְּחֹשֶׁת | לַכֶּסֶף |
|---|---|---|---|---|---|
| begin! | number | there-no-is | and-in-the-iron | and-in-the-bronze | in-the-silver |

| דָּוִיד | וַיְצַו | | עִמָּךְ׃ | יְהוָה | וִיהִי | וַעֲשֵׂה |
|---|---|---|---|---|---|---|
| David | then-he-ordered | (17) | with-you | Yahweh | and-may-he-be | and-do-work! |

| יְהוָה | הֲלֹא | | בְנוֹ׃ | לִשְׁלֹמֹה | לַעְזֹר | יִשְׂרָאֵל | שָׂרֵי | לְכָל־ |
|---|---|---|---|---|---|---|---|---|
| Yahweh | not? | (18) | son-of-him | to-Solomon | to-help | Israel | leaders-of | to-all-of |

| נָתַן | כִּי ׀ | מִסָּבִיב | לָכֶם | וְהֵנִיחַ | עִמָּכֶם | אֱלֹהֵיכֶם |
|---|---|---|---|---|---|---|
| he-gave | for | at-around | to-you | and-he-granted-rest | with-you | God-of-you |

| הָאָרֶץ | וְנִכְבְּשָׁה | הָאָרֶץ | יֹשְׁבֵי | אֵת | בְּיָדִי |
|---|---|---|---|---|---|
| the-land | and-she-is-subject | the-land | ones-inhabiting-of | *** | into-hand-of-me |

| לְבַבְכֶם | תְּנוּ | עַתָּה | | עַמּוֹ׃ | וְלִפְנֵי | יְהוָה | לִפְנֵי |
|---|---|---|---|---|---|---|---|
| heart-of-you | devote! | now | (19) | people-of-him | and-before | Yahweh | before |

| אֶת־ | וּבְנוּ | וְקוּמוּ | אֱלֹהֵיכֶם | לַיהוָה | לִדְרוֹשׁ | וְנַפְשְׁכֶם |
|---|---|---|---|---|---|---|
| *** | and-build! | and-begin! | God-of-you | to-Yahweh | to-seek | and-soul-of-you |

| יְהוָה | בְּרִית־ | אֲרוֹן | אֶת־ | לְהָבִיא | הָאֱלֹהִים | יְהוָה | מִקְדַּשׁ |
|---|---|---|---|---|---|---|---|
| Yahweh | covenant-of | ark-of | *** | to-bring | the-God | Yahweh | sanctuary-of |

| הַנִּבְנֶה | לַבַּיִת | הָאֱלֹהִים | קֹדֶשׁ | וּכְלֵי |
|---|---|---|---|---|
| the-one-being-built | into-the-temple | the-God | sacredness-of | and-articles-of |

| יָמִים | וְשָׂבַע | זָקֵן | וְדָוִיד | | יְהוָה׃ | לְשֵׁם־ |
|---|---|---|---|---|---|---|
| days | and-he-was-full | he-was-old | when-David | (23:1) | Yahweh | for-Name-of |

| וַיֶּאֱסֹף | | יִשְׂרָאֵל׃ | עַל־ | בְנוֹ | שְׁלֹמֹה | אֶת־ | וַיַּמְלֵךְ |
|---|---|---|---|---|---|---|---|
| and-he-gathered | (2) | Israel | over | son-of-him | Solomon | *** | then-he-made-king |

| וְהַלְוִיִּם׃ | וְהַכֹּהֲנִים | יִשְׂרָאֵל | שָׂרֵי | כָּל־ | אֶת־ |
|---|---|---|---|---|---|
| and-the-Levites | and-the-priests | Israel | leaders-of | all-of | *** |

strong and courageous. Do not
be afraid or discouraged.
14"I have taken great pains
to provide for the temple of
the LORD a hundred thousand
talents[b] of gold, a million talents[c] of silver, quantities of
bronze and iron too great to be
weighed, and wood and stone.
And you may add to them.
15You have many workmen:
stonecutters, masons and carpenters, as well as men skilled
in every kind of work 16in gold
and silver, bronze and iron—
craftsmen beyond number.
Now begin the work, and the
LORD be with you."
17Then David ordered all the
leaders of Israel to help his son
Solomon. 18He said to them,
"Is not the LORD your God
with you? And has he not
granted you rest on every
side? For he has handed the
inhabitants of the land over to
me, and the land is subject to
the LORD and to his people.
19Now devote your heart and
soul to seeking the LORD your
God. Begin to build the sanctuary of the LORD God, so that
you may bring the ark of the
covenant of the LORD and the
sacred articles belonging to
God into the temple that will
be built for the Name of the
LORD."

### *The Levites*

23 When David was old
and full of years, he
made his son Solomon king
over Israel.
2He also gathered together
all the leaders of Israel, as well
as the priests and Levites. 3The

[b]14 That is, about 3,750 tons (about 3,450 metric tons)
[c]14 That is, about 37,500 tons (about 34,500 metric tons)

וַיִּסָּפְרוּ֙ הַלְוִיִּ֔ם מִבֶּ֛ן שְׁלֹשִׁ֥ים שָׁנָ֖ה וָמָ֑עְלָה
and-upward  year  thirty  from-son-of  the-Levites  and-they-were-counted  (3)

וַיְהִ֣י מִסְפָּרָ֗ם לְגֻלְגְּלֹתָ֛ם לִגְבָרִ֖ים שְׁלֹשִׁ֥ים וּשְׁמוֹנָ֖ה אָֽלֶף׃
thousand  and-eight  thirty  of-men  by-totals-of-them  number-of-them  and-he-was

מֵאֵ֗לֶּה לְנַצֵּ֙חַ֙ עַל־מְלֶ֣אכֶת בֵּית־יְהוָ֔ה עֶשְׂרִ֥ים וְאַרְבָּעָ֖ה
and-four  twenty  Yahweh  temple-of  work-of  over  to-supervise  and-of-these  (4)

אָ֑לֶף וְשֹׁטְרִ֣ים וְשֹׁפְטִ֔ים שֵׁ֖שֶׁת אֲלָפִ֑ים׃ וְאַרְבַּ֥עַת
and-four-of  (5)  thousands  six-of  and-ones-being-judges  and-officials  thousand

אֲלָפִ֖ים שֹׁעֲרִ֑ים וְאַרְבַּ֣עַת אֲלָפִים֙ מְהַֽלְלִ֣ים לַֽיהוָ֔ה
to-Yahweh  ones-praising  thousands  and-four-of  gatekeepers  thousands

בַּכֵּלִ֕ים אֲשֶׁ֥ר עָשִׂ֖יתִי לְהַלֵּֽל׃ וַיֶּֽחָלְקֵ֥ם דָּוִ֖יד
David  and-he-divided-them  (6)  to-praise  I-provided  that  with-the-instruments

מַחְלְק֑וֹת לִבְנֵ֣י לֵוִ֔י לְגֵרְשׁ֖וֹן קְהָ֥ת וּמְרָרִֽי׃ לַגֵּרְשֻׁנִּ֖י
of-the-Gershonite  (7)  and-Merari  Kohath  of-Gershon  Levi  of-sons-of  groups

לַעְדָּ֣ן וְשִׁמְעִ֑י בְּנֵ֣י לַעְדָּ֗ן הָרֹ֛אשׁ יְחִיאֵ֥ל וְזֵתָ֖ם וְיוֹאֵ֥ל
and-Joel  and-Zetham  Jehiel  the-first  Ladan  sons-of  (8)  and-Shimei  Ladan

שְׁלֹשָֽׁה׃ בְּנֵ֣י שִׁמְעִ֗י שְׁלֹמוֹת֙ וַחֲזִיאֵ֣ל וְהָרָ֔ן שְׁלֹשָׁ֖ה אֵ֑לֶּה רָאשֵׁ֥י
heads-of  these  three  and-Haran  and-Haziel  Shelomoth  Shimei  sons-of  (9)  three

הָאָב֖וֹת לְלַעְדָּֽן׃ וּבְנֵ֣י שִׁמְעִ֔י יַ֥חַת זִינָ֖א וִיע֥וּשׁ
and-Jeush  Zina  Jahath  Shimei  and-sons-of  (10)  of-Ladan  the-fathers

וּבְרִיעָ֑ה אֵ֛לֶּה בְנֵֽי־שִׁמְעִ֖י אַרְבָּעָֽה׃ וַיְהִֽי־יַ֣חַת הָרֹ֔אשׁ
the-first  Jahath  and-he-was  (11)  four  Shimei  sons-of  these  and-Beriah

וְזִיזָ֖ה הַשֵּׁנִ֑י וִיע֤וּשׁ וּבְרִיעָה֙ לֹֽא־הִרְבּ֣וּ בָנִ֔ים וַיִּֽהְיוּ֙
so-they-were  sons  they-had-many  not  and-Beriah  but-Jeush  the-second  and-Ziza

לְבֵ֣ית אָ֔ב לִפְקֻדָּ֖ה אֶחָֽת׃ בְּנֵ֣י קְהָ֑ת עַמְרָ֥ם יִצְהָ֖ר
Izhar  Amram  Kohath  sons-of  (12)  one  as-assignment  father  as-family-of

חֶבְר֣וֹן וְעֻזִּיאֵ֖ל אַרְבָּעָֽה׃ בְּנֵ֣י עַמְרָ֗ם אַהֲרֹ֣ן וּמֹשֶׁ֑ה וַיִּבָּדֵ֡ל
and-he-was-set-apart  and-Moses  Aaron  Amram  sons-of  (13)  four  and-Uzziel  Hebron

אַהֲרֹן֩ לְהַקְדִּישׁ֨וֹ קֹ֜דֶשׁ קָֽדָשִׁ֥ים הֽוּא־וּבָנָ֖יו
and-descendants-of-him  he  holy-things  most-holy-of  to-consecrate-him  Aaron

עַד־עוֹלָ֗ם לְהַקְטִיר֩ לִפְנֵ֨י יְהוָ֤ה לְשָׁרְתוֹ֙ וּלְבָרֵ֣ךְ
and-to-bless  to-minister-to-him  Yahweh  before  to-sacrifice  forever  to

בִּשְׁמ֖וֹ עַד־עוֹלָֽם׃ וּמֹשֶׁ֖ה אִ֣ישׁ הָאֱלֹהִ֑ים בָּנָ֕יו
sons-of-him  the-God  man-of  and-Moses  (14)  forever  to  in-name-of-him

יִקָּרְא֖וּ עַל־שֵׁ֣בֶט הַלֵּוִֽי׃ בְּנֵ֣י מֹשֶׁ֔ה גֵּרְשֹׁ֖ם
Gershom  Moses  sons-of  (15)  the-Levi  tribe-of  as  they-were-counted

וֶאֱלִיעֶֽזֶר׃ בְּנֵ֖י גֵרְשׁ֑וֹם שְׁבוּאֵ֖ל הָרֹֽאשׁ׃ וַיִּֽהְי֥וּ
and-they-were  (17)  the-first  Shubael  Gershom  descendants-of  (16)  and-Eliezer

Levites thirty years old or more were counted, and the total number of men was thirty-eight thousand. [4]David said, "Of these, twenty-four thousand are to supervise the work of the temple of the LORD and six thousand are to be officials and judges. [5]Four thousand are to be gatekeepers and four thousand are to praise the LORD with the musical instruments I have provided for that purpose."

[6]David divided the Levites into groups corresponding to the sons of Levi: Gershon, Kohath and Merari.

*Gershonites*

[7]Belonging to the Gershonites:
   Ladan and Shimei.
[8]The sons of Ladan:
   Jehiel the first, Zetham and Joel—three in all.
[9]The sons of Shimei:
   Shelomoth, Haziel and Haran—three in all.
   These were the heads of the families of Ladan.
[10]And the sons of Shimei:
   Jahath, Ziza,[d] Jeush and Beriah.
   These were the sons of Shimei—four in all.
[11]Jahath was the first and Ziza the second, but Jeush and Beriah did not have many sons; so they were counted as one family with one assignment.

*Kohathites*

[12]The sons of Kohath:
   Amram, Izhar, Hebron and Uzziel—four in all.
[13]The sons of Amram:
   Aaron and Moses.
   Aaron was set apart, he and his descendants forever, to consecrate the most holy things, to offer sacrifices before the LORD, to minister before him and to pronounce blessings in his name forever. [14]The sons of Moses the man of God were counted as part of the tribe of Levi.
[15]The sons of Moses:
   Gershom and Eliezer.
[16]The descendants of Gershom:
   Shubael was the first.

*d10* One Hebrew manuscript, Septuagint and Vulgate (see also verse 11); most Hebrew manuscripts *Zina*

*9 ק שְׁלוֹמִית

בְנֵי־ אֱלִיעֶזֶר רְחַבְיָה הָרֹאשׁ וְלֹא־ הָיָה לֶאֱלִיעֶזֶר בָּנִים
sons to-Eliezer he-was but-not the-first Rehabiah Eliezer descendants-of

אֲחֵרִים וּבְנֵי רְחַבְיָה רָבוּ לְמָעְלָה׃ בְּנֵי
sons-of (18) to-above they-were-numerous Rehabiah but-sons-of other-ones

יִצְהָר שְׁלֹמִית הָרֹאשׁ׃ בְּנֵי חֶבְרוֹן יְרִיָּהוּ הָרֹאשׁ אֲמַרְיָה
Amariah the-first Jeriah Hebron sons-of (19) the-first Shelomith Izhar

הַשֵּׁנִי יַחֲזִיאֵל הַשְּׁלִישִׁי וִיקַמְעָם הָרְבִיעִי׃ בְּנֵי עֻזִּיאֵל
Uzziel sons-of (20) the-fourth and-Jekameam the-third Jahaziel the-second

מִיכָה הָרֹאשׁ וְיִשִּׁיָּה הַשֵּׁנִי׃ בְּנֵי מְרָרִי מַחְלִי וּמוּשִׁי
and-Mushi Mahli Merari sons-of (21) the-second and-Isshiah the-first Micah

בְּנֵי מַחְלִי אֶלְעָזָר וְקִישׁ׃ וַיָּמָת אֶלְעָזָר וְלֹא־ הָיוּ
they-were and-not Eleazar and-he-died (22) and-Kish Eleazar Mahli sons-of

לוֹ בָּנִים כִּי אִם־ בָּנוֹת וַיִּשָּׂאוּם בְּנֵי־ קִישׁ
Kish sons-of and-they-married-them daughters only but sons to-him

אֲחֵיהֶם׃ בְּנֵי מוּשִׁי מַחְלִי וְעֵדֶר וִירֵמוֹת שְׁלֹשָׁה׃
three and-Jeremoth and-Eder Mahli Mushi sons-of (23) cousins-of-them

אֵלֶּה בְנֵי־ לֵוִי לְבֵית אֲבֹתֵיהֶם רָאשֵׁי
heads-of fathers-of-them by-family-of Levi descendants-of these (24)

הָאָבוֹת לִפְקוּדֵיהֶם בְּמִסְפַּר שֵׁמוֹת לְגֻלְגְּלֹתָם
by-heads-of-them names by-count-of as-ones-being-registered-of-them the-fathers

עֹשֵׂה הַמְּלָאכָה לַעֲבֹדַת בֵּית יְהוָה מִבֶּן עֶשְׂרִים שָׁנָה
year twenty from-son-of Yahweh temple-of for-service-of the-work one-doing

וָמָעְלָה׃ כִּי אָמַר דָּוִיד הֵנִיחַ יְהוָה אֱלֹהֵי־יִשְׂרָאֵל
Israel God-of Yahweh he-granted-rest David he-said for (25) and-upward

לְעַמּוֹ וַיִּשְׁכֹּן בִּירוּשָׁלַםִ עַד־ לְעוֹלָם׃
to-forever to in-Jerusalem and-he-came-to-dwell to-people-of-him

וְגַם לַלְוִיִּם אֵין־ לָשֵׂאת אֶת־ הַמִּשְׁכָּן וְאֶת־
or the-tabernacle *** to-carry there-is-not to-the-Levites and-also (26)

כָּל־ כֵּלָיו לַעֲבֹדָתוֹ׃ כִּי בְדִבְרֵי
at-instructions-of indeed (27) for-service-of-him articles-of-him any-of

דָוִיד הָאַחֲרֹנִים הֵמָּה מִסְפַּר בְּנֵי־ לֵוִי מִבֶּן עֶשְׂרִים שָׁנָה
year twenty from-son-of Levi sons-of count-of they the-last-ones David

וּלְמָעְלָה׃ כִּי מַעֲמָדָם לְיַד־ בְּנֵי אַהֲרֹן
Aaron descendants-of at-hand-of duty-of-them indeed (28) and-to-upward

לַעֲבֹדַת בֵּית יְהוָה עַל־ הַחֲצֵרוֹת וְעַל־ הַלְּשָׁכוֹת
the-side-rooms and-over the-courtyards over Yahweh temple-of in-service-of

וְעַל־ טָהֳרַת לְכָל־ קֹדֶשׁ וּמַעֲשֵׂה עֲבֹדַת
duty-of and-performance-of sacred-thing of-all-of purification-of and-over

17 The descendants of Eliezer:
Rehabiah was the first.
Eliezer had no other
sons, but the sons of
Rehabiah were very numerous.
18 The sons of Izhar:
Shelomith was the first.
19 The sons of Hebron:
Jeriah the first, Amariah
the second, Jahaziel the
third and Jekameam the
fourth.
20 The sons of Uzziel:
Micah the first and Isshiah the second.

*Merarites*

21 The sons of Merari:
Mahli and Mushi.
The sons of Mahli:
Eleazar and Kish.
22 Eleazar died without
having sons: he had only
daughters. Their cousins,
the sons of Kish, married
them.
23 The sons of Mushi:
Mahli, Eder and Jeremoth—three in all.

24 These were the descendants of Levi by their families—
the heads of families as they
were registered under their
names and counted individually, that is, the workers
twenty years old or more who
served in the temple of the
LORD. 25 For David had said,
"Since the LORD, the God of Israel, has granted rest to his
people and has come to dwell
in Jerusalem forever, 26 the Levites no longer need to carry
the tabernacle or any of the articles used in its service." 27 According to the last instructions
of David, the Levites were
counted from those twenty
years old or more.
28 The duty of the Levites was
to help Aaron's descendants
in the service of the temple of
the LORD: to be in charge of the
courtyards, the side rooms, the
purification of all sacred
things and the performance of

בֵּית הָאֱלֹהִים׃ וּלְלֶחֶם הַמַּעֲרֶכֶת וּלְסֹלֶת
and-over-flour the-one-set-out and-over-bread-of (29) the-God house-of

לְמִנְחָה וְלִרְקִיקֵי הַמַּצּוֹת וְלַמַּחֲבַת
and-over-the-baking the-unleavened-ones and-over-wafers-of for-grain-offering

וְלַמֻּרְבֶּכֶת וּלְכָל־ מְשׂוּרָה וּמִדָּה׃ וְלַעֲמֹד
and-to-stand (30) and-size measurement and-over-all-of and-over-the-mixing

בַּבֹּקֶר בַּבֹּקֶר לְהֹדוֹת וּלְהַלֵּל לַיהוָה וְכֵן
and-same to-Yahweh and-to-praise to-thank in-the-morning in-the-morning

לָעָרֶב׃ וּלְכֹל הַעֲלוֹת עֹלוֹת לַיהוָה
to-Yahweh burnt-offerings to-present and-over-all-of (31) in-the-evening

לַשַּׁבָּתוֹת לֶחֳדָשִׁים וְלַמֹּעֲדִים בְּמִסְפָּר כְּמִשְׁפָּט
and-as-way in-number and-at-the-feasts at-the-New-Moons on-the-Sabbaths

עֲלֵיהֶם תָּמִיד לִפְנֵי יְהוָה׃ וְשָׁמְרוּ אֶת־
*** so-they-carried-out (32) Yahweh before regularly upon-them

מִשְׁמֶרֶת אֹהֶל־ מוֹעֵד וְאֵת מִשְׁמֶרֶת הַקֹּדֶשׁ
the-Holy-Place responsibility-of and Meeting Tent-of responsibility-of

וּמִשְׁמֶרֶת בְּנֵי אַהֲרֹן אֲחֵיהֶם לַעֲבֹדַת
for-service-of brothers-of-them Aaron descendants-of and-responsibility-of

בֵּית יְהוָה׃ וְלִבְנֵי אַהֲרֹן מַחְלְקוֹתָם בְּנֵי אַהֲרֹן
Aaron sons-of divisions-of-them Aaron and-of-sons-of (24:1) Yahweh temple-of

נָדָב וַאֲבִיהוּא אֶלְעָזָר וְאִיתָמָר׃ וַיָּמָת נָדָב וַאֲבִיהוּא לִפְנֵי
before and-Abihu Nadab but-he-died (2) and-Ithamar Eleazar and-Abihu Nadab

אֲבִיהֶם וּבָנִים לֹא־ הָיוּ לָהֶם וַיְכַהֲנוּ אֶלְעָזָר
Eleazar so-they-became-priests to-them they-were not and-sons father-of-them

וְאִיתָמָר׃ וַיֶּחָלְקֵם דָּוִיד וְצָדוֹק מִן־ בְּנֵי
descendants-of from and-Zadok David and-he-divided-them (3) and-Ithamar

אֶלְעָזָר וַאֲחִימֶלֶךְ מִן־ בְּנֵי אִיתָמָר לִפְקֻדָּתָם
for-order-of-them Ithamar descendants-of from and-Ahimelech Eleazar

בַּעֲבֹדָתָם׃ וַיִּמָּצְאוּ בְנֵי־ אֶלְעָזָר רַבִּים
many Eleazar descendants-of and-they-were-found (4) for-ministry-of-them

לְרָאשֵׁי הַגְּבָרִים מִן־ בְּנֵי אִיתָמָר וַיַּחְלְקוּם
and-they-divided-them Ithamar descendants-of more-than the-men of-leaders-of

לִבְנֵי אֶלְעָזָר רָאשִׁים לְבֵית־ אָבוֹת שִׁשָּׁה עָשָׂר
ten six fathers of-family-of heads Eleazar from-descendants-of

וְלִבְנֵי אִיתָמָר לְבֵית אֲבוֹתָם שְׁמוֹנָה׃
eight fathers-of-them of-family-of Ithamar and-from-descendants-of

וַיַּחְלְקוּם בְּגוֹרָלוֹת אֵלֶּה עִם־ אֵלֶּה כִּי־ הָיוּ שָׂרֵי־
officials-of they-were for these with these by-lots and-they-divided-them (5)

other duties at the house of
God. 29They were in charge of
the bread set out on the table,
the flour for the grain
offerings, the unleavened wafers, the baking and the mixing, and all measurements of
quantity and size. 30They were
also to stand every morning to
thank and praise the LORD.
They were to do the same in
the evening 31and whenever
burnt offerings were pre-
sented to the LORD on Sabbaths and at New Moon festivals and at appointed feasts.
They were to serve before the
LORD regularly in the proper
number and in the way prescribed for them.
32And so the Levites carried
out their responsibilities for
the Tent of Meeting, for the
Holy Place and, under their
brothers the descendants of
Aaron, for the service of the
temple of the LORD.

*The Divisions of Priests*

24 These were the divi-
sions of the sons of
Aaron:
The sons of Aaron were
Nadab, Abihu, Eleazar and
Ithamar. 2But Nadab and
Abihu died before their father
did, and they had no sons; so
Eleazar and Ithamar served as
the priests. 3With the help of
Zadok a descendant of Eleazar
and Ahimelech a descendant
of Ithamar, David separated
them into divisions for their
appointed order of ministering. 4A larger number of leaders were found among Eleazar's descendants than among
Ithamar's, and they were divided accordingly: sixteen
heads of families from Eleazar's descendants and eight
heads of families from Ithamar's descendants. 5They divided them impartially by
drawing lots, for there were

קֹדֶשׁ וְשָׂרֵי הָאֱלֹהִים מִבְּנֵי אֶלְעָזָר
Eleazar among-descendants-of the-God and-officials-of sanctuary

וּבִבְנֵי אִיתָמָר׃ וַיִּכְתְּבֵם שְׁמַעְיָה בֶן־
son-of Shemaiah and-he-recorded-them (6) Ithamar and-among-descendants-of

נְתַנְאֵל הַסּוֹפֵר מִן־ הַלֵּוִי לִפְנֵי הַמֶּלֶךְ וְהַשָּׂרִים
and-the-officials the-king in-presences-of the-Levite from the-scribe Nethanel

וְצָדוֹק הַכֹּהֵן וַאֲחִימֶלֶךְ בֶּן־ אֶבְיָתָר וְרָאשֵׁי הָאָבוֹת
the-fathers and-heads-of Abiathar son-of and-Ahimelech the-priest and-Zadok

לַכֹּהֲנִים וְלַלְוִיִּם בֵּית־ אָב אֶחָד אָחֻז
being-taken one father family-of and-of-the-Levites of-the-priests

לְאֶלְעָזָר וְאָחֻז ׀ אָחֻז לְאִיתָמָר׃ וַיֵּצֵא
and-he-fell (7) from-Ithamar being-taken and-being-taken from-Eleazar

הַגּוֹרָל הָרִאשׁוֹן לִיהוֹיָרִיב לִידַעְיָה הַשֵּׁנִי׃ לְחָרִם הַשְּׁלִשִׁי
the-third to-Harim (8) the-second to-Jedaiah to-Jehoiarib the-first the-lot

לִשְׂעֹרִים הָרְבִעִי׃ לְמַלְכִּיָּה הַחֲמִישִׁי לְמִיָּמִן הַשִּׁשִּׁי׃
the-sixth to-Mijamin the-fifth to-Malkijah (9) the-fourth to-Seorim

לְהַקּוֹץ הַשְּׁבִעִי לַאֲבִיָּה הַשְּׁמִינִי׃ לְיֵשׁוּעַ הַתְּשִׁעִי
the-ninth to-Jeshua (11) the-eighth to-Abijah the-seventh to-Hakkoz (10)

לִשְׁכַנְיָהוּ הָעֲשִׂרִי׃ לְאֶלְיָשִׁיב עַשְׁתֵּי עָשָׂר לְיָקִים שְׁנֵים עָשָׂר׃
ten two to-Jakim ten one to-Eliashib (12) the-tenth to-Shecaniah

לְחֻפָּה שְׁלֹשָׁה עָשָׂר לְיֶשֶׁבְאָב אַרְבָּעָה עָשָׂר׃ לְבִלְגָּה חֲמִשָּׁה עָשָׂר
ten five to-Bilgah (14) ten four to-Jeshebeab ten three to-Huppah (13)

לְאִמֵּר שִׁשָּׁה עָשָׂר׃ לְחֵזִיר שִׁבְעָה עָשָׂר לְהַפִּצֵּץ שְׁמוֹנָה עָשָׂר׃
ten eight to-Happizzez ten seven to-Hezir (15) ten six to-Immer

לִפְתַחְיָה תִּשְׁעָה עָשָׂר לִיחֶזְקֵאל הָעֶשְׂרִים׃ לְיָכִין אֶחָד
one to-Jakin (17) the-twenty to-Jehezkel ten nine to-Pethahiah (16)

וְעֶשְׂרִים לְגָמוּל שְׁנַיִם וְעֶשְׂרִים׃ לִדְלָיָהוּ שְׁלֹשָׁה וְעֶשְׂרִים
and-twenty three to-Delaiah (18) and-twenty two to-Gamul and-twenty

לְמַעַזְיָהוּ אַרְבָּעָה וְעֶשְׂרִים׃ אֵלֶּה פְקֻדָּתָם לַעֲבֹדָתָם
for-ministry-of-them order-of-them these (19) and-twenty four to-Maaziah

לָבוֹא לְבֵית־ יְהוָה כְּמִשְׁפָּטָם בְּיַד אַהֲרֹן
Aaron by-hand-of as-regulation-of-them Yahweh into-temple-of to-enter

אֲבִיהֶם כַּאֲשֶׁר צִוָּהוּ יְהוָה אֱלֹהֵי יִשְׂרָאֵל׃
Israel God-of Yahweh he-commanded-him just-as father-of-them

וְלִבְנֵי לֵוִי הַנּוֹתָרִים לִבְנֵי עַמְרָם
Amram from-sons-of the-ones-being-left Levi and-for-descendants-of (20)

שׁוּבָאֵל לִבְנֵי שׁוּבָאֵל יֶחְדְּיָהוּ׃ לִרְחַבְיָהוּ לִבְנֵי
from-sons-of for-Rehabiah (21) Jehdeiah Shubael from-sons-of Shubael

officials of the sanctuary and officials of God among the descendants of both Eleazar and Ithamar.

6The scribe Shemaiah son of Nethanel, a Levite, recorded their names in the presence of the king and of the officials: Zadok the priest, Ahimelech son of Abiathar and the heads of families of the priests and of the Levites—one family being taken from Eleazar and then one from Ithamar.

7The first lot fell to Jehoiarib,
the second to Jedaiah,
8the third to Harim,
the fourth to Seorim,
9the fifth to Malkijah,
the sixth to Mijamin,
10the seventh to Hakkoz,
the eighth to Abijah,
11the ninth to Jeshua,
the tenth to Shecaniah,
12the eleventh to Eliashib,
the twelfth to Jakim,
13the thirteenth to Huppah,
the fourteenth to Jeshebeab,
14the fifteenth to Bilgah,
the sixteenth to Immer,
15the seventeenth to Hezir,
the eighteenth to Happizzez,
16the nineteenth to Pethahiah,
the twentieth to Jehezkel,
17the twenty-first to Jakin,
the twenty-second to Gamul,
18the twenty-third to Delaiah
and the twenty-fourth to Maaziah.

19This was their appointed order of ministering when they entered the temple of the LORD, according to the regulations prescribed for them by their forefather Aaron, as the LORD, the God of Israel, had commanded him.

*The Rest of the Levites*

20As for the rest of the descendants of Levi:
from the sons of Amram: Shubael;
from the sons of Shubael: Jehdeiah.
21As for Rehabiah, from his sons:

רְחַבְיָהוּ הָרֹאשׁ יִשִּׁיָּה׃ לַיִּצְהָרִי שְׁלֹמוֹת לִבְנֵי

from-sons-of Shelomoth from-the-Izharite (22) Isshiah the-first Rehabiah

שְׁלֹמוֹת יָחַת׃ וּבְנֵי יְרִיָּהוּ אֲמַרְיָהוּ הַשֵּׁנִי יַחֲזִיאֵל

Jahaziel the-second Amariah Jeriah and-sons-of (23) Jahath Shelomoth

הַשְּׁלִישִׁי יְקַמְעָם הָרְבִיעִי׃ בְּנֵי עֻזִּיאֵל מִיכָה לִבְנֵי מִיכָה

Micah from-sons-of Micah Uzziel sons-of (24) the-fourth Jekameam the-third

שָׁמִּור׃ אֲחִי מִיכָה יִשִּׁיָּה לִבְנֵי יִשִּׁיָּה זְכַרְיָהוּ׃

Zechariah Isshiah from-sons-of Isshiah Micah brother-of (25) Shamir

בְּנֵי מְרָרִי מַחְלִי וּמוּשִׁי בְּנֵי יַעֲזִיָּהוּ בְנוֹ׃ בְּנֵי

sons-of (27) Beno Jaaziah sons-of and-Mushi Mahli Merari sons-of (26)

מְרָרִי לְיַעֲזִיָּהוּ בְּנוֹ וְשֹׁהַם וְזַכּוּר וְעִבְרִי׃ לְמַחְלִי

from-Mahli (28) and-Ibri and-Zaccur and-Shoham Beno from-Jaaziah Merari

אֶלְעָזָר וְלֹא־הָיָה לוֹ בָּנִים׃ לְקִישׁ בְּנֵי־קִישׁ יְרַחְמְאֵל׃

Jerahmeel Kish sons-of from-Kish (29) sons to-him he-was now-not Eleazar

וּבְנֵי מוּשִׁי מַחְלִי וְעֵדֶר וִירִימוֹת אֵלֶּה בְּנֵי הַלְוִיִּם

the-Levites sons-of these and-Jerimoth and-Eder Mahli Mushi and-sons-of (30)

לְבֵית אֲבֹתֵיהֶם׃ וַיַּפִּילוּ גַם־הֵם גּוֹרָלוֹת לְעֻמַּת

just-as lots they also and-they-cast (31) fathers-of-them by-family-of

אֲחֵיהֶם בְּנֵי־אַהֲרֹן לִפְנֵי דָּוִיד הַמֶּלֶךְ

the-king David in-presences-of Aaron descendants-of brothers-of-them

וְצָדוֹק וַאֲחִימֶלֶךְ וְרָאשֵׁי הָאָבוֹת לַכֹּהֲנִים

of-the-priests the-fathers and-heads-of and-Ahimelech and-Zadok

וְלַלְוִיִּם אָבוֹת הָרֹאשׁ לְעֻמַּת אָחִיו הַקָּטָן׃

the-young brother-of-him same-as the-head fathers and-of-the-Levites

וַיַּבְדֵּל דָּוִיד וְשָׂרֵי הַצָּבָא לַעֲבֹדָה

for-the-ministry the-army and-commanders-of David and-he-set-apart (25:1)

לִבְנֵי אָסָף וְהֵימָן וִידוּתוּן הַנִּבְּאִים בְּכִנֹּרוֹת

with-harps the-ones-prophesying and-Jeduthun and-Heman Asaph from-sons-of

בִּנְבָלִים וּבִמְצִלְתָּיִם וַיְהִי מִסְפָּרָם אַנְשֵׁי מְלָאכָה

work men-of list-of-them and-he-was and-with-cymbals with-lyres

לַעֲבֹדָתָם׃ לִבְנֵי אָסָף זַכּוּר וְיוֹסֵף וּנְתַנְיָה

and-Nethaniah and-Joseph Zaccur Asaph from-sons-of (2) of-service-of-them

וַאֲשַׂרְאֵלָה בְּנֵי אָסָף עַל יַד־אָסָף הַנִּבָּא עַל־

under the-one-prophesying Asaph hand-of under Asaph sons-of and-Asarelah

יְדֵי הַמֶּלֶךְ׃ לִידוּתוּן בְּנֵי יְדוּתוּן גְּדַלְיָהוּ וּצְרִי

and-Zeri Gedaliah Jeduthun sons-of for-Jeduthun (3) the-king hands-of

וִישַׁעְיָהוּ חֲשַׁבְיָהוּ וּמַתִּתְיָהוּ שִׁשָּׁה עַל יְדֵי אֲבִיהֶם

father-of-them hands-of under six and-Mattithiah Hashabiah and-Jeshaiah

Isshiah was the first.
22 From the Izharites: Shelomoth;
from the sons of Shelomoth: Jahath.
23 The sons of Hebron: Jeriah the first,[e] Amariah the second, Jahaziel the third and Jekameam the fourth.
24 The son of Uzziel: Micah; from the sons of Micah: Shamir.
25 The brother of Micah: Isshiah;
from the sons of Isshiah: Zechariah.
26 The sons of Merari: Mahli and Mushi.
The son of Jaaziah: Beno.
27 The sons of Merari:
from Jaaziah: Beno, Shoham, Zaccur and Ibri.
28 From Mahli: Eleazar, who had no sons.
29 From Kish: the son of Kish: Jerahmeel.
30 And the sons of Mushi: Mahli, Eder and Jerimoth.

These were the Levites, according to their families.
31 They also cast lots, just as their brothers the descendants of Aaron did, in the presence of King David and of Zadok, Ahimelech, and the heads of families of the priests and of the Levites. The families of the oldest brother were treated the same as those of the youngest.

*The Singers*

25 David, together with the commanders of the army, set apart some of the sons of Asaph, Heman and Jeduthun for the ministry of prophesying, accompanied by harps, lyres and cymbals. Here is the list of the men who performed this service:

2 From the sons of Asaph:
Zaccur, Joseph, Nethaniah and Asarelah. The sons of Asaph were under the supervision of Asaph, who prophesied under the king's supervision.
3 As for Jeduthun, from his sons:
Gedaliah, Zeri, Jeshaiah, Shimei,[f] Hashabiah and Mattithiah, six in all, under

[e] 23 Two Hebrew manuscripts and some Septuagint manuscripts (see also 1 Chron. 23:19); most Hebrew manuscripts *The sons of Jeriah:*

[f] 3 One Hebrew manuscript and some Septuagint manuscripts (see also verse 17); most Hebrew manuscripts do not have *Shimei.*

°24 ק שמיר

°1 ק הנבאים

יְדוּתוּן בַּכִּנּוֹר הַנִּבָּא עַל־ הֹדוֹת וְהַלֵּל
and-to-praise to-thank in the-one-prophesying with-the-harp Jeduthun

לַיהוָה׃ לְהֵימָן בְּנֵי הֵימָן בֻּקִּיָּהוּ מַתַּנְיָהוּ עֻזִּיאֵל שְׁבוּאֵל
Shubael Uzziel Mattaniah Bukkiah Heman sons-of for-Heman (4) to-Yahweh

וִירִימוֹת חֲנַנְיָה חֲנָנִי אֱלִיאָתָה גִדַּלְתִּי וְרֹמַמְתִּי עֶזֶר יָשְׁבְּקָשָׁה
Joshbekashah Ezer and-Romamti Giddalti Eliathah Hanani Hananiah and-Jerimoth

מַלּוֹתִי הוֹתִיר מַחֲזִיאוֹת׃ כָּל־ אֵלֶּה בָנִים לְהֵימָן חֹזֵה הַמֶּלֶךְ
the-king seer-of of-Heman sons these all-of (5) Mahazioth Hothir Mallothi

בְּדִבְרֵי הָאֱלֹהִים לְהָרִים קָרֶן וַיִּתֵּן הָאֱלֹהִים לְהֵימָן
to-Heman the-God and-he-gave horn to-exalt the-God through-promises-of

בָּנִים אַרְבָּעָה עָשָׂר וּבָנוֹת שָׁלוֹשׁ׃ כָּל־ אֵלֶּה עַל־ יְדֵי
hands-of under these all-of (6) three and-daughters ten four sons

אֲבִיהֶם בַּשִּׁיר בֵּית יְהוָה בִּמְצִלְתַּיִם נְבָלִים וְכִנֹּרוֹת
and-harps lyres with-cymbals Yahweh temple-of for-the-music father-of-them

לַעֲבֹדַת בֵּית הָאֱלֹהִים עַל יְדֵי הַמֶּלֶךְ אָסָף וִידוּתוּן
and-Jeduthun Asaph the-king hands-of under the-God house-of for-ministry-of

וְהֵימָן׃ וַיְהִי מִסְפָּרָם עִם־ אֲחֵיהֶם
relatives-of-them with number-of-them and-he-was (7) and-Heman

מְלֻמְּדֵי־ שִׁיר לַיהוָה כָּל־ הַמֵּבִין
the-one-being-skilled all-of for-Yahweh music ones-being-trained-of

מָאתַיִם שְׁמוֹנִים וּשְׁמוֹנָה׃ וַיַּפִּילוּ גּוֹרָלוֹת מִשְׁמֶרֶת לְעֻמַּת
just-as duty lots-of and-they-cast (8) and-eight eighty two-hundreds

כַּקָּטֹן כַּגָּדוֹל מֵבִין עִם־ תַּלְמִיד׃ וַיֵּצֵא הַגּוֹרָל
the-lot and-he-fell (9) student as one-teaching so-the-old as-the-young

הָרִאשׁוֹן לְאָסָף לְיוֹסֵף גְּדַלְיָהוּ הַשֵּׁנִי הוּא־ וְאֶחָיו
and-relatives-of-him he the-second Gedaliah to-Joseph for-Asaph the-first

וּבָנָיו שְׁנֵים עָשָׂר׃ הַשְּׁלִשִׁי זַכּוּר בָּנָיו וְאֶחָיו
and-relatives-of-him sons-of-him Zaccur the-third (10) ten two and-sons-of-him

שְׁנֵים עָשָׂר׃ הָרְבִיעִי לַיִּצְרִי בָּנָיו וְאֶחָיו
and-relatives-of-him sons-of-him to-the-Izrite the-fourth (11) ten two

שְׁנֵים עָשָׂר׃ הַחֲמִישִׁי נְתַנְיָהוּ בָּנָיו וְאֶחָיו שְׁנֵים עָשָׂר׃
ten two and-relatives-of-him sons-of-him Nethaniah the-fifth (12) ten two

הַשִּׁשִּׁי בֻקִּיָּהוּ בָּנָיו וְאֶחָיו שְׁנֵים עָשָׂר׃
ten two and-relatives-of-him sons-of-him Bukkiah the-sixth (13)

הַשְּׁבִעִי יְשַׂרְאֵלָה בָּנָיו וְאֶחָיו שְׁנֵים עָשָׂר׃
ten two and-relatives-of-him sons-of-him Jesarelah the-seventh (14)

הַשְּׁמִינִי יְשַׁעְיָהוּ בָּנָיו וְאֶחָיו שְׁנֵים עָשָׂר׃
ten two and-relatives-of-him sons-of-him Jeshaiah the-eighth (15)

the supervision of their father Jeduthun, who prophesied, using the harp in thanking and praising the LORD.
4 As for Heman, from his sons: Bukkiah, Mattaniah, Uzziel, Shubael and Jerimoth; Hananiah, Hanani, Eliathah, Giddalti and Romamti-Ezer; Joshbekashah, Mallothi, Hothir and Mahazioth. 5 All these were sons of Heman the king's seer. They were given him through the promises of God to exalt him.[g] God gave Heman fourteen sons and three daughters.

6 All these men were under the supervision of their fathers for the music of the temple of the LORD, with cymbals, lyres and harps, for the ministry at the house of God. Asaph, Jeduthun and Heman were under the supervision of the king. 7 Along with their relatives—all of them trained and skilled in music for the LORD—they numbered 288. 8 Young and old alike, teacher as well as student, cast lots for their duties.

9 The first lot, which was for Asaph, fell to Joseph,
his sons and relatives,[h] 12[i]
the second to Gedaliah,
he and his relatives and sons, 12
10 the third to Zaccur,
his sons and relatives, 12
11 the fourth to Izri,[j]
his sons and relatives, 12
12 the fifth to Nethaniah,
his sons and relatives, 12
13 the sixth to Bukkiah,
his sons and relatives, 12
14 the seventh to Jesarelah,[k]
his sons and relatives, 12
15 the eighth to Jeshaiah,
his sons and relatives, 12

g5 Hebrew *exalt the horn*
h9 See Septuagint; Hebrew does not have *his sons and relatives.*
i9 See the total in verse 7; Hebrew does not have *twelve.*
j11 A variant of *Zeri*
k14 A variant of *Asarelah*

הַתְּשִׁעִי מַתַּנְיָהוּ בָּנָיו וְאֶחָיו שְׁנֵים עָשָׂר׃
ten two and-relatives-of-him sons-of-him Mattaniah the-ninth (16)

הָעֲשִׂירִי שִׁמְעִי בָּנָיו וְאֶחָיו שְׁנֵים עָשָׂר׃
ten two and-relatives-of-him sons-of-him Shimei the-tenth (17)

עַשְׁתֵּי־עָשָׂר עֲזַרְאֵל בָּנָיו וְאֶחָיו שְׁנֵים עָשָׂר׃
ten two and-relatives-of-him sons-of-him Azarel ten one (18)

הַשְּׁנֵים עָשָׂר לַחֲשַׁבְיָה בָּנָיו וְאֶחָיו שְׁנֵים עָשָׂר׃
ten two and-relatives-of-him sons-of-him to-Hashabiah ten the-two (19)

לִשְׁלֹשָׁה עָשָׂר שׁוּבָאֵל בָּנָיו וְאֶחָיו שְׁנֵים עָשָׂר׃
ten two and-relatives-of-him sons-of-him Shubael ten to-three (20)

לְאַרְבָּעָה עָשָׂר מַתִּתְיָהוּ בָּנָיו וְאֶחָיו שְׁנֵים עָשָׂר׃
ten two and-relatives-of-him sons-of-him Mattithiah ten to-four (21)

לַחֲמִשָּׁה עָשָׂר לִירֵמוֹת בָּנָיו וְאֶחָיו שְׁנֵים עָשָׂר׃
ten two and-relatives-of-him sons-of-him to-Jerimoth ten to-five (22)

לְשִׁשָּׁה עָשָׂר לַחֲנַנְיָהוּ בָּנָיו וְאֶחָיו שְׁנֵים עָשָׂר׃
ten two and-relatives-of-him sons-of-him to-Hananiah ten to-six (23)

לְשִׁבְעָה עָשָׂר לְיָשְׁבְּקָשָׁה בָּנָיו וְאֶחָיו שְׁנֵים עָשָׂר׃
ten two and-relatives-of-him sons-of-him to-Joshbekashah ten to-seven (24)

לִשְׁמוֹנָה עָשָׂר לַחֲנָנִי בָּנָיו וְאֶחָיו שְׁנֵים עָשָׂר׃
ten two and-relatives-of-him sons-of-him to-Hanani ten to-eight (25)

לְתִשְׁעָה עָשָׂר לְמַלּוֹתִי בָּנָיו וְאֶחָיו שְׁנֵים עָשָׂר׃
ten two and-relatives-of-him sons-of-him to-Mallothi ten to-nine (26)

לְעֶשְׂרִים לֶאֱלִיָּתָה בָּנָיו וְאֶחָיו שְׁנֵים עָשָׂר׃
ten two and-relatives-of-him sons-of-him to-Eliathah to-twenty (27)

לְאֶחָד וְעֶשְׂרִים לְהוֹתִיר בָּנָיו וְאֶחָיו שְׁנֵים עָשָׂר׃
ten two and-relatives-of-him sons-of-him to-Hothir and-twenty to-one (28)

לִשְׁנַיִם וְעֶשְׂרִים לְגִדַּלְתִּי בָּנָיו וְאֶחָיו שְׁנֵים עָשָׂר׃
ten two and-relatives-of-him sons-of-him to-Giddalti and-twenty to-two (29)

לִשְׁלֹשָׁה וְעֶשְׂרִים לְמַחֲזִיאוֹת בָּנָיו וְאֶחָיו שְׁנֵים
two and-relatives-of-him sons-of-him to-Mahazioth and-twenty to-three (30)

עָשָׂר׃ לְאַרְבָּעָה וְעֶשְׂרִים לְרוֹמַמְתִּי עֶזֶר בָּנָיו וְאֶחָיו
and-relatives-of-him sons-of-him Ezer to-Romamti and-twenty to-four (31) ten

שְׁנֵים עָשָׂר׃ לְמַחְלְקוֹת לְשֹׁעֲרִים לְקָרְחִים מְשֶׁלֶמְיָהוּ
Meshelemiah from-the-Korahites of-gatekeepers of-divisions (26:1) ten two

בֶּן־קֹרֵא מִן־בְּנֵי אָסָף׃ וְלִמְשֶׁלֶמְיָהוּ בָּנִים זְכַרְיָהוּ
Zechariah sons and-to-Meshelemiah (2) Asaph sons-of from Kore son-of

הַבְּכוֹר יְדִיעֲאֵל הַשֵּׁנִי זְבַדְיָהוּ הַשְּׁלִישִׁי יַתְנִיאֵל הָרְבִיעִי׃
the-fourth Jathniel the-third Zebadiah the-second Jediael the-firstborn

[16]the ninth to Mattaniah,
his sons and relatives,
12
[17]the tenth to Shimei,
his sons and relatives,
12
[18]the eleventh to Azarel,[l]
his sons and relatives,
12
[19]the twelfth to
Hashabiah,
his sons and relatives,
12
[20]the thirteenth to
Shubael,
his sons and relatives,
12
[21]the fourteenth to
Mattithiah,
his sons and relatives,
12
[22]the fifteenth to Jerimoth,
his sons and relatives,
12
[23]the sixteenth to
Hananiah,
his sons and relatives,
12
[24]the seventeenth to
Joshbekashah,
his sons and relatives,
12
[25]the eighteenth to
Hanani,
his sons and relatives,
12
[26]the nineteenth to
Mallothi,
his sons and relatives,
12
[27]the twentieth to
Eliathah,
his sons and relatives,
12
[28]the twenty-first to
Hothir,
his sons and relatives,
12
[29]the twenty-second to
Giddalti,
his sons and relatives,
12
[30]the twenty-third to
Mahazioth,
his sons and relatives,
12
[31]the twenty-fourth to
Romamti-Ezer,
his sons and relatives,
12

*The Gatekeepers*

26 The divisions of the gatekeepers:

From the Korahites: Meshelemiah son of Kore, one of the sons of Asaph.
[2]Meshelemiah had sons:
Zechariah the firstborn,
Jediael the second,
Zebadiah the third,
Jathniel the fourth,

[l]18 A variant of *Uzziel*

עֵילָם הַחֲמִישִׁי יְהוֹחָנָן הַשִּׁשִּׁי אֶלְיְהוֹעֵינַי הַשְּׁבִיעִי׃ וּלְעֹבֵד
and-to-Obed (4) the-seventh Eliehoenai the-sixth Jehohanan the-fifth Elam (3)

אֱדֹם בָּנִים שְׁמַעְיָה הַבְּכוֹר יְהוֹזָבָד הַשֵּׁנִי יוֹאָח הַשְּׁלִשִׁי
the-third Joah the-second Jehozabad the-firstborn Shemaiah sons Edom

וְשָׂכָר הָרְבִיעִי וּנְתַנְאֵל הַחֲמִישִׁי׃ עַמִּיאֵל הַשִּׁשִּׁי יִשָּׂשכָר
Issachar the-sixth Ammiel (5) the-fifth and-Nethanel the-fourth and-Sacar

הַשְּׁבִיעִי פְּעֻלְּתַי הַשְּׁמִינִי כִּי בֵרֲכוֹ אֱלֹהִים׃ וְלִשְׁמַעְיָה
and-to-Shemaiah (6) God he-blessed-him for the-eighth Peullethai the-seventh

בְנוֹ נוֹלַד בָּנִים הַמִּמְשָׁלִים לְבֵית אֲבִיהֶם כִּי־
because father-of-them in-family-of the-leaders sons he-was-born son-of-him

גִבּוֹרֵי חַיִל הֵמָּה׃ בְּנֵי שְׁמַעְיָה עָתְנִי וּרְפָאֵל וְעוֹבֵד
and-Obed and-Rephael Othni Shemaiah sons-of (7) they capability men-of

אֶלְזָבָד אֶחָיו בְּנֵי־ חָיִל אֱלִיהוּ וּסְמַכְיָהוּ׃ כָּל־ אֵלֶּה
these all-of (8) and-Semakiah Elihu ability men-of relatives-of-him Elzabad

מִבְּנֵי ׀ עֹבֵד אֱדֹם הֵמָּה וּבְנֵיהֶם וַאֲחֵיהֶם
and-relatives-of-them and-sons-of-them they Edom Obed from-descendants-of

אִישׁ־ חַיִל בַּכֹּחַ לַעֲבֹדָה שִׁשִּׁים וּשְׁנַיִם לְעֹבֵד אֱדֹם׃
Edom of-Obed and-two sixty for-the-work with-the-strength capability man-of

וְלִמְשֶׁלֶמְיָהוּ בָּנִים וְאַחִים בְּנֵי־ חַיִל שְׁמוֹנָה עָשָׂר׃
ten eight ability men-of and-relatives sons and-to-Meshelemiah (9)

וּלְחֹסָה מִן־ בְּנֵי־ מְרָרִי בָּנִים שִׁמְרִי הָרֹאשׁ כִּי לֹא־
not although the-first Shimri sons Merari sons-of from and-to-Hosah (10)

הָיָה בְכוֹר וַיְשִׂימֵהוּ אָבִיהוּ לְרֹאשׁ׃ חִלְקִיָּהוּ
Hilkiah (11) as-first father-of-him but-he-appointed-him firstborn he-was

הַשֵּׁנִי טְבַלְיָהוּ הַשְּׁלִשִׁי זְכַרְיָהוּ הָרְבִעִי כָּל־ בָּנִים וְאַחִים
and-relatives sons all-of the-fourth Zechariah the-third Tabaliah the-second

לְחֹסָה שְׁלֹשָׁה עָשָׂר׃ לְאֵלֶּה מַחְלְקוֹת הַשֹּׁעֲרִים לְרָאשֵׁי
through-chiefs-of the-gatekeepers divisions-of to-these (12) ten three of-Hosah

הַגְּבָרִים מִשְׁמָרוֹת לְעֻמַּת אֲחֵיהֶם לְשָׁרֵת בְּבֵית יְהוָה׃
Yahweh in-temple-of to-minister relatives-of-them just-as duties the-men

וַיַּפִּילוּ גוֹרָלוֹת כַּקָּטֹן כַּגָּדוֹל לְבֵית אֲבוֹתָם
fathers-of-them by-family-of so-the-old as-the-young lots and-they-cast (13)

לְשַׁעַר וָשָׁעַר׃ וַיִּפֹּל הַגּוֹרָל מִזְרָחָה לְשֶׁלֶמְיָהוּ
for-Shelemiah to-East the-lot and-he-fell (14) and-gate for-gate

וּזְכַרְיָהוּ בְנוֹ יוֹעֵץ ׀ בְּשֶׂכֶל הִפִּילוּ גוֹרָלוֹת
lots they-cast with-wisdom one-counseling son-of-him then-Zechariah

וַיֵּצֵא גוֹרָלוֹ צָפוֹנָה׃ לְעֹבֵד אֱדֹם נֶגְבָּה וּלְבָנָיו
and-to-sons-of-him to-South Edom to-Obed (15) to-North lot-of-him and-he-fell

3Elam the fifth,
Jehohanan the sixth
and Eliehoenai the seventh.
4Obed-Edom also had sons:
Shemaiah the firstborn,
Jehozabad the second,
Joah the third,
Sacar the fourth,
Nethanel the fifth,
5Ammiel the sixth,
Issachar the seventh
and Peullethai the eighth.
(For God had blessed Obed-Edom.)

6His son Shemaiah also had sons, who were leaders in their father's family because they were very capable men.
7The sons of Shemaiah: Othni, Rephael, Obed and Elzabad; his relatives Elihu and Semakiah were also able men.
8All these were descendants of Obed-Edom; they and their sons and their relatives were capable men with the strength to do the work—descendants of Obed-Edom, 62 in all.
9Meshelemiah had sons and relatives, who were able men—18 in all.

10Hosah the Merarite had sons: Shimri the first (although he was not the firstborn, his father had appointed him the first),
11Hilkiah the second, Tabaliah the third and Zechariah the fourth. The sons and relatives of Hosah were 13 in all.
12These divisions of the gatekeepers, through their chief men, had duties for ministering in the temple of the LORD, just as their relatives had.
13Lots were cast for each gate, according to their families, young and old alike.
14The lot for the East Gate fell to Shelemiah.[m] Then lots were cast for his son Zechariah, a wise counselor, and the lot for the North Gate fell to him.
15The lot for the South Gate fell to Obed-Edom, and the lot for the storehouse fell to his sons.

m14 A variant of *Meshelemiah*

בֵּית הָאֲסֻפִּים׃ לְשֻׁפִּים וּלְחֹסָה לַמַּעֲרָב עִם שַׁעַר
Gate-of with for-the-West and-to-Hosah to-Shuppim (16) the-stores house-of

שַׁלֶּכֶת בַּמְסִלָּה הָעוֹלָה מִשְׁמָר לְעֻמַּת מִשְׁמָר׃
guard alongside-of guard the-one-going-up on-the-road Shalleketh

לַמִּזְרָח הַלְוִיִּם שִׁשָּׁה לַצָּפוֹנָה לַיּוֹם אַרְבָּעָה לַנֶּגְבָּה
on-the-south four for-the-day on-the-north six the-Levites on-the-east (17)

לַיּוֹם אַרְבָּעָה וְלָאֲסֻפִּים שְׁנַיִם שְׁנָיִם׃ לַפַּרְבָּר לַמַּעֲרָב
to-the-west for-the-court (18) two two and-at-the-storehouses four for-the-day

אַרְבָּעָה לַמְסִלָּה שְׁנַיִם לַפַּרְבָּר׃ אֵלֶּה מַחְלְקוֹת הַשֹּׁעֲרִים
the-gatekeepers divisions-of these (19) at-the-court two at-the-road four

לִבְנֵי הַקָּרְחִי וְלִבְנֵי מְרָרִי׃ וְהַלְוִיִּם
and-the-Levites (20) Merari and-of-descendants-of the-Korahite of-descendants-of

אֲחִיָּה עַל־ אוֹצְרוֹת בֵּית הָאֱלֹהִים וּלְאֹצְרוֹת
and-of-treasuries-of the-God house-of treasuries-of over Ahijah

הַקֳּדָשִׁים׃ בְּנֵי לַעְדָּן בְּנֵי הַגֵּרְשֻׁנִּי
the-Gershonite sons-of Ladan descendants-of (21) the-dedicated-things

לְלַעְדָּן רָאשֵׁי הָאָבוֹת לְלַעְדָּן הַגֵּרְשֻׁנִּי יְחִיאֵלִי׃
Jehieli the-Gershonite of-Ladan the-fathers heads-of through-Ladan

בְּנֵי יְחִיאֵלִי זֵתָם וְיוֹאֵל אָחִיו עַל־ אֹצְרוֹת
treasuries-of over brother-of-him and-Joel Zetham Jehieli sons-of (22)

בֵּית יְהוָה׃ לַעַמְרָמִי לַיִּצְהָרִי לַחֶבְרוֹנִי
from-the-Hebronite from-the-Izharite from-the-Amramite (23) Yahweh temple-of

לָעָזִּיאֵלִי׃ וּשְׁבֻאֵל בֶּן־ גֵּרְשׁוֹם בֶּן־ מֹשֶׁה
Moses son-of Gershom descendant-of and-Shubael (24) from-the-Uzzielite

נָגִיד עַל־ הָאֹצָרוֹת׃ וְאֶחָיו לֶאֱלִיעֶזֶר
through-Eliezer and-relatives-of-him (25) the-treasuries over officer

רְחַבְיָהוּ בְנוֹ וִישַׁעְיָהוּ בְנוֹ וְיֹרָם בְּנוֹ וְזִכְרִי
and-Zicri son-of-him and-Joram son-of-him and-Jeshaiah son-of-him Rehabiah

בְנוֹ וּשְׁלֹמוֹת בְּנוֹ׃ הוּא שְׁלֹמוֹת וְאֶחָיו
and-relatives-of-him Shelomith he (26) son-of-him and-Shelomith son-of-him

עַל כָּל־ אֹצְרוֹת הַקֳּדָשִׁים אֲשֶׁר הִקְדִּישׁ דָּוִיד
David he-dedicated that the-dedicated-things treasuries-of all-of over

הַמֶּלֶךְ וְרָאשֵׁי הָאָבוֹת לְשָׂרֵי־ הָאֲלָפִים
the-thousands of-commanders-of the-fathers and-heads-of the-king

וְהַמֵּאוֹת וְשָׂרֵי הַצָּבָא׃ מִן־ הַמִּלְחָמוֹת וּמִן־
and-from the-battles from (27) the-army and-commanders-of and-the-hundreds

הַשָּׁלָל הִקְדִּישׁוּ לְחַזֵּק לְבֵית יְהוָה׃ וְכֹל
and-all-of (28) Yahweh to-temple-of to-repair they-dedicated the-plunder

°25 ק ושלמית

[16]The lots for the West Gate and the Shalleketh Gate on the upper road fell to Shuppim and Hosah.

Guard was alongside of guard: [17]There were six Levites a day on the east, four a day on the north, four a day on the south and two at a time at the storehouse. [18]As for the court to the west, there were four at the road and two at the court itself.

[19]These were the divisions of the gatekeepers who were descendants of Korah and Merari.

*The Treasurers and Other Officials*

[20]Their fellow Levites were[a] in charge of the treasuries of the house of God and the treasuries for the dedicated things.

[21]The descendants of Ladan, who were Gershonites through Ladan and who were heads of families belonging to Ladan the Gershonite, were Jehieli, [22]the sons of Jehieli, Zetham and his brother Joel. They were in charge of the treasuries of the temple of the LORD.

[23]From the Amramites, the Izharites, the Hebronites and the Uzzielites:

[24]Shubael, a descendant of Gershom son of Moses, was the officer in charge of the treasuries. [25]His relatives through Eliezer: Rehabiah his son, Jeshaiah his son, Joram his son, Zicri his son and Shelomith his son. [26]Shelomith and his relatives were in charge of all the treasuries for the things dedicated by King David, by the heads of families who were the commanders of thousands and commanders of hundreds, and by the other army commanders. [27]Some of the plunder taken in battle they dedicated for the repair of the temple of the LORD. [28]And

[a]20 Septuagint; Hebrew *As for the Levites, Ahijah was*

הַהִקְדִּישׁ שְׁמוּאֵל הָרֹאֶה וְשָׁאוּל בֶּן־ קִישׁ וְאַבְנֵר בֶּן־ נֵר
Ner son-of and-Abner Kish son-of and-Saul the-seer Samuel what-he-dedicated

וְיוֹאָב בֶּן־ צְרוּיָה כֹּל הַמַּקְדִּישׁ עַל יַד־
hand-of in the-thing-being-dedicated all-of Zeruiah son-of and-Joab

שְׁלֹמִית וְאֶחָיו׃ לַיִּצְהָרִי כְּנַנְיָהוּ וּבָנָיו
and-sons-of-him Kenaniah from-the-Izharite (29) and-relatives-of-him Shelomith

לַמְּלָאכָה הַחִיצוֹנָה עַל־ יִשְׂרָאֵל לְשֹׁטְרִים וּלְשֹׁפְטִים׃
and-as-ones-being-judges as-officials Israel over at-the-outside for-the-duty

לַחֶבְרוֹנִי חֲשַׁבְיָהוּ וְאֶחָיו בְּנֵי־ חַיִל
ability men-of and-relatives-of-him Hashabiah from-the-Hebronite (30)

אֶלֶף וּשְׁבַע־ מֵאוֹת עַל פְּקֻדַּת יִשְׂרָאֵל מֵעֵבֶר
at-near Israel responsibility-of over hundreds and-seven-of thousand

לַיַּרְדֵּן מַעְרָבָה לְכֹל מְלֶאכֶת יְהוָה וְלַעֲבֹדַת הַמֶּלֶךְ׃
the-king and-for-service-of Yahweh work-of for-all-of at-west to-the-Jordan

לַחֶבְרוֹנִי יְרִיָּה הָרֹאשׁ לַחֶבְרוֹנִי לְתֹלְדֹתָיו
by-records-of-him of-the-Hebronite the-chief Jeriah for-the-Hebronite (31)

לְאָבוֹת בִּשְׁנַת הָאַרְבָּעִים לְמַלְכוּת דָּוִיד נִדְרָשׁוּ
they-were-searched David of-reign-of the-forty in-year-of of-fathers

וַיִּמָּצֵא בָהֶם גִּבּוֹרֵי חַיִל בְּיַעְזֵיר גִּלְעָד׃
Gilead at-Jazer-of capability men-of among-them and-he-was-found

וְאֶחָיו בְּנֵי־ חַיִל אַלְפַּיִם וּשְׁבַע מֵאוֹת
hundreds and-seven-of two-thousands ability men-of and-relatives-of-him (32)

רָאשֵׁי הָאָבוֹת וַיַּפְקִידֵם דָּוִיד הַמֶּלֶךְ עַל־
over the-king David and-he-put-in-charge-them the-fathers heads-of

הָראוּבֵנִי וְהַגָּדִי וַחֲצִי שֵׁבֶט הַמְנַשִּׁי לְכָל־
for-every-of the-Manassite tribe-of and-half-of and-the-Gadite the-Reubenite

דְּבַר הָאֱלֹהִים וּדְבַר הַמֶּלֶךְ׃ וּבְנֵי יִשְׂרָאֵל ׀
Israel and-sons-of (27:1) the-king and-affair-of the-God matter-of

לְמִסְפָּרָם רָאשֵׁי הָאָבוֹת וְשָׂרֵי הָאֲלָפִים ׀
the-thousands and-commanders-of the-fathers heads-of by-list-of-them

וְהַמֵּאוֹת וְשֹׁטְרֵיהֶם הַמְשָׁרְתִים אֶת־ הַמֶּלֶךְ
the-king *** the-ones-serving and-officers-of-them and-the-hundreds

לְכֹל ׀ דְּבַר הַמַּחְלְקוֹת הַבָּאָה וְהַיֹּצֵאת
and-the-one-going-out the-one-coming-in the-divisions concern-of in-every-of

חֹדֶשׁ בְּחֹדֶשׁ לְכֹל חָדְשֵׁי הַשָּׁנָה הַמַּחֲלֹקֶת הָאַחַת
the-each the-division the-year months-of through-all-of by-month month

עֶשְׂרִים וְאַרְבָּעָה אָלֶף׃ עַל הַמַּחֲלֹקֶת הָרִאשׁוֹנָה לַחֹדֶשׁ
for-the-month the-first the-division over (2) thousand and-four twenty

everything dedicated by
Samuel the seer and by
Saul son of Kish, Abner
son of Ner and Joab son
of Zeruiah, and all the
other dedicated things
were in the care of Shelomith and his relatives.
29 From the Izharites: Kenaniah and his sons were
assigned duties away
from the temple, as
officials and judges over
Israel.
30 From the Hebronites:
Hashabiah and his rela-
tives—seventeen hun-
dred able men—were re-
sponsible in Israel west
of the Jordan for all the
work of the LORD and for
the king's service. 31 As
for the Hebronites, Jeri-
ah was their chief ac-
cording to the genealogi-
cal records of their families. In the fortieth year
of David's reign a search
was made in the records,
and capable men among
the Hebronites were
found at Jazer in Gilead.
32 Jeriah had twenty-sev-
en hundred relatives,
who were able men and
heads of families, and
King David put them in
charge of the Reubenites,
the Gadites and the half-
tribe of Manasseh for
every matter pertaining
to God and for the affairs
of the king.

*Army Divisions*

27 This is the list of the Israelites—heads of fami-
lies, commanders of thou-
sands and commanders of
hundreds, and their officers,
who served the king in all that
concerned the army divisions
that were on duty month by
month throughout the year.
Each division consisted of 24,-
000 men.

2 In charge of the first division, for the first month,

הָרִאשׁוֹן יָשָׁבְעָם בֶּן־ זַבְדִּיאֵל וְעַל מַחֲלֻקְתּוֹ עֶשְׂרִים וְאַרְבָּעָה
and-four twenty division-of-him and-in Zabdiel son-of Jashobeam the-first

אָלֶף׃ מִן־ בְּנֵי־ פֶרֶץ הָרֹאשׁ לְכָל־ שָׂרֵי
officers-of of-all-of the-chief Perez descendants-of from (3) thousand

הַצְּבָאוֹת לַחֹדֶשׁ הָרִאשׁוֹן׃ וְעַל מַחֲלֹקֶת ׀ הַחֹדֶשׁ
the-month division-of and-over (4) the-first for-the-month the-armies

הַשֵּׁנִי דּוֹדַי הָאֲחוֹחִי וּמַחֲלֻקְתּוֹ וּמִקְלוֹת הַנָּגִיד
the-leader and-Mikloth and-division-of-him the-Ahohite Dodai the-second

וְעַל מַחֲלֻקְתּוֹ עֶשְׂרִים וְאַרְבָּעָה אָלֶף׃ שַׂר הַצָּבָא
the-army commander-of (5) thousand and-four twenty division-of-him and-in

הַשְּׁלִישִׁי לַחֹדֶשׁ הַשְּׁלִישִׁי בְּנָיָהוּ בֶּן־ יְהוֹיָדָע הַכֹּהֵן רֹאשׁ
chief the-priest Jehoiada son-of Benaiah the-third for-the-month the-third

וְעַל מַחֲלֻקְתּוֹ עֶשְׂרִים וְאַרְבָּעָה אָלֶף׃ הוּא בְנָיָהוּ גִּבּוֹר
mighty-man-of Benaiah this (6) thousand and-four twenty division-of-him and-in

הַשְּׁלֹשִׁים וְעַל־ הַשְּׁלֹשִׁים וּמַחֲלֻקְתּוֹ עַמִּיזָבָד בְּנוֹ׃
son-of-him Ammizabad and-division-of-him the-Thirty and-over the-Thirty

הָרְבִיעִי לַחֹדֶשׁ הָרְבִיעִי עֲשָׂה־אֵל אֲחִי יוֹאָב וּזְבַדְיָה
and-Zebadiah Joab brother-of El Asah the-fourth for-the-month the-fourth (7)

בְנוֹ אַחֲרָיו וְעַל מַחֲלֻקְתּוֹ עֶשְׂרִים וְאַרְבָּעָה אָלֶף׃
thousand and-four twenty division-of-him and-in after-him son-of-him

הַחֲמִישִׁי* לַחֹדֶשׁ הַחֲמִישִׁי הַשַּׂר שַׁמְהוּת הַיִּזְרָח
the-Izrahite Shamhuth the-commander the-fifth for-the-month the-fifth (8)

וְעַל מַחֲלֻקְתּוֹ עֶשְׂרִים וְאַרְבָּעָה אָלֶף׃ הַשִּׁשִּׁי לַחֹדֶשׁ
for-the-month the-sixth (9) thousand and-four twenty division-of-him and-in

הַשִּׁשִּׁי עִירָא בֶן־ עִקֵּשׁ הַתְּקוֹעִי וְעַל מַחֲלֻקְתּוֹ עֶשְׂרִים
twenty division-of-him and-in the-Tekoite Ikkesh son-of Ira the-sixth

וְאַרְבָּעָה אָלֶף׃ הַשְּׁבִיעִי לַחֹדֶשׁ הַשְּׁבִיעִי חֶלֶץ
Helez the-seventh for-the-month the-seventh (10) thousand and-four

הַפְּלוֹנִי מִן־ בְּנֵי אֶפְרָיִם וְעַל מַחֲלֻקְתּוֹ עֶשְׂרִים וְאַרְבָּעָה
and-four twenty division-of-him and-in Ephraim sons-of from the-Pelonite

אָלֶף׃ הַשְּׁמִינִי לַחֹדֶשׁ הַשְּׁמִינִי סִבְּכַי הַחֻשָׁתִי
the-Hushathite Sibbecai the-eighth for-the-month the-eighth (11) thousand

לַזַּרְחִי וְעַל מַחֲלֻקְתּוֹ עֶשְׂרִים וְאַרְבָּעָה אָלֶף׃
thousand and-four twenty division-of-him and-in of-the-Zerahite

הַתְּשִׁיעִי לַחֹדֶשׁ הַתְּשִׁיעִי אֲבִיעֶזֶר הָעַנְּתֹתִי
the-Anathothite Abiezer the-ninth for-the-month the-ninth (12)

לַבֶּנְיָמִינִי וְעַל מַחֲלֻקְתּוֹ עֶשְׂרִים וְאַרְבָּעָה אָלֶף׃
thousand and-four twenty division-of-him and-in of-the-Benjamite

was Jashobeam son of Zabdiel. There were 24,000 men in his division.
[3]He was a descendant of Perez and chief of all the army officers for the first month.
[4]In charge of the division for the second month was Dodai the Ahohite; Mikloth was the leader of his division. There were 24,000 men in his division.
[5]The third army commander, for the third month, was Benaiah son of Jehoiada the priest. He was chief and there were 24,000 men in his division. [6]This was the Benaiah who was a mighty man among the Thirty and was over the Thirty. His son Ammizabad was in charge of his division.
[7]The fourth, for the fourth month, was Asahel the brother of Joab; his son Zebadiah was his successor. There were 24,000 men in his division.
[8]The fifth, for the fifth month, was the commander Shamhuth the Izrahite. There were 24,000 men in his division.
[9]The sixth, for the sixth month, was Ira the son of Ikkesh the Tekoite. There were 24,000 men in his division.
[10]The seventh, for the seventh month, was Helez the Pelonite, an Ephraimite. There were 24,000 men in his division.
[11]The eighth, for the eighth month, was Sibbecai the Hushathite, a Zerahite. There were 24,000 men in his division.
[12]The ninth, for the ninth month, was Abiezer the Anathothite, a Benjamite. There were 24,000 men in his division.

*8 Most mss have *hateph pathah* under the *beth* (הַחֲ).

°12 ק לבן ימיני

הָעֲשִׂירִי לַחֹדֶשׁ הָעֲשִׂירִי מַהְרַי הַנְּטוֹפָתִי
the-Netophathite Maharai the-tenth for-the-month the-tenth (13)

לַזַּרְחִי וְעַל מַחֲלֻקְתּוֹ עֶשְׂרִים וְאַרְבָּעָה אָלֶף׃ עַשְׁתֵּי־
one (14) thousand and-four twenty division-of-him and-in of-the-Zerahite

עָשָׂר לְעַשְׁתֵּי־עָשָׂר הַחֹדֶשׁ בְּנָיָה הַפִּרְעָתוֹנִי מִן־ בְּנֵי אֶפְרָיִם
Ephraim sons-of from the-Pirathonite Benaiah the-month ten for-one ten

וְעַל מַחֲלֻקְתּוֹ עֶשְׂרִים וְאַרְבָּעָה אָלֶף׃ הַשְּׁנֵים עָשָׂר לִשְׁנֵים
for-two ten the-two (15) thousand and-four twenty division-of-him and-in

עָשָׂר הַחֹדֶשׁ חֶלְדַּי הַנְּטוֹפָתִי לְעָתְנִיאֵל וְעַל מַחֲלֻקְתּוֹ
division-of-him and-in of-Othniel the-Netophathite Heldai the-month ten

עֶשְׂרִים וְאַרְבָּעָה אָלֶף׃ וְעַל שִׁבְטֵי יִשְׂרָאֵל לָרְאוּבֵנִי
over-the-Reubenite Israel tribes-of and-over (16) thousand and-four twenty

נָגִיד אֱלִיעֶזֶר בֶּן־ זִכְרִי לַשִּׁמְעוֹנִי שְׁפַטְיָהוּ בֶּן־ מַעֲכָה׃
Maacah son-of Shephatiah over-the-Simeonite Zicri son-of Eliezer officer

לְלֵוִי חֲשַׁבְיָה בֶּן־ קְמוּאֵל לְאַהֲרֹן צָדוֹק׃ לִיהוּדָה
over-Judah (18) Zadok over-Aaron Kemuel son-of Hashabiah over-Levi (17)

אֱלִיהוּ מֵאֲחֵי דָוִיד לְיִשָּׂשכָר עָמְרִי בֶּן־ מִיכָאֵל׃
Michael son-of Omri over-Issachar David from-brothers-of Elihu

לִזְבוּלֻן יִשְׁמַעְיָהוּ בֶּן־ עֹבַדְיָהוּ לְנַפְתָּלִי יְרִימוֹת בֶּן־
son-of Jerimoth over-Naphtali Obadiah son-of Ishmaiah over-Zebulun (19)

עַזְרִיאֵל׃ לִבְנֵי אֶפְרַיִם הוֹשֵׁעַ בֶּן־ עֲזַזְיָהוּ לַחֲצִי שֵׁבֶט
tribe-of over-half-of Azaziah son-of Hoshea Ephraim over-sons-of (20) Azriel

מְנַשֶּׁה יוֹאֵל בֶּן־ פְּדָיָהוּ׃ לַחֲצִי הַמְנַשֶּׁה גִּלְעָדָה יִדּוֹ
Iddo in-Gilead the-Manasseh over-half-of (21) Pedaiah son-of Joel Manasseh

בֶּן־ זְכַרְיָהוּ לְבִנְיָמִן יַעֲשִׂיאֵל בֶּן־ אַבְנֵר׃ לְדָן עֲזַרְאֵל
Azarel over-Dan (22) Abner son-of Jaasiel over-Benjamin Zechariah son-of

בֶּן־ יְרֹחָם אֵלֶּה שָׂרֵי שִׁבְטֵי יִשְׂרָאֵל׃ וְלֹא־ נָשָׂא
he-took and-not (23) Israel tribes-of officers-of these Jeroham son-of

דָּוִיד מִסְפָּרָם לְמִבֶּן עֶשְׂרִים שָׁנָה וּלְמַטָּה כִּי
because or-of-less year twenty of-from-son-of from-number-of-them David

אָמַר יְהוָה לְהַרְבּוֹת אֶת־ יִשְׂרָאֵל כְּכוֹכְבֵי הַשָּׁמָיִם׃
the-skies as-stars-of Israel *** to-make-numerous Yahweh he-promised

יוֹאָב בֶּן־ צְרוּיָה הֵחֵל לִמְנוֹת וְלֹא כִלָּה וַיְהִי
and-he-came he-finished but-not to-count he-began Zeruiah son-of Joab (24)

בָּזֹאת קֶצֶף עַל־יִשְׂרָאֵל וְלֹא עָלָה הַמִּסְפָּר בְּמִסְפַּר
in-number-of the-number he-entered and-not Israel on wrath on-account-of-this

דִּבְרֵי־ הַיָּמִים לַמֶּלֶךְ דָּוִיד׃ וְעַל אֹצְרוֹת הַמֶּלֶךְ
the-king storehouses-of and-over (25) David of-the-king the-days annals-of

13 The tenth, for the tenth month, was Maharai the Netophathite, a Zerahite. There were 24,000 men in his division.
14 The eleventh, for the eleventh month, was Benaiah the Pirathonite, an Ephraimite. There were 24,000 men in his division.
15 The twelfth, for the twelfth month, was Heldai the Netophathite, from the family of Othniel. There were 24,000 men in his division.

*Officers of the Tribes*

16 The officers over the tribes of Israel:

over the Reubenites: Eliezer son of Zicri;
over the Simeonites: Shephatiah son of Maacah;
17 over Levi: Hashabiah son of Kemuel;
over Aaron: Zadok;
18 over Judah: Elihu, a brother of David;
over Issachar: Omri son of Michael;
19 over Zebulun: Ishmaiah son of Obadiah;
over Naphtali: Jerimoth son of Azriel;
20 over the Ephraimites: Hoshea son of Azaziah;
over half the tribe of Manasseh: Joel son of Pedaiah;
21 over the half-tribe of Manasseh in Gilead: Iddo son of Zechariah;
over Benjamin: Jaasiel son of Abner;
22 over Dan: Azarel son of Jeroham.

These were the officers over the tribes of Israel.

23 David did not take the number of the men twenty years old or less, because the LORD had promised to make Israel as numerous as the stars in the sky. 24 Joab son of Zeruiah began to count the men but did not finish. Wrath came on Israel on account of this numbering, and the number was not entered in the book[°] of the annals of King David.

*The King's Overseers*

25 Azmaveth son of Adiel was in charge of the royal storehouses.

[°]24 Septuagint; Hebrew *number*

עַזְמָוֶת בֶּן־ עֲדִיאֵל וְעַל הָאֹצָרוֹת בַּשָּׂדֶה בֶּעָרִים
in-the-towns in-the-field the-storehouses and-over Adiel son-of Azmaveth

וּבַכְּפָרִים וּבַמִּגְדָּלוֹת יְהוֹנָתָן בֶּן־ עֻזִּיָּהוּ׃
Uzziah son-of Jonathan and-in-the-watchtowers and-in-the-villages

(26) וְעַל עֹשֵׂי מְלֶאכֶת הַשָּׂדֶה לַעֲבֹדַת הָאֲדָמָה עֶזְרִי בֶּן־
son-of Ezri the-land to-farm the-field work-of ones-doing-of and-over (26)

כְּלוּב׃ (27) וְעַל־ הַכְּרָמִים שִׁמְעִי הָרָמָתִי וְעַל
and-over the-Ramathite Shimei the-vineyards and-over (27) Kelub

שֶׁבַּכְּרָמִים לְאֹצְרוֹת הַיַּיִן זַבְדִּי הַשִּׁפְמִי׃
the-Shiphmite Zabdi the-wine for-vats-of what-from-the-vineyards

(28) וְעַל־ הַזֵּיתִים וְהַשִּׁקְמִים אֲשֶׁר בַּשְּׁפֵלָה
in-the-foothill that and-the-sycamore-trees the-olive-trees and-over (28)

בַּעַל חָנָן הַגְּדֵרִי וְעַל־ אֹצְרוֹת הַשֶּׁמֶן יוֹעָשׁ׃
Joash the-olive-oil supplies-of and-over the-Gederite Hanan Baal

(29) וְעַל־ הַבָּקָר הָרֹעִים בַּשָּׁרוֹן שִׁטְרַי הַשָּׁרוֹנִי
the-Sharonite Shitrai in-the-Sharon the-ones-grazing the-herd and-over (29)

וְעַל־ הַבָּקָר בָּעֲמָקִים שָׁפָט בֶּן־ עַדְלָי׃ (30) וְעַל־
and-over (30) Adlai son-of Shaphat in-the-valleys the-herd and-over

הַגְּמַלִּים אוֹבִיל הַיִּשְׁמְעֵלִי וְעַל־ הָאֲתֹנוֹת יֶחְדְּיָהוּ הַמֵּרֹנֹתִי׃
the-Meronothite Jehdeiah the-donkeys and-over the-Ishmaelite Obil the-camels

(31) וְעַל־ הַצֹּאן יָזִיז הַהַגְרִי כָּל־ אֵלֶּה שָׂרֵי
officials-of these all-of the-Hagrite Jaziz the-flock and-over (31)

הָרְכוּשׁ אֲשֶׁר לַמֶּלֶךְ דָּוִיד׃ (32) וִיהוֹנָתָן דּוֹד־ דָּוִיד
David uncle-of and-Jonathan (32) David to-the-king that the-property

יוֹעֵץ אִישׁ־ מֵבִין וְסוֹפֵר הוּא וִיחִיאֵל בֶּן־ חַכְמוֹנִי
Hacmoni son-of and-Jehiel he and-scribe having-insight man-of one-counseling

עִם־ בְּנֵי הַמֶּלֶךְ׃ (33) וַאֲחִיתֹפֶל יוֹעֵץ לַמֶּלֶךְ
to-the-king one-counseling and-Ahithophel (33) the-king sons-of with

וְחוּשַׁי הָאַרְכִּי רֵעַ הַמֶּלֶךְ׃ (34) וְאַחֲרֵי אֲחִיתֹפֶל יְהוֹיָדָע
Jehoiada Ahithophel and-after (34) the-king friend-of the-Arkite and-Hushai

בֶּן־ בְּנָיָהוּ וְאֶבְיָתָר וְשַׂר־ צָבָא לַמֶּלֶךְ יוֹאָב׃
Joab of-the-king army and-commander-of and-Abiathar Benaiah son-of

(28:1) וַיַּקְהֵל דָּוִיד אֶת־ כָּל־ שָׂרֵי יִשְׂרָאֵל שָׂרֵי
officers-of Israel officials-of all-of *** David and-he-summoned (28:1)

הַשְּׁבָטִים וְשָׂרֵי הַמַּחְלְקוֹת הַמְשָׁרְתִים אֶת־ הַמֶּלֶךְ
the-king *** the-ones-serving the-divisions and-commanders-of the-tribes

וְשָׂרֵי הָאֲלָפִים וְשָׂרֵי הַמֵּאוֹת וְשָׂרֵי
and-officials-of the-hundreds and-commanders-of the-thousands and-commanders-of

Jonathan son of Uzziah was
in charge of the storehouses in
the outlying districts, in the
towns, the villages and the
watchtowers.
26 Ezri son of Kelub was in
charge of the field workers
who farmed the land.
27 Shimei the Ramathite was
in charge of the vineyards.
Zabdi the Shiphmite was in
charge of the produce of the
vineyards for the wine vats.
28 Baal-Hanan the Gederite
was in charge of the olive and
sycamore-fig trees in the western foothills.
Joash was in charge of the
supplies of olive oil.
29 Shitrai the Sharonite was
in charge of the herds grazing
in Sharon.
Shaphat son of Adlai was in
charge of the herds in the valleys.
30 Obil the Ishmaelite was in
charge of the camels.
Jehdeiah the Meronothite
was in charge of the donkeys.
31 Jaziz the Hagrite was in
charge of the flocks.
All these were the officials in
charge of King David's property.

32 Jonathan, David's uncle,
was a counselor, a man of insight and a scribe. Jehiel son of
Hacmoni took care of the
king's sons.
33 Ahithophel was the king's
counselor.
Hushai the Arkite was the
king's friend. 34 Ahithophel
was succeeded by Jehoiada
son of Benaiah and by Abiathar.
Joab was the commander of
the royal army.

*David's Plans for the Temple*

28 David summoned all
the officials of Israel to
assemble at Jerusalem: the
officers over the tribes, the
commanders of the divisions
in the service of the king, the
commanders of thousands
and commanders of hundreds,
and the officials in charge of

°29 ק שרטי

כָּל־ רְכוּשׁ־ וּמִקְנֶה ׀ לַמֶּלֶךְ וּלְבָנָיו עִם־
with and-of-sons-of-him of-the-king and-livestock property all-of

הַסָּרִיסִים וְהַגִּבּוֹרִים וּלְכָל־ גִּבּוֹר חָיִל
bravery warrior-of and-to-all-of and-the-mighty-men the-palace-officials

אֶל־ יְרוּשָׁלָ͏ִם׃ וַיָּקָם דָּוִיד הַמֶּלֶךְ עַל־ רַגְלָיו וַיֹּאמֶר
and-he-said feet-of-him to the-king David and-he-rose (2) Jerusalem to

שְׁמָעוּנִי אַחַי וְעַמִּי אֲנִי עִם־ לְבָבִי לִבְנוֹת
to-build heart-of-me in I and-people-of-me brothers-of-me listen-to-me!

בֵּית מְנוּחָה לַאֲרוֹן בְּרִית־ יְהוָה וְלַהֲדֹם רַגְלֵי
feet-of even-for-footstool-of Yahweh covenant-of for-ark-of rest house-of

אֱלֹהֵינוּ וַהֲכִינוֹתִי לִבְנוֹת׃ וְהָאֱלֹהִים אָמַר לִי לֹא־
not to-me he-said but-the-God (3) to-build and-I-made-plans God-of-us

תִבְנֶה בַיִת לִשְׁמִי כִּי אִישׁ מִלְחָמוֹת אַתָּה וְדָמִים
and-bloods you wars man-of because for-Name-of-me house you-will-build

שָׁפָכְתָּ׃ וַיִּבְחַר יְהוָה אֱלֹהֵי יִשְׂרָאֵל בִּי מִכֹּל בֵּית־
family-of from-whole-of to-me Israel God-of Yahweh yet-he-chose (4) you-shed

אָבִי לִהְיוֹת לְמֶלֶךְ עַל־ יִשְׂרָאֵל לְעוֹלָם כִּי בִיהוּדָה בָּחַר
he-chose to-Judah indeed to-forever Israel over as-king to-be father-of-me

לְנָגִיד וּבְבֵית יְהוּדָה בֵּית אָבִי וּבִבְנֵי
and-from-sons-of father-of-me family-of Judah and-from-house-of as-leader

אָבִי בִּי רָצָה לְהַמְלִיךְ עַל־ כָּל־יִשְׂרָאֵל׃
Israel all-of over to-make-king he-was-pleased with-me father-of-me

וּמִכָּל־ בָּנַי כִּי רַבִּים בָּנִים נָתַן לִי יְהוָה
Yahweh to-me he-gave sons many indeed sons-of-me and-of-all-of (5)

וַיִּבְחַר בִּשְׁלֹמֹה בְנִי לָשֶׁבֶת עַל־ כִּסֵּא מַלְכוּת יְהוָה
Yahweh kingdom-of throne-of on to-sit son-of-me to-Solomon now-he-chose

עַל־ יִשְׂרָאֵל׃ וַיֹּאמֶר לִי שְׁלֹמֹה בִנְךָ הוּא־ יִבְנֶה
he-will-build he son-of-you Solomon to-me and-he-said (6) Israel over

בֵיתִי וַחֲצֵרוֹתָי כִּי־ בָחַרְתִּי בוֹ לִי לְבֵן וַאֲנִי
and-I as-son for-me to-him I-chose for and-courts-of-me house-of-me

אֶהְיֶה־ לּוֹ לְאָב׃ וַהֲכִינוֹתִי אֶת־ מַלְכוּתוֹ עַד־
to kingdom-of-him *** and-I-will-establish (7) as-father to-him I-will-be

לְעוֹלָם אִם־ יֶחֱזַק לַעֲשׂוֹת מִצְוֹתַי וּמִשְׁפָּטַי
and-laws-of-me commands-of-me to-carry-out he-will-be-unswerving if to-forever

כַּיּוֹם הַזֶּה׃ וְעַתָּה לְעֵינֵי כָל־ יִשְׂרָאֵל קְהַל־ יְהוָה
Yahweh assembly-of Israel all-of in-eyes-of so-now (8) the-this as-the-day

וּבְאָזְנֵי אֱלֹהֵינוּ שִׁמְרוּ וְדִרְשׁוּ כָּל־ מִצְוֹת יְהוָה
Yahweh commands-of all-of and-follow! be-careful! God-of-us and-in-ears-of

all the property and livestock belonging to the king and his sons, together with the palace officials, the mighty men and all the brave warriors.
[2]King David rose to his feet and said: "Listen to me, my brothers and my people. I had it in my heart to build a house as a place of rest for the ark of the covenant of the LORD, for the footstool of our God, and I made plans to build it.
[3]But God said to me, 'You are not to build a house for my Name, because you are a warrior and have shed blood.'
[4]"Yet the LORD, the God of Israel, chose me from my whole family to be king over Israel forever. He chose Judah as leader, and from the house of Judah he chose my family, and from my father's sons he was pleased to make me king over all Israel.
[5]Of all my sons—and the LORD has given me many—he has chosen my son Solomon to sit on the throne of the kingdom of the LORD over Israel.
[6]He said to me: 'Solomon your son is the one who will build my house and my courts, for I have chosen him to be my son, and I will be his father.
[7]I will establish his kingdom forever if he is unswerving in carrying out my commands and laws, as is being done at this time.'
[8]"So now I charge you in the sight of all Israel and of the assembly of the LORD, and in the hearing of our God: Be careful to follow all the commands of the LORD your God,

אֱלֹהֵיכֶם לְמַעַן תִּירְשׁוּ אֶת־ הָאָרֶץ הַטּוֹבָה וְהִנְחַלְתֶּם
and-you-may-pass-on the-good the-land *** you-may-possess so-that God-of-you

לִבְנֵיכֶם אַחֲרֵיכֶם עַד־ עוֹלָם׃ וְאַתָּה שְׁלֹמֹה־ בְנִי
son-of-me Solomon and-you (9) forever to after-you to-descendants-of-you

דַּע אֶת־ אֱלֹהֵי אָבִיךָ וְעָבְדֵהוּ בְּלֵב שָׁלֵם
whole with-heart and-serve-him! father-of-you God-of *** acknowledge!

וּבְנֶפֶשׁ חֲפֵצָה כִּי כָל־ לְבָבוֹת דּוֹרֵשׁ יְהוָה וְכָל־
and-every-of Yahweh searching hearts all-of for willing and-with-mind

יֵצֶר מַחֲשָׁבוֹת מֵבִין אִם־ תִּדְרְשֶׁנּוּ יִמָּצֵא לָךְ
by-you he-will-be-found you-seek-him if understanding thoughts motive-of

וְאִם־ תַּעַזְבֶנּוּ יַזְנִיחֲךָ לָעַד׃ רְאֵה׀ עַתָּה כִּי־
for now consider! (10) for-ever he-will-reject-you you-forsake-him but-if

יְהוָה בָּחַר בְּךָ לִבְנוֹת־ בַּיִת לַמִּקְדָּשׁ חֲזַק
be-strong! as-the-sanctuary temple to-build to-you he-chose Yahweh

וַעֲשֵׂה׃ וַיִּתֵּן דָּוִיד לִשְׁלֹמֹה בְנוֹ אֶת־ תַּבְנִית
plan-of *** son-of-him to-Solomon David then-he-gave (11) and-do-work!

הָאוּלָם וְאֶת־ בָּתָּיו וְגַנְזַכָּיו וַעֲלִיֹּתָיו
and-upper-parts-of-him and-storerooms-of-him buildings-of-him and the-portico

וַחֲדָרָיו הַפְּנִימִים וּבֵית הַכַּפֹּרֶת׃ וְתַבְנִית
and-plan-of (12) the-atonement and-place-of the-inner-ones and-rooms-of-him

כֹּל אֲשֶׁר הָיָה בָרוּחַ עִמּוֹ לְחַצְרוֹת בֵּית־ יְהוָה
Yahweh temple-of for-courts-of in-him by-the-Spirit he-was that all

וּלְכָל־ הַלְּשָׁכוֹת סָבִיב לְאֹצְרוֹת בֵּית הָאֱלֹהִים
the-God temple-of for-treasuries-of surrounding the-rooms and-for-all-of

וּלְאֹצְרוֹת הַקֳּדָשִׁים׃ וּלְמַחְלְקוֹת
and-for-divisions-of (13) the-dedicated-things and-for-treasuries-of

הַכֹּהֲנִים וְהַלְוִיִּם וּלְכָל־ מְלֶאכֶת עֲבוֹדַת בֵּית־
temple-of service-of work-of and-for-all-of and-the-Levites the-priests

יְהוָה וּלְכָל־ כְּלֵי עֲבוֹדַת בֵּית־ יְהוָה׃
Yahweh temple-of service-of articles-of and-for-all-of Yahweh

לַזָּהָב בַּמִּשְׁקָל לַזָּהָב לְכָל־ כְּלֵי עֲבוֹדָה
service articles-of for-all-of for-the-gold by-the-weight for-the-gold (14)

וַעֲבוֹדָה לְכֹל כְּלֵי הַכֶּסֶף בְּמִשְׁקָל לְכָל־
for-all-of by-weight the-silver articles-of for-all-of and-service

כְּלֵי עֲבוֹדָה וַעֲבוֹדָה׃ וּמִשְׁקָל לִמְנֹרוֹת הַזָּהָב
the-gold for-lampstands-of and-weight (15) and-service service articles-of

וְנֵרֹתֵיהֶם זָהָב בְּמִשְׁקַל־ מְנוֹרָה וּמְנוֹרָה
and-lampstand lampstand with-weight-of gold and-lamps-of-them

that you may possess this
good land and pass it on as an
inheritance to your descendants forever.
9 "And you, my son Solo-
mon, acknowledge the God of
your father, and serve him
with wholehearted devotion
and with a willing mind, for
the LORD searches every heart
and understands every motive
behind the thoughts. If you
seek him, he will be found by
you; but if you forsake him, he
will reject you forever. 10 Consider now, for the LORD has
chosen you to build a temple
as a sanctuary. Be strong and
do the work."
11 Then David gave his son
Solomon the plans for the portico of the temple, its buildings, its storerooms, its upper
parts, its inner rooms and the
place of atonement. 12 He gave
him the plans of all that the
Spirit had put in his mind for
the courts of the temple of the
LORD and all the surrounding
rooms, for the treasuries of the
temple of God and for the
treasuries for the dedicated
things. 13 He gave him instructions for the divisions of the
priests and Levites, and for all
the work of serving in the
temple of the LORD, as well as
for all the articles to be used in
its service. 14 He designated the
weight of gold for all the gold
articles to be used in various
kinds of service, and the
weight of silver for all the silver articles to be used in various kinds of service: 15 the
weight of gold for the gold
lampstands and their lamps,
with the weight for each

וְנֵרֹתֶיהָ וְלִמְנֹרוֹת הַכֶּסֶף בְּמִשְׁקָל לִמְנוֹרָה
of-lampstand with-weight the-silver and-for-lampstands-of and-lamps-of-her

וְנֵרֹתֶיהָ כַּעֲבוֹדַת מְנוֹרָה וּמְנוֹרָה׃ (16) וְאֶת־ הַזָּהָב מִשְׁקָל
weight the-gold and (16) and-lampstand lampstand as-use-of and-lamps-of-her

לְשֻׁלְחֲנוֹת הַמַּעֲרֶכֶת לְשֻׁלְחַן* וְשֻׁלְחָן וְכֶסֶף
and-silver and-table for-table the-consecrated-bread for-tables-of

לְשֻׁלְחֲנוֹת הַכָּסֶף׃ (17) וְהַמִּזְלָגוֹת וְהַמִּזְרָקוֹת
and-the-sprinkling-bowls and-the-forks (17) the-silver for-tables-of

וְהַקְּשָׂוֹת זָהָב טָהוֹר וְלִכְפוֹרֵי הַזָּהָב בְּמִשְׁקָל לִכְפוֹר
for-dish by-weight the-gold and-for-dishes-of pure gold and-the-pitchers

וּכְפוֹר וְלִכְפוֹרֵי הַכֶּסֶף בְּמִשְׁקָל לִכְפוֹר וּכְפוֹר׃
and-dish for-dish by-weight the-silver and-for-dishes-of and-dish

(18) וּלְמִזְבַּח הַקְּטֹרֶת זָהָב מְזֻקָּק בַּמִּשְׁקָל
by-the-weight being-refined gold the-incense and-for-altar-of (18)

וּלְתַבְנִית הַמֶּרְכָּבָה הַכְּרֻבִים זָהָב לְפֹרְשִׂים
for-ones-spreading gold the-cherubim the-chariot and-for-plan-of

וְסֹכְכִים עַל־ אֲרוֹן בְּרִית־ יְהוָה׃ (19) הַכֹּל בִּכְתָב
in-writing the-whole (19) Yahweh covenant-of ark-of over and-ones-sheltering

מִיַּד יְהוָה עָלַי הִשְׂכִּיל כֹּל מַלְאֲכוֹת הַתַּבְנִית׃
the-plan details-of all-of he-gave-understanding on-me Yahweh because-hand-of

(20) וַיֹּאמֶר דָּוִיד לִשְׁלֹמֹה בְּנוֹ חֲזַק וֶאֱמַץ
and-be-courageous! be-strong! son-of-him to-Solomon David and-he-said (20)

וַעֲשֵׂה אַל־ תִּירָא וְאַל־ תֵּחָת כִּי יְהוָה אֱלֹהִים
God Yahweh for you-be-discouraged and-not you-be-afraid not and-do-work!

אֱלֹהַי עִמָּךְ לֹא יַרְפְּךָ וְלֹא יַעַזְבֶךָּ עַד־
until he-will-forsake-you and-not he-will-fail-you not with-you God-of-me

לִכְלוֹת כָּל־ מְלֶאכֶת עֲבוֹדַת בֵּית־ יְהוָה׃ (21) וְהִנֵּה
now-see! (21) Yahweh temple-of service-of work-of all-of to-be-finished

מַחְלְקוֹת הַכֹּהֲנִים וְהַלְוִיִּם לְכָל־ עֲבוֹדַת בֵּית
temple-of work-of for-all-of and-the-Levites the-priests divisions-of

הָאֱלֹהִים וְעִמְּךָ בְכָל־ מְלָאכָה לְכָל־ נָדִיב בַּחָכְמָה
with-the-skill one-willing from-every-of work in-all-of and-with-you the-God

לְכָל־ עֲבוֹדָה וְהַשָּׂרִים וְכָל־ הָעָם לְכָל־
in-all-of the-people and-all-of and-the-officials craft in-any-of

דְּבָרֶיךָ׃ (29:1) וַיֹּאמֶר דָּוִיד הַמֶּלֶךְ לְכָל־ הַקָּהָל
the-assembly to-whole-of the-king David then-he-said (29:1) commands-of-you

שְׁלֹמֹה בְנִי אֶחָד בָּחַר־ בּוֹ אֱלֹהִים נַעַר וָרָךְ
and-inexperienced young God to-him he-chose one son-of-me Solomon

lampstand and its lamps; and the weight of silver for each silver lampstand and its lamps, according to the use of each lampstand; [16]the weight of gold for each table for consecrated bread; the weight of silver for the silver tables; [17]the weight of pure gold for the forks, sprinkling bowls and pitchers; the weight of gold for each gold dish; the weight of silver for each silver dish; [18]and the weight of the refined gold for the altar of incense. He also gave him the plan for the chariot, that is, the cherubim of gold that spread their wings and shelter the ark of the covenant of the LORD.
[19]"All this is in writing," David said, "because the hand of the LORD was upon me, and he gave me understanding in all the details of the plan."
[20]David also said to Solomon his son, "Be strong and courageous, and do the work. Do not be afraid or discouraged, for the LORD God, my God, is with you. He will not fail you or forsake you until all the work for the service of the temple of the LORD is finished.
[21]The divisions of the priests and Levites are ready for all the work on the temple of God, and every willing man skilled in any craft will help you in all the work. The officials and all the people will obey your every command."

### *Gifts for Building the Temple*

29 Then King David said to the whole assembly: "My son Solomon, the one whom God has chosen, is young and inexperienced. The

*16 Most mss have *qamets* under the *beth* (חָן־).

וְהַמְּלָאכָה גְדוֹלָה כִּי לֹא לְאָדָם הַבִּירָה כִּי לַיהוָה אֱלֹהִים׃

God for-Yahweh but the-palace for-man not for great and-the-task

וּכְכָל־ כֹּחִי הֲכִינוֹתִי לְבֵית־ אֱלֹהַי

God-of-me for-temple-of I-provided resource-of-me and-with-all-of (2)

הַזָּהָב ׀ לַזָּהָב וְהַכֶּסֶף לַכֶּסֶף וְהַנְּחֹשֶׁת

and-the-bronze for-the-silver and-the-silver for-the-gold the-gold

לַנְּחֹשֶׁת הַבַּרְזֶל לַבַּרְזֶל וְהָעֵצִים לָעֵצִים אַבְנֵי־

stones-of for-the-woods and-the-woods for-the-iron the-iron for-the-bronze

שֹׁהַם וּמִלּוּאִים אַבְנֵי־ פוּךְ[a] וְרִקְמָה וְכֹל אֶבֶן

stone and-every-of and-colored-stone turquoise stones-of and-settings onyx

יְקָרָה וְאַבְנֵי־ שַׁיִשׁ לָרֹב׃ וְעוֹד בִּרְצוֹתִי

in-to-devote-me and-besides (3) as-many marble and-stones-of fine

בְּבֵית אֱלֹהַי יֶשׁ־ לִי סְגֻלָּה זָהָב וָכָסֶף נָתַתִּי

I-give and-silver gold treasure of-me there-is God-of-me to-temple-of

לְבֵית־ אֱלֹהַי לְמַעְלָה מִכָּל־ הֲכִינוֹתִי לְבֵית הַקֹּדֶשׁ׃

the-holiness for-temple-of I-provided over-all to-above God-of-me for-temple-of

שְׁלֹשֶׁת אֲלָפִים כִּכְּרֵי זָהָב מִזְּהַב אוֹפִיר וְשִׁבְעַת

and-seven-of Ophir of-gold-of gold talents-of thousands three-of (4)

אֲלָפִים כִּכַּר־ כֶּסֶף מְזֻקָּק לָטוּחַ קִירוֹת הַבָּתִּים׃

the-buildings walls-of to-overlay being-refined silver talent-of thousands

לַזָּהָב לַזָּהָב וְלַכֶּסֶף לַכֶּסֶף וּלְכָל־

and-for-all-of for-the-silver and-for-the-silver for-the-gold for-the-gold (5)

מְלָאכָה בְּיַד חָרָשִׁים וּמִי מִתְנַדֵּב לְמַלֹּאות יָדוֹ

hand-of-him to-consecrate one-willing now-who? craftsmen by-hand-of work

הַיּוֹם לַיהוָה׃ וַיִּתְנַדְּבוּ שָׂרֵי הָאָבוֹת

the-fathers leaders-of then-they-gave-willingly (6) to-Yahweh the-day

וְשָׂרֵי ׀ שִׁבְטֵי יִשְׂרָאֵל וְשָׂרֵי הָאֲלָפִים

the-thousands and-commanders-of Israel tribes-of and-officers-of

וְהַמֵּאוֹת וּלְשָׂרֵי מְלֶאכֶת הַמֶּלֶךְ׃ וַיִּתְּנוּ

and-they-gave (7) the-king work-of and-of-officials-of and-the-hundreds

לַעֲבוֹדַת בֵּית־ הָאֱלֹהִים זָהָב כִּכָּרִים חֲמֵשֶׁת־ אֲלָפִים וַאֲדַרְכֹנִים*

and-darics thousands five-of talents gold the-God temple-of to-work-of

רִבּוֹ וְכֶסֶף כִּכָּרִים עֲשֶׂרֶת אֲלָפִים וּנְחֹשֶׁת רִבּוֹ

ten-thousand and-bronze thousands ten-of talents and-silver ten-thousand

וּשְׁמוֹנַת אֲלָפִים כִּכָּרִים וּבַרְזֶל מֵאָה־ אֶלֶף כִּכָּרִים׃

talents thousand hundred and-iron talents thousands and-eight-of

וְהַנִּמְצָא אִתּוֹ אֲבָנִים נָתְנוּ לְאוֹצַר

to-treasury-of they-gave stones with-him and-the-one-being-found (8)

task is great, because this palatial structure is not for man but for the LORD God. [2]With all my resources I have provided for the temple of my God—gold for the gold work, silver for the silver, bronze for the bronze, iron for the iron and wood for the wood, as well as onyx for the settings, turquoise, stones of various colors, and all kinds of fine stone and marble—all of these in large quantities. [3]Besides, in my devotion to the temple of my God I now give my personal treasures of gold and silver for the temple of my God, over and above everything I have provided for this holy temple: [4]three thousand talents[p] of gold (gold of Ophir) and seven thousand talents[q] of refined silver, for the overlaying of the walls of the buildings, [5]for the gold work and the silver work, and for all the work to be done by the craftsmen. Now, who is willing to consecrate himself today to the LORD?"

[6]Then the leaders of families, the officers of the tribes of Israel, the commanders of thousands and commanders of hundreds, and the officials in charge of the king's work gave willingly. [7]They gave toward the work on the temple of God five thousand talents[r] and ten thousand darics[s] of gold, ten thousand talents[t] of silver, eighteen thousand talents[u] of bronze and a hundred thousand talents[v] of iron. [8]Any who had precious stones gave them to the treasury of

[p]4 That is, about 110 tons (about 100 metric tons)
[q]4 That is, about 260 tons (about 240 metric tons)
[r]7 That is, about 190 tons (about 170 metric tons)
[s]7 That is, about 185 pounds (about 84 kilograms)
[t]7 That is, about 375 tons (about 345 metric tons)
[u]7 That is, about 675 tons (about 610 metric tons)
[v]7 That is, about 3,750 tons (about 3,450 metric tons)

*7 Most mss have *dagesh* in the *kaph* (כֹּנִים—).

בֵּית־ יְהוָה עַל יַד־ יְחִיאֵל הַגֵּרְשֻׁנִּי׃ וַיִּשְׂמְחוּ
and-they-rejoiced (9) the-Gershonite Jehiel hand-of into Yahweh temple-of

הָעָם עַל־ הִתְנַדְּבָם כִּי בְּלֵב שָׁלֵם הִתְנַדְּבוּ
they-gave-freely whole with-heart for to-be-willing-them at the-people

לַיהוָה וְגַם דָּוִיד הַמֶּלֶךְ שָׂמַח שִׂמְחָה גְדוֹלָה׃ וַיְבָרֶךְ
and-he-praised (10) great joy he-rejoiced the-king David and-also to-Yahweh

דָּוִיד אֶת־ יְהוָה לְעֵינֵי כָּל־ הַקָּהָל וַיֹּאמֶר דָּוִיד
David and-he-said the-assembly whole-of in-eyes-of Yahweh *** David

בָּרוּךְ אַתָּה יְהוָה אֱלֹהֵי יִשְׂרָאֵל אָבִינוּ מֵעוֹלָם וְעַד־
and-to from-everlasting father-of-us Israel God-of Yahweh you being-praised

עוֹלָם׃ לְךָ יְהוָה הַגְּדֻלָּה וְהַגְּבוּרָה וְהַתִּפְאֶרֶת
and-the-glory and-the-power the-greatness Yahweh to-you (11) everlasting

וְהַנֵּצַח וְהַהוֹד כִּי־ כֹל בַּשָּׁמַיִם וּבָאָרֶץ
and-in-the-earth in-the-heavens all for and-the-splendor and-the-majesty

לְךָ יְהוָה הַמַּמְלָכָה וְהַמִּתְנַשֵּׂא לְכֹל ׀ לְרֹאשׁ׃
as-head over-all and-the-one-being-exalted the-kingdom Yahweh to-you

וְהָעֹשֶׁר וְהַכָּבוֹד מִלְּפָנֶיךָ וְאַתָּה מוֹשֵׁל
one-ruling and-you from-before-you and-the-honor and-the-wealth (12)

בַּכֹּל וּבְיָדְךָ כֹּחַ וּגְבוּרָה וּבְיָדְךָ
and-in-hand-of-you and-power strength and-in-hand-of-you over-the-all

לְגַדֵּל וּלְחַזֵּק לַכֹּל׃ וְעַתָּה אֱלֹהֵינוּ
God-of-us and-now (13) to-the-all and-to-give-strength to-exalt

מוֹדִים אֲנַחְנוּ לָךְ וּמְהַלְלִים לְשֵׁם תִּפְאַרְתֶּךָ׃
glory-of-you to-name-of and-ones-praising to-you we ones-giving-thanks

וְכִי מִי אֲנִי וּמִי עַמִּי כִּי־ נַעְצֹר כֹּחַ
ability we-should-have that people-of-me and-who? I who? but-indeed (14)

לְהִתְנַדֵּב כָּזֹאת כִּי־ מִמְּךָ הַכֹּל וּמִיָּדְךָ נָתַנּוּ
we-gave and-from-hand-of-you the-all from-you for as-this to-give-generously

לָךְ׃ כִּי־ גֵרִים אֲנַחְנוּ לְפָנֶיךָ וְתוֹשָׁבִים כְּכָל־ אֲבֹתֵינוּ
fathers-of-us as-all-of and-strangers before-you we aliens for (15) to-you

כַּצֵּל ׀ יָמֵינוּ עַל־ הָאָרֶץ וְאֵין מִקְוֶה׃ יְהוָה
Yahweh (16) hope and-there-is-no the-earth on days-of-us like-the-shadow

אֱלֹהֵינוּ כֹל* הֶהָמוֹן הַזֶּה אֲשֶׁר הֲכִינֹנוּ לִבְנוֹת־ לְךָ
for-you to-build we-provided that the-this the-abundance all-of God-of-us

בַיִת לְשֵׁם קָדְשֶׁךָ מִיָּדְךָ הִיא° וּלְךָ הַכֹּל׃
the-all and-to-you he from-hand-of-you Holiness-of-you for-Name-of temple

וְיָדַעְתִּי אֱלֹהַי כִּי אַתָּה בֹּחֵן לֵבָב וּמֵישָׁרִים תִּרְצֶה
you-enjoy and-integrities heart one-testing you that God-of-me and-I-know (17)

the temple of the LORD in the
custody of Jehiel the Gershonite. 9The people rejoiced
at the willing response of
their leaders, for they had
given freely and wholeheartedly to the LORD. David the
king also rejoiced greatly.

*David's Prayer*

10David praised the LORD in
the presence of the whole assembly, saying,

"Praise be to you, O LORD,
God of our father Israel,
from everlasting to
everlasting.
11Yours, O LORD, is the
greatness and the
power
and the glory and the
majesty and the
splendor,
for everything in heaven
and earth is yours.
Yours, O LORD, is the
kingdom;
you are exalted as head
over all.
12Wealth and honor come
from you;
you are the ruler of all
things.
In your hands are strength
and power
to exalt and give strength
to all.
13Now, our God, we give you
thanks,
and praise your glorious
name.

14"But who am I, and who
are my people, that we should
be able to give as generously
as this? Everything comes
from you, and we have given
you only what comes from
your hand. 15We are aliens and
strangers in your sight, as
were all our forefathers. Our
days on earth are like a shadow, without hope. 16O LORD
our God, as for all this abundance that we have provided
for building you a temple for
your Holy Name, it comes
from your hand, and all of it
belongs to you. 17I know, my
God, that you test the heart
and are pleased with integrity.

*16 Most mss have *dagesh* in the *kaph* (כֹּל).

°16 ק הוּא

אֲנִי בְּיֹשֶׁר לְבָבִי הִתְנַדַּבְתִּי כָל־ אֵלֶּה וְעַתָּה
and-now these all-of I-gave-willingly intent-of-me in-honesty-of I

עַמְּךָ הַנִּמְצְאוּ־ פֹה רָאִיתִי בְשִׂמְחָה לְהִתְנַדֶּב־ לָךְ׃
to-you to-give-willingly with-joy I-saw here who-they-are-found people-of-you

יְהוָה אֱלֹהֵי אַבְרָהָם יִצְחָק וְיִשְׂרָאֵל אֲבֹתֵינוּ שָׁמְרָה־זֹּאת
this keep! fathers-of-us and-Israel Isaac Abraham God-of Yahweh (18)

לְעוֹלָם לְיֵצֶר מַחְשְׁבוֹת לְבַב עַמֶּךָ וְהָכֵן
and-keep-loyal! people-of-you heart-of thoughts-of as-desire-of to-forever

לְבָבָם אֵלֶיךָ׃ וְלִשְׁלֹמֹה בְנִי תֵּן לֵבָב שָׁלֵם לִשְׁמוֹר
to-keep whole heart give! son-of-me and-to-Solomon (19) to-you heart-of-them

מִצְוֹתֶיךָ עֵדְוֹתֶיךָ וְחֻקֶּיךָ וְלַעֲשׂוֹת הַכֹּל
the-everything and-to-do and-decrees-of-you requirements-of-you commands-of-you

וְלִבְנוֹת הַבִּירָה אֲשֶׁר־ הֲכִינוֹתִי׃ וַיֹּאמֶר דָּוִיד לְכָל־
to-whole-of David then-he-said (20) I-provided which the-palace and-to-build

הַקָּהָל בָּרְכוּ־ נָא אֶת־ יְהוָה אֱלֹהֵיכֶם וַיְבָרְכוּ כָל־
whole-of so-they-praised God-of-you Yahweh *** now! praise! the-assembly

הַקָּהָל לַיהוָה אֱלֹהֵי אֲבֹתֵיהֶם וַיִּקְּדוּ
and-they-bowed-low fathers-of-them God-of to-Yahweh the-assembly

וַיִּשְׁתַּחֲווּ לַיהוָה וְלַמֶּלֶךְ׃
and-before-the-king before-Yahweh and-they-fell-prostrate

וַיִּזְבְּחוּ לַיהוָה ׀ זְבָחִים וַיַּעֲלוּ עֹלוֹת
burnt-offerings and-they-presented sacrifices to-Yahweh and-they-sacrificed (21)

לַיהוָה לְמָחֳרַת הַיּוֹם הַהוּא פָּרִים אֶלֶף אֵילִים אֶלֶף
thousand rams thousand bulls the-that the-day on-next-day-of to-Yahweh

כְּבָשִׂים אֶלֶף וְנִסְכֵּיהֶם וּזְבָחִים לָרֹב
in-abundance and-sacrifices and-drink-offerings-of-them thousand male-lambs

לְכָל־ יִשְׂרָאֵל׃ וַיֹּאכְלוּ וַיִּשְׁתּוּ לִפְנֵי יְהוָה
Yahweh in-presences-of and-they-drank and-they-ate (22) Israel for-all-of

בַּיּוֹם הַהוּא בְּשִׂמְחָה גְדוֹלָה וַיַּמְלִיכוּ שֵׁנִית
second-time then-they-acknowledged-as-king great with-joy the-that on-the-day

לִשְׁלֹמֹה בֶן־ דָּוִיד וַיִּמְשְׁחוּ לַיהוָה לְנָגִיד
as-ruler before-Yahweh and-they-anointed David son-of to-Solomon

וּלְצָדוֹק לְכֹהֵן׃ וַיֵּשֶׁב שְׁלֹמֹה עַל־ כִּסֵּא יְהוָה ׀ לְמֶלֶךְ
as-king Yahweh throne-of on Solomon so-he-sat (23) as-priest and-to-Zadok

תַּחַת־ דָּוִיד אָבִיו וַיַּצְלַח וַיִּשְׁמְעוּ אֵלָיו
to-him and-they-obeyed and-he-prospered father-of-him David in-place-of

כָּל־ יִשְׂרָאֵל׃ וְכָל־ הַשָּׂרִים וְהַגִּבֹּרִים וְגַם
and-also and-the-mighty-men the-officers and-all-of (24) Israel all-of

All these things have I given willingly and with honest intent. And now I have seen with joy how willingly your people who are here have given to you. 18 O LORD, God of our fathers Abraham, Isaac and Israel, keep this desire in the hearts of your people forever, and keep their hearts loyal to you. 19 And give my son Solomon the wholehearted devotion to keep your commands, requirements and decrees and to do everything to build the palatial structure for which I have provided."

20 Then David said to the whole assembly, "Praise the LORD your God." So they all praised the LORD, the God of their fathers; they bowed low and fell prostrate before the LORD and the king.

*Solomon Acknowledged as King*

21 The next day they made sacrifices to the LORD and presented burnt offerings to him: a thousand bulls, a thousand rams and a thousand male lambs, together with their drink offerings, and other sacrifices in abundance for all Israel. 22 They ate and drank with great joy in the presence of the LORD that day.

Then they acknowledged Solomon son of David as king a second time, anointing him before the LORD to be ruler and Zadok to be priest. 23 So Solomon sat on the throne of the LORD as king in place of his father David. He prospered and all Israel obeyed him. 24 All the officers and mighty men,

כָּל־ בְּנֵי הַמֶּלֶךְ דָּוִיד נָתְנוּ יָד תַּחַת שְׁלֹמֹה הַמֶּלֶךְ׃
the-king Solomon under hand they-put David the-king sons-of all-of

(25) וַיְגַדֵּל יְהוָה אֶת־ שְׁלֹמֹה לְמַעְלָה לְעֵינֵי כָּל־ יִשְׂרָאֵל
Israel all-of in-eyes-of to-upward Solomon *** Yahweh and-he-exalted (25)

וַיִּתֵּן עָלָיו הוֹד מַלְכוּת אֲשֶׁר לֹא־ הָיָה עַל־ כָּל־ מֶלֶךְ
king any-of on he-was not that royalty splendor-of on-him and-he-bestowed

לְפָנָיו עַל־יִשְׂרָאֵל׃ (26) וְדָוִיד בֶּן־ יִשַׁי מָלַךְ עַל־ כָּל־
all-of over he-was-king Jesse son-of and-David (26) Israel over before-him

יִשְׂרָאֵל׃ (27) וְהַיָּמִים אֲשֶׁר מָלַךְ עַל־יִשְׂרָאֵל אַרְבָּעִים שָׁנָה בְּחֶבְרוֹן
in-Hebron year forty Israel over he-ruled which and-the-days (27) Israel

מָלַךְ שֶׁבַע שָׁנִים וּבִירוּשָׁלַםִ מָלַךְ שְׁלֹשִׁים וְשָׁלוֹשׁ׃
and-three thirty he-ruled and-in-Jerusalem years seven he-ruled

(28) וַיָּמָת בְּשֵׂיבָה טוֹבָה שְׂבַע יָמִים עֹשֶׁר וְכָבוֹד
and-honor wealth days full-of good at-old-age and-he-died (28)

וַיִּמְלֹךְ שְׁלֹמֹה בְנוֹ תַּחְתָּיו׃ (29) וְדִבְרֵי
and-events-of (29) in-place-of-him son-of-him Solomon and-he-became-king

דָּוִיד הַמֶּלֶךְ הָרִאשֹׁנִים וְהָאֲחרֹנִים* הִנָּם כְּתוּבִים
ones-being-written see-they! and-the-ends the-beginnings the-king David

עַל־ דִּבְרֵי שְׁמוּאֵל הָרֹאֶה וְעַל־ דִּבְרֵי נָתָן הַנָּבִיא
the-prophet Nathan records-of and-in the-seer Samuel records-of in

וְעַל־ דִּבְרֵי גָּד הַחֹזֶה׃ (30) עִם כָּל־ מַלְכוּתוֹ
reign-of-him all-of with (30) the-seer Gad records-of and-in

וּגְבוּרָתוֹ וְהָעִתִּים אֲשֶׁר עָבְרוּ עָלָיו
around-him they-surrounded that and-the-circumstances and-power-of-him

וְעַל־ יִשְׂרָאֵל וְעַל כָּל־ מַמְלְכוֹת הָאֲרָצוֹת׃
the-lands kingdoms-of all-of and-around Israel and-around

as well as all of King David's sons, pledged their submission to King Solomon.
[25]The LORD highly exalted Solomon in the sight of all Israel and bestowed on him royal splendor such as no king over Israel ever had before.

*The Death of David*

[26]David son of Jesse was king over all Israel.
[27]He ruled over Israel forty years—seven in Hebron and thirty-three in Jerusalem.
[28]He died at a good old age, having enjoyed long life, wealth and honor. His son Solomon succeeded him as king.
[29]As for the events of King David's reign, from beginning to end, they are written in the records of Samuel the seer, the records of Nathan the prophet and the records of Gad the seer,
[30]together with the details of his reign and power, and the circumstances that surrounded him and Israel and the kingdoms of all the other lands.

*29 Most mss have *pathah* under the *aleph* and *hateph pathah* under the *beth* (אַחֲ–).

וַיִּתְחַזֵּק שְׁלֹמֹה בֶן־ דָּוִיד עַל־ מַלְכוּתוֹ
kingdom-of-him over David son-of Solomon and-he-established-himself (1:1)

וַיהוָה אֱלֹהָיו עִמּוֹ וַיְגַדְּלֵהוּ לְמָעְלָה׃
to-upward and-he-made-great-him with-him God-of-him for-Yahweh

וַיֹּאמֶר שְׁלֹמֹה לְכָל־ יִשְׂרָאֵל לְשָׂרֵי הָאֲלָפִים
the-thousands to-commanders-of Israel to-all-of Solomon then-he-spoke (2)

וְהַמֵּאוֹת וְלַשֹּׁפְטִים וּלְכֹל נָשִׂיא לְכָל־
in-all-of leader and-to-all-of and-to-the-ones-being-judges and-the-hundreds

יִשְׂרָאֵל רָאשֵׁי הָאָבוֹת׃ וַיֵּלְכוּ שְׁלֹמֹה וְכָל־ הַקָּהָל
the-assembly and-all-of Solomon and-they-went (3) the-fathers heads-of Israel

עִמּוֹ לַבָּמָה אֲשֶׁר בְּגִבְעוֹן כִּי־ שָׁם הָיָה אֹהֶל
Tent-of he-was there for at-Gibeon that to-the-high-place with-him

מוֹעֵד הָאֱלֹהִים אֲשֶׁר עָשָׂה מֹשֶׁה עֶבֶד־ יְהוָה בַּמִּדְבָּר׃
in-the-desert Yahweh servant-of Moses he-made which the-God Meeting-of

אֲבָל אֲרוֹן הָאֱלֹהִים הֶעֱלָה דָוִיד מִקִּרְיַת יְעָרִים
Jearim from-Kiriath David he-brought-up the-God ark-of now (4)

בַּהֵכִין לוֹ דָּוִיד כִּי נָטָה־ לוֹ אֹהֶל
tent for-him he-pitched because David for-him to-what-he-prepared

בִּירוּשָׁלִָם׃ וּמִזְבַּח הַנְּחֹשֶׁת אֲשֶׁר עָשָׂה בְּצַלְאֵל בֶּן־ אוּרִי
Uri son-of Bezalel he-made that the-bronze but-altar-of (5) in-Jerusalem

בֶן־ חוּר שָׁם* לִפְנֵי מִשְׁכַּן יְהוָה וַיִּדְרְשֵׁהוּ
and-he-inquired-of-him Yahweh tabernacle-of in-front-of he-put Hur son-of

שְׁלֹמֹה וְהַקָּהָל׃ וַיַּעַל שְׁלֹמֹה שָׁם עַל־ מִזְבַּח
altar-of to there Solomon and-he-went-up (6) and-the-assembly Solomon

הַנְּחֹשֶׁת לִפְנֵי יְהוָה אֲשֶׁר לְאֹהֶל מוֹעֵד וַיַּעַל עָלָיו
on-him and-he-offered Meeting in-Tent-of that Yahweh before the-bronze

עֹלוֹת אָלֶף׃ בַּלַּיְלָה הַהוּא נִרְאָה אֱלֹהִים
God he-appeared the-that in-the-night (7) thousand burnt-offerings

לִשְׁלֹמֹה וַיֹּאמֶר לוֹ שְׁאַל מָה אֶתֶּן־ לָךְ׃
to-you I-should-give whatever ask! to-him and-he-said to-Solomon

וַיֹּאמֶר שְׁלֹמֹה לֵאלֹהִים אַתָּה עָשִׂיתָ עִם־ דָּוִיד אָבִי
father-of-me David to you-showed you to-God Solomon and-he-answered (8)

חֶסֶד גָּדוֹל וְהִמְלַכְתַּנִי תַּחְתָּיו׃ עַתָּה יְהוָה אֱלֹהִים
God Yahweh now (9) in-place-of-him and-you-made-king-me great kindness

יֵאָמֵן דְּבָרְךָ עִם דָּוִיד אָבִי כִּי אַתָּה
you for father-of-me David to promise-of-you let-him-be-confirmed

הִמְלַכְתַּנִי עַל־ עַם רַב כַּעֲפַר הָאָרֶץ׃ עַתָּה חָכְמָה
wisdom now (10) the-earth as-dust-of numerous people over you-made-king-me

*Solomon Asks for Wisdom*

1 Solomon son of David
established himself firmly
over his kingdom, for the
LORD his God was with him
and made him exceedingly
great.
[2]Then Solomon spoke to all
Israel—to the commanders of
thousands and commanders
of hundreds, to the judges and
to all the leaders in Israel, the
heads of families— [3]and Solomon and the whole assembly
went to the high place at Gibeon, for God's Tent of Meeting
was there, which Moses the
LORD's servant had made in
the desert. [4]Now David had
brought up the ark of God
from Kiriath Jearim to the
place he had prepared for it,
because he had pitched a tent
for it in Jerusalem. [5]But the
bronze altar that Bezalel son of
Uri, the son of Hur, had made
was in Gibeon in front of the
tabernacle of the LORD; so
Solomon and the assembly inquired of him there. [6]Solomon
went up to the bronze altar before the LORD in the Tent of
Meeting and offered a thousand burnt offerings on it.
[7]That night God appeared to
Solomon and said to him,
"Ask for whatever you want
me to give you."
[8]Solomon answered God,
"You have shown great kindness to David my father and
have made me king in his
place. [9]Now, LORD God, let
your promise to my father David be confirmed, for you have
made me king over a people
who are as numerous as the
dust of the earth. [10]Give me

*5 The NIV reads this word as שָׂם, *there.*

וּמַדָּע תֶּן־ לִי וְאֵצְאָה לִפְנֵי הָעָם־ הַזֶּה
the-this the-people before that-I-may-go-out to-me give! and-knowledge

וְאָבוֹאָה כִּי־ מִי יִשְׁפֹּט אֶת־ עַמְּךָ הַזֶּה
the-this people-of-you *** he-can-govern who? for and-I-may-come-in

הַגָּדוֹל׃ (11) וַיֹּאמֶר־ אֱלֹהִים ׀ לִשְׁלֹמֹה יַעַן אֲשֶׁר הָיְתָה זֹאת עִם־
in this she-was that since to-Solomon God and-he-said (11) the-great

לְבָבֶךָ וְלֹא־ שָׁאַלְתָּ עֹשֶׁר נְכָסִים וְכָבוֹד וְאֵת נֶפֶשׁ
life-of nor or-honor riches wealth you-asked and-not heart-of-you

שֹׂנְאֶיךָ וְגַם־ יָמִים רַבִּים לֹא שָׁאָלְתָּ וַתִּשְׁאַל־
but-you-asked you-asked not many days and-also ones-being-enemies-of-you

לְּךָ חָכְמָה וּמַדָּע אֲשֶׁר תִּשְׁפּוֹט אֶת־ עַמִּי אֲשֶׁר
whom people-of-me *** you-will-govern which and-knowledge wisdom for-you

הִמְלַכְתִּיךָ עָלָיו׃ (12) הַחָכְמָה וְהַמַּדָּע נָתוּן
being-given and-the-knowledge the-wisdom (12) over-him I-made-king-you

לָךְ וְעֹשֶׁר וּנְכָסִים וְכָבוֹד אֶתֶּן־ לָךְ אֲשֶׁר ׀ לֹא־ הָיָה
he-was not that to-you I-will-give and-honor and-riches also-wealth to-you

כֵּן לַמְּלָכִים אֲשֶׁר לְפָנֶיךָ וְאַחֲרֶיךָ לֹא יִהְיֶה־ כֵּן׃
such he-will-be not and-after-you before-you who to-the-kings such

(13) וַיָּבֹא שְׁלֹמֹה לַבָּמָה אֲשֶׁר־ בְּגִבְעוֹן יְרוּשָׁלִַם
Jerusalem in-Gibeon that from-the-high-place Solomon then-he-went (13)

מִלִּפְנֵי אֹהֶל מוֹעֵד וַיִּמְלֹךְ עַל־ יִשְׂרָאֵל׃ (14) וַיֶּאֱסֹף
and-he-accumulated (14) Israel over and-he-reigned Meeting Tent-of from-before

שְׁלֹמֹה רֶכֶב וּפָרָשִׁים וַיְהִי־ לוֹ אֶלֶף וְאַרְבַּע־ מֵאוֹת
hundreds and-four-of thousand to-him and-he-was and-horses chariot Solomon

רֶכֶב וּשְׁנֵים־ עָשָׂר אֶלֶף פָּרָשִׁים וַיַּנִּיחֵם בְּעָרֵי הָרֶכֶב
the-chariot in-cities-of and-he-kept-them horses thousand ten and-two chariot

וְעִם־ הַמֶּלֶךְ בִּירוּשָׁלִָם׃ (15) וַיִּתֵּן הַמֶּלֶךְ אֶת־ הַכֶּסֶף
the-silver *** the-king and-he-made (15) in-Jerusalem the-king and-with

וְאֶת־ הַזָּהָב בִּירוּשָׁלִַם כָּאֲבָנִים וְאֵת הָאֲרָזִים נָתַן
he-made the-cedars and like-the-stones in-Jerusalem the-gold and

כַּשִּׁקְמִים אֲשֶׁר־ בַּשְּׁפֵלָה לָרֹב׃
as-plentiful in-the-foothill that like-the-sycamore-fig-trees

(16) וּמוֹצָא הַסּוּסִים אֲשֶׁר לִשְׁלֹמֹה מִמִּצְרָיִם וּמִקְוֵא
and-from-Kue from-Egypt of-Solomon that the-horses and-import-of (16)

סֹחֲרֵי הַמֶּלֶךְ מִקְוֵא יִקְחוּ בִּמְחִיר׃
by-purchase they-acquired from-Kue the-king ones-being-merchants-of

(17) וַיַּעֲלוּ וַיּוֹצִיאוּ מִמִּצְרַיִם מֶרְכָּבָה בְּשֵׁשׁ
for-six-of chariot from-Egypt and-they-brought-out and-they-brought-up (17)

wisdom and knowledge, that I may lead this people, for who is able to govern this great people of yours?"
[11]God said to Solomon, "Since this is your heart's desire and you have not asked for wealth, riches or honor, nor for the death of your enemies, and since you have not asked for a long life but for wisdom and knowledge to govern my people over whom I have made you king,
[12]therefore wisdom and knowledge will be given you. And I will also give you wealth, riches and honor, such as no king who was before you ever had and none after you will have."
[13]Then Solomon went to Jerusalem from the high place at Gibeon, from before the Tent of Meeting. And he reigned over Israel.
[14]Solomon accumulated chariots and horses; he had fourteen hundred chariots and twelve thousand horses,[a] which he kept in the chariot cities and also with him in Jerusalem.
[15]The king made silver and gold as common in Jerusalem as stones, and cedar as plentiful as sycamore-fig trees in the foothills.
[16]Solomon's horses were imported from Egypt[b] and from Kue[c]—the royal merchants purchased them from Kue.
[17]They imported a chariot from Egypt for six hundred

[a]14 Or *charioteers*
[b]16 Or possibly *Muzur*, a region in Cilicia; also in verse 17
[c]16 Probably Cilicia

מֵאוֹת כֶּסֶף וְסוּס בַּחֲמִשִּׁים וּמֵאָה וְכֵן לְכָל־
to-all-of and-same and-hundred for-fifty and-horse silver hundreds

מַלְכֵי הַחִתִּים וּמַלְכֵי אֲרָם בְּיָדָם יוֹצִיאוּ׃
they-exported by-hand-of-them Aram and-kings-of the-Hittites kings-of

וַיֹּאמֶר שְׁלֹמֹה לִבְנוֹת בַּיִת לְשֵׁם יְהוָה וּבַיִת
and-palace Yahweh for-Name-of temple to-build Solomon and-he-ordered *(18)

לְמַלְכוּתוֹ׃ וַיִּסְפֹּר שְׁלֹמֹה שִׁבְעִים אֶלֶף אִישׁ
man thousand seventy Solomon and-he-conscripted (2:1) for-royalty-of-him

סַבָּל וּשְׁמוֹנִים אֶלֶף אִישׁ חֹצֵב בָּהָר וּמְנַצְּחִים
and-ones-being-foremen in-the-hill cutting man thousand and-eighty carrier

עֲלֵיהֶם שְׁלֹשֶׁת אֲלָפִים וְשֵׁשׁ מֵאוֹת׃ וַיִּשְׁלַח שְׁלֹמֹה
Solomon and-he-sent (2) hundreds and-six-of thousands three-of over-them

אֶל־ חוּרָם מֶלֶךְ־ צֹר לֵאמֹר כַּאֲשֶׁר עָשִׂיתָ עִם־ דָּוִיד אָבִי
father-of-me David for you-did just-as to-say Tyre king-of Huram to

וַתִּשְׁלַח־ לוֹ אֲרָזִים לִבְנוֹת־ לוֹ בַיִת לָשֶׁבֶת בּוֹ׃ הִנֵּה
see! (3) in-him to-live palace for-him to-build cedars to-him when-you-sent

אֲנִי בוֹנֶה־ בַיִת לְשֵׁם׀ יְהוָה אֱלֹהָי לְהַקְדִּישׁ לוֹ לְהַקְטִיר
to-burn to-him to-dedicate God-of-me Yahweh for-Name-of temple building I

לְפָנָיו קְטֹרֶת־ סַמִּים וּמַעֲרֶכֶת תָּמִיד
regularly and-consecrated-bread fragrances incense-of before-him

וְעֹלוֹת לַבֹּקֶר וְלָעֶרֶב לַשַּׁבָּתוֹת
on-the-Sabbaths and-for-the-evening for-the-morning and-burnt-offerings

וְלֶחֳדָשִׁים וּלְמוֹעֲדֵי יְהוָה אֱלֹהֵינוּ לְעוֹלָם
to-forever God-of-us Yahweh and-at-appointed-feasts-of and-on-the-New-Moons

זֹאת עַל־ יִשְׂרָאֵל׃ וְהַבַּיִת אֲשֶׁר־אֲנִי בוֹנֶה גָּדוֹל כִּי־ גָדוֹל
great because great building I that and-the-temple (4) Israel over this

אֱלֹהֵינוּ מִכָּל־ הָאֱלֹהִים׃ וּמִי יַעֲצָר־ כֹּחַ לִבְנוֹת־
to-build ability he-has but-who? (5) the-gods more-than-all-of God-of-us

לוֹ בַיִת כִּי הַשָּׁמַיִם וּשְׁמֵי הַשָּׁמַיִם לֹא
not the-heavens even-heavens-of the-heavens since temple for-him

יְכַלְכְּלֻהוּ וּמִי אֲנִי אֲשֶׁר אֶבְנֶה־ לּוֹ בַיִת כִּי
except temple for-him I-should-build that I then-who? they-can-contain-him

אִם־ לְהַקְטִיר לְפָנָיו׃ וְעַתָּה שְׁלַח־ לִי אִישׁ־ חָכָם
skilled man to-me send! so-now (6) before-him to-burn-sacrifice only

לַעֲשׂוֹת בַּזָּהָב וּבַכֶּסֶף וּבַנְּחֹשֶׁת וּבַבַּרְזֶל
and-in-the-iron and-in-the-bronze and-in-the-silver in-the-gold to-work

וּבָאַרְגְּוָן וְכַרְמִיל וּתְכֵלֶת וְיֹדֵעַ לְפַתֵּחַ
to-engrave and-being-experienced and-blue-yarn and-crimson and-in-the-purple

shekels[d] of silver, and a horse for a hundred and fifty.[e] They also exported them to all the kings of the Hittites and of the Arameans.

*Preparations for Building the Temple*

2 Solomon gave orders to build a temple for the Name of the LORD and a royal palace for himself. 2He conscripted seventy thousand men as carriers and eighty thousand as stonecutters in the hills and thirty-six hundred as foremen over them.

3Solomon sent this message to Hiram[f] king of Tyre:

"Send me cedar logs as you did for my father David when you sent him cedar to build a palace to live in. 4Now I am about to build a temple for the Name of the LORD my God and to dedicate it to him for burning fragrant incense before him, for setting out the consecrated bread regularly, and for making burnt offerings every morning and evening and on Sabbaths and New Moons and at the appointed feasts of the LORD our God. This is a lasting ordinance for Israel.

5"The temple I am going to build will be great, because our God is greater than all other gods. 6But who is able to build a temple for him, since the heavens, even the highest heavens, cannot contain him? Who then am I to build a temple for him, except as a place to burn sacrifices before him?

7"Send me, therefore, a man skilled to work in gold and silver, bronze and iron, and in purple, crimson and blue yarn, and experienced

d17 That is, about 15 pounds (about 7 kilograms)
e17 That is, about 3 3/4 pounds (about 1.7 kilograms)
f3 Hebrew *Huram*, a variant of *Hiram*; also in verses 11 and 12

*18 The Hebrew numeration of chapter 2 begins with verse 2 in the English; thus, there is a one-verse discrepancy throughout the chapter.

פִּתּוּחִים עִם־ הַחֲכָמִים אֲשֶׁר עִמִּי בִּיהוּדָה וּבִירוּשָׁלִַם
and-in-Jerusalem in-Judah with-me who the-skilled-craftsmen with engravings

אֲשֶׁר הֵכִין דָּוִיד אָבִי׃ וּשְׁלַח־ לִי עֲצֵי אֲרָזִים
cedars logs-of to-me and-send! (7) father-of-me David he-provided whom

בְּרוֹשִׁים וְאַלְגּוּמִּים מֵהַלְּבָנוֹן כִּי אֲנִי יָדַעְתִּי אֲשֶׁר עֲבָדֶיךָ
men-of-you that I-know I for from-the-Lebanon and-algums pines

יוֹדְעִים לִכְרוֹת עֲצֵי לְבָנוֹן וְהִנֵּה עֲבָדַי עִם־
with men-of-me and-see! Lebanon timbers-of to-cut ones-being-skilled

עֲבָדֶיךָ׃ וּלְהָכִין לִי עֵצִים לָרֹב כִּי הַבַּיִת
the-temple because as-plenty lumbers to-me and-to-provide (8) men-of-you

אֲשֶׁר־ אֲנִי בוֹנֶה גָּדוֹל וְהַפְלֵא׃ וְהִנֵּה
and-see! (9) and-to-be-magnificent large building I that

לַחֹטְבִים ׀ לְכֹרְתֵי ׀ הָעֵצִים נָתַתִּי חִטִּים ׀
wheats I-will-give the-timbers to-ones-cutting-of to-the-ones-being-woodsmen

מַכּוֹת לַעֲבָדֶיךָ כֹּרִים עֶשְׂרִים אֶלֶף וּשְׂעֹרִים כֹּרִים עֶשְׂרִים
twenty cors and-barleys thousand twenty cors to-servants-of-you ones-ground

אֶלֶף וְיַיִן בַּתִּים עֶשְׂרִים אֶלֶף וְשֶׁמֶן בַּתִּים עֶשְׂרִים אָלֶף׃
thousand twenty baths and-olive-oil thousand twenty baths and-wine thousand

וַיֹּאמֶר חוּרָם מֶלֶךְ־ צֹר בִּכְתָב וַיִּשְׁלַח אֶל־ שְׁלֹמֹה
Solomon to and-he-sent by-letter Tyre king-of Huram and-he-replied (10)

בְּאַהֲבַת יְהוָה אֶת־ עַמּוֹ נְתָנְךָ עֲלֵיהֶם מֶלֶךְ׃
king over-them he-made-you people-of-him *** Yahweh because-to-love

וַיֹּאמֶר חוּרָם בָּרוּךְ יְהוָה אֱלֹהֵי יִשְׂרָאֵל אֲשֶׁר עָשָׂה אֶת־
*** he-made who Israel God-of Yahweh being-praised Huram and-he-said (11)

הַשָּׁמַיִם וְאֶת־ הָאָרֶץ אֲשֶׁר נָתַן לְדָוִיד הַמֶּלֶךְ בֵּן חָכָם יוֹדֵעַ
knowing-of wise son the-king to-David he-gave who the-earth and the-heavens

שֵׂכֶל וּבִינָה אֲשֶׁר יִבְנֶה־ בַּיִת לַיהוָה וּבַיִת
and-palace for-Yahweh temple he-will-build who and-discernment intelligence

לְמַלְכוּתוֹ׃ וְעַתָּה שָׁלַחְתִּי אִישׁ־ חָכָם יוֹדֵעַ בִּינָה
discernment knowing-of skilled man I-send and-now (12) for-kingdom-of-him

לְחוּרָם אָבִי׃ בֶּן־ אִשָּׁה מִן־ בְּנוֹת דָּן וְאָבִיו
and-father-of-him Dan daughters-of from woman son-of (13) Abi namely-Huram

אִישׁ־ צֹרִי יוֹדֵעַ לַעֲשׂוֹת בַּזָּהָב־ וּבַכֶּסֶף בַּנְּחֹשֶׁת
in-the-bronze and-in-the-silver in-the-gold to-work being-trained Tyrian man

בַּבַּרְזֶל בָּאֲבָנִים וּבָעֵצִים בָּאַרְגָּמָן בַּתְּכֵלֶת
with-the-blue-yarn with-the-purple and-in-the-woods in-the-stones in-the-iron

וּבַבּוּץ וּבַכַּרְמִיל וּלְפַתֵּחַ כָּל־ פִּתּוּחַ
engraving every-of and-to-engrave and-with-the-crimson and-with-the-fine-linen

in the art of engraving, to work in Judah and Jerusalem with my skilled craftsmen, whom my father David provided.

[8]"Send me also cedar, pine and algum[g] logs from Lebanon, for I know that your men are skilled in cutting timber there. My men will work with yours [9]to provide me with plenty of lumber, because the temple I build must be large and magnificent. [10]I will give your servants, the woodsmen who cut the timber, twenty thousand cors[h] of ground wheat, twenty thousand cors of barley, twenty thousand baths[i] of wine and twenty thousand baths of olive oil."

[11]Hiram king of Tyre replied by letter to Solomon:

"Because the LORD loves his people, he has made you their king."

[12]And Hiram added:

"Praise be to the LORD, the God of Israel, who made heaven and earth! He has given King David a wise son, endowed with intelligence and discernment, who will build a temple for the LORD and a palace for himself.

[13]"I am sending you Huram-Abi, a man of great skill, [14]whose mother was from Dan and whose father was from Tyre. He is trained to work in gold and silver, bronze and iron, stone and wood, and with purple and blue and crimson yarn and fine linen. He is experienced in all kinds

g8 Probably a variant of *almug;* possibly juniper
h10 That is, probably about 125,000 bushels (about 4,400 kiloliters)
i10 That is, probably about 115,000 gallons (about 440 kiloliters)

*See the note on page 85.

וְלַחְשֹׁב כָּל־ מַחֲשָׁבֶת אֲשֶׁר יִנָּתֶן־ לוֹ עִם־ חֲכָמֶיךָ
craftsmen-of-you with to-him he-is-given that design any-of and-to-execute

וְחַכְמֵי אֲדֹנִי דָּוִיד אָבִיךָ׃ וְעַתָּה הַחִטִּים
the-wheats and-now (14) father-of-you David lord-of-me and-craftsmen-of

וְהַשְּׂעֹרִים הַשֶּׁמֶן וְהַיַּיִן אֲשֶׁר אָמַר אֲדֹנִי
lord-of-me he-promised that and-the-wine the-olive-oil and-the-barleys

יִשְׁלַח לַעֲבָדָיו׃ וַאֲנַחְנוּ נִכְרֹת עֵצִים מִן־
from logs we-will-cut and-we (15) to-servants-of-him let-him-send

הַלְּבָנוֹן כְּכָל־ צָרְכֶּךָ וּנְבִיאֵם לְךָ רַפְסֹדוֹת עַל־יָם
sea by rafts to-you and-we-will-send-them need-of-you as-all-of the-Lebanon

יָפוֹ וְאַתָּה תַּעֲלֶה אֹתָם יְרוּשָׁלִָם׃ וַיִּסְפֹּר
then-he-took-census (16) Jerusalem them you-can-take-up then-you Joppa

שְׁלֹמֹה כָּל־ הָאֲנָשִׁים הַגֵּירִים אֲשֶׁר בְּאֶרֶץ יִשְׂרָאֵל אַחֲרֵי הַסְּפָר
the-census after Israel in-land-of who the-aliens the-men all-of Solomon

אֲשֶׁר סְפָרָם דָּוִיד אָבִיו וַיִּמָּצְאוּ מֵאָה
hundred and-they-were-found father-of-him David he-took-census-of-them that

וַחֲמִשִּׁים אֶלֶף וּשְׁלֹשֶׁת אֲלָפִים וְשֵׁשׁ מֵאוֹת׃
hundreds and-six-of thousands and-three-of thousand and-fifty

וַיַּעַשׂ מֵהֶם שִׁבְעִים אֶלֶף סַבָּל וּשְׁמֹנִים אֶלֶף
thousand and-eighty carrier thousand seventy of-them and-he-assigned (17)

חֹצֵב בָּהָר וּשְׁלֹשֶׁת אֲלָפִים וְשֵׁשׁ מֵאוֹת
hundreds and-six-of thousands and-three-of in-the-hill cutting

מְנַצְּחִים לְהַעֲבִיד אֶת־ הָעָם׃ וַיָּחֶל שְׁלֹמֹה
Solomon then-he-began (3:1) the-people *** to-make-work ones-being-foremen

לִבְנוֹת אֶת־ בֵּית־ יְהוָה בִּירוּשָׁלִַם בְּהַר הַמּוֹרִיָּה אֲשֶׁר
where the-Moriah on-Mount-of in-Jerusalem Yahweh temple-of *** to-build

נִרְאָה לְדָוִיד אָבִיהוּ אֲשֶׁר הֵכִין בִּמְקוֹם דָּוִיד
David on-place-of he-provided which father-of-him to-David he-appeared

בְּגֹרֶן אָרְנָן הַיְבוּסִי׃ וַיָּחֶל לִבְנוֹת
to-build and-he-began (2) the-Jebusite Ornan on-threshing-floor-of

בַּחֹדֶשׁ הַשֵּׁנִי בַּשֵּׁנִי בִּשְׁנַת אַרְבַּע לְמַלְכוּתוֹ׃
of-reign-of-him four in-year-of on-the-second the-second in-the-month

וְאֵלֶּה הוּסַד שְׁלֹמֹה לִבְנוֹת אֶת־ בֵּית הָאֱלֹהִים
the-God temple-of *** to-build Solomon to-be-founded and-these (3)

הָאֹרֶךְ אַמּוֹת בַּמִּדָּה הָרִאשׁוֹנָה אַמּוֹת שִׁשִּׁים וְרֹחַב אַמּוֹת
cubits and-width sixty cubits the-old by-the-standard cubits the-length

עֶשְׂרִים׃ וְהָאוּלָם אֲשֶׁר עַל־ פְּנֵי הָאֹרֶךְ עַל־ פְּנֵי רֹחַב־
width-of fronts-of at the-length fronts-of at that and-the-portico (4) twenty

of engraving and can execute any design given to him. He will work with your craftsmen and with those of my lord, David your father.

15"Now let my lord send his servants the wheat and barley and the olive oil and wine he promised, 16and we will cut all the logs from Lebanon that you need and will float them in rafts by sea down to Joppa. You can then take them up to Jerusalem."

17Solomon took a census of all the aliens who were in Israel, after the census his father David had taken; and they were found to be 153,600. 18He assigned 70,000 of them to be carriers and 80,000 to be stonecutters in the hills, with 3,600 foremen over them to keep the people working.

*Solomon Builds the Temple*

3 Then Solomon began to build the temple of the LORD in Jerusalem on Mount Moriah, where the LORD had appeared to his father David. It was on the threshing floor of Araunah[j] the Jebusite, the place provided by David. 2He began building on the second day of the second month in the fourth year of his reign.

3The foundation Solomon laid for building the temple of God was sixty cubits long and twenty cubits wide[k] (using the cubit of the old standard). 4The

j1 Hebrew *Ornan,* a variant of *Araunah*
k3 That is, about 90 feet (about 27 meters) long and 30 feet (about 9 meters) wide

*See the note on page 85.

הַבַּיִת אַמּוֹת עֶשְׂרִים וְהַגֹּבַהּ מֵאָה וְעֶשְׂרִים וַיְצַפֵּהוּ
and-he-overlaid-him and-twenty hundred and-the-height twenty cubits the-temple

מִפְּנִימָה זָהָב טָהוֹר׃ וְאֵת הַבַּיִת הַגָּדוֹל חִפָּה עֵץ בְּרוֹשִׁים
pines wood-of he-paneled the-main the-hall and (5) pure gold on-inside

וַיְחַפֵּהוּ זָהָב טוֹב וַיַּעַל עָלָיו תִּמֹרִים וְשַׁרְשְׁרוֹת׃
and-chains palm-trees on-him and-he-decorated fine gold and-he-covered-him

וַיְצַף אֶת־ הַבַּיִת אֶבֶן יְקָרָה לְתִפְאָרֶת וְהַזָּהָב
and-the-gold for-beauty precious stone the-temple *** and-he-adorned (6)

זְהַב פַּרְוָיִם׃ וַיְחַף אֶת־ הַבַּיִת הַקֹּרוֹת
the-ceiling-beams the-temple *** and-he-overlaid (7) Parvaim gold-of

הַסִּפִּים וְקִירוֹתָיו וְדַלְתוֹתָיו זָהָב וּפִתַּח כְּרוּבִים
cherubim and-he-carved gold and-doors-of-him and-walls-of-him the-doorframes

עַל־ הַקִּירוֹת׃ וַיַּעַשׂ אֶת־ בֵּית־ קֹדֶשׁ הַקֳּדָשִׁים
the-Holy-Ones Most-Holy-of Place-of *** and-he-built (8) the-walls on

אָרְכּוֹ עַל־ פְּנֵי רֹחַב־ הַבַּיִת אַמּוֹת עֶשְׂרִים
twenty cubits the-temple width-of dimensions-of as length-of-him

וְרָחְבּוֹ אַמּוֹת עֶשְׂרִים וַיְחַפֵּהוּ זָהָב טוֹב לְכִכָּרִים
with-talents fine gold and-he-overlaid-him twenty cubits and-width-of-him

שֵׁשׁ מֵאוֹת׃ וּמִשְׁקָל לְמִסְמְרוֹת לִשְׁקָלִים חֲמִשִּׁים זָהָב
gold fifty in-shekels of-nails and-weight (9) hundreds six-of

וְהָעֲלִיּוֹת חִפָּה זָהָב׃ וַיַּעַשׂ בְּבֵית־
in-Place-of and-he-made (10) gold he-overlaid and-the-upper-parts

קֹדֶשׁ הַקֳּדָשִׁים כְּרוּבִים שְׁנַיִם מַעֲשֵׂה צַעֲצֻעִים וַיְצַפּוּ
and-they-overlaid sculptures work-of pair cherubim the-Holy-Ones Most-Holy-of

אֹתָם זָהָב׃ וְכַנְפֵי הַכְּרוּבִים אָרְכָּם אַמּוֹת עֶשְׂרִים כְּנַף
wing-of twenty cubits span-of-them the-cherubim and-wings-of (11) gold them

הָאֶחָד לְאַמּוֹת חָמֵשׁ מַגַּעַת לְקִיר הַבַּיִת וְהַכָּנָף הָאַחֶרֶת
the-other and-the-wing the-temple on-wall-of touching five in-cubits the-one

אַמּוֹת חָמֵשׁ מַגִּיעַ לִכְנַף הַכְּרוּב הָאַחֵר׃ וּכְנַף
and-wing-of (12) the-other the-cherub on-wing-of touching five cubits

הַכְּרוּב הָאֶחָד* אַמּוֹת חָמֵשׁ מַגִּיעַ לְקִיר הַבַּיִת וְהַכָּנָף
and-the-wing the-temple on-wall-of touching five cubits *the-one the-cherub

הָאַחֶרֶת אַמּוֹת חָמֵשׁ דְּבֵקָה לִכְנַף הַכְּרוּב הָאַחֵר׃ כַּנְפֵי
wings-of (13) the-other the-cherub on-wing-of touching five cubits the-other

הַכְּרוּבִים הָאֵלֶּה פֹּרְשִׂים אַמּוֹת עֶשְׂרִים וְהֵם עֹמְדִים
ones-standing and-they twenty cubits ones-extending the-these the-cherubim

עַל־ רַגְלֵיהֶם וּפְנֵיהֶם לַבָּיִת׃ וַיַּעַשׂ אֶת־
*** and-he-made (14) toward-the-hall and-faces-of-them feet-of-them on

portico at the front of the temple was twenty cubits[l] long across the width of the building and twenty cubits[m] high.

He overlaid the inside with pure gold. [5]He paneled the main hall with pine and covered it with fine gold and decorated it with palm tree and chain designs. [6]He adorned the temple with precious stones. And the gold he used was gold of Parvaim. [7]He overlaid the ceiling beams, doorframes, walls and doors of the temple with gold, and he carved cherubim on the walls.

[8]He built the Most Holy Place, its length corresponding to the width of the temple—twenty cubits long and twenty cubits wide. He overlaid the inside with six hundred talents[n] of fine gold. [9]The gold nails weighed fifty shekels.[o] He also overlaid the upper parts with gold.

[10]In the Most Holy Place he made a pair of sculptured cherubim and overlaid them with gold. [11]The total wingspan of the cherubim was twenty cubits. One wing of the first cherub was five cubits[p] long and touched the temple wall, while its other wing, also five cubits long, touched the wing of the other cherub. [12]Similarly one wing of the second cherub was five cubits long and touched the other temple wall, and its other wing, also five cubits long, touched the wing of the first cherub. [13]The wings of these cherubim extended twenty cubits. They stood on their feet, facing the main hall.[q]

[14]He made the curtain of

[l]4 That is, about 30 feet (about 9 meters); also in verses 8, 11 and 13
[m]4 Some Septuagint and Syriac manuscripts; Hebrew *a hundred and twenty*
[n]8 That is, about 23 tons (about 21 metric tons)
[o]9 That is, about 1 1/4 pounds (about 0.6 kilogram)
[p]11 That is, about 7 1/2 feet (about 2.3 meters); also in verse 15
[q]13 Or *facing inward*

*12 The NIV reads this word as the last (and vice versa), assuming the confusion of similar final letters.

הַפָּרֹ֫כֶת תְּכֵ֫לֶת וְאַרְגָּמָ֫ן וְכַרְמִ֫יל וּבוּץ וַיַּ֫עַל
the-curtain | blue-yarn | and-purple | and-crimson | and-fine-linen | and-he-worked

עָלָ֑יו כְּרוּבִֽים׃ (15) וַיַּ֫עַשׂ לִפְנֵ֣י הַבַּ֔יִת עַמּוּדִ֖ים שְׁנַ֔יִם
into-him | cherubim | (15) | and-he-made | in-front-of | the-temple | pillars | two

אַמּ֥וֹת שְׁלֹשִׁ֖ים וְחָמֵ֣שׁ אֹ֑רֶךְ וְהַצֶּ֗פֶת אֲשֶׁר־עַל־רֹאשׁ֖וֹ אַמּ֥וֹת חָמֵֽשׁ׃
cubits | thirty | and-five | length | and-the-capital | that | on top-of-him | cubits | five

(16) וַיַּ֤עַשׂ שַׁרְשְׁרוֹת֙ בַּדְּבִ֔יר וַיִּתֵּ֖ן עַל־רֹ֣אשׁ
(16) | and-he-made | chains | *in-the-inner-sanctuary | and-he-put | on | top-of

הָעַמֻּדִ֑ים וַיַּ֤עַשׂ רִמּוֹנִים֙ מֵאָ֔ה וַיִּתֵּ֖ן בַּֽשַּׁרְשְׁרֽוֹת׃
the-pillars | and-he-made | pomegranates | hundred | and-he-attached | to-the-chains

(17) וַיָּ֙קֶם֙ אֶת־הָ֣עַמּוּדִ֔ים עַל־פְּנֵ֖י הַהֵיכָ֑ל אֶחָ֥ד מִיָּמִ֖ין
(17) | and-he-erected | *** | the-pillars | in | front-of | the-temple | one | to-south

וְאֶחָ֣ד מֵֽהַשְּׂמֹ֑אול וַיִּקְרָ֤א שֵׁם־[הַיְמָנִי֙] יָכִ֔ין וְשֵׁ֥ם
and-one | to-the-north | and-he-called | name-of | the-southern | Jakin | and-name-of

הַשְּׂמָאלִ֖י בֹּֽעַז׃ (4:1) וַיַּ֙עַשׂ֙ מִזְבַּ֣ח נְחֹ֔שֶׁת עֶשְׂרִ֤ים אַמָּה֙ אָרְכּ֔וֹ
the-northern | Boaz | (4:1) | and-he-made | altar-of | bronze | twenty | cubit | length-of-him

וְעֶשְׂרִ֤ים אַמָּה֙ רָחְבּ֔וֹ וְעֶ֥שֶׂר אַמּ֖וֹת קוֹמָתֽוֹ׃ (2) וַיַּ֥עַשׂ
and-twenty | cubit | width-of-him | and-ten | cubits | height-of-him | (2) | and-he-made

אֶת־הַיָּ֖ם מוּצָ֑ק עֶ֣שֶׂר בָּֽאַמָּ֞ה מִשְּׂפָת֤וֹ אֶל־שְׂפָתוֹ֙
*** | the-Sea | being-cast | ten | by-the-cubit | from-rim-of-him | to | rim-of-him

עָג֣וֹל ׀ סָבִ֔יב וְחָמֵ֤שׁ בָּֽאַמָּה֙ קוֹמָת֔וֹ וְקָו֙ שְׁלֹשִׁ֣ים
circular | around | and-five | by-the-cubit | height-of-him | and-line | thirty

בָּֽאַמָּ֔ה יָסֹ֥ב אֹת֖וֹ סָבִֽיב׃ (3) וּדְמ֣וּת בְּקָרִים֩ תַּ֨חַת
by-the-cubit | he-measured-around | him | around | (3) | and-figure-of | bulls | below

ל֜וֹ ׀ סָבִ֤יב ׀ סוֹבְבִ֣ים אֹת֗וֹ עֶ֚שֶׂר בָּֽאַמָּ֔ה מַקִּיפִ֥ים
to-him | around | around | ones-encircling | him | ten | to-the-cubit | ones-encircling

אֶת־הַיָּ֖ם סָבִ֑יב שְׁנַ֤יִם טוּרִים֙ הַבָּקָ֔ר יְצוּקִ֖ים בְּמֻצַקְתּֽוֹ׃
*** | the-Sea | around | two | rows | the-bull | ones-being-cast | with-casting-of-him

(4) עֹמֵ֞ד עַל־שְׁנֵ֧ים עָשָׂ֣ר בָּקָ֗ר שְׁלֹשָׁ֣ה פֹנִ֣ים ׀ צָפ֟וֹנָה וּשְׁלוֹשָׁה֩
standing | on | two | ten | bull | three | ones-facing | to-north | and-three

פֹנִ֨ים ׀ יָ֜מָּה וּשְׁלֹשָׁ֣ה ׀ פֹּנִ֣ים נֶ֗גְבָּה וּשְׁלֹשָׁה֙ פֹּנִ֣ים
ones-facing | to-west | and-three | ones-facing | to-south | and-three | ones-facing

מִזְרָ֔חָה וְהַיָּ֥ם עֲלֵיהֶ֖ם מִלְמָ֑עְלָה וְכָל־אֲחֹרֵיהֶ֖ם
to-east | and-the-Sea | on-them | on-top | and-all-of | hindquarters-of-them

בָּֽיְתָה׃ (5) וְעָבְי֣וֹ טֶ֔פַח וּשְׂפָתוֹ֙ כְּמַעֲשֵׂ֣ה
toward-center | (5) | and-thickness-of-him | handbreadth | and-rim-of-him | like-work-of

שְׂפַת־כּ֔וֹס פֶּ֖רַח שֽׁוֹשַׁנָּ֑ה מַחֲזִ֣יק בַּתִּ֗ים שְׁלֹ֤שֶׁת אֲלָפִים֙ יָכִֽיל׃
rim-of | cup | blossom-of | lily | holding | baths | three-of | thousands | he-contained

---

blue, purple and crimson yarn and fine linen, with cherubim worked into it.

[15] In the front of the temple he made two pillars, which ⌊together⌋ were thirty-five cubits[r] long, each with a capital on top measuring five cubits. [16] He made interwoven chains[s] and put them on top of the pillars. He also made a hundred pomegranates and attached them to the chains. [17] He erected the pillars in the front of the temple, one to the south and one to the north. The one to the south he named Jakin[t] and the one to the north Boaz.[u]

*The Temple's Furnishings*

**4** He made a bronze altar twenty cubits long, twenty cubits wide and ten cubits high.[v] [2] He made the Sea of cast metal, circular in shape, measuring ten cubits from rim to rim and five cubits[w] high. It took a line of thirty cubits[x] to measure around it. [3] Below the rim, figures of bulls encircled it—ten to a cubit.[y] The bulls were cast in two rows in one piece with the Sea.

[4] The Sea stood on twelve bulls, three facing north, three facing west, three facing south and three facing east. The Sea rested on top of them, and their hindquarters were toward the center. [5] It was a handbreadth in thickness, and its rim was like the rim of a cup, like a lily blossom. It held three thousand baths.[z]

[r]15 That is, about 52 feet (about 16 meters)
[s]16 Or possibly *made chains in the inner sanctuary;* the meaning of the Hebrew for this phrase is uncertain.
[t]17 *Jakin* probably means *he establishes.*
[u]17 *Boaz* probably means *in him is strength.*
[v]1 That is, about 30 feet (about 9 meters) long and wide, and about 15 feet (about 4.5 meters) high
[w]2 That is, about 7 1/2 feet (about 2.3 meters)
[x]2 That is, about 45 feet (about 13.5 meters)
[y]3 That is, about 1 1/2 feet (about 0.5 meter)
[z]5 That is, about 17,500 gallons (about 66 kiloliters)

*16 Or possibly ( כְּרָבִיד ), *like-a-necklace* or *-weaving.*

°17 ק הימני

וַיַּעַשׂ כִּיּוֹרִים עֲשָׂרָה וַיִּתֵּן חֲמִשָּׁה מִיָּמִין וַחֲמִשָּׁה מִשְּׂמֹאול
on-north and-five on-south five and-he-placed ten basins then-he-made (6)

לְרָחְצָה בָהֶם אֶת־ מַעֲשֵׂה הָעוֹלָה יָדִיחוּ בָם
in-them they-rinsed the-burnt-offering thing-of *** in-them to-wash

וְהַיָּם לְרָחְצָה לַכֹּהֲנִים בּוֹ׃ וַיַּעַשׂ אֶת־ מְנֹרוֹת
lampstands-of *** and-he-made (7) in-him by-the-priests to-wash but-the-Sea

הַזָּהָב עֶשֶׂר כְּמִשְׁפָּטָם וַיִּתֵּן בַּהֵיכָל חָמֵשׁ
five in-the-temple and-he-placed as-specification-of-them ten the-gold

מִיָּמִין וְחָמֵשׁ מִשְּׂמֹאול׃ וַיַּעַשׂ שֻׁלְחָנוֹת עֲשָׂרָה וַיַּנַּח
and-he-placed ten tables and-he-made (8) on-north and-five on-south

בַּהֵיכָל חֲמִשָּׁה מִיָּמִין וַחֲמִשָּׁה מִשְּׂמֹאול וַיַּעַשׂ מִזְרְקֵי
sprinkling-bowls-of and-he-made on-north and-five on-south five in-the-temple

זָהָב מֵאָה׃ וַיַּעַשׂ חֲצַר הַכֹּהֲנִים וְהָעֲזָרָה הַגְּדוֹלָה
the-large and-the-court the-priests courtyard-of and-he-made (9) hundred gold

וּדְלָתוֹת לָעֲזָרָה וְדַלְתוֹתֵיהֶם צִפָּה נְחֹשֶׁת׃ וְאֶת־
and (10) bronze he-overlaid and-doors-of-them for-the-court and-doors

הַיָּם נָתַן מִכֶּתֶף הַיְמָנִית קֵדְמָה מִמּוּל נֶגְבָּה׃
to-south in-front-of to-east the-south on-side-of he-placed the-Sea

וַיַּעַשׂ חוּרָם אֶת־הַסִּירוֹת וְאֶת־ הַיָּעִים וְאֶת־ הַמִּזְרָקוֹת
the-sprinkling-bowls and the-shovels and the-pots *** Huram and-he-made (11)

וַיְכַל חִירָם לַעֲשׂוֹת אֶת־ הַמְּלָאכָה אֲשֶׁר עָשָׂה לַמֶּלֶךְ
for-the-king he-undertook that the-work *** to-do Huram so-he-finished

שְׁלֹמֹה בְּבֵית הָאֱלֹהִים׃ עַמּוּדִים שְׁנַיִם וְהַגֻּלּוֹת
and-the-bowl-shapes two pillars (12) the-God in-temple-of Solomon

וְהַכֹּתָרוֹת עַל־ רֹאשׁ הָעַמֻּדִים שְׁתָּיִם וְהַשְּׂבָכוֹת שְׁתַּיִם לְכַסּוֹת
to-decorate two and-the-networks two the-pillars top-of on and-the-capitals

אֶת־ שְׁתֵּי גֻּלּוֹת הַכֹּתָרוֹת אֲשֶׁר עַל־ רֹאשׁ הָעַמּוּדִים׃ וְאֶת־
and (13) the-pillars top-of on that the-capitals bowl-shapes-of two-of ***

הָרִמּוֹנִים אַרְבַּע מֵאוֹת לִשְׁתֵּי הַשְּׂבָכוֹת שְׁנַיִם טוּרִים
rows two the-networks for-two-of hundreds four-of the-pomegranates

רִמּוֹנִים לַשְּׂבָכָה הָאֶחָת לְכַסּוֹת אֶת־ שְׁתֵּי גֻּלּוֹת
bowl-shapes-of two-of *** to-decorate the-each for-the-network pomegranates

הַכֹּתָרוֹת אֲשֶׁר עַל־ פְּנֵי הָעַמּוּדִים׃ וְאֶת־ הַמְּכֹנוֹת עָשָׂה וְאֶת־
and he-made the-stands and (14) the-pillars tops-of on that the-capitals

הַכִּיֹּרוֹת עָשָׂה עַל־ הַמְּכֹנוֹת׃ אֶת־הַיָּם אֶחָד וְאֶת־ הַבָּקָר שְׁנֵים־עָשָׂר
ten two the-bull and one the-Sea *** (15) the-stands on he-made the-basins

תַּחְתָּיו׃ וְאֶת־הַסִּירוֹת וְאֶת־ הַיָּעִים וְאֶת־ הַמִּזְלָגוֹת וְאֶת־ כָּל־
all-of and the-meat-forks and the-shovels and the-pots and (16) under-him

[6]He then made ten basins for washing and placed five on the south side and five on the north. In them the things to be used for the burnt offerings were rinsed, but the Sea was to be used by the priests for washing.

[7]He made ten gold lampstands according to the specifications for them and placed them in the temple, five on the south side and five on the north.

[8]He made ten tables and placed them in the temple, five on the south side and five on the north. He also made a hundred gold sprinkling bowls.

[9]He made the courtyard of the priests, and the large court and the doors for the court, and overlaid the doors with bronze. [10]He placed the Sea on the south side, at the southeast corner.

[11]He also made the pots and shovels and sprinkling bowls.

So Huram finished the work he had undertaken for King Solomon in the temple of God:

[12]the two pillars;
the two bowl-shaped capitals on top of the pillars;
the two sets of network decorating the two bowl-shaped capitals on top of the pillars;
[13]the four hundred pomegranates for the two sets of network (two rows of pomegranates for each network, decorating the bowl-shaped capitals on top of the pillars);
[14]the stands with their basins;
[15]the Sea and the twelve bulls under it;
[16]the pots, shovels, meat

°11 ק חורם

כְּלֵיהֶם עָשָׂה חוּרָם אָבִיו לַמֶּלֶךְ שְׁלֹמֹה
Solomon for-the-king Abi Huram he-made articles-of-them

לְבֵית יְהוָה נְחֹשֶׁת מָרוּק׃ בְּכִכַּר הַיַּרְדֵּן
the-Jordan in-plain-of (17) being-polished bronze Yahweh for-temple-of

יְצָקָם הַמֶּלֶךְ בַּעֲבִי הָאֲדָמָה בֵּין סֻכּוֹת וּבֵין
and-between Succoth between the-clay in-mold-of the-king he-cast-them

צְרֵדָתָה׃ וַיַּעַשׂ שְׁלֹמֹה כָּל־ הַכֵּלִים הָאֵלֶּה לָרֹב מְאֹד
very to-much the-these the-things all-of Solomon and-he-made (18) Zeredatha

כִּי לֹא נֶחְקַר מִשְׁקַל הַנְּחֹשֶׁת׃ וַיַּעַשׂ שְׁלֹמֹה אֵת
*** Solomon and-he-made (19) the-bronze weight-of he-was-determined not that

כָּל־ הַכֵּלִים אֲשֶׁר בֵּית הָאֱלֹהִים וְאֵת מִזְבַּח הַזָּהָב וְאֶת־
and the-gold altar-of and the-God house-of that the-furnishings all-of

הַשֻּׁלְחָנוֹת וַעֲלֵיהֶם לֶחֶם הַפָּנִים׃ וְאֶת־ הַמְּנֹרוֹת
the-lampstands and (20) the-Presences bread-of and-on-them the-tables

וְנֵרֹתֵיהֶם לְבַעֲרָם כַּמִּשְׁפָּט לִפְנֵי
in-front-of as-the-prescription to-burn-them and-lamps-of-them

הַדְּבִיר זָהָב סָגוּר׃ וְהַפֶּרַח וְהַנֵּרוֹת
and-the-lamps and-the-floral-work (21) pure gold the-inner-sanctuary

וְהַמֶּלְקַחַיִם* זָהָב הוּא מִכְלוֹת זָהָב׃ וְהַמְזַמְּרוֹת
and-the-wick-trimmers (22) gold ones-solid-of this gold and-the-tongs

וְהַמִּזְרָקוֹת וְהַכַּפּוֹת וְהַמַּחְתּוֹת זָהָב סָגוּר וּפֶתַח
and-door-of pure gold and-the-censers and-the-ladles and-the-sprinkling-bowls

הַבַּיִת דַּלְתוֹתָיו הַפְּנִימִיּוֹת לְקֹדֶשׁ הַקֳּדָשִׁים
the-Holy-Places to-Most-Holy-of the-inner-ones doors-of-him the-temple

וְדַלְתֵי הַבַּיִת לַהֵיכָל זָהָב׃ וַתִּשְׁלַם
when-she-was-finished (5:1) gold of-the-temple the-main-hall and-doors-of

כָּל־ הַמְּלָאכָה אֲשֶׁר־ עָשָׂה שְׁלֹמֹה לְבֵית יְהוָה וַיָּבֵא
and-he-brought Yahweh for-temple-of Solomon he-did that the-work all-of

שְׁלֹמֹה אֶת־ קָדְשֵׁי ׀ דָּוִיד אָבִיו וְאֶת־ הַכֶּסֶף וְאֶת־
and the-silver and father-of-him David dedicated-things-of *** Solomon

הַזָּהָב וְאֶת־ כָּל־ הַכֵּלִים נָתַן בְּאֹצְרוֹת בֵּית
temple-of in-treasuries-of he-placed the-furnishings all-of and the-gold

הָאֱלֹהִים׃ אָז יַקְהִיל שְׁלֹמֹה אֶת־ זִקְנֵי יִשְׂרָאֵל וְאֶת־ כָּל־
all-of and Israel elders-of *** Solomon he-summoned then (2) the-God

רָאשֵׁי הַמַּטּוֹת נְשִׂיאֵי הָאָבוֹת לִבְנֵי יִשְׂרָאֵל אֶל־ יְרוּשָׁלִָם
Jerusalem to Israel of-sons-of the-fathers chiefs-of the-tribes heads-of

לְהַעֲלוֹת אֶת־ אֲרוֹן בְּרִית־ יְהוָה מֵעִיר דָּוִיד הִיא צִיּוֹן׃
Zion that David from-City-of Yahweh covenant-of ark-of *** to-bring-up

*21 Most mss have *qamets* under the *qoph* ( קָחִים– ).

forks and all related articles.

All the objects that Huram-Abi made for King Solomon for the temple of the LORD
were of polished bronze. 17The
king had them cast in clay molds in the plain of the Jordan between Succoth and
Zarethan.[a] 18All these things
that Solomon made amounted to so much that the weight of the bronze was not determined.
19Solomon also made all the furnishings that were in God's temple:

the golden altar;
the tables on which was the bread of the Presence;
20the lampstands of pure gold with their lamps, to burn in front of the inner sanctuary as prescribed;
21the gold floral work and lamps and tongs (they were solid gold);
22the pure gold wick trimmers, sprinkling bowls, ladles and censers; and the gold doors of the temple: the inner doors to the Most Holy Place and the doors of the main hall.

5 When all the work Solomon had done for the temple of the LORD was finished, he brought in the things his father David had dedicated—the silver and gold and all the furnishings—and he placed them in the treasuries of God's temple.

*The Ark Brought to the Temple*

2Then Solomon summoned to Jerusalem the elders of Israel, all the heads of the tribes and the chiefs of the Israelite families, to bring up the ark of the LORD's covenant from
Zion, the City of David. 3And

[a]17 Hebrew *Zeredatha*, a variant of *Zarethan*

וַיִּקָּהֲלוּ֙   אֶל־   הַמֶּ֔לֶךְ   כָּל־   אִ֥ישׁ   יִשְׂרָאֵ֖ל   בֶּחָ֑ג
(3) and-they-came-together   to   the-king   all-of   man-of   Israel   at-the-festival

ה֖וּא   הַחֹ֥דֶשׁ   הַשְּׁבִעִֽי׃   וַיָּבֹ֕אוּ   כֹּ֖ל   זִקְנֵ֥י   יִשְׂרָאֵ֑ל
that   the-month   the-seventh   (4) when-they-arrived   all-of   elders-of   Israel

וַיִּשְׂא֥וּ   הַלְוִיִּ֖ם   אֶת־   הָאָרֽוֹן׃   (5)   וַיַּעֲל֣וּ   אֶת־
then-they-took-up   the-Levites   ***   the-ark   (5) and-they-brought-up   ***

הָאָר֗וֹן   וְאֶת־   אֹ֤הֶל   מוֹעֵד֙   וְאֶת־   כָּל־   כְּלֵ֣י   הַקֹּ֔דֶשׁ   אֲשֶׁ֖ר
the-ark   and   Tent-of   Meeting   and   all-of   furnishings-of   the-sacred   that

בָּאֹ֑הֶל   הֶעֱל֣וּ   אֹתָ֔ם   הַכֹּהֲנִ֖ים   הַלְוִיִּֽם׃   (6)   וְהַמֶּ֣לֶךְ
in-the-Tent   they-carried-up   them   the-priests   the-Levites   (6) and-the-king

שְׁלֹמֹ֗ה   וְכָל־   עֲדַ֤ת   יִשְׂרָאֵל֙   הַנּוֹעָדִ֣ים   עָלָ֔יו
Solomon   and-entire-of   assembly-of   Israel   the-ones-having-gathered   about-him

לִפְנֵ֖י   הָאָר֑וֹן   מְזַבְּחִים֙   צֹ֣אן   וּבָקָ֔ר   אֲשֶׁ֧ר   לֹֽא־   יִסָּפְר֛וּ
before   the-ark   ones-sacrificing   sheep   and-cattle   that   not   they-were-recorded

וְלֹ֥א   יִמָּנ֖וּ   מֵרֹֽב׃   (7)   וַיָּבִ֣יאוּ   הַכֹּהֲנִ֗ים
and-not   they-were-numbered   for-greatness   (7) then-they-brought   the-priests

אֶת־   אֲר֧וֹן   בְּרִית־   יְהוָ֛ה   אֶל־   מְקוֹמ֖וֹ   אֶל־   דְּבִ֥יר
***   ark-of   covenant-of   Yahweh   to   place-of-him   in   inner-sanctuary-of

הַבַּ֖יִת   אֶל־   קֹ֣דֶשׁ   הַקֳּדָשִׁ֑ים   אֶל־   תַּ֖חַת   כַּנְפֵ֥י   הַכְּרוּבִֽים׃
in   the-temple   Most-Holy-of   the-Holy-Places   at   beneath   wings-of   the-cherubim

(8)   וַיִּהְי֣וּ   הַכְּרוּבִים֙   פֹּרְשִׂ֣ים   כְּנָפַ֔יִם   עַל־   מְק֖וֹם   הָאָר֑וֹן
(8) and-they-were   the-cherubim   ones-spreading   wings   over   place-of   the-ark

וַיְכַסּ֧וּ   הַכְּרוּבִ֛ים   עַל־   הָאָר֖וֹן   וְעַל־   בַּדָּ֥יו   מִלְמָֽעְלָה׃
and-they-covered   the-cherubim   over   the-ark   and-over   poles-of-him   at-above

(9)   וַֽיַּאֲרִ֘יכוּ֙   הַבַּדִּ֔ים   וַיֵּרָאוּ֩   רָאשֵׁ֨י   הַבַּדִּ֤ים   מִן־
(9) and-they-were-long   the-poles   so-they-were-seen   ends-of   the-poles   from

הָאָרוֹן֙   עַל־   פְּנֵ֣י   הַדְּבִ֔יר   וְלֹ֥א   יֵרָא֖וּ   הַח֑וּצָה
the-ark   in   front-of   the-inner-sanctuary   but-not   they-were-seen   at-the-outside

וַֽיְהִי־   שָׁ֔ם   עַ֖ד   הַיּ֥וֹם   הַזֶּֽה׃   (10)   אֵ֚ין   בָּֽאָר֔וֹן   רַ֗ק
and-he-is   there   to   the-day   the-this   (10) there-was-nothing   in-the-ark   except

שְׁנֵ֣י   הַלֻּח֔וֹת   אֲשֶׁר־   נָתַ֥ן   מֹשֶׁ֖ה   בְּחֹרֵ֑ב   אֲשֶׁ֨ר   כָּרַ֤ת
two-of   the-tablets   that   he-placed   Moses   at-Horeb   where   he-made-covenant

יְהוָה֙   עִם־   בְּנֵ֣י   יִשְׂרָאֵ֔ל   בְּצֵאתָ֖ם   מִמִּצְרָֽיִם׃   (11)   וַיְהִ֕י
Yahweh   with   sons-of   Israel   after-to-come-them   from-Egypt   (11) then-he-was

בְּצֵ֥את   הַכֹּהֲנִ֖ים   מִן־   הַקֹּ֑דֶשׁ   כִּ֠י   כָּל־   הַכֹּהֲנִ֤ים
when-to-withdraw   the-priests   from   the-Holy-Place   for   all-of   the-priests

הַֽנִּמְצְאִים֙   הִתְקַדָּ֔שׁוּ   אֵ֥ין   לִשְׁמ֖וֹר   לְמַחְלְקֽוֹת׃
the-ones-being-found   they-consecrated-themselves   not   to-regard   for-divisions

---

all the men of Israel came together to the king at the time of the festival in the seventh month. [4]When all the elders of Israel had arrived, the Levites took up the ark, [5]and they brought up the ark and the Tent of Meeting and all the sacred furnishings in it. The priests, who were Levites, carried them up; [6]and King Solomon and the entire assembly of Israel that had gathered about him were before the ark, sacrificing so many sheep and cattle that they could not be recorded or counted.

[7]The priests then brought the ark of the Lord's covenant to its place in the inner sanctuary of the temple, the Most Holy Place, and put it beneath the wings of the cherubim. [8]The cherubim spread their wings over the place of the ark and covered the ark and its carrying poles. [9]These poles were so long that their ends, extending from the ark, could be seen from in front of the inner sanctuary, but not from outside the Holy Place; and they are still there today. [10]There was nothing in the ark except the two tablets that Moses had placed in it at Horeb, where the Lord made a covenant with the Israelites after they came out of Egypt.

[11]The priests then withdrew from the Holy Place. All the priests who were there had consecrated themselves, regardless of their divisions.

*7 Most mss have *hateph qamets* under the *qoph* (הַקֳּ).

והלוים המשררים לכלם לאסף
indeed-Asaph indeed-all-of-them the-ones-making-music and-the-Levites (12)

להימן לידתון ולבניהם ולאחיהם
and-indeed-relatives-of-them and-indeed-sons-of-them indeed-Jeduthun indeed-Heman

מלבשים בוץ במצלתים ובנבלים וכנרות
and-lyres and-with-harps with-cymbals fine-linen ones-being-dressed

עמדים מזרח למזבח ועמהם כהנים למאה
indeed-hundred priests and-with-them of-the-altar east ones-standing

ועשרים מחצררים° בחצצרות׃ ויהי כאחד
as-one and-he-was (13) on-the-trumpets ones-sounding and-twenty

למחצצרים° ולמשררים להשמיע
to-make-heard and-indeed-the-ones-singing indeed-the-ones-sounding-trumpets

קול־ אחד להלל ולהדות ליהוה וכהרים קול
voice and-as-to-raise to-Yahweh and-to-thank to-praise one voice

בחצצרות ובמצלתים ובכלי השיר
the-music and-with-instruments-of and-with-the-cymbals with-the-trumpets

ובהלל ליהוה כי טוב כי לעולם חסדו
love-of-him to-forever indeed good that to-Yahweh and-when-to-praise

והבית מלא ענן בית יהוה׃ ולא־ יכלו
they-could and-not (14) Yahweh temple-of cloud he-was-filled then-the-temple

הכהנים לעמוד לשרת מפני הענן כי־ מלא
he-filled for the-cloud because-of to-perform to-continue the-priests

כבוד־ יהוה את־ בית האלהים׃ אז אמר שלמה יהוה
Yahweh Solomon he-said then (6:1) the-God temple-of *** Yahweh glory-of

אמר לשכון בערפל׃ ואני בניתי בית־ זבל
magnificence temple-of I-built and-I (2) in-the-dark-cloud to-dwell he-said

לך ומכון לשבתך עולמים׃ ויסב המלך את־
*** the-king and-he-turned (3) forevers to-dwell-you even-place for-you

פניו ויברך את כל־ קהל ישראל וכל־
while-whole-of Israel assembly-of whole-of *** and-he-blessed faces-of-him

קהל ישראל עומד׃ ויאמר ברוך יהוה אלהי
God-of Yahweh being-praised then-he-said (4) standing Israel assembly-of

ישראל אשר דבר בפיו את דויד אבי
father-of-me David *** with-mouth-of-him he-promised who Israel

ובידיו מלא לאמר׃ מן־ היום אשר הוצאתי
I-brought when the-day since (5) to-say he-fulfilled and-with-hands-of-him

את־ עמי מארץ מצרים לא־ בחרתי בעיר מכל
from-any-of to-city I-chose not Egypt from-land-of people-of-me ***

[12]All the Levites who were musicians—Asaph, Heman, Jeduthun and their sons and relatives—stood on the east side of the altar, dressed in fine linen and playing cymbals, harps and lyres. They were accompanied by 120 priests sounding trumpets. [13]The trumpeters and singers joined in unison, as with one voice, to give praise and thanks to the LORD. Accompanied by trumpets, cymbals and other instruments, they raised their voices in praise to the LORD and sang:

> "He is good;
> his love endures
> forever."

Then the temple of the LORD was filled with a cloud, [14]and the priests could not perform their service because of the cloud, for the glory of the LORD filled the temple of God.

6 Then Solomon said, "The LORD has said that he would dwell in a dark cloud; [2]I have built a magnificent temple for you, a place for you to dwell forever."

[3]While the whole assembly of Israel was standing there, the king turned around and blessed them. [4]Then he said:

> "Praise be to the LORD, the God of Israel, who with his hands has fulfilled what he promised with his mouth to my father David. For he said, [5]'Since the day I brought my people out of Egypt, I have not chosen a city in any tribe of Israel to

°12 ק מחצרים
°13 ק למחצרים

שִׁבְטֵ֣י יִשְׂרָאֵ֔ל לִבְנ֣וֹת בַּ֔יִת לִהְי֥וֹת שְׁמִ֖י שָׁ֑ם וְלֹא־בָחַ֣רְתִּי
I-chose and-not there Name-of-me to-be temple to-build Israel tribes-of

בְאִ֔ישׁ לִהְי֥וֹת נָגִ֖יד עַל־עַמִּ֥י יִשְׂרָאֵֽל׃ וָאֶבְחַר֙ בִּיר֣וּשָׁלַ֔ם
to-Jerusalem but-I-chose (6) Israel people-of-me over leader to-be to-anyone

לִהְי֥וֹת שְׁמִ֖י שָׁ֑ם וָאֶבְחַ֣ר בְּדָוִ֔יד לִהְי֖וֹת עַל־עַמִּ֥י יִשְׂרָאֵֽל׃
Israel people-of-me over to-be to-David and-I-chose there Name-of-me to-be

וַיְהִ֕י עִם־לְבַ֖ב דָּוִ֣יד אָבִ֑י לִבְנ֣וֹת בַּ֔יִת לְשֵׁ֕ם
for-Name-of temple to-build father-of-me David heart-of in and-he-was (7)

יְהוָ֖ה אֱלֹהֵ֥י יִשְׂרָאֵֽל׃ וַיֹּ֤אמֶר יְהוָה֙ אֶל־דָּוִ֣יד אָבִ֔י יַ֗עַן
because father-of-me David to Yahweh but-he-said (8) Israel God-of Yahweh

אֲשֶׁ֤ר הָיָה֙ עִם־לְבָ֣בְךָ֔ לִבְנ֥וֹת בַּ֖יִת לִשְׁמִ֑י הֱטִיב֔וֹתָ
you-did-well for-Name-of-me temple to-build heart-of-you in he-was that

כִּ֥י הָיָ֖ה עִם־לְבָבֶֽךָ׃ רַ֣ק אַתָּ֔ה לֹ֥א תִבְנֶ֖ה
you-will-build not you nevertheless (9) heart-of-you in he-was because

הַבָּ֑יִת כִּ֤י בִנְךָ֙ הַיּוֹצֵ֣א מֵחֲלָצֶ֔יךָ הֽוּא־יִבְנֶ֥ה
he-will-build he from-loins-of-you the-one-coming son-of-you but the-temple

הַבַּ֖יִת לִשְׁמִֽי׃ וַיָּ֣קֶם יְהוָ֔ה אֶת־דְּבָר֖וֹ אֲשֶׁ֣ר
that promise-of-him *** Yahweh and-he-kept (10) for-Name-of-me the-temple

דִּבֵּ֑ר וָאָק֞וּם תַּ֣חַת דָּוִ֣יד אָבִ֗י וָאֵשֵׁ֣ב ׀ עַל־כִּסֵּ֣א
throne-of on and-I-sit father-of-me David after and-I-succeeded he-promised

יִשְׂרָאֵ֔ל כַּאֲשֶׁר֙ דִּבֶּ֣ר יְהוָ֔ה וָאֶבְנֶ֣ה הַבַּ֔יִת לְשֵׁ֖ם יְהוָ֥ה
Yahweh for-Name-of the-temple and-I-built Yahweh he-promised just-as Israel

אֱלֹהֵ֥י יִשְׂרָאֵֽל׃ וָאָשִׂ֥ים שָׁם֙ אֶת־הָ֣אָר֔וֹן אֲשֶׁר־שָׁ֖ם בְּרִ֣ית
covenant-of there which the-ark *** there and-I-placed (11) Israel God-of

יְהוָ֑ה אֲשֶׁ֥ר כָּרַ֖ת עִם־בְּנֵ֥י יִשְׂרָאֵֽל׃ וַֽיַּעֲמֹ֗ד לִפְנֵי֙ מִזְבַּ֣ח
altar-of before then-he-stood (12) Israel people-of with he-made that Yahweh

יְהוָ֔ה נֶ֖גֶד כָּל־קְהַ֣ל יִשְׂרָאֵ֑ל וַיִּפְרֹ֖שׂ כַּפָּֽיו׃
hands-of-him and-he-spread Israel assembly-of whole-of in-front-of Yahweh

כִּֽי־עָשָׂ֣ה שְׁלֹמֹ֡ה כִּיּ֣וֹר נְ֠חֹשֶׁת וַֽיִּתְּנֵ֞הוּ בְּת֣וֹךְ
in-center-of and-he-placed-him bronze platform-of Solomon he-made now (13)

הָֽעֲזָרָ֗ה חָמֵ֨שׁ אַמּ֜וֹת אָרְכּ֗וֹ וְחָמֵ֨שׁ אַמּ֤וֹת רָחְבּוֹ֙
width-of-him cubits and-five length-of-him cubits five the-outer-court

וְאַמּ֥וֹת שָׁל֖וֹשׁ קוֹמָת֑וֹ וַיַּעֲמֹ֣ד עָלָ֗יו וַיִּבְרַ֤ךְ עַל־
on then-he-knelt on-him and-he-stood height-of-him three and-cubits

בִּרְכָּיו֙ נֶ֚גֶד כָּל־קְהַ֣ל יִשְׂרָאֵ֔ל וַיִּפְרֹ֥שׂ כַּפָּ֖יו
hands-of-him and-he-spread Israel assembly-of whole-of before knees-of-him

הַשָּׁמָֽיְמָה׃ וַיֹּאמַ֗ר יְהוָ֞ה אֱלֹהֵ֤י יִשְׂרָאֵל֙ אֵין־
there-is-no Israel God-of Yahweh and-he-said (14) toward-the-heavens

have a temple built for my Name to be there, nor have I chosen anyone to be the leader over my people Israel. [6]But now I have chosen Jerusalem for my Name to be there, and I have chosen David to rule my people Israel.'

[7]"My father David had it in his heart to build a temple for the Name of the LORD, the God of Israel. [8]But the LORD said to my father David, 'Because it was in your heart to build a temple for my Name, you did well to have this in your heart. [9]Nevertheless, you are not the one to build the temple, but your son, who is your own flesh and blood—he is the one who will build the temple for my Name.'

[10]"The LORD has kept the promise he made. I have succeeded David my father and now I sit on the throne of Israel, just as the LORD promised, and I have built the temple for the Name of the LORD, the God of Israel. [11]There I have placed the ark, in which is the covenant of the LORD that he made with the people of Israel."

*Solomon's Prayer of Dedication*

[12]Then Solomon stood before the altar of the LORD in front of the whole assembly of Israel and spread out his hands. [13]Now he had made a bronze platform, five cubits[b] long, five cubits wide and three cubits[c] high, and had placed it in the center of the outer court. He stood on the platform and then knelt down before the whole assembly of Israel and spread out his hands toward heaven. [14]He said:

"O LORD, God of Israel,

[b]13 That is, about 7 1/2 feet (about 2.3 meters)
[c]13 That is, about 4 1/2 feet (about 1.3 meters)

כָּמוֹךָ אֱלֹהִים בַּשָּׁמַיִם וּבָאָרֶץ שֹׁמֵר הַבְּרִית וְהַחֶסֶד
and-the-love the-covenant keeping or-on-the-earth in-the-heavens God like-you

לַעֲבָדֶיךָ הַהֹלְכִים לְפָנֶיךָ בְּכָל־
with-whole-of before-you the-ones-continuing with-servants-of-you

לִבָּם׃ אֲשֶׁר שָׁמַרְתָּ לְעַבְדְּךָ דָּוִיד אָבִי אֵת
*** father-of-me David to-servant-of-you you-kept who (15) heart-of-them

אֲשֶׁר־ דִּבַּרְתָּ לוֹ וַתְּדַבֵּר בְּפִיךָ
with-mouth-of-you and-you-promised to-him you-promised what

וּבְיָדְךָ מִלֵּאתָ כַּיּוֹם הַזֶּה׃ וְעַתָּה יְהוָה ׀
Yahweh and-now (16) the-this as-the-day you-fulfilled and-with-hand-of-you

אֱלֹהֵי יִשְׂרָאֵל שְׁמֹר לְעַבְדְּךָ דָוִיד אָבִי אֵת אֲשֶׁר
what *** father-of-me David for-servant-of-you keep! Israel God-of

דִּבַּרְתָּ לּוֹ לֵאמֹר לֹא־ יִכָּרֵת לְךָ אִישׁ מִלְּפָנַי
from-before-me man of-you he-shall-be-cut-off not to-say to-him you-promised

יוֹשֵׁב עַל־ כִּסֵּא יִשְׂרָאֵל רַק אִם־ יִשְׁמְרוּ בָנֶיךָ אֶת־
*** sons-of-you they-are-careful if only Israel throne-of on sitting

דַּרְכָּם לָלֶכֶת בְּתוֹרָתִי כַּאֲשֶׁר הָלַכְתָּ לְפָנָי׃
before-me you-walked just-as according-to-law-of-me to-walk way-of-them

וְעַתָּה יְהוָה אֱלֹהֵי יִשְׂרָאֵל יֵאָמֵן דְּבָרְךָ אֲשֶׁר
that word-of-you let-him-come-true Israel God-of Yahweh and-now (17)

דִּבַּרְתָּ לְעַבְדְּךָ לְדָוִיד׃ כִּי הַאֻמְנָם יֵשֵׁב אֱלֹהִים
God will-he-dwell really? but (18) to-David to-servant-of-you you-promised

אֶת־ הָאָדָם עַל־ הָאָרֶץ הִנֵּה שָׁמַיִם וּשְׁמֵי הַשָּׁמַיִם לֹא
not the-heavens even-heavens-of heavens see! the-earth on the-man with

יְכַלְכְּלוּךָ אַף כִּי־ הַבַּיִת הַזֶּה אֲשֶׁר בָּנִיתִי׃
I-built that the-this the-temple indeed how-much-less they-can-contain-you

וּפָנִיתָ אֶל־ תְּפִלַּת עַבְדְּךָ וְאֶל־
and-to servant-of-you prayer-of to yet-you-give-attention (19)

תְּחִנָּתוֹ יְהוָה אֱלֹהָי לִשְׁמֹעַ אֶל־ הָרִנָּה וְאֶל־ הַתְּפִלָּה
the-prayer and-to the-cry to to-hear God-of-me Yahweh mercy-plea-of-him

אֲשֶׁר עַבְדְּךָ מִתְפַּלֵּל לְפָנֶיךָ׃ לִהְיוֹת עֵינֶיךָ
eyes-of-you to-be (20) in-presences-of-you praying servant-of-you that

פְּתֻחוֹת אֶל־ הַבַּיִת הַזֶּה יוֹמָם וָלַיְלָה אֶל־ הַמָּקוֹם
the-place toward and-night by-day the-this the-temple toward ones-being-open

אֲשֶׁר אָמַרְתָּ לָשׂוּם שִׁמְךָ שָׁם לִשְׁמוֹעַ אֶל־ הַתְּפִלָּה אֲשֶׁר יִתְפַּלֵּל
he-prays that the-prayer to to-hear there Name-of-you to-put you-said which

עַבְדְּךָ אֶל־ הַמָּקוֹם הַזֶּה׃ וְשָׁמַעְתָּ אֶל־ תַּחֲנוּנֵי
supplications-of to and-you-hear (21) the-this the-place toward servant-of-you

there is no God like you in
heaven or on earth—you
who keep your covenant of
love with your servants
who continue wholeheart-
edly in your way.
15You
have kept your promise to
your servant David my fa-
ther; with your mouth you
have promised and with
your hand you have
fulfilled it—as it is today.
16"Now LORD, God of Is-
rael, keep for your servant
David my father the prom-
ises you made to him when
you said, 'You shall never
fail to have a man to sit before me on the throne of Israel, if only your sons are
careful in all they do to
walk before me according
to my law, as you have
done.'
17And now, O LORD,
God of Israel, let your word
that you promised your servant David come true.
18"But will God really
dwell on earth with men?
The heavens, even the
highest heavens, cannot
contain you. How much
less this temple I have built!
19Yet give attention to your
servant's prayer and his
plea for mercy, O LORD my
God. Hear the cry and the
prayer that your servant is
praying in your presence.
20May your eyes be open
toward this temple day and
night, this place of which
you said you would put
your Name there. May you
hear the prayer your ser-
vant prays toward this
place.
21Hear the supplica-
tions of your servant and of

עַבְדְּךָ וְעַמְּךָ יִשְׂרָאֵל אֲשֶׁר יִתְפַּלְלוּ אֶל־ הַמָּקוֹם
the-place toward they-pray when Israel and-people-of-you servant-of-you

הַזֶּה וְאַתָּה תִּשְׁמַע מִמְּקוֹם שִׁבְתְּךָ מִן־ הַשָּׁמַיִם
the-heavens from to-dwell-you from-place-of you-hear and-you the-this

וְשָׁמַעְתָּ וְסָלָחְתָּ׃ אִם־ יֶחֱטָא אִישׁ לְרֵעֵהוּ
to-neighbor-of-him man he-wrongs when (22) then-you-forgive when-you-hear

וְנָשָׁא־ בוֹ אָלָה לְהַאֲלֹתוֹ וּבָא אָלָה לִפְנֵי
before he-swears-oath and-he-comes to-take-oath-him oath on-him and-he-takes

מִזְבַּחֲךָ בַּבַּיִת הַזֶּה׃ וְאַתָּה תִּשְׁמַע מִן־ הַשָּׁמַיִם
the-heavens from you-hear then-you (23) the-this in-the-temple altar-of-you

וְעָשִׂיתָ וְשָׁפַטְתָּ אֶת־ עֲבָדֶיךָ לְהָשִׁיב לְרָשָׁע לָתֵת
to-bring to-guilty to-repay servants-of-you *** and-you-judge and-you-act

דַּרְכּוֹ בְּרֹאשׁוֹ וּלְהַצְדִּיק צַדִּיק לָתֶת לוֹ
for-him to-establish innocent and-to-declare-innocent on-head-of-him way-of-him

כְּצִדְקָתוֹ׃ וְאִם־ יִנָּגֵף עַמְּךָ יִשְׂרָאֵל לִפְנֵי
before Israel people-of-you he-is-defeated and-when (24) as-innocence-of-him

אוֹיֵב כִּי יֶחֶטְאוּ־ לָךְ וְשָׁבוּ
when-they-turn-back against-you they-sinned because one-being-enemy

וְהוֹדוּ אֶת־ שְׁמֶךָ וְהִתְפַּלְלוּ וְהִתְחַנְּנוּ
and-they-make-supplication and-they-pray name-of-you *** and-they-confess

לְפָנֶיךָ בַּבַּיִת הַזֶּה׃ וְאַתָּה תִּשְׁמַע מִן־ הַשָּׁמַיִם
the-heavens from you-hear then-you (25) the-this in-the-temple before-you

וְסָלַחְתָּ לְחַטַּאת עַמְּךָ יִשְׂרָאֵל וַהֲשֵׁבוֹתָם אֶל־
to and-you-bring-back-them Israel people-of-you to-sin-of and-you-forgive

הָאֲדָמָה אֲשֶׁר־ נָתַתָּה לָהֶם וְלַאֲבֹתֵיהֶם׃ בְּהֵעָצֵר
when-to-be-shut-up (26) and-to-fathers-of-them to-them you-gave that the-land

הַשָּׁמַיִם וְלֹא־ יִהְיֶה מָטָר כִּי יֶחֶטְאוּ־ לָךְ וְהִתְפַּלְלוּ
when-they-pray against-you they-sinned because rain he-is and-not the-heavens

אֶל־ הַמָּקוֹם הַזֶּה וְהוֹדוּ אֶת־ שְׁמֶךָ מֵחַטָּאתָם
from-sin-of-them name-of-you *** and-they-confess the-this the-place toward

יְשׁוּבוּן כִּי תַעֲנֵם׃ וְאַתָּה תִּשְׁמַע הַשָּׁמַיִם
the-heavens you-hear then-you (27) you-afflicted-them because they-turn

וְסָלַחְתָּ לְחַטַּאת עֲבָדֶיךָ וְעַמְּךָ יִשְׂרָאֵל כִּי
indeed Israel and-people-of-you servants-of-you to-sin-of and-you-forgive

תוֹרֵם אֶל־ הַדֶּרֶךְ הַטּוֹבָה אֲשֶׁר יֵלְכוּ־ בָהּ
in-her they-should-walk that the-right the-way about you-teach-them

וְנָתַתָּה מָטָר עַל־ אַרְצְךָ אֲשֶׁר־ נָתַתָּה לְעַמְּךָ
to-people-of-you you-gave that land-of-you on rain and-you-send

your people Israel when they pray toward this place. Hear from heaven, your dwelling place; and when you hear, forgive.

[22]"When a man wrongs his neighbor and is required to take an oath and he comes and swears the oath before your altar in this temple, [23]then hear from heaven and act. Judge between your servants, repaying the guilty by bringing down on his own head what he has done. Declare the innocent not guilty and so establish his innocence.

[24]"When your people Israel have been defeated by an enemy because they have sinned against you and when they turn back and confess your name, praying and making supplication before you in this temple, [25]then hear from heaven and forgive the sin of your people Israel and bring them back to the land you gave to them and their fathers.

[26]"When the heavens are shut up and there is no rain because your people have sinned against you, and when they pray toward this place and confess your name and turn from their sin because you have afflicted them, [27]then hear from heaven and forgive the sin of your servants, your people Israel. Teach them the right way to live, and send rain on the land you gave your people for an

לְנַחֲלָה׃ רָעָב כִּי־ יִהְיֶה בָאָרֶץ דֶּבֶר כִּי־ יִהְיֶה
he-comes when plague to-the-land he-comes when famine (28) for-inheritance

שִׁדָּפוֹן וְיֵרָקוֹן אַרְבֶּה וְחָסִיל כִּי יִהְיֶה כִּי יָצַר־
he-besieges when he-comes when or-grasshopper locust or-mildew blight

לוֹ אוֹיְבָיו בְּאֶרֶץ שְׁעָרָיו כָּל־ נֶגַע
disaster any-of gates-of-him in-land-of ones-being-enemies-of-him against-him

וְכָל־ מַחֲלָה׃ כָּל־ תְּפִלָּה כָל־ תְּחִנָּה אֲשֶׁר יִהְיֶה לְכָל־
from-any-of he-comes that plea any-of prayer any-of (29) disease or-any-of

הָאָדָם וּלְכֹל עַמְּךָ יִשְׂרָאֵל אֲשֶׁר יֵדְעוּ אִישׁ
each they-are-aware who Israel people-of-you indeed-from-any-of the-person

נִגְעוֹ וּמַכְאֹבוֹ וּפָרַשׂ כַּפָּיו אֶל־
toward hands-of-him and-he-spreads-out and-pain-of-him affliction-of-him

הַבַּיִת הַזֶּה׃ וְאַתָּה תִּשְׁמַע מִן־ הַשָּׁמַיִם מְכוֹן
place-of the-heavens from you-hear then-you (30) the-this the-temple

שִׁבְתֶּךָ וְסָלַחְתָּ וְנָתַתָּה לָאִישׁ כְּכָל־ דְּרָכָיו
ways-of-him as-all-of with-the-each and-you-deal and-you-forgive to-dwell-you

אֲשֶׁר תֵּדַע אֶת־ לְבָבוֹ כִּי אַתָּה לְבַדְּךָ יָדַעְתָּ אֶת־ לְבַב
heart-of *** you-know by-yourself you for heart-of-him *** you-know since

בְּנֵי הָאָדָם׃ לְמַעַן יִירָאוּךָ לָלֶכֶת בִּדְרָכֶיךָ
in-ways-of-you to-walk they-will-fear-you so-that (31) the-man sons-of

כָּל־ הַיָּמִים אֲשֶׁר־ הֵם חַיִּים עַל־ פְּנֵי הָאֲדָמָה אֲשֶׁר נָתַתָּה
you-gave that the-land faces-of on ones-alive they that the-days all-of

לַאֲבֹתֵינוּ׃ וְגַם אֶל־ הַנָּכְרִי אֲשֶׁר לֹא מֵעַמְּךָ
from-people-of-you not who the-foreigner for and-also (32) to-fathers-of-us

יִשְׂרָאֵל הוּא וּבָא | מֵאֶרֶץ רְחוֹקָה לְמַעַן שִׁמְךָ הַגָּדוֹל
the-great name-of-you because-of distant from-land but-he-came he Israel

וְיָדְךָ הַחֲזָקָה וּזְרוֹעֲךָ הַנְּטוּיָה
the-one-being-outstretched and-arm-of-you the-mighty and-hand-of-you

וּבָאוּ וְהִתְפַּלְלוּ אֶל־ הַבַּיִת הַזֶּה׃ וְאַתָּה
then-you (33) the-this the-temple toward and-they-pray when-they-come

תִּשְׁמַע מִן־ הַשָּׁמַיִם מִמְּכוֹן שִׁבְתֶּךָ וְעָשִׂיתָ כְּכֹל אֲשֶׁר־
that as-all and-you-do to-dwell-you from-place-of the-heavens from you-hear

יִקְרָא אֵלֶיךָ הַנָּכְרִי לְמַעַן יֵדְעוּ כָל־ עַמֵּי
peoples-of all-of they-may-know so-that the-foreigner of-you he-asks

הָאָרֶץ אֶת־ שְׁמֶךָ וּלְיִרְאָה אֹתְךָ כְּעַמְּךָ יִשְׂרָאֵל
Israel as-people-of-you you and-to-fear name-of-you *** the-earth

וְלָדַעַת כִּי־ שִׁמְךָ נִקְרָא עַל־ הַבַּיִת הַזֶּה אֲשֶׁר בָּנִיתִי׃
I-built that the-this the-house to he-is-called Name-of-you that and-to-know

inheritance.
28 "When famine or
plague comes to the land, or
blight or mildew, locusts or
grasshoppers, or when enemies besiege them in any
of their cities, whatever
disaster or disease may
come, 29 and when a prayer
or plea is made by any of
your people Israel—each
one aware of his afflictions
and pains, and spreading
out his hands toward this
temple— 30 then hear from
heaven, your dwelling
place. Forgive, and deal
with each man according to
all he does, since you know
his heart (for you alone
know the hearts of men),
31 so that they will fear you
and walk in your ways all
the time they live in the
land you gave our fathers.
32 "As for the foreigner
who does not belong to
your people Israel but has
come from a distant land
because of your great name
and your mighty hand and
your outstretched arm—
when he comes and prays
toward this temple, 33 then
hear from heaven, your
dwelling place, and do
whatever the foreigner asks
of you, so that all the peoples of the earth may know
your name and fear you, as
do your own people Israel,
and may know that this
house I have built bears
your Name.

כִּי־ יֵצֵא עַמְּךָ לַמִּלְחָמָה עַל־ אֹיְבָיו

being-enemies-of-him against to-the-war people-of-you he-goes-out when (34)

בַּדֶּרֶךְ אֲשֶׁר תִּשְׁלָחֵם וְהִתְפַּלְלוּ אֵלֶיךָ דֶּרֶךְ הָעִיר

the-city direction-of to-you and-they-pray you-send-them that in-the-way

הַזֹּאת אֲשֶׁר בָּחַרְתָּ בָּהּ וְהַבַּיִת אֲשֶׁר־ בָּנִיתִי לִשְׁמֶךָ׃

for-Name-of-you I-built that and-the-temple to-her you-chose that the-this

וְשָׁמַעְתָּ מִן־ הַשָּׁמַיִם אֶת־ תְּפִלָּתָם וְאֶת־ תְּחִנָּתָם

plea-of-them and prayer-of-them *** the-heavens from then-you-hear (35)

וְעָשִׂיתָ מִשְׁפָּטָם׃ כִּי יֶחֶטְאוּ־ לָךְ כִּי אֵין אָדָם

person no for against-you they-sin when (36) cause-of-them and-you-uphold

אֲשֶׁר לֹא־ יֶחֱטָא וְאָנַפְתָּ בָם וּנְתַתָּם לִפְנֵי

over-to and-you-give-them with-them and-you-become-angry he-sins not who

אוֹיֵב וְשָׁבוּם שׁוֹבֵיהֶם אֶל־אֶרֶץ

land to ones-being-captive-of-them and-they-take-captive-them one-being-enemy

רְחוֹקָה אוֹ קְרוֹבָה׃ וְהֵשִׁיבוּ אֶל־ לְבָבָם בְּאֶרֶץ אֲשֶׁר

where in-the-land heart-of-them in and-they-change (37) near or far

נִשְׁבּוּ־ שָׁם וְשָׁבוּ ׀ וְהִתְחַנְּנוּ אֵלֶיךָ

with-you and-they-plead and-they-repent there they-are-held-captive

בְּאֶרֶץ שִׁבְיָם לֵאמֹר חָטָאנוּ הֶעֱוִינוּ וְרָשָׁעְנוּ׃

and-we-acted-wickedly we-did-wrong we-sinned to-say captivity-of-them in-land-of

וְשָׁבוּ אֵלֶיךָ בְּכָל־ לִבָּם וּבְכָל־

and-with-all-of heart-of-them with-all-of to-you and-they-turn (38)

נַפְשָׁם בְּאֶרֶץ שִׁבְיָם אֲשֶׁר־ שָׁבוּ אֹתָם

them they-took-captive where captivity-of-them in-land-of soul-of-them

וְהִתְפַּלְלוּ דֶּרֶךְ אַרְצָם אֲשֶׁר נָתַתָּה לַאֲבוֹתָם

to-fathers-of-them you-gave that land-of-them direction-of and-they-pray

וְהָעִיר אֲשֶׁר בָּחַרְתָּ וְלַבַּיִת אֲשֶׁר־ בָּנִיתִי

I-built that and-toward-the-temple you-chose that and-the-city

לִשְׁמֶךָ׃ וְשָׁמַעְתָּ מִן־ הַשָּׁמַיִם מִמְּכוֹן

from-place-of the-heavens from then-you-hear (39) for-Name-of-you

שִׁבְתְּךָ אֶת־ תְּפִלָּתָם וְאֶת־ תְּחִנֹּתֵיהֶם וְעָשִׂיתָ

and-you-uphold pleas-of-them and prayer-of-them *** to-dwell-you

מִשְׁפָּטָם וְסָלַחְתָּ לְעַמְּךָ אֲשֶׁר חָטְאוּ־ לָךְ׃

against-you they-sinned who to-people-of-you and-you-forgive cause-of-them

עַתָּה אֱלֹהַי יִהְיוּ־ נָא עֵינֶיךָ פְּתֻחוֹת

ones-being-open eyes-of-you now! may-they-be God-of-me now (40)

וְאָזְנֶיךָ קַשֻּׁבוֹת לִתְפִלַּת הַמָּקוֹם הַזֶּה׃ וְעַתָּה

and-now (41) the-this the-place to-prayer-of ones-attentive and-ears-of-you

34"When your people go to war against their enemies, wherever you send them, and when they pray to you toward this city you have chosen and the temple I have built for your Name, 35then hear from heaven their prayer and their plea, and uphold their cause.

36"When they sin against you—for there is no one who does not sin—and you become angry with them and give them over to the enemy, who takes them captive to a land far away or near; 37and if they have a change of heart in the land where they are held captive, and repent and plead with you in the land of their captivity and say, 'We have sinned, we have done wrong and acted wickedly'; 38and if they turn back to you with all their heart and soul in the land of their captivity where they were taken, and pray toward the land you gave their fathers, toward the city you have chosen and toward the temple I have built for your Name; 39then from heaven, your dwelling place, hear their prayer and their pleas, and uphold their cause. And forgive your people, who have sinned against you.

40"Now, my God, may your eyes be open and your ears attentive to the prayers offered in this place.

קוּמָה יְהוָה אֱלֹהִים לְנוּחֶךָ אַתָּה וַאֲרוֹן עֻזֶּךָ
might-of-you and-ark-of you to-resting-place-of-you God Yahweh arise!

כֹּהֲנֶיךָ יְהוָה אֱלֹהִים יִלְבְּשׁוּ תְשׁוּעָה וַחֲסִידֶיךָ
and-saints-of-you salvation may-they-be-clothed God Yahweh priests-of-you

יִשְׂמְחוּ בַטּוֹב׃ (42) יְהוָה אֱלֹהִים אַל־ תָּשֵׁב פְּנֵי
faces-of you-reject not God Yahweh (42) in-the-goodness may-they-rejoice

מְשִׁיחֶיךָ* זָכְרָה לְחַסְדֵי דָּוִיד עַבְדֶּךָ׃
servant-of-you David to-kindnesses-of remember! *anointed-ones-of-you

(7:1) וּכְכַלּוֹת שְׁלֹמֹה לְהִתְפַּלֵּל וְהָאֵשׁ יָרְדָה
she-came-down then-the-fire to-pray Solomon and-when-to-finish (7:1)

מֵהַשָּׁמַיִם וַתֹּאכַל הָעֹלָה וְהַזְּבָחִים
and-the-sacrifices the-burnt-offering and-she-consumed from-the-heavens

וּכְבוֹד יְהוָה מָלֵא אֶת־ הַבָּיִת׃ (2) וְלֹא יָכְלוּ
they-could and-not (2) the-temple *** he-filled Yahweh and-glory-of

הַכֹּהֲנִים לָבוֹא אֶל־ בֵּית יְהוָה כִּי־ מָלֵא כְבוֹד־ יְהוָה
Yahweh glory-of he-filled because Yahweh temple-of into to-enter the-priests

אֶת־ בֵּית יְהוָה׃ (3) וְכֹל | בְּנֵי יִשְׂרָאֵל רֹאִים
ones-seeing Israel sons-of when-all-of (3) Yahweh temple-of ***

בְּרֶדֶת הָאֵשׁ וּכְבוֹד יְהוָה עַל־ הַבָּיִת
the-temple above Yahweh and-glory-of the-fire when-to-come-down

וַיִּכְרְעוּ אַפַּיִם אַרְצָה עַל־ הָרִצְפָה וַיִּשְׁתַּחֲווּ
and-they-worshiped the-pavement on to-ground faces then-they-knelt

וְהוֹדוֹת לַיהוָה כִּי טוֹב כִּי לְעוֹלָם חַסְדּוֹ׃
love-of-him to-forever indeed good that to-Yahweh and-to-give-thanks

(4) וְהַמֶּלֶךְ וְכָל־ הָעָם זֹבְחִים זֶבַח לִפְנֵי יְהוָה׃
Yahweh before sacrifice ones-offering the-people and-all-of then-the-king (4)

(5) וַיִּזְבַּח הַמֶּלֶךְ שְׁלֹמֹה אֶת־ זֶבַח הַבָּקָר עֶשְׂרִים וּשְׁנַיִם
and-two twenty the-cattle sacrifice-of *** Solomon the-king and-he-offered (5)

אֶלֶף וְצֹאן מֵאָה וְעֶשְׂרִים אָלֶף וַיַּחְנְכוּ אֶת־
*** so-they-dedicated thousand and-twenty hundred and-sheep thousand

בֵּית הָאֱלֹהִים הַמֶּלֶךְ וְכָל־ הָעָם׃ (6) וְהַכֹּהֲנִים עַל־
at and-the-priests (6) the-people and-all-of the-king the-God temple-of

מִשְׁמְרוֹתָם עֹמְדִים וְהַלְוִיִּם בִּכְלֵי־ שִׁיר
music-of with-instruments-of and-the-Levites ones-standing positions-of-them

יְהוָה אֲשֶׁר עָשָׂה דָּוִיד הַמֶּלֶךְ לְהֹדוֹת לַיהוָה כִּי־ לְעוֹלָם
to-forever indeed to-Yahweh to-give-thanks the-king David he-made which Yahweh

חַסְדּוֹ בְּהַלֵּל דָּוִיד בְּיָדָם וְהַכֹּהֲנִים
and-the-priests by-hand-of-them David when-to-praise love-of-him

41"Now arise, O LORD
God, and come to
your resting place,
you and the ark of
your might.
May your priests, O
LORD God, be
clothed with
salvation,
may your saints
rejoice in your
goodness.
42O LORD God, do not
reject your anointed
one.
Remember the
kindnesses
promised to David
your servant."

*The Dedication of the Temple*

7 When Solomon finished praying, fire came down from heaven and consumed the burnt offering and the sacrifices, and the glory of the LORD filled the temple. 2The priests could not enter the temple of the LORD because the glory of the LORD filled it. 3When all the Israelites saw the fire coming down and the glory of the LORD above the temple, they knelt on the pavement with their faces to the ground, and they worshiped and gave thanks to the LORD, saying,

"He is good;
his love endures
forever."

4Then the king and all the people offered sacrifices before the LORD. 5And King Solomon offered a sacrifice of twenty-two thousand head of cattle and a hundred and twenty thousand sheep and goats. So the king and all the people dedicated the temple of God. 6The priests took their positions, as did the Levites with the LORD's musical instruments, which King David had made for praising the LORD and which were used when he gave thanks, saying, "His love endures forever." Opposite the Levites, the priests blew

**42* Many mss (and Ps. 132:10) have this word in the singular (חך—).

מַחְצְצְרִים נֶגְדָּם וְכָל־ יִשְׂרָאֵל עֹמְדִים׃
ones-standing Israel and-all-of opposite-them ones-blowing-trumpets

וַיְקַדֵּשׁ שְׁלֹמֹה אֶת־ תּוֹךְ הֶחָצֵר אֲשֶׁר לִפְנֵי
in-front-of that the-courtyard middle-of *** Solomon and-he-consecrated (7)

בֵית־ יְהוָה כִּי־ עָשָׂה שָׁם הָעֹלוֹת וְאֵת חֶלְבֵי
fat-parts-of and the-burnt-offerings here he-offered for Yahweh temple-of

הַשְּׁלָמִים כִּי־ מִזְבַּח הַנְּחֹשֶׁת אֲשֶׁר עָשָׂה שְׁלֹמֹה
Solomon he-made that the-bronze altar-of because the-fellowship-offerings

לֹא יָכוֹל לְהָכִיל אֶת־ הָעֹלָה וְאֶת־ הַמִּנְחָה וְאֶת־
and the-grain-offering and the-burnt-offering *** to-hold he-could not

הַחֲלָבִים׃ וַיַּעַשׂ שְׁלֹמֹה אֶת־ הֶחָג בָּעֵת
at-the-time the-festival *** Solomon so-he-observed (8) the-fat-portions

הַהִיא שִׁבְעַת יָמִים וְכָל־ יִשְׂרָאֵל עִמּוֹ קָהָל גָּדוֹל מְאֹד
very vast assembly with-him Israel and-all-of days seven-of the-that

מִלְּבוֹא חֲמָת עַד־ נַחַל מִצְרָיִם׃ וַיַּעֲשׂוּ בַּיּוֹם הַשְּׁמִינִי
the-eighth on-the-day and-they-held (9) Egypt Wadi-of to Hamath from-Lebo

עֲצָרֶת כִּי ׀ חֲנֻכַּת הַמִּזְבֵּחַ עָשׂוּ שִׁבְעַת יָמִים
days seven-of they-celebrated the-altar dedication-of for assembly

וְהֶחָג שִׁבְעַת יָמִים׃ וּבְיוֹם עֶשְׂרִים וּשְׁלֹשָׁה
and-three twenty and-on-day-of (10) days seven-of and-the-festival

לַחֹדֶשׁ הַשְּׁבִיעִי שִׁלַּח אֶת־ הָעָם לְאָהֳלֵיהֶם שְׂמֵחִים
ones-joyful to-homes-of-them the-people *** he-sent the-seventh of-the-month

וְטוֹבֵי לֵב עַל־ הַטּוֹבָה אֲשֶׁר עָשָׂה יְהוָה לְדָוִיד
for-David Yahweh he-did that the-good for heart and-ones-glad-of

וְלִשְׁלֹמֹה וּלְיִשְׂרָאֵל עַמּוֹ׃ וַיְכַל שְׁלֹמֹה
Solomon when-he-finished (11) people-of-him and-for-Israel and-for-Solomon

אֶת־ בֵּית יְהוָה וְאֶת־ בֵּית הַמֶּלֶךְ וְאֵת כָּל־ הַבָּא עַל־
into the-thing-coming all-of and the-king palace-of and Yahweh temple-of ***

לֵב שְׁלֹמֹה לַעֲשׂוֹת בְּבֵית־ יְהוָה וּבְבֵיתוֹ
and-in-palace-of-him Yahweh in-temple-of to-do Solomon mind-of

הִצְלִיחַ׃ וַיֵּרָא יְהוָה אֶל־ שְׁלֹמֹה בַּלָּיְלָה
in-the-night Solomon to Yahweh then-he-appeared (12) he-carried-out

וַיֹּאמֶר לוֹ שָׁמַעְתִּי אֶת־ תְּפִלָּתֶךָ וּבָחַרְתִּי בַּמָּקוֹם
to-the-place and-I-chose prayer-of-you *** I-heard to-him and-he-said

הַזֶּה לִי לְבֵית זָבַח׃ הֵן אֶעֱצֹר הַשָּׁמַיִם
the-heavens I-shut-up when (13) sacrifice as-temple-of for-me the-this

וְלֹא־ יִהְיֶה מָטָר וְהֵן־ אֲצַוֶּה עַל־ חָגָב לֶאֱכוֹל הָאָרֶץ וְאִם־
or-when the-land to-devour locust to I-command or-when rain he-is so-not

their trumpets, and all the Israelites were standing.

[7]Solomon consecrated the middle part of the courtyard in front of the temple of the LORD, and there he offered burnt offerings and the fat of the fellowship offerings,[d] because the bronze altar he had made could not hold the burnt offerings, the grain offerings and the fat portions.

[8]So Solomon observed the festival at that time for seven days, and all Israel with him—a vast assembly, people from Lebo[e] Hamath to the Wadi of Egypt. [9]On the eighth day they held an assembly, for they had celebrated the dedication of the altar for seven days and the festival for seven days more. [10]On the twenty-third day of the seventh month he sent the people to their homes, joyful and glad in heart for the good things the LORD had done for David and Solomon and for his people Israel.

*The LORD Appears to Solomon*

[11]When Solomon had finished the temple of the LORD and the royal palace, and had succeeded in carrying out all he had in mind to do in the temple of the LORD and in his own palace, [12]the LORD appeared to him at night and said:

"I have heard your prayer and have chosen this place for myself as a temple for sacrifices.

[13]"When I shut up the heavens so that there is no rain, or command locusts to devour the land or send a

[d]7 Traditionally *peace offerings*
[e]8 Or *from the entrance to*

°6 ק מחצרים

אֲשַׁלַּח דֶּבֶר בְּעַמִּי׃ וְיִכָּנְעוּ עַמִּי
people-of-me if-they-humble-themselves (14) among-people-of-me plague I-send

אֲשֶׁר נִקְרָא־ שְׁמִי עֲלֵיהֶם וְיִתְפַּלְלוּ וִיבַקְשׁוּ פָנַי
faces-of-me and-they-seek and-they-pray on-them name-of-me he-is-called who

וְיָשֻׁבוּ מִדַּרְכֵיהֶם הָרָעִים וַאֲנִי אֶשְׁמַע מִן־
from I-will-hear then-I the-wicked-ones from-ways-of-them and-they-turn

הַשָּׁמַיִם וְאֶסְלַח לְחַטָּאתָם וְאֶרְפָּא אֶת־ אַרְצָם׃
land-of-them *** and-I-will-heal to-sin-of-them and-I-will-forgive the-heavens

עַתָּה עֵינַי יִהְיוּ פְתֻחוֹת וְאָזְנַי קַשֻּׁבוֹת
ones-attentive and-ears-of-me ones-being-open they-will-be eyes-of-me now (15)

לִתְפִלַּת הַמָּקוֹם הַזֶּה׃ וְעַתָּה בָּחַרְתִּי וְהִקְדַּשְׁתִּי אֶת־
*** and-I-consecrated I-chose and-now (16) the-this the-place to-prayer-of

הַבַּיִת הַזֶּה לִהְיוֹת־ שְׁמִי שָׁם עַד־ עוֹלָם וְהָיוּ
and-they-will-be forever to there Name-of-me to-be the-this the-temple

עֵינַי וְלִבִּי שָׁם כָּל־ הַיָּמִים׃ וְאַתָּה אִם־ תֵּלֵךְ
you-walk if and-you (17) the-days all-of there and-heart-of-me eyes-of-me

לְפָנַי כַּאֲשֶׁר הָלַךְ דָּוִיד אָבִיךָ וְלַעֲשׂוֹת כְּכֹל אֲשֶׁר
that as-all and-to-do father-of-you David he-walked just-as before-me

צִוִּיתִיךָ וְחֻקַּי וּמִשְׁפָּטַי תִּשְׁמוֹר׃
you-observe and-laws-of-me and-decrees-of-me I-command-you

וַהֲקִימוֹתִי אֵת כִּסֵּא מַלְכוּתֶךָ כַּאֲשֶׁר כָּרַתִּי
I-covenanted just-as kingdom-of-you throne-of *** then-I-will-establish (18)

לְדָוִיד אָבִיךָ לֵאמֹר לֹא־ יִכָּרֵת לְךָ אִישׁ מוֹשֵׁל
ruling man of-you he-shall-be-cut-off not to-say father-of-you with-David

בְּיִשְׂרָאֵל׃ וְאִם־ תְּשׁוּבוּן אַתֶּם וַעֲזַבְתֶּם חֻקּוֹתַי
decrees-of-me and-you-forsake you you-turn but-if (19) over-Israel

וּמִצְוֹתַי אֲשֶׁר נָתַתִּי לִפְנֵיכֶם וַהֲלַכְתֶּם וַעֲבַדְתֶּם אֱלֹהִים
gods and-you-serve and-you-go before-you I-gave that and-commands-of-me

אֲחֵרִים וְהִשְׁתַּחֲוִיתֶם לָהֶם׃ וּנְתַשְׁתִּים מֵעַל
from-on then-I-will-uproot-them (20) to-them and-you-worship other-ones

אַדְמָתִי אֲשֶׁר נָתַתִּי לָהֶם וְאֶת־ הַבַּיִת הַזֶּה אֲשֶׁר הִקְדַּשְׁתִּי
I-consecrated that the-this the-temple and to-them I-gave which land-of-me

לִשְׁמִי אַשְׁלִיךְ מֵעַל פָּנָי וְאֶתְּנֶנּוּ
and-I-will-make-him faces-of-me from-before I-will-reject for-Name-of-me

לְמָשָׁל וְלִשְׁנִינָה בְּכָל־ הָעַמִּים׃
the-peoples among-all-of and-as-object-of-ridicule as-byword

וְהַבַּיִת הַזֶּה אֲשֶׁר הָיָה עֶלְיוֹן לְכָל־ עֹבֵר
one-passing to-every-of imposing he-is that the-this though-the-temple (21)

plague among my people,
[14]if my people, who are
called by my name, will
humble themselves and
pray and seek my face and
turn from their wicked
ways, then will I hear from
heaven and will forgive
their sin and will heal their
land. [15]Now my eyes will be
open and my ears attentive
to the prayers offered in
this place. [16]I have chosen
and consecrated this tem-
ple so that my Name may
be there forever. My eyes
and my heart will always
be there.
[17]"As for you, if you walk
before me as David your father did, and do all I command, and observe my de-
crees and laws, [18]I will
establish your royal throne,
as I covenanted with David
your father when I said,
'You shall never fail to have
a man to rule over Israel.'
[19]"But if you[f] turn away
and forsake the decrees and
commands I have given
you[f] and go off to serve
other gods and worship
them, [20]then I will uproot
Israel from my land, which
I have given them, and will
reject this temple I have
consecrated for my Name. I
will make it a byword and
an object of ridicule among
all peoples. [21]And though
this temple is now so im-
posing, all who pass by will

f19 The Hebrew is plural.

עָלָיו יִשֹּׁם וְאָמַר בַּמֶּה עָשָׂה יְהוָה כָּכָה
such Yahweh he-did for-the-why? and-he-will-say he-will-be-appalled by-him

לָאָרֶץ הַזֹּאת וְלַבַּיִת הַזֶּה׃ וְאָמְרוּ
and-they-will-answer (22) the-this and-to-the-temple the-this to-the-land

עַל אֲשֶׁר עָזְבוּ אֶת־ יְהוָה׀ אֱלֹהֵי אֲבֹתֵיהֶם אֲשֶׁר
who fathers-of-them God-of Yahweh *** they-forsook that because

הוֹצִיאָם מֵאֶרֶץ מִצְרַיִם וַיַּחֲזִיקוּ בֵּאלֹהִים אֲחֵרִים
other-ones on-gods and-they-embraced Egypt from-land-of he-brought-them

וַיִּשְׁתַּחֲווּ לָהֶם וַיַּעַבְדוּם עַל־ כֵּן הֵבִיא עֲלֵיהֶם
on-them he-brought this for and-they-served-them to-them and-they-worshiped

אֵת כָּל־ הָרָעָה הַזֹּאת׃ וַיְהִי מִקֵּץ׀ עֶשְׂרִים שָׁנָה אֲשֶׁר
when year twenty at-end-of and-he-was (8:1) the-this the-disaster all-of ***

בָּנָה שְׁלֹמֹה אֶת־ בֵּית יְהוָה וְאֶת־ בֵּיתוֹ׃ וְהֶעָרִים
and-the-villages (2) palace-of-him and Yahweh temple-of *** Solomon he-built

אֲשֶׁר נָתַן חוּרָם לִשְׁלֹמֹה בָּנָה שְׁלֹמֹה אֹתָם וַיּוֹשֶׁב שָׁם
there and-he-settled them Solomon he-rebuilt to-Solomon Huram he-gave that

אֶת־ בְּנֵי יִשְׂרָאֵל׃ וַיֵּלֶךְ שְׁלֹמֹה חֲמָת צוֹבָה וַיֶּחֱזַק
and-he-captured Zobah Hamath Solomon then-he-went (3) Israel sons-of ***

עָלֶיהָ׃ וַיִּבֶן אֶת־ תַּדְמֹר בַּמִּדְבָּר וְאֵת כָּל־ עָרֵי
cities-of all-of and in-the-desert Tadmor *** and-he-built-up (4) to-her

הַמִּסְכְּנוֹת אֲשֶׁר בָּנָה בַּחֲמָת׃ וַיִּבֶן אֶת־ בֵּית חוֹרוֹן
Horon Beth *** and-he-rebuilt (5) in-Hamath he-built that the-stores

הָעֶלְיוֹן וְאֶת־ בֵּית חוֹרוֹן הַתַּחְתּוֹן עָרֵי מָצוֹר חוֹמוֹת דְּלָתַיִם
gates walls fortification cities-of the-Lower Horon Beth and the-Upper

וּבְרִיחַ׃ וְאֶת־ בַּעֲלָת וְאֵת כָּל־ עָרֵי הַמִּסְכְּנוֹת אֲשֶׁר הָיוּ
they-were that the-stores cities-of all-of and Baalath and (6) and-bar

לִשְׁלֹמֹה וְאֵת כָּל־ עָרֵי הָרֶכֶב וְאֵת עָרֵי הַפָּרָשִׁים וְאֵת׀
and the-horses cities-of and the-chariot cities-of all-of and to-Solomon

כָּל־ חֵשֶׁק שְׁלֹמֹה אֲשֶׁר חָשַׁק לִבְנוֹת בִּירוּשָׁלַםִ
in-Jerusalem to-build he-desired that Solomon desire-of every-of

וּבַלְּבָנוֹן וּבְכֹל אֶרֶץ מֶמְשַׁלְתּוֹ׃ כָּל־
all-of (7) rule-of-him territory-of and-through-all-of and-in-the-Lebanon

הָעָם הַנּוֹתָר מִן־ הַחִתִּי וְהָאֱמֹרִי
and-the-Amorite the-Hittite from the-one-being-left the-people

וְהַפְּרִזִּי וְהַחִוִּי וְהַיְבוּסִי אֲשֶׁר לֹא מִיִּשְׂרָאֵל הֵמָּה׃
they from-Israel not who and-the-Jebusite and-the-Hivite and-the-Perizzite

מִן־ בְּנֵיהֶם אֲשֶׁר נוֹתְרוּ אַחֲרֵיהֶם בָּאָרֶץ אֲשֶׁר
who in-the-land after-them they-remained who descendants-of-them from (8)

be appalled and say, 'Why
has the LORD done such a
thing to this land and to
this temple?' [22]People will
answer, 'Because they have
forsaken the LORD, the God
of their fathers, who
brought them out of Egypt,
and have embraced other
gods, worshiping and serving them—that is why he
brought all this disaster on
them.' "

*Solomon's Other Activities*

8 At the end of twenty
years, during which Solo-
mon built the temple of the
LORD and his own palace,
[2]Solomon rebuilt the villages
that Hiram[g] had given him,
and settled Israelites in them.
[3]Solomon then went to
Hamath Zobah and captured
it. [4]He also built up Tadmor in
the desert and all the store cities he had built in Hamath.
[5]He rebuilt Upper Beth Horon
and Lower Beth Horon as fortified cities, with walls and
with gates and bars, [6]as well as
Baalath and all his store cities,
and all the cities for his
chariots and for his
horses[h]—whatever he desired
to build in Jerusalem, in Lebanon and throughout all the
territory he ruled.
[7]All the people left from the
Hittites, Amorites, Perizzites,
Hivites and Jebusites (these
peoples were not Israelites),
[8]that is, their descendants remaining in the land, whom

[g]2 Hebrew *Huram*, a variant of *Hiram*; also in verse 18
[h]6 Or *charioteers*

לֹא־ כִלּוּם בְּנֵי יִשְׂרָאֵל וַיַּעֲלֵם שְׁלֹמֹה
Solomon now-he-conscripted-them Israel sons-of they-destroyed-them not

לְמַס עַד הַיּוֹם הַזֶּה׃ וּמִן־ בְּנֵי יִשְׂרָאֵל אֲשֶׁר לֹא־
not who Israel sons-of but-from (9) the-this the-day to for-slave-labor

נָתַן שְׁלֹמֹה לַעֲבָדִים לִמְלַאכְתּוֹ כִּי־ הֵמָּה אַנְשֵׁי מִלְחָמָה
fight men-of they for for-work-of-him as-slaves Solomon he-made

וְשָׂרֵי שָׁלִישָׁיו וְשָׂרֵי רִכְבּוֹ
chariot-of-him and-commanders-of captains-of-him and-commanders-of

וּפָרָשָׁיו׃ וְאֵלֶּה שָׂרֵי הַנִּצִּיבִים°
the-ones-being-officials chiefs-of and-these (10) and-charioteers-of-him

אֲשֶׁר־ לַמֶּלֶךְ שְׁלֹמֹה חֲמִשִּׁים וּמָאתַיִם הָרֹדִים
the-ones-supervising and-two-hundreds fifty Solomon of-the-king who

בָּעָם׃ וְאֶת־ בַּת־ פַּרְעֹה הֶעֱלָה שְׁלֹמֹה
Solomon he-brought-up Pharaoh daughter-of and (11) over-the-people

מֵעִיר דָּוִיד לַבַּיִת אֲשֶׁר בָּנָה־ לָהּ כִּי אָמַר לֹא־
not he-said for for-her he-built that to-the-palace David from-City-of

תֵשֵׁב אִשָּׁה לִי בְּבֵית דָּוִיד מֶלֶךְ־ יִשְׂרָאֵל כִּי־ קֹדֶשׁ
holy because Israel king-of David in-palace-of of-me wife she-must-live

הֵמָּה אֲשֶׁר־ בָּאָה אֲלֵיהֶם אֲרוֹן יְהוָה׃ אָז הֶעֱלָה
he-sacrificed then (12) Yahweh ark-of into-them she-entered where they

שְׁלֹמֹה עֹלוֹת לַיהוָה עַל מִזְבַּח יְהוָה אֲשֶׁר בָּנָה לִפְנֵי
in-front-of he-built that Yahweh altar-of on to-Yahweh burnt-offerings Solomon

הָאוּלָם׃ וּבִדְבַר־ יוֹם בְּיוֹם לְהַעֲלוֹת
to-offer by-day day and-for-requirement-of (13) the-portico

כְּמִצְוַת מֹשֶׁה לַשַּׁבָּתוֹת וְלֶחֳדָשִׁים וְלַמּוֹעֲדוֹת
and-for-the-feasts and-for-the-New-Moons for-the-Sabbaths Moses as-command-of

שָׁלוֹשׁ פְּעָמִים בַּשָּׁנָה בְּחַג הַמַּצּוֹת
the-Unleavened-Breads for-Feast-of during-the-year times three

וּבְחַג הַשָּׁבֻעוֹת וּבְחַג הַסֻּכּוֹת׃
the-Tabernacles and-for-Feast-of the-Weeks and-for-Feast-of

וַיַּעֲמֵד כְּמִשְׁפַּט דָּוִיד־ אָבִיו אֶת־ מַחְלְקוֹת
divisions-of *** father-of-him David as-ordinance-of and-he-appointed (14)

הַכֹּהֲנִים עַל־ עֲבֹדָתָם וְהַלְוִיִּם עַל־ מִשְׁמְרוֹתָם
leaderships-of-them for and-the-Levites duty-of-them for the-priests

לְהַלֵּל וּלְשָׁרֵת נֶגֶד הַכֹּהֲנִים לִדְבַר־ יוֹם
day for-requirement-of the-priests before and-to-assist to-praise

בְּיוֹמוֹ וְהַשּׁוֹעֲרִים בְּמַחְלְקוֹתָם לְשַׁעַר וָשָׁעַר
and-gate for-gate by-divisions-of-them and-the-gatekeepers by-day-of-him

the Israelites had not destroyed—these Solomon conscripted for his slave labor
force, as it is to this day. 9But
Solomon did not make slaves
of the Israelites for his work;
they were his fighting men,
commanders of his captains,
and commanders of his chariots and charioteers. 10They
were also King Solomon's
chief officials—two hundred
and fifty officials supervising
the men.
11Solomon brought Phar-
aoh's daughter up from the
City of David to the palace he
had built for her, for he said,
"My wife must not live in the
palace of David king of Israel,
because the places the ark of
the LORD has entered are
holy."
12On the altar of the LORD
that he had built in front of
the portico, Solomon sac-
rificed burnt offerings to the
LORD, 13according to the daily
requirement for offerings
commanded by Moses for
Sabbaths, New Moons and the
three annual feasts—the Feast
of Unleavened Bread, the
Feast of Weeks and the Feast
of Tabernacles. 14Following
the ordinance of his father David, he appointed the divisions of the priests for their
duties, and the Levites to lead
the praise and to assist the
priests according to each day's
requirement. He also appointed the gatekeepers by divisions for the various gates, because this was what David the

°10 ק הנצבים

כִּי כֵן מִצְוַת דָּוִיד אִישׁ־הָאֱלֹהִים׃ וְלֹא סָרוּ
they-deviated and-not (15) the-God man-of David order-of this because

מִצְוַת הַמֶּלֶךְ עַל־הַכֹּהֲנִים וְהַלְוִיִּם לְכָל־דָּבָר
matter in-any-of and-the-Levites the-priests to the-king command-of

וְלָאֹצָרוֹת׃ וַתִּכֹּן כָּל־מְלֶאכֶת שְׁלֹמֹה
Solomon work-of all-of and-she-was-carried-out (16) even-about-the-treasuries

עַד־הַיּוֹם מוּסַד בֵּית־יְהוָה וְעַד־כְּלֹתוֹ
to-be-completed-him and-to Yahweh temple-of foundation-of the-day from

שָׁלֵם בֵּית יְהוָה׃ אָז הָלַךְ שְׁלֹמֹה לְעֶצְיוֹן־גֶּבֶר וְאֶל־
and-to Geber to-Ezion Solomon he-went then (17) Yahweh temple-of finished

אֵילוֹת עַל־שְׂפַת הַיָּם בְּאֶרֶץ אֱדוֹם׃ וַיִּשְׁלַח־לוֹ חוּרָם
Huram to-him and-he-sent (18) Edom in-land-of the-sea coast-of on Elath

בְּיַד־עֲבָדָיו אֳנִיּוֹת° וַעֲבָדִים יוֹדְעֵי יָם וַיָּבֹאוּ
and-they-sailed sea ones-knowing-of and-men ships officers-of-him by-hand-of

עִם־עַבְדֵי שְׁלֹמֹה אוֹפִירָה וַיִּקְחוּ מִשָּׁם אַרְבַּע־מֵאוֹת
hundreds four from-there and-they-brought to-Ophir Solomon men-of with

וַחֲמִשִּׁים כִּכַּר זָהָב וַיָּבִיאוּ אֶל־הַמֶּלֶךְ שְׁלֹמֹה׃
Solomon the-king to and-they-delivered gold talent-of and-fifty

וּמַלְכַּת־שְׁבָא שָׁמְעָה אֶת־שֵׁמַע שְׁלֹמֹה וַתָּבוֹא
then-she-came Solomon fame-of *** she-heard Sheba when-queen-of (9:1)

לְנַסּוֹת אֶת־שְׁלֹמֹה בְחִידוֹת בִּירוּשָׁלִַם בְּחַיִל כָּבֵד מְאֹד
very great with-caravan to-Jerusalem with-hard-questions Solomon *** to-test

וּגְמַלִּים נֹשְׂאִים בְּשָׂמִים וְזָהָב לָרֹב וְאֶבֶן יְקָרָה
precious and-stone in-quantity and-gold spices ones-carrying and-camels

וַתָּבוֹא אֶל־שְׁלֹמֹה וַתְּדַבֵּר עִמּוֹ אֵת כָּל־אֲשֶׁר הָיָה עִם־
on he-was that all *** with-him and-she-talked Solomon to and-she-came

לְבָבָהּ׃ וַיַּגֶּד־לָהּ שְׁלֹמֹה אֶת־כָּל־דְּבָרֶיהָ
questions-of-her all-of *** Solomon to-her and-he-answered (2) mind-of-her

וְלֹא־נֶעְלַם דָּבָר מִשְּׁלֹמֹה אֲשֶׁר לֹא הִגִּיד לָהּ׃
to-her he-explained not that for-Solomon question he-was-too-hard and-not

וַתֵּרֶא מַלְכַּת־שְׁבָא אֵת חָכְמַת שְׁלֹמֹה וְהַבַּיִת אֲשֶׁר
that and-the-palace Solomon wisdom-of *** Sheba queen-of when-she-saw (3)

בָּנָה׃ וּמַאֲכַל שֻׁלְחָנוֹ וּמוֹשַׁב עֲבָדָיו
officials-of-him and-seating-of table-of-him and-food-of (4) he-built

וּמַעֲמַד מְשָׁרְתָיו וּמַלְבּוּשֵׁיהֶם וּמַשְׁקָיו
and-cupbearers-of-him and-robes-of-them ones-attending-him and-station-of

וּמַלְבּוּשֵׁיהֶם וַעֲלִיָּתוֹ* אֲשֶׁר יַעֲלֶה בֵּית יְהוָה
Yahweh temple-of he-went-up which *and-ascent-of-him and-robes-of-them

man of God had ordered.
[15]They did not deviate from
the king's commands to the
priests or to the Levites in any
matter, including that of the
treasuries.
[16]All Solomon's work was
carried out, from the day the
foundation of the temple of
the LORD was laid until its
completion. So the temple of
the LORD was finished.
[17]Then Solomon went to
Ezion Geber and Elath on the
seacoast of Edom. [18]And
Hiram sent him ships com-
manded by his own officers,
men who knew the sea. These,
with Solomon's men, sailed to
Ophir and brought back four
hundred and fifty talents[i] of
gold, which they delivered to
King Solomon.

*The Queen of Sheba Visits Solomon*

9 When the queen of Sheba
heard of Solomon's fame,
she came to Jerusalem to test
him with hard questions. Arriving with a very great caravan—with camels carrying
spices, large quantities of gold,
and precious stones—she
came to Solomon and talked
with him about all she had on
her mind. [2]Solomon answered
all her questions; nothing was
too hard for him to explain to
her. [3]When the queen of
Sheba saw the wisdom of
Solomon, as well as the palace
he had built, [4]the food on his
table, the seating of his
officials, the attending servants in their robes, the cup-
bearers in their robes and the
burnt offerings he made at[j]
the temple of the LORD, she

[i]18 That is, about 17 tons (about 16 metric tons)
[j]4 Or *the ascent by which he went up to*

*4 The NIV reads this word as in 1 Kings 10:5 ( וְעֹלָתוֹ ), *and-burnt-offering-of-him.*

°18 ק אניות

וְלֹא־ הָיָה עוֹד בָּהּ רוּחַ׃ וַתֹּאמֶר אֶל־ הַמֶּלֶךְ אֱמֶת
true the-king to and-she-said (5) breath in-her longer he-was then-not

הַדָּבָר אֲשֶׁר שָׁמַעְתִּי בְּאַרְצִי עַל־ דְּבָרֶיךָ וְעַל־
and-about achievements-of-you about in-country-of-me I-heard that the-report

חָכְמָתֶךָ׃ וְלֹא־ הֶאֱמַנְתִּי לְדִבְרֵיהֶם עַד אֲשֶׁר־ בָּאתִי
I-came when until in-sayings-of-them I-believed but-not (6) wisdom-of-you

וַתִּרְאֶינָה עֵינַי וְהִנֵּה לֹא הֻגַּד־ לִי חֲצִי מַרְבִּית
greatness-of half-of to-me he-was-told not and-see! eyes-of-me and-they-saw

חָכְמָתֶךָ יָסַפְתָּ עַל־ הַשְּׁמוּעָה אֲשֶׁר שָׁמָעְתִּי׃ אַשְׁרֵי
happinesses-of (7) I-heard that the-report over you-exceeded wisdom-of-you

אֲנָשֶׁיךָ וְאַשְׁרֵי עֲבָדֶיךָ אֵלֶּה הָעֹמְדִים
the-ones-standing these officials-of-you and-happinesses-of men-of-you

לְפָנֶיךָ תָּמִיד וְשֹׁמְעִים אֶת־ חָכְמָתֶךָ׃ יְהִי
may-he-be (8) wisdom-of-you *** and-ones-hearing continually before-you

יְהוָה אֱלֹהֶיךָ בָּרוּךְ אֲשֶׁר ׀ חָפֵץ בְּךָ לְתִתְּךָ עַל־
on to-place-you in-you he-delighted who being-praised God-of-you Yahweh

כִּסְאוֹ לְמֶלֶךְ לַיהוָה אֱלֹהֶיךָ בְּאַהֲבַת אֱלֹהֶיךָ אֶת־
*** God-of-you because-to-love God-of-you for-Yahweh as-king throne-of-him

יִשְׂרָאֵל לְהַעֲמִידוֹ לְעוֹלָם וַיִּתֶּנְךָ עֲלֵיהֶם לְמֶלֶךְ לַעֲשׂוֹת
to-maintain as-king over-them then-he-made-you to-forever to-uphold-him Israel

מִשְׁפָּט וּצְדָקָה׃ וַתִּתֵּן לַמֶּלֶךְ מֵאָה וְעֶשְׂרִים ׀
and-twenty hundred to-the-king then-she-gave (9) and-righteousness justice

כִּכַּר זָהָב וּבְשָׂמִים לָרֹב מְאֹד וְאֶבֶן יְקָרָה וְלֹא
and-never precious and-stone large in-quantity and-spices gold talent-of

הָיָה כַּבֹּשֶׂם הַהוּא אֲשֶׁר־ נָתְנָה מַלְכַּת־ שְׁבָא לַמֶּלֶךְ
to-the-king Sheba queen-of she-gave that the-this like-the-spice he-was

שְׁלֹמֹה׃ וְגַם־ עַבְדֵי חִירָם° וְעַבְדֵי שְׁלֹמֹה אֲשֶׁר־ הֵבִיאוּ זָהָב
gold they-brought who Solomon and-men-of Hiram men-of and-also (10) Solomon

מֵאוֹפִיר הֵבִיאוּ עֲצֵי אַלְגּוּמִּים וְאֶבֶן יְקָרָה׃ וַיַּעַשׂ
and-he-made (11) precious and-stone algums woods-of they-brought from-Ophir

הַמֶּלֶךְ אֶת־ עֲצֵי הָאַלְגּוּמִּים מְסִלּוֹת לְבֵית־ יְהוָה וּלְבֵית
and-for-palace-of Yahweh for-temple-of steps the-algums woods-of *** the-king

הַמֶּלֶךְ וְכִנֹּרוֹת וּנְבָלִים לַשָּׁרִים וְלֹא־
and-never for-the-ones-making-music and-lyres and-harps the-king

נִרְאוּ כָהֵם לְפָנִים בְּאֶרֶץ יְהוּדָה׃ וְהַמֶּלֶךְ שְׁלֹמֹה
Solomon and-the-king (12) Judah in-land-of before like-them they-were-seen

נָתַן לְמַלְכַּת־ שְׁבָא אֶת־ כָּל־ חֶפְצָהּ אֲשֶׁר שָׁאָלָה
she-asked-for that desire-of-her all-of *** Sheba to-queen-of he-gave

was overwhelmed.

[5]She said to the king, "The report I heard in my own country about your achievements and your wisdom is true. [6]But I did not believe what they said until I came and saw with my own eyes. Indeed, not even half the greatness of your wisdom was told me; you have far exceeded the report I heard. [7]How happy your men must be! How happy your officials, who continually stand before you and hear your wisdom! [8]Praise be to the LORD your God, who has delighted in you and placed you on his throne as king to rule for the LORD your God. Because of the love of your God for Israel and his desire to uphold them forever, he has made you king over them, to maintain justice and righteousness."

[9]Then she gave the king 120 talents[k] of gold, large quantities of spices, and precious stones. There had never been such spices as those the queen of Sheba gave to King Solomon.

[10](The men of Hiram and the men of Solomon brought gold from Ophir; they also brought algumwood[l] and precious stones. [11]The king used the algumwood to make steps for the temple of the LORD and for the royal palace, and to make harps and lyres for the musicians. Nothing like them had ever been seen in Judah.)

[12]King Solomon gave the queen of Sheba all she desired and asked for; he gave her

[k]9 That is, about 4 1/2 tons (about 4 metric tons)

[l]10 Probably a variant of *almugwood*

°*10* ק חורם

מִלְּבַד אֲשֶׁר־הֵבִיאָה אֶל־הַמֶּלֶךְ וַתַּהֲפֹךְ וַתֵּלֶךְ
and-she-returned then-she-left the-king to she-brought what more-than

לְאַרְצָהּ הִיא וַעֲבָדֶיהָ׃ (13) וַיְהִי מִשְׁקַל הַזָּהָב
the-gold weight-of and-he-was (13) and-servants-of-her she to-country-of-her

אֲשֶׁר־בָּא לִשְׁלֹמֹה בְּשָׁנָה אֶחָת שֵׁשׁ מֵאוֹת וְשִׁשִּׁים וָשֵׁשׁ
and-six and-sixty hundreds six each in-year to-Solomon he-came that

כִּכְּרֵי זָהָב׃ (14) לְבַד מֵאַנְשֵׁי הַתָּרִים
the-ones-being-merchants from-men-of besides (14) gold talents-of

וְהַסֹּחֲרִים מְבִיאִים וְכָל־מַלְכֵי עֲרַב
Arabia kings-of and-all-of ones-bringing and-the-ones-trading

וּפַחוֹת הָאָרֶץ מְבִיאִים זָהָב וָכֶסֶף לִשְׁלֹמֹה׃
to-Solomon and-silver gold ones-bringing the-land and-governors-of

(15) וַיַּעַשׂ הַמֶּלֶךְ שְׁלֹמֹה מָאתַיִם צִנָּה זָהָב שָׁחוּט
being-hammered gold shield two-hundreds Solomon the-king and-he-made (15)

שֵׁשׁ מֵאוֹת זָהָב שָׁחוּט יַעֲלֶה עַל־הַצִּנָּה הָאֶחָת׃
the-each the-shield into he-went being-hammered gold hundreds six

(16) וּשְׁלֹשׁ־מֵאוֹת מָגִנִּים זָהָב שָׁחוּט שְׁלֹשׁ
three-of being-hammered gold small-shields hundreds and-three-of (16)

מֵאוֹת זָהָב יַעֲלֶה עַל־הַמָּגֵן הָאֶחָת וַיִּתְּנֵם הַמֶּלֶךְ
the-king and-he-put-them the-each the-shield into he-went gold hundreds

בְּבֵית יַעַר הַלְּבָנוֹן׃ (17) וַיַּעַשׂ הַמֶּלֶךְ כִּסֵּא־
throne-of the-king then-he-made (17) the-Lebanon Forest-of in-Palace-of

שֵׁן גָּדוֹל וַיְצַפֵּהוּ זָהָב טָהוֹר׃ (18) וְשֵׁשׁ מַעֲלוֹת לַכִּסֵּא
to-the-throne steps and-six-of (18) pure gold and-he-overlaid-him great ivory

וְכֶבֶשׁ בַּזָּהָב לַכִּסֵּא מָאֳחָזִים וְיָדוֹת
and-armrests ones-being-attached to-the-throne of-the-gold and-footstool

מִזֶּה וּמִזֶּה עַל־מְקוֹם הַשָּׁבֶת וּשְׁנַיִם אֲרָיוֹת
lions and-two the-seat place-of at and-on-that-side on-this-side

עֹמְדִים אֵצֶל הַיָּדוֹת׃ (19) וּשְׁנֵים עָשָׂר אֲרָיוֹת עֹמְדִים שָׁם
there ones-standing lions ten and-two (19) the-armrests beside ones-standing

עַל־שֵׁשׁ הַמַּעֲלוֹת מִזֶּה וּמִזֶּה לֹא־נַעֲשָׂה כֵן
like he-was-made not and-on-that-end on-this-end the-steps six-of on

לְכָל־מַמְלָכָה׃ (20) וְכֹל כְּלֵי מַשְׁקֵה הַמֶּלֶךְ שְׁלֹמֹה
Solomon the-king drinking-of goblets-of and-all-of (20) kingdom for-any-of

זָהָב וְכֹל כְּלֵי בֵית־יַעַר הַלְּבָנוֹן זָהָב סָגוּר
pure gold the-Lebanon Forest-of Palace-of articles-of and-all-of gold

אֵין כֶּסֶף נֶחְשָׁב בִּימֵי שְׁלֹמֹה לִמְאוּמָה׃ (21) כִּי־
indeed (21) as-anything Solomon in-days-of being-considered silver nothing-of

more than she had brought to him. Then she left and returned with her retinue to her own country.

*Solomon's Splendor*

13 The weight of the gold that Solomon received yearly was 666 talents,[m] 14 not including the revenues brought in by merchants and traders. Also all the kings of Arabia and the governors of the land brought gold and silver to Solomon.

15 King Solomon made two hundred large shields of hammered gold; six hundred bekas[n] of hammered gold went into each shield. 16 He also made three hundred small shields of hammered gold, with three hundred bekas[o] of gold in each shield. The king put them in the Palace of the Forest of Lebanon.

17 Then the king made a great throne inlaid with ivory and overlaid with pure gold. 18 The throne had six steps, and a footstool of gold was attached to it. On both sides of the seat were armrests, with a lion standing beside each of them. 19 Twelve lions stood on the six steps, one at either end of each step. Nothing like it had ever been made for any other kingdom. 20 All King Solomon's goblets were gold, and all the household articles in the Palace of the Forest of Lebanon were pure gold. Nothing was made of silver, because silver was considered of little value in Solomon's day. 21 The king

[m] *13* That is, about 25 tons (about 23 metric tons)
[n] *15* That is, about 7 1/2 pounds (about 3.5 kilograms)
[o] *16* That is, about 3 3/4 pounds (about 1.7 kilograms)

אֳנִיּוֹת לַמֶּלֶךְ הֹלְכוֹת תַּרְשִׁישׁ עִם עַבְדֵי חוּרָם אַחַת לְשָׁלוֹשׁ שָׁנִים
years in-three once Huram men-of with Tarshish ones-going to-the-king ships

תָּבוֹאנָה ׀ אֳנִיּוֹת תַּרְשִׁישׁ נֹשְׂאוֹת זָהָב וָכֶסֶף שֶׁנְהַבִּים וְקוֹפִים
and-apes ivories and-silver gold ones-carrying Tarshish ships-of they-returned

וְתוּכִּיִּים׃ וַיִּגְדַּל הַמֶּלֶךְ שְׁלֹמֹה מִכֹּל מַלְכֵי
kings-of more-than-all-of Solomon the-king and-he-was-great (22) and-baboons

הָאָרֶץ לְעֹשֶׁר וְחָכְמָה׃ וְכֹל מַלְכֵי הָאָרֶץ
the-earth kings-of and-all-of (23) and-wisdom in-wealth the-earth

מְבַקְשִׁים אֶת־ פְּנֵי שְׁלֹמֹה לִשְׁמֹעַ אֶת־ חָכְמָתוֹ אֲשֶׁר־ נָתַן
he-put that wisdom-of-him *** to-hear Solomon faces-of *** ones-seeking

הָאֱלֹהִים בְּלִבּוֹ׃ וְהֵם מְבִיאִים אִישׁ מִנְחָתוֹ
gift-of-him each ones-bringing and-they (24) in-heart-of-him the-God

כְּלֵי כֶסֶף וּכְלֵי זָהָב וּשְׂלָמוֹת נֵשֶׁק וּבְשָׂמִים סוּסִים
horses and-spices weapon and-robes gold and-articles-of silver articles-of

וּפְרָדִים דְּבַר־ שָׁנָה בְּשָׁנָה׃ וַיְהִי לִשְׁלֹמֹה אַרְבַּעַת
four-of to-Solomon and-he-was (25) after-year year event-of and-mules

אֲלָפִים אֻרְיוֹת סוּסִים וּמַרְכָּבוֹת וּשְׁנֵים־ עָשָׂר אֶלֶף פָּרָשִׁים
horses thousand ten and-two and-chariots horses stalls-of thousands

וַיַּנִּיחֵם בְּעָרֵי הָרֶכֶב וְעִם־ הַמֶּלֶךְ בִּירוּשָׁלָםִ׃
in-Jerusalem the-king and-with the-chariot in-cities-of and-he-kept-them

וַיְהִי מוֹשֵׁל בְּכָל־ הַמְּלָכִים מִן־ הַנָּהָר וְעַד־ אֶרֶץ
land-of even-to the-River from the-kings over-all-of ruling and-he-was (26)

פְּלִשְׁתִּים וְעַד גְּבוּל מִצְרָיִם׃ וַיִּתֵּן הַמֶּלֶךְ אֶת־ הַכֶּסֶף
the-silver *** the-king and-he-made (27) Egypt border-of and-to Philistines

בִּירוּשָׁלַםִ כָּאֲבָנִים וְאֵת הָאֲרָזִים נָתַן כַּשִּׁקְמִים
as-the-sycamore-trees he-made the-cedars and as-the-stones in-Jerusalem

אֲשֶׁר־ בַּשְּׁפֵלָה לָרֹב׃ וּמוֹצִיאִים סוּסִים מִמִּצְרַיִם
from-Egypt horses and-ones-importing (28) in-number in-the-foothill that

לִשְׁלֹמֹה וּמִכָּל־ הָאֲרָצוֹת׃ וּשְׁאָר דִּבְרֵי שְׁלֹמֹה
Solomon events-of and-other-of (29) the-countries and-from-all-of to-Solomon

הָרִאשֹׁנִים וְהָאַחֲרוֹנִים* הֲלֹא־ הֵם כְּתוּבִים עַל־ דִּבְרֵי
records-of in ones-being-written they not? and-the-ends the-beginnings

נָתָן הַנָּבִיא וְעַל־ נְבוּאַת אֲחִיָּה הַשִּׁילוֹנִי וּבַחֲזוֹת
and-in-visions-of the-Shilonite Ahijah prophecy-of and-in the-prophet Nathan

יֶעְדִּי° הַחֹזֶה עַל־ יָרָבְעָם בֶּן־ נְבָט׃ וַיִּמְלֹךְ שְׁלֹמֹה
Solomon and-he-reigned (30) Nebat son-of Jeroboam concerning the-seer Iddo

בִירוּשָׁלַםִ עַל־ כָּל־ יִשְׂרָאֵל אַרְבָּעִים שָׁנָה׃ וַיִּשְׁכַּב שְׁלֹמֹה עִם־
with Solomon then-he-rested (31) year forty Israel all-of over in-Jerusalem

had a fleet of trading ships[p] manned by Hiram's[q] men. Once every three years it returned, carrying gold, silver and ivory, and apes and baboons.

22King Solomon was greater in riches and wisdom than all the other kings of the earth. 23All the kings of the earth sought audience with Solomon to hear the wisdom God had put in his heart. 24Year after year, everyone who came brought a gift—articles of silver and gold, and robes, weapons and spices, and horses and mules.

25Solomon had four thousand stalls for horses and chariots, and twelve thousand horses,[r] which he kept in the chariot cities and also with him in Jerusalem. 26He ruled over all the kings from the River[s] to the land of the Philistines, as far as the border of Egypt. 27The king made silver as common in Jerusalem as stones, and cedar as plentiful as sycamore-fig trees in the foothills. 28Solomon's horses were imported from Egypt[t] and from all other countries.

*Solomon's Death*

29As for the other events of Solomon's reign, from beginning to end, are they not written in the records of Nathan the prophet, in the prophecy of Ahijah the Shilonite and in the visions of Iddo the seer concerning Jeroboam son of Nebat? 30Solomon reigned in Jerusalem over all Israel forty years. 31Then he rested with

p21 Hebrew *of ships that could go to Tarshish*
q21 Hebrew *Huram*, a variant of *Hiram*
r25 Or *charioteers*
s26 That is, the Euphrates
t28 Or possibly *Muzur*, a region in Cilicia

*29 Most mss have *pathah* under the *aleph* (וְהָאַחֲ).

°29 ק יעדו

אֲבֹתָיו וַיִּקְבְּרֻהוּ בְּעִיר דָּוִיד אָבִיו
father-of-him David in-city-of and-they-buried-him fathers-of-him

וַיִּמְלֹךְ רְחַבְעָם בְּנוֹ תַּחְתָּיו׃ וַיֵּלֶךְ
and-he-went (10:1) in-place-of-him son-of-him Rehoboam and-he-became-king

רְחַבְעָם שְׁכֶמָה כִּי שְׁכֶם בָּאוּ כָל־יִשְׂרָאֵל לְהַמְלִיךְ אֹתוֹ׃
him to-make-king Israel all-of they-went Shechem for to-Shechem Rehoboam

וַיְהִי כִּשְׁמֹעַ יָרָבְעָם בֶּן־נְבָט וְהוּא בְמִצְרַיִם אֲשֶׁר
where in-Egypt now-he Nebat son-of Jeroboam when-to-hear and-he-was (2)

בָּרַח מִפְּנֵי שְׁלֹמֹה הַמֶּלֶךְ וַיָּשָׁב יָרָבְעָם מִמִּצְרָיִם׃
from-Egypt Jeroboam then-he-returned the-king Solomon from-before he-fled

וַיִּשְׁלְחוּ וַיִּקְרְאוּ־לוֹ וַיָּבֹא יָרָבְעָם וְכָל־
and-all-of Jeroboam and-he-went for-him and-they-called so-they-sent (3)

יִשְׂרָאֵל וַיְדַבְּרוּ אֶל־רְחַבְעָם לֵאמֹר׃ אָבִיךָ הִקְשָׁה אֶת־
*** he-made-heavy father-of-you (4) to-say Rehoboam to and-they-said Israel

עֻלֵּנוּ וְעַתָּה הָקֵל מֵעֲבֹדַת אָבִיךָ הַקָּשָׁה
the-harsh father-of-you from-labor-of lighten! but-now yoke-of-us

וּמֵעֻלּוֹ הַכָּבֵד אֲשֶׁר־נָתַן עָלֵינוּ וְנַעַבְדֶךָּ׃
and-we-will-serve-you on-us he-put that the-heavy and-from-yoke-of-him

וַיֹּאמֶר אֲלֵהֶם עוֹד שְׁלֹשֶׁת יָמִים וְשׁוּבוּ אֵלָי
to-me then-come-back! days three-of still to-them and-he-answered (5)

וַיֵּלֶךְ הָעָם׃ וַיִּוָּעַץ הַמֶּלֶךְ רְחַבְעָם אֶת־
with Rehoboam the-king then-he-consulted (6) the-people so-he-went-away

הַזְּקֵנִים אֲשֶׁר־הָיוּ עֹמְדִים לִפְנֵי שְׁלֹמֹה אָבִיו
father-of-him Solomon before ones-serving they-were who the-elders

בִּהְיֹתוֹ חַי לֵאמֹר אֵיךְ אַתֶּם נוֹעָצִים לְהָשִׁיב לָעָם־
to-the-people to-return ones-advising you how? to-ask alive while-to-be-him

הַזֶּה דָּבָר׃ וַיְדַבְּרוּ אֵלָיו לֵאמֹר אִם־תִּהְיֶה לְטוֹב
as-kind you-will-be if to-say to-him and-they-replied (7) answer the-this

לְהָעָם הַזֶּה וּרְצִיתָם וְדִבַּרְתָּ אֲלֵהֶם דְּבָרִים
answers to-them and-you-give and-you-please-them the-this to-the-people

טוֹבִים וְהָיוּ לְךָ עֲבָדִים כָּל־הַיָּמִים׃
the-days all-of servants to-you and-they-will-be favorable-ones

וַיַּעֲזֹב אֶת־עֲצַת הַזְּקֵנִים אֲשֶׁר יְעָצֻהוּ
they-gave-him that the-elders advice-of with but-he-rejected (8)

וַיִּוָּעַץ אֶת־הַיְלָדִים אֲשֶׁר גָּדְלוּ אִתּוֹ הָעֹמְדִים
the-ones-serving with-him they-grew-up who the-young-men *** and-he-consulted

לְפָנָיו׃ וַיֹּאמֶר אֲלֵהֶם מָה אַתֶּם נוֹעָצִים וְנָשִׁיב
that-we-should-give ones-advising you what? to-them and-he-asked (9) before-him

his fathers and was buried in the city of David his father. And Rehoboam his son succeeded him as king.

*Israel Rebels Against Rehoboam*

**10** Rehoboam went to Shechem, for all the Israelites had gone there to make him king. 2When Jeroboam son of Nebat heard this (he was in Egypt, where he had fled from King Solomon), he returned from Egypt. 3So they sent for Jeroboam, and he and all Israel went to Rehoboam and said to him: 4"Your father put a heavy yoke on us, but now lighten the harsh labor and the heavy yoke he put on us, and we will serve you."

5Rehoboam answered, "Come back to me in three days." So the people went away.

6Then King Rehoboam consulted the elders who had served his father Solomon during his lifetime. "How would you advise me to answer these people?" he asked.

7They replied, "If you will be kind to these people and please them and give them a favorable answer, they will always be your servants."

8But Rehoboam rejected the advice the elders gave him and consulted the young men who had grown up with him and were serving him. 9He asked them, "What is your advice? How should we answer

דָּבָר אֶת־ הָעָם הַזֶּה אֲשֶׁר דִּבְּרוּ אֵלַי לֵאמֹר הָקֵל מִן־
from lighten! to-say to-me they-say who the-this the-people *** answer

הָעֹל אֲשֶׁר־ נָתַן אָבִיךָ עָלֵינוּ׃ וַיְדַבְּרוּ אִתּוֹ
to-him and-they-replied (10) on-us father-of-you he-put that the-yoke

הַיְלָדִים אֲשֶׁר גָּדְלוּ אִתּוֹ לֵאמֹר כֹּה־ תֹאמַר לָעָם
to-the-people you-tell this to-say with-him they-grew-up who the-young-men

אֲשֶׁר־ דִּבְּרוּ אֵלֶיךָ לֵאמֹר אָבִיךָ הִכְבִּיד אֶת־ עֻלֵּנוּ
yoke-of-us *** he-made-heavy father-of-you to-say to-you they-said who

וְאַתָּה הָקֵל מֵעָלֵינוּ כֹּה תֹאמַר אֲלֵהֶם קָטָנִּי
little-one-of-me to-them you-tell this from-on-us you-make-light but-you

עָבָה מִמָּתְנֵי אָבִי׃ וְעַתָּה אָבִי
father-of-me and-now (11) father-of-me more-than-waists-of he-is-thick

הֶעְמִיס עֲלֵיכֶם עֹל כָּבֵד וַאֲנִי אֹסִיף עַל־ עֻלְּכֶם אָבִי
father-of-me yoke-of-you to I-will-add but-I heavy yoke on-you he-laid

יִסַּר אֶתְכֶם בַּשּׁוֹטִים וַאֲנִי בָּעַקְרַבִּים*׃ וַיָּבֹא
and-he-returned (12) with-the-scorpions but-I with-the-whips you he-scourged

יָרָבְעָם וְכָל־ הָעָם אֶל־ רְחַבְעָם בַּיּוֹם הַשְּׁלִשִׁי כַּאֲשֶׁר
just-as the-third on-the-day Rehoboam to the-people and-all-of Jeroboam

דִּבֶּר הַמֶּלֶךְ לֵאמֹר שׁוּבוּ אֵלַי בַּיּוֹם הַשְּׁלִשִׁי׃
the-third on-the-day to-me come-back! to-say the-king he-said

וַיַּעֲנֵם הַמֶּלֶךְ קָשָׁה וַיַּעֲזֹב הַמֶּלֶךְ רְחַבְעָם
Rehoboam the-king and-he-rejected harshly the-king and-he-answered-them (13)

אֵת עֲצַת הַזְּקֵנִים׃ וַיְדַבֵּר אֲלֵהֶם כַּעֲצַת הַיְלָדִים
the-young-men as-advice-of to-them and-he-spoke (14) the-elders advice-of ***

לֵאמֹר אַכְבִּיד† אֶת־ עֻלְּכֶם וַאֲנִי אֹסִיף עָלָיו אָבִי
father-of-me to-him I-will-add but-I yoke-of-you *** †I-made-heavy to-say

יִסַּר אֶתְכֶם בַּשּׁוֹטִים וַאֲנִי בָּעַקְרַבִּים*׃ וְלֹא־
so-not (15) with-the-scorpions but-I with-the-whips you he-scourged

שָׁמַע הַמֶּלֶךְ אֶל־ הָעָם כִּי־ הָיְתָה נְסִבָּה מֵעִם
from-with turn-of-events she-was for the-people to the-king he-listened

הָאֱלֹהִים לְמַעַן הָקִים יְהוָה אֶת־ דְּבָרוֹ אֲשֶׁר דִּבֶּר
he-spoke that word-of-him *** Yahweh to-fulfill in-order-to the-God

בְּיַד אֲחִיָּהוּ הַשִּׁלוֹנִי אֶל־ יָרָבְעָם בֶּן־ נְבָט׃ וְכָל־
when-all-of (16) Nebat son-of Jeroboam to the-Shilonite Ahijah by-hand-of

יִשְׂרָאֵל כִּי לֹא־ שָׁמַע הַמֶּלֶךְ לָהֶם וַיָּשִׁיבוּ הָעָם
the-people then-they-answered to-them the-king he-listened not that Israel

אֶת־הַמֶּלֶךְ ׀ לֵאמֹר מַה־ לָּנוּ חֵלֶק בְּדָוִיד וְלֹא־ נַחֲלָה בְּבֶן־ יִשַׁי
Jesse in-son-of part and-not in-David share to-us what? to-say the-king ***

these people who say to me,
'Lighten the yoke your father
put on us'?"
[10]The young men who had
grown up with him replied,
"Tell the people who have said
to you, 'Your father put a
heavy yoke on us, but make
our yoke lighter'—tell them,
'My little finger is thicker than
my father's waist. [11]My father
laid on you a heavy yoke; I
will make it even heavier. My
father scourged you with
whips; I will scourge you with
scorpions.'"
[12]Three days later Jeroboam
and all the people returned to
Rehoboam, as the king had
said, "Come back to me in
three days." [13]The king answered them harshly. Re-
jecting the advice of the elders, [14]he followed the advice
of the young men and said,
"My father made your yoke
heavy; I will make it even
heavier. My father scourged
you with whips; I will scourge
you with scorpions." [15]So the
king did not listen to the
people, for this turn of events
was from God, to fulfill the
word the LORD had spoken to
Jeroboam son of Nebat
through Ahijah the Shilonite.
[16]When all Israel saw that
the king refused to listen to
them, they answered the king:

"What share do we have in
David,
what part in Jesse's son?

*11, 14 Most mss have *pathah* under the *ayin* (בַּעְ').

†14 Many mss read אָבִי הִכְבִּיד, *he-made-heavy father-of-me*

אִישׁ לְאֹהָלֶיךָ יִשְׂרָאֵל עַתָּה רְאֵה בֵיתְךָ דָּוִיד וַיֵּלֶךְ
so-he-went David house-of-you look-after! now Israel to-tents-of-you each

כָּל־ יִשְׂרָאֵל לְאֹהָלָיו׃ וּבְנֵי יִשְׂרָאֵל הַיֹּשְׁבִים
the-ones-living Israel but-sons-of (17) to-homes-of-him Israel all-of

בְּעָרֵי יְהוּדָה וַיִּמְלֹךְ עֲלֵיהֶם רְחַבְעָם׃ וַיִּשְׁלַח
and-he-sent-out (18) Rehoboam over-them and-he-ruled Judah in-towns-of

הַמֶּלֶךְ רְחַבְעָם אֶת־ הֲדֹרָם אֲשֶׁר עַל־ הַמַּס וַיִּרְגְּמוּ־
but-they-stoned the-forced-labor over who Hadoram *** Rehoboam the-king

בוֹ בְנֵי־ יִשְׂרָאֵל אֶבֶן וַיָּמֹת וְהַמֶּלֶךְ רְחַבְעָם הִתְאַמֵּץ
he-managed Rehoboam but-the-king and-he-died stone Israel sons-of on-him

לַעֲלוֹת בַּמֶּרְכָּבָה לָנוּס יְרוּשָׁלָם׃ וַיִּפְשְׁעוּ יִשְׂרָאֵל
Israel so-they-rebelled (19) Jerusalem to-escape into-the-chariot to-get-up

בְּבֵית דָּוִיד עַד הַיּוֹם הַזֶּה׃ וַיָּבֹא רְחַבְעָם
Rehoboam when-he-arrived (11:1) the-this the-day to David against-house-of

יְרוּשָׁלַם וַיַּקְהֵל אֶת־ בֵּית יְהוּדָה וּבִנְיָמִן מֵאָה וּשְׁמוֹנִים
and-eighty hundred and-Benjamin Judah house-of *** then-he-mustered Jerusalem

אֶלֶף בָּחוּר עֹשֵׂה מִלְחָמָה לְהִלָּחֵם עִם־ יִשְׂרָאֵל לְהָשִׁיב אֶת־
*** to-regain Israel against to-make-war fight doing being-chosen thousand

הַמַּמְלָכָה לִרְחַבְעָם׃ וַיְהִי דְּבַר־ יְהוָה אֶל־ שְׁמַעְיָהוּ אִישׁ־
man-of Shemaiah to Yahweh word-of but-he-came (2) for-Rehoboam the-kingdom

הָאֱלֹהִים לֵאמֹר׃ אֱמֹר אֶל־ רְחַבְעָם בֶּן־ שְׁלֹמֹה מֶלֶךְ יְהוּדָה וְאֶל
and-to Judah king-of Solomon son-of Rehoboam to say! (3) to-say the-God

כָּל־ יִשְׂרָאֵל בִּיהוּדָה וּבִנְיָמִן לֵאמֹר׃ כֹּה אָמַר יְהוָה לֹא־
not Yahweh he-says this (4) to-say and-Benjamin in-Judah Israel all-of

תַעֲלוּ וְלֹא־ תִלָּחֲמוּ עִם־ אֲחֵיכֶם שׁוּבוּ אִישׁ
each go-back! brothers-of-you against you-fight and-not you-go-up

לְבֵיתוֹ כִּי מֵאִתִּי נִהְיָה הַדָּבָר הַזֶּה וַיִּשְׁמְעוּ
so-they-obeyed the-this the-thing he-is-done from-with-me for to-home-of-him

אֶת־ דִּבְרֵי יְהוָה וַיָּשֻׁבוּ מִלֶּכֶת אֶל־ יָרָבְעָם׃
Jeroboam against from-to-march and-they-turned-back Yahweh words-of ***

וַיֵּשֶׁב רְחַבְעָם בִּירוּשָׁלָם וַיִּבֶן עָרִים לְמָצוֹר
for-defense towns and-he-built-up in-Jerusalem Rehoboam and-he-lived (5)

בִּיהוּדָה׃ וַיִּבֶן אֶת־ בֵּית־ לֶחֶם וְאֶת־ עֵיטָם וְאֶת־ תְּקוֹעַ׃ וְאֶת־
and (7) Tekoa and Etam and Lehem Beth *** and-he-built-up (6) in-Judah

בֵּית־צוּר וְאֶת־שׂוֹכוֹ וְאֶת־עֲדֻלָּם׃ וְאֶת־ גַּת וְאֶת־ מָרֵשָׁה וְאֶת־ זִיף׃ וְאֶת־
and (9) Ziph and Mareshah and Gath and (8) Adullam and Soco and Zur Beth

אֲדוֹרַיִם וְאֶת־ לָכִישׁ וְאֶת־ עֲזֵקָה׃ וְאֶת־צָרְעָה וְאֶת־אַיָּלוֹן וְאֶת־ חֶבְרוֹן אֲשֶׁר
that Hebron and Aijalon and Zorah and (10) Azekah and Lachish and Adoraim

To your tents, O Israel!
Look after your own
house, O David!"

So all the Israelites went home. [17]But as for the Israelites who were living in the towns of Judah, Rehoboam still ruled over them.

[18]King Rehoboam sent out Adoniram,[a] who was in charge of forced labor, but the Israelites stoned him to death. King Rehoboam, however, managed to get into his chariot and escape to Jerusalem. [19]So Israel has been in rebellion against the house of David to this day.

11 When Rehoboam arrived in Jerusalem, he mustered the house of Judah and Benjamin—a hundred and eighty thousand fighting men—to make war against Israel and to regain the kingdom for Rehoboam.

[2]But this word of the LORD came to Shemaiah the man of God: [3]"Say to Rehoboam son of Solomon king of Judah and to all the Israelites in Judah and Benjamin, [4]'This is what the LORD says: Do not go up to fight against your brothers. Go home, every one of you, for this is my doing.'" So they obeyed the words of the LORD and turned back from marching against Jeroboam.

*Rehoboam Fortifies Judah*

[5]Rehoboam lived in Jerusalem and built up towns for defense in Judah: [6]Bethlehem, Etam, Tekoa, [7]Beth Zur, Soco, Adullam, [8]Gath, Mareshah, Ziph, [9]Adoraim, Lachish, Azekah, [10]Zorah, Aijalon and Hebron. These were fortified cities in Judah and Benjamin.

[a]18 Hebrew *Hadoram*, a variant of *Adoniram*

בִּיהוּדָה וּבְבִנְיָמִן עָרֵי מְצֻרוֹת׃ וַיְחַזֵּק אֶת־
*** and-he-strengthened (11) fortifications cities-of and-in-Benjamin in-Judah

הַמְּצֻרוֹת וַיִּתֵּן בָּהֶם נְגִידִים וְאֹצְרוֹת מַאֲכָל וְשֶׁמֶן
and-olive-oil food and-supplies-of commanders in-them and-he-put the-defenses

וָיָיִן׃ וּבְכָל־ עִיר וָעִיר צִנּוֹת וּרְמָחִים וַיְחַזְּקֵם
and-he-made-strong-them and-spears shields and-city city and-in-all-of (12) and-wine

לְהַרְבֵּה מְאֹד וַיְהִי־ לוֹ יְהוּדָה וּבִנְיָמִן׃ וְהַכֹּהֲנִים
and-the-priests (13) and-Benjamin Judah to-him so-he-was very to-be-great

וְהַלְוִיִּם אֲשֶׁר בְּכָל־ יִשְׂרָאֵל הִתְיַצְּבוּ עָלָיו מִכָּל־
from-all-of with-him they-sided Israel in-all-of who and-the-Levites

גְּבוּלָם׃ כִּי־ עָזְבוּ הַלְוִיִּם אֶת־ מִגְרְשֵׁיהֶם
pastures-of-them *** the-Levites they-abandoned indeed (14) district-of-them

וַאֲחֻזָּתָם וַיֵּלְכוּ לִיהוּדָה וְלִירוּשָׁלִָם כִּי־
because and-to-Jerusalem to-Judah and-they-came and-property-of-them

הִזְנִיחָם יָרָבְעָם וּבָנָיו מִכַּהֵן לַיהוָה׃
of-Yahweh from-to-be-priest and-sons-of-him Jeroboam he-rejected-them

וַיַּעֲמֶד־ לוֹ כֹּהֲנִים לַבָּמוֹת וְלַשְּׂעִירִים
and-for-the-goat-idols for-the-high-places priests for-him and-he-appointed (15)

וְלָעֲגָלִים אֲשֶׁר עָשָׂה׃ וְאַחֲרֵיהֶם מִכֹּל שִׁבְטֵי
tribes-of from-all-of and-after-them (16) he-made that and-for-the-calf-idols

יִשְׂרָאֵל הַנֹּתְנִים אֶת־ לְבָבָם לְבַקֵּשׁ אֶת־ יְהוָה אֱלֹהֵי יִשְׂרָאֵל
Israel God-of Yahweh *** to-seek heart-of-them *** the-ones-setting Israel

בָּאוּ יְרוּשָׁלִַם לִזְבּוֹחַ לַיהוָה אֱלֹהֵי אֲבוֹתֵיהֶם׃
fathers-of-them God-of to-Yahweh to-sacrifice Jerusalem they-followed

וַיְחַזְּקוּ אֶת־ מַלְכוּת יְהוּדָה וַיְאַמְּצוּ אֶת־
*** and-they-supported Judah kingdom-of *** and-they-strengthened (17)

רְחַבְעָם בֶּן־ שְׁלֹמֹה לְשָׁנִים שָׁלוֹשׁ כִּי הָלְכוּ בְּדֶרֶךְ דָּוִיד
David in-way-of they-walked indeed three for-years Solomon son-of Rehoboam

וּשְׁלֹמֹה לְשָׁנִים שָׁלוֹשׁ׃ וַיִּקַּח־ לוֹ רְחַבְעָם אִשָּׁה אֶת־
*** wife Rehoboam for-him and-he-married (18) three for-years and-Solomon

מָחֲלַת בֶּן־° יְרִימוֹת בֶּן־ דָּוִיד אֲבִיהַיִל בַּת־ אֱלִיאָב בֶּן־
son-of Eliab daughter-of Abihail David son-of Jerimoth daughter-of Mahalath

יִשָׁי׃ וַתֵּלֶד לוֹ בָּנִים אֶת־ יְעוּשׁ וְאֶת־ שְׁמַרְיָה וְאֶת־ זָהַם׃
Zaham and Shemariah and Jeush *** sons to-him and-she-bore (19) Jesse

וְאַחֲרֶיהָ לָקַח אֶת־ מַעֲכָה בַּת־ אַבְשָׁלוֹם וַתֵּלֶד
and-she-bore Absalom daughter-of Maacah *** he-married then-after-her (20)

לוֹ אֶת־ אֲבִיָּה וְאֶת־ עַתַּי וְאֶת־ זִיזָא וְאֶת־ שְׁלֹמִית׃ וַיֶּאֱהַב
and-he-loved (21) Shelomith and Ziza and Attai and Abijah *** to-him

[11]He strengthened their defenses and put commanders in them, with supplies of food, olive oil and wine. [12]He put shields and spears in all the cities, and made them very strong. So Judah and Benjamin were his.

[13]The priests and Levites from all their districts sided with him. [14]The Levites even abandoned their pasturelands and property, and came to Judah and Jerusalem because Jeroboam and his sons had rejected them as priests of the LORD. [15]And he appointed his own priests for the high places and for the goat and calf idols he had made. [16]Those from every tribe of Israel who set their hearts on seeking the LORD, the God of Israel, followed the Levites to Jerusalem to offer sacrifices to the LORD, the God of their fathers. [17]They strengthened the kingdom of Judah and supported Rehoboam son of Solomon three years, walking in the ways of David and Solomon during this time.

*Rehoboam's Family*

[18]Rehoboam married Mahalath, who was the daughter of David's son Jerimoth and of Abihail, the daughter of Jesse's son Eliab. [19]She bore him sons: Jeush, Shemariah and Zaham. [20]Then he married Maacah daughter of Absalom, who bore him Abijah, Attai, Ziza and Shelomith. [21]Rehoboam loved Maacah daughter

°18 ק בת

רְחַבְעָם אֶת־ מַעֲכָה בַת־ אַבְשָׁלוֹם מִכָּל־ נָשָׁיו
wives-of-him more-than-any-of Absalom daughter-of Maacah *** Rehoboam

וּפִילַגְשָׁיו כִּי נָשִׁים שְׁמוֹנֶה־עֶשְׂרֵה נָשָׂא וּפִילַגְשִׁים שִׁשִּׁים
sixty and-concubines he-took ten eight wives indeed and-concubines-of-him

וַיּוֹלֶד עֶשְׂרִים וּשְׁמוֹנָה בָנִים וְשִׁשִּׁים בָּנוֹת׃ וַיַּעֲמֵד
and-he-appointed (22) daughters and-sixty sons and-eight twenty and-he-fathered

לָרֹאשׁ רְחַבְעָם אֶת־ אֲבִיָּה בֶן־ מַעֲכָה לְנָגִיד בְּאֶחָיו
among-brothers-of-him as-prince Maacah son-of Abijah *** Rehoboam as-chief

כִּי לְהַמְלִיכוֹ׃ וַיָּבֶן וַיִּפְרֹץ
and-he-dispersed and-he-acted-wisely (23) to-make-king-him in-order-to

מִכָּל־ בָּנָיו לְכָל־ אַרְצוֹת יְהוּדָה וּבִנְיָמִן
and-Benjamin Judah districts-of through-all-of sons-of-him from-all-of

לְכֹל עָרֵי הַמְּצֻרוֹת וַיִּתֵּן לָהֶם הַמָּזוֹן
the-provision to-them and-he-gave the-fortifications cities-of to-all-of

לָרֹב וַיִּשְׁאַל הֲמוֹן נָשִׁים׃ וַיְהִי כְּהָכִין
as-to-establish and-he-was (12:1) wives many-of and-he-took in-abundance

מַלְכוּת רְחַבְעָם וּכְחֶזְקָתוֹ עָזַב אֶת־ תּוֹרַת
law-of *** he-abandoned and-as-to-become-strong-him Rehoboam kingdom-of

יְהוָה וְכָל־ יִשְׂרָאֵל עִמּוֹ׃ וַיְהִי בַּשָּׁנָה הַחֲמִישִׁית
the-fifth in-the-year and-he-was (2) with-him Israel and-all-of Yahweh

לַמֶּלֶךְ רְחַבְעָם עָלָה שִׁישַׁק מֶלֶךְ־ מִצְרַיִם עַל־ יְרוּשָׁלִַם
Jerusalem against Egypt king-of Shishak he-attacked Rehoboam of-the-king

כִּי מָעֲלוּ בַּיהוָה׃ בְּאֶלֶף וּמָאתַיִם
and-two-hundreds with-thousand (3) to-Yahweh they-were-unfaithful because

רֶכֶב וּבְשִׁשִּׁים אֶלֶף פָּרָשִׁים וְאֵין מִסְפָּר לָעָם אֲשֶׁר־
that of-the-troop number and-not horsemen thousand and-with-sixty chariot

בָּאוּ עִמּוֹ מִמִּצְרַיִם לוּבִים סֻכִּיִּים וְכוּשִׁים׃ וַיִּלְכֹּד
and-he-captured (4) and-Cushites Sukkites Libyans from-Egypt with-him they-came

אֶת־ עָרֵי הַמְּצֻרוֹת אֲשֶׁר לִיהוּדָה וַיָּבֹא עַד־ יְרוּשָׁלִָם׃
Jerusalem as-far-as and-he-came in-Judah that the-fortifications cities-of ***

וּשְׁמַעְיָה הַנָּבִיא בָּא אֶל־ רְחַבְעָם וְשָׂרֵי יְהוּדָה אֲשֶׁר־
who Judah and-leaders-of Rehoboam to he-came the-prophet then-Shemaiah (5)

נֶאֶסְפוּ אֶל־ יְרוּשָׁלִָם מִפְּנֵי שִׁישָׁק וַיֹּאמֶר לָהֶם כֹּה־
this to-them and-he-said Shishak because-of Jerusalem in they-assembled

אָמַר יְהוָה אַתֶּם עֲזַבְתֶּם אֹתִי וְאַף־ אֲנִי עָזַבְתִּי אֶתְכֶם בְּיַד־
to-hand-of you I-abandon I now-therefore me you-abandoned you Yahweh he-says

שִׁישָׁק׃ וַיִּכָּנְעוּ שָׂרֵי־ יִשְׂרָאֵל וְהַמֶּלֶךְ
and-the-king Israel leaders-of and-they-humbled-themselves (6) Shishak

of Absalom more than any of his other wives and concubines. In all, he had eighteen wives and sixty concubines, twenty-eight sons and sixty daughters.

22 Rehoboam appointed Abijah son of Maacah to be the chief prince among his brothers, in order to make him king. 23 He acted wisely, dispersing some of his sons throughout the districts of Judah and Benjamin, and to all the fortified cities. He gave them abundant provisions and took many wives for them.

*Shishak Attacks Jerusalem*

12 After Rehoboam's position as king was established and he had become strong, he and all Israel[v] with him abandoned the law of the LORD. 2 Because they had been unfaithful to the LORD, Shishak king of Egypt attacked Jerusalem in the fifth year of King Rehoboam. 3 With twelve hundred chariots and sixty thousand horsemen and the innumerable troops of Libyans, Sukkites and Cushites[w] that came with him from Egypt, 4 he captured the fortified cities of Judah and came as far as Jerusalem.

5 Then the prophet Shemaiah came to Rehoboam and to the leaders of Judah who had assembled in Jerusalem for fear of Shishak, and he said to them, "This is what the LORD says, 'You have abandoned me; therefore, I now abandon you to Shishak.' "

6 The leaders of Israel and the king humbled themselves and

[v] *1* That is, Judah, as frequently in 2 Chronicles
[w] *3* That is, people from the upper Nile region

וַיֹּאמְרוּ צַדִּיק ׀ יְהוָה׃ (7) וּבִרְאוֹת יְהוָה כִּי
that Yahweh and-when-to-see (7) Yahweh just and-they-said

נִכְנָעוּ הָיָה דְבַר־ יְהוָה אֶל־ שְׁמַעְיָה ׀ לֵאמֹר
to-say Shemaiah to Yahweh word-of he-came they-humbled-themselves

נִכְנְעוּ לֹא אַשְׁחִיתֵם וְנָתַתִּי לָהֶם
to-them but-I-will-give I-will-destroy-them not they-humbled-themselves

כִּמְעַט לִפְלֵיטָה וְלֹא־ תִתַּךְ חֲמָתִי
wrath-of-me she-will-be-poured-out and-not for-deliverance as-soon

בִּירוּשָׁלִָם בְּיַד־ שִׁישָׁק׃ (8) כִּי יִהְיוּ־ לוֹ לַעֲבָדִים
as-subjects to-him they-will-be however (8) Shishak by-hand-of on-Jerusalem

וְיֵדְעוּ עֲבוֹדָתִי וַעֲבוֹדַת מַמְלְכוֹת הָאֲרָצוֹת׃
the-lands kingdoms-of and-service-of service-of-me so-they-may-learn

(9) וַיַּעַל שִׁישַׁק מֶלֶךְ־ מִצְרַיִם עַל־ יְרוּשָׁלִָם
Jerusalem against Egypt king-of Shishak when-he-attacked (9)

וַיִּקַּח אֶת־ אֹצְרוֹת בֵּית־ יְהוָה וְאֶת־ אֹצְרוֹת
treasures-of and Yahweh temple-of treasures-of *** then-he-carried-off

בֵּית הַמֶּלֶךְ אֶת־ הַכֹּל לָקָח וַיִּקַּח אֶת־ מָגִנֵּי הַזָּהָב
the-gold shields-of *** and-he-took he-took the-whole *** the-king palace-of

אֲשֶׁר עָשָׂה שְׁלֹמֹה׃ (10) וַיַּעַשׂ הַמֶּלֶךְ רְחַבְעָם תַּחְתֵּיהֶם
in-place-of-them Rehoboam the-king so-he-made (10) Solomon he-made that

מָגִנֵּי נְחֹשֶׁת וְהִפְקִיד עַל־ יַד שָׂרֵי
commanders-of hand-of under and-he-assigned bronze shields-of

הָרָצִים הַשֹּׁמְרִים פֶּתַח בֵּית הַמֶּלֶךְ׃
the-king palace-of entrance-of the-ones-being-on-duty the-ones-guarding

(11) וַיְהִי מִדֵּי־ בוֹא הַמֶּלֶךְ בֵּית יְהוָה בָּאוּ
they-went Yahweh temple-of the-king to-go as-often-as and-he-was (11)

הָרָצִים וּנְשָׂאוּם וֶהֱשִׁבוּם אֶל־ תָּא
room-of to then-they-returned-them and-they-bore-them the-ones-guarding

הָרָצִים׃ (12) וּבְהִכָּנְעוֹ שָׁב מִמֶּנּוּ
from-him he-turned and-because-to-be-humbled-him (12) the-ones-guarding

אַף־ יְהוָה וְלֹא לְהַשְׁחִית לְכָלָה וְגַם בִּיהוּדָה הָיָה
he-was in-Judah indeed-also to-totality to-destroy and-not Yahweh anger-of

דְּבָרִים טוֹבִים׃ (13) וַיִּתְחַזֵּק הַמֶּלֶךְ רְחַבְעָם
Rehoboam the-king and-he-established-himself (13) good-ones things

בִּירוּשָׁלִָם וַיִּמְלֹךְ כִּי בֶן־ אַרְבָּעִים וְאַחַת שָׁנָה רְחַבְעָם
Rehoboam year and-one forty son-of indeed and-he-was-king in-Jerusalem

בְּמָלְכוֹ וּשְׁבַע עֶשְׂרֵה שָׁנָה ׀ מָלַךְ בִּירוּשָׁלִָם
in-Jerusalem he-reigned year ten and-seven-of when-to-become-king-him

said, "The LORD is just."
7When the LORD saw that
they humbled themselves, this
word of the LORD came to
Shemaiah: "Since they have
humbled themselves, I will
not destroy them but will soon
give them deliverance. My
wrath will not be poured out
on Jerusalem through Shishak.
8They will, however, become
subject to him, so that they
may learn the difference between serving me and serving
the kings of other lands."
9When Shishak king of
Egypt attacked Jerusalem, he
carried off the treasures of the
temple of the LORD and the
treasures of the royal palace.
He took everything, including
the gold shields Solomon had
made. 10So King Rehoboam
made bronze shields to replace
them and assigned these to
the commanders of the guard
on duty at the entrance to the
royal palace. 11Whenever the
king went to the LORD's temple, the guards went with him,
bearing the shields, and afterward they returned them to
the guardroom.
12Because Rehoboam hum-
bled himself, the LORD's anger
turned from him, and he was
not totally destroyed. Indeed,
there was some good in Judah.
13King Rehoboam estab-
lished himself firmly in
Jerusalem and continued as
king. He was forty-one years
old when he became king, and
he reigned seventeen years in

הָעִיר אֲשֶׁר־ בָּחַר יְהוָה לָשׂוּם אֶת־ שְׁמוֹ שָׁם מִכֹּל
from-all-of there Name-of-him *** to-put Yahweh he-chose that the-city

שִׁבְטֵי יִשְׂרָאֵל וְשֵׁם אִמּוֹ נַעֲמָה הָעַמֹּנִית׃
the-Ammonite Naamah mother-of-him and-name-of Israel tribes-of

וַיַּעַשׂ הָרָע כִּי לֹא הֵכִין לִבּוֹ לִדְרוֹשׁ אֶת־ יְהוָה׃
Yahweh *** to-seek heart-of-him he-set not because the-evil and-he-did (14)

וְדִבְרֵי רְחַבְעָם הָרִאשֹׁנִים וְהָאַחֲרוֹנִים* הֲלֹא־ הֵם
they not? and-the-ends the-beginnings Rehoboam and-events-of (15)

כְּתוּבִים בְּדִבְרֵי שְׁמַעְיָה הַנָּבִיא וְעִדּוֹ הַחֹזֶה
the-seer and-Iddo the-prophet Shemaiah in-records-of ones-being-written

לְהִתְיַחֵשׂ וּמִלְחֲמוֹת רְחַבְעָם וְיָרָבְעָם כָּל־ הַיָּמִים׃
the-days all-of and-Jeroboam Rehoboam and-wars-of to-be-recorded

וַיִּשְׁכַּב רְחַבְעָם עִם־ אֲבֹתָיו וַיִּקָּבֵר בְּעִיר
in-City-of and-he-was-buried fathers-of-him with Rehoboam and-he-rested (16)

דָּוִיד וַיִּמְלֹךְ אֲבִיָּה בְנוֹ תַּחְתָּיו׃ בִּשְׁנַת
in-year-of (13:1) in-place-of-him son-of-him Abijah and-he-became-king David

שְׁמוֹנֶה עֶשְׂרֵה לַמֶּלֶךְ יָרָבְעָם וַיִּמְלֹךְ אֲבִיָּה עַל־ יְהוּדָה׃
Judah over Abijah then-he-became-king Jeroboam of-the-king ten eight

שָׁלוֹשׁ שָׁנִים מָלַךְ בִּירוּשָׁלִַם וְשֵׁם אִמּוֹ מִיכָיָהוּ
Micaiah mother-of-him and-name-of in-Jerusalem he-reigned years three (2)

בַּת־ אוּרִיאֵל מִן־ גִּבְעָה וּמִלְחָמָה הָיְתָה בֵּין אֲבִיָּה וּבֵין
and-between Abijah between she-was and-war Gibeah from Uriel daughter-of

יָרָבְעָם׃ וַיֶּאְסֹר אֲבִיָּה אֶת־ הַמִּלְחָמָה בְּחַיִל גִּבּוֹרֵי מִלְחָמָה
fight men-of with-force the-battle *** Abijah and-he-went-into (3) Jeroboam

אַרְבַּע־ מֵאוֹת אֶלֶף אִישׁ בָּחוּר וְיָרָבְעָם עָרַךְ עִמּוֹ
against-him he-drew and-Jeroboam being-able man thousand hundreds four-of

מִלְחָמָה בִּשְׁמוֹנֶה מֵאוֹת אֶלֶף אִישׁ בָּחוּר גִּבּוֹר חָיִל׃
valiant troop-of being-able man thousand hundreds with-eight battle-line

וַיָּקָם אֲבִיָּה מֵעַל לְהַר צְמָרַיִם אֲשֶׁר בְּהַר
in-hill-country-of that Zemaraim on-Mount-of at-upon Abijah and-he-stood (4)

אֶפְרָיִם וַיֹּאמֶר שְׁמָעוּנִי יָרָבְעָם וְכָל־ יִשְׂרָאֵל׃ הֲלֹא
not? (5) Israel and-all-of Jeroboam listen-to-me! and-he-said Ephraim

לָכֶם לָדַעַת כִּי יְהוָה׀ אֱלֹהֵי יִשְׂרָאֵל נָתַן מַמְלָכָה לְדָוִיד עַל־
over to-David kingship he-gave Israel God-of Yahweh that to-know to-you

יִשְׂרָאֵל לְעוֹלָם לוֹ וּלְבָנָיו בְּרִית מֶלַח׃
salt covenant-of and-to-descendants-of-him to-him to-forever Israel

וַיָּקָם יָרָבְעָם בֶּן־ נְבָט עֶבֶד שְׁלֹמֹה בֶן־ דָּוִיד
David son-of Solomon official-of Nebat son-of Jeroboam yet-he-rose (6)

Jerusalem, the city the LORD had chosen out of all the tribes of Israel in which to put his Name. His mother's name was Naamah; she was an Ammonite.
14 He did evil because he had not set his heart on seeking the LORD.
15 As for the events of Rehoboam's reign, from beginning to end, are they not written in the records of Shemaiah the prophet and of Iddo the seer that deal with genealogies? There was continual warfare between Rehoboam and Jeroboam.
16 Rehoboam rested with his fathers and was buried in the City of David. And Abijah his son succeeded him as king.

*Abijah King of Judah*

13 In the eighteenth year of the reign of Jeroboam, Abijah became king of Judah,
2 and he reigned in Jerusalem three years. His mother's name was Maacah,[x] a daughter[y] of Uriel of Gibeah.
There was war between Abijah and Jeroboam.
3 Abijah went into battle with a force of four hundred thousand able fighting men, and Jeroboam drew up a battle line against him with eight hundred thousand able troops.
4 Abijah stood on Mount Zemaraim, in the hill country of Ephraim, and said, "Jeroboam and all Israel, listen to me!
5 Don't you know that the LORD, the God of Israel, has given the kingship of Israel to David and his descendants forever by a covenant of salt?
6 Yet Jeroboam son of Nebat, an official of Solomon son of

x2 Septuagint and Syriac (see also 2 Chron. 11:20 and 1 Kings 15:2); Hebrew *Micaiah*
y2 Or *granddaughter*

*15 Most mss have *hateph pathah* under the *heth* and *pathah* under the *aleph* ( וְהָאַחַ׳ ).

וַיִּמְרֹד עַל־ אֲדֹנָיו׃ וַיִּקָּבְצוּ עָלָיו
around-him and-they-gathered (7) masters-of-him against and-he-rebelled

אֲנָשִׁים רֵקִים בְּנֵי בְלִיַּעַל וַיִּתְאַמְּצוּ עַל־ רְחַבְעָם
Rehoboam against and-they-opposed scoundrel sons-of worthless-ones men

בֶּן־ שְׁלֹמֹה וּרְחַבְעָם הָיָה נַעַר וְרַךְ־ לֵבָב וְלֹא
and-not heart and-indecisive-of young he-was when-Rehoboam Solomon son-of

הִתְחַזַּק לִפְנֵיהֶם׃ וְעַתָּה ׀ אַתֶּם אֹמְרִים לְהִתְחַזֵּק לִפְנֵי
against to-resist ones-planning you and-now (8) against-them he-was-strong

מַמְלֶכֶת יְהוָה בְּיַד בְּנֵי דָוִיד וְאַתֶּם הָמוֹן רָב
vast army and-you David descendants-of in-hand-of Yahweh kingdom-of

וְעִמָּכֶם עֶגְלֵי זָהָב אֲשֶׁר עָשָׂה לָכֶם יָרָבְעָם לֵאלֹהִים׃ הֲלֹא
not? (9) as-gods Jeroboam for-you he-made that gold calves-of and-with-you

הִדַּחְתֶּם אֶת־ כֹּהֲנֵי יְהוָה אֶת־ בְּנֵי אַהֲרֹן וְהַלְוִיִּם
and-the-Levites Aaron sons-of *** Yahweh priests-of *** you-drove-out

וַתַּעֲשׂוּ לָכֶם כֹּהֲנִים כְּעַמֵּי הָאֲרָצוֹת כָּל־ הַבָּא
the-one-coming any-of the-lands as-peoples-of priests of-you and-you-made

לְמַלֵּא יָדוֹ בְּפַר בֶּן־ בָּקָר וְאֵילִם שִׁבְעָה
seven and-rams cattle son-of with-bull hand-of-him to-consecrate

וְהָיָה כֹהֵן לְלֹא אֱלֹהִים׃ וַאֲנַחְנוּ יְהוָה אֱלֹהֵינוּ וְלֹא
and-not God-of-us Yahweh and-we (10) gods of-not priest and-he-may-become

עֲזַבְנֻהוּ וְכֹהֲנִים מְשָׁרְתִים לַיהוָה בְּנֵי אַהֲרֹן
Aaron sons-of to-Yahweh ones-serving and-priests we-forsook-him

וְהַלְוִיִּם בַּמְלָאכֶת׃ וּמַקְטִרִים לַיהוָה עֹלוֹת
burnt-offerings to-Yahweh and-ones-presenting (11) in-the-work and-the-Levites

בַּבֹּקֶר־ בַּבֹּקֶר וּבָעֶרֶב־ בָּעֶרֶב וּקְטֹרֶת־
and-incense-of in-the-evening and-in-the-evening in-the-morning in-the-morning

סַמִּים וּמַעֲרֶכֶת לֶחֶם עַל־ הַשֻּׁלְחָן הַטָּהוֹר וּמְנוֹרַת
and-lampstand-of the-clean the-table on bread and-setting-of fragrances

הַזָּהָב וְנֵרֹתֶיהָ לְבָעֵר בָּעֶרֶב בָּעֶרֶב כִּי־
indeed in-the-evening in-the-evening to-light and-lamps-of-her the-gold

שֹׁמְרִים אֲנַחְנוּ אֶת־ מִשְׁמֶרֶת יְהוָה אֱלֹהֵינוּ וְאַתֶּם עֲזַבְתֶּם
you-forsook but-you God-of-us Yahweh requirement-of *** we ones-observing

אֹתוֹ׃ וְהִנֵּה עִמָּנוּ בָרֹאשׁ הָאֱלֹהִים ׀ וְכֹהֲנָיו
and-priests-of-him the-God as-the-leader with-us and-see! (12) him

וַחֲצֹצְרוֹת הַתְּרוּעָה לְהָרִיעַ עֲלֵיכֶם בְּנֵי יִשְׂרָאֵל אַל־
not Israel men-of against-you to-sound the-battle-cry and-trumpets

תִּלָּחֲמוּ עִם־ יְהוָה אֱלֹהֵי־ אֲבֹתֵיכֶם כִּי־ לֹא תַצְלִיחוּ׃
you-will-succeed not for fathers-of-you God-of Yahweh against you-fight

David, rebelled against his master.
[7]Some worthless scoundrels gathered around him and opposed Rehoboam son of Solomon when he was young and indecisive and not strong enough to resist them.
[8]"And now you plan to resist the kingdom of the LORD, which is in the hands of David's descendants. You are indeed a vast army and have with you the golden calves that Jeroboam made to be your gods.
[9]But didn't you drive out the priests of the LORD, the sons of Aaron, and the Levites, and make priests of your own as the peoples of other lands do? Whoever comes to consecrate himself with a young bull and seven rams may become a priest of what are not gods.
[10]"As for us, the LORD is our God, and we have not forsaken him. The priests who serve the LORD are sons of Aaron, and the Levites assist them.
[11]Every morning and evening they present burnt offerings and fragrant incense to the LORD. They set out the bread on the ceremonially clean table and light the lamps on the gold lampstand every evening. We are observing the requirements of the LORD our God. But you have forsaken him.
[12]God is with us; he is our leader. His priests with their trumpets will sound the battle cry against you. Men of Israel, do not fight against the LORD, the God of your fathers, for you will not succeed."

וְיָרָבְעָם הֵסֵב אֶת־הַמַּאְרָב לָבוֹא מֵאַחֲרֵיהֶם

to-rear-of-them to-go the-troop *** he-sent-around now-Jeroboam (13)

וַיִּהְיוּ לִפְנֵי יְהוּדָה וְהַמַּאְרָב מֵאַחֲרֵיהֶם׃

at-behind-them and-the-ambush Judah in-front-of so-they-were

וַיִּפְנוּ יְהוּדָה וְהִנֵּה לָהֶם הַמִּלְחָמָה פָּנִים וְאָחוֹר

and-rear fronts the-attack against-them and-see! Judah and-they-turned (14)

וַיִּצְעֲקוּ לַיהוָה וְהַכֹּהֲנִים מַחְצְצְרִים בַּחֲצֹצְרוֹת׃

on-the-trumpets ones-blowing and-the-priests to-Yahweh then-they-cried

וַיָּרִיעוּ אִישׁ יְהוּדָה וַיְהִי בְּהָרִיעַ אִישׁ

man-of when-to-raise-cry and-he-was Judah man-of and-they-raised-cry (15)

יְהוּדָה וְהָאֱלֹהִים נָגַף אֶת־יָרָבְעָם וְכָל־יִשְׂרָאֵל לִפְנֵי אֲבִיָּה

Abijah before Israel and-all-of Jeroboam *** he-routed then-the-God Judah

וִיהוּדָה׃ וַיָּנוּסוּ בְנֵי־יִשְׂרָאֵל מִפְּנֵי יְהוּדָה

Judah from-before Israel sons-of and-they-fled (16) and-Judah

וַיִּתְּנֵם אֱלֹהִים בְּיָדָם׃ וַיַּכּוּ בָהֶם

on-them and-he-inflicted (17) into-hand-of-them God and-he-delivered-them

אֲבִיָּה וְעַמּוֹ מַכָּה רַבָּה וַיִּפְּלוּ חֲלָלִים מִיִּשְׂרָאֵל

from-Israel casualties so-they-fell heavy loss and-people-of-him Abijah

חֲמֵשׁ־מֵאוֹת אֶלֶף אִישׁ בָּחוּר׃ וַיִּכָּנְעוּ בְנֵי־

men-of and-they-were-subdued (18) being-able man thousand hundreds five-of

יִשְׂרָאֵל בָּעֵת הַהִיא וַיֶּאֶמְצוּ בְּנֵי יְהוּדָה כִּי

because Judah men-of and-they-were-victorious the-that on-the-occasion Israel

נִשְׁעֲנוּ עַל־יְהוָה אֱלֹהֵי אֲבוֹתֵיהֶם׃ וַיִּרְדֹּף אֲבִיָּה

Abijah and-he-pursued (19) fathers-of-them God-of Yahweh on they-relied

אַחֲרֵי יָרָבְעָם וַיִּלְכֹּד מִמֶּנּוּ עָרִים אֶת־בֵּית־אֵל וְאֶת־בְּנוֹתֶיהָ

villages-of-her and El Beth *** towns from-him and-he-took Jeroboam after

וְאֶת־יְשָׁנָה וְאֶת־בְּנוֹתֶיהָ וְאֶת־עֶפְרוֹן וּבְנֹתֶיהָ׃ וְלֹא־

and-not (20) and-villages-of-her Ephron and villages-of-her and Jeshanah and

עָצַר כֹּחַ־יָרָבְעָם עוֹד בִּימֵי אֲבִיָּהוּ וַיִּגְּפֵהוּ

and-he-struck-down-him Abijah in-days-of again Jeroboam power he-regained

יְהוָה וַיָּמֹת׃ וַיִּתְחַזֵּק אֲבִיָּהוּ וַיִּשָּׂא־לוֹ

to-him and-he-married Abijah but-he-gained-strength (21) and-he-died Yahweh

נָשִׁים אַרְבַּע עֶשְׂרֵה וַיּוֹלֶד עֶשְׂרִים וּשְׁנַיִם בָּנִים וְשֵׁשׁ עֶשְׂרֵה בָּנוֹת׃

daughters ten and-six sons and-two twenty and-he-fathered ten four wives

וְיֶתֶר דִּבְרֵי אֲבִיָּה וּדְרָכָיו וּדְבָרָיו

and-words-of-him and-deeds-of-him Abijah events-of and-other-of (22)

כְּתוּבִים בְּמִדְרַשׁ הַנָּבִיא עִדּוֹ׃ וַיִּשְׁכַּב

and-he-rested *(23) Iddo the-prophet in-annotation-of ones-being-written

13Now Jeroboam had sent troops around to the rear, so that while he was in front of Judah the ambush was behind them. 14Judah turned and saw that they were being attacked at both front and rear. Then they cried out to the LORD. The priests blew their trumpets 15and the men of Judah raised the battle cry. At the sound of their battle cry, God routed Jeroboam and all Israel before Abijah and Judah. 16The Israelites fled before Judah, and God delivered them into their hands. 17Abijah and his men inflicted heavy losses on them, so that there were five hundred thousand casualties among Israel's able men. 18The men of Israel were subdued on that occasion, and the men of Judah were victorious because they relied on the LORD, the God of their fathers.

19Abijah pursued Jeroboam and took from him the towns of Bethel, Jeshanah and Ephron, with their surrounding villages. 20Jeroboam did not regain power during the time of Abijah. And the LORD struck him down and he died.

21But Abijah grew in strength. He married fourteen wives and had twenty-two sons and sixteen daughters.

22The other events of Abijah's reign, what he did and what he said, are written in the annotations of the prophet Iddo.

*23 The Hebrew numeration of chapter 14 begins with verse 2 of the English; thus, there is a one-verse discrepancy throughout the chapter.

°14 ק מחצרים

°19 ק עפרין

אֲבִיָּה עִם־ אֲבֹתָיו וַיִּקְבְּרוּ אֹתוֹ בְּעִיר דָּוִיד
David in-City-of him and-they-buried fathers-of-him with Abijah

וַיִּמְלֹךְ אָסָא בְנוֹ תַּחְתָּיו בְּיָמָיו
in-days-of-him in-place-of-him son-of-him Asa and-he-became-king

שָׁקְטָה הָאָרֶץ עֶשֶׂר שָׁנִים׃ וַיַּעַשׂ אָסָא הַטּוֹב
the-good Asa and-he-did (14:1) years ten the-country she-was-at-peace

וְהַיָּשָׁר בְּעֵינֵי יְהוָה אֱלֹהָיו׃ וַיָּסַר אֶת־ מִזְבְּחוֹת
altars-of *** and-he-removed (2) God-of-him Yahweh in-eyes-of and-the-right

הַנֵּכָר וְהַבָּמוֹת וַיְשַׁבֵּר אֶת־ הַמַּצֵּבוֹת
the-sacred-stones *** and-he-smashed and-the-high-places the-foreign

וַיְגַדַּע אֶת־ הָאֲשֵׁרִים׃ וַיֹּאמֶר לִיהוּדָה לִדְרוֹשׁ
to-seek to-Judah and-he-commanded (3) the-Asherah-poles *** and-he-cut-down

אֶת־ יְהוָה אֱלֹהֵי אֲבוֹתֵיהֶם וְלַעֲשׂוֹת הַתּוֹרָה וְהַמִּצְוָה׃
and-the-command the-law and-to-obey fathers-of-them God-of Yahweh ***

וַיָּסַר מִכָּל־ עָרֵי יְהוּדָה אֶת־ הַבָּמוֹת וְאֶת־
and the-high-places *** Judah towns-of from-all-of and-he-removed (4)

הַחַמָּנִים וַתִּשְׁקֹט הַמַּמְלָכָה לְפָנָיו׃
under-him the-kingdom and-she-was-at-peace the-incense-altars

וַיִּבֶן עָרֵי מְצוּרָה בִּיהוּדָה כִּי־ שָׁקְטָה
she-was-at-peace since in-Judah fortification cities-of and-he-built-up (5)

הָאָרֶץ וְאֵין־ עִמּוֹ מִלְחָמָה בַּשָּׁנִים הָאֵלֶּה כִּי־ הֵנִיחַ
he-gave-rest for the-those during-the-years war with-him and-no-one the-land

יְהוָה לוֹ׃ וַיֹּאמֶר לִיהוּדָה נִבְנֶה ׀ אֶת־ הֶעָרִים
the-towns *** let-us-build-up to-Judah and-he-said (6) to-him Yahweh

הָאֵלֶּה וְנָסֵב חוֹמָה וּמִגְדָּלִים דְּלָתַיִם וּבְרִיחִים עוֹדֶנּוּ
still-he and-bars gates and-towers wall and-let-us-put-around the-these

הָאָרֶץ לְפָנֵינוּ כִּי דָרַשְׁנוּ אֶת־ יְהוָה אֱלֹהֵינוּ דָּרַשְׁנוּ
we-sought God-of-us Yahweh *** we-sought because before-us the-land

וַיָּנַח לָנוּ מִסָּבִיב וַיִּבְנוּ וַיַּצְלִיחוּ׃
and-they-prospered so-they-built at-around to-us and-he-gave-rest

וַיְהִי לְאָסָא חַיִל נֹשֵׂא צִנָּה וָרֹמַח מִיהוּדָה
from-Judah and-spear large-shield carrying army to-Asa and-he-was (7)

שְׁלֹשׁ מֵאוֹת אֶלֶף וּמִבִּנְיָמִן נֹשְׂאֵי מָגֵן
small-shield ones-carrying-of and-from-Benjamin thousand hundreds three-of

וְדֹרְכֵי קֶשֶׁת מָאתַיִם וּשְׁמוֹנִים אֶלֶף כָּל־ אֵלֶּה
these all-of thousand and-eighty two-hundreds bow and-ones-drawing-of

גִּבּוֹרֵי חָיִל׃ וַיֵּצֵא אֲלֵיהֶם זֶרַח הַכּוּשִׁי
the-Cushite Zerah against-them and-he-marched-out (8) bravery fighting-men-of

14 And Abijah rested
with his fathers and
was buried in the City of David. Asa his son succeeded
him as king, and in his days
the country was at peace for
ten years.

*Asa King of Judah*

2 Asa did what was good and
right in the eyes of the LORD
his God. 3 He removed the foreign altars and the high
places, smashed the sacred
stones and cut down the
Asherah poles.[z] 4 He commanded Judah to seek the
LORD, the God of their fathers,
and to obey his laws and commands. 5 He removed the high
places and incense altars in
every town in Judah, and the
kingdom was at peace under
him. 6 He built up the fortified
cities of Judah, since the land
was at peace. No one was at
war with him during those
years, for the LORD gave him
rest.

7 "Let us build up these
towns," he said to Judah, "and
put walls around them, with
towers, gates and bars. The
land is still ours, because we
have sought the LORD our God;
we sought him and he has giv-
en us rest on every side." So
they built and prospered.

8 Asa had an army of three
hundred thousand men from
Judah, equipped with large
shields and with spears, and
two hundred and eighty thousand from Benjamin, armed
with small shields and with
bows. All these were brave
fighting men.

9 Zerah the Cushite marched

z3 That is, symbols of the goddess Asherah; here and elsewhere in 2 Chronicles

*See the note on page 116.

בְּחַיִל אֶלֶף אֲלָפִים וּמַרְכָּבוֹת שְׁלֹשׁ מֵאוֹת וַיָּבֹא
and-he-came hundreds three-of and-chariots thousands thousand-of with-army

עַד־ מָרֵשָׁה׃ וַיֵּצֵא אָסָא לְפָנָיו וַיַּעַרְכוּ
and-they-took-up before-him Asa and-he-went-out (9) Mareshah as-far-as

מִלְחָמָה בְּגֵיא צְפָתָה לְמָרֵשָׁה׃ וַיִּקְרָא אָסָא
Asa then-he-called (10) near-Mareshah Zephathah in-Valley-of battle-position

אֶל־ יְהוָה אֱלֹהָיו וַיֹּאמַר יְהוָה אֵין־ עִמְּךָ לַעְזוֹר
to-help like-you there-is-no-one Yahweh and-he-said God-of-him Yahweh to

בֵּין רַב לְאֵין כֹּחַ עָזְרֵנוּ יְהוָה אֱלֹהֵינוּ כִּי־ עָלֶיךָ
on-you for God-of-us Yahweh help-us! power to-one-without mighty against

נִשְׁעַנּוּ וּבְשִׁמְךָ בָאנוּ עַל־ הֶהָמוֹן הַזֶּה יְהוָה
Yahweh the-this the-vast-army against we-came and-in-name-of-you we-rely

אֱלֹהֵינוּ אַתָּה אַל־ יַעְצֹר עִמְּךָ אֱנוֹשׁ׃ וַיִּגֹּף
and-he-struck-down (11) men against-you let-him-prevail not you God-of-us

יְהוָה אֶת־ הַכּוּשִׁים לִפְנֵי אָסָא וְלִפְנֵי יְהוּדָה וַיָּנֻסוּ הַכּוּשִׁים׃
the-Cushites and-they-fled Judah and-before Asa before the-Cushites *** Yahweh

וַיִּרְדְּפֵם אָסָא וְהָעָם אֲשֶׁר־ עִמּוֹ עַד־ לִגְרָר
to-Gerar as-far-as with-him who and-the-army Asa and-he-pursued-them (12)

וַיִּפֹּל מִכּוּשִׁים לְאֵין לָהֶם מִחְיָה כִּי־ נִשְׁבָּרוּ
they-were-crushed that recovery to-them so-not from-Cushites and-he-fell

לִפְנֵי־ יְהוָה וְלִפְנֵי מַחֲנֵהוּ וַיִּשְׂאוּ שָׁלָל
plunder and-they-carried-off force-of-him and-before Yahweh before

הַרְבֵּה מְאֹד׃ וַיַּכּוּ אֵת כָּל־ הֶעָרִים סְבִיבוֹת
ones-around the-villages all-of *** and-they-destroyed (13) very to-be-large

גְּרָר כִּי־ הָיָה פַחַד־ יְהוָה עֲלֵיהֶם וַיָּבֹזּוּ אֶת־ כָּל־
all-of *** and-they-plundered upon-them Yahweh terror-of he-fell for Gerar

הֶעָרִים כִּי־ בִזָּה רַבָּה הָיְתָה בָהֶם׃ וְגַם־ אָהֳלֵי
camps-of and-also (14) in-them she-was much booty since the-villages

מִקְנֶה הִכּוּ וַיִּשְׁבּוּ צֹאן לָרֹב וּגְמַלִּים
and-camels in-quantity flock and-they-carried-off they-attacked herdsman

וַיָּשֻׁבוּ יְרוּשָׁלִָם׃ וַעֲזַרְיָהוּ בֶּן־ עוֹדֵד הָיְתָה עָלָיו
upon-him she-came Oded son-of and-Azariah (15:1) Jerusalem then-they-returned

רוּחַ אֱלֹהִים׃ וַיֵּצֵא לִפְנֵי אָסָא וַיֹּאמֶר לוֹ שְׁמָעוּנִי
listen-to-me! to-him and-he-said Asa before and-he-went-out (2) God Spirit-of

אָסָא וְכָל־ יְהוּדָה וּבִנְיָמִן יְהוָה עִמָּכֶם בִּהְיוֹתְכֶם עִמּוֹ
with-him when-to-be-you with-you Yahweh and-Benjamin Judah and-all-of Asa

וְאִם־ תִּדְרְשֻׁהוּ יִמָּצֵא לָכֶם וְאִם־ תַּעַזְבֻהוּ
you-forsake-him but-if by-you he-will-be-found you-seek-him and-if

out against them with a vast army[a] and three hundred chariots, and came as far as Mareshah.
10Asa went out to meet him, and they took up battle positions in the Valley of Zephathah near Mareshah.
11Then Asa called to the LORD his God and said, "LORD, there is no one like you to help the powerless against the mighty. Help us, O LORD our God, for we rely on you, and in your name we have come against this vast army. O LORD, you are our God; do not let man prevail against you."
12The LORD struck down the Cushites before Asa and Judah. The Cushites fled,
13and Asa and his army pursued them as far as Gerar. Such a great number of Cushites fell that they could not recover; they were crushed before the LORD and his forces. The men of Judah carried off a large amount of plunder.
14They destroyed all the villages around Gerar, for the terror of the LORD had fallen upon them. They plundered all these villages, since there was much booty there.
15They also attacked the camps of the herdsmen and carried off droves of sheep and goats and camels. Then they returned to Jerusalem.

*Asa's Reform*

15 The Spirit of God came upon Azariah son of Oded.
2He went out to meet Asa and said to him, "Listen to me, Asa and all Judah and Benjamin. The LORD is with you when you are with him. If you seek him, he will be found by you, but if you forsake him,

[a]9 Hebrew *with an army of a thousand thousands* or *with an army of thousands upon thousands*

*See the note on page 116.

יַעֲזֹב אֶתְכֶם׃ וְיָמִים רַבִּים לְיִשְׂרָאֵל לְלֹא ׀ אֱלֹהֵי אֱמֶת
truth God-of that-not in-Israel many and-days (3) you he-will-forsake

וּלְלֹא כֹּהֵן מוֹרֶה וּלְלֹא תוֹרָה׃ וַיָּשָׁב
but-he-turned (4) law and-that-not teaching priest and-that-not

בַּצַּר־ לוֹ עַל־ יְהוָה אֱלֹהֵי יִשְׂרָאֵל וַיְבַקְשֻׁהוּ
and-they-sought-him Israel God-of Yahweh to of-him in-the-distress

וַיִּמָּצֵא לָהֶם׃ וּבָעִתִּים הָהֵם אֵין שָׁלוֹם
safe not the-those and-in-the-days (5) by-them and-he-was-found

לַיּוֹצֵא וְלַבָּא כִּי מְהוּמֹת רַבּוֹת עַל כָּל־
all-of to great-ones turmoils for and-for-the-one-coming for-the-one-going

יוֹשְׁבֵי הָאֲרָצוֹת׃ וְכֻתְּתוּ גוֹי־ בְּגוֹי
by-nation nation and-they-were-crushed (6) the-lands ones-inhabiting-of

וְעִיר בְּעִיר כִּי־ אֱלֹהִים הֲמָמָם בְּכָל־ צָרָה׃
distress with-every-of he-troubled-them God because by-city and-city

וְאַתֶּם חִזְקוּ וְאַל־ יִרְפּוּ יְדֵיכֶם כִּי יֵשׁ
there-is for hands-of-you let-them-give-up and-not be-strong! but-you (7)

שָׂכָר לִפְעֻלַּתְכֶם׃ וְכִשְׁמֹעַ אָסָא הַדְּבָרִים הָאֵלֶּה
the-these the-words Asa and-when-to-hear (8) for-work-of-you reward

וְהַנְּבוּאָה עֹדֵד הַנָּבִיא הִתְחַזַּק וַיַּעֲבֵר
and-he-removed he-took-courage the-prophet Oded and-the-prophecy

הַשִּׁקּוּצִים מִכָּל־ אֶרֶץ יְהוּדָה וּבִנְיָמִן וּמִן־
and-from and-Benjamin Judah land-of from-whole-of the-detestable-things

הֶעָרִים אֲשֶׁר לָכַד מֵהַר אֶפְרָיִם וַיְחַדֵּשׁ אֶת־ מִזְבַּח
altar-of *** and-he-repaired Ephraim in-hill-of he-captured that the-towns

יְהוָה אֲשֶׁר לִפְנֵי אוּלָם יְהוָה׃ וַיִּקְבֹּץ אֶת־ כָּל־
all-of *** then-he-assembled (9) Yahweh portico-of in-front-of that Yahweh

יְהוּדָה וּבִנְיָמִן וְהַגָּרִים עִמָּהֶם מֵאֶפְרַיִם וּמְנַשֶּׁה
and-Manasseh from-Ephraim among-them and-the-ones-settling and-Benjamin Judah

וּמִשִּׁמְעוֹן כִּי־ נָפְלוּ עָלָיו מִיִּשְׂרָאֵל לָרֹב
in-number from-Israel to-him they-came-over for and-from-Simeon

בִּרְאֹתָם כִּי־ יְהוָה אֱלֹהָיו עִמּוֹ׃ וַיִּקָּבְצוּ
and-they-assembled (10) with-him God-of-him Yahweh that when-to-see-them

יְרוּשָׁלִַם בַּחֹדֶשׁ הַשְּׁלִישִׁי לִשְׁנַת חֲמֵשׁ־ עֶשְׂרֵה לְמַלְכוּת אָסָא׃
Asa of-reign-of ten five-of of-year-of the-third in-the-month Jerusalem

וַיִּזְבְּחוּ לַיהוָה בַּיּוֹם הַהוּא מִן־ הַשָּׁלָל
the-plunder from the-that on-the-day to-Yahweh and-they-sacrificed (11)

הֵבִיאוּ בָּקָר שְׁבַע מֵאוֹת וְצֹאן שִׁבְעַת אֲלָפִים׃
thousands seven-of and-flock hundreds seven-of cattle they-brought-back

he will forsake you. 3For a long
time Israel was without the
true God, without a priest to
teach and without the law.
4But in their distress they
turned to the LORD, the God of
Israel, and sought him, and he
was found by them. 5In those
days it was not safe to travel
about, for all the inhabitants
of the lands were in great turmoil. 6One nation was being
crushed by another and one
city by another, because God
was troubling them with
every kind of distress. 7But as
for you, be strong and do not
give up, for your work will be
rewarded."
8When Asa heard these
words and the prophecy of
Azariah son of[b] Oded the
prophet, he took courage. He
removed the detestable idols
from the whole land of Judah
and Benjamin and from the
towns he had captured in the
hills of Ephraim. He repaired
the altar of the LORD that was
in front of the portico of the
LORD's temple.
9Then he assembled all
Judah and Benjamin and the
people from Ephraim, Manasseh and Simeon who had settled among them, for large
numbers had come over to
him from Israel when they
saw that the LORD his God was
with him.
10They assembled at Jerusalem in the third month of the
fifteenth year of Asa's reign.
11At that time they sacrificed
to the LORD seven hundred
head of cattle and seven thousand sheep and goats from the
plunder they had brought

[b]8 Vulgate and Syriac (see also Septuagint and verse 1); Hebrew does not have *Azariah son of.*

וַיָּבֹאוּ בַבְּרִית לִדְרוֹשׁ אֶת־ יְהוָה אֱלֹהֵי
God-of Yahweh *** to-seek into-the-covenant and-they-entered (12)

אֲבוֹתֵיהֶם בְּכָל־ לְבָבָם וּבְכָל־ נַפְשָׁם׃
soul-of-them and-with-all-of heart-of-them with-all-of fathers-of-them

וְכֹל אֲשֶׁר לֹא־ יִדְרֹשׁ לַיהוָה אֱלֹהֵי־יִשְׂרָאֵל יוּמָת
he-was-killed Israel God-of to-Yahweh he-would-seek not who and-all (13)

לְמִן־ קָטֹן וְעַד־ גָּדוֹל לְמֵאִישׁ וְעַד־ אִשָּׁה׃
woman or-to whether-from-man great or-to small whether-from

וַיִּשָּׁבְעוּ לַיהוָה בְּקוֹל גָּדוֹל וּבִתְרוּעָה
and-with-shouting loud with-acclamation to-Yahweh and-they-took-oath (14)

וּבַחֲצֹצְרוֹת וּבְשׁוֹפָרוֹת׃ וַיִּשְׂמְחוּ כָל־ יְהוּדָה עַל־
about Judah all-of and-they-rejoiced (15) and-with-horns and-with-trumpets

הַשְּׁבוּעָה כִּי בְכָל־ לְבָבָם נִשְׁבָּעוּ וּבְכָל־
and-with-all-of they-swore heart-of-them with-whole-of because the-oath

רְצוֹנָם בִּקְשֻׁהוּ וַיִּמָּצֵא לָהֶם וַיָּנַח
so-he-gave-rest by-them and-he-was-found they-sought-him eagerness-of-them

יְהוָה לָהֶם מִסָּבִיב׃ וְגַם־ מַעֲכָה אֵם ׀ אָסָא הַמֶּלֶךְ
the-king Asa grandmother-of Maacah and-also (16) at-around to-them Yahweh

הֱסִירָהּ מִגְּבִירָה אֲשֶׁר־ עָשְׂתָה לַאֲשֵׁרָה מִפְלָצֶת
repulsive-pole to-Asherah she-made because from-queen-mother he-deposed-her

וַיִּכְרֹת אָסָא אֶת־ מִפְלַצְתָּהּ וַיָּדֶק וַיִּשְׂרֹף
and-he-burned and-he-broke-up repulsive-pole-of-her *** Asa and-he-cut-down

בְּנַחַל קִדְרוֹן׃ וְהַבָּמוֹת לֹא־ סָרוּ מִיִּשְׂרָאֵל
from-Israel they-removed not but-the-high-places (17) Kidron in-Valley-of

רַק לְבַב־ אָסָא הָיָה שָׁלֵם כָּל־ יָמָיו׃
days-of-him all-of fully-committed he-was Asa heart-of however

וַיָּבֵא אֶת־ קָדְשֵׁי אָבִיו
father-of-him dedicated-things-of *** and-he-brought (18)

וְקָדָשָׁיו בֵּית הָאֱלֹהִים כֶּסֶף וְזָהָב וְכֵלִים׃
and-articles and-gold silver the-God temple-of and-dedicated-things-of-him

וּמִלְחָמָה לֹא הָיָתָה עַד שְׁנַת־ שְׁלֹשִׁים וְחָמֵשׁ לְמַלְכוּת אָסָא׃
Asa of-reign-of and-five thirty year-of until she-was not and-war (19)

בִּשְׁנַת שְׁלֹשִׁים וָשֵׁשׁ לְמַלְכוּת אָסָא עָלָה בַּעְשָׁא מֶלֶךְ־
king-of Baasha he-went-up Asa of-reign-of and-six thirty in-year-of (16:1)

יִשְׂרָאֵל עַל־ יְהוּדָה וַיִּבֶן אֶת־ הָרָמָה לְבִלְתִּי תֵּת יוֹצֵא
one-leaving to-allow not the-Ramah *** and-he-fortified Judah against Israel

וָבָא לְאָסָא מֶלֶךְ יְהוּדָה׃ וַיֹּצֵא אָסָא כֶּסֶף וְזָהָב
and-gold silver Asa then-he-took (2) Judah king-of to-Asa or-one-entering

back. 12They entered into a covenant to seek the LORD, the God of their fathers, with all their heart and soul. 13All who would not seek the LORD, the God of Israel, were to be put to death, whether small or great, man or woman. 14They took an oath to the LORD with loud acclamation, with shouting and with trumpets and horns. 15All Judah rejoiced about the oath because they had sworn it wholeheartedly. They sought God eagerly, and he was found by them. So the LORD gave them rest on every side.

16King Asa also deposed his grandmother Maacah from her position as queen mother, because she had made a repulsive Asherah pole. Asa cut the pole down, broke it up and burned it in the Kidron Valley. 17Although he did not remove the high places from Israel, Asa's heart was fully committed ⌞to the LORD⌟ all his life. 18He brought into the temple of God the silver and gold and the articles that he and his father had dedicated.

19There was no more war until the thirty-fifth year of Asa's reign.

*Asa's Last Years*

16 In the thirty-sixth year of Asa's reign Baasha king of Israel went up against Judah and fortified Ramah to prevent anyone from leaving or entering the territory of Asa king of Judah.

2Asa then took the silver and

מֵאֹצְרוֹת בֵּית יְהוָה וּבֵית הַמֶּלֶךְ וַיִּשְׁלַח אֶל־
to and-he-sent the-king and-palace-of Yahweh temple-of from-treasuries-of

בֶּן־הֲדַד מֶלֶךְ אֲרָם הַיּוֹשֵׁב בְּדַרְמֶשֶׂק לֵאמֹר׃ בְּרִית
treaty (3) to-say in-Damascus the-one-ruling Aram king-of Hadad Ben

בֵּינִי וּבֵינֶךָ וּבֵין אָבִי וּבֵין אָבִיךָ
father-of-you and-between father-of-me and-between and-between-you between-me

הִנֵּה שָׁלַחְתִּי לְךָ כֶּסֶף וְזָהָב לֵךְ הָפֵר בְּרִיתְךָ אֶת־בַּעְשָׁא
Baasha with treaty-of-you break! come! and-gold silver to-you I-send see!

מֶלֶךְ יִשְׂרָאֵל וְיַעֲלֶה מֵעָלָי׃ וַיִּשְׁמַע
and-he-agreed (4) from-against-me so-he-will-withdraw Israel king-of

*בֶּן הֲדַד אֶל־הַמֶּלֶךְ אָסָא וַיִּשְׁלַח אֶת־שָׂרֵי הַחֲיָלִים אֲשֶׁר־
that the-forces commanders-of *** and-he-sent Asa the-king with Hadad Ben

לוֹ אֶל־עָרֵי יִשְׂרָאֵל וַיַּכּוּ אֶת־עִיּוֹן וְאֶת־דָּן וְאֵת
and Dan and Ijon *** and-they-conquered Israel towns-of against to-him

אָבֵל מַיִם וְאֵת כָּל־מִסְכְּנוֹת עָרֵי נַפְתָּלִי׃ וַיְהִי כִּשְׁמֹעַ
when-to-hear and-he-was (5) Naphtali cities-of stores-of all-of and Maim Abel

בַּעְשָׁא וַיֶּחְדַּל מִבְּנוֹת אֶת־הָרָמָה וַיַּשְׁבֵּת אֶת־
*** and-he-abandoned the-Ramah *** from-to-build then-he-stopped Baasha

מְלַאכְתּוֹ׃ וְאָסָא הַמֶּלֶךְ לָקַח אֶת־כָּל־יְהוּדָה
Judah all-of *** he-brought the-king then-Asa (6) work-of-him

וַיִּשְׂאוּ אֶת־אַבְנֵי הָרָמָה וְאֶת־עֵצֶיהָ אֲשֶׁר
that timbers-of-her and the-Ramah stones-of *** and-they-carried-away

בָּנָה בַּעְשָׁא וַיִּבֶן בָּהֶם אֶת־גֶּבַע וְאֶת־הַמִּצְפָּה׃
the-Mizpah and Geba *** with-them and-he-built-up Baasha he-used

וּבָעֵת הַהִיא בָּא חֲנָנִי הָרֹאֶה אֶל־אָסָא מֶלֶךְ יְהוּדָה
Judah king-of Asa to the-seer Hanani he-came the-that and-at-the-time (7)

וַיֹּאמֶר אֵלָיו בְּהִשָּׁעֶנְךָ עַל־מֶלֶךְ אֲרָם וְלֹא נִשְׁעַנְתָּ
you-relied and-not Aram king-of on because-to-rely-you to-him and-he-said

עַל־יְהוָה אֱלֹהֶיךָ עַל־כֵּן נִמְלַט חֵיל מֶלֶךְ־אֲרָם מִיָּדֶךָ׃
from-hand-of-you Aram king-of army-of he-escaped this for God-of-you Yahweh on

הֲלֹא הַכּוּשִׁים וְהַלּוּבִים הָיוּ לְחַיִל ׀ לָרֹב
in-greatness as-army they-were and-the-Libyans the-Cushites not? (8)

לְרֶכֶב וּלְפָרָשִׁים לְהַרְבֵּה מְאֹד וּבְהִשָּׁעֶנְךָ עַל־
on yet-when-to-rely-you very to-be-great and-with-horsemen with-chariot

יְהוָה נְתָנָם בְּיָדֶךָ׃ כִּי יְהוָה עֵינָיו
eyes-of-him Yahweh for (9) into-hand-of-you he-delivered-them Yahweh

מְשֹׁטְטוֹת בְּכָל־הָאָרֶץ לְהִתְחַזֵּק עִם־לְבָבָם
heart-of-them to to-strengthen the-earth through-all-of ones-ranging

gold out of the treasuries of the
LORD's temple and of his own
palace and sent it to Ben-
Hadad king of Aram, who was
ruling in Damascus. 3"Let
there be a treaty between me
and you," he said, "as there
was between my father and
your father. See, I am sending
you silver and gold. Now
break your treaty with Baasha
king of Israel so he will withdraw from me."
4Ben-Hadad agreed with
King Asa and sent the commanders of his forces against
the towns of Israel. They conquered Ijon, Dan, Abel Maim[c]
and all the store cities of
Naphtali. 5When Baasha
heard this, he stopped building Ramah and abandoned
his work. 6Then King Asa
brought all the men of Judah,
and they carried away from
Ramah the stones and timber
Baasha had been using. With
them he built up Geba and
Mizpah.
7At that time Hanani the
seer came to Asa king of Judah
and said to him: "Because you
relied on the king of Aram and
not on the LORD your God, the
army of the king of Aram has
escaped from your hand.
8Were not the Cushites[d] and
Libyans a mighty army with
great numbers of chariots and
horsemen[e]? Yet when you relied on the LORD, he delivered
them into your hand. 9For the
eyes of the LORD range
throughout the earth to
strengthen those whose hearts

[c]4 Also known as *Abel Beth Maacah*
[d]8 That is, people from the upper Nile region
[e]8 Or *charioteers*

*4 Most mss connect these two words with *maqqeph* (בֶּן־הדד).

שָׁלֵם אֵלָיו נִסְכַּלְתָּ עַל־זֹאת כִּי מֵעַתָּה יֵשׁ
there-is from-now indeed this in you-acted-foolishly to-him fully-committed

עִמְּךָ מִלְחָמוֹת׃ וַיִּכְעַס אָסָא אֶל־הָרֹאֶה וַיִּתְּנֵהוּ
and-he-put-him the-seer with Asa and-he-was-angry (10) wars against-you

בֵּית הַמַּהְפֶּכֶת כִּי־בְזַעַף עִמּוֹ עַל־זֹאת וַיְרַצֵּץ
and-he-oppressed this for against-him of-rage because the-prisons house-of

אָסָא מִן־הָעָם בָּעֵת הַהִיא׃ וְהִנֵּה דִּבְרֵי אָסָא
Asa events-of and-see! (11) the-that at-the-time the-people from Asa

הָרִאשׁוֹנִים וְהָאַחֲרוֹנִים הִנָּם כְּתוּבִים עַל־סֵפֶר הַמְּלָכִים
the-kings book-of in ones-being-written see-they! and-the-ends the-beginnings

לִיהוּדָה וְיִשְׂרָאֵל׃ וַיֶּחֱלֶא אָסָא בִּשְׁנַת שְׁלוֹשִׁים
thirty in-year-of Asa and-he-became-diseased (12) and-Israel of-Judah

וָתֵשַׁע לְמַלְכוּתוֹ בְּרַגְלָיו עַד־לְמַעְלָה חָלְיוֹ
disease-of-him to-severity to in-feet-of-him of-reign-of-him and-nine

וְגַם־בְּחָלְיוֹ לֹא־דָרַשׁ אֶת־יְהוָה כִּי
only Yahweh *** he-sought not in-illness-of-him yet-even

בָּרֹפְאִים׃ וַיִּשְׁכַּב אָסָא עִם־אֲבֹתָיו
fathers-of-him with Asa then-he-rested (13) to-the-ones-being-physicians

וַיָּמָת בִּשְׁנַת אַרְבָּעִים וְאַחַת לְמָלְכוֹ׃ וַיִּקְבְּרֻהוּ
and-they-buried-him (14) of-reign-of-him and-one forty in-year-of and-he-died

בְקִבְרֹתָיו אֲשֶׁר כָּרָה־לוֹ בְּעִיר דָּוִיד וַיַּשְׁכִּיבֻהוּ
and-they-laid-him David in-City-of for-him he-cut-out that in-tombs-of-him

בַּמִּשְׁכָּב אֲשֶׁר מִלֵּא בְּשָׂמִים וּזְנִים מְרֻקָּחִים
ones-being-blended and-various-kinds spices he-was-covered that on-the-bier

בְּמִרְקַחַת מַעֲשֶׂה וַיִּשְׂרְפוּ־לוֹ שְׂרֵפָה גְּדוֹלָה עַד־לִמְאֹד׃
to-very to huge fire for-him and-they-burned mixture with-perfume-of

וַיִּמְלֹךְ יְהוֹשָׁפָט בְּנוֹ תַּחְתָּיו
in-place-of-him son-of-him Jehoshaphat and-he-became-king (17:1)

וַיִּתְחַזֵּק עַל־יִשְׂרָאֵל׃ וַיִּתֶּן־חַיִל
troop and-he-stationed (2) Israel against and-he-strengthened-himself

בְּכָל־עָרֵי יְהוּדָה הַבְּצֻרוֹת וַיִּתֵּן נְצִיבִים
garrisons and-he-put the-ones-being-fortified Judah cities-of in-all-of

בְּאֶרֶץ יְהוּדָה וּבְעָרֵי אֶפְרַיִם אֲשֶׁר לָכַד אָסָא אָבִיו׃
father-of-him Asa he-captured that Ephraim and-in-towns-of Judah in-land-of

וַיְהִי יְהוָה עִם־יְהוֹשָׁפָט כִּי הָלַךְ בְּדַרְכֵי דָּוִיד
David in-ways-of he-walked because Jehoshaphat with Yahweh and-he-was (3)

אָבִיו הָרִאשֹׁנִים וְלֹא דָרַשׁ לַבְּעָלִים׃ כִּי
but (4) to-the-Baals he-consulted and-not the-early-ones father-of-him

are fully committed to him. You have done a foolish thing, and from now on you will be at war."

10 Asa was angry with the seer because of this; he was so enraged that he put him in prison. At the same time Asa brutally oppressed some of the people.

11 The events of Asa's reign, from beginning to end, are written in the book of the kings of Judah and Israel.
12 In the thirty-ninth year of his reign Asa was afflicted with a disease in his feet. Though his disease was severe, even in his illness he did not seek help from the LORD, but only from the physicians.
13 Then in the forty-first year of his reign Asa died and rested with his fathers.
14 They buried him in the tomb that he had cut out for himself in the City of David. They laid him on a bier covered with spices and various blended perfumes, and they made a huge fire in his honor.

*Jehoshaphat King of Judah*

17 Jehoshaphat his son succeeded him as king and strengthened himself against Israel.
2 He stationed troops in all the fortified cities of Judah and put garrisons in Judah and in the towns of Ephraim that his father Asa had captured.

3 The LORD was with Jehoshaphat because in his early years he walked in the ways his father David had followed. He did not consult the Baals

לֵאלֹהֵי אָבִיו דָּרָשׁ וּבְמִצְוֺתָיו הָלָךְ וְלֹא
and-not he-followed and-to-commands-of-him he-sought father-of-him to-God-of

כְּמַעֲשֵׂה יִשְׂרָאֵל׃ וַיָּכֶן יְהוָה אֶת־ הַמַּמְלָכָה
the-kingdom *** Yahweh and-he-established (5) Israel as-practice-of

בְּיָדוֹ וַיִּתְּנוּ כָל־ יְהוּדָה מִנְחָה לִיהוֹשָׁפָט
to-Jehoshaphat gift Judah all-of and-they-brought under-hand-of-him

וַיְהִי־ לוֹ עֹשֶׁר־ וְכָבוֹד לָרֹב׃ וַיִּגְבַּה
and-he-was-devoted (6) in-greatness and-honor wealth to-him so-he-was

לִבּוֹ בְּדַרְכֵי יְהוָה וְעוֹד הֵסִיר אֶת־ הַבָּמוֹת
the-high-places *** he-removed and-furthermore Yahweh to-ways-of heart-of-him

וְאֶת־ הָאֲשֵׁרִים מִיהוּדָה׃ וּבִשְׁנַת שָׁלוֹשׁ לְמָלְכוֹ שָׁלַח
he-sent to-reign-him three in-year-of (7) from-Judah the-Asherah-poles and

לְשָׂרָיו לְבֶן־ חַיִל וּלְעֹבַדְיָה וְלִזְכַרְיָה
and-namely-Zechariah and-namely-Obadiah Hail namely-Ben of-officials-of-him

וְלִנְתַנְאֵל וּלְמִיכָיָהוּ לְלַמֵּד בְּעָרֵי יְהוּדָה׃
Judah in-cities-of to-teach and-namely-Micaiah and-namely-Nethanel

וְעִמָּהֶם הַלְוִיִּם שְׁמַעְיָהוּ וּנְתַנְיָהוּ וּזְבַדְיָהוּ וַעֲשָׂהאֵל
and-Asahel and-Zebadiah and-Nethaniah Shemaiah the-Levites and-with-them (8)

וּשְׁמִרָימוֹת וִיהוֹנָתָן וַאֲדֹנִיָּהוּ וְטוֹבִיָּהוּ וְטוֹב אֲדוֹנִיָּה
Adonijah and-Tob and-Tobijah and-Adonijah and-Jehonathan and-Shemiramoth

הַלְוִיִּם וְעִמָּהֶם אֱלִישָׁמָע וִיהוֹרָם הַכֹּהֲנִים׃ וַיְלַמְּדוּ
and-they-taught (9) the-priests and-Jehoram Elishama and-with-them the-Levites

בִּיהוּדָה וְעִמָּהֶם סֵפֶר תּוֹרַת יְהוָה וַיָּסֹבּוּ
and-they-went-around Yahweh Law-of Book-of and-with-them throughout-Judah

בְּכָל־ עָרֵי יְהוּדָה וַיְלַמְּדוּ בָּעָם׃ וַיְהִי ׀
and-he-fell (10) to-the-people and-they-taught Judah towns-of to-all-of

פַּחַד יְהוָה עַל כָּל־ מַמְלְכוֹת הָאֲרָצוֹת אֲשֶׁר סְבִיבוֹת יְהוּדָה
Judah ones-surrounding that the-lands kingdoms-of all-of on Yahweh fear-of

וְלֹא נִלְחֲמוּ עִם־ יְהוֹשָׁפָט׃ וּמִן־ פְּלִשְׁתִּים מְבִיאִים
ones-bringing Philistines and-from (11) Jehoshaphat with they-made-war so-not

לִיהוֹשָׁפָט מִנְחָה וְכֶסֶף מַשָּׂא גַּם הָעַרְבִיאִים מְבִיאִים לוֹ
to-him ones-bringing the-Arabs and tribute and-silver-of gift to-Jehoshaphat

צֹאן אֵילִים שִׁבְעַת אֲלָפִים וּשְׁבַע מֵאוֹת וּתְיָשִׁים שִׁבְעַת
seven-of and-goats hundreds and-seven-of thousands seven-of rams flock

אֲלָפִים וּשְׁבַע מֵאוֹת׃ וַיְהִי יְהוֹשָׁפָט הֹלֵךְ
growing Jehoshaphat and-he-was (12) hundreds and-seven-of thousands

וְגָדֵל עַד־ לְמָעְלָה וַיִּבֶן בִּיהוּדָה בִּירָנִיּוֹת וְעָרֵי
and-cities-of forts in-Judah and-he-built to-more to and-he-became-powerful

[4]but sought the God of his father and followed his commands rather than the practices of Israel. [5]The LORD established the kingdom under his control; and all Judah brought gifts to Jehoshaphat, so that he had great wealth and honor. [6]His heart was devoted to the ways of the LORD; furthermore, he removed the high places and the Asherah poles from Judah.

[7]In the third year of his reign he sent his officials Ben-Hail, Obadiah, Zechariah, Nethanel and Micaiah to teach in the towns of Judah. [8]With them were certain Levites—Shemaiah, Nethaniah, Zebadiah, Asahel, Shemiramoth, Jehonathan, Adonijah, Tobijah and Tob-Adonijah—and the priests Elishama and Jehoram. [9]They taught throughout Judah, taking with them the Book of the Law of the LORD; they went around to all the towns of Judah and taught the people.

[10]The fear of the LORD fell on all the kingdoms of the lands surrounding Judah, so that they did not make war with Jehoshaphat. [11]Some Philistines brought Jehoshaphat gifts and silver as tribute, and the Arabs brought him flocks: seven thousand seven hundred rams and seven thousand seven hundred goats.

[12]Jehoshaphat became more and more powerful; he built forts and store cities in Judah

°8 ק ושמירמות

מִסְכְּנוֹת׃ וּמְלָאכָה רַבָּה הָיָה לוֹ בְּעָרֵי יְהוּדָה וְאַנְשֵׁי
and-men-of Judah in-towns-of to-him he-was large and-supply (13) stores

מִלְחָמָה גִּבּוֹרֵי חַיִל בִּירוּשָׁלָם׃ וְאֵלֶּה פְּקֻדָּתָם
enrollment-of-them and-these (14) in-Jerusalem valor warriors-of fight

לְבֵית אֲבוֹתֵיהֶם לִיהוּדָה שָׂרֵי אֲלָפִים עַדְנָה
Adnah thousands commanders-of from-Judah fathers-of-them by-family-of

הַשָּׂר וְעִמּוֹ גִּבּוֹרֵי חַיִל שְׁלֹשׁ מֵאוֹת אָלֶף׃
thousand hundreds three-of fight men-of and-with-him the-commander

וְעַל־ יָדוֹ יְהוֹחָנָן הַשָּׂר וְעִמּוֹ מָאתַיִם
two-hundreds and-with-him the-commander Jehohanan hand-of-him and-at (15)

וּשְׁמוֹנִים אָלֶף׃ וְעַל־ יָדוֹ עֲמַסְיָה בֶן־ זִכְרִי
Zicri son-of Amasiah hand-of-him and-at (16) thousand and-eighty

הַמִּתְנַדֵּב לַיהוָה וְעִמּוֹ מָאתַיִם אֶלֶף
thousand two-hundreds and-with-him to-Yahweh the-one-volunteering-himself

גִּבּוֹר חָיִל׃ וּמִן־ בִּנְיָמִן גִּבּוֹר חַיִל אֶלְיָדָע וְעִמּוֹ
and-with-him Eliada valor soldier-of Benjamin and-from (17) fight man-of

נֹשְׁקֵי־ קֶשֶׁת וּמָגֵן מָאתַיִם אָלֶף׃ וְעַל־
and-at (18) thousand two-hundreds and-shield bow ones-being-armed-of

יָדוֹ יְהוֹזָבָד וְעִמּוֹ מֵאָה־ וּשְׁמוֹנִים אֶלֶף
thousand and-eighty hundred and-with-him Jehozabad hand-of-him

חֲלוּצֵי צָבָא׃ אֵלֶּה הַמְשָׁרְתִים אֶת־ הַמֶּלֶךְ מִלְּבַד
besides the-king *** the-ones-serving these (19) battle ones-being-armed-of

אֲשֶׁר־ נָתַן הַמֶּלֶךְ בְּעָרֵי הַמִּבְצָר בְּכָל־
through-all-of the-fortification in-cities-of the-king he-stationed whom

יְהוּדָה׃ וַיְהִי לִיהוֹשָׁפָט עֹשֶׁר וְכָבוֹד לָרֹב
in-greatness and-honor wealth to-Jehoshaphat now-he-was (18:1) Judah

וַיִּתְחַתֵּן לְאַחְאָב׃ וַיֵּרֶד לְקֵץ שָׁנִים אֶל־אַחְאָב
Ahab to years at-end-of and-he-went-down (2) with-Ahab and-he-allied-himself

לְשֹׁמְרוֹן וַיִּזְבַּח־ לוֹ אַחְאָב צֹאן וּבָקָר לָרֹב
in-quantity and-cattle sheep Ahab for-him and-he-slaughtered in-Samaria

וְלָעָם אֲשֶׁר עִמּוֹ וַיְסִיתֵהוּ לַעֲלוֹת אֶל־ רָמֹת גִּלְעָד׃
Gilead Ramoth *** to-attack and-he-urged-him with-him who and-for-the-people

וַיֹּאמֶר אַחְאָב מֶלֶךְ־ יִשְׂרָאֵל אֶל־ יְהוֹשָׁפָט מֶלֶךְ יְהוּדָה
Judah king-of Jehoshaphat to Israel king-of Ahab and-he-asked (3)

הֲתֵלֵךְ עִמִּי רָמֹת גִּלְעָד וַיֹּאמֶר לוֹ כָּמוֹנִי כָמוֹךָ
as-you so-me to-him and-he-replied Gilead Ramoth with-me will-you-go?

וּכְעַמְּךָ עַמִּי וְעִמְּךָ בַּמִּלְחָמָה׃ וַיֹּאמֶר
but-he-said (4) in-the-war and-with-you people-of-me and-as-people-of-you

[13]and had large supplies in the towns of Judah. He also kept experienced fighting men in Jerusalem. [14]Their enrollment by families was as follows:

From Judah, commanders of units of 1,000:
Adnah the commander, with 300,000 fighting men;
[15]next, Jehohanan the commander, with 280,000;
[16]next, Amasiah son of Zicri, who volunteered himself for the service of the LORD, with 200,000.
[17]From Benjamin:
Eliada, a valiant soldier, with 200,000 men armed with bows and shields;
[18]next, Jehozabad, with 180,000 men armed for battle.

[19]These were the men who served the king, besides those he stationed in the fortified cities throughout Judah.

*Micaiah Prophesies Against Ahab*

18 Now Jehoshaphat had great wealth and honor, and he allied himself with Ahab by marriage. [2]Some years later he went down to visit Ahab in Samaria. Ahab slaughtered many sheep and cattle for him and the people with him and urged him to attack Ramoth Gilead. [3]Ahab king of Israel asked Jehoshaphat king of Judah, "Will you go with me against Ramoth Gilead?"

Jehoshaphat replied, "I am as you are, and my people as your people; we will join you in the war." [4]But Jehoshaphat

יְהוֹשָׁפָט אֶל־ מֶלֶךְ יִשְׂרָאֵל דְּרָשׁ־ נָא כַיּוֹם אֶת־ דְּבַר יְהוָה׃
Yahweh counsel-of *** as-the-day now! seek! Israel king-of to Jehoshaphat

וַיִּקְבֹּץ מֶלֶךְ־יִשְׂרָאֵל אֶת־ הַנְּבִאִים אַרְבַּע מֵאוֹת אִישׁ
man hundreds four the-prophets *** Israel king-of so-he-brought-together (5)

וַיֹּאמֶר אֲלֵהֶם הֲנֵלֵךְ אֶל־ רָמֹת גִּלְעָד לַמִּלְחָמָה אִם־
or to-the-war Gilead Ramoth against shall-we-go? to-them and-he-asked

אֶחְדָּל וַיֹּאמְרוּ עֲלֵה וְיִתֵּן הָאֱלֹהִים בְּיַד
into-hand-of the-God for-he-will-give go! and-they-answered shall-I-refrain

הַמֶּלֶךְ׃ וַיֹּאמֶר יְהוֹשָׁפָט הַאֵין פֹּה נָבִיא לַיהוָה עוֹד
still of-Yahweh prophet here not? Jehoshaphat but-he-asked (6) the-king

וְנִדְרְשָׁה מֵאֹתוֹ׃ וַיֹּאמֶר מֶלֶךְ־ יִשְׂרָאֵל ׀ אֶל־ יְהוֹשָׁפָט
Jehoshaphat to Israel king-of and-he-answered (7) of-him that-we-can-inquire

עוֹד אִישׁ־ אֶחָד לִדְרוֹשׁ אֶת־ יְהוָה מֵאֹתוֹ וַאֲנִי שְׂנֵאתִיהוּ כִּי־
because I-hate-him but-I through-him Yahweh *** to-inquire one man still

אֵינֶנּוּ מִתְנַבֵּא עָלַי לְטוֹבָה כִּי כָל־ יָמָיו לְרָעָה הוּא
he for-bad days-of-him all-of but for-good about-me prophesying never-he

מִיכָיְהוּ בֶּן־ יִמְלָא וַיֹּאמֶר יְהוֹשָׁפָט אַל־ יֹאמַר הַמֶּלֶךְ
the-king he-should-say not Jehoshaphat and-he-replied Imlah son-of Micaiah

כֵּן׃ וַיִּקְרָא מֶלֶךְ יִשְׂרָאֵל אֶל־ סָרִיס אֶחָד וַיֹּאמֶר
and-he-said one official to Israel king-of so-he-called (8) that

מַהֵר מִיכָהוּ בֶן־ יִמְלָא׃ וּמֶלֶךְ יִשְׂרָאֵל וִיהוֹשָׁפָט
and-Jehoshaphat Israel and-king-of (9) Imlah son-of Micaiah bring-at-once!

מֶלֶךְ־ יְהוּדָה יוֹשְׁבִים אִישׁ עַל־ כִּסְאוֹ מְלֻבָּשִׁים בְּגָדִים
robes ones-being-dressed throne-of-him on each ones-sitting Judah king-of

וְיֹשְׁבִים בַּגֹּרֶן פֶּתַח שַׁעַר שֹׁמְרוֹן וְכָל־
and-all-of Samaria gate-of entrance-of at-threshing-floor and-ones-sitting

הַנְּבִיאִים מִתְנַבְּאִים לִפְנֵיהֶם׃ וַיַּעַשׂ לוֹ צִדְקִיָּהוּ
Zedekiah for-him now-he-made (10) before-them ones-prophesying the-prophets

בֶן־ כְּנַעֲנָה קַרְנֵי בַרְזֶל וַיֹּאמֶר כֹּה־ אָמַר יְהוָה בְּאֵלֶּה
with-these Yahweh he-says this and-he-declared iron horns-of Kenaanah son-of

תְּנַגַּח אֶת־ אֲרָם עַד־ כַּלּוֹתָם׃ וְכָל־ הַנְּבִאִים
the-prophets and-all-of (11) to-destroy-them until Aram *** you-will-gore

נִבְּאִים כֵּן לֵאמֹר עֲלֵה רָמֹת גִּלְעָד וְהַצְלַח
and-be-victorious! Gilead Ramoth attack! to-say same ones-prophesying

וְנָתַן יְהוָה בְּיַד הַמֶּלֶךְ׃ וְהַמַּלְאָךְ אֲשֶׁר־
who and-the-messenger (12) the-king into-hand-of Yahweh for-he-will-give

הָלַךְ ׀ לִקְרֹא לְמִיכָיְהוּ דִּבֶּר אֵלָיו לֵאמֹר הִנֵּה דִבְרֵי
words-of look! to-say to-him he-said to-Micaiah to-summon he-went

also said to the king of Israel,
"First seek the counsel of the
LORD."
5So the king of Israel
brought together the pro-
phets—four hundred men—
and asked them, "Shall we go
to war against Ramoth Gilead,
or shall I refrain?"
"Go," they answered, "for
God will give it into the king's
hand."
6But Jehoshaphat asked, "Is
there not a prophet of the LORD
here whom we can inquire
of?"
7The king of Israel answered
Jehoshaphat, "There is still
one man through whom we
can inquire of the LORD, but I
hate him because he never
prophesies anything good
about me, but always bad. He
is Micaiah son of Imlah."
"The king should not say
that," Jehoshaphat replied.
8So the king of Israel called
one of his officials and said,
"Bring Micaiah son of Imlah
at once."
9Dressed in their royal
robes, the king of Israel and
Jehoshaphat king of Judah
were sitting on their thrones
at the threshing floor by the
entrance to the gate of Samaria, with all the prophets
prophesying before them.
10Now Zedekiah son of Kenaanah had made iron horns, and
he declared, "This is what the
LORD says: 'With these you
will gore the Arameans until
they are destroyed.'"
11All the other prophets were
prophesying the same thing.
"Attack Ramoth Gilead and be
victorious," they said, "for the
LORD will give it into the
king's hand."
12The messenger who had
gone to summon Micaiah said
to him, "Look, as one man the

°8 ק מיכיהו

הַנְּבִאִים פֶּה־אֶחָד טוֹב אֶל־הַמֶּלֶךְ וִיהִי־נָא דְבָרְךָ
word-of-you now! so-let-him-be the-king for success one mouth the-prophets

כְּאַחַד מֵהֶם וְדִבַּרְתָּ טּוֹב׃ וַיֹּאמֶר מִיכָיְהוּ חַי־
life-of Micaiah but-he-said (13) favorably and-you-speak with-them as-one

יְהוָה כִּי אֶת־אֲשֶׁר־יֹאמַר אֱלֹהַי אֹתוֹ אֲדַבֵּר׃ וַיָּבֹא
when-he-arrived (14) I-can-tell him God-of-me he-says what *** only Yahweh

אֶל־הַמֶּלֶךְ וַיֹּאמֶר הַמֶּלֶךְ אֵלָיו מִיכָה הֲנֵלֵךְ אֶל־רָמֹת
Ramoth against shall-we-go? Micaiah to-him the-king then-he-asked the-king at

גִּלְעָד לַמִּלְחָמָה אִם־אֶחְדָּל וַיֹּאמֶר עֲלוּ
attack! and-he-answered shall-I-refrain or to-the-war Gilead

וְהַצְלִיחוּ וְיִנָּתְנוּ בְּיֶדְכֶם׃ וַיֹּאמֶר
but-he-said (15) into-hand-of-you for-they-will-be-given and-be-victorious!

אֵלָיו הַמֶּלֶךְ עַד־כַּמֶּה פְעָמִים אֲנִי מַשְׁבִּיעֶךָ אֲשֶׁר לֹא־
not that making-swear-you I times as-the-how-many? to the-king to-him

תְדַבֵּר אֵלַי רַק־אֱמֶת בְּשֵׁם יְהוָה׃ וַיֹּאמֶר רָאִיתִי אֶת־
*** I-saw then-he-answered (16) Yahweh in-name-of truth only to-me you-tell

כָּל־יִשְׂרָאֵל נְפוֹצִים עַל־הֶהָרִים כַּצֹּאן אֲשֶׁר אֵין־
not that like-the-sheep the-hills on ones-being-scattered Israel all-of

לָהֶן רֹעֶה וַיֹּאמֶר יְהוָה לֹא־אֲדֹנִים לָאֵלֶּה יָשׁוּבוּ
let-them-go to-these masters not Yahweh and-he-said one-shepherding to-them

אִישׁ־לְבֵיתוֹ בְּשָׁלוֹם׃ וַיֹּאמֶר מֶלֶךְ־יִשְׂרָאֵל אֶל־יְהוֹשָׁפָט
Jehoshaphat to Israel king-of and-he-said (17) in-peace to-home-of-him each

הֲלֹא אָמַרְתִּי אֵלֶיךָ לֹא־יִתְנַבֵּא עָלַי טוֹב כִּי אִם־לְרָע׃
for-bad only but good about-me he-prophesies not to-you I-told not?

וַיֹּאמֶר לָכֵן שִׁמְעוּ דְבַר־יְהוָה רָאִיתִי אֶת־יְהוָה יוֹשֵׁב
sitting Yahweh *** I-saw Yahweh word-of hear! therefore and-he-said (18)

עַל־כִּסְאוֹ וְכָל־צְבָא הַשָּׁמַיִם עֹמְדִים עַל־יְמִינוֹ
right-of-him on ones-standing the-heavens host-of and-all-of throne-of-him on

וּשְׂמֹאלוֹ׃ וַיֹּאמֶר יְהוָה מִי יְפַתֶּה אֶת־אַחְאָב מֶלֶךְ־
king-of Ahab *** he-will-lure who? Yahweh and-he-said (19) and-left-of-him

יִשְׂרָאֵל וְיַעַל וְיִפֹּל בְּרָמוֹת גִּלְעָד וַיֹּאמֶר זֶה
this and-he-said Gilead at-Ramoth and-he-falls so-he-attacks Israel

אֹמֵר כָּכָה וְזֶה אֹמֵר כָּכָה׃ וַיֵּצֵא הָרוּחַ
the-spirit and-he-came-forward (20) such suggesting and-that such suggesting

וַיַּעֲמֹד לִפְנֵי יְהוָה וַיֹּאמֶר אֲנִי אֲפַתֶּנּוּ וַיֹּאמֶר יְהוָה
Yahweh and-he-asked I-will-lure-him I and-he-said Yahweh before and-he-stood

אֵלָיו בַּמָּה׃ וַיֹּאמֶר אֵצֵא וְהָיִיתִי לְרוּחַ שֶׁקֶר
lying as-spirit and-I-will-be I-will-go and-he-said (21) by-the-how? to-him

other prophets are predicting
success for the king. Let your
word agree with theirs, and
speak favorably."
[13]But Micaiah said, "As surely as the LORD lives, I can tell
him only what my God says."
[14]When he arrived, the king
asked him, "Micaiah, shall we
go to war against Ramoth Gilead, or shall I refrain?"
"Attack and be victorious,"
he answered, "for they will be
given into your hand."
[15]The king said to him,
"How many times must I
make you swear to tell me
nothing but the truth in the
name of the LORD?"
[16]Then Micaiah answered,
"I saw all Israel scattered on
the hills like sheep without a
shepherd, and the LORD said,
'These people have no master.
Let each one go home in
peace.' "
[17]The king of Israel said to
Jehoshaphat, "Didn't I tell you
that he never prophesies anything good about me, but only
bad?"
[18]Micaiah continued,
"Therefore hear the word of
the LORD: I saw the LORD sitting on his throne with all the
host of heaven standing on
his right and on his left. [19]And
the LORD said, 'Who will lure
Ahab king of Israel into attacking Ramoth Gilead and
going to his death there?'
"One suggested this, and
another that. [20]Finally, a spirit
came forward, stood before
the LORD and said, 'I will lure
him.'
" 'By what means?' the LORD
asked.
[21]" 'I will go and be a lying

בְּפִי כָּל־ נְבִיאָיו וַיֹּאמֶר תְּפַתֶּה וְגַם־
and-also you-will-lure and-he-said prophets-of-him all-of in-mouth-of

תּוּכָל צֵא וַעֲשֵׂה־ כֵן׃ וְעַתָּה הִנֵּה נָתַן יְהוָה רוּחַ
spirit Yahweh he-put see! so-now (22) this and-do! go! you-will-succeed

שֶׁקֶר בְּפִי נְבִיאֶיךָ אֵלֶּה וַיהוָה דִּבֶּר עָלֶיךָ רָעָה׃
disaster for-you he-decreed and-Yahweh these prophets-of-you in-mouth-of lying

וַיִּגַּשׁ צִדְקִיָּהוּ בֶן־ כְּנַעֲנָה וַיַּךְ אֶת־מִיכָיְהוּ
Micaiah *** and-he-slapped Kenaanah son-of Zedekiah then-he-went-up (23)

עַל־ הַלֶּחִי וַיֹּאמֶר אֵי זֶה הַדֶּרֶךְ עָבַר רוּחַ־ יְהוָה
Yahweh spirit-of he-went the-way this where? and-he-asked the-cheek on

מֵאִתִּי לְדַבֵּר אֹתָךְ׃ וַיֹּאמֶר מִיכָיְהוּ הִנְּךָ רֹאֶה
finding-out see-you? Micaiah and-he-replied (24) to-you to-speak from-with-me

בַּיּוֹם הַהוּא אֲשֶׁר תָּבוֹא חֶדֶר בְּחֶדֶר לְהֵחָבֵא׃ וַיֹּאמֶר
then-he-ordered (25) to-hide in-room room you-go when the-that on-the-day

מֶלֶךְ יִשְׂרָאֵל קְחוּ אֶת־ מִיכָיְהוּ וַהֲשִׁיבֻהוּ אֶל־ אָמוֹן שַׂר־
ruler-of Amon to and-send-back-him! Micaiah *** take! Israel king-of

הָעִיר וְאֶל־ יוֹאָשׁ בֶּן־ הַמֶּלֶךְ׃ וַאֲמַרְתֶּם כֹּה אָמַר הַמֶּלֶךְ
the-king he-says this and-you-say (26) the-king son-of Joash and-to the-city

שִׂימוּ זֶה בֵּית הַכֶּלֶא וְהַאֲכִלֻהוּ לֶחֶם לַחַץ
scanty bread and-give-to-eat-him! the-prison house-of this-one put!

וּמַיִם לַחַץ עַד שׁוּבִי בְשָׁלוֹם׃ וַיֹּאמֶר מִיכָיְהוּ
Micaiah and-he-declared (27) in-safety to-return-me until scanty and-waters

אִם־ שׁוֹב תָּשׁוּב בְּשָׁלוֹם לֹא־ דִבֶּר יְהוָה בִּי וַיֹּאמֶר
then-he-said through-me Yahweh he-spoke not in-safety you-return to-return if

שִׁמְעוּ עַמִּים כֻּלָּם׃ וַיַּעַל מֶלֶךְ־ יִשְׂרָאֵל
Israel king-of so-he-went-up (28) all-of-them peoples mark-words!

וִיהוֹשָׁפָט מֶלֶךְ־ יְהוּדָה אֶל־ רָמֹת גִּלְעָד׃ וַיֹּאמֶר מֶלֶךְ
king-of and-he-said (29) Gilead Ramoth to Judah king-of and-Jehoshaphat

יִשְׂרָאֵל אֶל־ יְהוֹשָׁפָט הִתְחַפֵּשׂ וָבוֹא בַמִּלְחָמָה
into-the-battle and-to-enter to-disguise-himself Jehoshaphat to Israel

וְאַתָּה לְבַשׁ בְּגָדֶיךָ וַיִּתְחַפֵּשׂ מֶלֶךְ יִשְׂרָאֵל וַיָּבֹאוּ
and-he-went Israel king-of so-he-disguised-himself robes-of-you wear! but-you

בַּמִּלְחָמָה׃ וּמֶלֶךְ אֲרָם צִוָּה אֶת־ שָׂרֵי הָרֶכֶב
the-chariot commanders-of *** he-ordered Aram now-king-of (30) into-the-battle

אֲשֶׁר־ לוֹ לֵאמֹר לֹא תִּלָּחֲמוּ אֶת־ הַקָּטֹן אֶת־ הַגָּדוֹל כִּי אִם־
only except the-great *** the-small *** you-fight not to-say to-him that

אֶת־ מֶלֶךְ יִשְׂרָאֵל לְבַדּוֹ׃ וַיְהִי כִּרְאוֹת שָׂרֵי
commanders-of when-to-see and-he-was (31) by-himself Israel king-of ***

spirit in the mouths of all his prophets,' he said.

"'You will succeed in luring him,' said the LORD. 'Go and do it.'

[22]"So now the LORD has put a lying spirit in the mouths of these prophets of yours. The LORD has decreed disaster for you."

[23]Then Zedekiah son of Kenaanah went up and slapped Micaiah in the face. "Which way did the spirit from[f] the LORD go when he went from me to speak to you?" he asked.

[24]Micaiah replied, "You will find out on the day you go to hide in an inner room."

[25]The king of Israel then ordered, "Take Micaiah and send him back to Amon the ruler of the city and to Joash the king's son, [26]and say, 'This is what the king says: Put this fellow in prison and give him nothing but bread and water until I return safely.'"

[27]Micaiah declared, "If you ever return safely, the LORD has not spoken through me." Then he added, "Mark my words, all you people!"

### *Ahab Killed at Ramoth Gilead*

[28]So the king of Israel and Jehoshaphat king of Judah went up to Ramoth Gilead. [29]The king of Israel said to Jehoshaphat, "I will enter the battle in disguise, but you wear your royal robes." So the king of Israel disguised himself and went into battle.

[30]Now the king of Aram had ordered his chariot commanders, "Do not fight with anyone, small or great, except the king of Israel." [31]When the

f23 Or *Spirit of*

הָרֶכֶב אֶת־ יְהוֹשָׁפָט וְהֵמָּה אָמְרוּ מֶלֶךְ יִשְׂרָאֵל הוּא

this Israel king-of they-thought then-they Jehoshaphat *** the-chariot

וַיָּסֹבּוּ עָלָיו לְהִלָּחֵם וַיִּזְעַק יְהוֹשָׁפָט וַיהוָה

and-Yahweh Jehoshaphat but-he-cried-out to-attack against-him so-they-turned

עֲזָרוֹ וַיְסִיתֵם אֱלֹהִים מִמֶּנּוּ׃ וַיְהִי כִּרְאוֹת

when-to-see for-he-was (32) from-him God and-he-drew-away-them he-helped-him

שָׂרֵי הָרֶכֶב כִּי לֹא־ הָיָה מֶלֶךְ יִשְׂרָאֵל וַיָּשֻׁבוּ

then-they-turned Israel king-of he-was not that the-chariot commanders-of

מֵאַחֲרָיו׃ וְאִישׁ מָשַׁךְ בַּקֶּשֶׁת לְתֻמּוֹ וַיַּךְ

and-he-hit at-random-of-him on-the-bow he-drew but-someone (33) from-after-him

אֶת־ מֶלֶךְ יִשְׂרָאֵל בֵּין הַדְּבָקִים וּבֵין הַשִּׁרְיָן וַיֹּאמֶר

and-he-told the-armor and-between the-sections between Israel king-of ***

לָרַכָּב הֲפֹךְ יָדֶיךָ וְהוֹצֵאתַנִי מִן־ הַמַּחֲנֶה

the-fight from and-get-out-me! hand-of-you turn-around! to-the-chariot-driver

כִּי הָחֳלֵיתִי׃ וַתַּעַל הַמִּלְחָמָה בַּיּוֹם הַהוּא

the-that through-the-day the-battle and-she-raged (34) I-am-wounded for

וּמֶלֶךְ יִשְׂרָאֵל הָיָה מַעֲמִיד בַּמֶּרְכָּבָה נֹכַח אֲרָם עַד־

until Aram facing in-the-chariot being-propped-up he-was Israel and-king-of

הָעָרֶב וַיָּמָת לְעֵת בּוֹא הַשָּׁמֶשׁ׃ וַיָּשָׁב

when-he-returned (19:1) the-sun to-set at-time-of then-he-died the-evening

יְהוֹשָׁפָט מֶלֶךְ־ יְהוּדָה אֶל־ בֵּיתוֹ בְשָׁלוֹם לִירוּשָׁלִָם׃

in-Jerusalem in-safety palace-of-him to Judah king-of Jehoshaphat

וַיֵּצֵא אֶל־ פָּנָיו יֵהוּא בֶן־ חֲנָנִי הַחֹזֶה וַיֹּאמֶר

and-he-said the-seer Hanani son-of Jehu faces-of-him to then-he-went-out (2)

אֶל־ הַמֶּלֶךְ יְהוֹשָׁפָט הֲלָרָשָׁע לַעְזֹר וּלְשֹׂנְאֵי יְהוָה

Yahweh and-to-ones-hating-of to-help to-the-wicked? Jehoshaphat the-king to

תֶּאֱהָב וּבָזֹאת עָלֶיךָ קֶּצֶף מִלִּפְנֵי יְהוָה׃ אֲבָל

however (3) Yahweh from-before wrath upon-you and-because-of-this you-love

דְּבָרִים טוֹבִים נִמְצְאוּ עִמָּךְ כִּי־ בִעַרְתָּ הָאֲשֵׁרוֹת

the-Asherah-poles you-got-rid for in-you they-are-found good-ones things

מִן־ הָאָרֶץ וַהֲכִינוֹתָ לְבָבְךָ לִדְרֹשׁ הָאֱלֹהִים׃ וַיֵּשֶׁב

and-he-lived (4) the-God to-seek heart-of-you and-you-set the-land from

יְהוֹשָׁפָט בִּירוּשָׁלִָם וַיָּשָׁב וַיֵּצֵא בָעָם

among-the-people and-he-went-out and-he-returned in-Jerusalem Jehoshaphat

מִבְּאֵר שֶׁבַע עַד־ הַר אֶפְרַיִם וַיְשִׁיבֵם אֶל־ יְהוָה

Yahweh to and-he-turned-back-them Ephraim hill-country-of to Sheba from-Beer

אֱלֹהֵי אֲבוֹתֵיהֶם׃ וַיַּעֲמֵד שֹׁפְטִים בָּאָרֶץ

in-the-land ones-judging and-he-appointed (5) fathers-of-them God-of

chariot commanders saw Jehoshaphat, they thought, "This is the king of Israel." So they turned to attack him, but Jehoshaphat cried out, and the LORD helped him. God drew them away from him, [32]for when the chariot commanders saw that he was not the king of Israel, they stopped pursuing him.

[33]But someone drew his bow at random and hit the king of Israel between the sections of his armor. The king told the chariot driver, "Wheel around and get me out of the fighting. I've been wounded." [34]All day long the battle raged, and the king of Israel propped himself up in his chariot facing the Arameans until evening. Then at sunset he died.

**19** When Jehoshaphat king of Judah returned safely to his palace in Jerusalem, [2]Jehu the seer, the son of Hanani, went out to meet him and said to the king, "Should you help the wicked and love[g] those who hate the LORD? Because of this, the wrath of the LORD is upon you. [3]There is, however, some good in you, for you have rid the land of the Asherah poles and have set your heart on seeking God."

### *Jehoshaphat Appoints Judges*

[4]Jehoshaphat lived in Jerusalem, and he went out again among the people from Beersheba to the hill country of Ephraim and turned them back to the LORD, the God of their fathers. [5]He appointed judges in the land, in each of

[g]2 Or *and make alliances with*

°33 ידך ק

בְּכָל־ עָרֵי יְהוּדָה הַבְּצֻרוֹת לְעִיר וָעִיר׃
and-city in-city the-ones-being-fortified Judah cities-of in-each-of

וַיֹּאמֶר אֶל־ הַשֹּׁפְטִים רְאוּ מָה־ אַתֶּם עֹשִׂים כִּי
because ones-doing you what consider! the-ones-judging to and-he-told (6)

לֹא לְאָדָם תִּשְׁפְּטוּ כִּי לַיהוָה וְעִמָּכֶם בִּדְבַר מִשְׁפָּט׃
verdict in-word-of and-with-you for-Yahweh but you-judge for-man not

וְעַתָּה יְהִי־ פַחַד־ יְהוָה עֲלֵיכֶם שִׁמְרוּ וַעֲשׂוּ כִּי־ אֵין
there-is-no for and-do! judge! upon-you Yahweh fear-of let-him-be and-now (7)

עִם־ יְהוָה אֱלֹהֵינוּ עַוְלָה וּמַשֹּׂא פָנִים וּמִקַּח־ שֹׁחַד׃
bribe or-taking-of faces or-lifting-of injustice God-of-us Yahweh with

וְגַם בִּירוּשָׁלַםִ הֶעֱמִיד יְהוֹשָׁפָט מִן־ הַלְוִיִּם
the-Levites from Jehoshaphat he-appointed in-Jerusalem and-also (8)

וְהַכֹּהֲנִים וּמֵרָאשֵׁי הָאָבוֹת לְיִשְׂרָאֵל לְמִשְׁפַּט יְהוָה
Yahweh for-law-of of-Israel the-fathers and-from-heads-of and-the-priests

וְלָרִיב וַיָּשֻׁבוּ יְרוּשָׁלָםִ׃ וַיְצַו עֲלֵיהֶם לֵאמֹר
to-say to-them and-he-ordered (9) Jerusalem and-they-lived and-for-dispute

כֹּה תַעֲשׂוּן בְּיִרְאַת יְהוָה בֶּאֱמוּנָה וּבְלֵבָב שָׁלֵם׃
whole and-with-heart in-faith Yahweh in-fear-of you-must-serve thus

וְכָל־ רִיב אֲשֶׁר־ יָבוֹא עֲלֵיכֶם מֵאֲחֵיכֶם ׀
from-fellows-of-you before-you he-comes that case and-every-of (10)

הַיֹּשְׁבִים בְּעָרֵיהֶם בֵּין־ דָּם ׀ לְדָם בֵּין־ תּוֹרָה
law between to-blood blood between in-cities-of-them the-ones-living

לְמִצְוָה לְחֻקִּים וּלְמִשְׁפָּטִים וְהִזְהַרְתֶּם אֹתָם וְלֹא
so-not them and-you-must-warn or-to-ordinances to-decrees to-command

יֶאְשְׁמוּ לַיהוָה וְהָיָה־ קֶצֶף עֲלֵיכֶם וְעַל־ אֲחֵיכֶם כֹּה
this brothers-of-you and-on on-you wrath or-he-will-come against-Yahweh they-sin

תַעֲשׂוּן וְלֹא תֶאְשָׁמוּ׃ וְהִנֵּה אֲמַרְיָהוּ כֹהֵן הָרֹאשׁ עֲלֵיכֶם
over-you the-chief priest Amariah and-see! (11) you-will-sin and-not you-do

לְכֹל דְּבַר־ יְהוָה וּזְבַדְיָהוּ בֶן־ יִשְׁמָעֵאל הַנָּגִיד לְבֵית־
of-tribe-of the-leader Ishmael son-of and-Zebadiah Yahweh matter-of in-any-of

יְהוּדָה לְכֹל דְּבַר־ הַמֶּלֶךְ וְשֹׁטְרִים הַלְוִיִּם לִפְנֵיכֶם
before-you the-Levites and-officials the-king matter-of in-any-of Judah

חִזְקוּ וַעֲשׂוּ וִיהִי יְהוָה עִם־ הַטּוֹב׃ וַיְהִי
and-he-was (20:1) the-good with Yahweh and-may-he-be and-act! be-courageous!

אַחֲרֵיכֵן בָּאוּ בְנֵי־ מוֹאָב וּבְנֵי עַמּוֹן וְעִמָּהֶם ׀
and-with-them Ammon and-sons-of Moab sons-of they-came after-this

מֵהָעַמּוֹנִים עַל־ יְהוֹשָׁפָט לַמִּלְחָמָה׃ וַיָּבֹאוּ
and-they-came (2) to-the-war Jehoshaphat against from-the-Ammonites

the fortified cities of Judah.
6He told them, "Consider carefully what you do, because you
are not judging for man but
for the LORD, who is with you
whenever you give a verdict.
7Now let the fear of the LORD
be upon you. Judge carefully,
for with the LORD our God
there is no injustice or partiality or bribery."
8In Jerusalem also, Jehoshaphat appointed some of the
Levites, priests and heads of
Israelite families to administer
the law of the LORD and to settle disputes. And they lived in
Jerusalem. 9He gave them
these orders: "You must serve
faithfully and wholeheartedly
in the fear of the LORD. 10In
every case that comes before
you from your fellow countrymen who live in the cities—
whether bloodshed or other
concerns of the law, com-
mands, decrees or ordi-
nances—you are to warn them
not to sin against the LORD;
otherwise his wrath will come
on you and your brothers. Do
this, and you will not sin.
11"Amariah the chief priest
will be over you in any matter
concerning the LORD, and
Zebadiah son of Ishmael, the
leader of the tribe of Judah,
will be over you in any matter
concerning the king, and the
Levites will serve as officials
before you. Act with courage,
and may the LORD be with
those who do well."

*Jehoshaphat Defeats Moab and Ammon*

20 After this, the Moab-
ites and Ammonites
with some of the Meunites[h]
came to make war on Jehoshaphat.

h1 Some Septuagint manuscripts; Hebrew *Ammonites*

וַיַּגִּידוּ לִיהוֹשָׁפָט לֵאמֹר בָּא עָלֶיךָ הָמוֹן רָב
vast army against-you he-comes to-say to-Jehoshaphat and-they-told

מֵעֵבֶר לַיָּם מֵאֲרָם וְהִנָּם בְּחַצְצוֹן תָּמָר הִיא
that Tamar in-Hazazon and-see-they! from-Aram of-the-Sea from-other-side

עֵין גֶּדִי׃ (3) וַיִּרָא וַיִּתֵּן יְהוֹשָׁפָט אֶת־ פָּנָיו
faces-of-him *** Jehoshaphat and-he-set and-he-was-alarmed (3) Gedi En

לִדְרוֹשׁ לַיהוָה וַיִּקְרָא־ צוֹם עַל־ כָּל־ יְהוּדָה׃
Judah all-of for fast and-he-proclaimed of-Yahweh to-inquire

(4) וַיִּקָּבְצוּ יְהוּדָה לְבַקֵּשׁ מֵיְהוָה גַּם מִכָּל־
from-all-of indeed from-Yahweh to-seek-help Judah and-they-came-together (4)

עָרֵי יְהוּדָה בָּאוּ לְבַקֵּשׁ אֶת־ יְהוָה׃ (5) וַיַּעֲמֹד יְהוֹשָׁפָט
Jehoshaphat then-he-stood-up (5) Yahweh *** to-seek they-came Judah towns-of

בִּקְהַל יְהוּדָה וִירוּשָׁלִַם בְּבֵית יְהוָה לִפְנֵי
in-front-of Yahweh at-temple-of and-Jerusalem Judah in-assembly-of

הֶחָצֵר הַחֲדָשָׁה׃ (6) וַיֹּאמַר יְהוָה אֱלֹהֵי אֲבֹתֵינוּ הֲלֹא אַתָּה־
you not? fathers-of-us God-of Yahweh and-he-said (6) the-new the-courtyard

הוּא אֱלֹהִים בַּשָּׁמַיִם וְאַתָּה מוֹשֵׁל בְּכֹל מַמְלְכוֹת הַגּוֹיִם
the-nations kingdoms-of over-all-of ruling and-you in-the-heavens God he

וּבְיָדְךָ כֹּחַ וּגְבוּרָה וְאֵין עִמְּךָ לְהִתְיַצֵּב׃
to-withstand against-you and-no-one and-might power and-in-hand-of-you

(7) הֲלֹא ׀ אַתָּה אֱלֹהֵינוּ הוֹרַשְׁתָּ אֶת־ יֹשְׁבֵי הָאָרֶץ הַזֹּאת
the-this the-land ones-inhabiting-of *** you-drove-out God-of-us you not? (7)

מִלִּפְנֵי עַמְּךָ יִשְׂרָאֵל וַתִּתְּנָהּ לְזֶרַע אַבְרָהָם
Abraham to-descendant-of and-you-gave-her Israel people-of-you from-before

אֹהַבְךָ לְעוֹלָם׃ (8) וַיֵּשְׁבוּ־ בָהּ וַיִּבְנוּ לְךָ ׀
for-you and-they-built in-her and-they-lived (8) to-forever friend-of-you

בָּהּ מִקְדָּשׁ לְשִׁמְךָ לֵאמֹר׃ (9) אִם־ תָּבוֹא עָלֵינוּ רָעָה
calamity upon-us she-comes if (9) to-say for-Name-of-you sanctuary in-her

חֶרֶב שְׁפוֹט וְדֶבֶר וְרָעָב נַעַמְדָה לִפְנֵי הַבַּיִת
the-temple before we-will-stand or-famine or-plague judgment sword-of

הַזֶּה וּלְפָנֶיךָ כִּי שִׁמְךָ בַּבַּיִת הַזֶּה
the-this in-the-temple Name-of-you that and-in-presences-of-you the-this

וְנִזְעַק אֵלֶיךָ מִצָּרָתֵנוּ וְתִשְׁמַע וְתוֹשִׁיעַ׃
and-you-will-save and-you-will-hear in-distress-of-us to-you and-we-will-cry-out

(10) וְעַתָּה הִנֵּה בְנֵי־ עַמּוֹן וּמוֹאָב וְהַר־ שֵׂעִיר אֲשֶׁר לֹא־
not who Seir and-Mount-of and-Moab Ammon men-of see! but-now (10)

נָתַתָּה לְיִשְׂרָאֵל לָבוֹא בָהֶם בְּבֹאָם מֵאֶרֶץ
from-land-of when-to-come-them into-them to-invade to-Israel you-would-allow

2 Some men came and told Jehoshaphat, "A vast army is coming against you from Edom,[i] from the other side of the Sea.[j] It is already in Hazazon Tamar" (that is, En Gedi).
3 Alarmed, Jehoshaphat resolved to inquire of the LORD, and he proclaimed a fast for all Judah.
4 The people of Judah came together to seek help from the LORD; indeed, they came from every town in Judah to seek him.
5 Then Jehoshaphat stood up in the assembly of Judah and Jerusalem at the temple of the LORD in the front of the new courtyard
6 and said:

"O LORD, God of our fathers, are you not the God who is in heaven? You rule over all the kingdoms of the nations. Power and might are in your hand, and no one can withstand you.
7 O our God, did you not drive out the inhabitants of this land before your people Israel and give it forever to the descendants of Abraham your friend?
8 They have lived in it and have built in it a sanctuary for your Name, saying,
9 'If calamity comes upon us, whether the sword of judgment, or plague or famine, we will stand in your presence before this temple that bears your Name and will cry out to you in our distress, and you will hear us and save us.'

10 "But now here are men from Ammon, Moab and Mount Seir, whose territory you would not allow Israel to invade when they

[i] 2 One Hebrew manuscript; most Hebrew manuscripts, Septuagint and Vulgate *Aram*
[j] 2 That is, the Dead Sea

מִצְרָיִם כִּי סָרוּ מֵעֲלֵיהֶם וְלֹא הִשְׁמִידוּם׃
they-destroyed-them and-not from-against-them they-turned so Egypt

(11) וְהִנֵּה־ הֵם גֹּמְלִים עָלֵינוּ לָבוֹא לְגָרְשֵׁנוּ
to-drive-out-us to-come to-us ones-repaying they now-see! (11)

מִיְּרֻשָּׁתְךָ אֲשֶׁר הוֹרַשְׁתָּנוּ׃ (12) אֱלֹהֵינוּ הֲלֹא תִשְׁפָּט־
will-you-judge not? God-of-us (12) you-gave-us that from-possession-of-you

בָּם כִּי אֵין בָּנוּ כֹּחַ לִפְנֵי הֶהָמוֹן הָרָב הַזֶּה
the-this the-vast the-army before power to-us not for against-them

הַבָּא עָלֵינוּ וַאֲנַחְנוּ לֹא נֵדַע מַה־ נַּעֲשֶׂה כִּי
but we-should-do what we-know not and-we against-us the-one-attacking

עָלֶיךָ עֵינֵינוּ׃ (13) וְכָל־ יְהוּדָה עֹמְדִים לִפְנֵי יְהוָה גַּם־
also Yahweh before ones-standing Judah and-all-of (13) eyes-of-us upon-you

טַפָּם נְשֵׁיהֶם וּבְנֵיהֶם׃ (14) וְיַחֲזִיאֵל בֶּן־
son-of then-Jahaziel (14) and-little-ones-of-them wives-of-them child-of-them

זְכַרְיָהוּ בֶּן־ בְּנָיָה בֶּן־ יְעִיאֵל בֶּן־ מַתַּנְיָה הַלֵּוִי מִן־
from the-Levite Mattaniah son-of Jeiel son-of Benaiah son-of Zechariah

בְּנֵי אָסָף הָיְתָה עָלָיו רוּחַ יְהוָה בְּתוֹךְ הַקָּהָל׃
the-assembly in-midst-of Yahweh Spirit-of upon-him she-came Asaph sons-of

(15) וַיֹּאמֶר הַקְשִׁיבוּ כָל־ יְהוּדָה וְיֹשְׁבֵי יְרוּשָׁלִַם
Jerusalem and-ones-living-of Judah all-of listen! and-he-said (15)

וְהַמֶּלֶךְ יְהוֹשָׁפָט כֹּה־ אָמַר יְהוָה לָכֶם אַתֶּם אַל־ תִּירְאוּ
you-be-afraid not you to-you Yahweh he-says this Jehoshaphat and-the-king

וְאַל־ תֵּחַתּוּ מִפְּנֵי הֶהָמוֹן הָרָב הַזֶּה כִּי לֹא
not for the-this the-vast the-army because-of you-be-discouraged and-not

לָכֶם הַמִּלְחָמָה כִּי לֵאלֹהִים׃ (16) מָחָר רְדוּ עֲלֵיהֶם
against-them march-down! tomorrow (16) to-God but the-battle to-you

הִנָּם עֹלִים בְּמַעֲלֵה הַצִּיץ וּמְצָאתֶם אֹתָם
them and-you-will-find the-Ziz by-Pass-of ones-climbing-up see-they!

בְּסוֹף הַנַּחַל פְּנֵי מִדְבַּר יְרוּאֵל׃ (17) לֹא לָכֶם לְהִלָּחֵם בָּזֹאת
in-this to-fight to-you not (17) Jeruel Desert-of facing the-gorge at-end-of

הִתְיַצְּבוּ עִמְדוּ וּרְאוּ אֶת־ יְשׁוּעַת יְהוָה עִמָּכֶם יְהוּדָה
Judah with-you Yahweh deliverance-of *** and-see! stand-firm! take-positions!

וִירוּשָׁלִַם אַל־ תִּירְאוּ וְאַל־ תֵּחַתּוּ מָחָר צְאוּ
go-out! tomorrow you-be-discouraged and-not you-be-afraid not and-Jerusalem

לִפְנֵיהֶם וַיהוָה עִמָּכֶם׃ (18) וַיִּקֹּד יְהוֹשָׁפָט אַפַּיִם
faces Jehoshaphat and-he-bowed (18) with-you and-Yahweh to-faces-of-them

אַרְצָה וְכָל־ יְהוּדָה וְיֹשְׁבֵי יְרוּשָׁלִַם נָפְלוּ
they-fell-down Jerusalem and-ones-living-of Judah and-all-of to-ground

came from Egypt; so they
turned away from them
and did not destroy them.
11See how they are repaying
us by coming to drive us
out of the possession you
gave us as an inheritance.
12O our God, will you not
judge them? For we have
no power to face this vast
army that is attacking us.
We do not know what to
do, but our eyes are upon
you."

13All the men of Judah, with
their wives and children and
little ones, stood there before
the LORD.
14Then the Spirit of the LORD
came upon Jahaziel son of
Zechariah, the son of Benaiah,
the son of Jeiel, the son of Mattaniah, a Levite and descendant of Asaph, as he stood in
the assembly.
15He said: "Listen, King Jehoshaphat and all who live in
Judah and Jerusalem! This is
what the LORD says to you: 'Do
not be afraid or discouraged
because of this vast army. For
the battle is not yours, but
God's.
16Tomorrow march
down against them. They will
be climbing up by the Pass of
Ziz, and you will find them at
the end of the gorge in the
Desert of Jeruel.
17You will not
have to fight this battle. Take
up your positions; stand firm
and see the deliverance the
LORD will give you, O Judah
and Jerusalem. Do not be
afraid; do not be discouraged.
Go out to face them tomorrow,
and the LORD will be with
you.'"
18Jehoshaphat bowed with
his face to the ground, and all
the people of Judah and

לִפְנֵי יְהוָה לְהִשְׁתַּחֲוֺת לַיהוָה׃ (19) וַיָּקֻמוּ הַלְוִיִּם מִן־
from the-Levites then-they-stood-up (19) to-Yahweh to-worship Yahweh before

בְּנֵי הַקְּהָתִים וּמִן־ בְּנֵי הַקָּרְחִים לְהַלֵּל לַיהוָה אֱלֹהֵי
God-of to-Yahweh to-praise the-Korahites sons-of and-from the-Kohathites sons-of

יִשְׂרָאֵל בְּקוֹל גָּדוֹל לְמָעְלָה׃ (20) וַיַּשְׁכִּימוּ בַבֹּקֶר וַיֵּצְאוּ
and-they-left in-the-morning and-they-rose (20) to-upward loud with-voice Israel

לְמִדְבַּר תְּקוֹעַ וּבְצֵאתָם עָמַד יְהוֹשָׁפָט וַיֹּאמֶר
and-he-said Jehoshaphat he-stood and-as-to-set-out-them Tekoa for-Desert-of

שְׁמָעוּנִי יְהוּדָה וְיֹשְׁבֵי יְרוּשָׁלִַם הַאֲמִינוּ בַּיהוָה
in-Yahweh have-faith! Jerusalem and-ones-living-of Judah listen-to-me!

אֱלֹהֵיכֶם וְתֵאָמֵנוּ הַאֲמִינוּ בִנְבִיאָיו וְהַצְלִיחוּ׃
and-succeed! in-prophets-of-him have-faith! and-you-will-be-upheld God-of-you

(21) וַיִּוָּעַץ אֶל־ הָעָם וַיַּעֲמֵד מְשֹׁרְרִים
ones-singing then-he-appointed the-people with after-he-consulted (21)

לַיהוָה וּמְהַלְלִים לְהַדְרַת־ קֹדֶשׁ בְּצֵאת לִפְנֵי
before as-to-go-out holiness to-splendor-of and-ones-praising to-Yahweh

הֶחָלוּץ וְאֹמְרִים הוֹדוּ לַיהוָה כִּי לְעוֹלָם
to-forever for to-Yahweh give-thanks! and-ones-saying the-one-being-in-army

חַסְדּוֹ׃ (22) וּבְעֵת הֵחֵלּוּ בְרִנָּה וּתְהִלָּה נָתַן יְהוָה
Yahweh he-set and-praise with-song they-began and-at-time-of (22) love-of-him

מְאָרְבִים עַל־ בְּנֵי עַמּוֹן מוֹאָב וְהַר־ שֵׂעִיר
Seir and-Mount-of Moab Ammon men-of against ones-being-ambushes

הַבָּאִים לִיהוּדָה וַיִּנָּגֵפוּ׃ (23) וַיַּעַמְדוּ
and-they-rose-up (23) and-they-were-defeated into-Judah the-ones-invading

בְּנֵי עַמּוֹן וּמוֹאָב עַל־ יֹשְׁבֵי הַר־ שֵׂעִיר לְהַחֲרִים
to-destroy Seir Mount-of ones-living-of against and-Moab Ammon men-of

וּלְהַשְׁמִיד וּכְכַלּוֹתָם בְּיוֹשְׁבֵי שֵׂעִיר
Seir with-ones-living-of and-after-to-finish-them and-to-annihilate

עָזְרוּ אִישׁ־ בְּרֵעֵהוּ לְמַשְׁחִית׃ (24) וִיהוּדָה בָּא עַל־
to he-came when-Judah (24) to-destroy to-other-of-him each they-helped

הַמִּצְפֶּה לַמִּדְבָּר וַיִּפְנוּ אֶל־ הֶהָמוֹן
the-vast-army toward and-they-looked in-the-desert the-watchtower

וְהִנָּם פְּגָרִים נֹפְלִים אַרְצָה וְאֵין פְּלֵיטָה׃
escapee and-no-one on-ground ones-lying dead-bodies then-see-they!

(25) וַיָּבֹא יְהוֹשָׁפָט וְעַמּוֹ לָבֹז אֶת־ שְׁלָלָם
plunder-of-them *** to-carry-off and-people-of-him Jehoshaphat so-he-went (25)

וַיִּמְצְאוּ בָהֶם לָרֹב וּרְכוּשׁ וּפְגָרִים
and-corpses both-equipment in-quantity among-them and-they-found

Jerusalem fell down in worship before the LORD. 19Then
some Levites from the Kohathites and Korahites stood
up and praised the LORD, the God of Israel, with very loud
voice.

20Early in the morning they left for the Desert of Tekoa. As
they set out, Jehoshaphat stood and said, "Listen to me,
Judah and people of Jerusalem! Have faith in the LORD your
God and you will be upheld; have faith in his prophets and
you will be successful." 21After
consulting the people, Jehoshaphat appointed men to sing
to the LORD and to praise him for the splendor of his[k] holiness as they went out at the
head of the army, saying:

"Give thanks to the LORD,
for his love endures
forever."

22As they began to sing and praise, the LORD set ambushes
against the men of Ammon and Moab and Mount Seir
who were invading Judah, and they were defeated. 23The
men of Ammon and Moab rose up against the men from
Mount Seir to destroy and annihilate them. After they
finished slaughtering the men from Seir, they helped to destroy one another.

24When the men of Judah came to the place that overlooks the desert and looked
toward the vast army, they saw only dead bodies lying on
the ground; no one had escaped. 25So Jehoshaphat and
his men went to carry off their plunder, and they found
among them a great amount of equipment and clothing[l] and

[k]21 *Or him with the splendor of*
[l]25 Some Hebrew manuscripts and Vulgate; most Hebrew manuscripts *corpses*

וּכְלֵי חֲמֻדוֹת וַיְנַצְּלוּ לָהֶם לְאֵין מַשָּׂא

taking-away to-not for-them and-they-stripped values and-articles-of

וַיִּהְיוּ יָמִים שְׁלוֹשָׁה בֹּזְזִים אֶת־ הַשָּׁלָל כִּי רַב־הוּא׃

he much for the-plunder *** ones-collecting three days and-they-were

וּבַיּוֹם הָרְבִעִי נִקְהֲלוּ לְעֵמֶק בְּרָכָה כִּי־

for Beracah in-Valley-of they-assembled the-fourth and-on-the-day (26)

שָׁם בֵּרְכוּ אֶת־ יְהוָה עַל־ כֵּן קָרְאוּ אֶת־ שֵׁם הַמָּקוֹם

the-place name-of *** they-call this for Yahweh *** they-praised there

הַהוּא עֵמֶק בְּרָכָה עַד־ הַיּוֹם׃ וַיָּשֻׁבוּ כָּל־ אִישׁ

man-of all-of then-they-returned (27) the-day to Beracah Valley-of the-that

יְהוּדָה וִירוּשָׁלִַם וִיהוֹשָׁפָט בְּרֹאשָׁם לָשׁוּב אֶל־ יְרוּשָׁלִַם

Jerusalem to to-return at-head-of-them and-Jehoshaphat and-Jerusalem Judah

בְּשִׂמְחָה כִּי־ שִׂמְּחָם יְהוָה מֵאוֹיְבֵיהֶם׃

over-ones-being-enemies-of-them Yahweh he-made-rejoice-them for with-joy

וַיָּבֹאוּ יְרוּשָׁלִַם בִּנְבָלִים וּבְכִנֹּרוֹת וּבַחֲצֹצְרוֹת

and-with-trumpets and-with-lutes with-harps Jerusalem and-they-entered (28)

אֶל־ בֵּית יְהוָה׃ וַיְהִי פַּחַד אֱלֹהִים עַל כָּל־ מַמְלְכוֹת

kingdoms-of all-of upon God fear-of and-he-came (29) Yahweh temple-of to

הָאֲרָצוֹת בְּשָׁמְעָם כִּי נִלְחַם יְהוָה עִם

against Yahweh he-fought how when-to-hear-them the-countries

אוֹיְבֵי יִשְׂרָאֵל׃ וַתִּשְׁקֹט מַלְכוּת יְהוֹשָׁפָט

Jehoshaphat kingdom-of and-she-was-at-peace (30) Israel ones-being-enemies-of

וַיָּנַח לוֹ אֱלֹהָיו מִסָּבִיב׃ וַיִּמְלֹךְ יְהוֹשָׁפָט עַל־יְהוּדָה

Judah over Jehoshaphat so-he-reigned (31) at-around God-of-him to-him for-he-gave-rest

בֶּן־ שְׁלֹשִׁים וְחָמֵשׁ שָׁנָה בְּמָלְכוֹ וְעֶשְׂרִים וְחָמֵשׁ

and-five and-twenty when-to-become-king-him year and-five thirty son-of

שָׁנָה מָלַךְ בִּירוּשָׁלִַם וְשֵׁם אִמּוֹ עֲזוּבָה בַּת־

daughter-of Azubah mother-of-him and-name-of in-Jerusalem he-reigned year

שִׁלְחִי׃ וַיֵּלֶךְ בְּדֶרֶךְ אָבִיו אָסָא וְלֹא־ סָר

he-strayed and-not Asa father-of-him in-way-of and-he-walked (32) Shilhi

מִמֶּנָּה לַעֲשׂוֹת הַיָּשָׁר בְּעֵינֵי יְהוָה׃ אַךְ הַבָּמוֹת לֹא־

not the-high-places however (33) Yahweh in-eyes-of the-right to-do from-her

סָרוּ וְעוֹד הָעָם לֹא־ הֵכִינוּ לְבָבָם לֵאלֹהֵי

to-God-of heart-of-them they-set not the-people and-still they-removed

אֲבֹתֵיהֶם׃ וְיֶתֶר דִּבְרֵי יְהוֹשָׁפָט הָרִאשֹׁנִים

the-beginnings Jehoshaphat events-of and-other-of (34) fathers-of-them

וְהָאַחֲרֹנִים הִנָּם כְּתוּבִים בְּדִבְרֵי יֵהוּא בֶן־ חֲנָנִי

Hanani son-of Jehu in-annals-of ones-being-written see-they! and-the-ends

also articles of value—more than they could take away. There was so much plunder that it took three days to collect it. [26]On the fourth day they assembled in the Valley of Beracah, where they praised the LORD. This is why it is called the Valley of Beracah[m] to this day.

[27]Then, led by Jehoshaphat, all the men of Judah and Jerusalem returned joyfully to Jerusalem, for the LORD had given them cause to rejoice over their enemies. [28]They entered Jerusalem and went to the temple of the LORD with harps and lutes and trumpets.

[29]The fear of God came upon all the kingdoms of the countries when they heard how the LORD had fought against the enemies of Israel. [30]And the kingdom of Jehoshaphat was at peace, for his God had given him rest on every side.

*The End of Jehoshaphat's Reign*

[31]So Jehoshaphat reigned over Judah. He was thirty-five years old when he became king of Judah, and he reigned in Jerusalem twenty-five years. His mother's name was Azubah daughter of Shilhi. [32]He walked in the ways of his father Asa and did not stray from them; he did what was right in the eyes of the LORD. [33]The high places, however, were not removed, and the people still had not set their hearts on the God of their fathers.

[34]The other events of Jehoshaphat's reign, from beginning to end, are written in the annals of Jehu son of Hanani,

[m]26 *Beracah* means *praise.*

אֲשֶׁר הֹעֲלָה עַל־ סֵפֶר מַלְכֵי יִשְׂרָאֵל׃ וְאַחֲרֵי־כֵן

and-after-this (35) Israel kings-of book-of in he-is-recorded which

אֶתְחַבַּר יְהוֹשָׁפָט מֶלֶךְ־ יְהוּדָה עִם אֲחַזְיָה מֶלֶךְ־יִשְׂרָאֵל הוּא

he Israel king-of Ahaziah with Judah king-of Jehoshaphat he-made-alliance

הִרְשִׁיעַ לַעֲשׂוֹת׃ וַיְחַבְּרֵהוּ עִמּוֹ לַעֲשׂוֹת

to-construct with-him and-he-agreed-with-him (36) to-practice he-was-wicked

אֳנִיּוֹת לָלֶכֶת תַּרְשִׁישׁ וַיַּעֲשׂוּ אֳנִיּוֹת בְּעֶצְיוֹן גָּבֶר׃ וַיִּתְנַבֵּא

and-he-prophesied (37) Geber at-Ezion ships and-they-built Tarshish to-go ships

אֱלִיעֶזֶר בֶּן־ דֹּדָוָהוּ מִמָּרֵשָׁה עַל־ יְהוֹשָׁפָט לֵאמֹר

to-say Jehoshaphat against from-Mareshah Dodavahu son-of Eliezer

כְּהִתְחַבֶּרְךָ עִם־ אֲחַזְיָהוּ פָּרַץ יְהוָה אֶת־

*** Yahweh he-will-destroy Ahaziah with because-to-make-alliance-you

מַעֲשֶׂיךָ וַיִּשָּׁבְרוּ אֳנִיּוֹת וְלֹא עָצְרוּ לָלֶכֶת

to-sail they-were-able and-not ships and-they-were-wrecked works-of-you

אֶל־ תַּרְשִׁישׁ׃ וַיִּשְׁכַּב יְהוֹשָׁפָט עִם־ אֲבֹתָיו

fathers-of-him with Jehoshaphat then-he-rested (21:1) Tarshish to

וַיִּקָּבֵר עִם־ אֲבֹתָיו בְּעִיר דָּוִיד וַיִּמְלֹךְ

and-he-became-king David in-City-of fathers-of-him with and-he-was-buried

יְהוֹרָם בְּנוֹ תַּחְתָּיו׃ וְלוֹ־ אַחִים בְּנֵי

sons-of brothers and-to-him (2) in-place-of-him son-of-him Jehoram

יְהוֹשָׁפָט עֲזַרְיָה וִיחִיאֵל וּזְכַרְיָהוּ וַעֲזַרְיָהוּ וּמִיכָאֵל

and-Michael and-Azariahu and-Zechariah and-Jehiel Azariah Jehoshaphat

וּשְׁפַטְיָהוּ כָּל־ אֵלֶּה בְּנֵי יְהוֹשָׁפָט מֶלֶךְ־ יִשְׂרָאֵל׃ וַיִּתֵּן

and-he-gave (3) Israel king-of Jehoshaphat sons-of these all-of and-Shephatiah

לָהֶם אֲבִיהֶם מַתָּנוֹת רַבּוֹת לְכֶסֶף וּלְזָהָב

and-of-gold of-silver many-ones gifts father-of-them to-them

וּלְמִגְדָּנוֹת עִם־ עָרֵי מְצֻרוֹת בִּיהוּדָה וְאֶת־

but in-Judah fortifications cities-of as-well-as and-of-articles-of-value

הַמַּמְלָכָה נָתַן לִיהוֹרָם כִּי־ הוּא הַבְּכוֹר׃

the-firstborn he because to-Jehoram he-gave the-kingdom

וַיָּקָם יְהוֹרָם עַל־ מַמְלֶכֶת* אָבִיו

father-of-him kingdom-of over Jehoram when-he-was-established (4)

וַיִּתְחַזַּק וַיַּהֲרֹג אֶת־ כָּל־ אֶחָיו בֶּחָרֶב

with-the-sword brothers-of-him all-of *** then-he-killed and-he-was-firm

וְגַם מִשָּׂרֵי יִשְׂרָאֵל׃ בֶּן־ שְׁלֹשִׁים וּשְׁתַּיִם שָׁנָה יְהוֹרָם

Jehoram year and-two thirty son-of (5) Israel from-princes-of and-also

בְּמָלְכוֹ וּשְׁמוֹנֶה שָׁנִים מָלַךְ בִּירוּשָׁלָםִ׃

in-Jerusalem he-reigned years and-eight when-to-become-king-him

which are recorded in the book of the kings of Israel.

35 Later, Jehoshaphat king of Judah made an alliance with Ahaziah king of Israel, who was guilty of wickedness. 36 He agreed with him to construct a fleet of trading ships.[n] After these were built at Ezion Geber, 37 Eliezer son of Dodavahu of Mareshah prophesied against Jehoshaphat, saying, "Because you have made an alliance with Ahaziah, the LORD will destroy what you have made." The ships were wrecked and were not able to set sail to trade.[o]

21 Then Jehoshaphat rested with his fathers and was buried with them in the City of David. And Jehoram his son succeeded him as king. 2 Jehoram's brothers, the sons of Jehoshaphat, were Azariah, Jehiel, Zechariah, Azariahu, Michael and Shephatiah. All these were sons of Jehoshaphat king of Israel.[p] 3 Their father had given them many gifts of silver and gold and articles of value, as well as fortified cities in Judah, but he had given the kingdom to Jehoram because he was his firstborn son.

*Jehoram King of Judah*

4 When Jehoram established himself firmly over his father's kingdom, he put all his brothers to the sword along with some of the princes of Israel. 5 Jehoram was thirty-two years old when he became king, and he reigned in Jerusalem eight years. 6 He

[n]36 Hebrew *of ships that could go to Tarshish*
[o]37 Hebrew *sail for Tarshish*
[p]2 That is, Judah, as frequently in 2 Chronicles

*4 Most mss have *segol* under the *kaph* ( כֶת– ).

וַיֵּ֗לֶךְ בְּדֶ֣רֶךְ ׀ מַלְכֵ֣י יִשְׂרָאֵ֗ל כַּאֲשֶׁ֤ר עָשׂוּ֙ בֵּ֣ית אַחְאָ֔ב
Ahab house-of they-did just-as Israel kings-of in-way-of and-he-walked (6)

כִּ֚י בַּת־ אַחְאָ֔ב הָ֣יְתָה לּ֖וֹ אִשָּׁ֑ה וַיַּ֥עַשׂ הָרַ֖ע בְּעֵינֵ֥י
in-eyes-of the-evil and-he-did wife to-him she-was Ahab daughter-of for

יְהוָֽה: וְלֹא־ אָבָ֣ה יְהוָ֗ה לְהַשְׁחִית֙ אֶת־ בֵּ֣ית דָּוִ֔יד
David house-of *** to-destroy Yahweh he-was-willing but-not (7) Yahweh

לְמַ֣עַן הַבְּרִ֗ית אֲשֶׁ֤ר כָּרַת֙ לְדָוִ֔יד וְכַאֲשֶׁ֣ר אָמַ֔ר
he-promised and-just-as with-David he-made that the-covenant because-of

לָתֵ֥ת ל֛וֹ נִ֖יר וּלְבָנָ֑יו כָּל־ הַיָּמִֽים:
the-days all-of and-for-sons-of-him lamp for-him to-maintain

בְּיָמָיו֙ פָּשַׁ֣ע אֱד֔וֹם מִתַּ֖חַת יַד־ יְהוּדָ֑ה וַיַּמְלִ֖יכוּ
and-they-set-king Judah hand-of from-under Edom he-rebelled in-days-of-him (8)

עֲלֵיהֶ֖ם מֶֽלֶךְ: (9) וַיַּֽעֲבֹר֙ יְהוֹרָם֙ עִם־ שָׂרָ֔יו וְכָל־
and-all-of officers-of-him with Jehoram so-he-went (9) king over-them

הָרֶ֖כֶב עִמּ֑וֹ וַיְהִי֙ קָ֣ם לַ֔יְלָה וַיַּ֥ךְ אֶת־
*** and-he-broke-through night he-rose and-he-was with-him the-chariot

אֱד֗וֹם הַסּוֹבֵ֤ב אֵלָיו֙ וְאֵ֖ת שָׂרֵ֣י הָרָ֑כֶב:
the-chariot commanders-of and around-him the-one-surrounding Edom

וַיִּפְשַׁ֨ע אֱד֜וֹם מִתַּ֣חַת יַד־ יְהוּדָ֗ה עַ֚ד הַיּ֣וֹם הַזֶּ֔ה אָ֣ז
then the-this the-day to Judah hand-of from-under Edom and-he-rebels (10)

תִּפְשַׁ֤ע לִבְנָה֙ בָּעֵ֣ת הַהִ֔יא מִתַּ֖חַת יָד֑וֹ כִּ֣י
because hand-of-him from-under the-same at-the-time Libnah she-revolted

עָזַ֕ב אֶת־ יְהוָ֖ה אֱלֹהֵ֥י אֲבֹתָֽיו: (11) גַּם־ה֤וּא עָשָׂה֙ בָמ֔וֹת
high-places he-built he also (11) fathers-of-him God-of Yahweh *** he-forsook

בְּהָרֵ֣י יְהוּדָ֑ה וַיֶּ֛זֶן אֶת־ יֹשְׁבֵ֥י יְרוּשָׁלִַ֖ם
Jerusalem ones-living-of *** and-he-led-to-prostitution Judah on-hills-of

וַיַּדַּ֖ח אֶת־ יְהוּדָֽה: (12) וַיָּבֹ֤א אֵלָיו֙ מִכְתָּ֔ב מֵאֵלִיָּ֥הוּ
from-Elijah letter to-him and-he-came (12) Judah *** and-he-led-astray

הַנָּבִ֖יא לֵאמֹ֑ר כֹּ֣ה ׀ אָמַ֞ר יְהוָ֗ה אֱלֹהֵי֙ דָּוִ֣יד אָבִ֔יךָ תַּ֗חַת
because father-of-you David God-of Yahweh he-says this to-say the-prophet

אֲשֶׁ֤ר לֹא־ הָלַ֙כְתָּ֙ בְּדַרְכֵי֙ יְהוֹשָׁפָ֣ט אָבִ֔יךָ וּבְדַרְכֵ֖י אָסָ֥א
Asa or-in-ways-of father-of-you Jehoshaphat in-ways-of you-walked not that

מֶֽלֶךְ־ יְהוּדָֽה: (13) וַתֵּ֗לֶךְ בְּדֶ֙רֶךְ֙ מַלְכֵ֣י יִשְׂרָאֵ֔ל
Israel kings-of in-way-of but-you-walked (13) Judah king-of

וַתַּזְנֶ֤ה אֶת־ יְהוּדָה֙ וְאֶת־ יֹשְׁבֵ֣י יְרוּשָׁלִַ֔ם
Jerusalem ones-living-of and Judah *** and-you-led-to-prostitution

כְּהַזְנ֖וֹת בֵּ֣ית אַחְאָ֑ב וְגַ֛ם אֶת־ אַחֶ֥יךָ בֵית־
house-of brothers-of-you *** and-also Ahab house-of as-to-be-prostitutes

walked in the ways of the kings of Israel, as the house of Ahab had done, for he married a daughter of Ahab. He did evil in the eyes of the LORD. [7]Nevertheless, because of the covenant the LORD had made with him, the LORD was not willing to destroy the house of David. He had promised to maintain a lamp for David and his descendants forever.

[8]In the time of Jehoram, Edom rebelled against Judah and set up its own king. [9]So Jehoram went there with his officers and all his chariots. The Edomites surrounded him and his chariot commanders, but he rose up and broke through by night. [10]To this day Edom has been in rebellion against Judah.

Libnah revolted at the same time, because Jehoram had forsaken the LORD, the God of his fathers. [11]He had also built high places on the hills of Judah and had caused the people of Jerusalem to prostitute themselves and had led Judah astray.

[12]Jehoram received a letter from Elijah the prophet, which said:

"This is what the LORD, the God of your father David, says: 'You have not walked in the ways of your father Jehoshaphat or of Asa king of Judah. [13]But you have walked in the ways of the kings of Israel, and you have led Judah and the people of Jerusalem to prostitute themselves, just as the house of Ahab did. You have also murdered your own brothers, members of

אָבִיךָ הַטּוֹבִים מִמְּךָ הָרָגְתָּ׃ הִנֵּה יְהוָה
Yahweh see! (14) you-murdered than-you the-ones-better father-of-you

נֹגֵף מַגֵּפָה גְדוֹלָה בְּעַמֶּךָ וּבְבָנֶיךָ וּבְנָשֶׁיךָ
and-on-wives-of-you and-on-sons-of-you on-people-of-you heavy blow striking

וּבְכָל־ רְכוּשֶׁךָ׃ וְאַתָּה בָּחֳלָיִים רַבִּים
great-ones with-illnesses and-you (15) possession-of-you and-on-all-of

בְּמַחֲלַה מֵעֶיךָ עַד־ יֵצְאוּ מֵעֶיךָ מִן־
from bowels-of-you they-come-out until bowels-of-you with-disease-of

הַחֹלִי יָמִים עַל־ יָמִים׃ וַיָּעַר יְהוָה עַל־ יְהוֹרָם אֵת
*** Jehoram against Yahweh and-he-aroused (16) days after days the-disease

רוּחַ הַפְּלִשְׁתִּים וְהָעַרְבִים אֲשֶׁר עַל־ יַד כּוּשִׁים׃
Cushites hand-of at who and-the-Arabs the-Philistines hostility-of

וַיַּעֲלוּ בִיהוּדָה וַיְבַקְעוּהָ וַיִּשְׁבּוּ
and-they-carried-off and-they-invaded-her against-Judah and-they-attacked (17)

אֵת כָּל־ הָרְכוּשׁ הַנִּמְצָא לְבֵית־ הַמֶּלֶךְ וְגַם־
and-also the-king in-palace-of the-one-being-found the-possession all-of ***

בָּנָיו וְנָשָׁיו וְלֹא נִשְׁאַר־ לוֹ בֵּן כִּי אִם־
only except son to-him he-was-left and-not and-wives-of-him sons-of-him

יְהוֹאָחָז קְטֹן בָּנָיו׃ וְאַחֲרֵי כָּל־ זֹאת נְגָפוֹ
he-afflicted-him this all-of and-after (18) sons-of-him youngest-of Jehoahaz

יְהוָה ׀ בְּמֵעָיו לָחֳלִי לְאֵין מַרְפֵּא׃ וַיְהִי לְיָמִים ׀
in-days and-he-was (19) curing of-no with-disease in-bowels-of-him Yahweh

מִיָּמִים וּכְעֵת צֵאת הַקֵּץ לְיָמִים שְׁנַיִם יָצְאוּ
they-came-out two of-days the-end to-come and-about-time-of after-days

מֵעָיו עִם־ חָלְיוֹ וַיָּמָת בְּתַחֲלֻאִים רָעִים
severe-ones in-pains and-he-died disease-of-him because-of bowels-of-him

וְלֹא־ עָשׂוּ לוֹ עַמּוֹ שְׂרֵפָה כִּשְׂרֵפַת אֲבֹתָיו׃
fathers-of-him as-fire-of fire people-of-him for-him they-made but-not

בֶּן־ שְׁלֹשִׁים וּשְׁתַּיִם הָיָה בְמָלְכוֹ וּשְׁמוֹנֶה שָׁנִים
years and-eight when-to-become-king-him he-was and-two thirty son-of (20)

מָלַךְ בִּירוּשָׁלִַם וַיֵּלֶךְ בְּלֹא חֶמְדָּה וַיִּקְבְּרֻהוּ
and-they-buried-him regret with-no and-he-passed-away in-Jerusalem he-reigned

בְּעִיר דָּוִיד וְלֹא בְּקִבְרוֹת הַמְּלָכִים׃ וַיַּמְלִיכוּ
and-they-made-king (22:1) the-kings in-tombs-of but-not David in-City-of

יוֹשְׁבֵי יְרוּשָׁלִַם אֶת־ אֲחַזְיָהוּ בְּנוֹ הַקָּטֹן תַּחְתָּיו
in-place-of-him the-young son-of-him Ahaziah *** Jerusalem ones-living-of

כִּי כָל־ הָרִאשֹׁנִים הָרַג הַגְּדוּד הַבָּא בָעַרְבִים
with-the-Arabs the-one-coming the-raider he-killed the-older-ones all-of since

your father's house, men who were better than you. [14]So now the LORD is about to strike your people, your sons, your wives and everything that is yours, with a heavy blow. [15]You yourself will be very ill with a lingering disease of the bowels, until the disease causes your bowels to come out.' "

[16]The LORD aroused against Jehoram the hostility of the Philistines and of the Arabs who lived near the Cushites. [17]They attacked Judah, invaded it and carried off all the goods found in the king's palace, together with his sons and wives. Not a son was left to him except Ahaziah,[q] the youngest.

[18]After all this, the LORD afflicted Jehoram with an incurable disease of the bowels. [19]In the course of time, at the end of the second year, his bowels came out because of the disease, and he died in great pain. His people made no fire in his honor, as they had for his fathers.

[20]Jehoram was thirty-two years old when he became king, and he reigned in Jerusalem eight years. He passed away, to no one's regret, and was buried in the City of David, but not in the tombs of the kings.

*Ahaziah King of Judah*

**22** The people of Jerusalem made Ahaziah, Jehoram's youngest son, king in his place, since the raiders, who came with the Arabs into the camp, had killed all the

q17 Hebrew *Jehoahaz,* a variant of *Ahaziah*

לְמַּחֲנֶה וַיִּמְלֹךְ אֲחַזְיָהוּ בֶן־ יְהוֹרָם מֶלֶךְ יְהוּדָה׃ בֶּן־
son-of (2) Judah king-of Jehoram son-of Ahaziah so-he-reigned into-the-camp

אַרְבָּעִים וּשְׁתַּיִם שָׁנָה אֲחַזְיָהוּ בְמָלְכוֹ וְשָׁנָה אַחַת מָלַךְ
he-reigned one and-year when-to-become-king-him Ahaziah year and-two forty

בִּירוּשָׁלִָם וְשֵׁם אִמּוֹ עֲתַלְיָהוּ בַּת־ עָמְרִי׃ גַּם־
also (3) Omri daughter-of Athaliah mother-of-him and-name-of in-Jerusalem

הוּא הָלַךְ בְּדַרְכֵי בֵּית אַחְאָב כִּי אִמּוֹ הָיְתָה
she-was mother-of-him for Ahab house-of in-ways-of he-walked he

יוֹעַצְתּוֹ לְהַרְשִׁיעַ׃ וַיַּעַשׂ הָרַע בְּעֵינֵי יְהוָה
Yahweh in-eyes-of the-evil and-he-did (4) to-do-wrong encouraging-him

כְּבֵית אַחְאָב כִּי־ הֵמָּה הָיוּ־ לוֹ יוֹעֲצִים אַחֲרֵי מוֹת
death-of after ones-advising to-him they-became they for Ahab as-house-of

אָבִיו לְמַשְׁחִית לוֹ׃ גַּם בַּעֲצָתָם הָלַךְ
he-followed to-advice-of-them also (5) of-him to-undoing father-of-him

וַיֵּלֶךְ אֶת־ יְהוֹרָם בֶּן־ אַחְאָב מֶלֶךְ יִשְׂרָאֵל לַמִּלְחָמָה עַל־
against to-the-war Israel king-of Ahab son-of Jehoram with when-he-went

חֲזָאֵל מֶלֶךְ־ אֲרָם בְּרָמוֹת גִּלְעָד וַיַּכּוּ הָרַמִּים אֶת־
*** the-Arameans and-they-wounded Gilead at-Ramoth Aram king-of Hazael

יוֹרָם׃ וַיָּשָׁב לְהִתְרַפֵּא בְיִזְרְעֶאל כִּי הַמַּכִּים אֲשֶׁר
that the-wounds from to-Jezreel to-recover so-he-returned (6) Joram

הִכֻּהוּ בָרָמָה בְּהִלָּחֲמוֹ אֶת־ חֲזָהאֵל מֶלֶךְ אֲרָם
Aram king-of Hazael *** when-to-fight-him at-the-Ramah they-inflicted-on-him

וַעֲזַרְיָהוּ בֶן־ יְהוֹרָם מֶלֶךְ יְהוּדָה יָרַד לִרְאוֹת אֶת־ יְהוֹרָם
Jehoram *** to-see he-went-down Judah king-of Jehoram son-of then-Azariah

בֶּן־ אַחְאָב בְּיִזְרְעֶאל כִּי־ חֹלֶה הוּא׃ וּמֵאֱלֹהִים הָיְתָה
she-was and-from-God (7) he being-wounded for to-Jezreel Ahab son-of

תְּבוּסַת אֲחַזְיָהוּ לָבוֹא אֶל־ יוֹרָם וּבְבֹאוֹ יָצָא
he-went-out now-when-to-arrive-him Joram to to-visit Ahaziah downfall-of

עִם־ יְהוֹרָם אֶל־יֵהוּא בֶן־ נִמְשִׁי אֲשֶׁר מְשָׁחוֹ יְהוָה לְהַכְרִית
to-destroy Yahweh he-anointed-him whom Nimshi son-of Jehu to Jehoram with

אֶת־ בֵּית אַחְאָב׃ וַיְהִי כְּהִשָּׁפֵט יֵהוּא עִם־ בֵּית אַחְאָב
Ahab house-of against Jehu while-to-judge and-he-was (8) Ahab house-of ***

וַיִּמְצָא אֶת־ שָׂרֵי יְהוּדָה וּבְנֵי אֲחֵי אֲחַזְיָהוּ
Ahaziah relatives-of and-sons-of Judah princes-of *** then-he-found

מְשָׁרְתִים לַאֲחַזְיָהוּ וַיַּהַרְגֵם׃ וַיְבַקֵּשׁ אֶת־
*** then-he-searched (9) and-he-killed-them to-Ahaziah ones-attending

אֲחַזְיָהוּ וַיִּלְכְּדֻהוּ וְהוּא מִתְחַבֵּא בְשֹׁמְרוֹן וַיְבִאֻהוּ
and-they-brought-him in-Samaria hiding while-he and-they-captured-him Ahaziah

older sons. So Ahaziah son of
Jehoram king of Judah began
to reign.
[2]Ahaziah was twenty-two[r]
years old when he became
king, and he reigned in
Jerusalem one year. His
mother's name was Athaliah,
a granddaughter of Omri.
[3]He too walked in the ways
of the house of Ahab, for his
mother encouraged him in doing wrong. [4]He did evil in the
eyes of the LORD, as the house
of Ahab had done, for after his
father's death they became his
advisers, to his undoing. [5]He
also followed their counsel
when he went with Joram[s]
son of Ahab king of Israel to
war against Hazael king of
Aram at Ramoth Gilead. The
Arameans wounded Joram;
[6]so he returned to Jezreel to
recover from the wounds they
had inflicted on him at
Ramoth[t] in his battle with
Hazael king of Aram.
Then Ahaziah[u] son of Jehoram king of Judah went
down to Jezreel to see Joram
son of Ahab because he had
been wounded.
[7]Through Ahaziah's visit to
Joram, God brought about
Ahaziah's downfall. When
Ahaziah arrived, he went out
with Joram to meet Jehu son of
Nimshi, whom the LORD had
anointed to destroy the house
of Ahab. [8]While Jehu was ex-
ecuting judgment on the
house of Ahab, he found the
princes of Judah and the sons
of Ahaziah's relatives, who
had been attending Ahaziah,
and he killed them. [9]He then
went in search of Ahaziah,
and his men captured him
while he was hiding in Samaria. He was brought to Jehu

[r]2 Some Septuagint manuscripts and Syriac (see also 2 Kings 8:26); Hebrew *forty-two*
[s]5 Hebrew *Jehoram*, a variant of *Joram*; also in verses 6 and 7
[t]6 Hebrew *Ramah*, a variant of *Ramoth*
[u]6 Some Hebrew manuscripts, Septuagint, Vulgate and Syriac (see also 2 Kings 8:29); most Hebrew manuscripts *Azariah*

אֶל־יֵהוּא וַיְמִתֻהוּ וַֽיִּקְבְּרֻהוּ כִּי אָמְרוּ בֶּן־
son-of they-said for and-they-buried-him and-they-killed-him Jehu to

יְהוֹשָׁפָט הוּא אֲשֶׁר־דָּרַשׁ אֶת־יְהוָה בְּכָל־לְבָבוֹ וְאֵין
so-no-one heart-of-him with-all-of Yahweh *** he-sought who he Jehoshaphat

לְבֵית אֲחַזְיָהוּ לַעְצֹר כֹּחַ לְמַמְלָכָה׃ וַעֲתַלְיָהוּ אֵם
mother-of when-Athaliah (10) for-kingdom power to-have Ahaziah of-house-of

אֲחַזְיָהוּ רָאֲתָה כִּי מֵת בְּנָהּ וַתָּקָם
then-she-proceeded son-of-her he-was-dead that she-saw Ahaziah

וַתְּדַבֵּר אֶת־כָּל־זֶרַע הַמַּמְלָכָה לְבֵית יְהוּדָה׃
Judah of-house-of the-royal family-of whole-of *** and-she-destroyed

וַתִּקַּח יְהוֹשַׁבְעַת בַּת־הַמֶּלֶךְ אֶת־יוֹאָשׁ בֶּן־אֲחַזְיָהוּ
Ahaziah son-of Joash *** the-king daughter-of Jehoshabeath but-she-took (11)

וַתִּגְנֹב אֹתוֹ מִתּוֹךְ בְּנֵי־הַמֶּלֶךְ הַמּוּמָתִים
the-ones-being-murdered the-king sons-of from-among him and-she-stole-away

וַתִּתֵּן אֹתוֹ וְאֶת־מֵינִקְתּוֹ בַּחֲדַר הַמִּטּוֹת וַתַּסְתִּירֵהוּ
and-she-hid-him the-beds in-room-of one-nursing-him and him and-she-put

יְהוֹשַׁבְעַת בַּת־הַמֶּלֶךְ יְהוֹרָם אֵשֶׁת יְהוֹיָדָע הַכֹּהֵן
the-priest Jehoiada wife-of Jehoram the-king daughter-of Jehoshabeath

כִּי הִיא הָיְתָה אֲחוֹת אֲחַזְיָהוּ מִפְּנֵי עֲתַלְיָהוּ וְלֹא
so-not Athaliah from-before Ahaziah sister-of she-was she because

הֱמִיתָתְהוּ׃ וַיְהִי אִתָּם בְּבֵית הָאֱלֹהִים מִתְחַבֵּא
being-hidden the-God at-temple-of with-them and-he-was (12) she-killed-him

שֵׁשׁ שָׁנִים וַעֲתַלְיָה מֹלֶכֶת עַל־הָאָרֶץ׃ וּבַשָּׁנָה
and-in-the-year (23:1) the-land over ruling while-Athaliah years six

הַשְּׁבִעִית הִתְחַזַּק יְהוֹיָדָע וַיִּקַּח אֶת־שָׂרֵי
commanders-of with and-he-made Jehoiada he-showed-strength the-seventh

הַמֵּאוֹת לַעֲזַרְיָהוּ בֶן־יְרֹחָם וּלְיִשְׁמָעֵאל בֶּן־יְהוֹחָנָן
Jehohanan son-of and-with-Ishmael Jeroham son-of with-Azariah the-hundreds

וְלַעֲזַרְיָהוּ בֶן־עוֹבֵד וְאֶת־מַעֲשֵׂיָהוּ בֶן־עֲדָיָהוּ וְאֶת־
and-with Adaiah son-of Maaseiah and-with Obed son-of and-with-Azariah

אֱלִישָׁפָט בֶּן־זִכְרִי עִמּוֹ בַבְּרִית׃ וַיָּסֹבּוּ
and-they-went (2) in-the-covenant with-him Zicri son-of Elishaphat

בִּיהוּדָה וַיִּקְבְּצוּ אֶת־הַלְוִיִּם מִכָּל־עָרֵי
towns-of from-all-of the-Levites *** and-they-gathered throughout-Judah

יְהוּדָה וְרָאשֵׁי הָאָבוֹת לְיִשְׂרָאֵל וַיָּבֹאוּ אֶל־יְרוּשָׁלִָם׃
Jerusalem to when-they-came of-Israel the-fathers and-heads-of Judah

וַיִּכְרֹת כָּל־הַקָּהָל בְּרִית בְּבֵית הָאֱלֹהִים
the-God at-temple-of covenant the-assembly whole-of then-they-made (3)

and put to death. They buried him, for they said, "He was a son of Jehoshaphat, who sought the LORD with all his heart." So there was no one in the house of Ahaziah powerful enough to retain the kingdom.

*Athaliah and Joash*

10When Athaliah the mother of Ahaziah saw that her son was dead, she proceeded to destroy the whole royal family of the house of Judah. 11But Jehosheba,[v] the daughter of King Jehoram, took Joash son of Ahaziah and stole him away from among the royal princes who were about to be murdered and put him and his nurse in a bedroom. Because Jehosheba,[v] the daughter of King Jehoram and wife of the priest Jehoiada, was Ahaziah's sister, she hid the child from Athaliah so she could not kill him. 12He remained hidden with them at the temple of God for six years while Athaliah ruled the land.

23 In the seventh year Jehoiada showed his strength. He made a covenant with the commanders of units of a hundred: Azariah son of Jeroham, Ishmael son of Jehohanan, Azariah son of Obed, Maaseiah son of Adaiah, and Elishaphat son of Zicri. 2They went throughout Judah and gathered the Levites and the heads of Israelite families from all the towns. When they came to Jerusalem, 3the whole assembly made a covenant with the king at the temple of God.

[v]11 Hebrew *Jehoshabeath*, a variant of *Jehosheba*

עִם־ הַמֶּלֶךְ וַיֹּאמֶר לָהֶם הִנֵּה בֶן־ הַמֶּלֶךְ יִמְלֹךְ
he-shall-reign the-king son-of see! to-them and-he-said the-king with

כַּאֲשֶׁר דִּבֶּר יְהוָה עַל־ בְּנֵי דָוִיד׃ זֶה הַדָּבָר
the-thing this (4) David descendants-of concerning Yahweh he-promised just-as

אֲשֶׁר תַּעֲשׂוּ הַשְּׁלִשִׁית מִכֶּם בָּאֵי הַשַּׁבָּת
the-Sabbath ones-going-on-duty-of of-you the-third you-must-do that

לַכֹּהֲנִים וְלַלְוִיִּם לְשֹׁעֲרֵי הַסִּפִּים׃ וְהַשְּׁלִשִׁית
and-the-third (5) the-doors as-watchers-of and-of-the-Levites of-the-priests

בְּבֵית הַמֶּלֶךְ וְהַשְּׁלִשִׁית בְּשַׁעַר הַיְסוֹד וְכָל־
and-all-of the-Foundation at-Gate-of and-the-third the-king at-palace-of

הָעָם בְּחַצְרוֹת בֵּית יְהוָה׃ וְאַל־ יָבוֹא
he-may-enter and-not (6) Yahweh temple-of in-courtyards-of the-people

בֵית־ יְהוָה כִּי אִם־ הַכֹּהֲנִים וְהַמְשָׁרְתִים
and-the-ones-being-on-duty the-priests only except Yahweh temple-of

לַלְוִיִּם הֵמָּה יָבֹאוּ כִּי־ קֹדֶשׁ הֵמָּה וְכָל־
but-all-of they consecrated because they-may-enter they of-the-Levites

הָעָם יִשְׁמְרוּ מִשְׁמֶרֶת יְהוָה׃ וְהִקִּיפוּ
and-they-must-station-selves (7) Yahweh assignment-of they-must-guard the-people

הַלְוִיִּם אֶת־ הַמֶּלֶךְ סָבִיב אִישׁ וְכֵלָיו בְּיָדוֹ
in-hand-of-him with-weapons-of-him each around the-king *** the-Levites

וְהַבָּא אֶל־ הַבַּיִת יוּמָת וִהְיוּ אֶת־
with and-stay! he-must-be-killed the-temple into and-the-one-entering

הַמֶּלֶךְ בְּבֹאוֹ וּבְצֵאתוֹ׃ וַיַּעֲשׂוּ הַלְוִיִּם
the-Levites and-they-did (8) and-when-to-come-him when-to-go-him the-king

וְכָל־ יְהוּדָה כְּכֹל אֲשֶׁר־ צִוָּה יְהוֹיָדָע הַכֹּהֵן וַיִּקְחוּ
and-they-took the-priest Jehoiada he-ordered that as-all Judah and-all-of

אִישׁ אֶת־ אֲנָשָׁיו בָּאֵי הַשַּׁבָּת עִם
with the-Sabbath ones-going-on-duty-of men-of-him *** each

יוֹצְאֵי הַשַּׁבָּת כִּי לֹא פָטַר יְהוֹיָדָע הַכֹּהֵן
the-priest Jehoiada he-released not for the-Sabbath ones-going-off-duty-of

אֶת־ הַמַּחְלְקוֹת׃ וַיִּתֵּן יְהוֹיָדָע הַכֹּהֵן לְשָׂרֵי
to-commanders-of the-priest Jehoiada then-he-gave (9) the-divisions ***

הַמֵּאוֹת אֶת־ הַחֲנִיתִים וְאֶת־ הַמָּגִנּוֹת וְאֶת־ הַשְּׁלָטִים אֲשֶׁר
that the-small-shields and the-large-shields and the-spears *** the-hundreds

לַמֶּלֶךְ דָּוִיד אֲשֶׁר בֵּית הָאֱלֹהִים׃ וַיַּעֲמֵד אֶת־ כָּל־
all-of *** and-he-stationed (10) the-God temple-of that David to-the-king

הָעָם וְאִישׁ ׀ שִׁלְחוֹ בְּיָדוֹ מִכֶּתֶף הַבַּיִת
the-temple from-side-of in-hand-of-him weapon-of-him and-each the-people

Jehoiada said to them, "The king's son shall reign, as the LORD promised concerning the descendants of David. 4 Now this is what you are to do: A third of you priests and Levites who are going on duty on the Sabbath are to keep watch at the doors, 5 a third of you at the royal palace and a third at the Foundation Gate, and all the other men are to be in the courtyards of the temple of the LORD. 6 No one is to enter the temple of the LORD except the priests and Levites on duty; they may enter because they are consecrated, but all the other men are to guard what the LORD has assigned to them.[w] 7 The Levites are to station themselves around the king, each man with his weapons in his hand. Anyone who enters the temple must be put to death. Stay close to the king wherever he goes."

8 The Levites and all the men of Judah did just as Jehoiada the priest ordered. Each one took his men—those who were going on duty on the Sabbath and those who were going off duty—for Jehoiada the priest had not released any of the divisions. 9 Then he gave the commanders of units of a hundred the spears and the large and small shields that had belonged to King David and that were in the temple of God. 10 He stationed all the men, each with his weapon in his

w6 Or *to observe the LORD's command ⌞not to enter⌟*

הַיְמָנִית עַד־ כֶּתֶף הַבַּיִת הַשְּׂמָאלִית לַמִּזְבֵּחַ וְלַבָּיִת
and-near-the-temple near-the-altar the-north the-temple side-of to the-south

עַל־הַמֶּלֶךְ סָבִיב׃ וַיּוֹצִיאוּ אֶת־ בֶּן־ הַמֶּלֶךְ וַיִּתְּנוּ
and-they-put the-king son-of *** and-they-brought-out (11) around the-king by

עָלָיו אֶת־ הַנֵּזֶר וְאֶת־ הָעֵדוּת וַיַּמְלִיכוּ אֹתוֹ
him and-they-proclaimed-king the-covenant and the-crown *** on-him

וַיִּמְשָׁחֻהוּ יְהוֹיָדָע וּבָנָיו וַיֹּאמְרוּ יְחִי
may-he-live and-they-shouted and-sons-of-him Jehoiada and-they-anointed-him

הַמֶּלֶךְ׃ וַתִּשְׁמַע עֲתַלְיָהוּ אֶת־ קוֹל הָעָם
the-people noise-of *** Athaliah when-she-heard (12) the-king

הָרָצִים וְהַמְהַלְלִים אֶת־ הַמֶּלֶךְ וַתָּבוֹא אֶל־
to then-she-went the-king *** and-the-ones-cheering the-ones-running

הָעָם בֵּית יְהוָה׃ וַתֵּרֶא וְהִנֵּה הַמֶּלֶךְ עוֹמֵד
standing the-king and-see! and-she-looked (13) Yahweh temple-of the-people

עַל־ עַמּוּדוֹ בַּמָּבוֹא וְהַשָּׂרִים וְהַחֲצֹצְרוֹת עַל־
beside and-the-trumpeters and-the-officers at-the-entrance pillar-of-him by

הַמֶּלֶךְ וְכָל־ עַם הָאָרֶץ שָׂמֵחַ וְתוֹקֵעַ בַּחֲצֹצְרוֹת
on-the-trumpets and-blowing rejoicing the-land people-of and-all-of the-king

וְהַמְשׁוֹרְרִים בִּכְלֵי הַשִּׁיר וּמוֹדִיעִים לְהַלֵּל
to-praise and-ones-leading the-music with-instruments-of and-the-ones-singing

וַתִּקְרַע עֲתַלְיָהוּ אֶת־ בְּגָדֶיהָ וַתֹּאמֶר קֶשֶׁר קָשֶׁר׃
treason treason and-she-shouted robes-of-her *** Athaliah then-she-tore

וַיּוֹצֵא יְהוֹיָדָע הַכֹּהֵן אֶת־ שָׂרֵי הַמֵּאוֹת ׀
the-hundreds commanders-of *** the-priest Jehoiada and-he-sent-out (14)

פְּקוּדֵי הַחַיִל וַיֹּאמֶר אֲלֵהֶם הוֹצִיאוּהָ אֶל־
to bring-out-her! to-them and-he-said the-troop ones-being-in-charge-of

מִבֵּית הַשְּׂדֵרוֹת וְהַבָּא אַחֲרֶיהָ יוּמַת
he-must-be-killed after-her and-the-one-following the-ranks outside-of

בֶּחָרֶב כִּי אָמַר הַכֹּהֵן לֹא תְמִיתוּהָ בֵּית יְהוָה׃
Yahweh temple-of you-kill-her not the-priest he-said for with-the-sword

וַיָּשִׂמוּ לָהּ יָדַיִם וַתָּבוֹא אֶל־ מְבוֹא שַׁעַר־
Gate-of entrance-of to as-she-reached hands on-her so-they-laid (15)

הַסּוּסִים בֵּית הַמֶּלֶךְ וַיְמִיתוּהָ שָׁם׃ וַיִּכְרֹת
then-he-made (16) there and-they-killed-her the-king palace-of the-Horses

יְהוֹיָדָע בְּרִית בֵּינוֹ וּבֵין כָּל־ הָעָם וּבֵין
and-between the-people all-of and-between between-him covenant Jehoiada

הַמֶּלֶךְ לִהְיוֹת לְעָם לַיהוָה׃ וַיָּבֹאוּ כָל־ הָעָם
the-people all-of and-they-went (17) of-Yahweh as-people to-be the-king

hand, around the king—near
the altar and the temple, from
the south side to the north side
of the temple.
[11]Jehoiada and his sons
brought out the king's son and
put the crown on him; they
presented him with a copy of
the covenant and proclaimed
him king. They anointed him
and shouted, "Long live the
king!"
[12]When Athaliah heard the
noise of the people running
and cheering the king, she
went to them at the temple of
the LORD. [13]She looked, and
there was the king, standing
by his pillar at the entrance.
The officers and the trumpeters were beside the king, and
all the people of the land were
rejoicing and blowing trumpets, and singers with musical
instruments were leading the
praises. Then Athaliah tore
her robes and shouted, "Treason! Treason!"
[14]Jehoiada the priest sent out
the commanders of units of a
hundred, who were in charge
of the troops, and said to
them: "Bring her out between
the ranks[x] and put to the
sword anyone who follows
her." For the priest had said,
"Do not put her to death at the
temple of the LORD." [15]So they
seized her as she reached the
entrance of the Horse Gate on
the palace grounds, and there
they put her to death.
[16]Jehoiada then made a covenant that he and the people
and the king[y] would be the
LORD's people. [17]All the people

[x]14 *Or out from the precincts*
[y]16 *Or covenant between* ⌞*the* LORD⌟ *and the people and the king that they* (see 2 Kings 11:17)

בֵּית־ הַבַּעַל֒ וַֽיִּתְּצֻ֒הוּ וְאֶת־ מִזְבְּחֹתָ֣יו וְאֶת־ צְלָמָ֖יו
temple-of the-Baal and-and-they-tore-down-him and altars-of-him and idols-of-him

שִׁבֵּ֑רוּ וְאֵ֗ת מַתָּן֙ כֹּהֵ֣ן הַבַּ֔עַל הָרְג֖וּ לִפְנֵ֥י הַֽמִּזְבְּחֽוֹת׃
they-smashed and Mattan priest-of the-Baal they-killed in-front-of the-altars

וַיָּ֩שֶׂם֩ יְהוֹיָדָ֨ע פְּקֻדֹּ֜ת בֵּ֣ית יְהוָ֗ה בְּיַ֣ד
(18) then-he-placed Jehoiada oversights-of temple-of Yahweh in-hand-of

הַכֹּהֲנִ֣ים הַלְוִיִּ֔ם אֲשֶׁ֨ר חָלַ֤ק דָּוִיד֙ עַל־ בֵּ֣ית יְהוָ֔ה לְהַעֲל֥וֹת
the-priests the-Levites whom he-assigned David in temple-of Yahweh to-present

עֹל֣וֹת יְהוָ֗ה כַּכָּת֛וּב בְּתוֹרַ֥ת מֹשֶׁ֖ה בְּשִׂמְחָ֣ה
offerings-of Yahweh as-the-thing-being-written in-Law-of Moses with-rejoicing

וּבְשִׁ֑יר עַ֖ל יְדֵ֥י דָוִֽיד׃ (19) וַֽיַּעֲמֵד֙ הַשּׁ֣וֹעֲרִ֔ים עַל־
and-with-song as orders-of David and-he-stationed the-doorkeepers at

שַׁעֲרֵ֖י בֵּ֣ית יְהוָ֑ה וְלֹֽא־ יָבֹ֥א טָמֵ֖א לְכָל־ דָּבָֽר׃
gates-of temple-of Yahweh so-not he-might-enter unclean in-any-of way

(20) וַיִּקַּ֣ח אֶת־ שָׂרֵ֣י הַמֵּא֗וֹת וְאֶת־ הָֽאַדִּירִים֙ וְאֶת־
and-he-took *** commanders-of the-hundreds and the-nobles and

הַמּֽוֹשְׁלִים֙ בָּעָ֔ם וְאֵ֖ת ׀ כָּל־ עַ֣ם הָאָ֑רֶץ וַיּ֙וֹרֶד֙
the-ones-ruling of-the-people and all-of people-of the-land and-he-brought-down

אֶת־ הַמֶּ֔לֶךְ מִבֵּ֖ית יְהוָ֑ה וַיָּבֹ֛אוּ בְּתֽוֹךְ־ שַׁ֥עַר הָעֶלְי֖וֹן
*** the-king from-temple-of Yahweh and-they-went through Gate-of the-Upper

בֵּ֣ית הַמֶּ֔לֶךְ וַיּוֹשִׁ֙יבוּ֙ אֶת־ הַמֶּ֔לֶךְ עַ֖ל כִּסֵּ֥א הַמַּמְלָכָֽה׃
palace-of the-king and-they-seated *** the-king on throne-of the-royalty

וַיִּשְׂמְח֥וּ כָל־ עַם־ הָאָ֖רֶץ וְהָעִ֣יר שָׁקָ֑טָה
(21) and-they-rejoiced all-of people-of the-land and-the-city she-was-quiet

וְאֶת־ עֲתַלְיָ֖הוּ הֵמִ֥יתוּ בֶחָֽרֶב׃ (24:1) בֶּן־ שֶׁ֤בַע שָׁנִים֙ יֹאָ֔שׁ
and Athaliah they-killed with-the-sword son-of seven years Joash

בְּמָלְכ֔וֹ וְאַרְבָּעִ֣ים שָׁנָ֔ה מָלַ֖ךְ בִּירוּשָׁלָ֑͏ִם וְשֵׁ֣ם
when-to-become-king-him and-forty year he-reigned in-Jerusalem and-name-of

אִמּ֔וֹ צִבְיָ֖ה מִבְּאֵ֥ר שָׁ֑בַע (2) וַיַּ֧עַשׂ יוֹאָ֛שׁ הַיָּשָׁ֖ר
mother-of-him Zibiah from-Beer Sheba (2) and-he-did Joash the-right

בְּעֵינֵ֣י יְהוָ֑ה כָּל־ יְמֵ֖י יְהוֹיָדָ֥ע הַכֹּהֵֽן׃ (3) וַיִּשָּׂא־ ל֣וֹ
in-eyes-of Yahweh all-of days-of Jehoiada the-priest and-he-chose for-him

יְהוֹיָדָ֖ע נָשִׁ֣ים שְׁתָּ֑יִם וַיּ֖וֹלֶד בָּנִ֥ים וּבָנֽוֹת׃ (4) וַיְהִ֖י
Jehoiada wives two and-he-fathered sons and-daughters (4) and-he-was

אַחֲרֵי־ כֵ֑ן הָיָ֣ה עִם־ לֵ֣ב יוֹאָ֔שׁ לְחַדֵּ֖שׁ אֶת־ בֵּ֥ית יְהוָֽה׃
after-this he-was in heart-of Joash to-restore *** temple-of Yahweh

(5) וַיִּקְבֹּ֞ץ אֶת־ הַכֹּהֲנִ֤ים וְהַלְוִיִּם֙ וַיֹּ֣אמֶר
(5) and-he-called-together *** the-priests and-the-Levites and-he-said

went to the temple of Baal and tore it down. They smashed the altars and idols and killed Mattan the priest of Baal in front of the altars.

[18]Then Jehoiada placed the oversight of the temple of the LORD in the hands of the priests, who were Levites, to whom David had made assignments in the temple, to present the burnt offerings of the LORD as written in the Law of Moses, with rejoicing and singing, as David had ordered. [19]He also stationed doorkeepers at the gates of the LORD's temple so that no one who was in any way unclean might enter.

[20]He took with him the commanders of hundreds, the nobles, the rulers of the people and all the people of the land and brought the king down from the temple of the LORD. They went into the palace through the Upper Gate and seated the king on the royal throne, [21]and all the people of the land rejoiced. And the city was quiet, because Athaliah had been slain with the sword.

### Joash Repairs the Temple

**24** Joash was seven years old when he became king, and he reigned in Jerusalem forty years. His mother's name was Zibiah; she was from Beersheba. [2]Joash did what was right in the eyes of the LORD all the years of Jehoiada the priest. [3]Jehoiada chose two wives for him, and he had sons and daughters.

[4]Some time later Joash decided to restore the temple of the LORD. [5]He called together the priests and Levites and

לָהֶם צְאוּ לְעָרֵי יְהוּדָה וְקִבְצוּ מִכָּל־ יִשְׂרָאֵל כֶּסֶף
money Israel from-all-of and-collect! Judah to-towns-of go! to-them

לְחַזֵּק ׀ אֶת־ בֵּית אֱלֹהֵיכֶם מִדֵּי שָׁנָה בְּשָׁנָה וְאַתֶּם
and-you by-year year from-dues-of God-of-you temple-of *** to-repair

תְּמַהֲרוּ לַדָּבָר וְלֹא מִהֲרוּ הַלְוִיִּם׃
the-Levites they-acted-at-once but-not in-the-matter you-act-now

וַיִּקְרָא הַמֶּלֶךְ לִיהוֹיָדָע הָרֹאשׁ וַיֹּאמֶר לוֹ מַדּוּעַ
why? to-him and-he-said the-chief for-Jehoiada the-king so-he-summoned (6)

לֹא־ דָרַשְׁתָּ עַל־ הַלְוִיִּם לְהָבִיא מִיהוּדָה וּמִירוּשָׁלַםִ
and-from-Jerusalem from-Judah to-bring-in the-Levites from you-required not

אֶת־ מַשְׂאַת מֹשֶׁה עֶבֶד־ יְהוָה וְהַקָּהָל לְיִשְׂרָאֵל לְאֹהֶל
for-Tent-of of-Israel and-the-assembly Yahweh servant-of Moses tax-of ***

הָעֵדוּת׃ כִּי עֲתַלְיָהוּ הַמִּרְשַׁעַת בָּנֶיהָ פָרְצוּ אֶת־
*** they-broke-into sons-of-her the-wicked Athaliah now (7) the-Testimony

בֵּית הָאֱלֹהִים וְגַם כָּל־ קָדְשֵׁי בֵית־ יְהוָה
Yahweh temple-of sacred-objects-of all-of and-even the-God temple-of

עָשׂוּ לַבְּעָלִים׃ וַיֹּאמֶר הַמֶּלֶךְ וַיַּעֲשׂוּ אֲרוֹן
chest and-they-made the-king and-he-commanded (8) for-the-Baals they-used

אֶחָד וַיִּתְּנֻהוּ בְּשַׁעַר בֵּית־ יְהוָה חוּצָה׃
at-outside Yahweh temple-of at-gate-of and-they-placed-him one

וַיִּתְּנוּ־ קוֹל בִּיהוּדָה וּבִירוּשָׁלַםִ לְהָבִיא
to-bring and-in-Jerusalem in-Judah proclamation and-they-issued (9)

לַיהוָה מַשְׂאַת מֹשֶׁה עֶבֶד־ הָאֱלֹהִים עַל־ יִשְׂרָאֵל בַּמִּדְבָּר׃
in-the-desert Israel from the-God servant-of Moses tax-of to-Yahweh

וַיִּשְׂמְחוּ כָל־ הַשָּׂרִים וְכָל־ הָעָם
the-people and-all-of the-officials all-of and-they-were-glad (10)

וַיָּבִיאוּ וַיַּשְׁלִיכוּ לָאָרוֹן עַד־ לְכַלֵּה׃
to-fill until into-the-chest and-they-dropped and-they-brought

וַיְהִי בְּעֵת יָבִיא אֶת־ הָאָרוֹן אֶל־ פְּקֻדַּת הַמֶּלֶךְ
the-king official-of to the-chest *** he-brought-in at-time-of and-he-was (11)

בְּיַד הַלְוִיִּם וְכִרְאוֹתָם כִּי־ רַב הַכֶּסֶף
the-money large-amount that and-when-to-see-them the-Levites by-hand-of

וּבָא סוֹפֵר הַמֶּלֶךְ וּפְקִיד כֹּהֵן הָרֹאשׁ
the-chief priest and-officer-of the-king secretary-of then-he-came

וִיעָרוּ אֶת־ הָאָרוֹן וְיִשָּׂאֻהוּ וִישִׁבֻהוּ אֶל־
to and-they-returned-him and-they-carried-him the-chest *** and-they-emptied

מְקֹמוֹ כֹּה עָשׂוּ לְיוֹם ׀ בְּיוֹם וַיַּאַסְפוּ־ כֶסֶף
money and-they-collected after-day for-day they-did this place-of-him

said to them, "Go to the towns of Judah and collect the money due annually from all Israel, to repair the temple of your God. Do it now." But the Levites did not act at once.

6 Therefore the king summoned Jehoiada the chief priest and said to him, "Why haven't you required the Levites to bring in from Judah and Jerusalem the tax imposed by Moses the servant of the LORD and by the assembly of Israel for the Tent of the Testimony?"

7 Now the sons of that wicked woman Athaliah had broken into the temple of God and had used even its sacred objects for the Baals.

8 At the king's command, a chest was made and placed outside, at the gate of the temple of the LORD. 9 A proclamation was then issued in Judah and Jerusalem that they should bring to the LORD the tax that Moses the servant of God had required of Israel in the desert. 10 All the officials and all the people brought their contributions gladly, dropping them into the chest until it was full. 11 Whenever the chest was brought in by the Levites to the king's officials and they saw that there was a large amount of money, the royal secretary and the officer of the chief priest would come and empty the chest and carry it back to its place. They did this regularly and collected a great

לָרֹֽב׃ וַיִּתְּנֵ֨הוּ הַמֶּ֜לֶךְ וִיהוֹיָדָ֗ע אֶל־ עוֹשֵׂה֙
one-doing-of to and-Jehoiada the-king and-he-gave-him (12) in-great-amount

מְלֶ֙אכֶת֙ עֲבוֹדַ֣ת בֵּית־ יְהוָ֔ה וַיִּהְי֣וּ שֹׂכְרִ֗ים
ones-hiring and-they-were Yahweh temple-of requirement-of work-of

חֹצְבִ֤ים וְחָרָשִׁים֙ לְחַדֵּ֖שׁ בֵּ֣ית יְהוָ֑ה וְ֠גַם
and-also Yahweh temple-of to-restore and-carpenters ones-being-masons

לְחָרָשֵׁ֤י בַרְזֶל֙ וּנְחֹ֔שֶׁת לְחַזֵּ֖ק אֶת־ בֵּ֥ית יְהוָֽה׃
Yahweh temple-of *** to-repair and-bronze iron to-workers-of

וַֽיַּעֲשׂוּ֙ עֹשֵׂ֣י הַמְּלָאכָ֔ה וַתַּ֧עַל
and-she-progressed the-work ones-being-in-charge-of and-they-were-diligent (13)

אֲרוּכָ֛ה לַמְּלָאכָ֖ה בְּיָדָ֑ם וַיַּעֲמִ֜ידוּ אֶת־ בֵּ֧ית הָאֱלֹהִ֛ים
the-God temple-of *** and-they-rebuilt under-hand-of-them of-the-work repair

עַל־ מַתְכֻּנְתּ֖וֹ וַיְאַמְּצֻֽהוּ׃ וּֽכְכַלּוֹתָ֗ם
and-when-to-finish-them (14) and-they-reinforced-him design-of-him according-to

הֵבִ֣יאוּ לִ֠פְנֵי הַמֶּ֨לֶךְ וִיהוֹיָדָ֜ע אֶת־ שְׁאָ֣ר הַכֶּ֗סֶף וַיַּעֲשֵׂ֨הוּ
and-he-made-him the-money rest-of *** and-Jehoiada the-king to they-brought

כֵלִ֤ים לְבֵית־ יְהוָה֙ כְּלֵ֣י שָׁרֵ֔ת וְהַעֲל֔וֹת
and-the-burnt-offerings service articles-of Yahweh for-temple-of articles

וְכַפּ֕וֹת וּכְלֵ֖י זָהָ֣ב וָכָ֑סֶף וַ֠יִּהְיוּ מַעֲלִ֨ים
ones-presenting and-they-were and-silver gold and-objects-of and-ladles

עֹל֤וֹת בְּבֵית־ יְהוָה֙ תָּמִ֔יד כֹּ֖ל יְמֵ֥י יְהוֹיָדָֽע׃
Jehoiada days-of all-of continually Yahweh in-temple-of burnt-offerings

וַיִּזְקַ֧ן יְהוֹיָדָ֛ע וַיִּשְׂבַּ֥ע יָמִ֖ים וַיָּמֹ֑ת בֶּן־ מֵאָ֧ה
hundred son-of and-he-died days and-he-was-full Jehoiada now-he-was-old (15)

וּשְׁלֹשִׁ֛ים שָׁנָ֖ה בְּמוֹתֽוֹ׃ וַיִּקְבְּרֻ֥הוּ בְעִיר־ דָּוִ֖יד
David in-City-of and-they-buried-him (16) in-death-of-him year and-thirty

עִם־ הַמְּלָכִ֑ים כִּֽי־ עָשָׂ֨ה טוֹבָ֤ה בְּיִשְׂרָאֵל֙ וְעִ֥ם הָאֱלֹהִ֖ים וּבֵיתֽוֹ׃
and-temple-of-him the-God and-for in-Israel good he-did because the-kings with

וְאַחֲרֵי֙ מ֣וֹת יְהוֹיָדָ֔ע בָּ֚אוּ שָׂרֵ֣י יְהוּדָ֔ה
Judah officials-of they-came Jehoiada death-of and-after (17)

וַיִּֽשְׁתַּחֲווּ֙ לַמֶּ֔לֶךְ אָ֛ז שָׁמַ֥ע הַמֶּ֖לֶךְ אֲלֵיהֶֽם׃
to-them the-king he-listened then to-the-king and-they-paid-homage

וַיַּעַזְב֗וּ אֶת־ בֵּ֤ית יְהוָה֙ אֱלֹהֵ֣י אֲבוֹתֵיהֶ֔ם
fathers-of-them God-of Yahweh temple-of *** and-they-abandoned (18)

וַיַּעַבְד֥וּ אֶת־ הָאֲשֵׁרִ֖ים וְאֶת־ הָעֲצַבִּ֑ים וַֽיְהִי־ קֶ֗צֶף
anger and-he-came the-idols and the-Asherah-poles *** and-they-worshiped

עַל־ יְהוּדָה֙ וִיר֣וּשָׁלִַ֔ם בְּאַשְׁמָתָ֖ם זֹֽאת׃ וַיִּשְׁלַ֤ח
althought-he-sent (19) this because-of-guilt-of-them and-Jerusalem Judah upon

amount of money. [12]The king and Jehoiada gave it to the men who carried out the work required for the temple of the LORD. They hired masons and carpenters to restore the LORD's temple, and also workers in iron and bronze to repair the temple.

[13]The men in charge of the work were diligent, and the repairs progressed under them. They rebuilt the temple of God according to its original design and reinforced it. [14]When they had finished, they brought the rest of the money to the king and Jehoiada, and with it were made articles for the LORD's temple: articles for the service and for the burnt offerings, and also ladles and other objects of gold and silver. As long as Jehoiada lived, burnt offerings were presented continually in the temple of the LORD.

[15]Now Jehoiada was old and full of years, and he died at the age of a hundred and thirty. [16]He was buried with the kings in the City of David, because of the good he had done in Israel for God and his temple.

*The Wickedness of Joash*

[17]After the death of Jehoiada, the officials of Judah came and paid homage to the king, and he listened to them. [18]They abandoned the temple of the LORD, the God of their fathers, and worshiped Asherah poles and idols. Because of their guilt, God's anger came upon Judah and Jerusalem. [19]Although the LORD sent prophets

בָּהֶם נְבִאִים לַהֲשִׁיבָם אֶל־ יְהוָה וַיָּעִידוּ בָם
against-them and-they-testified Yahweh to to-bring-back-them prophets to-them

וְלֹא הֶאֱזִינוּ׃ וְרוּחַ אֱלֹהִים לָבְשָׁה אֶת־ זְכַרְיָה
Zechariah *** she-came-upon God then-Spirit-of (20) they-listened but-not

בֶּן־ יְהוֹיָדָע הַכֹּהֵן וַיַּעֲמֹד מֵעַל לָעָם וַיֹּאמֶר
and-he-said to-the-people at-before and-he-stood the-priest Jehoiada son-of

לָהֶם כֹּה ׀ אָמַר הָאֱלֹהִים לָמָה אַתֶּם עֹבְרִים אֶת־ מִצְוֹת יְהוָה
Yahweh commands-of *** ones-disobeying you why? the-God he-says this to-them

וְלֹא תַצְלִיחוּ כִּי־ עֲזַבְתֶּם אֶת־ יְהוָה וַיַּעֲזֹב אֶתְכֶם׃
you then-he-forsook Yahweh *** you-forsook because you-will-prosper now-not

וַיִּקְשְׁרוּ עָלָיו וַיִּרְגְּמֻהוּ אֶבֶן בְּמִצְוַת
by-order-of stone and-they-stoned-him against-him but-they-plotted (21)

הַמֶּלֶךְ בַּחֲצַר בֵּית יְהוָה׃ וְלֹא־ זָכַר יוֹאָשׁ
Joash he-remembered and-not (22) Yahweh temple-of in-courtyard-of the-king

הַמֶּלֶךְ הַחֶסֶד אֲשֶׁר עָשָׂה יְהוֹיָדָע אָבִיו עִמּוֹ
to-him father-of-him Jehoiada he-showed that the-kindness the-king

וַיַּהֲרֹג אֶת־ בְּנוֹ וּכְמוֹתוֹ אָמַר יֵרֶא יְהוָה
Yahweh may-he-see he-said and-as-to-die-him son-of-him *** but-he-killed

וְיִדְרֹשׁ׃ וַיְהִי ׀ לִתְקוּפַת הַשָּׁנָה עָלָה
he-marched the-year at-turn-of and-he-was (23) and-may-he-call-to-account

עָלָיו חֵיל אֲרָם וַיָּבֹאוּ אֶל־ יְהוּדָה וִירוּשָׁלִַם
and-Jerusalem Judah into and-they-invaded Aram army-of against-him

וַיַּשְׁחִיתוּ אֶת־ כָּל־ שָׂרֵי הָעָם מֵעָם וְכָל־
and-all-of from-people the-people leaders-of all-of *** and-they-killed

שְׁלָלָם שִׁלְּחוּ לְמֶלֶךְ דַּרְמָשֶׂק׃ כִּי בְמִצְעַר אֲנָשִׁים
men with-few-of although (24) Damascus to-king-of they-sent plunder-of-them

בָּאוּ ׀ חֵיל אֲרָם וַיהוָה נָתַן בְּיָדָם חַיִל
army into-hand-of-them he-delivered but-Yahweh Aram army-of they-came

לָרֹב מְאֹד כִּי עָזְבוּ אֶת־ יְהוָה אֱלֹהֵי אֲבוֹתֵיהֶם וְאֶת־
and fathers-of-them God-of Yahweh *** they-forsook because very as-large

יוֹאָשׁ עָשׂוּ שְׁפָטִים׃ וּבְלֶכְתָּם מִמֶּנּוּ כִּי־
then from-him and-when-to-withdraw-them (25) judgments they-executed Joash

עָזְבוּ אֹתוֹ בְּמַחֲלִיִּים° רַבִּים הִתְקַשְּׁרוּ עָלָיו
against-him and-they-conspired severe-ones with-wounds him they-left

עֲבָדָיו בִּדְמֵי בְּנֵי יְהוֹיָדָע הַכֹּהֵן וַיַּהַרְגֻהוּ
and-they-killed-him the-priest Jehoiada sons-of for-bloods-of officials-of-him

עַל־ מִטָּתוֹ וַיָּמֹת וַיִּקְבְּרֻהוּ בְּעִיר דָּוִיד וְלֹא
but-not David in-City-of and-they-buried-him so-he-died bed-of-him in

to the people to bring them back to him, and though they testified against them, they would not listen.
[20]Then the Spirit of God came upon Zechariah son of Jehoiada the priest. He stood before the people and said, "This is what God says: 'Why do you disobey the LORD's commands? You will not prosper. Because you have forsaken the LORD, he has forsaken you.' "
[21]But they plotted against him, and by order of the king they stoned him to death in the courtyard of the LORD's temple. [22]King Joash did not remember the kindness Zechariah's father Jehoiada had shown him but killed his son, who said as he lay dying, "May the LORD see this and call you to account."
[23]At the turn of the year,[z] the army of Aram marched against Joash; it invaded Judah and Jerusalem and killed all the leaders of the people. They sent all the plunder to their king in Damascus. [24]Although the Aramean army had come with only a few men, the LORD delivered into their hands a much larger army. Because Judah had forsaken the LORD, the God of their fathers, judgment was executed on Joash. [25]When the Arameans withdrew, they left Joash severely wounded. His officials conspired against him for murdering the son of Jehoiada the priest, and they killed him in his bed. So he died and was buried in the City of David, but not in the

[z]23 That is, in the spring

°25 ק במחלוים

קָבְרֻהוּ בְּקִבְרוֹת הַמְּלָכִים׃ וְאֵלֶּה הַמִּתְקַשְּׁרִים

the-ones-conspiring and-these (26) the-kings in-tombs-of they-buried-him

עָלָיו זָבָד בֶּן־ שִׁמְעָת הָעַמּוֹנִית וִיהוֹזָבָד בֶּן־

son-of and-Jehozabad the-Ammonite-woman Shimeath son-of Zabad against-him

שִׁמְרִית הַמּוֹאָבִית׃ וּבָנָיו וְרֹב הַמַּשָּׂא

the-prophecy he-was-many and-sons-of-him (27) the-Moabite-woman Shimrith

עָלָיו וִיסוֹד בֵּית הָאֱלֹהִים הִנָּם כְּתוּבִים

ones-being-written see-they! the-God temple-of and-restoration-of about-him

עַל־ מִדְרַשׁ סֵפֶר הַמְּלָכִים וַיִּמְלֹךְ אֲמַצְיָהוּ בְנוֹ

son-of-him Amaziah and-he-became-king the-kings book-of annotation-of in

תַּחְתָּיו׃ בֶּן־ עֶשְׂרִים וְחָמֵשׁ שָׁנָה מָלַךְ אֲמַצְיָהוּ

Amaziah he-became-king year and-five twenty son-of (25:1) in-place-of-him

וְעֶשְׂרִים וָתֵשַׁע שָׁנָה מָלַךְ בִּירוּשָׁלָםִ וְשֵׁם אִמּוֹ

mother-of-him and-name-of in-Jerusalem he-reigned year and-nine and-twenty

יְהוֹעַדָּן מִירוּשָׁלָםִ׃ וַיַּעַשׂ הַיָּשָׁר בְּעֵינֵי יְהוָה רַק לֹא

not but Yahweh in-eyes-of the-right and-he-did (2) from-Jerusalem Jehoaddan

בְּלֵבָב שָׁלֵם׃ וַיְהִי כַּאֲשֶׁר חָזְקָה הַמַּמְלָכָה עָלָיו

under-him the-kingdom she-was-firm just-as and-he-was (3) whole with-heart

וַיַּהֲרֹג אֶת־ עֲבָדָיו הַמַּכִּים אֶת־ הַמֶּלֶךְ

the-king *** the-ones-murdering officials-of-him *** then-he-executed

אָבִיו׃ וְאֶת־ בְּנֵיהֶם לֹא הֵמִית כִּי כַכָּתוּב

as-the-one-being-written but he-killed not sons-of-them yet (4) father-of-him

בַּתּוֹרָה בְּסֵפֶר מֹשֶׁה אֲשֶׁר־ צִוָּה יְהוָה לֵאמֹר לֹא־

not to-say Yahweh he-commanded where Moses in-Book-of in-the-Law

יָמוּתוּ אָבוֹת עַל־ בָּנִים וּבָנִים לֹא־ יָמוּתוּ

they-shall-be-killed not and-children children for fathers they-shall-be-killed

עַל־ אָבוֹת כִּי אִישׁ בְּחֶטְאוֹ יָמוּתוּ׃ וַיִּקְבֹּץ

and-he-called-together (5) they-must-die for-sin-of-him each but fathers for

אֲמַצְיָהוּ אֶת־יְהוּדָה וַיַּעֲמִידֵם לְבֵית־ אָבוֹת לְשָׂרֵי

by-commanders-of fathers by-family-of and-he-assigned-them Judah *** Amaziah

הָאֲלָפִים וּלְשָׂרֵי הַמֵּאוֹת לְכָל־ יְהוּדָה וּבִנְיָמִן

and-Benjamin Judah for-all-of the-hundreds and-by-commanders-of the-thousands

וַיִּפְקְדֵם לְמִבֶּן עֶשְׂרִים שָׁנָה וָמַעְלָה וַיִּמְצָאֵם

and-he-found-them and-upward year twenty to-from-son-of then-he-mustered-them

שְׁלֹשׁ־ מֵאוֹת אֶלֶף בָּחוּר יוֹצֵא צָבָא אֹחֵז

handling-of military serving-of being-ready thousand hundreds three-of

רֹמַח וְצִנָּה׃ וַיִּשְׂכֹּר מִיִּשְׂרָאֵל מֵאָה אֶלֶף גִּבּוֹר חָיִל

fight men-of thousand hundred from-Israel and-he-hired (6) and-shield spear

tombs of the kings.
26Those who conspired
against him were Zabad,[a] son
of Shimeath an Ammonite
woman, and Jehozabad, son of
Shimrith[b] a Moabite woman.
27The account of his sons, the
many prophecies about him,
and the record of the restoration of the temple of God are
written in the annotations on
the book of the kings. And
Amaziah his son succeeded
him as king.

*Amaziah King of Judah*

25 Amaziah was twenty-
five years old when he
became king, and he reigned
in Jerusalem twenty-nine
years. His mother's name was
Jehoaddin[c]; she was from
Jerusalem. 2He did what was
right in the eyes of the LORD,
but not wholeheartedly. 3After
the kingdom was firmly in his
control, he executed the
officials who had murdered
his father the king. 4Yet he did
not put their sons to death, but
acted in accordance with what
is written in the Law, in the
Book of Moses, where the
LORD commanded: "Fathers
shall not be put to death for
their children, nor children
put to death for their fathers;
each is to die for his own
sins."[d]
5Amaziah called the people
of Judah together and as-
signed them according to their
families to commanders of
thousands and commanders
of hundreds for all Judah and
Benjamin. He then mustered
those twenty years old or more
and found that there were
three hundred thousand men
ready for military service, able
to handle the spear and shield.
6He also hired a hundred thousand fighting men from Israel

[a]26 A variant of *Jozabad*
[b]26 A variant of *Shomer*
[c]1 Hebrew *Jehoaddan*, a variant of *Jehoaddin*
[d]4 Deut. 24:16

°27 ק ירב

בְּמֵאָה כִּכַּר־כָּסֶף׃ וְאִישׁ הָאֱלֹהִים בָּא אֵלָיו לֵאמֹר
to-say to-him he-came the-God but-man-of (7) silver talent-of with-hundred

הַמֶּלֶךְ אַל־יָבֹא עִמְּךָ צְבָא יִשְׂרָאֵל כִּי אֵין יְהוָה עִם־
with Yahweh not for Israel troop-of with-you he-must-march not the-king

יִשְׂרָאֵל כֹּל בְּנֵי אֶפְרָיִם׃ כִּי אִם־בֹּא אַתָּה עֲשֵׂה
fight! you go! if even (8) Ephraim people-of any-of Israel

חֲזַק לַמִּלְחָמָה יַכְשִׁילְךָ הָאֱלֹהִים לִפְנֵי
before the-God he-will-overthrow-you in-the-battle be-courageous!

אוֹיֵב כִּי יֶשׁ־כֹּחַ בֵּאלֹהִים לַעְזוֹר וּלְהַכְשִׁיל׃
or-to-overthrow to-help to-God power there-is for one-being-enemy

וַיֹּאמֶר אֲמַצְיָהוּ לְאִישׁ הָאֱלֹהִים וּמַה־לַּעֲשׂוֹת לִמְאַת
with-hundred-of to-do but-what? the-God to-man-of Amaziah and-he-asked (9)

הַכִּכָּר אֲשֶׁר נָתַתִּי לִגְדוּד יִשְׂרָאֵל וַיֹּאמֶר אִישׁ הָאֱלֹהִים
the-God man-of and-he-replied Israel for-troop-of I-paid that the-talent

יֵשׁ לַיהוָה לָתֶת לְךָ הַרְבֵּה מִזֶּה׃ וַיַּבְדִּילֵם
so-he-dismissed-them (10) than-that to-be-more to-you to-give to-Yahweh there-is

אֲמַצְיָהוּ לְהַגְּדוּד אֲשֶׁר־בָּא אֵלָיו מֵאֶפְרַיִם לָלֶכֶת לִמְקוֹמָם
to-home-of-them to-go from-Ephraim to-him he-came who to-the-troop Amaziah

וַיִּחַר אַפָּם מְאֹד בִּיהוּדָה וַיָּשׁוּבוּ לִמְקוֹמָם
for-home-of-them and-they-left with-Judah very rage-of-them and-he-was-furious

בָּחֳרִי־אָף׃ וַאֲמַצְיָהוּ הִתְחַזַּק וַיִּנְהַג אֶת־
*** and-he-led he-marshaled-strength then-Amaziah (11) rage in-heat-of

עַמּוֹ וַיֵּלֶךְ גֵּיא הַמֶּלַח וַיַּךְ אֶת־בְּנֵי־שֵׂעִיר
Seir men-of *** and-he-killed the-Salt Valley-of and-he-went army-of-him

עֲשֶׂרֶת אֲלָפִים׃ וַעֲשֶׂרֶת אֲלָפִים חַיִּים שָׁבוּ בְּנֵי
men-of they-captured ones-alive thousands and-ten-of (12) thousands ten-of

יְהוּדָה וַיְבִיאוּם לְרֹאשׁ הַסֶּלַע וַיַּשְׁלִיכוּם מֵרֹאשׁ־
from-top-of and-they-threw-them the-cliff to-top-of and-they-took-them Judah

הַסֶּלַע וְכֻלָּם נִבְקָעוּ׃ וּבְנֵי הַגְּדוּד
the-troop and-men-of (13) they-were-dashed-to-pieces so-all-of-them the-cliff

אֲשֶׁר הֵשִׁיב אֲמַצְיָהוּ מִלֶּכֶת עִמּוֹ לַמִּלְחָמָה וַיִּפְשְׁטוּ
and-they-raided in-the-war with-him from-to-take-part Amaziah he-sent-back that

בְּעָרֵי יְהוּדָה מִשֹּׁמְרוֹן וְעַד־בֵּית חוֹרוֹן וַיַּכּוּ מֵהֶם
from-them and-they-killed Horon Beth even-to from-Samaria Judah in-towns-of

שְׁלֹשֶׁת אֲלָפִים וַיָּבֹזּוּ בִּזָּה רַבָּה׃ וַיְהִי אַחֲרֵי
after and-he-was (14) great plunder and-they-carried-off thousands three-of

בוֹא אֲמַצְיָהוּ מֵהַכּוֹת אֶת־אֲדוֹמִים וַיָּבֵא אֶת־
*** then-he-brought-back Edomites *** from-to-slaughter Amaziah to-return

for a hundred talents[e] of silver.
7But a man of God came to
him and said, "O king, these
troops from Israel must not
march with you, for the LORD
is not with Israel—not with
any of the people of Ephraim.
8Even if you go and fight
courageously in battle, God
will overthrow you before the
enemy, for God has the power
to help or to overthrow."
9Amaziah asked the man of
God, "But what about the
hundred talents I paid for
these Israelite troops?"
The man of God replied,
"The LORD can give you much
more than that."
10So Amaziah dismissed the
troops who had come to him
from Ephraim and sent them
home. They were furious with
Judah and left for home in a
great rage.
11Amaziah then marshaled
his strength and led his army
to the Valley of Salt, where he
killed ten thousand men of
Seir. 12The army of Judah also
captured ten thousand men
alive, took them to the top of a
cliff and threw them down so
that all were dashed to pieces.
13Meanwhile the troops that
Amaziah had sent back and
had not allowed to take part in
the war raided Judean towns
from Samaria to Beth Horon.
They killed three thousand
people and carried off great
quantities of plunder.
14When Amaziah returned
from slaughtering the Edomites, he brought back the gods

[e]6 That is, about 3 3/4 tons (about 3.4 metric tons); also in verse 9

אֱלֹהֵי֙　בְּנֵ֣י　שֵׂעִ֔יר　וַיַּֽעֲמִידֵ֥ם　ל֖וֹ　לֵֽאלֹהִ֑ים　וְלִפְנֵיהֶ֥ם
gods-of　people-of　Seir　and-he-set-up-them　for-him　as-gods　and-before-them

יִֽשְׁתַּחֲוֶ֖ה　וְלָהֶ֥ם　יְקַטֵּֽר׃　(15)　וַיִּֽחַר־　אַ֥ף　יְהוָ֖ה
he-bowed　and-to-them　he-burned-sacrifice　(15)　and-he-burned　anger-of　Yahweh

בַּֽאֲמַצְיָ֑הוּ　וַיִּשְׁלַ֤ח　אֵלָיו֙　נָבִ֔יא　וַיֹּ֣אמֶר　ל֔וֹ　לָ֥מָה
against-Amaziah　and-he-sent　to-him　prophet　and-he-said　to-him　why?

דָרַ֨שְׁתָּ֙　אֶת־　אֱלֹהֵ֣י　הָעָ֔ם　אֲשֶׁ֛ר　לֹא־　הִצִּ֥ילוּ　אֶת־
you-consult　***　gods-of　the-people　which　not　they-could-save　***

עַמָּ֖ם　מִיָּדֶֽךָ׃　(16)　וַיְהִ֣י ׀　בְּדַבְּר֣וֹ　אֵלָ֗יו
people-of-them　from-hand-of-you　(16)　and-he-was　while-to-speak-him　to-him

וַיֹּ֤אמֶר　ל֙וֹ　הַלְיוֹעֵ֤ץ　לַמֶּ֨לֶךְ֙　נְתַנּ֔וּךָ　חֲדַל־
then-he-said　to-him　as-one-advising?　to-the-king　we-appointed-you　stop!

לְךָ֖　לָ֣מָּה　יַכּ֑וּךָ　וַיֶּחְדַּ֣ל　הַנָּבִ֗יא　וַיֹּ֨אמֶר֙
for-you　why?　they-should-strike-down-you　so-he-stopped　the-prophet　but-he-said

יָדַ֗עְתִּי　כִּֽי־　יָעַ֤ץ　אֱלֹהִים֙　לְהַשְׁחִיתֶ֔ךָ　כִּֽי־　עָשִׂ֣יתָ　זֹּ֔את　וְלֹ֥א
I-know　that　he-determined　God　to-destroy-you　because　you-did　this　and-not

שָׁמַ֖עְתָּ　לַֽעֲצָתִֽי׃　(17)　וַיִּוָּעַ֗ץ　אֲמַצְיָ֙הוּ֙　מֶ֣לֶךְ　יְהוּדָ֔ה
you-listened　to-counsel-of-me　(17)　after-he-consulted　Amaziah　king-of　Judah

וַ֠יִּשְׁלַח　אֶל־　יוֹאָ֨שׁ　בֶּן־　יְהוֹאָחָ֧ז　בֶּן־　יֵה֛וּא　מֶ֥לֶךְ　יִשְׂרָאֵ֖ל　לֵאמֹ֑ר
then-he-sent　to　Joash　son-of　Jehoahaz　son-of　Jehu　king-of　Israel　to-say

לְךָ֥　נִתְרָאֶ֖ה　פָנִֽים׃　(18)　וַיִּשְׁלַ֞ח　יוֹאָ֣שׁ　מֶֽלֶךְ־יִשְׂרָאֵ֗ל　אֶל־אֲמַצְיָ֣הוּ
come!　let-us-meet　faces　(18)　but-he-replied　Joash　king-of　Israel　to　Amaziah

מֶֽלֶךְ־　יְהוּדָ֣ה　לֵאמֹר֒　הַח֜וֹחַ　אֲשֶׁ֣ר　בַּלְּבָנ֗וֹן　שָׁ֠לַח　אֶל־　הָאֶ֤רֶז
king-of　Judah　to-say　the-thistle　that　in-the-Lebanon　he-sent　to　the-cedar

אֲשֶׁ֣ר　בַּלְּבָנוֹן֙　לֵאמֹ֔ר　תְּנָֽה־　אֶת־　בִּתְּךָ֥　לִבְנִ֖י　לְאִשָּׁ֑ה
that　in-the-Lebanon　to-say　give!　***　daughter-of-you　to-son-of-me　as-wife

וַֽתַּעֲבֹ֞ר　חַיַּ֤ת　הַשָּׂדֶה֙　אֲשֶׁ֣ר　בַּלְּבָנ֔וֹן　וַתִּרְמֹ֖ס
then-she-came-along　beast-of　the-field　that　in-the-Lebanon　and-she-trampled

אֶת־　הַחֽוֹחַ׃　(19)　אָמַ֗רְתָּ　הִנֵּ֤ה　הִכִּ֙יתָ֙　אֶת־　אֱד֔וֹם　וּנְשָׂאֲךָ֥
***　the-thistle　(19)　you-say　see!　you-defeated　***　Edom　and-he-lifted-you

לִבְּךָ֖　לְהַכְבִּ֑יד　עַתָּ֛ה　שְׁבָ֥ה　בְּבֵיתְךָ֖　לָ֤מָּה　תִתְגָּרֶה֙　בְּרָעָ֔ה
heart-of-you　to-be-proud　now　stay!　at-home-of-you　why?　you-ask　for-trouble

וְנָ֣פַלְתָּ֔　אַתָּ֖ה　וִיהוּדָ֥ה　עִמָּֽךְ׃　(20)　וְלֹא־　שָׁמַ֣ע　אֲמַצְיָ֔הוּ　כִּ֤י
so-you-fall　you　and-Judah　with-you　(20)　but-not　he-listened　Amaziah　for

מֵהָֽאֱלֹהִים֙　הִ֔יא　לְמַ֖עַן　תִּתָּ֣ם　בְּיָ֑ד　כִּ֣י　דָֽרְשׁ֔וּ　אֵ֖ת
from-the-God　this　so-that　to-give-them　into-hand　because　they-sought　***

אֱלֹהֵ֥י　אֱדֽוֹם׃　(21)　וַיַּ֨עַל　יוֹאָ֤שׁ　מֶֽלֶךְ־יִשְׂרָאֵל֙　וַיִּתְרָא֣וּ　פָנִ֔ים
gods-of　Edom　(21)　so-he-attacked　Joash　king-of　Israel　and-they-met　faces

ק　לכה　17°

of the people of Seir. He set them up as his own gods, bowed down to them and burned sacrifices to them. [15]The anger of the LORD burned against Amaziah, and he sent a prophet to him, who said, "Why do you consult this people's gods, which could not save their own people from your hand?"

[16]While he was still speaking, the king said to him, "Have we appointed you an adviser to the king? Stop! Why be struck down?"

So the prophet stopped but said, "I know that God has determined to destroy you, because you have done this and have not listened to my counsel."

[17]After Amaziah king of Judah consulted his advisers, he sent this challenge to Jehoash[f] son of Jehoahaz, the son of Jehu, king of Israel: "Come, meet me face to face."

[18]But Jehoash king of Israel replied to Amaziah king of Judah: "A thistle in Lebanon sent a message to a cedar in Lebanon, 'Give your daughter to my son in marriage.' Then a wild beast in Lebanon came along and trampled the thistle underfoot. [19]You say to yourself that you have defeated Edom, and now you are arrogant and proud. But stay at home! Why ask for trouble and cause your own downfall and that of Judah also?"

[20]Amaziah, however, would not listen, for God so worked that he might hand them over to Jehoash[f], because they sought the gods of Edom. [21]So Jehoash king of Israel attacked. He and Amaziah king

*f 17 Hebrew Joash, a variant of Jehoash; also in verses 18, 21, 23 and 25*

הוּא וַאֲמַצְיָהוּ מֶלֶךְ־ יְהוּדָה בְּבֵית שֶׁמֶשׁ אֲשֶׁר לִיהוּדָה׃

he / and-Amaziah / king-of / Judah / at-Beth / Shemesh / that / in-Judah

וַיִּנָּגֶף יְהוּדָה לִפְנֵי יִשְׂרָאֵל וַיָּנֻסוּ אִישׁ לְאֹהָלָיו׃

(22) / and-he-was-routed / Judah / before / Israel / and-they-fled / each / to-homes-of-him

וְאֵת אֲמַצְיָהוּ מֶלֶךְ־ יְהוּדָה בֶּן־ יוֹאָשׁ בֶּן־ יְהוֹאָחָז תָּפַשׂ

and (23) / Amaziah / king-of / Judah / son-of / Joash / son-of / Jehoahaz / he-captured

יוֹאָשׁ מֶלֶךְ־ יִשְׂרָאֵל בְּבֵית שֶׁמֶשׁ וַיְבִיאֵהוּ יְרוּשָׁלַם

Joash / king-of / Israel / at-Beth / Shemesh / then-he-brought-him / Jerusalem

וַיִּפְרֹץ בְּחוֹמַת יְרוּשָׁלַם מִשַּׁעַר אֶפְרַיִם עַד־ שַׁעַר

and-he-broke / through-wall-of / Jerusalem / from-Gate-of / Ephraim / to / Gate-of

הַפּוֹנֶה אַרְבַּע מֵאוֹת אַמָּה׃ וְכָל־ הַזָּהָב וְהַכֶּסֶף וְאֵת

the-Corner / four / hundreds / cubit / (24) / and-all-of / the-gold / and-the-silver / and

כָּל־ הַכֵּלִים הַנִּמְצְאִים בְּבֵית־ הָאֱלֹהִים עִם־ עֹבֵד אֱדוֹם

all-of / the-articles / the-ones-being-found / in-temple-of / the-God / with / Obed / Edom

וְאֵת אֹצְרוֹת בֵּית הַמֶּלֶךְ וְאֵת בְּנֵי הַתַּעֲרֻבוֹת וַיָּשָׁב

and / treasuries-of / palace-of / the-king / and / sons-of / the-hostages / and-he-returned

שֹׁמְרוֹן׃ וַיְחִי אֲמַצְיָהוּ בֶן־ יוֹאָשׁ מֶלֶךְ יְהוּדָה אַחֲרֵי מוֹת

Samaria / (25) / and-he-lived / Amaziah / son-of / Joash / king-of / Judah / after / death-of

יוֹאָשׁ בֶּן־ יְהוֹאָחָז מֶלֶךְ יִשְׂרָאֵל חֲמֵשׁ עֶשְׂרֵה שָׁנָה׃ וְיֶתֶר

Joash / son-of / Jehoahaz / king-of / Israel / five-of / ten / year / (26) / and-other-of

דִּבְרֵי אֲמַצְיָהוּ הָרִאשֹׁנִים וְהָאַחֲרוֹנִים הֲלֹא הִנָּם

events-of / Amaziah / the-beginnings / and-the-ends / not? / see-they!

כְּתוּבִים עַל־ סֵפֶר מַלְכֵי־ יְהוּדָה וְיִשְׂרָאֵל׃ וּמֵעֵת אֲשֶׁר־

ones-being-written / in / book-of / kings-of / Judah / and-Israel / (27) / and-from-time / that

סָר אֲמַצְיָהוּ מֵאַחֲרֵי יְהוָה וַיִּקְשְׁרוּ עָלָיו קֶשֶׁר

he-turned / Amaziah / from-after / Yahweh / then-they-conspired / against-him / conspiracy

בִּירוּשָׁלַם וַיָּנָס לָכִישָׁה וַיִּשְׁלְחוּ אַחֲרָיו לָכִישָׁה

in-Jerusalem / and-he-fled / to-Lachish / but-they-sent / after-him / to-Lachish

וַיְמִיתֻהוּ שָׁם׃ וַיִּשָּׂאֻהוּ עַל־ הַסּוּסִים

and-they-killed-him / there / (28) / and-they-brought-back-him / by / the-horses

וַיִּקְבְּרוּ אֹתוֹ עִם־ אֲבֹתָיו בְּעִיר יְהוּדָה׃ וַיִּקְחוּ

and-they-buried / him / with / fathers-of-him / in-City-of / Judah / (26:1) / then-they-took

כָּל־ עַם יְהוּדָה אֶת־ עֻזִּיָּהוּ וְהוּא בֶּן־ שֵׁשׁ עֶשְׂרֵה שָׁנָה

all-of / people-of / Judah / *** / Uzziah / now-he / son-of / six-of / ten / year

וַיַּמְלִיכוּ אֹתוֹ תַּחַת אָבִיו אֲמַצְיָהוּ׃ הוּא בָּנָה

and-they-made-king / him / in-place-of / father-of-him / Amaziah / (2) / he / he-rebuilt

אֶת־ אֵילוֹת וַיְשִׁיבֶהָ לִיהוּדָה אַחֲרֵי שְׁכַב־ הַמֶּלֶךְ עִם־

*** / Elath / and-he-restored-her / to-Judah / after / to-rest / the-king / with

---

of Judah faced each other at Beth Shemesh in Judah. [22]Judah was routed by Israel, and every man fled to his home. [23]Jehoash king of Israel captured Amaziah king of Judah, the son of Joash, the son of Ahaziah,[g] at Beth Shemesh. Then Jehoash brought him to Jerusalem and broke down the wall of Jerusalem from the Ephraim Gate to the Corner Gate—a section about six hundred feet[h] long. [24]He took all the gold and silver and all the articles found in the temple of God that had been in the care of Obed-Edom, together with the palace treasures and the hostages, and returned to Samaria.

[25]Amaziah son of Joash king of Judah lived for fifteen years after the death of Jehoash son of Jehoahaz king of Israel. [26]As for the other events of Amaziah's reign, from beginning to end, are they not written in the book of the kings of Judah and Israel? [27]From the time that Amaziah turned away from following the LORD, they conspired against him in Jerusalem and he fled to Lachish, but they sent men after him to Lachish and killed him there. [28]He was brought back by horse and was buried with his fathers in the City of Judah.

### Uzziah King of Judah

**26** Then all the people of Judah took Uzziah,[i] who was sixteen years old, and made him king in place of his father Amaziah. [2]He was the one who rebuilt Elath and restored it to Judah after Amaziah rested with his fathers.

---

g23 Hebrew *Jehoahaz*, a variant of *Ahaziah*
h23 Hebrew *four hundred cubits* (about 180 meters)
i1 Also called *Azariah*

אֲבֹתָיו׃ בֶּן־ שֵׁשׁ עֶשְׂרֵה שָׁנָה עֻזִּיָּהוּ בְמָלְכוֹ

when-to-become-king-him Uzziah year ten six-of son-of (3) fathers-of-him

וַחֲמִשִּׁים וּשְׁתַּיִם שָׁנָה מָלַךְ בִּירוּשָׁלִָם וְשֵׁם אִמּוֹ

mother-of-him and-name-of in-Jerusalem he-reigned year and-two and-fifty

יְכִילְיָה° מִן־ יְרוּשָׁלִָם׃ וַיַּעַשׂ הַיָּשָׁר בְּעֵינֵי יְהוָה כְּכֹל

as-all Yahweh in-eyes-of the-right and-he-did (4) Jerusalem from Jecoliah

אֲשֶׁר־עָשָׂה אֲמַצְיָהוּ אָבִיו׃ וַיְהִי לִדְרֹשׁ אֱלֹהִים בִּימֵי

during-days-of God to-seek and-he-was (5) father-of-him Amaziah he-did that

זְכַרְיָהוּ הַמֵּבִין בִּרְאֹת* הָאֱלֹהִים וּבִימֵי

and-in-days-of the-God *to-have-vision the-one-instructing Zechariah

דָּרְשׁוֹ אֶת־ יְהוָה הִצְלִיחוֹ הָאֱלֹהִים׃ וַיֵּצֵא

and-he-went-out (6) the-God he-gave-success-him Yahweh *** to-seek-him

וַיִּלָּחֶם בַּפְּלִשְׁתִּים וַיִּפְרֹץ אֶת־ חוֹמַת גַּת וְאֵת

and Gath wall-of *** and-he-broke-down against-the-Philistines and-he-warred

חוֹמַת יַבְנֵה וְאֵת חוֹמַת אַשְׁדּוֹד וַיִּבְנֶה עָרִים בְּאַשְׁדּוֹד

near-Ashdod towns then-he-rebuilt Ashdod wall-of and Jabneh wall-of

וּבַפְּלִשְׁתִּים׃ וַיַּעְזְרֵהוּ הָאֱלֹהִים עַל־ פְּלִשְׁתִּים

Philistines against the-God and-he-helped-him (7) and-among-the-Philistines

וְעַל־ הָעַרְבִיים° הַיֹּשְׁבִים בְּגוּר־ בָּעַל וְהַמְּעוּנִים׃

and-the-Meunites Baal in-Gur the-ones-living the-Arabs and-against

וַיִּתְּנוּ הָעַמּוֹנִים מִנְחָה לְעֻזִּיָּהוּ וַיֵּלֶךְ שְׁמוֹ

name-of-him and-he-spread to-Uzziah tribute the-Ammonites and-they-brought (8)

עַד־ לְבוֹא מִצְרַיִם כִּי הֶחֱזִיק עַד־ לְמָעְלָה׃

to-upward to he-became-powerful because Egypt to-enter as-far-as

וַיִּבֶן עֻזִּיָּהוּ מִגְדָּלִים בִּירוּשָׁלִַם עַל־ שַׁעַר הַפִּנָּה וְעַל־

and-at the-Corner Gate-of at in-Jerusalem towers Uzziah and-he-built (9)

שַׁעַר הַגַּיְא וְעַל־ הַמִּקְצוֹעַ וַיְחַזְּקֵם׃

and-he-fortified-them the-angle-of-the-wall and-at the-Valley Gate-of

וַיִּבֶן מִגְדָּלִים בַּמִּדְבָּר וַיַּחְצֹב בֹּרוֹת רַבִּים כִּי מִקְנֶה־

livestock because many cisterns and-he-dug in-the-desert towers and-he-built (10)

רַּב† הָיָה לוֹ וּבַשְּׁפֵלָה וּבַמִּישׁוֹר אִכָּרִים

field-workers and-in-the-plain and-in-the-foothill to-him he-was much

וְכֹרְמִים בֶּהָרִים וּבַכַּרְמֶל כִּי־ אֹהֵב

loving for and-in-the-fertile-land in-the-hills and-ones-working-vineyards

אֲדָמָה הָיָה׃ וַיְהִי לְעֻזִּיָּהוּ חַיִל° עֹשֵׂה מִלְחָמָה

war being-trained-of army to-Uzziah and-he-was (11) he-was soil

יוֹצְאֵי צָבָא לִגְדוּד בְּמִסְפַּר פְּקֻדָּתָם

mustering-of-them by-number-of by-division battle ones-going-out-of

[3]Uzziah was sixteen years
old when he became king, and
he reigned in Jerusalem fifty-
two years. His mother's name
was Jecoliah; she was from
Jerusalem. [4]He did what was
right in the eyes of the LORD,
just as his father Amaziah had
done. [5]He sought God during
the days of Zechariah, who instructed him in the fear[j] of
God. As long as he sought the
LORD, God gave him success.
[6]He went to war against the
Philistines and broke down
the walls of Gath, Jabneh and
Ashdod. He then rebuilt
towns near Ashdod and
elsewhere among the Philistines. [7]God helped him against
the Philistines and against the
Arabs who lived in Gur Baal
and against the Meunites.
[8]The Ammonites brought tribute to Uzziah, and his fame
spread as far as the border of
Egypt, because he had become
very powerful.
[9]Uzziah built towers in
Jerusalem at the Corner Gate,
at the Valley Gate and at the
angle of the wall, and he fortified them. [10]He also built
towers in the desert and dug
many cisterns, because he had
much livestock in the foothills
and in the plain. He had
people working his fields and
vineyards in the hills and in
the fertile lands, for he loved
the soil.
[11]Uzziah had a well-trained
army, ready to go out by divisions according to their numbers as mustered by Jeiel the

j5 Many Hebrew manuscripts, Septuagint and Syriac; other Hebrew manuscripts *vision*

*5 Many mss have ( בִּירְאַת ), *to-fears;* the versions read ( בְּיִרְאַת ), *in-fear-of*

†10 Most mss have no *dagesh* in the *resh* ( רַב ).

°3 ק יכליה

°7 ק הערבים

בְּיַד יְעוּאֵל הַסּוֹפֵר וּמַעֲשֵׂיָהוּ הַשּׁוֹטֵר עַל יַד־
hand-of under the-officer and-Maaseiah the-secretary Jeiel by-hand-of

חֲנַנְיָהוּ מִשָּׂרֵי הַמֶּלֶךְ׃ (12) כֹּל מִסְפַּר רָאשֵׁי
leaders-of number-of total-of (12) the-king from-officials-of Hananiah

הָאָבוֹת לְגִבּוֹרֵי חָיִל אַלְפַּיִם וְשֵׁשׁ מֵאוֹת׃
hundreds and-six-of two-thousands fight over-men-of the-fathers

(13) וְעַל־ יָדָם חֵיל צָבָא שְׁלֹשׁ מֵאוֹת אֶלֶף
thousand hundreds three-of battle army-of hand-of-them and-under (13)

וְשִׁבְעַת אֲלָפִים וַחֲמֵשׁ מֵאוֹת עוֹשֵׂי מִלְחָמָה
war ones-being-trained-of hundreds and-five-of thousands and-seven-of

בְּכֹחַ חָיִל לַעְזֹר לַמֶּלֶךְ עַל־ הָאוֹיֵב׃
the-one-being-enemy against to-the-king to-support force with-power-of

(14) וַיָּכֶן לָהֶם עֻזִּיָּהוּ לְכָל־ הַצָּבָא מָגִנִּים וּרְמָחִים
and-spears shields the-army for-entire-of Uzziah to-them and-he-provided (14)

וְכוֹבָעִים וְשִׁרְיֹנוֹת וּקְשָׁתוֹת וּלְאַבְנֵי קְלָעִים׃ (15) וַיַּעַשׂ ׀
and-he-made (15) slings and-for-stones-of and-bows and-coats-of-armor and-helmets

בִּירוּשָׁלַםִ חִשְּׁבֹנוֹת מַחֲשֶׁבֶת חוֹשֵׁב לִהְיוֹת עַל־ הַמִּגְדָּלִים
the-towers on to-use one-being-skillful design-of machines in-Jerusalem

וְעַל־ הַפִּנּוֹת לִירוֹא בַּחִצִּים וּבָאֲבָנִים גְּדֹלוֹת
large-ones and-with-the-stones with-the-arrows to-shoot the-corners and-on

וַיֵּצֵא שְׁמוֹ עַד־ לְמֵרָחוֹק כִּי־ הִפְלִיא לְהֵעָזֵר
to-be-helped he-was-great for to-at-distance to name-of-him and-he-spread

עַד כִּי־ חָזָק׃ (16) וּכְחֶזְקָתוֹ
but-after-to-become-powerful-him (16) he-became-powerful when until

גָּבַהּ לִבּוֹ עַד־ לְהַשְׁחִית וַיִּמְעַל בַּיהוָה
to-Yahweh and-he-was-unfaithful to-fall-down until heart-of-him he-lifted

אֱלֹהָיו וַיָּבֹא אֶל־ הֵיכַל יְהוָה לְהַקְטִיר עַל־ מִזְבַּח
altar-of on to-burn-incense Yahweh temple-of into and-he-entered God-of-him

הַקְּטֹרֶת׃ (17) וַיָּבֹא אַחֲרָיו עֲזַרְיָהוּ הַכֹּהֵן וְעִמּוֹ
and-with-him the-priest Azariah after-him and-he-followed (17) the-incense

כֹּהֲנִים ׀ לַיהוָה שְׁמוֹנִים בְּנֵי־ חָיִל׃ (18) וַיַּעַמְדוּ עַל־
against and-they-confronted (18) courage men-of eighty of-Yahweh priests

עֻזִּיָּהוּ הַמֶּלֶךְ וַיֹּאמְרוּ לוֹ לֹא־ לְךָ עֻזִּיָּהוּ לְהַקְטִיר
to-burn-incense Uzziah for-you not to-him and-they-said the-king Uzziah

לַיהוָה כִּי לַכֹּהֲנִים בְּנֵי־ אַהֲרֹן הַמְקֻדָּשִׁים
the-ones-being-consecrated Aaron descendants-of for-the-priests but to-Yahweh

לְהַקְטִיר צֵא מִן־ הַמִּקְדָּשׁ כִּי מָעַלְתָּ וְלֹא־
and-not you-were-unfaithful for the-sanctuary from leave! to-burn-incense

secretary and Maaseiah the officer under the direction of Hananiah, one of the royal officials. [12]The total number of family leaders over the fighting men was 2,600. [13]Under their command was an army of 307,500 men trained for war, a powerful force to support the king against his enemies. [14]Uzziah provided shields, spears, helmets, coats of armor, bows and slingstones for the entire army. [15]In Jerusalem he made machines designed by skillful men for use on the towers and on the corner defenses to shoot arrows and hurl large stones. His fame spread far and wide, for he was greatly helped until he became powerful.

[16]But after Uzziah became powerful, his pride led to his downfall. He was unfaithful to the LORD his God, and entered the temple of the LORD to burn incense on the altar of incense. [17]Azariah the priest with eighty other courageous priests of the LORD followed him in. [18]They confronted him and said, "It is not right for you, Uzziah, to burn incense to the LORD. That is for the priests, the descendants of Aaron, who have been consecrated to burn incense. Leave the sanctuary, for you have been unfaithful; and you will

°11 ק יעיאל

לְךָ לְכָבוֹד מֵיְהוָה אֱלֹהִים׃ וַיִּזְעַף עֻזִּיָּהוּ
Uzziah and-he-became-angry (19) God by-Yahweh for-honor to-you

וּבְיָדוֹ מִקְטֶרֶת לְהַקְטִיר וּבְזַעְפּוֹ עִם־ הַכֹּהֲנִים
the-priests at and-while-to-rage-him to-burn-incense censer and-in-hand-of-him

וְהַצָּרַעַת זָרְחָה בְמִצְחוֹ לִפְנֵי הַכֹּהֲנִים
the-priests in-presences-of on-forehead-of-him she-broke-out then-the-leprosy

בְּבֵית יְהוָה מֵעַל לְמִזְבַּח הַקְּטֹרֶת׃ וַיִּפֶן
when-he-looked (20) the-incense to-altar-of at-before Yahweh in-temple-of

אֵלָיו עֲזַרְיָהוּ כֹהֵן הָרֹאשׁ וְכָל־ הַכֹּהֲנִים וְהִנֵּה־ הוּא
he then-see! the-priests and-all-of the-chief priest Azariah at-him

מְצֹרָע בְּמִצְחוֹ וַיַּבְהִלוּהוּ מִשָּׁם וְגַם־
and-indeed from-there so-they-hurried-him on-forehead-of-him being-leprous

הוּא נִדְחַף לָצֵאת כִּי נִגְּעוֹ יְהוָה׃ וַיְהִי
and-he-was (21) Yahweh he-afflicted-him because to-leave he-was-eager he

עֻזִּיָּהוּ הַמֶּלֶךְ מְצֹרָע ׀ עַד־ יוֹם מוֹתוֹ וַיֵּשֶׁב
and-he-lived death-of-him day-of until being-leprous the-king Uzziah

בֵּית הַחָפְשׁוּת מְצֹרָע כִּי נִגְזַר מִבֵּית
from-temple-of he-was-excluded indeed being-leprous the-separate house-of

יְהוָה וְיוֹתָם בְּנוֹ עַל־ בֵּית הַמֶּלֶךְ שׁוֹפֵט אֶת־ עַם
people-of *** governing the-king palace-of over son-of-him and-Jotham Yahweh

הָאָרֶץ׃ וְיֶתֶר דִּבְרֵי עֻזִּיָּהוּ הָרִאשֹׁנִים וְהָאֲחֲרֹנִים*
and-the-ends the-beginnings Uzziah events-of and-other-of (22) the-land

כָּתַב יְשַׁעְיָהוּ בֶן־ אָמוֹץ הַנָּבִיא׃ וַיִּשְׁכַּב עֻזִּיָּהוּ עִם־
with Uzziah and-he-rested (23) the-prophet Amoz son-of Isaiah he-recorded

אֲבֹתָיו וַיִּקְבְּרוּ אֹתוֹ עִם־ אֲבֹתָיו בִּשְׂדֵה הַקְּבוּרָה
the-burial in-field-of fathers-of-him with him and-they-buried fathers-of-him

אֲשֶׁר לַמְּלָכִים כִּי אָמְרוּ מְצוֹרָע הוּא וַיִּמְלֹךְ יוֹתָם
Jotham and-he-became-king he having-leprosy they-said for to-the-kings that

בְּנוֹ תַּחְתָּיו׃ בֶּן־ עֶשְׂרִים וְחָמֵשׁ שָׁנָה יוֹתָם
Jotham year and-five twenty son-of (27:1) in-place-of-him son-of-him

בְּמָלְכוֹ וְשֵׁשׁ־ עֶשְׂרֵה שָׁנָה מָלַךְ בִּירוּשָׁלָםִ
in-Jerusalem he-reigned year ten and-six-of when-to-become-king-him

וְשֵׁם אִמּוֹ יְרוּשָׁה בַּת־ צָדוֹק׃ וַיַּעַשׂ הַיָּשָׁר
the-right and-he-did (2) Zadok daughter-of Jerusha mother-of-him and-name-of

בְּעֵינֵי יְהוָה כְּכֹל אֲשֶׁר־ עָשָׂה עֻזִּיָּהוּ אָבִיו רַק לֹא־ בָא
he-entered not but father-of-him Uzziah he-did that as-all Yahweh in-eyes-of

אֶל־ הֵיכַל יְהוָה וְעוֹד הָעָם מַשְׁחִיתִים׃ הוּא
he (3) ones-being-corrupt the-people but-still Yahweh temple-of into

not be honored by the LORD God."
[19]Uzziah, who had a censer in his hand ready to burn incense, became angry. While he was raging at the priests in their presence before the incense altar in the LORD's temple, leprosy[k] broke out on his forehead. [20]When Azariah the chief priest and all the other priests looked at him, they saw that he had leprosy on his forehead, so they hurried him out. Indeed, he himself was eager to leave, because the LORD had afflicted him.
[21]King Uzziah had leprosy until the day he died. He lived in a separate house[l] —leprous, and excluded from the temple of the LORD. Jotham his son had charge of the palace and governed the people of the land.
[22]The other events of Uzziah's reign, from beginning to end, are recorded by the prophet Isaiah son of Amoz. [23]Uzziah rested with his fathers and was buried near them in a field for burial that belonged to the kings, for people said, "He had leprosy." And Jotham his son succeeded him as king.

*Jotham King of Judah*

27 Jotham was twenty-five years old when he became king, and he reigned in Jerusalem sixteen years. His mother's name was Jerusha daughter of Zadok. [2]He did what was right in the eyes of the LORD, just as his father Uzziah had done, but unlike him he did not enter the temple of the LORD. The people, however, continued their corrupt

[k]19 The Hebrew word was used for various diseases affecting the skin—not necessarily leprosy; also in verses 20, 21 and 23.
[l]21 Or *in a house where he was relieved of responsibilities*

*22 Most mss have *pathah* under the *aleph* ( וְהָאַחֲ' ).

°21 ק החפשית

בָּנָה אֶת־ שַׁעַר בֵּית־ יְהוָה הָעֶלְיוֹן וּבְחוֹמַת הָעֹפֶל
the-Ophel and-on-wall-of the-Upper Yahweh temple-of Gate-of *** he-rebuilt

בָּנָה לָרֹב׃ וְעָרִים בָּנָה בְּהַר־ יְהוּדָה וּבֶחֳרָשִׁים
and-in-the-woods Judah in-hill-of he-built and-towns (4) to-extent he-worked

בָּנָה בִּירָנִיּוֹת וּמִגְדָּלִים׃ וְהוּא נִלְחַם עִם־ מֶלֶךְ בְּנֵי־ עַמּוֹן
Ammon sons-of king-of on he-made-war and-he (5) and-towers forts he-built

וַיֶּחֱזַק עֲלֵיהֶם וַיִּתְּנוּ־ לוֹ בְנֵי־ עַמּוֹן בַּשָּׁנָה
in-the-year Ammon sons-of to-him and-they-paid against-them and-he-conquered

הַהִיא מֵאָה כִּכַּר־ כֶּסֶף וַעֲשֶׂרֶת אֲלָפִים כֹּרִים חִטִּים
wheats cors thousands and-ten-of silver talent-of hundred the-that

וּשְׂעוֹרִים עֲשֶׂרֶת אֲלָפִים זֹאת הֵשִׁיבוּ לוֹ בְּנֵי עַמּוֹן
Ammon sons-of to-him they-brought same thousands ten-of and-barleys

וּבַשָּׁנָה הַשֵּׁנִית וְהַשְּׁלִישִׁית׃ וַיִּתְחַזֵּק יוֹתָם
Jotham and-he-grew-powerful (6) and-the-third the-second also-in-the-year

כִּי הֵכִין דְּרָכָיו לִפְנֵי יְהוָה אֱלֹהָיו׃
God-of-him Yahweh before ways-of-him he-made-steadfast because

וְיֶתֶר דִּבְרֵי יוֹתָם וְכָל־ מִלְחֲמֹתָיו וּדְרָכָיו
and-ways-of-him wars-of-him and-all-of Jotham events-of and-other-of (7)

הִנָּם כְּתוּבִים עַל־ סֵפֶר מַלְכֵי־ יִשְׂרָאֵל וִיהוּדָה׃ בֶּן־
son-of (8) and-Judah Israel kings-of book-of in ones-being-written see-they!

עֶשְׂרִים וְחָמֵשׁ שָׁנָה הָיָה בְמָלְכוֹ וְשֵׁשׁ־ עֶשְׂרֵה שָׁנָה
year ten and-six-of when-to-become-king-him he-was year and-five twenty

מָלַךְ בִּירוּשָׁלִָם׃ וַיִּשְׁכַּב יוֹתָם עִם־ אֲבֹתָיו
fathers-of-him with Jotham and-he-rested (9) in-Jerusalem he-reigned

וַיִּקְבְּרוּ אֹתוֹ בְּעִיר דָּוִיד וַיִּמְלֹךְ אָחָז בְּנוֹ
son-of-him Ahaz and-he-became-king David in-City-of him and-they-buried

תַּחְתָּיו׃ בֶּן־ עֶשְׂרִים שָׁנָה אָחָז בְּמָלְכוֹ
when-to-become-king-him Ahaz year twenty son-of (28:1) in-place-of-him

וְשֵׁשׁ־ עֶשְׂרֵה שָׁנָה מָלַךְ בִּירוּשָׁלִָם וְלֹא־ עָשָׂה הַיָּשָׁר
the-right he-did but-not in-Jerusalem he-reigned year ten and-six-of

בְּעֵינֵי יְהוָה כְּדָוִיד אָבִיו׃ וַיֵּלֶךְ בְּדַרְכֵי
in-ways-of and-he-walked (2) father-of-him like-David Yahweh in-eyes-of

מַלְכֵי יִשְׂרָאֵל וְגַם מַסֵּכוֹת עָשָׂה לַבְּעָלִים׃ וְהוּא
and-he (3) for-the-Baals he-made cast-idols and-also Israel kings-of

הִקְטִיר בְּגֵיא בֶן־ הִנֹּם וַיַּבְעֵר אֶת־ בָּנָיו
sons-of-him *** and-he-sacrificed Hinnom Ben in-Valley-of he-burned-sacrifice

בָּאֵשׁ כְּתֹעֲבוֹת הַגּוֹיִם אֲשֶׁר הֹרִישׁ יְהוָה
Yahweh he-drove-out that the-nations as-detestable-ways-of in-the-fire

practices. [3]Jotham rebuilt the
Upper Gate of the temple of
the LORD and did extensive
work on the wall at the hill of
Ophel. [4]He built towns in the
Judean hills and forts and towers in the wooded areas.
[5]Jotham made war on the
king of the Ammonites and
conquered them. That year the
Ammonites paid him a hun-
dred talents[m] of silver, ten
thousand cors[n] of wheat and
ten thousand cors of barley.
The Ammonites brought him
the same amount also in the
second and third years.
[6]Jotham grew powerful because he walked steadfastly
before the LORD his God.
[7]The other events in Jotham's reign, including all his
wars and the other things he
did, are written in the book of
the kings of Israel and Judah.
[8]He was twenty-five years old
when he became king, and he
reigned in Jerusalem sixteen
years. [9]Jotham rested with his
fathers and was buried in the
City of David. And Ahaz his
son succeeded him as king.

*Ahaz King of Judah*

28 Ahaz was twenty years
old when he became
king, and he reigned in
Jerusalem sixteen years. Unlike David his father, he did
not do what was right in the
eyes of the LORD. [2]He walked
in the ways of the kings of Israel and also made cast idols
for worshiping the Baals. [3]He
burned sacrifices in the Valley
of Ben Hinnom and sacrificed
his sons in the fire, following
the detestable ways of the nations the LORD had driven out

[m]5 That is, about 3 3/4 tons (about 3.4 metric tons)
[n]5 That is, probably about 62,000 bushels (about 2,200 kiloliters)

מִפְּנֵי בְּנֵי יִשְׂרָאֵל׃ וַיְזַבֵּחַ וַיְקַטֵּר

and-he-burned-incense and-he-sacrificed (4) Israel sons-of from-before

בַּבָּמוֹת וְעַל־ הַגְּבָעוֹת וְתַחַת כָּל־ עֵץ רַעֲנָן׃

spreading tree-of every-of and-under the-hilltops and-on at-the-high-places

וַיִּתְּנֵהוּ יְהוָה אֱלֹהָיו בְּיַד מֶלֶךְ אֲרָם

Aram king-of into-hand-of God-of-him Yahweh so-he-gave-him (5)

וַיַּכּוּ־ בוֹ וַיִּשְׁבּוּ מִמֶּנּוּ שִׁבְיָה גְדוֹלָה

many prisoner from-him and-they-took-prisoner against-him and-they-defeated

וַיָּבִיאוּ דַּרְמָשֶׂק וְגַם בְּיַד־ מֶלֶךְ יִשְׂרָאֵל נִתָּן

he-was-given Israel king-of into-hand-of and-also Damascus and-they-brought

וַיַּךְ־ בּוֹ מַכָּה גְדוֹלָה׃ וַיַּהֲרֹג פֶּקַח בֶּן־

son-of Pekah and-he-killed (6) heavy casualty on-him and-he-inflicted

רְמַלְיָהוּ בִּיהוּדָה מֵאָה וְעֶשְׂרִים אֶלֶף בְּיוֹם אֶחָד הַכֹּל בְּנֵי־

soldiers-of the-whole one in-day thousand and-twenty hundred in-Judah Remaliah

חָיִל בְּעָזְבָם אֶת־ יְהוָה אֱלֹהֵי אֲבוֹתָם׃

fathers-of-them God-of Yahweh *** because-to-forsake-them army

וַיַּהֲרֹג זִכְרִי ׀ גִּבּוֹר אֶפְרַיִם אֶת־ מַעֲשֵׂיָהוּ בֶּן־ הַמֶּלֶךְ

the-king son-of Maaseiah *** Ephraim warrior-of Zicri and-he-killed (7)

וְאֶת־ עַזְרִיקָם נְגִיד הַבָּיִת וְאֶת־ אֶלְקָנָה מִשְׁנֵה הַמֶּלֶךְ׃

the-king second-of Elkanah and the-palace officer-of Azrikam and

וַיִּשְׁבּוּ בְנֵי־ יִשְׂרָאֵל מֵאֲחֵיהֶם מָאתַיִם

two-hundreds from-kinsmen-of-them Israel sons-of and-they-took-captive (8)

אֶלֶף נָשִׁים בָּנִים וּבָנוֹת וְגַם־ שָׁלָל רָב בָּזְזוּ מֵהֶם

from-them they-took great plunder and-also and-daughters sons wives thousand

וַיָּבִיאוּ אֶת־ הַשָּׁלָל לְשֹׁמְרוֹן׃ וְשָׁם הָיָה

he-was but-there (9) to-Samaria the-plunder *** and-they-carried-back

נָבִיא לַיהוָה עֹדֵד שְׁמוֹ וַיֵּצֵא לִפְנֵי הַצָּבָא

the-army to-faces-of and-he-went-out name-of-him Oded of-Yahweh prophet

הַבָּא לְשֹׁמְרוֹן וַיֹּאמֶר לָהֶם הִנֵּה בַּחֲמַת

because-of-anger-of see! to-them and-he-said to-Samaria the-one-returning

יְהוָה אֱלֹהֵי־ אֲבוֹתֵיכֶם עַל־ יְהוּדָה נְתָנָם בְּיֶדְכֶם

into-hand-of-you he-gave-them Judah with fathers-of-you God-of Yahweh

וַתַּהַרְגוּ־ בָם בְּזַעַף* עַד לַשָּׁמַיִם הִגִּיעַ׃ וְעַתָּה

and-now (10) he-reaches to-the-heavens to in-rage of-them but-you-slaughtered

בְּנֵי־ יְהוּדָה וִירוּשָׁלִַם אַתֶּם אֹמְרִים לִכְבֹּשׁ לַעֲבָדִים

as-male-slaves to-make intending you and-Jerusalem Judah people-of

וְלִשְׁפָחוֹת לָכֶם הֲלֹא רַק־ אַתֶּם עִמָּכֶם אֲשָׁמוֹת לַיהוָה

against-Yahweh sins with-you you also not? for-you and-as-female-slaves

before the Israelites. [4]He offered sacrifices and burned incense at the high places, on the hilltops and under every spreading tree.

[5]Therefore the LORD his God handed him over to the king of Aram. The Arameans defeated him and took many of his people as prisoners and brought them to Damascus.

He was also given into the hands of the king of Israel, who inflicted heavy casualties on him. [6]In one day Pekah son of Remaliah killed a hundred and twenty thousand soldiers in Judah—because Judah had forsaken the LORD, the God of their fathers. [7]Zicri, an Ephraimite warrior, killed Maaseiah the king's son, Azrikam the officer in charge of the palace, and Elkanah, second to the king. [8]The Israelites took captive from their kinsmen two hundred thousand wives, sons and daughters. They also took a great deal of plunder, which they carried back to Samaria.

[9]But a prophet of the LORD named Oded was there, and he went out to meet the army when it returned to Samaria. He said to them, "Because the LORD, the God of your fathers, was angry with Judah, he gave them into your hand. But you have slaughtered them in a rage that reaches to heaven. [10]And now you intend to make the men and women of Judah and Jerusalem your slaves. But aren't you also guilty of sins against the LORD your God?

*9 Most mss have *dagesh* in the *beth* ( בְּ‎ ).

אֱלֹהֵיכֶם׃ וְעַתָּה שְׁמָעוּנִי וְהָשִׁיבוּ הַשִּׁבְיָה אֲשֶׁר
whom the-prisoner and-send-back! listen-to-me! and-now (11) God-of-you

שְׁבִיתֶם מֵאֲחֵיכֶם כִּי חֲרוֹן אַף־ יְהוָה
Yahweh anger-of fierceness-of for from-countrymen-of-you you-took-prisoner

עֲלֵיכֶם׃ וַיָּקֻמוּ אֲנָשִׁים מֵרָאשֵׁי בְנֵי־ אֶפְרַיִם עֲזַרְיָהוּ
Azariah Ephraim sons-of from-leaders-of men then-they-confronted (12) on-you

בֶן־ יְהוֹחָנָן בֶּרֶכְיָהוּ בֶן־ מְשִׁלֵּמוֹת וִיחִזְקִיָּהוּ בֶּן־ שַׁלֻּם
Shallum son-of and-Jehizkiah Meshillemoth son-of Berekiah Jehohanan son-of

וַעֲמָשָׂא בֶּן־ חַדְלָי עַל־ הַבָּאִים מִן־ הַצָּבָא׃ וַיֹּאמְרוּ
and-they-said (13) the-war from the-ones-arriving to Hadlai son-of and-Amasa

לָהֶם לֹא־ תָבִיאוּ אֶת־ הַשִּׁבְיָה הֵנָּה כִּי לְאַשְׁמַת יְהוָה
Yahweh as-guilt-of or to-here the-prisoner *** you-must-bring not to-them

עָלֵינוּ אַתֶּם אֹמְרִים לְהֹסִיף עַל־ חַטֹּאתֵינוּ וְעַל־ אַשְׁמָתֵנוּ כִּי־ רַבָּה
great for guilts-of-us and-to sins-of-us to to-add intending you to-us

אַשְׁמָה לָנוּ וַחֲרוֹן אָף עַל־ יִשְׂרָאֵל׃ וַיַּעֲזֹב
so-he-gave-up (14) Israel on anger and-fierceness-of of-us guilt

הֶחָלוּץ אֶת־ הַשִּׁבְיָה וְאֶת־ הַבִּזָּה לִפְנֵי
in-presences-of the-plunder and the-prisoner *** the-one-being-soldier

הַשָּׂרִים וְכָל־ הַקָּהָל׃ וַיָּקֻמוּ הָאֲנָשִׁים אֲשֶׁר־
who the-men and-they-rose (15) the-assembly and-all-of the-officials

נִקְּבוּ בְשֵׁמוֹת וַיַּחֲזִיקוּ בַשִּׁבְיָה וְכָל־
and-all-of of-the-prisoner and-they-took by-names they-were-designated

מַעֲרֻמֵּיהֶם הִלְבִּישׁוּ מִן־ הַשָּׁלָל וַיַּלְבִּשׁוּם
and-they-gave-clothes-them the-plunder from they-clothed ones-naked-of-them

וַיַּנְעִלוּם וַיַּאֲכִלוּם וַיַּשְׁקוּם
and-they-gave-drink-them and-they-gave-food-them and-they-gave-sandals-them

וַיְסֻכוּם וַיְנַהֲלוּם בַּחֲמֹרִים לְכָל־ כּוֹשֵׁל
being-weak for-all-of on-donkeys and-they-put-them and-they-gave-balm-them

וַיְבִיאוּם יְרֵחוֹ עִיר־ הַתְּמָרִים אֵצֶל אֲחֵיהֶם
countrymen-of-them to the-Palms City-of Jericho so-they-took-back-them

וַיָּשׁוּבוּ שֹׁמְרוֹן׃ בָּעֵת הַהִיא שָׁלַח הַמֶּלֶךְ אָחָז
Ahaz the-king he-sent the-that at-the-time (16) Samaria and-they-returned

עַל־ מַלְכֵי אַשּׁוּר לַעְזֹר לוֹ׃ וְעוֹד אֲדוֹמִים בָּאוּ
they-came Edomites and-again (17) to-him to-help Assyria kings-of to

וַיַּכּוּ בִיהוּדָה וַיִּשְׁבּוּ־ שֶׁבִי׃
prisoner and-they-carried-away against-Judah and-they-attacked

וּפְלִשְׁתִּים פָּשְׁטוּ בְּעָרֵי הַשְּׁפֵלָה וְהַנֶּגֶב
and-the-Negev the-foothill in-towns-of they-raided while-Philistines (18)

[11]Now listen to me! Send back
your fellow countrymen you
have taken as prisoners, for
the LORD's fierce anger rests on
you."
[12]Then some of the leaders in
Ephraim—Azariah son of
Jehohanan, Berekiah son of
Meshillemoth, Jehizkiah son
of Shallum, and Amasa son of
Hadlai—confronted those
who were arriving from the
war. [13]"You must not bring
those prisoners here," they
said, "or we will be guilty before the LORD. Do you intend
to add to our sin and guilt? For
our guilt is already great, and
his fierce anger rests on Israel."
[14]So the soldiers gave up the
prisoners and plunder in the
presence of the officials and all
the assembly. [15]The men
designated by name took the
prisoners, and from the plunder they clothed all who were
naked. They provided them
with clothes and sandals, food
and drink, and healing balm.
All those who were weak they
put on donkeys. So they took
them back to their fellow
countrymen at Jericho, the
City of Palms, and returned to
Samaria.
[16]At that time King Ahaz
sent to the king[o] of Assyria for
help. [17]The Edomites had
again come and attacked
Judah and carried away prisoners, [18]while the Philistines
had raided towns in the foothills and in the Negev of

[o]*16* One Hebrew manuscript, Septuagint and Vulgate (see also 2 Kings 16:7); most Hebrew manuscripts *kings*

לִֽיהוּדָה וַיִּלְכְּדוּ אֶת־בֵּית־שֶׁמֶשׁ וְאֶת־אַיָּלוֹן וְאֶת־הַגְּדֵרוֹת
the-Gederoth and Aijalon and Shemesh Beth *** and-they-captured of-Judah

וְאֶת־שׂוֹכוֹ וּבְנוֹתֶיהָ וְאֶת־תִּמְנָה וּבְנוֹתֶיהָ וְאֶת־גִּמְזוֹ וְאֶת־
and Gimzo and and-villages-of-her Timnah and and-villages-of-her Soco and

בְּנֹתֶיהָ וַיֵּשְׁבוּ שָׁם׃ כִּי־הִכְנִיעַ יְהוָה אֶת־
*** Yahweh he-humbled for (19) there and-they-occupied villages-of-her

יְהוּדָה בַּעֲבוּר אָחָז מֶלֶךְ־יִשְׂרָאֵל כִּי הִפְרִיעַ בִּיהוּדָה
in-Judah he-promoted-wickedness for Israel king-of Ahaz because-of Judah

וּמָעוֹל מַעַל בַּיהוָה׃ וַיָּבֹא עָלָיו תִּלְּגַת
Tilgath to-him and-he-came (20) to-Yahweh unfaithfulness and-to-be-unfaithful

פִּלְנְאֶסֶר מֶלֶךְ אַשּׁוּר וַיָּצַר לוֹ וְלֹא חֲזָקוֹ׃
he-helped-him and-not to-him but-he-troubled Assyria king-of Pilneser

כִּי־חָלַק אָחָז אֶת־בֵּית יְהוָה וְאֶת־בֵּית הַמֶּלֶךְ
the-king palace-of and Yahweh temple-of *** Ahaz he-took-from for (21)

וְהַשָּׂרִים וַיִּתֵּן לְמֶלֶךְ אַשּׁוּר וְלֹא לְעֶזְרָה לוֹ׃
for-him as-help but-not Assyria to-king-of and-he-presented and-the-princes

וּבְעֵת הָצֵר לוֹ וַיּוֹסֶף לִמְעוֹל
to-be-unfaithful then-he-continued to-him to-trouble and-in-time-of (22)

בַּיהוָה הוּא הַמֶּלֶךְ אָחָז׃ וַיִּזְבַּח לֵאלֹהֵי דַרְמֶשֶׂק
Damascus to-gods-of and-he-sacrificed (23) Ahaz the-king he to-Yahweh

הַמַּכִּים בּוֹ וַיֹּאמֶר כִּי אֱלֹהֵי מַלְכֵי־אֲרָם
Aram kings-of gods-of since for-he-thought against-him the-ones-defeating

הֵם מַעְזְרִים אוֹתָם לָהֶם אֲזַבֵּחַ וְיַעְזְרוּנִי
so-they-will-help-me I-will-sacrifice to-them them ones-helping they

וְהֵם הָיוּ־לוֹ לְהַכְשִׁילוֹ וּלְכָל־יִשְׂרָאֵל׃
Israel and-to-all-of to-cast-down-him to-him they-were but-they

וַיֶּאֱסֹף אָחָז אֶת־כְּלֵי בֵית־הָאֱלֹהִים
the-God temple-of furnishings-of *** Ahaz and-he-gathered (24)

וַיְקַצֵּץ אֶת־כְּלֵי בֵית־הָאֱלֹהִים וַיִּסְגֹּר אֶת־
*** and-he-shut the-God temple-of furnishings-of *** and-he-took-away

דַּלְתוֹת בֵּית־יְהוָה וַיַּעַשׂ לוֹ מִזְבְּחוֹת בְּכָל־פִּנָּה
corner at-every-of altars for-him and-he-set-up Yahweh temple-of doors-of

בִּירוּשָׁלִָם׃ וּבְכָל־עִיר וָעִיר לִיהוּדָה עָשָׂה בָמוֹת
high-places he-built in-Judah and-town town and-in-every-of (25) in-Jerusalem

לְקַטֵּר לֵאלֹהִים אֲחֵרִים וַיַּכְעֵס אֶת־יְהוָה אֱלֹהֵי
God-of Yahweh *** and-he-provoked other-ones to-gods to-burn-sacrifice

אֲבֹתָיו׃ וְיֶתֶר דְּבָרָיו וְכָל־דְּרָכָיו
ways-of-him and-all-of events-of-him and-other-of (26) fathers-of-him

Judah. They captured and occupied Beth Shemesh, Aijalon and Gederoth, as well as Soco, Timnah and Gimzo, with their surrounding villages. 19The LORD had humbled Judah because of Ahaz king of Israel,[p] for he had promoted wickedness in Judah and had been most unfaithful to the LORD. 20Tiglath-Pileser[q] king of Assyria came to him, but he gave him trouble instead of help. 21Ahaz took some of the things from the temple of the LORD and from the royal palace and from the princes and presented them to the king of Assyria, but that did not help him.

22In his time of trouble King Ahaz became even more unfaithful to the LORD. 23He offered sacrifices to the gods of Damascus, who had defeated him; for he thought, "Since the gods of the kings of Aram have helped them, I will sacrifice to them so they will help me." But they were his downfall and the downfall of all Israel.

24Ahaz gathered together the furnishings from the temple of God and took them away.[r] He shut the doors of the LORD's temple and set up altars at every street corner in Jerusalem. 25In every town in Judah he built high places to burn sacrifices to other gods and provoked the LORD, the God of his fathers, to anger.

26The other events of his reign and all his ways, from

p19 That is, Judah, as frequently in 2 Chronicles
q20 Hebrew *Tilgath-Pilneser*, a variant of *Tiglath-Pileser*
r24 Or *and cut them up*

הָרִאשֹׁנִים וְהָאַחֲרוֹנִים הִנָּם כְּתוּבִים עַל־ סֵפֶר מַלְכֵי־
kings-of book-of in ones-being-written see-they! and-the-ends the-beginnings

יְהוּדָה וְיִשְׂרָאֵל׃ וַיִּשְׁכַּב אָחָז עִם־ אֲבֹתָיו
fathers-of-him with Ahaz and-he-rested (27) and-Israel Judah

וַיִּקְבְּרֻהוּ בָעִיר בִּירוּשָׁלַםִ כִּי לֹא הֱבִיאֻהוּ
they-placed-him not but in-Jerusalem in-the-city and-they-buried-him

לְקִבְרֵי מַלְכֵי יִשְׂרָאֵל וַיִּמְלֹךְ יְחִזְקִיָּהוּ בְנוֹ
son-of-him Hezekiah and-he-became-king Israel kings-of in-tombs-of

תַּחְתָּיו׃ יְחִזְקִיָּהוּ מָלַךְ בֶּן־ עֶשְׂרִים וְחָמֵשׁ שָׁנָה
year and-five twenty son-of he-became-king Hezekiah (29:1) in-place-of-him

וְעֶשְׂרִים וָתֵשַׁע שָׁנָה מָלַךְ בִּירוּשָׁלָםִ וְשֵׁם אִמּוֹ
mother-of-him and-name-of in-Jerusalem he-reigned year and-nine and-twenty

אֲבִיָּה בַּת־ זְכַרְיָהוּ׃ וַיַּעַשׂ הַיָּשָׁר בְּעֵינֵי יְהוָה
Yahweh in-eyes-of the-right and-he-did (2) Zechariah daughter-of Abijah

כְּכֹל אֲשֶׁר־ עָשָׂה דָּוִיד אָבִיו׃ הוּא בַשָּׁנָה הָרִאשׁוֹנָה
the-first in-the-year he (3) father-of-him David he-did that as-all

לְמָלְכוֹ בַּחֹדֶשׁ הָרִאשׁוֹן פָּתַח אֶת־ דַּלְתוֹת בֵּית־ יְהוָה
Yahweh temple-of doors-of *** he-opened the-first in-the-month to-reign-him

וַיְחַזְּקֵם׃ וַיָּבֵא אֶת־ הַכֹּהֲנִים וְאֶת־ הַלְוִיִּם
the-Levites and the-priests *** and-he-brought-in (4) and-he-repaired-them

וַיַּאַסְפֵם לִרְחוֹב הַמִּזְרָח׃ וַיֹּאמֶר לָהֶם
to-them and-he-said (5) the-east in-square-of and-he-assembled-them

שְׁמָעוּנִי הַלְוִיִּם עַתָּה הִתְקַדְּשׁוּ וְקַדְּשׁוּ אֶת־
*** and-consecrate! consecrate-yourselves! now the-Levites listen-to-me!

בֵּית יְהוָה אֱלֹהֵי אֲבֹתֵיכֶם וְהוֹצִיאוּ אֶת־ הַנִּדָּה מִן־
from the-defilement *** and-remove! fathers-of-you God-of Yahweh temple-of

הַקֹּדֶשׁ׃ כִּי־ מָעֲלוּ אֲבֹתֵינוּ וְעָשׂוּ
and-they-did fathers-of-us they-were-unfaithful for (6) the-sanctuary

הָרַע בְּעֵינֵי יְהוָה־ אֱלֹהֵינוּ וַיַּעַזְבֻהוּ וַיַּסֵּבּוּ
and-they-turned-away and-they-forsook-him God-of-us Yahweh in-eyes-of the-evil

פְנֵיהֶם מִמִּשְׁכַּן יְהוָה וַיִּתְּנוּ־ עֹרֶף׃ גַּם סָגְרוּ
they-shut also (7) back and-they-turned Yahweh from-dwelling-of faces-of-them

דַּלְתוֹת הָאוּלָם וַיְכַבּוּ אֶת־ הַנֵּרוֹת וּקְטֹרֶת לֹא
not and-incense the-lamps *** and-they-put-out the-portico doors-of

הִקְטִירוּ וְעֹלָה לֹא־ הֶעֱלוּ בַקֹּדֶשׁ
at-the-sanctuary they-presented not and-burnt-offering they-burned

לֵאלֹהֵי יִשְׂרָאֵל׃ וַיְהִי קֶצֶף יְהוָה עַל־ יְהוּדָה וִירוּשָׁלִָם
and-Jerusalem Judah on Yahweh anger-of so-he-fell (8) Israel to-God-of

beginning to end, are written in the book of the kings of Judah and Israel.
27 Ahaz rested with his fathers and was buried in the city of Jerusalem, but he was not placed in the tombs of the kings of Israel. And Hezekiah his son succeeded him as king.

*Hezekiah Purifies the Temple*

29 Hezekiah was twenty-five years old when he became king, and he reigned in Jerusalem twenty-nine years. His mother's name was Abijah daughter of Zechariah.
2 He did what was right in the eyes of the LORD, just as his father David had done.
3 In the first month of the first year of his reign, he opened the doors of the temple of the LORD and repaired them.
4 He brought in the priests and the Levites, assembled them in the square on the east side
5 and said: "Listen to me, Levites! Consecrate yourselves now and consecrate the temple of the LORD, the God of your fathers. Remove all defilement from the sanctuary.
6 Our fathers were unfaithful; they did evil in the eyes of the LORD our God and forsook him. They turned their faces away from the LORD's dwelling place and turned their backs on him.
7 They also shut the doors of the portico and put out the lamps. They did not burn incense or present any burnt offerings at the sanctuary to the God of Israel.
8 Therefore, the anger of the LORD has fallen on Judah and Jerusalem;

וַיִּתְּנֵם לְזַוָּעָה לְשַׁמָּה וְלִשְׁרֵקָה כַּאֲשֶׁר
just-as and-as-object-of-scorn as-horror as-object-of-dread and-he-made-them

אַתֶּם רֹאִים בְּעֵינֵיכֶם׃ (9) וְהִנֵּה נָפְלוּ אֲבוֹתֵינוּ
fathers-of-us they-fell and-see! (9) with-eyes-of-you ones-seeing you

בֶּחָרֶב וּבָנֵינוּ וּבְנוֹתֵינוּ וְנָשֵׁינוּ
and-wives-of-us and-daughters-of-us and-sons-of-us by-the-sword

בַּשְּׁבִי עַל־זֹאת׃ (10) עַתָּה עִם־לְבָבִי לִכְרוֹת בְּרִית לַיהוָה
with-Yahweh covenant to-make heart-of-me in now (10) this for in-the-captivity

אֱלֹהֵי יִשְׂרָאֵל וְיָשֹׁב מִמֶּנּוּ חֲרוֹן אַפּוֹ׃
anger-of-him fierceness-of from-us so-he-will-turn Israel God-of

(11) בָּנַי עַתָּה אַל־תִּשָּׁלוּ כִּי־בָכֶם בָּחַר יְהוָה
Yahweh he-chose to-you for you-be-negligent not now sons-of-me (11)

לַעֲמֹד לְפָנָיו לְשָׁרְתוֹ וְלִהְיוֹת לוֹ מְשָׁרְתִים
ones-ministering before-him and-to-be to-serve-him before-him to-stand

וּמַקְטִרִים׃ (12) וַיָּקֻמוּ הַלְוִיִּם מַחַת בֶּן־
son-of Mahath the-Levites then-they-set-to-work (12) and-ones-burning-incense

עֲמָשַׂי וְיוֹאֵל בֶּן־עֲזַרְיָהוּ מִן־בְּנֵי הַקְּהָתִי וּמִן־בְּנֵי
sons-of and-from the-Kohathite sons-of from Azariah son-of and-Joel Amasai

מְרָרִי קִישׁ בֶּן־עַבְדִּי וַעֲזַרְיָהוּ בֶּן־יְהַלֶּלְאֵל וּמִן־הַגֵּרְשֻׁנִּי
the-Gershonite and-from Jehallelel son-of and-Azariah Abdi son-of Kish Merari

יוֹאָח בֶּן־זִמָּה וְעֵדֶן בֶּן־יוֹאָח׃ (13) וּמִן־בְּנֵי
descendants-of and-from (13) Joah son-of and-Eden Zimmah son-of Joah

אֱלִיצָפָן שִׁמְרִי וִיעוּאֵל וּמִן־בְּנֵי אָסָף זְכַרְיָהוּ
Zechariah Asaph descendants-of and-from and-Jeiel Shimri Elizaphan

וּמַתַּנְיָהוּ׃ (14) וּמִן־בְּנֵי הֵימָן יְחוּאֵל וְשִׁמְעִי וּמִן־
and-from and-Shimei Jehiel Heman descendants-of and-from (14) and-Mattaniah

בְּנֵי יְדוּתוּן שְׁמַעְיָה וְעֻזִּיאֵל׃ (15) וַיַּאַסְפוּ אֶת־
*** when-they-assembled (15) and-Uzziel Shemaiah Jeduthun descendants-of

אֲחֵיהֶם וַיִּתְקַדְּשׁוּ וַיָּבֹאוּ כְמִצְוַת־
as-order-of then-they-went-in and-they-consecrated-themselves brothers-of-them

הַמֶּלֶךְ בְּדִבְרֵי יְהוָה לְטַהֵר בֵּית יְהוָה׃ (16) וַיָּבֹאוּ
and-they-went (16) Yahweh temple-of to-purify Yahweh at-words-of the-king

הַכֹּהֲנִים לִפְנִימָה בֵית־יְהוָה לְטַהֵר וַיּוֹצִיאוּ
and-they-brought-out to-purify Yahweh sanctuary-of into-inside the-priests

אֵת כָּל־הַטֻּמְאָה אֲשֶׁר מָצְאוּ בְּהֵיכַל יְהוָה
Yahweh in-temple-of they-found that the-uncleanness all-of ***

לַחֲצַר בֵּית יְהוָה וַיְקַבְּלוּ הַלְוִיִּם לְהוֹצִיא
to-carry-out the-Levites and-they-took Yahweh temple-of to-courtyard-of

he has made them an object of
dread and horror and scorn, as
you can see with your own
eyes. 9This is why our fathers
have fallen by the sword and
why our sons and daughters
and our wives are in captivity.
10Now I intend to make a covenant with the LORD, the God
of Israel, so that his fierce anger will turn away from us.
11My sons, do not be negligent
now, for the LORD has chosen
you to stand before him and
serve him, to minister before
him and to burn incense."
12Then these Levites set to
work:
from the Kohathites,
Mahath son of Amasai
and Joel son of Aza-
riah;
from the Merarites,
Kish son of Abdi and
Azariah son of Je-
hallelel;
from the Gershonites,
Joah son of Zimmah
and Eden son of Joah;
13from the descendants of
Elizaphan,
Shimri and Jeiel;
from the descendants of
Asaph,
Zechariah and Mat-
taniah;
14from the descendants of
Heman,
Jehiel and Shimei;
from the descendants of
Jeduthun,
Shemaiah and Uzziel.
15When they had assembled
their brothers and consecrated
themselves, they went in to
purify the temple of the LORD,
as the king had ordered, following the word of the LORD.
16The priests went into the
sanctuary of the LORD to purify
it. They brought out to the
courtyard of the LORD's temple
everything unclean that they
found in the temple of the
LORD. The Levites took it and

°8 ק לזועה
°13 ק ויעיאל
°14 ק יחיאל

לְנַחַל־ קִדְרוֹן חוּצָה׃ (17) וַיָּחֵלּוּ בְּאֶחָד לַחֹדֶשׁ
of-the-month on-one and-they-began (17) to-outside Kidron to-Valley-of

הָרִאשׁוֹן לְקַדֵּשׁ וּבְיוֹם שְׁמוֹנָה לַחֹדֶשׁ בָּאוּ
they-reached of-the-month eight and-on-day to-consecrate the-first

לְאוּלָם יְהוָה וַיְקַדְּשׁוּ אֶת־ בֵּית־ יְהוָה לְיָמִים שְׁמוֹנָה
eight for-days Yahweh temple-of *** and-they-consecrated Yahweh to-portico-of

וּבְיוֹם שִׁשָּׁה עָשָׂר לַחֹדֶשׁ הָרִאשׁוֹן כִּלּוּ׃ (18) וַיָּבוֹאוּ
then-they-went (18) they-finished the-first of-the-month ten six and-on-day

פְנִימָה אֶל־ חִזְקִיָּהוּ הַמֶּלֶךְ וַיֹּאמְרוּ טִהַרְנוּ אֶת־ כָּל־
entire-of *** we-purified and-they-reported the-king Hezekiah to inside

בֵּית יְהוָה אֶת־ מִזְבַּח הָעוֹלָה וְאֶת־ כָּל־ כֵּלָיו
utensils-of-him all-of and the-burnt-offering altar-of *** Yahweh temple-of

וְאֶת־ שֻׁלְחַן הַמַּעֲרֶכֶת וְאֶת־ כָּל־ כֵּלָיו׃ (19) וְאֵת
and (19) articles-of-him all-of and the-consecrated-bread table-of and

כָּל־ הַכֵּלִים אֲשֶׁר הִזְנִיחַ הַמֶּלֶךְ אָחָז בְּמַלְכוּתוֹ
during-reign-of-him Ahaz the-king he-removed that the-articles all-of

בְּמַעֲלוֹ הֵכַנּוּ וְהִקְדָּשְׁנוּ וְהִנָּם לִפְנֵי
in-front-of now-see-they! and-we-consecrated we-prepared in-unfaithfulness-of-him

מִזְבַּח יְהוָה׃ (20) וַיַּשְׁכֵּם יְחִזְקִיָּהוּ הַמֶּלֶךְ וַיֶּאֱסֹף אֵת
*** and-he-gathered the-king Hezekiah and-he-got-up (20) Yahweh altar-of

שָׂרֵי הָעִיר וַיַּעַל בֵּית יְהוָה׃ (21) וַיָּבִיאוּ
and-they-brought (21) Yahweh temple-of and-he-went-up the-city officials-of

פָרִים־שִׁבְעָה וְאֵילִים שִׁבְעָה וּכְבָשִׂים שִׁבְעָה וּצְפִירֵי עִזִּים שִׁבְעָה
seven goats and-male-goats-of seven and-lambs seven and-rams seven bulls

לְחַטָּאת עַל־ הַמַּמְלָכָה וְעַל־ הַמִּקְדָּשׁ וְעַל־ יְהוּדָה
Judah and-for the-sanctuary and-for the-kingdom for as-sin-offering

וַיֹּאמֶר לִבְנֵי אַהֲרֹן הַכֹּהֲנִים לְהַעֲלוֹת עַל־ מִזְבַּח
altar-of on to-offer the-priests Aaron to-descendants-of and-he-commanded

יְהוָה׃ (22) וַיִּשְׁחֲטוּ הַבָּקָר וַיְקַבְּלוּ הַכֹּהֲנִים אֶת־
*** the-priests and-they-took the-bull so-they-slaughtered (22) Yahweh

הַדָּם וַיִּזְרְקוּ הַמִּזְבֵּחָה וַיִּשְׁחֲטוּ הָאֵלִים
the-rams then-they-slaughtered on-the-altar and-they-sprinkled the-blood

וַיִּזְרְקוּ הַדָּם הַמִּזְבֵּחָה וַיִּשְׁחֲטוּ הַכְּבָשִׂים
the-lambs then-they-slaughtered on-the-altar the-blood and-they-sprinkled

וַיִּזְרְקוּ הַדָּם הַמִּזְבֵּחָה׃ (23) וַיַּגִּישׁוּ אֶת־ שְׂעִירֵי
goats-of *** and-they-brought (23) on-the-altar the-blood and-they-sprinkled

הַחַטָּאת לִפְנֵי הַמֶּלֶךְ וְהַקָּהָל וַיִּסְמְכוּ יְדֵיהֶם
hands-of-them and-they-laid and-the-assembly the-king before the-sin-offering

carried it out to the Kidron
Valley. [17]They began the consecration on the first day of
the first month, and by the
eighth day of the month they
reached the portico of the
LORD. For eight more days
they consecrated the temple of
the LORD itself, finishing on
the sixteenth day of the first
month.

[18]Then they went in to King
Hezekiah and reported: "We
have purified the entire temple of the LORD, the altar of
burnt offering with all its
utensils, and the table for setting out the consecrated bread,
with all its articles. [19]We have
prepared and consecrated all
the articles that King Ahaz
removed in his unfaithfulness
while he was king. They are
now in front of the LORD's altar."

[20]Early the next morning
King Hezekiah gathered the
city officials together and
went up to the temple of the
LORD. [21]They brought seven
bulls, seven rams, seven male
lambs and seven male goats as
a sin offering for the kingdom,
for the sanctuary and for
Judah. The king commanded
the priests, the descendants of
Aaron, to offer these on the altar of the LORD. [22]So they
slaughtered the bulls, and the
priests took the blood and
sprinkled it on the altar; next
they slaughtered the rams and
sprinkled their blood on the
altar; then they slaughtered
the lambs and sprinkled their
blood on the altar. [23]The goats
for the sin offering were
brought before the king and
the assembly, and they laid
their hands on them. [24]The

עֲלֵיהֶֽם׃ וַיִּשְׁחָטוּם הַכֹּהֲנִים וַיְחַטְּאוּ
and-they-made-sin-offering the-priests then-they-slaughtered-them (24) on-them

אֶת־ דָּמָם הַמִּזְבֵּחָה לְכַפֵּר עַל־ כָּל־ יִשְׂרָאֵל כִּי לְכָל־
for-all-of because Israel all-of for to-atone on-the-altar blood-of-them ***

יִשְׂרָאֵל אָמַר הַמֶּלֶךְ הָעוֹלָה וְהַחַטָּֽאת׃
and-the-sin-offering the-burnt-offering the-king he-ordered Israel

וַיַּעֲמֵד אֶת־ הַלְוִיִּם בֵּית יְהוָה בִּמְצִלְתַּיִם
with-cymbals Yahweh temple-of the-Levites *** and-he-stationed (25)

בִּנְבָלִים וּבְכִנֹּרוֹת בְּמִצְוַת דָּוִיד וְגָד חֹזֵה־ הַמֶּלֶךְ
the-king seer-of and-Gad David as-prescription-of and-with-lyres with-harps

וְנָתָן הַנָּבִיא כִּי בְיַד־ יְהוָה הַמִּצְוָה בְּיַד־
through-hand-of the-command Yahweh by-hand-of for the-prophet and-Nathan

נְבִיאָֽיו׃ וַיַּעַמְדוּ הַלְוִיִּם בִּכְלֵי דָוִיד
David with-instruments-of the-Levites so-they-stood (26) prophets-of-him

וְהַכֹּהֲנִים בַּחֲצֹצְרֽוֹת׃ וַיֹּאמֶר חִזְקִיָּהוּ לְהַעֲלוֹת
to-sacrifice Hezekiah and-he-ordered (27) with-the-trumpets and-the-priests

הָעֹלָה לְהַמִּזְבֵּחַ וּבְעֵת הֵחֵל הָעוֹלָה הֵחֵל
he-began the-offering he-began and-at-time on-the-altar the-burnt-offering

שִׁיר־ יְהוָה וְהַחֲצֹצְרוֹת וְעַל־ יְדֵי כְּלֵי דָּוִיד מֶֽלֶךְ־
king-of David instruments-of hands-of and-with and-the-trumpets Yahweh song-of

יִשְׂרָאֵֽל׃ וְכָל־ הַקָּהָל מִֽשְׁתַּחֲוִים וְהַשִּׁיר מְשׁוֹרֵר
singing while-the-song ones-worshiping the-asssembly and-whole-of (28) Israel

וְהַחֲצֹצְרוֹת מַחְצְצְרִים הַכֹּל עַד לִכְלוֹת
to-be-completed until the-whole ones-playing and-the-trumpets

הָעֹלָֽה׃ וּכְכַלּוֹת לְהַעֲלוֹת כָּרְעוּ הַמֶּלֶךְ
the-king they-knelt to-offer and-when-to-be-finished (29) the-burnt-offering

וְכָל־ הַנִּמְצְאִים אִתּוֹ וַיִּֽשְׁתַּחֲוֽוּ׃ וַיֹּאמֶר
and-he-ordered (30) and-they-worshiped with-him the-ones-being-found and-all-of

יְחִזְקִיָּהוּ הַמֶּלֶךְ וְהַשָּׂרִים לַלְוִיִּם לְהַלֵּל לַיהוָה
to-Yahweh to-praise to-the-Levites and-the-officials the-king Hezekiah

בְּדִבְרֵי דָוִיד וְאָסָף הַחֹזֶה וַיְהַלְלוּ עַד־ לְשִׂמְחָה
with-gladness to so-they-sang-praises the-seer and-Asaph David with-words-of

וַיִּקְּדוּ וַיִּֽשְׁתַּחֲוֽוּ׃ וַיַּעַן יְחִזְקִיָּהוּ
Hezekiah then-he-answered (31) and-they-worshiped and-they-bowed-heads

וַיֹּאמֶר עַתָּה מִלֵּאתֶם יֶדְכֶם לַיהוָה גֹּשׁוּ וְהָבִיאוּ
and-bring! come! to-Yahweh hand-of-you you-dedicated now and-he-said

זְבָחִים וְתוֹדוֹת לְבֵית יְהוָה וַיָּבִיאוּ
so-they-brought Yahweh to-temple-of and-thank-offerings sacrifices

priests then slaughtered the goats and presented their blood on the altar for a sin offering to atone for all Israel, because the king had ordered the burnt offering and the sin offering for all Israel.

25 He stationed the Levites in the temple of the LORD with cymbals, harps and lyres in the way prescribed by David and Gad the king's seer and Nathan the prophet; this was commanded by the LORD through his prophets. 26 So the Levites stood ready with David's instruments, and the priests with their trumpets.

27 Hezekiah gave the order to sacrifice the burnt offering on the altar. As the offering began, singing to the LORD began also, accompanied by trumpets and the instruments of David king of Israel. 28 The whole assembly bowed in worship, while the singers sang and the trumpeters played. All this continued until the sacrifice of the burnt offering was completed.

29 When the offerings were finished, the king and everyone present with him knelt down and worshiped. 30 King Hezekiah and his officials ordered the Levites to praise the LORD with the words of David and of Asaph the seer. So they sang praises with gladness and bowed their heads and worshiped.

31 Then Hezekiah said, "You have now dedicated yourselves to the LORD. Come and bring sacrifices and thank offerings to the temple of the LORD." So the assembly

°28 ק מחצרים

הַקָּהָל֙ זְבָחִים וְתוֹדוֹת וְכָל־ נְדִיב לֵב
heart willing-of and-all-of and-thank-offerings sacrifices the-assembly

עֹלוֹת׃ (32) וַיְהִי מִסְפַּר הָעֹלָה אֲשֶׁר
that the-burnt-offering number-of and-he-was (32) burnt-offerings

הֵבִיאוּ הַקָּהָל֙ בָּקָר שִׁבְעִים אֵילִים מֵאָה כְּבָשִׂים מָאתָיִם
two-hundreds lambs hundred rams seventy bull the-assembly they-brought

לְעֹלָה לַיהוָה כָּל־ אֵלֶּה׃ (33) וְהַקֳּדָשִׁים בָּקָר
bull and-the-ones-consecrated (33) these all-of to-Yahweh for-burnt-offering

שֵׁשׁ מֵאוֹת וְצֹאן שְׁלֹשֶׁת אֲלָפִים׃ (34) רַק הַכֹּהֲנִים
the-priests however (34) thousands three-of and-sheep hundreds six-of

הָיוּ לִמְעָט וְלֹא יָכְלוּ לְהַפְשִׁיט אֶת־ כָּל־ הָעֹלוֹת
the-burnt-offerings all-of *** to-skin they-could and-not as-few they-were

וַיְחַזְּקוּם אֲחֵיהֶם הַלְוִיִּם עַד־ כְּלוֹת הַמְּלָאכָה
the-task to-be-finished until the-Levites kinsmen-of-them so-they-helped-them

וְעַד יִתְקַדְּשׁוּ הַכֹּהֲנִים כִּי הַלְוִיִּם
the-Levites for the-priests they-were-consecrated and-until

יִשְׁרֵי לֵבָב לְהִתְקַדֵּשׁ מֵהַכֹּהֲנִים׃
more-than-the-priests to-consecrate-themselves heart ones-conscientious-of

(35) וְגַם־ עֹלָה לָרֹב בְּחֶלְבֵי הַשְּׁלָמִים
the-fellowship-offerings with-fats-of in-abundance burnt-offering and-also (35)

וּבַנְּסָכִים לָעֹלָה וַתִּכּוֹן
so-she-was-reestablished with-the-burnt-offering and-with-the-drink-offerings

עֲבוֹדַת בֵּית־ יְהוָה׃ (36) וַיִּשְׂמַח יְחִזְקִיָּהוּ וְכָל־
and-all-of Hezekiah and-he-rejoiced (36) Yahweh temple-of service-of

הָעָם עַל הַהֵכִין הָאֱלֹהִים לָעָם כִּי
because for-the-people the-God what-he-brought-about at the-people

בְּפִתְאֹם הָיָה הַדָּבָר׃ (30:1) וַיִּשְׁלַח יְחִזְקִיָּהוּ עַל־ כָּל־ יִשְׂרָאֵל
Israel all-of to Hezekiah and-he-sent (30:1) the-thing he-was in-quickness

וִיהוּדָה וְגַם־ אִגְּרוֹת כָּתַב עַל־ אֶפְרַיִם וּמְנַשֶּׁה לָבוֹא
to-come and-Manasseh Ephraim to he-wrote letters and-also and-Judah

לְבֵית־ יְהוָה בִּירוּשָׁלָםִ לַעֲשׂוֹת פֶּסַח לַיהוָה אֱלֹהֵי
God-of to-Yahweh Passover to-celebrate in-Jerusalem Yahweh to-temple-of

יִשְׂרָאֵל׃ (2) וַיִּוָּעַץ הַמֶּלֶךְ וְשָׂרָיו וְכָל־
and-whole-of and-officials-of-him the-king and-he-decided (2) Israel

הַקָּהָל בִּירוּשָׁלָםִ לַעֲשׂוֹת הַפֶּסַח בַּחֹדֶשׁ הַשֵּׁנִי׃
the-second in-the-month the-Passover to-celebrate in-Jerusalem the-assembly

(3) כִּי לֹא יָכְלוּ לַעֲשֹׂתוֹ בָּעֵת הַהִיא כִּי
because the-that at-the-time to-celebrate-him they-were-able not for (3)

brought sacrifices and thank offerings, and all whose hearts were willing brought burnt offerings.

32 The number of burnt offerings the assembly brought was seventy bulls, a hundred rams and two hundred male lambs—all of them for burnt offerings to the LORD. 33 The animals consecrated as sacrifices amounted to six hundred bulls and three thousand sheep and goats. 34 The priests, however, were too few to skin all the burnt offerings; so their kinsmen the Levites helped them until the task was finished and until other priests had been consecrated, for the Levites had been more conscientious in consecrating themselves than the priests had been. 35 There were burnt offerings in abundance, together with the fat of the fellowship offerings[s] and the drink offerings that accompanied the burnt offerings.

So the service of the temple of the LORD was reestablished. 36 Hezekiah and all the people rejoiced at what God had brought about for his people, because it was done so quickly.

*Hezekiah Celebrates the Passover*

30 Hezekiah sent word to all Israel and Judah and also wrote letters to Ephraim and Manasseh, inviting them to come to the temple of the LORD in Jerusalem and celebrate the Passover to the LORD, the God of Israel. 2 The king and his officials and the whole assembly in Jerusalem decided to celebrate the Passover in the second month. 3 They had not been able to celebrate it at the regular time because not

[s]35 Traditionally *peace offerings*

הַכֹּהֲנִים לֹא־ הִתְקַדְּשׁוּ לְמַדַּי וְהָעָם לֹא־
not and-the-people as-what-enough they-consecrated-themselves not the-priests

נֶאֶסְפוּ לִירוּשָׁלִָם׃ וַיִּישַׁר הַדָּבָר בְּעֵינֵי הַמֶּלֶךְ
the-king in-eyes-of the-plan and-he-was-right (4) in-Jerusalem they-assembled

וּבְעֵינֵי כָּל־ הַקָּהָל׃ וַיַּעֲמִידוּ דָבָר לְהַעֲבִיר
to-send issue and-they-decided (5) the-assembly whole-of and-in-eyes-of

קוֹל בְּכָל־ יִשְׂרָאֵל מִבְּאֵר־ שֶׁבַע וְעַד־ דָּן לָבוֹא
to-come Dan even-to Sheba from-Beer Israel through-all-of proclamation

לַעֲשׂוֹת פֶּסַח לַיהוָה אֱלֹהֵי־ יִשְׂרָאֵל בִּירוּשָׁלִָם כִּי לֹא
not for to-Jerusalem Israel God-of to-Yahweh Passover to-celebrate

לָרֹב עָשׂוּ כַּכָּתוּב׃ וַיֵּלְכוּ
and-they-went (6) as-the-one-being-written they-celebrated in-large-number

הָרָצִים בָּאִגְּרוֹת מִיַּד הַמֶּלֶךְ
the-king from-hand-of with-the-letters the-ones-being-couriers

וְשָׂרָיו בְּכָל־ יִשְׂרָאֵל וִיהוּדָה וּכְמִצְוַת
and-at-command-of and-Judah Israel through-all-of and-officials-of-him

הַמֶּלֶךְ לֵאמֹר בְּנֵי יִשְׂרָאֵל שׁוּבוּ אֶל־ יְהוָה אֱלֹהֵי אַבְרָהָם יִצְחָק
Isaac Abraham God-of Yahweh to return! Israel people-of to-say the-king

וְיִשְׂרָאֵל וְיָשֹׁב אֶל־ הַפְּלֵיטָה הַנִּשְׁאֶרֶת לָכֶם
of-you the-one-being-left the-escapee to that-he-may-return and-Israel

מִכַּף מַלְכֵי אַשּׁוּר׃ וְאַל־ תִּהְיוּ כַּאֲבוֹתֵיכֶם
like-fathers-of-you you-be and-not (7) Assyria kings-of from-hand-of

וְכַאֲחֵיכֶם אֲשֶׁר מָעֲלוּ בַּיהוָה אֱלֹהֵי
God-of to-Yahweh they-were-unfaithful who and-like-brothers-of-you

אֲבוֹתֵיהֶם וַיִּתְּנֵם לְשַׁמָּה כַּאֲשֶׁר אַתֶּם רֹאִים׃
ones-seeing you just-as as-object-of-horror so-he-made-them fathers-of-them

עַתָּה אַל־ תַּקְשׁוּ עָרְפְּכֶם כַּאֲבוֹתֵיכֶם תְּנוּ־ יָד
hand submit! as-fathers-of-you neck-of-you you-make-stiff not now (8)

לַיהוָה וּבֹאוּ לְמִקְדָּשׁוֹ אֲשֶׁר הִקְדִּישׁ לְעוֹלָם
to-forever he-consecrated which to-sanctuary-of-him and-come! to-Yahweh

וְעִבְדוּ אֶת־ יְהוָה אֱלֹהֵיכֶם וְיָשֹׁב מִכֶּם חֲרוֹן
fierceness-of from-you so-he-will-turn God-of-you Yahweh *** and-serve!

אַפּוֹ׃ כִּי בְשׁוּבְכֶם עַל־ יְהוָה אֲחֵיכֶם
brothers-of-you Yahweh to when-to-return-you if (9) anger-of-him

וּבְנֵיכֶם לְרַחֲמִים לִפְנֵי שׁוֹבֵיהֶם וְלָשׁוּב
and-to-come-back ones-capturing-them before to-compassions and-children-of-you

לָאָרֶץ הַזֹּאת כִּי־ חַנּוּן וְרַחוּם יְהוָה אֱלֹהֵיכֶם וְלֹא־
and-not God-of-you Yahweh and-compassionate gracious for the-this to-the-land

enough priests had consecrated themselves and the people had not assembled in Jerusalem. 4The plan seemed right both to the king and to the whole assembly. 5They decided to send a proclamation throughout Israel, from Beersheba to Dan, calling the people to come to Jerusalem and celebrate the Passover to the LORD, the God of Israel. It had not been celebrated in large numbers according to what was written.

6At the king's command, couriers went throughout Israel and Judah with letters from the king and from his officials, which read:

"People of Israel, return to the LORD, the God of Abraham, Isaac and Israel, that he may return to you who are left, who have escaped from the hand of the kings of Assyria. 7Do not be like your fathers and brothers, who were unfaithful to the LORD, the God of their fathers, so that he made them an object of horror, as you see. 8Do not be stiff-necked, as your fathers were; submit to the LORD. Come to the sanctuary, which he has consecrated forever. Serve the LORD your God, so that his fierce anger will turn away from you. 9If you return to the LORD, then your brothers and your children will be shown compassion by their captors and will come back to this land, for the LORD your God is gracious and compassionate. He will not

יָסִיר פָּנִים מִכֶּם אִם־ תָּשׁוּבוּ אֵלָיו׃ וַיִּהְיוּ
and-they-were (10) to-him you-return if from-you faces he-will-turn

הָרָצִים עֹבְרִים מֵעִיר ׀ לָעִיר בְּאֶרֶץ־ אֶפְרַיִם
Ephraim in-land-of to-town from-town ones-going the-ones-being-couriers

וּמְנַשֶּׁה וְעַד־ זְבֻלוּן וַיִּהְיוּ מַשְׂחִיקִים עֲלֵיהֶם
against-them ones-scorning but-they-were Zebulun and-as-far-as and-Manasseh

וּמַלְעִגִים בָּם׃ אַךְ־ אֲנָשִׁים מֵאָשֵׁר וּמְנַשֶּׁה
and-Manasseh from-Asher men nevertheless (11) at-them and-ones-ridiculing

וּמִזְּבֻלוּן נִכְנְעוּ וַיָּבֹאוּ לִירוּשָׁלִָם׃ גַּם
also (12) to-Jerusalem and-they-went they-humbled-themselves and-from-Zebulun

בִּיהוּדָה הָיְתָה יַד הָאֱלֹהִים לָתֵת לָהֶם לֵב אֶחָד לַעֲשׂוֹת
to-carry-out one mind to-them to-give the-God hand-of she-was in-Judah

מִצְוַת הַמֶּלֶךְ וְהַשָּׂרִים בִּדְבַר יְהוָה׃ וַיֵּאָסְפוּ
and-they-assembled (13) Yahweh at-word-of and-the-officials the-king order-of

יְרוּשָׁלִַם עַם־ רָב לַעֲשׂוֹת אֶת־ חַג הַמַּצּוֹת
the-Unleavened-Breads Feast-of *** to-celebrate large people Jerusalem

בַּחֹדֶשׁ הַשֵּׁנִי קָהָל לָרֹב מְאֹד׃ וַיָּקֻמוּ
and-they-rose (14) very as-large crowd the-second in-the-month

וַיָּסִירוּ אֶת־ הַמִּזְבְּחוֹת אֲשֶׁר בִּירוּשָׁלִַם וְאֵת כָּל־
all-of and in-Jerusalem that the-altars *** and-they-removed

הַמְקַטְּרוֹת הֵסִירוּ וַיַּשְׁלִיכוּ לְנַחַל קִדְרוֹן׃
Kidron into-Valley-of and-they-threw they-cleared the-incense-altars

וַיִּשְׁחֲטוּ הַפֶּסַח בְּאַרְבָּעָה עָשָׂר לַחֹדֶשׁ
of-the-month ten on-four the-Passover-lamb and-they-slaughtered (15)

הַשֵּׁנִי וְהַכֹּהֲנִים וְהַלְוִיִּם נִכְלְמוּ
they-were-ashamed and-the-Levites and-the-priests the-second

וַיִּתְקַדְּשׁוּ וַיָּבִיאוּ עֹלוֹת בֵּית
temple-of burnt-offerings and-they-brought and-they-consecrated-themselves

יְהוָה׃ וַיַּעַמְדוּ עַל־ עָמְדָם כְּמִשְׁפָּטָם
as-prescription-of-them position-of-them at then-they-took-up (16) Yahweh

כְּתוֹרַת מֹשֶׁה אִישׁ־ הָאֱלֹהִים הַכֹּהֲנִים זֹרְקִים אֶת־ הַדָּם
the-blood *** ones-sprinkling the-priests the-God man-of Moses as-Law-of

מִיַּד הַלְוִיִּם׃ כִּי־ רַבַּת בַּקָּהָל אֲשֶׁר לֹא־
not who in-the-crowd many since (17) the-Levites from-hand-of

הִתְקַדָּשׁוּ וְהַלְוִיִּם עַל־ שְׁחִיטַת הַפְּסָחִים
the-Passover-lambs killing-of for then-the-Levites they-consecrated-themselves

לְכֹל לֹא טָהוֹר לְהַקְדִּישׁ לַיהוָה׃ כִּי מַרְבִּית הָעָם
the-people most-of although (18) to-Yahweh to-consecrate clean not for-all

turn his face from you if
you return to him."

10The couriers went from
town to town in Ephraim and
Manasseh, as far as Zebulun,
but the people scorned and
ridiculed them.
11Nevertheless, some men of Asher,
Manasseh and Zebulun humbled themselves and went to
Jerusalem.
12Also in Judah the
hand of God was on the
people to give them unity of
mind to carry out what the
king and his officials had ordered, following the word of
the LORD.

13A very large crowd of
people assembled in Jerusalem
to celebrate the Feast of Unleavened Bread in the second
month.
14They removed the altars in Jerusalem and cleared
away the incense altars and
threw them into the Kidron
Valley.

15They slaughtered the Passover lamb on the fourteenth
day of the second month. The
priests and the Levites were
ashamed and consecrated
themselves and brought burnt
offerings to the temple of the
LORD.
16Then they took up
their regular positions as prescribed in the Law of Moses
the man of God. The priests
sprinkled the blood handed to
them by the Levites.
17Since
many in the crowd had not
consecrated themselves, the
Levites had to kill the Passover
lambs for all those who were
not ceremonially clean and
could not consecrate ⌊their
lambs⌋ to the LORD.
18Although
most of the many people who

רַבַּת מֵאֶפְרַיִם וּמְנַשֶּׁה יִשָּׂשכָר וּזְבֻלוּן לֹא הִטֶּהָרוּ
they-purified-themselves not and-Zebulun Issachar and-Manasseh from-Ephraim many

כִּי־ אָכְלוּ אֶת־ הַפֶּסַח בְּלֹא כַכָּתוּב כִּי
but to-the-thing-being-written in-contrary the-Passover *** they-ate yet

הִתְפַּלֵּל יְחִזְקִיָּהוּ עֲלֵיהֶם לֵאמֹר יְהוָה הַטּוֹב יְכַפֵּר בְּעַד׃
to may-he-pardon the-good Yahweh to-say for-them Hezekiah he-prayed

כָּל־ לְבָבוֹ הֵכִין לִדְרוֹשׁ הָאֱלֹהִים ׀ יְהוָה אֱלֹהֵי אֲבוֹתָיו
fathers-of-him God-of Yahweh the-God to-seek he-set heart-of-him every-of (19)

וְלֹא כְּטָהֳרַת הַקֹּדֶשׁ׃ וַיִּשְׁמַע יְהוָה אֶל־ יְחִזְקִיָּהוּ
Hezekiah to Yahweh and-he-heard (20) the-sanctuary as-cleanness-of even-not

וַיִּרְפָּא אֶת־ הָעָם׃ וַיַּעֲשׂוּ בְנֵי־ יִשְׂרָאֵל
Israel sons-of and-they-celebrated (21) the-people *** and-he-healed

הַנִּמְצְאִים בִּירוּשָׁלִַם אֶת־ חַג הַמַּצּוֹת שִׁבְעַת
seven-of the-Unleavened-Breads Feast-of *** in-Jerusalem the-ones-being-found

יָמִים בְּשִׂמְחָה גְדוֹלָה וּמְהַלְלִים לַיהוָה יוֹם ׀ בְּיוֹם הַלְוִיִּם
the-Levites by-day day to-Yahweh while-ones-singing great with-rejoicing days

וְהַכֹּהֲנִים בִּכְלֵי־ עֹז לַיהוָה׃ וַיְדַבֵּר
and-he-spoke (22) to-Yahweh praise with-instruments-of and-the-priests

יְחִזְקִיָּהוּ עַל־ לֵב כָּל־ הַלְוִיִּם הַמַּשְׂכִּילִים
the-ones-showing-understanding the-Levites all-of heart-of to Hezekiah

שֵׂכֶל־ טוֹב לַיהוָה וַיֹּאכְלוּ אֶת־ הַמּוֹעֵד שִׁבְעַת
seven-of the-assigned-portion *** and-they-ate of-Yahweh good understanding-of

הַיָּמִים מְזַבְּחִים זִבְחֵי שְׁלָמִים וּמִתְוַדִּים לַיהוָה
to-Yahweh and-ones-praising fellowships offerings-of ones-offering the-days

אֱלֹהֵי אֲבוֹתֵיהֶם׃ וַיִּוָּעֲצוּ כָּל־ הַקָּהָל
the-assembly whole-of then-they-agreed (23) fathers-of-them God-of

לַעֲשׂוֹת שִׁבְעַת יָמִים אֲחֵרִים וַיַּעֲשׂוּ שִׁבְעַת־ יָמִים
days seven-of so-they-celebrated ones-more days seven-of to-celebrate

שִׂמְחָה׃ כִּי חִזְקִיָּהוּ מֶלֶךְ־ יְהוּדָה הֵרִים לַקָּהָל
for-the-assembly he-provided Judah king-of Hezekiah now (24) joyfully

אֶלֶף פָּרִים וְשִׁבְעַת אֲלָפִים צֹאן וְהַשָּׂרִים הֵרִימוּ
they-provided and-the-officials sheep thousands and-seven-of bulls thousand-of

לַקָּהָל פָּרִים אֶלֶף וְצֹאן עֲשֶׂרֶת אֲלָפִים
thousands ten-of and-sheep thousand bulls for-the-assembly

וַיִּתְקַדְּשׁוּ כֹהֲנִים לָרֹב׃ וַיִּשְׂמְחוּ ׀
and-they-rejoiced (25) in-number priests and-they-consecrated-themselves

כָּל־ קְהַל יְהוּדָה וְהַכֹּהֲנִים וְהַלְוִיִּם וְכָל־
and-all-of and-the-Levites and-the-priests Judah assembly-of entire-of

came from Ephraim, Manasseh, Issachar and Zebulun had not purified themselves, yet they ate the Passover, contrary to what was written. But Hezekiah prayed for them, saying, "May the LORD, who is good, pardon everyone [19]who sets his heart on seeking God—the LORD, the God of his fathers—even if he is not clean according to the rules of the sanctuary." [20]And the LORD heard Hezekiah and healed the people.

[21]The Israelites who were present in Jerusalem celebrated the Feast of Unleavened Bread for seven days with great rejoicing, while the Levites and priests sang to the LORD every day, accompanied by the LORD's instruments of praise.[t]

[22]Hezekiah spoke encouragingly to all the Levites, who showed good understanding of the service of the LORD. For the seven days they ate their assigned portion and offered fellowship offerings[u] and praised the LORD, the God of their fathers.

[23]The whole assembly then agreed to celebrate the festival seven more days; so for another seven days they celebrated joyfully. [24]Hezekiah king of Judah provided a thousand bulls and seven thousand sheep and goats for the assembly, and the officials provided them with a thousand bulls and ten thousand sheep and goats. A great number of priests consecrated themselves. [25]The entire assembly of Judah rejoiced,

t21 Or *priests praised the* LORD *every day with resounding instruments belonging to the* LORD
u22 Traditionally *peace offerings*

הַקָּהָל הַבָּאִים מִיִּשְׂרָאֵל וְהַגֵּרִים הַבָּאִים
the-ones-coming | and-the-aliens | from-Israel | the-ones-coming | the-assembly

מֵאֶרֶץ יִשְׂרָאֵל וְהַיּוֹשְׁבִים בִּיהוּדָה׃ וַתְּהִי שִׂמְחָה־
joy | and-she-was | (26) | in-Judah | and-the-ones-living | Israel | from-land-of

גְדוֹלָה בִּירוּשָׁלִָם כִּי מִימֵי שְׁלֹמֹה בֶן־ דָּוִיד מֶלֶךְ יִשְׂרָאֵל
Israel | king-of | David | son-of | Solomon | since-days-of | for | in-Jerusalem | great

לֹא כָזֹאת בִּירוּשָׁלִָם׃ וַיָּקֻמוּ הַכֹּהֲנִים הַלְוִיִּם
the-Levites | the-priests | and-they-stood | (27) | in-Jerusalem | like-this | not

וַיְבָרֲכוּ אֶת־ הָעָם וַיִּשָּׁמַע בְּקוֹלָם
to-voice-of-them | and-he-was-heard | the-people | *** | and-they-blessed

וַתָּבוֹא תְפִלָּתָם לִמְעוֹן קָדְשׁוֹ לַשָּׁמָיִם׃
to-the-heavens | holy-place-of-him | to-dwelling-of | prayer-of-them | for-she-reached

(31:1) וּכְכַלּוֹת כָּל־ זֹאת יָצְאוּ כָּל־ יִשְׂרָאֵל
Israel | all-of | they-went-out | this | all-of | and-when-to-end | (31:1)

הַנִּמְצְאִים לְעָרֵי יְהוּדָה וַיְשַׁבְּרוּ הַמַּצֵּבוֹת
the-sacred-stones | and-they-smashed | Judah | to-towns-of | the-ones-being-found

וַיְגַדְּעוּ הָאֲשֵׁרִים וַיְנַתְּצוּ אֶת־ הַבָּמוֹת
the-high-places | *** | and-they-destroyed | the-Asherah-poles | and-they-cut-down

וְאֶת־ הַמִּזְבְּחֹת מִכָּל־ יְהוּדָה וּבִנְיָמִן וּבְאֶפְרַיִם וּמְנַשֶּׁה
and-Manasseh | and-in-Ephraim | and-Benjamin | Judah | through-all-of | the-altars | and

עַד־ לְכַלֵּה וַיָּשׁוּבוּ כָּל־ בְּנֵי יִשְׂרָאֵל אִישׁ
each | Israel | sons-of | all-of | then-they-returned | to-finish | until

לַאֲחֻזָּתוֹ לְעָרֵיהֶם׃ וַיַּעֲמֵד יְחִזְקִיָּהוּ אֶת־
*** | Hezekiah | and-he-assigned | (2) | to-towns-of-them | to-property-of-him

מַחְלְקוֹת הַכֹּהֲנִים וְהַלְוִיִּם עַל־ מַחְלְקוֹתָם אִישׁ ׀
each | divisions-of-them | by | and-the-Levites | the-priests | divisions-of

כְּפִי עֲבֹדָתוֹ לַכֹּהֲנִים וְלַלְוִיִּם לְעֹלָה
for-burnt-offering | and-as-the-Levites | as-the-priests | duty-of-him | according-to

וְלִשְׁלָמִים לְשָׁרֵת וּלְהֹדוֹת וּלְהַלֵּל
and-to-praise | and-to-give-thanks | to-minister | and-for-fellowship-offerings

בְּשַׁעֲרֵי מַחֲנוֹת יְהוָה׃ וּמְנָת הַמֶּלֶךְ מִן־
from | the-king | and-contribution-of | (3) | Yahweh | dwellings-of | at-gates-of

רְכוּשׁוֹ לָעֹלוֹת לְעֹלוֹת הַבֹּקֶר
the-morning | for-burnt-offerings-of | for-the-burnt-offerings | possession-of-him

וְהָעֶרֶב וְהָעֹלוֹת לַשַּׁבָּתוֹת וְלֶחֳדָשִׁים
and-on-the-New-Moons | on-the-Sabbaths | and-the-burnt-offerings | and-the-evening

וְלַמֹּעֲדִים כַּכָּתוּב בְּתוֹרַת יְהוָה׃
Yahweh | in-Law-of | as-the-thing-being-written | and-on-the-appointed-feasts

along with the priests and Levites and all who had assembled from Israel, including the aliens who had come from Israel and those who lived in Judah.
26 There was great joy in Jerusalem, for since the days of Solomon son of David king of Israel there had been nothing like this in Jerusalem.
27 The priests and the Levites stood to bless the people, and God heard them, for their prayer reached heaven, his holy dwelling place.

31 When all this had ended, the Israelites who were there went out to the towns of Judah, smashed the sacred stones and cut down the Asherah poles. They destroyed the high places and the altars throughout Judah and Benjamin and in Ephraim and Manasseh. After they had destroyed all of them, the Israelites returned to their own towns and to their own property.

*Contributions for Worship*

2 Hezekiah assigned the priests and Levites to divisions—each of them according to their duties as priests or Levites—to offer burnt offerings and fellowship offerings,[v] to minister, to give thanks and to sing praises at the gates of the LORD's dwelling.
3 The king contributed from his own possessions for the morning and evening burnt offerings and for the burnt offerings on the Sabbaths, New Moons and appointed feasts as written in

[v] 2 Traditionally *peace offerings*

וַיֹּאמֶר לָעָם לְיוֹשְׁבֵי יְרוּשָׁלַםִ לָתֵת
to-give Jerusalem to-ones-living-of to-the-people and-he-ordered (4)

מְנָת הַכֹּהֲנִים וְהַלְוִיִּם לְמַעַן יֶחֶזְקוּ
they-could-devote-themselves so-that and-the-Levites the-priests portion-of

בְּתוֹרַת יְהוָה׃ וְכִפְרֹץ הַדָּבָר הִרְבּוּ בְנֵי־
sons-of they-gave-generously the-order and-as-to-go-out (5) Yahweh to-Law-of

יִשְׂרָאֵל רֵאשִׁית דָּגָן תִּירוֹשׁ וְיִצְהָר וּדְבַשׁ וְכֹל תְּבוּאַת
produce-of and-all-of and-honey and-oil new-wine grain firstfruit-of Israel

שָׂדֶה וּמַעְשַׂר הַכֹּל לָרֹב הֵבִיאוּ׃ וּבְנֵי
and-men-of (6) they-brought as-great-amount the-whole and-tithe-of field

יִשְׂרָאֵל וִיהוּדָה הַיּוֹשְׁבִים בְּעָרֵי יְהוּדָה גַּם־ הֵם מַעְשַׂר בָּקָר
herd tithe-of they also Judah in-towns-of the-ones-living and-Judah Israel

וָצֹאן וּמַעְשַׂר קָדָשִׁים הַמְקֻדָּשִׁים לַיהוָה
to-Yahweh the-ones-being-dedicated holy-things and-tithe-of and-flock

אֱלֹהֵיהֶם הֵבִיאוּ וַיִּתְּנוּ עֲרֵמוֹת עֲרֵמוֹת׃ בַּחֹדֶשׁ
in-the-month (7) heaps heaps and-they-piled they-brought God-of-them

הַשְּׁלִשִׁי הֵחֵלּוּ הָעֲרֵמוֹת לִיסּוֹד וּבַחֹדֶשׁ הַשְּׁבִיעִי
the-seventh and-in-the-month to-pile the-heaps they-began the-third

כִּלּוּ׃ וַיָּבֹאוּ יְחִזְקִיָּהוּ וְהַשָּׂרִים וַיִּרְאוּ
and-they-saw and-the-officials Hezekiah when-they-came (8) they-finished

אֶת־ הָעֲרֵמוֹת וַיְבָרְכוּ אֶת־ יְהוָה וְאֵת עַמּוֹ יִשְׂרָאֵל׃
Israel people-of-him and Yahweh *** then-they-blessed the-heaps ***

וַיִּדְרֹשׁ יְחִזְקִיָּהוּ עַל־ הַכֹּהֲנִים וְהַלְוִיִּם עַל־ הָעֲרֵמוֹת׃
the-heaps about and-the-Levites the-priests to Hezekiah and-he-asked (9)

וַיֹּאמֶר אֵלָיו עֲזַרְיָהוּ הַכֹּהֵן הָרֹאשׁ לְבֵית
from-family-of the-chief the-priest Azariah to-him and-he-answered (10)

צָדוֹק וַיֹּאמֶר מֵהָחֵל הַתְּרוּמָה לָבִיא בֵית־ יְהוָה
Yahweh temple-of to-bring the-contribution since-to-begin and-he-said Zadok

אָכוֹל וְשָׂבוֹעַ וְהוֹתֵר עַד־ לָרוֹב כִּי יְהוָה
Yahweh because as-plenty to and-to-have-spare and-to-have-enough to-eat

בֵּרַךְ אֶת־ עַמּוֹ וְהַנּוֹתָר אֶת־ הֶהָמוֹן
the-great-amount *** and-the-one-being-left-over people-of-him *** he-blessed

הַזֶּה׃ וַיֹּאמֶר יְחִזְקִיָּהוּ לְהָכִין לְשָׁכוֹת בְּבֵית
in-temple-of storerooms to-prepare Hezekiah and-he-ordered (11) the-this

יְהוָה וַיָּכִינוּ׃ וַיָּבִיאוּ אֶת־ הַתְּרוּמָה
the-contribution *** then-they-brought (12) and-they-prepared Yahweh

וְהַמַּעֲשֵׂר וְהַקֳּדָשִׁים בֶּאֱמוּנָה וַעֲלֵיהֶם נָגִיד
leader and-over-them in-faithfulness and-the-dedicated-gifts and-the-tithe

the Law of the LORD. 4He ordered the people living in
Jerusalem to give the portion
due the priests and Levites so
they could devote themselves
to the Law of the LORD. 5As
soon as the order went out, the
Israelites generously gave the
firstfruits of their grain, new
wine, oil and honey and all
that the fields produced. They
brought a great amount, a
tithe of everything. 6The men
of Israel and Judah who lived
in the towns of Judah also
brought a tithe of their herds
and flocks and a tithe of the
holy things dedicated to the
LORD their God, and they piled
them in heaps. 7They began
doing this in the third month
and finished in the seventh
month. 8When Hezekiah and
his officials came and saw the
heaps, they praised the LORD
and blessed his people Israel.
9Hezekiah asked the priests
and Levites about the heaps;
10and Azariah the chief priest,
from the family of Zadok, answered, "Since the people began to bring their contributions to the temple of the
LORD, we have had enough to
eat and plenty to spare, because the LORD has blessed his
people, and this great amount
is left over."
11Hezekiah gave orders to
prepare storerooms in the
temple of the LORD, and this
was done. 12Then they faithfully brought in the contributions, tithes and dedicated

כּוֹנַנְיָהוּ הַלֵּוִי וְשִׁמְעִי אָחִיהוּ מִשְׁנֶה׃ וִיחִיאֵל
Conaniah the-Levite and-Shimei brother-of-him next (13) and-Jehiel

וַעֲזַזְיָהוּ וְנַחַת וַעֲשָׂהאֵל וִירִימוֹת וְיוֹזָבָד וֶאֱלִיאֵל
and-Azaziah and-Nahath and-Asahel and-Jerimoth and-Jozabad and-Eliel

וְיִסְמַכְיָהוּ וּמַחַת וּבְנָיָהוּ פְּקִידִים מִיַּד כּוֹנַנְיָהוּ
and-Ismakiah and-Mahath and-Benaiah supervisors under-hand-of Conaniah

וְשִׁמְעִי אָחִיו בְּמִפְקַד יְחִזְקִיָּהוּ הַמֶּלֶךְ וַעֲזַרְיָהוּ
and-Shimei brother-of-him by-appointment-of Hezekiah the-king and-Azariah

נְגִיד בֵּית־ הָאֱלֹהִים׃ וְקוֹרֵא בֶן־ יִמְנָה הַלֵּוִי
official-of temple-of the-God (14) and-Kore son-of Imnah the-Levite

הַשּׁוֹעֵר לַמִּזְרָחָה עַל נִדְבוֹת הָאֱלֹהִים
the-gatekeeper of-to-the-east over freewill-offerings-of the-God

לָתֵת תְּרוּמַת יְהוָה וְקָדְשֵׁי
to-distribute contribution-of Yahweh and-consecrated-ones-of

הַקֳּדָשִׁים׃ וְעַל־ יָדוֹ עֵדֶן וּמִנְיָמִן וְיֵשׁוּעַ
the-consecrated-gifts (15) and-at hand-of-him Eden and-Miniamin and-Jeshua

וּשְׁמַעְיָהוּ אֲמַרְיָהוּ וּשְׁכַנְיָהוּ בְּעָרֵי הַכֹּהֲנִים בֶּאֱמוּנָה
and-Shemaiah Amariah and-Shecaniah in-towns-of the-priests in-faithfulness

לָתֵת לַאֲחֵיהֶם בְּמַחְלְקוֹת כַּגָּדוֹל כַּקָּטָן׃
to-distribute to-fellows-of-them by-divisions as-the-old so-the-young

מִלְּבַד הִתְיַחְשָׂם לִזְכָרִים מִבֶּן שָׁלוֹשׁ שָׁנִים
(16) in-addition-to to-be-recorded-them to-males from-son-of three years

וּלְמַעְלָה לְכָל־ הַבָּא לְבֵית־ יְהוָה לִדְבַר־
and-to-upward to-all-of the-one-entering into-temple-of Yahweh for-duty-of

יוֹם בְּיוֹמוֹ לַעֲבוֹדָתָם בְּמִשְׁמְרוֹתָם
day in-day-of-him for-task-of-them according-to-responsibilities-of-them

כְּמַחְלְקוֹתֵיהֶם׃ וְאֵת הִתְיַחֵשׂ הַכֹּהֲנִים לְבֵית
by-divisions-of-them (17) and to-be-enrolled the-priests by-family-of

אֲבוֹתֵיהֶם וְהַלְוִיִּם מִבֶּן עֶשְׂרִים שָׁנָה וּלְמָעְלָה
fathers-of-them and-the-Levites from-son-of twenty year and-to-upward

בְּמִשְׁמְרוֹתֵיהֶם בְּמַחְלְקוֹתֵיהֶם׃
according-to-responsibilities-of-them by-divisions-of-them

וּלְהִתְיַחֵשׂ בְּכָל־ טַפָּם נְשֵׁיהֶם
(18) and-to-be-recorded of-all-of little-one-of-them wives-of-them

וּבְנֵיהֶם וּבְנוֹתֵיהֶם לְכָל־ קָהָל כִּי
and-sons-of-them and-daughters-of-them of-whole-of community for

בֶאֱמוּנָתָם יִתְקַדְּשׁוּ־ קֹדֶשׁ׃
in-faithfulness-of-them they-consecrated-themselves consecration

gifts. Conaniah, a Levite, was in charge of these things, and his brother Shimei was next in rank. [13]Jehiel, Azaziah, Nahath, Asahel, Jerimoth, Jozabad, Eliel, Ismakiah, Mahath and Benaiah were supervisors under Conaniah and Shimei his brother, by appointment of King Hezekiah and Azariah the official in charge of the temple of God.

[14]Kore son of Imnah the Levite, keeper of the East Gate, was in charge of the freewill offerings given to God, distributing the contributions made to the LORD and also the consecrated gifts. [15]Eden, Miniamin, Jeshua, Shemaiah, Amariah and Shecaniah assisted him faithfully in the towns of the priests, distributing to their fellow priests according to their divisions, old and young alike.

[16]In addition, they distributed to the males three years old or more whose names were in the genealogical records—all who would enter the temple of the LORD to perform the daily duties of their various tasks, according to their responsibilities and their divisions. [17]And they distributed to the priests enrolled by their families in the genealogical records and likewise to the Levites twenty years old or more, according to their responsibilities and their divisions. [18]They included all the little ones, the wives, and the sons and daughters of the whole community listed in these genealogical records. For they were faithful in consecrating themselves.

°12 ק כנניהו
°13 ק כנניהו

וְלִבְנֵי אַהֲרֹן הַכֹּהֲנִים בִּשְׂדֵי מִגְרַשׁ עָרֵיהֶם
towns-of-them farm-of in-lands-of the-priests Aaron and-for-descendants-of (19)

בְּכָל־ עִיר וָעִיר אֲנָשִׁים אֲשֶׁר נִקְּבוּ בְּשֵׁמוֹת לָתֵת
to-distribute by-names they-were-designated who men or-town town in-any-of

מָנוֹת לְכָל־ זָכָר בַּכֹּהֲנִים וּלְכָל־ הִתְיַחֵשׂ
to-be-recorded and-to-all-of among-the-priests male to-every-of portions

בַּלְוִיִּם׃ וַיַּעַשׂ כָּזֹאת יְחִזְקִיָּהוּ בְּכָל־ יְהוּדָה
Judah through-all-of Hezekiah as-this and-he-did (20) of-the-Levites

וַיַּעַשׂ הַטּוֹב וְהַיָּשָׁר וְהָאֱמֶת לִפְנֵי יְהוָה אֱלֹהָיו׃
God-of-him Yahweh before and-the-faithful and-the-right the-good and-he-did

וּבְכָל־ מַעֲשֶׂה אֲשֶׁר־ הֵחֵל | בַּעֲבוֹדַת בֵּית־ הָאֱלֹהִים
the-God temple-of in-service-of he-undertook that deed and-in-all-of (21)

וּבַתּוֹרָה וּבַמִּצְוָה לִדְרֹשׁ לֵאלֹהָיו בְּכָל־
with-whole-of to-God-of-him to-seek and-for-the-command and-for-the-law

לְבָבוֹ עָשָׂה וְהִצְלִיחַ׃ אַחֲרֵי הַדְּבָרִים
the-things after (32:1) and-he-prospered he-worked heart-of-him

וְהָאֱמֶת הָאֵלֶּה בָּא סַנְחֵרִיב מֶלֶךְ־ אַשּׁוּר
Assyria king-of Sennacherib he-came the-these and-the-faithfulness

וַיָּבֹא בִיהוּדָה וַיִּחַן עַל־ הֶעָרִים
the-cities to and-he-laid-siege into-Judah and-he-invaded

הַבְּצֻרוֹת וַיֹּאמֶר לְבִקְעָם אֵלָיו׃ וַיַּרְא
when-he-saw (2) for-him to-conquer-them and-he-thought the-ones-being-fortified

יְחִזְקִיָּהוּ כִּי־ בָא סַנְחֵרִיב וּפָנָיו לַמִּלְחָמָה עַל־יְרוּשָׁלִָם׃
Jerusalem on to-the-war and-faces-of-him Sennacherib he-came that Hezekiah

וַיִּוָּעַץ עִם־ שָׂרָיו וְגִבֹּרָיו
and-military-staffs-of-him officials-of-him with then-he-consulted (3)

לִסְתּוֹם אֶת־ מֵימֵי הָעֲיָנוֹת אֲשֶׁר מִחוּץ לָעִיר
to-the-city at-outside-of that the-springs waters-of *** to-block-off

וַיַּעְזְרוּהוּ׃ וַיִּקָּבְצוּ עַם־ רָב וַיִּסְתְּמוּ אֶת־
*** and-they-blocked large force and-they-assembled (4) and-they-helped-him

כָּל־ הַמַּעְיָנוֹת וְאֶת־ הַנַּחַל הַשּׁוֹטֵף בְּתוֹךְ־ הָאָרֶץ לֵאמֹר
to-say the-land through the-one-flowing the-stream and the-springs all-of

לָמָּה יָבוֹאוּ מַלְכֵי אַשּׁוּר וּמָצְאוּ מַיִם רַבִּים׃
ones-plentiful waters and-they-find Assyria kings-of should-they-come why?

וַיִּתְחַזַּק וַיִּבֶן אֶת־ כָּל־ הַחוֹמָה
the-wall all-of *** and-he-repaired then-he-worked-hard (5)

הַפְּרוּצָה וַיַּעַל עַל־ הַמִּגְדָּלוֹת וְלַחוּצָה הַחוֹמָה
the-wall and-to-the-outside the-towers on and-he-built the-one-being-broken

19 As for the priests, the descendants of Aaron, who lived on the farm lands around their towns or in any other towns, men were designated by name to distribute portions to every male among them and to all who were recorded in the genealogies of the Levites.

20 This is what Hezekiah did throughout Judah, doing what was good and right and faithful before the LORD his God. 21 In everything that he undertook in the service of God's temple and in obedience to the law and the commands, he sought his God and worked wholeheartedly. And so he prospered.

*Sennacherib Threatens Jerusalem*

32 After all that Hezekiah had so faithfully done, Sennacherib king of Assyria came and invaded Judah. He laid siege to the fortified cities, thinking to conquer them for himself. 2 When Hezekiah saw that Sennacherib had come and that he intended to make war on Jerusalem, 3 he consulted with his officials and military staff about blocking off the water from the springs outside the city, and they helped him. 4 A large force of men assembled, and they blocked all the springs and the stream that flowed through the land. "Why should the kings[w] of Assyria come and find plenty of water?" they said. 5 Then he worked hard repairing all the broken sections of the wall and building towers on it. He built another wall

[w]4 Hebrew; Septuagint and Syriac *king*

אַחֶ֫רֶת וַיְחַזֵּק אֶת־ הַמִּלּוֹא עִיר דָּוִיד
David City-of the-supporting-terrace *** and-he-reinforced another

וַיַּעַשׂ שֶׁלַח לָרֹב וּמָגִנִּים׃ וַיִּתֵּן שָׂרֵי
officers-of and-he-appointed (6) and-shields in-number weapon and-he-made

מִלְחָמוֹת עַל־ הָעָם וַיִּקְבְּצֵם אֵלָיו אֶל־ רְחוֹב
square-of in before-him and-he-assembled-them the-people over militaries

שַׁעַר הָעִיר וַיְדַבֵּר עַל־ לְבָבָם לֵאמֹר׃ חִזְקוּ
be-strong! (7) to-say heart-of-them to and-he-spoke the-city gate-of

וְאִמְצוּ אַל־ תִּירְאוּ וְאַל־ תֵּחַתּוּ מִפְּנֵי
because-of you-be-discouraged and-not you-be-afraid not and-be-courageous!

מֶלֶךְ אַשּׁוּר וּמִלִּפְנֵי כָּל־ הֶהָמוֹן אֲשֶׁר־ עִמּוֹ כִּי־
for with-him that the-vast-army all-of and-because-of Assyria king-of

עִמָּנוּ רַב מֵעִמּוֹ׃ עִמּוֹ זְרוֹעַ בָּשָׂר וְעִמָּנוּ
but-with-us flesh arm-of with-him (8) more-than-with-him great-power with-us

יְהוָה אֱלֹהֵינוּ לְעָזְרֵנוּ וּלְהִלָּחֵם מִלְחֲמֹתֵנוּ וַיִּסָּמְכוּ
and-they-gained-confidence battles-of-us and-to-fight to-help-us God-of-us Yahweh

הָעָם עַל־ דִּבְרֵי יְחִזְקִיָּהוּ מֶלֶךְ־ יְהוּדָה׃ אַחַר זֶה שָׁלַח
he-sent this after (9) Judah king-of Hezekiah words-of from the-people

סַנְחֵרִיב מֶלֶךְ־ אַשּׁוּר עֲבָדָיו יְרוּשָׁלַיְמָה וְהוּא עַל־
against when-he to-Jerusalem officers-of-him Assyria king-of Sennacherib

לָכִישׁ וְכָל־ מֶמְשַׁלְתּוֹ עִמּוֹ עַל־ יְחִזְקִיָּהוּ מֶלֶךְ יְהוּדָה וְעַל־
and-to Judah king-of Hezekiah to with-him force-of-him and-all-of Lachish

כָּל־ יְהוּדָה אֲשֶׁר בִּירוּשָׁלִַם לֵאמֹר׃ כֹּה אָמַר סַנְחֵרִיב מֶלֶךְ
king-of Sennacherib he-says this (10) to-say in-Jerusalem who Judah all-of

אַשּׁוּר עַל־ מָה אַתֶּם בֹּטְחִים וְיֹשְׁבִים בְּמָצוֹר
under-siege and-ones-remaining ones-basing-confidence you what? on Assyria

בִּירוּשָׁלִָם׃ הֲלֹא יְחִזְקִיָּהוּ מַסִּית אֶתְכֶם לָתֵת אֶתְכֶם לָמוּת בְּרָעָב
of-hunger to-die you to-let you misleading Hezekiah not? (11) in-Jerusalem

וּבְצָמָא לֵאמֹר יְהוָה אֱלֹהֵינוּ יַצִּילֵנוּ מִכַּף מֶלֶךְ
king-of from-hand-of he-will-save-us God-of-us Yahweh to-say and-of-thirst

אַשּׁוּר׃ הֲלֹא־ הוּא יְחִזְקִיָּהוּ הֵסִיר אֶת־ בָּמֹתָיו וְאֶת־
and high-places-of-him *** he-removed Hezekiah himself not? (12) Assyria

מִזְבְּחֹתָיו וַיֹּאמֶר לִיהוּדָה וְלִירוּשָׁלִַם לֵאמֹר לִפְנֵי מִזְבֵּחַ אֶחָד
one altar before to-say and-to-Jerusalem to-Judah and-he-said altars-of-him

תִּשְׁתַּחֲווּ וְעָלָיו תַּקְטִירוּ׃ הֲלֹא תֵדְעוּ מָה
what you-know not? (13) you-must-burn-sacrifice and-on-him you-must-worship

עָשִׂיתִי אֲנִי וַאֲבוֹתַי לְכֹל עַמֵּי הָאֲרָצוֹת הֲיָכוֹל
to-be-able? the-lands peoples-of to-all-of and-fathers-of-me I I-did

outside that one and reinforced the supporting terraces[x]
of the City of David. He also
made large numbers of weapons and shields.
6He appointed military
officers over the people and assembled them before him in
the square at the city gate and
encouraged them with these
words: 7"Be strong and courageous. Do not be afraid or discouraged because of the king
of Assyria and the vast army
with him, for there is a greater
power with us than with him.
8With him is only the arm of
flesh, but with us is the LORD
our God to help us and to fight
our battles." And the people
gained confidence from what
Hezekiah the king of Judah
said.
9Later, when Sennacherib
king of Assyria and all his
forces were laying siege to Lachish, he sent his officers to
Jerusalem with this message
for Hezekiah king of Judah
and for all the people of Judah
who were there:

10"This is what Sennach-
erib king of Assyria says:
On what are you basing
your confidence, that you
remain in Jerusalem under
siege? 11When Hezekiah
says, 'The LORD our God
will save us from the hand
of the king of Assyria,' he is
misleading you, to let you
die of hunger and thirst.
12Did not Hezekiah himself
remove this god's high
places and altars, saying to
Judah and Jerusalem, 'You
must worship before one
altar and burn sacrifices on
it'?
13"Do you not know what
I and my fathers have done
to all the peoples of the other lands? Were the gods of

x5 Or *the Millo*

יָכְל֨וּ אֱלֹהֵ֜י גּוֹיֵ֤ הָאֲרָצוֹת֙ לְהַצִּ֥יל אֶת־ אַרְצָ֖ם
land-of-them *** to-deliver the-lands nations-of gods-of were-they-able

מִיָּדִֽי׃ (14) מִ֠י בְּכָל־ אֱלֹהֵ֞י הַגּוֹיִ֤ם הָאֵ֙לֶּה֙ אֲשֶׁ֣ר
that the-these the-nations gods-of of-all-of who? (14) from-hand-of-me

הֶחֱרִ֣ימוּ אֲבוֹתַ֔י אֲשֶׁ֣ר יָכ֔וֹל לְהַצִּ֥יל אֶת־ עַמּ֖וֹ
people-of-him *** to-save he-was-able who fathers-of-me they-destroyed

מִיָּדִ֑י כִּ֚י יוּכַל֙ אֱלֹ֣הֵיכֶ֔ם לְהַצִּ֥יל אֶתְכֶ֖ם מִיָּדִֽי׃
from-hand-of-me you to-deliver God-of-you is-he-able how from-hand-of-me

(15) וְעַתָּ֡ה אַל־ יַשִּׁיא֩ אֶתְכֶ֨ם חִזְקִיָּ֜הוּ וְאַל־ יַסִּ֧ית אֶתְכֶ֣ם
you let-him-mislead and-not Hezekiah you let-him-deceive not and-now (15)

כָּזֹאת֮ וְאַל־ תַּאֲמִ֣ינוּ לוֹ֒ כִּי־ לֹ֣א יוּכַ֗ל כָּל־ אֱל֙וֹהַּ֙*
god-of any-of he-was-able not for in-him you-believe and-not like-this

כָּל־ גּ֣וֹי וּמַמְלָכָ֔ה לְהַצִּ֥יל עַמּ֛וֹ מִיָּדִ֖י
from-hand-of-me people-of-him to-deliver or-kingdom nation any-of

וּמִיַּ֣ד אֲבוֹתָ֑י אַ֕ף כִּ֚י אֱלֹ֣הֵיכֶ֔ם לֹא־
not gods-of-you then how-much-less fathers-of-me or-from-hand-of

יַצִּ֥ילוּ אֶתְכֶ֖ם מִיָּדִֽי׃ (16) וְעוֹד֙ דִּבְּר֣וּ
they-spoke and-further (16) from-hand-of-me you they-will-deliver

עֲבָדָ֔יו עַל־ יְהוָ֖ה הָאֱלֹהִ֑ים וְעַ֖ל יְחִזְקִיָּ֥הוּ עַבְדּֽוֹ׃
servant-of-him Hezekiah and-against the-God Yahweh against officers-of-him

(17) וּסְפָרִ֣ים כָּתַ֔ב לְחָרֵ֕ף לַיהוָ֖ה אֱלֹהֵ֣י יִשְׂרָאֵ֑ל וְלֵאמֹ֨ר
and-to-say Israel God-of to-Yahweh to-insult he-wrote and-letters (17)

עָלָ֜יו לֵאמֹ֗ר כֵּאלֹהֵי֩ גּוֹיֵ֨ הָאֲרָצ֜וֹת אֲשֶׁ֧ר לֹא־ הִצִּ֣ילוּ
they-rescued not that the-lands peoples-of as-gods-of to-say against-him

עַמָּם֮ מִיָּדִי֒ כֵּ֡ן לֹא־ יַצִּ֞יל אֱלֹהֵ֧י יְחִזְקִיָּ֛הוּ
Hezekiah God-of he-will-rescue not so from-hand-of-me people-of-them

עַמּ֖וֹ מִיָּדִֽי׃ (18) וַיִּקְרְא֨וּ בְקוֹל־ גָּד֤וֹל יְהוּדִית֙
Hebrew loud with-voice then-they-called (18) from-hand-of-me people-of-him

עַל־ עַ֤ם יְרֽוּשָׁלִַ֙ם֙ אֲשֶׁ֣ר עַל־ הַחוֹמָ֔ה לְיָרְאָ֖ם וּֽלְבַהֲלָ֑ם
and-to-make-afraid-them to-terrify-them the-wall on who Jerusalem people-of to

לְמַ֖עַן יִלְכְּד֥וּ אֶת־ הָעִֽיר׃ (19) וַֽיְדַבְּר֔וּ אֶל־ אֱלֹהֵ֖י
God-of about and-they-spoke (19) the-city *** they-could-capture so-that

יְרוּשָׁלִָ֑ם כְּעַ֗ל אֱלֹהֵי֙ עַמֵּ֣י הָאָ֔רֶץ מַעֲשֵׂ֖ה יְדֵ֥י הָאָדָֽם׃
the-man hands-of work-of the-world peoples-of gods-of as-about Jerusalem

(20) וַיִּתְפַּלֵּ֞ל יְחִזְקִיָּ֣הוּ הַמֶּ֗לֶךְ וִֽישַׁעְיָ֧הוּ בֶן־ אָמ֛וֹץ הַנָּבִ֖יא
the-prophet Amoz son-of and-Isaiah the-king Hezekiah and-he-prayed (20)

עַל־ זֹ֑את וַֽיִּזְעֲק֖וּ הַשָּׁמָֽיִם׃ (21) וַיִּשְׁלַ֤ח יְהוָה֙ מַלְאָ֔ךְ
angel Yahweh and-he-sent (21) the-heavens and-they-cried-out this about

those nations ever able to
deliver their land from my
hand? [14]Who of all the gods
of these nations that my fathers destroyed has been
able to save his people from
me? How then can your
god deliver you from my
hand? [15]Now do not let
Hezekiah deceive you and
mislead you like this. Do
not believe him, for no god
of any nation or kingdom
has been able to deliver his
people from my hand or the
hand of my fathers. How
much less will your god deliver you from my hand!"

[16]Sennacherib's officers
spoke further against the LORD
God and against his servant
Hezekiah. [17]The king also
wrote letters insulting the
LORD, the God of Israel, and
saying this against him: "Just
as the gods of the peoples of
the other lands did not rescue
their people from my hand, so
the god of Hezekiah will not
rescue his people from my
hand." [18]Then they called out
in Hebrew to the people of
Jerusalem who were on the
wall, to terrify them and make
them afraid in order to capture
the city. [19]They spoke about
the God of Jerusalem as they
did about the gods of the other
peoples of the world—the
work of men's hands.

[20]King Hezekiah and the
prophet Isaiah son of Amoz
cried out in prayer to heaven
about this. [21]And the LORD

*15 Most mss have *mappiq* in the *he* (הּ).

וַיַּכְחֵד כָּל־ גִּבּוֹר חַיִל וְנָגִיד וְשַׂר בְּמַחֲנֵה
in-camp-of and-officer and-leader fight men-of all-of and-he-annihilated

מֶלֶךְ אַשּׁוּר וַיָּשָׁב בְּבֹשֶׁת פָּנִים לְאַרְצוֹ וַיָּבֹא
and-he-went to-land-of-him faces in-disgrace-of so-he-withdrew Assyria king-of

בֵּית אֱלֹהָיו וּמִיצִיאֵו מֵעָיו שָׁם הִפִּילֻהוּ
they-cut-down-him there loins-of-him and-from-sons-of gods-of-him temple-of

בֶחָרֶב׃ וַיּוֹשַׁע יְהוָה אֶת־ יְחִזְקִיָּהוּ וְאֵת ׀ יֹשְׁבֵי
ones-living-of and Hezekiah *** Yahweh so-he-saved (22) with-the-sword

יְרוּשָׁלִַם מִיַּד סַנְחֵרִיב מֶלֶךְ־ אַשּׁוּר וּמִיַּד־ כֹּל
all and-from-hand-of Assyria king-of Sennacherib from-hand-of Jerusalem

וַיְנַהֲלֵם מִסָּבִיב׃ וְרַבִּים מְבִיאִים מִנְחָה
offering ones-bringing and-many (23) at-around and-he-took-care-of-them

לַיהוָה לִירוּשָׁלִַם וּמִגְדָּנוֹת לִיחִזְקִיָּהוּ מֶלֶךְ יְהוּדָה
Judah king-of for-Hezekiah and-valuable-gifts to-Jerusalem for-Yahweh

וַיִּנַּשֵּׂא לְעֵינֵי כָל־ הַגּוֹיִם מֵאַחֲרֵי־ כֵן׃
then from-after the-nations all-of in-eyes-of and-he-was-regarded

בַּיָּמִים הָהֵם חָלָה יְחִזְקִיָּהוּ עַד־ לָמוּת וַיִּתְפַּלֵּל
and-he-prayed to-die until Hezekiah he-became-ill the-those in-the-days (24)

אֶל־ יְהוָה וַיֹּאמֶר לוֹ וּמוֹפֵת נָתַן לוֹ׃
to-him he-gave and-miraculous-sign to-him and-he-answered Yahweh to

וְלֹא־ כִגְמֻל עָלָיו הֵשִׁיב יְחִזְקִיָּהוּ כִּי גָבַהּ
he-was-proud but Hezekiah he-responded to-him as-kindness but-not (25)

לִבּוֹ וַיְהִי עָלָיו קֶצֶף וְעַל־ יְהוּדָה וִירוּשָׁלִָם׃
and-Jerusalem Judah and-on wrath on-him so-he-was heart-of-him

וַיִּכָּנַע יְחִזְקִיָּהוּ בְּגֹבַהּ לִבּוֹ הוּא וְיֹשְׁבֵי
and-ones-living-of he heart-of-him of-pride-of Hezekiah then-he-repented (26)

יְרוּשָׁלִַם וְלֹא־ בָא עֲלֵיהֶם קֶצֶף יְהוָה בִּימֵי יְחִזְקִיָּהוּ׃
Hezekiah during-days-of Yahweh wrath-of upon-them he-came so-not Jerusalem

וַיְהִי לִיחִזְקִיָּהוּ עֹשֶׁר וְכָבוֹד הַרְבֵּה מְאֹד וְאֹצָרוֹת
and-treasuries very to-be-great and-honor wealth to-Hezekiah and-he-was (27)

עָשָׂה־ לוֹ לְכֶסֶף וּלְזָהָב וּלְאֶבֶן יְקָרָה וְלִבְשָׂמִים
and-for-spices precious and-for-stone and-for-gold for-silver for-him he-made

וּלְמָגִנִּים וּלְכֹל כְּלֵי חֶמְדָּה׃ וּמִסְכְּנוֹת
and-buildings (28) value things-of and-for-all-of and-for-shields

לִתְבוּאַת דָּגָן וְתִירוֹשׁ וְיִצְהָר וְאֻרָוֹת לְכָל־ בְּהֵמָה
cattle for-every-of and-stalls and-oil and-new-wine grain for-harvest-of

וּבְהֵמָה וַעֲדָרִים לָאֲוֵרוֹת׃ וְעָרִים עָשָׂה לוֹ
for-him he-built and-villages (29) in-the-pens and-flocks and-cattle

sent an angel, who annihilated all the fighting men and the leaders and officers in the camp of the Assyrian king. So he withdrew to his own land in disgrace. And when he went into the temple of his god, some of his sons cut him down with the sword.

22 So the LORD saved Hezekiah and the people of Jerusalem from the hand of Sennacherib king of Assyria and from the hand of all others. He took care of them[y] on every side. 23 Many brought offerings to Jerusalem for the LORD and valuable gifts for Hezekiah king of Judah. From then on he was highly regarded by all the nations.

*Hezekiah's Pride, Success and Death*

24 In those days Hezekiah became ill and was at the point of death. He prayed to the LORD, who answered him and gave him a miraculous sign. 25 But Hezekiah's heart was proud and he did not respond to the kindness shown him; therefore the LORD's wrath was on him and on Judah and Jerusalem. 26 Then Hezekiah repented of the pride of his heart, as did the people of Jerusalem; therefore the LORD's wrath did not come upon them during the days of Hezekiah.

27 Hezekiah had very great riches and honor, and he made treasuries for his silver and gold and for his precious stones, spices, shields and all kinds of valuables. 28 He also made buildings to store the harvest of grain, new wine and oil; and he made stalls for various kinds of cattle, and pens for the flocks. 29 He built

[y]22 Hebrew; Septuagint and Vulgate *He gave them rest*

°21 ק ומיציאי

וּמִקְנֵה־ צֹאן וּבָקָר לָרֹב כִּי נָתַן־ לוֹ אֱלֹהִים רְכוּשׁ
richness God to-him he-gave for in-number and-herd flock and-acquisition-of

רַב מְאֹד׃ וְהוּא יְחִזְקִיָּהוּ סָתַם אֶת־ מוֹצָא מֵימֵי גִיחוֹן
Gihon springs-of outlet-of *** he-blocked Hezekiah now-he (30) very great

הָעֶלְיוֹן וַיַּישְּׁרֵם* לְמַטָּה־ מַּעְרָבָה לְעִיר דָּוִיד
David of-City-of to-west to-downward and-he-channeled-them the-upper

וַיַּצְלַח יְחִזְקִיָּהוּ בְּכָל־ מַעֲשֵׂהוּ׃ וְכֵן
but-this (31) undertaking-of-him in-all-of Hezekiah and-he-succeeded

בִּמְלִיצֵי ׀ שָׂרֵי בָבֶל הַמְשַׁלְּחִים עָלָיו
to-him the-ones-sending Babylon rulers-of when-ones-being-envoys-of

לִדְרֹשׁ הַמּוֹפֵת אֲשֶׁר הָיָה בָאָרֶץ עֲזָבוֹ
he-left-him in-the-land he-occurred that the-miraculous-sign to-ask-about

הָאֱלֹהִים לְנַסּוֹתוֹ לָדַעַת כָּל־ בִּלְבָבוֹ׃ וְיֶתֶר
and-other-of (32) in-heart-of-him all-of to-know to-test-him the-God

דִּבְרֵי יְחִזְקִיָּהוּ וַחֲסָדָיו הִנָּם כְּתוּבִים
ones-being-written see-they! and-acts-of-devotion-of-him Hezekiah events-of

בַּחֲזוֹן יְשַׁעְיָהוּ בֶן־ אָמוֹץ הַנָּבִיא עַל־ סֵפֶר מַלְכֵי־ יְהוּדָה
Judah kings-of book-of in the-prophet Amoz son-of Isaiah in-vision-of

וְיִשְׂרָאֵל׃ וַיִּשְׁכַּב יְחִזְקִיָּהוּ עִם־ אֲבֹתָיו וַיִּקְבְּרֻהוּ
and-they-buried-him fathers-of-him with Hezekiah and-he-rested (33) and-Israel

בְּמַעֲלֵה קִבְרֵי בְנֵי־ דָוִיד וְכָבוֹד עָשׂוּ־ לוֹ
to-him they-gave and-honor David descendants-of tombs-of on-hill-of

בְמוֹתוֹ כָּל־ יְהוּדָה וְיֹשְׁבֵי יְרוּשָׁלִַם וַיִּמְלֹךְ
and-he-became-king Jerusalem and-ones-living-of Judah all-of in-death-of-him

מְנַשֶּׁה בְנוֹ תַּחְתָּיו׃ בֶּן־ שְׁתֵּים עֶשְׂרֵה שָׁנָה מְנַשֶּׁה
Manasseh year ten two son-of (33:1) in-place-of-him son-of-him Manasseh

בְמָלְכוֹ וַחֲמִשִּׁים וְחָמֵשׁ שָׁנָה מָלַךְ בִּירוּשָׁלִָם׃
in-Jerusalem he-reigned year and-five and-fifty when-to-become-king-him

וַיַּעַשׂ הָרַע בְּעֵינֵי יְהוָה כְּתוֹעֲבוֹת
as-detestable-practices-of Yahweh in-eyes-of the-evil and-he-did (2)

הַגּוֹיִם אֲשֶׁר הוֹרִישׁ יְהוָה מִפְּנֵי בְּנֵי יִשְׂרָאֵל׃
Israel sons-of from-before Yahweh he-drove-out that the-nations

וַיָּשָׁב וַיִּבֶן אֶת־ הַבָּמוֹת אֲשֶׁר נִתַּץ
he-demolished that the-high-places *** and-he-rebuilt and-he-returned (3)

יְחִזְקִיָּהוּ אָבִיו וַיָּקֶם מִזְבְּחוֹת לַבְּעָלִים וַיַּעַשׂ
and-he-made to-the-Baals altars and-he-erected father-of-him Hezekiah

אֲשֵׁרוֹת וַיִּשְׁתַּחוּ לְכָל־ צְבָא הַשָּׁמַיִם וַיַּעֲבֹד אֹתָם׃
them and-he-worshiped the-heavens host-of to-all-of and-he-bowed Asherah-poles

villages and acquired great numbers of flocks and herds, for God had given him very great riches.
[30]It was Hezekiah who blocked the upper outlet of the Gihon spring and channeled the water down to the west side of the City of David. He succeeded in everything he undertook.
[31]But when envoys were sent by the rulers of Babylon to ask him about the miraculous sign that had occurred in the land, God left him to test him and to know everything that was in his heart.
[32]The other events of Hezekiah's reign and his acts of devotion are written in the vision of the prophet Isaiah son of Amoz in the book of the kings of Judah and Israel.
[33]Hezekiah rested with his fathers and was buried on the hill where the tombs of David's descendants are. All Judah and the people of Jerusalem honored him when he died. And Manasseh his son succeeded him as king.

*Manasseh King of Judah*

33 Manasseh was twelve years old when he became king, and he reigned in Jerusalem fifty-five years.
[2]He did evil in the eyes of the LORD, following the detestable practices of the nations the LORD had driven out before the Israelites.
[3]He rebuilt the high places his father Hezekiah had demolished; he also erected altars to the Baals and made Asherah poles. He bowed down to all the starry hosts and worshiped them.

*30 Most mss have *sheva* under the first *yod* and *pathah* under the second (וַיְיַשְׁ) as a *Kethib* form, and omit the first *yod* and *sheva* in the *Qere* (וַיַּשְׁ).

וּבָנָה מִזְבְּחוֹת בְּבֵית יְהוָה אֲשֶׁר אָמַר יְהוָה בִּירוּשָׁלִָם
in-Jerusalem Yahweh he-said which Yahweh in-temple-of altars and-he-built (4)

יִהְיֶה־ שְׁמִי לְעוֹלָם׃ וַיִּבֶן מִזְבְּחוֹת לְכָל־
to-all-of altars and-he-built (5) to-forever Name-of-me he-will-remain

צְבָא הַשָּׁמָיִם בִּשְׁתֵּי חַצְרוֹת בֵּית־ יְהוָה׃ וְהוּא
and-he (6) Yahweh temple-of courts-of in-both-of the-heavens host-of

הֶעֱבִיר אֶת־ בָּנָיו בָּאֵשׁ בְּגֵי בֶן־ הִנֹּם
Hinnom Ben in-Valley-of through-the-fire sons-of-him *** he-made-pass

וְעוֹנֵן וְנִחֵשׁ וְכִשֵּׁף
and-he-practiced-witchcraft and-he-practiced-divination and-he-practiced-sorcery

וְעָשָׂה אוֹב וְיִדְּעוֹנִי הִרְבָּה לַעֲשׂוֹת הָרַע בְּעֵינֵי
in-eyes-of the-evil to-do he-did-much and-spiritist medium and-he-consulted

יְהוָה לְהַכְעִיסוֹ׃ וַיָּשֶׂם אֶת־ פֶּסֶל הַסֶּמֶל אֲשֶׁר
that the-carving image-of *** and-he-put (7) to-provoke-to-anger-him Yahweh

עָשָׂה בְּבֵית הָאֱלֹהִים אֲשֶׁר אָמַר אֱלֹהִים אֶל־דָּוִיד וְאֶל־ שְׁלֹמֹה
Solomon and-to David to God he-said which the-God in-temple-of he-made

בְנוֹ בַּבַּיִת הַזֶּה וּבִירוּשָׁלִַם אֲשֶׁר בָּחַרְתִּי מִכֹּל
from-all-of I-chose which and-in-Jerusalem the-this in-the-temple son-of-him

שִׁבְטֵי יִשְׂרָאֵל אָשִׂים אֶת־ שְׁמִי לְעֵילוֹם׃ וְלֹא
and-not (8) to-forever Name-of-me *** I-will-put Israel tribes-of

אוֹסִיף לְהָסִיר אֶת־ רֶגֶל יִשְׂרָאֵל מֵעַל הָאֲדָמָה אֲשֶׁר
that the-land from-on Israel foot-of *** to-make-leave I-will-repeat

הֶעֱמַדְתִּי לַאֲבֹתֵיכֶם רַק ׀ אִם־ יִשְׁמְרוּ לַעֲשׂוֹת אֵת כָּל־ אֲשֶׁר
that all *** to-do they-are-careful if only to-fathers-of-you I-assigned

צִוִּיתִים לְכָל־ הַתּוֹרָה וְהַחֻקִּים וְהַמִּשְׁפָּטִים
and-the-ordinances and-the-decrees the-law about-all-of I-commanded-them

בְּיַד־ מֹשֶׁה׃ וַיֶּתַע מְנַשֶּׁה אֶת־יְהוּדָה וְיֹשְׁבֵי
and-ones-living-of Judah *** Manasseh but-he-led-astray (9) Moses by-hand-of

יְרוּשָׁלִָם לַעֲשׂוֹת רָע מִן־ הַגּוֹיִם אֲשֶׁר הִשְׁמִיד יְהוָה
Yahweh he-destroyed that the-nations more-than evil to-do Jerusalem

מִפְּנֵי בְּנֵי יִשְׂרָאֵל׃ וַיְדַבֵּר יְהוָה אֶל־ מְנַשֶּׁה וְאֶל־
and-to Manasseh to Yahweh and-he-spoke (10) Israel sons-of from-before

עַמּוֹ וְלֹא הִקְשִׁיבוּ׃ וַיָּבֵא יְהוָה
Yahweh so-he-brought (11) they-paid-attention but-not people-of-him

עֲלֵיהֶם אֶת־ שָׂרֵי הַצָּבָא אֲשֶׁר לְמֶלֶךְ אַשּׁוּר
Assyria of-king-of that the-army commanders-of *** against-them

וַיִּלְכְּדוּ אֶת־ מְנַשֶּׁה בַּחֹחִים וַיַּאַסְרֻהוּ
and-they-bound-him with-the-hooks Manasseh *** and-they-took-prisoner

[4]He built altars in the temple
of the LORD, of which the LORD
had said, "My Name will remain in Jerusalem forever."
[5]In both courts of the temple of
the LORD, he built altars to all
the starry hosts. [6]He sacrificed
his sons in[z] the fire in the Valley of Ben Hinnom, practiced
sorcery, divination and witchcraft, and consulted mediums
and spiritists. He did much
evil in the eyes of the LORD,
provoking him to anger.
[7]He took the carved image
he had made and put it in
God's temple, of which God
had said to David and to his
son Solomon, "In this temple
and in Jerusalem, which I
have chosen out of all the
tribes of Israel, I will put my
Name forever. [8]I will not again
make the feet of the Israelites
leave the land I assigned to
your forefathers, if only they
will be careful to do everything I commanded them concerning all the laws, decrees
and ordinances given through
Moses." [9]But Manasseh led
Judah and the people of
Jerusalem astray, so that they
did more evil than the nations
the LORD had destroyed before
the Israelites.
[10]The LORD spoke to Manasseh and his people, but they
paid no attention. [11]So the
LORD brought against them
the army commanders of the
king of Assyria, who took
Manasseh prisoner, put a
hook in his nose, bound him

[z]6 Or *He made his sons pass through*

בַּנְחֻשְׁתַּיִם וַיּוֹלִיכֻהוּ בָּבֶלָה׃ וּכְהָצֵר
and-in-to-distress (12) to-Babylon and-they-took-him with-the-bronze-shackles

לוֹ חִלָּה אֶת־ פְּנֵי יְהוָה אֱלֹהָיו וַיִּכָּנַע
and-he-humbled-himself God-of-him Yahweh faces-of *** he-sought to-him

מְאֹד מִלִּפְנֵי אֱלֹהֵי אֲבֹתָיו׃ וַיִּתְפַּלֵּל אֵלָיו
to-him when-he-prayed (13) fathers-of-him God-of at-before greatly

וַיֵּעָתֶר לוֹ וַיִּשְׁמַע תְּחִנָּתוֹ וַיְשִׁיבֵהוּ
so-he-brought-back-him plea-of-him and-he-listened-to by-him then-he-was-moved

יְרוּשָׁלַםִ לְמַלְכוּתוֹ וַיֵּדַע מְנַשֶּׁה כִּי יְהוָה הוּא הָאֱלֹהִים׃
the-God he Yahweh that Manasseh then-he-knew to-kingdom-of-him Jerusalem

וְאַחֲרֵי־ כֵן בָּנָה חוֹמָה חִיצוֹנָה ׀ לְעִיר־ דָּוִיד מַעְרָבָה לְגִיחוֹן
of-Gihon to-west David of-City-of outer wall he-rebuilt this and-after (14)

בַּנַּחַל וְלָבוֹא בְשַׁעַר הַדָּגִים וְסָבַב לָעֹפֶל
to-the-Ophel and-he-encircled the-Fishes to-Gate-of as-to-go in-the-valley

וַיַּגְבִּיהֶהָ מְאֹד וַיָּשֶׂם שָׂרֵי־ חַיִל בְּכָל־
in-all-of military commanders-of and-he-stationed much and-he-made-high-her

הֶעָרִים הַבְּצֻרוֹת בִּיהוּדָה׃ וַיָּסַר אֶת־ אֱלֹהֵי
gods-of *** and-he-got-rid (15) in-Judah the-ones-being-fortified the-cities

הַנֵּכָר וְאֶת־ הַסֶּמֶל מִבֵּית יְהוָה וְכָל־ הַמִּזְבְּחוֹת אֲשֶׁר
that the-altars and-all-of Yahweh from-temple-of the-image and the-foreign

בָּנָה בְּהַר בֵּית־ יְהוָה וּבִירוּשָׁלָםִ וַיַּשְׁלֵךְ חוּצָה
to-outside and-he-threw and-in-Jerusalem Yahweh temple-of on-hill-of he-built

לָעִיר׃ וַיִּכֶן אֶת־ מִזְבַּח יְהוָה וַיִּזְבַּח
and-he-sacrificed Yahweh altar-of *** then-he-restored (16) of-the-city

עָלָיו זִבְחֵי שְׁלָמִים וְתוֹדָה וַיֹּאמֶר לִיהוּדָה לַעֲבוֹד
to-serve to-Judah and-he-told and-thanksgiving fellowships offerings-of on-him

אֶת־ יְהוָה אֱלֹהֵי יִשְׂרָאֵל׃ אֲבָל עוֹד הָעָם זֹבְחִים
ones-sacrificing the-people still however (17) Israel God-of Yahweh ***

בַּבָּמוֹת רַק לַיהוָה אֱלֹהֵיהֶם׃ וְיֶתֶר דִּבְרֵי
events-of and-other-of (18) God-of-them to-Yahweh but at-the-high-places

מְנַשֶּׁה וּתְפִלָּתוֹ אֶל־ אֱלֹהָיו וְדִבְרֵי הַחֹזִים
the-seers and-words-of God-of-him to and-prayer-of-him Manasseh

הַמְדַבְּרִים אֵלָיו בְּשֵׁם יְהוָה אֱלֹהֵי יִשְׂרָאֵל הִנָּם עַל־
in see-they! Israel God-of Yahweh in-name-of to-him the-ones-speaking

דִּבְרֵי מַלְכֵי יִשְׂרָאֵל׃ וּתְפִלָּתוֹ וְהֵעָתֶר־ לוֹ
by-him and-to-be-moved and-prayer-of-him (19) Israel kings-of annals-of

וְכָל־ חַטָּאתוֹ וּמַעְלוֹ וְהַמְּקֹמוֹת אֲשֶׁר
where and-the-sites and-unfaithfulness-of-him sin-of-him and-all-of

with bronze shackles and took him to Babylon. [12]In his distress he sought the favor of the LORD his God and humbled himself greatly before the God of his fathers. [13]And when he prayed to him, the LORD was moved by his entreaty and listened to his plea; so he brought him back to Jerusalem and to his kingdom. Then Manasseh knew that the LORD is God.

[14]Afterward he rebuilt the outer wall of the City of David, west of the Gihon spring in the valley, as far as the entrance of the Fish Gate and encircling the hill of Ophel; he also made it much higher. He stationed military commanders in all the fortified cities in Judah.

[15]He got rid of the foreign gods and removed the image from the temple of the LORD, as well as all the altars he had built on the temple hill and in Jerusalem; and he threw them out of the city. [16]Then he restored the altar of the LORD and sacrificed fellowship[b] and thank offerings on it, and told Judah to serve the LORD, the God of Israel. [17]The people, however, continued to sacrifice at the high places, but only to the LORD their God.

[18]The other events of Manasseh's reign, including his prayer to his God and the words the seers spoke to him in the name of the LORD, the God of Israel, are written in the annals of the kings of Israel.[c] [19]His prayer and how God was moved by his entreaty, as well as all his sins and unfaithfulness, and the sites

[b]16 Traditionally *peace*
[c]18 That is, Judah, as frequently in 2 Chronicles

°16 ק ויבן

בָּנָה בָהֶם בָּמוֹת וְהֶעֱמִיד הָאֲשֵׁרִים וְהַפְּסִלִים

and-the-idols the-Asherah-poles and-he-set-up high-places on-them he-built

לִפְנֵי הִכָּנְעוֹ הִנָּם כְּתוּבִים עַל דִּבְרֵי חוֹזָי׃

Hozai records-of in ones-being-written see-they! to-be-humbled-him before

וַיִּשְׁכַּב מְנַשֶּׁה עִם־ אֲבֹתָיו וַיִּקְבְּרֻהוּ

and-they-buried-him fathers-of-him with Manasseh and-he-rested (20)

בֵּיתוֹ וַיִּמְלֹךְ אָמוֹן בְּנוֹ תַּחְתָּיו׃ בֶּן־

son-of (21) in-place-of-him son-of-him Amon and-he-became-king palace-of-him

עֶשְׂרִים וּשְׁתַּיִם שָׁנָה אָמוֹן בְּמָלְכוֹ וּשְׁתַּיִם שָׁנִים מָלַךְ

he-reigned years and-two when-to-become-king-him Amon year and-two twenty

בִּירוּשָׁלִָם׃ וַיַּעַשׂ הָרַע בְּעֵינֵי יְהוָה כַּאֲשֶׁר עָשָׂה

he-did just-as Yahweh in-eyes-of the-evil and-he-did (22) in-Jerusalem

מְנַשֶּׁה אָבִיו וּלְכָל־ הַפְּסִילִים אֲשֶׁר עָשָׂה מְנַשֶּׁה

Manasseh he-made that the-idols and-to-all-of father-of-him Manasseh

אָבִיו זִבַּח אָמוֹן וַיַּעַבְדֵם׃ וְלֹא

but-not (23) and-he-worshiped-them Amon he-sacrificed father-of-him

נִכְנַע מִלִּפְנֵי יְהוָה כְּהִכָּנַע מְנַשֶּׁה

Manasseh like-to-humble-himself Yahweh at-before he-humbled-himself

אָבִיו כִּי הוּא אָמוֹן הִרְבָּה אַשְׁמָה׃ וַיִּקְשְׁרוּ

and-they-conspired (24) guilt he-increased Amon he instead father-of-him

עָלָיו עֲבָדָיו וַיְמִיתֻהוּ בְּבֵיתוֹ׃

in-palace-of-him and-they-assassinated-him officials-of-him against-him

וַיַּכּוּ עַם־ הָאָרֶץ אֵת כָּל־ הַקֹּשְׁרִים עַל־

against the-ones-plotting all-of *** the-land people-of then-they-killed (25)

הַמֶּלֶךְ אָמוֹן וַיַּמְלִיכוּ עַם־ הָאָרֶץ אֶת־ יֹאשִׁיָּהוּ בְנוֹ

son-of-him Josiah *** the-land people-of and-they-made-king Amon the-king

תַּחְתָּיו׃ בֶּן־ שְׁמוֹנֶה שָׁנִים יֹאשִׁיָּהוּ בְמָלְכוֹ

when-to-become-king-him Josiah years eight son-of (34:1) in-place-of-him

וּשְׁלֹשִׁים וְאַחַת שָׁנָה מָלַךְ בִּירוּשָׁלִָם׃ וַיַּעַשׂ הַיָּשָׁר

the-right and-he-did (2) in-Jerusalem he-reigned year and-one and-thirty

בְּעֵינֵי יְהוָה וַיֵּלֶךְ בְּדַרְכֵי דָּוִיד אָבִיו וְלֹא־

and-not father-of-him David in-ways-of and-he-walked Yahweh in-eyes-of

סָר יָמִין וּשְׂמֹאול׃ וּבִשְׁמוֹנֶה שָׁנִים לְמָלְכוֹ וְהוּא

while-he to-reign-him years and-in-eight (3) or-left right he-turned

עוֹדֶנּוּ נַעַר הֵחֵל לִדְרוֹשׁ לֵאלֹהֵי דָּוִיד אָבִיו וּבִשְׁתֵּים

and-in-two father-of-him David to-God-of to-seek he-began young still-he

עֶשְׂרֵה שָׁנָה הֵחֵל לְטַהֵר אֶת־ יְהוּדָה וִירוּשָׁלִַם מִן־ הַבָּמוֹת

the-high-places of and-Jerusalem Judah *** to-purge he-began year ten

where he built high places and
set up Asherah poles and idols
before he humbled himself—
all are written in the records of
the seers.[d] 20Manasseh rested
with his fathers and was buried in his palace. And Amon
his son succeeded him as king.

*Amon King of Judah*

21Amon was twenty-two
years old when he became
king, and he reigned in
Jerusalem two years. 22He did
evil in the eyes of the LORD, as
his father Manasseh had
done. Amon worshiped and
offered sacrifices to all the
idols Manasseh had made.
23But unlike his father Manasseh, he did not humble himself before the LORD; Amon increased his guilt.

24Amon's officials conspired
against him and assassinated
him in his palace. 25Then the
people of the land killed all
who had plotted against King
Amon, and they made Josiah
his son king in his place.

*Josiah's Reforms*

34 Josiah was eight years
old when he became
king, and he reigned in
Jerusalem thirty-one years.
2He did what was right in the
eyes of the LORD and walked
in the ways of his father David, not turning aside to the
right or to the left.

3In the eighth year of his
reign, while he was still
young, he began to seek the
God of his father David. In his
twelfth year he began to purge
Judah and Jerusalem of high

[d]19 One Hebrew manuscript and Septuagint; most Hebrew manuscripts *of Hozai*

וְהָאֲשֵׁרִים וְהַפְּסִלִים וְהַמַּסֵּכוֹת׃
and-the-cast-images and-the-carved-idols and-the-Asherah-poles

וַיְנַתְּצוּ לְפָנָיו אֵת מִזְבְּחוֹת הַבְּעָלִים וְהַחַמָּנִים
and-the-incense-altars the-Baals altars-of *** before-him and-they-tore-down (4)

אֲשֶׁר־לְמַעְלָה מֵעֲלֵיהֶם גִּדֵּעַ וְהָאֲשֵׁרִים וְהַפְּסִלִים
and-the-idols and-the-Asherah-poles he-cut-to-pieces at-over-them at-above that

וְהַמַּסֵּכוֹת שִׁבַּר וְהֵדַק וַיִּזְרֹק עַל־
over and-he-scattered and-he-broke-to-pieces he-smashed and-the-images

פְּנֵי הַקְּבָרִים הַזֹּבְחִים לָהֶם׃ וְעַצְמוֹת כֹּהֲנִים
priests and-bones-of (5) to-them the-ones-sacrificing the-graves surfaces-of

שָׂרַף עַל־ מִזְבְּחוֹתֵים° וַיְטַהֵר אֶת־ יְהוּדָה וְאֶת־ יְרוּשָׁלִָם׃
Jerusalem and Judah *** so-he-purged altars-of-them on he-burned

וּבְעָרֵי מְנַשֶּׁה וְאֶפְרַיִם וְשִׁמְעוֹן וְעַד־ נַפְתָּלִי
Naphtali and-as-far-as and-Simeon and-Ephraim Manasseh and-in-towns-of (6)

בְּהַר ° בְּתֵיהֶם סָבִיב׃ וַיְנַתֵּץ אֶת־ הַמִּזְבְּחוֹת וְאֶת־
and the-altars *** then-he-tore-down (7) around in-ruins-of-them

הָאֲשֵׁרִים וְהַפְּסִלִים כִּתַּת לְהֵדַק וְכָל־
and-all-of to-be-powder he-crushed and-the-idols the-Asherah-poles

הַחַמָּנִים גִּדַּע בְּכָל־ אֶרֶץ יִשְׂרָאֵל
Israel land-of through-all-of he-cut-to-pieces the-incense-altars

וַיָּשָׁב לִירוּשָׁלִָם׃ וּבִשְׁנַת שְׁמוֹנֶה עֶשְׂרֵה לְמָלְכוֹ
to-reign-him ten eight and-in-year-of (8) to-Jerusalem then-he-went-back

לְטַהֵר הָאָרֶץ וְהַבָּיִת שָׁלַח אֶת־ שָׁפָן בֶּן־ אֲצַלְיָהוּ וְאֶת־
and Azaliah son-of Shaphan *** he-sent and-the-temple the-land to-purify

מַעֲשֵׂיָהוּ שַׂר־ הָעִיר וְאֵת יוֹאָח בֶּן־ יוֹאָחָז הַמַּזְכִּיר
the-one-recording Joahaz son-of Joah with the-city ruler-of Maaseiah

לְחַזֵּק אֶת־ בֵּית יְהוָה אֱלֹהָיו׃ וַיָּבֹאוּ אֶל־חִלְקִיָּהוּ
Hilkiah to and-they-went (9) God-of-him Yahweh temple-of *** to-repair

הַכֹּהֵן הַגָּדוֹל וַיִּתְּנוּ אֶת־ הַכֶּסֶף הַמּוּבָא
the-one-being-brought the-money *** and-they-gave the-high the-priest

בֵית־ אֱלֹהִים אֲשֶׁר אָסְפוּ־ הַלְוִיִּם שֹׁמְרֵי הַסַּף
the-door ones-keeping-of the-Levites they-collected which God temple-of

מִיַּד מְנַשֶּׁה וְאֶפְרַיִם וּמִכֹּל שְׁאֵרִית יִשְׂרָאֵל
Israel remnant-of and-from-entire-of and-Ephraim Manasseh from-hand-of

וּמִכָּל־ יְהוּדָה וּבִנְיָמִן וַיָּשֻׁבֵי° יְרוּשָׁלִָם׃
Jerusalem *and-they-returned and-Benjamin Judah and-from-all-of

וַיִּתְּנוּ עַל־ יַד עֹשֵׂה הַמְּלָאכָה
the-work one-supervising-of hand-of to then-they-entrusted (10)

places, Asherah poles, carved
idols and cast images. [4]Under
his direction the altars of the
Baals were torn down; he cut
to pieces the incense altars
that were above them, and
smashed the Asherah poles,
the idols and the images.
These he broke to pieces and
scattered over the graves of
those who had sacrificed to
them. [5]He burned the bones of
the priests on their altars, and
so he purged Judah and
Jerusalem. [6]In the towns of
Manasseh, Ephraim and
Simeon, as far as Naphtali,
and in the ruins around them,
[7]he tore down the altars and
the Asherah poles and crushed
the idols to powder and cut to
pieces all the incense altars
throughout Israel. Then he
went back to Jerusalem.
[8]In the eighteenth year of Josiah's reign, to purify the land
and the temple, he sent Shaphan son of Azaliah and Maaseiah the ruler of the city, with
Joah son of Joahaz, the
recorder, to repair the temple
of the LORD his God.
[9]They went to Hilkiah the
high priest and gave him the
money that had been brought
into the temple of God, which
the Levites who were the
doorkeepers had collected
from the people of Manasseh,
Ephraim and the entire remnant of Israel and from all the
people of Judah and Benjamin
and the inhabitants of Jerusalem. [10]Then they entrusted it
to the men appointed to supervise the work on the LORD's

*9 The interlinear translation follows the *Qere*; the NIV points the consonants of the *Ketib* as a Qal participle ( וְיֹשְׁבֵי ), *and-ones-inhabiting-of*.

°5 ק מזבחותם
°6 ק בחרבתיהם
°9 ק וישבו

הַמֻּפְקָדִים בְּבֵית יְהוָה וַיִּתְּנוּ אֹתוֹ עוֹשֵׂי

ones-doing-of him and-they-paid Yahweh to-temple-of the-ones-being-appointed

הַמְּלָאכָה אֲשֶׁר עֹשִׂים בְּבֵית יְהוָה לִבְדּוֹק וּלְחַזֵּק

and-to-restore to-repair Yahweh on-temple-of ones-working who the-work

הַבָּיִת׃ וַיִּתְּנוּ לֶחָרָשִׁים וְלַבֹּנִים

and-to-the-ones-building to-the-carpenters and-they-gave (11) the-temple

לִקְנוֹת אַבְנֵי מַחְצֵב וְעֵצִים לַמְחַבְּרוֹת וּלְקָרוֹת

and-to-furnish-beams for-the-joists and-timbers dressed stones-of to-purchase

אֶת־ הַבָּתִּים אֲשֶׁר הִשְׁחִיתוּ מַלְכֵי יְהוּדָה׃

Judah kings-of they-allowed-to-fall-into-ruin that the-buildings ***

וְהָאֲנָשִׁים עֹשִׂים בֶּאֱמוּנָה בַּמְּלָאכָה וַעֲלֵיהֶם ׀

and-over-them in-the-work in-faith ones-doing and-the-men (12)

מֻפְקָדִים יַחַת וְעֹבַדְיָהוּ הַלְוִיִּם מִן־ בְּנֵי מְרָרִי

Merari descendants-of from the-Levites and-Obadiah Jahath ones-being-appointed

וּזְכַרְיָה וּמְשֻׁלָּם מִן־ בְּנֵי הַקְּהָתִים לְנַצֵּחַ

to-direct the-Kohathites descendants-of from and-Meshullam and-Zechariah

וְהַלְוִיִּם כָּל־ מֵבִין בִּכְלֵי־ שִׁיר׃ וְעַל

and-over (13) music with-instruments-of being-skilled all-of and-the-Levites

הַסַּבָּלִים וּמְנַצְּחִים לְכֹל עֹשֵׂה מְלָאכָה לַעֲבוֹדָה

to-job work one-doing-of over-all-of and-ones-supervising the-laborers

וַעֲבוֹדָה וּמֵהַלְוִיִּם סוֹפְרִים וְשֹׁטְרִים וְשׁוֹעֲרִים׃

and-doorkeepers and-scribes secretaries and-from-the-Levites and-job

וּבְהוֹצִיאָם אֶת־ הַכֶּסֶף הַמּוּבָא בֵּית

temple-of the-one-being-taken the-money *** and-while-to-bring-out-them (14)

יְהוָה מָצָא חִלְקִיָּהוּ הַכֹּהֵן אֶת־ סֵפֶר תּוֹרַת־ יְהוָה בְּיַד־

through-hand-of Yahweh Law-of Book-of *** the-priest Hilkiah he-found Yahweh

מֹשֶׁה׃ וַיַּעַן חִלְקִיָּהוּ וַיֹּאמֶר אֶל־ שָׁפָן הַסּוֹפֵר סֵפֶר

Book-of the-secretary Shaphan to and-he-said Hilkiah and-he-spoke (15) Moses

הַתּוֹרָה מָצָאתִי בְּבֵית יְהוָה וַיִּתֵּן חִלְקִיָּהוּ אֶת־הַסֵּפֶר אֶל־ שָׁפָן׃

Shaphan to the-book *** Hilkiah and-he-gave Yahweh in-temple-of I-found the-Law

וַיָּבֵא שָׁפָן אֶת־ הַסֵּפֶר אֶל־ הַמֶּלֶךְ וַיָּשֶׁב עוֹד אֶת־

*** again and-he-gave the-king to the-book *** Shaphan then-he-took (16)

הַמֶּלֶךְ דָּבָר לֵאמֹר כֹּל אֲשֶׁר־ נִתַּן בְּיַד־ עֲבָדֶיךָ

officials-of-you into-hand-of he-was-committed that all to-say report the-king

הֵם עֹשִׂים׃ וַיַּתִּיכוּ אֶת־ הַכֶּסֶף הַנִּמְצָא

the-one-being-found the-money *** and-they-paid-out (17) ones-doing they

בְּבֵית־ יְהוָה וַיִּתְּנוּהוּ עַל־ יַד הַמֻּפְקָדִים

the-ones-supervising hand-of into and-they-entrusted-him Yahweh in-temple-of

temple. These men paid the
workers who repaired and restored the temple. [11]They also
gave money to the carpenters
and builders to purchase
dressed stone, and timber for
joists and beams for the buildings that the kings of Judah
had allowed to fall into ruin.
[12]The men did the work
faithfully. Over them to direct
them were Jahath and Oba-
diah, Levites descended from
Merari, and Zechariah and
Meshullam, descended from
Kohath. The Levites—all who
were skilled in playing musical instruments— [13]had charge
of the laborers and supervised
all the workers from job to job.
Some of the Levites were secretaries, scribes and doorkeepers.

*The Book of the Law Found*

[14]While they were bringing
out the money that had been
taken into the temple of the
LORD, Hilkiah the priest found
the Book of the Law of the
LORD that had been given
through Moses. [15]Hilkiah said
to Shaphan the secretary, "I
have found the Book of the
Law in the temple of the
LORD." He gave it to Shaphan.
[16]Then Shaphan took the
book to the king and reported
to him: "Your officials are doing everything that has been
committed to them. [17]They
have paid out the money that
was in the temple of the LORD
and have entrusted it to the

וְעַל־ יַד עוֹשֵׂי הַמְּלָאכָה׃ וַיַּגֵּד שָׁפָן

Shaphan then-he-informed (18) the-work ones-doing-of hand-of and-into

הַסּוֹפֵר לַמֶּלֶךְ לֵאמֹר סֵפֶר נָתַן לִי חִלְקִיָּהוּ הַכֹּהֵן

the-priest Hilkiah to-me he-gave book to-say to-the-king the-secretary

וַיִּקְרָא־ בוֹ שָׁפָן לִפְנֵי הַמֶּלֶךְ׃ וַיְהִי

and-he-was (19) the-king in-presences-of Shaphan from-him and-he-read

כִּשְׁמֹעַ הַמֶּלֶךְ אֵת דִּבְרֵי הַתּוֹרָה וַיִּקְרַע אֶת־ בְּגָדָיו׃

robes-of-him *** then-he-tore the-Law words-of *** the-king when-to-hear

וַיְצַו הַמֶּלֶךְ אֶת־ חִלְקִיָּהוּ וְאֶת־אֲחִיקָם בֶּן־ שָׁפָן וְאֶת־עַבְדּוֹן

Abdon and Shaphan son-of Ahikam and Hilkiah *** the-king and-he-ordered (20)

בֶּן־ מִיכָה וְאֵת ׀ שָׁפָן הַסּוֹפֵר וְאֵת עֲשָׂיָה עֶבֶד־ הַמֶּלֶךְ

the-king attendant-of Asaiah and the-secretary Shaphan and Micah son-of

לֵאמֹר׃ לְכוּ דִרְשׁוּ אֶת־ יְהוָה בַּעֲדִי וּבְעַד הַנִּשְׁאָר בְּיִשְׂרָאֵל

in-Israel the-one-remaining and-for for-me Yahweh *** inquire! go! (21) to-say

וּבִיהוּדָה עַל־ דִּבְרֵי הַסֵּפֶר אֲשֶׁר נִמְצָא כִּי־ גְדוֹלָה חֲמַת־

anger-of great for he-was-found that the-book words-of about and-in-Judah

יְהוָה אֲשֶׁר נִתְּכָה בָנוּ עַל אֲשֶׁר לֹא־ שָׁמְרוּ אֲבוֹתֵינוּ

fathers-of-us they-kept not that because on-us she-is-poured-out that Yahweh

אֶת־ דְּבַר יְהוָה לַעֲשׂוֹת כְּכָל־ הַכָּתוּב עַל־ הַסֵּפֶר

the-book in the-thing-being-written as-all-of to-act Yahweh word-of ***

הַזֶּה׃ וַיֵּלֶךְ חִלְקִיָּהוּ וַאֲשֶׁר הַמֶּלֶךְ אֶל־חֻלְדָּה הַנְּבִיאָה

the-prophetess Huldah to the-king and-who Hilkiah and-he-went (22) the-this

אֵשֶׁת ׀ שַׁלֻּם בֶּן־ תּוֹקְהַת בֶּן־ חַסְרָה שׁוֹמֵר הַבְּגָדִים

the-clothes one-keeping-of Hasrah son-of Tokhath son-of Shallum wife-of

וְהִיא יוֹשֶׁבֶת בִּירוּשָׁלַםִ בַּמִּשְׁנֶה וַיְדַבְּרוּ אֵלֶיהָ

to-her and-they-spoke in-the-Second-District in-Jerusalem living now-she

כָּזֹאת׃ וַתֹּאמֶר לָהֶם כֹּה־ אָמַר יְהוָה אֱלֹהֵי יִשְׂרָאֵל אִמְרוּ

tell! Israel God-of Yahweh he-says this to-them and-she-said (23) as-this

לָאִישׁ אֲשֶׁר־ שָׁלַח אֶתְכֶם אֵלָי׃ כֹּה אָמַר יְהוָה הִנְנִי מֵבִיא

bringing see-I! Yahweh he-says this (24) to-me you he-sent who to-the-man

רָעָה עַל־ הַמָּקוֹם הַזֶּה וְעַל־ יוֹשְׁבָיו אֵת כָּל־

all-of *** ones-living-of-him and-on the-this the-place on disaster

הָאָלוֹת הַכְּתוּבוֹת עַל־ הַסֵּפֶר אֲשֶׁר קָרְאוּ לִפְנֵי

in-presences-of they-read that the-book in the-ones-being-written the-curses

מֶלֶךְ יְהוּדָה׃ תַּחַת ׀ אֲשֶׁר עֲזָבוּנִי וַיְקַטִּירוּ

and-they-burned-incense they-forsook-me that because (25) Judah king-of

לֵאלֹהִים אֲחֵרִים לְמַעַן הַכְעִיסֵנִי בְּכֹל מַעֲשֵׂי יְדֵיהֶם

hands-of-them works-of by-all-of to-anger-me in-order-to other-ones to-gods

supervisors and workers."
18Then Shaphan the secretary informed the king, "Hilkiah the priest has given me a book." And Shaphan read from it in the presence of the king.

19When the king heard the words of the Law, he tore his robes. 20He gave these orders to Hilkiah, Ahikam son of Shaphan, Abdon son of Micah,[e] Shaphan the secretary and Asaiah the king's attendant: 21"Go and inquire of the LORD for me and for the remnant in Israel and Judah about what is written in this book that has been found. Great is the LORD's anger that is poured out on us because our fathers have not kept the word of the LORD; they have not acted in accordance with all that is written in this book."

22Hilkiah and those the king had sent with him[f] went to speak to the prophetess Huldah, who was the wife of Shallum son of Tokhath,[g] the son of Hasrah,[h] keeper of the wardrobe. She lived in Jerusalem, in the Second District.

23She said to them, "This is what the LORD, the God of Israel, says: Tell the man who sent you to me, 24'This is what the LORD says: I am going to bring disaster on this place and its people—all the curses written in the book that has been read in the presence of the king of Judah. 25Because they have forsaken me and burned incense to other gods and provoked me to anger by all that their hands have

[e]20 Also called *Acbor son of Micaiah*
[f]22 One Hebrew manuscript, Vulgate and Syriac; most Hebrew manuscripts do not have *had sent with him.*
[g]22 Also called *Tikvah*
[h]22 Also called *Harhas*

°22 ק תקהת
°25 ק ויקטרו

| וְלֹא | הַזֶּה | בַּמָּקוֹם | חֲמָתִי | וְתִתַּךְ |
|---|---|---|---|---|
| and-not | the-this | on-the-place | anger-of-me | and-she-will-be-poured-out |

| לִדְרוֹשׁ | אֶתְכֶם | הַשֹּׁלֵחַ | יְהוּדָה | מֶלֶךְ | וְאֶל־ | | תִכְבֶּה׃ |
|---|---|---|---|---|---|---|---|
| to-inquire | you | the-one-sending | Judah | king-of | and-to | (26) | she-will-be-quenched |

| הַדְּבָרִים | יִשְׂרָאֵל | אֱלֹהֵי | יְהוָה | אָמַר | כֹּה־ | אֵלָיו | תֹאמְרוּ | כֹּה | בַּיהוָה |
|---|---|---|---|---|---|---|---|---|---|
| the-words | Israel | God-of | Yahweh | he-says | this | to-him | you-tell | this | of-Yahweh |

| וַתִּכָּנַע | לְבָבְךָ | רַךְ־ | יַעַן | | שָׁמָעְתָּ׃ | אֲשֶׁר |
|---|---|---|---|---|---|---|
| and-you-humbled-self | heart-of-you | he-was-responsive | because | (27) | you-heard | that |

| הַזֶּה | הַמָּקוֹם | עַל־ | דְּבָרָיו | אֶת־ | בְּשָׁמְעֲךָ | אֱלֹהִים | מִלִּפְנֵי |
|---|---|---|---|---|---|---|---|
| the-this | the-place | against | words-of-him | *** | when-to-hear-you | God | at-before |

| וַתִּקְרַע | לְפָנַי | וַתִּכָּנַע | יֹשְׁבָיו | וְעַל־ |
|---|---|---|---|---|
| and-you-tore | before-me | and-you-humbled-self | ones-living-of-him | and-against |

| שָׁמַעְתִּי | אֲנִי | וְגַם־ | לְפָנָי | וַתֵּבְךְּ | בְּגָדֶיךָ | אֶת־ |
|---|---|---|---|---|---|---|
| I-heard | I | now-indeed | in-presences-of-me | and-you-wept | robes-of-you | *** |

| אֲבֹתֶיךָ | אֶל־ | אֹסִפְךָ | הִנְנִי | | יְהוָה׃ | נְאֻם־ |
|---|---|---|---|---|---|---|
| fathers-of-you | to | I-will-gather-you | see-I! | (28) | Yahweh | declaration-of |

| תִרְאֶינָה | וְלֹא־ | בְּשָׁלוֹם | קִבְרֹתֶיךָ | אֶל־ | וְנֶאֱסַפְתָּ |
|---|---|---|---|---|---|
| they-will-see | and-not | in-peace | tombs-of-you | in | and-you-will-be-buried |

| הַזֶּה | הַמָּקוֹם | עַל־ | מֵבִיא | אֲנִי | אֲשֶׁר | הָרָעָה | בְּכֹל | עֵינֶיךָ |
|---|---|---|---|---|---|---|---|---|
| the-this | the-place | on | bringing | I | that | the-disaster | to-all-of | eyes-of-you |

| דָּבָר׃ | הַמֶּלֶךְ | אֶת־ | וַיָּשִׁיבוּ | יֹשְׁבָיו | וְעַל־ |
|---|---|---|---|---|---|
| answer | the-king | *** | so-they-took-back | ones-living-of-him | and-on |

| יְהוּדָה | זִקְנֵי | כָּל־ | אֶת־ | וַיֶּאֱסֹף | הַמֶּלֶךְ | וַיִּשְׁלַח | |
|---|---|---|---|---|---|---|---|
| Judah | elders-of | all-of | *** | and-he-brought-together | the-king | then-he-called | (29) |

| וְכָל־ | יְהוָה | בֵּית־ | הַמֶּלֶךְ | וַיַּעַל | | וִירוּשָׁלִָם׃ |
|---|---|---|---|---|---|---|
| and-all-of | Yahweh | temple-of | the-king | and-he-went-up | (30) | and-Jerusalem |

| וְהַלְוִיִּם | וְהַכֹּהֲנִים | יְרוּשָׁלִַם | וְיֹשְׁבֵי | יְהוּדָה | אִישׁ |
|---|---|---|---|---|---|
| and-the-Levites | and-the-priests | Jerusalem | and-ones-living-of | Judah | man-of |

| בְאָזְנֵיהֶם | וַיִּקְרָא | קָטָן | וְעַד־ | מִגָּדוֹל | הָעָם | וְכָל־ |
|---|---|---|---|---|---|---|
| in-ears-of-them | and-he-read | least | even-to | from-greatest | the-people | and-all-of |

| יְהוָה׃ | בֵּית | הַנִּמְצָא | הַבְּרִית | סֵפֶר | דִּבְרֵי | כָּל־ | אֶת־ |
|---|---|---|---|---|---|---|---|
| Yahweh | temple-of | the-one-being-found | the-Covenant | Book-of | words-of | all-of | *** |

| הַבְּרִית | אֶת־ | וַיִּכְרֹת | עָמְדוֹ | עַל־ | הַמֶּלֶךְ | וַיַּעֲמֹד | |
|---|---|---|---|---|---|---|---|
| the-covenant | *** | and-he-renewed | pillar-of-him | by | the-king | and-he-stood | (31) |

| מִצְוֹתָיו | אֶת־ | וְלִשְׁמוֹר | יְהוָה | אַחֲרֵי | לָלֶכֶת | יְהוָה | לִפְנֵי |
|---|---|---|---|---|---|---|---|
| commands-of-him | *** | and-to-keep | Yahweh | after | to-follow | Yahweh | in-presences-of |

| לְבָבוֹ | בְּכָל־ | וְחֻקָּיו | וְעֵדְוֹתָיו |
|---|---|---|---|
| heart-of-him | with-all-of | and-decrees-of-him | and-regulations-of-him |

made,[i] my anger will be poured out on this place and will not be quenched.'
26Tell the king of Judah, who sent you to inquire of the LORD, 'This is what the LORD, the God of Israel, says concerning the words you heard:
27Because your heart was responsive and you humbled yourself before God when you heard what he spoke against this place and its people, and because you humbled yourself before me and tore your robes and wept in my presence, I have heard you, declares the LORD.
28Now I will gather you to your fathers, and you will be buried in peace. Your eyes will not see all the disaster I am going to bring on this place and on those who live here.' "

So they took her answer back to the king.

29Then the king called together all the elders of Judah and Jerusalem.
30He went up to the temple of the LORD with the men of Judah, the people of Jerusalem, the priests and the Levites—all the people from the least to the greatest. He read in their hearing all the words of the Book of the Covenant, which had been found in the temple of the LORD.
31The king stood by his pillar and renewed the covenant in the presence of the LORD—to follow the LORD and keep his commands, regulations and decrees with all his heart and

i25 Or *by everything they have done*

וּבְכָל־ נַפְשׁוֹ לַעֲשׂוֹת אֶת־ דִּבְרֵי הַבְּרִית
the-covenant words-of *** to-obey soul-of-him and-with-all-of

הַכְּתוּבִים עַל־ הַסֵּפֶר הַזֶּה׃ וַיַּעֲמֵד אֵת
*** and-he-made-pledge (32) the-this the-book in the-ones-being-written

כָּל־ הַנִּמְצָא בִירוּשָׁלִַם וּבִנְיָמִן וַיַּעֲשׂוּ
and-they-did and-Benjamin in-Jerusalem the-one-being-found all-of

יֹשְׁבֵי יְרוּשָׁלִַם כִּבְרִית אֱלֹהִים אֱלֹהֵי אֲבוֹתֵיהֶם׃
fathers-of-them God-of God as-covenant-of Jerusalem ones-living-of

וַיָּסַר יֹאשִׁיָּהוּ אֶת־ כָּל־ הַתּוֹעֵבוֹת מִכָּל־
from-all-of the-detestable-idols all-of *** Josiah and-he-removed (33)

הָאֲרָצוֹת אֲשֶׁר לִבְנֵי יִשְׂרָאֵל וַיַּעֲבֵד אֵת כָּל־
all-of *** and-he-had-serve Israel to-sons-of that the-territories

הַנִּמְצָא בְּיִשְׂרָאֵל לַעֲבוֹד אֶת־ יְהוָה אֱלֹהֵיהֶם כָּל־
all-of God-of-them Yahweh *** to-serve in-Israel the-one-being-present

יָמָיו לֹא סָרוּ מֵאַחֲרֵי יְהוָה אֱלֹהֵי אֲבוֹתֵיהֶם׃
fathers-of-them God-of Yahweh from-after they-turned not days-of-him

וַיַּעַשׂ יֹאשִׁיָּהוּ בִירוּשָׁלִַם פֶּסַח לַיהוָה
to-Yahweh Passover in-Jerusalem Josiah and-he-celebrated (35:1)

וַיִּשְׁחֲטוּ הַפֶּסַח בְּאַרְבָּעָה עָשָׂר לַחֹדֶשׁ הָרִאשׁוֹן׃
the-first of-the-month ten on-four the-Passover-lamb and-they-slaughtered

וַיַּעֲמֵד הַכֹּהֲנִים עַל־ מִשְׁמְרוֹתָם וַיְחַזְּקֵם
and-he-encouraged-them duties-of-them to the-priests and-he-appointed (2)

לַעֲבוֹדַת בֵּית יְהוָה׃ וַיֹּאמֶר לַלְוִיִּם
to-the-Levites and-he-said (3) Yahweh temple-of in-service-of

הַמְּבוֹנִים לְכָל־ יִשְׂרָאֵל הַקְּדוֹשִׁים לַיהוָה תְּנוּ
put! to-Yahweh the-ones-consecrated Israel to-all-of the-ones-instructing

אֶת־ אֲרוֹן־ הַקֹּדֶשׁ בַּבַּיִת אֲשֶׁר בָּנָה שְׁלֹמֹה בֶן־ דָּוִיד
David son-of Solomon he-built that in-the-temple the-sacred ark-of ***

מֶלֶךְ יִשְׂרָאֵל אֵין־ לָכֶם מַשָּׂא בַּכָּתֵף עַתָּה עִבְדוּ אֶת־
*** serve! now on-the-shoulder something-carried to-you not Israel king-of

יְהוָה אֱלֹהֵיכֶם וְאֵת עַמּוֹ יִשְׂרָאֵל׃ וְהִכּוֹנוּ
now-prepare-yourselves! (4) Israel people-of-him and God-of-you Yahweh

לְבֵית־ אֲבוֹתֵיכֶם כְּמַחְלְקוֹתֵיכֶם בִּכְתָב דָּוִיד מֶלֶךְ
king-of David as-writing-of in-divisions-of-you fathers-of-you by-family-of

יִשְׂרָאֵל וּבְמִכְתַּב שְׁלֹמֹה בְנוֹ׃ וְעִמְדוּ בַקֹּדֶשׁ
in-the-holy-place and-stand! (5) son-of-him Solomon and-as-writing-of Israel

לִפְלֻגּוֹת בֵּית הָאָבוֹת לַאֲחֵיכֶם בְּנֵי הָעָם
the-people sons-of of-fellows-of-you the-fathers family-of by-subdivisions-of

all his soul, and to obey the words of the covenant written in this book.

[32]Then he had everyone in Jerusalem and Benjamin pledge themselves to it; the people of Jerusalem did this in accordance with the covenant of God, the God of their fathers.

[33]Josiah removed all the detestable idols from all the territory belonging to the Israelites, and he had all who were present in Israel serve the LORD their God. As long as he lived, they did not fail to follow the LORD, the God of their fathers.

*Josiah Celebrates the Passover*

35 Josiah celebrated the Passover to the LORD in Jerusalem, and the Passover lamb was slaughtered on the fourteenth day of the first month. [2]He appointed the priests to their duties and encouraged them in the service of the LORD's temple. [3]He said to the Levites, who instructed all Israel and who had been consecrated to the LORD: "Put the sacred ark in the temple that Solomon son of David king of Israel built. It is not to be carried about on your shoulders. Now serve the LORD your God and his people Israel. [4]Prepare yourselves by families in your divisions, according to the directions written by David king of Israel and by his son Solomon.

[5]"Stand in the holy place with a group of Levites for

°3 ק המבינים
°4 ק והכינו

וַחֲלֻקַּת בֵּית־ אָב לַלְוִיִּם׃ וְשַׁחֲטוּ
and-slaughter! (6) of-the-Levites father family-of and-group-of

הַפָּסַח וְהִתְקַדְּשׁוּ וְהָכִינוּ לַאֲחֵיכֶם
for-fellows-of-you and-prepare! and-consecrate-yourselves! the-Passover-lamb

לַעֲשׂוֹת כִּדְבַר־ יְהוָה בְּיַד־ מֹשֶׁה׃ וַיָּרֶם יֹאשִׁיָּהוּ
Josiah and-he-provided (7) Moses by-hand-of Yahweh as-command-of to-do

לִבְנֵי הָעָם צֹאן כְּבָשִׂים וּבְנֵי־ עִזִּים הַכֹּל
the-total goats and-offsprings-of sheeps flock-of the-people for-sons-of

לַפְּסָחִים לְכָל־ הַנִּמְצָא לְמִסְפַּר שְׁלֹשִׁים
thirty in-number the-one-being-found for-all-of for-the-Passover-offerings

אֶלֶף וּבָקָר שְׁלֹשֶׁת אֲלָפִים אֵלֶּה מֵרְכוּשׁ הַמֶּלֶךְ׃
the-king from-possession-of these thousands three-of and-cattle thousand

וְשָׂרָיו לִנְדָבָה לָעָם
to-the-people with-volunteer-contribution and-officials-of-him (8)

לַכֹּהֲנִים וְלַלְוִיִּם הֵרִימוּ חִלְקִיָּה וּזְכַרְיָהוּ
and-Zechariah Hilkiah they-gave and-to-the-Levites to-the-priests

וִיחִיאֵל נְגִידֵי בֵּית הָאֱלֹהִים לַכֹּהֲנִים נָתְנוּ
they-gave to-the-priests the-God temple-of administrators-of and-Jehiel

לַפְּסָחִים אַלְפַּיִם וְשֵׁשׁ מֵאוֹת וּבָקָר
and-cattle hundreds and-six-of two-thousands for-the-Passover-offerings

שְׁלֹשׁ מֵאוֹת׃ וְכוֹנַנְיָהוּ וּשְׁמַעְיָהוּ וּנְתַנְאֵל אֶחָיו
brothers-of-him and-Nethanel and-Shemaiah also-Conaniah (9) hundreds three-of

וַחֲשַׁבְיָהוּ וִיעִיאֵל וְיוֹזָבָד שָׂרֵי הַלְוִיִּם הֵרִימוּ
they-provided the-Levites leaders-of and-Jozabad and-Jeiel and-Hashabiah

לַלְוִיִּם לַפְּסָחִים חֲמֵשֶׁת אֲלָפִים וּבָקָר
and-cattle thousands five-of for-the-Passover-offerings for-the-Levites

חֲמֵשׁ מֵאוֹת׃ וַתִּכּוֹן הָעֲבוֹדָה וַיַּעַמְדוּ
and-they-stood the-service and-she-was-arranged (10) hundreds five-of

הַכֹּהֲנִים עַל־ עָמְדָם וְהַלְוִיִּם עַל־ מַחְלְקוֹתָם כְּמִצְוַת
as-order-of divisions-of-them in and-the-Levites place-of-them in the-priests

הַמֶּלֶךְ׃ וַיִּשְׁחֲטוּ הַפָּסַח וַיִּזְרְקוּ
and-they-sprinkled the-Passover-lamb and-they-slaughtered (11) the-king

הַכֹּהֲנִים מִיָּדָם וְהַלְוִיִּם מַפְשִׁיטִים׃
ones-skinning while-the-Levites from-hand-of-them the-priests

וַיָּסִירוּ הָעֹלָה לְתִתָּם לְמִפְלַגּוֹת
to-subdivisions to-give-them the-burnt-offering and-they-set-aside (12)

לְבֵית־ אָבוֹת לִבְנֵי הָעָם לְהַקְרִיב לַיהוָה
to-Yahweh to-offer the-people of-sons-of fathers of-family-of

each subdivision of the families of your fellow countrymen, the lay people. [6]Slaughter the Passover lambs, consecrate yourselves and prepare ⌊the lambs⌋ for your fellow countrymen, doing what the LORD commanded through Moses."

[7]Josiah provided for all the lay people who were there a total of thirty thousand sheep and goats for the Passover offerings, and also three thousand cattle—all from the king's own possessions.

[8]His officials also contributed voluntarily to the people and the priests and Levites. Hilkiah, Zechariah and Jehiel, the administrators of God's temple, gave the priests twenty-six hundred Passover offerings and three hundred cattle. [9]Also Conaniah along with Shemaiah and Nethanel, his brothers, and Hashabiah, Jeiel and Jozabad, the leaders of the Levites, provided five thousand Passover offerings and five hundred head of cattle for the Levites.

[10]The service was arranged and the priests stood in their places with the Levites in their divisions as the king had ordered. [11]The Passover lambs were slaughtered, and the priests sprinkled the blood handed to them, while the Levites skinned the animals. [12]They set aside the burnt offerings to give them to the subdivisions of the families of the people to offer to the LORD,

°9 ק וכנניהו

כַּכָּתוּב בְּסֵפֶר מֹשֶׁה וְכֵן לַבָּקָר׃
with-the-cattle and-same Moses in-Book-of as-the-thing-being-written

וַיְבַשְּׁלוּ הַפֶּסַח בָּאֵשׁ כַּמִּשְׁפָּט
as-the-prescription over-the-fire the-Passover-animal and-they-roasted (13)

וְהַקֳּדָשִׁים בִּשְּׁלוּ בַּסִּירוֹת וּבַדְּוָדִים
and-in-the-caldrons in-the-pots they-boiled and-the-holy-offerings

וּבַצֵּלָחוֹת וַיָּרִיצוּ לְכָל־ בְּנֵי הָעָם׃
the-people sons-of to-all-of and-they-served-quickly and-in-the-pans

וְאַחַר הֵכִינוּ לָהֶם וְלַכֹּהֲנִים כִּי הַכֹּהֲנִים
the-priests because and-for-the-priests for-them they-prepared and-after (14)

בְּנֵי אַהֲרֹן בְּהַעֲלוֹת הָעוֹלָה וְהַחֲלָבִים
and-the-fat-portions the-burnt-offering in-to-sacrifice Aaron descendants-of

עַד־ לָיְלָה וְהַלְוִיִּם הֵכִינוּ לָהֶם וְלַכֹּהֲנִים
and-for-the-priests for-them they-prepared so-the-Levites nightfall until

בְּנֵי אַהֲרֹן׃ וְהַמְשֹׁרְרִים בְּנֵי־ אָסָף עַל־
in Asaph descendants-of and-the-ones-making-music (15) Aaron sons-of

מַעֲמָדָם כְּמִצְוַת דָּוִיד וְאָסָף וְהֵימָן וִידֻתוּן חוֹזֵה
seer-of and-Jeduthun and-Heman and-Asaph David as-prescription-of place-of-them

הַמֶּלֶךְ וְהַשֹּׁעֲרִים לְשַׁעַר וָשָׁעַר אֵין לָהֶם לָסוּר מֵעַל
from-at to-leave to-them not and-gate at-gate and-the-gatekeepers the-king

עֲבֹדָתָם כִּי־ אֲחֵיהֶם הַלְוִיִּם הֵכִינוּ לָהֶם׃
for-them they-prepared the-Levites fellows-of-them because post-of-them

וַתִּכּוֹן כָּל־ עֲבוֹדַת יְהוָה בַּיּוֹם הַהוּא
the-that on-the-day Yahweh service-of entire-of so-she-was-carried-out (16)

לַעֲשׂוֹת הַפֶּסַח וְהַעֲלוֹת עֹלוֹת עַל מִזְבַּח יְהוָה
Yahweh altar-of on burnt-offerings and-to-offer the-Passover to-celebrate

כְּמִצְוַת הַמֶּלֶךְ יֹאשִׁיָּהוּ׃ וַיַּעֲשׂוּ בְנֵי־ יִשְׂרָאֵל
Israel sons-of and-they-celebrated (17) Josiah the-king as-order-of

הַנִּמְצְאִים אֶת־ הַפֶּסַח בָּעֵת הַהִיא וְאֶת־ חַג
Feast-of and the-that at-the-time the-Passover *** the-ones-being-found

הַמַּצּוֹת שִׁבְעַת יָמִים׃ וְלֹא־ נַעֲשָׂה פֶסַח
Passover she-was-observed and-not (18) days seven-of the-Unleavened-Breads

כָּמֹהוּ בְּיִשְׂרָאֵל מִימֵי שְׁמוּאֵל הַנָּבִיא וְכָל־ מַלְכֵי
kings-of and-all-of the-prophet Samuel since-days-of in-Israel like-him

יִשְׂרָאֵל׀ לֹא־ עָשׂוּ כַּפֶּסַח אֲשֶׁר־ עָשָׂה יֹאשִׁיָּהוּ
Josiah he-did that like-the-Passover they-celebrated not Israel

וְהַכֹּהֲנִים וְהַלְוִיִּם וְכָל־ יְהוּדָה וְיִשְׂרָאֵל הַנִּמְצָא
the-one-being-found and-Israel Judah and-all-of and-the-Levites with-the-priests

as is written in the Book of Moses. They did the same with the cattle. [13]They roasted the Passover animals over the fire as prescribed, and boiled the holy offerings in pots, caldrons and pans and served them quickly to all the people. [14]After this, they made preparations for themselves and for the priests, because the priests, the descendants of Aaron, were sacrificing the burnt offerings and the fat portions until nightfall. So the Levites made preparations for themselves and for the Aaronic priests.

[15]The musicians, the descendants of Asaph, were in the places prescribed by David, Asaph, Heman and Jeduthun the king's seer. The gatekeepers at each gate did not need to leave their posts, because their fellow Levites made the preparations for them.

[16]So at that time the entire service of the LORD was carried out for the celebration of the Passover and the offering of burnt offerings on the altar of the LORD, as King Josiah had ordered. [17]The Israelites who were present celebrated the Passover at that time and observed the Feast of Unleavened Bread for seven days. [18]The Passover had not been observed like this in Israel since the days of the prophet Samuel; and none of the kings of Israel had ever celebrated such a Passover as did Josiah, with the priests, the Levites and all Judah and Israel who

וְיוֹשְׁבֵי יְרוּשָׁלִָם׃ בִּשְׁמוֹנֶה עֶשְׂרֵה שָׁנָה לְמַלְכוּת יֹאשִׁיָּהוּ

Josiah of-reign-of year ten in-eight (19) Jerusalem and-ones-living-of

נַעֲשָׂה הַפֶּסַח הַזֶּה׃ אַחֲרֵי כָל־ זֹאת אֲשֶׁר

when this all-of after (20) the-this the-Passover she-was-celebrated

הֵכִין יֹאשִׁיָּהוּ אֶת־ הַבַּיִת עָלָה נְכוֹ מֶלֶךְ־מִצְרַיִם לְהִלָּחֵם

to-fight Egypt king-of Neco he-went-up the-temple *** Josiah he-set-in-order

בְּכַרְכְּמִישׁ עַל־ פְּרָת וַיֵּצֵא לִקְרָאתוֹ יֹאשִׁיָּהוּ׃

Josiah to-meet-him and-he-marched-out Euphrates on at-Carchemish

וַיִּשְׁלַח אֵלָיו מַלְאָכִים ׀ לֵאמֹר ׀ מַה־ לִּי וָלָךְ

and-between-you between-me what? to-say messengers to-him but-he-sent (21)

מֶלֶךְ יְהוּדָה לֹא־ עָלֶיךָ אַתָּה הַיּוֹם כִּי אֶל־ בֵּית מִלְחַמְתִּי

war-of-me house-of against but the-day you against-you not Judah king-of

וֵאלֹהִים אָמַר לְבַהֲלֵנִי חֲדַל־ לְךָ מֵאֱלֹהִים אֲשֶׁר־ עִמִּי וְאַל־

so-not with-me who against-God for-you stop! to-hurry-me he-told and-God

יַשְׁחִיתֶךָ׃ וְלֹא־ הֵסֵב יֹאשִׁיָּהוּ פָּנָיו מִמֶּנּוּ

from-him faces-of-him Josiah he-turned-away but-not (22) he-destroys-you

כִּי לְהִלָּחֶם־ בּוֹ הִתְחַפֵּשׂ וְלֹא שָׁמַע אֶל־

to he-listened and-not he-disguised-himself against-him to-battle but

דִּבְרֵי נְכוֹ מִפִּי אֱלֹהִים וַיָּבֹא לְהִלָּחֵם בְּבִקְעַת מְגִדּוֹ׃

Megiddo on-plain-of to-fight but-he-went God at-command-of Neco words-of

וַיֹּרוּ הַיֹּרִים לַמֶּלֶךְ יֹאשִׁיָּהוּ וַיֹּאמֶר

and-he-told Josiah to-the-king the-ones-being-archers but-they-shot (23)

הַמֶּלֶךְ לַעֲבָדָיו הַעֲבִירוּנִי כִּי הָחֳלֵיתִי מְאֹד׃

badly I-am-wounded for take-away-me! to-officers-of-him the-king

וַיַּעֲבִירֻהוּ עֲבָדָיו מִן־ הַמֶּרְכָּבָה וַיַּרְכִּיבֻהוּ עַל

in and-they-put-him the-chariot from officers-of-him so-they-took-him (24)

רֶכֶב הַמִּשְׁנֶה אֲשֶׁר־ לוֹ וַיּוֹלִיכֻהוּ יְרוּשָׁלַםִ וַיָּמָת

and-he-died Jerusalem and-they-brought-him to-him that the-other chariot-of

וַיִּקָּבֵר בְּקִבְרוֹת אֲבֹתָיו וְכָל־ יְהוּדָה וִירוּשָׁלַםִ

and-Jerusalem Judah and-all-of fathers-of-him in-tombs-of and-he-was-buried

מִתְאַבְּלִים עַל־ יֹאשִׁיָּהוּ׃ וַיְקוֹנֵן יִרְמְיָהוּ עַל־יֹאשִׁיָּהוּ

Josiah for Jeremiah and-he-composed-lament (25) Josiah for ones-mourning

וַיֹּאמְרוּ כָל־ הַשָּׁרִים ׀ וְהַשָּׁרוֹת

and-the-women-singing the-men-singing all-of and-they-commemorate

בְּקִינוֹתֵיהֶם עַל־ יֹאשִׁיָּהוּ עַד־ הַיּוֹם וַיִּתְּנוּם לְחֹק עַל־

in as-tradition and-they-made-them the-day to Josiah for in-laments-of-them

יִשְׂרָאֵל וְהִנָּם כְּתוּבִים עַל־ הַקִּינוֹת׃ וְיֶתֶר

and-other-of (26) the-Laments in ones-being-written and-see-they! Israel

were there with the people of Jerusalem. [19]This Passover was celebrated in the eighteenth year of Josiah's reign.

*The Death of Josiah*

[20]After all this, when Josiah had set the temple in order, Neco king of Egypt went up to fight at Carchemish on the Euphrates, and Josiah marched out to meet him in battle. [21]But Neco sent messengers to him, saying, "What quarrel is there between you and me, O king of Judah? It is not you I am attacking at this time, but the house with which I am at war. God has told me to hurry; so stop opposing God, who is with me, or he will destroy you."

[22]Josiah, however, would not turn away from him, but disguised himself to engage him in battle. He would not listen to what Neco had said at God's command but went to fight him on the plain of Megiddo.

[23]Archers shot King Josiah, and he told his officers, "Take me away; I am badly wounded." [24]So they took him out of his chariot, put him in the other chariot he had and brought him to Jerusalem, where he died. He was buried in the tombs of his fathers, and all Judah and Jerusalem mourned for him.

[25]Jeremiah composed laments for Josiah, and to this day all the men and women singers commemorate Josiah in the laments. These became a tradition in Israel and are written in the Laments.

דִּבְרֵי יֹאשִׁיָּהוּ וַחֲסָדָיו כַּכָּתוּב
as-the-thing-being-written and-acts-of-devotion-of-him Josiah events-of

בְּתוֹרַת יְהוָה׃ וּדְבָרָיו הָרִאשֹׁנִים וְהָאַחֲרֹנִים הִנָּם
see-they! and-the-ends the-beginnings and-events-of-him (27) Yahweh in-Law-of

כְּתוּבִים עַל־סֵפֶר מַלְכֵי־יִשְׂרָאֵל וִיהוּדָה׃ וַיִּקְחוּ
and-they-took (36:1) and-Judah Israel kings-of book-of in ones-being-written

עַם־הָאָרֶץ אֶת־יְהוֹאָחָז בֶּן־יֹאשִׁיָּהוּ וַיַּמְלִיכֻהוּ
and-they-made-king-him Josiah son-of Jehoahaz *** the-land people-of

תַחַת־אָבִיו בִּירוּשָׁלִָם׃ בֶּן־שָׁלוֹשׁ וְעֶשְׂרִים שָׁנָה
year and-twenty three son-of (2) in-Jerusalem father-of-him in-place-of

יוֹאָחָז בְּמָלְכוֹ וּשְׁלֹשָׁה חֳדָשִׁים מָלַךְ בִּירוּשָׁלִָם׃
in-Jerusalem he-reigned months and-three when-to-become-king-him Joahaz

וַיְסִירֵהוּ מֶלֶךְ־מִצְרַיִם בִּירוּשָׁלִָם וַיַּעֲנֹשׁ אֶת־
*** and-he-imposed-levy in-Jerusalem Egypt king-of and-he-dethroned-him (3)

הָאָרֶץ מֵאָה כִכַּר־כֶּסֶף וְכִכַּר זָהָב׃ וַיַּמְלֵךְ
and-he-made-king (4) gold and-talent-of silver talent-of hundred the-land

מֶלֶךְ־מִצְרַיִם אֶת־אֶלְיָקִים אָחִיו עַל־יְהוּדָה וִירוּשָׁלִַם
and-Jerusalem Judah over brother-of-him Eliakim *** Egypt king-of

וַיַּסֵּב אֶת־שְׁמוֹ יְהוֹיָקִים וְאֶת־יוֹאָחָז אָחִיו לָקַח
he-took brother-of-him Joahaz but Jehoiakim name-of-him *** and-he-changed

נְכוֹ וַיְבִיאֵהוּ מִצְרָיְמָה׃ בֶּן־עֶשְׂרִים וְחָמֵשׁ שָׁנָה
year and-five twenty son-of (5) to-Egypt and-he-carried-off-him Neco

יְהוֹיָקִים בְּמָלְכוֹ וְאַחַת עֶשְׂרֵה שָׁנָה מָלַךְ בִּירוּשָׁלִָם
in-Jerusalem he-reigned year ten and-one-of when-to-become-king-him Jehoiakim

וַיַּעַשׂ הָרַע בְּעֵינֵי יְהוָה אֱלֹהָיו׃ עָלָיו עָלָה
he-attacked against-him (6) God-of-him Yahweh in-eyes-of the-evil and-he-did

נְבוּכַדְנֶאצַּר מֶלֶךְ בָּבֶל וַיַּאַסְרֵהוּ בַּנְחֻשְׁתַּיִם
with-the-bronze-shackles and-he-bound-him Babylon king-of Nebuchadnezzar

לְהֹלִיכוֹ בָּבֶלָה׃ וּמִכְּלֵי בֵּית יְהוָה הֵבִיא
he-took Yahweh temple-of and-from-articles-of (7) to-Babylon to-take-him

נְבוּכַדְנֶאצַּר לְבָבֶל וַיִּתְּנֵם בְּהֵיכָלוֹ בְּבָבֶל׃
in-Babylon in-temple-of-him and-he-put-them to-Babylon Nebuchadnezzar

וְיֶתֶר דִּבְרֵי יְהוֹיָקִים וְתֹעֲבֹתָיו אֲשֶׁר־עָשָׂה
he-did that and-detestable-things-of-him Jehoiakim events-of and-other-of (8)

וְהַנִּמְצָא עָלָיו הִנָּם כְּתוּבִים עַל־סֵפֶר
book-of in ones-being-written see-they! against-him and-the-thing-being-found

מַלְכֵי יִשְׂרָאֵל וִיהוּדָה וַיִּמְלֹךְ יְהוֹיָכִין בְּנוֹ
son-of-him Jehoiachin and-he-became-king and-Judah Israel kings-of

[26]The other events of Josiah's reign and his acts of devotion, according to what is written in the Law of the LORD— [27]all the events, from beginning to end, are written in the book of the kings of Israel and Judah.

36 [1]And the people of the land took Jehoahaz son of Josiah and made him king in Jerusalem in place of his father.

*Jehoahaz King of Judah*

[2]Jehoahaz[j] was twenty-three years old when he became king, and he reigned in Jerusalem three months. [3]The king of Egypt dethroned him in Jerusalem and imposed on Judah a levy of a hundred talents[k] of silver and a talent[l] of gold. [4]The king of Egypt made Eliakim, a brother of Jehoahaz, king over Judah and Jerusalem and changed Eliakim's name to Jehoiakim. But Neco took Eliakim's brother Jehoahaz and carried him off to Egypt.

*Jehoiakim King of Judah*

[5]Jehoiakim was twenty-five years old when he became king, and he reigned in Jerusalem eleven years. He did evil in the eyes of the LORD his God. [6]Nebuchadnezzar king of Babylon attacked him and bound him with bronze shackles to take him to Babylon. [7]Nebuchadnezzar also took to Babylon articles from the temple of the LORD and put them in his temple[m] there.

[8]The other events of Jehoiakim's reign, the detestable things he did and all that was found against him, are written in the book of the kings of Israel and Judah. And Jehoiachin his son succeeded him as king.

[j]2 Hebrew *Joahaz,* a variant of *Jehoahaz;* also in verse 4
[k]3 That is, about 3 3/4 tons (about 3.4 metric tons)
[l]3 That is, about 75 pounds (about 34 kilograms)
[m]7 Or *palace*

תַּחְתָּיו׃ בֶּן־ שְׁמוֹנֶה שָׁנִים יְהוֹיָכִין בְּמָלְכוֹ

when-to-become-king-him Jehoiachin years eight son-of (9) in-place-of-him

וּשְׁלֹשָׁה חֳדָשִׁים וַעֲשֶׂרֶת יָמִים מָלַךְ בִּירוּשָׁלִָם וַיַּעַשׂ הָרַע

the-evil and-he-did in-Jerusalem he-reigned days and-ten-of months and-three

בְּעֵינֵי יְהוָה׃ וְלִתְשׁוּבַת הַשָּׁנָה שָׁלַח הַמֶּלֶךְ נְבוּכַדְנֶאצַּר

Nebuchadnezzar the-king he-sent the-year and-at-turn-of (10) Yahweh in-eyes-of

וַיְבִאֵהוּ בָבֶלָה עִם־ כְּלֵי חֶמְדַּת בֵּית־ יְהוָה

Yahweh temple-of value-of articles-of with to-Babylon and-he-brought-him

וַיַּמְלֵךְ אֶת־ צִדְקִיָּהוּ אָחִיו עַל־ יְהוּדָה וִירוּשָׁלִָם׃

and-Jerusalem Judah over brother-of-him Zedekiah *** and-he-made-king

בֶּן־ עֶשְׂרִים וְאַחַת שָׁנָה צִדְקִיָּהוּ בְמָלְכוֹ וְאַחַת

and-one-of when-to-become-king-him Zedekiah year and-one twenty son-of (11)

עֶשְׂרֵה שָׁנָה מָלַךְ בִּירוּשָׁלִָם׃ וַיַּעַשׂ הָרַע בְּעֵינֵי יְהוָה

Yahweh in-eyes-of the-evil and-he-did (12) in-Jerusalem he-reigned year ten

אֱלֹהָיו לֹא נִכְנַע מִלִּפְנֵי יִרְמְיָהוּ הַנָּבִיא מִפִּי

at-word-of the-prophet Jeremiah at-before he-humbled-himself not God-of-him

יְהוָה׃ וְגַם בַּמֶּלֶךְ נְבוּכַדְנֶאצַּר מָרָד אֲשֶׁר

who he-rebelled Nebuchadnezzar against-the-king and-also (13) Yahweh

הִשְׁבִּיעוֹ בֵּאלֹהִים וַיֶּקֶשׁ אֶת־ עָרְפּוֹ וַיְאַמֵּץ

and-he-hardened neck-of-him *** and-he-became-stiff by-God he-made-take-oath

אֶת־ לְבָבוֹ מִשּׁוּב אֶל־ יְהוָה אֱלֹהֵי יִשְׂרָאֵל׃ גַּם כָּל־

all-of furthermore (14) Israel God-of Yahweh to from-to-turn heart-of-him ***

שָׂרֵי הַכֹּהֲנִים וְהָעָם הִרְבּוּ לִמְעָוֹל־

to-be-unfaithful they-became-more and-the-people the-priests leaders-of

מַעַל כְּכֹל תֹּעֲבוֹת הַגּוֹיִם וַיְטַמְּאוּ

and-they-defiled the-nations detestable-practices-of as-all-of unfaithfulness

אֶת־ בֵּית יְהוָה אֲשֶׁר הִקְדִּישׁ בִּירוּשָׁלִָם׃ וַיִּשְׁלַח יְהוָה

Yahweh and-he-sent (15) in-Jerusalem he-consecrated which Yahweh temple-of ***

אֱלֹהֵי אֲבוֹתֵיהֶם עֲלֵיהֶם בְּיַד מַלְאָכָיו הַשְׁכֵּם

to-get-up messengers-of-him by-hand-of to-them fathers-of-them God-of

וְשָׁלוֹחַ כִּי־ חָמַל עַל־ עַמּוֹ וְעַל־ מְעוֹנוֹ׃

dwelling-of-him and-on people-of-him on he-had-pity because and-to-send

וַיִּהְיוּ מַלְעִבִים בְּמַלְאֲכֵי הָאֱלֹהִים וּבוֹזִים

and-ones-despising the-God at-messengers-of ones-mocking but-they-were (16)

דְּבָרָיו וּמִתַּעְתְּעִים בִּנְבִאָיו עַד עֲלוֹת חֲמַת־

wrath-of to-be-aroused until at-prophets-of-him and-ones-scoffing words-of-him

יְהוָה בְּעַמּוֹ עַד־ לְאֵין מַרְפֵּא׃ וַיַּעַל

and-he-brought (17) remedy to-there-was-no until against-people-of-him Yahweh

*Jehoiachin King of Judah*

[9]Jehoiachin was eighteen[n]
years old when he became
king, and he reigned in
Jerusalem three months and
ten days. He did evil in the
eyes of the LORD. [10]At the turn
of the year,[o] King Nebuchadnezzar sent for him and
brought him to Babylon, together with articles of value
from the temple of the LORD,
and he made Jehoiachin's uncle,[p] Zedekiah, king over
Judah and Jerusalem.

*Zedekiah King of Judah*

[11]Zedekiah was twenty-one
years old when he became
king, and he reigned in
Jerusalem eleven years. [12]He
did evil in the eyes of the LORD
his God and did not humble
himself before Jeremiah the
prophet, who spoke the word
of the LORD. [13]He also rebelled
against King Nebuchadnez-
zar, who had made him take
an oath in God's name. He
became stiff-necked and hardened his heart and would not
turn to the LORD, the God of
Israel. [14]Furthermore, all the
leaders of the priests and the
people became more and more
unfaithful, following all the
detestable practices of the nations and defiling the temple
of the LORD, which he had
consecrated in Jerusalem.

*The Fall of Jerusalem*

[15]The LORD, the God of their
fathers, sent word to them
through his messengers again
and again, because he had
pity on his people and on his
dwelling place. [16]But they
mocked God's messengers, despised his words and scoffed
at his prophets until the wrath
of the LORD was aroused
against his people and there
was no remedy. [17]He brought

[n]9 One Hebrew manuscript, some Septuagint manuscripts and Syriac (see also 2 Kings 24:8); most Hebrew manuscripts *eight*

[o]10 That is, in the spring

[p]10 Hebrew *brother*, that is, relative (see 2 Kings 24:17)

°*14* ק למעל

עֲלֵיהֶם אֶת־ מֶלֶךְ כַּשְׂדִּיִּים° וַיַּהֲרֹג בַּחוּרֵיהֶם
young-men-of-them and-he-killed Chaldeans king-of *** against-them

בַּחֶרֶב בְּבֵית מִקְדָּשָׁם וְלֹא חָמַל עַל־ בָּחוּר
young-man to he-spared and-not sanctuary-of-them in-house-of with-the-sword

וּבְתוּלָה זָקֵן וְיָשֵׁשׁ הַכֹּל נָתַן בְּיָדוֹ׃
into-hand-of-him he-gave the-whole or-aged old-man or-young-woman

(18) וְכֹל כְּלֵי בֵּית הָאֱלֹהִים הַגְּדֹלִים וְהַקְּטַנִּים
and-the-small-ones the-large-ones the-God temple-of articles-of and-all-of (18)

וְאֹצְרוֹת בֵּית יְהוָה וְאֹצְרוֹת הַמֶּלֶךְ וְשָׂרָיו
and-officials-of-him the-king and-treasures-of Yahweh temple-of and-treasures-of

הַכֹּל הֵבִיא בָבֶל׃ (19) וַיִּשְׂרְפוּ אֶת־ בֵּית הָאֱלֹהִים
the-God temple-of *** and-they-set-fire (19) Babylon he-carried the-whole

וַיְנַתְּצוּ אֵת חוֹמַת יְרוּשָׁלָםִ וְכָל־ אַרְמְנוֹתֶיהָ
palaces-of-her and-all-of Jerusalem wall-of *** and-they-broke-down

שָׂרְפוּ בָאֵשׁ וְכָל־ כְּלֵי מַחֲמַדֶּיהָ לְהַשְׁחִית׃
to-destroy valuable-ones-of-her articles-of and-all-of with-fire they-burned

(20) וַיֶּגֶל הַשְּׁאֵרִית מִן־ הַחֶרֶב אֶל־ בָּבֶל וַיִּהְיוּ־
and-they-became Babylon to the-sword from the-remnant and-he-exiled (20)

לוֹ וּלְבָנָיו לַעֲבָדִים עַד־ מְלֹךְ מַלְכוּת פָּרָס׃
Persia kingdom-of to-come-to-power until as-servants and-to-sons-of-him to-him

(21) לְמַלֹּאות דְּבַר־ יְהוָה בְּפִי יִרְמְיָהוּ עַד־ רָצְתָה הָאָרֶץ
the-land she-enjoyed until Jeremiah by-mouth-of Yahweh word-of to-fulfill (21)

אֶת־ שַׁבְּתוֹתֶיהָ כָּל־ יְמֵי הָשַּׁמָּה שָׁבָתָה לְמַלֹּאות
to-complete she-rested to-be-desolate days-of all-of Sabbaths-of-her ***

שִׁבְעִים שָׁנָה׃ (22) וּבִשְׁנַת אַחַת לְכוֹרֶשׁ מֶלֶךְ פָּרַס לִכְלוֹת
to-fulfill Persia king-of of-Cyrus one now-in-year-of (22) year seventy

דְּבַר־ יְהוָה בְּפִי יִרְמְיָהוּ הֵעִיר יְהוָה אֶת־ רוּחַ כּוֹרֶשׁ מֶלֶךְ־
king-of Cyrus heart-of *** Yahweh he-moved Jeremiah by-mouth-of Yahweh word-of

פָּרַס וַיַּעֲבֶר־ קוֹל בְּכָל־ מַלְכוּתוֹ וְגַם־ בְּמִכְתָּב
in-writing and-also realm-of-him through-all-of proclamation so-he-made Persia

לֵאמֹר׃ (23) כֹּה־ אָמַר כּוֹרֶשׁ ׀ מֶלֶךְ פָּרַס כָּל־ מַמְלְכוֹת הָאָרֶץ
the-earth kingdoms-of all-of Persia king-of Cyrus he-says this (23) to-say

נָתַן לִי יְהוָה אֱלֹהֵי הַשָּׁמַיִם וְהוּא־ פָקַד עָלַי לִבְנוֹת־
to-build to-me he-appointed and-he the-heavens God-of Yahweh to-me he-gave

לוֹ בַיִת בִּירוּשָׁלַםִ אֲשֶׁר בִּיהוּדָה מִי־ בָכֶם מִכָּל־
from-all-of among-you anyone in-Judah that at-Jerusalem temple for-him

עַמּוֹ יְהוָה אֱלֹהָיו עִמּוֹ וְיָעַל׃
and-let-him-go-up with-him God-of-him Yahweh people-of-him

up against them the king of the Babylonians,[q] who killed their young men with the sword in the sanctuary, and spared neither young man nor young woman, old man or aged. God handed all of them over to Nebuchadnezzar. [18]He carried to Babylon all the articles from the temple of God, both large and small, and the treasures of the LORD's temple and the treasures of the king and his officials. [19]They set fire to God's temple and broke down the wall of Jerusalem; they burned all the palaces and destroyed everything of value there.

[20]He carried into exile to Babylon the remnant, who escaped from the sword, and they became servants to him and his sons until the kingdom of Persia came to power. [21]The land enjoyed its Sabbath rests; all the time of its desolation it rested, until the seventy years were completed in fulfillment of the word of the LORD spoken by Jeremiah.

[22]In the first year of Cyrus king of Persia, in order to fulfill the word of the LORD spoken by Jeremiah, the LORD moved the heart of Cyrus king of Persia to make a proclamation throughout his realm and to put it in writing:

[23]"This is what Cyrus king of Persia says:

"'The LORD, the God of heaven, has given me all the kingdoms of the earth and he has appointed me to build a temple for him at Jerusalem in Judah. Anyone of his people among you—may the LORD his God be with him, and let him go up.'"

q17 Or *Chaldeans*

°17 ק כשדים

וּבִשְׁנַת אַחַת לְכוֹרֶשׁ מֶלֶךְ פָּרַס לִכְלוֹת דְּבַר־ יְהוָה
Yahweh word-of to-fulfill Persia king-of of-Cyrus one now-in-year-of (1:1)

מִפִּי יִרְמְיָה הֵעִיר יְהוָה אֶת־ רוּחַ כֹּרֶשׁ מֶלֶךְ־ פָּרַס
Persia king-of Cyrus heart-of *** Yahweh he-moved Jeremiah by-mouth-of

וַיַּעֲבֶר־ קוֹל בְּכָל־ מַלְכוּתוֹ וְגַם־ בְּמִכְתָּב
in-writing and-also realm-of-him through-all-of proclamation so-he-made

לֵאמֹר׃ כֹּה אָמַר כֹּרֶשׁ מֶלֶךְ פָּרַס כֹּל מַמְלְכוֹת הָאָרֶץ
the-earth kingdoms-of all-of Persia king-of Cyrus he-says this (2) to-say

נָתַן לִי יְהוָה אֱלֹהֵי הַשָּׁמָיִם וְהוּא־ פָקַד עָלַי לִבְנוֹת־
to-build to-me he-appointed and-he the-heavens God-of Yahweh to-me he-gave

לוֹ בַיִת בִּירוּשָׁלִַם אֲשֶׁר בִּיהוּדָה׃ מִי־ בָכֶם מִכָּל־
from-all-of among-you anyone (3) in-Judah that at-Jerusalem temple for-him

עַמּוֹ יְהִי אֱלֹהָיו עִמּוֹ וְיַעַל לִירוּשָׁלִַם
to-Jerusalem and-let-him-go-up with-him God-of-him may-he-be people-of-him

אֲשֶׁר בִּיהוּדָה וְיִבֶן אֶת־ בֵּית יְהוָה אֱלֹהֵי יִשְׂרָאֵל הוּא
he Israel God-of Yahweh temple-of *** and-let-him-build in-Judah that

הָאֱלֹהִים אֲשֶׁר בִּירוּשָׁלִָם׃ וְכָל־ הַנִּשְׁאָר מִכָּל־
from-any-of the-one-surviving and-all-of (4) in-Jerusalem who the-God

הַמְּקֹמוֹת אֲשֶׁר הוּא גָר־ שָׁם יְנַשְּׂאוּהוּ אַנְשֵׁי מְקֹמוֹ
place-of-him people-of let-them-provide-him there living he where the-places

בְּכֶסֶף וּבְזָהָב וּבִרְכוּשׁ וּבִבְהֵמָה עִם־
with and-with-livestock and-with-goods and-with-gold with-silver

הַנְּדָבָה לְבֵית הָאֱלֹהִים אֲשֶׁר בִּירוּשָׁלִָם׃
in-Jerusalem that the-God for-temple-of the-freewill-offering

וַיָּקוּמוּ רָאשֵׁי הָאָבוֹת לִיהוּדָה וּבִנְיָמִן
and-Benjamin of-Judah the-fathers heads-of then-they-prepared (5)

וְהַכֹּהֲנִים וְהַלְוִיִּם לְכֹל הֵעִיר הָאֱלֹהִים אֶת־ רוּחוֹ
heart-of-him *** the-God he-moved to-everyone and-the-Levites and-the-priests

לַעֲלוֹת לִבְנוֹת אֶת־ בֵּית יְהוָה אֲשֶׁר בִּירוּשָׁלִָם׃ וְכָל־
and-all-of (6) in-Jerusalem that Yahweh temple-of *** and-to-build to-go-up

סְבִיבֹתֵיהֶם חִזְּקוּ בִידֵיהֶם בִּכְלֵי־ כֶסֶף
silver with-articles-of to-hands-of-them they-assisted neighbors-of-them

בַּזָּהָב בָּרְכוּשׁ וּבַבְּהֵמָה וּבַמִּגְדָּנוֹת
and-with-the-valuable-gifts and-with-the-livestock with-the-goods with-the-gold

לְבַד עַל־ כָּל־ הִתְנַדֵּב׃ וְהַמֶּלֶךְ כּוֹרֶשׁ
Cyrus and-the-king (7) to-be-freely-given all-of to in-addition-to

הוֹצִיא אֶת־ כְּלֵי בֵית־ יְהוָה אֲשֶׁר הוֹצִיא
he-carried-away which Yahweh temple-of articles-of *** he-brought-out

### *Cyrus Helps the Exiles to Return*

1 In the first year of Cyrus king of Persia, in order to fulfill the word of the LORD spoken by Jeremiah, the LORD moved the heart of Cyrus king of Persia to make a proclamation throughout his realm and to put it in writing:

2"This is what Cyrus king of Persia says:

" 'The LORD, the God of heaven, has given me all the kingdoms of the earth and he has appointed me to build a temple for him at Jerusalem in Judah.
3Anyone of his people among you—may his God be with him, and let him go up to Jerusalem in Judah and build the temple of the LORD, the God of Israel, the God who is in Jerusalem.
4And the people of any place where survivors may now be living are to provide him with silver and gold, with goods and livestock, and with freewill offerings for the temple of God in Jerusalem.' "

5Then the family heads of Judah and Benjamin, and the priests and Levites—everyone whose heart God had moved—prepared to go up and build the house of the LORD in Jerusalem.
6All their neighbors assisted them with articles of silver and gold, with goods and livestock, and with valuable gifts, in addition to all the freewill offerings.
7Moreover, King Cyrus brought out the articles belonging to the temple of the LORD, which Nebuchadnezzar had carried away

נְבוּכַדְנֶצַּר מִירוּשָׁלִַם וַיִּתְּנֵם בְּבֵית אֱלֹהָיו׃
gods-of-him in-temple-of and-he-placed-them from-Jerusalem Nebuchadnezzar

(8) וַיּוֹצִיאֵם כּוֹרֶשׁ מֶלֶךְ פָּרַס עַל־ יַד מִתְרְדָת
Mithredath hand-of by Persia king-of Cyrus and-he-had-brought-them (8)

הַגִּזְבָּר וַיִּסְפְּרֵם לְשֵׁשְׁבַּצַּר הַנָּשִׂיא לִיהוּדָה׃
of-Judah the-prince to-Sheshbazzar and-he-counted-them the-treasurer

(9) וְאֵלֶּה מִסְפָּרָם אֲגַרְטְלֵי זָהָב שְׁלֹשִׁים אֲגַרְטְלֵי־ כֶסֶף
silver dishes-of thirty gold dishes-of inventory-of-them and-these (9)

אֶלֶף מַחֲלָפִים תִּשְׁעָה וְעֶשְׂרִים׃ (10) כְּפוֹרֵי זָהָב שְׁלֹשִׁים כְּפוֹרֵי כֶסֶף
silver bowls-of thirty gold bowls-of (10) and-twenty nine pans thousand

מִשְׁנִים אַרְבַּע מֵאוֹת וַעֲשָׂרָה כֵּלִים אֲחֵרִים אָלֶף׃
thousand other-ones articles and-ten hundreds four-of matching-ones

(11) כָּל־ כֵּלִים לַזָּהָב וְלַכֶּסֶף חֲמֵשֶׁת אֲלָפִים
thousands five-of and-of-the-silver of-the-gold articles all-of (11)

וְאַרְבַּע מֵאוֹת הַכֹּל הֶעֱלָה שֵׁשְׁבַּצַּר עִם הֵעָלוֹת
to-come-up when Sheshbazzar he-brought-up the-whole hundreds and-four-of

הַגּוֹלָה מִבָּבֶל לִירוּשָׁלִָם׃ (2:1) וְאֵלֶּה ׀ בְּנֵי
people-of now-these (2:1) to-Jerusalem from-Babylon the-exile

הַמְּדִינָה הָעֹלִים מִשְּׁבִי הַגּוֹלָה אֲשֶׁר
whom the-exile from-captivity-of the-ones-coming-up the-province

הֶגְלָה נְבוּכַדְנֶצּוֹר מֶלֶךְ־ בָּבֶל לְבָבֶל וַיָּשׁוּבוּ
and-they-returned to-Babylon Babylon king-of Nebuchadnezzar he-took-captive

לִירוּשָׁלִַם וִיהוּדָה אִישׁ לְעִירוֹ׃ (2) אֲשֶׁר־ בָּאוּ עִם־ זְרֻבָּבֶל
Zerubbabel with they-came who (2) to-town-of-him each and-Judah to-Jerusalem

יֵשׁוּעַ נְחֶמְיָה שְׂרָיָה רְעֵלָיָה מָרְדֳּכַי בִּלְשָׁן מִסְפָּר בִּגְוַי רְחוּם
Rehum Bigvai Mispar Bilshan Mordecai Reelaiah Seraiah Nehemiah Jeshua

בַּעֲנָה מִסְפַּר אַנְשֵׁי עַם יִשְׂרָאֵל׃ (3) בְּנֵי פַרְעֹשׁ
Parosh descendants-of (3) Israel people-of men-of list-of Baanah

אַלְפַּיִם מֵאָה שִׁבְעִים וּשְׁנָיִם׃ (4) בְּנֵי שְׁפַטְיָה שְׁלֹשׁ
three-of Shephatiah descendants-of (4) and-two seventy hundred two-thousands

מֵאוֹת שִׁבְעִים וּשְׁנָיִם׃ (5) בְּנֵי אָרַח שְׁבַע מֵאוֹת חֲמִשָּׁה
five hundreds seven-of Arah descendants-of (5) and-two seventy hundreds

וְשִׁבְעִים׃ (6) בְּנֵי־ פַחַת מוֹאָב לִבְנֵי יֵשׁוּעַ
Jeshua through-descendants-of Moab Pahath descendants-of (6) and-seventy

יוֹאָב אַלְפַּיִם שְׁמֹנֶה מֵאוֹת וּשְׁנֵים עָשָׂר׃ (7) בְּנֵי עֵילָם
Elam descendants-of (7) ten and-two hundreds eight two-thousands Joab

אֶלֶף מָאתַיִם חֲמִשִּׁים וְאַרְבָּעָה׃ (8) בְּנֵי זַתּוּא תְּשַׁע
nine-of Zattu descendants-of (8) and-four fifty two-hundreds thousand

from Jerusalem and had placed in the temple of his god.[a]
8 Cyrus king of Persia had them brought by Mithredath the treasurer, who counted them out to Sheshbazzar the prince of Judah.

9 This was the inventory:

| | |
|---|---|
| gold dishes | 30 |
| silver dishes | 1,000 |
| silver pans[b] | 29 |
| 10 gold bowls | 30 |
| matching silver bowls | 410 |
| other articles | 1,000 |

11 In all, there were 5,400 articles of gold and of silver. Sheshbazzar brought all these along when the exiles came up from Babylon to Jerusalem.

*The List of the Exiles Who Returned*

2 Now these are the people of the province who came up from the captivity of the exiles, whom Nebuchadnezzar king of Babylon had taken captive to Babylon (they returned to Jerusalem and Judah, each to his own town,
2 in company with Zerubbabel, Jeshua, Nehemiah, Seraiah, Reelaiah, Mordecai, Bilshan, Mispar, Bigvai, Rehum and Baanah):

The list of the men of the people of Israel:

| | |
|---|---|
| 3 the descendants of Parosh | 2,172 |
| 4 of Shephatiah | 372 |
| 5 of Arah | 775 |
| 6 of Pahath-Moab (through the line of Jeshua and Joab) | 2,812 |
| 7 of Elam | 1,254 |
| 8 of Zattu | 945 |

a7 Or *gods*
b9 The meaning of the Hebrew for this word is uncertain.

°7 ק נבוכדנצר

מֵאוֹת וְאַרְבָּעִים וַחֲמִשָּׁה׃ בְּנֵי זַכָּי שְׁבַע מֵאוֹת
hundreds seven-of Zaccai descendants-of (9) and-five and-forty hundreds

וְשִׁשִּׁים׃ בְּנֵי בָנִי שֵׁשׁ מֵאוֹת אַרְבָּעִים וּשְׁנָיִם׃
and-two forty hundreds six-of Bani descendants-of (10) and-sixty

בְּנֵי בֵבָי שֵׁשׁ מֵאוֹת עֶשְׂרִים וּשְׁלֹשָׁה׃ בְּנֵי
descendants-of (12) and-three twenty hundreds six-of Bebai descendants-of (11)

עַזְגָּד אֶלֶף מָאתַיִם עֶשְׂרִים וּשְׁנָיִם׃ בְּנֵי אֲדֹנִיקָם
Adonikam descendants-of (13) and-two twenty two-hundreds thousand Azgad

שֵׁשׁ מֵאוֹת שִׁשִּׁים וְשִׁשָּׁה׃ בְּנֵי בִגְוָי אַלְפַּיִם חֲמִשִּׁים
fifty two-thousands Bigvai descendants-of (14) and-six sixty hundreds six-of

וְשִׁשָּׁה׃ בְּנֵי עָדִין אַרְבַּע מֵאוֹת חֲמִשִּׁים וְאַרְבָּעָה׃
and-four fifty hundreds four-of Adin descendants-of (15) and-six

בְּנֵי־ אָטֵר לִיחִזְקִיָּה תִּשְׁעִים וּשְׁמֹנָה׃ בְּנֵי
descendants-of (17) and-eight ninety through-Hezekiah Ater descendants-of (16)

בֵצָי שְׁלֹשׁ מֵאוֹת עֶשְׂרִים וּשְׁלֹשָׁה׃ בְּנֵי יוֹרָה מֵאָה
hundred Jorah descendants-of (18) and-three twenty hundreds three-of Bezai

וּשְׁנֵים עָשָׂר׃ בְּנֵי חָשֻׁם מָאתַיִם עֶשְׂרִים וּשְׁלֹשָׁה׃
and-three twenty two-hundreds Hashum descendants-of (19) ten and-two

בְּנֵי גִבָּר תִּשְׁעִים וַחֲמִשָּׁה׃ בְּנֵי בֵית־ לָחֶם מֵאָה
hundred Lehem Beth men-of (21) and-five ninety Gibbar descendants-of (20)

עֶשְׂרִים וּשְׁלֹשָׁה׃ אַנְשֵׁי נְטֹפָה חֲמִשִּׁים וְשִׁשָּׁה׃ אַנְשֵׁי עֲנָתוֹת
Anathoth men-of (23) and-six fifty Netophah men-of (22) and-three twenty

מֵאָה עֶשְׂרִים וּשְׁמֹנָה׃ בְּנֵי עַזְמָוֶת אַרְבָּעִים וּשְׁנָיִם׃ בְּנֵי
men-of (25) and-two forty Azmaveth men-of (24) and-eight twenty hundred

קִרְיַת עָרִים כְּפִירָה וּבְאֵרוֹת שְׁבַע מֵאוֹת וְאַרְבָּעִים וּשְׁלֹשָׁה׃
and-three and-forty hundreds seven-of and-Beeroth Kephirah Arim Kiriath

בְּנֵי הָרָמָה וָגָבַע שֵׁשׁ מֵאוֹת עֶשְׂרִים וְאֶחָד׃ אַנְשֵׁי
men-of (27) and-one twenty hundreds six-of and-Geba the-Ramah men-of (26)

מִכְמָס מֵאָה עֶשְׂרִים וּשְׁנָיִם׃ אַנְשֵׁי בֵית־אֵל וְהָעָי מָאתָיִם
two-hundreds and-the-Ai El Beth men-of (28) and-two twenty hundred Micmash

עֶשְׂרִים וּשְׁלֹשָׁה׃ בְּנֵי נְבוֹ חֲמִשִּׁים וּשְׁנָיִם׃ בְּנֵי מַגְבִּישׁ מֵאָה
hundred Magbish men-of (30) and-two fifty Nebo men-of (29) and-three twenty

חֲמִשִּׁים וְשִׁשָּׁה׃ בְּנֵי עֵילָם אַחֵר אֶלֶף מָאתַיִם חֲמִשִּׁים וְאַרְבָּעָה׃
and-four fifty two-hundreds thousand other Elam men-of (31) and-six fifty

בְּנֵי חָרִם שְׁלֹשׁ מֵאוֹת וְעֶשְׂרִים׃ בְּנֵי־ לֹד חָדִיד וְאוֹנוֹ
and-Ono Hadid Lod men-of (33) and-twenty hundreds three-of Harim men-of (32)

שְׁבַע מֵאוֹת עֶשְׂרִים וַחֲמִשָּׁה׃ בְּנֵי יְרֵחוֹ שְׁלֹשׁ מֵאוֹת
hundreds three-of Jericho men-of (34) and-five twenty hundreds seven-of

9 of Zaccai 760
10 of Bani 642
11 of Bebai 623
12 of Azgad 1,222
13 of Adonikam 666
14 of Bigvai 2,056
15 of Adin 454
16 of Ater (through Hezekiah) 98
17 of Bezai 323
18 of Jorah 112
19 of Hashum 223
20 of Gibbar 95

21 the men of Bethlehem 123
22 of Netophah 56
23 of Anathoth 128
24 of Azmaveth 42
25 of Kiriath Jearim,[c] Kephirah and Beeroth 743
26 of Ramah and Geba 621
27 of Micmash 122
28 of Bethel and Ai 223
29 of Nebo 52
30 of Magbish 156
31 of the other Elam 1,254
32 of Harim 320
33 of Lod, Hadid and Ono 725
34 of Jericho 345

[c] 25 See Septuagint (see also Neh. 7:29); Hebrew *Kiriath Arim.*

אַרְבָּעִים וַחֲמִשָּׁה׃ בְּנֵי סְנָאָה שְׁלֹשֶׁת אֲלָפִים וְשֵׁשׁ מֵאוֹת
hundreds and-six-of thousands three-of Senaah men-of (35) and-five forty

וּשְׁלֹשִׁים׃ הַכֹּהֲנִים בְּנֵי יְדַעְיָה לְבֵית יֵשׁוּעַ
Jeshua through-family-of Jedaiah descendants-of the-priests (36) and-thirty

תְּשַׁע מֵאוֹת שִׁבְעִים וּשְׁלֹשָׁה׃ בְּנֵי אִמֵּר אֶלֶף חֲמִשִּׁים
fifty thousand Immer descendants-of (37) and-three seventy hundreds nine-of

וּשְׁנָיִם׃ בְּנֵי פַשְׁחוּר אֶלֶף מָאתַיִם אַרְבָּעִים וְשִׁבְעָה׃
and-seven forty two-hundreds thousand Pashhur descendants-of (38) and-two

בְּנֵי חָרִם אֶלֶף וְשִׁבְעָה עָשָׂר׃ הַלְוִיִּם
the-Levites (40) ten and-seven thousand Harim descendants-of (39)

בְּנֵי־יֵשׁוּעַ וְקַדְמִיאֵל לִבְנֵי הוֹדַוְיָה שִׁבְעִים
seventy Hodaviah through-descendants-of and-Kadmiel Jeshua descendants-of

וְאַרְבָּעָה׃ הַמְשֹׁרְרִים בְּנֵי אָסָף מֵאָה עֶשְׂרִים וּשְׁמֹנָה׃
and-eight twenty hundred Asaph descendants-of the-ones-singing (41) and-four

בְּנֵי הַשֹּׁעֲרִים בְּנֵי־שַׁלּוּם בְּנֵי־
descendants-of Shallum descendants-of the-gatekeepers descendants-of (42)

אָטֵר בְּנֵי־טַלְמוֹן בְּנֵי־עַקּוּב בְּנֵי חֲטִיטָא
Hatita descendants-of Akkub descendants-of Talmon descendants-of Ater

בְּנֵי שֹׁבָי הַכֹּל מֵאָה שְׁלֹשִׁים וְתִשְׁעָה׃ הַנְּתִינִים
the-temple-servants (43) and-nine thirty hundred the-total Shobai descendants-of

בְּנֵי־צִיחָא בְנֵי־חֲשׂוּפָא בְּנֵי טַבָּעוֹת׃
Tabbaoth descendants-of Hasupha descendants-of Ziha descendants-of

בְּנֵי־קֵרֹס בְּנֵי־סִיעֲהָא בְּנֵי פָדוֹן׃
Padon descendants-of Siaha descendants-of Keros descendants-of (44)

בְּנֵי־לְבָנָה בְנֵי־חֲגָבָה בְּנֵי עַקּוּב׃
Akkub descendants-of Hagabah descendants-of Lebanah descendants-of (45)

בְּנֵי־חָגָב בְּנֵי־שַׁמְלַי בְּנֵי חָנָן׃
Hanan descendants-of Shalmai descendants-of Hagab descendants-of (46)

בְּנֵי־גִדֵּל בְּנֵי־גַחַר בְּנֵי רְאָיָה׃
Reaiah descendants-of Gahar descendants-of Giddel descendants-of (47)

בְּנֵי־רְצִין בְּנֵי־נְקוֹדָא בְּנֵי גַזָּם׃
Gazzam descendants-of Nekoda descendants-of Rezin descendants-of (48)

בְּנֵי־עֻזָּא בְנֵי־פָסֵחַ בְּנֵי בֵסָי׃
Besai descendants-of Paseah descendants-of Uzza descendants-of (49)

בְּנֵי־אַסְנָה בְנֵי־מְעִינִים בְּנֵי נְפִיסִים׃
Nephussim descendants-of Meunim descendants-of Asnah descendants-of (50)

בְּנֵי־בַקְבּוּק בְּנֵי־חֲקוּפָא בְּנֵי חַרְחוּר׃
Harhur descendants-of Hakupha descendants-of Bakbuk descendants-of (51)

---

35 of Senaah 3,630

36 The priests:

the descendants of Jedaiah (through the family of Jeshua) 973
37 of Immer 1,052
38 of Pashhur 1,247
39 of Harim 1,017

40 The Levites:

the descendants of Jeshua and Kadmiel (through the line of Hodaviah) 74

41 The singers:

the descendants of Asaph 128

42 The gatekeepers of the temple:

the descendants of Shallum, Ater, Talmon, Akkub, Hatita and Shobai 139

43 The temple servants:

the descendants of Ziha, Hasupha, Tabbaoth,
44 Keros, Siaha, Padon,
45 Lebanah, Hagabah, Akkub,
46 Hagab, Shalmai, Hanan,
47 Giddel, Gahar, Reaiah,
48 Rezin, Nekoda, Gazzam,
49 Uzza, Paseah, Besai,
50 Asnah, Meunim, Nephussim,
51 Bakbuk, Hakupha, Harhur,

°46 ק שלמי
°50a ק מעונים
°50b ק נפוסים

בְּנֵי־ בַצְלוּת בְּנֵי־ מְחִידָא בְּנֵי חַרְשָׁא׃
Harsha descendants-of Mehida descendants-of Bazluth descendants-of (52)

בְּנֵי־ בַרְקוֹס בְּנֵי־ סִֽיסְרָא בְּנֵי־ תָֽמַח׃
Temah descendants-of Sisera descendants-of Barkos descendants-of (53)

בְּנֵי נְצִיחַ בְּנֵי חֲטִיפָא׃ בְּנֵי
descendants-of (55) Hatipha descendants-of Neziah descendants-of (54)

עַבְדֵי שְׁלֹמֹה בְּנֵי־ סֹטַי בְּנֵי־ הַסֹּפֶרֶת
Hassophereth descendants-of Sotai descendants-of Solomon servants-of

בְּנֵי פְרוּדָא׃ בְּנֵי־ יַעְלָה בְּנֵי־ דַרְקוֹן
Darkon descendants-of Jaala descendants-of (56) Peruda descendants-of

בְּנֵי גִדֵּל׃ בְּנֵי שְׁפַטְיָה בְּנֵי־ חַטִּיל
Hattil descendants-of Shephatiah descendants-of (57) Giddel descendants-of

בְּנֵי פֹּכֶרֶת הַצְּבָיִים בְּנֵי אָמִי׃ כָּל־
total-of (58) Ami descendants-of Hazzebaim Pokereth descendants-of

הַנְּתִינִים וּבְנֵי עַבְדֵי שְׁלֹמֹה שְׁלֹשׁ מֵאוֹת
hundreds three-of Solomon servants-of and-descendants-of the-temple-servants

תִּשְׁעִים וּשְׁנָיִם׃ וְאֵלֶּה הָעֹלִים מִתֵּל מֶלַח תֵּל חַרְשָׁא כְּרוּב
Kerub Harsha Tel Melah from-Tel the-ones-coming these (59) and-two ninety

אַדָּן אִמֵּר וְלֹא יָכְלוּ לְהַגִּיד בֵּית־ אֲבוֹתָם
fathers-of-them family-of to-show they-could but-not Immer Addon

וְזַרְעָם אִם מִיִּשְׂרָאֵל הֵם׃ בְּנֵי־ דְלָיָה
Delaiah descendants-of (60) they from-Israel whether and-descent-of-them

בְּנֵי־ טוֹבִיָּה בְּנֵי נְקוֹדָא שֵׁשׁ מֵאוֹת חֲמִשִּׁים וּשְׁנָיִם׃
and-two fifty hundreds six-of Nekoda descendants-of Tobiah descendants-of

וּמִבְּנֵי הַכֹּהֲנִים בְּנֵי חֳבַיָּה
Hobaiah descendants-of the-priests and-from-descendants-of (61)

בְּנֵי הַקּוֹץ בְּנֵי בַרְזִלַּי אֲשֶׁר לָקַח מִבְּנוֹת
of-daughters-of he-married who Barzillai descendants-of Hakkoz descendants-of

בַּרְזִלַּי הַגִּלְעָדִי אִשָּׁה וַיִּקָּרֵא עַל־ שְׁמָם׃ אֵלֶּה
these (62) name-of-them by and-he-was-called wife the-Gileadite Barzillai

בִּקְשׁוּ כְתָבָם הַמִּתְיַחְשִׂים וְלֹא נִמְצָאוּ
they-could-find but-not the-ones-being-recorded record-of-them they-searched

וַיְגֹאֲלוּ מִן־ הַכְּהֻנָּה׃ וַיֹּאמֶר הַתִּרְשָׁתָא
the-governor and-he-ordered (63) the-priesthood from so-they-were-excluded

לָהֶם אֲשֶׁר לֹא־ יֹאכְלוּ מִקֹּדֶשׁ הַקֳּדָשִׁים עַד עֲמֹד
to-minister until the-holy-things from-most-holy-of they-eat not that to-them

כֹּהֵן לְאוּרִים וּלְתֻמִּים׃ כָּל־ הַקָּהָל כְּאֶחָד אַרְבַּע
four-of as-one the-company whole-of (64) and-with-Thummim with-Urim priest

---

52 Bazluth, Mehida, Harsha,
53 Barkos, Sisera, Temah,
54 Neziah and Hatipha

55 The descendants of the servants of Solomon:

the descendants of Sotai, Hassophereth, Peruda,
56 Jaala, Darkon, Giddel,
57 Shephatiah, Hattil, Pokereth-Hazzebaim and Ami

58 The temple servants and the descendants of the servants of Solomon 392

59 The following came up from the towns of Tel Melah, Tel Harsha, Kerub, Addon and Immer, but they could not show that their families were descended from Israel:

60 The descendants of Delaiah, Tobiah and Nekoda 652

61 And from among the priests:

The descendants of Hobaiah, Hakkoz and Barzillai (a man who had married a daughter of Barzillai the Gileadite and was called by that name).
62 These searched for their family records, but they could not find them and so were excluded from the priesthood as unclean.
63 The governor ordered them not to eat any of the most sacred food until there was a priest ministering with the Urim and Thummim.

64 The whole company

רִבּֽוֹא אֲלָפִ֔ים שְׁלֹשׁ־ מֵאֹ֖ות שִׁשִּֽׁים: מִלְּבַ֗ד
ten-thousand · two-thousands · three-of · hundreds · sixty · (65) · from-besides

עֲבָדֵיהֶם֙ וְאַמְהֹֽתֵיהֶ֔ם אֵ֖לֶּה שִׁבְעַ֥ת אֲלָפִ֖ים
menservants-of-them · and-maidservants-of-them · these · seven-of · thousands

שָׁלֹ֥שׁ מֵאֹ֛ות שְׁלֹשִׁ֥ים וְשִׁבְעָ֖ה וְלָהֶ֑ם מְשֹׁרְרִ֖ים וּֽמְשֹׁרֲרֹֽות
three-of · hundreds · thirty · and-seven · and-to-them · men-singing · and-women-singing

מָאתָֽיִם: סוּסֵיהֶ֕ם שְׁבַ֥ע מֵאֹ֖ות שְׁלֹשִׁ֥ים וְשִׁשָּׁ֑ה
two-hundreds · (66) · horses-of-them · seven-of · hundreds · thirty · and-six

פִּרְדֵיהֶ֕ם מָאתַ֖יִם אַרְבָּעִ֣ים וַחֲמִשָּֽׁה: גְּמַלֵּיהֶ֕ם אַרְבַּ֥ע
mules-of-them · two-hundreds · forty · and-five · (67) · camels-of-them · four-of

מֵאֹ֖ות שְׁלֹשִׁ֣ים וַחֲמִשָּׁ֑ה חֲמֹרִ֕ים שֵׁ֣שֶׁת אֲלָפִ֔ים שְׁבַ֥ע מֵאֹֽות
hundreds · thirty · and-five · donkeys · six-of · thousands · seven-of · hundreds

וְעֶשְׂרִֽים: וּֽמֵרָאשֵׁי֙ הָֽאָבֹ֔ות בְּבֹואָ֕ם
and-twenty · (68) · and-from-heads-of · the-fathers · when-to-arrive-them

לְבֵ֤ית יְהוָה֙ אֲשֶׁ֣ר בִּירוּשָׁלִָ֔ם הִֽתְנַדְּבוּ֙
at-house-of · Yahweh · that · in-Jerusalem · they-gave-freewill-offerings

לְבֵ֣ית הָֽאֱלֹהִ֔ים לְהַעֲמִידֹ֖ו עַל־ מְכֹונֹֽו: כְּכֹחָ֗ם
to-house-of · the-God · to-rebuild-him · on · site-of-him · (69) · as-ability-of-them

נָתְנוּ֙ לְאֹוצַ֣ר הַמְּלָאכָ֔ה זָהָ֕ב דַּרְכְּמֹונִים֙ שֵׁ֣שׁ רִבֹּ֔אות
they-gave · to-treasury-of · the-work · gold · drachmas · six-of · ten-thousands

וְאֶ֑לֶף וְכֶ֗סֶף מָנִים֙ חֲמֵ֣שֶׁת אֲלָפִ֔ים וְכָתְנֹ֥ת כֹּהֲנִ֖ים
and-thousand · and-silver · minas · five-of · thousands · and-garments-of · priests

מֵאָֽה: וַיֵּשְׁב֣וּ הַכֹּהֲנִ֣ים וְהַלְוִיִּ֗ם וּמִן־ הָעָ֡ם
hundred · (70) · and-they-settled · the-priests · and-the-Levites · and-from · the-people

וְֽהַמְשֹׁרְרִ֥ים וְהַשֹּׁועֲרִ֖ים וְהַנְּתִינִ֑ים
and-the-ones-singing · and-the-gatekeepers · and-the-temple-servants

בְּעָרֵיהֶ֑ם וְכָל־ יִשְׂרָאֵ֖ל בְּעָרֵיהֶֽם: וַיִּגַּע֙
in-towns-of-them · and-all-of · Israel · in-towns-of-them · (3:1) · when-he-came

הַחֹ֣דֶשׁ הַשְּׁבִיעִ֔י וּבְנֵ֥י יִשְׂרָאֵ֖ל בֶּעָרִ֑ים וַיֵּאָסְפ֥וּ
the-month · the-seventh · and-sons-of · Israel · in-the-towns · then-they-assembled

הָעָ֛ם כְּאִ֥ישׁ אֶחָ֖ד אֶל־ יְרוּשָׁלִָֽם: וַיָּ֡קָם יֵשׁ֣וּעַ בֶּן־ יֹֽוצָדָ֡ק
the-people · as-man · one · in · Jerusalem · (2) · then-he-began · Jeshua · son-of · Jozadak

וְאֶחָיו֩ הַכֹּהֲנִ֨ים וּזְרֻבָּבֶ֤ל בֶּן־ שְׁאַלְתִּיאֵל֙
and-fellows-of-him · the-priests · and-Zerubbabel · son-of · Shealtiel

וְאֶחָ֔יו וַיִּבְנ֕וּ אֶת־ מִזְבַּ֖ח אֱלֹהֵ֣י יִשְׂרָאֵ֑ל לְהַעֲלֹ֤ות
and-associates-of-him · and-they-built · *** · altar-of · God-of · Israel · to-sacrifice

עָלָיו֙ עֹלֹ֔ות כַּכָּת֕וּב בְּתֹורַ֖ת מֹשֶׁ֥ה אִישׁ־ הָאֱלֹהִֽים:
on-him · burnt-offerings · as-the-thing-written · in-Law-of · Moses · man-of · the-God

---

numbered 42,360, 65besides their 7,337 menservants and maidservants; and they also had 200 men and women singers. 66They had 736 horses, 245 mules, 67435 camels and 6,720 donkeys.

68When they arrived at the house of the LORD in Jerusalem, some of the heads of the families gave freewill offerings toward the rebuilding of the house of God on its site. 69According to their ability they gave to the treasury for this work 61,000 drachmasd of gold, 5,000 minase of silver and 100 priestly garments.

70The priests, the Levites, the singers, the gatekeepers and the temple servants settled in their own towns, along with some of the other people, and the rest of the Israelites settled in their towns.

### Rebuilding the Altar

3 When the seventh month came and the Israelites had settled in their towns, the people assembled as one man in Jerusalem. 2Then Jeshua son of Jozadak and his fellow priests and Zerubbabel son of Shealtiel and his associates began to build the altar of the God of Israel to sacrifice burnt offerings on it, in accordance with what is written in the Law of Moses the man of God.

d69 That is, about 1,100 pounds (about 500 kilograms)
e69 That is, about 3 tons (about 2.9 metric tons)

וַיָּכִינוּ הַמִּזְבֵּחַ עַל־ מְכוֹנֹתָיו כִּי בְּאֵימָה עֲלֵיהֶם
to-them of-fear despite foundations-of-him on the-altar and-they-built (3)

מֵעַמֵּי הָאֲרָצוֹת וַיַּעַל° עָלָיו עֹלוֹת לַיהוָה
to-Yahweh burnt-offerings on-him and-they-sacrificed the-lands from-peoples-of

עֹלוֹת לַבֹּקֶר וְלָעָרֶב׃ וַיַּעֲשׂוּ אֶת־
*** then-they-celebrated (4) and-for-the-evening for-the-morning sacrifices

חַג הַסֻּכּוֹת כַּכָּתוּב וְעֹלַת
and-burnt-offering-of as-the-thing-being-written the-Tabernacles Feast-of

יוֹם בְּיוֹם בְּמִסְפָּר כְּמִשְׁפַּט דְּבַר־ יוֹם בְּיוֹמוֹ׃
for-day-of-him day matter-of as-prescription-of by-number for-day day

וְאַחֲרֵיכֵן עֹלַת תָּמִיד וְלֶחֳדָשִׁים
and-for-the-New-Moons regular burnt-offering-of and-after-that (5)

וּלְכָל־ מוֹעֲדֵי יְהוָה הַמְקֻדָּשִׁים וּלְכֹל
and-for-all-of the-ones-being-sacred Yahweh appointed-feasts-of and-for-all-of

מִתְנַדֵּב נְדָבָה לַיהוָה׃ מִיּוֹם אֶחָד לַחֹדֶשׁ
of-the-month one on-day (6) to-Yahweh freewill-offering one-being-brought

הַשְּׁבִיעִי הֵחֵלּוּ לְהַעֲלוֹת עֹלוֹת לַיהוָה וְהֵיכַל
though-temple-of to-Yahweh burnt-offerings to-offer they-began the-seventh

יְהוָה לֹא יֻסָּד׃ וַיִּתְּנוּ־ כֶסֶף לַחֹצְבִים
to-the-ones-being-masons money then-they-gave (7) he-was-founded not Yahweh

וְלֶחָרָשִׁים וּמַאֲכָל וּמִשְׁתֶּה וָשֶׁמֶן לַצִּדֹנִים
to-the-Sidonians and-oil and-drink and-food and-to-the-carpenters

וְלַצֹּרִים לְהָבִיא עֲצֵי אֲרָזִים מִן־ הַלְּבָנוֹן אֶל־ יָם יָפוֹא
Joppa sea by the-Lebanon from cedars woods-of to-bring and-to-the-Tyrians

כְּרִשְׁיוֹן כּוֹרֶשׁ מֶלֶךְ־ פָּרַס עֲלֵיהֶם׃ וּבַשָּׁנָה
and-in-the-year (8) to-them Persia king-of Cyrus as-authorization-of

הַשֵּׁנִית לְבוֹאָם אֶל־ בֵּית הָאֱלֹהִים לִירוּשָׁלַםִ בַּחֹדֶשׁ
in-the-month in-Jerusalem the-God house-of at to-arrive-them the-second

הַשֵּׁנִי הֵחֵלּוּ זְרֻבָּבֶל בֶּן־ שְׁאַלְתִּיאֵל וְיֵשׁוּעַ בֶּן־ יוֹצָדָק
Jozadak son-of and-Jeshua Shealtiel son-of Zerubbabel they-began the-second

וּשְׁאָר אֲחֵיהֶם׀ הַכֹּהֲנִים וְהַלְוִיִּם וְכָל־
and-all-of and-the-Levites the-priests brothers-of-them and-rest-of

הַבָּאִים מֵהַשְּׁבִי יְרוּשָׁלַםִ וַיַּעֲמִידוּ אֶת־
*** and-they-appointed Jerusalem from-the-captivity the-ones-returning

הַלְוִיִּם מִבֶּן עֶשְׂרִים שָׁנָה וָמַעְלָה לְנַצֵּחַ עַל־ מְלֶאכֶת
building-of over to-supervise and-upward year twenty from-son-of the-Levites

בֵּית־ יְהוָה׃ וַיַּעֲמֹד יֵשׁוּעַ בָּנָיו וְאֶחָיו
and-brothers-of-him sons-of-him Jeshua and-he-joined (9) Yahweh house-of

°3 ק ויעלו

[3]Despite their fear of the peoples around them, they built the altar on its foundation and sacrificed burnt offerings on it to the LORD, both the morning and evening sacrifices. [4]Then in accordance with what is written, they celebrated the Feast of Tabernacles with the required number of burnt offerings prescribed for each day. [5]After that, they presented the regular burnt offerings, the New Moon sacrifices and the sacrifices for all the appointed feasts of the LORD, as well as those brought as freewill offerings to the LORD. [6]On the first day of the seventh month they began to offer burnt offerings to the LORD, though the foundation of the LORD's temple had not yet been laid.

*Rebuilding the Temple*

[7]Then they gave money to the masons and carpenters, and gave food and drink and oil to the people of Sidon and Tyre, so that they would bring cedar logs by sea from Lebanon to Joppa, as authorized by Cyrus king of Persia.

[8]In the second month of the second year after their arrival at the house of God in Jerusalem, Zerubbabel son of Shealtiel, Jeshua son of Jozadak and the rest of their brothers (the priests and the Levites and all who had returned from the captivity to Jerusalem) began the work, appointing Levites twenty years of age and older to supervise the building of the house of the LORD. [9]Jeshua and his sons and brothers and Kadmiel and his

קַדְמִיאֵל וּבָנָיו בְּנֵי־ יְהוּדָה כְּאֶחָד לְנַצֵּחַ עַל־
over to-supervise as-one Yehudah descendants-of and-sons-of-him Kadmiel

עֹשֵׂה הַמְּלָאכָה בְּבֵית הָאֱלֹהִים בְּנֵי חֵנָדָד בְּנֵיהֶם
sons-of-them Henadad sons-of the-God on-house-of the-work one-doing-of

וַאֲחֵיהֶם הַלְוִיִּם׃ וְיִסְּדוּ הַבֹּנִים
the-ones-building when-they-laid-foundation (10) the-Levites and-brothers-of-them

אֶת־ הֵיכַל יְהוָה וַיַּעֲמִידוּ הַכֹּהֲנִים מְלֻבָּשִׁים
ones-being-dressed the-priests then-they-took-places Yahweh temple-of ***

בַּחֲצֹצְרוֹת וְהַלְוִיִּם בְּנֵי־ אָסָף בַּמְצִלְתַּיִם לְהַלֵּל אֶת־
*** to-praise with-the-cymbals Asaph sons-of and-the-Levites with-the-trumpets

יְהוָה עַל־ יְדֵי דָּוִיד מֶלֶךְ־ יִשְׂרָאֵל׃ וַיַּעֲנוּ בְּהַלֵּל
when-to-praise and-they-sang (11) Israel king-of David hands-of at Yahweh

וּבְהוֹדֹת לַיהוָה כִּי טוֹב כִּי־ לְעוֹלָם חַסְדּוֹ
love-of-him to-forever indeed good indeed to-Yahweh and-when-to-give-thanks

עַל־יִשְׂרָאֵל וְכָל־ הָעָם הֵרִיעוּ תְרוּעָה גְדוֹלָה בְהַלֵּל
when-to-praise great shout they-shouted the-people and-all-of Israel to

לַיהוָה עַל הוּסַד בֵּית־ יְהוָה׃ וְרַבִּים מֵהַכֹּהֲנִים
of-the-priests but-many (12) Yahweh house-of he-was-founded because to-Yahweh

וְהַלְוִיִּם וְרָאשֵׁי הָאָבוֹת הַזְּקֵנִים אֲשֶׁר רָאוּ אֶת־
*** they-saw who the-older-ones the-fathers and-heads-of and-the-Levites

הַבַּיִת הָרִאשׁוֹן בְּיָסְדוֹ זֶה הַבַּיִת
the-temple this when-to-lay-foundation-of-him the-former the-temple

בְּעֵינֵיהֶם בֹּכִים בְּקוֹל גָּדוֹל וְרַבִּים בִּתְרוּעָה
with-shout while-many loud with-voice ones-weeping with-eyes-of-them

בְשִׂמְחָה לְהָרִים קוֹל׃ וְאֵין הָעָם מַכִּירִים
ones-distinguishing the-people and-no-one-of (13) voice to-raise with-joy

קוֹל תְּרוּעַת הַשִּׂמְחָה לְקוֹל בְּכִי הָעָם כִּי הָעָם
the-people because the-people weeping-of from-sound-of the-joy shout-of sound-of

מְרִיעִים תְּרוּעָה גְדוֹלָה וְהַקּוֹל נִשְׁמַע עַד־ לְמֵרָחוֹק׃
to-at-distance to he-was-heard and-the-sound much noise ones-making-noise

וַיִּשְׁמְעוּ צָרֵי יְהוּדָה וּבִנְיָמִן כִּי־ בְנֵי
sons-of that and-Benjamin Judah enemies-of when-they-heard (4:1)

הַגּוֹלָה בּוֹנִים הֵיכָל לַיהוָה אֱלֹהֵי יִשְׂרָאֵל׃
Israel God-of for-Yahweh temple ones-building the-exile

וַיִּגְּשׁוּ אֶל־ זְרֻבָּבֶל וְאֶל־ רָאשֵׁי הָאָבוֹת וַיֹּאמְרוּ
and-they-said the-fathers heads-of and-to Zerubbabel to then-they-came (2)

לָהֶם נִבְנֶה עִמָּכֶם כִּי כָכֶם נִדְרוֹשׁ לֵאלֹהֵיכֶם
to-God-of-you we-seek like-you because with-you let-us-build to-them

sons (descendants of Hodaviah[f]) and the sons of Henadad and their sons and brothers—all Levites—joined together in supervising those working on the house of God.
10 When the builders laid the foundation of the temple of the LORD, the priests in their vestments and with trumpets, and the Levites (the sons of Asaph) with cymbals, took their places to praise the LORD, as prescribed by David king of Israel.
11 With praise and thanksgiving they sang to the LORD:

"He is good;
his love to Israel endures forever."

And all the people gave a great shout of praise to the LORD, because the foundation of the house of the LORD was laid.
12 But many of the older priests and Levites and family heads, who had seen the former temple, wept aloud when they saw the foundation of this temple being laid, while many others shouted for joy.
13 No one could distinguish the sound of the shouts of joy from the sound of weeping, because the people made so much noise. And the sound was heard far away.

*Opposition to the Rebuilding*

4 When the enemies of Judah and Benjamin heard that the exiles were building a temple for the LORD, the God of Israel,
2 they came to Zerubbabel and to the heads of the families and said, "Let us help you build because, like you, we seek your God and

f9 Hebrew *Yehudah*, probably a variant of *Hodaviah*

וְלֹא | אֲנַחְנוּ זֹבְחִים מִימֵי אֵסַר חַדֹּן מֶלֶךְ אַשּׁוּר
Assyria king-of Haddon Esar since-days-of ones-sacrificing we and-to-him

הַמַּעֲלֶה אֹתָנוּ פֹּה׃ וַיֹּאמֶר לָהֶם זְרֻבָּבֶל וְיֵשׁוּעַ
and-Jeshua Zerubbabel to-them but-he-answered (3) here us the-one-bringing

וּשְׁאָר רָאשֵׁי הָאָבוֹת לְיִשְׂרָאֵל לֹא־ לָכֶם וָלָנוּ לִבְנוֹת
to-build and-to-us to-you not of-Israel the-fathers heads-of and-rest-of

בַּיִת לֵאלֹהֵינוּ כִּי אֲנַחְנוּ יַחַד נִבְנֶה לַיהוָה אֱלֹהֵי יִשְׂרָאֵל
Israel God-of for-Yahweh we-will-build alone we but to-God-of-us temple

כַּאֲשֶׁר צִוָּנוּ הַמֶּלֶךְ כּוֹרֶשׁ מֶלֶךְ־ פָּרָס׃ וַיְהִי
then-he-was (4) Persia king-of Cyrus the-king he-commanded-us just-as

עַם־ הָאָרֶץ מְרַפִּים יְדֵי עַם־ יְהוּדָה
Judah people-of hands-of ones-discouraging the-land people-of

וּמְבַלְּהִים אוֹתָם לִבְנוֹת׃ וְסֹכְרִים עֲלֵיהֶם
against-them and-ones-hiring (5) to-build them and-ones-making-afraid

יוֹעֲצִים לְהָפֵר עֲצָתָם כָּל־ יְמֵי כּוֹרֶשׁ מֶלֶךְ פָּרַס
Persia king-of Cyrus days-of all-of plan-of-them to-frustrate ones-counseling

וְעַד־ מַלְכוּת דָּרְיָוֶשׁ מֶלֶךְ־ פָּרָס׃ וּבְמַלְכוּת אֲחַשְׁוֵרוֹשׁ
Ahasuerus and-in-reign-of (6) Persia king-of Darius reign-of and-to

בִּתְחִלַּת מַלְכוּתוֹ כָּתְבוּ שִׂטְנָה עַל־ יֹשְׁבֵי
ones-living-of against accusation they-wrote reign-of-him at-beginning-of

יְהוּדָה וִירוּשָׁלִָם׃ וּבִימֵי אַרְתַּחְשַׁשְׂתָּא כָּתַב בִּשְׁלָם
Bishlam he-wrote Artaxerxes and-in-days-of (7) and-Jerusalem Judah

מִתְרְדָת טָבְאֵל וּשְׁאָר כְּנָוֹתָו עַל־אַרְתַּחְשַׁשְׂתָּא מֶלֶךְ פָּרָס
Persia king-of Artaxerxes to associates-of-him and-rest-of Tabeel Mithredath

וּכְתָב הַנִּשְׁתְּוָן כָּתוּב אֲרָמִית וּמְתֻרְגָּם אֲרָמִית׃
Aramaic and-being-translated Aramaic being-written the-letter and-writing-of

רְחוּם בְּעֵל־ טְעֵם וְשִׁמְשַׁי סָפְרָא כְּתַבוּ אִגְּרָה
letter they-wrote the-secretary and-Shimshai command officer-of Rehum (8)

חֲדָה עַל־ יְרוּשְׁלֶם לְאַרְתַּחְשַׁשְׂתָּא מַלְכָּא כְּנֵמָא׃ אֱדַיִן רְחוּם
Rehum then (9) as-follows the-king to-Artaxerxes Jerusalem against a

בְּעֵל־ טְעֵם וְשִׁמְשַׁי סָפְרָא וּשְׁאָר כְּנָוָתְהוֹן
associates-of-them and-rest-of the-secretary and-Shimshai command officer-of

דִּינָיֵא וַאֲפַרְסַתְכָיֵא טַרְפְּלָיֵא אֲפָרְסָיֵא אַרְכְּוָי
the-Erechites the-Persians the-men-from-Tripolis and-the-officials the-judges

בָבְלָיֵא שׁוּשַׁנְכָיֵא דֶּהָוֵא עֵלְמָיֵא׃ וּשְׁאָר
and-other-of (10) the-Elamites who-that the-Susaites the-Babylonians

אֻמַּיָּא דִּי הַגְלִי אָסְנַפַּר רַבָּא וְיַקִּירָא
and-the-honorable the-great Osnapper he-deported whom the-peoples

have been sacrificing to him
since the time of Esarhaddon
king of Assyria, who brought
us here."
3But Zerubbabel, Jeshua and
the rest of the heads of the
families of Israel answered,
"You have no part with us in
building a temple to our God.
We alone will build it for the
LORD, the God of Israel, as
King Cyrus, the king of Persia,
commanded us."
4Then the peoples around
them set out to discourage the
people of Judah and make
them afraid to go on building.[g]
5They hired counselors to
work against them and frustrate their plans during the entire reign of Cyrus king of
Persia and down to the reign
of Darius king of Persia.

### *Later Opposition Under Artaxerxes*

6At the beginning of the
reign of Xerxes,[h] they lodged
an accusation against the
people of Judah and Jerusalem.
7And in the days of Arta-
xerxes king of Persia, Bishlam,
Mithredath, Tabeel and the
rest of his associates wrote a
letter to Artaxerxes. The letter
was written in Aramaic script
and in the Aramaic
language.[i,j]
8Rehum the commanding
officer and Shimshai the secretary wrote a letter against
Jerusalem to Artaxerxes the
king as follows:

9Rehum the commanding
officer and Shimshai the
secretary, together with the
rest of their associates—the
judges and officials over the
men from Tripolis, Persia,[k]
Erech and Babylon, the
Elamites of Susa, 10and the
other people whom the
great and honorable Ashurbanipal[l] deported and settled in the city of Samaria

g4 Or *and troubled them as they built*
h6 Hebrew *Ahasuerus*, a variant of Xerxes' name
i7 Or *written in Aramaic and translated*
j7 The text of Ezra 4:8–6:18 is in Aramaic.
k9 Or *officials, magistrates and governors over the men from*
l10 Aramaic *Osnapper*, a variant of *Ashurbanipal*

°2 ק ולו
°4 ק ומבהלים
°7a ק כנותיו
°7b ק שת
°9a ק ארכויא
°9b ק דהיא

וְהוֹתֵב הִמּוֹ בְּקִרְיָה דִּי שָׁמְרָיִן וּשְׁאָר עֲבַר־ נַהֲרָה
the-River Beyond-of and-elsewhere-of Samaria of in-city them and-he-settled

וּכְעֶנֶת׃ דְּנָה פַּרְשֶׁגֶן אִגַּרְתָּא דִּי שְׁלַחוּ עֲלוֹהִי עַל־אַרְתַּחְשַׁשְׂתְּא
Artaxerxes to to-him they-sent that the-letter copy-of this (11) and-now

מַלְכָּא עַבְדָיךְ° אֱנָשׁ עֲבַר־ נַהֲרָה וּכְעֶנֶת׃ יְדִיעַ
being-known (12) and-now the-River Beyond-of man-of servant-of-you the-king

לֶהֱוֵא לְמַלְכָּא דִּי יְהוּדָיֵא דִּי סְלִקוּ מִן־ לְוָתָךְ עֲלֶינָא
to-us with-you from they-came-up who the-Jews that to-the-king let-him-be

אֲתוֹ לִירוּשְׁלֶם קִרְיְתָא מָרָדְתָּא וּבִאישְׁתָּא° בָּנַיִן
ones-rebuilding and-the-wicked the-rebellious the-city to-Jerusalem they-went

וְשׁוּרַיָּ° אֶשַׁכְלִלוּ° וְאֻשַּׁיָּא יַחִיטוּ׃ כְּעַן
furthermore (13) they-repair and-the-foundations they-restore and-the-walls

יְדִיעַ לֶהֱוֵא לְמַלְכָּא דִּי הֵן קִרְיְתָא דָךְ תִּתְבְּנֵא
she-is-built this the-city if that to-the-king let-him-be being-known

וְשׁוּרַיָּה יִשְׁתַּכְלְלוּן מִנְדָּה־ בְלוֹ וַהֲלָךְ לָא יִנְתְּנוּן
they-will-pay not or-duty tribute tax they-are-restored and-the-walls

וְאַפְּתֹם מַלְכִים תְּהַנְזִק׃ כְּעַן כָּל־ קֳבֵל דִּי־ מְלַח
salt-of that because since now (14) she-will-suffer royalties and-revenue-of

הֵיכְלָא מְלַחְנָא וְעַרְוַת מַלְכָּא לָא אֲרִיךְ לַנָא לְמֶחֱזֵא
to-see for-us proper not the-king and-dishonor-of we-ate-salt the-palace

עַל־ דְּנָה שְׁלַחְנָא וְהוֹדַעְנָא לְמַלְכָּא׃ דִּי יְבַקַּר
he-may-search that (15) to-the-king and-we-inform we-send this because-of

בִּסְפַר־ דָּכְרָנַיָּא דִּי אֲבָהָתָךְ וּתְהַשְׁכַּח בִּסְפַר
in-record-of and-you-will-find predecessors-of-you of the-archives in-record-of

דָּכְרָנַיָּא וְתִנְדַּע דִּי קִרְיְתָא דָךְ קִרְיָא מָרָדָא
rebellious city this the-city that and-you-will-know the-archives

וּמְהַנְזְקַת מַלְכִין וּמְדִנָן וְאֶשְׁתַּדּוּר עָבְדִין
ones-doing and-rebellion and-provinces kings and-one-troubling-of

בְּגַוַּהּ מִן־ יוֹמָת עָלְמָא עַל־ דְּנָה קִרְיְתָא דָךְ
this the-city this for the-ancient days-of from in-midst-of-her

הָחָרְבַת׃ מְהוֹדְעִין אֲנַחְנָה לְמַלְכָּא דִּי הֵן קִרְיְתָא דָךְ
this the-city if that to-the-king we ones-informing (16) she-was-destroyed

תִּתְבְּנֵא וְשׁוּרַיַּהּ יִשְׁתַּכְלְלוּן לָקֳבֵל דְּנָה חֲלָק
portion this because-of they-are-restored and-the-walls she-is-built

בַּעֲבַר נַהֲרָא לָא אִיתַי לָךְ׃ פִּתְגָמָא שְׁלַח מַלְכָּא
the-king he-sent the-reply (17) for-you there-is not the-River in-Beyond-of

עַל־ רְחוּם בְּעֵל־ טְעֵם וְשִׁמְשַׁי סָפְרָא וּשְׁאָר
and-rest-of the-secretary and-Shimshai command officer-of Rehum to

and elsewhere in Trans-Euphrates.

11(This is a copy of the letter they sent him.)

To King Artaxerxes,

From your servants, the men of Trans-Euphrates:

12The king should know
that the Jews who came up
to us from you have gone to
Jerusalem and are rebuilding that rebellious and
wicked city. They are restoring the walls and repairing the foundations.
13Furthermore, the king
should know that if this
city is built and its walls are
restored, no more taxes,
tribute or duty will be paid,
and the royal revenues will
suffer. 14Now since we are
under obligation to the palace and it is not proper for
us to see the king dishonored, we are sending this
message to inform the king,
15so that a search may be
made in the archives of
your predecessors. In these
records you will find that
this city is a rebellious city,
troublesome to kings and
provinces, a place of rebellion from ancient times.
That is why this city was
destroyed. 16We inform the
king that if this city is built
and its walls are restored,
you will be left with nothing in Trans-Euphrates.

17The king sent this reply:

To Rehum the command-
ing officer, Shimshai the
secretary and the rest of

°11 ק עבדך
°12a ק ובישתא
°12b ק ושוריא
°12c ק שכלילו

כנותהון די יתבין בשמרין ושאר עבר־

Beyond-of and-elsewhere-of in-Samaria ones-living who associates-of-them

נהרה שלם וכעת : נשתונא די שלחתון עלינא

to-us you-sent that the-letter (18) and-now greeting the-River

מפרש קרי קדמי : ומני שים

he-was-issued and-from-me (19) in-presence-of-me he-was-read being-translated

טעם ובקרו והשכחו די קריתא דך מן־ יומת

days-of from this the-city that and-they-found and-they-searched order

עלמא על־ מלכין מתנשאה ומרד ואשתדור מתעבד־

happening and-sedition and-rebellion one-revolting kings against the-ancient

בה : ומלכין תקיפין הוו על־ ירושלם ושליטין

and-rulers Jerusalem over they-were powerful-ones and-kings (20) in-her

בכל עבר נהרה ומדה בלו והלך מתיהב

being-paid and-duty tribute and-tax the-River Beyond-of over-whole-of

להון : כען שימו טעם לבטלא גבריא אלך וקריתא

so-the-city these the-men to-make-stop order issue! now (21) to-them

דך לא תתבנא עד־ מני טעמא יתשם :

he-is-issued the-order from-me until she-will-be-rebuilt not this

וזהירין הוו שלו למעבד על־ דנה למה ישגא

let-him-grow why? this in to-do neglect be! and-ones-being-careful (22)

חבלא להנזקת מלכין : אדין מן־ די פרשגן

copy-of when from as-soon-as (23) royalties to-be-detrimental the-threat

נשתונא די ארתחששתא מלכא קרי קדם־ רחום ושמשי

and-Shimshai Rehum to he-was-read the-king Artaxerxes of the-letter

ספרא וכנותהון אזלו בבהילו לירושלם על־

to to-Jerusalem in-immediacy they-went and-associates-of-them the-secretary

יהודיא ובטלו המו באדרע וחיל : באדין

by-thus (24) and-force by-compulsion them and-they-stopped the-Jews

בטלת עבידת בית־ אלהא די בירושלם והות

and-she-was in-Jerusalem that the-God house-of work-of she-stood-still

בטלא עד שנת תרתין למלכות דריוש מלך־ פרס :

Persia king-of Darius of-reign-of two year-of until standing-still

והתנבי חגי נביאה וזכריה בר־ עדוא

Iddo descendant-of and-Zechariah prophet Haggai now-he-prophesied (5:1)

נביאיא על־ יהודיא די ביהוד ובירושלם בשם אלה

God-of in-name-of and-in-Jerusalem in-Judah who the-Jews to the-prophets

ישראל עליהון : באדין קמו זרבבל בר־שאלתיאל

Shealtiel son-of Zerubbabel they-set-to-work at-then (2) over-them Israel

their associates living in
Samaria and elsewhere in
Trans-Euphrates:

Greetings.

18The letter you sent us
has been read and trans-
lated in my presence. 19I issued an order and a search
was made, and it was
found that this city has a
long history of revolt
against kings and has been
a place of rebellion and se-
dition. 20Jerusalem has had
powerful kings ruling over
the whole of Trans-Euph-
rates, and taxes, tribute and
duty were paid to them.
21Now issue an order to
these men to stop work, so
that this city will not be rebuilt until I so order. 22Be
careful not to neglect this
matter. Why let this threat
grow, to the detriment of
the royal interests?

23As soon as the copy of the
letter of King Artaxerxes was
read to Rehum and Shimshai
the secretary and their associates, they went immediately
to the Jews in Jerusalem and
compelled them by force to
stop.

24Thus the work on the
house of God in Jerusalem
came to a standstill until the
second year of the reign of
Darius king of Persia.

*Tattenai's Letter to Darius*

5 Now Haggai the prophet
and Zechariah the
prophet, a descendant of Iddo,
prophesied to the Jews in
Judah and Jerusalem in the
name of the God of Israel, who
was over them. 2Then Zerubbabel son of Shealtiel and

°23 ק ששת
°1a ק נביא
°1b ק נבייא

וְיֵשׁוּעַ בַּר־ יוֹצָדָק וְשָׁרִיו לְמִבְנֵא בֵּית אֱלָהָא דִּי

that the-God house-of to-rebuild and-they-began Jozadak son-of and-Jeshua

בִירוּשְׁלֶם וְעִמְּהוֹן נְבִיַּאיָּא° דִּי־ אֱלָהָא מְסָעֲדִין לְהוֹן׃

to-them ones-helping the-God of the-prophets and-with-them in-Jerusalem

בֵּהּ־ זִמְנָא אֲתָא עֲלֵיהוֹן תַּתְּנַי פַּחַת עֲבַר־ נַהֲרָה

the-River Beyond-of governor-of Tattenai to-them he-went the-time at-him (3)

וּשְׁתַר בּוֹזְנַי וּכְנָוָתְהוֹן וְכֵן אָמְרִין לְהֹם

to-them ones-asking and-this and-associates-of-them Bozenai and-Shethar

מַן־ שָׂם לְכֹם טְעֵם בַּיְתָא דְנָה לִבְּנֵא וְאֻשַּׁרְנָא

and-the-structure to-rebuild this the-temple authorization to-you he-gave who?

דְנָה לְשַׁכְלָלָה׃ אֱדַיִן כְּנֵמָא אֲמַרְנָא לְהֹם מַן־ אִנּוּן שְׁמָהָת

names-of they what? to-them we-told following also (4) to-restore this

גֻּבְרַיָּא דִּי־ דְנָה בִנְיָנָא בָּנַיִן׃ וְעֵין אֱלָהֲהֹם

God-of-them but-eye-of (5) ones-constructing the-building this who the-men

הֲוָת עַל־ שָׂבֵי יְהוּדָיֵא וְלָא־ בַטִּלוּ הִמּוֹ עַד־

until them they-stopped and-not the-Jews ones-being-elders-of over she-was

טַעְמָא לְדָרְיָוֶשׁ יְהָךְ וֶאֱדַיִן יְתִיבוּן נִשְׁתְּוָנָא

the-written-reply they-could-return and-then he-could-go to-Darius the-report

עַל־ דְּנָה׃ פַּרְשֶׁגֶן אִגַּרְתָּא דִּי־ שְׁלַח תַּתְּנַי ׀ פַּחַת

governor-of Tattenai he-sent that the-letter copy-of (6) this about

עֲבַר־ נַהֲרָה וּשְׁתַר בּוֹזְנַי וּכְנָוָתֵהּ אֲפַרְסְכָיֵא

the-officials and-associates-of-him Bozenai and-Shethar the-River Beyond-of

דִּי בַּעֲבַר נַהֲרָה עַל־דָּרְיָוֶשׁ מַלְכָּא׃ פִּתְגָמָא שְׁלַחוּ עֲלוֹהִי

to-him they-sent the-report (7) the-king Darius to the-River of-Beyond-of who

וְכִדְנָה כְּתִיב בְּגַוֵּהּ לְדָרְיָוֶשׁ מַלְכָּא שְׁלָמָא

the-greeting the-king to-Darius within-him he-was-written and-as-this

כֹלָּא׃ יְדִיעַ ׀ לֶהֱוֵא לְמַלְכָּא דִּי־ אֲזַלְנָא לִיהוּד

to-Judah we-went that to-the-king let-him-be being-known (8) the-cordial

מְדִינְתָּא לְבֵית אֱלָהָא רַבָּא וְהוּא מִתְבְּנֵא אֶבֶן גְּלָל

large stone being-built and-he the-great the-God to-temple-of the-district

וְאָע מִתְּשָׂם בְּכֻתְלַיָּא וַעֲבִידְתָּא דָךְ אָסְפַּרְנָא

diligently this and-the-work in-the-walls being-placed and-timber

מִתְעַבְדָא וּמַצְלַח בִּידְהֹם׃ אֱדַיִן שְׁאֵלְנָא

we-questioned then (9) under-hand-of-them and-making-progress being-carried-on

לְשָׂבַיָּא אִלֵּךְ כְּנֵמָא אֲמַרְנָא לְהֹם מַן־ שָׂם לְכֹם

to-you he-gave who? to-them we-asked this these to-the-ones-being-elders

טְעֵם בַּיְתָא דְנָה לְמִבְנְיָה וְאֻשַּׁרְנָא דְנָה לְשַׁכְלָלָה׃

to-restore this and-the-structure to-rebuild this the-temple authorization

Jeshua son of Jozadak set to work to rebuild the house of God in Jerusalem. And the prophets of God were with them, helping them.

[3]At that time Tattenai, governor of Trans-Euphrates, and Shethar-Bozenai and their associates went to them and asked, "Who authorized you to rebuild this temple and restore this structure?" [4]They also asked, "What are the names of the men constructing this building?"[m] [5]But the eye of their God was watching over the elders of the Jews, and they were not stopped until a report could go to Darius and his written reply be received.

[6]This is a copy of the letter that Tattenai, governor of Trans-Euphrates, and Shethar-Bozenai and their associates, the officials of Trans-Euphrates, sent to King Darius. [7]The report they sent him read as follows:

To King Darius:

Cordial greetings.

[8]The king should know that we went to the district of Judah, to the temple of the great God. The people are building it with large stones and placing the timbers in the walls. The work is being carried on with diligence and is making rapid progress under their direction.

[9]We questioned the elders and asked them, "Who authorized you to rebuild this temple and restore this

[m]4 See Septuagint; Aramaic [4]*We told them the names of the man constructing this building.*

°2 ק נביייא

וְאַף שְׁמָהָתְהֹם שְׁאֵלְנָא לְהֹם לְהוֹדָעוּתָךְ דִּי
that to-inform-you of-them we-asked names-of-them and-also (10)

נִכְתֻּב שֻׁם־ גֻּבְרַיָּא דִּי בְרָאשֵׁיהֹם׃ וּכְנֵמָא
and-this (11) over-heads-of-them who the-men name-of we-could-write-down

פִתְגָמָא הֲתִיבוּנָא לְמֵמַר אֲנַחְנָא הִמּוֹ עַבְדוֹהִי דִי־ אֱלָהּ שְׁמַיָּא
the-heavens God-of who servants-of-him they we to-say they-gave-us the-answer

וְאַרְעָא וּבָנַיִן בַּיְתָא דִּי־ הֲוָא בְנֵה
being-built he-was that the-temple and-ones-rebuilding and-the-earth

מִקַּדְמַת דְּנָה שְׁנִין שַׂגִּיאָן וּמֶלֶךְ לְיִשְׂרָאֵל רַב בְּנָהִי
he-built-him great of-Israel and-king many years this from-before-of

וְשַׁכְלְלֵהּ׃ לָהֵן מִן־ דִּי הַרְגִּזוּ אֲבָהֳתַנָא*
fathers-of-us they-angered that because but (12) and-he-finished-him

לֶאֱלָהּ שְׁמַיָּא יְהַב הִמּוֹ בְּיַד נְבוּכַדְנֶצַּר מֶלֶךְ־
king-of Nebuchadnezzar into-hand-of them he-gave the-heavens to-God-of

בָּבֶל כַּסְדָּיָא° וּבַיְתָה דְנָה סַתְרֵהּ וְעַמָּה
and-the-people he-destroyed-him this and-the-temple the-Chaldean Babylon

הַגְלִי לְבָבֶל׃ בְּרַם בִּשְׁנַת חֲדָה לְכוֹרֶשׁ מַלְכָּא דִּי
of the-king of-Cyrus one in-year-of however (13) to-Babylon he-deported

בָבֶל כּוֹרֶשׁ מַלְכָּא שָׂם טְעֵם בֵּית־ אֱלָהָא דְנָה לִבְּנֵא׃
to-rebuild this the-God house-of decree he-issued the-king Cyrus Babylon

וְאַף מָאנַיָּא דִי־ בֵית־ אֱלָהָא דִּי דַהֲבָה וְכַסְפָּא
and-the-silver the-gold of the-God house-of of the-articles and-even (14)

דִּי נְבוּכַדְנֶצַּר הַנְפֵּק מִן־ הֵיכְלָא דִּי בִירוּשְׁלֶם וְהֵיבֵל
and-he-brought in-Jerusalem that the-temple from he-took Nebuchadnezzar which

הִמּוֹ לְהֵיכְלָא דִּי בָבֶל הַנְפֵּק הִמּוֹ כּוֹרֶשׁ מַלְכָּא מִן־ הֵיכְלָא
the-temple from the-king Cyrus them he-removed Babylon in to-the-temple them

דִּי בָבֶל וִיהִיבוּ לְשֵׁשְׁבַּצַּר שְׁמֵהּ דִּי פֶחָה
governor who name-of-him to-Sheshbazzar then-they-were-given Babylon of

שָׂמֵהּ׃ וַאֲמַר־ לֵהּ אֵלֶּה° מָאנַיָּא שֵׂא אֵזֶל־
go! take! the-articles these to-him and-he-told (15) he-appointed-him

אֲחֵת הִמּוֹ בְּהֵיכְלָא דִּי בִירוּשְׁלֶם וּבֵית אֱלָהָא
the-God and-house-of in-Jerusalem that in-the-temple them deposit!

יִתְבְּנֵא עַל־ אַתְרֵהּ׃ אֱדַיִן שֵׁשְׁבַּצַּר דֵּךְ אֲתָא יְהַב
he-laid he-came this Sheshbazzar so (16) site-of-him on let-him-be-rebuilt

אֻשַּׁיָּא דִּי־ בֵית אֱלָהָא דִּי בִירוּשְׁלֶם וּמִן־ אֱדַיִן וְעַד־
and-to then and-from in-Jerusalem that the-God house-of of the-foundations

כְּעַן מִתְבְּנֵא וְלָא שְׁלִם׃ וּכְעַן הֵן עַל־ מַלְכָּא
the-king to if and-now (17) being-finished but-not being-constructed present

structure?" [10]We also asked them their names, so that we could write down the names of their leaders for your information.

[11]This is the answer they gave us:

"We are the servants of the God of heaven and earth, and we are rebuilding the temple that was built many years ago, one that a great king of Israel built and finished. [12]But because our fathers angered the God of heaven, he handed them over to Nebuchadnezzar the Chaldean, king of Babylon, who destroyed this temple and deported the people to Babylon.

[13]"However, in the first year of Cyrus king of Babylon, King Cyrus issued a decree to rebuild this house of God. [14]He even removed from the temple[n] of Babylon the gold and silver articles of the house of God, which Nebuchadnezzar had taken from the temple in Jerusalem and brought to the temple[n] in Babylon.

"Then King Cyrus gave them to a man named Sheshbazzar, whom he had appointed governor, [15]and he told him, 'Take these articles and go and deposit them in the temple in Jerusalem. And rebuild the house of God on its site.' [16]So this Sheshbazzar came and laid the foundations of the house of God in Jerusalem. From that day to the present it has been under construction but is not yet finished."

[17]Now if it pleases the

n14 Or *palace*

*12 Most mss have *qamets* under the *he* (הָ–).

°12 ק כסדאה

°15 ק אל

טָב יִתְבַּקַּר בְּבֵית גִּנְזַיָּא דִּי־ מַלְכָּא תַמָּה

there the-king of the-archives in-house-of let-him-be-searched pleasing

דִּי בְּבָבֶל הֵן אִיתַי דִּי־ מִן־ כּוֹרֶשׁ מַלְכָּא שִׂים טְעֵם

decree he-issued the-king Cyrus from of there-is if in-Babylon that

לְמִבְנֵא בֵּית־ אֱלָהָא דֵךְ בִּירוּשְׁלֶם וּרְעוּת מַלְכָּא עַל־

in the-king then-decision-of in-Jerusalem this the-God house-of to-rebuild

דְּנָה יִשְׁלַח עֲלֶינָא׃ בֵּאדַיִן דָּרְיָוֶשׁ מַלְכָּא שָׂם טְעֵם

order he-issued the-king Darius at-then (6:1) to-us let-him-send this

וּבַקַּרוּ ׀ בְּבֵית סִפְרַיָּא דִּי גִנְזַיָּא מְהַחֲתִין

ones-storing the-treasuries of the-archives in-house-of and-they-searched

תַּמָּה בְּבָבֶל׃ וְהִשְׁתְּכַח בְּאַחְמְתָא בְּבִירְתָא דִּי

that in-the-citadel in-Ecbatana and-he-was-found (2) at-Babylon there

בְּמָדַי מְדִינְתָּה מְגִלָּה חֲדָה וְכֵן־ כְּתִיב בְּגַוַּהּ

within-her he-was-written and-this a scroll the-province in-Media

דִּכְרוֹנָה׃ בִּשְׁנַת חֲדָה לְכוֹרֶשׁ מַלְכָּא כּוֹרֶשׁ מַלְכָּא שָׂם

he-issued the-king Cyrus the-king of-Cyrus one in-year-of (3) the-memorandum

טְעֵם בֵּית־ אֱלָהָא בִירוּשְׁלֶם בַּיְתָא יִתְבְּנֵא אֲתַר דִּי־

of place let-him-be-rebuilt the-temple in-Jerusalem the-God temple-of decree

דָבְחִין דִּבְחִין וְאֻשּׁוֹהִי מְסוֹבְלִין

ones-being-laid and-foundations-of-him sacrifices ones-presenting

רוּמֵהּ אַמִּין שִׁתִּין פְּתָיֵהּ אַמִּין שִׁתִּין׃ נִדְבָּכִין דִּי־ אֶבֶן

stone of courses (4) sixty cubits width-of-him sixty cubits height-of-him

גְּלָל תְּלָתָא וְנִדְבָּךְ דִּי־ אָע חֲדַת וְנִפְקְתָא מִן־ בֵּית מַלְכָּא

the-king treasury-of from and-the-cost one wood of and-course three large

תִּתְיְהִב׃ וְאַף מָאנֵי בֵית־ אֱלָהָא דִּי דַהֲבָה

the-gold of the-God house-of articles-of and-also (5) let-her-be-paid

וְכַסְפָּא דִּי נְבוּכַדְנֶצַּר הַנְפֵּק מִן־ הֵיכְלָא דִּי־ בִירוּשְׁלֶם

in-Jerusalem that the-temple from he-took Nebuchadnezzar which and-the-silver

וְהֵיבֵל לְבָבֶל יַהֲתִיבוּן וִיהָךְ לְהֵיכְלָא דִּי־

that to-the-temple and-let-him-go let-them-return to-Babylon and-he-brought

בִירוּשְׁלֶם לְאַתְרֵהּ וְתַחֵת בְּבֵית אֱלָהָא׃ כְּעַן

now (6) the-God in-house-of and-you-deposit to-place-of-him in-Jerusalem

תַּתְּנַי פַּחַת עֲבַר־ נַהֲרָה שְׁתַר בּוֹזְנַי וּכְנָוָתְהוֹן

and-fellows-of-them Bozenai Shethar the-River Beyond-of governor-of Tattenai

אֲפַרְסְכָיֵא דִּי בַּעֲבַר נַהֲרָה רַחִיקִין הֲווֹ מִן־ תַּמָּה׃

there from stay! ones-away the-River of-Beyond-of that the-officials

שְׁבֻקוּ לַעֲבִידַת בֵּית־ אֱלָהָא דֵךְ פַּחַת

governor-of this the-God temple-of with-work-of do-not-interfere! (7)

---

king, let a search be made in the royal archives of Babylon to see if King Cyrus did in fact issue a decree to rebuild this house of God in Jerusalem. Then let the king send us his decision in this matter.

*The Decree of Darius*

6 King Darius then issued an order, and they searched in the archives stored in the treasury at Babylon. 2A scroll was found in the citadel of Ecbatana in the province of Media, and this was written on it:

Memorandum:

3In the first year of King Cyrus, the king issued a decree concerning the temple of God in Jerusalem:

Let the temple be rebuilt as a place to present sacrifices, and let its foundations be laid. It is to be ninety feet[a] high and ninety feet wide, 4with three courses of large stones and one of timbers. The costs are to be paid by the royal treasury. 5Also, the gold and silver articles of the house of God, which Nebuchadnezzar took from the temple in Jerusalem and brought to Babylon, are to be returned to their places in the temple in Jerusalem; they are to be deposited in the house of God.

6Now then, Tattenai, governor of Trans-Euphrates, and Shethar-Bozenai and you, their fellow officials of that province, stay away from there. 7Do not interfere with the work on this temple of God. Let

[a]3 Aramaic *sixty cubits* (about 27 meters)

יְהוּדָיֵא וּלְשָׂבֵי יְהוּדָיֵא בֵּית־ אֱלָהָא דֵךְ

this the-God house-of the-Jews and-to-ones-being-elders-of the-Jews

יִבְנוֹן עַל־ אַתְרֵהּ׃ וּמִנִּי שִׂים טְעֵם לְמָא

of-what decree he-is-issued and-from-me (8) site-of-him on let-them-rebuild

דִּי־ תַעַבְדוּן עִם־ שָׂבֵי יְהוּדָיֵא אִלֵּךְ לְמִבְנֵא

to-construct these the-Jews ones-being-elders-of for you-must-do that

בֵּית־ אֱלָהָא דֵךְ וּמִנִּכְסֵי מַלְכָּא דִּי מִדַּת

revenue-of from the-king and-from-treasuries-of this the-God house-of

עֲבַר נַהֲרָה אָסְפַּרְנָא נִפְקְתָא תֶּהֱוֵא מִתְיַהֲבָא לְגֻבְרַיָּא

to-the-men being-paid she-must-be the-expense fully the-River Beyond-of

אִלֵּךְ דִּי־ לָא לְבַטָּלָא׃ וּמָה חַשְׁחָן וּבְנֵי

even-young-ones-of things-needed and-whatever (9) to-stop not that these

תוֹרִין וְדִכְרִין וְאִמְּרִין | לַעֲלָוָן | לֶאֱלָהּ שְׁמַיָּא חִנְטִין

wheats the-heavens to-God-of for-burnt-offerings and-lambs and-rams bulls

מְלַח | חֲמַר וּמְשַׁח כְּמֵאמַר כָּהֲנַיָּא דִּי־ בִירוּשְׁלֶם לֶהֱוֵא מִתְיְהֵב

being-given to-be in-Jerusalem who the-priests as-request-of and-oil wine salt

לְהֹם יוֹם | בְּיוֹם דִּי־ לָא שָׁלוּ׃ דִּי־ לֶהֱוֺן מְהַקְרְבִין

ones-sacrificing they-may-be that (10) fail without that by-day day to-them

נִיחוֹחִין לֶאֱלָהּ שְׁמַיָּא וּמְצַלַּיִן לְחַיֵּי מַלְכָּא

the-king for-lives-of and-ones-praying the-heavens to-God-of things-pleasing

וּבְנוֹהִי׃ וּמִנִּי שִׂים טְעֵם דִּי כָל־ אֱנָשׁ דִּי

who person any-of that decree he-is-issued and-from-me (11) and-sons-of-him

יְהַשְׁנֵא פִּתְגָמָא דְנָה יִתְנְסַח אָע מִן־ בַּיְתֵהּ

house-of-him from beam he-must-be-pulled this the-edict he-changes

וּזְקִיף יִתְמְחֵא עֲלֹהִי וּבַיְתֵהּ נְוָלוּ

rubble-pile and-house-of-him on-him he-must-be-impaled and-being-lifted-up

יִתְעֲבֵד עַל־ דְּנָה׃ וֵאלָהָא דִּי שַׁכִּן שְׁמֵהּ

name-of-him he-caused-to-dwell who and-the-God (12) this for he-must-be-made

תַּמָּה יְמַגַּר כָּל־ מֶלֶךְ וְעַם דִּי | יִשְׁלַח יְדֵהּ

hand-of-him he-lifts who or-people king any-of may-he-overthrow there

לְהַשְׁנָיָה לְחַבָּלָה בֵּית־ אֱלָהָא דֵךְ דִּי בִירוּשְׁלֶם אֲנָה דָרְיָוֶשׁ

Darius I in-Jerusalem that this the-God temple-of to-destroy to-change

שָׂמֶת טְעֵם אָסְפַּרְנָא יִתְעֲבִד׃ אֱדַיִן תַּתְּנַי

Tattenai then (13) let-him-be-carried-out diligently decree I-issued

פַּחַת עֲבַר־ נַהֲרָה שְׁתַר בּוֹזְנַי וּכְנָוָתְהוֹן

and-associates-of-them Bozenai Shethar the-River Beyond-of governor-of

לָקֳבֵל דִּי־ שְׁלַח דָּרְיָוֶשׁ מַלְכָּא כְּנֵמָא אָסְפַּרְנָא עֲבַדוּ׃

they-carried-out diligently this the-king Darius he-sent that because

the governor of the Jews and the Jewish elders rebuild this house of God on its site.

8 Moreover, I hereby decree what you are to do for these elders of the Jews in the construction of this house of God:

The expenses of these men are to be fully paid out of the royal treasury, from the revenues of Trans-Euphrates, so that the work will not stop. 9 Whatever is needed—young bulls, rams, male lambs for burnt offerings to the God of heaven, and wheat, salt, wine and oil, as requested by the priests in Jerusalem—must be given them daily without fail, 10 so that they may offer sacrifices pleasing to the God of heaven and pray for the well-being of the king and his sons.

11 Furthermore, I decree that if anyone changes this edict, a beam is to be pulled from his house and he is to be lifted up and impaled on it. And for this crime his house is to be made a pile of rubble. 12 May God, who has caused his Name to dwell there, overthrow any king or people who lifts a hand to change this decree or to destroy this temple in Jerusalem.

I Darius have decreed it. Let it be carried out with diligence.

### *Completion and Dedication of the Temple*

13 Then, because of the decree King Darius had sent, Tattenai, governor of Trans-Euphrates, and Shethar-Bozenai and their associates carried it out with diligence.

וְשָׂבֵי יְהוּדָיֵא בָּנַיִן וּמַצְלְחִין

and-ones-prospering ones-building the-Jews so-ones-being-elders-of (14)

בִּנְבוּאַת חַגַּי נְבִיָּאה וּזְכַרְיָה בַּר־ עִדּוֹא וּבְנוֹ

and-they-built Iddo son-of and-Zechariah prophet Haggai under-preaching-of

וְשַׁכְלִלוּ מִן־ טַעַם אֱלָהּ יִשְׂרָאֵל וּמִטְּעֵם

and-at-decree-of Israel God-of command-of according-to and-they-finished

כּוֹרֶשׁ וְדָרְיָוֶשׁ וְאַרְתַּחְשַׁשְׂתְּא מֶלֶךְ פָּרָס׃ וְשֵׁיצִיא

and-he-completed (15) Persia king-of and-Artaxerxes and-Darius Cyrus

בַּיְתָה דְנָה עַד יוֹם תְּלָתָה לִירַח אֲדָר דִּי־ הִיא שְׁנַת־ שֵׁת

six year-of this that Adar of-month-of three day-of on this the-temple

לְמַלְכוּת דָּרְיָוֶשׁ מַלְכָּא׃ וַעֲבַדוּ בְנֵי־ יִשְׂרָאֵל

Israel people-of then-they-celebrated (16) the-king Darius of-reign-of

כָּהֲנַיָּא וְלֵוָיֵא וּשְׁאָר בְּנֵי־ גָלוּתָא חֲנֻכַּת

dedication-of the-exile sons-of and-rest-of and-the-Levites the-priests

בֵּית־ אֱלָהָא דְנָה בְּחֶדְוָה׃ וְהַקְרִבוּ לַחֲנֻכַּת

for-dedication-of and-they-offered (17) with-joy this the-God house-of

בֵּית־ אֱלָהָא דְנָה תּוֹרִין מְאָה דִּכְרִין מָאתַיִן אִמְּרִין אַרְבַּע מְאָה

hundred four-of lambs two-hundreds rams hundred bulls this the-God house-of

וּצְפִירֵי עִזִּין לְחַטָּיָא עַל־ כָּל־ יִשְׂרָאֵל תְּרֵי־ עֲשַׂר

ten two-of Israel all-of for as-the-sin-offering goats and-male-goats-of

לְמִנְיָן שִׁבְטֵי יִשְׂרָאֵל׃ וַהֲקִימוּ כָהֲנַיָּא

the-priests and-they-installed (18) Israel tribes-of as-number-of

בִּפְלֻגָּתְהוֹן וְלֵוָיֵא בְּמַחְלְקָתְהוֹן עַל־ עֲבִידַת אֱלָהָא

the-God service-of for in-groups-of-them and-the-Levites in-divisions-of-them

דִּי בִירוּשְׁלֶם כִּכְתָב סְפַר מֹשֶׁה׃ וַיַּעֲשׂוּ

and-they-celebrated (19) Moses Book-of as-writing-of at-Jerusalem who

בְנֵי־ הַגּוֹלָה אֶת־ הַפָּסַח בְּאַרְבָּעָה עָשָׂר לַחֹדֶשׁ הָרִאשׁוֹן׃

the-first of-the-month ten on-four the-Passover *** the-exile sons-of

כִּי הִטַּהֲרוּ הַכֹּהֲנִים וְהַלְוִיִּם כְּאֶחָד

as-one and-the-Levites the-priests they-purified-themselves for (20)

כֻּלָּם טְהוֹרִים וַיִּשְׁחֲטוּ הַפֶּסַח לְכָל־

for-all-of the-Passover-lamb and-they-slaughtered ones-clean all-of-them

בְּנֵי הַגּוֹלָה וְלַאֲחֵיהֶם הַכֹּהֲנִים וְלָהֶם׃

and-for-themselves the-priests and-for-brothers-of-them the-exile sons-of

וַיֹּאכְלוּ בְנֵי־ יִשְׂרָאֵל הַשָּׁבִים מֵהַגּוֹלָה וְכֹל

and-all-of from-the-exile the-ones-returning Israel sons-of so-they-ate (21)

הַנִּבְדָּל מִטֻּמְאַת גּוֹיֵ־ הָאָרֶץ אֲלֵהֶם

around-them the-land Gentiles-of from-uncleanness-of the-one-separating-himself

14So the elders of the Jews continued to build and prosper under the preaching of Haggai the prophet and Zechariah, a descendant of Iddo. They finished building the temple according to the command of the God of Israel and the decrees of Cyrus, Darius and Artaxerxes, kings of Persia. 15The temple was completed on the third day of the month Adar, in the sixth year of the reign of King Darius.

16Then the people of Israel—the priests, the Levites and the rest of the exiles—celebrated the dedication of the house of God with joy. 17For the dedication of this house of God they offered a hundred bulls, two hundred rams, four hundred male lambs and, as a sin offering for all Israel, twelve male goats, one for each of the tribes of Israel. 18And they installed the priests in their divisions and the Levites in their groups for the service of God at Jerusalem, according to what is written in the Book of Moses.

*The Passover*

19On the fourteenth day of the first month, the exiles celebrated the Passover. 20The priests and Levites had purified themselves and were all ceremonially clean. The Levites slaughtered the Passover lamb for all the exiles, for their brothers the priests and for themselves. 21So the Israelites who had returned from the exile ate it, together with all who had separated themselves from the unclean practices of

°14 ק נביא
°17 ק לחטאה

לִדְרֹשׁ לַיהוָה אֱלֹהֵי יִשְׂרָאֵל׃ וַיַּעֲשׂוּ חַג־

Feast-of and-they-celebrated (22) Israel God-of to-Yahweh to-seek

מַצּוֹת שִׁבְעַת יָמִים בְּשִׂמְחָה כִּי שִׂמְּחָם

he-filled-with-joy-them because with-joy days seven-of Unleavened-Breads

יְהוָה וְהֵסֵב לֵב מֶלֶךְ־ אַשּׁוּר עֲלֵיהֶם לְחַזֵּק

to-assist for-them Assyria king-of heart-of and-he-changed Yahweh

יְדֵיהֶם בִּמְלֶאכֶת בֵּית־ הָאֱלֹהִים אֱלֹהֵי יִשְׂרָאֵל׃ וְאַחַר

and-after (7:1) Israel God-of the-God house-of in-work-of hands-of-them

הַדְּבָרִים הָאֵלֶּה בְּמַלְכוּת אַרְתַּחְשַׁסְתְּא מֶלֶךְ־ פָּרָס עֶזְרָא בֶּן־

son-of Ezra Persia king-of Artaxerxes during-reign-of the-these the-things

שְׂרָיָה בֶּן־ עֲזַרְיָה בֶּן־ חִלְקִיָּה׃ בֶּן־ שַׁלּוּם בֶּן־ צָדוֹק

Zadok son-of Shallum son-of (2) Hilkiah son-of Azariah son-of Seraiah

בֶּן־ אֲחִיטוּב׃ בֶּן־ אֲמַרְיָה בֶּן־ עֲזַרְיָה בֶּן־ מְרָיוֹת׃ בֶּן־

son-of (4) Meraioth son-of Azariah son-of Amariah son-of (3) Ahitub son-of

זְרַחְיָה בֶּן־ עֻזִּי בֶּן־ בֻּקִּי׃ בֶּן־ אֲבִישׁוּעַ בֶּן־ פִּינְחָס בֶּן־

son-of Phinehas son-of Abishua son-of (5) Bukki son-of Uzzi son-of Zerahiah

אֶלְעָזָר בֶּן־ אַהֲרֹן הַכֹּהֵן הָרֹאשׁ׃ הוּא עֶזְרָא עָלָה

he-came-up Ezra this (6) the-chief the-priest Aaron son-of Eleazar

מִבָּבֶל וְהוּא־ סֹפֵר מָהִיר בְּתוֹרַת מֹשֶׁה אֲשֶׁר־ נָתַן יְהוָה

Yahweh he-gave which Moses in-Law-of well-versed teacher now-he from-Babylon

אֱלֹהֵי יִשְׂרָאֵל וַיִּתֶּן־ לוֹ הַמֶּלֶךְ כְּיַד־ יְהוָה אֱלֹהָיו

God-of-him Yahweh for-hand-of the-king to-him and-he-granted Israel God-of

עָלָיו כֹּל בַּקָּשָׁתוֹ׃ וַיַּעֲלוּ מִבְּנֵי־ יִשְׂרָאֵל

Israel from-sons-of and-they-came-up (7) request-of-him every-of on-him

וּמִן־ הַכֹּהֲנִים וְהַלְוִיִּם וְהַמְשֹׁרְרִים וְהַשֹּׁעֲרִים

and-the-gatekeepers and-the-ones-singing and-the-Levites the-priests and-from

וְהַנְּתִינִים אֶל־ יְרוּשָׁלִָם בִּשְׁנַת־ שֶׁבַע לְאַרְתַּחְשַׁסְתְּא הַמֶּלֶךְ׃

the-king of-Artaxerxes seven in-year-of Jerusalem to and-the-temple-servants

וַיָּבֹא יְרוּשָׁלַםִ בַּחֹדֶשׁ הַחֲמִישִׁי הִיא שְׁנַת הַשְּׁבִיעִית

the-seventh year-of this the-fifth in-the-month Jerusalem and-he-arrived (8)

לַמֶּלֶךְ׃ כִּי בְּאֶחָד לַחֹדֶשׁ הָרִאשׁוֹן הוּא יְסֻד*

beginning-of this the-first of-the-month on-one now (9) of-the-king

הַמַּעֲלָה מִבָּבֶל וּבְאֶחָד לַחֹדֶשׁ הַחֲמִישִׁי בָּא אֶל־

in he-arrived the-fifth of-the-month and-on-one from-Babylon the-journey

יְרוּשָׁלַםִ כְּיַד־ אֱלֹהָיו הַטּוֹבָה עָלָיו׃ כִּי עֶזְרָא הֵכִין

he-devoted Ezra for (10) on-him the-good God-of-him for-hand-of Jerusalem

לְבָבוֹ לִדְרוֹשׁ אֶת־ תּוֹרַת יְהוָה וְלַעֲשֹׂת וּלְלַמֵּד

and-to-teach and-to-observe Yahweh Law-of *** to-study heart-of-him

their Gentile neighbors in order to seek the LORD, the God
of Israel. 22For seven days they
celebrated with joy the Feast
of Unleavened Bread, because
the LORD had filled them with
joy by changing the attitude of
the king of Assyria, so that he
assisted them in the work on
the house of God, the God of
Israel.

*Ezra Comes to Jerusalem*

7 After these things, during
the reign of Artaxerxes
king of Persia, Ezra son of Seraiah, the son of Azariah, the
son of Hilkiah, 2the son of
Shallum, the son of Zadok, the
son of Ahitub, 3the son of
Amariah, the son of Azariah,
the son of Meraioth, 4the son
of Zerahiah, the son of Uzzi,
the son of Bukki, 5the son of
Abishua, the son of Phinehas,
the son of Eleazar, the son of
Aaron the chief priest— 6this
Ezra came up from Babylon.
He was a teacher well versed
in the Law of Moses, which
the LORD, the God of Israel,
had given. The king had
granted him everything he
asked, for the hand of the
LORD his God was on him.
7Some of the Israelites, including priests, Levites, singers,
gatekeepers and temple servants, also came up to Jerusalem in the seventh year of
King Artaxerxes.
8Ezra arrived in Jerusalem in
the fifth month of the seventh
year of the king. 9He had
begun his journey from Babylon on the first day of the first
month, and he arrived in
Jerusalem on the first day of
the fifth month, for the good
hand of his God was on him.
10For Ezra had devoted himself
to the study and observance of
the Law of the LORD, and to

*9 The NIV repoints this word as יָסַד, he-began.

נָתַן אֲשֶׁר הַנִּשְׁתְּוָן פַּרְשֶׁגֶן וְזֶה ׀ וּמִשְׁפָּט׃ חֹק בְּיִשְׂרָאֵל
he-gave that the-letter copy-of now-this (11) and-law decree in-Israel

דִּבְרֵי סֹפֵר הַסֹּפֵר הַכֹּהֵן לְעֶזְרָא אַרְתַּחְשַׁסְתְּא הַמֶּלֶךְ
matters-of teacher-of the-teacher the-priest to-Ezra Artaxerxes the-king

מֶלֶךְ אַרְתַּחְשַׁסְתְּא עַל־יִשְׂרָאֵל׃ וְחֻקָּיו יְהוָה מִצְוֺת־
king-of Artaxerxes (12) Israel for and-decrees-of-him Yahweh commands-of

שְׁמַיָּא אֱלָהּ דִּי־ דָתָא סָפַר כָהֲנָא לְעֶזְרָא מַלְכַיָּא
the-heavens God-of of the-Law teacher-of the-priest to-Ezra the-kings

כָל־ דִּי טְעֵם שִׂים מִנִּי וּכְעֶנֶת׃ גְּמִיר
any-of that decree he-is-issued from-me (13) and-now being-greeted

וְכָהֲנוֹהִי יִשְׂרָאֵל עַמָּה מִן־ בְּמַלְכוּתִי מִתְנַדַּב
and-priests-of-him Israel the-people from in-kingdom-of-me one-wishing

דִּי קֳבֵל כָּל־ יְהָךְ׃ עִמָּךְ לִירוּשְׁלֶם לִמְהָךְ וְלֵוָיֵא
that because for (14) he-may-go with-you to-Jerusalem to-go and-the-Levites

עַל־ לְבַקָּרָא שְׁלִיחַ יָעֲטֹהִי וְשִׁבְעַת מַלְכָּא קֳדָם מִן־
about to-inquire being-sent advisers-of-him and-seven-of the-king before from

בִידָךְ׃ דִּי אֱלָהָךְ בְּדָת וְלִירוּשְׁלֶם יְהוּד
in-hand-of-you which God-of-you regarding-Law-of and-about-Jerusalem Judah

וְיָעֲטוֹהִי מַלְכָּא דִּי־ וּדְהַב כְּסַף וּלְהֵיבָלָה
and-advisers-of-him the-king that and-gold silver and-to-take (15)

מִשְׁכְּנֵהּ׃ בִירוּשְׁלֶם דִּי יִשְׂרָאֵל לֶאֱלָהּ הִתְנַדַּבוּ
dwelling-of-him in-Jerusalem who Israel to-God-of they-gave-freely

מְדִינַת בְּכֹל תְהַשְׁכַּח דִּי וּדְהַב כְּסַף וְכֹל
province-of from-all-of you-may-obtain that and-gold silver with-all-of (16)

מִתְנַדְּבִין וְכָהֲנַיָּא עַמָּא הִתְנַדָּבוּת עִם בָּבֶל
ones-offering-freely and-the-priests the-people to-offer-freely with Babylon

דְּנָה קֳבֵל כָּל־ בִירוּשְׁלֶם׃ דִּי אֱלָהֲהֹם לְבֵית
this because-of for (17) in-Jerusalem that God-of-them for-temple-of

אִמְּרִין דִּכְרִין ׀ תּוֹרִין דְנָה בְּכַסְפָּא תִקְנֵא אָסְפַּרְנָא
lambs rams bulls this with-the-money you-buy diligently

הִמּוֹ וּתְקָרֵב וְנִסְכֵּיהוֹן וּמִנְחָתְהוֹן
them and-you-sacrifice and-drink-offerings-of-them and-grain-offerings-of-them

וּמָה בִירוּשְׁלֶם׃ דִּי אֱלָהֲכֹם בֵּית דִּי עַל־מַדְבְּחָה
and-whatever (18) in-Jerusalem that God-of-you temple-of of the-altar on

כַּסְפָּא בִּשְׁאָר יֵיטַב אֶחָיךְ וְעַל־ עֲלָיךְ דִּי
the-silver with-rest-of he-seems-good brother-of-you and-to to-you that

וּמָאנַיָּא תַּעַבְדוּן׃ אֱלָהֲכֹם כִּרְעוּת לְמֶעְבַּד וְדַהֲבָה
and-the-articles (19) you-may-do God-of-you as-will-of to-do and-the-gold

teaching its decrees and laws in Israel.

*King Artaxerxes' Letter to Ezra*

11 This is a copy of the letter King Artaxerxes had given to Ezra the priest and teacher, a man learned in matters concerning the commands and decrees of the LORD for Israel:

12 [P] Artaxerxes, king of kings,

To Ezra the priest, a teacher of the Law of the God of heaven:

Greetings.

13 Now I decree that any of the Israelites in my kingdom, including priests and Levites, who wish to go to Jerusalem with you, may go. 14 You are sent by the king and his seven advisers to inquire about Judah and Jerusalem with regard to the Law of your God, which is in your hand. 15 Moreover, you are to take with you the silver and gold that the king and his advisers have freely given to the God of Israel, whose dwelling is in Jerusalem, 16 together with all the silver and gold you may obtain from the province of Babylon, as well as the freewill offerings of the people and priests for the temple of their God in Jerusalem. 17 With this money be sure to buy bulls, rams and male lambs, together with their grain offerings and drink offerings, and sacrifice them on the altar of the temple of your God in Jerusalem.

18 You and your brother Jews may then do whatever seems best with the rest of the silver and gold, in accordance with the will of your God. 19 Deliver to the

P12 The text of Ezra 7:12-26 is in Aramaic.

°18a ק עלך
°18b ק אחך

דִּי־ מִתְיַהֲבִין לָךְ לְפָלְחָן בֵּית אֱלָהָךְ
God-of-you temple-of for-worship-of to-you ones-being-entrusted that

הַשְׁלֵם קֳדָם אֱלָהּ יְרוּשְׁלֶם׃ וּשְׁאָר חַשְׁחוּת בֵּית
temple-of the-thing-needed-of and-rest-of (20) Jerusalem God-of to deliver!

אֱלָהָךְ דִּי יִפֶּל־ לָךְ לְמִנְתַּן תִּנְתֵּן מִן־ בֵּית
house-of from you-may-provide to-supply to-you he-may-fall that God-of-you

גִּנְזֵי מַלְכָּא׃ וּמִנִּי אֲנָה אַרְתַּחְשַׁסְתְּא מַלְכָּא שִׂים
he-is-issued the-king Artaxerxes I now-from-me (21) the-king treasuries-of

טְעֵם לְכֹל גִּזַּבְרַיָּא דִּי בַּעֲבַר נַהֲרָה דִּי כָל־ דִּי
that all that the-River of-Beyond-of who the-treasurers to-all-of order

יִשְׁאֲלֶנְכוֹן עֶזְרָא כָהֲנָה סָפַר דָּתָא דִּי־ אֱלָהּ שְׁמַיָּא
the-heavens God-of of the-Law teacher-of the-priest Ezra he-may-ask-you

אָסְפַּרְנָא יִתְעֲבֶד׃ עַד־ כְּסַף כַּכְּרִין מְאָה וְעַד־
and-up-to hundred talents silver up-to (22) let-him-provide diligently

חִנְטִין כֹּרִין מְאָה וְעַד־ חֲמַר בַּתִּין מְאָה וְעַד־ בַּתִּין מְשַׁח
olive-oil baths and-up-to hundred baths wine and-up-to hundred cors wheats

מְאָה וּמְלַח דִּי־ לָא כְתָב׃ כָּל־ דִּי מִן־ טַעַם
prescription-of from that all (23) limit without that and-salt hundred

אֱלָהּ שְׁמַיָּא יִתְעֲבֵד אַדְרַזְדָּא לְבֵית אֱלָהּ
God-of for-temple-of diligently let-him-be-done the-heavens God-of

שְׁמַיָּא דִּי־ לְמָה לֶהֱוֵא קְצַף עַל־ מַלְכוּת מַלְכָּא
the-king realm-of against wrath should-he-be why? for the-heavens

וּבְנוֹהִי׃ וּלְכֹם מְהוֹדְעִין דִּי כָל־ כָּהֲנַיָּא
the-priests any-of that ones-making-known and-to-you (24) and-sons-of-him

וְלֵוָיֵא זַמָּרַיָּא תָרָעַיָּא נְתִינַיָּא
the-temple-servants the-gatekeepers the-singers and-the-Levites

וּפָלְחֵי בֵּית אֱלָהָא דְנָה מִנְדָּה בְלוֹ וַהֲלָךְ לָא שַׁלִּיט
authority no or-duty tribute tax this the-God house-of and-ones-working-of

לְמִרְמֵא עֲלֵיהֹם׃ וְאַנְתְּ עֶזְרָא כְּחָכְמַת אֱלָהָךְ דִּי־
which God-of-you as-wisdom-of Ezra and-you (25) on-them to-impose

בִידָךְ מֶנִּי שָׁפְטִין וְדַיָּנִין דִּי־ לֶהֱוֺן
they-may-be that and-judges ones-being-magistrates appoint! in-hand-of-you

דָּאנִין לְכָל־ עַמָּה דִּי בַּעֲבַר נַהֲרָה לְכָל־
to-all-of the-River of-Beyond-of who the-people to-all-of ones-administering-justice

יָדְעֵי דָּתֵי אֱלָהָךְ וְדִי לָא יָדַע תְּהוֹדְעוּן׃ וְכָל־
and-any (26) you-teach knowing not and-who God-of-you laws-of ones-knowing-of

דִּי־ לָא לֶהֱוֵא עָבֵד דָּתָא דִּי־ אֱלָהָךְ וְדָתָא דִּי מַלְכָּא
the-king of and-the-law God-of-you of the-law obeying he-is not who

God of Jerusalem all the articles entrusted to you for worship in the temple of your God. [20]And anything else needed for the temple of your God that you may have occasion to supply, you may provide from the royal treasury.

[21]Now I, King Artaxerxes, order all the treasurers of Trans-Euphrates to provide with diligence whatever Ezra the priest, a teacher of the Law of the God of heaven, may ask of you— [22]up to a hundred talents[r] of silver, a hundred cors[s] of wheat, a hundred baths[t] of wine, a hundred baths[t] of olive oil, and salt without limit. [23]Whatever the God of heaven has prescribed, let it be done with diligence for the temple of the God of heaven. Why should there be wrath against the realm of the king and of his sons? [24]You are also to know that you have no authority to impose taxes, tribute or duty on any of the priests, Levites, singers, gatekeepers, temple servants or other workers at this house of God.

[25]And you, Ezra, in accordance with the wisdom of your God, which you possess, appoint magistrates and judges to administer justice to all the people of Trans-Euphrates—all who know the laws of your God. And you are to teach any who do not know them. [26]Whoever does not obey the law of your God and the law of the king

[r]22 That is, about 3 3/4 tons (about 3.4 metric tons)
[s]22 That is, probably about 600 bushels (about 22 kiloliters)
[t]22 That is, probably about 600 gallons (about 2.2 kiloliters)

°25 ק דאינין

אָסְפַּרְנָא דִּינָה לֶהֱוֵא מִתְעֲבֵד מִנֵּהּ הֵן לְמוֹת הֵן
or by-death whether to-him being-done he-must-be the-punishment diligently

לִשְׁרֹשׁוּ הֵן לַעֲנָשׁ נִכְסִין וְלֶאֱסוּרִין׃
or-by-imprisonments properties by-confiscation-of or by-banishment

בָּרוּךְ יְהוָה אֱלָהֵי אֲבוֹתֵינוּ אֲשֶׁר נָתַן כָּזֹאת בְּלֵב
in-heart-of as-this he-put who fathers-of-us God-of Yahweh being-blessed (27)

הַמֶּלֶךְ לְפָאֵר אֶת־ בֵּית יְהוָה אֲשֶׁר בִּירוּשָׁלִָם׃ וְעָלַי
and-to-me (28) in-Jerusalem that Yahweh house-of *** to-honor the-king

הִטָּה־ חֶסֶד לִפְנֵי הַמֶּלֶךְ וְיוֹעֲצָיו וּלְכָל־
and-before-all-of and-ones-advising-him the-king before favor he-extended

שָׂרֵי הַמֶּלֶךְ הַגִּבֹּרִים וַאֲנִי הִתְחַזַּקְתִּי כְּיַד־
because-hand-of I-took-courage and-I the-powerful-ones the-king officials-of

יְהוָה אֱלֹהַי עָלַי וָאֶקְבְּצָה מִיִּשְׂרָאֵל רָאשִׁים לַעֲלוֹת
to-go-up leading-men from-Israel and-I-gathered on-me God-of-me Yahweh

עִמִּי׃ וְאֵלֶּה רָאשֵׁי אֲבֹתֵיהֶם וְהִתְיַחְשָׂם
and-to-be-registered-them fathers-of-them heads-of and-these (8:1) with-me

הָעֹלִים עִמִּי בְּמַלְכוּת אַרְתַּחְשַׁסְתְּא הַמֶּלֶךְ מִבָּבֶל׃
from-Babylon the-king Artaxerxes during-reign-of with-me the-ones-coming-up

מִבְּנֵי פִינְחָס גֵּרְשֹׁם מִבְּנֵי אִיתָמָר דָּנִיֵּאל
Daniel Ithamar of-descendants-of Gershom Phinehas of-descendants-of (2)

מִבְּנֵי דָוִיד חַטּוּשׁ׃ מִבְּנֵי שְׁכַנְיָה
Shecaniah of-descendants-of (3) Hattush David of-descendants-of

מִבְּנֵי פַרְעֹשׁ זְכַרְיָה וְעִמּוֹ הִתְיַחֵשׂ לִזְכָרִים
of-men to-be-registered and-with-him Zechariah Parosh of-descendants-of

מֵאָה וַחֲמִשִּׁים׃ מִבְּנֵי פַּחַת מוֹאָב אֶלְיְהוֹעֵינַי בֶּן־
son-of Eliehoenai Moab Pahath of-descendants-of (4) and-fifty hundred

זְרַחְיָה וְעִמּוֹ מָאתַיִם הַזְּכָרִים׃ מִבְּנֵי שְׁכַנְיָה
Shecaniah of-descendants-of (5) the-men two-hundreds and-with-him Zerahiah

בֶּן־ יַחֲזִיאֵל וְעִמּוֹ שְׁלֹשׁ מֵאוֹת הַזְּכָרִים׃ וּמִבְּנֵי
and-of-descendants-of (6) the-men hundreds three-of and-with-him Jahaziel son-of

עָדִין עֶבֶד בֶּן־ יוֹנָתָן וְעִמּוֹ חֲמִשִּׁים הַזְּכָרִים׃ וּמִבְּנֵי
and-of-descendants-of (7) the-men fifty and-with-him Jonathan son-of Ebed Adin

עֵילָם יְשַׁעְיָה בֶּן־ עֲתַלְיָה וְעִמּוֹ שִׁבְעִים הַזְּכָרִים׃
the-men seventy and-with-him Athaliah son-of Jeshaiah Elam

וּמִבְּנֵי שְׁפַטְיָה זְבַדְיָה בֶן־ מִיכָאֵל וְעִמּוֹ
and-with-him Michael son-of Zebadiah Shephatiah and-of-descendants-of (8)

שְׁמֹנִים הַזְּכָרִים׃ מִבְּנֵי יוֹאָב עֹבַדְיָה בֶּן־ יְחִיאֵל וְעִמּוֹ
and-with-him Jehiel son-of Obadiah Joab of-descendants-of (9) the-men eighty

must surely be punished by death, banishment, confiscation of property, or imprisonment.

27 Praise be to the LORD, the God of our fathers, who has put it into the king's heart to bring honor to the house of the LORD in Jerusalem in this way 28 and who has extended his good favor to me before the king and his advisers and all the king's powerful officials. Because the hand of the LORD my God was on me, I took courage and gathered leading men from Israel to go up with me.

*List of the Family Heads Returning With Ezra*

8 These are the family heads and those registered with them who came up with me from Babylon during the reign of King Artaxerxes:

2 of the descendants of Phinehas, Gershom;
of the descendants of Ithamar, Daniel;
of the descendants of David, Hattush 3 of the descendants of Shecaniah;

of the descendants of Parosh, Zechariah, and with him were registered 150 men;
4 of the descendants of Pahath-Moab, Eliehoenai son of Zerahiah, and with him 200 men;
5 of the descendants of Zattu,[u] Shecaniah son of Jahaziel, and with him 300 men;
6 of the descendants of Adin, Ebed son of Jonathan, and with him 50 men;
7 of the descendants of Elam, Jeshaiah son of Athaliah, and with him 70 men;
8 of the descendants of Shephatiah, Zebadiah son of Michael, and with him 80 men;
9 of the descendants of Joab, Obadiah son of Jehiel,

[u] 5 Some Septuagint manuscripts (also 1 Esdras 8:32); Hebrew does not have *Zattu.*

°26 ק לשרשי

מָאתַיִם וּשְׁמֹנָה עָשָׂר הַזְּכָרִים׃ וּמִבְּנֵי שְׁלוֹמִית
Shelomith and-of-descendants-of (10) the-men ten and-eight two-hundreds

בֶּן־ יוֹסִפְיָה וְעִמּוֹ מֵאָה וְשִׁשִּׁים הַזְּכָרִים׃
the-men and-sixty hundred and-with-him Josiphiah son-of

וּמִבְּנֵי בֵּבָי זְכַרְיָה בֶּן־ בֵּבָי וְעִמּוֹ עֶשְׂרִים
twenty and-with-him Bebai son-of Zechariah Bebai and-of-descendants-of (11)

וּשְׁמֹנָה הַזְּכָרִים׃ וּמִבְּנֵי עַזְגָּד יוֹחָנָן בֶּן־ הַקָּטָן
Hakkatan son-of Johanan Azgad and-of-descendants-of (12) the-men and-eight

וְעִמּוֹ מֵאָה וַעֲשָׂרָה הַזְּכָרִים׃ וּמִבְּנֵי אֲדֹנִיקָם
Adonikam and-of-descendants-of (13) the-men and-ten hundred and-with-him

אַחֲרֹנִים וְאֵלֶּה שְׁמוֹתָם אֱלִיפֶלֶט יְעִיאֵל וּשְׁמַעְיָה וְעִמָּהֶם
and-with-them and-Shemaiah Jeuel Eliphelet names-of-them and-these last-ones

שִׁשִּׁים הַזְּכָרִים׃ וּמִבְּנֵי בִגְוַי עוּתַי וְזַבּוּד וְעִמּוֹ
and-with-him and-Zaccur Uthai Bigvai and-of-descendants-of (14) the-men sixty

שִׁבְעִים הַזְּכָרִים׃ וָאֶקְבְּצֵם אֶל־ הַנָּהָר הַבָּא
the-one-flowing the-canal at and-I-assembled-them (15) the-men seventy

אֶל־ אַהֲוָא וַנַּחֲנֶה שָׁם יָמִים שְׁלֹשָׁה וָאָבִינָה בָעָם
among-the-people when-I-checked three days there and-we-camped Ahava toward

וּבַכֹּהֲנִים וּמִבְּנֵי לֵוִי לֹא־ מָצָאתִי שָׁם׃
there I-found not Levi then-from-sons-of and-among-the-priests

וָאֶשְׁלְחָה לֶאֱלִיעֶזֶר לַאֲרִיאֵל לִשְׁמַעְיָה וּלְאֶלְנָתָן
and-for-Elnathan for-Shemaiah for-Ariel for-Eliezer so-I-summoned (16)

וּלְיָרִיב וּלְאֶלְנָתָן וּלְנָתָן וְלִזְכַרְיָה
and-for-Zechariah and-for-Nathan and-for-Elnathan and-for-Jarib

וְלִמְשֻׁלָּם רָאשִׁים וּלְיוֹיָרִיב וּלְאֶלְנָתָן מְבִינִים׃
ones-being-learned and-for-Elnathan and-for-Joiarib leaders and-for-Meshullam

וָאֲוַצֶּאָה אוֹתָם עַל־ אִדּוֹ הָרֹאשׁ בְּכָסִפְיָא הַמָּקוֹם וָאָשִׂימָה
and-I-put the-place in-Casiphia the-leader Iddo to them and-I-sent (17)

בְּפִיהֶם דְּבָרִים לְדַבֵּר אֶל־ אִדּוֹ אָחִיו הַנְּתוּנִים
the-temple-servants kin-of-him Iddo to to-say words in-mouth-of-them

בְּכָסִפְיָא הַמָּקוֹם לְהָבִיא־ לָנוּ מְשָׁרְתִים לְבֵית אֱלֹהֵינוּ׃
God-of-us for-house-of ones-attending to-us to-bring the-place in-Casiphia

וַיָּבִיאוּ לָנוּ כְּיַד־ אֱלֹהֵינוּ הַטּוֹבָה עָלֵינוּ אִישׁ
man on-us the-good God-of-us because-hand-of to-us and-they-brought (18)

שֶׂכֶל מִבְּנֵי מַחְלִי בֶּן־ לֵוִי בֶּן־ יִשְׂרָאֵל וְשֵׁרֵבְיָה
even-Sherebiah Israel son-of Levi son-of Mahli from-descendants-of capable

וּבָנָיו וְאֶחָיו שְׁמֹנָה עָשָׂר׃ וְאֶת־ חֲשַׁבְיָה וְאִתּוֹ
and-with-him Hashabiah and (19) ten eight and-brothers-of-him and-sons-of-him

and with him 218 men;
[10]of the descendants of Bani,[v]
Shelomith son of Josiphiah, and with him 160 men;
[11]of the descendants of Bebai, Zechariah son of Bebai, and with him 28 men;
[12]of the descendants of Azgad, Johanan son of Hakkatan, and with him 110 men;
[13]of the descendants of Adonikam, the last ones, whose names were Eliphelet, Jeuel and Shemaiah, and with them 60 men;
[14]of the descendants of Bigvai, Uthai and Zaccur, and with them 70 men.

*The Return to Jerusalem*

[15]I assembled them at the canal that flows toward Ahava, and we camped there three days. When I checked among the people and the priests, I found no Levites there.
[16]So I summoned Eliezer, Ariel, Shemaiah, Elnathan, Jarib, Elnathan, Nathan, Zechariah and Meshullam, who were leaders, and Joiarib and Elnathan, who were men of learning,
[17]and I sent them to Iddo, the leader in Casiphia. I told them what to say to Iddo and his kinsmen, the temple servants in Casiphia, so that they might bring attendants to us for the house of our God.
[18]Because the good hand of our God was on us, they brought us Sherebiah, a capable man, from the descendants of Mahli son of Levi, the son of Israel, and Sherebiah's sons and brothers, 18 men;
[19]and Hashabiah, together with Jeshaiah

[v]10 Some Septuagint manuscripts (also 1 Esdras 8:36); Hebrew does not have *Bani.*

°14 ק וזכור
°17a ק ואצוה
°17b ק הנתינים

יְשַׁעְיָה מִבְּנֵי מְרָרִי אֶחָיו וּבְנֵיהֶם עֶשְׂרִים׃

twenty and-sons-of-them brothers-of-him Merari from-descendants-of Jeshaiah

וּמִן־ הַנְּתִינִים שֶׁנָּתַן דָּוִיד וְהַשָּׂרִים

and-the-officials David whom-he-established the-temple-servants and-from (20)

לַעֲבֹדַת הַלְוִיִּם נְתִינִים מָאתַיִם וְעֶשְׂרִים

and-twenty two-hundreds temple-servants the-Levites for-assistance-of

כֻּלָּם נִקְּבוּ בְשֵׁמוֹת׃ וָאֶקְרָא שָׁם צוֹם

fast there and-I-proclaimed (21) by-names they-were-registered all-of-them

עַל־ הַנָּהָר אַהֲוָא לְהִתְעַנּוֹת לִפְנֵי אֱלֹהֵינוּ לְבַקֵּשׁ מִמֶּנּוּ דֶּרֶךְ

journey from-him to-ask God-of-us before to-be-humbled Ahava the-Canal by

יְשָׁרָה לָנוּ וּלְטַפֵּנוּ וּלְכָל־ רְכוּשֵׁנוּ׃ כִּי

indeed (22) possession-of-us and-with-all-of and-for-child-of-us for-us safe

בֹשְׁתִּי לִשְׁאוֹל מִן־ הַמֶּלֶךְ חַיִל וּפָרָשִׁים לְעָזְרֵנוּ

to-protect-us and-horsemen soldier the-king from to-ask I-was-ashamed

מֵאוֹיֵב בַּדָּרֶךְ כִּי־ אָמַרְנוּ לַמֶּלֶךְ לֵאמֹר יַד־

hand-of to-say to-the-king we-told because on-the-road from-one-being-enemy

אֱלֹהֵינוּ עַל־ כָּל־ מְבַקְשָׁיו לְטוֹבָה וְעֻזּוֹ

but-greatness-of-him for-good ones-looking-to-him all-of on God-of-us

וְאַפּוֹ עַל כָּל־ עֹזְבָיו׃ וַנָּצוּמָה

so-we-fasted (23) ones-forsaking-him all-of against and-anger-of-him

וַנְּבַקְשָׁה מֵאֱלֹהֵינוּ עַל־ זֹאת וַיֵּעָתֵר לָנוּ׃

to-us and-he-answered this about from-God-of-us and-we-petitioned

וָאַבְדִּילָה מִשָּׂרֵי הַכֹּהֲנִים שְׁנֵים עָשָׂר לְשֵׁרֵבְיָה

with-Sherebiah ten two the-priests from-leaders-of then-I-set-apart (24)

חֲשַׁבְיָה וְעִמָּהֶם מֵאֲחֵיהֶם עֲשָׂרָה׃ וָאֶשְׁקֳולָה°

and-I-weighed-out (25) ten from-brothers-of-them and-with-them Hashabiah

לָהֶם אֶת־ הַכֶּסֶף וְאֶת־ הַזָּהָב וְאֶת־ הַכֵּלִים תְּרוּמַת בֵּית־

house-of offering-of the-articles and the-gold and the-silver *** to-them

אֱלֹהֵינוּ הַהֵרִימוּ הַמֶּלֶךְ וְיֹעֲצָיו וְשָׂרָיו

and-officials-of-him and-ones-advising-him the-king that-they-donated God-of-us

וְכָל־ יִשְׂרָאֵל הַנִּמְצָאִים׃ וָאֶשְׁקֲלָה עַל־

to and-I-weighed-out (26) the-ones-being-present Israel and-all-of

יָדָם כֶּסֶף כִּכָּרִים שֵׁשׁ־ מֵאוֹת וַחֲמִשִּׁים וּכְלֵי־ כֶסֶף

silver and-articles-of and-fifty hundreds six-of talents silver hand-of-them

מֵאָה לְכִכָּרִים זָהָב מֵאָה כִכָּר׃ וּכְפֹרֵי זָהָב עֶשְׂרִים

twenty gold and-bowls-of (27) talent hundred gold of-talents hundred

לַאֲדַרְכֹנִים אָלֶף וּכְלֵי נְחֹשֶׁת מֻצְהָב טוֹבָה שְׁנַיִם

two fine being-polished bronze and-articles-of thousand in-darics

from the descendants of
Merari, and his brothers and
nephews, 20 men. [20]They also
brought 220 of the temple servants—a body that David and
the officials had established to
assist the Levites. All were registered by name.
[21]There, by the Ahava Canal,
I proclaimed a fast, so that we
might humble ourselves before our God and ask him for a
safe journey for us and our
children, with all our possessions. [22]I was ashamed to ask
the king for soldiers and
horsemen to protect us from
enemies on the road, because
we had told the king, "The
good hand of our God is on
everyone who looks to him,
but his great anger is against
all who forsake him." [23]So we
fasted and petitioned our God
about this, and he answered
our prayer.
[24]Then I set apart twelve of
the leading priests, together
with Sherebiah, Hashabiah
and ten of their brothers, [25]and
I weighed out to them the
offering of silver and gold and
the articles that the king, his
advisers, his officials and all
Israel present there had donat-
ed for the house of our God. [26]I
weighed out to them 650 talents[w] of silver, silver articles
weighing 100 talents,[x] 100 talents[x] of gold, [27]20 bowls of
gold valued at 1,000 darics,[y]
and two fine articles of polished bronze, as precious as

[w]26 That is, about 25 tons (about 22 metric tons)
[x]26 That is, about 3 3/4 tons (about 3.4 metric tons)
[y]27 That is, about 19 pounds (about 8.5 kilograms)

°25 ק ואשקלה

חֲמוּדֹת כַּזָּהָב׃ וָאֹמְרָה אֲלֵהֶם אַתֶּם קֹדֶשׁ לַיהוָה
to-Yahweh consecrated you to-them and-I-said (28) as-the-gold ones-precious

וְהַכֵּלִים קֹדֶשׁ וְהַכֶּסֶף וְהַזָּהָב נְדָבָה
freewill-offering and-the-gold and-the-silver consecrated and-the-articles

לַיהוָה אֱלֹהֵי אֲבֹתֵיכֶם׃ שִׁקְדוּ וְשִׁמְרוּ עַד־ תִּשְׁקְלוּ
you-weigh until and-be-careful! guard! (29) fathers-of-you God-of to-Yahweh

לִפְנֵי שָׂרֵי הַכֹּהֲנִים וְהַלְוִיִּם וְשָׂרֵי־ הָאָבוֹת
the-fathers and-heads-of and-the-Levites the-priests leaders-of before

לְיִשְׂרָאֵל בִּירוּשָׁלִָם הַלִּשְׁכוֹת בֵּית יְהוָה׃ וְקִבְּלוּ
then-they-received (30) Yahweh house-of the-chambers in-Jerusalem of-Israel

הַכֹּהֲנִים וְהַלְוִיִּם מִשְׁקַל הַכֶּסֶף וְהַזָּהָב וְהַכֵּלִים
and-the-articles and-the-gold the-silver weight-of and-the-Levites the-priests

לְהָבִיא לִירוּשָׁלִָם לְבֵית אֱלֹהֵינוּ׃ וַנִּסְעָה מִנְּהַר
from-Canal-of and-we-set-out (31) God-of-us to-house-of to-Jerusalem to-take

אַהֲוָא בִּשְׁנֵים עָשָׂר לַחֹדֶשׁ הָרִאשׁוֹן לָלֶכֶת יְרוּשָׁלִָם וְיַד־
and-hand-of Jerusalem to-go the-first of-the-month ten on-two Ahava

אֱלֹהֵינוּ הָיְתָה עָלֵינוּ וַיַּצִּילֵנוּ מִכַּף אוֹיֵב
one-being-enemy from-hand-of and-he-protected-us on-us she-was God-of-us

וְאוֹרֵב עַל־ הַדָּרֶךְ׃ וַנָּבוֹא יְרוּשָׁלִָם וַנֵּשֶׁב
and-we-rested Jerusalem so-we-arrived (32) the-way along and-one-being-bandit

שָׁם יָמִים שְׁלֹשָׁה׃ וּבַיּוֹם הָרְבִיעִי נִשְׁקַל הַכֶּסֶף
the-silver we-weighed-out the-fourth and-on-the-day (33) three days there

וְהַזָּהָב וְהַכֵּלִים בְּבֵית אֱלֹהֵינוּ עַל יַד־ מְרֵמוֹת
Meremoth hand-of into God-of-us in-house-of and-the-articles and-the-gold

בֶּן־ אוּרִיָּה הַכֹּהֵן וְעִמּוֹ אֶלְעָזָר בֶּן־ פִּינְחָס וְעִמָּהֶם
and-with-them Phinehas son-of Eleazar and-with-him the-priest Uriah son-of

יוֹזָבָד בֶּן־ יֵשׁוּעַ וְנוֹעַדְיָה בֶן־ בִּנּוּי הַלְוִיִּם׃ בְּמִסְפָּר
by-number (34) the-Levites Binnui son-of and-Noadiah Jeshua son-of Jozabad

בְּמִשְׁקָל לַכֹּל וַיִּכָּתֵב כָּל־ הַמִּשְׁקָל בָּעֵת
at-the-time the-weight entire-of and-he-was-recorded for-the-whole by-weight

הַהִיא׃ הַבָּאִים מֵהַשְּׁבִי בְנֵי־ הַגּוֹלָה
the-exile sons-of from-the-captivity the-ones-returning (35) the-that

הִקְרִיבוּ עֹלוֹת ׀ לֵאלֹהֵי יִשְׂרָאֵל פָּרִים שְׁנֵים־ עָשָׂר עַל־ כָּל־
all-of for ten two bulls Israel to-God-of burnt-offerings they-sacrificed

יִשְׂרָאֵל אֵילִים ׀ תִּשְׁעִים וְשִׁשָּׁה כְּבָשִׂים שִׁבְעִים וְשִׁבְעָה צְפִירֵי חַטָּאת
sin-offering goats-of and-seven seventy lambs and-six ninety rams Israel

שְׁנֵים עָשָׂר הַכֹּל עוֹלָה לַיהוָה׃ וַיִּתְּנוּ ׀ אֶת־
*** also-they-delivered (36) to-Yahweh burnt-offering the-whole ten two

gold.

28I said to them, "You as well as these articles are consecrated to the LORD. The silver and gold are a freewill offering to the LORD, the God of your fathers. 29Guard them carefully until you weigh them out in the chambers of the house of the LORD in Jerusalem before the leading priests and the Levites and the family heads of Israel." 30Then the priests and Levites received the silver and gold and sacred articles that had been weighed out to be taken to the house of our God in Jerusalem.

31On the twelfth day of the first month we set out from the Ahava Canal to go to Jerusalem. The hand of our God was on us, and he protected us from enemies and bandits along the way. 32So we arrived in Jerusalem, where we rested three days.

33On the fourth day, in the house of our God, we weighed out the silver and gold and the sacred articles into the hands of Meremoth son of Uriah, the priest. Eleazar son of Phinehas was with him, and so were the Levites Jozabad son of Jeshua and Noadiah son of Binnui. 34Everything was accounted for by number and weight, and the entire weight was recorded at that time.

35Then the exiles who had returned from captivity sacrificed burnt offerings to the God of Israel: twelve bulls for all Israel, ninety-six rams, seventy-seven male lambs, and as a sin offering, twelve male goats. All this was a burnt offering to the LORD. 36They

דָּתֵי הַמֶּלֶךְ לַאֲחַשְׁדַּרְפְּנֵי הַמֶּלֶךְ וּפַחֲוֹות עֵבֶר
Beyond-of and-governors-of the-king to-satraps-of the-king orders-of

הַנָּהָר וְנִשְּׂאוּ אֶת־ הָעָם וְאֶת־ בֵּית־ הָאֱלֹהִים׃
the-God house-of and the-people *** then-they-assisted the-River

(9:1) וּכְכַלּוֹת אֵלֶּה נִגְּשׁוּ אֵלַי הַשָּׂרִים לֵאמֹר לֹא־
not to-say the-leaders to-me they-came these and-after-to-complete (9:1)

נִבְדְּלוּ הָעָם יִשְׂרָאֵל וְהַכֹּהֲנִים וְהַלְוִיִּם
and-the-Levites and-the-priests Israel the-people they-kept-separate

מֵעַמֵּי הָאֲרָצוֹת כְּתוֹעֲבֹתֵיהֶם לַכְּנַעֲנִי
like-the-Canaanite with-detestable-practices-of-them the-lands from-peoples-of

הַחִתִּי הַפְּרִזִּי הַיְבוּסִי הָעַמֹּנִי הַמֹּאָבִי הַמִּצְרִי
the-Egyptian the-Moabite the-Ammonite the-Jebusite the-Perizzite the-Hittite

וְהָאֱמֹרִי׃ (2) כִּי־ נָשְׂאוּ מִבְּנֹתֵיהֶם לָהֶם
for-them from-daughters-of-them they-took indeed (2) and-the-Amorite

וְלִבְנֵיהֶם וְהִתְעָרְבוּ זֶרַע הַקֹּדֶשׁ בְּעַמֵּי
with-peoples-of the-holy race-of and-they-mingled and-for-sons-of-them

הָאֲרָצוֹת וְיַד הַשָּׂרִים וְהַסְּגָנִים הָיְתָה
she-was and-the-officials the-leaders and-hand-of the-lands

בַּמַּעַל הַזֶּה רִאשׁוֹנָה׃ (3) וּכְשָׁמְעִי אֶת־ הַדָּבָר
the-thing *** and-when-to-hear-me (3) leader the-this in-the-unfaithfulness

הַזֶּה קָרַעְתִּי אֶת־ בִּגְדִי וּמְעִילִי וָאֶמְרְטָה מִשְּׂעַר
from-hair-of and-I-pulled and-cloak-of-me tunic-of-me *** I-tore the-this

רֹאשִׁי וּזְקָנִי וָאֵשְׁבָה מְשׁוֹמֵם׃ (4) וְאֵלַי
then-around-me (4) being-appalled and-I-sat-down and-beard-of-me head-of-me

יֵאָסְפוּ כֹּל חָרֵד בְּדִבְרֵי אֱלֹהֵי־ יִשְׂרָאֵל עַל
because-of Israel God-of at-words-of trembler every-of they-gathered

מַעַל הַגּוֹלָה וַאֲנִי יֹשֵׁב מְשׁוֹמֵם עַד
until being-appalled sitting and-I the-exile unfaithfulness-of

לְמִנְחַת הָעָרֶב׃ (5) וּבְמִנְחַת הָעֶרֶב קַמְתִּי
I-rose the-evening then-at-sacrifice-of (5) the-evening at-sacrifice-of

מִתַּעֲנִיתִי וּבְקָרְעִי בִגְדִי וּמְעִילִי וָאֶכְרְעָה
and-I-knelt and-cloak-of-me tunic-of-me and-in-to-tear-me from-abasement-of-me

עַל־ בִּרְכַּי וָאֶפְרְשָׂה כַפַּי אֶל־ יְהוָה אֱלֹהָי׃ (6) וָאֹמְרָה
and-I-prayed (6) God-of-me Yahweh to hands-of-me and-I-spread knees-of-me on

אֱלֹהַי בֹּשְׁתִּי וְנִכְלַמְתִּי לְהָרִים אֱלֹהַי פָּנַי
faces-of-me God-of-me to-lift and-I-am-disgraced I-am-ashamed God-of-me

אֵלֶיךָ כִּי עֲוֺנֹתֵינוּ רָבוּ לְמַעְלָה רֹאשׁ וְאַשְׁמָתֵנוּ
and-guilt-of-us head to-over they-are-high sins-of-us because to-you

also delivered the king's orders to the royal satraps and to the governors of Trans-Euphrates, who then gave assistance to the people and to the house of God.

*Ezra's Prayer About Intermarriage*

9 After these things had been done, the leaders came to me and said, "The people of Israel, including the priests and the Levites, have not kept themselves separate from the neighboring peoples with their detestable practices, like those of the Canaanites, Hittites, Perizzites, Jebusites, Ammonites, Moabites, Egyptians and Amorites. [2]They have taken some of their daughters as wives for themselves and their sons, and have mingled the holy race with the peoples around them. And the leaders and officials have led the way in this unfaithfulness."

[3]When I heard this, I tore my tunic and cloak, pulled hair from my head and beard and sat down appalled. [4]Then everyone who trembled at the words of the God of Israel gathered around me because of this unfaithfulness of the exiles. And I sat there appalled until the evening sacrifice.

[5]Then, at the evening sacrifice, I rose from my self-abasement, with my tunic and cloak torn, and fell on my knees with my hands spread out to the LORD my God [6]and prayed:

"O my God, I am too ashamed and disgraced to lift up my face to you, my God, because our sins are higher than our heads and

גָדְלָה עַד לַשָּׁמָיִם׃ מִימֵי אֲבֹתֵינוּ אֲנַחְנוּ בְּאַשְׁמָה

in-guilt we forefathers-of-us from-days-of (7) to-the-heavens to she-reached

גְדֹלָה עַד הַיּוֹם הַזֶּה וּבַעֲוֺנֹתֵינוּ נִתַּנּוּ אֲנַחְנוּ

we we-were-subjected and-because-of-sins-of-us the-this the-day until great

מְלָכֵינוּ כֹהֲנֵינוּ בְּיַד ׀ מַלְכֵי הָאֲרָצוֹת בַּחֶרֶב

to-the-sword the-lands kings-of at-hand-of priests-of-us kings-of-us

בַּשְּׁבִי וּבַבִּזָּה וּבְבֹשֶׁת פָּנִים כְּהַיּוֹם

as-the-day faces and-to-humiliation-of and-to-the-pillage to-the-captivity

הַזֶּה׃ וְעַתָּה כִּמְעַט־ רֶגַע הָיְתָה תְחִנָּה מֵאֵת ׀ יְהוָה

Yahweh from grace she-was moment for-brief-of but-now (8) the-this

אֱלֹהֵינוּ לְהַשְׁאִיר לָנוּ פְּלֵיטָה וְלָתֶת־ לָנוּ יָתֵד

firm-place to-us and-to-give remnant for-us to-leave-remnant God-of-us

בִּמְקוֹם קָדְשׁוֹ לְהָאִיר עֵינֵינוּ אֱלֹהֵינוּ

God-of-us eyes-of-us to-give-light sanctuary-of-him in-place-of

וּלְתִתֵּנוּ מִחְיָה מְעַט בְּעַבְדֻתֵנוּ׃ כִּי־ עֲבָדִים אֲנַחְנוּ

we slaves though (9) in-bondage-of-us little relief and-to-give-us

וּבְעַבְדֻתֵנוּ לֹא עֲזָבָנוּ אֱלֹהֵינוּ וַיַּט־ עָלֵינוּ

to-us and-he-showed God-of-us he-deserted-us not yet-in-bondage-of-us

חֶסֶד לִפְנֵי מַלְכֵי פָרַס לָתֶת־ לָנוּ מִחְיָה לְרוֹמֵם אֶת־

*** to-rebuild new-life to-us to-grant Persia kings-of in-sights-of kindness

בֵּית אֱלֹהֵינוּ וּלְהַעֲמִיד אֶת־ חָרְבֹתָיו וְלָתֶת־ לָנוּ גָדֵר

wall to-us and-to-give ruins-of-him *** and-to-repair God-of-us house-of

בִּיהוּדָה וּבִירוּשָׁלִָם׃ וְעַתָּה מַה־ נֹּאמַר אֱלֹהֵינוּ אַחֲרֵי־זֹאת

this after God-of-us can-we-say what? but-now (10) and-in-Jerusalem in-Judah

כִּי עָזַבְנוּ מִצְוֺתֶיךָ׃ אֲשֶׁר צִוִּיתָ בְּיַד

through-hand-of you-gave that (11) commands-of-you we-disregarded for

עֲבָדֶיךָ הַנְּבִיאִים לֵאמֹר הָאָרֶץ אֲשֶׁר אַתֶּם בָּאִים

ones-entering you that the-land to-say the-prophets servants-of-you

לְרִשְׁתָּהּ אֶרֶץ נִדָּה הִיא בְּנִדַּת עַמֵּי הָאֲרָצוֹת

the-lands peoples-of by-corruption-of she pollution land-of to-possess-her

בְּתוֹעֲבֹתֵיהֶם אֲשֶׁר מִלְאוּהָ מִפֶּה אֶל־ פֶּה

end to from-end they-filled-her that by-detestable-practices-of-them

בְּטֻמְאָתָם׃ וְעַתָּה בְּנוֹתֵיכֶם אַל־ תִּתְּנוּ לִבְנֵיהֶם

to-sons-of-them you-give not daughters-of-you so-now (12) with-impurity-of-them

וּבְנֹתֵיהֶם אַל־ תִּשְׂאוּ לִבְנֵיכֶם וְלֹא־ תִדְרְשׁוּ

you-further and-not for-sons-of-you you-take not and-daughters-of-them

שְׁלֹמָם וְטוֹבָתָם עַד־ עוֹלָם לְמַעַן תֶּחֶזְקוּ

you-may-be-strong that forever to or-prosperity-of-them welfare-of-them

our guilt has reached to the heavens. [7]From the days of our forefathers until now, our guilt has been great. Because of our sins, we and our kings and our priests have been subjected to the sword and captivity, to pillage and humiliation at the hand of foreign kings, as it is today.

[8]"But now, for a brief moment, the LORD our God has been gracious in leaving us a remnant and giving us a firm place in his sanctuary, and so our God gives light to our eyes and a little relief in our bondage. [9]Though we are slaves, our God has not deserted us in our bondage. He has shown us kindness in the sight of the kings of Persia: He has granted us new life to rebuild the house of our God and repair its ruins, and he has given us a wall of protection in Judah and Jerusalem.

[10]"But now, O our God, what can we say after this? For we have disregarded the commands [11]you gave through your servants the prophets when you said: 'The land you are entering to possess is a land polluted by the corruption of its peoples. By their detestable practices they have filled it with their impurity from one end to the other. [12]Therefore, do not give your daughters in marriage to their sons or take their daughters for your sons. Do not further their welfare or prosperity at any time, that you may be strong and eat

וַאֲכַלְתֶּם אֶת־ טוּב הָאָרֶץ וְהוֹרַשְׁתֶּם לִבְנֵיכֶם
to-children-of-you and-you-may-leave the-land good-of *** and-you-may-eat

עַד־ עוֹלָם׃ וְאַחֲרֵי כָּל־ הַבָּא עָלֵינוּ בְּמַעֲשֵׂינוּ
for-deeds-of-us to-us the-thing-happening all-of and-after (13) everlasting to

הָרָעִים וּבְאַשְׁמָתֵנוּ הַגְּדֹלָה כִּי | אַתָּה אֱלֹהֵינוּ חָשַׂכְתָּ
you-withheld God-of-us you yet the-great and-for-guilt-of-us the-evil-ones

לְמַטָּה מֵעֲוֺנֵנוּ וְנָתַתָּה לָּנוּ פְּלֵיטָה כָּזֹאת׃
like-this remnant to-us and-you-gave than-sin-of-us to-less

הֲנָשׁוּב לְהָפֵר מִצְוֺתֶיךָ וּלְהִתְחַתֵּן
and-to-intermarry commands-of-you to-break shall-we-do-again? (14)

בְּעַמֵּי הַתֹּעֵבוֹת הָאֵלֶּה הֲלוֹא תֶאֱנַף־
would-you-be-angry not? the-these the-detestable-practices with-peoples-of

בָּנוּ עַד־ כַּלֵּה לְאֵין שְׁאֵרִית וּפְלֵיטָה׃ יְהוָה אֱלֹהֵי יִשְׂרָאֵל
Israel God-of Yahweh (15) or-survivor remnant to-no to-destroy to with-us

צַדִּיק אַתָּה כִּי־ נִשְׁאַרְנוּ פְּלֵיטָה כְּהַיּוֹם הַזֶּה הִנְנוּ
see-we! the-this as-the-day remnant we-are-left indeed you righteous

לְפָנֶיךָ בְּאַשְׁמָתֵינוּ כִּי אֵין לַעֲמוֹד לְפָנֶיךָ
in-presences-of-you to-stand none though in-guilt-of-us before-you

עַל־ זֹאת׃ וּכְהִתְפַּלֵּל עֶזְרָא וּכְהִתְוַדֹּתוֹ
and-while-to-confess-him Ezra and-while-to-pray (10:1) this because-of

בֹּכֶה וּמִתְנַפֵּל לִפְנֵי בֵּית הָאֱלֹהִים נִקְבְּצוּ אֵלָיו
around-him they-gathered the-God house-of before and-throwing-himself weeping

מִיִּשְׂרָאֵל קָהָל רַב־ מְאֹד אֲנָשִׁים וְנָשִׁים וִילָדִים כִּי־ בָכוּ
they-wept also and-children and-women men very large crowd from-Israel

הָעָם הַרְבֵּה־ בֶכֶה׃ וַיַּעַן שְׁכַנְיָה בֶן־ יְחִיאֵל
Jehiel son-of Shecaniah then-he-spoke (2) weeping to-be-bitter the-people

מִבְּנֵי עוֹלָם° וַיֹּאמֶר לְעֶזְרָא אֲנַחְנוּ מָעַלְנוּ בֵּאלֹהֵינוּ
to-God-of-us we-were-unfaithful we to-Ezra and-he-said Elam of-descendants-of

וַנֹּשֶׁב נָשִׁים נָכְרִיּוֹת מֵעַמֵּי הָאָרֶץ וְעַתָּה יֵשׁ־
there-is but-now the-land from-peoples-of foreigners women and-we-married

מִקְוֶה לְיִשְׂרָאֵל עַל־ זֹאת׃ וְעַתָּה נִכְרָת־ בְּרִית
covenant let-us-make and-now (3) this in-spite-of for-Israel hope

לֵאלֹהֵינוּ לְהוֹצִיא כָל־ נָשִׁים וְהַנּוֹלָד מֵהֶם
of-them and-the-one-being-born women all-of to-send-away before-God-of-us

בַּעֲצַת אֲדֹנָי וְהַחֲרֵדִים בְּמִצְוַת אֱלֹהֵינוּ
God-of-us to-command-of and-the-ones-who-fear lords-of-me as-counsel-of

וְכַתּוֹרָה יֵעָשֶׂה׃ קוּם כִּי־ עָלֶיךָ הַדָּבָר וַאֲנַחְנוּ
and-we the-matter to-you for rise-up! (4) let-him-be-done and-as-the-law

the good things of the land
and leave it to your children as an everlasting inheritance.'
13"What has happened to
us is a result of our evil
deeds and our great guilt,
and yet, our God, you have
punished us less than our
sins have deserved and
have given us a remnant
like this. 14Shall we again
break your commands and
intermarry with the peo-
ples who commit such de-
testable practices? Would
you not be angry enough
with us to destroy us, leaving us no remnant or survivor? 15O LORD, God of Israel,
you are righteous! We are
left this day as a remnant.
Here we are before you in
our guilt, though because of
it not one of us can stand in
your presence."

*The People's Confession of Sin*

10 While Ezra was pray-
ing and confessing,
weeping and throwing him-
self down before the house of
God, a large crowd of Israelites—men, women and chil-
dren—gathered around him.
They too wept bitterly. 2Then
Shecaniah son of Jehiel, one of
the descendants of Elam, said
to Ezra, "We have been unfaithful to our God by marrying foreign women from the
peoples around us. But in spite
of this, there is still hope for
Israel. 3Now let us make a covenant before our God to send
away all these women and
their children, in accordance
with the counsel of my lord
and of those who fear the
commands of our God. Let it
be done according to the Law.
4Rise up; this matter is in your

°2 ק עילם

עִמָּךְ חֲזַק וַעֲשֵׂה׃ וַיָּקָם עֶזְרָא וַיַּשְׁבַּע אֶת־

*** and-he-put-under-oath Ezra so-he-rose (5) and-do! take-courage! with-you

שָׂרֵי הַכֹּהֲנִים הַלְוִיִּם וְכָל־ יִשְׂרָאֵל לַעֲשׂוֹת כַּדָּבָר

as-the-suggestion to-do Israel and-all-of the-Levites the-priests leaders-of

הַזֶּה וַיִּשָּׁבֵעוּ׃ וַיָּקָם עֶזְרָא מִלִּפְנֵי בֵּית

house-of from-before Ezra then-he-withdrew (6) and-they-took-oath the-this

הָאֱלֹהִים וַיֵּלֶךְ אֶל־לִשְׁכַּת יְהוֹחָנָן בֶּן־ אֶלְיָשִׁיב וַיֵּלֶךְ שָׁם

there when-he-went Eliashib son-of Jehohanan room-of to and-he-went the-God

לֶחֶם לֹא־ אָכַל וּמַיִם לֹא־ שָׁתָה כִּי מִתְאַבֵּל עַל־

over mourning because he-drank not and-waters he-ate not food

מַעַל הַגּוֹלָה׃ וַיַּעֲבִירוּ קוֹל בִּיהוּדָה

in-Judah proclamation and-they-issued (7) the-exile unfaithfulness-of

וִירוּשָׁלַםִ לְכֹל בְּנֵי הַגּוֹלָה לְהִקָּבֵץ יְרוּשָׁלָםִ׃ וְכֹל

and-any (8) Jerusalem to-assemble the-exile sons-of for-all-of and-Jerusalem

אֲשֶׁר לֹא־ יָבוֹא לִשְׁלֹשֶׁת הַיָּמִים כַּעֲצַת הַשָּׂרִים

the-officials as-decision-of the-days in-three-of he-appeared not who

וְהַזְּקֵנִים יָחֳרַם כָּל־ רְכוּשׁוֹ וְהוּא

and-he property-of-him all-of he-would-forfeit and-the-elders

יִבָּדֵל מִקְּהַל הַגּוֹלָה׃ וַיִּקָּבְצוּ כָל־

all-of and-they-gathered (9) the-exile from-assembly-of he-would-be-expelled

אַנְשֵׁי־ יְהוּדָה וּבִנְיָמִן | יְרוּשָׁלַםִ לִשְׁלֹשֶׁת הַיָּמִים הוּא חֹדֶשׁ

month-of that the-days in-three-of Jerusalem and-Benjamin Judah men-of

הַתְּשִׁיעִי בְּעֶשְׂרִים בַּחֹדֶשׁ וַיֵּשְׁבוּ כָל־ הָעָם בִּרְחוֹב

in-square-of the-people all-of and-they-sat of-the-month on-twenty the-ninth

בֵּית הָאֱלֹהִים מַרְעִידִים עַל־ הַדָּבָר וּמֵהַגְּשָׁמִים׃

and-by-the-rains the-occasion by ones-being-distressed the-God house-of

וַיָּקָם עֶזְרָא הַכֹּהֵן וַיֹּאמֶר אֲלֵהֶם אַתֶּם

you to-them and-he-said the-priest Ezra then-he-stood-up (10)

מְעַלְתֶּם וַתֹּשִׁיבוּ נָשִׁים נָכְרִיּוֹת לְהוֹסִיף עַל־ אַשְׁמַת

guilt-of to to-add foreign-ones women and-you-married you-were-unfaithful

יִשְׂרָאֵל׃ וְעַתָּה תְּנוּ תוֹדָה לַיהוָה אֱלֹהֵי־ אֲבֹתֵיכֶם וַעֲשׂוּ

and-do! fathers-of-you God-of to-Yahweh confession make! and-now (11) Israel

רְצוֹנוֹ וְהִבָּדְלוּ מֵעַמֵּי הָאָרֶץ וּמִן־

and-from the-land from-peoples-of and-separate-yourselves! will-of-him

הַנָּשִׁים הַנָּכְרִיּוֹת׃ וַיַּעֲנוּ כָל־ הַקָּהָל

the-assembly whole-of and-they-responded (12) the-foreign-ones the-wives

וַיֹּאמְרוּ קוֹל גָּדוֹל כֵּן כִּדְבָרְיךָ עָלֵינוּ לַעֲשׂוֹת׃ אֲבָל הָעָם

the-people but (13) to-do to-us as-word-of-you right loud voice and-they-said

hands. We will support you, so take courage and do it."

5So Ezra rose up and put the leading priests and Levites and all Israel under oath to do what had been suggested. And they took the oath. 6Then Ezra withdrew from before the house of God and went to the room of Jehohanan son of Eliashib. While he was there, he ate no food and drank no water, because he continued to mourn over the unfaithfulness of the exiles.

7A proclamation was then issued throughout Judah and Jerusalem for all the exiles to assemble in Jerusalem. 8Anyone who failed to appear within three days would forfeit all his property, in accordance with the decision of the officials and elders, and would himself be expelled from the assembly of the exiles.

9Within the three days, all the men of Judah and Benjamin had gathered in Jerusalem. And on the twentieth day of the ninth month, all the people were sitting in the square before the house of God, greatly distressed by the occasion and because of the rain. 10Then Ezra the priest stood up and said to them, "You have been unfaithful; you have married foreign women, adding to Israel's guilt. 11Now make confession to the LORD, the God of your fathers, and do his will. Separate yourselves from the peoples around you and from your foreign wives."

12The whole assembly responded with a loud voice: "You are right! We must do as you say. 13But there are many

°12 ק כדברך

רַב וְהָעֵת גְּשָׁמִים וְאֵין כֹּחַ לַעֲמוֹד בַּחוּץ וְהַמְּלָאכָה
and-the-matter at-outside to-stand ability so-not rains and-the-season many

לֹא־לְיוֹם אֶחָד וְלֹא לִשְׁנַיִם כִּי־הִרְבִּינוּ לִפְשֹׁעַ בַּדָּבָר
in-the-thing to-sin we-made-great because in-two and-not one in-day not

הַזֶּה׃ יַעֲמְדוּ־נָא שָׂרֵינוּ לְכָל־הַקָּהָל
the-assembly for-whole-of officials-of-us now! let-them-act (14) the-this

וְכֹל ׀ אֲשֶׁר בֶּעָרֵינוּ הַהֹשִׁיב נָשִׁים נָכְרִיּוֹת
foreign-ones women who-he-married in-the-towns-of-us who then-all

יָבֹא לְעִתִּים מְזֻמָּנִים וְעִמָּהֶם זִקְנֵי־עִיר וָעִיר
and-town town elders-of and-with-them ones-being-set at-times let-him-come

וְשֹׁפְטֶיהָ עַד לְהָשִׁיב חֲרוֹן אַף־אֱלֹהֵינוּ
God-of-us anger-of fierceness-of to-turn until and-ones-judging-of-her

מִמֶּנּוּ עַד לַדָּבָר הַזֶּה׃ אַךְ יוֹנָתָן בֶּן־עֲשָׂהאֵל
Asahel son-of Jonathan only (15) the-this in-the-matter to from-us

וְיַחְזְיָה בֶּן־תִּקְוָה עָמְדוּ עַל־זֹאת וּמְשֻׁלָּם
and-Meshullam this against they-opposed Tikvah son-of and-Jahzeiah

וְשַׁבְּתַי הַלֵּוִי עֲזָרֻם׃ וַיַּעֲשׂוּ־כֵן בְּנֵי
sons-of so and-they-did (16) they-supported-them the-Levite and-Shabbethai

הַגּוֹלָה וַיִּבָּדְלוּ עֶזְרָא הַכֹּהֵן אֲנָשִׁים רָאשֵׁי הָאָבוֹת
the-fathers heads-of men the-priest Ezra and-they-were-selected the-exile

לְבֵית אֲבֹתָם וְכֻלָּם בְּשֵׁמוֹת וַיֵּשְׁבוּ
and-they-sat-down by-names and-all-of-them fathers-of-them by-family-of

בְּיוֹם אֶחָד לַחֹדֶשׁ הָעֲשִׂירִי לְדַרְיוֹשׁ הַדָּבָר׃
the-matter to-investigate the-tenth of-the-month one on-day

וַיְכַלּוּ בַכֹּל אֲנָשִׁים הַהֹשִׁיבוּ נָשִׁים נָכְרִיּוֹת
foreign-ones women who-they-married men with-the-all and-they-finished (17)

עַד יוֹם אֶחָד לַחֹדֶשׁ הָרִאשׁוֹן׃ וַיִּמָּצֵא מִבְּנֵי
among-descendants-of and-he-was-found (18) the-first of-the-month one day by

הַכֹּהֲנִים אֲשֶׁר הֹשִׁיבוּ נָשִׁים נָכְרִיּוֹת מִבְּנֵי יֵשׁוּעַ
Jeshua from-descendants-of foreign-ones women they-married who the-priests

בֶּן־יוֹצָדָק וְאֶחָיו מַעֲשֵׂיָה וֶאֱלִיעֶזֶר וְיָרִיב וּגְדַלְיָה׃
and-Gedaliah and-Jarib and-Eliezer Maaseiah and-brothers-of-him Jozadak son-of

וַיִּתְּנוּ יָדָם לְהוֹצִיא נְשֵׁיהֶם וַאֲשֵׁמִים
and-guilt-offerings wives-of-them to-put-away hand-of-them and-they-gave (19)

אֵיל־צֹאן עַל־אַשְׁמָתָם׃ וּמִבְּנֵי אִמֵּר חֲנָנִי
Hanani Immer and-from-descendants-of (20) guilt-of-them for flock ram-of

וּזְבַדְיָה׃ וּמִבְּנֵי חָרִם מַעֲשֵׂיָה וְאֵלִיָּה
and-Elijah Maaseiah Harim and-from-descendants-of (21) and-Zebadiah

people here and it is the rainy season; so we cannot stand outside. Besides, this matter cannot be taken care of in a day or two, because we have sinned greatly in this thing.
14Let our officials act for the whole assembly. Then let everyone in our towns who has married a foreign woman come at a set time, along with the elders and judges of each town, until the fierce anger of our God in this matter is turned away from us." 15Only
Jonathan son of Asahel and Jahzeiah son of Tikvah, supported by Meshullam and Shabbethai the Levite, opposed this.
16So the exiles did as was proposed. Ezra the priest selected men who were family heads, one from each family division, and all of them designated by name. On the first day of the tenth month they sat down to investigate the cases,
17and by the first day of the first month they finished dealing with all the men who had married foreign women.

*Those Guilty of Intermarriage*

18Among the descendants of the priests, the following had married foreign women:

From the descendants of Jeshua son of Jozadak, and his brothers: Maaseiah, Eliezer, Jarib and Gedaliah.
19(They all gave their hands in pledge to put away their wives, and for their guilt they each presented a ram from the flock as a guilt offering.)

20From the descendants of Immer:
Hanani and Zebadiah.

21From the descendants of Harim:
Maaseiah, Elijah, Shemaiah, Jehiel and Uzziah.

22From the descendants of Pashhur:
Elioenai, Maaseiah, Ishmael, Nethanel, Jozabad

*14 Most mss have *pathah* under the *ayin* (יַעַמְדוּ).

וּשְׁמַעְיָה וִיחִיאֵל וְעֻזִּיָּה׃ וּמִבְּנֵי פַּשְׁחוּר
Pashhur and-from-descendants-of (22) and-Uzziah and-Jehiel and-Shemaiah

אֶלְיוֹעֵינַי מַעֲשֵׂיָה יִשְׁמָעֵאל נְתַנְאֵל יוֹזָבָד וְאֶלְעָשָׂה׃ וּמִן־
and-among (23) and-Elasah Jozabad Nethanel Ishmael Maaseiah Elioenai

הַלְוִיִּם יוֹזָבָד וְשִׁמְעִי וְקֵלָיָה הוּא קְלִיטָא פְּתַחְיָה יְהוּדָה
Judah Pethahiah Kelita that and-Kelaiah and-Shimei Jozabad the-Levites

וֶאֱלִיעֶזֶר׃ וּמִן־ הַמְשֹׁרְרִים אֶלְיָשִׁיב וּמִן־ הַשֹּׁעֲרִים
the-gatekeepers and-from Eliashib the-ones-singing and-from (24) and-Eliezer

שַׁלֻּם וָטֶלֶם וְאוּרִי׃ וּמִיִּשְׂרָאֵל מִבְּנֵי פַרְעֹשׁ
Parosh from-descendants-of and-among-Israel (25) and-Uri and-Telem Shallum

רַמְיָה וְיִזִּיָּה וּמַלְכִּיָּה וּמִיָּמִן וְאֶלְעָזָר וּמַלְכִּיָּה
and-Malkijah and-Eleazar and-Mijamin and-Malkijah and-Izziah Ramiah

וּבְנָיָה׃ וּמִבְּנֵי עֵילָם מַתַּנְיָה זְכַרְיָה וִיחִיאֵל
and-Jehiel Zechariah Mattaniah Elam and-from-descendants-of (26) and-Benaiah

וְעַבְדִּי וִירֵמוֹת וְאֵלִיָּה׃ וּמִבְּנֵי זַתּוּא אֶלְיוֹעֵינַי
Elioenai Zattu and-from-descendants-of (27) and-Elijah and-Jeremoth and-Abdi

אֶלְיָשִׁיב מַתַּנְיָה וִירֵמוֹת וְזָבָד וַעֲזִיזָא׃ וּמִבְּנֵי
and-from-descendants-of (28) and-Aziza and-Zabad and-Jeremoth Mattaniah Eliashib

בֵּבָי יְהוֹחָנָן חֲנַנְיָה זַבַּי עַתְלָי׃ וּמִבְּנֵי בָּנִי
Bani and-from-descendants-of (29) Athlai Zabbai Hananiah Jehohanan Bebai

מְשֻׁלָּם מַלּוּךְ וַעֲדָיָה יָשׁוּב וּשְׁאָל יְרָמוֹת׃
Jeremoth and-Sheal Jashub and-Adaiah Malluch Meshullam

וּמִבְּנֵי פַּחַת מוֹאָב עַדְנָא וּכְלָל בְּנָיָה מַעֲשֵׂיָה
Maaseiah Benaiah and-Kelal Adna Moab Pahath and-from-descendants-of (30)

מַתַּנְיָה בְצַלְאֵל וּבִנּוּי וּמְנַשֶּׁה׃ וּבְנֵי חָרִם
Harim and-descendants-of (31) and-Manasseh and-Binnui Bezalel Mattaniah

אֱלִיעֶזֶר יִשִּׁיָּה מַלְכִּיָּה שְׁמַעְיָה שִׁמְעוֹן׃ בִּנְיָמִן* מַלּוּךְ שְׁמַרְיָה׃
Shemariah Malluch Benjamin (32) Shimeon Shemaiah Malkijah Ishijah Eliezer

מִבְּנֵי חָשֻׁם מַתְּנַי מַתַּתָּה זָבָד אֱלִיפֶלֶט יְרֵמַי
Jeremai Eliphelet Zabad Mattattah Mattenai Hashum from-descendants-of (33)

מְנַשֶּׁה שִׁמְעִי׃ מִבְּנֵי בָנִי מַעֲדַי עַמְרָם וְאוּאֵל׃
and-Uel Amram Maadai Bani from-descendants-of (34) Shimei Manasseh

בְּנָיָה בֵדְיָה כְּלֻהִי°׃ וַנְיָה מְרֵמוֹת אֶלְיָשִׁיב׃ מַתַּנְיָה
Mattaniah (37) Eliashib Meremoth Vaniah (36) Keluhi Bedeiah Benaiah (35)

מַתְּנַי וְיַעֲשׂוּ°׃ וּבָנִי† וּבִנּוּי שִׁמְעִי׃ וְשֶׁלֶמְיָה
and-Shelemiah (39) Shimei and-Binnui †and-Bani (38) and-Jaasu Mattenai

וְנָתָן וַעֲדָיָה׃ מַכְנַדְבַי שָׁשַׁי שָׁרָי׃ עֲזַרְאֵל
Azarel (41) Sharai Shashai Macnadebai (40) and-Adaiah and-Nathan

and Elasah.
[23]Among the Levites:
Jozabad, Shimei, Kelaiah (that is Kelita), Pethahiah, Judah and Eliezer.
[24]From the singers:
Eliashib.
From the gatekeepers:
Shallum, Telem and Uri.
[25]And among the other Israelites:
From the descendants of Parosh:
Ramiah, Izziah, Malkijah, Mijamin, Eleazar, Malkijah and Benaiah.
[26]From the descendants of Elam:
Mattaniah, Zechariah, Jehiel, Abdi, Jeremoth and Elijah.
[27]From the descendants of Zattu:
Elioenai, Eliashib, Mattaniah, Jeremoth, Zabad and Aziza.
[28]From the descendants of Bebai:
Jehohanan, Hananiah, Zabbai and Athlai.
[29]From the descendants of Bani:
Meshullam, Malluch, Adaiah, Jashub, Sheal and Jeremoth.
[30]From the descendants of Pahath-Moab:
Adna, Kelal, Benaiah, Maaseiah, Mattaniah, Bezalel, Binnui and Manasseh.
[31]From the descendants of Harim:
Eliezer, Ishijah, Malkijah, Shemaiah, Shimeon, [32]Benjamin, Malluch and Shemariah.
[33]From the descendants of Hashum:
Mattenai, Mattattah, Zabad, Eliphelet, Jeremai, Manasseh and Shimei.
[34]From the descendants of Bani:
Maadai, Amram and Uel, [35]Benaiah, Bedeiah, Keluhi, [36]Vaniah, Meremoth, Eliashib, [37]Mattaniah, Mattenai and Jaasu.
[38]From the descendants of Binnui:[a]

[a]37,38 See Septuagint (also 1 Esdras 9:34); Hebrew *Jaasu* [38]*and Bani and Binnui,*

*32 Most mss have *hireq* under the *beth* ( 'בִ ).

†38 The NIV, following the Septuagint (note *a* above), repoints this word to וּבְנֵי *and-descendants-of.*

°29 ק ורמות
°35 ק כלוהו
°37 ק ויעשי

| Joseph | Amariah | Shallum | (42) | Shemariah | and-Shelemiah |
|---|---|---|---|---|---|
| יוֹסֵף׃ | אֲמַרְיָה | שַׁלּוּם | | שְׁמַרְיָה׃ | וְשֶׁלֶמְיָהוּ |

| Jaddai | Zebina | Zabad | Mattithiah | Jeiel | Nebo | from-descendants-of | (43) |
|---|---|---|---|---|---|---|---|
| יַדּוֹ | זְבִינָא | זָבָד | מַתִּתְיָה | יְעִיאֵל | נְבוֹ | מִבְּנֵי | |

| foreign-ones | women | they-married | these | all-of | (44) | Benaiah | and-Joel |
|---|---|---|---|---|---|---|---|
| נָכְרִיּוֹת | נָשִׁים | נָשְׂאוּ* | אֵלֶּה | כָּל־ | | בְּנָיָה׃ | וְיוֹאֵל |

| children | that-they-had | wives | from-them | and-there-were |
|---|---|---|---|---|
| בָּנִים׃ | וַיָּשִׂימוּ | נָשִׁים | מֵהֶם | וְיֵשׁ |

Shimei, 39Shelemiah, Nathan, Adaiah, 40Macnadebai, Shashai, Sharai, 41Azarel, Shelemiah, Shemariah, 42Shallum, Amariah and Joseph.

43From the descendants of Nebo:
Jeiel, Mattithiah, Zabad, Zebina, Jaddai, Joel and Benaiah.

44All these had married foreign women, and some of them had children by these wives.[b]

[b]44 *Or and they sent them away with their children*

*44 The original text of L reads **נשאי** ; the text was later changed to match the *Qere* form.

°*43* ק ידי
°*44* ק נשאו

דִּבְרֵי נְחֶמְיָה בֶּן־ חֲכַלְיָה וַיְהִי בְחֹדֶשׁ־ כִּסְלֵו°
Kislev in-month-of and-he-was Hacaliah son-of Nehemiah words-of (1:1)

שְׁנַת עֶשְׂרִים וַאֲנִי הָיִיתִי בְּשׁוּשַׁן הַבִּירָה׃ וַיָּבֹא חֲנָנִי
Hanani then-he-came (2) the-citadel in-Susa I-was while-I twenty year-of

אֶחָד מֵאַחַי הוּא וַאֲנָשִׁים מִיהוּדָה וָאֶשְׁאָלֵם עַל־
about and-I-questioned-them from-Judah and-men he of-brothers-of-me one

הַיְּהוּדִים הַפְּלֵיטָה אֲשֶׁר־ נִשְׁאֲרוּ מִן־ הַשֶּׁבִי וְעַל־ יְרוּשָׁלִָם׃
Jerusalem and-about the-exile from they-survived that the-remnant the-Jews

וַיֹּאמְרוּ לִי הַנִּשְׁאָרִים אֲשֶׁר־ נִשְׁאֲרוּ מִן־ הַשְּׁבִי
the-exile from they-survived who the-ones-surviving to-me and-they-said (3)

שָׁם בַּמְּדִינָה בְּרָעָה גְדֹלָה וּבְחֶרְפָּה וְחוֹמַת יְרוּשָׁלִַם
Jerusalem and-wall-of and-in-disgrace great in-trouble in-the-province there

מְפֹרָצֶת וּשְׁעָרֶיהָ נִצְּתוּ בָאֵשׁ׃ וַיְהִי
and-he-was (4) with-fire they-were-burned and-gates-of-her being-broken-down

כְּשָׁמְעִי ׀ אֶת־ הַדְּבָרִים הָאֵלֶּה יָשַׁבְתִּי וָאֶבְכֶּה וָאֶתְאַבְּלָה
and-I-mourned and-I-wept I-sat-down the-these the-things *** when-to-hear-me

יָמִים וָאֱהִי צָם וּמִתְפַּלֵּל לִפְנֵי אֱלֹהֵי הַשָּׁמָיִם׃ וָאֹמַר
then-I-said (5) the-heavens God-of before and-praying fasting and-I-was days

אָנָּא יְהוָה אֱלֹהֵי הַשָּׁמַיִם הָאֵל הַגָּדוֹל וְהַנּוֹרָא
and-the-one-being-awesome the-great the-God the-heavens God-of Yahweh O!

שֹׁמֵר הַבְּרִית וָחֶסֶד לְאֹהֲבָיו וּלְשֹׁמְרֵי
and-with-ones-obeying-of with-ones-loving-him and-love the-covenant keeping-of

מִצְוֺתָיו׃ תְּהִי נָא אָזְנְךָ־ קַשֶּׁבֶת וְעֵינֶיךָ
and-eyes-of-you attentive ear-of-you now! let-her-be (6) commands-of-him

פְתוּחוֹת* לִשְׁמֹעַ אֶל־ תְּפִלַּת עַבְדְּךָ אֲשֶׁר אָנֹכִי מִתְפַּלֵּל
praying I that servant-of-you prayer-of to to-hear ones-being-open

לְפָנֶיךָ הַיּוֹם יוֹמָם וָלַיְלָה עַל־ בְּנֵי יִשְׂרָאֵל עֲבָדֶיךָ
servants-of-you Israel people-of for and-night by-day the-day before-you

וּמִתְוַדֶּה עַל־חַטֹּאות בְּנֵי־ יִשְׂרָאֵל אֲשֶׁר חָטָאנוּ לָךְ
against-you we-committed-sin that Israel people-of sins-of to and-confessing

וַאֲנִי וּבֵית־ אָבִי חָטָאנוּ׃ חֲבֹל
to-act-wickedly (7) we-committed-sin father-of-me and-house-of even-I

חָבַלְנוּ לָךְ וְלֹא־ שָׁמַרְנוּ אֶת־ הַמִּצְוֹת וְאֶת־
and the-commands *** we-obeyed and-not toward-you we-acted-wickedly

הַחֻקִּים וְאֶת־ הַמִּשְׁפָּטִים אֲשֶׁר צִוִּיתָ אֶת־ מֹשֶׁה עַבְדֶּךָ׃
servant-of-you Moses *** you-gave that the-laws and the-decrees

זְכָר־ נָא אֶת־ הַדָּבָר אֲשֶׁר צִוִּיתָ אֶת־ מֹשֶׁה עַבְדְּךָ
servant-of-you Moses *** you-gave that the-instruction *** now! remember! (8)

*Nehemiah's Prayer*

**1** The words of Nehemiah son of Hacaliah:

In the month of Kislev in the twentieth year, while I was in the citadel of Susa, [2]Hanani, one of my brothers, came from Judah with some other men, and I questioned them about the Jewish remnant that survived the exile, and also about Jerusalem.

[3]They said to me, "Those who survived the exile and are back in the province are in great trouble and disgrace. The wall of Jerusalem is broken down, and its gates have been burned with fire."

[4]When I heard these things, I sat down and wept. For some days I mourned and fasted and prayed before the God of heaven. [5]Then I said:

"O LORD, God of heaven, the great and awesome God, who keeps his covenant of love with those who love him and obey his commands, [6]let your ear be attentive and your eyes open to hear the prayer your servant is praying before you day and night for your servants, the people of Israel. I confess the sins we Israelites, including myself and my father's house, have committed against you. [7]We have acted very wickedly toward you. We have not obeyed the commands, decrees and laws you gave your servant Moses.

[8]"Remember the instruction you gave your servant

*6 Most mss have no *qibbuts* under the *tav* (פְּתֻ׳).

°*1* ק כסליו

לֵאמֹר אַתֶּם תִּמְעָלוּ אֲנִי אָפִיץ אֶתְכֶם בָּעַמִּים׃
among-the-nations you I-will-scatter I you-are-unfaithful you to-say

וְשַׁבְתֶּם אֵלַי וּשְׁמַרְתֶּם מִצְוֹתַי וַעֲשִׂיתֶם אֹתָם אִם־יִהְיֶה
he-is if them and-you-do commands-of-me and-you-obey to-me but-you-return (9)

נִדַּחֲכֶם בִּקְצֵה הַשָּׁמַיִם מִשָּׁם אֲקַבְּצֵם
I-will-gather-them from-there the-heavens at-horizon-of one-being-exiled-of-you

וַהֲבִוֹאתִים אֶל־הַמָּקוֹם אֲשֶׁר בָּחַרְתִּי לְשַׁכֵּן אֶת־שְׁמִי
Name-of-me *** to-make-dwell I-chose that the-place to and-I-will-bring-them

שָׁם׃ וְהֵם עֲבָדֶיךָ וְעַמֶּךָ אֲשֶׁר פָּדִיתָ
you-redeemed whom and-people-of-you servants-of-you and-they (10) there

בְּכֹחֲךָ הַגָּדוֹל וּבְיָדְךָ הַחֲזָקָה׃ אָנָּא אֲדֹנָי
Lord O! (11) the-mighty and-by-hand-of-you the-great by-strength-of-you

תְּהִי נָא אָזְנְךָ־קַשֶּׁבֶת אֶל־תְּפִלַּת עַבְדְּךָ וְאֶל־
and-to servant-of-you prayer-of to attentive ear-of-you now! let-her-be

תְּפִלַּת עֲבָדֶיךָ הַחֲפֵצִים לְיִרְאָה אֶת־שְׁמֶךָ
name-of-you *** to-revere the-ones-who-delight servants-of-you prayer-of

וְהַצְלִיחָה־נָּא לְעַבְדְּךָ הַיּוֹם וּתְנֵהוּ לְרַחֲמִים
with-favors and-grant-him! the-day to-servant-of-you now! and-give-success!

לִפְנֵי הָאִישׁ הַזֶּה וַאֲנִי הָיִיתִי מַשְׁקֶה לַמֶּלֶךְ׃
to-the-king cupbearer I-was now-I the-this the-man in-presences-of

וַיְהִי ׀ בְּחֹדֶשׁ נִיסָן שְׁנַת עֶשְׂרִים לְאַרְתַּחְשַׁסְתְּא הַמֶּלֶךְ
the-king of-Artaxerxes twenty year-of Nisan in-month-of and-he-was (2:1)

יַיִן לְפָנָיו וָאֶשָּׂא אֶת־הַיַּיִן וָאֶתְּנָה לַמֶּלֶךְ וְלֹא־הָיִיתִי
I-was now-not to-the-king and-I-gave the-wine *** and-I-took before-him wine

רַע לְפָנָיו׃ וַיֹּאמֶר לִי הַמֶּלֶךְ מַדּוּעַ ׀ פָּנֶיךָ
faces-of-you why? the-king to-me so-he-asked (2) in-presences-of-him sad

רָעִים וְאַתָּה אֵינְךָ חוֹלֶה אֵין זֶה כִּי־אִם רֹעַ לֵב
heart sadness-of only but this nothing being-ill not-you when-you ones-sad

וָאִירָא הַרְבֵּה מְאֹד׃ וָאֹמַר לַמֶּלֶךְ הַמֶּלֶךְ
the-king to-the-king but-I-said (3) very to-be-much and-I-was-afraid

לְעוֹלָם יִחְיֶה מַדּוּעַ לֹא־יֵרְעוּ פָנַי אֲשֶׁר
when faces-of-me they-should-look-sad not why? may-he-live to-forever

הָעִיר בֵּית־קִבְרוֹת אֲבֹתַי חֲרֵבָה וּשְׁעָרֶיהָ
and-gates-of-her she-lies-in-ruin fathers-of-me burials-of house-of the-city

אֻכְּלוּ בָאֵשׁ׃ וַיֹּאמֶר לִי הַמֶּלֶךְ עַל־מַה־זֶּה
this what? to the-king to-me and-he-said (4) by-fire they-were-destroyed

אַתָּה מְבַקֵּשׁ וָאֶתְפַּלֵּל אֶל־אֱלֹהֵי הַשָּׁמָיִם׃ וָאֹמַר לַמֶּלֶךְ
to-the-king and-I-answered (5) the-heavens God-of to then-I-prayed wanting you

Moses, saying, 'If you are unfaithful, I will scatter you among the nations, [9]but if you return to me and obey my commands, then even if your exiled people are at the farthest horizon, I will gather them from there and bring them to the place I have chosen as a dwelling for my Name.'

[10]"They are your servants and your people, whom you redeemed by your great strength and your mighty hand. [11]O Lord, let your ear be attentive to the prayer of this your servant and to the prayer of your servants who delight in revering your name. Give your servant success today by granting him favor in the presence of this man."

I was cupbearer to the king.

### *Artaxerxes Sends Nehemiah to Jerusalem*

**2** In the month of Nisan in the twentieth year of King Artaxerxes, when wine was brought for him, I took the wine and gave it to the king. I had not been sad in his presence before; [2]so the king asked me, "Why does your face look so sad when you are not ill? This can be nothing but sadness of heart."

I was very much afraid, [3]but I said to the king, "May the king live forever! Why should my face not look sad when the city where my fathers are buried lies in ruins, and its gates have been destroyed by fire?"

[4]The king said to me, "What is it you want?"

Then I prayed to the God of heaven, [5]and I answered the

°9 ק והביאותים

אִם־עַל־ הַמֶּלֶךְ טוֹב וְאִם־ יִיטַב עַבְדְּךָ לְפָנֶיךָ
before-you servant-of-you he-found-favor and-if pleasing the-king to if

אֲשֶׁר תִּשְׁלָחֵנִי אֶל־ יְהוּדָה אֶל־ עִיר קִבְרוֹת אֲבֹתַי
fathers-of-me burials-of city-of to Judah to you-send-me then

וְאֶבְנֶנָּה׃ וַיֹּאמֶר לִי הַמֶּלֶךְ וְהַשֵּׁגַל ׀ יוֹשֶׁבֶת
sitting with-the-queen the-king to-me then-he-asked (6) so-I-can-rebuild-her

אֶצְלוֹ עַד־ מָתַי יִהְיֶה מַהֲלָכְךָ וּמָתַי תָּשׁוּב
will-you-get-back and-when? journey-of-you will-he-be when? until beside-him

וַיִּיטַב לִפְנֵי־הַמֶּלֶךְ וַיִּשְׁלָחֵנִי וָאֶתְּנָה לוֹ זְמָן׃ וָאוֹמַר
also-I-said (7) time for-him so-I-set and-he-sent-me the-king to and-he-pleased

לַמֶּלֶךְ אִם־ עַל־ הַמֶּלֶךְ טוֹב אִגְּרוֹת יִתְּנוּ־ לִי עַל־
to to-me let-them-give letters pleasing the-king to if to-the-king

פַּחֲווֹת עֵבֶר הַנָּהָר אֲשֶׁר יַעֲבִירוּנִי
they-will-provide-safe-conduct-to-me that the-River Beyond-of governors-of

עַד אֲשֶׁר־ אָבוֹא אֶל־יְהוּדָה׃ וְאִגֶּרֶת אֶל־ אָסָף שֹׁמֵר
one-keeping-of Asaph to and-letter (8) Judah in I-arrive when until

הַפַּרְדֵּס אֲשֶׁר לַמֶּלֶךְ אֲשֶׁר יִתֶּן־ לִי עֵצִים לְקָרוֹת
to-make-beam timbers to-me he-will-give that to-the-king that the-forest

אֶת־ שַׁעֲרֵי הַבִּירָה אֲשֶׁר־ לַבַּיִת וּלְחוֹמַת הָעִיר
the-city and-for-wall-of by-the-temple that the-citadel gates-of ***

וְלַבַּיִת אֲשֶׁר־ אָבוֹא אֵלָיו וַיִּתֶּן־ לִי הַמֶּלֶךְ
the-king to-me and-he-granted in-him I-will-occupy that and-for-the-residence

כְּיַד־ אֱלֹהַי הַטּוֹבָה עָלָי׃ וָאָבוֹא אֶל־ פַּחֲווֹת
governors-of to so-I-went (9) upon-me the-gracious God-of-me because-hand-of

עֵבֶר הַנָּהָר וָאֶתְּנָה לָהֶם אֵת אִגְּרוֹת הַמֶּלֶךְ וַיִּשְׁלַח
also-he-sent the-king letters-of *** to-them and-I-gave the-River Beyond-of

עִמִּי הַמֶּלֶךְ שָׂרֵי חַיִל וּפָרָשִׁים׃ וַיִּשְׁמַע סַנְבַלַּט
Sanballat when-he-heard (10) and-cavalrymen army officers-of the-king with-me

הַחֹרֹנִי וְטוֹבִיָּה הָעֶבֶד הָעַמֹּנִי וַיֵּרַע לָהֶם
to-them and-he-disturbed the-Ammonite the-official and-Tobiah the-Horonite

רָעָה גְדֹלָה אֲשֶׁר־ בָּא אָדָם לְבַקֵּשׁ טוֹבָה לִבְנֵי יִשְׂרָאֵל׃
Israel of-sons-of welfare to-promote someone he-came that great disturbance

וָאָבוֹא אֶל־ יְרוּשָׁלִָם וָאֱהִי־ שָׁם יָמִים שְׁלֹשָׁה׃ וָאָקוּם ׀
and-I-set-out (12) three days there and-I-stayed Jerusalem to and-I-went (11)

לַיְלָה אֲנִי וַאֲנָשִׁים ׀ מְעַט עִמִּי וְלֹא־ הִגַּדְתִּי לְאָדָם מָה אֱלֹהַי נֹתֵן
putting God-of-me what to-anyone I-told and-not with-me few and-men I night

אֶל־ לִבִּי לַעֲשׂוֹת לִירוּשָׁלִָם וּבְהֵמָה אֵין עִמִּי כִּי
except with-me there-was-no and-mount for-Jerusalem to-do heart-of-me in

king, "If it pleases the king and if your servant has found favor in his sight, let him send me to the city in Judah where my fathers are buried so that I can rebuild it."

6 Then the king, with the queen sitting beside him, asked me, "How long will your journey take, and when will you get back?" It pleased the king to send me; so I set a time.

7 I also said to him, "If it pleases the king, may I have letters to the governors of Trans-Euphrates, so that they will provide me safe-conduct until I arrive in Judah?
8 And may I have a letter to Asaph, keeper of the king's forest, so he will give me timber to make beams for the gates of the citadel by the temple and for the city wall and for the residence I will occupy?" And because the gracious hand of my God was upon me, the king granted my requests.
9 So I went to the governors of Trans-Euphrates and gave them the king's letters. The king had also sent army officers and cavalry with me.

10 When Sanballat the Horonite and Tobiah the Ammonite official heard about this, they were very much disturbed that someone had come to promote the welfare of the Israelites.

### *Nehemiah Inspects Jerusalem's Walls*

11 I went to Jerusalem, and after staying there three days
12 I set out during the night with a few men. I had not told anyone what my God had put in my heart to do for Jerusalem. There were no mounts with

אִם־ הַבְּהֵמָה֙ אֲשֶׁ֣ר אֲנִ֣י רֹכֵ֣ב בָּ֑הּ: (13) וָאֵצְאָ֨ה בְשַֽׁעַר־
only — the-mount — that — I — riding — on-her — (13) — and-I-went-out — through-Gate-of

הַגַּ֜יְא לַ֗יְלָה וְאֶל־ פְּנֵי֙ עֵ֣ין הַתַּנִּ֔ין וְאֶל־ שַׁ֣עַר
the-Valley — night — and-toward — faces-of — Well-of — the-Jackal — and-toward — Gate-of

הָאַשְׁפֹּ֑ת וָאֱהִ֗י שֹׂבֵ֛ר בְּחוֹמֹ֥ת יְרוּשָׁלַ֖͏ִם אֲשֶׁר־
the-Dungs — and-I-was — examining — to-walls-of — Jerusalem — which

הַמְפֹרוָֹצִ֑ים וּשְׁעָרֶ֖יהָ אֻכְּל֥וּ בָאֵֽשׁ:
*they-ones-being-broken-down — and-gates-of-her — they-were-destroyed — by-fire

(14) וָאֶֽעֱבֹר֙ אֶל־ שַׁ֣עַר הָעַ֔יִן וְאֶל־ בְּרֵכַ֖ת הַמֶּ֑לֶךְ
(14) — then-I-moved-on — toward — Gate-of — the-Fountain — and-toward — Pool-of — the-King

וְאֵֽין־ מָק֥וֹם לַבְּהֵמָ֖ה לַעֲבֹ֥ר תַּחְתָּֽי: (15) וָאֱהִ֨י
but-there-was-no — room — for-the-mount — to-get-through — under-me — (15) — so-I-was

עֹלֶ֤ה בַנַּ֙חַל֙ לַ֔יְלָה וָאֱהִ֥י שֹׂבֵ֖ר בַּחוֹמָ֑ה וָאָשׁ֗וּב
going-up — in-the-valley — night — and-I-was — examining — to-the-wall — and-I-turned-back

וָאָב֛וֹא בְּשַׁ֥עַר הַגַּ֖יְא וָאָשֽׁוּב:
and-I-reentered — through-Gate-of — the-Valley — and-I-turned-back

(16) וְהַסְּגָנִ֗ים לֹ֤א יָדְעוּ֙ אָ֣נָה הָלַ֔כְתִּי וּמָ֖ה אֲנִ֣י עֹשֶׂ֑ה
(16) — and-the-officials — not — they-knew — to-where — I-went — or-what — I — doing

וְלַיְּהוּדִ֨ים וְלַכֹּהֲנִ֜ים וְלַחֹרִ֗ים וְלַסְּגָנִ֛ים
because-to-the-Jews — or-to-the-priests — or-to-the-nobles — or-to-the-officials

וּלְיֶ֨תֶר֙ עֹשֵׂ֣ה הַמְּלָאכָ֔ה עַד־ כֵּ֖ן לֹ֥א הִגַּֽדְתִּי: (17) וָאוֹמַ֣ר
or-to-other-of — one-doing-of — the-work — until — yet — nothing — I-said — (17) — then-I-said

אֲלֵהֶ֗ם אַתֶּ֤ם רֹאִים֙ הָרָעָה֙ אֲשֶׁ֣ר אֲנַ֣חְנוּ בָ֔הּ אֲשֶׁ֥ר יְרוּשָׁלַ֖͏ִם
to-them — you — ones-seeing — the-trouble — that — we — in-her — that — Jerusalem

חֲרֵבָ֔ה וּשְׁעָרֶ֖יהָ נִצְּת֣וּ בָאֵ֑שׁ לְכ֗וּ
she-lies-in-ruin — and-gates-of-her — they-were-burned — with-fire — come!

וְנִבְנֶה֙ אֶת־ חוֹמַ֣ת יְרוּשָׁלַ֔͏ִם וְלֹֽא־ נִהְיֶ֥ה ע֖וֹד חֶרְפָּֽה:
and-let-us-rebuild — *** — wall-of — Jerusalem — and-not — we-will-be — longer — disgrace

(18) וָאַגִּ֨יד לָהֶ֜ם אֶת־ יַ֣ד אֱלֹהַ֗י אֲשֶׁר־ הִיא֙ טוֹבָה֙ עָלַ֔י
(18) — also-I-told — to-them — *** — hand-of — God-of-me — that — she — gracious — upon-me

וְאַף־ דִּבְרֵ֥י הַמֶּ֖לֶךְ אֲשֶׁ֣ר אָֽמַר־ לִ֑י וַיֹּֽאמְרוּ֙ נָק֣וּם
and-also — words-of — the-king — that — he-said — to-me — and-they-replied — let-us-start

וּבָנִ֔ינוּ וַיְחַזְּק֥וּ יְדֵיהֶ֖ם לַטּוֹבָֽה: (19) וַיִּשְׁמַ֞ע
and-let-us-rebuild — so-they-began — hands-of-them — in-the-good — (19) — when-he-heard

סַנְבַלַּ֣ט הַחֹרֹנִ֗י וְטֹבִיָּה֙ הָעֶ֣בֶד הָֽעַמּוֹנִ֔י וְגֶ֙שֶׁם֙
Sanballat — the-Horonite — and-Tobiah — the-official — the-Ammonite — and-Geshem

הָֽעַרְבִ֔י וַיַּלְעִ֣גוּ לָ֔נוּ וַיִּבְז֖וּ עָלֵ֑ינוּ וַיֹּ֣אמְר֔וּ
the-Arab — then-they-mocked — at-us — and-they-ridiculed — at-us — and-they-asked

---

me except the one I was riding on.

[13]By night I went out through the Valley Gate toward the Jackal[a] Well and the Dung Gate, examining the walls of Jerusalem, which had been broken down, and its gates, which had been destroyed by fire. [14]Then I moved on toward the Fountain Gate and the King's Pool, but there was not enough room for my mount to get through; [15]so I went up the valley by night, examining the wall. Finally, I turned back and reentered through the Valley Gate. [16]The officials did not know where I had gone or what I was doing, because as yet I had said nothing to the Jews or the priests or nobles or officials or any others who would be doing the work.

[17]Then I said to them, "You see the trouble we are in: Jerusalem lies in ruins, and its gates have been burned with fire. Come, let us rebuild the wall of Jerusalem, and we will no longer be in disgrace." [18]I also told them about the gracious hand of my God upon me and what the king had said to me.

They replied, "Let us start rebuilding." So they began this good work.

[19]But when Sanballat the Horonite, Tobiah the Ammonite official and Geshem the Arab heard about it, they mocked and ridiculed us.

[a]13 Or Serpent or Fig

*13 The Qere reading separates the Kethib form into two words, the pronoun they preceding the participle ones-being-broken-down.

° 13 ק הַם | פְרוּצִים

מָה־ הַדָּבָר הַזֶּה אֲשֶׁר אַתֶּם עֹשִׂים הַעַל הַמֶּלֶךְ אַתֶּם
you the-king against? ones-doing you that the-this the-thing what?

מֹרְדִים׃ וָאָשִׁיב אוֹתָם דָּבָר וָאוֹמַר לָהֶם אֱלֹהֵי הַשָּׁמַיִם
the-heavens God-of to-them and-I-said answer them and-I-gave (20) ones-rebelling

הוּא יַצְלִיחַ לָנוּ וַאֲנַחְנוּ עֲבָדָיו נָקוּם
we-will-start servants-of-him and-we to-us he-will-give-success he

וּבָנִינוּ וְלָכֶם אֵין־ חֵלֶק וּצְדָקָה וְזִכָּרוֹן
or-historic-right or-claim share there-is-no but-for-you and-we-will-rebuild

בִּירוּשָׁלָ͏ִם׃ וַיָּקָם אֶלְיָשִׁיב הַכֹּהֵן הַגָּדוֹל
the-high the-priest Eliashib so-he-went-to-work (3:1) in-Jerusalem

וְאֶחָיו הַכֹּהֲנִים וַיִּבְנוּ אֶת־ שַׁעַר הַצֹּאן הֵמָּה
they the-Sheep Gate-of *** and-they-rebuilt the-priests and-fellows-of-him

קִדְּשׁוּהוּ וַיַּעֲמִידוּ דַּלְתֹתָיו וְעַד־ מִגְדַּל
Tower-of and-as-far-as doors-of-him and-they-set-in-place they-dedicated-him

הַמֵּאָה קִדְּשׁוּהוּ עַד מִגְדַּל חֲנַנְאֵל׃ וְעַל־
and-at (2) Hananel Tower-of as-far-as they-dedicated-him the-Hundred

יָדוֹ בָנוּ אַנְשֵׁי יְרֵחוֹ וְעַל־ יָדוֹ בָּנָה זַכּוּר
Zaccur he-built side-of-him and-at Jericho men-of they-built side-of-him

בֶּן־ אִמְרִי׃ וְאֵת שַׁעַר הַדָּגִים בָּנוּ בְּנֵי הַסְּנָאָה הֵמָּה
they Hassenaah sons-of they-rebuilt the-Fishes Gate-of and (3) Imri son-of

קֵרוּהוּ וַיַּעֲמִידוּ דַּלְתֹתָיו מַנְעוּלָיו
bolts-of-him doors-of-him and-they-put-in-place they-laid-beams-of-him

וּבְרִיחָיו׃ וְעַל־ יָדָם הֶחֱזִיק מְרֵמוֹת בֶּן־ אוּרִיָּה
Uriah son-of Meremoth he-repaired side-of-them and-at (4) and-bars-of-him

בֶּן־ הַקּוֹץ וְעַל־ יָדָם הֶחֱזִיק מְשֻׁלָּם בֶּן־ בֶּרֶכְיָה
Berekiah son-of Meshullam he-repaired side-of-them and-at Hakkoz son-of

בֶּן־ מְשֵׁיזַבְאֵל וְעַל־ יָדָם הֶחֱזִיק צָדוֹק בֶּן־ בַּעֲנָא׃
Baana son-of Zadok he-repaired side-of-them and-at Meshezabel son-of

וְעַל־ יָדָם הֶחֱזִיקוּ הַתְּקוֹעִים וְאַדִּירֵיהֶם לֹא־
not but-nobles-of-them the-Tekoaites they-repaired side-of-them and-at (5)

הֵבִיאוּ צַוָּרָם בַּעֲבֹדַת אֲדֹנֵיהֶם׃ וְאֵת שַׁעַר
Gate-of and (6) supervisors-of-them to-work-of shoulder-of-them they-put

הַיְשָׁנָה הֶחֱזִיקוּ יוֹיָדָע בֶּן־ פָּסֵחַ וּמְשֻׁלָּם בֶּן־
son-of and-Meshullam Paseah son-of Joiada they-repaired the-Jeshanah

בְּסוֹדְיָה הֵמָּה קֵרוּהוּ וַיַּעֲמִידוּ דַּלְתֹתָיו
doors-of-him and-they-put-in-place they-laid-beams-of-him they Besodeiah

וּמַנְעֻלָיו וּבְרִיחָיו׃ וְעַל־ יָדָם הֶחֱזִיק מְלַטְיָה
Melatiah he-repaired side-of-them and-at (7) and-bars-of-him and-bolts-of-him

"What is this you are doing?" they asked. "Are you rebelling against the king?"
20 I answered them by saying, "The God of heaven will give us success. We his servants will start rebuilding, but as for you, you have no share in Jerusalem or any claim or historic right to it."

*Builders of the Wall*

3 Eliashib the high priest and his fellow priests went to work and rebuilt the Sheep Gate. They dedicated it and set its doors in place, building as far as the Tower of the Hundred, which they dedicated, and as far as the Tower of Hananel.
2 The men of Jericho built the adjoining section, and Zaccur son of Imri built next to them.

3 The Fish Gate was rebuilt by the sons of Hassenaah. They laid its beams and put its doors and bolts and bars in place.
4 Meremoth son of Uriah, the son of Hakkoz, repaired the next section. Next to him Meshullam son of Berekiah, the son of Meshezabel, made repairs, and next to him Zadok son of Baana also made repairs.
5 The next section was repaired by the men of Tekoa, but their nobles would not put their shoulders to the work under their supervisors.[b]

6 The Jeshanah[c] Gate was repaired by Joiada son of Paseah and Meshullam son of Besodeiah. They laid its beams and put its doors and bolts and bars in place.
7 Next to them, repairs were made by men

[b] 5 Or *their Lord* or *the governor*
[c] 6 Or *Old*

הַגִּבְעֹנִי וְיָדוֹן הַמֵּרֹנֹתִי אַנְשֵׁי גִבְעוֹן וְהַמִּצְפָּה
and-the-Mizpah Gibeon men-of the-Meronothite and-Jadon the-Gibeonite

לְכִסֵּא פַּחַת עֵבֶר הַנָּהָר׃ עַל־ יָדוֹ
side-of-him at (8) the-River Beyond-of governor-of under-authority-of

הֶחֱזִיק עֻזִּיאֵל בֶּן־ חַרְהֲיָה צוֹרְפִים וְעַל־ יָדוֹ
side-of-him and-at ones-being-goldsmiths Harhaiah son-of Uzziel he-repaired

הֶחֱזִיק חֲנַנְיָה בֶּן־ הָרַקָּחִים וַיַּעַזְבוּ יְרוּשָׁלַםִ
Jerusalem and-they-restored the-perfume-makers son-of Hananiah he-repaired

עַד הַחוֹמָה הָרְחָבָה׃ וְעַל־ יָדָם הֶחֱזִיק רְפָיָה
Rephaiah he-repaired side-of-them and-at (9) the-Broad the-Wall as-far-as

בֶן־ חוּר שַׂר חֲצִי פֶּלֶךְ יְרוּשָׁלָםִ׃ וְעַל־ יָדָם
side-of-them and-at (10) Jerusalem district-of half-of ruler-of Hur son-of

הֶחֱזִיק יְדָיָה בֶן־ חֲרוּמַף וְנֶגֶד בֵּיתוֹ וְעַל־
and-at house-of-him and-opposite Harumaph son-of Jedaiah he-repaired

יָדוֹ הֶחֱזִיק חַטּוּשׁ בֶּן־ חֲשַׁבְנְיָה׃ מִדָּה שֵׁנִית
another section (11) Hashabneiah son-of Hattush he-repaired side-of-him

הֶחֱזִיק מַלְכִּיָּה בֶן־ חָרִם וְחַשּׁוּב בֶּן־ פַּחַת מוֹאָב וְאֵת
and Moab Pahath son-of and-Hasshub Harim son-of Malkijah he-repaired

מִגְדַּל הַתַּנּוּרִים׃ וְעַל־ יָדוֹ הֶחֱזִיק שַׁלּוּם בֶּן־
son-of Shallum he-repaired side-of-him and-at (12) the-Ovens Tower-of

הַלּוֹחֵשׁ שַׂר חֲצִי פֶּלֶךְ יְרוּשָׁלָםִ הוּא וּבְנוֹתָיו׃
and-daughters-of-him he Jerusalem district-of half-of ruler-of Hallohesh

אֵת שַׁעַר הַגַּיְא הֶחֱזִיק חָנוּן וְיֹשְׁבֵי זָנוֹחַ
Zanoah and-ones-residing-of Hanun he-repaired the-Valley Gate-of *** (13)

הֵמָּה בָנוּהוּ וַיַּעֲמִידוּ דַּלְתֹתָיו מַנְעֻלָיו
bolts-of-him doors-of-him and-they-put-in-place they-rebuilt-him they

וּבְרִיחָיו וְאֶלֶף אַמָּה בַּחוֹמָה עַד שַׁעַר הַשְׁפוֹת׃
the-Dungs Gate-of as-far-as of-the-wall cubit and-thousand-of and-bars-of-him

וְאֵת ׀ שַׁעַר הָאַשְׁפּוֹת הֶחֱזִיק מַלְכִּיָּה בֶן־ רֵכָב שַׂר
ruler-of Recab son-of Malkijah he-repaired the-Dungs Gate-of and (14)

פֶּלֶךְ בֵּית־ הַכָּרֶם הוּא יִבְנֶנּוּ וְיַעֲמִיד דַּלְתֹתָיו
doors-of-him and-he-put-in-place he-rebuilt-him he Haccerem Beth district-of

מַנְעֻלָיו וּבְרִיחָיו׃ וְאֵת שַׁעַר הָעַיִן הֶחֱזִיק
he-repaired the-Fountain Gate-of and (15) and-bars-of-him bolts-of-him

שַׁלּוּן בֶּן־ כָּל־ חֹזֶה שַׂר פֶּלֶךְ הַמִּצְפָּה הוּא יִבְנֶנּוּ
he-rebuilt-him he the-Mizpah district-of ruler-of Hozeh Col son-of Shallun

וִיטַלְלֶנּוּ וְיַעֲמִידוּ דַּלְתֹתָיו מַנְעֻלָיו
bolts-of-him doors-of-him and-he-put-in-place and-he-roofed-him

from Gibeon and Mizpah—Melatiah of Gibeon and Jadon of Meronoth—places under the authority of the governor of Trans-Euphrates. 8Uzziel son of Harhaiah, one of the goldsmiths, repaired the next section; and Hananiah, one of the perfume-makers, made repairs next to that. They restored[d] Jerusalem as far as the Broad Wall. 9Rephaiah son of Hur, ruler of a half-district of Jerusalem, repaired the next section. 10Adjoining this, Jedaiah son of Harumaph made repairs opposite his house, and Hattush son of Hashabneiah made repairs next to him. 11Malkijah son of Harim and Hasshub son of Pahath-Moab repaired another section and the Tower of the Ovens. 12Shallum son of Hallohesh, ruler of a half-district of Jerusalem, repaired the next section with the help of his daughters.

13The Valley Gate was repaired by Hanun and the residents of Zanoah. They rebuilt it and put its doors and bolts and bars in place. They also repaired five hundred yards[e] of the wall as far as the Dung Gate.

14The Dung Gate was repaired by Malkijah son of Recab, ruler of the district of Beth Haccerem. He rebuilt it and put its doors and bolts and bars in place.

15The Fountain Gate was repaired by Shallun son of Col-Hozeh, ruler of the district of Mizpah. He rebuilt it, roofing it over and putting its doors and bolts and bars in place. He

[d] 8 Or *They left out part of*
[e] 13 Hebrew *a thousand cubits* (about 450 meters)

°15 ק ויעמיד

וּבְרִיחָיו וְאֵת חוֹמַת בְּרֵכַת הַשֶּׁלַח לְגַן־הַמֶּלֶךְ
the-King by-Garden-of the-Shelah Pool-of wall-of also and-bars-of-him

וְעַד־הַמַּעֲלוֹת הַיּוֹרְדוֹת מֵעִיר דָּוִיד׃ אַחֲרָיו
beyond-him (16) David from-City-of the-ones-going-down the-steps and-as-far-as

הֶחֱזִיק נְחֶמְיָה בֶן־עַזְבּוּק שַׂר חֲצִי פֶּלֶךְ בֵּית־צוּר
Zur Beth district-of half-of ruler-of Azbuk son-of Nehemiah he-repaired

עַד־נֶגֶד קִבְרֵי דָוִיד וְעַד־הַבְּרֵכָה הָעֲשׂוּיָה
the-one-being-artificial the-pool and-as-far-as David tombs-of opposite up-to

וְעַד בֵּית הַגִּבֹּרִים׃ אַחֲרָיו הֶחֱזִיקוּ הַלְוִיִּם
the-Levites they-repaired next-to-him (17) the-Heroes House-of and-as-far-as

רְחוּם בֶּן־בָּנִי עַל־יָדוֹ הֶחֱזִיק חֲשַׁבְיָה שַׂר־חֲצִי־
half-of ruler-of Hashabiah he-repaired side-of-him at Bani son-of Rehum

פֶלֶךְ קְעִילָה לְפִלְכּוֹ׃ אַחֲרָיו הֶחֱזִיקוּ
they-repaired next-to-him (18) for-district-of-him Keilah district-of

אֲחֵיהֶם בַּוַּי בֶּן־חֵנָדָד שַׂר חֲצִי פֶּלֶךְ קְעִילָה׃
Keilah district-of half-of ruler-of Henadad son-of Bavvai countrymen-of-them

וַיְחַזֵּק עַל־יָדוֹ עֵזֶר בֶּן־יֵשׁוּעַ שַׂר הַמִּצְפָּה
the-Mizpah ruler-of Jeshua son-of Ezer side-of-him at and-he-repaired (19)

מִדָּה שֵׁנִית מִנֶּגֶד עֲלֹת הַנֶּשֶׁק הַמִּקְצֹעַ׃ אַחֲרָיו
next-to-him (20) the-angle the-armory to-ascend from-facing another section

הֶחֱרָה הֶחֱזִיק בָּרוּךְ בֶּן־זַבַּי° מִדָּה שֵׁנִית מִן־
from another section Zabbai son-of Baruch he-repaired he-was-zealous

הַמִּקְצוֹעַ עַד־פֶּתַח בֵּית אֶלְיָשִׁיב הַכֹּהֵן הַגָּדוֹל׃
the-high the-priest Eliashib house-of entrance-of to the-angle

אַחֲרָיו הֶחֱזִיק מְרֵמוֹת בֶּן־אוּרִיָּה בֶּן־הַקּוֹץ מִדָּה
section Hakkoz son-of Uriah son-of Meremoth he-repaired next-to-him (21)

שֵׁנִית מִפֶּתַח בֵּית אֶלְיָשִׁיב וְעַד־תַּכְלִית בֵּית אֶלְיָשִׁיב׃
Eliashib house-of end-of and-to Eliashib house-of from-entrance-of another

וְאַחֲרָיו הֶחֱזִיקוּ הַכֹּהֲנִים אַנְשֵׁי הַכִּכָּר׃
the-surrounding-region men-of the-priests they-repaired and-next-to-him (22)

אַחֲרָיו הֶחֱזִיק בִּנְיָמִן וְחַשּׁוּב נֶגֶד בֵּיתָם
house-of-them in-front-of and-Hasshub Benjamin he-repaired beyond-him (23)

אַחֲרָיו הֶחֱזִיק עֲזַרְיָה בֶן־מַעֲשֵׂיָה בֶּן־עֲנַנְיָה אֵצֶל
beside Ananiah son-of Maaseiah son-of Azariah he-repaired next-to-him

בֵּיתוֹ׃ אַחֲרָיו הֶחֱזִיק בִּנּוּי בֶּן־חֵנָדָד מִדָּה
section Henadad son-of Binnui he-repaired next-to-him (24) house-of-him

שֵׁנִית מִבֵּית עֲזַרְיָה עַד־הַמִּקְצוֹעַ וְעַד־הַפִּנָּה׃ פָּלָל
Palal (25) the-corner and-to the-angle to Azariah from-house-of another

also repaired the wall of the Pool of Siloam,[f] by the King's Garden, as far as the steps going down from the City of David. [16]Beyond him, Nehemiah son of Azbuk, ruler of a half-district of Beth Zur, made repairs up to a point opposite the tombs[g] of David, as far as the artificial pool and the House of the Heroes.

[17]Next to him, the repairs were made by the Levites under Rehum son of Bani. Beside him, Hashabiah, ruler of half the district of Keilah, carried out repairs for his district. [18]Next to him, the repairs were made by their countrymen under Binnui[h] son of Henadad, ruler of the other half-district of Keilah. [19]Next to him, Ezer son of Jeshua, ruler of Mizpah, repaired another section, from a point facing the ascent to the armory as far as the angle. [20]Next to him, Baruch son of Zabbai zealously repaired another section, from the angle to the entrance of the house of Eliashib the high priest. [21]Next to him, Meremoth son of Uriah, the son of Hakkoz, repaired another section, from the entrance of Eliashib's house to the end of it.

[22]The repairs next to him were made by the priests from the surrounding region. [23]Beyond them, Benjamin and Hasshub made repairs in front of their house; and next to them, Azariah son of Maaseiah, the son of Ananiah, made repairs beside his house. [24]Next to him, Binnui son of Henadad repaired another section, from Azariah's house to the angle and the corner,

[f]15 Hebrew *Shelah*, a variant of *Shiloah*, that is, Siloam
[g]16 Hebrew; Septuagint, some Vulgate manuscripts and Syriac *tomb*
[h]18 Two Hebrew manuscripts, some Septuagint manuscripts and Syriac (see also verse 24); most Hebrew manuscripts *Bavvai*

°*20* ק זכי

בֶּן־ אוּזַי מִנֶּגֶד הַמִּקְצוֹעַ וְהַמִּגְדָּל הַיּוֹצֵא
the-one-projecting and-the-tower the-angle at-opposite Uzai son-of

מִבֵּית הַמֶּלֶךְ הָעֶלְיוֹן אֲשֶׁר לַחֲצַר הַמַּטָּרָה אַחֲרָיו
next-to-him the-guard near-court-of that the-upper the-king from-palace-of

פְּדָיָה בֶן־ פַּרְעֹשׁ׃ וְהַנְּתִינִים הָיוּ יֹשְׁבִים
ones-living they-were and-the-temple-servants (26) Parosh son-of Pedaiah

בָּעֹפֶל עַד נֶגֶד שַׁעַר הַמַּיִם לַמִּזְרָח וְהַמִּגְדָּל
and-the-tower toward-the-east the-Waters Gate-of opposite up-to on-the-Ophel

הַיּוֹצֵא׃ אַחֲרָיו הֶחֱזִיקוּ הַתְּקֹעִים מִדָּה
section the-Tekoaites they-repaired next-to-him (27) the-one-projecting

שֵׁנִית מִנֶּגֶד הַמִּגְדָּל הַגָּדוֹל הַיּוֹצֵא וְעַד חוֹמַת
wall-of and-to the-one-projecting the-great the-tower from-before another

הָעֹפֶל׃ מֵעַל ׀ שַׁעַר הַסּוּסִים הֶחֱזִיקוּ הַכֹּהֲנִים אִישׁ
each the-priests they-repaired the-Horses Gate-of at-above (28) the-Ophel

לְנֶגֶד בֵּיתוֹ׃ אַחֲרָיו הֶחֱזִיק צָדוֹק בֶּן־ אִמֵּר
Immer son-of Zadok he-repaired next-to-him (29) house-of-him in-front-of

נֶגֶד בֵּיתוֹ וְאַחֲרָיו הֶחֱזִיק שְׁמַעְיָה בֶן־ שְׁכַנְיָה
Shecaniah son-of Shemaiah he-repaired and-next-to-him house-of-him opposite

שֹׁמֵר שַׁעַר הַמִּזְרָח׃ אַחֲרָי° הֶחֱזִיק חֲנַנְיָה
Hananiah he-repaired next-to-him (30) the-East Gate-of one-guarding-of

בֶן־ שֶׁלֶמְיָה וְחָנוּן בֶּן־ צָלָף הַשִּׁשִּׁי מִדָּה שֵׁנִי
another section the-sixth Zalaph son-of and-Hanun Shelemiah son-of

אַחֲרָיו הֶחֱזִיק מְשֻׁלָּם בֶּן־ בֶּרֶכְיָה נֶגֶד נִשְׁכָּתוֹ׃
living-quarter-of-him opposite Berekiah son-of Meshullam he-repaired next-to-him

אַחֲרָי° הֶחֱזִיק מַלְכִּיָּה בֶּן־ הַצֹּרְפִי עַד־
as-far-as the-goldsmith son-of Malkijah he-repaired next-to-him (31)

בֵּית הַנְּתִינִים וְהָרֹכְלִים נֶגֶד שַׁעַר
Gate-of opposite and-the-ones-being-merchants the-temple-servants house-of

הַמִּפְקָד וְעַד עֲלִיַּת הַפִּנָּה׃ וּבֵין
and-between (32) the-corner room-above-of and-as-far-as the-Inspection

עֲלִיַּת הַפִּנָּה לְשַׁעַר הַצֹּאן הֶחֱזִיקוּ
they-repaired the-Sheep to-Gate-of the-corner room-above-of

הַצֹּרְפִים וְהָרֹכְלִים׃ וַיְהִי
and-he-was *(33[1]) and-the-ones-being-merchants the-ones-being-goldsmiths

כַּאֲשֶׁר שָׁמַע סַנְבַלַּט כִּי־ אֲנַחְנוּ בוֹנִים אֶת־ הַחוֹמָה וַיִּחַר
then-he-angered the-wall *** ones-rebuilding we that Sanballat he-heard as-when

לוֹ וַיִּכְעַס הַרְבֵּה וַיַּלְעֵג עַל־ הַיְּהוּדִים׃
the-Jews at and-he-ridiculed to-be-great and-he-was-incensed to-him

[25]and Palal son of Uzai worked opposite the angle and the tower projecting from the upper palace near the court of the guard. Next to him, Pedaiah son of Parosh [26]and the temple servants living on the hill of Ophel made repairs up to a point opposite the Water Gate toward the east and the projecting tower. [27]Next to them, the men of Tekoa repaired another section, from the great projecting tower to the wall of Ophel.

[28]Above the Horse Gate, the priests made repairs, each in front of his own house. [29]Next to them, Zadok son of Immer made repairs opposite his house. Next to him, Shemaiah son of Shecaniah, the guard at the East Gate, made repairs. [30]Next to him, Hananiah son of Shelemiah, and Hanun, the sixth son of Zalaph, repaired another section. Next to them, Meshullam son of Berekiah made repairs opposite his living quarters. [31]Next to him, Malkijah, one of the goldsmiths, made repairs as far as the house of the temple servants and the merchants, opposite the Inspection Gate, and as far as the room above the corner; [32]and between the room above the corner and the Sheep Gate the goldsmiths and merchants made repairs.

*Opposition to the Rebuilding*

**4** When Sanballat heard that we were rebuilding the wall, he became angry and was greatly incensed. He ridiculed the Jews, [2]and in the

*33 The Hebrew numeration of chapter 4 begins with verse 7 in the English; the number in brackets indicates the English numeration.

°30 ק אחריו
°31 ק אחריו

(34[2]) וַיֹּאמֶר ׀ לִפְנֵי אֶחָיו וְחֵיל שֹׁמְרוֹן
Samaria and-army-of associates-of-him in-presences-of and-he-said (34[2])

וַיֹּאמֶר מָה הַיְּהוּדִים הָאֲמֵלָלִים עֹשִׂים הֲיַעַזְבוּ
will-they-restore? ones-doing the-feeble-ones the-Jews what? and-he-said

לָהֶם הֲיִזְבָּחוּ הַיְכַלּוּ בַיּוֹם
in-the-day will-they-finish? will-they-offer-sacrifices? for-them

הַיְחַיּוּ אֶת־ הָאֲבָנִים מֵעֲרֵמוֹת הֶעָפָר וְהֵמָּה
for-they the-rubble from-heaps-of the-stones *** can-they-bring-to-life?

שְׂרוּפוֹת׃ (35[3]) וְטוֹבִיָּה הָעַמֹּנִי אֶצְלוֹ וַיֹּאמֶר
and-he-said at-side-of-him the-Ammonite and-Tobiah (35[3]) ones-being-burned

גַּם אֲשֶׁר־ הֵם בּוֹנִים אִם־ יַעֲלֶה שׁוּעָל וּפָרַץ
then-he-would-break-down fox he-climbed-up if ones-building they what indeed

חוֹמַת אַבְנֵיהֶם׃ (36[4]) שְׁמַע אֱלֹהֵינוּ כִּי־ הָיִינוּ בוּזָה וְהָשֵׁב
and-turn! despised we-are for God-of-us hear! (36[4]) stones-of-them wall-of

חֶרְפָּתָם אֶל־ רֹאשָׁם וּתְנֵם לְבִזָּה בְּאֶרֶץ
in-land-of as-plunder and-give-them! head-of-them on insult-of-them

שִׁבְיָה׃ (37[5]) וְאַל־ תְּכַס עַל־ עֲוֺנָם וְחַטָּאתָם
or-sin-of-them guilt-of-them over you-cover and-not (37[5]) captivity

מִלְּפָנֶיךָ אַל־ תִּמָּחֶה כִּי הִכְעִיסוּ לְנֶגֶד
in-face-of they-threw-insults for you-blot-out not from-before-you

הַבּוֹנִים׃ (38[6]) וַנִּבְנֶה אֶת־ הַחוֹמָה וַתִּקָּשֵׁר
and-she-reached-height the-wall *** so-we-rebuilt (38[6]) the-ones-building

כָּל־ הַחוֹמָה עַד־ חֶצְיָהּ וַיְהִי לֵב לָעָם לַעֲשׂוֹת׃
to-work of-the-people heart for-he-was half-of-her to the-wall all-of

(4:1[7]) וַיְהִי כַאֲשֶׁר שָׁמַע סַנְבַלַּט וְטוֹבִיָּה וְהָעַרְבִים
and-the-Arabs and-Tobiah Sanballat he-heard as-when but-he-was (4:1[7])

וְהָעַמֹּנִים וְהָאַשְׁדּוֹדִים כִּי־ עָלְתָה אֲרוּכָה לְחֹמוֹת
of-walls-of repair she-went-ahead that and-the-Ashdodites and-the-Ammonites

יְרוּשָׁלִַם כִּי־ הֵחֵלּוּ הַפְּרֻצִים לְהִסָּתֵם וַיִּחַר
then-he-angered to-be-closed the-ones-being-gaps they-began that Jerusalem

לָהֶם מְאֹד׃ (2[8]) וַיִּקְשְׁרוּ כֻלָּם יַחְדָּו לָבוֹא לְהִלָּחֵם
to-fight to-come together all-of-them and-they-plotted (2[8]) very to-them

בִּירוּשָׁלִָם וְלַעֲשׂוֹת לוֹ תּוֹעָה׃ (3[9]) וַנִּתְפַּלֵּל
but-we-prayed (3[9]) trouble against-him and-to-stir-up against-Jerusalem

אֶל־ אֱלֹהֵינוּ וַנַּעֲמִיד מִשְׁמָר עֲלֵיהֶם יוֹמָם וָלַיְלָה מִפְּנֵיהֶם׃
because-of-them and-night by-day for-them guard and-we-posted God-of-us to

(4[10]) וַיֹּאמֶר יְהוּדָה כָּשַׁל כֹּחַ הַסַּבָּל וְהֶעָפָר
and-the-rubble the-laborer strength-of he-gives-out Judah and-he-said (4[10])

presence of his associates and the army of Samaria, he said, "What are those feeble Jews doing? Will they restore their wall? Will they offer sacrifices? Will they finish in a day? Can they bring the stones back to life from those heaps of rubble—burned as they are?"

[3]Tobiah the Ammonite, who was at his side, said, "What they are building—if even a fox climbed up on it, he would break down their wall of stones!"

[4]Hear us, O our God, for we are despised. Turn their insults back on their own heads. Give them over as plunder in a land of captivity. [5]Do not cover up their guilt or blot out their sins from your sight, for they have thrown insults in the face of[i] the builders.

[6]So we rebuilt the wall till all of it reached half its height, for the people worked with all their heart.

[7]But when Sanballat, Tobiah, the Arabs, the Ammonites and the men of Ashdod heard that the repairs to Jerusalem's walls had gone ahead and that the gaps were being closed, they were very angry. [8]They all plotted together to come and fight against Jerusalem and stir up trouble against it. [9]But we prayed to our God and posted a guard day and night to meet this threat.

[10]Meanwhile, the people in Judah said, "The strength of the laborers is giving out, and

[i]5 Or *have provoked you to anger before*

*See the note on page 223.

הַרְבֵּה וַאֲנַחְנוּ לֹא נוּכַל לִבְנוֹת בַּחוֹמָה׃ וַיֹּאמְרוּ
also-they-said (5[11]) on-the-wall to-rebuild we-are-able not that-we to-be-much

צָרֵינוּ לֹא יֵדְעוּ וְלֹא יִרְאוּ עַד אֲשֶׁר־ נָבוֹא
we-will-be when until they-will-see and-not they-will-know not enemies-of-us

אֶל־ תּוֹכָם וַהֲרַגְנוּם וְהִשְׁבַּתְנוּ אֶת־הַמְּלָאכָה׃
the-work *** and-we-will-end and-we-will-kill-them among-them in

וַיְהִי כַּאֲשֶׁר־ בָּאוּ הַיְּהוּדִים הַיֹּשְׁבִים אֶצְלָם
near-them the-ones-living the-Jews they-came as-when then-he-was (6[12])

וַיֹּאמְרוּ לָנוּ עֶשֶׂר פְּעָמִים מִכָּל־ הַמְּקֹמוֹת אֲשֶׁר־ תָּשׁוּבוּ עָלֵינוּ׃
against-us you-turn where the-places at-any-of times ten to-us and-they-told

וָאַעֲמִיד מִתַּחְתִּיּוֹת לַמָּקוֹם מֵאַחֲרֵי לַחוֹמָה
of-the-wall at-behind at-the-point at-lowest-ones so-I-stationed (7[13])

בַּצְּחִחִיִּים וָאַעֲמִיד אֶת־ הָעָם לְמִשְׁפָּחוֹת עִם־
with by-families the-people *** and-I-posted at-the-exposed-places

חַרְבֹתֵיהֶם רָמְחֵיהֶם וְקַשְּׁתֹתֵיהֶם׃ וָאֵרֶא
after-I-looked-over (8[14]) and-bows-of-them spears-of-them swords-of-them

וָאָקוּם וָאֹמַר אֶל־ הַחֹרִים וְאֶל־ הַסְּגָנִים וְאֶל־ יֶתֶר
rest-of and-to the-officials and-to the-nobles to and-I-said then-I-stood-up

הָעָם אַל־ תִּירְאוּ מִפְּנֵיהֶם אֶת־ אֲדֹנָי הַגָּדוֹל
the-great Lord *** because-of-them you-be-afraid not the-people

וְהַנּוֹרָא זְכֹרוּ וְהִלָּחֲמוּ עַל־ אֲחֵיכֶם בְּנֵיכֶם
sons-of-you brothers-of-you for and-fight! remember! and-the-one-being-awesome

וּבְנֹתֵיכֶם נְשֵׁיכֶם וּבָתֵּיכֶם׃ וַיְהִי
and-he-was (9[15]) and-homes-of-you wives-of-you and-daughters-of-you

כַּאֲשֶׁר־ שָׁמְעוּ אוֹיְבֵינוּ כִּי־ נוֹדַע לָנוּ
to-us he-was-aware that ones-being-enemies-of-us they-heard as-when

וַיָּפֶר הָאֱלֹהִים אֶת־ עֲצָתָם וַנָּשָׁוב כֻּלָּנוּ אֶל־
to all-of-us then-we-returned plot-of-them *** the-God and-he-frustrated

הַחוֹמָה אִישׁ אֶל־ מְלַאכְתּוֹ׃ וַיְהִי ׀ מִן־ הַיּוֹם הַהוּא
the-that the-day from and-he-was (10[16]) work-of-him to each the-wall

חֲצִי נְעָרַי עֹשִׂים בַּמְּלָאכָה וְחֶצְיָם מַחֲזִיקִים
ones-being-equipped while-half-of-them in-the-work ones-doing men-of-me half-of

וְהָרְמָחִים הַמָּגִנִּים וְהַקְּשָׁתוֹת וְהַשִּׁרְיֹנִים וְהַשָּׂרִים
and-the-officers and-the-armors and-the-bows the-shields with-the-spears

אַחֲרֵי כָּל־ בֵּית יְהוּדָה׃ הַבּוֹנִים בַּחוֹמָה
on-the-wall the-ones-building (11[17]) Judah house-of all-of behind

וְהַנֹּשְׂאִים בַּסֶּבֶל עֹמְשִׂים בְּאַחַת יָדוֹ
hand-of-him with-one-of ones-loading of-the-material and-the-ones-carrying

there is so much rubble that
we cannot rebuild the wall."
[11]Also our enemies said,
"Before they know it or see us,
we will be right there among
them and will kill them and
put an end to the work."
[12]Then the Jews who lived
near them came and told us
ten times over, "Wherever you
turn, they will attack us."
[13]Therefore I stationed some
of the people behind the lowest points of the wall at the exposed places, posting them by
families, with their swords,
spears and bows. [14]After I
looked things over, I stood up
and said to the nobles, the
officials and the rest of the
people, "Don't be afraid of
them. Remember the Lord,
who is great and awesome,
and fight for your brothers,
your sons and your daughters,
your wives and your homes."
[15]When our enemies heard
that we were aware of their
plot and that God had frustrated it, we all returned to the
wall, each to his own work.
[16]From that day on, half of
my men did the work, while
the other half were equipped
with spears, shields, bows and
armor. The officers posted
themselves behind all the
people of Judah [17]who were
building the wall. Those who
carried materials did their
work with one hand and held

*See the note on page 223.

°7 ק בצחיחים

°9 ק ונשב

עֹשֶׂה בַמְּלָאכָה וְאַחַת מַחֲזֶקֶת הַשָּׁלַח׃ וְהַבּוֹנִים
and-the-ones-building (12[18]) the-weapon holding and-one in-the-work doing

אִישׁ חַרְבּוֹ אֲסוּרִים עַל־ מָתְנָיו וּבוֹנִים
and-ones-working sides-of-him at ones-being-worn sword-of-him each

וְהַתּוֹקֵעַ בַּשּׁוֹפָר אֶצְלִי׃ וָאֹמַר אֶל־ הַחֹרִים
the-nobles to then-I-said (13[19]) with-me on-the-trumpet but-the-one-sounding

וְאֶל־ הַסְּגָנִים וְאֶל־ יֶתֶר הָעָם הַמְּלָאכָה הַרְבֵּה
to-be-extensive the-work the-people rest-of and-to the-officials and-to

וּרְחָבָה וַאֲנַחְנוּ נִפְרָדִים עַל־ הַחוֹמָה רְחוֹקִים אִישׁ
each ones-distant the-wall along ones-being-separated and-we and-spread-out

מֵאָחִיו׃ בִּמְקוֹם אֲשֶׁר תִּשְׁמְעוּ אֶת־ קוֹל הַשּׁוֹפָר
the-trumpet sound-of *** you-hear where at-place-of (14[20]) from-fellows-of-him

שָׁמָּה תִּקָּבְצוּ אֵלֵינוּ אֱלֹהֵינוּ יִלָּחֶם לָנוּ׃ וַאֲנַחְנוּ
so-we (15[21]) for-us he-will-fight God-of-us with-us you-join at-there

עֹשִׂים בַּמְּלָאכָה וְחֶצְיָם מַחֲזִיקִים בָּרְמָחִים
on-the-spears ones-holding with-half-of-them in-the-work ones-doing

מֵעֲלוֹת הַשַּׁחַר עַד צֵאת הַכּוֹכָבִים׃ גַּם בָּעֵת
at-the-time also (16[22]) the-stars to-come-out till the-dawn from-to-come-up

הַהִיא אָמַרְתִּי לָעָם אִישׁ וְנַעֲרוֹ יָלִינוּ
have-them-spend-night and-helper-of-him man to-the-people I-said the-that

בְּתוֹךְ יְרוּשָׁלִַם וְהָיוּ־ לָנוּ הַלַּיְלָה מִשְׁמָר וְהַיּוֹם
and-the-day guard the-night for-us so-they-can-serve Jerusalem inside-of

מְלָאכָה׃ וְאֵין אֲנִי וְאַחַי וּנְעָרַי וְאַנְשֵׁי
nor-men-of nor-men-of-me nor-brothers-of-me I and-neither (17[23]) workman

הַמִּשְׁמָר אֲשֶׁר אַחֲרַי אֵין־אֲנַחְנוּ פֹשְׁטִים בְּגָדֵינוּ אִישׁ שִׁלְחוֹ
weapon-of-him each clothes-of-us ones-taking-off we not with-me who the-guard

הַמָּיִם׃ וַתְּהִי צַעֲקַת הָעָם וּנְשֵׁיהֶם גְּדוֹלָה
great and-wives-of-them the-people outcry-of now-she-was (5:1) the-waters

אֶל־ אֲחֵיהֶם הַיְּהוּדִים׃ וְיֵשׁ אֲשֶׁר אֹמְרִים
ones-saying who and-there-was (2) the-Jewish-ones brothers-of-them against

בָּנֵינוּ וּבְנֹתֵינוּ אֲנַחְנוּ רַבִּים וְנִקְחָה דָגָן
grain and-we-must-get ones-numerous we and-daughters-of-us sons-of-us

וְנֹאכְלָה וְנִחְיֶה׃ וְיֵשׁ אֲשֶׁר אֹמְרִים שְׂדֹתֵינוּ
fields-of-us ones-saying who and-there-was (3) and-we-may-live so-we-may-eat

וּכְרָמֵינוּ וּבָתֵּינוּ אֲנַחְנוּ עֹרְבִים וְנִקְחָה דָגָן
grain so-we-can-get ones-mortgaging we and-homes-of-us and-vineyards-of-us

בָּרָעָב׃ וְיֵשׁ אֲשֶׁר אֹמְרִים לָוִינוּ כֶסֶף
money we-borrowed ones-saying who and-there-was (4) during-the-famine

a weapon in the other, [18]and each of the builders wore his sword at his side as he worked. But the man who sounded the trumpet stayed with me.

[19]Then I said to the nobles, the officials and the rest of the people, "The work is extensive and spread out, and we are widely separated from each other along the wall. [20]Wherever you hear the sound of the trumpet, join us there. Our God will fight for us!"

[21]So we continued the work with half the men holding spears, from the first light of dawn till the stars came out. [22]At that time I also said to the people, "Have every man and his helper stay inside Jerusalem at night, so they can serve us as guards by night and workmen by day." [23]Neither I nor my brothers nor my men nor the guards with me took off our clothes; each had his weapon, even when he went for water.[j]

*Nehemiah Helps the Poor*

5 Now the men and their wives raised a great outcry against their Jewish brothers. [2]Some were saying, "We and our sons and daughters are numerous; in order for us to eat and stay alive, we must get grain."

[3]Others were saying, "We are mortgaging our fields, our vineyards and our homes to get grain during the famine."

[4]Still others were saying, "We have had to borrow

[j]23 The meaning of the Hebrew for this clause is uncertain.

*See the note on page 223.

לְמִדַּת הַמֶּלֶךְ שְׂדֹתֵינוּ וּכְרָמֵינוּ׃ וְעַתָּה
although-now (5) and-vineyards-of-us fields-of-us the-king for-tax-of

כִּבְשַׂר אַחֵינוּ בְּשָׂרֵנוּ כִּבְנֵיהֶם בָּנֵינוּ וְהִנֵּה
yet-see! sons-of-us as-sons-of-them flesh-of-us countrymen-of-us as-flesh-of

אֲנַחְנוּ כֹבְשִׁים אֶת־ בָּנֵינוּ וְאֶת־ בְּנֹתֵינוּ לַעֲבָדִים וְיֵשׁ
and-there-is as-slaves daughters-of-us and sons-of-us *** ones-subjecting we

מִבְּנֹתֵינוּ נִכְבָּשׁוֹת וְאֵין לְאֵל יָדֵנוּ
hand-of-us in-power-of but-not ones-being-enslaved from-daughters-of-us

וּשְׂדֹתֵינוּ וּכְרָמֵינוּ לַאֲחֵרִים׃ וַיִּחַר לִי
to-me and-he-angered (6) to-others and-vineyards-of-us because-fields-of-us

מְאֹד כַּאֲשֶׁר שָׁמַעְתִּי אֶת־ זַעֲקָתָם וְאֵת הַדְּבָרִים הָאֵלֶּה׃
the-these the-charges and outcry-of-them *** I-heard as-when very

וַיִּמָּלֵךְ לִבִּי עָלַי וָאָרִיבָה אֶת־ הַחֹרִים וְאֶת־
and the-nobles *** then-I-accused with-me mind-of-me and-he-pondered (7)

הַסְּגָנִים וָאֹמְרָה לָהֶם מַשָּׁא אִישׁ־ בְּאָחִיו אַתֶּם
you from-countryman-of-him each usury to-them and-I-told the-officials

נֹשְׁאִים וָאֶתֵּן עֲלֵיהֶם קְהִלָּה גְדוֹלָה׃ וָאֹמְרָה לָהֶם
to-them and-I-said (8) large meeting against-them so-I-called ones-exacting

אֲנַחְנוּ קָנִינוּ אֶת־ אַחֵינוּ הַיְּהוּדִים הַנִּמְכָּרִים
the-ones-being-sold the-Jewish-ones brothers-of-us *** we-bought-back we

לַגּוֹיִם כְּדֵי בָנוּ וְגַם־ אַתֶּם תִּמְכְּרוּ אֶת־ אֲחֵיכֶם
brothers-of-you *** you-sell you now-indeed to-us as-possible-of to-the-Gentiles

וְנִמְכְּרוּ־ לָנוּ וַיַּחֲרִישׁוּ וְלֹא מָצְאוּ
they-found because-not and-they-kept-quiet to-us but-they-were-sold-back

דָּבָר׃ וַיֹּאמֶר לֹא־ טוֹב הַדָּבָר אֲשֶׁר־אַתֶּם עֹשִׂים הֲלוֹא בְּיִרְאַת
in-fear-of not? ones-doing you that the-thing right not so-I-said (9) word

אֱלֹהֵינוּ תֵּלֵכוּ מֵחֶרְפַּת הַגּוֹיִם אוֹיְבֵינוּ׃
being-enemies-of-us the-Gentiles from-reproach-of you-should-walk God-of-us

וְגַם־ אֲנִי אַחַי וּנְעָרַי נֹשִׁים בָּהֶם כֶּסֶף
money to-them ones-lending and-men-of-me brothers-of-me I and-also (10)

וְדָגָן נַעַזְבָה־ נָּא אֶת־ הַמַּשָּׁא הַזֶּה׃ הָשִׁיבוּ נָא
now! give-back! (11) the-this the-usury *** now! let-us-stop and-grain

לָהֶם כְּהַיּוֹם שְׂדֹתֵיהֶם כַּרְמֵיהֶם זֵיתֵיהֶם
olive-groves-of-them vineyards-of-them fields-of-them as-the-day to-them

וּבָתֵּיהֶם וּמְאַת הַכֶּסֶף וְהַדָּגָן הַתִּירוֹשׁ
the-new-wine and-the-grain the-money and-hundredth-of and-houses-of-them

וְהַיִּצְהָר אֲשֶׁר אַתֶּם נֹשִׁים בָּהֶם׃ וַיֹּאמְרוּ נָשִׁיב
we-will-give-back and-they-said (12) to-them ones-charging you that and-the-oil

money to-pay the king's tax on
our fields and vineyards. 5Al-
though we are of the same
flesh and blood as our countrymen and though our sons
are as good as theirs, yet we
have to subject our sons and
daughters to slavery. Some of
our daughters have already
been enslaved, but we are
powerless, because our fields
and our vineyards belong to
others."
6When I heard their outcry
and these charges, I was very
angry. 7I pondered them in my
mind and then accused the
nobles and officials. I told
them, "You are exacting usury
from your own countrymen!"
So I called together a large
meeting to deal with them
8and said: "As far as possible,
we have bought back our
Jewish brothers who were sold
to the Gentiles. Now you are
selling your brothers, only for
them to be sold back to us!"
They kept quiet, because they
could find nothing to say.
9So I continued, "What you
are doing is not right.
Shouldn't you walk in the fear
of our God to avoid the reproach of our Gentile enemies? 10I and my brothers and
my men are also lending the
people money and grain. But
let the exacting of usury stop!
11Give back to them immediately their fields, vineyards,
olive groves and houses, and
also the usury you are charging them—the hundredth part
of the money, grain, new
wine and oil."
12"We will give it back,"

9° ק ואמר

וּמֵהֶם לֹא נְבַקֵּשׁ כֵּן נַעֲשֶׂה כַּאֲשֶׁר אַתָּה אוֹמֵר
saying you just-as we-will-do same we-will-demand not and-from-them

וָאֶקְרָא אֶת־ הַכֹּהֲנִים וָאַשְׁבִּיעֵם לַעֲשׂוֹת כַּדָּבָר
as-the-promise to-do and-I-made-take-oath-them the-priests *** then-I-summoned

הַזֶּה׃ גַּם־ חָצְנִי נָעַרְתִּי וָאֹמְרָה כָּכָה
this-way and-I-said I-shook-out fold-of-robe-of-me also (13) the-this

יְנַעֵר הָאֱלֹהִים אֶת־ כָּל־ הָאִישׁ אֲשֶׁר לֹא־ יָקִים אֶת־
*** he-keeps not who the-man every-of *** the-God may-he-shake-out

הַדָּבָר הַזֶּה מִבֵּיתוֹ וּמִיגִיעוֹ וְכָכָה
and-so and-from-possession-of-him from-house-of-him the-this the-promise

יִהְיֶה נָעוּר וָרֵק וַיֹּאמְרוּ כָל־ הַקָּהָל
the-assembly whole-of and-they-said and-empty being-shaken-out may-he-be

אָמֵן וַיְהַלְלוּ אֶת־ יְהוָה וַיַּעַשׂ הָעָם כַּדָּבָר
as-the-promise the-people and-he-did Yahweh *** and-they-praised amen

הַזֶּה׃ גַּם מִיּוֹם אֲשֶׁר־ צִוָּה אֹתִי לִהְיוֹת פֶּחָם
governor-of-them to-be me he-appointed when from-day moreover (14) the-this

בְּאֶרֶץ יְהוּדָה מִשְּׁנַת עֶשְׂרִים וְעַד שְׁנַת שְׁלֹשִׁים וּשְׁתַּיִם
and-two thirty year-of and-until twenty from-year-of Judah in-land-of

לְאַרְתַּחְשַׁסְתְּא הַמֶּלֶךְ שָׁנִים שְׁתֵּים עֶשְׂרֵה אֲנִי וְאַחַי לֶחֶם
food-of and-brothers-of-me I ten two years the-king of-Artaxerxes

הַפֶּחָה לֹא אָכַלְתִּי׃ וְהַפַּחוֹת הָרִאשֹׁנִים אֲשֶׁר־ לְפָנַי
before-me who the-earlier-ones but-the-governors (15) I-ate not the-governor

הִכְבִּידוּ עַל־ הָעָם וַיִּקְחוּ מֵהֶם בְּלֶחֶם
with-food from-them and-they-took the-people on they-placed-heavy-burden

וָיַיִן אַחַר כֶּסֶף־ שְׁקָלִים אַרְבָּעִים גַּם נַעֲרֵיהֶם
assistants-of-them also forty shekels silver-of in-addition-to and-wine

שָׁלְטוּ עַל־ הָעָם וַאֲנִי לֹא־ עָשִׂיתִי כֵן מִפְּנֵי יִרְאַת
reverence-of because-of same I-acted not but-I the-people over they-lorded

אֱלֹהִים׃ וְגַם בִּמְלֶאכֶת הַחוֹמָה הַזֹּאת הֶחֱזַקְתִּי וְשָׂדֶה
and-land I-devoted-myself the-this the-wall to-work-of but-instead (16) God

לֹא קָנִינוּ וְכָל־ נְעָרַי קְבוּצִים שָׁם עַל־
for there ones-being-assembled men-of-me and-all-of we-acquired not

הַמְּלָאכָה׃ וְהַיְּהוּדִים וְהַסְּגָנִים מֵאָה וַחֲמִשִּׁים אִישׁ
man and-fifty hundred and-the-officials furthermore-the-Jews (17) the-work

וְהַבָּאִים אֵלֵינוּ מִן־ הַגּוֹיִם אֲשֶׁר־ סְבִיבֹתֵינוּ עַל־ שֻׁלְחָנִי׃
table-of-me at ones-around-us who the-nations from to-us and-the-ones-coming

וַאֲשֶׁר הָיָה נַעֲשֶׂה לְיוֹם אֶחָד שׁוֹר אֶחָד צֹאן שֵׁשׁ־
six-of sheep one ox each for-day being-prepared he-was and-what (18)

they said. "And we will not
demand anything more from
them. We will do as you say."
Then I summoned the
priests and made the nobles
and officials take an oath to do
what they had promised. 13I
also shook out the folds of my
robe and said, "In this way
may God shake out of his
house and possessions every
man who does not keep this
promise. So may such a man
be shaken out and emptied!"
At this the whole assembly
said, "Amen," and praised the
LORD. And the people did as
they had promised.
14Moreover, from the twentieth year of King Artaxerxes,
when I was appointed to be
their governor in the land of
Judah, until his thirty-second
year—twelve years—neither I
nor my brothers ate the food
allotted to the governor. 15But
the earlier governors—those
preceding me—placed a heavy
burden on the people and took
forty shekels[k] of silver from
them in addition to food and
wine. Their assistants also
lorded it over the people. But
out of reverence for God I did
not act like that. 16Instead, I
devoted myself to the work on
this wall. All my men were assembled there for the work;
we[l] did not acquire any land.
17Furthermore, a hundred
and fifty Jews and officials ate
at my table, as well as those
who came to us from the surrounding nations. 18Each day
one ox, six choice sheep and

[k]15 That is, about 1 pound (about 0.5 kilogram)

[l]16 Most Hebrew manuscripts; some Hebrew manuscripts, Septuagint, Vulgate and Syriac *I*

בְּרֻרוֹת וְצִפֳּרִים נַעֲשׂוּ־ לִי וּבֵין עֲשֶׂרֶת
ten-of and-between for-me they-were-prepared and-poultry ones-being-chosen

יָמִים בְּכָל־ יַיִן לְהַרְבֵּה וְעִם־ זֶה לֶחֶם
food-of this but-in-spite-of to-be-abundant wine with-all-of days

הַפֶּחָה לֹא בִקַּשְׁתִּי כִּי־ כָבְדָה הָעֲבֹדָה עַל־ הָעָם
the-people on the-demand she-was-heavy because I-demanded never the-governor

הַזֶּה׃ זָכְרָה־ לִּי אֱלֹהַי לְטוֹבָה כֹּל אֲשֶׁר־עָשִׂיתִי עַל־
for I-did that all with-favor God-of-me to-me remember! (19) the-this

הָעָם הַזֶּה׃ וַיְהִי כַאֲשֶׁר נִשְׁמַע לְסַנְבַלַּט
by-Sanballat he-was-heard as-when and-he-was (6:1) the-this the-people

וְטוֹבִיָּה וּלְגֶשֶׁם הָעַרְבִי וּלְיֶתֶר אֹיְבֵינוּ
ones-being-enemies-of-us and-by-rest-of the-Arab and-by-Geshem and-Tobiah

כִּי בָנִיתִי אֶת־ הַחוֹמָה וְלֹא־ נוֹתַר בָּהּ פָּרֶץ גַּם עַד־
up-to though gap in-her he-was-left and-not the-wall *** I-rebuilt that

הָעֵת הַהִיא דְּלָתוֹת לֹא־הֶעֱמַדְתִּי בַשְּׁעָרִים׃ וַיִּשְׁלַח סַנְבַלַּט
Sanballat then-he-sent (2) in-the-gates I-set not doors the-that the-time

וְגֶשֶׁם אֵלַי לֵאמֹר לְכָה וְנִוָּעֲדָה יַחְדָּו בַּכְּפִירִים
in-the-villages together and-let-us-meet come! to-say to-me and-Geshem

בְּבִקְעַת אוֹנוֹ וְהֵמָּה חֹשְׁבִים לַעֲשׂוֹת לִי רָעָה׃ וָאֶשְׁלְחָה
so-I-sent (3) harm to-me to-do ones-scheming but-they Ono on-plain-of

עֲלֵיהֶם מַלְאָכִים לֵאמֹר מְלָאכָה גְדוֹלָה אֲנִי עֹשֶׂה וְלֹא אוּכַל
I-can and-not carrying-on I great project to-say messengers to-them

לָרֶדֶת לָמָּה תִשְׁבַּת הַמְּלָאכָה כַּאֲשֶׁר אַרְפֶּהָ וְיָרַדְתִּי
and-I-go-down I-leave-her as-while the-work should-she-stop why? to-go-down

אֲלֵיכֶם׃ וַיִּשְׁלְחוּ אֵלַי כַּדָּבָר הַזֶּה אַרְבַּע פְּעָמִים וָאָשִׁיב
and-I-gave times four the-this as-the-message to-me and-they-sent (4) to-you

אוֹתָם כַּדָּבָר הַזֶּה׃ וַיִּשְׁלַח אֵלַי סַנְבַלַּט כַּדָּבָר
as-the-message Sanballat to-me then-he-sent (5) the-this as-the-answer them

הַזֶּה פַּעַם חֲמִישִׁית אֶת־ נַעֲרוֹ וְאִגֶּרֶת פְּתוּחָה בְּיָדוֹ׃
in-hand-of-him being-unsealed and-letter aide-of-him with fifth time the-this

כָּתוּב בָּהּ בַּגּוֹיִם נִשְׁמָע וְגַשְׁמוּ אֹמֵר
saying and-Gashmu he-is-reported among-the-nations in-her being-written (6)

אַתָּה וְהַיְּהוּדִים חֹשְׁבִים לִמְרוֹד עַל־ כֵּן אַתָּה בוֹנֶה הַחוֹמָה
the-wall building you this for to-revolt ones-plotting and-the-Jews you

וְאַתָּה הֹוֶה לָהֶם לְמֶלֶךְ כַּדְּבָרִים הָאֵלֶּה׃ וְגַם־
and-even (7) the-these as-the-reports as-king to-them becoming moreover-you

נְבִיאִים הֶעֱמַדְתָּ לִקְרֹא עָלֶיךָ בִירוּשָׁלִַם לֵאמֹר מֶלֶךְ
king to-say in-Jerusalem about-you to-proclaim you-appointed prophets

some poultry were prepared for me, and every ten days an abundant supply of wine of all kinds. In spite of all this, I never demanded the food allotted to the governor, because the demands were heavy on these people.

[19]Remember me with favor, O my God, for all I have done for these people.

*Further Opposition to the Rebuilding*

6 When word came to Sanballat, Tobiah, Geshem the Arab and the rest of our enemies that I had rebuilt the wall and not a gap was left in it—though up to that time I had not set the doors in the gates— [2]Sanballat and Geshem sent me this message: "Come, let us meet together in one of the villages[m] on the plain of Ono."

But they were scheming to harm me; [3]so I sent messengers to them with this reply: "I am carrying on a great project and cannot go down. Why should the work stop while I leave it and go down to you?" [4]Four times they sent me the same message, and each time I gave them the same answer.

[5]Then, the fifth time, Sanballat sent his aide to me with the same message, and in his hand was an unsealed letter [6]in which was written:

> "It is reported among the nations—and Geshem[n] says it is true—that you and the Jews are plotting to revolt, and therefore you are building the wall. Moreover, according to these reports you are about to become their king [7]and have even appointed prophets to make this proclamation about you in Jerusalem: 'There is a king

[m]2 Or *in Kephirim*
[n]6 Hebrew *Gashmu*, a variant of *Geshem*

ביהודה ועתה ישמע למלך כדברים האלה
the-these as-the-reports to-the-king he-will-be-reported and-now in-Judah

ועתה לכה ונועצה יחדו: (8) ואשלחה אליו לאמר לא
not to-say to-him and-I-sent (8) together and-let-us-confer come! so-now

נהיה כדברים האלה אשר אתה אומר כי מלבך
from-mind-of-you but saying you that the-these like-the-things he-happens

אתה בודאם: (9) כי כלם מיראים אותנו לאמר
to-say us ones-frightening all-of-them for (9) making-up-them you

ירפו ידיהם מן־ המלאכה ולא תעשה
she-will-be-completed and-not the-work for hands-of-them they-will-get-weak

ועתה חזק את־ ידי: (10) ואני־ באתי בית שמעיה
Shemaiah house-of I-went and-I (10) hands-of-me *** strengthen! so-now

בן־ דליה בן־ מהיטבאל והוא עצור ויאמר נועד
let-us-meet and-he-said being-shut-in now-he Mehetabel son-of Delaiah son-of

אל־ בית האלהים אל־ תוך ההיכל ונסגרה דלתות
doors-of and-let-us-close the-temple inside-of at the-God house-of in

ההיכל כי באים להרגך ולילה באים להרגך:
to-kill-you men-coming and-night to-kill-you men-coming because the-temple

(11) ואמרה האיש כמוני יברח ומי כמוני אשר־ יבוא
he-should-go who like-me or-who? should-he-run like-me man? but-I-said (11)

אל־ ההיכל וחי לא אבוא: (12) ואכירה והנה
that-see! and-I-realized (12) I-will-go not so-he-might-live the-temple into

לא־ אלהים שלחו כי הנבואה דבר עלי וטוביה
because-Tobiah against-me he-spoke the-prophecy but he-sent-him God not

וסנבלט שכרו: (13) למען שכור הוא למען־
so-that he being-hired so-that (13) he-hired-him and-Sanballat

אירא ואעשה־ כן וחטאתי והיה
then-he-would-be so-I-would-sin this and-I-would-do I-would-be-intimidated

להם לשם רע למען יחרפוני: (14) זכרה אלהי
God-of-me remember! (14) they-could-discredit-me so-that bad for-name to-them

לטוביה ולסנבלט כמעשיו אלה וגם לנועדיה
to-Noadiah and-also these as-deeds-of-him and-to-Sanballat to-Tobiah

הנביאה וליתר הנביאים אשר היו מיראים
ones-intimidating they-were who the-prophets and-to-rest-of the-prophetess

אותי: (15) ותשלם החומה בעשרים וחמשה לאלול לחמשים
in-fifty of-Elul and-five on-twenty the-wall so-she-was-completed (15) me

ושנים יום: (16) ויהי כאשר שמעו כל־ אויבינו
being-enemies-of-us all-of they-heard as-when and-he-was (16) day and-two

in Judah!' Now this report will get back to the king; so come, let us confer together."

8 I sent him this reply: "Nothing like what you are saying is happening; you are just making it up out of your head."

9 They were all trying to frighten us, thinking, "Their hands will get too weak for the work, and it will not be completed."

⌞But I prayed,⌟ "Now strengthen my hands."

10 One day I went to the house of Shemaiah son of Delaiah, the son of Mehetabel, who was shut in at his home. He said, "Let us meet in the house of God, inside the temple, and let us close the temple doors, because men are coming to kill you—by night they are coming to kill you."

11 But I said, "Should a man like me run away? Or should one like me go into the temple to save his life? I will not go!" 12 I realized that God had not sent him, but that he had prophesied against me because Tobiah and Sanballat had hired him. 13 He had been hired to intimidate me so that I would commit a sin by doing this, and then they would give me a bad name to discredit me.

14 Remember Tobiah and Sanballat, O my God, because of what they have done; remember also the prophetess Noadiah and the rest of the prophets who have been trying to intimidate me.

*The Completion of the Wall*

15 So the wall was completed on the twenty-fifth of Elul, in fifty-two days. 16 When all our enemies heard about this and

וַיִּרְאוּ כָּל־ הַגּוֹיִם אֲשֶׁר סְבִיבֹתֵינוּ וַיִּפְּלוּ מְאֹד
greatly then-they-fell ones-around-us that the-nations all-of and-they-saw

בְּעֵינֵיהֶם וַיֵּדְעוּ כִּי מֵאֵת אֱלֹהֵינוּ נֶעֶשְׂתָה
she-was-done God-of-us from-with that because-they-realized in-eyes-of-them

הַמְּלָאכָה הַזֹּאת׃ גַּם בַּיָּמִים הָהֵם מַרְבִּים חֹרֵי
nobles-of ones-sending-many the-those in-the-days also (17) the-this the-work

יְהוּדָה אִגְּרֹתֵיהֶם הוֹלְכוֹת עַל־טוֹבִיָּה וַאֲשֶׁר לְטוֹבִיָּה בָּאוֹת
ones-coming from-Tobiah and-that Tobiah to ones-going letters-of-them Judah

אֲלֵיהֶם׃ כִּי־ רַבִּים בִּיהוּדָה בַּעֲלֵי שְׁבוּעָה לוֹ כִּי־ חָתָן הוּא
he son-in-law since to-him oath masters-of in-Judah many for (18) to-them

לִשְׁכַנְיָה בֶן־ אָרַח וִיהוֹחָנָן בְּנוֹ לָקַח אֶת־ בַּת־
daughter-of *** he-married son-of-him and-Jehohanan Arah son-of to-Shecaniah

מְשֻׁלָּם בֶּן בֶּרֶכְיָה׃ גַּם טוֹבֹתָיו הָיוּ
they-were good-deeds-of-him moreover (19) Berekiah son-of Meshullam

אֹמְרִים לְפָנַי וּדְבָרַי הָיוּ מוֹצִיאִים לוֹ אִגְּרוֹת
letters to-him ones-telling they-were then-words-of-me to-me ones-reporting

שָׁלַח טוֹבִיָּה לְיָרְאֵנִי׃ וַיְהִי כַּאֲשֶׁר נִבְנְתָה
she-was-rebuilt as-when and-he-was (7:1) to-intimidate-me Tobiah he-sent

הַחוֹמָה וָאַעֲמִיד הַדְּלָתוֹת וַיִּפָּקְדוּ הַשּׁוֹעֲרִים
the-gatekeepers then-they-were-appointed the-doors and-I-set-in-place the-wall

וְהַמְשֹׁרְרִים וְהַלְוִיִּם׃ וָאֲצַוֶּה אֶת־ חֲנָנִי
Hanani *** and-I-put-in-charge (2) and-the-Levites and-the-ones-singing

אָחִי וְאֶת־ חֲנַנְיָה שַׂר הַבִּירָה עַל־ יְרוּשָׁלִַם כִּי־
because Jerusalem over the-citadel commander-of Hananiah and brother-of-me

הוּא כְּאִישׁ אֱמֶת וְיָרֵא אֶת־ הָאֱלֹהִים מֵרַבִּים׃ וַיֹּאמֶר
and-I-said (3) more-than-most the-God *** and-he-feared integrity as-man-of he

לָהֶם לֹא יִפָּתְחוּ שַׁעֲרֵי יְרוּשָׁלִַם עַד־ חֹם הַשֶּׁמֶשׁ
the-sun to-be-hot until Jerusalem gates-of they-must-be-opened not to-them

וְעַד הֵם עֹמְדִים יָגִיפוּ הַדְּלָתוֹת וֶאֱחֹזוּ
and-bar! the-doors let-them-shut ones-being-on-duty they and-while

וְהַעֲמֵיד מִשְׁמְרוֹת יֹשְׁבֵי יְרוּשָׁלִַם אִישׁ בְּמִשְׁמָרוֹ
at-post-of-him one Jerusalem ones-residing-of guards also-appoint!

וְאִישׁ נֶגֶד בֵּיתוֹ׃ וְהָעִיר רַחֲבַת יָדַיִם וּגְדוֹלָה
and-large hands spacious-of now-the-city (4) house-of-him near and-one

וְהָעָם מְעַט בְּתוֹכָהּ וְאֵין בָּתִּים בְּנוּיִם׃
ones-being-rebuilt houses and-not within-her few but-the-people

וַיִּתֵּן אֱלֹהַי אֶל־ לִבִּי וָאֶקְבְּצָה אֶת־ הַחֹרִים וְאֶת־
and the-nobles *** and-I-assembled heart-of-me into God-of-me so-he-put (5)

all the surrounding nations saw it, our enemies lost their self-confidence, because they realized that this work had been done with the help of our God.

[17]Also, in those days the nobles of Judah were sending many letters to Tobiah, and replies from Tobiah kept coming to them. [18]For many in Judah were under oath to him, since he was son-in-law to Shecaniah son of Arah, and his son Jehohanan had married the daughter of Meshullam son of Berekiah. [19]Moreover, they kept reporting to me his good deeds and then telling him what I said. And Tobiah sent letters to intimidate me.

7 After the wall had been rebuilt and I had set the doors in place, the gatekeepers and the singers and the Levites were appointed. [2]I put in charge of Jerusalem my brother Hanani, along with° Hananiah the commander of the citadel, because he was a man of integrity and feared God more than most men do. [3]I said to them, "The gates of Jerusalem are not to be opened until the sun is hot. While the gatekeepers are still on duty, have them shut the doors and bar them. Also appoint residents of Jerusalem as guards, some at their posts and some near their own houses."

*The List of the Exiles Who Returned*

[4]Now the city was large and spacious, but there were few people in it, and the houses had not yet been rebuilt. [5]So my God put it into my heart to assemble the nobles, the

°2 Or *Hanani, that is,*

°3 ק ואמר

הַסְּגָנִים וְאֶת־ הָעָם לְהִתְיַחֵשׂ וָאֶמְצָא סֵפֶר
record-of and-I-found to-be-registered the-people and the-officials

הַיַּחַשׂ הָעוֹלִים בָּרִאשׁוֹנָה וָאֶמְצָא כָּתוּב
being-written and-I-found at-the-first the-ones-returning the-genealogy

בּוֹ׃ אֵלֶּה ׀ בְּנֵי הַמְּדִינָה הָעֹלִים מִשְּׁבִי
from-captivity-of the-ones-coming-up the-province people-of these (6) in-him

הַגּוֹלָה אֲשֶׁר הֶגְלָה נְבוּכַדְנֶצַּר מֶלֶךְ בָּבֶל וַיָּשׁוּבוּ
and-they-returned Babylon king-of Nebuchadnezzar he-took-captive whom the-exile

לִירוּשָׁלִַם וְלִיהוּדָה אִישׁ לְעִירוֹ׃ הַבָּאִים עִם־
with the-ones-coming (7) to-town-of-him each and-to-Judah to-Jerusalem

זְרֻבָּבֶל יֵשׁוּעַ נְחֶמְיָה עֲזַרְיָה רַעַמְיָה נַחֲמָנִי מָרְדֳּכַי בִּלְשָׁן
Bilshan Mordecai Nahamani Raamiah Azariah Nehemiah Jeshua Zerubbabel

מִסְפֶּרֶת בִּגְוַי נְחוּם בַּעֲנָה מִסְפַּר אַנְשֵׁי עַם יִשְׂרָאֵל׃
Israel people-of men-of list-of Baanah Nehum Bigvai Mispereth

בְּנֵי פַרְעֹשׁ אַלְפַּיִם מֵאָה וְשִׁבְעִים וּשְׁנָיִם׃
and-two and-seventy hundred two-thousands Parosh descendants-of (8)

בְּנֵי שְׁפַטְיָה שְׁלֹשׁ מֵאוֹת שִׁבְעִים וּשְׁנָיִם׃
and-two seventy hundreds three-of Shephatiah descendants-of (9)

בְּנֵי אָרַח שֵׁשׁ מֵאוֹת חֲמִשִּׁים וּשְׁנָיִם׃ בְּנֵי־
descendants-of (11) and-two fifty hundreds six-of Arah descendants-of (10)

פַחַת מוֹאָב לִבְנֵי יֵשׁוּעַ וְיוֹאָב אַלְפַּיִם וּשְׁמֹנֶה מֵאוֹת
hundreds and-eight-of two-thousands and-Joab Jeshua through-sons-of Moab Pahath

שְׁמֹנָה עָשָׂר׃ בְּנֵי עֵילָם אֶלֶף מָאתַיִם חֲמִשִּׁים וְאַרְבָּעָה׃
and-four fifty two-hundreds thousand Elam descendants-of (12) ten eight

בְּנֵי זַתּוּא שְׁמֹנֶה מֵאוֹת אַרְבָּעִים וַחֲמִשָּׁה׃ בְּנֵי
descendants-of (14) and-five forty hundreds eight-of Zattu descendants-of (13)

זַכָּי שְׁבַע מֵאוֹת וְשִׁשִּׁים׃ בְּנֵי בִנּוּי שֵׁשׁ מֵאוֹת
hundreds six-of Binnui descendants-of (15) and-sixty hundreds seven-of Zaccai

אַרְבָּעִים וּשְׁמֹנָה׃ בְּנֵי בֵבָי שֵׁשׁ מֵאוֹת עֶשְׂרִים וּשְׁמֹנָה׃
and-eight twenty hundreds six-of Bebai descendants-of (16) and-eight forty

בְּנֵי עַזְגָּד אַלְפַּיִם שְׁלֹשׁ מֵאוֹת עֶשְׂרִים וּשְׁנָיִם׃
and-two twenty hundreds three-of two-thousands Azgad descendants-of (17)

בְּנֵי אֲדֹנִיקָם שֵׁשׁ מֵאוֹת שִׁשִּׁים וְשִׁבְעָה׃
and-seven sixty hundreds six-of Adonikam descendants-of (18)

בְּנֵי בִגְוָי אַלְפַּיִם שִׁשִּׁים וְשִׁבְעָה׃ בְּנֵי
descendants-of (20) and-seven sixty two-thousands Bigvai descendants-of (19)

עָדִין שֵׁשׁ מֵאוֹת חֲמִשִּׁים וַחֲמִשָּׁה׃ בְּנֵי־ אָטֵר לְחִזְקִיָּה
through-Hezekiah Ater descendants-of (21) and-five fifty hundreds six-of Adin

officials and the common people for registration by families. I found the genealogical record of those who had been the first to return. This is what I found written there:

[6]These are the people of the province who came up from the captivity of the exiles whom Nebuchadnezzar king of Babylon had taken captive (they returned to Jerusalem and Judah, each to his own town, [7]in company with Zerubbabel, Jeshua, Nehemiah, Azariah, Raamiah, Nahamani, Mordecai, Bilshan, Mispereth, Bigvai, Nehum and Baanah):

The list of the men of Israel:

| | |
|---|---|
| [8]the descendants of Parosh | 2,172 |
| [9]of Shephatiah | 372 |
| [10]of Arah | 652 |
| [11]of Pahath-Moab (through the line of Jeshua and Joab) | 2,818 |
| [12]of Elam | 1,254 |
| [13]of Zattu | 845 |
| [14]of Zaccai | 760 |
| [15]of Binnui | 648 |
| [16]of Bebai | 628 |
| [17]of Azgad | 2,322 |
| [18]of Adonikam | 667 |
| [19]of Bigvai | 2,067 |
| [20]of Adin | 655 |
| [21]of Ater (through Hezekiah) | 98 |

תִּשְׁעִים וּשְׁמֹנָה׃ בְּנֵי חָשֻׁם שְׁלֹשׁ מֵאוֹת עֶשְׂרִים
twenty hundreds three-of Hashum descendants-of (22) and-eight ninety

וּשְׁמֹנָה׃ בְּנֵי בֵצָי שְׁלֹשׁ מֵאוֹת עֶשְׂרִים וְאַרְבָּעָה׃
and-four twenty hundreds three-of Bezai descendants-of (23) and-eight

בְּנֵי חָרִיף מֵאָה שְׁנֵים עָשָׂר׃ בְּנֵי גִבְעוֹן
Gibeon descendants-of (25) ten two hundred Hariph descendants-of (24)

תִּשְׁעִים וַחֲמִשָּׁה׃ אַנְשֵׁי בֵית־לֶחֶם וּנְטֹפָה מֵאָה שְׁמֹנִים וּשְׁמֹנָה׃
and-eight eighty hundred and-Netophah Lehem Beth men-of (26) and-five ninety

אַנְשֵׁי עֲנָתוֹת מֵאָה עֶשְׂרִים וּשְׁמֹנָה׃ אַנְשֵׁי בֵית־עַזְמָוֶת
Azmaveth Beth men-of (28) and-eight twenty hundred Anathoth men-of (27)

אַרְבָּעִים וּשְׁנָיִם׃ אַנְשֵׁי קִרְיַת יְעָרִים כְּפִירָה וּבְאֵרוֹת שְׁבַע
seven-of and-Beeroth Kephirah Jearim Kiriath men-of (29) and-two forty

מֵאוֹת אַרְבָּעִים וּשְׁלֹשָׁה׃ אַנְשֵׁי הָרָמָה וָגָבַע שֵׁשׁ מֵאוֹת
hundreds six-of and-Geba the-Ramah men-of (30) and-three forty hundreds

עֶשְׂרִים וְאֶחָד׃ אַנְשֵׁי מִכְמָס מֵאָה וְעֶשְׂרִים וּשְׁנָיִם׃ אַנְשֵׁי
men-of (32) and-two and-twenty hundred Micmash men-of (31) and-one twenty

בֵית־אֵל וְהָעָי מֵאָה עֶשְׂרִים וּשְׁלֹשָׁה׃ אַנְשֵׁי נְבוֹ אַחֵר חֲמִשִּׁים
fifty other Nebo men-of (33) and-three twenty hundred and-the-Ai El Beth

וּשְׁנָיִם׃ בְּנֵי עֵילָם אַחֵר אֶלֶף מָאתַיִם חֲמִשִּׁים וְאַרְבָּעָה׃
and-four fifty two-hundreds thousand other Elam men-of (34) and-two

בְּנֵי חָרִם שְׁלֹשׁ מֵאוֹת וְעֶשְׂרִים׃ בְּנֵי יְרֵחוֹ שְׁלֹשׁ
three-of Jericho men-of (36) and-twenty hundreds three-of Harim men-of (35)

מֵאוֹת אַרְבָּעִים וַחֲמִשָּׁה׃ בְּנֵי־לֹד חָדִיד וְאוֹנוֹ שְׁבַע מֵאוֹת
hundreds seven-of and-Ono Hadid Lod men-of (37) and-five forty hundreds

וְעֶשְׂרִים וְאֶחָד׃ בְּנֵי סְנָאָה שְׁלֹשֶׁת אֲלָפִים תְּשַׁע מֵאוֹת
hundreds nine-of thousands three-of Senaah men-of (38) and-one and-twenty

וּשְׁלֹשִׁים׃ הַכֹּהֲנִים בְּנֵי יְדַעְיָה לְבֵית יֵשׁוּעַ
Jeshua through-family-of Jedaiah descendants-of the-priests (39) and-thirty

תְּשַׁע מֵאוֹת שִׁבְעִים וּשְׁלֹשָׁה׃ בְּנֵי אִמֵּר אֶלֶף
thousand Immer descendants-of (40) and-three seventy hundreds nine-of

חֲמִשִּׁים וּשְׁנָיִם׃ בְּנֵי פַשְׁחוּר אֶלֶף מָאתַיִם אַרְבָּעִים
forty two-hundreds thousand Pashhur descendants-of (41) and-two fifty

וְשִׁבְעָה׃ בְּנֵי חָרִם אֶלֶף שִׁבְעָה עָשָׂר׃ הַלְוִיִּם
the-Levites (43) ten seven thousand Harim descendants-of (42) and-seven

בְּנֵי־יֵשׁוּעַ לְקַדְמִיאֵל לִבְנֵי לְהוֹדְוָה שִׁבְעִים
seventy of-Hodaviah through-sons-of through-Kadmiel Jeshua descendants-of

וְאַרְבָּעָה׃ הַמְשֹׁרְרִים בְּנֵי אָסָף מֵאָה אַרְבָּעִים וּשְׁמֹנָה׃
and-eight forty hundred Asaph descendants-of the-ones-singing (44) and-four

22 of Hashum 328
23 of Bezai 324
24 of Hariph 112
25 of Gibeon 95

26 the men of Bethlehem and Netophah 188
27 of Anathoth 128
28 of Beth Azmaveth 42
29 of Kiriath Jearim, Kephirah and Beeroth 743
30 of Ramah and Geba 621
31 of Micmash 122
32 of Bethel and Ai 123
33 of the other Nebo 52
34 of the other Elam 1,254
35 of Harim 320
36 of Jericho 345
37 of Lod, Hadid and Ono 721
38 of Senaah 3,930

39 The priests:

the descendants of Jedaiah (through the family of Jeshua) 973
40 of Immer 1,052
41 of Pashhur 1,247
42 of Harim 1,017

43 The Levites:

the descendants of Jeshua (through Kadmiel through the line of Hodaviah) 74

44 The singers:

the descendants of Asaph 148

(45) הַשֹּׁעֲרִים בְּנֵי־ שַׁלּוּם בְּנֵי־ אָטֵר
Ater descendants-of Shallum descendants-of the-gatekeepers (45)

בְּנֵי־ טַלְמֹן בְּנֵי־ עַקּוּב בְּנֵי חֲטִיטָא
Hatita descendants-of Akkub descendants-of Talmon descendants-of

בְּנֵי שֹׁבָי מֵאָה שְׁלֹשִׁים וּשְׁמֹנָה׃ (46) הַנְּתִינִים
the-temple-servants (46) and-eight thirty hundred Shobai descendants-of

בְּנֵי־ צִחָא בְּנֵי־ חֲשֻׂפָא בְּנֵי טַבָּעוֹת׃
Tabbaoth descendants-of Hasupha descendants-of Ziha descendants-of

(47) בְּנֵי־ קֵירֹס בְּנֵי־ סִיעָא בְּנֵי פָדוֹן׃
Padon descendants-of Sia descendants-of Keros descendants-of (47)

(48) בְּנֵי־ לְבָנָה בְנֵי־ חֲגָבָה בְּנֵי שַׁלְמָי׃
Shalmai descendants-of Hagaba descendants-of Lebana descendants-of (48)

(49) בְּנֵי־ חָנָן בְּנֵי־ גִדֵּל בְּנֵי־ גָחַר׃
Gaher descendants-of Giddel descendants-of Hanan descendants-of (49)

(50) בְּנֵי־ רְאָיָה בְנֵי־ רְצִין בְּנֵי נְקוֹדָא׃
Nekoda descendants-of Rezin descendants-of Reaiah descendants-of (50)

(51) בְּנֵי־ גַזָּם בְּנֵי־ עֻזָּא בְּנֵי פָסֵחַ׃
Paseah descendants-of Uzza descendants-of Gazzam descendants-of (51)

(52) בְּנֵי־ בֵסַי בְּנֵי־ מְעוּנִים בְּנֵי נְפוּשְׁסִים°׃
Nephussim descendants-of Meunim descendants-of Besai descendants-of (52)

(53) בְּנֵי־ בַקְבּוּק בְּנֵי־ חֲקוּפָא בְּנֵי חַרְחוּר׃
Harhur descendants-of Hakupha descendants-of Bakbuk descendants-of (53)

(54) בְּנֵי־ בַצְלִית בְּנֵי־ מְחִידָא בְּנֵי חַרְשָׁא׃
Harsha descendants-of Mehida descendants-of Bazluth descendants-of (54)

(55) בְּנֵי־ בַרְקוֹס בְּנֵי־ סִיסְרָא בְּנֵי־ תָמַח׃
Temah descendants-of Sisera descendants-of Barkos descendants-of (55)

(56) בְּנֵי נְצִיחַ בְּנֵי חֲטִיפָא׃ (57) בְּנֵי
descendants-of (57) Hatipha descendants-of Neziah descendants-of (56)

עַבְדֵי שְׁלֹמֹה בְּנֵי־ סוֹטַי בְּנֵי־ סוֹפֶרֶת
Sophereth descendants-of Sotai descendants-of Solomon servants-of

בְּנֵי פְרִידָא׃ (58) בְּנֵי־ יַעְלָא בְּנֵי־ דַרְקוֹן
Darkon descendants-of Jaala descendants-of (58) Perida descendants-of

בְּנֵי גִדֵּל׃ (59) בְּנֵי שְׁפַטְיָה בְּנֵי־ חַטִּיל
Hattil descendants-of Shephatiah descendants-of (59) Giddel descendants-of

בְּנֵי פֹּכֶרֶת הַצְּבָיִים בְּנֵי אָמוֹן׃ (60) כָּל־
total-of (60) Amon descendants-of Hazzebaim Pokereth descendants-of

הַנְּתִינִים וּבְנֵי עַבְדֵי שְׁלֹמֹה שְׁלֹשׁ מֵאוֹת
hundreds three-of Solomon servants-of and-descendants-of the-temple-servants

°52 ק נפישסים

[45]The gatekeepers:

the descendants of
Shallum, Ater,
Talmon, Akkub, Hatita
and Shobai 138

[46]The temple servants:

the descendants of
Ziha, Hasupha,
Tabbaoth,
[47]Keros, Sia, Padon,
[48]Lebana, Hagaba,
Shalmai,
[49]Hanan, Giddel, Gaher,
[50]Reaiah, Rezin,
Nekoda,
[51]Gazzam, Uzza, Paseah,
[52]Besai, Meunim,
Nephussim,
[53]Bakbuk, Hakupha,
Harhur,
[54]Bazluth, Mehida,
Harsha,
[55]Barkos, Sisera, Temah,
[56]Neziah and Hatipha

[57]The descendants of the servants of Solomon:

the descendants of
Sotai, Sophereth,
Perida,
[58]Jaala, Darkon, Giddel,
[59]Shephatiah, Hattil,
Pokereth-Hazzebaim
and Amon

[60]The temple servants and
the descendants of the
servants of Solomon
392

תִּשְׁעִים וּשְׁנָיִם׃ וְאֵלֶּה הָעוֹלִים מִתֵּל מֶלַח תֵּל חַרְשָׁא
Harsha Tel Melah from-Tel the-ones-coming-up and-these (61) and-two ninety

כְּרוּב אַדּוֹן וְאִמֵּר וְלֹא יָכְלוּ לְהַגִּיד בֵּית־ אֲבוֹתָם
fathers-of-them family-of to-show they-could but-not and-Immer Addon Kerub

וְזַרְעָם אִם מִיִּשְׂרָאֵל הֵם׃ בְּנֵי־ דְלָיָה
Delaiah descendants-of (62) they from-Israel whether and-descent-of-them

בְנֵי־ טוֹבִיָּה בְּנֵי נְקוֹדָא שֵׁשׁ מֵאוֹת וְאַרְבָּעִים
and-forty hundreds six-of Nekoda descendants-of Tobiah descendants-of

וּשְׁנָיִם׃ וּמִן־ הַכֹּהֲנִים בְּנֵי חֳבַיָּה בְּנֵי
descendants-of Hobaiah descendants-of the-priests and-from (63) and-two

הַקּוֹץ בְּנֵי בַרְזִלַּי אֲשֶׁר לָקַח מִבְּנוֹת בַּרְזִלַּי
Barzillai of-daughters-of he-married who Barzillai descendants-of Hakkoz

הַגִּלְעָדִי אִשָּׁה וַיִּקָּרֵא עַל־ שְׁמָם׃ אֵלֶּה בִּקְשׁוּ
they-searched these (64) name-of-them by and-he-was-called wife the-Gileadite

כְתָבָם הַמִּתְיַחְשִׂים וְלֹא נִמְצָא
he-was-found but-not the-ones-being-enrolled-by-family record-of-them

וַיְגֹאֲלוּ מִן־ הַכְּהֻנָּה׃ וַיֹּאמֶר
so-he-ordered (65) the-priesthood from so-they-were-excluded-as-unclean

הַתִּרְשָׁתָא לָהֶם אֲשֶׁר לֹא־ יֹאכְלוּ מִקֹּדֶשׁ
from-most-sacred-of they-could-eat not that to-them the-governor

הַקֳּדָשִׁים עַד עֲמֹד הַכֹּהֵן לְאוּרִים וְתוּמִּים׃
and-Thummim with-Urim the-priest to-minister until the-sacred-things

כָּל־ הַקָּהָל כְּאֶחָד אַרְבַּע רִבּוֹא אַלְפַּיִם שְׁלֹשׁ־
three-of two-thousands ten-thousand four-of as-one the-company whole-of (66)

מֵאוֹת וְשִׁשִּׁים׃ מִלְּבַד עַבְדֵיהֶם וְאַמְהֹתֵיהֶם
and-maidservants-of-them menservants-of-them from-besides (67) and-sixty hundreds

אֵלֶּה שִׁבְעַת אֲלָפִים שְׁלֹשׁ מֵאוֹת שְׁלֹשִׁים וְשִׁבְעָה וְלָהֶם
also-to-them and-seven thirty hundreds three-of thousands seven-of these

מְשֹׁרְרִים וּמְשֹׁרְרוֹת מָאתַיִם וְאַרְבָּעִים וַחֲמִשָּׁה׃ גְּמַלִּים
camels *(68) and-five and-forty two-hundreds and-women-singing men-singing

אַרְבַּע מֵאוֹת שְׁלֹשִׁים וַחֲמִשָּׁה חֲמֹרִים שֵׁשֶׁת אֲלָפִים שְׁבַע מֵאוֹת
hundreds seven-of thousands six-of donkeys and-five thirty hundreds four-of

וְעֶשְׂרִים׃ וּמִקְצָת רָאשֵׁי הָאָבוֹת נָתְנוּ
they-contributed the-fathers heads-of and-from-end-of (69) and-twenty

לַמְּלָאכָה הַתִּרְשָׁתָא נָתַן לָאוֹצָר זָהָב דַּרְכְּמֹנִים אֶלֶף
thousand drachmas gold to-the-treasury he-gave the-governor to-the-work

מִזְרָקוֹת חֲמִשִּׁים כָּתְנוֹת כֹּהֲנִים שְׁלֹשִׁים וַחֲמֵשׁ מֵאוֹת׃
hundreds and-five-of thirty priests garments-of fifty bowls

[61]The following came up from the towns of Tel Melah, Tel Harsha, Kerub, Addon and Immer, but they could not show that their families were descended from Israel:

[62]the descendants of
Delaiah, Tobiah and Nekoda 642

[63]And from among the priests:

the descendants of
Hobaiah, Hakkoz and Barzillai (a man who had married a daughter of Barzillai the Gileadite and was called by that name).

[64]These searched for their family records, but they could not find them and so were excluded from the priesthood as unclean. [65]The governor, therefore, ordered them not to eat any of the most sacred food until there should be a priest ministering with the Urim and Thummim.

[66]The whole company numbered 42,360, [67]besides their 7,337 menservants and maidservants; and they also had 245 men and women singers. [68]There were 736 horses, 245 mules,[p] [69]435 camels and 6,720 donkeys.

[70]Some of the heads of the families contributed to the work. The governor gave to the treasury 1,000 drachmas[q] of gold, 50 bowls and 530 garments for priests.

[p]68 Some Hebrew manuscripts (see also Ezra 2:66); most Hebrew manuscripts do not have this verse.
[q]70 That is, about 19 pounds (about 8.5 kilograms)

*68 Most mss do not have this verse; thus, there is a one-verse discrepancy through the rest of chapter 7.

וּמֵרָאשֵׁי הָאָבוֹת נָתְנוּ לְאוֹצַר הַמְּלָאכָה זָהָב
gold the-work to-treasury-of they-gave the-fathers and-from-heads-of (70)

דַּרְכְּמוֹנִים שְׁתֵּי רִבּוֹת וְכֶסֶף מָנִים אַלְפַּיִם וּמָאתָיִם׃
and-two-hundreds two-thousands minas and-silver ten-thousands two-of drachmas

וַאֲשֶׁר נָתְנוּ שְׁאֵרִית הָעָם זָהָב דַּרְכְּמוֹנִים שְׁתֵּי רִבּוֹא
ten-thousand two-of drachmas gold the-people rest-of they-gave and-what (71)

וְכֶסֶף מָנִים אַלְפָּיִם וְכָתְנֹת כֹּהֲנִים שִׁשִּׁים וְשִׁבְעָה׃
and-seven sixty priests and-garments-of two-thousands minas and-silver

וַיֵּשְׁבוּ הַכֹּהֲנִים וְהַלְוִיִּם וְהַשּׁוֹעֲרִים
and-the-gatekeepers and-the-Levites the-priests and-they-settled (72)

וְהַמְשֹׁרְרִים וּמִן־ הָעָם וְהַנְּתִינִים וְכָל־
and-all-of and-the-temple-servants the-people and-from and-the-ones-singing

יִשְׂרָאֵל בְּעָרֵיהֶם וַיִּגַּע הַחֹדֶשׁ הַשְּׁבִיעִי וּבְנֵי
and-sons-of the-seventh the-month when-he-came in-towns-of-them Israel

יִשְׂרָאֵל בְּעָרֵיהֶם׃ וַיֵּאָסְפוּ כָל־ הָעָם כְּאִישׁ
as-man the-people all-of and-they-assembled (8:1) in-towns-of-them Israel

אֶחָד אֶל־ הָרְחוֹב אֲשֶׁר לִפְנֵי שַׁעַר־ הַמָּיִם וַיֹּאמְרוּ לְעֶזְרָא
to-Ezra and-they-told the-Waters Gate-of before that the-square in one

הַסֹּפֵר לְהָבִיא אֶת־ סֵפֶר תּוֹרַת מֹשֶׁה אֲשֶׁר־ צִוָּה יְהוָה
Yahweh he-commanded which Moses Law-of Book-of *** to-bring-out the-scribe

אֶת־יִשְׂרָאֵל׃ וַיָּבִיא עֶזְרָא הַכֹּהֵן אֶת־ הַתּוֹרָה לִפְנֵי הַקָּהָל
the-assembly before the-Law *** the-priest Ezra so-he-brought (2) Israel ***

מֵאִישׁ וְעַד־ אִשָּׁה וְכֹל מֵבִין לִשְׁמֹעַ בְּיוֹם אֶחָד לַחֹדֶשׁ
of-the-month one on-day to-hear understanding and-all-of woman and-to from-man

הַשְּׁבִיעִי׃ וַיִּקְרָא־ בוֹ לִפְנֵי הָרְחוֹב אֲשֶׁר ׀ לִפְנֵי שַׁעַר־
Gate-of before that the-square facing from-him and-he-read (3) the-seventh

הַמַּיִם מִן־ הָאוֹר עַד־ מַחֲצִית הַיּוֹם נֶגֶד הָאֲנָשִׁים
the-men in-presence-of the-day noon-of till the-daybreak from the-Waters

וְהַנָּשִׁים וְהַמְּבִינִים וְאָזְנֵי כָל־ הָעָם אֶל־
to the-people all-of and-ears-of and-the-ones-understanding and-the-women

סֵפֶר הַתּוֹרָה׃ וַיַּעֲמֹד עֶזְרָא הַסֹּפֵר עַל־ מִגְדַּל־ עֵץ
wood high-platform-of on the-scribe Ezra and-he-stood (4) the-Law Book-of

אֲשֶׁר עָשׂוּ לַדָּבָר וַיַּעֲמֹד אֶצְלוֹ מַתִּתְיָה
Mattithiah beside-him and-he-stood for-the-occasion they-built that

וְשֶׁמַע וַעֲנָיָה וְאוּרִיָּה וְחִלְקִיָּה וּמַעֲשֵׂיָה עַל־ יְמִינוֹ
right-of-him on and-Maaseiah and-Hilkiah and-Uriah and-Anaiah and-Shema

וּמִשְּׂמֹאלוֹ פְּדָיָה וּמִישָׁאֵל וּמַלְכִּיָּה וְחָשֻׁם וְחַשְׁבַּדָּנָה
and-Hashbaddanah and-Hashum and-Malkijah and-Mishael Pedaiah and-on-left-of-him

71 Some of the heads of the families gave to the treasury for the work 20,000 drachmas[r] of gold and 2,200 minas[s] of silver.
72 The total given by the rest of the people was 20,000 drachmas of gold, 2,000 minas[t] of silver and 67 garments for priests.
73 The priests, the Levites, the gatekeepers, the singers and the temple servants, along with certain of the people and the rest of the Israelites, settled in their own towns.

*Ezra Reads the Law*

When the seventh month came and the Israelites had
8 settled in their towns, 1 all the people assembled as one man in the square before the Water Gate. They told Ezra the scribe to bring out the Book of the Law of Moses, which the LORD had commanded for Israel.
2 So on the first day of the seventh month Ezra the priest brought the Law before the assembly, which was made up of men and women and all who were able to understand.
3 He read it aloud from daybreak till noon as he faced the square before the Water Gate in the presence of the men, women and others who could understand. And all the people listened attentively to the Book of the Law.
4 Ezra the scribe stood on a high wooden platform built for the occasion. Beside him on his right stood Mattithiah, Shema, Anaiah, Uriah, Hilkiah and Maaseiah; and on his left were Pedaiah, Mishael,

[r] 71 That is, about 375 pounds (about 170 kilograms); also in verse 72
[s] 71 That is, about 1 1/3 tons (about 1.2 metric tons)
[t] 72 That is, about 1 1/4 tons (about 1.1 metric tons)

*See the note on page 235.

זְכַרְיָה מְשֻׁלָּם׃ (5) וַיִּפְתַּח עֶזְרָא הַסֵּפֶר לְעֵינֵי כָל־
all-of before-eyes-of the-book Ezra and-he-opened (5) Meshullam Zechariah

הָעָם כִּי־ מֵעַל כָּל־ הָעָם הָיָה וּכְפִתְחוֹ
and-as-to-open-him he-was the-people all-of at-above because the-people

עָמְדוּ כָל־ הָעָם׃ (6) וַיְבָרֶךְ עֶזְרָא אֶת־ יְהוָה הָאֱלֹהִים
the-God Yahweh *** Ezra and-he-praised (6) the-people all-of they-stood-up

הַגָּדוֹל וַיַּעֲנוּ כָל־ הָעָם אָמֵן | אָמֵן בְּמֹעַל
with-lifting-of amen amen the-people all-of and-they-responded the-great

יְדֵיהֶם וַיִּקְּדוּ וַיִּשְׁתַּחֲוֻּ* לַיהוָה אַפַּיִם אָרְצָה׃
to-ground faces to-Yahweh and-they-worshiped then-they-bowed hands-of-them

(7) וְיֵשׁוּעַ וּבָנִי וְשֵׁרֵבְיָה | יָמִין עַקּוּב שַׁבְּתַי | הוֹדִיָּה מַעֲשֵׂיָה
Maaseiah Hodiah Shabbethai Akkub Jamin and-Sherebiah and-Bani and-Jeshua (7)

קְלִיטָא עֲזַרְיָה יוֹזָבָד חָנָן פְּלָאיָה וְהַלְוִיִּם מְבִינִים אֶת־
*** ones-instructing namely-the-Levites Pelaiah Hanan Jozabad Azariah Kelita

הָעָם לַתּוֹרָה וְהָעָם עַל־ עָמְדָם׃
standing-place-of-them at while-the-people in-the-Law the-people

(8) וַיִּקְרְאוּ בַסֵּפֶר בְּתוֹרַת הָאֱלֹהִים מְפֹרָשׁ וְשׂוֹם
and-to-give making-clear the-God of-Law-of from-the-Book and-they-read (8)

שֶׂכֶל וַיָּבִינוּ בַּמִּקְרָא׃ (9) וַיֹּאמֶר נְחֶמְיָה
Nehemiah then-he-said (9) to-the-reading so-they-could-understand meaning

הוּא הַתִּרְשָׁתָא וְעֶזְרָא הַכֹּהֵן | הַסֹּפֵר וְהַלְוִיִּם
and-the-Levites the-scribe the-priest and-Ezra the-governor he

הַמְּבִינִים אֶת־ הָעָם לְכָל־ הָעָם הַיּוֹם קָדֹשׁ־ הוּא
this sacred the-day the-people to-all-of the-people *** the-ones-instructing

לַיהוָה אֱלֹהֵיכֶם אַל־ תִּתְאַבְּלוּ וְאַל־ תִּבְכּוּ כִּי בוֹכִים כָּל־
all-of ones-weeping for you-weep and-not you-mourn not God-of-you to-Yahweh

הָעָם כְּשָׁמְעָם אֶת־ דִּבְרֵי הַתּוֹרָה׃ (10) וַיֹּאמֶר לָהֶם
to-them and-he-said (10) the-Law words-of *** as-to-listen-them the-people

לְכוּ אִכְלוּ מַשְׁמַנִּים וּשְׁתוּ מַמְתַקִּים וְשִׁלְחוּ מָנוֹת לְאֵין
to-nothing portions and-send! sweet-things and-drink! choice-foods eat! go!

נָכוֹן לוֹ כִּי־ קָדוֹשׁ הַיּוֹם לַאֲדֹנֵינוּ וְאַל־ תֵּעָצֵבוּ
you-grieve and-not to-Lord-of-us the-day sacred for for-him being-prepared

כִּי־ חֶדְוַת יְהוָה הִיא מָעֻזְּכֶם׃ (11) וְהַלְוִיִּם מַחְשִׁים
ones-calming and-the-Levites (11) strength-of-you she Yahweh joy-of for

לְכָל־ הָעָם לֵאמֹר הַסּוּ כִּי הַיּוֹם קָדֹשׁ וְאַל־ תֵּעָצֵבוּ׃
you-grieve and-not sacred the-day for be-still! to-say the-people to-all-of

(12) וַיֵּלְכוּ כָל־ הָעָם לֶאֱכֹל וְלִשְׁתּוֹת וּלְשַׁלַּח
and-to-send and-to-drink to-eat the-people all-of then-they-went-away (12)

*6 Most mss have no *dagesh* in the *vav* and *shureq* in place of the *qibbuts* ( וּ— ).

Malkijah, Hashum, Hashbad-
danah, Zechariah and Me-
shullam.
5 Ezra opened the book. All
the people could see him because he was standing above
them; and as he opened it, the
people all stood up. 6 Ezra
praised the LORD, the great
God; and all the people lifted
their hands and responded,
"Amen! Amen!" Then they
bowed down and worshiped
the LORD with their faces to
the ground.
7 The Levites—Jeshua, Bani,
Sherebiah, Jamin, Akkub,
Shabbethai, Hodiah, Maa-
seiah, Kelita, Azariah, Jozabad, Hanan and Pelaiah—
instructed the people in the
Law while the people were
standing there. 8 They read
from the Book of the Law of
God, making it clear[v] and giving the meaning so that the
people could understand what
was being read.
9 Then Nehemiah the governor, Ezra the priest and scribe,
and the Levites who were in-
structing the people said to
them all, "This day is sacred to
the LORD your God. Do not
mourn or weep." For all the
people had been weeping as
they listened to the words of
the Law.
10 Nehemiah said, "Go and
enjoy choice food and sweet
drinks, and send some to
those who have nothing prepared. This day is sacred to our
Lord. Do not grieve, for the joy
of the LORD is your strength."
11 The Levites calmed all the
people, saying, "Be still, for
this is a sacred day. Do not
grieve."
12 Then all the people went
away to eat and drink, to send

[v] 8 Or *God, translating it*

מָנוֹת וּלַעֲשׂוֹת שִׂמְחָה גְדוֹלָה כִּי הֵבִינוּ בַּדְּבָרִים אֲשֶׁר
that to-the-words they-understood because great joy and-to-celebrate portions

הוֹדִיעוּ לָהֶם׃ וּבַיּוֹם הַשֵּׁנִי נֶאֶסְפוּ רָאשֵׁי
heads-of they-gathered the-second and-on-the-day (13) to-them they-made-known

הָאָבוֹת לְכָל־ הָעָם הַכֹּהֲנִים וְהַלְוִיִּם אֶל־ עֶזְרָא
Ezra around and-the-Levites the-priests the-people of-all-of the-fathers

הַסֹּפֵר וּלְהַשְׂכִּיל אֶל־ דִּבְרֵי הַתּוֹרָה׃ וַיִּמְצְאוּ
and-they-found (14) the-Law words-of to and-to-give-attention the-scribe

כָּתוּב בַּתּוֹרָה אֲשֶׁר צִוָּה יְהוָה בְּיַד־ מֹשֶׁה אֲשֶׁר
that Moses by-hand-of Yahweh he-commanded which in-the-Law being-written

יֵשְׁבוּ בְנֵי־ יִשְׂרָאֵל בַּסֻּכּוֹת בֶּחָג בַּחֹדֶשׁ
of-the-month during-the-feast in-the-booths Israel sons-of they-live

הַשְּׁבִיעִי׃ וַאֲשֶׁר יַשְׁמִיעוּ וְיַעֲבִירוּ קוֹל בְּכָל־
through-all-of word and-they-spread they-proclaim and-that (15) the-seventh

עָרֵיהֶם וּבִירוּשָׁלִַם לֵאמֹר צְאוּ הָהָר וְהָבִיאוּ
and-bring! the-hill-country go-out! to-say and-in-Jerusalem towns-of-them

עֲלֵי־ זַיִת וַעֲלֵי־ עֵץ שֶׁמֶן וַעֲלֵי הֲדַס
myrtle and-branches-of wild-olive tree-of and-branches-of olive branches-of

וַעֲלֵי תְמָרִים וַעֲלֵי עֵץ עָבֹת לַעֲשֹׂת סֻכֹּת
booths to-make shade tree-of and-branches-of palms and-branches-of

כַּכָּתוּב׃ וַיֵּצְאוּ הָעָם וַיָּבִיאוּ
and-they-brought the-people so-they-went-out (16) as-the-thing-being-written

וַיַּעֲשׂוּ לָהֶם סֻכּוֹת אִישׁ עַל־ גַּגּוֹ וּבְחַצְרֹתֵיהֶם
and-in-courtyards-of-them roof-of-him on each booths for-them and-they-built

וּבְחַצְרוֹת בֵּית הָאֱלֹהִים וּבִרְחוֹב שַׁעַר הַמַּיִם
the-Waters Gate-of and-in-square-of the-God house-of and-in-courts-of

וּבִרְחוֹב שַׁעַר אֶפְרָיִם׃ וַיַּעֲשׂוּ כָל־ הַקָּהָל
the-company whole-of and-they-built (17) Ephraim Gate-of and-in-square-of

הַשָּׁבִים מִן־ הַשְּׁבִי ׀ סֻכּוֹת וַיֵּשְׁבוּ בַסֻּכּוֹת כִּי
indeed in-the-booths and-they-lived booths the-exile from the-ones-returning

לֹא־ עָשׂוּ מִימֵי יֵשׁוּעַ בִּן־ נוּן כֵּן בְּנֵי יִשְׂרָאֵל עַד
until Israel sons-of thus Nun son-of Joshua from-days-of they-celebrated not

הַיּוֹם הַהוּא וַתְּהִי שִׂמְחָה גְּדוֹלָה מְאֹד׃ וַיִּקְרָא בְּסֵפֶר
from-Book-of and-he-read (18) very great joy and-she-was the-that the-day

תּוֹרַת הָאֱלֹהִים יוֹם ׀ בְּיוֹם מִן־ הַיּוֹם הָרִאשׁוֹן עַד הַיּוֹם הָאַחֲרוֹן
the-last the-day to the-first the-day from after-day day the-God Law-of

וַיַּעֲשׂוּ־ חָג שִׁבְעַת יָמִים וּבַיּוֹם הַשְּׁמִינִי עֲצֶרֶת
assembly the-eighth and-on-the-day days seven-of feast and-they-celebrated

portions of food and to celebrate with great joy, because they now understood the words that had been made known to them.

13On the second day of the month, the heads of all the families, along with the priests and the Levites, gathered around Ezra the scribe to give attention to the words of
the Law. 14They found written in the Law, which the LORD had commanded through Moses, that the Israelites were to live in booths during the feast of the seventh month
15and that they should proclaim this word and spread it throughout their towns and in Jerusalem: "Go out into the hill country and bring back branches from olive and wild olive trees, and from myrtles, palms and shade trees, to make booths"—as it is written.[w]

16So the people went out and brought back branches and built themselves booths on their own roofs, in their courtyards, in the courts of the house of God and in the square by the Water Gate and the one by the Gate of
Ephraim. 17The whole company that had returned from exile built booths and lived in them. From the days of Joshua son of Nun until that day, the Israelites had not celebrated it like this. And their joy was very great.

18Day after day, from the first day to the last, Ezra read from the Book of the Law of God. They celebrated the feast for seven days, and on the eighth day, in accordance

[w]15 See Lev. 23:37-40.

כַּמִּשְׁפָּט׃ (9:1) וּבְיוֹם עֶשְׂרִים וְאַרְבָּעָה לַחֹדֶשׁ הַזֶּה
the-same of-the-month and-four twenty and-on-day-of (9:1) as-the-regulation

נֶאֶסְפוּ בְנֵי־ יִשְׂרָאֵל בְּצוֹם וּבְשַׂקִּים וַאֲדָמָה
and-dust and-with-sackcloths with-fasting Israel sons-of they-gathered

עֲלֵיהֶם׃ (2) וַיִּבָּדְלוּ זֶרַע יִשְׂרָאֵל מִכֹּל
from-all-of Israel descendant-of and-they-separated-themselves (2) on-them

בְּנֵי נֵכָר וַיַּעַמְדוּ וַיִּתְוַדּוּ עַל־ חַטֹּאתֵיהֶם
sins-of-them to and-they-confessed and-they-stood foreigner sons-of

וַעֲוֹנוֹת אֲבֹתֵיהֶם׃ (3) וַיָּקוּמוּ עַל־ עָמְדָם
place-of-them at and-they-stood (3) fathers-of-them and-wickednesses-of

וַיִּקְרְאוּ בְּסֵפֶר תּוֹרַת יְהוָה אֱלֹהֵיהֶם רְבִעִית הַיּוֹם
the-day fourth-of God-of-them Yahweh Law-of from-Book-of and-they-read

וּרְבִעִית מִתְוַדִּים וּמִשְׁתַּחֲוִים לַיהוָה אֱלֹהֵיהֶם׃
God-of-them to-Yahweh and-ones-worshiping ones-confessing and-fourth

(4) וַיָּקָם עַל־ מַעֲלֵה הַלְוִיִּם יֵשׁוּעַ וּבָנִי קַדְמִיאֵל
and-Kadmiel and-Bani Jeshua the-Levites stair-of on and-he-stood (4)

שְׁבַנְיָה בֻּנִּי שֵׁרֵבְיָה בָּנִי כְנָנִי וַיִּזְעֲקוּ בְּקוֹל גָּדוֹל אֶל־
to loud with-voice and-they-called Kenani Bani Sherebiah Bunni Shebaniah

יְהוָה אֱלֹהֵיהֶם׃ (5) וַיֹּאמְרוּ הַלְוִיִּם יֵשׁוּעַ וְקַדְמִיאֵל בָּנִי
Bani and-Kadmiel Jeshua the-Levites and-they-said (5) God-of-them Yahweh

חֲשַׁבְנְיָה שֵׁרֵבְיָה הוֹדִיָּה שְׁבַנְיָה פְתַחְיָה קוּמוּ בָּרְכוּ אֶת־
*** praise! stand-up! Pethahiah Shebaniah Hodiah Sherebiah Hashabneiah

יְהוָה אֱלֹהֵיכֶם מִן־ הָעוֹלָם עַד־ הָעוֹלָם וִיבָרְכוּ
and-may-they-bless the-everlasting to the-everlasting from God-of-you Yahweh

שֵׁם כְּבֹדֶךָ וּמְרוֹמַם עַל־ כָּל־ בְּרָכָה וּתְהִלָּה׃
and-praise blessing all-of above and-being-exalted glory-of-you name-of

(6) אַתָּה־הוּא יְהוָה לְבַדֶּךָ אַתָּ° עָשִׂיתָ אֶת־ הַשָּׁמַיִם שְׁמֵי
heavens-of the-heavens *** you-made you by-yourself Yahweh he you (6)

הַשָּׁמַיִם וְכָל־ צְבָאָם הָאָרֶץ וְכָל־ אֲשֶׁר עָלֶיהָ הַיַּמִּים
the-seas on-her that and-all-of the-earth host-of-them and-all-of the-heavens

וְכָל־ אֲשֶׁר בָּהֶם וְאַתָּה מְחַיֶּה אֶת־ כֻּלָּם וּצְבָא
and-multitude-of all-of-them *** giving-life and-you in-them that and-all-of

הַשָּׁמַיִם לְךָ מִשְׁתַּחֲוִים׃ (7) אַתָּה־הוּא יְהוָה הָאֱלֹהִים אֲשֶׁר בָּחַרְתָּ
you-chose who the-God Yahweh he you (7) ones-worshiping to-you the-heavens

בְּאַבְרָם וְהוֹצֵאתוֹ מֵאוּר כַּשְׂדִּים וְשַׂמְתָּ שְּׁמוֹ
name-of-him and-you-made Chaldeans from-Ur-of and-you-brought-him to-Abram

אַבְרָהָם׃ (8) וּמָצָאתָ אֶת־ לְבָבוֹ נֶאֱמָן לְפָנֶיךָ וְכָרוֹת
and-to-make to-you being-faithful heart-of-him *** and-you-found (8) Abraham

°6 ק אתה

with the regulation, there was an assembly.

*The Israelites Confess Their Sins*

9 On the twenty-fourth day of the same month, the Israelites gathered together, fasting and wearing sackcloth and having dust on their heads. 2Those of Israelite descent had separated themselves from all foreigners. They stood in their places and confessed their sins and the wickedness of their fathers. 3They stood where they were and read from the Book of the Law of the LORD their God for a fourth of the day, and spent another fourth in confession and in worshiping the LORD their God. 4Standing on the stairs were the Levites—Jeshua, Bani, Kadmiel, Shebaniah, Bunni, Sherebiah, Bani and Kenani—who called with loud voices to the LORD their God. 5And the Levites—Jeshua, Kadmiel, Bani, Hashabneiah, Sherebiah, Hodiah, Shebaniah and Pethahiah—said: "Stand up and praise the LORD your God, who is from everlasting to everlasting.[x]"

"Blessed be your glorious name, and may it be exalted above all blessing and praise. 6You alone are the LORD. You made the heavens, even the highest heavens, and all their starry host, the earth and all that is on it, the seas and all that is in them. You give life to everything, and the multitudes of heaven worship you.

7"You are the LORD God, who chose Abram and brought him out of Ur of the Chaldeans and named him Abraham. 8You found his heart faithful to you, and you made a covenant

x5 Or *God for ever and ever*

עִמּוֹ הַבְּרִית לָתֵת אֶת־ אֶרֶץ הַכְּנַעֲנִי הַחִתִּי

the-Hittite the-Canaanite land-of *** to-give the-covenant with-him

הָאֱמֹרִי וְהַפְּרִזִּי וְהַיְבוּסִי וְהַגִּרְגָּשִׁי לָתֵת

to-give and-the-Girgashite and-the-Jebusite and-the-Perizzite the-Amorite

לְזַרְעוֹ וַתָּקֶם אֶת־ דְּבָרֶיךָ כִּי צַדִּיק אָתָּה׃

you righteous because promises-of-you *** and-you-kept to-descendant-of-him

(9) וַתֵּרֶא אֶת־ עֳנִי אֲבֹתֵינוּ בְּמִצְרָיִם וְאֶת־ זַעֲקָתָם

cry-of-them and in-Egypt fathers-of-us suffering-of *** and-you-saw (9)

שָׁמַעְתָּ עַל־ יַם־ סוּף׃ (10) וַתִּתֵּן אֹתֹת וּמֹפְתִים בְּפַרְעֹה

against-Pharaoh and-wonders signs and-you-sent (10) Reed Sea-of at you-heard

וּבְכָל־ עֲבָדָיו וּבְכָל־ עַם אַרְצוֹ

land-of-him people-of and-against-all-of officials-of-him and-against-all-of

כִּי יָדַעְתָּ כִּי הֵזִידוּ עֲלֵיהֶם וַתַּעַשׂ־ לְךָ שֵׁם

name for-you and-you-made to-them they-treated-arrogantly how you-knew for

כְּהַיּוֹם הַזֶּה׃ (11) וְהַיָּם בָּקַעְתָּ לִפְנֵיהֶם וַיַּעַבְרוּ

so-they-passed before-them you-divided and-the-sea (11) the-this to-the-day

בְתוֹךְ־ הַיָּם בַּיַּבָּשָׁה וְאֶת־ רֹדְפֵיהֶם הִשְׁלַכְתָּ

you-hurled ones-pursuing-them but on-the-dry-ground the-sea through-midst-of

בִמְצוֹלֹת כְּמוֹ־ אֶבֶן בְּמַיִם עַזִּים׃ (12) וּבְעַמּוּד עָנָן

cloud and-with-pillar-of (12) mighty-ones into-waters stone like into-depths

הִנְחִיתָם יוֹמָם וּבְעַמּוּד אֵשׁ לַיְלָה לְהָאִיר לָהֶם

to-them to-give-light night fire and-with-pillar-of by-day you-led-them

אֶת־הַדֶּרֶךְ אֲשֶׁר יֵלְכוּ־ בָהּ׃ (13) וְעַל הַר־ סִינַי יָרַדְתָּ

you-came-down Sinai Mount-of and-on (13) on-her they-walked which the-way ***

וְדַבֵּר עִמָּהֶם מִשָּׁמָיִם וַתִּתֵּן לָהֶם מִשְׁפָּטִים יְשָׁרִים

just-ones regulations to-them and-you-gave from-heavens to-them and-to-speak

וְתוֹרוֹת אֱמֶת חֻקִּים וּמִצְוֹת טוֹבִים׃ (14) וְאֶת־ שַׁבַּת

Sabbath-of and (14) good-ones and-commands decrees right and-laws-of

קָדְשְׁךָ הוֹדַעְתָּ* לָהֶם וּמִצְווֹת וְחֻקִּים וְתוֹרָה

and-law and-decrees and-commands to-them you-made-known holiness-of-you

צִוִּיתָ לָהֶם בְּיַד מֹשֶׁה עַבְדֶּךָ׃ (15) וְלֶחֶם מִשָּׁמַיִם

from-heavens and-bread (15) servant-of-you Moses by-hand-of to-them you-gave

נָתַתָּה לָהֶם לִרְעָבָם וּמַיִם מִסֶּלַע הוֹצֵאתָ לָהֶם

to-them you-brought from-rock and-waters in-hunger-of-them to-them you-gave

לִצְמָאָם וַתֹּאמֶר לָהֶם לָבוֹא לָרֶשֶׁת אֶת־ הָאָרֶץ אֲשֶׁר־

that the-land *** to-possess to-go-in to-them and-you-told in-thirst-of-them

נָשָׂאתָ אֶת־ יָדְךָ לָתֵת לָהֶם׃ (16) וְהֵם וַאֲבֹתֵינוּ

indeed-fathers-of-us but-they (16) to-them to-give hand-of-you *** you-lifted

with him to give to his descendants the land of the Canaanites, Hittites, Amorites, Perizzites, Jebusites and Girgashites. You have kept your promise because you are righteous.
9"You saw the suffering of our forefathers in Egypt; you heard their cry at the Red Sea.[a]
10You sent miraculous signs and wonders against Pharaoh, against all his officials and all the people of his land, for you knew how arrogantly the Egyptians treated them. You made a name for yourself, which remains to this day.
11You divided the sea before them, so that they passed through it on dry ground, but you hurled their pursuers into the depths, like a stone into mighty waters.
12By day you led them with a pillar of cloud, and by night with a pillar of fire to give them light on the way they were to take.
13"You came down on Mount Sinai; you spoke to them from heaven. You gave them regulations and laws that are just and right, and decrees and commands that are good.
14You made known to them your holy Sabbath and gave them commands, decrees and laws through your servant Moses.
15In their hunger you gave them bread from heaven and in their thirst you brought them water from the rock; you told them to go in and take possession of the land you had sworn with uplifted hand to give them.
16"But they, our forefathers, became arrogant and

[a]9 Hebrew *Yam Suph;* that is, Sea of Reeds

*14 Most mss have *sheva* under the *ayin* and *dagesh* in the *tav* ( עְתָּ— ).

הֵזִידוּ וַיַּקְשׁוּ אֶת־ עָרְפָּם וְלֹא

and-not neck-of-them *** and-they-made-stiff they-became-arrogant

שָׁמְעוּ אֶל־ מִצְוֺתֶיךָ׃ וַיְמָאֲנוּ לִשְׁמֹעַ וְלֹא־

and-not to-listen and-they-refused (17) commands-of-you to they-obeyed

זָכְרוּ נִפְלְאֹתֶיךָ אֲשֶׁר עָשִׂיתָ עִמָּהֶם

among-them you-performed that ones-being-miracles-of-you they-remembered

וַיַּקְשׁוּ אֶת־ עָרְפָּם וַיִּתְּנוּ־ רֹאשׁ לָשׁוּב

to-return leader and-they-appointed neck-of-them *** and-they-made-stiff

לְעַבְדֻתָם בְּמִרְיָם וְאַתָּה אֱלוֹהַּ סְלִיחוֹת חַנּוּן

gracious forgivings God-of but-you in-rebellion-of-them to-slavery-of-them

וְרַחוּם אֶרֶךְ־ אַפַּיִם וְרַב־ וחֶסֶד וְלֹא עֲזַבְתָּם׃

you-deserted-them so-not love and-abundant-of angers slow-of and-compassionate

אַף כִּי־ עָשׂוּ לָהֶם עֵגֶל מַסֵּכָה וַיֹּאמְרוּ זֶה אֱלֹהֶיךָ

god-of-you this and-they-said image calf-of for-them they-cast when even (18)

אֲשֶׁר הֶעֶלְךָ מִמִּצְרָיִם וַיַּעֲשׂוּ נֶאָצוֹת גְּדֹלוֹת׃

awful-ones blasphemies or-they-committed from-Egypt he-brought-up-you who

וְאַתָּה בְּרַחֲמֶיךָ הָרַבִּים לֹא עֲזַבְתָּם

you-abandoned-them not the-great-ones because-of-compassions-of-you and-you (19)

בַּמִּדְבָּר אֶת־ עַמּוּד הֶעָנָן לֹא־ סָר מֵעֲלֵיהֶם

from-before-them he-ceased not the-cloud pillar-of *** in-the-desert

בְּיוֹמָם לְהַנְחֹתָם בְּהַדֶּרֶךְ וְאֶת־ עַמּוּד הָאֵשׁ בְּלַיְלָה לְהָאִיר

to-shine by-night the-fire pillar-of nor on-the-path to-guide-them at-by-day

לָהֶם וְאֶת ־הַדֶּרֶךְ אֲשֶׁר יֵלְכוּ־ בָהּ׃ וְרוּחֲךָ הַטּוֹבָה

the-good and-Spirit-of-you (20) on-her they-walked that the-way and on-them

נָתַתָּ לְהַשְׂכִּילָם וּמַנְךָ לֹא־ מָנַעְתָּ מִפִּיהֶם

from-mouth-of-them you-withheld not and-manna-of-you to-instruct-them you-gave

וּמַיִם נָתַתָּה לָהֶם לִצְמָאָם׃ וְאַרְבָּעִים שָׁנָה

year and-forty (21) for-thirst-of-them to-them you-gave and-waters

כִּלְכַּלְתָּם בַּמִּדְבָּר לֹא חָסֵרוּ שַׂלְמֹתֵיהֶם לֹא

not clothes-of-them they-lacked nothing in-the-desert you-sustained-them

בָלוּ וְרַגְלֵיהֶם לֹא בָצֵקוּ׃ וַתִּתֵּן

and-you-gave (22) they-became-swollen not and-feet-of-them they-wore-out

לָהֶם מַמְלָכוֹת וַעֲמָמִים וַתַּחְלְקֵם לְפֵאָה

for-remote-frontier and-you-allotted-them and-nations kingdoms to-them

וַיִּירְשׁוּ אֶת־ אֶרֶץ סִיחוֹן וְאֶת־ אֶרֶץ מֶלֶךְ חֶשְׁבּוֹן וְאֶת־

and Heshbon king-of country-of namely Sihon country-of *** and-they-took-over

אֶרֶץ עוֹג מֶלֶךְ־ הַבָּשָׁן׃ וּבְנֵיהֶם הִרְבִּיתָ

you-made-numerous and-sons-of-them (23) the-Bashan king-of Og country-of

stiff-necked, and did not obey your commands.
17They refused to listen and failed to remember the miracles you performed among them. They became stiff-necked and in their rebellion appointed a leader in order to return to their slavery. But you are a forgiving God, gracious and compassionate, slow to anger and abounding in love. Therefore you did not desert them, 18even when they cast for themselves an image of a calf and said, 'This is your god, who brought you up out of Egypt,' or when they committed awful blasphemies.
19"Because of your great compassion you did not abandon them in the desert. By day the pillar of cloud did not cease to guide them on their path, nor the pillar of fire by night to shine on the way they were to take. 20You gave your good Spirit to instruct them. You did not withhold your manna from their mouths, and you gave them water for their thirst. 21For forty years you sustained them in the desert; they lacked nothing, their clothes did not wear out nor did their feet become swollen.
22"You gave them kingdoms and nations, allotting to them even the remotest frontiers. They took over the country of Sihon[b] king of Heshbon and the country of Og king of Bashan. 23You made their sons as

[b]22 One Hebrew manuscript and Septuagint; most Hebrew manuscripts *Sihon, that is, the country of the*

°17 ק חסד

כְּכֹכְבֵי הַשָּׁמָיִם וַתְּבִיאֵם אֶל־ הָאָרֶץ אֲשֶׁר־ אָמַרְתָּ
you-told that the-land into and-you-brought-them the-skies as-stars-of

לַאֲבֹתֵיהֶם לָבוֹא לָרָשֶׁת׃ וַיָּבֹאוּ הַבָּנִים
the-sons and-they-went-in (24) to-possess to-enter to-fathers-of-them

וַיִּירְשׁוּ אֶת־ הָאָרֶץ וַתַּכְנַע לִפְנֵיהֶם אֶת־ יֹשְׁבֵי
ones-living-of *** before-them and-you-subdued the-land *** and-they-possessed

הָאָרֶץ הַכְּנַעֲנִים וַתִּתְּנֵם בְּיָדָם וְאֶת־ מַלְכֵיהֶם
kings-of-them and into-hand-of-them and-you-gave-them the-Canaanites the-land

וְאֶת־ עַמְמֵי הָאָרֶץ לַעֲשׂוֹת בָּהֶם כִּרְצוֹנָם׃
as-pleasure-of-them with-them to-deal the-land peoples-of and

וַיִּלְכְּדוּ עָרִים בְּצֻרוֹת וַאֲדָמָה שְׁמֵנָה
fertile and-land ones-being-fortified cities and-they-captured (25)

וַיִּירְשׁוּ בָּתִּים מְלֵאִים־ כָּל־ טוּב בֹּרוֹת חֲצוּבִים
ones-being-dug wells good all-of ones-filled houses and-they-possessed

כְּרָמִים וְזֵיתִים וְעֵץ מַאֲכָל לָרֹב וַיֹּאכְלוּ
and-they-ate in-abundance fruit and-tree-of and-olive-groves vineyards

וַיִּשְׂבְּעוּ וַיַּשְׁמִינוּ וַיִּתְעַדְּנוּ
and-they-reveled and-they-were-well-nourished and-they-were-full

בְּטוּבְךָ הַגָּדוֹל׃ וַיַּמְרוּ וַיִּמְרְדוּ
and-they-rebelled but-they-were-disobedient (26) the-great in-goodness-of-you

בָּךְ וַיַּשְׁלִכוּ אֶת־ תּוֹרָתְךָ אַחֲרֵי גַוָּם וְאֶת־
and back-of-them behind law-of-you *** and-they-put against-you

נְבִיאֶיךָ הָרָגוּ אֲשֶׁר־ הֵעִידוּ בָם לַהֲשִׁיבָם
to-turn-back-them to-them they-admonished who they-killed prophets-of-you

אֵלֶיךָ וַיַּעֲשׂוּ נֶאָצוֹת גְּדוֹלֹת׃ וַתִּתְּנֵם
so-you-gave-them (27) awful-ones blasphemies and-they-committed to-you

בְּיַד צָרֵיהֶם וַיָּצֵרוּ לָהֶם וּבְעֵת
but-at-time-of to-them and-they-oppressed enemies-of-them into-hand-of

צָרָתָם יִצְעֲקוּ אֵלֶיךָ וְאַתָּה מִשָּׁמַיִם תִּשְׁמָע
you-heard from-heavens and-you to-you they-cried-out oppression-of-them

וּכְרַחֲמֶיךָ הָרַבִּים תִּתֵּן לָהֶם מוֹשִׁיעִים
ones-delivering to-them you-gave the-great-ones and-in-compassions-of-you

וְיוֹשִׁיעוּם מִיַּד צָרֵיהֶם׃ וּכְנוֹחַ
but-as-to-be-rest (28) enemies-of-them from-hand-of and-they-rescued-them

לָהֶם יָשׁוּבוּ לַעֲשׂוֹת רַע לְפָנֶיךָ וַתַּעַזְבֵם
then-you-abandoned-them before-you evil to-do they-did-again to-them

בְּיַד אֹיְבֵיהֶם וַיִּרְדּוּ בָהֶם
over-them so-they-ruled ones-being-enemies-of-them into-hand-of

numerous as the stars in the sky, and you brought them into the land that you told their fathers to enter and possess. [24]Their sons went in and took possession of the land. You subdued before them the Canaanites, who lived in the land; you handed the Canaanites over to them, along with their kings and the peoples of the land, to deal with them as they pleased. [25]They captured fortified cities and fertile land; they took possession of houses filled with all kinds of good things, wells already dug, vineyards, olive groves and fruit trees in abundance. They ate to the full and were well-nourished; they reveled in your great goodness.

[26]"But they were disobedient and rebelled against you; they put your law behind their backs. They killed your prophets, who had admonished them in order to turn them back to you; they committed awful blasphemies. [27]So you handed them over to their enemies, who oppressed them. But when they were oppressed they cried out to you. From heaven you heard them, and in your great compassion you gave them deliverers, who rescued them from the hand of their enemies.

[28]"But as soon as they were at rest, they again did what was evil in your sight. Then you abandoned them to the hand of their enemies so that they ruled over

וַיָּשׁוּבוּ וַיִּזְעָקוּךָ וְאַתָּה מִשָּׁמַיִם תִּשְׁמַע
you-heard from-heavens then-you and-they-cried-out-to-you when-they-did-again

וְתַצִּילֵם כְּרַחֲמֶיךָ רַבּוֹת עִתִּים׃ וַתָּעַד
and-you-warned (29) times many-of in-compassions-of-you and-you-delivered-them

בָּהֶם לַהֲשִׁיבָם אֶל־ תּוֹרָתֶךָ וְהֵמָּה הֵזִידוּ וְלֹא־
and-not they-became-arrogant but-they law-of-you to to-return-them to-them

שָׁמְעוּ לְמִצְוֹתֶיךָ וּבְמִשְׁפָּטֶיךָ חָטְאוּ־
they-sinned and-against-ordinances-of-you to-commands-of-you they-obeyed

בָם אֲשֶׁר־ יַעֲשֶׂה אָדָם וְחָיָה בָהֶם וַיִּתְּנוּ
and-they-turned by-them then-he-will-live man he-obeys which against-them

כָתֵף סוֹרֶרֶת וְעָרְפָּם הִקְשׁוּ וְלֹא שָׁמֵעוּ׃
they-listened and-not they-made-stiff and-neck-of-them being-stubborn back

וַתִּמְשֹׁךְ עֲלֵיהֶם שָׁנִים רַבּוֹת וַתָּעַד בָּם
to-them and-you-admonished many years with-them and-you-were-patient (30)

בְּרוּחֲךָ בְּיַד־ נְבִיאֶיךָ וְלֹא הֶאֱזִינוּ
they-paid-attention yet-not prophets-of-you by-hand-of by-Spirit-of-you

וַתִּתְּנֵם בְּיַד עַמֵּי הָאֲרָצֹת׃ וּבְרַחֲמֶיךָ
but-in-mercies-of-you (31) the-lands peoples-of into-hand-of so-you-gave-them

הָרַבִּים לֹא־ עֲשִׂיתָם כָּלָה וְלֹא עֲזַבְתָּם כִּי אֵל־
God-of for you-abandoned-them and-not end you-put-them not the-great-ones

חַנּוּן וְרַחוּם אָתָּה׃ וְעַתָּה אֱלֹהֵינוּ הָאֵל הַגָּדוֹל הַגִּבּוֹר
the-mighty the-great the-God God-of-us so-now (32) you and-mercy grace

וְהַנּוֹרָא שׁוֹמֵר הַבְּרִית וְהַחֶסֶד אַל־
not and-the-love the-covenant keeping and-the-one-being-awesome

יִמְעַט לְפָנֶיךָ אֵת כָּל־ הַתְּלָאָה אֲשֶׁר־
that the-hardship all-of *** before-you let-him-seem-trifling

מְצָאַתְנוּ לִמְלָכֵינוּ לְשָׂרֵינוּ וּלְכֹהֲנֵינוּ
and-upon-priests-of-us upon-leaders-of-us upon-kings-of-us she-came-upon-us

וְלִנְבִיאֵנוּ וְלַאֲבֹתֵינוּ וּלְכָל־ עַמֶּךָ
people-of-you and-upon-all-of and-upon-fathers-of-us and-upon-prophets-of-us

מִימֵי מַלְכֵי אַשּׁוּר עַד הַיּוֹם הַזֶּה׃ וְאַתָּה צַדִּיק עַל
in just and-you (33) the-this the-day until Assyria kings-of from-days-of

כָּל־ הַבָּא עָלֵינוּ כִּי־ אֱמֶת עָשִׂיתָ וַאֲנַחְנוּ הִרְשָׁעְנוּ׃
we-did-wrong while-we you-acted faithfully for to-us the-thing-happening all-of

וְאֶת־ מְלָכֵינוּ שָׂרֵינוּ כֹּהֲנֵינוּ וַאֲבֹתֵינוּ לֹא
not and-fathers-of-us priests-of-us leaders-of-us kings-of-us and (34)

עָשׂוּ תּוֹרָתֶךָ וְלֹא הִקְשִׁיבוּ אֶל־ מִצְוֹתֶיךָ
commands-of-you to they-paid-attention and-not law-of-you they-followed

them. And when they cried
out to you again, you heard
from heaven, and in your
compassion you delivered
them time after time.
29"You warned them to
return to your law, but they
became arrogant and dis-
obeyed your commands.
They sinned against your
ordinances, by which a
man will live if he obeys
them. Stubbornly they
turned their backs on you,
became stiff-necked and
refused to listen. 30For
many years you were pa-
tient with them. By your
Spirit you admonished
them through your proph-
ets. Yet they paid no attention, so you handed them
over to the neighboring
peoples. 31But in your great
mercy you did not put an
end to them or abandon
them, for you are a gracious
and merciful God.
32"Now therefore, O our
God, the great, mighty and
awesome God, who keeps
his covenant of love, do not
let all this hardship seem
trifling in your eyes—the
hardship that has come
upon us, upon our kings
and leaders, upon our
priests and prophets, upon
our fathers and all your
people, from the days of the
kings of Assyria until today. 33In all that has happened to us, you have been
just; you have acted faithfully, while we did wrong.
34Our kings, our leaders,
our priests and our fathers
did not follow your law;
they did not pay attention
to your commands or the

וּלְעֵדְוֹתֶיךָ אֲשֶׁר הַעִידֹתָ בָּהֶם׃ וְהֵם בְּמַלְכוּתָם
in-kingdom-of-them while-they (35) to-them you-gave that or-to-warnings-of-you

וּבְטוּבְךָ הָרָב אֲשֶׁר־ נָתַתָּ לָהֶם וּבְאֶרֶץ
and-in-land-of to-them you-gave that the-great and-in-goodness-of-you

הָרְחָבָה וְהַשְּׁמֵנָה אֲשֶׁר־ נָתַתָּ לִפְנֵיהֶם לֹא עֲבָדוּךָ
they-served-you not to-them you-gave that and-the-fertile the-spacious

וְלֹא־ שָׁבוּ מִמַּעַלְלֵיהֶם הָרָעִים׃ הִנֵּה אֲנַחְנוּ הַיּוֹם
the-day we see! (36) the-evil-ones from-ways-of-them they-turned and-not

עֲבָדִים וְהָאָרֶץ אֲשֶׁר־ נָתַתָּה לַאֲבֹתֵינוּ לֶאֱכֹל אֶת־ פִּרְיָהּ
fruit-of-her *** to-eat to-forefathers-of-us you-gave that and-the-land slaves

וְאֶת־ טוּבָהּ הִנֵּה אֲנַחְנוּ עֲבָדִים עָלֶיהָ׃ וּתְבוּאָתָהּ מַרְבָּה
being-abundant and-harvest-of-her (37) in-her slaves we see! good-of-her and

לַמְּלָכִים אֲשֶׁר־ נָתַתָּה עָלֵינוּ בְּחַטֹּאותֵינוּ וְעַל
and-over because-of-sins-of-us over-us you-placed whom to-the-kings

גְּוִיֹּתֵינוּ מֹשְׁלִים וּבִבְהֶמְתֵּנוּ כִּרְצוֹנָם
as-pleasure-of-them and-over-cattle-of-us ones-ruling bodies-of-us

וּבְצָרָה גְדוֹלָה אֲנָחְנוּ׃ וּבְכָל־ זֹאת אֲנַחְנוּ
we this and-because-of-all-of *(10:1) we great and-in-distress

כֹּרְתִים אֲמָנָה וְכֹתְבִים וְעַל הֶחָתוּם
the-one-being-sealed and-to and-ones-writing binding ones-making-agreement

שָׂרֵינוּ לְוִיֵּנוּ כֹּהֲנֵינוּ׃ וְעַל הַחֲתוּמִים
the-ones-being-sealed and-to (2) priests-of-us Levites-of-us leaders-of-us

נְחֶמְיָה הַתִּרְשָׁתָא בֶּן־ חֲכַלְיָה וְצִדְקִיָּה׃ שְׂרָיָה עֲזַרְיָה
Azariah Seraiah (3) and-Zedekiah Hacaliah son-of the-governor Nehemiah

יִרְמְיָה׃ פַּשְׁחוּר אֲמַרְיָה מַלְכִּיָּה׃ חַטּוּשׁ שְׁבַנְיָה מַלּוּךְ׃
Malluch Shebaniah Hattush (5) Malkijah Amariah Pashhur (4) Jeremiah

חָרִם מְרֵמוֹת עֹבַדְיָה׃ דָּנִיֵּאל גִּנְּתוֹן בָּרוּךְ׃ מְשֻׁלָּם אֲבִיָּה
Abijah Meshullam (8) Baruch Ginnethon Daniel (7) Obadiah Meremoth Harim (6)

מִיָּמִן׃ מַעַזְיָה בִלְגַּי שְׁמַעְיָה אֵלֶּה הַכֹּהֲנִים׃ וְהַלְוִיִּם
and-the-Levites (10) the-priests these Shemaiah Bilgai Maaziah (9) Mijamin

וְיֵשׁוּעַ בֶּן־ אֲזַנְיָה בִּנּוּי מִבְּנֵי חֵנָדָד קַדְמִיאֵל׃
Kadmiel Henadad of-sons-of Binnui Azaniah son-of and-Jeshua

וַאֲחֵיהֶם שְׁבַנְיָה הוֹדִיָּה קְלִיטָא פְּלָאיָה חָנָן׃ מִיכָא
Mica (12) Hanan Pelaiah Kelita Hodiah Shebaniah and-associates-of-them (11)

רְחוֹב חֲשַׁבְיָה׃ זַכּוּר שֵׁרֵבְיָה שְׁבַנְיָה׃ הוֹדִיָּה בָנִי בְּנִינוּ׃
Beninu Bani Hodiah (14) Shebaniah Sherebiah Zaccur (13) Hashabiah Rehob

רָאשֵׁי הָעָם פַּרְעֹשׁ פַּחַת מוֹאָב עֵילָם זַתּוּא בָּנִי׃ בֻּנִּי
Bunni (16) Bani Zattu Elam Moab Pahath Parosh the-people leaders-of (15)

warnings you gave them. [35]Even while they were in their kingdom, enjoying your great goodness to them in the spacious and fertile land you gave them, they did not serve you or turn from their evil ways.

[36]"But see, we are slaves today, slaves in the land you gave our forefathers so they could eat its fruit and the other good things it produces. [37]Because of our sins, its abundant harvest goes to the kings you have placed over us. They rule over our bodies and our cattle as they please. We are in great distress.

*The Agreement of the People*

[38]"In view of all this, we are making a binding agreement, putting it in writing, and our leaders, our Levites and our priests are affixing their seals to it."

**10** Those who sealed it were:

Nehemiah the governor, the son of Hacaliah.

Zedekiah, [2]Seraiah, Azariah, Jeremiah,
[3]Pashhur, Amariah, Malkijah,
[4]Hattush, Shebaniah, Malluch,
[5]Harim, Meremoth, Obadiah,
[6]Daniel, Ginnethon, Baruch,
[7]Meshullam, Abijah, Mijamin,
[8]Maaziah, Bilgai and Shemaiah.
These were the priests.

[9]The Levites:

Jeshua son of Azaniah, Binnui of the sons of Henadad, Kadmiel,
[10]and their associates: Shebaniah,
Hodiah, Kelita, Pelaiah, Hanan,
[11]Mica, Rehob, Hashabiah,
[12]Zaccur, Sherebiah, Shebaniah,
[13]Hodiah, Bani and Beninu.

[14]The leaders of the people:

Parosh, Pahath-Moab, Elam, Zattu, Bani,

*1 The Hebrew numeration of chapter 10 begins with verse 38 of chapter 9 in English; thus, there is a one-verse discrepancy throughout chapter 10.

עַזְגָּד בֵּבָי׃ אֲדֹנִיָּה בִּגְוַי עָדִין׃ אָטֵר חִזְקִיָּה עַזּוּר׃ הוֹדִיָּה
Hodiah (19) Azzur Hezekiah Ater (18) Adin Bigvai Adonijah (17) Bebai Azgad

חָשֻׁם בֵּצָי׃ חָרִיף עֲנָתוֹת נֵובָי׃ מַגְפִּיעָשׁ מְשֻׁלָּם חֵזִיר׃
Hezir Meshullam Magpiash (21) Nebai Anathoth Hariph (20) Bezai Hashum

מְשֵׁיזַבְאֵל צָדוֹק יַדּוּעַ׃ פְּלַטְיָה חָנָן עֲנָיָה׃ הוֹשֵׁעַ
Hoshea (24) Anaiah Hanan Pelatiah (23) Jaddua Zadok Meshezabel (22)

חֲנַנְיָה חַשּׁוּב׃ הַלּוֹחֵשׁ פִּלְחָא שׁוֹבֵק׃ רְחוּם חֲשַׁבְנָה מַעֲשֵׂיָה׃
Maaseiah Hashabnah Rehum (26) Shobek Pilha Hallohesh (25) Hasshub Hananiah

וַאֲחִיָּה חָנָן עָנָן׃ מַלּוּךְ חָרִם בַּעֲנָה׃ וּשְׁאָר
and-rest-of (29) Baanah Harim Malluch (28) Anan Hanan and-Ahiah (27)

הָעָם הַכֹּהֲנִים הַלְוִיִּם הַשּׁוֹעֲרִים הַמְשֹׁרְרִים
the-ones-singing the-gatekeepers the-Levites the-priests the-people

הַנְּתִינִים וְכָל־ הַנִּבְדָּל מֵעַמֵּי
from-peoples-of the-one-separating-himself and-all-of the-temple-servants

הָאֲרָצוֹת אֶל־ תּוֹרַת הָאֱלֹהִים נְשֵׁיהֶם בְּנֵיהֶם וּבְנֹתֵיהֶם
and-daughters-of-them sons-of-them wives-of-them the-God Law-of for the-lands

כֹּל יוֹדֵעַ מֵבִין׃ מַחֲזִקִים עַל־ אֲחֵיהֶם
brothers-of-them with ones-joining (30) one-understanding one-knowing all-of

אַדִּירֵיהֶם וּבָאִים בְּאָלָה וּבִשְׁבוּעָה לָלֶכֶת בְּתוֹרַת
to-Law-of to-follow and-with-oath with-curse and-ones-binding nobles-of-them

הָאֱלֹהִים אֲשֶׁר נִתְּנָה בְּיַד מֹשֶׁה עֶבֶד־ הָאֱלֹהִים
the-God servant-of Moses by-hand-of she-was-given that the-God

וְלִשְׁמוֹר וְלַעֲשׂוֹת אֶת־ כָּל־ מִצְוֹת יְהוָה אֲדֹנֵינוּ
Lord-of-us Yahweh commands-of all-of *** and-to-obey and-to-be-careful

וּמִשְׁפָּטָיו וְחֻקָּיו׃ וַאֲשֶׁר לֹא־ נִתֵּן
we-will-give not and-that (31) and-decrees-of-him and-regulations-of-him

בְּנֹתֵינוּ לְעַמֵּי הָאָרֶץ וְאֶת־ בְּנֹתֵיהֶם לֹא נִקַּח
we-will-take not daughters-of-them and the-land to-peoples-of daughters-of-us

לְבָנֵינוּ׃ וְעַמֵּי הָאָרֶץ הַמְבִיאִים אֶת־
*** the-ones-bringing the-land when-peoples-of (32) for-sons-of-us

הַמַּקָּחוֹת וְכָל־ שֶׁבֶר בְּיוֹם הַשַּׁבָּת לִמְכּוֹר לֹא־
not to-sell the-Sabbath on-day-of grain or-any-of the-merchandises

נִקַּח מֵהֶם בַּשַּׁבָּת וּבְיוֹם קֹדֶשׁ וְנִטֹּשׁ
and-we-will-forgo holy or-on-day-of on-the-Sabbath from-them we-will-buy

אֶת־ הַשָּׁנָה הַשְּׁבִיעִית וּמַשָּׁא כָל־ יָד׃ וְהֶעֱמַדְנוּ
and-we-will-assume (33) hand all-of and-debt-of the-seventh the-year ***

עָלֵינוּ מִצְוֹת לָתֵת עָלֵינוּ שְׁלִשִׁית הַשֶּׁקֶל בַּשָּׁנָה לַעֲבֹדַת
for-service-of in-the-year the-shekel third-of of-us to-give commands on-us

15Bunni, Azgad, Bebai,
16Adonijah, Bigvai, Adin,
17Ater, Hezekiah, Azzur,
18Hodiah, Hashum, Bezai,
19Hariph, Anathoth, Nebai,
20Magpiash, Meshullam, Hezir,
21Meshezabel, Zadok, Jaddua,
22Pelatiah, Hanan, Anaiah,
23Hoshea, Hananiah, Hasshub,
24Hallohesh, Pilha, Shobek,
25Rehum, Hashabnah, Maaseiah,
26Ahiah, Hanan, Anan,
27Malluch, Harim and Baanah.

28"The rest of the people—priests, Levites, gatekeepers, singers, temple servants and all who separated themselves from the neighboring peoples for the sake of the Law of God, together with their wives and all their sons and daughters who are able to understand—
29all these now join their brothers the nobles, and bind themselves with a curse and an oath to follow the Law of God given through Moses the servant of God and to obey carefully all the commands, regulations and decrees of the LORD our God.
30"We promise not to give our daughters in marriage to the peoples around us or take their daughters for our sons.
31"When the neighboring peoples bring merchandise or grain to sell on the Sabbath, we will not buy from them on the Sabbath or on any holy day. Every seventh year we will forgo working the land and will cancel all debts.
32"We assume the responsibility for carrying out the commands to give a third of a shekel[c] each year for the service of the house of

[c]32 That is, about 1/8 ounce (about 4 grams)

*See the note on page 244.

°20 ק ניבי

בֵּית אֱלֹהֵינוּ׃ לְלֶחֶם הַמַּעֲרֶכֶת וּמִנְחַת
and-grain-offering-of the-one-set-out for-bread-of (34) God-of-us house-of

הַתָּמִיד וּלְעוֹלַת הַתָּמִיד הַשַּׁבָּתוֹת הֶחֳדָשִׁים
the-New-Moons the-Sabbaths the-regular and-for-burnt-offering-of the-regular

לַמּוֹעֲדִים וְלַקֳּדָשִׁים וְלַחַטָּאוֹת
and-for-the-sin-offerings and-for-the-holy-offerings for-the-appointed-feasts

לְכַפֵּר עַל־יִשְׂרָאֵל וְכֹל מְלֶאכֶת בֵּית־ אֱלֹהֵינוּ׃ וְהַגּוֹרָלוֹת
and-the-lots (35) God-of-us house-of duty-of and-all-of Israel for to-atone

הִפַּלְנוּ עַל־ קֻרְבַּן הָעֵצִים הַכֹּהֲנִים הַלְוִיִּם וְהָעָם
and-the-people the-Levites the-priests the-woods contribution-of for we-cast

לְהָבִיא לְבֵית אֱלֹהֵינוּ לְבֵית־ אֲבֹתֵינוּ לְעִתִּים
at-times fathers-of-us by-family-of God-of-us to-house-of to-bring

מְזֻמָּנִים שָׁנָה בְשָׁנָה לְבַעֵר עַל־ מִזְבַּח יְהוָה אֱלֹהֵינוּ
God-of-us Yahweh altar-of on to-burn by-year year ones-being-set

כַּכָּתוּב בַּתּוֹרָה׃ וּלְהָבִיא אֶת־ בִּכּוּרֵי
firstfruits-of *** and-to-bring (36) in-the-Law as-the-thing-being-written

אַדְמָתֵנוּ וּבִכּוּרֵי כָּל־ פְּרִי כָּל ־עֵץ שָׁנָה בְשָׁנָה
by-year year tree every-of fruit-of every-of and-firstfruits-of land-of-us

לְבֵית יְהוָה׃ וְאֶת־ בְּכֹרוֹת בָּנֵינוּ וּבְהֶמְתֵּינוּ
and-cattles-of-us sons-of-us ones-firstborn-of and (37) Yahweh to-house-of

כַּכָּתוּב בַּתּוֹרָה וְאֶת־ בְּכוֹרֵי בְקָרֵינוּ
herds-of-us ones-firstborn-of and in-the-Law as-the-thing-being-written

וְצֹאנֵינוּ לְהָבִיא לְבֵית אֱלֹהֵינוּ לַכֹּהֲנִים
to-the-priests God-of-us to-house-of to-bring and-flocks-of-us

הַמְשָׁרְתִים בְּבֵית אֱלֹהֵינוּ׃ וְאֶת־ רֵאשִׁית
first-of moreover (38) God-of-us at-house-of the-ones-ministering

עֲרִיסֹתֵינוּ וּתְרוּמֹתֵינוּ וּפְרִי כָל־ עֵץ תִּירוֹשׁ
new-wine tree all-of and-fruit-of and-offerings-of-us ground-meals-of-us

וְיִצְהָר נָבִיא לַכֹּהֲנִים אֶל־ לִשְׁכוֹת בֵּית־ אֱלֹהֵינוּ
God-of-us house-of storerooms-of to to-the-priests we-will-bring and-oil

וּמַעְשַׂר אַדְמָתֵנוּ לַלְוִיִּם וְהֵם הַלְוִיִּם
the-Levites for-they to-the-Levites land-of-us and-tithe-of

הַמְעַשְּׂרִים בְּכֹל עָרֵי עֲבֹדָתֵנוּ׃ וְהָיָה
and-he-must-be (39) work-of-us towns-of in-all-of the-ones-collecting-tithes

הַכֹּהֵן בֶּן־ אַהֲרֹן עִם־ הַלְוִיִּם בַּעְשֹׂר
when-to-receive-tithe the-Levites with Aaron descendant-of the-priest

הַלְוִיִּם וְהַלְוִיִּם יַעֲלוּ אֶת־ מַעֲשַׂר הַמַּעֲשֵׂר
the-tithe tenth-of *** they-must-bring-up and-the-Levites the-Levites

our God: [33]for the bread set out on the table; for the regular grain offerings and burnt offerings; for the offerings on the Sabbaths, New Moon festivals and appointed feasts; for the holy offerings; for sin offerings to make atonement for Israel; and for all the duties of the house of our God.

[34]"We—the priests, the Levites and the people—have cast lots to determine when each of our families is to bring to the house of our God at set times each year a contribution of wood to burn on the altar of the LORD our God, as it is written in the Law.

[35]"We also assume responsibility for bringing to the house of the LORD each year the firstfruits of our crops and of every fruit tree.

[36]"As it is also written in the Law, we will bring the firstborn of our sons and of our cattle, of our herds and of our flocks to the house of our God, to the priests ministering there.

[37]"Moreover, we will bring to the storerooms of the house of our God, to the priests, the first of our ground meal, of our ⌞grain⌟ offerings, of the fruit of all our trees and of our new wine and oil. And we will bring a tithe of our crops to the Levites, for it is the Levites who collect the tithes in all the towns where we work. [38]A priest descended from Aaron is to accompany the Levites when they receive the tithes, and the Levites are to bring a tenth of the tithes up to the house

*See the note on page 244.

לְבֵית אֱלֹהֵינוּ אֶל־ הַלְּשָׁכוֹת לְבֵית הָאוֹצָר׃ כִּי
for (40) the-treasury of-house-of the-storerooms to God-of-us to-house-of

אֶל־ הַלְּשָׁכוֹת יָבִיאוּ בְנֵי־ יִשְׂרָאֵל וּבְנֵי הַלֵּוִי
the-Levite and-people-of Israel people-of they-must-bring the-storerooms to

אֶת־ תְּרוּמַת הַדָּגָן הַתִּירוֹשׁ וְהַיִּצְהָר וְשָׁם כְּלֵי
articles-of and-there and-the-oil the-new-wine the-grain contribution-of ***

הַמִּקְדָּשׁ וְהַכֹּהֲנִים הַמְשָׁרְתִים וְהַשּׁוֹעֲרִים
and-the-gatekeepers the-ones-ministering and-the-priests the-sanctuary

וְהַמְשֹׁרְרִים וְלֹא נַעֲזֹב אֶת־ בֵּית אֱלֹהֵינוּ׃
God-of-us house-of *** we-will-neglect and-not and-the-ones-singing

וַיֵּשְׁבוּ שָׂרֵי־ הָעָם בִּירוּשָׁלָ͏ִם וּשְׁאָר
and-rest-of in-Jerusalem the-people leaders-of now-they-settled (11:1)

הָעָם הִפִּילוּ גוֹרָלוֹת לְהָבִיא ׀ אֶחָד מִן־ הָעֲשָׂרָה לָשֶׁבֶת בִּירוּשָׁלַ͏ִם
in-Jerusalem to-live the-ten of one to-bring lots they-cast the-people

עִיר הַקֹּדֶשׁ וְתֵשַׁע הַיָּדוֹת בֶּעָרִים׃ וַיְבָרְכוּ
and-they-commended (2) in-the-towns the-others and-nine the-holy city-of

הָעָם לְכֹל הָאֲנָשִׁים הַמִּתְנַדְּבִים לָשֶׁבֶת בִּירוּשָׁלָ͏ִם׃
in-Jerusalem to-live the-ones-volunteering the-men to-all-of the-people

וְאֵלֶּה רָאשֵׁי הַמְּדִינָה אֲשֶׁר יָשְׁבוּ בִּירוּשָׁלָ͏ִם
in-Jerusalem they-settled who the-province leaders-of and-these (3)

וּבְעָרֵי יְהוּדָה יָשְׁבוּ אִישׁ בַּאֲחֻזָּתוֹ בְּעָרֵיהֶם
in-towns-of-them on-property-of-him each they-lived Judah now-in-towns-of

יִשְׂרָאֵל הַכֹּהֲנִים וְהַלְוִיִּם וְהַנְּתִינִים וּבְנֵי
and-descendants-of and-the-temple-servants and-the-Levites the-priests Israel

עַבְדֵי שְׁלֹמֹה׃ וּבִירוּשָׁלַ͏ִם יָשְׁבוּ מִבְּנֵי יְהוּדָה
Judah from-people-of they-lived while-in-Jerusalem (4) Solomon servants-of

וּמִבְּנֵי בִנְיָמִן מִבְּנֵי יְהוּדָה עֲתָיָה בֶן־ עֻזִּיָּה
Uzziah son-of Athaiah Judah from-descendants-of Benjamin and-from-people-of

בֶּן־ זְכַרְיָה בֶן־ אֲמַרְיָה בֶן־ שְׁפַטְיָה בֶּן־ מַהֲלַלְאֵל
Mahalalel son-of Shephatiah son-of Amariah son-of Zechariah son-of

מִבְּנֵי־ פָרֶץ׃ וּמַעֲשֵׂיָה בֶן־ בָּרוּךְ בֶּן־ כָּל־ חֹזֶה בֶּן־
son-of Hozeh Col son-of Baruch son-of and-Maaseiah (5) Perez from-descendants-of

חֲזָיָה בֶן־ עֲדָיָה בֶן־ יוֹיָרִיב בֶּן־ זְכַרְיָה בֶּן־ הַשִּׁלֹנִי׃
the-Shilonite descendant-of Zechariah son-of Joiarib son-of Adaiah son-of Hazaiah

כָּל־ בְּנֵי־ פֶרֶץ הַיֹּשְׁבִים בִּירוּשָׁלָ͏ִם אַרְבַּע
four-of in-Jerusalem the-ones-living Perez descendants-of total-of (6)

מֵאוֹת שִׁשִּׁים וּשְׁמֹנָה אַנְשֵׁי־ חָיִל׃ וְאֵלֶּה בְּנֵי בִנְיָמִן
Benjamin descendants-of and-these (7) bravery men-of and-eight sixty hundreds

of our God, to the store-
rooms of the treasury. 39The
people of Israel, including
the Levites, are to bring
their contributions of
grain, new wine and oil to
the storerooms where the
articles for the sanctuary
are kept and where the
ministering priests, the
gatekeepers and the singers
stay.

"We will not neglect the
house of our God."

*The New Residents of Jerusalem*

11 Now the leaders of the
people settled in
Jerusalem, and the rest of the
people cast lots to bring one
out of every ten to live in
Jerusalem, the holy city, while
the remaining nine were to
stay in their own towns. 2The
people commended all the
men who volunteered to live
in Jerusalem.

3These are the provincial
leaders who settled in Jerusalem (now some Israelites,
priests, Levites, temple servants and descendants of
Solomon's servants lived in
the towns of Judah, each on
his own property in the various towns, 4while other people
from both Judah and Benjamin lived in Jerusalem):

From the descendants of
Judah:

Athaiah son of Uzziah, the
son of Zechariah, the son of
Amariah, the son of Shephatiah, the son of Mahalalel,
a descendant of Perez; 5and
Maaseiah son of Baruch,
the son of Col-Hozeh, the
son of Hazaiah, the son of
Adaiah, the son of Joiarib,
the son of Zechariah, a descendant of Shelah. 6The
descendants of Perez who
lived in Jerusalem totaled
468 brave men.

7From the descendants of Benjamin:

*See the note on page 244.

סַלֻּא בֶּן־ מְשֻׁלָּם בֶּן־ יוֹעֵד בֶּן־ פְּדָיָה בֶּן־ קוֹלָיָה בֶּן־
son-of Kolaiah son-of Pedaiah son-of Joed son-of Meshullam son-of Sallu

מַעֲשֵׂיָה בֶּן־ אִיתִיאֵל בֶּן־ יְשַׁעְיָה׃ וְאַחֲרָיו גַּבַּי סַלָּי
Sallai Gabbai and-after-him (8) Jeshaiah son-of Ithiel son-of Maaseiah

תְּשַׁע מֵאוֹת עֶשְׂרִים וּשְׁמֹנָה׃ וְיוֹאֵל בֶּן־ זִכְרִי פָּקִיד
chief-officer Zicri son-of and-Joel (9) and-eight twenty hundreds nine-of

עֲלֵיהֶם וִיהוּדָה בֶן־ הַסְּנוּאָה עַל־ הָעִיר מִשְׁנֶה׃ מִן־
from (10) Second-District the-city over Hassenuah son-of and-Judah over-them

הַכֹּהֲנִים יְדַעְיָה בֶן־ יוֹיָרִיב יָכִין׃ שְׂרָיָה בֶּן־ חִלְקִיָּה בֶּן־
son-of Hilkiah son-of Seraiah (11) Jakin Joiarib son-of Jedaiah the-priests

מְשֻׁלָּם בֶּן־ צָדוֹק בֶּן־ מְרָיוֹת בֶּן־ אֲחִיטוּב נְגִד בֵּית
house-of supervisor-of Ahitub son-of Meraioth son-of Zadok son-of Meshullam

הָאֱלֹהִים׃ וַאֲחֵיהֶם עֹשֵׂי הַמְּלָאכָה
the-work ones-carrying-on-of and-associates-of-them (12) the-God

לַבַּיִת שְׁמֹנֶה מֵאוֹת עֶשְׂרִים וּשְׁנָיִם וַעֲדָיָה בֶּן־ יְרֹחָם
Jeroham son-of and-Adaiah and-two twenty hundreds eight-of for-the-temple

בֶּן־ פְּלַלְיָה בֶּן־ אַמְצִי בֶּן־ זְכַרְיָה בֶּן־ פַשְׁחוּר בֶּן־ מַלְכִּיָּה׃
Malkijah son-of Pashhur son-of Zechariah son-of Amzi son-of Pelaliah son-of

וְאֶחָיו רָאשִׁים לְאָבוֹת מָאתַיִם אַרְבָּעִים וּשְׁנָיִם
and-two forty two-hundreds of-fathers heads and-associates-of-him (13)

וַעֲמַשְׁסַי בֶּן־ עֲזַרְאֵל בֶּן־ אַחְזַי בֶּן־ מְשִׁלֵּמוֹת בֶּן־ אִמֵּר׃
Immer son-of Meshillemoth son-of Ahzai son-of Azarel son-of and-Amashsai

וַאֲחֵיהֶם גִּבֹּרֵי חַיִל מֵאָה עֶשְׂרִים וּשְׁמֹנָה
and-eight twenty hundred bravery warriors-of and-associates-of-them (14)

וּפָקִיד עֲלֵיהֶם זַבְדִּיאֵל בֶּן־ הַגְּדוֹלִים׃ וּמִן־
and-from (15) Haggedolim son-of Zabdiel over-them and-chief-officer

הַלְוִיִּם שְׁמַעְיָה בֶן־ חַשּׁוּב בֶּן־ עַזְרִיקָם בֶּן־ חֲשַׁבְיָה בֶּן־
son-of Hashabiah son-of Azrikam son-of Hasshub son-of Shemaiah the-Levites

בּוּנִּי׃ וְשַׁבְּתַי וְיוֹזָבָד עַל־ הַמְּלָאכָה הַחִיצֹנָה לְבֵית
of-house-of the-outside the-work over and-Jozabad and-Shabbethai (16) Bunni

הָאֱלֹהִים מֵרָאשֵׁי הַלְוִיִּם׃ וּמַתַּנְיָה בֶן־ מִיכָה° בֶּן־ זַבְדִּי
Zabdi son-of Mica son-of and-Mattaniah (17) the-Levites from-heads-of the-God

בֶּן־ אָסָף רֹאשׁ הַתְּחִלָּה יְהוֹדֶה לַתְּפִלָּה וּבַקְבֻּקְיָה
and-Bakbukiah to-the-prayer he-led the-thanksgiving director-of Asaph son-of

מִשְׁנֶה מֵאֶחָיו וְעַבְדָּא בֶּן־ שַׁמּוּעַ בֶּן־ גָּלָל בֶּן־
son-of Galal son-of Shammua son-of and-Abda among-associates-of-him second

יְדִיתוּן׃ כָּל־ הַלְוִיִּם בְּעִיר הַקֹּדֶשׁ מָאתַיִם שְׁמֹנִים
eighty two-hundreds the-holy in-city-of the-Levites total-of (18) Jeduthun

Sallu son of Meshullam, the
son of Joed, the son of Pedaiah, the son of Kolaiah,
the son of Maaseiah, the
son of Ithiel, the son of Jeshaiah, 8and his followers,
Gabbai and Sallai—928
men. 9Joel son of Zicri was
their chief officer, and
Judah son of Hassenuah
was over the Second Dis-
trict of the city.

10From the priests:

Jedaiah; the son[d] of Joiarib;
Jakin; 11Seraiah son of Hilkiah, the son of Meshullam,
the son of Zadok, the son of
Meraioth, the son of Ahi-
tub, supervisor in the
house of God, 12and their
associates, who carried on
work for the temple—822
men; Adaiah son of Jero-
ham, the son of Pelaliah,
the son of Amzi, the son of
Zechariah, the son of Pashhur, the son of Malkijah,
13and his associates, who
were heads of families—
242 men; Amashsai son of
Azarel, the son of Ahzai,
the son of Meshillemoth,
the son of Immer, 14and
his[e] associates, who were
brave warriors—128 men.
Their chief officer was Zabdiel son of Haggedolim.

15From the Levites:

Shemaiah son of Hasshub,
the son of Azrikam, the son
of Hashabiah, the son of
Bunni; 16Shabbethai and
Jozabad, two of the heads
of the Levites, who had
charge of the outside work
of the house of God; 17Mat-
taniah son of Mica, the son
of Zabdi, the son of Asaph,
the director who led in
thanksgiving and prayer;
Bakbukiah, second among
his associates; and Abda
son of Shammua, the son of
Galal, the son of Jeduthun.
18The Levites in the holy
city totaled 284.

[d]10 Or *Jedaiah*
[e]14 Most Septuagint manuscripts; Hebrew *their*

°17 ק ידותון

וְאַרְבָּעָה׃ וְהַשּׁוֹעֲרִים עַקּוּב טַלְמוֹן וַאֲחֵיהֶם
and-associates-of-them Talmon Akkub and-the-gatekeepers (19) and-four

הַשֹּׁמְרִים בַּשְּׁעָרִים מֵאָה שִׁבְעִים וּשְׁנָיִם׃ וּשְׁאָר
and-rest-of (20) and-two seventy hundred at-the-gates the-ones-watching

יִשְׂרָאֵל הַכֹּהֲנִים הַלְוִיִּם בְּכָל־ עָרֵי יְהוּדָה אִישׁ
each Judah towns-of in-all-of the-Levites the-priests Israel

בְּנַחֲלָתוֹ׃ וְהַנְּתִינִים יֹשְׁבִים בָּעֹפֶל
on-the-Ophel ones-living and-the-temple-servants (21) on-property-of-him

וְצִיחָא וְגִשְׁפָּא עַל־ הַנְּתִינִים׃ וּפְקִיד
and-chief-officer-of (22) the-temple-servants over and-Gishpa and-Ziha

הַלְוִיִּם בִּירוּשָׁלִַם עֻזִּי בֶּן־ בָּנִי בֶּן־ חֲשַׁבְיָה בֶּן־ מַתַּנְיָה
Mattaniah son-of Hashabiah son-of Bani son-of Uzzi in-Jerusalem the-Levites

בֶּן־ מִיכָא מִבְּנֵי אָסָף הַמְשֹׁרְרִים לְנֶגֶד מְלֶאכֶת
service-of in-front-of the-ones-singing Asaph from-descendants-of Mica son-of

בֵּית־ הָאֱלֹהִים׃ כִּי־ מִצְוַת הַמֶּלֶךְ עֲלֵיהֶם וַאֲמָנָה
and-regulation over-them the-king order-of indeed (23) the-God house-of

עַל־ הַמְשֹׁרְרִים דְּבַר־ יוֹם בְּיוֹמוֹ׃ וּפְתַחְיָה בֶּן־
son-of and-Pethahiah (24) in-day-of-him day activity-of the-ones-singing for

מְשֵׁיזַבְאֵל מִבְּנֵי־ זֶרַח בֶּן־ יְהוּדָה לְיַד הַמֶּלֶךְ לְכָל־
in-all-of the-king at-hand-of Judah son-of Zerah of-descendants-of Meshezabel

דָּבָר לָעָם׃ וְאֶל־ הַחֲצֵרִים בִּשְׂדֹתָם
with-fields-of-them the-villages and-for (25) of-the-people affair

מִבְּנֵי יְהוּדָה יָשְׁבוּ בְּקִרְיַת הָאַרְבַּע וּבְנֹתֶיהָ
and-settlements-of-her the-Arba in-Kiriath they-lived Judah from-people-of

וּבְדִיבֹן וּבְנֹתֶיהָ וּבִיקַּבְצְאֵל וַחֲצֵרֶיהָ׃
and-villages-of-her and-in-Jekabzeel and-settlements-of-her and-in-Dibon

וּבְיֵשׁוּעַ וּבְמוֹלָדָה וּבְבֵית פֶּלֶט׃ וּבַחֲצַר שׁוּעָל
Shual and-in-Hazar (27) Pelet and-in-Beth and-in-Moladah and-in-Jeshua (26)

וּבִבְאֵר שֶׁבַע וּבְנֹתֶיהָ׃ וּבְצִקְלַג וּבִמְכֹנָה
and-in-Meconah and-in-Ziklag (28) and-settlements-of-her Sheba and-in-Beer

וּבִבְנֹתֶיהָ׃ וּבְעֵין רִמּוֹן וּבְצָרְעָה וּבְיַרְמוּת׃
and-in-Jarmuth and-in-Zorah Rimmon and-in-En (29) and-in-settlements-of-her

זָנֹחַ עֲדֻלָּם וְחַצְרֵיהֶם לָכִישׁ וּשְׂדֹתֶיהָ עֲזֵקָה
Azekah and-fields-of-her Lachish and-villages-of-them Adullam Zanoah (30)

וּבְנֹתֶיהָ וַיַּחֲנוּ מִבְּאֵר־ שֶׁבַע עַד־ גֵּיא־ הִנֹּם׃
Hinnom Valley-of to Sheba from-Beer so-they-lived and-settlements-of-her

וּבְנֵי בִנְיָמִן מִגָּבַע מִכְמָשׂ וְעַיָּה וּבֵית־ אֵל
El and-Beth and-Aija Micmash from-Geba Benjamin and-descendants-of (31)

19 The gatekeepers:

Akkub, Talmon and their
associates, who kept watch
at the gates—172 men.

20 The rest of the Israelites,
with the priests and Levites,
were in all the towns of Judah,
each on his ancestral property.
21 The temple servants lived
on the hill of Ophel, and Ziha
and Gishpa were in charge of
them.

22 The chief officer of the Levites in Jerusalem was Uzzi
son of Bani, the son of Hashabiah, the son of Mattaniah,
the son of Mica. Uzzi was one
of Asaph's descendants, who
were the singers responsible
for the service of the house of
God. 23 The singers were under
the king's orders, which regu-
lated their daily activity.

24 Pethahiah son of Meshezabel, one of the descendants of
Zerah son of Judah, was the
king's agent in all affairs relating to the people.

25 As for the villages with
their fields, some of the people
of Judah lived in Kiriath Arba
and its surrounding settlements, in Dibon and its settlements, in Jekabzeel and its villages, 26 in Jeshua, in Moladah,
in Beth Pelet, 27 in Hazar Shual,
in Beersheba and its settlements, 28 in Ziklag, in Meco-
nah and its settlements, 29 in
En Rimmon, in Zorah, in Jarmuth, 30 Zanoah, Adullam and
their villages, in Lachish and
its fields, and in Azekah and
its settlements. So they were
living all the way from Beersheba to the Valley of Hinnom.

31 The descendants of the
Benjamites from Geba lived in
Micmash, Aija, Bethel and its

וּבְנֹתֶיהָ׃ עֲנָתוֹת נֹב עֲנָנְיָה׃ חָצוֹר ׀ רָמָה גִּתָּיִם׃

Gittaim Ramah Hazor (33) Ananiah Nob Anathoth (32) and-settlements-of-her

חָדִיד צְבֹעִים נְבַלָּט׃ לֹד וְאוֹנוֹ גֵּי הַחֲרָשִׁים׃

the-Craftsmen Valley-of and-Ono Lod (35) Neballat Zeboim Hadid (34)

וּמִן־ הַלְוִיִּם מַחְלְקוֹת יְהוּדָה לְבִנְיָמִין׃ וְאֵלֶּה

and-these (12:1) in-Benjamin Judah divisions-of the-Levites and-of (36)

הַכֹּהֲנִים וְהַלְוִיִּם אֲשֶׁר עָלוּ עִם־ זְרֻבָּבֶל בֶּן־

son-of Zerubbabel with they-returned who and-the-Levites the-priests

שְׁאַלְתִּיאֵל וְיֵשׁוּעַ שְׂרָיָה יִרְמְיָה עֶזְרָא׃ אֲמַרְיָה מַלּוּךְ חַטּוּשׁ׃

Hattush Malluch Amariah (2) Ezra Jeremiah Seraiah and-Jeshua Shealtiel

שְׁכַנְיָה רְחֻם מְרֵמֹת׃ עִדּוֹא גִנְּתוֹי אֲבִיָּה׃ מִיָּמִין מַעַדְיָה

Maadiah Mijamin (5) Abijah Ginnethoi Iddo (4) Meremoth Rehum Shecaniah (3)

בִּלְגָּה׃ שְׁמַעְיָה וְיוֹיָרִיב יְדַעְיָה׃ סַלּוּ עָמוֹק חִלְקִיָּה יְדַעְיָה

Jedaiah Hilkiah Amok Sallu (7) Jedaiah and-Joiarib Shemaiah (6) Bilgah

אֵלֶּה רָאשֵׁי הַכֹּהֲנִים וַאֲחֵיהֶם בִּימֵי יֵשׁוּעַ׃

Jeshua in-days-of and-associates-of-them the-priests leaders-of these

וְהַלְוִיִּם יֵשׁוּעַ בִּנּוּי קַדְמִיאֵל שֵׁרֵבְיָה יְהוּדָה מַתַּנְיָה עַל־

over Mattaniah Judah Sherebiah Kadmiel Binnui Jeshua and-the-Levites (8)

הֻיְּדוֹת הוּא וְאֶחָיו׃ וּבַקְבֻּקְיָה וְעֻנּוֹ

and-Unni and-Bakbukiah (9) and-associates-of-him he songs-of-thanksgiving

אֲחֵיהֶם לְנֶגְדָּם לְמִשְׁמָרוֹת׃ וְיֵשׁוּעַ הוֹלִיד

he-fathered and-Jeshua (10) in-services at-opposite-them associates-of-them

אֶת־ יוֹיָקִים וְיוֹיָקִים הוֹלִיד אֶת־ אֶלְיָשִׁיב וְאֶלְיָשִׁיב אֶת־יוֹיָדָע׃

Joiada *** and-Eliashib Eliashib *** he-fathered and-Joiakim Joiakim ***

וְיוֹיָדָע הוֹלִיד אֶת־ יוֹנָתָן וְיוֹנָתָן הוֹלִיד אֶת־ יַדּוּעַ׃

Jaddua *** he-fathered and-Jonathan Jonathan *** he-fathered and-Joiada (11)

וּבִימֵי יוֹיָקִים הָיוּ כֹהֲנִים רָאשֵׁי הָאָבוֹת לִשְׂרָיָה

of-Seraiah the-fathers heads-of priests they-were Joiakim and-in-days-of (12)

מְרָיָה לְיִרְמְיָה חֲנַנְיָה׃ לְעֶזְרָא מְשֻׁלָּם לַאֲמַרְיָה יְהוֹחָנָן׃

Jehohanan of-Amariah Meshullam of-Ezra (13) Hananiah of-Jeremiah Meraiah

לִמְלוּכִי יוֹנָתָן לִשְׁבַנְיָה יוֹסֵף׃ לְחָרִם עַדְנָא לִמְרָיוֹת

of-Meraioth Adna of-Harim (15) Joseph of-Shebaniah Jonathan of-Malluch (14)

חֶלְקָי׃ לְעִדְּיָא זְכַרְיָה לְגִנְּתוֹן מְשֻׁלָּם׃ לַאֲבִיָּה זִכְרִי

Zicri of-Abijah (17) Meshullam of-Ginnethon Zechariah of-Iddo (16) Helkai

לְמִנְיָמִין לְמוֹעַדְיָה פִּלְטָי׃ לְבִלְגָּה שַׁמּוּעַ לִשְׁמַעְיָה יְהוֹנָתָן׃

Jehonathan of-Shemaiah Shammua of-Bilgah (18) Piltai of-Maadiah of-Miniamin

וּלְיוֹיָרִיב מַתְּנַי לִידַעְיָה עֻזִּי׃ לְסַלַּי קַלָּי לְעָמוֹק

of-Amok Kallai of-Sallu (20) Uzzi of-Jedaiah Mattenai and-of-Joiarib (19)

settlements, [32]in Anathoth,
Nob and Ananiah, [33]in Hazor,
Ramah and Gittaim, [34]in Hadid, Zeboim and Neballat, [35]in
Lod and Ono, and in the Valley of the Craftsmen.
[36]Some of the divisions of the Levites of Judah settled in Benjamin.

*Priests and Levites*

**12** These were the priests and Levites who returned with Zerubbabel son of Shealtiel and with Jeshua:

Seraiah, Jeremiah, Ezra,
[2]Amariah, Malluch, Hattush,
[3]Shecaniah, Rehum, Meremoth,
[4]Iddo, Ginnethon,[f] Abijah,
[5]Mijamin, Maadiah, Bilgah,
[6]Shemaiah, Joiarib, Jedaiah,
[7]Sallu, Amok, Hilkiah and Jedaiah.

These were the leaders of the priests and their associates in the days of Jeshua.

[8]The Levites were Jeshua, Binnui, Kadmiel, Sherebiah, Judah, and also Mattaniah, who, together with his associates, was in charge of the songs of thanksgiving.
[9]Bakbukiah and Unni, their associates, stood opposite them in the services.

[10]Jeshua was the father of Joiakim, Joiakim the father of Eliashib, Eliashib the father of Joiada,
[11]Joiada the father of Jonathan, and Jonathan the father of Jaddua.

[12]In the days of Joiakim, these were the heads of the priestly families:

of Seraiah's family, Meraiah;
of Jeremiah's, Hananiah;
[13]of Ezra's, Meshullam;
of Amariah's, Jehohanan;
[14]of Malluch's, Jonathan;
of Shecaniah's,[g] Joseph;
[15]of Harim's, Adna;
of Meremoth's,[h] Helkai;
[16]of Iddo's, Zechariah;
of Ginnethon's, Meshullam;
[17]of Abijah's, Zicri;
of Miniamin's and of Maadiah's, Piltai;
[18]of Bilgah's, Shammua;
of Shemaiah's, Jehonathan;
[19]of Joiarib's, Mattenai;
of Jedaiah's, Uzzi;
[20]of Sallu's, Kallai;

[f]4 Many Hebrew manuscripts and Vulgate (see also Neh. 12:16); most Hebrew manuscripts *Ginnethoi*

[g]14 Very many Hebrew manuscripts, some Septuagint manuscripts and Syriac (see also Neh. 12:3); most Hebrew manuscripts *Shebaniah's*

[h]15 Some Septuagint manuscripts (see also Neh. 12:3); Hebrew *Meraioth's*

°9 ק ועני , °14 ק למליכו

°16 ק לעדוא

| הַלְוִיִּֽם | נְתַנְאֵֽל׃ | לִידַעְיָ֖ה | חֲשַׁבְיָ֔ה | לְחִלְקִיָּ֣ה | עֵ֔בֶר |
|---|---|---|---|---|---|
| the-Levites (22) | Nethanel | of-Jedaiah | Hashabiah | of-Hilkiah (21) | Eber |

| כְּתוּבִ֣ים | וְיַדּ֗וּעַ | וְיֽוֹחָנָ֣ן | יוֹיָדָ֣ע | אֶלְיָשִׁ֣יב | בִּימֵ֣י |
|---|---|---|---|---|---|
| ones-being-recorded | and-Jaddua | and-Johanan | Joiada | Eliashib | in-days-of |

| הַפָּרְסִֽי׃ | דָּרְיָ֖וֶשׁ | מַלְכ֥וּת | עַל־ | וְהַכֹּ֣הֲנִ֔ים | אָב֑וֹת | רָאשֵׁ֣י |
|---|---|---|---|---|---|---|
| the-Persian | Darius | reign-of | in | and-the-priests | fathers | heads-of |

| סֵ֖פֶר | עַל־ | כְּתוּבִ֔ים | הָֽאָבוֹת֙ | רָאשֵׁ֤י | לֵוִ֗י | בְּנֵ֣י | |
|---|---|---|---|---|---|---|---|
| book-of | in | ones-being-recorded | the-fathers | heads-of | Levi | descendants-of | (23) |

| אֶלְיָשִֽׁיב׃ | בֶּן־ | יֽוֹחָנָ֖ן | יְמֵ֥י | וְעַד־ | הַיָּמִ֑ים | דִּבְרֵ֖י |
|---|---|---|---|---|---|---|
| Eliashib | son-of | Johanan | days-of | and-up-to | the-days | annals-of |

| קַדְמִיאֵ֗ל | בֶּן־ | וְיֵשׁ֣וּעַ | שֵׁרֵ֣בְיָ֔ה | חֲשַׁבְיָ֣ה | הַלְוִיִּ֜ם | וְרָאשֵׁ֨י |
|---|---|---|---|---|---|---|
| Kadmiel | son-of | and-Jeshua | Sherebiah | Hashabiah | the-Levites | and-leaders-of (24) |

| לְהוֹד֣וֹת | לְהַלֵּ֣ל | לְנֶגְדָּ֑ם | וַאֲחֵיהֶ֣ם |
|---|---|---|---|
| to-give-thanks | to-give-praise | at-opposite-them | and-associates-of-them |

| מִשְׁמָֽר׃ | לְעֻמַּ֥ת | מִשְׁמָ֖ר | הָֽאֱלֹהִ֑ים | אִישׁ־ | דָּוִ֣יד | בְּמִצְוַ֖ת |
|---|---|---|---|---|---|---|
| section | responding-to | section | the-God | man-of | David | as-prescription-of |

| שֹׁמְרִ֥ים | עַקּ֣וּב | טַלְמ֧וֹן | מְשֻׁלָּ֖ם | עֹבַדְיָ֛ה | וּבַקְבֻּקְיָ֔ה | מַתַּנְיָ֣ה |
|---|---|---|---|---|---|---|
| ones-guarding | Akkub | Talmon | Meshullam | Obadiah | and-Bakbukiah | Mattaniah (25) |

| יֽוֹיָקִ֑ים | בִּימֵ֖י | אֵ֔לֶּה | הַשְּׁעָרִ֑ים | בְּאַסֻּפֵּ֖י | מִשְׁמָ֔ר | שֽׁוֹעֲרִים֙ |
|---|---|---|---|---|---|---|
| Joiakim | in-days-of | these (26) | the-gates | over-storerooms-of | guard | gatekeepers |

| וְעֶזְרָ֖א | הַפֶּחָ֑ה | נְחֶמְיָ֣ה | וּבִימֵי֙ | יֽוֹצָדָ֔ק | בֶּן־ | יֵשׁ֣וּעַ | בֶּן־ |
|---|---|---|---|---|---|---|---|
| and-Ezra | the-governor | Nehemiah | and-in-days-of | Jozadak | son-of | Jeshua | son-of |

| בִּקְשׁ֣וּ | יְרוּשָׁלִַ֗ם | חוֹמַ֣ת | וּבַחֲנֻכַּ֞ת | הַסֹּפֵֽר׃ | הַכֹּהֵ֖ן |
|---|---|---|---|---|---|
| they-sought | Jerusalem | wall-of | and-at-dedication-of (27) | the-scribe | the-priest |

| לִירֽוּשָׁלִַ֔ם | לַהֲבִיאָ֖ם | מְקֽוֹמֹתָ֔ם | מִכָּל־ | הַלְוִיִּם֙ | אֶת־ |
|---|---|---|---|---|---|
| to-Jerusalem | to-bring-them | dwellings-of-them | from-all-of | the-Levites | *** |

| וּבְשִׁ֑יר | וּבְתוֹד֣וֹת | וְשִׂמְחָ֔ה | חֲנֻכָּ֣ה | לַעֲשֹׂ֧ת |
|---|---|---|---|---|
| and-with-music | and-with-songs-of-thanksgiving | and-joy | dedication | to-celebrate |

| בְּנֵ֣י | וַיֵּאָ֣סְפ֔וּ | וּבְכִנֹּרֽוֹת׃ | נְבָלִ֖ים | מְצִלְתַּ֥יִם |
|---|---|---|---|---|
| sons-of | and-they-were-brought-together (28) | and-with-lyres | harps | cymbals |

| וּמִן־ | יְרוּשָׁלָ֑͏ִם | סְבִיב֖וֹת | הַכִּכָּ֕ר | וּמִן־ | הַמְשֹׁרְרִ֑ים |
|---|---|---|---|---|---|
| and-from | Jerusalem | ones-around-of | the-region | and-from | the-ones-singing |

| וּמִשְּׂדֽוֹת | הַגִּלְגָּ֗ל | וּמִבֵּית֙ | נְטֹפָתִֽי׃ | חַצְרֵ֖י |
|---|---|---|---|---|
| and-from-areas-of | the-Gilgal | and-from-Beth (29) | Netophathite | villages-of |

| הַֽמְשֹׁרֲרִ֖ים | לָהֶ֔ם | בָּנ֣וּ | חֲצֵרִ֣ים | כִּ֤י | וְעַזְמָ֑וֶת | גֶּ֖בַע |
|---|---|---|---|---|---|---|
| the-ones-singing | for-them | they-built | villages | for | and-Azmaveth | Geba |

| הַכֹּהֲנִ֖ים | וַיִּֽטַּהֲר֔וּ | יְרוּשָׁלָֽͅם׃ | סְבִיב֖וֹת |
|---|---|---|---|
| the-priests | when-they-purified-themselves (30) | Jerusalem | ones-around-of |

of Amok's, Eber; [21]of Hilkiah's, Hashabiah; of Jedaiah's, Nethanel. [22]The family heads of the Levites in the days of Eliashib, Joiada, Johanan and Jaddua, as well as those of the priests, were recorded in the reign of Darius the Persian. [23]The family heads among the descendants of Levi up to the time of Johanan son of Eliashib were recorded in the book of the annals. [24]And the leaders of the Levites were Hashabiah, Sherebiah, Jeshua son of Kadmiel, and their associates, who stood opposite them to give praise and thanksgiving, one section responding to the other, as prescribed by David the man of God. [25]Mattaniah, Bakbukiah, Obadiah, Meshullam, Talmon and Akkub were gatekeepers who guarded the storerooms at the gates. [26]They served in the days of Joiakim son of Jeshua, the son of Jozadak, and in the days of Nehemiah the governor and of Ezra the priest and scribe.

*Dedication of the Wall of Jerusalem*

[27]At the dedication of the wall of Jerusalem, the Levites were sought out from where they lived and were brought to Jerusalem to celebrate joyfully the dedication with songs of thanksgiving and with the music of cymbals, harps and lyres. [28]The singers also were brought together from the region around Jerusalem—from the villages of the Netophathites, [29]from Beth Gilgal, and from the area of Geba and Azmaveth, for the singers had built villages for themselves around Jerusalem. [30]When the priests and Levites had

וְהַלְוִיִּם וַיְטַהֲרוּ אֶת־ הָעָם וְאֶת־ הַשְּׁעָרִים וְאֶת־
and the-gates and the-people *** then-they-purified and-the-Levites

הַחוֹמָה׃ וָאַעֲלֶה אֶת־ שָׂרֵי יְהוּדָה מֵעַל לַחוֹמָה
of-the-wall on-top Judah leaders-of *** and-I-made-go-up (31) the-wall

וָאַעֲמִידָה שְׁתֵּי תוֹדֹת גְּדוֹלֹת וְתַהֲלֻכֹת לַיָּמִין מֵעַל
on-top to-the-right and-processions large-ones choirs two-of also-I-assigned

לַחוֹמָה לְשַׁעַר הָאַשְׁפֹּת׃ וַיֵּלֶךְ אַחֲרֵיהֶם הוֹשַׁעְיָה
Hoshaiah after-them and-he-followed (32) the-Dungs toward-Gate-of of-the-wall

וַחֲצִי שָׂרֵי יְהוּדָה׃ וַעֲזַרְיָה עֶזְרָא וּמְשֻׁלָּם׃ יְהוּדָה
Judah (34) and-Meshullam Ezra with-Azariah (33) Judah leaders-of and-half-of

וּבִנְיָמִן וּשְׁמַעְיָה וְיִרְמְיָה׃ וּמִבְּנֵי הַכֹּהֲנִים
the-priests and-from-sons-of (35) and-Jeremiah and-Shemaiah and-Benjamin

בַּחֲצֹצְרוֹת זְכַרְיָה בֶן־ יוֹנָתָן בֶּן־ שְׁמַעְיָה בֶּן־ מַתַּנְיָה
Mattaniah son-of Shemaiah son-of Jonathan son-of Zechariah with-trumpets

בֶּן־ מִיכָיָה בֶּן־ זַכּוּר בֶּן־ אָסָף׃ וְאֶחָיו שְׁמַעְיָה
Shemaiah and-associates-of-him (36) Asaph son-of Zaccur son-of Micaiah son-of

וַעֲזַרְאֵל מִלֲלַי גִּלֲלַי מָעַי נְתַנְאֵל וִיהוּדָה חֲנָנִי בִּכְלֵי־
with-instruments-of Hanani and-Judah Nethanel Maai Gilalai Milalai and-Azarel

שִׁיר דָּוִיד אִישׁ הָאֱלֹהִים וְעֶזְרָא הַסּוֹפֵר לִפְנֵיהֶם׃ וְעַל
and-at (37) before-them the-scribe and-Ezra the-God man-of David music-of

שַׁעַר הָעַיִן וְנֶגְדָּם עָלוּ עַל־ מַעֲלוֹת עִיר דָּוִיד
David City-of steps-of on they-went-up and-before-them the-Fountain Gate-of

בַּמַּעֲלֶה לַחוֹמָה מֵעַל לְבֵית דָּוִיד וְעַד שַׁעַר
Gate-of and-to David of-house-of at-above to-the-wall on-the-ascent

הַמַּיִם מִזְרָח׃ וְהַתּוֹדָה הַשֵּׁנִית הַהוֹלֶכֶת לְמוֹאל
in-opposite the-one-proceeding the-second and-the-choir (38) east the-Waters

וַאֲנִי אַחֲרֶיהָ וַחֲצִי הָעָם מֵעַל לְהַחוֹמָה מֵעַל
to-past of-the-wall on-top the-people with-half-of after-her and-I

לְמִגְדַּל הַתַּנּוּרִים וְעַד הַחוֹמָה הָרְחָבָה׃ וּמֵעַל לְשַׁעַר־
to-Gate-of and-to-over (39) the-Broad the-Wall and-to the-Ovens to-Tower-of

אֶפְרַיִם וְעַל־ שַׁעַר הַיְשָׁנָה וְעַל־ שַׁעַר הַדָּגִים וּמִגְדַּל
and-Tower-of the-Fishes Gate-of and-over the-Jeshanah Gate-of and-over Ephraim

חֲנַנְאֵל וּמִגְדַּל הַמֵּאָה וְעַד שַׁעַר הַצֹּאן
the-Sheep Gate-of and-as-far-as the-Hundred and-Tower-of Hananel

וְעָמְדוּ בְּשַׁעַר הַמַּטָּרָה׃ וַתַּעֲמֹדְנָה שְׁתֵּי
two-of then-they-took-places (40) the-Guard at-Gate-of and-they-stopped

הַתּוֹדֹת בְּבֵית הָאֱלֹהִים וַאֲנִי וַחֲצִי הַסְּגָנִים עִמִּי׃
with-me the-officials and-half-of and-I the-God in-house-of the-choirs

purified themselves ceremonially, they purified the people, the gates and the wall.

31 I had the leaders of Judah go up on top[i] of the wall. I also assigned two large choirs to give thanks. One was to proceed on top[j] of the wall to the right, toward the Dung Gate.
32 Hoshaiah and half the leaders of Judah followed them,
33 along with Azariah, Ezra,
Meshullam, 34 Judah, Benjamin, Shemaiah, Jeremiah, as
well 35 as some priests with trumpets, and also Zechariah son of Jonathan, the son of Shemaiah, the son of Mattaniah, the son of Micaiah, the son of Zaccur, the son of
Asaph, 36 and his associates—Shemaiah, Azarel, Milalai, Gilalai, Maai, Nethanel, Judah and Hanani—with musical instruments ⌞prescribed by⌟ David the man of God. Ezra the scribe led the procession. 37 At the Fountain Gate they continued directly up the steps of the City of David on the ascent to the wall and passed above the house of David to the Water Gate on the east.

38 The second choir proceeded in the opposite direction. I followed them on top[k] of the wall, together with half the people—past the Tower of the Ovens to the Broad Wall,
39 over the Gate of Ephraim, the Jeshanah[l] Gate, the Fish Gate, the Tower of Hananel and the Tower of the Hundred, as far as the Sheep Gate. At the Gate of the Guard they stopped.

40 The two choirs that gave thanks then took their places in the house of God; so did I, together with half the officials,

[i] 31 Or *go alongside*
[j] 31 Or *proceed alongside*
[k] 38 Or *them alongside*
[l] 39 Or *Old*

וְהַכֹּהֲנִים אֶלְיָקִים מַעֲשֵׂיָה מִנְיָמִין מִיכָיָה אֶלְיוֹעֵינַי זְכַרְיָה
Zechariah Elioenai Micaiah Mijamin Maaseiah Eliakim and-the-priests (41)

חֲנַנְיָה בַּחֲצֹצְרוֹת׃ וּמַעֲשֵׂיָה וּשְׁמַעְיָה וְאֶלְעָזָר וְעֻזִּי
and-Uzzi and-Eleazar and-Shemaiah also-Maaseiah (42) with-trumpets Hananiah

וִיהוֹחָנָן וּמַלְכִּיָּה וְעֵילָם וָעָזֶר וַיַּשְׁמִיעוּ הַמְשֹׁרְרִים
the-ones-singing and-they-sang and-Ezer and-Elam and-Malkijah and-Jehohanan

וְיִזְרַחְיָה הַפָּקִיד׃ וַיִּזְבְּחוּ בַיּוֹם־ הַהוּא
the-that on-the-day and-they-offered (43) the-director and-Jezrahiah

זְבָחִים גְּדוֹלִים וַיִּשְׂמָחוּ כִּי הָאֱלֹהִים שִׂמְּחָם
he-gave-joy-to-them the-God because and-they-rejoiced great-ones sacrifices

שִׂמְחָה גְדוֹלָה וְגַם הַנָּשִׁים וְהַיְלָדִים שָׂמֵחוּ וַתִּשָּׁמַע
and-she-was-heard they-rejoiced and-the-children the-women and-also great joy

שִׂמְחַת יְרוּשָׁלִַם מֵרָחוֹק׃ וַיִּפָּקְדוּ בַיּוֹם
at-the-time and-they-were-appointed (44) at-far Jerusalem rejoicing-of

הַהוּא אֲנָשִׁים עַל־ הַנְּשָׁכוֹת לָאוֹצָרוֹת לַתְּרוּמוֹת
for-the-contributions of-the-treasuries the-storerooms over men the-that

לָרֵאשִׁית וְלַמַּעַשְׂרוֹת לִכְנוֹס בָּהֶם לִשְׂדֵי
from-fields-of into-them to-bring and-for-the-tithes for-the-firstfruit

הֶעָרִים מְנָאוֹת הַתּוֹרָה לַכֹּהֲנִים וְלַלְוִיִּם כִּי
for and-for-the-Levites for-the-priests the-Law portions-of the-towns

שִׂמְחַת יְהוּדָה עַל־ הַכֹּהֲנִים וְעַל־ הַלְוִיִּם הָעֹמְדִים׃
the-ones-ministering the-Levites and-with the-priests with Judah pleasure-of

וַיִּשְׁמְרוּ מִשְׁמֶרֶת אֱלֹהֵיהֶם וּמִשְׁמֶרֶת הַטָּהֳרָה
the-purification and-service-of God-of-them service-of and-they-performed (45)

וְהַמְשֹׁרְרִים וְהַשֹּׁעֲרִים כְּמִצְוַת דָּוִיד שְׁלֹמֹה
Solomon David as-command-of and-the-gatekeepers also-the-ones-singing

בְנוֹ׃ כִּי־ בִימֵי דָוִיד וְאָסָף מִקֶּדֶם רָאשׁ°
directors-of at-long-ago and-Asaph David in-days-of for (46) son-of-him

הַמְשֹׁרְרִים וְשִׁיר־ תְּהִלָּה וְהֹדוֹת לֵאלֹהִים׃ וְכָל־
so-all-of (47) to-God and-thanksgivings praise and-song-of the-ones-singing

יִשְׂרָאֵל בִּימֵי זְרֻבָּבֶל וּבִימֵי נְחֶמְיָה נֹתְנִים
ones-contributing Nehemiah and-in-days-of Zerubbabel in-days-of Israel

מְנָיוֹת הַמְשֹׁרְרִים וְהַשֹּׁעֲרִים דְּבַר־ יוֹם בְּיוֹמוֹ
in-day-of-him day amount-of and-the-gatekeepers the-ones-singing portions-of

וּמַקְדִּשִׁים לַלְוִיִּם וְהַלְוִיִּם מַקְדִּשִׁים
ones-setting-aside and-the-Levites for-the-Levites and-ones-setting-aside

לִבְנֵי אַהֲרֹן׃ בַּיּוֹם הַהוּא נִקְרָא בְּסֵפֶר
in-Book-of he-was-read the-that on-the-day (13:1) Aaron for-descendants-of

°46 ק ראשי

[41]as well as the priests—Eliakim, Maaseiah, Mijamin, Micaiah, Elioenai, Zechariah and Hananiah with their trumpets— [42]and also Maaseiah, Shemaiah, Eleazar, Uzzi, Jehohanan, Malkijah, Elam and Ezer. The choirs sang under the direction of Jezrahiah. [43]And on that day they offered great sacrifices, rejoicing because God had given them great joy. The women and children also rejoiced. The sound of rejoicing in Jerusalem could be heard far away.

[44]At that time men were appointed to be in charge of the storerooms for the contributions, firstfruits and tithes. From the fields around the towns they were to bring into the storerooms the portions required by the Law for the priests and the Levites, for Judah was pleased with the ministering priests and Levites. [45]They performed the service of their God and the service of purification, as did also the singers and gatekeepers, according to the commands of David and his son Solomon. [46]For long ago, in the days of David and Asaph, there had been directors for the singers and for the songs of praise and thanksgiving to God. [47]So in the days of Zerubbabel and of Nehemiah, all Israel contributed the daily portions for the singers and gatekeepers. They also set aside the portion for the other Levites, and the Levites set aside the portion for the descendants of Aaron.

*Nehemiah's Final Reforms*

13 On that day the Book of Moses was read

מֹשֶׁה בְּאָזְנֵי הָעָם וְנִמְצָא כָּתוּב בּוֹ אֲשֶׁר לֹא־
not that in-him being-written and-he-was-found the-people in-ears-of Moses

יָבוֹא עַמֹּנִי וּמֹאָבִי בִּקְהַל הָאֱלֹהִים עַד־עוֹלָם׃
ever to the-God into-assembly-of or-Moabite Ammonite he-should-enter

כִּי לֹא קִדְּמוּ אֶת־ בְּנֵי יִשְׂרָאֵל בַּלֶּחֶם וּבַמָּיִם
and-with-the-waters with-the-food Israel sons-of *** they-met not because (2)

וַיִּשְׂכֹּר עָלָיו אֶת־ בִּלְעָם לְקַלְלוֹ וַיַּהֲפֹךְ אֱלֹהֵינוּ
God-of-us but-he-turned to-curse-him Balaam *** against-him but-they-hired

הַקְּלָלָה לִבְרָכָה׃ וַיְהִי כְּשָׁמְעָם אֶת־ הַתּוֹרָה
the-law *** when-to-hear-them and-he-was (3) into-blessing the-curse

וַיַּבְדִּילוּ כָל־ עֵרֶב מִיִּשְׂרָאֵל׃ וְלִפְנֵי מִזֶּה
to-this and-before (4) from-Israel foreign-descent all-of then-they-excluded

אֶלְיָשִׁיב הַכֹּהֵן נָתוּן בְּלִשְׁכַּת בֵּית־ אֱלֹהֵינוּ קָרוֹב
close God-of-us house-of over-storeroom-of being-put the-priest Eliashib

לְטוֹבִיָּה׃ וַיַּעַשׂ לוֹ לִשְׁכָּה גְדוֹלָה וְשָׁם הָיוּ
they-were and-there large room to-him and-he-provided (5) to-Tobiah

לְפָנִים נֹתְנִים אֶת־ הַמִּנְחָה הַלְּבוֹנָה וְהַכֵּלִים
and-the-articles the-incense the-grain-offering *** ones-storing formerly

וּמַעְשַׂר הַדָּגָן הַתִּירוֹשׁ וְהַיִּצְהָר מִצְוַת הַלְוִיִּם
the-Levites prescription-of and-the-oil the-new-wine the-grain also-tithe-of

וְהַמְשֹׁרְרִים וְהַשֹּׁעֲרִים וּתְרוּמַת הַכֹּהֲנִים׃
the-priests and-contribution-of and-the-gatekeepers and-the-ones-singing

וּבְכָל־ זֶה לֹא הָיִיתִי בִּירוּשָׁלָםִ כִּי בִּשְׁנַת שְׁלֹשִׁים
thirty in-year-of for in-Jerusalem I-was not this but-while-all-of (6)

וּשְׁתַּיִם לְאַרְתַּחְשַׁסְתְּא מֶלֶךְ־ בָּבֶל בָּאתִי אֶל־ הַמֶּלֶךְ וּלְקֵץ
and-at-end-of the-king to I-returned Babylon king-of of-Artaxerxes and-two

יָמִים נִשְׁאַלְתִּי מִן־ הַמֶּלֶךְ׃ וָאָבוֹא לִירוּשָׁלָםִ וָאָבִינָה
and-I-learned to-Jerusalem and-I-came-back (7) the-king from I-asked days

בָרָעָה אֲשֶׁר עָשָׂה אֶלְיָשִׁיב לְטוֹבִיָּה לַעֲשׂוֹת לוֹ נִשְׁכָּה
room to-him to-provide to-Tobiah Eliashib he-did that about-the-evil-thing

בְּחַצְרֵי בֵּית הָאֱלֹהִים׃ וַיֵּרַע לִי מְאֹד
greatly to-me and-he-displeased (8) the-God house-of in-courts-of

וָאַשְׁלִיכָה אֶת־ כָּל־ כְּלֵי בֵית־ טוֹבִיָּה הַחוּץ מִן־
from the-outside Tobiah house-of goods-of all-of *** and-I-threw-out

הַלִּשְׁכָּה׃ וָאֹמְרָה וַיְטַהֲרוּ הַלְּשָׁכוֹת וָאָשִׁיבָה
then-I-put-back the-rooms and-they-purified and-I-ordered (9) the-room

שָּׁם כְּלֵי בֵּית הָאֱלֹהִים אֶת־ הַמִּנְחָה וְהַלְּבוֹנָה׃
and-the-incense the-grain-offering with the-God house-of equipments-of there

aloud in the hearing of the people and there it was found written that no Ammonite or Moabite should ever be admitted into the assembly of God, [2]because they had not met the Israelites with food and water but had hired Balaam to call a curse down on them. (Our God, however, turned the curse into a blessing.) [3]When the people heard this law, they excluded from Israel all who were of foreign descent.

[4]Before this, Eliashib the priest had been put in charge of the storerooms of the house of our God. He was closely associated with Tobiah, and he had [5]provided him with a large room formerly used to store the grain offerings and incense and temple articles, and also the tithes of grain, new wine and oil prescribed for the Levites, singers and gatekeepers, as well as the contributions for the priests.

[6]But while all this was going on, I was not in Jerusalem, for in the thirty-second year of Artaxerxes king of Babylon I had returned to the king. Some time later I asked his permission [7]and came back to Jerusalem. Here I learned about the evil thing Eliashib had done in providing Tobiah a room in the courts of the house of God. [8]I was greatly displeased and threw all Tobiah's household goods out of the room. [9]I gave orders to purify the rooms, and then I put back into them the equipment of the house of God, with the grain offerings and the incense.

וָאֵדְעָה כִּי־ מְנָיוֹת הַלְוִיִּם לֹא נִתָּנָה
she-was-given not the-Levites portions-of that also-I-learned (10)

וַיִּבְרְחוּ אִישׁ־ לְשָׂדֵהוּ הַלְוִיִּם וְהַמְשֹׁרְרִים
and-the-ones-singing the-Levites to-field-of-him each and-they-went-back

עֹשֵׂי הַמְּלָאכָה׃ וָאָרִיבָה אֶת־ הַסְּגָנִים
the-officials *** so-I-rebuked (11) the-service ones-being-responsible-of

וָאֹמְרָה מַדּוּעַ נֶעֱזַב בֵּית־ הָאֱלֹהִים וָאֶקְבְּצֵם
then-I-called-together-them the-God house-of he-is-neglected why? and-I-asked

וָאַעֲמִדֵם עַל־ עָמְדָם׃ וְכָל־ יְהוּדָה הֵבִיאוּ
they-brought Judah and-all-of (12) post-of-them at and-I-stationed-them

מַעְשַׂר הַדָּגָן וְהַתִּירוֹשׁ וְהַיִּצְהָר לָאוֹצָרוֹת׃
into-the-storerooms and-the-oil and-the-new-wine the-grain tithe-of

וָאוֹצְרָה עַל־ אוֹצָרוֹת שֶׁלֶמְיָה הַכֹּהֵן וְצָדוֹק הַסּוֹפֵר
the-scribe and-Zadok the-priest Shelemiah storerooms over and-I-put (13)

וּפְדָיָה מִן־ הַלְוִיִּם וְעַל־ יָדָם חָנָן בֶּן־ זַכּוּר בֶּן־
son-of Zaccur son-of Hanan hand-of-them and-at the-Levites from and-Pedaiah

מַתַּנְיָה כִּי נֶאֱמָנִים נֶחְשָׁבוּ וַעֲלֵיהֶם
and-to-them they-were-considered ones-being-trustworthy because Mattaniah

לַחֲלֹק לַאֲחֵיהֶם׃ זָכְרָה־ לִּי אֱלֹהַי עַל־ זֹאת
this for God-of-me to-me remember! (14) to-brothers-of-them to-distribute

וְאַל־ תֶּמַח חֲסָדַי אֲשֶׁר עָשִׂיתִי בְּבֵית אֱלֹהַי
God-of-me for-house-of I-did that faithful-deeds-of-me you-blot-out and-not

וּבְמִשְׁמָרָיו׃ בַּיָּמִים הָהֵמָּה רָאִיתִי בִיהוּדָה ׀
in-Judah I-saw the-those in-the-days (15) and-for-services-of-him

דֹּרְכִים־ גִּתּוֹת ׀ בַּשַּׁבָּת וּמְבִיאִים הָעֲרֵמוֹת
the-grains and-ones-bringing-in on-the-Sabbath winepresses men-treading

וְעֹמְסִים עַל־ הַחֲמֹרִים וְאַף־ יַיִן עֲנָבִים וּתְאֵנִים וְכָל־
and-all-of and-figs grapes wine and-also the-donkeys on and-ones-loading

מַשָּׂא וּמְבִיאִים יְרוּשָׁלִַם בְּיוֹם הַשַּׁבָּת וָאָעִיד בְּיוֹם
on-day so-I-warned the-Sabbath on-day-of Jerusalem and-ones-bringing load

מִכְרָם צַיִד׃ וְהַצֹּרִים יָשְׁבוּ בָהּ מְבִיאִים דָּאג
fish ones-bringing in-her they-lived and-the-Tyrians (16) food to-sell-them

וְכָל־ מֶכֶר וּמֹכְרִים בַּשַּׁבָּת לִבְנֵי יְהוּדָה
Judah to-people-of on-the-Sabbath and-ones-selling merchandise and-all-of

וּבִירוּשָׁלִָם׃ וָאָרִיבָה אֵת חֹרֵי יְהוּדָה וָאֹמְרָה לָהֶם
to-them and-I-said Judah nobles-of *** and-I-rebuked (17) and-in-Jerusalem

מָה־ הַדָּבָר הָרָע הַזֶּה אֲשֶׁר אַתֶּם עֹשִׂים וּמְחַלְּלִים
and-ones-desecrating ones-doing you that the-this the-wicked the-thing what?

10I also learned that the portions assigned to the Levites had not been given to them, and that all the Levites and singers responsible for the service had gone back to their own fields.
11So I rebuked the officials and asked them, "Why is the house of God neglected?" Then I called them together and stationed them at their posts.
12All Judah brought the tithes of grain, new wine and oil into the storerooms.
13I put Shelemiah the priest, Zadok the scribe, and a Levite named Pedaiah in charge of the storerooms and made Hanan son of Zaccur, the son of Mattaniah, their assistant, because these men were considered trustworthy. They were made responsible for distributing the supplies to their brothers.

14Remember me for this, O my God, and do not blot out what I have so faithfully done for the house of my God and its services.

15In those days I saw men in Judah treading winepresses on the Sabbath and bringing in grain and loading it on donkeys, together with wine, grapes, figs and all other kinds of loads. And they were bringing all this into Jerusalem on the Sabbath. Therefore I warned them against selling food on that day.
16Men from Tyre who lived in Jerusalem were bringing in fish and all kinds of merchandise and selling them in Jerusalem on the Sabbath to the people of Judah.
17I rebuked the nobles of Judah and said to them, "What is this wicked thing you are doing—desecrating

אֶת־ יוֹם הַשַּׁבָּת׃ הֲלוֹא כֹה עָשׂוּ אֲבֹתֵיכֶם וַיָּבֵא
so-he-brought forefathers-of-you they-did same not? (18) the-Sabbath day-of ***

אֱלֹהֵינוּ עָלֵינוּ אֵת כָּל־ הָרָעָה הַזֹּאת וְעַל הָעִיר הַזֹּאת
the-this the-city and-upon the-this the-calamity all-of *** upon-us God-of-us

וְאַתֶּם מוֹסִיפִים חָרוֹן עַל־ יִשְׂרָאֵל לְחַלֵּל אֶת־ הַשַּׁבָּת׃
the-Sabbath *** to-desecrate Israel against wrath ones-stirring-up-more now-you

וַיְהִי כַּאֲשֶׁר צָלֲלוּ שַׁעֲרֵי יְרוּשָׁלִַם לִפְנֵי
before Jerusalem gates-of they-became-shadowed as-when and-he-was (19)

הַשַּׁבָּת וָאֹמְרָה וַיִּסָּגְרוּ הַדְּלָתוֹת וָאֹמְרָה אֲשֶׁר לֹא
not that and-I-ordered the-doors and-they-were-shut then-I-ordered the-Sabbath

יִפְתָּחוּם עַד אַחַר הַשַּׁבָּת וּמִנְּעָרַי הֶעֱמַדְתִּי עַל־
at I-stationed and-from-men-of-me the-Sabbath after until they-open-them

הַשְּׁעָרִים לֹא־ יָבוֹא מַשָּׂא בְּיוֹם הַשַּׁבָּת׃
the-Sabbath on-day-of load they-could-bring-in not the-gates

וַיָּלִינוּ הָרֹכְלִים וּמֹכְרֵי כָל־
all-of and-ones-selling-of the-ones-being-merchants and-they-spent-night (20)

מִמְכָּר מִחוּץ לִירוּשָׁלִָם פַּעַם וּשְׁתָּיִם׃ וָאָעִידָה בָהֶם
to-them but-I-warned (21) or-twice once of-Jerusalem at-outside good

וָאֹמְרָה אֲלֵיהֶם מַדּוּעַ אַתֶּם לֵנִים נֶגֶד הַחוֹמָה אִם־ תִּשְׁנוּ
you-do-again if the-wall by ones-spending-night you why? to-them and-I-said

יָד אֶשְׁלַח בָּכֶם מִן־ הָעֵת הַהִיא לֹא־ בָאוּ בַּשַּׁבָּת׃
on-the-Sabbath they-came not the-that the-time from on-you I-will-lay hand

וָאֹמְרָה לַלְוִיִּם אֲשֶׁר יִהְיוּ מִטַּהֲרִים
ones-purifying-themselves they-must-be that to-the-Levites then-I-commanded (22)

וּבָאִים שֹׁמְרִים הַשְּׁעָרִים לְקַדֵּשׁ אֶת־ יוֹם
day-of *** to-keep-holy the-gates and-ones-guarding and-ones-going

הַשַּׁבָּת גַּם־ זֹאת זָכְרָה־ לִּי אֱלֹהַי וְחוּסָה עָלַי
to-me and-show-mercy! God-of-me to-me remember! this also the-Sabbath

כְּרֹב חַסְדֶּךָ׃ גַּם ׀ בַּיָּמִים הָהֵם רָאִיתִי אֶת־
*** I-saw the-those in-the-days moreover (23) love-of-you as-greatness-of

הַיְּהוּדִים הֹשִׁיבוּ נָשִׁים אַשְׁדֳּדִיּוֹת עַמֳּנִיּוֹת מוֹאֲבִיּוֹת׃
Moabites Ammonites Ashdodites women they-married the-Judahites

וּבְנֵיהֶם חֲצִי מְדַבֵּר אַשְׁדּוֹדִית וְאֵינָם
and-not-they Ashdodite one-speaking half-of and-children-of-them (24)

מַכִּירִים לְדַבֵּר יְהוּדִית וְכִלְשׁוֹן עַם וָעָם׃
or-people people or-as-language-of Judahite to-speak ones-knowing

וָאָרִיב עִמָּם וָאֲקַלְלֵם וָאַכֶּה מֵהֶם אֲנָשִׁים
men of-them and-I-beat and-I-cursed-them to-them and-I-rebuked (25)

the Sabbath day? [18]Didn't your
forefathers do the same
things, so that our God
brought all this calamity upon
us and upon this city? Now
you are stirring up more wrath
against Israel by desecrating
the Sabbath."
[19]When evening shadows
fell on the gates of Jerusalem
before the Sabbath, I ordered
the doors to be shut and not
opened until the Sabbath was
over. I stationed some of my
own men at the gates so that
no load could be brought in on
the Sabbath day. [20]Once or
twice the merchants and sell-
ers of all kinds of goods spent
the night outside Jerusalem.
[21]But I warned them and said,
"Why do you spend the night
by the wall? If you do this
again, I will lay hands on
you." From that time on they
no longer came on the Sabbath. [22]Then I commanded the
Levites to purify themselves
and go and guard the gates in
order to keep the Sabbath day
holy.

Remember me for this also,
O my God, and show mercy to
me according to your great
love.

[23]Moreover, in those days I
saw men of Judah who had
married women from Ashdod,
Ammon and Moab. [24]Half of
their children spoke the language of Ashdod or the language of one of the other peoples, and did not know how to
speak the language of Judah.
[25]I rebuked them and called
curses down on them. I beat
some of the men and pulled

°23a ק אשדדיות
°23b ק עמניות

וָאֶמְרְטֵם וָאַשְׁבִּיעֵם בֵּאלֹהִים אִם־
not by-God and-I-made-take-oath-them and-I-pulled-out-hair-of-them

תִּתְּנוּ בְנֹתֵיכֶם לִבְנֵיהֶם וְאִם־ תִּשְׂאוּ
you-shall-take and-not to-sons-of-them daughters-of-you you-shall-give

מִבְּנֹתֵיהֶם לִבְנֵיכֶם וְלָכֶם׃ הֲלוֹא עַל־ אֵלֶּה
these because-of not? (26) or-for-you for-sons-of-you from-daughters-of-them

חָטָא־ שְׁלֹמֹה מֶלֶךְ יִשְׂרָאֵל וּבַגּוֹיִם הָרַבִּים לֹא־ הָיָה
he-was not the-many and-among-the-nations Israel king-of Solomon he-sinned

מֶלֶךְ כָּמֹהוּ וְאָהוּב לֵאלֹהָיו הָיָה וַיִּתְּנֵהוּ אֱלֹהִים
God and-he-made-him he-was by-God-of-him and-being-loved like-him king

מֶלֶךְ עַל־ כָּל־ יִשְׂרָאֵל גַּם־ אוֹתוֹ הֶחֱטִיאוּ הַנָּשִׁים הַנָּכְרִיּוֹת׃
the-foreigners the-women they-led-to-sin him even Israel all-of over king

וְלָכֶם הֲנִשְׁמַע לַעֲשֹׂת אֵת כָּל־ הָרָעָה
the-wickedness all-of *** to-do must-we-hear? now-about-you (27)

הַגְּדוֹלָה הַזֹּאת לִמְעֹל בֵּאלֹהֵינוּ לְהֹשִׁיב נָשִׁים
women to-marry to-God-of-us to-be-unfaithful the-this the-terrible

נָכְרִיּוֹת׃ וּמִבְּנֵי יוֹיָדָע בֶּן־ אֶלְיָשִׁיב הַכֹּהֵן הַגָּדוֹל
the-high the-priest Eliashib son-of Joiada and-from-sons-of (28) foreigners

חָתָן לְסַנְבַלַּט הַחֹרֹנִי וָאַבְרִיחֵהוּ מֵעָלָי׃
from-with-me and-I-drove-away-him the-Horonite of-Sanballat son-in-law

זָכְרָה לָהֶם אֱלֹהָי עַל גָּאֳלֵי הַכְּהֻנָּה
the-priesthood defilements-of because-of God-of-me to-them remember! (29)

וּבְרִית הַכְּהֻנָּה וְהַלְוִיִּם׃ וְטִהַרְתִּים
so-I-purified-them (30) and-the-Levites the-priesthood and-covenant-of

מִכָּל־ נֵכָר וָאַעֲמִידָה מִשְׁמָרוֹת לַכֹּהֲנִים
to-the-priests duties and-I-assigned foreign from-every-of

וְלַלְוִיִּם אִישׁ בִּמְלַאכְתּוֹ׃ וּלְקֻרְבַּן
and-for-contribution-of (31) to-task-of-him each and-to-the-Levites

הָעֵצִים בְּעִתִּים מְזֻמָּנוֹת וְלַבִּכּוּרִים
and-for-the-firstfruits ones-being-designated at-times the-woods

זָכְרָה־ לִּי אֱלֹהַי לְטוֹבָה׃
with-favor God-of-me to-me remember!

out their hair. I made them take an oath in God's name and said: "You are not to give your daughters in marriage to their sons, nor are you to take their daughters in marriage for your sons or for yourselves. [26]Was it not because of marriages like these that Solomon king of Israel sinned? Among the many nations there was no king like him. He was loved by his God, and God made him king over all Israel, but even he was led into sin by foreign women. [27]Must we hear now that you too are doing all this terrible wickedness and are being unfaithful to our God by marrying foreign women?"

[28]One of the sons of Joiada son of Eliashib the high priest was son-in-law to Sanballat the Horonite. And I drove him away from me.

[29]Remember them, O my God, because they defiled the priestly office and the covenant of the priesthood and of the Levites.

[30]So I purified the priests and the Levites of everything foreign, and assigned them duties, each to his own task. [31]I also made provision for contributions of wood at designated times, and for the firstfruits.

Remember me with favor, O my God.

וַיְהִי בִּימֵי אֲחַשְׁוֵרוֹשׁ הוּא אֲחַשְׁוֵרוֹשׁ הַמֹּלֵךְ מֵהֹדּוּ
from-India the-one-ruling Ahasuerus he Ahasuerus in-days-of and-he-was (1:1)

וְעַד־ כּוּשׁ שֶׁבַע וְעֶשְׂרִים וּמֵאָה מְדִינָה׃ בַּיָּמִים הָהֵם
the-those in-the-days (2) province and-hundred and-twenty seven Cush even-to

כְּשֶׁבֶת ׀ הַמֶּלֶךְ אֲחַשְׁוֵרוֹשׁ עַל כִּסֵּא מַלְכוּתוֹ אֲשֶׁר בְּשׁוּשַׁן
in-Susa that royalty-of-him throne-of from Ahasuerus the-king as-to-reign

הַבִּירָה׃ בִּשְׁנַת שָׁלוֹשׁ לְמָלְכוֹ עָשָׂה מִשְׁתֶּה לְכָל־
for-all-of banquet he-gave to-reign-him three in-year-of (3) the-citadel

שָׂרָיו וַעֲבָדָיו חֵיל ׀ פָּרַס וּמָדַי
and-Media Persia military-leader-of and-officials-of-him nobles-of-him

הַפַּרְתְּמִים וְשָׂרֵי הַמְּדִינוֹת לְפָנָיו׃ בְּהַרְאֹתוֹ אֶת־
*** when-to-display-him (4) before-him the-provinces and-nobles-of the-princes

עֹשֶׁר כְּבוֹד מַלְכוּתוֹ וְאֶת־ יְקָר תִּפְאֶרֶת גְּדוּלָּתוֹ
majesty-of-him glory-of splendor-of and kingdom-of-him vastness-of wealth-of

יָמִים רַבִּים שְׁמוֹנִים וּמְאַת יוֹם׃ וּבִמְלוֹאת ׀ הַיָּמִים
the-days and-when-to-be-over (5) day and-hundred-of eighty many days

הָאֵלֶּה עָשָׂה הַמֶּלֶךְ לְכָל־ הָעָם הַנִּמְצְאִים בְּשׁוּשַׁן
in-Susa the-ones-being-found the-people for-all-of the-king he-gave the-these

הַבִּירָה לְמִגָּדוֹל וְעַד־ קָטָן מִשְׁתֶּה שִׁבְעַת יָמִים
days seven-of banquet least even-to for-from-greatest the-citadel

בַּחֲצַר גִּנַּת בִּיתַן הַמֶּלֶךְ׃ חוּר ׀ כַּרְפַּס וּתְכֵלֶת
and-blue linen white (6) the-king palace-of garden-of in-enclosure-of

אָחוּז בְּחַבְלֵי־ בוּץ וְאַרְגָּמָן עַל־ גְּלִילֵי כֶסֶף
silver rings-of to and-purple white-linen with-cords-of being-fastened

וְעַמּוּדֵי שֵׁשׁ מִטּוֹת ׀ זָהָב וָכֶסֶף עַל רִצְפַת בַּהַט־
porphyry pavement-of on and-silver gold couches-of marble and-pillars-of

וָשֵׁשׁ וְדַר וְסֹחָרֶת׃ וְהַשְׁקוֹת
and-to-serve-wine (7) and-costly-stone and-mother-of-pearl and-marble

בִּכְלֵי זָהָב וְכֵלִים מִכֵּלִים שׁוֹנִים וְיֵין
and-wine-of ones-differing from-goblets and-goblets gold in-goblets-of

מַלְכוּת רָב כְּיַד הַמֶּלֶךְ׃ וְהַשְּׁתִיָּה כַדָּת
by-the-command and-the-drinking (8) the-king as-hand-of abundant royalty

אֵין אֹנֵס כִּי־ כֵן ׀ יִסַּד הַמֶּלֶךְ עַל כָּל־ רַב
wine-steward-of all-of to the-king he-instructed so for compelling no

בֵּיתוֹ לַעֲשׂוֹת כִּרְצוֹן אִישׁ־ וָאִישׁ׃ גַּם וַשְׁתִּי הַמַּלְכָּה
the-queen Vashti also (9) and-man man as-wish-of to-serve palace-of-him

עָשְׂתָה מִשְׁתֵּה נָשִׁים בֵּית הַמַּלְכוּת אֲשֶׁר לַמֶּלֶךְ אֲחַשְׁוֵרוֹשׁ׃
Ahasuerus of-the-king that the-royalty palace-of women banquet-of she-gave

### *Queen Vashti Deposed*

1 This is what happened during the time of Xerxes,[a] the Xerxes who ruled over 127 provinces stretching from India to Cush[b]:
2At that time
King Xerxes reigned from his royal throne in the citadel of Susa,
3and in the third year of his reign he gave a banquet for all his nobles and officials. The military leaders of Persia and Media, the princes, and the nobles of the provinces were present.
4For a full 180 days he displayed the vast wealth of his kingdom and the splendor and glory of his majesty.
5When these days were over,
the king gave a banquet, lasting seven days, in the enclosed garden of the king's palace, for all the people from the least to the greatest, who were in the citadel of Susa.
6The garden had hangings of
white and blue linen, fastened with cords of white linen and purple material to silver rings on marble pillars. There were couches of gold and silver on a mosaic pavement of porphyry, marble, mother-of-pearl and other costly stones.
7Wine
was served in goblets of gold, each one different from the other, and the royal wine was abundant, in keeping with the king's liberality.
8By the king's
command each guest was allowed to drink in his own way, for the king instructed all the wine stewards to serve each man what he wished.
9Queen Vashti also gave a
banquet for the women in the royal palace of King Xerxes.

[a]1 Hebrew *Ahasuerus,* a variant of Xerxes' name; here and throughout Esther
[b]1 That is, the upper Nile region

בַּיּוֹם הַשְּׁבִיעִי כְּטוֹב לֵב־הַמֶּלֶךְ בַּיָּיִן
from-the-wine the-king spirit-of when-high the-seventh on-the-day (10)

אָמַר לִמְהוּמָן בִּזְּתָא חַרְבוֹנָא בִּגְתָא וַאֲבַגְתָא זֵתַר וְכַרְכַּס
and-Carcas Zethar and-Abagtha Bigtha Harbona Biztha to-Mehuman he-commanded

שִׁבְעַת הַסָּרִיסִים הַמְשָׁרְתִים אֶת־פְּנֵי הַמֶּלֶךְ אֲחַשְׁוֵרוֹשׁ׃
Ahasuerus the-king before *** the-ones-serving the-eunuchs seven-of

לְהָבִיא אֶת־וַשְׁתִּי הַמַּלְכָּה לִפְנֵי הַמֶּלֶךְ בְּכֶתֶר מַלְכוּת
royalty with-crown-of the-king before the-queen Vashti *** to-bring (11)

לְהַרְאוֹת הָעַמִּים וְהַשָּׂרִים אֶת־יָפְיָהּ כִּי־טוֹבַת
lovely-of for beauty-of-her *** and-the-nobles the-peoples to-display

מַרְאֶה הִיא׃ וַתְּמָאֵן הַמַּלְכָּה וַשְׁתִּי לָבוֹא בִּדְבַר
at-command-of to-come Vashti the-queen but-she-refused (12) she appearance

הַמֶּלֶךְ אֲשֶׁר בְּיַד הַסָּרִיסִים וַיִּקְצֹף הַמֶּלֶךְ מְאֹד
very the-king then-he-became-furious the-attendants by-hand-of that the-king

וַחֲמָתוֹ בָּעֲרָה בוֹ׃ וַיֹּאמֶר הַמֶּלֶךְ לַחֲכָמִים
with-wise-men the-king and-he-spoke (13) in-him she-burned and-anger-of-him

יֹדְעֵי הָעִתִּים כִּי־כֵן דְּבַר הַמֶּלֶךְ לִפְנֵי כָּל־
all-of before the-king custom-of so since the-times ones-understanding-of

יֹדְעֵי דָּת וָדִין׃ וְהַקָּרֹב אֵלָיו כַּרְשְׁנָא
Carshena to-him and-the-one-close (14) and-justice law ones-being-expert-of

שֵׁתָר אַדְמָתָא תַרְשִׁישׁ מֶרֶס מַרְסְנָא מְמוּכָן שִׁבְעַת שָׂרֵי ׀ פָּרַס
Persia nobles-of seven-of Memucan Marsena Meres Tarshish Admatha Shethar

וּמָדַי רֹאֵי פְּנֵי הַמֶּלֶךְ הַיֹּשְׁבִים רִאשֹׁנָה
highest the-ones-being the-king faces-of ones-seeing-of and-Media

בַּמַּלְכוּת׃ כְּדָת מַה־לַּעֲשׂוֹת בַּמַּלְכָּה וַשְׁתִּי עַל ׀
because Vashti to-the-queen to-do what? according-to-law (15) in-the-kingdom

אֲשֶׁר לֹא־עָשְׂתָה אֶת־מַאֲמַר הַמֶּלֶךְ אֲחַשְׁוֵרוֹשׁ בְּיַד הַסָּרִיסִים׃
the-eunuchs by-hand-of Ahasuerus the-king command-of *** she-obeyed not that

וַיֹּאמֶר מוּמְכָן° לִפְנֵי הַמֶּלֶךְ וְהַשָּׂרִים לֹא
not and-the-nobles the-king in-presences-of Memucan then-he-replied (16)

עַל־הַמֶּלֶךְ לְבַדּוֹ עָוְתָה וַשְׁתִּי הַמַּלְכָּה כִּי עַל־
against but the-queen Vashti she-did-wrong by-himself the-king against

כָּל־הַשָּׂרִים וְעַל־כָּל־הָעַמִּים אֲשֶׁר בְּכָל־מְדִינוֹת
provinces-of in-all-of who the-peoples all-of and-against the-nobles all-of

הַמֶּלֶךְ אֲחַשְׁוֵרוֹשׁ׃ כִּי־יֵצֵא דְבַר־הַמַּלְכָּה עַל־כָּל־
all-of to the-queen conduct-of he-will-go-out for (17) Ahasuerus the-king

הַנָּשִׁים לְהַבְזוֹת בַּעְלֵיהֶן בְּעֵינֵיהֶן בְּאָמְרָם
when-to-say-them in-eyes-of-them husbands-of-them to-despise the-women

10On the seventh day, when King Xerxes was in high spirits from wine, he commanded the seven eunuchs who served him—Mehuman, Biztha, Harbona, Bigtha, Abagtha, Zethar and Carcas— 11to bring before him Queen Vashti, wearing her royal crown, in order to display her beauty to the people and nobles, for she was lovely to look at. 12But when the attendants delivered the king's command, Queen Vashti refused to come. Then the king became furious and burned with anger.

13Since it was customary for the king to consult experts in matters of law and justice, he spoke with the wise men who understood the laws 14and were closest to the king—Carshena, Shethar, Admatha, Tarshish, Meres, Marsena and Memucan, the seven nobles of Persia and Media who had special access to the king and were highest in the kingdom.

15"According to law, what must be done to Queen Vashti?" he asked. "She has not obeyed the command of King Xerxes that the eunuchs have taken to her."

16Then Memucan replied in the presence of the king and the nobles, "Queen Vashti has done wrong, not only against the king but also against all the nobles and the peoples of all the provinces of King Xerxes. 17For the queen's conduct will become known to all the women, and so they will despise their husbands and

°16 ק ממוכן

הַמֶּלֶךְ אֲחַשְׁוֵרוֹשׁ אָמַר לְהָבִיא אֶת־ וַשְׁתִּי הַמַּלְכָּה לְפָנָיו
before-him the-queen Vashti *** to-bring he-commanded Ahasuerus the-king

וְלֹא־ בָאָה׃ וְהַיּוֹם הַזֶּה תֹּאמַרְנָה | שָׂרוֹת
noble-women-of they-will-respond the-this and-the-day (18) she-came but-not

פָּרַס־ וּמָדַי אֲשֶׁר שָׁמְעוּ אֶת־ דְּבַר הַמַּלְכָּה לְכֹל שָׂרֵי
nobles-of of-all-of the-queen conduct-of *** they-heard who and-Media Persia

הַמֶּלֶךְ וּכְדַי בִּזָּיוֹן וָקָצֶף׃ אִם־עַל־ הַמֶּלֶךְ טוֹב
pleasing the-king to if (19) and-discord disrespect and-as-no-end-of the-king

יֵצֵא דְבַר־ מַלְכוּת מִלְּפָנָיו וְיִכָּתֵב
and-let-him-be-written from-before-him royalty decree-of let-him-issue

בְּדָתֵי פָרַס־ וּמָדַי וְלֹא יַעֲבוֹר אֲשֶׁר לֹא־ תָבוֹא
she-may-enter never that he-can-be-repealed that-not and-Media Persia in-laws-of

וַשְׁתִּי לִפְנֵי הַמֶּלֶךְ אֲחַשְׁוֵרוֹשׁ וּמַלְכוּתָהּ יִתֵּן
let-him-give also-royal-position-of-her Ahasuerus the-king presences-of Vashti

הַמֶּלֶךְ לִרְעוּתָהּ הַטּוֹבָה מִמֶּנָּה׃ וְנִשְׁמַע
when-he-is-heard (20) than-her the-one-better to-contemporary-of-her the-king

פִּתְגָם הַמֶּלֶךְ אֲשֶׁר־ יַעֲשֶׂה בְּכָל־ מַלְכוּתוֹ כִּי
indeed realm-of-him through-all-of he-proclaims that the-king edict-of

רַבָּה הִיא וְכָל־ הַנָּשִׁים יִתְּנוּ יְקָר לְבַעְלֵיהֶן
to-husbands-of-them respect they-will-give the-women and-all-of she vast

לְמִגָּדוֹל וְעַד־ קָטָן׃ וַיִּיטַב הַדָּבָר בְּעֵינֵי
in-eyes-of the-advice and-he-was-pleasing (21) least even-to to-from-greatest

הַמֶּלֶךְ וְהַשָּׂרִים וַיַּעַשׂ הַמֶּלֶךְ כִּדְבַר מְמוּכָן׃
Memucan as-proposal-of the-king so-he-did and-the-nobles the-king

וַיִּשְׁלַח סְפָרִים אֶל־ כָּל־ מְדִינוֹת הַמֶּלֶךְ אֶל־ מְדִינָה
province to the-king provinces-of all-of to dispatches and-he-sent (22)

וּמְדִינָה כִּכְתָבָהּ וְאֶל־ עַם וָעָם כִּלְשׁוֹנוֹ
in-language-of-him and-people people and-to in-script-of-her and-province

לִהְיוֹת כָּל־ אִישׁ שֹׂרֵר בְּבֵיתוֹ וּמְדַבֵּר כִּלְשׁוֹן
in-tongue-of and-proclaiming over-household-of-him ruling man every-of to-be

עַמּוֹ׃ אַחַר הַדְּבָרִים הָאֵלֶּה כְּשֹׁךְ חֲמַת
anger-of when-to-subside the-these the-things after (2:1) people-of-him

הַמֶּלֶךְ אֲחַשְׁוֵרוֹשׁ זָכַר אֶת־ וַשְׁתִּי וְאֵת אֲשֶׁר־ עָשָׂתָה וְאֵת אֲשֶׁר־
what and she-did what and Vashti *** he-remembered Ahasuerus the-king

נִגְזַר עָלֶיהָ׃ וַיֹּאמְרוּ נַעֲרֵי־ הַמֶּלֶךְ
the-king attendants-of then-they-proposed (2) about-her he-was-decreed

מְשָׁרְתָיו יְבַקְשׁוּ לַמֶּלֶךְ נְעָרוֹת בְּתוּלוֹת
virgins young-women for-the-king let-them-search ones-serving-him

say, 'King Xerxes commanded Queen Vashti to be brought before him, but she would not come.' [18]This very day the Persian and Median women of the nobility who have heard about the queen's conduct will respond to all the king's nobles in the same way. There will be no end of disrespect and discord.

[19]"Therefore, if it pleases the king, let him issue a royal decree and let it be written in the laws of Persia and Media, which cannot be repealed, that Vashti is never again to enter the presence of King Xerxes. Also let the king give her royal position to someone else who is better than she. [20]Then when the king's edict is proclaimed throughout all his vast realm, all the women will respect their husbands, from the least to the greatest."

[21]The king and his nobles were pleased with this advice, so the king did as Memucan proposed. [22]He sent dispatches to all parts of the kingdom, to each province in its own script and to each people in its own language, proclaiming in each people's tongue that every man should be ruler over his own household.

*Esther Made Queen*

2 Later when the anger of King Xerxes had subsided, he remembered Vashti and what she had done and what he had decreed about her. [2]Then the king's personal attendants proposed, "Let a search be made for beautiful young virgins for the king.

טוֹבוֹת מַרְאֶה׃ וְיַפְקֵד הַמֶּלֶךְ פְּקִידִים
commissioners the-king and-let-him-appoint (3) appearance ones-beautiful-of

בְּכָל־ מְדִינוֹת מַלְכוּתוֹ וְיִקְבְּצוּ אֶת־ כָּל־ נַעֲרָה־
girl all-of *** and-let-them-bring realm-of-him provinces-of in-all-of

בְתוּלָה טוֹבַת מַרְאֶה אֶל־שׁוּשַׁן הַבִּירָה אֶל־ בֵּית הַנָּשִׁים
the-women harem-of into the-citadel Susa to appearance beautiful-of virgin

אֶל־ יַד הֵגֶא סְרִיס הַמֶּלֶךְ שֹׁמֵר הַנָּשִׁים
the-women one-having-charge-of the-king eunuch-of Hegai hand-of under

וְנָתוֹן תַּמְרוּקֵיהֶן׃ וְהַנַּעֲרָה אֲשֶׁר תִּיטַב
she-is-pleasing who then-the-girl (4) beauty-treatments-of-them and-to-give

בְּעֵינֵי הַמֶּלֶךְ תִּמְלֹךְ תַּחַת וַשְׁתִּי וַיִּיטַב
and-he-was-appealing Vashti instead-of let-her-be-queen the-king in-eyes-of

הַדָּבָר בְּעֵינֵי הַמֶּלֶךְ וַיַּעַשׂ כֵּן׃ אִישׁ יְהוּדִי הָיָה בְּשׁוּשַׁן
in-Susa he-was Jew man (5) this and-he-did the-king in-eyes-of the-advice

הַבִּירָה וּשְׁמוֹ מָרְדֳּכַי בֶּן יָאִיר בֶּן־ שִׁמְעִי בֶּן־ קִישׁ
Kish son-of Shimei son-of Jair son-of Mordecai and-name-of-him the-citadel

אִישׁ יְמִינִי׃ אֲשֶׁר הָגְלָה מִירוּשָׁלַיִם עִם־ הַגֹּלָה אֲשֶׁר
who the-captive among from-Jerusalem he-was-exiled who (6) Benjamite man

הָגְלְתָה עִם יְכָנְיָה מֶלֶךְ־ יְהוּדָה אֲשֶׁר הֶגְלָה נְבוּכַדְנֶאצַּר
Nebuchadnezzar he-captured whom Judah king-of Jeconiah with she-was-captured

מֶלֶךְ בָּבֶל׃ וַיְהִי אֹמֵן אֶת־ הֲדַסָּה הִיא אֶסְתֵּר בַּת־
daughter-of Esther she Hadassah *** bringing-up and-he-was (7) Babylon king-of

דֹּדוֹ כִּי אֵין לָהּ אָב וָאֵם וְהַנַּעֲרָה יְפַת־ תֹּאַר
form lovely-of and-the-girl or-mother father to-her not because uncle-of-him

וְטוֹבַת מַרְאֶה וּבְמוֹת אָבִיהָ וְאִמָּהּ
and-mother-of-her father-of-her and-at-death-of feature and-fine-of

לְקָחָהּ מָרְדֳּכַי לוֹ לְבַת׃ וַיְהִי בְּהִשָּׁמַע
when-to-be-heard and-he-was (8) as-daughter to-him Mordecai he-took-her

דְּבַר־ הַמֶּלֶךְ וְדָתוֹ וּבְהִקָּבֵץ נְעָרוֹת רַבּוֹת אֶל־
to many girls and-when-to-be-brought and-edict-of-him the-king order-of

שׁוּשַׁן הַבִּירָה אֶל־ יַד הֵגָי וַתִּלָּקַח אֶסְתֵּר אֶל־ בֵּית
palace-of to Esther also-she-was-taken Hegai hand-of under the-citadel Susa

הַמֶּלֶךְ אֶל־ יַד הֵגַי שֹׁמֵר הַנָּשִׁים׃ וַתִּיטַב
and-she-was-pleasing (9) the-women one-having-charge-of Hegai hand-of to the-king

הַנַּעֲרָה בְעֵינָיו וַתִּשָּׂא חֶסֶד לְפָנָיו וַיְבַהֵל אֶת־
*** and-he-was-immediate before-him favor and-she-won in-eyes-of-him the-girl

תַּמְרוּקֶיהָ וְאֶת־ מָנוֹתֶהָ לָתֵת לָהּ וְאֵת שֶׁבַע
seven-of and to-her to-provide foods-of-her and beauty-treatments-of-her

3Let the king appoint commissioners in every province of
his realm to bring all these
beautiful girls into the harem
at the citadel of Susa. Let them
be placed under the care of
Hegai, the king's eunuch, who
is in charge of the women; and
let beauty treatments be given
to them. 4Then let the girl who
pleases the king be queen instead of Vashti." This advice
appealed to the king, and he
followed it.

5Now there was in the citadel of Susa a Jew of the tribe of
Benjamin, named Mordecai
son of Jair, the son of Shimei,
the son of Kish, 6who had
been carried into exile from
Jerusalem by Nebuchadnezzar
king of Babylon, among those
taken captive with Jehoiachin[c] king of Judah. 7Mordecai
had a cousin named Hadas-
sah, whom he had brought up
because she had neither father
nor mother. This girl, who was
also known as Esther, was
lovely in form and features,
and Mordecai had taken her as
his own daughter when her
father and mother died.

8When the king's order and
edict had been proclaimed,
many girls were brought to the
citadel of Susa and put under
the care of Hegai. Esther also
was taken to the king's palace
and entrusted to Hegai, who
had charge of the harem. 9The
girl pleased him and won his
favor. Immediately he provided her with her beauty
treatments and special food.

[c]6 Hebrew *Jeconiah*, a variant of *Jehoiachin*

הַנְּעָרוֹת הָרְאֻיוֹת לָתֶת־ לָהּ מִבֵּית הַמֶּלֶךְ
the-king from-palace-of to-her to-assign the-ones-being-selected the-maids

וַיְשַׁנֶּהָ וְאֶת־ נַעֲרוֹתֶיהָ לְטוֹב בֵּית הַנָּשִׁים׃ (10) לֹא־
not (10) the-women harem-of to-best-of maids-of-her and and-he-moved-her

הִגִּידָה אֶסְתֵּר אֶת־ עַמָּהּ וְאֶת־ מוֹלַדְתָּהּ כִּי מָרְדֳּכַי
Mordecai because family-of-her and nationality-of-her *** Esther she-revealed

צִוָּה עָלֶיהָ אֲשֶׁר לֹא־ תַגִּיד׃ (11) וּבְכָל־ יוֹם
day and-on-every-of (11) she-should-reveal not that to-her he-commanded

וָיוֹם מָרְדֳּכַי מִתְהַלֵּךְ לִפְנֵי חֲצַר בֵּית־ הַנָּשִׁים לָדַעַת
to-find-out the-women harem-of courtyard-of near walking Mordecai and-day

אֶת־ שְׁלוֹם אֶסְתֵּר וּמַה־ יֵּעָשֶׂה בָּהּ׃ (12) וּבְהַגִּיעַ
and-before-to-come (12) to-her he-happened and-what Esther welfare-of ***

תֹּר נַעֲרָה וְנַעֲרָה לָבוֹא אֶל־ הַמֶּלֶךְ אֲחַשְׁוֵרוֹשׁ מִקֵּץ הֱיוֹת
to-be when-completion Ahasuerus the-king to to-go-in and-girl girl turn-of

לָהּ כְּדָת הַנָּשִׁים שְׁנֵים עָשָׂר חֹדֶשׁ כִּי כֵּן יִמְלְאוּ
they-were-completed so for month ten two the-women as-prescription-of to-her

יְמֵי מְרוּקֵיהֶן שִׁשָּׁה חֳדָשִׁים בְּשֶׁמֶן הַמֹּר וְשִׁשָּׁה
and-six the-myrrh with-oil-of months six beauty-treatments-of-her days-of

חֳדָשִׁים בַּבְּשָׂמִים וּבְתַמְרוּקֵי הַנָּשִׁים׃ (13) וּבָזֶה
and-as-this (13) the-women and-with-cosmetics-of with-the-perfumes months

הַנַּעֲרָה בָּאָה אֶל־ הַמֶּלֶךְ אֵת כָּל־ אֲשֶׁר תֹּאמַר יִנָּתֵן לָהּ
to-her he-was-given she-wanted that anything *** the-king to going the-girl

לָבוֹא עִמָּהּ מִבֵּית הַנָּשִׁים עַד־ בֵּית הַמֶּלֶךְ׃
the-king palace-of to the-women from-harem-of with-her to-take

(14) בָּעֶרֶב הִיא בָאָה וּבַבֹּקֶר הִיא שָׁבָה אֶל־ בֵּית
harem-of to returning she and-in-the-morning going she in-the-evening (14)

הַנָּשִׁים שֵׁנִי אֶל־ יַד שַׁעַשְׁגַז סְרִיס הַמֶּלֶךְ
the-king eunuch-of Shaashgaz hand-of to another-part the-women

שֹׁמֵר הַפִּילַגְשִׁים לֹא־ תָבוֹא עוֹד אֶל־ הַמֶּלֶךְ
the-king to again she-returned not the-concubines one-being-in-charge-of

כִּי אִם־ חָפֵץ בָּהּ הַמֶּלֶךְ וְנִקְרְאָה בְשֵׁם׃
by-name and-she-was-summoned the-king with-her he-was-pleased if unless

(15) וּבְהַגִּיעַ תֹּר־ אֶסְתֵּר בַּת־ אֲבִיחַיִל דֹּד מָרְדֳּכַי
Mordecai uncle-of Abihail daughter-of Esther turn-of and-when-to-come (15)

אֲשֶׁר לָקַח־ לוֹ לְבַת לָבוֹא אֶל־ הַמֶּלֶךְ לֹא בִקְשָׁה
she-asked-for not the-king to to-go as-daughter for-him he-adopted whom

דָּבָר כִּי אִם אֶת־ אֲשֶׁר יֹאמַר הֵגַי סְרִיס־ הַמֶּלֶךְ
the-king eunuch-of Hegai he-suggested what *** than other anything

He assigned to her seven maids selected from the king's palace and moved her and her maids into the best place in the harem.

10 Esther had not revealed her nationality and family background, because Mordecai had forbidden her to do
so. 11 Every day he walked back and forth near the courtyard of the harem to find out how Esther was and what was happening to her.

12 Before a girl's turn came to go in to King Xerxes, she had to complete twelve months of beauty treatments prescribed for the women, six months with oil of myrrh and six with perfumes and cosmetics.
13 And this is how she would go to the king: Anything she wanted was given her to take with her from the harem to the king's palace. 14 In the evening
she would go there and in the morning return to another part of the harem to the care of Shaashgaz, the king's eunuch who was in charge of the concubines. She would not return to the king unless he was pleased with her and summoned her by name.

15 When the turn came for Esther (the girl Mordecai had adopted, the daughter of his uncle Abihail) to go to the king, she asked for nothing other than what Hegai, the king's eunuch who was in

שֹׁמֵר הַנָּשִׁים וַתְּהִי אֶסְתֵּר נֹשֵׂאת חֵן בְּעֵינֵי
in-eyes-of favor winning Esther and-she-was the-women one-being-in-charge-of

כָּל־ רֹאֶיהָ׃ וַתִּלָּקַח אֶסְתֵּר אֶל־ הַמֶּלֶךְ אֲחַשְׁוֵרוֹשׁ
Ahasuerus the-king to Esther and-she-was-taken (16) ones-seeing-her all-of

אֶל־ בֵּית מַלְכוּתוֹ בַּחֹדֶשׁ הָעֲשִׂירִי הוּא־ חֹדֶשׁ טֵבֵת
Tebeth month-of that the-tenth in-the-month royalty-of-him residence-of in

בִּשְׁנַת־ שֶׁבַע לְמַלְכוּתוֹ׃ וַיֶּאֱהַב הַמֶּלֶךְ אֶת־
*** the-king now-he-was-attracted (17) of-reign-of-him seven in-year-of

אֶסְתֵּר מִכָּל־ הַנָּשִׁים וַתִּשָּׂא־ חֵן וָחֶסֶד לְפָנָיו
before-him and-approval favor and-she-won the-women more-than-any-of Esther

מִכָּל־ הַבְּתוּלֹת וַיָּשֶׂם כֶּתֶר־ מַלְכוּת בְּרֹאשָׁהּ
on-head-of-her royalty crown-of so-he-set the-virgins more-than-any-of

וַיַּמְלִיכֶהָ תַּחַת וַשְׁתִּי׃ וַיַּעַשׂ הַמֶּלֶךְ מִשְׁתֶּה
banquet the-king and-he-gave (18) Vashti instead-of and-he-made-queen-her

גָדוֹל לְכָל־ שָׂרָיו וַעֲבָדָיו אֵת מִשְׁתֵּה אֶסְתֵּר
Esther banquet-of *** and-officials-of-him nobles-of-him for-all-of great

וַהֲנָחָה לַמְּדִינוֹת עָשָׂה וַיִּתֵּן מַשְׂאֵת
gift and-he-distributed he-proclaimed throughout-the-provinces and-holiday

כְּיַד הַמֶּלֶךְ׃ וּבְהִקָּבֵץ בְּתוּלוֹת שֵׁנִית
second-time virgins and-when-to-be-assembled (19) the-king as-hand-of

וּמָרְדֳּכַי יֹשֵׁב בְּשַׁעַר־ הַמֶּלֶךְ׃ אֵין אֶסְתֵּר מַגֶּדֶת
revealing Esther not (20) the-king at-gate-of sitting then-Mordecai

מוֹלַדְתָּהּ וְאֶת־ עַמָּהּ כַּאֲשֶׁר צִוָּה עָלֶיהָ מָרְדֳּכָי וְאֶת־
and Mordecai to-her he-told just-as nationality-of-her or family-of-her

מַאֲמַר מָרְדֳּכַי אֶסְתֵּר עֹשָׂה כַּאֲשֶׁר הָיְתָה בְאָמְנָה
when-bringing-up she-did just-as following Esther Mordecai instruction-of

אִתּוֹ׃ בַּיָּמִים הָהֵם וּמָרְדֳּכַי יֹשֵׁב בְּשַׁעַר־
at-gate-of sitting when-Mordecai the-those during-the-days (21) with-him

הַמֶּלֶךְ קָצַף בִּגְתָן וָתֶרֶשׁ שְׁנֵי־ סָרִיסֵי הַמֶּלֶךְ
the-king officers-of two-of and-Teresh Bigthan he-became-angry the-king

מִשֹּׁמְרֵי הַסַּף וַיְבַקְשׁוּ לִשְׁלֹחַ יָד
hand to-send and-they-conspired the-doorway from-ones-guarding-of

בַּמֶּלֶךְ אֲחַשְׁוֵרֹשׁ׃ וַיִּוָּדַע הַדָּבָר לְמָרְדֳּכַי
by-Mordecai the-plot but-he-was-found-out (22) Ahasuerus against-the-king

וַיַּגֵּד לְאֶסְתֵּר הַמַּלְכָּה וַתֹּאמֶר אֶסְתֵּר לַמֶּלֶךְ בְּשֵׁם
in-name-of to-the-king Esther and-she-reported the-queen to-Esther and-he-told

מָרְדֳּכָי׃ וַיְבֻקַּשׁ הַדָּבָר וַיִּמָּצֵא
and-he-was-found the-report when-he-was-investigated (23) Mordecai

charge of the harem, sug-
gested. And Esther won the favor of everyone who saw her.
16She was taken to King Xerxes
in the royal residence in the
tenth month, the month of
Tebeth, in the seventh year of
his reign.
17Now the king was attracted to Esther more than to any
of the other women, and she
won his favor and approval
more than any of the other
virgins. So he set a royal
crown on her head and made
her queen instead of Vashti.
18And the king gave a great
banquet, Esther's banquet, for
all his nobles and officials. He
proclaimed a holiday throughout the provinces and distributed gifts with royal liberality.

*Mordecai Uncovers a Conspiracy*

19When the virgins were assembled a second time, Mordecai was sitting at the king's
gate. 20But Esther had kept secret her family background
and nationality just as Mordecai had told her to do, for
she continued to follow Mordecai's instructions as she had
done when he was bringing
her up.
21During the time Mordecai
was sitting at the king's gate,
Bigthana[d] and Teresh, two of
the king's officers who guarded the doorway, became angry
and conspired to assassinate
King Xerxes. 22But Mordecai
found out about the plot and
told Queen Esther, who in
turn reported it to the king,
giving credit to Mordecai.
23And when the report was in-
vestigated and found to be

[d]21 Hebrew *Bigthan*, a variant of *Bigthana*

וַיִּתָּלוּ שְׁנֵיהֶם עַל־ עֵץ וַיִּכָּתֵב בְּסֵפֶר
in-book-of and-he-was-recorded gallows on two-of-them then-they-were-hanged

דִּבְרֵי הַיָּמִים לִפְנֵי הַמֶּלֶךְ׃ אַחַר | הַדְּבָרִים הָאֵלֶּה
the-these the-events after (3:1) the-king in-presences-of the-days annals-of

גִּדַּל° הַמֶּלֶךְ אֲחַשְׁוֵרוֹשׁ אֶת־ הָמָן בֶּן־ הַמְּדָתָא הָאֲגָגִי
the-Agagite Hammedatha son-of Haman *** Ahasuerus the-king he-honored

וַיְנַשְּׂאֵהוּ וַיָּשֶׂם אֶת־ כִּסְאוֹ מֵעַל כָּל־ הַשָּׂרִים
the-nobles all-of at-above seat-of-him *** and-he-gave and-he-elevated-him

אֲשֶׁר אִתּוֹ׃ וְכָל־ עַבְדֵי הַמֶּלֶךְ אֲשֶׁר־ בְּשַׁעַר הַמֶּלֶךְ
the-king at-gate-of who the-king officials-of and-all-of (2) with-him who

כֹּרְעִים וּמִשְׁתַּחֲוִים לְהָמָן כִּי־ כֵן צִוָּה־ לוֹ
about-him he-commanded this for to-Haman and-ones-paying-honor ones-kneeling

הַמֶּלֶךְ וּמָרְדֳּכַי לֹא יִכְרַע וְלֹא יִשְׁתַּחֲוֶה׃ וַיֹּאמְרוּ
then-they-asked (3) he-paid-honor and-not he-knelt not but-Mordecai the-king

עַבְדֵי הַמֶּלֶךְ אֲשֶׁר־ בְּשַׁעַר הַמֶּלֶךְ לְמָרְדֳּכַי מַדּוּעַ אַתָּה
you why? to-Mordecai the-king at-gate-of who the-king officials-of

עוֹבֵר אֵת מִצְוַת הַמֶּלֶךְ׃ וַיְהִי בְּאָמְרָם° אֵלָיו
to-him when-to-speak-them and-he-was (4) the-king command-of *** disobeying

יוֹם וָיוֹם וְלֹא שָׁמַע אֲלֵיהֶם וַיַּגִּידוּ לְהָמָן לִרְאוֹת
to-see to-Haman so-they-told with-them he-complied but-not after-day day

הֲיַעַמְדוּ דִּבְרֵי מָרְדֳּכַי כִּי־ הִגִּיד לָהֶם אֲשֶׁר־
that to-them he-told for Mordecai behaviors-of whether-they-would-be-tolerated

הוּא יְהוּדִי׃ וַיַּרְא הָמָן כִּי־ אֵין מָרְדֳּכַי כֹּרֵעַ וּמִשְׁתַּחֲוֶה
or-paying-honor kneeling Mordecai not that Haman when-he-saw (5) Jew he

לוֹ וַיִּמָּלֵא הָמָן חֵמָה׃ וַיִּבֶז בְּעֵינָיו
in-eyes-of-him yet-he-scorned (6) rage Haman then-he-was-filled to-him

לִשְׁלֹח* יָד בְּמָרְדֳּכַי לְבַדּוֹ כִּי־ הִגִּידוּ לוֹ אֶת־ עַם
people-of *** to-him they-told for by-himself against-Mordecai hand to-send

מָרְדֳּכָי וַיְבַקֵּשׁ הָמָן לְהַשְׁמִיד אֶת־ כָּל־ הַיְּהוּדִים אֲשֶׁר בְּכָל־
in-whole-of who the-Jews all-of *** to-destroy Haman so-he-looked Mordecai

מַלְכוּת אֲחַשְׁוֵרוֹשׁ עַם מָרְדֳּכָי׃ בַּחֹדֶשׁ הָרִאשׁוֹן הוּא־
that the-first in-the-month (7) Mordecai people-of Ahasuerus kingdom-of

חֹדֶשׁ נִיסָן בִּשְׁנַת שְׁתֵּים עֶשְׂרֵה לַמֶּלֶךְ אֲחַשְׁוֵרוֹשׁ הִפִּיל פּוּר הוּא°
that pur he-cast Ahasuerus of-the-king ten two in-year-of Nisan month-of

הַגּוֹרָל לִפְנֵי הָמָן מִיּוֹם | לְיוֹם וּמֵחֹדֶשׁ לְחֹדֶשׁ שְׁנֵים־
two to-month and-from-month to-day from-day Haman in-presences-of the-lot

עָשָׂר הוּא־ חֹדֶשׁ אֲדָר׃ וַיֹּאמֶר הָמָן לַמֶּלֶךְ אֲחַשְׁוֵרוֹשׁ
Ahasuerus to-the-king Haman then-he-said (8) Adar month-of that ten

true, the two officials were hanged on a gallows.[e] All this was recorded in the book of the annals in the presence of the king.

*Haman's Plot to Destroy the Jews*

3 After these events, King Xerxes honored Haman son of Hammedatha, the Agagite, elevating him and giving him a seat of honor higher than that of all the other nobles. [2]All the royal officials at the king's gate knelt down and paid honor to Haman, for the king had commanded this concerning him. But Mordecai would not kneel down or pay him honor.

[3]Then the royal officials at the king's gate asked Mordecai, "Why do you disobey the king's command?" [4]Day after day they spoke to him but he refused to comply. Therefore they told Haman about it to see whether Mordecai's behavior would be tolerated, for he had told them he was a Jew.

[5]When Haman saw that Mordecai would not kneel down or pay him honor, he was enraged. [6]Yet having learned who Mordecai's people were, he scorned the idea of killing only Mordecai. Instead Haman looked for a way to destroy all Mordecai's people, the Jews, throughout the whole kingdom of Xerxes.

[7]In the twelfth year of King Xerxes, in the first month, the month of Nisan, they cast the *pur* (that is, the lot) in the presence of Haman to select a day and month. And the lot fell on[f] the twelfth month, the month of Adar.

[8]Then Haman said to King

e23 Or *were hung on a post;* here and elsewhere in Esther
f7 Septuagint; Hebrew does not have *And the lot fell on.*

*6 Most mss have *pathah* under the *beth* (לַח–).

°4 כאמרם ק

יֶשְׁנוֹ עַם־ אֶחָד מְפֻזָּר וּמְפֹרָד בֵּין
there-is-he people certain being-dispersed and-being-scattered among

הָעַמִּים בְּכֹל מְדִינוֹת מַלְכוּתֶךָ וְדָתֵיהֶם
the-peoples in-all-of provinces-of kingdom-of-you and-customs-of-them

שֹׁנוֹת מִכָּל־ עָם וְאֶת־ דָּתֵי הַמֶּלֶךְ אֵינָם עֹשִׂים
ones-differing from-all-of people and laws-of the-king not-they ones-obeying

וְלַמֶּלֶךְ אֵין־ שֹׁוֶה לְהַנִּיחָם׃ אִם־עַל־ הַמֶּלֶךְ
and-to-the-king not being-in-best-interest to-tolerate-them (9) if to the-king

טוֹב יִכָּתֵב לְאַבְּדָם וַעֲשֶׂרֶת אֲלָפִים כִּכַּר־
pleasing let-him-be-decreed to-destroy-them and-ten-of thousands talent-of

כֶּסֶף אֶשְׁקוֹל עַל־ יְדֵי עֹשֵׂי הַמְּלָאכָה לְהָבִיא אֶל־
silver I-will-put in hands-of ones-carrying-out-of the-business to-put into

גִּנְזֵי הַמֶּלֶךְ׃ וַיָּסַר הַמֶּלֶךְ אֶת־ טַבַּעְתּוֹ
treasuries-of the-king (10) so-he-took-off the-king *** signet-ring-of-him

מֵעַל יָדוֹ וַיִּתְּנָהּ לְהָמָן בֶּן־ הַמְּדָתָא הָאֲגָגִי
from-on hand-of-him and-he-gave-her to-Haman son-of Hammedatha the-Agagite

צֹרֵר הַיְּהוּדִים׃ וַיֹּאמֶר הַמֶּלֶךְ לְהָמָן הַכֶּסֶף
being-enemy-of the-Jews (11) and-he-said the-king to-Haman the-money

נָתוּן לָךְ וְהָעָם לַעֲשׂוֹת בּוֹ כַּטּוֹב בְּעֵינֶיךָ׃
being-kept by-you and-the-people to-do with-him as-the-pleasing in-eyes-of-you

וַיִּקָּרְאוּ סֹפְרֵי הַמֶּלֶךְ בַּחֹדֶשׁ הָרִאשׁוֹן
(12) then-they-were-summoned secretaries-of the-king in-the-month the-first

בִּשְׁלוֹשָׁה עָשָׂר יוֹם בּוֹ וַיִּכָּתֵב כְּכָל־אֲשֶׁר־ צִוָּה הָמָן אֶל
on-three ten day of-him and-he-was-written as-all that he-ordered Haman to

אֲחַשְׁדַּרְפְּנֵי־הַמֶּלֶךְ וְאֶל־ הַפַּחוֹת אֲשֶׁר ׀ עַל־ מְדִינָה וּמְדִינָה
satraps-of the-king and-to the-governors who over province and-province

וְאֶל־ שָׂרֵי עַם וָעָם מְדִינָה וּמְדִינָה כִּכְתָבָהּ
and-to nobles-of people and-people province and-province in-script-of-her

וְעַם וָעָם כִּלְשׁוֹנוֹ בְּשֵׁם הַמֶּלֶךְ אֲחַשְׁוֵרֹשׁ
and-people and-people in-language-of-him in-name-of the-king Ahasuerus

נִכְתָּב וְנֶחְתָּם בְּטַבַּעַת הַמֶּלֶךְ׃ וְנִשְׁלוֹחַ
being-written and-being-sealed with-signet-ring-of the-king (13) and-to-be-sent

סְפָרִים בְּיַד הָרָצִים אֶל־ כָּל־ מְדִינוֹת הַמֶּלֶךְ
dispatches by-hand-of the-ones-being-couriers to all-of provinces-of the-king

לְהַשְׁמִיד לַהֲרֹג וּלְאַבֵּד אֶת־ כָּל־ הַיְּהוּדִים מִנַּעַר וְעַד־
to-destroy to-kill and-to-annihilate *** all-of the-Jews from-young and-to

זָקֵן טַף וְנָשִׁים בְּיוֹם אֶחָד בִּשְׁלוֹשָׁה עָשָׂר לְחֹדֶשׁ שְׁנֵים־עָשָׂר
old little-child and-women on-day single on-three ten of-month-of two ten

Xerxes, "There is a certain people dispersed and scattered among the peoples in all the provinces of your kingdom who keep themselves separate. Their customs are different from those of all other people, and they do not obey the king's laws; it is not in the king's best interest to tolerate them. 9If it pleases the king, let a decree be issued to destroy them, and I will put ten thousand talents[g] of silver into the royal treasury for the men who carry out this business."

10So the king took the signet ring off his finger and gave it to Haman son of Hammedatha, the Agagite, the enemy of the Jews. 11"Keep the money," the king said to Haman, "and do with the people as you please."

12Then on the thirteenth day of the first month the royal secretaries were summoned. They wrote out in the script of each province and in the language of each people all Haman's orders to the king's satraps, the governors of the various provinces and the nobles of the various peoples. These were written in the name of King Xerxes himself and sealed with his own ring. 13Dispatches were sent by couriers to all the king's provinces with the order to destroy, kill and annihilate all the Jews—young and old, women and little children—on a single day, the thirteenth day of the twelfth month, the

g9 That is, about 375 tons (about 345 metric tons)

הוּא־ חֹדֶשׁ אֲדָר וּשְׁלָלָם לָבוֹז׃ פַּתְשֶׁגֶן הַכְּתָב
the-edict copy-of (14) to-plunder and-good-of-them Adar month-of that

לְהִנָּתֵן דָּת בְּכָל־ מְדִינָה וּמְדִינָה גָּלוּי
being-made-known and-province province in-every-of law to-be-issued

לְכָל־ הָעַמִּים לִהְיוֹת עֲתִדִים לַיּוֹם הַזֶּה׃
the-that for-the-day ones-ready to-be the-peoples to-every-of

(15) הָרָצִים יָצְאוּ דְחוּפִים
ones-being-spurred-on they-went-out the-ones-being-couriers (15)

בִּדְבַר הַמֶּלֶךְ וְהַדָּת נִתְּנָה בְּשׁוּשַׁן הַבִּירָה
the-citadel in-Susa she-was-issued and-the-edict the-king by-command-of

וְהַמֶּלֶךְ וְהָמָן יָשְׁבוּ לִשְׁתּוֹת וְהָעִיר שׁוּשָׁן נָבוֹכָה׃
she-was-bewildered Susa but-the-city to-drink they-sat and-Haman and-the-king

(4:1) וּמָרְדֳּכַי יָדַע אֶת־כָּל־אֲשֶׁר נַעֲשָׂה וַיִּקְרַע מָרְדֳּכַי
Mordecai then-he-tore being-done that all *** he-learned when-Mordecai (4:1)

אֶת־ בְּגָדָיו וַיִּלְבַּשׁ שַׂק וָאֵפֶר וַיֵּצֵא בְּתוֹךְ
in-midst-of and-he-went-out and-ash sackcloth and-he-put-on clothes-of-him ***

הָעִיר וַיִּזְעַק זְעָקָה גְדֹלָה וּמָרָה׃ וַיָּבוֹא עַד
as-far-as but-he-went (2) and-bitter loud wailing and-he-wailed the-city

לִפְנֵי שַׁעַר־ הַמֶּלֶךְ כִּי אֵין לָבוֹא אֶל־ שַׁעַר הַמֶּלֶךְ
the-king gate-of into to-enter no-one because the-king gate-of before

בִּלְבוּשׁ שָׂק׃ וּבְכָל־ מְדִינָה וּמְדִינָה מְקוֹם
place-of and-province province and-in-every-of (3) sackcloth in-clothing-of

אֲשֶׁר דְּבַר־ הַמֶּלֶךְ וְדָתוֹ מַגִּיעַ אֵבֶל גָּדוֹל לַיְּהוּדִים
among-the-Jews great mourning coming and-order-of-him the-king edict-of which

וְצוֹם וּבְכִי וּמִסְפֵּד שַׂק וָאֵפֶר יֻצַּע
he-was-laid-on and-ash sackcloth and-wailing and-weeping with-fasting

לָרַבִּים׃ (4) °וַתָּבוֹאינָה נַעֲרוֹת אֶסְתֵּר וְסָרִיסֶיהָ
and-eunuchs-of-her Esther maids-of when-they-came (4) by-the-many

וַיַּגִּידוּ לָהּ וַתִּתְחַלְחַל הַמַּלְכָּה מְאֹד וַתִּשְׁלַח
and-she-sent great the-queen then-she-was-in-distress to-her and-they-told

בְּגָדִים לְהַלְבִּישׁ אֶת־ מָרְדֳּכַי וּלְהָסִיר שַׂקּוֹ מֵעָלָיו
from-on-him sackcloth-of-him and-to-take-off Mordecai *** to-put-on clothes

וְלֹא קִבֵּל׃ (5) וַתִּקְרָא אֶסְתֵּר לַהֲתָךְ מִסָּרִיסֵי
from-eunuchs-of to-Hathach Esther then-she-summoned (5) he-accepted but-not

הַמֶּלֶךְ אֲשֶׁר הֶעֱמִיד לְפָנֶיהָ וַתְּצַוֵּהוּ עַל־ מָרְדֳּכָי
Mordecai about and-she-ordered-him to-her he-assigned whom the-king

לָדַעַת מַה־ זֶּה וְעַל־ מַה־ זֶּה׃ (6) וַיֵּצֵא הֲתָךְ אֶל־
to Hathach so-he-went-out (6) this what? and-for this what? to-find-out

°4 ק ותבאוה

month of Adar, and to plunder their goods. [14]A copy of the text of the edict was to be issued as law in every province and made known to the people of every nationality so they would be ready for that day.

[15]Spurred on by the king's command, the couriers went out, and the edict was issued in the citadel of Susa. The king and Haman sat down to drink, but the city of Susa was bewildered.

*Mordecai Persuades Esther to Help*

4 When Mordecai learned of all that had been done, he tore his clothes, put on sackcloth and ashes, and went out into the city, wailing loudly and bitterly. [2]But he went only as far as the king's gate, because no one clothed in sackcloth was allowed to enter it. [3]In every province to which the edict and order of the king came, there was great mourning among the Jews, with fasting, weeping and wailing. Many lay on sackcloth and ashes.

[4]When Esther's maids and eunuchs came and told her about Mordecai, she was in great distress. She sent clothes for him to put on instead of his sackcloth, but he would not accept them. [5]Then Esther summoned Hathach, one of the king's eunuchs assigned to attend her, and ordered him to find out what was troubling Mordecai and why.

[6]So Hathach went out to

מָרְדֳּכָי אֶל־ רְחוֹב הָעִיר אֲשֶׁר לִפְנֵי שַׁעַר־ הַמֶּלֶךְ׃

the-king gate-of in-front-of that the-city open-square-of in Mordecai

וַיַּגֶּד־ לוֹ מָרְדֳּכַי אֵת כָּל־ אֲשֶׁר קָרָהוּ וְאֵת ׀

and he-happened-to-him that everything *** Mordecai to-him and-he-told (7)

פָּרָשַׁת הַכֶּסֶף אֲשֶׁר אָמַר הָמָן לִשְׁקוֹל עַל־ גִּנְזֵי

treasuries-of into to-pay Haman he-promised that the-money exact-amount-of

הַמֶּלֶךְ בַּיְּהוּדִיים לְאַבְּדָם׃ וְאֶת־ פַּתְשֶׁגֶן כְּתָב־ הַדָּת

the-edict text-of copy-of also (8) to-destroy-them for-the-Jews the-king

אֲשֶׁר־ נִתַּן בְּשׁוּשָׁן לְהַשְׁמִידָם נָתַן לוֹ לְהַרְאוֹת

to-show to-him he-gave to-annihilate-them in-Susa he-was-published which

אֶת־ אֶסְתֵּר וּלְהַגִּיד לָהּ וּלְצַוּוֹת עָלֶיהָ לָבוֹא אֶל־ הַמֶּלֶךְ

the-king to to-go to-her and-to-urge to-her and-to-explain Esther ***

לְהִתְחַנֶּן־ לוֹ וּלְבַקֵּשׁ מִלְּפָנָיו עַל־ עַמָּהּ׃

people-of-her for from-before-him and-to-plead with-him to-beg-for-mercy

וַיָּבוֹא הֲתָךְ וַיַּגֵּד לְאֶסְתֵּר אֵת דִּבְרֵי מָרְדֳּכָי׃

Mordecai words-of *** to-Esther and-he-reported Hathach then-he-went-back (9)

וַתֹּאמֶר אֶסְתֵּר לַהֲתָךְ וַתְּצַוֵּהוּ אֶל־מָרְדֳּכָי׃

Mordecai to and-she-instructed-him to-Hathach Esther then-she-said (10)

כָּל־ עַבְדֵי הַמֶּלֶךְ וְעַם־ מְדִינוֹת הַמֶּלֶךְ

the-king provinces-of and-people-of the-king officials-of all-of (11)

יֹדְעִים אֲשֶׁר כָּל־ אִישׁ וְאִשָּׁה אֲשֶׁר יָבוֹא־ אֶל־הַמֶּלֶךְ אֶל־

in the-king to he-approaches who or-woman man any-of that ones-knowing

הֶחָצֵר הַפְּנִימִית אֲשֶׁר לֹא־ יִקָּרֵא אַחַת דָּתוֹ לְהָמִית לְבַד

except to-kill law-of-him one he-was-summoned not who the-inner the-court

מֵאֲשֶׁר יוֹשִׁיט־ לוֹ הַמֶּלֶךְ אֶת־ שַׁרְבִיט הַזָּהָב וְחָיָה

and-he-lives the-gold scepter-of *** the-king to-him he-extends from-whom

וַאֲנִי לֹא נִקְרֵאתִי לָבוֹא אֶל־ הַמֶּלֶךְ זֶה שְׁלוֹשִׁים יוֹם׃ וַיַּגִּידוּ

when-they-reported (12) day thirty this the-king to to-go I-was-called not but-I

לְמָרְדֳּכָי אֵת דִּבְרֵי אֶסְתֵּר׃ וַיֹּאמֶר מָרְדֳּכַי לְהָשִׁיב

to-send-back Mordecai and-he-answered (13) Esther words-of *** to-Mordecai

אֶל־אֶסְתֵּר אַל־ תְּדַמִּי בְנַפְשֵׁךְ לְהִמָּלֵט בֵּית־ הַמֶּלֶךְ מִכָּל־

of-all-of the-king house-of to-escape in-self-of-you you-think not Esther to

הַיְּהוּדִים׃ כִּי אִם־ הַחֲרֵשׁ תַּחֲרִישִׁי בָּעֵת הַזֹּאת

the-this at-the-time you-remain-silent to-remain-silent if for (14) the-Jews

רֶוַח וְהַצָּלָה יַעֲמוֹד לַיְּהוּדִים מִמָּקוֹם אַחֵר

another from-place for-the-Jews he-will-arise and-deliverance relief

וְאַתְּ וּבֵית־ אָבִיךְ תֹּאבֵדוּ וּמִי יוֹדֵעַ אִם־

but knowing and-who? you-will-perish father-of-you and-family-of but-you

°7 ק ביהודים

Mordecai in the open square of the city in front of the king's gate. [7]Mordecai told him everything that had happened to him, including the exact amount of money Haman had promised to pay into the royal treasury for the destruction of the Jews. [8]He also gave him a copy of the text of the edict for their annihilation, which had been published in Susa, to show to Esther and explain it to her, and he told him to urge her to go into the king's presence to beg for mercy and plead with him for her people.

[9]Hathach went back and reported to Esther what Mordecai had said. [10]Then she instructed him to say to Mordecai, [11]"All the king's officials and the people of the royal provinces know that for any man or woman who approaches the king in the inner court without being summoned the king has but one law: that he be put to death. The only exception to this is for the king to extend the gold scepter to him and spare his life. But thirty days have passed since I was called to go to the king."

[12]When Esther's words were reported to Mordecai, [13]he sent back this answer: "Do not think that because you are in the king's house you alone of all the Jews will escape. [14]For if you remain silent at this time, relief and deliverance for the Jews will arise from another place, but you and your father's family will perish. And

לְעֵת כָּזֹאת הִגַּעַתְּ לַמַּלְכוּת׃ וַתֹּאמֶר אֶסְתֵּר לְהָשִׁיב אֶל־
to to-send Esther then-she-replied (15) to-the-royalty you-came as-this for-time

מָרְדֳּכָי׃ לֵךְ כְּנוֹס אֶת־ כָּל־ הַיְּהוּדִים הַנִּמְצְאִים
the-ones-being-found the-Jews all-of *** gather-together! go! (16) Mordecai

בְּשׁוּשָׁן וְצוּמוּ עָלַי וְאַל־ תֹּאכְלוּ וְאַל־ תִּשְׁתּוּ שְׁלֹשֶׁת יָמִים
days three-of you-drink and-not you-eat and-not for-me and-fast! in-Susa

לַיְלָה וָיוֹם גַּם־אֲנִי וְנַעֲרֹתַי אָצוּם כֵּן וּבְכֵן אָבוֹא
I-will-go and-when-so same I-will-fast and-maids-of-me I and or-day night

אֶל־ הַמֶּלֶךְ אֲשֶׁר לֹא־ כַדָּת וְכַאֲשֶׁר אָבַדְתִּי אָבָדְתִּי׃
I-perish I-perish and-as-if according-to-the-law not though the-king to

וַיַּעֲבֹר מָרְדֳּכָי וַיַּעַשׂ כְּכֹל אֲשֶׁר־ צִוְּתָה
she-instructed that as-all and-he-carried-out Mordecai so-he-went-away (17)

עָלָיו אֶסְתֵּר׃ וַיְהִי ׀ בַּיּוֹם הַשְּׁלִישִׁי וַתִּלְבַּשׁ אֶסְתֵּר
Esther then-she-put-on the-third on-the-day and-he-was (5:1) Esther to-him

מַלְכוּת וַתַּעֲמֹד בַּחֲצַר בֵּית־ הַמֶּלֶךְ הַפְּנִימִית נֹכַח
in-front-of the-inner the-king palace-of in-court-of and-she-stood royalty

בֵּית הַמֶּלֶךְ וְהַמֶּלֶךְ יוֹשֵׁב עַל־ כִּסֵּא מַלְכוּתוֹ בְּבֵית
in-hall-of royalty-of-him throne-of on sitting and-the-king the-king hall-of

הַמַּלְכוּת נֹכַח פֶּתַח הַבָּיִת׃ וַיְהִי כִרְאוֹת הַמֶּלֶךְ
the-king when-to-see and-he-was (2) the-hall entrance-of facing the-royalty

אֶת־אֶסְתֵּר הַמַּלְכָּה עֹמֶדֶת בֶּחָצֵר נָשְׂאָה חֵן בְּעֵינָיו
in-eyes-of-him pleasure she-found in-the-court standing the-queen Esther ***

וַיּוֹשֶׁט הַמֶּלֶךְ לְאֶסְתֵּר אֶת־ שַׁרְבִיט הַזָּהָב אֲשֶׁר
that the-gold scepter-of *** to-Esther the-king and-he-held-out

בְּיָדוֹ וַתִּקְרַב אֶסְתֵּר וַתִּגַּע בְּרֹאשׁ הַשַּׁרְבִיט׃
the-scepter on-tip-of and-she-touched Esther so-she-approached in-hand-of-him

וַיֹּאמֶר לָהּ הַמֶּלֶךְ מַה־ לָּךְ אֶסְתֵּר הַמַּלְכָּה וּמַה־
and-what? the-queen Esther to-you what? the-king to-her then-he-asked (3)

בַּקָּשָׁתֵךְ עַד־ חֲצִי הַמַּלְכוּת וְיִנָּתֵן לָךְ׃
to-you and-he-will-be-given the-kingdom half-of up-to request-of-you

וַתֹּאמֶר אֶסְתֵּר אִם־ עַל־ הַמֶּלֶךְ טוֹב יָבוֹא הַמֶּלֶךְ
the-king let-him-come pleasing the-king to if Esther and-she-replied (4)

וְהָמָן הַיּוֹם אֶל־ הַמִּשְׁתֶּה אֲשֶׁר־ עָשִׂיתִי לוֹ׃ וַיֹּאמֶר
and-he-said (5) for-him I-prepared that the-banquet to the-day with-Haman

הַמֶּלֶךְ מַהֲרוּ אֶת־ הָמָן לַעֲשׂוֹת אֶת־ דְּבַר אֶסְתֵּר וַיָּבֹא
so-he-went Esther request-of *** to-do Haman *** bring-at-once! the-king

הַמֶּלֶךְ וְהָמָן אֶל־ הַמִּשְׁתֶּה אֲשֶׁר־ עָשְׂתָה אֶסְתֵּר׃ וַיֹּאמֶר
and-he-asked (6) Esther she-prepared that the-banquet to and-Haman the-king

who knows but that you have come to royal position for such a time as this?"

15Then Esther sent this reply to Mordecai: 16"Go, gather together all the Jews who are in Susa, and fast for me. Do not eat or drink for three days, night or day. I and my maids will fast as you do. When this is done, I will go to the king, even though it is against the law. And if I perish, I perish."

17So Mordecai went away and carried out all of Esther's instructions.

*Esther's Request to the King*

5 On the third day Esther put on her royal robes and stood in the inner court of the palace, in front of the king's hall. The king was sitting on his royal throne in the hall, facing the entrance. 2When he saw Queen Esther standing in the court, he was pleased with her and held out to her the gold scepter that was in his hand. So Esther approached and touched the tip of the scepter.

3Then the king asked, "What is it, Queen Esther? What is your request? Even up to half the kingdom, it will be given you."

4"If it pleases the king," replied Esther, "let the king, together with Haman, come today to a banquet I have prepared for him."

5"Bring Haman at once," the king said, "so that we may do what Esther asks."

So the king and Haman went to the banquet Esther had prepared. 6As they were

הַמֶּ֨לֶךְ לְאֶסְתֵּר֙ בְּמִשְׁתֵּ֣ה הַיַּ֔יִן מַה־ שְּׁאֵלָתֵ֖ךְ
petition-of-you what? the-wine as-drinking-of to-Esther the-king

וְיִנָּ֣תֵֽן לָ֑ךְ וּמַה־ בַּקָּשָׁתֵ֛ךְ עַד־ חֲצִ֥י
half-of up-to request-of-you and-what? to-you and-he-will-be-given

הַמַּלְכ֖וּת וְתֵעָֽשׂ׃ וַתַּ֥עַן אֶסְתֵּ֖ר וַתֹּאמַ֑ר
and-she-said Esther and-she-replied (7) and-she-will-be-granted the-kingdom

שְׁאֵלָתִ֖י וּבַקָּשָׁתִֽי׃ אִם־מָצָ֨אתִי חֵ֜ן בְּעֵינֵ֣י הַמֶּ֗לֶךְ
the-king in-eyes-of favor I-find if (8) and-request-of-me petition-of-me

וְאִם־ עַל־ הַמֶּ֙לֶךְ֙ ט֔וֹב לָתֵת֙ אֶת־ שְׁאֵ֣לָתִ֔י וְלַעֲשׂ֖וֹת אֶת־
*** and-to-fulfill petition-of-me *** to-grant pleasing the-king to and-if

בַּקָּשָׁתִ֑י יָב֧וֹא הַמֶּ֣לֶךְ וְהָמָ֗ן אֶל־ הַמִּשְׁתֶּה֙ אֲשֶׁ֣ר
that the-banquet to and-Haman the-king let-him-come request-of-me

אֶֽעֱשֶׂ֣ה לָהֶ֔ם וּמָחָ֥ר אֶֽעֱשֶׂ֖ה כִּדְבַ֥ר הַמֶּֽלֶךְ׃
the-king as-question-of I-will-answer then-tomorrow for-them I-will-prepare

וַיֵּצֵ֤א הָמָן֙ בַּיּ֣וֹם הַה֔וּא שָׂמֵ֖חַ וְט֣וֹב לֵ֑ב
spirit and-high-of happy the-that on-the-day Haman and-he-went-out (9)

וְכִרְאוֹת֩ הָמָ֨ן אֶֽת־ מָרְדֳּכַ֜י בְּשַׁ֣עַר הַמֶּ֗לֶךְ וְלֹא־ קָם֙
he-rose and-not the-king at-gate-of Mordecai *** Haman but-when-to-see

וְלֹא־ זָ֣ע מִמֶּ֔נּוּ וַיִּמָּלֵ֥א הָמָ֛ן עַל־ מָרְדֳּכַ֖י חֵמָֽה׃
rage Mordecai against Haman then-he-was-filled of-him he-showed-fear and-not

וַיִּתְאַפַּ֣ק הָמָ֔ן וַיָּב֖וֹא אֶל־ בֵּית֑וֹ וַיִּשְׁלַ֛ח
and-he-called home-of-him to and-he-went Haman but-he-restrained-himself (10)

וַיָּבֵ֥א אֶת־ אֹהֲבָ֖יו וְאֶת־ זֶ֥רֶשׁ אִשְׁתּֽוֹ׃
wife-of-him Zeresh and ones-being-friends-of-him *** and-he-brought

וַיְסַפֵּ֨ר לָהֶ֥ם הָמָ֛ן אֶת־ כְּב֥וֹד עָשְׁר֖וֹ וְרֹ֣ב
and-many-of wealth-of-him vastness-of *** Haman to-them and-he-boasted (11)

בָּנָ֑יו וְאֵת֩ כָּל־ אֲשֶׁ֨ר גִּדְּל֤וֹ הַמֶּ֙לֶךְ֙ וְאֵ֣ת אֲשֶׁ֣ר נִשְּׂא֔וֹ
he-elevated-him how and the-king he-honored-him that all and sons-of-him

עַל־ הַשָּׂרִ֖ים וְעַבְדֵ֥י הַמֶּֽלֶךְ׃ וַיֹּאמֶר֮ הָמָן֒ אַ֣ף לֹא־
not also Haman and-he-said (12) the-king and-officials-of the-nobles above

הֵבִ֣יאָה֩ אֶסְתֵּ֨ר הַמַּלְכָּ֧ה עִם־ הַמֶּ֛לֶךְ אֶל־ הַמִּשְׁתֶּ֥ה אֲשֶׁר־ עָשָׂ֖תָה כִּ֣י
but she-gave that the-banquet to the-king with the-queen Esther she-invited

אִם־ אוֹתִ֑י וְגַם־ לְמָחָ֛ר אֲנִ֥י קָֽרוּא־ לָ֖הּ עִם־ הַמֶּֽלֶךְ׃
the-king with by-her being-invited I for-tomorrow and-also me only

וְכָל־ זֶ֕ה אֵינֶ֥נּוּ שֹׁוֶ֖ה לִ֑י בְּכָל־ עֵ֗ת אֲשֶׁ֨ר אֲנִ֤י
I that time at-every-of to-me satisfying not-he this but-all-of (13)

רֹאֶה֙ אֶת־ מָרְדֳּכַ֣י הַיְּהוּדִ֔י יוֹשֵׁ֖ב בְּשַׁ֥עַר הַמֶּֽלֶךְ׃ וַתֹּ֨אמֶר
and-she-said (14) the-king at-gate-of sitting the-Jew Mordecai *** seeing

drinking wine, the king again asked Esther, "Now what is your petition? It will be given you. And what is your request? Even up to half the kingdom, it will be granted."

[7]Esther replied, "My petition and my request is this: [8]If the king regards me with favor and if it pleases the king to grant my petition and fulfill my request, let the king and Haman come tomorrow to the banquet I will prepare for them. Then I will answer the king's question."

*Haman's Rage Against Mordecai*

[9]Haman went out that day happy and in high spirits. But when he saw Mordecai at the king's gate and observed that he neither rose nor showed fear in his presence, he was filled with rage against Mordecai. [10]Nevertheless, Haman restrained himself and went home.

Calling together his friends and Zeresh, his wife, [11]Haman boasted to them about his vast wealth, his many sons, and all the ways the king had honored him and how he had elevated him above the other nobles and officials. [12]"And that's not all," Haman added. "I'm the only person Queen Esther invited to accompany the king to the banquet she gave. And she has invited me along with the king tomorrow. [13]But all this gives me no satisfaction as long as I see that Jew Mordecai sitting at the king's gate."

לוֹ זֶרֶשׁ אִשְׁתּוֹ וְכָל־ אֹהֲבָיו יַעֲשׂוּ־
to-him Zeresh wife-of-him and-all-of ones-being-friends-of-him let-them-build

עֵץ גָּבֹהַּ חֲמִשִּׁים אַמָּה וּבַבֹּקֶר ׀ אֱמֹר לַמֶּלֶךְ
gallows height fifty cubit and-in-the-morning ask! to-the-king

וְיִתְלוּ אֶת־ מָרְדֳּכַי עָלָיו וּבֹא־ עִם־ הַמֶּלֶךְ אֶל־ הַמִּשְׁתֶּה
and-let-them-hang *** Mordecai on-him then-go! with the-king to the-dinner

שָׂמֵחַ וַיִּיטַב הַדָּבָר לִפְנֵי הָמָן וַיַּעַשׂ הָעֵץ׃
happy and-he-was-delightful the-suggestion before Haman and-he-built the-gallows

בַּלַּיְלָה הַהוּא נָדְדָה שְׁנַת הַמֶּלֶךְ וַיֹּאמֶר
(6:1) in-the-night the-that she-fled sleep-of the-king so-he-ordered

לְהָבִיא אֶת־ סֵפֶר הַזִּכְרֹנוֹת דִּבְרֵי הַיָּמִים וַיִּהְיוּ
to-bring *** book-of the-chronicles records-of the-days and-they-were

נִקְרָאִים לִפְנֵי הַמֶּלֶךְ׃ וַיִּמָּצֵא כָתוּב אֲשֶׁר
ones-being-read before the-king (2) and-he-was-found being-recorded that

הִגִּיד מָרְדֳּכַי עַל־ בִּגְתָנָא וָתֶרֶשׁ שְׁנֵי סָרִיסֵי הַמֶּלֶךְ
he-exposed Mordecai about Bigthana and-Teresh two-of officers-of the-king

מִשֹּׁמְרֵי הַסַּף אֲשֶׁר בִּקְשׁוּ לִשְׁלֹחַ יָד
from-ones-guarding-of the-doorway who they-conspired to-send hand

בַּמֶּלֶךְ אֲחַשְׁוֵרוֹשׁ׃ וַיֹּאמֶר הַמֶּלֶךְ מַה־ נַּעֲשָׂה
against-the-king Ahasuerus (3) and-he-asked the-king what? he-was-done

יְקָר וּגְדוּלָּה לְמָרְדֳּכַי עַל־ זֶה וַיֹּאמְרוּ נַעֲרֵי הַמֶּלֶךְ
honor and-recognition for-Mordecai for this and-they-answered men-of the-king

מְשָׁרְתָיו לֹא־ נַעֲשָׂה עִמּוֹ דָּבָר׃ וַיֹּאמֶר הַמֶּלֶךְ
ones-attending-him not he-was-done for-him anything (4) and-he-said the-king

מִי בֶחָצֵר וְהָמָן בָּא לַחֲצַר בֵּית־ הַמֶּלֶךְ
who? in-the-court now-Haman he-entered into-court-of palace-of the-king

הַחִיצוֹנָה לֵאמֹר לַמֶּלֶךְ לִתְלוֹת אֶת־ מָרְדֳּכַי עַל־ הָעֵץ אֲשֶׁר־
the-outer to-speak to-the-king to-hang *** Mordecai on the-gallows that

הֵכִין לוֹ׃ וַיֹּאמְרוּ נַעֲרֵי הַמֶּלֶךְ אֵלָיו הִנֵּה
he-erected for-him (5) and-they-answered attendants-of the-king to-him see!

הָמָן עֹמֵד בֶּחָצֵר וַיֹּאמֶר הַמֶּלֶךְ יָבוֹא׃
Haman standing in-the-court and-he-ordered the-king let-him-come-in

וַיָּבוֹא הָמָן וַיֹּאמֶר לוֹ הַמֶּלֶךְ מַה־לַעֲשׂוֹת*
(6) when-he-entered Haman then-he-asked to-him the-king what? to-do

בָּאִישׁ אֲשֶׁר הַמֶּלֶךְ חָפֵץ בִּיקָרוֹ וַיֹּאמֶר הָמָן
for-the-man whom the-king he-delights in-honor-of-him now-he-thought Haman

בְּלִבּוֹ לְמִי יַחְפֹּץ הַמֶּלֶךְ לַעֲשׂוֹת יְקָר יוֹתֵר מִמֶּנִּי׃
to-self-of-him to-whom? he-would-rather the-king to-do honor other than-me

14 His wife Zeresh and all his friends said to him, "Have a gallows built, seventy-five feet[h] high, and ask the king in the morning to have Mordecai hanged on it.[i] Then go with the king to the dinner and be happy." This suggestion delighted Haman, and he had the gallows built.

*Mordecai Honored*

6 That night the king could not sleep; so he ordered the book of the chronicles, the record of his reign, to be brought in and read to him. 2 It was found recorded there that Mordecai had exposed Bigthana and Teresh, two of the king's officers, who guarded the doorway and who had conspired to assassinate King Xerxes.

3 "What honor and recognition has Mordecai received for this?" the king asked.

"Nothing has been done for him," his attendants answered.

4 The king said, "Who is in the court?" Now Haman had just entered the outer court of the palace to speak to the king about hanging Mordecai on the gallows he had erected for him.

5 His attendants answered, "Haman is standing in the court."

"Bring him in," the king ordered.

6 When Haman entered, the king asked him, "What should be done for the man the king delights to honor?"

Now Haman thought to himself, "Who is there that the king would rather honor

h 14 Hebrew *fifty cubits* (about 23 meters)
i 14 Or *Have poles erected . . . Mordecai hung on it*

*6 Most mss have *dagesh* in the *lamed* (לּ).

וַיֹּאמֶר הָמָן אֶל־הַמֶּלֶךְ אִישׁ אֲשֶׁר הַמֶּלֶךְ חָפֵץ
he-delights the-king whom man the-king to Haman so-he-answered (7)

בִּיקָרוֹ׃ יָבִיאוּ לְבוּשׁ מַלְכוּת אֲשֶׁר לָבַשׁ־בּוֹ
on-him he-wore that royalty robe-of have-them-bring (8) in-honor-of-him

הַמֶּלֶךְ וְסוּס אֲשֶׁר רָכַב עָלָיו הַמֶּלֶךְ וַאֲשֶׁר נִתַּן
he-was-placed and-that the-king on-him he-rode that and-horse the-king

כֶּתֶר מַלְכוּת בְּרֹאשׁוֹ׃ וְנָתוֹן הַלְּבוּשׁ וְהַסּוּס
and-the-horse the-robe and-to-entrust (9) on-head-of-him royalty crest-of

עַל־יַד־אִישׁ מִשָּׂרֵי הַמֶּלֶךְ הַפַּרְתְּמִים וְהִלְבִּישׁוּ אֶת־
*** and-let-them-robe the-nobles the-king from-princes-of man hand-of to

הָאִישׁ אֲשֶׁר הַמֶּלֶךְ חָפֵץ בִּיקָרוֹ וְהִרְכִּיבֻהוּ עַל־
on and-let-them-lead-him in-honor-of-him he-delights the-king whom the-man

הַסּוּס בִּרְחוֹב הָעִיר וְקָרְאוּ לְפָנָיו כָּכָה
this before-him and-let-them-proclaim the-city through-street-of the-horse

יֵעָשֶׂה לָאִישׁ אֲשֶׁר הַמֶּלֶךְ חָפֵץ בִּיקָרוֹ׃
in-honor-of-him he-delights the-king whom for-the-man he-is-done

וַיֹּאמֶר הַמֶּלֶךְ לְהָמָן מַהֵר קַח אֶת־הַלְּבוּשׁ וְאֶת־
and the-robe *** get! go-at-once! to-Haman the-king and-he-commanded (10)

הַסּוּס כַּאֲשֶׁר דִּבַּרְתָּ וַעֲשֵׂה־כֵן לְמָרְדֳּכַי הַיְּהוּדִי
the-Jew for-Mordecai this and-do! you-suggested just-as the-horse

הַיּוֹשֵׁב בְּשַׁעַר הַמֶּלֶךְ אַל־תַּפֵּל דָּבָר מִכֹּל אֲשֶׁר
that of-all anything you-neglect not the-king at-gate-of the-one-sitting

דִּבַּרְתָּ׃ וַיִּקַּח הָמָן אֶת־הַלְּבוּשׁ וְאֶת־הַסּוּס וַיַּלְבֵּשׁ
and-he-robed the-horse and the-robe *** Haman so-he-got (11) you-recommended

אֶת־מָרְדֳּכָי וַיַּרְכִּיבֵהוּ בִּרְחוֹב הָעִיר
the-city through-street-of and-he-led-on-horse-him Mordecai ***

וַיִּקְרָא לְפָנָיו כָּכָה יֵעָשֶׂה לָאִישׁ אֲשֶׁר חָפֵץ
the-king whom for-the-man he-is-done this before-him and-he-proclaimed

הַמֶּלֶךְ בִּיקָרוֹ׃ וַיָּשָׁב מָרְדֳּכַי אֶל־שַׁעַר
gate-of to Mordecai then-he-returned (12) in-honor-of-him he-delights

הַמֶּלֶךְ וְהָמָן נִדְחַף אֶל־בֵּיתוֹ אָבֵל וַחֲפוּי רֹאשׁ׃
head and-being-covered-of grief home-of-him to he-rushed but-Haman the-king

וַיְסַפֵּר הָמָן לְזֶרֶשׁ אִשְׁתּוֹ וּלְכָל־
and-to-all-of wife-of-him to-Zeresh Haman and-he-told (13)

אֹהֲבָיו אֵת כָּל־אֲשֶׁר קָרָהוּ וַיֹּאמְרוּ לוֹ
to-him and-they-said he-happened-to-him that all *** ones-being-friends-of-him

חֲכָמָיו וְזֶרֶשׁ אִשְׁתּוֹ אִם מִזֶּרַע הַיְּהוּדִים
the-Jews from-descendant-of since wife-of-him and-Zeresh advisers-of-him

than me?" 7So he answered
the king, "For the man the
king delights to honor, 8have
them bring a royal robe the
king has worn and a horse the
king has ridden, one with a
royal crest placed on its head.
9Then let the robe and horse
be entrusted to one of the
king's most noble princes. Let
them robe the man the king
delights to honor, and lead
him on the horse through the
city streets, proclaiming before him, 'This is what is done
for the man the king delights
to honor!' "

10"Go at once," the king
commanded Haman. "Get the
robe and the horse and do just
as you have suggested for
Mordecai the Jew, who sits at
the king's gate. Do not neglect
anything you have recommended."

11So Haman got the robe and
the horse. He robed Mordecai,
and led him on horseback
through the city streets, proclaiming before him, "This is
what is done for the man the
king delights to honor!"

12Afterward Mordecai returned to the king's gate. But
Haman rushed home, with his
head covered in grief, 13and
told Zeresh his wife and all his
friends everything that had
happened to him.

His advisers and his wife
Zeresh said to him, "Since

מָרְדֳּכַי אֲשֶׁר הַחִלּוֹתָ לִנְפֹּל לְפָנָיו לֹא־ תוּכַל לוֹ כִּי־
surely against-him you-can-stand not before-him to-fall you-began whom Mordecai

נָפוֹל תִּפּוֹל לְפָנָיו׃ עוֹדָם מְדַבְּרִים
ones-talking still-they (14) before-him you-will-come-to-ruin to-come-to-ruin

עִמּוֹ וְסָרִיסֵי הַמֶּלֶךְ הִגִּיעוּ וַיַּבְהִלוּ לְהָבִיא אֶת־
*** to-take and-they-hurried they-arrived the-king and-eunuchs-of with-him

הָמָן אֶל־ הַמִּשְׁתֶּה אֲשֶׁר־ עָשְׂתָה אֶסְתֵּר׃ וַיָּבֹא הַמֶּלֶךְ
the-king so-he-went (7:1) Esther she-prepared that the-banquet to Haman

וְהָמָן לִשְׁתּוֹת עִם־ אֶסְתֵּר הַמַּלְכָּה׃ וַיֹּאמֶר הַמֶּלֶךְ לְאֶסְתֵּר
to-Esther the-king and-he-asked (2) the-queen Esther with to-dine and-Haman

גַּם בַּיּוֹם הַשֵּׁנִי בְּמִשְׁתֵּה הַיַּיִן מַה־ שְּׁאֵלָתֵךְ
petition-of-you what? the-wine as-drinking-of the-second on-the-day again

אֶסְתֵּר הַמַּלְכָּה וְתִנָּתֵן לָךְ וּמַה־ בַּקָּשָׁתֵךְ
request-of-you and-what? to-you and-she-will-be-given the-queen Esther

עַד־ חֲצִי הַמַּלְכוּת וְתֵעָשׂ׃ וַתַּעַן אֶסְתֵּר
Esther then-she-answered (3) and-she-will-be-granted the-kingdom half-of up-to

הַמַּלְכָּה וַתֹּאמַר אִם־ מָצָאתִי חֵן בְּעֵינֶיךָ הַמֶּלֶךְ וְאִם־ עַל־
to and-if the-king in-eyes-of-you favor I-found if and-she-said the-queen

הַמֶּלֶךְ טוֹב תִּנָּתֶן־ לִי נַפְשִׁי בִּשְׁאֵלָתִי
as-petition-of-me life-of-me to-me let-her-be-granted pleasing the-king

וְעַמִּי בְּבַקָּשָׁתִי׃ כִּי נִמְכַּרְנוּ אֲנִי וְעַמִּי
and-people-of-me I we-were-sold for (4) as-request-of-me and-people-of-me

לְהַשְׁמִיד לַהֲרוֹג וּלְאַבֵּד וְאִלּוּ לַעֲבָדִים
as-male-slaves and-if and-to-annihilate and-to-slaughter to-destroy

וְלִשְׁפָחוֹת נִמְכַּרְנוּ הֶחֱרַשְׁתִּי כִּי אֵין הַצָּר
the-distress not because I-would-keep-quiet we-were-sold and-as-female-slaves

שֹׁוֶה בְּנֵזֶק הַמֶּלֶךְ׃ וַיֹּאמֶר הַמֶּלֶךְ אֲחַשְׁוֵרוֹשׁ
Ahasuerus the-king and-he-asked (5) the-king for-disturbance-of justifying

וַיֹּאמֶר לְאֶסְתֵּר הַמַּלְכָּה מִי הוּא זֶה וְאֵי־ זֶה הוּא אֲשֶׁר־
who he this and-where? this he who? the-queen to-Esther and-he-said

מְלָאוֹ לִבּוֹ לַעֲשׂוֹת כֵּן׃ וַתֹּאמֶר־* אֶסְתֵּר אִישׁ צַר
adversary man Esther and-she-said (6) such to-do heart-of-him he-filled-him

וְאוֹיֵב הָמָן הָרָע הַזֶּה וְהָמָן נִבְעַת
he-was-terrified then-Haman the-this the-vile Haman and-being-enemy

מִלִּפְנֵי הַמֶּלֶךְ וְהַמַּלְכָּה׃ וְהַמֶּלֶךְ קָם בַּחֲמָתוֹ
in-rage-of-him he-got-up and-the-king (7) and-the-queen the-king from-before

מִמִּשְׁתֵּה הַיַּיִן אֶל־ גִּנַּת הַבִּיתָן וְהָמָן עָמַד
he-stayed but-Haman the-palace garden-of into the-wine from-drinking-of

Mordecai, before whom your downfall has started, is of Jewish origin, you cannot stand against him—you will surely come to ruin!" 14While they were still talking with him, the king's eunuchs arrived and hurried Haman away to the banquet Esther had prepared.

*Haman Hanged*

7 So the king and Haman went to dine with Queen Esther, 2and as they were drinking wine on that second day, the king again asked, "Queen Esther, what is your petition? It will be given you. What is your request? Even up to half the kingdom, it will be granted."

3Then Queen Esther answered, "If I have found favor with you, O king, and if it pleases your majesty, grant me my life—this is my petition. And spare my people—this is my request. 4For I and my people have been sold for destruction and slaughter and annihilation. If we had merely been sold as male and female slaves, I would have kept quiet, because no such distress would justify disturbing the king.[j]"

5King Xerxes asked Queen Esther, "Who is he? Where is the man who has dared to do such a thing?"

6Esther said, "The adversary and enemy is this vile Haman."

Then Haman was terrified before the king and queen. 7The king got up in a rage, left his wine and went out into the palace garden. But Haman,

*j4 Or quiet, but the compensation our adversary offers cannot be compared with the loss the king would suffer*

*6 Most mss have no *maqqeph* after this word ( ותאמר ).

לְבַקֵּשׁ עַל־ נַפְשׁוֹ מֵאֶסְתֵּר הַמַּלְכָּה כִּי רָאָה כִּי־
that he-realized for the-queen from-Esther life-of-him for to-beg

כָלְתָה אֵלָיו הָרָעָה מֵאֵת הַמֶּלֶךְ׃ וְהַמֶּלֶךְ
and-the-king (8) the-king from-with the-fate about-him she-was-decided

שָׁב מִגִּנַּת הַבִּיתָן אֶל־ בֵּית ׀ מִשְׁתֵּה הַיַּיִן וְהָמָן
and-Haman the-wine banquet-of hall-of to the-palace from-garden-of returning

נֹפֵל עַל־ הַמִּטָּה אֲשֶׁר אֶסְתֵּר עָלֶיהָ וַיֹּאמֶר הַמֶּלֶךְ הֲגַם
even? the-king and-he-exclaimed on-her Esther where the-couch on falling

לִכְבּוֹשׁ אֶת־ הַמַּלְכָּה עִמִּי בַּבָּיִת הַדָּבָר יָצָא מִפִּי
from-mouth-of he-left the-word in-the-house with-me the-queen *** to-molest

הַמֶּלֶךְ וּפְנֵי הָמָן חָפוּ׃ וַיֹּאמֶר חַרְבוֹנָה אֶחָד מִן־
from one Harbona then-he-said (9) they-covered Haman and-faces-of the-king

הַסָּרִיסִים לִפְנֵי הַמֶּלֶךְ גַּם הִנֵּה־ הָעֵץ אֲשֶׁר־ עָשָׂה הָמָן
Haman he-made that the-gallows see! also the-king before the-eunuchs

לְמָרְדֳּכַי אֲשֶׁר דִּבֶּר־ טוֹב עַל־ הַמֶּלֶךְ עֹמֵד בְּבֵית הָמָן
Haman by-house-of standing the-king for help he-spoke-up who for-Mordecai

גָּבֹהַּ חֲמִשִּׁים אַמָּה וַיֹּאמֶר הַמֶּלֶךְ תְּלֻהוּ עָלָיו׃ וַיִּתְלוּ
so-they-hanged (10) on-him hang-him! the-king and-he-said cubit fifty height

אֶת־ הָמָן עַל־ הָעֵץ אֲשֶׁר־ הֵכִין לְמָרְדֳּכָי וַחֲמַת הַמֶּלֶךְ
the-king then-fury-of for-Mordecai he-prepared that the-gallows on Haman ***

שָׁכָכָה׃ בַּיּוֹם הַהוּא נָתַן הַמֶּלֶךְ אֲחַשְׁוֵרוֹשׁ לְאֶסְתֵּר
to-Esther Ahasuerus the-king he-gave the-same on-the-day (8:1) she-subsided

הַמַּלְכָּה אֶת־ בֵּית הָמָן צֹרֵר הַיְּהוּדִיים וּמָרְדֳּכַי
and-Mordecai the-Jews one-being-enemy-of Haman estate-of *** the-queen

בָּא לִפְנֵי הַמֶּלֶךְ כִּי־ הִגִּידָה אֶסְתֵּר מַה הוּא־ לָהּ׃
to-her he how Esther she-told for the-king into-presences-of he-came

וַיָּסַר הַמֶּלֶךְ אֶת־ טַבַּעְתּוֹ אֲשֶׁר הֶעֱבִיר
he-reclaimed which signet-ring-of-him *** the-king and-he-took-off (2)

מֵהָמָן וַיִּתְּנָהּ לְמָרְדֳּכָי וַתָּשֶׂם אֶסְתֵּר אֶת־
*** Esther and-she-appointed to-Mordecai and-he-presented-her from-Haman

מָרְדֳּכַי עַל־ בֵּית הָמָן׃ וַתּוֹסֶף אֶסְתֵּר וַתְּדַבֵּר
and-she-pleaded Esther and-she-did-again (3) Haman estate-of over Mordecai

לִפְנֵי הַמֶּלֶךְ וַתִּפֹּל לִפְנֵי רַגְלָיו וַתֵּבְךְּ וַתִּתְחַנֶּן־
and-she-begged and-she-wept feet-of-him before and-she-fell the-king before

לוֹ לְהַעֲבִיר אֶת־ רָעַת הָמָן הָאֲגָגִי וְאֵת מַחֲשַׁבְתּוֹ אֲשֶׁר
which plan-of-him and the-Agagite Haman evil-of *** to-put-end to-him

חָשַׁב עַל־ הַיְּהוּדִים׃ וַיּוֹשֶׁט הַמֶּלֶךְ לְאֶסְתֵּר אֵת
*** to-Esther the-king then-he-extended (4) the-Jews against he-devised

realizing that the king had already decided his fate, stayed behind to beg Queen Esther for his life.

8 Just as the king returned from the palace garden to the banquet hall, Haman was falling on the couch where Esther was reclining.

The king exclaimed, "Will he even molest the queen while she is with me in the house?"

As soon as the word left the king's mouth, they covered Haman's face. 9 Then Harbona, one of the eunuchs attending the king, said, "A gallows seventy-five feet[k] high stands by Haman's house. He had it made for Mordecai, who spoke up to help the king."

The king said, "Hang him on it!" 10 So they hanged Haman on the gallows he had prepared for Mordecai. Then the king's fury subsided.

*The King's Edict in Behalf of the Jews*

8 That same day King Xerxes gave Queen Esther the estate of Haman, the enemy of the Jews. And Mordecai came into the presence of the king, for Esther had told how he was related to her. 2 The king took off his signet ring, which he had reclaimed from Haman, and presented it to Mordecai. And Esther appointed him over Haman's estate.

3 Esther again pleaded with the king, falling at his feet and weeping. She begged him to put an end to the evil plan of Haman the Agagite, which he had devised against the Jews. 4 Then the king extended the

k9 Hebrew *fifty cubits* (about 23 meters)

°1 ק היהודים

שַׁרְבִט הַזָּהָב וַתָּקָם אֶסְתֵּר וַתַּעֲמֹד לִפְנֵי הַמֶּלֶךְ׃
scepter-of the-gold and-she-arose Esther and-she-stood before the-king

(5) וַתֹּאמֶר אִם־עַל־הַמֶּלֶךְ טוֹב וְאִם־מָצָאתִי חֵן לְפָנָיו
(5) and-she-said if to the-king pleasing and-if I-find favor before-him

וְכָשֵׁר הַדָּבָר לִפְנֵי הַמֶּלֶךְ וְטוֹבָה אֲנִי בְּעֵינָיו
and-he-is-right the-thing before the-king and-pleasing I in-eyes-of-him

יִכָּתֵב לְהָשִׁיב אֶת־הַסְּפָרִים מַחֲשֶׁבֶת הָמָן בֶּן־
let-him-be-written to-overrule *** the-dispatches device-of Haman son-of

הַמְּדָתָא הָאֲגָגִי אֲשֶׁר כָּתַב לְאַבֵּד אֶת־הַיְּהוּדִים אֲשֶׁר בְּכָל־
Hammedatha the-Agagite that he-wrote to-destroy *** the-Jews who in-all-of

מְדִינוֹת הַמֶּלֶךְ׃ (6) כִּי אֵיכָכָה אוּכַל וְרָאִיתִי בָּרָעָה אֲשֶׁר־
provinces-of the-king (6) for how? can-I-bear and-I-see to-the-disaster that

יִמְצָא אֶת־עַמִּי וְאֵיכָכָה אוּכַל וְרָאִיתִי בְּאָבְדַן
he-will-fall-on *** people-of-me and-how? can-I-bear and-I-see to-destruction-of

מוֹלַדְתִּי׃ (7) וַיֹּאמֶר הַמֶּלֶךְ אֲחַשְׁוֵרֹשׁ לְאֶסְתֵּר הַמַּלְכָּה
family-of-me (7) and-he-replied the-king Ahasuerus to-Esther the-queen

וּלְמָרְדֳּכַי הַיְּהוּדִי הִנֵּה בֵית־הָמָן נָתַתִּי לְאֶסְתֵּר וְאֹתוֹ
and-to-Mordecai the-Jew see! estate-of Haman I-gave to-Esther and-him

תָּלוּ עַל־הָעֵץ עַל אֲשֶׁר־שָׁלַח יָדוֹ בַּיְּהוּדִיים׃
they-hanged on the-gallows because that he-sent hand-of-him against-the-Jews

(8) וְאַתֶּם כִּתְבוּ עַל־הַיְּהוּדִים כַּטּוֹב בְּעֵינֵיכֶם
(8) now-you write! in-behalf-of the-Jews as-the-best in-eyes-of-you

בְּשֵׁם הַמֶּלֶךְ וְחִתְמוּ בְּטַבַּעַת הַמֶּלֶךְ כִּי־כְתָב
in-name-of the-king and-seal! with-signet-ring-of the-king for document

אֲשֶׁר־נִכְתָּב בְּשֵׁם־הַמֶּלֶךְ וְנַחְתּוֹם בְּטַבַּעַת
which being-written in-name-of the-king and-to-be-sealed with-signet-ring-of

הַמֶּלֶךְ אֵין לְהָשִׁיב׃ (9) וַיִּקָּרְאוּ סֹפְרֵי־הַמֶּלֶךְ
the-king not to-revoke (9) and-they-were-summoned secretaries-of the-king

בָּעֵת־הַהִיא בַּחֹדֶשׁ הַשְּׁלִישִׁי הוּא־חֹדֶשׁ סִיוָן בִּשְׁלוֹשָׁה
at-the-time the-that in-the-month the-third that month-of Sivan on-three

וְעֶשְׂרִים בּוֹ וַיִּכָּתֵב כְּכָל־אֲשֶׁר־צִוָּה מָרְדֳּכַי אֶל־
and-twenty of-him and-he-was-written as-all that he-ordered Mordecai to

הַיְּהוּדִים וְאֶל הָאֲחַשְׁדַּרְפְּנִים־וְהַפַּחוֹת וְשָׂרֵי הַמְּדִינוֹת
the-Jews and-to the-satraps and-the-governors and-nobles-of the-provinces

אֲשֶׁר ׀ מֵהֹדּוּ וְעַד־כּוּשׁ שֶׁבַע וְעֶשְׂרִים וּמֵאָה מְדִינָה מְדִינָה
that from-India and-to Cush seven and-twenty and-hundred province province

וּמְדִינָה כִּכְתָבָהּ וְעַם וָעָם כִּלְשֹׁנוֹ וְאֶל־
and-province in-script-of-her and-people and-people in-language-of-him and-to

gold scepter to Esther and she
arose and stood before him.
5"If it pleases the king," she
said, "and if he regards me
with favor and thinks it the
right thing to do, and if he is
pleased with me, let an order
be written overruling the dispatches that Haman son of
Hammedatha, the Agagite,
devised and wrote to destroy
the Jews in all the king's provinces. 6For how can I bear to
see disaster fall on my people?
How can I bear to see the destruction of my family?"
7King Xerxes replied to
Queen Esther and to Mordecai
the Jew, "Because Haman attacked the Jews, I have given
his estate to Esther, and they
have hanged him on the gallows.[l] 8Now write another decree in the king's name in behalf of the Jews as seems best
to you, and seal it with the
king's signet ring—for no
document written in the
king's name and sealed with
his ring can be revoked."
9At once the royal secretaries
were summoned—on the
twenty-third day of the third
month, the month of Sivan.
They wrote out all Mordecai's
orders to the Jews, and to the
satraps, governors and nobles
of the 127 provinces stretching from India to Cush.[m] These
orders were written in the
script of each province and the
language of each people and

[l]7 Or *have hung him on a pole*
[m]9 That is, the upper Nile region

°7 ק ביהודים

הַיְּהוּדִים כִּכְתָבָם וְכִלְשׁוֹנָם׃ וַיִּכְתֹּב
and-he-wrote (10) and-in-language-of-them in-script-of-them the-Jews

בְּשֵׁם הַמֶּלֶךְ אֲחַשְׁוֵרֹשׁ וַיַּחְתֹּם בְּטַבַּעַת הַמֶּלֶךְ
the-king with-signet-ring-of and-he-sealed Ahasuerus the-king in-name-of

וַיִּשְׁלַח סְפָרִים בְּיַד הָרָצִים בַּסּוּסִים
on-the-mounts the-ones-being-couriers by-hand-of dispatches and-he-sent

רֹכְבֵי הָרֶכֶשׁ הָאֲחַשְׁתְּרָנִים בְּנֵי הָרַמָּכִים׃
the-studs ones-bred-of the-royal-ones the-fast-horse ones-riding-of

(11) אֲשֶׁר נָתַן הַמֶּלֶךְ לַיְּהוּדִים ׀ אֲשֶׁר בְּכָל־ עִיר־ וָעִיר
and-city city in-every-of who to-the-Jews the-king he-granted that (11)

לְהִקָּהֵל וְלַעֲמֹד עַל־ נַפְשָׁם לְהַשְׁמִיד וְלַהֲרֹג
and-to-kill to-destroy self-of-them to and-to-protect to-assemble

וּלְאַבֵּד אֶת־ כָּל־ חֵיל עַם וּמְדִינָה
or-province nation armed-force-of any-of *** and-to-annihilate

הַצָּרִים אֹתָם טַף וְנָשִׁים וּשְׁלָלָם לָבוֹז׃
to-plunder and-property-of-them and-women child them the-ones-attacking

(12) בְּיוֹם אֶחָד בְּכָל־ מְדִינוֹת הַמֶּלֶךְ אֲחַשְׁוֵרוֹשׁ בִּשְׁלוֹשָׁה עָשָׂר
ten on-three Ahasuerus the-king provinces-of in-all-of one on-day (12)

לְחֹדֶשׁ שְׁנֵים־עָשָׂר הוּא־ חֹדֶשׁ אֲדָר׃ (13) פַּתְשֶׁגֶן הַכְּתָב לְהִנָּתֵן
to-be-issued the-text copy-of (13) Adar month-of that ten two of-month-of

דָּת בְּכָל־ מְדִינָה וּמְדִינָה גָּלוּי לְכָל־ הָעַמִּים
the-peoples to-all-of being-made-known and-province province in-every-of law

וְלִהְיוֹת הַיְּהוּדִיים° עֲתוֹדִים° לַיּוֹם הַזֶּה לְהִנָּקֵם
to-avenge-self the-this on-the-day ones-ready the-Jews so-to-be

מֵאֹיְבֵיהֶם׃ (14) הָרָצִים רֹכְבֵי
ones-riding-of the-ones-being-couriers (14) on-ones-being-enemies-of-them

הָרֶכֶשׁ הָאֲחַשְׁתְּרָנִים יָצְאוּ מְבֹהָלִים וּדְחוּפִים
and-ones-being-spurred-on ones-racing they-went-out the-royal-ones the-horse

בִּדְבַר הַמֶּלֶךְ וְהַדָּת נִתְּנָה בְּשׁוּשַׁן הַבִּירָה׃
the-citadel in-Susa she-was-issued and-the-edict the-king by-command-of

(15) וּמָרְדֳּכַי יָצָא ׀ מִלִּפְנֵי הַמֶּלֶךְ בִּלְבוּשׁ מַלְכוּת
royalty in-garment-of the-king from-presences-of he-left and-Mordecai (15)

תְּכֵלֶת וָחוּר וַעֲטֶרֶת זָהָב גְּדוֹלָה וְתַכְרִיךְ בּוּץ וְאַרְגָּמָן
and-purple fine-linen and-robe-of large gold and-crown-of and-white blue

וְהָעִיר שׁוּשָׁן צָהֲלָה וְשָׂמֵחָה׃ (16) לַיְּהוּדִים הָיְתָה
she-was for-the-Jews (16) and-she-rejoiced she-celebrated Susa and-the-city

אוֹרָה וְשִׂמְחָה וְשָׂשֹׂן וִיקָר׃ (17) וּבְכָל־ מְדִינָה
province and-in-every-of (17) and-honor and-gladness and-joy happiness

also to the Jews in their own
script and language. [10]Mor-
decai wrote in the name of
King Xerxes, sealed the dispatches with the king's signet
ring, and sent them by mounted couriers, who rode fast
horses especially bred for the
king.
[11]The king's edict granted
the Jews in every city the right
to assemble and protect themselves; to destroy, kill and annihilate any armed force of
any nationality or province
that might attack them and
their women and children;
and to plunder the property of
their enemies. [12]The day appointed for the Jews to do this
in all the provinces of King
Xerxes was the thirteenth day
of the twelfth month, the
month of Adar. [13]A copy of the
text of the edict was to be issued as law in every province
and made known to the
people of every nationality so
that the Jews would be ready
on that day to avenge themselves on their enemies.
[14]The couriers, riding the
royal horses, raced out,
spurred on by the king's command. And the edict was also
issued in the citadel of Susa.
[15]Mordecai left the king's
presence wearing royal garments of blue and white, a
large crown of gold and a purple robe of fine linen. And the
city of Susa held a joyous celebration. [16]For the Jews it was a
time of happiness and joy,
gladness and honor. [17]In every

°13a ק היהודים
°13b ק עתידים

וּמְדִינָה וּבְכָל־ עִיר וָעִיר מְקוֹם אֲשֶׁר דְּבַר־ הַמֶּלֶךְ
the-king command-of where place-of and-city city and-in-every-of and-province

וְדָתוֹ מַגִּיעַ שִׂמְחָה וְשָׂשׂוֹן לַיְּהוּדִים מִשְׁתֶּה וְיוֹם
and-day-of feast among-the-Jews and-gladness joy going and-edict-of-him

טוֹב וְרַבִּים מֵעַמֵּי הָאָרֶץ מִתְיַהֲדִים כִּי־
because ones-becoming-Jews the-nation from-peoples-of and-many celebration

נָפַל פַּחַד־ הַיְּהוּדִים עֲלֵיהֶם׃ וּבִשְׁנֵים עָשָׂר חֹדֶשׁ הוּא־ חֹדֶשׁ
month-of that month ten and-in-two (9:1) to-them the-Jews fear-of he-seized

אֲדָר בִּשְׁלוֹשָׁה עָשָׂר יוֹם בּוֹ אֲשֶׁר הִגִּיעַ דְּבַר־ הַמֶּלֶךְ וְדָתוֹ
and-command-of-him the-king edict-of he-came when of-him day ten on-three Adar

לְהֵעָשׂוֹת בַּיּוֹם אֲשֶׁר שִׂבְּרוּ אֹיְבֵי הַיְּהוּדִים
the-Jews ones-being-enemies-of they-hoped when on-the-day to-be-carried-out

לִשְׁלוֹט בָּהֶם וְנַהֲפוֹךְ הוּא אֲשֶׁר יִשְׁלְטוּ
they-got-upper-hand for this but-to-be-overturned over-them to-overpower

הַיְּהוּדִים הֵמָּה בְּשֹׂנְאֵיהֶם׃ נִקְהֲלוּ הַיְּהוּדִים
the-Jews and-they-assembled (2) over-ones-hating-them they the-Jews

בְּעָרֵיהֶם בְּכָל־ מְדִינוֹת הַמֶּלֶךְ אֲחַשְׁוֵרוֹשׁ* לִשְׁלֹחַ יָד
hand to-send Ahasuerus the-king provinces-of in-all-of in-cities-of-them

בִּמְבַקְשֵׁי רָעָתָם וְאִישׁ לֹא־ עָמַד
he-could-stand not and-man destruction-of-them against-ones-seeking-of

לִפְנֵיהֶם כִּי־ נָפַל פַּחְדָּם עַל־ כָּל־ הָעַמִּים׃
the-peoples all-of on fear-of-them he-fell because against-them

וְכָל־ שָׂרֵי הַמְּדִינוֹת וְהָאֲחַשְׁדַּרְפְּנִים וְהַפַּחוֹת
and-the-governors and-the-satraps the-provinces nobles-of and-all-of (3)

וְעֹשֵׂי הַמְּלָאכָה אֲשֶׁר לַמֶּלֶךְ מְנַשְּׂאִים אֶת־הַיְּהוּדִים
the-Jews *** ones-helping of-the-king who the-work and-ones-administering-of

כִּי־ נָפַל פַּחַד־ מָרְדֳּכַי עֲלֵיהֶם׃ כִּי־ גָדוֹל מָרְדֳּכַי
Mordecai prominent for (4) to-them Mordecai fear-of he-seized because

בְּבֵית הַמֶּלֶךְ וְשָׁמְעוֹ הוֹלֵךְ בְּכָל־
through-all-of spreading and-reputation-of-him the-king in-palace-of

הַמְּדִינוֹת כִּי־ הָאִישׁ מָרְדֳּכַי הוֹלֵךְ וְגָדוֹל׃
and-powerful becoming-more Mordecai the-man for the-provinces

וַיַּכּוּ הַיְּהוּדִים בְּכָל־ אֹיְבֵיהֶם
ones-being-enemies-of-them to-all-of the-Jews and-they-struck-down (5)

מַכַּת־ חֶרֶב וְהֶרֶג וְאַבְדָן וַיַּעֲשׂוּ בְשֹׂנְאֵיהֶם
to-ones-hating-them and-they-did and-destruction and-killing sword striking-of

כִּרְצוֹנָם׃ וּבְשׁוּשַׁן הַבִּירָה הָרְגוּ הַיְּהוּדִים
the-Jews they-killed the-citadel and-in-Susa (6) as-pleasure-of-them

province and in every city, wherever the edict of the king went, there was joy and gladness among the Jews, with feasting and celebrating. And many people of other nationalities became Jews because fear of the Jews had seized them.

*Triumph of the Jews*

9 On the thirteenth day of the twelfth month, the month of Adar, the edict commanded by the king was to be carried out. On this day the enemies of the Jews had hoped to overpower them, but now the tables were turned and the Jews got the upper hand over those who hated them. 2The Jews assembled in their cities in all the provinces of King Xerxes to attack those seeking their destruction. No one could stand against them, because the people of all the other nationalities were afraid of them. 3And all the nobles of the provinces, the satraps, the governors and the king's administrators helped the Jews, because fear of Mordecai had seized them. 4Mordecai was prominent in the palace; his reputation spread throughout the provinces, and he became more and more powerful.

5The Jews struck down all their enemies with the sword, killing and destroying them, and they did what they pleased to those who hated them. 6In the citadel of Susa, the Jews killed and destroyed

*2 Most mss have *hateph pathah* under the *aleph* (אֲ).

וְאַבֵּד חֲמֵשׁ מֵאוֹת אִישׁ׃ וְאֵת ׀ פַּרְשַׁנְדָּתָא וְאֵת ׀ דַּלְפוֹן וְאֵת ׀
and Dalphon and Parshandatha also (7) man hundreds five-of and-to-destroy

אַסְפָּתָא׃ וְאֵת ׀ פּוֹרָתָא וְאֵת ׀ אֲדַלְיָא וְאֵת ׀ אֲרִידָתָא׃ וְאֵת ׀ פַּרְמַשְׁתָּא וְאֵת ׀ אֲרִיסַי
Arisai and Parmashta and (9) Aridatha and Adalia and Poratha and (8) Aspatha

וְאֵת ׀ אֲרִדַי וְאֵת ׀ וַיְזָתָא׃ עֲשֶׂרֶת בְּנֵי הָמָן בֶּן־ הַמְּדָתָא
Hammedatha son-of Haman sons-of ten-of (10) Vaizatha and Aridai and

צֹרֵר הַיְּהוּדִים הָרָגוּ וּבַבִּזָּה לֹא שָׁלְחוּ אֶת־
*** they-laid not but-on-the-plunder they-killed the-Jews one-being-enemy-of

יָדָם׃ בַּיּוֹם הַהוּא בָּא מִסְפַּר הַהֲרוּגִים
the-ones-being-slain number-of he-came the-same on-the-day (11) hand-of-them

בְּשׁוּשַׁן הַבִּירָה לִפְנֵי הַמֶּלֶךְ׃ וַיֹּאמֶר הַמֶּלֶךְ לְאֶסְתֵּר
to-Esther the-king and-he-said (12) the-king before the-citadel in-Susa

הַמַּלְכָּה בְּשׁוּשַׁן הַבִּירָה הָרְגוּ הַיְּהוּדִים וְאַבֵּד חֲמֵשׁ
five-of and-to-destroy the-Jews they-killed the-citadel in-Susa the-queen

מֵאוֹת אִישׁ וְאֵת עֲשֶׂרֶת בְּנֵי־ הָמָן בִּשְׁאָר מְדִינוֹת הַמֶּלֶךְ
the-king provinces-of in-rest-of Haman sons-of ten-of and man hundreds

מֶה עָשׂוּ וּמַה־ שְּׁאֵלָתֵךְ וְיִנָּתֵן לָךְ
to-you and-he-will-be-given petition-of-you now-what? they-did what?

וּמַה־ בַּקָּשָׁתֵךְ עוֹד וְתֵעָשׂ׃ וַתֹּאמֶר
and-she-answered (13) and-she-will-be-granted also request-of-you and-what?

אֶסְתֵּר אִם־ עַל־ הַמֶּלֶךְ טוֹב יִנָּתֵן גַּם־ מָחָר לַיְּהוּדִים
to-the-Jews tomorrow also let-him-be-given pleasing the-king to if Esther

אֲשֶׁר בְּשׁוּשָׁן לַעֲשׂוֹת כְּדָת הַיּוֹם וְאֵת עֲשֶׂרֶת בְּנֵי־ הָמָן
Haman sons-of ten-of and the-day as-edict-of to-carry-out in-Susa who

יִתְלוּ עַל־ הָעֵץ׃ וַיֹּאמֶר הַמֶּלֶךְ לְהֵעָשׂוֹת כֵּן
this to-be-done the-king so-he-commanded (14) the-gallows on let-them-hang

וַתִּנָּתֵן דָּת בְּשׁוּשָׁן וְאֵת עֲשֶׂרֶת בְּנֵי־ הָמָן תָּלוּ׃
they-hanged Haman sons-of ten-of and in-Susa edict and-she-was-issued

וַיִּקָּהֲלוּ הַיְּהוּדִיִּים אֲשֶׁר־ בְּשׁוּשָׁן גַּם בְּיוֹם אַרְבָּעָה עָשָׂר
ten four on-day-of also in-Susa who the-Jews and-they-came-together (15)

לְחֹדֶשׁ אֲדָר וַיַּהַרְגוּ בְשׁוּשָׁן שְׁלֹשׁ מֵאוֹת אִישׁ
man hundreds three-of in-Susa and-they-killed Adar of-month-of

וּבַבִּזָּה לֹא שָׁלְחוּ אֶת־ יָדָם׃ וּשְׁאָר
and-remainder-of (16) hand-of-them *** they-laid not but-on-the-plunder

הַיְּהוּדִים אֲשֶׁר בִּמְדִינוֹת הַמֶּלֶךְ נִקְהֲלוּ ׀ וְעָמֹד עַל־
to and-to-protect they-assembled the-king in-provinces-of who the-Jews

נַפְשָׁם וְנוֹחַ מֵאֹיְבֵיהֶם וְהָרֹג
and-to-kill from-ones-being-enemies-of-them and-to-get-relief self-of-them

five hundred men. [7]They also killed Parshandatha, Dalphon, Aspatha, [8]Poratha, Adalia, Aridatha, [9]Parmashta, Arisai, Aridai and Vaizatha, [10]the ten sons of Haman son of Hammedatha, the enemy of the Jews. But they did not lay their hands on the plunder.

[11]The number of those slain in the citadel of Susa was reported to the king that same day. [12]The king said to Queen Esther, "The Jews have killed five hundred men and the ten sons of Haman in the citadel of Susa. What have they done in the rest of the king's provinces? Now what is your petition? It will be given you. What is your request? It will also be granted."

[13]"If it pleases the king," Esther answered, "give the Jews in Susa permission to carry out this day's edict tomorrow also, and let Haman's ten sons be hanged on gallows.[n]"

[14]So the king commanded that this be done. An edict was issued in Susa, and they hanged[o] the ten sons of Haman. [15]The Jews in Susa came together on the fourteenth day of the month of Adar, and they put to death in Susa three hundred men, but they did not lay their hands on the plunder.

[16]Meanwhile, the remainder of the Jews who were in the king's provinces also assembled to protect themselves and get relief from their enemies.

[n]13 Or *be hung on poles;* also in verse 25
[o]14 Or *hung*

°15 ק היהודים

בְּשֹׂנְאֵיהֶם חֲמִשָּׁה וְשִׁבְעִים אָלֶף וּבַבִּזָּה לֹא
not but-on-the-plunder thousand and-seventy five of-ones-hating-them

שָׁלְחוּ אֶת־ יָדָם׃ בְּיוֹם־שְׁלֹשָׁה עָשָׂר לְחֹדֶשׁ אֲדָר וְנוֹחַ
and-to-rest Adar of-month-of ten three on-day-of (17) hand-of-them *** they-laid

בְּאַרְבָּעָה עָשָׂר בּוֹ וְעָשֹׂה אֹתוֹ יוֹם מִשְׁתֶּה וְשִׂמְחָה׃ וְהַיְּהוּדִיים
but-the-Jews (18) and-joy feasting day-of him and-to-make of-him ten on-four

אֲשֶׁר־ בְּשׁוּשָׁן נִקְהֲלוּ בִּשְׁלֹשָׁה עָשָׂר בּוֹ וּבְאַרְבָּעָה עָשָׂר בּוֹ
of-him ten and-on-four of-him ten on-three they-assembled in-Susa who

וְנוֹחַ בַּחֲמִשָּׁה עָשָׂר בּוֹ וְעָשֹׂה אֹתוֹ יוֹם מִשְׁתֶּה וְשִׂמְחָה׃
and-joy feasting day-of him and-to-make of-him ten on-five and-to-rest

עַל־ כֵּן הַיְּהוּדִים הַפְּרָוזִים הַיֹּשְׁבִים בְּעָרֵי
in-villages-of the-ones-living the-rural-ones the-Jews this for (19)

הַפְּרָזוֹת עֹשִׂים אֵת יוֹם אַרְבָּעָה עָשָׂר לְחֹדֶשׁ אֲדָר שִׂמְחָה
joy Adar of-month-of ten four day-of *** ones-observing the-rural-areas

וּמִשְׁתֶּה וְיוֹם טוֹב וּמִשְׁלוֹחַ מָנוֹת אִישׁ לְרֵעֵהוּ׃
to-fellow-of-him each presents and-giving good and-day-of and-feasting

וַיִּכְתֹּב מָרְדֳּכַי אֶת־ הַדְּבָרִים הָאֵלֶּה וַיִּשְׁלַח סְפָרִים
letters and-he-sent the-these the-events *** Mordecai and-he-recorded (20)

אֶל־ כָּל־ הַיְּהוּדִים אֲשֶׁר בְּכָל־ מְדִינוֹת הַמֶּלֶךְ אֲחַשְׁוֵרוֹשׁ
Ahasuerus the-king provinces-of in-all-of who the-Jews all-of to

הַקְּרוֹבִים וְהָרְחוֹקִים׃ לְקַיֵּם עֲלֵיהֶם לִהְיוֹת
to-be on-them to-impose (21) and-the-ones-far the-ones-near

עֹשִׂים אֵת יוֹם אַרְבָּעָה עָשָׂר לְחֹדֶשׁ אֲדָר וְאֵת יוֹם־חֲמִשָּׁה עָשָׂר
ten five day-of and Adar of-month-of ten four day-of *** ones-celebrating

בּוֹ בְּכָל־ שָׁנָה וְשָׁנָה׃ כַּיָּמִים אֲשֶׁר־ נָחוּ
they-got-relief when as-the-days (22) and-year year in-every-of of-him

בָהֶם הַיְּהוּדִים מֵאוֹיְבֵיהֶם וְהַחֹדֶשׁ אֲשֶׁר
when and-the-month from-ones-being-enemies-of-them the-Jews for-them

נֶהְפַּךְ לָהֶם מִיָּגוֹן לְשִׂמְחָה וּמֵאֵבֶל לְיוֹם
to-day-of and-from-mourning to-joy from-sorrow for-them he-was-turned

טוֹב לַעֲשׂוֹת אוֹתָם יְמֵי מִשְׁתֶּה וְשִׂמְחָה וּמִשְׁלוֹחַ מָנוֹת
food-presents and-giving and-joy feasting days-of them to-observe celebration

אִישׁ לְרֵעֵהוּ וּמַתָּנוֹת לָאֶבְיוֹנִים׃ וְקִבֵּל הַיְּהוּדִים
the-Jews so-he-agreed (23) to-the-poor-ones and-gifts to-fellow-of-him one

אֵת אֲשֶׁר־ הֵחֵלּוּ לַעֲשׂוֹת וְאֵת אֲשֶׁר־ כָּתַב מָרְדֳּכַי אֲלֵיהֶם׃ כִּי
for (24) to-them Mordecai he-wrote what and to-celebrate they-began what ***

הָמָן בֶּן־ הַמְּדָתָא הָאֲגָגִי צֹרֵר כָּל־ הַיְּהוּדִים חָשַׁב
he-plotted the-Jews all-of being-enemy-of the-Agagite Hammedatha son-of Haman

They killed seventy-five thousand of them but did not lay their hands on the plunder. [17]This happened on the thirteenth day of the month of Adar, and on the fourteenth they rested and made it a day of feasting and joy.

*Purim Celebrated*

[18]The Jews in Susa, however, had assembled on the thirteenth and fourteenth, and then on the fifteenth they rested and made it a day of feasting and joy.

[19]That is why rural Jews—those living in villages—observe the fourteenth of the month of Adar as a day of joy and feasting, a day for giving presents to each other.

[20]Mordecai recorded these events, and he sent letters to all the Jews throughout the provinces of King Xerxes, near and far, [21]to have them celebrate annually the fourteenth and fifteenth days of the month of Adar [22]as the time when the Jews got relief from their enemies, and as the month when their sorrow was turned into joy and their mourning into a day of celebration. He wrote them to observe the days as days of feasting and joy and giving presents of food to one another and gifts to the poor.

[23]So the Jews agreed to continue the celebration they had begun, doing what Mordecai had written to them. [24]For Haman son of Hammedatha, the Agagite, the enemy of all the Jews, had plotted against the

°18 ק והיהודים
°19 ק הפרזים

עַל־הַיְּהוּדִים לְאַבְּדָם וְהִפִּל פּוּר הוּא הַגּוֹרָל לְהֻמָּם
to-ruin-them the-lot that pur and-he-cast to-destroy-them the-Jews against

וּלְאַבְּדָם׃ וּבְבֹאָהּ לִפְנֵי הַמֶּלֶךְ אָמַר
he-ordered the-king before but-when-to-come-her (25) and-to-destroy-them

עִם־הַסֵּפֶר יָשׁוּב מַחֲשַׁבְתּוֹ הָרָעָה אֲשֶׁר־חָשַׁב
he-devised that the-evil scheme-of-him he-should-come-back the-writing with

עַל־הַיְּהוּדִים עַל־רֹאשׁוֹ וְתָלוּ אֹתוֹ וְאֶת־בָּנָיו עַל־
on sons-of-him and him and-they-should-hang head-of-him on the-Jews against

הָעֵץ׃ עַל־כֵּן קָרְאוּ לַיָּמִים הָאֵלֶּה פוּרִים עַל־שֵׁם
name-of from Purim the-these to-the-days they-called this for (26) the-gallows

הַפּוּר עַל־כֵּן עַל־כָּל־דִּבְרֵי הָאִגֶּרֶת הַזֹּאת וּמָה־
and-what the-this the-letter words-of all-of because-of this for the-pur

רָאוּ עַל־כָּכָה וּמָה הִגִּיעַ אֲלֵיהֶם׃ קִיְּמוּ
they-established (27) to-them he-happened and-what this because-of they-saw

וְקִבְּל° הַיְּהוּדִים ׀ עֲלֵיהֶם ׀ וְעַל־זַרְעָם וְעַל כָּל־
all-of and-upon descendant-of-them and-upon upon-them the-Jews and-they-took

הַנִּלְוִים עֲלֵיהֶם וְלֹא יַעֲבוֹר לִהְיוֹת עֹשִׂים אֵת
*** ones-observing to-be they-should-fail so-not with-them the-ones-joining

שְׁנֵי הַיָּמִים הָאֵלֶּה כִּכְתָבָם וְכִזְמַנָּם
and-as-appointed-time-of-them as-prescription-of-them the-these the-days two-of

בְּכָל־שָׁנָה וְשָׁנָה׃ וְהַיָּמִים הָאֵלֶּה נִזְכָּרִים
ones-being-remembered the-these and-the-days (28) and-year year in-every-of

וְנַעֲשִׂים בְּכָל־דּוֹר וָדוֹר מִשְׁפָּחָה
family and-generation generation in-every-of and-ones-being-observed

וּמִשְׁפָּחָה מְדִינָה וּמְדִינָה וְעִיר וָעִיר וִימֵי הַפּוּרִים
the-Purim and-days-of and-city and-city and-province province and-family

הָאֵלֶּה לֹא יַעַבְרוּ מִתּוֹךְ הַיְּהוּדִים וְזִכְרָם
and-memory-of-them the-Jews from-among they-should-cease never the-these

לֹא־יָסוּף מִזַּרְעָם׃ וַתִּכְתֹּב
so-she-wrote (29) among-descendant-of-them he-should-die-out not

אֶסְתֵּר הַמַּלְכָּה בַת־אֲבִיחַיִל וּמָרְדֳּכַי הַיְּהוּדִי אֶת־כָּל־
full-of with the-Jew and-Mordecai Abihail daughter-of the-queen Esther

תֹּקֶף לְקַיֵּם אֵת אִגֶּרֶת הַפֻּרִים הַזֹּאת הַשֵּׁנִית׃
the-second the-this the-Purim letter-of *** to-confirm authority

וַיִּשְׁלַח סְפָרִים אֶל־כָּל־הַיְּהוּדִים אֶל־שֶׁבַע וְעֶשְׂרִים וּמֵאָה
and-hundred and-twenty seven in the-Jews all-of to letters and-he-sent (30)

מְדִינָה מַלְכוּת אֲחַשְׁוֵרוֹשׁ דִּבְרֵי שָׁלוֹם וֶאֱמֶת׃
and-assurance good-will words-of Ahasuerus kingdom-of province

°27 ק וקבלו

Jews to destroy them and had
cast the *pur* (that is, the lot) for
their ruin and destruction.
25But when the plot came to
the king's attention,[p] he issued written orders that the
evil scheme Haman had de-
vised against the Jews should
come back onto his own head,
and that he and his sons
should be hanged on the gallows. 26(Therefore these days
were called Purim, from the
word *pur*.) Because of everything written in this letter and
because of what they had seen
and what had happened to
them, 27the Jews took it upon
themselves to establish the
custom that they and their descendants and all who join
them should without fail observe these two days every
year, in the way prescribed
and at the time appointed.
28These days should be
remembered and observed in
every generation by every
family, and in every province
and in every city. And these
days of Purim should never
cease to be celebrated by the
Jews, nor should the memory
of them die out among their
descendants.
29So Queen Esther, daughter
of Abihail, along with Mordecai the Jew, wrote with full
authority to confirm this second letter concerning Purim.
30And Mordecai sent letters to
all the Jews in the 127 provinces of the kingdom of
Xerxes—words of good will
and assurance— 31to establish

p25 Or *when Esther came before the king*

לְקַיֵּם אַת־* יְמֵי הַפֻּרִים הָאֵלֶּה בִּזְמַנֵּיהֶם
(31) to-establish *** days-of the-Purim the-these at-designated-times-of-them

כַּאֲשֶׁר קִיַּם עֲלֵיהֶם מָרְדֳּכַי הַיְּהוּדִי וְאֶסְתֵּר הַמַּלְכָּה
just-as he-decreed for-them Mordecai the-Jew and-Esther the-queen

וְכַאֲשֶׁר קִיְּמוּ עַל־ נַפְשָׁם וְעַל־ זַרְעָם
and-just-as they-established for self-of-them and-for descendant-of-them

דִּבְרֵי הַצּוֹמוֹת וְזַעֲקָתָם׃ וּמַאֲמַר אֶסְתֵּר
times-of the-fastings and-lamentation-of-them (32) and-decree-of Esther

קִיַּם דִּבְרֵי הַפֻּרִים הָאֵלֶּה וְנִכְתָּב
he-confirmed regulations-of the-Purim the-these and-being-written

בַּסֵּפֶר׃ וַיָּשֶׂם הַמֶּלֶךְ אֲחַשְׁרֵשׁ° ׀ מַס עַל־
in-the-record (10:1) and-he-imposed the-king Ahasuerus tribute throughout

הָאָרֶץ וְאִיֵּי הַיָּם׃ וְכָל־ מַעֲשֵׂה תָקְפּוֹ
the-empire and-shores-of the-sea (2) and-all-of act-of power-of-him

וּגְבוּרָתוֹ וּפָרָשַׁת גְּדֻלַּת מָרְדֳּכַי אֲשֶׁר
and-might-of-him with-full-account-of greatness-of Mordecai which

גִּדְּלוֹ הַמֶּלֶךְ הֲלוֹא־ הֵם כְּתוּבִים עַל־ סֵפֶר דִּבְרֵי
he-raised-him the-king not? they ones-being-written in book-of annals-of

הַיָּמִים לְמַלְכֵי מָדַי וּפָרָס׃ כִּי ׀ מָרְדֳּכַי הַיְּהוּדִי מִשְׁנֶה
the-days of-kings-of Media and-Persia (3) indeed Mordecai the-Jew second

לַמֶּלֶךְ אֲחַשְׁוֵרוֹשׁ וְגָדוֹל לַיְּהוּדִים וְרָצוּי
to-the-king Ahasuerus and-preeminent among-the-Jews and-being-esteemed

לְרֹב אֶחָיו דֹּרֵשׁ טוֹב לְעַמּוֹ
by-many-of fellows-of-him working-for good of-people-of-him

וְדֹבֵר שָׁלוֹם לְכָל־ זַרְעוֹ׃
and-speaking-up welfare of-all-of relative-of-him

these days of Purim at their designated times, as Mordecai the Jew and Queen Esther had decreed for them, and as they had established for themselves and their descendants in regard to their times of fasting and lamentation. 32 Esther's decree confirmed these regulations about Purim, and it was written down in the records.

*The Greatness of Mordecai*

10 King Xerxes imposed tribute throughout the empire, to its distant shores. 2 And all his acts of power and might, together with a full account of the greatness of Mordecai to which the king had raised him, are they not written in the book of the annals of the kings of Media and Persia? 3 Mordecai the Jew was second in rank to King Xerxes, preeminent among the Jews, and held in high esteem by his many fellow Jews, because he worked for the good of his people and spoke up for the welfare of all the Jews.

*31 Most mss have *segol* under the *aleph* ( אֶת ).

°1 ק אחשורוש

איש היה בארץ־ עוץ איוב שמו והיה | האיש ההוא
the-this the-man and-he-was name-of-him Job Uz in-land-of he-lived man (1:1)

תם וישר וירא אלהים וסר מרע׃
from-evil and-shunning God and-fearing-of and-upright blameless

ויולדו לו שבעה בנים ושלוש בנות׃ ויהי
and-he-was (3) daughters and-three sons seven to-him and-they-were-born (2)

מקנהו שבעת אלפי־ צאן ושלשת אלפי
thousands-of and-three-of sheep thousands-of seven-of possession-of-him

גמלים וחמש מאות צמד־ בקר וחמש מאות אתונות
donkeys hundreds and-five-of oxen yoke-of hundreds and-five-of camels

ועבדה רבה מאד ויהי האיש ההוא גדול
great the-this the-man and-he-was very large-number and-servant

מכל־ בני־ קדם׃ והלכו בניו
sons-of-him and-they-took-turns (4) East peoples-of more-than-all-of

ועשו משתה בית איש יומו ושלחו וקראו
and-they-invited and-they-sent day-of-him each home-of feast and-they-held

לשלשת אחיתיהם° לאכל ולשתות עמהם׃ ויהי
and-he-was (5) with-them and-to-drink to-eat sisters-of-them to-three-of

כי הקיפו ימי המשתה וישלח איוב ויקדשם
and-he-purified-them Job then-he-sent the-feast days-of they-ran-course when

והשכים בבקר והעלה עלות מספר
number-of burnt-offerings and-he-sacrificed in-the-morning then-he-got-up

כלם כי אמר איוב אולי חטאו בני
children-of-me they-sinned perhaps Job he-thought for each-of-them

וברכו אלהים בלבבם ככה יעשה איוב כל־ הימים׃
the-days all-of Job he-did this in-heart-of-them God and-they-cursed

ויהי היום ויבאו בני האלהים להתיצב על־
before to-present-self the-God sons-of that-they-came the-day and-he-was (6)

יהוה ויבוא גם־ השטן בתוכם׃ ויאמר יהוה אל־
to Yahweh and-he-said (7) in-among-them the-Satan also and-he-came Yahweh

השטן מאין תבא ויען השטן את־ יהוה
Yahweh *** the-Satan and-he-answered you-came from-where? the-Satan

ויאמר משוט בארץ ומהתהלך בה׃ ויאמר
then-he-said (8) in-her and-from-to-go through-the-earth from-to-roam and-he-said

יהוה אל־ השטן השמת לבך על־ עבדי איוב
Job servant-of-me to heart-of-you have-you-considered? the-Satan to Yahweh

כי אין כמהו בארץ איש תם וישר ירא
fearing-of and-upright blameless man on-the-earth like-him there-is-no-one for

*Prologue*

1 In the land of Uz there lived a man whose name was Job. This man was blameless and upright; he feared God and shunned evil. 2He had seven sons and three daughters, 3and he owned seven thousand sheep, three thousand camels, five hundred yoke of oxen and five hundred donkeys, and had a large number of servants. He was the greatest man among all the people of the East.

4His sons used to take turns holding feasts in their homes, and they would invite their three sisters to eat and drink with them. 5When a period of feasting had run its course, Job would send and have them purified. Early in the morning he would sacrifice a burnt offering for each of them, thinking, "Perhaps my children have sinned and cursed God in their hearts." This was Job's regular custom.

*Job's First Test*

6One day the angels[a] came to present themselves before the LORD, and Satan[b] also came with them. 7The LORD said to Satan, "Where have you come from?"

Satan answered the LORD, "From roaming through the earth and going back and forth in it."

8Then the LORD said to Satan, "Have you considered my servant Job? There is no one on earth like him; he is blameless and upright,

[a]6 Hebrew *the sons of God*
[b]6 *Satan* means *accuser.*

°4 ק אחיותיהם

אֱלֹהִים וְסָר מֵרָע׃ וַיַּעַן הַשָּׂטָן אֶת־ יְהוָה
Yahweh *** the-Satan and-he-replied (9) from-evil and-shunning God

וַיֹּאמַר הַחִנָּם יָרֵא אִיּוֹב אֱלֹהִים׃ הֲלֹא־ אַתְּ° שַׂכְתָּ
you-put-hedge you not? (10) God Job fearing for-nothing? and-he-said

בַעֲדוֹ וּבְעַד־ בֵּיתוֹ וּבְעַד כָּל־אֲשֶׁר־ לוֹ מִסָּבִיב
at-around to-him that all and-around household-of-him and-around around-him

מַעֲשֵׂה יָדָיו בֵּרַכְתָּ וּמִקְנֵהוּ פָּרַץ בָּאָרֶץ׃
through-the-land he-spreads so-flock-of-him you-blessed hands-of-him work-of

וְאוּלָם שְׁלַח־ נָא יָדְךָ וְגַע בְּכָל־ אֲשֶׁר־ לוֹ
to-him that against-all and-strike! hand-of-you now! stretch! now-but (11)

אִם־ לֹא עַל־ פָּנֶיךָ יְבָרְכֶךָּ׃ וַיֹּאמֶר יְהוָה אֶל־
to Yahweh and-he-said (12) he-will-curse-you faces-of-you to surely indeed

הַשָּׂטָן הִנֵּה כָל־אֲשֶׁר־ לוֹ בְּיָדֶךָ רַק אֵלָיו אַל־ תִּשְׁלַח
you-lay not on-him but in-hand-of-you to-him that all see! the-Satan

יָדֶךָ וַיֵּצֵא הַשָּׂטָן מֵעִם פְּנֵי יְהוָה׃
Yahweh presences-of from-in the-Satan then-he-went-out hand-of-you

וַיְהִי הַיּוֹם וּבָנָיו וּבְנֹתָיו אֹכְלִים
ones-feasting and-daughters-of-him when-sons-of-him the-day and-he-was (13)

וְשֹׁתִים יַיִן בְּבֵית אֲחִיהֶם הַבְּכוֹר׃ וּמַלְאָךְ
then-messenger (14) the-oldest brother-of-them at-house-of wine and-ones-drinking

בָּא אֶל־אִיּוֹב וַיֹּאמַר הַבָּקָר הָיוּ חֹרְשׁוֹת וְהָאֲתֹנוֹת
and-the-donkeys ones-plowing they-were the-oxen and-he-said Job to he-came

רֹעוֹת עַל־ יְדֵיהֶם׃ וַתִּפֹּל שְׁבָא וַתִּקָּחֵם
and-she-carried-away-them Sabean and-she-attacked (15) hands-of-them at ones-grazing

וְאֶת־ הַנְּעָרִים הִכּוּ לְפִי־ חָרֶב וָאִמָּלְטָה רַק־אֲנִי לְבַדִּי
by-myself I only and-I-escaped sword with-edge-of they-killed the-servants and

לְהַגִּיד לָךְ׃ עוֹד ׀ זֶה מְדַבֵּר וְזֶה בָּא וַיֹּאמַר אֵשׁ
fire-of and-he-said he-came then-this speaking this while (16) to-you to-tell

אֱלֹהִים נָפְלָה מִן־ הַשָּׁמַיִם וַתִּבְעַר בַּצֹּאן וּבַנְּעָרִים
and-to-the-servants to-the-sheep and-she-burned the-skies from she-fell God

וַתֹּאכְלֵם וָאִמָּלְטָה רַק־ אֲנִי לְבַדִּי לְהַגִּיד לָךְ׃
to-you to-tell by-myself I only and-I-escaped and-she-consumed-them

עוֹד ׀ זֶה מְדַבֵּר וְזֶה בָּא וַיֹּאמַר כַּשְׂדִּים שָׂמוּ ׀
they-formed Chaldeans and-he-said he-came then-this speaking this while (17)

שְׁלֹשָׁה רָאשִׁים וַיִּפְשְׁטוּ עַל־ הַגְּמַלִּים וַיִּקָּחוּם
and-she-carried-off-them the-camels on and-they-swept-down raiding-parties three

וְאֶת־ הַנְּעָרִים הִכּוּ לְפִי־ חָרֶב וָאִמָּלְטָה רַק־אֲנִי
I only and-I-escaped sword with-edge-of they-killed the-servants and

a man who fears God and shuns
evil."
[9]"Does Job fear God for nothing?" Satan replied. [10]"Have you
not put a hedge around him and
his household and everything he
has? You have blessed the work of
his hands, so that his flocks and
herds are spread throughout the
land. [11]But stretch out your hand
and strike everything he has, and
he will surely curse you to your
face."
[12]The LORD said to Satan, "Very
well, then, everything he has is in
your hands, but on the man himself do not lay a finger."
Then Satan went out from the
presence of the LORD.
[13]One day when Job's sons and
daughters were feasting and
drinking wine at the oldest brother's house, [14]a messenger came to
Job and said, "The oxen were
plowing and the donkeys were
grazing nearby, [15]and the Sabeans
attacked and carried them off.
They put the servants to the
sword, and I am the only one who
has escaped to tell you!"
[16]While he was still speaking,
another messenger came and said,
"The fire of God fell from the sky
and burned up the sheep and the
servants, and I am the only one
who has escaped to tell you!"
[17]While he was still speaking,
another messenger came and said,
"The Chaldeans formed three
raiding parties and swept down
on your camels and carried them
off. They put the servants to the
sword, and I am the only one who

°10 ק אתה

לְבַדִּי לְהַגִּיד לָךְ׃ עַד זֶה מְדַבֵּר וְזֶה בָּא
he-came then-this speaking this while (18) to-you to-tell by-myself

וַיֹּאמַר בָּנֶיךָ וּבְנוֹתֶיךָ אֹכְלִים וְשֹׁתִים
and-ones-drinking ones-feasting and-daughters-of-you sons-of-you and-he-said

יַיִן בְּבֵית אֲחִיהֶם הַבְּכוֹר׃ וְהִנֵּה רוּחַ גְּדוֹלָה
mighty wind when-see! (19) the-oldest brother-of-them at-house-of wine

בָּאָה מֵעֵבֶר הַמִּדְבָּר וַיִּגַּע בְּאַרְבַּע פִּנּוֹת
corners-of on-four-of and-he-struck the-desert from-across-of she-swept-in

הַבַּיִת וַיִּפֹּל עַל־ הַנְּעָרִים וַיָּמוּתוּ וָאִמָּלְטָה
and-I-escaped and-they-are-dead the-youths on and-he-collapsed the-house

רַק־ אֲנִי לְבַדִּי לְהַגִּיד לָךְ׃ וַיָּקָם אִיּוֹב וַיִּקְרַע אֶת־
*** and-he-tore Job and-he-got-up (20) to-you to-tell by-myself I only

מְעִלוֹ וַיָּגָז אֶת־ רֹאשׁוֹ וַיִּפֹּל אַרְצָה
to-ground then-he-fell head-of-him *** and-he-shaved robe-of-him

וַיִּשְׁתָּחוּ׃ וַיֹּאמֶר עָרֹם יָצָתִי מִבֶּטֶן אִמִּי
mother-of-me from-womb-of I-came naked and-he-said (21) and-he-worshiped

וְעָרֹם אָשׁוּב שָׁמָה* יְהוָה נָתַן וַיהוָה לָקָח
he-took-away and-Yahweh he-gave Yahweh to-there I-will-depart and-naked

יְהִי שֵׁם יְהוָה מְבֹרָךְ׃ בְּכָל־ זֹאת לֹא־ חָטָא
he-sinned not this in-all-of (22) being-praised Yahweh name-of may-he-be

אִיּוֹב וְלֹא־ נָתַן תִּפְלָה לֵאלֹהִים׃ וַיְהִי הַיּוֹם
the-day and-he-was (2:1) to-God wrongdoing he-charged for-not Job

וַיָּבֹאוּ בְּנֵי הָאֱלֹהִים לְהִתְיַצֵּב עַל־ יְהוָה וַיָּבוֹא
and-he-came Yahweh before to-present-self the-God sons-of then-they-came

גַם־ הַשָּׂטָן בְּתֹכָם לְהִתְיַצֵּב עַל־ יְהוָה׃ וַיֹּאמֶר
and-he-said (2) Yahweh before to-present-self in-among-them the-Satan also

יְהוָה אֶל־ הַשָּׂטָן אֵי מִזֶּה תָּבֹא וַיַּעַן הַשָּׂטָן
the-Satan and-he-answered you-came from-there where? the-Satan to Yahweh

אֶת־ יְהוָה וַיֹּאמַר מִשּׁוּט בָּאָרֶץ וּמֵהִתְהַלֵּךְ בָּהּ׃
in-her and-from-to-go through-the-earth from-to-roam and-he-said Yahweh ***

וַיֹּאמֶר יְהוָה אֶל־ הַשָּׂטָן הֲשַׂמְתָּ לִבְּךָ אֶל־
to heart-of-you have-you-considered? the-Satan to Yahweh then-he-said (3)

עַבְדִּי אִיּוֹב כִּי אֵין כָּמֹהוּ בָּאָרֶץ אִישׁ תָּם
blameless man on-the-earth like-him there-is-no-one for Job servant-of-me

וְיָשָׁר יְרֵא אֱלֹהִים וְסָר מֵרָע וְעֹדֶנּוּ מַחֲזִיק
maintaining and-still-he from-evil and-shunning God fearing-of and-upright

בְּתֻמָּתוֹ וַתְּסִיתֵנִי בוֹ לְבַלְּעוֹ חִנָּם׃
without-reason to-ruin-him against-him though-you-incited-me to-integrity-of-him

has escaped to tell you!"

18 While he was still speaking, yet another messenger came and said, "Your sons and daughters were feasting and drinking wine at the oldest brother's house, 19 when suddenly a mighty wind swept in from the desert and struck the four corners of the house. It collapsed on them and they are dead, and I am the only one who has escaped to tell you!"

20 At this, Job got up and tore his robe and shaved his head. Then he fell to the ground in worship 21 and said:

"Naked I came from my
mother's womb,
and naked I will depart.[c]
The LORD gave and the LORD
has taken away;
may the name of the LORD
be praised."

22 In all this, Job did not sin by charging God with wrongdoing.

*Job's Second Test*

2 On another day the angels[d] came to present themselves before the LORD, and Satan also came with them to present himself before him. 2 And the LORD said to Satan, "Where have you come from?"

Satan answered the LORD, "From roaming through the earth and going back and forth in it."

3 Then the LORD said to Satan, "Have you considered my servant Job? There is no one on earth like him; he is blameless and upright, a man who fears God and shuns evil. And he still maintains his integrity, though you incited me against him to ruin him without any reason."

c 21 Or *will return there*
d 1 Hebrew *the sons of God*

*21 Most mss have *dagesh* in the *mem* ( שׁמּה ).

°21 ק יצאתי

וַיַּעַן הַשָּׂטָן אֶת־יְהוָה וַיֹּאמַר עוֹר בְּעַד־עוֹר וְכָל
and-all skin for skin and-he-said Yahweh *** the-Satan and-he-replied (4)

אֲשֶׁר לָאִישׁ יִתֵּן בְּעַד נַפְשׁוֹ׃ אוּלָם שְׁלַח־נָא יָדְךָ
hand-of-you now! stretch! but (5) life-of-him for he-will-give to-man that

וְגַע אֶל־עַצְמוֹ וְאֶל־בְּשָׂרוֹ אִם־לֹא אֶל־פָּנֶיךָ
faces-of-you to surely indeed flesh-of-him and-to bone-of-him to and-strike!

יְבָרְכֶךָּ׃ וַיֹּאמֶר יְהוָה אֶל־הַשָּׂטָן הִנּוֹ בְיָדֶךָ
in-hand-of-you see-he! the-Satan to Yahweh and-he-said (6) he-will-curse-you

אַךְ אֶת־נַפְשׁוֹ שְׁמֹר׃ וַיֵּצֵא הַשָּׂטָן מֵאֵת פְּנֵי
presences-of from the-Satan so-he-went-out (7) spare! life-of-him *** but

יְהוָה וַיַּךְ אֶת־אִיּוֹב בִּשְׁחִין רָע מִכַּף רַגְלוֹ
foot-of-him from-sole-of painful with-sore Job *** and-he-afflicted Yahweh

°עַד קָדְקֳדוֹ׃ וַיִּקַּח־לוֹ חֶרֶשׂ לְהִתְגָּרֵד
to-scrape-himself broken-pottery for-him then-he-took (8) head-of-him and-to

בּוֹ וְהוּא יֹשֵׁב בְּתוֹךְ־הָאֵפֶר׃ וַתֹּאמֶר לוֹ אִשְׁתּוֹ
wife-of-him to-him and-she-said (9) the-ash in-among sitting as-he with-him

עֹדְךָ מַחֲזִיק בְּתֻמָּתֶךָ בָּרֵךְ אֱלֹהִים וָמֻת׃ וַיֹּאמֶר
and-he-replied (10) and-die! God curse! to-integrity-of-you holding still-you

אֵלֶיהָ כְּדַבֵּר אַחַת הַנְּבָלוֹת תְּדַבֵּרִי גַּם אֶת־הַטּוֹב
the-good *** indeed you-talk the-foolish-women one-of like-to-talk to-her

נְקַבֵּל מֵאֵת הָאֱלֹהִים וְאֶת־הָרָע לֹא נְקַבֵּל בְּכָל־
in-all-of we-shall-accept not the-trouble and the-God from we-shall-accept

זֹאת לֹא־חָטָא אִיּוֹב בִּשְׂפָתָיו׃ וַיִּשְׁמְעוּ שְׁלֹשֶׁת ׀
three-of when-they-heard (11) with-sayings-of-him Job he-sinned not this

רֵעֵי אִיּוֹב אֵת כָּל־הָרָעָה הַזֹּאת הַבָּאָה עָלָיו
upon-him that-she-came the-this the-trouble all-of *** Job friends-of

וַיָּבֹאוּ אִישׁ מִמְּקֹמוֹ אֱלִיפַז הַתֵּימָנִי וּבִלְדַּד
and-Bildad the-Temanite Eliphaz from-home-of-him each then-they-set-out

הַשּׁוּחִי וְצוֹפַר הַנַּעֲמָתִי וַיִּוָּעֲדוּ יַחְדָּו לָבוֹא
to-go together and-they-met the-Naamathite and-Zophar the-Shuhite

לָנוּד־לוֹ וּלְנַחֲמוֹ׃ וַיִּשְׂאוּ אֶת־
*** when-they-raised (12) and-to-comfort-him with-him to-sympathize

עֵינֵיהֶם מֵרָחוֹק וְלֹא הִכִּירֻהוּ וַיִּשְׂאוּ
and-they-raised they-recognized-him then-not from-distance eyes-of-them

קוֹלָם וַיִּבְכּוּ וַיִּקְרְעוּ אִישׁ מְעִלוֹ וַיִּזְרְקוּ
and-they-sprinkled robe-of-him each and-they-tore and-they-wept voice-of-them

עָפָר עַל־רָאשֵׁיהֶם הַשָּׁמָיְמָה׃ וַיֵּשְׁבוּ אִתּוֹ לָאָרֶץ
on-the-ground with-him then-they-sat (13) to-the-skies heads-of-them on dust

4"Skin for skin!" Satan replied. "A man will give all he has for his own life. 5But stretch out your hand and strike his flesh and bones, and he will surely curse you to your face."

6The LORD said to Satan, "Very well, then, he is in your hands; but you must spare his life."

7So Satan went out from the presence of the LORD and afflicted Job with painful sores from the soles of his feet to the top of his head. 8Then Job took a piece of broken pottery and scraped himself with it as he sat among the ashes.

9His wife said to him, "Are you still holding on to your integrity? Curse God and die!"

10He replied, "You are talking like a foolish[c] woman. Shall we accept good from God, and not trouble?"

In all this, Job did not sin in what he said.

*Job's Three Friends*

11When Job's three friends, Eliphaz the Temanite, Bildad the Shuhite and Zophar the Naamathite, heard about all the troubles that had come upon him, they set out from their homes and met together by agreement to go and sympathize with him and comfort him. 12When they saw him from a distance, they could hardly recognize him; they began to weep aloud, and they tore their robes and sprinkled dust on their heads. 13Then they sat on the ground

[c]10 The Hebrew word rendered *foolish* denotes moral deficiency.

°7 ק ועד

שִׁבְעַת יָמִים וְשִׁבְעַת לֵילוֹת וְאֵין־ דֹּבֵר אֵלָיו דָּבָר כִּי

because word to-him saying and-no-one nights and-seven-of days seven-of

רָאוּ כִּי־ גָדַל הַכְּאֵב מְאֹד׃ אַחֲרֵי־ כֵן פָּתַח

he-opened this after (3:1) very the-suffering he-was-great how they-saw

אִיּוֹב אֶת־ פִּיהוּ וַיְקַלֵּל אֶת־ יוֹמוֹ׃ וַיַּעַן אִיּוֹב

Job and-he-spoke (2) day-of-him *** and-he-cursed mouth-of-him *** Job

וַיֹּאמַר׃ יֹאבַד יוֹם אִוָּלֶד בּוֹ וְהַלַּיְלָה אָמַר

he-said and-the-night on-him I-was-born day may-he-perish (3) and-he-said

הֹרָה גָבֶר׃ הַיּוֹם הַהוּא יְהִי חֹשֶׁךְ אַל־ יִדְרְשֵׁהוּ

may-he-care-for-him not dark may-he-turn the-that the-day (4) boy he-is-born

אֱלוֹהַּ מִמָּעַל וְאַל־ תּוֹפַע עָלָיו נְהָרָה׃ יִגְאָלֻהוּ

may-they-claim-him (5) light upon-him may-she-shine and-not at-above God

חֹשֶׁךְ וְצַלְמָוֶת תִּשְׁכָּן־ עָלָיו עֲנָנָה יְבַעֲתֻהוּ

may-they-overwhelm-him cloud over-him may-she-settle and-deep-shadow darkness

כִּמְרִירֵי יוֹם׃ הַלַּיְלָה הַהוּא יִקָּחֵהוּ אֹפֶל

thick-darkness may-he-seize-him the-that the-night (6) day as-blacknesses-of

אַל־ יִחַדְּ בִּימֵי שָׁנָה בְּמִסְפַּר יְרָחִים אַל־ יָבֹא׃

may-he-enter not months in-number-of year among-days-of may-he-be-included not

הִנֵּה הַלַּיְלָה הַהוּא יְהִי גַלְמוּד אַל־ תָּבֹא רְנָנָה

shout-of-joy may-she-come not barren may-he-be the-that the-night see! (7)

בוֹ׃ יִקְּבֻהוּ אֹרְרֵי־ יוֹם הָעֲתִידִים עֹרֵר

to-rouse the-ones-ready day ones-cursing-of may-they-curse-him (8) into-him

לִוְיָתָן׃ יֶחְשְׁכוּ כּוֹכְבֵי נִשְׁפּוֹ יְקַו־

may-he-wait morning-of-him stars-of may-they-become-dark (9) Leviathan

לְאוֹר וָאַיִן וְאַל־ יִרְאֶה בְּעַפְעַפֵּי־ שָׁחַר׃

dawn to-first-rays-of may-he-see and-not but-there-is-not for-daylight

כִּי לֹא סָגַר דַּלְתֵי בִטְנִי וַיַּסְתֵּר עָמָל מֵעֵינָי׃

from-eyes-of-me trouble nor-he-hid womb-of-me doors-of he-shut not for (10)

לָמָּה לֹּא מֵרֶחֶם אָמוּת מִבֶּטֶן יָצָאתִי וְאֶגְוָע׃ מַדּוּעַ

why? (12) and-I-died I-came from-womb did-I-perish at-birth not why? (11)

קִדְּמוּנִי בִרְכָּיִם וּמַה־ שָּׁדַיִם כִּי אִינָק׃ כִּי־ עַתָּה

now for (13) I-was-nursed that breasts and-why? knees they-received-me

שָׁכַבְתִּי וְאֶשְׁקוֹט יָשַׁנְתִּי אָז יָנוּחַ

he-would-be-rest then I-would-sleep and-I-would-be-at-peace I-would-lie

לִי׃ עִם־ מְלָכִים וְיֹעֲצֵי אָרֶץ הַבֹּנִים

the-ones-building earth and-ones-counseling-of kings with (14) to-me

חֳרָבוֹת לָמוֹ׃ אוֹ עִם־ שָׂרִים זָהָב לָהֶם הַמְמַלְאִים בָּתֵּיהֶם

houses-of-them the-ones-filling to-them gold rulers with or (15) for-them ruins

with him for seven days and seven nights. No one said a word to him, because they saw how great his suffering was.

*Job Speaks*

3 After this, Job opened his mouth and cursed the day of his birth. [2]He said:

[3]"May the day of my birth perish,
and the night it was said, 'A boy is born!'
[4]That day—may it turn to darkness;
may God above not care about it;
may no light shine upon it.
[5]May darkness and deep shadow[f] claim it once more;
may a cloud settle over it;
may blackness overwhelm its light.
[6]That night—may thick darkness seize it;
may it not be included among the days of the year
nor be entered in any of the months.
[7]May that night be barren;
may no shout of joy be heard in it.
[8]May those who curse days[g] curse that day,
those who are ready to rouse Leviathan.
[9]May its morning stars become dark;
may it wait for daylight in vain
and not see the first rays of dawn,
[10]for it did not shut the doors of the womb on me
to hide trouble from my eyes.

[11]"Why did I not perish at birth,
and die as I came from the womb?
[12]Why were there knees to receive me
and breasts that I might be nursed?
[13]For now I would be lying down in peace;
I would be asleep and at rest
[14]with kings and counselors of the earth,
who built for themselves places now lying in ruins,
[15]with rulers who had gold,
who filled their houses with

[f]5 Or *and the shadow of death*
[g]8 Or *the sea*

כָּֽסֶף׃ אוֹ כְנֵפֶל טָמוּן לֹא אֶהְיֶה כְּעֹלְלִים
like-infants I-was not being-hidden like-stillborn-child or (16) silver

לֹא־ רָאוּ אוֹר׃ שָׁם רְשָׁעִים חָדְלוּ רֹגֶז וְשָׁם
and-there turmoil they-cease wicked-ones there (17) light they-saw never

יָנוּחוּ יְגִיעֵי כֹחַ׃ יַחַד אֲסִירִים שַׁאֲנָנוּ לֹא
not they-enjoy-ease captives together (18) strength ones-weary-of they-rest

שָׁמְעוּ קוֹל נֹגֵשׂ׃ קָטֹן וְגָדוֹל שָׁם הוּא וְעֶבֶד חָפְשִׁי
free and-slave he there and-great small (19) one-driving shout-of they-hear

מֵאֲדֹנָיו׃ לָמָּה יִתֵּן לְעָמֵל אוֹר וְחַיִּים
and-lives light to-miserable he-gives why? (20) from-masters-of-him

לְמָרֵי נָפֶשׁ׃ הַמְחַכִּים לַמָּוֶת וְאֵינֶנּוּ
and-not-he for-the-death the-ones-longing (21) soul to-ones-bitter-of

וַיַּחְפְּרֻהוּ מִמַּטְמוֹנִים׃ הַשְּׂמֵחִים אֱלֵי־
to the-ones-joyful (22) more-than-hidden-treasures and-they-search-for-him

גִיל יָשִׂישׂוּ כִּי יִמְצְאוּ־ קָבֶר׃ לְגֶבֶר אֲשֶׁר־ דַּרְכּוֹ
way-of-him who to-man (23) grave they-reach when they-rejoice gladness

נִסְתָּרָה וַיָּסֶךְ אֱלוֹהַּ בַּעֲדוֹ׃ כִּי־ לִפְנֵי לַחְמִי
food-of-me instead-of for (24) around-him God and-he-hedged-in she-is-hidden

אַנְחָתִי תָבֹא וַיִּתְּכוּ כַמַּיִם שַׁאֲגֹתָי׃
groans-of-me like-waters and-they-pour-out she-comes sighing-of-me

כִּי פַחַד פָּחַדְתִּי וַיֶּאֱתָיֵנִי וַאֲשֶׁר יָגֹרְתִּי יָבֹא
he-happened I-dreaded and-what and-he-came-upon-me I-feared fear for (25)

לִי׃ לֹא שָׁלַוְתִּי ׀ וְלֹא שָׁקַטְתִּי וְלֹא־ נָחְתִּי
I-have-rest and-not I-have-quiet and-not I-have-peace not (26) to-me

וַיָּבֹא רֹגֶז׃ וַיַּעַן אֱלִיפַז הַתֵּימָנִי וַיֹּאמַר׃
and-he-said the-Temanite Eliphaz then-he-replied (4:1) turmoil but-he-came

הֲנִסָּה דָבָר אֵלֶיךָ תִּלְאֶה וַעְצֹר בְּמִלִּין
from-words but-to-keep will-you-be-impatient with-you word he-ventures? (2)

מִי יוּכָל׃ הִנֵּה יִסַּרְתָּ רַבִּים וְיָדַיִם רָפוֹת
feeble-ones and-hands many you-instructed see! (3) he-can who?

תְּחַזֵּק׃ כּוֹשֵׁל יְקִימוּן מִלֶּיךָ וּבִרְכַּיִם
and-knees words-of-you they-supported one-stumbling (4) you-strengthened

כֹּרְעוֹת תְּאַמֵּץ׃ כִּי עַתָּה ׀ תָּבוֹא אֵלֶיךָ
to-you she-comes now but (5) you-strengthened ones-faltering

וַתֵּלֶא תִּגַּע עָדֶיךָ וַתִּבָּהֵל׃ הֲלֹא
not? (6) and-you-are-dismayed against-you she-strikes and-you-are-discouraged

יִרְאָתְךָ כִּסְלָתֶךָ תִּקְוָתְךָ וְתֹם דְּרָכֶיךָ׃
ways-of-you and-blamelessness-of hope-of-you confidence-of-you piety-of-you

silver.
16 Or why was I not hidden in the ground like a stillborn child,
like an infant who never saw the light of day?
17 There the wicked cease from turmoil,
and there the weary are at rest.
18 Captives also enjoy their ease;
they no longer hear the slave driver's shout.
19 The small and the great are there,
and the slave is freed from his master.

20 "Why is light given to those in misery,
and life to the bitter of soul,
21 to those who long for death that does not come,
who search for it more than for hidden treasure,
22 who are filled with gladness and rejoice when they reach the grave?
23 Why is life given to a man whose way is hidden,
whom God has hedged in?
24 For sighing comes to me instead of food;
my groans pour out like water.
25 What I feared has come upon me;
what I dreaded has happened to me.
26 I have no peace, no quietness;
I have no rest, but only turmoil."

*Eliphaz*

4 Then Eliphaz the Temanite replied:

2 "If someone ventures a word with you, will you be impatient?
But who can keep from speaking?
3 Think how you have instructed many,
how you have strengthened feeble hands.
4 Your words have supported those who stumbled;
you have strengthened faltering knees.
5 But now trouble comes to you, and you are discouraged;
it strikes you, and you are dismayed.
6 Should not your piety be your confidence
and your blameless ways your hope?

זְכָר־ נָא מִי הוּא נָקִי אָבָד וְאֵיפֹה יְשָׁרִים
upright-ones and-where? he-perished innocent he who? now! consider! (7)

נִכְחָדוּ׃ כַּאֲשֶׁר רָאִיתִי חֹרְשֵׁי אָוֶן
evil ones-plowing-of I-observed just-as (8) they-were-destroyed

וְזֹרְעֵי עָמָל יִקְצְרֻהוּ׃ מִנִּשְׁמַת אֱלוֹהַּ
God at-breath-of (9) they-reap-him trouble and-ones-sowing-of

יֹאבֵדוּ וּמֵרוּחַ אַפּוֹ יִכְלוּ׃ שַׁאֲגַת
roar-of (10) they-perish anger-of-him and-at-blast-of they-are-destroyed

אַרְיֵה וְקוֹל שָׁחַל וְשִׁנֵּי כְפִירִים נִתָּעוּ׃ לַיִשׁ
lion (11) they-are-broken lions yet-teeth-of lion and-growl-of lion

אֹבֵד מִבְּלִי־ טָרֶף וּבְנֵי לָבִיא יִתְפָּרָדוּ׃
they-are-scattered lioness and-cubs-of prey from-lack-of perishing

וְאֵלַי דָּבָר יְגֻנָּב וַתִּקַּח אָזְנִי שֵׁמֶץ
whisper ear-of-me and-she-caught he-was-secretly-brought word now-to-me (12)

מֶנְהוּ׃ בִּשְׂעִפִּים מֵחֶזְיֹנוֹת לָיְלָה בִּנְפֹל תַּרְדֵּמָה
deep-sleep when-to-fall night of-dreams-of amid-disquieting-ones (13) of-him

עַל־אֲנָשִׁים׃ פַּחַד קְרָאַנִי וּרְעָדָה וְרֹב עַצְמוֹתַי
bones-of-me and-all-of and-trembling he-seized-me fear (14) men on

הִפְחִיד׃ וְרוּחַ עַל־ פָּנַי יַחֲלֹף תְּסַמֵּר
she-stood-on-end he-glided faces-of-me by and-spirit (15) he-made-shake

שַׂעֲרַת בְּשָׂרִי׃ יַעֲמֹד ׀ וְלֹא־ אַכִּיר מַרְאֵהוּ
appearance-of-him I-could-tell but-not he-stopped (16) body-of-me hair-of

תְּמוּנָה לְנֶגֶד עֵינָי דְּמָמָה וָקוֹל אֶשְׁמָע׃ הַאֱנוֹשׁ
mortal? (17) I-heard and-voice hushed eyes-of-me at-before form

מֵאֱלוֹהַּ יִצְדָּק אִם מֵעֹשֵׂהוּ יִטְהַר־ גָּבֶר׃
man is-he-pure more-than-one-making-him or is-he-righteous more-than-God

הֵן בַּעֲבָדָיו לֹא יַאֲמִין וּבְמַלְאָכָיו
and-to-angels-of-him he-places-trust not in-servants-of-him if (18)

יָשִׂים תָּהֳלָה׃ אַף ׀ שֹׁכְנֵי בָתֵּי־ חֹמֶר אֲשֶׁר־
which clay houses-of ones-living-of how-much-more (19) error he-charges

בֶּעָפָר יְסוֹדָם יְדַכְּאוּם לִפְנֵי־ עָשׁ׃ מִבֹּקֶר
from-dawn (20) moth before they-crush-them foundation-of-them in-the-dust

לָעֶרֶב יֻכַּתּוּ מִבְּלִי מֵשִׂים לָנֶצַח יֹאבֵדוּ׃
they-perish to-forever being-noticed from-not they-are-broken to-the-dusk

הֲלֹא־ נִסַּע יִתְרָם בָּם יָמוּתוּ וְלֹא
and-not they-die from-them tent-cord-of-them he-is-pulled-up not? (21)

בְּחָכְמָה׃ קְרָא־ נָא הֲיֵשׁ עוֹנֶךָּ וְאֶל־ מִי
which? and-to one-answering-you is-there? now! call! (5:1) with-wisdom

7 "Consider now: Who, being innocent, has ever perished?
Where were the upright ever destroyed?
8 As I have observed, those who plow evil
and those who sow trouble reap it.
9 At the breath of God they are destroyed;
at the blast of his anger they perish.
10 The lions may roar and growl,
yet the teeth of the great lions are broken.
11 The lion perishes for lack of prey,
and the cubs of the lioness are scattered.

12 "A word was secretly brought to me,
my ears caught a whisper of it.
13 Amid disquieting dreams in the night,
when deep sleep falls on men,
14 fear and trembling seized me
and made all my bones shake.
15 A spirit glided past my face,
and the hair on my body stood on end.
16 It stopped,
but I could not tell what it was.
A form stood before my eyes,
and I heard a hushed voice:
17 'Can a mortal be more righteous than God?
Can a man be more pure than his Maker?
18 If God places no trust in his servants,
if he charges his angels with error,
19 how much more those who live in houses of clay,
whose foundations are in the dust,
who are crushed more readily than a moth!
20 Between dawn and dusk they are broken to pieces;
unnoticed, they perish forever.
21 Are not the cords of their tent pulled up,
so that they die without wisdom?'

5 "Call if you will, but who will answer you?

מִקְּדֹשִׁים תִּפְנֶה׃ (2) כִּי־ לֶאֱוִיל יַהֲרָג־ כָּעַשׂ

resentment he-kills to-fool for (2) will-you-turn of-holy-ones

וּפֹתֶה תָּמִית קִנְאָה׃ (3) אֲנִי־ רָאִיתִי אֱוִיל מַשְׁרִישׁ וָאֶקּוֹב

but-I-cursed taking-root fool I-saw I (3) envy she-slays and-one-being-simple

נָוֵהוּ פִתְאֹם׃ (4) יִרְחֲקוּ בָנָיו מִיֶּשַׁע

from-safety children-of-him they-are-far (4) suddenly house-of-him

וְיִדַּכְּאוּ בַשַּׁעַר וְאֵין מַצִּיל׃ (5) אֲשֶׁר קְצִירוֹ ׀

harvest-of-him who (5) one-defending and-no in-the-court and-they-are-crushed

רָעֵב יֹאכֵל וְאֶל־ מִצִּנִּים יִקָּחֵהוּ וְשָׁאַף צַמִּים

ones-thirsty and-he-pants he-takes-him from-thorns even-to he-consumes hungry

חֵילָם׃ (6) כִּי ׀ לֹא־ יֵצֵא מֵעָפָר אָוֶן וּמֵאֲדָמָה לֹא־

not or-from-ground hardship from-soil he-springs not for (6) wealth-of-them

יִצְמַח עָמָל׃ (7) כִּי־ אָדָם לְעָמָל יוּלָּד וּבְנֵי־ רֶשֶׁף

flame as-sons-of he-is-born to-trouble man yet (7) trouble he-sprouts

יַגְבִּיהוּ עוּף׃ (8) אוּלָם אֲנִי אֶדְרֹשׁ אֶל־ אֵל וְאֶל־ אֱלֹהִים

God and-before God to I-would-appeal I but-if (8) to-fly they-go-upward

אָשִׂים דִּבְרָתִי׃ (9) עֹשֶׂה גְדֹלוֹת וְאֵין חֵקֶר

fathomable and-not wonders performing (9) cause-of-me I-would-lay

נִפְלָאוֹת עַד־ אֵין מִסְפָּר׃ (10) הַנֹּתֵן מָטָר עַל־

on rain the-one-bestowing (10) count no to things-being-miraculous

פְּנֵי־ אָרֶץ וְשֹׁלֵחַ מַיִם* עַל־ פְּנֵי חוּצוֹת׃

countrysides surfaces-of on waters and-sending earth surfaces-of

(11) לָשׂוּם שְׁפָלִים לְמָרוֹם וְקֹדְרִים שָׂגְבוּ יֶשַׁע׃

safety they-are-lifted and-ones-mourning on-high lowly-ones to-set (11)

(12) מֵפֵר מַחְשְׁבוֹת עֲרוּמִים וְלֹא־ תַעֲשֶׂינָה יְדֵיהֶם תּוּשִׁיָּה׃

success hands-of-them they-achieve so-not crafty-ones plans-of thwarting (12)

(13) לֹכֵד חֲכָמִים בְּעָרְמָם וַעֲצַת נִפְתָּלִים

ones-being-wily and-scheme-of in-craftiness-of-them wise-ones catching (13)

נִמְהָרָה׃ (14) יוֹמָם יְפַגְּשׁוּ־ חֹשֶׁךְ וְכַלַּיְלָה

and-as-the-night darkness they-are-overcome by-day (14) she-is-swept-away

יְמַשְׁשׁוּ בַצָּהֳרָיִם׃ (15) וַיֹּשַׁע מֵחֶרֶב מִפִּיהֶם

in-mouth-of-them from-sword and-he-saves (15) at-the-noon they-grope

וּמִיַּד חָזָק אֶבְיוֹן׃ (16) וַתְּהִי לַדַּל תִּקְוָה

hope to-the-poor so-she-is (16) needy powerful and-from-clutch-of

וְעֹלָתָה קָפְצָה פִּיהָ׃ (17) הִנֵּה אַשְׁרֵי אֱנוֹשׁ

man blessings-of see! (17) mouth-of-her she-shuts and-injustice

יוֹכִחֶנּוּ אֱלוֹהַּ וּמוּסַר שַׁדַּי אַל־ תִּמְאָס׃ (18) כִּי הוּא

he for (18) you-despise not Almighty so-discipline-of God he-corrects-him

To which of the holy ones
will you turn?
2Resentment kills a fool,
and envy slays the simple.
3I myself have seen a fool
taking root,
but suddenly his house was
cursed.
4His children are far from
safety,
crushed in court without a
defender.
5The hungry consume his
harvest,
taking it even from among
thorns,
and the thirsty pant after
his wealth.
6For hardship does not spring
from the soil,
nor does trouble sprout from
the ground.
7Yet man is born to trouble
as surely as sparks fly
upward.
8"But if it were I, I would
appeal to God;
I would lay my cause before
him.
9He performs wonders that
cannot be fathomed,
miracles that cannot be
counted.
10He bestows rain on the earth;
he sends water upon the
countryside.
11The lowly he sets on high,
and those who mourn are
lifted to safety.
12He thwarts the plans of the
crafty,
so that their hands achieve
no success.
13He catches the wise in their
craftiness,
and the schemes of the wily
are swept away.
14Darkness comes upon them in
the daytime;
at noon they grope as in the
night.
15He saves the needy from the
sword in their mouth;
he saves them from the
clutches of the powerful.
16So the poor have hope,
and injustice shuts its
mouth.

17"Blessed is the man whom
God corrects;
so do not despise the
discipline of the
Almighty.[h]

[h] 17 Hebrew *Shaddai*; here and throughout Job

*10 Most mss have the accent *rebia mugrash* (·́).

יַכְאִיב וְיֶחְבָּשׁ יִמְחַץ וְיָדָו° תִּרְפֶּינָה׃
they-heal but-hands-of-him he-injures but-he-binds-up he-wounds

(19) בְּשֵׁשׁ צָרוֹת יַצִּילֶךָּ וּבְשֶׁבַע ׀ לֹא־ יִגַּע
he-will-befall not and-in-seven he-will-rescue-you calamities from-six-of (19)

בְּךָ רָע׃ (20) בְּרָעָב פָּדְךָ מִמָּוֶת וּבְמִלְחָמָה
and-in-battle from-death he-will-ransom-you in-famine (20) harm on-you

מִידֵי חָרֶב׃ (21) בְּשׁוֹט לָשׁוֹן תֵּחָבֵא וְלֹא־
and-not you-will-be-protected tongue from-lash-of (21) sword from-strokes-of

תִירָא מִשֹּׁד כִּי יָבוֹא׃ (22) לְשֹׁד וּלְכָפָן
and-at-famine at-destruction (22) he-comes when of-destruction you-will-fear

תִּשְׂחָק וּמֵחַיַּת הָאָרֶץ אַל־ תִּירָא׃ (23) כִּי עִם־
with for (23) you-will-fear not the-earth and-of-beast-of you-will-laugh

אַבְנֵי הַשָּׂדֶה בְרִיתֶךָ וְחַיַּת הַשָּׂדֶה הָשְׁלְמָה־
she-will-be-at-peace the-wild and-animal-of covenant-of-you the-field stones-of

לָךְ׃ (24) וְיָדַעְתָּ כִּי־ שָׁלוֹם אָהֳלֶךָ וּפָקַדְתָּ
and-you-will-take-stock tent-of-you secure that and-you-will-know (24) with-you

נָוְךָ וְלֹא תֶחֱטָא׃ (25) וְיָדַעְתָּ כִּי־ רַב
many that and-you-will-know (25) you-will-miss and-nothing property-of-you

זַרְעֶךָ וְצֶאֱצָאֶיךָ כְּעֵשֶׂב הָאָרֶץ׃ (26) תָּבוֹא
you-will-come (26) the-earth like-grass-of and-descendants-of-you child-of-you

בְכֶלַח אֱלֵי־ קָבֶר כַּעֲלוֹת גָּדִישׁ בְּעִתּוֹ׃ (27) הִנֵּה־זֹאת
this see! (27) in-season-of-him sheaf like-to-gather grave to in-vigor

חֲקַרְנוּהָ כֶּן־ הִיא שְׁמָעֶנָּה וְאַתָּה דַע־ לָךְ׃ (6:1) וַיַּעַן
then-he-replied (6:1) to-you apply! and-you hear-her! she true we-examined-her

אִיּוֹב וַיֹּאמַר׃ (2) לוּ שָׁקוֹל יִשָּׁקֵל כַּעְשִׂי
anguish-of-me he-was-weighed to-be-weighed if-only (2) and-he-said Job

וְהַיָּתִי° בְּמֹאזְנַיִם יִשְׂאוּ־ יָחַד׃ (3) כִּי־ עַתָּה
now surely (3) together they-placed on-scales and-misery-of-me

מֵחוֹל יַמִּים יִכְבָּד עַל־ כֵּן דְּבָרַי לָעוּ׃
they-were-impetuous words-of-me this for he-would-weigh seas more-than-sand-of

(4) כִּי חִצֵּי שַׁדַּי עִמָּדִי אֲשֶׁר חֲמָתָם שֹׁתָה רוּחִי
spirit-of-me drinking poison-of-them that in-me Almighty arrows-of indeed (4)

בִּעוּתֵי אֱלוֹהַּ יַעַרְכוּנִי׃ (5) הֲיִנְהַק־ פֶּרֶא עֲלֵי־
over wild-donkey does-he-bray? (5) they-are-marshaled-against-me God terrors-of

דֶשֶׁא אִם יִגְעֶה־ שּׁוֹר עַל־ בְּלִילוֹ׃ (6) הֲיֵאָכֵל תָּפֵל
tasteless-food is-he-eaten? (6) fodder-of-him over ox does-he-bellow or grass

מִבְּלִי־ מֶלַח אִם־ יֶשׁ־ טַעַם בְּרִיר חַלָּמוּת׃ (7) מֵאֲנָה
she-refuses (7) egg-white in-slime-of flavor is-there or salt without

---

18For he wounds, but he also binds up;
he injures, but his hands also heal.
19From six calamities he will rescue you;
in seven no harm will befall you.
20In famine he will ransom you from death,
and in battle from the stroke of the sword.
21You will be protected from the lash of the tongue,
and need not fear when destruction comes.
22You will laugh at destruction and famine
and need not fear the beasts of the earth.
23For you will have a covenant with the stones of the field,
and the wild animals will be at peace with you.
24You will know that your tent is secure;
you will take stock of your property and find nothing missing.
25You will know that your children will be many,
and your descendants like the grass of the earth.
26You will come to the grave in full vigor,
like sheaves gathered in season.

27"We have examined this, and it is true.
So hear it and apply it to yourself."

*Job*

6 Then Job replied:

2"If only my anguish could be weighed
and all my misery be placed on the scales!
3It would surely outweigh the sand of the seas—
no wonder my words have been impetuous.
4The arrows of the Almighty are in me,
my spirit drinks in their poison;
God's terrors are marshaled against me.
5Does a wild donkey bray when it has grass,
or an ox bellow when it has fodder?
6Is tasteless food eaten without salt,
or is there flavor in the white of an egg[i]?

[i]6 The meaning of the Hebrew for this phrase is uncertain.

°18 ק וידיו
°2 ק והותי

לִנְגּוֹעַ נַפְשִׁי הֵמָּה כִּדְוֵי לַחְמִי׃ מִי־ יִתֵּן
he-will-grant who? (8) food-of-me illnessess-of they self-of-me to-touch

תָּבוֹא שֶׁאֱלָתִי וְתִקְוָתִי יִתֵּן אֱלוֹהַּ׃
God he-would-grant and-hope-of-me request-of-me she-will-come

וְיֹאֵל אֱלוֹהַּ וִידַכְּאֵנִי יַתֵּר
he-would-let-loose and-he-would-crush-me God and-he-was-willing (9)

יָדוֹ וִיבַצְּעֵנִי׃ *וּתְהִי עוֹד
still then-she-would-be (10) and-he-would-cut-off-me hand-of-him

נֶחָמָתִי וַאֲסַלְּדָה בְחִילָה לֹא יַחְמוֹל כִּי־ לֹא
not that he-would-relent not in-pain and-I-would-rejoice consolation-of-me

כִחַדְתִּי אִמְרֵי קָדוֹשׁ׃ מַה־ כֹּחִי כִּי־ אֲיַחֵל
I-should-hope that strength-of-me what? (11) Holy-One words-of I-denied

וּמַה־ קִּצִּי כִּי־ אַאֲרִיךְ נַפְשִׁי׃ אִם־
indeed (12) soul-of-me I-should-make-patient that prospect-of-me and-what?

כֹּחַ אֲבָנִים כֹּחִי אִם־ בְּשָׂרִי נָחוּשׁ׃ הַאִם אֵין
no indeed? (13) bronze flesh-of-me or strength-of-me stones strength-of

עֶזְרָתִי בִי וְתֻשִׁיָּה נִדְּחָה מִמֶּנִּי׃ לַמָּס
for-the-desperate (14) from-me she-was-driven now-success for-me help-of-me

מֵרֵעֵהוּ חָסֶד וְיִרְאַת שַׁדַּי יַעֲזוֹב׃
he-forsakes Almighty though-fear-of devotion from-friends-of-him

אַחַי בָּגְדוּ כְמוֹ־ נָחַל
intermittent-stream as they-are-undependable brothers-of-me (15)

כַּאֲפִיק נְחָלִים יַעֲבֹרוּ׃ הַקֹּדְרִים מִנִּי־קָרַח עָלֵימוֹ
with-them ice by the-ones-being-dark (16) they-overflow streams as-channel-of

יִתְעַלֶּם־ שָׁלֶג׃ בְּעֵת יְזֹרְבוּ נִצְמָתוּ
they-cease-to-flow they-are-dry by-season (17) snow he-is-swollen

בְּחֻמּוֹ נִדְעֲכוּ מִמְּקוֹמָם׃ יִלָּפְתוּ
they-turn-aside (18) from-channel-of-them they-vanish when-to-be-hot-him

אָרְחוֹת דַּרְכָּם יַעֲלוּ בַתֹּהוּ וְיֹאבֵדוּ׃
and-they-perish into-the-wasteland they-go-up route-of-them caravans

הִבִּיטוּ אָרְחוֹת תֵּמָא הֲלִיכֹת שְׁבָא קִוּוּ־
they-hope Sheba traveling-merchants-of Tema caravans-of they-look (19)

לָמוֹ׃ בֹּשׁוּ כִּי־ בָטָח בָּאוּ עָדֶיהָ
at-her they-arrive he-was-confident because they-are-distressed (20) for-them

וַיֶּחְפָּרוּ׃ כִּי־ עַתָּה הֱיִיתֶם °לֹא תִּרְאוּ חֲתַת
dreadful you-see nothing you-were you too (21) but-they-are-disappointed

וַתִּירָאוּ׃ הֲכִי־ אָמַרְתִּי הָבוּ לִי וּמִכֹּחֲכֶם
and-from-wealth-of-you to-me give! I-said ever? (22) and-you-are-afraid

7 I refuse to touch it;
such food makes me ill.
8 "Oh, that I might have my request,
that God would grant what I hope for,
9 that God would be willing to crush me,
to let loose his hand and cut me off!
10 Then I would still have this consolation—
my joy in unrelenting pain—
that I had not denied the words of the Holy One.
11 "What strength do I have, that I should still hope?
What prospects, that I should be patient?
12 Do I have the strength of stone?
Is my flesh bronze?
13 Do I have any power to help myself,
now that success has been driven from me?
14 "A despairing man should have the devotion of his friends,
even though he forsakes the fear of the Almighty.
15 But my brothers are as undependable as intermittent streams,
as the streams that overflow
16 when darkened by thawing ice
and swollen with melting snow,
17 but that cease to flow in the dry season,
and in the heat vanish from their channels.
18 Caravans turn aside from their routes;
they go up into the wasteland and perish.
19 The caravans of Tema look for water,
the traveling merchants of Sheba look in hope.
20 They are distressed, because they had been confident;
they arrive there, only to be disappointed.
21 Now you too have proved to be of no help;
you see something dreadful and are afraid.
22 Have I ever said, 'Give something on my behalf,

**10* Most mss connect these two words with *maqqeph* (ותהי־עוד).

°21 ק לו

שִׁחֲדוּ בַּעֲדִי׃ וּמַלְּטוּנִי מִיַּד־ צָר וּמִיַּד

and-from-clutch-of enemy from-hand-of and-deliver-me! (23) for-me pay-ransom!

עָרִיצִים תִּפְדּוּנִי׃ הוֹרוּנִי וַאֲנִי אַחֲרִישׁ וּמַה־

and-what I-will-be-quiet and-I teach-me! (24) you-ransom-me ruthless-ones

שָּׁגִיתִי הָבִינוּ לִי׃ מַה־ נִּמְרְצוּ אִמְרֵי־ יֹשֶׁר וּמַה־

but-what? honesty words-of they-are-painful how! (25) to-me show! I-did-wrong

יּוֹכִיחַ הוֹכֵחַ מִכֶּם׃ הַלְהוֹכַח מִלִּים תַּחְשֹׁבוּ וּלְרוּחַ

and-as-wind do-you-mean sayings to-correct? (26) from-you to-prove he-proves

אִמְרֵי נֹאָשׁ׃ אַף־ עַל־ יָתוֹם תַּפִּילוּ

you-would-cast-lot fatherless for even (27) despairing-man words-of

וְתִכְרוּ עַל־ רֵיעֲכֶם׃ וְעַתָּה הוֹאִילוּ פְנוּ־ בִי

at-me look! be-kind! but-now (28) friend-of-you over and-you-would-barter

וְעַל־ פְּנֵיכֶם אִם־ אֲכַזֵּב׃ שֻׁבוּ־ נָא אַל־ תְּהִי עַוְלָה

unjust you-be not now! relent! (29) would-I-lie indeed faces-of-you and-to

וְשָׁבִי עוֹד צִדְקִי־ בָהּ׃ הֲיֵשׁ־ בִּלְשׁוֹנִי

on-lip-of-me is-there? (30) in-her integrity-of-me again and-consider!

עַוְלָה אִם־ חִכִּי לֹא־ יָבִין הַוּוֹת׃ הֲלֹא־

not? (7:1) malice he-can-discern not mouth-of-me indeed wickedness

צָבָא לֶאֱנוֹשׁ עֲלֵ־ אֶרֶץ וְכִימֵי שָׂכִיר יָמָיו׃

days-of-him hired-man and-like-days-of earth on to-man hard-service

כְּעֶבֶד יִשְׁאַף־ צֵל וּכְשָׂכִיר יְקַוֶּה פָעֳלוֹ׃

wage-of-him he-waits-for or-like-hired-man shadow he-longs-for like-slave (2)

כֵּן הָנְחַלְתִּי לִי יַרְחֵי־ שָׁוְא וְלֵילוֹת עָמָל

misery and-nights-of futility months-of to-me I-was-allotted so (3)

מִנּוּ־ לִי׃ אִם־ שָׁכַבְתִּי וְאָמַרְתִּי מָתַי

how-long? then-I-think I-lie-down when (4) to-me they-assigned

אָקוּם וּמִדַּד־ עָרֶב וְשָׂבַעְתִּי נְדֻדִים עֲדֵי־ נָשֶׁף׃

dawn till tossings and-I-am-full night now-he-drags-on will-I-get-up

לָבַשׁ בְּשָׂרִי רִמָּה וְגִישׁ עָפָר עוֹרִי רָגַע

he-is-broken skin-of-me dust and-scab-of worm body-of-me he-is-clothed (5)

וַיִּמָּאֵס׃ יָמַי קַלּוּ מִנִּי־ אָרֶג

shuttle-of-weaver more-than they-are-swift days-of-me (6) and-he-festers

וַיִּכְלוּ בְּאֶפֶס תִּקְוָה׃ זְכֹר כִּי־ רוּחַ חַיָּי לֹא־

never lives-of-me breath that remember! (7) hope with-no and-they-end

תָשׁוּב עֵינִי לִרְאוֹת טוֹב׃ לֹא־ תְשׁוּרֵנִי עֵין

eye-of she-will-see-me not (8) happiness to-see eye-of-me she-will-do-again

רֹאִי עֵינֶיךָ בִּי וְאֵינֶנִּי׃ כָּלָה עָנָן וַיֵּלַךְ

and-he-goes cloud he-vanishes (9) but-no-more-I to-me eyes-of-you seeing-me

°29 ק ושבו
°1 ק עלי
°5 ק וגוש

pay a ransom for me from
your wealth,
23 deliver me from the hand of
the enemy,
ransom me from the
clutches of the ruthless'?
24 "Teach me, and I will be quiet;
show me where I have been
wrong.
25 How painful are honest words!
But what do your arguments
prove?
26 Do you mean to correct what I
say,
and treat the words of a
despairing man as wind?
27 You would even cast lots for
the fatherless
and barter away your friend.
28 "But now be so kind as to look
at me.
Would I lie to your face?
29 Relent, do not be unjust;
reconsider, for my integrity
is at stake.[j]
30 Is there any wickedness on my
lips?
Can my mouth not discern
malice?

7 "Does not man have hard
service on earth?
Are not his days like those
of a hired man?
2 Like a slave longing for the
evening shadows,
or a hired man waiting
eagerly for his wages,
3 so I have been allotted months
of futility,
and nights of misery have
been assigned to me.
4 When I lie down I think,
'How long before I get
up?'
The night drags on, and I
toss till dawn.
5 My body is clothed with
worms and scabs,
my skin is broken and
festering.
6 "My days are swifter than a
weaver's shuttle,
and they come to an end
without hope.
7 Remember, O God, that my
life is but a breath;
my eyes will never see
happiness again.
8 The eye that now sees me will
see me no longer;
you will look for me, but I
will be no more.
9 As a cloud vanishes and is
gone,

j29 Or *my righteousness still stands*

כֵּן יוֹרֵד שְׁאוֹל לֹא יַעֲלֶה׃ לֹא־ יָשׁוּב עוֹד

again he-will-come never (10) he-returns not Sheol one-going-down so

לְבֵיתוֹ וְלֹא־ יַכִּירֶנּוּ עוֹד מְקֹמוֹ׃ גַּם־ אֲנִי

I therefore (11) place-of-him more he-will-know-him and-not to-house-of-him

לֹא אֶחֱשָׂךְ פִּי אֲדַבְּרָה בְּצַר רוּחִי

spirit-of-me in-anguish-of I-will-speak-out mouth-of-me I-will-keep-silent not

אָשִׂיחָה בְּמַר נַפְשִׁי׃ הֲיָם־אָנִי אִם־ תַּנִּין

monster-of-the-deep or I sea? (12) soul-of-me in-bitterness-of I-will-complain

כִּי־ תָשִׂים עָלַי מִשְׁמָר׃ כִּי־ אָמַרְתִּי תְּנַחֲמֵנִי עַרְשִׂי

bed-of-me she-will-comfort-me I-think when (13) guard over-me you-put that

יִשָּׂא בְשִׂיחִי מִשְׁכָּבִי׃ וְחִתַּתַּנִי

then-you-frighten-me (14) couch-of-me to-complaint-of-me he-will-ease

בַחֲלֹמוֹת וּמֵחֶזְיֹנוֹת תְּבַעֲתַנִּי׃ וַתִּבְחַר מַחֲנָק

strangling so-she-prefers (15) you-terrify-me and-with-visions with-dreams

נַפְשִׁי מָוֶת מֵעַצְמוֹתָי׃ מָאַסְתִּי לֹא־ לְעֹלָם

to-forever not I-despise (16) rather-than-bodies-of-me death life-of-me

אֶחְיֶה חֲדַל מִמֶּנִּי כִּי־ הֶבֶל יָמָי׃ מָה־ אֱנוֹשׁ

man what? (17) days-of-me meaningless for from-me let-alone! I-would-live

כִּי תְגַדְּלֶנּוּ וְכִי־ תָשִׁית אֵלָיו לִבֶּךָ׃

heart-of-you to-him you-give-attention and-that you-make-much-of-him that

וַתִּפְקְדֶנּוּ לִבְקָרִים לִרְגָעִים תִּבְחָנֶנּוּ׃

you-test-him in-moments in-mornings that-you-examine-him (18)

כַּמָּה לֹא־ תִשְׁעֶה מִמֶּנִּי לֹא־ תַרְפֵּנִי

you-will-let-alone-me not from-me you-will-look-away not as-the-when? (19)

עַד־ בִּלְעִי רֻקִּי׃ חָטָאתִי מָה אֶפְעַל ׀ לָךְ

to-you I-did what? I-sinned (20) spittle-of-me to-swallow-me even

נֹצֵר הָאָדָם לָמָה שַׂמְתַּנִי לְמִפְגָּע לָךְ וָאֶהְיֶה עָלַי

to-me and-I-became of-you as-target you-made-me why? the-man one-watching

לְמַשָּׂא׃ וּמֶה ׀ לֹא־ תִשָּׂא פִשְׁעִי וְתַעֲבִיר אֶת־

*** and-you-forgive offense-of-me you-pardon not and-why? (21) as-burden

עֲוֹנִי כִּי־ עַתָּה לֶעָפָר אֶשְׁכָּב וְשִׁחַרְתַּנִי*

and-you-will-search-for-me I-will-lie-down in-the-dust soon for sin-of-me

וְאֵינֶנִּי׃ וַיַּעַן בִּלְדַּד הַשּׁוּחִי וַיֹּאמַר׃† עַד־

until (2) and-he-said the-Shuhite Bildad then-he-replied (8:1) but-no-more-I

אָן תְּמַלֶּל־ אֵלֶּה וְרוּחַ כַּבִּיר אִמְרֵי־ פִיךָ׃

mouth-of-you words-of blustering now-wind these-things will-you-say when?

הַאֵל יְעַוֵּת מִשְׁפָּט וְאִם־ שַׁדַּי יְעַוֵּת־ צֶדֶק׃ אִם־

when (4) right he-perverts Almighty or-indeed justice he-perverts God? (3)

so he who goes down to the
grave[k] does not return.
10 He will never come to his
house again;
his place will know him no
more.

11 "Therefore I will not keep
silent;
I will speak out in the
anguish of my spirit,
I will complain in the
bitterness of my soul.
12 Am I the sea, or the monster
of the deep,
that you put me under
guard?
13 When I think my bed will
comfort me
and my couch will ease my
complaint,
14 even then you frighten me
with dreams
and terrify me with visions,
15 so that I prefer strangling and
death,
rather than this body of
mine.
16 I despise my life; I would not
live forever.
Let me alone; my days have
no meaning.

17 "What is man that you make
so much of him,
that you give him so much
attention,
18 that you examine him every
morning
and test him every moment?
19 Will you never look away from
me,
or let me alone even for an
instant?
20 If I have sinned, what have I
done to you,
O watcher of men?
Why have you made me your
target?
Have I become a burden to
you?[l]
21 Why do you not pardon my
offenses
and forgive my sins?
For I will soon lie down in the
dust;
you will search for me, but I
will be no more."

*Bildad*

8 Then Bildad the Shuhite replied:

2 "How long will you say such
things?
Your words are a blustering
wind.
3 Does God pervert justice?
Does the Almighty pervert
what is right?

[k] 9 Hebrew *Sheol*

[l] 20 A few manuscripts of the Masoretic Text, an ancient Hebrew scribal tradition and Septuagint; most manuscripts of the Masoretic Text *I have become a burden to myself.*

*21 Most mss have *pathah* under the *beth* (וְשִׁחַרְ).

†1 Most mss have *dagesh* in the *yod* (וַיּ).

בָּנֶיךָ חָטְאוּ־ לוֹ וַיְשַׁלְּחֵם בְּיַד־
into-hand-of then-he-gave-over-them against-him they-sinned children-of-you

פִּשְׁעָם׃ (5) אִם־אַתָּה תְּשַׁחֵר אֶל־ אֵל וְאֶל־ שַׁדַּי תִּתְחַנָּן׃
you-will-plead Almighty and-with God to you-will-look you if (5) sin-of-them

(6) אִם־זַךְ וְיָשָׁר אָתָּה כִּי־ עַתָּה יָעִיר עָלֶיךָ
on-behalf-of-you he-will-rouse-himself now even you and-upright pure if (6)

וְשִׁלַּם נְוַת צִדְקֶךָ׃ (7) וְהָיָה רֵאשִׁיתְךָ
beginning-of-you and-he-will-be (7) right-of-you place-of and-he-will-restore

מִצְעָר וְאַחֲרִיתְךָ יִשְׂגֶּה מְאֹד׃ (8) כִּי־ שְׁאַל־ נָא
now! ask! indeed (8) greatly he-will-prosper and-future-of-you humble

לְדֹר רִישׁוֹן וְכוֹנֵן לְחֵקֶר אֲבוֹתָם׃
fathers-of-them about-learning-of and-find-out! former to-generation

(9) כִּי־ תְמוֹל אֲנַחְנוּ וְלֹא נֵדָע כִּי צֵל יָמֵינוּ עֲלֵי־אָרֶץ׃
earth on days-of-us shadow for we-know and-nothing we yesterday for (9)

(10) הֲלֹא־ הֵם יוֹרוּךָ יֹאמְרוּ לָךְ
to-you they-will-tell they-will-instruct-you they not? (10)

וּמִלִּבָּם יוֹצִאוּ מִלִּים׃ (11) הֲיִגְאֶה־
can-he-grow? (11) words they-will-bring-forth and-from-understanding-of-them

גֹּמֶא בְּלֹא בִצָּה יִשְׂגֶּה־ אָחוּ בְלִי־ מָיִם׃ (12) עֹדֶנּוּ
still-he (12) waters without reed can-he-thrive marsh with-no papyrus

בְּאִבּוֹ לֹא יִקָּטֵף וְלִפְנֵי כָל־ חָצִיר יִיבָשׁ׃ (13) כֵּן
such (13) he-withers grass all-of yet-before he-was-cut not in-growth-of-him

אָרְחוֹת כָּל־ שֹׁכְחֵי אֵל וְתִקְוַת חָנֵף תֹּאבֵד׃
she-perishes godless so-hope-of God ones-forgetting-of all-of destinies-of

(14) אֲשֶׁר־ יָקוֹט כִּסְלוֹ וּבֵית עַכָּבִישׁ מִבְטַחוֹ׃
reliance-of-him spider and-web-of trust-of-him he-is-fragile what (14)

(15) יִשָּׁעֵן עַל־ בֵּיתוֹ וְלֹא יַעֲמֹד יַחֲזִיק בּוֹ וְלֹא
but-not to-him he-clings he-stands but-not web-of-him on he-leans (15)

יָקוּם׃ (16) רָטֹב הוּא לִפְנֵי־ שָׁמֶשׁ וְעַל־ גַּנָּתוֹ
garden-of-him and-over sunshine in he watered-plant (16) he-holds

יֹנַקְתּוֹ תֵצֵא׃ (17) עַל־ גַּל שָׁרָשָׁיו יְסֻבָּכוּ
they-entwine roots-of-him rock-pile around (17) she-spreads shoot-of-him

בֵּית אֲבָנִים יֶחֱזֶה׃ (18) אִם־ יְבַלְּעֶנּוּ מִמְּקוֹמוֹ
from-spot-of-him he-tears-him when (18) he-looks-for stones place-of

וְכִחֶשׁ בּוֹ לֹא רְאִיתִיךָ׃ (19) הֶן־ הוּא מְשׂוֹשׂ דַּרְכּוֹ
way-of-him joy-of this surely (19) I-saw-you never to-him then-he-disowns

וּמֵעָפָר אַחֵר יִצְמָחוּ׃ (20) הֶן־ אֵל לֹא יִמְאַס־ תָּם
blameless-man he-rejects not God surely (20) they-grow other and-from-soil

4When your children sinned
against him,
he gave them over to the
penalty of their sin.
5But if you will look to God
and plead with the
Almighty,
6if you are pure and upright,
even now he will rouse
himself on your behalf
and restore you to your
rightful place.
7Your beginnings will seem
humble,
so prosperous will your
future be.

8"Ask the former generations
and find out what their
fathers learned,
9for we were born only
yesterday and know
nothing,
and our days on earth are
but a shadow.
10Will they not instruct you and
tell you?
Will they not bring forth
words from their
understanding?
11Can papyrus grow tall where
there is no marsh?
Can reeds thrive without
water?
12While still growing and uncut,
they wither more quickly
than grass.
13Such is the destiny of all who
forget God;
so perishes the hope of the
godless.
14What he trusts in is fragile[m];
what he relies on is a
spider's web.
15He leans on his web, but it
gives way;
he clings to it, but it does
not hold.
16He is like a well-watered plant
in the sunshine,
spreading its shoots over the
garden;
17it entwines its roots around a
pile of rocks
and looks for a place among
the stones.
18But when it is torn from its
spot,
that place disowns it and
says, 'I never saw you.'
19Surely its life withers away,
and[n] from the soil other
plants grow.
20"Surely God does not reject a
blameless man

[m]14 The meaning of the Hebrew for this word is uncertain.
[n]19 Or *Surely all the joy it has / is that*

וְלֹא־ יַחֲזִיק בְּיַד־ מְרֵעִים׃ עַד־ יְמַלֵּה
he-will-fill yet (21) ones-doing-evil to-hand-of he-strengthens and-not

שְׂחוֹק פִּיךָ וּשְׂפָתֶיךָ תְרוּעָה׃ שֹׂנְאֶיךָ
ones-hating-you (22) shout-of-joy and-lips-of-you mouth-of-you laughter

יִלְבְּשׁוּ־ בֹשֶׁת וְאֹהֶל רְשָׁעִים אֵינֶנּוּ׃
no-more-he wicked-ones and-tent-of shame they-will-be-clothed

וַיַּעַן אִיּוֹב וַיֹּאמַר׃ אָמְנָם יָדַעְתִּי כִי־ כֵן וּמַה־
but-how? true that I-know indeed (2) and-he-said Job then-he-replied (9:1)

יִּצְדַּק אֱנוֹשׁ עִם־ אֵל׃ אִם־ יַחְפֹּץ לָרִיב
to-dispute he-wished though (3) God before mortal can-he-be-righteous

עִמּוֹ לֹא־ יַעֲנֶנּוּ אַחַת מִנִּי־ אָלֶף׃ חֲכַם לֵבָב
heart wise-of (4) thousand out-of one he-could-answer-him not with-him

וְאַמִּיץ כֹּחַ מִי־ הִקְשָׁה אֵלָיו וַיִּשְׁלָם׃
and-he-was-unscathed against-him he-resisted who? power and-vast-of

הַמַּעְתִּיק הָרִים וְלֹא יָדָעוּ אֲשֶׁר הֲפָכָם
he-overturns-them who they-know so-not mountains the-one-moving (5)

בְּאַפּוֹ׃ הַמַּרְגִּיז אֶרֶץ מִמְּקוֹמָהּ וְעַמּוּדֶיהָ
and-pillars-of-her from-place-of-her earth the-one-shaking (6) in-anger-of-him

יִתְפַלָּצוּן׃ הָאֹמֵר לַחֶרֶס וְלֹא יִזְרָח וּבְעַד
and-behind he-shines and-not to-the-sun the-one-speaking (7) they-tremble

כּוֹכָבִים יַחְתֹּם׃ נֹטֶה שָׁמַיִם לְבַדּוֹ וְדוֹרֵךְ
and-one-treading by-himself heavens one-stretching-out (8) he-seals-off stars

עַל־ בָּמֳתֵי יָם׃ עֹשֶׂה־ עָשׁ כְּסִיל וְכִימָה וְחַדְרֵי
and-constellations-of and-Pleiades Orion Bear One-Making (9) sea waves-of on

תֵמָן׃ עֹשֶׂה גְדֹלוֹת עַד־אֵין חֵקֶר וְנִפְלָאוֹת
and-things-being-miracles fathomable not to wonders one-performing (10) south

עַד־אֵין מִסְפָּר׃ הֵן יַעֲבֹר עָלַי וְלֹא אֶרְאֶה וְיַחֲלֹף וְלֹא־
and-not and-he-goes-by I-see and-not by-me he-passes see! (11) number no to

אָבִין לוֹ׃ הֵן יַחְתֹּף מִי יְשִׁיבֶנּוּ מִי־
who? he-can-stop-him who? he-snatches-away if (12) to-him I-perceive

יֹאמַר אֵלָיו מַה־ תַּעֲשֶׂה׃ אֱלוֹהַּ לֹא־ יָשִׁיב אַפּוֹ
anger-of-him he-restrains not God (13) you-do what? to-him he-can-say

תַּחְתָּו שָׁחֲחוּ עֹזְרֵי רָהַב׃ אַף כִּי־אָנֹכִי
I then how (14) Rahab ones-being-cohorts-of they-cower under-him

אֶעֱנֶנּוּ אֶבְחֲרָה דְבָרַי עִמּוֹ׃ אֲשֶׁר אִם־
though that (15) with-him words-of-me can-I-find I-can-dispute-with-him

צָדַקְתִּי לֹא אֶעֱנֶה לִמְשֹׁפְטִי אֶתְחַנָּן׃
I-could-plead-for-mercy to-one-judging-me I-could-answer not I-were-innocent

or strengthen the hands of evildoers.
21 He will yet fill your mouth with laughter
and your lips with shouts of joy.
22 Your enemies will be clothed in shame,
and the tents of the wicked will be no more."

*Job*

9 Then Job replied:
2 "Indeed, I know that this is true.
But how can a mortal be righteous before God?
3 Though one wished to dispute with him,
he could not answer him one time out of a thousand.
4 His wisdom is profound, his power is vast.
Who has resisted him and come out unscathed?
5 He moves mountains without their knowing it
and overturns them in his anger.
6 He shakes the earth from its place
and makes its pillars tremble.
7 He speaks to the sun and it does not shine;
he seals off the light of the stars.
8 He alone stretches out the heavens
and treads on the waves of the sea.
9 He is the Maker of the Bear and Orion,
the Pleiades and the constellations of the south.
10 He performs wonders that cannot be fathomed,
miracles that cannot be numbered.
11 When he passes me, I cannot see him;
when he goes by, I cannot perceive him.
12 If he snatches away, who can stop him?
Who can say to him, 'What are you doing?'
13 God does not restrain his anger;
even the cohorts of Rahab cowered at his feet.

14 "How then can I dispute with him?
How can I find words to argue with him?
15 Though I were innocent, I could not answer him;
I could only plead with my Judge for mercy.

°13 ק תחתיו

אִם־ קָרָאתִי וַיַּעֲנֵנִי לֹא־ אַאֲמִין כִּי־ יַאֲזִין

he-would-hear that I-believe not and-he-responded-to-me I-summoned if (16)

קוֹלִי׃ אֲשֶׁר־ בִּשְׂעָרָה יְשׁוּפֵנִי וְהִרְבָּה

and-he-would-multiply he-would-crush-me with-storm who (17) voice-of-me

פְצָעַי חִנָּם׃ לֹא־ יִתְּנֵנִי הָשֵׁב רוּחִי כִּי

but breath-of-me to-regain he-would-let-me not (18) no-reason wounds-of-me

יַשְׂבִּעַנִי מַמְּרֹרִים׃ אִם־ לְכֹחַ אַמִּיץ הִנֵּה וְאִם־

and-if see! mighty of-strength if (19) miseries he-would-overwhelm-me

לְמִשְׁפָּט מִי יוֹעִידֵנִי׃ אִם־ אֶצְדָּק פִּי

mouth-of-me I-were-innocent if (20) he-will-summon-me who? of-justice

יַרְשִׁיעֵנִי תָּם־ אָנִי וַיַּעְקְשֵׁנִי׃ תָּם־

blameless (21) then-he-would-pronounce-guilty-me I blameless he-would-condemn-me

אָנִי לֹא־ אֵדַע נַפְשִׁי אֶמְאַס חַיָּי׃ אַחַת הִיא עַל־

for she same (22) lives-of-me I-despise self-of-me I-am-concerned not I

כֵּן אָמַרְתִּי תָּם וְרָשָׁע הוּא מְכַלֶּה׃ אִם־ שׁוֹט

scourge when (23) destroying he and-wicked blameless I-say this

יָמִית פִּתְאֹם לְמַסַּת נְקִיִּם יִלְעָג׃ אֶרֶץ

land (24) he-mocks innocent-ones at-despair-of sudden he-brings-death

נִתְּנָה בְיַד־ רָשָׁע פְּנֵי־ שֹׁפְטֶיהָ יְכַסֶּה אִם־

if he-blindfolds ones-judging-her faces-of wicked into-hand-of she-falls

לֹא אֵפוֹא מִי־ הוּא׃ וְיָמַי קַלּוּ מִנִּי־ רָץ

one-running more-than they-are-swift and-days-of-me (25) he who? then not

בָּרְחוּ לֹא־ רָאוּ טוֹבָה׃ חָלְפוּ עִם־ אֳנִיּוֹת אֵבֶה

papyrus boats-of like they-skim-past (26) joy they-glimpse not they-fly-away

כְּנֶשֶׁר יָטוּשׂ עֲלֵי־ אֹכֶל׃ אִם־ אָמְרִי אֶשְׁכְּחָה

I-will-forget to-say-me if (27) prey on he-swoops-down like-eagle

שִׂיחִי אֶעֶזְבָה פָנַי וְאַבְלִיגָה׃ יָגֹרְתִּי

I-dread (28) and-I-will-smile expressions-of-me I-will-change complaint-of-me

כָל־ עַצְּבֹתָי יָדַעְתִּי כִּי־ לֹא תְנַקֵּנִי׃ אָנֹכִי

I (29) you-will-hold-innocent-me not that I-know sufferings-of-me all-of

אֶרְשָׁע לָמָּה־ זֶּה הֶבֶל אִיגָע׃ אִם־ הִתְרָחַצְתִּי

I-washed-myself if (30) I-should-struggle in-vain this why? I-am-guilty

בְמוֹ־ שָׁלֶג וַהֲזִכּוֹתִי בְּבֹר כַּפָּי׃ אָז

then (31) hands-of-me with-washing-soda and-I-washed soap *with

בַּשַּׁחַת תִּטְבְּלֵנִי וְתִעֲבוּנִי שַׂלְמוֹתָי׃

clothes-of-me so-they-would-detest-me you-would-plunge-me in-the-slime-pit

כִּי־ לֹא־ אִישׁ כָּמֹנִי אֶעֱנֶנּוּ נָבוֹא יַחְדָּו

together we-might-come I-might-answer-him like-me man not for (32)

16 Even if I summoned him and
he responded,
I do not believe he would
give me a hearing.
17 He would crush me with a
storm
and multiply my wounds for
no reason.
18 He would not let me regain
my breath
but would overwhelm me
with misery.
19 If it is a matter of strength, he
is mighty!
And if it is a matter of
justice, who will summon
him[o]?
20 Even if I were innocent, my
mouth would condemn
me;
if I were blameless, it would
pronounce me guilty.

21 "Although I am blameless,
I have no concern for
myself;
I despise my own life.
22 It is all the same; that is why I
say,
'He destroys both the
blameless and the
wicked.'
23 When a scourge brings sudden
death,
he mocks the despair of the
innocent.
24 When a land falls into the
hands of the wicked,
he blindfolds its judges.
If it is not he, then who is
it?

25 "My days are swifter than a
runner;
they fly away without a
glimpse of joy.
26 They skim past like boats of
papyrus,
like eagles swooping down
on their prey.
27 If I say, 'I will forget my
complaint,
I will change my expression,
and smile,'
28 I still dread all my sufferings,
for I know you will not hold
me innocent.
29 Since I am already found
guilty,
why should I struggle in
vain?
30 Even if I washed myself with
soap[p]
and my hands with
washing soda,
31 you would plunge me into a
slime pit
so that even my clothes
would detest me.

32 "He is not a man like me that
I might answer him,
that we might confront each

[o]19 See Septuagint; Hebrew *me.*
[p]30 Or *snow*

*30 The *Qere* reads *with-waters-of.*

°30 ק במי

בַּמִּשְׁפָּט׃ (33) לֹא יֵשׁ־ בֵּינֵינוּ מוֹכִיחַ יָשֵׁת
he-may-lay one-arbitrating between-us there-is *not (33) in-the-court

יָדוֹ עַל־ שְׁנֵינוּ׃ (34) יָסֵר מֵעָלַי שִׁבְטוֹ
rod-of-him from-against-me he-might-remove (34) both-of-us on hand-of-him

וְאֵמָתוֹ אַל־ תְּבַעֲתַנִּי׃ (35) אֲדַבְּרָה† וְלֹא
and-not I-would-speak-up (35) she-would-frighten-me not so-terror-of-him

אִירָאֶנּוּ כִּי לֹא־ כֵן אָנֹכִי עִמָּדִי׃ (10:1) נָקְטָה נַפְשִׁי
soul-of-me she-loathes (10:1) with-me I so not but I-would-fear-him

בְּחַיָּי אֶעֶזְבָה עָלַי שִׂיחִי אֲדַבְּרָה††
I-will-speak-out complaint-of-me to-me I-will-give-free-rein to-lives-of-me

בְּמַר נַפְשִׁי׃ (2) אֹמַר אֶל־ אֱלוֹהַּ אַל־ תַּרְשִׁיעֵנִי
you-condemn-me not God to I-will-say (2) soul-of-me in-bitterness-of

הוֹדִיעֵנִי עַל מַה־ תְּרִיבֵנִי׃ (3) הֲטוֹב לְךָ כִּי־ תַעֲשֹׁק
you-oppress that to-you pleasing? (3) you-charge-me what about tell-me!

כִּי־ תִמְאַס יְגִיעַ כַּפֶּיךָ וְעַל־ עֲצַת רְשָׁעִים הוֹפָעְתָּ׃
you-smile wicked-ones scheme-of while-on hands-of-you work-of you-spurn that

(4) הַעֵינֵי בָשָׂר לָךְ אִם־ כִּרְאוֹת אֱנוֹשׁ תִּרְאֶה׃ (5) הֲכִימֵי
like-days-of? (5) you-see mortal as-to-see indeed to-you flesh eyes-of? (4)

אֱנוֹשׁ יָמֶיךָ אִם־ שְׁנוֹתֶיךָ כִּימֵי גָבֶר׃ (6) כִּי־ תְבַקֵּשׁ
you-must-search that (6) man like-days-of years-of-you or days-of-you mortal

לַעֲוֺנִי וּלְחַטָּאתִי תִדְרוֹשׁ׃ (7) עַל־ דַּעְתְּךָ
knowledge-of-you though (7) you-must-probe and-after-sin-of-me to-fault-of-me

כִּי־ לֹא אֶרְשָׁע וְאֵין מִיָּדְךָ מַצִּיל׃ (8) יָדֶיךָ
hands-of-you (8) rescuing from-hand-of-you and-no-one I-am-guilty not that

עִצְּבוּנִי וַיַּעֲשׂוּנִי יַחַד סָבִיב וַתְּבַלְּעֵנִי׃
and-you-will-swallow-me around altogether and-they-made-me they-shaped-me

(9) זְכָר־ נָא כִּי־ כַחֹמֶר עֲשִׂיתָנִי וְאֶל־ עָפָר
dust now-to you-molded-me like-the-clay that now! remember! (9)

תְּשִׁיבֵנִי׃ (10) הֲלֹא כֶחָלָב תַּתִּיכֵנִי וְכַגְּבִנָּה
and-like-the-cheese you-poured-out-me like-the-milk not? (10) will-you-turn-me

תַּקְפִּיאֵנִי׃ (11) עוֹר וּבָשָׂר תַּלְבִּישֵׁנִי וּבַעֲצָמוֹת וְגִידִים
and-sinews and-with-bones you-clothed-me and-flesh skin (11) you-curdled-me

תְּסֹכְכֵנִי׃ (12) חַיִּים וָחֶסֶד עָשִׂיתָ עִמָּדִי
to-me you-gave and-kindness lives (12) you-knit-together-me

וּפְקֻדָּתְךָ שָׁמְרָה רוּחִי׃ (13) וְאֵלֶּה
but-these (13) spirit-of-me she-watched-over and-providence-of-you

צָפַנְתָּ בִלְבָבֶךָ יָדַעְתִּי כִּי־ זֹאת עִמָּךְ׃ (14) אִם־ חָטָאתִי
I-sinned if (14) in-you this that I-know in-heart-of-you you-concealed

other in court.
33 If only there were someone to
arbitrate between us,
to lay his hand upon us
both,
34 someone to remove God's rod
from me,
so that his terror would
frighten me no more.
35 Then I would speak up
without fear of him,
but as it now stands with
me, I cannot.

10 "I loathe my very life;
therefore I will give free
rein to my complaint
and speak out in the
bitterness of my soul.
2 I will say to God: Do not
condemn me,
but tell me what charges
you have against me.
3 Does it please you to oppress
me,
to spurn the work of your
hands,
while you smile on the
schemes of the wicked?
4 Do you have eyes of flesh?
Do you see as a mortal sees?
5 Are your days like those of a
mortal
or your years like those of a
man,
6 that you must search out my
faults
and probe after my sin—
7 though you know that I am
not guilty
and that no one can rescue
me from your hand?

8 "Your hands shaped me and
made me.
Will you now turn and
destroy me?
9 Remember that you molded
me like clay.
Will you now turn me to
dust again?
10 Did you not pour me out like
milk
and curdle me like cheese,
11 clothe me with skin and flesh
and knit me together with
bones and sinews?
12 You gave me life and showed
me kindness,
and in your providence
watched over my spirit.

13 "But this is what you
concealed in your heart,
and I know that this was in
your mind:
14 If I sinned, you would be
watching me

*33 The NIV reads לֻא, *if-only*, with the Septuagint and Syriac versions.

†35 Most mss have *hateph pathah* under the *aleph* (אֲ).

††1 Most mss have the accent over the *resh* (רָה—).

וּשְׁמַרְתָּנִי וּמֵעֲוֺנִי לֹא תְנַקֵּנִי׃

you-would-let-go-unpunished-me not and-from-offense-of-me then-you-would-watch-me

אִם־רָשַׁעְתִּי אַלְלַי לִי וְצָדַקְתִּי לֹא־אֶשָּׂא רֹאשִׁי

head-of-me I-can-lift not if-I-am-innocent to-me woe! I-am-guilty if (15)

שְׂבַע קָלוֹן וּרְאֵה* עָנְיִי׃ וְיִגְאֶה כַּשַּׁחַל

like-the-lion if-he-is-high (16) affliction-of-me *and-aware-of shame full-of

תְּצוּדֵנִי וְתָשֹׁב תִּתְפַּלָּא־בִי׃

against-me you-display-awesome-power and-you-do-again you-stalk-me

תְּחַדֵּשׁ עֵדֶיךָ׀ נֶגְדִּי וְתֶרֶב כַּעַשְׂךָ

anger-of-you and-you-increase against-me witnesses-of-you you-make-new (17)

עִמָּדִי חֲלִיפוֹת וְצָבָא עִמִּי׃ וְלָמָּה מֵרֶחֶם הֹצֵאתָנִי

you-brought-me from-womb then-why? (18) against-me and-force waves toward-me

אֶגְוַע וְעַיִן לֹא־תִרְאֵנִי׃ כַּאֲשֶׁר לֹא־הָיִיתִי

I-came-to-be never if-only (19) she-saw-me never and-eye I-should-have-died

אֶהְיֶה מִבֶּטֶן לַקֶּבֶר אוּבָל׃ הֲלֹא־מְעַט יָמַי

days-of-me few-of not? (20) I-was-carried to-the-grave from-womb I-came-to-be

°יַחְדָּל °יָשִׁית מִמֶּנִּי וְאַבְלִיגָה מְּעָט׃ בְּטֶרֶם

at-before (21) momentary so-I-can-have-joy from-me now-turn-away! he-is-over

אֵלֵךְ וְלֹא אָשׁוּב אֶל־אֶרֶץ חֹשֶׁךְ וְצַלְמָוֶת׃ אֶרֶץ עֵיפָתָה׀

darkness land-of (22) and-deep-shadow gloom land-of to I-return and-not I-go

כְּמוֹ אֹפֶל צַלְמָוֶת וְלֹא סְדָרִים וַתֹּפַע כְּמוֹ־אֹפֶל׃

darkness like and-she-is-light orders and-no deep-shadow night like

וַיַּעַן צֹפַר הַנַּעֲמָתִי וַיֹּאמַר׃ הֲרֹב דְּבָרִים

words all-of? (2) and-he-said the-Naamathite Zophar then-he-replied (11:1)

לֹא יֵעָנֶה וְאִם־אִישׁ שְׂפָתַיִם יִצְדָּק׃

is-he-vindicated speeches man-of and-indeed he-is-answered not

בַּדֶּיךָ מְתִים יַחֲרִישׁוּ וַתִּלְעַג וְאֵין מַכְלִם׃

rebuking then-no-one when-you-mock will-they-silence men idle-talks-of-you (3)

וַתֹּאמֶר זַךְ לִקְחִי וּבַר הָיִיתִי בְעֵינֶיךָ׃ וְאוּלָם

if-only (5) in-eyes-of-you I-am and-pure belief-of-me flawless and-you-say (4)

מִי־יִתֵּן אֱלוֹהַּ דַּבֵּר וְיִפְתַּח שְׂפָתָיו עִמָּךְ׃

against-you lips-of-him and-he-would-open to-speak God he-would-give someone

וְיַגֶּד־לְךָ׀ תַּעֲלֻמוֹת חָכְמָה כִּי־כִפְלַיִם לְתוּשִׁיָּה†

to-true-wisdom two-sides for wisdom secrets-of to-you and-he-would-disclose (6)

וְדַע כִּי־יַשֶּׁה לְךָ אֱלוֹהַּ† מֵעֲוֺנֶךָ׃ הַחֵקֶר אֱלוֹהַּ†

God mystery-of? (7) from-sin-of-you God of-you he-forgot that and-know!

תִּמְצָא אִם עַד־תַּכְלִית שַׁדַּי תִּמְצָא׃ גָּבְהֵי

ones-higher-of (8) can-you-probe Almighty limit-of to or can-you-fathom

and would not let my
offense go unpunished.
15 If I am guilty—woe to me!
Even if I am innocent, I
cannot lift my head,
for I am full of shame
and drowned in[q] my
affliction.
16 If I hold my head high, you
stalk me like a lion
and again display your
awesome power against
me.
17 You bring new witnesses
against me
and increase your anger
toward me;
your forces come against me
wave upon wave.

18 "Why then did you bring me
out of the womb?
I wish I had died before any
eye saw me.
19 If only I had never come into
being,
or had been carried straight
from the womb to the
grave!
20 Are not my few days almost
over?
Turn away from me so I can
have a moment's joy
21 before I go to the place of no
return,
to the land of gloom and
deep shadow,[r]
22 to the land of deepest night,
of deep shadow and
disorder,
where even the light is like
darkness."

*Zophar*

**11** Then Zophar the Naamathite replied:

2 "Are all these words to go
unanswered?
Is this talker to be
vindicated?
3 Will your idle talk reduce men
to silence?
Will no one rebuke you
when you mock?
4 You say to God, 'My beliefs
are flawless
and I am pure in your
sight.'
5 Oh, how I wish that God
would speak,
that he would open his lips
against you
6 and disclose to you the secrets
of wisdom,
for true wisdom has two
sides.
Know this: God has even
forgotten some of your
sin.

7 "Can you fathom the
mysteries of God?
Can you probe the limits of
the Almighty?

q15 Or *and aware of*
r21 Or *and the shadow of death*; also in verse 22

*15 The NIV reads וּרְוֵה, *and-drowned-of.*

†6, 7 Most mss have *mappiq* in the *he* (הּ).

°20a ק וחדל

°20b ק ושית

שָׁמַיִם מַה־ תִּפְעָל עֲמֻקָּה מִשְּׁאוֹל מַה־ תֵּדָע׃ אֲרֻכָּה
long (9) can-you-know what? more-than-Sheol deep can-you-do what? heavens

מֵאֶרֶץ מִדָּה וּרְחָבָה מִנִּי־ יָם׃ אִם־ יַחֲלֹף
he-comes-along if (10) sea more-than and-wide measure more-than-earth

וְיַסְגִּיר וְיַקְהִיל וּמִי יְשִׁיבֶנּוּ׃ כִּי־
surely (11) he-can-oppose-him then-who? and-he-convenes-court and-he-confines

הוּא יָדַע מְתֵי־ שָׁוְא וַיַּרְא־ אָוֶן וְלֹא יִתְבּוֹנָן׃
does-he-take-note then-not evil when-he-sees deceit men-of he-recognizes he

וְאִישׁ נָבוּב יִלָּבֵב וְעַיִר פֶּרֶא אָדָם
man wild-donkey if-colt he-can-become-wise being-witless but-man (12)

יִוָּלֵד׃ אִם־אַתָּה הֲכִינוֹתָ לִבֶּךָ וּפָרַשְׂתָּ אֵלָיו
to-him and-you-stretch-out heart-of-you you-devote you if (13) he-can-be-born

כַּפֶּךָ׃ אִם־ אָוֶן בְּיָדְךָ הַרְחִיקֵהוּ וְאַל־ תַּשְׁכֵּן
you-let-dwell and-not put-away-him! in-hand-of-you sin if (14) hand-of-you

בְּאֹהָלֶיךָ עַוְלָה׃ כִּי־ אָז תִּשָּׂא פָנֶיךָ מִמּוּם
without-shame faces-of-you you-will-lift then surely (15) evil in-tents-of-you

וְהָיִיתָ מֻצָק וְלֹא תִירָא׃ כִּי־ אַתָּה עָמָל
trouble you surely (16) you-will-fear and-not standing-firm and-you-will-be

תִּשְׁכָּח כְּמַיִם עָבְרוּ תִזְכֹּר׃ וּמִצָּהֳרַיִם
and-more-than-noonday (17) you-will-recall they-go-by as-waters you-will-forget

יָקוּם חָלֶד תָּעֻפָה כַּבֹּקֶר תִּהְיֶה׃
she-will-become like-the-morning darkness life he-will-be-bright

וּבָטַחְתָּ כִּי־ יֵשׁ תִּקְוָה וְחָפַרְתָּ
and-you-will-look-around hope there-is because and-you-will-be-secure (18)

לָבֶטַח תִּשְׁכָּב׃ וְרָבַצְתָּ וְאֵין מַחֲרִיד
making-afraid with-no-one and-you-will-lie-down (19) you-will-rest in-safety

וְחִלּוּ פָנֶיךָ רַבִּים׃ וְעֵינֵי רְשָׁעִים
wicked-ones but-eyes-of (20) many faces-of-you and-they-will-court-favor

תִּכְלֶינָה וּמָנוֹס אָבַד מִנְהֶם וְתִקְוָתָם מַפַּח־
gasp-of and-hope-of-them from-them he-will-elude and-escape they-will-fail

נָפֶשׁ׃ וַיַּעַן אִיּוֹב וַיֹּאמַר׃ אָמְנָם כִּי אַתֶּם־ עָם
people you that doubtless (2) and-he-said Job then-he-replied (12:1) life

וְעִמָּכֶם תָּמוּת חָכְמָה׃ גַּם־ לִי לֵבָב כְּמוֹכֶם לֹא־
not as-well-as-you mind to-me but (3) wisdom she-will-die and-with-you

נֹפֵל אָנֹכִי מִכֶּם וְאֶת־ מִי־ אֵין כְּמוֹ־ אֵלֶּה׃ שְׂחֹק
laughingstock (4) these-things like not whom? and-with to-you I being-inferior

לְרֵעֵהוּ אֶהְיֶה קֹרֵא לֶאֱלוֹהַּ וַיַּעֲנֵהוּ שְׂחוֹק
laughingstock and-he-answered-him to-God calling I-became to-friends-of-him

8They are higher than the heavens—what can you do?
They are deeper than the depths of the grave[s]—what can you know?
9Their measure is longer than the earth
and wider than the sea.

10"If he comes along and confines you in prison
and convenes a court, who can oppose him?
11Surely he recognizes deceitful men;
and when he sees evil, does he not take note?
12But a witless man can no more become wise
than a wild donkey's colt can be born a man.[t]

13"Yet if you devote your heart to him
and stretch out your hands to him,
14if you put away the sin that is in your hand
and allow no evil to dwell in your tent,
15then you will lift up your face without shame;
you will stand firm and without fear.
16You will surely forget your trouble,
recalling it only as waters gone by.
17Life will be brighter than noonday,
and darkness will become like morning.
18You will be secure, because there is hope;
you will look about you and take your rest in safety.
19You will lie down, with no one to make you afraid,
and many will court your favor.
20But the eyes of the wicked will fail,
and escape will elude them;
their hope will become a dying gasp."

*Job*

12 Then Job replied:
2"Doubtless you are the people,
and wisdom will die with you!
3But I have a mind as well as you;
I am not inferior to you.
Who does not know all these things?

4"I have become a laughingstock to my friends,
though I called upon God and he answered—
a mere laughingstock,

s8 Hebrew *than Sheol*
t12 Or *wild donkey can be born tame*

צַדִּיק תָּמִים׃ לַפִּיד בּוּז לְעַשְׁתּוּת
in-thinking-of contempt for-the-misfortune (5) blameless righteous

שַׁאֲנָן נָכוֹן לְמוֹעֲדֵי רָגֶל׃ יִשְׁלָיוּ אֹהָלִים
tents they-are-undisturbed (6) foot of-ones-slipping-of fate man-at-ease

לְשֹׁדְדִים וּבַטֻּחוֹת לְמַרְגִּיזֵי אֵל לַאֲשֶׁר
to-whom God to-ones-provoking-of and-securities of-ones-marauding

הֵבִיא אֱלוֹהַּ בְּיָדוֹ׃ וְאוּלָם שְׁאַל־נָא בְהֵמוֹת
animals now! ask! but-however (7) in-hand-of-him god he-carries

וְתֹרֶךָּ וְעוֹף הַשָּׁמַיִם וְיַגֶּד־לָךְ׃ אוֹ
or (8) to-you and-he-will-tell the-airs or-bird-of and-she-will-teach-you

שִׂיחַ לָאָרֶץ וְתֹרֶךָּ וִיסַפְּרוּ לְךָ דְּגֵי
fishes-of to-you or-let-them-inform and-she-will-teach-you to-the-earth speak!

הַיָּם׃ מִי לֹא־יָדַע בְּכָל־אֵלֶּה כִּי יַד־יְהוָה עָשְׂתָה
she-did Yahweh hand-of that these of-all-of he-knows not which? (9) the-sea

זֹּאת׃ אֲשֶׁר בְּיָדוֹ נֶפֶשׁ כָּל־חָי וְרוּחַ כָּל־
all-of and-breath-of creature every-of life-of in-hand-of-him that (10) this

בְּשַׂר־אִישׁ׃ הֲלֹא־אֹזֶן מִלִּין תִּבְחָן וְחֵךְ אֹכֶל יִטְעַם־
he-tastes food as-tongue she-tests words ear not? (11) mankind flesh-of

לוֹ׃ בִּישִׁישִׁים חָכְמָה וְאֹרֶךְ יָמִים תְּבוּנָה׃
understanding days and-length-of wisdom among-aged-ones (12) for-him

עִמּוֹ חָכְמָה וּגְבוּרָה לוֹ עֵצָה וּתְבוּנָה׃ הֵן
see! (14) and-understanding counsel to-him and-power wisdom to-him (13)

יַהֲרוֹס וְלֹא יִבָּנֶה יִסְגֹּר עַל־אִישׁ וְלֹא
and-not man to he-imprisons he-can-be-rebuilt and-not he-tears-down

יִפָּתֵחַ׃ הֵן יַעְצֹר בַּמַּיִם וְיִבָשׁוּ
and-they-have-drought to-the-waters he-holds-back see! (15) he-can-be-released

וִישַׁלְּחֵם וְיַהַפְכוּ אָרֶץ׃ עִמּוֹ עֹז
strength to-him (16) land then-they-devastate if-he-lets-loose-them

וְתוּשִׁיָּה לוֹ שֹׁגֵג וּמַשְׁגֶּה׃ מוֹלִיךְ
leading-away (17) and-one-deceiving one-being-deceived to-him and-victory

יוֹעֲצִים שׁוֹלָל וְשֹׁפְטִים יְהוֹלֵל׃ מוּסַר מְלָכִים
kings shackle-of (18) he-makes-fool and-ones-judging stripped ones-counseling

פִּתֵּחַ וַיֶּאְסֹר אֵזוֹר בְּמָתְנֵיהֶם׃ מוֹלִיךְ
leading-away (19) around-waists-of-them loincloth and-he-ties he-takes-off

כֹּהֲנִים שׁוֹלָל וְאֵתָנִים יְסַלֵּף׃ מֵסִיר שָׂפָה
lip silencing (20) he-overthrows and-established-men stripped priests

לְנֶאֱמָנִים וְטַעַם זְקֵנִים יִקָּח׃ שׁוֹפֵךְ
pouring (21) he-takes-away elders and-discernment-of of-ones-being-trusted

though righteous and
blameless!
5 Men at ease have contempt for
misfortune
as the fate of those whose
feet are slipping.
6 The tents of marauders are
undisturbed,
and those who provoke God
are secure—
those who carry their god in
their hands.[u]

7 "But ask the animals, and they
will teach you,
or the birds of the air, and
they will tell you;
8 or speak to the earth, and it
will teach you,
or let the fish of the sea
inform you.
9 Which of all these does not
know
that the hand of the LORD
has done this?
10 In his hand is the life of every
creature
and the breath of all
mankind.
11 Does not the ear test words
as the tongue tastes food?
12 Is not wisdom found among
the aged?
Does not long life bring
understanding?

13 "To God belong wisdom and
power;
counsel and understanding
are his.
14 What he tears down cannot be
rebuilt;
the man he imprisons
cannot be released.
15 If he holds back the waters,
there is drought;
if he lets them loose, they
devastate the land.
16 To him belong strength and
victory;
both deceived and deceiver
are his.
17 He leads counselors away
stripped
and makes fools of judges.
18 He takes off the shackles put
on by kings
and ties a loincloth[v] around
their waist.
19 He leads priests away stripped
and overthrows men long
established.
20 He silences the lips of trusted
advisers
and takes away the
discernment of elders.

[u]6 Or *secure / in what God's hand brings them*
[v]18 Or *shackles of kings / and ties a belt*

בּוּז עַל־ נְדִיבִים וּמְזִיחַ אֲפִיקִים רִפָּה׃ מְגַלֶּה
revealing (22) he-disarms mighty-ones and-belt-of nobles on contempt

עֲמֻקוֹת מִנִּי־ חֹשֶׁךְ וַיֹּצֵא לָאוֹר צַלְמָוֶת׃ מַשְׂגִּיא
making-great (23) deep-shadow to-light and-he-brings darkness from deep-things

לַגּוֹיִם וַיְאַבְּדֵם שֹׁטֵחַ לַגּוֹיִם
to-the-nations enlarging and-he-destroys-them to-the-nations

וַיַּנְחֵם׃ מֵסִיר לֵב רָאשֵׁי עַם־ הָאָרֶץ
the-earth people-of leaders-of reason-of depriving (24) and-he-disperses-them

וַיַּתְעֵם בְּתֹהוּ לֹא־ דָרֶךְ׃ יְמַשְׁשׁוּ־ חֹשֶׁךְ וְלֹא־
with-no darkness they-grope (25) track no through-waste and-he-sends-them

אוֹר וַיַּתְעֵם כַּשִּׁכּוֹר׃ הֶן־ כֹּל רָאֲתָה
she-saw all see! (13:1) like-the-drunkard and-he-makes-stagger-them light

עֵינִי שָׁמְעָה אָזְנִי וַתָּבֶן לָהּ׃ כְּדַעְתְּכֶם
as-knowledge-of-you (2) to-her and-she-understood ear-of-me she-heard eye-of-me

יָדַעְתִּי גַם־ אָנִי לֹא־ נֹפֵל אָנֹכִי מִכֶּם׃ אוּלָם אֲנִי אֶל־ שַׁדַּי
Almighty to I but (3) to-you I being-inferior not I also I-know

אֲדַבֵּר וְהוֹכֵחַ אֶל־ אֵל אֶחְפָּץ׃ וְאוּלָם אַתֶּם
you but-however (4) I-desire God with and-to-argue-case I-would-speak

טֹפְלֵי־ שָׁקֶר רֹפְאֵי אֱלִל כֻּלְּכֶם׃ מִי־
who? (5) all-of-you worthlessness ones-being-physicians-of lie ones-smearing-of

יִתֵּן הַחֲרֵשׁ תַּחֲרִישׁוּן וּתְהִי לָכֶם
for-you and-she-would-be you-would-be-silent to-be-silent he-would-make

לְחָכְמָה׃ שִׁמְעוּ־ נָא תוֹכַחְתִּי וְרִבוֹת שְׂפָתַי הַקְשִׁיבוּ׃
listen! lips-of-me and-pleas-of argument-of-me now! hear! (6) as-wisdom

הַלְאֵל תְּדַבְּרוּ עַוְלָה וְלוֹ תְּדַבְּרוּ
will-you-speak and-for-him wickedly will you-speak on-behalf-of-God? (7)

רְמִיָּה׃ הֲפָנָיו תִּשָּׂאוּן אִם־ לָאֵל
for-God or will-you-show-partiality faces-of-him? (8) deceitfully

תְּרִיבוּן׃ הֲטוֹב כִּי־ יַחְקֹר אֶתְכֶם אִם־ כְּהָתֵל בֶּאֱנוֹשׁ
to-man as-to-deceive or you he-examined if well? (9) will-you-argue-case

תְּהָתֵלּוּ בוֹ׃ הוֹכֵחַ יוֹכִיחַ אֶתְכֶם אִם־ בַּסֵּתֶר
in-the-secret if you he-would-rebuke to-rebuke (10) to-him could-you-deceive

פָּנִים תִּשָּׂאוּן׃ הֲלֹא שְׂאֵתוֹ תְּבַעֵת אֶתְכֶם
you she-would-terrify splendor-of-him not? (11) you-showed-partiality faces

וּפַחְדּוֹ יִפֹּל עֲלֵיכֶם׃ זִכְרֹנֵיכֶם מִשְׁלֵי־ אֵפֶר
ash proverbs-of maxims-of-you (12) on-you he-would-fall and-dread-of-him

לְגַבֵּי־ חֹמֶר גַּבֵּיכֶם׃ הַחֲרִישׁוּ מִמֶּנִּי
from-me keep-silent! (13) defenses-of-you clay as-defenses-of

21 He pours contempt on nobles
and disarms the mighty.
22 He reveals the deep things of darkness
and brings deep shadows into the light.
23 He makes nations great, and destroys them;
he enlarges nations, and disperses them.
24 He deprives the leaders of the earth of their reason;
he sends them wandering through a trackless waste.
25 They grope in darkness with no light;
he makes them stagger like drunkards.

13 "My eyes have seen all this,
my ears have heard and understood it.
2 What you know, I also know;
I am not inferior to you.
3 But I desire to speak to the Almighty
and to argue my case with God.
4 You, however, smear me with lies;
you are worthless physicians, all of you!
5 If only you would be altogether silent!
For you, that would be wisdom.
6 Hear now my argument;
listen to the plea of my lips.
7 Will you speak wickedly on God's behalf?
Will you speak deceitfully for him?
8 Will you show him partiality?
Will you argue the case for God?
9 Would it turn out well if he examined you?
Could you deceive him as you might deceive men?
10 He would surely rebuke you
if you secretly showed partiality.
11 Would not his splendor terrify you?
Would not the dread of him fall on you?
12 Your maxims are proverbs of ashes;
your defenses are defenses of clay.
13 "Keep silent and let me speak;

וְאֲדַבְּרָה־ אָנִי וְיַעֲבֹר עָלַי מָה׃ עַל־ מָה ׀ אֶשָּׂא

I-put why? for (14) whatever to-me then-let-him-come I and-let-me-speak

בְשָׂרִי בְשִׁנָּי וְנַפְשִׁי אָשִׂים בְּכַפִּי׃ הֵן

though (15) in-hands-of-me I-take and-life-of-me in-teeth-of-me flesh-of-me

יִקְטְלֵנִי לֹא° אֲיַחֵל אַךְ־ דְּרָכַי אֶל־ פָּנָיו אוֹכִיחַ׃

I-will-defend faces-of-him to ways-of-me surely I-will-hope in-him he-slay-me

(16) גַּם־ הוּא־ לִי לִישׁוּעָה כִּי־ לֹא לְפָנָיו חָנֵף

godless-man before-him not for for-deliverance to-me this indeed (16)

יָבוֹא׃ (17) שִׁמְעוּ שָׁמוֹעַ מִלָּתִי וְאַחֲוָתִי

and-saying-of-me word-of-me to-listen listen! (17) he-would-come

בְּאָזְנֵיכֶם׃ (18) הִנֵּה־ נָא עָרַכְתִּי מִשְׁפָּט יָדַעְתִּי כִּי־ אֲנִי

I that I-know case I-prepared now! see! (18) in-ears-of-you

אֶצְדָּק׃ (19) מִי־ הוּא יָרִיב עִמָּדִי כִּי־ עַתָּה

now if-so against-me can-he-bring-charges he who? (19) I-will-be-vindicated

אַחֲרִישׁ וְאֶגְוָע׃ (20) אַךְ־ שְׁתַּיִם אַל־* תַּעַשׂ עִמָּדִי אָז

then to-me you-do *not two only (20) and-I-will-die I-will-be-silent

מִפָּנֶיךָ לֹא אֶסָּתֵר׃ (21) כַּפְּךָ מֵעָלַי הַרְחַק

withdraw-far! from-upon-me hand-of-you (21) I-will-hide not from-before-you

וְאֵמָתְךָ אַל־ תְּבַעֲתַנִּי׃ (22) וּקְרָא וְאָנֹכִי אֶעֱנֶה

I-will-answer and-I then-summon! (22) you-frighten-me not and-terror-of-you

אוֹ־ אֲדַבֵּר וַהֲשִׁיבֵנִי׃ (23) כַּמָּה לִי עֲוֺנוֹת וְחַטָּאוֹת

and-sins wrongs to-me as-the-how-many? (23) and-reply-to-me! let-me-speak or

פִּשְׁעִי וְחַטָּאתִי הֹדִיעֵנִי׃ (24) לָמָּה־ פָנֶיךָ תַסְתִּיר

you-hide faces-of-you why? (24) show-me! and-sin-of-me offense-of-me

וְתַחְשְׁבֵנִי לְאוֹיֵב לָךְ׃ (25) הֶעָלֶה נִדָּף

being-wind-blown leaf? (25) to-you as-being-enemy and-you-consider-me

תַּעֲרוֹץ וְאֶת־ קַשׁ יָבֵשׁ תִּרְדֹּף׃ (26) כִּי־ תִכְתֹּב

you-write-down for (26) will-you-chase dry chaff and will-you-torment

עָלַי מְרֹרוֹת וְתוֹרִישֵׁנִי עֲוֺנוֹת נְעוּרָי׃

youths-of-me sins-of and-you-make-inherit-me bitter-things against-me

(27) וְתָשֵׂם בַּסַּד ׀ רַגְלַי וְתִשְׁמוֹר כָּל־

all-of and-you-watch feet-of-me in-the-shackle and-you-fasten (27)

אָרְחוֹתָי עַל־ שָׁרְשֵׁי רַגְלַי תִּתְחַקֶּה׃ (28) וְהוּא כְּרָקָב

like-rotten-thing so-he (28) you-put-mark feet-of-me soles-of on paths-of-me

יִבְלֶה כְּבֶגֶד אֲכָלוֹ עָשׁ׃ (14:1) אָדָם יְלוּד אִשָּׁה

woman being-born-of man (14:1) moth he-eats-him like-garment he-wastes-away

קְצַר יָמִים וּשְׂבַע־ רֹגֶז׃ (2) כְּצִיץ יָצָא וַיִּמָּל

and-he-withers he-springs-up like-flower (2) trouble and-full-of days few-of

then let come to me what
may.
14Why do I put myself in
jeopardy
and take my life in my
hands?
15Though he slay me, yet will I
hope in him;
I will surely[w] defend my
ways to his face.
16Indeed, this might turn out for
my deliverance,
for no godless man would
dare come before him!
17Listen carefully to my words;
let your ears take in what I
say.
18Now that I have prepared my
case,
I know I will be vindicated.
19Can anyone bring charges
against me?
If so, I will be silent and
die.
20"Only grant me these two
things, O God,
and then I will not hide
from you:
21Withdraw your hand far from
me,
and stop frightening me
with your terrors.
22Then summon me and I will
answer,
or let me speak, and you
reply.
23How many wrongs and sins
have I committed?
Show me my offense and
my sin.
24Why do you hide your face
and consider me your
enemy?
25Will you torment a
wind-blown leaf?
Will you chase after dry
chaff?
26For you write down bitter
things against me
and make me inherit the
sins of my youth.
27You fasten my feet in shackles;
you keep close watch on all
my paths
by putting marks on the
soles of my feet.
28"So man wastes away like
something rotten,
like a garment eaten by
moths.

14 "Man born of woman
is of few days and full of
trouble.
2He springs up like a flower
and withers away;

w15 Or *He will surely slay me; I have no hope — / yet I will*

*20 The NIV repoints this word as אֵל־, *God.*

°15 ק לוֹ

וַיִּבְרַח כַּצֵּל וְלֹא יַעֲמוֹד׃ אַף־עַל־זֶה פָּקַחְתָּ

do-you-fix this on indeed (3) he-endures and-not like-the-shadow and-he-flees

עֵינֶךָ וְאֹתִי תָבִיא בְמִשְׁפָּט עִמָּךְ׃ מִי־יִתֵּן

he-can-bring who? (4) before-you for-judgment will-you-bring and-me eye-of-you

טָהוֹר מִטָּמֵא לֹא אֶחָד׃ אִם חֲרוּצִים ׀ יָמָיו

days-of-him ones-being-determined indeed (5) one no from-impure pure

מִסְפַּר־חֳדָשָׁיו אִתָּךְ חֻקָּו עָשִׂיתָ וְלֹא יַעֲבוֹר׃

he-can-exceed and-not you-set limits-of-him with-you months-of-him number-of

שְׁעֵה מֵעָלָיו וְיֶחְדָּל עַד־יִרְצֶה כְּשָׂכִיר

like-hired-man he-enjoys till and-let-him-be-alone away-from-him look! (6)

יוֹמוֹ׃ כִּי יֵשׁ לָעֵץ תִּקְוָה אִם־יִכָּרֵת

he-is-cut-down if hope for-tree there-is at-least (7) time-of-him

וְעוֹד יַחֲלִיף וְיֹנַקְתּוֹ לֹא תֶחְדָּל׃ אִם־

if (8) she-will-fail not and-new-shoot-of-him he-will-sprout then-again

יַזְקִין בָּאָרֶץ שָׁרְשׁוֹ וּבֶעָפָר יָמוּת גִּזְעוֹ׃

stump-of-him he-dies and-in-the-soil root-of-him in-the-ground he-grows-old

מֵרֵיחַ מַיִם יַפְרִחַ וְעָשָׂה קָצִיר כְּמוֹ־נָטַע׃

plant like shoot and-he-will-put-forth he-will-bud waters at-scent-of (9)

וְגֶבֶר יָמוּת וַיֶּחֱלָשׁ וַיִּגְוַע אָדָם וְאַיּוֹ׃

and-no-more-he man and-he-breathes-last and-he-is-laid-low he-dies but-man (10)

אָזְלוּ־מַיִם מִנִּי־יָם וְנָהָר יֶחֱרַב

he-becomes-parched or-riverbed sea from waters they-disappear (11)

וְיָבֵשׁ׃ וְאִישׁ שָׁכַב וְלֹא־יָקוּם עַד־בִּלְתִּי

no-longer till he-rises and-not he-lies-down so-man (12) and-he-becomes-dry

שָׁמַיִם לֹא יָקִיצוּ וְלֹא־יֵעֹרוּ מִשְּׁנָתָם׃

from-sleep-of-them they-will-be-roused and-not they-will-awake not heavens

מִי יִתֵּן ׀ בִּשְׁאוֹל תַּצְפִּנֵנִי תַּסְתִּירֵנִי

you-would-conceal-me you-would-hide-me in-Sheol he-would-grant who? (13)

עַד־שׁוּב אַפֶּךָ תָּשִׁית לִי חֹק וְתִזְכְּרֵנִי׃

then-you-would-remember-me time for-me you-would-set anger-of-you to-pass till

אִם־יָמוּת גֶּבֶר הֲיִחְיֶה כָּל־יְמֵי צְבָאִי

hard-service-of-me days-of all-of will-he-live-again? man he-dies if (14)

אֲיַחֵל עַד־בּוֹא חֲלִיפָתִי׃ תִּקְרָא וְאָנֹכִי

and-I you-will-call (15) renewal-of-me to-come until I-will-wait

אֶעֱנֶךָּ לְמַעֲשֵׂה יָדֶיךָ תִכְסֹף׃ כִּי־

surely (16) you-will-long hands-of-you for-creature-of I-will-answer-you

עַתָּה צְעָדַי תִּסְפּוֹר לֹא־תִשְׁמוֹר עַל־חַטָּאתִי׃

sin-of-me of you-will-keep-track not you-will-count steps-of-me then

like a fleeting shadow, he
does not endure.
3Do you fix your eye on such a
one?
Will you bring him[x] before
you for judgment?
4Who can bring what is pure
from the impure?
No one!
5Man's days are determined;
you have decreed the
number of his months
and have set limits he
cannot exceed.
6So look away from him and let
him alone,
till he has put in his time
like a hired man.

7"At least there is hope for a
tree:
If it is cut down, it will
sprout again,
and its new shoots will not
fail.
8Its roots may grow old in the
ground
and its stump die in the
soil,
9yet at the scent of water it will
bud
and put forth shoots like a
plant.
10But man dies and is laid low;
he breathes his last and is
no more.
11As water disappears from the
sea
or a riverbed becomes
parched and dry,
12so man lies down and does
not rise;
till the heavens are no more,
men will not awake
or be roused from their
sleep.

13"If only you would hide me in
the grave[y]
and conceal me till your
anger has passed!
If only you would set me a
time
and then remember me!
14If a man dies, will he live
again?
All the days of my hard
service
I will wait for my renewal[z]
to come.
15You will call and I will answer
you;
you will long for the
creature your hands have
made.
16Surely then you will count my
steps
but not keep track of my
sin.

x3 Septuagint, Vulgate and Syriac; Hebrew *me*
y13 Hebrew *Sheol* z14 Or *release*

°5 ק חקיו

חָתֻם בִּצְרוֹר פִּשְׁעִי וַתִּטְפֹּל עַל־ עֲוֺנִי׃
sin-of-me over and-you-will-cover offense-of-me in-bag being-sealed (17)

וְאוּלָם הַר־ נוֹפֵל יִבּוֹל וְצוּר יֶעְתַּק
he-moves and-rock he-crumbles eroding mountain but-however (18)

מִמְּקֹמוֹ׃ אֲבָנִים ׀ שָׁחֲקוּ מַיִם תִּשְׁטֹף־
she-washes-away waters they-wear-away stones (19) from-place-of-him

סְפִיחֶיהָ עֲפַר־ אֶרֶץ וְתִקְוַת אֱנוֹשׁ הֶאֱבַדְתָּ׃ תִּתְקְפֵהוּ
you-overpower-him (20) you-destroy man so-hope-of land soil-of torrents-of-her

לָנֶצַח וַיַּהֲלֹךְ מְשַׁנֶּה פָנָיו וַתְּשַׁלְּחֵהוּ׃
and-you-send-away-him countenances-of-him changing and-he-is-gone for-ever

יִכְבְּדוּ בָנָיו וְלֹא יֵדָע וְיִצְעֲרוּ
if-they-are-brought-low he-knows but-not sons-of-him they-are-honored (21)

וְלֹא־ יָבִין לָמוֹ׃ אַךְ־ בְּשָׂרוֹ עָלָיו יִכְאָב
he-feels-pain to-him body-of-him only (22) to-them he-sees then-not

וְנַפְשׁוֹ עָלָיו תֶּאֱבָל׃ וַיַּעַן אֱלִיפַז הַתֵּימָנִי
the-Temanite Eliphaz then-he-replied (15:1) she-mourns for-him and-self-of-him

וַיֹּאמַר׃ הֶחָכָם יַעֲנֶה דַעַת־ רוּחַ וִימַלֵּא
or-would-he-fill empty notion-of would-he-answer wise-man? (2) and-he-said

קָדִים בִּטְנוֹ׃ הוֹכֵחַ בְּדָבָר לֹא יִסְכּוֹן
he-would-be-useful not with-word to-argue (3) belly-of-him hot-east-wind

וּמִלִּים לֹא־ יוֹעִיל בָּם׃ אַף־אַתָּה תָּפֵר
you-undermine you but (4) with-them he-would-have-value not and-speeches

יִרְאָה וְתִגְרַע שִׂיחָה לִפְנֵי־ אֵל׃ כִּי יְאַלֵּף עֲוֺנְךָ
sin-of-you he-prompts for (5) God to devotion and-you-hinder piety

פִיךָ וְתִבְחַר לְשׁוֹן עֲרוּמִים׃ יַרְשִׁיעֲךָ
he-condemns-you (6) crafty-ones tongue-of and-you-adopt mouth-of-you

פִיךָ וְלֹא־ אָנִי וּשְׂפָתֶיךָ יַעֲנוּ־ בָךְ׃ הֲרִאישׁוֹן
first? (7) against-you they-testify and-lips-of-you I and-not mouth-of-you

אָדָם תִּוָּלֵד וְלִפְנֵי גְבָעוֹת חוֹלָלְתָּ׃ הַבְסוֹד
on-council-of? (8) you-were-brought-forth hills and-before you-were-born man

אֱלוֹהַ* תִּשְׁמָע וְתִגְרַע אֵלֶיךָ חָכְמָה׃ מַה־ יָּדַעְתָּ וְלֹא
that-not you-know what? (9) wisdom to-you and-you-limit you-listen God

נֵדָע תָּבִין וְלֹא־ עִמָּנוּ הוּא׃ גַּם־ שָׂב גַּם־
also gray-haired also (10) he with-us that-not you-have-insight we-know

יָשִׁישׁ בָּנוּ כַּבִּיר מֵאָבִיךָ יָמִים׃ הַמְעַט מִמְּךָ
for-you not-enough? (11) days more-than-father-of-you great with-us aged

תַּנְחֻמוֹת אֵל וְדָבָר לָאַט עִמָּךְ׃ מַה־ יִּקָּחֲךָ
he-carried-away-you why? (12) to-you in-gentleness and-word God consolations-of

[17]My offenses will be sealed up
in a bag;
you will cover over my sin.
[18]"But as a mountain erodes and
crumbles
and as a rock is moved from
its place,
[19]as water wears away stones
and torrents wash away the
soil,
so you destroy man's hope.
[20]You overpower him once for
all, and he is gone;
you change his countenance
and send him away.
[21]If his sons are honored, he
does not know it;
if they are brought low, he
does not see it.
[22]He feels but the pain of his
own body
and mourns only for
himself."

*Eliphaz*

15 Then Eliphaz the Temanite
replied:
[2]"Would a wise man answer
with empty notions
or fill his belly with the hot
east wind?
[3]Would he argue with useless
words,
with speeches that have no
value?
[4]But you even undermine piety
and hinder devotion to God.
[5]Your sin prompts your mouth;
you adopt the tongue of the
crafty.
[6]Your own mouth condemns
you, not mine;
your own lips testify against
you.

[7]"Are you the first man ever
born?
Were you brought forth
before the hills?
[8]Do you listen in on God's
council?
Do you limit wisdom to
yourself?
[9]What do you know that we do
not know?
What insights do you have
that we do not have?
[10]The gray-haired and the aged
are on our side,
men even older than your
father.
[11]Are God's consolations not
enough for you,
words spoken gently to you?
[12]Why has your heart carried
you away,

*8 Most mss have *mappiq* in the *he* (הּ).

לִבֶּךָ וּמַה־ יִּרְזְמוּן עֵינֶיךָ׃ כִּי־ תָשִׁיב אֶל־
against you-vent that (13) eyes-of-you they-flash and-why? heart-of-you

אֵל רוּחֶךָ וְהֹצֵאתָ מִפִּיךָ מִלִּין׃ מָה־ אֱנוֹשׁ
man what? (14) words from-mouth-of-you and-you-pour-out rage-of-you God

כִּי־ יִזְכֶּה וְכִי־ יִצְדַּק יְלוּד אִשָּׁה׃
woman one-being-born-of he-could-be-righteous or-that he-could-be-pure that

הֵן בִּקְדֹשָׁו לֹא יַאֲמִין וְשָׁמַיִם לֹא־ זַכּוּ
they-are-pure not if-heavens he-places-trust not in-holy-ones-of-him if (15)

בְעֵינָיו׃ אַף כִּי־ נִתְעָב וְנֶאֱלָח
and-one-being-corrupt one-being-vile indeed how-much-less (16) in-eyes-of-him

אִישׁ־ שֹׁתֶה כַמַּיִם עַוְלָה׃ אֲחַוְךָ שְׁמַע־ לִי
to-me listen! I-will-explain-to-you (17) evil like-the-waters drinking-up man

וְזֶה־ חָזִיתִי וַאֲסַפֵּרָה׃ אֲשֶׁר־ חֲכָמִים יַגִּידוּ וְלֹא
and-nothing they-declared wise-men what (18) so-let-me-tell I-saw and-this

כִחֲדוּ מֵאֲבוֹתָם׃ לָהֶם לְבַדָּם נִתְּנָה
she-was-given by-themselves to-them (19) from-fathers-of-them they-hid

הָאָרֶץ וְלֹא־ עָבַר זָר בְּתוֹכָם׃ כָּל־ יְמֵי
days-of all-of (20) among-them one-being-alien he-passed when-not the-land

רָשָׁע הוּא מִתְחוֹלֵל וּמִסְפַּר שָׁנִים נִצְפְּנוּ
they-are-stored-up years and-number-of suffering-torment he wicked-man

לֶעָרִיץ׃ קוֹל־ פְּחָדִים בְּאָזְנָיו בַּשָּׁלוֹם
during-the-peace in-ears-of-him terrifying-things sound-of (21) for-the-ruthless

שׁוֹדֵד יְבוֹאֶנּוּ׃ לֹא־ יַאֲמִין שׁוּב מִנִּי־ חֹשֶׁךְ
darkness from to-escape he-trusts not (22) he-attacks-him one-marauding

וְצָפוּ הוּא אֱלֵי־חָרֶב׃ נֹדֵד הוּא לַלֶּחֶם אַיֵּה* יָדַע |
he-knows *where? for-the-food he wandering (23) sword for he and-being-marked

כִּי־ נָכוֹן בְּיָדוֹ יוֹם־ חֹשֶׁךְ׃ יְבַעֲתֻהוּ צַר
distress they-terrify-him (24) darkness day-of at-hand-of-him he-is-set that

וּמְצוּקָה תִּתְקְפֵהוּ כְּמֶלֶךְ | עָתִיד לַכִּידוֹר׃ כִּי־
because (25) for-the-attack poised like-king she-overwhelms-him and-anguish

נָטָה אֶל־ אֵל יָדוֹ וְאֶל־ שַׁדַּי יִתְגַּבָּר׃
he-vaunts-himself Almighty and-against fist-of-him God at he-shakes

יָרוּץ אֵלָיו בְּצַוָּאר בַּעֲבִי גַּבֵּי
backs-of with-thickness-of in-defiance against-him he-charges (26)

מָגִנָּיו׃ כִּי־ כִסָּה פָנָיו בְּחֶלְבּוֹ
with-fat-of-him faces-of-him he-covers though (27) shields-of-him

וַיַּעַשׂ פִּימָה עֲלֵי־כָסֶל׃ וַיִּשְׁכּוֹן | עָרִים נִכְחָדוֹת
ones-being-ruined towns yet-he-will-inhabit (28) waist at bulge and-he-makes

and why do your eyes flash,
13 so that you vent your rage
against God
and pour out such words
from your mouth?

14 "What is man, that he could
be pure,
or one born of woman, that
he could be righteous?
15 If God places no trust in his
holy ones,
if even the heavens are not
pure in his eyes,
16 how much less man, who is
vile and corrupt,
who drinks up evil like
water!

17 "Listen to me and I will
explain to you;
let me tell you what I have
seen,
18 what wise men have declared,
hiding nothing received
from their fathers
19 (to whom alone the land was
given
when no alien passed
among them):
20 All his days the wicked man
suffers torment,
the ruthless through all the
years stored up for him.
21 Terrifying sounds fill his ears;
when all seems well,
marauders attack him.
22 He despairs of escaping the
darkness;
he is marked for the sword.
23 He wanders about—food for
vultures[a];
he knows the day of
darkness is at hand.
24 Distress and anguish fill him
with terror;
they overwhelm him, like a
king poised to attack,
25 because he shakes his fist at
God
and vaunts himself against
the Almighty,
26 defiantly charging against him
with a thick, strong shield.

27 "Though his face is covered
with fat
and his waist bulges with
flesh,
28 he will inhabit ruined towns

[a]23 *Or about, looking for food*

*23 The NIV repoints this word as אַיָּה, *vulture*.

°15 ק בקדשיו

°22 ק וצפוי

בָּתִּים לֹא־יֵשְׁבוּ לָמוֹ אֲשֶׁר הִתְעַתְּדוּ לְגַלִּים׃ לֹא־
not (29) to-rubbles they-crumble that in-them they-live not houses

יֶעְשַׁר וְלֹא־יָקוּם חֵילוֹ וְלֹא־יִטֶּה
he-will-spread and-not wealth-of-him he-will-endure and-not he-will-be-rich

לָאָרֶץ מִנְלָם׃ לֹא־יָסוּר ׀ מִנִּי־חֹשֶׁךְ
darkness from he-will-escape not (30) possession-of-them over-the-land

יֹנַקְתּוֹ תְּיַבֵּשׁ שַׁלְהָבֶת וְיָסוּר בְּרוּחַ
by-breath-of and-he-will-be-carried-away flame she-will-wither shoot-of-him

פִּיו׃ אַל־יַאֲמֵן °בַּשָּׁו נִתְעָה כִּי־
for deceiving-himself in-the-worthless let-him-trust not (31) mouth-of-him

שָׁוְא תִּהְיֶה תְמוּרָתוֹ׃ בְּלֹא־יוֹמוֹ תִּמָּלֵא
she-will-be-paid day-of-him when-not (32) return-of-him she-will-be nothing

וְכִפָּתוֹ לֹא רַעֲנָנָה׃ יַחְמֹס כַּגֶּפֶן
like-the-vine he-will-be-stripped (33) she-will-flourish not and-branch-of-him

בִּסְרוֹ וְיַשְׁלֵךְ כַּזַּיִת נִצָּתוֹ׃
blossom-of-him like-the-olive-tree and-he-will-shed unripe-grape-of-him

כִּי־עֲדַת חָנֵף גַּלְמוּד וְאֵשׁ אָכְלָה אָהֳלֵי־
tents-of she-will-consume and-fire barren godless company-of for (34)

שֹׁחַד׃ הָרֹה עָמָל וְיָלֹד אָוֶן וּבִטְנָם
and-womb-of-them evil and-to-bear trouble to-conceive (35) bribe

תָּכִין מִרְמָה׃ וַיַּעַן אִיּוֹב וַיֹּאמַר׃ שָׁמַעְתִּי
I-heard (2) and-he-said Job then-he-replied (16:1) deceit she-fashions

כְאֵלֶּה רַבּוֹת מְנַחֲמֵי עָמָל כֻּלְּכֶם׃ הֲקֵץ
end? (3) all-of-you misery ones-comforting-of many-things like-these

לְדִבְרֵי־רוּחַ אוֹ מַה־יַּמְרִיצְךָ כִּי תַעֲנֶה׃ גַּם ׀ אָנֹכִי כָּכֶם
like-you I also (4) you-argue that he-ails-you what? or wind of-speeches-of

אֲדַבֵּרָה לוּ־יֵשׁ נַפְשְׁכֶם תַּחַת נַפְשִׁי אַחְבִּירָה
I-could-make-fine self-of-me in-place-of self-of-you there-was if I-could-speak

עֲלֵיכֶם בְּמִלִּים וְאָנִיעָה עֲלֵיכֶם בְּמוֹ רֹאשִׁי׃
head-of-me with at-you and-I-could-shake with-speeches against-you

אֲאַמִּצְכֶם בְּמוֹ־פִי וְנִיד שְׂפָתַי
lips-of-me and-comfort-of mouth-of-me with I-would-encourage-you (5)

יַחְשֹׂךְ׃ אִם־אֲדַבְּרָה לֹא־יֵחָשֵׂךְ כְּאֵבִי
pain-of-me he-is-relieved not I-speak if (6) he-would-bring-relief

וְאַחְדְּלָה מַה־מִנִי* יַהֲלֹךְ׃ אַךְ־עַתָּה הֶלְאָנִי
he-wore-out-me now surely (7) he-goes-away from-me what? if-I-refrain

הֲשִׁמּוֹתָ כָּל־עֲדָתִי׃ וַתִּקְמְטֵנִי לְעֵד
as-witness and-you-bound-me (8) household-of-me entire-of you-devastated

and houses where no one lives,
houses crumbling to rubble.
[29]He will no longer be rich and his wealth will not endure,
nor will his possessions spread over the land.
[30]He will not escape the darkness;
a flame will wither his shoots,
and the breath of God's mouth will carry him away.
[31]Let him not deceive himself by trusting what is worthless,
for he will get nothing in return.
[32]Before his time he will be paid in full,
and his branches will not flourish.
[33]He will be like a vine stripped of its unripe grapes,
like an olive tree shedding its blossoms.
[34]For the company of the godless will be barren,
and fire will consume the tents of those who love bribes.
[35]They conceive trouble and give birth to evil;
their womb fashions deceit."

*Job*

16 Then Job replied:
[2]"I have heard many things like these;
miserable comforters are you all!
[3]Will your long-winded speeches never end?
What ails you that you keep on arguing?
[4]I also could speak like you,
if you were in my place;
I could make fine speeches against you
and shake my head at you.
[5]But my mouth would encourage you;
comfort from my lips would bring you relief.

[6]"Yet if I speak, my pain is not relieved;
and if I refrain, it does not go away.
[7]Surely, O God, you have worn me out;
you have devastated my entire household.
[8]You have bound me—and it has become a witness;

*6 Most mss have *dagesh* in the *mem* (מּ׳).

°*31* ק בשיו

הָיָה וַיָּקָם בִּי כַחֲשִׁי בְּפָנַי
against-faces-of-me gauntness-of-me against-me and-he-rises he-became

יַעֲנֶה׃ אַפּוֹ טָרַף | וַיִּשְׂטְמֵנִי חָרַק עָלַי
at-me he-gnashes and-he-assails-me he-tears anger-of-him (9) he-testifies

בְּשִׁנָּיו צָרִי | יִלְטוֹשׁ עֵינָיו לִי׃ פָּעֲרוּ
they-open (10) on-me eyes-of-him he-pierces opponent-of-me with-teeth-of-him

עָלַי | בְּפִיהֶם בְּחֶרְפָּה הִכּוּ לְחָיָי יַחַד
together cheeks-of-me they-strike in-scorn with-mouth-of-them against-me

עָלַי יִתְמַלָּאוּן׃ יַסְגִּירֵנִי אֵל אֶל עֲוִיל וְעַל־
and-into evil-man to God he-turned-over-me (11) they-unite against-me

יְדֵי רְשָׁעִים יִרְטֵנִי׃ שָׁלֵו הָיִיתִי | וַיְפַרְפְּרֵנִי
but-he-shattered-me I-was well (12) he-threw-me wicked-ones clutches-of

וְאָחַז בְּעָרְפִּי וַיְפַצְפְּצֵנִי וַיְקִימֵנִי לוֹ
for-him and-he-made-me and-he-crushed-me by-neck-of-me and-he-seized

לְמַטָּרָה׃ יָסֹבּוּ עָלַי | רַבָּיו יְפַלַּח
he-pierces archers-of-him around-me they-surround (13) as-target

כִּלְיוֹתַי וְלֹא יַחְמוֹל יִשְׁפֹּךְ לָאָרֶץ מְרֵרָתִי׃
gall-of-me on-the-ground he-spills he-pities and-not kidneys-of-me

יִפְרְצֵנִי פֶרֶץ עַל־ פְּנֵי־ פָרֶץ יָרֻץ עָלַי כְּגִבּוֹר׃
like-warrior at-me he-rushes burst faces-of upon burst he-bursts-upon-me (14)

שַׂק תָּפַרְתִּי עֲלֵי גִלְדִּי וְעֹלַלְתִּי בֶעָפָר קַרְנִי׃
brow-of-me in-the-dust and-I-buried skin-of-me over I-sewed sackcloth (15)

פָּנַי חֳמַרְמְרָה מִנִּי־ בֶכִי וְעַל עַפְעַפַּי צַלְמָוֶת׃
deep-shadow eyes-of-me and-around weeping with they-are-red faces-of-me (16)

עַל לֹא־ חָמָס בְּכַפָּי וּתְפִלָּתִי זַכָּה׃ אֶרֶץ אַל־
not earth (18) pure and-prayer-of-me in-hands-of-me violence not yet (17)

תְּכַסִּי דָמִי וְאַל־ יְהִי מָקוֹם לְזַעֲקָתִי׃ גַּם־
even (19) to-cry-of-me place-of-rest may-he-be and-not blood-of-me you-cover

עַתָּה הִנֵּה־ בַשָּׁמַיִם עֵדִי וְשָׂהֲדִי בַּמְּרוֹמִים׃
in-the-high-places and-advocate-of-me witness-of-me in-the-heavens see! now

*מְלִיצַי רֵעָי* אֶל־ אֱלוֹהַּ† דָּלְפָה עֵינִי׃
eye-of-me she-pours-tears God to *friends-of-me ones-scorning-me* (20)

וְיוֹכַח לְגֶבֶר עִם־ אֱלוֹהַּ וּבֶן־ אָדָם לְרֵעֵהוּ׃
for-friend-of-him man and-son-of God with on-behalf-of-man and-he-pleads (21)

כִּי־ שְׁנוֹת מִסְפָּר יֶאֱתָיוּ וְאֹרַח לֹא־ אָשׁוּב אֶהֱלֹךְ׃
I-will-go I-will-return not and-journey they-will-pass few years-of for (22)

רוּחִי חֻבָּלָה יָמַי נִזְעָכוּ קְבָרִים לִי׃
for-me graves they-are-cut-short days-of-me she-is-broken spirit-of-me (17:1)

my gauntness rises up and
testifies against me.
9 God assails me and tears me
in his anger
and gnashes his teeth at me;
my opponent fastens on me
his piercing eyes.
10 Men open their mouths to jeer
at me;
they strike my cheek in
scorn
and unite together against
me.
11 God has turned me over to evil
men
and thrown me into the
clutches of the wicked.
12 All was well with me, but he
shattered me;
he seized me by the neck
and crushed me.
He has made me his target;
13 his archers surround me.
Without pity, he pierces my
kidneys
and spills my gall on the
ground.
14 Again and again he bursts
upon me;
he rushes at me like a
warrior.

15 "I have sewed sackcloth over
my skin
and buried my brow in the
dust.
16 My face is red with weeping,
deep shadows ring my eyes;
17 yet my hands have been free
of violence
and my prayer is pure.

18 "O earth, do not cover my
blood;
may my cry never be laid to
rest!
19 Even now my witness is in
heaven;
my advocate is on high.
20 My intercessor is my friend[b]
as my eyes pour out tears to
God;
21 on behalf of a man he pleads
with God
as a man pleads for his
friend.

22 "Only a few years will pass
before I go on the journey
of no return.
17 My spirit is broken,
my days are cut short,
the grave awaits me.

[b]20 Or *My friends treat me with scorn*

*20 With singular forms (as in the versions, to stand in concord with vss. 19 and 21), מְלִיצִי רֵעִי, *one-interceding-for-me friend-of-me.*

†20 Most mss have *mappiq* in the *he* (הּ).

°16 ק חמרמרו

אִם־ לֹא הֲתֻלִים עִמָּדִי וּבְהַמְּרוֹתָם תָּלַן
she-must-dwell and-on-to-be-hostile-them around-me mockers surely indeed (2)

עֵינִי׃ שִׂימָה־ נָּא עָרְבֵנִי עִמָּךְ *מִי הוּא* לְיָדִי
into-hand-of-me he who? for-you pledge-of-me now! give! (3) eye-of-me

יִתָּקֵעַ׃ כִּי־ לִבָּם צָפַנְתָּ מִשָּׂכֶל עַל־
for to-understanding you-closed mind-of-them for (4) he-will-put-security

כֵּן לֹא תְרֹמֵם׃ לְחֵלֶק יַגִּיד רֵעִים וְעֵינֵי
and-eyes-of friends he-denounces for-reward (5) you-will-let-triumph not this

בָנָיו תִּכְלֶנָה׃ וְהִצִּגַנִי לִמְשֹׁל עַמִּים
peoples to-be-byword and-he-made-me (6) they-will-fail children-of-him

וְתֹפֶת לְפָנִים אֶהְיֶה׃ וַתֵּכַהּ מִכַּעַשׂ עֵינִי
eye-of-me with-grief and-she-grew-dim (7) I-am in-faces and-one-spitting

וִיצֻרַי כַּצֵּל כֻּלָּם׃ יָשֹׁמּוּ
they-are-appalled (8) all-of-them like-the-shadow and-frames-of-me

יְשָׁרִים עַל־ זֹאת וְנָקִי עַל־ חָנֵף יִתְעֹרָר׃
he-is-aroused ungodly against and-innocent this at upright-men

וְיֹאחֵז צַדִּיק דַּרְכּוֹ וּטֳהָר־ יָדַיִם יֹסִיף
he-will-grow hands and-clean-of way-of-him righteous but-he-will-hold (9)

אֹמֶץ׃ וְאוּלָם כֻּלָּם תָּשֻׁבוּ וּבֹאוּ נָא וְלֹא־
and-not now! and-come! you-do-again all-of-them but-now (10) strong

אֶמְצָא בָכֶם חָכָם׃ יָמַי עָבְרוּ זִמֹּתַי
plans-of-me they-passed days-of-me (11) wise-man among-you I-will-find

נִתְּקוּ מוֹרָשֵׁי לְבָבִי׃ לַיְלָה לְיוֹם יָשִׂימוּ
they-turn into-day night (12) heart-of-me desires-of they-are-shattered

אוֹר קָרוֹב מִפְּנֵי־ חֹשֶׁךְ׃ אִם־ אֲקַוֶּה שְׁאוֹל בֵּיתִי
home-of-me Sheol I-hope if (13) darkness in-faces-of near light

בַּחֹשֶׁךְ רִפַּדְתִּי יְצוּעָי׃ לַשַּׁחַת קָרָאתִי אָבִי
father-of-me I-say to-the-corruption (14) beds-of-me I-spread in-the-darkness

אָתָּה אִמִּי וַאֲחֹתִי לָרִמָּה׃ וְאַיֵּה אֵפוֹ תִקְוָתִי
hope-of-me then and-where? (15) to-the-worm sister-of-me mother-of-me you

וְתִקְוָתִי מִי יְשׁוּרֶנָּה׃ בַּדֵּי שְׁאֹל תֵּרַדְנָה
will-they-go-down Sheol gates-of (16) he-can-see-her who? and-hope-of-me

אִם־ יַחַד עַל־ עָפָר נָחַת׃ וַיַּעַן בִּלְדַּד
Bildad then-he-replied (18:1) will-we-descend dust into together or

הַשֻּׁחִי וַיֹּאמַר׃ עַד־ אָנָה ׀ תְּשִׂימוּן קִנְצֵי לְמִלִּין
of-speeches ends-of will-you-make when? until (2) and-he-said the-Shuhite

תָּבִינוּ וְאַחַר נְדַבֵּר׃ מַדּוּעַ נֶחְשַׁבְנוּ כַּבְּהֵמָה
as-the-cattle are-we-regarded why? (3) we-can-talk and-then be-sensible!

[2]Surely mockers surround me;
my eyes must dwell on their hostility.
[3]"Give me, O God, the pledge you demand.
Who else will put up security for me?
[4]You have closed their minds to understanding;
therefore you will not let them triumph.
[5]If a man denounces his friends for reward,
the eyes of his children will fail.

[6]"God has made me a byword to everyone,
a man in whose face people spit.
[7]My eyes have grown dim with grief;
my whole frame is but a shadow.
[8]Upright men are appalled at this;
the innocent are aroused against the ungodly.
[9]Nevertheless, the righteous will hold to their ways,
and those with clean hands will grow stronger.

[10]"But come on, all of you, try again!
I will not find a wise man among you.
[11]My days have passed, my plans are shattered,
and so are the desires of my heart.
[12]These men turn night into day;
in the face of darkness they say, 'Light is near.'
[13]If the only home I hope for is the grave,[c]
if I spread out my bed in darkness,
[14]if I say to corruption, 'You are my father,'
and to the worm, 'My mother' or 'My sister,'
[15]where then is my hope?
Who can see any hope for me?
[16]Will it go down to the gates of death[c]?
Will we descend together into the dust?"

*Bildad*

18 Then Bildad the Shuhite replied:

[2]"When will you end these speeches?
Be sensible, and then we can talk.
[3]Why are we regarded as cattle

[c] *13,16* Hebrew *Sheol*

*3 Most mss connect these two words with *maqqeph* מִי־הוּא.

נִטְמִינוּ בְּעֵינֵיכֶם׃ (4) טֹרֵף נַפְשׁוֹ בְּאַפּוֹ
in-anger-of-him self-of-him tearing (4) in-eyes-of-you we-are-stupid

הֲלְמַעַנְךָ תֵּעָזַב אָרֶץ וְיֶעְתַּק־ צוּר מִמְּקֹמוֹ׃
from-place-of-him rock or-he-is-moved earth she-is-abandoned for-sake-of-you?

(5) גַּם אוֹר רְשָׁעִים יִדְעָךְ וְלֹא־ יִגַּהּ שְׁבִיב
flame-of he-burns and-not he-is-snuffed-out wicked-ones lamp-of indeed (5)

אִשּׁוֹ׃ (6) אוֹר חָשַׁךְ בְּאָהֳלוֹ וְנֵרוֹ
and-lamp-of-him in-tent-of-him he-becomes-dark light (6) fire-of-him

עָלָיו יִדְעָךְ׃ (7) יֵצְרוּ צַעֲדֵי אוֹנוֹ
vigor-of-him steps-of they-are-weakened (7) he-goes-out beside-him

וְתַשְׁלִיכֵהוּ עֲצָתוֹ׃ (8) כִּי־ שֻׁלַּח בְרֶשֶׁת
into-net he-was-thrust indeed (8) scheme-of-him and-she-throws-down-him

בְּרַגְלָיו וְעַל־ שְׂבָכָה יִתְהַלָּךְ׃ (9) יֹאחֵז בְּעָקֵב פָּח
trap by-heel he-seizes (9) he-wanders mesh and-into by-feet-of-him

יַחֲזֵק עָלָיו צַמִּים׃ (10) טָמוּן בָּאָרֶץ חַבְלוֹ
noose-of-him on-the-ground being-hidden (10) snare to-him he-holds-fast

וּמַלְכֻּדְתּוֹ עֲלֵי נָתִיב׃ (11) סָבִיב בִּעֲתֻהוּ בַלָּהוֹת
terrors they-startle-him every-side (11) path in and-trap-of-him

וֶהֱפִיצֻהוּ לְרַגְלָיו׃ (12) יְהִי־ רָעֵב אֹנוֹ
calamity-of-him hungry he-is (12) at-steps-of-him and-they-dog-him

וְאֵיד נָכוֹן לְצַלְעוֹ׃ (13) יֹאכַל בַּדֵּי
parts-of he-eats-away (13) for-fall-of-him he-is-ready and-disaster

עוֹרוֹ יֹאכַל בַּדָּיו בְּכֹר מָוֶת׃ (14) יִנָּתֵק
he-is-torn (14) death firstborn-of limbs-of-him he-devours skin-of-him

מֵאָהֳלוֹ מִבְטַחוֹ וְתַצְעִדֵהוּ לְמֶלֶךְ בַּלָּהוֹת׃
terrors to-king-of and-she-marches-him security-of-him from-tent-of-him

(15) תִּשְׁכּוֹן בְּאָהֳלוֹ מִבְּלִי־ לוֹ יְזֹרֶה עַל־
over he-is-scattered to-him from-nothing in-tent-of-him she-resides (15)

נָוֵהוּ גָפְרִית׃ (16) מִתַּחַת שָׁרָשָׁיו יִבָשׁוּ
they-dry-up roots-of-him at-below (16) burning-sulfur dwelling-of-him

וּמִמַּעַל יִמַּל קְצִירוֹ׃ (17) זִכְרוֹ־ אָבַד מִנִּי־
from he-perishes memory-of-him (17) branch-of-him he-withers and-at-above

אֶרֶץ וְלֹא־ שֵׁם לוֹ עַל־ פְּנֵי־ חוּץ׃ (18) יֶהְדְּפֻהוּ מֵאוֹר
from-light they-drive-him (18) land surfaces-of in for-him name and-no earth

אֶל־ חֹשֶׁךְ וּמִתֵּבֵל יְנִדֻּהוּ׃ (19) לֹא נִין לוֹ וְלֹא־
and-no to-him offspring no (19) they-banish-him and-from-world darkness into

נֶכֶד בְּעַמּוֹ וְאֵין שָׂרִיד בִּמְגוּרָיו׃
in-living-places-of-him survivor and-no among-people-of-him descendant

and considered stupid in
your sight?
4You who tear yourself to
pieces in your anger,
is the earth to be abandoned
for your sake?
Or must the rocks be moved
from their place?

5"The lamp of the wicked is
snuffed out;
the flame of his fire stops
burning.
6The light in his tent becomes
dark;
the lamp beside him goes
out.
7The vigor of his step is
weakened;
his own schemes throw him
down.
8His feet thrust him into a net
and he wanders into its
mesh.
9A trap seizes him by the heel;
a snare holds him fast.
10A noose is hidden for him on
the ground;
a trap lies in his path.
11Terrors startle him on every
side
and dog his every step.
12Calamity is hungry for him;
disaster is ready for him
when he falls.
13It eats away parts of his skin;
death's firstborn devours his
limbs.
14He is torn from the security of
his tent
and marched off to the king
of terrors.
15Fire resides[d] in his tent;
burning sulfur is scattered
over his dwelling.
16His roots dry up below
and his branches wither
above.
17The memory of him perishes
from the earth;
he has no name in the land.
18He is driven from light into
darkness
and is banished from the
world.
19He has no offspring or
descendants among his
people,
no survivor where once he
lived.

[d]15 Or *Nothing he had remains*

עַל־ יוֹמוֹ נָשַׁמּוּ אַחֲרֹנִים וְקַדְמֹנִים אָחֲזוּ
they-seize and-men-of-east men-of-west they-are-appalled day-of-him at (20)

שָׂעַר׃ אַךְ־ אֵלֶּה מִשְׁכְּנוֹת עַוָּל וְזֶה מְקוֹם לֹא־
not place-of and-this evil-man dwellings-of these surely (21) horror

יָדַע־ אֵל׃ וַיַּעַן אִיּוֹב וַיֹּאמַר׃ עַד־ אָנָה
when? until (2) and-he-said Job then-he-replied (19:1) God he-knows

תּוֹגְיוּן נַפְשִׁי וּתְדַכְּאוּנַנִי בְמִלִּים׃ זֶה
this (3) with-words and-you-will-crush-me self-of-me you-will-torment

עֶשֶׂר פְּעָמִים תַּכְלִימוּנִי לֹא־ תֵבֹשׁוּ תַּהְכְּרוּ־ לִי׃
against-me you-attack you-are-ashamed not you-reproached-me times ten-of

וְאַף־ אָמְנָם שָׁגִיתִי אִתִּי תָּלִין מְשׁוּגָתִי׃ אִם־
if (5) error-of-me she-remains with-me I-went-astray true if-indeed (4)

אָמְנָם עָלַי תַּגְדִּילוּ וְתוֹכִיחוּ עָלַי
against-me and-you-would-use you-would-exalt-yourselves above-me indeed

חֶרְפָּתִּי*׃ דְּעוּ־ אֵפוֹ כִּי־ אֱלוֹהַּ עִוְּתָנִי וּמְצוּדוֹ
and-net-of-him he-wronged-me God that then know! (6) humiliation-of-me

עָלַי הִקִּיף׃ הֵן אֶצְעַק חָמָס וְלֹא אֵעָנֶה
I-get-response then-not wrong I-cry though (7) he-drew-around around-me

אֲשַׁוַּע וְאֵין מִשְׁפָּט׃ אָרְחִי גָדַר וְלֹא
so-not he-blocked way-of-me (8) justice but-there-is-no I-call-for-help

אֶעֱבוֹר וְעַל נְתִיבוֹתַי חֹשֶׁךְ יָשִׂים׃ כְּבוֹדִי
honor-of-me (9) he-shrouded darkness paths-of-me and-over I-can-pass

מֵעָלַי הִפְשִׁיט וַיָּסַר עֲטֶרֶת רֹאשִׁי׃ יִתְּצֵנִי
he-tears-down-me (10) head-of-me crown-of and-he-removed he-stripped from-on-me

סָבִיב וָאֵלַךְ וַיַּסַּע כָּעֵץ תִּקְוָתִי׃ וַיַּחַר
and-he-burns (11) hope-of-me like-tree and-he-uproots till-I-am-gone on-every-side

עָלַי אַפּוֹ וַיַּחְשְׁבֵנִי לוֹ כְצָרָיו׃
among-enemies-of-him to-him and-he-counts-me anger-of-him against-me

יַחַד ׀ יָבֹאוּ גְדוּדָיו וַיָּסֹלּוּ עָלַי
against-me and-they-build troops-of-him they-advance in-force (12)

דַּרְכָּם וַיַּחֲנוּ סָבִיב לְאָהֳלִי׃ אַחַי
brothers-of-me (13) at-tent-of-me around and-they-encamp siege-ramp-of-them

מֵעָלַי הִרְחִיק וְיֹדְעַי אַךְ־
also and-ones-being-acquainted-with-me he-alienated from-with-me

זָרוּ מִמֶּנִּי׃ חָדְלוּ קְרוֹבָי
kinsmen-of-me they-went-away (14) from-me they-are-estranged

וּמְיֻדָּעַי שְׁכֵחוּנִי׃ גָּרֵי בֵיתִי
house-of-me ones-being-guests-of (15) they-forgot-me and-ones-being-friends-of-me

20 Men of the west are appalled
at his fate;
men of the east are seized
with horror.
21 Surely such is the dwelling of
an evil man;
such is the place of one who
knows not God."

*Job*

19 Then Job replied:
2 "How long will you
torment me
and crush me with words?
3 Ten times now you have
reproached me;
shamelessly you attack me.
4 If it is true that I have gone
astray,
my error remains my
concern alone.
5 If indeed you would exalt
yourselves above me
and use my humiliation
against me,
6 then know that God has
wronged me
and drawn his net around
me.

7 "Though I cry, 'I've been
wronged!' I get no
response;
though I call for help, there
is no justice.
8 He has blocked my way so I
cannot pass;
he has shrouded my paths
in darkness.
9 He has stripped me of my
honor
and removed the crown
from my head.
10 He tears me down on every
side till I am gone;
he uproots my hope like a
tree.
11 His anger burns against me;
he counts me among his
enemies.
12 His troops advance in force;
they build a siege ramp
against me
and encamp around my
tent.

13 "He has alienated my brothers
from me;
my acquaintances are
completely estranged from
me.
14 My kinsmen have gone away;
my friends have forgotten
me.
15 My guests and my

*5 Most mss have no *dagesh* in the *tav* (תִי־).

וְאַמְהֹתַי לְזָר תַּחְשְׁבֻנִי נָכְרִי הָיִיתִי
I-am alien they-count-me as-being-stranger and-maidservants-of-me

בְּעֵינֵיהֶם׃ לְעַבְדִּי קָרָאתִי וְלֹא יַעֲנֶה בְּמוֹ־
with he-answers but-not I-summon to-servant-of-me (16) in-eyes-of-them

פִּי אֶתְחַנֶּן־ לוֹ׃ רוּחִי זָרָה לְאִשְׁתִּי
to-wife-of-me she-is-offensive breath-of-me (17) with-him I-beg mouth-of-me

וְחַנֹּתִי לִבְנֵי בִטְנִי׃ גַּם־ עֲוִילִים מָאֲסוּ
they-scorn little-boys even (18) womb-of-me to-sons-of and-I-am-loathsome

בִּי אָקוּמָה וַיְדַבְּרוּ־ בִי׃ תִּעֲבוּנִי
they-detest-me (19) against-me and-they-ridicule I-appear against-me

כָּל־ מְתֵי סוֹדִי וְזֶה־ אָהַבְתִּי נֶהְפְּכוּ־ בִי׃
against-me they-turned I-love and-this intimacy-of-me friends-of all-of

בְּעוֹרִי וּבִבְשָׂרִי דָּבְקָה עַצְמִי וָאֶתְמַלְּטָה
and-I-escaped bone-of-me she-sticks and-to-flesh-of-me to-skin-of-me (20)

בְּעוֹר שִׁנָּי׃ חָנֻּנִי חָנֻּנִי אַתֶּם רֵעָי כִּי
for friends-of-me you pity-me! pity-me! (21) teeth-of-me with-skin-of

יַד־ אֱלוֹהַּ נָגְעָה בִּי׃ לָמָּה תִּרְדְּפֻנִי כְמוֹ־ אֵל
God as you-pursue-me why? (22) against-me she-struck God hand-of

וּמִבְּשָׂרִי לֹא תִשְׂבָּעוּ׃ מִי־ יִתֵּן אֵפוֹ
then he-would-give who? (23) you-get-enough never and-of-flesh-of-me

וְיִכָּתְבוּן מִלָּי מִי־ יִתֵּן בַּסֵּפֶר
on-the-scroll he-would-give who? words-of-me that-they-were-recorded

וְיֻחָקוּ׃ בְּעֵט־ בַּרְזֶל וְעֹפָרֶת לָעַד בַּצּוּר
in-the-rock to-forever and-lead iron with-tool-of (24) that-they-were-written

יֵחָצְבוּן׃ וַאֲנִי יָדַעְתִּי גֹּאֲלִי חָי וְאַחֲרוֹן עַל־
upon and-end alive One-Redeeming-me I-know and-I (25) they-were-engraved

עָפָר יָקוּם׃ וְאַחַר עוֹרִי נִקְּפוּ־ זֹאת
this they-destroy skin-of-me and-after (26) he-will-stand earth

וּמִבְּשָׂרִי אֶחֱזֶה אֱלוֹהַּ׃ אֲשֶׁר אֲנִי | אֶחֱזֶה־ לִּי
indeed-I I-will-see I that (27) God I-will-see yet-in-flesh-of-me

וְעֵינַי רָאוּ וְלֹא־ זָר כָּלוּ כִלְיֹתַי
hearts-of-me they-yearn one-being-other and-not they-will-see and-eyes-of-me

בְּחֵקִי׃ כִּי תֹאמְרוּ מַה־ נִּרְדָּף־ לוֹ וְשֹׁרֶשׁ
since-root-of after-him we-will-hound how? you-say if (28) in-breast-of-me

דָּבָר נִמְצָא־ בִי׃ גּוּרוּ לָכֶם ׀ מִפְּנֵי־ חֶרֶב כִּי־ חֵמָה
wrath for sword because-of for-you fear! (29) in-me he-lies trouble

עֲוֹנוֹת חֶרֶב לְמַעַן תֵּדְעוּן שַׁדִּין׃ וַיַּעַן
then-he-replied (20:1) that-judgment you-will-know that sword punishments-of

maidservants count me a
stranger;
they look upon me as an
alien.
16I summon my servant, but he
does not answer,
though I beg him with my
own mouth.
17My breath is offensive to my
wife;
I am loathsome to my own
brothers.
18Even the little boys scorn me;
when I appear, they ridicule
me.
19All my intimate friends detest
me;
those I love have turned
against me.
20I am nothing but skin and
bones;
I have escaped with only
the skin of my teeth.[e]

21"Have pity on me, my friends,
have pity,
for the hand of God has
struck me.
22Why do you pursue me as God
does?
Will you never get enough
of my flesh?

23"Oh, that my words were
recorded,
that they were written on a
scroll,
24that they were inscribed with
an iron tool on[f] lead,
or engraved in rock forever!
25I know that my Redeemer[g]
lives,
and that in the end he will
stand upon the earth.[h]
26And after my skin has been
destroyed,
yet[i] in[j] my flesh I will see
God;
27I myself will see him
with my own eyes—I, and
not another.
How my heart yearns
within me!

28"If you say, 'How we will
hound him,
since the root of the trouble
lies in him,'
29you should fear the sword
yourselves;
for wrath will bring
punishment by the
sword,
and then you will know that
there is judgment.[k]"

e20 Or *only my gums*  f24 Or *and*
g25 Or *defender*  h25 Or *upon my grave*
i26 Or *And after I awake, / though this ⌞body⌟ has been destroyed, / then*
j26 Or */ apart from*
k29 Or */ that you may come to know the Almighty*

°29 ק שדון

צֹפַר הַנַּעֲמָתִי וַיֹּאמַר׃ לָכֵן שְׂעִפַּי
troubled-thoughts-of-me therefore (2) and-he-said the-Naamathite Zophar

יְשִׁיבוּנִי וּבַעֲבוּר חוּשִׁי בִי׃ מוּסַר
rebuke-of (3) in-me disturbance-of-me and-because-of they-prompt-me

כְּלִמָּתִי אֶשְׁמָע וְרוּחַ מִבִּינָתִי יַעֲנֵנִי׃
he-makes-reply-me from-understanding-of-me and-spirit I-hear dishonor-of-me

הֲזֹאת יָדַעְתָּ מִנִּי־ עַד מִנִּי שִׂים אָדָם עֲלֵי־ אָרֶץ׃ כִּי
that (5) earth on man to-place since of-old from you-know this? (4)

רִנְנַת רְשָׁעִים מִקָּרוֹב וְשִׂמְחַת חָנֵף עֲדֵי־ רָגַע׃ אִם־
though (6) moment to godless and-joy-of at-near wicked-ones mirth-of

יַעֲלֶה לַשָּׁמַיִם שִׂיאוֹ וְרֹאשׁוֹ לָעָב
to-the-cloud and-head-of-him pride-of-him to-the-heavens he-reaches

יַגִּיעַ׃ כְּגֶלֲלוֹ לָנֶצַח יֹאבֵד רֹאָיו
ones-seeing-him he-will-perish to-forever like-dung-of-him (7) he-touches

יֹאמְרוּ אַיּוֹ׃ כַּחֲלוֹם יָעוּף וְלֹא יִמְצָאֻהוּ
they-find-him and-not he-flies-away like-dream (8) where-he? they-will-say

וְיֻדַּד כְּחֶזְיוֹן לָיְלָה׃ עַיִן שְׁזָפַתּוּ וְלֹא
then-not she-sees-him eye (9) night like-vision-of and-he-is-banished

תוֹסִיף וְלֹא־ עוֹד תְּשׁוּרֶנּוּ מְקוֹמוֹ׃
place-of-him she-will-look-on-him more and-no she-will-do-again

בָּנָיו יְרַצּוּ דַלִּים וְיָדָיו
and-hands-of-him poor-ones they-must-make-amends children-of-him (10)

תָּשֵׁבְנָה אוֹנוֹ׃ עַצְמוֹתָיו מָלְאוּ
they-are-filled bones-of-him (11) wealth-of-him they-must-give-back

עֲלוּמָו° וְעִמּוֹ עַל־ עָפָר תִּשְׁכָּב׃ אִם־
though (12) she-will-lie dust in and-with-him youthful-vigors-of-him

תַּמְתִּיק בְּפִיו רָעָה יַכְחִידֶנָּה תַּחַת לְשׁוֹנוֹ׃
tongue-of-him under he-hides-her evil in-mouth-of-him she-is-sweet

יַחְמֹל עָלֶיהָ וְלֹא יַעַזְבֶנָּה וְיִמְנָעֶנָּה בְּתוֹךְ חִכּוֹ׃
mouth-of-him in and-he-keeps-her he-lets-go-her and-not to-her he-spares (13)

לַחְמוֹ בְּמֵעָיו נֶהְפָּךְ מְרוֹרַת פְּתָנִים
serpents venom-of he-will-turn-sour in-stomachs-of-him food-of-him (14)

בְּקִרְבּוֹ׃ חַיִל בָּלַע וַיְקִאֶנּוּ
then-he-will-spit-out-him he-swallowed richness (15) in-inside-of-him

מִבִּטְנוֹ יֹרִשֶׁנּוּ אֵל׃ רֹאשׁ־ פְּתָנִים
serpents poison-of (16) God he-will-make-vomit-him from-stomach-of-him

יִינָק תַּהַרְגֵהוּ לְשׁוֹן אֶפְעֶה׃ אַל־ יֵרֶא
he-will-enjoy not (17) adder fang-of she-will-kill-him he-will-suck

*Zophar*

**20** Then Zophar the Naamathite replied:

2"My troubled thoughts prompt me to answer
because I am greatly disturbed.
3I hear a rebuke that dishonors me,
and my understanding inspires me to reply.

4"Surely you know how it has been from of old,
ever since man[l] was placed on the earth,
5that the mirth of the wicked is brief,
the joy of the godless lasts but a moment.
6Though his pride reaches to the heavens
and his head touches the clouds,
7he will perish forever, like his own dung;
those who have seen him will say, 'Where is he?'
8Like a dream he flies away, no more to be found,
banished like a vision of the night.
9The eye that saw him will not see him again;
his place will look on him no more.
10His children must make amends to the poor;
his own hands must give back his wealth.
11The youthful vigor that fills his bones
will lie with him in the dust.

12"Though evil is sweet in his mouth
and he hides it under his tongue,
13though he cannot bear to let it go
and keeps it in his mouth,
14yet his food will turn sour in his stomach;
it will become the venom of serpents within him.
15He will spit out the riches he swallowed;
God will make his stomach vomit them up.
16He will suck the poison of serpents;
the fangs of an adder will kill him.
17He will not enjoy the streams,

[l]4 Or *Adam*

°11 ק עלומיו

בִּפְלַגּוֹת נַהֲרֵי נַחֲלֵי דְּבַשׁ וְחֶמְאָה׃ מֵשִׁיב יָגָע
produce-of-toil giving-back (18) and-cream honey flows-of rivers-of to-streams

וְלֹא יִבְלָע כְּחֵיל תְּמוּרָתוֹ וְלֹא יַעֲלֹס׃ כִּי־
for (19) he-will-enjoy and-not trade-of-him as-profit-of he-ate and-not

רִצַּץ עָזַב דַּלִּים בַּיִת גָּזַל וְלֹא
that-not he-seized house poor-ones he-left-destitute he-oppressed

יִבְנֵהוּ׃ כִּי לֹא־ יָדַע שָׁלֵו בְּבִטְנוֹ
from-craving-of-him respite he-will-know not surely (20) he-built-him

בַּחֲמוּדוֹ לֹא יְמַלֵּט׃ אֵין־ שָׂרִיד
left nothing (21) he-can-save-himself not by-one-being-treasured-of-him

לְאָכְלוֹ עַל־ כֵּן לֹא־ יָחִיל טוּבוֹ׃
prosperity-of-him he-will-endure not this for to-devour-him

בִּמְלֹאות שִׂפְקוֹ יֵצֶר לוֹ כָּל־ יַד
force-of full-of to-him he-will-be-in-distress plenty-of-him in-to-be-full (22)

עָמֵל תְּבוֹאֶנּוּ׃ יְהִי לְמַלֵּא בִטְנוֹ יְשַׁלַּח־
he-will-vent belly-of-him to-fill he-is (23) she-will-come-upon-him misery

בּוֹ חֲרוֹן אַפּוֹ וְיַמְטֵר עָלֵימוֹ
upon-him and-he-will-rain-down anger-of-him burning-of against-him

בִּלְחוּמוֹ׃ יִבְרַח מִנֵּשֶׁק בַּרְזֶל תַּחְלְפֵהוּ קֶשֶׁת
arrow-of she-pierces-him iron from-weapon-of he-flees (24) with-blow-of-him

נְחוּשָׁה׃ שָׁלַף וַיֵּצֵא מִגֵּוָה וּבָרָק
and-gleaming-point from-back and-he-comes-out he-pulls-out (25) bronze

מִמְּרֹרָתוֹ יַהֲלֹךְ עָלָיו אֵמִים׃ כָּל־ חֹשֶׁךְ
darkness total-of (26) terrors over-him he-will-come from-liver-of-him

טָמוּן לִצְפּוּנָיו תְּאָכְלֵהוּ אֵשׁ לֹא־
not fire she-will-consume-him for-ones-being-treasured-of-him lying-in-wait

נֻפָּח יֵרַע שָׂרִיד בְּאָהֳלוֹ׃ יְגַלּוּ
they-will-expose (27) in-tent-of-him left he-will-devour he-was-fanned

שָׁמַיִם עֲוֹנוֹ וְאֶרֶץ מִתְקוֹמָמָה לוֹ׃ יִגֶל
he-will-carry-off (28) against-him rising-up and-earth guilt-of-him heavens

יְבוּל בֵּיתוֹ נִגָּרוֹת בְּיוֹם אַפּוֹ׃ זֶה
such (29) wrath-of-him on-day-of ones-rushing house-of-him possession-of

חֵלֶק־ אָדָם רָשָׁע מֵאֱלֹהִים וְנַחֲלַת אִמְרוֹ מֵאֵל׃
by-God appointment-of-him and-heritage-of from-God wicked man fate-of

וַיַּעַן אִיּוֹב וַיֹּאמַר׃ שִׁמְעוּ שָׁמוֹעַ מִלָּתִי
word-of-me to-listen listen! (2) and-he-said Job then-he-replied (21:1)

וּתְהִי־ זֹאת תַּנְחוּמֹתֵיכֶם׃ שָׂאוּנִי וְאָנֹכִי אֲדַבֵּר
I-speak while-I bear-with-me! (3) consolations-of-you this and-let-her-be

the rivers flowing with
honey and cream.
18 What he toiled for he must
give back uneaten;
he will not enjoy the profit
from his trading.
19 For he has oppressed the poor
and left them destitute;
he has seized houses he did
not build.
20 "Surely he will have no respite
from his craving;
he cannot save himself by
his treasure.
21 Nothing is left for him to
devour;
his prosperity will not
endure.
22 In the midst of his plenty,
distress will overtake him;
the full force of misery will
come upon him.
23 When he has filled his belly,
God will vent his burning
anger against him
and rain down his blows
upon him.
24 Though he flees from an iron
weapon,
a bronze-tipped arrow
pierces him.
25 He pulls it out of his back,
the gleaming point out of
his liver.
Terrors will come over him;
26 total darkness lies in wait
for his treasures.
A fire unfanned will consume
him
and devour what is left in
his tent.
27 The heavens will expose his
guilt;
the earth will rise up against
him.
28 A flood will carry off his
house,
rushing waters[m] on the day
of God's wrath.
29 Such is the fate God allots the
wicked,
the heritage appointed for
them by God."

*Job*

**21** Then Job replied:
2 "Listen carefully to my
words;
let this be the consolation
you give me.
3 Bear with me while I speak,

[m]28 Or *The possessions in his house will be carried off, / washed away*

וְאַחַ֥ר דַּבְּרִ֗י תַלְעִֽיג׃ הֶ֭אָנֹכִי לְאָדָ֣ם שִׂיחִ֑י וְאִם־מַ֝דּ֗וּעַ
why? and-if complaint-of-me to-man I? (4) you-mock-on to-speak-me and-after

לֹא־תִקְצַ֥ר רוּחִֽי׃ פְּנוּ־אֵלַ֥י וְהָשַׁ֑מּוּ
and-be-astonished! at-me look! (5) spirit-of-me she-should-be-impatient not

וְשִׂ֖ימוּ יָ֣ד עַל־פֶּֽה׃ וְאִם־זָכַ֥רְתִּי וְנִבְהָ֑לְתִּי
then-I-am-terrified I-think and-when (6) mouth over hand and-clap!

וְאָחַ֥ז בְּ֝שָׂרִ֗י פַּלָּצֽוּת׃ מַדּ֣וּעַ רְשָׁעִ֣ים יִחְי֑וּ
they-live-on wicked-ones why? (7) trembling body-of-me and-he-seizes

עָ֝תְק֗וּ גַּם־גָּ֥בְרוּ חָֽיִל׃ זַ֝רְעָ֗ם נָכ֣וֹן
he-is-established child-of-them (8) power they-increase and they-grow-old

לִפְנֵיהֶ֣ם עִמָּ֑ם וְ֝צֶאֱצָאֵיהֶ֗ם לְעֵינֵיהֶֽם׃
before-eyes-of-them and-offsprings-of-them around-them before-them

בָּתֵּיהֶ֣ם שָׁל֣וֹם מִפָּ֑חַד וְלֹ֤א שֵׁ֖בֶט אֱל֣וֹהַּ עֲלֵיהֶֽם׃
upon-them God rod-of and-not from-fear safe homes-of-them (9)

שׁוֹר֣וֹ עִ֭בַּר וְלֹ֣א יַגְעִ֑ל תְּפַלֵּ֥ט פָּ֝רָת֗וֹ וְלֹ֣א
and-not cow-of-him she-calves he-fails and-never he-breeds bull-of-him (10)

תְשַׁכֵּֽל׃ יְשַׁלְּח֣וּ כַ֭צֹּאן עֲוִילֵיהֶ֑ם
children-of-them as-the-flock they-send-forth (11) she-miscarries

וְ֝יַלְדֵיהֶ֗ם יְרַקֵּדֽוּן׃ יִ֭שְׂאוּ כְּתֹ֣ף וְכִנּ֑וֹר
and-harp with-tambourine they-sing (12) they-dance-about and-little-ones-of-them

וְ֝יִשְׂמְח֗וּ לְק֣וֹל עוּגָֽב׃ יְבַלּ֣וּ בַטּ֣וֹב
in-the-prosperity they-spend (13) flute to-sound-of and-they-make-merry

יְמֵיהֶ֑ם וּ֝בְרֶ֗גַע שְׁא֣וֹל יֵחָֽתּוּ׃ וַיֹּאמְר֣וּ לָ֭אֵל
to-God yet-they-say (14) they-go-down Sheol and-in-instant days-of-them

ס֣וּר מִמֶּ֑נּוּ וְדַ֥עַת דְּ֝רָכֶ֗יךָ לֹ֣א חָפָֽצְנוּ׃ מַה־
who? (15) we-desire not ways-of-you and-to-know from-us leave-alone!

שַׁדַּ֥י* כִּֽי־נַעַבְדֶ֑נּוּ וּמַה־נּ֝וֹעִ֗יל כִּ֣י נִפְגַּע־
we-should-pray that would-we-gain and-what? we-should-serve-him that Almighty

בּֽוֹ׃ הֵ֤ן לֹ֣א בְיָדָ֣ם טוּבָ֑ם עֲצַ֥ת רְ֝שָׁעִ֗ים
wicked-ones counsel-of prosperity-of-them in-hand-of-them not see! (16) to-him

רָ֣חֲקָה מֶֽנִּי׃ כַּמָּ֤ה ׀ נֵר־רְשָׁעִ֬ים
wicked-ones lamp-of as-the-how-often? (17) from-me she-is-distant

יִדְעָ֗ךְ וְיָבֹ֣א עָלֵ֣ימוֹ אֵידָ֑ם חֲ֝בָלִ֗ים יְחַלֵּ֥ק
he-allots fates calamity-of-them upon-them and-he-comes he-is-snuffed-out

בְּאַפּֽוֹ׃ יִ֭הְיוּ כְּתֶ֣בֶן לִפְנֵי־ר֑וּחַ וּ֝כְמֹ֗ץ
and-like-chaff wind before like-straw they-are (18) in-anger-of-him

גְּנָבַ֥תּוּ סוּפָֽה׃ אֱ֭לוֹהַּ יִצְפֹּן־לְבָנָ֣יו אוֹנ֑וֹ
punishment-of-him for-sons-of-him he-stores-up God (19) gale she-sweeps-away-him

and after I have spoken,
mock on.
4"Is my complaint directed to
man?
Why should I not be
impatient?
5Look at me and be astonished;
clap your hand over your
mouth.
6When I think about this, I am
terrified;
trembling seizes my body.
7Why do the wicked live on,
growing old and increasing
in power?
8They see their children
established around them,
their offspring before their
eyes.
9Their homes are safe and free
from fear;
the rod of God is not upon
them.
10Their bulls never fail to breed;
their cows calve and do not
miscarry.
11They send forth their children
as a flock;
their little ones dance about.
12They sing to the music of
tambourine and harp;
they make merry to the
sound of the flute.
13They spend their years in
prosperity
and go down to the grave[n]
in peace.[o]
14Yet they say to God, 'Leave us
alone!
We have no desire to know
your ways.
15Who is the Almighty, that we
should serve him?
What would we gain by
praying to him?'
16But their prosperity is not in
their own hands,
so I stand aloof from the
counsel of the wicked.
17"Yet how often is the lamp of
the wicked snuffed out?
How often does calamity
come upon them,
the fate God allots in his
anger?
18How often are they like straw
before the wind,
like chaff swept away by a
gale?
19⌊It is said,⌋ 'God stores up a
man's punishment for his
sons.'

n13 Hebrew *Sheol* o13 Or *in an instant*
p17-20 Verses 17 and 18 may be taken as exclamations and 19 and 20 as declarations.

*15 Most mss have *dagesh* in the *shin* (שּׁ).

°13 ק יכלו

יְשַׁלֵּם אֵלָיו וְיֵדָע׃ (20) יִרְאוּ עֵינָו°
eyes-of-him let-them-see (20) so-he-will-know to-him let-him-repay

כִּידוֹ וּמֵחֲמַת שַׁדַּי יִשְׁתֶּה׃ (21) כִּי מַה־
what? for (21) let-him-drink Almighty and-of-wrath-of destruction-of-him

חֶפְצוֹ בְּבֵיתוֹ אַחֲרָיו וּמִסְפַּר חֳדָשָׁיו
months-of-him when-allotment-of behind-him about-family-of-him care-of-him

חֻצָּצוּ׃ (22) הַלְאֵל יְלַמֶּד־ דָּעַת וְהוּא רָמִים
ones-being-high since-he knowledge can-he-teach to-God? (22) they-end

יִשְׁפּוֹט׃ (23) זֶה יָמוּת בְּעֶצֶם תֻּמּוֹ כֻּלּוֹ
whole-of-him fullness-of-him in-vigor-of he-dies this-one (23) he-judges

שַׁלְאֲנַן וְשָׁלֵיו׃ (24) עֲטִינָיו מָלְאוּ חָלָב
nourishment they-are-full bodies-of-him (24) and-at-ease secure

וּמֹחַ עַצְמוֹתָיו יְשֻׁקֶּה׃ (25) וְזֶה יָמוּת בְּנֶפֶשׁ
in-soul he-dies and-another (25) he-is-rich bones-of-him and-marrow-of

מָרָה וְלֹא־ אָכַל בַּטּוֹבָה׃ (26) יַחַד עַל־ עָפָר יִשְׁכָּבוּ
they-lie dust in together (26) of-the-good he-enjoyed but-never bitter

וְרִמָּה תְּכַסֶּה עֲלֵיהֶם׃ (27) הֵן יָדַעְתִּי מַחְשְׁבוֹתֵיכֶם וּמְזִמּוֹת
and-schemes thoughts-of-you I-know see! (27) over-them she-covers and-worm

עָלַי תַּחְמֹסוּ׃ (28) כִּי תֹאמְרוּ אַיֵּה בֵית־ נָדִיב
great-man house-of where? you-say for (28) you-would-do-wrong against-me

וְאַיֵּה אֹהֶל ׀ מִשְׁכְּנוֹת רְשָׁעִים׃ (29) הֲלֹא שְׁאֶלְתֶּם
you-questioned never? (29) wicked-men living-places-of tent-of and-where?

עוֹבְרֵי דָרֶךְ וְאֹתֹתָם לֹא תְנַכֵּרוּ׃ (30) כִּי
that (30) you-regarded not and-accounts-of-them way ones-traveling-of

לְיוֹם אֵיד יֵחָשֶׂךְ רָע לְיוֹם עֲבָרוֹת
wraths from-day-of evil-man he-is-spared calamity from-day-of

יוּבָלוּ׃ (31) מִי־ יַגִּיד עַל־ פָּנָיו דַּרְכּוֹ
conduct-of-him faces-of-him to he-denounces who? (31) they-are-delivered

וְהוּא־ עָשָׂה מִי יְשַׁלֶּם־ לוֹ׃ (32) וְהוּא לִקְבָרוֹת יוּבָל
he-is-carried to-graves and-he (32) to-him he-repays who? he-did and-he

וְעַל־ גָּדִישׁ יִשְׁקוֹד׃ (33) מָתְקוּ־ לוֹ רִגְבֵי נָחַל
valley soils-of to-him they-are-sweet (33) he-watches tomb and-over

וְאַחֲרָיו כָּל־ אָדָם יִמְשׁוֹךְ וּלְפָנָיו אֵין מִסְפָּר׃
count there-is-no and-before-him he-follows man all-of and-after-him

(34) וְאֵיךְ תְּנַחֲמוּנִי הָבֶל וּתְשׁוּבֹתֵיכֶם נִשְׁאַר־
he-is-left and-answers-of-you nonsense can-you-console-me so-how? (34)

מָעַל׃ (22:1) וַיַּעַן אֱלִיפַז הַתֵּמָנִי וַיֹּאמַר׃
and-he-said the-Temanite Eliphaz then-he-replied (22:1) falsehood

Let him repay the man
himself, so that he will
know it!
20 Let his own eyes see his
destruction;
let him drink of the wrath
of the Almighty.[p]
21 For what does he care about
the family he leaves
behind
when his allotted months
come to an end?

22 "Can anyone teach knowledge
to God,
since he judges even the
highest?
23 One man dies in full vigor,
completely secure and at
ease,
24 his body[q] well nourished,
his bones rich with marrow.
25 Another man dies in bitterness
of soul,
never having enjoyed
anything good.
26 Side by side they lie in the
dust,
and worms cover them both.

27 "I know full well what you are
thinking,
the schemes by which you
would wrong me.
28 You say, 'Where now is the
great man's house,
the tents where wicked men
lived?'
29 Have you never questioned
those who travel?
Have you paid no regard to
their accounts—
30 that the evil man is spared
from the day of calamity,
that he is delivered from[r]
the day of wrath?
31 Who denounces his conduct to
his face?
Who repays him for what
he has done?
32 He is carried to the grave,
and watch is kept over his
tomb.
33 The soil in the valley is sweet
to him;
all men follow after him,
and a countless throng goes[s]
before him.

34 "So how can you console me
with your nonsense?
Nothing is left of your
answers but falsehood!"

*Eliphaz*

22 Then Eliphaz the Temanite
replied:

q24 The meaning of the Hebrew for this word is uncertain.
r30 Or *man is reserved for the day of calamity, / that he is brought forth to*
s33 Or */ as a countless throng went*

°20 ק עיניו

(2) הַלְאֵל יִסְכָּן־ גָּבֶר כִּי־ יִסְכֹּן עָלֵימוֹ מַשְׂכִּיל׃
one-being-wise to-him can-he-benefit even man can-he-be-of-benefit to-God? (2)

(3) הַחֵפֶץ לְשַׁדַּי כִּי תִצְדָּק וְאִם־ בֶּצַע כִּי־
if gain and-if you-were-righteous if to-Almighty pleasure? (3)

תַתֵּם דְּרָכֶיךָ׃ (4) הֲמִיִּרְאָתְךָ יֹכִיחֶךָ יָבוֹא
he-brings he-rebukes-you for-piety-of-you? (4) ways-of-you she-was-blameless

עִמְּךָ בַּמִּשְׁפָּט׃ (5) הֲלֹא רָעָתְךָ רַבָּה וְאֵין־ קֵץ
end and-not great wickedness-of-you not? (5) with-the-charge against-you

לַעֲוֺנֹתֶיךָ׃ (6) כִּי־ תַחְבֹּל אַחֶיךָ חִנָּם
for-no-reason brothers-of-you you-demanded-security for (6) to-sins-of-you

וּבִגְדֵי עֲרוּמִּים תַּפְשִׁיט׃ (7) לֹא־ מַיִם עָיֵף תַּשְׁקֶה
you-gave-drink weary waters no (7) you-stripped naked-ones and-clothings-of

וּמֵרָעֵב תִּמְנַע־ לָחֶם׃ (8) וְאִישׁ זְרוֹעַ לוֹ הָאָרֶץ
the-land to-him power though-man-of (8) food you-withheld and-from-hungry

וּנְשׂוּא פָנִים יֵשֶׁב בָּהּ׃ (9) אַלְמָנוֹת שִׁלַּחְתָּ
you-sent-away widows (9) on-her he-lived faces and-being-honored-of

רֵיקָם וּזְרֹעוֹת יְתֹמִים יְדֻכָּא׃ (10) עַל־ כֵּן
this for (10) he-was-broken fatherless-ones and-strengths-of empty-handed

סְבִיבוֹתֶיךָ פַחִים וִיבַהֶלְךָ פַּחַד פִּתְאֹם׃ (11) אוֹ־ חֹשֶׁךְ לֹא־
not dark or (11) sudden peril and-he-terrifies-you snares ones-around-you

תִרְאֶה וְשִׁפְעַת־ מַיִם תְּכַסֶּךָּ׃ (12) הֲלֹא־אֱלוֹהַּ גֹּבַהּ שָׁמָיִם
heavens height-of God not? (12) she-covers-you waters and-flood-of you-see

וּרְאֵה רֹאשׁ כּוֹכָבִים כִּי־ רָמּוּ׃ (13) וְאָמַרְתָּ מַה־ יָּדַע
he-knows what? yet-you-say (13) they-are-lofty how! stars height-of and-see!

אֵל הַבְעַד עֲרָפֶל יִשְׁפּוֹט׃ (14) עָבִים סֵתֶר־ לוֹ וְלֹא יִרְאֶה
he-sees so-not to-him veil thick-clouds (14) he-judges darkness through? God

וְחוּג שָׁמַיִם יִתְהַלָּךְ׃ (15) הַאֹרַח עוֹלָם תִּשְׁמֹר אֲשֶׁר
that will-you-keep old path-of? (15) he-goes-about heavens and-vault-of

דָּרְכוּ מְתֵי־ אָוֶן׃ (16) אֲשֶׁר־ קֻמְּטוּ וְלֹא־ עֵת נָהָר
flood time and-no they-were-carried-off that (16) evil men-of they-trod

יוּצַק יְסוֹדָם׃ (17) הָאֹמְרִים לָאֵל סוּר
leave-alone! to-God the-ones-saying (17) foundation-of-them he-was-washed-away

מִמֶּנּוּ וּמַה־ יִּפְעַל שַׁדַּי לָמוֹ׃ (18) וְהוּא מִלֵּא
he-filled yet-he (18) to-us Almighty can-he-do and-what? from-us

בָתֵּיהֶם טוֹב וַעֲצַת רְשָׁעִים רָחֲקָה מֶנִּי׃
from-me she-is-distant wicked-ones and-counsel-of good houses-of-them

(19) יִרְאוּ צַדִּיקִים וְיִשְׂמָחוּ וְנָקִי יִלְעַג־ לָמוֹ׃
at-them he-mocks and-innocent and-they-rejoice righteous-ones they-see (19)

2 "Can a man be of benefit to God?
Can even a wise man benefit him?
3 What pleasure would it give the Almighty if you were righteous?
What would he gain if your ways were blameless?
4 "Is it for your piety that he rebukes you
and brings charges against you?
5 Is not your wickedness great?
Are not your sins endless?
6 You demanded security from your brothers for no reason;
you stripped men of their clothing, leaving them naked.
7 You gave no water to the weary
and you withheld food from the hungry,
8 though you were a powerful man, owning land—
an honored man, living on it.
9 And you sent widows away empty-handed
and broke the strength of the fatherless.
10 That is why snares are all around you,
why sudden peril terrifies you,
11 why it is so dark you cannot see,
and why a flood of water covers you.
12 "Is not God in the heights of heaven?
And see how lofty are the highest stars!
13 Yet you say, 'What does God know?
Does he judge through such darkness?
14 Thick clouds veil him, so he does not see us
as he goes about in the vaulted heavens.'
15 Will you keep to the old path
that evil men have trod?
16 They were carried off before their time,
their foundations washed away by a flood.
17 They said to God, 'Leave us alone!
What can the Almighty do to us?'
18 Yet it was he who filled their houses with good things,
so I stand aloof from the counsel of the wicked.
19 "The righteous see their ruin and rejoice;
the innocent mock them, saying,

אִם־ לֹא נִכְחַד קִימָנוּ וְיִתְרָם אָכְלָה

she-devours and-wealth-of-them foe-of-us he-is-destroyed indeed surely (20)

אֵשׁ׃ הַסְכֶּן־ נָא עִמּוֹ וּשְׁלֵם* בָּהֶם תְּבוֹאַתְךָ

she-will-come-to-you in-them and-be-at-peace! with-him now! submit! (21) fire

טוֹבָה׃ קַח־ נָא מִפִּיו תּוֹרָה וְשִׂים

and-lay-up! instruction from-mouth-of-him now! accept! (22) prosperity

אֲמָרָיו בִּלְבָבֶךָ׃ אִם־ תָּשׁוּב עַד־ שַׁדַּי תִּבָּנֶה

you-will-be-restored Almighty to you-return if (23) in-heart-of-you words-of-him

תַּרְחִיק עַוְלָה מֵאָהֳלֶךָ׃ וְשִׁית־ עַל־ עָפָר בָּצֶר

nugget dust to and-assign! (24) from-tent-of-you wickedness you-remove-far

וּבְצוּר נְחָלִים אוֹפִיר׃ וְהָיָה שַׁדַּי בְּצָרֶיךָ

golds-of-you Almighty then-he-will-be (25) Ophir ravines and-to-rock-of

וְכֶסֶף תּוֹעָפוֹת לָךְ׃ כִּי־ אָז עַל־ שַׁדַּי

Almighty in then surely (26) for-you choicest-ones and-silver-of

תִּתְעַנָּג וְתִשָּׂא אֶל־אֱלוֹהַּ פָּנֶיךָ׃ תַּעְתִּיר

you-will-pray (27) faces-of-you God to and-you-will-lift-up you-will-delight

אֵלָיו וְיִשְׁמָעֶךָּ וּנְדָרֶיךָ תְשַׁלֵּם׃

you-will-fulfill and-vows-of-you and-he-will-hear-you to-him

וְתִגְזַר־ אוֹמֶר וְיָקָם לָךְ וְעַל־ דְּרָכֶיךָ

ways-of-you and-on for-you then-he-will-be-done matter when-you-decide (28)

נָגַהּ אוֹר׃ כִּי־ הִשְׁפִּילוּ וַתֹּאמֶר גֵּוָה

lifting-up and-you-say they-bring-low when (29) light he-will-shine

וְשַׁח עֵינַיִם יוֹשִׁעַ׃ יְמַלֵּט אִי־ נָקִי

innocent not he-will-deliver (30) he-will-save eyes then-downcast-of

וְנִמְלַט בְּבֹר כַּפֶּיךָ׃ וַיַּעַן

then-he-replied (23:1) hands-of-you through-cleanness-of and-he-will-be-delivered

אִיּוֹב וַיֹּאמַר׃ גַּם־ הַיּוֹם מְרִי שִׂחִי יָדִי כָּבְדָה

she-is-heavy hand-of-me complaint-of-me bitter the-day even (2) and-he-said Job

עַל־ אַנְחָתִי׃ מִי־ יִתֵּן יָדַעְתִּי וְאֶמְצָאֵהוּ

so-I-could-find-him I-knew he-would-allow who? (3) groaning-of-me in

אָבוֹא עַד־ תְּכוּנָתוֹ׃ אֶעֶרְכָה לְפָנָיו מִשְׁפָּט וּפִי

and-mouth-of-me case before-him I-would-state (4) dwelling-of-him to I-could-go

אֲמַלֵּא תוֹכָחוֹת׃ אֵדְעָה מִלִּים יַעֲנֵנִי

he-would-answer-me words I-would-find-out (5) arguments I-would-fill

וְאָבִינָה מַה־ יֹּאמַר לִי׃ הַבְּרָב־ כֹּחַ

power with-greatness-of? (6) to-me he-would-say what and-I-would-consider

יָרִיב עִמָּדִי לֹא אַךְ־ הוּא יָשִׂם בִּי׃

against-me he-would-press-charges he indeed no against-me would-he-oppose

20 'Surely our foes are destroyed,
and fire devours their wealth.'

21 "Submit to God and be at peace with him;
in this way prosperity will come to you.
22 Accept instruction from his mouth
and lay up his words in your heart.
23 If you return to the Almighty, you will be restored:
If you remove wickedness far from your tent
24 and assign your nuggets to the dust,
your gold of Ophir to the rocks in the ravines,
25 then the Almighty will be your gold,
the choicest silver for you.
26 Surely then you will find delight in the Almighty
and will lift up your face to God.
27 You will pray to him, and he will hear you,
and you will fulfill your vows.
28 What you decide on will be done,
and light will shine on your ways.
29 When men are brought low and you say, 'Lift them up!'
then he will save the downcast.
30 He will deliver even one who is not innocent,
who will be delivered through the cleanness of your hands."

*Job*

23 Then Job replied:

2 "Even today my complaint is bitter;
his hand[t] is heavy in spite of[u] my groaning.
3 If only I knew where to find him;
if only I could go to his dwelling!
4 I would state my case before him
and fill my mouth with arguments.
5 I would find out what he would answer me,
and consider what he would say.
6 Would he oppose me with great power?
No, he would not press charges against me.

[t] 2 Septuagint and Syriac; Hebrew / *the hand on me*
[u] 2 Or *heavy on me in*

**21* Most mss have *qamets* and *atnah* under the *lamed* ( וּשְׁלָ֑ם ).

שָׁם יָשָׁר נוֹכָח עִמּוֹ וַאֲפַלְּטָה
and-I-would-be-delivered before-him he-could-present-case upright-man there (7)

לָנֶצַח מִשֹּׁפְטִי׃ הֵן קֶדֶם אֶהֱלֹךְ וְאֵינֶנּוּ וְאָחוֹר וְלֹא־
then-not if-west then-not-he I-go east if (8) from-one-judging-me to-forever

אָבִין לוֹ׃ שְׂמֹאול בַּעֲשֹׂתוֹ וְלֹא־ אָחַז יַעְטֹף יָמִין
south he-turns I-see then-not when-to-work-him north (9) to-him I-find

וְלֹא אֶרְאֶה׃ כִּי־ יָדַע דֶּרֶךְ עִמָּדִי בְּחָנַנִי כַּזָּהָב
as-the-gold he-tests-me with-me way he-knows but (10) I-glimpse and-not

אֵצֵא׃ בַּאֲשֻׁרוֹ אָחֲזָה רַגְלִי דַּרְכּוֹ
way-of-him foot-of-me she-follows at-step-of-him (11) I-will-come-forth

שָׁמַרְתִּי וְלֹא־ אָט׃ מִצְוַת שְׂפָתָיו וְלֹא אָמִישׁ
I-departed and-not lips-of-him command-of (12) I-turned-aside and-not I-kept

מֵחֻקִּי צָפַנְתִּי אִמְרֵי־ פִיו׃ וְהוּא
but-he (13) mouth-of-him words-of I-treasured more-than-daily-bread-of-me

בְאֶחָד וּמִי יְשִׁיבֶנּוּ וְנַפְשׁוֹ אִוְּתָה וַיָּעַשׂ׃
and-he-does she-pleases and-self-of-him he-can-oppose-him and-who? as-alone

כִּי יַשְׁלִים חֻקִּי וְכָהֵנָּה רַבּוֹת עִמּוֹ׃
with-him many and-like-them decree-of-me he-carries-out indeed (14)

עַל־ כֵּן מִפָּנָיו אֶבָּהֵל אֶתְבּוֹנֵן וְאֶפְחַד מִמֶּנּוּ׃
from-him and-I-fear I-think I-am-terrified from-before-him this for (15)

וְאֵל הֵרַךְ לִבִּי וְשַׁדַּי הִבְהִילָנִי׃ כִּי־
yet (17) he-terrified-me and-Almighty heart-of-me he-made-faint and-God (16)

לֹא נִצְמַתִּי מִפְּנֵי־ חֹשֶׁךְ וּמִפָּנַי כִּסָּה־
she-covers and-over-faces-of-me darkness by-presences-of I-am-silenced not

אֹפֶל׃ מַדּוּעַ מִשַּׁדַּי לֹא־ נִצְפְּנוּ עִתִּים
times they-are-set not from-Almighty why? (24:1) thick-darkness

וְיֹדְעָו° לֹא־ חָזוּ יָמָיו׃ גְּבֻלוֹת יַשִּׂיגוּ
they-move boundary-stones (2) days-of-him they-see not and-ones-knowing-him

עֵדֶר גָּזְלוּ וַיִּרְעוּ׃ חֲמוֹר יְתוֹמִים יִנְהָגוּ
they-drive-away orphans donkey-of (3) and-they-pasture they-stole flock

יַחְבְּלוּ שׁוֹר אַלְמָנָה׃ יַטּוּ אֶבְיֹנִים מִדָּרֶךְ
from-path needy-ones they-thrust (4) widow ox-of they-take-in-pledge

יַחַד חֻבְּאוּ עֲנִיֵּי־ אָרֶץ׃ הֵן פְּרָאִים ׀
wild-donkeys see! (5) land poor-ones-of they-are-forced-to-hide together

בַּמִּדְבָּר יָצְאוּ בְּפָעֳלָם מְשַׁחֲרֵי לַטָּרֶף
for-the-food ones-foraging-of in-labor-of-them they-go-about in-the-desert

עֲרָבָה לוֹ לֶחֶם לַנְּעָרִים׃ בַּשָּׂדֶה בְּלִילוֹ
fodder-of-him in-the-field (6) for-the-children food for-him wasteland

7There an upright man could
present his case before
him,
and I would be delivered
forever from my judge.
8"But if I go to the east, he is
not there;
if I go to the west, I do not
find him.
9When he is at work in the
north, I do not see him;
when he turns to the south,
I catch no glimpse of
him.
10But he knows the way that I
take;
when he has tested me, I
will come forth as gold.
11My feet have closely followed
his steps;
I have kept to his way
without turning aside.
12I have not departed from the
commands of his lips;
I have treasured the words
of his mouth more than
my daily bread.
13"But he stands alone, and who
can oppose him?
He does whatever he
pleases.
14He carries out his decree
against me,
and many such plans he still
has in store.
15That is why I am terrified
before him;
when I think of all this, I
fear him.
16God has made my heart faint;
the Almighty has terrified
me.
17Yet I am not silenced by the
darkness,
by the thick darkness that
covers my face.

24 "Why does the Almighty
not set times for
judgment?
Why must those who know
him look in vain for such
days?
2Men move boundary stones;
they pasture flocks they
have stolen.
3They drive away the orphan's
donkey
and take the widow's ox in
pledge.
4They thrust the needy from
the path
and force all the poor of the
land into hiding.
5Like wild donkeys in the
desert,
the poor go about their labor
of foraging food;
the wasteland provides food
for their children.
6They gather fodder in the
fields

°1 ק וידעיו

יַקְצִירוּ וְכֶרֶם רָשָׁע יְלַקֵּשׁוּ׃ עָרוֹם יָלִינוּ
they-spend-night naked (7) they-glean wicked and-vineyard-of they-gather

מִבְּלִי לְבוּשׁ וְאֵין כְּסוּת בַּקָּרָה׃ מִזֶּרֶם
from-rain-of (8) in-the-cold covering and-nothing clothing from-lack-of

הָרִים יִרְטָבוּ וּמִבְּלִי מַחְסֶה חִבְּקוּ־צוּר׃
rock they-hug shelter and-from-lack-of they-are-drenched mountains

יִגְזְלוּ מִשֹּׁד יָתוֹם וְעַל־* עָנִי
poor *and-infant-of fatherless-child from-breast they-snatch (9)

יַחְבֹּלוּ׃ עָרוֹם הִלְּכוּ בְּלִי לְבוּשׁ וּרְעֵבִים
and-hungry-ones clothing lacking-of they-go-about naked (10) they-seize-for-debt

נָשְׂאוּ עֹמֶר׃ בֵּין־ שׁוּרֹתָם יַצְהִירוּ יְקָבִים
winepresses they-crush-olives terraces-of-them among (11) sheaf they-carry

דָּרְכוּ וַיִּצְמָאוּ׃ מֵעִיר מְתִים† ׀ יִנְאָקוּ וְנֶפֶשׁ־
and-soul-of they-groan †men from-city (12) yet-they-thirst they-tread

חֲלָלִים תְּשַׁוֵּעַ וֶאֱלוֹהַּ לֹא־ יָשִׂים תִּפְלָה׃ הֵמָּה ׀
those (13) wrongdoing he-charges not but-God she-cries-for-help wounded-ones

הָיוּ בְּמֹרְדֵי־ אוֹר לֹא־ הִכִּירוּ דְרָכָיו וְלֹא
and-not ways-of-him they-know not light among-ones-rebelling-of they-are

יָשְׁבוּ בִּנְתִיבֹתָיו׃ לָאוֹר יָקוּם רוֹצֵחַ
one-murdering he-rises-up after-daylight (14) in-paths-of-him they-stay

יִקְטָל־ עָנִי וְאֶבְיוֹן וּבַלַּיְלָה יְהִי כַגַּנָּב׃ וְעֵין
and-eye-of (15) like-the-thief he-is and-in-the-night and-needy poor he-kills

נֹאֵף ׀ שָׁמְרָה נֶשֶׁף לֵאמֹר לֹא־ תְשׁוּרֵנִי עָיִן
eye she-will-see-me not to-think dusk she-watches one-commiting-adultery

וְסֵתֶר פָּנִים יָשִׂים׃ חָתַר בַּחֹשֶׁךְ בָּתִּים
houses in-the-dark they-break-into (16) he-keeps faces and-concealing-of

יוֹמָם חִתְּמוּ־ לָמוֹ לֹא־ יָדְעוּ אוֹר׃ כִּי יַחְדָּו ׀ בֹּקֶר
morning together for (17) light they-know not for-them they-shut-in by-day

לָמוֹ צַלְמָוֶת כִּי־ יַכִּיר בַּלְהוֹת צַלְמָוֶת׃ קַל־הוּא ׀
he foam (18) darkness terrors-of he-befriends for deep-darkness to-them

עַל־ פְּנֵי־ מַיִם תְּקֻלַּל חֶלְקָתָם בָּאָרֶץ לֹא־
no-one in-the-land portion-of-them she-is-cursed waters surfaces-of on

יִפְנֶה דֶּרֶךְ כְּרָמִים׃ צִיָּה גַם־ חֹם יִגְזְלוּ מֵימֵי־
waters-of they-snatch-away heat and drought (19) vineyards way-of he-goes

שֶׁלֶג שְׁאוֹל חָטָאוּ׃ יִשְׁכָּחֵהוּ רֶחֶם ׀ מְתָקוֹ רִמָּה עוֹד
longer worm he-feasts-on-him womb he-forgets-him (20) they-sinned Sheol snow

לֹא־ יִזָּכֵר וַתִּשָּׁבֵר כָּעֵץ עַוְלָה׃ רֹעֶה עֲקָרָה
barren preying-of (21) evil like-tree but-she-is-broken he-is-remembered not

and glean in the vineyards
of the wicked.
7 Lacking clothes, they spend
the night naked;
they have nothing to cover
themselves in the cold.
8 They are drenched by
mountain rains
and hug the rocks for lack of
shelter.
9 The fatherless child is
snatched from the breast;
the infant of the poor is
seized for a debt.
10 Lacking clothes, they go about
naked;
they carry the sheaves, but
still go hungry.
11 They crush olives among the
terraces[v];
they tread the winepresses,
yet suffer thirst.
12 The groans of the dying rise
from the city,
and the souls of the
wounded cry out for help.
But God charges no one
with wrongdoing.

13 "There are those who rebel
against the light,
who do not know its ways
or stay in its paths.
14 When daylight is gone, the
murderer rises up
and kills the poor and
needy;
in the night he steals forth
like a thief.
15 The eye of the adulterer
watches for dusk;
he thinks, 'No eye will see
me,'
and he keeps his face
concealed.
16 In the dark, men break into
houses,
but by day they shut
themselves in;
they want nothing to do
with the light.
17 For all of them, deep darkness
is their morning[w];
they make friends with the
terrors of darkness.[x]

18 "Yet they are foam on the
surface of the water;
their portion of the land is
cursed,
so that no one goes to the
vineyards.
19 As heat and drought snatch
away the melted snow,
so the grave[y] snatches away
those who have sinned.
20 The womb forgets them,
the worm feasts on them;
evil men are no longer
remembered
but are broken like a tree.
21 They prey on the barren and

v 11 Or *olives between the millstones;* the meaning of the Hebrew for this word is uncertain.
w 17 Or *them, their morning is like the shadow of death*
x 17 Or *of the shadow of death*
y 19 Hebrew *Sheol*

*9 The NIV repoints this word as וְעַל; the text as pointed reads *and-over.*

†12 The NIV repoints this word with *tsere* under the *mem* מֵ, *dying-ones.*

°6 ק יקצורו

לֹא תֵלֵד וְאַלְמָנָה לֹא יְיֵטִיב׃ וּמָשַׁךְ
but-he-drags-away (22) he-shows-kindness not and-widow she-bore-child not

אַבִּירִים בְּכֹחוֹ יָקוּם וְלֹא־ יַאֲמִין
he-has-assurance but-not he-becomes-established by-power-of-him mighty-ones

בַּחַיִּין׃ יִתֶּן־ לוֹ לָבֶטַח וְיִשָּׁעֵן וְעֵינֵיהוּ
but-eyes-of-him and-may-he-rest in-security to-him he-may-let (23) of-the-lives

עַל־ דַּרְכֵיהֶם׃ רוֹמּוּ מְּעַט וְאֵינֶנּוּ
then-not-he little-while they-are-exalted (24) ways-of-them on

וְהֻמְּכוּ כַּכֹּל יִקָּפְצוּן וּכְרֹאשׁ
and-like-head-of they-are-gathered-up like-the-all and-they-are-brought-low

שִׁבֹּלֶת יִמָּלוּ׃ וְאִם־ לֹא אֵפוֹ מִי יַכְזִיבֵנִי
he-can-prove-false-me who? then not and-if (25) they-are-cut-off grain

וְיָשֵׂם לְאַל מִלָּתִי׃ וַיַּעַן בִּלְדַּד
Bildad then-he-replied (25:1) word-of-me to-nothing and-he-can-reduce

הַשֻּׁחִי וַיֹּאמַר׃ הַמְשֵׁל וָפַחַד עִמּוֹ עֹשֶׂה
establishing to-him and-awe to-have-dominion (2) and-he-said the-Shuhite

שָׁלוֹם בִּמְרוֹמָיו׃ הֲיֵשׁ מִסְפָּר לִגְדוּדָיו וְעַל־ מִי
whom? and-upon to-forces-of-him number is-there? (3) in-heights-of-him order

לֹא־ יָקוּם אוֹרֵהוּ׃ וּמַה־ יִּצְדַּק אֱנוֹשׁ עִם־ אֵל
God before man can-he-be-righteous then-how? (4) light-of-him he-rises not

וּמַה־ יִּזְכֶּה יְלוּד אִשָּׁה׃ הֵן עַד־ יָרֵחַ וְלֹא
and-not moon even if (5) woman one-being-born-of can-he-be-pure and-how?

יַאֲהִיל וְכוֹכָבִים לֹא־ זַכּוּ בְעֵינָיו׃ אַף
how-much-less (6) in-eyes-of-him they-are-pure not and-stars he-is-bright

כִּי־ אֱנוֹשׁ רִמָּה וּבֶן־ אָדָם תּוֹלֵעָה׃ וַיַּעַן אִיּוֹב וַיֹּאמַר׃
and-he-said Job then-he-replied (26:1) worm man and-son-of maggot man then

מֶה־ עָזַרְתָּ לְלֹא־ כֹחַ הוֹשַׁעְתָּ זְרוֹעַ לֹא־ עֹז׃ מַה־
what! (3) strength no arm you-saved power to-no you-helped how! (2)

יָּעַצְתָּ לְלֹא חָכְמָה וְתוּשִׁיָּה לָרֹב הוֹדָעְתָּ׃ אֶת־
with (4) you-displayed in-greatness and-insight wisdom to-no you-advised

מִי הִגַּדְתָּ מִלִּין וְנִשְׁמַת־ מִי יָצְאָה מִמֶּךָּ׃
from-you she-came-out who? and-spirit-of words you-uttered whom?

הָרְפָאִים יְחוֹלָלוּ מִתַּחַת מַיִם וְשֹׁכְנֵיהֶם׃
and-ones-living-of-them waters at-beneath they-are-in-anguish the-dead-ones (5)

עָרוֹם שְׁאוֹל נֶגְדּוֹ וְאֵין כְּסוּת לָאֲבַדּוֹן׃* נֹטֶה צָפוֹן
north spreading-out (7) to-Abaddon cover and-no before-him Sheol naked (6)

עַל־ תֹּהוּ תֹּלֶה אֶרֶץ עַל־ בְּלִי־ מָה׃ צֹרֵר־ מַיִם
waters wrapping-up (8) what not over earth suspending empty-space over

childless woman,
and to the widow show no kindness.
22 But God drags away the mighty by his power;
though they become established, they have no assurance of life.
23 He may let them rest in a feeling of security,
but his eyes are on their ways.
24 For a little while they are exalted, and then they are gone;
they are brought low and gathered up like all others;
they are cut off like heads of grain.
25 "If this is not so, who can prove me false
and reduce my words to nothing?"

*Bildad*

## 25
Then Bildad the Shuhite replied:

2 "Dominion and awe belong to God;
he establishes order in the heights of heaven.
3 Can his forces be numbered?
Upon whom does his light not rise?
4 How then can a man be righteous before God?
How can one born of woman be pure?
5 If even the moon is not bright
and the stars are not pure in his eyes,
6 how much less man, who is but a maggot—
a son of man, who is only a worm!"

*Job*

## 26
Then Job replied:

2 "How you have helped the powerless!
How you have saved the arm that is feeble!
3 What advice you have offered to one without wisdom!
And what great insight you have displayed!
4 Who has helped you utter these words?
And whose spirit spoke from your mouth?
5 "The dead are in deep anguish,
those beneath the waters and all that live in them.
6 Death[z] is naked before God;
Destruction[a] lies uncovered.
7 He spreads out the northern ⌊skies⌋ over empty space;
he suspends the earth over nothing.
8 He wraps up the waters in his

[z] 6 Hebrew *Sheol* [a] 6 Hebrew *Abaddon*

*6 Most mss have *pathah* under the *lamed* (לַ).

בְּעָבָיו וְלֹא־ נִבְקַע עָנָן תַּחְתָּם׃ מְאַחֵז פְּנֵי־
faces-of covering (9) under-them cloud he-bursts yet-not in-clouds-of-him

כִסֵּה* פַּרְשֵׁז עָלָיו עֲנָנוֹ׃ חֹק־ חָג עַל־
on he-marks-out horizon (10) cloud-of-him over-him to-spread *full-moon

פְּנֵי־ מָיִם עַד־ תַּכְלִית אוֹר עִם־ חֹשֶׁךְ׃ עַמּוּדֵי
pillars-of (11) darkness between light boundary-of for waters faces-of

שָׁמַיִם יְרוֹפָפוּ וְיִתְמְהוּ מִגַּעֲרָתוֹ׃ בְּכֹחוֹ
by-power-of-him (12) at-rebuke-of-him and-they-are-aghast they-quake heavens

רָגַע הַיָּם °וּבִתְוּבְנָתוֹ מָחַץ רָהַב׃
Rahab he-cut-to-pieces and-by-wisdom-of-him the-sea he-churned-up

בְּרוּחוֹ שָׁמַיִם שִׁפְרָה חֹלְלָה יָדוֹ נָחָשׁ בָּרִיחַ׃
gliding serpent hand-of-him piercing fair skies by-breath-of-him (13)

הֶן־ אֵלֶּה׀ קְצוֹת °דְּרָכוֹ וּמַה־ שֵּׁמֶץ דָּבָר
whisper faint-of and-how! ways-of-him outer-fringes-of these see! (14)

נִשְׁמַע־ בּוֹ וְרַעַם °גְּבוּרֹתוֹ מִי יִתְבּוֹנָן׃
he-can-understand who? powers-of-him then-thunder-of of-him we-hear

וַיֹּסֶף אִיּוֹב שְׂאֵת מְשָׁלוֹ וַיֹּאמַר׃
and-he-said discourse-of-him to-take-up Job and-he-continued (27:1)

חַי־ אֵל הֵסִיר מִשְׁפָּטִי וְשַׁדַּי הֵמַר
he-made-bitter and-Almighty justice-of-me he-denied God life-of (2)

נַפְשִׁי׃ כִּי־ כָל־ עוֹד נִשְׁמָתִי בִי וְרוּחַ אֱלוֹהַּ
God and-breath-of in-me life-of-me length-of all-of for (3) soul-of-me

בְּאַפִּי׃ אִם־ תְּדַבֵּרְנָה שְׂפָתַי עַוְלָה וּלְשׁוֹנִי
and-tongue-of-me wickedness lips-of-me she-will-speak not (4) in-nostril-of-me

אִם־ יֶהְגֶּה רְמִיָּה׃ חָלִילָה לִּי אִם־ אַצְדִּיק
I-will-declare-right never from-me far-be-it! (5) deceit he-will-utter not

אֶתְכֶם עַד־אֶגְוָע לֹא־אָסִיר תֻּמָּתִי מִמֶּנִּי׃ בְּצִדְקָתִי
to-righteousness-of-me (6) from-me integrity-of-me I-will-deny not I-die till you

הֶחֱזַקְתִּי וְלֹא אַרְפֶּהָ לֹא־ יֶחֱרַף
he-will-reproach not I-will-let-go-of-her and-never I-will-maintain

לְבָבִי מִיָּמָי׃ יְהִי כְרָשָׁע אֹיְבִי
being-enemy-of-me like-wicked may-he-be (7) from-days-of-me conscience-of-me

וּמִתְקוֹמְמִי כְעַוָּל׃ כִּי מַה־ תִּקְוַת חָנֵף כִּי
when godless hope-of what? for (8) like-unjust and-one-being-adversary-of-me

יִבְצָע כִּי יֵשֶׁל אֱלוֹהַּ נַפְשׁוֹ׃ הֲצַעֲקָתוֹ יִשְׁמַע׀
he-listens cry-of-him? (9) life-of-him God he-takes-away when he-is-cut-off

אֵל כִּי־ תָבוֹא עָלָיו צָרָה׃ אִם־עַל־ שַׁדַּי יִתְעַנָּג
will-he-delight Almighty in or (10) distress upon-him she-comes when God

clouds,
yet the clouds do not burst
under their weight.
9He covers the face of the full
moon,
spreading his clouds over it.
10He marks out the horizon on
the face of the waters
for a boundary between
light and darkness.
11The pillars of the heavens
quake,
aghast at his rebuke.
12By his power he churned up
the sea;
by his wisdom he cut Rahab
to pieces.
13By his breath the skies became
fair;
his hand pierced the gliding
serpent.
14And these are but the outer
fringe of his works;
how faint the whisper we
hear of him!
Who then can understand
the thunder of his
power?"

27 And Job continued his discourse:

2"As surely as God lives, who
has denied me justice,
the Almighty, who has
made me taste bitterness
of soul,
3as long as I have life within
me,
the breath of God in my
nostrils,
4my lips will not speak
wickedness,
and my tongue will utter no
deceit.
5I will never admit you are in
the right;
till I die, I will not deny my
integrity.
6I will maintain my
righteousness and never
let go of it;
my conscience will not
reproach me as long as I
live.

7"May my enemies be like the
wicked,
my adversaries like the
unjust!
8For what hope has the godless
when he is cut off,
when God takes away his
life?
9Does God listen to his cry
when distress comes upon
him?
10Will he find delight in the
Almighty?

*9 The NIV repoints this word as כֶּסֶה; the text as pointed reads *throne.*

°*12* ק ובתבונתו
°*14a* ק דרכיו
°*14b* ק גבורתיו

יִקְרָא אֱלוֹהַּ בְּכָל־ עֵת: אוֹרֶה אֶתְכֶם בְּיַד־ אֵל
God about-power-of you I-will-teach (11) time at-all-of God will-he-call-upon

אֲשֶׁר עִם־ שַׁדַּי לֹא אֲכַחֵד: הֵן־ אַתֶּם כֻּלְּכֶם חֲזִיתֶם
you-saw all-of-you you see! (12) I-will-conceal not Almighty with what

וְלָמָּה־ זֶּה הֶבֶל תֶּהְבָּלוּ: זֶה ׀ חֵלֶק־ אָדָם
man allotment-of this (13) you-talk-meaninglessly meaningless this then-why?

רָשָׁע ׀ עִם־ אֵל וְנַחֲלַת עָרִיצִים מִשַּׁדַּי יִקָּחוּ:
they-receive from-Almighty ruthless-ones and-heritage-of God from wicked

אִם־ יִרְבּוּ בָנָיו לְמוֹ־ חָרֶב וְצֶאֱצָאָיו
and-offsprings-of-him sword to children-of-him they-are-many if (14)

לֹא יִשְׂבְּעוּ־ לָחֶם: שְׂרִידָו בַּמָּוֶת
by-the-plague survivors-of-him (15) food they-will-have-enough never

יִקָּבֵרוּ וְאַלְמְנֹתָיו לֹא תִבְכֶּינָה: אִם־
though (16) they-will-weep not and-widows-of-him they-will-be-buried

יִצְבֹּר כֶּעָפָר כָּסֶף וְכַחֹמֶר יָכִין מַלְבּוּשׁ:
clothing he-piles and-like-the-clay silver like-the-dust he-heaps-up

יָכִין וְצַדִּיק יִלְבָּשׁ וְכֶסֶף נָקִי יַחֲלֹק:
he-will-divide innocent and-silver he-will-wear but-righteous he-lays-up (17)

בָּנָה כָעָשׁ בֵּיתוֹ וּכְסֻכָּה עָשָׂה נֹצֵר:
man-watching he-made and-like-hut house-of-him like-the-moth he-builds (18)

עָשִׁיר יִשְׁכַּב וְלֹא יֵאָסֵף עֵינָיו פָּקַח
he-opens eyes-of-him he-will-do-again but-not he-lies-down wealthy (19)

וְאֵינֶנּוּ: תַּשִּׂיגֵהוּ כַמַּיִם בַּלָּהוֹת לַיְלָה
night terrors like-the-floods she-overtakes-him (20) and-not-he

גְּנָבַתּוּ סוּפָה: יִשָּׂאֵהוּ קָדִים וְיֵלַךְ
and-he-is-gone east-wind he-carries-off-him (21) tempest she-snatches-him

וִישָׂעֲרֵהוּ מִמְּקֹמוֹ: וְיַשְׁלֵךְ עָלָיו וְלֹא
and-not against-him and-he-hurls (22) from-place-of-him and-he-sweeps-him

יַחְמֹל מִיָּדוֹ בָּרוֹחַ יִבְרָח: יִשְׂפֹּק עָלֵימוֹ
against-him he-claps (23) he-flees to-flee from-power-of-him he-shows-mercy

כַפֵּימוֹ וְיִשְׁרֹק עָלָיו מִמְּקֹמוֹ: כִּי
indeed (28:1) from-place-of-him against-him and-he-hisses hands-of-him

יֵשׁ לַכֶּסֶף מוֹצָא וּמָקוֹם לַזָּהָב יָזֹקּוּ: בַּרְזֶל
iron (2) they-refine for-the-gold and-place mine for-the-silver there-is

מֵעָפָר יֻקָּח וְאֶבֶן יָצוּק נְחוּשָׁה: קֵץ ׀ שָׂם לַחֹשֶׁךְ
to-the-darkness he-puts end (3) copper being-smelted and-ore he-is-taken from-earth

וּלְכָל־ תַּכְלִית הוּא חוֹקֵר אֶבֶן אֹפֶל וְצַלְמָוֶת: פָּרַץ
he-cuts (4) and-darkness blackness ore searching he recess and-to-every-of

Will he call upon God at all times?

11"I will teach you about the power of God;
the ways of the Almighty I will not conceal.
12You have all seen this yourselves.
Why then this meaningless talk?

13"Here is the fate God allots to the wicked,
the heritage a ruthless man receives from the Almighty:
14However many his children, their fate is the sword;
his offspring will never have enough to eat.
15The plague will bury those who survive him,
and their widows will not weep for them.
16Though he heaps up silver like dust
and clothes like piles of clay,
17what he lays up the righteous will wear,
and the innocent will divide his silver.
18The house he builds is like a moth's cocoon,
like a hut made by a watchman.
19He lies down wealthy, but will do so no more;
when he opens his eyes, all is gone.
20Terrors overtake him like a flood;
a tempest snatches him away in the night.
21The east wind carries him off, and he is gone;
it sweeps him out of his place.
22It hurls itself against him without mercy
as he flees headlong from its power.
23It claps its hands in derision
and hisses him out of his place.

28 "There is a mine for silver and a place where gold is refined.
2Iron is taken from the earth,
and copper is smelted from ore.
3Man puts an end to the darkness;
he searches the farthest recesses
for ore in the blackest darkness.

°15 ק שרידיו

נָחַל | מֵעִם־ גָּר הַנִּשְׁכָּחִים מִנִּי־ רָגֶל דַּלּוּ
they-dangle foot by the-ones-being-forgotten one-dwelling from-with shaft

מֵאֱנוֹשׁ נָעוּ׃ אֶרֶץ מִמֶּנָּה יֵצֵא־ לָחֶם וְתַחְתֶּיהָ
and-below-her food he-comes from-her earth (5) they-sway from-man

נֶהְפַּךְ כְּמוֹ־ אֵשׁ׃ מְקוֹם־ סַפִּיר אֲבָנֶיהָ וְעַפְרֹת
and-dusts-of rocks-of-her sapphire place-of (6) fire as he-is-transformed

זָהָב לוֹ׃ נָתִיב לֹא־ יְדָעוֹ עַיִט וְלֹא
and-not bird-of-prey he-knows-him not hidden-path (7) to-him gold

שְׁזָפַתּוּ עֵין אַיָּה׃ לֹא־ הִדְרִיכֻהוּ בְנֵי־ שָׁחַץ לֹא־
not pride sons-of they-set-foot-on-him not (8) falcon eye-of she-saw-him

עָדָה עָלָיו שָׁחַל׃ בַּחַלָּמִישׁ שָׁלַח יָדוֹ
hand-of-him he-assaults against-the-flinty-rock (9) lion on-him he-prowls

הָפַךְ מִשֹּׁרֶשׁ הָרִים׃ בַּצּוּרוֹת יְאֹרִים בִּקֵּעַ
he-digs tunnels through-the-rocks (10) mountains from-root-of he-lays-bare

וְכָל־ יְקָר רָאֲתָה עֵינוֹ׃ מִבְּכִי נְהָרוֹת חִבֵּשׁ
he-searches rivers *sources-of (11) eye-of-him she-sees treasure and-all-of

וְתַעֲלֻמָהּ יֹצִא אוֹר׃ וְהַחָכְמָה מֵאַיִן
at-where? but-the-wisdom (12) light he-brings and-hidden-thing-of-her

תִּמָּצֵא וְאֵי זֶה מְקוֹם בִּינָה׃ לֹא־
not (13) understanding dwelling-of this and-where? can-she-be-found

יָדַע אֱנוֹשׁ עֶרְכָּהּ וְלֹא תִמָּצֵא בְּאֶרֶץ
in-land-of she-can-be-found and-not worth-of-her man he-comprehends

הַחַיִּים׃ תְּהוֹם אָמַר לֹא בִי־ הִיא וְיָם אָמַר אֵין עִמָּדִי׃
with-me not he-says and-sea she in-me not he-says deep (14) the-living-ones

לֹא־ יֻתַּן סְגוֹר תַּחְתֶּיהָ וְלֹא יִשָּׁקֵל
he-can-be-weighed and-not with-her fine-gold he-can-be-bought not (15)

כֶּסֶף מְחִירָהּ׃ לֹא־ תְסֻלֶּה בְּכֶתֶם אוֹפִיר בְּשֹׁהַם
with-onyx Ophir with-gold-of she-can-be-bought not (16) price-of-her silver

יָקָר וְסַפִּיר׃ לֹא־ יַעַרְכֶנָּה זָהָב וּזְכוֹכִית
or-crystal gold he-can-compare-with-her not (17) or-sapphire precious

וּתְמוּרָתָהּ כְּלִי־ פָז׃ רָאמוֹת וְגָבִישׁ לֹא יִזָּכֵר
he-is-mentioned not and-jasper corals (18) gold jewel-of or-having-of-her

וּמֶשֶׁךְ חָכְמָה מִפְּנִינִים׃ לֹא־ יַעַרְכֶנָּה פִּטְדַת־
topaz-of he-can-compare-with-her not (19) beyond-rubies wisdom and-price-of

כּוּשׁ בְּכֶתֶם טָהוֹר לֹא תְסֻלֶּה׃ וְהַחָכְמָה מֵאַיִן
from-where? and-the-wisdom (20) she-can-be-bought not pure with-gold Cush

תָּבוֹא וְאֵי זֶה מְקוֹם בִּינָה׃ וְנֶעֶלְמָה
and-she-is-hidden (21) understanding dwelling-of this and-where? she-comes

[4]Far from where people dwell
he cuts a shaft,
in places forgotten by the
foot of man;
far from men he dangles
and sways.
[5]The earth, from which food
comes,
is transformed below as by
fire;
[6]sapphires[b] come from its rocks,
and its dust contains
nuggets of gold.
[7]No bird of prey knows that
hidden path,
no falcon's eye has seen it.
[8]Proud beasts do not set foot on
it,
and no lion prowls there.
[9]Man's hand assaults the flinty
rock
and lays bare the roots of
the mountains.
[10]He tunnels through the rock;
his eyes see all its treasures.
[11]He searches[c] the sources of the
rivers
and brings hidden things to
light.

[12]"But where can wisdom be
found?
Where does understanding
dwell?
[13]Man does not comprehend its
worth;
it cannot be found in the
land of the living.
[14]The deep says, 'It is not in
me';
the sea says, 'It is not with
me.'
[15]It cannot be bought with the
finest gold,
nor can its price be weighed
in silver.
[16]It cannot be bought with the
gold of Ophir,
with precious onyx or
sapphires.
[17]Neither gold nor crystal can
compare with it,
nor can it be had for jewels
of gold.
[18]Coral and jasper are not
worthy of mention;
the price of wisdom is
beyond rubies.
[19]The topaz of Cush cannot
compare with it;
it cannot be bought with
pure gold.

[20]"Where then does wisdom
come from?
Where does understanding
dwell?
[21]It is hidden from the eyes of

[b]6 Or *lapis lazuli;* also in verse 16
[c]11 Septuagint, Aquila and Vulgate; Hebrew *He dams up*

**11* The NIV repoints this word as מִבְּכֵי; the text as pointed reads *from-weeping-of.*

מֵעֵינֵי כָל־ חָי וּמֵעוֹף הַשָּׁמַיִם נִסְתָּרָה׃

she-is-concealed the-airs and-from-bird-of living-thing every-of from-eyes-of

אֲבַדּוֹן וָמָוֶת אָמְרוּ בְּאָזְנֵינוּ שָׁמַעְנוּ שִׁמְעָהּ׃

rumor-of-her we-heard with-ears-of-us they-say and-Death Abaddon (22)

אֱלֹהִים הֵבִין דַּרְכָּהּ וְהוּא יָדַע אֶת־ מְקוֹמָהּ׃

dwelling-of-her *** he-knows and-he way-of-her he-understands God (23)

כִּי־ הוּא לִקְצוֹת־ הָאָרֶץ יַבִּיט תַּחַת כָּל־ הַשָּׁמַיִם יִרְאֶה׃

he-sees the-heavens all-of under he-views the-earth to-ends-of he for (24)

לַעֲשׂוֹת לָרוּחַ מִשְׁקָל וּמַיִם תִּכֵּן בְּמִדָּה׃

by-measure he-measured and-waters force of-the-wind to-establish (25)

בַּעֲשֹׂתוֹ לַמָּטָר חֹק וְדֶרֶךְ לַחֲזִיז קֹלוֹת׃

thunders for-storm-of and-path decree for-the-rain when-to-make-him (26)

אָז רָאָהּ וַיְסַפְּרָהּ הֱכִינָהּ וְגַם־

and-also he-confirmed-her and-he-appraised-her he-looked-at-her then (27)

חֲקָרָהּ׃ וַיֹּאמֶר ׀ לָאָדָם הֵן יִרְאַת אֲדֹנָי הִיא חָכְמָה

wisdom that Lord fear-of see! to-the-man and-he-said (28) he-tested-her

וְסוּר מֵרָע בִּינָה׃ וַיֹּסֶף אִיּוֹב שְׂאֵת

to-take-up Job and-he-continued (29:1) understanding from-evil and-to-shun

מְשָׁלוֹ וַיֹּאמַר׃ מִי־ יִתְּנֵנִי כְיַרְחֵי־ קֶדֶם

gone-by as-months-of he-would-grant-me who? (2) and-he-said discourse-of-him

כִּימֵי אֱלוֹהַ יִשְׁמְרֵנִי׃ בְּהִלּוֹ נֵרוֹ עֲלֵי

upon lamp-of-him when-to-shine-him (3) he-watched-over-me God as-days-of

רֹאשִׁי לְאוֹרוֹ אֵלֶךְ חֹשֶׁךְ׃ כַּאֲשֶׁר הָיִיתִי בִּימֵי

in-days-of I-was as-when (4) darkness I-walked by-light-of-him head-of-me

חָרְפִּי בְּסוֹד אֱלוֹהַ עֲלֵי אָהֳלִי׃ בְּעוֹד שַׁדַּי

Almighty when-still (5) house-of-me on God when-friendship-of prime-of-me

עִמָּדִי סְבִיבוֹתַי נְעָרָי׃ בִּרְחוֹץ הֲלִיכַי

paths-of-me when-to-be-drenched (6) children-of-me ones-around-me with-me

בְּחֵמָה וְצוּר יָצוּק עִמָּדִי פַּלְגֵי־ שָׁמֶן׃ בְּצֵאתִי

when-to-go-me (7) olive-oil streams-of for-me being-poured-out and-rock with-cream

שַׁעַר עֲלֵי־קָרֶת בָּרְחוֹב אָכִין מוֹשָׁבִי׃ רָאוּנִי נְעָרִים

young-men they-saw-me (8) seat-of-me I-took in-the-public-square city of gate

וְנֶחְבָּאוּ וִישִׁישִׁים קָמוּ עָמָדוּ׃ שָׂרִים

chief-men (9) they-stood they-rose and-old-men and-they-stepped-aside

עָצְרוּ בְמִלִּים וְכַף יָשִׂימוּ לְפִיהֶם׃ קוֹל־

voice-of (10) over-mouth-of-them they-covered and-hand from-speeches they-refrained

נְגִידִים נֶחְבָּאוּ וּלְשׁוֹנָם לְחִכָּם דָּבֵקָה׃

she-stuck to-roof-of-mouth-of-them and-tongue-of-them they-were-hushed nobles

every living thing,
concealed even from the
birds of the air.
22 Destruction[d] and Death say,
'Only a rumor of it has
reached our ears.'
23 God understands the way to it
and he alone knows where
it dwells,
24 for he views the ends of the
earth
and sees everything under
the heavens.
25 When he established the force
of the wind
and measured out the
waters,
26 when he made a decree for the
rain
and a path for the
thunderstorm,
27 then he looked at wisdom and
appraised it;
he confirmed it and tested
it.
28 And he said to man,
'The fear of the Lord—that is
wisdom,
and to shun evil is
understanding.' "

29 Job continued his discourse:

2 "How I long for the months
gone by,
for the days when God
watched over me,
3 when his lamp shone upon
my head
and by his light I walked
through darkness!
4 Oh, for the days when I was
in my prime,
when God's intimate
friendship blessed my
house,
5 when the Almighty was still
with me
and my children were
around me,
6 when my path was drenched
with cream
and the rock poured out for
me streams of olive oil.

7 "When I went to the gate of
the city
and took my seat in the
public square,
8 the young men saw me and
stepped aside
and the old men rose to
their feet;
9 the chief men refrained from
speaking
and covered their mouths
with their hands;
10 the voices of the nobles were
hushed,
and their tongues stuck to
the roof of their mouths.

[d] 22 Hebrew *Abaddon*

כִּ֤י אֹ֣זֶן שָׁ֭מְעָה וַתְּאַשְּׁרֵ֑נִי וְעַ֥יִן רָ֝אֲתָה
she-saw and-eye then-she-spoke-well-of-me she-heard ear when (11)

וַתְּעִידֵֽנִי׃ כִּֽי־אֲ֭מַלֵּט עָנִ֣י מְשַׁוֵּ֑עַ וְ֝יָת֗וֹם
and-fatherless crying-out poor I-rescued because (12) then-she-commended-me

וְֽלֹא־עֹזֵ֥ר לֽוֹ׃ בִּרְכַּ֣ת אֹ֭בֵד עָלַ֣י תָּבֹ֑א
she-came on-me man-dying blessing-of (13) to-him one-assisting and-not

וְלֵ֖ב אַלְמָנָ֣ה אַרְנִֽן׃ צֶ֣דֶק לָ֭בַשְׁתִּי וַיִּלְבָּשֵׁ֑נִי
and-he-clothed-me I-put-on righteousness (14) I-made-sing widow and-heart-of

כִּמְעִ֥יל וְ֝צָנִ֗יף מִשְׁפָּטִֽי׃ עֵ֭ינַיִם הָיִ֣יתִי לַֽעִוֵּ֑ר וְרַגְלַ֖יִם
and-feet to-the-blind I-was eyes (15) justice-of-me and-turban as-robe

לַפִּסֵּ֣חַ אָֽנִי׃ אָ֣ב אָנֹכִ֣י לָֽאֶבְיוֹנִ֑ים וְרִ֥ב לֹא־יָ֝דַ֗עְתִּי
I-knew not and-case to-the-needy-ones I father (16) I to-the-lame

אֶחְקְרֵֽהוּ׃ וָֽ֭אֲשַׁבְּרָה מְתַלְּע֣וֹת עַוָּ֑ל וּ֝מִשִּׁנָּ֗יו
and-from-teeth-of-him wicked fangs-of and-I-broke (17) I-took-up-him

אַשְׁלִ֥יךְ טָֽרֶף׃ וָ֭אֹמַר עִם־קִנִּ֣י אֶגְוָ֑ע
I-will-die house-of-me in and-I-thought (18) victim I-snatched

וְ֝כַח֗וֹל אַרְבֶּ֥ה יָמִֽים׃ שָׁרְשִׁ֣י פָת֣וּחַ אֱלֵי־מָ֑יִם וְ֝טַ֗ל
and-dew waters to reaching root-of-me (19) days I-number and-as-the-sand

יָלִ֥ין בִּקְצִירִֽי׃ כְּ֭בוֹדִי חָדָ֣שׁ עִמָּדִ֑י
with-me fresh glory-of-me (20) on-branch-of-me he-will-spend-night

וְ֝קַשְׁתִּ֗י בְּיָדִ֥י תַחֲלִֽיף׃ לִֽי־שָׁמְע֥וּ
they-listened to-me (21) she-will-be-new in-hand-of-me and-bow-of-me

וְיִחֵ֑לּוּ וְ֝יִדְּמ֗וּ לְמ֣וֹ עֲצָתִֽי׃
counsel-of-me for and-they-waited-in-silence and-they-were-expectant

אַחֲרֵ֣י דְ֭בָרִי לֹ֣א יִשְׁנ֑וּ וְ֝עָלֵ֗ימוֹ תִּטֹּ֥ף מִלָּתִֽי׃
word-of-me she-fell and-on-them they-spoke-more not speech-of-me after (22)

וְיִחֲל֣וּ כְמָטָ֣ר לִ֑י וּ֝פִיהֶ֗ם פָּעֲר֥וּ
they-drank and-mouth-of-them for-me as-the-shower and-they-waited (23)

לְמַלְקֽוֹשׁ׃ אֶשְׂחַ֣ק אֲ֭לֵהֶם לֹ֣א יַאֲמִ֑ינוּ וְא֥וֹר
and-light-of they-believed not at-them I-smiled (24) as-spring-rain

פָּ֝נַ֗י לֹ֣א יַפִּילֽוּן׃ אֶֽבֲחַ֣ר דַּ֭רְכָּם וְאֵשֵׁ֣ב רֹ֑אשׁ
chief and-I-sat way-of-them I-chose (25) they-rejected not faces-of-me

וְ֝אֶשְׁכּ֗וֹן כְּמֶ֥לֶךְ בַּגְּד֑וּד כַּאֲשֶׁ֖ר אֲבֵלִ֣ים יְנַחֵֽם׃ וְעַתָּ֤ה ׀
but-now (30:1) he-comforts mourners as-like among-the-troop as-king and-I-dwelt

שָׂחֲק֬וּ עָלַ֗י צְעִירִ֥ים מִמֶּ֗נִּי לְיָ֫מִ֥ים אֲשֶׁר־מָאַ֥סְתִּי
I-would-have-disdained whom in-days more-than-me men-young at-me they-mock

אֲ֝בוֹתָ֗ם לָ֝שִׁ֗ית עִם־כַּלְבֵ֥י צֹאנִֽי׃ גַּם־כֹּ֣חַ
strength-of also (2) sheep-of-me dogs-of with to-put fathers-of-them

[11]Whoever heard me spoke well
of me,
and those who saw me
commended me,
[12]because I rescued the poor
who cried for help,
and the fatherless who had
none to assist him.
[13]The man who was dying
blessed me;
I made the widow's heart
sing.
[14]I put on righteousness as my
clothing;
justice was my robe and my
turban.
[15]I was eyes to the blind
and feet to the lame.
[16]I was a father to the needy;
I took up the case of the
stranger.
[17]I broke the fangs of the
wicked
and snatched the victims
from their teeth.

[18]"I thought, 'I will die in my
own house,
my days as numerous as the
grains of sand.
[19]My roots will reach to the
water,
and the dew will lie all
night on my branches.
[20]My glory will remain fresh in
me,
the bow ever new in my
hand.'

[21]"Men listened to me
expectantly,
waiting in silence for my
counsel.
[22]After I had spoken, they spoke
no more;
my words fell gently on
their ears.
[23]They waited for me as for
showers
and drank in my words as
the spring rain.
[24]When I smiled at them, they
scarcely believed it;
the light of my face was
precious to them.[e]
[25]I chose the way for them and
sat as their chief;
I dwelt as a king among his
troops;
I was like one who comforts
mourners.

30 "But now they mock me,
men younger than I,
whose fathers I would have
disdained
to put with my sheep dogs.
[2]Of what use was the strength

[e]24 The meaning of the Hebrew for this clause is uncertain.

*11 Most mss have *bireq* under the *yod* (יִ–).

יְדֵיהֶם לָמָּה לִּי עָלֵימוֹ אָבַד כָּלַח׃ בְּחֶסֶר
from-want (3) vigor he-went from-them to-me what? hands-of-them

וּבְכָפָן גַּלְמוּד הַעֹרְקִים צִיָּה אֶמֶשׁ שׁוֹאָה
desolation night parched-land the-ones-roaming haggard and-from-hunger

וּמְשֹׁאָה׃ הַקֹּטְפִים מַלּוּחַ עֲלֵי־ שִׂיחַ וְשֹׁרֶשׁ
and-root-of brush in salt-herb the-ones-gathering (4) and-wasteland

רְתָמִים לַחְמָם׃ מִן־ גֵּו יְגֹרָשׁוּ יָרִיעוּ
they-shouted they-were-banished fellowship from (5) food-of-them broom-trees

עָלֵימוֹ כַּגַּנָּב׃ בַּעֲרוּץ נְחָלִים לִשְׁכֹּן חֹרֵי עָפָר
ground holes-of to-live stream-beds in-dryness-of (6) as-the-thief at-them

וְכֵפִים׃ בֵּין־ שִׂיחִים יִנְהָקוּ תַּחַת חָרוּל יְסֻפָּחוּ׃
they-huddled underbrush under they-brayed bushes among (7) and-rocks

בְּנֵי־ נָבָל גַּם־ בְּנֵי בְלִי־ שֵׁם נִכְּאוּ מִן־
from they-were-driven name without broods-of and baseness broods-of (8)

הָאָרֶץ׃ וְעַתָּה נְגִינָתָם הָיִיתִי וָאֱהִי לָהֶם
among-them and-I-became I-am mocking-song-of-them and-now (9) the-land

לְמִלָּה׃ תִּעֲבוּנִי רָחֲקוּ מֶנִּי וּמִפָּנַי
and-in-faces-of-me from-me they-keep-distance they-detest-me (10) as-byword

לֹא־ חָשְׂכוּ רֹק׃ כִּי־ יִתְרָו° פִּתַּח וַיְעַנֵּנִי
and-he-afflicted-me he-unstrung bow-of-me now (11) spit they-hesitate not

וְרֶסֶן מִפָּנַי שִׁלֵּחוּ׃ עַל־ יָמִין פִּרְחַח
tribe right on (12) they-throw-off in-presences-of-me and-restraint

יָקוּמוּ רַגְלַי שִׁלֵּחוּ וַיָּסֹלּוּ עָלַי אָרְחוֹת
ramps-of against-me and-they-build they-lay-snare feet-of-me they-attack

אֵידָם׃ נָתְסוּ נְתִיבָתִי לְהַוָּתִי־ יֹעִילוּ
they-succeed in-destruction-of-me road-of-me they-break-up (13) siege-of-them

לֹא עֹזֵר לָמוֹ׃ כְּפֶרֶץ רָחָב יֶאֱתָיוּ תַּחַת שֹׁאָה
ruin amid they-advance gaping as-breach (14) to-them one-helping not

הִתְגַּלְגָּלוּ׃ הָהְפַּךְ עָלַי בַּלָּהוֹת תִּרְדֹּף כָּרוּחַ
like-the-wind she-drives-away terrors over-me he-is-overwhelmed (15) they-roll-in

נְדִבָתִי וּכְעָב עָבְרָה יְשֻׁעָתִי׃ וְעַתָּה עָלַי
from-me and-now (16) safety-of-me she-vanishes and-like-cloud dignity-of-me

תִּשְׁתַּפֵּךְ נַפְשִׁי יֹאחֲזוּנִי יְמֵי־ עֹנִי׃ לַיְלָה
night (17) suffering-of-me days-of they-grip-me life-of-me she-ebbs-away

עֲצָמַי נִקַּר מֵעָלָי וְעֹרְקַי לֹא יִשְׁכָּבוּן׃
they-rest never and-ones-gnawing-me from-upon-me he-pierces bones-of-me

בְּרָב־ כֹּחַ יִתְחַפֵּשׂ לְבוּשִׁי כְּפִי
like-neck-of clothing-of-me he-becomes-like power in-greatness-of (18)

of their hands to me,
since their vigor had gone
from them?
3 Haggard from want and
hunger,
they roamed[f] the parched
land
in desolate wastelands at
night.
4 In the brush they gathered salt
herbs,
and their food[g] was the root
of the broom tree.
5 They were banished from their
fellow men,
shouted at as if they were
thieves.
6 They were forced to live in the
dry stream beds,
among the rocks and in
holes in the ground.
7 They brayed among the
bushes
and huddled in the
underbrush.
8 A base and nameless brood,
they were driven out of the
land.

9 "And now their sons mock me
in song;
I have become a byword
among them.
10 They detest me and keep their
distance;
they do not hesitate to spit
in my face.
11 Now that God has unstrung
my bow and afflicted me,
they throw off restraint in
my presence.
12 On my right the tribe[h] attacks;
they lay snares for my feet,
they build their siege ramps
against me.
13 They break up my road;
they succeed in destroying
me—
without anyone's helping
them.[i]
14 They advance as through a
gaping breach;
amid the ruins they come
rolling in.
15 Terrors overwhelm me;
my dignity is driven away
as by the wind,
my safety vanishes like a
cloud.

16 "And now my life ebbs away;
days of suffering grip me.
17 Night pierces my bones;
my gnawing pains never
rest.
18 In his great power ⌊God⌋
becomes like clothing to
me[j];

f3 Or *gnawed* g4 Or *fuel*
h12 The meaning of the Hebrew for this word is uncertain.
i13 Or *me.* / *'No one can help him,' ⌊they say⌋.*
j18 Hebrew; Septuagint *⌊God⌋ grasps my clothing*

°11 ק יתרי

כֻּתָּנְתִּי יַאַזְרֵנִי׃ הֹרָנִי לַחֹמֶר וָאֶתְמַשֵּׁל
and-I-am-reduced into-the-mud he-throws-me (19) he-binds-me garment-of-me

כֶּעָפָר וָאֵפֶר׃ אֲשַׁוַּע אֵלֶיךָ וְלֹא תַעֲנֵנִי עָמַדְתִּי
I-stand-up you-answer-me but-not to-you I-cry-out (20) and-ash to-the-dust

וַתִּתְבֹּנֶן בִּי׃ תֵּהָפֵךְ לְאַכְזָר לִי בְּעֹצֶם
with-might-of on-me with-ruthlessness you-turn (21) at-me but-you-look

יָדְךָ תִשְׂטְמֵנִי׃ תִּשָּׂאֵנִי אֶל־רוּחַ תַּרְכִּיבֵנִי
you-drive-me wind before you-snatch-up-me (22) you-attack-me hand-of-you

וּתְמֹגְגֵנִי תְּשֻׁוָּה׃ כִּי־יָדַעְתִּי מָוֶת תְּשִׁיבֵנִי
you-will-bring-down-me death I-know for (23) storm and-you-toss-about-me

וּבֵית מוֹעֵד לְכָל־חָי׃ אַךְ לֹא־בְעִי
on-broken-man no-one surely (24) living for-all-of appointed and-place-of

יִשְׁלַח־יָד אִם־בְּפִידוֹ לָהֶן שׁוּעַ׃ אִם־לֹא
not indeed (25) cry-for-help to-them in-distress-of-him when hand he-lays

בָכִיתִי לִקְשֵׁה־יוֹם עָגְמָה נַפְשִׁי לָאֶבְיוֹן׃ כִּי
when (26) for-the-poor soul-of-me she-grieved day for-troubled-of I-wept

טוֹב קִוִּיתִי וַיָּבֹא רָע וַאֲיַחֲלָה לְאוֹר וַיָּבֹא
then-he-came for-light when-I-looked evil then-he-came I-hoped-for good

אֹפֶל׃ מֵעַי רֻתְּחוּ וְלֹא־דָמּוּ קִדְּמֻנִי
they-confront-me they-stop and-never they-churn insides-of-me (27) darkness

יְמֵי־עֹנִי׃ קֹדֵר הִלַּכְתִּי בְּלֹא חַמָּה קַמְתִּי
I-stand-up sun by-not I-go-about being-blackened (28) suffering-of-me days-of

בַקָּהָל אֲשַׁוֵּעַ׃ אָח הָיִיתִי לְתַנִּים וְרֵעַ
and-companion of-jackals I-became brother (29) I-cry-for-help in-the-assembly

לִבְנוֹת יַעֲנָה׃ עוֹרִי שָׁחַר מֵעָלָי וְעַצְמִי־
and-body-of-me from-on-me she-grows-black skin-of-me (30) owl to-daughters-of

חָרָה מִנִּי־חֹרֶב׃ וַיְהִי לְאֵבֶל כִּנֹּרִי וְעֻגָבִי
and-flute-of-me harp-of-me to-mourning and-he-is (31) fever with she-burns

לְקוֹל בֹּכִים׃ בְּרִית כָּרַתִּי לְעֵינָי וּמָה
so-how? with-eyes-of-me I-made covenant (31:1) ones-wailing to-sound-of

אֶתְבּוֹנֵן עַל־בְּתוּלָה׃ וּמֶה ׀ חֵלֶק אֱלוֹהַּ מִמָּעַל וְנַחֲלַת
and-heritage-of from-above God lot-of for-what? (2) girl at can-I-look

שַׁדַּי מִמְּרֹמִים׃ הֲלֹא־אֵיד לְעַוָּל וְנֵכֶר לְפֹעֲלֵי
for-ones-doing-of and-disaster for-wicked ruin not? (3) from-heights Almighty

אָוֶן׃ הֲלֹא־הוּא יִרְאֶה דְרָכָי וְכָל־צְעָדַי יִסְפּוֹר׃
he-counts steps-of-me and-every-of ways-of-me he-sees he not? (4) wrong

אִם־הָלַכְתִּי עִם־שָׁוְא וַתַּחַשׁ עַל־מִרְמָה רַגְלִי׃
foot-of-me deceit after or-she-hurried falsehood in I-walked if (5)

he binds me like the neck of
my garment.
19 He throws me into the mud,
and I am reduced to dust
and ashes.

20 "I cry out to you, O God, but
you do not answer;
I stand up, but you merely
look at me.
21 You turn on me ruthlessly;
with the might of your hand
you attack me.
22 You snatch me up and drive
me before the wind;
you toss me about in the
storm.
23 I know you will bring me
down to death,
to the place appointed for all
the living.

24 "Surely no one lays a hand on
a broken man
when he cries for help in
his distress.
25 Have I not wept for those in
trouble?
Has not my soul grieved for
the poor?
26 Yet when I hoped for good,
evil came;
when I looked for light,
then came darkness.
27 The churning inside me never
stops;
days of suffering confront
me.
28 I go about blackened, but not
by the sun;
I stand up in the assembly
and cry for help.
29 I have become a brother of
jackals,
a companion of owls.
30 My skin grows black and
peels;
my body burns with fever.
31 My harp is tuned to mourning,
and my flute to the sound of
wailing.

31 "I made a covenant with
my eyes
not to look lustfully at a girl.
2 For what is man's lot from
God above,
his heritage from the
Almighty on high?
3 Is it not ruin for the wicked,
disaster for those who do
wrong?
4 Does he not see my ways
and count my every step?

5 "If I have walked in falsehood
or my foot has hurried after
deceit—

°22 ק תושיה

יִשְׁקְלֵנִי בְמֹאזְנֵי־צֶדֶק וְיֵדַע אֱלוֹהַּ
God and-he-will-know honesty in-scales-of let-him-weigh-me (6)

תֻּמָּתִי׃ אִם תִּטֶּה אַשֻּׁרִי מִנִּי הַדָּרֶךְ וְאַחַר
if-after the-path from step-of-me she-turned if (7) blamelessness-of-me

עֵינַי הָלַךְ לִבִּי וּבְכַפַּי דָּבַק מְאוּם׃
defilement he-clings if-to-hands-of-me heart-of-me he-followed eyes-of-me

אֶזְרְעָה וְאַחֵר יֹאכֵל וְצֶאֱצָאַי יְשֹׁרָשׁוּ׃ אִם־
if (9) may-they-be-uprooted and-crops-of-me may-he-eat but-other I-sow (8)

נִפְתָּה לִבִּי עַל־אִשָּׁה וְעַל־פֶּתַח רֵעִי אָרָבְתִּי׃
I-lurked neighbor-of-me door-of or-at woman by heart-of-me he-was-enticed

תִּטְחַן לְאַחֵר אִשְׁתִּי וְעָלֶיהָ יִכְרְעוּן אֲחֵרִין׃
others may-they-sleep and-with-her wife-of-me for-another may-she-grind (10)

כִּי־הוּא זִמָּה וְהִיא עָוֺן פְּלִילִים׃ כִּי אֵשׁ הִיא עַד־אֲבַדּוֹן
Abaddon to she fire for (12) judgments sin and-that shameful that for (11)

תֹּאכֵל וּבְכָל־תְּבוּאָתִי תְשָׁרֵשׁ׃ אִם־אֶמְאַס
I-denied if (13) she-would-uproot harvest-of-me and-to-all-of she-burns

מִשְׁפַּט עַבְדִּי וַאֲמָתִי בְּרִבָם
when-grievance-of-them and-maidservant-of-me manservant-of-me justice-of

עִמָּדִי׃ וּמָה אֶעֱשֶׂה כִּי־יָקוּם אֵל וְכִי־יִפְקֹד
he-calls and-when God he-confronts when will-I-do then-what? (14) against-me

מָה אֲשִׁיבֶנּוּ׃ הֲלֹא־בַבֶּטֶן עֹשֵׂנִי עָשָׂהוּ
he-made-him one-making-me in-the-womb not? (15) will-I-answer-him what?

וַיְכֻנֶנּוּ בָּרֶחֶם אֶחָד׃ אִם־אֶמְנַע מֵחֵפֶץ דַּלִּים
poor-ones from-desire-of I-denied if (16) same in-the-womb and-he-formed-us

וְעֵינֵי אַלְמָנָה אֲכַלֶּה׃ וְאֹכַל פִּתִּי לְבַדִּי וְלֹא־
and-not by-myself bread-of-me if-I-ate (17) I-let-grow-weary widow or-eyes-of

אָכַל יָתוֹם מִמֶּנָּה׃ כִּי מִנְּעוּרַי גְּדֵלַנִי כְאָב
as-father he-was-reared-by-me from-youths-of-me but (18) of-her fatherless he-ate

וּמִבֶּטֶן אִמִּי אַנְחֶנָּה׃ אִם־אֶרְאֶה אוֹבֵד
one-perishing I-saw if (19) I-guided-her mother-of-me and-from-womb-of

מִבְּלִי לְבוּשׁ וְאֵין כְּסוּת לָאֶבְיוֹן׃ אִם־לֹא
not if (20) to-the-needy-man garment or-no clothing from-lack-of

בֵרְכוּנִי חֲלָצָו וּמִגֵּז כְּבָשַׂי יִתְחַמָּם׃
he-was-warmed sheeps-of-me or-with-fleece-of hearts-of-him they-blessed-me

אִם־הֲנִיפוֹתִי עַל־יָתוֹם יָדִי כִּי־אֶרְאֶה בַשַּׁעַר
in-the-court I-knew when hand-of-me fatherless against I-raised if (21)

עֶזְרָתִי׃ כְּתֵפִי מִשִּׁכְמָה תִפּוֹל וְאֶזְרֹעִי
and-arm-of-me let-her-fall from-shoulder arm-of-me (22) influence-of-me

6let God weigh me in honest scales
and he will know that I am blameless—
7if my steps have turned from the path,
if my heart has been led by my eyes,
or if my hands have been defiled,
8then may others eat what I have sown,
and may my crops be uprooted.

9"If my heart has been enticed by a woman,
or if I have lurked at my neighbor's door,
10then may my wife grind another man's grain,
and may other men sleep with her.
11For that would have been shameful,
a sin to be judged.
12It is a fire that burns to Destruction[k];
it would have uprooted my harvest.

13"If I have denied justice to my menservants and maidservants
when they had a grievance against me,
14what will I do when God confronts me?
What will I answer when called to account?
15Did not he who made me in the womb make them?
Did not the same one form us both within our mothers?

16"If I have denied the desires of the poor
or let the eyes of the widow grow weary,
17if I have kept my bread to myself,
not sharing it with the fatherless—
18but from my youth I reared him as would a father,
and from my birth I guided the widow—
19if I have seen anyone perishing for lack of clothing,
or a needy man without a garment,
20and his heart did not bless me
for warming him with the fleece from my sheep,
21if I have raised my hand against the fatherless,
knowing that I had influence in court,
22then let my arm fall from the shoulder,

[k]12 Hebrew *Abaddon*

*7 Most mss have no *qibbuts* under the *mem* (מְאוּם)

°11a ק היא
°11b ק והוא
°20 ק חלציו

מִקָּנָה תִּשָּׁבֵר׃ כִּי פַחַד אֵלַי אֵיד אֵל
God destruction-of to-me dread for (23) let-her-be-broken-off at-joint

וּמִשְּׂאֵתוֹ לֹא אוּכָל׃ אִם־שַׂמְתִּי זָהָב כִּסְלִי
trust-of-me gold I-put if (24) I-could-do not and-because-of-splendor-of-him

וְלַכֶּתֶם אָמַרְתִּי מִבְטַחִי׃ אִם־אֶשְׂמַח כִּי־רַב
great that I-rejoiced if (25) security-of-me I-said or-to-the-pure-gold

חֵילִי וְכִי־כַבִּיר מָצְאָה יָדִי׃ אִם־אֶרְאֶה אוֹר
sun I-regarded if (26) hand-of-me she-gained fortune and-that wealth-of-me

כִּי יָהֵל וְיָרֵחַ יָקָר הֹלֵךְ׃ וַיִּפְתְּ
so-he-was-enticed (27) moving splendor or-moon he-was-radiant that

בַּסֵּתֶר לִבִּי וַתִּשַּׁק יָדִי לְפִי׃
to-mouth-of-me hand-of-me and-she-kissed heart-of-me in-the-secret

גַּם־הוּא עָוֺן פְּלִילִי כִּי־כִחַשְׁתִּי לָאֵל מִמָּעַל׃
on-high to-God I-would-be-unfaithful for judgment sin this also (28)

אִם־אֶשְׂמַח בְּפִיד מְשַׂנְאִי וְהִתְעֹרַרְתִּי כִּי־
that or-I-gloated one-being-enemy-of-me at-misfortune-of I-rejoiced if (29)

מְצָאוֹ רָע׃ וְלֹא־נָתַתִּי לַחֲטֹא חִכִּי לִשְׁאֹל
to-invoke mouth-of-me to-sin I-allowed now-not (30) trouble he-came-to-him

בְאָלָה נַפְשׁוֹ׃ אִם־לֹא אָמְרוּ מְתֵי אָהֳלִי מִי־
who? house-of-me men-of they-said never if (31) life-of-him to-curse

יִתֵּן מִבְּשָׂרוֹ לֹא נִשְׂבָּע׃ בַּחוּץ לֹא־
not in-the-street (32) he-had-fill not from-meat-of-him he-would-give

יָלִין גֵּר דְּלָתַי לָאֹרַח* אֶפְתָּח׃ אִם־כִּסִּיתִי
I-concealed if (33) I-opened *to-the-road doors-of-me stranger he-spent-night

כְאָדָם פְּשָׁעָי לִטְמוֹן בְּחֻבִּי עֲוֺנִי׃ כִּי אֶעֱרוֹץ ׀
I-feared because (34) guilt-of-me in-heart-of-me to-hide sins-of-me as-man

הָמוֹן רַבָּה וּבוּז־מִשְׁפָּחוֹת יְחִתֵּנִי וָאֶדֹּם לֹא־
not that-I-kept-silent he-made-dread-me clans and-contempt-of greatly crowd

אֵצֵא פָתַח׃ מִי יִתֶּן־לִי ׀ שֹׁמֵעַ לִי הֶן־
see! to-me one-hearing to-me he-would-give who? (35) door I-went-out

תָּוִי שַׁדַּי יַעֲנֵנִי וְסֵפֶר כָּתַב
let-him-write and-indictment let-him-answer-me Almighty signature-of-me

אִישׁ רִיבִי׃ אִם־לֹא עַל־שִׁכְמִי אֶשָּׂאֶנּוּ
I-would-wear-him shoulder-of-me on surely indeed (36) accusation-of-me man-of

אֶעֶנְדֶנּוּ עֲטָרוֹת לִי׃ מִסְפַּר צְעָדַי אַגִּידֶנּוּ
I-would-give-him steps-of-me account-of (37) on-me crowns I-would-put-on-him

כְּמוֹ־נָגִיד אֲקָרְבֶנּוּ׃ אִם־עָלַי אַדְמָתִי תִזְעָק
she-cries-out land-of-me against-me if (38) I-would-approach-him prince like

let it be broken off at the joint.
23 For I dreaded destruction from God,
and for fear of his splendor I could not do such things.

24 "If I have put my trust in gold
or said to pure gold, 'You are my security,'
25 if I have rejoiced over my great wealth,
the fortune my hands had gained,
26 if I have regarded the sun in its radiance
or the moon moving in splendor,
27 so that my heart was secretly enticed
and my hand offered them a kiss of homage,
28 then these also would be sins to be judged,
for I would have been unfaithful to God on high.

29 "If I have rejoiced at my enemy's misfortune
or gloated over the trouble that came to him—
30 I have not allowed my mouth to sin
by invoking a curse against his life—
31 if the men of my household have never said,
'Who has not had his fill of Job's meat?'—
32 but no stranger had to spend the night in the street,
for my door was always open to the traveler—
33 if I have concealed my sin as men do,[l]
by hiding my guilt in my heart
34 because I so feared the crowd
and so dreaded the contempt of the clans
that I kept silent and would not go outside

35 ("Oh, that I had someone to hear me!
I sign now my defense—let the Almighty answer me;
let my accuser put his indictment in writing.
36 Surely I would wear it on my shoulder,
I would put it on like a crown.
37 I would give him an account of my every step;
like a prince I would approach him.)—

38 "if my land cries out against me

[l] 33 *Or as Adam did*

*32 The NIV repoints the word as לָאֹרֵחַ, *to-the-one-traveling.*

וְיַחַד תְּלָמֶיהָ יִבְכָּיוּן׃ אִם־ כֹּחָהּ אָכַלְתִּי
I-devoured yield-of-her if (39) they-weep furrows-of-her and-together

בְלִי־ כֶסֶף וְנֶפֶשׁ בְּעָלֶיהָ הִפָּחְתִּי׃ תַּחַת חִטָּה
wheat instead-of (40) I-broke tenants-of-her or-spirit-of payment without

יֵצֵא חוֹחַ וְתַחַת־ שְׂעֹרָה בָאְשָׁה תַּמּוּ דִּבְרֵי אִיּוֹב׃
Job words-of they-are-ended weed barley and-instead-of brier let-him-come-up

וַיִּשְׁבְּתוּ שְׁלֹשֶׁת הָאֲנָשִׁים הָאֵלֶּה מֵעֲנוֹת אֶת־אִיּוֹב
Job *** from-to-answer the-these the-men three-of so-they-stopped (32:1)

כִּי הוּא צַדִּיק בְּעֵינָיו׃ וַיִּחַר אַף אֱלִיהוּא
Elihu anger-of but-he-burned (2) in-eyes-of-him righteous he because

בֶּן־ בַּרַכְאֵל הַבּוּזִי מִמִּשְׁפַּחַת רָם בְּאִיּוֹב חָרָה אַפּוֹ
anger-of-him he-burned against-Job Ram of-family-of the-Buzite Barakel son-of

עַל־ צַדְּקוֹ נַפְשׁוֹ מֵאֱלֹהִים׃ וּבִשְׁלֹשֶׁת
also-against-three-of (93) rather-than-God self-of-him to-justify-him because

רֵעָיו חָרָה אַפּוֹ עַל אֲשֶׁר לֹא־ מָצְאוּ מַעֲנֶה
refutation they-found not that because anger-of-him he-burned friends-of-him

וַיַּרְשִׁיעוּ אֶת־אִיּוֹב׃ וֶאֱלִיהוּ חִכָּה אֶת־אִיּוֹב בִּדְבָרִים
with-speeches Job *** he-waited now-Elihu (4) Job *** yet-they-condemned

כִּי זְקֵנִים־ הֵמָּה מִמֶּנּוּ לְיָמִים׃ וַיַּרְא אֱלִיהוּא כִּי אֵין
no that Elihu when-he-saw (5) in-days more-than-he they ones-old because

מַעֲנֶה בְּפִי שְׁלֹשֶׁת הָאֲנָשִׁים וַיִּחַר אַפּוֹ׃
anger-of-him then-he-was-aroused the-men three-of in-mouth-of saying

וַיַּעַן אֱלִיהוּא בֶן־ בַּרַכְאֵל הַבּוּזִי וַיֹּאמַר צָעִיר אֲנִי
I young and-he-said the-Buzite Barakel son-of Elihu so-he-responded (6)

לְיָמִים וְאַתֶּם יְשִׁישִׁים עַל־ כֵּן זָחַלְתִּי וָאִירָא מֵחַוֺּת
from-to-tell and-I-feared I-was-afraid this for old-ones and-you in-days

דֵּעִי אֶתְכֶם׃ אָמַרְתִּי יָמִים יְדַבֵּרוּ וְרֹב שָׁנִים
years and-many-of they-should-speak days I-thought (7) you knowledge-of-me

יֹדִיעוּ חָכְמָה׃ אָכֵן רוּחַ־ הִיא בֶאֱנוֹשׁ וְנִשְׁמַת שַׁדַּי
Almighty even-breath-of in-man she spirit but (8) wisdom they-should-teach

תְּבִינֵם׃ לֹא־ רַבִּים יֶחְכָּמוּ וּזְקֵנִים
nor-aged-ones they-are-wise many not (9) she-gives-understanding-to-them

יָבִינוּ מִשְׁפָּט׃ לָכֵן אָמַרְתִּי שִׁמְעָה־ לִּי אֲחַוֶּה
I-will-tell to-me listen! I-say therefore (10) right they-understand

דֵעִי אַף־אָנִי׃ הֵן הוֹחַלְתִּי לְדִבְרֵיכֶם אָזִין
I-listened through-speeches-of-you I-waited see! (11) I also knowledge-of-me

עַד־ תְּבוּנֹתֵיכֶם עַד־ תַּחְקְרוּן מִלִּין׃ וְעָדֵיכֶם
and-to-you (12) words you-searched-for while reasonings-of-you to

---

and all its furrows are wet
with tears,
39 if I have devoured its yield
without payment
or broken the spirit of its
tenants,
40 then let briers come up instead
of wheat
and weeds instead of
barley."

The words of Job are ended.

*Elihu*

32 So these three men stopped
answering Job, because he
was righteous in his own eyes.
2 But Elihu son of Barakel the Bu-
zite, of the family of Ram, became
very angry with Job for justifying
himself rather than God. 3 He was
also angry with the three friends,
because they had found no way to
refute Job, and yet had condemned him.[m] 4 Now Elihu had
waited before speaking to Job because they were older than he.
5 But when he saw that the three
men had nothing more to say, his
anger was aroused.
6 So Elihu son of Barakel the Bu-
zite said:

"I am young in years,
and you are old;
that is why I was fearful,
not daring to tell you what I
know.
7 I thought, 'Age should speak;
advanced years should teach
wisdom.'
8 But it is the spirit[n] in a man,
the breath of the Almighty,
that gives him
understanding.
9 It is not only the old[o] who are
wise,
not only the aged who
understand what is right.

10 "Therefore I say: Listen to me;
I too will tell you what I
know.
11 I waited while you spoke,
I listened to your reasoning;
while you were searching for
words,

m3 Masoretic Text; an ancient Hebrew scribal tradition *Job, and so had condemned God*
n8 Or *Spirit;* also in verse 18
o9 Or *many;* or *great*

אֶתְבּוֹנָן וְהִנֵּה אֵין לְאִיּוֹב מוֹכִיחַ עוֹנֶה
answering proving-wrong to-Job no-one but-see! I-gave-attention

אֲמָרָיו מִכֶּם: (13) פֶּן־ תֹּאמְרוּ מָצָאנוּ חָכְמָה אֵל
God wisdom we-found you-say not (13) of-you arguments-of-him

יִדְּפֶנּוּ לֹא־ אִישׁ: (14) וְלֹא־ עָרַךְ אֵלַי מִלִּין
words against-me he-marshaled but-not (14) man not let-him-refute-him

וּבְאִמְרֵיכֶם לֹא אֲשִׁיבֶנּוּ: (15) חַתּוּ לֹא־
not they-are-dismayed (15) I-will-answer-him not and-with-arguments-of-you

עָנוּ עוֹד הֶעְתִּיקוּ מֵהֶם מִלִּים: (16) וְהוֹחַלְתִּי כִּי־ לֹא
not because now-must-I-wait (16) words from-them they-failed more they-say

יְדַבֵּרוּ כִּי עָמְדוּ לֹא־ עָנוּ עוֹד: (17) אַעֲנֶה אַף־אֲנִי
I also I-will-say (17) more they-reply not they-stand because they-speak

חֶלְקִי אֲחַוֶּה דֵעִי אַף־אָנִי: (18) כִּי מָלֵתִי מִלִּים
words I-am-full for (18) I also knowledge-of-me I-will-tell portion-of-me

הֱצִיקַתְנִי רוּחַ בִּטְנִי: (19) הִנֵּה־ בִטְנִי כְּיַיִן לֹא־
not like-wine inside-of-me see! (19) inside-of-me spirit-of she-compels-me

יִפָּתֵחַ כְּאֹבוֹת חֲדָשִׁים יִבָּקֵעַ: (20) אֲדַבְּרָה
I-must-speak (20) he-bursts new-ones like-wineskins he-is-open

וְיִרְוַח־ לִי אֶפְתַּח שְׂפָתַי וְאֶעֱנֶה: (21) אַל־
not (21) and-I-must-reply lips-of-me I-must-open to-me and-he-will-relieve

נָא אֶשָּׂא פְנֵי־ אִישׁ וְאֶל־ אָדָם לֹא אֲכַנֶּה:
I-will-flatter not man or-to man faces-of I-will-show-partiality now!

(22) כִּי לֹא יָדַעְתִּי אֲכַנֶּה כִּמְעַט יִשָּׂאֵנִי
he-would-take-away-me as-soon I-can-flatter I-am-skilled not for (22)

עֹשֵׂנִי: (33:1) וְאוּלָם שְׁמַע־ נָא אִיּוֹב מִלָּי וְכָל־
and-all-of words-of-me Job now! listen! but-now (33:1) One-Making-me

דְּבָרַי הַאֲזִינָה: (2) הִנֵּה־ נָא פָּתַחְתִּי פִי דִּבְּרָה
she-speaks mouth-of-me I-open now! see! (2) pay-attention! sayings-of-me

לְשׁוֹנִי בְחִכִּי: (3) יֹשֶׁר־ לִבִּי אֲמָרָי
words-of-me heart-of-me uprightness-of (3) in-mouth-of-me tongue-of-me

וְדַעַת שְׂפָתַי בָּרוּר מִלֵּלוּ: (4) רוּחַ־ אֵל
God Spirit-of (4) they-speak being-sincere lips-of-me and-knowledge-of

עָשָׂתְנִי וְנִשְׁמַת שַׁדַּי תְּחַיֵּנִי: (5) אִם־ תּוּכַל
you-can if (5) she-gives-life-to-me Almighty and-breath-of she-made-me

הֲשִׁיבֵנִי עֶרְכָה לְפָנַי הִתְיַצָּבָה: (6) הֵן־אֲנִי כְפִיךָ
like-mouth-of-you I see! (6) prepare-yourself! before-me confront! answer-me!

לָאֵל מֵחֹמֶר קֹרַצְתִּי גַם־ אָנִי: (7) הִנֵּה אֵמָתִי לֹא
not fear-of-me see! (7) I also I-was-taken from-clay before-God

12 I gave you my full attention.
But not one of you has proved Job wrong;
none of you has answered his arguments.
13 Do not say, 'We have found wisdom;
let God refute him, not man.'
14 But Job has not marshaled his words against me,
and I will not answer him with your arguments.

15 "They are dismayed and have no more to say;
words have failed them.
16 Must I wait, now that they are silent,
now that they stand there with no reply?
17 I too will have my say;
I too will tell what I know.
18 For I am full of words,
and the spirit within me compels me;
19 inside I am like bottled-up wine,
like new wineskins ready to burst.
20 I must speak and find relief;
I must open my lips and reply.
21 I will show partiality to no one,
nor will I flatter any man;
22 for if I were skilled in flattery,
my Maker would soon take me away.

33 "But now, Job, listen to my words;
pay attention to everything I say.
2 I am about to open my mouth;
my words are on the tip of my tongue.
3 My words come from an upright heart;
my lips sincerely speak what I know.
4 The Spirit of God has made me;
the breath of the Almighty gives me life.
5 Answer me then, if you can;
prepare yourself and confront me.
6 I am just like you before God;
I too have been taken from clay.
7 No fear of me should alarm you,

תְבַעֲתֶךָ וְאַכְפִּי עָלֶיךָ לֹא־ יִכְבָּד׃
he-should-be-heavy not upon-you or-hand-of-me she-should-alarm-you

אַךְ אָמַרְתָּ בְאָזְנָי וְקוֹל מִלִּין אֶשְׁמָע׃ זַךְ אֲנִי
I pure (9) I-heard words and-sound-of in-ears-of-me you-said but (8)

בְּלִי פָשַׁע חַף אָנֹכִי וְלֹא עָוֹן לִי׃ הֵן תְּנוּאוֹת עָלַי יִמְצָא
he-found with-me faults yet (10) to-me guilt and-not I clean sin without

יַחְשְׁבֵנִי לְאוֹיֵב לוֹ׃ יָשֵׂם בַּסַּד רַגְלָי
feet-of-me in-the-shackle he-fastens (11) of-him as-being-enemy he-considers-me

יִשְׁמֹר כָּל־ אָרְחֹתָי׃ הֶן־ זֹאת לֹא־ צָדַקְתָּ אֶעֱנֶךָּ
I-tell-you you-are-right not this but (12) paths-of-me all-of he-watches

כִּי־ יִרְבֶּה אֱלוֹהַּ* מֵאֱנוֹשׁ׃ מַדּוּעַ אֵלָיו רִיבוֹתָ כִּי כָל־
any-of that you-complain to-him why? (13) more-than-man God he-is-great for

דְּבָרָיו לֹא־ יַעֲנֶה׃ כִּי־ בְאַחַת יְדַבֶּר־ אֵל וּבִשְׁתַּיִם לֹא
not now-in-two God he-speaks in-one for (14) he-answers not words-of-him

יְשׁוּרֶנָּה׃ בַּחֲלוֹם ׀ חֶזְיוֹן לַיְלָה בִּנְפֹל תַּרְדֵּמָה עַל־
on deep-sleep when-to-fall night vision-of in-dream (15) he-perceives-her

אֲנָשִׁים בִּתְנוּמוֹת עֲלֵי מִשְׁכָּב׃ אָז יִגְלֶה אֹזֶן אֲנָשִׁים וּבְמֹסָרָם
and-with-warning-of-them men ear-of he-may-open then (16) bed in in-slumbers men

יַחְתֹּם† לְהָסִיר אָדָם מַעֲשֶׂה וְגֵוָה מִגֶּבֶר יְכַסֶּה׃
he-keeps from-man and-pride deed man to-turn (17) †he-may-seal

יַחְשֹׂךְ נַפְשׁוֹ מִנִּי־ שָׁחַת וְחַיָּתוֹ מֵעֲבֹר
from-to-perish and-life-of-him pit from soul-of-him he-preserves (18)

בַּשָּׁלַח׃ וְהוּכַח בְמַכְאוֹב עַל־ מִשְׁכָּבוֹ וְרִיב°
with-distress-of bed-of-him on by-pain or-he-is-chastened (19) by-the-sword

עֲצָמָיו אֵתָן׃ וְזִהֲמַתּוּ חַיָּתוֹ לָחֶם
food being-of-him so-she-finds-repulsive-him (20) constant bones-of-him

וְנַפְשׁוֹ מַאֲכַל תַּאֲוָה׃ יִכֶל בְּשָׂרוֹ מֵרֹאִי
from-sight flesh-of-him he-wastes-away (21) choice meal-of and-soul-of-him

וְשֻׁפִּי° עַצְמוֹתָיו לֹא רֻאוּ׃ וַתִּקְרַב
and-she-draws-near (22) they-were-seen not bones-of-him now-they-stick-out

לַשַּׁחַת נַפְשׁוֹ וְחַיָּתוֹ לַמְמִתִים׃ אִם־
if (23) to-the-ones-bringing-death and-life-of-him soul-of-him to-the-pit

יֵשׁ עָלָיו ׀ מַלְאָךְ מֵלִיץ אֶחָד מִנִּי־ אָלֶף לְהַגִּיד לְאָדָם
to-man to-tell thousand from one one-mediating angel beside-him there-is

יָשְׁרוֹ׃ וַיְחֻנֶּנּוּ וַיֹּאמֶר
and-he-should-say then-he-should-be-gracious-to-him (24) right-of-him

פְּדָעֵהוּ מֵרֶדֶת שַׁחַת מָצָאתִי כֹפֶר׃ רֻטֲפַשׁ
he-is-renewed (25) ransom I-found pit from-to-go-down spare-him!

nor should my hand be
heavy upon you.

8"But you have said in my
hearing—
I heard the very words—
9"I am pure and without sin;
I am clean and free from
guilt.
10Yet God has found fault with
me;
he considers me his enemy.
11He fastens my feet in shackles;
he keeps close watch on all
my paths.'

12"But I tell you, in this you are
not right,
for God is greater than man.
13Why do you complain to him
that he answers none of
man's words[p]?
14For God does speak—now one
way, now another—
though man may not
perceive it.
15In a dream, in a vision of the
night,
when deep sleep falls on
men
as they slumber in their
beds,
16he may speak in their ears
and terrify them with
warnings,
17to turn man from wrongdoing
and keep him from pride,
18to preserve his soul from the
pit,[q]
his life from perishing by
the sword.[r]
19Or a man may be chastened
on a bed of pain
with constant distress in his
bones,
20so that his very being finds
food repulsive
and his soul loathes the
choicest meal.
21His flesh wastes away to
nothing,
and his bones, once hidden,
now stick out.
22His soul draws near to the
pit,[s]
and his life to the
messengers of death.[t]

23"Yet if there is an angel on his
side
as a mediator, one out of a
thousand,
to tell a man what is right
for him,
24to be gracious to him and say,
'Spare him from going
down to the pit[u]';
I have found a ransom for
him'—
25then his flesh is renewed like

[p]13 *Or that he does not answer for any of his actions*
[q]18 *Or preserve him from the grave*
[r]18 *Or from crossing the River*
[s]22 *Or He draws near to the grave*
[t]22 *Or to the dead* [u]24 *Or grave*

*12 Most mss have *mappiq* in the *he* (הּ-).

†16 The NIV repoints this word as יְחִתֵּם, *he-may-terrify-them.*

°19 ק ורוב

°21 ק ושפו

בְּשָׂרוֹ מִנֹּעַר יָשׁוּב לִימֵי עֲלוּמָיו׃
youths-of-him to-days-of he-is-restored like-child flesh-of-him

יֶעְתַּר אֶל־אֱלוֹהַּ ׀ וַיִּרְצֵהוּ וַיַּרְא פָּנָיו
faces-of-him and-he-sees and-he-finds-favor-with-him God to he-prays (26)

בִּתְרוּעָה וַיָּשֶׁב לֶאֱנוֹשׁ צִדְקָתוֹ׃ יָשֹׁר ׀
he-comes (27) righteous-state-of-him to-man and-he-restores with-shout-of-joy

עַל־אֲנָשִׁים וַיֹּאמֶר חָטָאתִי וְיָשָׁר הֶעֱוֵיתִי וְלֹא־ שָׁוָה
he-gave-desert but-not I-perverted and-right I-sinned and-he-says men to

לִי׃ פָּדָה נַפְשִׁי מֵעֲבֹר בַּשָּׁחַת וְחַיָּתִי
and-life-of-me to-the-pit from-to-go-down soul-of-me he-redeemed (28) to-me

בָּאוֹר תִּרְאֶה׃ הֶן־ כָּל־ אֵלֶּה יִפְעַל־ אֵל פַּעֲמַיִם שָׁלוֹשׁ
thrice twice God he-does these all-of see! (29) she-will-see to-the-light

עִם־גָּבֶר׃ לְהָשִׁיב נַפְשׁוֹ מִנִּי־ שָׁחַת לֵאוֹר בְּאוֹר
by-light-of to-be-shined-on pit from soul-of-him to-turn-back (30) man to

הַחַיִּים*׃ הַקְשֵׁב אִיּוֹב שְׁמַע־ לִי הַחֲרֵשׁ וְאָנֹכִי אֲדַבֵּר׃
I-will-speak and-I be-silent! to-me listen! Job pay-attention! (31) the-lives

אִם־ יֶשׁ־ מִלִּין הֲשִׁיבֵנִי דַּבֵּר כִּי־ חָפַצְתִּי צַדְּקֶךָּ׃
to-clear-you I-want for speak-up! answer-me! words there-are if (32)

אִם־ אַיִן אַתָּה שְׁמַע־ לִי הַחֲרֵשׁ וַאֲאַלֶּפְךָ חָכְמָה׃
wisdom and-I-will-teach-you be-silent! to-me listen! you not if (33)

וַיַּעַן אֱלִיהוּא וַיֹּאמַר׃ שִׁמְעוּ חֲכָמִים מִלָּי
words-of-me wise-men hear! (2) and-he-said Elihu then-he-spoke (34:1)

וְיֹדְעִים הַאֲזִינוּ לִי׃ כִּי־ אֹזֶן מִלִּין תִּבְחָן וְחֵךְ
and-tongue she-tests words ear for (3) to-me listen! and-ones-learning

יִטְעַם לֶאֱכֹל׃ מִשְׁפָּט נִבְחֲרָה־ לָּנוּ נֵדְעָה בֵינֵינוּ מַה־
what among-us let-us-learn for-us let-us-discern right (4) to-eat he-tastes

טּוֹב׃ כִּי־ אָמַר אִיּוֹב צָדַקְתִּי וְאֵל הֵסִיר מִשְׁפָּטִי׃
justice-of-me he-denies but-God I-am-innocent Job he-says for (5) good

עַל־ מִשְׁפָּטִי אֲכַזֵּב אָנוּשׁ חִצִּי בְלִי־ פָשַׁע׃
guilt without arrow-of-me being-incurable I-lie right-of-me although (6)

מִי־ גֶבֶר כְּאִיּוֹב יִשְׁתֶּה־ לַּעַג כַּמָּיִם׃ וְאָרַח
and-he-keeps (8) like-the-waters scorn he-drinks like-Job man what? (7)

לְחֶבְרָה עִם־ פֹּעֲלֵי אָוֶן וְלָלֶכֶת עִם־ אַנְשֵׁי־ רֶשַׁע׃
wickedness men-of with and-to-associate evil ones-doing-of with in-company

כִּי־ אָמַר לֹא יִסְכָּן־ גָּבֶר בִּרְצֹתוֹ עִם־אֱלֹהִים׃ לָכֵן ׀
so (10) God to when-to-please-him man he-profits nothing he-says for (9)

אַנְשֵׁי לֵבָב שִׁמְעוּ לִי חָלִלָה לָאֵל מֵרֶשַׁע וְשַׁדַּי
and-Almighty from-evil from-God far-be-it! to-me listen! understanding men-of

a child's;
it is restored as in the days
of his youth.
26 He prays to God and finds
favor with him,
he sees God's face and
shouts for joy;
he is restored by God to his
righteous state.
27 Then he comes to men and
says,
'I sinned, and perverted
what was right,
but I did not get what I
deserved.
28 He redeemed my soul from
going down to the pit,[v]
and I will live to enjoy the
light.'

29 "God does all these things to a
man—
twice, even three times—
30 to turn back his soul from the
pit,[w]
that the light of life may
shine on him.

31 "Pay attention, Job, and listen
to me;
be silent, and I will speak.
32 If you have anything to say,
answer me;
speak up, for I want you to
be cleared.
33 But if not, then listen to me;
be silent, and I will teach
you wisdom."

## 34

Then Elihu said:
2 "Hear my words, you
wise men;
listen to me, you men of
learning.
3 For the ear tests words
as the tongue tastes food.
4 Let us discern for ourselves
what is right;
let us learn together what is
good.

5 "Job says, 'I am innocent,
but God denies me justice.
6 Although I am right,
I am considered a liar;
although I am guiltless,
his arrow inflicts an
incurable wound.'
7 What man is like Job,
who drinks scorn like water?
8 He keeps company with
evildoers;
he associates with wicked
men.
9 For he says, 'It profits a man
nothing
when he tries to please
God.'
10 "So listen to me, you men of
understanding.
Far be it from God to do
evil,
from the Almighty to do

v28 Or *redeemed me from going down to the grave*
w30 Or *turn him back from the grave*

*30 Most mss have the accent on the final syllable (הַחַיִּים).

°28a ק נפשו
°28b ק וחיתו

מֵעָוֶל׃ כִּי פֹעַל אָדָם יְשַׁלֶּם־ לוֹ וּכְאֹרַח אִישׁ

man and-as-conduct-of to-him he-repays man deed-of for (11) from-wrong

יַמְצִאֶנּוּ׃ אַף־ אָמְנָם אֵל לֹא־ יַרְשִׁיעַ וְשַׁדַּי לֹא־

not and-Almighty he-does-wrong not God indeed surely (12) he-brings-upon-him

יְעַוֵּת מִשְׁפָּט׃ מִי־ פָקַד עָלָיו אָרְצָה וּמִי

and-who? over-earth to-him he-appointed who? (13) justice he-perverts

שָׂם תֵּבֵל כֻּלָּהּ׃ אִם־ יָשִׂים אֵלָיו לִבּוֹ

heart-of-him to-him he-intended if (14) whole-of-her world he-put-in-charge

רוּחוֹ וְנִשְׁמָתוֹ אֵלָיו יֶאֱסֹף׃ יִגְוַע

he-would-perish (15) he-withdrew to-him and-breath-of-him spirit-of-him

כָּל־ בָּשָׂר יַחַד וְאָדָם עַל־ עָפָר יָשׁוּב׃ וְאִם־

and-if (16) he-would-return dust to and-man together mankind all-of

בִּינָה שִׁמְעָה־ זֹּאת הַאֲזִינָה לְקוֹל מִלָּי׃ הַאַף

indeed? (17) sayings-of-me to-sound-of listen! this hear! understanding

שׂוֹנֵא מִשְׁפָּט יַחֲבוֹשׁ וְאִם־ צַדִּיק כַּבִּיר תַּרְשִׁיעַ׃

will-you-condemn Mighty-One Just-One or-indeed can-he-govern justice one-hating

הַאֲמֹר לְמֶלֶךְ בְּלִיָּעַל רָשָׁע אֶל־ נְדִיבִים׃ אֲשֶׁר לֹא־

not who (19) nobles to wicked worthless to-king to-say? (18)

נָשָׂא ׀ פְּנֵי שָׂרִים וְלֹא נִכַּר־ שׁוֹעַ לִפְנֵי־ דָל כִּי־

for poor over rich he-favors and-not princes faces-of he-shows-partiality

מַעֲשֵׂה יָדָיו כֻּלָּם׃ רֶגַע ׀ יָמֻתוּ וַחֲצוֹת לָיְלָה

night and-middle-of they-die instant (20) all-of-them hands-of-him work-of

יְגֹעֲשׁוּ עָם וְיַעֲבֹרוּ וְיָסִירוּ אַבִּיר לֹא בְיָד׃

by-hand not mighty and-they-remove and-they-pass-away people they-are-shaken

כִּי־ עֵינָיו עַל־ דַּרְכֵי־ אִישׁ וְכָל־ צְעָדָיו יִרְאֶה׃

he-sees steps-of-him and-every-of man ways-of on eyes-of-him for (21)

אֵין־ חֹשֶׁךְ וְאֵין צַלְמָוֶת לְהִסָּתֶר שָׁם

there to-be-hidden deep-shadow and-there-is-no dark-place there-is-no (22)

פֹּעֲלֵי אָוֶן׃ כִּי לֹא עַל־אִישׁ יָשִׂים עוֹד לַהֲלֹךְ אֶל־

before to-come further he-examines man to not for (23) evil ones-doing-of

אֵל בַּמִּשְׁפָּט׃ יָרֹעַ כַּבִּירִים לֹא־ חֵקֶר

inquiry without mighty-ones he-shatters (24) for-the-judgment God

וַיַּעֲמֵד אֲחֵרִים תַּחְתָּם׃ לָכֵן יַכִּיר מַעְבָּדֵיהֶם

deeds-of-them he-notes because (25) in-place-of-them others and-he-sets-up

וְהָפַךְ לַיְלָה וְיִדַּכָּאוּ׃ תַּחַת־ רְשָׁעִים

wickednesses for (26) and-they-are-crushed night then-he-overthrows

סְפָקָם בִּמְקוֹם רֹאִים׃ אֲשֶׁר עַל־ כֵּן סָרוּ

they-turned that because for (27) ones-seeing in-place-of he-punishes-them

wrong.
11 He repays a man for what he
has done;
he brings upon him what
his conduct deserves.
12 It is unthinkable that God
would do wrong,
that the Almighty would
pervert justice.
13 Who appointed him over the
earth?
Who put him in charge of
the whole world?
14 If it were his intention
and he withdrew his spirit[x]
and breath,
15 all mankind would perish
together
and man would return to
the dust.

16 "If you have understanding,
hear this;
listen to what I say.
17 Can he who hates justice
govern?
Will you condemn the just
and mighty One?
18 Is he not the One who says to
kings, 'You are worthless,'
and to nobles, 'You are
wicked,'
19 who shows no partiality to
princes
and does not favor the rich
over the poor,
for they are all the work of
his hands?
20 They die in an instant, in the
middle of the night;
the people are shaken and
they pass away;
the mighty are removed
without human hand.

21 "His eyes are on the ways of
men;
he sees their every step.
22 There is no dark place, no
deep shadow,
where evildoers can hide.
23 God has no need to examine
men further,
that they should come
before him for judgment.
24 Without inquiry he shatters
the mighty
and sets up others in their
place.
25 Because he takes note of their
deeds,
he overthrows them in the
night and they are
crushed.
26 He punishes them for their
wickedness
where everyone can see
them,
27 because they turned from

[x] 14 Or *Spirit*

מֵאַחֲרָיו וְכָל־ דְּרָכָיו לֹא הִשְׂכִּילוּ׃ לְהָבִיא
to-make-come (28) they-regarded not ways-of-him and-any-of from-after-him

עָלָיו צַעֲקַת־ דָּל וְצַעֲקַת עֲנִיִּים יִשְׁמָע׃ וְהוּא
but-he (29) he-heard needy-ones so-cry-of poor cry-of before-him

יַשְׁקִט | וּמִי יַרְשִׁעַ וְיַסְתֵּר פָּנִים וּמִי
then-who? faces if-he-hides he-can-condemn then-who? he-remains-silent

יְשׁוּרֶנּוּ וְעַל־ גּוֹי וְעַל־ אָדָם יָחַד׃ מִמְּלֹךְ אָדָם
man from-to-rule (30) alike man and-over nation yet-over he-can-see-him

חָנֵף מִמֹּקְשֵׁי עָם׃ כִּי־ אֶל־ אֵל הֶאָמַר נָשָׂאתִי
I-am-guilty he-says? God to suppose (31) people from-snares-of godless

לֹא אֶחְבֹּל׃ בִּלְעֲדֵי אֶחֱזֶה אַתָּה הֹרֵנִי אִם־ עָוֶל פָּעַלְתִּי
I-did wrong if teach-me! you I-see what-not (32) I-will-offend no-more

לֹא אֹסִיף׃ הַמֵעִמְּךָ יְשַׁלְמֶנָּה*† כִּי־ מָאַסְתָּ
you-refuse when should-he-reward-her from-with-you? (33) I-will-do-again not

כִּי־ אַתָּה תִבְחַר וְלֹא־ אָנִי וּמַה־ יָדַעְתָּ דַבֵּר׃ אַנְשֵׁי
men-of (34) tell! you-know so-what I and-not you-decide you for

לֵבָב יֹאמְרוּ לִי וְגֶבֶר חָכָם שֹׁמֵעַ לִי׃ אִיּוֹב לֹא־
not Job (35) to-me hearing wise and-man to-me they-declare understanding

בְדַעַת יְדַבֵּר וּדְבָרָיו לֹא בְהַשְׂכֵּיל׃ אָבִי
oh! (36) with-to-have-insight not and-words-of-him he-speaks with-knowledge

יִבָּחֵן אִיּוֹב עַד־ נֶצַח עַל־ תְּשֻׁבֹת בְּאַנְשֵׁי־ אָוֶן׃ כִּי
for (37) wickedness of-men-of answers for utmost to Job he-might-be-tested

יֹסִיף עַל־ חַטָּאתוֹ פֶשַׁע בֵּינֵינוּ יִסְפּוֹק וְיֶרֶב
and-he-multiplies he-claps among-us rebellion sin-of-him to he-adds

אֲמָרָיו לָאֵל׃ וַיַּעַן אֱלִיהוּ וַיֹּאמַר׃ הֲזֹאת
this? (2) and-he-said Elihu then-he-spoke (35:1) against-God words-of-him

חָשַׁבְתָּ לְמִשְׁפָּט אָמַרְתָּ צִדְקִי מֵאֵל׃ כִּי־ תֹאמַר מַה־
what? you-ask yet (3) by-God clearing-of-me you-say as-just you-think

יִסְכָּן־ לָךְ מָה־ אֹעִיל מֵחַטָּאתִי׃ אֲנִי אֲשִׁיבְךָ
I-would-reply-to-you I (4) from-sin-of-me I-gain what? to-you he-profits

מִלִּין וְאֶת־ רֵעֶיךָ עִמָּךְ׃ הַבֵּט שָׁמַיִם וּרְאֵה וְשׁוּר
and-gaze! and-see! heavens look! (5) with-you friends-of-you and words

שְׁחָקִים גָּבְהוּ מִמֶּךָּ׃ אִם־ חָטָאתָ מַה־ תִּפְעָל־ בּוֹ
to-him she-affects how? you-sin if (6) above-you they-are-high clouds

וְרַבּוּ פְשָׁעֶיךָ מַה־ תַּעֲשֶׂה־ לּוֹ׃ אִם־ צָדַקְתָּ
you-are-righteous if (7) to-him she-does what? sins-of-you if-they-are-many

מַה־ תִּתֶּן־ לוֹ אוֹ מַה־ מִיָּדְךָ יִקָּח׃ לְאִישׁ־
to-man (8) he-receives from-hand-of-you what? or to-him you-give what?

following him
and had no regard for any
of his ways.
[28]They caused the cry of the
poor to come before him,
so that he heard the cry of
the needy.
[29]But if he remains silent, who
can condemn him?
If he hides his face, who
can see him?
Yet he is over man and nation
alike,
[30] to keep a godless man from
ruling,
from laying snares for the
people.

[31]"Suppose a man says to God,
'I am guilty but will offend
no more.
[32]Teach me what I cannot see;
if I have done wrong, I will
not do so again.'
[33]Should God then reward you
on your terms,
when you refuse to repent?
You must decide, not I;
so tell me what you know.

[34]"Men of understanding
declare,
wise men who hear me say
to me,
[35]'Job speaks without
knowledge;
his words lack insight.'
[36]Oh, that Job might be tested to
the utmost
for answering like a wicked
man!
[37]To his sin he adds rebellion;
scornfully he claps his
hands among us
and multiplies his words
against God."

35 Then Elihu said:
[2]"Do you think this is
just?
You say, 'I will be cleared
by God.[y]'
[3]Yet you ask him, 'What profit
is it to me,[z]
and what do I gain by not
sinning?'

[4]"I would like to reply to you
and to your friends with
you.
[5]Look up at the heavens and
see;
gaze at the clouds so high
above you.
[6]If you sin, how does that
affect him?
If your sins are many, what
does that do to him?
[7]If you are righteous, what do
you give to him,
or what does he receive
from your hand?

y2 Or *My righteousness is more than God's*
z3 Or *you*

*33a Most mss have *dagesh* in the lamed (יְשַׁלְּ).
†33b Most mss have dagesh in the *yod* ( יּ ).

כָּמוֹךָ רִשְׁעֶךָ וּלְבֶן־ אָדָם צִדְקָתֶךָ׃
righteousness-of-you man and-to-son-of wickedness-of-you like-you

(9) מֵרֹב עֲשׁוּקִים יַזְעִיקוּ יְשַׁוְּעוּ מִזְּרוֹעַ
from-arm-of they-plead-for-relief they-cry-out oppressions under-load-of (9)

רַבִּים׃ (10) וְלֹא־ אָמַר אַיֵּה אֱלוֹהַּ עֹשָׂי נֹתֵן זְמִרוֹת
songs giving Ones-Making-me God where? he-says but-no-one (10) powerful-ones

בַּלָּיְלָה׃ (11) מַלְּפֵנוּ מִבַּהֲמוֹת אֶרֶץ וּמֵעוֹף
and-more-than-bird-of earth more-than-beasts-of teaching-us (11) in-the-night

הַשָּׁמַיִם יְחַכְּמֵנוּ׃ (12) שָׁם יִצְעֲקוּ וְלֹא יַעֲנֶה
he-answers then-not they-cry-out when (12) he-makes-wise-us the-airs

מִפְּנֵי גְּאוֹן רָעִים׃ (13) אַךְ־ שָׁוְא לֹא־ יִשְׁמַע ׀ אֵל
God he-listens not emptiness indeed (13) wicked-ones arrogance-of because-of

וְשַׁדַּי לֹא יְשׁוּרֶנָּה׃ (14) אַף כִּי־ תֹאמַר
you-say when how-much-less (14) he-pays-attention-to-her not and-Almighty

לֹא תְשׁוּרֶנּוּ דִּין לְפָנָיו וּתְחוֹלֵל לוֹ׃ (15) וְעַתָּה
and-further (15) for-him and-you-must-wait before-him case you-see-him not

כִּי־ אַיִן פָּקַד אַפּוֹ וְלֹא־ יָדַע בַּפַּשׁ
to-the-wickedness he-notices and-not anger-of-him he-punishes never that

מְאֹד׃ (16) וְאִיּוֹב הֶבֶל יִפְצֶה־ פִּיהוּ בִּבְלִי־ דַעַת מִלִּין
words knowledge with-no mouth-of-him he-opens emptiness so-Job (16) least

יַכְבִּר׃ (36:1) וַיֹּסֶף אֱלִיהוּא וַיֹּאמַר׃ (2) כַּתַּר־ לִי
with-me bear! (2) and-he-said Elihu and-he-continued (36:1) he-multiplies

זְעֵיר וַאֲחַוֶּךָּ כִּי עוֹד לֶאֱלוֹהַּ מִלִּים׃
sayings in-behalf-of-God more that and-I-will-show-you little-longer

(3) אֶשָּׂא דֵעִי לְמֵרָחוֹק וּלְפֹעֲלִי אֶתֵּן־
I-ascribe and-to-One-Making-me at-from-afar knowledge-of-me I-get (3)

צֶדֶק׃ (4) כִּי־ אָמְנָם לֹא־ שֶׁקֶר מִלָּי תְּמִים דֵּעוֹת
knowledges perfect-of words-of-me false not assuredly for (4) justice

עִמָּךְ׃ (5) הֶן־ אֵל כַּבִּיר וְלֹא יִמְאָס כַּבִּיר כֹּחַ לֵב׃
purpose firm-of mighty he-despises but-not mighty God see! (5) with-you

(6) לֹא־ יְחַיֶּה רָשָׁע וּמִשְׁפַּט עֲנִיִּים יִתֵּן׃ (7) לֹא־
not (7) he-gives afflicted-ones but-right-of wicked he-keeps-alive not (6)

יִגְרַע מִצַּדִּיק עֵינָיו וְאֶת־ מְלָכִים לַכִּסֵּא
on-the-throne kings and-with eyes-of-him from-righteous he-takes

וַיֹּשִׁיבֵם לָנֶצַח וַיִּגְבָּהוּ׃ (8) וְאִם־
but-if (8) and-they-are-exalted to-forever and-he-enthrones-them

אֲסוּרִים בַּזִּקִּים יִלָּכְדוּן בְּחַבְלֵי־ עֹנִי׃
affliction by-cords-of and-they-are-held-fast in-the-chains ones-being-bound

8 Your wickedness affects only a
man like yourself,
and your righteousness only
the sons of men.

9 "Men cry out under a load of
oppression;
they plead for relief from
the arm of the powerful.
10 But no one says, 'Where is
God my Maker,
who gives songs in the
night,
11 who teaches more to us than
to[a] the beasts of the earth
and makes us wiser than[b]
the birds of the air?'
12 He does not answer when
men cry out
because of the arrogance of
the wicked.
13 Indeed, God does not listen to
their empty plea;
the Almighty pays no
attention to it.
14 How much less, then, will he
listen
when you say that you do
not see him,
that your case is before him
and you must wait for him,
15 and further, that his anger
never punishes
and he does not take the
least notice of
wickedness.[c]
16 So Job opens his mouth with
empty talk;
without knowledge he
multiplies words."

36 Elihu continued:
2 "Bear with me a little
longer and I will show
you
that there is more to be said
in God's behalf.
3 I get my knowledge from afar;
I will ascribe justice to my
Maker.
4 Be assured that my words are
not false;
one perfect in knowledge is
with you.

5 "God is mighty, but does not
despise men;
he is mighty, and firm in
his purpose.
6 He does not keep the wicked
alive
but gives the afflicted their
rights.
7 He does not take his eyes off
the righteous;
he enthrones them with
kings
and exalts them forever.
8 But if men are bound in
chains,
held fast by cords of
affliction,

[a] 11 Or *teaches us by*
[b] 11 Or *us wise by*
[c] 15 Symmachus, Theodotion and Vulgate; the meaning of the Hebrew for this word is uncertain.

וַיַּגֵּד לָהֶם פָּעֳלָם וּפִשְׁעֵיהֶם כִּי יִתְגַּבָּרוּ׃
they-did-arrogantly that and-sins-of-them deed-of-them to-them then-he-tells (9)

וַיִּגֶל אָזְנָם לַמּוּסָר וַיֹּאמֶר כִּי־יְשֻׁבוּן
they-repent that and-he-commands to-the-correction ear-of-them and-he-opens (10)

מֵאָוֶן׃ אִם־יִשְׁמְעוּ וְיַעַבְדוּ יְכַלּוּ יְמֵיהֶם
days-of-them they-will-finish and-they-serve they-obey if (11) of-evil

בַּטּוֹב וּשְׁנֵיהֶם בַּנְּעִימִים׃ וְאִם־לֹא
not but-if (12) in-the-contentments and-years-of-them in-the-prosperity

יִשְׁמְעוּ בְּשֶׁלַח יַעֲבֹרוּ וְיִגְוְעוּ כִּבְלִי־דָעַת׃
knowledge as-without and-they-will-die they-will-perish by-sword they-listen

וְחַנְפֵי־לֵב יָשִׂימוּ אָף לֹא יְשַׁוְּעוּ
they-cry-for-help not resentment they-harbor heart and-ones-godless-of (13)

כִּי אֲסָרָם׃ תָּמֹת בַּנֹּעַר נַפְשָׁם וְחַיָּתָם
and-life-of-them soul-of-them in-the-youth she-dies (14) he-fetters-them when

בַּקְּדֵשִׁים׃ יְחַלֵּץ עָנִי בְעָנְיוֹ
in-suffering-of-him sufferer he-delivers (15) among-the-male-prostitutes

וְיִגֶל בַּלַּחַץ אָזְנָם׃ וְאַף הֲסִיתְךָ
he-woos-you and-also (16) ear-of-them in-the-affliction and-he-opens

מִפִּי־צָר רַחַב לֹא־מוּצָק תַּחְתֶּיהָ וְנַחַת
and-comfort-of to-her restriction no spacious-place distress from-jaw-of

שֻׁלְחָנְךָ מָלֵא דָשֶׁן׃ וְדִין־רָשָׁע
wicked but-judgment-of (17) choice-food he-is-laden table-of-you

מָלֵאתָ דִּין וּמִשְׁפָּט יִתְמֹכוּ׃ כִּי־חֵמָה פֶּן־
not †wrath for (18) they-took-hold and-justice judgment you-are-laden

יְסִיתְךָ בְסֵפֶק וְרָב־כֹּפֶר אַל־יַטֶּךָּ׃
let-him-turn-you not bribe and-largeness-of by-richness he-should-entice-you

הֲיַעֲרֹךְ שׁוּעֲךָ לֹא בְצָר וְכֹל מַאֲמַצֵּי־
efforts-of or-all-of in-distress not wealth-of-you would-he-sustain? (19)

כֹחַ׃ אַל־תִּשְׁאַף הַלָּיְלָה לַעֲלוֹת עַמִּים תַּחְתָּם׃
place-of-them peoples to-drag-away the-night you-long-for not (20) might

הִשָּׁמֶר אַל־תֵּפֶן אֶל־אָוֶן כִּי־עַל־זֶה בָּחַרְתָּ מֵעֹנִי׃
to-affliction you-prefer this to for evil to you-turn not beware! (21)

הֶן־אֵל יַשְׂגִּיב בְּכֹחוֹ מִי כָמֹהוּ מוֹרֶה׃
teacher like-him who? in-power-of-him he-is-exalted God see! (22)

מִי־פָקַד עָלָיו דַּרְכּוֹ וּמִי־אָמַר פָּעַלְתָּ עַוְלָה׃
wrong you-did he-said or-who? way-of-him for-him he-prescribed who? (23)

זְכֹר כִּי־תַשְׂגִּיא פָעֳלוֹ אֲשֶׁר שֹׁרְרוּ אֲנָשִׁים׃
men they-praised which work-of-him you-must-extol that remember! (24)

[9]he tells them what they have
done—
that they have sinned
arrogantly.
[10]He makes them listen to
correction
and commands them to
repent of their evil.
[11]If they obey and serve him,
they will spend the rest of
their days in prosperity
and their years in
contentment.
[12]But if they do not listen,
they will perish by the
sword[d]
and die without knowledge.

[13]"The godless in heart harbor
resentment;
even when he fetters them,
they do not cry for help.
[14]They die in their youth,
among male prostitutes of
the shrines.
[15]But those who suffer he
delivers in their suffering;
he speaks to them in their
affliction.

[16]"He is wooing you from the
jaws of distress
to a spacious place free from
restriction,
to the comfort of your table
laden with choice food.
[17]But now you are laden with
the judgment due the
wicked;
judgment and justice have
taken hold of you.
[18]Be careful that no one entices
you by riches;
do not let a large bribe turn
you aside.
[19]Would your wealth
or even all your mighty
efforts
sustain you so you would
not be in distress?
[20]Do not long for the night
to drag people away from
their homes.[e]
[21]Beware of turning to evil,
which you seem to prefer to
affliction.

[22]"God is exalted in his power.
Who is a teacher like him?
[23]Who has prescribed his ways
for him,
or said to him, 'You have
done wrong'?
[24]Remember to extol his work,
which men have praised in
song.

[d]*12 Or will cross the River*
[e]20 The meaning of the Hebrew for verses 18-20 is uncertain.

*12 Many mss have *beth* instead of *kaph* (בִּבְ׳).

†18 The NIV repoints this word as חֲמֵה, *be-careful!*

כָּל־ אָדָם חָזוּ־ בוֹ אֱנוֹשׁ יַבִּיט מֵרָחוֹק׃ הֶן־ אֵל
God see! (26) from-afar he-gazes man to-him they-saw mankind all-of (25)

שַׂגִּיא וְלֹא נֵדָע מִסְפַּר שָׁנָיו וְלֹא־ חֵקֶר׃
finding-out and-no years-of-him number-of we-comprehend and-not great

כִּי יְגָרַע נִטְפֵי־ מָיִם יָזֹקּוּ מָטָר לְאֵדוֹ׃
to-stream-of-him rain they-distill waters drops-of he-draws-up for (27)

אֲשֶׁר־ יִזְּלוּ שְׁחָקִים יִרְעֲפוּ עֲלֵי אָדָם רָב׃
abundance mankind on they-shower clouds they-pour-moisture that (28)

אַף אִם־ יָבִין מִפְרְשֵׂי־ עָב תְּשֻׁאוֹת
thunders-of cloud spreadings-out-of he-understands if indeed (29)

סֻכָּתוֹ׃ הֵן־ פָּרַשׂ עָלָיו אוֹרוֹ וְשָׁרְשֵׁי
and-depths-of lightning-of-him about-him he-scatters see! (30) pavilion-of-him

הַיָּם כִּסָּה׃ כִּי־ בָם יָדִין עַמִּים יִתֶּן־ אֹכֶל
food he-provides nations he-governs by-them for (31) he-bathes the-sea

לְמַכְבִּיר׃ עַל־ כַּפַּיִם כִּסָּה־ אוֹר וַיְצַו עָלֶיהָ
to-her and-he-commands lightning he-fills hands in (32) to-be-abundant

בְמַפְגִּיעַ׃ יַגִּיד עָלָיו רֵעוֹ מִקְנֶה אַף עַל־
about even cattle thunder-of-him about-him he-announces (33) to-one-striking

עוֹלֶה׃ אַף־ לְזֹאת יֶחֱרַד לִבִּי וְיִתַּר
and-he-leaps heart-of-me he-pounds at-this indeed (37:1) approaching

מִמְּקוֹמוֹ׃ שִׁמְעוּ שָׁמוֹעַ בְּרֹגֶז קֹלוֹ וְהֶגֶה
and-rumbling voice-of-him to-roar-of to-listen listen! (2) from-place-of-him

מִפִּיו יֵצֵא׃ תַּחַת־ כָּל־ הַשָּׁמַיִם יִשְׁרֵהוּ
he-unleashes-him the-heavens whole-of beneath (3) he-comes from-mouth-of-him

וְאוֹרוֹ עַל־ כַּנְפוֹת הָאָרֶץ׃ אַחֲרָיו ׀ יִשְׁאַג־ קוֹל
sound he-roars after-him (4) the-earth ends-of to and-lightning-of-him

יַרְעֵם בְּקוֹל גְּאוֹנוֹ וְלֹא יְעַקְּבֵם
he-holds-back-them and-nothing majesty-of-him with-voice-of he-thunders

כִּי־ יִשָּׁמַע קוֹלוֹ׃ יַרְעֵם אֵל בְּקוֹלוֹ
with-voice-of-him God he-thunders (5) voice-of-him he-is-heard when

נִפְלָאוֹת עֹשֶׂה גְדֹלוֹת וְלֹא נֵדָע׃ כִּי
for (6) we-understand and-not great-things doing ways-being-marvelous

לַשֶּׁלַג* ׀ יֹאמַר הֱוֵא אֶרֶץ וְגֶשֶׁם מָטָר וְגֶשֶׁם מִטְרוֹת
rains and-downpour-of rain and-shower-of earth fall! he-says to-the-snow

עֻזּוֹ׃† בְּיַד־ כָּל־ אָדָם יַחְתּוֹם לָדַעַת כָּל־ אַנְשֵׁי
men-of all-of to-know he-stops man every-of to-labor-of (7) †might-of-him

מַעֲשֵׂהוּ׃ וַתָּבֹא חַיָּה בְמוֹ־ אָרֶב וּבִמְעוֹנֹתֶיהָ תִשְׁכֹּן׃
she-remains and-in-dens-of-her cover into animal and-she-goes (8) work-of-him

25 All mankind has seen it;
men gaze on it from afar.
26 How great is God—beyond our understanding!
The number of his years is past finding out.
27 "He draws up the drops of water,
which distill as rain to the streams[f];
28 the clouds pour down their moisture
and abundant showers fall on mankind.
29 Who can understand how he spreads out the clouds,
how he thunders from his pavilion?
30 See how he scatters his lightning about him,
bathing the depths of the sea.
31 This is the way he governs[g] the nations
and provides food in abundance.
32 He fills his hands with lightning
and commands it to strike its mark.
33 His thunder announces the coming storm;
even the cattle make known its approach.[h]

37 "At this my heart pounds
and leaps from its place.
2 Listen! Listen to the roar of his voice,
to the rumbling that comes from his mouth.
3 He unleashes his lightning beneath the whole heaven
and sends it to the ends of the earth.
4 After that comes the sound of his roar;
he thunders with his majestic voice.
When his voice resounds,
he holds nothing back.
5 God's voice thunders in marvelous ways;
he does great things beyond our understanding.
6 He says to the snow, 'Fall on the earth,'
and to the rain shower, 'Be a mighty downpour.'
7 So that all men he has made may know his work,
he stops every man from his labor.[i]
8 The animals take cover;
they remain in their dens.

f27 Or *distill from the mist as rain*
g31 Or *nourishes*
h33 Or *announces his coming— / the One zealous against evil*
i7 Or / *he fills all men with fear by his power*

*6a Most mss have *segol* under the *lamed* (לֶג־).

†6b The NIV repoints this word as עֹז, *be-mighty!*

מִן־ הַחֶדֶר תָּבוֹא סוּפָה וּמִמְּזָרִים קָרָה׃
cold and-from-ones-driving tempest she-comes the-chamber from (9)

מִנִּשְׁמַת־ אֵל יִתֶּן־ קָרַח וְרֹחַב מַיִם בְּמוּצָק׃
in-frozenness waters and-breadth-of ice he-produces God from-breath-of (10)

אַף־ בְּרִי יַטְרִיחַ עָב יָפִיץ עֲנַן אוֹרוֹ׃
lightning-of-him cloud-of he-scatters cloud he-loads with-moisture also (11)

וְהוּא מְסִבּוֹת ׀ מִתְהַפֵּךְ בְּתַחְבּוּלֹתָו לְפָעֳלָם כֹּל אֲשֶׁר
that all to-do-them at-directions-of-him swirling ones-around and-he (12)

יְצַוֵּם ׀ עַל־ פְּנֵי תֵבֵל אָרְצָה׃ אִם־ לְשֵׁבֶט אִם־
or as-rod whether (13) to-earth world-of faces-of over he-commands-them

לְאַרְצוֹ אִם־ לְחֶסֶד יַמְצִאֵהוּ׃ הַאֲזִינָה זֹּאת אִיּוֹב עֲמֹד
stop! Job this listen! (14) he-brings-him for-love or for-earth-of-him

וְהִתְבּוֹנֵן ׀ נִפְלְאוֹת אֵל׃ הֲתֵדַע בְּשׂוּם־
how-to-control do-you-know? (15) God things-being-wonders-of and-consider!

אֱלוֹהַ עֲלֵיהֶם וְהוֹפִיעַ אוֹר עֲנָנוֹ׃ הֲתֵדַע
do-you-know? (16) cloud-of-him lightning-of and-he-makes-flash over-them God

עַל־ מִפְלְשֵׂי־ עָב מִפְלְאוֹת תְּמִים דֵּעִים׃ אֲשֶׁר־
who (17) knowledges one-perfect-of wonders-of cloud hangings-of how

בְּגָדֶיךָ חַמִּים בְּהַשְׁקִט אֶרֶץ מִדָּרוֹם׃
under-south-wind land when-to-lie-hushed ones-sweltering clothes-of-you

תַּרְקִיעַ עִמּוֹ לִשְׁחָקִים חֲזָקִים כִּרְאִי מוּצָק׃
being-cast as-mirror-of ones-hard to-skies with-him can-you-spread-out (18)

הוֹדִיעֵנוּ מַה־ נֹּאמַר לוֹ לֹא־ נַעֲרֹךְ מִפְּנֵי־
because-of we-can-draw-up-case not to-him we-should-say what tell-us! (19)

חֹשֶׁךְ׃ הַיְסֻפַּר־ לוֹ כִּי אֲדַבֵּר אִם־ אָמַר
would-he-ask or I-would-speak that to-him should-he-be-told? (20) darkness

אִישׁ כִּי יְבֻלָּע׃ וְעַתָּה ׀ לֹא רָאוּ אוֹר בָּהִיר הוּא
he bright sun they-look-at not and-now (21) he-be-swallowed-up that man

בַּשְּׁחָקִים וְרוּחַ עָבְרָה וַתְּטַהֲרֵם׃ מִצָּפוֹן זָהָב
gold from-north (22) and-she-cleans-them she-sweeps after-wind in-the-skies

יֶאֱתֶה עַל־אֱלוֹהַ נוֹרָא הוֹד׃ שַׁדַּי לֹא־ מְצָאנֻהוּ
we-can-reach-him not Almighty (23) majesty being-awesome-of God to he-comes

שַׂגִּיא־ כֹחַ וּמִשְׁפָּט וְרֹב־ צְדָקָה לֹא יְעַנֶּה׃
he-oppresses not righteousness and-greatness-of and-justice power exalted-of

לָכֵן יְרֵאוּהוּ אֲנָשִׁים לֹא־ יִרְאֶה כָּל־ חַכְמֵי־ לֵב׃
heart ones-wise-of all-of he-regards not men they-revere-him therefore (24)

וַיַּעַן־ יְהוָה אֶת־אִיּוֹב מִנְ ° הַסְּעָרָה וַיֹּאמַר׃ מִי
who? (2) and-he-said the-storm from Job *** Yahweh then-he-answered (38:1)

9 The tempest comes out from its chamber,
the cold from the driving winds.
10 The breath of God produces ice,
and the broad waters become frozen.
11 He loads the clouds with moisture;
he scatters his lightning through them.
12 At his direction they swirl around
over the face of the whole earth
to do whatever he commands them.
13 He brings the clouds to punish men,
or to water his earth[l] and show his love.

14 "Listen to this, Job;
stop and consider God's wonders.
15 Do you know how God controls the clouds
and makes his lightning flash?
16 Do you know how the clouds hang poised,
those wonders of him who is perfect in knowledge?
17 You who swelter in your clothes
when the land lies hushed under the south wind,
18 can you join him in spreading out the skies,
hard as a mirror of cast bronze?

19 "Tell us what we should say to him;
we cannot draw up our case because of our darkness.
20 Should he be told that I want to speak?
Would any man ask to be swallowed up?
21 Now no one can look at the sun,
bright as it is in the skies
after the wind has swept them clean.
22 Out of the north he comes in golden splendor;
God comes in awesome majesty.
23 The Almighty is beyond our reach and exalted in power;
in his justice and great righteousness, he does not oppress.
24 Therefore, men revere him,
for does he not have regard for all the wise in heart?[k]"

*The LORD Speaks*

38 Then the LORD answered Job out of the storm. He said:

[l] 13 *Or to favor them*
[k] 24 *Or for he does not have regard for any who think they are wise*

° *12* ק בתחבולתיו
° *1* ק מן הסערה

זֶה׀ מַחְשִׁיךְ עֵצָה בְמִלִּין בְּלִי־ דָעַת׃ אֱזָר־ נָא

now! brace-yourself! (3) knowledge without with-words counsel darkening this

כְגֶבֶר חֲלָצֶיךָ וְאֶשְׁאָלְךָ וְהוֹדִיעֵנִי׃ אֵיפֹה

where? (4) then-answer-me! and-I-will-question-you loins-of-you like-man

הָיִיתָ בְּיָסְדִי־ אָרֶץ הַגֵּד אִם־ יָדַעְתָּ בִינָה׃ מִי־

who? (5) understanding you-know if tell! earth when-to-found-me were-you

שָׂם מְמַדֶּיהָ כִּי תֵדָע אוֹ מִי־ נָטָה

he-stretched who? or you-know surely dimensions-of-her he-marked-off

עָלֶיהָ קָּו׃ עַל־ מָה אֲדָנֶיהָ הָטְבָּעוּ אוֹ

or they-were-set footings-of-her what? on (6) measuring-line across-her

מִי־ יָרָה אֶבֶן פִּנָּתָהּ׃ בְּרָן־ יַחַד כּוֹכְבֵי

stars-of together while-to-sing (7) corner-of-her stone-of he-laid who?

בֹקֶר וַיָּרִיעוּ כָּל־ בְּנֵי אֱלֹהִים׃ וַיָּסֶךְ

and-he-shut-up (8) God sons-of all-of and-they-shouted-for-joy morning

בִּדְלָתַיִם יָם בְּגִיחוֹ מֵרֶחֶם יֵצֵא׃ בְּשׂוּמִי

when-to-make-me (9) he-came-forth from-womb when-to-burst-him sea behind-doors

עָנָן לְבֻשׁוֹ וַעֲרָפֶל חֲתֻלָּתוֹ׃ וָאֶשְׁבֹּר

when-I-fixed (10) wrapping-of-him and-thick-darkness garment-of-him cloud

עָלָיו חֻקִּי וָאָשִׂים בְּרִיחַ וּדְלָתָיִם׃ וָאֹמַר עַד־ פֹּה

here to when-I-said (11) and-doors bar and-I-set-in-place limit-of-me for-him

תָבוֹא וְלֹא תֹסִיף וּפֹא־ יָשִׁית בִּגְאוֹן גַּלֶּיךָ׃

waves-of-you to-pride-of he-halts and-here you-go-farther and-not you-may-come

הֲמִיָּמֶיךָ* צִוִּיתָ בֹּקֶר יִדַּעְתָּה° שַׁחַר מְקֹמוֹ׃

place-of-him the-dawn you-showed morning you-ordered in-days-of-you? (12)

לֶאֱחֹז בְּכַנְפוֹת הָאָרֶץ וְיִנָּעֲרוּ רְשָׁעִים מִמֶּנָּה׃

from-her wicked-ones that-they-be-shaken the-earth by-edges-of to-take (13)

תִּתְהַפֵּךְ כְּחֹמֶר חוֹתָם וְיִתְיַצְּבוּ כְּמוֹ לְבוּשׁ׃

garment like and-they-stand-out seal like-clay-of she-takes-shape (14)

וְיִמָּנַע מֵרְשָׁעִים אוֹרָם וּזְרוֹעַ רָמָה

being-upraised and-arm light-of-them from-wicked-ones and-he-is-denied (15)

תִּשָּׁבֵר׃ הֲבָאתָ עַד־ נִבְכֵי־ יָם וּבְחֵקֶר תְּהוֹם

deep or-in-recess-of sea springs-of to you-journeyed? (16) she-is-broken

הִתְהַלָּכְתָּ׃ הֲנִגְלוּ לְךָ שַׁעֲרֵי־ מָוֶת וְשַׁעֲרֵי

or-gates-of death gates-of to-you were-they-shown? (17) you-walked

צַלְמָוֶת תִּרְאֶה׃ הִתְבֹּנַנְתָּ עַד־ רַחֲבֵי־ אָרֶץ הַגֵּד

tell! earth vast-expanses-of to you-comprehended (18) you-saw deep-shadow

אִם־ יָדַעְתָּ כֻלָּהּ׃ אֵי־ זֶה הַדֶּרֶךְ יִשְׁכָּן־ אוֹר וְחֹשֶׁךְ

and-darkness light he-abides the-way this what? (19) all-of-her you-know if

2 "Who is this that darkens my counsel
with words without knowledge?
3 Brace yourself like a man;
I will question you,
and you shall answer me.

4 "Where were you when I laid the earth's foundation?
Tell me, if you understand.
5 Who marked off its dimensions? Surely you know!
Who stretched a measuring line across it?
6 On what were its footings set,
or who laid its cornerstone—
7 while the morning stars sang together
and all the angels[l] shouted for joy?

8 "Who shut up the sea behind doors
when it burst forth from the womb,
9 when I made the clouds its garment
and wrapped it in thick darkness,
10 when I fixed limits for it
and set its doors and bars in place,
11 when I said, 'This far you may come and no farther;
here is where your proud waves halt'?

12 "Have you ever given orders to the morning,
or shown the dawn its place,
13 that it might take the earth by the edges
and shake the wicked out of it?
14 The earth takes shape like clay under a seal;
its features stand out like those of a garment.
15 The wicked are denied their light,
and their upraised arm is broken.

16 "Have you journeyed to the springs of the sea
or walked in the recesses of the deep?
17 Have the gates of death been shown to you?
Have you seen the gates of the shadow of death[m]?
18 Have you comprehended the vast expanses of the earth?
Tell me, if you know all this.
19 "What is the way to the abode of light?

l 7 Hebrew *the sons of God*
m 17 Or *gates of deep shadows*

*12 Most mss have *hateph pathah* under the *he* (הֲ).

°12 ק ידעת השחר

אֵי־ זֶה מְקֹמוֹ׃ כִּי תִקָּחֶנּוּ אֶל־ גְּבוּלוֹ
place-of-him to can-you-take-him indeed (20) residence-of-him this where?

וְכִי תָבִין נְתִיבוֹת בֵּיתוֹ׃ יָדַעְתָּ כִּי־ אָז
then surely you-know (21) dwelling-of-him paths-of do-you-know and-indeed

תִּוָּלֵד וּמִסְפַּר יָמֶיךָ רַבִּים׃ הֲבָאתָ אֶל־
into you-entered? (22) many days-of-you and-number-of you-were-born

אֹצְרוֹת שָׁלֶג וְאֹצְרוֹת בָּרָד תִּרְאֶה׃ אֲשֶׁר־ חָשַׂכְתִּי
I-reserve which (23) you-saw hail or-storehouses-of snow storehouses-of

לְעֶת־ צָר לְיוֹם קְרָב וּמִלְחָמָה׃ אֵי־ זֶה הַדֶּרֶךְ
the-way this what? (24) and-battle war for-day-of trouble for-time-of

יֵחָלֶק אוֹר יָפֵץ קָדִים עֲלֵי־ אָרֶץ׃ מִי־ פִלַּג
he-cuts who? (25) earth over east-wind he-scatters lightning he-is-dispersed

לַשֶּׁטֶף תְּעָלָה וְדֶרֶךְ לַחֲזִיז קֹלוֹת׃ לְהַמְטִיר
to-water (26) thunders for-storm-of and-path channel for-the-rain-torrent

עַל־אֶרֶץ לֹא־ אִישׁ מִדְבָּר לֹא־אָדָם בּוֹ׃ לְהַשְׂבִּיעַ שֹׁאָה
desolation to-satisfy (27) in-him one no desert man without land on

וּמְשֹׁאָה וּלְהַצְמִיחַ מֹצָא דֶשֶׁא׃ הֲיֵשׁ־ לַמָּטָר
to-the-rain is-there? (28) grass shoot-of and-to-make-sprout and-wasteland

אָב אוֹ מִי־ הוֹלִיד אֶגְלֵי־ טָל׃ מִבֶּטֶן מִי יָצָא
he-comes whom? from-womb-of (29) dew drops-of he-fathers who? or father

הַקֶּרַח וּכְפֹר שָׁמַיִם מִי יְלָדוֹ׃ כָּאֶבֶן מַיִם
waters as-the-stone (30) he-bears-him who? heavens and-frost-of the-ice

יִתְחַבָּאוּ וּפְנֵי תְהוֹם יִתְלַכָּדוּ׃ הַתְקַשֵּׁר
can-you-bind? (31) they-freeze deep when-surfaces-of they-become-hard

מַעֲדַנּוֹת כִּימָה אוֹ־ מֹשְׁכוֹת כְּסִיל תְּפַתֵּחַ׃ הֲתֹצִיא
can-you-bring-forth? (32) can-you-loose Orion cords-of or Pleiades beauties-of

מַזָּרוֹת בְּעִתּוֹ וְעַיִשׁ עַל־ בָּנֶיהָ תַנְחֵם׃
can-you-lead-out-them cubs-of-her with or-Bear in-season-of-him constellations

הֲיָדַעְתָּ חֻקּוֹת שָׁמָיִם אִם־ תָּשִׂים מִשְׁטָרוֹ
dominion-of-him can-you-set-up or heavens laws-of do-you-know? (33)

בָאָרֶץ׃ הֲתָרִים לָעָב קוֹלֶךָ וְשִׁפְעַת־
and-flood-of voice-of-you to-the-cloud can-you-raise? (34) over-the-earth

מַיִם תְּכַסֶּךָּ׃ הַתְשַׁלַּח בְּרָקִים וְיֵלֵכוּ
so-they-go lightning-bolts do-you-send? (35) can-you-cover-yourself waters

וְיֹאמְרוּ לְךָ הִנֵּנוּ׃ מִי־ שָׁת בַּטֻּחוֹת חָכְמָה
wisdom to-the-hearts he-endowed who? (36) here-we! to-you and-do-they-report

אוֹ מִי־ נָתַן לַשֶּׂכְוִי בִינָה׃ מִי־ יְסַפֵּר שְׁחָקִים
clouds he-counts who? (37) understanding to-the-mind he-gave who? or

And where does darkness reside?
20 Can you take them to their places?
Do you know the paths to their dwellings?
21 Surely you know, for you were already born!
You have lived so many years!

22 "Have you entered the storehouses of the snow
or seen the storehouses of the hail,
23 which I reserve for times of trouble,
for days of war and battle?
24 What is the way to the place where the lightning is dispersed,
or the place where the east winds are scattered over the earth?
25 Who cuts a channel for the torrents of rain,
and a path for the thunderstorm,
26 to water a land where no man lives,
a desert with no one in it,
27 to satisfy a desolate wasteland
and make it sprout with grass?
28 Does the rain have a father?
Who fathers the drops of dew?
29 From whose womb comes the ice?
Who gives birth to the frost from the heavens
30 when the waters become hard as stone,
when the surface of the deep is frozen?

31 "Can you bind the beautiful[n] Pleiades?
Can you loose the cords of Orion?
32 Can you bring forth the constellations in their seasons[o]
or lead out the Bear[p] with its cubs?
33 Do you know the laws of the heavens?
Can you set up ⌊God's[q]⌋ dominion over the earth?

34 "Can you raise your voice to the clouds
and cover yourself with a flood of water?
35 Do you send the lightning bolts on their way?
Do they report to you, 'Here we are'?
36 Who endowed the heart[r] with wisdom
or gave understanding to the mind[r]?
37 Who has the wisdom to count the clouds?

n31 Or *the twinkling*; or *the chains of the*
o32 Or *the morning star in its season*
p32 Or *out Leo* q33 Or *his*; or *their*
r36 The meaning of the Hebrew for this word is uncertain.

בְּחָכְמָה וְנִבְלֵי שָׁמַיִם מִי יַשְׁכִּיב׃ בְּצֶקֶת עָפָר
dust when-to-harden (38) he-can-tip-over who? heavens or-jars-of in-wisdom

לַמּוּצָק וּרְגָבִים יְדֻבָּקוּ׃ הֲתָצוּד
do-you-hunt? (39) they-stick-together and-clods-of-earth into-the-hard-thing

לְלָבִיא טָרֶף וְחַיַּת כְּפִירִים תְּמַלֵּא׃ כִּי־ יָשֹׁחוּ
they-crouch when (40) you-satisfy lions and-hunger-of prey for-lioness

בַמְּעוֹנוֹת יֵשְׁבוּ בַסֻּכָּה לְמוֹ־ אָרֶב׃ מִי יָכִין
he-provides who? (41) wait in in-the-thicket they-lie in-the-dens

לָעֹרֵב צֵידוֹ כִּי־ יְלָדָו° אֶל־ אֵל יְשַׁוֵּעוּ
they-cry-out God to young-ones-of-him when food-of-him for-the-raven

יִתְעוּ לִבְלִי־ אֹכֶל׃ הֲיָדַעְתָּ עֵת לֶדֶת יַעֲלֵי־
goats-of to-give-birth time-of do-you-know? (39:1) food for-lack-of they-wander

סָלַע חֹלֵל אַיָּלוֹת תִּשְׁמֹר׃ תִּסְפֹּר יְרָחִים תְּמַלֶּאנָה
they-complete-term months do-you-count (2) do-you-watch fawns to-bear mountain

וְיָדַעְתָּ עֵת לִדְתָּנָה׃ תִּכְרַעְנָה יַלְדֵיהֶן
young-ones-of-them they-crouch-down (3) to-give-birth-them time-of and-do-you-know

תְּפַלַּחְנָה חֶבְלֵיהֶם תְּשַׁלַּחְנָה׃ יַחְלְמוּ בְנֵיהֶם
young-ones-of-them they-thrive (4) they-end labor-pains-of-them they-bring-forth

יִרְבּוּ בַבָּר יָצְאוּ וְלֹא־ שָׁבוּ לָמוֹ׃ מִי־
who? (5) to-them they-return and-not they-leave in-the-wild they-grow-strong

שִׁלַּח פֶּרֶא חָפְשִׁי וּמֹסְרוֹת עָרוֹד מִי פִתֵּחַ׃ אֲשֶׁר־
that (6) he-untied who? donkey and-ropes-of free wild-donkey he-let-go

שַׂמְתִּי עֲרָבָה בֵיתוֹ וּמִשְׁכְּנוֹתָיו מְלֵחָה׃ יִשְׂחַק
he-laughs (7) salt-flat and-habitats-of-him home-of-him wasteland I-gave

לַהֲמוֹן קִרְיָה תְּשֻׁאוֹת נוֹגֵשׂ לֹא יִשְׁמָע׃ יְתוּר הָרִים
hills he-ranges (8) he-hears not one-driving shouts-of town at-commotion-of

מִרְעֵהוּ וְאַחַר כָּל־ יָרוֹק יִדְרוֹשׁ׃ הֲיֹאבֶה
will-he-consent? (9) he-searches green-thing any-of and-for pasture-of-him

רֵים עָבְדֶךָ אִם־ יָלִין עַל־ אֲבוּסֶךָ׃ הֲתִקְשָׁר־
can-you-hold? (10) manger-of-you by will-he-stay-night or to-serve-you wild-ox

רֵים בְּתֶלֶם עֲבֹתוֹ אִם־ יְשַׂדֵּד עֲמָקִים אַחֲרֶיךָ׃
behind-you valleys will-he-till or harness-of-him to-furrow-of wild-ox

הֲתִבְטַח־ בּוֹ כִּי־ רַב כֹּחוֹ וְתַעֲזֹב
and-will-you-leave strength-of-him greatness-of for on-him will-you-rely? (11)

אֵלָיו יְגִיעֶךָ׃ הֲתַאֲמִין בּוֹ כִּי־ יָשׁוּב°
he-will-bring-in that in-him can-you-trust? (12) heavy-work-of-you to-him

זַרְעֶךָ וְגָרְנְךָ יֶאֱסֹף׃ כְּנַף־ רְנָנִים
ostriches wing-of (13) he-will-gather and-threshing-floor-of-you grain-of-you

Who can tip over the water
jars of the heavens
38 when the dust becomes hard
and the clods of earth stick
together?

39 "Do you hunt the prey for the
lioness
and satisfy the hunger of
the lions
40 when they crouch in their
dens
or lie in wait in a thicket?
41 Who provides food for the
raven
when its young cry out to
God
and wander about for lack
of food?

39 "Do you know when the
mountain goats give
birth?
Do you watch when the doe
bears her fawn?
2 Do you count the months till
they bear?
Do you know the time they
give birth?
3 They crouch down and bring
forth their young;
their labor pains are ended.
4 Their young thrive and grow
strong in the wilds;
they leave and do not
return.

5 "Who let the wild donkey go
free?
Who untied his ropes?
6 I gave him the wasteland as
his home,
the salt flats as his habitat.
7 He laughs at the commotion in
the town;
he does not hear a driver's
shout.
8 He ranges the hills for his
pasture
and searches for any green
thing.

9 "Will the wild ox consent to
serve you?
Will he stay by your manger
at night?
10 Can you hold him to the
furrow with a harness?
Will he till the valleys
behind you?
11 Will you rely on him for his
great strength?
Will you leave your heavy
work to him?
12 Can you trust him to bring in
your grain
and gather it to your
threshing floor?

13 "The wings of the ostrich flap

°41 ק ילדיו
°12 ק ישיב

נֶעֱלָסָה אִם־ אֶבְרָה חֲסִידָה וְנֹצָה׃ כִּי־ תַעֲזֹב
she-lays indeed (14) and-feather stork pinion not she-flaps-joyfully

לָאָרֶץ בֵּצֶיהָ וְעַל־ עָפָר תְּחַמֵּם׃ וַתִּשְׁכַּח
and-she-is-unmindful (15) she-warms-them sand and-in eggs-of-her on-the-ground

כִּי־ רֶגֶל תְּזוּרֶהָ וְחַיַּת הַשָּׂדֶה תְּדוּשֶׁהָ׃
she-may-trample-her the-wild or-animal-of she-may-crush-her foot that

הִקְשִׁיחַ בָּנֶיהָ לְּלֹא־ לָהּ לְרִיק יְגִיעָהּ
labor-of-her in-vain to-her as-not young-ones-of-her he-treats-harshly (16)

בְּלִי־ פָחַד׃ כִּי־ הִשָּׁהּ אֱלוֹהַּ חָכְמָה וְלֹא־ חָלַק
he-gave-share and-not wisdom God he-did-not-endow-her for (17) care without

לָהּ בַּבִּינָה׃ כָּעֵת בַּמָּרוֹם תַּמְרִיא
she-spreads-feathers to-the-height yet-the-time (18) of-the-good-sense to-her

תִּשְׂחַק לַסּוּס וּלְרֹכְבוֹ׃ הֲתִתֵּן לַסּוּס
to-the-horse do-you-give? (19) and-at-one-riding-him at-the-horse she-laughs

גְּבוּרָה הֲתַלְבִּישׁ צַוָּארוֹ רַעְמָה׃ הְתַרְעִישֶׁנּוּ*
do-you-make-leap-him? (20) flowing-mane neck-of-him do-you-clothe? strength

כָּאַרְבֶּה הוֹד נַחְרוֹ אֵימָה׃ יַחְפְּרוּ
they-paw (21) terror snorting-of-him pride-of like-the-locust

בָעֵמֶק וְיָשִׂישׂ בְּכֹחַ יֵצֵא לִקְרַאת־ נָשֶׁק׃
fray to-meet he-charges in-strength and-he-rejoices with-the-fierceness

יִשְׂחַק לְפַחַד וְלֹא יֵחָת וְלֹא־ יָשׁוּב מִפְּנֵי־
from-edges-of he-shys-away and-not he-fears and-nothing at-fear he-laughs (22)

חָרֶב׃ עָלָיו תִּרְנֶה אַשְׁפָּה לַהַב חֲנִית וְכִידוֹן׃
and-lance spear flash-of quiver she-rattles beside-him (23) sword

בְּרַעַשׁ וְרֹגֶז יְגַמֶּא־ אָרֶץ וְלֹא־ יַאֲמִין כִּי־
when he-stands-still and-not ground he-eats-up and-excitement in-frenzy (24)

קוֹל שׁוֹפָר׃ בְּדֵי שֹׁפָר ׀ יֹאמַר הֶאָח וּמֵרָחוֹק
and-from-afar aha! he-snorts trumpet as-often-as (25) trumpet sound-of

יָרִיחַ מִלְחָמָה רַעַם שָׂרִים וּתְרוּעָה׃
and-battle-cry commanders shout-of battle he-catches-scent

הֲמִבִּינָתְךָ יַאֲבֶר־ נֵץ יִפְרֹשׂ כְּנָפָו°
wings-of-him he-spreads hawk he-takes-flight by-wisdom-of-you? (26)

לְתֵימָן׃ אִם־עַל־ פִּיךָ יַגְבִּיהַּ נָשֶׁר וְכִי יָרִים
he-builds-high and-indeed eagle he-soars command-of-you at or (27) toward-south

קִנּוֹ׃ סֶלַע יִשְׁכֹּן וְיִתְלֹנָן עַל־ שֶׁן־ סֶלַע
rock crag-of on and-he-stays-night he-dwells cliff (28) nest-of-him

וּמְצוּדָה׃ מִשָּׁם חָפַר־ אֹכֶל לְמֵרָחוֹק עֵינָיו
eyes-of-him at-from-afar food he-seeks-out from-there (29) and-stronghold

joyfully,
but they cannot compare
with the pinions and
feathers of the stork.
14 She lays her eggs on the
ground
and lets them warm in the
sand,
15 unmindful that a foot may
crush them,
that some wild animal may
trample them.
16 She treats her young harshly,
as if they were not hers;
she cares not that her labor
was in vain,
17 for God did not endow her
with wisdom
or give her a share of good
sense.
18 Yet when she spreads her
feathers to run,
she laughs at horse and
rider.

19 "Do you give the horse his
strength
or clothe his neck with a
flowing mane?
20 Do you make him leap like a
locust,
striking terror with his
proud snorting?
21 He paws fiercely, rejoicing in
his strength,
and charges into the fray.
22 He laughs at fear, afraid of
nothing;
he does not shy away from
the sword.
23 The quiver rattles against his
side,
along with the flashing
spear and lance.
24 In frenzied excitement he eats
up the ground;
he cannot stand still when
the trumpet sounds.
25 At the blast of the trumpet he
snorts, 'Aha!'
He catches the scent of
battle from afar,
the shout of commanders
and the battle cry.

26 "Does the hawk take flight by
your wisdom
and spread his wings
toward the south?
27 Does the eagle soar at your
command
and build his nest on high?
28 He dwells on a cliff and stays
there at night;
a rocky crag is his
stronghold.
29 From there he seeks out his
food;

*20 Most mss have *hateph pathah* under the *he* (הֲ).

°26 ק כנפיו

יַבִּיטוּ׃ וְאֶפְרֹחָו יְעַלְעוּ־דָם וּבַאֲשֶׁר חֲלָלִים

slain-ones and-at-where blood they-feast and-young-ones-of-him (30) they-detect

שָׁם הוּא׃ וַיַּעַן יְהוָה אֶת־אִיּוֹב וַיֹּאמַר׃ הֲרֹב

to-contend? (2) and-he-said Job *** Yahweh and-he-spoke (40:1) he there

עִם־שַׁדַּי יִסּוֹר מוֹכִיחַ אֱלוֹהַּ יַעֲנֶנָּה׃

let-him-answer-her God one-accusing will-he-correct Almighty with

וַיַּעַן אִיּוֹב אֶת־יְהוָה וַיֹּאמַר׃ הֵן קַלֹּתִי מָה

how? I-am-unworthy see! (4) and-he-said Yahweh *** Job then-he-answered (3)

אֲשִׁיבֶךָּ יָדִי שַׂמְתִּי לְמוֹ־פִי׃ אַחַת דִּבַּרְתִּי וְלֹא

but-not I-spoke once (5) mouth-of-me over I-put hand-of-me can-I-reply-to-you

אֶעֱנֶה וּשְׁתַּיִם וְלֹא אוֹסִיף׃ וַיַּעַן־יְהוָה אֶת־אִיּוֹב

Job *** Yahweh then-he-spoke (6) I-will-say-more but-not and-twice I-answer

מִן ׀ סְעָרָה וַיֹּאמַר׃ אֱזָר־נָא כְגֶבֶר חֲלָצֶיךָ

loins-of-you like-man now! brace-yourself! (7) and-he-said storm from

אֶשְׁאָלְךָ וְהוֹדִיעֵנִי׃ הַאַף תָּפֵר מִשְׁפָּטִי

justice-of-me would-you-discredit indeed? (8) and-answer-me! I-will-question-you

תַּרְשִׁיעֵנִי לְמַעַן תִּצְדָּק׃ וְאִם־זְרוֹעַ

arm now-indeed (9) you-would-justify-yourself so-that would-you-condemn-me

כָּאֵל ׀ לָךְ וּבְקוֹל כָּמֹהוּ תַרְעֵם׃ עֲדֵה

adorn-yourself! (10) can-you-thunder like-his and-with-voice to-you like-God

נָא גָאוֹן וָגֹבַהּ וְהוֹד וְהָדָר תִּלְבָּשׁ׃

you-clothe-yourself and-majesty and-honor and-splendor glory now!

הָפֵץ עֶבְרוֹת אַפֶּךָ וּרְאֵה כָל־גֵּאֶה

proud-man every-of and-look! wrath-of-you furies-of unleash! (11)

וְהַשְׁפִּילֵהוּ׃ רְאֵה כָל־גֵּאֶה הַכְנִיעֵהוּ וַהֲדֹךְ

and-crush! humble-him! proud-man every-of look! (12) and-bring-low-him!

רְשָׁעִים תַּחְתָּם׃ טָמְנֵם בֶּעָפָר יָחַד פְּנֵיהֶם

faces-of-them together in-the-dust bury-them! (13) in-place-of-them wicked-ones

חֲבֹשׁ בַּטָּמוּן׃ וְגַם־אֲנִי אוֹדֶךָּ כִּי־תוֹשִׁעַ

she-can-save that I-will-admit-to-you I then-also (14) in-the-grave shroud!

לְךָ יְמִינֶךָ׃ הִנֵּה־נָא בְהֵמוֹת אֲשֶׁר־עָשִׂיתִי עִמָּךְ חָצִיר

grass with-you I-made which behemoth now! see! (15) right-hand-of-you to-you

כַּבָּקָר יֹאכֵל׃ הִנֵּה־נָא כֹחוֹ בְמָתְנָיו

in-loins-of-him strength-of-him now! see! (16) he-feeds-on like-the-ox

וְאֹנוֹ בִּשְׁרִירֵי בִטְנוֹ׃ יַחְפֹּץ זְנָבוֹ כְמוֹ־

like tail-of-him he-sways (17) belly-of-him in-muscles-of and-power-of-him

אֶרֶז גִּידֵי פַחֲדָו יְשֹׂרָגוּ׃ עֲצָמָיו אֲפִיקֵי

tubes-of bones-of-him (18) they-are-close-knit thighs-of-him sinews-of cedar

his eyes detect it from afar.
30 His young ones feast on blood,
and where the slain are,
there is he."

40 The LORD said to Job:
2 "Will the one who contends with the Almighty correct him?
Let him who accuses God answer him!"

3 Then Job answered the LORD:

4 "I am unworthy—how can I reply to you?
I put my hand over my mouth.
5 I spoke once, but I have no answer—
twice, but I will say no more."

6 Then the LORD spoke to Job out of the storm:

7 "Brace yourself like a man;
I will question you,
and you shall answer me.

8 "Would you discredit my justice?
Would you condemn me to justify yourself?
9 Do you have an arm like God's,
and can your voice thunder like his?
10 Then adorn yourself with glory and splendor,
and clothe yourself in honor and majesty.
11 Unleash the fury of your wrath,
look at every proud man and bring him low,
12 look at every proud man and humble him,
crush the wicked where they stand.
13 Bury them all in the dust together;
shroud their faces in the grave.
14 Then I myself will admit to you
that your own right hand can save you.

15 "Look at the behemoth,[s]
which I made along with you
and which feeds on grass like an ox.
16 What strength he has in his loins,
what power in the muscles of his belly!
17 His tail[t] sways like a cedar;
the sinews of his thighs are close-knit.
18 His bones are tubes of bronze,

[s] 15 Possibly the hippopotamus or the elephant
[t] 17 Possibly trunk

°30 ק ואפרחיו
°6 ק מן סערה
°17 ק פחדיו

נְחוּשָׁה גְּרָמָיו כִּמְטִיל בַּרְזֶל׃ הוּא רֵאשִׁית דַּרְכֵי־אֵל
God works-of first-of he (19) iron like-rod-of limbs-of-him bronze

הָעֹשׂוֹ יַגֵּשׁ חַרְבּוֹ׃ כִּי־בוּל הָרִים
hills produce-of indeed (20) sword-of-him he-can-approach the-One-Making-him

יִשְׂאוּ־לוֹ וְכָל־חַיַּת הַשָּׂדֶה יְשַׂחֲקוּ־שָׁם׃ תַּחַת־
under (21) nearby they-play the-wild animal-of and-all-of to-him they-bring

צֶאֱלִים יִשְׁכָּב בְּסֵתֶר קָנֶה וּבִצָּה׃ יְסֻכֻּהוּ
they-conceal-him (22) and-marsh reed in-hiding-of he-lies lotus-plants

צֶאֱלִים צִלֲלוֹ יְסֻבּוּהוּ עַרְבֵי־נָחַל׃ הֵן יַעֲשֹׁק
he-rages see! (23) stream poplars-of they-surround-him shadow-of-him lotuses

נָהָר לֹא יַחְפּוֹז יִבְטַח כִּי־יָגִיחַ יַרְדֵּן אֶל־
against Jordan he-should-surge though he-is-secure he-is-alarmed not river

פִּיהוּ׃ בְּעֵינָיו יִקָּחֶנּוּ בְּמוֹקְשִׁים יִנְקָב־
can-he-pierce with-traps can-he-capture-him by-eyes-of-him (24) mouth-of-him

אָף׃ תִּמְשֹׁךְ לִוְיָתָן בְּחַכָּה וּבְחֶבֶל
or-with-rope with-fishhook leviathan can-you-pull-in *(25[1]) nose

תַּשְׁקִיעַ לְשֹׁנוֹ׃ הֲתָשִׂים אַגְמֹן בְּאַפּוֹ
through-nose-of-him cord can-you-put? (26[2]) tongue-of-him can-you-tie-down

וּבְחוֹחַ תִּקּוֹב לֶחֱיוֹ׃† הֲיַרְבֶּה אֵלֶיךָ
to-you will-he-continue? (27[3]) jaw-of-him can-you-pierce or-with-hook

תַּחֲנוּנִים אִם־יְדַבֵּר אֵלֶיךָ רַכּוֹת׃ הֲיִכְרֹת
will-he-make? (28[4]) gentle-words to-you will-he-speak or beggings-for-mercy

בְּרִית עִמָּךְ תִּקָּחֶנּוּ לְעֶבֶד עוֹלָם׃ הַתְשַׂחֶק־
can-you-make-pet? (29[5]) for-life as-slave will-you-take-him with-you agreement

בּוֹ כַּצִּפּוֹר וְתִקְשְׁרֶנּוּ לְנַעֲרוֹתֶיךָ׃
for-girls-of-you or-will-you-put-leash-on-him like-the-bird of-him

יִכְרוּ עָלָיו חַבָּרִים יֶחֱצוּהוּ בֵּין כְּנַעֲנִים׃
merchants among will-they-divide-him traders for-him will-they-barter (30[6])

הַתְמַלֵּא בְשֻׂכּוֹת עוֹרוֹ וּבְצִלְצַל דָּגִים
fishes or-with-spear-of hide-of-him with-harpoons can-you-fill? (31[7])

רֹאשׁוֹ׃ שִׂים־עָלָיו כַּפֶּךָ זְכֹר מִלְחָמָה אַל־
never struggle remember! hand-of-you on-him lay! (32[8]) head-of-him

תּוֹסַף׃ הֵן־תֹּחַלְתּוֹ נִכְזָבָה הֲגַם אֶל־
at indeed? she-is-false hope-of-him see! (41:1[9]) you-will-do-again

מַרְאָיו יֻטָל׃ לֹא־אַכְזָר כִּי יְעוּרֶנּוּ
he-can-rouse-him that fierce no-one (2[10]) he-is-overpowered sights-of-him

וּמִי הוּא לְפָנַי יִתְיַצָּב׃ מִי הִקְדִּימַנִי
he-has-claim-against-me who? (3[11]) he-can-stand against-me he then-who?

his limbs like rods of iron.
19 He ranks first among the works of God,
yet his Maker can approach him with his sword.
20 The hills bring him their produce,
and all the wild animals play nearby.
21 Under the lotus plants he lies,
hidden among the reeds in the marsh.
22 The lotuses conceal him in their shadow;
the poplars by the stream surround him.
23 When the river rages, he is not alarmed;
he is secure, though the Jordan should surge against his mouth.
24 Can anyone capture him by the eyes,[u]
or trap him and pierce his nose?

41 "Can you pull in the leviathan[v] with a fishhook
or tie down his tongue with a rope?
2 Can you put a cord through his nose
or pierce his jaw with a hook?
3 Will he keep begging you for mercy?
Will he speak to you with gentle words?
4 Will he make an agreement with you
for you to take him as your slave for life?
5 Can you make a pet of him like a bird
or put him on a leash for your girls?
6 Will traders barter for him?
Will they divide him up among the merchants?
7 Can you fill his hide with harpoons
or his head with fishing spears?
8 If you lay a hand on him,
you will remember the struggle and never do it again!
9 Any hope of subduing him is false;
the mere sight of him is overpowering.
10 No one is fierce enough to rouse him.
Who then is able to stand against me?
11 Who has a claim against me

[u]24 Or *by a water hole*
[v]1 Possibly the crocodile

*25 The Hebrew numeration of chapter 41 begins with verse 9 in English; the number in brackets indicates the English numeration.

†26 Most mss have the accent on the final syllable (יוֹ—).

וַאֲשַׁלֵּם תַּחַת כָּל־ הַשָּׁמַיִם לִי־ הוּא׃ לֹא־ אַחֲרִישׁ
I-will-not-speak not (4[12]) he to-me the-heavens all-of under that-I-must-pay

בַּדָּיו וּדְבַר־ גְּבוּרוֹת וְחִין עֶרְכּוֹ׃ מִי־
who? (5[13]) form-of-him and-grace-of strengths or-account-of limbs-of-him

גִלָּה פְּנֵי לְבוּשׁוֹ בְּכֶפֶל רִסְנוֹ
bridle-of-him with-double-of coat-of-him outer-parts-of he-can-strip-off

מִי יָבוֹא׃ דַּלְתֵי פָנָיו מִי פִתֵּחַ
he-would-open who? mouths-of-him doors-of (6[14]) he-would-approach who?

סְבִיבוֹת שִׁנָּיו אֵימָה׃ גַּאֲוָה† אֲפִיקֵי מָגִנִּים
shields rows-of †pride (7[15]) fearsome teeth-of-him ones-ringed-about-of

סָגוּר חוֹתָם צָר׃ אֶחָד בְּאֶחָד יִגַּשׁוּ וְרוּחַ לֹא־
not that-air they-are-close to-next each (8[16]) tight seal being-closed

יָבוֹא בֵינֵיהֶם׃ אִישׁ־ בְּאָחִיהוּ יְדֻבָּקוּ
they-are-joined-fast to-other-of-him one (9[17]) between-them he-passes

יִתְלַכְּדוּ וְלֹא יִתְפָּרָדוּ׃ עֲטִישֹׁתָיו
sneezings-of-him (10[18]) they-can-be-parted and-not they-cling-together

תָּהֶל אוֹר וְעֵינָיו כְּעַפְעַפֵּי־ שָׁחַר׃ מִפִּיו
from-mouth-of-him (11[19]) dawn like-rays-of and-eyes-of-him light she-flashes

לַפִּידִים יַהֲלֹכוּ כִּידוֹדֵי אֵשׁ יִתְמַלָּטוּ׃
they-shoot-out fire sparks-of they-stream firebrands

מִנְּחִירָיו יֵצֵא עָשָׁן כְּדוּד נָפוּחַ וְאַגְמֹן׃
and-reed boiling as-pot smoke he-pours from-nostrils-of-him (12[20])

נַפְשׁוֹ גֶּחָלִים תְּלַהֵט וְלַהַב מִפִּיו
mouth-of-him and-flame-of she-sets-ablaze coals breath-of-him (13[21])

יֵצֵא׃ בְּצַוָּארוֹ יָלִין עֹז וּלְפָנָיו
and-before-him strength he-resides in-neck-of-him (14[22]) he-darts-out

תָּדוּץ דְּאָבָה׃ מַפְּלֵי בְשָׂרוֹ דָבֵקוּ
they-are-tightly-joined flesh-of-him folds-of (15[23]) dismay she-goes

יָצוּק עָלָיו בַּל־ יִמּוֹט׃ לִבּוֹ יָצוּק כְּמוֹ־אָבֶן
rock as being-hard chest-of-him (16[24]) he-is-moved not on-him being-firm

וְיָצוּק כְּפֶלַח תַּחְתִּית׃ מִשֵּׂתוֹ יָגוּרוּ
they-are-terrified when-to-rise-him (17[25]) lower as-millstone and-being-hard

אֵלִים מִשְּׁבָרִים יִתְחַטָּאוּ׃ מַשִּׂיגֵהוּ חֶרֶב
sword one-reaching-him (18[26]) they-retreat from-thrashings mighty-ones

בְּלִי תָקוּם חֲנִית מַסָּע וְשִׁרְיָה׃ יַחְשֹׁב לְתֶבֶן בַּרְזֶל
iron like-straw he-treats (19[27]) or-javelin dart spear she-has-effect not

לְעֵץ רִקָּבוֹן נְחוּשָׁה׃ לֹא־ יַבְרִיחֶנּוּ בֶן־ קֶשֶׁת לְקַשׁ
like-chaff bow son-of he-makes-flee-him not (20[28]) bronze rottenness like-wood-of

that I must pay?
Everything under heaven belongs to me.
12"I will not fail to speak of his limbs,
his strength and his graceful form.
13Who can strip off his outer coat?
Who would approach him with a bridle?
14Who dares open the doors of his mouth,
ringed about with his fearsome teeth?
15His back has[w] rows of shields tightly sealed together;
16each is so close to the next that no air can pass between.
17They are joined fast to one another;
they cling together and cannot be parted.
18His sneezing throws out flashes of light;
his eyes are like the rays of dawn.
19Firebrands stream from his mouth;
sparks of fire shoot out.
20Smoke pours from his nostrils as from a boiling pot over a fire of reeds.
21His breath sets coals ablaze,
and flames dart from his mouth.
22Strength resides in his neck;
dismay goes before him.
23The folds of his flesh are tightly joined;
they are firm and immovable.
24His chest is hard as rock,
hard as a lower millstone.
25When he rises up, the mighty are terrified;
they retreat before his thrashing.
26The sword that reaches him has no effect,
nor does the spear or the dart or the javelin.
27Iron he treats like straw
and bronze like rotten wood.
28Arrows do not make him flee;

w15 Or *His pride is his*

*See the note on page 344.

†7 The NIV reads this word as גֵּוֹה, *back-of-him*.

°4 ק לוֹ

נֶהְפְּכוּ־ לוֹ אַבְנֵי־ קָלַע׃ כְּקַשׁ נֶחְשְׁבוּ תוֹתָח
club they-seem like-straw (21[29]) sling stones-of to-him they-are-turned

וְיִשְׂחַק לְרַעַשׁ כִּידוֹן׃ תַּחְתָּיו חַדּוּדֵי
jagged-pieces-of undersides-of-him (22[30]) lance at-rattling-of and-he-laughs

חָרֶשׂ יִרְפַּד חָרוּץ עֲלֵי־ טִיט׃ יַרְתִּיחַ
he-makes-churn (23[31]) mud in threshing-sledge he-leaves-trail potsherd

כַּסִּיר מְצוּלָה יָם יָשִׂים כַּמֶּרְקָחָה׃ אַחֲרָיו
behind-him (24[32]) like-the-ointment-pot he-stirs sea depth like-the-caldron

יָאִיר נָתִיב יַחְשֹׁב תְּהוֹם לְשֵׂיבָה׃ אֵין־ עַל־
on nothing (25[33]) as-white-haired deep he-would-think wake he-makes-glisten

עָפָר מָשְׁלוֹ הֶעָשׂוּ לִבְלִי־ חָת׃ אֵת־ כָּל־
all-of *** (26[34]) fear without the-one-being-created equal-of-him earth

גָּבֹהַּ יִרְאֶה הוּא מֶלֶךְ עַל־ כָּל־ בְּנֵי־ שָׁחַץ׃ וַיַּעַן
then-he-replied (42:1) pride sons-of all-of over king he he-looks haughty

אִיּוֹב אֶת־ יְהוָה וַיֹּאמַר׃ יָדַעְתָּ כִּי־ כֹל תּוּכָל וְלֹא־
and-not you-can-do all that I-know (2) and-he-said Yahweh *** Job

יִבָּצֵר מִמְּךָ מְזִמָּה׃ מִי זֶה ׀ מַעְלִים עֵצָה בְּלִי
without counsel obscuring this who? (3) plan of-you he-can-be-thwarted

דָעַת לָכֵן הִגַּדְתִּי וְלֹא אָבִין נִפְלָאוֹת
things-being-wonderful I-understood and-not I-spoke surely knowledge

מִמֶּנִּי וְלֹא אֵדָע׃ שְׁמַע־ נָא וְאָנֹכִי אֲדַבֵּר
I-will-speak and-I now! listen! (4) I-knew and-not more-than-me

אֶשְׁאָלְךָ וְהוֹדִיעֵנִי׃ לְשֵׁמַע־ אֹזֶן שְׁמַעְתִּיךָ
I-heard-of-you ear with-hearing-of (5) and-answer-me! I-will-question-you

וְעַתָּה עֵינִי רָאָתְךָ׃ עַל־ כֵּן אֶמְאַס וְנִחַמְתִּי עַל־
in and-I-repent I-despise-myself this for (6) she-saw-you eye-of-me but-now

עָפָר וָאֵפֶר׃ וַיְהִי אַחַר דִּבֶּר יְהוָה אֶת־ הַדְּבָרִים הָאֵלֶּה
the-these the-things *** Yahweh he-said after and-he-was (7) and-ash dust

אֶל־ אִיּוֹב וַיֹּאמֶר יְהוָה אֶל־ אֱלִיפַז הַתֵּימָנִי חָרָה אַפִּי
anger-of-me he-burns the-Temanite Eliphaz to Yahweh then-he-said Job to

בְךָ וּבִשְׁנֵי רֵעֶיךָ כִּי לֹא דִבַּרְתֶּם אֵלַי
of-me you-spoke not because friends-of-you and-against-two-of against-you

נְכוֹנָה כְּעַבְדִּי אִיּוֹב׃ וְעַתָּה קְחוּ־ לָכֶם שִׁבְעָה־ פָרִים
bulls seven for-you take! so-now (8) Job as-servant-of-me being-right

וְשִׁבְעָה אֵילִים וּלְכוּ ׀ אֶל־ עַבְדִּי אִיּוֹב וְהַעֲלִיתֶם עוֹלָה
burnt-offering and-you-sacrifice Job servant-of-me to and-go! rams and-seven

בַּעַדְכֶם וְאִיּוֹב עַבְדִּי יִתְפַּלֵּל עֲלֵיכֶם כִּי אִם־ פָּנָיו
faces-of-him surely indeed for-you he-will-pray servant-of-me and-Job for-you

slingstones are like chaff to
him.
[29]A club seems to him but a
piece of straw;
he laughs at the rattling of
the lance.
[30]His undersides are jagged
potsherds,
leaving a trail in the mud
like a threshing sledge.
[31]He makes the depths churn
like a boiling caldron
and stirs up the sea like a
pot of ointment.
[32]Behind him he leaves a
glistening wake;
one would think the deep
had white hair.
[33]Nothing on earth is his
equal—
a creature without fear.
[34]He looks down on all that are
haughty;
he is king over all that are
proud."

*Job*

42 Then Job replied to the
LORD:

[2]"I know that you can do all
things;
no plan of yours can be
thwarted.
[3]⌞You asked,⌟ 'Who is this that
obscures my counsel
without knowledge?'
Surely I spoke of things I
did not understand,
things too wonderful for me
to know.

[4]⌞"You said,⌟ 'Listen now, and I
will speak;
I will question you,
and you shall answer me.'
[5]My ears had heard of you
but now my eyes have seen
you.
[6]Therefore I despise myself
and repent in dust and
ashes."

*Epilogue*

[7]After the LORD had said these things to Job, he said to Eliphaz the Temanite, "I am angry with you and your two friends, because you have not spoken of me what is right, as my servant Job has. [8]So now take seven bulls and seven rams and go to my servant Job and sacrifice a burnt offering for yourselves. My servant Job will pray for you, and I will accept his

*See the note on page 344.

°2 ק ידעתי

אֶשָּׂא לְבִלְתִּי עֲשׂוֹת עִמָּכֶם נְבָלָה כִּי לֹא דִבַּרְתֶּם אֵלַי נְכוֹנָה
being-right of-me you-spoke not for folly with-you to-deal not I-will-accept

כְּעַבְדִּי אִיּוֹב׃ וַיֵּלְכוּ אֱלִיפַז הַתֵּימָנִי וּבִלְדַּד
and-Bildad the-Temanite Eliphaz so-they-went (9) Job as-servant-of-me

הַשּׁוּחִי צֹפַר הַנַּעֲמָתִי וַיַּעֲשׂוּ כַּאֲשֶׁר דִּבֶּר אֲלֵיהֶם יְהוָה
Yahweh to-them he-told as-what and-they-did the-Naamathite Zophar the-Shuhite

וַיִּשָּׂא יְהוָה אֶת־ פְּנֵי אִיּוֹב׃ וַיהוָה שָׁב אֶת־
*** he-returned then-Yahweh (10) Job faces-of *** Yahweh and-he-accepted

שְׁבִית אִיּוֹב בְּהִתְפַּלְלוֹ בְּעַד רֵעֵהוּ וַיֹּסֶף יְהוָה
Yahweh and-he-increased friends-of-him for after-to-pray-him Job prosperity-of

אֶת־כָּל־אֲשֶׁר לְאִיּוֹב לְמִשְׁנֶה׃ וַיָּבֹאוּ אֵלָיו כָּל־ אֶחָיו
brothers-of-him all-of to-him and-they-came (11) by-twice to-Job that all ***

וְכָל־ אַחְיֹתָיו וְכָל־ יֹדְעָיו לְפָנִים וַיֹּאכְלוּ
and-they-ate before ones-knowing-him and-all-of sisters-of-him and-all-of

עִמּוֹ לֶחֶם בְּבֵיתוֹ וַיָּנֻדוּ לוֹ וַיְנַחֲמוּ אֹתוֹ
him and-they-consoled to-him and-they-comforted in-house-of-him food with-him

עַל כָּל־ הָרָעָה אֲשֶׁר־ הֵבִיא יְהוָה עָלָיו וַיִּתְּנוּ־ לוֹ
to-him and-they-gave upon-him Yahweh he-brought that the-trouble all-of over

אִישׁ קְשִׂיטָה אֶחָת וְאִישׁ נֶזֶם זָהָב אֶחָד׃ וַיהוָה בֵּרַךְ אֶת־
*** he-blessed and-Yahweh (12) one gold ring-of and-each one kesitah each

אַחֲרִית אִיּוֹב מֵרֵאשִׁתוֹ וַיְהִי־ לוֹ אַרְבָּעָה עָשָׂר אֶלֶף
thousand ten four to-him and-he-was more-than-first-of-him Job latter-part-of

צֹאן וְשֵׁשֶׁת אֲלָפִים גְּמַלִּים וְאֶלֶף־ צֶמֶד בָּקָר וְאֶלֶף אֲתוֹנוֹת׃
donkeys and-thousand ox yoke-of and-thousand camels thousands and-six-of sheep

וַיְהִי־ לוֹ שִׁבְעָנָה בָנִים וְשָׁלוֹשׁ בָּנוֹת׃ וַיִּקְרָא
and-he-called (14) daughters and-three sons seven to-him also-he-was (13)

שֵׁם־ הָאַחַת יְמִימָה וְשֵׁם הַשֵּׁנִית קְצִיעָה וְשֵׁם הַשְּׁלִישִׁית
the-third and-name-of Keziah the-second and-name-of Jemimah the-first name-of

קֶרֶן הַפּוּךְ׃ וְלֹא נִמְצָא נָשִׁים יָפוֹת כִּבְנוֹת
as-daughters-of beautiful-ones women he-was-found and-not (15) Happuch Keren

אִיּוֹב בְּכָל־ הָאָרֶץ וַיִּתֵּן לָהֶם אֲבִיהֶם נַחֲלָה בְּתוֹךְ
with inheritance father-of-them to-them and-he-granted the-land in-all-of Job

אֲחֵיהֶם׃ וַיְחִי אִיּוֹב אַחֲרֵי־ זֹאת מֵאָה וְאַרְבָּעִים שָׁנָה
year and-forty hundred this after Job and-he-lived (16) brothers-of-them

וַיִּרְאֶ אֶת־ בָּנָיו וְאֶת־ בְּנֵי בָנָיו אַרְבָּעָה
four children-of-him children-of and children-of-him *** and-he-saw

דֹּרוֹת׃ וַיָּמָת אִיּוֹב זָקֵן וּשְׂבַע יָמִים׃
days and-full-of old Job so-he-died (17) generations

°10 ק שבות
°11 ק אחיותיו
°16 ק וירא

prayer and not deal with you according to your folly. You have not spoken of me what is right, as my servant Job has." [9]So Eliphaz the Temanite, Bildad the Shuhite and Zophar the Naamathite did what the LORD told them; and the LORD accepted Job's prayer.

[10]After Job had prayed for his friends, the LORD made him prosperous again and gave him twice as much as he had before. [11]All his brothers and sisters and everyone who had known him before came and ate with him in his house. They comforted and consoled him over all the trouble the LORD had brought upon him, and each one gave him a piece of silver[x] and a gold ring.

[12]The LORD blessed the latter part of Job's life more than the first. He had fourteen thousand sheep, six thousand camels, a thousand yoke of oxen and a thousand donkeys. [13]And he also had seven sons and three daughters. [14]The first daughter he named Jemimah, the second Keziah and the third Keren-Happuch. [15]Nowhere in all the land were there found women as beautiful as Job's daughters, and their father granted them an inheritance along with their brothers.

[16]After this, Job lived a hundred and forty years; he saw his children and their children to the fourth generation. [17]And so he died, old and full of years.

[x]*11* Hebrew *him a kesitah;* a kesitah was a unit of money of unknown weight and value.

אַשְׁרֵי הָאִישׁ אֲשֶׁר ׀ לֹא הָלַךְ בַּעֲצַת רְשָׁעִים
wicked-ones in-counsel-of he-walks not who the-man blessednesses-of (1:1)

וּבְדֶרֶךְ חַטָּאִים לֹא עָמָד וּבְמוֹשַׁב לֵצִים לֹא יָשָׁב׃
he-sits not ones-mocking or-in-seat-of he-stands not sinners or-in-way-of

כִּי אִם בְּתוֹרַת יְהוָה חֶפְצוֹ וּבְתוֹרָתוֹ יֶהְגֶּה
he-meditates and-on-law-of-him delight-of-him Yahweh in-law-of rather but (2)

יוֹמָם וָלָיְלָה׃ וְהָיָה כְּעֵץ שָׁתוּל עַל־ פַּלְגֵי מָיִם
waters streams-of by being-planted like-tree and-he-is (3) and-night by-day

אֲשֶׁר פִּרְיוֹ ׀ יִתֵּן בְּעִתּוֹ וְעָלֵהוּ לֹא־ יִבּוֹל
he-withers not and-leaf-of-him in-season-of-him he-yields fruit-of-him which

וְכֹל אֲשֶׁר־ יַעֲשֶׂה יַצְלִיחַ׃ לֹא־ כֵן הָרְשָׁעִים כִּי אִם־
rather but the-wicked-ones so not (4) he-prospers he-does that and-all

כַּמֹּץ אֲשֶׁר־ תִּדְּפֶנּוּ רוּחַ׃ עַל־ כֵּן ׀ לֹא־ יָקֻמוּ
they-will-stand not this for (5) wind she-blows-away-him that like-the-chaff

רְשָׁעִים בַּמִּשְׁפָּט וְחַטָּאִים בַּעֲדַת צַדִּיקִים׃ כִּי־
for (6) righteous-ones in-assembly-of or-sinners in-the-judgment wicked-ones

יוֹדֵעַ יְהוָה דֶּרֶךְ צַדִּיקִים וְדֶרֶךְ רְשָׁעִים
wicked-ones but-way-of righteous-ones way-of Yahweh watching-over

תֹּאבֵד׃ לָמָּה רָגְשׁוּ גוֹיִם וּלְאֻמִּים יֶהְגּוּ־ רִיק׃
vanity they-plot and-peoples nations they-rage why? (2:1) she-will-perish

יִתְיַצְּבוּ ׀ מַלְכֵי־ אֶרֶץ וְרוֹזְנִים נוֹסְדוּ־ יָחַד
together they-gather and-ones-ruling earth kings-of they-take-stand (2)

עַל־ יְהוָה* וְעַל־ מְשִׁיחוֹ׃ נְנַתְּקָה אֶת־
*** let-us-break (3) anointed-one-of-him and-against Yahweh against

מוֹסְרוֹתֵימוֹ וְנַשְׁלִיכָה מִמֶּנּוּ עֲבֹתֵימוֹ׃
fetters-of-them from-us and-let-us-throw-off chains-of-them

יוֹשֵׁב בַּשָּׁמַיִם יִשְׂחָק אֲדֹנָי יִלְעַג־ לָמוֹ׃
at-them he-scoffs Lord he-laughs in-the-heavens One-being-enthroned (4)

אָז יְדַבֵּר אֵלֵימוֹ בְאַפּוֹ וּבַחֲרוֹנוֹ
and-in-wrath-of-him in-anger-of-him against-them he-rebukes then (5)

יְבַהֲלֵמוֹ׃ וַאֲנִי נָסַכְתִּי מַלְכִּי עַל־ צִיּוֹן הַר־
hill-of Zion on king-of-me I-installed indeed-I (6) he-terrifies-them

קָדְשִׁי׃ אֲסַפְּרָה אֶל חֹק יְהוָה אָמַר אֵלַי
to-me he-said Yahweh decree-of to I-will-proclaim (7) holiness-of-me

בְּנִי אַתָּה אֲנִי הַיּוֹם יְלִדְתִּיךָ׃ שְׁאַל מִמֶּנִּי
of-me ask! (8) I-became-father-of-you the-day I you son-of-me

וְאֶתְּנָה גוֹיִם נַחֲלָתֶךָ וַאֲחֻזָּתְךָ אַפְסֵי־ אָרֶץ׃
earth ends-of and-possession-of-you inheritance-of-you nations and-I-will-make

**BOOK I**

*Psalms 1-41*

**Psalm 1**

1 Blessed is the man
who does not walk in the counsel of the wicked
or stand in the way of sinners
or sit in the seat of mockers.
2 But his delight is in the law of the LORD,
and on his law he meditates day and night.
3 He is like a tree planted by streams of water,
which yields its fruit in season
and whose leaf does not wither.
Whatever he does prospers.

4 Not so the wicked!
They are like chaff
that the wind blows away.
5 Therefore the wicked will not stand in the judgment,
nor sinners in the assembly of the righteous.

6 For the LORD watches over the way of the righteous,
but the way of the wicked will perish.

**Psalm 2**

1 Why do the nations rage
and the peoples plot in vain?
2 The kings of the earth take their stand
and the rulers gather together
against the LORD
and against his Anointed One.[a]
3 "Let us break their chains," they say,
"and throw off their fetters."

4 The One enthroned in heaven laughs;
the Lord scoffs at them.
5 Then he rebukes them in his anger
and terrifies them in his wrath, saying,
6 "I have installed my King[b]
on Zion, my holy hill."

7 I will proclaim the decree of the LORD:

He said to me, "You are my Son[c];
today I have become your Father.[d]
8 Ask of me,
and I will make the nations your inheritance,
the ends of the earth your possession.

[a]2 Or *anointed one*
[b]6 Or *king* [c]7 Or *son*; also in verse 12
[d]7 Or *have begotten you*

*2 Most mss have the accent *rebia mugrash* ( ֗ ).

תְּרֹעֵם בְּשֵׁבֶט בַּרְזֶל כִּכְלִי יוֹצֵר
one-making-pottery like-article-of iron with-scepter-of you-will-rule-them (9)

תְּנַפְּצֵם׃ וְעַתָּה מְלָכִים הַשְׂכִּילוּ הִוָּסְרוּ
be-warned! be-wise! kings therefore-now (10) you-will-dash-to-pieces-them

שֹׁפְטֵי אָרֶץ׃ עִבְדוּ אֶת־יְהוָה בְּיִרְאָה וְגִילוּ בִּרְעָדָה׃
with-trembling and-rejoice! with-fear Yahweh *** serve! (11) earth ones-ruling-of

נַשְּׁקוּ־בַר פֶּן־יֶאֱנַף ׀ וְתֹאבְדוּ דֶרֶךְ כִּי־יִבְעַר
he-can-flare-up for way and-you-be-destroyed he-be-angry lest son kiss! (12)

כִּמְעַט אַפּוֹ אַשְׁרֵי כָּל־חוֹסֵי בוֹ׃
in-him ones-taking-refuge-of all-of blessednesses-of wrath-of-him in-moment

מִזְמוֹר לְדָוִד בְּבָרְחוֹ מִפְּנֵי ׀ אַבְשָׁלוֹם בְּנוֹ׃
son-of-him Absalom from-faces-of when-to-flee-him of-David psalm *(3:1)

יְהוָה מָה־רַבּוּ צָרָי רַבִּים קָמִים עָלָי׃
against-me ones-rising-up many foes-of-me they-are-many how! Yahweh (2)

רַבִּים אֹמְרִים לְנַפְשִׁי אֵין יְשׁוּעָתָה לּוֹ בֵאלֹהִים סֶלָה׃
selah by-God for-him deliverance no of-self-of-me ones-saying many (3)

וְאַתָּה יְהוָה מָגֵן בַּעֲדִי כְּבוֹדִי וּמֵרִים
and-one-lifting Glorious-One-of-me around-me shield Yahweh but-you (4)

רֹאשִׁי׃ קוֹלִי אֶל־יְהוָה אֶקְרָא וַיַּעֲנֵנִי מֵהַר
from-hill-of and-he-answers-me I-cry Yahweh to voice-of-me (5) head-of-me

קָדְשׁוֹ סֶלָה׃ אֲנִי שָׁכַבְתִּי וָאִישָׁנָה הֱקִיצוֹתִי כִּי יְהוָה
Yahweh because I-wake and-I-sleep I-lie-down I (6) selah holiness-of-him

יִסְמְכֵנִי׃ לֹא־אִירָא מֵרִבְבוֹת עָם אֲשֶׁר
who people of-tens-of-thousands-of I-will-fear not (7) he-sustains-me

סָבִיב שָׁתוּ עָלָי׃ קוּמָה יְהוָה ׀ הוֹשִׁיעֵנִי אֱלֹהַי
God-of-me deliver-me! Yahweh arise! (8) against-me they-are-drawn-up every-side

כִּי־הִכִּיתָ אֶת־כָּל־אֹיְבַי לֶחִי שִׁנֵּי רְשָׁעִים
wicked-ones teeth-of jaw ones-being-enemies-of-me all-of *** you-struck for

שִׁבַּרְתָּ׃ לַיהוָה הַיְשׁוּעָה עַל־עַמְּךָ בִרְכָתֶךָ
blessing-of-you people-of-you on the-deliverance from-Yahweh (9) you-broke

סֶלָה׃ לַמְנַצֵּחַ בִּנְגִינוֹת מִזְמוֹר לְדָוִד׃
of-David psalm with-stringed-instruments for-the-one-directing *(4:1) selah

בְּקָרְאִי עֲנֵנִי ׀ אֱלֹהֵי צִדְקִי בַּצָּר
from-the-distress righteousness-of-me God-of answer-me! when-to-call-me (2)

הִרְחַבְתָּ לִּי חָנֵּנִי וּשְׁמַע תְּפִלָּתִי׃ בְּנֵי
sons-of (3) prayer-of-me and-hear! be-merciful-to-me! to-me you-give-relief

אִישׁ עַד־מֶה כְבוֹדִי לִכְלִמָּה תֶּאֱהָבוּן רִיק תְּבַקְשׁוּ
will-you-seek delusion will-you-love into-shame glory-of-me when? until man

9 You will rule them with an
iron scepter[e];
you will dash them to pieces
like pottery."

10 Therefore, you kings, be wise;
be warned, you rulers of the
earth.
11 Serve the LORD with fear
and rejoice with trembling.
12 Kiss the Son, lest he be angry
and you be destroyed in
your way,
for his wrath can flare up in a
moment.
Blessed are all who take
refuge in him.

**Psalm 3**

A psalm of David. When he fled from his son Absalom.

1 O LORD, how many are my
foes!
How many rise up against
me!
2 Many are saying of me,
"God will not deliver him."
*Selah*[f]

3 But you are a shield around
me, O LORD,
my Glorious One, who lifts
up my head.
4 To the LORD I cry aloud,
and he answers me from his
holy hill. *Selah*

5 I lie down and sleep;
I wake again, because the
LORD sustains me.
6 I will not fear the tens of
thousands
drawn up against me on
every side.

7 Arise, O LORD!
Deliver me, O my God!
For you have struck all my
enemies on the jaw;
you have broken the teeth
of the wicked.

8 From the LORD comes
deliverance.
May your blessing be on
your people. *Selah*

**Psalm 4**

For the director of music. With stringed instruments. A psalm of David.

1 Answer me when I call to you,
O my righteous God.
Give me relief from my
distress;
be merciful to me and hear
my prayer.

2 How long, O men, will you
turn my glory into
shame[g]?
How long will you love
delusions and seek false

e9 Or *will break them with a rod of iron*
f2 A word of uncertain meaning, occurring frequently in the Psalms; possibly a musical term
g2 Or *you dishonor my Glorious One*

***1** The Hebrew numeration of this psalm begins with the "superscription" of the English translation; thus there is a one-verse discrepancy throughout the psalm.

כָזָב סֶלָה׃ (4) וּדְעוּ כִּי־ הִפְלָה יְהוָה חָסִיד לוֹ יְהוָה
Yahweh for-him godly Yahweh he-set-apart that and-know! (4) selah lie

יִשְׁמַע בְּקָרְאִי אֵלָיו׃ (5) רִגְזוּ וְאַל־ תֶּחֱטָאוּ אִמְרוּ
search! you-sin and-not be-angry! (5) to-him when-to-call-me he-will-hear

בִלְבַבְכֶם עַל־ מִשְׁכַּבְכֶם וְדֹמּוּ סֶלָה׃ (6) זִבְחוּ זִבְחֵי־
sacrifices-of offer! (6) selah and-be-silent! bed-of-you on in-heart-of-you

צֶדֶק וּבִטְחוּ אֶל־ יְהוָה׃ (7) רַבִּים אֹמְרִים מִי־ יַרְאֵנוּ טוֹב
good he-can-show-us who? ones-asking many (7) Yahweh in and-trust! right

נְסָה־ עָלֵינוּ אוֹר פָּנֶיךָ יְהוָה׃ (8) נָתַתָּה שִׂמְחָה
joy you-put (8) Yahweh faces-of-you light-of upon-us let-shine!

בְלִבִּי מֵעֵת דְּגָנָם וְתִירוֹשָׁם
and-new-wine-of-them grain-of-them more-than-time-of in-heart-of-me

רָבּוּ׃ (9) בְּשָׁלוֹם יַחְדָּו אֶשְׁכְּבָה וְאִישָׁן כִּי־ אַתָּה
you for and-I-will-sleep I-will-lie-down together in-peace (9) they-abound

יְהוָה לְבָדָד לָבֶטַח תּוֹשִׁיבֵנִי׃ *(5:1) לַמְנַצֵּחַ אֶל־
for for-the-one-directing *(5:1) you-make-dwell-me in-safety alone Yahweh

הַנְּחִילוֹת מִזְמוֹר לְדָוִד׃ (2) אֲמָרַי הַאֲזִינָה ׀ יְהוָה בִּינָה
consider! Yahweh give-ear! words-of-me (2) of-David psalm the-flutes

הֲגִיגִי׃ (3) הַקְשִׁיבָה ׀ לְקוֹל שַׁוְעִי מַלְכִּי
King-of-me cry-for-help-of-me to-sound-of listen! (3) sighing-of-me

וֵאלֹהָי כִּי־ אֵלֶיךָ אֶתְפַּלָּל׃ (4) יְהוָה בֹּקֶר תִּשְׁמַע קוֹלִי
voice-of-me you-hear morning Yahweh (4) I-pray to-you for and-God-of-me

בֹּקֶר אֶעֱרָךְ־ לְךָ וַאֲצַפֶּה׃ (5) כִּי ׀ לֹא אֵל־ חָפֵץ
pleased-in God-of not for (5) and-I-wait before-you I-lay-request morning

רֶשַׁע ׀ אָתָּה לֹא יְגֻרְךָ רָע׃ (6) לֹא־ יִתְיַצְּבוּ
they-can-stand not (6) wicked he-can-dwell-with-you not you evil

הוֹלְלִים לְנֶגֶד עֵינֶיךָ שָׂנֵאתָ כָּל־ פֹּעֲלֵי אָוֶן׃
wrong ones-doing-of all-of you-hate eyes-of-you at-before ones-being-arrogant

(7) תְּאַבֵּד דֹּבְרֵי כָזָב אִישׁ־ דָּמִים וּמִרְמָה יְתָעֵב ׀
he-abhors and-deceit bloods man-of lie ones-telling-of you-destroy (7)

יְהוָה׃ (8) וַאֲנִי בְּרֹב חַסְדְּךָ אָבוֹא בֵיתֶךָ
house-of-you I-will-come-into mercy-of-you by-greatness-of but-I (8) Yahweh

אֶשְׁתַּחֲוֶה אֶל־ הֵיכַל־ קָדְשְׁךָ בְּיִרְאָתֶךָ׃ (9) יְהוָה ׀
Yahweh (9) in-reverence-of-you holiness-of-you temple-of toward I-will-bow

נְחֵנִי בְצִדְקָתֶךָ לְמַעַן שׁוֹרְרָי
ones-being-enemies-of-me because-of in-righteousness-of-you lead-me!

הַוְשַׁר לְפָנַי דַּרְכֶּךָ׃ (10) כִּי אֵין בְּפִיהוּ נְכוֹנָה
being-trusted from-mouth-of-him not for (10) way-of-you before-me make-straight!

gods[h]? *Selah*
3 Know that the LORD has set
apart the godly for
himself;
the LORD will hear when I
call to him.

4 In your anger do not sin;
when you are on your beds,
search your hearts and be
silent. *Selah*
5 Offer right sacrifices
and trust in the LORD.

6 Many are asking, "Who can
show us any good?"
Let the light of your face
shine upon us, O LORD.
7 You have filled my heart with
greater joy
than when their grain and
new wine abound.
8 I will lie down and sleep in
peace,
for you alone, O LORD,
make me dwell in safety.

**Psalm 5**

For the director of music. For flutes. A psalm of David.

1 Give ear to my words, O LORD,
consider my sighing.
2 Listen to my cry for help,
my King and my God,
for to you I pray.
3 Morning by morning, O LORD,
you hear my voice;
morning by morning I lay
my requests before you
and wait in expectation.

4 You are not a God who takes
pleasure in evil;
with you the wicked cannot
dwell.
5 The arrogant cannot stand in
your presence;
you hate all who do wrong.
6 You destroy those who tell lies;
bloodthirsty and deceitful
men
the LORD abhors.

7 But I, by your great mercy,
will come into your house;
in reverence will I bow down
toward your holy temple.
8 Lead me, O LORD, in your
righteousness
because of my enemies—
make straight your way
before me.

9 Not a word from their mouth
can be trusted;

[h]2 Hebrew *seek lies*

*Heading, *1* See the note on page 349.

9 ק הישר

קִרְבָּם הַוּוֹת קֶבֶר־ פָּתוּחַ גְּרוֹנָם לְשׁוֹנָם
tongue-of-them throat-of-them being-open grave destructions heart-of-them

יַחֲלִיקוּן׃† הַאֲשִׁימֵם׀ אֱלֹהִים יִפְּלוּ
let-them-fall God declare-guilty-them! (11) they-speak-deceit

מִמֹּעֲצוֹתֵיהֶם בְּרֹב פִּשְׁעֵיהֶם הַדִּיחֵמוֹ כִּי־ מָרוּ
they-rebelled for banish-them! sins-of-them for-many-of by-intrigues-of-them

בָךְ׃ וְיִשְׂמְחוּ כָל־ חוֹסֵי בָךְ
in-you ones-taking-refuge-of all-of but-let-them-be-glad (12) against-you

לְעוֹלָם יְרַנֵּנוּ וְתָסֵךְ עָלֵימוֹ
over-them and-you-spread-protection let-them-sing-for-joy for-ever

וְיַעְלְצוּ בְךָ אֹהֲבֵי שְׁמֶךָ׃ כִּי־ אַתָּה
you for (13) name-of-you ones-loving-of in-you that-they-may-rejoice

תְּבָרֵךְ צַדִּיק יְהוָה כַּצִּנָּה רָצוֹן תַּעְטְרֶנּוּ׃
you-surround-him favor as-the-shield Yahweh righteous you-bless

לַמְנַצֵּחַ בִּנְגִינוֹת עַל־ הַשְּׁמִינִית
the-sheminith according-to with-stringed-instruments for-the-one-directing *(6:1)

מִזְמוֹר לְדָוִד׃ יְהוָה אַל־ בְּאַפְּךָ תוֹכִיחֵנִי וְאַל־
or-not you-rebuke-me in-anger-of-you not Yahweh (2) of-David psalm

בַּחֲמָתְךָ תְיַסְּרֵנִי׃ חָנֵּנִי יְהוָה כִּי אֻמְלַל
faint for Yahweh be-merciful-to-me! (3) you-discipline-me in-wrath-of-you

אָנִי רְפָאֵנִי יְהוָה כִּי נִבְהֲלוּ עֲצָמָי׃ וְנַפְשִׁי
and-soul-of-me (4) bones-of-me they-are-in-agony for Yahweh heal-me! I

נִבְהֲלָה מְאֹד וְאַתְּ° יְהוָה עַד־ מָתָי׃ שׁוּבָה יְהוָה חַלְּצָה
deliver! Yahweh turn! (5) when? until Yahweh but-you great she-is-in-anguish

נַפְשִׁי הוֹשִׁיעֵנִי לְמַעַן חַסְדֶּךָ׃ כִּי אֵין בַּמָּוֶת
in-the-death not for (6) unfailing-love-of-you because-of save-me! soul-of-me

זִכְרֶךָ בִּשְׁאוֹל מִי יוֹדֶה־ לָּךְ׃ יָגַעְתִּי
I-am-worn-out (7) to-you he-praises who? from-Sheol remembrance-of-you

בְאַנְחָתִי אַשְׂחֶה בְכָל־ לַיְלָה מִטָּתִי בְּדִמְעָתִי
with-tear-of-me bed-of-me night through-all-of I-flood from-groaning-of-me

עַרְשִׂי אַמְסֶה׃ עָשְׁשָׁה מִכַּעַס עֵינִי עָתְקָה
she-fails eye-of-me with-sorrow she-grows-weak (8) I-drench couch-of-me

בְּכָל־ צוֹרְרָי׃ סוּרוּ מִמֶּנִּי כָּל־ פֹּעֲלֵי
ones-doing-of all-of from-me away! (9) ones-being-foes-of-me because-of-all-of

אָוֶן כִּי־ שָׁמַע יְהוָה קוֹל בִּכְיִי׃ שָׁמַע יְהוָה
Yahweh he-heard (10) weeping-of-me sound-of Yahweh he-heard for evil

תְּחִנָּתִי יְהוָה תְּפִלָּתִי יִקָּח׃ יֵבֹשׁוּ׀
may-they-be-ashamed (11) he-accepts prayer-of-me Yahweh cry-for-mercy-of-me

their heart is filled with
destruction.
Their throat is an open grave;
with their tongue they speak
deceit.
10Declare them guilty, O God!
Let their intrigues be their
downfall.
Banish them for their many
sins,
for they have rebelled
against you.
11But let all who take refuge in
you be glad;
let them ever sing for joy.
Spread your protection over
them,
that those who love your
name may rejoice in you.
12For surely, O LORD, you bless
the righteous;
you surround them with
your favor as with a
shield.

### Psalm 6

For the director of music. With stringed instruments. According to *sheminith.*[t] A psalm of David.

1O LORD, do not rebuke me in
your anger
or discipline me in your
wrath.
2Be merciful to me, LORD, for I
am faint;
O LORD, heal me, for my
bones are in agony.
3My soul is in anguish.
How long, O LORD, how
long?

4Turn, O LORD, and deliver me;
save me because of your
unfailing love.
5No one remembers you when
he is dead.
Who praises you from the
grave[j]?

6I am worn out from groaning;
all night long I flood my bed
with weeping
and drench my couch with
tears.
7My eyes grow weak with
sorrow;
they fail because of all my
foes.

8Away from me, all you who
do evil,
for the LORD has heard my
weeping.
9The LORD has heard my cry for
mercy;
the LORD accepts my prayer.

tTitle: Probably a musical term
j5 Hebrew *Sheol*

*Heading, *1* See the note on page 349.

†*10* Most mss have the accent on the final syllable.

°*4* ק ואתה

וְיִבָּהֲלוּ מְאֹד כָּל־ אֹיְבָי

ones-being-enemies-of-me all-of greatly and-may-they-be-dismayed

יָשֻׁבוּ יֵבֹשׁוּ רָגַע׃ שִׁגָּיוֹן לְדָוִד

of-David shiggaion *(7:1) suddenly may-they-be-disgraced may-they-turn-back

אֲשֶׁר־ שָׁר לַיהוָה עַל־ דִּבְרֵי־ כוּשׁ בֶּן־יְמִינִי׃ יְהוָה

Yahweh (2) Benjamite Cush matters-of concerning to-Yahweh he-sang which

אֱלֹהַי בְּךָ חָסִיתִי הוֹשִׁיעֵנִי מִכָּל־ רֹדְפַי

ones-pursuing-me from-all-of save-me! I-take-refuge in-you God-of-me

וְהַצִּילֵנִי׃ פֶּן־ יִטְרֹף כְּאַרְיֵה נַפְשִׁי פֹּרֵק

ripping-to-pieces self-of-me like-lion he-will-tear or (3) and-deliver-me!

וְאֵין מַצִּיל׃ יְהוָה אֱלֹהַי אִם־עָשִׂיתִי זֹאת אִם־ יֶשׁ־ עָוֶל

guilt there-is if this I-did if God-of-me Yahweh (4) rescuing and-no-one

בְּכַפָּי׃ אִם־גָּמַלְתִּי שׁוֹלְמִי רָע וָאֲחַלְּצָה

or-I-robbed evil one-being-at-peace-with-me I-did if (5) on-hands-of-me

צוֹרְרִי רֵיקָם׃ יִרַדֹּף אוֹיֵב ׀

one-being-enemy let-him-pursue (6) without-cause one-being-foe-of-me

נַפְשִׁי וְיַשֵּׂג וְיִרְמֹס לָאָרֶץ חַיָּי

lives-of-me to-the-ground and-let-him-trample and-let-him-overtake self-of-me

וּכְבוֹדִי ׀ לֶעָפָר יַשְׁכֵּן סֶלָה׃ קוּמָה יְהוָה ׀

Yahweh arise! (7) selah let-him-make-sleep in-the-dust and-honor-of-me

בְּאַפֶּךָ הִנָּשֵׂא בְּעַבְרוֹת צוֹרְרָי וְעוּרָה

and-awake! ones-being-enemies-of-me against-rages-of rise-up! in-anger-of-you

אֵלַי מִשְׁפָּט צִוִּיתָ׃ וַעֲדַת לְאֻמִּים תְּסוֹבְבֶךָּ

let-her-surround-you peoples and-assembly-of (8) you-decree justice God-of-me

וְעָלֶיהָ לַמָּרוֹם שׁוּבָה׃ יְהוָה יָדִין עַמִּים

peoples let-him-judge Yahweh (9) rule! from-the-height and-over-her

שָׁפְטֵנִי יְהוָה כְּצִדְקִי וּכְתֻמִּי עָלָי׃

Most-High and-as-integrity-of-me as-righteousness-of-me Yahweh judge-me!

יִגְמָר־ נָא רַע ׀ רְשָׁעִים וּתְכוֹנֵן צַדִּיק

righteous and-you-make-secure wicked-ones violence-of now! may-he-end (10)

וּבֹחֵן לִבּוֹת וּכְלָיוֹת אֱלֹהִים צַדִּיק׃ מָגִנִּי עַל־אֱלֹהִים

God Most-High shield-of-me (11) righteous God and-hearts minds and-searching

מוֹשִׁיעַ יִשְׁרֵי־ לֵב׃ אֱלֹהִים שׁוֹפֵט צַדִּיק וְאֵל

and-God righteous judging God (12) heart ones-upright-of saving

זֹעֵם בְּכָל־ יוֹם׃ אִם־ לֹא יָשׁוּב חַרְבּוֹ

sword-of-him he-relents not if (13) day in-every-of expressing-wrath

יִלְטוֹשׁ קַשְׁתּוֹ דָרַךְ וַיְכוֹנְנֶהָ׃

and-he-will-string-her he-will-bend bow-of-him he-will-sharpen

---

10 May all my enemies be
ashamed and dismayed;
may they turn back in
sudden disgrace.

**Psalm 7**

A *shiggaion*[k] of David, which he sang to the LORD concerning Cush, a Benjamite.

1 O LORD my God, I take refuge
in you;
save and deliver me from all
who pursue me,
2 or they will tear me like a lion
and rip me to pieces with
no one to rescue me.

3 O LORD my God, if I have
done this
and there is guilt on my
hands—
4 if I have done evil to him who
is at peace with me
or without cause have
robbed my foe—
5 then let my enemy pursue and
overtake me;
let him trample my life to
the ground
and make me sleep in the
dust. *Selah*

6 Arise, O LORD, in your anger;
rise up against the rage of
my enemies.
Awake, my God; decree
justice.
7 Let the assembled peoples
gather around you.
Rule over them from on
high;
8 let the LORD judge the
peoples.
Judge me, O LORD, according
to my righteousness,
according to my integrity, O
Most High.
9 O righteous God,
who searches minds and
hearts,
bring to an end the violence of
the wicked
and make the righteous
secure.

10 My shield[l] is God Most High,
who saves the upright in
heart.
11 God is a righteous judge,
a God who expresses his
wrath every day.
12 If he does not relent,
he[m] will sharpen his sword;
he will bend and string his
bow.

[k] Title: Probably a literary or musical term
[l] 10 Or *sovereign*
[m] 12 Or *If a man does not repent, / God*

*Heading, *1* See the note on page 349.

וְלוֹ הֵכִין כְּלֵי־ מָוֶת חִצָּיו לְדֹלְקִים
of-ones-flaming arrows-of-him death weapons-of he-prepared and-for-him (14)

יִפְעָל׃ הִנֵּה יְחַבֶּל־ אָוֶן וְהָרָה עָמָל
trouble and-he-conceives evil he-is-pregnant see! (15) he-makes-ready

וְיָלַד שָׁקֶר׃ בּוֹר כָּרָה וַיַּחְפְּרֵהוּ
and-he-scoops-out-him he-digs hole (16) disillusionment then-he-gives-birth

וַיִּפֹּל בְּשַׁחַת יִפְעָל׃ יָשׁוּב עֲמָלוֹ בְרֹאשׁוֹ
on-head-of-him trouble-of-him he-recoils (17) he-made into-pit but-he-falls

וְעַל קָדְקֳדוֹ חֲמָסוֹ יֵרֵד׃ אוֹדֶה יְהוָה
Yahweh I-will-thank (18) he-comes-down violence-of-him head-of-him and-on

כְּצִדְקוֹ וַאֲזַמְּרָה שֵׁם־ יְהוָה עֶלְיוֹן׃
Most-High Yahweh name-of and-I-will-sing-praise because-of-righteousness-of-him

לַמְנַצֵּחַ עַל־ הַגִּתִּית מִזְמוֹר לְדָוִד׃
of-David psalm the-gittith according-to for-the-one-directing *(8:1)

יְהוָה אֲדֹנֵינוּ מָה־ אַדִּיר שִׁמְךָ בְּכָל־ הָאָרֶץ אֲשֶׁר
who the-earth in-all-of name-of-you majestic how! Lord-of-us Yahweh (2)

תְּנָה הוֹדְךָ עַל־ הַשָּׁמָיִם׃ מִפִּי עוֹלְלִים ׀
children from-lip-of (3) the-heavens above glory-of-you set!

וְיֹנְקִים יִסַּדְתָּ עֹז לְמַעַן צוֹרְרֶיךָ
ones-being-enemies-of-you because-of strength you-ordained and-ones-being-infants

לְהַשְׁבִּית אוֹיֵב וּמִתְנַקֵּם׃ כִּי־ אֶרְאֶה שָׁמֶיךָ
heavens-of-you I-consider when (4) and-one-avenging one-being-foe to-silence

מַעֲשֵׂי אֶצְבְּעֹתֶיךָ יָרֵחַ וְכוֹכָבִים אֲשֶׁר כּוֹנָנְתָּה׃ מָה־
what? (5) you-set-in-place which and-stars moon fingers-of-you works-of

אֱנוֹשׁ כִּי־ תִזְכְּרֶנּוּ וּבֶן־ אָדָם כִּי תִפְקְדֶנּוּ׃
you-care-for-him that man and-son-of you-are-mindful-of-him that man

וַתְּחַסְּרֵהוּ מְּעַט מֵאֱלֹהִים וְכָבוֹד וְהָדָר תְּעַטְּרֵהוּ׃
you-crowned-him and-honor and-glory than-God little and-you-made-lower-him (6)

תַּמְשִׁילֵהוּ בְּמַעֲשֵׂי יָדֶיךָ כֹּל שַׁתָּה תַחַת־
under you-put everything hands-of-you over-works-of you-made-ruler-him (7)

רַגְלָיו׃ צֹנֶה וַאֲלָפִים כֻּלָּם וְגַם בַּהֲמוֹת שָׂדָי׃
field beasts-of and-also all-of-them and-herds flock (8) feet-of-him

צִפּוֹר שָׁמַיִם וּדְגֵי הַיָּם עֹבֵר אָרְחוֹת יַמִּים׃
seas paths-of swimming-through the-sea and-fishes-of airs bird-of (9)

יְהוָה אֲדֹנֵינוּ מָה־ אַדִּיר שִׁמְךָ בְּכָל־ הָאָרֶץ׃
the-earth in-all-of name-of-you majestic how! Lord-of-us Yahweh (10)

לַמְנַצֵּחַ עַלְמוּת לַבֵּן מִזְמוֹר לְדָוִד׃
of-David psalm of-the-son to-death-of for-the-one-directing *(9:1)

13 He has prepared his deadly
weapons;
he makes ready his flaming
arrows.

14 He who is pregnant with evil
and conceives trouble gives
birth to disillusionment.
15 He who digs a hole and scoops
it out
falls into the pit he has
made.
16 The trouble he causes recoils
on himself;
his violence comes down on
his own head.

17 I will give thanks to the LORD
because of his
righteousness
and will sing praise to the
name of the LORD Most
High.

### Psalm 8

For the director of music. According to *gittith*.[n] A psalm of David.

1 O LORD, our Lord,
how majestic is your name
in all the earth!

You have set your glory
above the heavens.
2 From the lips of children and
infants
you have ordained praise[o]
because of your enemies,
to silence the foe and the
avenger.

3 When I consider your heavens,
the work of your fingers,
the moon and the stars,
which you have set in place,
4 what is man that you are
mindful of him,
the son of man that you
care for him?
5 You made him a little lower
than the heavenly beings[p]
and crowned him with glory
and honor.

6 You made him ruler over the
works of your hands;
you put everything under
his feet:
7 all flocks and herds,
and the beasts of the field,
8 the birds of the air,
and the fish of the sea,
all that swim the paths of
the seas.

9 O LORD, our Lord,
how majestic is your name
in all the earth!

### Psalm 9[q]

For the director of music. To ⌞the tune of⌟ "The Death of the Son." A psalm of David.

[n]Title: Probably a musical term
[o]2 Or *strength*
[p]5 Or *than God*
[q]Psalms 9 and 10 may have been originally a single acrostic poem, the stanzas of which begin with the successive letters of the Hebrew alphabet. In the Septuagint they constitute one psalm.

*Heading, *1* See the note on page 349.

אוֹדֶה יְהוָה בְּכָל־ לִבִּי אֲסַפְּרָה כָּל־
all-of I-will-tell heart-of-me with-all-of Yahweh I-will-praise (2)

נִפְלְאוֹתֶיךָ׃ אֶשְׂמְחָה וְאֶעֶלְצָה בָךְ
in-you and-I-will-rejoice I-will-be-glad (3) things-being-wonders-of-you

אֲזַמְּרָה שִׁמְךָ עֶלְיוֹן׃ בְּשׁוּב־ אוֹיְבַי
being-enemies-of-me when-to-turn (4) Most-High name-of-you I-will-sing-praise

אָחוֹר יִכָּשְׁלוּ וְיֹאבְדוּ מִפָּנֶיךָ׃ כִּי־ עָשִׂיתָ מִשְׁפָּטִי
right-of-me you-upheld for (5) at-before-you and-they-perish they-stumble back

וְדִינִי יָשַׁבְתָּ לְכִסֵּא שׁוֹפֵט צֶדֶק׃ גָּעַרְתָּ גוֹיִם
nations you-rebuked (6) righteous judging on-throne you-sat and-cause-of-me

אִבַּדְתָּ רָשָׁע שְׁמָם מָחִיתָ לְעוֹלָם וָעֶד׃
and-ever to-forever you-blotted-out name-of-them wicked you-destroyed

הָאוֹיֵב ׀ תַּמּוּ חֳרָבוֹת לָנֶצַח וְעָרִים
and-cities to-endless ruins they-are-overtaken the-one-being-enemy (7)

נָתַשְׁתָּ אָבַד זִכְרָם הֵמָּה׃ וַיהוָה לְעוֹלָם
to-forever and-Yahweh (8) they memory-of-them he-perished you-uprooted

יֵשֵׁב כּוֹנֵן לַמִּשְׁפָּט כִּסְאוֹ׃ וְהוּא
and-he (9) throne-of-him for-the-judgment he-established he-reigns

יִשְׁפֹּט־ תֵּבֵל בְּצֶדֶק יָדִין לְאֻמִּים בְּמֵישָׁרִים׃
with-justices peoples he-will-govern in-righteousness world he-will-judge

וִיהִי יְהוָה מִשְׂגָּב לַדָּךְ מִשְׂגָּב לְעִתּוֹת
in-times stronghold for-the-oppressed refuge Yahweh and-he-is (10)

בַּצָּרָה׃ וְיִבְטְחוּ בְךָ יוֹדְעֵי שְׁמֶךָ כִּי
for name-of-you ones-knowing-of in-you and-they-will-trust (11) of-the-trouble

לֹא־ עָזַבְתָּ דֹרְשֶׁיךָ יְהוָה׃ זַמְּרוּ לַיהוָה
to-Yahweh sing-praises! (12) Yahweh ones-seeking-of-you you-forsook never

יֹשֵׁב צִיּוֹן הַגִּידוּ בָעַמִּים עֲלִילוֹתָיו׃ כִּי־
for (13) deeds-of-him among-the-nations proclaim! Zion one-being-enthroned-of

דֹרֵשׁ דָּמִים אוֹתָם זָכָר לֹא־ שָׁכַח צַעֲקַת עֲנָיִים׃
afflicted-ones cry-of he-ignores not he-remembers them bloods one-avenging

חָנְנֵנִי יְהוָה רְאֵה עָנְיִי מִשֹּׂנְאָי
by-ones-being-enemies-of-me persecution-of-me see! Yahweh have-mercy-on-me! (14)

מְרוֹמְמִי מִשַּׁעֲרֵי מָוֶת׃ לְמַעַן אֲסַפְּרָה כָּל־
all-of I-may-declare that (15) death from-gates-of lifting-up-me

תְּהִלָּתֶיךָ בְּשַׁעֲרֵי בַת־ צִיּוֹן אָגִילָה בִּישׁוּעָתֶךָ׃
in-salvation-of-you I-will-rejoice Zion daughter-of in-gates-of praises-of-you

טָבְעוּ גוֹיִם בְּשַׁחַת עָשׂוּ בְּרֶשֶׁת־ זוּ טָמָנוּ נִלְכְּדָה
she-is-caught they-hid that in-net they-dug into-pit nations they-fell (16)

1 I will praise you, O LORD, with
all my heart;
I will tell of all your
wonders.
2 I will be glad and rejoice in
you;
I will sing praise to your
name, O Most High.

3 My enemies turn back;
they stumble and perish
before you.
4 For you have upheld my right
and my cause;
you have sat on your
throne, judging
righteously.
5 You have rebuked the nations
and destroyed the wicked;
you have blotted out their
name for ever and ever.
6 Endless ruin has overtaken the
enemy,
you have uprooted their
cities;
even the memory of them
has perished.

7 The LORD reigns forever;
he has established his
throne for judgment.
8 He will judge the world in
righteousness;
he will govern the peoples
with justice.
9 The LORD is a refuge for the
oppressed,
a stronghold in times of
trouble.
10 Those who know your name
will trust in you,
for you, LORD, have never
forsaken those who seek
you.

11 Sing praises to the LORD,
enthroned in Zion;
proclaim among the nations
what he has done.
12 For he who avenges blood
remembers;
he does not ignore the cry
of the afflicted.

13 O LORD, see how my enemies
persecute me!
Have mercy and lift me up
from the gates of death,
14 that I may declare your praises
in the gates of the Daughter
of Zion
and there rejoice in your
salvation.
15 The nations have fallen into
the pit they have dug;
their feet are caught in the
net they have hidden.

*See the note on page 349.

°13 ק ענוים

רַגְלָם׃ נוֹדַע ׀ יְהוָה מִשְׁפָּט עָשָׂה בְּפֹעַל כַּפָּיו
hands-of-him by-work-of he-does justice Yahweh he-is-known (17) foot-of-them

נוֹקֵשׁ רָשָׁע הִגָּיוֹן סֶלָה׃ יָשׁוּבוּ רְשָׁעִים לִשְׁאוֹלָה
to-Sheol wicked-ones they-return (18) selah higgaion wicked being-ensnared

כָּל־ גּוֹיִם שְׁכֵחֵי אֱלֹהִים׃ כִּי לֹא לָנֶצַח
to-always not but (19) God ones-forgetful-of nations all-of

יִשָּׁכַח אֶבְיוֹן תִּקְוַת °עֲנָוִים תֹּאבַד לָעַד׃
to-ever she-will-perish afflicted-ones hope-of needy he-will-be-forgotten

קוּמָה יְהוָה אַל־ יָעֹז אֱנוֹשׁ יִשָּׁפְטוּ גוֹיִם עַל־
in nations let-them-be-judged man let-him-triumph not Yahweh arise! (20)

פָּנֶיךָ׃ שִׁיתָה יְהוָה ׀ מוֹרָה לָהֶם יֵדְעוּ גוֹיִם
nations let-them-know to-them terror Yahweh strike! (21) presences-of-you

אֱנוֹשׁ הֵמָּה סֶּלָה׃ לָמָה יְהוָה תַּעֲמֹד בְּרָחוֹק תַּעְלִים לְעִתּוֹת
in-times you-hide at-far-off you-stand Yahweh why? (10:1) selah they man

בַּצָּרָה׃ בְּגַאֲוַת רָשָׁע יִדְלַק עָנִי יִתָּפְשׂוּ ׀
they-are-caught weak he-hunts wicked in-arrogance-of (2) of-the-trouble

בִּמְזִמּוֹת זוּ חָשָׁבוּ׃ כִּי־ הִלֵּל רָשָׁע עַל־ תַּאֲוַת
craving-of about wicked he-boasts for (3) they-devise that in-schemes

נַפְשׁוֹ וּבֹצֵעַ בֵּרֵךְ נִאֵץ ׀ יְהוָה׃ רָשָׁע
wicked (4) Yahweh he-reviles he-blesses and-one-being-greedy heart-of-him

כְּגֹבַהּ אַפּוֹ בַּל־ יִדְרֹשׁ אֵין אֱלֹהִים כָּל־ מְזִמּוֹתָיו׃
thoughts-of-him all-of God not he-seeks not nose-of-him in-pride-of

יָחִילוּ °דְרָכָו ׀ בְּכָל־ עֵת מָרוֹם מִשְׁפָּטֶיךָ מִנֶּגְדּוֹ
from-near-him laws-of-you haughty time at-all-of ways-of-him they-prosper (5)

כָּל־ צוֹרְרָיו יָפִיחַ בָּהֶם׃ אָמַר בְּלִבּוֹ
to-self-of-him he-says (6) at-them he-sneers ones-being-enemies-of-him all-of

בַּל־ אֶמּוֹט לְדֹר וָדֹר אֲשֶׁר לֹא־ בְרָע׃
in-trouble not happy and-generation to-generation I-will-be-shaken not

אָלָה פִּיהוּ מָלֵא וּמִרְמוֹת וָתֹךְ תַּחַת לְשׁוֹנוֹ
tongue-of-him under and-threat and-lies he-is-full mouth-of-him curse (7)

עָמָל וָאָוֶן׃ יֵשֵׁב ׀ בְּמַאְרַב חֲצֵרִים בַּמִּסְתָּרִים יַהֲרֹג
he-murders from-the-ambushes villages in-wait-of he-lies (8) and-evil trouble

נָקִי עֵינָיו לְחֵלְכָה יִצְפֹּנוּ׃ יֶאֱרֹב
he-lies-in-wait (9) they-are-secret for-victim eyes-of-him innocent

בַּמִּסְתָּר ׀ כְּאַרְיֵה בְסֻכֹּה יֶאֱרֹב לַחֲטוֹף עָנִי
helpless to-catch he-lies-in-wait in-cover-of-him like-lion in-the-ambush

יַחְטֹף עָנִי בְּמָשְׁכוֹ בְרִשְׁתּוֹ׃ °וְדָכֶה
he-is-crushed (10) in-net-of-him when-to-drag-off-him helpless he-catches

16 The LORD is known by his justice;
the wicked are ensnared by the work of their hands.
*Higgaion.*[r] *Selah*
17 The wicked return to the grave,[s]
all the nations that forget God.
18 But the needy will not always be forgotten,
nor the hope of the afflicted ever perish.
19 Arise, O LORD, let not man triumph;
let the nations be judged in your presence.
20 Strike them with terror, O LORD;
let the nations know they are but men. *Selah*

**Psalm 10**[t]

1 Why, O LORD, do you stand far off?
Why do you hide yourself in times of trouble?
2 In his arrogance the wicked man hunts down the weak,
who are caught in the schemes he devises.
3 He boasts of the cravings of his heart;
he blesses the greedy and reviles the LORD.
4 In his pride the wicked does not seek him;
in all his thoughts there is no room for God.
5 His ways are always prosperous;
he is haughty and your laws are far from him;
he sneers at all his enemies.
6 He says to himself, "Nothing will shake me;
I'll always be happy and never have trouble."
7 His mouth is full of curses and lies and threats;
trouble and evil are under his tongue.
8 He lies in wait near the villages;
from ambush he murders the innocent,
watching in secret for his victims.
9 He lies in wait like a lion in cover;
he lies in wait to catch the helpless;
he catches the helpless and drags them off in his net.

[r] 16 Or *Meditation;* possibly a musical notation
[s] 17 Hebrew *Sheol*
[t] Psalms 9 and 10 may have been originally a single acrostic poem, the stanzas of which begin with the successive letters of the Hebrew alphabet. In the Septuagint they constitute one psalm.

*See the note on page 349.

°*19* ק עניים
°*5* ק דרכיו
°*10* ק ידכה

יָשֹׁחַ וְנָפַל בַּעֲצוּמָיו חֵלְכָּאִים׃ אָמַר
he-says (11) *victims under-strengths-of-him and-he-falls he-collapses

בְּלִבּוֹ שָׁכַח אֵל הִסְתִּיר פָּנָיו בַּל־ רָאָה לָנֶצַח׃
to-ever he-sees not faces-of-him he-covers God he-forgot to-self-of-him

קוּמָה יְהוָה אֵל נְשָׂא יָדֶךָ אַל־ תִּשְׁכַּח עֲנָיִים׃
helpless-ones you-forget not hand-of-you lift-up! God Yahweh arise! (12)

עַל־ מֶה׀ נִאֵץ רָשָׁע׀ אֱלֹהִים אָמַר בְּלִבּוֹ לֹא
not to-self-of-him he-says God wicked he-reviles why? for (13)

תִּדְרֹשׁ׃ רָאִתָה כִּי־ אַתָּה׀ עָמָל׀ וָכַעַס׀ תַּבִּיט
you-consider and-grief trouble you but you-see (14) you-will-call-account

לָתֵת בְּיָדֶךָ עָלֶיךָ יַעֲזֹב חֵלֵכָה יָתוֹם אַתָּה׀ הָיִיתָ
you-are you fatherless victim he-commits to-you into-hand-of-you to-take

עוֹזֵר׃ שְׁבֹר זְרוֹעַ רָשָׁע וָרָע תִּדְרוֹשׁ־ רִשְׁעוֹ
wickedness-of-him you-call-account and-evil wicked arm-of break! (15) one-helping

בַל־ תִּמְצָא׃ יְהוָה מֶלֶךְ עוֹלָם וָעֶד אָבְדוּ
they-will-perish and-ever forever King Yahweh (16) she-would-be-found-out not

גוֹיִם מֵאַרְצוֹ׃ תַּאֲוַת עֲנָוִים שָׁמַעְתָּ יְהוָה
Yahweh you-hear afflicted-ones desire-of (17) from-land-of-him nations

תָּכִין לִבָּם תַּקְשִׁיב אָזְנֶךָ׃ לִשְׁפֹּט
to-defend (18) ear-of-you you-make-listen heart-of-them you-encourage

יָתוֹם וָדָךְ בַּל־ יוֹסִיף עוֹד לַעֲרֹץ אֱנוֹשׁ מִן־ הָאָרֶץ׃
the-earth from man to-terrify more he-may-repeat not and-oppressed fatherless

לַמְנַצֵּחַ לְדָוִד בַּיהוָה׀ חָסִיתִי אֵיךְ תֹּאמְרוּ
can-you-say how? I-take-refuge in-Yahweh of-David for-the-one-directing (11:1)

לְנַפְשִׁי נוּדוּ הַרְכֶם צִפּוֹר׃ כִּי הִנֵּה הָרְשָׁעִים
the-wicked-ones look! for (2) bird mountain-of-you flee! to-self-of-me

יִדְרְכוּן קֶשֶׁת כּוֹנְנוּ חִצָּם עַל־ יֶתֶר לִירוֹת בְּמוֹ־ אֹפֶל
shadow from to-shoot string against arrow-of-them they-set bow they-bend

לְיִשְׁרֵי־ לֵב׃ כִּי הַשָּׁתוֹת יֵהָרֵסוּן צַדִּיק
righteous they-are-destroyed the-foundations when (3) heart at-ones-upright-of

מַה־ פָּעָל׃ יְהוָה׀ בְּהֵיכַל קָדְשׁוֹ יְהוָה בַּשָּׁמַיִם
in-the-heavens Yahweh holiness-of-him in-temple-of Yahweh (4) can-he-do what?

כִּסְאוֹ עֵינָיו יֶחֱזוּ עַפְעַפָּיו יִבְחֲנוּ בְּנֵי
sons-of they-examine eyes-of-him they-observe eyes-of-him throne-of-him

אָדָם׃ יְהוָה צַדִּיק יִבְחָן וְרָשָׁע וְאֹהֵב חָמָס
violence and-one-loving but-wicked he-examines righteous Yahweh (5) man

שָׂנְאָה נַפְשׁוֹ׃ יַמְטֵר עַל־ רְשָׁעִים פַּחִים אֵשׁ וְגָפְרִית
and-sulfur fire coal-of wicked-ones on he-will-rain (6) soul-of-him she-hates

10 His victims are crushed, they collapse;
they fall under his strength.
11 He says to himself, "God has forgotten;
he covers his face and never sees."

12 Arise, LORD! Lift up your hand, O God.
Do not forget the helpless.
13 Why does the wicked man revile God?
Why does he say to himself, "He won't call me to account"?
14 But you, O God, do see trouble and grief;
you consider it to take it in hand.
The victim commits himself to you;
you are the helper of the fatherless.
15 Break the arm of the wicked and evil man;
call him to account for his wickedness
that would not be found out.

16 The LORD is King for ever and ever;
the nations will perish from his land.
17 You hear, O LORD, the desire of the afflicted;
you encourage them, and you listen to their cry,
18 defending the fatherless and the oppressed,
in order that man, who is of the earth, may terrify no more.

### Psalm 11

For the director of music. Of David.

1 In the LORD I take refuge.
How then can you say to me:
"Flee like a bird to your mountain.
2 For look, the wicked bend their bows;
they set their arrows against the strings
to shoot from the shadows at the upright in heart.
3 When the foundations are being destroyed,
what can the righteous do[u]?"

4 The LORD is in his holy temple;
the LORD is on his heavenly throne.
He observes the sons of men;
his eyes examine them.
5 The LORD examines the righteous,
but the wicked[v] and those who love violence
his soul hates.
6 On the wicked he will rain
fiery coals and burning sulfur;

u3 Or *what is the Righteous One doing*
v5 Or *The LORD, the Righteous One, examines the wicked, /*

*10 The *Qere* reads *host-of afflicted-ones.*

°10 ק חיל כאים °12 ק ענוים
°1 ק נודי

וְרוּחַ זִלְעָפוֹת מְנָת כּוֹסָם׃ כִּי־ צַדִּיק יְהוָה צְדָקוֹת
justices Yahweh righteous for (7) cup-of-them lot-of scorchings and-wind-of

אָהֵב יָשָׁר יֶחֱזוּ פָנֵימוֹ׃ לַמְנַצֵּחַ
for-the-one-directing *(12:1) faces-of-him they-will-see upright he-loves

עַל־ הַשְּׁמִינִית מִזְמוֹר לְדָוִד׃ הוֹשִׁיעָה יְהוָה כִּי־ גָמַר
he-is-no-more for Yahweh help! (2) of-David psalm the-sheminith according-to

חָסִיד כִּי־ פַסּוּ אֱמוּנִים מִבְּנֵי אָדָם׃ שָׁוְא ׀
lie (3) man from-sons-of ones-being-faithful they-vanished for godly

יְדַבְּרוּ אִישׁ אֶת־ רֵעֵהוּ שְׂפַת חֲלָקוֹת בְּלֵב וָלֵב
and-heart with-heart flatterings lip-of neighbor-of-him *** each they-speak

יְדַבֵּרוּ׃ יַכְרֵת יְהוָה כָּל־ שִׂפְתֵי חֲלָקוֹת לָשׁוֹן
tongue flatterings lips-of all-of Yahweh may-he-cut-off (4) they-speak

מְדַבֶּרֶת גְּדֹלוֹת׃ אֲשֶׁר אָמְרוּ ׀ לִלְשֹׁנֵנוּ נַגְבִּיר
we-will-triumph with-tongue-of-us they-say that (5) boasts speaking

שְׂפָתֵינוּ אִתָּנוּ מִי אָדוֹן לָנוּ׃ מִשֹּׁד עֲנִיִּים
weak-ones because-of-oppression-of (6) of-us master who? with-us lips-of-us

מֵאַנְקַת אֶבְיוֹנִים עַתָּה אָקוּם יֹאמַר יְהוָה אָשִׁית
I-will-put Yahweh he-says I-will-arise now needy-ones because-of-groaning-of

בְּיֵשַׁע יָפִיחַ לוֹ׃ אִמֲרוֹת יְהוָה אֲמָרוֹת טְהֹרוֹת
flawless-ones words Yahweh words-of (7) against-him he-maligns in-protection

כֶּסֶף צָרוּף בַּעֲלִיל לָאָרֶץ מְזֻקָּק שִׁבְעָתָיִם׃
seven-times being-purified of-the-clay in-furnace being-refined silver

אַתָּה־ יְהוָה תִּשְׁמְרֵם תִּצְּרֶנּוּ ׀ מִן־ הַדּוֹר
the-people from you-will-protect-us you-will-keep-safe-them Yahweh you (8)

זוּ לְעוֹלָם׃ סָבִיב רְשָׁעִים יִתְהַלָּכוּן כְּרֻם זֻלּוּת
vileness when-to-be-honored they-strut wicked-ones about (9) to-forever such

לִבְנֵי אָדָם׃ לַמְנַצֵּחַ מִזְמוֹר לְדָוִד׃ עַד־
until (2) of-David psalm for-the-one-directing *(13:1) man among-sons-of

אָנָה יְהוָה תִּשְׁכָּחֵנִי נֶצַח עַד־ אָנָה ׀ תַּסְתִּיר אֶת־
*** will-you-hide when? until forever will-you-forget-me Yahweh when?

פָּנֶיךָ מִמֶּנִּי׃ עַד־ אָנָה אָשִׁית עֵצוֹת בְּנַפְשִׁי
of-soul-of-me thoughts must-I-wrestle when? until (3) from-me faces-of-you

יָגוֹן בִּלְבָבִי יוֹמָם עַד־ אָנָה ׀ יָרוּם אֹיְבִי
one-being-enemy-of-me will-he-triumph when? until by-day in-heart-of-me sorrow

עָלָי׃ הַבִּיטָה עֲנֵנִי יְהוָה אֱלֹהָי הָאִירָה עֵינַי פֶּן־
or eyes-of-me give-light! God-of-me Yahweh answer-me! look! (4) over-me

אִישַׁן הַמָּוֶת׃ פֶּן־ יֹאמַר אֹיְבִי יְכָלְתִּיו
I-overcame-him one-being-enemy-of-me he-will-say or (5) the-death I-will-sleep

a scorching wind will be
their lot.

7 For the LORD is righteous,
he loves justice;
upright men will see his
face.

### Psalm 12

For the director of music. According to *sheminith*.[w] A psalm of David.

1 Help, LORD, for the godly are
no more;
the faithful have vanished
from among men.
2 Everyone lies to his neighbor;
their flattering lips speak
with deception.
3 May the LORD cut off all
flattering lips
and every boastful tongue
4 that says, "We will triumph
with our tongues;
we own our lips[x]—who is
our master?"

5 "Because of the oppression of
the weak
and the groaning of the
needy,
I will now arise," says the
LORD.
"I will protect them from
those who malign them."
6 And the words of the LORD are
flawless,
like silver refined in a
furnace of clay,
purified seven times.
7 O LORD, you will keep us safe
and protect us from such
people forever.
8 The wicked freely strut about
when what is vile is
honored among men.

### Psalm 13

For the director of music. A psalm of David.

1 How long, O LORD? Will you
forget me forever?
How long will you hide
your face from me?
2 How long must I wrestle with
my thoughts
and every day have sorrow
in my heart?
How long will my enemy
triumph over me?
3 Look on me and answer, O
LORD my God.
Give light to my eyes, or I
will sleep in death;
4 my enemy will say, "I have
overcome him,"

[w] Title: Probably a musical term
[x] 4 Or */ our lips are our plowshares*

*Heading, *1* See the note on page 349.

צָרַי   יָגִ֣ילוּ   כִּ֣י אֶמּ֑וֹט:   וַאֲנִ֤י ׀   בְּחַסְדְּךָ֣
foes-of-me   they-will-rejoice   when   I-fall   (6)   but-I   in-unfailing-love-of-you

בָטַ֗חְתִּי   יָ֘גֵ֤ל   לִבִּ֗י   בִּ֥ישׁוּעָתֶ֑ךָ   אָשִׁ֥ירָה   לַיהוָ֑ה
I-trust   he-rejoices   heart-of-me   in-salvation-of-you   I-will-sing   to-Yahweh

כִּ֖י   גָמַ֣ל   עָלָֽי:   (14:1)   לַמְנַצֵּ֗חַ   לְדָוִ֥ד   אָמַ֬ר   נָבָ֨ל
for   he-was-good   to-me   (14:1)   for-the-one-directing   of-David   he-says   fool

בְּ֭לִבּוֹ   אֵ֣ין   אֱלֹהִ֑ים   הִֽשְׁחִ֗יתוּ   הִֽתְעִ֥יבוּ   עֲלִילָ֗ה
in-heart-of-him   there-is-no   God   they-are-corrupt   they-are-vile   deed

אֵ֣ין   עֹֽשֵׂה־   ט֑וֹב:   (2)   יְֽהוָ֗ה   מִשָּׁמַיִם֮   הִשְׁקִ֪יף   עַֽל־בְּנֵי־
there-is-no   one-doing-of   good   (2)   Yahweh   from-heavens   he-looks-down   on sons-of

אָ֫דָ֥ם   לִ֭רְאוֹת   הֲיֵ֣שׁ   מַשְׂכִּ֑יל   דֹּ֝רֵ֗שׁ   אֶת־אֱלֹהִֽים:   (3)   הַכֹּ֪ל
man   to-see   if-there-is   one-understanding   one-seeking   *** God   (3)   the-all

סָ֡ר   יַחְדָּ֪ו   נֶ֫אֱלָ֥חוּ   אֵ֤ין   עֹֽשֵׂה־   ט֑וֹב   אֵ֣ין
he-turned-aside   together   they-became-corrupt   there-is-no   one-doing-of   good   not

גַּם־אֶחָֽד:   (4)   הֲלֹ֥א   יָדְעוּ֮   כָּל־   פֹּ֪עֲלֵ֫י   אָ֥וֶן   אֹכְלֵ֣י
one even   (4)   never?   will-they-learn   all-of   ones-doing-of   evil   ones-devouring-of

עַ֭מִּי   אָ֣כְלוּ   לֶ֑חֶם   יְ֝הוָ֗ה   לֹ֣א   קָרָֽאוּ:   (5)   שָׁ֤ם ׀   פָּ֣חֲדוּ
people-of-me   they-eat   bread   Yahweh   not   they-call-on   (5)   there   they-dread

פָ֑חַד   כִּֽי־אֱ֭לֹהִים   בְּד֣וֹר   צַדִּֽיק:   (6)   עֲצַת־   עָנִ֥י   תָבִ֑ישׁוּ   כִּ֖י
dread   for God   in-company-of   righteous   (6)   plan-of   poor   you-frustrate   but

יְהוָ֣ה   מַחְסֵֽהוּ:   (7)   מִ֥י   יִתֵּ֣ן   מִצִּיּוֹן֮   יְשׁוּעַ֪ת   יִשְׂרָ֫אֵ֥ל
Yahweh   refuge-of-him   (7)   who?   he-would-bring   from-Zion   salvation-of   Israel

בְּשׁ֣וּב   יְ֭הוָה   שְׁב֣וּת   עַמּ֑וֹ   יָגֵ֥ל   יַֽעֲקֹ֗ב
when-to-restore   Yahweh   fortune-of   people-of-him   let-him-rejoice   Jacob

יִשְׂמַ֥ח   יִשְׂרָאֵֽל:   (15:1)   מִזְמ֗וֹר   לְדָ֫וִ֥ד   יְהוָ֗ה   מִי־   יָג֥וּר
let-him-be-glad   Israel   (15:1)   psalm   of-David   Yahweh   who?   he-may-dwell

בְּאָהֳלֶ֑ךָ   מִֽי־   יִ֝שְׁכֹּ֗ן   בְּהַ֣ר   קָדְשֶֽׁךָ:  
in-sanctuary-of-you   who?   he-may-live   on-hill-of   holiness-of-you

הוֹלֵ֣ךְ   תָּ֭מִים   וּפֹעֵ֥ל   צֶ֑דֶק   וְדֹבֵ֥ר   אֱמֶ֗ת
one-walking   (2)   blamelessly   and-one-doing   righteousness   and-one-speaking   truth

בִּלְבָבֽוֹ:   (3)   לֹֽא־   רָגַ֨ל ׀   עַל־   לְשֹׁנ֗וֹ   לֹא־   עָשָׂ֣ה
from-heart-of-him   (3)   not   he-slanders   with   tongue-of-him   not   he-does

לְרֵעֵ֣הוּ   רָעָ֑ה   וְ֝חֶרְפָּ֗ה   לֹא־   נָשָׂ֥א   עַל־   קְרֹבֽוֹ:
to-neighbor-of-him   wrong   and-slur   not   he-casts   on   fellow-man-of-him

נִבְזֶ֤ה ׀   (4)   בְּֽעֵ֘ינָ֤יו   נִמְאָ֗ס   וְאֶת־   יִרְאֵ֣י   יְהוָ֣ה
(4)   he-is-despised   in-eyes-of-him   man-being-vile   but   ones-fearing-of   Yahweh

יְכַבֵּ֑ד   נִשְׁבַּ֥ע   לְ֝הָרַ֗ע   וְלֹ֣א   יָמִֽר:   (5)   כַּסְפּ֤וֹ ׀   לֹא־
he-honors   he-swears-oath   to-hurt   and-not   he-changes   (5)   money-of-him   not

and my foes will rejoice
   when I fall.
[5]But I trust in your unfailing
   love;
   my heart rejoices in your
     salvation.
[6]I will sing to the LORD,
   for he has been good to me.

## Psalm 14

For the director of music. Of David.

[1]The fool[y] says in his heart,
   "There is no God."
They are corrupt, their deeds
   are vile;
   there is no one who does
     good.
[2]The LORD looks down from
   heaven
   on the sons of men
to see if there are any who
   understand,
   any who seek God.
[3]All have turned aside,
   they have together become
     corrupt;
there is no one who does
   good,
   not even one.
[4]Will evildoers never learn—
   those who devour my
     people as men eat bread
   and who do not call on the
     LORD?
[5]There they are, overwhelmed
   with dread,
   for God is present in the
     company of the righteous.
[6]You evildoers frustrate the
   plans of the poor,
   but the LORD is their refuge.
[7]Oh, that salvation for Israel
   would come out of Zion!
When the LORD restores the
   fortunes of his people,
   let Jacob rejoice and Israel
     be glad!

## Psalm 15

A psalm of David.

[1]LORD, who may dwell in your
   sanctuary?
   Who may live on your holy
     hill?
[2]He whose walk is blameless
   and who does what is
     righteous,
who speaks the truth from his
   heart
[3] and has no slander on his
   tongue,
who does his neighbor no
   wrong
   and casts no slur on his
     fellow man,
[4]who despises a vile man
   but honors those who fear
     the LORD,
who keeps his oath
   even when it hurts,
[5]who lends his money without

*y1* The Hebrew words rendered *fool* in
Psalms denote one who is morally deficient.

*See the note on page 349.

נָתַן בְּנֶשֶׁךְ וְשֹׁחַד עַל־ נָקִי לֹא לָקָח עֹשֵׂה־
one-doing-of he-accepts not innocent against and-bribe with-usury he-lends

אֵלֶּה לֹא יִמּוֹט לְעוֹלָם׃ מִכְתָּם לְדָוִד שָׁמְרֵנִי
keep-safe-me! of-David miktam (16:1) to-forever he-will-be-shaken not these

אֵל כִּי־ חָסִיתִי בָךְ׃ אָמַרְתְּ* לַיהוָה אֲדֹנָי אָתָּה טוֹבָתִי
good-of-me you Lord-of-me to-Yahweh *I-said (2) in-you I-take-refuge for God

בַּל־ עָלֶיךָ׃ לִקְדוֹשִׁים אֲשֶׁר־ בָּאָרֶץ הֵמָּה וְאַדִּירֵי
even-glorious-ones-of they in-the-land who as-for-saints (3) apart-from-you not

כָּל־ חֶפְצִי־ בָם׃ יִרְבּוּ עַצְּבוֹתָם אַחֵר
other sorrows-of-them they-will-increase (4) in-them delight-of-me all-of

מָהָרוּ בַּל־ אַסִּיךְ נִסְכֵּיהֶם מִדָּם וּבַל־
and-not of-blood libations-of-them I-will-pour-out not they-run-after

אֶשָּׂא אֶת־ שְׁמוֹתָם עַל־ שְׂפָתָי׃ יְהוָה מְנָת־
assignment-of Yahweh (5) lips-of-me on names-of-them *** I-will-take-up

חֶלְקִי וְכוֹסִי אַתָּה תּוֹמִיךְ גּוֹרָלִי׃ חֲבָלִים
boundary-lines (6) lot-of-me you-made-secure you and-cup-of-me portion-of-me

נָפְלוּ־ לִי בַּנְּעִמִים אַף־ נַחֲלָת שָׁפְרָה
she-is-delightful inheritance surely in-the-pleasant-places for-me they-fell

עָלָי׃ אֲבָרֵךְ אֶת־ יְהוָה אֲשֶׁר יְעָצָנִי אַף־ לֵילוֹת
nights even he-counsels-me who Yahweh *** I-will-praise (7) to-me

יִסְּרוּנִי כִלְיוֹתָי׃ שִׁוִּיתִי יְהוָה לְנֶגְדִּי תָמִיד כִּי
because always at-before-me Yahweh I-set (8) hearts-of-me they-instruct-me

מִימִינִי בַּל־ אֶמּוֹט׃ לָכֵן שָׂמַח לִבִּי
heart-of-me he-is-glad therefore (9) I-will-be-shaken not at-right-hand-of-me

וַיָּגֶל כְּבוֹדִי אַף־ בְּשָׂרִי יִשְׁכֹּן לָבֶטַח׃
in-security he-will-rest body-of-me also tongue-of-me and-he-rejoices

כִּי לֹא־ תַעֲזֹב נַפְשִׁי לִשְׁאוֹל לֹא־ תִתֵּן
you-will-let not to-Sheol self-of-me you-will-abandon not because (10)

חֲסִידְךָ לִרְאוֹת שָׁחַת׃ תּוֹדִיעֵנִי אֹרַח חַיִּים
lives path-of you-will-make-known-to-me (11) decay to-see holy-one-of-you

שֹׂבַע שְׂמָחוֹת אֶת־ פָּנֶיךָ נְעִמוֹת בִּימִינְךָ נֶצַח׃
eternally at-right-hand-of-you pleasures presences-of-you in joys fullness-of

תְּפִלָּה לְדָוִד שִׁמְעָה יְהוָה צֶדֶק הַקְשִׁיבָה רִנָּתִי
cry-of-me listen! righteous-plea Yahweh hear! of-David prayer (17:1)

הַאֲזִינָה תְפִלָּתִי בְּלֹא שִׂפְתֵי מִרְמָה׃ מִלְּפָנֶיךָ
from-before-you (2) deceit lips-of from-not prayer-of-me give-ear!

מִשְׁפָּטִי יֵצֵא עֵינֶיךָ תֶּחֱזֶינָה מֵישָׁרִים׃
right-ones may-they-see eyes-of-you may-he-come vindication-of-me

usury
and does not accept a bribe
against the innocent.

He who does these things
will never be shaken.

### Psalm 16

A *miktam*[z] of David.

1 Keep me safe, O God,
for in you I take refuge.

2 I said to the LORD, "You are
my Lord;
apart from you I have no
good thing."
3 As for the saints who are in
the land,
they are the glorious ones in
whom is all my delight.[a]
4 The sorrows of those will
increase
who run after other gods.
I will not pour out their
libations of blood
or take up their names on
my lips.

5 LORD, you have assigned me
my portion and my cup;
you have made my lot
secure.
6 The boundary lines have fallen
for me in pleasant places;
surely I have a delightful
inheritance.

7 I will praise the LORD, who
counsels me;
even at night my heart
instructs me.
8 I have set the LORD always
before me.
Because he is at my right
hand,
I will not be shaken.

9 Therefore my heart is glad and
my tongue rejoices;
my body also will rest
secure,
10 because you will not abandon
me to the grave,[b]
nor will you let your Holy
One[c] see decay.
11 You have made[d] known to me
the path of life;
you will fill me with joy in
your presence,
with eternal pleasures at
your right hand.

### Psalm 17

A prayer of David.

1 Hear, O LORD, my righteous
plea;
listen to my cry.
Give ear to my prayer—
it does not rise from
deceitful lips.
2 May my vindication come
from you;
may your eyes see what is
right.

[z] Title: Probably a literary or musical term
[a] 3 Or *As for the pagan priests who are in the land / and the nobles in whom all delight, I said:*
[b] 10 Hebrew *Sheol*
[c] 10 Or *your faithful one*
[d] 11 Or *You will make*

***2 Most mss have *bireq yod* with the *tav* (תִּי־).**

בָּחַנְתָּ לִבִּי ׀ פָּקַדְתָּ לַּיְלָה צְרַפְתַּנִי בַל־ תִּמְצָא

you-will-find not you-test-me night you-examine heart-of-me you-probe (3)

זַמֹּתִי בַּל־ יַעֲבָר־ פִּי׃ לִפְעֻלּוֹת אָדָם בִּדְבַר

by-word-of man for-deeds-of (4) mouth-of-me he-will-sin not I-resolved

שְׂפָתֶיךָ אֲנִי שָׁמַרְתִּי אָרְחוֹת פָּרִיץ׃ תָּמֹךְ אֲשֻׁרַי

steps-of-me to-hold (5) violent ways-of I-kept I lips-of-you

בְּמַעְגְּלוֹתֶיךָ בַּל־ נָמוֹטּוּ פְעָמָי׃ אֲנִי־ קְרָאתִיךָ כִי־

for I-call-on-you I (6) feet-of-me they-slipped not to-paths-of-you

תַעֲנֵנִי אֵל הַט־ אָזְנְךָ לִי שְׁמַע אִמְרָתִי׃

prayer-of-me hear! to-me ear-of-you give! God you-will-answer-me

הַפְלֵה חֲסָדֶיךָ מוֹשִׁיעַ חוֹסִים

ones-taking-refuge one-saving great-loves-of-you show-wonder! (7)

מִמִּתְקוֹמְמִים בִּימִינֶךָ׃ שָׁמְרֵנִי כְּאִישׁוֹן בַּת־

daughter-of as-apple-of keep-me! (8) by-right-hand-of-you from-ones-being-foes

עָיִן בְּצֵל כְּנָפֶיךָ תַּסְתִּירֵנִי׃ מִפְּנֵי רְשָׁעִים זוּ

who wicked-ones from-before (9) you-hide-me wings-of-you in-shadow-of eye

שַׁדּוּנִי אֹיְבַי בְּנֶפֶשׁ יַקִּיפוּ עָלָי׃

around-me they-surround of-life ones-being-enemies-of-me they-assail-me

חֶלְבָּמוֹ סָּגְרוּ פִּימוֹ דִּבְּרוּ בְגֵאוּת׃

with-arrogance they-speak mouth-of-them they-close callous-heart-of-them (10)

אַשֻּׁרֵינוּ עַתָּה °סְבָבוּנִי עֵינֵיהֶם יָשִׁיתוּ לִנְטוֹת

to-throw they-are-alert eyes-of-them they-surround-us now tracks-of-us (11)

בָּאָרֶץ׃ דִּמְיֹנוֹ כְּאַרְיֵה יִכְסוֹף לִטְרוֹף

to-tear-prey he-is-hungry like-lion likeness-of-him (12) to-the-ground

וְכִכְפִיר יֹשֵׁב בְּמִסְתָּרִים׃ קוּמָה יְהוָה קַדְּמָה

confront! Yahweh rise-up! (13) in-covers crouching and-like-great-lion

פָנָיו הַכְרִיעֵהוּ פַּלְּטָה נַפְשִׁי מֵרָשָׁע חַרְבֶּךָ׃

sword-of-you from-wicked self-of-me rescue! bring-down-him! before-him

מִמְתִים יָדְךָ ׀ יְהוָה מִמְתִים מֵחֶלֶד חֶלְקָם

reward-of-them from-world from-men Yahweh hand-of-you from-men (14)

בַּחַיִּים °וּצְפִינְךָ תְּמַלֵּא בִטְנָם

belly-of-them you-fill and-one-being-cherished-of-you in-the-lives

יִשְׂבְּעוּ בָנִים וְהִנִּיחוּ יִתְרָם לְעוֹלְלֵיהֶם׃

for-children-of-them wealth-of-them and-they-store-up sons they-have-plenty

אֲנִי בְּצֶדֶק אֶחֱזֶה פָנֶיךָ אֶשְׂבְּעָה בְהָקִיץ

when-to-wake I-will-be-satisfied faces-of-you I-will-see in-righteousness I (15)

תְּמוּנָתֶךָ׃ לַמְנַצֵּחַ ׀ לְעֶבֶד יְהוָה לְדָוִד

of-David Yahweh of-servant-of for-the-one-directing *(18:1) likeness-of-you

3Though you probe my heart
and examine me at night,
though you test me, you will
find nothing;
I have resolved that my
mouth will not sin.
4As for the deeds of men—
by the word of your lips
I have kept myself
from the ways of the
violent.
5My steps have held to your
paths;
my feet have not slipped.

6I call on you, O God, for you
will answer me;
give ear to me and hear my
prayer.
7Show the wonder of your great
love,
you who save by your right
hand
those who take refuge in
you from their foes.
8Keep me as the apple of your
eye;
hide me in the shadow of
your wings
9from the wicked who assail
me,
from my mortal enemies
who surround me.

10They close up their callous
hearts,
and their mouths speak with
arrogance.
11They have tracked me down,
they now surround me,
with eyes alert, to throw me
to the ground.
12They are like a lion hungry for
prey,
like a great lion crouching
in cover.

13Rise up, O LORD, confront
them, bring them down;
rescue me from the wicked
by your sword.
14O LORD, by your hand save me
from such men,
from men of this world
whose reward is in this
life.

You still the hunger of those
you cherish;
their sons have plenty,
and they store up wealth for
their children.
15And I—in righteousness I will
see your face;
when I awake, I will be
satisfied with seeing your
likeness.

**Psalm 18**

For the director of music. Of David the servant of the LORD. He sang to

*Heading, *1* See the note on page 349.

°*11* ק סבבונו

°*14* ק וצפונך

אֲשֶׁר דִּבֶּר ׀ לַיהוָה אֶת־ דִּבְרֵי הַשִּׁירָה הַזֹּאת בְּיוֹם הִצִּיל־
he-delivered on-day the-this the-song words-of *** to-Yahweh he-sang who

יְהוָה אוֹתוֹ מִכַּף כָּל־ אֹיְבָיו וּמִיַּד
and-from-hand-of ones-being-enemies-of-him all-of from-hand-of him Yahweh

שָׁאוּל׃ (2) וַיֹּאמַר אֶרְחָמְךָ יְהוָה חִזְקִי׃ (3) יְהוָה ׀ סַלְעִי
rock-of-me Yahweh (3) strength-of-me Yahweh I-love-you and-he-said (2) Saul

וּמְצוּדָתִי וּמְפַלְטִי אֵלִי צוּרִי אֶחֱסֶה־
I-take-refuge rock-of-me God-of-me and-one-delivering-me and-fortress-of-me

בּוֹ מָגִנִּי וְקֶרֶן־ יִשְׁעִי מִשְׂגַּבִּי׃
stronghold-of-me salvation-of-me and-horn-of shield-of-me in-him

(4) מְהֻלָּל אֶקְרָא יְהוָה וּמִן־ אֹיְבַי
ones-being-enemies-of-me and-from Yahweh I-call one-being-praised (4)

אִוָּשֵׁעַ׃ (5) אֲפָפוּנִי חֶבְלֵי־ מָוֶת וְנַחֲלֵי בְלִיַּעַל
destruction and-torrents-of death cords-of they-entangled-me (5) I-am-saved

יְבַעֲתוּנִי׃ (6) חֶבְלֵי שְׁאוֹל סְבָבוּנִי קִדְּמוּנִי
they-confronted-me they-coiled-around-me Sheol cords-of (6) they-overwhelmed-me

מוֹקְשֵׁי מָוֶת׃ (7) בַּצַּר־ לִי ׀ אֶקְרָא יְהוָה וְאֶל־ אֱלֹהַי
God-of-me and-to Yahweh I-called of-me in-the-distress (7) death snares-of

אֲשַׁוֵּעַ יִשְׁמַע מֵהֵיכָלוֹ קוֹלִי וְשַׁוְעָתִי
and-cry-of-me voice-of-me from-temple-of-him he-heard I-cried-for-help

לְפָנָיו ׀ תָּבוֹא בְאָזְנָיו׃ (8) וַתִּגְעַשׁ וַתִּרְעַשׁ ׀
and-she-quaked and-she-trembled (8) into-ears-of-him she-came before-him

הָאָרֶץ וּמוֹסְדֵי הָרִים יִרְגָּזוּ וַיִּתְגָּעֲשׁוּ כִּי־
because and-they-trembled they-shook mountains and-foundations-of the-earth

חָרָה לוֹ׃ (9) עָלָה עָשָׁן ׀ בְּאַפּוֹ וְאֵשׁ־
and-fire from-nostril-of-him smoke he-rose (9) to-him he-was-angry

מִפִּיו תֹּאכֵל גֶּחָלִים בָּעֲרוּ מִמֶּנּוּ׃ (10) וַיֵּט
and-he-parted (10) from-him they-blazed coals she-consumed from-mouth-of-him

שָׁמַיִם וַיֵּרַד וַעֲרָפֶל תַּחַת רַגְלָיו׃ (11) וַיִּרְכַּב
and-he-mounted (11) feet-of-him under and-dark-cloud and-he-came-down heavens

עַל־כְּרוּב וַיָּעֹף וַיֵּדֶא עַל־ כַּנְפֵי־ רוּחַ׃ (12) יָשֶׁת חֹשֶׁךְ ׀
darkness he-made (12) wind wings-of on and-he-soared and-he-flew cherub on

סִתְרוֹ סְבִיבוֹתָיו סֻכָּתוֹ חֶשְׁכַת־ מַיִם עָבֵי
clouds-of waters darkness-of canopy-of-him ones-around-him covering-of-him

שְׁחָקִים׃ (13) מִנֹּגַהּ נֶגְדּוֹ עָבָיו עָבְרוּ
they-advanced clouds-of-him presence-of-him from-brightness-of (13) skies

בָּרָד וְגַחֲלֵי־ אֵשׁ׃ (14) וַיַּרְעֵם בַּשָּׁמַיִם ׀
from-the-heavens and-he-thundered (14) lightning and-bolts-of hailstone

the LORD the words of this song when the LORD delivered him from the hand of all his enemies and from the hand of Saul. He said:

1 I love you, O LORD, my strength.
2 The LORD is my rock, my fortress and my deliverer;
my God is my rock, in whom I take refuge.
He is my shield and the horn[e] of my salvation, my stronghold.
3 I call to the LORD, who is worthy of praise,
and I am saved from my enemies.
4 The cords of death entangled me;
the torrents of destruction overwhelmed me.
5 The cords of the grave[f] coiled around me;
the snares of death confronted me.
6 In my distress I called to the LORD;
I cried to my God for help.
From his temple he heard my voice;
my cry came before him, into his ears.
7 The earth trembled and quaked,
and the foundations of the mountains shook;
they trembled because he was angry.
8 Smoke rose from his nostrils;
consuming fire came from his mouth,
burning coals blazed out of it.
9 He parted the heavens and came down;
dark clouds were under his feet.
10 He mounted the cherubim and flew;
he soared on the wings of the wind.
11 He made darkness his covering, his canopy around him—
the dark rain clouds of the sky.
12 Out of the brightness of his presence clouds advanced,
with hailstones and bolts of lightning.
13 The LORD thundered from heaven;

e2 *Horn* here symbolizes strength.
f5 Hebrew *Sheol*

*See the note on page 349.

יְהוָה וְעֶלְיוֹן יִתֵּן קֹלוֹ בָּרָד וְגַחֲלֵי־ אֵשׁ׃

lightning and-bolts-of hailstone voice-of-him he-resounded and-Most-High Yahweh

וַיִּשְׁלַח חִצָּיו וַיְפִיצֵם וּבְרָקִים

and-lightning-bolts and-he-scattered-them arrows-of-him and-he-shot (15)

רָב וַיְהֻמֵּם׃ וַיֵּרָאוּ אֲפִיקֵי מַיִם

waters valleys-of and-they-were-exposed (16) and-he-routed-them great

וַיִּגָּלוּ מוֹסְדוֹת תֵּבֵל מִגַּעֲרָתְךָ יְהוָה

Yahweh at-rebuke-of-you earth foundations-of and-they-were-laid-bare

מִנִּשְׁמַת רוּחַ אַפֶּךָ׃ יִשְׁלַח מִמָּרוֹם

from-on-high he-reached (17) nostril-of-you breath-of at-blast-of

יִקָּחֵנִי יַמְשֵׁנִי מִמַּיִם רַבִּים׃ יַצִּילֵנִי

he-rescued-me (18) deep-ones from-waters he-drew-out-me he-took-hold-of-me

מֵאֹיְבִי עָז וּמִשֹּׂנְאַי כִּי־

for and-from-ones-being-foes-of-me powerful from-one-being-enemy-of-me

אָמְצוּ מִמֶּנִּי׃ יְקַדְּמוּנִי בְיוֹם־ אֵידִי

disaster-of-me in-day-of they-confronted-me (19) for-me they-were-too-strong

וַיְהִי־ יְהוָה לְמִשְׁעָן לִי׃ וַיּוֹצִיאֵנִי

and-he-brought-out-me (20) to-me as-support Yahweh but-he-was

לַמֶּרְחָב יְחַלְּצֵנִי כִּי חָפֵץ בִּי׃

in-me he-delighted because he-rescued-me to-the-spacious-place

יִגְמְלֵנִי יְהוָה כְּצִדְקִי כְּבֹר יָדַי

hands-of-me as-cleanness-of as-righteousness-of-me Yahweh he-dealt-with-me (21)

יָשִׁיב לִי׃ כִּי־ שָׁמַרְתִּי דַּרְכֵי יְהוָה וְלֹא־ רָשַׁעְתִּי

I-did-evil and-not Yahweh ways-of I-kept for (22) to-me he-rewarded

מֵאֱלֹהָי׃ כִּי כָל־ מִשְׁפָּטָיו לְנֶגְדִּי וְחֻקֹּתָיו

and-decrees-of-him at-before-me laws-of-him all-of indeed (23) from-God-of-me

לֹא־ אָסִיר מֶנִּי׃ וָאֱהִי תָמִים עִמּוֹ וָאֶשְׁתַּמֵּר

and-I-kept-myself before-him blameless and-I-was (24) from-me I-turned not

מֵעֲוֹנִי׃ וַיָּשֶׁב־ יְהוָה לִי כְצִדְקִי

as-righteousness-of-me to-me Yahweh and-he-rewarded (25) from-sin-of-me

כְּבֹר יָדַי לְנֶגֶד עֵינָיו׃ עִם־ חָסִיד

faithful to (26) eyes-of-him at-before hands-of-me as-cleanness-of

תִּתְחַסָּד עִם־ גְּבַר תָּמִים תִּתַּמָּם׃

you-show-yourself-blameless blameless man-of to you-show-yourself-faithful

עִם־ נָבָר תִּתְבָּרָר וְעִם־ עִקֵּשׁ תִּתְפַּתָּל׃

you-show-yourself-shrewd crooked but-to you-show-yourself-pure one-being-pure to (27)

כִּי־ אַתָּה עַם־ עָנִי תוֹשִׁיעַ וְעֵינַיִם רָמוֹת

ones-being-haughty but-eyes you-save humble people you for (28)

the voice of the Most High
resounded.[g]
14 He shot his arrows and
scattered ⌞the enemies⌟,
great bolts of lightning and
routed them.
15 The valleys of the sea were
exposed
and the foundations of the
earth laid bare
at your rebuke, O LORD,
at the blast of breath from
your nostrils.
16 He reached down from on
high and took hold of me;
he drew me out of deep
waters.
17 He rescued me from my
powerful enemy,
from my foes, who were too
strong for me.
18 They confronted me in the day
of my disaster,
but the LORD was my
support.
19 He brought me out into a
spacious place;
he rescued me because he
delighted in me.
20 The LORD has dealt with me
according to my
righteousness;
according to the cleanness of
my hands he has
rewarded me.
21 For I have kept the ways of
the LORD;
I have not done evil by
turning from my God.
22 All his laws are before me;
I have not turned away
from his decrees.
23 I have been blameless before
him
and have kept myself from
sin.
24 The LORD has rewarded me
according to my
righteousness,
according to the cleanness of
my hands in his sight.
25 To the faithful you show
yourself faithful,
to the blameless you show
yourself blameless,
26 to the pure you show yourself
pure,
but to the crooked you show
yourself shrewd.
27 You save the humble
but bring low those whose
eyes are haughty.

[g] 13 Some Hebrew manuscripts and Septuagint (see also 2 Samuel 22:14); most Hebrew manuscripts *resounded, / amid hailstones and bolts of lightning*

*See the note on page 349.

תַּשְׁפִּיל׃ (29) כִּי־אַתָּה תָּאִיר נֵרִי יְהוָה אֱלֹהַי
God-of-me Yahweh lamp-of-me you-make-burn you indeed (29) you-bring-low

יַגִּיהַּ חָשְׁכִּי׃ (30) כִּי־בְךָ אָרֻץ גְּדוּד
troop I-can-advance with-you indeed (30) darkness-of-me he-makes-light

וּבֵאלֹהַי אֲדַלֶּג־שׁוּר׃ (31) הָאֵל תָּמִים דַּרְכּוֹ אִמְרַת־
word-of way-of-him perfect the-God (31) wall I-can-scale and-with-God-of-me

יְהוָה צְרוּפָה מָגֵן הוּא לְכֹל ׀ הַחֹסִים בּוֹ׃
in-him the-ones-taking-refuge to-all-of he shield being-flawless Yahweh

(32) כִּי מִי אֱלוֹהַּ מִבַּלְעֲדֵי יְהוָה וּמִי צוּר זוּלָתִי אֱלֹהֵינוּ׃ (33) הָאֵל
the-God (33) God-of-us except Rock and-who? Yahweh besides God who? for (32)

הַמְאַזְּרֵנִי חָיִל וַיִּתֵּן תָּמִים דַּרְכִּי׃ (34) מְשַׁוֶּה
one-making (34) way-of-me perfect and-he-makes strength the-one-arming-me

רַגְלַי כָּאַיָּלוֹת וְעַל בָּמֹתַי יַעֲמִידֵנִי׃ (35) מְלַמֵּד
training (35) he-makes-stand-me heights-of-me and-on like-the-deer feet-of-me

יָדַי לַמִּלְחָמָה וְנִחֲתָה קֶשֶׁת־נְחוּשָׁה זְרוֹעֹתָי׃
arms-of-me bronze bow-of and-she-can-bend for-the-battle hands-of-me

(36) וַתִּתֶּן־לִי מָגֵן יִשְׁעֶךָ וִימִינְךָ
and-right-hand-of-you victory-of-you shield-of to-me and-you-give (36)

תִסְעָדֵנִי וְעַנְוַתְךָ תַרְבֵּנִי׃ (37) תַּרְחִיב
you-broaden (37) you-make-great-me and-stooping-of-you she-sustains-me

צַעֲדִי תַחְתָּי וְלֹא מָעֲדוּ קַרְסֻלָּי׃ (38) אֶרְדּוֹף
I-pursued (38) ankles-of-me they-turn so-not beneath-me path-of-me

אוֹיְבַי וְאַשִּׂיגֵם וְלֹא־אָשׁוּב עַד־
till I-turned-back and-not and-I-overtook-them ones-being-enemies-of-me

כַּלּוֹתָם׃ (39) אֶמְחָצֵם וְלֹא־יֻכְלוּ קוּם יִפְּלוּ
they-fell to-rise they-could so-not I-crushed-them (39) to-destroy-them

תַּחַת רַגְלָי׃ (40) וַתְּאַזְּרֵנִי חַיִל לַמִּלְחָמָה תַּכְרִיעַ
you-made-bow for-the-battle strength and-you-armed-me (40) feet-of-me beneath

קָמַי תַּחְתָּי׃ (41) וְאֹיְבַי נָתַתָּה
you-turned and-ones-being-enemies-of-me (41) beneath-me adversaries-of-me

לִּי עֹרֶף וּמְשַׂנְאַי אַצְמִיתֵם׃ (42) יְשַׁוְּעוּ
they-cried-for-help (42) I-destroyed-them and-ones-being-foes-of-me back to-me

וְאֵין־מוֹשִׁיעַ עַל־יְהוָה וְלֹא עָנָם׃ (43) וְאֶשְׁחָקֵם
and-I-beat-them (43) he-answered-them but-not Yahweh to saving but-no-one

כְּעָפָר עַל־פְּנֵי־רוּחַ כְּטִיט חוּצוֹת אֲרִיקֵם׃
I-poured-out-them streets like-mud-of wind surfaces-of on as-dust

(44) תְּפַלְּטֵנִי מֵרִיבֵי עָם תְּשִׂימֵנִי לְרֹאשׁ גּוֹיִם
nations as-head-of you-made-me people from-attacks-of you-delivered-me (44)

28 You, O LORD, keep my lamp burning;
my God turns my darkness into light.
29 With your help I can advance against a troop[h];
with my God I can scale a wall.

30 As for God, his way is perfect;
the word of the LORD is flawless.
He is a shield
for all who take refuge in him.
31 For who is God besides the LORD?
And who is the Rock except our God?
32 It is God who arms me with strength
and makes my way perfect.
33 He makes my feet like the feet of a deer;
he enables me to stand on the heights.
34 He trains my hands for battle;
my arms can bend a bow of bronze.
35 You give me your shield of victory,
and your right hand sustains me;
you stoop down to make me great.
36 You broaden the path beneath me,
so that my ankles do not turn.

37 I pursued my enemies and overtook them;
I did not turn back till they were destroyed.
38 I crushed them so that they could not rise;
they fell beneath my feet.
39 You armed me with strength for battle;
you made my adversaries bow at my feet.
40 You made my enemies turn their backs in flight,
and I destroyed my foes.
41 They cried for help, but there was no one to save them—
to the LORD, but he did not answer.
42 I beat them as fine as dust borne on the wind;
I poured them out like mud in the streets.

43 You have delivered me from the attacks of the people;
you have made me the head of nations;

h29 Or *can run through a barricade*

*See the note on page 349.

עַם לֹא־יָדַעְתִּי יַעַבְדוּנִי׃ לְשֵׁמַע אֹזֶן יִשָּׁמְעוּ לִי
to-me they-obey ear in-hearing-of (45) they-are-subject-to-me I-knew not people

בְּנֵי־נֵכָר יְכַחֲשׁוּ־לִי׃ בְּנֵי־נֵכָר יִבֹּלוּ
they-lose-heart foreigner sons-of (46) before-me they-cringe foreigner sons-of

וְיַחְרְגוּ מִמִּסְגְּרוֹתֵיהֶם׃ חַי־יְהוָה וּבָרוּךְ
and-being-praised Yahweh alive (47) from-strongholds-of-them and-they-tremble

צוּרִי וְיָרוּם אֱלוֹהֵי יִשְׁעִי׃ הָאֵל
the-God (48) salvation-of-me God-of and-may-he-be-exalted Rock-of-me

הַנּוֹתֵן נְקָמוֹת לִי וַיַּדְבֵּר עַמִּים תַּחְתָּי׃
under-me nations and-he-subdues to-me vengeances the-one-giving

מְפַלְּטִי מֵאֹיְבָי אַף מִן־קָמַי תְּרוֹמְמֵנִי
you-exalted-me foes-of-me above also from-being-enemies-of-me one-saving-me (49)

מֵאִישׁ חָמָס תַּצִּילֵנִי׃ עַל־כֵּן׀ אוֹדְךָ
I-will-praise-you this for (50) you-rescued-me violence from-man-of

בַגּוֹיִם׀ יְהוָה וּלְשִׁמְךָ אֲזַמֵּרָה׃
I-will-sing-praise and-to-name-of-you Yahweh among-the-nations

מַגְדִּל יְשׁוּעוֹת מַלְכּוֹ וְעֹשֶׂה חֶסֶד׀
unfailing-kindness and-showing king-of-him victories-of making-great (51)

לִמְשִׁיחוֹ לְדָוִד וּלְזַרְעוֹ עַד־עוֹלָם׃
forever to and-to-descendant-of-him to-David to-anointed-of-him

לַמְנַצֵּחַ מִזְמוֹר לְדָוִד׃ הַשָּׁמַיִם מְסַפְּרִים
ones-declaring the-heavens (2) of-David psalm for-the-one-directing *(19:1)

כְּבוֹד־אֵל וּמַעֲשֵׂה יָדָיו מַגִּיד הָרָקִיעַ׃ יוֹם לְיוֹם
after-day day (3) the-sky proclaiming hands-of-him and-work-of God glory-of

יַבִּיעַ אֹמֶר וְלַיְלָה לְּלַיְלָה יְחַוֶּה־דָּעַת׃
knowledge he-displays after-night and-night speech he-pours-forth

אֵין־אֹמֶר וְאֵין דְּבָרִים בְּלִי נִשְׁמָע קוֹלָם׃
sound-of-them he-is-heard not languages and-there-are-no speech there-is-no (4)

בְּכָל־הָאָרֶץ׀ יָצָא קַוָּם וּבִקְצֵה תֵבֵל
world and-to-end-of line-of-them he-goes-out the-earth into-all-of (5)

מִלֵּיהֶם לַשֶּׁמֶשׁ שָׂם־אֹהֶל בָּהֶם׃ וְהוּא כְּחָתָן
like-bridegroom and-he (6) in-them tent he-pitched for-the-sun words-of-them

יֹצֵא מֵחֻפָּתוֹ יָשִׂישׂ כְּגִבּוֹר לָרוּץ אֹרַח׃
course to-run like-champion he-rejoices from-pavilion-of-him coming-forth

מִקְצֵה הַשָּׁמַיִם׀ מוֹצָאוֹ וּתְקוּפָתוֹ עַל־קְצוֹתָם
ends-of-them to and-circuit-of-him rise-of-him the-heavens at-end-of (7)

וְאֵין נִסְתָּר מֵחַמָּתוֹ׃ תּוֹרַת יְהוָה תְּמִימָה
perfect Yahweh law-of (8) from-heat-of-him being-hidden and-nothing

people I did not know are
subject to me.
44 As soon as they hear me, they
obey me;
foreigners cringe before me.
45 They all lose heart;
they come trembling from
their strongholds.

46 The LORD lives! Praise be to my
Rock!
Exalted be God my Savior!
47 He is the God who avenges
me,
who subdues nations under
me,
48 who saves me from my
enemies.
You exalted me above my foes;
from violent men you
rescued me.
49 Therefore I will praise you
among the nations, O
LORD;
I will sing praises to your
name.
50 He gives his king great
victories;
he shows unfailing kindness
to his anointed,
to David and his
descendants forever.

**Psalm 19**

For the director of music. A psalm of David.

1 The heavens declare the glory
of God;
the skies proclaim the work
of his hands.
2 Day after day they pour forth
speech;
night after night they
display knowledge.
3 There is no speech or language
where their voice is not
heard.[i]
4 Their voice[j] goes out into all
the earth,
their words to the ends of
the world.

In the heavens he has pitched
a tent for the sun,
5 which is like a bridegroom
coming forth from his
pavilion,
like a champion rejoicing to
run his course.
6 It rises at one end of the
heavens
and makes its circuit to the
other;
nothing is hidden from its
heat.
7 The law of the LORD is perfect,

i3 Or *They have no speech, there are no words; / no sound is heard from them*
j4 Septuagint, Jerome and Syriac; Hebrew *line*

*Heading, *1* See the note on page 349.

°51 ק מגדיל

מְשִׁיבַת נָפֶשׁ עֵדוּת יְהוָה נֶאֱמָנָה מַחְכִּימַת פֶּתִי׃

simple making-wise-of being-trustworthy Yahweh statute-of soul reviving-of

פִּקּוּדֵי יְהוָה יְשָׁרִים מְשַׂמְּחֵי־לֵב מִצְוַת יְהוָה

Yahweh command-of heart ones-giving-joy-of right-ones Yahweh precepts-of (9)

בָּרָה מְאִירַת עֵינָיִם׃ יִרְאַת יְהוָה ׀ טְהוֹרָה עוֹמֶדֶת לָעַד

to-forever enduring pure Yahweh fear-of (10) eyes giving-light-of radiant

מִשְׁפְּטֵי־ יְהוָה אֱמֶת צָדְקוּ יַחְדָּו׃

altogether they-are-righteous sure Yahweh ordinances-of

הַנֶּחֱמָדִים מִזָּהָב וּמִפַּז רָב

much and-more-than-pure-gold more-than-gold the-ones-being-precious (11)

וּמְתוּקִים מִדְּבַשׁ וְנֹפֶת צוּפִים׃ גַּם־

also (12) honeycombs and-honey-of more-than-honey and-ones-sweet

עַבְדְּךָ נִזְהָר בָּהֶם בְּשָׁמְרָם עֵקֶב רָב׃ שְׁגִיאוֹת

errors (13) great reward in-to-keep-them by-them being-warned servant-of-you

מִי־ יָבִין מִנִּסְתָּרוֹת נַקֵּנִי׃ גַּם

also (14) forgive-me! from-ones-being-hidden he-can-discern who?

מִזֵּדִים ׀ חֲשֹׂךְ עַבְדֶּךָ אַל־ יִמְשְׁלוּ־ בִי אָז

then over-me may-they-rule not servant-of-you keep! from-willful-sins

אֵיתָם וְנִקֵּיתִי מִפֶּשַׁע רָב׃

great of-transgression and-I-will-be-innocent I-will-be-blameless

יִהְיוּ לְרָצוֹן ׀ אִמְרֵי־ פִי וְהֶגְיוֹן

and-meditation-of mouth-of-me words-of as-pleasing may-they-be (15)

לִבִּי לְפָנֶיךָ יְהוָה צוּרִי וְגֹאֲלִי׃

and-One-Redeeming-me Rock-of-me Yahweh before-you heart-of-me

לַמְנַצֵּחַ מִזְמוֹר לְדָוִד׃ יַעַנְךָ יְהוָה

Yahweh may-he-answer-you (2) of-David psalm for-the-one-directing *(20:1)

בְּיוֹם צָרָה יְשַׂגֶּבְךָ שֵׁם ׀ אֱלֹהֵי יַעֲקֹב׃ יִשְׁלַח־

may-he-send (3) Jacob God-of name-of may-he-protect-you distress on-day-of

עֶזְרְךָ מִקֹּדֶשׁ וּמִצִּיּוֹן יִסְעָדֶךָּ׃ יִזְכֹּר

may-he-remember (4) may-he-support-you and-from-Zion from-sanctuary help-of-you

כָּל־ מִנְחֹתֶךָ וְעוֹלָתְךָ יְדַשְּׁנֶה סֶלָה׃

selah may-he-accept and-burnt-offering-of-you sacrifices-of-you all-of

יִתֶּן־ לְךָ כִלְבָבֶךָ וְכָל־ עֲצָתְךָ

plan-of-you and-all-of as-heart-of-you to-you may-he-give (5)

יְמַלֵּא׃ נְרַנְּנָה ׀ בִּישׁוּעָתֶךָ וּבְשֵׁם־

and-in-name-of at-victory-of-you we-will-shout-for-joy (6) may-he-make-succeed

אֱלֹהֵינוּ נִדְגֹּל יְמַלֵּא יְהוָה כָּל־ מִשְׁאֲלוֹתֶיךָ׃

requests-of-you all-of Yahweh may-he-grant we-will-lift-banner God-of-us

reviving the soul.
The statutes of the LORD are
trustworthy,
making wise the simple.
8The precepts of the LORD are
right,
giving joy to the heart.
The commands of the LORD are
radiant,
giving light to the eyes.
9The fear of the LORD is pure,
enduring forever.
The ordinances of the LORD are
sure
and altogether righteous.
10They are more precious than
gold,
than much pure gold;
they are sweeter than honey,
than honey from the comb.
11By them is your servant
warned;
in keeping them there is
great reward.

12Who can discern his errors?
Forgive my hidden faults.
13Keep your servant also from
willful sins;
may they not rule over me.
Then will I be blameless,
innocent of great
transgression.

14May the words of my mouth
and the meditation of my
heart
be pleasing in your sight,
O LORD, my Rock and my
Redeemer.

### Psalm 20

For the director of music. A psalm of David.

1May the LORD answer you
when you are in distress;
may the name of the God of
Jacob protect you.
2May he send you help from
the sanctuary
and grant you support from
Zion.
3May he remember all your
sacrifices
and accept your burnt
offerings. *Selah*
4May he give you the desire of
your heart
and make all your plans
succeed.
5We will shout for joy when
you are victorious
and will lift up our banners
in the name of our God.
May the LORD grant all your
requests.

*Heading, *1* See the note on page 349.

עַתָּה יָדַעְתִּי כִּי הוֹשִׁיעַ ׀ יְהוָה מְשִׁיחוֹ יַעֲנֵהוּ
he-answers-him anointed-of-him Yahweh he-saves that I-know now (7)

מִשְּׁמֵי קָדְשׁוֹ בִּגְבֻרוֹת יֵשַׁע יְמִינוֹ׃
right-hand-of-him salvation-of with-powers-of holiness-of-him from-heavens-of

אֵלֶּה בָרֶכֶב וְאֵלֶּה בַסּוּסִים וַאֲנַחְנוּ ׀ בְּשֵׁם־ יְהוָה
Yahweh in-name-of but-we in-the-horses and-these in-the-chariot these (8)

אֱלֹהֵינוּ נַזְכִּיר׃ הֵמָּה כָּרְעוּ וְנָפָלוּ וַאֲנַחְנוּ קַּמְנוּ†
we-rise-up but-we and-they-fall they-kneel they (9) we-trust God-of-us

וַנִּתְעוֹדָד׃ יְהוָה הוֹשִׁיעָה הַמֶּלֶךְ יַעֲנֵנוּ בְיוֹם־
on-day-of may-he-answer-us the-king save! Yahweh (10) and-we-stand-firm

קָרְאֵנוּ׃ לַמְנַצֵּחַ מִזְמוֹר לְדָוִד׃ יְהוָה
Yahweh (2) of-David psalm for-the-one-directing *(21:1) to-call-us

בְּעָזְּךָ יִשְׂמַח־ מֶלֶךְ וּבִישׁוּעָתְךָ מַה־ יָּגֶיל
he-has-joy how! and-in-victory-of-you king he-rejoices in-strength-of-you

מְאֹד׃ תַּאֲוַת לִבּוֹ נָתַתָּה לּוֹ וַאֲרֶשֶׁת שְׂפָתָיו
lips-of-him and-request-of to-him you-granted heart-of-him desire-of (3) great

בַּל־ מָנַעְתָּ סֶּלָה׃ כִּי־ תְקַדְּמֶנּוּ בִּרְכוֹת טוֹב תָּשִׁית
you-placed richness blessings-of you-welcomed-him indeed (4) selah you-withheld not

לְרֹאשׁוֹ עֲטֶרֶת פָּז׃ חַיִּים ׀ שָׁאַל מִמְּךָ נָתַתָּה לּוֹ
to-him you-gave from-you he-asked lives (5) pure-gold crown-of on-head-of-him

אֹרֶךְ יָמִים עוֹלָם וָעֶד׃ גָּדוֹל כְּבוֹדוֹ בִּישׁוּעָתֶךָ
through-victory-of-you glory-of-him great (6) and-ever forever days length-of

הוֹד וְהָדָר תְּשַׁוֶּה עָלָיו׃ כִּי־ תְשִׁיתֵהוּ
you-granted-him surely (7) on-him you-bestowed and-majesty splendor

בְרָכוֹת לָעַד תְּחַדֵּהוּ בְשִׂמְחָה אֶת־ פָּנֶיךָ׃
presences-of-you in with-joy you-made-glad-him for-eternity blessings

כִּי־ הַמֶּלֶךְ בֹּטֵחַ בַּיהוָה וּבְחֶסֶד עֶלְיוֹן
Most-High and-through-unfailing-love-of in-Yahweh trusting the-king for (8)

בַּל־ יִמּוֹט׃ תִּמְצָא יָדְךָ לְכָל־
on-all-of hand-of-you she-will-lay-hold (9) he-will-be-shaken not

אֹיְבֶיךָ יְמִינְךָ תִּמְצָא שֹׂנְאֶיךָ׃
ones-being-foes-of-you she-will-seize right-hand-of-you ones-being-enemies-of-you

תְּשִׁיתֵמוֹ ׀ כְּתַנּוּר אֵשׁ לְעֵת פָּנֶיךָ
appearances-of-you at-time-of fire like-furnace-of you-will-make-them (10)

יְהוָה בְּאַפּוֹ יְבַלְּעֵם וְתֹאכְלֵם אֵשׁ׃
fire and-she-will-consume-them he-will-swallow-them in-wrath-of-him Yahweh

פִּרְיָמוֹ מֵאֶרֶץ תְּאַבֵּד וְזַרְעָם
and-posterity-of-them you-will-destroy from-earth descendant-of-them (11)

6Now I know that the LORD
saves his anointed;
he answers him from his
holy heaven
with the saving power of
his right hand.
7Some trust in chariots and
some in horses,
but we trust in the name of
the LORD our God.
8They are brought to their
knees and fall,
but we rise up and stand
firm.
9O LORD, save the king!
Answer[k] us when we call!

### Psalm 21

For the director of music. A psalm of David.

1O LORD, the king rejoices in
your strength.
How great is his joy in the
victories you give!
2You have granted him the
desire of his heart
and have not withheld the
request of his lips. *Selah*
3You welcomed him with rich
blessings
and placed a crown of pure
gold on his head.
4He asked you for life, and you
gave it to him—
length of days, for ever and
ever.
5Through the victories you
gave, his glory is great;
you have bestowed on him
splendor and majesty.
6Surely you have granted him
eternal blessings
and made him glad with the
joy of your presence.
7For the king trusts in the
LORD;
through the unfailing love
of the Most High
he will not be shaken.
8Your hand will lay hold on all
your enemies;
your right hand will seize
your foes.
9At the time of your appearing
you will make them like a
fiery furnace.
In his wrath the LORD will
swallow them up,
and his fire will consume
them.
10You will destroy their
descendants from the
earth,
their posterity from

k9 Or *save! / O King, answer*

*Heading, *1* See the note on page 349.

†9 Most mss have no *dagesh* in the *qoph* (ק‎).

מִבְּנֵי אָדָם׃ כִּי־ נָטוּ עָלֶיךָ רָעָה חָשְׁבוּ
they-devise evil against-you they-plot though (12) mankind from-sons-of

מְזִמָּה בַּל־ יוּכָלוּ׃ כִּי תְּשִׁיתֵמוֹ שֶׁכֶם
back you-will-make-turn-them for (13) they-can-succeed not scheme

בְּמֵיתָרֶיךָ תְּכוֹנֵן עַל־ פְּנֵיהֶם׃ רוּמָה יְהוָה
Yahweh be-exalted! (14) faces-of-them at you-aim when-bowstrings-of-you

בְעֻזֶּךָ נָשִׁירָה וּנְזַמְּרָה גְּבוּרָתֶךָ׃
might-of-you and-we-will-praise we-will-sing in-strength-of-you

לַמְנַצֵּחַ עַל־ אַיֶּלֶת הַשַּׁחַר מִזְמוֹר לְדָוִד׃
of-David psalm the-morning doe-of to for-the-one-directing *(22:1)

אֵלִי אֵלִי לָמָה עֲזַבְתָּנִי רָחוֹק מִישׁוּעָתִי דִּבְרֵי
words-of from-salvation-of-me far you-forsook-me why? God-of-me God-of-me (2)

שַׁאֲגָתִי׃ אֱלֹהַי אֶקְרָא יוֹמָם וְלֹא תַעֲנֶה וְלַיְלָה
and-night you-answer but-not by-day I-cry-out God-of-me (3) groan-of-me

וְלֹא־ דוּמִיָּה לִי׃ וְאַתָּה קָדוֹשׁ יוֹשֵׁב תְּהִלּוֹת יִשְׂרָאֵל׃
Israel praises-of being-enthroned Holy-One yet-you (4) to-me silence and-not

בְּךָ בָּטְחוּ אֲבֹתֵינוּ בָּטְחוּ וַתְּפַלְּטֵמוֹ׃
and-you-delivered-them they-trusted fathers-of-us they-trusted in-you (5)

אֵלֶיךָ זָעֲקוּ וְנִמְלָטוּ בְּךָ בָטְחוּ וְלֹא־
and-not they-trusted in-you and-they-were-saved they-cried to-you (6)

בוֹשׁוּ׃ וְאָנֹכִי תוֹלַעַת וְלֹא־ אִישׁ חֶרְפַּת אָדָם
man scorn-of man and-not worm but-I (7) they-were-disappointed

וּבְזוּי עָם׃ כָּל־ רֹאַי יַלְעִגוּ לִי
at-me they-mock ones-seeing-me all-of (8) people and-being-despised-of

יַפְטִירוּ בְשָׂפָה יָנִיעוּ רֹאשׁ׃ גֹּל† אֶל־ יְהוָה יְפַלְּטֵהוּ
let-him-rescue-him Yahweh in trust! (9) head they-shake with-lip they-insult

יַצִּילֵהוּ כִּי חָפֵץ בּוֹ׃ כִּי־ אַתָּה גֹחִי
one-bringing-out-me you yet (10) in-him he-delights since let-him-deliver-him

מִבָּטֶן מַבְטִיחִי עַל־ שְׁדֵי אִמִּי׃ עָלֶיךָ
upon-you (11) mother-of-me breasts-of at one-making-trust-me from-womb

הָשְׁלַכְתִּי מֵרָחֶם מִבֶּטֶן אִמִּי אֵלִי אָתָּה׃ אַל־
not (12) you God-of-me mother-of-me from-womb-of from-womb I-was-cast

תִּרְחַק מִמֶּנִּי כִּי־ צָרָה קְרוֹבָה כִּי־ אֵין עוֹזֵר׃
one-helping there-is-not for near trouble for from-me you-be-far

סְבָבוּנִי פָּרִים רַבִּים אַבִּירֵי בָשָׁן כִּתְּרוּנִי׃
they-encircle-me Bashan strong-ones-of many bulls they-surround-me (13)

פָּצוּ עָלַי פִּיהֶם אַרְיֵה טֹרֵף וְשֹׁאֵג׃
and-roaring tearing-prey lion mouth-of-them against-me they-open-wide (14)

mankind.
11 Though they plot evil against you
and devise wicked schemes,
they cannot succeed;
12 for you will make them turn their backs
when you aim at them with drawn bow.

13 Be exalted, O LORD, in your strength;
we will sing and praise your might.

### Psalm 22

For the director of music. To the tune of "The Doe of the Morning." A psalm of David.

1 My God, my God, why have you forsaken me?
Why are you so far from saving me,
so far from the words of my groaning?
2 O my God, I cry out by day,
but you do not answer,
by night, and am not silent.

3 Yet you are enthroned as the Holy One;
you are the praise of Israel.[l]
4 In you our fathers put their trust;
they trusted and you delivered them.
5 They cried to you and were saved;
in you they trusted and were not disappointed.

6 But I am a worm and not a man,
scorned by men and despised by the people.
7 All who see me mock me;
they hurl insults, shaking their heads:
8 "He trusts in the LORD;
let the LORD rescue him.
Let him deliver him,
since he delights in him."

9 Yet you brought me out of the womb;
you made me trust in you
even at my mother's breast.
10 From birth I was cast upon you;
from my mother's womb
you have been my God.
11 Do not be far from me,
for trouble is near
and there is no one to help.

12 Many bulls surround me;
strong bulls of Bashan encircle me.
13 Roaring lions tearing their prey
open their mouths wide against me.

l3 Or *Yet you are holy, / enthroned on the praises of Israel*

*Heading, *1* See the note on page 349.
†9 The NIV repoints as גַּל, *be-trusts.*

| כָּל־ | וְהִתְפָּרְדוּ | נִשְׁפַּכְתִּי | כַּמַּיִם | |
|---|---|---|---|---|
| all-of | and-they-are-out-of-joint | I-am-poured-out | like-the-waters | (15) |

| בְּתוֹךְ | נָמֵס | כַּדּוֹנָג | לִבִּי | הָיָה | עַצְמוֹתָי |
|---|---|---|---|---|---|
| within | he-melted-away | like-the-wax | heart-of-me | he-is | bones-of-me |

| כֹּחִי | כַּחֶרֶשׂ ׀ | יָבֵשׁ | | מֵעָי׃ |
|---|---|---|---|---|
| strength-of-me | like-the-potsherd | he-is-dried-up | (16) | insides-of-me |

| תִּשְׁפְּתֵנִי׃ | מָוֶת | וְלַעֲפַר־ | מַלְקוֹחָי | מֻדְבָּק | וּלְשׁוֹנִי |
|---|---|---|---|---|---|
| you-lay-me | death | and-in-dust-of | roofs-of-mouth-of-me | being-stuck | and-tongue-of-me |

| הִקִּיפוּנִי | מְרֵעִים | עֲדַת | כְּלָבִים | סְבָבוּנִי | כִּי | |
|---|---|---|---|---|---|---|
| they-encircled-me | men-being-evil | band-of | dogs | they-surrounded-me | indeed | (17) |

| עַצְמוֹתָי | כָּל־ | אֲסַפֵּר | | וְרַגְלָי׃ | יָדַי | כָּאֲרִי† |
|---|---|---|---|---|---|---|
| bones-of-me | all-of | I-can-count | (18) | and-feet-of-me | hands-of-me | †like-the-lion |

| לָהֶם | בְגָדַי | יְחַלְּקוּ | | בִי׃ | יִרְאוּ־ | יַבִּיטוּ | הֵמָּה |
|---|---|---|---|---|---|---|---|
| among-them | garments-of-me | they-divide | (19) | over-me | they-gloat | they-stare | they |

| תִּרְחָק | אַל־ | יְהוָה | וְאַתָּה | | גוֹרָל׃ | יַפִּילוּ | לְבוּשִׁי | וְעַל־ |
|---|---|---|---|---|---|---|---|---|
| you-be-far-off | not | Yahweh | but-you | (20) | lot | they-cast | clothing-of-me | and-for |

| מֵחֶרֶב | הַצִּילָה | | חוּשָׁה׃ | לְעֶזְרָתִי | אֱיָלוּתִי |
|---|---|---|---|---|---|
| from-sword | deliver! | (21) | come-quickly! | as-help-of-me | Strength-of-me |

| מִפִּי | הוֹשִׁיעֵנִי | | יְחִידָתִי׃ | כֶּלֶב | מִיַּד־ | נַפְשִׁי |
|---|---|---|---|---|---|---|
| from-mouth-of | rescue-me! | (22) | precious-one-of-me | dog | from-power-of | life-of-me |

| שִׁמְךָ | אֲסַפְּרָה | | עֲנִיתָנִי׃ | רֵמִים | וּמִקַּרְנֵי | אַרְיֵה |
|---|---|---|---|---|---|---|
| name-of-you | I-will-declare | (23) | you-heard-me | wild-oxen | and-from-horns-of | lion |

| יִרְאֵי | | אֲהַלְלֶךָּ׃ | קָהָל | בְּתוֹךְ | לְאֶחָי |
|---|---|---|---|---|---|
| ones-fearing-of | (24) | I-will-praise-you | congregation | within | to-brothers-of-me |

| וְגוּרוּ | כַּבְּדוּהוּ | יַעֲקֹב | זֶרַע | כָּל־ | הַלְלוּהוּ | יְהוָה ׀ |
|---|---|---|---|---|---|---|
| and-revere! | honor-him! | Jacob | descendant-of | all-of | praise-him! | Yahweh |

| וְלֹא | בָזָה | לֹא־ | כִּי | | יִשְׂרָאֵל׃ | זֶרַע | כָּל־ | מִמֶּנּוּ |
|---|---|---|---|---|---|---|---|---|
| and-not | he-despised | not | for | (25) | Israel | descendant-of | all-of | before-him |

| מִמֶּנּוּ | פָּנָיו | הִסְתִּיר | וְלֹא־ | עָנִי | עֱנוּת | שִׁקַּץ |
|---|---|---|---|---|---|---|
| from-him | faces-of-him | he-hid | and-not | afflicted | suffering-of | he-disdained |

| תְהִלָּתִי | מֵאִתְּךָ | | שָׁמֵעַ׃ | אֵלָיו | וּבְשַׁוְּעוֹ |
|---|---|---|---|---|---|
| praise-of-me | from-with-you | (26) | he-heard | to-him | but-when-to-cry-for-help-him |

| יְרֵאָיו׃ | נֶגֶד | אֲשַׁלֵּם | נְדָרַי | רָב | בְּקָהָל |
|---|---|---|---|---|---|
| ones-fearing-him | before | I-will-fulfill | vows-of-me | great | in-assembly |

| יְהוָה | יְהַלְלוּ | וְיִשְׂבָּעוּ | עֲנָוִים ׀ | יֹאכְלוּ | |
|---|---|---|---|---|---|
| Yahweh | they-will-praise | and-they-will-be-satisfied | poor-ones | they-will-eat | (27) |

| יִזְכְּרוּ ׀ | | לָעַד׃ | לְבַבְכֶם | יְחִי | דֹּרְשָׁיו |
|---|---|---|---|---|---|
| they-will-remember | (28) | to-forever | heart-of-you | may-he-live | ones-seeking-him |

14 I am poured out like water,
and all my bones are out of joint.
My heart has turned to wax;
it has melted away within me.
15 My strength is dried up like a potsherd,
and my tongue sticks to the roof of my mouth;
you lay me[m] in the dust of death.
16 Dogs have surrounded me;
a band of evil men has encircled me,
they have pierced[n] my hands and my feet.
17 I can count all my bones;
people stare and gloat over me.
18 They divide my garments among them
and cast lots for my clothing.

19 But you, O LORD, be not far off;
O my Strength, come quickly to help me.
20 Deliver my life from the sword,
my precious life from the power of the dogs.
21 Rescue me from the mouth of the lions;
save[o] me from the horns of the wild oxen.

22 I will declare your name to my brothers;
in the congregation I will praise you.
23 You who fear the LORD, praise him!
All you descendants of Jacob, honor him!
Revere him, all you descendants of Israel!
24 For he has not despised or disdained
the suffering of the afflicted one;
he has not hidden his face from him
but has listened to his cry for help.

25 From you comes my praise in the great assembly;
before those who fear you[p] will I fulfill my vows.
26 The poor will eat and be satisfied;
they who seek the LORD will praise him—
may your hearts live forever!

[m] 15 Or / *I am laid*
[n] 16 Some Hebrew manuscripts, Septuagint and Syriac; most Hebrew manuscripts / *like the lion,*
[o] 21 Or *lions;* / *you have heard*
[p] 25 Hebrew *him*

*See the note on page 349.

†17 The NIV reads with some mss כָּרוּ or כארו, *they-pierced.*

וְיָשֻׁבוּ אֶל־ יְהוָה כָּל־ אַפְסֵי־ אָרֶץ וְיִשְׁתַּחֲווּ
and-they-will-bow-down earth ends-of all-of Yahweh to and-they-will-turn

לְפָנֶיךָ כָּל־ מִשְׁפְּחוֹת גּוֹיִם׃ כִּי לַיהוָה הַמְּלוּכָה
the-dominion to-Yahweh for (29) nations families-of all-of before-you

וּמֹשֵׁל בַּגּוֹיִם׃ אָכְלוּ וַיִּשְׁתַּחֲווּ ׀
and-they-will-worship they-will-feast (30) over-the-nations and-ruling

כָּל־ דִּשְׁנֵי־ אֶרֶץ לְפָנָיו יִכְרְעוּ כָּל־ יוֹרְדֵי
ones-going-down-of all-of they-will-kneel before-him earth rich-ones-of all-of

עָפָר וְנַפְשׁוֹ לֹא חִיָּה׃ זֶרַע יַעַבְדֶנּוּ
he-will-serve-him posterity (31) he-keeps-alive not and-self-of-him dust

יְסֻפַּר לַאדֹנָי לַדּוֹר׃ יָבֹאוּ
they-will-come (32) to-the-generation about-Lord he-will-be-told

וְיַגִּידוּ צִדְקָתוֹ לְעַם נוֹלָד כִּי עָשָׂה׃
he-did for being-born to-people righteousness-of-him and-they-will-proclaim

מִזְמוֹר לְדָוִד יְהוָה רֹעִי לֹא אֶחְסָר׃
I-shall-lack nothing one-being-shepherd-of-me Yahweh of-David psalm (23:1)

בִּנְאוֹת דֶּשֶׁא יַרְבִּיצֵנִי עַל־ מֵי מְנֻחוֹת
quiet-ones waters-of beside he-makes-lie-down-me greenness in-pastures-of (2)

יְנַהֲלֵנִי׃ נַפְשִׁי יְשׁוֹבֵב יַנְחֵנִי בְמַעְגְּלֵי־ צֶדֶק
righteousness in-paths-of he-guides-me he-restores soul-of-me (3) he-leads-me

לְמַעַן שְׁמוֹ׃ גַּם כִּי־ אֵלֵךְ בְּגֵיא צַלְמָוֶת
deep-darkness in-valley-of I-walk though even (4) name-of-him for-sake-of

לֹא־ אִירָא רָע כִּי־ אַתָּה עִמָּדִי שִׁבְטְךָ וּמִשְׁעַנְתֶּךָ הֵמָּה
they and-staff-of-you rod-of-you with-me you for evil I-will-fear not

יְנַחֲמֻנִי׃ תַּעֲרֹךְ לְפָנַי ׀ שֻׁלְחָן נֶגֶד
in-presence-of table before-me you-prepare (5) they-comfort-me

צֹרְרָי דִּשַּׁנְתָּ בַשֶּׁמֶן רֹאשִׁי כּוֹסִי
cup-of-me head-of-me with-the-oil you-anoint ones-being-enemies-of-me

רְוָיָה׃ אַךְ ׀ טוֹב וָחֶסֶד יִרְדְּפוּנִי כָּל־ יְמֵי
days-of all-of they-will-follow-me and-love goodness surely (6) overflow

חַיָּי וְשַׁבְתִּי בְּבֵית־ יְהוָה לְאֹרֶךְ יָמִים׃
days for-length-of Yahweh in-house-of and-I-will-dwell lives-of-me

לְדָוִד מִזְמוֹר לַיהוָה הָאָרֶץ וּמְלוֹאָהּ תֵּבֵל
world and-everything-in-her the-earth to-Yahweh psalm of-David (24:1)

וְיֹשְׁבֵי בָהּ׃ כִּי־ הוּא עַל־ יַמִּים יְסָדָהּ וְעַל־
and-upon he-founded-her seas upon he for (2) in-her and-ones-living-of

נְהָרוֹת יְכוֹנְנֶהָ׃ מִי־ יַעֲלֶה בְהַר־ יְהוָה וּמִי־
and-who? Yahweh to-hill-of he-may-ascend who? (3) he-established-her waters

---

27 All the ends of the earth
will remember and turn to
the LORD,
and all the families of the
nations
will bow down before him,
28 for dominion belongs to the
LORD
and he rules over the
nations.

29 All the rich of the earth will
feast and worship;
all who go down to the dust
will kneel before him—
those who cannot keep
themselves alive.
30 Posterity will serve him;
future generations will be
told about the Lord.
31 They will proclaim his
righteousness
to a people yet unborn—
for he has done it.

### Psalm 23

A psalm of David.

1 The LORD is my shepherd, I
shall lack nothing.
2 He makes me lie down in
green pastures,
he leads me beside quiet
waters,
3 he restores my soul.
He guides me in paths of
righteousness
for his name's sake.
4 Even though I walk
through the valley of the
shadow of death,[q]
I will fear no evil,
for you are with me;
your rod and your staff,
they comfort me.

5 You prepare a table before me
in the presence of my
enemies.
You anoint my head with oil;
my cup overflows.
6 Surely goodness and love will
follow me
all the days of my life,
and I will dwell in the house
of the LORD
forever.

### Psalm 24

Of David. A psalm.

1 The earth is the LORD's, and
everything in it,
the world, and all who live
in it;
2 for he founded it upon the
seas
and established it upon the
waters.
3 Who may ascend the hill of
the LORD?

q4 Or *through the darkest valley*

*See the note on page 349.

יָקוּם בִּמְקוֹם קָדְשׁוֹ׃ נְקִי כַפַּיִם וּבַר־
and-pure-of hands clean-of (4) holiness-of-him in-place-of he-may-stand

לֵבָב אֲשֶׁר ׀ לֹא־ נָשָׂא לַשָּׁוְא נַפְשִׁי וְלֹא נִשְׁבַּע
he-swears and-not soul-of-me to-the-idol he-lifts-up not who heart

לְמִרְמָה׃ יִשָּׂא בְרָכָה מֵאֵת יְהוָה וּצְדָקָה
and-vindication Yahweh from-with blessing he-will-receive (5) by-falsehood

מֵאֱלֹהֵי יִשְׁעוֹ׃ זֶה דּוֹר דֹּרְשָׁו
ones-seeking-him generation-of such (6) salvation-of-him from-God-of

מְבַקְשֵׁי פָנֶיךָ יַעֲקֹב סֶלָה׃ שְׂאוּ שְׁעָרִים ׀ רָאשֵׁיכֶם
heads-of-you gates lift-up! (7) selah Jacob faces-of-you ones-seeking-of

וְהִנָּשְׂאוּ פִּתְחֵי עוֹלָם וְיָבוֹא מֶלֶךְ הַכָּבוֹד׃
the-glory King-of that-he-may-come-in ancient doors-of and-be-lifted-up!

מִי זֶה מֶלֶךְ הַכָּבוֹד יְהוָה עִזּוּז וְגִבּוֹר יְהוָה גִּבּוֹר
mighty-of Yahweh and-mighty strong Yahweh the-glory King-of this who? (8)

מִלְחָמָה׃ שְׂאוּ שְׁעָרִים ׀ רָאשֵׁיכֶם וּשְׂאוּ פִּתְחֵי עוֹלָם
ancient doors-of and-lift-up! heads-of-you gates lift-up! (9) battle

וְיָבֹא מֶלֶךְ הַכָּבוֹד׃ מִי הוּא זֶה מֶלֶךְ הַכָּבוֹד
the-glory King-of this he who? (10) the-glory King-of that-he-may-come-in

יְהוָה צְבָאוֹת הוּא מֶלֶךְ הַכָּבוֹד סֶלָה׃ לְדָוִד אֵלֶיךָ יְהוָה
Yahweh to-you of-David (25:1) selah the-glory King-of he Hosts Yahweh-of

נַפְשִׁי אֶשָּׂא׃ אֱלֹהַי בְּךָ בָטַחְתִּי אַל־ אֵבוֹשָׁה אַל־
not let-me-be-shamed not I-trust in-you God-of-me (2) I-lift-up soul-of-me

יַעַלְצוּ אֹיְבַי לִי׃ גַּם כָּל־
all-of indeed (3) over-me ones-being-enemies-of-me let-them-triumph

קֹוֶיךָ לֹא יֵבֹשׁוּ יֵבֹשׁוּ
they-will-be-shamed they-will-be-shamed not ones-hoping-in-you

הַבּוֹגְדִים רֵיקָם׃ דְּרָכֶיךָ יְהוָה הוֹדִיעֵנִי
show-me! Yahweh ways-of-you (4) without-excuse the-ones-being-treacherous

אֹרְחוֹתֶיךָ לַמְּדֵנִי׃ הַדְרִיכֵנִי בַאֲמִתֶּךָ ׀ וְלַמְּדֵנִי כִּי־ אַתָּה
you for and-teach-me! in-truth-of-you guide-me! (5) teach-me! paths-of-you

אֱלֹהֵי יִשְׁעִי אוֹתְךָ קִוִּיתִי כָּל־ הַיּוֹם׃ זְכֹר־ רַחֲמֶיךָ
mercies-of-you remember! (6) the-day all-of I-hope-in you salvation-of-me God-of

יְהוָה וַחֲסָדֶיךָ כִּי מֵעוֹלָם הֵמָּה׃ חַטֹּאות נְעוּרַי ׀
youths-of-me sins-of (7) they from-of-old for and-loves-of-you Yahweh

וּפְשָׁעַי אַל־ תִּזְכֹּר כְּחַסְדְּךָ זְכָר־ לִי־
to-me remember! as-love-of-you you-remember not and-rebellious-ways-of-me

אַתָּה לְמַעַן טוּבְךָ יְהוָה׃ טוֹב־ וְיָשָׁר יְהוָה עַל־ כֵּן
this for Yahweh and-upright good (8) Yahweh goodness-of-you for you

Who may stand in his holy place?
4 He who has clean hands and a pure heart,
who does not lift up his soul to an idol
or swear by what is false.
5 He will receive blessing from the LORD
and vindication from God his Savior.
6 Such is the generation of those who seek him,
who seek your face, O God of Jacob.[r] *Selah*

7 Lift up your heads, O you gates;
be lifted up, you ancient doors,
that the King of glory may come in.
8 Who is this King of glory?
The LORD strong and mighty,
the LORD mighty in battle.
9 Lift up your heads, O you gates;
lift them up, you ancient doors,
that the King of glory may come in.
10 Who is he, this King of glory?
The LORD Almighty—
he is the King of glory. *Selah*

**Psalm 25**[s]

Of David.

1 To you, O LORD, I lift up my soul;
2 in you I trust, O my God.
Do not let me be put to shame,
nor let my enemies triumph over me.
3 No one whose hope is in you
will ever be put to shame,
but they will be put to shame
who are treacherous without excuse.

4 Show me your ways, O LORD,
teach me your paths;
5 guide me in your truth and teach me,
for you are God my Savior,
and my hope is in you all day long.
6 Remember, O LORD, your great mercy and love,
for they are from of old.
7 Remember not the sins of my youth
and my rebellious ways;
according to your love remember me,
for you are good, O LORD.

8 Good and upright is the LORD;

[r]6 Two Hebrew manuscripts and Syriac (see also Septuagint); most Hebrew manuscripts *face, Jacob*
[s]This psalm is an acrostic poem, the verses of which begin with the successive letters of the Hebrew alphabet.

°6 ק דרשיו

יוֹרֶה חַטָּאִים בַּדָּרֶךְ׃ יַדְרֵךְ עֲנָוִים בַּמִּשְׁפָּט

in-the-right humble-ones he-guides (9) in-the-way sinners he-instructs

וִילַמֵּד עֲנָוִים דַּרְכּוֹ׃ כָּל־ אָרְחוֹת יְהוָה חֶסֶד

loving Yahweh ways-of all-of (10) way-of-him humble-ones and-he-teaches

וֶאֱמֶת לְנֹצְרֵי בְרִיתוֹ וְעֵדֹתָיו׃

and-demands-of-him covenant-of-him for-ones-keeping-of and-faithful

לְמַעַן־ שִׁמְךָ יְהוָה וְסָלַחְתָּ לַעֲוֹנִי כִּי

though to-iniquity-of-me now-you-forgive Yahweh name-of-you for-sake-of (11)

רַב־ הוּא׃ מִי־ זֶה הָאִישׁ יְרֵא יְהוָה יוֹרֶנּוּ

he-will-instruct-him Yahweh fearing-of the-man this who? (12) he great

בְּדֶרֶךְ יִבְחָר׃ נַפְשׁוֹ בְּטוֹב תָּלִין

she-will-spend-days in-prosperity life-of-him (13) he-chooses in-way

וְזַרְעוֹ יִירַשׁ אָרֶץ׃ סוֹד יְהוָה

Yahweh confidence-of (14) land he-will-inherit and-descendant-of-him

לִירֵאָיו וּבְרִיתוֹ לְהוֹדִיעָם׃ עֵינַי

eyes-of-me (15) to-make-known-to-them and-covenant-of-him in-ones-fearing-him

תָּמִיד אֶל־ יְהוָה כִּי הוּא־ יוֹצִיא מֵרֶשֶׁת רַגְלָי׃ פְּנֵה־

turn! (16) feet-of-me from-snare he-will-release he for Yahweh on ever

אֵלַי וְחָנֵּנִי כִּי־ יָחִיד וְעָנִי אָנִי׃ צָרוֹת

troubles-of (17) I and-afflicted lonely for and-be-gracious-to-me! to-me

לְבָבִי הִרְחִיבוּ מִמְּצוּקוֹתַי הוֹצִיאֵנִי׃ רְאֵה

look-upon! (18) free-me! from-anguishes-of-me they-multiplied heart-of-me

עָנְיִי וַעֲמָלִי וְשָׂא לְכָל־ חַטֹּאותָי׃

sins-of-me to-all-of and-take-away! and-distress-of-me affliction-of-me

רְאֵה־ אוֹיְבַי כִּי־ רַבּוּ וְשִׂנְאַת חָמָס

fierceness and-hate-of they-increased how! ones-being-enemies-of-me see! (19)

שְׂנֵאוּנִי׃ שָׁמְרָה נַפְשִׁי וְהַצִּילֵנִי אַל־ אֵבוֹשׁ כִּי־

for let-me-be-shamed not and-rescue-me! life-of-me guard! (20) they-hate-me

חָסִיתִי בָךְ׃ תֹּם־ וָיֹשֶׁר יִצְּרוּנִי כִּי

because may-they-protect-me and-uprightness integrity (21) in-you I-take-refuge

קִוִּיתִיךָ׃ פְּדֵה אֱלֹהִים אֶת־ יִשְׂרָאֵל מִכֹּל צָרוֹתָיו׃

troubles-of-him from-all-of Israel *** God redeem! (22) I-hope-in-you

לְדָוִד ׀ שָׁפְטֵנִי יְהוָה כִּי־ אֲנִי בְּתֻמִּי הָלַכְתִּי

I-walked in-blameless-life-of-me I for Yahweh vindicate-me! of-David (26:1)

וּבַיהוָה בָּטַחְתִּי לֹא אֶמְעָד׃ בְּחָנֵנִי יְהוָה וְנַסֵּנִי

and-try-me! Yahweh test-me! (2) I-wavered not I-trusted and-in-Yahweh

צְרוֹפָה כִלְיוֹתַי וְלִבִּי׃ כִּי־ חַסְדְּךָ לְנֶגֶד עֵינָי

eyes-of-me at-before love-of-you for (3) and-mind-of-me hearts-of-me examine!

therefore he instructs
sinners in his ways.
[9]He guides the humble in what is right
and teaches them his way.
[10]All the ways of the LORD are loving and faithful
for those who keep the demands of his covenant.
[11]For the sake of your name, O LORD,
forgive my iniquity, though it is great.
[12]Who, then, is the man that fears the LORD?
He will instruct him in the way chosen for him.
[13]He will spend his days in prosperity,
and his descendants will inherit the land.
[14]The LORD confides in those who fear him;
he makes his covenant known to them.
[15]My eyes are ever on the LORD,
for only he will release my feet from the snare.

[16]Turn to me and be gracious to me,
for I am lonely and afflicted.
[17]The troubles of my heart have multiplied;
free me from my anguish.
[18]Look upon my affliction and my distress
and take away all my sins.
[19]See how my enemies have increased
and how fiercely they hate me!
[20]Guard my life and rescue me;
let me not be put to shame,
for I take refuge in you.
[21]May integrity and uprightness protect me,
because my hope is in you.

[22]Redeem Israel, O God,
from all their troubles!

**Psalm 26**

Of David.

[1]Vindicate me, O LORD,
for I have led a blameless life;
I have trusted in the LORD
without wavering.
[2]Test me, O LORD, and try me,
examine my heart and my mind;
[3]for your love is ever before me,

°2 ק צרפה

וְהִתְהַלַּכְתִּי בַּאֲמִתֶּךָ׃ לֹא־יָשַׁבְתִּי עִם־מְתֵי־שָׁוְא וְעִם
or-with deceit men-of with I-sit not (4) in-truth-of-you and-I-walk

נַעֲלָמִים לֹא אָבוֹא׃ שָׂנֵאתִי קְהַל מְרֵעִים
ones-doing-evil assembly-of I-abhor (5) I-consort not ones-being-hypocrites

וְעִם־רְשָׁעִים לֹא אֵשֵׁב׃ אֶרְחַץ בְּנִקָּיוֹן כַּפָּי
hands-of-me in-innocence I-wash (6) I-sit not wicked-ones and-with

וַאֲסֹבְבָה אֶת־מִזְבַּחֲךָ יְהוָה׃ לַשְׁמִעַ בְּקוֹל תּוֹדָה
praise with-voice-of to-proclaim (7) Yahweh altar-of-you *** and-I-go-about

וּלְסַפֵּר כָּל־נִפְלְאוֹתֶיךָ׃ יְהוָה אָהַבְתִּי
I-love Yahweh (8) deeds-being-wonderful-of-you all-of and-to-tell

מְעוֹן בֵּיתֶךָ וּמְקוֹם מִשְׁכַּן כְּבוֹדֶךָ׃ אַל־
not (9) glory-of-you dwelling-of and-place-of house-of-you living-place-of

תֶּאֱסֹף עִם־חַטָּאִים נַפְשִׁי וְעִם־אַנְשֵׁי דָמִים חַיָּי׃
lives-of-me bloods men-of or-with soul-of-me sinners with you-take-away

אֲשֶׁר־בִּידֵיהֶם זִמָּה וִימִינָם מָלְאָה שֹּׁחַד׃
bribe she-is-full and-right-hand-of-them scheme in-hands-of-them who (10)

וַאֲנִי בְּתֻמִּי אֵלֵךְ פְּדֵנִי וְחָנֵּנִי׃
and-be-merciful-to-me! redeem-me! I-walk in-blameless-life-of-me but-I (11)

רַגְלִי עָמְדָה בְמִישׁוֹר בְּמַקְהֵלִים אֲבָרֵךְ
I-will-praise in-great-assemblies on-level-ground she-stands foot-of-me (12)

יְהוָה׃ לְדָוִד ׀ יְהוָה ׀ אוֹרִי וְיִשְׁעִי מִמִּי
of-whom? and-salvation-of-me light-of-me Yahweh of-David (27:1) Yahweh

אִירָא יְהוָה מָעוֹז־חַיַּי מִמִּי אֶפְחָד׃
shall-I-be-afraid of-whom? lives-of-me stronghold-of Yahweh shall-I-fear

בִּקְרֹב עָלַי ׀ מְרֵעִים לֶאֱכֹל אֶת־בְּשָׂרִי
flesh-of-me *** to-devour men-being-evil against-me when-to-advance (2)

צָרַי וְאֹיְבַי לִי הֵמָּה כָשְׁלוּ
they-will-stumble they against-me and-ones-being-foes-of-me enemies-of-me

וְנָפָלוּ׃ אִם־תַּחֲנֶה עָלַי ׀ מַחֲנֶה לֹא־יִירָא
he-will-fear not army against-me she-besiege though (3) and-they-will-fall

לִבִּי אִם־תָּקוּם עָלַי מִלְחָמָה בְּזֹאת אֲנִי בוֹטֵחַ׃
being-confident I in-this war against-me she-break-out though heart-of-me

אַחַת ׀ שָׁאַלְתִּי מֵאֵת־יְהוָה אוֹתָהּ אֲבַקֵּשׁ שִׁבְתִּי בְּבֵית־יְהוָה
Yahweh in-house-of to-dwell-me I-seek her Yahweh from-with I-ask one (4)

כָּל־יְמֵי חַיַּי לַחֲזוֹת בְּנֹעַם־יְהוָה וּלְבַקֵּר
and-to-seek Yahweh upon-beauty-of to-gaze lives-of-me days-of all-of

בְּהֵיכָלוֹ׃ כִּי יִצְפְּנֵנִי ׀ בְּסֻכֹּה בְּיוֹם
in-day-of in-dwelling-of-him he-will-keep-safe-me for (5) in-temple-of-him

and I walk continually in
your truth.
4 I do not sit with deceitful
men,
nor do I consort with
hypocrites;
5 I abhor the assembly of
evildoers
and refuse to sit with the
wicked.
6 I wash my hands in
innocence,
and go about your altar, O
LORD,
7 proclaiming aloud your praise
and telling of all your
wonderful deeds.
8 I love the house where you
live, O LORD,
the place where your glory
dwells.

9 Do not take away my soul
along with sinners
or my life with bloodthirsty
men,
10 in whose hands are wicked
schemes,
whose right hands are full
of bribes.
11 But I lead a blameless life;
redeem me and be merciful
to me.

12 My feet stand on level ground;
in the great assembly I will
praise the LORD.

## Psalm 27

Of David.

1 The LORD is my light and my
salvation—
whom shall I fear?
The LORD is the stronghold of
my life—
of whom shall I be afraid?
2 When evil men advance
against me
to devour my flesh,[1]
when my enemies and my
foes attack me,
they will stumble and fall.
3 Though an army besiege me,
my heart will not fear;
though war break out against
me,
even then will I be
confident.

4 One thing I ask of the LORD,
this is what I seek:
that I may dwell in the house
of the LORD
all the days of my life,
to gaze upon the beauty of the
LORD
and to seek him in his
temple.
5 For in the day of trouble
he will keep me safe in his
dwelling;

[1] 2 Or *to slander me*

רָעָה יַסְתִּרֵנִי בְּסֵתֶר אָהֳלוֹ בְּצוּר
upon-rock tabernacle-of-him in-shelter-of he-will-hide-me trouble

יְרוֹמְמֵנִי׃ וְעַתָּה יָרוּם רֹאשִׁי עַל
above head-of-me he-will-be-exalted and-then (6) he-will-set-high-me

אֹיְבַי סְבִיבוֹתַי וְאֶזְבְּחָה בְאָהֳלוֹ
at-tabernacle-of-him and-I-will-sacrifice ones-around-me ones-being-enemies-of-me

זִבְחֵי תְרוּעָה אָשִׁירָה וַאֲזַמְּרָה לַיהוָה׃
to-Yahweh and-I-will-make-music I-will-sing shout-of-joy sacrifices-of

שְׁמַע־ יְהוָה קוֹלִי אֶקְרָא וְחָנֵּנִי וַעֲנֵנִי׃
and-answer-me! and-be-merciful-to-me! I-call voice-of-me Yahweh hear! (7)

לְךָ׀ אָמַר לִבִּי בַּקְּשׁוּ פָנָי אֶת־ פָּנֶיךָ יְהוָה
Yahweh faces-of-you *** faces-of-me seek! heart-of-me he-says of-you (8)

אֲבַקֵּשׁ׃ אַל־ תַּסְתֵּר פָּנֶיךָ׀ מִמֶּנִּי אַל־ תַּט־ בְּאַף
in-anger you-turn-away not from-me faces-of-you you-hide not (9) I-will-seek

עַבְדֶּךָ עֶזְרָתִי הָיִיתָ אַל־ תִּטְּשֵׁנִי וְאַל־ תַּעַזְבֵנִי
you-forsake-me and-not you-reject-me not you-are help-of-me servant-of-you

אֱלֹהֵי יִשְׁעִי׃ כִּי־ אָבִי וְאִמִּי עֲזָבוּנִי
they-forsake-me and-mother-of-me father-of-me though (10) salvation-of-me God-of

וַיהוָה יַאַסְפֵנִי׃ הוֹרֵנִי יְהוָה דַּרְכֶּךָ וּנְחֵנִי
and-lead-me! way-of-you Yahweh teach-me! (11) he-will-receive-me yet-Yahweh

בְּאֹרַח מִישׁוֹר לְמַעַן שׁוֹרְרָי׃ אַל־ תִּתְּנֵנִי
you-turn-over-me not (12) oppressors-of-me because-of straight in-path-of

בְּנֶפֶשׁ צָרָי כִּי קָמוּ־ בִי עֵדֵי־ שֶׁקֶר
falsehood witnesses-of against-me they-rise-up for foes-of-me to-desire-of

וִיפֵחַ חָמָס׃ לוּלֵא הֶאֱמַנְתִּי לִרְאוֹת בְּטוּב־
on-goodness-of to-see I-am-confident still (13) violence and-breather-of

יְהוָה בְּאֶרֶץ חַיִּים׃ קַוֵּה אֶל־ יְהוָה חֲזַק וְיַאֲמֵץ
and-strengthen! be-strong! Yahweh for wait! (14) live-ones in-land-of Yahweh

לִבֶּךָ וְקַוֵּה אֶל־ יְהוָה׃ לְדָוִד אֵלֶיךָ יְהוָה׀ אֶקְרָא
I-call Yahweh to-you of-David (28:1) Yahweh for and-wait! heart-of-you

צוּרִי אַל־ תֶּחֱרַשׁ מִמֶּנִּי פֶּן־ תֶּחֱשֶׁה מִמֶּנִּי
from-me you-remain-silent for-if to-me you-turn-deaf-ear not Rock-of-me

וְנִמְשַׁלְתִּי עִם־ יוֹרְדֵי בוֹר׃ שְׁמַע קוֹל
sound-of hear! (2) pit ones-going-down-of with then-I-will-be-like

תַּחֲנוּנַי בְּשַׁוְּעִי אֵלֶיךָ בְּנָשְׂאִי יָדַי
hands-of-me as-to-lift-me to-you as-to-call-for-help-me cries-for-mercy-of-me

אֶל־ דְּבִיר קָדְשֶׁךָ׃ אַל־ תִּמְשְׁכֵנִי עִם־ רְשָׁעִים
wicked-ones with you-drag-away-me not (3) Holiness-of-you Holy-Place-of toward

he will hide me in the shelter
of his tabernacle
and set me high upon a
rock.
6Then my head will be exalted
above the enemies who
surround me;
at his tabernacle will I sacrifice
with shouts of joy;
I will sing and make music
to the LORD.

7Hear my voice when I call, O
LORD;
be merciful to me and
answer me.
8My heart says of you, "Seek
his[a] face!"
Your face, LORD, I will seek.
9Do not hide your face from
me,
do not turn your servant
away in anger;
you have been my helper.
Do not reject me or forsake
me,
O God my Savior.
10Though my father and mother
forsake me,
the LORD will receive me.
11Teach me your way, O LORD;
lead me in a straight path
because of my oppressors.
12Do not turn me over to the
desire of my foes,
for false witnesses rise up
against me,
breathing out violence.

13I am still confident of this:
I will see the goodness of
the LORD
in the land of the living.
14Wait for the LORD;
be strong and take heart
and wait for the LORD.

## Psalm 28

Of David.

1To you I call, O LORD my
Rock;
do not turn a deaf ear to me.
For if you remain silent,
I will be like those who
have gone down to the
pit.
2Hear my cry for mercy
as I call to you for help,
as I lift up my hands
toward your Most Holy
Place.

3Do not drag me away with the
wicked,

[a]8 Or *To you, O my heart, he has said, "Seek my*

וְעִם־ פֹּעֲלֵי אָוֶן דֹּבְרֵי שָׁלוֹם עִם־ רֵעֵיהֶם

neighbors-of-them with cordiality ones-speaking-of evil ones-doing-of even-with

וְרָעָה בִּלְבָבָם׃ תֶּן־ לָהֶם כְּפָעֳלָם וּכְרֹעַ

and-as-evil-of as-deed-of-them to-them repay! (4) in-heart-of-them but-malice

מַעַלְלֵיהֶם כְּמַעֲשֵׂה יְדֵיהֶם תֵּן לָהֶם הָשֵׁב

bring-back! to-them repay! hands-of-them as-deed-of works-of-them

גְּמוּלָם לָהֶם׃ כִּי לֹא יָבִינוּ אֶל־ פְּעֻלֹּת יְהוָה

Yahweh works-of for they-show-regard not since (5) upon-them desert-of-them

וְאֶל־ מַעֲשֵׂה יָדָיו יֶהֶרְסֵם וְלֹא יִבְנֵם׃

he-will-rebuild-them and-never he-will-tear-down-them hands-of-him deed-of and-for

בָּרוּךְ יְהוָה כִּי־ שָׁמַע* קוֹל תַּחֲנוּנָי׃

cries-for-mercy-of-me sound-of he-heard for Yahweh being-praised (6)

יְהוָה׀ עֻזִּי וּמָגִנִּי בּוֹ בָטַח לִבִּי

heart-of-me he-trusts in-him and-shield-of-me strength-of-me Yahweh (7)

וְנֶעֱזָרְתִּי וַיַּעֲלֹז לִבִּי וּמִשִּׁירִי

and-in-song-of-me heart-of-me and-he-leaps-for-joy and-I-am-helped

אֲהוֹדֶנּוּ׃ יְהוָה עֹז־ לָמוֹ וּמָעוֹז יְשׁוּעוֹת

salvations-of and-fortress-of of-them strength Yahweh (8) I-will-thank-him

מְשִׁיחוֹ הוּא׃ הוֹשִׁיעָה׀ אֶת־ עַמֶּךָ וּבָרֵךְ אֶת־

*** and-bless! people-of-you *** save! (9) he anointed-of-him

נַחֲלָתֶךָ וּרְעֵם וְנַשְּׂאֵם עַד־ הָעוֹלָם׃

the-forever to and-carry-them! and-be-shepherd-of-them! inheritance-of-you

מִזְמוֹר לְדָוִד הָבוּ לַיהוָה בְּנֵי אֵלִים הָבוּ

ascribe! mighty-ones sons-of to-Yahweh ascribe! of-David psalm (29:1)

לַיהוָה כָּבוֹד וָעֹז׃ הָבוּ לַיהוָה כְּבוֹד שְׁמוֹ

name-of-him glory-of to-Yahweh ascribe! (2) and-strength glory to-Yahweh

הִשְׁתַּחֲווּ לַיהוָה בְּהַדְרַת־ קֹדֶשׁ׃ קוֹל יְהוָה עַל־

over Yahweh voice-of (3) holiness in-splendor-of to-Yahweh worship!

הַמָּיִם אֵל־ הַכָּבוֹד הִרְעִים יְהוָה עַל־ מַיִם רַבִּים׃

mighty-ones waters over Yahweh he-thunders the-glory God-of the-waters

קוֹל־ יְהוָה בַּכֹּחַ קוֹל יְהוָה בֶּהָדָר׃ קוֹל

voice-of (5) in-the-majesty Yahweh voice-of in-the-power Yahweh voice-of (4)

יְהוָה שֹׁבֵר אֲרָזִים וַיְשַׁבֵּר יְהוָה אֶת־ אַרְזֵי הַלְּבָנוֹן׃

the-Lebanon cedars-of *** Yahweh and-he-breaks cedars breaking Yahweh

וַיַּרְקִידֵם כְּמוֹ־ עֵגֶל לְבָנוֹן וְשִׂרְיֹן כְּמוֹ בֶן־ רְאֵמִים׃

wild-oxen son-of like and-Sirion Lebanon calf like and-he-makes-skip (6)

קוֹל־ יְהוָה חֹצֵב לַהֲבוֹת אֵשׁ׃ קוֹל יְהוָה

Yahweh voice-of (8) lightning flashes-of striking Yahweh voice-of (7)

with those who do evil,
who speak cordially with their neighbors
but harbor malice in their hearts.
4 Repay them for their deeds
and for their evil work;
repay them for what their hands have done
and bring back upon them what they deserve.
5 Since they show no regard for the works of the LORD
and what his hands have done,
he will tear them down
and never build them up again.

6 Praise be to the LORD,
for he has heard my cry for mercy.
7 The LORD is my strength and my shield;
my heart trusts in him, and I am helped.
My heart leaps for joy
and I will give thanks to him in song.

8 The LORD is the strength of his people,
a fortress of salvation for his anointed one.
9 Save your people and bless your inheritance;
be their shepherd and carry them forever.

### Psalm 29

A psalm of David.

1 Ascribe to the LORD, O mighty ones,
ascribe to the LORD glory and strength.
2 Ascribe to the LORD the glory due his name;
worship the LORD in the splendor of his[v] holiness.

3 The voice of the LORD is over the waters;
the God of glory thunders,
the LORD thunders over the mighty waters.
4 The voice of the LORD is powerful;
the voice of the LORD is majestic.
5 The voice of the LORD breaks the cedars;
the LORD breaks in pieces the cedars of Lebanon.
6 He makes Lebanon skip like a calf,
Sirion[w] like a young wild ox.
7 The voice of the LORD strikes
with flashes of lightning.
8 The voice of the LORD shakes

[v] 2 Or *LORD with the splendor of*
[w] 6 That is, Mount Hermon

*6 Most mss have the accent *rebia mugrash* (◌֗).

יָחִיל מִדְבָּר יָחִיל יְהוָה מִדְבַּר קָדֵשׁ׃ קוֹל יְהוָה׀
Yahweh voice-of (9) Kadesh Desert-of Yahweh he-shakes desert he-shakes

יְחוֹלֵל אַיָּלוֹת וַיֶּחֱשֹׂף־ יְעָרוֹת וּבְהֵיכָלוֹ
and-temple-of-him forests and-he-strips-bare †deers he-makes-give-birth†

כֻּלּוֹ אֹמֵר כָּבוֹד׃ יְהוָה לַמַּבּוּל יָשָׁב וַיֵּשֶׁב
and-he-is-enthroned he-sits over-the-flood Yahweh (10) glory crying all-of-him

יְהוָה מֶלֶךְ לְעוֹלָם׃ יְהוָה עֹז לְעַמּוֹ יִתֵּן יְהוָה׀
Yahweh he-gives to-people-of-him strength Yahweh (11) to-forever King Yahweh

יְבָרֵךְ אֶת־ עַמּוֹ בַשָּׁלוֹם׃ מִזְמוֹר שִׁיר־ חֲנֻכַּת
dedication-of song-of psalm *(30:1) with-the-peace people-of-him *** he-blesses

הַבַּיִת לְדָוִד׃ אֲרוֹמִמְךָ יְהוָה כִּי דִלִּיתָנִי וְלֹא־
and-not you-lifted-me for Yahweh I-will-exalt-you (2) of-David the-temple

שִׂמַּחְתָּ אֹיְבַי לִי׃ יְהוָה אֱלֹהָי
God-of-me Yahweh (3) over-me ones-being-enemies-of-me you-let-gloat

שִׁוַּעְתִּי אֵלֶיךָ וַתִּרְפָּאֵנִי׃ יְהוָה הֶעֱלִיתָ מִן־
from you-brought-up Yahweh (4) and-you-healed-me to-you I-cried-for-help

שְׁאוֹל נַפְשִׁי חִיִּיתַנִי מִיָּורְדִי־° בוֹר׃ זַמְּרוּ לַיהוָה
to-Yahweh sing! (5) pit from-to-go-down-me you-spared-me self-of-me Sheol

חֲסִידָיו וְהוֹדוּ לְזֵכֶר קָדְשׁוֹ׃ כִּי רֶגַע׀
moment for (6) holiness-of-him to-name-of and-praise! saints-of-him

בְּאַפּוֹ חַיִּים בִּרְצוֹנוֹ בָּעֶרֶב יָלִין בֶּכִי
weeping he-remains in-the-night in-favor-of-him lifetimes in-anger-of-him

וְלַבֹּקֶר רִנָּה׃ וַאֲנִי אָמַרְתִּי בְשַׁלְוִי בַּל־
not in-security-of-me I-said when-I (7) rejoicing but-in-the-morning

אֶמּוֹט לְעוֹלָם׃ יְהוָה בִּרְצוֹנְךָ הֶעֱמַדְתָּה
you-made-stand in-favor-of-you Yahweh (8) to-forever I-will-be-shaken

לְהַרְרִי עֹז הִסְתַּרְתָּ פָנֶיךָ הָיִיתִי נִבְהָל׃ אֵלֶיךָ
to-you (9) being-dismayed I-was faces-of-you you-hid firm to-mountain-of-me

יְהוָה אֶקְרָא וְאֶל־ אֲדֹנָי אֶתְחַנָּן׃ מַה־ בֶּצַע בְּדָמִי
in-destruction-of-me gain what? (10) I-cried-for-mercy Lord and-to I-called Yahweh

בְּרִדְתִּי אֶל־ שָׁחַת הֲיוֹדְךָ עָפָר הֲיַגִּיד
will-he-proclaim? dust will-he-praise-you? pit into in-to-go-down-me

אֲמִתֶּךָ׃ שְׁמַע־ יְהוָה וְחָנֵּנִי יְהוָה הֱיֵה־
be! Yahweh and-be-merciful-to-me! Yahweh hear! (11) faithfulness-of-you

עֹזֵר לִי׃ הָפַכְתָּ מִסְפְּדִי לְמָחוֹל לִי
for-me into-dancing wailing-of-me you-turned (12) to-me one-helping

פִּתַּחְתָּ שַׂקִּי וַתְּאַזְּרֵנִי שִׂמְחָה׃ לְמַעַן׀
so-that (13) joy and-you-clothed-me sackcloth-of-me you-removed

the desert;
the LORD shakes the Desert
of Kadesh.
9 The voice of the LORD twists
the oaks[x]
and strips the forests bare.
And in his temple all cry,
"Glory!"

10 The LORD sits[y] enthroned over
the flood;
the LORD is enthroned as
King forever.
11 The LORD gives strength to his
people;
the LORD blesses his people
with peace.

### Psalm 30

A psalm. A song. For the dedication of the temple.[z] Of David.

1 I will exalt you, O LORD,
for you lifted me out of the
depths
and did not let my enemies
gloat over me.
2 O LORD my God, I called to
you for help
and you healed me.
3 O LORD, you brought me up
from the grave[a];
you spared me from going
down into the pit.

4 Sing to the LORD, you saints of
his;
praise his holy name.
5 For his anger lasts only a
moment,
but his favor lasts a lifetime;
weeping may remain for a
night,
but rejoicing comes in the
morning.

6 When I felt secure, I said,
"I will never be shaken."
7 O LORD, when you favored me,
you made my mountain[b]
stand firm;
but when you hid your face,
I was dismayed.

8 To you, O LORD, I called;
to the Lord I cried for
mercy:
9 "What gain is there in my
destruction,[c]
in my going down into the
pit?
Will the dust praise you?
Will it proclaim your
faithfulness?
10 Hear, O LORD, and be merciful
to me;
O LORD, be my help."

11 You turned my wailing into
dancing;
you removed my sackcloth
and clothed me with joy,

x9 Or *LORD makes the deer give birth*
y10 Or *sat* z Title: Or *palace*
a3 Hebrew *Sheol* b7 Or *hill country*
c9 Or *there if I am silenced*

*Heading, *1* See the note on page 349.
†9 The NIV reads the second word as אֵילוֹת, and translates the phrase *be-twists oaks*.

°4 ק מירדי

יְזַמֶּרְךָ כָבוֹד וְלֹא יִדֹּם יְהוָה אֱלֹהַי לְעוֹלָם
to-forever God-of-me Yahweh he-may-be-silent and-not heart he-may-sing-to-you

אוֹדֶךָּ׃ לַמְנַצֵּחַ מִזְמוֹר לְדָוִד׃ בְּךָ
in-you (2) of-David psalm for-the-one-directing *(31:1) I-will-thank-you

יְהוָה חָסִיתִי אַל־ אֵבוֹשָׁה לְעוֹלָם בְּצִדְקָתְךָ
in-righteousness-of-you to-forever let-me-be-shamed not I-took-refuge Yahweh

פַּלְּטֵנִי׃ הַטֵּה אֵלַי ׀ אָזְנְךָ מְהֵרָה הַצִּילֵנִי הֱיֵה לִי ׀
for-me be! rescue-me! quickly ear-of-you to-me turn! (3) deliver-me!

לְצוּר־ מָעוֹז לְבֵית מְצוּדוֹת לְהוֹשִׁיעֵנִי׃ כִּי־ סַלְעִי
rock-of-me since (4) to-save-me fortresses as-house-of refuge as-rock-of

וּמְצוּדָתִי אָתָּה וּלְמַעַן שִׁמְךָ תַּנְחֵנִי וּתְנַהֲלֵנִי׃
and-you-guide-me you-lead-me name-of-you and-for-sake-of you and-fortress-of-me

תּוֹצִיאֵנִי מֵרֶשֶׁת זוּ טָמְנוּ לִי כִּי־ אַתָּה מָעוּזִּי׃
refuge-of-me you for for-me they-set that from-trap you-free-me (5)

בְּיָדְךָ אַפְקִיד רוּחִי פָּדִיתָה אוֹתִי יְהוָה אֵל אֱמֶת׃
truth God-of Yahweh me you-redeem spirit-of-me I-commit into-hand-of-you (6)

שָׂנֵאתִי הַשֹּׁמְרִים הַבְלֵי־ שָׁוְא וַאֲנִי אֶל־ יְהוָה בָּטָחְתִּי׃
I-trust Yahweh in and-I worthlessness idols-of the-ones-clinging-to I-hate (7)

אָגִילָה וְאֶשְׂמְחָה בְּחַסְדֶּךָ אֲשֶׁר רָאִיתָ אֶת־
*** you-saw for in-love-of-you and-I-will-rejoice I-will-be-glad (8)

עָנְיִי יָדַעְתָּ בְּצָרוֹת נַפְשִׁי׃ וְלֹא הִסְגַּרְתַּנִי
you-put-me and-not (9) soul-of-me to-anguishes-of you-knew affliction-of-me

בְּיַד־ אוֹיֵב הֶעֱמַדְתָּ בַמֶּרְחָב רַגְלָי׃
feet-of-me in-the-spacious-place you-set one-being-enemy into-hand-of

חָנֵּנִי יְהוָה כִּי צַר־ לִי עָשְׁשָׁה בְכַעַס
with-sorrow she-grows-weak to-me distress for Yahweh be-merciful-to-me! (10)

עֵינִי נַפְשִׁי וּבִטְנִי׃ כִּי כָלוּ בְיָגוֹן
by-anguish they-are-consumed for (11) and-body-of-me soul-of-me eye-of-me

חַיַּי וּשְׁנוֹתַי בַּאֲנָחָה כָּשַׁל בַּעֲוֹנִי
†because-of-guilt-of-me he-fails by-groaning and-years-of-me lives-of-me

כֹחִי וַעֲצָמַי עָשֵׁשׁוּ׃ מִכָּל־
because-of-all-of (12) they-grow-weak and-bones-of-me strength-of-me

צֹרְרַי הָיִיתִי חֶרְפָּה וְלִשְׁכֵנַי ׀ מְאֹד
utterly even-of-neighbors-of-me contempt I-am ones-being-enemies-of-me

וּפַחַד לִמְיֻדָּעַי רֹאַי בַּחוּץ נָדְדוּ
they-flee on-the-street ones-seeing-me to-ones-being-friends-of-me and-dread

מִמֶּנִּי׃ נִשְׁכַּחְתִּי כְּמֵת מִלֵּב הָיִיתִי כִּכְלִי
like-pottery I-became from-heart as-dead I-am-forgotten (13) from-me

[12]that my heart may sing to you
and not be silent.
O LORD my God, I will give
you thanks forever.

### Psalm 31

For the director of music. A psalm of David.

[1]In you, O LORD, I have taken
refuge;
let me never be put to
shame;
deliver me in your
righteousness.
[2]Turn your ear to me,
come quickly to my rescue;
be my rock of refuge,
a strong fortress to save me.
[3]Since you are my rock and my
fortress,
for the sake of your name
lead and guide me.
[4]Free me from the trap that is
set for me,
for you are my refuge.
[5]Into your hands I commit my
spirit;
redeem me, O LORD, the
God of truth.

[6]I hate those who cling to
worthless idols;
I trust in the LORD.
[7]I will be glad and rejoice in
your love,
for you saw my affliction
and knew the anguish of
my soul.
[8]You have not handed me over
to the enemy
but have set my feet in a
spacious place.

[9]Be merciful to me, O LORD, for
I am in distress;
my eyes grow weak with
sorrow,
my soul and my body with
grief.
[10]My life is consumed by
anguish
and my years by groaning;
my strength fails because of
my affliction,[d]
and my bones grow weak.
[11]Because of all my enemies,
I am the utter contempt of
my neighbors;
I am a dread to my friends—
those who see me on the
street flee from me.
[12]I am forgotten by them as
though I were dead;
I have become like broken
pottery.

[d]10 Or *guilt*

*Heading, *1* See the note on page 349.
†*11* The NIV reads this word as בְּעָנְיִי, *from-affliction-of-me*.

אֹבֵד׃ כִּי שָׁמַעְתִּי ׀ דִּבַּת רַבִּים מָגוֹר מִסָּבִיב

on-every-side terror many slander-of I-hear for (14) being-broken

בְּהִוָּסְדָם יַחַד עָלַי לָקַחַת נַפְשִׁי זָמָמוּ׃

they-plot life-of-me to-take against-me together when-to-conspire-them

וַאֲנִי ׀ עָלֶיךָ בָטַחְתִּי יְהוָה אָמַרְתִּי אֱלֹהַי אָתָּה׃ בְּיָדְךָ

in-hand-of-you (16) you God-of-me I-say Yahweh I-trust in-you but-I (15)

עִתֹּתָי הַצִּילֵנִי מִיַּד־ אוֹיְבַי

ones-being-enemies-of-me from-hand-of deliver-me! times-of-me

וּמֵרֹדְפָי׃ הָאִירָה פָנֶיךָ עַל־ עַבְדֶּךָ הוֹשִׁיעֵנִי

save-me! servant-of-you on faces-of-you shine! (17) and-from-ones-pursuing-me

בְחַסְדֶּךָ׃ יְהוָה אַל־ אֵבוֹשָׁה כִּי קְרָאתִיךָ

I-cried-to-you for let-me-be-shamed not Yahweh (18) in-unfailing-love-of-you

יֵבֹשׁוּ רְשָׁעִים יִדְּמוּ לִשְׁאוֹל׃

in-Sheol let-them-lie-silent wicked-ones let-them-be-shamed

תֵּאָלַמְנָה שִׂפְתֵי שָׁקֶר הַדֹּבְרוֹת עַל־ צַדִּיק

righteous against the-ones-speaking lying lips-of let-them-be-silenced (19)

עָתָק בְּגַאֲוָה וָבוּז׃ מָה רַב־ טוּבְךָ אֲשֶׁר־

which goodness-of-you great how! (20) and-contempt with-pride arrogance

צָפַנְתָּ לִּירֵאֶיךָ פָּעַלְתָּ לַחֹסִים

on-the-ones-taking-refuge you-bestow for-ones-fearing-you you-stored-up

בָּךְ נֶגֶד בְּנֵי אָדָם׃ תַּסְתִּירֵם ׀ בְּסֵתֶר פָּנֶיךָ

presences-of-you in-shelter-of you-hide-them (21) man sons-of in-sight-of in-you

מֵרֻכְסֵי אִישׁ תִּצְפְּנֵם בְּסֻכָּה מֵרִיב לְשֹׁנוֹת׃

tongues from-strife-of in-dwelling you-keep-safe-them man from-intrigues-of

בָּרוּךְ יְהוָה כִּי הִפְלִיא חַסְדּוֹ לִי בְּעִיר

in-city-of to-me love-of-him he-showed-wonderful for Yahweh being-praised (22)

מָצוֹר׃ וַאֲנִי ׀ אָמַרְתִּי בְחָפְזִי נִגְרַזְתִּי מִנֶּגֶד

from-before I-am-cut-off when-to-be-alarmed-me I-said and-I (23) siege

עֵינֶיךָ אָכֵן שָׁמַעְתָּ קוֹל תַּחֲנוּנַי בְּשַׁוְּעִי

when-to-call-for-help-me cries-for-mercy-of-me sound-of you-heard yet eyes-of-you

אֵלֶיךָ׃ אֶהֱבוּ אֶת־ יְהוָה כָּל־ חֲסִידָיו אֱמוּנִים

ones-being-faithful saints-of-him all-of Yahweh *** love! (24) to-you

נֹצֵר יְהוָה וּמְשַׁלֵּם עַל־ יֶתֶר עֹשֵׂה גַאֲוָה׃

pride one-acting-of full in but-one-paying-back Yahweh one-preserving

חִזְקוּ וְיַאֲמֵץ לְבַבְכֶם כָּל־ הַמְיַחֲלִים לַיהוָה׃

in-Yahweh the-ones-hoping all-of heart-of-you and-strengthen! be-strong! (25)

לְדָוִד מַשְׂכִּיל אַשְׁרֵי נְשׂוּי־ פֶּשַׁע

transgression one-being-forgiven-of blessednesses-of maskil of-David (32:1)

13 For I hear the slander of many;
there is terror on every side;
they conspire against me
and plot to take my life.

14 But I trust in you, O LORD;
I say, "You are my God."
15 My times are in your hands;
deliver me from my enemies
and from those who pursue me.
16 Let your face shine on your servant;
save me in your unfailing love.
17 Let me not be put to shame, O LORD,
for I have cried out to you;
but let the wicked be put to shame
and lie silent in the grave.[e]
18 Let their lying lips be silenced,
for with pride and contempt
they speak arrogantly
against the righteous.

19 How great is your goodness,
which you have stored up
for those who fear you,
which you bestow in the sight of men
on those who take refuge in you.
20 In the shelter of your presence
you hide them
from the intrigues of men;
in your dwelling you keep them safe
from the strife of tongues.

21 Praise be to the LORD,
for he showed his wonderful love to me
when I was in a besieged city.
22 In my alarm I said,
"I am cut off from your sight!"
Yet you heard my cry for mercy
when I called to you for help.

23 Love the LORD, all his saints!
The LORD preserves the faithful,
but the proud he pays back in full.
24 Be strong and take heart,
all you who hope in the LORD.

### Psalm 32

*Of David. A maskil.*[f]

1 Blessed is he
whose transgressions are forgiven,

[e] 17 Hebrew *Sheol*
[f] Title: Probably a literary or musical term

*See the note on page 349.

כְּסוּי חֲטָאָה׃ אַשְׁרֵי אָדָם לֹא יַחְשֹׁב יְהוָה
Yahweh he-counts not man blessednesses-of (2) sin one-being-covered-of

לוֹ עָוֺן וְאֵין בְּרוּחוֹ רְמִיָּה׃ כִּי־
when (3) deceit in-spirit-of-him and-there-is-not sin against-him

הֶחֱרַשְׁתִּי בָּלוּ עֲצָמָי בְּשַׁאֲגָתִי כָּל־
all-of through-groaning-of-me bones-of-me they-wasted-away I-kept-silent

הַיּוֹם׃ כִּי יוֹמָם וָלַיְלָה תִּכְבַּד עָלַי יָדֶךָ
hand-of-you upon-me she-was-heavy and-night by-day for (4) the-day

נֶהְפַּךְ לְשַׁדִּי בְּחַרְבֹנֵי קַיִץ סֶלָה׃ חַטָּאתִי
sin-of-me (5) selah summer in-heats-of strength-of-me he-was-sapped

אוֹדִיעֲךָ וַעֲוֺנִי לֹא־ כִסִּיתִי אָמַרְתִּי אוֹדֶה
I-will-confess I-said I-covered-up not and-iniquity-of-me I-acknowledged-to-you

עֲלֵי פְשָׁעַי לַיהוָה וְאַתָּה נָשָׂאתָ עֲוֺן חַטָּאתִי
sin-of-me guilt-of you-forgave and-you to-Yahweh transgressions-of-me to

סֶלָה׃ עַל־זֹאת יִתְפַּלֵּל כָּל־ חָסִיד אֵלֶיךָ לְעֵת מְצֹא
to-find at-time-of to-you godly-one every-of let-him-pray this for (6) selah

רַק לְשֵׁטֶף מַיִם רַבִּים אֵלָיו לֹא יַגִּיעוּ׃ אַתָּה
you (7) they-will-reach not to-him mighty-ones waters at-rising-of surely

סֵתֶר לִי מִצַּר תִּצְּרֵנִי רָנֵּי פַלֵּט
to-deliver songs-of you-will-protect-me from-trouble for-me hiding-place

תְּסוֹבְבֵנִי סֶלָה׃ אַשְׂכִּילְךָ וְאוֹרְךָ
and-I-will-teach-you I-will-instruct-you (8) selah you-will-surround-me

בְּדֶרֶךְ־ זוּ תֵלֵךְ אִיעֲצָה עָלֶיךָ עֵינִי׃ אַל־תִּהְיוּ
you-be not (9) eye-of-me over-you I-will-counsel you-should-go that in-way

כְּסוּס כְּפֶרֶד אֵין הָבִין בְּמֶתֶג־ וָרֶסֶן עֶדְיוֹ
harness-of-him and-bridle by-bit to-understand not like-mule like-horse

לִבְלוֹם בַּל קְרֹב אֵלֶיךָ׃ רַבִּים מַכְאוֹבִים לָרָשָׁע
of-the-wicked woes many (10) to-you to-come not to-control

וְהַבּוֹטֵחַ בַּיהוָה חֶסֶד יְסוֹבְבֶנּוּ׃ שִׂמְחוּ
rejoice! (11) he-surrounds-him unfailing-love in-Yahweh but-the-one-trusting

בַּיהוָה וְגִילוּ צַדִּיקִים וְהַרְנִינוּ כָּל־ יִשְׁרֵי־ לֵב׃
heart ones-upright-of all-of and-sing! righteous-ones and-be-glad! in-Yahweh

רַנְּנוּ צַדִּיקִים בַּיהוָה לַיְשָׁרִים נָאוָה
fitting for-the-upright-ones to-Yahweh righteous-ones sing-joyfully! (33:1)

תְהִלָּה׃ הוֹדוּ לַיהוָה בְּכִנּוֹר בְּנֵבֶל עָשׂוֹר זַמְּרוּ־ לוֹ׃
to-him make-music! ten on-lyre-of with-harp to-Yahweh praise! (2) praise

שִׁירוּ־ לוֹ שִׁיר חָדָשׁ הֵיטִיבוּ נַגֵּן בִּתְרוּעָה׃
with-shout-of-joy to-play be-skillful! new song to-him sing! (3)

whose sins are covered.
2 Blessed is the man
whose sin the LORD does not count against him
and in whose spirit is no deceit.

3 When I kept silent,
my bones wasted away
through my groaning all day long.
4 For day and night
your hand was heavy upon me;
my strength was sapped
as in the heat of summer. *Selah*
5 Then I acknowledged my sin to you
and did not cover up my iniquity.
I said, "I will confess
my transgressions to the LORD"—
and you forgave
the guilt of my sin. *Selah*

6 Therefore let everyone who is godly pray to you
while you may be found;
surely when the mighty waters rise,
they will not reach him.
7 You are my hiding place;
you will protect me from trouble
and surround me with songs of deliverance. *Selah*

8 I will instruct you and teach you in the way you should go;
I will counsel you and watch over you.
9 Do not be like the horse or the mule,
which have no understanding
but must be controlled by bit and bridle
or they will not come to you.
10 Many are the woes of the wicked,
but the LORD's unfailing love
surrounds the man who trusts in him.

11 Rejoice in the LORD and be glad, you righteous;
sing, all you who are upright in heart!

**Psalm 33**

1 Sing joyfully to the LORD, you righteous;
it is fitting for the upright to praise him.
2 Praise the LORD with the harp;
make music to him on the ten-stringed lyre.
3 Sing to him a new song;
play skillfully, and shout for joy.

כִּֽי־ יָשָׁר דְּבַר־ יְהוָה וְכָל־ מַעֲשֵׂהוּ בֶּאֱמוּנָה׃ אֹהֵב
one-loving (5) in-faithfulness deed-of-him and-all-of Yahweh word-of right for (4)

צְדָקָה וּמִשְׁפָּט חֶסֶד יְהוָה מָלְאָה הָאָֽרֶץ׃
the-earth she-is-full Yahweh unfailing-love-of and-justice righteousness

בִּדְבַר יְהוָה שָׁמַיִם נַעֲשׂוּ וּבְרוּחַ פִּיו
mouth-of-him and-by-breath-of they-were-made heavens Yahweh by-word-of (6)

כָּל־ צְבָאָֽם׃ כֹּנֵס כַּנֵּד* מֵי הַיָּם
the-sea waters-of *as-the-heap one-gathering (7) host-of-them all-of

נֹתֵן בְּאֹצָרוֹת תְּהוֹמֽוֹת׃ יִֽירְאוּ מֵיְהוָה כָּל־
all-of of-Yahweh let-them-fear (8) deeps into-storehouses one-putting

הָאָרֶץ מִמֶּנּוּ יָגוּרוּ כָּל־ יֹשְׁבֵי תֵבֵֽל׃ כִּי הוּא
he for (9) world ones-living-of all-of let-them-revere of-him the-earth

אָמַר וַיֶּהִי הֽוּא־ צִוָּה וַֽיַּעֲמֹֽד׃ יְהוָה
Yahweh (10) and-he-stood-firm he-commanded he and-he-came-to-be he-spoke

הֵפִיר עֲצַת־ גּוֹיִם הֵנִיא מַחְשְׁבוֹת עַמִּֽים׃ עֲצַת יְהוָה
Yahweh plan-of (11) peoples purposes-of he-thwarts nations plan-of he-foils

לְעוֹלָם תַּעֲמֹד מַחְשְׁבוֹת לִבּוֹ לְדֹר
to-generation heart-of-him purposes-of she-stands-firm to-forever

וָדֹֽר׃ אַשְׁרֵי הַגּוֹי אֲשֶׁר־ יְהוָה אֱלֹהָיו
God-of-him Yahweh who the-nation blessednesses-of (12) and-generation

הָעָם ׀ בָּחַר לְנַחֲלָה לֽוֹ׃ מִשָּׁמַיִם הִבִּיט
he-looks-down from-heavens (13) of-him for-inheritance he-chose the-people

יְהוָה רָאָה אֶֽת־ כָּל־ בְּנֵי הָאָדָֽם׃ מִמְּכוֹן־ שִׁבְתּוֹ
to-dwell-him from-place-of (14) the-mankind sons-of all-of *** he-sees Yahweh

הִשְׁגִּיחַ אֶל כָּל־ יֹשְׁבֵי הָאָֽרֶץ׃ הַיֹּצֵר יַחַד
together the-one-forming (15) the-earth ones-living-of all-of on he-watches

לִבָּם הַמֵּבִין אֶל־ כָּל־ מַעֲשֵׂיהֶֽם׃ אֵין־
there-is-no (16) deeds-of-them all-of to the-one-considering heart-of-them

הַמֶּלֶךְ נוֹשָׁע בְּרָב־ חָיִל גִּבּוֹר לֹֽא־ יִנָּצֵל בְּרָב־
by-greatness-of he-escapes not warrior army by-size-of being-saved the-king

כֹּֽחַ׃ שֶׁקֶר הַסּוּס לִתְשׁוּעָה וּבְרֹב
and-despite-greatness-of for-deliverance the-horse vain-hope (17) strength

חֵילוֹ לֹא יְמַלֵּֽט׃ הִנֵּה עֵין יְהוָה אֶל־ יְרֵאָיו
ones-fearing-him on Yahweh eye-of see! (18) he-can-save not strength-of-him

לַֽמְיַחֲלִים לְחַסְדּֽוֹ׃ לְהַצִּיל מִמָּוֶת נַפְשָׁם
self-of-them from-death to-deliver (19) in-unfailing-love-of-him on-ones-hoping

וּֽלְחַיּוֹתָם בָּרָעָֽב׃ נַפְשֵׁנוּ חִכְּתָה לַיהוָה
for-Yahweh she-waits self-of-us (20) in-the-famine and-to-keep-alive-them

*7 The NIV reads כַּנֹּ(א)ד, *into-jar.*

4 For the word of the LORD is
right and true;
he is faithful in all he does.
5 The LORD loves righteousness
and justice;
the earth is full of his
unfailing love.

6 By the word of the LORD were
the heavens made,
their starry host by the
breath of his mouth.
7 He gathers the waters of the
sea into jars[g];
he puts the deep into
storehouses.
8 Let all the earth fear the LORD;
let all the people of the
world revere him.
9 For he spoke, and it came to
be;
he commanded, and it stood
firm.
10 The LORD foils the plans of the
nations;
he thwarts the purposes of
the peoples.
11 But the plans of the LORD
stand firm forever,
the purposes of his heart
through all generations.

12 Blessed is the nation whose
God is the LORD,
the people he chose for his
inheritance.
13 From heaven the LORD looks
down
and sees all mankind;
14 from his dwelling place he
watches
all who live on earth—
15 he who forms the hearts of all,
who considers everything
they do.
16 No king is saved by the size of
his army;
no warrior escapes by his
great strength.
17 A horse is a vain hope for
deliverance;
despite all its great strength
it cannot save.
18 But the eyes of the LORD are
on those who fear him,
on those whose hope is in
his unfailing love,
19 to deliver them from death
and keep them alive in
famine.

20 We wait in hope for the LORD;

g7 Or *sea as into a heap*

עֶזְרֵנוּ וּמָגִנֵּנוּ הוּא׃ כִּי־ בוֹ יִשְׂמַח לִבֵּנוּ כִּי
for heart-of-us he-rejoices in-him for (21) he and-shield-of-us help-of-us

בְשֵׁם קָדְשׁוֹ בָטָחְנוּ׃ יְהִי־ חַסְדְּךָ
unfailing-love-of-you may-he-rest (22) we-trust holiness-of-him in-name-of

יְהוָה עָלֵינוּ כַּאֲשֶׁר יִחַלְנוּ לָךְ׃ לְדָוִד בְּשַׁנּוֹתוֹ
when-to-feign-him of-David *(34:1) in-you we-hope even-as upon-us Yahweh

אֶת־ טַעְמוֹ לִפְנֵי אֲבִימֶלֶךְ וַיְגָרְשֵׁהוּ וַיֵּלַךְ׃
and-he-left and-he-drove-away-him Abimelech before insanity-of-him ***

אֲבָרֲכָה אֶת־ יְהוָה בְּכָל־ עֵת תָּמִיד תְּהִלָּתוֹ בְּפִי׃
on-lip-of-me praise-of-him always time at-all-of Yahweh *** I-will-extol (2)

בַּיהוָה תִּתְהַלֵּל נַפְשִׁי יִשְׁמְעוּ עֲנָוִים
afflicted-ones let-them-hear soul-of-me she-will-boast in-Yahweh (3)

וְיִשְׂמָחוּ׃ גַּדְּלוּ לַיהוָה אִתִּי וּנְרוֹמְמָה
and-let-us-exalt with-me to-Yahweh glorify! (4) and-let-them-rejoice

שְׁמוֹ יַחְדָּו׃ דָּרַשְׁתִּי אֶת־ יְהוָה וְעָנָנִי
and-he-answered-me Yahweh *** I-sought (5) together name-of-him

וּמִכָּל־ מְגוּרוֹתַי הִצִּילָנִי׃ הִבִּיטוּ אֵלָיו
to-him they-look (6) he-delivered-me fears-of-me and-from-all-of

וְנָהָרוּ וּפְנֵיהֶם אַל־ יֶחְפָּרוּ׃ זֶה
this (7) they-are-covered-with-shame never and-faces-of-them and-they-are-radiant

עָנִי קָרָא וַיהוָה שָׁמֵעַ וּמִכָּל־ צָרוֹתָיו
troubles-of-him and-from-all-of he-heard and-Yahweh he-called poor-man

הוֹשִׁיעוֹ׃ חֹנֶה מַלְאַךְ־ יְהוָה סָבִיב לִירֵאָיו
about-ones-fearing-him around Yahweh angel-of one-encamping (8) he-saved-him

וַיְחַלְּצֵם׃ טַעֲמוּ וּרְאוּ כִּי־ טוֹב יְהוָה אַשְׁרֵי
blessednesses-of Yahweh good that and-see! taste! (9) and-he-delivers-them

הַגֶּבֶר יֶחֱסֶה־ בּוֹ׃ יְראוּ אֶת־ יְהוָה קְדֹשָׁיו כִּי־
for saints-of-him Yahweh *** fear! (10) in-him he-takes-refuge the-man

אֵין מַחְסוֹר לִירֵאָיו׃ כְּפִירִים רָשׁוּ
they-may-grow-weak lions (11) for-ones-fearing-him lack there-is-no

וְרָעֵבוּ וְדֹרְשֵׁי יְהוָה לֹא־ יַחְסְרוּ כָל־
any-of they-lack not Yahweh but-ones-seeking-of and-they-may-grow-hungry

טוֹב׃ לְכוּ־ בָנִים שִׁמְעוּ־ לִי יִרְאַת יְהוָה אֲלַמֶּדְכֶם׃
I-will-teach-you Yahweh fear-of to-me listen! children come! (12) good

מִי־ הָאִישׁ הֶחָפֵץ חַיִּים אֹהֵב יָמִים לִרְאוֹת טוֹב׃
good to-see days one-desiring lives the-one-loving the-man who? (13)

נְצֹר לְשׁוֹנְךָ מֵרָע וּשְׂפָתֶיךָ מִדַּבֵּר מִרְמָה׃
lie from-to-speak and-lips-of-you from-evil tongue-of-you keep! (14)

---

he is our help and our
shield.
21 In him our hearts rejoice,
for we trust in his holy
name.
22 May your unfailing love rest
upon us, O LORD,
even as we put our hope in
you.

### Psalm 34[h]

Of David. When he feigned insanity before Abimelech, who drove him away, and he left.

1 I will extol the LORD at all
times;
his praise will always be on
my lips.
2 My soul will boast in the
LORD;
let the afflicted hear and
rejoice.
3 Glorify the LORD with me;
let us exalt his name
together.

4 I sought the LORD, and he
answered me;
he delivered me from all my
fears.
5 Those who look to him are
radiant;
their faces are never covered
with shame.
6 This poor man called, and the
LORD heard him;
he saved him out of all his
troubles.
7 The angel of the LORD encamps
around those who fear
him,
and he delivers them.

8 Taste and see that the LORD is
good;
blessed is the man who
takes refuge in him.
9 Fear the LORD, you his saints,
for those who fear him lack
nothing.
10 The lions may grow weak and
hungry,
but those who seek the LORD
lack no good thing.

11 Come, my children, listen to
me;
I will teach you the fear of
the LORD.
12 Whoever of you loves life
and desires to see many
good days,
13 keep your tongue from evil
and your lips from speaking
lies.

[h] This psalm is an acrostic poem, the verses of which begin with the successive letters of the Hebrew alphabet.

*Heading, *1* See the note on page 349.

סוּר מֵרָע וַעֲשֵׂה־ טוֹב בַּקֵּשׁ שָׁלוֹם וְרָדְפֵהוּ׃ עֵינֵי
eyes-of (16) and-pursue-him! peace seek! good and-do! from-evil turn! (15)

יְהוָה אֶל־ צַדִּיקִים וְאָזְנָיו אֶל־ שַׁוְעָתָם׃ פְּנֵי יְהוָה
Yahweh faces-of (17) cry-of-them to and-ears-of-him righteous-ones on Yahweh

בְּעֹשֵׂי רָע לְהַכְרִית מֵאֶרֶץ זִכְרָם׃ צָעֲקוּ
they-cry (18) memory-of-them from-earth to-cut-off evil against-ones-doing-of

וַיהוָה שָׁמֵעַ וּמִכָּל־ צָרוֹתָם הִצִּילָם׃
he-delivers-them troubles-of-them and-from-all-of he-hears and-Yahweh

קָרוֹב יְהוָה לְנִשְׁבְּרֵי־ לֵב וְאֶת־ דַּכְּאֵי־
ones-crushed-of and heart to-ones-being-broken-of Yahweh close (19)

רוּחַ יוֹשִׁיעַ׃ רַבּוֹת רָעוֹת צַדִּיק וּמִכֻּלָּם
but-from-all-of-them righteous troubles-of many (20) he-saves spirit

יַצִּילֶנּוּ יְהוָה׃ שֹׁמֵר כָּל־ עַצְמוֹתָיו אַחַת מֵהֵנָּה
of-them one bones-of-him all-of one-protecting (21) Yahweh he-delivers-him

לֹא נִשְׁבָּרָה׃ תְּמוֹתֵת רָשָׁע רָעָה וְשֹׂנְאֵי
and-ones-being-foes-of evil wicked she-will-slay (22) she-will-be-broken not

צַדִּיק יֶאְשָׁמוּ׃ פּוֹדֶה יְהוָה נֶפֶשׁ
life-of Yahweh one-redeeming (23) they-will-be-condemned righteous

עֲבָדָיו וְלֹא יֶאְשְׁמוּ כָּל־ הַחֹסִים
the-ones-taking-refuge any-of they-will-be-condemned and-not servants-of-him

בּוֹ׃ לְדָוִד ׀ רִיבָה יְהוָה אֶת־ יְרִיבַי לְחַם אֶת־
against fight! contenders-of-me with Yahweh contend! of-David (35:1) in-him

לֹחֲמָי׃ הַחֲזֵק מָגֵן וְצִנָּה וְקוּמָה
and-arise! and-buckler shield take-up! (2) ones-fighting-against-me

בְּעֶזְרָתִי׃ וְהָרֵק חֲנִית וּסְגֹר† לִקְרַאת רֹדְפָי
ones-pursuing-me to-encounter †and-block! spear and-brandish! (3) to-aid-of-me

אֱמֹר לְנַפְשִׁי יְשֻׁעָתֵךְ אָנִי׃ יֵבֹשׁוּ
may-they-be-disgraced (4) I salvation-of-you to-soul-of-me say!

וְיִכָּלְמוּ מְבַקְשֵׁי נַפְשִׁי יִסֹּגוּ
may-they-be-turned life-of-me ones-seeking-of and-may-they-be-put-to-shame

אָחוֹר וְיַחְפְּרוּ חֹשְׁבֵי רָעָתִי׃ יִהְיוּ
may-they-be (5) ruin-of-me ones-plotting-of and-may-they-be-dismayed back

כְּמֹץ לִפְנֵי־ רוּחַ וּמַלְאַךְ יְהוָה דּוֹחֶה׃ יְהִי־
may-he-be (6) driving-away Yahweh with-angel-of wind before like-chaff

דַרְכָּם חֹשֶׁךְ וַחֲלַקְלַקּוֹת וּמַלְאַךְ יְהוָה רֹדְפָם׃
pursuing-them Yahweh with-angel-of and-slippery-ones dark way-of-them

כִּי־ חִנָּם טָמְנוּ־ לִי שַׁחַת רִשְׁתָּם חִנָּם
without-cause net-of-them pit for-me they-hid without-cause since (7)

[14]Turn from evil and do good;
seek peace and pursue it.
[15]The eyes of the LORD are on
the righteous
and his ears are attentive to
their cry;
[16]the face of the LORD is against
those who do evil,
to cut off the memory of
them from the earth.
[17]The righteous cry out, and the
LORD hears them;
he delivers them from all
their troubles.
[18]The LORD is close to the
brokenhearted
and saves those who are
crushed in spirit.
[19]A righteous man may have
many troubles,
but the LORD delivers him
from them all;
[20]he protects all his bones,
not one of them will be
broken.
[21]Evil will slay the wicked;
the foes of the righteous will
be condemned.
[22]The LORD redeems his
servants;
no one who takes refuge in
him will be condemned.

## Psalm 35

Of David.

[1]Contend, O LORD, with those
who contend with me;
fight against those who
fight against me.
[2]Take up shield and buckler;
arise and come to my aid.
[3]Brandish spear and javelin[i]
against those who pursue
me.
Say to my soul,
"I am your salvation."
[4]May those who seek my life
be disgraced and put to
shame;
may those who plot my ruin
be turned back in dismay.
[5]May they be like chaff before
the wind,
with the angel of the LORD
driving them away;
[6]may their path be dark and
slippery,
with the angel of the LORD
pursuing them.
[7]Since they hid their net for me
without cause

[i]3 Or *and block the way*

*See the note on page 349.

†3 The NIV repoints this word as וּסְגֹר or וְסֶגֶר, *and-javelin.*

חָפְרוּ לְנַפְשִׁי׃ תְּבוֹאֵהוּ שׁוֹאָה לֹא־יֵדָע
he-knows not ruin may-she-overtake-him (8) for-self-of-me they-dug

וְרִשְׁתּוֹ אֲשֶׁר־טָמַן תִּלְכְּדוֹ בְּשׁוֹאָה יִפָּל־בָּהּ׃
into-her may-he-fall to-ruin may-she-entangle-him he-hid that and-net-of-him

וְנַפְשִׁי תָּגִיל בַּיהוָה תָּשִׂישׂ
she-will-delight in-Yahweh she-will-rejoice then-soul-of-me (9)

בִּישׁוּעָתוֹ׃ כָּל עַצְמוֹתַי ׀ תֹּאמַרְנָה יְהוָה מִי
who? Yahweh they-will-exclaim bones-of-me all-of (10) in-salvation-of-him

כָמוֹךָ מַצִּיל עָנִי מֵחָזָק מִמֶּנּוּ וְעָנִי וְאֶבְיוֹן
and-needy even-poor more-than-him from-one-strong poor one-rescuing like-you

מִגֹּזְלוֹ׃ יְקוּמוּן עֵדֵי חָמָס אֲשֶׁר
which ruthlessness witnesses-of they-come-forward (11) from-one-robbing-him

לֹא־יָדַעְתִּי יִשְׁאָלוּנִי׃ יְשַׁלְּמוּנִי רָעָה תַּחַת טוֹבָה שְׁכוֹל
forlornness good for evil they-repay-me (12) they-question-me I-know not

לְנַפְשִׁי׃ וַאֲנִי ׀ בַּחֲלוֹתָם לְבוּשִׁי שָׂק
sackcloth clothing-of-me when-to-be-ill-them yet-I (13) of-soul-of-me

עִנֵּיתִי בַצּוֹם נַפְשִׁי וּתְפִלָּתִי עַל־חֵיקִי
breast-of-me to when-prayer-of-me self-of-me with-the-fasting I-humbled

תָשׁוּב׃ כְּרֵעַ־כְּאָח לִי הִתְהַלָּכְתִּי כַּאֲבֶל־
like-weeping-of I-went-about of-me as-brother as-friend (14) she-returned

אֵם קֹדֵר שַׁחוֹתִי׃ וּבְצַלְעִי שָׂמְחוּ
they-were-gleeful but-at-stumbling-of-me (15) I-bowed grieving mother

וְנֶאֶסָפוּ נֶאֶסְפוּ עָלַי נֵכִים וְלֹא יָדַעְתִּי
I-was-aware when-not attackers against-me they-gathered and-they-gathered

קָרְעוּ וְלֹא־דָמּוּ׃ בְּחַנְפֵי לַעֲגֵי מָעוֹג
circle mockers-of like-ungodly-ones-of (16) they-ceased and-not they-slandered

חָרֹק עָלַי שִׁנֵּימוֹ׃ אֲדֹנָי כַּמָּה תִּרְאֶה
will-you-look-on until-the-when? Lord (17) teeth-of-them against-me to-gnash

הָשִׁיבָה נַפְשִׁי מִשֹּׁאֵיהֶם מִכְּפִירִים יְחִידָתִי׃
precious-one-of-me from-lions from-ravages-of-them life-of-me rescue!

אוֹדְךָ בְּקָהָל רָב בְּעָם עָצוּם
thronging among-people great in-assembly I-will-give-thanks-to-you (18)

אֲהַלְלֶךָּ׃ אַל־יִשְׂמְחוּ־לִי אֹיְבַי
ones-being-enemies-of-me over-me let-them-gloat not (19) I-will-praise-you

שֶׁקֶר שֹׂנְאַי חִנָּם יִקְרְצוּ־עָיִן׃ כִּי לֹא
not for (20) eye let-them-wink without-reason ones-hating-me without-cause

שָׁלוֹם יְדַבֵּרוּ וְעַל רִגְעֵי־אֶרֶץ דִּבְרֵי מִרְמוֹת
false-ones accusations-of land quiet-ones-of but-against they-speak peaceably

and without cause dug a pit
for me,
8 may ruin overtake them by
surprise—
may the net they hid
entangle them,
may they fall into the pit, to
their ruin.
9 Then my soul will rejoice in
the LORD
and delight in his salvation.
10 My whole being will exclaim,
"Who is like you, O LORD?
You rescue the poor from
those too strong for them,
the poor and needy from
those who rob them."
11 Ruthless witnesses come
forward;
they question me on things
I know nothing about.
12 They repay me evil for good
and leave my soul forlorn.
13 Yet when they were ill, I put
on sackcloth
and humbled myself with
fasting.
When my prayers returned to
me unanswered,
14 I went about mourning
as though for my friend or
brother.
I bowed my head in grief
as though weeping for my
mother.
15 But when I stumbled, they
gathered in glee;
attackers gathered against
me when I was unaware.
They slandered me without
ceasing.
16 Like the ungodly they
maliciously mocked[j];
they gnashed their teeth at
me.
17 O LORD, how long will you
look on?
Rescue my life from their
ravages,
my precious life from these
lions.
18 I will give you thanks in the
great assembly;
among throngs of people I
will praise you.
19 Let not those gloat over me
who are my enemies
without cause;
let not those who hate me
without reason
maliciously wink the eye.
20 They do not speak peaceably,
but devise false accusations
against those who live
quietly in the land.

j16 Septuagint; Hebrew may mean *ungodly circle of mockers.*

יַחֲשֹׁבוּן׃ וַיַּרְחִיבוּ עָלַי פִּיהֶם אָמְרוּ הֶאָח ׀ הֶאָח
aha! aha! they-say mouth-of-them at-me and-they-open-wide (21) they-devise

רָאֲתָה עֵינֵינוּ׃ רָאִיתָה יְהוָה אַל־ תֶּחֱרַשׁ אֲדֹנָי אַל־† תִּרְחַק
you-be-far not Lord you-be-silent not Yahweh you-saw (22) eyes-of-us she-saw

מִמֶּנִּי׃ הָעִירָה וְהָקִיצָה לְמִשְׁפָּטִי אֱלֹהַי וַאדֹנָי
and-Lord God-of-me to-defense-of-me and-rise! awake! (23) from-me

לְרִיבִי׃ שָׁפְטֵנִי כְצִדְקְךָ יְהוָה אֱלֹהָי
God-of-me Yahweh in-righteousness-of-you vindicate-me! (24) to-contention-of-me

וְאַל־ יִשְׂמְחוּ־ לִי׃ אַל־ יֹאמְרוּ בְלִבָּם הֶאָח
aha! in-heart-of-them let-them-think not (25) over-me let-them-gloat and-not

נַפְשֵׁנוּ אַל־ יֹאמְרוּ בִּלַּעֲנוּהוּ׃ יֵבֹשׁוּ
may-they-be-put-to-shame (26) we-swallowed-him let-them-say not want-of-us

וְיַחְפְּרוּ ׀ יַחְדָּו שְׂמֵחֵי רָעָתִי יִלְבְּשׁוּ־
may-they-be-clothed distress-of-me gloaters-of together and-may-they-be-confused

בֹשֶׁת וּכְלִמָּה הַמַּגְדִּילִים עָלָי׃ יָרֹנּוּ
may-they-shout (27) over-me the-ones-exalting-themselves and-disgrace shame

וְיִשְׂמְחוּ חֲפֵצֵי צִדְקִי וְיֹאמְרוּ תָמִיד
always and-may-they-say vindication-of-me delighters-of and-may-they-be-glad

יִגְדַּל יְהוָה הֶחָפֵץ שְׁלוֹם עַבְדּוֹ׃
servant-of-him well-being-of the-one-delighting Yahweh may-he-be-exalted

וּלְשׁוֹנִי תֶּהְגֶּה צִדְקֶךָ כָּל־ הַיּוֹם
the-day all-of righteousness-of-you she-will-speak and-tongue-of-me (28)

תְּהִלָּתֶךָ׃ לַמְנַצֵּחַ ׀ לְעֶבֶד־ יְהוָה לְדָוִד׃
of-David Yahweh of-servant-of for-the-one-directing *(36:1) praise-of-you

נְאֻם־ פֶּשַׁע לָרָשָׁע בְּקֶרֶב לִבִּי אֵין־
there-is-no heart-of-me in-midst-of of-the-wicked sinfulness oracle-of (2)

פַּחַד אֱלֹהִים לְנֶגֶד עֵינָיו׃ כִּי־ הֶחֱלִיק אֵלָיו בְּעֵינָיו
in-eyes-of-him to-him he-flatters for (3) eyes-of-him at-before God fear-of

לִמְצֹא עֲוֹנוֹ לִשְׂנֹא׃ דִּבְרֵי־ פִיו אָוֶן וּמִרְמָה
and-deceitful wicked mouth-of-him words-of (4) to-hate sin-of-him to-detect

חָדַל לְהַשְׂכִּיל לְהֵיטִיב׃ אָוֶן ׀ יַחְשֹׁב עַל־ מִשְׁכָּבוֹ
bed-of-him on he-plots evil (5) to-do-good to-be-wise he-ceased

יִתְיַצֵּב עַל־ דֶּרֶךְ לֹא־ טוֹב רָע לֹא יִמְאָס׃ יְהוָה
Yahweh (6) he-rejects not wrong good not course to he-commits-himself

בְּהַשָּׁמַיִם חַסְדֶּךָ אֱמוּנָתְךָ עַד־ שְׁחָקִים׃
skies to faithfulness-of-you love-of-you to-the-heavens

צִדְקָתְךָ ׀ כְּהַרְרֵי־ אֵל מִשְׁפָּטְךָ תְּהוֹם רַבָּה
great deep justice-of-you might like-mountains-of righteousness-of-you (7)

21 They gape at me and say,
"Aha! Aha!
With our own eyes we have seen it."
22 O LORD, you have seen this; be not silent.
Do not be far from me, O Lord.
23 Awake, and rise to my defense!
Contend for me, my God and Lord.
24 Vindicate me in your righteousness, O LORD my God;
do not let them gloat over me.
25 Do not let them think, "Aha, just what we wanted!"
or say, "We have swallowed him up."
26 May all who gloat over my distress
be put to shame and confusion;
may all who exalt themselves over me
be clothed with shame and disgrace.
27 May those who delight in my vindication
shout for joy and gladness;
may they always say, "The LORD be exalted,
who delights in the well-being of his servant."
28 My tongue will speak of your righteousness
and of your praises all day long.

### Psalm 36

For the director of music. Of David the servant of the LORD.

1 An oracle is within my heart
concerning the sinfulness of the wicked:[k]
There is no fear of God
before his eyes.
2 For in his own eyes he flatters himself
too much to detect or hate his sin.
3 The words of his mouth are wicked and deceitful;
he has ceased to be wise and to do good.
4 Even on his bed he plots evil;
he commits himself to a sinful course
and does not reject what is wrong.
5 Your love, O LORD, reaches to the heavens,
your faithfulness to the skies.
6 Your righteousness is like the mighty mountains,
your justice like the great deep.

[k] 1 Or *heart: / Sin proceeds from the wicked.*

*Heading, *1* See the note on page 349.

†*22* Most mss have *pathah* under the *aleph* (אַל).

אָדָם־וּבְהֵמָה תוֹשִׁיעַ יְהוָה׃ מַה־יָּקָר חַסְדְּךָ
unfailing-love-of-you priceless how! (8) Yahweh you-preserve and-beast man

אֱלֹהִים וּבְנֵי אָדָם בְּצֵל כְּנָפֶיךָ יֶחֱסָיוּן׃
they-find-refuge wings-of-you in-shadow-of man and-sons-of high-ones

יִרְוְיֻן מִדֶּשֶׁן בֵּיתֶךָ וְנַחַל עֲדָנֶיךָ
delights-of-you and-river-of house-of-you on-abundance-of they-feast (9)

תַשְׁקֵם׃ כִּי־עִמְּךָ מְקוֹר חַיִּים בְּאוֹרְךָ
in-light-of-you lives fountain-of with-you for (10) you-give-drink-them

נִרְאֶה־אוֹר׃ מְשֹׁךְ חַסְדְּךָ לְיֹדְעֶיךָ
to-ones-knowing-you love-of-you continue! (11) light we-see

וְצִדְקָתְךָ לְיִשְׁרֵי־לֵב׃ אַל־תְּבוֹאֵנִי
let-her-come-to-me not (12) heart to-ones-upright-of and-righteousness-of-you

רֶגֶל גַּאֲוָה וְיַד־רְשָׁעִים אַל־תְּנִדֵנִי׃ שָׁם
see! (13) let-her-drive-away-me not wicked-ones or-hand-of pride foot-of

נָפְלוּ פֹּעֲלֵי אָוֶן דֹּחוּ וְלֹא־יָכְלוּ
they-are-able and-not they-are-thrown-down evil ones-doing-of they-lie-fallen

קוּם׃ לְדָוִד ׀ אַל־תִּתְחַר בַּמְּרֵעִים אַל־
not because-of-the-men-being-evil you-fret not of-David (37:1) to-rise

תְּקַנֵּא בְּעֹשֵׂי עַוְלָה׃ כִּי כֶחָצִיר מְהֵרָה
soon like-the-grass for (2) wrong of-ones-doing-of you-be-envious

יִמָּלוּ וּכְיֶרֶק דֶּשֶׁא יִבּוֹלוּן׃ בְּטַח
trust! (3) they-will-die-away plant and-like-green-of they-will-wither

בַּיהוָה וַעֲשֵׂה־טוֹב שְׁכָן־אֶרֶץ וּרְעֵה אֱמוּנָה׃ וְהִתְעַנַּג
and-delight! (4) safe and-enjoy-pasture! land dwell! good and-do! in-Yahweh

עַל־יְהוָה וְיִתֶּן־לְךָ מִשְׁאֲלֹת לִבֶּךָ׃ גּוֹל עַל־
to commit! (5) heart-of-you desires-of to-you and-he-will-give Yahweh in

יְהוָה דַּרְכֶּךָ וּבְטַח עָלָיו וְהוּא יַעֲשֶׂה׃ וְהוֹצִיא
and-he-will-make-shine (6) he-will-do and-he in-him and-trust! way-of-you Yahweh

כָאוֹר צִדְקֶךָ וּמִשְׁפָּטֶךָ כַּצָּהֳרָיִם׃
like-the-noonday-sun and-justice-of-you righteousness-of-you like-the-dawn

דּוֹם ׀ לַיהוָה וְהִתְחוֹלֵל לוֹ אַל־תִּתְחַר
you-fret not for-him and-wait-patiently! before-Yahweh be-still! (7)

בְּמַצְלִיחַ דַּרְכּוֹ בְּאִישׁ עֹשֶׂה מְזִמּוֹת׃ הֶרֶף
refrain! (8) schemes carrying-out over-man way-of-him over-one-making-succeed

מֵאַף וַעֲזֹב חֵמָה אַל־תִּתְחַר אַךְ־לְהָרֵעַ׃ כִּי־
for (9) to-bring-evil only you-fret not wrath and-turn-from! from-anger

מְרֵעִים יִכָּרֵתוּן וְקוֹיֵ יְהוָה הֵמָּה
they Yahweh but-ones-hoping-of they-will-be-cut-off men-being-evil

---

O LORD, you preserve both
man and beast.
7 How priceless is your
unfailing love!
Both high and low among
men
find[l] refuge in the shadow
of your wings.
8 They feast on the abundance
of your house;
you give them drink from
your river of delights.
9 For with you is the fountain of
life;
in your light we see light.
10 Continue your love to those
who know you,
your righteousness to the
upright in heart.
11 May the foot of the proud not
come against me,
nor the hand of the wicked
drive me away.
12 See how the evildoers lie
fallen—
thrown down, not able to
rise!

**Psalm 37[m]**

Of David.

1 Do not fret because of evil
men
or be envious of those who
do wrong;
2 for like the grass they will
soon wither,
like green plants they will
soon die away.
3 Trust in the LORD and do good;
dwell in the land and enjoy
safe pasture.
4 Delight yourself in the LORD
and he will give you the
desires of your heart.
5 Commit your way to the LORD;
trust in him and he will do
this:
6 He will make your
righteousness shine like
the dawn,
the justice of your cause like
the noonday sun.
7 Be still before the LORD and
wait patiently for him;
do not fret when men
succeed in their ways,
when they carry out their
wicked schemes.
8 Refrain from anger and turn
from wrath;
do not fret—it leads only to
evil.
9 For evil men will be cut off,
but those who hope in the

[l]7 Or *love, O God! / Men find;* or *love! / Both heavenly beings and men / find*
[m]This psalm is an acrostic poem, the stanzas of which begin with the successive letters of the Hebrew alphabet.

*See the note on page 349.

| | | | | | | |
|---|---|---|---|---|---|---|
| רָשָׁע | וְאֵין | מְעַט | וְעוֹד | | אָרֶץ׃ | יִירְשׁוּ־ |
| wicked | and-there-is-no | little | and-while | (10) | land | they-will-inherit |

| | | | | | |
|---|---|---|---|---|---|
| וַעֲנָוִים | | וְאֵינֶנּוּ׃ | מְקוֹמוֹ | עַל־ | וְהִתְבּוֹנַנְתָּ |
| but-meek-ones | (11) | then-not-he | place-of-him | for | though-you-look |

| | | | | | | | |
|---|---|---|---|---|---|---|---|
| זֹמֵם | | שָׁלוֹם׃ | רֹב | עַל־ | וְהִתְעַנְּגוּ | אָרֶץ | יִירְשׁוּ־ |
| plotting | (12) | peace | greatness-of | to | and-they-will-enjoy | land | they-will-inherit |

| | | | | | | |
|---|---|---|---|---|---|---|
| אֲדֹנָי | | שִׁנָּיו׃ | עָלָיו | וְחֹרֵק | לַצַּדִּיק | רָשָׁע |
| Lord | (13) | teeth-of-him | at-him | and-gnashing | against-the-righteous | wicked |

| | | | | | | | | | | |
|---|---|---|---|---|---|---|---|---|---|---|
| פָּתְחוּ | חֶרֶב ׀ | | יוֹמוֹ׃ | יָבֹא | כִּי־ | רָאָה | כִּי־ | לוֹ | יִשְׂחַק־ |
| they-draw | sword | (14) | day-of-him | he-comes | that | he-knows | for | at-him | he-laughs |

| | | | | | | |
|---|---|---|---|---|---|---|
| לִטְבוֹחַ | וְאֶבְיוֹן | עָנִי | לְהַפִּיל | קַשְׁתָּם | וְדָרְכוּ | רְשָׁעִים |
| to-slay | and-needy | poor | to-bring-down | bow-of-them | and-they-bend | wicked-ones |

| | | | | | |
|---|---|---|---|---|---|
| בְלִבָּם | תָּבוֹא | חַרְבָּם | | דָרֶךְ׃ | יִשְׁרֵי־ |
| into-heart-of-them | she-will-pierce | sword-of-them | (15) | way | ones-upright-of |

| | | | | | |
|---|---|---|---|---|---|
| לַצַּדִּיק | מְעַט | טוֹב־ | | תִּשָּׁבַרְנָה׃ | וְקַשְּׁתוֹתָם |
| of-the-righteous | little | better | (16) | they-will-be-broken | and-bows-of-them |

| | | | | | | |
|---|---|---|---|---|---|---|
| רְשָׁעִים | זְרוֹעוֹת | כִּי | | רַבִּים׃ | רְשָׁעִים | מֵהֲמוֹן |
| wicked-ones | powers-of | for | (17) | many | wicked-ones | than-wealth-of |

| | | | | | |
|---|---|---|---|---|---|
| יוֹדֵעַ | | יְהוָה׃ | צַדִּיקִים | וְסוֹמֵךְ | תִּשָּׁבַרְנָה |
| one-knowing | (18) | Yahweh | righteous-ones | but-one-upholding | they-will-be-broken |

| | | | | | |
|---|---|---|---|---|---|
| תִּהְיֶה׃ | לְעוֹלָם | וְנַחֲלָתָם | תְמִימִם | יְמֵי | יְהוָה |
| she-will-endure | to-forever | and-inheritance-of-them | blameless-ones | days-of | Yahweh |

| | | | | | | |
|---|---|---|---|---|---|---|
| רְעָבוֹן | וּבִימֵי | רָעָה | בְּעֵת | יֵבֹשׁוּ | לֹא־ | |
| famine | and-in-days-of | disaster | in-time-of | they-will-wither | not | (19) |

| | | | | |
|---|---|---|---|---|
| יֹאבֵדוּ | רְשָׁעִים ׀ | כִּי | | יִשְׂבָּעוּ׃ |
| they-will-perish | wicked-ones | but | (20) | they-will-enjoy-plenty |

| | | | | |
|---|---|---|---|---|
| כָּלוּ | כָּרִים | כִּיקַר | יְהוָה | וְאֹיְבֵי |
| they-will-vanish | fields | like-beauty-of | Yahweh | and-ones-being-enemies-of |

| | | | | | | |
|---|---|---|---|---|---|---|
| יְשַׁלֵּם | וְלֹא | רָשָׁע | לֹוֶה | | כָּלוּ׃ | בֶעָשָׁן |
| he-repays | and-not | wicked | borrowing | (21) | they-will-vanish | like-the-smoke |

| | | | | | |
|---|---|---|---|---|---|
| מְבֹרָכָיו | כִּי | | וְנוֹתֵן׃ | חוֹנֵן | וְצַדִּיק |
| ones-being-blessed-of-him | indeed | (22) | and-giving | being-generous | but-righteous |

| | | | |
|---|---|---|---|
| יִכָּרֵתוּ׃ | וּמְקֻלָּלָיו | אָרֶץ | יִירְשׁוּ |
| they-will-be-cut-off | but-ones-being-cursed-of-him | land | they-will-inherit |

| | | | | | | |
|---|---|---|---|---|---|---|
| יֶחְפָּץ׃ | וְדַרְכּוֹ | כּוֹנָנוּ | גֶבֶר | מִצְעֲדֵי־ | מֵיְהוָה | |
| he-delights-in | and-way-of-him | they-are-made-firm | man | steps-of | by-Yahweh | (23) |

| | | | | | | | | |
|---|---|---|---|---|---|---|---|---|
| יָדוֹ׃ | סוֹמֵךְ | יְהוָה | כִּי־ | יוּטָל | לֹא־ | יִפֹּל | כִּי־ | |
| hand-of-him | one-upholding | Yahweh | for | he-will-fall | not | he-stumble | though | (24) |

LORD will inherit the
land.
[10]A little while, and the wicked
will be no more;
though you look for them,
they will not be found.
[11]But the meek will inherit the
land
and enjoy great peace.
[12]The wicked plot against the
righteous
and gnash their teeth at
them;
[13]but the Lord laughs at the
wicked,
for he knows their day is
coming.
[14]The wicked draw the sword
and bend the bow
to bring down the poor and
needy,
to slay those whose ways
are upright.
[15]But their swords will pierce
their own hearts,
and their bows will be
broken.
[16]Better the little that the
righteous have
than the wealth of many
wicked;
[17]for the power of the wicked
will be broken,
but the LORD upholds the
righteous.
[18]The days of the blameless are
known to the LORD,
and their inheritance will
endure forever.
[19]In times of disaster they will
not wither;
in days of famine they will
enjoy plenty.
[20]But the wicked will perish:
The LORD's enemies will be
like the beauty of the
fields,
they will vanish—vanish
like smoke.
[21]The wicked borrow and do not
repay,
but the righteous give
generously;
[22]those the LORD blesses will
inherit the land,
but those he curses will be
cut off.
[23]The LORD delights in the way
of the man
whose steps he has made
firm;
[24]though he stumble, he will not
fall,
for the LORD upholds him
with his hand.

נַעַר ׀ הָיִיתִי גַּם־ זָקַנְתִּי וְלֹא־ רָאִיתִי צַדִּיק נֶעֱזָב
being-forsaken righteous I-saw yet-never I-am-old now I-was young (25)

וְזַרְעוֹ מְבַקֶּשׁ־ לָחֶם׃ כָּל־ הַיּוֹם חוֹנֵן וּמַלְוֶה
and-lending being-generous the-day all-of (26) bread begging or-child-of-him

וְזַרְעוֹ לִבְרָכָה׃ סוּר מֵרָע וַעֲשֵׂה־ טוֹב וּשְׁכֹן
then-live! good and-do! from-evil turn! (27) for-blessing and-child-of-him

לְעוֹלָם׃ כִּי יְהוָה ׀ אֹהֵב מִשְׁפָּט וְלֹא־ יַעֲזֹב אֶת־
*** he-will-forsake and-not just one-loving Yahweh for (28) to-always

חֲסִידָיו לְעוֹלָם נִשְׁמָרוּ וְזֶרַע
but-offspring-of they-will-be-protected to-forever faithful-ones-of-him

רְשָׁעִים נִכְרָת׃ צַדִּיקִים יִירְשׁוּ־ אָרֶץ
land they-will-inherit righteous-ones (29) he-will-be-cut-off wicked-ones

וְיִשְׁכְּנוּ לָעַד עָלֶיהָ׃ פִּי־ צַדִּיק יֶהְגֶּה
he-utters righteous mouth-of (30) in-her to-forever and-they-will-dwell

חָכְמָה וּלְשׁוֹנוֹ תְּדַבֵּר מִשְׁפָּט׃ תּוֹרַת אֱלֹהָיו
God-of-him law-of (31) justice she-speaks and-tongue-of-him wisdom

בְּלִבּוֹ לֹא תִמְעַד אֲשֻׁרָיו׃ צוֹפֶה רָשָׁע
wicked one-lying-in-wait (32) feet-of-him she-slips not in-heart-of-him

לַצַּדִּיק וּמְבַקֵּשׁ לַהֲמִיתוֹ׃ יְהוָה לֹא־ יַעַזְבֶנּוּ
he-will-leave-him not Yahweh (33) to-kill-him and-one-seeking for-the-righteous

בְיָדוֹ וְלֹא יַרְשִׁיעֶנּוּ בְּהִשָּׁפְטוֹ׃ קַוֵּה
wait! (34) when-to-be-on-trial-him he-will-condemn-him or-not in-power-of-him

אֶל־ יְהוָה ׀ וּשְׁמֹר דַּרְכּוֹ וִירוֹמִמְךָ לָרֶשֶׁת אָרֶץ
land to-possess and-he-will-exalt-you way-of-him and-keep! Yahweh for

בְּהִכָּרֵת רְשָׁעִים תִּרְאֶה׃ רָאִיתִי רָשָׁע עָרִיץ
ruthless-man wicked-man I-saw (35) you-will-see wicked-ones when-to-be-cut-off

וּמִתְעָרֶה כְּאֶזְרָח רַעֲנָן׃ וַיַּעֲבֹר וְהִנֵּה
and-see! but-he-passed-away (36) green-tree like-native and-flourishing

אֵינֶנּוּ וָאֲבַקְשֵׁהוּ וְלֹא נִמְצָא׃ שְׁמָר־
consider! (37) he-was-found then-not though-I-looked-for-him no-more-he

תָּם וּרְאֵה יָשָׁר כִּי־ אַחֲרִית לְאִישׁ שָׁלוֹם׃
peace for-man-of future for upright and-observe! blameless

וּפֹשְׁעִים נִשְׁמְדוּ יַחְדָּו אַחֲרִית רְשָׁעִים
wicked-ones future-of together they-will-be-destroyed but-ones-sinning (38)

נִכְרָתָה׃ וּתְשׁוּעַת צַדִּיקִים מֵיְהוָה
from-Yahweh righteous-ones and-salvation-of (39) she-will-be-cut-off

מָעוּזָּם בְּעֵת צָרָה׃ וַיַּעְזְרֵם יְהוָה
Yahweh and-he-helps-them (40) trouble in-time-of stronghold-of-them

25 I was young and now I am old,
yet I have never seen the righteous forsaken
or their children begging bread.
26 They are always generous and lend freely;
their children will be blessed.

27 Turn from evil and do good;
then you will always live securely.
28 For the LORD loves the just
and will not forsake his faithful ones.

They will be protected forever,
but the offspring of the wicked will be cut off;
29 the righteous will inherit the land
and dwell in it forever.

30 The mouth of the righteous man utters wisdom,
and his tongue speaks what is just.
31 The law of his God is in his heart;
his feet do not slip.

32 The wicked lie in wait for the righteous,
seeking their very lives;
33 but the LORD will not leave them in their power
or let them be condemned when brought to trial.

34 Wait for the LORD
and keep his way.
He will exalt you to possess the land;
when the wicked are cut off, you will see it.

35 I have seen a wicked and ruthless man
flourishing like a green tree in its native soil,
36 but he soon passed away and was no more;
though I looked for him, he could not be found.

37 Consider the blameless, observe the upright;
there is a future[n] for the man of peace.
38 But all sinners will be destroyed;
the future[o] of the wicked will be cut off.

39 The salvation of the righteous comes from the LORD;
he is their stronghold in time of trouble.
40 The LORD helps them and

[n]37 Or *there will be posterity*
[o]38 Or *posterity*

וַיְפַלְּטֵם יְפַלְּטֵם מֵרְשָׁעִים וְיוֹשִׁיעֵם
and-he-saves-them from-wicked-ones he-delivers-them and-he-delivers-them

כִּֽי־ חָסוּ בוֹ׃ מִזְמוֹר לְדָוִד לְהַזְכִּיר׃
to-make-petition of-David psalm *(38:1) in-him they-take-refuge because

יְהוָה אַל־ בְּקֶצְפְּךָ תוֹכִיחֵנִי וּבַחֲמָתְךָ תְיַסְּרֵנִי׃
you-discipline-me or-in-wrath-of-you you-rebuke-me in-anger-of-you not Yahweh (2)

כִּֽי־ חִצֶּיךָ נִחֲתוּ בִי וַתִּנְחַת עָלַי
upon-me and-she-came-down into-me they-pierced arrows-of-you for (3)

יָדֶךָ׃ אֵין־ מְתֹם בִּבְשָׂרִי מִפְּנֵי זַעְמֶךָ
wrath-of-you because-of in-body-of-me health there-is-no (4) hand-of-you

אֵין־ שָׁלוֹם בַּעֲצָמַי מִפְּנֵי חַטָּאתִי׃ כִּי
indeed (5) sin-of-me because-of in-bones-of-me soundness there-is-no

עֲוֺנֹתַי עָבְרוּ רֹאשִׁי כְּמַשָּׂא כָבֵד יִכְבְּדוּ
they-are-too-heavy heavy like-burden head-of-me they-overwhelmed guilts-of-me

מִמֶּנִּי׃ הִבְאִישׁוּ נָמַקּוּ חַבּוּרֹתָי מִפְּנֵי
because-of wounds-of-me they-fester they-are-loathsome (6) for-me

אִוַּלְתִּי׃ נַעֲוֵיתִי שַׁחֹתִי עַד־ מְאֹד כָּל־
all-of very-much to I-am-brought-low I-am-bowed-down (7) sinful-folly-of-me

הַיּוֹם קֹדֵר הִלָּכְתִּי׃ כִּֽי־ כְסָלַי מָלְאוּ נִקְלֶה
one-searing they-are-filled backs-of-me indeed (8) I-go-about mourning the-day

וְאֵין מְתֹם בִּבְשָׂרִי׃ נְפוּגוֹתִי וְנִדְכֵּיתִי עַד־
to and-I-am-crushed I-am-feeble (9) in-body-of-me health and-there-is-no

מְאֹד שָׁאַגְתִּי מִנַּהֲמַת לִבִּי׃ אֲדֹנָי† נֶגְדְּךָ כָל־
all-of before-you Lord (10) heart-of-me in-anguish-of I-groan utterly

תַּאֲוָתִי וְאַנְחָתִי מִמְּךָ לֹא־ נִסְתָּרָה׃ לִבִּי
heart-of-me (11) she-is-hidden not from-you and-sighing-of-me longing-of-me

סְחַרְחַר עֲזָבַנִי כֹחִי וְאוֹר־ עֵינַי גַּם־ הֵם
they even eyes-of-me and-light-of strength-of-me he-fails-me he-pounds

אֵין אִתִּי׃ אֹהֲבַי ׀ וְרֵעַי מִנֶּגֶד
from-before and-companions-of-me ones-being-friends-of-me (12) with-me not

נִגְעִי יַעֲמֹדוּ וּקְרוֹבַי מֵרָחֹק עָמָדוּ׃
they-stay at-far-away and-neighbors-of-me they-avoid wound-of-me

וַיְנַקְשׁוּ ׀ מְבַקְשֵׁי נַפְשִׁי וְדֹרְשֵׁי
and-ones-wanting-of life-of-me ones-seeking-of and-they-set-traps (13)

רָעָתִי דִּבְּרוּ הַוּוֹת וּמִרְמוֹת כָּל־ הַיּוֹם יֶהְגּוּ׃
they-plot the-day all-of and-deceptions ruins they-talk-of harm-of-me

וַאֲנִי כְחֵרֵשׁ לֹא אֶשְׁמָע וּכְאִלֵּם לֹא יִפְתַּח־
he-can-open not and-like-mute I-can-hear not like-deaf-man and-I (14)

delivers them;
he delivers them from the wicked and saves them,
because they take refuge in him.

**Psalm 38**

A psalm of David. A petition.

1 O LORD, do not rebuke me in your anger
or discipline me in your wrath.
2 For your arrows have pierced me,
and your hand has come down upon me.
3 Because of your wrath there is no health in my body;
my bones have no soundness because of my sin.
4 My guilt has overwhelmed me
like a burden too heavy to bear.

5 My wounds fester and are loathsome
because of my sinful folly.
6 I am bowed down and brought very low;
all day long I go about mourning.
7 My back is filled with searing pain;
there is no health in my body.
8 I am feeble and utterly crushed;
I groan in anguish of heart.

9 All my longings lie open before you, O Lord;
my sighing is not hidden from you.
10 My heart pounds, my strength fails me;
even the light has gone from my eyes.
11 My friends and companions avoid me because of my wounds;
my neighbors stay far away.
12 Those who seek my life set their traps,
those who would harm me talk of my ruin;
all day long they plot deception.

13 I am like a deaf man, who cannot hear,
like a mute, who cannot open his mouth;

*Heading, *1* See the note on page 349.
†*10* Most mss have the accent *rebia* (נִי־).

פיו׃ ואהי כאיש אשר לא־ שמע ואין
and-there-are-not one-hearing not who like-man and-I-became (15) mouth-of-him

בפיו תוכחות׃ כי־ לך יהוה הוחלתי אתה תענה
you-will-answer you I-wait Yahweh for-you indeed (16) replies in-mouth-of-him

אדני אלהי׃ כי־ אמרתי פן־ ישמחו־ לי במוט
when-to-slip over-me let-them-gloat not I-said for (17) God-of-me Lord

רגלי עלי הגדילו׃ כי־ אני לצלע נכון
being-ready for-fall I for (18) let-them-exalt-themselves over-me foot-of-me

ומכאובי נגדי תמיד׃ כי־ עוני אגיד אדאג
I-am-troubled I-confess iniquity-of-me indeed (19) ever with-me and-pain-of-me

מחטאתי׃ ואיבי חיים עצמו
they-are-many vigorous-ones and-ones-being-enemies-of-me (20) by-sin-of-me

ורבו שנאי שקר׃ ומשלמי
and-ones-repaying-of (21) without-reason ones-hating-me and-they-are-numerous

רעה תחת טובה ישטנוני תחת רדופי־ טוב׃ אל־ תעזבני
you-forsake-me not (22) good to-seek-me when they-slander-me good for evil

יהוה אלהי אל־ תרחק ממני׃ חושה לעזרתי
to-help-of-me come-quickly! (23) from-me you-be-far not God-of-me Yahweh

אדני תשועתי׃ למנצח לידיתון מזמור לדוד׃
of-David psalm for-Jeduthun for-the-one-directing *(39:1) salvation-of-me Lord

אמרתי אשמרה דרכי מחטוא בלשוני אשמרה
I-will-put with-tongue-of-me from-to-sin ways-of-me I-will-watch I-said (2)

לפי מחסום בעד רשע לנגדי׃ נאלמתי
I-was-silent (3) in-presence-of-me wicked as-long-as muzzle on-mouth-of-me

דומיה החשיתי מטוב וכאבי נעכר׃ חם־
he-grew-hot (4) he-increased and-anguish-of-me of-good I-said-nothing still

לבי׀ בקרבי בהגיגי תבער־ אש דברתי
I-spoke fire she-burned in-meditation-of-me in-inside-of-me heart-of-me

בלשוני׃ הודיעני יהוה׀ קצי ומדת ימי
days-of-me and-number-of end-of-me Yahweh show-me! (5) with-tongue-of-me

מה־ היא אדעה מה־ חדל אני׃ הנה טפחות׀ נתתה
you-made handbreadths see! (6) I fleeting how let-me-know she what?

ימי וחלדי כאין נגדך אך־ כל־ הבל
breath all-of indeed before-you as-nothing and-span-of-me days-of-me

כל־ אדם נצב סלה׃ אך־ בצלם׀ יתהלך־ איש אך־
indeed man he-goes-about as-phantom indeed (7) selah he-stands man each-of

הבל יהמיון יצבר ולא־ ידע מי־
who? he-knows but-not he-heaps-up-wealth they-bustle-about vainly

14 I have become like a man who
does not hear,
whose mouth can offer no
reply.
15 I wait for you, O LORD;
you will answer, O Lord my
God.
16 For I said, "Do not let them
gloat
or exalt themselves over me
when my foot slips."
17 For I am about to fall,
and my pain is ever with
me.
18 I confess my iniquity;
I am troubled by my sin.
19 Many are those who are my
vigorous enemies;
those who hate me without
reason are numerous.
20 Those who repay my good
with evil
slander me when I seek
what is good.
21 O LORD, do not forsake me;
be not far from me, O my
God.
22 Come quickly to help me,
O Lord my Savior.

### Psalm 39

For the director of music. For Jeduthun. A psalm of David.

1 I said, "I will watch my ways
and keep my tongue from
sin;
I will put a muzzle on my
mouth
as long as the wicked are in
my presence."
2 But when I was silent and
still,
not even saying anything
good,
my anguish increased.
3 My heart grew hot within me,
and as I meditated, the fire
burned;
then I spoke with my
tongue:
4 "Show me, O LORD, my life's
end
and the number of my days;
let me know how fleeting is
my life.
5 You have made my days a
mere handbreadth;
the span of my years is as
nothing before you.
Each man's life is but a
breath. *Selah*
6 Man is a mere phantom as he
goes to and fro:
He bustles about, but only
in vain;
he heaps up wealth, not
knowing who will get it.

*Heading, *1* See the note on page 349.

°*21* ק רדפי

°*1* ק לידותון

אֹסְפָם׃ וְעַתָּה מַה־ קִּוִּיתִי אֲדֹנָי תּוֹחַלְתִּי לְךָ הִיא׃
she in-you hope-of-me Lord do-I-look-for what? but-now (8) one-getting-them

מִכָּל־ פְּשָׁעַי הַצִּילֵנִי חֶרְפַּת נָבָל אַל־ תְּשִׂימֵנִי׃
you-make-me not fool scorn-of save-me! transgressions-of-me from-all-of (9)

נֶאֱלַמְתִּי לֹא אֶפְתַּח־ פִּי כִּי אַתָּה עָשִׂיתָ׃ הָסֵר
remove! (11) you-did you for mouth-of-me I-opened not I-was-silent (10)

מֵעָלַי נִגְעֶךָ מִתִּגְרַת יָדְךָ אֲנִי כָלִיתִי׃
I-am-overcome I hand-of-you from-blow-of scourge-of-you from-upon-me

בְּתוֹכָחוֹת עַל־ עָוֺן ׀ יִסַּרְתָּ אִישׁ וַתֶּמֶס כָּעָשׁ
like-the-moth and-you-consume man you-discipline sin for with-rebukes (12)

חֲמוּדוֹ אַךְ הֶבֶל כָּל־ אָדָם סֶלָה׃ שִׁמְעָה־ תְפִלָּתִי ׀
prayer-of-me hear! (13) selah man each-of breath indeed wealth-of-him

יְהוָה וְשַׁוְעָתִי ׀ הַאֲזִינָה אֶל־ דִּמְעָתִי אַל־ תֶּחֱרַשׁ כִּי
for you-be-deaf not weeping-of-me to listen! and-cry-for-help-of-me Yahweh

גֵר אָנֹכִי עִמָּךְ תּוֹשָׁב כְּכָל־ אֲבוֹתָי׃ הָשַׁע מִמֶּנִּי
away-from-me look! (14) fathers-of-me as-all-of stranger with-you I alien

וְאַבְלִיגָה בְּטֶרֶם אֵלֵךְ וְאֵינֶנִּי׃ לַמְנַצֵּחַ
for-the-one-directing *(40:1) and-no-more-I I-depart at-before that-I-may-rejoice

לְדָוִד מִזְמוֹר׃ קַוֹּה קִוִּיתִי יְהוָה וַיֵּט אֵלַי
to-me and-he-turned Yahweh I-waited-for to-wait-for (2) psalm of-David

וַיִּשְׁמַע שַׁוְעָתִי׃ וַיַּעֲלֵנִי ׀ מִבּוֹר שָׁאוֹן מִטִּיט
from-mud-of slime from-pit-of and-he-lifted-me (3) cry-of-me and-he-heard

הַיָּוֵן וַיָּקֶם עַל־ סֶלַע רַגְלַי כּוֹנֵן אֲשֻׁרָי׃
standing-places-of-me making-firm feet-of-me rock on and-he-set the-mire

וַיִּתֵּן בְּפִי ׀ שִׁיר חָדָשׁ תְּהִלָּה לֵאלֹהֵינוּ
to-God-of-us hymn-of-praise new song in-mouth-of-me and-he-put (4)

יִרְאוּ רַבִּים וְיִירָאוּ וְיִבְטְחוּ בַּיהוָה׃
in-Yahweh and-they-will-trust and-they-will-fear many they-will-see

אַשְׁרֵי הַגֶּבֶר אֲשֶׁר־ שָׂם יְהוָה מִבְטַחוֹ וְלֹא־
and-not trust-of-him Yahweh he-makes who the-man blessednesses-of (5)

פָנָה אֶל־ רְהָבִים וְשָׂטֵי כָזָב׃ רַבּוֹת עָשִׂיתָ ׀ אַתָּה ׀
you you-did many (6) false-god and-ones-turning-of proud-ones to he-looks

יְהוָה אֱלֹהַי נִפְלְאֹתֶיךָ וּמַחְשְׁבֹתֶיךָ אֵלֵינוּ אֵין ׀
no-one for-us and-plans-of-you things-being-wonders-of-you God-of-me Yahweh

עֲרֹךְ אֵלֶיךָ אַגִּידָה וַאֲדַבֵּרָה עָצְמוּ
they-would-be-too-many and-should-I-tell should-I-speak to-you to-recount

מִסַּפֵּר׃ זֶבַח וּמִנְחָה ׀ לֹא־ חָפַצְתָּ אָזְנַיִם כָּרִיתָ
you-pierced ears you-desired not and-offering sacrifice (7) than-to-declare

7"But now, Lord, what do I look for?
My hope is in you.
8Save me from all my transgressions;
do not make me the scorn of fools.
9I was silent; I would not open my mouth,
for you are the one who has done this.
10Remove your scourge from me;
I am overcome by the blow of your hand.
11You rebuke and discipline men for their sin;
you consume their wealth like a moth—
each man is but a breath.
*Selah*

12"Hear my prayer, O LORD,
listen to my cry for help;
be not deaf to my weeping.
For I dwell with you as an alien,
a stranger, as all my fathers were.
13Look away from me, that I may rejoice again
before I depart and am no more."

**Psalm 40**

For the director of music. Of David. A psalm.

1I waited patiently for the LORD;
he turned to me and heard my cry.
2He lifted me out of the slimy pit,
out of the mud and mire;
he set my feet on a rock
and gave me a firm place to stand.
3He put a new song in my mouth,
a hymn of praise to our God.
Many will see and fear
and put their trust in the LORD.

4Blessed is the man
who makes the LORD his trust,
who does not look to the proud,
to those who turn aside to false gods.[p]
5Many, O LORD my God,
are the wonders you have done.
The things you planned for us
no one can recount to you;
were I to speak and tell of them,
they would be too many to declare.
6Sacrifice and offering you did not desire,
but my ears you have pierced[q,r];

p4 Or *to falsehood*
q6 Hebrew; Septuagint *but a body you have prepared for me* (see also Symmachus and Theodotion)
r6 Or *opened*

***Heading, *1* See the note on page 349.**

לִי עוֹלָה וַחֲטָאָה לֹא שָׁאָלְתָּ׃ אָז אָמַרְתִּי
I-said then (8) you-required not and-sin-offering burnt-offering for-me

הִנֵּה־בָאתִי בִּמְגִלַּת־סֵפֶר כָּתוּב עָלָי׃ לַעֲשׂוֹת־רְצוֹנְךָ
will-of-you to-do (9) about-me one-being-written book in-scroll-of I-came here!

אֱלֹהַי חָפָצְתִּי וְתוֹרָתְךָ בְּתוֹךְ מֵעָי׃ בִּשַּׂרְתִּי
I-proclaim (10) hearts-of-me within and-law-of-you I-desire God-of-me

צֶדֶק ׀ בְּקָהָל רָב הִנֵּה שְׂפָתַי לֹא אֶכְלָא יְהוָה אַתָּה
you Yahweh I-seal not lips-of-me see! great in-assembly righteousness

יָדָעְתָּ׃ צִדְקָתְךָ לֹא־כִסִּיתִי ׀ בְּתוֹךְ לִבִּי
heart-of-me within I-hide not righteousness-of-you (11) you-know

אֱמוּנָתְךָ וּתְשׁוּעָתְךָ אָמָרְתִּי לֹא־כִחַדְתִּי חַסְדְּךָ
love-of-you I-conceal not I-speak and-salvation-of-you faithfulness-of-you

וַאֲמִתְּךָ לְקָהָל רָב׃ אַתָּה יְהוָה לֹא־תִכְלָא
you-withhold not Yahweh you (12) great from-assembly and-truth-of-you

רַחֲמֶיךָ מִמֶּנִּי חַסְדְּךָ וַאֲמִתְּךָ תָּמִיד יִצְּרוּנִי׃
may-they-protect-me always and-truth-of-you love-of-you from-me mercies-of-you

כִּי אָפְפוּ־עָלַי ׀ רָעוֹת עַד־אֵין מִסְפָּר
number there-is-no to troubles around-me they-surround for (13)

הִשִּׂיגוּנִי עֲוֺנֹתַי וְלֹא־יָכֹלְתִּי לִרְאוֹת עָצְמוּ מִשַּׂעֲרוֹת
than-hairs-of they-are-more to-see I-can and-not sins-of-me they-overtook-me

רֹאשִׁי וְלִבִּי עֲזָבָנִי׃ רְצֵה יְהוָה לְהַצִּילֵנִי
to-save-me Yahweh be-pleased! (14) he-fails-me and-heart-of-me head-of-me

יְהוָה לְעֶזְרָתִי חוּשָׁה׃ יֵבֹשׁוּ
may-they-be-shamed (15) come-quickly! to-help-of-me Yahweh

וְיַחְפְּרוּ ׀ יַחַד מְבַקְשֵׁי נַפְשִׁי לִסְפּוֹתָהּ
to-take-her life-of-me ones-seeking-of together and-may-they-be-confused

יִסֹּגוּ אָחוֹר וְיִכָּלְמוּ חֲפֵצֵי רָעָתִי׃
ruin-of-me desirers-of and-may-they-be-disgraced back may-they-be-turned

יָשֹׁמּוּ עַל־עֵקֶב בָּשְׁתָּם הָאֹמְרִים לִי
to-me the-ones-saying shame-of-them cause-of for may-they-be-appalled (16)

הֶאָח ׀ הֶאָח׃ יָשִׂישׂוּ וְיִשְׂמְחוּ ׀ בְּךָ כָּל־
all-of in-you and-may-they-be-glad may-they-rejoice (17) aha! aha!

מְבַקְשֶׁיךָ יֹאמְרוּ תָמִיד יִגְדַּל יְהוָה אֹהֲבֵי
ones-loving-of Yahweh may-he-be-exalted always may-they-say ones-seeking-you

תְּשׁוּעָתֶךָ׃ וַאֲנִי ׀ עָנִי וְאֶבְיוֹן אֲדֹנָי יַחֲשָׁב לִי
of-me may-he-think Lord and-needy poor yet-I (18) salvation-of-you

עֶזְרָתִי וּמְפַלְטִי אַתָּה אֱלֹהַי אַל־תְּאַחַר׃
you-delay not God-of-me you and-one-delivering-me help-of-me

burnt offerings and sin
offerings
you did not require.
7 Then I said, "Here I am, I
have come—
it is written about me in the
scroll.[s]
8 I desire to do your will, O my
God;
your law is within my
heart."

9 I proclaim righteousness in the
great assembly;
I do not seal my lips,
as you know, O LORD.
10 I do not hide your
righteousness in my
heart;
I speak of your faithfulness
and salvation.
I do not conceal your love and
your truth
from the great assembly.

11 Do not withhold your mercy
from me, O LORD;
may your love and your
truth always protect me.
12 For troubles without number
surround me;
my sins have overtaken me,
and I cannot see.
They are more than the hairs
of my head,
and my heart fails within
me.

13 Be pleased, O LORD, to save
me;
O LORD, come quickly to
help me.
14 May all who seek to take my
life
be put to shame and
confusion;
may all who desire my ruin
be turned back in disgrace.
15 May those who say to me,
"Aha! Aha!"
be appalled at their own
shame.
16 But may all who seek you
rejoice and be glad in you;
may those who love your
salvation always say,
"The LORD be exalted!"

17 Yet I am poor and needy;
may the Lord think of me.
You are my help and my
deliverer;
O my God, do not delay.

s7 *Or come / with the scroll written for me*

*See the note on page 349.

לַמְנַצֵּחַ מִזְמוֹר לְדָוִד׃ אַשְׁרֵי מַשְׂכִּיל
one-regarding blessednesses-of (2) of-David psalm for-the-one-directing *(41:1)

אֶל־דָּל בְּיוֹם רָעָה יְמַלְּטֵהוּ יְהוָה׃ יְהוָה ׀
Yahweh (3) Yahweh he-delivers-him trouble in-time-of weak to

יִשְׁמְרֵהוּ וִיחַיֵּהוּ יְאֻשַּׁר°
and-he-is-blessed and-he-will-preserve-life-of-him he-will-protect-him

בָּאָרֶץ וְאַל־תִּתְּנֵהוּ בְּנֶפֶשׁ אֹיְבָיו׃
ones-being-foes-of-him to-desire-of he-will-surrender-him and-not in-the-land

יְהוָה יִסְעָדֶנּוּ עַל־עֶרֶשׂ דְּוָי כָּל־מִשְׁכָּבוֹ
bed-of-him all-of sickness bed-of on he-will-sustain-him Yahweh (4)

הָפַכְתָּ בְחָלְיוֹ׃ אֲנִי־אָמַרְתִּי יְהוָה חָנֵּנִי
have-mercy-on-me! Yahweh I-said I (5) from-illness-of-him you-will-restore

רְפָאָה נַפְשִׁי כִּי־חָטָאתִי לָךְ׃ אוֹיְבַי
ones-being-enemies-of-me (6) against-you I-sinned for self-of-me heal!

יֹאמְרוּ רַע לִי מָתַי יָמוּת וְאָבַד שְׁמוֹ׃
name-of-him and-will-he-perish will-he-die when? of-me malice they-say

וְאִם־בָּא לִרְאוֹת ׀ שָׁוְא יְדַבֵּר לִבּוֹ יִקְבָּץ־
he-gathers heart-of-him he-speaks falsely to-see he-comes when-ever (7)

אָוֶן לוֹ יֵצֵא לַחוּץ יְדַבֵּר׃ יַחַד
together (8) he-speaks to-the-outside he-goes-out for-him slander

עָלַי יִתְלַחֲשׁוּ כָּל־שֹׂנְאָי עָלַי ׀ יַחְשְׁבוּ
they-imagine for-me ones-being-enemies-of-me all-of they-whisper against-me

רָעָה לִי׃ דְּבַר־בְּלִיַּעַל יָצוּק בּוֹ וַאֲשֶׁר שָׁכַב לֹא־
not he-lies and-where upon-him being-set vileness disease-of (9) for-me worst

יוֹסִיף לָקוּם׃ גַּם־אִישׁ שְׁלוֹמִי ׀ אֲשֶׁר־בָּטַחְתִּי
I-trusted whom close-friend-of-me man even (10) to-get-up he-will-do-again

בוֹ אוֹכֵל לַחְמִי הִגְדִּיל עָלַי עָקֵב׃ וְאַתָּה יְהוָה
Yahweh but-you (11) heel against-me he-lifted bread-of-me one-eating in-him

חָנֵּנִי וַהֲקִימֵנִי וַאֲשַׁלְּמָה לָהֶם׃ בְּזֹאת
in-this (12) to-them that-I-may-repay and-raise-up-me! have-mercy-on-me!

יָדַעְתִּי כִּי־חָפַצְתָּ בִּי כִּי לֹא־יָרִיעַ אֹיְבִי
one-being-enemy-of-me he-triumphs not for with-me you-are-pleased that I-know

עָלָי׃ וַאֲנִי בְּתֻמִּי תָּמַכְתָּ בִּי וַתַּצִּיבֵנִי
and-you-set-me to-me you-uphold in-integrity-of-me and-I (13) over-me

לְפָנֶיךָ לְעוֹלָם׃ בָּרוּךְ יְהוָה ׀ אֱלֹהֵי יִשְׂרָאֵל
Israel God-of Yahweh being-praised (14) to-forever in-presences-of-you

מֵהָעוֹלָם וְעַד הָעוֹלָם אָמֵן ׀ וְאָמֵן׃
and-amen amen the-everlasting and-to from-the-everlasting

**Psalm 41**

For the director of music. A psalm of David.

1Blessed is he who has regard
for the weak;
the LORD delivers him in
times of trouble.
2The LORD will protect him and
preserve his life;
he will bless him in the
land
and not surrender him to
the desire of his foes.
3The LORD will sustain him on
his sickbed
and restore him from his
bed of illness.

4I said, "O LORD, have mercy
on me;
heal me, for I have sinned
against you."
5My enemies say of me in
malice,
"When will he die and his
name perish?"
6Whenever one comes to see
me,
he speaks falsely, while his
heart gathers slander;
then he goes out and
spreads it abroad.

7All my enemies whisper
together against me;
they imagine the worst for
me, saying,
8"A vile disease has beset him;
he will never get up from
the place where he lies."
9Even my close friend, whom I
trusted,
he who shared my bread,
has lifted up his heel against
me.

10But you, O LORD, have mercy
on me;
raise me up, that I may
repay them.
11I know that you are pleased
with me,
for my enemy does not
triumph over me.
12In my integrity you uphold me
and set me in your presence
forever.

13Praise be to the LORD, the God
of Israel,
from everlasting to
everlasting.
Amen and Amen.

*Heading, *1* See the note on page 349.

°3 ק ואשר

לַמְנַצֵּחַ מַשְׂכִּיל לִבְנֵי־ קֹרַח׃ כְּאַיָּל תַּעֲרֹג
she-pants as-deer (2) Korah of-sons-of maskil for-the-one-directing *(42:1)

עַל־ אֲפִיקֵי־ מָיִם כֵּן נַפְשִׁי תַעֲרֹג אֵלֶיךָ אֱלֹהִים׃ צָמְאָה
she-thirsts (3) God for-you she-pants soul-of-me so waters streams-of for

נַפְשִׁי ׀ לֵאלֹהִים לְאֵל חָי מָתַי אָבוֹא וְאֵרָאֶה פְּנֵי
faces-of and-can-I-be-met can-I-go when? living for-God for-God soul-of-me

אֱלֹהִים׃ הָיְתָה־ לִּי דִמְעָתִי לֶחֶם יוֹמָם וָלָיְלָה בֶּאֱמֹר אֵלַי
to-me while-to-say and-night by-day food tear-of-me for-me she-was (4) God

כָּל־ הַיּוֹם אַיֵּה אֱלֹהֶיךָ׃ אֵלֶּה אֶזְכְּרָה ׀ וְאֶשְׁפְּכָה עָלַי ׀
before-me as-I-pour-out I-remember these (5) God-of-you where? the-day all-of

נַפְשִׁי כִּי אֶעֱבֹר ׀ בַּסָּךְ אֶדַּדֵּם עַד־ בֵּית
house-of to I-would-lead-them with-the-multitude I-would-go how! soul-of-me

אֱלֹהִים בְּקוֹל־ רִנָּה וְתוֹדָה הָמוֹן חוֹגֵג׃
being-festive throng and-thanksgiving shout-of-joy with-sound-of God

מַה־ תִּשְׁתּוֹחֲחִי ׀ נַפְשִׁי וַתֶּהֱמִי עָלָי
within-me and-are-you-disturbed soul-of-me are-you-downcast why? (6)

הוֹחִילִי לֵאלֹהִים כִּי־ עוֹד אוֹדֶנּוּ יְשׁוּעוֹת †פָּנָיו׃
presences-of-him† saving-helps-of I-will-praise-him yet for in-God put-hope!

אֱלֹהַי† עָלַי נַפְשִׁי תִשְׁתּוֹחָח עַל־ כֵּן אֶזְכָּרְךָ
I-will-remember-you this for she-is-downcast soul-of-me within-me †God-of-me (7)

מֵאֶרֶץ יַרְדֵּן וְחֶרְמוֹנִים מֵהַר מִצְעָר׃ תְּהוֹם־אֶל־
to deep (8) Mizar from-Mount-of and-heights-of-Hermon Jordan from-land-of

תְּהוֹם קוֹרֵא לְקוֹל צִנּוֹרֶיךָ כָּל־ מִשְׁבָּרֶיךָ
waves-of-you all-of waterfalls-of-you in-roar-of one-calling deep

וְגַלֶּיךָ עָלַי עָבָרוּ׃ יוֹמָם ׀ יְצַוֶּה יְהוָה ׀
Yahweh he-directs by-day (9) they-swept over-me and-breakers-of-you

חַסְדּוֹ וּבַלַּיְלָה שִׁירֹה עִמִּי תְּפִלָּה לְאֵל
to-God-of prayer with-me song-of-him and-at-the-night love-of-him

חַיָּי׃ אוֹמְרָה ׀ לְאֵל סַלְעִי לָמָה שְׁכַחְתָּנִי לָמָּה־ קֹדֵר
mourning why? you-forgot-me why? Rock-of-me to-God I-say (10) lives-of-me

אֵלֵךְ בְּלַחַץ אוֹיֵב׃ בְּרֶצַח ׀
with-mortal-agony (11) one-being-enemy in-oppression-of I-must-go-about

בְּעַצְמוֹתַי חֵרְפוּנִי צוֹרְרָי בְּאָמְרָם אֵלַי
to-me as-to-say-them ones-being-foes-of-me they-taunt-me in-bones-of-me

כָּל־ הַיּוֹם אַיֵּה אֱלֹהֶיךָ׃ מַה־ תִּשְׁתּוֹחֲחִי ׀ נַפְשִׁי
soul-of-me are-you-downcast why? (12) God-of-you where? the-day all-of

וּמַה־ תֶּהֱמִי עָלָי הוֹחִילִי לֵאלֹהִים כִּי־עוֹד אוֹדֶנּוּ
I-will-praise-him yet for in-God put-hope! within-me are-you-disturbed and-why?

## BOOK II

*Psalms 42-72*

### Psalm 42[f]

For the director of music. A *maskil*[u] of the Sons of Korah.

[1]As the deer pants for streams
of water,
so my soul pants for you, O
God.
[2]My soul thirsts for God, for the
living God.
When can I go and meet
with God?
[3]My tears have been my food
day and night,
while men say to me all day
long,
"Where is your God?"
[4]These things I remember
as I pour out my soul:
how I used to go with the
multitude,
leading the procession to the
house of God,
with shouts of joy and
thanksgiving
among the festive throng.

[5]Why are you downcast, O my
soul?
Why so disturbed within
me?
Put your hope in God,
for I will yet praise him,
my Savior and [6]my God.
My[v] soul is downcast within
me;
therefore I will remember
you
from the land of the Jordan,
the heights of
Hermon—from Mount
Mizar.
[7]Deep calls to deep
in the roar of your
waterfalls;
all your waves and breakers
have swept over me.

[8]By day the LORD directs his
love,
at night his song is with
me—
a prayer to the God of my
life.

[9]I say to God my Rock,
"Why have you forgotten
me?
Why must I go about
mourning,
oppressed by the enemy?"
[10]My bones suffer mortal agony
as my foes taunt me,
saying to me all day long,
"Where is your God?"

[11]Why are you downcast, O my

[f]In many Hebrew manuscripts Psalms 42 and 43 constitute one psalm.
[u]Title: Probably a literary or musical term
[v]5,6 A few Hebrew manuscripts, Septuagint and Syriac; most Hebrew manuscripts *praise him for his saving help. / [6]O my God, my*

*Heading, *1* See the note on page 349.

†6,7 The NIV reads with some mss and versions פְּנֵי וֵאלֹהָי׃ *and-God-of-me faces-of-me* as in verse 12.

°9 ק שירו

יְשׁוּעֹת פָּנַי וֵאלֹהָי׃ שָׁפְטֵנִי אֱלֹהִים ׀
God vindicate-me! (43:1) and-God-of-me faces-of-me saving-helps-of

וְרִיבָה רִיבִי מִגּוֹי לֹא־ חָסִיד מֵאִישׁ־ מִרְמָה
deceit from-man-of godly not against-nation cause-of-me and-plead!

וְעַוְלָה תְפַלְּטֵנִי׃ כִּי־ אַתָּה ׀ אֱלֹהֵי מָעוּזִּי לָמָה
why? stronghold-of-me God-of you indeed (2) you-rescue-me and-wickedness

זְנַחְתָּנִי לָמָּה־ קֹדֵר אֶתְהַלֵּךְ בְּלַחַץ אוֹיֵב׃
one-being-enemy in-oppression-of must-I-go-about mourning why? you-rejected-me

שְׁלַח־ אוֹרְךָ וַאֲמִתְּךָ הֵמָּה יַנְחוּנִי
let-them-guide-me they and-truth-of-you light-of-you send-forth! (3)

יְבִיאוּנִי אֶל־ הַר־ קָדְשְׁךָ וְאֶל־ מִשְׁכְּנוֹתֶיךָ׃
dwellings-of-you and-to holiness-of-you mountain-of to let-them-bring-me

וְאָבוֹאָה ׀ אֶל־ מִזְבַּח אֱלֹהִים אֶל־ אֵל שִׂמְחַת גִּילִי
delight-of-me joy-of God to God altar-of to then-I-will-go (4)

וְאוֹדְךָ בְכִנּוֹר אֱלֹהִים אֱלֹהָי׃ מַה־ תִּשְׁתּוֹחֲחִי ׀
are-you-downcast why? (5) God-of-me God with-harp and-I-will-praise-you

נַפְשִׁי וּמַה־ תֶּהֱמִי עָלָי הוֹחִילִי לֵאלֹהִים כִּי־ עוֹד
yet for in-God put-hope! within-me are-you-disturbed and-why? soul-of-me

אוֹדֶנּוּ יְשׁוּעֹת פָּנַי וֵאלֹהָי׃
and-God-of-me faces-of-me saving-helps-of I-will-praise-him

לַמְנַצֵּחַ לִבְנֵי־ קֹרַח מַשְׂכִּיל׃ אֱלֹהִים ׀ בְּאָזְנֵינוּ
with-ears-of-us God (2) maskil Korah of-sons-of for-the-one-directing *(44:1)

שָׁמַעְנוּ אֲבוֹתֵינוּ סִפְּרוּ־ לָנוּ פֹּעַל פָּעַלְתָּ בִימֵיהֶם
in-days-of-them you-did deed to-us they-told fathers-of-us we-heard

בִּימֵי קֶדֶם׃ אַתָּה ׀ יָדְךָ גּוֹיִם הוֹרַשְׁתָּ
you-drove-out nations hand-of-you you (3) long-ago in-days-of

וַתִּטָּעֵם תָּרַע לְאֻמִּים וַתְּשַׁלְּחֵם׃
and-you-made-flourish-them to-peoples you-crushed and-you-planted-them

כִּי לֹא בְחַרְבָּם יָרְשׁוּ אָרֶץ וּזְרוֹעָם לֹא־
not and-arm-of-them land they-won by-sword-of-them not for (4)

הוֹשִׁיעָה לָּמוֹ כִּי־ יְמִינְךָ וּזְרוֹעֲךָ וְאוֹר
and-light-of and-arm-of-you right-hand-of-you but to-them she-brought-victory

פָּנֶיךָ כִּי רְצִיתָם׃ אַתָּה־ הוּא מַלְכִּי אֱלֹהִים ׀ צַוֵּה
decree! God King-of-me he you (5) you-loved-them for faces-of-you

יְשׁוּעוֹת יַעֲקֹב׃ בְּךָ צָרֵינוּ נְנַגֵּחַ
we-push-back enemies-of-us through-you (6) Jacob victories-of

בְּשִׁמְךָ נָבוּס קָמֵינוּ׃ כִּי לֹא
not indeed (7) ones-being-foes-of-us we-trample through-name-of-you

soul?
Why so disturbed within me?
Put your hope in God,
for I will yet praise him,
my Savior and my God.

## Psalm 43[w]

1 Vindicate me, O God,
and plead my cause against an ungodly nation;
rescue me from deceitful and wicked men.
2 You are God my stronghold.
Why have you rejected me?
Why must I go about mourning,
oppressed by the enemy?
3 Send forth your light and your truth,
let them guide me;
let them bring me to your holy mountain,
to the place where you dwell.
4 Then will I go to the altar of God,
to God, my joy and my delight.
I will praise you with the harp,
O God, my God.

5 Why are you downcast, O my soul?
Why so disturbed within me?
Put your hope in God,
for I will yet praise him,
my Savior and my God.

## Psalm 44

For the director of music. Of the Sons of Korah. A *maskil*.[x]

1 We have heard with our ears, O God;
our fathers have told us
what you did in their days,
in days long ago.
2 With your hand you drove out the nations
and planted our fathers;
you crushed the peoples
and made our fathers flourish.
3 It was not by their sword that they won the land,
nor did their arm bring them victory;
it was your right hand, your arm,
and the light of your face,
for you loved them.
4 You are my King and my God,
who decrees[y] victories for Jacob.
5 Through you we push back our enemies;
through your name we trample our foes.

[w] In many Hebrew manuscripts Psalms 42 and 43 constitute one psalm.
[x] Title: Probably a literary or musical term
[y] 4 Septuagint, Aquila and Syriac; Hebrew *King, O God; / command*

*Heading, *1* See the note on page 349.

בְקַשְׁתִּי אֶבְטָח וְחַרְבִּי לֹא תוֹשִׁיעֵנִי׃ כִּי
but (8) she-brings-victory-to-me not and-sword-of-me I-trust in-bow-of-me

הוֹשַׁעְתָּנוּ מִצָּרֵינוּ וּמְשַׂנְאֵינוּ
and-ones-being-adversaries-of-us over-enemies-of-us you-give-victory-to-us

הֱבִישׁוֹתָ׃ בֵּאלֹהִים הִלַּלְנוּ כָל־ הַיּוֹם וְשִׁמְךָ ׀ לְעוֹלָם
to-forever and-name-of-you the-day all-of we-boast in-God (9) you-shame

נוֹדֶה סֶלָה׃ אַף־ זָנַחְתָּ וַתַּכְלִימֵנוּ וְלֹא־
and-not and-you-humbled-us you-rejected but (10) selah we-will-praise

תֵצֵא בְּצִבְאוֹתֵינוּ׃ תְּשִׁיבֵנוּ אָחוֹר מִנִּי־ צָר
enemy before back you-turned-us (11) with-armies-of-us you-go-out

וּמְשַׂנְאֵינוּ שָׁסוּ לָמוֹ׃ תִּתְּנֵנוּ
you-gave-up-us (12) from-us they-plundered and-ones-being-adversaries-of-us

כְּצֹאן מַאֲכָל וּבַגּוֹיִם זֵרִיתָנוּ׃ תִּמְכֹּר־
you-sold (13) you-scattered-us and-among-the-nations devouring like-sheep-of

עַמְּךָ בְלֹא־ הוֹן וְלֹא־ רִבִּיתָ בִּמְחִירֵיהֶם׃
from-sales-of-them you-gained and-nothing great-price for-no people-of-you

תְּשִׂימֵנוּ חֶרְפָּה לִשְׁכֵנֵינוּ לַעַג וָקֶלֶס
and-derision scorn to-neighbors-of-us reproach you-made-us (14)

לִסְבִיבוֹתֵינוּ׃ תְּשִׂימֵנוּ מָשָׁל בַּגּוֹיִם מְנוֹד־ רֹאשׁ
head shaking-of among-the-nations byword you-made-us (15) to-ones-around-us

†בַל־אֻמִּים׃ כָּל־ הַיּוֹם כְּלִמָּתִי נֶגְדִּי וּבֹשֶׁת
and-shame-of before-me disgrace-of-me the-day all-of (16) †among-the-peoples

פָּנַי כִּסָּתְנִי׃ מִקּוֹל מְחָרֵף וּמְגַדֵּף
and-one-reviling one-reproaching at-taunt-of (17) she-covers-me faces-of-me

מִפְּנֵי אוֹיֵב וּמִתְנַקֵּם׃ כָּל־ זֹאת
this all-of (18) even-one-avenging one-being-enemy because-of

בָּאַתְנוּ וְלֹא שְׁכַחֲנוּךָ וְלֹא־ שִׁקַּרְנוּ
we-were-false and-not we-forgot-you though-not she-happened-to-us

בִּבְרִיתֶךָ׃ לֹא־ נָסוֹג אָחוֹר לִבֵּנוּ וַתֵּט
or-she-strayed heart-of-us back he-turned not (19) to-covenant-of-you

אֲשֻׁרֵינוּ מִנִּי אָרְחֶךָ׃ כִּי דִכִּיתָנוּ בִּמְקוֹם תַּנִּים
jackals into-haunt-of you-crushed-us but (20) path-of-you from feet-of-us

וַתְּכַס עָלֵינוּ בְצַלְמָוֶת׃ אִם־ שָׁכַחְנוּ שֵׁם
name-of we-forgot if (21) with-deep-darkness over-us and-you-covered

אֱלֹהֵינוּ וַנִּפְרֹשׂ כַּפֵּינוּ לְאֵל זָר׃ הֲלֹא
not? (22) being-foreign to-god hands-of-us or-we-spread-out God-of-us

אֱלֹהִים יַחֲקָר־ זֹאת כִּי־ הוּא יֹדֵעַ תַּעֲלֻמוֹת לֵב׃
heart secrets-of one-knowing he since this would-he-have-discovered God

6 I do not trust in my bow,
my sword does not bring me victory;
7 but you give us victory over our enemies,
you put our adversaries to shame.
8 In God we make our boast all day long,
and we will praise your name forever. *Selah*
9 But now you have rejected and humbled us;
you no longer go out with our armies.
10 You made us retreat before the enemy,
and our adversaries have plundered us.
11 You gave us up to be devoured like sheep
and have scattered us among the nations.
12 You sold your people for a pittance,
gaining nothing from their sale.
13 You have made us a reproach to our neighbors,
the scorn and derision of those around us.
14 You have made us a byword among the nations;
the peoples shake their heads at us.
15 My disgrace is before me all day long,
and my face is covered with shame
16 at the taunts of those who reproach and revile me,
because of the enemy, who is bent on revenge.

17 All this happened to us,
though we had not forgotten you
or been false to your covenant.
18 Our hearts had not turned back;
our feet had not strayed from your path.
19 But you crushed us and made us a haunt for jackals
and covered us over with deep darkness.

20 If we had forgotten the name of our God
or spread out our hands to a foreign god,
21 would not God have discovered it,
since he knows the secrets of the heart?

*See the note on page 349.

†*15* Most mss read these two words as one with *sheva* under the *lamed* (בְּלאֻ').

(23) כִּי־ עָלֶיךָ הֹרַגְנוּ כָל־ הַיּוֹם נֶחְשַׁבְנוּ כְּצֹאן

as-sheep-of we-are-considered the-day all-of we-face-death for-you yet (23)

טִבְחָה׃ (24) עוּרָה ׀ לָמָּה תִישַׁן ׀ אֲדֹנָי הָקִיצָה אַל־ תִּזְנַח

you-reject not rouse-yourself! Lord you-sleep why? awake! (24) slaughter

לָנֶצַח׃ (25) לָמָּה־ פָנֶיךָ תַסְתִּיר תִּשְׁכַּח עָנְיֵנוּ

misery-of-us you-forget you-hide faces-of-you why? (25) to-forever

וְלַחֲצֵנוּ׃ (26) כִּי שָׁחָה לֶעָפָר נַפְשֵׁנוּ

self-of-us to-the-dust she-is-brought-down indeed (26) and-oppression-of-us

דָּבְקָה לָאָרֶץ בִּטְנֵנוּ׃ (27) קוּמָה עֶזְרָתָה לָּנוּ

to-us as-help rise-up! (27) body-of-us to-the-ground she-clings

וּפְדֵנוּ לְמַעַן חַסְדֶּךָ׃ *(45:1) לַמְנַצֵּחַ

for-the-one-directing *(45:1) unfailing-love-of-you because-of and-redeem-us!

עַל־שֹׁשַׁנִּים לִבְנֵי־ קֹרַח מַשְׂכִּיל שִׁיר יְדִידֹת׃ (2) רָחַשׁ

he-is-stirred (2) weddings song-of maskil Korah of-sons-of lilies to

לִבִּי ׀ דָּבָר טוֹב אֹמֵר אָנִי מַעֲשַׂי לְמֶלֶךְ לְשׁוֹנִי

tongue-of-me for-king verses-of-me I one-reciting noble theme heart-of-me

עֵט ׀ סוֹפֵר מָהִיר׃ (3) יָפְיָפִיתָ מִבְּנֵי אָדָם

man more-than-sons-of you-are-excellent (3) skillful writer pen-of

הוּצַק חֵן בְּשִׂפְתוֹתֶיךָ† עַל־ כֵּן בֵּרַכְךָ אֱלֹהִים לְעוֹלָם׃

to-forever God he-blessed-you this for on-lips-of-you grace he-was-anointed

(4) חֲגוֹר־ חַרְבְּךָ עַל־ יָרֵךְ גִּבּוֹר הוֹדְךָ וַהֲדָרֶךָ׃

and-majesty-of-you splendor-of-you mighty-one side upon sword-of-you gird! (4)

(5) וַהֲדָרְךָ ׀ צְלַח רְכַב עַל־ דְּבַר־ אֱמֶת

truth behalf-of in ride-forth! be-victorious! and-majesty-of-you (5)

וְעַנְוָה־ צֶדֶק וְתוֹרְךָ נוֹרָאוֹת

deeds-being-awesome and-let-her-display-you righteousness and-humility

יְמִינֶךָ׃ (6) חִצֶּיךָ שְׁנוּנִים עַמִּים תַּחְתֶּיךָ

beneath-you nations ones-being-sharp arrows-of-you (6) right-hand-of-you

יִפְּלוּ בְּלֵב אוֹיְבֵי הַמֶּלֶךְ׃ (7) כִּסְאֲךָ

throne-of-you (7) the-king ones-being-enemies-of into-heart-of let-them-fall

אֱלֹהִים עוֹלָם וָעֶד שֵׁבֶט מִישֹׁר שֵׁבֶט מַלְכוּתֶךָ׃

kingdom-of-you scepter-of justice scepter-of and-ever forever God

(8) אָהַבְתָּ צֶּדֶק וַתִּשְׂנָא רֶשַׁע עַל־ כֵּן ׀ מְשָׁחֲךָ

he-anointed-you this for wickedness and-you-hate righteousness you-love (8)

אֱלֹהִים אֱלֹהֶיךָ שֶׁמֶן שָׂשׂוֹן מֵחֲבֵרֶיךָ׃ (9) מֹר־ וַאֲהָלוֹת

and-aloes myrrh (9) above-companions-of-you joy oil-of God-of-you God

קְצִיעוֹת כָּל־ בִּגְדֹתֶיךָ מִן־ הֵיכְלֵי שֵׁן מִנִּי שִׂמְּחוּךָ׃

they-made-glad-you strings ivory palaces-of from robes-of-you all-of cassias

---

22Yet for your sake we face
death all day long;
we are considered as sheep
to be slaughtered.
23Awake, O Lord! Why do you
sleep?
Rouse yourself! Do not reject
us forever.
24Why do you hide your face
and forget our misery and
oppression?
25We are brought down to the
dust;
our bodies cling to the
ground.
26Rise up and help us;
redeem us because of your
unfailing love.

**Psalm 45**

For the director of music. To the tune of "Lilies." Of the Sons of Korah. A *maskil*.[z] A wedding song.

1My heart is stirred by a noble
theme
as I recite my verses for the
king;
my tongue is the pen of a
skillful writer.
2You are the most excellent of
men
and your lips have been
anointed with grace,
since God has blessed you
forever.
3Gird your sword upon your
side, O mighty one;
clothe yourself with
splendor and majesty.
4In your majesty ride forth
victoriously
in behalf of truth, humility
and righteousness;
let your right hand display
awesome deeds.
5Let your sharp arrows pierce
the hearts of the king's
enemies;
let the nations fall beneath
your feet.
6Your throne, O God, will last
for ever and ever;
a scepter of justice will be
the scepter of your
kingdom.
7You love righteousness and
hate wickedness;
therefore God, your God,
has set you above your
companions
by anointing you with the
oil of joy.
8All your robes are fragrant
with myrrh and aloes and
cassia;
from palaces adorned with
ivory
the music of the strings
makes you glad.

zTitle: Probably a literary or musical term

*Heading, *1* See the note on page 349.

†3 Most mss have *hireq* under the *sin* ( בְּשִׂפְ׳ ).

בְּנוֹת מְלָכִים בְּיִקְּרוֹתֶיךָ נִצְּבָה שֵׁגַל
royal-bride she-stands among-honored-women-of-you kings daughters-of (10)

לִימִינְךָ בְּכֶתֶם אוֹפִיר׃ שִׁמְעִי־בַת וּרְאִי
and-consider! daughter listen! (11) Ophir in-gold-of at-right-hand-of-you

וְהַטִּי אָזְנֵךְ וְשִׁכְחִי עַמֵּךְ וּבֵית אָבִיךְ׃
father-of-you and-house-of people-of-you and-forget! ear-of-you and-give!

וְיִתְאָו הַמֶּלֶךְ יָפְיֵךְ כִּי־הוּא אֲדֹנַיִךְ
lords-of-you he for beauty-of-you the-king and-he-is-enthralled (12)

וְהִשְׁתַּחֲוִי־לוֹ׃ וּבַת־צֹר ׀ בְּמִנְחָה פָּנַיִךְ יְחַלּוּ
they-will-seek faces-of-you with-gift Tyre and-Daughter-of (13) to-him so-honor!

עֲשִׁירֵי עָם׃ כָּל־כְּבוּדָּה בַת־מֶלֶךְ פְּנִימָה
at-within king daughter-of glorious all-of (14) people wealthy-men-of

מִמִּשְׁבְּצוֹת זָהָב לְבוּשָׁהּ׃ לִרְקָמוֹת תּוּבַל
she-is-led in-embroidered-garments (15) gown-of-her gold with-interweavings-of

לַמֶּלֶךְ בְּתוּלוֹת אַחֲרֶיהָ רֵעוֹתֶיהָ מוּבָאוֹת לָךְ׃
to-you ones-being-brought companions-of-her following-her virgins to-the-king

תּוּבַלְנָה בִּשְׂמָחֹת וָגִיל תְּבֹאֶינָה בְּהֵיכַל מֶלֶךְ׃
king into-palace-of they-enter and-gladness with-joy they-are-led-in (16)

תַּחַת אֲבֹתֶיךָ יִהְיוּ בָנֶיךָ תְּשִׁיתֵמוֹ
you-will-make-them sons-of-you they-will-be fathers-of-you in-place-of (17)

לְשָׂרִים בְּכָל־הָאָרֶץ׃ אַזְכִּירָה שִׁמְךָ
name-of-you I-will-perpetuate-memory (18) the-land through-all-of as-princes

בְּכָל־דֹּר וָדֹר עַל־כֵּן עַמִּים יְהוֹדֻךָ
they-will-praise-you nations this for and-generation generation through-all-of

לְעֹלָם וָעֶד׃ לַמְנַצֵּחַ לִבְנֵי־קֹרַח
Korah of-sons-of for-the-one-directing *(46:1) and-ever to-forever

עַל־עֲלָמוֹת שִׁיר׃ אֱלֹהִים לָנוּ מַחֲסֶה וָעֹז עֶזְרָה בְצָרוֹת
in-troubles help and-strength refuge to-us God (2) song alamoth according-to

נִמְצָא מְאֹד׃ עַל־כֵּן לֹא־נִירָא בְּהָמִיר אָרֶץ
earth through-to-give-way we-will-fear not this for (3) ever one-being-present

וּבְמוֹט הָרִים בְּלֵב יַמִּים׃ יֶהֱמוּ יֶחְמְרוּ
they-foam they-roar (4) seas into-heart-of mountains and-though-to-fall

מֵימָיו יִרְעֲשׁוּ־הָרִים בְּגַאֲוָתוֹ סֶלָה׃ נָהָר
river (5) selah with-surging-of-him mountains they-quake waters-of-him

פְּלָגָיו יְשַׂמְּחוּ עִיר־אֱלֹהִים קְדֹשׁ מִשְׁכְּנֵי עֶלְיוֹן׃
Most-High dwellings-of holy-place-of God city-of they-make-glad streams-of-him

אֱלֹהִים בְּקִרְבָּהּ בַּל־תִּמּוֹט יַעְזְרֶהָ אֱלֹהִים לִפְנוֹת
to-come God he-will-help-her she-will-fall not in-inside-of-her God (6)

9 Daughters of kings are among your honored women;
at your right hand is the royal bride in gold of Ophir.
10 Listen, O daughter, consider and give ear:
Forget your people and your father's house.
11 The king is enthralled by your beauty;
honor him, for he is your lord.
12 The Daughter of Tyre will come with a gift,[a]
men of wealth will seek your favor.
13 All glorious is the princess within ⌊her chamber⌋;
her gown is interwoven with gold.
14 In embroidered garments she is led to the king;
her virgin companions follow her
and are brought to you.
15 They are led in with joy and gladness;
they enter the palace of the king.
16 Your sons will take the place of your fathers;
you will make them princes throughout the land.
17 I will perpetuate your memory through all generations;
therefore the nations will praise you for ever and ever.

### Psalm 46

For the director of music. Of the Sons of Korah. According to *alamoth*.[b] A song.

1 God is our refuge and strength,
an ever present help in trouble.
2 Therefore we will not fear, though the earth give way
and the mountains fall into the heart of the sea,
3 though its waters roar and foam
and the mountains quake with their surging. *Selah*
4 There is a river whose streams make glad the city of God,
the holy place where the Most High dwells.
5 God is within her, she will not fall;
God will help her at break of day.

[a]12 Or *A Tyrian robe is among the gifts*
[b]Title: Probably a musical term

*Heading, *1* See the note on page 349.

בֹּקֶר׃ הָמוּ גוֹיִם מָטוּ מַמְלָכוֹת נָתַן
he-lifts kingdoms they-fall nations they-are-in-uproar (7) daybreak

בְּקוֹלוֹ תָּמוּג אָרֶץ׃ יְהוָה צְבָאוֹת עִמָּנוּ מִשְׂגָּב־לָנוּ
to-us fortress with-us Hosts Yahweh-of (8) earth she-melts to-voice-of-him

אֱלֹהֵי יַעֲקֹב סֶלָה׃ לְכוּ־חֲזוּ מִפְעֲלוֹת יְהוָה אֲשֶׁר־שָׂם שַׁמּוֹת
desolations he-brought that Yahweh works-of see! come! (9) selah Jacob God-of

בָּאָרֶץ׃ מַשְׁבִּית מִלְחָמוֹת עַד־קְצֵה הָאָרֶץ קֶשֶׁת יְשַׁבֵּר
he-breaks bow the-earth end-of to wars one-making-cease (10) on-the-earth

וְקִצֵּץ חֲנִית עֲגָלוֹת† יִשְׂרֹף בָּאֵשׁ׃ הַרְפּוּ וּדְעוּ
and-know! be-still! (11) with-fire he-burns †chariots spear and-he-shatters

כִּי־אָנֹכִי אֱלֹהִים אָרוּם בַּגּוֹיִם אָרוּם בָּאָרֶץ׃
in-the-earth I-will-be-exalted among-the-nations I-will-be-exalted God I that

יְהוָה צְבָאוֹת עִמָּנוּ מִשְׂגָּב־לָנוּ אֱלֹהֵי יַעֲקֹב סֶלָה׃
selah Jacob God-of to-us fortress with-us Hosts Yahweh-of (12)

לַמְנַצֵּחַ ׀ לִבְנֵי־קֹרַח מִזְמוֹר׃ כָּל־הָעַמִּים
the-nations all-of (2) psalm Korah of-sons-of for-the-one-directing *(47:1)

תִּקְעוּ־כָף הָרִיעוּ לֵאלֹהִים בְּקוֹל רִנָּה׃ כִּי־יְהוָה עֶלְיוֹן
Most-High Yahweh how! (3) joy with-cry-of to-God shout! hand clap!

נוֹרָא מֶלֶךְ גָּדוֹל עַל־כָּל־הָאָרֶץ׃ יַדְבֵּר עַמִּים
nations he-subdued (4) the-earth all-of over great King one-being-awesome

תַּחְתֵּינוּ וּלְאֻמִּים תַּחַת רַגְלֵינוּ׃ יִבְחַר־לָנוּ אֶת־נַחֲלָתֵנוּ
inheritance-of-us *** for-us he-chose (5) feet-of-us under and-peoples under-us

אֶת גְּאוֹן יַעֲקֹב אֲשֶׁר־אָהֵב סֶלָה׃ עָלָה אֱלֹהִים בִּתְרוּעָה
with-shout-of-joy God he-ascended (6) selah he-loved whom Jacob pride-of ***

יְהוָה בְּקוֹל שׁוֹפָר׃ זַמְּרוּ אֱלֹהִים זַמֵּרוּ
sing-praises! God sing-praises! (7) trumpet amid-sound-of Yahweh

זַמְּרוּ לְמַלְכֵּנוּ זַמֵּרוּ׃ כִּי מֶלֶךְ כָּל־הָאָרֶץ
the-earth all-of King-of for (8) sing-praises! to-King-of-us sing-praises!

אֱלֹהִים זַמְּרוּ מַשְׂכִּיל׃ מָלַךְ אֱלֹהִים עַל־גּוֹיִם אֱלֹהִים יָשַׁב ׀
he-sits God nations over God he-reigns (9) maskil sing-praise! God

עַל־כִּסֵּא קָדְשׁוֹ׃ נְדִיבֵי עַמִּים ׀ נֶאֱסָפוּ עַם
people-of they-assemble nations nobles-of (10) holiness-of-him throne-of on

אֱלֹהֵי אַבְרָהָם כִּי לֵאלֹהִים מָגִנֵּי־אֶרֶץ מְאֹד נַעֲלָה׃
he-is-exalted greatly earth shields-of to-God for Abraham God-of

שִׁיר מִזְמוֹר לִבְנֵי־קֹרַח׃ גָּדוֹל יְהוָה וּמְהֻלָּל
and-one-being-praised Yahweh great (2) Korah of-sons-of psalm song *(48:1)

מְאֹד בְּעִיר אֱלֹהֵינוּ הַר־קָדְשׁוֹ׃ יְפֵה
beautiful-of (3) holiness-of-him mountain-of God-of-us in-city-of greatly

6 Nations are in uproar,
kingdoms fall;
he lifts his voice, the earth
melts.
7 The LORD Almighty is with us;
the God of Jacob is our
fortress. *Selah*
8 Come and see the works of the
LORD,
the desolations he has
brought on the earth.
9 He makes wars cease to the
ends of the earth;
he breaks the bow and
shatters the spear,
he burns the shields[c] with
fire.
10 "Be still, and know that I am
God;
I will be exalted among the
nations,
I will be exalted in the
earth."
11 The LORD Almighty is with us;
the God of Jacob is our
fortress. *Selah*

## Psalm 47

For the director of music. Of the Sons of Korah. A psalm.

1 Clap your hands, all you
nations;
shout to God with cries of
joy.
2 How awesome is the LORD
Most High,
the great King over all the
earth!
3 He subdued nations under us,
peoples under our feet.
4 He chose our inheritance for
us,
the pride of Jacob, whom he
loved. *Selah*
5 God has ascended amid shouts
of joy,
the LORD amid the sounding
of trumpets.
6 Sing praises to God, sing
praises;
sing praises to our King,
sing praises.
7 For God is the King of all the
earth;
sing to him a psalm[d] of
praise.
8 God reigns over the nations;
God is seated on his holy
throne.
9 The nobles of the nations
assemble
as the people of the God of
Abraham,
for the kings[e] of the earth
belong to God;
he is greatly exalted.

## Psalm 48

A song. A psalm of the Sons of Korah.

1 Great is the LORD, and most

c9 Or *chariots*
d7 Or *a maskil* (probably a literary or musical term)
e9 Or *shields*

*Heading, *1* See the note on page 349.
†*10* The NIV repoints this word as וַעֲגָלוֹת, *and-shields.*

נוֹף מְשׂוֹשׂ כָּל־ הָאָרֶץ הַר־ צִיּוֹן יַרְכְּתֵי צָפוֹן
Zaphon utmost-heights-of Zion Mount-of the-earth whole-of joy-of loftiness

קִרְיַת מֶלֶךְ רָב׃ אֱלֹהִים בְּאַרְמְנוֹתֶיהָ נוֹדַע לְמִשְׂגָּב׃
as-fortress he-showed-himself in-citadels-of-her God (4) Great King city-of

כִּי־ הִנֵּה הַמְּלָכִים נוֹעֲדוּ עָבְרוּ יַחְדָּו׃
together they-advanced they-joined-forces the-kings see! when (5)

הֵמָּה רָאוּ כֵּן תָּמָהוּ נִבְהֲלוּ נֶחְפָּזוּ׃
they-fled they-were-terrified they-were-astounded thus they-saw they (6)

רְעָדָה אֲחָזָתַם שָׁם חִיל כַּיּוֹלֵדָה׃
like-the-woman-being-in-labor pain there she-seized-them trembling (7)

בְּרוּחַ קָדִים תְּשַׁבֵּר אֳנִיּוֹת תַּרְשִׁישׁ׃ כַּאֲשֶׁר שָׁמַעְנוּ ׀
we-heard just-as (9) Tarshish ships-of you-destroyed east by-wind-of (8)

כֵּן רָאִינוּ בְּעִיר־ יְהוָה צְבָאוֹת בְּעִיר אֱלֹהֵינוּ אֱלֹהִים
God God-of-us in-city-of Hosts Yahweh-of in-city-of we-saw so

יְכוֹנְנֶהָ עַד־ עוֹלָם סֶלָה׃ דִּמִּינוּ אֱלֹהִים חַסְדֶּךָ
unfailing-love-of-you God we-meditate (10) selah forever to he-makes-secure-her

בְּקֶרֶב הֵיכָלֶךָ׃ כְּשִׁמְךָ אֱלֹהִים כֵּן תְּהִלָּתְךָ עַל־
to praise-of-you so God like-name-of-you (11) temple-of-you at-within

קַצְוֵי־ אֶרֶץ צֶדֶק מָלְאָה יְמִינֶךָ׃ יִשְׂמַח ׀
he-rejoices (12) right-hand-of-you she-is-filled righteousness earth ends-of

הַר־ צִיּוֹן תָּגֵלְנָה בְּנוֹת יְהוּדָה לְמַעַן מִשְׁפָּטֶיךָ׃
judgments-of-you because-of Judah villages-of they-are-glad Zion Mount-of

סֹבּוּ צִיּוֹן וְהַקִּיפוּהָ סִפְרוּ מִגְדָּלֶיהָ׃ שִׁיתוּ
consider! (14) towers-of-her count! and-go-around-her! Zion walk-about! (13)

לִבְּכֶם ׀ לְחֵילָה פַּסְּגוּ אַרְמְנוֹתֶיהָ לְמַעַן תְּסַפְּרוּ
you-may-tell so-that citadels-of-her view! to-rampart-of-her heart-of-you

לְדוֹר אַחֲרוֹן׃ כִּי זֶה ׀ אֱלֹהִים אֱלֹהֵינוּ עוֹלָם וָעֶד הוּא
he and-ever forever God-of-us God this for (15) next to-generation

יְנַהֲגֵנוּ עַל־ מוּת׃ לַמְנַצֵּחַ ׀ לִבְנֵי־ קֹרַח
Korah of-sons-of for-the-one-directing *(49:1) to-die to he-will-guide-us

מִזְמוֹר׃ שִׁמְעוּ־זֹאת כָּל־ הָעַמִּים הַאֲזִינוּ כָּל־ יֹשְׁבֵי חָלֶד׃
world ones-living-of all-of listen! the-peoples all-of this hear! (2) psalm

גַּם־ בְּנֵי אָדָם גַּם־ בְּנֵי־ אִישׁ יַחַד עָשִׁיר וְאֶבְיוֹן׃ פִּי
mouth-of-me (4) and-poor rich alike man sons-of both mankind sons-of both (3)

יְדַבֵּר חָכְמוֹת וְהָגוּת לִבִּי תְבוּנוֹת׃
understanding-things heart-of-me and-utterance-of words-of-wisdom he-will-speak

אַטֶּה לְמָשָׁל אָזְנִי אֶפְתַּח בְּכִנּוֹר חִידָתִי׃
riddle-of-me with-harp I-will-expound ear-of-me to-proverb I-will-turn (5)

worthy of praise,
in the city of our God, his holy mountain.
2 It is beautiful in its loftiness,
the joy of the whole earth.
Like the utmost heights of Zaphon[f] is Mount Zion,
the[g] city of the Great King.
3 God is in her citadels;
he has shown himself to be her fortress.

4 When the kings joined forces,
when they advanced together,
5 they saw ⌊her⌋ and were astounded;
they fled in terror.
6 Trembling seized them there,
pain like that of a woman in labor.
7 You destroyed them like ships of Tarshish
shattered by an east wind.

8 As we have heard,
so have we seen
in the city of the LORD Almighty,
in the city of our God:
God makes her secure forever. *Selah*

9 Within your temple, O God,
we meditate on your unfailing love.
10 Like your name, O God,
your praise reaches to the ends of the earth;
your right hand is filled with righteousness.
11 Mount Zion rejoices,
the villages of Judah are glad
because of your judgments.

12 Walk about Zion, go around her,
count her towers,
13 consider well her ramparts,
view her citadels,
that you may tell of them to the next generation.
14 For this God is our God for ever and ever;
he will be our guide even to the end.

**Psalm 49**

For the director of music. Of the Sons of Korah. A psalm.

1 Hear this, all you peoples;
listen, all who live in this world,
2 both low and high,
rich and poor alike:
3 My mouth will speak words of wisdom;
the utterance from my heart will give understanding.
4 I will turn my ear to a proverb;
with the harp I will expound my riddle:

f2 *Zaphon* can refer to a sacred mountain or the direction north.
g2 Or *earth, / Mount Zion, on the northern side / of the*

*Heading, *1* See the note on page 349.

(6) לָמָּה אִירָא בִּימֵי רָע עֲוֺן עֲקֵבַי
deceivers-of-me wickedness-of evil in-days-of should-I-fear why? (6)

יְסוּבֵּנִי׃ (7) הַבֹּטְחִים עַל־ חֵילָם וּבְרֹב
and-in-greatness-of wealth-of-them in the-ones-trusting (7) he-surrounds-me

עָשְׁרָם יִתְהַלָּלוּ׃ (8) אָח לֹא־ פָדֹה יִפְדֶּה אִישׁ
man he-can-redeem to-redeem not another (8) they-boast richness-of-them

לֹא־ יִתֵּן לֵאלֹהִים כָּפְרוֹ׃ (9) וְיֵקַר פִּדְיוֹן
ransom-of for-he-is-costly (9) ransom-of-him to-God he-can-give not

נַפְשָׁם וְחָדַל לְעוֹלָם׃ (10) וִיחִי־ עוֹד
on that-he-should-live (10) to-forever and-he-is-not-enough life-of-them

לָנֶצַח לֹא יִרְאֶה הַשָּׁחַת׃ (11) כִּי יִרְאֶה ׀ חֲכָמִים יָמוּתוּ
they-die wise-men he-sees for (11) the-decay he-should-see not to-forever

יַחַד כְּסִיל וָבַעַר יֹאבֵדוּ וְעָזְבוּ לַאֲחֵרִים
to-others and-they-leave they-perish and-senseless foolish alike

חֵילָם׃ (12) קִרְבָּם† בָּתֵּימוֹ ׀ לְעוֹלָם מִשְׁכְּנֹתָם
dwellings-of-them to-forever houses-of-them †thought-of-them (12) wealth-of-them

לְדֹר וָדֹר קָרְאוּ בִשְׁמוֹתָם עֲלֵי אֲדָמוֹת׃
lands to by-names-of-them they-called and-generation for-generation

(13) וְאָדָם בִּיקָר בַּל־ יָלִין נִמְשַׁל כַּבְּהֵמוֹת
like-the-beasts he-is-like he-endures not despite-richness but-man (13)

נִדְמוּ׃ (14) זֶה דַרְכָּם כֵּסֶל לָמוֹ וְאַחֲרֵיהֶם ׀
and-follower-of-them in-themselves trust fate-of-them this (14) they-perish

בְּפִיהֶם יִרְצוּ סֶלָה׃ (15) כַּצֹּאן ׀ לִשְׁאוֹל
for-Sheol like-the-sheep (15) selah they-approve to-saying-of-them

שַׁתּוּ מָוֶת יִרְעֵם וַיִּרְדּוּ בָם
over-them and-they-will-rule he-will-feed-on-them death they-are-destined

יְשָׁרִים ׀ לַבֹּקֶר וְצִירָם° לְבַלּוֹת שְׁאוֹל מִזְּבֻל
from-mansion Sheol to-decay and-form-of-them in-the-morning upright-ones

לוֹ׃ (16) אַךְ־אֱלֹהִים יִפְדֶּה נַפְשִׁי מִיַּד־ שְׁאוֹל כִּי
surely Sheol from-hand-of soul-of-me he-will-redeem God but (16) of-him

יִקָּחֵנִי סֶלָה׃ (17) אַל־ תִּירָא כִּי־ יַעֲשִׁר אִישׁ כִּי־
when man he-grows-rich when you-be-overawed not (17) selah he-will-take-me

יִרְבֶּה כְּבוֹד בֵּיתוֹ׃ (18) כִּי לֹא בְמוֹתוֹ
in-death-of-him not for (18) house-of-him splendor-of he-increases

יִקַּח הַכֹּל לֹא־ יֵרֵד אַחֲרָיו כְּבוֹדוֹ׃
splendor-of-him with-him he-will-descend not the-whole he-will-take

(19) כִּי־ נַפְשׁוֹ בְּחַיָּיו יְבָרֵךְ וְיוֹדֻךָ
and-they-praise-you he-blessed during-lives-of-him self-of-him though (19)

5Why should I fear when evil
days come,
when wicked deceivers
surround me—
6those who trust in their wealth
and boast of their great
riches?
7No man can redeem the life of
another
or give to God a ransom for
him—
8the ransom for a life is costly,
no payment is ever
enough—
9that he should live on forever
and not see decay.
10For all can see that wise men
die;
the foolish and the senseless
alike perish
and leave their wealth to
others.
11Their tombs will remain their
houses[h] forever,
their dwellings for endless
generations,
though they had[i] named
lands after themselves.
12But man, despite his riches,
does not endure;
he is[j] like the beasts that
perish.
13This is the fate of those who
trust in themselves,
and of their followers, who
approve their sayings.
*Selah*
14Like sheep they are destined
for the grave,[k]
and death will feed on
them.
The upright will rule over
them in the morning;
their forms will decay in the
grave,[k]
far from their princely
mansions.
15But God will redeem my soul[l]
from the grave;
he will surely take me to
himself. *Selah*
16Do not be overawed when a
man grows rich,
when the splendor of his
house increases;
17for he will take nothing with
him when he dies,
his splendor will not
descend with him.
18Though while he lived he
counted himself blessed—
and men praise you when

[h]11 Septuagint and Syriac; Hebrew *In their thoughts their houses will remain*
[i]11 Or */ for they have*
[j]12 Hebrew; Septuagint and Syriac *But a man who has riches without understanding / is*
[k]14 Hebrew *Sheol*; also in verse 15
[l]15 Or *redeem me*

*See the note on page 349.

†12 The NIV reads with some versions קִבְרָם, *tomb-of-them*.

°15 ק וצורם

כִּֽי־ תֵיטִיב לָֽךְ׃ תָּבוֹא עַד־ דּוֹר אֲבוֹתָיו
fathers-of-him generation-of to she-will-go (20) to-you you-prosper when

עַד־נֵצַח לֹא יִרְאוּ־ אֽוֹר׃ אָדָם בִּיקָר וְלֹא יָבִין
he-understands but-not with-richness man (21) light they-see not forever to

נִמְשַׁל כַּבְּהֵמוֹת נִדְמֽוּ׃ מִזְמוֹר לְאָסָף אֵל ׀ אֱלֹהִים
God Mighty-One of-Asaph psalm (50:1) they-perish like-the-beasts he-is-like

יְהוָה דִּבֶּר וַיִּקְרָא־ אָרֶץ מִמִּזְרַח־ שֶׁמֶשׁ עַד־ מְבֹאֽוֹ׃
setting-of-him to sun from-rising-of earth and-he-summons he-speaks Yahweh

מִצִּיּוֹן מִכְלַל־ יֹפִי אֱלֹהִים הוֹפִֽיעַ׃ יָבֹא אֱלֹהֵינוּ
God-of-us he-comes (3) he-shines-forth God beauty perfect-of from-Zion (2)

וְאַל־ יֶחֱרַשׁ אֵשׁ־ לְפָנָיו תֹּאכֵל וּסְבִיבָיו
and-ones-around-him she-devours before-him fire he-will-be-silent and-not

נִשְׂעֲרָה מְאֹֽד׃ יִקְרָא אֶל־ הַשָּׁמַיִם מֵעָל וְאֶל־ הָאָרֶץ
the-earth and-to at-above the-heavens to he-summons (4) greatly she-storms

לָדִין עַמּֽוֹ׃ אִסְפוּ־ לִי חֲסִידָי כֹּרְתֵי
ones-making-of consecrated-ones-of-me to-me gather! (5) people-of-him to-judge

בְרִיתִי עֲלֵי־ זָֽבַח׃ וַיַּגִּידוּ שָׁמַיִם צִדְקוֹ
righteousness-of-him heavens and-they-proclaim (6) sacrifice by covenant-of-me

כִּֽי־ אֱלֹהִים ׀ שֹׁפֵט הוּא סֶלָה׃ שִׁמְעָה עַמִּי ׀ וַאֲדַבֵּרָה יִשְׂרָאֵל
Israel and-I-will-speak people-of-me hear! (7) selah he one-judging God for

וְאָעִידָה בָּךְ אֱלֹהִים אֱלֹהֶיךָ אָנֹֽכִי׃ לֹא עַל־ זְבָחֶיךָ
sacrifices-of-you for not (8) I God-of-you God against-you and-I-will-testify

אוֹכִיחֶךָ וְעוֹלֹתֶיךָ לְנֶגְדִּי תָמִֽיד׃ לֹא־ אֶקַּח
I-need not (9) ever at-before-me or-burnt-offerings-of-you I-rebuke-you

מִבֵּיתְךָ פָר מִמִּכְלְאֹתֶיךָ עַתּוּדִֽים׃ כִּֽי־ לִי כָל־
every-of to-me for (10) goats from-pens-of-you bull from-stall-of-you

חַיְתוֹ־ יָעַר בְּהֵמוֹת בְּהַרְרֵי־ אָֽלֶף׃ יָדַעְתִּי כָּל־ עוֹף
bird-of every-of I-know (11) thousand on-hills-of cattles forest animal-of

הָרִים וְזִיז שָׂדַי עִמָּדִֽי׃ אִם־ אֶרְעַב לֹא־ אֹמַר
I-would-tell not I-were-hungry if (12) to-me field and-creature-of mountains

לָךְ כִּי־ לִי תֵבֵל וּמְלֹאָֽהּ׃ הַאוֹכַל בְּשַׂר אַבִּירִים
bulls flesh-of do-I-eat? (13) and-all-in-her world to-me for to-you

וְדַם עַתּוּדִים אֶשְׁתֶּֽה׃ זְבַח לֵאלֹהִים תּוֹדָה
thank-offering to-God sacrifice! (14) do-I-drink goats or-blood-of

וְשַׁלֵּם לְעֶלְיוֹן נְדָרֶֽיךָ׃ וּקְרָאֵנִי בְּיוֹם צָרָה
trouble in-day-of and-call-upon-me! (15) vows-of-you to-Most-High and-fulfill!

אֲחַלֶּצְךָ וּתְכַבְּדֵֽנִי׃ וְלָרָשָׁע ׀ אָמַר
he-says but-to-the-wicked (16) and-you-will-honor-me I-will-deliver-you

you prosper—
19 he will join the generation of his fathers,
who will never see the light ⌊of life⌋.
20 A man who has riches without understanding
is like the beasts that perish.

### Psalm 50

A psalm of Asaph.

1 The Mighty One, God, the LORD,
speaks and summons the earth
from the rising of the sun to the place where it sets.
2 From Zion, perfect in beauty,
God shines forth.
3 Our God comes and will not be silent;
a fire devours before him,
and around him a tempest rages.
4 He summons the heavens above,
and the earth, that he may judge his people:
5 "Gather to me my consecrated ones,
who made a covenant with me by sacrifice."
6 And the heavens proclaim his righteousness,
for God himself is judge.
*Selah*

7 "Hear, O my people, and I will speak,
O Israel, and I will testify against you:
I am God, your God.
8 I do not rebuke you for your sacrifices
or your burnt offerings, which are ever before me.
9 I have no need of a bull from your stall
or of goats from your pens,
10 for every animal of the forest is mine,
and the cattle on a thousand hills.
11 I know every bird in the mountains,
and the creatures of the field are mine.
12 If I were hungry I would not tell you,
for the world is mine, and all that is in it.
13 Do I eat the flesh of bulls
or drink the blood of goats?
14 Sacrifice thank offerings to God,
fulfill your vows to the Most High,
15 and call upon me in the day of trouble;
I will deliver you, and you will honor me."

16 But to the wicked, God says:

*See the note on page 349.

אֱלֹהִים מַה־ לְּךָ לְסַפֵּר חֻקָּי וַתִּשָּׂא בְרִיתִי עֲלֵי־
on covenant-of-me or-you-take laws-of-me to-recite to-you what? God

פִיךָ׃ וְאַתָּה שָׂנֵאתָ מוּסָר וַתַּשְׁלֵךְ דְּבָרַי
words-of-me and-you-cast instruction you-hate for-you (17) lip-of-you

אַחֲרֶיךָ׃ אִם־ רָאִיתָ גַנָּב וַתִּרֶץ עִמּוֹ וְעִם
and-with with-him then-you-join thief you-see when (18) behind-you

מְנָאֲפִים חֶלְקֶךָ׃ פִּיךָ שָׁלַחְתָּ בְרָעָה
for-evil you-use mouth-of-you (19) lot-of-you ones-committing-adultery

וּלְשׁוֹנְךָ תַּצְמִיד מִרְמָה׃ תֵּשֵׁב בְּאָחִיךָ
against-brother-of-you you-sit (20) deceit you-harness-to and-tongue-of-you

תְדַבֵּר בְּבֶן־ אִמְּךָ תִּתֶּן־ דֹּפִי׃ אֵלֶּה עָשִׂיתָ
you-did these (21) slander you-give mother-of-you against-son-of you-speak

וְהֶחֱרַשְׁתִּי דִּמִּיתָ הֱיוֹת־ אֶהְיֶה כָמוֹךָ אוֹכִיחֲךָ
I-will-rebuke-you like-you I-was to-be you-thought and-I-kept-silent

וְאֶעֶרְכָה לְעֵינֶיךָ׃ בִּינוּ־ נָא זֹאת
this now! consider! (22) before-eyes-of-you and-I-will-accuse

שֹׁכְחֵי אֱלוֹהַּ פֶּן־ אֶטְרֹף וְאֵין מַצִּיל׃
one-rescuing and-there-is-not I-will-tear-to-pieces or God ones-forgetting-of

זֹבֵחַ תּוֹדָה יְכַבְּדָנְנִי וְשָׂם דֶּרֶךְ
way and-he-prepares he-honors-me thank-offering one-sacrificing (23)

אַרְאֶנּוּ בְּיֵשַׁע אֱלֹהִים׃ לַמְנַצֵּחַ מִזְמוֹר
psalm for-the-one-directing *(51:1) God to-salvation-of I-will-show-him

לְדָוִד׃ בְּבוֹא־ אֵלָיו נָתָן הַנָּבִיא כַּאֲשֶׁר־ בָּא אֶל־
into he-went after-when the-prophet Nathan to-him when-to-come (2) of-David

בַּת־ שָׁבַע׃ חָנֵּנִי אֱלֹהִים כְּחַסְדֶּךָ
according-to-unfailing-love-of-you God have-mercy-on-me! (3) Sheba Bath

כְּרֹב רַחֲמֶיךָ מְחֵה פְשָׁעָי׃
transgressions-of-me blot-out! compassions-of-you according-to-greatness-of

הֶרֶבה° כַּבְּסֵנִי מֵעֲוֹנִי וּמֵחַטָּאתִי טַהֲרֵנִי׃
cleanse-me! and-from-sin-of-me of-iniquity-of-me wash-me! †make-many! (4)

כִּי־ פְשָׁעַי אֲנִי אֵדָע וְחַטָּאתִי נֶגְדִּי תָמִיד׃
always before-me and-sin-of-me I-know I transgressions-of-me for (5)

לְךָ לְבַדְּךָ חָטָאתִי וְהָרַע בְּעֵינֶיךָ עָשִׂיתִי
I-did in-eyes-of-you and-the-evil I-sinned by-yourself against-you (6)

לְמַעַן תִּצְדַּק בְּדָבְרֶךָ תִּזְכֶּה
you-are-justified when-to-speak-you you-are-proved-right so-that

בְשָׁפְטֶךָ׃ הֵן־ בְּעָווֹן חוֹלָלְתִּי וּבְחֵטְא יֶחֱמַתְנִי
she-conceived-me and-in-sin I-was-born in-sin surely (7) when-to-judge-you

"What right have you to recite my laws
or take my covenant on your lips?
17You hate my instruction
and cast my words behind you.
18When you see a thief, you join with him;
you throw in your lot with adulterers.
19You use your mouth for evil
and harness your tongue to deceit.
20You speak continually against your brother
and slander your own mother's son.
21These things you have done
and I kept silent;
you thought I was altogether[m] like you.
But I will rebuke you
and accuse you to your face.

22"Consider this, you who forget God,
or I will tear you to pieces, with none to rescue:
23He who sacrifices thank offerings honors me,
and he prepares the way
so that I may show him[n] the salvation of God."

### Psalm 51

For the director of music. A psalm of David. When the prophet Nathan came to him after David had committed adultery with Bathsheba.

1Have mercy on me, O God,
according to your unfailing love;
according to your great compassion
blot out my transgressions.
2Wash away all my iniquity
and cleanse me from my sin.

3For I know my transgressions,
and my sin is always before me.
4Against you, you only, have I sinned
and done what is evil in your sight,
so that you are proved right when you speak
and justified when you judge.
5Surely I have been a sinner from birth,

[m]21 Or *thought the 'I AM' was*
[n]23 Or *and to him who considers his way / I will show*

*Heading, *1* The Hebrew numeration of this psalm begins with the "superscription" in English; thus there is a two-verse discrepancy throughout the psalm.

†4 The Kethib form (הַרְבֵּה) is an infinitive, *to-be-many.*

°4 ק הרב

אִמִּי׃ הֵן־ אֱמֶת חָפַצְתָּ בַטֻּחוֹת
in-the-inner-parts you-desire truth surely (8) mother-of-me

וּבְסָתֻם חָכְמָה תוֹדִיעֵנִי׃ תְּחַטְּאֵנִי בְאֵזוֹב
with-hyssop you-cleanse-me (9) you-teach-me wisdom and-in-place-being-inmost

וְאֶטְהָר תְּכַבְּסֵנִי וּמִשֶּׁלֶג אַלְבִּין׃
I-will-be-white and-more-than-snow you-wash-me and-I-will-be-clean

תַּשְׁמִיעֵנִי שָׂשׂוֹן וְשִׂמְחָה תָּגֵלְנָה עֲצָמוֹת דִּכִּיתָ׃
you-crushed bones let-them-rejoice and-gladness joy you-let-hear-me (10)

הַסְתֵּר פָּנֶיךָ מֵחֲטָאָי וְכָל־ עֲוֺנֹתַי מְחֵה׃
blot-out! iniquities-of-me and-all-of from-sins-of-me faces-of-you hide! (11)

לֵב טָהוֹר בְּרָא־ לִי אֱלֹהִים וְרוּחַ נָכוֹן חַדֵּשׁ
renew! being-steadfast and-spirit God in-me create! pure heart (12)

בְּקִרְבִּי׃ אַל־ תַּשְׁלִיכֵנִי מִלְּפָנֶיךָ וְרוּחַ
or-Spirit-of from-in-presences-of-you you-cast-me not (13) in-inside-of-me

קָדְשְׁךָ אַל־ תִּקַּח מִמֶּנִּי׃ הָשִׁיבָה לִּי שְׂשׂוֹן
joy-of to-me restore! (14) from-me you-take not Holiness-of-you

יִשְׁעֶךָ וְרוּחַ נְדִיבָה תִסְמְכֵנִי׃
you-sustain-me willing and-spirit salvation-of-you

אֲלַמְּדָה פֹשְׁעִים דְּרָכֶיךָ וְחַטָּאִים אֵלֶיךָ
to-you and-sinners ways-of-you ones-transgressing I-will-teach (15)

יָשׁוּבוּ׃ הַצִּילֵנִי מִדָּמִים ׀ אֱלֹהִים אֱלֹהֵי תְּשׁוּעָתִי
salvation-of-me God-of God from-bloodguilts save-me! (16) they-will-turn-back

תְּרַנֵּן לְשׁוֹנִי צִדְקָתֶךָ׃ אֲדֹנָי שְׂפָתַי תִּפְתָּח
you-open lips-of-me Lord (17) righteousness-of-you tongue-of-me she-will-sing

וּפִי יַגִּיד תְּהִלָּתֶךָ׃ כִּי ׀ לֹא־ תַחְפֹּץ
you-delight-in not for (18) praise-of-you he-will-declare and-mouth-of-me

זֶבַח וְאֶתֵּנָה עוֹלָה לֹא תִרְצֶה׃
you-take-pleasure-in not burnt-offering or-I-would-bring sacrifice

זִבְחֵי אֱלֹהִים רוּחַ נִשְׁבָּרָה לֵב־ נִשְׁבָּר וְנִדְכֶּה
and-being-contrite being-broken heart being-broken spirit God sacrifices-of (19)

אֱלֹהִים לֹא תִבְזֶה׃ הֵיטִיבָה בִרְצוֹנְךָ אֶת־ צִיּוֹן
Zion *** in-pleasure-of-you make-prosper! (20) you-will-despise not God

תִּבְנֶה חוֹמוֹת יְרוּשָׁלִָם׃ אָז תַּחְפֹּץ זִבְחֵי־
sacrifices-of you-will-delight-in then (21) Jerusalem walls-of you-build-up

צֶדֶק עוֹלָה וְכָלִיל אָז יַעֲלוּ עַל־
on they-will-offer then and-whole-offering burnt-offering righteous

מִזְבַּחֲךָ פָרִים׃ לַמְנַצֵּחַ מַשְׂכִּיל לְדָוִד׃ בְּבוֹא ׀
when-to-go (2) of-David maskil for-the-one-directing *(52:1) bulls altar-of-you

sinful from the time my
mother conceived me.
6 Surely you desire truth in the
inner parts[o];
you teach[p] me wisdom in
the inmost place.
7 Cleanse me with hyssop, and I
will be clean;
wash me, and I will be
whiter than snow.
8 Let me hear joy and gladness;
let the bones you have
crushed rejoice.
9 Hide your face from my sins
and blot out all my iniquity.
10 Create in me a pure heart, O
God,
and renew a steadfast spirit
within me.
11 Do not cast me from your
presence
or take your Holy Spirit
from me.
12 Restore to me the joy of your
salvation
and grant me a willing
spirit, to sustain me.
13 Then I will teach transgressors
your ways,
and sinners will turn back
to you.
14 Save me from bloodguilt, O
God,
the God who saves me,
and my tongue will sing of
your righteousness.
15 O Lord, open my lips,
and my mouth will declare
your praise.
16 You do not delight in sacrifice,
or I would bring it;
you do not take pleasure in
burnt offerings.
17 The sacrifices of God are[q] a
broken spirit;
a broken and contrite heart,
O God, you will not despise.
18 In your good pleasure make
Zion prosper;
build up the walls of
Jerusalem.
19 Then there will be righteous
sacrifices,
whole burnt offerings to
delight you;
then bulls will be offered on
your altar.

**Psalm 52**

For the director of music. A *maskil*[r] of

o6 The meaning of the Hebrew for this phrase is uncertain.
p6 Or *you desired ... ; / you taught*
q17 Or *My sacrifice, O God, is*
rTitle: Probably a literary or musical term

*Heading, *1* See the note on page 401.

דּוֹאֵג הָאֲדֹמִי וַיַּגֵּד לְשָׁאוּל וַיֹּאמֶר לוֹ בָּא דָוִד
David he-went to-him and-he-said to-Saul and-he-told the-Edomite Doeg

אֶל־ בֵּית אֲחִימֶלֶךְ׃ מַה־ תִּתְהַלֵּל בְּרָעָה הַגִּבּוֹר חֶסֶד
disgrace-of the-mighty-man of-evil you-boast why? (3) Ahimelech house-of to

אֵל כָּל־ הַיּוֹם׃ הַוּוֹת תַּחְשֹׁב לְשׁוֹנֶךָ כְּתַעַר
like-razor tongue-of-you she-plots destructions (4) the-day all-of God

מְלֻטָּשׁ עֹשֵׂה רְמִיָּה׃ אָהַבְתָּ רָּע מִטּוֹב
rather-than-good evil you-love (5) deceit one-practicing-of being-sharpened

שֶׁקֶר ׀ מִדַּבֵּר צֶדֶק סֶלָה׃ אָהַבְתָּ כָל־ דִּבְרֵי־
words-of all-of you-love (6) selah truth rather-than-to-speak falsehood

בָלַע לְשׁוֹן מִרְמָה׃ גַּם־ אֵל יִתָּצְךָ לָנֶצַח
to-everlasting he-will-bring-down-you God surely (7) deceit tongue-of harmful

יַחְתְּךָ וְיִסָּחֲךָ מֵאֹהֶל וְשֵׁרֶשְׁךָ
and-he-will-uproot-you from-tent and-he-will-tear-you he-will-snatch-up-you

מֵאֶרֶץ חַיִּים סֶלָה׃ וְיִרְאוּ צַדִּיקִים
righteous-ones then-they-will-see (8) selah living-ones from-land-of

וְיִירָאוּ וְעָלָיו יִשְׂחָקוּ׃ הִנֵּה הַגֶּבֶר לֹא יָשִׂים
he-made not the-man see! (9) they-will-laugh and-at-him and-they-will-fear

אֱלֹהִים מָעוּזּוֹ וַיִּבְטַח בְּרֹב עָשְׁרוֹ
wealth-of-him in-greatness-of but-he-trusted stronghold-of-him God

יָעֹז בְּהַוָּתוֹ׃ וַאֲנִי ׀ כְּזַיִת רַעֲנָן
flourishing like-olive-tree but-I (10) by-destruction-of-him he-grew-strong

בְּבֵית אֱלֹהִים בָּטַחְתִּי בְחֶסֶד־ אֱלֹהִים עוֹלָם וָעֶד׃
and-ever forever God in-unfailing-love-of I-trust God in-house-of

אוֹדְךָ לְעוֹלָם כִּי עָשִׂיתָ וַאֲקַוֶּה שִׁמְךָ
name-of-you and-I-will-hope-in you-did for to-forever I-will-praise-you (11)

כִּי־ טוֹב נֶגֶד חֲסִידֶיךָ׃ לַמְנַצֵּחַ
for-the-one-directing †(53:1) saints-of-you in-presence-of good for

עַל־ מָחֲלַת מַשְׂכִּיל לְדָוִד׃ אָמַר נָבָל בְּלִבּוֹ
in-heart-of-him fool he-says (2) of-David maskil mahalath according-to

אֵין אֱלֹהִים הִשְׁחִיתוּ וְהִתְעִיבוּ עָוֶל אֵין
there-is-no evil-way and-they-are-vile they-are-corrupt God there-is-no

עֹשֵׂה־ טוֹב׃ אֱלֹהִים מִשָּׁמַיִם הִשְׁקִיף עַל־ בְּנֵי אָדָם לִרְאוֹת
to-see man sons-of on he-looks from-heavens God (3) good one-doing-of

הֲיֵשׁ מַשְׂכִּיל דֹּרֵשׁ אֶת־ אֱלֹהִים׃ כֻּלּוֹ
all-of-him (4) God *** one-seeking one-understanding if-there-is

סָג יַחְדָּו נֶאֱלָחוּ אֵין עֹשֵׂה־ טוֹב
good one-doing-of there-is-no they-became-corrupt together he-turned-away

David. When Doeg the Edomite had gone to Saul and told him: "David has gone to the house of Ahimelech."

1 Why do you boast of evil, you mighty man?
Why do you boast all day long,
you who are a disgrace in the eyes of God?
2 Your tongue plots destruction;
it is like a sharpened razor,
you who practice deceit.
3 You love evil rather than good,
falsehood rather than speaking the truth. *Selah*
4 You love every harmful word,
O you deceitful tongue!

5 Surely God will bring you down to everlasting ruin:
He will snatch you up and tear you from your tent;
he will uproot you from the land of the living. *Selah*
6 The righteous will see and fear;
they will laugh at him, saying,
7 "Here now is the man
who did not make God his stronghold
but trusted in his great wealth
and grew strong by destroying others!"

8 But I am like an olive tree
flourishing in the house of God;
I trust in God's unfailing love
for ever and ever.
9 I will praise you forever for what you have done;
in your name I will hope,
for your name is good.
I will praise you in the presence of your saints.

## Psalm 53

For the director of music. According to *mahalath*.[s] A *maskil*[t] of David.

1 The fool says in his heart,
"There is no God."
They are corrupt, and their ways are vile;
there is no one who does good.
2 God looks down from heaven
on the sons of men
to see if there are any who understand,
any who seek God.
3 Everyone has turned away,
they have together become corrupt;
there is no one who does good,

[s]Title: Probably a musical term
[t]Title: Probably a literary or musical term

*See the note on page 401.
†Heading, *1* See the note on page 349.

אֵין גַּם־אֶחָד׃ הֲלֹא יָדְעוּ פֹּעֲלֵי אָוֶן אֹכְלֵי
ones-devouring-of evil ones-doing-of will-they-learn never? (5) one even not

עַמִּי אָכְלוּ לֶחֶם אֱלֹהִים לֹא קָרָאוּ׃ שָׁם ׀ פָּחֲדוּ־
they-dreaded there (6) they-call-on not God bread they-eat people-of-me

פַחַד לֹא־הָיָה פָחַד כִּי־אֱלֹהִים פִּזַּר עַצְמוֹת חֹנָךְ
one-attacking-you bones-of he-scattered God for dread he-was not dread

הֱבִשֹׁתָה כִּי־אֱלֹהִים מְאָסָם׃ מִי יִתֵּן מִצִּיּוֹן
from-Zion he-would-bring who? (7) he-despised-them God for you-put-to-shame

יְשֻׁעוֹת יִשְׂרָאֵל בְּשׁוּב אֱלֹהִים שְׁבוּת עַמּוֹ
people-of-him fortune-of God when-to-restore Israel salvations-of

יָגֵל יַעֲקֹב יִשְׂמַח יִשְׂרָאֵל׃ לַמְנַצֵּחַ
for-the-one-directing †(54:1) Israel let-him-be-glad Jacob let-him-rejoice

בִּנְגִינֹת מַשְׂכִּיל לְדָוִד׃ בְּבֹא הַזִּיפִים
the-Ziphites when-to-go (2) of-David maskil with-stringed-instruments

וַיֹּאמְרוּ לְשָׁאוּל הֲלֹא דָוִד מִסְתַּתֵּר עִמָּנוּ׃ אֱלֹהִים בְּשִׁמְךָ
by-name-of-you God (3) among-us hiding David not? to-Saul and-they-said

הוֹשִׁיעֵנִי וּבִגְבוּרָתְךָ תְדִינֵנִי׃ אֱלֹהִים שְׁמַע תְּפִלָּתִי
prayer-of-me hear! God (4) you-vindicate-me and-by-might-of-you save-me!

הַאֲזִינָה לְאִמְרֵי־פִי׃ כִּי זָרִים ׀ קָמוּ
they-attack ones-being-strangers for (5) mouth-of-me to-words-of listen!

עָלַי וְעָרִיצִים בִּקְשׁוּ נַפְשִׁי לֹא שָׂמוּ אֱלֹהִים
God they-regard not life-of-me they-seek and-ruthless-men against-me

לְנֶגְדָּם סֶלָה׃ הִנֵּה אֱלֹהִים עֹזֵר לִי אֲדֹנָי בְּסֹמְכֵי
among-ones-sustaining-of Lord to-me one-helping God see! (6) selah at-before-them

נַפְשִׁי׃ יָשׁוּב° הָרַע לְשֹׁרְרָי בַּאֲמִתְּךָ
in-faithfulness-of-you on-slanderers-of-me the-evil let-him-recoil (7) self-of-me

הַצְמִיתֵם׃ בִּנְדָבָה אֶזְבְּחָה־לָּךְ אוֹדֶה
I-will-praise to-you I-will-sacrifice with-freewill-offering (8) destroy-them!

שִׁמְךָ יְהוָה כִּי־טוֹב׃ כִּי מִכָּל־צָרָה הִצִּילָנִי
he-delivered-me trouble from-all-of for (9) good for Yahweh name-of-you

וּבְאֹיְבַי רָאֲתָה עֵינִי׃ לַמְנַצֵּחַ
for-the-one-directing *(55:1) eye-of-me she-looked and-on-ones-being-foes-of-me

בִּנְגִינֹת מַשְׂכִּיל לְדָוִד׃ הַאֲזִינָה אֱלֹהִים תְּפִלָּתִי
prayer-of-me God listen! (2) of-David maskil with-stringed-instruments

וְאַל־תִּתְעַלַּם מִתְּחִנָּתִי׃ הַקְשִׁיבָה לִּי וַעֲנֵנִי אָרִיד
I-am-troubled and-answer-me! to-me hear! (3) to-plea-of-me you-ignore and-not

בְּשִׂיחִי וְאָהִימָה׃ מִקּוֹל אוֹיֵב
one-being-enemy at-voice-of (4) and-I-am-distraught by-thought-of-me

not even one.
[4]Will the evildoers never
learn—
those who devour my
people as men eat bread
and who do not call on
God?
[5]There they were, overwhelmed
with dread,
where there was nothing to
dread.
God scattered the bones of
those who attacked you;
you put them to shame, for
God despised them.
[6]Oh, that salvation for Israel
would come out of Zion!
When God restores the
fortunes of his people,
let Jacob rejoice and Israel
be glad!

**Psalm 54**

For the director of music. With stringed instruments. A *maskil*[u] of David. When the Ziphites had gone to Saul and said, "Is not David hiding among us?"

[1]Save me, O God, by your
name;
vindicate me by your might.
[2]Hear my prayer, O God;
listen to the words of my
mouth.
[3]Strangers are attacking me;
ruthless men seek my life—
men without regard for God.
*Selah*
[4]Surely God is my help;
the Lord is the one who
sustains me.
[5]Let evil recoil on those who
slander me;
in your faithfulness destroy
them.
[6]I will sacrifice a freewill
offering to you;
I will praise your name, O
LORD,
for it is good.
[7]For he has delivered me from
all my troubles,
and my eyes have looked in
triumph on my foes.

**Psalm 55**

For the director of music. With stringed instruments. A *maskil*[u] of David.

[1]Listen to my prayer, O God,
do not ignore my plea;
[2] hear me and answer me.
My thoughts trouble me and I
am distraught
[3] at the voice of the enemy,

[u]Title: Probably a literary or musical term

*Heading, *1* See the note on page 349.
†*1* See the note on page 401.
°7 ק ישיב

מִפְּנֵי עָקַת רָשָׁע כִּי־ יָמִיטוּ עָלַי אָוֶן וּבְאַף
and-in-anger suffering upon-me they-bring-down for wicked stare-of at-faces-of

יִשְׂטְמוּנִי׃ לִבִּי יָחִיל בְּקִרְבִּי וְאֵימוֹת
and-terrors-of at-within-me he-is-in-anguish heart-of-me (5) they-revile-me

מָוֶת נָפְלוּ עָלָי׃ יִרְאָה וָרַעַד יָבֹא בִי
against-me he-beset and-trembling fear (6) on-me they-assail death

וַתְּכַסֵּנִי פַּלָּצוּת׃ וָאֹמַר מִי־ יִתֶּן־ לִּי
to-me he-would-allow who? and-I-said (7) horror and-she-overwhelmed-me

אֵבֶר כַּיּוֹנָה אָעוּפָה וְאֶשְׁכֹּנָה׃ הִנֵּה אַרְחִיק
I-would-be-far see! (8) and-I-would-rest I-would-fly-away like-the-dove wing

נְדֹד אָלִין בַּמִּדְבָּר סֶלָה׃ אָחִישָׁה מִפְלָט
place-of-shelter I-would-hurry (9) selah in-the-desert I-would-stay to-flee

לִי מֵרוּחַ סֹעָה מִסָּעַר׃ בַּלַּע אֲדֹנָי פַּלַּג
confound! Lord confuse! (10) from-storm being-tempestuous from-wind to-me

לְשׁוֹנָם כִּי־ רָאִיתִי חָמָס וְרִיב בָּעִיר׃ יוֹמָם
by-day (11) in-the-city and-strife violence I-see for speech-of-them

וָלַיְלָה יְסוֹבְבֻהָ עַל־ חוֹמֹתֶיהָ וְאָוֶן וְעָמָל
and-abuse and-malice walls-of-her on they-prowl-about-her and-night

בְּקִרְבָּהּ׃ הַוּוֹת בְּקִרְבָּהּ וְלֹא־ יָמִישׁ
he-leaves and-never at-within-her destructive-forces (12) at-within-her

מֵרְחֹבָהּ תֹּךְ וּמִרְמָה׃ כִּי לֹא־ אוֹיֵב יְחָרְפֵנִי
he-insults-me one-being-enemy †not for (13) and-lie threat from-street-of-her

וְאֶשָּׂא לֹא־ מְשַׂנְאִי עָלַי הִגְדִּיל וְאֶסָּתֵר מִמֶּנּוּ׃
from-him and-I-hide he-raises against-me one-being-foe-of-me †not and-I-endure

וְאַתָּה אֱנוֹשׁ כְּעֶרְכִּי אַלּוּפִי וּמְיֻדָּעִי׃
and-one-being-friend-of-me companion-of-me as-order-of-me man but-you (14)

אֲשֶׁר יַחְדָּו נַמְתִּיק סוֹד בְּבֵית אֱלֹהִים נְהַלֵּךְ
we-walked God at-house-of fellowship we-made-sweet together who (15)

בְּרָגֶשׁ׃ יַשִּׁימָוֶת ׀ עָלֵימוֹ יֵרְדוּ שְׁאוֹל חַיִּים
alive-ones Sheol let-them-go-down to-them death let-him-take (16) with-throng

כִּי־רָעוֹת בִּמְגוּרָם בְּקִרְבָּם׃ אֲנִי אֶל־אֱלֹהִים אֶקְרָא וַיהוָה
and-Yahweh I-call God to I (17) in-among-them in-lodging-of-them evils for

יוֹשִׁיעֵנִי׃ עֶרֶב וָבֹקֶר וְצָהֳרַיִם אָשִׂיחָה וְאֶהֱמֶה
and-I-tell-distress I-cry-out and-noon and-morning evening (18) he-saves-me

וַיִּשְׁמַע קוֹלִי׃ פָּדָה בְשָׁלוֹם נַפְשִׁי מִקְּרָב־
from-battle self-of-me in-wholeness he-ransoms (19) voice-of-me and-he-hears

לִי כִּי־ בְרַבִּים הָיוּ עִמָּדִי׃ יִשְׁמַע ׀ אֵל ׀
God he-will-hear (20) opposite-me they-are among-many though against-me

at the stares of the wicked;
for they bring down suffering upon me
and revile me in their anger.

[4]My heart is in anguish within me;
the terrors of death assail me.
[5]Fear and trembling have beset me;
horror has overwhelmed me.
[6]I said, "Oh, that I had the wings of a dove!
I would fly away and be at rest—
[7]I would flee far away
and stay in the desert; *Selah*
[8]I would hurry to my place of shelter,
far from the tempest and storm."

[9]Confuse the wicked, O Lord, confound their speech,
for I see violence and strife in the city.
[10]Day and night they prowl about on its walls;
malice and abuse are within it.
[11]Destructive forces are at work in the city;
threats and lies never leave its streets.
[12]If an enemy were insulting me,
I could endure it;
if a foe were raising himself against me,
I could hide from him.
[13]But it is you, a man like myself,
my companion, my close friend,
[14]with whom I once enjoyed sweet fellowship
as we walked with the throng at the house of God.

[15]Let death take my enemies by surprise;
let them go down alive to the grave,[v]
for evil finds lodging among them.
[16]But I call to God,
and the LORD saves me.
[17]Evening, morning and noon
I cry out in distress,
and he hears my voice.
[18]He ransoms me unharmed
from the battle waged against me,
even though many oppose me.

[v]15 Hebrew *Sheol*

*See the note on page 349.

†13 The NIV points this word as לֻא, *if.*

°16 ישי מות ק

וְיַעֲנֵם וְיֹשֵׁב קֶדֶם סֶלָה אֲשֶׁר אֵין
never who selah forever even-one-being-enthroned and-he-will-afflict-them

חֲלִיפוֹת לָמוֹ וְלֹא יָרְאוּ אֱלֹהִים׃ (21) שָׁלַח יָדָיו
hands-of-him he-sends (21) God they-fear and-not to-them changes

בִּשְׁלֹמָיו חִלֵּל בְּרִיתוֹ׃ (22) חָלְקוּ ׀
they-are-smooth (22) covenant-of-him he-violates against-friends-of-him

מַחְמָאֹת פִּיו וּקְרָב־ לִבּוֹ רַכּוּ
they-are-soothing heart-of-him yet-war-of mouth-of-him butters-of

דְבָרָיו מִשֶּׁמֶן וְהֵמָּה פְתִחוֹת׃ (23) הַשְׁלֵךְ עַל־ יְהוָה ׀
Yahweh on cast! (23) drawn-swords yet-they more-than-oil words-of-him

יְהָבְךָ וְהוּא יְכַלְכְּלֶךָ לֹא־ יִתֵּן לְעוֹלָם מוֹט
fall to-forever he-will-let not he-will-sustain-you and-he care-of-you

לַצַּדִּיק׃ (24) וְאַתָּה אֱלֹהִים ׀ תּוֹרִדֵם ׀ לִבְאֵר
into-pit-of you-will-bring-down-them God but-you (24) of-the-righteous

שַׁחַת אַנְשֵׁי דָמִים וּמִרְמָה לֹא־ יֶחֱצוּ יְמֵיהֶם
days-of-them they-will-live-half not and-deceit bloods men-of corruption

וַאֲנִי אֶבְטַח־ בָּךְ׃ *(56:1) לַמְנַצֵּחַ ׀ עַל־ יוֹנַת אֵלֶם†
†silence-of dove-of to for-the-one-directing *(56:1) in-you I-will-trust but-I

רְחֹקִים לְדָוִד מִכְתָּם בֶּאֱחֹז אֹתוֹ פְלִשְׁתִּים בְּגַת׃
in-Gath Philistines him when-to-seize miktam of-David distant-ones

(2) חָנֵּנִי אֱלֹהִים כִּי־ שְׁאָפַנִי אֱנוֹשׁ כָּל־ הַיּוֹם לֹחֵם
one-attacking the-day all-of man he-pursues-me for God be-merciful-to-me! (2)

יִלְחָצֵנִי׃ (3) שָׁאֲפוּ שׁוֹרְרַי כָּל־ הַיּוֹם כִּי־ רַבִּים
many indeed the-day all-of ones-slandering-me they-pursue (3) he-oppresses-me

לֹחֲמִים לִי מָרוֹם׃ (4) יוֹם אִירָא אֲנִי אֵלֶיךָ אֶבְטָח׃
I-trust in-you I I-am-afraid day (4) pride against-me ones-attacking

(5) בֵּאלֹהִים אֲהַלֵּל דְּבָרוֹ בֵּאלֹהִים בָּטַחְתִּי לֹא אִירָא מַה־
what? I-will-be-afraid not I-trust in-God word-of-him I-praise in-God (5)

יַּעֲשֶׂה בָשָׂר לִי׃ (6) כָּל־ הַיּוֹם דְּבָרַי יְעַצֵּבוּ עָלַי
against-me they-twist words-of-me the-day all-of (6) to-me mortal can-he-do

כָּל־ מַחְשְׁבֹתָם לָרָע׃ (7) יָגוּרוּ ׀ יִצְפּוֹנוּ הֵמָּה עֲקֵבַי
steps-of-me they they-lurk they-conspire (7) for-harm plots-of-them all-of

יִשְׁמֹרוּ כַּאֲשֶׁר קִוּוּ נַפְשִׁי׃ (8) עַל־ אָוֶן
no-account on (8) life-of-me they-are-eager-for as-that they-watch

פַּלֶּט־ לָמוֹ בְּאַף עַמִּים ׀ הוֹרֵד אֱלֹהִים׃ (9) נֹדִי
lament-of-me (9) God bring-down! nations in-anger to-them let-escape!

סָפַרְתָּה אַתָּה שִׂימָה דִמְעָתִי בְנֹאדֶךָ הֲלֹא בְּסִפְרָתֶךָ׃
in-record-of-you not? in-wineskin-of-you tear-of-me put! you you-record

19God, who is enthroned
forever,
will hear them and afflict
them— *Selah*
men who never change their
ways
and have no fear of God.

20My companion attacks his
friends;
he violates his covenant.
21His speech is smooth as butter,
yet war is in his heart;
his words are more soothing
than oil,
yet they are drawn swords.

22Cast your cares on the LORD
and he will sustain you;
he will never let the
righteous fall.
23But you, O God, will bring
down the wicked
into the pit of corruption;
bloodthirsty and deceitful men
will not live out half their
days.

But as for me, I trust in you.

**Psalm 56**

For the director of music. To the tune of, "A Dove on Distant Oaks." Of David. A *miktam*.[w] When the Philistines had seized him in Gath.

1Be merciful to me, O God, for
men hotly pursue me;
all day long they press their
attack.
2My slanderers pursue me all
day long;
many are attacking me in
their pride.

3When I am afraid,
I will trust in you.
4In God, whose word I praise,
in God I trust; I will not be
afraid.
What can mortal man do to
me?

5All day long they twist my
words;
they are always plotting to
harm me.
6They conspire, they lurk,
they watch my steps,
eager to take my life.

7On no account let them
escape;
in your anger, O God, bring
down the nations.
8Record my lament;
list my tears on your
scroll[x]—
are they not in your record?

[w]Title: Probably a literary or musical term
[x]8 Or *I put my tears in your wineskin*

*Heading, *1* See the note on page 349.
†*1* The NIV repoints this word as אֵלִם, *oaks*.

°7 ק יִצְפֹּנוּ

אָז יָשׁוּבוּ אוֹיְבַי אָחוֹר בְּיוֹם אֶקְרָא זֶה־

this I-call on-day back ones-being-enemies-of-me they-will-turn then (10)

יָדַעְתִּי כִּי־אֱלֹהִים לִי׃ בֵּאלֹהִים אֲהַלֵּל דָּבָר בַּיהוָה אֲהַלֵּל

I-praise in-Yahweh word I-praise in-God (1) for-me God that I-will-know

דָּבָר׃ בֵּאלֹהִים בָּטַחְתִּי לֹא אִירָא מַה־ יַּעֲשֶׂה אָדָם לִי׃

to-me man can-he-do what? I-will-be-afraid not I-trust in-God (12) word

עָלַי אֱלֹהִים נְדָרֶיךָ אֲשַׁלֵּם תּוֹדֹת לָךְ׃

to-you thank-offerings I-will-present vows-of-you God upon-me (13)

כִּי הִצַּלְתָּ נַפְשִׁי מִמָּוֶת הֲלֹא רַגְלַי מִדֶּחִי

from-stumbling feet-of-me not? from-death soul-of-me you-delivered for (14)

לְהִתְהַלֵּךְ לִפְנֵי אֱלֹהִים בְּאוֹר הַחַיִּים׃ לַמְנַצֵּחַ אַל־

not for-the-one-directing *(57:1) the-lives in-light-of God before to-walk

תַּשְׁחֵת לְדָוִד מִכְתָּם בְּבָרְחוֹ מִפְּנֵי־ שָׁאוּל בַּמְּעָרָה׃

into-the-cave Saul from-before when-to-flee-him miktam of-David you-destroy

חָנֵּנִי אֱלֹהִים | חָנֵּנִי כִּי בְךָ חָסָיָה

she-takes-refuge in-you for have-mercy-on-me! God have-mercy-on-me! (2)

נַפְשִׁי וּבְצֵל־ כְּנָפֶיךָ אֶחְסֶה עַד יַעֲבֹר

he-passed until I-will-take-refuge wings-of-you and-in-shadow-of soul-of-me

הַוּוֹת׃ אֶקְרָא לֵאלֹהִים עֶלְיוֹן לָאֵל גֹּמֵר עָלָי׃

for-me one-fulfilling to-God Most-High to-God I-cry-out (3) disasters

יִשְׁלַח מִשָּׁמַיִם | וְיוֹשִׁיעֵנִי חֵרֵף שֹׁאֲפִי סֶלָה

selah one-pursuing-me he-rebukes and-he-saves-me from-heavens he-sends (4)

יִשְׁלַח אֱלֹהִים חַסְדּוֹ וַאֲמִתּוֹ׃ נַפְשִׁי | בְּתוֹךְ

in-midst-of self-of-me (5) and-faithfulness-of-him love-of-him God he-sends

לְבָאִם אֶשְׁכְּבָה לֹהֲטִים בְּנֵי־ אָדָם שִׁנֵּיהֶם חֲנִית וְחִצִּים

and-arrows spear teeth-of-them man sons-of ones-being-ravenous I-lie lions

וּלְשׁוֹנָם חֶרֶב חַדָּה׃ רוּמָה עַל־ הַשָּׁמַיִם אֱלֹהִים עַל

over God the-heavens above be-exalted! (6) sharp sword and-tongue-of-them

כָּל־ הָאָרֶץ כְּבוֹדֶךָ׃ רֶשֶׁת | הֵכִינוּ לִפְעָמַי כָּפַף

he-was-bowed for-feet-of-me they-spread net (7) glory-of-you the-earth all-of

נַפְשִׁי כָּרוּ לְפָנַי שִׁיחָה נָפְלוּ בְתוֹכָהּ סֶלָה׃

selah into-inside-of-her they-fell pit before-me they-dug self-of-me

נָכוֹן לִבִּי אֱלֹהִים נָכוֹן לִבִּי אָשִׁירָה

I-will-sing heart-of-me he-is-steadfast God heart-of-me he-is-steadfast (8)

וַאֲזַמֵּרָה׃ עוּרָה כְבוֹדִי עוּרָה הַנֵּבֶל וְכִנּוֹר

and-lyre the-harp awake! soul-of-me awake! (9) and-I-will-make-music

אָעִירָה שָּׁחַר׃ אוֹדְךָ בָעַמִּים | אֲדֹנָי

Lord among-the-nations I-will-praise-you (10) dawn I-will-awaken

[9]Then my enemies will turn back
when I call for help.
By this I will know that God is for me.
[10]In God, whose word I praise,
in the LORD, whose word I praise—
[11]in God I trust; I will not be afraid.
What can man do to me?

[12]I am under vows to you, O God;
I will present my thank offerings to you.
[13]For you have delivered my soul from death
and my feet from stumbling,
that I may walk before God
in the light of life.[y]

### Psalm 57

For the director of music. ⌊To the tune of⌋ "Do Not Destroy." Of David. A *miktam*.[z] When he had fled from Saul into the cave.

[1]Have mercy on me, O God, have mercy on me,
for in you my soul takes refuge.
I will take refuge in the shadow of your wings
until the disaster has passed.

[2]I cry out to God Most High,
to God, who fulfills ⌊his purpose⌋ for me.
[3]He sends from heaven and saves me,
rebuking those who hotly pursue me; *Selah*
God sends his love and his faithfulness.

[4]I am in the midst of lions;
I lie among ravenous beasts—
men whose teeth are spears and arrows,
whose tongues are sharp swords.

[5]Be exalted, O God, above the heavens;
let your glory be over all the earth.

[6]They spread a net for my feet—
I was bowed down in distress.
They dug a pit in my path—
but they have fallen into it themselves. *Selah*

[7]My heart is steadfast, O God,
my heart is steadfast;
I will sing and make music.
[8]Awake, my soul!
Awake, harp and lyre!
I will awaken the dawn.

[9]I will praise you, O Lord, among the nations;

[y]13 Or *the land of the living*
[z]Title: Probably a literary or musical term

*Heading, *1* See the note on page 349.

אֲזַמֶּרְךָ בַּל־אֻמִּים׃† כִּי־גָדֹל עַד־שָׁמַיִם חַסְדֶּךָ
love-of-you heavens to great for (11) †among-the-peoples I-will-sing-of-you

וְעַד־שְׁחָקִים אֲמִתֶּךָ׃ רוּמָה עַל־שָׁמַיִם אֱלֹהִים עַל
over God heavens above be-exalted! (12) faithfulness-of-you skies and-to

כָּל־הָאָרֶץ כְּבוֹדֶךָ׃ לַמְנַצֵּחַ אַל־תַּשְׁחֵת
you-destroy not for-the-one-directing *(58:1) glory-of-you the-earth all-of

לְדָוִד מִכְתָּם׃ הַאֻמְנָם אֵלֶם†† צֶדֶק תְּדַבֵּרוּן מֵישָׁרִים תִּשְׁפְּטוּ
you-judge ones-upright you-speak justly ††silence indeed? (2) miktam of-David

בְּנֵי אָדָם׃ אַף־בְּלֵב עוֹלֹת תִּפְעָלוּן בָּאָרֶץ חֲמַס
violence-of on-the-earth you-devise injustices in-heart no (3) man sons-of

יְדֵיכֶם תְּפַלֵּסוּן׃ זֹרוּ רְשָׁעִים מֵרָחֶם
from-birth wicked-ones they-go-astray (4) you-mete-out hands-of-you

תָּעוּ מִבֶּטֶן דֹּבְרֵי כָזָב׃ חֲמַת־לָמוֹ
of-them venom-of (5) lie ones-speaking-of from-womb they-are-wayward

כִּדְמוּת חֲמַת־נָחָשׁ כְּמוֹ־פֶתֶן חֵרֵשׁ יַאְטֵם אָזְנוֹ׃
ear-of-him he-stopped deaf cobra like snake venom-of as-likeness-of

אֲשֶׁר לֹא־יִשְׁמַע לְקוֹל מְלַחֲשִׁים חוֹבֵר חֲבָרִים
enchantments one-enchanting ones-charming to-tune-of he-heeds not that (6)

מְחֻכָּם׃ אֱלֹהִים הֲרָס־שִׁנֵּימוֹ בְּפִימוֹ מַלְתְּעוֹת כְּפִירִים
lions fangs-of in-mouth-of-them teeth-of-them break! God (7) being-skillful

נְתֹץ ׀ יְהוָה׃ יִמָּאֲסוּ כְמוֹ־מַיִם יִתְהַלְּכוּ־לָמוֹ
of-themselves they-flow-away waters like let-them-vanish (8) Yahweh tear-out!

יִדְרֹךְ °חִצָּו כְּמוֹ יִתְמֹלָלוּ׃ כְּמוֹ שַׁבְּלוּל תֶּמֶס
melting-away slug like (9) let-them-be-blunted so arrows-of-him he-draws-bow

יַהֲלֹךְ נֵפֶל אֵשֶׁת בַּל־חָזוּ שָׁמֶשׁ׃ בְּטֶרֶם
at-before (10) sun may-they-see not woman-of stillborn-child-of he-moves-along

יָבִינוּ סִּירֹתֵיכֶם אָטָד כְּמוֹ־חַי כְּמוֹ־חָרוֹן יִשְׂעָרֶנּוּ׃
he-will-sweep-away-him dry whether green whether thorn pots-of-you they-feel

יִשְׂמַח צַדִּיק כִּי־חָזָה נָקָם פְּעָמָיו יִרְחַץ
he-bathes feet-of-him vengeance he-sees when righteous he-will-be-glad (11)

בְּדַם הָרָשָׁע׃ וְיֹאמַר אָדָם אַךְ־פְּרִי לַצַּדִּיק
for-the-righteous reward surely man then-he-will-say (12) the-wicked in-blood-of

אַךְ יֵשׁ־אֱלֹהִים שֹׁפְטִים בָּאָרֶץ׃ לַמְנַצֵּחַ
for-the-one-directing *(59:1) over-the-earth ones-judging God there-is surely

אַל־תַּשְׁחֵת לְדָוִד מִכְתָּם בִּשְׁלֹחַ שָׁאוּל וַיִּשְׁמְרוּ אֶת־
*** and-they-watched Saul when-to-send miktam of-David you-destroy not

הַבַּיִת לַהֲמִיתוֹ׃ הַצִּילֵנִי מֵאֹיְבַי ׀ אֱלֹהָי
God-of-me from-ones-being-enemies-of-me deliver-me! (2) to-kill-him the-house

I will sing of you among the peoples.
10For great is your love, reaching to the heavens;
your faithfulness reaches to the skies.
11Be exalted, O God, above the heavens;
let your glory be over all the earth.

### Psalm 58

For the director of music. ⌊To the tune of⌋ "Do Not Destroy." Of David. A *miktam*.[a]

1Do you rulers indeed speak justly?
Do you judge uprightly among men?
2No, in your heart you devise injustice,
and your hands mete out violence on the earth.
3Even from birth the wicked go astray;
from the womb they are wayward and speak lies.
4Their venom is like the venom of a snake,
like that of a cobra that has stopped its ears,
5that will not heed the tune of the charmer,
however skillful the enchanter may be.
6Break the teeth in their mouths, O God;
tear out, O LORD, the fangs of the lions!
7Let them vanish like water that flows away;
when they draw the bow, let their arrows be blunted.
8Like a slug melting away as it moves along,
like a stillborn child, may they not see the sun.
9Before your pots can feel ⌊the heat of⌋ the thorns—
whether they be green or dry—the wicked will be swept away.[b]
10The righteous will be glad when they are avenged,
when they bathe their feet in the blood of the wicked.
11Then men will say,
"Surely the righteous still are rewarded;
surely there is a God who judges the earth."

### Psalm 59

For the director of music. ⌊To the tune of⌋ "Do Not Destroy." Of David. A *miktam*.[c] When Saul had sent men to watch David's house in order to kill him.

[a]Title: Probably a literary or musical term
[b]9 The meaning of the Hebrew for this verse is uncertain.
[c]Title: Probably a literary or musical term

*Heading, *1* See the note on page 349.

†*10* Most mss read these two words as one (בְלָא׳).

††*2* The NIV reads this word as אֵלִם, *rams = leaders.*

°8 ק חציו

מִמִּתְקוֹמְמַי† תְּשַׂגְּבֵנִי׃ הַצִּילֵנִי מִפֹּעֲלֵי
from-ones-doing-of deliver-me! (3) you-protect-me from-ones-rising-up-against-me

אָוֶן וּמֵאַנְשֵׁי דָמִים הוֹשִׁיעֵנִי׃ כִּי הִנֵּה אָרְבוּ
they-lie-in-wait see! for (4) save-me! bloods and-from-men-of evil

לְנַפְשִׁי יָגוּרוּ עָלַי עַזִּים†† לֹא־ פִשְׁעִי וְלֹא־
and-no offense-of-me no fierce-men against-me they-conspire for-self-of-me

חַטָּאתִי יְהוָה׃ בְּלִי־ עָוֺן יְרוּצוּן וְיִכּוֹנָנוּ עוּרָה לִקְרָאתִי
to-help-me arise! and-they-are-ready they-attack wrong no (5) Yahweh sin-of-me

וּרְאֵה׃ וְאַתָּה יְהוָה־אֱלֹהִים צְבָאוֹת אֱלֹהֵי יִשְׂרָאֵל הָקִיצָה
rouse-yourself! Israel God-of Hosts God Yahweh and-you (6) and-look!

לִפְקֹד כָּל־ הַגּוֹיִם אַל־ תָּחֹן כָּל־ בֹּגְדֵי
ones-being-traitors-of all-of you-show-mercy not the-nations all-of to-punish

אָוֶן סֶלָה׃ יָשׁוּבוּ לָעֶרֶב יֶהֱמוּ כַכָּלֶב
like-the-dog they-snarl at-the-evening they-return (7) selah wickedness

וִיסוֹבְבוּ עִיר׃ הִנֵּה ׀ יַבִּיעוּן בְּפִיהֶם חֲרָבוֹת
swords from-mouth-of-them they-spew see! (8) city and-they-prowl-about

בְּשִׂפְתוֹתֵיהֶם כִּי־ מִי שֹׁמֵעַ׃ וְאַתָּה יְהוָה תִּשְׂחַק־
you-laugh Yahweh but-you (9) one-hearing who? that from-lips-of-them

לָמוֹ תִּלְעַג לְכָל־ גּוֹיִם׃ עֻזּוֹ אֵלֶיךָ אֶשְׁמֹרָה
I-watch for-you Strength-of-him (10) nations at-all-of you-scoff at-them

כִּי־אֱלֹהִים מִשְׂגַּבִּי׃ אֱלֹהֵי חַסְדּוֹ° יְקַדְּמֵנִי אֱלֹהִים
God he-will-go-before-me love-of-me God-of (11) fortress-of-me God for

יַרְאֵנִי בְשֹׁרְרָי׃ אַל־ תַּהַרְגֵם ׀ פֶּן־
or you-kill-them not (12) over-ones-slandering-me he-will-let-gloat-me

יִשְׁכְּחוּ עַמִּי הֲנִיעֵמוֹ בְחֵילְךָ
in-might-of-you make-wander-them! people-of-me they-will-forget

וְהוֹרִידֵמוֹ מָגִנֵּנוּ אֲדֹנָי׃ חַטַּאת־ פִּימוֹ דְּבַר־
word-of mouth-of-them sin-of (13) Lord shield-of-us and-bring-down-them!

שְׂפָתֵימוֹ וְיִלָּכְדוּ בִגְאוֹנָם וּמֵאָלָה וּמִכַּחַשׁ
and-for-lie and-for-curse in-pride-of-them and-let-them-be-caught lips-of-them

יְסַפֵּרוּ׃ כַּלֵּה בְחֵמָה כַּלֵּה וְאֵינֵמוֹ וְיֵדְעוּ
then-they-will-know and-no-more-they consume! in-wrath consume! (14) they-utter

כִּי־אֱלֹהִים מֹשֵׁל בְּיַעֲקֹב לְאַפְסֵי הָאָרֶץ סֶלָה׃ וְיָשֻׁבוּ
now-they-return (15) selah the-earth to-ends-of over-Jacob ruling God that

לָעֶרֶב יֶהֱמוּ כַכָּלֶב וִיסוֹבְבוּ עִיר׃ הֵמָּה
they (16) city and-they-prowl-about like-the-dog they-snarl at-the-evening

יְנוּעוּן° לֶאֱכֹל אִם־ לֹא יִשְׂבְּעוּ וַיָּלִינוּ׃
then-they-howl they-are-satisfied not if to-eat they-wander-about

1 Deliver me from my enemies, O God;
protect me from those who rise up against me.
2 Deliver me from evildoers
and save me from bloodthirsty men.
3 See how they lie in wait for me!
Fierce men conspire against me
for no offense or sin of mine, O LORD.
4 I have done no wrong, yet they are ready to attack me.
Arise to help me; look on my plight!
5 O LORD God Almighty, the God of Israel,
rouse yourself to punish all the nations;
show no mercy to wicked traitors. *Selah*

6 They return at evening,
snarling like dogs,
and prowl about the city.
7 See what they spew from their mouths—
they spew out swords from their lips,
and they say, "Who can hear us?"
8 But you, O LORD, laugh at them;
you scoff at all those nations.
9 O my Strength, I watch for you;
you, O God, are my fortress,
10 my loving God.

God will go before me
and will let me gloat over those who slander me.
11 But do not kill them, O Lord our shield,[d]
or my people will forget.
In your might make them wander about,
and bring them down.
12 For the sins of their mouths,
for the words of their lips,
let them be caught in their pride.
For the curses and lies they utter,
13 consume them in wrath,
consume them till they are no more.
Then it will be known to the ends of the earth
that God rules over Jacob. *Selah*

14 They return at evening,
snarling like dogs,
and prowl about the city.
15 They wander about for food
and howl if not satisfied.

[d] *11 Or sovereign*

*See the note on page 349.

†2 Most mss have *dagesh* in the second *mem* ( 'מּ ).

††4 Most mss have *dagesh* in the *zayin* ( עזּים ).

°*11* ק חסדי

°*16* ק יניעון

וַאֲנִי ׀ אָשִׁיר עֻזֶּךָ וַאֲרַנֵּן לַבֹּקֶר
in-the-morning and-I-will-sing strength-of-you I-will-sing but-I (17)

חַסְדֶּךָ כִּי־ הָיִיתָ מִשְׂגָּב לִי וּמָנוֹס בְּיוֹם צַר־ לִי׃
to-me trouble in-time-of and-refuge of-me fortress you-are for love-of-you

עֻזִּי אֵלֶיךָ אֲזַמֵּרָה כִּי־אֱלֹהִים מִשְׂגַּבִּי אֱלֹהֵי
God-of fortress-of-me God for I-sing-praise to-you Strength-of-me (18)

חַסְדִּי׃ לַמְנַצֵּחַ עַל־ שׁוּשַׁן עֵדוּת מִכְתָּם לְדָוִד
of-David miktam covenant lily-of to for-the-one-directing †(60:1) love-of-me

לְלַמֵּד׃ בְּהַצּוֹתוֹ ׀ אֶת אֲרַם נַהֲרַיִם וְאֶת־ אֲרַם צוֹבָה
Zobah Aram-of and Naharaim Aram-of *** when-to-fight-him (2) to-teach

וַיָּשָׁב יוֹאָב וַיַּךְ אֶת־ אֱדוֹם בְּגֵיא־ מֶלַח שְׁנֵים
two Salt in-Valley-of Edom *** and-he-struck-down Joab when-he-returned

עָשָׂר אָלֶף׃ אֱלֹהִים זְנַחְתָּנוּ פְרַצְתָּנוּ אָנַפְתָּ
you-were-angry you-burst-forth-upon-us you-rejected-us God (3) thousand ten

תְּשׁוֹבֵב לָנוּ׃ הִרְעַשְׁתָּה אֶרֶץ פְּצַמְתָּהּ רְפָה שְׁבָרֶיהָ
fractures-of-her mend! you-tore-open-her land you-shook (4) to-us you-restore

כִי־ מָטָה׃ הִרְאִיתָה עַמְּךָ קָשָׁה הִשְׁקִיתָנוּ
you-made-drink-us desperate-time people-of-you you-showed (5) she-quakes for

יַיִן תַּרְעֵלָה׃ נָתַתָּה לִּירֵאֶיךָ נֵּס לְהִתְנוֹסֵס
to-be-unfurled banner for-ones-fearing-you you-raised (6) staggering wine

מִפְּנֵי קֹשֶׁט סֶלָה׃ לְמַעַן יֵחָלְצוּן יְדִידֶיךָ הוֹשִׁיעָה
save! loved-ones-of-you they-may-be-delivered so-that (7) selah bow against

יְמִינְךָ וַעֲנֵנוּ׃ אֱלֹהִים ׀ דִּבֶּר בְּקָדְשׁוֹ
from-sanctuary-of-him he-spoke God (8) and-help-us! right-hand-of-you

אֶעְלֹזָה אֲחַלְּקָה שְׁכֶם וְעֵמֶק סֻכּוֹת אֲמַדֵּד׃
I-will-measure Succoth and-Valley-of Shechem I-will-parcel-out I-will-triumph

לִי גִלְעָד ׀ וְלִי מְנַשֶּׁה וְאֶפְרַיִם מָעוֹז רֹאשִׁי יְהוּדָה
Judah head-of-me helmet-of and-Ephraim Manasseh and-to-me Gilead to-me (9)

מְחֹקְקִי׃ מוֹאָב ׀ סִיר רַחְצִי עַל־אֱדוֹם אַשְׁלִיךְ
I-toss Edom upon washing-of-me basin-of Moab (10) one-being-scepter-of-me

נַעֲלִי עָלַי פְּלֶשֶׁת הִתְרֹעָעִי׃ מִי יֹבִלֵנִי
he-will-bring-in-me who? (11) I-shout-in-triumph Philistia over sandal-of-me

עִיר מָצוֹר מִי נָחַנִי עַד־ אֱדוֹם׃ הֲלֹא־אַתָּה אֱלֹהִים
God you not? (12) Edom to he-will-lead-me who? fortification city-of

זְנַחְתָּנוּ וְלֹא־ תֵצֵא אֱלֹהִים בְּצִבְאוֹתֵינוּ׃ הָבָה־ לָּנוּ
to-us give! (13) with-armies-of-us God you-go-out and-not you-rejected-us

עֶזְרָת מִצָּר וְשָׁוְא תְּשׁוּעַת אָדָם׃ בֵּאלֹהִים נַעֲשֶׂה־
we-will-gain with-God (14) man help-of for-worthless against-enemy aid

[16]But I will sing of your strength,
in the morning I will sing of your love;
for you are my fortress,
my refuge in times of trouble.

[17]O my Strength, I sing praise to you;
you, O God, are my fortress,
my loving God.

**Psalm 60**

For the director of music. To ⌊the tune of⌋ "The Lily of the Covenant." A *miktam*[e] of David. For teaching. When he fought Aram Naharaim[f] and Aram Zobah,[g] and when Joab returned and struck down twelve thousand Edomites in the Valley of Salt.

[1]You have rejected us, O God,
and burst forth upon us;
you have been angry—now restore us!
[2]You have shaken the land and torn it open;
mend its fractures, for it is quaking.
[3]You have shown your people desperate times;
you have given us wine that makes us stagger.

[4]But for those who fear you,
you have raised a banner
to be unfurled against the bow. *Selah*

[5]Save us and help us with your right hand,
that those you love may be delivered.
[6]God has spoken from his sanctuary:
"In triumph I will parcel out Shechem
and measure off the Valley of Succoth.
[7]Gilead is mine, and Manasseh is mine;
Ephraim is my helmet,
Judah my scepter.
[8]Moab is my washbasin,
upon Edom I toss my sandal;
over Philistia I shout in triumph."

[9]Who will bring me to the fortified city?
Who will lead me to Edom?
[10]Is it not you, O God, you who have rejected us
and no longer go out with our armies?
[11]Give us aid against the enemy,
for the help of man is worthless.
[12]With God we will gain the

[e]Title: Probably a literary or musical term
[f]Title: That is, Arameans of Northwest Mesopotamia
[g]Title: That is, Arameans of central Syria

*See the note on page 349.
†Heading, 1 See the note on page 401.

°7 ק ועננו

חַיִל וְהוּא יָבוּס צָרֵינוּ׃ לַמְנַצֵּחַ ׀
for-the-one-directing †(61:1) enemies-of-us he-will-trample and-he victory

עַל־ נְגִינַת לְדָוִד׃ שִׁמְעָה אֱלֹהִים רִנָּתִי הַקְשִׁיבָה
listen-to! cry-of-me God hear! (2) of-David stringed-instrument with

תְּפִלָּתִי׃ מִקְצֵה הָאָרֶץ ׀ אֵלֶיךָ אֶקְרָא בַּעֲטֹף
as-to-grow-faint I-call to-you the-earth from-end-of (3) prayer-of-me

לִבִּי בְּצוּר־ יָרוּם מִמֶּנִּי תַנְחֵנִי׃ כִּי־ הָיִיתָ
you-are for (4) you-lead-me more-than-me he-is-high to-rock heart-of-me

מַחְסֶה לִי מִגְדַּל־ עֹז מִפְּנֵי אוֹיֵב׃ אָגוּרָה
I-would-dwell (5) one-being-foe at-against strength tower-of to-me refuge

בְאָהָלְךָ עוֹלָמִים אֶחֱסֶה בְסֵתֶר כְּנָפֶיךָ סֶּלָה׃
selah wings-of-you in-shelter-of I-would-take-refuge forevers in-tent-of-you

כִּי־אַתָּה אֱלֹהִים שָׁמַעְתָּ לִנְדָרָי נָתַתָּ יְרֻשַּׁת יִרְאֵי
ones-fearing-of inheritance-of you-gave to-vows-of-me you-heard God you for (6)

שְׁמֶךָ׃ יָמִים עַל־ יְמֵי־ מֶלֶךְ תּוֹסִיף שְׁנוֹתָיו כְּמוֹ־
for years-of-him you-increase king days-of upon days (7) name-of-you

דֹר וָדֹר׃ יֵשֵׁב עוֹלָם לִפְנֵי
in-presences-of forever may-he-be-enthroned (8) and-generation generation

אֱלֹהִים חֶסֶד וֶאֱמֶת מַן יִנְצְרֻהוּ׃ כֵּן
then (9) they-will-protect-him appoint! and-faithfulness love God

אֲזַמְּרָה שִׁמְךָ לָעַד לְשַׁלְּמִי נְדָרַי יוֹם ׀ יוֹם׃
day day vows-of-me to-fulfill-me for-ever name-of-you I-will-sing-praise

לַמְנַצֵּחַ עַל־ יְדוּתוּן מִזְמוֹר לְדָוִד׃ אַךְ אֶל־אֱלֹהִים
God in alone (2) of-David psalm Jeduthun to for-the-one-directing †(62:1)

דּוּמִיָּה נַפְשִׁי מִמֶּנּוּ יְשׁוּעָתִי׃ אַךְ־ הוּא צוּרִי
rock-of-me he alone (3) salvation-of-me from-him soul-of-me rest

וִישׁוּעָתִי מִשְׂגַּבִּי לֹא־ אֶמּוֹט רַבָּה׃ עַד־
until (4) greatly I-will-be-shaken never fortress-of-me and-salvation-of-me

אָנָה ׀ תְּהוֹתְתוּ עַל אִישׁ תְּרָצְּחוּ כֻלְּכֶם כְּקִיר
like-wall all-of-you you-would-throw-down man on you-will-assault to-when?

נָטוּי גָּדֵר הַדְּחוּיָה׃ אַךְ מִשְּׂאֵתוֹ ׀
from-lofty-place-of-him fully (5) the-one-tottering fence one-leaning

יָעֲצוּ לְהַדִּיחַ יִרְצוּ כָזָב בְּפִיו יְבָרֵכוּ
they-bless with-mouth-of-him lie they-delight-in to-topple they-intend

וּבְקִרְבָּם יְקַלְלוּ־ סֶלָה׃ אַךְ לֵאלֹהִים דּוֹמִּי נַפְשִׁי
soul-of-me find-rest! in-God alone (6) selah they-curse but-in-heart-of-them

כִּי־ מִמֶּנּוּ תִּקְוָתִי׃ אַךְ־ הוּא צוּרִי וִישׁוּעָתִי
and-salvation-of-me rock-of-me he alone (7) hope-of-me from-him for

victory,
and he will trample down our enemies.

**Psalm 61**

For the director of music. With stringed instruments. Of David.

1 Hear my cry, O God;
listen to my prayer.
2 From the ends of the earth I call to you,
I call as my heart grows faint;
lead me to the rock that is higher than I.

3 For you have been my refuge,
a strong tower against the foe.
4 I long to dwell in your tent forever
and take refuge in the shelter of your wings. *Selah*

5 For you have heard my vows, O God;
you have given me the heritage of those who fear your name.

6 Increase the days of the king's life,
his years for many generations.
7 May he be enthroned in God's presence forever;
appoint your love and faithfulness to protect him.

8 Then will I ever sing praise to your name
and fulfill my vows day after day.

**Psalm 62**

For the director of music. To Jeduthun. A psalm of David.

1 My soul finds rest in God alone;
my salvation comes from him.
2 He alone is my rock and my salvation;
he is my fortress, I will never be shaken.

3 How long will you assault a man?
Would all of you throw him down—
this leaning wall, this tottering fence?
4 They fully intend to topple him
from his lofty place;
they take delight in lies.
With their mouths they bless,
but in their hearts they curse. *Selah*

5 Find rest, O my soul, in God alone;
my hope comes from him.
6 He alone is my rock and my salvation;

*See the note on page 401.
†Heading, *1* See the note on page 349.

מִשְׂגַּבִּי לֹא אֶמּוֹט׃ עַל־אֱלֹהִים יִשְׁעִי וּכְבוֹדִי
and-honor-of-me salvation-of-me God on (8) I-will-be-shaken not fortress-of-me

צוּר־עֻזִּי מַחְסִי בֵּאלֹהִים׃ בִּטְחוּ בוֹ בְכָל־עֵת ׀
time at-all-of in-him trust! (9) in-God refuge-of-me might-of-me rock-of

עָם שִׁפְכוּ־לְפָנָיו לְבַבְכֶם אֱלֹהִים מַחֲסֶה־לָּנוּ סֶלָה׃ אַךְ ׀ הֶבֶל
breath but (10) selah to-us refuge God heart-of-you to-him pour-out! people

בְּנֵי־אָדָם כָּזָב בְּנֵי אִישׁ בְּמֹאזְנַיִם לַעֲלוֹת הֵמָּה מֵהֶבֶל יָחַד׃
together only-breath they to-go-up on-balances man sons-of lie mankind sons-of

אַל־תִּבְטְחוּ בְעֹשֶׁק וּבְגָזֵל אַל־תֶּהְבָּלוּ
you-take-pride not or-in-stolen-thing in-extortion you-trust not (11)

חַיִל ׀ כִּי־יָנוּב אַל־תָּשִׁיתוּ לֵב׃ אַחַת ׀ דִּבֶּר אֱלֹהִים
God he-spoke one-thing (12) heart you-set not he-increases though richness

שְׁתַּיִם־זוּ שָׁמָעְתִּי כִּי עֹז לֵאלֹהִים׃ וּלְךָ־אֲדֹנָי חָסֶד
love Lord and-to-you (13) to-God strength that I-heard which two-things

כִּי־אַתָּה תְשַׁלֵּם לְאִישׁ כְּמַעֲשֵׂהוּ׃ מִזְמוֹר לְדָוִד
of-David psalm *(63:1) as-deed-of-him to-each you-will-reward you surely

בִּהְיוֹתוֹ בְּמִדְבַּר יְהוּדָה׃ אֱלֹהִים ׀ אֵלִי אַתָּה אֲשַׁחֲרֶךָּ
I-earnestly-seek-you you God-of-me God (2) Judah in-desert-of when-to-be-him

צָמְאָה לְךָ ׀ נַפְשִׁי כָּמַהּ לְךָ בְשָׂרִי בְּאֶרֶץ־צִיָּה
dry in-land body-of-me for-you he-longs soul-of-me for-you she-thirsts

וְעָיֵף בְּלִי־מָיִם׃ כֵּן בַּקֹּדֶשׁ חֲזִיתִךָ לִרְאוֹת עֻזְּךָ
power-of-you to-behold I-saw-you in-the-sanctuary so (3) waters no and-weary

וּכְבוֹדֶךָ׃ כִּי־טוֹב חַסְדְּךָ מֵחַיִּים שְׂפָתַי
lips-of-me than-lives love-of-you better because (4) and-glory-of-you

יְשַׁבְּחוּנְךָ׃ כֵּן אֲבָרֶכְךָ בְחַיָּי בְּשִׁמְךָ
in-name-of-you in-lives-of-me I-will-praise-you so (5) they-will-glorify-you

אֶשָּׂא כַפָּי׃ כְּמוֹ חֵלֶב וָדֶשֶׁן תִּשְׂבַּע
she-will-be-satisfied and-richness fatness as (6) hands-of-me I-will-lift-up

נַפְשִׁי וְשִׂפְתֵי רְנָנוֹת יְהַלֶּל־פִּי׃ אִם־
when (7) mouth-of-me he-will-praise singings and-lips-of soul-of-me

זְכַרְתִּיךָ עַל־יְצוּעָי בְּאַשְׁמֻרוֹת אֶהְגֶּה־בָּךְ׃ כִּי־
because (8) of-you I-think through-night-watches beds-of-me on I-remember-you

הָיִיתָ עֶזְרָתָה לִּי וּבְצֵל כְּנָפֶיךָ אֲרַנֵּן׃ דָּבְקָה
she-stays (9) I-sing wings-of-you then-in-shadow-of to-me help you-are

נַפְשִׁי אַחֲרֶיךָ בִּי תָּמְכָה יְמִינֶךָ׃ וְהֵמָּה
and-they (10) right-hand-of-you she-upholds to-me close-to-you self-of-me

לְשׁוֹאָה יְבַקְשׁוּ נַפְשִׁי יָבֹאוּ בְּתַחְתִּיּוֹת הָאָרֶץ׃
the-earth to-depths-of they-will-go life-of-me they-seek for-destruction

he is my fortress, I will not
be shaken.
[7]My salvation and my honor
depend on God[h];
he is my mighty rock, my
refuge.
[8]Trust in him at all times, O
people;
pour out your hearts to him,
for God is our refuge. *Selah*
[9]Lowborn men are but a
breath,
the highborn are but a lie;
if weighed on a balance, they
are nothing;
together they are only a
breath.
[10]Do not trust in extortion
or take pride in stolen
goods;
though your riches increase,
do not set your heart on
them.
[11]One thing God has spoken,
two things have I heard:
that you, O God, are strong,
[12] and that you, O Lord, are
loving.
Surely you will reward each
person
according to what he has
done.

**Psalm 63**

A psalm of David. When he was in the desert of Judah.

[1]O God, you are my God,
earnestly I seek you;
my soul thirsts for you,
my body longs for you,
in a dry and weary land
where there is no water.
[2]I have seen you in the
sanctuary
and beheld your power and
your glory.
[3]Because your love is better
than life,
my lips will glorify you.
[4]I will praise you as long as I
live,
and in your name I will lift
up my hands.
[5]My soul will be satisfied as
with the richest of foods;
with singing lips my mouth
will praise you.
[6]On my bed I remember you;
I think of you through the
watches of the night.
[7]Because you are my help,
I sing in the shadow of your
wings.
[8]I stay close to you;
your right hand upholds me.
[9]They who seek my life will be
destroyed;
they will go down to the
depths of the earth.

[h]7 Or *I God Most High is my salvation and my honor*

*Heading, *1* See the note on page 349.

יַגִּירֻהוּ עַל־ יְדֵי־ חָרֶב מְנָת שֻׁעָלִים יִהְיוּ׃

they-will-become jackals food-of sword hands-of to they-will-give-him (11)

וְהַמֶּלֶךְ יִשְׂמַח בֵּאלֹהִים יִתְהַלֵּל כָּל־ הַנִּשְׁבָּע

the-one-swearing all-of he-will-praise in-God he-will-rejoice but-the-king (12)

בּוֹ כִּי יִסָּכֵר פִּי דוֹבְרֵי־ שָׁקֶר׃

lie ones-speaking-of mouth-of he-will-be-silenced while by-him

לַמְנַצֵּחַ מִזְמוֹר לְדָוִד׃ שְׁמַע־אֱלֹהִים קוֹלִי

voice-of-me God hear! (2) of-David psalm for-the-one-directing *(64:1)

בְשִׂיחִי מִפַּחַד אוֹיֵב תִּצֹּר חַיָּי׃

lives-of-me you-protect one-being-enemy from-threat-of in-complaint-of-me

תַּסְתִּירֵנִי מִסּוֹד מְרֵעִים מֵרִגְשַׁת

from-noisy-crowd-of ones-being-wicked from-conspiracy-of you-hide-me (3)

פֹּעֲלֵי אָוֶן׃ אֲשֶׁר שָׁנְנוּ כַחֶרֶב לְשׁוֹנָם

tongue-of-them like-the-sword they-sharpen who (4) evil ones-doing-of

דָּרְכוּ חִצָּם דָּבָר מָר׃ לִירוֹת בַּמִּסְתָּרִים תָּם

innocent-man from-the-ambushes to-shoot (5) deadly word arrow-of-them they-aim

פִּתְאֹם יֹרֻהוּ וְלֹא יִירָאוּ׃ יְחַזְּקוּ־ לָמוֹ דָּבָר

plan to-them they-encourage (6) they-fear and-not they-shoot-him suddenly

רָע יְסַפְּרוּ לִטְמוֹן מוֹקְשִׁים אָמְרוּ מִי יִרְאֶה־ לָּמוֹ׃ יַחְפְּשׂוּ־

they-plot (7) to-them he-will-see who? they-say snares to-hide they-talk evil

עוֹלֹת תַּמְנוּ חֵפֶשׂ מְחֻפָּשׂ וְקֶרֶב אִישׁ

man surely-mind-of one-being-planned plan we-made-perfect injustices

וְלֵב עָמֹק׃ וַיֹּרֵם אֱלֹהִים חֵץ פִּתְאוֹם הָיוּ

they-will-be suddenly arrow God but-he-will-shoot-them (8) cunning and-heart

מַכּוֹתָם׃ וַיַּכְשִׁילוּהוּ עָלֵימוֹ לְשׁוֹנָם

tongue-of-them against-them and-they-will-ruin-him (9) strikings-down-of-them

יִתְנֹדֲדוּ כָּל־ רֹאֵה בָם׃ וַיִּירְאוּ

and-they-will-fear (10) to-them one-seeing-of all-of they-will-shake-head

כָּל־ אָדָם וַיַּגִּידוּ פֹּעַל אֱלֹהִים וּמַעֲשֵׂהוּ

and-deed-of-him God work-of and-they-will-proclaim mankind all-of

הִשְׂכִּילוּ׃ יִשְׂמַח צַדִּיק בַּיהוָה וְחָסָה

and-let-him-take-refuge in-Yahweh righteous let-him-rejoice (11) they-will-ponder

בוֹ וְיִתְהַלְלוּ כָּל־ יִשְׁרֵי־ לֵב׃

heart ones-upright-of all-of and-let-them-praise in-him

לַמְנַצֵּחַ מִזְמוֹר לְדָוִד שִׁיר׃ לְךָ דֻמִיָּה תְהִלָּה

praise silence for-you (2) song of-David psalm for-the-one-directing *(65:1)

אֱלֹהִים בְּצִיּוֹן וּלְךָ יְשֻׁלַּם־ נֶדֶר׃ שֹׁמֵעַ תְּפִלָּה

prayer one-hearing (3) vow he-will-be-fulfilled and-to-you in-Zion God

[10]They will be given over to the sword
and become food for jackals.

[11]But the king will rejoice in God;
all who swear by God's name will praise him,
while the mouths of liars will be silenced.

## Psalm 64

For the director of music. A psalm of David.

[1]Hear me, O God, as I voice my complaint;
protect my life from the threat of the enemy.

[2]Hide me from the conspiracy of the wicked,
from that noisy crowd of evildoers,
[3]who sharpen their tongues like swords
and aim their words like deadly arrows.
[4]They shoot from ambush at the innocent man;
they shoot at him suddenly, without fear.

[5]They encourage each other in evil plans,
they talk about hiding their snares;
they say, "Who will see them[i]?"
[6]They plot injustice and say,
"We have devised a perfect plan!"
Surely the mind and heart of man are cunning.

[7]But God will shoot them with arrows;
suddenly they will be struck down.
[8]He will turn their own tongues against them
and bring them to ruin;
all who see them will shake their heads in scorn.
[9]All mankind will fear;
they will proclaim the works of God
and ponder what he has done.

[10]Let the righteous rejoice in the LORD
and take refuge in him;
let all the upright in heart praise him!

## Psalm 65

For the director of music. A psalm of David. A song.

[1]Praise awaits[j] you, O God, in Zion;
to you our vows will be fulfilled.
[2]O you who hear prayer,

i5 Or *us*
j1 Or *befits;* the meaning of the Hebrew for this word is uncertain.

*Heading, *1* See the note on page 349.

עָדֶיךָ כָּל־ בָּשָׂר יָבֹאוּ׃ דִּבְרֵי עֲוֺנֹת גָּבְרוּ מֶנִּי
over-me they-overwhelmed sins matters-of (4) they-will-come man all-of to-you

פְּשָׁעֵינוּ אַתָּה תְכַפְּרֵם׃ אַשְׁרֵי ׀ תִּבְחַר
you-choose blessednesses-of (5) you-atoned-for-them you transgressions-of-us

וּתְקָרֵב יִשְׁכֹּן חֲצֵרֶיךָ נִשְׂבְּעָה בְּטוּב
with-goodness-of we-are-filled courts-of-you he-lives and-you-bring-near

בֵּיתֶךָ קְדֹשׁ הֵיכָלֶךָ׃ נוֹרָאוֹת ׀
deeds-being-awesome (6) temple-of-you holiness-of house-of-you

בְּצֶדֶק תַּעֲנֵנוּ אֱלֹהֵי יִשְׁעֵנוּ מִבְטָח כָּל־ קַצְוֵי־ אֶרֶץ
earth ends-of all-of hope salvation-of-us God-of you-answer-us of-righteousness

וְיָם רְחֹקִים׃ מֵכִין הָרִים בְּכֹחוֹ נֶאְזָר
one-arming-himself by-power-of-him mountains one-forming (7) far-ones and-sea-of

בִּגְבוּרָה׃ מַשְׁבִּיחַ ׀ שְׁאוֹן יַמִּים שְׁאוֹן גַּלֵּיהֶם
waves-of-them roar-of seas roar-of one-stilling (8) with-strength

וַהֲמוֹן לְאֻמִּים׃ וַיִּירְאוּ ׀ יֹשְׁבֵי קְצָוֺת
places-far-away ones-living-of and-they-fear (9) nations and-turmoil-of

מֵאוֹתֹתֶיךָ מוֹצָאֵי־ בֹקֶר וָעֶרֶב תַּרְנִין׃
you-call-forth-songs-of-joy and-evening morning dawns-of of-wonders-of-you

פָּקַדְתָּ הָאָרֶץ ׀ וַתְּשֹׁקְקֶהָ רַבַּת תַּעְשְׁרֶנָּה
you-enrich-her abundantly and-you-water-her the-land you-care-for (10)

פֶּלֶג אֱלֹהִים מָלֵא מָיִם תָּכִין דְּגָנָם כִּי־ כֵן
so for grain-of-them you-provide waters filled-of God stream-of

תְּכִינֶהָ׃ תְּלָמֶיהָ רַוֵּה נַחֵת גְּדוּדֶיהָ
ridges-of-her to-level to-drench furrows-of-her (11) you-ordained-her

בִּרְבִיבִים תְּמֹגְגֶנָּה צִמְחָהּ תְּבָרֵךְ׃ עִטַּרְתָּ שְׁנַת
year-of you-crown (12) you-bless crop-of-her you-soften-her with-showers

טוֹבָתֶךָ וּמַעְגָּלֶיךָ יִרְעֲפוּן דָּשֶׁן׃ יִרְעֲפוּ
they-overflow (13) abundance they-overflow and-carts-of-you bounty-of-you

נְאוֹת מִדְבָּר וְגִיל גְּבָעוֹת תַּחְגֹּרְנָה׃ לָבְשׁוּ
they-are-covered (14) they-are-clothed hills and-gladness desert grasslands-of

כָרִים ׀ הַצֹּאן וַעֲמָקִים יַעַטְפוּ־ בָר יִתְרוֹעֲעוּ
they-shout-for-joy grain they-are-mantled and-valleys the-flock meadows

אַף־ יָשִׁירוּ׃ לַמְנַצֵּחַ שִׁיר מִזְמוֹר הָרִיעוּ לֵאלֹהִים
to-God shout! psalm song for-the-one-directing (66:1) they-sing also

כָּל־ הָאָרֶץ׃ זַמְּרוּ כְבוֹד־ שְׁמוֹ שִׂימוּ כָבוֹד תְּהִלָּתוֹ׃
praise-of-him glory offer! name-of-him glory-of sing! (2) the-earth all-of

אִמְרוּ לֵאלֹהִים מַה־ נּוֹרָא מַעֲשֶׂיךָ בְּרֹב
in-greatness-of deeds-of-you one-being-awesome how! to-God say! (3)

to you all men will come.
3 When we were overwhelmed by sins,
you atoned for our transgressions.
4 Blessed is the man you choose
and bring near to live in your courts!
We are filled with the good things of your house,
of your holy temple.

5 You answer us with awesome deeds of righteousness,
O God our Savior,
the hope of all the ends of the earth
and of the farthest seas,
6 who formed the mountains by your power,
having armed yourself with strength,
7 who stilled the roaring of the seas,
the roaring of their waves,
and the turmoil of the nations.
8 Those living far away fear your wonders;
where morning dawns and evening fades
you call forth songs of joy.

9 You care for the land and water it;
you enrich it abundantly.
The streams of God are filled with water
to provide the people with grain,
for so you have ordained it.[k]
10 You drench its furrows
and level its ridges;
you soften it with showers
and bless its crops.
11 You crown the year with your bounty,
and your carts overflow with abundance.
12 The grasslands of the desert overflow;
the hills are clothed with gladness.
13 The meadows are covered with flocks
and the valleys are mantled with grain;
they shout for joy and sing.

### Psalm 66

For the director of music. A song. A psalm.

1 Shout with joy to God, all the earth!
2 Sing to the glory of his name;
offer him glory and praise!
3 Say to God, "How awesome are your deeds!

k9 Or *for that is how you prepare the land*

*See the note on page 349.

עֻזְּךָ יְכַחֲשׁוּ לְךָ אֹיְבֶיךָ׃ כָּל־

all-of (4) ones-being-enemies-of-you before-you they-cringe power-of-you

הָאָרֶץ ׀ יִשְׁתַּחֲווּ לְךָ וִיזַמְּרוּ־ לָךְ יְזַמְּרוּ

they-sing-praise to-you and-they-sing-praise to-you they-bow-down the-earth

שִׁמְךָ סֶלָה׃ לְכוּ וּרְאוּ מִפְעֲלוֹת אֱלֹהִים נוֹרָא עֲלִילָה

work one-being-awesome God deeds-of and-see! come! (5) selah name-of-you

עַל־ בְּנֵי אָדָם׃ הָפַךְ יָם ׀ לְיַבָּשָׁה בַּנָּהָר

through-the-river into-dry-land sea he-turned (6) man sons-of in-behalf-of

יַעַבְרוּ בְרָגֶל שָׁם נִשְׂמְחָה־ בּוֹ׃ מֹשֵׁל בִּגְבוּרָתוֹ ׀

by-power-of-him one-ruling (7) in-him let-us-rejoice there on-foot they-passed

עוֹלָם עֵינָיו בַּגּוֹיִם תִּצְפֶּינָה הַסּוֹרְרִים ׀ אַל־

not the-ones-rebelling they-watch on-the-nations eyes-of-him forever

יָרִימוּ° לָמוֹ סֶלָה׃ בָּרְכוּ עַמִּים ׀ אֱלֹהֵינוּ

God-of-us peoples praise! (8) selah against-him let-them-rise-up

וְהַשְׁמִיעוּ קוֹל תְּהִלָּתוֹ׃ הַשָּׂם נַפְשֵׁנוּ

life-of-us the-one-preserving (9) praise-of-him sound-of and-make-heard!

בַּחַיִּים וְלֹא־ נָתַן לַמּוֹט רַגְלֵנוּ׃

foot-of-us for-the-slipping he-allowed and-not among-the-living-ones

כִּי־ בְחַנְתָּנוּ אֱלֹהִים צְרַפְתָּנוּ כִּצְרָף־ כָּסֶף׃

silver like-to-refine you-refined-us God you-tested-us for (10)

הֲבֵאתָנוּ בַמְּצוּדָה שַׂמְתָּ מוּעָקָה בְמָתְנֵינוּ׃

on-backs-of-us burden you-laid into-the-prison you-brought-us (11)

הִרְכַּבְתָּ אֱנוֹשׁ לְרֹאשֵׁנוּ בָּאנוּ־ בָאֵשׁ

through-the-fire we-went over-head-of-us man you-let-ride (12)

וּבַמַּיִם וַתּוֹצִיאֵנוּ לָרְוָיָה׃

to-the-place-of-abundance and-you-brought-us and-through-the-waters

אָבוֹא בֵיתְךָ בְעוֹלוֹת אֲשַׁלֵּם לְךָ

to-you I-will-fulfill with-burnt-offerings temple-of-you I-will-come (13)

נְדָרָי׃ אֲשֶׁר־ פָּצוּ שְׂפָתָי וְדִבֶּר־ פִּי

mouth-of-me and-he-spoke lips-of-me they-promised which (14) vows-of-me

בַּצַּר־ לִי׃ עֹלוֹת מֵחִים אַעֲלֶה־ לָּךְ

to-you I-will-sacrifice fat-animals sacrifices-of (15) of-me in-the-trouble

עִם־ קְטֹרֶת אֵילִים אֶעֱשֶׂה בָקָר עִם־עַתּוּדִים סֶלָה׃ לְכוּ־ שִׁמְעוּ

listen! come! (16) selah goats with bull I-will-offer rams offering-of with

וַאֲסַפְּרָה כָּל־ יִרְאֵי אֱלֹהִים אֲשֶׁר עָשָׂה לְנַפְשִׁי׃

for-self-of-me he-did what God ones-fearing-of all-of and-let-me-tell

אֵלָיו פִּי־ קָרָאתִי וְרוֹמַם תַּחַת לְשׁוֹנִי׃ אָוֶן אִם־

if sin (18) tongue-of-me on and-praise I-cried-out mouth-of-me to-him (17)

So great is your power
that your enemies cringe
before you.
4All the earth bows down to
you;
they sing praise to you,
they sing praise to your
name." *Selah*

5Come and see what God has
done,
how awesome his works in
man's behalf!
6He turned the sea into dry
land,
they passed through the
river on foot—
come, let us rejoice in him.
7He rules forever by his power,
his eyes watch the nations—
let not the rebellious rise up
against him. *Selah*

8Praise our God, O peoples,
let the sound of his praise
be heard;
9he has preserved our lives
and kept our feet from
slipping.
10For you, O God, tested us;
you refined us like silver.
11You brought us into prison
and laid burdens on our
backs.
12You let men ride over our
heads;
we went through fire and
water,
but you brought us to a
place of abundance.

13I will come to your temple
with burnt offerings
and fulfill my vows to you—
14vows my lips promised and
my mouth spoke
when I was in trouble.
15I will sacrifice fat animals to
you
and an offering of rams;
I will offer bulls and goats.
*Selah*

16Come and listen, all you who
fear God;
let me tell you what he has
done for me.
17I cried out to him with my
mouth;
his praise was on my
tongue.

°7 ק ירומו

רָאִיתִי בְלִבִּי לֹא יִשְׁמַע ׀ אֲדֹנָי׃ אָכֵן
surely (19) Lord he-would-have-listened not in-heart-of-me I-cherished

שָׁמַע אֱלֹהִים הִקְשִׁיב בְּקוֹל תְּפִלָּתִי׃ בָּרוּךְ אֱלֹהִים
God being-praised (20) prayer-of-me to-voice-of he-heard God he-listened

אֲשֶׁר לֹא־ הֵסִיר תְּפִלָּתִי וְחַסְדּוֹ מֵאִתִּי׃
from-with-me or-love-of-him prayer-of-me he-rejected not who

לַמְנַצֵּחַ† בִּנְגִינֹת מִזְמוֹר שִׁיר׃ אֱלֹהִים
God (2) song psalm with-stringed-instruments for-the-one-directing *(67:1)

יְחָנֵּנוּ וִיבָרְכֵנוּ יָאֵר פָּנָיו
faces-of-him may-he-make-shine and-may-he-bless-us may-he-be-gracious-to-us

אִתָּנוּ סֶלָה׃ לָדַעַת בָּאָרֶץ דַּרְכֶּךָ בְּכָל־ גּוֹיִם
nations among-all-of way-of-you on-the-earth to-know (3) selah upon-us

יְשׁוּעָתֶךָ׃ יוֹדוּךָ עַמִּים ׀ אֱלֹהִים יוֹדוּךָ
may-they-praise-you God peoples may-they-praise-you (4) salvation-of-you

עַמִּים כֻּלָּם׃ יִשְׂמְחוּ וִירַנְּנוּ לְאֻמִּים
nations and-may-they-sing-for-joy may-they-be-glad (5) all-of-them peoples

כִּי־ תִשְׁפֹּט עַמִּים מִישׁוֹר וּלְאֻמִּים ׀ בָּאָרֶץ תַּנְחֵם סֶלָה׃
selah you-guide-them of-the-earth and-nations justly peoples you-rule for

יוֹדוּךָ עַמִּים ׀ אֱלֹהִים יוֹדוּךָ עַמִּים כֻּלָּם׃
all-of-them peoples may-they-praise-you God peoples may-they-praise-you (6)

אֶרֶץ נָתְנָה יְבוּלָהּ יְבָרְכֵנוּ אֱלֹהִים אֱלֹהֵינוּ׃
God-of-us God he-will-bless-us harvest-of-her she-will-yield land (7)

יְבָרְכֵנוּ אֱלֹהִים וְיִירְאוּ אֹתוֹ כָּל־ אַפְסֵי־ אָרֶץ׃
earth ends-of all-of him and-they-will-fear God he-will-bless-us (8)

לַמְנַצֵּחַ לְדָוִד מִזְמוֹר שִׁיר׃ יָקוּם אֱלֹהִים
God may-he-arise (2) song psalm of-David for-the-one-directing *(68:1)

יָפוּצוּ אוֹיְבָיו וְיָנוּסוּ
and-may-they-flee ones-being-enemies-of-him may-they-be-scattered

מְשַׂנְאָיו מִפָּנָיו׃ כְּהִנְדֹּף עָשָׁן תִּנְדֹּף
may-you-blow smoke as-to-be-blown (3) from-before-him ones-being-foes-of-him

כְּהִמֵּס דּוֹנַג מִפְּנֵי־ אֵשׁ יֹאבְדוּ רְשָׁעִים מִפְּנֵי אֱלֹהִים׃
God from-before wicked-ones may-they-perish fire at-before wax as-to-melt

וְצַדִּיקִים יִשְׂמְחוּ יַעַלְצוּ לִפְנֵי אֱלֹהִים
God before may-they-rejoice may-they-be-glad but-righteous-ones (4)

וְיָשִׂישׂוּ בְשִׂמְחָה׃ שִׁירוּ ׀ לֵאלֹהִים זַמְּרוּ שְׁמוֹ
name-of-him sing-praise! to-God sing! (5) with-joy and-may-they-be-happy

סֹלּוּ לָרֹכֵב בָּעֲרָבוֹת בְּיָהּ שְׁמוֹ וְעִלְזוּ
and-rejoice! name-of-him to-Yahweh on-the-clouds to-the-one-riding extol!

18If I had cherished sin in my heart,
the Lord would not have listened;
19but God has surely listened
and heard my voice in prayer.
20Praise be to God,
who has not rejected my prayer
or withheld his love from me!

**Psalm 67**

For the director of music. With stringed instruments. A psalm. A song.

1May God be gracious to us and bless us
and make his face shine upon us; *Selah*
2may your ways be known on earth,
your salvation among all nations.

3May the peoples praise you, O God;
may all the peoples praise you.
4May the nations be glad and sing for joy,
for you rule the peoples justly
and guide the nations of the earth. *Selah*
5May the peoples praise you, O God;
may all the peoples praise you.

6Then the land will yield its harvest,
and God, our God, will bless us.
7God will bless us,
and all the ends of the earth will fear him.

**Psalm 68**

For the director of music. Of David. A psalm. A song.

1May God arise, may his enemies be scattered;
may his foes flee before him.
2As smoke is blown away by the wind,
may you blow them away;
as wax melts before the fire,
may the wicked perish before God.
3But may the righteous be glad
and rejoice before God;
may they be happy and joyful.

4Sing to God, sing praise to his name,
extol him who rides on the clouds[l] —
his name is the LORD—
and rejoice before him.

[l]4 Or / *prepare the way for him who rides through the deserts*

*Heading, *1* See the note on page 349.

†*1* Most mss have *pathah* under the *beth* (צַח–).

לְפָנָיו׃ אֲבִי יְתוֹמִים וְדַיַּן אַלְמָנוֹת אֱלֹהִים
God widows and-defender-of fatherless-ones father-of (6) before-him

בִּמְעוֹן קָדְשׁוֹ׃ אֱלֹהִים ׀ מוֹשִׁיב יְחִידִים ׀ בַּיְתָה
in-family lonely-ones one-setting God (7) holiness-of-him in-dwelling-of

מוֹצִיא אֲסִירִים בַּכּוֹשָׁרוֹת אַךְ סוֹרְרִים שָׁכְנוּ
they-live ones-rebelling but with-the-songs prisoners one-leading-forth

צְחִיחָה׃ אֱלֹהִים בְּצֵאתְךָ לִפְנֵי עַמֶּךָ
people-of-you before when-to-go-out-you God (8) sun-scorched-land

בְּצַעְדְּךָ בִישִׁימוֹן סֶלָה׃ אֶרֶץ רָעָשָׁה ׀ אַף־ שָׁמַיִם
heavens also she-shook earth (9) selah through-wasteland when-to-march-you

נָטְפוּ מִפְּנֵי אֱלֹהִים זֶה סִינַי מִפְּנֵי אֱלֹהִים אֱלֹהֵי יִשְׂרָאֵל׃
Israel God-of God at-before Sinai One-of God at-before they-poured-rain

גֶּשֶׁם נְדָבוֹת תָּנִיף אֱלֹהִים נַחֲלָתְךָ וְנִלְאָה
even-one-being-weary inheritance-of-you God you-gave abundances shower-of (10)

אַתָּה כוֹנַנְתָּהּ׃ חַיָּתְךָ יָשְׁבוּ־ בָהּ תָּכִין
you-provided in-her they-settled people-of-you (11) you-refreshed-her you

בְּטוֹבָתְךָ לֶעָנִי אֱלֹהִים׃ אֲדֹנָי יִתֶּן־ אֹמֶר
word he-announced Lord (12) God for-the-poor from-bounty-of-you

הַמְבַשְּׂרוֹת צָבָא רָב׃ מַלְכֵי צְבָאוֹת יִדֹּדוּן יִדֹּדוּן
they-flee they-flee armies kings-of (13) great company the-ones-proclaiming

וּנְוַת בַּיִת תְּחַלֵּק שָׁלָל׃ אִם־ תִּשְׁכְּבוּן בֵּין
among you-sleep while (14) plunder she-divides residence and-camp-of

שְׁפַתָּיִם כַּנְפֵי יוֹנָה נֶחְפָּה בַכֶּסֶף וְאֶבְרוֹתֶיהָ
and-feathers-of-her with-the-silver being-sheathed dove wings-of campfires

בִּירַקְרַק חָרוּץ׃ בְּפָרֵשׂ שַׁדַּי מְלָכִים בָּהּ תַּשְׁלֵג
she-snowed in-her kings Almighty when-to-scatter (15) gold with-shine-of

בְּצַלְמוֹן׃ הַר־ אֱלֹהִים הַר־ בָּשָׁן הַר
mountain-of Bashan mountain-of majesties mountain-of (16) on-Zalmon

גַּבְנֻנִּים הַר־ בָּשָׁן׃ לָמָּה ׀ תְּרַצְּדוּן הָרִים
mountains you-gaze-in-envy why? (17) Bashan mountain-of rugged-ones

גַּבְנֻנִּים הָהָר חָמַד אֱלֹהִים לְשִׁבְתּוֹ אַף־ יְהוָה
Yahweh indeed to-reign-him God he-chooses the-mountain rugged-ones

יִשְׁכֹּן לָנֶצַח׃ רֶכֶב אֱלֹהִים רִבֹּתַיִם אַלְפֵי
thousands-of tens-of-thousands God chariot-of (18) to-forever he-will-dwell

שִׁנְאָן אֲדֹנָי בָם סִינַי בַּקֹּדֶשׁ׃ עָלִיתָ לַמָּרוֹם ׀
to-the-height you-ascended (19) into-the-sanctuary Sinai †in-them Lord multitude

שָׁבִיתָ שֶּׁבִי לָקַחְתָּ מַתָּנוֹת בָּאָדָם וְאַף סוֹרְרִים
ones-rebelling even-also from-the-man gifts you-received captive you-led

5 A father to the fatherless, a
defender of widows,
is God in his holy dwelling.
6 God sets the lonely in
families,[m]
he leads forth the prisoners
with singing;
but the rebellious live in a
sun-scorched land.
7 When you went out before
your people, O God,
when you marched through
the wasteland, *Selah*
8 the earth shook,
the heavens poured down
rain,
before God, the One of Sinai,
before God, the God of
Israel.
9 You gave abundant showers,
O God;
you refreshed your weary
inheritance.
10 Your people settled in it,
and from your bounty, O
God, you provided for the
poor.
11 The Lord announced the word,
and great was the company
of those who proclaimed
it:
12 "Kings and armies flee in
haste;
in the camps men divide the
plunder.
13 Even while you sleep among
the campfires,[n]
the wings of ⌊my⌋ dove are
sheathed with silver,
its feathers with shining
gold."
14 When the Almighty[o] scattered
the kings in the land,
it was like snow fallen on
Zalmon.
15 The mountains of Bashan are
majestic mountains;
rugged are the mountains of
Bashan.
16 Why gaze in envy, O rugged
mountains,
at the mountain where God
chooses to reign,
where the LORD himself will
dwell forever?
17 The chariots of God are tens of
thousands
and thousands of thousands;
the Lord ⌊has come⌋ from
Sinai into his sanctuary.
18 When you ascended on high,
you led captives in your
train;
you received gifts from men,
even from[p] the rebellious—

[m] 6 *Or the desolate in a homeland*
[n] 13 *Or saddlebags*
[o] 14 Hebrew *Shaddai*
[p] 18 *Or gifts for men, / even*

*See the note on page 349.
†18 The NIV repoints this word as (בְּמוֹ) בָּם, *from*.

לִשְׁכֹּן | יָהּ אֱלֹהִים׃ בָּרוּךְ אֲדֹנָי יוֹם | יוֹם יַעֲמָס־לָנוּ
for-us he-bears-burden day day Lord being-praised (20) God Yahweh to-dwell

הָאֵל יְשׁוּעָתֵנוּ סֶלָה׃ הָאֵל | לָנוּ אֵל לְמוֹשָׁעוֹת וְלֵיהוִה
and-from-Yahweh of-salvations God of-us the-God (21) selah salvation-of-us the-God

אֲדֹנָי לַמָּוֶת תּוֹצָאוֹת׃ אַךְ־אֱלֹהִים יִמְחַץ רֹאשׁ
head-of he-will-crush God surely (22) escapes from-the-death Lord

אֹיְבָיו קָדְקֹד שֵׂעָר מִתְהַלֵּךְ בַּאֲשָׁמָיו׃
in-sins-of-him one-going-on hair crown-of ones-being-enemies-of-him

אָמַר אֲדֹנָי מִבָּשָׁן אָשִׁיב אָשִׁיב מִמְּצֻלוֹת יָם׃
sea from-depths-of I-will-bring I-will-bring from-Bashan Lord he-says (23)

לְמַעַן | תִּמְחַץ† רַגְלְךָ בְּדָם לְשׁוֹן כְּלָבֶיךָ
dogs-of-you tongue-of in-blood foot-of-you †you-may-shatter so-that (24)

מֵאֹיְבִים מִנֵּהוּ׃ רָאוּ הֲלִיכוֹתֶיךָ אֱלֹהִים
God processions-of-you they-view (25) share-of-him from-ones-being-foes

הֲלִיכוֹת אֵלִי מַלְכִּי בַקֹּדֶשׁ׃ קִדְּמוּ
they-are-in-front (26) into-the-sanctuary King-of-me God-of-me processions-of

שָׁרִים אַחַר נֹגְנִים בְּתוֹךְ עֲלָמוֹת תּוֹפֵפוֹת׃
ones-playing-tambourines maidens in-among ones-playing-music after ones-singing

בְּמַקְהֵלוֹת בָּרְכוּ אֱלֹהִים יְהוָה מִמְּקוֹר יִשְׂרָאֵל׃
Israel in-assembly-of Yahweh God praise! in-great-congregations (27)

שָׁם בִּנְיָמִן | צָעִיר רֹדֵם שָׂרֵי יְהוּדָה רִגְמָתָם
throng-of-them Judah princes-of one-leading-them little Benjamin there (28)

שָׂרֵי זְבֻלוּן שָׂרֵי נַפְתָּלִי׃ צִוָּה אֱלֹהֶיךָ
God-of-you he-summoned (29) Naphtali princes-of Zebulun princes-of

עֻזֶּךָ עוּזָּה אֱלֹהִים זוּ פָּעַלְתָּ לָּנוּ׃ מֵהֵיכָלֶךָ
because-of-temple-of-you (30) for-us you-did as God show-strength! power-of-you

עַל־יְרוּשָׁלָםִ לְךָ יוֹבִילוּ מְלָכִים שָׁי׃ גְּעַר חַיַּת קָנֶה
reed beast-of rebuke! (31) gift kings they-will-bring to-you Jerusalem at

עֲדַת אַבִּירִים | בְּעֶגְלֵי עַמִּים מִתְרַפֵּס בְּרַצֵּי־כָסֶף
silver with-bars-of one-being-humbled nations among-calves-of bulls herd-of

בִּזַּר עַמִּים קְרָבוֹת יֶחְפָּצוּ׃ יֶאֱתָיוּ חַשְׁמַנִּים מִנִּי
from envoys they-will-come (32) they-delight-in wars nations he-scatters

מִצְרָיִם כּוּשׁ תָּרִיץ יָדָיו לֵאלֹהִים׃ מַמְלְכוֹת הָאָרֶץ
the-earth kingdoms-of (33) to-God hands-of-him she-will-submit Cush Egypt

שִׁירוּ לֵאלֹהִים זַמְּרוּ אֲדֹנָי סֶלָה׃ לָרֹכֵב בִּשְׁמֵי
in-skies-of to-the-one-riding (34) selah Lord sing-praise! to-God sing!

שְׁמֵי־קֶדֶם הֵן יִתֵּן בְּקוֹלוֹ קוֹל עֹז׃
might voice-of with-voice-of-him he-thunders see! ancient skies-of

that you,[q] O LORD God,
might dwell there.

19 Praise be to the Lord, to God our Savior,
who daily bears our burdens. *Selah*

20 Our God is a God who saves;
from the Sovereign LORD comes escape from death.

21 Surely God will crush the heads of his enemies,
the hairy crowns of those who go on in their sins.

22 The Lord says, "I will bring you from Bashan;
I will bring you from the depths of the sea,

23 that you may plunge your feet in the blood of your foes,
while the tongues of your dogs have their share."

24 Your procession has come into view, O God,
the procession of my God and King into the sanctuary.

25 In front are the singers, after them the musicians;
with them are the maidens playing tambourines.

26 Praise God in the great congregation;
praise the LORD in the assembly of Israel.

27 There is the little tribe of Benjamin, leading them,
there the great throng of Judah's princes,
and there the princes of Zebulun and of Naphtali.

28 Summon your power, O God ;
show us your strength, O God, as you have done before.

29 Because of your temple at Jerusalem
kings will bring you gifts.

30 Rebuke the beast among the reeds,
the herd of bulls among the calves of the nations.
Humbled, may it bring bars of silver.
Scatter the nations who delight in war.

31 Envoys will come from Egypt;
Cush[s] will submit herself to God.

32 Sing to God, O kingdoms of the earth,
sing praise to the Lord, *Selah*

33 to him who rides the ancient skies above,
who thunders with mighty voice.

q18 Or *they*
r28 Many Hebrew manuscripts, Septuagint and Syriac; most Hebrew manuscripts *Your God has summoned power for you*
s31 That is, the upper Nile region

*See the note on page 349.

†24 The NIV reads this word as תִּרְחַץ, *you-may-wash.*

תְּנוּ עֹז לֵֽאלֹהִים עַל־ יִשְׂרָאֵל גַּאֲוָתוֹ וְעֻזּוֹ
and-power-of-him majesty-of-him Israel over of-God power proclaim! (35)

בַּשְּׁחָקִים׃ נוֹרָא אֱלֹהִים מִֽמִּקְדָּשֶׁיךָ אֵל יִשְׂרָאֵל
Israel God-of in-sanctuaries-of-you God one-being-awesome (36) in-the-skies

הוּא נֹתֵן ׀ עֹז וְתַעֲצֻמוֹת לָעָם בָּרוּךְ אֱלֹהִים׃
God being-praised to-the-people and-strengths power one-giving he

לַמְנַצֵּחַ עַל־שׁוֹשַׁנִּים לְדָוִד׃ הוֹשִׁיעֵנִי אֱלֹהִים כִּי
for God save-me! (2) of-David lilies to for-the-one-directing *(69:1)

בָאוּ מַיִם עַד־ נָפֶשׁ׃ טָבַעְתִּי ׀ בִּיוֵן מְצוּלָה וְאֵין
and-there-is-no depth into-mire-of I-sink (3) neck to waters they-came

מָעֳמָד בָּאתִי בְמַעֲמַקֵּי־ מַיִם וְשִׁבֹּלֶת שְׁטָפָתְנִי׃
she-engulfs-me and-flood waters into-depths-of I-came foothold

יָגַעְתִּי בְקָרְאִי נִחַר גְּרוֹנִי כָּלוּ
they-fail throat-of-me he-is-parched from-to-call-out-me I-am-worn-out (4)

עֵינַי מְיַחֵל לֵאלֹהָי׃ רַבּוּ ׀ מִשַּׂעֲרוֹת
more-than-hairs-of they-are-numerous (5) for-God-of-me one-looking eyes-of-me

רֹאשִׁי שֹׂנְאַי חִנָּם עָצְמוּ מַצְמִיתַי
ones-destroying-me they-are-many without-reason ones-hating-me head-of-me

אֹיְבַי שֶׁקֶר אֲשֶׁר לֹא־ גָזַלְתִּי אָז אָשִׁיב׃
I-must-restore then I-stole not what without-cause ones-being-enemies-of-me

אֱלֹהִים אַתָּה יָדַעְתָּ לְאִוַּלְתִּי וְאַשְׁמוֹתַי מִמְּךָ לֹא־
not from-you and-guilts-of-me to-folly-of-me you-know you God (6)

נִכְחָדוּ׃ אַל־ יֵבֹשׁוּ בִי ׀ קֹוֶיךָ
ones-hoping-of-you because-of-me may-they-be-disgraced not (7) they-are-hidden

אֲדֹנָי יְהוִה צְבָאוֹת אַל־ יִכָּלְמוּ בִי מְבַקְשֶׁיךָ
ones-seeking-you because-of-me may-they-be-shamed not Hosts Yahweh-of Lord

אֱלֹהֵי יִשְׂרָאֵל׃ כִּי־ עָלֶיךָ נָשָׂאתִי חֶרְפָּה כִּסְּתָה כְלִמָּה
shame she-covers scorn I-endure for-sake-of-you for (8) Israel God-of

פָנָי׃ מוּזָר הָיִיתִי לְאֶחָי וְנָכְרִי לִבְנֵי
to-sons-of and-alien to-brothers-of-me I-am one-being-stranger (9) faces-of-me

אִמִּי׃ כִּי־ קִנְאַת בֵּיתְךָ אֲכָלָתְנִי וְחֶרְפּוֹת
and-insults-of she-consumes-me house-of-you zeal-of for (10) mother-of-me

חוֹרְפֶיךָ נָפְלוּ עָלָי׃ וָאֶבְכֶּה בַצּוֹם נַפְשִׁי
self-of-me in-the-fast when-I-weep (11) on-me they-fall ones-insulting-you

וַתְּהִי לַחֲרָפוֹת לִי׃ וָאֶתְּנָה לְבוּשִׁי שָׂק
sackcloth clothing-of-me when-I-put-on (12) to-me of-scorns then-she-is

וָאֱהִי לָהֶם לְמָשָׁל׃ יָשִׂיחוּ בִי יֹשְׁבֵי שָׁעַר
gate ones-sitting-of at-me they-mock (13) as-sport to-them then-I-am

34 Proclaim the power of God,
whose majesty is over Israel,
whose power is in the skies.
35 You are awesome, O God, in
your sanctuary;
the God of Israel gives
power and strength to his
people.

Praise be to God!

### Psalm 69

For the director of music. To the tune of "Lilies." Of David.

1 Save me, O God,
for the waters have come up
to my neck.
2 I sink in the miry depths,
where there is no foothold.
I have come into the deep
waters;
the floods engulf me.
3 I am worn out calling for help;
my throat is parched.
My eyes fail,
looking for my God.
4 Those who hate me without
reason
outnumber the hairs of my
head;
many are my enemies without
cause,
those who seek to destroy
me.
I am forced to restore
what I did not steal.

5 You know my folly, O God;
my guilt is not hidden from
you.

6 May those who hope in you
not be disgraced because of
me,
O Lord, the LORD Almighty;
may those who seek you
not be put to shame because
of me,
O God of Israel.
7 For I endure scorn for your
sake,
and shame covers my face.
8 I am a stranger to my brothers,
an alien to my own
mother's sons;
9 for zeal for your house
consumes me,
and the insults of those who
insult you fall on me.
10 When I weep and fast,
I must endure scorn;
11 when I put on sackcloth,
people make sport of me.
12 Those who sit at the gate mock
me,

*Heading, *1* See the note on page 349.

וּנְגִינוֹת שׁוֹתֵי שֵׁכָר׃ וַאֲנִי תְפִלָּתִי־
prayer-of-me but-I (14) strong-drink ones-drinking-of and-songs-of

לְךָ ׀ יְהוָה עֵת רָצוֹן אֱלֹהִים בְּרָב־ חַסְדֶּךָ עֲנֵנִי
answer-me! love-of-you in-greatness-of God favor time-of Yahweh to-you

בֶּאֱמֶת יִשְׁעֶךָ׃ הַצִּילֵנִי מִטִּיט וְאַל־ אֶטְבָּעָה
let-me-sink and-not from-mire rescue-me! (15) salvation-of-you with-sureness-of

אִנָּצְלָה מִשֹּׂנְאַי וּמִמַּעֲמַקֵּי־ מָיִם׃ אַל־
not (16) waters and-from-depths-of from-ones-hating-me let-me-be-delivered

תִּשְׁטְפֵנִי ׀ שִׁבֹּלֶת מַיִם וְאַל־ תִּבְלָעֵנִי מְצוּלָה וְאַל־
and-not depth let-her-swallow-me and-not waters flood-of let-her-engulf-me

תֶּאְטַר־ עָלַי בְּאֵר פִּיהָ׃ עֲנֵנִי יְהוָה כִּי־ טוֹב
good for Yahweh answer-me! (17) mouth-of-her pit over-me let-her-close

חַסְדֶּךָ כְּרֹב רַחֲמֶיךָ פְּנֵה אֵלָי׃ וְאַל־ תַּסְתֵּר
you-hide and-not (18) to-me turn! mercies-of-you in-greatness-of love-of-you

פָּנֶיךָ מֵעַבְדֶּךָ כִּי־ צַר־ לִי מַהֵר עֲנֵנִי׃
answer-me! be-quick! to-me trouble for from-servant-of-you faces-of-you

קָרְבָה אֶל־ נַפְשִׁי גְאָלָהּ לְמַעַן אֹיְבַי
ones-being-foes-of-me because-of rescue-her! self-of-me to come-near! (19)

פְּדֵנִי׃ אַתָּה יָדַעְתָּ חֶרְפָּתִי וּבָשְׁתִּי וּכְלִמָּתִי
and-shame-of-me and-disgrace-of-me scorn-of-me you-know you (20) redeem-me!

נֶגְדְּךָ כָּל־ צוֹרְרָי׃ חֶרְפָּה ׀ שָׁבְרָה לִבִּי
heart-of-me she-broke scorn (21) ones-being-enemies-of-me all-of before-you

וָאָנוּשָׁה וָאֲקַוֶּה לָנוּד וָאַיִן
but-there-was-none to-have-sympathy and-I-looked and-I-became-helpless

וְלַמְנַחֲמִים וְלֹא מָצָאתִי׃ וַיִּתְּנוּ בְּבָרוּתִי
in-food-of-me and-they-put (22) I-found but-none and-for-ones-comforting

רֹאשׁ וְלִצְמָאִי יַשְׁקוּנִי חֹמֶץ׃ יְהִי־
may-he-become (23) vinegar they-gave-drink-me and-for-thirst-of-me gall

שֻׁלְחָנָם לִפְנֵיהֶם לְפָח וְלִשְׁלוֹמִים לְמוֹקֵשׁ׃
as-trap and-as-retributions as-snare before-them table-of-them

תֶּחְשַׁכְנָה עֵינֵיהֶם מֵרְאוֹת וּמָתְנֵיהֶם תָּמִיד
forever and-backs-of-them from-to-see eyes-of-them may-they-be-darkened (24)

הַמְעַד׃ שְׁפָךְ־ עֲלֵיהֶם זַעְמֶךָ וַחֲרוֹן אַפְּךָ
anger-of-you and-fierceness-of wrath-of-you on-them pour-out! (25) bend!

יַשִּׂיגֵם׃ תְּהִי־ טִירָתָם נְשַׁמָּה
one-being-deserted place-of-them may-she-be (26) let-him-overtake-them

בְּאָהֳלֵיהֶם אַל־ יְהִי יֹשֵׁב׃ כִּי־ אַתָּה אֲשֶׁר־ הִכִּיתָ
you-wound whom you for (27) one-dwelling let-him-be not in-tents-of-them

and I am the song of the
drunkards.
13 But I pray to you, O LORD,
in the time of your favor;
in your great love, O God,
answer me with your sure
salvation.
14 Rescue me from the mire,
do not let me sink;
deliver me from those who
hate me,
from the deep waters.
15 Do not let the floodwaters
engulf me
or the depths swallow me
up
or the pit close its mouth
over me.
16 Answer me, O LORD, out of the
goodness of your love;
in your great mercy turn to
me.
17 Do not hide your face from
your servant;
answer me quickly, for I am
in trouble.
18 Come near and rescue me;
redeem me because of my
foes.
19 You know how I am scorned,
disgraced and shamed;
all my enemies are before
you.
20 Scorn has broken my heart
and has left me helpless;
I looked for sympathy, but
there was none,
for comforters, but I found
none.
21 They put gall in my food
and gave me vinegar for my
thirst.
22 May the table set before them
become a snare;
may it become retribution
and[t] a trap.
23 May their eyes be darkened so
they cannot see,
and their backs be bent
forever.
24 Pour out your wrath on them;
let your fierce anger
overtake them.
25 May their place be deserted;
let there be no one to dwell
in their tents.
26 For they persecute those you
wound

[t]22 Or *snare / and their fellowship become*

*See the note on page 349.

רָדָפוּ וְאֶל־ מַכְאוֹב חֲלָלֶיךָ יְסַפֵּרוּ׃ תְּנָה־

charge! (28) they-talk ones-hurt-of-you pain-of and-about they-persecute

עָוֺן עַל־ עֲוֺנָם וְאַל־ יָבֹאוּ בְּצִדְקָתֶךָ׃

in-salvation-of-you let-them-share and-not crime-of-them upon crime

יִמָּחוּ מִסֵּפֶר חַיִּים וְעִם צַדִּיקִים אַל־

not righteous-ones and-with lives of-book-of may-they-be-blotted-out (29)

יִכָּתֵבוּ׃ וַאֲנִי עָנִי וְכוֹאֵב יְשׁוּעָתְךָ אֱלֹהִים

God salvation-of-you and-one-suffering pain and-I (30) may-they-be-listed

תְּשַׂגְּבֵנִי׃ אֲהַלְלָה שֵׁם־ אֱלֹהִים בְּשִׁיר וַאֲגַדְּלֶנּוּ

and-I-will-glorify-him in-song God name-of I-will-praise (31) may-she-protect-me

בְתוֹדָה׃ וְתִיטַב לַיהוָה מִשּׁוֹר פָּר

bull more-than-ox to-Yahweh and-she-will-please (32) with-thanksgiving

מַקְרִן מַפְרִיס׃ רָאוּ עֲנָוִים יִשְׂמָחוּ

they-will-be-glad poor-ones they-will-see (33) one-having-hoof one-having-horn

דֹּרְשֵׁי אֱלֹהִים וִיחִי לְבַבְכֶם׃ כִּי־ שֹׁמֵעַ אֶל־

to one-hearing for (34) heart-of-you now-may-he-live God ones-seeking-of

אֶבְיוֹנִים יְהוָה וְאֶת־ אֲסִירָיו לֹא בָזָה׃ יְהַלְלוּהוּ

let-them-praise-him (35) he-despises not captives-of-him and Yahweh needy-ones

שָׁמַיִם וָאָרֶץ יַמִּים וְכָל־ רֹמֵשׂ בָּם׃ כִּי אֱלֹהִים ׀

God for (36) in-them one-moving and-all-of seas and-earth heavens

יוֹשִׁיעַ צִיּוֹן וְיִבְנֶה עָרֵי יְהוּדָה וְיָשְׁבוּ

then-they-will-settle Judah cities-of and-he-will-rebuild Zion he-will-save

שָׁם וִירֵשׁוּהָ׃ וְזֶרַע עֲבָדָיו

servants-of-him and-child-of (37) and-they-will-possess-her there

יִנְחָלוּהָ וְאֹהֲבֵי שְׁמוֹ יִשְׁכְּנוּ־ בָהּ׃

in-her they-will-dwell name-of-him and-ones-loving-of they-will-inherit-her

לַמְנַצֵּחַ לְדָוִד לְהַזְכִּיר׃ אֱלֹהִים לְהַצִּילֵנִי

to-save-me God (2) to-make-petition of-David for-the-one-directing *(70:1)

יְהוָה לְעֶזְרָתִי חוּשָׁה׃ יֵבֹשׁוּ וְיַחְפְּרוּ

and-may-they-be-confused may-they-be-shamed (3) hasten! to-help-of-me Yahweh

מְבַקְשֵׁי נַפְשִׁי יִסֹּגוּ אָחוֹר וְיִכָּלְמוּ

and-may-they-be-disgraced back may-they-be-turned life-of-me ones-seeking-of

חֲפֵצֵי רָעָתִי׃ יָשׁוּבוּ עַל־ עֵקֶב בָּשְׁתָּם

shame-of-them cause-of at may-they-turn-back (4) ruin-of-me ones-desirous-of

הָאֹמְרִים הֶאָח ׀ הֶאָח׃ יָשִׂישׂוּ וְיִשְׂמְחוּ ׀ בְּךָ

in-you and-may-they-be-glad may-they-rejoice (5) aha! aha! the-ones-saying

כָּל־ מְבַקְשֶׁיךָ וְיֹאמְרוּ תָמִיד יִגְדַּל אֱלֹהִים

God let-him-be-exalted always and-may-they-say ones-seeking-you all-of

and talk about the pain of
those you hurt.
27 Charge them with crime upon
crime;
do not let them share in
your salvation.
28 May they be blotted out of the
book of life
and not be listed with the
righteous.

29 I am in pain and distress;
may your salvation, O God,
protect me.
30 I will praise God's name in
song
and glorify him with
thanksgiving.
31 This will please the Lord more
than an ox,
more than a bull with its
horns and hoofs.
32 The poor will see and be
glad—
you who seek God, may
your hearts live!
33 The Lord hears the needy
and does not despise his
captive people.

34 Let heaven and earth praise
him,
the seas and all that move
in them,
35 for God will save Zion
and rebuild the cities of
Judah.
Then people will settle there
and possess it;
36 the children of his servants
will inherit it,
and those who love his
name will dwell there.

**Psalm 70**

For the director of music. Of David. A petition.

1 Hasten, O God, to save me;
O Lord, come quickly to
help me.
2 May those who seek my life
be put to shame and
confusion;
may all who desire my ruin
be turned back in disgrace.
3 May those who say to me,
"Aha! Aha!"
turn back because of their
shame.
4 But may all who seek you
rejoice and be glad in you;
may those who love your
salvation always say,
"Let God be exalted!"

*Heading, *1* See the note on page 349.

אֹהֲבֵי יְשׁוּעָתֶךָ׃ וַאֲנִי׀ עָנִי וְאֶבְיוֹן אֱלֹהִים חוּשָׁה־

come-quickly! God and-needy poor yet-I (6) salvation-of-you ones-loving-of

לִּי עֶזְרִי וּמְפַלְטִי אַתָּה יְהוָה אַל־תְּאַחַר׃ בְּךָ־

in-you (71:1) you-delay not Yahweh you and-one-delivering-me help-of-me to-me

יְהוָה חָסִיתִי אַל־אֵבוֹשָׁה לְעוֹלָם׃ בְּצִדְקָתְךָ

in-righteousness-of-you (2) to-forever let-me-be-shamed not I-took-refuge Yahweh

תַּצִּילֵנִי וּתְפַלְּטֵנִי הַטֵּה־אֵלַי אָזְנְךָ וְהוֹשִׁיעֵנִי׃ הֱיֵה

be! (3) and-save-me! ear-of-you to-me turn! and-you-deliver-me you-rescue-me

לִי׀ לְצוּר מָעוֹן לָבוֹא תָּמִיד צִוִּיתָ לְהוֹשִׁיעֵנִי כִּי־סַלְעִי

rock-of-me for to-save-me you-command always to-go refuge as-rock-of to-me

וּמְצוּדָתִי אָתָּה׃ אֱלֹהַי פַּלְּטֵנִי מִיַּד רָשָׁע

wicked from-hand-of deliver-me! God-of-me (4) you and-fortress-of-me

מִכַּף מְעַוֵּל וְחוֹמֵץ׃ כִּי־אַתָּה תִקְוָתִי אֲדֹנָי

Lord hope-of-me you for (5) and-one-being-cruel one-being-evil from-grasp-of

יְהוָה מִבְטַחִי מִנְּעוּרָי׃ עָלֶיךָ׀ נִסְמַכְתִּי מִבֶּטֶן

from-birth I-relied on-you (6) since-youths-of-me confidence-of-me Yahweh

מִמְּעֵי אִמִּי אַתָּה גוֹזִי בְּךָ תְהִלָּתִי

praise-of-me to-you one-bringing-forth-me you mother-of-me from-wombs-of

תָמִיד׃ כְּמוֹפֵת הָיִיתִי לְרַבִּים וְאַתָּה מַחֲסִי־עֹז׃

strong refuge-of-me but-you to-many I-became like-portent (7) ever

יִמָּלֵא פִי תְּהִלָּתֶךָ כָּל־הַיּוֹם תִּפְאַרְתֶּךָ׃

splendor-of-you the-day all-of praise-of-you mouth-of-me he-is-filled (8)

אַל־תַּשְׁלִיכֵנִי לְעֵת זִקְנָה כִּכְלוֹת כֹּחִי

strength-of-me when-to-be-gone old-age at-time-of you-cast-away-me not (9)

אַל־תַּעַזְבֵנִי׃ כִּי־אָמְרוּ אוֹיְבַי לִי

against-me ones-being-enemies-of-me they-speak for (10) you-forsake-me not

וְשֹׁמְרֵי נַפְשִׁי נוֹעֲצוּ יַחְדָּו׃ לֵאמֹר אֱלֹהִים

God to-say (11) together they-conspire life-of-me and-ones-waiting-of

עֲזָבוֹ רִדְפוּ וְתִפְשׂוּהוּ כִּי־אֵין מַצִּיל׃

one-rescuing there-is-not for and-seize-him! pursue! he-forsook-him

אֱלֹהִים אַל־תִּרְחַק מִמֶּנִּי אֱלֹהַי לְעֶזְרָתִי חִישָׁה׃

come-quickly! to-help-of-me God-of-me from-me you-be-far not God (12)

יֵבֹשׁוּ יִכְלוּ שֹׂטְנֵי נַפְשִׁי

self-of-me ones-accusing-of may-they-perish may-they-be-shamed (13)

יַעֲטוּ חֶרְפָּה וּכְלִמָּה מְבַקְשֵׁי רָעָתִי׃ וַאֲנִי

but-I (14) harm-of-me ones-wanting-of and-disgrace scorn may-they-be-covered

תָּמִיד אֲיַחֵל וְהוֹסַפְתִּי עַל־כָּל־תְּהִלָּתֶךָ׃ פִּי׀

mouth-of-me (15) praise-of-you all-of to and-I-will-add I-will-hope always

[5]Yet I am poor and needy;
come quickly to me, O God.
You are my help and my deliverer;
O LORD, do not delay.

**Psalm 71**

[1]In you, O LORD, I have taken refuge;
let me never be put to shame.
[2]Rescue me and deliver me in your righteousness;
turn your ear to me and save me.
[3]Be my rock of refuge,
to which I can always go;
give the command to save me,
for you are my rock and my fortress.
[4]Deliver me, O my God, from the hand of the wicked,
from the grasp of evil and cruel men.

[5]For you have been my hope, O Sovereign LORD,
my confidence since my youth.
[6]From birth I have relied on you;
you brought me forth from my mother's womb.
I will ever praise you.
[7]I have become like a portent to many,
but you are my strong refuge.
[8]My mouth is filled with your praise,
declaring your splendor all day long.

[9]Do not cast me away when I am old;
do not forsake me when my strength is gone.
[10]For my enemies speak against me;
those who wait to kill me conspire together.
[11]They say, "God has forsaken him;
pursue him and seize him,
for no one will rescue him."
[12]Be not far from me, O God;
come quickly, O my God, to help me.
[13]May my accusers perish in shame;
may those who want to harm me
be covered with scorn and disgrace.

[14]But as for me, I will always have hope;
I will praise you more and more.

*See the note on page 349.

°12 ק חושה

יְסַפֵּר צִדְקָתֶךָ כָּל־ הַיּוֹם תְּשׁוּעָתֶךָ כִּי לֹא
not though salvation-of-you the-day all-of righteousness-of-you he-will-tell

יָדַעְתִּי סְפֹרוֹת׃ אָבוֹא בִּגְבֻרוֹת אֲדֹנָי יְהוִה אַזְכִּיר
I-will-proclaim Yahweh Lord in-mighty-acts-of I-will-come (16) measures I-know

צִדְקָתְךָ לְבַדֶּךָ׃ אֱלֹהִים לִמַּדְתַּנִי מִנְּעוּרָי
since-youths-of-me you-taught-me God (17) by-yourself righteousness-of-you

וְעַד־ הֵנָּה אַגִּיד נִפְלְאוֹתֶיךָ׃ וְגַם עַד־ זִקְנָה ׀
old-age in and-even (18) deeds-being-marvelous-of-you I-declare to-now and-to

וְשֵׂיבָה אֱלֹהִים אַל־ תַּעַזְבֵנִי עַד־ אַגִּיד זְרוֹעֲךָ
power-of-you I-declare till you-forsake-me not God and-gray-hair

לְדוֹר לְכָל־ יָבוֹא גְּבוּרָתֶךָ׃ וְצִדְקָתְךָ
and-righteousness-of-you (19) might-of-you he-will-come to-all-of to-generation

אֱלֹהִים עַד־מָרוֹם אֲשֶׁר־עָשִׂיתָ גְדֹלוֹת אֱלֹהִים מִי כָמוֹךָ׃ אֲשֶׁר
though (20) like-you who? God great-things you-did who sky to God

הִרְאִיתַנוּ ׀ צָרוֹת רַבּוֹת וְרָעוֹת תָּשׁוּב
you-will-do-again and-bitter-ones many troubles you-made-see-me

תְּחַיֵּינוּ וּמִתְּהֹמוֹת הָאָרֶץ תָּשׁוּב
you-will-do-again the-earth and-from-depths-of you-will-let-live-me

תַּעֲלֵנִי׃ תֶּרֶב ׀ גְּדֻלָּתִי וְתִסֹּב
and-you-will-do-again honor-of-me you-will-increase (21) you-will-bring-up-me

תְּנַחֲמֵנִי׃ גַּם־ אֲנִי ׀ אוֹדְךָ בִכְלִי־ נֶבֶל
harp with-instrument-of I-will-praise-you I also (22) you-will-comfort-me

אֲמִתְּךָ אֱלֹהָי אֲזַמְּרָה לְךָ בְכִנּוֹר קְדוֹשׁ
Holy-One-of with-lyre to-you I-will-sing-praise God-of-me faithfulness-of-you

יִשְׂרָאֵל׃ תְּרַנֵּנָּה שְׂפָתַי כִּי אֲזַמְּרָה־ לָּךְ
to-you I-sing-praise when lips-of-me they-will-shout-for-joy (23) Israel

וְנַפְשִׁי אֲשֶׁר פָּדִיתָ׃ גַּם־ לְשׁוֹנִי כָּל־ הַיּוֹם
the-day all-of tongue-of-me also (24) you-redeemed whom even-self-of-me

תֶּהְגֶּה צִדְקָתֶךָ כִּי־ בֹשׁוּ כִּי־
for they-have-been-shamed for righteousness-of-you she-will-tell

חָפְרוּ מְבַקְשֵׁי רָעָתִי׃ לִשְׁלֹמֹה ׀ אֱלֹהִים
God of-Solomon (72:1) harm-of-me ones-wanting-of they-have-been-confused

מִשְׁפָּטֶיךָ לְמֶלֶךְ תֵּן וְצִדְקָתְךָ לְבֶן־ מֶלֶךְ׃
royalty to-son-of and-righteousness-of-you endow! to-king justices-of-you

יָדִין עַמְּךָ בְצֶדֶק וַעֲנִיֶּיךָ
and-afflicted-ones-of-you in-righteousness people-of-you he-will-judge (2)

בְמִשְׁפָּט׃ יִשְׂאוּ הָרִים שָׁלוֹם לָעָם וּגְבָעוֹת
and-hills to-the-people prosperity mountains they-will-bring (3) with-justice

15 My mouth will tell of your
righteousness,
of your salvation all day
long,
though I know not its
measure.
16 I will come and proclaim your
mighty acts, O Sovereign
LORD;
I will proclaim your
righteousness, yours
alone.
17 Since my youth, O God, you
have taught me,
and to this day I declare
your marvelous deeds.
18 Even when I am old and gray,
do not forsake me, O God,
till I declare your power to the
next generation,
your might to all who are to
come.

19 Your righteousness reaches to
the skies, O God,
you who have done great
things.
Who, O God, is like you?
20 Though you have made me see
troubles, many and bitter,
you will restore my life
again;
from the depths of the earth
you will again bring me up.
21 You will increase my honor
and comfort me once again.

22 I will praise you with the harp
for your faithfulness, O my
God;
I will sing praise to you with
the lyre,
O Holy One of Israel.
23 My lips will shout for joy
when I sing praise to you—
I, whom you have
redeemed.
24 My tongue will tell of your
righteous acts
all day long,
for those who wanted to harm
me
have been put to shame and
confusion.

## Psalm 72

Of Solomon.

1 Endow the king with your
justice, O God,
the royal son with your
righteousness.
2 He will[u] judge your people in
righteousness,
your afflicted ones with
justice.
3 The mountains will bring
prosperity to the people,

[u]2 Or *May he*; similarly in verses 3-11 and 17

°20a ק הראיתני
°20b ק תחייני

בִּצְדָקָה׃ יִשְׁפֹּט ׀ עֲנִיֵּי־ עָם יוֹשִׁיעַ
he-will-save people afflicted-ones-of he-will-defend (4) in-righteousness

לִבְנֵי אֶבְיוֹן וִידַכֵּא עוֹשֵׁק׃ יִירָאוּךָ
they-will-fear-you (5) one-oppressing and-he-will-crush needy to-children-of

עִם־ שָׁמֶשׁ וְלִפְנֵי יָרֵחַ דּוֹר דּוֹרִים׃ יֵרֵד
he-will-fall (6) generations generation-of moon and-as-long-as sun as-long-as

כְּמָטָר עַל־ גֵּז כִּרְבִיבִים זַרְזִיף אָרֶץ׃ יִפְרַח־
he-will-flourish (7) earth watering-of like-showers mown-field on like-rain

בְּיָמָיו צַדִּיק וְרֹב שָׁלוֹם עַד־ בְּלִי יָרֵחַ׃
moon no-more till prosperity and-abundance-of righteous in-days-of-him

וְיֵרְדְּ מִיָּם עַד־ יָם וּמִנָּהָר עַד־ אַפְסֵי־ אָרֶץ׃
earth ends-of to and-from-River sea to from-sea and-he-will-rule (8)

לְפָנָיו יִכְרְעוּ צִיִּים וְאֹיְבָיו
and-ones-being-enemies-of-him desert-tribes they-will-bow before-him (9)

עָפָר יְלַחֵכוּ׃ מַלְכֵי תַרְשִׁישׁ וְאִיִּים מִנְחָה
tribute and-distant-shores Tarshish kings-of (10) they-will-lick dust

יָשִׁיבוּ מַלְכֵי שְׁבָא וּסְבָא אֶשְׁכָּר יַקְרִיבוּ׃
they-will-present gift and-Seba Sheba kings-of they-will-bring

וְיִשְׁתַּחֲווּ־ לוֹ כָל־ מְלָכִים כָּל־ גּוֹיִם יַעַבְדוּהוּ׃
they-will-serve-him nations all-of kings all-of to-him and-they-will-bow (11)

כִּי־ יַצִּיל אֶבְיוֹן מְשַׁוֵּעַ וְעָנִי וְאֵין־
when-there-is-not and-afflicted one-crying-out needy he-will-deliver for (12)

עֹזֵר לוֹ׃ יָחֹס עַל־ דַּל וְאֶבְיוֹן וְנַפְשׁוֹת
and-lives-of and-needy weak on he-will-take-pity (13) to-him one-helping

אֶבְיוֹנִים יוֹשִׁיעַ׃ מִתּוֹךְ וּמֵחָמָס יִגְאַל
he-will-rescue and-from-violence from-oppression (14) he-will-save needy-ones

נַפְשָׁם וְיֵיקַר דָּמָם בְּעֵינָיו׃
in-eyes-of-him blood-of-them for-he-is-precious life-of-them

וִיחִי וְיִתֶּן־ לוֹ מִזְּהַב שְׁבָא וְיִתְפַּלֵּל
and-may-he-pray Sheba from-gold-of to-him and-may-he-give and-may-he-live (15)

בַּעֲדוֹ תָמִיד כָּל־ הַיּוֹם יְבָרֲכֶנְהוּ׃ יְהִי פִסַּת־
abundance-of let-him-be (16) may-he-bless-him the-day all-of ever for-him

בַּר ׀ בָּאָרֶץ בְּרֹאשׁ הָרִים יִרְעַשׁ כַּלְּבָנוֹן
like-the-Lebanon let-him-sway hills on-top-of throughout-the-land grain

פִּרְיוֹ וְיָצִיצוּ מֵעִיר כְּעֵשֶׂב הָאָרֶץ׃
the-field like-grass-of one-thriving and-let-them-flourish fruit-of-him

יְהִי שְׁמוֹ לְעוֹלָם לִפְנֵי־ שֶׁמֶשׁ יִנּוֹן
may-he-continue sun as-long-as to-forever name-of-him may-he-endure (17)

°17 ק ינון

the hills the fruit of
righteousness.
4 He will defend the afflicted
among the people
and save the children of the
needy;
he will crush the oppressor.
5 He will endure[v] as long as the
sun,
as long as the moon,
through all generations.
6 He will be like rain falling on
a mown field,
like showers watering the
earth.
7 In his days the righteous will
flourish;
prosperity will abound till
the moon is no more.
8 He will rule from sea to sea
and from the River[w] to the
ends of the earth.[x]
9 The desert tribes will bow
before him
and his enemies will lick the
dust.
10 The kings of Tarshish and of
distant shores
will bring tribute to him;
the kings of Sheba and Seba
will present him gifts.
11 All kings will bow down to
him
and all nations will serve
him.
12 For he will deliver the needy
who cry out,
the afflicted who have no
one to help.
13 He will take pity on the weak
and the needy
and save the needy from
death.
14 He will rescue them from
oppression and violence,
for precious is their blood in
his sight.
15 Long may he live!
May gold from Sheba be
given him.
May people ever pray for him
and bless him all day long.
16 Let grain abound throughout
the land;
on the tops of the hills may
it sway.
Let its fruit flourish like
Lebanon;
let it thrive like the grass of
the field.
17 May his name endure forever;
may it continue as long as
the sun.

v5 Septuagint; Hebrew / *You will be feared*
w8 That is, the Euphrates
x8 Or *the end of the land*

שְׁמוֹ וְיִתְבָּרְכוּ בוֹ כָּל־ גּוֹיִם
nations all-of through-him and-they-will-be-blessed name-of-him

יְאַשְּׁרֽוּהוּ׃ בָּרוּךְ ׀ יְהוָה אֱלֹהִים אֱלֹהֵי יִשְׂרָאֵל
Israel God-of God Yahweh being-praised (18) they-will-call-blessed-him

עֹשֵׂה נִפְלָאוֹת לְבַדּֽוֹ׃ וּבָרוּךְ ׀ שֵׁם
name-of and-being-praised (19) by-himself deeds-being-marvelous one-doing-of

כְּבוֹדוֹ לְעוֹלָם וְיִמָּלֵא כְבוֹדוֹ אֶת־ כֹּל
whole-of *** glory-of-him and-may-he-be-filled to-forever glory-of-him

הָאָרֶץ אָמֵן ׀ וְאָמֵֽן׃ כָּלּוּ תְפִלּוֹת דָּוִד בֶּן־ יִשָֽׁי׃
Jesse son-of David prayers-of they-are-concluded (20) and-amen amen the-earth

מִזְמוֹר לְאָסָף אַךְ טוֹב לְיִשְׂרָאֵל אֱלֹהִים לְבָרֵי לֵבָֽב׃
heart to-ones-pure-of God to-Israel good surely of-Asaph psalm (73:1)

וַאֲנִי כִּמְעַט נָטָיוּ רַגְלָי כְּאַיִן שֻׁפְּכָה
they-were-lost as-nearly feet-of-me they-slipped as-almost but-I (2)

אֲשֻׁרָֽי׃ כִּי־ קִנֵּאתִי בַּהוֹלְלִים שְׁלוֹם
prosperity-of to-the-ones-being-arrogant I-envied for (3) footholds-of-me

רְשָׁעִים אֶרְאֶֽה׃ כִּי אֵין חַרְצֻבּוֹת לְמוֹתָם וּבָרִיא
and-healthy at-death-of-them struggles no for (4) I-saw wicked-ones

אוּלָֽם׃ בַּעֲמַל אֱנוֹשׁ אֵינֵמוֹ וְעִם־ אָדָם לֹא
not human and-by not-of-them man from-burden-of (5) body-of-them

יְנֻגָּֽעוּ׃ לָכֵן עֲנָקַתְמוֹ גַאֲוָה יַעֲטָף־
he-wraps pride she-is-a-necklace-to-them therefore (6) they-are-plagued

שִׁית חָמָס לָֽמוֹ׃ יָצָא מֵחֵלֶב עֵינֵמוֹ עָבְרוּ
they-pass-limits eye-of-them with-fat he-bulges (7) on-them violence clothing

מַשְׂכִּיּוֹת לֵבָֽב׃ יָמִיקוּ ׀ וִידַבְּרוּ בְרָע עֹשֶׁק
oppression with-malice and-they-speak they-scoff (8) mind conceits-of

מִמָּרוֹם יְדַבֵּֽרוּ׃ שַׁתּוּ בַשָּׁמַיִם פִּיהֶם
mouth-of-them to-the-heavens they-lay-claim (9) they-threaten in-arrogance

וּלְשׁוֹנָם תִּהֲלַךְ בָּאָֽרֶץ׃ לָכֵן ׀ יָשִׁיב
he-turns therefore (10) to-the-earth she-possesses and-tongue-of-them

עַמּוֹ הֲלֹם וּמֵי מָלֵא יִמָּצוּ לָֽמוֹ׃
for-them they-drink-up abundance and-waters-of to-here people-of-him

וְאָמְרוּ אֵיכָה יָדַע־ אֵל וְיֵשׁ דֵּעָה בְעֶלְיֽוֹן׃
to-Most-High knowledge and-is-there God he-knows how? and-they-say (11)

הִנֵּה־ אֵלֶּה רְשָׁעִים וְשַׁלְוֵי עוֹלָם הִשְׂגּוּ־ חָֽיִל׃
wealth they-increase always even-ones-carefree-of wicked-ones these see! (12)

אַךְ־ רִיק זִכִּיתִי לְבָבִי וָאֶרְחַץ בְּנִקָּיוֹן
in-innocence and-I-washed heart-of-me I-kept-pure in-vain surely (13)

All nations will be blessed
through him,
and they will call him
blessed.

18 Praise be to the LORD God, the
God of Israel,
who alone does marvelous
deeds.
19 Praise be to his glorious name
forever;
may the whole earth be
filled with his glory.
Amen and Amen.

20 This concludes the prayers of
David son of Jesse.

## BOOK III

*Psalms 73-89*

### Psalm 73

A psalm of Asaph.

1 Surely God is good to Israel,
to those who are pure in
heart.

2 But as for me, my feet had
almost slipped;
I had nearly lost my
foothold.
3 For I envied the arrogant
when I saw the prosperity
of the wicked.

4 They have no struggles;
their bodies are healthy and
strong.[y]
5 They are free from the burdens
common to man;
they are not plagued by
human ills.
6 Therefore pride is their
necklace;
they clothe themselves with
violence.
7 From their callous hearts
comes iniquity[z];
the evil conceits of their
minds know no limits.
8 They scoff, and speak with
malice;
in their arrogance they
threaten oppression.
9 Their mouths lay claim to
heaven,
and their tongues take
possession of the earth.
10 Therefore their people turn to
them
and drink up waters in
abundance.[a]
11 They say, "How can God
know?
Does the Most High have
knowledge?"
12 This is what the wicked are
like—
always carefree, they
increase in wealth.

13 Surely in vain have I kept my

y4 With a different word division of the Hebrew; Masoretic Text *struggles at their death; / their bodies are healthy*
z7 Syriac (see also Septuagint); Hebrew *Their eyes bulge with fat*
a10 The meaning of the Hebrew for this verse is uncertain.

°2a ק נטיו
°2b ק שפכו
°10 ק ישוב

כַּפָּי׃ וָאֱהִי נָגוּעַ כָּל־ הַיּוֹם וְתוֹכַחְתִּי
and-punishment-of-me the-day all-of being-plagued but-I-am (14) hands-of-me

לַבְּקָרִים׃ אִם־ אָמַרְתִּי אֲסַפְּרָה כְמוֹ הִנֵּה דוֹר
generation-of see! thus I-will-speak I-said if (15) in-the-mornings

בָּנֶיךָ בָגָדְתִּי׃ וָאֲחַשְּׁבָה לָדַעַת זֹאת
this to-understand when-I-tried (16) I-would-have-betrayed children-of-you

עָמָל הִיא בְעֵינָי׃ עַד־ אָבוֹא אֶל־ מִקְדְּשֵׁי־ אֵל
God sanctuaries-of into I-entered till (17) to-eyes-of-me he oppressive

אָבִינָה לְאַחֲרִיתָם׃ אַךְ בַּחֲלָקוֹת
on-slippery-grounds surely (18) about-final-destiny-of-them I-understood

תָּשִׁית לָמוֹ הִפַּלְתָּם לְמַשּׁוּאוֹת׃ אֵיךְ הָיוּ
they-are how! (19) to-ruins you-cast-down-them to-them you-place

לְשַׁמָּה כְרָגַע סָפוּ תַּמּוּ מִן־
by they-are-completed they-are-swept-away in-suddenness for-destruction

בַלָּהוֹת׃ כַּחֲלוֹם מֵהָקִיץ אֲדֹנָי בָּעִיר ׀ צַלְמָם
fantasy-of-them when-to-arise Lord when-to-awaken as-dream (20) terrors

תִּבְזֶה׃ כִּי יִתְחַמֵּץ לְבָבִי וְכִלְיוֹתַי
and-spirits-of-me heart-of-me he-was-grieved when (21) you-will-despise

אֶשְׁתּוֹנָן׃ וַאֲנִי־ בַעַר וְלֹא אֵדָע בְּהֵמוֹת הָיִיתִי
I-was brute-beasts I-knew and-not senseless and-I (22) I-was-embittered

עִמָּךְ׃ וַאֲנִי תָמִיד עִמָּךְ אָחַזְתָּ בְּיַד־ יְמִינִי׃
right-of-me by-hand-of you-hold with-you always yet-I (23) before-you

בַּעֲצָתְךָ תַנְחֵנִי וְאַחַר כָּבוֹד תִּקָּחֵנִי׃
you-will-take-me glory and-afterward you-guide-me with-counsel-of-you (24)

מִי־ לִי בַשָּׁמָיִם וְעִמְּךָ לֹא־ חָפַצְתִּי בָאָרֶץ׃
on-the-earth I-desire nothing and-with-you in-the-heavens to-me who? (25)

כָּלָה שְׁאֵרִי וּלְבָבִי צוּר־ לְבָבִי
heart-of-me strength-of and-heart-of-me flesh-of-me he-may-fail (26)

וְחֶלְקִי אֱלֹהִים לְעוֹלָם׃ כִּי־ הִנֵּה רְחֵקֶיךָ
ones-far-from-you see! for (27) to-forever God and-portion-of-me

יֹאבֵדוּ הִצְמַתָּה כָּל־ זוֹנֶה מִמֶּךָּ׃ וַאֲנִי ׀
but-I (28) to-you one-being-unfaithful all-of you-destroy they-will-perish

קִרֲבַת אֱלֹהִים לִי־ טוֹב שַׁתִּי ׀ בַּאדֹנָי יְהוִה מַחְסִי לְסַפֵּר
to-tell refuge-of-me Yahweh to-Lord I-made good to-me God nearness-of

כָּל־ מַלְאֲכוֹתֶיךָ׃ מַשְׂכִּיל לְאָסָף לָמָה אֱלֹהִים זָנַחְתָּ לָנֶצַח
to-forever you-rejected God why? of-Asaph maskil (74:1) deeds-of-you all-of

יֶעְשַׁן אַפְּךָ בְּצֹאן מַרְעִיתֶךָ׃ זְכֹר
remember! (2) pasture-of-you against-sheep-of anger-of-you he-smolders

heart pure;
in vain have I washed my hands in innocence.
[14]All day long I have been plagued;
I have been punished every morning.

[15]If I had said, "I will speak thus,"
I would have betrayed this generation of your children.
[16]When I tried to understand all this,
it was oppressive to me
[17]till I entered the sanctuary of God;
then I understood their final destiny.

[18]Surely you place them on slippery ground;
you cast them down to ruin.
[19]How suddenly are they destroyed,
completely swept away by terrors!
[20]As a dream when one awakes,
so when you arise, O Lord,
you will despise them as fantasies.

[21]When my heart was grieved
and my spirit embittered,
[22]I was senseless and ignorant;
I was a brute beast before you.

[23]Yet I am always with you;
you hold me by my right hand.
[24]You guide me with your counsel,
and afterward you will take me into glory.
[25]Whom have I in heaven but you?
And being with you, I desire nothing on earth.
[26]My flesh and my heart may fail,
but God is the strength of my heart
and my portion forever.

[27]Those who are far from you will perish;
you destroy all who are unfaithful to you.
[28]But as for me, it is good to be near God.
I have made the Sovereign LORD my refuge;
I will tell of all your deeds.

### Psalm 74

A *maskil*[b] of Asaph.

[1]Why have you rejected us forever, O God?
Why does your anger smolder against the sheep of your pasture?

[b]Title: Probably a literary or musical term

°*16* ק הוא

עֲדָתְךָ׀ קָנִיתָ קֶּדֶם גָּאַלְתָּ שֵׁבֶט נַחֲלָתֶךָ
inheritance-of-you tribe-of you-redeemed of-old you-purchased people-of-you

הַר־ צִיּוֹן זֶה׀ שָׁכַנְתָּ בּוֹ׃ הָרִימָה פְעָמֶיךָ
steps-of-you lift-high! (3) in-him you-dwelt where Zion Mount-of

לְמַשֻּׁאוֹת נֶצַח כָּל־ הֵרַע אוֹיֵב בַּקֹּדֶשׁ׃
to-the-sanctuary one-being-enemy to-destroy all-of everlasting through-ruins-of

שָׁאֲגוּ צֹרְרֶיךָ בְּקֶרֶב מוֹעֲדֶךָ שָׂמוּ
they-set-up meeting-of-you in-place-of ones-being-foes-of-you they-roared (4)

אוֹתֹתָם אֹתוֹת׃ יִוָּדַע כְּמֵבִיא לְמָעְלָה
at-above like-one-wielding he-behaved (5) signs standards-of-them

בִּסֲבָךְ־ עֵץ קַרְדֻּמּוֹת׃ וְעַת° פִּתּוּחֶיהָ יָּחַד
together carved-panels-of-her and-now (6) axes tree through-thicket-of

בְּכַשִּׁיל וְכֵילַפֹּת יַהֲלֹמוּן׃ שִׁלְחוּ בָאֵשׁ
with-fire they-sent-down (7) they-smashed and-hatchets with-axe

מִקְדָּשֶׁךָ לָאָרֶץ חִלְּלוּ מִשְׁכַּן־ שְׁמֶךָ׃
Name-of-you dwelling-place-of they-defiled to-the-ground sanctuary-of-you

אָמְרוּ בְלִבָּם נִינָם יָחַד שָׂרְפוּ
they-burned completely we-will-crush-them in-heart-of-them they-said (8)

כָל־ מוֹעֲדֵי־ אֵל בָּאָרֶץ׃ אוֹתֹתֵינוּ לֹא רָאִינוּ
we-see not miraculous-signs-of-us (9) in-the-land God worship-places-of all-of

אֵין־ עוֹד נָבִיא וְלֹא־ אִתָּנוּ יֹדֵעַ עַד־ מָה׃
when? until one-knowing among-us and-not prophet longer there-is-no

עַד־ מָתַי אֱלֹהִים יְחָרֶף צָר יְנָאֵץ אוֹיֵב
one-being-foe will-he-revile enemy will-he-mock God when? until (10)

שִׁמְךָ לָנֶצַח׃ לָמָּה תָשִׁיב יָדְךָ
hand-of-you you-hold-back why? (11) to-forever name-of-you

וִימִינֶךָ מִקֶּרֶב חֵוקְךָ° כַלֵּה׃ וֵאלֹהִים
but-God (12) destroy! bosom-of-you from-fold-of even-right-hand-of-you

מַלְכִּי מִקֶּדֶם פֹּעֵל יְשׁוּעוֹת בְּקֶרֶב הָאָרֶץ׃
the-earth upon-midst-of salvations one-bringing from-of-old king-of-me

אַתָּה פוֹרַרְתָּ בְעָזְּךָ יָם שִׁבַּרְתָּ רָאשֵׁי תַנִּינִים עַל־
in monsters heads-of you-broke sea by-power-of-you you-split-open you (13)

הַמָּיִם׃ אַתָּה רִצַּצְתָּ רָאשֵׁי לִוְיָתָן תִּתְּנֶנּוּ מַאֲכָל
food you-gave-him Leviathan heads-of you-crushed you (14) the-waters

לְעָם לְצִיִּים׃ אַתָּה בָקַעְתָּ מַעְיָן וָנָחַל אַתָּה
you and-stream spring you-opened-up you (15) to-desert-creatures to-people

הוֹבַשְׁתָּ נַהֲרוֹת אֵיתָן׃ לְךָ יוֹם אַף־ לְךָ לָיְלָה
night to-you also day to-you (16) ever-flowing rivers-of you-dried-up

2Remember the people you
purchased of old,
the tribe you redeemed as
your inheritance—
Mount Zion, where you
dwelt.
3Pick your way through these
everlasting ruins,
all this destruction the
enemy has brought on
the sanctuary.
4Your foes roared in the place
where you met with us;
they set up their standards
as signs.
5They behaved like men
wielding axes
to cut through a thicket of
trees.
6They smashed all the carved
paneling
with their axes and hatchets.
7They burned your sanctuary to
the ground;
they defiled the dwelling
place of your Name.
8They said in their hearts, "We
will crush them
completely!"
They burned every place
where God was
worshiped in the land.
9We are given no miraculous
signs;
no prophets are left,
and none of us knows how
long this will be.
10How long will the enemy
mock you, O God?
Will the foe revile your
name forever?
11Why do you hold back your
hand, your right hand?
Take it from the folds of
your garment and destroy
them!
12But you, O God, are my king
from of old;
you bring salvation upon
the earth.
13It was you who split open the
sea by your power;
you broke the heads of the
monster in the waters.
14It was you who crushed the
heads of Leviathan
and gave him as food to the
creatures of the desert.
15It was you who opened up
springs and streams;
you dried up the ever
flowing rivers.
16The day is yours, and yours
also the night;

°6 ק ועתה
°11 ק חיקך

אַתָּה הֲכִינוֹתָ מָאוֹר וָשָׁמֶשׁ׃ אַתָּה הִצַּבְתָּ כָּל־ גְּבוּלוֹת אָרֶץ
earth boundaries-of all-of you-set you (17) and-sun moon you-established you

קַיִץ וָחֹרֶף אַתָּה יְצַרְתָּם׃ זְכָר־ זֹאת אוֹיֵב
one-being-enemy this remember! (18) you-made-them you and-winter summer

חֵרֵף ׀ יְהוָה וְעַם נָבָל נִאֲצוּ שְׁמֶךָ׃ אַל־
not (19) name-of-you they-reviled foolish and-people Yahweh he-mocked

תִּתֵּן לְחַיַּת נֶפֶשׁ תּוֹרֶךָ חַיַּת עֲנִיֶּיךָ
afflicted-ones-of-you life-of dove-of-you life-of to-wild-beast you-hand-over

אַל־ תִּשְׁכַּח לָנֶצַח׃ הַבֵּט לַבְּרִית כִּי מָלְאוּ
they-fill because for-the-covenant have-regard! (20) to-forever you-forget not

מַחֲשַׁכֵּי־ אֶרֶץ נְאוֹת חָמָס׃ אַל־ יָשֹׁב דַּךְ
oppressed let-him-retreat not (21) violence haunts-of land dark-places-of

נִכְלָם עָנִי וְאֶבְיוֹן יְהַלְלוּ שְׁמֶךָ׃ קוּמָה
rise-up! (22) name-of-you may-they-praise and-needy poor one-being-disgraced

אֱלֹהִים רִיבָה רִיבֶךָ זְכֹר חֶרְפָּתְךָ מִנִּי־נָבָל כָּל־ הַיּוֹם׃
the-day all-of fool by mocking-of-you remember! cause-of-you defend! God

אַל־ תִּשְׁכַּח קוֹל צֹרְרֶיךָ שְׁאוֹן
uproar-of ones-being-adversaries-of-you clamor-of you-ignore not (23)

קָמֶיךָ עֹלֶה תָמִיד׃ לַמְנַצֵּחַ
for-the-one-directing *(75:1) continually one-rising ones-being-enemies-of-you

אַל־ תַּשְׁחֵת מִזְמוֹר לְאָסָף שִׁיר׃ הוֹדִינוּ לְּךָ ׀ אֱלֹהִים
God to-you we-give-thanks (2) song of-Asaph psalm you-destroy not

הוֹדִינוּ וְקָרוֹב שְׁמֶךָ סִפְּרוּ נִפְלְאוֹתֶיךָ׃
deeds-being-wonderful-of-you they-tell Name-of-you for-near we-give-thanks

כִּי אֶקַּח מוֹעֵד אֲנִי מֵישָׁרִים אֶשְׁפֹּט׃ נְמֹגִים
ones-quaking (4) I-judge upright-ones I appointed-time I-choose that (3)

אֶרֶץ וְכָל־ יֹשְׁבֶיהָ אָנֹכִי תִכַּנְתִּי עַמּוּדֶיהָ סֶּלָה׃
selah pillars-of-her I-hold-firm I ones-being-people-of-her and-all-of earth

אָמַרְתִּי לַהוֹלְלִים אַל־ תָּהֹלּוּ וְלָרְשָׁעִים
and-to-the-wicked-ones you-boast not to-the-ones-being-arrogant I-say (5)

אַל־ תָּרִימוּ קָרֶן׃ אַל־ תָּרִימוּ לַמָּרוֹם קַרְנְכֶם
horn-of-you against-the-heaven you-lift not (6) horn you-lift-up not

תְּדַבְּרוּ בְצַוָּאר עָתָק׃ כִּי לֹא מִמּוֹצָא וּמִמַּעֲרָב
or-from-west from-east no-one for (7) outstretched with-neck you-speak

וְלֹא מִמִּדְבַּר הָרִים׃ כִּי־ אֱלֹהִים שֹׁפֵט זֶה
this-one one-judging God but (8) to-exalt from-desert and-no-one

יַשְׁפִּיל וְזֶה יָרִים׃ כִּי כוֹס בְּיַד־ יְהוָה וְיַיִן
and-wine Yahweh in-hand-of cup for (9) he-exalts and-this-one he-brings-down

you established the sun and
moon.
17It was you who set all the
boundaries of the earth;
you made both summer and
winter.
18Remember how the enemy has
mocked you, O LORD,
how foolish people have
reviled your name.
19Do not hand over the life of
your dove to wild beasts;
do not forget the lives of
your afflicted people
forever.
20Have regard for your
covenant,
because haunts of violence
fill the dark places of the
land.
21Do not let the oppressed
retreat in disgrace;
may the poor and needy
praise your name.
22Rise up, O God, and defend
your cause;
remember how fools mock
you all day long.
23Do not ignore the clamor of
your adversaries,
the uproar of your enemies,
which rises continually.

**Psalm 75**

For the director of music. ⌞To the tune of⌟ "Do Not Destroy." A psalm of Asaph. A song.

1We give thanks to you, O God,
we give thanks, for your
Name is near;
men tell of your wonderful
deeds.
2You say, "I choose the
appointed time;
it is I who judge uprightly.
3When the earth and all its
people quake,
it is I who hold its pillars
firm. *Selah*
4To the arrogant I say, 'Boast
no more,'
and to the wicked, 'Do not
lift up your horns.
5Do not lift your horns against
heaven;
do not speak with
outstretched neck.' "
6No one from the east or the
west
or from the desert can exalt
a man.
7But it is God who judges:
He brings one down, he
exalts another.
8In the hand of the LORD is a
cup

*Heading, *1* See the note on page 349.

חָמַר | מָלֵא מֶסֶךְ וַיַּגֵּר מִזֶּה אַךְ־ שְׁמָרֶיהָ
dregs-of-her indeed from-this and-he-pours-out mixed-spice he-is-full he-foams

יָמֹצּוּ יִשְׁתּוּ כֹּל רִשְׁעֵי־ אָרֶץ׃ וַאֲנִי אַגִּיד
I-will-declare and-I (10) earth wicked-ones-of all-of they-drink they-drink

לְעֹלָם אֲזַמְּרָה לֵאלֹהֵי יַעֲקֹב׃ וְכָל־ קַרְנֵי
horns-of and-all-of (11) Jacob to-God-of I-will-sing-praise to-forever

רְשָׁעִים אֲגַדֵּעַ תְּרוֹמַמְנָה קַרְנוֹת צַדִּיק׃
righteous horns-of they-will-be-lifted-up I-will-cut-off wicked-ones

לַמְנַצֵּחַ בִּנְגִינֹת מִזְמוֹר לְאָסָף שִׁיר׃
song of-Asaph psalm with-stringed-instruments for-the-one-directing *(76:1)

נוֹדָע בִּיהוּדָה אֱלֹהִים בְּיִשְׂרָאֵל גָּדוֹל שְׁמוֹ׃ וַיְהִי
and-he-is (3) name-of-him great in-Israel God in-Judah one-being-known (2)

בְשָׁלֵם סֻכּוֹ וּמְעוֹנָתוֹ בְצִיּוֹן׃ שָׁמָּה שִׁבַּר
he-broke at-there (4) in-Zion and-dwelling-place-of-him tent-of-him in-Salem

רִשְׁפֵי־ קָשֶׁת מָגֵן וְחֶרֶב וּמִלְחָמָה סֶלָה׃ נָאוֹר
one-giving-light (5) selah and-weapon-of-war and-sword shield arrow flashes-of

אַתָּה אַדִּיר מֵהַרְרֵי־ טָרֶף׃ אֶשְׁתּוֹלְלוּ | אַבִּירֵי
men-valiant-of they-lie-plundered (6) game more-than-mountains-of majestic you

לֵב נָמוּ שְׁנָתָם וְלֹא־ מָצְאוּ כָל־ אַנְשֵׁי־ חַיִל
war men-of any-of they-can-lift and-not sleep-of-them they-sleep heart

יְדֵיהֶם׃ מִגַּעֲרָתְךָ אֱלֹהֵי יַעֲקֹב נִרְדָּם וְרֶכֶב
both-chariot one-lying-still Jacob God-of at-rebuke-of-you (7) hands-of-them

וָסוּס׃ אַתָּה | נוֹרָא אַתָּה וּמִי־ יַעֲמֹד לְפָנֶיךָ
before-you he-can-stand and-who? you one-being-feared you (8) and-horse

מֵאָז אַפֶּךָ׃ מִשָּׁמַיִם הִשְׁמַעְתָּ דִּין אֶרֶץ יָרְאָה
she-feared land judgment you-pronounced from-heavens (9) anger-of-you at-when

וְשָׁקָטָה׃ בְּקוּם־ לַמִּשְׁפָּט אֱלֹהִים לְהוֹשִׁיעַ כָּל־
all-of to-save God for-the-judgment when-to-rise (10) and-she-was-quiet

עַנְוֵי־ אֶרֶץ סֶלָה׃ כִּי־ חֲמַת אָדָם תּוֹדֶךָּ
she-praises-you man wrath-of surely (11) selah land afflicted-ones-of

שְׁאֵרִית חֵמֹת תַּחְגֹּר׃ נִדְרוּ וְשַׁלְּמוּ לַיהוָה
to-Yahweh and-fulfill! make-vows! (12) you-restrain wraths survivor-of

אֱלֹהֵיכֶם כָּל־ סְבִיבָיו יוֹבִילוּ שַׁי לַמּוֹרָא׃
to-the-One-being-feared gift let-them-bring neighbors-of-him all-of God-of-you

יִבְצֹר רוּחַ נְגִידִים נוֹרָא לְמַלְכֵי־ אָרֶץ׃
earth by-kings-of one-being-feared rulers spirit-of he-breaks (13)

לַמְנַצֵּחַ עַל־ יְדִיתוּן לְאָסָף מִזְמוֹר׃ קוֹלִי
cry-of-me (2) psalm of-Asaph Jeduthun to for-the-one-directing *(77:1)

full of foaming wine mixed
with spices;
he pours it out, and all the
wicked of the earth
drink it down to its very
dregs.
9 As for me, I will declare this
forever;
I will sing praise to the God
of Jacob.
10 I will cut off the horns of all
the wicked,
but the horns of the
righteous will be lifted
up.

### Psalm 76

For the director of music. With stringed instruments. A psalm of Asaph. A song.

1 In Judah God is known;
his name is great in Israel.
2 His tent is in Salem,
his dwelling place in Zion.
3 There he broke the flashing
arrows,
the shields and the swords,
the weapons of war. *Selah*
4 You are resplendent with light,
more majestic than
mountains rich with
game.
5 Valiant men lie plundered,
they sleep their last sleep;
not one of the warriors
can lift his hands.
6 At your rebuke, O God of
Jacob,
both horse and chariot lie
still.
7 You alone are to be feared.
Who can stand before you
when you are angry?
8 From heaven you pronounced
judgment,
and the land feared and was
quiet—
9 when you, O God, rose up to
judge,
to save all the afflicted of
the land. *Selah*
10 Surely your wrath against men
brings you praise,
and the survivors of your
wrath are restrained.[c]
11 Make vows to the LORD your
God and fulfill them;
let all the neighboring lands
bring gifts to the One to be
feared.
12 He breaks the spirit of rulers;
he is feared by the kings of
the earth.

### Psalm 77

For the director of music. To Jeduthun. Of Asaph. A psalm.

c10 Or *Surely the wrath of men brings you praise, / and with the remainder of wrath you arm yourself*

*Heading, *1* See the note on page 349.

°1 ק ידותון

אֶל־אֱלֹהִים וְאֶצְעָקָה קוֹלִי אֶל־אֱלֹהִים וְהַאֲזִין אֵלָי׃
to-me and-to-hear God to cry-of-me indeed-I-cried-for-help God to

בְּיוֹם צָרָתִי אֲדֹנָי דָּרָשְׁתִּי יָדִי ׀ לַיְלָה נִגְּרָה
she-was-stretched night hand-of-me I-sought Lord distress-of-me in-day-of (3)

וְלֹא תָפוּג מֵאֲנָה הִנָּחֵם נַפְשִׁי׃ אֶזְכְּרָה
I-remembered (4) soul-of-me to-be-comforted she-refused she-became-tired and-not

אֱלֹהִים וְאֶהֱמָיָה אָשִׂיחָה ׀ וְתִתְעַטֵּף רוּחִי סֶלָה׃ אָחַזְתָּ
you-kept (5) selah spirit-of-me and-she-grew-faint I-mused and-I-groaned God

שְׁמֻרוֹת עֵינָי נִפְעַמְתִּי וְלֹא אֲדַבֵּר׃ חִשַּׁבְתִּי יָמִים
days I-thought-of (6) I-could-speak and-not I-was-troubled eyes-of-me lids-of

מִקֶּדֶם שְׁנוֹת עוֹלָמִים׃ אֶזְכְּרָה נְגִינָתִי בַּלָּיְלָה
in-the-night song-of-me I-remembered (7) ones-long-ago years-of at-formerly

עִם־לְבָבִי אָשִׂיחָה וַיְחַפֵּשׂ רוּחִי׃ הַלְעוֹלָמִים
to-forevers? (8) spirit-of-me and-he-inquired I-mused heart-of-me in

יִזְנַח ׀ אֲדֹנָי וְלֹא־יֹסִיף לִרְצוֹת עוֹד׃
again to-show-favor he-will-do-again and-never Lord will-he-reject

הֶאָפֵס לָנֶצַח חַסְדּוֹ גָּמַר אֹמֶר
promise he-failed unfailing-love-of-him to-forever he-vanished? (9)

לְדֹר וָדֹר׃ הֲשָׁכַח חַנּוֹת אֵל אִם־
or God to-be-merciful he-forgot? (10) and-generation for-generation

קָפַץ בְּאַף רַחֲמָיו סֶלָה׃ וָאֹמַר
then-I-thought (11) selah compassions-of-him in-anger he-withheld

חַלּוֹתִי הִיא שְׁנוֹת יְמִין עֶלְיוֹן׃ אֶזְכּוֹר
I-will-remember (12) Most-High right-hand-of years-of this to-appeal-me

מַעַלְלֵי־יָהּ כִּי־אֶזְכְּרָה מִקֶּדֶם פִּלְאֶךָ׃
miracle-of-you of-long-ago I-will-remember yes Yahweh deeds-of

וְהָגִיתִי בְכָל־פָּעֳלֶךָ וּבַעֲלִילוֹתֶיךָ
and-to-mighty-deeds-of-you work-of-you on-all-of and-I-will-meditate (13)

אָשִׂיחָה׃ אֱלֹהִים בַּקֹּדֶשׁ דַּרְכֶּךָ מִי־אֵל גָּדוֹל
great god what? way-of-you in-the-holiness God (14) I-will-consider

כֵּאלֹהִים׃ אַתָּה הָאֵל עֹשֵׂה פֶלֶא הוֹדַעְתָּ בָעַמִּים
among-the-peoples you-display miracle one-performing-of the-God you (15) as-God

עֻזֶּךָ׃ גָּאַלְתָּ בִּזְרוֹעַ עַמֶּךָ בְּנֵי־יַעֲקֹב
Jacob descendants-of people-of-you with-arm you-redeemed (16) power-of-you

וְיוֹסֵף סֶלָה׃ רָאוּךָ מַּיִם ׀ אֱלֹהִים רָאוּךָ מַּיִם יָחִילוּ
they-writhed waters they-saw-you God waters they-saw-you (17) selah and-Joseph

אַף יִרְגְּזוּ תְהֹמוֹת׃ זֹרְמוּ מַיִם ׀ עָבוֹת
clouds waters they-poured-down (18) depths they-were-convulsed indeed

1 I cried out to God for help;
I cried out to God to hear me.
2 When I was in distress, I sought the Lord;
at night I stretched out untiring hands
and my soul refused to be comforted.

3 I remembered you, O God, and I groaned;
I mused, and my spirit grew faint. *Selah*
4 You kept my eyes from closing;
I was too troubled to speak.
5 I thought about the former days,
the years of long ago;
6 I remembered my songs in the night.
My heart mused and my spirit inquired:

7 "Will the Lord reject us forever?
Will he never show his favor again?
8 Has his unfailing love vanished forever?
Has his promise failed for all time?
9 Has God forgotten to be merciful?
Has he in anger withheld his compassion?" *Selah*

10 Then I thought, "To this I will appeal:
the years of the right hand of the Most High."
11 I will remember the deeds of the LORD;
yes, I will remember your miracles of long ago.
12 I will meditate on all your works
and consider all your mighty deeds.

13 Your ways, O God, are holy.
What god is so great as our God?
14 You are the God who performs miracles;
you display your power among the peoples.
15 With your mighty arm you redeemed your people,
the descendants of Jacob and Joseph. *Selah*

16 The waters saw you, O God,
the waters saw you and writhed;
the very depths were convulsed.
17 The clouds poured down water,

*See the note on page 349.

°12 ק אזכור

קֹול נָתְנוּ שְׁחָקִים אַף־ חֲצָצֶיךָ יִתְהַלָּכוּ׃
they-flashed-around arrows-of-you also skies they-resounded thunder

(19) קֹול רַעַמְךָ ׀ בַּגַּלְגַּל הֵאִירוּ בְרָקִים תֵּבֵל
world lightnings they-lit-up in-the-whirlwind thunder-of-you sound-of (19)

רָגְזָה וַתִּרְעַשׁ הָאָרֶץ׃ (20) בַּיָּם דַּרְכֶּךָ
path-of-you through-the-sea (20) the-earth and-she-quaked she-trembled

וּשְׁבִילְךָ° בְּמַיִם רַבִּים וְעִקְּבֹותֶיךָ לֹא
not though-footprints-of-you mighty-ones through-waters and-way-of-you

נֹדָעוּ׃ (21) נָחִיתָ כַצֹּאן עַמֶּךָ בְּיַד־ מֹשֶׁה
Moses by-hand-of people-of-you like-the-flock you-led (21) they-were-seen

וְאַהֲרֹן׃ (78:1) מַשְׂכִּיל לְאָסָף הַאֲזִינָה עַמִּי תֹּורָתִי הַטּוּ
turn! teaching-of-me people-of-me hear! of-Asaph maskil (78:1) and-Aaron

אָזְנְכֶם לְאִמְרֵי־ פִי׃ (2) אֶפְתְּחָה בְמָשָׁל פִּי
mouth-of-me in-parable I-will-open (2) mouth-of-me to-words-of ear-of-you

אַבִּיעָה חִידֹות מִנִּי־ קֶדֶם׃ (3) אֲשֶׁר שָׁמַעְנוּ וַנֵּדָעֵם
and-we-knew-them we-heard that (3) of-old from things-hidden I-will-utter

וַאֲבֹותֵינוּ סִפְּרוּ־ לָנוּ׃ (4) לֹא נְכַחֵד ׀ מִבְּנֵיהֶם
from-children-of-them we-will-hide not (4) to-us they-told and-fathers-of-us

לְדֹור אַחֲרֹון מְסַפְּרִים תְּהִלֹּות יְהוָה וֶעֱזוּזֹו
and-power-of-him Yahweh praiseworthy-deeds-of ones-telling next to-generation

וְנִפְלְאֹותָיו אֲשֶׁר עָשָׂה׃ (5) וַיָּקֶם עֵדוּת ׀
statute and-he-decreed (5) he-did that and-deeds-being-wonders-of-him

בְּיַעֲקֹב וְתֹורָה שָׂם בְּיִשְׂרָאֵל אֲשֶׁר צִוָּה אֶת־
*** he-commanded which in-Israel he-established and-law for-Jacob

אֲבֹותֵינוּ לְהֹודִיעָם לִבְנֵיהֶם׃ (6) לְמַעַן יֵדְעוּ ׀
they-would-know so-that (6) to-children-of-them to-teach-them forefathers-of-us

דֹּור אַחֲרֹון בָּנִים יִוָּלֵדוּ יָקֻמוּ וִיסַפְּרוּ
and-they-will-tell they-will-rise they-will-be-born children next generation

לִבְנֵיהֶם׃ (7) וְיָשִׂימוּ בֵאלֹהִים כִּסְלָם וְלֹא
and-not trust-of-them in-God then-they-would-put (7) to-children-of-them

יִשְׁכְּחוּ מַעַלְלֵי־ אֵל וּמִצְוֹתָיו יִנְצֹרוּ׃ (8) וְלֹא
and-not (8) they-would-keep but-commands-of-him God deeds-of they-would-forget

יִהְיוּ ׀ כַּאֲבֹותָם דֹּור סֹורֵר
one-being-stubborn generation like-forefathers-of-them they-would-be

וּמֹרֶה דֹּור לֹא־ הֵכִין לִבֹּו וְלֹא־
and-not heart-of-him he-was-loyal not generation and-one-rebelling

נֶאֶמְנָה אֶת־ אֵל רוּחֹו׃ (9) בְּנֵי־ אֶפְרַיִם נֹושְׁקֵי
ones-being-armed-of Ephraim men-of (9) spirit-of-him God to she-was-faithful

the skies resounded with
thunder;
your arrows flashed back
and forth.
18Your thunder was heard in the
whirlwind,
your lightning lit up the
world;
the earth trembled and
quaked.
19Your path led through the sea,
your way through the
mighty waters,
though your footprints were
not seen.

20You led your people like a
flock
by the hand of Moses and
Aaron.

### Psalm 78

A *maskil*[d] of Asaph.

1O my people, hear my
teaching;
listen to the words of my
mouth.
2I will open my mouth in
parables,
I will utter things hidden
from of old—
3things we have heard and
known,
things our fathers have told
us.
4We will not hide them from
their children;
we will tell the next
generation
the praiseworthy deeds of the
LORD,
his power, and the wonders
he has done.
5He decreed statutes for Jacob
and established the law in
Israel,
which he commanded our
forefathers
to teach their children,
6so the next generation would
know them,
even the children yet to be
born,
and they in turn would tell
their children.
7Then they would put their
trust in God
and would not forget his
deeds
but would keep his
commands.
8They would not be like their
forefathers—
a stubborn and rebellious
generation,
whose hearts were not loyal to
God,
whose spirits were not
faithful to him.

9The men of Ephraim, though
armed with bows,

[d] Title: Probably a literary or musical term

*See the note on page 349.

°20 ק ושבילך

רוֹמֵי־ קֶשֶׁת הָפְכוּ בְיוֹם קְרָב: לֹא שָׁמְרוּ
ones-shooting-of · bow · they-turned-back · on-day-of · battle · (10) · not · they-kept

בְּרִית אֱלֹהִים וּבְתוֹרָתוֹ מֵאֲנוּ לָלֶכֶת: וַיִּשְׁכְּחוּ
covenant-of · God · and-by-law-of-him · they-refused · to-live · (11) · and-they-forgot

עֲלִילוֹתָיו וְנִפְלְאוֹתָיו אֲשֶׁר הֶרְאָם:
deeds-of-him · and-deeds-being-wonders-of-him · which · he-showed-them

נֶגֶד אֲבוֹתָם עָשָׂה פֶלֶא בְּאֶרֶץ מִצְרַיִם שְׂדֵה־
in-sight-of · (12) · fathers-of-them · he-did · miracle · in-land-of · Egypt · region-of

צֹעַן: בָּקַע יָם וַיַּעֲבִירֵם וַיַּצֶּב־ מַיִם
Zoan · (13) · he-divided · sea · and-he-led-through-them · and-he-made-stand · waters

וַיַּנְחֵם בֶּעָנָן יוֹמָם וְכָל־ הַלַּיְלָה
wall · like · (14) · and-he-guided-them · with-the-cloud · by-day · and-all-of · the-night

בְּאוֹר אֵשׁ: יְבַקַּע צֻרִים בַּמִּדְבָּר וַיַּשְׁקְ
with-light-of · fire · (15) · he-split · rocks · in-the-desert · and-he-gave-water

כִּתְהֹמוֹת רַבָּה: וַיּוֹצִא נוֹזְלִים מִסָּלַע
as-seas · abundant · (16) · and-he-brought-out · ones-streaming · from-rocky-crag

וַיּוֹרִד כַּנְּהָרוֹת מָיִם: וַיּוֹסִיפוּ עוֹד
and-he-made-flow-down · like-the-rivers · waters · (17) · but-they-continued · again

לַחֲטֹא־ לוֹ לַמְרוֹת עֶלְיוֹן בַּצִּיָּה: וַיְנַסּוּ־
to-sin · against-him · to-rebel-against · Most-High · in-the-desert · (18) · and-they-tested

אֵל בִּלְבָבָם לִשְׁאָל־ אֹכֶל לְנַפְשָׁם: וַיְדַבְּרוּ
God · by-will-of-them · to-demand · food · for-craving-of-them · (19) · and-they-spoke

בֵּאלֹהִים אָמְרוּ הֲיוּכַל אֵל לַעֲרֹךְ שֻׁלְחָן בַּמִּדְבָּר: הֵן
against-God · they-said · can-he? · God · to-spread · table · in-the-desert · (20) · see!

הִכָּה צוּר וַיָּזוּבוּ מַיִם וּנְחָלִים יִשְׁטֹפוּ הֲגַם־
he-struck · rock · and-they-gushed-out · waters · and-streams · they-flowed · also?

לֶחֶם יוּכַל תֵּת אִם־ יָכִין שְׁאֵר לְעַמּוֹ: לָכֵן
food · can-he · to-give · or · can-he-supply · meat · for-people-of-him · (21) · when

שָׁמַע יְהוָה וַיִּתְעַבָּר וְאֵשׁ נִשְּׂקָה בְיַעֲקֹב
he-heard · Yahweh · then-he-was-angry · and-fire · she-broke-out · against-Jacob

וְגַם־ אַף עָלָה בְיִשְׂרָאֵל: כִּי לֹא הֶאֱמִינוּ בֵּאלֹהִים
and-also · wrath · he-rose · against-Israel · (22) · for · not · they-believed · in-God

וְלֹא בָטְחוּ בִּישׁוּעָתוֹ: וַיְצַו שְׁחָקִים
and-not · they-trusted · in-deliverance-of-him · (23) · yet-he-commanded · skies

מִמַּעַל וְדַלְתֵי שָׁמַיִם פָּתָח: וַיַּמְטֵר עֲלֵיהֶם
at-above · and-doors-of · heavens · he-opened · (24) · and-he-rained-down · for-them

מָן לֶאֱכֹל וּדְגַן־ שָׁמַיִם נָתַן לָמוֹ: לֶחֶם אַבִּירִים
manna · to-eat · and-grain-of · heavens · he-gave · to-them · (25) · bread-of · angels

turned back on the day of battle;

[10] they did not keep God's covenant
and refused to live by his law.

[11] They forgot what he had done,
the wonders he had shown them.

[12] He did miracles in the sight of their fathers
in the land of Egypt, in the region of Zoan.

[13] He divided the sea and led them through;
he made the water stand firm like a wall.

[14] He guided them with the cloud by day
and with light from the fire all night.

[15] He split the rocks in the desert
and gave them water as abundant as the seas;

[16] he brought streams out of a rocky crag
and made water flow down like rivers.

[17] But they continued to sin against him,
rebelling in the desert against the Most High.

[18] They willfully put God to the test
by demanding the food they craved.

[19] They spoke against God, saying,
"Can God spread a table in the desert?

[20] When he struck the rock, water gushed out,
and streams flowed abundantly.
But can he also give us food?
Can he supply meat for his people?"

[21] When the LORD heard them, he was very angry;
his fire broke out against Jacob,
and his wrath rose against Israel,

[22] for they did not believe in God
or trust in his deliverance.

[23] Yet he gave a command to the skies above
and opened the doors of the heavens;

[24] he rained down manna for the people to eat,
he gave them the grain of heaven.

[25] Men ate the bread of angels;

אָכַל אִישׁ צֵידָה שָׁלַח לָהֶם לָשֹׂבַע׃ יַסַּע קָדִים
east-wind he-let-loose (26) in-abundance to-them he-sent food man he-ate

בַּשָּׁמָיִם וַיְנַהֵג בְּעֻזּוֹ תֵימָן׃
south-wind by-power-of-him and-he-led-forth from-the-heavens

וַיַּמְטֵר עֲלֵיהֶם כֶּעָפָר שְׁאֵר וּכְחוֹל יַמִּים
seas and-like-sand-of meat like-the-dust on-them and-he-rained-down (27)

עוֹף כָּנָף׃ וַיַּפֵּל בְּקֶרֶב מַחֲנֵהוּ סָבִיב
around camp-of-him to-inside-of and-he-made-come-down (28) flight bird-of

לְמִשְׁכְּנֹתָיו׃ וַיֹּאכְלוּ וַיִּשְׂבְּעוּ מְאֹד וְתַאֲוָתָם
for-craving-of-them more and-they-had-enough and-they-ate (29) about-tents-of-him

יָבִא לָהֶם׃ לֹא־ זָרוּ מִתַּאֲוָתָם עוֹד אָכְלָם
food-of-them still from-craving-of-them they-turned not (30) to-them he-gave

בְּפִיהֶם׃ וְאַף אֱלֹהִים ׀ עָלָה בָהֶם וַיַּהֲרֹג
and-he-killed against-them he-rose God and-anger-of (31) in-mouth-of-them

בְּמִשְׁמַנֵּיהֶם וּבַחוּרֵי יִשְׂרָאֵל הִכְרִיעַ׃ בְּכָל־
in-all-of (32) he-cut-down Israel and-men-being-young-of to-sturdy-ones-of-them

זֹאת חָטְאוּ־ עוֹד וְלֹא־ הֶאֱמִינוּ בְּנִפְלְאוֹתָיו׃
in-deeds-being-wonders-of-him they-believed and-not still they-sinned this

וַיְכַל־ בַּהֶבֶל יְמֵיהֶם וּשְׁנוֹתָם בַּבֶּהָלָה׃
in-the-terror and-years-of-them days-of-them in-the-futility so-he-ended (33)

אִם־ הֲרָגָם וּדְרָשׁוּהוּ וְשָׁבוּ
and-they-turned then-they-would-seek-him he-slew-them whenever (34)

וְשִׁחֲרוּ־ אֵל׃ וַיִּזְכְּרוּ כִּי־אֱלֹהִים צוּרָם
Rock-of-them God that and-they-remembered (35) God and-they-were-eager-for

וְאֵל עֶלְיוֹן גֹּאֲלָם׃ וַיְפַתּוּהוּ
but-they-would-flatter-him (36) One-Redeeming-them Most-High and-God

בְּפִיהֶם וּבִלְשׁוֹנָם יְכַזְּבוּ־ לוֹ׃
to-him they-lied and-with-tongue-of-them with-mouth-of-them

וְלִבָּם לֹא־ נָכוֹן עִמּוֹ וְלֹא נֶאֶמְנוּ
they-were-faithful and-not to-him he-was-loyal not and-heart-of-them (37)

בִּבְרִיתוֹ׃ וְהוּא רַחוּם ׀ יְכַפֵּר עָוֹן וְלֹא־
and-not iniquity he-atoned-for merciful yet-he (38) to-covenant-of-him

יַשְׁחִית וְהִרְבָּה לְהָשִׁיב אַפּוֹ וְלֹא־ יָעִיר
he-stirred-up and-not anger-of-him to-restrain and-he-did-often he-destroyed

כָּל־ חֲמָתוֹ׃ וַיִּזְכֹּר כִּי־ בָשָׂר הֵמָּה רוּחַ הוֹלֵךְ
passing breeze they flesh that and-he-remembered (39) wrath-of-him fullness-of

וְלֹא יָשׁוּב׃ כַּמָּה יַמְרוּהוּ בַמִּדְבָּר
in-the-desert they-rebelled-against-him as-the-how! (40) he-returns and-not

he sent them all the food
they could eat.
26 He let loose the east wind
from the heavens
and led forth the south
wind by his power.
27 He rained meat down on them
like dust,
flying birds like sand on the
seashore.
28 He made them come down
inside their camp,
all around their tents.
29 They ate till they had more
than enough,
for he had given them what
they craved.
30 But before they turned from
the food they craved,
even while it was still in
their mouths,
31 God's anger rose against them;
he put to death the sturdiest
among them,
cutting down the young
men of Israel.
32 In spite of all this, they kept
on sinning;
in spite of his wonders, they
did not believe.
33 So he ended their days in
futility
and their years in terror.
34 Whenever God slew them,
they would seek him;
they eagerly turned to him
again.
35 They remembered that God
was their Rock,
that God Most High was
their Redeemer.
36 But then they would flatter
him with their mouths,
lying to him with their
tongues;
37 their hearts were not loyal to
him,
they were not faithful to his
covenant.
38 Yet he was merciful;
he atoned for their
iniquities
and did not destroy them.
Time after time he restrained
his anger
and did not stir up his full
wrath.
39 He remembered that they were
but flesh,
a passing breeze that does
not return.
40 How often they rebelled
against him in the desert

יַעֲצִיבוּהוּ בִּישִׁימוֹן׃ וַיָּשׁוּבוּ וַיְנַסּוּ אֵל
God and-they-tested and-they-did-again (41) in-wasteland they-grieved-him

וּקְדוֹשׁ יִשְׂרָאֵל הִתְווּ׃ לֹא־ זָכְרוּ אֶת־ יָדוֹ
power-of-him *** they-remembered not (42) they-vexed Israel and-Holy-One-of

יוֹם אֲשֶׁר־ פָּדָם מִנִּי־ צָר׃ אֲשֶׁר־ שָׂם בְּמִצְרַיִם
in-Egypt he-displayed when (43) oppressor from he-redeemed-them that day

אֹתוֹתָיו וּמוֹפְתָיו בִּשְׂדֵה־ צֹעַן׃ וַיַּהֲפֹךְ
and-he-turned (44) Zoan in-region-of and-wonders-of-him miraculous-signs-of-him

לְדָם יְאֹרֵיהֶם וְנֹזְלֵיהֶם בַּל־ יִשְׁתָּיוּן׃
they-could-drink not and-ones-streaming-of-them rivers-of-them to-blood

יְשַׁלַּח בָּהֶם עָרֹב וַיֹּאכְלֵם וּצְפַרְדֵּעַ וַתַּשְׁחִיתֵם׃
and-he-devastated-them and-frog and-he-devoured-them swarm to-them he-sent (45)

וַיִּתֵּן לֶחָסִיל יְבוּלָם וִיגִיעָם
and-produce-of-them crop-of-them to-the-grasshopper and-he-gave (46)

לָאַרְבֶּה׃ יַהֲרֹג בַּבָּרָד גַּפְנָם
vine-of-them with-the-hail he-destroyed (47) to-the-locust

וְשִׁקְמוֹתָם בַּחֲנָמַל׃ וַיַּסְגֵּר לַבָּרָד
to-the-hail and-he-gave-over (48) with-the-sleet and-sycamore-figs-of-them

בְּעִירָם וּמִקְנֵיהֶם לָרְשָׁפִים׃ יְשַׁלַּח־
he-unleashed (49) to-the-lightning-bolts and-livestocks-of-them cattle-of-them

בָּם ׀ חֲרוֹן אַפּוֹ עֶבְרָה וָזַעַם וְצָרָה מִשְׁלַחַת
band-of and-hostility and-indignation wrath anger-of-him heat-of against-them

מַלְאֲכֵי רָעִים׃ יְפַלֵּס נָתִיב לְאַפּוֹ לֹא־ חָשַׂךְ
he-spared not for-anger-of-him path he-prepared (50) destructions angels-of

מִמָּוֶת נַפְשָׁם וְחַיָּתָם לַדֶּבֶר הִסְגִּיר׃
he-gave-over to-the-plague but-life-of-them self-of-them from-death

וַיַּךְ כָּל־ בְּכוֹר בְּמִצְרָיִם רֵאשִׁית אוֹנִים
manhoods firstfruit-of of-Egypt firstborn all-of and-he-struck-down (51)

בְּאָהֳלֵי־ חָם׃ וַיַּסַּע כַּצֹּאן עַמּוֹ
people-of-him like-the-flock but-he-brought-out (52) Ham in-tents-of

וַיְנַהֲגֵם כַּעֵדֶר בַּמִּדְבָּר׃ וַיַּנְחֵם
and-he-guided-them (53) through-the-desert like-the-sheep and-he-led-them

לָבֶטַח וְלֹא פָחָדוּ וְאֶת־ אוֹיְבֵיהֶם כִּסָּה
he-engulfed ones-being-enemies-of-them but they-were-afraid so-not in-safety

הַיָּם׃ וַיְבִיאֵם אֶל־ גְּבוּל קָדְשׁוֹ הַר־
hill-country holiness-of-him border-of to thus-he-brought-them (54) the-sea

זֶה קָנְתָה יְמִינוֹ׃ וַיְגָרֶשׁ מִפְּנֵיהֶם ׀ גּוֹיִם
nations from-before-them and-he-drove-out (55) right-hand-of-him she-took this

and grieved him in the
wasteland!
41 Again and again they put God
to the test;
they vexed the Holy One of
Israel.
42 They did not remember his
power—
the day he redeemed them
from the oppressor,
43 the day he displayed his
miraculous signs in
Egypt,
his wonders in the region of
Zoan.
44 He turned their rivers to
blood;
they could not drink from
their streams.
45 He sent swarms of flies that
devoured them
and frogs that devastated
them.
46 He gave their crops to the
grasshopper,
their produce to the locust.
47 He destroyed their vines with
hail
and their sycamore-figs with
sleet.
48 He gave over their cattle to the
hail,
their livestock to bolts of
lightning.
49 He unleashed against them his
hot anger,
his wrath, indignation and
hostility—
a band of destroying angels.
50 He prepared a path for his
anger;
he did not spare them from
death
but gave them over to the
plague.
51 He struck down all the
firstborn of Egypt,
the firstfruits of manhood in
the tents of Ham.
52 But he brought his people out
like a flock;
he led them like sheep
through the desert.
53 He guided them safely, so they
were unafraid;
but the sea engulfed their
enemies.
54 Thus he brought them to the
border of his holy land,
to the hill country his right
hand had taken.
55 He drove out nations before
them

וַיַּפִּילֵם בְּחֶבֶל נַחֲלָה וַיַּשְׁכֵּן בְּאָהֳלֵיהֶם
and-he-allotted-them from-land inheritance and-he-settled in-homes-of-them

שִׁבְטֵי יִשְׂרָאֵל׃ (56) וַיְנַסּוּ וַיַּמְרוּ אֶת־אֱלֹהִים
tribes-of Israel (56) but-they-tested and-they-rebelled-against *** God

עֶלְיוֹן וְעֵדוֹתָיו לֹא שָׁמָרוּ׃ (57) וַיִּסֹּגוּ
Most-High and-statutes-of-him not they-kept (57) and-they-were-disloyal

וַיִּבְגְּדוּ כַּאֲבוֹתָם נֶהְפְּכוּ כְּקֶשֶׁת רְמִיָּה׃
and-they-were-faithless like-fathers-of-them they-were-unreliable as-bow-of faultiness

(58) וַיַּכְעִיסוּהוּ בְּבָמוֹתָם וּבִפְסִילֵיהֶם
(58) and-they-angered-him with-high-places-of-them and-with-idols-of-them

יַקְנִיאוּהוּ׃ (59) שָׁמַע אֱלֹהִים וַיִּתְעַבָּר וַיִּמְאַס
they-made-jealous-him (59) he-heard God and-he-was-angry and-he-rejected

מְאֹד בְּיִשְׂרָאֵל׃ (60) וַיִּטֹּשׁ מִשְׁכַּן שִׁלוֹ אֹהֶל
completely to-Israel (60) and-he-abandoned tabernacle-of Shiloh tent

שִׁכֵּן בָּאָדָם׃ (61) וַיִּתֵּן לַשְּׁבִי עֻזּוֹ
he-set-up among-the-man (61) and-he-sent into-the-captivity might-of-him

וְתִפְאַרְתּוֹ בְיַד־צָר׃ (62) וַיַּסְגֵּר לַחֶרֶב
and-splendor-of-him into-hand-of enemy (62) and-he-gave-over to-the-sword

עַמּוֹ וּבְנַחֲלָתוֹ הִתְעַבָּר׃ (63) בַּחוּרָיו
people-of-him and-with-inheritance-of-him he-was-angry (63) and-young-men-of-him

אָכְלָה־אֵשׁ וּבְתוּלֹתָיו לֹא הוּלָּלוּ׃
she-consumed fire and-maidens-of-him not they-were-sung-about

(64) כֹּהֲנָיו בַּחֶרֶב נָפָלוּ וְאַלְמְנֹתָיו לֹא
(64) priests-of-him by-the-sword they-fell and-widows-of-him not

תִבְכֶּינָה׃ (65) וַיִּקַץ כְּיָשֵׁן | אֲדֹנָי כְּגִבּוֹר מִתְרוֹנֵן
they-could-weep (65) then-he-awoke as-sleep Lord as-man one-being-in-stupor

מִיָּיִן׃ (66) וַיַּךְ־צָרָיו אָחוֹר חֶרְפַּת עוֹלָם
from-wine (66) and-he-beat enemies-of-him back shame-of everlasting

נָתַן לָמוֹ׃ (67) וַיִּמְאַס בְּאֹהֶל יוֹסֵף וּבְשֵׁבֶט
he-put to-them (67) then-he-rejected to-tent-of Joseph and-to-tribe-of

אֶפְרַיִם לֹא בָחָר׃ (68) וַיִּבְחַר אֶת־שֵׁבֶט יְהוּדָה אֶת־הַר צִיּוֹן
Ephraim not he-chose (68) but-he-chose *** tribe-of Judah *** Mount-of Zion

אֲשֶׁר אָהֵב׃ (69) וַיִּבֶן כְּמוֹ־רָמִים מִקְדָּשׁוֹ
which he-loved (69) and-he-built like ones-being-high sanctuary-of-him

כְּאֶרֶץ יְסָדָהּ לְעוֹלָם׃ (70) וַיִּבְחַר בְּדָוִד
like-earth he-established-her to-forever (70) and-he-chose to-David

עַבְדּוֹ וַיִּקָּחֵהוּ מִמִּכְלְאֹת צֹאן׃ (71) מֵאַחַר עָלוֹת
servant-of-him and-he-took-him from-pens-of sheep (71) from-after to-tend

and allotted their lands to
them as an inheritance;
he settled the tribes of Israel
in their homes.
56But they put God to the test
and rebelled against the
Most High;
they did not keep his
statutes.
57Like their fathers they were
disloyal and faithless,
as unreliable as a faulty
bow.
58They angered him with their
high places;
they aroused his jealousy
with their idols.
59When God heard them, he was
very angry;
he rejected Israel completely.
60He abandoned the tabernacle
of Shiloh,
the tent he had set up
among men.
61He sent ⌊the ark of⌋ his might
into captivity,
his splendor into the hands
of the enemy.
62He gave his people over to the
sword;
he was very angry with his
inheritance.
63Fire consumed their young
men,
and their maidens had no
wedding songs;
64their priests were put to the
sword,
and their widows could not
weep.
65Then the Lord awoke as from
sleep,
as a man wakes from the
stupor of wine.
66He beat back his enemies;
he put them to everlasting
shame.
67Then he rejected the tents of
Joseph,
he did not choose the tribe
of Ephraim;
68but he chose the tribe of
Judah,
Mount Zion, which he
loved.
69He built his sanctuary like the
high mountains,
like the earth that he
established forever.
70He chose David his servant
and took him from the
sheep pens;
71from tending the sheep he

הֱבִיאוֹ לִרְעוֹת בְּיַעֲקֹב עַמּוֹ וּבְיִשְׂרָאֵל
he-brought-him to-shepherd to-Jacob people-of-him even-to-Israel

נַחֲלָתוֹ׃ וַיִּרְעֵם כְּתֹם לְבָבוֹ
inheritance-of-him (72) and-he-shepherded-them with-integrity-of heart-of-him

וּבִתְבוּנוֹת כַּפָּיו יַנְחֵם׃ מִזְמוֹר לְאָסָף אֱלֹהִים
and-with-skills-of hands-of-him he-led-them (79:1) psalm of-Asaph God

בָּאוּ גוֹיִם ׀ בְּנַחֲלָתֶךָ טִמְּאוּ אֶת־ הֵיכַל
they-invaded nations into-inheritance-of-you they-defiled *** temple-of

קָדְשֶׁךָ שָׂמוּ אֶת־ יְרוּשָׁלִַם לְעִיִּים׃ נָתְנוּ אֶת־
holiness-of-you they-reduced *** Jerusalem to-rubbles (2) they-gave ***

נִבְלַת עֲבָדֶיךָ מַאֲכָל לְעוֹף הַשָּׁמָיִם בְּשַׂר חֲסִידֶיךָ
body-of servants-of-you food to-bird-of the-airs flesh-of saints-of-you

לְחַיְתוֹ־ אָרֶץ׃ שָׁפְכוּ דָמָם ׀ כַּמַּיִם
to-beast-of earth (3) they-poured-out blood-of-them like-the-waters

סְבִיבוֹת יְרוּשָׁלִָם וְאֵין קוֹבֵר׃ הָיִינוּ חֶרְפָּה
ones-around-of Jerusalem and-there-is-not one-burying (4) we-are reproach

לִשְׁכֵנֵינוּ לַעַג וָקֶלֶס לִסְבִיבוֹתֵינוּ׃ עַד־ מָה
to-neighbors-of-us scorn and-derision to-ones-around-us (5) until when?

יְהוָה תֶּאֱנַף לָנֶצַח תִּבְעַר כְּמוֹ־ אֵשׁ קִנְאָתֶךָ׃
Yahweh will-you-be-angry to-forever will-she-burn like fire jealousy-of-you

שְׁפֹךְ חֲמָתְךָ אֶל־ הַגּוֹיִם אֲשֶׁר לֹא־ יְדָעוּךָ
(6) pour-out! wrath-of-you on the-nations that not they-acknowledge-you

וְעַל מַמְלָכוֹת אֲשֶׁר בְּשִׁמְךָ לֹא קָרָאוּ׃ כִּי אָכַל אֶת־
and-on kingdoms that on-name-of-you not they-call (7) for he-devoured ***

יַעֲקֹב וְאֶת־ נָוֵהוּ הֵשַׁמּוּ׃ אַל־ תִּזְכָּר־ לָנוּ עֲוֹנֹת
Jacob and homeland-of-him they-destroyed (8) not you-hold against-us sins-of

רִאשֹׁנִים מַהֵר יְקַדְּמוּנוּ רַחֲמֶיךָ כִּי דַלּוֹנוּ
fathers to-be-quick may-they-meet-us mercies-of-you for we-are-in-need

מְאֹד׃ עָזְרֵנוּ ׀ אֱלֹהֵי יִשְׁעֵנוּ עַל־ דְּבַר כְּבוֹד־
desperately (9) help-us! God-of salvation-of-us for account-of glory-of

שְׁמֶךָ וְהַצִּילֵנוּ וְכַפֵּר עַל־ חַטֹּאתֵינוּ לְמַעַן שְׁמֶךָ׃
name-of-you and-deliver-us! and-atone! for sins-of-us for-sake-of name-of-you

לָמָּה ׀ יֹאמְרוּ הַגּוֹיִם אַיֵּה אֱלֹהֵיהֶם יִוָּדַע
(10) why? should-they-say the-nations where? God-of-them let-him-be-known

בַּגּיִים° לְעֵינֵינוּ נִקְמַת דַּם־ עֲבָדֶיךָ
among-the-nations before-eyes-of-us vengeance-of blood-of servants-of-you

הַשָּׁפוּךְ׃ תָּבוֹא לְפָנֶיךָ אֶנְקַת אָסִיר
the-one-being-poured-out (11) may-she-come before-you groan-of prisoner

°10 ק בגוים

brought him
to be the shepherd of his people Jacob,
of Israel his inheritance.
72 And David shepherded them with integrity of heart;
with skillful hands he led them.

### Psalm 79

A psalm of Asaph.

1 O God, the nations have invaded your inheritance;
they have defiled your holy temple,
they have reduced Jerusalem to rubble.
2 They have given the dead bodies of your servants
as food to the birds of the air,
the flesh of your saints to the beasts of the earth.
3 They have poured out blood like water
all around Jerusalem,
and there is no one to bury the dead.
4 We are objects of reproach to our neighbors,
of scorn and derision to those around us.

5 How long, O LORD? Will you be angry forever?
How long will your jealousy burn like fire?
6 Pour out your wrath on the nations
that do not acknowledge you,
on the kingdoms
that do not call on your name;
7 for they have devoured Jacob
and destroyed his homeland.
8 Do not hold against us the sins of the fathers;
may your mercy come quickly to meet us,
for we are in desperate need.

9 Help us, O God our Savior,
for the glory of your name;
deliver us and atone for our sins
for your name's sake.
10 Why should the nations say,
"Where is their God?"
Before our eyes, make known among the nations
that you avenge the outpoured blood of your servants.
11 May the groans of the prisoners come before you;

כְּגֹדֶל זְרוֹעֲךָ הוֹתֵר בְּנֵי תְמוּתָה׃ וְהָשֵׁב

and-pay-back! (12) death men-of preserve! arm-of-you by-strength-of

לִשְׁכֵנֵינוּ שִׁבְעָתַיִם אֶל־ חֵיקָם חֶרְפָּתָם אֲשֶׁר

that reproach-of-them lap-of-them into seven-times to-neighbors-of-us

חֵרְפוּךָ אֲדֹנָי׃ וַאֲנַחְנוּ עַמְּךָ ׀ וְצֹאן

and-sheep-of people-of-you then-we (13) Lord they-reproached-you

מַרְעִיתֶךָ נוֹדֶה לְּךָ לְעוֹלָם לְדֹר וָדֹר

and-generation to-generation to-forever to-you we-will-praise pasture-of-you

נְסַפֵּר תְּהִלָּתֶךָ׃ לַמְנַצֵּחַ אֶל־שֹׁשַׁנִּים עֵדוּת

covenant lilies to for-the-one-directing *(80:1) praise-of-you we-will-recount

לְאָסָף מִזְמוֹר׃ רֹעֵה יִשְׂרָאֵל ׀ הַאֲזִינָה נֹהֵג כַּצֹּאן

like-the-flock one-leading hear! Israel One-Shepherding-of (2) psalm of-Asaph

יוֹסֵף יֹשֵׁב הַכְּרוּבִים הוֹפִיעָה׃ לִפְנֵי אֶפְרַיִם ׀

Ephraim before (3) shine-forth! the-cherubim one-being-enthroned-of Joseph

וּבִנְיָמִן וּמְנַשֶּׁה עוֹרְרָה אֶת־ גְּבוּרָתֶךָ וּלְכָה לִישֻׁעָתָה

to-salvation and-come! might-of-you *** awaken! and-Manasseh and-Benjamin

לָּנוּ׃ אֱלֹהִים הֲשִׁיבֵנוּ וְהָאֵר פָּנֶיךָ וְנִוָּשֵׁעָה׃

that-we-may-be-saved faces-of-you and-make-shine! restore-us! God (4) of-us

יְהוָה אֱלֹהִים צְבָאוֹת עַד־ מָתַי עָשַׁנְתָּ בִּתְפִלַּת

against-prayer-of will-you-smolder when? until Hosts God Yahweh (5)

עַמֶּךָ׃ הֶאֱכַלְתָּם לֶחֶם דִּמְעָה וַתַּשְׁקֵמוֹ

and-you-made-drink-them tear bread-of you-fed-them (6) people-of-you

בִּדְמָעוֹת שָׁלִישׁ׃ תְּשִׂימֵנוּ מָדוֹן לִשְׁכֵנֵינוּ

to-neighbors-of-us contention you-made-us (7) bowlful of-tears-of

וְאֹיְבֵינוּ יִלְעֲגוּ־ לָמוֹ׃ אֱלֹהִים צְבָאוֹת הֲשִׁיבֵנוּ

restore-us! Hosts God (8) at-us they-mock and-ones-being-enemies-of-us

וְהָאֵר פָּנֶיךָ וְנִוָּשֵׁעָה׃ גֶּפֶן מִמִּצְרַיִם

from-Egypt vine (9) that-we-may-be-saved faces-of-you and-make-shine!

תַּסִּיעַ תְּגָרֵשׁ גּוֹיִם וַתִּטָּעֶהָ׃ פִּנִּיתָ

you-cleared (10) and-you-planted-her nations you-drove-out you-brought

לְפָנֶיהָ וַתַּשְׁרֵשׁ שָׁרָשֶׁיהָ וַתְּמַלֵּא־ אָרֶץ׃

land and-she-filled roots-of-her and-she-took-root before-her

כָּסּוּ הָרִים צִלָּהּ וַעֲנָפֶיהָ אַרְזֵי־

cedars-of and-branches-of-her shade-of-her mountains they-were-covered (11)

אֵל׃ תְּשַׁלַּח קְצִירֶהָ עַד־ יָם וְאֶל־ נָהָר יוֹנְקוֹתֶיהָ׃

shoots-of-her River and-as-far-as Sea to bough-of-her she-sent-out (12) mighty

לָמָּה פָּרַצְתָּ גְדֵרֶיהָ וְאָרוּהָ כָּל־ עֹבְרֵי

ones-passing-of all-of so-they-pick-her walls-of-her you-broke-down why? (13)

by the strength of your arm
preserve those condemned
to die.

12 Pay back into the laps of our
neighbors seven times
the reproach they have
hurled at you, O Lord.
13 Then we your people, the
sheep of your pasture,
will praise you forever;
from generation to generation
we will recount your praise.

### Psalm 80

For the director of music. To the tune of "The Lilies of the Covenant." Of Asaph. A psalm.

1 Hear us, O Shepherd of Israel,
you who lead Joseph like a
flock;
you who sit enthroned
between the cherubim,
shine forth
2 before Ephraim, Benjamin
and Manasseh.
Awaken your might;
come and save us.

3 Restore us, O God;
make your face shine upon
us,
that we may be saved.

4 O LORD God Almighty,
how long will your anger
smolder
against the prayers of your
people?
5 You have fed them with the
bread of tears;
you have made them drink
tears by the bowlful.
6 You have made us a source of
contention to our
neighbors,
and our enemies mock us.

7 Restore us, O God Almighty;
make your face shine upon
us,
that we may be saved.

8 You brought a vine out of
Egypt;
you drove out the nations
and planted it.
9 You cleared the ground for it,
and it took root and filled
the land.
10 The mountains were covered
with its shade,
the mighty cedars with its
branches.
11 It sent out its boughs to the
Sea,[e]
its shoots as far as the
River.[f]

12 Why have you broken down
its walls
so that all who pass by pick
its grapes?

[e] 11 Probably the Mediterranean
[f] 11 That is, the Euphrates

*Heading, 1 See the note on page 349.

דָּֽרֶךְ׃ יְכַרְסְמֶנָּה חֲזִיר מִיָּעַר וְזִיז שָׂדַי
field and-creature-of from-forest boar and-he-ravages-her (14) way

יִרְעֶנָּה׃ אֱלֹהִים צְבָאוֹת שׁוּב־ נָא הַבֵּט מִשָּׁמַיִם וּרְאֵה
and-see! from-heavens look-down! now! return! Hosts God (15) he-feeds-on-her

וּפְקֹד גֶּפֶן זֹאת׃ וְכַנָּה אֲשֶׁר־ נָטְעָה יְמִינֶךָ
right-hand-of-you she-planted that and-root (16) this vine and-watch-over!

וְעַל־ בֵּן אִמַּצְתָּה לָּךְ׃ שְׂרֻפָה בָאֵשׁ
with-fire one-being-burned (17) for-you you-raised-up son and-over

כְּסוּחָה מִגַּעֲרַת פָּנֶיךָ יֹאבֵדוּ׃ תְּהִי־
let-her-be (18) they-perish faces-of-you at-rebuke-of one-being-cut-down

יָדְךָ עַל־ אִישׁ יְמִינֶךָ עַל־ בֶּן־ אָדָם אִמַּצְתָּ לָּךְ׃
for-you you-raised-up man son-of on right-hand-of-you man-of on hand-of-you

וְלֹא־ נָסוֹג מִמֶּךָּ תְּחַיֵּנוּ וּבְשִׁמְךָ
and-on-name-of-you you-revive-us from-you we-will-turn-away then-not (19)

נִקְרָא׃ יְהוָה אֱלֹהִים צְבָאוֹת הֲשִׁיבֵנוּ הָאֵר פָּנֶיךָ
faces-of-you make-shine! restore-us! Hosts God Yahweh (20) we-will-call

וְנִוָּשֵׁעָה׃ לַמְנַצֵּחַ עַל־ הַגִּתִּית
the-gittith according-to for-the-one-directing *(81:1) that-we-may-be-saved

לְאָסָף׃ הַרְנִינוּ לֵאלֹהִים עוּזֵּנוּ הָרִיעוּ לֵאלֹהֵי יַעֲקֹב׃
Jacob to-God-of shout! strength-of-us to-God sing-for-joy! (2) of-Asaph

שְׂאוּ־ זִמְרָה וּתְנוּ־ תֹף כִּנּוֹר נָעִים עִם־ נָבֶל׃ תִּקְעוּ
sound! (4) lyre and melodious harp tambourine and-strike! music begin! (3)

בַחֹדֶשׁ שׁוֹפָר בַּכֶּסֶה לְיוֹם חַגֵּנוּ׃ כִּי
for (5) Feast-of-us on-day-of at-the-full-moon horn-of-ram at-the-New-Moon

חֹק לְיִשְׂרָאֵל הוּא מִשְׁפָּט לֵאלֹהֵי יַעֲקֹב׃ עֵדוּת בִּיהוֹסֵף
for-Joseph statute (6) Jacob of-God-of ordinance this for-Israel decree

שָׂמוֹ בְּצֵאתוֹ עַל־ אֶרֶץ מִצְרָיִם שְׂפַת לֹא־
not language-of Egypt land-of against when-to-go-out-him he-established-him

יָדַעְתִּי אֶשְׁמָע׃ הֲסִירוֹתִי מִסֵּבֶל שִׁכְמוֹ כַּפָּיו
hands-of-him shoulder-of-him from-burden I-removed (7) I-heard I-understood

מִדּוּד תַּעֲבֹרְנָה׃ בַּצָּרָה קָרָאתָ וָאֲחַלְּצֶךָּ
and-I-rescued-you you-called in-the-distress (8) they-were-freed from-basket

אֶעֶנְךָ בְּסֵתֶר רַעַם אֶבְחָנְךָ עַל־ מֵי מְרִיבָה סֶלָה׃
selah Meribah waters-of at I-tested-you thunder from-cloud-of I-answered-you

שְׁמַע עַמִּי וְאָעִידָה בָּךְ יִשְׂרָאֵל אִם־ תִּשְׁמַע־
you-would-listen if Israel to-you and-I-will-warn people-of-me hear! (9)

לִי׃ לֹא־ יִהְיֶה בְךָ אֵל זָר וְלֹא תִשְׁתַּחֲוֶה
you-shall-bow and-not being-foreign god among-you he-shall-be not (10) to-me

13 Boars from the forest ravage it
and the creatures of the field feed on it.
14 Return to us, O God Almighty!
Look down from heaven and see!
Watch over this vine,
15 the root your right hand has planted,
the son[g] you have raised up for yourself.

16 Your vine is cut down, it is burned with fire;
at your rebuke your people perish.
17 Let your hand rest on the man at your right hand,
the son of man you have raised up for yourself.
18 Then we will not turn away from you;
revive us, and we will call on your name.

19 Restore us, O LORD God Almighty;
make your face shine upon us,
that we may be saved.

## Psalm 81

For the director of music. According to *gittith*.[h] Of Asaph.

1 Sing for joy to God our strength;
shout aloud to the God of Jacob!
2 Begin the music, strike the tambourine,
play the melodious harp and lyre.

3 Sound the ram's horn at the New Moon,
and when the moon is full, on the day of our Feast;
4 this is a decree for Israel,
an ordinance of the God of Jacob.
5 He established it as a statute for Joseph
when he went out against Egypt,
where we heard a language we did not understand.[i]

6 He says, "I removed the burden from their shoulders;
their hands were set free from the basket.
7 In your distress you called and I rescued you,
I answered you out of a thundercloud;
I tested you at the waters of Meribah. *Selah*

8 "Hear, O my people, and I will warn you—
if you would but listen to me, O Israel!
9 You shall have no foreign god among you;
you shall not bow down to

g15 Or *branch*
hTitle: Probably a musical term
i5 Or / *and we heard a voice we had not known*

*Heading, *1* See the note on page 349.

לְאֵל נֵכָר׃ אָנֹכִי ׀ יְהוָה אֱלֹהֶיךָ הַֽמַּעַלְךָ מֵאֶרֶץ
from-land-of the-one-bringing-up-you God-of-you Yahweh I (11) alien to-god

מִצְרָיִם הַרְחֶב־ פִּיךָ וַאֲמַלְאֵהוּ׃ וְלֹא־ שָׁמַע
he-listened but-not (12) and-I-will-fill-him mouth-of-you open-wide! Egypt

עַמִּי לְקוֹלִי וְיִשְׂרָאֵל לֹא־ אָבָה לִי׃ וָאֲשַׁלְּחֵהוּ
so-I-gave-him (13) to-me he-submitted not and-Israel to-voice-of-me people-of-me

בִּשְׁרִירוּת לִבָּם יֵלְכוּ בְּמוֹעֲצוֹתֵיהֶם׃ לוּ
if (14) to-devices-of-them they-followed heart-of-them to-stubbornness-of

עַמִּי שֹׁמֵעַ לִי יִשְׂרָאֵל בִּדְרָכַי יְהַלֵּכוּ׃
they-would-follow to-ways-of-me Israel to-me one-listening people-of-me

כִּמְעַט אוֹיְבֵיהֶם אַכְנִיעַ וְעַל
and-against I-would-subdue ones-being-enemies-of-them as-quickly (15)

צָרֵיהֶם אָשִׁיב יָדִי׃ מְשַׂנְאֵי יְהוָה
Yahweh ones-hating-of (16) hand-of-me I-would-turn foes-of-them

יְכַחֲשׁוּ־ לוֹ וִיהִי עִתָּם לְעוֹלָם׃
to-forever punishment-of-them and-he-would-last before-him they-would-cringe

וַיַּאֲכִילֵהוּ מֵחֵלֶב חִטָּה וּמִצּוּר דְּבַשׁ
honey and-from-rock wheat with-finest-of but-he-would-feed-him (17)

אַשְׂבִּיעֶךָ׃ מִזְמוֹר לְאָסָף אֱלֹהִים נִצָּב בַּעֲדַת־
in-assembly-of one-presiding God of-Asaph psalm (82:1) I-would-satisfy-you

אֵל בְּקֶרֶב אֱלֹהִים יִשְׁפֹּט׃ עַד־ מָתַי תִּשְׁפְּטוּ־ עָוֶל
unjust will-you-defend when? until (2) he-gives-judgment gods in-among great

וּפְנֵי רְשָׁעִים תִּשְׂאוּ־ סֶלָה׃ שִׁפְטוּ־ דַל
weak defend! (3) selah you-will-show-partiality wicked-ones and-faces-of

וְיָתוֹם עָנִי וָרָשׁ הַצְדִּיקוּ׃ פַּלְּטוּ־
rescue! (4) maintain-rights! and-one-being-oppressed poor and-fatherless

דַל וְאֶבְיוֹן מִיַּד רְשָׁעִים הַצִּילוּ׃ לֹא יָדְעוּ
they-know nothing (5) deliver! wicked-ones from-hand-of and-needy weak

וְלֹא יָבִינוּ בַּחֲשֵׁכָה יִתְהַלָּכוּ יִמּוֹטוּ כָּל־
all-of they-are-shaken they-walk in-darkness they-understand and-nothing

מוֹסְדֵי אָרֶץ׃ אֲנִי־אָמַרְתִּי אֱלֹהִים אַתֶּם וּבְנֵי עֶלְיוֹן כֻּלְּכֶם׃
all-of-you Most-High and-sons-of you gods I-said I (6) earth foundations-of

אָכֵן כְּאָדָם תְּמוּתוּן וּכְאַחַד הַשָּׂרִים תִּפֹּלוּ׃
you-will-fall the-rulers and-like-other-of you-will-die like-man but (7)

קוּמָה אֱלֹהִים שָׁפְטָה הָאָרֶץ כִּי־ אַתָּה תִנְחַל בְּכָל־ הַגּוֹיִם׃
the-nations of-all-of you-inherit you for the-earth judge! God rise-up! (8)

שִׁיר מִזְמוֹר לְאָסָף׃ אֱלֹהִים אַל־ דֳּמִי־ לָךְ אַל־ תֶּחֱרַשׁ
you-be-quiet not to-you silence not God (2) of-Asaph psalm song *(83:1)

an alien god.
10 I am the LORD your God,
who brought you up out of Egypt.
Open wide your mouth and I will fill it.

11 "But my people would not listen to me;
Israel would not submit to me.
12 So I gave them over to their stubborn hearts
to follow their own devices.

13 "If my people would but listen to me,
if Israel would follow my ways,
14 how quickly would I subdue their enemies
and turn my hand against their foes!
15 Those who hate the LORD would cringe before him,
and their punishment would last forever.
16 But you would be fed with the finest of wheat;
with honey from the rock I would satisfy you."

## Psalm 82

A psalm of Asaph.

1 God presides in the great assembly;
he gives judgment among the "gods":

2 "How long will you[j] defend the unjust
and show partiality to the wicked? *Selah*
3 Defend the cause of the weak and fatherless;
maintain the rights of the poor and oppressed.
4 Rescue the weak and needy;
deliver them from the hand of the wicked.

5 "They know nothing, they understand nothing.
They walk about in darkness;
all the foundations of the earth are shaken.

6 "I said, 'You are "gods";
you are all sons of the Most High.'
7 But you will die like mere men;
you will fall like every other ruler."

8 Rise up, O God, judge the earth,
for all the nations are your inheritance.

## Psalm 83

A song. A psalm of Asaph.

1 O God, do not keep silent;

j2 The Hebrew is plural.

*Heading, *1* See the note on page 349.

וְאַל־ תִּשְׁקֹט אֵל׃ כִּֽי־ הִנֵּה אוֹיְבֶיךָ יֶהֱמָיוּן
they-are-astir ones-being-enemies-of-you see! for (3) God you-be-still and-not

וּמְשַׂנְאֶיךָ נָשְׂאוּ רֹאשׁ׃ עַל־ עַמְּךָ
people-of-you against (4) head they-rear and-ones-being-foes-of-you

יַעֲרִימוּ סוֹד וְיִתְיָעֲצוּ עַל־ צְפוּנֶיךָ׃
ones-being-cherished-of-you against and-they-plot conspiracy they-make-cunning

אָמְרוּ לְכוּ וְנַכְחִידֵם מִגּוֹי וְלֹא־
that-not as-nation and-let-us-destroy-them come! they-say (5)

יִזָּכֵר שֵׁם־ יִשְׂרָאֵל עוֹד׃ כִּי נוֹעֲצוּ לֵב יַחְדָּו
together mind they-plot for (6) more Israel name-of he-will-be-remembered

עָלֶיךָ בְּרִית יִכְרֹתוּ׃ אָהֳלֵי אֱדוֹם וְיִשְׁמְעֵאלִים מוֹאָב
Moab and-Ishmaelites Edom tents-of (7) they-form alliance against-you

וְהַגְרִים׃ גְּבָל וְעַמּוֹן וַעֲמָלֵק פְּלֶשֶׁת עִם־ יֹשְׁבֵי
ones-living-of with Philistia and-Amalek and-Ammon Gebal (8) and-Hagrites

צוֹר׃ גַּם־ אַשּׁוּר נִלְוָה עִמָּם הָיוּ זְרוֹעַ לִבְנֵי־
to-descendants-of strength they-are with-them he-joined Assyria even (9) Tyre

לוֹט סֶלָה׃ עֲשֵׂה־ לָהֶם כְּמִדְיָן כְּסִיסְרָא כְיָבִין בְּנַחַל קִישׁוֹן׃
Kishon at-river-of as-Jabin as-Sisera as-Midian to-them do! (10) selah Lot

נִשְׁמְדוּ בְעֵין־דֹּאר הָיוּ דֹּמֶן לָאֲדָמָה׃ שִׁיתֵמוֹ
make-them! (12) on-the-ground refuse they-became Dor at-En they-perished (11)

נְדִיבֵמוֹ כְּעֹרֵב וְכִזְאֵב וּכְזֶבַח וּכְצַלְמֻנָּע
and-like-Zalmunna and-like-Zebah and-like-Zeeb like-Oreb nobles-of-them

כָּל־ נְסִיכֵמוֹ׃ אֲשֶׁר אָמְרוּ נִירֲשָׁה לָּנוּ אֵת
*** for-us let-us-take-possession they-said who (13) princes-of-them all-of

נְאוֹת אֱלֹהִים׃ אֱלֹהַי שִׁיתֵמוֹ כַגַּלְגַּל כְּקַשׁ
like-chaff like-the-tumbleweed make-them! God-of-me (14) God pasturelands-of

לִפְנֵי־ רוּחַ׃ כְּאֵשׁ תִּבְעַר־ יָעַר וּכְלֶהָבָה תְּלַהֵט
she-sets-ablaze or-as-flame forest she-consumes as-fire (15) wind before

הָרִים׃ כֵּן תִּרְדְּפֵם בְּסַעֲרֶךָ וּבְסוּפָתְךָ
and-with-storm-of-you with-tempest-of-you you-pursue-them so (16) mountains

תְבַהֲלֵם׃ מַלֵּא פְנֵיהֶם קָלוֹן וִיבַקְשׁוּ
so-they-will-seek shame faces-of-them cover! (17) you-terrify-them

שִׁמְךָ יְהוָה׃ יֵבֹשׁוּ וְיִבָּהֲלוּ עֲדֵי־
to and-may-they-be-dismayed may-they-be-ashamed (18) Yahweh name-of-you

עַד וְיַחְפְּרוּ וְיֹאבֵדוּ׃ וְיֵדְעוּ
and-let-them-know (19) and-may-they-perish and-may-they-be-disgraced ever

כִּי־ אַתָּה שִׁמְךָ יְהוָה לְבַדֶּךָ עֶלְיוֹן עַל־ כָּל־ הָאָרֶץ׃
the-earth all-of over Most-High by-yourself Yahweh name-of-you you that

be not quiet, O God, be not
still.
2See how your enemies are
astir,
how your foes rear their
heads.
3With cunning they conspire
against your people;
they plot against those you
cherish.
4"Come," they say, "let us
destroy them as a nation,
that the name of Israel be
remembered no more."
5With one mind they plot
together;
they form an alliance
against you—
6the tents of Edom and the
Ishmaelites,
of Moab and the
descendants of Hagar,
7Gebal,[k] Ammon and Amalek,
Philistia, with the people of
Tyre.
8Even Assyria has joined them
to lend strength to the
descendants of Lot. *Selah*
9Do to them as you did to
Midian,
as you did to Sisera and
Jabin at the river Kishon,
10who perished at Endor
and became like refuse on
the ground.
11Make their nobles like Oreb
and Zeeb,
all their princes like Zebah
and Zalmunna,
12who said, "Let us take
possession
of the pasturelands of God."
13Make them like tumbleweed,
O my God,
like chaff before the wind.
14As fire consumes the forest
or a flame sets the
mountains ablaze,
15so pursue them with your
tempest
and terrify them with your
storm.
16Cover their faces with shame
so that men will seek your
name, O LORD.
17May they ever be ashamed
and dismayed;
may they perish in disgrace.
18Let them know that you,
whose name is the LORD—
that you alone are the Most
High over all the earth.

k7 That is, Byblos

*See the note on page 349.

לַמְנַצֵּחַ עַל־הַגִּתִּית לִבְנֵי־קֹרַח מִזְמוֹר׃

psalm Korah of-Sons-of the-gittith according-to for-the-one-directing *(84:1)

מַה־יְּדִידוֹת מִשְׁכְּנוֹתֶיךָ יְהוָה צְבָאוֹת׃ נִכְסְפָה וְגַם־

and-even she-yearns (3) Hosts Yahweh-of dwellings-of-you lovely-ones how! (2)

כָּלְתָה ׀ נַפְשִׁי לְחַצְרוֹת יְהוָה לִבִּי וּבְשָׂרִי

and-flesh-of-me heart-of-me Yahweh for-courts-of soul-of-me she-faints

יְרַנְּנוּ אֶל אֵל־חָי׃ גַּם־צִפּוֹר ׀ מָצְאָה בַיִת וּדְרוֹר ׀ קֵן

nest and-swallow home she-found sparrow even (4) living God for they-cry-out

לָהּ אֲשֶׁר־שָׁתָה אֶפְרֹחֶיהָ אֶת־מִזְבְּחוֹתֶיךָ יְהוָה

Yahweh-of altars-of-you near young-ones-of-her she-may-have where for-her

צְבָאוֹת מַלְכִּי וֵאלֹהָי׃ אַשְׁרֵי יוֹשְׁבֵי

ones-dwelling-of blessednesses-of (5) and-God-of-me King-of-me Hosts

בֵיתֶךָ עוֹד יְהַלְלוּךָ סֶּלָה׃ אַשְׁרֵי אָדָם עוֹז־

strength man blessednesses-of (6) selah they-praise-you ever house-of-you

לוֹ בָךְ מְסִלּוֹת בִּלְבָבָם׃ עֹבְרֵי ׀ בְּעֵמֶק

through-Valley-of ones-passing-of (7) in-heart-of-them pilgrimages in-you of-him

הַבָּכָא מַעְיָן יְשִׁיתוּהוּ גַּם־בְּרָכוֹת יַעְטֶה מוֹרֶה׃ יֵלְכוּ

they-go (8) autumn-rain he-covers pools also they-make-him spring the-Baca

מֵחַיִל אֶל־חָיִל יֵרָאֶה אֶל־אֱלֹהִים בְּצִיּוֹן׃ יְהוָה אֱלֹהִים

God Yahweh (9) in-Zion God before he-appears strength to from-strength

צְבָאוֹת שִׁמְעָה תְפִלָּתִי הַאֲזִינָה אֱלֹהֵי יַעֲקֹב סֶלָה׃ מָגִנֵּנוּ רְאֵה

look! shield-of-us (10) selah Jacob God-of listen! prayer-of-me hear! Hosts

אֱלֹהִים וְהַבֵּט פְּנֵי מְשִׁיחֶךָ׃ כִּי טוֹב־יוֹם בַּחֲצֵרֶיךָ

in-courts-of-you day better for (11) anointed-one-of-you faces-of and-look! God

מֵאָלֶף בָּחַרְתִּי הִסְתּוֹפֵף בְּבֵית אֱלֹהַי

God-of-me in-house-of to-be-doorkeeper I-would-rather than-thousand

מִדּוּר בְּאָהֳלֵי־רֶשַׁע׃ כִּי שֶׁמֶשׁ ׀ וּמָגֵן יְהוָה אֱלֹהִים חֵן

favor God Yahweh and-shield sun for (12) wicked in-tents-of than-to-dwell

וְכָבוֹד יִתֵּן יְהוָה לֹא יִמְנַע־טוֹב לַהֹלְכִים

from-ones-walking good-thing he-withholds not Yahweh he-bestows and-honor

בְּתָמִים׃ יְהוָה צְבָאוֹת אַשְׁרֵי אָדָם בֹּטֵחַ בָּךְ׃

in-you one-trusting man blessednesses-of Hosts Yahweh-of (13) in-blamelessness

לַמְנַצֵּחַ ׀ לִבְנֵי־קֹרַח מִזְמוֹר׃ רָצִיתָ

you-showed-favor (2) psalm Korah of-Sons-of for-the-one-directing *(85:1)

יְהוָה אַרְצֶךָ שַׁבְתָּ שְׁבוּת יַעֲקֹב׃ נָשָׂאתָ עֲוֹן

iniquity-of you-forgave (3) Jacob fortune-of you-restored land-of-you Yahweh

עַמֶּךָ כִּסִּיתָ כָל־חַטָּאתָם סֶלָה׃ אָסַפְתָּ כָל־

all-of you-set-aside (4) selah sin-of-them all-of you-covered people-of-you

**Psalm 84**

For the director of music. According to *gittith*.[l] Of the Sons of Korah. A psalm.

1 How lovely is your dwelling place,
O LORD Almighty!
2 My soul yearns, even faints
for the courts of the LORD;
my heart and my flesh cry out
for the living God.

3 Even the sparrow has found a home,
and the swallow a nest for herself,
where she may have her young—
a place near your altar,
O LORD Almighty, my King and my God.
4 Blessed are those who dwell in your house;
they are ever praising you. *Selah*

5 Blessed are those whose strength is in you,
who have set their hearts on pilgrimage.
6 As they pass through the Valley of Baca,
they make it a place of springs;
the autumn rains also cover it with pools.[m]
7 They go from strength to strength
till each appears before God in Zion.

8 Hear my prayer, O LORD God Almighty;
listen to me, O God of Jacob. *Selah*
9 Look upon our shield,[n] O God;
look with favor on your anointed one.

10 Better is one day in your courts
than a thousand elsewhere;
I would rather be a doorkeeper in the house of my God
than dwell in the tents of the wicked.
11 For the LORD God is a sun and shield;
the LORD bestows favor and honor;
no good thing does he withhold
from those whose walk is blameless.

12 O LORD Almighty,
blessed is the man who trusts in you.

**Psalm 85**

For the director of music. Of the Sons of Korah. A psalm.

1 You showed favor to your land, O LORD;
you restored the fortunes of Jacob.
2 You forgave the iniquity of

[l] Title: Probably a musical term
[m] 6 Or *blessings*
[n] 9 Or *sovereign*

*Heading, *1* See the note on page 349.

°2 ק שבית

עֶבְרָתֶךָ הֱשִׁיבוֹתָ מֵחֲרוֹן אַפֶּךָ׃ שׁוּבֵנוּ
restore-us! (5) anger-of-you from-fierceness-of you-turned wrath-of-you

אֱלֹהֵי יִשְׁעֵנוּ וְהָפֵר כַּעַסְךָ עִמָּנוּ׃ הַלְעוֹלָם
to-forever? (6) toward-us displeasure-of-you and-put-away! salvation-of-us God-of

תֶּאֱנַף־ בָּנוּ תִּמְשֹׁךְ אַפְּךָ לְדֹר
to-generation anger-of-you will-you-prolong with-us will-you-be-angry

וָדֹר׃ הֲלֹא־ אַתָּה תָּשׁוּב תְּחַיֵּנוּ
will-you-revive-us will-you-do-again you not? (7) and-generation

וְעַמְּךָ יִשְׂמְחוּ־ בָךְ׃ הַרְאֵנוּ יְהוָה
Yahweh show-us! (8) in-you they-may-rejoice that-people-of-you

חַסְדֶּךָ וְיֶשְׁעֲךָ תִּתֶּן־ לָנוּ׃ אֶשְׁמְעָה
I-will-listen (9) to-us you-grant and-salvation-of-you unfailing-love-of-you

מַה־ יְדַבֵּר הָאֵל ׀ יְהוָה כִּי ׀ יְדַבֵּר שָׁלוֹם אֶל־ עַמּוֹ
people-of-him to peace he-promises for Yahweh the-God he-will-say what

וְאֶל־ חֲסִידָיו וְאַל־ יָשׁוּבוּ לְכִסְלָה׃ אַךְ ׀ קָרוֹב
near surely (10) to-folly let-them-return but-not saints-of-him even-to

לִירֵאָיו יִשְׁעוֹ לִשְׁכֹּן כָּבוֹד בְּאַרְצֵנוּ׃ חֶסֶד־
love (11) in-land-of-us glory to-dwell salvation-of-him to-ones-fearing-him

וֶאֱמֶת נִפְגָּשׁוּ צֶדֶק וְשָׁלוֹם נָשָׁקוּ׃ אֱמֶת
faithfulness (12) they-kiss and-peace righteousness they-meet and-faithfulness

מֵאֶרֶץ תִּצְמָח וְצֶדֶק מִשָּׁמַיִם נִשְׁקָף׃
he-looks-down from-heavens and-righteousness she-springs-forth from-earth

גַּם־ יְהוָה יִתֵּן הַטּוֹב וְאַרְצֵנוּ תִּתֵּן
she-will-yield and-land-of-us the-good he-will-give Yahweh indeed (13)

יְבוּלָהּ׃ צֶדֶק לְפָנָיו יְהַלֵּךְ וְיָשֵׂם לְדֶרֶךְ
for-way and-he-prepares he-goes before-him righteousness (14) harvest-of-her

פְּעָמָיו׃ תְּפִלָּה לְדָוִד הַטֵּה־ יְהוָה אָזְנְךָ עֲנֵנִי
answer-me! ear-of-you Yahweh hear! of-David prayer (86:1) steps-of-him

כִּי־ עָנִי וְאֶבְיוֹן אָנִי׃ שָׁמְרָה נַפְשִׁי כִּי־ חָסִיד אָנִי הוֹשַׁע
save! I devoted for life-of-me guard! (2) I and-needy poor for

עַבְדְּךָ אַתָּה אֱלֹהַי הַבּוֹטֵחַ אֵלֶיךָ׃ חָנֵּנִי
have-mercy-on-me! (3) in-you the-one-trusting God-of-me you servant-of-you

אֲדֹנָי כִּי אֵלֶיךָ אֶקְרָא כָּל־ הַיּוֹם׃ שַׂמֵּחַ נֶפֶשׁ עַבְדֶּךָ
servant-of-you self-of bring-joy! (4) the-day all-of I-call to-you for Lord

כִּי אֵלֶיךָ אֲדֹנָי נַפְשִׁי אֶשָּׂא׃ כִּי־ אַתָּה אֲדֹנָי טוֹב וְסַלָּח
and-forgiving kind Lord you indeed (5) I-lift-up soul-of-me Lord to-you for

וְרַב־ חֶסֶד לְכָל־ קֹרְאֶיךָ׃ הַאֲזִינָה יְהוָה
Yahweh hear! (6) ones-calling-to-you to-all-of love and-abundant-of

your people
and covered all their sins.
*Selah*
3 You set aside all your wrath
and turned from your fierce
anger.
4 Restore us again, O God our
Savior,
and put away your
displeasure toward us.
5 Will you be angry with us
forever?
Will you prolong your anger
through all generations?
6 Will you not revive us again,
that your people may rejoice
in you?
7 Show us your unfailing love,
O LORD,
and grant us your salvation.
8 I will listen to what God the
LORD will say;
he promises peace to his
people, his saints—
but let them not return to
folly.
9 Surely his salvation is near
those who fear him,
that his glory may dwell in
our land.
10 Love and faithfulness meet
together;
righteousness and peace kiss
each other.
11 Faithfulness springs forth from
the earth,
and righteousness looks
down from heaven.
12 The LORD will indeed give
what is good,
and our land will yield its
harvest.
13 Righteousness goes before him
and prepares the way for his
steps.

### Psalm 86

A prayer of David.

1 Hear, O LORD, and answer me,
for I am poor and needy.
2 Guard my life, for I am
devoted to you.
You are my God; save your
servant
who trusts in you.
3 Have mercy on me, O Lord,
for I call to you all day long.
4 Bring joy to your servant,
for to you, O Lord,
I lift up my soul.
5 You are kind and forgiving, O
Lord,
abounding in love to all
who call to you.
6 Hear my prayer, O LORD;

*See the note on page 349.

תְּפִלָּתִ֑י וְֽהַקְשִׁיבָה בְּקֹ֥ול תַּחֲנוּנֹותָֽי׃ בְּי֣וֹם
in-day-of (7) cries-for-mercy-of-me to-sound-of and-listen! prayer-of-me

צָרָתִ֣י אֶקְרָאֶ֑ךָּ כִּ֣י תַעֲנֵֽנִי׃ אֵין־
there-is-none (8) you-will-answer-me for I-will-call-to-you trouble-of-me

כָּמֹ֖וךָ בָאֱלֹהִ֥ים ׀ אֲדֹנָ֗י וְאֵ֣ין כְּֽמַעֲשֶֽׂיךָ׃ כָּל־
all-of (9) like-deeds-of-you and-there-is-not Lord among-the-gods like-you

גֹּויִ֤ם ׀ אֲשֶׁ֬ר עָשִׂ֗יתָ יָבֹ֤ואוּ ׀ וְיִשְׁתַּחֲו֣וּ לְפָנֶ֣יךָ אֲדֹנָ֑י
Lord before-you and-they-will-worship they-will-come you-made that nations

וִֽיכַבְּד֥וּ לִשְׁמֶֽךָ׃ כִּֽי־גָדֹ֣ול אַ֭תָּה וְעֹשֵׂ֣ה
and-one-doing-of you great for (10) to-name-of-you and-they-will-bring-glory

נִפְלָאֹ֑ות אַתָּ֖ה אֱלֹהִ֣ים לְבַדֶּֽךָ׃ הֹ֘ורֵ֤נִי יְהוָ֨ה ׀ דַּרְכֶּ֗ךָ
way-of-you Yahweh teach-me! (11) by-yourself God you deeds-being-marvelous

אֲהַלֵּ֥ךְ בַּאֲמִתֶּ֑ךָ יַחֵ֥ד לְ֝בָבִ֗י לְיִרְאָ֥ה שְׁמֶֽךָ׃
name-of-you to-fear heart-of-me make-undivided! in-truth-of-you I-will-walk

אֹודְךָ֤ ׀ אֲדֹנָ֣י אֱ֭לֹהַי בְּכָל־לְבָבִ֑י וַאֲכַבְּדָ֖ה
and-I-will-glorify heart-of-me with-all-of God-of-me Lord I-will-praise-you (12)

שִׁמְךָ֣ לְעֹולָֽם׃ כִּֽי־חַ֭סְדְּךָ גָּדֹ֣ול עָלָ֑י וְהִצַּ֥לְתָּ
and-you-delivered toward-me great love-of-you for (13) to-forever name-of-you

נַ֝פְשִׁ֗י מִשְּׁאֹ֥ול תַּחְתִּיָּֽה׃ אֱלֹהִ֤ים ׀ זֵ֘דִ֤ים קָֽמוּ־עָלַ֗י
against-me they-attack arrogant-ones God (14) depth from-Sheol soul-of-me

וַעֲדַ֣ת עָ֭רִיצִים בִּקְשׁ֣וּ נַפְשִׁ֑י וְלֹ֖א שָׂמ֣וּךָ
they-regard-you and-not life-of-me they-seek ruthless-men and-band-of

לְנֶגְדָּֽם׃ וְאַתָּ֣ה אֲ֭דֹנָי אֵל־רַח֣וּם וְחַנּ֑וּן אֶ֥רֶךְ
slow-of and-gracious compassionate God Lord but-you (15) at-before-them

אַ֝פַּ֗יִם וְרַב־חֶ֥סֶד וֶאֱמֶֽת׃ פְּנֵ֥ה אֵלַ֗י
to-me turn! (16) and-faithfulness love and-abundant-of angers

וְחָ֫נֵּ֥נִי תְּנָֽה־עֻזְּךָ֥ לְעַבְדֶּ֑ךָ וְ֝הֹושִׁ֗יעָה
and-save! to-servant-of-you strength-of-you grant! and-have-mercy-on-me!

לְבֶן־אֲמָתֶֽךָ׃ עֲשֵֽׂה־עִמִּ֥י אֹות֮ לְטֹ֫ובָ֥ה וְיִרְא֣וּ
that-they-may-see of-goodness sign to-me give! (17) maidservant-of-you to-son-of

שֹׂנְאַ֣י וְיֵבֹ֑שׁוּ כִּֽי־אַתָּ֥ה יְ֝הוָ֗ה עֲזַרְתַּ֥נִי
you-helped-me Yahweh you for and-they-may-be-shamed ones-being-enemies-of-me

וְנִחַמְתָּֽנִי׃ לִבְנֵי־קֹ֭רַח מִזְמֹ֣ור שִׁ֑יר יְ֝סוּדָתֹ֗ו
foundation-of-him song psalm Korah of-Sons-of (87:1) and-you-comforted-me

בְּהַרְרֵי־קֹֽדֶשׁ׃ אֹהֵ֣ב יְ֭הוָה שַׁעֲרֵ֣י צִיֹּ֑ון מִ֝כֹּ֗ל
more-than-all-of Zion gates-of Yahweh one-loving (2) holiness on-mountains-of

מִשְׁכְּנֹ֥ות יַעֲקֹֽב׃ נִ֭כְבָּדֹות מְדֻבָּ֣ר בָּ֑ךְ עִ֥יר
city-of of-you one-being-said things-being-glorious (3) Jacob dwellings-of

listen to my cry for mercy.
7 In the day of my trouble I will call to you,
for you will answer me.

8 Among the gods there is none like you, O Lord;
no deeds can compare with yours.
9 All the nations you have made will come and worship before you, O Lord;
they will bring glory to your name.
10 For you are great and do marvelous deeds;
you alone are God.

11 Teach me your way, O LORD,
and I will walk in your truth;
give me an undivided heart,
that I may fear your name.
12 I will praise you, O Lord my God, with all my heart;
I will glorify your name forever.
13 For great is your love toward me;
you have delivered my soul from the depths of the grave.[o]

14 The arrogant are attacking me, O God;
a band of ruthless men seeks my life—
men without regard for you.
15 But you, O Lord, are a compassionate and gracious God,
slow to anger, abounding in love and faithfulness.
16 Turn to me and have mercy on me;
grant your strength to your servant
and save the son of your maidservant.[p]
17 Give me a sign of your goodness,
that my enemies may see it and be put to shame,
for you, O LORD, have helped me and comforted me.

### Psalm 87

Of the Sons of Korah. A psalm. A song.

1 He has set his foundation on the holy mountain;
2 the LORD loves the gates of Zion
more than all the dwellings of Jacob.
3 Glorious things are said of you,

o13 Hebrew *Sheol*
p16 Or *save your faithful son*

הָאֱלֹהִים סֶלָה׃ אַזְכִּיר ׀ רַהַב וּבָבֶל לְיֹדְעָי
among-ones-acknowledging-me and-Babylon Rahab I-will-record (4) selah the-God

הִנֵּה פְלֶשֶׁת וְצוֹר עִם־כּוּשׁ זֶה יֻלַּד־שָׁם׃ וּֽלְצִיּוֹן ׀
indeed-of-Zion (5) there he-was-born this-one Cush with and-Tyre Philistia see!

יֵאָמַר אִישׁ וְאִישׁ יֻלַּד־בָּהּ וְהוּא יְכוֹנְנֶהָ
he-will-establish-her and-he in-her he-was-born and-one one he-will-be-said

עֶלְיוֹן׃ יְהוָה יִסְפֹּר בִּכְתוֹב עַמִּים זֶה
this-one peoples when-to-register he-will-write Yahweh (6) Most-High

יֻלַּד־שָׁם סֶלָה׃ וְשָׁרִים כְּחֹלְלִים כָּל־
all-of as-ones-making-music and-ones-singing (7) selah there he-was-born

מַעְיָנַי בָּךְ׃ שִׁיר מִזְמוֹר לִבְנֵי קֹרַח לַמְנַצֵּחַ
for-the-one-directing Korah of-Sons-of psalm song *(88:1) in-you fountains-of-me

עַל־ מָחֲלַת לְעַנּוֹת מַשְׂכִּיל לְהֵימָן הָאֶזְרָחִי׃ יְהוָה
Yahweh (2) the-Ezrahite of-Heman maskil leannoth mahalath according-to

אֱלֹהֵי יְשׁוּעָתִי יוֹם־צָעַקְתִּי בַלַּיְלָה נֶגְדֶּךָ׃ תָּבוֹא
may-she-come (3) before-you in-the-night I-cry-out day salvation-of-me God-of

לְפָנֶיךָ תְּפִלָּתִי הַטֵּה־אָזְנְךָ לְרִנָּתִי׃ כִּי־ שָׂבְעָה
she-is-full for (4) to-cry-of-me ear-of-you turn! prayer-of-me before-you

בְרָעוֹת נַפְשִׁי וְחַיַּי לִשְׁאוֹל הִגִּיעוּ׃ נֶחְשַׁבְתִּי
I-am-counted (5) they-draw-near to-Sheol and-lives-of-me soul-of-me of-troubles

עִם־ יוֹרְדֵי בוֹר הָיִיתִי כְּגֶבֶר אֵין־ אֱיָל׃
strength without like-man I-am pit ones-going-down-of among

בַּמֵּתִים חָפְשִׁי כְּמוֹ חֲלָלִים ׀ שֹׁכְבֵי קֶבֶר אֲשֶׁר
whom grave ones-lying-of slain-ones like set-apart with-the-dead-ones (6)

לֹא זְכַרְתָּם עוֹד וְהֵמָּה מִיָּדְךָ נִגְזָרוּ׃
they-are-cut-off from-care-of-you and-they more you-remember-them not

שַׁתַּנִי בְּבוֹר תַּחְתִּיּוֹת בְּמַחֲשַׁכִּים בִּמְצֹלוֹת׃ עָלַי
upon-me (8) in-depths in-darkest-ones lowest-ones in-pit-of you-put-me (7)

סָמְכָה חֲמָתֶךָ וְכָל־ מִשְׁבָּרֶיךָ עִנִּיתָ סֶּלָה׃
selah you-overwhelmed waves-of-you and-all-of wrath-of-you she-lies-heavily

הִרְחַקְתָּ מְיֻדָּעַי מִמֶּנִּי שַׁתַּנִי תוֹעֵבוֹת
repulsive-ones you-made-me from-me ones-being-friends-of-me you-took-away (9)

לָמוֹ כָּלֻא וְלֹא אֵצֵא׃ עֵינִי דָאֲבָה
she-is-dim eye-of-me (10) I-can-escape and-not one-being-confined to-them

מִנִּי עֹנִי קְרָאתִיךָ יְהוָה בְּכָל־ יוֹם שִׁטַּחְתִּי אֵלֶיךָ
to-you I-spread-out day in-every-of Yahweh I-call-to-you grief from

כַפָּי׃ הֲלַמֵּתִים תַּעֲשֶׂה־ פֶּלֶא אִם־ רְפָאִים יָקוּמוּ ׀
they-rise-up dead-ones or wonder you-show to-the-dead-ones? (11) hands-of-me

O city of God: *Selah*
4 "I will record Rahab[q] and
Babylon
among those who
acknowledge me—
Philistia too, and Tyre, along
with Cush[r]—
and will say, 'This[s] one was
born in Zion.' "
5 Indeed, of Zion it will be said,
"This one and that one were
born in her,
and the Most High himself
will establish her."
6 The LORD will write in the
register of the peoples:
"This one was born in
Zion." *Selah*
7 As they make music they will
sing,
"All my fountains are in
you."

**Psalm 88**

A song. A psalm of the Sons of Korah. For the director of music. According to *mahalath leannoth*.[t] A *maskil*[u] of Heman the Ezrahite.

1 O LORD, the God who saves
me,
day and night I cry out
before you.
2 May my prayer come before
you;
turn your ear to my cry.
3 For my soul is full of trouble
and my life draws near the
grave.[v]
4 I am counted among those
who go down to the pit;
I am like a man without
strength.
5 I am set apart with the dead,
like the slain who lie in the
grave,
whom you remember no more,
who are cut off from your
care.
6 You have put me in the lowest
pit,
in the darkest depths.
7 Your wrath lies heavily upon
me;
you have overwhelmed me
with all your waves. *Selah*
8 You have taken from me my
closest friends
and have made me repulsive
to them.
I am confined and cannot
escape;
9 my eyes are dim with grief.
I call to you, O LORD, every
day;
I spread out my hands to
you.
10 Do you show your wonders to
the dead?
Do those who are dead rise

q4 A poetic name for Egypt
r4 That is, the upper Nile region
s4 Or *"O Rahab and Babylon, / Philistia, Tyre and Cush, / I will record concerning those who acknowledge me: / 'This*
tTitle: Possibly a tune, "The Suffering of Affliction"
uTitle: Probably a literary or musical term
v3 Hebrew *Sheol*

*Heading, *1* See the note on page 349.

יוֹדוּךָ סֶּלָה׃ הַיְסֻפַּר בַּקֶּבֶר חַסְדֶּךָ
they-praise-you selah (12) is-he-declared? in-the-grave love-of-you

אֱמוּנָתְךָ בָּאֲבַדּוֹן׃ הֲיִוָּדַע בַּחֹשֶׁךְ פִּלְאֶךָ
faithfulness-of-you in-Abaddon (13) is-he-known? in-the-darkness wonder-of-you

וְצִדְקָתְךָ בְּאֶרֶץ נְשִׁיָּה׃ וַאֲנִי ׀ אֵלֶיךָ יְהוָה
or-righteous-deed-of-you in-land-of oblivion (14) but-I to-you Yahweh

שִׁוַּעְתִּי וּבַבֹּקֶר תְּפִלָּתִי תְקַדְּמֶךָּ׃ לָמָה
I-cry-for-help and-in-the-morning prayer-of-me she-comes-before-you (15) why?

יְהוָה תִּזְנַח נַפְשִׁי תַּסְתִּיר פָּנֶיךָ מִמֶּנִּי׃ עָנִי
Yahweh you-reject self-of-me you-hide faces-of-you from-me (16) afflicted

אֲנִי וְגֹוֵעַ מִנֹּעַר נָשָׂאתִי אֵמֶיךָ
I and-one-being-close-to-death from-youth I-suffered terrors-of-you

אָפוּנָה׃ עָלַי עָבְרוּ חֲרוֹנֶיךָ בִּעוּתֶיךָ
and-I-am-in-despair (17) over-me they-swept wraths-of-you terrors-of-you

צִמְּתוּתֻנִי׃ סַבּוּנִי כַמַּיִם כָּל־ הַיּוֹם
they-destroyed-me (18) they-surround-me like-the-floods all-of the-day

הִקִּיפוּ עָלַי יָחַד׃ הִרְחַקְתָּ מִמֶּנִּי אֹהֵב
they-engulfed over-me completely (19) you-took-far from-me one-loving

וָרֵעַ מְיֻדָּעַי מַחְשָׁךְ׃ מַשְׂכִּיל לְאֵיתָן
and-companion ones-being-friends-of-me darkness *(89:1) maskil of-Ethan

הָאֶזְרָחִי׃ חַסְדֵי יְהוָה עוֹלָם אָשִׁירָה לְדֹר
the-Ezrahite (2) great-loves-of Yahweh forever I-will-sing to-generation

וָדֹר ׀ אוֹדִיעַ אֱמוּנָתְךָ בְּפִי׃
and-generation I-will-make-known faithfulness-of-you with-mouth-of-me

כִּי־ אָמַרְתִּי עוֹלָם חֶסֶד יִבָּנֶה שָׁמַיִם ׀ תָּכִן
(3) indeed I-will-declare forever love he-stands-firm heavens you-established

אֱמוּנָתְךָ בָהֶם׃ כָּרַתִּי בְרִית לִבְחִירִי
faithfulness-of-you in-them (4) I-made covenant with-chosen-one-of-me

נִשְׁבַּעְתִּי לְדָוִד עַבְדִּי׃ עַד־ עוֹלָם אָכִין זַרְעֶךָ
I-swore to-David servant-of-me (5) to forever I-will-establish line-of-you

וּבָנִיתִי לְדֹר־ וָדוֹר כִּסְאֲךָ סֶלָה׃
and-I-will-make-firm to-generation and-generation throne-of-you selah

וְיוֹדוּ שָׁמַיִם פִּלְאֲךָ יְהוָה אַף־ אֱמוּנָתְךָ
(6) and-they-praise heavens wonder-of-you Yahweh also faithfulness-of-you

בִּקְהַל קְדֹשִׁים׃ כִּי מִי בַשַּׁחַק יַעֲרֹךְ לַיהוָה
in-assembly-of holy-ones (7) for who? in-the-sky he-can-compare to-Yahweh

יִדְמֶה לַיהוָה בִּבְנֵי אֵלִים׃ אֵל נַעֲרָץ
he-is-like to-Yahweh among-sons-of heavenly-beings (8) God one-being-feared

up and praise you? *Selah*
11 Is your love declared in the grave,
your faithfulness in Destruction[w]?
12 Are your wonders known in the place of darkness,
or your righteous deeds in the land of oblivion?

13 But I cry to you for help, O LORD;
in the morning my prayer comes before you.
14 Why, O LORD, do you reject me
and hide your face from me?

15 From my youth I have been afflicted and close to death;
I have suffered your terrors and am in despair.
16 Your wrath has swept over me;
your terrors have destroyed me.
17 All day long they surround me like a flood;
they have completely engulfed me.
18 You have taken my companions and loved ones from me;
the darkness is my closest friend.

## Psalm 89

A *maskil*[x] of Ethan the Ezrahite.

1 I will sing of the LORD's great love forever;
with my mouth I will make your faithfulness known through all generations.
2 I will declare that your love stands firm forever,
that you established your faithfulness in heaven itself.

3 You said, "I have made a covenant with my chosen one,
I have sworn to David my servant,
4 'I will establish your line forever
and make your throne firm through all generations.' "
*Selah*

5 The heavens praise your wonders, O LORD,
your faithfulness too, in the assembly of the holy ones.
6 For who in the skies above can compare with the LORD?
Who is like the LORD among the heavenly beings?

w11 Hebrew *Abaddon*
xTitle: Probably a literary or musical term

*Heading, *1* See the note on page 349.

בְּסוֹד־ קְדֹשִׁים רַבָּה וְנוֹרָא עַל־ כָּל־
all-of over and-one-being-awesome greatly holy-ones in-council-of

סְבִיבָיו׃ יְהוָה׀ אֱלֹהֵי צְבָאוֹת מִי־ כָמוֹךָ חֲסִין׀ יָהּ
Yahweh mighty like-you who? Hosts God-of Yahweh (9) ones-surrounding-him

וֶאֱמוּנָתְךָ סְבִיבוֹתֶיךָ׃ אַתָּה מוֹשֵׁל בְּגֵאוּת
over-surging-of one-ruling you (10) ones-around-you and-faithfulness-of-you

הַיָּם בְּשׂוֹא גַלָּיו אַתָּה תְשַׁבְּחֵם׃ אַתָּה
you (11) you-still-them you waves-of-him when-to-mount-up the-sea

דִכִּאתָ כֶחָלָל רָהַב בִּזְרוֹעַ עֻזְּךָ פִּזַּרְתָּ
you-scattered strength-of-you with-arm-of Rahab like-the-slain you-crushed

אוֹיְבֶיךָ׃ לְךָ שָׁמַיִם אַף־ לְךָ אֶרֶץ תֵּבֵל
world earth to-you also heavens to-you (12) ones-being-enemies-of-you

וּמְלֹאָהּ אַתָּה יְסַדְתָּם׃ צָפוֹן וְיָמִין אַתָּה
you and-south north (13) you-founded-them you and-fullness-of-her

בְּרָאתָם תָּבוֹר וְחֶרְמוֹן בְּשִׁמְךָ יְרַנֵּנוּ׃ לְךָ
to-you (14) they-sing-for-joy at-name-of-you and-Hermon Tabor you-created-them

זְרוֹעַ עִם־ גְּבוּרָה תָּעֹז יָדְךָ תָּרוּם יְמִינֶךָ׃
right-hand-of-you she-is-exalted hand-of-you she-is-strong power with arm

צֶדֶק וּמִשְׁפָּט מְכוֹן כִּסְאֶךָ חֶסֶד וֶאֱמֶת
and-faithfulness love throne-of-you foundation-of and-justice righteousness (15)

יְקַדְּמוּ פָנֶיךָ׃ אַשְׁרֵי הָעָם יוֹדְעֵי
ones-learning-of the-people blessednesses-of (16) faces-of-you they-go-before

תְרוּעָה יְהוָה בְּאוֹר־ פָּנֶיךָ יְהַלֵּכוּן׃ בְּשִׁמְךָ
in-name-of-you (17) they-walk presences-of-you in-light-of Yahweh acclamation

יְגִילוּן כָּל־ הַיּוֹם וּבְצִדְקָתְךָ יָרוּמוּ׃ כִּי־
for (18) they-exult and-in-righteousness-of-you the-day all-of they-rejoice

תִפְאֶרֶת עֻזָּמוֹ אָתָּה וּבִרְצֹנְךָ תָּרִים° קַרְנֵנוּ׃
horn-of-us you-exalt and-by-favor-of-you you strength-of-them glory-of

כִּי לַיהוָה מָגִנֵּנוּ וְלִקְדוֹשׁ יִשְׂרָאֵל מַלְכֵּנוּ׃
king-of-us Israel and-to-Holy-One-of shield-of-us to-Yahweh indeed (19)

אָז דִּבַּרְתָּ־ בְחָזוֹן לַחֲסִידֶיךָ וַתֹּאמֶר שִׁוִּיתִי
I-bestowed and-you-said to-faithful-ones-of-you in-vision you-spoke once (20)

עֵזֶר עַל־ גִּבּוֹר הֲרִימוֹתִי בָחוּר מֵעָם׃ מָצָאתִי דָּוִד
David I-found (21) from-people man-being-young I-exalted warrior on strength

עַבְדִּי בְּשֶׁמֶן קָדְשִׁי מְשַׁחְתִּיו׃ אֲשֶׁר יָדִי
hand-of-me that (22) I-anointed-him sacredness-of-me with-oil-of servant-of-me

תִּכּוֹן עִמּוֹ אַף־ זְרוֹעִי תְאַמְּצֶנּוּ׃ לֹא־
not (23) she-will-strengthen-him arm-of-me surely to-him she-will-sustain

7 In the council of the holy ones
God is greatly feared;
he is more awesome than all
who surround him.
8 O LORD God Almighty, who is
like you?
You are mighty, O LORD,
and your faithfulness
surrounds you.
9 You rule over the surging sea;
when its waves mount up,
you still them.
10 You crushed Rahab like one of
the slain;
with your strong arm you
scattered your enemies.
11 The heavens are yours, and
yours also the earth;
you founded the world and
all that is in it.
12 You created the north and the
south;
Tabor and Hermon sing for
joy at your name.
13 Your arm is endued with
power;
your hand is strong, your
right hand exalted.
14 Righteousness and justice are
the foundation of your
throne;
love and faithfulness go
before you.
15 Blessed are those who have
learned to acclaim you,
who walk in the light of
your presence, O LORD.
16 They rejoice in your name all
day long;
they exult in your
righteousness.
17 For you are their glory and
strength,
and by your favor you exalt
our horn.[y]
18 Indeed, our shield[z] belongs to
the LORD,
our king to the Holy One of
Israel.
19 Once you spoke in a vision,
to your faithful people you
said:
"I have bestowed strength on
a warrior;
I have exalted a young man
from among the people.
20 I have found David my
servant;
with my sacred oil I have
anointed him.
21 My hand will sustain him;
surely my arm will
strengthen him.

y17 *Horn* here symbolizes strong one.
z18 Or *sovereign*

*See the note on page 349.

°18 ק תרום

יַשִּׁא אוֹיֵב בּוֹ וּבֶן־ עַוְלָה לֹא

not wickedness and-man-of to-him one-being-enemy he-will-subject-to-tribute

יְעַנֶּנּוּ׃ (24) וְכַתּוֹתִי מִפָּנָיו צָרָיו

foes-of-him at-before-him and-I-will-crush (24) he-will-oppress-him

וּמְשַׂנְאָיו אֶגּוֹף׃ (25) וֶאֱמוּנָתִי†

and-faithfulness-of-me (25) I-will-strike-down and-ones-being-adversaries-of-him

וְחַסְדִּי עִמּוֹ וּבִשְׁמִי תָּרוּם קַרְנוֹ׃

horn-of-him she-will-be-exalted and-through-name-of-me with-him and-love-of-me

(26) וְשַׂמְתִּי בַיָּם יָדוֹ וּבַנְּהָרוֹת

and-over-the-rivers hand-of-him over-the-sea and-I-will-set (26)

יְמִינוֹ׃ (27) הוּא יִקְרָאֵנִי אָבִי אָתָּה אֵלִי

God-of-me you Father-of-me he-will-call-out-to-me he (27) right-hand-of-him

וְצוּר יְשׁוּעָתִי׃ (28) אַף־אָנִי בְּכוֹר אֶתְּנֵהוּ עֶלְיוֹן

most-exalted I-will-appoint-him firstborn I also (28) salvation-of-me and-Rock-of

לְמַלְכֵי־ אָרֶץ׃ (29) לְעוֹלָם אֶשְׁמָור־ לוֹ חַסְדִּי

love-of-me to-him I-will-maintain to-forever (29) earth of-kings-of

וּבְרִיתִי נֶאֱמֶנֶת לוֹ׃ (30) וְשַׂמְתִּי

and-I-will-establish (30) with-him one-unfailing and-covenant-of-me

לָעַד זַרְעוֹ וְכִסְאוֹ כִּימֵי שָׁמָיִם׃ (31) אִם־

if (31) heavens as-days-of and-throne-of-him line-of-him to-forever

יַעַזְבוּ בָנָיו תּוֹרָתִי וּבְמִשְׁפָּטַי לֹא יֵלֵכוּן׃

they-follow not and-to-statutes-of-me law-of-me sons-of-him they-forsake

(32) אִם־ חֻקֹּתַי יְחַלֵּלוּ וּמִצְוֺתַי לֹא יִשְׁמֹרוּ׃

they-keep not and-commands-of-me they-violate decrees-of-me if (32)

(33) וּפָקַדְתִּי בְשֵׁבֶט פִּשְׁעָם וּבִנְגָעִים

and-with-floggings sin-of-them with-rod then-I-will-punish (33)

עֲוֺנָם׃ (34) וְחַסְדִּי לֹא־ אָפִיר מֵעִמּוֹ וְלֹא־

and-never from-with-him I-will-take not but-love-of-me (34) iniquity-of-them

אֲשַׁקֵּר בֶּאֱמוּנָתִי׃ (35) לֹא־ אֲחַלֵּל בְּרִיתִי

covenant-of-me I-will-violate not (35) to-faithfulness-of-me I-will-betray

וּמוֹצָא שְׂפָתַי לֹא אֲשַׁנֶּה׃ (36) אַחַת נִשְׁבַּעְתִּי בְקָדְשִׁי

by-holiness-of-me I-swore once (36) I-will-alter not lips-of-me or-utterance-of

אִם־ לְדָוִד אֲכַזֵּב׃ (37) זַרְעוֹ לְעוֹלָם יִהְיֶה

he-will-continue to-forever line-of-him (37) I-will-lie to-David not

וְכִסְאוֹ כַשֶּׁמֶשׁ נֶגְדִּי׃ (38) כְּיָרֵחַ יִכּוֹן

he-will-be-established like-moon (38) before-me like-the-sun and-throne-of-him

עוֹלָם וְעֵד בַּשַּׁחַק נֶאֱמָן סֶלָה׃ (39) וְאַתָּה

but-you (39) selah one-being-faithful in-the-sky and-witness forever

22 No enemy will subject him to tribute;
no wicked man will oppress him.
23 I will crush his foes before him
and strike down his adversaries.
24 My faithful love will be with him,
and through my name his horn[a] will be exalted.
25 I will set his hand over the sea,
his right hand over the rivers.
26 He will call out to me, 'You are my Father,
my God, the Rock my Savior.'
27 I will also appoint him my firstborn,
the most exalted of the kings of the earth.
28 I will maintain my love to him forever,
and my covenant with him will never fail.
29 I will establish his line forever,
his throne as long as the heavens endure.

30 "If his sons forsake my law
and do not follow my statutes,
31 if they violate my decrees
and fail to keep my commands,
32 I will punish their sin with the rod,
their iniquity with flogging;
33 but I will not take my love from him,
nor will I ever betray my faithfulness.
34 I will not violate my covenant
or alter what my lips have uttered.
35 Once for all, I have sworn by my holiness—
and I will not lie to David—
36 that his line will continue forever
and his throne endure before me like the sun;
37 it will be established forever like the moon,
the faithful witness in the sky." *Selah*

[a]24 *Horn* here symbolizes strength.

*See the note on page 349.

†25 Most mss have *hateph segol* under the *aleph* (וֶאֱ).

°29 ק אשמר

זָנַחְתָּ וַתִּמְאָס הִתְעַבַּרְתָּ עִם־ מְשִׁיחֶךָ׃
anointed-one-of-you with you-were-angry and-you-spurned you-rejected

נֵאַרְתָּה בְּרִית עַבְדֶּךָ חִלַּלְתָּ לָאָרֶץ
in-the-dust you-defiled servant-of-you covenant-of you-renounced (40)

נִזְרוֹ׃ פָּרַצְתָּ כָל־ גְּדֵרֹתָיו שַׂמְתָּ
you-reduced walls-of-him all-of you-broke-through (41) crown-of-him

מִבְצָרָיו מְחִתָּה׃ שַׁסֻּהוּ כָּל־ עֹבְרֵי דָרֶךְ
way ones-passing-of all-of they-plundered-him (42) ruin strongholds-of-him

הָיָה חֶרְפָּה לִשְׁכֵנָיו׃ הֲרִימוֹתָ יְמִין צָרָיו
foes-of-him right-hand-of you-exalted (43) of-neighbors-of-him scorn he-became

הִשְׂמַחְתָּ כָּל־ אוֹיְבָיו׃ אַף־ תָּשִׁיב
you-turned-back also (44) ones-being-enemies-of-him all-of you-made-rejoice

צוּר חַרְבּוֹ וְלֹא הֲקֵימֹתוֹ בַּמִּלְחָמָה׃ הִשְׁבַּתָּ
you-ended (45) in-the-battle you-supported-him and-not sword-of-him edge-of

מִטְּהָרוֹ וְכִסְאוֹ לָאָרֶץ מִגַּרְתָּה׃ הִקְצַרְתָּ
you-cut-short (46) you-cast to-the-ground and-throne-of-him to-splendor-of-him

יְמֵי עֲלוּמָיו הֶעֱטִיתָ עָלָיו בּוּשָׁה סֶלָה׃ עַד־ מָה
when? until (47) selah shame over-him you-covered youths-of-him days-of

יְהוָה תִּסָּתֵר לָנֶצַח תִּבְעַר כְּמוֹ־ אֵשׁ חֲמָתֶךָ׃
wrath-of-you fire like will-she-burn to-forever will-you-hide-yourself Yahweh

זְכָר־ אֲנִי מֶה־ חָלֶד עַל־ מַה־ שָּׁוְא בָּרָאתָ כָל־ בְּנֵי־
sons-of all-of you-created futility what for fleeting how I remember! (48)

אָדָם׃ מִי גֶבֶר יִחְיֶה וְלֹא יִרְאֶה־ מָּוֶת יְמַלֵּט
he-can-save death he-can-see and-not he-can-live man what? (49) man

נַפְשׁוֹ מִיַּד־ שְׁאוֹל סֶלָה׃ אַיֵּה ׀ חֲסָדֶיךָ
great-loves-of-you where? (50) selah Sheol from-power-of self-of-him

הָרִאשֹׁנִים ׀ אֲדֹנָי נִשְׁבַּעְתָּ לְדָוִד בֶּאֱמוּנָתֶךָ׃ זְכֹר
remember! (51) in-faithfulness-of-you to-David you-swore Lord the-former-ones

אֲדֹנָי חֶרְפַּת עֲבָדֶיךָ שְׂאֵתִי בְחֵיקִי כָּל־ רַבִּים ׀ עַמִּים׃
nations †many all-of in-heart-of-me to-bear-me servants-of-you mocking-of Lord

אֲשֶׁר חֵרְפוּ אוֹיְבֶיךָ ׀ יְהוָה אֲשֶׁר חֵרְפוּ
they-mocked which Yahweh ones-being-enemies-of-you they-mocked which (52)

עִקְּבוֹת מְשִׁיחֶךָ׃ בָּרוּךְ יְהוָה לְעוֹלָם אָמֵן ׀
amen to-forever Yahweh one-being-praised (53) anointed-one-of-you steps-of

וְאָמֵן׃ תְּפִלָּה לְמֹשֶׁה אִישׁ־ הָאֱלֹהִים אֲדֹנָי מָעוֹן אַתָּה
you dwelling-place Lord the-God man-of of-Moses prayer (90:1) and-amen

הָיִיתָ לָּנוּ בְּדֹר וָדֹר׃ בְּטֶרֶם ׀ הָרִים
mountains at-before (2) and-generation through-generation to-us you-are

38But you have rejected, you have spurned,
you have been very angry with your anointed one.
39You have renounced the covenant with your servant
and have defiled his crown in the dust.
40You have broken through all his walls
and reduced his strongholds to ruins.
41All who pass by have plundered him;
he has become the scorn of his neighbors.
42You have exalted the right hand of his foes;
you have made all his enemies rejoice.
43You have turned back the edge of his sword
and have not supported him in battle.
44You have put an end to his splendor
and cast his throne to the ground.
45You have cut short the days of his youth;
you have covered him with a mantle of shame. *Selah*

46How long, O LORD? Will you hide yourself forever?
How long will your wrath burn like fire?
47Remember how fleeting is my life.
For what futility you have created all men!
48What man can live and not see death,
or save himself from the power of the grave[b]? *Selah*
49O Lord, where is your former great love,
which in your faithfulness you swore to David?
50Remember, Lord, how your servant has[c] been mocked,
how I bear in my heart the taunts of all the nations,
51the taunts with which your enemies have mocked, O LORD,
with which they have mocked every step of your anointed one.

52Praise be to the LORD forever!
Amen and Amen.

## BOOK IV

*Psalms 90-106*

### Psalm 90

A prayer of Moses the man of God.

1Lord, you have been our dwelling place
throughout all generations.
2Before the mountains were

[b] *48* Hebrew *Sheol*
[c] *50* Or *your servants have*

*See the note on page 349.
†*51* The NIV reads this word as (רִבֵּים), *taunts-of*.

יֻלָּדוּ וַתְּחוֹלֵל אֶרֶץ וְתֵבֵל וּמֵעוֹלָם עַד־
to and-from-everlasting and-world earth or-you-brought-forth they-were-born

עוֹלָם אַתָּה אֵל׃ תָּשֵׁב אֱנוֹשׁ עַד־דַּכָּא וַתֹּאמֶר שׁוּבוּ
return! and-you-say dust to man you-turn-back (3) God you everlasting

בְנֵי־אָדָם׃ כִּי אֶלֶף שָׁנִים בְּעֵינֶיךָ כְּיוֹם אֶתְמוֹל כִּי
that yesterday like-day-of in-eyes-of-you years thousand-of for (4) man sons-of

יַעֲבֹר וְאַשְׁמוּרָה בַלָּיְלָה׃ זְרַמְתָּם שֵׁנָה יִהְיוּ
they-are sleep you-sweep-away-them (5) in-the-night or-watch he-went-by

בַּבֹּקֶר כֶּחָצִיר יַחֲלֹף׃ בַּבֹּקֶר יָצִיץ
he-springs-up in-the-morning (6) he-sprouts like-the-new-grass in-the-morning

וְחָלָף לָעֶרֶב יְמוֹלֵל וְיָבֵשׁ׃ כִּי־
indeed (7) and-he-is-dry he-is-withered by-the-evening and-he-sprouts

כָלִינוּ בְאַפֶּךָ וּבַחֲמָתְךָ נִבְהָלְנוּ׃
we-are-terrified and-by-indignation-of-you by-anger-of-you we-are-consumed

שַׁתָּ עֲוֺנֹתֵינוּ לְנֶגְדֶּךָ עֲלֻמֵנוּ לִמְאוֹר
in-light-of one-being-secret-of-us at-before-you iniquities-of-us you-set (8)

פָּנֶיךָ׃ כִּי כָל־יָמֵינוּ פָּנוּ בְעֶבְרָתֶךָ
under-wrath-of-you they-pass-away days-of-us all-of indeed (9) presences-of-you

כִּלִּינוּ שָׁנֵינוּ כְמוֹ־הֶגֶה׃ יְמֵי־שְׁנוֹתֵינוּ בָהֶם שִׁבְעִים
seventy of-them years-of-us days-of (10) moan with years-of-us we-finish

שָׁנָה וְאִם בִּגְבוּרֹת שְׁמוֹנִים שָׁנָה וְרָהְבָּם* עָמָל וָאָוֶן
and-sorrow trouble *yet-best-of-them year eighty in-strengths or-if year

כִּי־גָז חִישׁ וַנָּעֻפָה׃ מִי־יוֹדֵעַ עֹז
power-of one-knowing who? (11) and-we-fly-away quickly he-passes for

אַפֶּךָ וּכְיִרְאָתְךָ עֶבְרָתֶךָ׃ לִמְנוֹת יָמֵינוּ כֵּן
aright days-of-us to-number (12) wrath-of-you for-as-fear-of-you anger-of-you

הוֹדַע וְנָבִא לְבַב חָכְמָה׃ שׁוּבָה יְהוָה עַד־מָתָי
when? until Yahweh relent! (13) wisdom heart-of that-we-may-gain teach!

וְהִנָּחֵם עַל־עֲבָדֶיךָ׃ שַׂבְּעֵנוּ בַבֹּקֶר
in-the-morning satisfy-us! (14) servants-of-you on and-have-compassion!

חַסְדֶּךָ וּנְרַנְּנָה וְנִשְׂמְחָה בְּכָל־
for-all-of and-we-may-be-glad that-we-may-sing-for-joy unfailing-love-of-you

יָמֵינוּ׃ שַׂמְּחֵנוּ כִּימוֹת עִנִּיתָנוּ שְׁנוֹת רָאִינוּ
we-saw years-of you-afflicted-us as-days-of make-glad-us! (15) days-of-us

רָעָה׃ יֵרָאֶה אֶל־עֲבָדֶיךָ פָעֳלֶךָ וַהֲדָרְךָ
and-splendor-of-you deed-of-you servants-of-you to may-he-be-shown (16) trouble

עַל־בְּנֵיהֶם׃ וִיהִי נֹעַם אֲדֹנָי אֱלֹהֵינוּ עָלֵינוּ
upon-us God-of-us Lord favor-of and-may-he-rest (17) children-of-them to

born
or you brought forth the
earth and the world,
from everlasting to
everlasting you are God.
3 You turn men back to dust,
saying, "Return to dust, O
sons of men."
4 For a thousand years in your
sight
are like a day that has just
gone by,
or like a watch in the night.
5 You sweep men away in the
sleep of death;
they are like the new grass
of the morning—
6 though in the morning it
springs up new,
by evening it is dry and
withered.
7 We are consumed by your
anger
and terrified by your
indignation.
8 You have set our iniquities
before you,
our secret sins in the light
of your presence.
9 All our days pass away under
your wrath;
we finish our years with a
moan.
10 The length of our days is
seventy years—
or eighty, if we have the
strength;
yet their span[d] is but trouble
and sorrow,
for they quickly pass, and
we fly away.
11 Who knows the power of your
anger?
For your wrath is as great as
the fear that is due you.
12 Teach us to number our days
aright,
that we may gain a heart of
wisdom.
13 Relent, O LORD! How long will
it be?
Have compassion on your
servants.
14 Satisfy us in the morning with
your unfailing love,
that we may sing for joy
and be glad all our days.
15 Make us glad for as many days
as you have afflicted us,
for as many years as we
have seen trouble.
16 May your deeds be shown to
your servants,
your splendor to their
children.
17 May the favor[e] of the Lord our
God rest upon us;

[d]*10* *Or yet the best of them* [e]*17* Or *beauty*

*10 The NIV reads this word as וְרָחְבָּם, *yet-span-of-them.*

°8 ק שׁתה

| יָדֵינוּ | וּמַעֲשֵׂה | עָלֵינוּ | כּוֹנְנָה | יָדֵינוּ | וּמַעֲשֵׂה |
|---|---|---|---|---|---|
| hands-of-us | yes-work-of | for-us | establish! | hands-of-us | and-work-of |

| בְּצֵל | עֶלְיוֹן | בְּסֵתֶר | יֹשֵׁב | | כּוֹנְנֵהוּ׃ |
|---|---|---|---|---|---|
| in-shadow-of | Most-High | in-shelter-of | one-dwelling | (91:1) | establish-him! |

| וּמְצוּדָתִי | מַחְסִי | לַיהוָה | אֹמַר | | יִתְלוֹנָן׃ | שַׁדַּי |
|---|---|---|---|---|---|---|
| and-fortress-of-me | refuge-of-me | of-Yahweh | I-will-say | (2) | he-will-rest | Almighty |

| מִפַּח | יַצִּילְךָ | הוּא | כִּי | | בּוֹ׃ | אֶבְטַח־ | אֱלֹהַי |
|---|---|---|---|---|---|---|---|
| from-snare-of | he-will-save-you | he | surely | (3) | in-him | I-trust | God-of-me |

| יָסֶךְ | בְּאֶבְרָתוֹ ׀ | | הַוּוֹת׃ | מִדֶּבֶר | יָקוּשׁ |
|---|---|---|---|---|---|
| he-will-cover | with-feather-of-him | (4) | deadly-ones | from-pestilence-of | fowler |

| וְסֹחֵרָה | צִנָּה | תֶּחְסֶה | כְּנָפָיו | וְתַחַת־ | לָךְ |
|---|---|---|---|---|---|
| and-rampart | shield | you-will-find-refuge | wings-of-him | and-under | over-you |

| מֵחֵץ | לַיְלָה | מִפַּחַד | תִירָא | לֹא־ | | אֲמִתּוֹ׃ |
|---|---|---|---|---|---|---|
| of-arrow | night | of-terror-of | you-will-fear | not | (5) | faithfulness-of-him |

| מִקֶּטֶב | יַהֲלֹךְ | בָּאֹפֶל | מִדֶּבֶר | | יוֹמָם׃ | יָעוּף |
|---|---|---|---|---|---|---|
| of-plague | he-stalks | in-the-darkness | of-pestilence | (6) | by-day | he-flies |

| וּרְבָבָה | אֶלֶף | מִצִּדְּךָ ׀ | יִפֹּל | | צָהֳרָיִם׃ | יָשׁוּד |
|---|---|---|---|---|---|---|
| and-ten-thousand | thousand | at-side-of-you | he-may-fall | (7) | midday | he-destroys |

| בְּעֵינֶיךָ | רַק | | יִגָּשׁ׃ | לֹא | אֵלֶיךָ | מִימִינֶךָ |
|---|---|---|---|---|---|---|
| with-eyes-of-you | only | (8) | he-will-come-near | not | to-you | at-right-hand-of-you |

| כִּי־אַתָּה | | תִּרְאֶה׃ | רְשָׁעִים | וְשִׁלֻּמַת | תַבִּיט |
|---|---|---|---|---|---|
| you if | (9) | you-will-see | wicked-ones | and-punishment-of | you-will-observe |

| תְאֻנֶּה | לֹא־ | | מְעוֹנֶךָ׃ | שַׂמְתָּ | עֶלְיוֹן | מַחְסִי | יְהוָה |
|---|---|---|---|---|---|---|---|
| she-will-befall | not | (10) | dwelling-of-you | you-make | Most-High | refuge-of-me | Yahweh |

| כִּי | | בְּאָהֳלֶךָ׃ | יִקְרַב | לֹא־ | וְנֶגַע | רָעָה | אֵלֶיךָ |
|---|---|---|---|---|---|---|---|
| for | (11) | to-tent-of-you | he-will-come-near | not | and-disaster | harm | to-you |

| דְּרָכֶיךָ׃ | בְּכָל־ | לִשְׁמָרְךָ | לָּךְ | יְצַוֶּה־ | מַלְאָכָיו |
|---|---|---|---|---|---|
| ways-of-you | in-all-of | to-guard-you | concerning-you | he-will-command | angels-of-him |

| בָּאֶבֶן | תִּגֹּף | פֶּן־ | יִשָּׂאוּנְךָ | כַּפַּיִם | עַל־ | |
|---|---|---|---|---|---|---|
| against-the-stone | you-will-strike | so-not | they-will-lift-up-you | hands | in | (12) |

| תִּרְמֹס | תִּדְרֹךְ | וָפֶתֶן | שַׁחַל | עַל־ | | רַגְלֶךָ׃ |
|---|---|---|---|---|---|---|
| you-will-trample | you-will-tread | and-cobra | lion | upon | (13) | foot-of-you |

| וַאֲפַלְּטֵהוּ | חָשַׁק | בִי | כִּי | | וְתַנִּין׃ | כְּפִיר |
|---|---|---|---|---|---|---|
| then-I-will-rescue-him | he-loves | to-me | because | (14) | and-serpent | great-lion |

| יִקְרָאֵנִי ׀ | | שְׁמִי׃ | יָדַע | כִּי־ | אֲשַׂגְּבֵהוּ |
|---|---|---|---|---|---|
| he-will-call-upon-me | (15) | name-of-me | he-acknowledges | for | I-will-protect-him |

| אֲחַלְּצֵהוּ | בְצָרָה | אָנֹכִי | עִמּוֹ־ | וְאֶעֱנֵהוּ |
|---|---|---|---|---|
| I-will-deliver-him | in-trouble | I | with-him | and-I-will-answer-him |

establish the work of our hands for us—
yes, establish the work of our hands.

**Psalm 91**

1 He who dwells in the shelter of the Most High
will rest in the shadow of the Almighty.[f]
2 I will say of the LORD, "He is my refuge and my fortress,
my God, in whom I trust."
3 Surely he will save you from the fowler's snare
and from the deadly pestilence.
4 He will cover you with his feathers,
and under his wings you will find refuge;
his faithfulness will be your shield and rampart.
5 You will not fear the terror of night,
nor the arrow that flies by day,
6 nor the pestilence that stalks in the darkness,
nor the plague that destroys at midday.
7 A thousand may fall at your side,
ten thousand at your right hand,
but it will not come near you.
8 You will only observe with your eyes
and see the punishment of the wicked.

9 If you make the Most High your dwelling—
even the LORD, who is my refuge—
10 then no harm will befall you,
no disaster will come near your tent.
11 For he will command his angels concerning you
to guard you in all your ways;
12 they will lift you up in their hands,
so that you will not strike your foot against a stone.
13 You will tread upon the lion and the cobra;
you will trample the great lion and the serpent.

14 "Because he loves me," says the LORD, "I will rescue him;
I will protect him, for he acknowledges my name.
15 He will call upon me, and I will answer him;
I will be with him in trouble,

f1 Hebrew *Shaddai*

וַאֲכַבְּדֵהוּ׃ אֹרֶךְ יָמִים אַשְׂבִּיעֵהוּ וְאַרְאֵהוּ
and-I-will-show-him I-will-satisfy-him days length-of (16) and-I-will-honor-him

בִּישׁוּעָתִי׃ מִזְמוֹר שִׁיר לְיוֹם הַשַּׁבָּת׃ טוֹב
good (2) the-Sabbath for-day-of song psalm *(92:1) to-salvation-of-me

לְהֹדוֹת לַיהוָה וּלְזַמֵּר לְשִׁמְךָ עֶלְיוֹן׃ לְהַגִּיד
to-proclaim (3) Most-High to-name-of-you and-to-make-music to-Yahweh to-praise

בַּבֹּקֶר חַסְדֶּךָ וֶאֱמוּנָתְךָ בַּלֵּילוֹת׃ עֲלֵי־
to (4) at-the-nights and-faithfulness-of-you love-of-you in-the-morning

עָשׂוֹר וַעֲלֵי־נָבֶל עֲלֵי הִגָּיוֹן בְּכִנּוֹר׃ כִּי שִׂמַּחְתַּנִי יְהוָה
Yahweh you-make-glad-me for (5) of-harp melody to lyre and-to ten-stringed

בְּפָעֳלֶךָ בְּמַעֲשֵׂי יָדֶיךָ אֲרַנֵּן׃ מַה־ גָּדְלוּ
they-are-great how (6) I-sing-for-joy hands-of-you at-works-of by-deed-of-you

מַעֲשֶׂיךָ יְהוָה מְאֹד עָמְקוּ מַחְשְׁבֹתֶיךָ׃ אִישׁ־ בַּעַר
senseless man (7) thoughts-of-you they-are-profound very Yahweh works-of-you

לֹא יֵדָע וּכְסִיל לֹא־ יָבִין אֶת־ זֹאת׃ בִּפְרֹחַ
though-to-spring-up (8) this *** he-understands not and-fool he-knows not

רְשָׁעִים׀ כְּמוֹ עֵשֶׂב וַיָּצִיצוּ כָּל־ פֹּעֲלֵי אָוֶן
evil ones-doing-of all-of and-they-flourish grass like wicked-ones

לְהִשָּׁמְדָם עֲדֵי־ עַד׃ וְאַתָּה מָרוֹם לְעֹלָם יְהוָה׃
Yahweh to-forever exalted but-you (9) forever to to-be-destroyed-them

כִּי הִנֵּה אֹיְבֶיךָ׀ יְהוָה כִּי־ הִנֵּה
surely! for Yahweh ones-being-enemies-of-you surely! for (10)

אֹיְבֶיךָ יֹאבֵדוּ יִתְפָּרְדוּ כָּל־
all-of they-will-be-scattered they-will-perish ones-being-enemies-of-you

פֹּעֲלֵי אָוֶן׃ וַתָּרֶם כִּרְאֵים קַרְנִי בַּלֹּתִי
I-was-anointed horn-of-me like-wild-ox for-you-exalted (11) evil ones-doing-of

בְּשֶׁמֶן רַעֲנָן׃ וַתַּבֵּט עֵינִי בְּשׁוּרָי†
†to-walls-of-me eye-of-me and-she-saw (12) fineness with-oil-of

בַּקָּמִים עָלַי מְרֵעִים תִּשְׁמַעְנָה אָזְנָי׃
ears-of-me they-heard ones-being-wicked against-me on-the-ones-being-foes

צַדִּיק כַּתָּמָר יִפְרָח כְּאֶרֶז בַּלְּבָנוֹן
of-the-Lebanon like-cedar he-will-flourish like-the-palm-tree righteous (13)

יִשְׂגֶּה׃ שְׁתוּלִים בְּבֵית יְהוָה בְּחַצְרוֹת אֱלֹהֵינוּ
God-of-us in-courts-of Yahweh in-house-of ones-being-planted (14) he-will-grow

יַפְרִיחוּ׃ עוֹד יְנוּבוּן בְּשֵׂיבָה דְּשֵׁנִים
fresh-ones in-old-age they-will-bear-fruit still (15) they-will-flourish

וְרַעֲנַנִּים יִהְיוּ׃ לְהַגִּיד כִּי־ יָשָׁר יְהוָה צוּרִי
Rock-of-me Yahweh upright that to-proclaim (16) they-will-stay and-green-ones

I will deliver him and honor him.
[16]With long life will I satisfy him
and show him my salvation."

### Psalm 92

A psalm. A song. For the Sabbath day.

[1]It is good to praise the LORD
and make music to your name, O Most High,
[2]to proclaim your love in the morning
and your faithfulness at night,
[3]to the music of the ten-stringed lyre
and the melody of the harp.
[4]For you make me glad by your deeds, O LORD;
I sing for joy at the works of your hands.
[5]How great are your works, O LORD,
how profound your thoughts!
[6]The senseless man does not know,
fools do not understand,
[7]that though the wicked spring up like grass
and all evildoers flourish,
they will be forever destroyed.
[8]But you, O LORD, are exalted forever.
[9]For surely your enemies, O LORD,
surely your enemies will perish;
all evildoers will be scattered.
[10]You have exalted my horn[g]
like that of a wild ox;
fine oils have been poured upon me.
[11]My eyes have seen the defeat of my adversaries;
my ears have heard the rout of my wicked foes.
[12]The righteous will flourish like a palm tree,
they will grow like a cedar of Lebanon;
[13]planted in the house of the LORD,
they will flourish in the courts of our God.
[14]They will still bear fruit in old age,
they will stay fresh and green,
[15]proclaiming, "The LORD is upright;
he is my Rock, and there is

g10 *Horn* here symbolizes strength.

*Heading, *1* See the note on page 349.
†*12* The NIV reads this word as בְּשׁוֹרְרַי, *on-adversaries-of-me.*

וְלֹא־ עַלְתָה בּוֹ׃ יְהוָה מָלָךְ גֵּאוּת לָבֵשׁ לָבֵשׁ
he-is-robed he-is-robed majesty he-reigns Yahweh (93:1) in-him wickedness and-no

יְהוָה עֹז הִתְאַזָּר אַף־ תִּכּוֹן תֵּבֵל בַּל־ תִּמּוֹט׃
she-can-be-moved not world she-is-established firmly he-is-armed strength Yahweh

נָכוֹן כִּסְאֲךָ מֵאָז מֵעוֹלָם אָתָּה׃
you from-eternity from-long-ago throne-of-you he-was-established (2)

נָשְׂאוּ נְהָרוֹת ׀ יְהוָה נָשְׂאוּ נְהָרוֹת קוֹלָם יִשְׂאוּ
they-lifted-up voice-of-them seas they-lifted-up Yahweh seas they-lifted-up (3)

נְהָרוֹת דָּכְיָם׃ מִקֹּלוֹת ׀ מַיִם רַבִּים אַדִּירִים
mighty-ones great-ones waters more-than-thunders-of (4) pounding-of-them seas

מִשְׁבְּרֵי־ יָם אַדִּיר בַּמָּרוֹם יְהוָה׃ עֵדֹתֶיךָ ׀ נֶאֶמְנוּ
they-stand-firm statutes-of-you (5) Yahweh in-the-height mighty sea breakers-of

מְאֹד לְבֵיתְךָ נַאֲוָה־ קֹדֶשׁ יְהוָה לְאֹרֶךְ יָמִים׃
days for-length-of Yahweh holiness adornment to-house-of-you very

אֵל־ נְקָמוֹת יְהוָה אֵל נְקָמוֹת הוֹפִיעַ׃ הִנָּשֵׂא
rise-up! (2) shine-forth! vengeances God-of Yahweh vengeances God-of (94:1)

שֹׁפֵט הָאָרֶץ הָשֵׁב גְּמוּל עַל־ גֵּאִים׃ עַד־ מָתַי
when? until (3) proud-ones to desert pay-back! the-earth One-Judging

רְשָׁעִים ׀ יְהוָה עַד־ מָתַי רְשָׁעִים יַעֲלֹזוּ׃
will-they-be-jubilant wicked-ones when? until Yahweh wicked-ones

יַבִּיעוּ יְדַבְּרוּ עָתָק יִתְאַמְּרוּ כָּל־ פֹּעֲלֵי אָוֶן׃
evil ones-doing-of all-of they-boast arrogance they-speak they-pour-out (4)

עַמְּךָ יְהוָה יְדַכְּאוּ וְנַחֲלָתְךָ יְעַנּוּ׃
they-oppress and-inheritance-of-you they-crush Yahweh people-of-you (5)

אַלְמָנָה וְגֵר יַהֲרֹגוּ וִיתוֹמִים יְרַצֵּחוּ׃ וַיֹּאמְרוּ
and-they-say (7) they-murder and-fatherless-ones they-slay and-alien widow (6)

לֹא יִרְאֶה־ יָּהּ וְלֹא־ יָבִין אֱלֹהֵי יַעֲקֹב׃ בִּינוּ
take-heed! (8) Jacob God-of he-heeds and-not Yahweh he-sees not

בֹּעֲרִים בָּעָם וּכְסִילִים מָתַי תַּשְׂכִּילוּ׃
will-you-become-wise when? and-fools among-the-people ones-being-senseless

הֲנֹטַע אֹזֶן הֲלֹא יִשְׁמָע אִם־ יֹצֵר עַיִן הֲלֹא יַבִּיט׃
he-sees not? eye one-forming or he-hears not? ear one-implanting? (9)

הֲיֹסֵר גּוֹיִם הֲלֹא יוֹכִיחַ הַמְלַמֵּד אָדָם דָּעַת׃
knowledge man one-teaching? will-he-punish not? nations one-disciplining (10)

יְהוָה יֹדֵעַ מַחְשְׁבוֹת אָדָם כִּי־ הֵמָּה הָבֶל׃ אַשְׁרֵי ׀
blessednesses-of (12) futile they that man thoughts-of knowing Yahweh (11)

הַגֶּבֶר אֲשֶׁר־ תְּיַסְּרֶנּוּ יָּהּ וּמִתּוֹרָתְךָ תְלַמְּדֶנּוּ׃
you-teach-him and-from-law-of-you Yahweh you-discipline-him whom the-man

no wickedness in him."

**Psalm 93**

1The LORD reigns, he is robed
in majesty;
the LORD is robed in majesty
and is armed with strength.
The world is firmly
established;
it cannot be moved.
2Your throne was established
long ago;
you are from all eternity.
3The seas have lifted up, O
LORD,
the seas have lifted up their
voice;
the seas have lifted up their
pounding waves.
4Mightier than the thunder of
the great waters,
mightier than the breakers
of the sea—
the LORD on high is mighty.
5Your statutes stand firm;
holiness adorns your house
for endless days, O LORD.

**Psalm 94**

1O LORD, the God who avenges,
O God who avenges, shine
forth.
2Rise up, O Judge of the earth;
pay back to the proud what
they deserve.
3How long will the wicked, O
LORD,
how long will the wicked be
jubilant?
4They pour out arrogant words;
all the evildoers are full of
boasting.
5They crush your people, O
LORD;
they oppress your
inheritance.
6They slay the widow and the
alien;
they murder the fatherless.
7They say, "The LORD does not
see;
the God of Jacob pays no
heed."
8Take heed, you senseless ones
among the people;
you fools, when will you
become wise?
9Does he who implanted the
ear not hear?
Does he who formed the eye
not see?
10Does he who disciplines
nations not punish?
Does he who teaches man
lack knowledge?
11The LORD knows the thoughts
of man;
he knows that they are
futile.
12Blessed is the man you
discipline, O LORD,
the man you teach from
your law;

*See the note on page 349.

°16 ק עולתה

לְהַשְׁקִיט לוֹ מִימֵי רָע עַד יִכָּרֶה
he-is-dug till trouble from-days-of to-him to-grant-relief (13)

לָרָשָׁע שָׁחַת׃ כִּי ׀ לֹא־ יִטֹּשׁ יְהוָה עַמּוֹ
people-of-him Yahweh he-will-reject not for (14) pit for-the-wicked

וְנַחֲלָתוֹ לֹא יַעֲזֹב׃ כִּי־ עַד־ צֶדֶק
righteousness on for (15) he-will-forsake never and-inheritance-of-him

יָשׁוּב מִשְׁפָּט וְאַחֲרָיו כָּל־ יִשְׁרֵי־ לֵב׃ מִי־
who? (16) heart ones-upright-of all-of and-after-him judgment he-will-be-again

יָקוּם לִי עִם־ מְרֵעִים מִי־ יִתְיַצֵּב
he-will-take-stand who? ones-being-wicked against for-me he-will-rise-up

לִי עִם־ פֹּעֲלֵי אָוֶן׃ לוּלֵי יְהוָה עֶזְרָתָה לִּי כִּמְעַט ׀
as-soon to-me help Yahweh unless (17) evil ones-doing-of against for-me

שָׁכְנָה דוּמָה נַפְשִׁי׃ אִם־ אָמַרְתִּי מָטָה רַגְלִי
foot-of-me she-slips I-said when (18) self-of-me silence she-would-have-dwelt

חַסְדְּךָ יְהוָה יִסְעָדֵנִי׃ בְּרֹב שַׂרְעַפַּי
anxieties-of-me when-to-be-great (19) he-supported-me Yahweh love-of-you

בְּקִרְבִּי תַּנְחוּמֶיךָ יְשַׁעַשְׁעוּ נַפְשִׁי׃
soul-of-me they-brought-joy consolations-of-you at-inside-of-me

הַיְחָבְרְךָ כִּסֵּא הַוּוֹת יֹצֵר עָמָל
misery one-bringing-on corruptions throne-of can-he-be-allied-with-you? (20)

עֲלֵי־ חֹק׃ יָגוֹדּוּ עַל־ נֶפֶשׁ צַדִּיק וְדָם
and-blood righteous life-of against they-band-together (21) decree by

נָקִי יַרְשִׁיעוּ׃ וַיְהִי יְהוָה לִי לְמִשְׂגָּב וֵאלֹהַי
and-God-of-me as-fortress to-me Yahweh but-he-became (22) they-condemn innocent

לְצוּר מַחְסִי׃ וַיָּשֶׁב עֲלֵיהֶם ׀ אֶת־ אוֹנָם
sin-of-them *** to-them and-he-will-repay (23) refuge-of-me as-rock-of

וּבְרָעָתָם יַצְמִיתֵם יַצְמִיתֵם יְהוָה
Yahweh he-will-destroy-them he-will-destroy-them and-for-wickedness-of-them

אֱלֹהֵינוּ׃ לְכוּ נְרַנְּנָה לַיהוָה נָרִיעָה לְצוּר
to-Rock-of let-us-shout to-Yahweh let-us-sing come! (95:1) God-of-us

יִשְׁעֵנוּ׃ נְקַדְּמָה פָנָיו בְּתוֹדָה
with-thanksgiving faces-of-him let-us-come-before (2) salvation-of-us

בִּזְמִרוֹת נָרִיעַ לוֹ׃ כִּי אֵל גָּדוֹל יְהוָה וּמֶלֶךְ גָּדוֹל
great and-King Yahweh great God for (3) to-him let-us-extol with-songs

עַל־ כָּל־ אֱלֹהִים׃ אֲשֶׁר בְּיָדוֹ מֶחְקְרֵי־ אָרֶץ וְתוֹעֲפוֹת
and-peaks-of earth depths-of in-hand-of-him who (4) gods all-of above

הָרִים לוֹ׃ אֲשֶׁר־ לוֹ הַיָּם וְהוּא עָשָׂהוּ וְיַבֶּשֶׁת
and-dry-land he-made-him for-he the-sea to-him who (5) to-him mountains

[13]you grant him relief from days of trouble,
till a pit is dug for the wicked.
[14]For the LORD will not reject his people;
he will never forsake his inheritance.
[15]Judgment will again be founded on righteousness,
and all the upright in heart will follow it.

[16]Who will rise up for me against the wicked?
Who will take a stand for me against evildoers?
[17]Unless the LORD had given me help,
I would soon have dwelt in the silence of death.
[18]When I said, "My foot is slipping,"
your love, O LORD, supported me.
[19]When anxiety was great within me,
your consolation brought joy to my soul.

[20]Can a corrupt throne be allied with you—
one that brings on misery by its decrees?
[21]They band together against the righteous
and condemn the innocent to death.
[22]But the LORD has become my fortress,
and my God the rock in whom I take refuge.
[23]He will repay them for their sins
and destroy them for their wickedness;
the LORD our God will destroy them.

## Psalm 95

[1]Come, let us sing for joy to the LORD;
let us shout aloud to the Rock of our salvation.
[2]Let us come before him with thanksgiving
and extol him with music and song.

[3]For the LORD is the great God,
the great King above all gods.
[4]In his hand are the depths of the earth,
and the mountain peaks belong to him.
[5]The sea is his, for he made it,

יָדָ֥יו יָצָֽרוּ׃ בֹּ֭אוּ נִשְׁתַּחֲוֶ֣ה וְנִכְרָ֑עָה נִ֝בְרְכָ֗ה
let-us-kneel and-let-us-bow let-us-worship come! (6) they-formed hands-of-him

לִֽפְנֵי־ יְהוָ֥ה עֹשֵֽׂנוּ׃ כִּ֤י ה֬וּא אֱלֹהֵ֗ינוּ וַאֲנַ֤חְנוּ עַ֣ם
people-of and-we God-of-us he for (7) One-Making-us Yahweh before

מַ֭רְעִיתוֹ וְצֹ֣אן יָד֑וֹ הַ֝יּ֗וֹם אִֽם־ בְּקֹל֥וֹ תִשְׁמָֽעוּ׃
you-hear to-voice-of-him if the-day care-of-him and-flock-of pasture-of-him

אַל־ תַּקְשׁ֣וּ לְ֭בַבְכֶם כִּמְרִיבָ֑ה כְּי֥וֹם מַ֝סָּ֗ה בַּמִּדְבָּֽר׃
in-the-desert Massah as-day-of as-Meribah heart-of-you you-harden not (8)

אֲשֶׁ֣ר נִ֭סּוּנִי אֲבוֹתֵיכֶ֑ם בְּ֝חָנ֗וּנִי גַּם־ רָא֥וּ
they-saw though they-tried-me fathers-of-you they-tested-me where (9)

פָעֳלִֽי׃ אַרְבָּ֘עִ֤ים שָׁנָ֨ה ׀ אָ֘ק֤וּט בְּד֗וֹר וָאֹמַ֗ר עַ֤ם
people and-I-said with-generation I-was-angry year forty (10) deed-of-me

תֹּעֵ֣י לֵבָ֣ב הֵ֑ם וְ֝הֵ֗ם לֹא־ יָדְע֥וּ דְרָכָֽי׃ אֲשֶׁר־
so (11) ways-of-me they-knew not and-they they heart ones-straying-of

נִשְׁבַּ֥עְתִּי בְאַפִּ֑י אִם־ יְ֝בֹא֗וּן אֶל־ מְנוּחָתִֽי׃
rest-of-me into they-shall-enter never in-anger-of-me I-declared-on-oath

שִׁ֣ירוּ לַ֭יהוָה שִׁ֣יר חָדָ֑שׁ שִׁ֥ירוּ לַ֝יהוָ֗ה כָּל־ הָאָֽרֶץ׃ שִׁ֣ירוּ
sing! (2) the-earth all-of to-Yahweh sing! new song to-Yahweh sing! (96:1)

לַ֭יהוָה בָּרְכ֣וּ שְׁמ֑וֹ בַּשְּׂר֥וּ מִיּֽוֹם־ לְ֝י֗וֹם יְשׁוּעָתֽוֹ׃
salvation-of-him to-day from-day proclaim! name-of-him praise! to-Yahweh

סַפְּר֣וּ בַגּוֹיִ֣ם כְּבוֹד֑וֹ בְּכָל־ הָ֝עַמִּ֗ים
the-peoples among-all-of glory-of-him among-the-nations declare! (3)

נִפְלְאוֹתָֽיו׃ כִּ֥י גָ֘ד֤וֹל יְהוָ֣ה וּמְהֻלָּ֣ל מְאֹ֑ד
greatly and-one-being-praised Yahweh great for (4) deeds-being-marvelous-of-him

נ֥וֹרָא ה֝֗וּא עַל־ כָּל־ אֱלֹהִֽים׃ כִּ֤י ׀ כָּל־ אֱלֹהֵ֣י הָעַמִּ֣ים
the-nations gods-of all-of for (5) gods all-of above he one-being-feared

אֱלִילִ֑ים וַ֝יהוָ֗ה שָׁמַ֥יִם עָשָֽׂה׃ הוֹד־ וְהָדָ֥ר לְפָנָ֑יו עֹ֥ז
strength before-him and-majesty splendor (6) he-made heavens but-Yahweh idols

וְ֝תִפְאֶ֗רֶת בְּמִקְדָּשֽׁוֹ׃ הָב֣וּ לַ֭יהוָה מִשְׁפְּח֣וֹת עַמִּ֑ים
nations families-of to-Yahweh ascribe! (7) in-sanctuary-of-him and-glory

הָב֥וּ לַ֝יהוָ֗ה כָּב֥וֹד וָעֹֽז׃ הָב֣וּ לַ֭יהוָה כְּב֣וֹד
glory-of to-Yahweh ascribe! (8) and-strength glory to-Yahweh ascribe!

שְׁמ֑וֹ שְׂאֽוּ־ מִ֝נְחָ֗ה וּבֹ֥אוּ לְחַצְרוֹתָֽיו׃ הִשְׁתַּחֲו֣וּ
worship! (9) into-courts-of-him and-come! offering bring! name-of-him

לַ֭יהוָה בְּהַדְרַת־ קֹ֑דֶשׁ חִ֥ילוּ מִ֝פָּנָ֗יו כָּל־ הָאָֽרֶץ׃
the-earth all-of at-before-him tremble! holiness in-splendor-of to-Yahweh

אִמְר֤וּ בַגּוֹיִ֨ם ׀ יְה֘וָ֤ה מָלָ֗ךְ אַף־ תִּכּ֣וֹן תֵּ֭בֵל
world she-is-established firmly he-reigns Yahweh among-the-nations say! (10)

and his hands formed the
dry land.

6Come, let us bow down in
worship,
let us kneel before the LORD
our Maker;
7for he is our God
and we are the people of his
pasture,
the flock under his care.

Today, if you hear his voice,
8 do not harden your hearts as
you did at Meribah,[h]
as you did that day at
Massah[i] in the desert,
9where your fathers tested and
tried me,
though they had seen what
I did.
10For forty years I was angry
with that generation;
I said, "They are a people
whose hearts go astray,
and they have not known
my ways."
11So I declared on oath in my
anger,
"They shall never enter my
rest."

**Psalm 96**

1Sing to the LORD a new song;
sing to the LORD, all the
earth.
2Sing to the LORD, praise his
name;
proclaim his salvation day
after day.
3Declare his glory among the
nations,
his marvelous deeds among
all peoples.

4For great is the LORD and most
worthy of praise;
he is to be feared above all
gods.
5For all the gods of the nations
are idols,
but the LORD made the
heavens.
6Splendor and majesty are
before him;
strength and glory are in his
sanctuary.

7Ascribe to the LORD, O families
of nations,
ascribe to the LORD glory
and strength.
8Ascribe to the LORD the glory
due his name;
bring an offering and come
into his courts.
9Worship the LORD in the
splendor of his[j] holiness;
tremble before him, all the
earth.

10Say among the nations, "The
LORD reigns."
The world is firmly

h8 *Meribah* means *quarreling*.
i8 *Massah* means *testing*.
j9 Or *LORD with the splendor of*

בַּל־ תִּמּוֹט יָדִין עַמִּים בְּמֵישָׁרִים׃ יִשְׂמְחוּ
let-them-rejoice (11) with-equities peoples he-will-judge she-can-be-moved not

הַשָּׁמַיִם וְתָגֵל הָאָרֶץ יִרְעַם הַיָּם
the-sea let-him-resound the-earth and-let-her-be-glad the-heavens

וּמְלֹאוֹ׃ יַעֲלֹז שָׂדַי וְכָל־ אֲשֶׁר־ בּוֹ
in-him that and-all field let-him-be-jubilant (12) and-fullness-of-him

אָז יְרַנְּנוּ כָּל־ עֲצֵי־ יָעַר׃ לִפְנֵי יְהוָה כִּי
for Yahweh before (13) forest trees-of all-of they-will-sing-for-joy then

בָא כִּי בָא לִשְׁפֹּט הָאָרֶץ יִשְׁפֹּט־ תֵּבֵל בְּצֶדֶק
in-righteousness world he-will-judge the-earth to-judge he-comes for he-comes

וְעַמִּים בֶּאֱמוּנָתוֹ׃ יְהוָה מָלָךְ תָּגֵל הָאָרֶץ
the-earth let-her-be-glad he-reigns Yahweh (97:1) in-truth-of-him and-peoples

יִשְׂמְחוּ אִיִּים רַבִּים׃ עָנָן וַעֲרָפֶל
and-thick-darkness cloud (2) distant-ones shores let-them-rejoice

סְבִיבָיו צֶדֶק וּמִשְׁפָּט מְכוֹן כִּסְאוֹ׃
throne-of-him foundation-of and-justice righteousness ones-around-him

אֵשׁ לְפָנָיו תֵּלֵךְ וּתְלַהֵט סָבִיב צָרָיו׃
foes-of-him on-every-side and-she-consumes she-goes before-him fire (3)

הֵאִירוּ בְרָקָיו תֵּבֵל רָאֲתָה וַתָּחֵל הָאָרֶץ׃
the-earth and-she-trembles she-sees world lightnings-of-him they-light-up (4)

הָרִים כַּדּוֹנַג נָמַסּוּ מִלִּפְנֵי יְהוָה מִלִּפְנֵי אֲדוֹן
Lord-of at-before Yahweh at-before they-melt like-the-wax mountains (5)

כָּל־ הָאָרֶץ׃ הִגִּידוּ הַשָּׁמַיִם צִדְקוֹ וְרָאוּ
and-they-see righteousness-of-him the-heavens they-proclaim (6) the-earth all-of

כָל־ הָעַמִּים כְּבוֹדוֹ׃ יֵבֹשׁוּ כָּל־ עֹבְדֵי
ones-worshiping-of all-of let-them-be-shamed (7) glory-of-him the-peoples all-of

פֶסֶל הַמִּתְהַלְלִים בָּאֱלִילִים הִשְׁתַּחֲווּ־ לוֹ כָּל־ אֱלֹהִים׃ שָׁמְעָה
she-hears (8) gods all-of to-him worship! in-the-idols the-ones-boasting image

וַתִּשְׂמַח צִיּוֹן וַתָּגֵלְנָה בְּנוֹת יְהוּדָה לְמַעַן
because-of Judah villages-of and-they-are-glad Zion and-she-rejoices

מִשְׁפָּטֶיךָ יְהוָה׃ כִּי־אַתָּה יְהוָה עֶלְיוֹן עַל־ כָּל־ הָאָרֶץ
the-earth all-of over Most-High Yahweh you for (9) Yahweh judgments-of-you

מְאֹד נַעֲלֵיתָ עַל־ כָּל־ אֱלֹהִים׃ אֹהֲבֵי יְהוָה שִׂנְאוּ
hate! Yahweh ones-loving-of (10) gods all-of above you-are-exalted far

רָע שֹׁמֵר נַפְשׁוֹת חֲסִידָיו מִיַּד רְשָׁעִים
wicked-ones from-hand-of faithful-ones-of-him lives-of one-guarding evil

יַצִּילֵם׃ אוֹר זָרֻעַ לַצַּדִּיק וּלְיִשְׁרֵי־
and-on-ones-upright-of upon-the-righteous being-shed light (11) he-delivers-them

established, it cannot be moved;
he will judge the peoples with equity.
11 Let the heavens rejoice, let the earth be glad;
let the sea resound, and all that is in it;
12 let the fields be jubilant, and everything in them.
Then all the trees of the forest will sing for joy;
13 they will sing before the LORD, for he comes,
he comes to judge the earth.
He will judge the world in righteousness
and the peoples in his truth.

## Psalm 97

1 The LORD reigns, let the earth be glad;
let the distant shores rejoice.
2 Clouds and thick darkness surround him;
righteousness and justice are the foundation of his throne.
3 Fire goes before him
and consumes his foes on every side.
4 His lightning lights up the world;
the earth sees and trembles.
5 The mountains melt like wax before the LORD,
before the Lord of all the earth.
6 The heavens proclaim his righteousness,
and all the peoples see his glory.
7 All who worship images are put to shame,
those who boast in idols—
worship him, all you gods!
8 Zion hears and rejoices
and the villages of Judah are glad
because of your judgments, O LORD.
9 For you, O LORD, are the Most High over all the earth;
you are exalted far above all gods.
10 Let those who love the LORD hate evil,
for he guards the lives of his faithful ones
and delivers them from the hand of the wicked.
11 Light is shed upon the righteous
and joy on the upright in

לֵב שִׂמְחָה׃ שִׂמְחוּ צַדִּיקִים בַּיהוָה וְהוֹדוּ לְזֵכֶר
to-name-of and-praise! in-Yahweh righteous-ones rejoice! (12) joy heart

קָדְשׁוֹ׃ מִזְמוֹר שִׁירוּ לַיהוָה׀ שִׁיר חָדָשׁ כִּי־ נִפְלָאוֹת
things-being-marvelous for new song to-Yahweh sing! psalm (98:1) holiness-of-him

עָשָׂה הוֹשִׁיעָה־ לּוֹ יְמִינוֹ וּזְרוֹעַ
and-arm-of right-hand-of-him for-him she-worked-salvation he-did

קָדְשׁוֹ׃ הוֹדִיעַ יְהוָה יְשׁוּעָתוֹ לְעֵינֵי
before-eyes-of salvation-of-him Yahweh he-made-known (2) holiness-of-him

הַגּוֹיִם גִּלָּה צִדְקָתוֹ׃ זָכַר חַסְדּוֹ׀
love-of-him he-remembered (3) righteousness-of-him he-revealed the-nations

וֶאֱמוּנָתוֹ לְבֵית יִשְׂרָאֵל רָאוּ כָל־ אַפְסֵי־ אָרֶץ
earth ends-of all-of they-saw Israel to-house-of and-faithfulness-of-him

אֵת יְשׁוּעַת אֱלֹהֵינוּ׃ הָרִיעוּ לַיהוָה כָּל־ הָאָרֶץ
the-earth all-of to-Yahweh shout-for-joy! (4) God-of-us salvation-of ***

פִּצְחוּ וְרַנְּנוּ וְזַמֵּרוּ׃ זַמְּרוּ לַיהוָה בְּכִנּוֹר
with-harp to-Yahweh make-music! (5) and-make-music! and-sing! burst-forth!

בְּכִנּוֹר וְקוֹל זִמְרָה׃ בַּחֲצֹצְרוֹת וְקוֹל שׁוֹפָר
horn-of-ram and-blast-of with-trumpets (6) singing and-sound-of with-harp

הָרִיעוּ לִפְנֵי׀ הַמֶּלֶךְ יְהוָה׃ יִרְעַם הַיָּם
the-sea let-him-resound (7) Yahweh the-King before shout-for-joy!

וּמְלֹאוֹ תֵּבֵל וְיֹשְׁבֵי בָהּ׃ נְהָרוֹת יִמְחֲאוּ־
let-them-clap rivers (8) in-her and-ones-living-of world and-fullness-of-him

כָף יַחַד הָרִים יְרַנֵּנוּ׃ לִפְנֵי־ יְהוָה כִּי בָא
he-comes for Yahweh before (9) let-them-sing-for-joy mountains together hand

לִשְׁפֹּט הָאָרֶץ יִשְׁפֹּט־ תֵּבֵל בְּצֶדֶק וְעַמִּים
and-peoples in-righteousness world he-will-judge the-earth to-judge

בְּמֵישָׁרִים׃ יְהוָה מָלָךְ יִרְגְּזוּ עַמִּים
nations let-them-tremble he-reigns Yahweh (99:1) with-equities

יֹשֵׁב כְּרוּבִים תָּנוּט הָאָרֶץ׃ יְהוָה בְּצִיּוֹן
in-Zion Yahweh (2) the-earth let-her-shake cherubim one-sitting-enthroned-of

גָּדוֹל וְרָם הוּא עַל־ כָּל־ הָעַמִּים׃ יוֹדוּ
let-them-praise (3) the-nations all-of over he and-one-being-exalted great

שִׁמְךָ גָּדוֹל וְנוֹרָא קָדוֹשׁ הוּא׃ וְעֹז מֶלֶךְ מִשְׁפָּט
justice King and-mighty (4) he holy and-one-being-awesome great name-of-you

אָהֵב אַתָּה כּוֹנַנְתָּ מֵישָׁרִים מִשְׁפָּט וּצְדָקָה בְּיַעֲקֹב׀ אַתָּה עָשִׂיתָ׃
you-did you in-Jacob and-right just equities you-established you he-loves

רוֹמְמוּ יְהוָה אֱלֹהֵינוּ וְהִשְׁתַּחֲווּ לַהֲדֹם רַגְלָיו קָדוֹשׁ הוּא׃
he holy feet-of-him at-footstool-of and-worship! God-of-us Yahweh exalt! (5)

heart.
12 Rejoice in the LORD, you who
are righteous,
and praise his holy name.

### Psalm 98

A psalm.

1 Sing to the LORD a new song,
for he has done marvelous
things;
his right hand and his holy
arm
have worked salvation for
him.
2 The LORD has made his
salvation known
and revealed his
righteousness to the
nations.
3 He has remembered his love
and his faithfulness to the
house of Israel;
all the ends of the earth have
seen
the salvation of our God.

4 Shout for joy to the LORD, all
the earth,
burst into jubilant song with
music;
5 make music to the LORD with
the harp,
with the harp and the sound
of singing,
6 with trumpets and the blast of
the ram's horn—
shout for joy before the
LORD, the King.

7 Let the sea resound, and
everything in it,
the world, and all who live
in it.
8 Let the rivers clap their hands,
let the mountains sing
together for joy;
9 let them sing before the LORD,
for he comes to judge the
earth.
He will judge the world in
righteousness
and the peoples with equity.

### Psalm 99

1 The LORD reigns,
let the nations tremble;
he sits enthroned between the
cherubim,
let the earth shake.
2 Great is the LORD in Zion;
he is exalted over all the
nations.
3 Let them praise your great and
awesome name—
he is holy.

4 The King is mighty, he loves
justice—
you have established equity;
in Jacob you have done
what is just and right.
5 Exalt the LORD our God
and worship at his footstool;
he is holy.

מֹשֶׁה וְאַהֲרֹן בְּכֹהֲנָיו וּשְׁמוּאֵל בְּקֹרְאֵי
among-ones-calling-of and-Samuel among-priests-of-him and-Aaron Moses (6)

שְׁמוֹ קֹרִאים אֶל־ יְהוָה וְהוּא יַעֲנֵם׃ בְּעַמּוּד
from-pillar-of (7) he-answered-them and-he Yahweh on ones-calling name-of-him

עָנָן יְדַבֵּר אֲלֵיהֶם שָׁמְרוּ עֵדֹתָיו וְחֹק נָתַן־
he-gave and-decree statutes-of-him they-kept to-them he-spoke cloud

לָמוֹ׃ יְהוָה אֱלֹהֵינוּ אַתָּה עֲנִיתָם אֵל נֹשֵׂא הָיִיתָ
you-were one-forgiving God you-answered-them you God-of-us Yahweh (8) to-them

לָהֶם וְנֹקֵם עַל־ עֲלִילוֹתָם׃ רוֹמְמוּ יְהוָה אֱלֹהֵינוּ
God-of-us Yahweh exalt! (9) misdeeds-of-them to though-one-punishing to-them

וְהִשְׁתַּחֲווּ לְהַר קָדְשׁוֹ כִּי־ קָדוֹשׁ יְהוָה אֱלֹהֵינוּ׃
God-of-us Yahweh holy for holiness-of-him at-mountain-of and-worship!

מִזְמוֹר לְתוֹדָה הָרִיעוּ לַיהוָה כָּל־ הָאָרֶץ׃
the-earth all-of to-Yahweh shout-for-joy! for-thanksgiving psalm (100:1)

עִבְדוּ אֶת־ יְהוָה בְּשִׂמְחָה בֹּאוּ לְפָנָיו בִּרְנָנָה׃
with-joyful-song before-him come! with-gladness Yahweh *** serve! (2)

דְּעוּ כִּי־ יְהוָה הוּא אֱלֹהִים הוּא־ עָשָׂנוּ °וְלֹא אֲנַחְנוּ עַמּוֹ
people-of-him we and-to-him he-made-us he God he Yahweh that know! (3)

וְצֹאן מַרְעִיתוֹ׃ בֹּאוּ שְׁעָרָיו בְּתוֹדָה
with-thanksgiving gates-of-him enter! (4) pasture-of-him and-sheep-of

חֲצֵרֹתָיו בִּתְהִלָּה הוֹדוּ־ לוֹ בָּרְכוּ שְׁמוֹ׃ כִּי־
for (5) name-of-him praise! to-him give-thanks! with-praise courts-of-him

טוֹב יְהוָה לְעוֹלָם חַסְדּוֹ וְעַד־ דֹּר וָדֹר
and-generation generation and-through love-of-him to-forever Yahweh good

אֱמוּנָתוֹ׃ לְדָוִד מִזְמוֹר חֶסֶד־ וּמִשְׁפָּט אָשִׁירָה
I-will-sing and-justice love psalm of-David (101:1) faithfulness-of-him

לְךָ יְהוָה אֲזַמֵּרָה׃ אַשְׂכִּילָה בְּדֶרֶךְ תָּמִים מָתַי
when? blameless in-life I-will-be-careful (2) I-will-sing-praise Yahweh to-you

תָּבוֹא אֵלָי אֶתְהַלֵּךְ בְּתָם־ לְבָבִי בְּקֶרֶב
in-midst-of heart-of-me with-blamelessness-of I-will-walk to-me will-you-come

בֵּיתִי׃ לֹא־ אָשִׁית לְנֶגֶד עֵינַי דְּבַר־ בְּלִיָּעַל עֲשֹׂה־
to-do vileness thing-of eyes-of-me at-before I-will-set not (3) house-of-me

סֵטִים שָׂנֵאתִי לֹא יִדְבַּק בִּי׃ לֵבָב עִקֵּשׁ
perverse heart (4) to-me he-will-cling not I-hate faithless-men

יָסוּר מִמֶּנִּי רָע לֹא אֵדָע׃ °מְלוֹשְׁנִי בַסֵּתֶר
in-the-secret one-slandering (5) I-know not evil from-me he-shall-be-far

רֵעֵהוּ אוֹתוֹ אַצְמִית גְּבַהּ־ עֵינַיִם וּרְחַב לֵבָב אֹתוֹ
him heart and-proud-of eyes haughty-of I-will-silence him neighbor-of-him

6Moses and Aaron were among
his priests,
Samuel was among those
who called on his name;
they called on the LORD
and he answered them.
7He spoke to them from the
pillar of cloud;
they kept his statutes and
the decrees he gave them.

8O LORD our God,
you answered them;
you were to Israel[k] a forgiving
God,
though you punished their
misdeeds.[l]

9Exalt the LORD our God
and worship at his holy
mountain,
for the LORD our God is
holy.

### Psalm 100

A psalm. For giving thanks.

1Shout for joy to the LORD, all
the earth.
2 Serve the LORD with
gladness;
come before him with joyful
songs.
3Know that the LORD is God.
It is he who made us, and
we are his[m];
we are his people, the sheep
of his pasture.

4Enter his gates with
thanksgiving
and his courts with praise;
give thanks to him and
praise his name.
5For the LORD is good and his
love endures forever;
his faithfulness continues
through all generations.

### Psalm 101

Of David. A psalm.

1I will sing of your love and
justice;
to you, O LORD, I will sing
praise.
2I will be careful to lead a
blameless life—
when will you come to me?

I will walk in my house
with blameless heart.
3I will set before my eyes
no vile thing.

The deeds of faithless men I
hate;
they will not cling to me.
4Men of perverse heart shall be
far from me;
I will have nothing to do
with evil.
5Whoever slanders his neighbor
in secret,
him will I put to silence;
whoever has haughty eyes and
a proud heart,

k8 Hebrew *them*
l8 Or / *an avenger of the wrongs done to them*
m3 Or *and not we ourselves*

°3 ק ולו
°5 ק מלשני

לֹא אוּכָל: (6) עֵינַי | בְּנֶאֶמְנֵי־ אֶרֶץ לָשֶׁבֶת
to-dwell land on-ones-being-faithful-of eyes-of-me (6) I-will-endure not

עִמָּדִי הֹלֵךְ בְּדֶרֶךְ תָּמִים הוּא יְשָׁרְתֵנִי: (7) לֹא־
not (7) he-will-minister-to-me he blameless in-way one-walking with-me

יֵשֵׁב | בְּקֶרֶב בֵּיתִי עֹשֵׂה רְמִיָּה דֹּבֵר
one-speaking deceit one-practicing-of house-of-me in-midst-of he-will-dwell

שְׁקָרִים לֹא־ יִכּוֹן לְנֶגֶד עֵינָי: (8) לַבְּקָרִים
in-the-mornings (8) eyes-of-me at-before he-will-stand not falsehoods

אַצְמִית כָּל־ רִשְׁעֵי־ אָרֶץ לְהַכְרִית מֵעִיר־ יְהוָה
Yahweh from-city-of to-cut-off land wicked-ones-of all-of I-will-silence

כָּל־ פֹּעֲלֵי אָוֶן: *(102:1) תְּפִלָּה לְעָנִי כִּי־ יַעֲטֹף
he-is-faint when of-afflicted-man prayer *(102:1) evil ones-doing-of all-of

וְלִפְנֵי יְהוָה יִשְׁפֹּךְ שִׂיחוֹ: (2) יְהוָה שִׁמְעָה תְפִלָּתִי
prayer-of-me hear! Yahweh (2) lament-of-him he-pours-out Yahweh and-before

וְשַׁוְעָתִי אֵלֶיךָ תָבוֹא: (3) אַל־ תַּסְתֵּר פָּנֶיךָ |
faces-of-you you-hide not (3) let-her-come to-you and-cry-for-help-of-me

מִמֶּנִּי בְּיוֹם צַר לִי הַטֵּה־ אֵלַי אָזְנֶךָ בְּיוֹם אֶקְרָא
I-call on-day ear-of-you to-me turn! of-me distress on-day-of from-me

מַהֵר עֲנֵנִי: (4) כִּי־ כָלוּ בְעָשָׁן יָמָי וְעַצְמוֹתַי
and-bones-of-me days-of-me like-smoke they-vanish for (4) answer-me! quickly

כְּמוֹ־קֵד נִחָרוּ: (5) הוּכָּה־ כָעֵשֶׂב
like-the-grass he-is-blighted (5) they-burn like-glowing-ember

וַיִּבַשׁ לִבִּי כִּי־ שָׁכַחְתִּי מֵאֲכֹל לַחְמִי:
food-of-me from-to-eat I-forget that heart-of-me and-he-is-withered

(6) מִקּוֹל אַנְחָתִי דָּבְקָה עַצְמִי לִבְשָׂרִי:
to-skin-of-me bone-of-me she-clings groaning-of-me because-of-loudness-of (6)

(7) דָּמִיתִי לִקְאַת מִדְבָּר הָיִיתִי כְּכוֹס חֳרָבוֹת: (8) שָׁקַדְתִּי
I-lie-awake (8) ruins like-owl-of I-am desert to-owl-of I-am-like (7)

וָאֶהְיֶה כְּצִפּוֹר בּוֹדֵד עַל־ גָּג: (9) כָּל־ הַיּוֹם
the-day all-of (9) housetop on one-being-alone like-bird and-I-became

חֵרְפוּנִי אוֹיְבָי מְהוֹלָלַי בִּי
by-me ones-railing-against-me ones-being-enemies-of-me they-taunt-me

נִשְׁבָּעוּ: (10) כִּי־ אֵפֶר כַּלֶּחֶם אָכָלְתִּי וְשִׁקֻּוַי בִּבְכִי
with-tear and-drinks-of-me I-eat as-the-food ash for (10) they-curse

מָסָכְתִּי: (11) מִפְּנֵי־ זַעַמְךָ וְקִצְפֶּךָ כִּי נְשָׂאתַנִי
you-took-up-me for and-wrath-of-you anger-of-you because-of (11) I-mingle

וַתַּשְׁלִיכֵנִי: (12) יָמַי כְּצֵל נָטוּי וַאֲנִי
and-I one-being-long like-shadow days-of-me (12) and-you-threw-aside-me

him will I not endure.

6 My eyes will be on the faithful
in the land,
that they may dwell with
me;
he whose walk is blameless
will minister to me.

7 No one who practices deceit
will dwell in my house;
no one who speaks falsely
will stand in my presence.

8 Every morning I will put to
silence
all the wicked in the land;
I will cut off every evildoer
from the city of the LORD.

### Psalm 102

A prayer of an afflicted man. When he is faint and pours out his lament before the LORD.

1 Hear my prayer, O LORD;
let my cry for help come to
you.
2 Do not hide your face from me
when I am in distress.
Turn your ear to me;
when I call, answer me
quickly.

3 For my days vanish like
smoke;
my bones burn like glowing
embers.
4 My heart is blighted and
withered like grass;
I forget to eat my food.
5 Because of my loud groaning
I am reduced to skin and
bones.
6 I am like a desert owl,
like an owl among the ruins.
7 I lie awake; I have become
like a bird alone on a
housetop.
8 All day long my enemies taunt
me;
those who rail against me
use my name as a curse.
9 For I eat ashes as my food
and mingle my drink with
tears
10 because of your great wrath,
for you have taken me up
and thrown me aside.
11 My days are like the evening
shadow;

*Heading, 1 See the note on page 349.

[4] Most mss treat these two words as one ( כמוקד ).

כְּעֵשֶׂב אִיבָשׁ׃ וְאַתָּה יְהוָה לְעוֹלָם תֵּשֵׁב
you-sit-enthroned to-forever Yahweh but-you (13) I-wither-away like-the-grass

וְזִכְרְךָ לְדֹר וָדֹר׃ אַתָּה תָקוּם
you-will-arise you (14) and-generation to-generation and-renown-of-you

תְּרַחֵם צִיּוֹן כִּי־ עֵת לְחֶנְנָהּ כִּי־ בָא
he-came for to-show-favor-to-her time for Zion you-will-have-compassion-on

מוֹעֵד׃ כִּי־ רָצוּ עֲבָדֶיךָ אֶת־ אֲבָנֶיהָ וְאֶת־
and stones-of-her *** servants-of-you they-are-dear for (15) appointed-time

עֲפָרָהּ יְחֹנֵנוּ׃ וְיִירְאוּ גוֹיִם אֶת־ שֵׁם
name-of *** nations and-they-will-fear (16) they-move-to-pity dust-of-her

יְהוָה וְכָל־ מַלְכֵי הָאָרֶץ אֶת־ כְּבוֹדֶךָ׃ כִּי־ בָנָה
he-will-rebuild for (17) glory-of-you *** the-earth kings-of and-all-of Yahweh

יְהוָה צִיּוֹן נִרְאָה בִּכְבוֹדוֹ׃ פָּנָה אֶל־ תְּפִלַּת
prayer-of to he-will-respond (18) in-glory-of-him he-will-appear Zion Yahweh

הָעַרְעָר וְלֹא־ בָזָה אֶת־ תְּפִלָּתָם׃ תִּכָּתֶב
let-her-be-written (19) plea-of-them *** he-will-despise and-not the-destitute

זֹאת לְדוֹר אַחֲרוֹן וְעַם נִבְרָא יְהַלֶּל־
he-may-praise one-being-created that-people future for-generation this

יָהּ׃ כִּי־ הִשְׁקִיף מִמְּרוֹם קָדְשׁוֹ יְהוָה
Yahweh sanctuary-of-him from-high-place-of he-looked-down that (20) Yahweh

מִשָּׁמַיִם׀ אֶל־ אֶרֶץ הִבִּיט׃ לִשְׁמֹעַ אֶנְקַת אָסִיר לְפַתֵּחַ
to-release prisoner groan-of to-hear (21) he-viewed earth to from-heavens

בְּנֵי תְמוּתָה׃ לְסַפֵּר בְּצִיּוֹן שֵׁם יְהוָה וּתְהִלָּתוֹ
and-praise-of-him Yahweh name-of in-Zion to-declare (22) death men-of

בִּירוּשָׁלָם׃ בְּהִקָּבֵץ עַמִּים יַחְדָּו וּמַמְלָכוֹת לַעֲבֹד
to-worship and-kingdoms together peoples when-to-assemble (23) in-Jerusalem

אֶת־ יְהוָה׃ עִנָּה בַדֶּרֶךְ כֹּחוֹ° קִצַּר יָמָי׃
days-of-me he-cut-short strength-of-me in-the-course he-broke (24) Yahweh ***

אֹמַר אֵלִי אַל־ תַּעֲלֵנִי בַּחֲצִי יָמָי
days-of-me in-midst-of you-take-away-me not God-of-me I-said (25)

בְּדוֹר דּוֹרִים שְׁנוֹתֶיךָ׃ לְפָנִים הָאָרֶץ
the-earth in-beginning (26) years-of-you generations through-generation-of

יָסַדְתָּ וּמַעֲשֵׂה יָדֶיךָ שָׁמָיִם׃ הֵמָּה׀ יֹאבֵדוּ
they-will-perish they (27) heavens hands-of-you and-work-of you-founded

וְאַתָּה תַעֲמֹד וְכֻלָּם כַּבֶּגֶד יִבְלוּ
they-will-wear-out like-the-garment and-all-of-them you-remain but-you

כַּלְּבוּשׁ תַּחֲלִיפֵם וְיַחֲלֹפוּ׃ וְאַתָּה־
but-you (28) and-they-will-be-discarded you-will-change-them like-the-clothing

I wither away like grass.

12 But you, O LORD, sit enthroned forever;
your renown endures through all generations.
13 You will arise and have compassion on Zion,
for it is time to show favor to her;
the appointed time has come.
14 For her stones are dear to your servants;
her very dust moves them to pity.
15 The nations will fear the name of the LORD,
all the kings of the earth will revere your glory.
16 For the LORD will rebuild Zion
and appear in his glory.
17 He will respond to the prayer of the destitute;
he will not despise their plea.

18 Let this be written for a future generation,
that a people not yet created may praise the LORD:
19 "The LORD looked down from his sanctuary on high,
from heaven he viewed the earth,
20 to hear the groans of the prisoners
and release those condemned to death."
21 So the name of the LORD will be declared in Zion
and his praise in Jerusalem
22 when the peoples and the kingdoms
assemble to worship the LORD.

23 In the course of my life[n] he broke my strength;
he cut short my days.
24 So I said:
"Do not take me away, O my God, in the midst of my days;
your years go on through all generations.
25 In the beginning you laid the foundations of the earth,
and the heavens are the work of your hands.
26 They will perish, but you remain;
they will all wear out like a garment.
Like clothing you will change them
and they will be discarded.

[n] 23 Or *By his power*

*See the note on page 349.

°24 ק כחי

הוּא וּשְׁנוֹתֶיךָ לֹא יִתָּמּוּ׃ בְּנֵי־ עֲבָדֶיךָ

servants-of-you children-of (29) they-end never and-years-of-you same

יִשְׁכּוֹנוּ וְזַרְעָם לְפָנֶיךָ יִכּוֹן׃

he-will-be-established before-you and-descendant-of-them they-will-live

לְדָוִד ׀ בָּרְכִי נַפְשִׁי אֶת־ יְהוָה וְכָל־ קְרָבַי

inmost-beings-of-me and-all-of Yahweh *** soul-of-me praise! of-David (103:1)

אֶת־ שֵׁם קָדְשׁוֹ׃ בָּרְכִי נַפְשִׁי אֶת־ יְהוָה וְאַל־

and-not Yahweh *** soul-of-me praise! (2) holiness-of-him name-of ***

תִּשְׁכְּחִי כָּל־ גְּמוּלָיו׃ הַסֹּלֵחַ לְכָל־ עֲוֺנֵכִי

sin-of-you to-all-of the-one-forgiving (3) benefits-of-him all-of you-forget

הָרֹפֵא לְכָל־ תַּחֲלֻאָיְכִי׃ הַגּוֹאֵל מִשַּׁחַת

from-pit the-one-redeeming (4) diseases-of-you to-all-of the-one-healing

חַיָּיְכִי הַמְעַטְּרֵכִי חֶסֶד וְרַחֲמִים׃ הַמַּשְׂבִּיעַ

the-one-satisfying (5) and-compassions love the-one-crowning-you lives-of-you

בַּטּוֹב עֶדְיֵךְ תִּתְחַדֵּשׁ כַּנֶּשֶׁר נְעוּרָיְכִי׃

youths-of-you like-the-eagle she-is-renewed desire-of-you with-the-good

עֹשֵׂה צְדָקוֹת יְהוָה וּמִשְׁפָּטִים לְכָל־

for-all-of and-justices Yahweh righteousnesses one-working-of (6)

עֲשׁוּקִים׃ יוֹדִיעַ דְּרָכָיו לְמֹשֶׁה לִבְנֵי

to-peoples-of to-Moses ways-of-him he-made-known (7) ones-being-oppressed

יִשְׂרָאֵל עֲלִילוֹתָיו׃ רַחוּם וְחַנּוּן יְהוָה אֶרֶךְ אַפַּיִם

angers slow-of Yahweh and-gracious compassionate (8) deeds-of-him Israel

וְרַב־ חָסֶד׃ לֹא־ לָנֶצַח יָרִיב וְלֹא לְעוֹלָם

to-forever and-not he-will-accuse to-always not (9) love and-abundant-of

יִטּוֹר׃ לֹא כַחֲטָאֵינוּ עָשָׂה לָנוּ וְלֹא

and-not to-us he-treats as-sins-of-us not (10) he-will-harbor-anger

כַעֲוֺנֹתֵינוּ גָּמַל עָלֵינוּ׃ כִּי כִגְבֹהַּ שָׁמַיִם עַל־

above heavens as-to-be-high for (11) to-us he-repays as-iniquities-of-us

הָאָרֶץ גָּבַר חַסְדּוֹ עַל־ יְרֵאָיו׃ כִּרְחֹק

as-to-be-far (12) ones-fearing-him for love-of-him he-is-great the-earth

מִזְרָח מִמַּעֲרָב הִרְחִיק מִמֶּנּוּ אֶת־ פְּשָׁעֵינוּ׃

transgressions-of-us *** from-us he-removed-far from-west east

כְּרַחֵם אָב עַל־ בָּנִים רִחַם יְהוָה עַל־

on Yahweh he-has-compassion children on father as-to-have-compassion (13)

יְרֵאָיו׃ כִּי־ הוּא יָדַע יִצְרֵנוּ זָכוּר כִּי־

that one-being-reminded form-of-us he-knows he for (14) ones-fearing-him

עָפָר אֲנָחְנוּ׃ אֱנוֹשׁ כֶּחָצִיר יָמָיו כְּצִיץ הַשָּׂדֶה כֵּן

so the-field like-flower-of days-of-him like-the-grass man (15) we dust

27But you remain the same,
and your years will never end.
28The children of your servants will live in your presence;
their descendants will be established before you."

### Psalm 103

Of David.

1Praise the LORD, O my soul;
all my inmost being, praise his holy name.
2Praise the LORD, O my soul,
and forget not all his benefits.
3He forgives all my[o] sins
and heals all my diseases;
4he redeems my life from the pit
and crowns me with love and compassion.
5He satisfies my desires with good things,
so that my youth is renewed like the eagle's.
6The LORD works righteousness
and justice for all the oppressed.
7He made known his ways to Moses,
his deeds to the people of Israel:
8The LORD is compassionate and gracious,
slow to anger, abounding in love.
9He will not always accuse,
nor will he harbor his anger forever;
10he does not treat us as our sins deserve
or repay us according to our iniquities.
11For as high as the heavens are above the earth,
so great is his love for those who fear him;
12as far as the east is from the west,
so far has he removed our transgressions from us.
13As a father has compassion on his children,
so the LORD has compassion on those who fear him;
14for he knows how we are formed,
he remembers that we are dust.
15As for man, his days are like grass,
he flourishes like a flower of the field;

o3 Hebrew *your* (referring to *my soul*); also in verses 3b-5

*See the note on page 349.

יָצִֽיץ׃ (16) כִּי רוּחַ עָבְרָה־ בּוֹ וְאֵינֶנּוּ וְלֹא־
and-not and-not-he over-him she-blows wind for (16) he-flourishes

יַכִּירֶנּוּ עוֹד מְקוֹמוֹ׃ (17) וְחֶסֶד יְהוָה ׀ מֵעוֹלָם
from-everlasting Yahweh but-love-of (17) place-of-him more he-remembers-him

וְעַד־ עוֹלָם עַל־ יְרֵאָיו וְצִדְקָתוֹ
and-righteousness-of-him ones-fearing-him with everlasting and-to

לִבְנֵי בָנִים׃ (18) לְשֹׁמְרֵי בְרִיתוֹ
covenant-of-him with-ones-keeping-of (18) children with-children-of

וּלְזֹכְרֵי פִקֻּדָיו לַעֲשׂוֹתָם׃ (19) יְהוָה
Yahweh (19) to-obey-them precepts-of-him and-with-ones-remembering-of

בַּשָּׁמַיִם הֵכִין כִּסְאוֹ וּמַלְכוּתוֹ בַּכֹּל
over-the-all and-kingdom-of-him throne-of-him he-established in-the-heavens

מָשָׁלָה׃ (20) בָּרְכוּ יְהוָה מַלְאָכָיו גִּבֹּרֵי כֹחַ
strength mighty-ones-of angels-of-him Yahweh praise! (20) she-rules

עֹשֵׂי דְבָרוֹ לִשְׁמֹעַ בְּקוֹל דְּבָרוֹ׃ (21) בָּרְכוּ
praise! (21) word-of-him to-voice-of to-obey bidding-of-him ones-doing-of

יְהוָה כָּל־ צְבָאָיו מְשָׁרְתָיו עֹשֵׂי רְצוֹנוֹ׃
will-of-him ones-doing-of ones-serving-him hosts-of-him all-of Yahweh

(22) בָּרְכוּ יְהוָה ׀ כָּל־ מַעֲשָׂיו בְּכָל־ מְקֹמוֹת מֶמְשַׁלְתּוֹ
dominion-of-him places-of in-all-of works-of-him all-of Yahweh praise! (22)

בָּרְכִי נַפְשִׁי אֶת־ יְהוָה׃ (104:1) בָּרְכִי נַפְשִׁי אֶת־ יְהוָה יְהוָה
Yahweh Yahweh *** soul-of-me praise! (104:1) Yahweh *** soul-of-me praise!

אֱלֹהַי גָּדַלְתָּ מְּאֹד הוֹד וְהָדָר לָבָשְׁתָּ׃
you-are-clothed and-majesty splendor very you-are-great God-of-me

(2) עֹטֶה־ אוֹר כַּשַּׂלְמָה נוֹטֶה שָׁמַיִם
heavens one-stretching-out as-the-garment light one-wrapping-himself (2)

כַּיְרִיעָה׃ (3) הַמְקָרֶה בַמַּיִם עֲלִיּוֹתָיו
upper-chambers-of-him on-the-waters the-one-laying-beams (3) like-the-tent

הַשָּׂם־ עָבִים רְכוּבוֹ הַמְהַלֵּךְ עַל־ כַּנְפֵי־ רוּחַ׃
wind wings-of on the-one-riding chariot-of-him clouds the-one-making

(4) עֹשֶׂה מַלְאָכָיו רוּחוֹת מְשָׁרְתָיו אֵשׁ לֹהֵט׃
flaming fire ones-serving-him winds messengers-of-him one-making (4)

(5) יָסַד־ אֶרֶץ עַל־ מְכוֹנֶיהָ בַּל־ תִּמּוֹט עוֹלָם וָעֶד׃
and-ever for-ever she-can-be-moved not foundations-of-her on earth he-set (5)

(6) תְּהוֹם כַּלְּבוּשׁ כִּסִּיתוֹ עַל־ הָרִים יַעַמְדוּ־ מָיִם׃
waters they-stood mountains above you-covered-him as-the-garment deep (6)

(7) מִן־ גַּעֲרָתְךָ יְנוּסוּן מִן־ קוֹל רַעַמְךָ יֵחָפֵזוּן׃
they-took-to-flight thunder-of-you sound-of at they-fled rebuke-of-you at (7)

16 the wind blows over it and it is gone,
and its place remembers it no more.
17 But from everlasting to everlasting
the LORD's love is with those who fear him,
and his righteousness with their children's children—
18 with those who keep his covenant
and remember to obey his precepts.

19 The LORD has established his throne in heaven,
and his kingdom rules over all.

20 Praise the LORD, you his angels,
you mighty ones who do his bidding,
who obey his word.
21 Praise the LORD, all his heavenly hosts,
you his servants who do his will.
22 Praise the LORD, all his works
everywhere in his dominion.

Praise the LORD, O my soul.

### Psalm 104

1 Praise the LORD, O my soul.

O LORD my God, you are very great;
you are clothed with splendor and majesty.
2 He wraps himself in light as with a garment;
he stretches out the heavens like a tent
3 and lays the beams of his upper chambers on their waters.
He makes the clouds his chariot
and rides on the wings of the wind.
4 He makes winds his messengers,[p]
flames of fire his servants.

5 He set the earth on its foundations;
it can never be moved.
6 You covered it with the deep as with a garment;
the waters stood above the mountains.
7 But at your rebuke the waters fled,
at the sound of your thunder they took to flight;

p4 Or *angels*

יַעֲלוּ הָרִים יֵרְדוּ בְקָעוֹת אֶל־מְקוֹם זֶה ׀
which place-of to valleys they-went-down mountains they-flowed-over (8)

יָסַדְתָּ לָהֶם׃ גְּבוּל־שַׂמְתָּ בַּל־יַעֲבֹרוּן בַּל־
never they-can-cross not you-set boundary (9) for-them you-assigned

יְשׁוּבוּן לְכַסּוֹת הָאָרֶץ׃ הַמְשַׁלֵּחַ מַעְיָנִים
springs the-one-making-pour (10) the-earth to-cover they-will-come-again

בַּנְּחָלִים בֵּין הָרִים יְהַלֵּכוּן׃ יַשְׁקוּ כָּל־
all-of they-give-water (11) they-flow mountains between into-the-ravines

חַיְתוֹ שָׂדָי יִשְׁבְּרוּ פְרָאִים צְמָאָם׃ עֲלֵיהֶם עוֹף־
bird-of by-them (12) thirst-of-them donkeys they-quench field beast-of

הַשָּׁמַיִם יִשְׁכּוֹן מִבֵּין עֳפָאיִם יִתְּנוּ־קוֹל׃ מַשְׁקֶה
one-watering (13) song they-give branches in-among they-nest the-airs

הָרִים מֵעֲלִיּוֹתָיו מִפְּרִי מַעֲשֶׂיךָ תִּשְׂבַּע
she-is-satisfied works-of-you by-fruit-of from-upper-chambers-of-him mountains

הָאָרֶץ׃ מַצְמִיחַ חָצִיר ׀ לַבְּהֵמָה וְעֵשֶׂב לַעֲבֹדַת
for-cultivation-of and-plant for-the-cattle grass one-making-grow (14) the-earth

הָאָדָם לְהוֹצִיא לֶחֶם מִן־הָאָרֶץ׃ וְיַיִן ׀ יְשַׂמַּח
he-makes-glad and-wine (15) the-earth from food to-bring-forth the-man

לְבַב־אֱנוֹשׁ לְהַצְהִיל פָּנִים מִשָּׁמֶן וְלֶחֶם לְבַב־אֱנוֹשׁ יִסְעָד׃
he-sustains man heart-of and-bread with-oil faces to-make-shine man heart-of

יִשְׂבְּעוּ עֲצֵי יְהוָה אַרְזֵי לְבָנוֹן אֲשֶׁר נָטָע׃
he-planted that Lebanon cedars-of Yahweh trees-of they-are-well-watered (16)

אֲשֶׁר־שָׁם צִפֳּרִים יְקַנֵּנוּ חֲסִידָה בְּרוֹשִׁים בֵּיתָהּ׃
home-of-her pine-trees stork they-make-nests birds there where (17)

הָרִים הַגְּבֹהִים לַיְּעֵלִים סְלָעִים מַחְסֶה לַשְׁפַנִּים׃
for-the-coneys refuge crags to-the-wild-goats the-high-ones mountains (18)

עָשָׂה יָרֵחַ לְמוֹעֲדִים שֶׁמֶשׁ יָדַע מְבוֹאוֹ׃
going-down-of-him he-knows sun to-seasons moon he-marks-off (19)

תָּשֶׁת־חֹשֶׁךְ וִיהִי לָיְלָה בּוֹ־תִרְמֹשׂ כָּל־
all-of she-prowls in-him night and-he-becomes darkness you-bring (20)

חַיְתוֹ־יָעַר׃ הַכְּפִירִים שֹׁאֲגִים לַטָּרֶף וּלְבַקֵּשׁ מֵאֵל
from-God and-to-seek for-the-prey ones-roaring the-lions (21) forest beast-of

אָכְלָם׃ תִּזְרַח הַשֶּׁמֶשׁ יֵאָסֵפוּן וְאֶל־מְעוֹנֹתָם
dens-of-them and-into they-steal-away the-sun she-rises (22) food-of-them

יִרְבָּצוּן׃ יֵצֵא אָדָם לְפָעֳלוֹ וְלַעֲבֹדָתוֹ עֲדֵי־
until and-to-labor-of-him to-work-of-him man he-goes-out (23) they-lie-down

עָרֶב׃ מָה־רַבּוּ מַעֲשֶׂיךָ ׀ יְהוָה כֻּלָּם בְּחָכְמָה
in-wisdom all-of-them Yahweh works-of-you they-are-many how! (24) evening

8 they flowed over the mountains,
they went down into the valleys,
to the place you assigned for them.
9 You set a boundary they cannot cross;
never again will they cover the earth.

10 He makes springs pour water into the ravines;
it flows between the mountains.
11 They give water to all the beasts of the field;
the wild donkeys quench their thirst.
12 The birds of the air nest by the waters;
they sing among the branches.
13 He waters the mountains from his upper chambers;
the earth is satisfied by the fruit of his work.
14 He makes grass grow for the cattle,
and plants for man to cultivate—
bringing forth food from the earth:
15 wine that gladdens the heart of man,
oil to make his face shine,
and bread that sustains his heart.
16 The trees of the LORD are well watered,
the cedars of Lebanon that he planted.
17 There the birds make their nests;
the stork has its home in the pine trees.
18 The high mountains belong to the wild goats;
the crags are a refuge for the coneys.[q]

19 The moon marks off the seasons,
and the sun knows when to go down.
20 You bring darkness, it becomes night,
and all the beasts of the forest prowl.
21 The lions roar for their prey
and seek their food from God.
22 The sun rises, and they steal away;
they return and lie down in their dens.
23 Then man goes out to his work,
to his labor until evening.

24 How many are your works, O LORD!
In wisdom you made them all;

q18 That is, the hyrax or rock badger

עָשִׂיתָ מָלְאָה הָאָרֶץ קִנְיָנֶךָ׃ (25) זֶה ׀ הַיָּם גָּדוֹל
vast the-sea there (25) creature-of-you the-earth she-is-full you-made

וּרְחַב יָדָיִם שָׁם־ רֶמֶשׂ וְאֵין מִסְפָּר חַיּוֹת קְטַנּוֹת
small-ones living-things number and-no creature there hands and-spacious-of

עִם־ גְּדֹלוֹת׃ (26) שָׁם אֳנִיּוֹת יְהַלֵּכוּן לִוְיָתָן זֶה־ יָצַרְתָּ
you-formed which leviathan they-go-about ships there (26) large-ones and

לְשַׂחֶק־ בּוֹ׃ (27) כֻּלָּם אֵלֶיךָ יְשַׂבֵּרוּן לָתֵת אָכְלָם
food-of-them to-give they-look to-you all-of-them (27) in-him to-frolic

בְּעִתּוֹ׃ (28) תִּתֵּן לָהֶם יִלְקֹטוּן תִּפְתַּח יָדְךָ
hand-of-you you-open they-gather to-them you-give (28) at-time-of-him

יִשְׂבְּעוּן טוֹב׃ (29) תַּסְתִּיר פָּנֶיךָ יִבָּהֵלוּן
they-are-terrified faces-of-you you-hide (29) good they-are-satisfied

תֹּסֵף רוּחָם יִגְוָעוּן וְאֶל־ עֲפָרָם יְשׁוּבוּן׃
they-return dust-of-them and-to they-die breath-of-them you-take-away

(30) תְּשַׁלַּח רוּחֲךָ יִבָּרֵאוּן וּתְחַדֵּשׁ פְּנֵי אֲדָמָה׃
earth faces-of and-you-renew they-are-created Spirit-of-you you-send (30)

(31) יְהִי כְבוֹד יְהוָה לְעוֹלָם יִשְׂמַח יְהוָה
Yahweh may-he-rejoice to-forever Yahweh glory-of may-he-endure (31)

בְּמַעֲשָׂיו׃ (32) הַמַּבִּיט לָאָרֶץ וַתִּרְעָד יִגַּע
he-touches and-she-trembles at-the-earth the-one-looking (32) in-works-of-him

בֶּהָרִים וְיֶעֱשָׁנוּ׃ (33) אָשִׁירָה לַיהוָה בְּחַיָּי
during-lives-of-me to-Yahweh I-will-sing (33) and-they-smoke on-the-mountains

אֲזַמְּרָה לֵאלֹהַי בְּעוֹדִי׃ (34) יֶעֱרַב עָלָיו
to-him may-he-be-pleasing (34) while-still-I to-God-of-me I-will-sing-praise

שִׂיחִי אָנֹכִי אֶשְׂמַח בַּיהוָה׃ (35) יִתַּמּוּ חַטָּאִים ׀
sinners may-they-vanish (35) in-Yahweh I-rejoice I meditation-of-me

מִן־ הָאָרֶץ וּרְשָׁעִים ׀ עוֹד אֵינָם בָּרְכִי נַפְשִׁי אֶת־ יְהוָה
Yahweh *** soul-of-me praise! not-they more and-wicked-ones the-earth from

הַלְלוּ־ יָהּ׃ (105:1) הוֹדוּ לַיהוָה קִרְאוּ בִּשְׁמוֹ
on-name-of-him call! to-Yahweh give-thanks! (105:1) Yahweh praise!

הוֹדִיעוּ בָעַמִּים עֲלִילוֹתָיו׃ (2) שִׁירוּ־ לוֹ זַמְּרוּ־
sing-praise! to-him sing! (2) deeds-of-him among-the-nations make-known!

לוֹ שִׂיחוּ בְּכָל־ נִפְלְאוֹתָיו׃ (3) הִתְהַלְלוּ בְּשֵׁם
in-name-of glory! (3) acts-being-wonderful-of-him of-all-of tell! to-him

קָדְשׁוֹ יִשְׂמַח לֵב ׀ מְבַקְשֵׁי יְהוָה׃ (4) דִּרְשׁוּ
look-to! (4) Yahweh ones-seeking-of heart-of let-him-rejoice holiness-of-him

יְהוָה וְעֻזּוֹ בַּקְּשׁוּ פָנָיו תָּמִיד׃ (5) זִכְרוּ
remember! (5) always faces-of-him seek! and-strength-of-him Yahweh

the earth is full of your
creatures.
25 There is the sea, vast and
spacious,
teeming with creatures
beyond number—
living things both large and
small.
26 There the ships go to and fro,
and the leviathan, which
you formed to frolic there.
27 These all look to you
to give them their food at
the proper time.
28 When you give it to them,
they gather it up;
when you open your hand,
they are satisfied with good
things.
29 When you hide your face,
they are terrified;
when you take away their
breath,
they die and return to the
dust.
30 When you send your Spirit,
they are created,
and you renew the face of
the earth.
31 May the glory of the LORD
endure forever;
may the LORD rejoice in his
works.
32 He looks at the earth, and it
trembles;
he touches the mountains,
and they smoke.
33 I will sing to the LORD all my
life;
I will sing praise to my God
as long as I live.
34 May my meditation be
pleasing to him,
as I rejoice in the LORD.
35 But may sinners vanish from
the earth
and the wicked be no more.
Praise the LORD, O my soul.
Praise the LORD.[r]

**Psalm 105**

1 Give thanks to the LORD, call
on his name;
make known among the
nations what he has
done.
2 Sing to him, sing praise to
him;
tell of all his wonderful acts.
3 Glory in his holy name;
let the hearts of those who
seek the LORD rejoice.
4 Look to the LORD and his
strength;
seek his face always.

[r]35 Hebrew *Hallelu Yah*

נִפְלְאוֹתָיו אֲשֶׁר־ עָשָׂה מֹפְתָיו וּמִשְׁפְּטֵי־
and-judgments-of miracles-of-him he-did that deeds-being-wonders-of-him

פִיו׃ זֶרַע אַבְרָהָם עַבְדּוֹ בְּנֵי יַעֲקֹב
Jacob sons-of servant-of-him Abraham descendant-of (6) mouth-of-him

בְּחִירָיו׃ הוּא יְהוָה אֱלֹהֵינוּ בְּכָל־ הָאָרֶץ מִשְׁפָּטָיו׃
judgments-of-him the-earth in-all-of God-of-us Yahweh he (7) chosen-ones-of-him

זָכַר לְעוֹלָם בְּרִיתוֹ דָּבָר צִוָּה לְאֶלֶף
for-thousand-of he-commanded word covenant-of-him to-forever he-remembers (8)

דּוֹר׃ אֲשֶׁר כָּרַת אֶת־ אַבְרָהָם וּשְׁבוּעָתוֹ לְיִשְׂחָק׃
to-Isaac and-oath-of-him Abraham with he-made that (9) generation

וַיַּעֲמִידֶהָ לְיַעֲקֹב לְחֹק לְיִשְׂרָאֵל בְּרִית עוֹלָם׃
everlasting covenant-of to-Israel as-decree to-Jacob and-he-confirmed-her (10)

לֵאמֹר לְךָ אֶתֵּן אֶת־ אֶרֶץ־ כְּנָעַן חֶבֶל נַחֲלַתְכֶם׃
inheritance-of-you portion-of Canaan land-of *** I-will-give to-you to-say (11)

בִּהְיוֹתָם מְתֵי מִסְפָּר כִּמְעַט וְגָרִים בָּהּ׃
in-her and-ones-being-strangers as-few number ones-few-of when-to-be-them (12)

וַיִּתְהַלְּכוּ מִגּוֹי אֶל־ גּוֹי מִמַּמְלָכָה אֶל־ עַם אַחֵר׃
another people to from-kingdom nation to from-nation then-they-wandered (13)

לֹא־ הִנִּיחַ אָדָם לְעָשְׁקָם וַיּוֹכַח עֲלֵיהֶם
for-sake-of-them and-he-rebuked to-oppress-them anyone he-allowed not (14)

מְלָכִים׃ אַל־ תִּגְּעוּ בִמְשִׁיחָי וְלִנְבִיאַי אַל־
not or-to-prophets-of-me on-anointed-ones-of-me you-touch not (15) kings

תָּרֵעוּ׃ וַיִּקְרָא רָעָב עַל־ הָאָרֶץ כָּל־ מַטֵּה־ לֶחֶם
food supply-of all-of the-land on famine and-he-called (16) you-harm

שָׁבָר׃ שָׁלַח לִפְנֵיהֶם אִישׁ לְעֶבֶד נִמְכַּר יוֹסֵף׃
Joseph he-was-sold as-slave man before-them he-sent (17) he-destroyed

עִנּוּ בַכֶּבֶל רַגְלָיו° בַּרְזֶל בָּאָה נַפְשׁוֹ׃
neck-of-him she-entered iron foot-of-him with-the-shackle they-bruised (18)

עַד־ עֵת בֹּא־ דְבָרוֹ אִמְרַת יְהוָה
Yahweh word-of foretelling-of-him to-come-to-pass time-of till (19)

צְרָפָתְהוּ׃ שָׁלַח מֶלֶךְ וַיַּתִּירֵהוּ מֹשֵׁל עַמִּים
peoples one-ruling and-he-released-him king he-sent (20) she-proved-true-him

וַיְפַתְּחֵהוּ׃ שָׂמוֹ אָדוֹן לְבֵיתוֹ וּמֹשֵׁל
and-one-ruling of-household-of-him master he-made-him (21) and-he-set-free-him

בְּכָל־ קִנְיָנוֹ׃ לֶאְסֹר שָׂרָיו
princes-of-him to-discipline (22) possession-of-him over-all-of

בְּנַפְשׁוֹ וּזְקֵנָיו יְחַכֵּם׃ וַיָּבֹא
then-he-entered (23) he-taught-wisdom and-elders-of-him as-pleasure-of-him

5 Remember the wonders he has done,
his miracles, and the judgments he pronounced,
6 O descendants of Abraham his servant,
O sons of Jacob, his chosen ones.
7 He is the LORD our God;
his judgments are in all the earth.
8 He remembers his covenant forever,
the word he commanded, for a thousand generations,
9 the covenant he made with Abraham,
the oath he swore to Isaac.
10 He confirmed it to Jacob as a decree,
to Israel as an everlasting covenant:
11 "To you I will give the land of Canaan
as the portion you will inherit."
12 When they were but few in number,
few indeed, and strangers in it,
13 they wandered from nation to nation,
from one kingdom to another.
14 He allowed no one to oppress them;
for their sake he rebuked kings:
15 "Do not touch my anointed ones;
do my prophets no harm."
16 He called down famine on the land
and destroyed all their supplies of food;
17 and he sent a man before them—
Joseph, sold as a slave.
18 They bruised his feet with shackles,
his neck was put in irons,
19 till what he foretold came to pass,
till the word of the LORD proved him true.
20 The king sent and released him,
the ruler of peoples set him free.
21 He made him master of his household,
ruler over all he possessed,
22 to discipline his princes as he pleased
and teach his elders wisdom.

°18 ק רגלו

יִשְׂרָאֵל מִצְרָיִם וְיַעֲקֹב גָּר בְּאֶרֶץ־ חָם׃ וַיֶּפֶר
and-he-made-fruitful (24) Ham in-land-of he-lived-as-alien and-Jacob Egypt Israel

אֶת־ עַמּוֹ מְאֹד וַיַּעֲצִמֵהוּ מִצָּרָיו׃
more-than-foes-of-him and-he-made-numerous-him very people-of-him ***

הָפַךְ לִבָּם לִשְׂנֹא עַמּוֹ לְהִתְנַכֵּל
to-conspire people-of-him to-hate heart-of-them he-turned (25)

בַּעֲבָדָיו׃ שָׁלַח מֹשֶׁה עַבְדּוֹ אַהֲרֹן אֲשֶׁר בָּחַר־
he-chose whom Aaron servant-of-him Moses he-sent (26) against-servants-of-him

בּוֹ׃ שָׂמוּ־ בָם דִּבְרֵי אֹתוֹתָיו וּמֹפְתִים
and-wonders signs-of-him deeds-of among-them they-performed (27) to-him

בְּאֶרֶץ חָם׃ שָׁלַח חֹשֶׁךְ וַיַּחְשִׁךְ וְלֹא־ מָרוּ
they-rebelled for-not and-he-made-dark darkness he-sent (28) Ham in-land-of

אֶת־ דְּבָרוֹו׃ הָפַךְ אֶת־ מֵימֵיהֶם לְדָם
into-blood waters-of-them *** he-turned (29) *word-of-him against

וַיָּמֶת אֶת־ דְּגָתָם׃ שָׁרַץ אַרְצָם צְפַרְדְּעִים
frogs land-of-them he-teemed (30) fish-of-them *** and-he-caused-to-die

בְּחַדְרֵי מַלְכֵיהֶם׃ אָמַר וַיָּבֹא עָרֹב כִּנִּים
gnats swarm-of-flies and-he-came he-spoke (31) rulers-of-them into-bedrooms-of

בְּכָל־ גְּבוּלָם׃ נָתַן גִּשְׁמֵיהֶם בָּרָד אֵשׁ
flame-of hail rains-of-them he-turned (32) country-of-them through-all-of

לֶהָבוֹת בְּאַרְצָם׃ וַיַּךְ גַּפְנָם
vine-of-them and-he-struck-down (33) through-land-of-them lightnings

וּתְאֵנָתָם וַיְשַׁבֵּר עֵץ גְּבוּלָם׃ אָמַר
he-spoke (34) country-of-them tree-of and-he-shattered and-fig-tree-of-them

וַיָּבֹא אַרְבֶּה וְיֶלֶק וְאֵין מִסְפָּר׃ וַיֹּאכַל כָּל־
every-of and-he-ate-up (35) number with-no and-grasshopper locust and-he-came

עֵשֶׂב בְּאַרְצָם וַיֹּאכַל פְּרִי אַדְמָתָם׃
soil-of-them produce-of and-he-ate-up in-land-of-them green-thing

וַיַּךְ כָּל־ בְּכוֹר בְּאַרְצָם רֵאשִׁית לְכָל־
of-all-of firstfruit in-land-of-them firstborn all-of then-he-struck-down (36)

אוֹנָם׃ וַיּוֹצִיאֵם בְּכֶסֶף וְזָהָב וְאֵין
and-no-one and-gold with-silver and-he-brought-out-them (37) manhood-of-them

בִּשְׁבָטָיו כּוֹשֵׁל׃ שָׂמַח מִצְרַיִם בְּצֵאתָם
when-to-leave-them Egypt he-was-glad (38) faltering among-tribes-of-him

כִּי־ נָפַל פַּחְדָּם עֲלֵיהֶם׃ פָּרַשׂ עָנָן לְמָסָךְ
as-covering cloud he-spread-out (39) on-them dread-of-them he-fell because

וְאֵשׁ לְהָאִיר לָיְלָה׃ שָׁאַל וַיָּבֵא שְׂלָו וְלֶחֶם
and-bread-of quail and-he-brought he-asked (40) night to-give-light and-fire

23 Then Israel entered Egypt;
Jacob lived as an alien in the land of Ham.
24 The LORD made his people very fruitful;
he made them too numerous for their foes,
25 whose hearts he turned to hate his people,
to conspire against his servants.
26 He sent Moses his servant,
and Aaron, whom he had chosen.
27 They performed his miraculous signs among them,
his wonders in the land of Ham.
28 He sent darkness and made the land dark—
for had they not rebelled against his words?
29 He turned their waters into blood,
causing their fish to die.
30 Their land teemed with frogs,
which went up into the bedrooms of their rulers.
31 He spoke, and there came swarms of flies,
and gnats throughout their country.
32 He turned their rain into hail,
with lightning throughout their land;
33 he struck down their vines and fig trees
and shattered the trees of their country.
34 He spoke, and the locusts came,
grasshoppers without number;
35 they ate up every green thing in their land,
ate up the produce of their soil.
36 Then he struck down all the firstborn in their land,
the firstfruits of all their manhood.
37 He brought out Israel, laden with silver and gold,
and from among their tribes no one faltered.
38 Egypt was glad when they left,
because dread of Israel had fallen on them.
39 He spread out a cloud as a covering,
and a fire to give light at night.
40 They asked, and he brought them quail

*28 Many mss point the *Kethib* form as a plural (ָ־יו).

°28 ק דברו

שָׁמַיִם יַשְׂבִּיעֵם׃ פָּתַח צוּר וַיָּזוּבוּ מָיִם
waters and-they-gushed-out rock he-opened (41) he-satisfied-them heavens

הָלְכוּ בַּצִּיּוֹת נָהָר׃ כִּי־ זָכַר אֶת־ דְּבַר
promise-of *** he-remembered for (42) river in-the-deserts they-flowed

קָדְשׁוֹ אֶת־ אַבְרָהָם עַבְדּוֹ׃ וַיּוֹצִא
and-he-brought-out (43) servant-of-him Abraham with holiness-of-him

עַמּוֹ בְשָׂשׂוֹן בְּרִנָּה אֶת־ בְּחִירָיו׃
chosen-ones-of-him *** with-shout-of-joy with-rejoicing people-of-him

וַיִּתֵּן לָהֶם אַרְצוֹת גּוֹיִם וַעֲמַל לְאֻמִּים יִירָשׁוּ׃
they-inherited peoples and-toil-of nations lands-of to-them and-he-gave (44)

בַּעֲבוּר ׀ יִשְׁמְרוּ חֻקָּיו וְתוֹרֹתָיו יִנְצֹרוּ
they-might-observe and-laws-of-him precepts-of-him they-might-keep so-that (45)

הַלְלוּ־ יָהּ׃ הַלְלוּיָהּ ׀ הוֹדוּ לַיהוָה כִּי־ טוֹב כִּי
for good for to-Yahweh give-thanks! praise-Yahweh! (106:1) Yahweh praise!

לְעוֹלָם חַסְדּוֹ׃ מִי יְמַלֵּל גְּבוּרוֹת יְהוָה
Yahweh mighty-acts-of he-can-proclaim who? (2) love-of-him to-forever

יַשְׁמִיעַ כָּל־ תְּהִלָּתוֹ׃ אַשְׁרֵי
blessednesses-of (3) praise-of-him fullness-of he-can-declare

שֹׁמְרֵי מִשְׁפָּט עֹשֵׂה צְדָקָה בְכָל־ עֵת׃ זָכְרֵנִי
remember-me! (4) time at-all-of right one-doing-of justice ones-maintaining-of

יְהוָה בִּרְצוֹן עַמֶּךָ פָּקְדֵנִי בִּישׁוּעָתֶךָ׃
in-salvation-of-you come-to-aid-of-me! people-of-you in-favor-of Yahweh

לִרְאוֹת ׀ בְּטוֹבַת בְּחִירֶיךָ לִשְׂמֹחַ בְּשִׂמְחַת
in-joy-of to-have-joy chosen-ones-of-you to-prosperity-of to-enjoy (5)

גּוֹיֶךָ לְהִתְהַלֵּל עִם־ נַחֲלָתֶךָ׃ חָטָאנוּ עִם־
with we-sinned (6) inheritance-of-you with to-give-praise nation-of-you

אֲבוֹתֵינוּ הֶעֱוִינוּ הִרְשָׁעְנוּ׃ אֲבוֹתֵינוּ בְמִצְרַיִם ׀ לֹא־
not in-Egypt fathers-of-us (7) we-acted-wickedly we-did-wrong fathers-of-us

הִשְׂכִּילוּ נִפְלְאוֹתֶיךָ לֹא זָכְרוּ אֶת־ רֹב
many-of *** they-remembered not deeds-being-miracles-of-you they-gave-thought

חֲסָדֶיךָ וַיַּמְרוּ עַל־ יָם בְּיַם־ סוּף׃ וַיּוֹשִׁיעֵם
yet-he-saved-them (8) Reed by-Sea-of sea by and-they-rebelled kindnesses-of-you

לְמַעַן שְׁמוֹ לְהוֹדִיעַ אֶת־ גְּבוּרָתוֹ׃ וַיִּגְעַר
and-he-rebuked (9) power-of-him *** to-make-known name-of-him for-sake-of

בְּיַם־ סוּף וַיֶּחֱרָב וַיּוֹלִיכֵם בַּתְּהֹמוֹת
through-the-depths and-he-led-them and-he-dried-up Reed to-Sea-of

כַּמִּדְבָּר׃ וַיּוֹשִׁיעֵם מִיַּד שׂוֹנֵא
one-being-foe from-hand-of and-he-saved-them (10) as-the-desert

and satisfied them with the
bread of heaven.
41 He opened the rock, and water
gushed out;
like a river it flowed in the
desert.
42 For he remembered his holy
promise
given to his servant
Abraham.
43 He brought out his people
with rejoicing,
his chosen ones with shouts
of joy;
44 he gave them the lands of the
nations,
and they fell heir to what
others had toiled for—
45 that they might keep his
precepts
and observe his laws.

Praise the LORD.[s]

## Psalm 106

1 Praise the LORD.[t]

Give thanks to the LORD, for
he is good;
his love endures forever.
2 Who can proclaim the mighty
acts of the LORD
or fully declare his praise?
3 Blessed are they who maintain
justice,
who constantly do what is
right.
4 Remember me, O LORD, when
you show favor to your
people,
come to my aid when you
save them,
5 that I may enjoy the
prosperity of your chosen
ones,
that I may share in the joy
of your nation
and join your inheritance in
giving praise.

6 We have sinned, even as our
fathers did;
we have done wrong and
acted wickedly.
7 When our fathers were in
Egypt,
they gave no thought to
your miracles;
they did not remember your
many kindnesses,
and they rebelled by the sea,
the Red Sea.[u]
8 Yet he saved them for his
name's sake,
to make his mighty power
known.
9 He rebuked the Red Sea, and
it dried up;
he led them through the
depths as through a
desert.
10 He saved them from the hand
of the foe;

[s] 45 Hebrew *Hallelu Yah*
[t] 1 Hebrew *Hallelu Yah*; also in verse 48
[u] 7 Hebrew *Yam Suph*; that is, Sea of Reeds; also in verses 9 and 22

וַיִּגְאָלֵם מִיַּד אוֹיֵב׃ וַיְכַסּוּ־
and-they-covered (11) one-being-enemy from-hand-of and-he-redeemed-them

מַיִם צָרֵיהֶם אֶחָד מֵהֶם לֹא נוֹתָר׃ וַיַּאֲמִינוּ
then-they-believed (12) he-survived not of-them one adversaries-of-them waters

בִדְבָרָיו יָשִׁירוּ תְּהִלָּתוֹ׃ מִהֲרוּ שָׁכְחוּ
they-forgot they-did-soon (13) praise-of-him they-sang in-promises-of-him

מַעֲשָׂיו לֹא־ חִכּוּ לַעֲצָתוֹ׃ וַיִּתְאַוּוּ תַאֲוָה
craving and-they-craved (14) for-counsel-of-him they-waited not deeds-of-him

בַּמִּדְבָּר וַיְנַסּוּ־ אֵל בִּישִׁימוֹן׃ וַיִּתֵּן לָהֶם
to-them so-he-gave (15) in-wasteland God and-they-tested in-the-desert

שֶׁאֱלָתָם וַיְשַׁלַּח רָזוֹן בְּנַפְשָׁם׃
upon-life-of-them wasting-disease but-he-sent request-of-them

וַיְקַנְאוּ לְמֹשֶׁה בַּמַּחֲנֶה לְאַהֲרֹן קְדוֹשׁ יְהוָה׃
Yahweh consecrated-of to-Aaron in-the-camp to-Moses and-they-envied (16)

תִּפְתַּח־ אֶרֶץ וַתִּבְלַע דָּתָן וַתְּכַס עַל־
over and-she-buried Dathan and-she-swallowed earth she-opened-up (17)

עֲדַת אֲבִירָם׃ וַתִּבְעַר־ אֵשׁ בַּעֲדָתָם לֶהָבָה
flame among-follower-of-them fire and-she-blazed (18) Abiram company-of

תְּלַהֵט רְשָׁעִים׃ יַעֲשׂוּ־ עֵגֶל בְּחֹרֵב וַיִּשְׁתַּחֲווּ
and-they-worshiped at-Horeb calf they-made (19) wicked-ones she-consumed

לְמַסֵּכָה׃ וַיָּמִירוּ אֶת־ כְּבוֹדָם בְּתַבְנִית שׁוֹר
bull for-image-of Glory-of-them *** and-they-exchanged (20) to-cast-idol

אֹכֵל עֵשֶׂב׃ שָׁכְחוּ אֵל מוֹשִׁיעָם עֹשֶׂה גְדֹלוֹת
great-things one-doing one-saving-them God they-forgot (21) grass one-eating

בְּמִצְרָיִם׃ נִפְלָאוֹת בְּאֶרֶץ חָם נוֹרָאוֹת עַל־
by deeds-being-awesome Ham in-land-of deeds-being-miracles (22) in-Egypt

יַם־ סוּף׃ וַיֹּאמֶר לְהַשְׁמִידָם לוּלֵי מֹשֶׁה בְּחִירוֹ
chosen-one-of-him Moses if-not to-destroy-them so-he-said (23) Reed Sea-of

עָמַד בַּפֶּרֶץ לְפָנָיו לְהָשִׁיב חֲמָתוֹ מֵהַשְׁחִית׃
from-to-destroy wrath-of-him to-keep before-him in-the-breach he-stood

וַיִּמְאֲסוּ בְּאֶרֶץ חֶמְדָּה לֹא־ הֶאֱמִינוּ לִדְבָרוֹ׃
to-promise-of-him they-believed not pleasantness to-land-of then-they-despised (24)

וַיֵּרָגְנוּ בְאָהֳלֵיהֶם לֹא שָׁמְעוּ בְּקוֹל יְהוָה׃
Yahweh to-voice-of they-obeyed not in-tents-of-them and-they-grumbled (25)

וַיִּשָּׂא יָדוֹ לָהֶם לְהַפִּיל אוֹתָם בַּמִּדְבָּר׃
in-the-desert them to-make-fall to-them hand-of-him so-he-lifted (26)

וּלְהַפִּיל זַרְעָם בַּגּוֹיִם וּלְזָרוֹתָם
and-to-scatter-them among-the-nations descendant-of-them and-to-make-fall (27)

---

from the hand of the enemy
he redeemed them.
11 The waters covered their
adversaries;
not one of them survived.
12 Then they believed his
promises
and sang his praise.

13 But they soon forgot what he
had done
and did not wait for his
counsel.
14 In the desert they gave in to
their craving;
in the wasteland they put
God to the test.
15 So he gave them what they
asked for,
but sent a wasting disease
upon them.

16 In the camp they grew envious
of Moses
and of Aaron, who was
consecrated to the LORD.
17 The earth opened up and
swallowed Dathan;
it buried the company of
Abiram.
18 Fire blazed among their
followers;
a flame consumed the
wicked.

19 At Horeb they made a calf
and worshiped an idol cast
from metal.
20 They exchanged their Glory
for an image of a bull,
which eats grass.
21 They forgot the God who
saved them,
who had done great things
in Egypt,
22 miracles in the land of Ham
and awesome deeds by the
Red Sea.
23 So he said he would destroy
them—
had not Moses, his chosen
one,
stood in the breach before him
to keep his wrath from
destroying them.

24 Then they despised the
pleasant land;
they did not believe his
promise.
25 They grumbled in their tents
and did not obey the LORD.
26 So he swore to them with
uplifted hand
that he would make them
fall in the desert,
27 make their descendants fall
among the nations
and scatter them throughout

בָּאֲרָצוֹת׃ וַיִּצָּמְדוּ לְבַעַל פְּעוֹר וַיֹּאכְלוּ
and-they-ate Peor to-Baal-of and-they-yoked-themselves (28) through-the-lands

זִבְחֵי מֵתִים׃ וַיַּכְעִיסוּ בְּמַעַלְלֵיהֶם
by-deeds-of-them and-they-provoked-anger (29) lifeless-ones sacrifices-of

וַתִּפְרָץ־ בָּם מַגֵּפָה׃ וַיַּעֲמֹד פִּינְחָס
Phinehas but-he-stood-up (30) plague among-them and-she-broke-out

וַיְפַלֵּל וַתֵּעָצַר הַמַּגֵּפָה׃ וַתֵּחָשֶׁב
and-she-was-credited (31) the-plague and-she-was-checked and-he-intervened

לוֹ לִצְדָקָה לְדֹר וָדֹר עַד־ עוֹלָם׃
forever to and-generation for-generation as-righteousness to-him

וַיַּקְצִיפוּ עַל־ מֵי מְרִיבָה וַיֵּרַע לְמֹשֶׁה
to-Moses and-he-was-trouble Meribah waters-of by and-they-angered (32)

בַּעֲבוּרָם׃ כִּי־ הִמְרוּ אֶת־ רוּחוֹ וַיְבַטֵּא
and-he-spoke-rashly Spirit-of-him against they-rebelled for (33) because-of-them

בִּשְׂפָתָיו׃ לֹא־ הִשְׁמִידוּ אֶת־ הָעַמִּים אֲשֶׁר אָמַר
he-commanded as the-peoples *** they-destroyed not (34) with-lips-of-him

יְהוָה לָהֶם׃ וַיִּתְעָרְבוּ בַגּוֹיִם וַיִּלְמְדוּ
and-they-adopted with-the-nations but-they-mingled (35) to-them Yahweh

מַעֲשֵׂיהֶם׃ וַיַּעַבְדוּ אֶת־ עֲצַבֵּיהֶם וַיִּהְיוּ
and-they-became idols-of-them *** and-they-worshiped (36) customs-of-them

לָהֶם לְמוֹקֵשׁ׃ וַיִּזְבְּחוּ אֶת־ בְּנֵיהֶם וְאֶת־ בְּנוֹתֵיהֶם
daughters-of-them and sons-of-them *** and-they-sacrificed (37) as-snare to-them

לַשֵּׁדִים׃ וַיִּשְׁפְּכוּ דָם נָקִי דַּם־ בְּנֵיהֶם
sons-of-them blood-of innocent blood and-they-shed (38) to-the-demons

וּבְנוֹתֵיהֶם אֲשֶׁר זִבְּחוּ לַעֲצַבֵּי כְנָעַן
Canaan to-idols-of they-sacrificed whom and-daughters-of-them

וַתֶּחֱנַף הָאָרֶץ בַּדָּמִים׃ וַיִּטְמְאוּ
and-they-defiled-themselves (39) by-the-bloods the-land and-she-was-desecrated

בְמַעֲשֵׂיהֶם וַיִּזְנוּ בְּמַעַלְלֵיהֶם׃
by-deeds-of-them and-they-prostituted-themselves by-deeds-of-them

וַיִּחַר־ אַף יְהוָה בְּעַמּוֹ וַיְתָעֵב אֶת־
*** and-he-abhorred against-people-of-him Yahweh anger-of so-he-burned (40)

נַחֲלָתוֹ׃ וַיִּתְּנֵם בְּיַד־ גּוֹיִם וַיִּמְשְׁלוּ
and-they-ruled nations into-hand-of and-he-gave-them (41) inheritance-of-him

בָהֶם שֹׂנְאֵיהֶם׃ וַיִּלְחָצוּם
and-they-oppressed-them (42) ones-being-foes-of-them over-them

אוֹיְבֵיהֶם וַיִּכָּנְעוּ תַּחַת יָדָם׃ פְּעָמִים
times (43) power-of-them to and-they-were-subjected ones-being-enemies-of-them

the lands.
28They yoked themselves to the
Baal of Peor
and ate sacrifices offered to
lifeless gods;
29they provoked the LORD to
anger by their wicked
deeds,
and a plague broke out
among them.
30But Phinehas stood up and
intervened,
and the plague was checked.
31This was credited to him as
righteousness
for endless generations to
come.
32By the waters of Meribah they
angered the LORD,
and trouble came to Moses
because of them;
33for they rebelled against the
Spirit of God,
and rash words came from
Moses' lips.[v]
34They did not destroy the
peoples
as the LORD had commanded
them,
35but they mingled with the
nations
and adopted their customs.
36They worshiped their idols,
which became a snare to
them.
37They sacrificed their sons
and their daughters to
demons.
38They shed innocent blood,
the blood of their sons and
daughters,
whom they sacrificed to the
idols of Canaan,
and the land was desecrated
by their blood.
39They defiled themselves by
what they did;
by their deeds they
prostituted themselves.
40Therefore the LORD was angry
with his people
and abhorred his
inheritance.
41He handed them over to the
nations,
and their foes ruled over
them.
42Their enemies oppressed them
and subjected them to their
power.

[v]33 Or *against his spirit, / and rash words came from his lips*

רַבּוֹת יַצִּילֵם וְהֵמָּה יַמְרוּ בַּעֲצָתָם
as-decision-of-them they-rebelled but-they he-delivered-them many

וַיָּמֹכּוּ בַּעֲוֺנָם׃ וַיַּרְא בַּצַּר
of-the-distress but-he-took-note (44) in-sin-of-them and-they-wasted-away

לָהֶם בְּשָׁמְעוֹ אֶת־ רִנָּתָם׃ וַיִּזְכֹּר לָהֶם
for-them and-he-remembered (45) cry-of-them *** when-to-hear-him of-them

בְּרִיתוֹ וַיִּנָּחֵם כְּרֹב חֲסָדָו׃ וַיִּתֵּן
and-he-made (46) loves-of-him as-greatness-of and-he-relented covenant-of-him

אוֹתָם לְרַחֲמִים לִפְנֵי כָּל־ שׁוֹבֵיהֶם׃ הוֹשִׁיעֵנוּ ׀
save-us! (47) ones-capturing-them all-of by to-pities them

יְהוָה אֱלֹהֵינוּ וְקַבְּצֵנוּ מִן־ הַגּוֹיִם לְהֹדוֹת לְשֵׁם
to-name-of to-give-thanks the-nations from and-gather-us! God-of-us Yahweh

קָדְשֶׁךָ לְהִשְׁתַּבֵּחַ בִּתְהִלָּתֶךָ׃ בָּרוּךְ־ יְהוָה אֱלֹהֵי
God-of Yahweh being-praised (48) in-praise-of-you to-glory holiness-of-you

יִשְׂרָאֵל מִן־ הָעוֹלָם ׀ וְעַד הָעוֹלָם וְאָמַר כָּל־
all-of and-let-him-say the-everlasting and-to the-everlasting from Israel

הָעָם אָמֵן הַלְלוּ־ יָהּ׃ הֹדוּ לַיהוָה כִּי־ טוֹב
good for to-Yahweh give-thanks! (107:1) Yahweh praise! amen the-people

כִּי לְעוֹלָם חַסְדּוֹ׃ יֹאמְרוּ גְּאוּלֵי יְהוָה
Yahweh ones-being-redeemed-of let-them-say (2) love-of-him to-forever for

אֲשֶׁר גְּאָלָם מִיַּד־ צָר׃ וּמֵאֲרָצוֹת קִבְּצָם
he-gathered-them and-from-lands (3) foe from-hand-of he-redeemed-them whom

מִמִּזְרָח וּמִמַּעֲרָב מִצָּפוֹן וּמִיָּם׃ תָּעוּ בַמִּדְבָּר
in-the-desert they-wandered (4) and-from-sea from-north and-from-west from-east

בִּישִׁימוֹן דָּרֶךְ עִיר מוֹשָׁב לֹא מָצָאוּ׃ רְעֵבִים גַּם־
and ones-hungry (5) they-found not settlement city-of way in-wasteland

צְמֵאִים נַפְשָׁם בָּהֶם תִּתְעַטָּף׃ וַיִּצְעֲקוּ
then-they-cried-out (6) she-ebbed-away in-them life-of-them ones-thirsty

אֶל־ יְהוָה בַּצַּר לָהֶם מִמְּצוּקוֹתֵיהֶם יַצִּילֵם׃
he-delivered-them from-distresses-of-them of-them in-the-trouble Yahweh to

וַיַּדְרִיכֵם בְּדֶרֶךְ יְשָׁרָה לָלֶכֶת אֶל־ עִיר מוֹשָׁב׃
settlement city-of to to-go straight by-way and-he-led-them (7)

יוֹדוּ לַיהוָה חַסְדּוֹ
unfailing-love-of-him to-Yahweh let-them-give-thanks (8)

וְנִפְלְאוֹתָיו לִבְנֵי אָדָם׃ כִּי־ הִשְׂבִּיעַ נֶפֶשׁ
throat he-satisfies for (9) man for-sons-of and-deeds-being-wonderful-of-him

שֹׁקֵקָה וְנֶפֶשׁ רְעֵבָה מִלֵּא־ טוֹב׃ יֹשְׁבֵי חֹשֶׁךְ
darkness ones-sitting-of (10) good he-fills hungry and-throat one-thirsting

[43]Many times he delivered them,
but they were bent on rebellion
and they wasted away in their sin.
[44]But he took note of their distress
when he heard their cry;
[45]for their sake he remembered his covenant
and out of his great love he relented.
[46]He caused them to be pitied
by all who held them captive.

[47]Save us, O LORD our God,
and gather us from the nations,
that we may give thanks to your holy name
and glory in your praise.

[48]Praise be to the LORD, the God of Israel,
from everlasting to everlasting.
Let all the people say, "Amen!"
Praise the LORD.

## BOOK V

*Psalms 107-150*

### Psalm 107

[1]Give thanks to the LORD, for he is good;
his love endures forever.
[2]Let the redeemed of the LORD say this—
those he redeemed from the hand of the foe,
[3]those he gathered from the lands,
from east and west, from north and south.[w]

[4]Some wandered in desert wastelands,
finding no way to a city where they could settle.
[5]They were hungry and thirsty,
and their lives ebbed away.
[6]Then they cried out to the LORD in their trouble,
and he delivered them from their distress.
[7]He led them by a straight way
to a city where they could settle.
[8]Let them give thanks to the LORD for his unfailing love
and his wonderful deeds for men,
[9]for he satisfies the thirsty
and fills the hungry with good things.

[10]Some sat in darkness and the

w3 Hebrew *north and the sea*

°45 ק חסדיו

וְצַלְמָוֶת אֲסִירֵי עֳנִי וּבַרְזֶל׃ כִּי־ הִמְרוּ
they-rebelled-against for (11) and-iron suffering prisoners-of and-deepest-gloom

אִמְרֵי־ אֵל וַעֲצַת עֶלְיוֹן נָאָצוּ׃ וַיַּכְנַע
so-he-subjected (12) they-despised Most-High and-counsel-of God words-of

בֶּעָמָל לִבָּם כָּשְׁלוּ וְאֵין עֹזֵר׃
helping and-there-was-no-one they-stumbled heart-of-them to-the-bitter-labor

וַיִּזְעֲקוּ אֶל־ יְהוָה בַּצַּר לָהֶם מִמְּצֻקוֹתֵיהֶם
from-distresses-of-them of-them in-the-trouble Yahweh to then-they-cried (13)

יוֹשִׁיעֵם׃ יוֹצִיאֵם מֵחֹשֶׁךְ וְצַלְמָוֶת
and-deepest-gloom from-darkness he-brought-out-them (14) he-saved-them

וּמוֹסְרוֹתֵיהֶם יְנַתֵּק׃ יוֹדוּ לַיהוָה
to-Yahweh let-them-give-thanks (15) he-broke-away and-chains-of-them

חַסְדּוֹ וְנִפְלְאוֹתָיו לִבְנֵי אָדָם׃
man for-sons-of and-deeds-being-wonderful-of-him unfailing-love-of-him

כִּי־ שִׁבַּר דַּלְתוֹת נְחֹשֶׁת וּבְרִיחֵי בַרְזֶל גִּדֵּעַ׃
he-cuts-through iron and-bars-of bronze gates-of he-breaks-down for (16)

אֱוִלִים מִדֶּרֶךְ פִּשְׁעָם וּמֵעֲוֹנֹתֵיהֶם
and-because-of-iniquities-of-them rebellion-of-them through-way-of fools (17)

יִתְעַנּוּ׃ כָּל־ אֹכֶל תְּתַעֵב נַפְשָׁם וַיַּגִּיעוּ
and-they-drew-near self-of-them she-loathed food all-of (18) they-were-afflicted

עַד־ שַׁעֲרֵי מָוֶת׃ וַיִּזְעֲקוּ אֶל־ יְהוָה בַּצַּר לָהֶם
of-them in-the-trouble Yahweh to then-they-cried (19) death gates-of to

מִמְּצֻקוֹתֵיהֶם יוֹשִׁיעֵם׃ יִשְׁלַח דְּבָרוֹ
word-of-him he-sent-forth (20) he-saved-them from-distresses-of-them

וְיִרְפָּאֵם וִימַלֵּט מִשְּׁחִיתוֹתָם׃ יוֹדוּ
let-them-give-thanks (21) from-graves-of-them and-he-rescued and-he-healed-them

לַיהוָה חַסְדּוֹ וְנִפְלְאוֹתָיו לִבְנֵי
for-sons-of and-deeds-being-wonders-of-him unfailing-love-of-him to-Yahweh

אָדָם׃ וְיִזְבְּחוּ זִבְחֵי תוֹדָה וִיסַפְּרוּ
and-let-them-tell thanksgiving offerings-of and-let-them-sacrifice (22) man

מַעֲשָׂיו בְּרִנָּה׃ יוֹרְדֵי הַיָּם בָּאֳנִיּוֹת
in-the-ships the-sea ones-going-down-of (23) with-song-of-joy works-of-him

עֹשֵׂי מְלָאכָה בְּמַיִם רַבִּים׃ הֵמָּה רָאוּ מַעֲשֵׂי יְהוָה
Yahweh works-of they-saw they (24) mighty-ones on-waters trade ones-doing-of

וְנִפְלְאוֹתָיו בִּמְצוּלָה׃ וַיֹּאמֶר וַיַּעֲמֵד
and-he-stirred-up for-he-spoke (25) in-deep and-deeds-being-wonderful-of-him

רוּחַ סְעָרָה וַתְּרוֹמֵם גַּלָּיו׃ יַעֲלוּ שָׁמַיִם
heavens they-mounted-up (26) waves-of-him and-she-lifted tempest wind

deepest gloom,
prisoners suffering in iron chains,
11 for they had rebelled against the words of God
and despised the counsel of the Most High.
12 So he subjected them to bitter labor;
they stumbled, and there was no one to help.
13 Then they cried to the LORD in their trouble,
and he saved them from their distress.
14 He brought them out of darkness and the deepest gloom
and broke away their chains.
15 Let them give thanks to the LORD for his unfailing love
and his wonderful deeds for men,
16 for he breaks down gates of bronze
and cuts through bars of iron.

17 Some became fools through their rebellious ways
and suffered affliction because of their iniquities.
18 They loathed all food
and drew near the gates of death.
19 Then they cried to the LORD in their trouble,
and he saved them from their distress.
20 He sent forth his word and healed them;
he rescued them from the grave.
21 Let them give thanks to the LORD for his unfailing love
and his wonderful deeds for men.
22 Let them sacrifice thank offerings
and tell of his works with songs of joy.

23 Others went out on the sea in ships;
they were merchants on the mighty waters.
24 They saw the works of the LORD,
his wonderful deeds in the deep.
25 For he spoke and stirred up a tempest
that lifted high the waves.
26 They mounted up to the

יֵרְדוּ תְהוֹמוֹת נַפְשָׁם בְּרָעָה תִתְמוֹגָג׃ יָחוֹגּוּ

they-reeled (27) she-melted-away in-peril courage-of-them depths they-went-down

וְיָנוּעוּ כַּשִּׁכּוֹר וְכָל־ חָכְמָתָם תִּתְבַּלָּע׃

she-ended wit-of-them and-all-of like-the-drunkard and-they-staggered

וַיִּצְעֲקוּ אֶל־ יְהוָה בַּצַּר לָהֶם וּמִמְּצוּקֹתֵיהֶם

and-from-distresses-of-them of-them in-the-trouble Yahweh to then-they-cried (28)

יוֹצִיאֵם׃ יָקֵם סְעָרָה לִדְמָמָה וַיֶּחֱשׁוּ

and-they-were-hushed to-whisper storm he-stilled (29) he-brought-out-them

גַּלֵּיהֶם׃ וַיִּשְׂמְחוּ כִי־ יִשְׁתֹּקוּ וַיַּנְחֵם

and-he-guided-them they-grew-calm when and-they-were-glad (30) waves-of-them

אֶל־ מְחוֹז חֶפְצָם׃ יוֹדוּ לַיהוָה

to-Yahweh let-them-give-thanks (31) desire-of-them haven-of to

חַסְדּוֹ וְנִפְלְאוֹתָיו לִבְנֵי אָדָם׃

man for-sons-of and-deeds-being-wonderful-of-him unfailing-love-of-him

וִירֹמְמוּהוּ בִּקְהַל־ עָם וּבְמוֹשַׁב זְקֵנִים

elders and-in-council-of people in-assembly-of and-let-them-exalt-him (32)

יְהַלְלוּהוּ׃ יָשֵׂם נְהָרוֹת לְמִדְבָּר וּמֹצָאֵי מַיִם

waters and-springs-of into-desert rivers he-turned (33) let-them-praise-him

לְצִמָּאוֹן׃ אֶרֶץ פְּרִי לִמְלֵחָה מֵרָעַת

because-of-wickedness-of into-salt-waste fruit land-of (34) into-thirsty-ground

יֹשְׁבֵי בָהּ׃ יָשֵׂם מִדְבָּר לַאֲגַם־ מַיִם וְאֶרֶץ

and-ground-of waters into-pool-of desert he-turned (35) in-her ones-living-of

צִיָּה לְמֹצָאֵי מָיִם׃ וַיּוֹשֶׁב שָׁם רְעֵבִים

hungry-ones there and-he-brought-to-live (36) waters into-springs-of parched

וַיְכוֹנְנוּ עִיר מוֹשָׁב׃ וַיִּזְרְעוּ שָׂדוֹת וַיִּטְּעוּ

and-they-planted fields and-they-sowed (37) settlement city-of and-they-founded

כְרָמִים וַיַּעֲשׂוּ פְּרִי תְבוּאָה׃ וַיְבָרְכֵם

and-he-blessed-them (38) harvest fruit-of and-they-yielded vineyards

וַיִּרְבּוּ מְאֹד וּבְהֶמְתָּם לֹא יַמְעִיט׃

he-let-diminish not and-herd-of-them greatly and-they-increased

וַיִּמְעֲטוּ וַיָּשֹׁחוּ מֵעֹצֶר רָעָה וְיָגוֹן׃

and-sorrow calamity by-oppression and-they-were-humbled then-they-decreased (39)

שֹׁפֵךְ בּוּז עַל־ נְדִיבִים וַיַּתְעֵם בְּתֹהוּ

in-waste and-he-made-wander-them nobles on contempt one-pouring (40)

לֹא־ דָרֶךְ׃ וַיְשַׂגֵּב אֶבְיוֹן מֵעוֹנִי וַיָּשֶׂם

and-he-increased from-affliction needy but-he-lifted (41) track without

כַּצֹּאן מִשְׁפָּחוֹת׃ יִרְאוּ יְשָׁרִים וְיִשְׂמָחוּ וְכָל־

but-all-of and-they-rejoice upright-ones they-see (42) families like-the-flock

heavens and went down
to the depths;
in their peril their courage
melted away.
27 They reeled and staggered like
drunken men;
they were at their wits' end.
28 Then they cried out to the
LORD in their trouble,
and he brought them out of
their distress.
29 He stilled the storm to a
whisper;
the waves of the sea were
hushed.
30 They were glad when it grew
calm,
and he guided them to their
desired haven.
31 Let them give thanks to the
LORD for his unfailing
love
and his wonderful deeds for
men.
32 Let them exalt him in the
assembly of the people
and praise him in the
council of the elders.

33 He turned rivers into a desert,
flowing springs into thirsty
ground,
34 and fruitful land into a salt
waste,
because of the wickedness of
those who lived there.
35 He turned the desert into pools
of water
and the parched ground into
flowing springs;
36 there he brought the hungry to
live,
and they founded a city
where they could settle.
37 They sowed fields and planted
vineyards
that yielded a fruitful
harvest;
38 he blessed them, and their
numbers greatly
increased,
and he did not let their
herds diminish.

39 Then their numbers decreased,
and they were humbled
by oppression, calamity and
sorrow;
40 he who pours contempt on
nobles
made them wander in a
trackless waste.
41 But he lifted the needy out of
their affliction
and increased their families
like flocks.
42 The upright see and rejoice,

עֹ֫וְלָה קָ֣פְצָה פִּֽיהָ׃ מִי־ חָכָם וְיִשְׁמָר־ אֵ֑לֶּה

these then-let-him-heed wise whoever (43) mouth-of-her she-shuts wicked

וְ֝יִתְבּ֣וֹנְנ֗וּ חַֽסְדֵ֥י יְהוָֽה׃ שִׁ֖יר מִזְמ֣וֹר לְדָוִֽד׃

of-David psalm song *(108:1) Yahweh great-loves-of and-let-them-consider

נָכ֣וֹן לִבִּ֣י אֱלֹהִ֑ים אָשִׁ֥ירָה וַ֝אֲזַמְּרָ֗ה אַף־

even and-I-will-make-music I-will-sing God heart-of-me he-is-steadfast (2)

כְּבוֹדִֽי׃ ע֭וּרָה הַנֵּ֣בֶל וְכִנּ֑וֹר אָעִ֥ירָה שָּֽׁחַר׃

dawn I-will-awaken and-lyre the-harp awake! (3) soul-of-me

אוֹדְךָ֖ בָעַמִּ֥ים ׀ יְהוָ֑ה וַ֝אֲזַמֶּרְךָ֗

and-I-will-sing-of-you Yahweh among-the-nations I-will-praise-you (4)

בַּל־אֻמִּֽים׃ כִּֽי־ גָד֣וֹל מֵֽעַל־ שָׁמַ֣יִם חַסְדֶּ֑ךָ וְֽעַד־שְׁחָקִ֥ים

skies and-to love-of-you heavens than-above greater for (5) †among-the-peoples

אֲמִתֶּֽךָ׃ ר֣וּמָה עַל־ שָׁמַ֣יִם אֱלֹהִ֑ים וְעַ֖ל כָּל־ הָאָ֣רֶץ

the-earth all-of and-over God heavens above be-exalted! (6) faithfulness-of-you

כְּבוֹדֶֽךָ׃ לְ֭מַעַן יֵחָלְצ֣וּן יְדִידֶ֑יךָ הוֹשִׁ֖יעָה

save! loved-ones-of-you they-may-be-delivered so-that (7) glory-of-you

יְמִֽינְךָ֣ וַעֲנֵֽנִי׃ אֱלֹהִ֤ים ׀ דִּבֶּ֥ר בְּקָדְשׁ֗וֹ

from-sanctuary-of-him he-spoke God (8) and-help-me! right-hand-of-you

אֶעְלֹ֗זָה אֲחַלְּקָ֥ה שְׁכֶ֑ם וְעֵ֖מֶק סֻכּ֣וֹת אֲמַדֵּֽד׃

I-will-measure Succoth and-Valley-of Shechem I-will-parcel-out I-will-triumph

לִ֤י גִלְעָ֨ד ׀ לִ֬י מְנַשֶּׁ֗ה וְ֭אֶפְרַיִם מָע֣וֹז רֹאשִׁ֑י יְ֝הוּדָ֗ה

Judah head-of-me helmet-of and-Ephraim Manasseh to-me Gilead to-me (9)

מְחֹקְקִֽי׃ מוֹאָ֤ב ׀ סִ֬יר רַחְצִ֗י עַל־אֱ֭דוֹם אַשְׁלִ֣יךְ

I-toss Edom upon washing-of-me basin-of Moab (10) one-being-scepter-of-me

נַעֲלִ֑י עֲלֵֽי־ פְ֝לֶ֗שֶׁת אֶתְרוֹעָֽע׃ מִ֣י יֹ֭בִלֵנִי

he-will-bring-me who? (11) I-shout-in-triumph Philistia over sandal-of-me

עִ֣יר מִבְצָ֑ר מִ֝י נָחַ֗נִי עַד־ אֱדֽוֹם׃ הֲלֹֽא־אֱלֹהִ֥ים

God not? (12) Edom to he-will-lead-me who? fortification city-of

זְנַחְתָּ֑נוּ וְֽלֹא־ תֵצֵ֥א אֱ֝לֹהִ֗ים בְּצִבְאֹתֵֽינוּ׃ הָֽבָה־ לָּ֣נוּ

to-us give! (13) with-armies-of-us God you-go-out and-not you-rejected-us

עֶזְרָ֣ת מִצָּ֑ר וְ֝שָׁ֗וְא תְּשׁוּעַ֥ת אָדָֽם׃ בֵּאלֹהִ֥ים נַעֲשֶׂה־

we-will-gain with-God (14) man help-of for-worthless against-enemy aid

חָ֑יִל וְ֝ה֗וּא יָב֥וּס צָרֵֽינוּ׃ לַמְנַצֵּ֥חַ

for-the-one-directing (109:1) enemies-of-us he-will-trample and-he victory

לְדָוִ֥ד מִזְמ֑וֹר אֱלֹהֵ֥י תְ֝הִלָּתִ֗י אַֽל־ תֶּחֱרַֽשׁ׃ כִּ֤י פִ֪י

mouth-of for (2) you-remain-silent not praise-of-me God-of psalm of-David

רָשָׁ֡ע וּֽפִי־ מִ֭רְמָה עָלַ֣י פָּתָ֑חוּ דִּבְּר֥וּ אִ֝תִּ֗י

against-me they-spoke they-opened against-me deceit and-mouth-of wicked

---

but all the wicked shut their
  mouths.

43 Whoever is wise, let him heed
  these things
and consider the great love
  of the LORD.

### Psalm 108

A song. A psalm of David.

1 My heart is steadfast, O God;
  I will sing and make music
    with all my soul.
2 Awake, harp and lyre!
  I will awaken the dawn.
3 I will praise you, O LORD,
    among the nations;
  I will sing of you among the
    peoples.
4 For great is your love, higher
    than the heavens;
  your faithfulness reaches to
    the skies.
5 Be exalted, O God, above the
    heavens,
  and let your glory be over
    all the earth.

6 Save us and help us with your
    right hand,
  that those you love may be
    delivered.
7 God has spoken from his
    sanctuary:
  "In triumph I will parcel out
    Shechem
  and measure off the Valley
    of Succoth.
8 Gilead is mine, Manasseh is
    mine;
  Ephraim is my helmet,
  Judah my scepter.
9 Moab is my washbasin,
  upon Edom I toss my
    sandal;
  over Philistia I shout in
    triumph."

10 Who will bring me to the
    fortified city?
  Who will lead me to Edom?
11 Is it not you, O God, you who
    have rejected us
  and no longer go out with
    our armies?
12 Give us aid against the enemy,
  for the help of man is
    worthless.
13 With God we will gain the
    victory,
  and he will trample down
    our enemies.

### Psalm 109

For the director of music. Of David. A psalm.

1 O God, whom I praise,
  do not remain silent,
2 for wicked and deceitful men
  have opened their mouths
    against me;
  they have spoken against

*1 See the note on page 349.

†4 Most mss read these two words as one (בַּלְ׳).

לְשׁוֹן שָׁקֶר׃ וְדִבְרֵי שִׂנְאָה סְבָבוּנִי וַיִּלָּחֲמוּנִי
and-they-attack-me they-surround-me hatred and-words-of (3) lie tongue-of

חִנָּם׃ תַּחַת־ אַהֲבָתִי יִשְׂטְנוּנִי וַאֲנִי תְפִלָּה׃
prayer but-I they-accuse-me friendship-of-me in-return-for (4) without-cause

וַיָּשִׂימוּ עָלַי רָעָה תַּחַת טוֹבָה וְשִׂנְאָה תַּחַת אַהֲבָתִי׃
friendship-of-me for and-hatred good for evil to-me and-they-repay (5)

הַפְקֵד עָלָיו רָשָׁע וְשָׂטָן יַעֲמֹד עַל־ יְמִינוֹ׃
right-hand-of-him at let-him-stand and-accuser evil against-him appoint! (6)

בְּהִשָּׁפְטוֹ יֵצֵא רָשָׁע וּתְפִלָּתוֹ תִּהְיֶה
may-she-be and-prayer-of-him guilty let-him-be-found when-to-be-tried-him (7)

לַחֲטָאָה׃ יִהְיוּ־ יָמָיו מְעַטִּים פְּקֻדָּתוֹ
leadership-of-him few-ones days-of-him may-they-be (8) as-condemnation

יִקַּח אַחֵר׃ יִהְיוּ־ בָנָיו יְתוֹמִים
fatherless-ones children-of-him may-they-be (9) another may-he-take

וְאִשְׁתּוֹ אַלְמָנָה׃ וְנוֹעַ יָנוּעוּ בָנָיו
children-of-him may-they-wander and-to-wander (10) widow and-wife-of-him

וְשִׁאֵלוּ וְדָרְשׁוּ מֵחָרְבוֹתֵיהֶם׃ יְנַקֵּשׁ
may-he-seize (11) from-ruins-of-them and-may-they-be-sought and-may-they-beg

נוֹשֶׁה לְכָל־ אֲשֶׁר־ לוֹ וְיָבֹזּוּ זָרִים
ones-being-strangers and-may-they-plunder to-him that to-all one-being-creditor

יְגִיעוֹ׃ אַל־ יְהִי־ לוֹ מֹשֵׁךְ חָסֶד וְאַל־
and-not kindness one-extending to-him may-he-be not (12) labor-of-him

יְהִי חוֹנֵן לִיתוֹמָיו׃ יְהִי־
may-he-be (13) on-fatherless-ones-of-him one-taking-pity may-he-be

אַחֲרִיתוֹ לְהַכְרִית בְּדוֹר אַחֵר יִמַּח
may-he-be-blotted-out next from-generation to-cut-off descendant-of-him

שְׁמָם׃ יִזָּכֵר ׀ עֲוֺן אֲבֹתָיו אֶל־
before fathers-of-him iniquity-of may-he-be-remembered (14) name-of-them

יְהוָה וְחַטַּאת אִמּוֹ אַל־ תִּמָּח׃ יִהְיוּ
may-they-be (15) may-she-be-blotted-out never mother-of-him and-sin-of Yahweh

נֶגֶד־ יְהוָה תָּמִיד וְיַכְרֵת מֵאֶרֶץ זִכְרָם׃
memory-of-them from-earth that-he-may-cut-off always Yahweh before

יַעַן אֲשֶׁר ׀ לֹא זָכַר עֲשׂוֹת חָסֶד וַיִּרְדֹּף אִישׁ־ עָנִי
poor man but-he-hounded kindness to-do he-thought never that for (16)

וְאֶבְיוֹן וְנִכְאֵה לֵבָב לְמוֹתֵת׃ וַיֶּאֱהַב קְלָלָה
curse and-he-loved (17) to-kill heart and-one-being-broken-of and-needy

וַתְּבוֹאֵהוּ וְלֹא־ חָפֵץ בִּבְרָכָה וַתִּרְחַק
so-may-she-be-far in-blessing he-found-pleasure and-not so-may-she-come-on-him

me with lying tongues.
3 With words of hatred they surround me;
they attack me without cause.
4 In return for my friendship they accuse me,
but I am a man of prayer.
5 They repay me evil for good,
and hatred for my friendship.

6 Appoint[x] an evil man[y] to oppose him;
let an accuser[z] stand at his right hand.
7 When he is tried, let him be found guilty,
and may his prayers condemn him.
8 May his days be few;
may another take his place of leadership.
9 May his children be fatherless
and his wife a widow.
10 May his children be wandering beggars;
may they be driven[a] from their ruined homes.
11 May a creditor seize all he has;
may strangers plunder the fruits of his labor.
12 May no one extend kindness to him
or take pity on his fatherless children.
13 May his descendants be cut off,
their names blotted out from the next generation.
14 May the iniquity of his fathers be remembered before the LORD;
may the sin of his mother never be blotted out.
15 May their sins always remain before the LORD,
that he may cut off the memory of them from the earth.

16 For he never thought of doing a kindness,
but hounded to death the poor
and the needy and the brokenhearted.
17 He loved to pronounce a curse—
may it[b] come on him;
he found no pleasure in blessing—
may it be[c] far from him.

x6 Or *They say:* "*Appoint* (with quotation marks at the end of verse 19)
y6 Or *the Evil One*
z6 Or *let Satan*
a10 Septuagint; Hebrew *sought*
b17 Or *curse, / and it has*
c17 Or *blessing, / and it is*

מִמֶּנּוּ׃ וַיִּלְבַּשׁ קְלָלָה כְּמַדּוֹ וַתָּבֹא
and-she-entered as-garment-of-him cursing and-he-wore (18) from-him

כַמַּיִם בְּקִרְבּוֹ וְכַשֶּׁמֶן בְּעַצְמוֹתָיו׃
into-bones-of-him and-like-the-oil into-body-of-him as-the-waters

תְּהִי־ לוֹ כְּבֶגֶד יַעְטֶה וּלְמֵזַח תָּמִיד
forever and-like-belt he-wraps like-cloak about-him may-she-be (19)

יַחְגְּרֶהָ׃ זֹאת פְּעֻלַּת שֹׂטְנַי מֵאֵת יְהוָה
Yahweh from-with ones-accusing-me payment-of this (20) he-ties-her

וְהַדֹּבְרִים רָע עַל־ נַפְשִׁי׃ וְאַתָּה׀ יְהוִה אֲדֹנָי
Lord Yahweh but-you (21) self-of-me against evil and-the-ones-speaking

עֲשֵׂה־ אִתִּי לְמַעַן שְׁמֶךָ כִּי־ טוֹב חַסְדְּךָ
love-of-you goodness-of out-of name-of-you for-sake-of with-me deal!

הַצִּילֵנִי׃ כִּי־ עָנִי וְאֶבְיוֹן אָנֹכִי וְלִבִּי חָלַל
he-is-wounded and-heart-of-me I and-needy poor for (22) deliver-me!

בְּקִרְבִּי׃ כְּצֵל־ כִּנְטוֹתוֹ נֶהֱלָכְתִּי
I-fade-away when-to-stretch-him like-shadow-of (23) at-within-me

נִנְעַרְתִּי כָּאַרְבֶּה׃ בִּרְכַּי כָּשְׁלוּ מִצּוֹם
from-fasting they-give-way knees-of-me (24) like-the-locust I-am-shaken-off

וּבְשָׂרִי כָּחַשׁ מִשָּׁמֶן׃ וַאֲנִי׀ הָיִיתִי חֶרְפָּה לָהֶם יִרְאוּנִי
they-see-me to-them scorn I-am and-I (25) from-fat he-is-thin and-body-of-me

יְנִיעוּן רֹאשָׁם׃ עָזְרֵנִי יְהוָה אֱלֹהָי הוֹשִׁיעֵנִי
save-me! God-of-me Yahweh help-me! (26) head-of-them they-shake

כְחַסְדֶּךָ׃ וְיֵדְעוּ כִּי־ יָדְךָ זֹּאת אַתָּה יְהוָה
Yahweh you this hand-of-you that and-let-them-know (27) as-love-of-you

עָשִׂיתָהּ׃ יְקַלְלוּ־ הֵמָּה וְאַתָּה תְבָרֵךְ קָמוּ׀
they-may-attack you-will-bless but-you they they-may-curse (28) you-did-her

וַיֵּבֹשׁוּ וְעַבְדְּךָ יִשְׂמָח׃
he-will-rejoice and-servant-of-you but-they-will-be-shamed

יִלְבְּשׁוּ שׂוֹטְנַי כְּלִמָּה וְיַעֲטוּ
and-they-will-be-wrapped disgrace ones-accusing-me they-will-be-clothed (29)

כַמְעִיל בָּשְׁתָּם׃ אוֹדֶה יְהוָה מְאֹד בְּפִי
with-mouth-of-me greatly Yahweh I-will-extol (30) shame-of-them as-the-cloak

וּבְתוֹךְ רַבִּים אֲהַלְלֶנּוּ׃ כִּי־ יַעֲמֹד
he-stands for (31) I-will-praise-him great-throngs and-in-midst-of

לִימִין אֶבְיוֹן לְהוֹשִׁיעַ מִשֹּׁפְטֵי נַפְשׁוֹ׃
life-of-him from-ones-condemning-of to-save needy at-right-hand-of

לְדָוִד מִזְמוֹר נְאֻם יְהוָה׀ לַאדֹנִי שֵׁב לִימִינִי
at-right-hand-of-me sit! to-Lord-of-me Yahweh saying-of psalm of-David (110:1)

18 He wore cursing as his
garment;
it entered into his body like
water,
into his bones like oil.
19 May it be like a cloak wrapped
about him,
like a belt tied forever
around him.
20 May this be the LORD's
payment to my accusers,
to those who speak evil of
me.
21 But you, O Sovereign LORD,
deal well with me for your
name's sake;
out of the goodness of your
love, deliver me.
22 For I am poor and needy,
and my heart is wounded
within me.
23 I fade away like an evening
shadow;
I am shaken off like a locust.
24 My knees give way from
fasting;
my body is thin and gaunt.
25 I am an object of scorn to my
accusers;
when they see me, they
shake their heads.

26 Help me, O LORD my God;
save me in accordance with
your love.
27 Let them know that it is your
hand,
that you, O LORD, have done
it.
28 They may curse, but you will
bless;
when they attack they will
be put to shame,
but your servant will rejoice.
29 My accusers will be clothed
with disgrace
and wrapped in shame as in
a cloak.

30 With my mouth I will greatly
extol the LORD;
in the great throng I will
praise him.
31 For he stands at the right
hand of the needy one,
to save his life from those
who condemn him.

**Psalm 110**

Of David. A psalm.

1 The LORD says to my Lord:
"Sit at my right hand

עַד־ אָשִׁית אֹיְבֶיךָ הֲדֹם לְרַגְלֶיךָ׃
for-feet-of-you footstool ones-being-enemies-of-you I-make until

מַטֵּה־ עֻזְּךָ יִשְׁלַח יְהוָה מִצִּיּוֹן רְדֵה בְּקֶרֶב
in-midst-of rule! from-Zion Yahweh he-will-extend might-of-you scepter-of (2)

אֹיְבֶיךָ׃ עַמְּךָ נְדָבֹת בְּיוֹם חֵילֶךָ
battle-of-you on-day-of willing-ones troop-of-you (3) ones-being-enemies-of-you

בְּהַדְרֵי־ קֹדֶשׁ מֵרֶחֶם מִשְׁחָר לְךָ טַל יַלְדֻתֶיךָ׃
youths-of-you dew-of to-you dawn from-womb-of holiness in-majesties-of

נִשְׁבַּע יְהוָה׀ וְלֹא יִנָּחֵם אַתָּה־ כֹהֵן לְעוֹלָם עַל־
in to-forever priest you he-will-change-mind and-not Yahweh he-swore (4)

דִּבְרָתִי מַלְכִּי־ צֶדֶק׃ אֲדֹנָי עַל־ יְמִינְךָ מָחַץ בְּיוֹם־
on-day-of he-will-crush right-hand-of-you at Lord (5) Zedek Melchi order-of

אַפּוֹ מְלָכִים׃ יָדִין בַּגּוֹיִם מָלֵא גְוִיּוֹת
dead-ones he-will-heap-up to-the-nations he-will-judge (6) kings wrath-of-him

מָחַץ רֹאשׁ עַל־אֶרֶץ רַבָּה׃ מִנַּחַל בַּדֶּרֶךְ יִשְׁתֶּה
he-will-drink beside-the-way from-brook (7) whole earth of ruler he-will-crush

עַל־ כֵּן יָרִים רֹאשׁ׃ הַלְלוּ יָהּ׀ אוֹדֶה
I-will-extol Yahweh praise! (111:1) head he-will-lift-up this because-of

יְהוָה בְּכָל־ לֵבָב בְּסוֹד יְשָׁרִים וְעֵדָה׃ גְּדֹלִים
great-ones (2) and-assembly upright-ones in-council-of heart with-all-of Yahweh

מַעֲשֵׂי יְהוָה דְּרוּשִׁים לְכָל־ חֶפְצֵיהֶם׃ הוֹד־
glorious (3) delighters-of-them by-all-of ones-being-pondered Yahweh works-of

וְהָדָר פָּעֳלוֹ וְצִדְקָתוֹ עֹמֶדֶת לָעַד׃
to-forever one-enduring and-righteousness-of-him deed-of-him and-majestic

זֵכֶר עָשָׂה לְנִפְלְאֹתָיו חַנּוּן
gracious for-deeds-being-wonders-of-him he-caused remembrance (4)

וְרַחוּם יְהוָה׃ טֶרֶף נָתַן לִירֵאָיו יִזְכֹּר
he-remembers for-ones-fearing-him he-provides food (5) Yahweh and-compassionate

לְעוֹלָם בְּרִיתוֹ׃ כֹּחַ מַעֲשָׂיו הִגִּיד לְעַמּוֹ
to-people-of-him he-showed works-of-him power-of (6) covenant-of-him to-forever

לָתֵת לָהֶם נַחֲלַת גּוֹיִם׃ מַעֲשֵׂי יָדָיו אֱמֶת וּמִשְׁפָּט׀
and-just faithful hands-of-him works-of (7) nations land-of to-them to-give

נֶאֱמָנִים כָּל־ פִּקּוּדָיו׃ סְמוּכִים
ones-being-steadfast (8) precepts-of-him all-of ones-being-trustworthy

לָעַד לְעוֹלָם עֲשׂוּיִם בֶּאֱמֶת וְיָשָׁר׃
and-uprightness in-faithfulness ones-being-done to-forever for-ever

פְּדוּת׀ שָׁלַח לְעַמּוֹ צִוָּה־ לְעוֹלָם
to-forever he-ordained for-people-of-him he-provided redemption (9)

until I make your enemies
a footstool for your feet."

2 The LORD will extend your
mighty scepter from Zion;
you will rule in the midst of
your enemies.
3 Your troops will be willing
on your day of battle.
Arrayed in holy majesty,
from the womb of the dawn
you will receive the dew of
your youth.[d]

4 The LORD has sworn
and will not change his
mind:
"You are a priest forever,
in the order of
Melchizedek."

5 The Lord is at your right hand;
he will crush kings on the
day of his wrath.
6 He will judge the nations,
heaping up the dead
and crushing the rulers of
the whole earth.
7 He will drink from a brook
beside the way[e];
therefore he will lift up his
head.

**Psalm 111**[f]

1 Praise the LORD.[g]

I will extol the LORD with all
my heart
in the council of the upright
and in the assembly.

2 Great are the works of the
LORD;
they are pondered by all
who delight in them.
3 Glorious and majestic are his
deeds,
and his righteousness
endures forever.
4 He has caused his wonders to
be remembered;
the LORD is gracious and
compassionate.
5 He provides food for those
who fear him;
he remembers his covenant
forever.
6 He has shown his people the
power of his works,
giving them the lands of
other nations.
7 The works of his hands are
faithful and just;
all his precepts are
trustworthy.
8 They are steadfast for ever and
ever,
done in faithfulness and
uprightness.
9 He provided redemption for
his people;
he ordained his covenant
forever—

[d] 3 Or / *your young men will come to you like the dew*
[e] 7 Or / *The One who grants succession will set him in authority*
[f] This psalm is an acrostic poem, the lines of which begin with the successive letters of the Hebrew alphabet.
[g] 1 Hebrew *Hallelu Yah*

בריתו קדוש ונורא שמו׃ ראשית חכמה׀
wisdom beginning-of (10) name-of-him and-being-awesome holy covenant-of-him

יראת יהוה שכל טוב לכל־ עשיהם תהלתו
praise-of-him ones-following-them to-all-of good understanding Yahweh fear-of

עמדת לעד׃ הללו יה׀ אשרי־ איש ירא
he-fears man blessednesses-of Yahweh praise! (112:1) to-eternity one-enduring

את־ יהוה במצותיו חפץ מאד׃ גבור בארץ
in-the-land mighty (2) greatly he-delights in-commands-of-him Yahweh ***

יהיה זרעו דור ישרים יברך׃
he-will-be-blessed upright-ones generation-of child-of-him he-will-be

הון־ ועשר בביתו וצדקתו עמדת
one-enduring and-righteousness-of-him in-house-of-him and-richness wealth (3)

לעד׃ זרח בחשך אור לישרים חנון
gracious for-the-upright-ones light in-the-darkness he-dawns (4) to-forever

ורחום וצדיק׃ טוב־ איש חונן ומלוה
and-lending being-generous man good-of (5) and-righteous and-compassionate

יכלכל דבריו במשפט׃ כי־ לעולם לא־
not to-forever surely (6) with-justice affairs-of-him he-conducts

ימוט לזכר עולם יהיה צדיק׃
righteous he-will-be forever for-remembrance-of he-will-be-shaken

משמועה רעה לא יירא נכון לבו בטח
one-trusting heart-of-him one-being-steadfast he-will-fear not bad of-news (7)

ביהוה׃ סמוך לבו לא יירא עד אשר־
when end he-will-fear not heart-of-him one-being-secure (8) in-Yahweh

יראה בצריו׃ פזר נתן לאביונים
to-the-poor-ones he-gave he-scattered (9) on-foes-of-him he-will-look

צדקתו עמדת לעד קרנו תרום
she-will-be-lifted horn-of-him to-forever one-enduring righteousness-of-him

בכבוד׃ רשע יראה׀ וכעס שניו
teeth-of-him and-he-will-be-vexed he-will-see wicked (10) in-honor

יחרק ונמס תאות רשעים תאבד׃
she-comes-to-nothing wicked-ones longing-of and-he-will-waste-away he-will-gnash

הללו יה׀ הללו עבדי יהוה הללו את־ שם יהוה׃
Yahweh name-of *** praise! Yahweh servants-of praise! Yahweh praise! (113:1)

יהי שם יהוה מברך מעתה ועד־ עולם׃
forevermore and-to from-now one-being-praised Yahweh name-of let-him-be (2)

ממזרח־ שמש עד־ מבואו מהלל שם יהוה׃
Yahweh name-of being-praised setting-of-him to sun from-rising-of (3)

holy and awesome is his
name.
10 The fear of the LORD is the
beginning of wisdom;
all who follow his precepts
have good understanding.
To him belongs eternal
praise.

### Psalm 112[h]

1 Praise the LORD.[i]

Blessed is the man who fears
the LORD,
who finds great delight in
his commands.
2 His children will be mighty in
the land;
each generation of the
upright will be blessed.
3 Wealth and riches are in his
house,
and his righteousness
endures forever.
4 Even in darkness light dawns
for the upright,
for the gracious and
compassionate and
righteous man.[j]
5 Good will come to him who is
generous and lends freely,
who conducts his affairs
with justice.
6 Surely he will never be
shaken;
a righteous man will be
remembered forever.
7 He will have no fear of bad
news;
his heart is steadfast,
trusting in the LORD.
8 His heart is secure, he will
have no fear;
in the end he will look in
triumph on his foes.
9 He has scattered abroad his
gifts to the poor,
his righteousness endures
forever;
his horn[k] will be lifted high
in honor.
10 The wicked man will see and
be vexed,
he will gnash his teeth and
waste away;
the longings of the wicked
will come to nothing.

### Psalm 113

1 Praise the LORD.[l]

Praise, O servants of the LORD,
praise the name of the LORD.
2 Let the name of the LORD be
praised,
both now and forevermore.
3 From the rising of the sun to
the place where it sets
the name of the LORD is to
be praised.

[h] This psalm is an acrostic poem, the lines of which begin with the successive letters of the Hebrew alphabet.
[i] 1 Hebrew *Hallelu Yah*
[j] 4 Or / *for* ⌊*the LORD*⌋ *is gracious and compassionate and righteous*
[k] 9 *Horn* here symbolizes dignity.
[l] 1 Hebrew *Hallelu Yah*; also in verse 9

רָם עַל־כָּל־גּוֹיִם ׀ יְהוָה עַל הַשָּׁמַיִם כְּבוֹדוֹ׃
glory-of-him the-heavens above Yahweh nations all-of over he-is-exalted (4)

מִי כַּיהוָה אֱלֹהֵינוּ הַמַּגְבִּיהִי לָשָׁבֶת׃
to-sit-enthroned the-one-being-on-high God-of-us like-Yahweh who? (5)

הַמַּשְׁפִּילִי לִרְאוֹת בַּשָּׁמַיִם וּבָאָרֶץ׃
and-on-the-earth on-the-heavens to-look the-one-stooping-down (6)

מְקִימִי מֵעָפָר דָּל מֵאַשְׁפֹּת יָרִים אֶבְיוֹן׃ לְהוֹשִׁיבִי
to-seat (8) needy he-lifts from-ash-heaps poor from-dust one-raising (7)

עִם־נְדִיבִים עִם נְדִיבֵי עַמּוֹ׃ מוֹשִׁיבִי ׀
one-settling (9) people-of-him princes-of with princes with

עֲקֶרֶת הַבַּיִת אֵם־הַבָּנִים שְׂמֵחָה הַלְלוּ־יָהּ׃
Yahweh praise! happy the-children mother-of the-home barren-woman-of

בְּצֵאת יִשְׂרָאֵל מִמִּצְרָיִם בֵּית יַעֲקֹב מֵעַם
from-people Jacob house-of from-Egypt Israel when-to-come-out (114:1)

לֹעֵז׃ הָיְתָה יְהוּדָה לְקָדְשׁוֹ יִשְׂרָאֵל
Israel as-sanctuary-of-him Judah she-became (2) one-having-foreign-tongue

מַמְשְׁלוֹתָיו׃ הַיָּם רָאָה וַיָּנֹס הַיַּרְדֵּן יִסֹּב
he-turned the-Jordan and-he-fled he-looked the-sea (3) dominions-of-him

לְאָחוֹר׃ הֶהָרִים רָקְדוּ כְאֵילִים גְּבָעוֹת כִּבְנֵי־צֹאן׃
flock like-lambs-of hills like-rams they-skipped the-mountains (4) to-back

מַה־לְּךָ הַיָּם כִּי תָנוּס הַיַּרְדֵּן תִּסֹּב לְאָחוֹר׃
to-back you-turned the-Jordan you-fled that the-sea to-you what? (5)

הֶהָרִים תִּרְקְדוּ כְאֵילִים גְּבָעוֹת כִּבְנֵי־צֹאן׃
flock like-lambs-of hills like-rams you-skipped the-mountains (6)

מִלִּפְנֵי אָדוֹן חוּלִי אָרֶץ מִלִּפְנֵי אֱלוֹהַּ יַעֲקֹב׃
Jacob God-of at-presences-of earth tremble! Lord at-presences-of (7)

הַהֹפְכִי הַצּוּר אֲגַם־מָיִם חַלָּמִישׁ לְמַעְיְנוֹ־מָיִם׃
waters into-spring-of hard-rock waters pool-of the-rock the-one-turning (8)

לֹא לָנוּ יְהוָה לֹא לָנוּ כִּי־לְשִׁמְךָ תֵּן כָּבוֹד עַל־
because-of glory give! to-name-of-you but to-us not Yahweh to-us not (115:1)

חַסְדְּךָ עַל־אֲמִתֶּךָ׃ לָמָּה יֹאמְרוּ הַגּוֹיִם
the-nations they-say why? (2) faithfulness-of-you because-of love-of-you

אַיֵּה־נָא אֱלֹהֵיהֶם׃ וֵאלֹהֵינוּ בַשָּׁמָיִם כֹּל אֲשֶׁר־חָפֵץ
he-pleases that all in-the-heavens now-God-of-us (3) God-of-them now! where?

עָשָׂה׃ עֲצַבֵּיהֶם כֶּסֶף וְזָהָב מַעֲשֵׂה יְדֵי אָדָם׃ פֶּה־
mouth (5) man hands-of making-of and-gold silver idols-of-them (4) he-does

לָהֶם וְלֹא יְדַבֵּרוּ עֵינַיִם לָהֶם וְלֹא יִרְאוּ׃
they-can-see but-not to-them eyes they-can-speak but-not to-them

4The Lord is exalted over all the nations,
his glory above the heavens.
5Who is like the Lord our God,
the One who sits enthroned on high,
6who stoops down to look
on the heavens and the earth?

7He raises the poor from the dust
and lifts the needy from the ash heap;
8he seats them with princes,
with the princes of their people.
9He settles the barren woman in her home
as a happy mother of children.

Praise the Lord.

### Psalm 114

1When Israel came out of Egypt,
the house of Jacob from a people of foreign tongue,
2Judah became God's sanctuary,
Israel his dominion.

3The sea looked and fled,
the Jordan turned back;
4the mountains skipped like rams,
the hills like lambs.

5Why was it, O sea, that you fled,
O Jordan, that you turned back,
6you mountains, that you skipped like rams,
you hills, like lambs?

7Tremble, O earth, at the presence of the Lord,
at the presence of the God of Jacob,
8who turned the rock into a pool,
the hard rock into springs of water.

### Psalm 115

1Not to us, O Lord, not to us
but to your name be the glory,
because of your love and faithfulness.

2Why do the nations say,
"Where is their God?"
3Our God is in heaven;
he does whatever pleases him.
4But their idols are silver and gold,
made by the hands of men.
5They have mouths, but cannot speak,
eyes, but they cannot see;

אָזְנַיִם לָהֶם וְלֹא יִשְׁמָעוּ אַף לָהֶם וְלֹא יְרִיחוּן׃
they-can-smell but-not to-them nose they-can-hear but-not to-them ears (6)

יְדֵיהֶם ׀ וְלֹא יְמִישׁוּן רַגְלֵיהֶם וְלֹא יְהַלֵּכוּ
they-can-walk but-not feet-of-them they-can-feel but-not hands-of-them (7)

לֹא־ יֶהְגּוּ בִּגְרוֹנָם׃ כְּמוֹהֶם יִהְיוּ
they-will-be like-them (8) with-throat-of-them they-can-utter-sound not

עֹשֵׂיהֶם כֹּל אֲשֶׁר־ בֹּטֵחַ בָּהֶם׃ יִשְׂרָאֵל בְּטַח בַּיהוָה
in-Yahweh trust! Israel (9) in-them one-trusting who all ones-making-them

עֶזְרָם וּמָגִנָּם הוּא׃ בֵּית אַהֲרֹן בִּטְחוּ בַיהוָה
in-Yahweh trust! Aaron house-of (10) he and-shield-of-them help-of-them

עֶזְרָם וּמָגִנָּם הוּא׃ יִרְאֵי יְהוָה בִּטְחוּ
trust! Yahweh ones-fearing-of (11) he and-shield-of-them help-of-them

בַיהוָה עֶזְרָם וּמָגִנָּם הוּא׃ יְהוָה זְכָרָנוּ
he-remembers-us Yahweh (12) he and-shield-of-them help-of-them in-Yahweh

יְבָרֵךְ יְבָרֵךְ אֶת־ בֵּית יִשְׂרָאֵל יְבָרֵךְ אֶת־ בֵּית
house-of *** he-will-bless Israel house-of *** he-will-bless he-will-bless

אַהֲרֹן׃ יְבָרֵךְ יִרְאֵי יְהוָה הַקְּטַנִּים עִם־
with the-small-ones Yahweh ones-fearing-of he-will-bless (13) Aaron

הַגְּדֹלִים׃ יֹסֵף יְהוָה עֲלֵיכֶם עֲלֵיכֶם וְעַל־
and-to to-you to-you Yahweh may-he-make-increase (14) the-great-ones

בְּנֵיכֶם׃ בְּרוּכִים אַתֶּם לַיהוָה עֹשֵׂה שָׁמַיִם
heavens One-Making-of by-Yahweh you ones-being-blessed (15) children-of-you

וָאָרֶץ׃ הַשָּׁמַיִם שָׁמַיִם לַיהוָה וְהָאָרֶץ נָתַן
he-gave but-the-earth to-Yahweh heavens the-heavens (16) and-earth

לִבְנֵי־ אָדָם׃ לֹא הַמֵּתִים יְהַלְלוּ־ יָהּ וְלֹא כָּל־
all-of and-not Yahweh they-praise the-dead-ones not (17) man to-sons-of

יֹרְדֵי דוּמָה׃ וַאֲנַחְנוּ ׀ נְבָרֵךְ יָהּ מֵעַתָּה וְעַד־
and-to from-now Yahweh we-extol but-we (18) silence ones-going-down-of

עוֹלָם הַלְלוּ־ יָהּ׃ אָהַבְתִּי כִּי־ יִשְׁמַע ׀ יְהוָה אֶת־
*** Yahweh he-heard because I-love (116:1) Yahweh praise! forevermore

קוֹלִי תַּחֲנוּנָי׃ כִּי־ הִטָּה אָזְנוֹ לִי
to-me ear-of-him he-turned because (2) cries-for-mercy-of-me voice-of-me

וּבְיָמַי אֶקְרָא׃ אֲפָפוּנִי ׀ חֶבְלֵי־ מָוֶת
death cords-of they-entangled-me (3) I-will-call then-during-days-of-me

וּמְצָרֵי שְׁאוֹל מְצָאוּנִי צָרָה וְיָגוֹן אֶמְצָא׃
I-was-overcome and-sorrow trouble they-came-upon-me Sheol and-anguishes-of

וּבְשֵׁם־ יְהוָה אֶקְרָא אָנָּה יְהוָה מַלְּטָה נַפְשִׁי׃ חַנּוּן
gracious (5) self-of-me save! Yahweh oh! I-called Yahweh then-on-name-of (4)

6 they have ears, but cannot hear,
noses, but they cannot smell;
7 they have hands, but cannot feel,
feet, but they cannot walk;
nor can they utter a sound with their throats.
8 Those who make them will be like them,
and so will all who trust in them.

9 O house of Israel, trust in the LORD—
he is their help and shield.
10 O house of Aaron, trust in the LORD—
he is their help and shield.
11 You who fear him, trust in the LORD—
he is their help and shield.

12 The LORD remembers us and will bless us:
He will bless the house of Israel,
he will bless the house of Aaron,
13 he will bless those who fear the LORD—
small and great alike.

14 May the LORD make you increase,
both you and your children.
15 May you be blessed by the LORD,
the Maker of heaven and earth.

16 The highest heavens belong to the LORD,
but the earth he has given to man.
17 It is not the dead who praise the LORD,
those who go down to silence;
18 it is we who extol the LORD,
both now and forevermore.

Praise the LORD.[m]

### Psalm 116

1 I love the LORD, for he heard my voice;
he heard my cry for mercy.
2 Because he turned his ear to me,
I will call on him as long as I live.

3 The cords of death entangled me,
the anguish of the grave[n] came upon me;
I was overcome by trouble and sorrow.
4 Then I called on the name of the LORD:
"O LORD, save me!"

[m] 18 Hebrew *Hallelu Yah*
[n] 3 Hebrew *Sheol*

יְהוָה וְצַדִּיק וֵאלֹהֵינוּ מְרַחֵם׃ שֹׁמֵר

one-protecting (6) one-being-compassionate and-God-of-us and-righteous Yahweh

פְּתָאיִם* יְהוָה דַּלּוֹתִי וְלִי יְהוֹשִׁיעַ׃ שׁוּבִי

return! (7) he-saved and-to-me I-was-in-need Yahweh simplehearted-ones

נַפְשִׁי לִמְנוּחָיְכִי כִּי־ יְהוָה גָּמַל עָלָיְכִי׃ כִּי חִלַּצְתָּ

you-delivered for (8) to-you he-was-good Yahweh for to-rests-of-you soul-of-me

נַפְשִׁי מִמָּוֶת אֶת־ עֵינִי מִן־דִּמְעָה אֶת־ רַגְלִי מִדֶּחִי׃

from-stumbling foot-of-me *** tear from eye-of-me *** from-death soul-of-me

אֶתְהַלֵּךְ לִפְנֵי יְהוָה בְּאַרְצוֹת הַחַיִּים׃ הֶאֱמַנְתִּי

I-believed (10) the-living-ones in-lands-of Yahweh before I-may-walk (9)

כִּי אֲדַבֵּר אֲנִי עָנִיתִי מְאֹד׃ אֲנִי אָמַרְתִּי בְחָפְזִי

when-to-be-dismayed-me I-said I (11) greatly I-am-afflicted I I-said therefore

כָּל־ הָאָדָם כֹּזֵב׃ מָה־ אָשִׁיב לַיהוָה כָּל־ תַּגְמוּלוֹהִי

goodness-of-him all-of to-Yahweh can-I-repay how? (12) one-lying the-man all-of

עָלָי׃ כּוֹס־ יְשׁוּעוֹת אֶשָּׂא וּבְשֵׁם יְהוָה אֶקְרָא׃

I-will-call Yahweh and-on-name-of I-will-lift salvations cup-of (13) to-me

נְדָרַי לַיהוָה אֲשַׁלֵּם נֶגְדָה־ נָּא לְכָל־

of-all-of now! in-presence I-will-fulfill to-Yahweh vows-of-me (14)

עַמּוֹ׃ יָקָר בְּעֵינֵי יְהוָה הַמָּוְתָה לַחֲסִידָיו׃

of-saints-of-him to-the-death Yahweh in-eyes-of precious (15) people-of-him

אָנָּה יְהוָה כִּי־ אֲנִי עַבְדֶּךָ אֲנִי־ עַבְדְּךָ בֶּן־

son-of servant-of-you I servant-of-you I truly Yahweh oh! (16)

אֲמָתֶךָ פִּתַּחְתָּ לְמוֹסֵרָי׃ לְךָ־ אֶזְבַּח

I-will-sacrifice to-you (17) from-chains-of-me you-freed maidservant-of-you

זֶבַח תּוֹדָה וּבְשֵׁם יְהוָה אֶקְרָא׃ נְדָרַי

vows-of-me (18) I-will-call Yahweh and-on-name-of thanksgiving offering-of

לַיהוָה אֲשַׁלֵּם נֶגְדָה־ נָּא לְכָל־ עַמּוֹ׃

people-of-him of-all-of now! in-presence I-will-fulfill to-Yahweh

בְּחַצְרוֹת׀ בֵּית יְהוָה בְּתוֹכֵכִי יְרוּשָׁלָםִ הַלְלוּ־ יָהּ׃

Yahweh praise! Jerusalem in-midst-of-you Yahweh house-of in-courts-of (19)

הַלְלוּ אֶת־ יְהוָה כָּל־ גּוֹיִם שַׁבְּחוּהוּ כָּל־ הָאֻמִּים׃

the-peoples all-of extol-him! nations all-of Yahweh *** praise! (117:1)

כִּי גָבַר עָלֵינוּ׀ חַסְדּוֹ וֶאֱמֶת־ יְהוָה

Yahweh and-faithfulness-of love-of-him toward-us he-is-great for (2)

לְעוֹלָם הַלְלוּ־ יָהּ׃ הוֹדוּ לַיהוָה כִּי־ טוֹב כִּי

for good for to-Yahweh give-thanks! (118:1) Yahweh praise! to-forever

לְעוֹלָם חַסְדּוֹ׃ יֹאמַר־ נָא יִשְׂרָאֵל כִּי לְעוֹלָם חַסְדּוֹ׃

love-of-him to-forever that Israel now! let-him-say (2) love-of-him to-forever

5 The LORD is gracious and
righteous;
our God is full of
compassion.
6 The LORD protects the
simplehearted;
when I was in great need,
he saved me.

7 Be at rest once more, O my
soul,
for the LORD has been good
to you.

8 For you, O LORD, have
delivered my soul from
death,
my eyes from tears,
my feet from stumbling,
9 that I may walk before the
LORD
in the land of the living.
10 I believed; therefore[o] I said,
"I am greatly afflicted."
11 And in my dismay I said,
"All men are liars."

12 How can I repay the LORD
for all his goodness to me?
13 I will lift up the cup of
salvation
and call on the name of the
LORD.
14 I will fulfill my vows to the
LORD
in the presence of all his
people.

15 Precious in the sight of the
LORD
is the death of his saints.
16 O LORD, truly I am your
servant;
I am your servant, the son
of your maidservant[p];
you have freed me from my
chains.

17 I will sacrifice a thank offering
to you
and call on the name of the
LORD.
18 I will fulfill my vows to the
LORD
in the presence of all his
people,
19 in the courts of the house of
the LORD—
in your midst, O Jerusalem.

Praise the LORD.[q]

**Psalm 117**

1 Praise the LORD, all you
nations;
extol him, all you peoples.
2 For great is his love toward us,
and the faithfulness of the
LORD endures forever.

Praise the LORD.[r]

**Psalm 118**

1 Give thanks to the LORD, for
he is good;
his love endures forever.

2 Let Israel say:
"His love endures forever."

[o]10 Or *believed even when*
[p]16 Or *servant, your faithful son*
[q]19 Hebrew *Hallelu Yah*
[r]2 Hebrew *Hallelu Yah*

*6 Most mss have *hireq* under the *aleph* (אִים—).

יֹאמְרוּ־ נָא בֵית־ אַהֲרֹן כִּי לְעוֹלָם חַסְדּוֹ׃

love-of-him to-forever that Aaron house-of now! let-them-say (3)

יֹאמְרוּ־ נָא יִרְאֵי יְהוָה כִּי לְעוֹלָם חַסְדּוֹ׃

love-of-him to-forever that Yahweh ones-fearing-of now! let-them-say (4)

מִן־ הַמֵּצַר קָרָאתִי יָּהּ עָנָנִי בַמֶּרְחָב יָהּ׃

Yahweh with-the-freedom he-answered-me Yahweh I-cried-to the-anguish in (5)

יְהוָה לִי לֹא אִירָא מַה־ יַּעֲשֶׂה לִי אָדָם׃ יְהוָה

Yahweh (7) man to-me can-he-do what? I-will-be-afraid not with-me Yahweh (6)

לִי בְּעֹזְרָי וַאֲנִי אֶרְאֶה בְשֹׂנְאָי׃

on-ones-being-enemies-of-me I-will-look and-I as-ones-helping-me with-me

טוֹב לַחֲסוֹת בַּיהוָה מִבְּטֹחַ בָּאָדָם׃ טוֹב

better (9) in-the-man than-to-trust in-Yahweh to-take-refuge better (8)

לַחֲסוֹת בַּיהוָה מִבְּטֹחַ בִּנְדִיבִים׃ כָּל־ גּוֹיִם

nations all-of (10) in-princes than-to-trust in-Yahweh to-take-refuge

סְבָבוּנִי בְּשֵׁם יְהוָה כִּי אֲמִילַם׃

I-cut-off-them indeed Yahweh in-name-of they-surrounded-me

סַבּוּנִי גַם־ סְבָבוּנִי בְּשֵׁם יְהוָה כִּי

indeed Yahweh in-name-of they-surrounded-me indeed they-surrounded-me (11)

אֲמִילַם׃ סַבּוּנִי כִדְבוֹרִים דֹּעֲכוּ כְּאֵשׁ

like-fire-of they-died-out like-bees they-swarmed-around-me (12) I-cut-off-them

קוֹצִים בְּשֵׁם יְהוָה כִּי אֲמִילַם׃ דַּחֹה

to-push-back (13) I-cut-off-them indeed Yahweh in-name-of thorns

דְחִיתַנִי לִנְפֹּל וַיהוָה עֲזָרָנִי׃ עָזִּי

strength-of-me (14) he-helped-me but-Yahweh to-fall you-pushed-back-me

וְזִמְרָת יָהּ וַיְהִי־ לִי לִישׁוּעָה׃ קוֹל רִנָּה וִישׁוּעָה

and-victory joy shout-of (15) as-salvation to-me and-he-became Yahweh and-song

בְּאָהֳלֵי צַדִּיקִים יְמִין יְהוָה עֹשָׂה חָיִל׃

mighty-thing one-doing Yahweh right-hand-of righteous-ones in-tents-of

יְמִין יְהוָה רוֹמֵמָה יְמִין יְהוָה עֹשָׂה

one-doing Yahweh right-hand-of one-being-lifted-high Yahweh right-hand-of (16)

חָיִל׃ לֹא אָמוּת כִּי־ אֶחְיֶה וַאֲסַפֵּר מַעֲשֵׂי

deeds-of and-I-will-proclaim I-will-live but I-will-die not (17) mighty-thing

יָהּ׃ יַסֹּר יִסְּרַנִּי יָּהּ וְלַמָּוֶת לֹא נְתָנָנִי׃

he-gave-me not but-to-the-death Yahweh he-chastened-me to-chasten (18) Yahweh

פִּתְחוּ־ לִי שַׁעֲרֵי־ צֶדֶק אָבֹא־ בָם

through-them I-will-enter righteousness gates-of for-me open! (19)

אוֹדֶה יָהּ׃ זֶה־ הַשַּׁעַר לַיהוָה צַדִּיקִים

righteous-ones of-Yahweh the-gate this (20) Yahweh I-will-give-thanks

3 Let the house of Aaron say:
"His love endures forever."
4 Let those who fear the LORD say:
"His love endures forever."

5 In my anguish I cried to the LORD,
and he answered by setting me free.
6 The LORD is with me; I will not be afraid.
What can man do to me?
7 The LORD is with me; he is my helper.
I will look in triumph on my enemies.

8 It is better to take refuge in the LORD
than to trust in man.
9 It is better to take refuge in the LORD
than to trust in princes.

10 All the nations surrounded me,
but in the name of the LORD I cut them off.
11 They surrounded me on every side,
but in the name of the LORD I cut them off.
12 They swarmed around me like bees,
but they died out as quickly as burning thorns;
in the name of the LORD I cut them off.

13 I was pushed back and about to fall,
but the LORD helped me.
14 The LORD is my strength and my song;
he has become my salvation.

15 Shouts of joy and victory resound in the tents of the righteous:
"The LORD's right hand has done mighty things!
16 The LORD's right hand is lifted high;
the LORD's right hand has done mighty things!"

17 I will not die but live,
and will proclaim what the LORD has done.
18 The LORD has chastened me severely,
but he has not given me over to death.

19 Open for me the gates of righteousness;
I will enter and give thanks to the LORD.
20 This is the gate of the LORD
through which the righteous

יָבֹאוּ בוֹ׃ אוֹדְךָ כִּי עֲנִיתָנִי
you-answered-me for I-will-give-thanks-to-you (21) through-him they-may-enter

וַתְּהִי־ לִי לִישׁוּעָה׃ אֶבֶן מָאֲסוּ הַבּוֹנִים
the-ones-building they-rejected stone (22) as-salvation to-me and-you-became

הָיְתָה לְרֹאשׁ פִּנָּה׃ מֵאֵת יְהוָה הָיְתָה זֹּאת הִיא
she this she-happened Yahweh from-with (23) corner as-capstone-of she-became

נִפְלָאת בְּעֵינֵינוּ׃ זֶה־ הַיּוֹם עָשָׂה יְהוָה
Yahweh he-made the-day this (24) in-eyes-of-us one-being-marvelous

נָגִילָה וְנִשְׂמְחָה בוֹ׃ אָנָּא יְהוָה הוֹשִׁיעָה נָּא אָנָּא יְהוָה
Yahweh oh! now! save! Yahweh oh! (25) in-him and-let-us-be-glad let-us-rejoice

הַצְלִיחָה נָּא׃ בָּרוּךְ הַבָּא בְּשֵׁם יְהוָה
Yahweh in-name-of the-one-coming being-blessed (26) now! grant-success!

בֵּרַכְנוּכֶם מִבֵּית יְהוָה׃ אֵל ׀ יְהוָה וַיָּאֶר לָנוּ
on-us and-he-shined-light Yahweh God (27) Yahweh from-house-of we-bless-you

אִסְרוּ־ חַג בַּעֲבֹתִים עַד־ קַרְנוֹת הַמִּזְבֵּחַ׃ אֵלִי
God-of-me (28) the-altar horns-of up-to with-boughs festal-procession join!

אַתָּה וְאוֹדֶךָּ אֱלֹהַי אֲרוֹמְמֶךָּ׃
and-I-will-exalt-you God-of-me and-I-will-give-thanks-to-you you

הוֹדוּ לַיהוָה כִּי־ טוֹב כִּי לְעוֹלָם חַסְדּוֹ׃
love-of-him to-forever for good for to-Yahweh give-thanks! (29)

אַשְׁרֵי תְמִימֵי־ דָרֶךְ הַהֹלְכִים בְּתוֹרַת
by-law-of the-ones-walking way ones-blameless-of blessednesses-of (119:1)

יְהוָה׃ אַשְׁרֵי נֹצְרֵי עֵדֹתָיו בְּכָל־ לֵב
heart with-all-of statutes-of-him ones-keeping-of blessednesses-of (2) Yahweh

יִדְרְשׁוּהוּ׃ אַף לֹא־ פָעֲלוּ עַוְלָה בִּדְרָכָיו הָלָכוּ׃ אַתָּה
you (4) they-walk in-ways-of-him wrong they-do nothing also (3) they-seek-him

צִוִּיתָה פִקֻּדֶיךָ לִשְׁמֹר מְאֹד׃ אַחֲלַי יִכֹּנוּ
they-were-steadfast oh-that! (5) fully to-obey precepts-of-you you-laid-down

דְרָכָי לִשְׁמֹר חֻקֶּיךָ׃ אָז לֹא־ אֵבוֹשׁ
I-would-be-shamed not then (6) decrees-of-you to-obey ways-of-me

בְּהַבִּיטִי אֶל־ כָּל־ מִצְוֹתֶיךָ׃ אוֹדְךָ
I-will-praise-you (7) commands-of-you all-of to when-to-consider-me

בְּיֹשֶׁר לֵבָב בְּלָמְדִי מִשְׁפְּטֵי צִדְקֶךָ׃
righteousness-of-you laws-of as-to-learn-me heart with-uprightness-of

אֶת־ חֻקֶּיךָ אֶשְׁמֹר אַל־ תַּעַזְבֵנִי עַד־ מְאֹד׃ בַּמֶּה
by-the-how? (9) utterly to you-forsake-me not I-will-obey decrees-of-you *** (8)

יְזַכֶּה־ נַּעַר אֶת־ אָרְחוֹ לִשְׁמֹר כִּדְבָרֶךָ׃
as-word-of-you to-live way-of-him *** young-man he-can-keep-pure

may enter.
21 I will give you thanks, for you
answered me;
you have become my
salvation.

22 The stone the builders rejected
has become the capstone;
23 the LORD has done this,
and it is marvelous in our
eyes.
24 This is the day the LORD has
made;
let us rejoice and be glad in
it.

25 O LORD, save us;
O LORD, grant us success.
26 Blessed is he who comes in
the name of the LORD.
From the house of the LORD
we bless you.[s]
27 The LORD is God,
and he has made his light
shine upon us.
With boughs in hand, join in
the festal procession
up[t] to the horns of the altar.

28 You are my God, and I will
give you thanks;
you are my God, and I will
exalt you.

29 Give thanks to the LORD, for
he is good;
his love endures forever.

### Psalm 119[u]

#### א Aleph

1 Blessed are they whose ways
are blameless,
who walk according to the
law of the LORD.
2 Blessed are they who keep his
statutes
and seek him with all their
heart.
3 They do nothing wrong;
they walk in his ways.
4 You have laid down precepts
that are to be fully obeyed.
5 Oh, that my ways were
steadfast
in obeying your decrees!
6 Then I would not be put to
shame
when I consider all your
commands.
7 I will praise you with an
upright heart
as I learn your righteous
laws.
8 I will obey your decrees;
do not utterly forsake me.

#### ב Beth

9 How can a young man keep
his way pure?
By living according to your
word.

[s]26 The Hebrew is plural.
[t]27 Or *Bind the festal sacrifice with ropes / and take it*
[u]This psalm is an acrostic poem; the verses of each stanza begin with the same letter of the Hebrew alphabet.

בְּכָל־ לִבִּי דְרַשְׁתִּיךָ אַל־ תַּשְׁגֵּנִי

(10) with-all-of heart-of-me I-seek-you not you-let-stray-me

מִמִּצְוֺתֶיךָ׃ בְּלִבִּי צָפַנְתִּי אִמְרָתֶךָ לְמַעַן לֹא

from-commands-of-you (11) in-heart-of-me I-hid word-of-you so-that not

אֶחֱטָא־ לָךְ׃ בָּרוּךְ אַתָּה יְהוָה לַמְּדֵנִי חֻקֶּיךָ׃

I-might-sin against-you (12) being-praised you Yahweh teach-me! decrees-of-you

בִּשְׂפָתַי סִפַּרְתִּי כֹּל מִשְׁפְּטֵי־ פִיךָ׃ בְּדֶרֶךְ

(13) with-lips-of-me I-recount all-of laws-of mouth-of-you (14) in-way-of

עֵדְוֺתֶיךָ שַׂשְׂתִּי כְּעַל כָּל־ הוֹן׃ בְּפִקֻּדֶיךָ

statutes-of-you I-rejoice as-in greatness-of richness (15) on-precepts-of-you

אָשִׂיחָה וְאַבִּיטָה אֹרְחֹתֶיךָ׃ בְּחֻקֹּתֶיךָ אֶשְׁתַּעֲשָׁע לֹא

I-meditate and-I-consider ways-of-you (16) in-decrees-of-you I-delight not

אֶשְׁכַּח דְּבָרֶךָ׃ גְּמֹל עַל־ עַבְדְּךָ אֶחְיֶה

and-I-will-neglect word-of-you (17) do-good! to servant-of-you I-will-live

וְאֶשְׁמְרָה דְבָרֶךָ׃ גַּל־ עֵינַי וְאַבִּיטָה

and-I-will-obey word-of-you (18) open! eyes-of-me that-I-may-see

נִפְלָאוֹת מִתּוֹרָתֶךָ׃ גֵּר אָנֹכִי בָאָרֶץ אַל־ תַּסְתֵּר

things-being-wonderful in-law-of-you (19) stranger I on-the-earth not you-hide

מִמֶּנִּי מִצְוֺתֶיךָ׃ גָּרְסָה נַפְשִׁי לְתַאֲבָה אֶל־

from-me commands-of-you (20) she-is-consumed soul-of-me with-longing for

מִשְׁפָּטֶיךָ בְכָל־ עֵת׃ גָּעַרְתָּ זֵדִים אֲרוּרִים

laws-of-you at-all-of time (21) you-rebuke arrogant-ones ones-being-cursed

הַשֹּׁגִים מִמִּצְוֺתֶיךָ׃ גַּל מֵעָלַי חֶרְפָּה

the-ones-straying from-commands-of-you (22) remove! from-upon-me scorn

וָבוּז כִּי עֵדֹתֶיךָ נָצָרְתִּי׃ גַּם יָשְׁבוּ שָׂרִים בִּי

and-contempt for statutes-of-you I-keep (23) though they-sit princes against-me

נִדְבָּרוּ עַבְדְּךָ יָשִׂיחַ בְּחֻקֶּיךָ׃ גַּם־

they-slander servant-of-you he-will-meditate on-decrees-of-you (24) indeed

עֵדֹתֶיךָ שַׁעֲשֻׁעָי אַנְשֵׁי עֲצָתִי׃ דָּבְקָה

statutes-of-you delights-of-me men-of counsel-of-me (25) she-is-laid-low

לֶעָפָר נַפְשִׁי חַיֵּנִי כִּדְבָרֶךָ׃ דְּרָכַי

in-the-dust self-of-me make-alive-me! as-word-of-you (26) ways-of-me

סִפַּרְתִּי וַתַּעֲנֵנִי לַמְּדֵנִי חֻקֶּיךָ׃ דֶּרֶךְ־

I-recounted and-you-answered-me teach-me! decrees-of-you (27) teaching-of

פִּקּוּדֶיךָ הֲבִינֵנִי וְאָשִׂיחָה בְּנִפְלְאוֹתֶיךָ׃

precepts-of-you let-understand-me! then-I-will-meditate on-ones-being-wonders-of-you

דָּלְפָה נַפְשִׁי מִתּוּגָה קַיְּמֵנִי כִּדְבָרֶךָ׃

(28) she-is-weary soul-of-me with-sorrow strengthen-me! as-word-of-you

10 I seek you with all my heart;
do not let me stray from your commands.
11 I have hidden your word in my heart
that I might not sin against you.
12 Praise be to you, O LORD;
teach me your decrees.
13 With my lips I recount
all the laws that come from your mouth.
14 I rejoice in following your statutes
as one rejoices in great riches.
15 I meditate on your precepts
and consider your ways.
16 I delight in your decrees;
I will not neglect your word.

ג Gimel

17 Do good to your servant, and I will live;
I will obey your word.
18 Open my eyes that I may see
wonderful things in your law.
19 I am a stranger on earth;
do not hide your commands from me.
20 My soul is consumed with longing
for your laws at all times.
21 You rebuke the arrogant, who are cursed
and who stray from your commands.
22 Remove from me scorn and contempt,
for I keep your statutes.
23 Though princes sit together and slander me,
your servant will meditate on your decrees.
24 Your statutes are my delight;
they are my counselors.

ד Daleth

25 I am laid low in the dust;
renew my life according to your word.
26 I recounted my ways and you answered me;
teach me your decrees.
27 Let me understand the teaching of your precepts;
then I will meditate on your wonders.
28 My soul is weary with sorrow;
strengthen me according to your word.

דֶּֽרֶךְ־ שֶׁקֶר הָסֵר מִמֶּנִּי וְתוֹרָתְךָ חָנֵּנִי׃ דֶּֽרֶךְ־
way-of (30) be-gracious-to-me! and-law-of-you from-me keep! deceit way-of (29)

אֱמוּנָה בָחָרְתִּי מִשְׁפָּטֶיךָ שִׁוִּיתִי׃ דָּבַקְתִּי בְעֵדְוֺתֶיךָ
to-statutes-of-you I-hold-fast (31) I-set-heart laws-of-you I-chose truth

יְהוָה אַל־ תְּבִישֵׁנִי׃ דֶּֽרֶךְ־ מִצְוֺתֶיךָ אָרוּץ כִּי
for I-run commands-of-you path-of (32) you-let-be-shamed-me not Yahweh

תַרְחִיב לִבִּי׃ הוֹרֵנִי יְהוָה דֶּרֶךְ חֻקֶּיךָ
decrees-of-you way-of Yahweh teach-me! (33) heart-of-me you-set-free

וְאֶצְּרֶנָּה עֵקֶב׃ הֲבִינֵנִי וְאֶצְּרָה תוֹרָתֶךָ
law-of-you and-I-will-keep make-understand-me! (34) end then-I-will-keep-her

וְאֶשְׁמְרֶנָּה בְכָל־ לֵב׃ הַדְרִיכֵנִי בִּנְתִיב
in-path-of direct-me! (35) heart with-all-of and-I-will-obey-her

מִצְוֺתֶיךָ כִּי־ בוֹ חָפָצְתִּי׃ הַט־ לִבִּי אֶל־ עֵדְוֺתֶיךָ
statutes-of-you to heart-of-me turn! (36) I-delight in-him for commands-of-you

וְאַל אֶל־ בָּצַע׃ הַעֲבֵר עֵינַי מֵרְאוֹת שָׁוְא
worthless-thing from-to-see eyes-of-me turn! (37) selfish-gain toward and-not

בִּדְרָכֶךָ חַיֵּנִי׃ הָקֵם לְעַבְדְּךָ אִמְרָתֶךָ
promise-of-you to-servant-of-you fulfill! (38) make-alive-me! in-way-of-you

אֲשֶׁר לְיִרְאָתֶךָ׃ הַעֲבֵר חֶרְפָּתִי אֲשֶׁר יָגֹרְתִּי כִּי מִשְׁפָּטֶיךָ
laws-of-you for I-dread that disgrace-of-me take-away! (39) to-fear-you that

טוֹבִים׃ הִנֵּה תָּאַבְתִּי לְפִקֻּדֶיךָ בְּצִדְקָתְךָ
in-righteousness-of-you for-precepts-of-you I-long see! (40) good-ones

חַיֵּנִי׃ וִיבֹאֻנִי חֲסָדֶךָ יְהוָה
Yahweh unfailing-loves-of-you and-may-they-come-to-me (41) make-alive-me!

תְּשׁוּעָתְךָ כְּאִמְרָתֶךָ׃ וְאֶעֱנֶה חֹרְפִי
one-taunting-me then-I-will-answer (42) as-promise-of-you salvation-of-you

דָבָר כִּי־ בָטַחְתִּי בִּדְבָרֶךָ׃ וְאַל־ תַּצֵּל מִפִּי
from-mouth-of-me you-snatch and-not (43) in-word-of-you I-trust for word

דְבַר־ אֱמֶת עַד־ מְאֹד כִּי לְמִשְׁפָּטֶךָ יִחָלְתִּי׃ וְאֶשְׁמְרָה
and-I-will-obey (44) I-put-hope in-laws-of-you for indeed to truth word-of

תוֹרָתְךָ תָמִיד לְעוֹלָם וָעֶד׃ וְאֶתְהַלְּכָה בָרְחָבָה כִּי
for in-the-freedom and-I-will-walk (45) and-ever to-forever always law-of-you

פִקֻּדֶיךָ דָרָשְׁתִּי׃ וַאֲדַבְּרָה בְעֵדֹתֶיךָ נֶגֶד
before of-statutes-of-you and-I-will-speak (46) I-sought-out precepts-of-you

מְלָכִים וְלֹא אֵבוֹשׁ׃ וְאֶשְׁתַּעֲשַׁע בְּמִצְוֺתֶיךָ אֲשֶׁר
because in-commands-of-you for-I-delight (47) I-will-be-shamed and-not kings

אָהָבְתִּי׃ וְאֶשָּׂא־ כַפַּי אֶל־ מִצְוֺתֶיךָ אֲשֶׁר אָהָבְתִּי
I-love which commands-of-you for hands-of-me and-I-reach-out (48) I-love

29 Keep me from deceitful ways;
be gracious to me through
your law.
30 I have chosen the way of
truth;
I have set my heart on your
laws.
31 I hold fast to your statutes, O
LORD;
do not let me be put to
shame.
32 I run in the path of your
commands,
for you have set my heart
free.

ה He

33 Teach me, O LORD, to follow
your decrees;
then I will keep them to the
end.
34 Give me understanding, and I
will keep your law
and obey it with all my
heart.
35 Direct me in the path of your
commands,
for there I find delight.
36 Turn my heart toward your
statutes
and not toward selfish gain.
37 Turn my eyes away from
worthless things;
renew my life according to
your word.[v]
38 Fulfill your promise to your
servant,
so that you may be feared.
39 Take away the disgrace I
dread,
for your laws are good.
40 How I long for your precepts!
Renew my life in your
righteousness.

ו Waw

41 May your unfailing love come
to me, O LORD,
your salvation according to
your promise;
42 then I will answer the one
who taunts me,
for I trust in your word.
43 Do not snatch the word of
truth from my mouth,
for I have put my hope in
your laws.
44 I will always obey your law,
for ever and ever.
45 I will walk about in freedom,
for I have sought out your
precepts.
46 I will speak of your statutes
before kings
and will not be put to
shame,
47 for I delight in your
commandments
because I love them.
48 I reach out my hands for your
commandments, which I
love,

[v]37 Two manuscripts of the Masoretic Text and Dead Sea Scrolls; most manuscripts of the Masoretic Text *life in your way*

וְאָשִׂיחָה בְחֻקֶּיךָ׃ זְכָר־דָּבָר לְעַבְדֶּךָ עַל
for to-servant-of-you word remember! (49) on-decrees-of-you and-I-meditate

אֲשֶׁר יִחַלְתָּנִי׃ זֹאת נֶחָמָתִי בְעָנְיִי כִּי
that in-suffering-of-me comfort-of-me this (50) you-gave-hope-to-me that

אִמְרָתְךָ חִיָּתְנִי׃ זֵדִים הֱלִיצֻנִי עַד־מְאֹד
excess to they-mock-me arrogant-ones (51) she-makes-alive-me promise-of-you

מִתּוֹרָתְךָ לֹא נָטִיתִי׃ זָכַרְתִּי מִשְׁפָּטֶיךָ מֵעוֹלָם ׀ יְהוָה
Yahweh from-ancient laws-of-you I-remember (52) I-turn not from-law-of-you

וָאֶתְנֶחָם׃ זַלְעָפָה אֲחָזַתְנִי מֵרְשָׁעִים
because-of-wicked-ones she-grips-me indignation (53) and-I-find-comfort

עֹזְבֵי תּוֹרָתֶךָ׃ זְמִרוֹת הָיוּ־לִי חֻקֶּיךָ
decrees-of-you to-me they-are songs (54) law-of-you ones-forsaking-of

בְּבֵית מְגוּרָי׃ זָכַרְתִּי בַלַּיְלָה שִׁמְךָ יְהוָה
Yahweh name-of-you in-the-night I-remember (55) lodgings-of-me in-house-of

וָאֶשְׁמְרָה תּוֹרָתֶךָ׃ זֹאת הָיְתָה־לִּי כִּי פִקֻּדֶיךָ נָצָרְתִּי׃
I-obey precepts-of-you that to-me she-is this (56) law-of-you and-I-will-keep

חֶלְקִי יְהוָה אָמַרְתִּי לִשְׁמֹר דְּבָרֶיךָ׃ חִלִּיתִי
I-sought (58) words-of-you to-obey I-promised Yahweh portion-of-me (57)

פָנֶיךָ בְכָל־לֵב חָנֵּנִי כְּאִמְרָתֶךָ׃
as-promise-of-you be-gracious-to-me! heart with-all-of faces-of-you

חִשַּׁבְתִּי דְרָכָי וָאָשִׁיבָה רַגְלַי אֶל־עֵדֹתֶיךָ׃
statutes-of-you to steps-of-me and-I-turned ways-of-me I-considered (59)

חַשְׁתִּי וְלֹא הִתְמַהְמָהְתִּי לִשְׁמֹר מִצְוֺתֶיךָ׃ חֶבְלֵי
ropes-of (61) commands-of-you to-obey I-will-delay and-not I-will-hasten (60)

רְשָׁעִים עִוְּדֻנִי תּוֹרָתְךָ לֹא שָׁכָחְתִּי׃ חֲצוֹת־
middles-of (62) I-will-forget not law-of-you they-bind-me wicked-ones

לַיְלָה אָקוּם לְהוֹדוֹת לָךְ עַל מִשְׁפְּטֵי צִדְקֶךָ׃
righteousness-of-you laws-of for to-you to-give-thanks I-rise night

חָבֵר אָנִי לְכָל־אֲשֶׁר יְרֵאוּךָ וּלְשֹׁמְרֵי פִּקּוּדֶיךָ׃
precepts-of-you and-to-ones-following-of they-fear-you who to-all I friend (63)

חַסְדְּךָ יְהוָה מָלְאָה הָאָרֶץ חֻקֶּיךָ לַמְּדֵנִי׃
teach-me! decrees-of-you the-earth she-is-filled Yahweh love-of-you (64)

טוֹב עָשִׂיתָ עִם־עַבְדְּךָ יְהוָה כִּדְבָרֶךָ׃ טוּב
goodness-of (66) as-word-of-you Yahweh servant-of-you to you-do good (65)

טַעַם וָדַעַת לַמְּדֵנִי כִּי בְמִצְוֺתֶיךָ הֶאֱמָנְתִּי׃ טֶרֶם
before (67) I-believe in-commands-of-you for teach-me! and-knowledge judgment

אֶעֱנֶה אֲנִי שֹׁגֵג וְעַתָּה אִמְרָתְךָ שָׁמָרְתִּי׃ טוֹב־אַתָּה
you good (68) I-obey word-of-you but-now one-going-astray I I-was-afflicted

and I meditate on your
decrees.

ז Zayin

49 Remember your word to your
servant,
for you have given me hope.
50 My comfort in my suffering is
this:
Your promise renews my
life.
51 The arrogant mock me without
restraint,
but I do not turn from your
law.
52 I remember your ancient laws,
O LORD,
and I find comfort in them.
53 Indignation grips me because
of the wicked,
who have forsaken your
law.
54 Your decrees are the theme of
my song
wherever I lodge.
55 In the night I remember your
name, O LORD,
and I will keep your law.
56 This has been my practice:
I obey your precepts.

ח Heth

57 You are my portion, O LORD;
I have promised to obey
your words.
58 I have sought your face with
all my heart;
be gracious to me according
to your promise.
59 I have considered my ways
and have turned my steps to
your statutes.
60 I will hasten and not delay
to obey your commands.
61 Though the wicked bind me
with ropes,
I will not forget your law.
62 At midnight I rise to give you
thanks
for your righteous laws.
63 I am a friend to all who fear
you,
to all who follow your
precepts.
64 The earth is filled with your
love, O LORD;
teach me your decrees.

ט Teth

65 Do good to your servant
according to your word, O
LORD.
66 Teach me knowledge and good
judgment,
for I believe in your
commands.
67 Before I was afflicted I went
astray,
but now I obey your word.
68 You are good, and what you

וּמֵטִיב לַמְּדֵנִי חֻקֶּיךָ׃ טָפְלוּ עָלַי שֶׁקֶר
lie upon-me they-smeared (69) decrees-of-you teach-me! and-one-doing-good

זֵדִים אֲנִי בְּכָל־ לֵב ׀ אֶצֹּר פִּקּוּדֶיךָ׃
precepts-of-you I-keep heart with-all-of I arrogant-ones

טָפַשׁ כַּחֵלֶב לִבָּם אֲנִי תּוֹרָתְךָ שִׁעֲשָׁעְתִּי׃
I-delight-in law-of-you I heart-of-them as-the-fat he-is-callous (70)

טוֹב־ לִי כִי־ עֻנֵּיתִי לְמַעַן אֶלְמַד חֻקֶּיךָ׃
decrees-of-you I-might-learn so-that I-was-afflicted that to-me good (71)

טוֹב־ לִי תוֹרַת־ פִּיךָ מֵאַלְפֵי זָהָב וָכָסֶף׃
and-silver gold more-than-thousands-of mouth-of-you law-of to-me precious (72)

יָדֶיךָ עָשׂוּנִי וַיְכוֹנְנוּנִי הֲבִינֵנִי
make-understand-me! and-they-formed-me they-made-me hands-of-you (73)

וְאֶלְמְדָה מִצְוֺתֶיךָ׃ יְרֵאֶיךָ יִרְאוּנִי
they-see-me ones-fearing-you (74) commands-of-you that-I-might-learn

וְיִשְׂמָחוּ כִּי לִדְבָרְךָ יִחָלְתִּי׃ יָדַעְתִּי יְהוָה כִּי־
that Yahweh I-know (75) I-hope in-word-of-you for and-they-rejoice

צֶדֶק מִשְׁפָּטֶיךָ וֶאֱמוּנָה עִנִּיתָנִי׃ יְהִי־ נָא
now! may-he-be (76) you-afflicted-me and-faithfulness laws-of-you righteous

חַסְדְּךָ לְנַחֲמֵנִי כְּאִמְרָתְךָ לְעַבְדֶּךָ׃
to-servant-of-you as-promise-of-you to-comfort-me unfailing-love-of-you

יְבֹאוּנִי רַחֲמֶיךָ וְאֶחְיֶה כִּי־ תוֹרָתְךָ
law-of-you for that-I-may-live compassions-of-you let-them-come-to-me (77)

שַׁעֲשֻׁעָי׃ יֵבֹשׁוּ זֵדִים כִּי־ שֶׁקֶר
without-cause for arrogant-ones may-they-be-shamed (78) delights-of-me

עִוְּתוּנִי אֲנִי אָשִׂיחַ בְּפִקּוּדֶיךָ׃ יָשׁוּבוּ
may-they-turn (79) on-precepts-of-you I-will-meditate I they-wronged-me

לִי יְרֵאֶיךָ °וְיֹדְעֵו עֵדֹתֶיךָ׃ יְהִי־
may-he-be (80) statutes-of-you and-ones-understanding-of ones-fearing-you to-me

לִבִּי תָמִים בְּחֻקֶּיךָ לְמַעַן לֹא אֵבוֹשׁ׃
I-may-be-shamed not so-that toward-decrees-of-you blameless heart-of-me

כָּלְתָה לִתְשׁוּעָתְךָ נַפְשִׁי לִדְבָרְךָ יִחָלְתִּי׃
I-put-hope in-word-of-you soul-of-me for-salvation-of-you she-faints (81)

כָּלוּ עֵינַי לְאִמְרָתֶךָ לֵאמֹר מָתַי תְּנַחֲמֵנִי׃
will-you-comfort-me when? to-say for-promise-of-you eyes-of-me they-fail (82)

כִּי־ הָיִיתִי כְּנֹאד בְּקִיטוֹר חֻקֶּיךָ לֹא שָׁכָחְתִּי׃
I-forget not decrees-of-you in-smoke like-wineskin I-am though (83)

כַּמָּה יְמֵי־ עַבְדֶּךָ מָתַי תַּעֲשֶׂה
will-you-execute when? servant-of-you days-of as-the-what? (84)

do is good;
teach me your decrees.
69Though the arrogant have smeared me with lies,
I keep your precepts with all my heart.
70Their hearts are callous and unfeeling,
but I delight in your law.
71It was good for me to be afflicted
so that I might learn your decrees.
72The law from your mouth is more precious to me
than thousands of pieces of silver and gold.

י Yodh

73Your hands made me and formed me;
give me understanding to learn your commands.
74May they who fear you rejoice when they see me,
for I have put my hope in your word.
75I know, O LORD, that your laws are righteous,
and in faithfulness you have afflicted me.
76May your unfailing love be my comfort,
according to your promise to your servant.
77Let your compassion come to me that I may live,
for your law is my delight.
78May the arrogant be put to shame for wronging me without cause;
but I will meditate on your precepts.
79May those who fear you turn to me,
those who understand your statutes.
80May my heart be blameless toward your decrees,
that I may not be put to shame.

כ Kaph

81My soul faints with longing for your salvation,
but I have put my hope in your word.
82My eyes fail, looking for your promise;
I say, "When will you comfort me?"
83Though I am like a wineskin in the smoke,
I do not forget your decrees.
84How long must your servant wait?
When will you punish my

*69 Most mss have *segol* under the *aleph* (אֶ).

°79 ק וידעי

רֹדְפַי מִשְׁפָּט׃ כָּרוּ־ לִי זֵדִים שִׁיחוֹת
pitfalls arrogant-ones for-me they-dig (85) punishment on-ones-persecuting-me

אֲשֶׁר לֹא כְתוֹרָתֶךָ׃ כָּל־ מִצְוֺתֶיךָ אֱמוּנָה שֶׁקֶר
without-cause trustworthy commands-of-you all-of (86) as-law-of-you not that

רְדָפוּנִי עָזְרֵנִי׃ כִּמְעַט כִּלּוּנִי בָאָרֶץ וַאֲנִי
but-I from-the-earth they-wiped-me as-almost (87) help-me! they-persecute-me

לֹא־ עָזַבְתִּי פִקֻּדֶיךָ׃ כְּחַסְדְּךָ חַיֵּנִי
preserve-alive-me! as-love-of-you (88) precepts-of-you I-forsook not

וְאֶשְׁמְרָה עֵדוּת פִּיךָ׃ לְעוֹלָם יְהוָה דְּבָרְךָ
word-of-you Yahweh to-eternity (89) mouth-of-you statute-of and-I-will-obey

נִצָּב בַּשָּׁמָיִם׃ לְדֹר וָדֹר
and-generation to-generation (90) in-the-heavens one-standing-firm

אֱמוּנָתֶךָ כּוֹנַנְתָּ אֶרֶץ וַתַּעֲמֹד׃ לְמִשְׁפָּטֶיךָ
as-laws-of-you (91) and-she-endures earth you-established faithfulness-of-you

עָמְדוּ הַיּוֹם כִּי הַכֹּל עֲבָדֶיךָ׃ לוּלֵי תוֹרָתְךָ
law-of-you if-not (92) servants-of-you the-all for the-day they-endure

שַׁעֲשֻׁעָי אָז אָבַדְתִּי בְעָנְיִי׃ לְעוֹלָם
to-forever (93) in-affliction-of-me I-would-have-perished then delights-of-me

לֹא־ אֶשְׁכַּח פִּקּוּדֶיךָ כִּי בָם חִיִּיתָנִי׃ לְךָ־
to-you (94) you-made-alive-me by-them for precepts-of-you I-will-forget not

אֲנִי הוֹשִׁיעֵנִי כִּי פִקּוּדֶיךָ דָרָשְׁתִּי׃ לִי קִוּוּ
they-wait for-me (95) I-sought-out precepts-of-you for save-me! I

רְשָׁעִים לְאַבְּדֵנִי עֵדֹתֶיךָ אֶתְבּוֹנָן׃ לְכָל
to-all-of (96) I-will-ponder statutes-of-you to-destroy-me wicked-ones

תִּכְלָה רָאִיתִי קֵץ רְחָבָה מִצְוָתְךָ מְאֹד׃ מָה־אָהַבְתִּי
I-love how! (97) very command-of-you boundless limit I-see perfection

תוֹרָתֶךָ כָּל־ הַיּוֹם הִיא שִׂיחָתִי׃ מֵאֹיְבַי
than-ones-being-enemies-of-me (98) meditation-of-me she the-day all-of law-of-you

תְּחַכְּמֵנִי מִצְוֺתֶךָ כִּי לְעוֹלָם הִיא־ לִי׃
with-me she to-forever for commands-of-you she-makes-wiser-me

מִכָּל־ מְלַמְּדַי הִשְׂכַּלְתִּי כִּי עֵדְוֺתֶיךָ
statutes-of-you for I-have-insight ones-teaching-me more-than-all-of (99)

שִׂיחָה לִי׃ מִזְּקֵנִים אֶתְבּוֹנָן כִּי פִקּוּדֶיךָ
precepts-of-you for I-understand more-than-elders (100) of-me meditation

נָצָרְתִּי׃ מִכָּל־ אֹרַח רָע כָּלִאתִי רַגְלָי לְמַעַן אֶשְׁמֹר
I-might-obey so-that feet-of-me I-kept evil path from-every-of (101) I-obey

דְּבָרֶךָ׃ מִמִּשְׁפָּטֶיךָ לֹא־ סָרְתִּי כִּי־ אַתָּה הוֹרֵתָנִי׃
you-taught-me you for I-departed not from-laws-of-you (102) word-of-you

persecutors?
85 The arrogant dig pitfalls for
me,
contrary to your law.
86 All your commands are
trustworthy;
help me, for men persecute
me without cause.
87 They almost wiped me from
the earth,
but I have not forsaken your
precepts.
88 Preserve my life according to
your love,
and I will obey the statutes
of your mouth.

ל Lamedh

89 Your word, O LORD, is eternal;
it stands firm in the
heavens.
90 Your faithfulness continues
through all generations;
you established the earth,
and it endures.
91 Your laws endure to this day,
for all things serve you.
92 If your law had not been my
delight,
I would have perished in
my affliction.
93 I will never forget your
precepts,
for by them you have
renewed my life.
94 Save me, for I am yours;
I have sought out your
precepts.
95 The wicked are waiting to
destroy me,
but I will ponder your
statutes.
96 To all perfection I see a limit;
but your commands are
boundless.

מ Mem

97 Oh, how I love your law!
I meditate on it all day long.
98 Your commands make me
wiser than my enemies,
for they are ever with me.
99 I have more insight than all
my teachers,
for I meditate on your
statutes.
100 I have more understanding
than the elders,
for I obey your precepts.
101 I have kept my feet from every
evil path
so that I might obey your
word.
102 I have not departed from your
laws,
for you yourself have taught
me.

מַה־ נִּמְלְצוּ לְחִכִּי אִמְרָתֶךָ מִדְּבַשׁ
more-than-honey promise-of-you to-taste-of-me they-are-sweet how! (103)

לְפִי׃ מִפִּקּוּדֶיךָ אֶתְבּוֹנָן עַל־ כֵּן
this for I-gain-understanding from-precepts-of-you (104) to-mouth-of-me

שָׂנֵאתִי ׀ כָּל־ אֹרַח שָׁקֶר׃ נֵר־ לְרַגְלִי דְבָרֶךָ וְאוֹר
and-light word-of-you to-foot-of-me lamp (105) wrongness path-of every-of I-hate

לִנְתִיבָתִי׃ נִשְׁבַּעְתִּי וָאֲקַיֵּמָה לִשְׁמֹר מִשְׁפְּטֵי
laws-of to-follow and-I-confirmed I-took-oath (106) for-path-of-me

צִדְקֶךָ׃ נַעֲנֵיתִי עַד־ מְאֹד יְהוָה חַיֵּנִי
make-alive-me! Yahweh much to I-suffered (107) righteousness-of-you

כִדְבָרֶךָ׃ נִדְבוֹת פִּי רְצֵה־ נָא יְהוָה
Yahweh now! accept! mouth-of-me willing-praises-of (108) as-word-of-you

וּמִשְׁפָּטֶיךָ לַמְּדֵנִי׃ נַפְשִׁי בְכַפִּי תָמִיד
constantly in-hand-of-me life-of-me (109) teach-me! and-laws-of-you

וְתוֹרָתְךָ לֹא שָׁכָחְתִּי׃ נָתְנוּ רְשָׁעִים פַּח לִי
for-me snare wicked-ones they-set (110) I-will-forget not but-law-of-you

וּמִפִּקּוּדֶיךָ לֹא תָעִיתִי׃ נָחַלְתִּי עֵדְוֺתֶיךָ
statutes-of-you I-have-heritage (111) I-strayed not but-from-precepts-of-you

לְעוֹלָם כִּי־ שְׂשׂוֹן לִבִּי הֵמָּה׃ נָטִיתִי לִבִּי לַעֲשׂוֹת
to-keep heart-of-me I-set (112) they heart-of-me joy-of indeed to-forever

חֻקֶּיךָ לְעוֹלָם עֵקֶב׃ סֵעֲפִים שָׂנֵאתִי
I-hate double-minded-men (113) very-end to-forever decrees-of-you

וְתוֹרָתְךָ אָהָבְתִּי׃ סִתְרִי וּמָגִנִּי אָתָּה לִדְבָרְךָ
in-word-of-you you and-shield-of-me refuge-of-me (114) I-love but-law-of-you

יִחָלְתִּי׃ סוּרוּ־ מִמֶּנִּי מְרֵעִים וְאֶצְּרָה מִצְוֺת
commands-of that-I-may-keep ones-doing-evil from-me be-away! (115) I-put-hope

אֱלֹהָי׃ סָמְכֵנִי כְאִמְרָתְךָ וְאֶחְיֶה וְאַל־
and-not and-I-will-live as-promise-of-you sustain-me! (116) God-of-me

תְּבִישֵׁנִי מִשִּׂבְרִי׃ סְעָדֵנִי וְאִוָּשֵׁעָה
and-I-will-be-delivered uphold-me! (117) from-hope-of-me you-shame-me

וְאֶשְׁעָה בְחֻקֶּיךָ תָמִיד׃ סָלִיתָ כָּל־
all-of you-reject (118) always for-decrees-of-you and-I-will-have-regard

שׁוֹגִים מֵחֻקֶּיךָ כִּי־ שֶׁקֶר תַּרְמִיתָם׃ סִגִים
drosses (119) deceitfulness-of-them vain for from-decrees-of-you ones-straying

הִשְׁבַּתָּ כָל־ רִשְׁעֵי־ אָרֶץ לָכֵן אָהַבְתִּי עֵדֹתֶיךָ׃
statutes-of-you I-love therefore earth wicked-ones-of all-of you-discard

סָמַר מִפַּחְדְּךָ בְשָׂרִי וּמִמִּשְׁפָּטֶיךָ יָרֵאתִי׃
I-stand-in-awe and-of-laws-of-you flesh-of-me in-fear-of-you he-trembles (120)

103 How sweet are your promises
to my taste,
sweeter than honey to my
mouth!
104 I gain understanding from
your precepts;
therefore I hate every wrong
path.

נ Nun

105 Your word is a lamp to my
feet
and a light for my path.
106 I have taken an oath and
confirmed it,
that I will follow your
righteous laws.
107 I have suffered much;
renew my life, O LORD,
according to your word.
108 Accept, O LORD, the willing
praise of my mouth,
and teach me your laws.
109 Though I constantly take my
life in my hands,
I will not forget your law.
110 The wicked have set a snare
for me,
but I have not strayed from
your precepts.
111 Your statutes are my heritage
forever;
they are the joy of my heart.
112 My heart is set on keeping
your decrees
to the very end.

ס Samekh

113 I hate double-minded men,
but I love your law.
114 You are my refuge and my
shield;
I have put my hope in your
word.
115 Away from me, you evildoers,
that I may keep the
commands of my God!
116 Sustain me according to your
promise, and I will live;
do not let my hopes be
dashed.
117 Uphold me, and I will be
delivered;
I will always have regard for
your decrees.
118 You reject all who stray from
your decrees,
for their deceitfulness is in
vain.
119 All the wicked of the earth you
discard like dross;
therefore I love your
statutes.
120 My flesh trembles in fear of
you;
I stand in awe of your laws.

עָשִׂיתִי מִשְׁפָּט וָצֶדֶק בַּל־תַּנִּיחֵנִי לְעֹשְׁקָי׃
to-ones-oppressing-me you-leave-me not and-justice righteousness I-did (121)

עֲרֹב עַבְדְּךָ לְטוֹב אַל־יַעַשְׁקֻנִי
let-them-oppress-me not of-well-being servant-of-you ensure! (122)

זֵדִים׃ עֵינַי כָּלוּ לִישׁוּעָתֶךָ וּלְאִמְרַת
and-for-promise-of for-salvation-of-you they-fail eyes-of-me (123) arrogant-ones

צִדְקֶךָ׃ עֲשֵׂה עִם־עַבְדְּךָ כְחַסְדֶּךָ
as-love-of-you servant-of-you with deal! (124) righteousness-of-you

וְחֻקֶּיךָ לַמְּדֵנִי׃ עַבְדְּךָ־אָנִי הֲבִינֵנִי
make-discern-me! I servant-of-you (125) teach-me! and-decrees-of-you

וְאֵדְעָה עֵדֹתֶיךָ׃ עֵת לַעֲשׂוֹת לַיהוָה הֵפֵרוּ
they-break O-Yahweh to-act time (126) statutes-of-you that-I-may-understand

תּוֹרָתֶךָ׃ עַל־כֵּן אָהַבְתִּי מִצְוֹתֶיךָ מִזָּהָב
more-than-gold commands-of-you I-love this for (127) law-of-you

וּמִפָּז׃ עַל־כֵּן ׀ כָּל־פִּקּוּדֵי כֹל יִשָּׁרְתִּי
I-consider-right all precepts-of all-of this for (128) even-more-than-pure-gold

כָּל־אֹרַח שֶׁקֶר שָׂנֵאתִי׃ פְּלָאוֹת עֵדְוֺתֶיךָ עַל־כֵּן
this for statutes-of-you wonderful-ones (129) I-hate wrongness path-of every-of

נְצָרָתַם נַפְשִׁי׃ פֵּתַח דְּבָרֶיךָ יָאִיר
he-gives-light words-of-you entrance-of (130) self-of-me she-obeys-them

מֵבִין פְּתָיִים׃ פִּי־פָעַרְתִּי וָאֶשְׁאָפָה כִּי
for and-I-pant I-open mouth-of-me (131) simple-ones one-giving-understanding

לְמִצְוֹתֶיךָ יָאָבְתִּי׃ פְּנֵה־אֵלַי וְחָנֵּנִי כְּמִשְׁפָּט
as-custom and-have-mercy-on-me! to-me turn! (132) I-long for-commands-of-you

לְאֹהֲבֵי שְׁמֶךָ׃ פְּעָמַי הָכֵן בְּאִמְרָתֶךָ
as-word-of-you direct! footsteps-of-me (133) name-of-you to-ones-loving-of

וְאַל־תַּשְׁלֶט־בִּי כָל־אָוֶן׃ פְּדֵנִי מֵעֹשֶׁק
from-oppression-of redeem-me! (134) sin any-of over-me you-let-rule and-not

אָדָם וְאֶשְׁמְרָה פִּקּוּדֶיךָ׃ פָּנֶיךָ הָאֵר
make-shine! faces-of-you (135) precepts-of-you that-I-may-obey man

בְּעַבְדֶּךָ וְלַמְּדֵנִי אֶת־חֻקֶּיךָ׃ פַּלְגֵי־מַיִם
tears streams-of (136) decrees-of-you *** and-teach-me! upon-servant-of-you

יָרְדוּ עֵינָי עַל לֹא־שָׁמְרוּ תוֹרָתֶךָ׃ צַדִּיק אַתָּה
you righteous (137) law-of-you they-obey not for eyes-of-me they-flow-down

יְהוָה וְיָשָׁר מִשְׁפָּטֶיךָ׃ צִוִּיתָ צֶדֶק עֵדֹתֶיךָ
statutes-of-you righteous you-laid-down (138) laws-of-you and-right Yahweh

וֶאֱמוּנָה מְאֹד׃ צִמְּתַתְנִי קִנְאָתִי כִּי־שָׁכְחוּ
they-ignore for zeal-of-me she-wears-out-me (139) fully and-trustworthy

ע Ayin

121 I have done what is righteous
and just;
do not leave me to my
oppressors.
122 Ensure your servant's
well-being;
let not the arrogant oppress
me.
123 My eyes fail, looking for your
salvation,
looking for your righteous
promise.
124 Deal with your servant
according to your love
and teach me your decrees.
125 I am your servant; give me
discernment
that I may understand your
statutes.
126 It is time for you to act, O
LORD;
your law is being broken.
127 Because I love your commands
more than gold, more than
pure gold,
128 and because I consider all your
precepts right,
I hate every wrong path.

פ Pe

129 Your statutes are wonderful;
therefore I obey them.
130 The entrance of your words
gives light;
it gives understanding to
the simple.
131 I open my mouth and pant,
longing for your commands.
132 Turn to me and have mercy on
me,
as you always do to those
who love your name.
133 Direct my footsteps according
to your word;
let no sin rule over me.
134 Redeem me from the
oppression of men,
that I may obey your
precepts.
135 Make your face shine upon
your servant
and teach me your decrees.
136 Streams of tears flow from my
eyes,
for your law is not obeyed.

צ Tsadhe

137 Righteous are you, O LORD,
and your laws are right.
138 The statutes you have laid
down are righteous;
they are fully trustworthy.
139 My zeal wears me out,

דְּבָרֶיךָ צָרָי׃ (140) צְרוּפָה אִמְרָתְךָ מְאֹד
thoroughly promise-of-you one-being-tested (140) enemies-of-me words-of-you

וְעַבְדְּךָ אֲהֵבָהּ׃ (141) צָעִיר אָנֹכִי וְנִבְזֶה
and-one-being-despised I lowly (141) he-loves-her and-servant-of-you

פִּקֻּדֶיךָ לֹא שָׁכָחְתִּי׃ (142) צִדְקָתְךָ צֶדֶק לְעוֹלָם
to-everlasting righteousness righteousness-of-you (142) I-forget not precepts-of-you

וְתוֹרָתְךָ אֱמֶת׃ (143) צַר־ וּמָצוֹק מְצָאוּנִי
they-came-upon-me and-distress trouble (143) true and-law-of-you

מִצְוֹתֶיךָ שַׁעֲשֻׁעָי׃ (144) צֶדֶק עֵדְוֹתֶיךָ לְעוֹלָם
to-forever statutes-of-you right (144) delights-of-me commands-of-you

הֲבִינֵנִי וְאֶחְיֶה׃ (145) קָרָאתִי בְכָל־ לֵב עֲנֵנִי
answer-me! heart with-all-of I-call (145) that-I-may-live make-understand-me!

יְהוָה חֻקֶּיךָ אֶצֹּרָה׃ (146) קְרָאתִיךָ הוֹשִׁיעֵנִי וְאֶשְׁמְרָה
and-I-will-keep save-me! I-call-to-you (146) I-will-obey decrees-of-you Yahweh

עֵדֹתֶיךָ׃ (147) קִדַּמְתִּי בַנֶּשֶׁף וָאֲשַׁוֵּעָה לִדְבָרְיךָ°
in-word-of-you and-I-cry-for-help before-the-dawn I-rise (147) statutes-of-you

יִחָלְתִּי׃ (148) קִדְּמוּ עֵינַי אַשְׁמֻרוֹת לָשִׂיחַ
to-meditate night-watches eyes-of-me they-stay-open (148) I-put-hope

בְּאִמְרָתֶךָ׃ (149) קוֹלִי שִׁמְעָה כְחַסְדֶּךָ יְהוָה כְּמִשְׁפָּטֶךָ
as-law-of-you Yahweh as-love-of-you hear! voice-of-me (149) on-promise-of-you

חַיֵּנִי׃ (150) קָרְבוּ רֹדְפֵי זִמָּה מִתּוֹרָתְךָ
from-law-of-you scheme ones-devising-of they-are-near (150) make-alive-me!

רָחָקוּ׃ (151) קָרוֹב אַתָּה יְהוָה וְכָל־ מִצְוֹתֶיךָ אֱמֶת׃
true commands-of-you and-all-of Yahweh you near (151) they-are-far

(152) קֶדֶם יָדַעְתִּי מֵעֵדֹתֶיךָ כִּי לְעוֹלָם
to-forever that from-statutes-of-you I-learned long-ago (152)

יְסַדְתָּם׃ (153) רְאֵה־ עָנְיִי וְחַלְּצֵנִי כִּי־
for and-deliver-me! suffering-of-me look-upon! (153) you-established-them

תוֹרָתְךָ לֹא שָׁכָחְתִּי׃ (154) רִיבָה רִיבִי וּגְאָלֵנִי
and-redeem-me! cause-of-me defend! (154) I-forgot not law-of-you

לְאִמְרָתְךָ חַיֵּנִי׃ (155) רָחוֹק מֵרְשָׁעִים יְשׁוּעָה כִּי־
for salvation from-wicked-ones far (155) make-alive-me! as-promise-of-you

חֻקֶּיךָ לֹא דָרָשׁוּ׃ (156) רַחֲמֶיךָ רַבִּים׀ יְהוָה
Yahweh great-ones compassions-of-you (156) they-seek-out not decrees-of-you

כְּמִשְׁפָּטֶיךָ חַיֵּנִי׃ (157) רַבִּים רֹדְפַי וְצָרָי
even-foes-of-me ones-persecuting-me many (157) make-alive-me! as-laws-of-you

מֵעֵדְוֹתֶיךָ לֹא נָטִיתִי׃ (158) רָאִיתִי בֹגְדִים
ones-being-faithless I-look-on (158) I-turned not from-statutes-of-you

for my enemies ignore your
words.
140 Your promises have been
thoroughly tested,
and your servant loves
them.
141 Though I am lowly and
despised,
I do not forget your
precepts.
142 Your righteousness is
everlasting
and your law is true.
143 Trouble and distress have
come upon me,
but your commands are my
delight.
144 Your statutes are forever right;
give me understanding that
I may live.

ק Qoph

145 I call with all my heart;
answer me, O LORD,
and I will obey your
decrees.
146 I call out to you; save me
and I will keep your
statutes.
147 I rise before dawn and cry for
help;
I have put my hope in your
word.
148 My eyes stay open through the
watches of the night,
that I may meditate on your
promises.
149 Hear my voice in accordance
with your love;
renew my life, O LORD,
according to your laws.
150 Those who devise wicked
schemes are near,
but they are far from your
law.
151 Yet you are near, O LORD,
and all your commands are
true.
152 Long ago I learned from your
statutes
that you established them to
last forever.

ר Resh

153 Look upon my suffering and
deliver me,
for I have not forgotten your
law.
154 Defend my cause and redeem
me;
renew my life according to
your promise.
155 Salvation is far from the
wicked,
for they do not seek out
your decrees.
156 Your compassion is great, O
LORD;
renew my life according to
your laws.
157 Many are the foes who
persecute me,
but I have not turned from
your statutes.
158 I look on the faithless with

°147 ק לדברך

וָאֶתְקוֹטָטָה אֲשֶׁר אִמְרָתְךָ לֹא שָׁמָרוּ׃ רְאֵה כִּי־ פִקּוּדֶיךָ
precepts-of-you how see! (159) they-obey not word-of-you for and-I-loathe

אָהָבְתִּי יְהוָה כְּחַסְדְּךָ חַיֵּנִי׃ רֹאשׁ־ דְּבָרְךָ אֱמֶת
true word-of-you all-of (160) keep-alive-me! as-love-of-you Yahweh I-love

וּלְעוֹלָם כָּל־ מִשְׁפַּט צִדְקֶךָ׃ שָׂרִים
rulers (161) righteousness-of-you law-of all-of and-to-eternity

רְדָפוּנִי חִנָּם וּמִדְּבָרְיךָ° פָּחַד לִבִּי׃
heart-of-me he-trembles but-at-word-of-you without-cause they-persecute-me

שָׂשׂ אָנֹכִי עַל־ אִמְרָתֶךָ כְּמוֹצֵא שָׁלָל רָב׃
great spoil like-one-finding promise-of-you in I one-rejoicing (162)

שֶׁקֶר שָׂנֵאתִי וַאֲתַעֵבָה תּוֹרָתְךָ אָהָבְתִּי׃ שֶׁבַע בַּיּוֹם
in-the-day seven (164) I-love law-of-you and-I-abhor I-hate falsehood (163)

הִלַּלְתִּיךָ עַל מִשְׁפְּטֵי צִדְקֶךָ׃ שָׁלוֹם רָב
great peace (165) righteousness-of-you laws-of for I-praise-you

לְאֹהֲבֵי תוֹרָתֶךָ וְאֵין־ לָמוֹ מִכְשׁוֹל׃ שִׂבַּרְתִּי
I-wait (166) stumbling to-them and-nothing law-of-you to-ones-loving-of

לִישׁוּעָתְךָ יְהוָה וּמִצְוֹתֶיךָ עָשִׂיתִי׃ שָׁמְרָה
she-obeys (167) I-follow and-commands-of-you Yahweh for-salvation-of-you

נַפְשִׁי עֵדֹתֶיךָ וָאֹהֲבֵם מְאֹד׃ שָׁמַרְתִּי פִקּוּדֶיךָ
precepts-of-you I-obey (168) greatly for-I-love-them statutes-of-you self-of-me

וְעֵדֹתֶיךָ כִּי כָל־ דְּרָכַי נֶגְדֶּךָ׃ תִּקְרַב
may-she-come (169) before-you ways-of-me all-of for and-statutes-of-you

רִנָּתִי לְפָנֶיךָ יְהוָה כִּדְבָרְךָ הֲבִינֵנִי׃
make-understand-me! as-word-of-you Yahweh before-you cry-of-me

תָּבוֹא תְּחִנָּתִי לְפָנֶיךָ כְּאִמְרָתְךָ הַצִּילֵנִי׃
deliver-me! as-promise-of-you before-you supplication-of-me may-she-come (170)

תַּבַּעְנָה שְׂפָתַי תְּהִלָּה כִּי תְלַמְּדֵנִי חֻקֶּיךָ׃
decrees-of-you you-teach-me for praise lips-of-me may-they-overflow (171)

תַּעַן לְשׁוֹנִי אִמְרָתֶךָ כִּי כָל־ מִצְוֹתֶיךָ
commands-of-you all-of for word-of-you tongue-of-me may-she-sing (172)

צֶּדֶק׃ תְּהִי־ יָדְךָ לְעָזְרֵנִי כִּי פִקּוּדֶיךָ בָחָרְתִּי׃
I-chose precepts-of-you for to-help-me hand-of-you may-she-be (173) righteous

תָּאַבְתִּי לִישׁוּעָתְךָ יְהוָה וְתוֹרָתְךָ שַׁעֲשֻׁעָי׃
delights-of-me and-law-of-you Yahweh for-salvation-of-you I-long (174)

תְּחִי־ נַפְשִׁי וּתְהַלְלֶךָּ וּמִשְׁפָּטֶךָ
and-laws-of-you that-she-may-praise-you self-of-me let-her-live (175)

יַעְזְרֻנִי׃ תָּעִיתִי כְּשֶׂה אֹבֵד בַּקֵּשׁ
seek! one-being-lost like-sheep I-strayed (176) may-they-sustain-me

loathing,
for they do not obey your word.
159 See how I love your precepts;
preserve my life, O LORD, according to your love.
160 All your words are true;
all your righteous laws are eternal.

ש Sin and Shin

161 Rulers persecute me without cause,
but my heart trembles at your word.
162 I rejoice in your promise
like one who finds great spoil.
163 I hate and abhor falsehood
but I love your law.
164 Seven times a day I praise you
for your righteous laws.
165 Great peace have they who love your law,
and nothing can make them stumble.
166 I wait for your salvation, O LORD,
and I follow your commands.
167 I obey your statutes,
for I love them greatly.
168 I obey your precepts and your statutes,
for all my ways are known to you.

ת Taw

169 May my cry come before you, O LORD;
give me understanding according to your word.
170 May my supplication come before you;
deliver me according to your promise.
171 May my lips overflow with praise,
for you teach me your decrees.
172 May my tongue sing of your word,
for all your commands are righteous.
173 May your hand be ready to help me,
for I have chosen your precepts.
174 I long for your salvation, O LORD,
and your law is my delight.
175 Let me live that I may praise you,
and may your laws sustain me.
176 I have strayed like a lost sheep.

°161 ק ומדברך

עַבְדֶּךָ כִּי מִצְוֹתֶיךָ לֹא שָׁכָחְתִּי׃ שִׁיר הַמַּעֲלוֹת
the-ascents song-of (120:1) I-forgot not commands-of-you for servant-of-you

אֶל־יְהוָה בַּצָּרָתָה לִּי קָרָאתִי וַיַּעֲנֵנִי׃ יְהוָה הַצִּילָה
save! Yahweh (2) and-he-answers-me I-call of-me in-the-distress Yahweh on

נַפְשִׁי מִשְּׂפַת־שֶׁקֶר מִלָּשׁוֹן רְמִיָּה׃ מַה־יִּתֵּן לְךָ
to-you will-he-do what? (3) deceitful from-tongue lie from-lip-of self-of-me

וּמַה־יֹּסִיף לָךְ לָשׁוֹן רְמִיָּה׃ חִצֵּי גִבּוֹר
warrior arrows-of (4) deceitful tongue to-you will-he-do-more and-what?

שְׁנוּנִים עִם גַּחֲלֵי רְתָמִים׃ אוֹיָה־לִי כִּי־גַרְתִּי
I-dwell that to-me woe! (5) broom-trees coals-of with ones-being-sharp

מֶשֶׁךְ שָׁכַנְתִּי עִם־אָהֳלֵי קֵדָר׃ רַבַּת שָׁכְנָה־לָּהּ נַפְשִׁי
self-of-me to-her she-lived too-long (6) Kedar tents-of among I-live Meshech

עִם שׂוֹנֵא שָׁלוֹם׃ אֲנִי־שָׁלוֹם וְכִי אֲדַבֵּר הֵמָּה לַמִּלְחָמָה׃
for-the-war they I-speak but-when peaceful I (7) peace one-hating among

שִׁיר לַמַּעֲלוֹת אֶשָּׂא עֵינַי אֶל־הֶהָרִים מֵאַיִן
from-where? the-hills to eyes-of-me I-will-lift-up of-the-ascents song (121:1)

יָבֹא עֶזְרִי׃ עֶזְרִי מֵעִם יְהוָה עֹשֵׂה שָׁמַיִם
heavens One-Making-of Yahweh from-with help-of-me (2) help-of-me he-comes

וָאָרֶץ׃ אַל־יִתֵּן לַמּוֹט רַגְלֶךָ אַל־יָנוּם
he-will-slumber not foot-of-you for-the-slipping he-will-let not (3) and-earth

שֹׁמְרֶךָ׃ הִנֵּה לֹא־יָנוּם וְלֹא יִישָׁן
he-will-sleep and-not he-will-slumber not indeed! (4) one-watching-over-you

שׁוֹמֵר יִשְׂרָאֵל׃ יְהוָה שֹׁמְרֶךָ יְהוָה צִלְּךָ
shade-of-you Yahweh one-watching-over-you Yahweh (5) Israel one-watching-over

עַל־יַד יְמִינֶךָ׃ יוֹמָם הַשֶּׁמֶשׁ לֹא־יַכֶּכָּה וְיָרֵחַ
or-moon he-will-harm-you not the-sun by-day (6) right-of-you hand-of at

בַּלָּיְלָה׃ יְהוָה יִשְׁמָרְךָ מִכָּל־רָע יִשְׁמֹר
he-will-watch-over harm from-all-of he-will-keep-you Yahweh (7) by-the-night

אֶת־נַפְשֶׁךָ׃ יְהוָה יִשְׁמָר־צֵאתְךָ וּבוֹאֶךָ
and-to-come-you to-go-you he-will-watch-over Yahweh (8) life-of-you ***

מֵעַתָּה וְעַד־עוֹלָם׃ שִׁיר הַמַּעֲלוֹת לְדָוִד שָׂמַחְתִּי
I-rejoiced of-David the-ascents song-of (122:1) forevermore and-to from-now

בְּאֹמְרִים לִי בֵּית יְהוָה נֵלֵךְ׃ עֹמְדוֹת הָיוּ
they-are ones-standing (2) let-us-go Yahweh house-of to-me with-ones-saying

רַגְלֵינוּ בִּשְׁעָרַיִךְ יְרוּשָׁלָםִ׃ יְרוּשָׁלַםִ הַבְּנוּיָה
the-one-being-built Jerusalem (3) Jerusalem in-gates-of-you feet-of-us

כְּעִיר שֶׁחֻבְּרָה־לָּהּ יַחְדָּו׃ שֶׁשָּׁם עָלוּ
they-go-up that-there (4) together to-her that-she-is-compacted like-city

Seek your servant,
for I have not forgotten your commandments.

### Psalm 120

A song of ascents.

1 I call on the LORD in my distress,
and he answers me.
2 Save me, O LORD, from lying lips
and from deceitful tongues.

3 What will he do to you,
and what more besides, O deceitful tongue?
4 He will punish you with a warrior's sharp arrows,
with burning coals of the broom tree.

5 Woe to me that I dwell in Meshech,
that I live among the tents of Kedar!
6 Too long have I lived
among those who hate peace.
7 I am a man of peace;
but when I speak, they are for war.

### Psalm 121

A song of ascents.

1 I lift up my eyes to the hills—
where does my help come from?
2 My help comes from the LORD,
the Maker of heaven and earth.

3 He will not let your foot slip—
he who watches over you will not slumber;
4 indeed, he who watches over Israel
will neither slumber nor sleep.

5 The LORD watches over you—
the LORD is your shade at your right hand;
6 the sun will not harm you by day,
nor the moon by night.

7 The LORD will keep you from all harm—
he will watch over your life;
8 the LORD will watch over your coming and going
both now and forevermore.

### Psalm 122

A song of ascents. Of David.

1 I rejoiced with those who said to me,
"Let us go to the house of the LORD."
2 Our feet are standing
in your gates, O Jerusalem.

3 Jerusalem is built like a city
that is closely compacted together.
4 That is where the tribes go up,

שְׁבָטִים שִׁבְטֵי־יָהּ עֵדוּת לְיִשְׂרָאֵל לְהֹדוֹת לְשֵׁם יְהוָה׃
Yahweh to-name-of to-praise to-Israel statute Yahweh tribes-of tribes

כִּי שָׁמָּה ׀ יָשְׁבוּ כִסְאוֹת לְמִשְׁפָּט כִּסְאוֹת לְבֵית דָּוִיד׃
David of-house-of thrones for-judgment thrones they-stand at-there for (5)

שַׁאֲלוּ שְׁלוֹם יְרוּשָׁלִָם יִשְׁלָיוּ אֹהֲבָיִךְ׃ יְהִי־
may-he-be (7) ones-loving-you may-they-be-secure Jerusalem peace-of pray! (6)

שָׁלוֹם בְּחֵילֵךְ שַׁלְוָה בְּאַרְמְנוֹתָיִךְ׃ לְמַעַן
for-sake-of (8) within-citadels-of-you security within-wall-of-you peace

אַחַי וְרֵעָי אֲדַבְּרָה־נָּא שָׁלוֹם בָּךְ׃
within-you peace now! I-will-say and-friends-of-me brothers-of-me

לְמַעַן בֵּית־יְהוָה אֱלֹהֵינוּ אֲבַקְשָׁה טוֹב לָךְ׃
of-you prosperity I-will-seek God-of-us Yahweh house-of for-sake-of (9)

שִׁיר הַמַּעֲלוֹת אֵלֶיךָ נָשָׂאתִי אֶת־עֵינַי הַיֹּשְׁבִי
the-one-sitting eyes-of-me *** I-lift-up to-you the-ascents song-of (123:1)

בַּשָּׁמָיִם׃ הִנֵּה כְעֵינֵי עֲבָדִים אֶל־יַד אֲדוֹנֵיהֶם
masters-of-them hand-of to slaves as-eyes-of see! (2) in-the-heavens

כְּעֵינֵי שִׁפְחָה אֶל־יַד גְּבִרְתָּהּ כֵּן עֵינֵינוּ אֶל־יְהוָה אֱלֹהֵינוּ
God-of-us Yahweh to eyes-of-us so mistress-of-her hand-of to maid as-eyes-of

עַד שֶׁיְּחָנֵּנוּ׃ חָנֵּנוּ יְהוָה חָנֵּנוּ
have-mercy-on-us! Yahweh have-mercy-on-us! (3) when-he-shows-mercy-to-us till

כִּי־רַב שָׂבַעְנוּ בוּז׃ רַבַּת שָׂבְעָה־לָּהּ נַפְשֵׁנוּ
self-of-us to-her she-endured much (4) contempt we-endured much for

הַלַּעַג הַשַּׁאֲנַנִּים הַבּוּז לִגְאֵיוֹנִים׃ שִׁיר
song-of (124:1) *of-arrogant-ones the-contempt the-proud-ones the-ridicule

הַמַּעֲלוֹת לְדָוִד לוּלֵי יְהוָה שֶׁהָיָה לָנוּ יֹאמַר־נָא יִשְׂרָאֵל׃
Israel now! let-him-say for-us who-he-was Yahweh if-not of-David the-ascents

לוּלֵי יְהוָה שֶׁהָיָה לָנוּ בְּקוּם עָלֵינוּ אָדָם׃ אֲזַי
then (3) man against-us when-to-attack for-us who-he-was Yahweh if-not (2)

חַיִּים בְּלָעוּנוּ בַּחֲרוֹת אַפָּם בָּנוּ׃
against-us anger-of-them when-to-flare they-would-have-swallowed-us ones-alive

אֲזַי הַמַּיִם שְׁטָפוּנוּ נַחְלָה עָבַר
he-would-have-swept torrent they-would-have-engulfed-us the-floods then (4)

עַל־נַפְשֵׁנוּ׃ אֲזַי עָבַר עַל־נַפְשֵׁנוּ הַמַּיִם
the-waters self-of-us over he-would-have-swept then (5) self-of-us over

הַזֵּידוֹנִים׃ בָּרוּךְ יְהוָה שֶׁלֹּא נְתָנָנוּ טֶרֶף
one-torn he-let-us who-not Yahweh being-praised (6) the-raging-ones

לְשִׁנֵּיהֶם׃ נַפְשֵׁנוּ כְּצִפּוֹר נִמְלְטָה מִפַּח
from-snare-of she-escaped like-bird self-of-us (7) by-teeth-of-them

the tribes of the LORD,
to praise the name of the LORD
according to the statute
given to Israel.
5 There the thrones for
judgment stand,
the thrones of the house of
David.
6 Pray for the peace of
Jerusalem:
"May those who love you be
secure.
7 May there be peace within
your walls
and security within your
citadels."
8 For the sake of my brothers
and friends,
I will say, "Peace be within
you."
9 For the sake of the house of
the LORD our God,
I will seek your prosperity.

**Psalm 123**

A song of ascents.

1 I lift up my eyes to you,
to you whose throne is in
heaven.
2 As the eyes of slaves look to
the hand of their master,
as the eyes of a maid look to
the hand of her mistress,
so our eyes look to the LORD
our God,
till he shows us his mercy.
3 Have mercy on us, O LORD,
have mercy on us,
for we have endured much
contempt.
4 We have endured much
ridicule from the proud,
much contempt from the
arrogant.

**Psalm 124**

A song of ascents. Of David.

1 If the LORD had not been on
our side—
let Israel say—
2 if the LORD had not been on
our side
when men attacked us,
3 when their anger flared
against us,
they would have swallowed
us alive;
4 the flood would have engulfed
us,
the torrent would have
swept over us,
5 the raging waters would
have swept us away.
6 Praise be to the LORD,
who has not let us be torn
by their teeth.
7 We have escaped like a bird
out of the fowler's snare;

*4 The *Qere* reads the word as two, *ones-arrogant-of things-being-cruel.*

°4 ק לגאי יונים

| נִמְלָֽטְנוּ׃ | וַאֲנַחְנוּ | נִשְׁבָּר | הַפַּח | יוֹקְשִׁים |
|---|---|---|---|---|
| we-escaped | and-we | one-being-broken | the-snare | ones-being-fowlers |

| שִׁיר | | וָאָֽרֶץ׃ | שָׁמַיִם | עֹשֵׂה | יְהוָה | בְּשֵׁם | עֶזְרֵנוּ | |
|---|---|---|---|---|---|---|---|---|
| song-of | (125:1) | and-earth | heavens | One-Making-of | Yahweh | in-name-of | help-of-us | (8) |

| יִמּוֹט | לֹא־ | צִיּוֹן | כְּהַר־ | בַּיהוָה | הַבֹּטְחִים | הַֽמַּעֲלוֹת |
|---|---|---|---|---|---|---|
| he-can-be-shaken | not | Zion | like-Mount-of | in-Yahweh | the-ones-trusting | the-ascents |

| וַיהוָה | לָהּ | סָבִיב | הָרִים | יְרוּשָׁלַ͏ִם | | יֵשֵׁב׃ | לְעוֹלָם |
|---|---|---|---|---|---|---|---|
| so-Yahweh | around-her | surrounding | mountains | Jerusalem | (2) | he-endures | to-forever |

| לֹא | כִּי | | עוֹלָם׃ | וְעַד־ | מֵעַתָּה | לְעַמּוֹ | סָבִיב |
|---|---|---|---|---|---|---|---|
| not | indeed | (3) | forevermore | and-to | from-now | around-people-of-him | surrounding |

| הַצַּדִּיקִים | גּוֹרַל | עַל | הָרֶשַׁע | שֵׁבֶט | יָנוּחַ |
|---|---|---|---|---|---|
| the-righteous-ones | allotment-of | over | the-wicked | scepter-of | he-will-remain |

| יְדֵיהֶם׃ | בְּעַוְלָתָה | הַצַּדִּיקִים | יִשְׁלְחוּ | לֹא־ | לְמַעַן |
|---|---|---|---|---|---|
| hands-of-them | for-evil | the-righteous-ones | they-might-use | not | so-that |

| בְּלִבּוֹתָם׃ | וְלִישָׁרִים | לַטּוֹבִים | יְהוָה | הֵיטִיבָה | |
|---|---|---|---|---|---|
| in-hearts-of-them | even-to-ones-upright | to-the-good-ones | Yahweh | do-good! | (4) |

| יְהוָה | יוֹלִיכֵם | עֲקַלְקַלּוֹתָם | וְהַמַּטִּים | |
|---|---|---|---|---|
| Yahweh | he-will-banish-them | crooked-ways-of-them | but-the-ones-turning | (5) |

| הַמַּעֲלוֹת | שִׁיר | | יִשְׂרָאֵל׃ | עַל־ | שָׁלוֹם | הָאָוֶן | פֹּעֲלֵי | אֶת־ |
|---|---|---|---|---|---|---|---|---|
| the-ascents | song-of | (126:1) | Israel | upon | peace | the-evil | ones-doing-of | with |

| כְּחֹלְמִים׃ | הָיִינוּ | צִיּוֹן | שִׁיבַת | אֶת־ | יְהוָה | בְּשׁוּב |
|---|---|---|---|---|---|---|
| like-ones-dreaming | we-were | Zion | captive-of | *** | Yahweh | when-to-bring-back |

| רִנָּה | וּלְשׁוֹנֵנוּ | פִּינוּ | שְׂחוֹק | יִמָּלֵא | אָז | |
|---|---|---|---|---|---|---|
| song-of-joy | and-tongue-of-us | mouth-of-us | laughter-of | he-was-filled | then | (2) |

| אֵלֶּה׃ | עִם־ | לַעֲשׂוֹת | יְהוָה | הִגְדִּיל | בַגּוֹיִם | יֹאמְרוּ | אָז |
|---|---|---|---|---|---|---|---|
| these | for | to-do | Yahweh | he-made-great | among-the-nations | they-said | then |

| שׁוּבָה | | שְׂמֵחִים׃ | הָיִינוּ | עִמָּנוּ | לַעֲשׂוֹת | יְהוָה | הִגְדִּיל | |
|---|---|---|---|---|---|---|---|---|
| restore! | (4) | ones-being-joyful | we-are | for-us | to-do | Yahweh | he-made-great | (3) |

| הַזֹּרְעִים | | בַּנֶּגֶב׃ | כַּאֲפִיקִים | °שְׁבוֹתֵנוּ | אֶת־ | יְהוָה |
|---|---|---|---|---|---|---|
| the-ones-sowing | (5) | in-the-Negev | like-streams | fortune-of-us | *** | Yahweh |

| וּבָכֹה | יֵלֵךְ׀ | הָלוֹךְ | | יִקְצֹרוּ׃ | בְּרִנָּה | בְּדִמְעָה |
|---|---|---|---|---|---|---|
| and-to-weep | he-goes-out | to-go-out | (6) | they-will-reap | with-song-of-joy | in-tear |

| נֹשֵׂא | בְרִנָּה | יָבוֹא | בֹּא־ | הַזָּרַע | מֶשֶׁךְ־ | נֹשֵׂא |
|---|---|---|---|---|---|---|
| carrying | with-song-of-joy | he-will-return | to-return | the-sowing | seed-of | carrying |

| יִבְנֶה | לֹא־ | יְהוָה׀ | אִם־ | לִשְׁלֹמֹה | הַמַּעֲלוֹת | שִׁיר | | אֲלֻמֹּתָיו׃ |
|---|---|---|---|---|---|---|---|---|
| he-builds | not | Yahweh | if | of-Solomon | the-ascents | song-of | (127:1) | sheaves-of-him |

| יִשְׁמָר־ | לֹא־ | יְהוָה | אִם־ | בוֹ | בוֹנָיו | עָמְלוּ | שָׁוְא׀ | בַּיִת |
|---|---|---|---|---|---|---|---|---|
| he-watches-over | not | Yahweh | if | on-him | ones-building-him | they-labor | vanity | house |

the snare has been broken,
and we have escaped.
8 Our help is in the name of the LORD,
the Maker of heaven and earth.

## Psalm 125

A song of ascents.

1 Those who trust in the LORD
are like Mount Zion,
which cannot be shaken but endures forever.
2 As the mountains surround Jerusalem,
so the LORD surrounds his people
both now and forevermore.

3 The scepter of the wicked will not remain
over the land allotted to the righteous,
for then the righteous might use
their hands to do evil.

4 Do good, O LORD, to those who are good,
to those who are upright in heart.
5 But those who turn to crooked ways
the LORD will banish with the evildoers.

Peace be upon Israel.

## Psalm 126

A song of ascents.

1 When the LORD brought back the captives to[w] Zion,
we were like men who dreamed.[x]
2 Our mouths were filled with laughter,
our tongues with songs of joy.
Then it was said among the nations,
"The LORD has done great things for them."
3 The LORD has done great things for us,
and we are filled with joy.

4 Restore our fortunes,[y] O LORD,
like streams in the Negev.
5 Those who sow in tears
will reap with songs of joy.
6 He who goes out weeping,
carrying seed to sow,
will return with songs of joy,
carrying sheaves with him.

## Psalm 127

A song of ascents. Of Solomon.

1 Unless the LORD builds the house,
its builders labor in vain.
Unless the LORD watches over

w1 Or *LORD restored the fortunes of*
x1 Or *men restored to health*
y4 Or *Bring back our captives*

°4 ק שביתנו

עִיר שָׁוְא | שָׁקַד שׁוֹמֵר׃ (2) שָׁוְא לָכֶם | מַשְׁכִּימֵי
ones-being-early-of to-you vanity (2) one-watching he-stands-guard vanity city

קוּם מְאַחֲרֵי־ שֶׁבֶת אֹכְלֵי לֶחֶם הָעֲצָבִים כֵּן
for the-toils bread-of ones-eating-of to-stay-up ones-being-late-of to-rise

יִתֵּן לִידִידוֹ שֵׁנָא׃ (3) הִנֵּה נַחֲלַת יְהוָה בָּנִים שָׂכָר
reward sons Yahweh heritage-of see! (3) sleep to-loved-one-of-him he-grants

פְּרִי הַבָּטֶן׃ (4) כְּחִצִּים בְּיַד־ גִּבּוֹר כֵּן בְּנֵי הַנְּעוּרִים׃
the-youths sons-of so warrior in-hand-of like-arrows (4) the-womb child-of

(5) אַשְׁרֵי הַגֶּבֶר אֲשֶׁר מִלֵּא אֶת־ אַשְׁפָּתוֹ מֵהֶם
with-them quiver-of-him *** he-is-full who the-man blessednesses-of (5)

לֹא־ יֵבֹשׁוּ כִּי־ יְדַבְּרוּ אֶת־ אוֹיְבִים בַּשָּׁעַר׃
in-the-gate ones-being-enemies with they-contend when they-will-be-shamed not

(128:1) שִׁיר הַמַּעֲלוֹת אַשְׁרֵי כָּל־ יְרֵא יְהוָה
Yahweh one-fearing-of all-of blessednesses-of the-ascents song-of (128:1)

הַהֹלֵךְ בִּדְרָכָיו׃ (2) יְגִיעַ כַּפֶּיךָ כִּי תֹאכֵל
you-will-eat indeed hands-of-you labor-of (2) in-ways-of-him the-one-walking

אַשְׁרֶיךָ וְטוֹב לָךְ׃ (3) אֶשְׁתְּךָ | כְּגֶפֶן
like-vine wife-of-you (3) to-you and-prosperity blessings-of-you

פֹּרִיָּה בְּיַרְכְּתֵי בֵיתֶךָ בָּנֶיךָ כִּשְׁתִלֵי זֵיתִים
olives like-shoots-of sons-of-you house-of-you at-insides-of one-being-fruitful

סָבִיב לְשֻׁלְחָנֶךָ׃ (4) הִנֵּה כִי־ כֵן יְבֹרַךְ גָּבֶר יְרֵא
one-fearing-of man he-is-blessed thus that see! (4) about-table-of-you around

יְהוָה׃ (5) יְבָרֶכְךָ יְהוָה מִצִּיּוֹן וּרְאֵה בְּטוּב
to-prosperity-of and-see! from-Zion Yahweh may-he-bless-you (5) Yahweh

יְרוּשָׁלִָם כֹּל יְמֵי חַיֶּיךָ׃ (6) וּרְאֵה־ בָנִים לְבָנֶיךָ
of-children-of-you children and-see! (6) lives-of-you days-of all-of Jerusalem

שָׁלוֹם עַל־ יִשְׂרָאֵל׃ (129:1) שִׁיר הַמַּעֲלוֹת רַבַּת צְרָרוּנִי
they-oppressed-me greatly the-ascents song-of (129:1) Israel upon peace

מִנְּעוּרָי יֹאמַר־ נָא יִשְׂרָאֵל׃ (2) רַבַּת צְרָרוּנִי
they-oppressed-me greatly (2) Israel now! let-him-say from-youths-of-me

מִנְּעוּרָי גַּם לֹא־ יָכְלוּ לִי׃ (3) עַל־ גַּבִּי
back-of-me on (3) over-me they-gained-victory not but from-youths-of-me

חָרְשׁוּ חֹרְשִׁים הֶאֱרִיכוּ לְמַעֲנוֹתָם׃ (4) יְהוָה צַדִּיק
righteous Yahweh (4) to-furrow-of-them they-made-long ones-plowing they-plowed

קִצֵּץ עֲבוֹת רְשָׁעִים׃ (5) יֵבֹשׁוּ וְיִסֹּגוּ
and-may-they-be-turned may-they-be-shamed (5) wicked-ones cords-of he-cut-free

אָחוֹר כֹּל שֹׂנְאֵי צִיּוֹן׃ (6) יִהְיוּ כַּחֲצִיר גַּגּוֹת
housetops like-grass-of may-they-be (6) Zion ones-hating-of all-of back

the city,
the watchmen stand guard
in vain.
2 In vain you rise early
and stay up late,
toiling for food to eat—
for he grants sleep to[a] those
he loves.

3 Sons are a heritage from the
Lord,
children a reward from him.
4 Like arrows in the hands of a
warrior
are sons born in one's
youth.
5 Blessed is the man
whose quiver is full of them.
They will not be put to shame
when they contend with
their enemies in the gate.

## Psalm 128

A song of ascents.

1 Blessed are all who fear the
Lord,
who walk in his ways.
2 You will eat the fruit of your
labor;
blessings and prosperity will
be yours.
3 Your wife will be like a fruitful
vine
within your house;
your sons will be like olive
shoots
around your table.
4 Thus is the man blessed
who fears the Lord.

5 May the Lord bless you from
Zion
all the days of your life;
may you see the prosperity of
Jerusalem,
6 and may you live to see
your children's children.

Peace be upon Israel.

## Psalm 129

A song of ascents.

1 They have greatly oppressed
me from my youth—
let Israel say—
2 they have greatly oppressed
me from my youth,
but they have not gained
the victory over me.
3 Plowmen have plowed my
back
and made their furrows
long.
4 But the Lord is righteous;
he has cut me free from the
cords of the wicked.

5 May all who hate Zion
be turned back in shame.
6 May they be like grass on the
housetops,

[a]2 Or *eat— / for while they sleep he provides for*

[3] ק למעניתם

שֶׁקַּדְמַת שָׁלַף יָבֵשׁ׃ (7) שֶׁלֹּא מִלֵּא כַפּוֹ
hand-of-him he-can-fill which-not (7) he-withers he-grows which-before

קוֹצֵר וְחִצְנוֹ מְעַמֵּר׃ (8) וְלֹא אָמְרוּ
may-they-say and-not (8) one-gathering or-arm-of-him one-reaping

הָעֹבְרִים בִּרְכַּת־ יְהוָה אֲלֵיכֶם בֵּרַכְנוּ אֶתְכֶם בְּשֵׁם
in-name-of you we-bless upon-you Yahweh blessing-of the-ones-passing-by

יְהוָה׃ (130:1) שִׁיר הַמַּעֲלוֹת מִמַּעֲמַקִּים קְרָאתִיךָ יְהוָה׃ (2) אֲדֹנָי
Lord (2) Yahweh I-cry-to-you from-depths the-ascents song-of (130:1) Yahweh

שִׁמְעָה בְקוֹלִי תִּהְיֶינָה אָזְנֶיךָ קַשֻּׁבוֹת לְקוֹל
to-cry-of attentive-ones ears-of-you let-them-be to-voice-of-me hear!

תַּחֲנוּנָי׃ (3) אִם־ עֲוֺנוֹת תִּשְׁמָר־ יָהּ אֲדֹנָי מִי יַעֲמֹד׃
he-could-stand who? Lord Yahweh you-recorded sins if (3) cries-for-mercy-of-me

(4) כִּי־ עִמְּךָ הַסְּלִיחָה לְמַעַן תִּוָּרֵא׃ (5) קִוִּיתִי
I-wait-for (5) you-are-feared therefore the-forgiveness with-you but (4)

יְהוָה קִוְּתָה נַפְשִׁי וְלִדְבָרוֹ הוֹחָלְתִּי׃ (6) נַפְשִׁי
soul-of-me (6) I-put-hope and-in-word-of-him soul-of-me she-waits Yahweh

לַאדֹנָי מִשֹּׁמְרִים לַבֹּקֶר שֹׁמְרִים לַבֹּקֶר׃
for-the-morning men-watching for-the-morning more-than-men-watching for-Lord

(7) יַחֵל יִשְׂרָאֵל אֶל־ יְהוָה כִּי־ עִם־ יְהוָה הַחֶסֶד
the-unfailing-love Yahweh with for Yahweh in Israel put-hope! (7)

וְהַרְבֵּה עִמּוֹ פְדוּת׃ (8) וְהוּא יִפְדֶּה אֶת־ יִשְׂרָאֵל
Israel *** he-will-redeem and-he (8) redemption with-him and-to-be-full

מִכֹּל עֲוֺנֹתָיו׃ (131:1) שִׁיר הַמַּעֲלוֹת לְדָוִד יְהוָה לֹא־
not Yahweh of-David the-ascents song-of (131:1) sins-of-him from-all-of

גָבַהּ לִבִּי וְלֹא־ רָמוּ עֵינַי וְלֹא־
and-not eyes-of-me they-are-haughty and-not heart-of-me he-is-proud

הִלַּכְתִּי בִּגְדֹלוֹת וּבְנִפְלָאוֹת מִמֶּנִּי׃
more-than-me or-with-things-being-wonderful with-great-matters I-am-concerned

(2) אִם־ לֹא שִׁוִּיתִי וְדוֹמַמְתִּי נַפְשִׁי כְּגָמֻל עֲלֵי
with like-one-being-weaned soul-of-me and-I-quieted I-stilled indeed but (2)

אִמּוֹ כַּגָּמֻל עָלַי נַפְשִׁי׃ (3) יַחֵל יִשְׂרָאֵל
Israel put-hope! (3) soul-of-me in-me like-the-one-being-weaned mother-of-him

אֶל־ יְהוָה מֵעַתָּה וְעַד־ עוֹלָם׃ (132:1) שִׁיר הַמַּעֲלוֹת זְכוֹר־
remember! the-ascents song-of (132:1) forevermore and-to from-now Yahweh in

יְהוָה לְדָוִד אֵת כָּל־ עֻנּוֹתוֹ׃ (2) אֲשֶׁר נִשְׁבַּע
he-swore-oath that (2) to-endure-hardship-him all-of *** to-David Yahweh

לַיהוָה נָדַר לַאֲבִיר יַעֲקֹב׃ (3) אִם־ אָבֹא
I-will-enter not (3) Jacob to-Mighty-One-of he-made-vow to-Yahweh

which withers before it can grow;
7 with it the reaper cannot fill his hands,
nor the one who gathers fill his arms.
8 May those who pass by not say,
"The blessing of the LORD be upon you;
we bless you in the name of the LORD."

## Psalm 130

A song of ascents.

1 Out of the depths I cry to you, O LORD;
2 O Lord, hear my voice.
Let your ears be attentive to my cry for mercy.

3 If you, O LORD, kept a record of sins,
O Lord, who could stand?
4 But with you there is forgiveness;
therefore you are feared.

5 I wait for the LORD, my soul waits,
and in his word I put my hope.
6 My soul waits for the Lord
more than watchmen wait for the morning,
more than watchmen wait for the morning.

7 O Israel, put your hope in the LORD,
for with the LORD is unfailing love
and with him is full redemption.
8 He himself will redeem Israel from all their sins.

## Psalm 131

A song of ascents. Of David.

1 My heart is not proud, O LORD,
my eyes are not haughty;
I do not concern myself with great matters
or things too wonderful for me.
2 But I have stilled and quieted my soul;
like a weaned child with its mother,
like a weaned child is my soul within me.

3 O Israel, put your hope in the LORD
both now and forevermore.

## Psalm 132

A song of ascents.

1 O LORD, remember David
and all the hardships he endured.

2 He swore an oath to the LORD
and made a vow to the Mighty One of Jacob:
3 "I will not enter my house

בְּאֹהֶל בֵּיתִי אִם־ אֶעֱלֶה עַל־ עֶרֶשׂ יְצוּעָי׃ אִם־
not (4) beds-of-me mat-of to I-will-go not house-of-me into-structure-of

אֶתֵּן שְׁנַת לְעֵינַי לְעַפְעַפַּי תְּנוּמָה׃ עַד־אֶמְצָא
I-find till (5) slumber to-eyelids-of-me to-eyes-of-me sleep-of I-will-allow

מָקוֹם לַיהוָה מִשְׁכָּנוֹת לַאֲבִיר יַעֲקֹב׃ הִנֵּה־ שְׁמַעֲנוּהָ
we-heard-her see! (6) Jacob for-Mighty-One-of dwellings for-Yahweh place

בְאֶפְרָתָה מְצָאנוּהָ בִּשְׂדֵי־ יָעַר׃ נָבוֹאָה לְמִשְׁכְּנוֹתָיו
to-dwellings-of-him let-us-go (7) Jaar in-fields-of we-came-upon-her in-Ephrathah

נִשְׁתַּחֲוֶה לַהֲדֹם רַגְלָיו׃ קוּמָה יְהוָה לִמְנוּחָתֶךָ
to-rest-of-you Yahweh arise! (8) feet-of-him at-footstool-of let-us-worship

אַתָּה וַאֲרוֹן עֻזֶּךָ׃ כֹּהֲנֶיךָ יִלְבְּשׁוּ־
may-they-be-clothed priests-of-you (9) might-of-you and-ark-of you

צֶדֶק וַחֲסִידֶיךָ יְרַנֵּנוּ׃ בַּעֲבוּר דָּוִד
David for-sake-of (10) may-they-sing-for-joy and-saints-of-you righteousness

עַבְדֶּךָ אַל־ תָּשֵׁב פְּנֵי מְשִׁיחֶךָ׃ נִשְׁבַּע־
he-swore-oath (11) anointed-one-of-you faces-of you-reject not servant-of-you

יְהוָה ׀ לְדָוִד אֱמֶת לֹא־ יָשׁוּב מִמֶּנָּה מִפְּרִי
from-descendant-of from-her he-will-revoke not sure to-David Yahweh

בִטְנְךָ אָשִׁית לְכִסֵּא־ לָךְ׃ אִם־ יִשְׁמְרוּ בָנֶיךָ ׀
sons-of-you they-keep if (12) of-you on-throne I-will-place body-of-you

בְּרִיתִי וְעֵדֹתִי זוֹ אֲלַמְּדֵם גַּם־ בְּנֵיהֶם עֲדֵי־
to sons-of-them then I-teach-them that and-statutes-of-me covenant-of-me

עַד יֵשְׁבוּ לְכִסֵּא־ לָךְ׃ כִּי־ בָחַר יְהוָה בְּצִיּוֹן
to-Zion Yahweh he-chose for (13) of-you on-throne they-will-sit forever

אִוָּהּ לְמוֹשָׁב לוֹ׃ זֹאת־ מְנוּחָתִי עֲדֵי־ עַד
forever to resting-place-of-me this (14) for-him for-dwelling he-desired-her

פֹּה־ אֵשֵׁב כִּי אִוִּתִיהָ׃ צֵידָהּ בָּרֵךְ אֲבָרֵךְ
I-will-bless to-bless provision-of-her (15) I-desired-her for I-will-sit here

אֶבְיוֹנֶיהָ אַשְׂבִּיעַ לָחֶם׃ וְכֹהֲנֶיהָ אַלְבִּישׁ
I-will-clothe and-priests-of-her (16) food I-will-satisfy poor-ones-of-her

יֶשַׁע וַחֲסִידֶיהָ רַנֵּן יְרַנֵּנוּ׃ שָׁם
here (17) they-will-sing-for-joy to-sing-for-joy and-saints-of-her salvation

אַצְמִיחַ קֶרֶן לְדָוִד עָרַכְתִּי נֵר לִמְשִׁיחִי׃
for-anointed-one-of-me lamp I-will-set-up for-David horn I-will-make-grow

אוֹיְבָיו אַלְבִּישׁ בֹּשֶׁת וְעָלָיו
but-on-him shame I-will-clothe ones-being-enemies-of-him (18)

יָצִיץ נִזְרוֹ׃ שִׁיר הַמַּעֲלוֹת לְדָוִד
of-David the-ascents song-of (133:1) crown-of-him he-will-be-resplendent

or go to my bed—
4I will allow no sleep to my eyes,
no slumber to my eyelids,
5till I find a place for the LORD,
a dwelling for the Mighty One of Jacob."

6We heard it in Ephrathah,
we came upon it in the fields of Jaar[a]:[b]
7"Let us go to his dwelling place;
let us worship at his footstool—
8arise, O LORD, and come to your resting place,
you and the ark of your might.
9May your priests be clothed with righteousness;
may your saints sing for joy."

10For the sake of David your servant,
do not reject your anointed one.

11The LORD swore an oath to David,
a sure oath that he will not revoke:
"One of your own descendants
I will place on your throne—
12if your sons keep my covenant
and the statutes I teach them,
then their sons will sit
on your throne for ever and ever."

13For the LORD has chosen Zion,
he has desired it for his dwelling:
14"This is my resting place for ever and ever;
here I will sit enthroned, for I have desired it—
15I will bless her with abundant provisions;
her poor will I satisfy with food.
16I will clothe her priests with salvation,
and her saints will ever sing for joy.

17"Here I will make a horn[c] grow for David
and set up a lamp for my anointed one.
18I will clothe his enemies with shame,
but the crown on his head will be resplendent."

### Psalm 133

A song of ascents. Of David.

[a]6 That is, Kiriath Jearim
[b]6 Or *heard of it in Ephrathah, / we found it in the fields of Jaar.* (And no quotes around verses 7-9)
[c]17 *Horn* here symbolizes strong one, that is, king.

הִנֵּה מַה־טּוֹב וּמַה־נָּעִים שֶׁבֶת אַחִים גַּם־יָחַד׃
together united brothers to-live pleasant and-how! good how! see!

כַּשֶּׁמֶן הַטּוֹב ׀ עַל־הָרֹאשׁ יֹרֵד עַל־הַזָּקָן זְקַן־
beard-of the-beard on running-down the-head on the-precious like-the-oil (2)

אַהֲרֹן שֶׁיֹּרֵד עַל־פִּי מִדּוֹתָיו׃ כְּטַל־חֶרְמוֹן
Hermon as-dew-of (3) robes-of-him collar-of on that-running-down Aaron

שֶׁיֹּרֵד עַל־הַרְרֵי צִיּוֹן כִּי שָׁם ׀ צִוָּה יְהוָה אֶת־הַבְּרָכָה
the-blessing *** Yahweh he-bestows there for Zion Mounts-of on that-falling

חַיִּים עַד־הָעוֹלָם׃ שִׁיר הַמַּעֲלוֹת הִנֵּה ׀ בָּרְכוּ אֶת־יְהוָה
Yahweh *** praise! see! the-ascents song-of (134:1) the-forever to lives

כָּל־עַבְדֵי יְהוָה הָעֹמְדִים בְּבֵית־יְהוָה
Yahweh in-house-of the-ones-ministering Yahweh servants-of all-of

בַּלֵּילוֹת׃ שְׂאוּ־יְדֵכֶם קֹדֶשׁ וּבָרְכוּ אֶת־יְהוָה׃
Yahweh *** and-praise! sanctuary hand-of-you lift-up! (2) in-the-nights

יְבָרֶכְךָ יְהוָה מִצִּיּוֹן עֹשֵׂה שָׁמַיִם וָאָרֶץ׃
and-earth heavens One-Making-of from-Zion Yahweh may-he-bless-you (3)

הַלְלוּ יָהּ ׀ הַלְלוּ אֶת־שֵׁם יְהוָה הַלְלוּ עַבְדֵי יְהוָה׃
Yahweh servants-of praise! Yahweh name-of *** praise! Yahweh praise! (135:1)

שֶׁעֹמְדִים בְּבֵית יְהוָה בְּחַצְרוֹת בֵּית אֱלֹהֵינוּ׃
God-of-us house-of in-courts-of Yahweh in-house-of who-ones-ministering (2)

הַלְלוּ־יָהּ כִּי־טוֹב יְהוָה זַמְּרוּ לִשְׁמוֹ כִּי נָעִים׃
pleasant for to-name-of-him sing-praise! Yahweh good for Yahweh praise! (3)

כִּי־יַעֲקֹב בָּחַר לוֹ יָהּ יִשְׂרָאֵל לִסְגֻלָּתוֹ׃ כִּי אֲנִי
I for (5) as-treasure-of-him Israel Yahweh for-him he-chose Jacob for (4)

יָדַעְתִּי כִּי־גָדוֹל יְהוָה וַאֲדֹנֵינוּ מִכָּל־אֱלֹהִים׃ כֹּל
all (6) gods greater-than-all-of and-Lord-of-us Yahweh great that I-know

אֲשֶׁר־חָפֵץ יְהוָה עָשָׂה בַּשָּׁמַיִם וּבָאָרֶץ בַּיַּמִּים
in-the-seas and-on-the-earth in-the-heavens he-does Yahweh he-pleases that

וְכָל־תְּהוֹמוֹת׃ מַעֲלֶה נְשִׂאִים מִקְצֵה הָאָרֶץ בְּרָקִים
lightnings the-earth from-end-of clouds one-making-rise (7) depths and-all-of

לַמָּטָר עָשָׂה מוֹצֵא־רוּחַ מֵאוֹצְרוֹתָיו׃
from-storehouses-of-him wind one-bringing-out he-sends with-the-rain

שֶׁהִכָּה בְּכוֹרֵי מִצְרָיִם מֵאָדָם עַד־בְּהֵמָה׃
animal to from-man Egypt firstborn-ones-of who-he-struck-down (8)

שָׁלַח ׀ אֹתוֹת וּמֹפְתִים בְּתוֹכֵכִי מִצְרָיִם בְּפַרְעֹה
against-Pharaoh Egypt into-midst-of-you and-wonders signs he-sent (9)

וּבְכָל־עֲבָדָיו׃ שֶׁהִכָּה גּוֹיִם רַבִּים
many nations who-he-struck-down (10) servants-of-him and-against-all-of

1 How good and pleasant it is
when brothers live together
in unity!
2 It is like precious oil poured
on the head,
running down on the beard,
running down on Aaron's
beard,
down upon the collar of his
robes.
3 It is as if the dew of Hermon
were falling on Mount Zion.
For there the LORD bestows his
blessing,
even life forevermore.

**Psalm 134**

A song of ascents.

1 Praise the LORD, all you
servants of the LORD
who minister by night in
the house of the LORD.
2 Lift up your hands in the
sanctuary
and praise the LORD.

3 May the LORD, the Maker of
heaven and earth,
bless you from Zion.

**Psalm 135**

1 Praise the LORD.[d]

Praise the name of the LORD;
Praise him, you servants of
the LORD,
2 you who minister in the house
of the LORD,
in the courts of the house of
our God.

3 Praise the LORD, for the LORD
is good;
sing praise to his name, for
that is pleasant.
4 For the LORD has chosen Jacob
to be his own,
Israel to be his treasured
possession.

5 I know that the LORD is great,
that our Lord is greater than
all gods.
6 The LORD does whatever
pleases him,
in the heavens and on the
earth,
in the seas and all their
depths.
7 He makes clouds rise from the
ends of the earth;
he sends lightning with the
rain
and brings out the wind
from his storehouses.

8 He struck down the firstborn
of Egypt,
the firstborn of men and
animals.
9 He sent his signs and wonders
into your midst, O Egypt,
against Pharaoh and all his
servants.
10 He struck down many nations

[d]1 Hebrew *Hallelu Yah*; also in verses 3 and 21

וְהָרַג מְלָכִים עֲצוּמִים׃ לְסִיחוֹן ׀ מֶלֶךְ הָאֱמֹרִי
the-Amorite king-of namely-Sihon (11) mighty-ones kings and-he-killed

וּלְעוֹג מֶלֶךְ הַבָּשָׁן וּלְכֹל מַמְלְכוֹת כְּנָעַן׃
Canaan kingdoms-of and-namely-all-of the-Bashan king-of and-namely-Og

(12) וְנָתַן אַרְצָם נַחֲלָה נַחֲלָה לְיִשְׂרָאֵל עַמּוֹ׃
people-of-him to-Israel inheritance inheritance land-of-them and-he-gave (12)

(13) יְהוָה שִׁמְךָ לְעוֹלָם יְהוָה זִכְרְךָ לְדֹר־
to-generation renown-of-you Yahweh to-forever name-of-you Yahweh (13)

וָדֹר׃ (14) כִּי־ יָדִין יְהוָה עַמּוֹ וְעַל־
and-on people-of-him Yahweh he-will-vindicate for (14) and-generation

עֲבָדָיו יִתְנֶחָם׃ (15) עֲצַבֵּי הַגּוֹיִם כֶּסֶף
silver the-nations idols-of (15) he-will-have-compassion servants-of-him

וְזָהָב מַעֲשֵׂה יְדֵי אָדָם׃ (16) פֶּה־ לָהֶם וְלֹא יְדַבֵּרוּ
they-can-speak but-not to-them mouth (16) man hands-of making-of and-gold

עֵינַיִם לָהֶם וְלֹא יִרְאוּ׃ (17) אָזְנַיִם לָהֶם וְלֹא יַאֲזִינוּ
they-can-hear but-not to-them ears (17) they-can-see but-not to-them eyes

אַף אֵין־ יֶשׁ־ רוּחַ בְּפִיהֶם׃ (18) כְּמוֹהֶם יִהְיוּ
they-will-be like-them (18) in-mouth-of-them breath there-is not or

עֹשֵׂיהֶם כֹּל אֲשֶׁר־ בֹּטֵחַ בָּהֶם׃ (19) בֵּית יִשְׂרָאֵל בָּרְכוּ אֶת־
*** praise! Israel house-of (19) in-them trusting who all ones-making-them

יְהוָה בֵּית אַהֲרֹן בָּרְכוּ אֶת־ יְהוָה׃ (20) בֵּית הַלֵּוִי בָּרְכוּ אֶת־
*** praise! the-Levite house-of (20) Yahweh *** praise! Aaron house-of Yahweh

יְהוָה יִרְאֵי יְהוָה בָּרְכוּ אֶת־ יְהוָה׃ (21) בָּרוּךְ יְהוָה ׀
Yahweh being-praised (21) Yahweh *** praise! Yahweh ones-fearing-of Yahweh

מִצִּיּוֹן שֹׁכֵן יְרוּשָׁלִָם הַלְלוּ־ יָהּ׃ (136:1) הוֹדוּ
give-thanks! (136:1) Yahweh praise! Jerusalem one-dwelling-of from-Zion

לַיהוָה כִּי־ טוֹב כִּי לְעוֹלָם חַסְדּוֹ׃ (2) הוֹדוּ לֵאלֹהֵי
to-God-of give-thanks! (2) love-of-him to-forever for good for to-Yahweh

הָאֱלֹהִים כִּי לְעוֹלָם חַסְדּוֹ׃ (3) הוֹדוּ לַאֲדֹנֵי הָאֲדֹנִים
the-lords to-Lord-of give-thanks! (3) love-of-him to-forever for the-gods

כִּי לְעֹלָם חַסְדּוֹ׃ (4) לְעֹשֵׂה נִפְלָאוֹת גְּדֹלוֹת
great-ones things-being-wonders to-one-doing-of (4) love-of-him to-forever for

לְבַדּוֹ כִּי לְעוֹלָם חַסְדּוֹ׃ (5) לְעֹשֵׂה הַשָּׁמַיִם
the-heavens to-one-making-of (5) love-of-him to-forever for by-himself

בִּתְבוּנָה כִּי לְעוֹלָם חַסְדּוֹ׃ (6) לְרֹקַע הָאָרֶץ
the-earth to-one-spreading-out (6) love-of-him to-forever for by-understanding

עַל־ הַמָּיִם כִּי לְעוֹלָם חַסְדּוֹ׃ (7) לְעֹשֵׂה אוֹרִים גְּדֹלִים
great-ones lights to-one-making-of (7) love-of-him to-forever for the-waters upon

---

and killed mighty kings—
11 Sihon king of the Amorites,
Og king of Bashan
and all the kings of Canaan—
12 and he gave their land as an inheritance,
an inheritance to his people Israel.

13 Your name, O LORD, endures forever,
your renown, O LORD, through all generations.
14 For the LORD will vindicate his people
and have compassion on his servants.

15 The idols of the nations are silver and gold,
made by the hands of men.
16 They have mouths, but cannot speak,
eyes, but they cannot see;
17 they have ears, but cannot hear,
nor is there breath in their mouths.
18 Those who make them will be like them,
and so will all who trust in them.

19 O house of Israel, praise the LORD;
O house of Aaron, praise the LORD;
20 O house of Levi, praise the LORD;
you who fear him, praise the LORD.
21 Praise be to the LORD from Zion,
to him who dwells in Jerusalem.

Praise the LORD.

**Psalm 136**

1 Give thanks to the LORD, for he is good.
*His love endures forever.*
2 Give thanks to the God of gods.
*His love endures forever.*
3 Give thanks to the Lord of lords:
*His love endures forever.*

4 to him who alone does great wonders,
*His love endures forever.*
5 who by his understanding made the heavens,
*His love endures forever.*
6 who spread out the earth upon the waters,
*His love endures forever.*
7 who made the great lights—

כִּי לְעוֹלָם חַסְדּוֹ׃ (8) אֶת־הַשֶּׁמֶשׁ לְמֶמְשֶׁלֶת בַּיּוֹם כִּי
for over-the-day as-governor the-sun *** (8) love-of-him to-forever for

לְעוֹלָם חַסְדּוֹ׃ (9) אֶת־הַיָּרֵחַ וְכוֹכָבִים לְמֶמְשְׁלוֹת
as-governors and-stars the-moon *** (9) love-of-him to-forever

בַּלָּיְלָה כִּי לְעוֹלָם חַסְדּוֹ׃ (10) לְמַכֵּה מִצְרַיִם
Egypt to-one-striking-down (10) love-of-him to-forever for over-the-night

בִּבְכוֹרֵיהֶם כִּי לְעוֹלָם חַסְדּוֹ׃ (11) וַיּוֹצֵא
and-he-brought-out (11) love-of-him to-forever for in-firstborn-ones-of-them

יִשְׂרָאֵל מִתּוֹכָם כִּי לְעוֹלָם חַסְדּוֹ׃ (12) בְּיָד חֲזָקָה
mighty with-hand (12) love-of-him to-forever for from-among-them Israel

וּבִזְרוֹעַ נְטוּיָה כִּי לְעוֹלָם חַסְדּוֹ׃
love-of-him to-forever for one-being-outstretched and-with-arm

(13) לְגֹזֵר יַם־סוּף לִגְזָרִים כִּי לְעוֹלָם חַסְדּוֹ׃
love-of-him to-forever for into-halves Reed Sea-of to-one-dividing (13)

(14) וְהֶעֱבִיר יִשְׂרָאֵל בְּתוֹכוֹ כִּי לְעוֹלָם חַסְדּוֹ׃
love-of-him to-forever for through-midst-of-him Israel and-he-brought (14)

(15) וְנִעֵר פַּרְעֹה וְחֵילוֹ בְיַם־סוּף כִּי לְעוֹלָם
to-forever for Reed into-Sea-of and-army-of-him Pharoah but-he-swept (15)

חַסְדּוֹ׃ (16) לְמוֹלִיךְ עַמּוֹ בַּמִּדְבָּר כִּי
for through-the-desert people-of-him to-one-leading (16) love-of-him

לְעוֹלָם חַסְדּוֹ׃ (17) לְמַכֵּה מְלָכִים גְּדֹלִים כִּי
for great-ones kings to-one-striking-down (17) love-of-him to-forever

לְעוֹלָם חַסְדּוֹ׃ (18) וַיַּהֲרֹג מְלָכִים אַדִּירִים כִּי לְעוֹלָם
to-forever for mighty-ones kings and-he-killed (18) love-of-him to-forever

חַסְדּוֹ׃ (19) לְסִיחוֹן מֶלֶךְ הָאֱמֹרִי כִּי לְעוֹלָם חַסְדּוֹ׃
love-of-him to-forever for the-Amorite king-of namely-Sihon (19) love-of-him

(20) וּלְעוֹג מֶלֶךְ הַבָּשָׁן כִּי לְעוֹלָם חַסְדּוֹ׃
love-of-him to-forever for the-Bashan king-of and-namely-Og (20)

(21) וְנָתַן אַרְצָם לְנַחֲלָה כִּי לְעוֹלָם חַסְדּוֹ׃
love-of-him to-forever for as-inheritance land-of-them and-he-gave (21)

(22) נַחֲלָה לְיִשְׂרָאֵל עַבְדּוֹ כִּי לְעוֹלָם חַסְדּוֹ׃
love-of-him to-forever for servant-of-him to-Israel inheritance (22)

(23) שֶׁבְּשִׁפְלֵנוּ זָכַר לָנוּ כִּי לְעוֹלָם חַסְדּוֹ׃
love-of-him to-forever for to-us he-remembered who-in-low-estate-of-us (23)

(24) וַיִּפְרְקֵנוּ מִצָּרֵינוּ כִּי לְעוֹלָם חַסְדּוֹ׃
love-of-him to-forever for from-enemies-of-us and-he-freed-us (24)

(25) נֹתֵן לֶחֶם לְכָל־בָּשָׂר כִּי לְעוֹלָם חַסְדּוֹ׃
love-of-him to-forever for creature to-every-of food one-giving (25)

*His love endures forever.*
8 the sun to govern the day,
*His love endures forever.*
9 the moon and stars to govern the night;
*His love endures forever.*

10 to him who struck down the firstborn of Egypt
*His love endures forever.*
11 and brought Israel out from among them
*His love endures forever.*
12 with a mighty hand and outstretched arm;
*His love endures forever.*

13 to him who divided the Red Sea[e] asunder
*His love endures forever.*
14 and brought Israel through the midst of it,
*His love endures forever.*
15 but swept Pharaoh and his army into the Red Sea;
*His love endures forever.*

16 to him who led his people through the desert,
*His love endures forever.*
17 who struck down great kings,
*His love endures forever.*
18 and killed mighty kings—
*His love endures forever.*
19 Sihon king of the Amorites
*His love endures forever.*
20 and Og king of Bashan—
*His love endures forever.*
21 and gave their land as an inheritance,
*His love endures forever.*
22 an inheritance to his servant Israel;
*His love endures forever.*

23 to the One who remembered us in our low estate
*His love endures forever.*
24 and freed us from our enemies,
*His love endures forever.*
25 and who gives food to every creature.
*His love endures forever.*

[e] 13 Hebrew *Yam Suph;* that is, Sea of Reeds; also in verse 15

הוֹדוּ לְאֵל הַשָּׁמָיִם כִּי לְעוֹלָם חַסְדּוֹ׃ עַל
by (137:1) love-of-him to-forever for the-heavens to-God-of give-thanks! (26)

נַהֲרוֹת׀ בָּבֶל שָׁם יָשַׁבְנוּ גַּם־ בָּכִינוּ בְּזָכְרֵנוּ אֶת־צִיּוֹן׃
Zion *** when-to-remember-us we-wept and we-sat there Babylon rivers-of

עַל־עֲרָבִים בְּתוֹכָהּ תָּלִינוּ כִּנֹּרוֹתֵינוּ׃ כִּי שָׁם שְׁאֵלוּנוּ
they-asked-us there for (3) harps-of-us we-hung in-midst-of-her poplars on (2)

שׁוֹבֵינוּ דִּבְרֵי־ שִׁיר וְתוֹלָלֵינוּ שִׂמְחָה שִׁירוּ לָנוּ
for-us sing! joy and-ones-tormenting-us song words-of ones-capturing-us

מִשִּׁיר צִיּוֹן׃ אֵיךְ נָשִׁיר אֶת־ שִׁיר־ יְהוָה עַל אַדְמַת
land-of in Yahweh song-of *** can-we-sing how? (4) Zion from-song-of

נֵכָר׃ אִם־ אֶשְׁכָּחֵךְ יְרוּשָׁלִָם תִּשְׁכַּח יְמִינִי׃
right-hand-of-me may-she-forget Jerusalem I-forget-you if (5) foreigner

תִּדְבַּק־ לְשׁוֹנִי׀ לְחִכִּי אִם־לֹא אֶזְכְּרֵכִי
I-remember-you not if to-roof-of-mouth-of-me tongue-of-me may-she-cling (6)

אִם־לֹא אַעֲלֶה אֶת־ יְרוּשָׁלִַם עַל רֹאשׁ שִׂמְחָתִי׃ זְכֹר יְהוָה׀
Yahweh remember! (7) joy-of-me height-of at Jerusalem *** I-consider not if

לִבְנֵי אֱדוֹם אֵת יוֹם יְרוּשָׁלִָם הָאֹמְרִים עָרוּ׀ עָרוּ
tear-down! tear-down! the-ones-crying Jerusalem day-of *** Edom about-sons-of

עַד הַיְסוֹד בָּהּ׃ בַּת־ בָּבֶל הַשְּׁדוּדָה
the-one-being-destroyed Babylon Daughter-of (8) of-her the-foundation to

אַשְׁרֵי שֶׁיְשַׁלֶּם־ לָךְ אֶת־ גְּמוּלֵךְ שֶׁגָּמַלְתְּ לָנוּ׃
to-us that-you-did deed-of-you *** to-you who-he-repays happinesses-of

אַשְׁרֵי׀ שֶׁיֹּאחֵז וְנִפֵּץ אֶת־ עֹלָלַיִךְ אֶל־
against infants-of-you *** and-he-dashes who-he-seizes happinesses-of (9)

הַסָּלַע׃ לְדָוִד׀ אוֹדְךָ בְכָל־ לִבִּי נֶגֶד
before heart-of-me with-all-of I-will-praise-you of-David (138:1) the-rock

אֱלֹהִים אֲזַמְּרֶךָּ׃ אֶשְׁתַּחֲוֶה אֶל־ הֵיכַל קָדְשְׁךָ
holiness-of-you temple-of toward I-will-bow (2) I-will-sing-praise-of-you gods

וְאוֹדֶה אֶת־ שְׁמֶךָ עַל־ חַסְדְּךָ וְעַל־ אֲמִתֶּךָ
faithfulness-of-you and-for love-of-you for name-of-you *** and-I-will-praise

כִּי־ הִגְדַּלְתָּ עַל־ כָּל־ שִׁמְךָ אִמְרָתֶךָ׃ בְּיוֹם קָרָאתִי
I-called on-day-of (3) word-of-you name-of-you all-of above you-exalted for

וַתַּעֲנֵנִי תַּרְהִבֵנִי בְנַפְשִׁי עֹז׃
stoutness in-heart-of-me you-made-bold-me then-you-answered-me

יוֹדוּךָ יְהוָה כָּל־ מַלְכֵי־ אָרֶץ כִּי שָׁמְעוּ אִמְרֵי־
words-of they-hear when earth kings-of all-of Yahweh may-they-praise-you (4)

פִיךָ׃ וְיָשִׁירוּ בְּדַרְכֵי יְהוָה כִּי גָדוֹל כְּבוֹד יְהוָה׃
Yahweh glory-of great for Yahweh of-ways-of and-may-they-sing (5) mouth-of-you

[26]Give thanks to the God of
heaven.
*His love endures forever.*

**Psalm 137**

[1]By the rivers of Babylon we
sat and wept
when we remembered Zion.
[2]There on the poplars
we hung our harps,
[3]for there our captors asked us
for songs,
our tormentors demanded
songs of joy;
they said, "Sing us one of
the songs of Zion!"

[4]How can we sing the songs of
the LORD
while in a foreign land?
[5]If I forget you, O Jerusalem,
may my right hand forget
⌊its skill⌋.
[6]May my tongue cling to the
roof of my mouth
if I do not remember you,
if I do not consider Jerusalem
my highest joy.

[7]Remember, O LORD, what the
Edomites did
on the day Jerusalem fell.
"Tear it down," they cried,
"tear it down to its
foundations!"

[8]O Daughter of Babylon,
doomed to destruction,
happy is he who repays you
for what you have done to
us—
[9]he who seizes your infants
and dashes them against the
rocks.

**Psalm 138**

Of David.

[1]I will praise you, O LORD, with
all my heart;
before the "gods" I will sing
your praise.
[2]I will bow down toward your
holy temple
and will praise your name
for your love and your
faithfulness,
for you have exalted above all
things
your name and your word.
[3]When I called, you answered
me;
you made me bold and
stouthearted.

[4]May all the kings of the earth
praise you, O LORD,
when they hear the words
of your mouth.
[5]May they sing of the ways of
the LORD,
for the glory of the LORD is
great.

כִּֽי־ רָם יְהוָה וְשָׁפָל יִרְאֶה וְגָבֹהַּ מִמֶּרְחָק
from-afar but-proud he-looks-upon yet-lowly Yahweh he-is-on-high though (6)

יְיֵדָֽע׃ אִם־ אֵלֵךְ ׀ בְּקֶרֶב צָרָה תְּחַיֵּנִי עַל
against you-keep-alive-me trouble in-midst-of I-walk though (7) he-knows

אַף אֹיְבַי תִּשְׁלַח יָדֶךָ וְתוֹשִׁיעֵנִי
and-you-save-me hand-of-you you-stretch-out ones-being-foes-of-me anger-of

יְמִינֶֽךָ׃ יְהוָה יִגְמֹר בַּעֲדִי יְהוָה חַסְדְּךָ
love-of-you Yahweh for-me he-will-fulfill Yahweh (8) right-hand-of-you

לְעוֹלָם מַעֲשֵׂי יָדֶיךָ אַל־ תֶּֽרֶף׃ לַמְנַצֵּחַ
for-the-one-directing (139:1) you-abandon not hands-of-you works-of to-forever

לְדָוִד מִזְמוֹר יְהוָה חֲקַרְתַּנִי וַתֵּדָֽע׃ אַתָּה יָדַעְתָּ שִׁבְתִּי
to-sit-me you-know you (2) and-you-know you-searched-me Yahweh psalm of-David

וְקוּמִי בַּנְתָּה לְרֵעִי מֵרָחֽוֹק׃ אָרְחִי
to-go-me (3) from-afar to-thought-of-me you-perceive and-to-rise-me

וְרִבְעִי זֵרִיתָ וְכָל־ דְּרָכַי הִסְכַּֽנְתָּה׃
you-are-familiar-with ways-of-me and-all-of you-discern and-to-lie-down-me

כִּי אֵין מִלָּה בִּלְשׁוֹנִי הֵן יְהוָה יָדַעְתָּ כֻלָּֽהּ׃ אָחוֹר
behind (5) all-of-her you-know Yahweh see! on-tongue-of-me word not for (4)

וָקֶדֶם צַרְתָּנִי וַתָּשֶׁת עָלַי כַּפֶּֽכָה׃ פְּלִאיָה
wonderful (6) hand-of-you upon-me and-you-laid you-hem-in-me and-before

דַעַת מִמֶּנִּי נִשְׂגְּבָה לֹא־ אוּכַל לָֽהּ׃ אָנָה
to-where? (7) to-her I-can-attain not one-being-lofty more-than-me knowledge

אֵלֵךְ מֵרוּחֶךָ וְאָנָה מִפָּנֶיךָ אֶבְרָֽח׃
can-I-flee from-presences-of-you and-to-where? from-Spirit-of-you can-I-go

אִם־ אֶסַּק שָׁמַיִם שָׁם אָתָּה וְאַצִּיעָה שְּׁאוֹל הִנֶּֽךָּ׃ אֶשָּׂא
I-rise (9) see-you! Sheol if-I-make-bed you there heavens I-go-up if (8)

כַנְפֵי־ שָׁחַר אֶשְׁכְּנָה בְּאַחֲרִית יָֽם׃ גַּם־ שָׁם יָדְךָ
hand-of-you there even (10) sea on-far-side-of I-settle dawn wings-of

תַנְחֵנִי וְתֹאחֲזֵנִי יְמִינֶֽךָ׃ וָאֹמַר
if-I-say (11) right-hand-of-you and-she-will-hold-me she-will-guide-me

אַךְ־ חֹשֶׁךְ יְשׁוּפֵנִי וְלַיְלָה אוֹר בַּעֲדֵֽנִי׃ גַּם־ חֹשֶׁךְ
darkness even (12) around-me light and-night he-will-hide-me darkness surely

לֹא־ יַחְשִׁיךְ מִמֶּךָ וְלַיְלָה כַּיּוֹם יָאִיר כַּחֲשֵׁיכָה
as-the-darkness he-will-shine as-the-day and-night to-you he-will-be-dark not

כָּאוֹרָֽה׃ כִּֽי־ אַתָּה קָנִיתָ כִלְיֹתָי תְּסֻכֵּנִי
you-knit-together-me inmost-beings-of-me you-created you for (13) so-the-light

בְּבֶטֶן אִמִּֽי׃ אוֹדְךָ עַל כִּי נוֹרָאוֹת
ones-being-fearful that because I-praise-you (14) mother-of-me in-womb-of

6Though the LORD is on high,
he looks upon the lowly,
but the proud he knows
from afar.
7Though I walk in the midst of
trouble,
you preserve my life;
you stretch out your hand
against the anger of my
foes,
with your right hand you
save me.
8The LORD will fulfill ⌊his
purpose⌋ for me;
your love, O LORD, endures
forever—
do not abandon the works
of your hands.

### Psalm 139

For the director of music. Of David. A psalm.

1O LORD, you have searched me
and you know me.
2You know when I sit and
when I rise;
you perceive my thoughts
from afar.
3You discern my going out and
my lying down;
you are familiar with all my
ways.
4Before a word is on my tongue
you know it completely, O
LORD.
5You hem me in—behind and
before;
you have laid your hand
upon me.
6Such knowledge is too
wonderful for me,
too lofty for me to attain.

7Where can I go from your
Spirit?
Where can I flee from your
presence?
8If I go up to the heavens, you
are there;
if I make my bed in the
depths,[f] you are there.
9If I rise on the wings of the
dawn,
if I settle on the far side of
the sea,
10even there your hand will
guide me,
your right hand will hold
me fast.
11If I say, "Surely the darkness
will hide me
and the light become night
around me,"
12even the darkness will not be
dark to you;
the night will shine like the
day,
for darkness is as light to
you.
13For you created my inmost
being;
you knit me together in my
mother's womb.
14I praise you because I am
fearfully and wonderfully
made;

f8 Hebrew *Sheol*

°6 ק פליאה

נִפְלֵיתִי נִפְלָאִים מַעֲשֶׂיךָ וְנַפְשִׁי יֹדַעַת
one-knowing and-self-of-me works-of-you ones-being-wonderful I-am-wonderful

מְאֹד׃ לֹא־ נִכְחַד עָצְמִי מִמֶּךָּ אֲשֶׁר־ עֻשֵּׂיתִי
I-was-made when from-you frame-of-me he-was-hidden not (15) well

בַסֵּתֶר רֻקַּמְתִּי בְּתַחְתִּיּוֹת אָרֶץ׃ גָּלְמִי ׀
body-of-me (16) earth in-depths-of I-was-woven-together in-the-secret-place

רָאוּ עֵינֶיךָ וְעַל־ סִפְרְךָ כֻּלָּם יִכָּתֵבוּ יָמִים
days they-were-written all-of-them book-of-you and-in eyes-of-you they-saw

יֻצָּרוּ °וְלֹא אֶחָד בָּהֶם׃ וְלִי מַה־ יָּקְרוּ
they-are-precious how! and-to-me (17) of-them one and-not they-were-ordained

רֵעֶיךָ אֵל מֶה עָצְמוּ רָאשֵׁיהֶם׃ אֶסְפְּרֵם
should-I-count-them (18) sums-of-them they-are-vast how! God thoughts-of-you

מֵחוֹל יִרְבּוּן הֱקִיצֹתִי וְעוֹדִי עִמָּךְ׃ אִם־
if (19) with-you and-still-I I-am-awake they-would-number more-than-sand

תִּקְטֹל אֱלוֹהַּ ׀ רָשָׁע וְאַנְשֵׁי דָמִים סוּרוּ מֶנִּי׃ אֲשֶׁר
who (20) from-me be-away! bloods and-men-of wicked God you-would-slay

יֹאמְרֻךָ לִמְזִמָּה נָשֻׂא† לַשָּׁוְא
for-the-misuse †one-being-used with-evil-intent they-speak-of-you

עָרֶיךָ׃ הֲלוֹא־ מְשַׂנְאֶיךָ יְהוָה ׀ אֶשְׂנָא
I-hate Yahweh ones-hating-you not? (21) adversaries-of-you

וּבִתְקוֹמְמֶיךָ אֶתְקוֹטָט׃ תַּכְלִית שִׂנְאָה שְׂנֵאתִים
I-hate-them hatred completeness-of (22) I-abhor and-to-ones-who-rise-against-you

לְאוֹיְבִים הָיוּ לִי׃ חָקְרֵנִי אֵל וְדַע לְבָבִי
heart-of-me and-know! God search-me! (23) to-me they-are as-ones-being-enemies

בְּחָנֵנִי וְדַע שַׂרְעַפָּי׃ וּרְאֵה אִם־ דֶּרֶךְ־ עֹצֶב
offense way-of if and-see! (24) anxious-thoughts-of-me and-know! test-me!

בִּי וּנְחֵנִי בְּדֶרֶךְ עוֹלָם׃ לַמְנַצֵּחַ מִזְמוֹר
psalm for-the-one-directing *(140:1) everlasting in-way-of and-lead-me! in-me

לְדָוִד׃ חַלְּצֵנִי יְהוָה מֵאָדָם רָע מֵאִישׁ חֲמָסִים
violences from-man-of evil from-man Yahweh rescue-me! (2) of-David

תִּנְצְרֵנִי׃ אֲשֶׁר חָשְׁבוּ רָעוֹת בְּלֵב כָּל־ יוֹם יָגוּרוּ
they-stir-up day every-of in-heart evils they-devise who (3) you-protect-me

מִלְחָמוֹת׃ שָׁנְנוּ לְשׁוֹנָם כְּמוֹ־ נָחָשׁ חֲמַת עַכְשׁוּב תַּחַת
on viper poison-of serpent as tongue-of-them they-make-sharp (4) wars

שְׂפָתֵימוֹ סֶלָה׃ שָׁמְרֵנִי יְהוָה ׀ מִידֵי רָשָׁע מֵאִישׁ
from-man-of wicked from-hands-of Yahweh keep-me! (5) selah lips-of-them

חֲמָסִים תִּנְצְרֵנִי אֲשֶׁר חָשְׁבוּ לִדְחוֹת פְּעָמָי׃ טָמְנוּ־
they-hid (6) feet-of-me to-trip they-plan who you-protect-me violences

your works are wonderful,
I know that full well.
15 My frame was not hidden
from you
when I was made in the
secret place.
When I was woven together in
the depths of the earth,
16 your eyes saw my unformed
body.
All the days ordained for me
were written in your book
before one of them came to
be.
17 How precious to[g] me are your
thoughts, O God!
How vast is the sum of
them!
18 Were I to count them,
they would outnumber the
grains of sand.
When I awake,
I am still with you.
19 If only you would slay the
wicked, O God!
Away from me, you
bloodthirsty men!
20 They speak of you with evil
intent;
your adversaries misuse
your name.
21 Do I not hate those who hate
you, O LORD,
and abhor those who rise up
against you?
22 I have nothing but hatred for
them;
I count them my enemies.
23 Search me, O God, and know
my heart;
test me and know my
anxious thoughts.
24 See if there is any offensive
way in me,
and lead me in the way
everlasting.

### Psalm 140

For the director of music. A psalm of David.

1 Rescue me, O LORD, from evil
men;
protect me from men of
violence,
2 who devise evil plans in their
hearts
and stir up war every day.
3 They make their tongues as
sharp as a serpent's;
the poison of vipers is on
their lips. *Selah*
4 Keep me, O LORD, from the
hands of the wicked;
protect me from men of
violence
who plan to trip my feet.

g17 Or *concerning*

*Heading, *1* See the note on page 349.

†*20* The NIV repoints this word as נָשְׂאוּ, *they-use*.

°*16* ק ולו

גֵאִים ׀ פַּח לִי וַחֲבָלִים פָּרְשׂוּ רֶשֶׁת לְיַד־ מַעְגָּל מֹקְשִׁים
traps path at-side-of net they-spread and-cords for-me snare proud-ones

שָׁתוּ־ לִי סֶלָה׃ אָמַרְתִּי לַיהוָה אֵלִי אָתָּה הַאֲזִינָה יְהוָה
Yahweh hear! you God-of-me to-Yahweh I-say (7) selah for-me they-set

קוֹל תַּחֲנוּנָי׃ יְהוִה אֲדֹנָי עֹז יְשׁוּעָתִי
deliverance-of-me strength-of Lord Yahweh (8) cries-for-mercy-of-me cry-of

סַכֹּתָה לְרֹאשִׁי בְּיוֹם נָשֶׁק׃ אַל־ תִּתֵּן יְהוָה
Yahweh you-grant not (9) battle in-day-of over-head-of-me you-shield

מַאֲוַיֵּי רָשָׁע זְמָמוֹ אַל־ תָּפֵק יָרוּמוּ סֶלָה׃
selah they-will-become-proud you-let-succeed not plan-of-him wicked desires-of

רֹאשׁ מְסִבָּי עֲמַל שְׂפָתֵימוֹ יְכַסֵּמוֹ׃
let-him-cover-them lips-of-them trouble-of ones-surrounding-me head-of (10)

יִמּוֹטוּ עֲלֵיהֶם גֶּחָלִים בָּאֵשׁ יַפִּלֵם
may-they-throw-them into-the-fire coals upon-them let-them-fall (11)

בְּמַהֲמֹרוֹת בַּל־ יָקוּמוּ׃ אִישׁ לָשׁוֹן בַּל־ יִכּוֹן
may-he-be-established not slander man-of (12) may-they-rise never into-miry-pits

בָּאָרֶץ אִישׁ־ חָמָס רָע יְצוּדֶנּוּ לְמַדְחֵפֹת׃
in-thrusts may-he-hunt-down-him disaster violence man-of in-the-land

יָדַעְתָּ כִּי־ יַעֲשֶׂה יְהוָה דִּין עָנִי מִשְׁפַּט אֶבְיֹנִים׃
needy-ones cause-of poor justice-of Yahweh he-secures that I-know (13)

אַךְ צַדִּיקִים יוֹדוּ לִשְׁמֶךָ יֵשְׁבוּ
they-will-live to-name-of-you they-will-praise righteous-ones surely (14)

יְשָׁרִים אֶת־ פָּנֶיךָ׃ מִזְמוֹר לְדָוִד יְהוָה קְרָאתִיךָ
I-call-to-you Yahweh of-David psalm (141:1) faces-of-you before upright-ones

חוּשָׁה לִּי הַאֲזִינָה קוֹלִי בְּקָרְאִי־ לָךְ׃ תִּכּוֹן
may-she-be-set (2) to-you when-to-call-me voice-of-me hear! to-me be-quick!

תְּפִלָּתִי קְטֹרֶת לְפָנֶיךָ מַשְׂאַת כַּפַּי מִנְחַת־ עָרֶב׃
evening sacrifice-of hands-of-me lifting-of before-you incense prayer-of-me

שִׁיתָה יְהוָה שָׁמְרָה לְפִי נִצְּרָה עַל־ דַּל שְׂפָתָי׃
lips-of-me door-of over keep-watch! over-mouth-of-me guard Yahweh set! (3)

אַל־ תַּט־ לִבִּי לְדָבָר ׀ רָע לְהִתְעוֹלֵל עֲלִלוֹת ׀
deeds to-take-part evil to-matter heart-of-me you-let-be-drawn not (4)

בְּרֶשַׁע אֶת־אִישִׁים פֹּעֲלֵי־ אָוֶן וּבַל־ אֶלְחַם בְּמַנְעַמֵּיהֶם׃
of-delicacies-of-them let-me-eat and-not evil ones-doing-of men with of-wickedness

יֶהֶלְמֵנִי־ צַדִּיק ׀ חֶסֶד וְיוֹכִיחֵנִי שֶׁמֶן
oil-of and-let-him-rebuke-me kindness righteous-man let-him-strike-me (5)

רֹאשׁ אַל־ יָנִי רֹאשִׁי כִּי־ עוֹד וּתְפִלָּתִי
also-prayer-of-me ever yet head-of-me he-will-refuse not head

5Proud men have hidden a snare for me;
they have spread out the cords of their net
and have set traps for me along my path. *Selah*

6O LORD, I say to you, "You are my God."
Hear, O LORD, my cry for mercy.
7O Sovereign LORD, my strong deliverer,
who shields my head in the day of battle—
8do not grant the wicked their desires, O LORD;
do not let their plans succeed,
or they will become proud. *Selah*

9Let the heads of those who surround me
be covered with the trouble their lips have caused.
10Let burning coals fall upon them;
may they be thrown into the fire,
into miry pits, never to rise.
11Let slanderers not be established in the land;
may disaster hunt down men of violence.

12I know that the LORD secures justice for the poor
and upholds the cause of the needy.
13Surely the righteous will praise your name
and the upright will live before you.

**Psalm 141**

A psalm of David.

1O LORD, I call to you; come quickly to me.
Hear my voice when I call to you.
2May my prayer be set before you like incense;
may the lifting up of my hands be like the evening sacrifice.

3Set a guard over my mouth, O LORD;
keep watch over the door of my lips.
4Let not my heart be drawn to what is evil,
to take part in wicked deeds
with men who are evildoers;
let me not eat of their delicacies.

5Let a righteous man strike me—it is a kindness;
let him rebuke me—it is oil on my head.
My head will not refuse it.

Yet my prayer is ever against

*See the note on page 349.

°10 ק יכסימו
°11 ק ימוטו
°13 ק ידעתי

בְּרָעוֹתֵיהֶם׃ נִשְׁמְטוּ בִידֵי־ סֶלַע
cliff from-edges-of they-will-be-thrown-down (6) against-evil-deeds-of-them

שֹׁפְטֵיהֶם וְשָׁמְעוּ אֲמָרַי כִּי נָעֵמוּ׃
they-were-well-spoken that words-of-me and-they-will-learn ones-ruling-them

כְּמוֹ פֹלֵחַ וּבֹקֵעַ בָּאָרֶץ נִפְזְרוּ
they-were-scattered to-the-earth and-one-breaking-up one-plowing as (7)

עֲצָמֵינוּ לְפִי שְׁאוֹל׃ כִּי אֵלֶיךָ ׀ יְהוִה אֲדֹנָי עֵינָי בְּכָה
in-you eyes-of-me Lord Yahweh on-you but (8) Sheol at-mouth-of bones-of-us

חָסִיתִי אַל־ תְּעַר נַפְשִׁי׃ שָׁמְרֵנִי מִידֵי
from-hands-of keep-me! (9) self-of-me you-give-over-to-death not I-take-refuge

פַּח יָקְשׁוּ לִי וּמֹקְשׁוֹת פֹּעֲלֵי אָוֶן׃ יִפְּלוּ
let-them-fall (10) evil ones-doing-of and-traps-of for-me they-laid snare

בְמַכְמֹרָיו רְשָׁעִים יַחַד אָנֹכִי עַד־ אֶעֱבוֹר׃ מַשְׂכִּיל
maskil *(142:1) I-pass-by while I together wicked-ones into-nets-of-him

לְדָוִד בִּהְיוֹתוֹ בַמְּעָרָה תְפִלָּה׃ קוֹלִי אֶל־ יְהוָה אֶזְעָק
I-cry Yahweh to voice-of-me (2) prayer in-the-cave when-to-be-him of-David

קוֹלִי אֶל־ יְהוָה אֶתְחַנָּן׃ אֶשְׁפֹּךְ לְפָנָיו שִׂיחִי
complaint-of-me before-him I-pour-out (3) I-ask-for-mercy Yahweh to voice-of-me

צָרָתִי לְפָנָיו אַגִּיד׃ בְּהִתְעַטֵּף עָלַי ׀ רוּחִי
spirit-of-me within-me when-to-grow-faint (4) I-tell before-him trouble-of-me

וְאַתָּה יָדַעְתָּ נְתִיבָתִי בְּאֹרַח־ זוּ אֲהַלֵּךְ טָמְנוּ פַח לִי׃
for-me snare they-hid I-walk where in-path way-of-me you-know then-you

הַבֵּיט יָמִין ׀ וּרְאֵה וְאֵין־ לִי מַכִּיר אָבַד
he-fled one-being-concerned for-me that-there-is-not and-see! right look! (5)

מָנוֹס מִמֶּנִּי אֵין דּוֹרֵשׁ לְנַפְשִׁי׃ זָעַקְתִּי אֵלֶיךָ יְהוָה
Yahweh to-you I-cry (6) for-life-of-me one-caring there-is-not from-me refuge

אָמַרְתִּי אַתָּה מַחְסִי חֶלְקִי בְּאֶרֶץ הַחַיִּים׃ הַקְשִׁיבָה ׀ אֶל־
to listen! (7) living-ones in-land-of portion-of-me refuge-of-me you I-say

רִנָּתִי כִּי־ דַלּוֹתִי מְאֹד הַצִּילֵנִי מֵרֹדְפַי כִּי
for from-ones-pursuing-me rescue-me! desperate I-am-in-need for cry-of-me

אָמְצוּ מִמֶּנִּי׃ הוֹצִיאָה מִמַּסְגֵּר ׀ נַפְשִׁי לְהוֹדוֹת
to-praise self-of-me from-prison set-free! (8) more-than-me they-are-strong

אֶת־ שְׁמֶךָ בִּי יַכְתִּרוּ צַדִּיקִים כִּי
because righteous-ones they-will-gather-about to-me name-of-you ***

תִגְמֹל עָלָי׃ מִזְמוֹר לְדָוִד יְהוָה ׀ שְׁמַע תְּפִלָּתִי
prayer-of-me hear! Yahweh of-David psalm (143:1) to-me you-will-be-good

הַאֲזִינָה אֶל־ תַּחֲנוּנַי בֶּאֱמֻנָתְךָ עֲנֵנִי
relieve-me! in-faithfulness-of-you cries-for-mercy-of-me to listen!

the deeds of evildoers;
6 their rulers will be thrown
down from the cliffs,
and the wicked will learn
that my words were well
spoken.
7 They will say, "As one plows
and breaks up the earth,
so our bones have been
scattered at the mouth of
the grave.[h]"

8 But my eyes are fixed on you,
O Sovereign LORD;
in you I take refuge—do not
give me over to death.
9 Keep me from the snares they
have laid for me,
from the traps set by
evildoers.
10 Let the wicked fall into their
own nets,
while I pass by in safety.

## Psalm 142

A *maskil*[i] of David. When he was in the cave. A prayer.

1 I cry aloud to the LORD;
I lift up my voice to the
LORD for mercy.
2 I pour out my complaint
before him;
before him I tell my trouble.
3 When my spirit grows faint
within me,
it is you who know my
way.
In the path where I walk
men have hidden a snare
for me.
4 Look to my right and see;
no one is concerned for me.
I have no refuge;
no one cares for my life.
5 I cry to you, O LORD;
I say, "You are my refuge,
my portion in the land of
the living."
6 Listen to my cry,
for I am in desperate need;
rescue me from those who
pursue me,
for they are too strong for
me.
7 Set me free from my prison,
that I may praise your
name.

Then the righteous will gather
about me
because of your goodness to
me.

## Psalm 143

A psalm of David.

1 O LORD, hear my prayer,
listen to my cry for mercy;
in your faithfulness and
righteousness
come to my relief.

h7 Hebrew *Sheol*
i Title: Probably a literary or musical term

***1 See the note on page 349.**

בְּצִדְקָתֶךָ׃ וְאַל־ תָּבוֹא בְמִשְׁפָּט אֶת־ עַבְדֶּךָ
servant-of-you *** into-judgment you-bring and-not (2) in-righteousness-of-you

כִּי לֹא־ יִצְדַּק לְפָנֶיךָ כָל־ חָי׃ כִּי רָדַף
he-pursues indeed (3) one-alive any-of before-you he-is-righteous not for

אוֹיֵב ׀ נַפְשִׁי דִּכָּא לָאָרֶץ חַיָּתִי הוֹשִׁיבַנִי
he-makes-dwell-me life-of-me to-the-ground he-crushes self-of-me one-being-enemy

בְמַחֲשַׁכִּים כְּמֵתֵי עוֹלָם׃ וַתִּתְעַטֵּף עָלַי
within-me so-she-grows-faint (4) long-ago like-dead-ones-of in-dark-places

רוּחִי בְּתוֹכִי יִשְׁתּוֹמֵם לִבִּי׃ זָכַרְתִּי יָמִים ׀
days I-remember (5) heart-of-me he-is-dismayed at-within-me spirit-of-me

מִקֶּדֶם הָגִיתִי בְכָל־ פָּעֳלֶךָ בְּמַעֲשֵׂה יָדֶיךָ
hands-of-you on-deed-of work-of-you on-all-of I-meditate of-long-ago

אֲשׂוֹחֵחַ׃ פֵּרַשְׂתִּי יָדַי אֵלֶיךָ נַפְשִׁי ׀ כְּאֶרֶץ־ עֲיֵפָה
parched like-land soul-of-me to-you hands-of-me I-spread-out (6) I-consider

לְךָ סֶלָה׃ מַהֵר עֲנֵנִי ׀ יְהוָה כָּלְתָה רוּחִי אַל־
not spirit-of-me she-faints Yahweh answer-me! be-quick! (7) selah for-you

תַּסְתֵּר פָּנֶיךָ מִמֶּנִּי וְנִמְשַׁלְתִּי עִם־ יֹרְדֵי בוֹר׃
pit ones-going-down-of with or-I-will-be-like from-me faces-of-you you-hide

הַשְׁמִיעֵנִי בַבֹּקֶר ׀ חַסְדֶּךָ כִּי־ בְךָ
in-you for unfailing-love-of-you in-the-morning bring-word-to-me! (8)

בָטָחְתִּי הוֹדִיעֵנִי דֶּרֶךְ־ זוּ אֵלֵךְ כִּי־ אֵלֶיךָ נָשָׂאתִי נַפְשִׁי׃
soul-of-me I-lift-up to-you for I-should-go that way show-me! I-put-trust

הַצִּילֵנִי מֵאֹיְבַי ׀ יְהוָה אֵלֶיךָ כִסִּתִי׃
I-hide in-you Yahweh from-ones-being-enemies-of-me rescue-me! (9)

לַמְּדֵנִי ׀ לַעֲשׂוֹת רְצוֹנֶךָ כִּי־ אַתָּה אֱלוֹהָי רוּחֲךָ טוֹבָה
good Spirit-of-you God-of-me you for will-of-you to-do teach-me! (10)

תַּנְחֵנִי בְּאֶרֶץ מִישׁוֹר׃ לְמַעַן־ שִׁמְךָ יְהוָה
Yahweh name-of-you for-sake-of (11) levelness on-ground-of may-she-lead-me

תְּחַיֵּנִי בְּצִדְקָתְךָ ׀ תוֹצִיא מִצָּרָה נַפְשִׁי׃
self-of-me from-trouble you-bring-out in-righteousness-of-you you-keep-alive-me

וּבְחַסְדְּךָ תַּצְמִית אֹיְבָי וְהַאֲבַדְתָּ
and-you-destroy ones-being-enemies-of-me you-silence and-in-love-of-you (12)

כָּל־ צֹרְרֵי נַפְשִׁי כִּי אֲנִי עַבְדֶּךָ׃ לְדָוִד ׀
of-David (144:1) servant-of-you I for self-of-me ones-being-foes-of all-of

בָּרוּךְ יְהוָה ׀ צוּרִי הַמְלַמֵּד יָדַי לַקְרָב
for-the-war hands-of-me the-one-training Rock-of-me Yahweh being-praised

אֶצְבְּעוֹתַי לַמִּלְחָמָה׃ חַסְדִּי וּמְצוּדָתִי מִשְׂגַּבִּי
stronghold-of-me and-fortress-of-me love-of-me (2) for-the-battle fingers-of-me

2 Do not bring your servant into judgment,
for no one living is righteous before you.
3 The enemy pursues me,
he crushes me to the ground;
he makes me dwell in darkness
like those long dead.
4 So my spirit grows faint within me;
my heart within me is dismayed.
5 I remember the days of long ago;
I meditate on all your works
and consider what your hands have done.
6 I spread out my hands to you;
my soul thirsts for you like a parched land. *Selah*
7 Answer me quickly, O LORD;
my spirit faints with longing.
Do not hide your face from me
or I will be like those who go down to the pit.
8 Let the morning bring me word of your unfailing love,
for I have put my trust in you.
Show me the way I should go,
for to you I lift up my soul.
9 Rescue me from my enemies, O LORD,
for I hide myself in you.
10 Teach me to do your will,
for you are my God;
may your good Spirit
lead me on level ground.
11 For your name's sake, O LORD, preserve my life;
in your righteousness, bring me out of trouble.
12 In your unfailing love, silence my enemies;
destroy all my foes,
for I am your servant.

**Psalm 144**

Of David.

1 Praise be to the LORD, my Rock,
who trains my hands for war,
my fingers for battle.
2 He is my loving God and my fortress,
my stronghold and my

וּמְפַלְטִי לִי מָגִנִּי וּבוֹ חָסִיתִי
I-take-refuge and-in-him shield-of-me to-me and-one-delivering-me

הָרוֹדֵד עַמִּי תַחְתָּי׃ (3) יְהוָה מָה־ אָדָם
man what? Yahweh (3) under-me people-of-me the-one-subduing

וַתֵּדָעֵהוּ בֶּן־ אֱנוֹשׁ וַתְּחַשְּׁבֵהוּ׃ (4) אָדָם לַהֶבֶל
to-the-breath man (4) that-you-think-of-him man son-of that-you-care-for-him

דָּמָה יָמָיו כְּצֵל עוֹבֵר׃ (5) יְהוָה הַט־ שָׁמֶיךָ
heavens-of-you part! Yahweh (5) one-fleeting like-shadow days-of-him he-is-like

וְתֵרֵד גַּע בֶּהָרִים וְיֶעֱשָׁנוּ׃ (6) בְּרוֹק
send-lightning! (6) so-they-smoke to-the-mountains touch! and-you-come-down

בָּרָק וּתְפִיצֵם שְׁלַח חִצֶּיךָ וּתְהֻמֵּם׃
and-you-rout-them arrows-of-you shoot! and-you-scatter-them lightning

(7) שְׁלַח יָדֶיךָ מִמָּרוֹם פְּצֵנִי וְהַצִּילֵנִי מִמַּיִם
from-waters and-rescue-me! deliver-me! from-on-high hands-of-you reach! (7)

רַבִּים מִיַּד בְּנֵי נֵכָר׃ (8) אֲשֶׁר פִּיהֶם דִּבֶּר־ שָׁוְא
lie he-speaks mouth-of-them who (8) foreign men-of from-hand-of mighty-ones

וִימִינָם יְמִין שָׁקֶר׃ (9) אֱלֹהִים שִׁיר חָדָשׁ אָשִׁירָה
I-will-sing new song God (9) deceit right-hand-of and-right-hand-of-them

לָךְ בְּנֵבֶל עָשׂוֹר אֲזַמְּרָה־ לָּךְ׃ (10) הַנּוֹתֵן תְּשׁוּעָה
victory the-One-giving (10) to-you I-will-make-music ten on-lyre-of to-you

לַמְּלָכִים הַפּוֹצֶה אֶת־ דָּוִד עַבְדּוֹ מֵחֶרֶב רָעָה׃
deadly from-sword servant-of-him David *** the-One-delivering to-the-kings

(11) פְּצֵנִי וְהַצִּילֵנִי מִיַּד בְּנֵי־ נֵכָר אֲשֶׁר פִּיהֶם
mouth-of-them who foreign men-of from-hand-of and-rescue-me! deliver-me! (11)

דִּבֶּר־ שָׁוְא וִימִינָם יְמִין שָׁקֶר׃ (12) אֲשֶׁר בָּנֵינוּ
sons-of-us then (12) deceit right-hand-of and-right-hand-of-them lie he-speaks

כִּנְטִעִים מְגֻדָּלִים בִּנְעוּרֵיהֶם בְּנוֹתֵינוּ
daughters-of-us in-youths-of-them ones-being-well-nurtured like-plants

כְזָוִיֹּת מְחֻטָּבוֹת תַּבְנִית הֵיכָל׃ (13) מְזָוֵינוּ
barns-of-us (13) palace adornment-of ones-being-carved like-pillars

מְלֵאִים מְפִיקִים מִזַּן אֶל־ זַן צֹאונֵנוּ
sheep-of-us kind to from-kind things-being-provided ones-filled

מַאֲלִיפוֹת מְרֻבָּבוֹת בְּחוּצוֹתֵינוּ׃
in-fields-of-us ones-becoming-tens-of-thousands ones-becoming-thousands

(14) אַלּוּפֵינוּ מְסֻבָּלִים אֵין־ פֶּרֶץ וְאֵין יוֹצֵאת וְאֵין
and-no going-away and-no breach no ones-drawing-loads oxen-of-us (14)

צְוָחָה בִּרְחֹבֹתֵינוּ׃ (15) אַשְׁרֵי הָעָם שֶׁכָּכָה
who-true the-people blessednesses-of (15) in-streets-of-us cry-of-distress

deliverer,
my shield, in whom I take refuge,
who subdues peoples[j] under me.

[3]O LORD, what is man that you care for him,
the son of man that you think of him?
[4]Man is like a breath;
his days are like a fleeting shadow.

[5]Part your heavens, O LORD, and come down;
touch the mountains, so that they smoke.
[6]Send forth lightning and scatter ⌊the enemies⌋;
shoot your arrows and rout them.
[7]Reach down your hand from on high;
deliver me and rescue me
from the mighty waters,
from the hands of foreigners
[8]whose mouths are full of lies,
whose right hands are deceitful.

[9]I will sing a new song to you, O God;
on the ten-stringed lyre I will make music to you,
[10]to the One who gives victory to kings,
who delivers his servant David from the deadly sword.

[11]Deliver me and rescue me
from the hands of foreigners
whose mouths are full of lies,
whose right hands are deceitful.

[12]Then our sons in their youth
will be like well-nurtured plants,
and our daughters will be like pillars
carved to adorn a palace.
[13]Our barns will be filled
with every kind of provision.
Our sheep will increase by thousands,
by tens of thousands in our fields;
[14] our oxen will draw heavy loads.[k]
There will be no breaching of walls,
no going into captivity,
no cry of distress in our streets.

[15]Blessed are the people of whom this is true;

[j]2 Many manuscripts of the Masoretic Text, Dead Sea Scrolls, Aquila, Jerome and Syriac; most manuscripts of the Masoretic Text *subdues my people*

[k]14 Or *our chieftains will be firmly established*

| | | | | | | |
|---|---|---|---|---|---|---|
| תְּהִלָּה | | אֱלֹהָיו׃ | שֶׁיְהוָה | הָעָם | אַשְׁרֵי | לוֹ |
| praise-psalm | (145:1) | God-of-him | who-Yahweh | the-people | blessednesses-of | of-him |

| | | | | | |
|---|---|---|---|---|---|
| שִׁמְךָ | וַאֲבָרְכָה | הַמֶּלֶךְ | אֱלוֹהַי | אֲרוֹמִמְךָ | לְדָוִד |
| name-of-you | and-I-will-praise | the-King | God-of-me | I-will-exalt-you | of-David |

| | | | | | | |
|---|---|---|---|---|---|---|
| וַאֲהַלְלָה | אֲבָרְכֶךָּ | יוֹם | בְּכָל־ | | וָעֶד׃ | לְעוֹלָם |
| and-I-will-extol | I-will-praise-you | day | in-every-of | (2) | and-ever | to-forever |

| | | | | | | | |
|---|---|---|---|---|---|---|---|
| מְאֹד | וּמְהֻלָּל | יְהוָה | גָּדוֹל | | וָעֶד׃ | לְעוֹלָם | שִׁמְךָ |
| greatly | and-one-being-praised | Yahweh | great | (3) | and-ever | to-forever | name-of-you |

| | | | | | |
|---|---|---|---|---|---|
| לְדוֹר | דּוֹר | | חֵקֶר׃ | אֵין | וְלִגְדֻלָּתוֹ |
| to-generation | generation | (4) | fathoming | there-is-no | and-to-greatness-of-him |

| | | | |
|---|---|---|---|
| יַגִּידוּ׃ | וּגְבוּרֹתֶיךָ | מַעֲשֶׂיךָ | יְשַׁבַּח |
| they-will-tell | and-mighty-acts-of-you | works-of-you | he-will-commend |

| | | | | | |
|---|---|---|---|---|---|
| נִפְלְאוֹתֶיךָ | וְדִבְרֵי | הוֹדֶךָ | כְּבוֹד | הֲדַר | |
| works-being-wonderful-of-you | and-deeds-of | majesty-of-you | glory-of | splendor-of | (5) |

| | | | | |
|---|---|---|---|---|
| יֹאמֵרוּ | נוֹרְאֹתֶיךָ | וֶעֱזוּז | | אָשִׂיחָה׃ |
| they-will-tell | works-being-awesome-of-you | and-power-of | (6) | I-will-meditate |

| | | | | | |
|---|---|---|---|---|---|
| טוּבְךָ | רַב־ | זֵכֶר | | אֲסַפְּרֶנָּה׃ | °וּגְדוּלֹּתְךָ |
| goodness-of-you | abundance-of | memory-of | (7) | I-will-proclaim | and-great-deed-of-you |

| | | | | |
|---|---|---|---|---|
| חַנּוּן | | יְרַנֵּנוּ׃ | וְצִדְקָתְךָ | יַבִּיעוּ |
| gracious | (8) | they-will-sing | and-righteousness-of-you | they-will-celebrate |

| | | | | | | | | | |
|---|---|---|---|---|---|---|---|---|---|
| יְהוָה | טוֹב־ | | חָסֶד׃ | וּגְדָל־ | אַפַּיִם | אֶרֶךְ | יְהוָה | וְרַחוּם |
| Yahweh | good | (9) | love | and-rich-of | angers | slow-of | Yahweh | and-compassionate |

| | | | | |
|---|---|---|---|---|
| מַעֲשָׂיו׃ | כָּל־ | עַל־ | וְרַחֲמָיו | לַכֹּל |
| makings-of-him | all-of | on | and-compassions-of-him | to-the-all |

| | | | | | |
|---|---|---|---|---|---|
| וַחֲסִידֶיךָ | מַעֲשֶׂיךָ | כָּל־ | יְהוָה | יוֹדוּךָ | |
| and-saints-of-you | makings-of-you | all-of | Yahweh | they-will-praise-you | (10) |

| | | | | |
|---|---|---|---|---|
| יֹאמֵרוּ | מַלְכוּתְךָ | כְּבוֹד | | יְבָרְכוּכָה׃ |
| they-will-tell | kingdom-of-you | glory-of | (11) | they-will-extol-you |

| | | | | | |
|---|---|---|---|---|---|
| הָאָדָם | לִבְנֵי | לְהוֹדִיעַ ׀ | | יְדַבֵּרוּ׃ | וּגְבוּרָתְךָ |
| the-man | to-sons-of | to-make-known | (12) | they-will-speak | and-might-of-you |

| | | | | | |
|---|---|---|---|---|---|
| מַלְכוּתְךָ | | מַלְכוּתוֹ׃ | הֲדַר | וּכְבוֹד | גְּבוּרֹתָיו |
| kingdom-of-you | (13) | kingdom-of-him | splendor-of | and-glory-of | mighty-acts-of-him |

| | | | | | |
|---|---|---|---|---|---|
| דּוֹר | בְּכָל־ | וּמֶמְשַׁלְתְּךָ | עֹלָמִים | כָּל־ | מַלְכוּת |
| generation | through-all-of | and-dominion-of-you | everlastings | all-of | kingdom-of |

| | | | | | | |
|---|---|---|---|---|---|---|
| וְזוֹקֵף | הַנֹּפְלִים | לְכָל־ | יְהוָה | סוֹמֵךְ | | וָדֹר׃ |
| and-lifting | the-ones-falling | to-all-of | Yahweh | upholding | (14) | *and-generation |

| | | | | | | | |
|---|---|---|---|---|---|---|---|
| וְאַתָּה | יְשַׂבֵּרוּ | אֵלֶיךָ | כֹל | עֵינֵי־ | | הַכְּפוּפִים׃ | לְכָל־ |
| and-you | they-look | to-you | all | eyes-of | (15) | the-ones-being-bowed | to-all-of |

blessed are the people whose
God is the LORD.

**Psalm 145**[l]

A psalm of praise. Of David.

1 I will exalt you, my God the King;
I will praise your name for ever and ever.
2 Every day I will praise you
and extol your name for ever and ever.

3 Great is the LORD and most worthy of praise;
his greatness no one can fathom.
4 One generation will commend your works to another;
they will tell of your mighty acts.
5 They will speak of the glorious splendor of your majesty,
and I will meditate on your wonderful works.[m]
6 They will tell of the power of your awesome works,
and I will proclaim your great deeds.
7 They will celebrate your abundant goodness
and joyfully sing of your righteousness.

8 The LORD is gracious and compassionate,
slow to anger and rich in love.
9 The LORD is good to all;
he has compassion on all he has made.
10 All you have made will praise you, O LORD;
your saints will extol you.
11 They will tell of the glory of your kingdom
and speak of your might,
12 so that all men may know of your mighty acts
and the glorious splendor of your kingdom.
13 Your kingdom is an everlasting kingdom,
and your dominion endures through all generations.

The LORD is faithful to all his promises
and loving toward all he has made.[n]
14 The LORD upholds all those who fall
and lifts up all who are bowed down.

[l] This psalm is an acrostic poem, the verses of which (including verse 13b) begin with the successive letters of the Hebrew alphabet.
[m] 5 Dead Sea Scrolls and Syriac (see also Septuagint); Masoretic Text *On the glorious splendor of your majesty / and on your wonderful works I will meditate*
[n] 13 One manuscript of the Masoretic Text, Dead Sea Scrolls, Septuagint and Syriac; most manuscripts of the Masoretic Text do not have the last two lines of verse 13.

*13 The NIV reads with the mss and versions listed above in footnote *n*:

| | | |
|---|---|---|
| בְּכָל־ | יהוה | נֶאֱמָן |
| *to-all-of* | *Yahweh* | *one-being-faithful* |
| בְּכָל־ | וְחָסִיד | דְּבָרָיו |
| *toward-all-of* | *and-loving* | *promises-of-him* |
| | | מַעֲשָׂיו |
| | | *makings-of-him.* |

°6 ק וגדולתך

נוֹתֵן־ לָהֶם אֶת־ אָכְלָם בְּעִתּוֹ׃ פּוֹתֵחַ אֶת־ יָדֶךָ
hand-of-you *** opening (16) at-time-of-him food-of-them *** to-them giving

וּמַשְׂבִּיעַ לְכָל־ חַי רָצוֹן׃ צַדִּיק יְהוָה
Yahweh righteous (17) desire living-thing to-every-of and-satisfying

בְּכָל־ דְּרָכָיו וְחָסִיד בְּכָל־ מַעֲשָׂיו׃ קָרוֹב
near (18) makings-of-him toward-all-of and-loving ways-of-him in-all-of

יְהוָה לְכָל־ קֹרְאָיו לְכֹל אֲשֶׁר יִקְרָאֻהוּ בֶאֱמֶת׃
in-truth they-call-on-him who to-all ones-calling-on-him to-all-of Yahweh

רְצוֹן־ יְרֵאָיו יַעֲשֶׂה וְאֶת־ שַׁוְעָתָם יִשְׁמַע
he-hears cry-of-them and he-fulfills ones-fearing-him desire-of (19)

וְיוֹשִׁיעֵם׃ שׁוֹמֵר יְהוָה אֶת־ כָּל־ אֹהֲבָיו וְאֵת
but ones-loving-him all-of *** Yahweh watching-over (20) and-he-saves-them

כָּל־ הָרְשָׁעִים יַשְׁמִיד׃ תְּהִלַּת יְהוָה יְדַבֶּר־
he-will-speak Yahweh praise-of (21) he-will-destroy the-wicked-ones all-of

פִּי וִיבָרֵךְ כָּל־ בָּשָׂר שֵׁם קָדְשׁוֹ
holiness-of-him name-of creature every-of and-let-him-praise mouth-of-me

לְעוֹלָם וָעֶד׃ הַלְלוּ־ יָהּ הַלְלִי נַפְשִׁי אֶת־ יְהוָה׃
Yahweh *** soul-of-me praise! Yahweh praise! (146:1) and-ever to-forever

אֲהַלְלָה יְהוָה בְּחַיָּי אֲזַמְּרָה לֵאלֹהַי
to-God-of-me I-will-sing-praise during-lives-of-me Yahweh I-will-praise (2)

בְּעוֹדִי׃ אַל־ תִּבְטְחוּ בִנְדִיבִים בְּבֶן־ אָדָם׀ שֶׁאֵין לוֹ
in-him who-not man in-son-of in-princes you-trust not (3) while-still-I

תְשׁוּעָה׃ תֵּצֵא רוּחוֹ יָשֻׁב לְאַדְמָתוֹ בַּיּוֹם
on-the-day to-ground-of-him he-returns spirit-of-him she-departs (4) salvation

הַהוּא אָבְדוּ עֶשְׁתֹּנֹתָיו׃ אַשְׁרֵי שֶׁאֵל
who-God-of blessednesses-of (5) plans-of-him they-come-to-nothing the-that

יַעֲקֹב בְּעֶזְרוֹ שִׂבְרוֹ עַל־ יְהוָה אֱלֹהָיו׃ עֹשֶׂה׀ שָׁמַיִם
heavens One-Making (6) God-of-him Yahweh in hope-of-him as-help-of-him Jacob

וָאָרֶץ אֶת־ הַיָּם וְאֶת־ כָּל־ אֲשֶׁר־ בָּם הַשֹּׁמֵר אֱמֶת
faithful the-one-remaining in-them that all and the-sea *** and-earth

לְעוֹלָם׃ עֹשֶׂה מִשְׁפָּט׀ לָעֲשׁוּקִים נֹתֵן לֶחֶם
food giving of-the-ones-being-oppressed cause upholding (7) to-forever

לָרְעֵבִים יְהוָה מַתִּיר אֲסוּרִים׃ יְהוָה׀
Yahweh (8) ones-being-prisoners setting-free Yahweh to-the-hungry-ones

פֹּקֵחַ עִוְרִים יְהוָה זֹקֵף כְּפוּפִים יְהוָה אֹהֵב
loving Yahweh ones-being-bowed lifting Yahweh blind-ones giving-sight

צַדִּיקִים׃ יְהוָה׀ שֹׁמֵר אֶת־ גֵּרִים יָתוֹם וְאַלְמָנָה
and-widow fatherless aliens *** watching-over Yahweh (9) righteous-ones

15 The eyes of all look to you,
and you give them their food at the proper time.
16 You open your hand
and satisfy the desires of every living thing.

17 The LORD is righteous in all his ways
and loving toward all he has made.
18 The LORD is near to all who call on him,
to all who call on him in truth.
19 He fulfills the desires of those who fear him;
he hears their cry and saves them.
20 The LORD watches over all who love him,
but all the wicked he will destroy.

21 My mouth will speak in praise of the LORD.
Let every creature praise his holy name
for ever and ever.

**Psalm 146**

1 Praise the LORD.[o]

Praise the LORD, O my soul.
2 I will praise the LORD all my life;
I will sing praise to my God as long as I live.

3 Do not put your trust in princes,
in mortal men, who cannot save.
4 When their spirit departs, they return to the ground;
on that very day their plans come to nothing.

5 Blessed is he whose help is the God of Jacob,
whose hope is in the LORD his God,
6 the Maker of heaven and earth,
the sea, and everything in them—
the LORD, who remains faithful forever.
7 He upholds the cause of the oppressed
and gives food to the hungry.
The LORD sets prisoners free,
8 the LORD gives sight to the blind,
the LORD lifts up those who are bowed down,
the LORD loves the righteous.
9 The LORD watches over the alien
and sustains the fatherless and the widow,

[o] 1 Hebrew *Hallelu Yah*; also in verse 10

יְעוֹדֵד וְדֶרֶךְ רְשָׁעִים יְעַוֵּת׃ יִמְלֹךְ יְהוָה ׀
Yahweh he-reigns (10) he-frustrates wicked-ones but-way-of he-sustains

לְעוֹלָם אֱלֹהַיִךְ צִיּוֹן לְדֹר וָדֹר הַלְלוּ־יָהּ׃
Yahweh praise! and-generation for-generation Zion God-of-you to-forever

הַלְלוּ יָהּ ׀ כִּי־טוֹב זַמְּרָה אֱלֹהֵינוּ כִּי־נָעִים
pleasant how! God-of-us to-sing-praise good how! Yahweh praise! (147:1)

נָאוָה תְהִלָּה׃ בּוֹנֵה יְרוּשָׁלַםִ יְהוָה נִדְחֵי יִשְׂרָאֵל
Israel ones-being-exiled-of Yahweh Jerusalem one-building-of (2) praise fitting

יְכַנֵּס׃ הָרֹפֵא לִשְׁבוּרֵי לֵב וּמְחַבֵּשׁ
and-one-binding heart to-ones-being-broken-of the-one-healing (3) he-gathers

לְעַצְּבוֹתָם׃ מוֹנֶה מִסְפָּר לַכּוֹכָבִים לְכֻלָּם
to-each-of-them of-the-stars number one-determining (4) to-wounds-of-them

שֵׁמוֹת יִקְרָא׃ גָּדוֹל אֲדוֹנֵינוּ וְרַב־כֹּחַ לִתְבוּנָתוֹ
to-understanding-of-him power and-mighty-of Lord-of-us great (5) he-calls names

אֵין מִסְפָּר׃ מְעוֹדֵד עֲנָוִים יְהוָה מַשְׁפִּיל רְשָׁעִים עֲדֵי־
to wicked-ones one-casting Yahweh humble-ones one-sustaining (6) limit no

אָרֶץ׃ עֱנוּ לַיהוָה בְּתוֹדָה זַמְּרוּ לֵאלֹהֵינוּ בְכִנּוֹר׃
on-harp to-God-of-us make-music! with-thanksgiving to-Yahweh sing! (7) ground

הַמְכַסֶּה שָׁמַיִם ׀ בְּעָבִים הַמֵּכִין לָאָרֶץ מָטָר
rain to-the-earth the-one-supplying with-clouds skies the-one-covering (8)

הַמַּצְמִיחַ הָרִים חָצִיר׃ נוֹתֵן לִבְהֵמָה לַחְמָהּ
food-of-her for-cattle the-one-providing (9) grass hills the-one-making-grow

לִבְנֵי עֹרֵב אֲשֶׁר יִקְרָאוּ׃ לֹא בִגְבוּרַת הַסּוּס
the-horse in-strength-of not (10) they-call when raven for-young-ones-of

יֶחְפָּץ לֹא־בְשׁוֹקֵי הָאִישׁ יִרְצֶה׃ רוֹצֶה יְהוָה
Yahweh one-delighting (11) he-delights the-man in-legs-of not he-is-pleased

אֶת־יְרֵאָיו אֶת־הַמְיַחֲלִים לְחַסְדּוֹ׃ שַׁבְּחִי
extol! (12) in-unfailing-love-of-him the-ones-hoping in ones-fearing-him in

יְרוּשָׁלַםִ אֶת־יְהוָה הַלְלִי אֱלֹהַיִךְ צִיּוֹן׃ כִּי־חִזַּק בְּרִיחֵי
bars-of he-strengthens for (13) Zion God-of-you praise! Yahweh *** Jerusalem

שְׁעָרָיִךְ בֵּרַךְ בָּנַיִךְ בְּקִרְבֵּךְ׃ הַשָּׂם־
the-one-granting (14) at-within-you peoples-of-you he-blesses gates-of-you

גְּבוּלֵךְ שָׁלוֹם חֵלֶב חִטִּים יַשְׂבִּיעֵךְ׃ הַשֹּׁלֵחַ
the-one-sending (15) he-satisfies-you wheats finest-of peace border-of-you

אִמְרָתוֹ אָרֶץ עַד־מְהֵרָה יָרוּץ דְּבָרוֹ׃ הַנֹּתֵן
the-one-spreading (16) word-of-him he-runs swiftness to earth command-of-him

שֶׁלֶג כַּצָּמֶר כְּפוֹר כָּאֵפֶר יְפַזֵּר׃ מַשְׁלִיךְ קַרְחוֹ
hail-of-him one-hurling (17) he-scatters like-the-ash frost like-the-wool snow

---

but he frustrates the ways of
the wicked.

10 The LORD reigns forever,
your God, O Zion, for all
generations.

Praise the LORD.

**Psalm 147**

1 Praise the LORD.[p]

How good it is to sing praises
to our God,
how pleasant and fitting to
praise him!

2 The LORD builds up Jerusalem;
he gathers the exiles of
Israel.
3 He heals the brokenhearted
and binds up their wounds.

4 He determines the number of
the stars
and calls them each by
name.
5 Great is our Lord and mighty
in power;
his understanding has no
limit.
6 The LORD sustains the humble
but casts the wicked to the
ground.

7 Sing to the LORD with
thanksgiving;
make music to our God on
the harp.
8 He covers the sky with clouds;
he supplies the earth with
rain
and makes grass grow on
the hills.
9 He provides food for the cattle
and for the young ravens
when they call.

10 His pleasure is not in the
strength of the horse,
nor his delight in the legs of
a man;
11 the LORD delights in those who
fear him,
who put their hope in his
unfailing love.

12 Extol the LORD, O Jerusalem;
praise your God, O Zion,
13 for he strengthens the bars of
your gates
and blesses your people
within you.
14 He grants peace to your
borders
and satisfies you with the
finest of wheat.

15 He sends his command to the
earth;
his word runs swiftly.
16 He spreads the snow like wool
and scatters the frost like
ashes.
17 He hurls down his hail like

p1 Hebrew *Hallelu Yah*; also in verse 20

כְפִתִּים לִפְנֵי קָרָתוֹ מִי יַעֲמֹד׃ יִשְׁלַח דְּבָרוֹ
word-of-him he-sends (18) he-can-stand who? icy-blast-of-him before like-pebbles

וְיַמְסֵם יַשֵּׁב רוּחוֹ יִזְּלוּ־ מָיִם׃ מַגִּיד
revealing (19) waters they-flow breeze-of-him he-stirs-up and-he-melts-them

דְּבָרָו לְיַעֲקֹב חֻקָּיו וּמִשְׁפָּטָיו לְיִשְׂרָאֵל׃ לֹא
not (20) to-Israel and-laws-of-him decrees-of-him to-Jacob words-of-him

עָשָׂה כֵן ׀ לְכָל־ גּוֹי וּמִשְׁפָּטִים בַּל־ יְדָעוּם הַלְלוּ־ יָהּ׃
Yahweh praise! they-know-them not and-laws nation for-any-of this he-did

הַלְלוּ יָהּ ׀ הַלְלוּ אֶת־ יְהוָה מִן־ הַשָּׁמַיִם הַלְלוּהוּ
praise-him! the-heavens from Yahweh *** praise! Yahweh praise! (148:1)

בַּמְּרוֹמִים׃ הַלְלוּהוּ כָל־ מַלְאָכָיו הַלְלוּהוּ כָּל־
all-of praise-him! angels-of-him all-of praise-him! (2) in-the-heights

צְבָאָו׃ הַלְלוּהוּ שֶׁמֶשׁ וְיָרֵחַ הַלְלוּהוּ כָּל־ כּוֹכְבֵי אוֹר׃
shining stars-of all-of praise-him! and-moon sun praise-him! (3) hosts-of-him

הַלְלוּהוּ שְׁמֵי הַשָּׁמָיִם וְהַמַּיִם אֲשֶׁר ׀ מֵעַל הַשָּׁמָיִם׃
the-skies at-above that and-the-waters the-heavens heavens-of praise-him! (4)

יְהַלְלוּ אֶת־ שֵׁם יְהוָה כִּי הוּא צִוָּה וְנִבְרָאוּ׃
and-they-were-created he-commanded he for Yahweh name-of *** let-them-praise (5)

וַיַּעֲמִידֵם לָעַד לְעוֹלָם חָק־ נָתַן וְלֹא
and-not he-gave decree to-forever for-ever and-he-set-in-place-them (6)

יַעֲבוֹר׃ הַלְלוּ אֶת־ יְהוָה מִן־ הָאָרֶץ תַּנִּינִים וְכָל־
and-all-of sea-creatures the-earth from Yahweh *** praise! (7) he-will-pass-away

תְּהֹמוֹת׃ אֵשׁ וּבָרָד שֶׁלֶג וְקִיטוֹר רוּחַ סְעָרָה עֹשָׂה
one-doing storm wind-of and-cloud snow and-hail lightning (8) depths

דְבָרוֹ׃ הֶהָרִים וְכָל־ גְּבָעוֹת עֵץ פְּרִי וְכָל־
and-all-of fruit tree-of hills and-all-of the-mountains (9) bidding-of-him

אֲרָזִים׃ הַחַיָּה וְכָל־ בְּהֵמָה רֶמֶשׂ וְצִפּוֹר כָּנָף׃
flight and-bird-of small-creature cattle and-all-of the-wild-animal (10) cedars

מַלְכֵי־ אֶרֶץ וְכָל־ לְאֻמִּים שָׂרִים וְכָל־ שֹׁפְטֵי אָרֶץ׃
earth ones-ruling-of and-all-of princes nations and-all-of earth kings-of (11)

בַּחוּרִים וְגַם־ בְּתוּלוֹת זְקֵנִים עִם־ נְעָרִים׃ יְהַלְלוּ ׀ אֶת־
*** let-them-praise (13) children and old-men maidens and-also young-men (12)

שֵׁם יְהוָה כִּי־ נִשְׂגָּב שְׁמוֹ לְבַדּוֹ הוֹדוֹ
splendor-of-him by-himself name-of-him one-being-exalted for Yahweh name-of

עַל־ אֶרֶץ וְשָׁמָיִם׃ וַיָּרֶם קֶרֶן ׀ לְעַמּוֹ תְּהִלָּה
praise for-people-of-him horn and-he-raised (14) and-heavens earth above

לְכָל־ חֲסִידָיו לִבְנֵי יִשְׂרָאֵל עַם־ קְרֹבוֹ הַלְלוּ־ יָהּ׃
Yahweh praise! close-to-him people-of Israel of-sons-of saints-of-him of-all-of

pebbles.
Who can withstand his icy blast?
18He sends his word and melts them;
he stirs up his breezes, and the waters flow.
19He has revealed his word to Jacob,
his laws and decrees to Israel.
20He has done this for no other nation;
they do not know his laws.

Praise the LORD.

**Psalm 148**

1Praise the LORD.[q]

Praise the LORD from the heavens,
praise him in the heights above.
2Praise him, all his angels,
praise him, all his heavenly hosts.
3Praise him, sun and moon,
praise him, all you shining stars.
4Praise him, you highest heavens
and you waters above the skies.
5Let them praise the name of the LORD,
for he commanded and they were created.
6He set them in place for ever and ever;
he gave a decree that will never pass away.

7Praise the LORD from the earth,
you great sea creatures and all ocean depths,
8lightning and hail, snow and clouds,
stormy winds that do his bidding,
9you mountains and all hills,
fruit trees and all cedars,
10wild animals and all cattle,
small creatures and flying birds,
11kings of the earth and all nations,
you princes and all rulers on earth,
12young men and maidens,
old men and children.

13Let them praise the name of the LORD,
for his name alone is exalted;
his splendor is above the earth and the heavens.
14He has raised up for his people a horn,[r]
the praise of all his saints,
of Israel, the people close to his heart.

Praise the LORD.

q1 Hebrew *Hallelu Yah*; also in verse 14
r14 *Horn* here symbolizes strong one, that is, king.

°19 ק דבריו
°2 ק צבאיו

הַלְלוּ יָהּ ׀ שִׁירוּ לַיהוָה שִׁיר חָדָשׁ תְּהִלָּתוֹ בִּקְהַל
in-assembly-of praise-of-him new song to-Yahweh sing! Yahweh praise! (149:1)

חֲסִידִים׃ יִשְׂמַח יִשְׂרָאֵל בְּעֹשָׂיו בְּנֵי־ צִיּוֹן
Zion peoples-of in-Ones-Making-him Israel let-him-rejoice (2) saints

יָגִילוּ בְמַלְכָּם׃ יְהַלְלוּ שְׁמוֹ בְמָחוֹל
with-dance name-of-him let-them-praise (3) in-King-of-them let-them-be-glad

בְּתֹף וְכִנּוֹר יְזַמְּרוּ־ לוֹ׃ כִּי־ רוֹצֶה יְהוָה
Yahweh delighting for (4) to-him let-them-make-music and-harp with-tambourine

בְּעַמּוֹ יְפָאֵר עֲנָוִים בִּישׁוּעָה׃ יַעְלְזוּ
let-them-rejoice (5) with-salvation humble-ones he-crowns in-people-of-him

חֲסִידִים בְּכָבוֹד יְרַנְּנוּ עַל־ מִשְׁכְּבוֹתָם׃ רוֹמְמוֹת אֵל
God praises-of (6) beds-of-them on let-them-sing-for-joy in-honor saints

בִּגְרוֹנָם וְחֶרֶב פִּיפִיּוֹת בְּיָדָם׃ לַעֲשׂוֹת
to-inflict (7) in-hand-of-them double-edges and-sword-of in-mouth-of-them

נְקָמָה בַּגּוֹיִם תּוֹכֵחֹת בַּל־אֻמִּים׃ לֶאְסֹר מַלְכֵיהֶם
kings-of-them to-bind (8) *on-the-peoples punishments on-the-nations vengeance

בְּזִקִּים וְנִכְבְּדֵיהֶם בְּכַבְלֵי בַרְזֶל׃ לַעֲשׂוֹת
to-carry-out (9) iron with-shackles-of and-ones-being-nobles-of-them with-fetters

בָּהֶם ׀ מִשְׁפָּט כָּתוּב הָדָר הוּא לְכָל־ חֲסִידָיו
saints-of-him of-all-of this glory one-being-written sentence against-them

הַלְלוּ־ יָהּ׃ הַלְלוּ יָהּ ׀ הַלְלוּ־ אֵל בְּקָדְשׁוֹ
in-sanctuary-of-him God praise! Yahweh praise! (150:1) Yahweh praise!

הַלְלוּהוּ בִּרְקִיעַ עֻזּוֹ׃ הַלְלוּהוּ בִגְבוּרֹתָיו
for-works-of-power-of-him praise-him! (2) might-of-him in-heaven-of praise-him!

הַלְלוּהוּ כְּרֹב גֻּדְלוֹ׃ הַלְלוּהוּ בְּתֵקַע
with-sounding-of praise-him! (3) greatness-of-him for-surpassing-of praise-him!

שׁוֹפָר הַלְלוּהוּ בְּנֵבֶל וְכִנּוֹר׃ הַלְלוּהוּ בְתֹף
with-tambourine praise-him! (4) and-lyre with-harp praise-him! trumpet

וּמָחוֹל הַלְלוּהוּ בְּמִנִּים וְעוּגָב׃ הַלְלוּהוּ בְצִלְצְלֵי־
with-cymbals-of praise-him! (5) and-flute with-strings praise-him! and-dance

שָׁמַע הַלְלוּהוּ בְּצִלְצְלֵי תְרוּעָה׃ כֹּל הַנְּשָׁמָה
the-breath all-of (6) resounding with-cymbals-of praise-him! clashing

תְּהַלֵּל יָהּ הַלְלוּ־ יָהּ׃
Yahweh praise! Yahweh let-her-praise

**Psalm 149**

1Praise the LORD.[s]

Sing to the LORD a new song,
his praise in the assembly of the saints.

2Let Israel rejoice in their Maker;
let the people of Zion be glad in their King.
3Let them praise his name with dancing
and make music to him with tambourine and harp.
4For the LORD takes delight in his people;
he crowns the humble with salvation.
5Let the saints rejoice in this honor
and sing for joy on their beds.

6May the praise of God be in their mouths
and a double-edged sword in their hands,
7to inflict vengeance on the nations
and punishment on the peoples,
8to bind their kings with fetters,
their nobles with shackles of iron,
9to carry out the sentence written against them.
This is the glory of all his saints.

Praise the LORD.

**Psalm 150**

1Praise the LORD.[t]

Praise God in his sanctuary;
praise him in his mighty heavens.
2Praise him for his acts of power;
praise him for his surpassing greatness.
3Praise him with the sounding of the trumpet,
praise him with the harp and lyre,
4praise him with tambourine and dancing,
praise him with the strings and flute,
5praise him with the clash of cymbals,
praise him with resounding cymbals.

6Let everything that has breath praise the LORD.

Praise the LORD.

[s]1 Hebrew *Hallelu Yah*; also in verse 9
[t]1 Hebrew *Hallelu Yah*; also in verse 6

*7 Most mss treat these two words as one ( בַּלְאֻמִּים ).

מִשְׁלֵי שְׁלֹמֹה בֶן־ דָּוִד מֶלֶךְ יִשְׂרָאֵל׃ לָדַעַת חָכְמָה
wisdom to-attain (2) Israel king-of David son-of Solomon proverbs-of (1:1)

וּמוּסָר לְהָבִין אִמְרֵי בִינָה׃ לָקַחַת מוּסַר
discipline-of to-acquire (3) insight words-of to-understand and-discipline

הַשְׂכֵּל צֶדֶק וּמִשְׁפָּט וּמֵישָׁרִים׃ לָתֵת לִפְתָאיִם עָרְמָה
prudence to-simple-ones to-give (4) and-fair-ones and-just right to-be-prudent

לְנַעַר דַּעַת וּמְזִמָּה׃ יִשְׁמַע חָכָם וְיוֹסֶף
and-let-him-add wise let-him-listen (5) and-discretion knowledge to-young

לֶקַח וְנָבוֹן תַּחְבֻּלוֹת יִקְנֶה׃ לְהָבִין מָשָׁל
proverb to-understand (6) let-him-get guidances and-one-discerning learning

וּמְלִיצָה דִּבְרֵי חֲכָמִים וְחִידֹתָם׃ יִרְאַת יְהוָה
Yahweh fear-of (7) and-riddles-of-them wise-ones sayings-of and-parable

**רֵאשִׁית דָּעַת חָכְמָה וּמוּסָר אֱוִילִים בָּזוּ׃ שְׁמַע**
**listen! (8) they-despise fools and-discipline wisdom knowledge beginning-of**

בְּנִי מוּסַר אָבִיךָ וְאַל־ תִּטֹּשׁ תּוֹרַת
teaching-of you-forsake and-not father-of-you instruction-of son-of-me

אִמֶּךָ׃ כִּי ׀ לִוְיַת חֵן הֵם לְרֹאשֶׁךָ וַעֲנָקִים
and-chains to-head-of-you they grace garland-of for (9) mother-of-you

לְגַרְגְּרֹתֶךָ׃ בְּנִי אִם־ יְפַתּוּךָ חַטָּאִים אַל־ תֹּבֵא׃
you-give-in not sinners they-entice-you if son-of-me (10) for-necks-of-you

אִם־ יֹאמְרוּ לְכָה אִתָּנוּ נֶאֶרְבָה לְדָם נִצְפְּנָה
let-us-hide for-blood let-us-lie-in-wait with-us come! they-say if (11)

לְנָקִי חִנָּם׃ נִבְלָעֵם כִּשְׁאוֹל חַיִּים
alive-ones like-Sheol let-us-swallow-them (12) without-cause for-harmless-soul

וּתְמִימִים כְּיוֹרְדֵי בוֹר׃ כָּל־ הוֹן יָקָר
value wealth-of all-of (13) pit like-ones-going-down-of and-whole-ones

נִמְצָא נְמַלֵּא בָתֵּינוּ שָׁלָל׃ גּוֹרָלְךָ תַּפִּיל
you-throw lot-of-you (14) plunder houses-of-us we-will-fill we-will-get

בְּתוֹכֵנוּ כִּיס אֶחָד יִהְיֶה לְכֻלָּנוּ׃ בְּנִי אַל־ תֵּלֵךְ
you-go not son-of-me (15) for-all-of-us he-will-be common purse in-among-us

בְּדֶרֶךְ אִתָּם מְנַע רַגְלְךָ מִנְּתִיבָתָם׃ כִּי רַגְלֵיהֶם
feet-of-them for (16) from-path-of-them foot-of-you withhold! with-them in-way

לָרַע יָרוּצוּ וִימַהֲרוּ לִשְׁפָּךְ־ דָּם׃ כִּי־ חִנָּם
useless how! (17) blood to-shed and-they-are-swift they-rush into-sin

מְזֹרָה הָרָשֶׁת בְּעֵינֵי כָּל־ בַּעַל כָּנָף׃ וְהֵם
and-they (18) wing master-of all-of before-eyes-of the-net being-spread

לְדָמָם יֶאֱרֹבוּ יִצְפְּנוּ לְנַפְשֹׁתָם׃ כֵּן
such (19) for-self-of-them they-hide they-lie-in-wait for-blood-of-them

### *Prologue: Purpose and Theme*

1 The proverbs of Solomon son
of David, king of Israel:

2for attaining wisdom and
discipline;
for understanding words of
insight;
3for acquiring a disciplined and
prudent life,
doing what is right and just
and fair;
4for giving prudence to the
simple,
knowledge and discretion to
the young—
5let the wise listen and add to
their learning,
and let the discerning get
guidance—
6for understanding proverbs
and parables,
the sayings and riddles of
the wise.

7The fear of the LORD is the
beginning of knowledge,
but fools[a] despise wisdom
and discipline.

### *Exhortations to Embrace Wisdom*

### *Warning Against Enticement*

8Listen, my son, to your
father's instruction
and do not forsake your
mother's teaching.
9They will be a garland to grace
your head
and a chain to adorn your
neck.

10My son, if sinners entice you,
do not give in to them.
11If they say, "Come along with
us;
let's lie in wait for
someone's blood,
let's waylay some harmless
soul;
12let's swallow them alive, like
the grave,[b]
and whole, like those who
go down to the pit;
13we will get all sorts of valuable
things
and fill our houses with
plunder;
14throw in your lot with us,
and we will share a
common purse"—
15my son, do not go along with
them,
do not set foot on their
paths;
16for their feet rush into sin,
they are swift to shed blood.
17How useless to spread a net
in full view of all the birds!
18These men lie in wait for their
own blood;
they waylay only
themselves!

[a]7 The Hebrew words rendered *fool* in Proverbs, and often elsewhere in the Old Testament, denote one who is morally deficient.
[b]12 Hebrew *Sheol*

אָרְחוֹת כָּל־ בֹּצֵעַ בָּצַע אֶת־ נֶפֶשׁ בְּעָלָיו
owners-of-him life-of *** ill-gotten-gain one-gaining all-of ends-of

יִקָּח׃ (20) חָכְמוֹת בַּחוּץ תָּרֹנָּה בָּרְחֹבוֹת
in-the-public-squares she-calls-aloud in-the-street wisdoms (20) he-takes-away

תִּתֵּן קוֹלָהּ׃ (21) בְּרֹאשׁ הֹמִיּוֹת תִּקְרָא
she-cries-out ones-being-noisy at-head-of (21) voice-of-her she-raises

בְּפִתְחֵי שְׁעָרִים בָּעִיר אֲמָרֶיהָ תֹאמֵר׃ (22) עַד־ מָתַי ׀
when? until (22) she-says speeches-of-her of-the-city gates in-gateways-of

פְּתָיִם תְּאֵהֲבוּ פֶתִי וְלֵצִים לָצוֹן
mockery and-ones-mocking simple-way will-you-love simple-ones

חָמְדוּ לָהֶם וּכְסִילִים יִשְׂנְאוּ־ דָעַת׃
knowledge will-they-hate and-fools for-them will-they-delight

(23) תָּשׁוּבוּ לְתוֹכַחְתִּי הִנֵּה אַבִּיעָה לָכֶם
to-you I-would-have-poured-out see! to-rebuke-of-me had-you-responded (23)

רוּחִי אוֹדִיעָה דְבָרַי אֶתְכֶם׃ (24) יַעַן קָרָאתִי
I-called since (24) to-you thoughts-of-me I-would-have-made-known heart-of-me

וַתְּמָאֵנוּ נָטִיתִי יָדִי וְאֵין מַקְשִׁיב׃
giving-heed and-no-one hand-of-me I-stretched-out and-you-rejected

(25) וַתִּפְרְעוּ כָל־ עֲצָתִי וְתוֹכַחְתִּי לֹא אֲבִיתֶם׃
you-accepted not and-rebuke-of-me advice-of-me all-of and-you-ignored (25)

(26) גַּם־ אֲנִי בְּאֵידְכֶם אֶשְׂחָק אֶלְעַג בְּבֹא
when-to-overtake I-will-mock I-will-laugh at-disaster-of-you I also (26)

פַחְדְּכֶם׃ (27) בְּבֹא כְשַׁאֲוָה ׀ פַּחְדְּכֶם
calamity-of-you like-storm when-to-overtake (27) calamity-of-you

וְאֵידְכֶם כְּסוּפָה יֶאֱתֶה בְּבֹא עֲלֵיכֶם
over-you when-to-come he-sweeps-over like-whirlwind and-disaster-of-you

צָרָה וְצוּקָה׃ (28) אָז יִקְרָאֻנְנִי וְלֹא אֶעֱנֶה
I-will-answer but-not they-will-call-to-me then (28) and-trouble distress

יְשַׁחֲרֻנְנִי וְלֹא יִמְצָאֻנְנִי׃ (29) תַּחַת כִּי־ שָׂנְאוּ
they-hated that since (29) they-will-find-me but-not they-will-look-for-me

דַעַת וְיִרְאַת יְהוָה לֹא בָחָרוּ׃ (30) לֹא־ אָבוּ
they-would-accept not (30) they-chose not Yahweh and-fear-of knowledge

לַעֲצָתִי נָאֲצוּ כָּל־ תּוֹכַחְתִּי׃ (31) וְיֹאכְלוּ
and-they-will-eat (31) rebuke-of-me all-of they-spurned to-advice-of-me

מִפְּרִי דַרְכָּם וּמִמֹּעֲצֹתֵיהֶם יִשְׂבָּעוּ׃
they-will-be-filled and-from-schemes-of-them way-of-them from-fruit-of

(32) כִּי מְשׁוּבַת פְּתָיִם תַּהַרְגֵם וְשַׁלְוַת
and-complacency-of she-will-kill-them simple-ones waywardness-of for (32)

°27 קְ כשׁואה

[19]Such is the end of all who go
after ill-gotten gain;
it takes away the lives of
those who get it.

*Warning Against Rejecting Wisdom*

[20]Wisdom calls aloud in the
street,
she raises her voice in the
public squares;
[21]at the head of the noisy
streets[c] she cries out,
in the gateways of the city
she makes her speech:

[22]"How long will you simple
ones[d] love your simple
ways?
How long will mockers
delight in mockery
and fools hate knowledge?
[23]If you had responded to my
rebuke,
I would have poured out my
heart to you
and made my thoughts
known to you.
[24]But since you rejected me
when I called
and no one gave heed when
I stretched out my hand,
[25]since you ignored all my
advice
and would not accept my
rebuke,
[26]I in turn will laugh at your
disaster;
I will mock when calamity
overtakes you—
[27]when calamity overtakes you
like a storm,
when disaster sweeps over
you like a whirlwind,
when distress and troubles
overwhelm you.

[28]"Then they will call to me but
I will not answer;
they will look for me but
will not find me.
[29]Since they hated knowledge
and did not choose to fear
the LORD,
[30]since they would not accept
my advice
and spurned my rebuke,
[31]they will eat the fruit of their
ways
and be filled with the fruit
of their schemes.
[32]For the waywardness of the
simple will kill them,
and the complacency of

c21 Hebrew; Septuagint / *on the tops of the walls*
d22 The Hebrew word rendered *simple* in Proverbs generally denotes one without moral direction and inclined to evil.

כְּסִילִים תְּאַבְּדֵם׃ וְשֹׁמֵעַ לִי יִשְׁכָּן־בֶּטַח
safety he-will-live to-me but-one-listening (33) she-will-destroy-them fools

וְשַׁאֲנַן מִפַּחַד רָעָה׃ בְּנִי אִם־תִּקַּח
you-accept if son-of-me (2:1) harm without-fear-of and-he-will-be-at-ease

אֲמָרָי וּמִצְוֹתַי תִּצְפֹּן אִתָּךְ׃ לְהַקְשִׁיב
to-turn (2) within-you you-store-up and-commands-of-me words-of-me

לַחָכְמָה אָזְנֶךָ תַּטֶּה לִבְּךָ לַתְּבוּנָה׃ כִּי
for (3) to-the-understanding heart-of-you you-apply ear-of-you to-the-wisdom

אִם לַבִּינָה תִקְרָא לַתְּבוּנָה תִּתֵּן קוֹלֶךָ׃
voice-of-you you-raise for-the-understanding you-call-out for-the-insight if

אִם־תְּבַקְשֶׁנָּה כַכָּסֶף וְכַמַּטְמוֹנִים
and-as-the-hidden-treasures as-the-silver you-look-for-her if (4)

תַּחְפְּשֶׂנָּה׃ אָז תָּבִין יִרְאַת יְהוָה וְדַעַת
**and-knowledge-of Yahweh fear-of you-will-understand then (5) you-search-for-her**

אֱלֹהִים תִּמְצָא׃ כִּי־יְהוָה יִתֵּן חָכְמָה מִפִּיו דַּעַת
knowledge from-mouth-of-him wisdom he-gives Yahweh for (6) you-will-find God

וּתְבוּנָה׃ וּצְפֹּן לַיְשָׁרִים תּוּשִׁיָּה מָגֵן
shield victory for-the-upright-ones and-he-stores (7) and-understanding

לְהֹלְכֵי תֹם׃ לִנְצֹר אָרְחוֹת מִשְׁפָּט וְדֶרֶךְ
and-way-of just courses-of to-guard (8) blamelessness to-ones-walking-of

חֲסִידָו יִשְׁמֹר׃ אָז תָּבִין צֶדֶק וּמִשְׁפָּט
and-just right you-will-understand then (9) he-protects faithful-ones-of-him

וּמֵישָׁרִים כָּל־מַעְגַּל־טוֹב׃ כִּי־תָבוֹא חָכְמָה
wisdom she-will-enter for (10) good path-of every-of and-fair-ones

בְלִבֶּךָ וְדַעַת לְנַפְשְׁךָ יִנְעָם׃
he-will-be-pleasant to-soul-of-you and-knowledge into-heart-of-you

מְזִמָּה תִּשְׁמֹר עָלֶיךָ תְּבוּנָה תִנְצְרֶכָּה׃
she-will-guard-you understanding to-you she-will-protect discretion (11)

לְהַצִּילְךָ מִדֶּרֶךְ רָע מֵאִישׁ מְדַבֵּר תַּהְפֻּכוֹת׃
perverse-words speaking from-man wicked-man from-way-of to-save-you (12)

הַעֹזְבִים אָרְחוֹת יֹשֶׁר לָלֶכֶת בְּדַרְכֵי־חֹשֶׁךְ׃
darkness in-ways-of to-walk straightness paths-of the-ones-leaving (13)

הַשְּׂמֵחִים לַעֲשׂוֹת רָע יָגִילוּ בְּתַהְפֻּכוֹת רָע׃
evil in-perversenesses-of they-rejoice wrong to-do the-ones-delighting (14)

אֲשֶׁר אָרְחֹתֵיהֶם עִקְּשִׁים וּנְלוֹזִים בְּמַעְגְּלוֹתָם׃
in-ways-of-them and-ones-being-devious crooked-ones paths-of-them who (15)

לְהַצִּילְךָ מֵאִשָּׁה זָרָה מִנָּכְרִיָּה
from-wayward-woman one-being-adulteress from-woman to-save-you (16)

fools will destroy them;
33 but whoever listens to me will
live in safety
and be at ease, without fear
of harm."

*Moral Benefits of Wisdom*

2 My son, if you accept my
words
and store up my commands
within you,
2 turning your ear to wisdom
and applying your heart to
understanding,
3 and if you call out for insight
and cry aloud for
understanding,
4 and if you look for it as for
silver
and search for it as for
hidden treasure,
5 then you will understand the
fear of the LORD
and find the knowledge of
God.
6 For the LORD gives wisdom,
and from his mouth come
knowledge and
understanding.
7 He holds victory in store for
the upright,
he is a shield to those
whose walk is blameless,
8 for he guards the course of the
just
and protects the way of his
faithful ones.

9 Then you will understand
what is right and just
and fair—every good path.
10 For wisdom will enter your
heart,
and knowledge will be
pleasant to your soul.
11 Discretion will protect you,
and understanding will
guard you.

12 Wisdom will save you from
the ways of wicked men,
from men whose words are
perverse,
13 who leave the straight paths
to walk in dark ways,
14 who delight in doing wrong
and rejoice in the
perverseness of evil,
15 whose paths are crooked
and who are devious in
their ways.

16 It will save you also from the
adulteress,
from the wayward wife with

°7 ק יצפן
°8 ק חסידיו

אֲמָרֶיהָ הֶחֱלִיקָה׃ הַעֹזֶבֶת אַלּוּף נְעוּרֶיהָ
youths-of-her partner-of the-one-leaving (17) she-makes-seductive words-of-her

וְאֶת־ בְּרִית אֱלֹהֶיהָ שָׁכֵחָה׃ כִּי שָׁחָה אֶל־ מָוֶת
death to she-leads-down for (18) she-ignored God-of-her covenant-of and

בֵּיתָהּ וְאֶל־ רְפָאִים מַעְגְּלֹתֶיהָ׃ כָּל־ בָּאֶיהָ
ones-going-to-her all-of (19) paths-of-her spirits-of-dead and-to house-of-her

לֹא יְשׁוּבוּן וְלֹא־ יַשִּׂיגוּ אָרְחוֹת חַיִּים׃ לְמַעַן תֵּלֵךְ
you-will-walk so-thus (20) lives paths-of they-attain and-not they-return not

בְּדֶרֶךְ טוֹבִים וְאָרְחוֹת צַדִּיקִים תִּשְׁמֹר׃ כִּי־
for (21) you-will-keep-to righteous-ones and-paths-of good-men in-way-of

יְשָׁרִים יִשְׁכְּנוּ־ אָרֶץ וּתְמִימִים יִוָּתְרוּ בָהּ׃
in-her they-will-remain and-blameless-ones land they-will-live upright-ones

וּרְשָׁעִים מֵאֶרֶץ יִכָּרֵתוּ וּבוֹגְדִים
and-ones-being-unfaithful they-will-be-cut-off from-land but-wicked-ones (22)

יִסְּחוּ מִמֶּנָּה׃ בְּנִי תּוֹרָתִי אַל־ תִּשְׁכָּח
you-forget not teaching-of-me son-of-me (3:1) from-her they-will-be-torn

וּמִצְוֺתַי יִצֹּר לִבֶּךָ׃ כִּי אֹרֶךְ יָמִים
days length-of for (2) heart-of-you let-him-keep but-commands-of-me

וּשְׁנוֹת חַיִּים וְשָׁלוֹם יוֹסִיפוּ לָךְ׃ חֶסֶד
love (3) to-you they-will-bring and-prosperity lives and-years-of

וֶאֱמֶת אַל־ יַעַזְבֻךָ קָשְׁרֵם עַל־ גַּרְגְּרוֹתֶיךָ
necks-of-you around bind-them! let-them-leave-you never and-faithfulness

כָּתְבֵם עַל־ לוּחַ לִבֶּךָ׃ וּמְצָא־ חֵן וְשֵׂכֶל־ טוֹב
good and-name favor then-win! (4) heart-of-you tablet-of on write-them!

בְּעֵינֵי אֱלֹהִים וְאָדָם׃ בְּטַח אֶל־ יְהוָה בְּכָל־ לִבֶּךָ וְאֶל־
and-on heart-of-you with-all-of Yahweh in trust! (5) and-man God in-eyes-of

בִּינָתְךָ אַל־ תִּשָּׁעֵן׃ בְּכָל־ דְּרָכֶיךָ דָעֵהוּ
acknowledge-him! ways-of-you in-all-of (6) you-lean not understanding-of-you

וְהוּא יְיַשֵּׁר אֹרְחֹתֶיךָ׃ אַל־ תְּהִי חָכָם בְּעֵינֶיךָ
in-eyes-of-you wise you-be not (7) paths-of-you he-will-make-straight and-he

יְרָא אֶת־ יְהוָה וְסוּר מֵרָע׃ רִפְאוּת תְּהִי לְשָׁרֶּךָ
to-body-of-you she-will-be health (8) from-evil and-shun! Yahweh *** fear!

וְשִׁקּוּי לְעַצְמוֹתֶיךָ׃ כַּבֵּד אֶת־ יְהוָה מֵהוֹנֶךָ
with-wealth-of-you Yahweh *** honor! (9) to-bones-of-you and-nourishment

וּמֵרֵאשִׁית כָּל־ תְּבוּאָתֶךָ׃ וְיִמָּלְאוּ
then-they-will-be-filled (10) crop-of-you all-of and-with-firstfruit-of

אֲסָמֶיךָ שָׂבָע וְתִירוֹשׁ יְקָבֶיךָ יִפְרֹצוּ׃
they-will-brim-over vats-of-you and-new-wine overflowing barns-of-you

her seductive words,
17 who has left the partner of her youth
and ignored the covenant she made before God.[e]
18 For her house leads down to death
and her paths to the spirits of the dead.
19 None who go to her return
or attain the paths of life.

20 Thus you will walk in the ways of good men
and keep to the paths of the righteous.
21 For the upright will live in the land,
and the blameless will remain in it;
22 but the wicked will be cut off from the land,
and the unfaithful will be torn from it.

*Further Benefits of Wisdom*

3 My son, do not forget my teaching,
but keep my commands in your heart,
2 for they will prolong your life many years
and bring you prosperity.

3 Let love and faithfulness never leave you;
bind them around your neck,
write them on the tablet of your heart.
4 Then you will win favor and a good name
in the sight of God and man.

5 Trust in the LORD with all your heart
and lean not on your own understanding;
6 in all your ways acknowledge him,
and he will make your paths straight.[f]

7 Do not be wise in your own eyes;
fear the LORD and shun evil.
8 This will bring health to your body
and nourishment to your bones.

9 Honor the LORD with your wealth,
with the firstfruits of all your crops;
10 then your barns will be filled to overflowing,
and your vats will brim over with new wine.

e 17 Or *covenant of her God*
f 6 Or *will direct your paths*

מוּסַר יְהוָה בְּנִי אַל־תִּמְאָס וְאַל־תָּקֹץ
you-resent and-not you-despise not son-of-me Yahweh discipline-of (11)

בְּתוֹכַחְתּוֹ׃ כִּי אֶת אֲשֶׁר יֶאֱהַב יְהוָה יוֹכִיחַ וּכְאָב
and-as-father he-disciplines Yahweh he-loves whom *** for (12) to-rebuke-of-him

אֶת־בֵּן יִרְצֶה׃ אַשְׁרֵי אָדָם מָצָא חָכְמָה וְאָדָם
and-man wisdom he-finds man blessednesses-of (13) he-delights-in son ***

יָפִיק תְּבוּנָה׃ כִּי טוֹב סַחְרָהּ מִסְּחַר־כָּסֶף
silver more-than-profit-of profit-of-her good for (14) understanding he-gains

וּמֵחָרוּץ תְּבוּאָתָהּ׃ יְקָרָה הִיא מִפְּנִיִּים°
more-than-rubies she precious (15) return-of-her and-more-than-gold

וְכָל־חֲפָצֶיךָ לֹא יִשְׁווּ־בָהּ׃ אֹרֶךְ יָמִים
days length-of (16) with-her they-can-compare not desires-of-you and-all-of

בִּימִינָהּ בִּשְׂמֹאולָהּ עֹשֶׁר וְכָבוֹד׃ דְּרָכֶיהָ
ways-of-her (17) and-honor richness and-in-left-hand-of-her in-right-hand-of-her

דַרְכֵי־נֹעַם וְכָל־נְתִיבוֹתֶיהָ שָׁלוֹם׃ עֵץ־חַיִּים הִיא
she lives tree-of (18) peace paths-of-her and-all-of pleasantness ways-of

לַמַּחֲזִיקִים בָּהּ וְתֹמְכֶיהָ מְאֻשָּׁר׃
being-blessed and-ones-laying-hold-of-her to-her to-the-ones-embracing

יְהוָה בְּחָכְמָה יָסַד־אָרֶץ כּוֹנֵן שָׁמַיִם
heavens he-set-in-place earth he-founded by-wisdom Yahweh (19)

בִּתְבוּנָה׃ בְּדַעְתּוֹ תְּהוֹמוֹת נִבְקָעוּ וּשְׁחָקִים
and-clouds they-were-divided deeps by-knowledge-of-him (20) by-understanding

יִרְעֲפוּ־טָל׃ בְּנִי אַל־יָלֻזוּ מֵעֵינֶיךָ
from-eyes-of-you let-them-depart not son-of-me (21) dew they-let-drop

נְצֹר תֻּשִׁיָּה וּמְזִמָּה׃ וְיִהְיוּ חַיִּים
lives and-they-will-be (22) and-discernment sound-judgment preserve!

לְנַפְשֶׁךָ וְחֵן לְגַרְגְּרֹתֶיךָ׃ אָז תֵּלֵךְ לָבֶטַח
in-safety you-will-go then (23) for-necks-of-you and-grace for-self-of-you

דַּרְכֶּךָ וְרַגְלְךָ לֹא תִגּוֹף׃ אִם־תִּשְׁכַּב לֹא־
not you-lie-down when (24) she-will-stumble not and-foot-of-you way-of-you

תִפְחָד וְשָׁכַבְתָּ וְעָרְבָה שְׁנָתֶךָ׃
sleep-of-you then-she-will-be-sweet when-you-lie-down you-will-be-afraid

אַל־תִּירָא מִפַּחַד פִּתְאֹם וּמִשֹּׁאַת רְשָׁעִים כִּי
that wicked-ones or-of-ruin-of sudden of-disaster you-fear not (25)

תָבֹא׃ כִּי־יְהוָה יִהְיֶה בְכִסְלֶךָ וְשָׁמַר
and-he-will-keep as-confidence-of-you he-will-be Yahweh for (26) she-overtakes

רַגְלְךָ מִלָּכֶד׃ אַל־תִּמְנַע־טוֹב מִבְּעָלָיו בִּהְיוֹת
when-to-be from-owners-of-him good you-withhold not (27) from-snare foot-of-you

11 My son, do not despise the LORD's discipline
and do not resent his rebuke,
12 because the LORD disciplines those he loves,
as a father[g] the son he delights in.

13 Blessed is the man who finds wisdom,
the man who gains understanding,
14 for she is more profitable than silver
and yields better returns than gold.
15 She is more precious than rubies;
nothing you desire can compare with her.
16 Long life is in her right hand;
in her left hand are riches and honor.
17 Her ways are pleasant ways,
and all her paths are peace.
18 She is a tree of life to those who embrace her;
those who lay hold of her will be blessed.

19 By wisdom the LORD laid the earth's foundations,
by understanding he set the heavens in place;
20 by his knowledge the deeps were divided,
and the clouds let drop the dew.

21 My son, preserve sound judgment and discernment,
do not let them out of your sight;
22 they will be life for you,
an ornament to grace your neck.
23 Then you will go on your way in safety,
and your foot will not stumble;
24 when you lie down, you will not be afraid;
when you lie down, your sleep will be sweet.
25 Have no fear of sudden disaster
or of the ruin that overtakes the wicked,
26 for the LORD will be your confidence
and will keep your foot from being snared.

27 Do not withhold good from those who deserve it,

*g12* Hebrew; Septuagint / *and he punishes*

°*15* ק מפנינים

לְאֵל יָדֶיךָ לַעֲשׂוֹת׃ אַל־ תֹּאמַר לְרֵעֶיךָ ׀ לֵךְ

come! to-neighbor-of-you you-say not (28) to-act hand-of-you in-power-of

וָשׁוּב וּמָחָר אֶתֵּן וְיֵשׁ אִתָּךְ׃ אַל־ תַּחֲרֹשׁ

you-plot not (29) with-you when-there-is I-will-give and-tomorrow and-return!

עַל־ רֵעֲךָ רָעָה וְהוּא־ יוֹשֵׁב לָבֶטַח אִתָּךְ׃ אַל־

not (30) near-you in-trust one-living when-he harm neighbor-of-you against

תָּרוֹב עִם־אָדָם חִנָּם אִם־לֹא גְמָלְךָ רָעָה׃ אַל־ תְּקַנֵּא

you-envy not (31) harm he-did-you not when without-reason man to you-accuse

בְּאִישׁ חָמָס וְאַל־ תִּבְחַר בְּכָל־ דְּרָכָיו׃ כִּי

for (32) ways-of-him to-any-of you-choose and-not violence to-man-of

תוֹעֲבַת יְהוָה נָלוֹז וְאֶת־ יְשָׁרִים סוֹדוֹ׃

confidence-of-him upright-ones but man-being-perverse Yahweh detestable-of

מְאֵרַת יְהוָה בְּבֵית רָשָׁע וּנְוֵה צַדִּיקִים יְבָרֵךְ׃

he-blesses righteous-ones but-home-of wicked on-house-of Yahweh curse-of (33)

אִם־ לַלֵּצִים הוּא־ יָלִיץ וְלַעֲנָיִים יִתֶּן־

he-gives but-to-the-humble-ones he-mocks he to-the-ones-mocking indeed (34)

חֵן׃ כָּבוֹד חֲכָמִים יִנְחָלוּ וּכְסִילִים מֵרִים קָלוֹן׃

shame one-holding-up but-fools they-inherit wise-ones honor (35) grace

שִׁמְעוּ בָנִים מוּסַר אָב וְהַקְשִׁיבוּ לָדַעַת

to-gain and-pay-attention! father instruction-of sons listen! (4:1)

בִּינָה׃ כִּי לֶקַח טוֹב נָתַתִּי לָכֶם תּוֹרָתִי אַל־

not teaching-of-me to-you I-give sound learning for (2) understanding

תַּעֲזֹבוּ׃ כִּי־ בֵן הָיִיתִי לְאָבִי רַךְ וְיָחִיד לִפְנֵי

before and-only-child tender with-father-of-me I-was boy when (3) you-forsake

אִמִּי׃ וַיֹּרֵנִי וַיֹּאמֶר לִי יִתְמָךְ־

let-him-lay-hold to-me and-he-said then-he-taught-me (4) mother-of-me

דְּבָרַי לִבֶּךָ שְׁמֹר מִצְוֹתַי וֶחְיֵה׃ קְנֵה חָכְמָה

wisdom get! (5) and-live! commands-of-me keep! heart-of-you words-of-me

קְנֵה בִינָה אַל־ תִּשְׁכַּח וְאַל־ תֵּט מֵאִמְרֵי־ פִי׃

mouth-of-me from-words-of you-swerve and-not you-forget not understanding get!

אַל־ תַּעַזְבֶהָ וְתִשְׁמְרֶךָּ אֱהָבֶהָ וְתִצְּרֶךָּ׃

and-she-will-watch-you love-her! and-she-will-protect-you you-forsake-her not (6)

רֵאשִׁית חָכְמָה קְנֵה חָכְמָה וּבְכָל־ קִנְיָנְךָ קְנֵה

get! possession-of-you though-with-all-of wisdom get! wisdom supreme (7)

בִינָה׃ סַלְסְלֶהָ וּתְרוֹמְמֶךָּ תְּכַבֵּדְךָ כִּי

if she-will-honor-you and-she-will-exalt-you esteem-her! (8) understanding

תְּחַבְּקֶנָּה׃ תִּתֵּן לְרֹאשְׁךָ לִוְיַת־ חֵן עֲטֶרֶת

crown-of grace garland-of on-head-of-you she-will-set (9) you-embrace-her

when it is in your power to
act.
28 Do not say to your neighbor,
"Come back later; I'll give it
tomorrow"—
when you now have it with
you.
29 Do not plot harm against your
neighbor,
who lives trustfully near
you.
30 Do not accuse a man for no
reason—
when he has done you no
harm.

31 Do not envy a violent man
or choose any of his ways,
32 for the LORD detests a perverse
man
but takes the upright into
his confidence.

33 The LORD's curse is on the
house of the wicked,
but he blesses the home of
the righteous.
34 He mocks proud mockers
but gives grace to the
humble.
35 The wise inherit honor,
but fools he holds up to
shame.

### *Wisdom Is Supreme*

4 Listen, my sons, to a father's
instruction;
pay attention and gain
understanding.
2 I give you sound learning,
so do not forsake my
teaching.
3 When I was a boy in my
father's house,
still tender, and an only
child of my mother,
4 he taught me and said,
"Lay hold of my words with
all your heart;
keep my commands and you
will live.
5 Get wisdom, get
understanding;
do not forget my words or
swerve from them.
6 Do not forsake wisdom, and
she will protect you;
love her, and she will watch
over you.
7 Wisdom is supreme; therefore
get wisdom.
Though it cost all you have,[h]
get understanding.
8 Esteem her, and she will exalt
you;
embrace her, and she will
honor you.
9 She will set a garland of grace
on your head

[h] 7 Or *Whatever else you get*

°27 ק ידך
°28 ק לרעך
°30 ק תריב
°34 ק ולענוים

תִּפְאֶרֶת תְּמַגְּנֶךָּ׃ שְׁמַע בְּנִי וְקַח אֲמָרָי
sayings-of-me and-accept! son-of-me listen! (10) she-will-present-you splendor

וְיִרְבּוּ לְךָ שְׁנוֹת חַיִּים׃ בְּדֶרֶךְ חָכְמָה הֹרֵתִיךָ
I-guide-you wisdom in-way-of (11) lives years-of to-you and-they-will-be-many

הִדְרַכְתִּיךָ בְּמַעְגְּלֵי־ יֹשֶׁר׃ בְּלֶכְתְּךָ לֹא־
not when-to-walk-you (12) straightness along-paths-of I-lead-you

יֵצַר צַעֲדֶךָ וְאִם־ תָּרוּץ לֹא תִכָּשֵׁל׃
you-will-stumble not you-run and-when step-of-you he-will-be-hampered

הַחֲזֵק בַּמּוּסָר אַל־ תֶּרֶף נִצְּרֶהָ כִּי־ הִיא
she for guard-her! you-let-go not to-the-instruction hold-on! (13)

חַיֶּיךָ׃ בְּאֹרַח רְשָׁעִים אַל־ תָּבֹא וְאַל־ תְּאַשֵּׁר בְּדֶרֶךְ
in-way-of you-walk and-not you-go not wicked-ones on-path-of (14) lives-of-you

רָעִים׃ פְּרָעֵהוּ אַל־ תַּעֲבָר־ בּוֹ שְׂטֵה מֵעָלָיו וַעֲבוֹר׃
and-go-on-way! from-on-him turn! on-him you-travel not avoid-him! (15) evil-men

כִּי לֹא יִשְׁנוּ אִם־לֹא יָרֵעוּ וְנִגְזְלָה שְׁנָתָם
slumber-of-them and-she-is-robbed they-do-evil not if they-can-sleep not for (16)

אִם־לֹא יַכְשׁוֹלוּ׃ כִּי לָחֲמוּ לֶחֶם רֶשַׁע וְיֵין
and-wine-of wickedness bread-of they-eat indeed (17) they-make-fall not if

חֲמָסִים יִשְׁתּוּ׃ וְאֹרַח צַדִּיקִים כְּאוֹר נֹגַהּ
dawn like-gleam-of righteous-ones and-path-of (18) they-drink violences

הוֹלֵךְ וָאוֹר עַד־ נְכוֹן הַיּוֹם׃ דֶּרֶךְ רְשָׁעִים
wicked-ones way-of (19) the-day being-full-of till and-to-be-bright continuing

כָּאֲפֵלָה לֹא יָדְעוּ בַּמֶּה יִכָּשֵׁלוּ׃ בְּנִי
son-of-me (20) they-stumble by-the-what they-know not like-the-deep-darkness

לִדְבָרַי הַקְשִׁיבָה לַאֲמָרַי הַט־ אָזְנֶךָ׃ אַל־
not (21) ear-of-you give! to-words-of-me pay-attention! to-sayings-of-me

יַלִּיזוּ מֵעֵינֶיךָ שָׁמְרֵם בְּתוֹךְ לְבָבֶךָ׃ כִּי־ חַיִּים
lives for (22) heart-of-you within keep-them! from-eyes-of-you let-them-go

הֵם לְמֹצְאֵיהֶם וּלְכָל־ בְּשָׂרוֹ מַרְפֵּא׃ מִכָּל־
above-all-of (23) health body-of-him and-to-whole-of to-ones-finding-them they

מִשְׁמָר נְצֹר לִבֶּךָ כִּי־ מִמֶּנּוּ תּוֹצְאוֹת חַיִּים׃ הָסֵר
put-away! (24) lives wellsprings-of from-him for heart-of-you guard! watching

מִמְּךָ עִקְּשׁוּת פֶּה וּלְזוּת שְׂפָתַיִם הַרְחֵק מִמֶּךָּ׃
from-you keep-far! lips and-corruptness-of mouth perversity-of from-you

עֵינֶיךָ לְנֹכַח יַבִּיטוּ וְעַפְעַפֶּיךָ יַיְשִׁרוּ
let-them-be-direct and-gazes-of-you let-them-look to-ahead eyes-of-you (25)

נֶגְדֶּךָ׃ פַּלֵּס מַעְגַּל רַגְלֶךָ וְכָל־ דְּרָכֶיךָ
ways-of-you and-all-of foot-of-you path-of make-level! (26) before-you

and present you with a crown of splendor."

10 Listen, my son, accept what I say,
and the years of your life will be many.
11 I guide you in the way of wisdom
and lead you along straight paths.
12 When you walk, your steps will not be hampered;
when you run, you will not stumble.
13 Hold on to instruction, do not let it go;
guard it well, for it is your life.
14 Do not set foot on the path of the wicked
or walk in the way of evil men.
15 Avoid it, do not travel on it;
turn from it and go on your way.
16 For they cannot sleep till they do evil;
they are robbed of slumber till they make someone fall.
17 They eat the bread of wickedness
and drink the wine of violence.

18 The path of the righteous is like the first gleam of dawn,
shining ever brighter till the full light of day.
19 But the way of the wicked is like deep darkness;
they do not know what makes them stumble.

20 My son, pay attention to what I say;
listen closely to my words.
21 Do not let them out of your sight,
keep them within your heart;
22 for they are life to those who find them
and health to a man's whole body.
23 Above all else, guard your heart,
for it is the wellspring of life.
24 Put away perversity from your mouth;
keep corrupt talk far from your lips.
25 Let your eyes look straight ahead,
fix your gaze directly before you.
26 Make level[1] paths for your feet
and take only ways that are

[1] 26 Or *Consider the*

°16 ק יכשילו

יִכֹּנוּ׃ אַל־ תֵּט־ יָמִין וּשְׂמֹאול הָסֵר רַגְלְךָ

foot-of-you keep! or-left right you-swerve not (27) let-them-be-firm

מֵרָע׃ בְּנִי לְחָכְמָתִי הַקְשִׁיבָה לִתְבוּנָתִי

to-insight-of-me pay-attention! to-wisdom-of-me son-of-me (5:1) from-evil

הַט־ אָזְנֶךָ׃ לִשְׁמֹר מְזִמּוֹת וְדַעַת שְׂפָתֶיךָ

lips-of-you and-knowledge discretions to-maintain (2) ear-of-you give!

יִנְצֹרוּ׃ כִּי נֹפֶת תִּטֹּפְנָה שִׂפְתֵי זָרָה

one-being-adulteress lips-of they-drip honey for (3) they-may-preserve

וְחָלָק מִשֶּׁמֶן חִכָּהּ׃ וְאַחֲרִיתָהּ מָרָה כַלַּעֲנָה

as-the-gall bitter but-end-of-her (4) speech-of-her more-than-oil and-smooth

חַדָּה כְּחֶרֶב פִּיּוֹת׃ רַגְלֶיהָ יֹרְדוֹת מָוֶת

death ones-going-down-of feet-of-her (5) double-edges as-sword-of sharp

שְׁאוֹל צְעָדֶיהָ יִתְמֹכוּ׃ אֹרַח חַיִּים פֶּן־ תְּפַלֵּס

she-gives-thought not lives way-of (6) they-lead steps-of-her Sheol

נָעוּ מַעְגְּלֹתֶיהָ לֹא תֵדָע׃ וְעַתָּה בָנִים שִׁמְעוּ־ לִי

to-me listen! sons so-now (7) she-knows not paths-of-her they-are-crooked

וְאַל־ תָּסוּרוּ מֵאִמְרֵי־ פִי׃ הַרְחֵק מֵעָלֶיהָ

from-by-her keep-far! (8) mouth-of-me from-sayings-of you-turn and-not

דַּרְכֶּךָ וְאַל־ תִּקְרַב אֶל־ פֶּתַח בֵּיתָהּ׃ פֶּן־ תִּתֵּן

you-give lest (9) house-of-her door-of to you-go-near and-not path-of-you

לַאֲחֵרִים הוֹדֶךָ וּשְׁנֹתֶיךָ לְאַכְזָרִי׃ פֶּן־ יִשְׂבְּעוּ

they-feast lest (10) to-cruel-one and-years-of-you strength-of-you to-others

זָרִים כֹּחֶךָ וַעֲצָבֶיךָ בְּבֵית נָכְרִי׃

another to-house-of and-toils-of-you wealth-of-you ones-being-strangers

וְנָהַמְתָּ בְאַחֲרִיתֶךָ בִּכְלוֹת בְּשָׂרְךָ

flesh-of-you when-to-be-spent at-end-of-you and-you-will-groan (11)

וּשְׁאֵרֶךָ׃ וְאָמַרְתָּ אֵיךְ שָׂנֵאתִי מוּסָר וְתוֹכַחַת

and-correction discipline I-hated how! and-you-will-say (12) and-body-of-you

נָאַץ לִבִּי׃ וְלֹא־ שָׁמַעְתִּי בְּקוֹל מוֹרָי

teachers-of-me to-voice-of I-obeyed and-not (13) heart-of-me he-spurned

וְלִמְלַמְּדַי לֹא־ הִטִּיתִי אָזְנִי׃ כִּמְעַט הָיִיתִי

I-was at-brink (14) ear-of-me I-turned not and-to-ones-instructing-me

בְכָל־ רָע בְּתוֹךְ קָהָל וְעֵדָה׃ שְׁתֵה־

drink! (15) even-congregation assembly in-midst-of ruin of-utterness-of

מַיִם מִבּוֹרֶךָ וְנֹזְלִים מִתּוֹךְ בְּאֵרֶךָ׃

well-of-you from-inside-of and-ones-running from-cistern-of-you waters

יָפוּצוּ מַעְיְנֹתֶיךָ חוּצָה בָּרְחֹבוֹת פַּלְגֵי־

streams-of in-the-squares in-street springs-of-you should-they-overflow (16)

firm.
27 Do not swerve to the right or
the left;
keep your foot from evil.

*Warning Against Adultery*

5 My son, pay attention to my
wisdom,
listen well to my words of
insight,
2 that you may maintain
discretion
and your lips may preserve
knowledge.
3 For the lips of an adulteress
drip honey,
and her speech is smoother
than oil;
4 but in the end she is bitter as
gall,
sharp as a double-edged
sword.
5 Her feet go down to death;
her steps lead straight to the
grave.
6 She gives no thought to the
way of life;
her paths are crooked, but
she knows it not.

7 Now then, my sons, listen to
me;
do not turn aside from what
I say.
8 Keep to a path far from her,
do not go near the door of
her house,
9 lest you give your best
strength to others
and your years to one who
is cruel,
10 lest strangers feast on your
wealth
and your toil enrich another
man's house.
11 At the end of your life you
will groan,
when your flesh and body
are spent.
12 You will say, "How I hated
discipline!
How my heart spurned
correction!
13 I would not obey my teachers
or listen to my instructors.
14 I have come to the brink of
utter ruin
in the midst of the whole
assembly."

15 Drink water from your own
cistern,
running water from your
own well.
16 Should your springs overflow
in the streets,

5 Hebrew *Sheol*

מָיִם׃ (17) יִהְיוּ־ לְךָ לְבַדֶּךָ וְאֵין לְזָרִים
to-ones-being-strangers and-never by-yourself for-you let-them-be (17) waters

אִתָּךְ׃ (18) יְהִי־ מְקוֹרְךָ בָרוּךְ וּשְׂמַח
and-rejoice! one-being-blessed fountain-of-you may-he-be (18) with-you

מֵאֵשֶׁת נְעוּרֶךָ׃ (19) אַיֶּלֶת אֲהָבִים וְיַעֲלַת־ חֵן דַּדֶּיהָ
breasts-of-her grace and-deer-of loves doe-of (19) youths-of-you in-wife-of

יְרַוֻּךָ בְכָל־ עֵת בְּאַהֲבָתָהּ תִּשְׁגֶּה
may-you-be-captivated by-love-of-her time at-all-of may-they-satisfy-you

תָמִיד׃ (20) וְלָמָּה תִשְׁגֶּה בְנִי בְזָרָה
by-one-being-adulteress son-of-me you-be-captivated and-why? (20) ever

וּתְחַבֵּק חֵק נָכְרִיָּה׃ (21) כִּי נֹכַח׀ עֵינֵי יְהוָה דַּרְכֵי־
ways-of Yahweh eyes-of in-front-of for (21) another bosom-of and-you-embrace

אִישׁ וְכָל־ מַעְגְּלֹתָיו מְפַלֵּס׃ (22) עֲוֺנוֹתָיו*
evil-deeds-of-him (22) one-examining paths-of-him and-all-of man

יִלְכְּדֻנוֹ אֶת־ הָרָשָׁע וּבְחַבְלֵי חַטָּאתוֹ יִתָּמֵךְ׃
he-is-held-fast sin-of-him and-by-cords-of the-wicked *** they-ensnare-him

(23) הוּא יָמוּת בְּאֵין מוּסָר וּבְרֹב אִוַּלְתּוֹ
folly-of-him and-by-greatness-of discipline for-lack-of he-will-die he (23)

יִשְׁגֶּה׃ (6:1) בְּנִי אִם־ עָרַבְתָּ לְרֵעֶךָ
for-neighbor-of-you you-put-up-security if son-of-me (6:1) he-will-be-led-astray

תָּקַעְתָּ† לַזָּר כַּפֶּיךָ׃ (2) נוֹקַשְׁתָּ
you-were-trapped (2) hands-of-you for-the-one-being-other you-struck

בְאִמְרֵי־ פִיךָ נִלְכַּדְתָּ בְּאִמְרֵי־ פִיךָ׃
mouth-of-you by-words-of you-were-ensnared mouth-of-you by-sayings-of

(3) עֲשֵׂה זֹאת אֵפוֹא׀ בְּנִי וְהִנָּצֵל כִּי בָאתָ בְכַף־
into-hand-of you-fell since and-free-yourself! son-of-me then this do! (3)

רֵעֶךָ לֵךְ הִתְרַפֵּס וּרְהַב רֵעֶיךָ׃ (4) אַל־
not (4) neighbors-of-you and-plead! humble-yourself! go! neighbor-of-you

תִּתֵּן שֵׁנָה לְעֵינֶיךָ וּתְנוּמָה לְעַפְעַפֶּיךָ׃ (5) הִנָּצֵל
free-yourself! (5) to-eyelids-of-you and-slumber to-eyes-of-you sleep you-allow

כִּצְבִי מִיָּד וּכְצִפּוֹר מִיַּד יָקוּשׁ׃ (6) לֵךְ־אֶל־נְמָלָה
ant to go! (6) fowler from-snare-of and-like-bird from-hand like-gazelle

עָצֵל רְאֵה דְרָכֶיהָ וַחֲכָם׃ (7) אֲשֶׁר אֵין־ לָהּ
to-her there-is-not that (7) and-be-wise! ways-of-her consider! sluggard

קָצִין שֹׁטֵר וּמֹשֵׁל׃ (8) תָּכִין בַּקַּיִץ לַחְמָהּ
provision-of-her in-the-summer she-stores (8) or-one-ruling overseer commander

אָגְרָה בַקָּצִיר מַאֲכָלָהּ׃ (9) עַד־ מָתַי עָצֵל׀ תִּשְׁכָּב
will-you-lie sluggard when? until (9) food-of-her at-the-harvest she-gathers

your streams of water in the
public squares?
17Let them be yours alone,
never to be shared with
strangers.
18May your fountain be blessed,
and may you rejoice in the
wife of your youth.
19A loving doe, a graceful deer—
may her breasts satisfy you
always,
may you ever be captivated
by her love.
20Why be captivated, my son, by
an adulteress?
Why embrace the bosom of
another man's wife?

21For a man's ways are in full
view of the LORD,
and he examines all his
paths.
22The evil deeds of a wicked
man ensnare him;
the cords of his sin hold
him fast.
23He will die for lack of
discipline,
led astray by his own great
folly.

*Warnings Against Folly*

6 My son, if you have put up
security for your neighbor,
if you have struck hands in
pledge for another,
2if you have been trapped by
what you said,
ensnared by the words of
your mouth,
3then do this, my son, to free
yourself,
since you have fallen into
your neighbor's hands:
Go and humble yourself;
press your plea with your
neighbor!
4Allow no sleep to your eyes,
no slumber to your eyelids.
5Free yourself, like a gazelle
from the hand of the
hunter,
like a bird from the snare of
the fowler.

6Go to the ant, you sluggard;
consider its ways and be
wise!
7It has no commander,
no overseer or ruler,
8yet it stores its provisions in
summer
and gathers its food at
harvest.

9How long will you lie there,
you sluggard?

*22 Most mss have *hateph pathah* under the *ayin* (עֲ).

†*1* Most mss have *dagesh* in the *tav* (תָּ—).

מָתַי תָּקוּם מִשְּׁנָתֶךָ׃ (10) מְעַט שֵׁנוֹת מְעַט
little-of sleeps little-of (10) from-sleep-of-you will-you-get-up when?

תְּנוּמוֹת מְעַט ׀ חִבֻּק יָדַיִם לִשְׁכָּב׃ (11) וּבָא־
and-he-will-come (11) to-rest hands folding-of little-of slumbers

כִמְהַלֵּךְ רֵאשֶׁךָ וּמַחְסֹרְךָ כְּאִישׁ מָגֵן׃
armor like-man-of and-scarcity-of-you poverty-of-you like-one-being-bandit

(12) אָדָם בְּלִיַּעַל אִישׁ אָוֶן הוֹלֵךְ עִקְּשׁוּת פֶּה׃
mouth corruptness-of one-going-about villainy man-of scoundrel man (12)

(13) קֹרֵץ בְּעֵינָו מֹלֵל בְּרַגְלָו מֹרֶה
one-motioning with-feet-of-him one-signaling with-eyes-of-him one-winking (13)

בְּאֶצְבְּעֹתָיו׃ (14) תַּהְפֻּכוֹת ׀ בְּלִבּוֹ חֹרֵשׁ רָע בְּכָל־
at-all-of evil one-plotting in-heart-of-him deceits (14) with-fingers-of-him

עֵת מִדְנִים יְשַׁלֵּחַ׃ (15) עַל־ כֵּן פִּתְאֹם יָבוֹא
he-will-overtake instantly this for (15) he-stirs-up dissensions time

אֵידוֹ פֶּתַע יִשָּׁבֵר וְאֵין מַרְפֵּא׃ (16) שֶׁשׁ־ הֵנָּה
they six (16) remedy with-no he-will-be-destroyed suddenly disaster-of-him

שָׂנֵא יְהוָה וְשֶׁבַע תּוֹעֲבוֹת נַפְשׁוֹ׃ (17) עֵינַיִם רָמוֹת
ones-being-haughty eyes (17) self-of-him detestable-of and-seven Yahweh he-hates

לְשׁוֹן שָׁקֶר וְיָדַיִם שֹׁפְכוֹת דָּם־ נָקִי׃ (18) לֵב חֹרֵשׁ
one-devising heart (18) innocent blood ones-shedding and-hands lie tongue-of

מַחְשְׁבוֹת אָוֶן רַגְלַיִם מְמַהֲרוֹת לָרוּץ לָרָעָה*׃
into-the-evil to-rush ones-being-quick feet wickedness schemes-of

(19) יָפִיחַ כְּזָבִים עֵד שָׁקֶר וּמְשַׁלֵּחַ מְדָנִים בֵּין
among dissensions and-one-stirring-up falsehood witness-of lies he-pours-out (19)

אַחִים׃ (20) נְצֹר בְּנִי מִצְוַת אָבִיךָ וְאַל־ תִּטֹּשׁ
you-forsake and-not father-of-you command-of son-of-me keep! (20) brothers

תּוֹרַת אִמֶּךָ׃ (21) קָשְׁרֵם עַל־ לִבְּךָ תָמִיד
forever heart-of-you upon bind-them! (21) mother-of-you teaching-of

עָנְדֵם עַל־ גַּרְגְּרֹתֶךָ׃ (22) בְּהִתְהַלֶּכְךָ ׀ תַּנְחֶה אֹתָךְ
you she-will-guide when-to-walk-you (22) necks-of-you around fasten-them!

בְּשָׁכְבְּךָ תִּשְׁמֹר עָלֶיךָ וַהֲקִיצוֹתָ הִיא
she when-you-awake over-you she-will-watch when-to-sleep-you

תְשִׂיחֶךָ׃ (23) כִּי נֵר מִצְוָה וְתוֹרָה אוֹר וְדֶרֶךְ
and-way-of light and-teaching command lamp for (23) she-will-speak-to-you

חַיִּים תּוֹכְחוֹת מוּסָר׃ (24) לִשְׁמָרְךָ מֵאֵשֶׁת רָע
immorality from-woman-of to-keep-you (24) discipline corrections-of lives

מֵחֶלְקַת לָשׁוֹן נָכְרִיָּה׃ (25) אַל־ תַּחְמֹד יָפְיָהּ
beauty-of-her you-lust-after not (25) wayward-woman tongue from-smoothness-of

When will you get up from
your sleep?
10 A little sleep, a little slumber,
a little folding of the hands
to rest—
11 and poverty will come on you
like a bandit
and scarcity like an armed
man.[k]
12 A scoundrel and villain,
who goes about with a
corrupt mouth,
13 who winks with his eye,
signals with his feet
and motions with his
fingers,
14 who plots evil with deceit in
his heart—
he always stirs up
dissension.
15 Therefore disaster will overtake
him in an instant;
he will suddenly be
destroyed—without
remedy.
16 There are six things the LORD
hates,
seven that are detestable to
him:
17 haughty eyes,
a lying tongue,
hands that shed innocent
blood,
18 a heart that devises
wicked schemes,
feet that are quick to rush
into evil,
19 a false witness who pours
out lies
and a man who stirs up
dissension among
brothers.

*Warning Against Adultery*

20 My son, keep your father's
commands
and do not forsake your
mother's teaching.
21 Bind them upon your heart
forever;
fasten them around your
neck.
22 When you walk, they will
guide you;
when you sleep, they will
watch over you;
when you awake, they will
speak to you.
23 For these commands are a
lamp,
this teaching is a light,
and the corrections of
discipline
are the way to life,
24 keeping you from the immoral
woman,
from the smooth tongue of
the wayward wife.
25 Do not lust in your heart after
her beauty

[k] 11 Or *like a vagrant / and scarcity like a beggar*

*18 Most mss have the accent *silluq* on the final syllable (עָה־).

°*13a* ק בעיניו
°*13b* ק ברגליו
°*14* ק מדינים
°*16* ק תועבת

בִּלְבָבֶךָ וְאַל־ תִּקָּחֲךָ בְּעַפְעַפֶּיהָ׃ כִּי
for (26) with-eyes-of-her let-her-captivate-you and-not in-heart-of-you

בְּעַד־ אִשָּׁה זוֹנָה עַד־ כִּכַּר לָחֶם וְאֵשֶׁת אִישׁ
man and-wife-of bread loaf-of to one-being-prostitute woman because-of

נֶפֶשׁ יְקָרָה תָצוּד׃ הֲיַחְתֶּה אִישׁ אֵשׁ בְּחֵיקוֹ
into-lap-of-him fire man can-he-scoop? (27) she-preys-upon precious life

וּבְגָדָיו לֹא תִשָּׂרַפְנָה׃ אִם־ יְהַלֵּךְ אִישׁ עַל־הַגֶּחָלִים
the-coals on man can-he-walk or (28) they-are-burned not and-clothes-of-him

וְרַגְלָיו לֹא תִכָּוֶינָה׃ כֵּן הַבָּא אֶל־ אֵשֶׁת
wife-of into the-one-going so (29) they-are-scorched not and-feet-of-him

רֵעֵהוּ לֹא יִנָּקֶה כָּל־ הַנֹּגֵעַ בָּהּ׃
on-her the-one-touching any-of he-will-go-unpunished not neighbor-of-him

לֹא־ יָבוּזוּ לַגַּנָּב כִּי יִגְנוֹב לְמַלֵּא נַפְשׁוֹ
hunger-of-him to-satisfy he-steals if to-the-thief they-despise not (30)

כִּי יִרְעָב׃ וְנִמְצָא יְשַׁלֵּם שִׁבְעָתָיִם אֶת־ כָּל־
all-of *** seven-times he-must-pay if-he-is-caught (31) he-starves when

הוֹן בֵּיתוֹ יִתֵּן׃ נֹאֵף אִשָּׁה
woman one-committing-adultery (32) he-must-give house-of-him wealth-of

חֲסַר־ לֵב מַשְׁחִית נַפְשׁוֹ הוּא יַעֲשֶׂנָּה׃ נֶגַע־
blow (33) he-does-her he self-of-him one-destroying judgment lacking-of

וְקָלוֹן יִמְצָא וְחֶרְפָּתוֹ לֹא תִמָּחֶה׃
he-will-be-wiped-away never and-shame-of-him he-will-find and-disgrace

כִּי־ קִנְאָה חֲמַת־ גָּבֶר וְלֹא־ יַחְמוֹל בְּיוֹם
on-day-of he-will-show-mercy and-not husband fury-of jealousy for (34)

נָקָם׃ לֹא־ יִשָּׂא פְּנֵי כָל־ כֹּפֶר וְלֹא־
and-not compensation any-of presences-of he-will-accept not (35) revenge

יֹאבֶה כִּי תַרְבֶּה־ שֹׁחַד׃ בְּנִי שְׁמֹר אֲמָרָי
words-of-me keep! son-of-me (7:1) bribe she-is-great though he-will-accept

וּמִצְוֹתַי תִּצְפֹּן אִתָּךְ׃ שְׁמֹר מִצְוֹתַי וֶחְיֵה
and-live! commands-of-me keep! (2) within-you you-store-up and-commands-of-me

וְתוֹרָתִי כְּאִישׁוֹן עֵינֶיךָ׃ קָשְׁרֵם עַל־ אֶצְבְּעֹתֶיךָ
fingers-of-you on bind-them! (3) eyes-of-you as-apple-of and-teaching-of-me

כָּתְבֵם עַל־ לוּחַ לִבֶּךָ׃ אֱמֹר לַחָכְמָה אֲחֹתִי אָתְּ
you sister-of-me to-wisdom say! (4) heart-of-you tablet-of on write-them!

וּמֹדָע לַבִּינָה תִקְרָא׃ לִשְׁמָרְךָ מֵאִשָּׁה
from-woman to-keep-you (5) you-call to-the-understanding and-kinsman

זָרָה מִנָּכְרִיָּה אֲמָרֶיהָ הֶחֱלִיקָה׃
she-makes-seductive words-of-her from-wayward-woman one-being-adulteress

or let her captivate you with
her eyes,
26 for the prostitute reduces you
to a loaf of bread,
and the adulteress preys
upon your very life.
27 Can a man scoop fire into his
lap
without his clothes being
burned?
28 Can a man walk on hot coals
without his feet being
scorched?
29 So is he who sleeps with
another man's wife;
no one who touches her will
go unpunished.

30 Men do not despise a thief if
he steals
to satisfy his hunger when
he is starving.
31 Yet if he is caught, he must
pay sevenfold,
though it costs him all the
wealth of his house.
32 But a man who commits
adultery lacks judgment;
whoever does so destroys
himself.
33 Blows and disgrace are his lot,
and his shame will never be
wiped away;
34 for jealousy arouses a
husband's fury,
and he will show no mercy
when he takes revenge.
35 He will not accept any
compensation;
he will refuse the bribe,
however great it is.

### *Warning Against the Adulteress*

7 My son, keep my words
and store up my commands
within you.
2 Keep my commands and you
will live;
guard my teachings as the
apple of your eye.
3 Bind them on your fingers;
write them on the tablet of
your heart.
4 Say to wisdom, "You are my
sister,"
and call understanding your
kinsman;
5 they will keep you from the
adulteress,
from the wayward wife with
her seductive words.

כִּי בְּחַלּוֹן בֵּיתִי בְּעַד אֶשְׁנַבִּי נִשְׁקָפְתִּי׃
I-looked-out lattice-of-me through house-of-me at-window-of for (6)

וָאֵרֶא בַפְּתָאִים אָבִינָה בַבָּנִים נַעַר
youth among-the-young-men I-noticed among-the-simple-ones and-I-saw (7)

חֲסַר־לֵב׃ עֹבֵר בַּשּׁוּק אֵצֶל פִּנָּהּ
corner-of-her near down-the-street one-going (8) judgment lacking-of

וְדֶרֶךְ בֵּיתָהּ יִצְעָד׃ בְּנֶשֶׁף־בְּעֶרֶב יוֹם
day at-evening-of at-twilight (9) he-walked house-of-her and-direction-of

בְּאִישׁוֹן לַיְלָה וַאֲפֵלָה׃ וְהִנֵּה אִשָּׁה לִקְרָאתוֹ שִׁית
dress-of to-meet-him woman then-see! (10) and-darkness night at-middle-of

זוֹנָה וּנְצֻרַת לֵב׃ הֹמִיָּה הִיא
she one-being-loud (11) intent and-one-being-crafty-of one-being-prostitute

וְסֹרָרֶת בְּבֵיתָהּ לֹא־יִשְׁכְּנוּ רַגְלֶיהָ׃ פַּעַם׀
now (12) feet-of-her they-stay never at-home-of-her and-one-being-defiant

בַּחוּץ פַּעַם בָּרְחֹבוֹת וְאֵצֶל כָּל־פִּנָּה תֶאֱרֹב׃
she-lurks corner every-of and-at in-the-squares now in-the-street

וְהֶחֱזִיקָה בּוֹ וְנָשְׁקָה־לּוֹ הֵעֵזָה
she-made-brazen to-him and-she-kissed of-him and-she-took-hold (13)

פָנֶיהָ וַתֹּאמַר לוֹ׃ זִבְחֵי שְׁלָמִים עָלָי
with-me fellowships offerings-of (14) to-him and-she-said faces-of-her

הַיּוֹם שִׁלַּמְתִּי נְדָרָי׃ עַל־כֵּן יָצָאתִי לִקְרָאתֶךָ
to-meet-you I-came-out this for (15) vows-of-me I-fulfilled the-day

לְשַׁחֵר פָּנֶיךָ וָאֶמְצָאֶךָּ׃ מַרְבַדִּים רָבַדְתִּי עַרְשִׂי
bed-of-me I-covered coverings (16) and-I-found-you faces-of-you to-look-for

חֲטֻבוֹת אֵטוּן מִצְרָיִם׃ נַפְתִּי מִשְׁכָּבִי מֹר אֲהָלִים וְקִנָּמוֹן׃
and-cinnamon aloes myrrh bed-of-me I-perfumed (17) Egypt linen-of colors-of

לְכָה נִרְוֶה דֹדִים עַד־הַבֹּקֶר נִתְעַלְּסָה
let-us-enjoy-ourselves the-morning till loves let-us-drink-deep come! (18)

בָּאֳהָבִים׃ כִּי אֵין הָאִישׁ בְּבֵיתוֹ הָלַךְ בְּדֶרֶךְ
on-journey he-went at-home-of-him the-husband not for (19) with-loves

מֵרָחוֹק׃ צְרוֹר־הַכֶּסֶף לָקַח בְּיָדוֹ לְיוֹם
on-day-of in-hand-of-him he-took the-money purse-of (20) at-distance

הַכֵּסֶא* יָבֹא בֵיתוֹ׃ הִטַּתּוּ בְּרֹב
with-quantity-of she-led-astray-him (21) home-of-him he-will-come the-full-moon

לִקְחָהּ בְּחֵלֶק שְׂפָתֶיהָ תַּדִּיחֶנּוּ׃ הוֹלֵךְ
following (22) she-seduced-him lips-of-her with-smoothness-of persuasion-of-her

אַחֲרֶיהָ פִּתְאֹם כְּשׁוֹר אֶל־טָבַח† יָבוֹא וּכְעֶכֶס אֶל־מוּסַר
discipline-of for and-like-noose he-goes slaughter to like-ox at-once after-her

[6]At the window of my house
I looked out through the lattice.
[7]I saw among the simple,
I noticed among the young men,
a youth who lacked judgment.
[8]He was going down the street near her corner,
walking along in the direction of her house
[9]at twilight, as the day was fading,
as the dark of night set in.

[10]Then out came a woman to meet him,
dressed like a prostitute and with crafty intent.
[11](She is loud and defiant,
her feet never stay at home;
[12]now in the street, now in the squares,
at every corner she lurks.)
[13]She took hold of him and kissed him
and with a brazen face she said:

[14]"I have fellowship offerings[l] at home;
today I fulfilled my vows.
[15]So I came out to meet you;
I looked for you and have found you!
[16]I have covered my bed
with colored linens from Egypt.
[17]I have perfumed my bed
with myrrh, aloes and cinnamon.
[18]Come, let's drink deep of love till morning;
let's enjoy ourselves with love!
[19]My husband is not at home;
he has gone on a long journey.
[20]He took his purse filled with money
and will not be home till full moon."

[21]With persuasive words she led him astray;
she seduced him with her smooth talk.
[22]All at once he followed her
like an ox going to the slaughter,
like a deer[m] stepping into a noose[n]

[l]14 Traditionally *peace offerings*
[m]22 Syriac (see also Septuagint); Hebrew *fool*
[n]22 The meaning of the Hebrew for this line is uncertain.

*20 Most mss have *segol* under the *kaph* (הַכֶּ).

†22 Most mss have *segol* under the *teth* (טֶ).

אֱוִֽיל׃ עַד יְפַלַּח חֵץ כְּבֵדוֹ כְּמַהֵר צִפּוֹר אֶל־פָּח
snare into bird like-to-dart liver-of-him arrow he-pierces till (23) fool

וְלֹֽא־יָדַע כִּֽי־בְנַפְשׁוֹ הֽוּא׃ וְעַתָּה בָנִים שִׁמְעוּ־לִי
to-me listen! sons so-now (24) this for-life-of-him that he-knows and-not

וְהַקְשִׁיבוּ לְאִמְרֵי־פִֽי׃ אַל־יֵשְׂטְ* אֶל־
to let-him-turn not (25) mouth-of-me to-sayings-of and-pay-attention!

דְּרָכֶיהָ לִבֶּךָ אַל־תֵּתַע בִּנְתִיבוֹתֶֽיהָ׃ כִּֽי־רַבִּים
many for (26) into-paths-of-her you-stray not heart-of-you ways-of-her

חֲלָלִים הִפִּילָה וַעֲצֻמִים כָּל־הֲרֻגֶֽיהָ׃
ones-being-slain-of-her all-of and-mighty-ones she-brought-down victims

דַּרְכֵי שְׁאוֹל בֵּיתָהּ יֹרְדוֹת אֶל־חַדְרֵי־מָֽוֶת׃
death chambers-of to ones-leading-down house-of-her Sheol highways-of (27)

הֲלֹא־חָכְמָה תִקְרָא וּתְבוּנָה תִּתֵּן קוֹלָֽהּ׃
voice-of-her she-raises and-understanding she-calls-out wisdom not? (8:1)

בְּרֹאשׁ־מְרוֹמִים עֲלֵי־דָרֶךְ בֵּית נְתִיבוֹת נִצָּֽבָה׃
she-takes-stand paths meeting-place-of way along heights on-top-of (2)

לְיַד־שְׁעָרִים לְפִי־קָרֶת מְבוֹא פְתָחִים תָּרֹֽנָּה׃
she-cries-aloud doors entrance-of city at-entrance-of gates at-side-of (3)

אֲלֵיכֶם אִישִׁים אֶקְרָא וְקוֹלִי אֶל־בְּנֵי אָדָֽם׃ הָבִינוּ
gain! (5) mankind sons-of to and-voice-of-me I-call-out men to-you (4)

פְתָאיִם עָרְמָה וּכְסִילִים הָבִינוּ לֵֽב׃ שִׁמְעוּ כִּֽי־
for listen! (6) understanding gain! and-foolish-ones prudence simple-ones

נְגִידִים אֲדַבֵּר וּמִפְתַּח שְׂפָתַי מֵישָׁרִֽים׃ כִּֽי־אֱמֶת
truth for (7) right-ones lips-of-me and-opening-of I-say worthy-things

יֶהְגֶּה חִכִּי וְתוֹעֲבַת שְׂפָתַי רֶֽשַׁע׃ בְּצֶדֶק
in-justice (8) wickedness lips-of-me and-detestable-of mouth-of-me he-speaks

כָּל־אִמְרֵי־פִי אֵין בָּהֶם נִפְתָּל וְעִקֵּֽשׁ׃
or-perverse one-being-crooked of-them none mouth-of-me words-of all-of

כֻּלָּם נְכֹחִים לַמֵּבִין וִישָׁרִים
and-faultless-ones to-the-one-discerning right-ones all-of-them (9)

לְמֹצְאֵי דָֽעַת׃ קְחוּ־מוּסָרִי וְאַל־כָּסֶף
silver and-not instruction-of-me choose! (10) knowledge to-ones-having-of

וְדַעַת מֵחָרוּץ נִבְחָֽר׃ כִּי־טוֹבָה חָכְמָה
wisdom precious for (11) one-being-choice rather-than-gold and-knowledge

מִפְּנִינִים וְכָל־חֲפָצִים לֹא יִשְׁווּ־בָֽהּ׃ אֲנִי־
I (12) with-her they-can-compare not desires and-all-of more-than-rubies

חָכְמָה שָׁכַנְתִּי עָרְמָה וְדַעַת מְזִמּוֹת אֶמְצָא׃ יִרְאַת
fear-of (13) I-possess discretions knowledge-of prudence I-dwell wisdom

23 till an arrow pierces his liver,
like a bird darting into a snare,
little knowing it will cost him his life.

24 Now then, my sons, listen to me;
pay attention to what I say.
25 Do not let your heart turn to her ways
or stray into her paths.
26 Many are the victims she has brought down;
her slain are a mighty throng.
27 Her house is a highway to the grave,°
leading down to the chambers of death.

*Wisdom's Call*

8 Does not wisdom call out?
Does not understanding raise her voice?
2 On the heights along the way,
where the paths meet, she takes her stand;
3 beside the gates leading into the city,
at the entrances, she cries aloud:
4 "To you, O men, I call out;
I raise my voice to all mankind.
5 You who are simple, gain prudence;
you who are foolish, gain understanding.
6 Listen, for I have worthy things to say;
I open my lips to speak what is right.
7 My mouth speaks what is true,
for my lips detest wickedness.
8 All the words of my mouth are just;
none of them is crooked or perverse.
9 To the discerning all of them are right;
they are faultless to those who have knowledge.
10 Choose my instruction instead of silver,
knowledge rather than choice gold,
11 for wisdom is more precious than rubies,
and nothing you desire can compare with her.

12 "I, wisdom, dwell together with prudence;
I possess knowledge and discretion.

°27 Hebrew *Sheol*

*25 Most mss have the accent *rebia mugrash* ( ֗ ).

יְהוָה שְׂנֹאת רָע גֵּאָה וְגָאוֹן | וְדֶרֶךְ רָע וּפִי
and-speech-of evil and-behavior-of and-arrogance pride evil to-hate Yahweh

תַּהְפֻּכוֹת שָׂנֵאתִי׃ לִי־ עֵצָה וְתוּשִׁיָּה אֲנִי בִינָה
understanding I and-sound-judgment counsel to-me (14) I-hate perversities

לִי גְבוּרָה׃ בִּי מְלָכִים יִמְלֹכוּ וְרוֹזְנִים יְחֹקְקוּ צֶדֶק׃
just they-make-laws and-ones-ruling they-reign kings by-me (15) power to-me

בִּי שָׂרִים יָשֹׂרוּ וּנְדִיבִים כָּל־ שֹׁפְטֵי צֶדֶק׃
righteousness ones-ruling-of all-of and-nobles they-govern princes by-me (16)

אֲנִי °אֹהֲבַיה אֵהָב וּמְשַׁחֲרַי יִמְצָאֻנְנִי׃ עֹשֶׁר־
richness (18) they-find-me and-ones-seeking-me I-love ones-loving-me I (17)

וְכָבוֹד אִתִּי הוֹן עָתֵק וּצְדָקָה׃ טוֹב פִּרְיִי
fruit-of-me good (19) and-prosperity enduring wealth-of with-me and-honor

מֵחָרוּץ וּמִפָּז וּתְבוּאָתִי מִכֶּסֶף
more-than-silver and-yield-of-me even-more-than-fine-gold more-than-gold

נִבְחָר׃ בְּאֹרַח־ צְדָקָה אֲהַלֵּךְ* בְּתוֹךְ נְתִיבוֹת מִשְׁפָּט׃
justice paths-of at-along I-walk righteousness in-way-of (20) being-choice

לְהַנְחִיל אֹהֲבַי | יֵשׁ וְאֹצְרֹתֵיהֶם אֲמַלֵּא׃ יְהוָה
Yahweh (22) I-fill and-treasuries-of-them wealth ones-loving-me to-bestow (21)

קָנָנִי רֵאשִׁית דַּרְכּוֹ קֶדֶם מִפְעָלָיו מֵאָז׃
from-of-old deeds-of-him before way-of-him beginning-of he-possessed-me

מֵעוֹלָם נִסַּכְתִּי מֵרֹאשׁ מִקַּדְמֵי־ אָרֶץ׃
world from-beginnings-of from-beginning I-was-appointed from-eternity (23)

בְּאֵין־ תְּהֹמוֹת חוֹלָלְתִּי בְּאֵין מַעְיָנוֹת נִכְבַּדֵּי־
ones-abounding-of springs when-no I-was-given-birth oceans when-no (24)

מָיִם׃ בְּטֶרֶם הָרִים הָטְבָּעוּ לִפְנֵי גְבָעוֹת חוֹלָלְתִּי׃
I-was-born hills before they-were-settled mountains at-before (25) waters

עַד־ לֹא עָשָׂה אֶרֶץ וְחוּצוֹת וְרֹאשׁ עַפְרוֹת† תֵּבֵל׃
world dusts-of or-any-of or-fields earth he-made not when (26)

בַּהֲכִינוֹ שָׁמַיִם שָׁם אָנִי בְּחוּקוֹ חוּג
horizon when-to-mark-out-him I there heavens when-to-set-in-place-him (27)

עַל־ פְּנֵי תְהוֹם׃ בְּאַמְּצוֹ שְׁחָקִים מִמָּעַל בַּעֲזוֹז
when-to-secure at-above clouds when-to-establish-him (28) deep faces-of on

עִינוֹת תְּהוֹם††׃ בְּשׂוּמוֹ לַיָּם | חֻקּוֹ וּמַיִם
so-waters boundary-of-him to-the-sea when-to-give-him (29) deep fountains-of

לֹא יַעַבְרוּ־ פִיו בְּחוּקוֹ מוֹסְדֵי
foundations-of when-to-mark-out-him command-of-him they-would-overstep not

אָרֶץ׃ וָאֶהְיֶה אֶצְלוֹ אָמוֹן וָאֶהְיֶה שַׁעֲשֻׁעִים יוֹם | יוֹם
day day delights and-I-was craftsman beside-him then-I-was (30) earth

13 To fear the LORD is to hate
evil;
I hate pride and arrogance,
evil behavior and perverse
speech.
14 Counsel and sound judgment
are mine;
I have understanding and
power.
15 By me kings reign
and rulers make laws that
are just;
16 by me princes govern,
and all nobles who rule on
earth.[p]
17 I love those who love me,
and those who seek me find
me.
18 With me are riches and honor,
enduring wealth and
prosperity.
19 My fruit is better than fine
gold;
what I yield surpasses
choice silver.
20 I walk in the way of
righteousness,
along the paths of justice,
21 bestowing wealth on those
who love me
and making their treasuries
full.
22 "The LORD possessed me[q] at
the beginning of his
work,[r]
before his deeds of old;
23 I was appointed[s] from
eternity,
from the beginning, before
the world began.
24 When there were no oceans, I
was given birth,
when there were no springs
abounding with water;
25 before the mountains were
settled in place,
before the hills, I was given
birth,
26 before he made the earth or its
fields
or any of the dust of the
world.
27 I was there when he set the
heavens in place,
when he marked out the
horizon on the face of the
deep,
28 when he established the clouds
above
and fixed securely the
fountains of the deep,
29 when he gave the sea its
boundary
so the waters would not
overstep his command,
and when he marked out the
foundations of the earth.
30 Then I was the craftsman at
his side.
I was filled with delight day

p16 Many Hebrew manuscripts and Septuagint; most Hebrew manuscripts *all righteous rulers*
q22 Or *The LORD brought me forth*
r22 Or *way;* or *dominion*
s23 Or *fashioned*

*20 Most mss have *sheva* in the *kaph* (ךְ—).

†26 Most mss have *pathah* under the *ayin* (עַ׳).

††28 Most mss have the accent *silluq* on the final syllable (תְּהוֹם).

°17 ק אהבי

מְשַׂחֶקֶת לְפָנָיו בְּכָל־ עֵת׃ מְשַׂחֶקֶת בְּתֵבֵל

in-whole-of one-rejoicing (31) time at-all-of in-presences-of-him one-rejoicing

אַרְצוֹ וְשַׁעֲשֻׁעַי אֶת־ בְּנֵי אָדָם׃ וְעַתָּה בָנִים שִׁמְעוּ־

listen! sons so-now (32) mankind sons-of *** and-delights-of-me world-of-him

לִי וְאַשְׁרֵי דְּרָכַי יִשְׁמֹרוּ׃ שִׁמְעוּ מוּסָר

instruction listen! (33) they-keep ways-of-me and-blessednesses-of to-me

וַחֲכָמוּ וְאַל־ תִּפְרָעוּ׃ אַשְׁרֵי אָדָם שֹׁמֵעַ לִי

to-me one-listening man blessednesses-of (34) you-ignore and-not and-be-wise!

לִשְׁקֹד עַל־ דַּלְתֹתַי יוֹם ׀ יוֹם לִשְׁמֹר מְזוּזֹת פְּתָחָי׃ כִּי

for (35) doors-of-me doorways-of to-wait day day doors-of-me at to-watch

מֹצְאִי מָצָאי חַיִּים וַיָּפֶק רָצוֹן מֵיְהוָה׃

from-Yahweh favor and-he-receives lives he-finds one-finding-me

וְחֹטְאִי חֹמֵס נַפְשׁוֹ כָּל־ מְשַׂנְאַי אָהֲבוּ

they-love ones-hating-me all-of self-of-him harming but-one-missing-me (36)

מָוֶת׃ חָכְמוֹת בָּנְתָה בֵיתָהּ חָצְבָה עַמּוּדֶיהָ שִׁבְעָה׃

seven pillars-of-her she-hewed-out house-of-her she-built wisdoms (9:1) death

טָבְחָה טִבְחָהּ מָסְכָה יֵינָהּ אַף עָרְכָה שֻׁלְחָנָהּ׃

table-of-her she-set also wine-of-her she-mixed meat-of-her she-prepared (2)

שָׁלְחָה נַעֲרֹתֶיהָ תִקְרָא עַל־ גַּפֵּי מְרֹמֵי קָרֶת׃

city high-points-of heights-of from she-calls maids-of-her she-sent-out (3)

מִי־ פֶתִי יָסֻר הֵנָּה חֲסַר־ לֵב אָמְרָה לּוֹ׃

to-him she-says judgment lacking-of to-here let-him-come simple whoever (4)

לְכוּ לַחֲמוּ בְלַחֲמִי וּשְׁתוּ בְּיַיִן מָסָכְתִּי׃ עִזְבוּ

leave! (6) I-mixed of-wine and-drink! of-food-of-me eat! come! (5)

פְתָאיִם וִחְיוּ וְאִשְׁרוּ בְּדֶרֶךְ בִּינָה׃ יֹסֵר ׀

one-correcting (7) understanding in-way-of and-walk! and-live! simple-ways

לֵץ לֹקֵחַ לוֹ קָלוֹן וּמוֹכִיחַ לְרָשָׁע מוּמוֹ׃

abuse-of-him to-wicked-man and-one-rebuking insult to-him inviting one-mocking

אַל־ תּוֹכַח לֵץ פֶּן־ יִשְׂנָאֶךָּ הוֹכַח לְחָכָם

to-wise-man rebuke! he-will-hate-you or one-mocking you-rebuke not (8)

וְיֶאֱהָבֶךָּ׃ תֵּן לְחָכָם וְיֶחְכַּם־ עוֹד

still and-he-will-be-wiser to-wise-man instruct! (9) and-he-will-love-you

הוֹדַע לְצַדִּיק וְיוֹסֶף לֶקַח׃ תְּחִלַּת חָכְמָה

wisdom beginning-of (10) learning and-he-will-add to-righteous-man teach!

יִרְאַת יְהוָה וְדַעַת קְדֹשִׁים בִּינָה׃ כִּי־ בִי

through-me for (11) understanding Holy-Ones and-knowledge-of Yahweh fear-of

יִרְבּוּ יָמֶיךָ וְיוֹסִיפוּ לְּךָ שְׁנוֹת חַיִּים׃

lives years-of to-you and-they-will-add days-of-you they-will-be-many

after day,
rejoicing always in his
presence,
31 rejoicing in his whole world
and delighting in mankind.
32 "Now then, my sons, listen to
me;
blessed are those who keep
my ways.
33 Listen to my instruction and
be wise;
do not ignore it.
34 Blessed is the man who listens
to me,
watching daily at my doors,
waiting at my doorway.
35 For whoever finds me finds
life
and receives favor from the
LORD.
36 But whoever fails to find me
harms himself;
all who hate me love death."

*Invitations of Wisdom and of Folly*

9 Wisdom has built her house;
she has hewn out its seven
pillars.
2 She has prepared her meat and
mixed her wine;
she has also set her table.
3 She has sent out her maids,
and she calls
from the highest point of
the city.
4 "Let all who are simple come
in here!"
she says to those who lack
judgment.
5 "Come, eat my food
and drink the wine I have
mixed.
6 Leave your simple ways and
you will live;
walk in the way of
understanding.

7 "Whoever corrects a mocker
invites insult;
whoever rebukes a wicked
man incurs abuse.
8 Do not rebuke a mocker or he
will hate you;
rebuke a wise man and he
will love you.
9 Instruct a wise man and he
will be wiser still;
teach a righteous man and
he will add to his
learning.

10 "The fear of the LORD is the
beginning of wisdom,
and knowledge of the Holy
One is understanding.
11 For through me your days will
be many,
and years will be added to
your life.

°35 ק מצא

אִם־ חָכַמְתָּ חָכַמְתָּ לָּךְ וְלַצְתָּ לְבַדְּךָ

by-yourself if-you-mock for-you you-are-wise you-are-wise if (12)

תִּשָּׂא׃ אֵשֶׁת כְּסִילוּת הֹמִיָּה פְּתַיּוּת וּבַל־

and-not undisciplined one-being-loud Folly woman-of (13) you-will-suffer

יָדְעָה מָּה׃ וְיָשְׁבָה לְפֶתַח בֵּיתָהּ עַל־ כִּסֵּא

seat-of on house-of-her at-door-of and-she-sits (14) anything she-knows

מְרֹמֵי קָרֶת׃ לִקְרֹא לְעֹבְרֵי־ דָרֶךְ הַמְיַשְּׁרִים

the-ones-going-straight road to-ones-passing-of to-call (15) city heights-of

אֹרְחוֹתָם׃ מִי־ פֶתִי יָסֻר הֵנָּה וַחֲסַר־ לֵב

judgment and-lacking-of to-here let-him-come simple whoever (16) ways-of-them

וְאָמְרָה לּוֹ׃ מַיִם־ גְּנוּבִים יִמְתָּקוּ וְלֶחֶם

and-food-of they-are-sweet ones-being-stolen waters (17) to-him and-she-says

סְתָרִים יִנְעָם׃ וְלֹא־ יָדַע כִּי־ רְפָאִים שָׁם

there dead-ones that he-knows but-not (18) he-is-delicious secrets

בְּעִמְקֵי שְׁאוֹל קְרֻאֶיהָ׃ מִשְׁלֵי שְׁלֹמֹה בֵּן

son Solomon proverbs-of (10:1) ones-being-guests-of-her Sheol in-depths-of

חָכָם יְשַׂמַּח־ אָב וּבֵן כְּסִיל תּוּגַת אִמּוֹ׃ לֹא־

not (2) mother-of-him grief-of foolish but-son father he-brings-joy wise

יוֹעִילוּ אוֹצְרוֹת רֶשַׁע וּצְדָקָה תַּצִּיל

she-delivers but-righteousness ill-gotten treasures-of they-are-valuable

מִמָּוֶת׃ לֹא־ יַרְעִיב יְהוָה נֶפֶשׁ צַדִּיק וְהַוַּת

but-craving-of righteous life-of Yahweh he-lets-go-hungry not (3) from-death

רְשָׁעִים יֶהְדֹּף׃ רָאשׁ עֹשֶׂה כַף־ רְמִיָּה

laziness hand-of one-making man-being-poor (4) he-thwarts wicked-ones

וְיַד חָרוּצִים תַּעֲשִׁיר׃ אֹגֵר בַּקַּיִץ בֵּן

son in-the-summer one-gathering (5) she-brings-wealth diligent-ones but-hand-of

מַשְׂכִּיל נִרְדָּם בַּקָּצִיר בֵּן מֵבִישׁ׃ בְּרָכוֹת

blessings (6) bringing-disgrace son during-the-harvest one-sleeping being-wise

לְרֹאשׁ צַדִּיק וּפִי רְשָׁעִים יְכַסֶּה חָמָס׃

violence he-overwhelms wicked-ones but-mouth-of righteous on-head-of

זֵכֶר צַדִּיק לִבְרָכָה וְשֵׁם רְשָׁעִים יִרְקָב׃

he-will-rot wicked-ones but-name-of as-blessing righteous memory-of (7)

חֲכַם־ לֵב יִקַּח מִצְוֹת וֶאֱוִיל שְׂפָתַיִם יִלָּבֵט׃

he-comes-to-ruin chatterings but-fool-of commands he-accepts heart wise-of (8)

הוֹלֵךְ בַּתֹּם יֵלֶךְ בֶּטַח וּמְעַקֵּשׁ

but-one-crooked-of security he-walks in-the-integrity one-walking (9)

דְּרָכָיו יִוָּדֵעַ׃ קֹרֵץ עַיִן יִתֵּן עַצָּבֶת

grief he-causes eye one-winking (10) he-will-be-found-out paths-of-him

12If you are wise, your wisdom
will reward you;
if you are a mocker, you
alone will suffer."
13The woman Folly is loud;
she is undisciplined and
without knowledge.
14She sits at the door of her
house,
on a seat at the highest
point of the city,
15calling out to those who pass
by,
who go straight on their
way.
16"Let all who are simple come
in here!"
she says to those who lack
judgment.
17"Stolen water is sweet;
food eaten in secret is
delicious!"
18But little do they know that
the dead are there,
that her guests are in the
depths of the grave.[t]

*Proverbs of Solomon*

10 The proverbs of Solomon:
A wise son brings joy to
his father,
but a foolish son grief to his
mother.
2Ill-gotten treasures are of no
value,
but righteousness delivers
from death.
3The LORD does not let the
righteous go hungry
but he thwarts the craving
of the wicked.
4Lazy hands make a man poor,
but diligent hands bring
wealth.
5He who gathers crops in
summer is a wise son,
but he who sleeps during
harvest is a disgraceful
son.
6Blessings crown the head of
the righteous,
but violence overwhelms the
mouth of the wicked.[u]
7The memory of the righteous
will be a blessing,
but the name of the wicked
will rot.
8The wise in heart accept
commands,
but a chattering fool comes
to ruin.
9The man of integrity walks
securely,
but he who takes crooked
paths will be found out.
10He who winks maliciously
causes grief,

[t]18 Hebrew *Sheol*
[u]6 Or *but the mouth of the wicked conceals violence*; also in verse 11

וֶאֱוִיל שְׂפָתַיִם יִלָּבֵט׃ מְקוֹר חַיִּים פִּי
mouth-of lives fountain-of (11) he-comes-to-ruin chatterings and-fool-of

צַדִּיק וּפִי רְשָׁעִים יְכַסֶּה חָמָס׃ שִׂנְאָה
hatred (12) violence he-overwhelms wicked-ones but-mouth-of righteous

תְּעוֹרֵר מְדָנִים וְעַל כָּל־פְּשָׁעִים תְּכַסֶּה אַהֲבָה׃ בְּשִׂפְתֵי
on-lips-of (13) love she-covers wrongs all-of but-over dissensions she-stirs-up

נָבוֹן תִּמָּצֵא חָכְמָה וְשֵׁבֶט לְגֵו חֲסַר־לֵב׃
judgment lacking-of for-back-of but-rod wisdom she-is-found discerning

חֲכָמִים יִצְפְּנוּ־דָעַת וּפִי־אֱוִיל מְחִתָּה קְרֹבָה׃
near ruin fool but-mouth-of knowledge they-store-up wise-men (14)

הוֹן עָשִׁיר קִרְיַת עֻזּוֹ מְחִתַּת דַּלִּים
poor-ones ruin-of fortification-of-him city-of rich wealth-of (15)

רֵישָׁם׃ פְּעֻלַּת צַדִּיק לְחַיִּים תְּבוּאַת רָשָׁע לְחַטָּאת׃
as-punishment wicked income-of as-lives righteous wage-of (16) poverty-of-them

אֹרַח לְחַיִּים שׁוֹמֵר מוּסָר וְעוֹזֵב תּוֹכַחַת
correction but-one-ignoring discipline one-heeding to-lives way (17)

מַתְעֶה׃ מְכַסֶּה שִׂנְאָה שִׂפְתֵי־שָׁקֶר וּמוֹצִא
and-one-spreading lie lips-of hatred one-concealing (18) one-leading-astray

דִבָּה הוּא כְסִיל׃ בְּרֹב דְּבָרִים לֹא יֶחְדַּל־פָּשַׁע וְחֹשֵׂךְ
but-one-holding sin he-is-absent not words when-many-of (19) fool he slander

שְׂפָתָיו מַשְׂכִּיל׃ כֶּסֶף נִבְחָר לְשׁוֹן צַדִּיק לֵב
heart-of righteous tongue-of being-choice silver (20) being-wise lips-of-him

רְשָׁעִים כִּמְעָט׃ שִׂפְתֵי צַדִּיק יִרְעוּ רַבִּים וֶאֱוִילִים
but-fools many they-nourish righteous lips-of (21) as-little wicked-ones

בַּחֲסַר־לֵב יָמוּתוּ׃ בִּרְכַּת יְהוָה הִיא תַעֲשִׁיר
she-brings-wealth she Yahweh blessing-of (22) they-die judgment for-lack-of

וְלֹא־יוֹסִף עֶצֶב עִמָּהּ׃ כִּשְׂחוֹק לִכְסִיל עֲשׂוֹת זִמָּה וְחָכְמָה
but-wisdom evil to-do to-fool as-pleasure (23) to-her trouble he-adds and-not

לְאִישׁ תְּבוּנָה׃ מְגוֹרַת רָשָׁע הִיא תְבוֹאֶנּוּ
she-will-overtake-him she wicked dread-of (24) understanding to-man-of

וְתַאֲוַת צַדִּיקִים יִתֵּן׃ כַּעֲבוֹר סוּפָה
storm when-to-sweep-by (25) he-will-grant righteous-ones but-desire-of

וְאֵין רָשָׁע וְצַדִּיק יְסוֹד עוֹלָם׃ כַּחֹמֶץ
as-the-vinegar (26) forever firm but-righteous wicked then-not

לַשִּׁנַּיִם וְכֶעָשָׁן לָעֵינָיִם כֵּן הֶעָצֵל לְשֹׁלְחָיו׃
to-ones-sending-him the-sluggard so to-the-eyes and-as-the-smoke to-the-teeth

יִרְאַת יְהוָה תּוֹסִיף יָמִים וּשְׁנוֹת רְשָׁעִים תִּקְצֹרְנָה׃
they-are-cut-short wicked-ones but-years-of days she-adds Yahweh fear-of (27)

and a chattering fool comes
to ruin.

11 The mouth of the righteous is
a fountain of life,
but violence overwhelms the
mouth of the wicked.

12 Hatred stirs up dissension,
but love covers over all
wrongs.

13 Wisdom is found on the lips
of the discerning,
but a rod is for the back of
him who lacks judgment.

14 Wise men store up knowledge,
but the mouth of a fool
invites ruin.

15 The wealth of the rich is their
fortified city,
but poverty is the ruin of
the poor.

16 The wages of the righteous
bring them life
but the income of the
wicked brings them
punishment.

17 He who heeds discipline
shows the way to life,
but whoever ignores
correction leads others
astray.

18 He who conceals his hatred
has lying lips,
and whoever spreads
slander is a fool.

19 When words are many, sin is
not absent,
but he who holds his tongue
is wise.

20 The tongue of the righteous is
choice silver,
but the heart of the wicked
is of little value.

21 The lips of the righteous
nourish many,
but fools die for lack of
judgment.

22 The blessing of the LORD
brings wealth,
and he adds no trouble to it.

23 A fool finds pleasure in evil
conduct,
but a man of understanding
delights in wisdom.

24 What the wicked dreads will
overtake him;
what the righteous desire
will be granted.

25 When the storm has swept by,
the wicked are gone,
but the righteous stand firm
forever.

26 As vinegar to the teeth and
smoke to the eyes,
so is a sluggard to those
who send him.

27 The fear of the LORD adds
length to life,
but the years of the wicked
are cut short.

תּוֹחֶלֶת צַדִּיקִים שִׂמְחָה וְתִקְוַת רְשָׁעִים תֹּאבֵד׃
(28) prospect-of righteous-ones joy but-hope-of wicked-ones she-perishes

מָעוֹז לַתֹּם דֶּרֶךְ יְהוָה וּמְחִתָּה לְפֹעֲלֵי אָוֶן׃
(29) refuge for-the-righteous way-of Yahweh but-ruin to-ones-doing-of evil

צַדִּיק לְעוֹלָם בַּל־יִמּוֹט וּרְשָׁעִים לֹא
(30) righteous to-forever not he-will-be-uprooted but-wicked-ones not

יִשְׁכְּנוּ־אָרֶץ׃ פִּי־צַדִּיק יָנוּב חָכְמָה
they-will-remain land (31) mouth-of righteous he-brings-forth wisdom

וּלְשׁוֹן תַּהְפֻּכוֹת תִּכָּרֵת׃ שִׂפְתֵי צַדִּיק
but-tongue-of perversities she-will-be-cut-out (32) lips-of righteous

יֵדְעוּן רָצוֹן וּפִי רְשָׁעִים תַּהְפֻּכוֹת׃ מֹאזְנֵי
they-know fitting but-mouth-of wicked-ones perversities (11:1) scales-of

מִרְמָה תּוֹעֲבַת יְהוָה וְאֶבֶן שְׁלֵמָה רְצוֹנוֹ׃
dishonesty abhorrence-of Yahweh but-weight accurate delight-of-him

בָּא־זָדוֹן וַיָּבֹא קָלוֹן וְאֶת־צְנוּעִים חָכְמָה׃
(2) he-comes pride then-he-comes disgrace but-with humilities wisdom

תֻּמַּת יְשָׁרִים תַּנְחֵם וְסֶלֶף
(3) integrity-of upright-ones she-guides-them but-duplicity-of

בּוֹגְדִים וְשַׁדֵּם׃ לֹא־יוֹעִיל הוֹן בְּיוֹם
ones-being-unfaithful he-destroys-them (4) not he-has-worth wealth in-day-of

עֶבְרָה וּצְדָקָה תַּצִּיל מִמָּוֶת׃ צִדְקַת
wrath but-righteousness she-delivers from-death (5) righteousness-of

תָּמִים תְּיַשֵּׁר דַּרְכּוֹ וּבְרִשְׁעָתוֹ יִפֹּל
blameless-ones he-makes-straight way-of-him but-by-wickedness-of-him he-falls

רָשָׁע׃ צִדְקַת יְשָׁרִים תַּצִּילֵם וּבְהַוַּת
wicked (6) righteousness-of upright-ones she-delivers-them but-by-evil-desire-of

בֹּגְדִים יִלָּכֵדוּ׃ בְּמוֹת אָדָם רָשָׁע תֹּאבַד
ones-being-unfaithful they-are-trapped (7) in-death-of man wicked she-perishes

תִּקְוָה וְתוֹחֶלֶת אוֹנִים אָבָדָה׃ צַדִּיק מִצָּרָה
hope and-expectation-of powers she-comes-to-nothing (8) righteous from-trouble

נֶחֱלָץ וַיָּבֹא רָשָׁע תַּחְתָּיו׃ בְּפֶה חָנֵף
he-is-rescued he-comes-on wicked instead-of-him (9) with-mouth godless

יַשְׁחִת רֵעֵהוּ וּבְדַעַת צַדִּיקִים יֵחָלֵצוּ׃
he-destroys neighbor-of-him but-through-knowledge righteous-ones they-escape

בְּטוּב צַדִּיקִים תַּעֲלֹץ קִרְיָה וּבַאֲבֹד
(10) in-prosperity-of righteous-ones she-rejoices city but-when-to-perish

רְשָׁעִים רִנָּה׃ בְּבִרְכַּת יְשָׁרִים תָּרוּם
wicked-ones shout-of-joy (11) through-blessing-of upright-ones she-is-exalted

°3 ק ישדם

28 The prospect of the righteous
is joy,
but the hopes of the wicked
come to nothing.

29 The way of the LORD is a
refuge for the righteous,
but it is the ruin of those
who do evil.

30 The righteous will never be
uprooted,
but the wicked will not
remain in the land.

31 The mouth of the righteous
brings forth wisdom,
but a perverse tongue will
be cut out.

32 The lips of the righteous know
what is fitting,
but the mouth of the wicked
only what is perverse.

11 The LORD abhors
dishonest scales,
but accurate weights are his
delight.

2 When pride comes, then
comes disgrace,
but with humility comes
wisdom.

3 The integrity of the upright
guides them,
but the unfaithful are
destroyed by their
duplicity.

4 Wealth is worthless in the day
of wrath,
but righteousness delivers
from death.

5 The righteousness of the
blameless makes a
straight way for them,
but the wicked are brought
down by their own
wickedness.

6 The righteousness of the
upright delivers them,
but the unfaithful are
trapped by evil desires.

7 When a wicked man dies, his
hope perishes;
all he expected from his
power comes to nothing.

8 The righteous man is rescued
from trouble,
and it comes on the wicked
instead.

9 With his mouth the godless
destroys his neighbor,
but through knowledge the
righteous escape.

10 When the righteous prosper,
the city rejoices;
when the wicked perish,
there are shouts of joy.

11 Through the blessing of the
upright a city is exalted,

קֶרֶת וּבְפִי רְשָׁעִים תֵּהָרֵס׃ בָּז־

he-derides (12) she-is-destroyed wicked-ones but-by-mouth-of city

לְרֵעֵהוּ חֲסַר־ לֵב וְאִישׁ תְּבוּנוֹת יַחֲרִישׁ׃

he-holds-tongue understandings but-man-of judgment lacking-of to-neighbor-of-him

(13) הוֹלֵךְ רָכִיל מְגַלֶּה־ סּוֹד וְנֶאֱמַן־

but-one-being-trustworthy-of confidence one-betraying gossip one-bringing (13)

רוּחַ מְכַסֶּה דָבָר׃ (14) בְּאֵין תַּחְבֻּלוֹת יִפָּל־ עָם

nation he-falls guidances for-lack-of (14) secret one-keeping spirit

וּתְשׁוּעָה בְּרֹב יוֹעֵץ׃ (15) רַע־ יֵרוֹעַ כִּי־

if he-will-suffer suffering (15) one-advising in-many-of but-victory

עָרַב זָר וְשֹׂנֵא תֹקְעִים בּוֹטֵחַ׃

one-being-safe strikings but-one-refusing one-being-other he-puts-up-security

(16) אֵשֶׁת־ חֵן תִּתְמֹךְ כָּבוֹד וְעָרִיצִים יִתְמְכוּ־ עֹשֶׁר׃

wealth they-gain but-ruthless-men respect she-gains kindhearted woman-of (16)

(17) גֹּמֵל נַפְשׁוֹ אִישׁ חָסֶד וְעֹכֵר שְׁאֵרוֹ

self-of-him but-one-harming kindness man-of self-of-him one-benefitting (17)

אַכְזָרִי׃ (18) רָשָׁע עֹשֶׂה פְעֻלַּת־ שָׁקֶר וְזֹרֵעַ צְדָקָה

righteousness but-one-sowing deception wage-of earning wicked (18) cruel-man

שֶׂכֶר אֱמֶת׃ (19) כֵּן־ צְדָקָה לְחַיִּים וּמְרַדֵּף רָעָה

evil but-one-pursuing to-lives righteous truly (19) sure reward-of

לְמוֹתוֹ׃ (20) תּוֹעֲבַת יְהוָה עִקְּשֵׁי־ לֵב

heart men-perverse-of Yahweh detesting-of (20) to-death-of-him

וּרְצוֹנוֹ תְּמִימֵי דָרֶךְ׃ (21) יָד לְיָד לֹא־

not upon-hand hand (21) way ones-blameless-of but-delight-of-him

יִנָּקֶה רָּע וְזֶרַע צַדִּיקִים נִמְלָט׃

he-will-go-free righteous-ones but-descendant-of wicked he-will-go-unpunished

(22) נֶזֶם זָהָב בְּאַף חֲזִיר אִשָּׁה יָפָה וְסָרַת טָעַם׃

discretion but-turning-away-of beautiful woman pig in-snout-of gold ring-of (22)

(23) תַּאֲוַת צַדִּיקִים אַךְ־ טוֹב תִּקְוַת רְשָׁעִים עֶבְרָה׃

wrath wicked-ones hope-of good only righteous-ones desire-of (23)

(24) יֵשׁ מְפַזֵּר וְנוֹסָף עוֹד וְחוֹשֵׂךְ

and-one-withholding more yet-one-gaining one-giving-freely there-is (24)

מִיֹּשֶׁר אַךְ־ לְמַחְסוֹר׃ (25) נֶפֶשׁ־ בְּרָכָה תְדֻשָּׁן

she-will-prosper generosity person-of (25) to-poverty but without-right

וּמַרְוֶה גַּם־ הוּא יוֹרֶא׃ (26) מֹנֵעַ בָּר

grain one-hoarding (26) he-will-be-refreshed he also and-one-refreshing

יִקְּבֻהוּ לְאוֹם וּבְרָכָה לְרֹאשׁ מַשְׁבִּיר׃ (27) שֹׁחֵר

one-seeking (27) one-selling on-head-of but-blessing people they-curse-him

but by the mouth of the
wicked it is destroyed.

12 A man who lacks judgment
derides his neighbor,
but a man of understanding
holds his tongue.

13 A gossip betrays a confidence,
but a trustworthy man keeps
a secret.

14 For lack of guidance a nation
falls,
but many advisers make
victory sure.

15 He who puts up security for
another will surely suffer,
but whoever refuses to strike
hands in pledge is safe.

16 A kindhearted woman gains
respect,
but ruthless men gain only
wealth.

17 A kind man benefits himself,
but a cruel man brings
himself harm.

18 The wicked man earns
deceptive wages,
but he who sows
righteousness reaps a sure
reward.

19 The truly righteous man
attains life,
but he who pursues evil
goes to his death.

20 The LORD detests men of
perverse heart
but he delights in those
whose ways are
blameless.

21 Be sure of this: The wicked
will not go unpunished,
but those who are righteous
will go free.

22 Like a gold ring in a pig's
snout
is a beautiful woman who
shows no discretion.

23 The desire of the righteous
ends only in good,
but the hope of the wicked
only in wrath.

24 One man gives freely, yet
gains even more;
another withholds unduly,
but comes to poverty.

25 A generous man will prosper;
he who refreshes others will
himself be refreshed.

26 People curse the man who
hoards grain,
but blessing crowns him
who is willing to sell.

טוֹב יְבַקֵּשׁ רָצוֹן וְדֹרֵשׁ רָעָה תְבוֹאֶנּוּ׃
she-will-come-to-him evil but-one-searching-for good-will he-finds good

(28) בּוֹטֵחַ בְּעָשְׁרוֹ הוּא יִפֹּל וְכֶעָלֶה
but-like-the-green-leaf he-will-fall he in-richness-of-him one-trusting (28)

צַדִּיקִים יִפְרָחוּ׃ (29) עוֹכֵר בֵּיתוֹ יִנְחַל־
he-will-inherit family-of-him one-troubling (29) they-will-thrive righteous-ones

רוּחַ וְעֶבֶד אֱוִיל לַחֲכַם־לֵב׃ (30) פְּרִי־צַדִּיק עֵץ חַיִּים
lives tree-of righteous fruit-of (30) heart to-wise-of fool and-servant wind

וְלֹקֵחַ נְפָשׁוֹת* חָכָם׃ (31) הֵן צַדִּיק בָּאָרֶץ יְשֻׁלָּם
he-receives-due on-the-earth righteous if (31) wise souls and-one-winning

אַף כִּי־רָשָׁע וְחוֹטֵא׃ (12:1) אֹהֵב מוּסָר
discipline one-loving (12:1) and-one-sinning ungodly indeed how-much-more

אֹהֵב דָּעַת וְשׂוֹנֵא תוֹכַחַת בָּעַר׃ (2) טוֹב יָפִיק
he-obtains good-man (2) stupid correction but-one-hating knowledge one-loving

רָצוֹן מֵיְהוָה וְאִישׁ מְזִמּוֹת יַרְשִׁיעַ׃ (3) לֹא־
not (3) he-condemns craftinesses but-man-of from-Yahweh favor

יִכּוֹן אָדָם בְּרֶשַׁע וְשֹׁרֶשׁ צַדִּיקִים בַּל־
not righteous-ones but-root-of through-wickedness man he-can-be-established

יִמּוֹט׃ (4) אֵשֶׁת־חַיִל עֲטֶרֶת בַּעְלָהּ וּכְרָקָב
but-like-decay husband-of-her crown-of nobility wife-of (4) he-can-be-moved

בְּעַצְמוֹתָיו מְבִישָׁה׃ (5) מַחְשְׁבוֹת צַדִּיקִים מִשְׁפָּט
just righteous-ones plans-of (5) one-bringing-disgrace in-bones-of-him

תַּחְבֻּלוֹת רְשָׁעִים מִרְמָה׃ (6) דִּבְרֵי רְשָׁעִים אֱרָב־
to-lie-in-wait wicked-ones words-of (6) deceitful wicked-ones advices-of

דָּם וּפִי יְשָׁרִים יַצִּילֵם׃ (7) הָפוֹךְ
to-overthrow (7) he-rescues-them upright-ones but-speech-of blood

רְשָׁעִים וְאֵינָם וּבֵית צַדִּיקִים יַעֲמֹד׃
he-stands-firm righteous-ones but-house-of and-no-more-they wicked-ones

(8) לְפִי־שִׂכְלוֹ יְהֻלַּל־אִישׁ וְנַעֲוֵה־
but-one-being-warped-of man he-is-praised wisdom-of-him as-speech-of (8)

לֵב יִהְיֶה לָבוּז׃ (9) טוֹב נִקְלֶה וְעֶבֶד לוֹ
to-him yet-servant one-being-nobody good (9) for-despising he-is mind

מִמְּתַכַּבֵּד† וַחֲסַר־לָחֶם׃ (10) יוֹדֵעַ
one-caring-for (10) food and-lacking-of more-than-one-pretending-greatness

צַדִּיק נֶפֶשׁ בְּהֶמְתּוֹ וְרַחֲמֵי רְשָׁעִים אַכְזָרִי׃
cruel wicked-ones but-kind-acts-of animal-of-him need-of righteous

(11) עֹבֵד אַדְמָתוֹ יִשְׂבַּע־לָחֶם וּמְרַדֵּף
but-one-chasing food he-will-have-abundance land-of-him one-working (11)

---

27 He who seeks good finds good will,
but evil comes to him who searches for it.

28 Whoever trusts in his riches will fall,
but the righteous will thrive like a green leaf.

29 He who brings trouble on his family will inherit only wind,
and the fool will be servant to the wise.

30 The fruit of the righteous is a tree of life,
and he who wins souls is wise.

31 If the righteous receive their due on earth,
how much more the ungodly and the sinner!

12 Whoever loves discipline loves knowledge,
but he who hates correction is stupid.

2 A good man obtains favor from the LORD,
but the LORD condemns a crafty man.

3 A man cannot be established through wickedness,
but the righteous cannot be uprooted.

4 A wife of noble character is her husband's crown,
but a disgraceful wife is like decay in his bones.

5 The plans of the righteous are just,
but the advice of the wicked is deceitful.

6 The words of the wicked lie in wait for blood,
but the speech of the upright rescues them.

7 Wicked men are overthrown and are no more,
but the house of the righteous stands firm.

8 A man is praised according to his wisdom,
but men with warped minds are despised.

9 Better to be a nobody and yet have a servant
than pretend to be somebody and have no food.

10 A righteous man cares for the needs of his animal,
but the kindest acts of the wicked are cruel.

11 He who works his land will have abundant food,

*30 Most mss have *shin* for *sin* (שׁוֹת—).

†9 Most mss have *hireq* under the *mem* and *sheva* under the *tav* (מִמְּתַ׳).

רֵיקִים חֲסַר־ לֵב׃ (12) חָמַד רָשָׁע מְצוֹד רָעִים
evil-men plunder-of wicked he-desires (12) judgment lacking-of fantasies

וְשֹׁרֶשׁ צַדִּיקִים יִתֵּן׃ (13) בְּפֶשַׁע שְׂפָתַיִם מוֹקֵשׁ
trap-of lips by-sinfulness-of (13) he-flourishes righteous-ones but-root-of

רָע וַיֵּצֵא מִצָּרָה צַדִּיק׃ (14) מִפְּרִי פִי־
lip-of from-fruit-of (14) righteous-man from-trouble but-he-escapes evil-man

אִישׁ יִשְׂבַּע־ טוֹב וּגְמוּל יְדֵי־ אָדָם יָשׁוּב לוֹ׃ (15) דֶּרֶךְ
way-of (15) to-him he-rewards man hands-of and-work-of good he-is-filled man

אֱוִיל יָשָׁר בְּעֵינָיו וְשֹׁמֵעַ לְעֵצָה חָכָם׃ (16) אֱוִיל
fool (16) wise-man to-advice but-one-listening in-eyes-of-him right fool

בַּיּוֹם יִוָּדַע כַּעְסוֹ וְכֹסֶה קָלוֹן עָרוּם׃
prudent-man insult but-one-overlooking annoyance-of-him he-shows in-the-day

(17) יָפִיחַ אֱמוּנָה יַגִּיד צֶדֶק וְעֵד שְׁקָרִים מִרְמָה׃
lie fallacies but-witness-of honesty he-testifies truthfulness he-gives (17)

(18) יֵשׁ בּוֹטֶה כְּמַדְקְרוֹת חָרֶב וּלְשׁוֹן
but-tongue-of sword like-piercings-of one-speaking-recklessly there-is (18)

חֲכָמִים מַרְפֵּא׃ (19) שְׂפַת־ אֱמֶת תִּכּוֹן לָעַד וְעַד־
but-while to-forever she-endures truth lip-of (19) healing wise-men

אַרְגִּיעָה לְשׁוֹן שָׁקֶר׃ (20) מִרְמָה בְּלֶב־ חֹרְשֵׁי רָע
evil ones-plotting-of in-heart-of deceit (20) lie tongue-of I-make-momentary

וּלְיֹעֲצֵי שָׁלוֹם שִׂמְחָה׃ (21) לֹא־ יְאֻנֶּה לַצַּדִּיק
to-the-righteous-one he-befalls not (21) joy peace but-to-ones-promoting-of

כָּל־ אָוֶן וּרְשָׁעִים מָלְאוּ רָע׃ (22) תּוֹעֲבַת יְהוָה
Yahweh detesting-of (22) trouble they-are-filled but-wicked-ones harm any-of

שִׂפְתֵי־שָׁקֶר וְעֹשֵׂי אֱמוּנָה רְצוֹנוֹ׃ (23) אָדָם עָרוּם כֹּסֶה
keeping prudent man (23) delight-of-him truth but-ones-doing-of lie lips-of

דָּעַת וְלֵב כְּסִילִים יִקְרָא אִוֶּלֶת׃ (24) יַד־ חָרוּצִים
diligent-ones hand-of (24) folly he-blurts-out fools but-heart-of knowledge

תִּמְשׁוֹל וּרְמִיָּה תִּהְיֶה לָמַס׃ (25) דְּאָגָה בְלֶב־
in-heart-of anxiety (25) in-slave-labor she-ends but-laziness she-will-rule

אִישׁ יַשְׁחֶנָּה וְדָבָר טוֹב יְשַׂמְּחֶנָּה׃ (26) יָתֵר
he-is-cautious (26) he-cheers-her kind but-word he-weighs-down-her man

מֵרֵעֵהוּ צַדִּיק וְדֶרֶךְ רְשָׁעִים תַּתְעֵם׃
she-leads-astray-them wicked-ones but-way-of righteous with-friend-of-him

(27) לֹא־ יַחֲרֹךְ רְמִיָּה צֵידוֹ וְהוֹן־ אָדָם יָקָר חָרוּץ׃
diligent prized man but-possession-of game-of-him lazy-man he-roasts not (27)

(28) בְּאֹרַח־ צְדָקָה חַיִּים וְדֶרֶךְ נְתִיבָה אַל־מָוֶת׃ (13:1) בֵּן חָכָם
wise son (13:1) death no path and-way-of lives righteousness in-way-of (28)

but he who chases fantasies
lacks judgment.

12The wicked desire the plunder
of evil men,
but the root of the righteous
flourishes.

13An evil man is trapped by his
sinful talk,
but a righteous man escapes
trouble.

14From the fruit of his lips a
man is filled with good
things
as surely as the work of his
hands rewards him.

15The way of a fool seems right
to him,
but a wise man listens to
advice.

16A fool shows his annoyance at
once,
but a prudent man overlooks
an insult.

17A truthful witness gives
honest testimony,
but a false witness tells lies.

18Reckless words pierce like a
sword,
but the tongue of the wise
brings healing.

19Truthful lips endure forever,
but a lying tongue lasts only
a moment.

20There is deceit in the hearts of
those who plot evil,
but joy for those who
promote peace.

21No harm befalls the righteous,
but the wicked have their
fill of trouble.

22The LORD detests lying lips,
but he delights in men who
are truthful.

23A prudent man keeps his
knowledge to himself,
but the heart of fools blurts
out folly.

24Diligent hands will rule,
but laziness ends in slave
labor.

25An anxious heart weighs a
man down,
but a kind word cheers him
up.

26A righteous man is cautious in
friendship,[v]
but the way of the wicked
leads them astray.

27The lazy man does not roast[w]
his game,
but the diligent man prizes
his possessions.

28In the way of righteousness
there is life;
along that path is
immortality.

v26 Or *man is a guide to his neighbor*
w27 The meaning of the Hebrew for this word is uncertain.

o14 ק ישיב

מוּסַר אָב וְלֵץ לֹא־שָׁמַע גְּעָרָה׃ מִפְּרִי
from-fruit-of (2) rebuke he-listens not but-one-mocking father instruction-of

פִּי־אִישׁ יֹאכַל טוֹב וְנֶפֶשׁ בֹּגְדִים חָמָס׃
violence ones-being-unfaithful but-craving-of good he-enjoys man lip-of

נֹצֵר פִּיו שֹׁמֵר נַפְשׁוֹ פֹּשֵׂק
one-opening-wide soul-of-him one-guarding lip-of-him one-guarding (3)

שְׂפָתָיו מְחִתָּה־לוֹ׃ מִתְאַוָּה וָאַיִן נַפְשׁוֹ עָצֵל
sluggard desire-of-him and-nothing one-craving (4) to-him ruin lips-of-him

וְנֶפֶשׁ חָרֻצִים תְּדֻשָּׁן׃ דְּבַר־שֶׁקֶר יִשְׂנָא
he-hates falsehood thing-of (5) she-is-satisfied diligent-ones but-desire-of

צַדִּיק וְרָשָׁע יַבְאִישׁ וְיַחְפִּיר׃ צְדָקָה
righteousness (6) and-he-brings-disgrace he-brings-shame but-wicked righteous

תִּצֹּר תָּם־דָּרֶךְ וְרִשְׁעָה תְּסַלֵּף חַטָּאת׃ יֵשׁ
there-is (7) sinner she-overthrows but-wickedness way integrity-of she-guards

מִתְעַשֵּׁר וְאֵין כֹּל מִתְרוֹשֵׁשׁ וְהוֹן רָב׃
great yet-wealth one-pretending-poverty anything yet-not one-pretending-wealth

כֹּפֶר נֶפֶשׁ־אִישׁ עָשְׁרוֹ וְרָשׁ לֹא־שָׁמַע
he-hears not but-one-being-poor wealth-of-him man life-of ransom-of (8)

גְּעָרָה׃ אוֹר־צַדִּיקִים יִשְׂמָח וְנֵר רְשָׁעִים
wicked-ones but-lamp-of he-shines righteous-ones light-of (9) threat

יִדְעָךְ׃ רַק־בְּזָדוֹן יִתֵּן מַצָּה וְאֶת־
but-in quarrel he-breeds by-pride only (10) he-is-snuffed-out

נוֹעָצִים חָכְמָה׃ הוֹן מֵהֶבֶל יִמְעָט
he-dwindles-away from-dishonesty money (11) wisdom ones-taking-advice

וְקֹבֵץ עַל־יָד יַרְבֶּה׃ תּוֹחֶלֶת מְמֻשָּׁכָה מַחֲלָה־
making-sick being-deferred hope (12) he-makes-grow hand by but-one-gathering

לֵב וְעֵץ חַיִּים תַּאֲוָה בָאָה׃ בָּז לְדָבָר
to-instruction one-scorning (13) being-fulfilled longing lives but-tree-of heart

יֵחָבֶל לוֹ וִירֵא מִצְוָה הוּא יְשֻׁלָּם׃
he-will-be-rewarded he command but-one-respecting-of for-him he-will-pay

תּוֹרַת חָכָם מְקוֹר חַיִּים לָסוּר מִמֹּקְשֵׁי מָוֶת׃
death from-snares-of to-turn lives fountain-of wise teaching-of (14)

שֵׂכֶל־טוֹב יִתֶּן־חֵן וְדֶרֶךְ בֹּגְדִים אֵיתָן׃
hard ones-being-unfaithful but-way-of favor he-wins good understanding (15)

כָּל־עָרוּם יַעֲשֶׂה בְדָעַת וּכְסִיל יִפְרֹשׂ אִוֶּלֶת׃
folly he-exposes but-fool from-knowledge he-acts prudent-man every-of (16)

מַלְאָךְ רָשָׁע יִפֹּל בְּרָע וְצִיר אֱמוּנִים מַרְפֵּא׃
healing trusts but-envoy-of into-trouble he-falls wicked messenger (17)

13 A wise son heeds his father's instruction,
but a mocker does not listen to rebuke.

2 From the fruit of his lips a man enjoys good things,
but the unfaithful have a craving for violence.

3 He who guards his lips guards his soul,
but he who speaks rashly will come to ruin.

4 The sluggard craves and gets nothing,
but the desires of the diligent are fully satisfied.

5 The righteous hate what is false,
but the wicked bring shame and disgrace.

6 Righteousness guards the man of integrity,
but wickedness overthrows the sinner.

7 One man pretends to be rich, yet has nothing;
another pretends to be poor, yet has great wealth.

8 A man's riches may ransom his life,
but a poor man hears no threat.

9 The light of the righteous shines brightly,
but the lamp of the wicked is snuffed out.

10 Pride only breeds quarrels,
but wisdom is found in those who take advice.

11 Dishonest money dwindles away,
but he who gathers money little by little makes it grow.

12 Hope deferred makes the heart sick,
but a longing fulfilled is a tree of life.

13 He who scorns instruction will pay for it,
but he who respects a command is rewarded.

14 The teaching of the wise is a fountain of life,
turning a man from the snares of death.

15 Good understanding wins favor,
but the way of the unfaithful is hard.[x]

16 Every prudent man acts out of knowledge,
but a fool exposes his folly.

17 A wicked messenger falls into trouble,
but a trustworthy envoy brings healing.

x15 Or *unfaithful does not endure*

רֵישׁ וְקָלוֹן פּוֹרֵעַ מוּסָר וְשׁוֹמֵר תּוֹכַחַת
correction but-one-heeding discipline one-ignoring and-shame poverty (18)

יְכֻבָּד׃ תַּאֲוָה נִהְיָה תֶּעֱרַב לְנָפֶשׁ
to-soul she-is-sweet being-fulfilled longing (19) he-is-honored

וְתוֹעֲבַת כְּסִילִים סוּר מֵרָע׃ הָלוֹךְ אֶת־ חֲכָמִים
wise-men with one-walking (20) from-evil to-turn fools but-detesting-of

וְחָכָם וְרֹעֶה כְסִילִים יֵרוֹעַ׃ חַטָּאִים
sinners (21) he-suffers-harm fools but-one-being-companion he-grows-wise

תְּרַדֵּף רָעָה וְאֶת־ צַדִּיקִים יְשַׁלֶּם־ טוֹב׃ טוֹב
good-man (22) prosperity he-rewards righteous-ones but misfortune she-pursues

יַנְחִיל בְּנֵי־ בָנִים וְצָפוּן לַצַּדִּיק
for-the-righteous but-one-being-stored children children-of he-leaves-inheritance

חֵיל חוֹטֵא׃ רָב־ אֹכֶל נִיר רָאשִׁים
men-being-poor field-of food abundance-of (23) one-sinning wealth-of

וְיֵשׁ נִסְפֶּה בְּלֹא מִשְׁפָּט׃ חוֹשֵׂךְ שִׁבְטוֹ
rod-of-him one-sparing (24) justice by-not being-swept-away but-there-is

שׂוֹנֵא בְנוֹ וְאֹהֲבוֹ שִׁחֲרוֹ מוּסָר׃
discipline he-is-careful-about-him but-one-loving-him son-of-him one-hating

צַדִּיק אֹכֵל לְשֹׂבַע נַפְשׁוֹ וּבֶטֶן רְשָׁעִים
wicked-ones but-stomach-of heart-of-him to-contentment-of eating righteous (25)

תֶּחְסָר׃ חַכְמוֹת נָשִׁים בָּנְתָה בֵיתָהּ וְאִוֶּלֶת
but-foolish house-of-her she-builds women wise-ones (14:1) she-goes-hungry

בְּיָדֶיהָ תֶהֶרְסֶנּוּ׃ הוֹלֵךְ בְּיָשְׁרוֹ
in-uprightness-of-him one-walking (2) she-tears-down-him with-hands-of-her

יְרֵא יְהוָה וּנְלוֹז דְּרָכָיו בּוֹזֵהוּ׃
one-despising-him ways-of-him but-one-being-devious-of Yahweh one-fearing-of

בְּפִי־ אֱוִיל חֹטֶר גַּאֲוָה וְשִׂפְתֵי חֲכָמִים תִּשְׁמוּרֵם׃
she-protects-them wise-ones but-lips-of back rod-of fool by-talk-of (3)

בְּאֵין אֲלָפִים אֵבוּס בָּר וְרָב־ תְּבוּאוֹת בְּכֹחַ
from-strength-of harvests but-abundance-of empty manger oxen when-no (4)

שׁוֹר׃ עֵד אֱמוּנִים לֹא יְכַזֵּב וְיָפִיחַ כְּזָבִים עֵד
witness-of lies but-he-pours-out he-deceives not truths witness-of (5) ox

שָׁקֶר׃ בִּקֶּשׁ־ לֵץ חָכְמָה וָאָיִן וְדַעַת
but-knowledge and-there-is-none wisdom one-mocking he-seeks (6) falsehood

לְנָבוֹן נָקָל׃ לֵךְ מִנֶּגֶד לְאִישׁ כְּסִיל
foolish to-man from-near stay-away! (7) he-comes-easily to-one-discerning

וּבַל־ יָדַעְתָּ שִׂפְתֵי־ דָעַת׃ חָכְמַת עָרוּם הָבִין
he-gives-thought prudent wisdom-of (8) knowledge lips-of you-will-find for-not

[18]He who ignores discipline
comes to poverty and
shame,
but whoever heeds
correction is honored.

[19]A longing fulfilled is sweet to
the soul,
but fools detest turning from
evil.

[20]He who walks with the wise
grows wise,
but a companion of fools
suffers harm.

[21]Misfortune pursues the sinner,
but prosperity is the reward
of the righteous.

[22]A good man leaves an
inheritance for his
children's children,
but a sinner's wealth is
stored up for the
righteous.

[23]A poor man's field may
produce abundant food,
but injustice sweeps it away.

[24]He who spares the rod hates
his son,
but he who loves him is
careful to discipline him.

[25]The righteous eat to their
hearts' content,
but the stomach of the
wicked goes hungry.

14 The wise woman builds
her house,
but with her own hands the
foolish one tears hers
down.

[2]He whose walk is upright fears
the LORD,
but he whose ways are
devious despises him.

[3]A fool's talk brings a rod to his
back,
but the lips of the wise
protect them.

[4]Where there are no oxen, the
manger is empty,
but from the strength of an
ox comes an abundant
harvest.

[5]A truthful witness does not
deceive,
but a false witness pours out
lies.

[6]The mocker seeks wisdom and
finds none,
but knowledge comes easily
to the discerning.

[7]Stay away from a foolish man,
for you will not find
knowledge on his lips.

[8]The wisdom of the prudent is
to give thought to their

20a ק הלך
20b ק יחכם

דַּרְכּוֹ וְאִוֶּלֶת כְּסִילִים מִרְמָה׃ אֱוִלִים יָלִיץ אָשָׁם
amends-for-sin he-mocks fools (9) deception fools but-folly-of way-of-him

וּבֵין יְשָׁרִים רָצוֹן׃ לֵב יוֹדֵעַ מָרַּת נַפְשׁוֹ
self-of-him bitterness-of knowing heart (10) good-will upright-ones but-among

וּבְשִׂמְחָתוֹ לֹא־ יִתְעָרַב זָר׃ בֵּית
house-of (11) one-being-stranger he-will-share not and-in-joy-of-him

רְשָׁעִים יִשָּׁמֵד וְאֹהֶל יְשָׁרִים יַפְרִיחַ׃
he-will-flourish upright-ones but-tent-of he-will-be-destroyed wicked-ones

יֵשׁ דֶּרֶךְ יָשָׁר לִפְנֵי־ אִישׁ וְאַחֲרִיתָהּ דַּרְכֵי־ מָוֶת׃ גַּם־
even (13) death ways-of but-end-of-her man before right way there-is (12)

בִּשְׂחוֹק יִכְאַב־ לֵב וְאַחֲרִיתָהּ* שִׂמְחָה תוּגָה׃ מִדְּרָכָיו
for-ways-of-him (14) grief joy and-end-of-her heart he-may-ache in-laughter

יִשְׂבַּע סוּג לֵב וּמֵעָלָיו אִישׁ טוֹב׃
good man and-for-with-him heart one-being-faithless-of he-will-be-repaid

פֶּתִי יַאֲמִין לְכָל־ דָּבָר וְעָרוּם יָבִין
he-gives-thought but-prudent-man thing to-any-of he-believes simple-man (15)

לַאֲשֻׁרוֹ׃ חָכָם יָרֵא וְסָר מֵרָע וּכְסִיל
but-fool from-evil and-shunning fearing wise-man (16) to-step-of-him

מִתְעַבֵּר וּבוֹטֵחַ׃ קְצַר־ אַפַּיִם יַעֲשֶׂה אִוֶּלֶת
folly he-does tempers quickness-of (17) and-being-reckless being-hotheaded

וְאִישׁ מְזִמּוֹת יִשָּׂנֵא׃ נָחֲלוּ פְתָאיִם אִוֶּלֶת
folly simple-ones they-inherit (18) he-is-hated craftinesses and-man-of

וַעֲרוּמִים יַכְתִּרוּ דָעַת׃ שַׁחוּ רָעִים
evil-men they-will-bow (19) knowledge they-crown but-prudent-ones

לִפְנֵי טוֹבִים וּרְשָׁעִים עַל־ שַׁעֲרֵי צַדִּיק׃ גַּם־
even (20) righteous gates-of at and-wicked-men good-men in-presences-of

לְרֵעֵהוּ יִשָּׂנֵא רָשׁ וְאֹהֲבֵי
but-ones-being-friends-of one-being-poor he-is-shunned by-neighbor-of-him

עָשִׁיר רַבִּים׃ בָּז־ לְרֵעֵהוּ חוֹטֵא וּמְחוֹנֵן
but-one-being-kind sinning to-neighbor-of-him one-despising (21) many rich

עֲנָיִים° אַשְׁרָיו׃ הֲלוֹא־ יִתְעוּ חֹרְשֵׁי רָע
evil ones-plotting-of they-go-astray not? (22) blessednesses-of-him needy-ones

וְחֶסֶד וֶאֱמֶת חֹרְשֵׁי טוֹב׃ בְּכָל־ עֶצֶב
hard-work by-all-of (23) good ones-planning-of and-faithfulness but-love

יִהְיֶה מוֹתָר וּדְבַר־ שְׂפָתַיִם אַךְ־ לְמַחְסוֹר׃ עֲטֶרֶת חֲכָמִים
wise-ones crown-of (24) to-poverty only lips but-talk-of profit he-comes

עָשְׁרָם אִוֶּלֶת כְּסִילִים אִוֶּלֶת׃ מַצִּיל נְפָשׁוֹת עֵד אֱמֶת
truth witness-of lives one-saving (25) folly fools folly-of wealth-of-them

ways,
but the folly of fools is deception.

9 Fools mock at making amends for sin,
but good will is found among the upright.

10 Each heart knows its own bitterness,
and no one else can share its joy.

11 The house of the wicked will be destroyed,
but the tent of the upright will flourish.

12 There is a way that seems right to a man,
but in the end it leads to death.

13 Even in laughter the heart may ache,
and joy may end in grief.

14 The faithless will be fully repaid for their ways,
and the good man rewarded for his.

15 A simple man believes anything,
but a prudent man gives thought to his steps.

16 A wise man fears the LORD and shuns evil,
but a fool is hotheaded and reckless.

17 A quick-tempered man does foolish things,
and a crafty man is hated.

18 The simple inherit folly,
but the prudent are crowned with knowledge.

19 Evil men will bow down in the presence of the good,
and the wicked at the gates of the righteous.

20 The poor are shunned even by their neighbors,
but the rich have many friends.

21 He who despises his neighbor sins,
but blessed is he who is kind to the needy.

22 Do not those who plot evil go astray?
But those who plan what is good find[y] love and faithfulness.

23 All hard work brings a profit,
but mere talk leads only to poverty.

24 The wealth of the wise is their crown,
but the folly of fools yields folly.

25 A truthful witness saves lives,

[y]22 Or *show*

*13 Most mss have the accent *rebia* on the final syllable (תָ֗הּ–).

°21 ק ענוים

וְיָפִחַ כְּזָבִים מִרְמָה׃ בְּיִרְאַת יְהוָה מִבְטַח־
security-of Yahweh in-fear-of (26) deceitful falsehoods but-he-witnesses

עֹז וּלְבָנָיו יִהְיֶה מַחְסֶה׃ יִרְאַת יְהוָה
Yahweh fear-of (27) refuge he-will-be and-for-children-of-him fortress

מְקוֹר חַיִּים לָסוּר מִמֹּקְשֵׁי מָוֶת׃ בְּרָב־ עָם
population in-largeness-of (28) death from-snares-of to-turn lives fountain-of

הַדְרַת־ מֶלֶךְ וּבְאֶפֶס לְאֹם מְחִתַּת רָזוֹן׃ אֶרֶךְ אַפַּיִם
angers long-of (29) prince ruin-of subject but-in-without king glory-of

רַב־ תְּבוּנָה וּקְצַר־ רוּחַ מֵרִים אִוֶּלֶת׃ חַיֵּי
lives-of (30) folly one-displaying temper but-quick-of understanding great-of

בְשָׂרִים לֵב מַרְפֵּא וּרְקַב עֲצָמוֹת קִנְאָה׃ עֹשֵׁק־ דָּל
poor one-oppressing (31) envy bones but-rot-of peace heart-of bodies

חֵרֵף עֹשֵׂהוּ וּמְכַבְּדוֹ חֹנֵן אֶבְיוֹן׃
needy one-being-kind but-honoring-him One-Making-him he-shows-contempt

בְּרָעָתוֹ יִדָּחֶה רָשָׁע וְחֹסֶה
but-one-having-refuge wicked he-is-brought-down in-calamity-of-him (32)

בְמוֹתוֹ צַדִּיק׃ בְּלֵב נָבוֹן תָּנוּחַ חָכְמָה
wisdom she-reposes one-discerning in-heart-of (33) righteous in-death-of-him

וּבְקֶרֶב כְּסִילִים תִּוָּדֵעַ׃ צְדָקָה תְּרוֹמֵם־
she-exalts righteousness (34) she-lets-herself-be-known fools even-in-among

גּוֹי וְחֶסֶד לְאֻמִּים חַטָּאת׃ רְצוֹן־ מֶלֶךְ לְעֶבֶד מַשְׂכִּיל
being-wise in-servant king delight-of (35) sin peoples but-disgrace-of nation

וְעֶבְרָתוֹ תִּהְיֶה מֵבִישׁ׃ מַעֲנֶה־ רַּךְ יָשִׁיב
he-turns-away gentle answer (15:1) one-bringing-shame she-is but-wrath-of-him

חֵמָה וּדְבַר־ עֶצֶב יַעֲלֶה־ אָף׃ לְשׁוֹן חֲכָמִים
wise-ones tongue-of (2) anger he-stirs-up harshness but-word-of wrath

תֵּיטִיב דָּעַת וּפִי כְסִילִים יַבִּיעַ אִוֶּלֶת׃ בְּכָל־
at-every-of (3) folly he-gushes fools but-mouth-of knowledge she-commends

מָקוֹם עֵינֵי יְהוָה צֹפוֹת רָעִים וטוֹבִים*׃ מַרְפֵּא
healing-of (4) and-good-ones wicked-ones ones-watching Yahweh eyes-of place

לָשׁוֹן עֵץ חַיִּים וְסֶלֶף בָּהּ שֶׁבֶר בְּרוּחַ׃ אֱוִיל יִנְאַץ
he-spurns fool (5) to-spirit crushing in-her but-deceit lives tree-of tongue

מוּסַר אָבִיו וְשֹׁמֵר תּוֹכַחַת יַעְרִם׃
he-shows-prudence correction but-one-heeding father-of-him discipline-of

בֵּית צַדִּיק חֹסֶן רָב וּבִתְבוּאַת רָשָׁע
wicked but-in-income-of great treasure righteous house-of (6)

נֶעְכָּרֶת׃ שִׂפְתֵי חֲכָמִים יְזָרוּ דָעַת וְלֵב
but-heart-of knowledge they-spread wise-ones lips-of (7) one-bringing-trouble

but a false witness is
deceitful.

26 He who fears the LORD has a
secure fortress,
and for his children it will
be a refuge.

27 The fear of the LORD is a
fountain of life,
turning a man from the
snares of death.

28 A large population is a king's
glory,
but without subjects a
prince is ruined.

29 A patient man has great
understanding,
but a quick-tempered man
displays folly.

30 A heart at peace gives life to
the body,
but envy rots the bones.

31 He who oppresses the poor
shows contempt for their
Maker,
but whoever is kind to the
needy honors God.

32 When calamity comes, the
wicked are brought down,
but even in death the
righteous have a refuge.

33 Wisdom reposes in the heart
of the discerning
and even among fools she
lets herself be known.[z]

34 Righteousness exalts a nation,
but sin is a disgrace to any
people.

35 A king delights in a wise
servant,
but a shameful servant
incurs his wrath.

15 A gentle answer turns
away wrath,
but a harsh word stirs up
anger.

2 The tongue of the wise
commends knowledge,
but the mouth of the fool
gushes folly.

3 The eyes of the LORD are
everywhere,
keeping watch on the
wicked and the good.

4 The tongue that brings healing
is a tree of life,
but a deceitful tongue
crushes the spirit.

5 A fool spurns his father's
discipline,
but whoever heeds
correction shows
prudence.

6 The house of the righteous
contains great treasure,
but the income of the
wicked brings them
trouble.

7 The lips of the wise spread
knowledge;

z33 Hebrew; Septuagint and Syriac / *but in the heart of fools she is not known*

*3 Most mss have *sheva* under the *vav* (וְט).

כְּסִילִים לֹא־כֵן׃ זֶבַח רְשָׁעִים תּוֹעֲבַת יְהוָה וּתְפִלַּת
but-prayer-of Yahweh detesting-of wicked-ones sacrifice-of (8) so not fools

יְשָׁרִים רְצוֹנוֹ׃ תּוֹעֲבַת יְהוָה דֶּרֶךְ רָשָׁע
wicked way-of Yahweh detesting-of (9) pleasure-of-him upright-ones

וּמְרַדֵּף צְדָקָה יֶאֱהָב׃ מוּסָר רָע לְעֹזֵב
for-one-leaving stern discipline (10) he-loves righteousness but-one-pursuing

אֹרַח שׂוֹנֵא תוֹכַחַת יָמוּת׃ שְׁאוֹל וַאֲבַדּוֹן נֶגֶד יְהוָה
Yahweh before and-Abaddon Sheol (11) he-will-die correction one-hating path

אַף כִּי־לִבּוֹת בְּנֵי־אָדָם׃ לֹא יֶאֱהַב־לֵץ
one-mocking he-loves not (12) man sons-of hearts-of indeed how-much-more

הוֹכֵחַ לוֹ אֶל־חֲכָמִים לֹא יֵלֵךְ׃ לֵב שָׂמֵחַ יֵיטִב
he-cheers happy heart (13) he-will-go not wise-ones to to-him to-correct

פָּנִים וּבְעַצְּבַת־לֵב רוּחַ נְכֵאָה׃ לֵב נָבוֹן יְבַקֶּשׁ־
he-seeks one-discerning heart (14) crushed spirit heart but-in-ache-of faces

דָּעַת וּפְנֵי° כְסִילִים יִרְעֶה אִוֶּלֶת׃ כָּל־יְמֵי עָנִי
oppressed days-of all-of (15) folly he-feeds-on fools but-mouth-of knowledge

רָעִים וְטוֹב־לֵב מִשְׁתֶּה תָמִיד׃ טוֹב־מְעַט
little good (16) continual feast heart but-cheerfulness-of wretched-ones

בְּיִרְאַת יְהוָה מֵאוֹצָר רָב וּמְהוּמָה בוֹ׃ טוֹב
good (17) with-him and-turmoil great more-than-wealth Yahweh with-fear-of

אֲרֻחַת יָרָק וְאַהֲבָה־שָׁם מִשּׁוֹר אָבוּס וְשִׂנְאָה־
and-hatred one-being-fattened more-than-calf there and-love vegetable meal-of

בוֹ׃ אִישׁ חֵמָה יְגָרֶה מָדוֹן וְאֶרֶךְ* אַפַּיִם
angers but-long-of dissension he-stirs-up hot-temper man-of (18) with-him

יַשְׁקִיט רִיב׃ דֶּרֶךְ עָצֵל כִּמְשֻׂכַת חָדֶק וְאֹרַח
but-path-of thorn like-blocking-of sluggard way-of (19) quarrel he-calms

יְשָׁרִים סְלֻלָה׃ בֵּן חָכָם יְשַׂמַּח־אָב וּכְסִיל
but-fool-of father he-brings-joy wise son (20) one-being-highway upright-ones

אָדָם בּוֹזֶה אִמּוֹ׃ אִוֶּלֶת שִׂמְחָה לַחֲסַר־לֵב
judgment to-lacking-of delight folly (21) mother-of-him one-despising man

וְאִישׁ תְּבוּנָה יְיַשֶּׁר־לָכֶת׃ הָפֵר מַחֲשָׁבוֹת
plans he-fails (22) to-go he-keeps-straight understanding but-man-of

בְּאֵין סוֹד וּבְרֹב יוֹעֲצִים תָּקוּם׃ שִׂמְחָה
joy (23) she-succeeds ones-advising but-with-many-of counsel for-lack-of

לָאִישׁ בְּמַעֲנֵה־פִיו וְדָבָר בְּעִתּוֹ מַה־טּוֹב׃
good how! in-time-of-him and-word mouth-of-him with-reply-of to-the-man

אֹרַח חַיִּים לְמַעְלָה לְמַשְׂכִּיל לְמַעַן סוּר מִשְּׁאוֹל
from-Sheol to-keep in-order-to for-one-being-wise to-upward lives path-of (24)

not so the hearts of fools.

8 The LORD detests the sacrifice
of the wicked,
but the prayer of the upright
pleases him.

9 The LORD detests the way of
the wicked
but he loves those who
pursue righteousness.

10 Stern discipline awaits him
who leaves the path;
he who hates correction will
die.

11 Death and Destruction[a] lie
open before the LORD—
how much more the hearts
of men!

12 A mocker resents correction;
he will not consult the wise.

13 A happy heart makes the face
cheerful,
but heartache crushes the
spirit.

14 The discerning heart seeks
knowledge,
but the mouth of a fool
feeds on folly.

15 All the days of the oppressed
are wretched,
but the cheerful heart has a
continual feast.

16 Better a little with the fear of
the LORD
than great wealth with
turmoil.

17 Better a meal of vegetables
where there is love
than a fattened calf with
hatred.

18 A hot-tempered man stirs up
dissension,
but a patient man calms a
quarrel.

19 The way of the sluggard is
blocked with thorns,
but the path of the upright
is a highway.

20 A wise son brings joy to his
father,
but a foolish man despises
his mother.

21 Folly delights a man who lacks
judgment,
but a man of understanding
keeps a straight course.

22 Plans fail for lack of counsel,
but with many advisers they
succeed.

23 A man finds joy in giving an
apt reply—
and how good is a timely
word!

24 The path of life leads upward
for the wise
to keep him from going
down to the grave.[b]

[a] *11* Hebrew *Sheol and Abaddon*
[b] *24* Hebrew *Sheol*

***18 Most mss have *sheva* in the *kaph* (ךְ—).**

°*14* ק ופי

מָטָּה׃ בֵּית גֵּאִים יִסַּח יְהוָה וְיַצֵּב
but-he-keeps-intact Yahweh he-tears-down proud-men house-of (25) downward

גְּבוּל אַלְמָנָה׃ תּוֹעֲבַת יְהוָה מַחְשְׁבוֹת רָע וּטְהֹרִים
but-pure-ones wicked thoughts-of Yahweh detesting-of (26) widow boundary-of

אִמְרֵי־נֹעַם׃ עֹכֵר בֵּיתוֹ בּוֹצֵעַ בָּצַע
greed one-being-greedy family-of-him one-troubling (27) pleasing thoughts-of

וְשׂוֹנֵא מַתָּנֹת יִחְיֶה׃ לֵב צַדִּיק יֶהְגֶּה
he-weighs righteous heart-of (28) he-will-live bribes but-one-hating

לַעֲנוֹת וּפִי רְשָׁעִים יַבִּיעַ רָעוֹת׃ רָחוֹק יְהוָה
Yahweh far (29) evils he-gushes wicked-ones but-mouth-of to-answer

מֵרְשָׁעִים וּתְפִלַּת צַדִּיקִים יִשְׁמָע׃ מְאוֹר־עֵינַיִם
eyes brightness-of (30) he-hears righteous-ones but-prayer-of from-wicked-ones

יְשַׂמַּח־לֵב שְׁמוּעָה טוֹבָה תְּדַשֶּׁן־עָצֶם׃ אֹזֶן שֹׁמַעַת
hearing-of ear (31) bone she-gives-health good news heart he-brings-joy

תּוֹכַחַת חַיִּים בְּקֶרֶב חֲכָמִים תָּלִין׃ פּוֹרֵעַ
one-ignoring (32) she-will-be-at-home wise-ones in-among lives rebuke-of

מוּסָר מוֹאֵס נַפְשׁוֹ וְשׁוֹמֵעַ תּוֹכַחַת קוֹנֶה
gaining correction but-one-heeding self-of-him despising discipline

לֵב׃ יִרְאַת יְהוָה מוּסַר חָכְמָה וְלִפְנֵי כָבוֹד
honor and-before wisdom teaching-of Yahweh fear-of (33) understanding

עֲנָוָה׃ לְאָדָם מַעַרְכֵי־לֵב וּמֵיְהוָה מַעֲנֵה לָשׁוֹן׃
tongue reply-of but-from-Yahweh heart plans-of to-man (16:1) humility

כָּל־דַּרְכֵי־אִישׁ זַךְ בְּעֵינָיו וְתֹכֵן רוּחוֹת
motives but-one-weighing in-eyes-of-him innocent man ways-of all-of (2)

יְהוָה׃ גֹּל אֶל־יְהוָה מַעֲשֶׂיךָ וְיִכֹּנוּ מַחְשְׁבֹתֶיךָ׃
plans-of-you and-they-will-succeed deeds-of-you Yahweh to commit! (3) Yahweh

כֹּל פָּעַל יְהוָה לַמַּעֲנֵהוּ וְגַם־רָשָׁע
wicked and-even for-the-end-of-him Yahweh he-works-out everything (4)

לְיוֹם רָעָה׃ תּוֹעֲבַת יְהוָה כָּל־גְּבַהּ־לֵב יָד
hand heart proud-of all-of Yahweh detesting-of (5) disaster for-day-of

לְיָד לֹא יִנָּקֶה׃ בְּחֶסֶד וֶאֱמֶת
and-faithfulness through-love (6) he-will-go-unpunished not upon-hand

יְכֻפַּר עָוֺן וּבְיִרְאַת יְהוָה סוּר מֵרָע׃
from-evil to-avoid Yahweh and-through-fear-of sin he-is-atoned

בִּרְצוֹת יְהוָה דַּרְכֵי־אִישׁ גַּם־אוֹיְבָיו
ones-being-enemies-of-him even man ways-of Yahweh when-to-please (7)

יַשְׁלִם אִתּוֹ׃ טוֹב־מְעַט בִּצְדָקָה מֵרֹב
more-than-much-of with-righteousness little good (8) with-him he-makes-at-peace

25The LORD tears down the proud man's house
but he keeps the widow's boundaries intact.
26The LORD detests the thoughts of the wicked,
but those of the pure are pleasing to him.
27A greedy man brings trouble to his family,
but he who hates bribes will live.
28The heart of the righteous weighs its answers,
but the mouth of the wicked gushes evil.
29The LORD is far from the wicked
but he hears the prayer of the righteous.
30A cheerful look brings joy to the heart,
and good news gives health to the bones.
31He who listens to a life-giving rebuke
will be at home among the wise.
32He who ignores discipline despises himself,
but whoever heeds correction gains understanding.
33The fear of the LORD teaches a man wisdom,[c]
and humility comes before honor.

16 To man belong the plans of the heart,
but from the LORD comes the reply of the tongue.
2All a man's ways seem innocent to him,
but motives are weighed by the LORD.
3Commit to the LORD whatever you do,
and your plans will succeed.
4The LORD works out everything for his own ends—
even the wicked for a day of disaster.
5The LORD detests all the proud of heart.
Be sure of this: They will not go unpunished.
6Through love and faithfulness sin is atoned for;
through the fear of the LORD a man avoids evil.
7When a man's ways are pleasing to the LORD,
he makes even his enemies live at peace with him.
8Better a little with righteousness

c33 Or *Wisdom teaches the fear of the LORD*

***31 Most mss have the accent *munah* on the first syllable (אָ֣).**

תְּבוּאוֹת בְּלֹא מִשְׁפָּט׃ לֵב אָדָם יְחַשֵּׁב דַּרְכּוֹ וַיהוָה
but-Yahweh course-of-him he-plans man heart-of (9) justice with-no gains

יָכִין צַעֲדוֹ׃ קֶסֶם ׀ עַל־ שִׂפְתֵי־ מֶלֶךְ בְּמִשְׁפָּט לֹא
not to-justice king lips-of on oracle (10) step-of-him he-determines

יִמְעַל־ פִּיו׃ פֶּלֶס ׀ וּמֹאזְנֵי מִשְׁפָּט לַיהוָה
from-Yahweh honesty and-balances-of scale (11) mouth-of-him he-should-betray

מַעֲשֵׂהוּ כָּל־ אַבְנֵי־ כִיס׃ תּוֹעֲבַת מְלָכִים עֲשׂוֹת רֶשַׁע
wrong to-do kings detesting-of (12) bag weights-of all-of making-of-him

כִּי בִצְדָקָה יִכּוֹן כִּסֵּא׃ רְצוֹן מְלָכִים
kings pleasure-of (13) throne he-is-established through-righteousness for

שִׂפְתֵי־ צֶדֶק וְדֹבֵר יְשָׁרִים יֶאֱהָב׃ חֲמַת־ מֶלֶךְ
king wrath-of (14) he-values truths and-one-speaking honesty lips-of

מַלְאֲכֵי־ מָוֶת וְאִישׁ חָכָם יְכַפְּרֶנָּה׃ בְּאוֹר־
when-to-brighten (15) he-will-appease-her wise but-man death messengers-of

פְּנֵי־ מֶלֶךְ חַיִּים וּרְצוֹנוֹ כְּעָב מַלְקוֹשׁ׃ קְנֹה־
get! (16) spring-rain like-cloud-of and-favor-of-him lives king faces-of

חָכְמָה מַה־ טּוֹב מֵחָרוּץ וּקְנוֹת בִּינָה נִבְחָר
one-being-choice understanding and-to-get more-than-gold good how! wisdom

מִכָּסֶף׃ מְסִלַּת יְשָׁרִים סוּר מֵרָע שֹׁמֵר
guarding from-evil to-avoid upright-ones highway-of (17) more-than-silver

נַפְשׁוֹ נֹצֵר דַּרְכּוֹ׃ לִפְנֵי־ שֶׁבֶר גָּאוֹן וְלִפְנֵי
and-before pride destruction before (18) way-of-him one-guarding soul-of-him

כִשָּׁלוֹן גֹּבַהּ רוּחַ׃ טוֹב שְׁפַל־ רוּחַ אֶת־ עֲנָיִים°
oppressed-ones among spirit lowliness-of good (19) spirit haughtiness-of fall

מֵחַלֵּק שָׁלָל אֶת־ גֵּאִים׃ מַשְׂכִּיל עַל־ דָּבָר
instruction to one-heeding (20) proud-ones with plunder more-than-to-share

יִמְצָא־ טוֹב וּבוֹטֵחַ בַּיהוָה אַשְׁרָיו׃
blessednesses-of-him in-Yahweh and-one-trusting prosperity he-finds

לַחֲכַם־ לֵב יִקָּרֵא נָבוֹן וּמֶתֶק שְׂפָתַיִם
lips and-pleasantness-of one-discerning he-is-called heart to-wise-of (21)

יֹסִיף לֶקַח׃ מְקוֹר חַיִּים שֵׂכֶל בְּעָלָיו
owners-of-him understanding-of lives fountain-of (22) instruction he-promotes

וּמוּסַר אֱוִלִים אִוֶּלֶת׃ לֵב חָכָם יַשְׂכִּיל פִּיהוּ
mouth-of-him he-guides wise-man heart-of (23) folly fools but-punishment-of

וְעַל־ שְׂפָתָיו יֹסִיף לֶקַח׃ צוּף־ דְּבַשׁ אִמְרֵי־
words-of honey honeycomb-of (24) instruction he-promotes lips-of-him and-on

נֹעַם מָתוֹק לַנֶּפֶשׁ וּמַרְפֵּא לָעָצֶם׃ יֵשׁ דֶּרֶךְ
way there-is (25) to-the-bone and-healing to-the-soul sweet pleasantness

°19 ק ענוים

than much gain with
injustice.

9 In his heart a man plans his
course,
but the LORD determines his
steps.

10 The lips of a king speak as an
oracle,
and his mouth should not
betray justice.

11 Honest scales and balances are
from the LORD;
all the weights in the bag
are of his making.

12 Kings detest wrongdoing,
for a throne is established
through righteousness.

13 Kings take pleasure in honest
lips;
they value a man who
speaks the truth.

14 A king's wrath is a messenger
of death,
but a wise man will appease
it.

15 When a king's face brightens,
it means life;
his favor is like a rain cloud
in spring.

16 How much better to get
wisdom than gold,
to choose understanding
rather than silver!

17 The highway of the upright
avoids evil;
he who guards his way
guards his soul.

18 Pride goes before destruction,
a haughty spirit before a
fall.

19 Better to be lowly in spirit and
among the oppressed
than to share plunder with
the proud.

20 Whoever gives heed to
instruction prospers,
and blessed is he who trusts
in the LORD.

21 The wise in heart are called
discerning,
and pleasant words promote
instruction.[d]

22 Understanding is a fountain of
life to those who have it,
but folly brings punishment
to fools.

23 A wise man's heart guides his
mouth, .
and his lips promote
instruction.[e]

24 Pleasant words are a
honeycomb,
sweet to the soul and
healing to the bones.

25 There is a way that seems

[d] 21 Or *words make a man persuasive*
[e] 23 Or *mouth / and makes his lips persuasive*

יָשָׁר לִפְנֵי־ אִישׁ וְאַחֲרִיתָהּ דַּרְכֵי־ מָוֶת׃ נֶפֶשׁ עָמֵל
laborer appetite-of (26) death ways-of but-end-of-her man before right

עָמְלָה לּוֹ כִּי־ אָכַף עָלָיו פִּיהוּ׃ אִישׁ בְּלִיַּעַל
scoundrel man (27) hunger-of-him to-him she-drives indeed for-him she-works

כֹּרֶה רָעָה וְעַל־ שְׂפָתָיו כְּאֵשׁ צָרָבֶת׃ אִישׁ
man-of (28) scorching like-fire lip-of-him and-on evil one-plotting

תַּהְפֻּכוֹת יְשַׁלַּח מָדוֹן וְנִרְגָּן מַפְרִיד אַלּוּף׃
friend separating and-one-gossiping dissension he-stirs-up perversities

אִישׁ חָמָס יְפַתֶּה רֵעֵהוּ וְהוֹלִיכוֹ בְּדֶרֶךְ
down-path and-he-leads-him neighbor-of-him he-entices violence man-of (29)

לֹא־ טוֹב׃ עֹצֶה עֵינָיו לַחְשֹׁב תַּהְפֻּכוֹת קֹרֵץ
one-pursing perversities to-plot eyes-of-him one-winking (30) good not

שְׂפָתָיו כִּלָּה רָעָה׃ עֲטֶרֶת תִּפְאֶרֶת שֵׂיבָה בְּדֶרֶךְ
by-life-of gray-hair splendor crown-of (31) evil he-is-bent-on lips-of-him

צְדָקָה תִּמָּצֵא׃ טוֹב אֶרֶךְ אַפַּיִם מִגִּבּוֹר
more-than-warrior angers long-of good (32) she-is-attained righteousness

וּמֹשֵׁל בְּרוּחוֹ מִלֹּכֵד עִיר׃ בַּחֵיק
into-the-lap (33) city more-than-one-taking over-temper-of-him and-one-controlling

יוּטַל אֶת־ הַגּוֹרָל וּמֵיְהוָה כָּל־ מִשְׁפָּטוֹ׃ טוֹב
good (17:1) decision-of-him every-of but-from-Yahweh the-lot *** he-is-cast

פַּת חֲרֵבָה וְשַׁלְוָה־ בָהּ מִבַּיִת מָלֵא זִבְחֵי־ רִיב׃
strife sacrifices-of full more-than-house with-her and-quiet dry crust

עֶבֶד־ מַשְׂכִּיל יִמְשֹׁל בְּבֵן מֵבִישׁ
one-bringing-disgrace over-son he-will-rule one-being-wise servant (2)

וּבְתוֹךְ אַחִים יַחֲלֹק נַחֲלָה׃ מַצְרֵף לַכֶּסֶף
for-the-silver crucible (3) inheritance he-will-share brothers and-in-among

וְכוּר לַזָּהָב וּבֹחֵן לִבּוֹת יְהוָה׃ מֵרַע
man-being-wicked (4) Yahweh hearts but-testing for-the-gold and-furnace

מַקְשִׁיב עַל־ שְׂפַת־ אָוֶן שֶׁקֶר מֵזִין עַל־ לְשׁוֹן הַוֺּת׃
malices tongue-of to paying-attention liar evil lip-of to listening

לֹעֵג לָרָשׁ חֵרֵף עֹשֵׂהוּ
One-Making-him he-shows-contempt to-the-one-being-poor one-mocking (5)

שָׂמֵחַ לְאֵיד לֹא יִנָּקֶה׃ עֲטֶרֶת זְקֵנִים
aged-ones crown-of (6) he-will-go-unpunished not over-disaster gloater

בְּנֵי בָנִים וְתִפְאֶרֶת בָּנִים אֲבוֹתָם׃ לֹא־ נָאוָה
suitable not (7) parents-of-them children and-pride-of children children-of

לְנָבָל שְׂפַת־ יֶתֶר אַף כִּי־ לְנָדִיב שְׂפַת־שָׁקֶר׃ אֶבֶן־
stone-of (8) lie lip-of to-ruler indeed how-much-more arrogance lip-of to-fool

°27 ק שפתו

right to a man
but in the end it leads to
death.

26 The laborer's appetite works
for him;
his hunger drives him on.

27 A scoundrel plots evil,
and his speech is like a
scorching fire.

28 A perverse man stirs up
dissension,
and a gossip separates close
friends.

29 A violent man entices his
neighbor
and leads him down a path
that is not good.

30 He who winks with his eye is
plotting perversity;
he who purses his lips is
bent on evil.

31 Gray hair is a crown of
splendor;
it is attained by a righteous
life.

32 Better a patient man than a
warrior,
a man who controls his
temper than one who
takes a city.

33 The lot is cast into the lap,
but its every decision is
from the LORD.

17 Better a dry crust with
peace and quiet
than a house full of
feasting,[f] with strife.

2 A wise servant will rule over a
disgraceful son,
and will share the
inheritance as one of the
brothers.

3 The crucible for silver and the
furnace for gold,
but the LORD tests the heart.

4 A wicked man listens to evil
lips;
a liar pays attention to a
malicious tongue.

5 He who mocks the poor shows
contempt for their Maker;
whoever gloats over disaster
will not go unpunished.

6 Children's children are a
crown to the aged,
and parents are the pride of
their children.

7 Arrogant[g] lips are unsuited to
a fool—
how much worse lying lips
to a ruler!

f1 Hebrew *sacrifices*
g7 Or *Eloquent*

חֵן הַשֹּׁחַד בְּעֵינֵי בְעָלָיו אֶל־ כָּל־ אֲשֶׁר יִפְנֶה
he-turns that everywhere to givers-of-him in-eyes-of the-bribe charm

יַשְׂכִּיל׃ מְכַסֶּה־ פֶּשַׁע מְבַקֵּשׁ אַהֲבָה וְשֹׁנֶה
but-one-repeating love promoting offense one-covering (9) he-succeeds

בְדָבָר מַפְרִיד אַלּוּף׃ תֵּחַת גְּעָרָה בְמֵבִין
to-man-discerning rebuke she-impresses (10) friend separating about-matter

מֵהַכּוֹת כְּסִיל מֵאָה׃ אַךְ־ מְרִי יְבַקֶּשׁ־ רָע
evil-man he-is-bent-on rebellion only (11) hundred fool more-than-to-lash

וּמַלְאָךְ אַכְזָרִי יְשֻׁלַּח־ בּוֹ׃ פָּגוֹשׁ דֹּב שַׁכּוּל
one-robbed bear to-meet (12) to-him he-will-be-sent merciless and-official

בְּאִישׁ וְאַל־ כְּסִיל בְּאִוַּלְתּוֹ׃ מֵשִׁיב רָעָה תַּחַת טוֹבָה
good for evil one-paying-back (13) in-folly-of-him fool and-not of-cub

לֹא־ תָמִישׁ רָעָה מִבֵּיתוֹ׃ פּוֹטֵר מַיִם רֵאשִׁית
start-of waters breaching-of (14) from-house-of-him evil she-will-leave not

מָדוֹן וְלִפְנֵי הִתְגַּלַּע הָרִיב נְטוֹשׁ׃ מַצְדִּיק רָשָׁע
guilty one-acquitting (15) drop! the-dispute he-breaks-out so-before quarrel

וּמַרְשִׁיעַ צַדִּיק תּוֹעֲבַת יְהוָה גַּם־ שְׁנֵיהֶם׃
both-of-them indeed Yahweh detesting-of innocent and-one-condemning

לָמָּה־ זֶּה מְחִיר בְּיַד־ כְּסִיל לִקְנוֹת חָכְמָה וְלֶב־ אָיִן׃
nothing since-desire-of wisdom to-get fool in-hand-of money this what? (16)

בְּכָל־ עֵת אֹהֵב הָרֵעַ וְאָח לְצָרָה יִוָּלֵד׃
he-is-born for-adversity and-brother the-friend loving time at-all-of (17)

אָדָם חֲסַר־ לֵב תּוֹקֵעַ כָּף עֹרֵב
one-putting-up-security hand one-striking judgment lacking-of man (18)

עֲרֻבָּה לִפְנֵי רֵעֵהוּ׃ אֹהֵב פֶּשַׁע אֹהֵב מַצָּה מַגְבִּיהַּ
one-making-high quarrel one-loving sin loving (19) neighbor-of-him for security

פִּתְחוֹ מְבַקֶּשׁ־ שָׁבֶר׃ עִקֶּשׁ־ לֵב לֹא יִמְצָא־
he-finds not heart perverse-of (20) destruction inviting gate-of-him

טוֹב וְנֶהְפָּךְ בִּלְשׁוֹנוֹ יִפּוֹל בְּרָעָה׃
into-trouble he-falls in-tongue-of-him and-one-being-deceitful prosperity

יֹלֵד כְּסִיל לְתוּגָה לוֹ וְלֹא־ יִשְׂמַח אֲבִי נָבָל׃
fool father-of he-has-joy and-not of-him to-grief fool one-bearing (21)

לֵב שָׂמֵחַ יֵיטִב גֵּהָה וְרוּחַ נְכֵאָה תְּיַבֶּשׁ־
she-dries-up crushed but-spirit medicine he-makes-good cheerful heart (22)

גָּרֶם׃ שֹׁחַד מֵחֵיק רָשָׁע יִקָּח לְהַטּוֹת אָרְחוֹת מִשְׁפָּט׃
justice courses-of to-pervert he-accepts wicked-man in-secret bribe (23) bone

אֶת־ פְּנֵי מֵבִין חָכְמָה וְעֵינֵי כְסִיל בִּקְצֵה־ אָרֶץ׃
earth to-end-of fool but-eyes-of wisdom one-discerning faces-of *** (24)

8 A bribe is a charm to the one who gives it;
wherever he turns, he succeeds.

9 He who covers over an offense promotes love,
but whoever repeats the matter separates close friends.

10 A rebuke impresses a man of discernment
more than a hundred lashes a fool.

11 An evil man is bent only on rebellion;
a merciless official will be sent against him.

12 Better to meet a bear robbed of her cubs
than a fool in his folly.

13 If a man pays back evil for good,
evil will never leave his house.

14 Starting a quarrel is like breaching a dam;
so drop the matter before a dispute breaks out.

15 Acquitting the guilty and condemning the innocent—
the LORD detests them both.

16 Of what use is money in the hand of a fool,
since he has no desire to get wisdom?

17 A friend loves at all times,
and a brother is born for adversity.

18 A man lacking in judgment strikes hands in pledge
and puts up security for his neighbor.

19 He who loves a quarrel loves sin;
he who builds a high gate invites destruction.

20 A man of perverse heart does not prosper;
he whose tongue is deceitful falls into trouble.

21 To have a fool for a son brings grief;
there is no joy for the father of a fool.

22 A cheerful heart is good medicine,
but a crushed spirit dries up the bones.

23 A wicked man accepts a bribe in secret
to pervert the course of justice.

24 A discerning man keeps wisdom in view,
but a fool's eyes wander to the ends of the earth.

°13 ק תמוש

כַּעַס לְאָבִיו בֵּן כְּסִיל וּמֶמֶר לְיוֹלַדְתּוֹ׃
to-one-bearing-him and-bitterness foolish son to-father-of-him grief (25)

גַּם עֲנוֹשׁ לַצַּדִּיק לֹא־ טוֹב לְהַכּוֹת נְדִיבִים עַל־ יֹשֶׁר׃
integrity for officials to-flog good not to-the-innocent to-punish also (26)

חוֹשֵׂךְ אֲמָרָיו יוֹדֵעַ דָּעַת וְקַר־° רוּחַ
temper and-even-of knowledge man-knowing words-of-him one-restraining (27)

אִישׁ תְּבוּנָה׃ גַּם אֱוִיל מַחֲרִישׁ חָכָם יֵחָשֵׁב
he-is-thought wise one-keeping-silent fool even (28) understanding man-of

אֹטֵם שְׂפָתָיו נָבוֹן׃ לְתַאֲוָה יְבַקֵּשׁ
he-pursues to-selfishness (18:1) one-discerning lips-of-him one-holding

נִפְרָד בְּכָל־ תּוּשִׁיָּה יִתְגַּלָּע׃ לֹא־
not (2) he-defies sound-judgment against-all-of man-being-unfriendly

יַחְפֹּץ כְּסִיל בִּתְבוּנָה כִּי אִם־ בְּהִתְגַּלּוֹת לִבּוֹ׃
opinion-of-him in-to-air rather but in-understanding fool he-finds-pleasure

בְּבוֹא־ רָשָׁע בָּא גַם־ בּוּז וְעִם־ קָלוֹן חֶרְפָּה׃
disgrace shame and-with contempt also he-comes wickedness when-to-come (3)

מַיִם עֲמֻקִּים דִּבְרֵי פִי־ אִישׁ נַחַל נֹבֵעַ מְקוֹר
fountain-of one-bubbling brook man mouth-of words-of deep-ones waters (4)

חָכְמָה׃ שְׂאֵת פְּנֵי־ רָשָׁע לֹא־ טוֹב לְהַטּוֹת צַדִּיק
innocent to-deprive good not wicked faces-of to-be-partial (5) wisdom

בַּמִּשְׁפָּט׃ שִׂפְתֵי כְסִיל יָבֹאוּ בְרִיב וּפִיו
and-mouth-of-him into-strife they-come fool lips-of (6) of-the-justice

לְמַהֲלֻמוֹת יִקְרָא׃ פִּי־ כְסִיל מְחִתָּה־ לוֹ וּשְׂפָתָיו
and-lips-of-him of-him undoing fool mouth-of (7) he-invites to-beatings

מוֹקֵשׁ נַפְשׁוֹ׃ דִּבְרֵי נִרְגָּן כְּמִתְלַהֲמִים
like-morsels-being-choice one-gossiping words-of (8) soul-of-him snare-of

וְהֵם יָרְדוּ חַדְרֵי־ בָטֶן׃ גַּם מִתְרַפֶּה
one-being-slack also (9) inmost-part chambers-of they-go-down and-they

בִּמְלַאכְתּוֹ אָח הוּא לְבַעַל מַשְׁחִית׃ מִגְדַּל־ עֹז
strength tower-of (10) destruction to-master-of he brother in-work-of-him

שֵׁם יְהוָה בּוֹ־ יָרוּץ צַדִּיק וְנִשְׂגָּב׃ הוֹן
wealth-of (11) and-he-is-safe righteous he-runs to-him Yahweh name-of

עָשִׁיר קִרְיַת עֻזּוֹ וּכְחוֹמָה נִשְׂגָּבָה
one-being-unscalable and-like-wall fortification-of-him city-of rich

בְּמַשְׂכִּיתוֹ׃ לִפְנֵי־ שֶׁבֶר יִגְבַּהּ לֶב־ אִישׁ
man heart-of he-is-proud downfall before (12) in-imagination-of-him

וְלִפְנֵי כָבוֹד עֲנָוָה׃ מֵשִׁיב דָּבָר בְּטֶרֶם יִשְׁמַע אִוֶּלֶת
folly he-listens at-before answer one-giving (13) humility honor but-before

25 A foolish son brings grief to his father and bitterness to the one who bore him.

26 It is not good to punish an innocent man, or to flog officials for their integrity.

27 A man of knowledge uses words with restraint, and a man of understanding is even-tempered.

28 Even a fool is thought wise if he keeps silent, and discerning if he holds his tongue.

18 An unfriendly man pursues selfish ends; he defies all sound judgment.

2 A fool finds no pleasure in understanding but delights in airing his own opinions.

3 When wickedness comes, so does contempt, and with shame comes disgrace.

4 The words of a man's mouth are deep waters, but the fountain of wisdom is a bubbling brook.

5 It is not good to be partial to the wicked or to deprive the innocent of justice.

6 A fool's lips bring him strife, and his mouth invites a beating.

7 A fool's mouth is his undoing, and his lips are a snare to his soul.

8 The words of a gossip are like choice morsels; they go down to a man's inmost parts.

9 One who is slack in his work is brother to one who destroys.

10 The name of the LORD is a strong tower; the righteous run to it and are safe.

11 The wealth of the rich is their fortified city; they imagine it an unscalable wall.

12 Before his downfall a man's heart is proud, but humility comes before honor.

13 He who answers before listening—

°27 ק יקר

הִיא־ לוֹ וּכְלִמָּה׃ (14) רוּחַ־ אִישׁ יְכַלְכֵּל מַחֲלֵהוּ
sickness-of-him he-sustains man spirit-of (14) and-shame to-him that

וְרוּחַ נְכֵאָה מִי יִשָּׂאֶנָּה׃ (15) לֵב נָבוֹן
one-discerning heart-of (15) he-can-bear-her who? crushed but-spirit

יִקְנֶה־ דָּעַת וְאֹזֶן חֲכָמִים תְּבַקֶּשׁ־ דָּעַת׃
knowledge she-seeks-out wise-ones and-ear-of knowledge he-acquires

(16) מַתָּן אָדָם יַרְחִיב לוֹ וְלִפְנֵי גְדֹלִים
great-ones and-into-presences-of for-him he-opens-way man gift-of (16)

יַנְחֶנּוּ׃ (17) צַדִּיק הָרִאשׁוֹן בְּרִיבוֹ יָבֹא־°
until-he-comes with-case-of-him the-first right (17) he-ushers-him

רֵעֵהוּ וַחֲקָרוֹ׃ (18) מִדְיָנִים יַשְׁבִּית הַגּוֹרָל
the-lot he-settles disputes (18) and-he-questions-him another-of-him

וּבֵין עֲצוּמִים יַפְרִיד׃ (19) אָח נִפְשָׁע
one-being-offended brother (19) he-keeps-apart strong-ones and-between

מִקִּרְיַת־ עֹז וּמִדְוָנִים° כִּבְרִיחַ אַרְמוֹן׃
citadel like-bar-of and-disputes fortification more-than-city-of

(20) מִפְּרִי פִי־ אִישׁ תִּשְׂבַּע בִּטְנוֹ תְּבוּאַת
harvest-of stomach-of-him he-is-filled man mouth-of from-fruit-of (20)

שְׂפָתָיו יִשְׂבָּע׃ (21) מָוֶת וְחַיִּים בְּיַד־ לָשׁוֹן
tongue in-power-of and-lives death (21) he-is-satisfied lips-of-him

וְאֹהֲבֶיהָ יֹאכַל פִּרְיָהּ׃ (22) מָצָא אִשָּׁה מָצָא
he-finds wife he-finds (22) fruit-of-her he-will-eat and-ones-loving-her

טוֹב וַיָּפֶק רָצוֹן מֵיְהוָה׃ (23) תַּחֲנוּנִים יְדַבֶּר־
he-speaks pleas-for-mercy (23) from-Yahweh favor and-he-receives good

רָשׁ וְעָשִׁיר יַעֲנֶה עַזּוֹת׃ (24) אִישׁ רֵעִים
companions man-of (24) harsh-things he-answers but-rich man-being-poor

לְהִתְרֹעֵעַ וְיֵשׁ אֹהֵב דָּבֵק מֵאָח׃
more-than-brother he-sticks-close one-being-friend but-there-is to-be-ruined

(19:1) טוֹב־ רָשׁ הוֹלֵךְ בְּתֻמּוֹ
in-blamelessness-of-him one-walking one-being-poor good (19:1)

מֵעִקֵּשׁ שְׂפָתָיו וְהוּא כְסִיל׃ (2) גַּם בְּלֹא־ דַעַת
knowledge with-no also (2) fool and-he lips-of-him more-than-one-perverse-of

נֶפֶשׁ לֹא־ טוֹב וְאָץ בְּרַגְלַיִם חוֹטֵא׃ (3) אִוֶּלֶת אָדָם
man folly-of (3) one-missing-way with-feet or-one-being-hasty good not zeal

תְּסַלֵּף דַּרְכּוֹ וְעַל־ יְהוָה יִזְעַף לִבּוֹ׃ (4) הוֹן
wealth (4) heart-of-him he-rages Yahweh yet-against life-of-him she-ruins

יֹסִיף רֵעִים רַבִּים וְדָל מֵרֵעֵהוּ* יִפָּרֵד׃
he-is-deserted by-friend-of-him but-poor-man many friends he-brings

that is his folly and his shame.

[14]A man's spirit sustains him in sickness,
but a crushed spirit who can bear?

[15]The heart of the discerning acquires knowledge;
the ears of the wise seek it out.

[16]A gift opens the way for the giver
and ushers him into the presence of the great.

[17]The first to present his case seems right,
till another comes forward and questions him.

[18]Casting the lot settles disputes
and keeps strong opponents apart.

[19]An offended brother is more unyielding than a fortified city,
and disputes are like the barred gates of a citadel.

[20]From the fruit of his mouth a man's stomach is filled;
with the harvest from his lips he is satisfied.

[21]The tongue has the power of life and death,
and those who love it will eat its fruit.

[22]He who finds a wife finds what is good
and receives favor from the LORD.

[23]A poor man pleads for mercy,
but a rich man answers harshly.

[24]A man of many companions may come to ruin,
but there is a friend who sticks closer than a brother.

19 Better a poor man whose walk is blameless
than a fool whose lips are perverse.

[2]It is not good to have zeal without knowledge,
nor to be hasty and miss the way.

[3]A man's own folly ruins his life,
yet his heart rages against the LORD.

[4]Wealth brings many friends,
but a poor man's friend deserts him.

*4 Most mss have *sheva* under the *mem* and *tsere* under the *ayin* (מְרֵעֵהוּ).

°17 ק ובא

°19 ק מדינים

עֵד שְׁקָרִים לֹא יִנָּקֶה וְיָפִיחַ כְּזָבִים
lies and-he-pours-out he-will-go-unpunished not falsehoods witness-of (5)

לֹא יִמָּלֵט׃ רַבִּים יְחַלּוּ פְנֵי־ נָדִיב וְכָל־
and-all-of ruler faces-of they-curry-favor many (6) he-will-go-free not

הָרֵעַ לְאִישׁ מַתָּן׃ כָּל אֲחֵי־ רָשׁ שְׂנֵאֻהוּ
they-shun-him man-being-poor relatives-of all-of (7) gift to-man-of the-friend

אַף כִּי מְרֵעֵהוּ רָחֲקוּ מִמֶּנּוּ מְרַדֵּף אֲמָרִים
pleas one-pursuing from-him they-avoid friend-of-him indeed how-much-more

לֹא־הֵמָּה׃ קֹנֶה־ לֵּב אֹהֵב נַפְשׁוֹ שֹׁמֵר תְּבוּנָה
understanding one-cherishing soul-of-him loving wisdom one-getting (8) they not

לִמְצֹא־ טוֹב׃ עֵד שְׁקָרִים לֹא יִנָּקֶה
he-will-go-unpunished not falsehoods witness-of (9) prosperity to-find

וְיָפִיחַ כְּזָבִים יֹאבֵד׃ לֹא־ נָאוֶה לִכְסִיל תַּעֲנוּג
luxury for-fool fitting not (10) he-will-perish lies and-he-pours-out

אַף כִּי־ לְעֶבֶד׀ מְשֹׁל בְּשָׂרִים׃ שֵׂכֶל אָדָם
man wisdom-of (11) over-princes to-rule for-slave indeed how-much-worse

הֶאֱרִיךְ אַפּוֹ וְתִפְאַרְתּוֹ* עֲבֹר עַל־ פָּשַׁע׃
offense by to-overlook and-glory-of-him anger-of-him he-makes-long

נַהַם כַּכְּפִיר זַעַף מֶלֶךְ וּכְטַל עַל־ עֵשֶׂב רְצוֹנוֹ׃
favor-of-him grass on but-like-dew king rage-of like-the-lion roar (12)

הַוֺּת לְאָבִיו בֵּן כְּסִיל וְדֶלֶף טֹרֵד
being-constant and-dripping foolish son to-father-of-him ruins (13)

מִדְיְנֵי אִשָּׁה׃ בַּיִת וָהוֹן נַחֲלַת אָבוֹת וּמֵיְהוָה
but-from-Yahweh parents inheritance-of and-wealth house (14) wife quarrels-of

אִשָּׁה מַשְׂכָּלֶת׃ עַצְלָה תַּפִּיל תַּרְדֵּמָה וְנֶפֶשׁ
but-self-of deep-sleep she-brings-on laziness (15) one-being-prudent wife

רְמִיָּה תִרְעָב׃ שֹׁמֵר מִצְוָה שֹׁמֵר נַפְשׁוֹ
soul-of-him guarding instruction one-obeying (16) she-goes-hungry shiftless-man

בּוֹזֵה דְרָכָיו יוּמָת׃ מַלְוֵה יְהוָה
Yahweh one-lending-of (17) he-will-die ways-of-him one-being-contemptuous-of

חוֹנֵן דָּל וּגְמֻלוֹ יְשַׁלֶּם־ לוֹ׃ יַסֵּר
discipline! (18) to-him he-will-reward and-deed-of-him poor one-being-kind

בִּנְךָ כִּי־ יֵשׁ תִּקְוָה וְאֶל־ הֲמִיתוֹ אַל־ תִּשָּׂא נַפְשֶׁךָ׃
will-of-you you-give not to-kill-him and-in hope there-is for son-of-you

גְּרָל־ חֵמָה נֹשֵׂא עֹנֶשׁ כִּי אִם־ תַּצִּיל וְעוֹד
then-again you-rescue if indeed penalty one-paying temper great-of (19)

תּוֹסִף׃ שְׁמַע עֵצָה וְקַבֵּל מוּסָר לְמַעַן
so-that instruction and-accept! advice listen! (20) you-must-do-again

5 A false witness will not go unpunished,
and he who pours out lies will not go free.

6 Many curry favor with a ruler,
and everyone is the friend of a man who gives gifts.

7 A poor man is shunned by all his relatives—
how much more do his friends avoid him!
Though he pursues them with pleading,
they are nowhere to be found.[h]

8 He who gets wisdom loves his own soul;
he who cherishes understanding prospers.

9 A false witness will not go unpunished,
and he who pours out lies will perish.

10 It is not fitting for a fool to live in luxury—
how much worse for a slave to rule over princes!

11 A man's wisdom gives him patience;
it is to his glory to overlook an offense.

12 A king's rage is like the roar of a lion,
but his favor is like dew on the grass.

13 A foolish son is his father's ruin,
and a quarrelsome wife is like a constant dripping.

14 Houses and wealth are inherited from parents,
but a prudent wife is from the LORD.

15 Laziness brings on deep sleep,
and the shiftless man goes hungry.

16 He who obeys instructions guards his soul,
but he who is contemptuous of his ways will die.

17 He who is kind to the poor lends to the LORD,
and he will reward him for what he has done.

18 Discipline your son, for in that there is hope;
do not be a willing party to his death.

19 A hot-tempered man must pay the penalty;
if you rescue him, you will have to do it again.

20 Listen to advice and accept instruction,

[h] 7 The meaning of the Hebrew for this sentence is uncertain.

*11 Most mss have *sheva* under the *pe* ('פְּ—).

°7 ק לו
°16 ק ימות
°19 ק גדל

תֶּחְכַּם בְּאַחֲרִיתֶךָ׃ רַבּוֹת מַחֲשָׁבוֹת בְּלֶב־ אִישׁ וַעֲצַת
but-purpose-of man in-heart-of plans many (21) in-end-of-you you-will-be-wise

יְהוָה הִיא תָקוּם׃ תַּאֲוַת אָדָם חַסְדּוֹ וְטוֹב־
and-good unfailing-love-of-him man desire-of (22) she-prevails she Yahweh

רָשׁ מֵאִישׁ כָּזָב׃ יִרְאַת יְהוָה לְחַיִּים וְשָׂבֵעַ
then-content to-lives Yahweh fear-of (23) lie more-than-man-of being-poor

יָלִין בַּל־ יִפָּקֶד רָע׃ טָמַן עָצֵל יָדוֹ
hand-of-him sluggard he-buries (24) trouble he-is-touched not he-rests

בַּצַּלָּחַת גַּם־ אֶל־ פִּיהוּ לֹא יְשִׁיבֶנָּה׃ לֵץ
one-mocking (25) he-will-bring-back-her not mouth-of-him to even in-the-dish

תַּכֶּה וּפֶתִי יַעְרִם וְהוֹכִיחַ לְנָבוֹן
to-one-discerning and-rebuke! he-will-learn-prudence and-simple you-flog

יָבִין דָּעַת׃ מְשַׁדֶּד־ אָב יַבְרִיחַ אֵם בֵּן
son mother he-drives-out father one-robbing (26) knowledge he-will-gain

מֵבִישׁ וּמַחְפִּיר׃ חֲדַל־* בְּנִי לִשְׁמֹעַ
to-listen son-of-me stop! (27) and-bringing-disgrace bringing-shame

מוּסָר לִשְׁגּוֹת† מֵאִמְרֵי־ דָעַת׃ עֵד בְּלִיַּעַל
corruptness witness-of (28) knowledge from-words-of to-stray instruction

יָלִיץ מִשְׁפָּט וּפִי רְשָׁעִים יְבַלַּע־ אָוֶן׃
evil he-gulps-down wicked-ones and-mouth-of justice he-mocks

נָכוֹנוּ לַלֵּצִים שְׁפָטִים וּמַהֲלֻמוֹת לְגֵו
for-back-of and-beatings penalties for-the-ones-mocking they-are-prepared (29)

כְּסִילִים׃ לֵץ הַיַּיִן†† הֹמֶה שֵׁכָר וְכָל־
and-every-of beer one-brawling the-wine one-mocking (20:1) fools

שֹׁגֶה בּוֹ לֹא יֶחְכָּם׃ נַהַם כַּכְּפִיר אֵימַת
wrath-of like-the-lion roar (2) he-is-wise not by-him one-being-led-astray

מֶלֶךְ מִתְעַבְּרוֹ חוֹטֵא נַפְשׁוֹ׃ כָּבוֹד לָאִישׁ שֶׁבֶת
avoidance to-man honor (3) life-of-him forfeiting one-angering-him king

מֵרִיב וְכָל־ אֱוִיל יִתְגַּלָּע׃ מֵחֹרֶף עָצֵל לֹא־ יַחֲרֹשׁ
he-plows not sluggard in-season (4) he-quarrels fool but-every-of from-strife

יִשְׁאַל° בַּקָּצִיר וָאָיִן׃ מַיִם עֲמֻקִּים עֵצָה
purpose deep-ones waters (5) but-nothing at-the-harvest so-he-looks

בְלֶב־ אִישׁ וְאִישׁ תְּבוּנָה יִדְלֶנָּה׃ רָב־ אָדָם
man many-of (6) he-draws-out-her understanding but-man-of man of-heart-of

יִקְרָא אִישׁ חַסְדּוֹ וְאִישׁ אֱמוּנִים מִי
who? faithfulnesses but-man-of unfailing-love-of-him man-of he-claims

יִמְצָא׃ מִתְהַלֵּךְ בְּתֻמּוֹ צַדִּיק אַשְׁרֵי
blessednesses-of righteous in-blamelessness-of-him one-walking (7) he-can-find

and in the end you will be wise.

21 Many are the plans in a man's heart,
but it is the LORD's purpose that prevails.

22 What a man desires is unfailing love[i];
better to be poor than a liar.

23 The fear of the LORD leads to life:
Then one rests content, untouched by trouble.

24 The sluggard buries his hand in the dish;
he will not even bring it back to his mouth!

25 Flog a mocker, and the simple will learn prudence;
rebuke a discerning man, and he will gain knowledge.

26 He who robs his father and drives out his mother
is a son who brings shame and disgrace.

27 Stop listening to instruction, my son,
and you will stray from the words of knowledge.

28 A corrupt witness mocks at justice,
and the mouth of the wicked gulps down evil.

29 Penalties are prepared for mockers,
and beatings for the backs of fools.

20 Wine is a mocker and beer a brawler;
whoever is led astray by them is not wise.

2 A king's wrath is like the roar of a lion;
he who angers him forfeits his life.

3 It is to a man's honor to avoid strife,
but every fool is quick to quarrel.

4 A sluggard does not plow in season;
so at harvest time he looks but finds nothing.

5 The purposes of a man's heart are deep waters,
but a man of understanding draws them out.

6 Many a man claims to have unfailing love,
but a faithful man who can find?

7 The righteous man leads a blameless life;

i22 Or *A man's greed is his shame*

*27 Most mss have *hateph pathah* under the *beth* (חֲ).

†27 Most mss have *dagesh* in the *gimel* (גּ—).

††1 Most mss have *hireq* under the second *yod* (יִן—).

°4 ק ושאל

בָנָיו אַחֲרָיו׃ מֶלֶךְ יוֹשֵׁב עַל־ כִּסֵּא־ דִין

judgment throne-of on sitting king (8) after-him children-of-him

מְזָרֶה בְעֵינָיו כָּל־ רָע׃ מִי־ יֹאמַר

he-can-say who? (9) evil all-of with-eyes-of-him one-winnowing-out

זִכִּיתִי לִבִּי טָהַרְתִּי מֵחַטָּאתִי׃ אֶבֶן וָאֶבֶן

and-weight weight (10) without-sin-of-me I-am-clean heart-of-me I-kept-pure

אֵיפָה וְאֵיפָה תּוֹעֲבַת יְהוָה גַּם־ שְׁנֵיהֶם׃ גַּם

even (11) both-of-them indeed Yahweh detesting-of and-measure measure

בְּמַעֲלָלָיו יִתְנַכֶּר־ נָעַר אִם־ זַךְ וְאִם־ יָשָׁר

right and-whether pure whether child he-is-known by-actions-of-him

פָּעֳלוֹ׃ אֹזֶן שֹׁמַעַת וְעַיִן רֹאָה יְהוָה עָשָׂה גַם־

indeed he-made Yahweh seeing and-eye hearing ear (12) conduct-of-him

שְׁנֵיהֶם׃ אַל־ תֶּאֱהַב שֵׁנָה פֶּן־ תִּוָּרֵשׁ פְּקַח

keep-open! you-will-grow-poor or sleep you-love not (13) both-of-them

עֵינֶיךָ שְׂבַע־ לָחֶם׃ רַע רַע יֹאמַר הַקּוֹנֶה

the-one-buying he-says no-good no-good (14) food have-spare! eyes-of-you

וְאֹזֵל לוֹ אָז יִתְהַלָּל׃ יֵשׁ זָהָב וְרָב־ פְּנִינִים

rubies and-abundance-of gold there-is (15) he-boasts then to-him then-going

וּכְלִי יְקָר שִׂפְתֵי־ דָעַת׃ לְקַח־ בִּגְדוֹ כִּי־

when garment-of-him take! (16) knowledge lips-of rarity but-jewel-of

עָרַב זָר וּבְעַד נָכְרִים° חַבְלֵהוּ׃

hold-in-pledge-him! wayward-woman and-for one-being-stranger he-puts-up-security

עָרֵב לָאִישׁ לֶחֶם שָׁקֶר וְאַחַר יִמָּלֵא־ פִיהוּ

mouth-of-him he-is-full but-afterward fraud food-of to-man sweet (17)

חָצָץ׃ מַחֲשָׁבוֹת בְּעֵצָה תִכּוֹן וּבְתַחְבֻּלוֹת עֲשֵׂה מִלְחָמָה׃

war wage! and-by-guidances you-make by-advice plans (18) gravel

גּוֹלֶה־ סּוֹד הוֹלֵךְ רָכִיל וּלְפֹתֶה שְׂפָתָיו

lips-of-him so-with-one-opening gossip one-spreading confidence betraying (19)

לֹא תִתְעָרָב׃ מְקַלֵּל אָבִיו וְאִמּוֹ

or-mother-of-him father-of-him one-cursing (20) you-share not

יִדְעַךְ נֵרוֹ בֶּאֱשׁוּן° חֹשֶׁךְ׃ נַחֲלָה

inheritance (21) darkness in-deepest-of lamp-of-him he-will-be-snuffed-out

מְבֹחֶלֶת° בָּרִאשֹׁנָה וְאַחֲרִיתָהּ לֹא תְבֹרָךְ׃

she-will-be-blessed not and-end-of-her at-the-beginning being-quickly-gained

אַל־ תֹּאמַר אֲשַׁלְּמָה־ רָע קַוֵּה לַיהוָה וְיֹשַׁע

and-he-will-deliver for-Yahweh wait! wrong I-will-pay-back you-say not (22)

לָךְ׃ תּוֹעֲבַת יְהוָה אֶבֶן וָאָבֶן וּמֹאזְנֵי מִרְמָה

dishonesty and-scales-of and-weight weight Yahweh detesting-of (23) to-you

blessed are his children after him.

8When a king sits on his throne to judge,
he winnows out all evil with his eyes.

9Who can say, "I have kept my heart pure;
I am clean and without sin"?

10Differing weights and differing measures—
the LORD detests them both.

11Even a child is known by his actions,
by whether his conduct is pure and right.

12Ears that hear and eyes that see—
the LORD has made them both.

13Do not love sleep or you will grow poor;
stay awake and you will have food to spare.

14"It's no good, it's no good!" says the buyer;
then off he goes and boasts about his purchase.

15Gold there is, and rubies in abundance,
but lips that speak knowledge are a rare jewel.

16Take the garment of one who puts up security for a stranger;
hold it in pledge if he does it for a wayward woman.

17Food gained by fraud tastes sweet to a man,
but he ends up with a mouth full of gravel.

18Make plans by seeking advice;
if you wage war, obtain guidance.

19A gossip betrays a confidence;
so avoid a man who talks too much.

20If a man curses his father or mother,
his lamp will be snuffed out in pitch darkness.

21An inheritance quickly gained at the beginning
will not be blessed at the end.

22Do not say, "I'll pay you back for this wrong!"
Wait for the LORD, and he will deliver you.

23The LORD detests differing weights,
and dishonest scales do not

°16 ק נכריה
°20 ק באשון
°21 ק מבהלת

לֹא־ טוֹב׃ מֵיְהוָה מִצְעֲדֵי־גָבֶר וְאָדָם מַה־ יָּבִין

can-he-understand how? and-anyone man steps-of from-Yahweh (24) pleasing not

דַּרְכּוֹ׃ מוֹקֵשׁ אָדָם יָלַע קֹדֶשׁ וְאַחַר נְדָרִים

vows and-later dedication he-makes-rash man trap-of (25) way-of-him

לְבַקֵּר׃ מְזָרֶה רְשָׁעִים מֶלֶךְ חָכָם וַיָּשֶׁב

and-he-drives wise king wicked-ones one-winnowing-out (26) to-consider

עֲלֵיהֶם אוֹפָן׃ נֵר יְהוָה נִשְׁמַת אָדָם חֹפֵשׂ

one-searching man spirit-of Yahweh lamp-of (27) threshing-wheel over-them

כָּל־ חַדְרֵי־ בָטֶן׃ חֶסֶד וֶאֱמֶת יִצְּרוּ־ מֶלֶךְ

king they-keep-safe and-faithfulness love (28) inmost-being parts-of all-of

וְסָעַד בַּחֶסֶד כִּסְאוֹ׃ תִּפְאֶרֶת

glory-of (29) throne-of-him through-the-love and-he-is-made-secure

בַּחוּרִים כֹּחָם וַהֲדַר זְקֵנִים שֵׂיבָה׃

gray-hair old-men and-splendor-of strength-of-them the-young-men

חַבֻּרוֹת פֶּצַע תַּמְרִיק בְּרָע וּמַכּוֹת חַדְרֵי־ בָטֶן׃

inmost-being parts-of and-beatings of-evil cleansing wound blows-of (30)

פַּלְגֵי־ מַיִם לֶב־ מֶלֶךְ בְּיַד־ יְהוָה עַל־ כָּל־ אֲשֶׁר

that everywhere to Yahweh in-hand-of king heart-of waters courses-of (21:1)

יַחְפֹּץ יַטֶּנּוּ׃ כָּל־ דֶּרֶךְ־ אִישׁ יָשָׁר בְּעֵינָיו

in-eyes-of-him right man way-of every-of (2) he-directs-him he-pleases

וְתֹכֵן לִבּוֹת יְהוָה׃ עֲשֹׂה צְדָקָה וּמִשְׁפָּט נִבְחָר

being-acceptable and-justice right to-do (3) Yahweh hearts but-one-weighing

לַיהוָה מִזָּבַח׃ רוּם־ עֵינַיִם וּרְחַב־ לֵב

heart and-pride-of eyes haughtiness-of (4) more-than-sacrifice to-Yahweh

נֵר רְשָׁעִים חַטָּאת׃ מַחְשְׁבוֹת חָרוּץ אַךְ־ לְמוֹתָר וְכָל־

and-all-of to-profit surely diligent plans-of (5) sin wicked-ones lamp-of

אָץ אַךְ־ לְמַחְסוֹר׃ פֹּעַל אוֹצָרוֹת בִּלְשׁוֹן שָׁקֶר

lie by-tongue-of fortunes making-of (6) to-poverty surely one-hastening

הֶבֶל נִדָּף מְבַקְשֵׁי־ מָוֶת׃ שֹׁד־ רְשָׁעִים

wicked-ones violence-of (7) death ones-seeking-of one-fleeting vapor

יְגוֹרֵם כִּי מֵאֲנוּ לַעֲשׂוֹת מִשְׁפָּט׃ הֲפַכְפַּךְ דֶּרֶךְ אִישׁ

man way-of devious (8) right to-do they-refuse for he-will-drag-away-them

וָזָר וְזַךְ יָשָׁר פָּעֳלוֹ׃ טוֹב לָשֶׁבֶת עַל־ פִּנַּת־

corner-of on to-live good (9) conduct-of-him upright but-innocent guilty

גָּג מֵאֵשֶׁת מִדְוָנִים וּבֵית חָבֶר׃ נֶפֶשׁ רָשָׁע

wicked self-of (10) sharing and-house-of quarrels more-than-wife-of roof

אִוְּתָה־ רָע לֹא־ יֻחַן בְּעֵינָיו רֵעֵהוּ׃

neighbor-of-him in-eyes-of-him he-gets-mercy not evil she-craves

please him.

24 A man's steps are directed by
the LORD.
How then can anyone
understand his own way?

25 It is a trap for a man to
dedicate something rashly
and only later to consider
his vows.

26 A wise king winnows out the
wicked;
he drives the threshing
wheel over them.

27 The lamp of the LORD searches
the spirit of a man[j];
it searches out his inmost
being.

28 Love and faithfulness keep a
king safe;
through love his throne is
made secure.

29 The glory of young men is
their strength,
gray hair the splendor of the
old.

30 Blows and wounds cleanse
away evil,
and beatings purge the
inmost being.

21 The king's heart is in the
hand of the LORD;
he directs it like a
watercourse wherever he
pleases.

2 All a man's ways seem right to
him,
but the LORD weighs the
heart.

3 To do what is right and just
is more acceptable to the
LORD than sacrifice.

4 Haughty eyes and a proud
heart,
the lamp of the wicked, are
sin!

5 The plans of the diligent lead
to profit
as surely as haste leads to
poverty.

6 A fortune made by a lying
tongue
is a fleeting vapor and a
deadly snare.[k]

7 The violence of the wicked
will drag them away,
for they refuse to do what is
right.

8 The way of the guilty is
devious,
but the conduct of the
innocent is upright.

9 Better to live on a corner of
the roof
than share a house with a
quarrelsome wife.

10 The wicked man craves evil;
his neighbor gets no mercy
from him.

j27 Or *The spirit of man is the LORD's lamp*
k6 Some Hebrew manuscripts, Septuagint and Vulgate; most Hebrew manuscripts *vapor for those who seek death*

°30 ק תמרוק

בַּעְנָשׁ־* לֵץ יֶחְכַּם־ פֶּתִי וּבְהַשְׂכִּיל
and-when-to-instruct simple he-gains-wisdom one-mocking when-to-punish (11)

לְחָכָם יִקַּח־ דָּעַת׃ מַשְׂכִּיל צַדִּיק לְבֵית
of-house-of Righteous-One one-taking-note (12) knowledge he-gets to-wise

רָשָׁע מְסַלֵּף רְשָׁעִים לָרָע׃ אֹטֵם אָזְנוֹ
ear-of-him one-shutting (13) to-ruin wicked-ones one-bringing wicked

מִזַּעֲקַת־ דָּל גַּם־ הוּא יִקְרָא וְלֹא יֵעָנֶה׃ מַתָּן
gift (14) he-will-be-answered and-not he-will-cry-out he also poor to-cry-of

בַּסֵּתֶר יִכְפֶּה־ אָף וְשֹׁחַד בַּחֵק חֵמָה עַזָּה׃ שִׂמְחָה
joy (15) great wrath in-the-cloak and-bribe anger he-soothes in-the-secret

לַצַּדִּיק עֲשׂוֹת מִשְׁפָּט וּמְחִתָּה לְפֹעֲלֵי אָוֶן׃ אָדָם
man (16) evil to-ones-doing-of but-terror justice to-do to-the-righteous

תּוֹעֶה מִדֶּרֶךְ הַשְׂכֵּל בִּקְהַל רְפָאִים יָנוּחַ׃
he-rests dead-ones in-company-of to-understand from-path-of one-straying

אִישׁ מַחְסוֹר אֹהֵב שִׂמְחָה אֹהֵב יַיִן־ וָשֶׁמֶן לֹא
never and-oil wine one-loving pleasure one-loving poverty man-of (17)

יַעֲשִׁיר׃ כֹּפֶר לַצַּדִּיק רָשָׁע וְתַחַת יְשָׁרִים
upright-ones and-for wicked for-the-righteous ransom (18) he-will-be-rich

בּוֹגֵד׃ טוֹב שֶׁבֶת בְּאֶרֶץ־ מִדְבָּר מֵאֵשֶׁת
more-than-wife-of desert in-land-of to-live good (19) one-being-unfaithful

מִדְוָנִים° וָכָעַס׃ אוֹצָר | נֶחְמָד וָשֶׁמֶן בִּנְוֵה חָכָם
wise in-house-of and-oil one-being-choice store (20) and-ill-temper quarrels

וּכְסִיל אָדָם יְבַלְּעֶנּוּ׃ רֹדֵף צְדָקָה וָחָסֶד יִמְצָא
he-finds and-love righteousness one-pursuing (21) he-devours-him man but-fool

חַיִּים צְדָקָה וְכָבוֹד׃ עִיר גִּבֹּרִים עָלָה חָכָם
wise he-attacks mighty-ones city-of (22) and-honor righteousness lives

וַיֹּרֶד עֹז מִבְטֶחָה׃ שֹׁמֵר פִּיו
mouth-of-him one-guarding (23) trust stronghold-of and-he-pulls-down

וּלְשׁוֹנוֹ שֹׁמֵר מִצָּרוֹת נַפְשׁוֹ׃ זֵד
proud (24) self-of-him from-calamities one-keeping and-tongue-of-him

יָהִיר לֵץ שְׁמוֹ עוֹשֶׂה בְּעֶבְרַת זָדוֹן׃
pride with-excess-of one-behaving name-of-him one-mocking arrogant

תַּאֲוַת עָצֵל תְּמִיתֶנּוּ כִּי־ מֵאֲנוּ יָדָיו
hands-of-him they-refuse because she-will-kill-him sluggard craving-of (25)

לַעֲשׂוֹת׃ כָּל־ הַיּוֹם הִתְאַוָּה תַאֲוָה וְצַדִּיק יִתֵּן וְלֹא
and-not he-gives but-righteous craving he-craves the-day all-of (26) to-work

יַחְשֹׂךְ׃ זֶבַח רְשָׁעִים תּוֹעֵבָה אַף כִּי־
when how-much-more detestable wicked-ones sacrifice-of (27) he-spares

11 When a mocker is punished,
the simple gain wisdom;
when a wise man is
instructed, he gets
knowledge.
12 The Righteous One[l] takes note
of the house of the
wicked
and brings the wicked to
ruin.
13 If a man shuts his ears to the
cry of the poor,
he too will cry out and not
be answered.
14 A gift given in secret soothes
anger,
and a bribe concealed in the
cloak pacifies great wrath.
15 When justice is done, it brings
joy to the righteous
but terror to evildoers.
16 A man who strays from the
path of understanding
comes to rest in the
company of the dead.
17 He who loves pleasure will
become poor;
whoever loves wine and oil
will never be rich.
18 The wicked become a ransom
for the righteous,
and the unfaithful for the
upright.
19 Better to live in a desert
than with a quarrelsome
and ill-tempered wife.
20 In the house of the wise are
stores of choice food and
oil,
but a foolish man devours
all he has.
21 He who pursues righteousness
and love
finds life, prosperity[m] and
honor.
22 A wise man attacks the city of
the mighty
and pulls down the
stronghold in which they
trust.
23 He who guards his mouth and
his tongue
keeps himself from calamity.
24 The proud and arrogant
man—"Mocker" is his
name;
he behaves with
overweening pride.
25 The sluggard's craving will be
the death of him,
because his hands refuse to
work.
26 All day long he craves for
more,
but the righteous give
without sparing.
27 The sacrifice of the wicked is
detestable—
how much more so when

[l] *12* Or *The righteous man*
[m] *21* Or *righteousness*

***11* Most mss have *hateph pathah* under the *ayin* (בַּעֲ).**

°*19* ק מדינים

בְזִמָּה יְבִיאֶנּוּ׃ עֵד־ כְּזָבִים יֹאבֵד

he-will-perish falsehoods witness-of (28) he-brings-him with-evil-intent

וְאִישׁ שׁוֹמֵעַ לָנֶצַח יְדַבֵּר׃ הֵעֵז אִישׁ רָשָׁע

wicked man he-makes-bold (29) he-will-speak to-forever listening and-man

בְּפָנָיו וְיָשָׁר הוּא ׀ יָכִין דַּרְכָּיו׃ אֵין

there-is-no (30) way-of-him he-gives-thought he but-upright with-fronts-of-him

חָכְמָה וְאֵין תְּבוּנָה וְאֵין עֵצָה לְנֶגֶד יְהוָה׃

Yahweh at-against plan and-there-is-no insight and-there-is-no wisdom

סוּס מוּכָן לְיוֹם מִלְחָמָה וְלַיהוָה הַתְּשׁוּעָה׃

the-victory but-with-Yahweh battle for-day-of being-made-ready horse (31)

נִבְחָר שֵׁם מֵעֹשֶׁר רָב מִכֶּסֶף

more-than-silver great more-than-richness name one-being-desirable (22:1)

וּמִזָּהָב חֵן טוֹב׃ עָשִׁיר וָרָשׁ נִפְגָּשׁוּ

they-have-in-common and-one-being-poor rich (2) good esteem and-more-than-gold

עֹשֵׂה כֻלָּם יְהוָה׃ עָרוּם ׀ רָאָה רָעָה וְיִסְתָּר

and-he-takes-refuge danger he-sees prudent (3) Yahweh all-of-them One-Making-of

וּפְתָיִים עָבְרוּ וְנֶעֱנָשׁוּ׃ עֵקֶב עֲנָוָה יִרְאַת

and-fear-of humility result-of (4) and-they-suffer they-go-on but-simple-ones

יְהוָה עֹשֶׁר וְכָבוֹד וְחַיִּים׃ צִנִּים פַּחִים בְּדֶרֶךְ עִקֵּשׁ

wicked in-path-of snares thorns (5) and-lives and-honor wealth Yahweh

שׁוֹמֵר נַפְשׁוֹ יִרְחַק מֵהֶם׃ חֲנֹךְ לַנַּעַר עַל־

in to-the-child train! (6) from-them he-stays-far soul-of-him one-guarding

פִּי דַרְכּוֹ גַּם כִּי־ יַזְקִין לֹא־ יָסוּר מִמֶּנָּה׃ עָשִׁיר

rich (7) from-him he-will-turn not he-is-old when and way-of-him according-to

בְּרָשִׁים יִמְשׁוֹל וְעֶבֶד לֹוֶה לְאִישׁ מַלְוֶה׃

one-lending of-man one-borrowing and-servant he-rules over-ones-being-poor

זוֹרֵעַ עַוְלָה יִקְצוֹר־ אָוֶן וְשֵׁבֶט עֶבְרָתוֹ

fury-of-him and-rod-of trouble he-reaps wickedness one-sowing (8)

יִכְלֶה׃ טוֹב־ עַיִן הוּא יְבֹרָךְ כִּי־ נָתַן

he-shares for he-will-be-blessed he eye generous-of (9) he-will-be-destroyed

מִלַּחְמוֹ לַדָּל׃ גָּרֵשׁ לֵץ וְיֵצֵא

and-he-goes-out one-mocking drive-out! (10) with-the-poor from-food-of-him

מָדוֹן וְיִשְׁבֹּת דִּין וְקָלוֹן׃ אֹהֵב טְהוֹר־ לֵב

heart purity-of one-loving (11) and-insult quarrel and-he-ends strife

חֵן שְׂפָתָיו רֵעֵהוּ מֶלֶךְ׃ עֵינֵי יְהוָה נָצְרוּ

they-watch-over Yahweh eyes-of (12) king friend-of-him speeches-of-him grace-of

דַּעַת וַיְסַלֵּף דִּבְרֵי בֹגֵד׃ אָמַר

he-says (13) one-being-unfaithful words-of but-he-frustrates knowledge

---

brought with evil intent!

28 A false witness will perish,
and whoever listens to him
will be destroyed forever.[n]

29 A wicked man puts up a bold
front,
but an upright man gives
thought to his ways.

30 There is no wisdom, no
insight, no plan
that can succeed against the
LORD.

31 The horse is made ready for
the day of battle,
but victory rests with the
LORD.

22 A good name is more
desirable than great
riches;
to be esteemed is better than
silver or gold.

2 Rich and poor have this in
common:
The LORD is the Maker of
them all.

3 A prudent man sees danger
and takes refuge,
but the simple keep going
and suffer for it.

4 Humility and the fear of the
LORD
bring wealth and honor and
life.

5 In the paths of the wicked lie
thorns and snares,
but he who guards his soul
stays far from them.

6 Train a child in the way he
should go,
and when he is old he will
not turn from it.

7 The rich rule over the poor,
and the borrower is servant
to the lender.

8 He who sows wickedness
reaps trouble,
and the rod of his fury will
be destroyed.

9 A generous man will himself
be blessed,
for he shares his food with
the poor.

10 Drive out the mocker, and out
goes strife;
quarrels and insults are
ended.

11 He who loves a pure heart and
whose speech is gracious
will have the king for his
friend.

12 The eyes of the LORD keep
watch over knowledge,
but he frustrates the words
of the unfaithful.

[n]28 Or / *but the words of an obedient man will live on*

°29a ק יבין
°29b ק דרכו
°3 ק ונסתר
°8 ק יקצר
°11 ק טהר

עָצֵל אֲרִי בַחוּץ בְּתוֹךְ רְחֹבוֹת אֵרָצֵחַ׃ שׁוּחָה
pit (14) I-will-be-murdered streets in-midst-of at-the-outside lion sluggard

עֲמֻקָּה פִּי זָרוֹת זְעוּם יְהוָה
Yahweh one-being-under-wrath-of ones-being-adulteresses mouth-of deep

יִפּוֹל־ שָׁם׃ אִוֶּלֶת קְשׁוּרָה בְלֶב־ נָעַר שֵׁבֶט מוּסָר
discipline rod-of child in-heart-of being-bound folly (15) there he-will-fall

יַרְחִיקֶנָּה מִמֶּנּוּ׃ עֹשֵׁק דָּל לְהַרְבּוֹת לוֹ
for-him to-increase poor one-oppressing (16) from-him he-will-drive-far-her

נֹתֵן לְעָשִׁיר אַךְ־ לְמַחְסוֹר׃ הַט אָזְנְךָ וּשְׁמַע
and-listen! ear-of-you pay-attention! (17) to-poverty both to-rich one-giving

דִּבְרֵי חֲכָמִים וְלִבְּךָ תָּשִׁית לְדַעְתִּי׃ כִּי־
for (18) to-teaching-of-me you-apply and-heart-of-you wise-ones sayings-of

נָעִים כִּי־ תִשְׁמְרֵם בְּבִטְנֶךָ יִכֹּנוּ יַחְדָּו עַל־
on all they-are-ready in-heart-of-you you-keep-them when pleasing

שְׂפָתֶיךָ׃ לִהְיוֹת בַּיהוָה מִבְטַחֶךָ הוֹדַעְתִּיךָ הַיּוֹם אַף־אָתָּה׃
you even the-day I-teach-you trust-of-you in-Yahweh to-be (19) lips-of-you

הֲלֹא כָתַבְתִּי לְךָ שָׁלִשׁוֹם בְּמֹעֵצוֹת וָדָעַת׃ לְהוֹדִיעֲךָ
to-teach-you (21) and-knowledge of-counsels thirty to-you I-wrote not? (20)

קֹשְׁטְ אִמְרֵי אֱמֶת לְהָשִׁיב אֲמָרִים אֱמֶת לְשֹׁלְחֶיךָ׃ אַל־
not (22) to-ones-sending-you sound answers to-give reliability words-of truth

תִּגְזָל־ דָּל כִּי דַל־ הוּא וְאַל־ תְּדַכֵּא עָנִי בַשָּׁעַר׃
in-the-court needy you-crush and-not he poor because poor you-exploit

כִּי־ יְהוָה יָרִיב רִיבָם וְקָבַע אֶת־
*** and-he-will-plunder case-of-them he-will-take-case Yahweh for (23)

קֹבְעֵיהֶם נָפֶשׁ׃ אַל־ תִּתְרַע אֶת־ בַּעַל אָף וְאֶת־
and-with hot-temper man-of *** you-befriend not (24) life ones-plundering-them

אִישׁ חֵמוֹת לֹא תָבוֹא׃ פֶּן־ תֶּאֱלַף אֹרְחֹתָו
ways-of-him you-may-learn or (25) you-associate not angers man-of

וְלָקַחְתָּ מוֹקֵשׁ לְנַפְשֶׁךָ׃ אַל־ תְּהִי בְתֹקְעֵי־
among-ones-striking-of you-be not (26) for-self-of-you snare and-you-may-get

כָף בַּעֹרְבִים מַשָּׁאוֹת׃ אִם־ אֵין־ לְךָ לְשַׁלֵּם
to-pay to-you not if (27) debts among-the-ones-putting-up-security hand

לָמָּה יִקַּח מִשְׁכָּבְךָ מִתַּחְתֶּיךָ׃ אַל־ תַּסֵּג
you-move not (28) from-under-you bed-of-you will-he-snatch why?

גְּבוּל עוֹלָם אֲשֶׁר עָשׂוּ אֲבוֹתֶיךָ׃ חָזִיתָ
you-see (29) forefathers-of-you they-set-up that ancient boundary-stone-of

אִישׁ מָהִיר בִּמְלַאכְתּוֹ לִפְנֵי־ מְלָכִים יִתְיַצָּב בַּל־ יִתְיַצֵּב
he-will-serve not he-will-serve kings before in-work-of-him skilled man

13 The sluggard says, "There is a
lion outside!"
or, "I will be murdered in
the streets!"

14 The mouth of an adulteress is
a deep pit;
he who is under the LORD's
wrath will fall into it.

15 Folly is bound up in the heart
of a child,
but the rod of discipline will
drive it far from him.

16 He who oppresses the poor to
increase his wealth
and he who gives gifts to
the rich—both come to
poverty.

*Sayings of the Wise*

17 Pay attention and listen to the
sayings of the wise;
apply your heart to what I
teach,
18 for it is pleasing when you
keep them in your heart
and have all of them ready
on your lips.
19 So that your trust may be in
the LORD,
I teach you today, even you.
20 Have I not written thirty°
sayings for you,
sayings of counsel and
knowledge,
21 teaching you true and reliable
words,
so that you can give sound
answers
to him who sent you?

22 Do not exploit the poor
because they are poor
and do not crush the needy
in court,
23 for the LORD will take up their
case
and will plunder those who
plunder them.

24 Do not make friends with a
hot-tempered man,
do not associate with one
easily angered,
25 or you may learn his ways
and get yourself ensnared.

26 Do not be a man who strikes
hands in pledge
or puts up security for debts;
27 if you lack the means to pay,
your very bed will be
snatched from under you.

28 Do not move an ancient
boundary stone
set up by your forefathers.

29 Do you see a man skilled in
his work?
He will serve before kings;
he will not serve before

°20 Or *not formerly written*; or *not written excellent*

°*15* ק יפל
°*20* ק שלישים
°*25* ק ארחתיו

לִפְנֵי חֲשֻׁכִּים׃ (23:1) כִּֽי־ תֵשֵׁב לִלְחוֹם אֶת־ מוֹשֵׁל בִּין
to-note one-ruling with to-dine you-sit when (23:1) men-being-obscure before

תָּבִין אֶת־ אֲשֶׁר לְפָנֶיךָ׃ (2) וְשַׂמְתָּ שַׂכִּין בְּלֹעֶךָ אִם־
if to-throat-of-you knife and-you-put (2) before-you what *** you-note

בַּעַל נֶפֶשׁ אָתָּה׃ (3) אַל־ תִּתְאָו לְמַטְעַמּוֹתָיו וְהוּא לֶחֶם
food-of for-that to-delicacies-of-him you-crave not (3) you gluttony man-of

כְּזָבִים׃ (4) אַל־ תִּיגַע לְהַעֲשִׁיר מִבִּינָתְךָ
in-wisdom-of-you to-get-rich you-wear-yourself-out not (4) deceits

חֲדָל׃ (5) הֲתָעוּף עֵינֶיךָ בּוֹ וְאֵינֶנּוּ כִּי עָשֹׂה
to-sprout for and-not-he at-him eyes-of-you you-cast? (5) show-restraint!

יַעֲשֶׂה־ לּוֹ כְנָפַיִם כְּנֶשֶׁר וְעָיף הַשָּׁמָיִם׃ (6) אַל־
not (6) the-skies he-will-fly like-eagle wings for-him he-will-sprout

תִּלְחַם אֶת־ לֶחֶם רַע עָיִן וְאַל־ תִּתְאָו לְמַטְעַמֹּתָיו׃
to-delicacies-of-him you-crave and-not eye stingy-of food-of *** you-eat

(7) כִּי ׀ כְּמוֹ־ שָׁעַר בְּנַפְשׁוֹ כֶּן־ הוּא אֱכוֹל וּשְׁתֵה יֹאמַר
he-says and-drink! eat! he so about-cost-of-him he-thinks like for (7)

לָךְ וְלִבּוֹ בַּל־ עִמָּךְ׃ (8) פִּתְּךָ־ אָכַלְתָּ
you-ate little-of-you (8) with-you not but-heart-of-him to-you

תְקִיאֶנָּה וְשִׁחַתָּ דְּבָרֶיךָ הַנְּעִימִים׃
the-good-ones words-of-you and-you-will-waste you-will-vomit-up-her

(9) בְּאָזְנֵי כְסִיל אַל־ תְּדַבֵּר כִּֽי־ יָבוּז לְשֵׂכֶל מִלֶּיךָ׃
words-of-you to-wisdom-of he-will-scorn for you-speak not fool in-ears-of (9)

(10) אַל־ תַּסֵּג גְּבוּל עוֹלָם וּבִשְׂדֵי יְתוֹמִים
fatherless-ones or-into-fields-of ancient boundary-stone-of you-move not (10)

אַל־ תָּבֹא׃ (11) כִּֽי־ גֹאֲלָם חָזָק הוּא־ יָרִיב
he-will-take-up-case he strong One-Defending-them for (11) you-encroach not

אֶת־ רִיבָם אִתָּךְ׃ (12) הָבִיאָה לַמּוּסָר לִבֶּךָ
heart-of-you to-the-instruction apply! (12) against-you case-of-them ***

וְאָזְנֶךָ לְאִמְרֵי־ דָעַת׃ (13) אַל־ תִּמְנַע מִנַּעַר
from-child you-withhold not (13) knowledge to-words-of and-ear-of-you

מוּסָר כִּֽי־ תַכֶּנּוּ בַשֵּׁבֶט לֹא יָמוּת׃ (14) אַתָּה
you (14) he-will-die not with-the-rod you-punish-him if discipline

בַּשֵּׁבֶט תַּכֶּנּוּ וְנַפְשׁוֹ מִשְּׁאוֹל תַּצִּיל׃ (15) בְּנִי
son-of-me (15) you-save from-Sheol and-soul-of-him you-punish-him with-the-rod

אִם־ חָכַם לִבֶּךָ יִשְׂמַח לִבִּי גַם־ אָנִי׃
I also heart-of-me he-will-be-glad heart-of-you he-is-wise if

(16) וְתַעְלֹזְנָה כִלְיוֹתָי בְּדַבֵּר שְׂפָתֶיךָ
lips-of-you when-to-speak inmost-beings-of-me and-they-will-rejoice (16)

obscure men.

23 When you sit to dine with a ruler,
note well what[p] is before you,
[2]and put a knife to your throat
if you are given to gluttony.
[3]Do not crave his delicacies,
for that food is deceptive.

[4]Do not wear yourself out to get rich;
have the wisdom to show restraint.
[5]Cast but a glance at riches,
and they are gone,
for they will surely sprout wings
and fly off to the sky like an eagle.

[6]Do not eat the food of a stingy man,
do not crave his delicacies;
[7]for he is the kind of man
who is always thinking about the cost.[q]
"Eat and drink," he says to you,
but his heart is not with you.
[8]You will vomit up the little you have eaten
and will have wasted your compliments.

[9]Do not speak to a fool,
for he will scorn the wisdom of your words.

[10]Do not move an ancient boundary stone
or encroach on the fields of the fatherless,
[11]for their Defender is strong;
he will take up their case against you.

[12]Apply your heart to instruction
and your ears to words of knowledge.

[13]Do not withhold discipline from a child;
if you punish him with the rod, he will not die.
[14]Punish him with the rod
and save his soul from death.[r]

[15]My son, if your heart is wise,
then my heart will be glad;
[16]my inmost being will rejoice
when your lips speak what

[p]1 Or *who*
[q]7 Or *for as he thinks within himself, / so he is*; or *for as he puts on a feast, / so he is*
[r]14 Hebrew *Sheol*

°3 ק תתאיו
°5a ק התעיף
°5b ק יעוף
°6 ק תתאיו

מֵישָׁרִים׃ (17) אַל־ יְקַנֵּא לִבְּךָ בַּחַטָּאִים כִּי אִם־
rather but to-the-sinners heart-of-you let-him-envy not (17) right-things

בְּיִרְאַת־ יְהוָה כָּל־ הַיּוֹם׃ (18) כִּי אִם־ יֵשׁ אַחֲרִית
future-hope there-is surely indeed (18) the-day all-of Yahweh for-fear-of

וְתִקְוָתְךָ לֹא תִכָּרֵת׃ (19) שְׁמַע־ אַתָּה בְנִי
son-of-me you listen! (19) she-will-be-cut-off not and-hope-of-you

וַחֲכָם וְאַשֵּׁר בַּדֶּרֶךְ לִבֶּךָ׃ (20) אַל־ תְּהִי
you-be not (20) heart-of-you to-the-path and-keep-right! and-be-wise!

בְּסֹבְאֵי־ יָיִן בְּזֹלְלֵי בָשָׂר לָמוֹ׃
for-them meat among-ones-gorging-of wine among-ones-drinking-too-much-of

(21) כִּי־ סֹבֵא וְזוֹלֵל יִוָּרֵשׁ וּקְרָעִים
and-rags he-will-become-poor and-one-being-glutton one-being-drunkard for (21)

תַּלְבִּישׁ נוּמָה׃ (22) שְׁמַע לְאָבִיךָ זֶה יְלָדֶךָ
he-gave-life-you who to-father-of-you listen! (22) drowsiness she-clothes

וְאַל־ תָּבוּז כִּי־ זָקְנָה אִמֶּךָ׃ (23) אֱמֶת קְנֵה וְאַל־
and-not buy! truth (23) mother-of-you she-is-old when you-despise and-not

תִּמְכֹּר חָכְמָה וּמוּסָר וּבִינָה׃ (24) גּוֹל יָגוֹל
he-has-joy to-have-joy (24) and-understanding and-discipline wisdom you-sell

אֲבִי צַדִּיק יוֹלֵד חָכָם וְיִשְׂמַח־ בּוֹ׃
in-him he-delights wise-man and-one-fathering righteous-man father-of

(25) יִשְׂמַח־ אָבִיךָ וְאִמֶּךָ וְתָגֵל
and-may-she-rejoice and-mother-of-you father-of-you may-he-be-glad (25)

יוֹלַדְתֶּךָ׃ (26) תְּנָה־ בְנִי לִבְּךָ לִי וְעֵינֶיךָ
and-eyes-of-you to-me heart-of-you son-of-me give! (26) one-bearing-you

דְּרָכַי תִּרְצֹנָה׃ (27) כִּי־ שׁוּחָה עֲמֻקָּה זוֹנָה וּבְאֵר
and-well one-being-prostitute deep pit for (27) let-them-keep ways-of-me

צָרָה נָכְרִיָּה׃ (28) אַף־ הִיא כְּחֶתֶף תֶּאֱרֹב
she-lies-in-wait like-bandit she also (28) wayward-wife narrow

וּבוֹגְדִים בְּאָדָם תּוֹסִף׃ (29) לְמִי אוֹי
woe to-whom? (29) she-multiplies among-men and-ones-being-unfaithful

לְמִי אֲבוֹי לְמִי מִדְוָנִים ׀ לְמִי שִׂיחַ לְמִי פְּצָעִים חִנָּם
needless bruises to-whom? complaint to-whom? strifes to-whom? sorrow to-whom?

לְמִי חַכְלִלוּת עֵינָיִם׃ (30) לַמְאַחֲרִים עַל־ הַיָּיִן
the-wine over to-the-ones-lingering (30) eyes bloodshot-of to-whom?

לַבָּאִים לַחְקֹר מִמְסָךְ׃ (31) אַל־ תֵּרֶא יַיִן כִּי יִתְאַדָּם
he-is-red when wine you-gaze not (31) mixed-wine to-sample to-the-ones-going

כִּי־ יִתֵּן בַּכִּיס עֵינוֹ יִתְהַלֵּךְ בְּמֵישָׁרִים׃
with-smoothnesses he-goes-down sparkle-of-him in-the-cup he-gives when

is right.

17 Do not let your heart envy sinners,
but always be zealous for the fear of the LORD.
18 There is surely a future hope for you,
and your hope will not be cut off.

19 Listen, my son, and be wise,
and keep your heart on the right path.
20 Do not join those who drink too much wine
or gorge themselves on meat,
21 for drunkards and gluttons become poor,
and drowsiness clothes them in rags.

22 Listen to your father, who gave you life,
and do not despise your mother when she is old.
23 Buy the truth and do not sell it;
get wisdom, discipline and understanding.
24 The father of a righteous man has great joy;
he who has a wise son delights in him.
25 May your father and mother be glad;
may she who gave you birth rejoice!

26 My son, give me your heart
and let your eyes keep to my ways,
27 for a prostitute is a deep pit
and a wayward wife is a narrow well.
28 Like a bandit she lies in wait,
and multiplies the unfaithful among men.

29 Who has woe? Who has sorrow?
Who has strife? Who has complaints?
Who has needless bruises?
Who has bloodshot eyes?
30 Those who linger over wine,
who go to sample bowls of mixed wine.
31 Do not gaze at wine when it is red,
when it sparkles in the cup,
when it goes down smoothly!

°24a ק יגיל °24b ק גיל
°24c ק ויולד °24d ק ישמח
°26 ק תצרנה °29 ק מדינים
°30 ק בכוס

אַחֲרִיתוֹ כְּנָחָשׁ יִשָּׁךְ וּכְצִפְעֹנִי יַפְרִשׁ׃ עֵינֶיךָ
eyes-of-you (33) he-poisons and-like-viper he-bites like-snake end-of-him (32)

יִרְאוּ זָרוֹת וְלִבְּךָ יְדַבֵּר
he-will-imagine and-mind-of-you things-being-strange they-will-see

תַּהְפֻּכוֹת׃ וְהָיִיתָ כְּשֹׁכֵב בְּלֶב־ יָם
sea on-heart-of like-one-sleeping and-you-will-be (34) confusing-things

וּכְשֹׁכֵב בְּרֹאשׁ חִבֵּל׃ הִכּוּנִי בַל־ חָלִיתִי
I-am-hurt not they-hit-me (35) rigging on-top-of and-like-one-lying

הֲלָמוּנִי בַּל־ יָדָעְתִּי מָתַי אָקִיץ אוֹסִיף אֲבַקְשֶׁנּוּ
I-can-find-him I-can-do-again will-I-wake-up when? I-feel not they-beat-me

עוֹד׃ אַל־ תְּקַנֵּא בְּאַנְשֵׁי רָעָה וְאַל־ תִּתְאָו[1] לִהְיוֹת
to-be you-desire and-not wickedness to-men-of you-envy not (24:1) another

אִתָּם׃ כִּי־ שֹׁד יֶהְגֶּה לִבָּם וְעָמָל שִׂפְתֵיהֶם
lips-of-them and-trouble heart-of-them he-plots violence for (2) with-them

תְּדַבֵּרְנָה׃ בְּחָכְמָה יִבָּנֶה בָּיִת וּבִתְבוּנָה
and-through-understanding house he-is-built by-wisdom (3) they-talk

יִתְכּוֹנָן׃ וּבְדַעַת חֲדָרִים יִמָּלְאוּ כָּל־
all-of they-are-filled rooms and-through-knowledge (4) he-is-established

הוֹן יָקָר וְנָעִים׃ גֶּבֶר־חָכָם בַּעוֹז וְאִישׁ־ דַּעַת
knowledge and-man-of in-the-power wise man (5) and-beautiful rare treasure

מְאַמֶּץ־ כֹּחַ׃ כִּי בְתַחְבֻּלוֹת תַּעֲשֶׂה־ לְּךָ מִלְחָמָה וּתְשׁוּעָה
and-victory war for-you you-wage by-guidances for (6) strength increasing

בְּרֹב יוֹעֵץ׃ רָאמוֹת לֶאֱוִיל חָכְמוֹת בַּשַּׁעַר לֹא
not at-the-gate wisdoms for-fool ones-being-high (7) one-advising in-many-of

יִפְתַּח־ פִּיהוּ׃ מְחַשֵּׁב לְהָרֵעַ לוֹ בַּעַל־ מְזִמּוֹת
schemes master-of to-him to-do-evil one-plotting (8) mouth-of-him he-opens

יִקְרָאוּ׃ זִמַּת אִוֶּלֶת חַטָּאת וְתוֹעֲבַת לְאָדָם לֵץ׃
one-mocking to-man and-detesting-of sin folly scheme-of (9) they-will-call

הִתְרַפִּיתָ בְּיוֹם צָרָה צַר כֹּחֶכָה׃ הַצֵּל
rescue! (11) strength-of-you small trouble in-time-of you-falter (10)

לְקֻחִים לַמָּוֶת וּמָטִים לַהֶרֶג אִם־
indeed to-the-slaughter and-ones-staggering to-the-death ones-being-led-away

תַּחְשׂוֹךְ׃ כִּי־ תֹאמַר הֵן לֹא־ יָדַעְנוּ זֶה הֲלֹא־ תֹכֵן לִבּוֹת
hearts one-weighing not? this we-knew not see! you-say if (12) you-hold-back

הוּא־ יָבִין וְנֹצֵר נַפְשְׁךָ הוּא יֵדָע וְהֵשִׁיב
and-he-will-repay he-knows he life-of-you and-one-guarding he-perceives he

לְאָדָם כְּפָעֳלוֹ׃ אֱכָל־ בְּנִי דְבַשׁ כִּי־ טוֹב וְנֹפֶת
and-honey-of-comb good for honey son-of-me eat! (13) as-deed-of-him to-person

[1] ק תתאיו

32In the end it bites like a snake
and poisons like a viper.
33Your eyes will see strange
sights
and your mind imagine
confusing things.
34You will be like one sleeping
on the high seas,
lying on top of the rigging.
35"They hit me," you will say,
"but I'm not hurt!
They beat me, but I don't
feel it!
When will I wake up
so I can find another
drink?"

24 Do not envy wicked men,
do not desire their
company;
2for their hearts plot violence,
and their lips talk about
making trouble.

3By wisdom a house is built,
and through understanding
it is established;
4through knowledge its rooms
are filled
with rare and beautiful
treasures.

5A wise man has great power,
and a man of knowledge
increases strength;
6for waging war you need
guidance,
and for victory many
advisers.

7Wisdom is too high for a fool;
in the assembly at the gate
he has nothing to say.

8He who plots evil
will be known as a schemer.
9The schemes of folly are sin,
and men detest a mocker.

10If you falter in times of
trouble,
how small is your strength!

11Rescue those being led away
to death;
hold back those staggering
toward slaughter.
12If you say, "But we knew
nothing about this,"
does not he who weighs the
heart perceive it?
Does not he who guards your
life know it?
Will he not repay each
person according to what
he has done?

13Eat honey, my son, for it is
good;
honey from the comb is

מָתוֹק עַל־ חִכֶּךָ׃ כֵּן ׀ דְּעֶה חָכְמָה לְנַפְשֶׁךָ אִם־ מָצָאתָ
you-find if to-soul-of-you wisdom know! also (14) taste-of-you to sweet

וְיֵשׁ אַחֲרִית וְתִקְוָתְךָ לֹא תִכָּרֵת׃ אַל־
not (15) she-will-be-cut-off not and-hope-of-you future-hope then-there-is

תֶּאֱרֹב רָשָׁע לִנְוֵה צַדִּיק אַל־ תְּשַׁדֵּד רִבְצוֹ׃
dwelling-of-him you-raid not righteous against-house-of outlaw you-lie-in-wait

כִּי שֶׁבַע ׀ יִפּוֹל צַדִּיק וָקָם וּרְשָׁעִים
but-wicked-ones but-he-rises-again righteous he-falls seven for (16)

יִכָּשְׁלוּ בְרָעָה׃ בִּנְפֹּל אֹויִבְךָ°
one-being-enemy-of-you when-to-fall (17) by-calamity they-are-brought-down

אַל־ תִּשְׂמָח וּבִכָּשְׁלוֹ אַל־ יָגֵל לִבֶּךָ׃
heart-of-you let-him-rejoice not and-when-to-stumble-him you-gloat not

פֶּן־ יִרְאֶה יְהוָה וְרַע בְּעֵינָיו
in-eyes-of-him and-he-will-be-disapproved Yahweh he-will-see or (18)

וְהֵשִׁיב מֵעָלָיו אַפּוֹ׃ אַל־ תִּתְחַר
you-fret not (19) wrath-of-him from-against-him and-he-will-turn-away

בַּמְּרֵעִים אַל־ תְּקַנֵּא בָּרְשָׁעִים׃ כִּי ׀ לֹא־
not for (20) to-the-wicked-ones you-envy not because-of-the-men-being-evil

תִהְיֶה אַחֲרִית לָרָע נֵר רְשָׁעִים יִדְעָךְ׃
he-will-be-snuffed-out wicked-men lamp-of for-the-evil-man future-hope she-is

יְרָא־ אֶת־ יְהוָה בְּנִי וָמֶלֶךְ עִם־ שׁוֹנִים אַל־תִּתְעָרָב׃
you-join not ones-rebelling with and-king son-of-me Yahweh *** fear! (21)

כִּי־ פִתְאֹם יָקוּם אֵידָם וּפִיד שְׁנֵיהֶם
two-of-them and-calamity-of destruction-of-them he-will-rise suddenly for (22)

מִי יוֹדֵעַ׃ גַּם־ אֵלֶּה לַחֲכָמִים הַכֵּר־ פָּנִים
faces to-show-partiality of-wise-men these also (23) knowing who?

בְּמִשְׁפָּט בַּל־ טוֹב׃ אֹמֵר ׀ לְרָשָׁע צַדִּיק אָתָּה יִקְּבֻהוּ
they-will-curse-him you innocent to-guilty one-saying (24) good not in-judgment

עַמִּים יִזְעָמוּהוּ לְאֻמִּים׃ וְלַמּוֹכִיחִים
but-to-the-ones-convicting (25) nations they-will-denounce-him peoples

יִנְעָם וַעֲלֵיהֶם תָּבוֹא בִרְכַּת־ טוֹב׃ שְׂפָתַיִם
lips (26) richness blessing-of she-will-come and-upon-them he-will-go-well

יִשָּׁק מֵשִׁיב דְּבָרִים נְכֹחִים׃ הָכֵן בַּחוּץ ׀
at-the-outside finish! (27) honest-ones answers one-giving he-kisses

מְלַאכְתֶּךָ וְעַתְּדָהּ בַּשָּׂדֶה לָךְ אַחַר וּבָנִיתָ
then-you-build afterward of-you in-the-field and-get-ready-her! work-of-you

בֵיתֶךָ׃ אַל־ תְּהִי עֵד־ חִנָּם בְּרֵעֶךָ
against-neighbor-of-you without-cause testifier you-be not (28) house-of-you

°17 ק אויבך

sweet to your taste.
14 Know also that wisdom is sweet to your soul;
if you find it, there is a future hope for you,
and your hope will not be cut off.

15 Do not lie in wait like an outlaw against a righteous man's house,
do not raid his dwelling place;
16 for though a righteous man falls seven times, he rises again,
but the wicked are brought down by calamity.

17 Do not gloat when your enemy falls;
when he stumbles, do not let your heart rejoice,
18 or the LORD will see and disapprove
and turn his wrath away from him.

19 Do not fret because of evil men
or be envious of the wicked,
20 for the evil man has no future hope,
and the lamp of the wicked will be snuffed out.

21 Fear the LORD and the king, my son,
and do not join with the rebellious,
22 for those two will send sudden destruction upon them,
and who knows what calamities they can bring?

### *Further Sayings of the Wise*

23 These also are sayings of the wise:

To show partiality in judging is not good:
24 Whoever says to the guilty, "You are innocent"—
peoples will curse him and nations denounce him.
25 But it will go well with those who convict the guilty,
and rich blessing will come upon them.

26 An honest answer
is like a kiss on the lips.

27 Finish your outdoor work
and get your fields ready;
after that, build your house.

28 Do not testify against your neighbor without cause,

וְהֲפִתִּיתָ בִּשְׂפָתֶיךָ׃ אַל־ תֹּאמַר כַּאֲשֶׁר עָשָׂה־ לִי כֵּן
so to-me he-did just-as you-say not (29) with-lips-of-you or-you-deceive?

אֶעֱשֶׂה־ לּוֹ אָשִׁיב לָאִישׁ כְּפָעֳלוֹ׃ עַל־ שְׂדֵה
field-of by (30) as-deed-of-him to-the-man I-will-pay-back to-him I-will-do

אִישׁ־ עָצֵל עָבַרְתִּי וְעַל־ כֶּרֶם אָדָם חֲסַר־ לֵב׃
judgment lacking-of man vineyard-of and-by I-went-past sluggard man

וְהִנֵּה עָלָה כֻלּוֹ ׀ קִמְּשֹׂנִים כָּסּוּ פָנָיו
surfaces-of-him they-covered thorns all-of-him he-came-up and-see! (31)

חֲרֻלִּים וְגֶדֶר אֲבָנָיו נֶהֱרָסָה׃ וָאֶחֱזֶה אָנֹכִי
I and-I-observed (32) she-was-in-ruins stones-of-him and-wall-of weeds

אָשִׁית לִבִּי רָאִיתִי לָקַחְתִּי מוּסָר׃ מְעַט שֵׁנוֹת מְעַט
little-of sleeps little-of (33) lesson I-learned I-saw heart-of-me I-applied

תְּנוּמוֹת מְעַט ׀ חִבֻּק יָדַיִם לִשְׁכָּב׃ וּבָא־
and-he-will-come (34) to-rest hands folding-of little-of slumbers

מִתְהַלֵּךְ רֵישֶׁךָ וּמַחְסֹרֶיךָ כְּאִישׁ מָגֵן׃
armor like-man-of and-scarcities-of-you poverty-of-you one-being-bandit

גַּם־ אֵלֶּה מִשְׁלֵי שְׁלֹמֹה אֲשֶׁר הֶעְתִּיקוּ אַנְשֵׁי ׀ חִזְקִיָּה
Hezekiah men-of they-copied that Solomon proverbs-of these also (25:1)

מֶלֶךְ־ יְהוּדָה׃ כְּבֹד אֱלֹהִים הַסְתֵּר דָּבָר וּכְבֹד מְלָכִים
kings and-glory-of matter to-conceal God glory-of (2) Judah king-of

חֲקֹר דָּבָר׃ שָׁמַיִם לָרוּם וָאָרֶץ לָעֹמֶק
to-the-depth and-earth to-the-height heavens (3) matter to-search-out

וְלֵב מְלָכִים אֵין חֵקֶר׃ הָגוֹ סִיגִים מִכָּסֶף
from-silver drosses to-remove (4) searching there-is-no kings so-heart-of

וַיֵּצֵא לַצֹּרֵף כֶּלִי׃ הָגוֹ רָשָׁע
wicked to-remove (5) material for-the-one-being-silversmith and-he-comes-out

לִפְנֵי־ מֶלֶךְ וְיִכּוֹן בַּצֶּדֶק
through-the-righteousness and-he-will-be-established king from-presences-of

כִּסְאוֹ׃ אַל־ תִּתְהַדַּר לִפְנֵי־ מֶלֶךְ וּבִמְקוֹם
or-to-place-of king in-presences-of you-exalt-yourself not (6) throne-of-him

גְּדֹלִים אַל־ תַּעֲמֹד׃ כִּי טוֹב אֲמָר־ לְךָ עֲלֵה הֵנָּה
to-here come-up! to-you to-say good for (7) you-claim not great-men

מֵהַשְׁפִּילְךָ לִפְנֵי נָדִיב אֲשֶׁר רָאוּ עֵינֶיךָ׃ אַל־
not (8) eyes-of-you they-saw what nobleman before more-than-to-humiliate-you

תֵּצֵא לָרִב מַהֵר פֶּן מַה־ תַּעֲשֶׂה בְּאַחֲרִיתָהּ בְּהַכְלִים
when-to-shame in-end-of-her will-you-do what? for hastily to-the-court you-bring

אֹתְךָ רֵעֶךָ׃ רִיבְךָ רִיב אֶת־ רֵעֲךָ
neighbor-of-you with argue-case! case-of-you (9) neighbor-of-you you

or use your lips to deceive.
29Do not say, "I'll do to him as
he has done to me;
I'll pay that man back for
what he did."

30I went past the field of the
sluggard,
past the vineyard of the
man who lacks judgment;
31thorns had come up
everywhere,
the ground was covered
with weeds,
and the stone wall was in
ruins.
32I applied my heart to what I
observed
and learned a lesson from
what I saw:
33A little sleep, a little slumber,
a little folding of the hands
to rest—
34and poverty will come on you
like a bandit
and scarcity like an armed
man.[s]

*More Proverbs of Solomon*

25 These are more proverbs of Solomon, copied by the men of Hezekiah king of Judah:

2It is the glory of God to
conceal a matter;
to search out a matter is the
glory of kings.

3As the heavens are high and
the earth is deep,
so the hearts of kings are
unsearchable.

4Remove the dross from the
silver,
and out comes material for[t]
the silversmith;
5remove the wicked from the
king's presence,
and his throne will be
established through
righteousness.

6Do not exalt yourself in the
king's presence,
and do not claim a place
among great men;
7it is better for him to say to
you, "Come up here,"
than for him to humiliate
you before a nobleman.

8What you have seen with your
eyes
do not bring[u] hastily to
court,
for what will you do in the
end
if your neighbor puts you to
shame?

9If you argue your case with a
neighbor,

s34 Or *like a vagrant / and scarcity like a beggar*
t4 Or *comes a vessel from*
u7,8 Or *nobleman / 8on whom you had set your eyes. / Do not go*

וְסוֹד אַחֵר אַל־ תְּגָל׃ פֶּן־ יְחַסֶּדְךָ שֹׁמֵעַ

one-hearing he-may-shame-you or (10) you-betray not another but-confidence-of

וְדִבָּתְךָ לֹא תָשׁוּב׃ תַּפּוּחֵי זָהָב בְּמַשְׂכִּיּוֹת

in-settings-of gold apples-of (11) she-will-go never and-bad-reputation-of-you

כָּסֶף דָּבָר דָּבֻר עַל־ אָפְנָיו׃ נֶזֶם זָהָב

gold earring-of (12) aptnesses-of-him in being-spoken word silver

וַחֲלִי־ כָתֶם מוֹכִיחַ חָכָם עַל־ אֹזֶן שֹׁמָעַת׃

one-listening ear to wise one-rebuking fine-gold or-ornament-of

כְּצִנַּת־ שֶׁלֶג ׀ בְּיוֹם קָצִיר צִיר נֶאֱמָן

one-being-trustworthy messenger harvest at-time-of snow like-coolness-of (13)

לְשֹׁלְחָיו וְנֶפֶשׁ אֲדֹנָיו יָשִׁיב׃ נְשִׂיאִים

clouds (14) he-refreshes masters-of-him and-spirit-of to-ones-sending-him

וְרוּחַ וְגֶשֶׁם אָיִן אִישׁ מִתְהַלֵּל בְּמַתַּת־ שָׁקֶר׃

deception of-gift-of boasting man there-is-none but-rain and-wind

בְּאֹרֶךְ אַפַּיִם יְפֻתֶּה קָצִין וְלָשׁוֹן רַכָּה

gentle and-tongue ruler he-can-be-persuaded tempers through-length-of (15)

תִּשְׁבָּר־ גָּרֶם׃ דְּבַשׁ מָצָאתָ אֱכֹל דַּיֶּךָּ פֶּן־

lest just-enough-of-you eat! you-find honey (16) bone she-can-break

תִּשְׂבָּעֶנּוּ וַהֲקֵאתוֹ׃ הֹקַר רַגְלְךָ

foot-of-you make-seldom! (17) and-you-vomit-out-him you-eat-too-much-of-him

מִבֵּית רֵעֶךָ פֶּן־ יִשְׂבָּעֲךָ וּשְׂנֵאֶךָ׃

and-he-hates-you he-have-too-much-of-you lest neighbor-of-you in-house-of

מֵפִיץ וְחֶרֶב וְחֵץ שָׁנוּן אִישׁ* עֹנֶה בְרֵעֵהוּ

against-neighbor-of-him giving man one-being-sharp or-arrow or-sword club (18)

עֵד שָׁקֶר׃ שֵׁן רֹעָה וְרֶגֶל מוּעָדֶת

one-being-lame or-foot one-being-bad tooth (19) falsehood testimony-of

מִבְטָח בּוֹגֵד בְּיוֹם צָרָה׃ מַעֲדֶה

one-taking-away (20) trouble in-time-of one-being-unfaithful reliance

בֶּגֶד ׀ בְּיוֹם קָרָה חֹמֶץ עַל־ נָתֶר וְשָׁר בַּשִּׁרִים עַל

to with-the-songs also-one-singing soda on vinegar cold on-day-of garment

לֶב־ רָע׃ אִם־ רָעֵב שֹׂנַאֲךָ הַאֲכִלֵהוּ

give-to-eat-him! one-being-enemy-of-you hungry if (21) heaviness heart-of

לָחֶם וְאִם־ צָמֵא הַשְׁקֵהוּ מָיִם׃ כִּי גֶחָלִים אַתָּה חֹתֶה

heaping you coals for (22) waters give-to-drink-him! thirsty and-if food

עַל־ רֹאשׁוֹ וַיהוָה יְשַׁלֶּם־ לָךְ׃ רוּחַ צָפוֹן תְּחוֹלֵל

she-brings north wind-of (23) to-you he-will-reward and-Yahweh head-of-him on

גֶּשֶׁם וּפָנִים נִזְעָמִים לְשׁוֹן סָתֶר׃ טוֹב שֶׁבֶת עַל־

on to-live good (24) slyness tongue-of ones-being-angry and-looks rain

do not betray another man's
confidence,
10 or he who hears it may shame
you
and you will never lose your
bad reputation.

11 A word aptly spoken
is like apples of gold in
settings of silver.

12 Like an earring of gold or an
ornament of fine gold
is a wise man's rebuke to a
listening ear.

13 Like the coolness of snow at
harvest time
is a trustworthy messenger
to those who send him;
he refreshes the spirit of his
masters.

14 Like clouds and wind without
rain
is a man who boasts of gifts
he does not give.

15 Through patience a ruler can
be persuaded,
and a gentle tongue can
break a bone.

16 If you find honey, eat just
enough—
too much of it, and you will
vomit.

17 Seldom set foot in your
neighbor's house—
too much of you, and he
will hate you.

18 Like a club or a sword or a
sharp arrow
is the man who gives false
testimony against his
neighbor.

19 Like a bad tooth or a lame foot
is reliance on the unfaithful
in times of trouble.

20 Like one who takes away a
garment on a cold day,
or like vinegar poured on
soda,
is one who sings songs to a
heavy heart.

21 If your enemy is hungry, give
him food to eat;
if he is thirsty, give him
water to drink.

22 In doing this, you will heap
burning coals on his
head,
and the LORD will reward
you.

23 As a north wind brings rain,
so a sly tongue brings angry
looks.

24 Better to live on a corner of

**18* Most mss have *maqqeph* (אִישׁ־).

פִּנַּת־ גָּג מֵאֵשֶׁת מִדְוָנִים וּבֵית חָבֶר׃ מַיִם
waters (25) sharing with-house-of quarrels more-than-wife-of roof corner-of

קָרִים עַל־נֶפֶשׁ עֲיֵפָה וּשְׁמוּעָה טוֹבָה מֵאֶרֶץ מֶרְחָק׃ מַעְיָן
spring (26) distance from-land-of good also-news weary soul to cold-ones

נִרְפָּשׂ וּמָקוֹר מָשְׁחָת צַדִּיק מָט
one-giving-way righteous-man one-being-polluted or-well one-being-muddied

לִפְנֵי־ רָשָׁע׃ אָכֹל דְּבַשׁ הַרְבּוֹת לֹא־ טוֹב וְחֵקֶר
or-seeking-of good not to-be-much honey to-eat (27) wicked before

כְּבֹדָם כָּבוֹד׃ עִיר פְּרוּצָה אֵין חוֹמָה אִישׁ אֲשֶׁר
who man wall no one-being-broken-down city (28) honorable honor-of-them

אֵין מַעְצָר לְרוּחוֹ׃ כַּשֶּׁלֶג ׀ בַּקַּיִץ וְכַמָּטָר
or-like-the-rain in-the-summer like-the-snow (26:1) of-self-of-him control no

בַּקָּצִיר כֵּן לֹא־ נָאוֶה לִכְסִיל כָּבוֹד׃ כַּצִּפּוֹר לָנוּד
to-flutter like-the-sparrow (2) honor for-fool fitting not so in-the-harvest

כַּדְּרוֹר לָעוּף כֵּן קִלְלַת חִנָּם לֹא° תָבֹא׃
she-comes-to-rest not undeserved curse-of so to-dart like-the-swallow

שׁוֹט לַסּוּס מֶתֶג לַחֲמוֹר וְשֵׁבֶט לְגֵו כְּסִילִים׃
fools for-back-of and-rod for-the-donkey halter for-the-horse whip (3)

אַל־ תַּעַן כְּסִיל כְּאִוַּלְתּוֹ פֶּן־ תִּשְׁוֶה־ לּוֹ גַם־אָתָּה׃
you also to-him you-will-be-like or as-folly-of-him fool you-answer not (4)

עֲנֵה כְסִיל כְּאִוַּלְתּוֹ פֶּן־ יִהְיֶה חָכָם בְּעֵינָיו׃
in-eyes-of-him wise he-will-be or as-folly-of-him fool answer! (5)

מְקַצֶּה רַגְלַיִם חָמָס שֹׁתֶה שֹׁלֵחַ דְּבָרִים בְּיַד־ כְּסִיל׃
fool by-hand-of messages one-sending drinking violence feet one-cutting-off (6)

דַּלְיוּ שֹׁקַיִם מִפִּסֵּחַ וּמָשָׁל בְּפִי כְּסִילִים׃
fools in-mouth-of also-proverb of-lame-man legs they-hang-limp (7)

כִּצְרוֹר אֶבֶן בְּמַרְגֵּמָה כֵּן־ נוֹתֵן לִכְסִיל כָּבוֹד׃ חוֹחַ
thornbush (9) honor to-fool giving so in-sling stone like-to-tie (8)

עָלָה בְיַד־ שִׁכּוֹר וּמָשָׁל בְּפִי כְסִילִים׃ רַב
archer (10) fools in-mouth-of also-proverb drunkard into-hand-of he-goes

מְחוֹלֵל־ כֹּל וְשֹׂכֵר כְּסִיל וְשֹׂכֵר עֹבְרִים׃
ones-passing-by or-one-hiring fool also-one-hiring all one-wounding

כְּכֶלֶב שָׁב עַל־ קֵאוֹ כְּסִיל שׁוֹנֶה בְאִוַּלְתּוֹ׃
to-folly-of-him repeating fool vomit-of-him to returning as-dog (11)

רָאִיתָ אִישׁ חָכָם בְּעֵינָיו תִּקְוָה לִכְסִיל מִמֶּנּוּ׃ אָמַר
he-says (13) more-than-him for-fool hope in-eyes-of-him wise man you-see (12)

עָצֵל שַׁחַל בַּדָּרֶךְ אֲרִי בֵּין הָרְחֹבוֹת׃ הַדֶּלֶת
the-door (14) the-streets among fierce-lion in-the-road lion sluggard

°24 ק מדינים
°2 ק לו

the roof
than share a house with a quarrelsome wife.

25 Like cold water to a weary soul
is good news from a distant land.

26 Like a muddied spring or a polluted well
is a righteous man who gives way to the wicked.

27 It is not good to eat too much honey,
nor is it honorable to seek one's own honor.

28 Like a city whose walls are broken down
is a man who lacks self-control.

26 Like snow in summer or rain in harvest,
honor is not fitting for a fool.

2 Like a fluttering sparrow or a darting swallow,
an undeserved curse does not come to rest.

3 A whip for the horse, a halter for the donkey,
and a rod for the backs of fools!

4 Do not answer a fool according to his folly,
or you will be like him yourself.

5 Answer a fool according to his folly,
or he will be wise in his own eyes.

6 Like cutting off one's feet or drinking violence
is the sending of a message by the hand of a fool.

7 Like a lame man's legs that hang limp
is a proverb in the mouth of a fool.

8 Like tying a stone in a sling
is the giving of honor to a fool.

9 Like a thornbush in a drunkard's hand
is a proverb in the mouth of a fool.

10 Like an archer who wounds at random
is he who hires a fool or any passer-by.

11 As a dog returns to its vomit,
so a fool repeats his folly.

12 Do you see a man wise in his own eyes?
There is more hope for a fool than for him.

13 The sluggard says, "There is a lion in the road,
a fierce lion roaming the streets!"

תִּסּוֹב עַל־ צִירָהּ וְעָצֵל עַל־ מִטָּתוֹ׃ טָמַן עָצֵל

sluggard he-buries (15) bed-of-him on also-sluggard hinge-of-her on she-turns

יָדוֹ בַּצַּלָּחַת נִלְאָה לַהֲשִׁיבָהּ אֶל־ פִּיו׃

mouth-of-him to to-bring-back-her he-is-too-lazy in-the-dish hand-of-him

חָכָם עָצֵל בְּעֵינָיו מִשִּׁבְעָה מְשִׁיבֵי טָעַם׃

discretion men-answering-of more-than-seven in-eyes-of-him sluggard wise (16)

מַחֲזִיק בְּאָזְנֵי־ כָלֶב עֹבֵר מִתְעַבֵּר עַל־ רִיב לֹּא־

not quarrel in meddling one-passing-by dog onto-ears-of one-seizing (17)

לוֹ׃ כְּמִתְלַהְלֵהַּ הַיֹּרֶה זִקִּים חִצִּים וָמָוֶת׃

and-death arrows firebrands the-one-shooting like-man-being-mad (18) to-him

כֵּן־ אִישׁ רִמָּה אֶת־ רֵעֵהוּ וְאָמַר הֲלֹא־ מְשַׂחֵק אָנִי׃

I one-joking not? and-he-says neighbor-of-him *** he-deceives man so (19)

בְּאֶפֶס עֵצִים תִּכְבֶּה־ אֵשׁ וּבְאֵין נִרְגָּן

one-gossiping also-when-without fire she-goes-out woods when-without (20)

יִשְׁתֹּק מָדוֹן׃ פֶּחָם לְגֶחָלִים וְעֵצִים לְאֵשׁ וְאִישׁ

also-man-of to-fire and-woods to-embers charcoal (21) quarrel he-dies-down

°מִדְוָנִים לְחַרְחַר־ רִיב׃ דִּבְרֵי נִרְגָּן כְּמִתְלַהֲמִים

like-morsels-being-choice one-gossiping words-of (22) strife to-kindle quarrels

וְהֵם יָרְדוּ חַדְרֵי־ בָטֶן׃ *כֶּסֶף סִיגִים*

*drosses silver-of* (23) inmost-part chambers-of they-go-down and-they

מְצֻפֶּה עַל־ חָרֶשׂ שְׂפָתַיִם דֹּלְקִים וְלֶב־ רָע׃

evil with-heart-of ones-being-fervent lips earthenware over being-coated

°בִּשְׂפָתָו יִנָּכֵר שׂוֹנֵא וּבְקִרְבּוֹ

but-in-heart-of-him man-being-malicious he-disguises-himself with-lips-of-him (24)

יָשִׁית מִרְמָה׃ כִּי־ יְחַנֵּן קוֹלוֹ אַל־ תַּאֲמֶן־

you-believe not speech-of-him he-is-charming though (25) deceit he-harbors

בּוֹ כִּי שֶׁבַע תּוֹעֵבוֹת בְּלִבּוֹ׃ תִּכַּסֶּה

she-may-be-concealed (26) in-heart-of-him abominations seven for in-him

שִׂנְאָה בְּמַשָּׁאוֹן תִּגָּלֶה רָעָתוֹ בְקָהָל׃

in-assembly wickedness-of-him she-will-be-exposed by-deception malice

כֹּרֶה־ שַּׁחַת בָּהּ יִפֹּל וְגֹלֵל אֶבֶן אֵלָיו

on-him stone and-one-rolling he-will-fall into-her pit one-digging (27)

תָּשׁוּב׃ לְשׁוֹן־ שֶׁקֶר יִשְׂנָא דַכָּיו וּפֶה

and-mouth ones-hurt-of-him he-hates lie tongue-of (28) she-will-come-back

חָלָק יַעֲשֶׂה מִדְחֶה׃ אַל־ תִּתְהַלֵּל בְּיוֹם מָחָר כִּי לֹא־

not for tomorrow about-day-of you-boast not (27:1) ruin he-works flattering

תֵדַע מַה־ יֵּלֶד יוֹם׃ יְהַלֶּלְךָ זָר

one-being-other let-him-praise-you (2) day he-may-bring-forth what you-know

---

14 As a door turns on its hinges,
so a sluggard turns on his bed.

15 The sluggard buries his hand in the dish;
he is too lazy to bring it back to his mouth.

16 The sluggard is wiser in his own eyes
than seven men who answer discreetly.

17 Like one who seizes a dog by the ears
is a passer-by who meddles in a quarrel not his own.

18 Like a madman shooting firebrands or deadly arrows
19 is a man who deceives his neighbor
and says, "I was only joking!"

20 Without wood a fire goes out;
without gossip a quarrel dies down.

21 As charcoal to embers and as wood to fire,
so is a quarrelsome man for kindling strife.

22 The words of a gossip are like choice morsels;
they go down to a man's inmost parts.

23 Like a coating of glaze[v] over earthenware
are fervent lips with an evil heart.

24 A malicious man disguises himself with his lips,
but in his heart he harbors deceit.
25 Though his speech is charming, do not believe him,
for seven abominations fill his heart.
26 His malice may be concealed by deception,
but his wickedness will be exposed in the assembly.

27 If a man digs a pit, he will fall into it;
if a man rolls a stone, it will roll back on him.

28 A lying tongue hates those it hurts,
and a flattering mouth works ruin.

# 27

1 Do not boast about tomorrow,
for you do not know what a day may bring forth.

2 Let another praise you, and

v23 With a different word division of the Hebrew; Masoretic Text *of silver dross*

*23 The NIV reads these words as כְּסַפְסִגִים, *like-glazes.*

°21 ק מדינים

°24 ק בשפתיו

וְלֹא־ פִיךָ נָכְרִי וְאַל־ שְׂפָתֶיךָ׃ (3) כֹּבֶד־ אֶבֶן
and-not mouth-of-you someone-else and-not lips-of-you (3) heavy stone

וְנֵטֶל הַחוֹל וְכַעַס אֱוִיל כָּבֵד מִשְּׁנֵיהֶם׃
and-burden the-sand but-provocation-of fool heavy more-than-both-of-them

(4) אַכְזְרִיּוּת חֵמָה וְשֶׁטֶף אָף וּמִי יַעֲמֹד לִפְנֵי קִנְאָה׃
(4) cruel anger and-overwhelming fury but-who? he-can-stand before jealousy

(5) טוֹבָה תּוֹכַחַת מְגֻלָּה מֵאַהֲבָה מְסֻתָּרֶת׃
(5) good rebuke one-being-open more-than-love one-being-hidden

(6) נֶאֱמָנִים פִּצְעֵי אוֹהֵב וְנַעְתָּרוֹת
(6) ones-being-faithful wounds-of one-being-friend though-ones-being-profuse

נְשִׁיקוֹת שׂוֹנֵא׃ (7) נֶפֶשׁ שְׂבֵעָה תָּבוּס נֹפֶת וְנֶפֶשׁ
kisses-of one-being-enemy (7) person full she-loathes honey but-person

רְעֵבָה כָּל־ מַר מָתוֹק׃ (8) כְּצִפּוֹר נוֹדֶדֶת מִן־ קִנָּהּ
hungry all-of bitterness sweet (8) like-bird one-straying from nest-of-her

כֵּן־ אִישׁ נוֹדֵד מִמְּקוֹמוֹ׃ (9) שֶׁמֶן וּקְטֹרֶת יְשַׂמַּח־
so man one-straying from-home-of-him (9) perfume and-incense he-brings-joy

לֵב וּמֶתֶק רֵעֵהוּ מֵעֲצַת־ נָפֶשׁ׃
heart also-pleasantness-of friend-of-him from-counsel-of earnestness

(10) רֵעֲךָ וְרֵעֶה° אָבִיךָ אַל־ תַּעֲזֹב וּבֵית
(10) friend-of-you and-friend-of father-of-you not you-forsake and-house-of

אָחִיךָ אַל־ תָּבוֹא בְּיוֹם אֵידֶךָ טוֹב שָׁכֵן קָרוֹב
brother-of-you not you-go in-day-of disaster-of-you good neighbor nearby

מֵאָח רָחוֹק׃ (11) חֲכַם בְּנִי וְשַׂמַּח לִבִּי
more-than-brother far (11) be-wise! son-of-me and-bring-joy! heart-of-me

וְאָשִׁיבָה חֹרְפִי דָבָר׃ (12) עָרוּם רָאָה
then-I-can-return one-treating-with-contempt-me answer (12) prudent he-sees

רָעָה נִסְתָּר פְּתָאיִם עָבְרוּ נֶעֱנָשׁוּ׃ (13) קַח־
danger he-takes-refuge simple-ones they-go-on they-suffer (13) take!

בִּגְדוֹ כִּי־ עָרַב זָר וּבְעַד
garment-of-him when he-puts-up-security one-being-stranger and-for

נָכְרִיָּה חַבְלֵהוּ׃ (14) מְבָרֵךְ רֵעֵהוּ בְּקוֹל גָּדוֹל
wayward-woman hold-him! (14) one-blessing neighbor-of-him with-voice loud

בַּבֹּקֶר הַשְׁכֵּים קְלָלָה תֵּחָשֶׁב לוֹ׃ (15) דֶּלֶף
in-the-morning to-be-early curse she-will-be-taken by-him (15) dripping

טוֹרֵד בְּיוֹם סַגְרִיר וְאֵשֶׁת מִדְוָנִים° נִשְׁתָּוָה׃
one-being-constant on-day-of rain also-wife-of quarrels she-is-like

(16) צֹפְנֶיהָ צָפַן־ רוּחַ וְשֶׁמֶן יְמִינוֹ
(16) ones-restraining-her he-restrains wind or-oil-of right-hand-of-him

°10 ק ורע
°15 ק מדינים

not your own mouth;
someone else, and not your own lips.

3 Stone is heavy and sand a burden,
but provocation by a fool is heavier than both.

4 Anger is cruel and fury overwhelming,
but who can stand before jealousy?

5 Better is open rebuke
than hidden love.

6 The kisses of an enemy may be profuse,
but faithful are the wounds of a friend.

7 He who is full loathes honey,
but to the hungry even what is bitter tastes sweet.

8 Like a bird that strays from its nest
is a man who strays from his home.

9 Perfume and incense bring joy to the heart,
and the pleasantness of one's friend springs from his earnest counsel.

10 Do not forsake your friend and the friend of your father,
and do not go to your brother's house when disaster strikes you—
better a neighbor nearby than a brother far away.

11 Be wise, my son, and bring joy to my heart;
then I can answer anyone who treats me with contempt.

12 The prudent see danger and take refuge,
but the simple keep going and suffer for it.

13 Take the garment of one who puts up security for a stranger;
hold it in pledge if he does it for a wayward woman.

14 If a man loudly blesses his neighbor early in the morning,
it will be taken as a curse.

15 A quarrelsome wife is like
a constant dripping on a rainy day;
16 restraining her is like restraining the wind
or grasping oil with the hand.

יִקְרָא׃ בַּרְזֶל בְּבַרְזֶל יָחַד וְאִישׁ יַחַד פְּנֵי־
faces-of he-sharpens so-man he-sharpens to-iron iron (17) he-grasps

רֵעֵהוּ׃ נֹצֵר תְּאֵנָה יֹאכַל פִּרְיָהּ
fruit-of-her he-will-eat fig-tree one-tending (18) other-of-him

וְשֹׁמֵר אֲדֹנָיו יְכֻבָּד׃ כַּמַּיִם
as-the-waters (19) he-will-be-honored masters-of-him and-one-looking-after

הַפָּנִים לַפָּנִים כֵּן לֵב־ הָאָדָם לָאָדָם׃ שְׁאוֹל וַאֲבַדֹּה
and-Abaddon Sheol (20) to-the-man the-man heart-of so to-the-faces the-faces

לֹא תִשְׂבַּעְנָה וְעֵינֵי הָאָדָם לֹא תִשְׂבַּעְנָה׃
they-are-satisfied never the-man and-eyes-of they-are-satisfied never

מַצְרֵף לַכֶּסֶף וְכוּר לַזָּהָב וְאִישׁ לְפִי
by-mouth-of but-man for-the-gold and-furnace for-the-silver crucible (21)

מַהֲלָלוֹ׃ אִם תִּכְתּוֹשׁ־ אֶת־ הָאֱוִיל | בַּמַּכְתֵּשׁ בְּתוֹךְ
in-among in-the-mortar the-fool *** you-grind though (22) praise-of-him

הָרִיפוֹת בַּעֱלִי לֹא־ תָסוּר מֵעָלָיו אִוַּלְתּוֹ׃
folly-of-him from-with-him she-will-be-removed not with-the-pestle the-grains

יָדֹעַ תֵּדַע פְּנֵי צֹאנֶךָ שִׁית לִבְּךָ
heart-of-you attend! flock-of-you conditions-of you-know to-know (23)

לַעֲדָרִים׃ כִּי לֹא לְעוֹלָם חֹסֶן וְאִם־ נֵזֶר לְדוֹר
for-generation crown or-even richness to-forever not for (24) to-the-herds

דּוֹר׃ גָּלָה חָצִיר וְנִרְאָה־ דֶשֶׁא
new-growth and-he-appears hay he-is-removed (25) and-generation

וְנֶאֶסְפוּ עִשְּׂבוֹת הָרִים׃ כְּבָשִׂים לִלְבוּשֶׁךָ
for-clothing-of-you lambs (26) hills grasses-of and-they-are-gathered

וּמְחִיר שָׂדֶה עַתּוּדִים׃ וְדֵי | חֲלֵב עִזִּים לְלַחְמְךָ
for-food-of-you goats milk-of and-plenty-of (27) goats field and-price-of

לְלֶחֶם בֵּיתֶךָ וְחַיִּים לְנַעֲרוֹתֶיךָ׃
to-servant-girls-of-you and-nourishments family-of-you for-food-of

נָסוּ וְאֵין־ רֹדֵף רָשָׁע וְצַדִּיקִים כִּכְפִיר
as-lion but-righteous-ones wicked one-pursuing though-not they-flee (28:1)

יִבְטָח׃ בְּפֶשַׁע אֶרֶץ רַבִּים שָׂרֶיהָ וּבְאָדָם
but-by-man rulers-of-her many country in-rebellion-of (2) he-is-bold

מֵבִין יֹדֵעַ כֵּן יַאֲרִיךְ׃ גֶּבֶר רָשׁ
one-being-poor man (3) he-maintains-order so one-knowing one-understanding

וְעֹשֵׁק דַּלִּים מָטָר סֹחֵף וְאֵין לָחֶם׃
crop so-there-is-no driving rain poor-ones also-one-oppressing

עֹזְבֵי תוֹרָה יְהַלְלוּ רָשָׁע וְשֹׁמְרֵי תוֹרָה
law but-ones-keeping-of wicked they-praise law ones-forsaking-of (4)

[17]As iron sharpens iron,
so one man sharpens another.

[18]He who tends a fig tree will eat its fruit,
and he who looks after his master will be honored.

[19]As water reflects a face,
so a man's heart reflects the man.

[20]Death and Destruction[w] are never satisfied,
and neither are the eyes of man.

[21]The crucible for silver and the furnace for gold,
but man is tested by the praise he receives.

[22]Though you grind a fool in a mortar,
grinding him like grain with a pestle,
you will not remove his folly from him.

[23]Be sure you know the condition of your flocks,
give careful attention to your herds;
[24]for riches do not endure forever,
and a crown is not secure for all generations.
[25]When the hay is removed and new growth appears
and the grass from the hills is gathered in,
[26]the lambs will provide you with clothing,
and the goats with the price of a field.
[27]You will have plenty of goats' milk
to feed you and your family
and to nourish your servant girls.

28 The wicked man flees though no one pursues,
but the righteous are as bold as a lion.

[2]When a country is rebellious, it has many rulers,
but a man of understanding and knowledge maintains order.

[3]A ruler[x] who oppresses the poor
is like a driving rain that leaves no crops.

[4]Those who forsake the law praise the wicked,
but those who keep the law

w20 Hebrew *Sheol and Abaddon*
x3 Or *A poor man*

°20 ק ואבדו
°24 ק ודור

יִתְגָּרוּ בָם׃ (5) אַנְשֵׁי־רָע לֹא־יָבִינוּ מִשְׁפָּט
justice they-understand not evil men-of (5) against-them they-resist

וּמְבַקְשֵׁי יְהוָה יָבִינוּ כֹל׃ (6) טוֹב־רָשׁ
one-being-poor good (6) fully they-understand Yahweh but-ones-seeking-of

הוֹלֵךְ בְּתֻמּוֹ מֵעִקֵּשׁ דְּרָכַיִם וְהוּא עָשִׁיר׃
rich and-he ways more-than-perverse-of in-blamelessness-of-him walking

(7) נוֹצֵר תּוֹרָה בֵּן מֵבִין וְרֹעֶה
but-one-being-companion-of one-discerning son law one-keeping (7)

זוֹלְלִים יַכְלִים אָבִיו׃ (8) מַרְבֶּה הוֹנוֹ
wealth-of-him one-increasing (8) father-of-him he-disgraces ones-being-gluttons

בְּנֶשֶׁךְ וּבְתַרְבִּית° לְחוֹנֵן דַּלִּים יִקְבְּצֶנּוּ׃
he-amasses-him poor-ones for-one-being-kind and-interest by-interest

(9) מֵסִיר אָזְנוֹ מִשְּׁמֹעַ תּוֹרָה גַּם־תְּפִלָּתוֹ תּוֹעֵבָה׃
detestable prayer-of-him even law from-to-hear ear-of-him one-turning (9)

(10) מַשְׁגֶּה יְשָׁרִים בְּדֶרֶךְ רָע בִּשְׁחוּתוֹ הוּא־יִפּוֹל
he-will-fall he into-trap-of-him evil along-path upright-ones one-leading (10)

וּתְמִימִים יִנְחֲלוּ־טוֹב׃ (11) חָכָם בְּעֵינָיו אִישׁ
man in-eyes-of-him wise (11) good they-will-inherit but-blameless-ones

עָשִׁיר וְדַל מֵבִין יַחְקְרֶנּוּ׃ (12) בַּעֲלֹץ
when-to-triumph (12) he-sees-through-him one-discerning but-poor rich

צַדִּיקִים רַבָּה תִפְאָרֶת וּבְקוּם רְשָׁעִים יְחֻפַּשׂ אָדָם׃
man he-is-hidden wicked-ones but-when-to-rise elation great righteous-ones

(13) מְכַסֶּה פְשָׁעָיו לֹא יַצְלִיחַ וּמוֹדֶה
but-one-confessing he-prospers not sins-of-him one-concealing (13)

וְעֹזֵב יְרֻחָם׃ (14) אַשְׁרֵי אָדָם מְפַחֵד
one-fearing man blessednesses-of (14) he-finds-mercy and-one-renouncing

תָּמִיד וּמַקְשֶׁה לִבּוֹ יִפּוֹל בְּרָעָה׃ (15) אֲרִי־
lion (15) into-trouble he-falls heart-of-him but-one-hardening always

נֹהֵם וְדֹב שׁוֹקֵק מֹשֵׁל רָשָׁע עַל עַם־דָּל׃ (16) נָגִיד
ruler (16) helpless people over wicked ruling charging or-bear roaring

חֲסַר תְּבוּנוֹת וְרַב מַעֲשַׁקּוֹת שֹׂנֵא° בֶצַע
ill-gotten-gain one-hating tyrannies and-great-of judgments lacking-of

יַאֲרִיךְ יָמִים׃ (17) אָדָם עָשֻׁק בְּדַם־נָפֶשׁ עַד־
till life by-blood-of being-tormented man (17) days he-will-have-long

בּוֹר יָנוּס אַל־יִתְמְכוּ־בוֹ׃ (18) הוֹלֵךְ
one-walking (18) to-him they-will-support not he-will-be-fugitive death

תָּמִים יִוָּשֵׁעַ וְנֶעְקַשׁ דְּרָכַיִם יִפּוֹל
he-will-fall ways but-one-being-perverse-of he-is-kept-safe blamelessly

resist them.

5 Evil men do not understand justice,
but those who seek the LORD understand it fully.

6 Better a poor man whose walk is blameless
than a rich man whose ways are perverse.

7 He who keeps the law is a discerning son,
but a companion of gluttons disgraces his father.

8 He who increases his wealth by exorbitant interest
amasses it for another, who will be kind to the poor.

9 If anyone turns a deaf ear to the law,
even his prayers are detestable.

10 He who leads the upright along an evil path
will fall into his own trap,
but the blameless will receive a good inheritance.

11 A rich man may be wise in his own eyes,
but a poor man who has discernment sees through him.

12 When the righteous triumph, there is great elation;
but when the wicked rise to power, men go into hiding.

13 He who conceals his sins does not prosper,
but whoever confesses and renounces them finds mercy.

14 Blessed is the man who always fears the LORD,
but he who hardens his heart falls into trouble.

15 Like a roaring lion or a charging bear
is a wicked man ruling over a helpless people.

16 A tyrannical ruler lacks judgment,
but he who hates ill-gotten gain will enjoy a long life.

17 A man tormented by the guilt of murder
will be a fugitive till death;
let no one support him.

18 He whose walk is blameless is kept safe,
but he whose ways are perverse will suddenly fall.

°8 ק ותרבית
°16 ק שנא

בְּאַחַת׃ (19) עֹבֵד אַדְמָתוֹ יִשְׂבַּע־לָחֶם
food he-will-have-abundance land-of-him one-working (19) in-suddenness

וּמְרַדֵּף רֵקִים יִשְׂבַּע־רִישׁ׃ (20) אִישׁ
man-of (20) poverty he-will-have-fill fantasies but-one-chasing

אֱמוּנוֹת רַב־בְּרָכוֹת וְאָץ לְהַעֲשִׁיר לֹא
not to-get-rich but-one-being-eager blessings rich-of faithfulnesses

יִנָּקֶה׃ (21) הַכֵּר־פָּנִים לֹא־טוֹב וְעַל־פַּת־
piece-of yet-for good not faces to-show-partiality (21) he-will-go-unpunished

לֶחֶם יִפְשַׁע־גָּבֶר׃ (22) נִבֳהָל לַהוֹן אִישׁ רַע עָיִן
eye stingy-of man for-the-wealth he-is-eager (22) man he-will-do-wrong bread

וְלֹא־יֵדַע כִּי־חֶסֶר יְבֹאֶנּוּ׃ (23) מוֹכִיחַ אָדָם אַחֲרַי
in-end man one-rebuking (23) he-awaits-him poverty that he-is-aware and-not

חֵן יִמְצָא מִמַּחֲלִיק לָשׁוֹן׃ (24) גּוֹזֵל ׀
one-robbing (24) tongue more-than-one-flattering he-will-gain favor

אָבִיו וְאִמּוֹ וְאֹמֵר אֵין־פָּשַׁע חָבֵר הוּא לְאִישׁ
to-man he partner wrong not and-one-saying or-mother-of-him father-of-him

מַשְׁחִית׃ (25) רְחַב־נֶפֶשׁ יְגָרֶה מָדוֹן וּבוֹטֵחַ
but-one-trusting dissension he-stirs-up greed broad-of (25) one-destroying

עַל־יְהוָה יְדֻשָּׁן׃ (26) בּוֹטֵחַ בְּלִבּוֹ הוּא כְסִיל
fool he in-self-of-him one-trusting (26) he-will-prosper Yahweh in

וְהוֹלֵךְ בְּחָכְמָה הוּא יִמָּלֵט׃ (27) נוֹתֵן
one-giving (27) he-is-kept-safe he in-wisdom but-one-walking

לָרָשׁ אֵין מַחְסוֹר וּמַעְלִים עֵינָיו רַב־מְאֵרוֹת׃
curses many-of eyes-of-him but-one-closing lack no to-the-one-being-poor

(28) בְּקוּם רְשָׁעִים יִסָּתֵר אָדָם וּבְאָבְדָם
but-when-to-perish-them person he-is-ridden wicked-ones when-to-rise (28)

יִרְבּוּ צַדִּיקִים׃ (29:1) אִישׁ תּוֹכָחוֹת מַקְשֶׁה־עֹרֶף פֶּתַע
suddenly neck making-stiff rebukes man-of (29:1) righteous-ones they-thrive

יִשָּׁבֵר וְאֵין מַרְפֵּא׃ (2) בִּרְבוֹת צַדִּיקִים
righteous-ones when-to-thrive (2) remedy with-no he-will-be-destroyed

יִשְׂמַח הָעָם וּבִמְשֹׁל רָשָׁע יֵאָנַח עָם׃ (3) אִישׁ־
man (3) people he-groans wicked but-when-to-rule the-people he-rejoices

אֹהֵב חָכְמָה יְשַׂמַּח אָבִיו וְרֹעֶה
but-one-being-companion-of father-of-him he-brings-joy wisdom loving

זוֹנוֹת יְאַבֶּד־הוֹן׃ (4) מֶלֶךְ בְּמִשְׁפָּט יַעֲמִיד
he-makes-stable by-justice king (4) wealth he-squanders ones-being-prostitutes

אֶרֶץ וְאִישׁ תְּרוּמוֹת יֶהֶרְסֶנָּה׃ (5) גֶּבֶר מַחֲלִיק עַל־
to flattering man (5) he-tears-down-her bribes but-man-of country

[19]He who works his land will
have abundant food,
but the one who chases
fantasies will have his fill
of poverty.

[20]A faithful man will be richly
blessed,
but one eager to get rich
will not go unpunished.

[21]To show partiality is not
good—
yet a man will do wrong for
a piece of bread.

[22]A stingy man is eager to get
rich
and is unaware that poverty
awaits him.

[23]He who rebukes a man will in
the end gain more favor
than he who has a flattering
tongue.

[24]He who robs his father or
mother
and says, "It's not wrong"—
he is partner to him who
destroys.

[25]A greedy man stirs up
dissension,
but he who trusts in the
LORD will prosper.

[26]He who trusts in himself is a
fool,
but he who walks in
wisdom is kept safe.

[27]He who gives to the poor will
lack nothing,
but he who closes his eyes
to them receives many
curses.

[28]When the wicked rise to
power, people go into
hiding;
but when the wicked perish,
the righteous thrive.

29 A man who remains
stiff-necked after many
rebukes
will suddenly be
destroyed—without
remedy.

[2]When the righteous thrive, the
people rejoice;
when the wicked rule, the
people groan.

[3]A man who loves wisdom
brings joy to his father,
but a companion of
prostitutes squanders his
wealth.

[4]By justice a king gives a
country stability,
but one who is greedy for
bribes tears it down.

[5]Whoever flatters his neighbor

רֵעֵהוּ רֶשֶׁת פּוֹרֵשׂ עַל־פְּעָמָיו׃ בְּפֶשַׁע אִישׁ רָע מוֹקֵשׁ
neighbor-of-him net spreading for feet-of-him (6) by-sin man evil snare

וְצַדִּיק יָרוּן וְשָׂמֵחַ׃ יֹדֵעַ צַדִּיק
but-righteous he-can-sing and-he-can-be-glad (7) one-caring-about righteous

דִּין דַּלִּים רָשָׁע לֹא־יָבִין דָּעַת׃ אַנְשֵׁי לָצוֹן
justice-of poor-ones wicked not he-is-concerned knowledge (8) men-of mockery

יָפִיחוּ קִרְיָה וַחֲכָמִים יָשִׁיבוּ אָף׃ אִישׁ־חָכָם
they-stir-up city but-wise-men they-turn-away anger (9) man wise

נִשְׁפָּט אֶת־אִישׁ אֱוִיל וְרָגַז וְשָׂחַק וְאֵין נָחַת׃
one-going-to-court with man fool and-he-rages and-he-scoffs but-no peace

אַנְשֵׁי דָמִים יִשְׂנְאוּ־תָם וִישָׁרִים יְבַקְשׁוּ נַפְשׁוֹ׃
(10) men-of bloods they-hate integrity and-upright-ones they-seek life-of-him

כָּל־רוּחוֹ יוֹצִיא כְסִיל וְחָכָם בְּאָחוֹר
(11) fullness-of anger-of-him he-gives fool but-wise at-last

יְשַׁבְּחֶנָּה׃ מֹשֵׁל מַקְשִׁיב עַל־דְּבַר־שָׁקֶר כָּל־
he-controls-her (12) one-ruling listening to word-of lie all-of

מְשָׁרְתָיו רְשָׁעִים׃ רָשׁ וְאִישׁ
ones-being-officials-of-him wicked-ones (13) man-being-poor and-man-of

תְּכָכִים נִפְגָּשׁוּ מֵאִיר־עֵינֵי שְׁנֵיהֶם יְהוָה׃
oppressions they-have-in-common one-giving-sight eyes-of both-of-them Yahweh

מֶלֶךְ שׁוֹפֵט בֶּאֱמֶת דַּלִּים כִּסְאוֹ לָעַד
(14) king judging with-fairness poor-ones throne-of-him to-always

יִכּוֹן׃ שֵׁבֶט וְתוֹכַחַת יִתֵּן חָכְמָה וְנַעַר
he-will-be-secure (15) rod and-correction he-imparts wisdom but-child

מְשֻׁלָּח מֵבִישׁ אִמּוֹ׃ בִּרְבוֹת רְשָׁעִים
one-being-left disgracing mother-of-him (16) when-to-thrive wicked-ones

יִרְבֶּה־פָּשַׁע וְצַדִּיקִים בְּמַפַּלְתָּם יִרְאוּ׃
he-thrives sin but-righteous-ones to-downfall-of-them they-will-see

יַסֵּר בִּנְךָ וִינִיחֶךָ וְיִתֵּן
(17) discipline! son-of-you and-he-will-give-peace-you and-he-will-bring

מַעֲדַנִּים לְנַפְשֶׁךָ׃ בְּאֵין חָזוֹן יִפָּרַע
delights to-soul-of-you (18) where-there-is-no revelation he-casts-off-restraint

עָם וְשֹׁמֵר תּוֹרָה אַשְׁרֵהוּ׃ בִּדְבָרִים לֹא־
people but-one-keeping law blessedness-of-him (19) by-words not

יִוָּסֶר עָבֶד כִּי־יָבִין וְאֵין מַעֲנֶה׃
he-can-be-corrected servant though he-understands yet-there-is-no response

חָזִיתָ אִישׁ אָץ בִּדְבָרָיו תִּקְוָה לִכְסִיל מִמֶּנּוּ׃
(20) you-see man one-being-hasty with-words-of-him hope for-fool more-than-him

is spreading a net for his feet.

6 An evil man is snared by his own sin,
but a righteous one can sing and be glad.

7 The righteous care about justice for the poor,
but the wicked have no such concern.

8 Mockers stir up a city,
but wise men turn away anger.

9 If a wise man goes to court with a fool,
the fool rages and scoffs, and there is no peace.

10 Bloodthirsty men hate a man of integrity
and seek to kill the upright.

11 A fool gives full vent to his anger,
but a wise man keeps himself under control.

12 If a ruler listens to lies,
all his officials become wicked.

13 The poor man and the oppressor have this in common:
The LORD gives sight to the eyes of both.

14 If a king judges the poor with fairness,
his throne will always be secure.

15 The rod of correction imparts wisdom,
but a child left to itself disgraces his mother.

16 When the wicked thrive, so does sin,
but the righteous will see their downfall.

17 Discipline your son, and he will give you peace;
he will bring delight to your soul.

18 Where there is no revelation, the people cast off restraint;
but blessed is he who keeps the law.

19 A servant cannot be corrected by mere words;
though he understands, he will not respond.

20 Do you see a man who speaks in haste?
There is more hope for a fool than for him.

מְפַנֵּק מִנֹּעַר עַבְדּוֹ וְאַחֲרִיתוֹ יִהְיֶה
he-will-be and-end-of-him servant-of-him from-youth one-pampering (21)

מָנוֹן: אִישׁ־ אַף יְגָרֶה מָדוֹן וּבַעַל חֵמָה
hot-temper and-man-of dissension he-stirs-up anger man-of (22) grief

רַב־ פָּשַׁע: גַּאֲוַת אָדָם תַּשְׁפִּילֶנּוּ וּשְׁפַל־ רוּחַ
spirit but-lowly-of she-brings-low-him man pride-of (23) sin many-of

יִתְמֹךְ כָּבוֹד: חוֹלֵק עִם־ גַּנָּב שׂוֹנֵא נַפְשׁוֹ
self-of-him being-enemy-of thief with one-being-accomplice (24) honor he-gains

אָלָה יִשְׁמַע וְלֹא יַגִּיד: חֶרְדַּת אָדָם יִתֵּן
he-will-prove-to-be man fear-of (25) he-dares-testify but-not he-takes oath

מוֹקֵשׁ וּבוֹטֵחַ בַּיהוָה יְשֻׂגָּב: רַבִּים מְבַקְשִׁים
ones-seeking many (26) he-is-kept-safe in-Yahweh but-one-trusting snare

פְּנֵי־ מוֹשֵׁל וּמֵיְהוָה מִשְׁפַּט־ אִישׁ: תּוֹעֲבַת
detesting-of (27) man justice-of but-from-Yahweh one-ruling faces-of

צַדִּיקִים אִישׁ עָוֶל וְתוֹעֲבַת רָשָׁע יְשַׁר־ דָּרֶךְ:
way upright-of wicked and-detesting-of dishonesty man-of righteous-ones

דִּבְרֵי׀ אָגוּר בִּן־ יָקֶה הַמַּשָּׂא נְאֻם הַגֶּבֶר
the-man declaration-of the-oracle Jakeh son-of Agur sayings-of (30:1)

לְאִיתִיאֵל לְאִיתִיאֵל וְאֻכָל: כִּי בַעַר אָנֹכִי מֵאִישׁ וְלֹא־
and-not more-than-man I ignorant indeed (2) and-Ucal to-Ithiel to-Ithiel

בִינַת אָדָם לִי: וְלֹא־ לָמַדְתִּי חָכְמָה וְדַעַת
or-knowledge-of wisdom I-learned and-not (3) to-me man understanding-of

קְדֹשִׁים אֵדָע: מִי עָלָה־ שָׁמַיִם׀ וַיֵּרַד מִי
who? and-he-came-down heavens he-went-up who? (4) I-know Holy-Ones

אָסַף־ רוּחַ׀ בְּחָפְנָיו מִי צָרַר־ מַיִם׀ בַּשִּׂמְלָה
in-the-cloak waters he-wrapped who? in-hollow-of-hands-of-him wind he-gathered

מִי הֵקִים כָּל־ אַפְסֵי־אָרֶץ מַה־ שְּׁמוֹ וּמַה־ שֶּׁם־
name-of and-what? name-of-him what? earth ends-of all-of he-established who?

בְּנוֹ כִּי תֵדָע: כָּל־ אִמְרַת אֱלוֹהַּ צְרוּפָה מָגֵן
shield one-being-flawless God word-of every-of (5) you-know if son-of-him

הוּא לַחֹסִים בּוֹ: אַל־ תּוֹסְףְּ עַל־ דְּבָרָיו פֶּן־
or words-of-him to you-add not (6) in-him to-ones-taking-refuge he

יוֹכִיחַ בְּךָ וְנִכְזָבְתָּ: שְׁתַּיִם שָׁאַלְתִּי מֵאִתָּךְ
from-with-you I-ask two (7) and-you-will-be-proved-liar to-you he-will-rebuke

אַל־ תִּמְנַע מִמֶּנִּי בְּטֶרֶם אָמוּת: שָׁוְא׀ וּדְבַר־ כָּזָב
lie and-word-of falsehood (8) I-die at-before from-me you-refuse not

הַרְחֵק מִמֶּנִּי רֵאשׁ וָעֹשֶׁר אַל־ תִּתֶּן־ לִי הַטְרִיפֵנִי
give-me! to-me you-give not or-richness poverty from-me keep-far!

21 If a man pampers his servant
from youth,
he will bring grief[y] in the
end.
22 An angry man stirs up
dissension,
and a hot-tempered one
commits many sins.
23 A man's pride brings him low,
but a man of lowly spirit
gains honor.
24 The accomplice of a thief is his
own enemy;
he is put under oath and
dare not testify.
25 Fear of man will prove to be a
snare,
but whoever trusts in the
LORD is kept safe.
26 Many seek an audience with a
ruler,
but it is from the LORD that
man gets justice.
27 The righteous detest the
dishonest;
the wicked detest the
upright.

*Sayings of Agur*

30 The sayings of Agur son of
Jakeh—an oracle[z]:
This man declared to Ithiel,
to Ithiel and to Ucal:[a]
2 "I am the most ignorant of
men;
I do not have a man's
understanding.
3 I have not learned wisdom,
nor have I knowledge of the
Holy One.
4 Who has gone up to heaven
and come down?
Who has gathered up the
wind in the hollow of his
hands?
Who has wrapped up the
waters in his cloak?
Who has established all the
ends of the earth?
What is his name, and the
name of his son?
Tell me if you know!

5 "Every word of God is
flawless;
he is a shield to those who
take refuge in him.
6 Do not add to his words,
or he will rebuke you and
prove you a liar.
7 "Two things I ask of you, O
LORD;
do not refuse me before I
die:
8 Keep falsehood and lies far
from me;
give me neither poverty nor
riches,

y21 The meaning of the Hebrew for this word is uncertain.
z1 Or *Jakeh of Massa*
a1 Masoretic Text; with a different word division of the Hebrew *declared, "I am weary, O God; / I am weary, O God, and faint.*

לֶחֶם חֻקִּי׃ פֶּן* אֶשְׂבַּע ׀ וְכִחַשְׁתִּי
and-I-may-disown I-may-have-too-much otherwise (9) portion-of-me bread-of

וְאָמַרְתִּי מִי יְהוָה וּפֶן־ אִוָּרֵשׁ וְגָנַבְתִּי
and-I-may-steal I-may-become-poor or-otherwise Yahweh who? and-I-may-say

וְתָפַשְׂתִּי שֵׁם אֱלֹהָי׃ אַל־ תַּלְשֵׁן עֶבֶד אֶל־
to servant you-slander not (10) God-of-me name-of so-I-would-dishonor

אֲדֹנָו° פֶּן־ יְקַלֶּלְךָ וְאָשָׁמְתָּ׃ דּוֹר
generation (11) and-you-will-pay he-will-curse-you or masters-of-him

אָבִיו יְקַלֵּל וְאֶת־ אִמּוֹ לֹא יְבָרֵךְ׃ דּוֹר
generation (12) he-blesses not mother-of-him and he-curses father-of-him

טָהוֹר בְּעֵינָיו וּמִצֹּאָתוֹ לֹא רֻחָץ׃ דּוֹר
generation (13) he-is-cleansed not yet-from-filth-of-him in-eyes-of-him pure

מָה־ רָמוּ עֵינָיו וְעַפְעַפָּיו יִנָּשֵׂאוּ׃
they-are-disdainful and-glances-of-him eyes-of-him they-are-haughty how!

דּוֹר ׀ חֲרָבוֹת שִׁנָּיו וּמַאֲכָלוֹת מְתַלְּעֹתָיו לֶאֱכֹל
to-devour jaws-of-him and-knives teeth-of-him swords generation (14)

עֲנִיִּים מֵאֶרֶץ וְאֶבְיוֹנִים מֵאָדָם׃ לַעֲלוּקָה ׀ שְׁתֵּי
two-of to-leech (15) from-mankind and-needy-ones from-earth poor-ones

בָנוֹת הַב ׀ הַב שָׁלוֹשׁ הֵנָּה לֹא תִשְׂבַּעְנָה אַרְבַּע לֹא־
never four they-are-satisfied never they three give! give! daughters

אָמְרוּ הוֹן׃ שְׁאוֹל וְעֹצֶר רָחַם אֶרֶץ לֹא־ שָׂבְעָה
she-is-satisfied never land womb and-barrenness-of Sheol (16) enough they-say

מַּיִם וְאֵשׁ לֹא־ אָמְרָה הוֹן׃ עַיִן ׀ תִּלְעַג לְאָב
at-father she-mocks eye (17) enough she-says never and-fire waters

וְתָבוּז לִיקֲּהַת־ אֵם יִקְּרוּהָ עֹרְבֵי־
ravens-of they-will-peck-out-her mother at-obedience-of and-she-scorns

נַחַל וְיֹאכְלוּהָ בְנֵי־ נָשֶׁר׃ שְׁלֹשָׁה הֵמָּה
they three (18) vulture young-ones-of and-they-will-eat-her valley

נִפְלְאוּ מִמֶּנִּי וְאַרְבָּעָ° לֹא יְדַעְתִּים׃ דֶּרֶךְ
way-of (19) I-understand-them not and-four more-than-me they-are-amazing

הַנֶּשֶׁר ׀ בַּשָּׁמַיִם דֶּרֶךְ נָחָשׁ עֲלֵי צוּר דֶּרֶךְ־ אֳנִיָּה בְלֶב־ יָם
sea on-heart-of ship way-of rock on snake way-of in-the-skies the-eagle

וְדֶרֶךְ גֶּבֶר בְּעַלְמָה׃ כֵּן ׀ דֶּרֶךְ אִשָּׁה מְנָאָפֶת
one-being-adulteress woman way-of this (20) with-maiden man and-way-of

אָכְלָה וּמָחֲתָה פִיהָ וְאָמְרָה לֹא־ פָעַלְתִּי אָוֶן׃ תַּחַת
under (21) wrong I-did not and-she-says mouth-of-her and-she-wipes she-eats

שָׁלוֹשׁ רָגְזָה אֶרֶץ וְתַחַת אַרְבַּע לֹא־ תוּכַל שְׂאֵת׃ תַּחַת־
under (22) to-bear-up she-can not four and-under earth she-trembles three

but give me only my daily
bread.
9 Otherwise, I may have too
much and disown you
and say, 'Who is the LORD?'
Or I may become poor and
steal,
and so dishonor the name
of my God.

10 "Do not slander a servant to
his master,
or he will curse you, and
you will pay for it.

11 "There are those who curse
their fathers
and do not bless their
mothers;
12 those who are pure in their
own eyes
and yet are not cleansed of
their filth;
13 those whose eyes are ever so
haughty,
whose glances are so
disdainful;
14 those whose teeth are swords
and whose jaws are set with
knives
to devour the poor from the
earth,
the needy from among
mankind.

15 "The leech has two daughters.
'Give! Give!' they cry.

"There are three things that
are never satisfied,
four that never say,
'Enough!':
16 the grave,[b] the barren womb,
land, which is never
satisfied with water,
and fire, which never says,
'Enough!'

17 "The eye that mocks a father,
that scorns obedience to a
mother,
will be pecked out by the
ravens of the valley,
will be eaten by the
vultures.

18 "There are three things that
are too amazing for me,
four that I do not
understand:
19 the way of an eagle in the sky,
the way of a snake on a
rock,
the way of a ship on the high
seas,
and the way of a man with
a maiden.

20 "This is the way of an
adulteress:
She eats and wipes her
mouth
and says, 'I've done nothing
wrong.'

21 "Under three things the earth
trembles,
under four it cannot bear
up:

b16 Hebrew *Sheol*

*9 Most mss have *maqqeph* after this word (פֶּן־).

°*10* ק אדניו

°*18* ק וארבעה

עֶבֶד כִּי יִמְלוֹךְ וְנָבָל כִּי יִשְׂבַּע־לָחֶם׃ תַּחַת
under (23) food he-is-full who and-fool he-becomes-king who servant

שְׂנוּאָה כִּי תִבָּעֵל וְשִׁפְחָה כִּי־תִירַשׁ
she-displaces who and-maidservant she-is-married who woman-being-unloved

גְּבִרְתָּהּ׃ אַרְבָּעָה הֵם קְטַנֵּי־אָרֶץ וְהֵמָּה חֲכָמִים
wise-ones yet-they earth small-ones-of they four (24) mistress-of-her

מְחֻכָּמִים׃ הַנְּמָלִים עַם לֹא־עָז וַיָּכִינוּ
yet-they-store-up strong not creature the-ants (25) ones-being-made-wise

בַקַּיִץ לַחְמָם׃ שְׁפַנִּים עַם לֹא־עָצוּם וַיָּשִׂימוּ
yet-they-make powerful not creature conies (26) food-of-them in-the-summer

בַסֶּלַע בֵּיתָם׃ מֶלֶךְ אֵין לָאַרְבֶּה וַיֵּצֵא
yet-he-advances to-the-locust there-is-no king (27) home-of-them in-the-crag

חֹצֵץ כֻּלּוֹ׃ שְׂמָמִית בְּיָדַיִם תְּתַפֵּשׂ וְהִיא
yet-she you-may-catch in-hands lizard (28) all-of-him one-being-in-ranks

בְּהֵיכְלֵי מֶלֶךְ׃ שְׁלֹשָׁה הֵמָּה מֵיטִיבֵי צָעַד וְאַרְבָּעָה
and-four stride ones-being-stately-of they three (29) king in-palaces-of

מֵיטִבֵי לָכֶת׃ לַיִשׁ גִּבּוֹר בַּבְּהֵמָה וְלֹא־
but-not among-the-beast mighty lion (30) to-move ones-being-stately-of

יָשׁוּב מִפְּנֵי־כֹל׃ זַרְזִיר מָתְנַיִם אוֹ־תַיִשׁ וּמֶלֶךְ
and-king he-goat or loins one-girded-of (31) anything from-before he-retreats

אַלְקוּם עִמּוֹ׃ אִם־נָבַלְתָּ בְהִתְנַשֵּׂא וְאִם־
or-if when-to-exalt-yourself you-played-fool if (32) around-him army

זַמּוֹתָ יָד לְפֶה׃ כִּי מִיץ חָלָב יוֹצִיא
he-produces milk churning-of for (33) over-mouth hand you-planned-evil

חֶמְאָה וּמִיץ־אַף יוֹצִיא דָם וּמִיץ אַפַּיִם
angers so-stirring-up-of blood he-produces nose and-twisting-of butter

יוֹצִיא רִיב׃ דִּבְרֵי לְמוּאֵל מֶלֶךְ מַשָּׂא אֲשֶׁר־יִסְּרַתּוּ
she-taught-him that oracle king Lemuel sayings-of (31:1) strife he-produces

אִמּוֹ׃ מַה־בְּרִי וּמַה־בַּר־בִּטְנִי וּמֶה בַּר־
son-of and-oh! womb-of-me son-of and-oh! son-of-me oh! (2) mother-of-him

נְדָרָי׃ אַל־תִּתֵּן לַנָּשִׁים חֵילֶךָ וּדְרָכֶיךָ
and-vigors-of-you strength-of-you on-the-women you-spend not (3) vows-of-me

לַמְחוֹת מְלָכִין׃ אַל לַמְלָכִים ׀ לְמוֹאֵל אַל לַמְלָכִים שְׁתוֹ־יָיִן
wine to-drink for-the-kings not Lemuel for-the-kings not (4) kings to-ruin

וּלְרוֹזְנִים אֵו שֵׁכָר׃ פֶּן־יִשְׁתֶּה וְיִשְׁכַּח
and-he-forgets he-drinks lest (5) beer craving-of or-for-ones-ruling

מְחֻקָּק וִישַׁנֶּה דִּין כָּל־בְּנֵי־עֹנִי׃
oppression people-of all-of right-of and-he-deprives one-being-decreed

°4 ק אי

[22]a servant who becomes king,
a fool who is full of food,
[23]an unloved woman who is married,
and a maidservant who displaces her mistress.

[24]"Four things on earth are small,
yet they are extremely wise:
[25]Ants are creatures of little strength,
yet they store up their food in the summer;
[26]conies[c] are creatures of little power,
yet they make their home in the crags;
[27]locusts have no king,
yet they advance together in ranks;
[28]a lizard can be caught with the hand,
yet it is found in kings' palaces.

[29]"There are three things that are stately in their stride,
four that move with stately bearing:
[30]a lion, mighty among beasts,
who retreats before nothing;
[31]a strutting rooster, a he-goat,
and a king with his army around him.[d]

[32]"If you have played the fool and exalted yourself,
or if you have planned evil,
clap your hand over your mouth!
[33]For as churning the milk produces butter,
and as twisting the nose produces blood,
so stirring up anger produces strife."

*Sayings of King Lemuel*

31 The sayings of King Lemuel—an oracle[e] his mother taught him:

[2]"O my son, O son of my womb,
O son of my vows,[f]
[3]do not spend your strength on women,
your vigor on those who ruin kings.

[4]"It is not for kings, O Lemuel—
not for kings to drink wine,
not for rulers to crave beer,
[5]lest they drink and forget what the law decrees,
and deprive all the oppressed of their rights.

c26 That is, the hyrax or rock badger
d31 Or *king secure against revolt*
e1 Or *of Lemuel king of Massa, which*
f2 Or / *the answer to my prayers*

תְּנוּ־ שֵׁכָר לְאוֹבֵד וְיַיִן לְמָרֵי נָפֶשׁ׃
soul to-ones-anguished-of and-wine to-one-perishing beer give! (6)

יִשְׁתֶּה וְיִשְׁכַּח רִישׁוֹ וַעֲמָלוֹ לֹא
not and-misery-of-him poverty-of-him and-let-him-forget let-him-drink (7)

יִזְכָּר־ עוֹד׃ פְּתַח־ פִּיךָ לְאִלֵּם אֶל־ דִּין כָּל־
all-of right-of for for-mute mouth-of-you open! (8) more let-him-remember

בְּנֵי חֲלוֹף׃ פְּתַח־ פִּיךָ שְׁפָט־ צֶדֶק וְדִין
and-defend-right! fairly judge! mouth-of-you open! (9) destitution people-of

עָנִי וְאֶבְיוֹן׃ אֵשֶׁת־ חַיִל מִי יִמְצָא וְרָחֹק מִפְּנִינִים
more-than-rubies and-far he-can-find who? nobility wife-of (10) and-needy poor

מִכְרָהּ׃ בָּטַח בָּהּ לֵב בַּעְלָהּ וְשָׁלָל
and-valuable husband-of-her heart-of in-her confidence (11) worth-of-her

לֹא יֶחְסָר׃ גְּמָלַתְהוּ טוֹב וְלֹא־ רָע כֹּל יְמֵי חַיֶּיהָ*׃
lives-of-her days-of all-of harm and-not good she-brings-him (12) he-lacks not

דָּרְשָׁה צֶמֶר וּפִשְׁתִּים וַתַּעַשׂ בְּחֵפֶץ כַּפֶּיהָ׃
hands-of-her with-eagerness-of and-she-works and-flaxes wool she-selects (13)

הָיְתָה כָּאֳנִיּוֹת סוֹחֵר מִמֶּרְחָק תָּבִיא לַחְמָהּ׃
food-of-her she-brings from-afar one-being-merchant like-ships-of she-is (14)

וַתָּקָם׀ בְּעוֹד לַיְלָה וַתִּתֵּן טֶרֶף לְבֵיתָהּ
for-family-of-her food and-she-provides dark while-still and-she-gets-up (15)

וְחֹק לְנַעֲרֹתֶיהָ׃ זָמְמָה שָׂדֶה וַתִּקָּחֵהוּ
and-she-buys-him field she-considers (16) for-servant-girls-of-her and-portion

מִפְּרִי כַפֶּיהָ נָטְעָ° כָּרֶם׃ חָגְרָה בְעוֹז
with-vigor she-girds (17) vineyard she-plants hands-of-her from-earning-of

מָתְנֶיהָ וַתְּאַמֵּץ זְרוֹעֹתֶיהָ׃ טָעֲמָה כִּי־ טוֹב
profitable that she-sees (18) arms-of-her and-she-strengthens loins-of-her

סַחְרָהּ לֹא־ יִכְבֶּה בַלַּיְל° נֵרָהּ׃ יָדֶיהָ
hands-of-her (19) lamp-of-her at-the-night she-goes-out not trading-of-her

שִׁלְּחָה בַכִּישׁוֹר וְכַפֶּיהָ תָּמְכוּ פָלֶךְ׃
spindle they-grasp and-fingers-of-her onto-the-distaff she-holds

כַּפָּהּ פָּרְשָׂה לֶעָנִי וְיָדֶיהָ שִׁלְּחָה
she-extends and-hands-of-her to-the-poor she-opens arm-of-her (20)

לָאֶבְיוֹן׃ לֹא־ תִירָא לְבֵיתָהּ מִשָּׁלֶג כִּי כָל־
all-of for from-snow for-household-of-her she-fears not (21) to-the-needy

בֵּיתָהּ לָבֻשׁ שָׁנִים׃ מַרְבַדִּים עָשְׂתָה־ לָּהּ
for-her she-makes coverings (22) scarlets one-being-clothed household-of-her

שֵׁשׁ וְאַרְגָּמָן לְבוּשָׁהּ׃ נוֹדָע בַּשְּׁעָרִים
at-the-gates one-being-respected (23) clothing-of-her and-purple fine-linen

6 Give beer to those who are perishing,
wine to those who are in anguish;
7 let them drink and forget their poverty
and remember their misery no more.

8 "Speak up for those who cannot speak for themselves,
for the rights of all who are destitute.
9 Speak up and judge fairly;
defend the rights of the poor and needy."

*Epilogue: The Wife of Noble Character*[g]

10 A wife of noble character who can find?
She is worth far more than rubies.
11 Her husband has full confidence in her
and lacks nothing of value.
12 She brings him good, not harm,
all the days of her life.
13 She selects wool and flax
and works with eager hands.
14 She is like the merchant ships,
bringing her food from afar.
15 She gets up while it is still dark;
she provides food for her family
and portions for her servant girls.
16 She considers a field and buys it;
out of her earnings she plants a vineyard.
17 She sets about her work vigorously;
her arms are strong for her tasks.
18 She sees that her trading is profitable,
and her lamp does not go out at night.
19 In her hand she holds the distaff
and grasps the spindle with her fingers.
20 She opens her arms to the poor
and extends her hands to the needy.
21 When it snows, she has no fear for her household;
for all of them are clothed in scarlet.
22 She makes coverings for her bed;
she is clothed in fine linen and purple.
23 Her husband is respected at the city gate,

g10 Verses 10-31 are an acrostic, each verse beginning with a successive letter of the Hebrew alphabet.

*12 Most mss have *qamets* under the *he* (הָ—).

°16 ק נטעה
°18 ק בלילה

| | | | | | | |
|---|---|---|---|---|---|---|
| סָדִין | | אָרֶץ׃ | זִקְנֵי־ | עִם־ | בְּשִׁבְתּוֹ | בַּעְלָהּ |
| linen-garment | (24) | land | elders-of | among | when-to-sit-him | husband-of-her |

| | | | | | | |
|---|---|---|---|---|---|---|
| עֹז־ | | לַכְּנַעֲנִי׃ | נָתְנָה | וַחֲגוֹר | וַתִּמְכֹּר | עָשְׂתָה |
| strength | (25) | to-the-merchant | she-supplies | and-sash | and-she-sells | she-makes |

| | | | | | | |
|---|---|---|---|---|---|---|
| פִּיהָ | | אַחֲרוֹן׃ | לְיוֹם | וַתִּשְׂחַק | לְבוּשָׁהּ | וְהָדָר |
| mouth-of-her | (26) | coming | at-day | and-she-can-laugh | clothing-of-her | and-dignity |

| | | | | | |
|---|---|---|---|---|---|
| לְשׁוֹנָהּ׃ | עַל־ | חֶסֶד | וְתוֹרַת־ | בְחָכְמָה | פָּתְחָה |
| tongue-of-her | on | faithfulness | and-instruction-of | with-wisdom | she-opens |

| | | | | | |
|---|---|---|---|---|---|
| עַצְלוּת | וְלֶחֶם | בֵּיתָהּ | הֲלִיכוֹת | צוֹפִיָּה | |
| idleness | and-bread-of | household-of-her | affairs-of | one-watching-over | (27) |

| | | | | | |
|---|---|---|---|---|---|
| וַיְאַשְּׁרוּהָ | בָנֶיהָ | קָמוּ | | תֹאכֵל׃ | לֹא |
| and-they-call-blessed-her | children-of-her | they-arise | (28) | she-eats | not |

| | | | | | | |
|---|---|---|---|---|---|---|
| חָיִל | עָשׂוּ | בָּנוֹת | רַבּוֹת | | וַיְהַלְלָהּ׃ | בַּעְלָהּ |
| noble-thing | they-do | women | many | (29) | also-he-praises-her | husband-of-her |

| | | | | | | | |
|---|---|---|---|---|---|---|---|
| וְהֶבֶל | הַחֵן | שֶׁקֶר | | כֻּלָּנָה׃ | עַל־ | עָלִית | וְאַתְּ |
| and-fleeting | the-charm | deceptive | (30) | all-of-them | over | you-surpass | but-you |

| | | | | | | | | |
|---|---|---|---|---|---|---|---|---|
| לָהּ | תְּנוּ־ | | תִתְהַלָּל׃ | הִיא | יְהוָה | יִרְאַת־ | אִשָּׁה | הַיֹּפִי |
| to-her | give! | (31) | she-is-praised | she | Yahweh | fearer-of | woman | the-beauty |

| | | | | |
|---|---|---|---|---|
| מַעֲשֶׂיהָ׃ | בַשְּׁעָרִים | וִיהַלְלוּהָ | יָדֶיהָ | מִפְּרִי |
| works-of-her | at-the-gates | and-let-them-praise-her | hands-of-her | from-earning-of |

where he takes his seat
among the elders of the
land.
24 She makes linen garments and
sells them,
and supplies the merchants
with sashes.
25 She is clothed with strength
and dignity;
she can laugh at the days to
come.
26 She speaks with wisdom,
and faithful instruction is
on her tongue.
27 She watches over the affairs of
her household
and does not eat the bread
of idleness.
28 Her children arise and call her
blessed;
her husband also, and he
praises her:
29 "Many women do noble
things,
but you surpass them all."
30 Charm is deceptive, and
beauty is fleeting;
but a woman who fears the
LORD is to be praised.
31 Give her the reward she has
earned,
and let her works bring her
praise at the city gate.

דִּבְרֵי קֹהֶלֶת בֶּן־ דָּוִד מֶלֶךְ בִּירוּשָׁלִָם׃ הֲבֵל
meaninglessness-of (2) in-Jerusalem king David son-of Teacher words-of (1:1)

הֲבָלִים אָמַר קֹהֶלֶת הֲבֵל הֲבָלִים הַכֹּל
the-whole meaninglessnesses meaninglessness-of Teacher he-says meaninglessnesses

הָבֶל׃ מַה־ יִּתְרוֹן לָאָדָם בְּכָל־ עֲמָלוֹ שֶׁיַּעֲמֹל
which-he-toils labor-of-him from-all-of to-the-man gain what? (3) meaningless

תַּחַת הַשָּׁמֶשׁ׃ דּוֹר הֹלֵךְ וְדוֹר בָּא וְהָאָרֶץ
but-the-earth going and-generation coming generation (4) the-sun under

לְעוֹלָם עֹמָדֶת׃ וְזָרַח הַשֶּׁמֶשׁ וּבָא הַשָּׁמֶשׁ וְאֶל־
and-to the-sun and-he-sets the-sun and-he-rises (5) remaining to-forever

מְקוֹמוֹ שׁוֹאֵף זוֹרֵחַ הוּא שָׁם׃ הוֹלֵךְ אֶל־דָּרוֹם וְסוֹבֵב אֶל־
to and-turning south to blowing (6) there he rising hurrying place-of-him

צָפוֹן סוֹבֵב ׀ סֹבֵב הוֹלֵךְ הָרוּחַ וְעַל־ סְבִיבֹתָיו
courses-of-him and-on the-wind going turning-round turning-round north

שָׁב הָרוּחַ׃ כָּל־ הַנְּחָלִים הֹלְכִים אֶל־ הַיָּם וְהַיָּם
yet-the-sea the-sea to ones-flowing the-streams all-of (7) the-wind returning

אֵינֶנּוּ מָלֵא אֶל־ מְקוֹם שֶׁהַנְּחָלִים הֹלְכִים שָׁם הֵם
they there ones-coming where-the-streams place-of to full never-he

שָׁבִים לָלָכֶת׃ כָּל־ הַדְּבָרִים יְגֵעִים לֹא־ יוּכַל אִישׁ
one he-can not wearisome-ones the-things all-of (8) to-go ones-returning

לְדַבֵּר לֹא־ תִשְׂבַּע עַיִן לִרְאוֹת וְלֹא־ תִמָּלֵא אֹזֶן מִשְּׁמֹעַ׃
from-to-hear ear she-has-fill or-never to-see eye she-has-enough never to-say

מַה־ שֶּׁהָיָה הוּא שֶׁיִּהְיֶה וּמַה־ שֶּׁנַּעֲשָׂה הוּא
he that-he-was-done and-what that-he-will-be he that-he-was what (9)

שֶׁיֵּעָשֶׂה וְאֵין כָּל־ חָדָשׁ תַּחַת הַשָּׁמֶשׁ׃ יֵשׁ
is-there (10) the-sun under new any-of and-there-is-not that-he-will-be-done

דָּבָר שֶׁיֹּאמַר רְאֵה־ זֶה חָדָשׁ הוּא כְּבָר הָיָה לְעֹלָמִים
from-ones-long-ago he-was already he new this look! which-he-can-say anything

אֲשֶׁר הָיָה מִלְּפָנֵנוּ׃ אֵין זִכְרוֹן לָרִאשֹׁנִים
of-the-men-of-old remembrance there-is-no (11) from-before-us he-was that

וְגַם לָאַחֲרֹנִים שֶׁיִּהְיוּ לֹא־ יִהְיֶה לָהֶם
of-them he-will-be not who-they-will-be of-the-coming-ones and-even

זִכָּרוֹן עִם שֶׁיִּהְיוּ לָאַחֲרֹנָה׃ אֲנִי קֹהֶלֶת הָיִיתִי
I-was Teacher I (12) in-the-following-time who-they-will-be by remembrance

מֶלֶךְ עַל־ יִשְׂרָאֵל בִּירוּשָׁלִָם׃ וְנָתַתִּי אֶת־ לִבִּי לִדְרוֹשׁ
to-study self-of-me *** and-I-devoted (13) in-Jerusalem Israel over king

וְלָתוּר בַּחָכְמָה עַל כָּל־ אֲשֶׁר נַעֲשָׂה תַּחַת הַשָּׁמָיִם הוּא ׀
this the-heavens under he-is-done that all to by-the-wisdom and-to-explore

*Everything Is Meaningless*

1 The words of the Teacher,[a] son of David, king in Jerusalem:

[2] "Meaningless! Meaningless!"
says the Teacher.
"Utterly meaningless!
Everything is meaningless."
[3] What does man gain from all his labor
at which he toils under the sun?
[4] Generations come and generations go,
but the earth remains forever.
[5] The sun rises and the sun sets,
and hurries back to where it rises.
[6] The wind blows to the south
and turns to the north;
round and round it goes,
ever returning on its course.
[7] All streams flow into the sea,
yet the sea is never full.
To the place the streams come from,
there they return again.
[8] All things are wearisome,
more than one can say.
The eye never has enough of seeing,
or the ear its fill of hearing.
[9] What has been will be again,
what has been done will be done again;
there is nothing new under the sun.
[10] Is there anything of which one can say,
"Look! This is something new"?
It was here already, long ago;
it was here before our time.
[11] There is no remembrance of men of old,
and even those who are yet to come
will not be remembered
by those who follow.

*Wisdom Is Meaningless*

[12] I, the Teacher, was king over Israel in Jerusalem. [13] I devoted myself to study and to explore by wisdom all that is done under

[a] 1 Or *leader of the assembly;* also in verses 2 and 12

עִנְיַן רָע נָתַן אֱלֹהִים לִבְנֵי הָאָדָם לַעֲנוֹת בּוֹ׃ רָאִיתִי

I-saw (14) to-him to-afflict the-man on-sons-of God he-laid heaviness burden-of

אֶת־ כָּל־ הַמַּעֲשִׂים שֶׁנַּעֲשׂוּ תַּחַת הַשָּׁמֶשׁ וְהִנֵּה

and-see! the-sun under that-they-are-done the-things-being-done all-of ***

הַכֹּל הֶבֶל וּרְעוּת רוּחַ׃ מְעֻוָּת לֹא־ יוּכַל

he-can not one-being-twisted (15) wind and-chasing-of meaningless the-all

לִתְקֹן וְחֶסְרוֹן לֹא־ יוּכַל לְהִמָּנוֹת׃ דִּבַּרְתִּי אֲנִי עִם־

in I I-thought (16) to-be-counted he-can not and-lack to-be-straightened

לִבִּי לֵאמֹר אֲנִי הִנֵּה הִגְדַּלְתִּי וְהוֹסַפְתִּי חָכְמָה עַל כָּל־ אֲשֶׁר־

who anyone above wisdom and-I-increased I-grew look! I to-say self-of-me

הָיָה לְפָנַי עַל־ יְרוּשָׁלִָם וְלִבִּי רָאָה הַרְבֵּה

to-be-much he-experienced and-heart-of-me Jerusalem over before-me he-was

חָכְמָה וָדָעַת׃ וָאֶתְּנָה לִבִּי לָדַעַת חָכְמָה

wisdom to-understand self-of-me then-I-applied (17) and-knowledge wisdom

וְדַעַת הוֹלֵלוֹת וְשִׂכְלוּת יָדַעְתִּי שֶׁגַּם־ זֶה הוּא רַעְיוֹן

chasing-of he this that-also I-learned and-folly madnesses and-to-understand

רוּחַ׃ כִּי בְּרֹב חָכְמָה רָב־ כָּעַס וְיוֹסִיף

when-he-becomes-more sorrow much-of wisdom with-much-of for (18) wind

דַּעַת יוֹסִיף מַכְאוֹב׃ אָמַרְתִּי אֲנִי בְּלִבִּי

in-heart-of-me I I-thought (2:1) grief then-he-becomes-more knowledge

לְכָה־ נָּא אֲנַסְּכָה* בְשִׂמְחָה וּרְאֵה בְטוֹב וְהִנֵּה

but-see! about-good and-find-out! with-pleasure I-will-test-you now! come!

גַם־ הוּא הָבֶל׃ לִשְׂחוֹק אָמַרְתִּי מְהוֹלָל וּלְשִׂמְחָה

and-with-pleasure being-foolish I-said to-laugh (2) meaningless that also

מַה־ זֹּה עֹשָׂה׃ תַּרְתִּי בְלִבִּי לִמְשׁוֹךְ בַּיַּיִן

with-the-wine to-cheer in-heart-of-me I-tried (3) accomplishing this what?

אֶת־ בְּשָׂרִי וְלִבִּי נֹהֵג בַּחָכְמָה וְלֶאֱחֹז בְּסִכְלוּת

to-folly and-to-embrace with-wisdom one-guiding and-mind-of-me self-of-me ***

עַד אֲשֶׁר־אֶרְאֶה אֵי־ זֶה טוֹב לִבְנֵי הָאָדָם אֲשֶׁר יַעֲשׂוּ

they-do that the-man for-sons-of worthwhile this what I-saw when until

תַּחַת הַשָּׁמַיִם מִסְפַּר יְמֵי חַיֵּיהֶם׃ הִגְדַּלְתִּי מַעֲשָׂי

projects-of-me I-made-great (4) lives-of-them days-of few-of the-heavens under

בָּנִיתִי לִי בָּתִּים נָטַעְתִּי לִי כְּרָמִים׃ עָשִׂיתִי לִי גַּנּוֹת

gardens for-me I-made (5) vineyards for-me I-planted houses for-me I-built

וּפַרְדֵּסִים וְנָטַעְתִּי בָהֶם עֵץ כָּל־ פֶּרִי׃ עָשִׂיתִי לִי

for-me I-made (6) fruit all-of tree-of in-them and-I-planted and-parks

בְּרֵכוֹת מַיִם לְהַשְׁקוֹת מֵהֶם יַעַר צוֹמֵחַ עֵצִים׃

trees one-flourishing-of grove from-them to-water waters reservoirs-of

heaven. What a heavy burden God has laid on men! 14I have seen all the things that are done under the sun; all of them are meaningless, a chasing after the wind.

15What is twisted cannot be
straightened;
what is lacking cannot be
counted.

16I thought to myself, "Look, I have grown and increased in wisdom more than anyone who has ruled over Jerusalem before me; I have experienced much of wisdom and knowledge." 17Then I applied myself to the understanding of wisdom, and also of madness and folly, but I learned that this, too, is a chasing after the wind.

18For with much wisdom comes
much sorrow;
the more knowledge, the
more grief.

*Pleasures Are Meaningless*

2 I thought in my heart, "Come now, I will test you with pleasure to find out what is good." But that also proved to be meaningless. 2"Laughter," I said, "is foolish. And what does pleasure accomplish?" 3I tried cheering myself with wine, and embracing folly—my mind still guiding me with wisdom. I wanted to see what was worthwhile for men to do under heaven during the few days of their lives.

4I undertook great projects: I built houses for myself and planted vineyards. 5I made gardens and parks and planted all kinds of fruit trees in them. 6I made reservoirs to water groves of flourishing trees. 7I bought male

*1 Most mss have the accent *mereka* (כָּ֥ה).

קָנִיתִי עֲבָדִים וּשְׁפָחוֹת וּבְנֵי־ בַיִת הָיָה
he-was house and-ones-born-of and-female-slaves male-slaves I-bought (7)

לִי גַּם מִקְנֶה בָקָר וָצֹאן הַרְבֵּה הָיָה לִי מִכֹּל
more-than-anyone to-me he-was to-be-many and-flock herd cattle also to-me

שֶׁהָיוּ לְפָנַי בִּירוּשָׁלִָם׃ כָּנַסְתִּי לִי גַּם־ כֶּסֶף וְזָהָב
and-gold silver also for-me I-amassed (8) in-Jerusalem before-me who-they-are

וּסְגֻלַּת מְלָכִים וְהַמְּדִינוֹת עָשִׂיתִי לִי שָׁרִים
men-singing for-me I-acquired and-the-provinces kings and-treasure-of

וְשָׁרוֹת וְתַעֲנוּגֹת בְּנֵי הָאָדָם שִׁדָּה וְשִׁדּוֹת׃
and-women woman the-man sons-of and-delights-of and-women-singing

וְגָדַלְתִּי וְהוֹסַפְתִּי מִכֹּל שֶׁהָיָה לְפָנַי
before-me who-he-was more-than-anyone and-I-grew and-I-became-great (9)

בִּירוּשָׁלִָם אַף חָכְמָתִי עָמְדָה לִּי׃ וְכֹל אֲשֶׁר
that and-all (10) with-me she-stayed wisdom-of-me indeed in-Jerusalem

שָׁאֲלוּ עֵינַי לֹא אָצַלְתִּי מֵהֶם לֹא־ מָנַעְתִּי אֶת־ לִבִּי
heart-of-me *** I-refused not from-them I-denied not eyes-of-me they-desired

מִכָּל־ שִׂמְחָה כִּי־ לִבִּי שָׂמֵחַ מִכָּל־ עֲמָלִי
work-of-me in-all-of delighted heart-of-me indeed pleasure from-any-of

וְזֶה־ הָיָה חֶלְקִי מִכָּל־ עֲמָלִי׃ וּפָנִיתִי אֲנִי
I when-I-surveyed (11) labor-of-me for-all-of reward-of-me he-was and-this

בְּכָל־ מַעֲשַׂי שֶׁעָשׂוּ יָדַי וּבֶעָמָל שֶׁעָמַלְתִּי
that-I-toiled and-to-the-toil hands-of-me that-they-did deeds-of-me to-all-of

לַעֲשׂוֹת וְהִנֵּה הַכֹּל הֶבֶל וּרְעוּת רוּחַ וְאֵין יִתְרוֹן
gain and-no wind and-chasing-of meaningless the-all that-see! to-achieve

תַּחַת הַשָּׁמֶשׁ׃ וּפָנִיתִי אֲנִי לִרְאוֹת חָכְמָה וְהוֹלֵלוֹת
also-madnesses wisdom to-consider I then-I-turned (12) the-sun under

וְסִכְלוּת כִּי ׀ מֶה הָאָדָם שֶׁיָּבוֹא אַחֲרֵי הַמֶּלֶךְ אֵת אֲשֶׁר־ כְּבָר
already what *** the-king after who-he-succeeds the-man what? for and-folly

עָשׂוּהוּ׃ וְרָאִיתִי אָנִי שֶׁיֵּשׁ יִתְרוֹן לַחָכְמָה מִן־
more-than to-the-wisdom value that-there-is I and-I-saw (13) they-did-him

הַסִּכְלוּת כִּיתְרוֹן* הָאוֹר מִן־ הַחֹשֶׁךְ׃ הֶחָכָם
the-wise-man (14) the-darkness more-than the-light as-value-of the-folly

עֵינָיו בְּרֹאשׁוֹ וְהַכְּסִיל בַּחֹשֶׁךְ הוֹלֵךְ
walking in-the-darkness while-the-fool in-head-of-him eyes-of-him

וְיָדַעְתִּי גַם־ אָנִי שֶׁמִּקְרֶה אֶחָד יִקְרֶה אֶת־ כֻּלָּם׃
all-of-them *** he-overtakes same that-fate I indeed but-I-realized

וְאָמַרְתִּי אֲנִי בְּלִבִּי כְּמִקְרֵה הַכְּסִיל גַּם־ אֲנִי
I also the-fool as-fate-of in-heart-of-me I then-I-thought (15)

and female slaves and had other slaves who were born in my house. I also owned more herds and flocks than anyone in Jerusalem before me. [8]I amassed silver and gold for myself, and the treasure of kings and provinces. I acquired men and women singers, and a harem[b] as well—the delights of the heart of man. [9]I became greater by far than anyone in Jerusalem before me. In all this my wisdom stayed with me.

[10]I denied myself nothing my
eyes desired;
I refused my heart no
pleasure.
My heart took delight in all
my work,
and this was the reward for
all my labor.
[11]Yet when I surveyed all that
my hands had done
and what I had toiled to
achieve,
everything was meaningless, a
chasing after the wind;
nothing was gained under
the sun.

### *Wisdom and Folly Are Meaningless*

[12]Then I turned my thoughts to
consider wisdom,
and also madness and folly.
What more can the king's
successor do
than what has already been
done?
[13]I saw that wisdom is better
than folly,
just as light is better than
darkness.
[14]The wise man has eyes in his
head,
while the fool walks in the
darkness;
but I came to realize
that the same fate overtakes
them both.
[15]Then I thought in my heart,
"The fate of the fool will

[b]8 The meaning of the Hebrew for this phrase is uncertain.

*13 Most mss have *sheva* under the *kaph* and *hireq* under the *yod* (כְּיִ).

יִקְרֵנִי וְלָמָּה חָכַמְתִּי אֲנִי אָז יוֹתֵר וְדִבַּרְתִּי
and-I-said gain then I should-I-be-wise then-why? he-will-overtake-me

בְלִבִּי שֶׁגַּם־ זֶה הָבֶל׃ כִּי אֵין זִכְרוֹן
remembrance-of there-is-no for (16) meaningless this that-also in-heart-of-me

לֶחָכָם עִם־ הַכְּסִיל לְעוֹלָם בְּשֶׁכְּבָר הַיָּמִים
the-days in-that-already to-forever the-fool like for-the-wise-man

הַבָּאִים הַכֹּל נִשְׁכָּח וְאֵיךְ יָמוּת
he-must-die and-indeed! he-will-be-forgotten the-all the-coming-ones

הֶחָכָם עִם־ הַכְּסִיל׃ וְשָׂנֵאתִי אֶת־ הַחַיִּים כִּי רַע
grievous because the-lives *** so-I-hated (17) the-fool like the-wise-man

עָלַי הַמַּעֲשֶׂה שֶׁנַּעֲשָׂה תַּחַת הַשָּׁמֶשׁ כִּי־ הַכֹּל הָבֶל
meaningless the-all for the-sun under that-he-is-done the-work to-me

וּרְעוּת רוּחַ׃ וְשָׂנֵאתִי אֲנִי אֶת־ כָּל־ עֲמָלִי שֶׁאֲנִי עָמֵל
toiling that-I toil-of-me all-of *** I and-I-hated (18) wind and-chasing-of

תַּחַת הַשָּׁמֶשׁ שֶׁאַנִּיחֶנּוּ לָאָדָם שֶׁיִּהְיֶה אַחֲרָי׃
after-me who-he-comes to-the-one that-I-must-leave-him the-sun under

וּמִי יוֹדֵעַ הֶחָכָם יִהְיֶה אוֹ סָכָל וְיִשְׁלַט
yet-he-will-control fool or he-will-be whether-wise-man knowing and-who? (19)

בְּכָל־ עֲמָלִי שֶׁעָמַלְתִּי וְשֶׁחָכַמְתִּי תַּחַת
under and-which-I-poured-skill which-I-poured-effort work-of-me over-all-of

הַשָּׁמֶשׁ גַּם־ זֶה הָבֶל׃ וְסַבּוֹתִי אֲנִי לְיַאֵשׁ אֶת־ לִבִּי
heart-of-me *** to-despair I so-I-began (20) meaningless this also the-sun

עַל כָּל־ הֶעָמָל שֶׁעָמַלְתִּי תַּחַת הַשָּׁמֶשׁ׃ כִּי־ יֵשׁ אָדָם
man there-is for (21) the-sun under which-I-labored the-toil all-of over

שֶׁעֲמָלוֹ בְּחָכְמָה וּבְדַעַת וּבְכִשְׁרוֹן וּלְאָדָם
then-to-man and-with-skill and-with-knowledge with-wisdom that-work-of-him

שֶׁלֹּא עָמַל־ בּוֹ יִתְּנֶנּוּ חֶלְקוֹ גַּם־ זֶה
this also property-of-him he-must-leave-him for-him he-worked who-not

הֶבֶל וְרָעָה רַבָּה׃ כִּי מֶה־ הֹוֶה לָאָדָם בְּכָל־
for-all-of to-the-man coming what? for (22) great and-misfortune meaningless

עֲמָלוֹ וּבְרַעְיוֹן לִבּוֹ שֶׁהוּא עָמֵל תַּחַת הַשָּׁמֶשׁ׃
the-sun under laboring which-he heart-of-him and-for-striving-of toil-of-him

כִּי כָל־ יָמָיו מַכְאֹבִים וָכַעַס עִנְיָנוֹ גַּם־ בַּלַּיְלָה
at-the-night even work-of-him and-grief-of pains days-of-him all-of for (23)

לֹא־ שָׁכַב לִבּוֹ גַּם־ זֶה הֶבֶל הוּא׃ אֵין־ טוֹב
better nothing (24) he meaningless this also mind-of-him he-rests not

בָּאָדָם שֶׁיֹּאכַל וְשָׁתָה וְהֶרְאָה אֶת־
*** and-he-should-find and-he-should-drink than-he-should-eat for-the-man

overtake me also.
What then do I gain by
being wise?"
I said in my heart,
"This too is meaningless."
16 For the wise man, like the
fool, will not be long
remembered;
in days to come both will be
forgotten.
Like the fool, the wise man too
must die!

*Toil Is Meaningless*

17 So I hated life, because the
work that is done under the sun
was grievous to me. All of it is
meaningless, a chasing after the
wind. 18 I hated all the things I had
toiled for under the sun, because I
must leave them to the one who
comes after me. 19 And who knows
whether he will be a wise man or
a fool? Yet he will have control
over all the work into which I
have poured my effort and skill
under the sun. This too is meaningless. 20 So my heart began to despair over all my toilsome labor
under the sun. 21 For a man may do
his work with wisdom, knowledge and skill, and then he must
leave all he owns to someone who
has not worked for it. This too is
meaningless and a great misfortune. 22 What does a man get for all
the toil and anxious striving with
which he labors under the sun?
23 All his days his work is pain and
grief; even at night his mind does
not rest. This too is meaningless.
24 A man can do nothing better
than to eat and drink and find

נַפְשׁוֹ טוֹב בַּעֲמָלוֹ גַּם־ זֹה רָאִיתִי אָנִי כִּי מִיַּד
from-hand-of that I I-see this also in-work-of-him satisfaction self-of-him

הָאֱלֹהִים הִיא׃ כִּי מִי יֹאכַל וּמִי יָחוּשׁ חוּץ
without he-can-find-enjoyment and-who? he-can-eat who? for (25) she the-God

מִמֶּנִּי׃ כִּי לְאָדָם שֶׁטּוֹב לְפָנָיו נָתַן חָכְמָה וְדַעַת
and-knowledge wisdom he-gives before-him who-pleasing to-man for (26) from-me

וְשִׂמְחָה וְלַחוֹטֶא נָתַן עִנְיָן לֶאֱסוֹף וְלִכְנוֹס
and-to-store to-gather task he-gives but-to-the-one-sinning and-happiness

לָתֵת לְטוֹב לִפְנֵי הָאֱלֹהִים גַּם־ זֶה הֶבֶל וּרְעוּת
and-chasing-of meaningless this also the-God before to-one-pleasing to-hand

רוּחַ׃ לַכֹּל זְמָן וְעֵת לְכָל־ חֵפֶץ תַּחַת
under activity for-every-of and-season time for-the-everything (3:1) wind

הַשָּׁמָיִם׃ עֵת לָלֶדֶת וְעֵת לָמוּת עֵת לָטַעַת
to-plant time-of to-die and-time-of to-be-born time-of (2) the-heavens

וְעֵת לַעֲקוֹר נָטוּעַ׃ עֵת לַהֲרוֹג וְעֵת
and-time-of to-kill time-of (3) one-being-planted to-uproot and-time-of

לִרְפּוֹא עֵת לִפְרוֹץ וְעֵת לִבְנוֹת׃ עֵת לִבְכּוֹת
to-weep time-of (4) to-build and-time-of to-tear-down time-of to-heal

וְעֵת לִשְׂחוֹק עֵת סְפוֹד וְעֵת רְקוֹד׃ עֵת
time-of (5) to-dance and-time-of to-mourn time-of to-laugh and-time-of

לְהַשְׁלִיךְ אֲבָנִים וְעֵת כְּנוֹס אֲבָנִים עֵת לַחֲבוֹק וְעֵת
and-time-of to-embrace time-of stones to-gather and-time-of stones to-scatter

לִרְחֹק מֵחַבֵּק׃ עֵת לְבַקֵּשׁ וְעֵת לְאַבֵּד
to-give-up and-time-of to-search time-of (6) from-to-embrace to-refrain

עֵת לִשְׁמוֹר וְעֵת לְהַשְׁלִיךְ׃ עֵת לִקְרוֹעַ וְעֵת
and-time-of to-tear time-of (7) to-throw-away and-time-of to-keep time-of

לִתְפּוֹר עֵת לַחֲשׁוֹת וְעֵת לְדַבֵּר׃ עֵת לֶאֱהֹב
to-love time-of (8) to-speak and-time-of to-be-silent time-of to-mend

וְעֵת לִשְׂנֹא עֵת מִלְחָמָה וְעֵת שָׁלוֹם׃ מַה־ יִּתְרוֹן
gain-of what? (9) peace and-time-of war time-of to-hate and-time-of

הָעוֹשֶׂה בַּאֲשֶׁר הוּא עָמֵל׃ רָאִיתִי אֶת־ הָעִנְיָן אֲשֶׁר נָתַן
he-laid that the-burden *** I-saw (10) toiling he from-what the-one-working

אֱלֹהִים לִבְנֵי הָאָדָם לַעֲנוֹת בּוֹ׃ אֶת־ הַכֹּל עָשָׂה יָפֶה
beautiful he-made the-all *** (11) to-him to-afflict the-man on-sons-of God

בְעִתּוֹ גַּם אֶת־ הָעֹלָם נָתַן בְּלִבָּם מִבְּלִי אֲשֶׁר
that yet-not in-heart-of-them he-set the-eternity *** also in-time-of-him

לֹא־ יִמְצָא הָאָדָם אֶת־הַמַּעֲשֶׂה אֲשֶׁר־ עָשָׂה הָאֱלֹהִים מֵרֹאשׁ
from-beginning the-God he-did that the-deed *** the-man he-can-fathom not

satisfaction in his work. This too,
I see, is from the hand of God, [25]for
without him, who can eat or find
enjoyment? [26]To the man who
pleases him, God gives wisdom,
knowledge and happiness, but to
the sinner he gives the task of
gathering and storing up wealth
to hand it over to the one who
pleases God. This too is meaningless, a chasing after the wind.

*A Time for Everything*

3 There is a time for everything,
and a season for every activity under heaven:

2 a time to be born and a time to die,
a time to plant and a time to uproot,
3 a time to kill and a time to heal,
a time to tear down and a time to build,
4 a time to weep and a time to laugh,
a time to mourn and a time to dance,
5 a time to scatter stones and a time to gather them,
a time to embrace and a time to refrain,
6 a time to search and a time to give up,
a time to keep and a time to throw away,
7 a time to tear and a time to mend,
a time to be silent and a time to speak,
8 a time to love and a time to hate,
a time for war and a time for peace.

[9]What does the worker gain
from his toil? [10]I have seen the burden God has laid on men. [11]He has
made everything beautiful in its
time. He has also set eternity in
the hearts of men; yet they cannot
fathom what God has done from

וְעַד־סֽוֹף׃ יָדַעְתִּי כִּי אֵין טוֹב בָּם כִּי אִם־
if than for-them better there-is-nothing that I-know (12) end and-to

לִשְׂמוֹחַ וְלַעֲשׂוֹת טוֹב בְּחַיָּיו׃ וְגַם כָּל־הָאָדָם
the-man every-of and-also (13) in-lives-of-him good and-to-do to-be-happy

שֶׁיֹּאכַל וְשָׁתָה וְרָאָה טוֹב בְּכָל־
in-all-of satisfaction and-he-may-find and-he-may-drink that-he-may-eat

עֲמָלוֹ מַתַּת אֱלֹהִים הִיא׃ יָדַעְתִּי כִּי כָּל־אֲשֶׁר יַעֲשֶׂה הָאֱלֹהִים הוּא
he the-God he-does that all that I-know (14) this God gift-of toil-of-him

יִהְיֶה לְעוֹלָם עָלָיו אֵין לְהוֹסִיף וּמִמֶּנּוּ אֵין לִגְרֹעַ
to-take nothing and-from-him to-add nothing to-him to-forever he-will-endure

וְהָאֱלֹהִים עָשָׂה שֶׁיִּרְאוּ מִלְּפָנָיו׃ מַה־
whatever (15) at-before-him who-they-will-revere he-does and-the-God

שֶּׁהָיָה כְּבָר הוּא וַאֲשֶׁר לִהְיוֹת כְּבָר הָיָה וְהָאֱלֹהִים
and-the-God he-was already to-be and-what he already that-he-was

יְבַקֵּשׁ אֶת־נִרְדָּף׃ וְעוֹד רָאִיתִי תַּחַת הַשָּׁמֶשׁ
the-sun under I-saw and-more (16) one-being-past *** he-calls-to-account

מְקוֹם הַמִּשְׁפָּט שָׁמָּה הָרֶשַׁע וּמְקוֹם הַצֶּדֶק
the-justice and-place-of the-wickedness at-there the-judgment place-of

שָׁמָּה הָרָשַׁע׃ אָמַרְתִּי אֲנִי בְּלִבִּי אֶת־הַצַּדִּיק
the-righteous *** in-heart-of-me I I-thought (17) the-wickedness at-there

וְאֶת־הָרָשָׁע יִשְׁפֹּט הָאֱלֹהִים כִּי־עֵת לְכָל־חֵפֶץ וְעַל
and-for activity for-every-of time for the-God he-will-judge the-wicked and

כָּל־הַמַּעֲשֶׂה שָׁם׃ אָמַרְתִּי אֲנִי בְּלִבִּי עַל־דִּבְרַת בְּנֵי
sons-of matter-of for in-heart-of-me I I-thought (18) there the-deed every-of

הָאָדָם לְבָרָם הָאֱלֹהִים וְלִרְאוֹת שְׁהֶם־בְּהֵמָה הֵמָּה לָהֶם׃
like-them they animal that-they and-to-see the-God to-test-them the-man

כִּי מִקְרֶה בְנֵי־הָאָדָם וּמִקְרֶה הַבְּהֵמָה וּמִקְרֶה אֶחָד
same also-fate the-animal and-fate the-man sons-of fate for (19)

לָהֶם כְּמוֹת זֶה כֵּן מוֹת זֶה וְרוּחַ אֶחָד לַכֹּל
to-the-all same and-spirit other death-of so one as-death-of for-them

וּמוֹתַר הָאָדָם מִן־הַבְּהֵמָה אָיִן כִּי הַכֹּל הָבֶל׃
meaningless the-all for there-is-no the-animal over the-man and-advantage-of

הַכֹּל הוֹלֵךְ אֶל־מָקוֹם אֶחָד הַכֹּל הָיָה מִן־הֶעָפָר וְהַכֹּל
and-the-all the-dust from he-comes the-all same place to going the-all (20)

שָׁב אֶל־הֶעָפָר׃ מִי יוֹדֵעַ רוּחַ בְּנֵי הָאָדָם
the-man sons-of spirit-of knowing who? (21) the-dust to he-returns

הָעֹלָה הִיא לְמָעְלָה וְרוּחַ הַבְּהֵמָה הַיֹּרֶדֶת הִיא
she the-one-going-down the-animal and-spirit-of to-upward she the-one-rising

beginning to end. [12]I know that there is nothing better for men than to be happy and do good while they live. [13]That every man may eat and drink, and find satisfaction in all his toil—this is the gift of God. [14]I know that everything God does will endure forever; nothing can be added to it and nothing taken from it. God does it, so men will revere him.

[15]Whatever is has already been,
and what will be has been before;
and God will call the past to account.[c]

[16]And I saw something else under the sun:

In the place of judgment—wickedness was there,
in the place of justice—wickedness was there.

[17]I thought in my heart,

"God will bring to judgment both the righteous and the wicked,
for there will be a time for every activity,
a time for every deed."

[18]I also thought, "As for men, God tests them so that they may see that they are like the animals. [19]Man's fate is like that of the animals; the same fate awaits them both: As one dies, so dies the other. All have the same breath[d]; man has no advantage over the animal. Everything is meaningless. [20]All go to the same place; all come from dust, and to dust all return. [21]Who knows if the spirit of man rises upward and if the spirit of the animal goes down into the earth[e]?"

[c]15 Or *God calls back the past*
[d]19 Or *spirit*
[e]21 Or *Who knows the spirit of man, which rises upward, or the spirit of the animal, which goes down into the earth*

לְמָטָּה לָאָרֶץ׃ וְרָאִיתִי כִּי אֵין טוֹב

good there-is-nothing that so-I-saw (22) into-the-earth to-downward

מֵאֲשֶׁר יִשְׂמַח הָאָדָם בְּמַעֲשָׂיו כִּי־ הוּא חֶלְקוֹ כִּי

for lot-of-him that because to-works-of-him the-man he-enjoy more-than-that

מִי יְבִיאֶנּוּ לִרְאוֹת בְּמֶה שֶׁיִּהְיֶה אַחֲרָיו׃

after-him that-he-will-happen to-what to-see he-can-bring-him who?

וְשַׁבְתִּי אֲנִי וָאֶרְאֶה אֶת־ כָּל־ הָעֲשֻׁקִים אֲשֶׁר

that the-ones-being-oppressed all-of *** and-I-saw I then-I-returned (4:1)

נַעֲשִׂים תַּחַת הַשָּׁמֶשׁ וְהִנֵּה ׀ דִּמְעַת הָעֲשֻׁקִים

the-ones-being-oppressed tear-of and-see! the-sun under ones-taking-place

וְאֵין לָהֶם מְנַחֵם וּמִיַּד עֹשְׁקֵיהֶם

ones-oppressing-them and-on-side-of one-comforting to-them and-there-was-not

כֹּחַ וְאֵין לָהֶם מְנַחֵם׃ וְשַׁבֵּחַ אֲנִי אֶת־

*** I and-to-declare (2) one-comforting to-them and-there-was-not power

הַמֵּתִים שֶׁכְּבָר מֵתוּ מִן־ הַחַיִּים אֲשֶׁר הֵמָּה

they who the-living-ones more-than they-died who-already the-dead-ones

חַיִּים עֲדֶנָה׃ וְטוֹב מִשְּׁנֵיהֶם אֵת אֲשֶׁר־ עֲדֶן לֹא

not yet who *** more-than-both-of-them but-good (3) still alive-ones

הָיָה אֲשֶׁר לֹא־ רָאָה אֶת־ הַמַּעֲשֶׂה הָרָע אֲשֶׁר נַעֲשָׂה תַּחַת הַשָּׁמֶשׁ׃

the-sun under he-is-done that the-evil the-deed *** he-saw not who he-is

וְרָאִיתִי אֲנִי אֶת־ כָּל־ עָמָל וְאֵת כָּל־ כִּשְׁרוֹן הַמַּעֲשֶׂה כִּי

that the-work achievement-of all-of and labor all-of *** I and-I-saw (4)

הִיא קִנְאַת־ אִישׁ מֵרֵעֵהוּ גַּם־ זֶה הֶבֶל וּרְעוּת רוּחַ׃

wind and-chasing-of meaningless this also of-neighbor-of-him man envy-of she

הַכְּסִיל חֹבֵק אֶת־ יָדָיו וְאֹכֵל אֶת־ בְּשָׂרוֹ׃ טוֹב

good (6) self-of-him *** and-ruining hands-of-him *** folding the-fool (5)

מְלֹא כַף נָחַת מִמְּלֹא חָפְנַיִם עָמָל

toil two-hands more-than-fullness-of tranquility hand fullness-of

וּרְעוּת רוּחַ׃ וְשַׁבְתִּי אֲנִי וָאֶרְאֶה הֶבֶל תַּחַת

under meaninglessness and-I-saw I and-I-did-again (7) wind and-chasing-of

הַשָּׁמֶשׁ׃ יֵשׁ אֶחָד וְאֵין שֵׁנִי גַּם בֵּן וָאָח

or-brother son also other and-there-was-not man there-was (8) the-sun

אֵין־ לוֹ וְאֵין קֵץ לְכָל־ עֲמָלוֹ גַּם־

yet toil-of-him to-all-of end and-there-was-no to-him there-was-not

עֵינָיו° לֹא־ תִשְׂבַּע עֹשֶׁר וּלְמִי ׀ אֲנִי עָמֵל וּמְחַסֵּר

and-depriving toiling I and-for-whom? wealth she-was-content not eye-of-him

אֶת־ נַפְשִׁי מִטּוֹבָה גַּם־ זֶה הֶבֶל וְעִנְיַן רָע הוּא׃

he misery and-business-of meaningless this also of-enjoyment self-of-me ***

°8 ק עינו

[22]So I saw that there is nothing better for a man than to enjoy his work, because that is his lot. For who can bring him to see what will happen after him?

*Oppression, Toil, Friendlessness*

**4** Again I looked and saw all the oppression that was taking place under the sun:

I saw the tears of the oppressed—
and they have no comforter;
power was on the side of their oppressors—
and they have no comforter.
[2]And I declared that the dead,
who had already died,
are happier than the living,
who are still alive.
[3]But better than both
is he who has not yet been,
who has not seen the evil
that is done under the sun.

[4]And I saw that all labor and all achievement spring from man's envy of his neighbor. This too is meaningless, a chasing after the wind.

[5]The fool folds his hands
and ruins himself.
[6]Better one handful with tranquillity
than two handfuls with toil
and chasing after the wind.

[7]Again I saw something meaningless under the sun:

[8]There was a man all alone;
he had neither son nor brother.
There was no end to his toil,
yet his eyes were not content with his wealth.
"For whom am I toiling," he asked,
"and why am I depriving myself of enjoyment?"
This too is meaningless—
a miserable business!

טוֹבִים הַשְּׁנַיִם מִן־ הָאֶחָד אֲשֶׁר יֵשׁ־ לָהֶם שָׂכָר טוֹב
good return to-them there-is because the-one more-than the-two good-ones (9)

בַּעֲמָלָם׃ כִּי אִם־ יִפֹּלוּ הָאֶחָד יָקִים אֶת־
*** he-can-help-up the-one they-fall if for (10) for-work-of-them

חֲבֵרוֹ וְאִילוֹ הָאֶחָד שֶׁיִּפּוֹל וְאֵין שֵׁנִי
other and-there-is-no who-he-falls the-one but-pity-to-him! friend-of-him

לַהֲקִימוֹ׃ גַּם אִם־ יִשְׁכְּבוּ שְׁנַיִם וְחַם לָהֶם וּלְאֶחָד
but-to-one to-them then-he-is-warm two they-lie-down if also (11) to-help-up-him

אֵיךְ יֵחָם׃ וְאִם־ יִתְקְפוֹ הָאֶחָד הַשְּׁנַיִם
the-two the-one they-may-overpower and-though (12) can-he-keep-warm how?

יַעַמְדוּ נֶגְדּוֹ וְהַחוּט הַמְשֻׁלָּשׁ לֹא בִמְהֵרָה
in-quickness not the-one-being-tripled and-the-cord before-him they-can-stand

יִנָּתֵק׃ טוֹב יֶלֶד מִסְכֵּן וְחָכָם מִמֶּלֶךְ זָקֵן וּכְסִיל
but-foolish old more-than-king but-wise poor youth good (13) he-is-broken

אֲשֶׁר לֹא־ יָדַע לְהִזָּהֵר עוֹד׃ כִּי־ מִבֵּית
from-house-of indeed (14) longer to-take-warning he-knows not who

הָסוּרִים יָצָא לִמְלֹךְ כִּי גַּם בְּמַלְכוּתוֹ
within-kingdom-of-him rather or to-be-king he-came the-ones-being-imprisoned

נוֹלַד רָשׁ׃ רָאִיתִי אֶת־ כָּל־ הַחַיִּים
the-ones-alive all-of *** I-saw (15) one-being-poor he-was-born

הַמְהַלְּכִים תַּחַת הַשָּׁמֶשׁ עִם הַיֶּלֶד הַשֵּׁנִי אֲשֶׁר יַעֲמֹד
he-succeeded who the-other the-youth with the-sun under the-ones-walking

תַּחְתָּיו׃ אֵין־ קֵץ לְכָל־ הָעָם לְכֹל אֲשֶׁר־ הָיָה
he-was who to-all the-people to-all-of end there-was-no (16) after-him

לִפְנֵיהֶם גַּם הָאַחֲרוֹנִים לֹא יִשְׂמְחוּ־ בוֹ כִּי־ גַם־
also indeed with-him they-were-pleased not the-later-ones but before-them

זֶה הֶבֶל וְרַעְיוֹן רוּחַ׃ שְׁמֹר רַגְלְיךָ° כַּאֲשֶׁר תֵּלֵךְ
you-go as-when step-of-you guard! *(17) wind and-chasing-of meaningless this

אֶל־ בֵּית הָאֱלֹהִים וְקָרוֹב לִשְׁמֹעַ מִתֵּת הַכְּסִילִים
the-fools rather-than-to-offer to-listen then-to-go-near the-God house-of to

זָבַח כִּי־ אֵינָם יוֹדְעִים לַעֲשׂוֹת רָע׃ אַל־ תְּבַהֵל עַל־
with you-be-quick not (5:1) wrong to-do ones-knowing not-they for sacrifice

פִּיךָ וְלִבְּךָ אַל־ יְמַהֵר לְהוֹצִיא דָבָר לִפְנֵי
before anything to-utter let-him-be-hasty not and-heart-of-you mouth-of-you

הָאֱלֹהִים כִּי הָאֱלֹהִים בַּשָּׁמַיִם וְאַתָּה עַל־ הָאָרֶץ עַל־ כֵּן יִהְיוּ
let-them-be this for the-earth on and-you in-the-heavens the-God for the-God

דְבָרֶיךָ מְעַטִּים׃ כִּי בָא הַחֲלוֹם בְּרֹב עִנְיָן
care when-many-of the-dream he-comes as (2) few-ones words-of-you

[9]Two are better than one,
because they have a good
return for their work:
[10]If one falls down,
his friend can help him up.
But pity the man who falls
and has no one to help him
up!
[11]Also, if two lie down together,
they will keep warm.
But how can one keep warm
alone?
[12]Though one may be
overpowered,
two can defend themselves.
A cord of three strands is not
quickly broken.

*Advancement Is Meaningless*

[13]Better a poor but wise youth
than an old but foolish king who
no longer knows how to take
warning. [14]The youth may have
come from prison to the kingship,
or he may have been born in poverty within his kingdom. [15]I saw
that all who lived and walked under the sun followed the youth,
the king's successor. [16]There was
no end to all the people who were
before them. But those who came
later were not pleased with the
successor. This too is meaningless,
a chasing after the wind.

*Stand in Awe of God*

5 Guard your steps when you go
to the house of God. Go near to
listen rather than to offer the sacrifice of fools, who do not know
that they do wrong.

[2]Do not be quick with your
mouth,
do not be hasty in your
heart
to utter anything before
God.
God is in heaven
and you are on earth,
so let your words be few.
[3]As a dream comes when there
are many cares,

***17 The Hebrew numeration of chapter 5 begins with verse two of the English; thus, there is a one-verse discrepancy throughout the chapter.**

°*17* ק רגלךָ

וְקוֹל כְּסִיל בְּרֹב דְּבָרִים׃ כַּאֲשֶׁר תִּדֹּר נֶדֶר לֵאלֹהִים
to-God vow you-make-vow as-when (3) words when-many-of fool so-speech-of

אַל־ תְּאַחֵר לְשַׁלְּמוֹ כִּי אֵין חֵפֶץ בַּכְּסִילִים אֵת אֲשֶׁר־
what *** in-the-fools pleasure there-is-no for to-fulfill-him you-delay not

תִּדֹּר שַׁלֵּם׃ טוֹב אֲשֶׁר לֹא־ תִדֹּר מִשֶּׁתִּדּוֹר
more-than-that-you-make-vow you-make-vow not that good (4) fulfill! you-vow

וְלֹא תְשַׁלֵּם׃ אַל־ תִּתֵּן אֶת־ פִּיךָ לַחֲטִיא אֶת־
*** to-lead-into-sin mouth-of-you *** you-let not (5) you-fulfill and-not

בְּשָׂרֶךָ וְאַל־ תֹּאמַר לִפְנֵי הַמַּלְאָךְ כִּי שְׁגָגָה הִיא
she mistake that the-messenger before you-protest and-not self-of-you

לָמָּה יִקְצֹף הָאֱלֹהִים עַל־ קוֹלֶךָ וְחִבֵּל אֶת־ מַעֲשֵׂה
work-of *** and-he-destroy saying-of-you at the-God should-he-be-angry why?

יָדֶיךָ׃ כִּי בְרֹב חֲלֹמוֹת וַהֲבָלִים וּדְבָרִים
and-words also-meaninglessnesses dreams in-much-of for (6) hands-of-you

הַרְבֵּה כִּי אֶת־הָאֱלֹהִים יְרָא׃ אִם־ עֹשֶׁק רָשׁ
one-being-poor oppression-of if (7) fear! the-God *** therefore to-be-many

וְגֵזֶל מִשְׁפָּט וָצֶדֶק תִּרְאֶה בַמְּדִינָה אַל־ תִּתְמַהּ
you-be-surprised not in-the-district you-see and-right justice and-denial-of

עַל־ הַחֵפֶץ כִּי גָבֹהַּ מֵעַל גָּבֹהַּ שֹׁמֵר וּגְבֹהִים
and-officials one-eyeing official at-above official for the-thing at

עֲלֵיהֶם׃ וְיִתְרוֹן אֶרֶץ בַּכֹּל הִיא מֶלֶךְ לְשָׂדֶה נֶעֱבָד׃
he-profits from-field king he to-the-all land and-increase-of (8) over-them

אֹהֵב כֶּסֶף לֹא־ יִשְׂבַּע כֶּסֶף וּמִי־ אֹהֵב
one-loving and-whoever money he-has-enough never money one-loving (9)

בֶּהָמוֹן לֹא תְבוּאָה גַּם־ זֶה הָבֶל׃ בִּרְבוֹת
when-to-increase (10) meaningless this also income never to-the-wealth

הַטּוֹבָה רַבּוּ אוֹכְלֶיהָ וּמַה־ כִּשְׁרוֹן לִבְעָלֶיהָ
to-owners-of-her benefit and-what? ones-consuming-her they-increase the-good

כִּי אִם־ רְאִית עֵינָיו׃ מְתוּקָה שְׁנַת הָעֹבֵד
the-one-laboring sleep-of sweet (11) eyes-of-him feasting-of if except

אִם־ מְעַט וְאִם־ הַרְבֵּה יֹאכֵל וְהַשָּׂבָע לֶעָשִׁיר
of-the-rich but-the-abundance he-eats to-be-much or-whether little whether

אֵינֶנּוּ מַנִּיחַ לוֹ לִישׁוֹן׃ יֵשׁ רָעָה חוֹלָה
one-being-grievous evil there-is (12) to-sleep to-him one-permitting not-he

רָאִיתִי תַּחַת הַשָּׁמֶשׁ עֹשֶׁר שָׁמוּר לִבְעָלָיו לְרָעָתוֹ׃
to-harm-of-him by-owners-of-him being-hoarded wealth the-sun under I-saw

וְאָבַד הָעֹשֶׁר הַהוּא בְּעִנְיַן רָע
misfortune through-event-of the-this the-wealth or-he-is-lost (13)

so the speech of a fool when
there are many words.

4 When you make a vow to God, do not delay in fulfilling it. He has no pleasure in fools; fulfill your vow. 5 It is better not to vow than to make a vow and not fulfill it. 6 Do not let your mouth lead you into sin. And do not protest to the ⌞temple⌟ messenger, "My vow was a mistake." Why should God be angry at what you say and destroy the work of your hands? 7 Much dreaming and many words are meaningless. Therefore stand in awe of God.

*Riches Are Meaningless*

8 If you see the poor oppressed in a district, and justice and rights denied, do not be surprised at such things; for one official is eyed by a higher one, and over them both are others higher still. 9 The increase from the land is taken by all; the king himself profits from the fields.

10 Whoever loves money never
has money enough;
whoever loves wealth is
never satisfied with his
income.
This too is meaningless.

11 As goods increase,
so do those who consume
them.
And what benefit are they to
the owner
except to feast his eyes on
them?

12 The sleep of a laborer is sweet,
whether he eats little or
much,
but the abundance of a rich
man
permits him no sleep.

13 I have seen a grievous evil under the sun:

wealth hoarded to the harm of
its owner,
14 or wealth lost through some
misfortune,

*See the note on page 576.

°8 ק הוא
°10 ק ראות

וְהוֹלִיד בֵּן וְאֵין בְּיָדוֹ מְאוּמָה׃ כַּאֲשֶׁר
just-as (14) anything for-hand-of-him and-there-is-not son so-he-fathers

יָצָא מִבֶּטֶן אִמּוֹ עָרוֹם יָשׁוּב לָלֶכֶת כְּשֶׁבָּא
as-that-he-comes to-go he-departs naked mother-of-him from-womb-of he-comes

וּמְאוּמָה לֹא־ יִשָּׂא בַעֲמָלוֹ שֶׁיֹּלֵךְ בְּיָדוֹ׃
in-hand-of-him that-he-can-carry from-labor-of-him he-takes not and-anything

וְגַם־ זֹה רָעָה חוֹלָה כָּל־ עֻמַּת שֶׁבָּא כֵּן
so that-he-comes as-of all-of being-grievous evil this and-also (15)

יֵלֵךְ וּמַה־ יִּתְרוֹן לוֹ שֶׁיַּעֲמֹל לָרוּחַ׃ גַּם
also (16) for-the-wind since-he-toils for-him gain and-what? he-departs

כָּל־ יָמָיו בַּחֹשֶׁךְ יֹאכֵל וְכָעַס הַרְבֵּה
to-be-great and-he-is-frustrated he-eats in-the-darkness days-of-him all-of

וְחָלְיוֹ וָקָצֶף׃ הִנֵּה אֲשֶׁר־ רָאִיתִי אָנִי טוֹב אֲשֶׁר־
that good I I-realized then see! (17) and-anger and-affliction-of-him

יָפֶה לֶאֱכוֹל־† וְלִשְׁתּוֹת וְלִרְאוֹת טוֹבָה בְּכָל־ עֲמָלוֹ ׀
labor-of-him in-all-of satisfaction and-to-find and-to-drink to-eat proper

שֶׁיַּעֲמֹל תַּחַת־ הַשֶּׁמֶשׁ מִסְפַּר יְמֵי־ חַיָּו אֲשֶׁר־ נָתַן־ לוֹ
to-him he-gave that lives-of-him days-of few-of the-sun under that-he-toils

הָאֱלֹהִים כִּי־ הוּא חֶלְקוֹ׃ גַּם כָּל־ הָאָדָם אֲשֶׁר נָתַן־
he-gives whom the-man any-of moreover (18) lot-of-him this for the-God

לוֹ הָאֱלֹהִים עֹשֶׁר וּנְכָסִים וְהִשְׁלִיטוֹ לֶאֱכֹל מִמֶּנּוּ
from-him to-enjoy and-he-enables-him and-possessions wealth the-God to-him

וְלָשֵׂאת אֶת־ חֶלְקוֹ וְלִשְׂמֹחַ בַּעֲמָלוֹ זֹה מַתַּת
gift-of this in-work-of-him and-to-be-happy lot-of-him *** and-to-accept

אֱלֹהִים הִיא׃ כִּי לֹא הַרְבֵּה יִזְכֹּר אֶת־ יְמֵי חַיָּיו
lives-of-him days-of *** he-reflects-on to-be-often not indeed (19) she God

כִּי הָאֱלֹהִים מַעֲנֶה בְּשִׂמְחַת לִבּוֹ׃ יֵשׁ
there-is (6:1) heart-of-him with-gladness-of one-occupying the-God because

רָעָה אֲשֶׁר רָאִיתִי תַּחַת הַשָּׁמֶשׁ וְרַבָּה הִיא עַל־הָאָדָם׃ אִישׁ אֲשֶׁר יִתֶּן־
he-gives whom man (2) the-man on she and-heavy the-sun under I-saw that evil

לוֹ הָאֱלֹהִים עֹשֶׁר וּנְכָסִים וְכָבוֹד וְאֵינֶנּוּ חָסֵר לְנַפְשׁוֹ ׀
to-heart-of-him lack so-not-he and-honor and-possessions wealth the-God to-him

מִכֹּל אֲשֶׁר־ יִתְאַוֶּה וְלֹא־ יַשְׁלִיטֶנּוּ הָאֱלֹהִים לֶאֱכֹל מִמֶּנּוּ
from-him to-enjoy the-God he-enables-him but-not he-desires that from-all

כִּי אִישׁ נָכְרִי יֹאכְלֶנּוּ זֶה הֶבֶל וָחֳלִי רָע הוּא׃
he grievous and-evil meaningless this he-enjoys-him stranger man but

אִם־ יוֹלִיד אִישׁ מֵאָה וְשָׁנִים רַבּוֹת יִחְיֶה וְרַב ׀
yet-many he-lives many and-years hundred man he-has-children if (3)

so that when he has a son
there is nothing left for him.
15 Naked a man comes from his
mother's womb,
and as he comes, so he
departs.
He takes nothing from his
labor
that he can carry in his
hand.

16 This too is a grievous evil:

As a man comes, so he
departs,
and what does he gain,
since he toils for the wind?
17 All his days he eats in
darkness,
with great frustration,
affliction and anger.

18 Then I realized that it is good and proper for a man to eat and drink, and to find satisfaction in his toilsome labor under the sun during the few days of life God has given him—for this is his lot.
19 Moreover, when God gives any man wealth and possessions, and enables him to enjoy them, to accept his lot and be happy in his work—this is a gift of God.
20 He seldom reflects on the days of his life, because God keeps him occupied with gladness of heart.

6 I have seen another evil under the sun, and it weighs heavily on men:
2 God gives a man wealth, possessions and honor, so that he lacks nothing his heart desires, but God does not enable him to enjoy them, and a stranger enjoys them instead. This is meaningless, a grievous evil.
3 A man may have a hundred children and live many years; yet no matter how long he lives, if he

*See the note on page 576.

†17 Most mss have *hateph segol* under the *aleph* (לֶאֱ).

שֶׁיִּהְיוּ יְמֵי־ שָׁנָיו וְנַפְשׁוֹ לֹא־ תִשְׂבַּע מִן־
from she-enjoys not if-self-of-him years-of-him days-of that-they-are

הַטּוֹבָה וְגַם־ קְבוּרָה לֹא־ הָיְתָה לּוֹ אָמַרְתִּי טוֹב מִמֶּנּוּ
more-than-him good I-say to-him she-is not burial and-also the-prosperity

הַנָּפֶל׃ (4) כִּי־ בַהֶבֶל בָּא וּבַחֹשֶׁךְ
and-in-the-darkness he-comes in-the-meaninglessness indeed (4) the-stillborn-child

יֵלֵךְ וּבַחֹשֶׁךְ שְׁמוֹ יְכֻסֶּה׃ (5) גַּם־ שֶׁמֶשׁ
sun though (5) he-is-shrouded name-of-him and-in-the-darkness he-departs

לֹא־ רָאָה וְלֹא יָדָע נַחַת לָזֶה מִזֶּה׃
more-than-that-one to-this-one rest he-knew and-never he-saw never

(6) וְאִלּוּ חָיָה אֶלֶף שָׁנִים פַּעֲמַיִם וְטוֹבָה לֹא רָאָה
he-enjoys not but-prosperity twice years thousand-of he-lives even-if (6)

הֲלֹא אֶל־ מָקוֹם אֶחָד הַכֹּל הוֹלֵךְ׃ (7) כָּל־ עֲמַל הָאָדָם לְפִיהוּ
for-mouth-of-him the-man effort-of all-of (7) going the-all same place to not?

וְגַם־ הַנֶּפֶשׁ לֹא תִמָּלֵא׃ (8) כִּי מַה־ יּוֹתֵר
advantage what? indeed (8) she-is-satisfied never the-appetite yet-also

לֶחָכָם מִן־ הַכְּסִיל מַה־ לֶּעָנִי יוֹדֵעַ לַהֲלֹךְ
to-conduct-himself knowing to-the-poor-man what? the-fool over to-the-wise

נֶגֶד הַחַיִּים׃ (9) טוֹב מַרְאֵה עֵינַיִם מֵהֲלָךְ־ נָפֶשׁ גַּם־
also appetite more-than-to-rove eyes sight-of good (9) the-others before

זֶה הֶבֶל וּרְעוּת רוּחַ׃ (10) מַה־ שֶּׁהָיָה כְּבָר
already that-he-exists whatever (10) wind and-chasing-of meaningless this

נִקְרָא שְׁמוֹ וְנוֹדָע אֲשֶׁר־ הוּא אָדָם וְלֹא־ יוּכַל
he-can and-not man he what and-being-known name-of-him he-was-called

לָדִין עִם שֶׁהתַּקִּיף מִמֶּנּוּ׃ (11) כִּי יֵשׁ־ דְּבָרִים הַרְבֵּה
to-be-many words there-are for (11) more-than-he who-strong with to-contend

מַרְבִּים הָבֶל מַה־ יֹּתֵר לָאָדָם׃ (12) כִּי מִי־
who? for (12) to-the-man profit what? meaninglessness ones-making-many

יוֹדֵעַ מַה־ טּוֹב לָאָדָם בַּחַיִּים מִסְפַּר יְמֵי־ חַיֵּי
lives-of days-of few-of in-the-lives for-the-man good what? knowing

הֶבְלוֹ וְיַעֲשֵׂם כַּצֵּל אֲשֶׁר מִי־
who? that like-the-shadow and-he-passes-through-them meaninglessness-of-him

יַגִּיד לָאָדָם מַה־ יִּהְיֶה אַחֲרָיו תַּחַת הַשָּׁמֶשׁ׃
the-sun under after-him he-will-happen what? to-the-man he-can-tell

(7:1) טוֹב שֵׁם מִשֶּׁמֶן טוֹב וְיוֹם הַמָּוֶת מִיּוֹם
more-than-day-of the-death and-day-of fine more-than-perfume name good (7:1)

הִוָּלְדוֹ׃ (2) טוֹב לָלֶכֶת אֶל־ בֵּית־ אֵבֶל מִלֶּכֶת אֶל־
to more-than-to-go mourning house-of to to-go good (2) to-be-born-him

cannot enjoy his prosperity and does not receive proper burial, I say that a stillborn child is better off than he. [4]It comes without meaning, it departs in darkness, and in darkness its name is shrouded. [5]Though it never saw the sun or knew anything, it has more rest than does that man—[6]even if he lives a thousand years twice over but fails to enjoy his prosperity. Do not all go to the same place?

[7]All man's efforts are for his
mouth,
yet his appetite is never
satisfied.
[8]What advantage has a wise
man
over a fool?
What does a poor man gain
by knowing how to conduct
himself before others?
[9]Better what the eye sees
than the roving of the
appetite.
This too is meaningless,
a chasing after the wind.

[10]Whatever exists has already
been named,
and what man is has been
known;
no man can contend
with one who is stronger
than he.
[11]The more the words,
the less the meaning,
and how does that profit
anyone?

[12]For who knows what is good for a man in life, during the few and meaningless days he passes through like a shadow? Who can tell him what will happen under the sun after he is gone?

*Wisdom*

7 A good name is better than
fine perfume,
and the day of death better
than the day of birth.
[2]It is better to go to a house of
mourning

°10 ק שתקיף

בֵּית מִשְׁתֶּה בַּאֲשֶׁר הוּא סוֹף כָּל־ הָאָדָם וְהַחַי
and-the-living the-man every-of destiny-of he for-that feasting house-of

יִתֵּן אֶל־ לִבּוֹ׃ טוֹב כַּעַס מִשְּׂחֹק כִּי־
because more-than-laughter sorrow good (3) heart-of-him to he-should-take

בְרֹעַ פָּנִים יִיטַב לֵב׃ לֵב חֲכָמִים בְּבֵית
in-house-of wise-men heart-of (4) heart he-is-good faces by-sadness-of

אֵבֶל וְלֵב כְּסִילִים בְּבֵית שִׂמְחָה׃ טוֹב לִשְׁמֹעַ גַּעֲרַת
rebuke-of to-heed good (5) pleasure in-house-of fools but-heart-of mourning

חָכָם מֵאִישׁ שֹׁמֵעַ שִׁיר כְּסִילִים׃ כִּי כְקוֹל
like-crackling-of indeed (6) fools song-of listening more-than-man wise

הַסִּירִים תַּחַת הַסִּיר כֵּן שְׂחֹק הַכְּסִיל וְגַם־ זֶה הָבֶל׃
meaningless this and-also the-fool laughter-of so the-pot under the-thorns

כִּי הָעֹשֶׁק יְהוֹלֵל חָכָם וִיאַבֵּד אֶת־ לֵב
heart *** and-he-corrupts wise-man he-makes-foolish the-extortion for (7)

מַתָּנָה׃ טוֹב אַחֲרִית דָּבָר מֵרֵאשִׁיתוֹ טוֹב אֶרֶךְ־
patience-of good more-than-beginning-of-him matter end-of good (8) bribe

רוּחַ מִגְּבַהּ־ רוּחַ׃ אַל־ תְּבַהֵל בְּרוּחֲךָ
in-spirit-of-you you-be-quick not (9) spirit more-than-pride-of spirit

לִכְעוֹס כִּי כַעַס בְּחֵיק כְּסִילִים יָנוּחַ׃ אַל־ תֹּאמַר מֶה
why? you-say not (10) he-resides fools in-lap-of anger for to-be-provoked

הָיָה שֶׁהַיָּמִים הָרִאשֹׁנִים הָיוּ טוֹבִים מֵאֵלֶּה כִּי לֹא
not for more-than-these good-ones they-were the-old-ones that-the-days he-was

מֵחָכְמָה שָׁאַלְתָּ עַל־ זֶה׃ טוֹבָה חָכְמָה עִם־ נַחֲלָה וְיֹתֵר
and-benefit inheritance like wisdom good (11) such about you-ask from-wisdom

לְרֹאֵי הַשָּׁמֶשׁ׃ כִּי בְּצֵל הַחָכְמָה בְּצֵל
in-shelter-of the-wisdom in-shelter-of for (12) the-sun to-ones-seeing-of

הַכָּסֶף וְיִתְרוֹן דַּעַת הַחָכְמָה תְּחַיֶּה
she-keeps-alive the-wisdom knowledge but-advantage-of the-money

בְעָלֶיהָ׃ רְאֵה אֶת־ מַעֲשֵׂה הָאֱלֹהִים כִּי מִי יוּכַל
he-can who? for the-God deed-of *** consider! (13) possessors-of-her

לְתַקֵּן אֵת אֲשֶׁר עִוְּתוֹ׃ בְּיוֹם טוֹבָה הֱיֵה
be! good in-time-of (14) he-made-crooked-him what *** to-straighten

בְטוֹב וּבְיוֹם רָעָה רְאֵה גַּם אֶת־ זֶה לְעֻמַּת־ זֶה
other as-well-as this *** also consider! bad but-in-time-of in-happiness

עָשָׂה הָאֱלֹהִים עַל־ דִּבְרַת שֶׁלֹּא יִמְצָא הָאָדָם אַחֲרָיו
after-him the-man he-can-discover that-not account-of on the-God he-made

מְאוּמָה׃ אֶת־ הַכֹּל רָאִיתִי בִּימֵי הֶבְלִי יֵשׁ
there-is meaninglessness-of-me in-days-of I-saw the-all *** (15) anything

than to go to a house of
feasting,
for death is the destiny of
every man;
the living should take this to
heart.
3 Sorrow is better than laughter,
because a sad face is good
for the heart.
4 The heart of the wise is in the
house of mourning,
but the heart of fools is in
the house of pleasure.
5 It is better to heed a wise
man's rebuke
than to listen to the song of
fools.
6 Like the crackling of thorns
under the pot,
so is the laughter of fools.
This too is meaningless.
7 Extortion turns a wise man
into a fool,
and a bribe corrupts the
heart.
8 The end of a matter is better
than its beginning,
and patience is better than
pride.
9 Do not be quickly provoked in
your spirit,
for anger resides in the lap
of fools.
10 Do not say, "Why were the
old days better than
these?"
For it is not wise to ask
such questions.
11 Wisdom, like an inheritance,
is a good thing
and benefits those who see
the sun.
12 Wisdom is a shelter
as money is a shelter,
but the advantage of
knowledge is this:
that wisdom preserves the
life of its possessor.
13 Consider what God has done:
Who can straighten
what he has made crooked?
14 When times are good, be
happy;
but when times are bad,
consider:
God has made the one
as well as the other.
Therefore, a man cannot
discover
anything about his future.
15 In this meaningless life of
mine I have seen both of these:

צַדִּיק אֹבֵד בְּצִדְקוֹ וְיֵשׁ רָשָׁע
wicked-man and-there-is in-righteousness-of-him perishing righteous-man

מַאֲרִיךְ בְּרָעָתוֹ׃ אַל־ תְּהִי צַדִּיק הַרְבֵּה וְאַל־
and-not to-be-much righteous you-be not (16) in-wickedness-of-him living-long

תִּתְחַכַּם יוֹתֵר לָמָּה תִּשּׁוֹמֵם׃ אַל־ תִּרְשַׁע
you-be-wicked not (17) you-destroy-yourself why? much you-be-overwise

הַרְבֵּה וְאַל־ תְּהִי סָכָל לָמָּה תָמוּת בְּלֹא עִתֶּךָ׃ טוֹב
good (18) time-of-you when-not you-die why? fool you-be and-not to-be-much

אֲשֶׁר תֶּאֱחֹז בָּזֶה וְגַם־ מִזֶּה אַל־ תַּנַּח אֶת־ יָדֶךָ כִּי־
for hand-of-you *** you-let-go not of-other and-also to-one you-grasp that

יְרֵא אֱלֹהִים יֵצֵא אֶת־ כֻּלָּם׃ הַחָכְמָה
the-wisdom (19) all-of-them *** he-will-avoid God one-fearing-of

תָּעֹז לֶחָכָם מֵעֲשָׂרָה שַׁלִּיטִים אֲשֶׁר הָיוּ
they-are who rulers more-than-ten to-the-wise-man she-is-powerful

בָּעִיר׃ כִּי אָדָם אֵין צַדִּיק בָּאָרֶץ אֲשֶׁר יַעֲשֶׂה־
he-does who on-the-earth righteous there-is-not man for (20) in-the-city

טּוֹב וְלֹא יֶחֱטָא׃ גַּם לְכָל־ הַדְּבָרִים אֲשֶׁר יְדַבֵּרוּ אַל־
not they-say that the-words to-all-of also (21) he-sins and-never right

תִּתֵּן לִבֶּךָ אֲשֶׁר לֹא־ תִשְׁמַע אֶת־ עַבְדְּךָ מְקַלְלֶךָ׃
cursing-you servant-of-you *** you-hear not that attention-of-you you-give

כִּי גַּם־פְּעָמִים רַבּוֹת יָדַע לִבֶּךָ אֲשֶׁר גַּם־ אַתָּ קִלַּלְתָּ
you-cursed you also that heart-of-you he-knows many times also for (22)

אֲחֵרִים׃ כָּל־ זֹה נִסִּיתִי בַחָכְמָה אָמַרְתִּי אֶחְכָּמָה וְהִיא
but-this I-will-be-wise I-said by-the-wisdom I-tested this all-of (23) others

רְחוֹקָה מִמֶּנִּי׃ רָחוֹק מַה־ שֶּׁהָיָה וְעָמֹק | עָמֹק
profound and-profound that-he-may-be whatever far-off (24) from-me beyond

מִי יִמְצָאֶנּוּ׃ סַבּוֹתִי אֲנִי וְלִבִּי לָדַעַת
to-understand also-mind-of-me I I-turned (25) he-can-discover-him who?

וְלָתוּר וּבַקֵּשׁ חָכְמָה וְחֶשְׁבּוֹן וְלָדַעַת
and-to-understand and-scheme wisdom and-to-search-out and-to-investigate

רֶשַׁע כֶּסֶל וְהַסִּכְלוּת הוֹלֵלוֹת׃ וּמוֹצֶא אֲנִי מַר
bitter I and-finding (26) madnesses and-the-folly stupidity wickedness-of

מִמָּוֶת אֶת־ הָאִשָּׁה אֲשֶׁר־הִיא מְצוֹדִים וַחֲרָמִים לִבָּהּ אֲסוּרִים
chains heart-of-her and-traps snares she who the-woman *** more-than-death

יָדֶיהָ טוֹב לִפְנֵי הָאֱלֹהִים יִמָּלֵט מִמֶּנָּה
from-her he-will-escape the-God before one-pleasing hands-of-her

וְחוֹטֵא יִלָּכֶד בָּהּ׃ רְאֵה זֶה מָצָאתִי
I-discovered this look! (27) by-her he-will-be-ensnared but-one-sinning

a righteous man perishing in
his righteousness,
and a wicked man living
long in his wickedness.
16 Do not be overrighteous,
neither be overwise—
why destroy yourself?
17 Do not be overwicked,
and do not be a fool—
why die before your time?
18 It is good to grasp the one
and not let go of the other.
The man who fears God will
avoid all ⌊extremes⌋.[f]
19 Wisdom makes one wise man
more powerful
than ten rulers in a city.
20 There is not a righteous man
on earth
who does what is right and
never sins.
21 Do not pay attention to every
word people say,
or you may hear your
servant cursing you—
22 for you know in your heart
that many times you
yourself have cursed
others.
23 All this I tested by wisdom and
I said,
"I am determined to be
wise"—
but this was beyond me.
24 Whatever wisdom may be,
it is far off and most
profound—
who can discover it?
25 So I turned my mind to
understand,
to investigate and to search
out wisdom and the
scheme of things
and to understand the
stupidity of wickedness
and the madness of folly.
26 I find more bitter than death
the woman who is a snare,
whose heart is a trap
and whose hands are
chains.
The man who pleases God will
escape her,
but the sinner she will
ensnare.
27 "Look," says the Teacher,[g]
"this is what I have discovered:

f18 Or *will follow them both*
g27 Or *leader of the assembly*

°22 ק אתה

אָמְרָה קֹהֶלֶת אַחַת לְאַחַת לִמְצֹא חֶשְׁבּוֹן׃ אֲשֶׁר עוֹד־
still that (28) scheme to-discover to-another one Teacher she-says

בִּקְשָׁה נַפְשִׁי וְלֹא מָצָאתִי אָדָם אֶחָד מֵאֶלֶף מָצָאתִי
I-found among-thousand one man I-found but-not self-of-me she-searched

וְאִשָּׁה בְכָל־ אֵלֶּה לֹא מָצָאתִי׃ לְבַד רְאֵה־ זֶה מָצָאתִי אֲשֶׁר
that I-found this see! only (29) I-found not these among-all-of but-woman

עָשָׂה הָאֱלֹהִים אֶת־ הָאָדָם יָשָׁר וְהֵמָּה בִקְשׁוּ חִשְּׁבֹנוֹת רַבִּים׃
many schemes they-search-for but-they upright the-mankind *** the-God he-made

מִי כְּהֶחָכָם וּמִי יוֹדֵעַ פֵּשֶׁר דָּבָר חָכְמַת
wisdom-of thing explanation-of knowing and-who? like-the-wise-man who? (8:1)

אָדָם תָּאִיר פָּנָיו וְעֹז פָּנָיו יְשֻׁנֶּא׃
he-is-changed appearances-of-him and-hardness-of faces-of-him she-brightens man

אֲנִי פִּי־ מֶלֶךְ שְׁמוֹר וְעַל דִּבְרַת שְׁבוּעַת אֱלֹהִים׃ אַל־
not (3) God oath-of word-of and-because-of obey! king command-of I (2)

תִּבָּהֵל מִפָּנָיו תֵּלֵךְ אַל־ תַּעֲמֹד בְּדָבָר רָע
bad for-cause you-stand-up not you-leave from-presences-of-him you-hurry

כִּי כָּל־ אֲשֶׁר יַחְפֹּץ יַעֲשֶׂה׃ בַּאֲשֶׁר דְּבַר־ מֶלֶךְ שִׁלְטוֹן
supreme king word-of since-that (4) he-will-do he-pleases that all-of for

וּמִי יֹאמַר־ לוֹ מַה־ תַּעֲשֶׂה׃ שׁוֹמֵר מִצְוָה לֹא
not command one-obeying (5) you-do what? to-him he-can-say then-who?

יֵדַע דָּבָר רָע וְעֵת וּמִשְׁפָּט יֵדַע לֵב
heart he-will-know and-procedure and-time harmful matter he-will-come-to

חָכָם׃ כִּי לְכָל־ חֵפֶץ יֵשׁ עֵת וּמִשְׁפָּט כִּי־
though and-procedure time there-is matter for-every-of for (6) wise

רָעַת הָאָדָם רַבָּה עָלָיו׃ כִּי־ אֵינֶנּוּ יֹדֵעַ מַה־
what knowing not-he since (7) upon-him heavy the-man misery-of

שֶׁיִּהְיֶה כִּי כַּאֲשֶׁר יִהְיֶה מִי יַגִּיד לוֹ׃
to-him he-can-tell who? he-will-come as-what for that-he-will-come

אֵין אָדָם שַׁלִּיט בָּרוּחַ לִכְלוֹא אֶת־ הָרוּחַ וְאֵין שִׁלְטוֹן
powerful so-no-one the-wind *** to-contain over-the-wind powerful man no (8)

בְּיוֹם הַמָּוֶת וְאֵין מִשְׁלַחַת בַּמִּלְחָמָה וְלֹא־ יְמַלֵּט
he-will-release so-not in-the-war discharged and-no-one the-death over-day-of

רֶשַׁע אֶת־ בְּעָלָיו׃ אֶת־ כָּל־ זֶה רָאִיתִי וְנָתוֹן
as-to-apply I-saw this all-of *** (9) practitioners-of-him *** wickedness

אֶת־ לִבִּי לְכָל־ מַעֲשֶׂה אֲשֶׁר נַעֲשָׂה תַּחַת הַשָּׁמֶשׁ עֵת אֲשֶׁר
when time the-sun under he-is-done that deed to-every-of mind-of-me ***

שָׁלַט הָאָדָם בְּאָדָם לְרַע לוֹ׃ וּבְכֵן רָאִיתִי
I-saw and-then-this (10) of-him to-hurt over-other the-man he-lords

"Adding one thing to another
to discover the scheme of things—
28 while I was still searching
but not finding—
I found one ⌊upright⌋ man
among a thousand,
but not one ⌊upright⌋ woman
among them all.
29 This only have I found:
God made mankind upright,
but men have gone in
search of many schemes."

8 Who is like the wise man?
Who knows the explanation
of things?
Wisdom brightens a man's
face
and changes its hard
appearance.

*Obey the King*

2 Obey the king's command, I say, because you took an oath before God. 3 Do not be in a hurry to leave the king's presence. Do not stand up for a bad cause, for he will do whatever he pleases. 4 Since a king's word is supreme, who can say to him, "What are you doing?"

5 Whoever obeys his command
will come to no harm,
and the wise heart will
know the proper time and
procedure.
6 For there is a proper time and
procedure for every
matter,
though a man's misery
weighs heavily upon him.

7 Since no man knows the
future,
who can tell him what is to
come?
8 No man has power over the
wind to contain it[h];
so no one has power over
the day of his death.
As no one is discharged in
time of war,
so wickedness will not
release those who practice
it.

9 All this I saw, as I applied my mind to everything done under the sun. There is a time when a man lords it over others to his own[i] hurt. 10 Then too, I saw the

h8 Or *over his spirit to retain it*
i9 Or *to their*

רְשָׁעִים קְבֻרִים וָבָאוּ וּמִמְּקוֹם קָדוֹשׁ
holiness also-from-place-of indeed-they-came ones-being-buried wicked-ones

יְהַלֵּכוּ וְיִשְׁתַּכְּחוּ בָעִיר אֲשֶׁר כֵּן־ עָשׂוּ גַּם־ זֶה
this also they-did this where in-the-city and-they-are-forgotten they-went

הָבֶל׃ אֲשֶׁר אֵין־ נַעֲשָׂה פִתְגָם מַעֲשֵׂה הָרָעָה
the-crime deed-of sentence he-is-carried-out not when (11) meaningless

מְהֵרָה עַל־ כֵּן מָלֵא לֵב בְּנֵי־ הָאָדָם בָּהֶם לַעֲשׂוֹת רָע׃
wrong to-do in-them the-man sons-of heart-of he-is-filled this for quickly

אֲשֶׁר חֹטֶא עֹשֶׂה רָע מְאַת וּמַאֲרִיךְ
and-living-long hundred-of crime committing man-being-wicked although (12)

לוֹ כִּי גַּם־ יוֹדֵעַ אָנִי אֲשֶׁר יִהְיֶה־ טּוֹב לְיִרְאֵי
with-ones-fearing-of better he-will-be that I knowing also indeed to-him

הָאֱלֹהִים אֲשֶׁר יִירְאוּ מִלְּפָנָיו׃ וְטוֹב לֹא־ יִהְיֶה
he-will-be not yet-well (13) at-before-him they-are-reverent who the-God

לָרָשָׁע וְלֹא־ יַאֲרִיךְ יָמִים כַּצֵּל אֲשֶׁר אֵינֶנּוּ
not-he because like-the-shadow days he-will-lengthen and-not with-the-wicked

יָרֵא מִלִּפְנֵי אֱלֹהִים׃ יֵשׁ־ הֶבֶל אֲשֶׁר נַעֲשָׂה עַל־
on he-occurs that meaninglessness there-is (14) God at-before fearing

הָאָרֶץ אֲשֶׁר ׀ יֵשׁ צַדִּיקִים אֲשֶׁר מַגִּיעַ אֲלֵהֶם כְּמַעֲשֵׂה
as-desert-of to-them happening that righteous-men there-are that the-earth

הָרְשָׁעִים וְיֵשׁ רְשָׁעִים שֶׁמַּגִּיעַ אֲלֵהֶם כְּמַעֲשֵׂה
as-desert-of to-them that-happening wicked-men and-there-are the-wicked-men

הַצַּדִּיקִים אָמַרְתִּי שֶׁגַּם־ זֶה הָבֶל׃ וְשִׁבַּחְתִּי אֲנִי אֶת־
*** I so-I-commend (15) meaningless this that-also I-say the-righteous-men

הַשִּׂמְחָה אֲשֶׁר אֵין־ טוֹב לָאָדָם תַּחַת הַשֶּׁמֶשׁ כִּי אִם־
if than the-sun under for-the-man better nothing because the-enjoyment

לֶאֱכוֹל וְלִשְׁתּוֹת וְלִשְׂמוֹחַ וְהוּא יִלְוֶנּוּ
he-will-accompany-him then-he and-to-be-glad and-to-drink to-eat

בַעֲמָלוֹ יְמֵי חַיָּיו אֲשֶׁר־ נָתַן־ לוֹ הָאֱלֹהִים תַּחַת הַשָּׁמֶשׁ׃
the-sun under the-God to-him he-gave that lives-of-him days-of in-work-of-him

כַּאֲשֶׁר נָתַתִּי אֶת־ לִבִּי לָדַעַת חָכְמָה וְלִרְאוֹת אֶת־
*** and-to-observe wisdom to-know mind-of-me *** I-applied as-when (16)

הָעִנְיָן אֲשֶׁר נַעֲשָׂה עַל־ הָאָרֶץ כִּי גַם בַּיּוֹם וּבַלַּיְלָה
or-in-the-night in-the-day also indeed the-earth on he-is-done that the-labor

שֵׁנָה בְּעֵינָיו אֵינֶנּוּ רֹאֶה׃ וְרָאִיתִי אֶת־ כָּל־ מַעֲשֵׂה
deed-of all-of *** then-I-saw (17) seeing not-he with-eyes-of-him sleep

הָאֱלֹהִים כִּי לֹא יוּכַל הָאָדָם לִמְצוֹא אֶת־ הַמַּעֲשֶׂה אֲשֶׁר נַעֲשָׂה
he-goes-on that the-deed *** to-comprehend the-man he-can not that the-God

wicked buried—those who used to come and go from the holy place and receive praise[j] in the city where they did this. This too is meaningless.

[11]When the sentence for a crime is not quickly carried out, the hearts of the people are filled with schemes to do wrong. [12]Although a wicked man commits a hundred crimes and still lives a long time, I know that it will go better with God-fearing men, who are reverent before God. [13]Yet because the wicked do not fear God, it will not go well with them, and their days will not lengthen like a shadow.

[14]There is something else meaningless that occurs on earth: righteous men who get what the wicked deserve, and wicked men who get what the righteous deserve. This too, I say, is meaningless. [15]So I commend the enjoyment of life, because nothing is better for a man under the sun than to eat and drink and be glad. Then joy will accompany him in his work all the days of the life God has given him under the sun.

[16]When I applied my mind to know wisdom and to observe man's labor on earth—his eyes not seeing sleep day or night— [17]then I saw all that God has done. No one can comprehend what goes

*j10* Some Hebrew manuscripts and Septuagint (Aquila); most Hebrew manuscripts *and are forgotten*

תַּחַת־ הַשָּׁמֶשׁ בְּשֶׁל אֲשֶׁר יַעֲמֹל הָאָדָם לְבַקֵּשׁ וְלֹא
but-not to-search-out the-man he-tries which in-spite-of the-sun under

יִמְצָא וְגַם אִם־ יֹאמַר הֶחָכָם לָדַעַת לֹא יוּכַל
he-can not to-know the-wise-man he-claims if and-even he-can-discover

לִמְצֹא׃ כִּי אֶת־ כָּל־ זֶה נָתַתִּי אֶל־ לִבִּי וְלָבוּר
and-to-conclude heart-of-me in I-put this all-of *** so (9:1) to-comprehend

אֶת־ כָּל־ זֶה אֲשֶׁר הַצַּדִּיקִים וְהַחֲכָמִים וַעֲבָדֵיהֶם
and-deeds-of-them and-the-wise-men the-righteous-men that this all-of ***

בְּיַד הָאֱלֹהִים גַּם־ אַהֲבָה גַם־שִׂנְאָה אֵין יוֹדֵעַ הָאָדָם הַכֹּל
the-whole the-man knowing not hate or love whether the-God in-hand-of

לִפְנֵיהֶם׃ הַכֹּל כַּאֲשֶׁר לַכֹּל מִקְרֶה אֶחָד לַצַּדִּיק
to-the-righteous common destiny to-the-all just-as the-all (2) awaiting-him

וְלָרָשָׁע לַטּוֹב וְלַטָּהוֹר וְלַטָּמֵא
and-to-the-unclean and-to-the-clean to-the-good and-to-the-wicked

וְלַזֹּבֵחַ וְלַאֲשֶׁר אֵינֶנּוּ זֹבֵחַ כַּטּוֹב
as-the-good-man sacrificing not-he and-to-whom and-to-the-one-sacrificing

כַּחֹטֶא הַנִּשְׁבָּע כַּאֲשֶׁר שְׁבוּעָה יָרֵא׃ זֶה ׀
this (3) one-fearing oath just-as the-one-taking-oath so-the-one-sinning

רָע בְּכֹל אֲשֶׁר־ נַעֲשָׂה תַּחַת הַשֶּׁמֶשׁ כִּי־ מִקְרֶה אֶחָד
same destiny indeed the-sun under he-happens that in-everything evil

לַכֹּל וְגַם לֵב בְּנֵי־ הָאָדָם מָלֵא־ רָע וְהוֹלֵלוֹת
and-madnesses evil he-is-full the-man sons-of heart-of and-also to-the-all

בִּלְבָבָם בְּחַיֵּיהֶם וְאַחֲרָיו אֶל־ הַמֵּתִים׃
the-dead-ones to and-after-him during-lives-of-them in-heart-of-them

כִּי־ מִי אֲשֶׁר יְבֻחַר אֶל כָּל־ הַחַיִּים יֵשׁ בִּטָּחוֹן
hope there-is the-living-ones all-of with he-is-among who anyone indeed (4)

כִּי־ לְכֶלֶב חַי הוּא טוֹב מִן־ הָאַרְיֵה הַמֵּת׃ כִּי הַחַיִּים
the-living-ones for (5) the-dead the-lion more-than good he live to-dog even

יוֹדְעִים שֶׁיָּמֻתוּ וְהַמֵּתִים אֵינָם יוֹדְעִים
ones-knowing not-they but-the-dead-ones that-they-will-die ones-knowing

מְאוּמָה וְאֵין־ עוֹד לָהֶם שָׂכָר כִּי נִשְׁכַּח זִכְרָם׃
memory-of-them he-is-forgotten even reward to-them further and-not anything

גַּם אַהֲבָתָם גַּם־ שִׂנְאָתָם גַּם־ קִנְאָתָם כְּבָר
long-since jealousy-of-them and hate-of-them and love-of-them also (6)

אָבָדָה וְחֵלֶק אֵין־ לָהֶם עוֹד לְעוֹלָם בְּכֹל אֲשֶׁר־ נַעֲשָׂה
he-happens that in-anything to-ever again to-them not and-part she-vanished

תַּחַת הַשָּׁמֶשׁ׃ לֵךְ אֱכֹל בְּשִׂמְחָה לַחְמֶךָ וּשְׁתֵה בְלֶב־
with-heart-of and-drink! food-of-you with-gladness eat! go! (7) the-sun under

on under the sun. Despite all his efforts to search it out, man cannot discover its meaning. Even if a wise man claims he knows, he cannot really comprehend it.

*A Common Destiny for All*

9 So I reflected on all this and concluded that the righteous and the wise and what they do are in God's hands, but no man knows whether love or hate awaits him. [2]All share a common destiny—the righteous and the wicked, the good and the bad,[k] the clean and the unclean, those who offer sacrifices and those who do not.

As it is with the good man,
so with the sinner;
as it is with those who take oaths,
so with those who are afraid to take them.

[3]This is the evil in everything that happens under the sun: The same destiny overtakes all. The hearts of men, moreover, are full of evil and there is madness in their hearts while they live, and afterward they join the dead. [4]Anyone who is among the living has hope[l]—even a live dog is better off than a dead lion!

[5]For the living know that they will die,
but the dead know nothing;
they have no further reward,
and even the memory of them is forgotten.
[6]Their love, their hate
and their jealousy have long since vanished;
never again will they have a part
in anything that happens under the sun.
[7]Go, eat your food with gladness,
and drink your wine with a joyful heart,

[k]2 Septuagint (Aquila), Vulgate and Syriac; Hebrew does not have *and the bad.*
[l]4 Or *What then is to be chosen? With all who live, there is hope*

°4 ק יחבר

טוֹב יֵינֶךָ כִּי כְבָר רָצָה הָאֱלֹהִים אֶת־ מַעֲשֶׂיךָ׃ בְּכָל־
at-all-of (8) deeds-of-you *** the-God he-favors now for wine-of-you joy

עֵת יִהְיוּ בְגָדֶיךָ לְבָנִים וְשֶׁמֶן עַל־ רֹאשְׁךָ אַל־
not head-of-you on and-oil white-ones clothes-of-you let-them-be time

יֶחְסָר׃ רְאֵה חַיִּים עִם־ אִשָּׁה אֲשֶׁר־ אָהַבְתָּ כָּל־ יְמֵי
days-of all-of you-love whom wife with lives enjoy! (9) let-him-be-lacking

חַיֵּי הֶבְלֶךָ אֲשֶׁר נָתַן־ לְךָ תַּחַת הַשֶּׁמֶשׁ כֹּל
all-of the-sun under to-you he-gave that meaninglessness-of-you lives-of

יְמֵי הֶבְלֶךָ כִּי הוּא חֶלְקְךָ בַּחַיִּים
in-the-lives lot-of-you this for meaninglessness-of-you days-of

וּבַעֲמָלְךָ אֲשֶׁר־אַתָּה עָמֵל תַּחַת הַשָּׁמֶשׁ׃ כֹּל אֲשֶׁר תִּמְצָא
she-finds that all (10) the-sun under toiling you that and-in-labor-of-you

יָדְךָ לַעֲשׂוֹת בְּכֹחֲךָ עֲשֵׂה כִּי אֵין מַעֲשֶׂה וְחֶשְׁבּוֹן
or-plan work there-is-no for do! with-might-of-you to-do hand-of-you

וְדַעַת וְחָכְמָה בִּשְׁאוֹל אֲשֶׁר אַתָּה הֹלֵךְ שָׁמָּה׃ שַׁבְתִּי
I-did-again (11) to-there going you where in-Sheol or-wisdom or-knowledge

וְרָאֹה תַחַת־ הַשֶּׁמֶשׁ כִּי לֹא לַקַּלִּים הַמֵּרוֹץ וְלֹא
or-not the-race to-the-swift-ones not that the-sun under and-to-see

לַגִּבּוֹרִים הַמִּלְחָמָה וְגַם לֹא לַחֲכָמִים לֶחֶם וְגַם לֹא
not and-also food to-the-wise-ones not and-also the-battle to-the-strong-ones

לַנְּבֹנִים עֹשֶׁר וְגַם לֹא לַיֹּדְעִים חֵן
favor to-the-ones-being-learned not and-also wealth to-the-ones-being-brilliant

כִּי־ עֵת וָפֶגַע יִקְרֶה אֶת־ כֻּלָּם׃ כִּי גַּם לֹא־
not also moreover (12) all-of-them *** he-happens and-chance time but

יֵדַע הָאָדָם אֶת־ עִתּוֹ כַּדָּגִים שֶׁנֶּאֱחָזִים
that-ones-being-caught as-the-fishes hour-of-him *** the-man he-knows

בִּמְצוֹדָה רָעָה וְכַצִּפֳּרִים הָאֲחֻזוֹת* בַּפָּח כָּהֵם
so-they in-the-snare the-ones-being-taken or-as-the-birds cruel in-net

יוּקָשִׁים בְּנֵי הָאָדָם לְעֵת רָעָה כְּשֶׁתִּפּוֹל עֲלֵיהֶם
upon-them as-that-she-falls evil by-time-of the-man sons-of ones-being-trapped

פִּתְאֹם׃ גַּם־ זֹה רָאִיתִי חָכְמָה תַּחַת הַשָּׁמֶשׁ וּגְדוֹלָה הִיא אֵלָי׃
to-me she and-great the-sun under wisdom I-saw this also (13) unexpectedly

עִיר קְטַנָּה וַאֲנָשִׁים בָּהּ מְעָט וּבָא־ אֵלֶיהָ מֶלֶךְ
king against-her and-he-came few in-her with-peoples small city (14)

גָּדוֹל וְסָבַב אֹתָהּ וּבָנָה עָלֶיהָ מְצוֹדִים גְּדֹלִים׃
huge-ones siegeworks against-her and-he-built her and-he-surrounded powerful

וּמָצָא בָהּ אִישׁ מִסְכֵּן חָכָם וּמִלַּט־ הוּא אֶת־ הָעִיר
the-city *** he and-he-saved wise poor man in-her now-he-found (15)

for it is now that God favors
what you do.
8Always be clothed in white,
and always anoint your
head with oil.

9Enjoy life with your wife, whom you love, all the days of this meaningless life that God has given you under the sun— all your meaningless days. For this is your lot in life and in your toilsome labor under the sun. 10Whatever your hand finds to do, do it with all your might, for in the grave,[m] where you are going, there is neither working nor planning nor knowledge nor wisdom.

11I have seen something else under the sun:

The race is not to the swift
or the battle to the strong,
nor does food come to the
wise
or wealth to the brilliant
or favor to the learned;
but time and chance happen
to them all.

12Moreover, no man knows when his hour will come:

As fish are caught in a cruel
net,
or birds are taken in a
snare,
so men are trapped by evil
times
that fall unexpectedly upon
them.

*Wisdom Better Than Folly*

13I also saw under the sun this example of wisdom that greatly impressed me: 14There was once a small city with only a few people in it. And a powerful king came against it, surrounded it and built huge siegeworks against it. 15Now there lived in that city a man poor but wise, and he saved the city by

*m10* Hebrew *Sheol*

**12* Most mss have *dagesh* in the *zayin* (זּוֹת־).

בְּחָכְמָתוֹ וְאָדָם לֹא זָכַר אֶת־ הָאִישׁ הַמִּסְכֵּן הַהוּא׃
the-that the-poor the-man *** he-remembered not but-man by-wisdom-of-him

וְאָמַרְתִּי אָנִי טוֹבָה חָכְמָה מִגְּבוּרָה וְחָכְמַת הַמִּסְכֵּן
the-poor-man but-wisdom-of more-than-strength wisdom good I so-I-said (16)

בְּזוּיָה וּדְבָרָיו אֵינָם נִשְׁמָעִים׃ דִּבְרֵי
words-of (17) ones-being-heeded not-they and-words-of-him being-despised

חֲכָמִים בְּנַחַת נִשְׁמָעִים מִזַּעֲקַת מוֹשֵׁל
one-ruling more-than-shout-of ones-being-heeded in-quietness wise-ones

בַּכְּסִילִים׃ טוֹבָה חָכְמָה מִכְּלֵי קְרָב וְחוֹטֶא אֶחָד
one but-one-sinning war more-than-weapons-of wisdom good (18) of-the-fools

יְאַבֵּד טוֹבָה הַרְבֵּה׃ זְבוּבֵי מָוֶת יַבְאִישׁ
he-gives-bad-smell death flies-of (10:1) to-be-much good he-destroys

יַבִּיעַ שֶׁמֶן רוֹקֵחַ יָקָר מֵחָכְמָה
more-than-wisdom weighty one-making-perfume oil-of he-makes-reek

מִכָּבוֹד סִכְלוּת מְעָט׃ לֵב חָכָם לִימִינוֹ וְלֵב
but-heart-of to-right-of-him wise heart-of (2) little folly more-than-honor

כְּסִיל לִשְׂמֹאלוֹ׃ וְגַם־ בַּדֶּרֶךְ כְּשֶׁהַסָּכָל הֹלֵךְ לִבּוֹ
sense-of-him walking as-that-fool on-the-road and-even (3) to-left-of-him fool

חָסֵר וְאָמַר לַכֹּל סָכָל הוּא׃ אִם־ רוּחַ הַמּוֹשֵׁל
the-one-ruling anger-of if (4) he stupid to-the-all and-he-shows lacking

תַּעֲלֶה עָלֶיךָ מְקוֹמְךָ אַל־ תַּנַּח כִּי מַרְפֵּא יַנִּיחַ
he-can-lay-to-rest calmness for you-leave not post-of-you against-you she-rises

חֲטָאִים גְּדוֹלִים׃ יֵשׁ רָעָה רָאִיתִי תַּחַת הַשָּׁמֶשׁ כִּשְׁגָגָה
as-error the-sun under I-saw evil there-is (5) great-ones errors

שֶׁיֹּצָא מִלִּפְנֵי הַשַּׁלִּיט׃ נִתַּן הַסֶּכֶל בַּמְּרוֹמִים
in-the-high-positions the-fool he-is-put (6) the-ruler from-before that-arising

רַבִּים וַעֲשִׁירִים בַּשֵּׁפֶל יֵשֵׁבוּ׃ רָאִיתִי עֲבָדִים עַל־סוּסִים
horses on slaves I-saw (7) they-occupy in-the-low-one while-rich-ones many

וְשָׂרִים הֹלְכִים כַּעֲבָדִים עַל־ הָאָרֶץ׃ חֹפֵר גּוּמָּץ
pit one-digging (8) the-ground on like-slaves ones-walking while-princes

בּוֹ יִפּוֹל וּפֹרֵץ גָּדֵר יִשְּׁכֶנּוּ נָחָשׁ׃
snake he-may-bite-him wall and-one-breaking-through he-may-fall into-him

מַסִּיעַ אֲבָנִים יֵעָצֵב בָּהֶם בּוֹקֵעַ עֵצִים
logs one-splitting by-them he-may-be-injured stones one-quarrying (9)

יִסָּכֶן בָּם׃ אִם־ קֵהָה הַבַּרְזֶל וְהוּא לֹא־פָנִים
edges not and-he the-axe he-is-dull if (10) by-them he-may-be-endangered

קִלְקַל וַחֲיָלִים יְגַבֵּר וְיִתְרוֹן הַכְשֵׁיר חָכְמָה׃
skill to-bring but-success he-must-empower then-strengths he-sharpened

his wisdom. But nobody remembered that poor man. 16So I said, "Wisdom is better than strength." But the poor man's wisdom is despised, and his words are no longer heeded.

17The quiet words of the wise
are more to be heeded
than the shouts of a ruler of fools.
18Wisdom is better than weapons of war,
but one sinner destroys much good.

10 As dead flies give perfume a bad smell,
so a little folly outweighs wisdom and honor.
2The heart of the wise inclines to the right,
but the heart of the fool to the left.
3Even as he walks along the road,
the fool lacks sense
and shows everyone how stupid he is.
4If a ruler's anger rises against you,
do not leave your post;
calmness can lay great errors to rest.

5There is an evil I have seen under the sun,
the sort of error that arises from a ruler:
6Fools are put in many high positions,
while the rich occupy the low ones.
7I have seen slaves on horseback,
while princes go on foot like slaves.

8Whoever digs a pit may fall into it;
whoever breaks through a wall may be bitten by a snake.
9Whoever quarries stones may be injured by them;
whoever splits logs may be endangered by them.

10If the ax is dull
and its edge unsharpened,
more strength is needed
but skill will bring success.

°3 ק כשסכל
°10 ק הכשר

אִם־ יִשֹּׁךְ הַנָּחָשׁ בְּלוֹא־ לָחַשׁ וְאֵין יִתְרוֹן
profit then-there-is-no charmed when-not the-snake he-bites if (11)

לְבַעַל הַלָּשׁוֹן׃ דִּבְרֵי פִי־ חָכָם חֵן וְשִׂפְתוֹת
but-lips-of gracious wise-man mouth-of words-of (12) the-tongue for-charmer-of

כְּסִיל תְּבַלְּעֶנּוּ׃ תְּחִלַּת דִּבְרֵי־ פִיהוּ סִכְלוּת וְאַחֲרִית
and-end-of folly mouth-of-him words-of beginning-of (13) she-consumes-him fool

פִּיהוּ הוֹלֵלוּת רָעָה׃ וְהַסָּכָל יַרְבֶּה דְבָרִים לֹא־ יֵדַע
he-knows not words he-multiplies and-the-fool (14) wicked madness mouth-of-him

הָאָדָם מַה־ שֶׁיִּהְיֶה וַאֲשֶׁר יִהְיֶה מֵאַחֲרָיו מִי
who? at-arter-him he-will-happen and-what that-he-comes what the-man

יַגִּיד לוֹ׃ עֲמַל הַכְּסִילִים תְּיַגְּעֶנּוּ אֲשֶׁר לֹא־ יָדַע
he-knows not that she-wearies-him the-fools work-of (15) to-him he-can-tell

לָלֶכֶת אֶל־עִיר׃ אִי־ לָךְ אֶרֶץ שֶׁמַּלְכֵּךְ נָעַר וְשָׂרַיִךְ
and-princes-of-you servant that-king-of-you land to-you woe! (16) town to to-go

בַּבֹּקֶר יֹאכֵלוּ׃ אַשְׁרֵיךְ אֶרֶץ שֶׁמַּלְכֵּךְ
that-king-of-you land blessednesses-of-you (17) they-feast in-the-morning

בֶּן־ חוֹרִים וְשָׂרַיִךְ בָּעֵת יֹאכֵלוּ בִּגְבוּרָה
for-strength they-eat at-the-time and-princes-of-you nobilities son-of

וְלֹא בַשְּׁתִי׃ בַּעֲצַלְתַּיִם יִמַּךְ הַמְּקָרֶה
the-rafter he-sags when-lazinesses (18) for-the-drunkenness and-not

וּבְשִׁפְלוּת יָדַיִם יִדְלֹף הַבָּיִת׃ לִשְׂחוֹק עֹשִׂים
ones-making for-laughter (19) the-house he-leaks hands and-when-idleness-of

לֶחֶם וְיַיִן יְשַׂמַּח חַיִּים וְהַכֶּסֶף יַעֲנֶה אֶת־ הַכֹּל׃
the-all *** he-answers but-the-money lives he-makes-merry and-wine feast

גַּם בְּמַדָּעֲךָ מֶלֶךְ אַל־ תְּקַלֵּל וּבְחַדְרֵי מִשְׁכָּבְךָ
bed-of-you or-in-rooms-of you-revile not king in-thought-of-you even (20)

אַל־ תְּקַלֵּל עָשִׁיר כִּי עוֹף הַשָּׁמַיִם יוֹלִיךְ אֶת־ הַקּוֹל
the-word *** he-may-carry the-airs bird-of because rich you-curse not

וּבַעַל הַכְּנָפַיִם יַגֵּיד דָּבָר׃ שַׁלַּח לַחְמְךָ עַל־
on bread-of-you cast! (11:1) saying he-may-report wings and-owner-of

פְּנֵי הַמָּיִם כִּי־ בְרֹב הַיָּמִים תִּמְצָאֶנּוּ׃ תֶּן־
give! (2) you-will-find-him the-days after-many-of for the-waters surfaces-of

חֵלֶק לְשִׁבְעָה וְגַם לִשְׁמוֹנָה כִּי לֹא תֵדַע מַה־ יִּהְיֶה רָעָה
disaster he-may-come what you-know not for to-eight and-also to-seven portion

עַל־ הָאָרֶץ׃ אִם־ יִמָּלְאוּ הֶעָבִים גֶּשֶׁם עַל־ הָאָרֶץ יָרִיקוּ
they-pour the-earth upon rain the-clouds they-are-full if (3) the-land upon

וְאִם־ יִפּוֹל עֵץ בַּדָּרוֹם וְאִם בַּצָּפוֹן מְקוֹם
place-of to-the-north or-whether to-the-south tree he-falls and-whether

[11]If a snake bites before it is charmed,
there is no profit for the charmer.
[12]Words from a wise man's mouth are gracious,
but a fool is consumed by his own lips.
[13]At the beginning his words are folly;
at the end they are wicked madness—
[14] and the fool multiplies words.
No one knows what is coming—
who can tell him what will happen after him?
[15]A fool's work wearies him;
he does not know the way to town.
[16]Woe to you, O land whose king was a servant[n]
and whose princes feast in the morning.
[17]Blessed are you, O land whose king is of noble birth
and whose princes eat at a proper time—
for strength and not for drunkenness.
[18]If a man is lazy, the rafters sag;
if his hands are idle, the house leaks.
[19]A feast is made for laughter,
and wine makes life merry,
but money is the answer for everything.
[20]Do not revile the king even in your thoughts,
or curse the rich in your bedroom,
because a bird of the air may carry your words,
and a bird on the wing may report what you say.

*Bread Upon the Waters*

11 Cast your bread upon the waters,
for after many days you will find it again.
[2]Give portions to seven, yes to eight,
for you do not know what disaster may come upon the land.
[3]If clouds are full of water,
they pour rain upon the earth.
Whether a tree falls to the south or to the north,

[n]16 Or *king is a child*

°20 ק כנפים

שֶׁיִּפּוֹל הָעֵץ שָׁם יְהוּא׃ שֹׁמֵר רוּחַ לֹא
not wind one-watching (4) he-will-lie there the-tree that-he-falls

יִזְרָע וְרֹאֶה בֶעָבִים לֹא יִקְצוֹר׃ כַּאֲשֶׁר
just-as (5) he-will-reap not at-the-clouds and-one-looking he-will-plant

אֵינְךָ יוֹדֵעַ מַה־ דֶּרֶךְ הָרוּחַ כַּעֲצָמִים בְּבֶטֶן הַמְּלֵאָה כָּכָה
so the-full in-womb-of as-bodies the-wind path-of what knowing not-you

לֹא תֵדַע אֶת־ מַעֲשֵׂה הָאֱלֹהִים אֲשֶׁר יַעֲשֶׂה אֶת־ הַכֹּל׃
the-all *** he-makes who the-God work-of *** you-can-understand not

בַּבֹּקֶר זְרַע אֶת־ זַרְעֶךָ וְלָעֶרֶב אַל־ תַּנַּח
you-let-be-idle not and-at-the-evening seed-of-you *** sow! in-the-morning (6)

יָדֶךָ כִּי אֵינְךָ יוֹדֵעַ* אֵי זֶה יִכְשָׁר† הֲזֶה אוֹ־
or whether-this he-will-succeed this which knowing not-you for hand-of-you

זֶה וְאִם־ שְׁנֵיהֶם כְּאֶחָד טוֹבִים׃ וּמָתוֹק הָאוֹר
the-light indeed-sweet (7) ones-well as-equal both-of-them or-whether that

וְטוֹב לַעֵינַיִם לִרְאוֹת אֶת־ הַשָּׁמֶשׁ׃ כִּי אִם־שָׁנִים הַרְבֵּה
to-be-many years if however (8) the-sun *** to-see to-the-eyes and-pleasing

יִחְיֶה הָאָדָם בְּכֻלָּם יִשְׂמָח וְיִזְכֹּר אֶת־
*** but-let-him-remember let-him-enjoy to-all-of-them the-man he-may-live

יְמֵי הַחֹשֶׁךְ כִּי־ הַרְבֵּה יִהְיוּ כָּל־ שֶׁבָּא
what-he-comes all-of they-will-be to-be-many for the-darkness days-of

הָבֶל׃ שְׂמַח בָּחוּר בְּיַלְדוּתֶיךָ וִיטִיבְךָ
and-let-him-give-joy-to-you in-youths-of-you young-man be-happy! (9) meaningless

לִבְּךָ בִּימֵי בְחוּרוֹתֶךָ וְהַלֵּךְ בְּדַרְכֵי לִבְּךָ
heart-of-you after-ways-of and-follow! youths-of-you in-days-of heart-of-you

וּבְמַרְאֵי עֵינֶיךָ וְדָע כִּי עַל־ כָּל־ אֵלֶּה
these all-of for that but-know! eyes-of-you and-after-sights-of

יְבִיאֲךָ הָאֱלֹהִים בַּמִּשְׁפָּט׃ וְהָסֵר כַּעַס
anxiety so-banish! (10) to-the-judgment the-God he-will-bring-you

מִלִּבֶּךָ וְהַעֲבֵר רָעָה מִבְּשָׂרֶךָ כִּי־ הַיַּלְדוּת
the-youth for from-body-of-you trouble and-cast-off! from-heart-of-you

וְהַשַּׁחֲרוּת הָבֶל׃ וּזְכֹר אֶת־ בּוֹרְאֶיךָ
Ones-Creating-you *** and-remember! (12:1) meaningless and-the-vigor

בִּימֵי בְּחוּרֹתֶיךָ עַד אֲשֶׁר לֹא־ יָבֹאוּ יְמֵי הָרָעָה
the-trouble days-of they-come not when before youths-of-you in-days-of

וְהִגִּיעוּ שָׁנִים אֲשֶׁר תֹּאמַר אֵין־ לִי בָהֶם חֵפֶץ׃
pleasure in-them to-me there-is-not you-will-say when years and-they-approach

עַד אֲשֶׁר לֹא־ תֶחְשַׁךְ הַשֶּׁמֶשׁ וְהָאוֹר וְהַיָּרֵחַ
and-the-moon and-the-light the-sun she-grows-dark not when before (2)

---

in the place where it falls,
there will it lie.
4 Whoever watches the wind
will not plant;
whoever looks at the clouds
will not reap.
5 As you do not know the path
of the wind,
or how the body is formed
in a mother's womb,
so you cannot understand the
work of God,
the Maker of all things.
6 Sow your seed in the morning,
and at evening let not your
hands be idle,
for you do not know which
will succeed,
whether this or that,
or whether both will do
equally well.

*Remember Your Creator While Young*

7 Light is sweet,
and it pleases the eyes to see
the sun.
8 However many years a man
may live,
let him enjoy them all.
But let him remember the days
of darkness,
for they will be many.
Everything to come is
meaningless.
9 Be happy, young man, while
you are young,
and let your heart give you
joy in the days of your
youth.
Follow the ways of your heart
and whatever your eyes see,
but know that for all these
things
God will bring you to
judgment.
10 So then, banish anxiety from
your heart
and cast off the troubles of
your body,
for youth and vigor are
meaningless.

12 Remember your Creator
in the days of your youth,
before the days of trouble
come
and the years approach
when you will say,
"I find no pleasure in
them"—
2 before the sun and the light
and the moon and the stars
grow dark,

*6 Most mss have *pathah* under the *ayin* (יוֹדֵעַ).

†6 Most mss have *pathah* under the *shin* (יִכְשַׁר).

וְהַכּוֹכָבִים וְשָׁבוּ הֶעָבִים אַחַר הַגָּשֶׁם׃ בַּיּוֹם
on-the-day (3) the-rain after the-clouds and-they-return and-the-stars

שֶׁיָּזֻעוּ שֹׁמְרֵי הַבַּיִת וְהִתְעַוְּתוּ אַנְשֵׁי הֶחָיִל
the-strength men-of and-they-stoop the-house ones-keeping-of that-they-tremble

וּבָטְלוּ הַטֹּחֲנוֹת כִּי מִעֵטוּ וְחָשְׁכוּ
and-they-grow-dim they-are-few because the-ones-grinding when-they-cease

הָרֹאוֹת בָּאֲרֻבּוֹת׃ וְסֻגְּרוּ דְלָתַיִם
doors when-they-are-closed (4) through-the-windows the-ones-looking

בַּשּׁוּק בִּשְׁפַל קוֹל הַטַּחֲנָה וְיָקוּם לְקוֹל
at-sound-of when-he-rises the-grinding sound-of when-to-fade to-the-street

הַצִּפּוֹר וְיִשַּׁחוּ כָּל־ בְּנוֹת הַשִּׁיר׃ גַּם מִגָּבֹהַּ
of-height when (5) the-song daughters-of all-of and-they-grow-faint the-bird

יִרָאוּ וְחַתְחַתִּים בַּדֶּרֶךְ וְיָנֵאץ הַשָּׁקֵד
the-almond-tree when-he-blossoms in-the-street and-dangers they-are-afraid

וְיִסְתַּבֵּל הֶחָגָב וְתָפֵר הָאֲבִיּוֹנָה
the-desire and-she-is-unstirred the-grasshopper and-he-drags-himself-along

כִּי־ הֹלֵךְ הָאָדָם אֶל־ בֵּית עוֹלָמוֹ וְסָבְבוּ בַשּׁוּק
in-the-street and-they-go-about eternity-of-him home-of to the-man going then

הַסֹּפְדִים׃ עַד אֲשֶׁר לֹא־ יֵרָחֵק° חֶבֶל הַכֶּסֶף
the-silver cord-of he-is-severed not when before (6) the-ones-mourning

וְתָרֻץ גֻּלַּת הַזָּהָב וְתִשָּׁבֶר כַּד עַל־ הַמַּבּוּעַ
the-spring at pitcher and-she-is-shattered the-gold bowl-of or-she-is-broken

וְנָרֹץ הַגַּלְגַּל אֶל־ הַבּוֹר׃ וְיָשֹׁב הֶעָפָר עַל־
to the-dust and-he-returns (7) the-well at the-wheel or-he-is-broken

הָאָרֶץ כְּשֶׁהָיָה וְהָרוּחַ תָּשׁוּב אֶל־ הָאֱלֹהִים אֲשֶׁר
who the-God to she-returns and-the-spirit as-which-he-came the-ground

נְתָנָהּ׃ הֲבֵל הֲבָלִים אָמַר הַקּוֹהֶלֶת
the-Teacher he-says meaninglessnesses meaninglessness-of (8) he-gave-her

הַכֹּל הָבֶל׃ וְיֹתֵר שֶׁהָיָה קֹהֶלֶת חָכָם עוֹד לִמַּד־
he-imparted also wise Teacher that-he-was and-not-only (9) meaningless the-whole

דַּעַת אֶת־ הָעָם וְאִזֵּן וְחִקֵּר תִּקֵּן
he-set-in-order and-he-searched-out and-he-pondered the-people *** knowledge

מְשָׁלִים הַרְבֵּה׃ בִּקֵּשׁ קֹהֶלֶת לִמְצֹא דִּבְרֵי־ חֵפֶץ
right words-of to-find Teacher he-searched (10) to-be-many proverbs

וְכָתוּב יֹשֶׁר דִּבְרֵי אֱמֶת׃ דִּבְרֵי חֲכָמִים
wise-men words-of (11) truth words-of upright and-one-being-written

כַּדָּרְבֹנוֹת וּכְמַשְׂמְרוֹת נְטוּעִים בַּעֲלֵי אֲסֻפּוֹת
collections masters-of ones-being-embedded and-like-nails like-the-goads

and the clouds return after
the rain;
3when the keepers of the house
tremble,
and the strong men stoop,
when the grinders cease
because they are few,
and those looking through
the windows grow dim;
4when the doors to the street
are closed
and the sound of grinding
fades;
when men rise up at the
sound of birds,
but all their songs grow
faint;
5when men are afraid of
heights
and of dangers in the
streets;
when the almond tree
blossoms
and the grasshopper drags
himself along
and desire no longer is
stirred.
Then man goes to his eternal
home
and mourners go about the
streets.

6Remember him—before the
silver cord is severed,
or the golden bowl is
broken;
before the pitcher is shattered
at the spring,
or the wheel broken at the
well,
7and the dust returns to the
ground it came from,
and the spirit returns to God
who gave it.

8"Meaningless! Meaningless!"
says the Teacher.°
"Everything is
meaningless!"

*The Conclusion of the Matter*

9Not only was the Teacher wise,
but also he imparted knowledge to
the people. He pondered and
searched out and set in order
many proverbs. 10The Teacher
searched to find just the right
words, and what he wrote was upright and true.
11The words of the wise are like
goads, their collected sayings like
firmly embedded nails—given by

°8 Or *the leader of the assembly;* also in verses 9 and 10

°6 ק ירתק

| | | | | |
|---|---|---|---|---|
| מֵהֵ֖מָּה | וְיֹתֵ֥ר | אֶחָֽד׃ | מֵרֹעֶ֣ה | נִתְּנ֖וּ |
| to-them | and-addition | (12) one | by-One-Being-Shepherd | they-are-given |

| | | | | | | | | |
|---|---|---|---|---|---|---|---|---|
| וְלַ֥הַג | קֵ֔ץ | אֵ֣ין | הַרְבֵּה֙ | סְפָרִ֤ים | עֲשׂ֨וֹת | הִזָּהֵ֑ר | בְּנִ֥י | |
| and-study | end | there-is-no | to-be-many | books | to-make | be-warned! | son-of-me | |

| | | | | | | | |
|---|---|---|---|---|---|---|---|
| נִשְׁמָ֑ע | הַכֹּ֣ל | דָּבָ֖ר | ס֥וֹף | בָּשָֽׂר׃ | יְגִעַ֥ת | הַרְבֵּ֖ה | |
| he-was-heard | the-all | matter | conclusion-of (13) | body | weariness-of | to-be-much | |

| | | | | | | | | |
|---|---|---|---|---|---|---|---|---|
| כָּל־ | זֶ֖ה | כִּי־ | שְׁמ֔וֹר | מִצְוֺתָ֣יו | וְאֶת־ | יְרָא֙ | אֶת־הָאֱלֹהִ֤ים | |
| whole-of | this | for | keep! | commandments-of-him | and | fear! | the-God *** | |

| | | | | | | | |
|---|---|---|---|---|---|---|---|
| בְמִשְׁפָּ֖ט | יָבִ֥א | הָאֱלֹהִים֙ | מַעֲשֶׂ֔ה | כָּל־ | אֶת־ | כִּ֤י | הָאָדָֽם׃ |
| into-judgment | he-will-bring | the-God | deed | every-of | *** | for (14) | the-man |

| | | | | | | |
|---|---|---|---|---|---|---|
| רָֽע׃ | וְאִם־ | ט֖וֹב | אִם־ | נֶעְלָ֑ם | כָּל־ | עַ֣ל |
| evil | or-whether | good | whether | thing-being-hidden | every-of | including |

one Shepherd. [12]Be warned, my son, of anything in addition to them.

Of making many books there is no end, and much study wearies the body.

[13]Now all has been heard;
   here is the conclusion of the matter:
Fear God and keep his commandments,
   for this is the whole duty of man.
[14]For God will bring every deed into judgment,
   including every hidden thing,
   whether it is good or evil.

שִׁיר הַשִּׁירִים אֲשֶׁר לִשְׁלֹמֹה׃ יִשָּׁקֵנִי מִנְּשִׁיקוֹת
with-kisses-of let-him-kiss-me (2) of-Solomon that the-Songs Song-of (1:1)

פִּיהוּ כִּי־ טוֹבִים דֹּדֶיךָ מִיָּיִן׃ לְרֵיחַ
in-fragrance-of (3) more-than-wine loves-of-you delightful-ones for mouth-of-him

שְׁמָנֶיךָ טוֹבִים שֶׁמֶן תּוּרַק שְׁמֶךָ עַל־ כֵּן
this for name-of-you she-is-poured-out perfume pleasing-ones perfumes-of-you

עֲלָמוֹת אֲהֵבוּךָ׃ מָשְׁכֵנִי אַחֲרֶיךָ נָּרוּצָה הֱבִיאַנִי
he-brought-me let-us-hurry with-you take-away-me! (4) they-love-you maidens

הַמֶּלֶךְ חֲדָרָיו נָגִילָה וְנִשְׂמְחָה בָּךְ נַזְכִּירָה
we-will-praise in-you and-we-delight we-rejoice chambers-of-him the-king

דֹדֶיךָ מִיַּיִן מֵישָׁרִים אֲהֵבוּךָ׃ שְׁחוֹרָה אֲנִי וְנָאוָה
yet-lovely I dark (5) they-adore-you right-ones more-than-wine loves-of-you

בְּנוֹת יְרוּשָׁלִָם כְּאָהֳלֵי קֵדָר כִּירִיעוֹת שְׁלֹמֹה׃
Solomon like-tent-curtains-of Kedar like-tents-of Jerusalem daughters-of

אַל־ תִּרְאוּנִי שֶׁאֲנִי שְׁחַרְחֹרֶת שֶׁשֱּׁזָפַתְנִי הַשָּׁמֶשׁ בְּנֵי
sons-of the-sun because-she-darkened-me dark because-I you-stare-at-me not (6)

אִמִּי נִחֲרוּ־ בִי שָׂמֻנִי נֹטֵרָה אֶת־
*** one-caring-for they-made-me with-me they-were-angry mother-of-me

הַכְּרָמִים כַּרְמִי שֶׁלִּי לֹא נָטָרְתִּי׃ הַגִּידָה לִּי
to-me tell! (7) I-cared-for not that-to-me vineyard-of-me the-vineyards

שֶׁאָהֲבָה נַפְשִׁי אֵיכָה תִרְעֶה אֵיכָה תַּרְבִּיץ
you-give-rest where? you-graze-flock where? self-of-me whom-she-loves

בַּצָּהֳרָיִם שַׁלָּמָה אֶהְיֶה כְּעֹטְיָה עַל עֶדְרֵי
flocks-of beside like-one-being-veiled I-should-be that-why? at-the-middays

חֲבֵרֶיךָ׃ אִם־לֹא תֵדְעִי לָךְ הַיָּפָה בַּנָּשִׁים
among-the-women the-beautiful-one to-you you-know not if (8) friends-of-you

צְאִי־ לָךְ בְּעִקְבֵי הַצֹּאן וּרְעִי אֶת־ גְּדִיֹּתַיִךְ
young-goats-of-you *** and-graze! the-sheep after-tracks-of to-you follow!

עַל מִשְׁכְּנוֹת הָרֹעִים׃ לְסֻסָתִי בְּרִכְבֵי פַרְעֹה
Pharaoh in-chariots-of to-mare-of-me (9) the-ones-being-shepherds tents-of by

דִּמִּיתִיךְ רַעְיָתִי׃ נָאווּ לְחָיַיִךְ
cheeks-of-you they-are-beautiful (10) darling-of-me I-liken-you

בַּתֹּרִים צַוָּארֵךְ בַּחֲרוּזִים׃ תּוֹרֵי זָהָב
gold earrings-of (11) with-the-strings-of-jewels neck-of-you with-the-earrings

נַעֲשֶׂה־ לָּךְ עִם נְקֻדּוֹת הַכָּסֶף׃ עַד־ שֶׁהַמֶּלֶךְ
that-the-king while (12) the-silver studs-of with for-you we-will-make

בִּמְסִבּוֹ נִרְדִּי נָתַן רֵיחוֹ׃ צְרוֹר
sachet-of (13) fragrance-of-him he-spread perfume-of-me at-table-of-him

**1** Solomon's Song of Songs.

*Beloved*[a]

2 Let him kiss me with the kisses of his mouth—
for your love is more delightful than wine.
3 Pleasing is the fragrance of your perfumes;
your name is like perfume poured out.
No wonder the maidens love you!
4 Take me away with you—let us hurry!
The king has brought me into his chambers.

*Friends*

We rejoice and delight in you[b];
we will praise your love more than wine.

*Beloved*

How right they are to adore you!
5 Dark am I, yet lovely,
O daughters of Jerusalem,
dark like the tents of Kedar,
like the tent curtains of Solomon.
6 Do not stare at me because I am dark,
because I am darkened by the sun.
My mother's sons were angry with me
and made me take care of the vineyards;
my own vineyard I have neglected.
7 Tell me, you whom I love,
where you graze your flock
and where you rest your sheep at midday.
Why should I be like a veiled woman
beside the flocks of your friends?

*Lover*

8 If you do not know, most beautiful of women,
follow the tracks of the sheep
and graze your young goats
by the tents of the shepherds.
9 I liken you, my darling, to a mare
harnessed to one of the chariots of Pharaoh.
10 Your cheeks are beautiful with earrings,
your neck with strings of jewels.
11 We will make you earrings of gold,
studded with silver.

*Beloved*

12 While the king was at his table,
my perfume spread its fragrance.

[a] Primarily on the basis of the gender of the Hebrew pronouns used, male and female speakers are indicated in the margins by the captions *Lover* and *Beloved* respectively. The words of others are marked *Friends*. In some instances the divisions and their captions are debatable.
[b] 4 The Hebrew is masculine singular.
[c] 5 Or *Salma*

הַמֹּר | דּוֹדִי לִי בֵּין שָׁדַי יָלִין׃ אֶשְׁכֹּל

cluster-of (14) he-rests breasts-of-me between to-me lover-of-me the-myrrh

הַכֹּפֶר | דּוֹדִי לִי בְּכַרְמֵי עֵין גֶּדִי׃ הִנָּךְ

see-you! (15) Gedi En from-vineyards-of to-me lover-of-me the-henna-blossom

יָפָה רַעְיָתִי הִנָּךְ יָפָה עֵינַיִךְ יוֹנִים׃ הִנְּךָ

see-you! (16) doves eyes-of-you beautiful see-you! darling-of-me beautiful

יָפֶה דוֹדִי אַף נָעִים אַף־ עַרְשֵׂנוּ רַעֲנָנָה׃ קֹרוֹת

beams-of (17) verdant bed-of-us indeed charming how! lover-of-me handsome

בָּתֵּינוּ אֲרָזִים רַחִיטֵנוּ בְּרוֹתִים׃ אֲנִי חֲבַצֶּלֶת הַשָּׁרוֹן שׁוֹשַׁנַּת

lily-of the-Sharon rose-of I (2:1) firs rafter-of-us cedars houses-of-us

הָעֲמָקִים׃ כְּשׁוֹשַׁנָּה בֵּין הַחוֹחִים כֵּן רַעְיָתִי בֵּין הַבָּנוֹת׃

the-maidens among darling-of-me so the-thorns among like-lily (2) the-valleys

כְּתַפּוּחַ בַּעֲצֵי הַיַּעַר כֵּן דּוֹדִי בֵּין

among lover-of-me so the-forest among-trees-of like-apple-tree (3)

הַבָּנִים בְּצִלּוֹ חִמַּדְתִּי וְיָשַׁבְתִּי וּפִרְיוֹ מָתוֹק

sweet and-fruit-of-him and-I-sit I-delight in-shade-of-him the-young-men

לְחִכִּי׃ הֱבִיאַנִי אֶל־ בֵּית הַיָּיִן וְדִגְלוֹ

and-banner-of-him the-banquet hall-of to he-took-me (4) to-taste-of-me

עָלַי אַהֲבָה׃ סַמְּכוּנִי בָּאֲשִׁישׁוֹת רַפְּדוּנִי בַּתַּפּוּחִים

with-the-apples refresh-me! with-the-raisins strengthen-me! (5) love over-me

כִּי־ חוֹלַת אַהֲבָה אָנִי׃ שְׂמֹאלוֹ תַּחַת לְרֹאשִׁי

to-head-of-me under left-arm-of-him (6) I love being-faint-of for

וִימִינוֹ תְּחַבְּקֵנִי׃ הִשְׁבַּעְתִּי אֶתְכֶם בְּנוֹת יְרוּשָׁלִַם

Jerusalem daughters-of you I-charge (7) she-embraces-me and-right-arm-of-him

בִּצְבָאוֹת אוֹ בְּאַיְלוֹת הַשָּׂדֶה אִם־ תָּעִירוּ | וְאִם־ תְּעוֹרְרוּ אֶת־

*** you-awaken and-not you-arouse not the-field by-does-of and by-gazelles

הָאַהֲבָה עַד שֶׁתֶּחְפָּץ׃ קוֹל דּוֹדִי הִנֵּה־ זֶה בָּא

he-comes there look! lover-of-me sound-of (8) that-she-desires until the-love

מְדַלֵּג עַל־ הֶהָרִים מְקַפֵּץ עַל־ הַגְּבָעוֹת׃ דּוֹמֶה

one-being-like (9) the-hills over bounding the-mountains across leaping

דוֹדִי לִצְבִי אוֹ לְעֹפֶר הָאַיָּלִים הִנֵּה־ זֶה עוֹמֵד

standing here look! the-stags to-young-deer-of or to-gazelle lover-of-me

אַחַר כָּתְלֵנוּ מַשְׁגִּיחַ מִן־ הַחַלֹּנוֹת* מֵצִיץ מִן־ הַחֲרַכִּים׃

the-lattices through peering the-windows through gazing wall-of-us behind

עָנָה דוֹדִי וְאָמַר לִי קוּמִי לָךְ רַעְיָתִי

darling-of-me to-you arise! to-me and-he-said lover-of-me he-spoke (10)

יָפָתִי וּלְכִי־ לָךְ׃ כִּי־ הִנֵּה הַסְּתָו עָבָר

he-passed the-winter see! for (11) to-you and-come! beautiful-one-of-me

13My lover is to me a sachet of myrrh
resting between my breasts.
14My lover is to me a cluster of henna blossoms
from the vineyards of En Gedi.

*Lover*

15How beautiful you are, my darling!
Oh, how beautiful!
Your eyes are doves.

*Beloved*

16How handsome you are, my lover!
Oh, how charming!
And our bed is verdant.

*Lover*

17The beams of our house are cedars;
our rafters are firs.

*Beloved*[d]

2 I am a rose[e] of Sharon,
a lily of the valleys.

*Lover*

2Like a lily among thorns
is my darling among the maidens.

*Beloved*

3Like an apple tree among the trees of the forest
is my lover among the young men.
I delight to sit in his shade,
and his fruit is sweet to my taste.
4He has taken me to the banquet hall,
and his banner over me is love.
5Strengthen me with raisins,
refresh me with apples,
for I am faint with love.
6His left arm is under my head,
and his right arm embraces me.
7Daughters of Jerusalem, I charge you
by the gazelles and by the does of the field:
Do not arouse or awaken love
until it so desires.

8Listen! My lover!
Look! Here he comes,
leaping across the mountains,
bounding over the hills.
9My lover is like a gazelle or a young stag.
Look! There he stands
behind our wall,
gazing through the windows,
peering through the lattice.
10My lover spoke and said to me,
"Arise, my darling,
my beautiful one, and come with me.
11See! The winter is past;

[d] 1 Or *Lover*
[e] 1 Possibly a member of the crocus family

*9 Most mss have *pathah* under the *beth* (הַחַלֹּנוֹת).

°17 ק רהיטנו
°11 ק הסתיו

הַגֶּשֶׁם חָלַף הָלַךְ לוֹ׃ (12) הַנִּצָּנִים נִרְאוּ בָאָרֶץ
the-rain he-is-over he-went to-him (12) the-flowers they-appear on-the-earth

עֵת הַזָּמִיר הִגִּיעַ וְקוֹל הַתּוֹר נִשְׁמַע בְּאַרְצֵנוּ׃
season-of the-song he-came and-sound-of the-dove he-is-heard in-land-of-us

(13) הַתְּאֵנָה חָנְטָה פַגֶּיהָ וְהַגְּפָנִים ׀ סְמָדַר
(13) the-fig-tree she-forms early-fruits-of-her and-the-vines blossom

נָתְנוּ רֵיחַ קוּמִי לְכִי רַעְיָתִי יָפָתִי
they-spread fragrance arise! come! darling-of-me beautiful-one-of-me

וּלְכִי־לָךְ׃ (14) יוֹנָתִי בְּחַגְוֵי הַסֶּלַע בְּסֵתֶר
and-come! to-you (14) dove-of-me in-clefts-of the-rock in-hiding-place-of

הַמַּדְרֵגָה הַרְאִינִי אֶת־מַרְאַיִךְ הַשְׁמִיעִינִי אֶת־קוֹלֵךְ כִּי־
the-mountainside show-me! *** faces-of-you let-hear-me! *** voice-of-you for

קוֹלֵךְ עָרֵב וּמַרְאֵיךְ נָאוֶה׃ (15) אֶחֱזוּ־לָנוּ שׁוּעָלִים שׁוּעָלִים
voice-of-you sweet and-faces-of-you lovely (15) catch! for-us foxes foxes

קְטַנִּים מְחַבְּלִים כְּרָמִים וּכְרָמֵינוּ סְמָדַר׃
little-ones ones-ruining vineyards indeed-vineyards-of-us bloom

(16) דּוֹדִי לִי וַאֲנִי לוֹ הָרֹעֶה בַּשּׁוֹשַׁנִּים׃
(16) lover-of-me to-me and-I to-him the-one-browsing among-the-lilies

(17) עַד שֶׁיָּפוּחַ הַיּוֹם וְנָסוּ הַצְּלָלִים סֹב דְּמֵה־
(17) until when-he-breaks the-day and-they-flee the-shadows turn! be-like!

לְךָ דוֹדִי לִצְבִי אוֹ לְעֹפֶר הָאַיָּלִים עַל־הָרֵי
to-you lover-of-me to-gazelle or to-young-deer-of the-stags on hills-of

בָתֶר׃ (3:1) עַל־מִשְׁכָּבִי בַּלֵּילוֹת בִּקַּשְׁתִּי אֵת שֶׁאָהֲבָה
ruggedness (3:1) on bed-of-me in-the-nights I-looked-for *** whom-she-loves

נַפְשִׁי בִּקַּשְׁתִּיו וְלֹא מְצָאתִיו׃ (2) אָקוּמָה נָּא
heart-of-me I-looked-for-him but-not I-found-him (2) I-will-get-up now!

וַאֲסוֹבְבָה בָעִיר בַּשְּׁוָקִים וּבָרְחֹבוֹת
and-I-will-go-about through-the-city through-the-streets and-through-the-squares

אֲבַקְשָׁה אֵת שֶׁאָהֲבָה נַפְשִׁי בִּקַּשְׁתִּיו וְלֹא
I-will-search-for *** whom-she-loves heart-of-me I-looked-for-him but-not

מְצָאתִיו׃ (3) מְצָאוּנִי הַשֹּׁמְרִים הַסֹּבְבִים
I-found-him (3) they-found-me the-men-watching the-ones-going-round

בָּעִיר אֵת שֶׁאָהֲבָה נַפְשִׁי רְאִיתֶם׃ (4) כִּמְעַט
in-the-city *** whom-she-loves heart-of-me you-saw (4) as-scarcely

שֶׁעָבַרְתִּי מֵהֶם עַד שֶׁמָּצָאתִי אֵת שֶׁאָהֲבָה נַפְשִׁי
that-I-passed from-them when that-I-found *** whom-she-loves heart-of-me

אֲחַזְתִּיו וְלֹא אַרְפֶּנּוּ עַד־שֶׁהֲבֵיאתִיו אֶל־בֵּית
I-held-him and-not I-would-let-go-him till when-I-brought-him to house-of

the rains are over and gone.
12 Flowers appear on the earth;
the season of singing has come,
the cooing of doves
is heard in our land.
13 The fig tree forms its early fruit;
the blossoming vines spread their fragrance.
Arise, come, my darling;
my beautiful one, come with me."

*Lover*

14 My dove in the clefts of the rock,
in the hiding places on the mountainside,
show me your face,
let me hear your voice;
for your voice is sweet,
and your face is lovely.
15 Catch for us the foxes,
the little foxes
that ruin the vineyards,
our vineyards that are in bloom.

*Beloved*

16 My lover is mine and I am his;
he browses among the lilies.
17 Until the day breaks
and the shadows flee,
turn, my lover,
and be like a gazelle
or like a young stag
on the rugged hills.[f]

3 All night long on my bed
I looked for the one my heart loves;
I looked for him but did not find him.
2 I will get up now and go about the city,
through its streets and squares;
I will search for the one my heart loves.
So I looked for him but did not find him.
3 The watchmen found me
as they made their rounds in the city.
"Have you seen the one my heart loves?"
4 Scarcely had I passed them
when I found the one my heart loves.
I held him and would not let him go
till I had brought him to my mother's house,

f17 Or *the hills of Bether*

°13 ק לך

אִמִּי וְאֶל־ חֶדֶר הוֹרָתִי׃ הִשְׁבַּעְתִּי אֶתְכֶם בְּנוֹת
daughters-of you I-charge (5) one-conceiving-me room-of and-to mother-of-me

יְרוּשָׁלַ͏ִם בִּצְבָאוֹת אוֹ בְּאַיְלוֹת הַשָּׂדֶה אִם־ תָּעִירוּ ׀ וְאִם־
and-not you-arouse not the-field by-does-of and by-gazelles Jerusalem

תְּעוֹרְרוּ אֶת־הָאַהֲבָה עַד שֶׁתֶּחְפָּץ׃ מִי זֹאת עֹלָה מִן־
from coming-up this who? (6) that-she-desires until the-love *** you-awaken

הַמִּדְבָּר כְּתִימֲרוֹת עָשָׁן מְקֻטֶּרֶת מוֹר וּלְבוֹנָה
and-incense myrrh being-perfumed-of smoke like-columns-of the-desert

מִכֹּל אַבְקַת רוֹכֵל׃ הִנֵּה מִטָּתוֹ
carriage-of-him look! (7) one-being-merchant spice-of from-all-of

שֶׁלִּשְׁלֹמֹה שִׁשִּׁים גִּבֹּרִים סָבִיב לָהּ מִגִּבֹּרֵי יִשְׂרָאֵל׃
Israel from-noble-ones-of about-her around warriors sixty that-to-Solomon

כֻּלָּם אֲחֻזֵי חֶרֶב מְלֻמְּדֵי מִלְחָמָה אִישׁ
each battle ones-being-experienced-of sword ones-wearing-of all-of-them (8)

חַרְבּוֹ עַל־ יְרֵכוֹ מִפַּחַד בַּלֵּילוֹת׃ אַפִּרְיוֹן עָשָׂה
he-made carriage (9) of-the-nights for-terror side-of-him at sword-of-him

לוֹ הַמֶּלֶךְ שְׁלֹמֹה מֵעֲצֵי הַלְּבָנוֹן׃ עַמּוּדָיו עָשָׂה
he-made posts-of-him (10) the-Lebanon from-woods-of Solomon the-king for-him

כֶּסֶף רְפִידָתוֹ זָהָב מֶרְכָּבוֹ אַרְגָּמָן תּוֹכוֹ רָצוּף
being-inlaid interior-of-him purple seat-of-him gold base-of-him silver

אַהֲבָה מִבְּנוֹת יְרוּשָׁלָ͏ִם׃ צְאֶינָה ׀ וּרְאֶינָה בְּנוֹת צִיּוֹן
Zion daughters-of and-look! come-out! (11) Jerusalem by-daughters-of love

בַּמֶּלֶךְ שְׁלֹמֹה בָּעֲטָרָה שֶׁעִטְּרָה־ לּוֹ אִמּוֹ
mother-of-him upon-him which-she-crowned with-the-crown Solomon at-the-king

בְּיוֹם חֲתֻנָּתוֹ וּבְיוֹם שִׂמְחַת לִבּוֹ׃ הִנָּךְ
see-you! (4:1) heart-of-him rejoicing-of on-day-of wedding-of-him on-day-of

יָפָה רַעְיָתִי הִנָּךְ יָפָה עֵינַיִךְ יוֹנִים מִבַּעַד
at-behind doves eyes-of-you beautiful see-you! darling-of-me beautiful

לְצַמָּתֵךְ שַׂעְרֵךְ כְּעֵדֶר הָעִזִּים שֶׁגָּלְשׁוּ
that-they-descend the-goats like-flock-of hair-of-you to-veil-of-you

מֵהַר גִּלְעָד׃ שִׁנַּיִךְ כְּעֵדֶר הַקְּצוּבוֹת
the-ones-being-shorn like-flock-of teeth-of-you (2) Gilead from-Mount-of

שֶׁעָלוּ מִן־ הָרַחְצָה שֶׁכֻּלָּם מַתְאִימוֹת
ones-having-twins that-each-of-them the-washing from that-they-come-up

וְשַׁכֻּלָה אֵין בָּהֶם׃ כְּחוּט הַשָּׁנִי שִׂפְתֹתַיִךְ
lips-of-you the-scarlet like-ribbon-of (3) of-them there-is-not and-alone

וּמִדְבָּרֵיךְ נָאוֶה כְּפֶלַח הָרִמּוֹן רַקָּתֵךְ מִבַּעַד
at-behind temple-of-you the-pomegranate like-half-of lovely and-mouths-of-you

to the room of the one who
conceived me.
5 Daughters of Jerusalem, I
charge you
by the gazelles and by the
does of the field:
Do not arouse or awaken love
until it so desires.

6 Who is this coming up from
the desert
like a column of smoke,
perfumed with myrrh and
incense
made from all the spices of
the merchant?
7 Look! It is Solomon's carriage,
escorted by sixty warriors,
the noblest of Israel,
8 all of them wearing the sword,
all experienced in battle,
each with his sword at his
side,
prepared for the terrors of
the night.
9 King Solomon made for
himself the carriage;
he made it of wood from
Lebanon.
10 Its posts he made of silver,
its base of gold.
Its seat was upholstered with
purple,
its interior lovingly inlaid
by[g] the daughters of
Jerusalem.
11 Come out, you daughters of
Zion,
and look at King Solomon
wearing the crown,
the crown with which his
mother crowned him
on the day of his wedding,
the day his heart rejoiced.

*Lover*

4 How beautiful you are, my
darling!
Oh, how beautiful!
Your eyes behind your veil
are doves.
Your hair is like a flock of
goats
descending from Mount
Gilead.
2 Your teeth are like a flock of
sheep just shorn,
coming up from the
washing.
Each has its twin;
not one of them is alone.
3 Your lips are like a scarlet
ribbon;
your mouth is lovely.
Your temples behind your veil
are like the halves of a
pomegranate.

g10 *Or its inlaid interior a gift of love / from*

| בָּנוּי | צַוָּארֵךְ | דָּוִיד | כְּמִגְדַּל | | לְצַמָּתֵךְ: |
|---|---|---|---|---|---|
| one-being-built | neck-of-you | David | like-tower-of | (4) | to-veil-of-you |

| שִׁלְטֵי | כֹּל | עָלָיו | תָּלוּי | הַמָּגֵן | אֶלֶף | לְתַלְפִּיּוֹת |
|---|---|---|---|---|---|---|
| shields-of | all-of | on-him | being-hung | the-shield | thousand-of | with-elegances |

| צְבִיָּה | תְּאוֹמֵי | עֳפָרִים | כִּשְׁנֵי | שָׁדַיִךְ | שְׁנֵי | | הַגִּבּוֹרִים: |
|---|---|---|---|---|---|---|---|
| gazelle | twins-of | fawns | like-two-of | breasts-of-you | two-of | (5) | the-warriors |

| הַיּוֹם | שֶׁיָּפוּחַ | עַד | | בַּשּׁוֹשַׁנִּים: | הָרוֹעִים |
|---|---|---|---|---|---|
| the-day | when-he-breaks | until | (6) | among-the-lilies | the-ones-browsing |

| וְאֶל־ | הַמּוֹר | הַר | אֶל־ | לִי | אֵלֶךְ | הַצְּלָלִים | וְנָסוּ |
|---|---|---|---|---|---|---|---|
| and-to | the-myrrh | mountain-of | to | to-me | I-will-go | the-shadows | and-they-flee |

| וּמוּם | רַעְיָתִי | יָפָה | כֻּלָּךְ | | הַלְּבוֹנָה: | גִּבְעַת |
|---|---|---|---|---|---|---|
| and-flaw | darling-of-me | beautiful | all-of-you | (7) | the-incense | hill-of |

| מִלְּבָנוֹן | אִתִּי | כַּלָּה | מִלְּבָנוֹן | אִתִּי | | בָּךְ: | אֵין |
|---|---|---|---|---|---|---|---|
| from-Lebanon | with-me | bride | from-Lebanon | with-me | (8) | in-you | there-is-not |

| וְחֶרְמוֹן | שְׂנִיר | מֵרֹאשׁ | אֲמָנָה | מֵרֹאשׁ | תָּשׁוּרִי ׀ | תָּבוֹאִי |
|---|---|---|---|---|---|---|
| even-Hermon | Senir | from-top-of | Amana | from-crest-of | you-descend | you-come |

| לִבַּבְתִּנִי | | נְמֵרִים: | מֵהַרְרֵי | אֲרָיוֹת | מִמְּעֹנוֹת |
|---|---|---|---|---|---|
| you-stole-heart-of-me | (9) | leopards | from-mountains-of | lions | from-dens-of |

| מֵעֵינַיִךְ | בְּאַחַד | לִבַּבְתִּינִי | כַלָּה | אֲחֹתִי |
|---|---|---|---|---|
| from-eyes-of-you | with-one | you-stole-heart-of-me | bride | sister-of-me |

| יָּפוּ | מַה־ | | מִצַּוְּרֹנָיִךְ: | עֲנָק | בְּאַחַד |
|---|---|---|---|---|---|
| they-are-delightful | how! | (10) | of-necklaces-of-you | jewel-of | with-one-of |

| דֹּדַיִךְ | טֹּבוּ | מַה־ | כַלָּה | אֲחֹתִי | דֹדַיִךְ |
|---|---|---|---|---|---|
| loves-of-you | they-are-pleasing | how! | bride | sister-of-me | loves-of-you |

| בְּשָׂמִים: | מִכָּל־ | שְׁמָנַיִךְ | וְרֵיחַ | מִיַּיִן |
|---|---|---|---|---|
| spices | more-than-any-of | perfumes-of-you | and-fragrance-of | more-than-wine |

| לְשׁוֹנֵךְ | תַּחַת | וְחָלָב | דְּבַשׁ | כַּלָּה | שִׂפְתוֹתַיִךְ | תִּטֹּפְנָה | נֹפֶת | |
|---|---|---|---|---|---|---|---|---|
| tongue-of-you | under | and-milk | honey | bride | lips-of-you | they-drop | honeycomb | (11) |

| גַּן ׀ | | לְבָנוֹן: | כְּרֵיחַ | שַׂלְמֹתַיִךְ | וְרֵיחַ |
|---|---|---|---|---|---|
| garden | (12) | Lebanon | like-fragrance-of | garments-of-you | and-fragrance-of |

| חָתוּם: | מַעְיָן | נָעוּל | גַּל | כַּלָּה | אֲחֹתִי | נָעוּל |
|---|---|---|---|---|---|---|
| being-sealed | fountain | being-enclosed | spring | bride | sister-of-me | being-locked |

| כְּפָרִים | מְגָדִים | פְּרִי | עִם | רִמּוֹנִים | פַּרְדֵּס | שְׁלָחַיִךְ | |
|---|---|---|---|---|---|---|---|
| hennas | choice-ones | fruit-of | with | pomegranates | orchard-of | plants-of-you | (13) |

| עֲצֵי | כָּל־ | עִם | וְקִנָּמוֹן | קָנֶה | וְכַרְכֹּם | נֵרְדְּ ׀ | | נְרָדִים: | עִם־ |
|---|---|---|---|---|---|---|---|---|---|
| trees-of | all-of | with | and-cinnamon | calamus | and-saffron | nard | (14) | nards | with |

| מַעְיַן | | בְּשָׂמִים: | רָאשֵׁי | כָּל־ | עִם | וַאֲהָלוֹת | מֹר | לְבוֹנָה |
|---|---|---|---|---|---|---|---|---|
| fountain-of | (15) | spices | finest-ones-of | all-of | and | and-aloes | myrrh | incense |

4 Your neck is like the tower of David,
built with elegance[h];
on it hang a thousand shields,
all of them shields of warriors.
5 Your two breasts are like two fawns,
like twin fawns of a gazelle
that browse among the lilies.
6 Until the day breaks
and the shadows flee,
I will go to the mountain of myrrh
and to the hill of incense.
7 All beautiful you are, my darling;
there is no flaw in you.

8 Come with me from Lebanon, my bride,
come with me from Lebanon.
Descend from the crest of Amana,
from the top of Senir, the summit of Hermon,
from the lions' dens
and the mountain haunts of the leopards.
9 You have stolen my heart, my sister, my bride;
you have stolen my heart
with one glance of your eyes,
with one jewel of your necklace.
10 How delightful is your love, my sister, my bride!
How much more pleasing is your love than wine,
and the fragrance of your perfume than any spice!
11 Your lips drop sweetness as the honeycomb, my bride;
milk and honey are under your tongue.
The fragrance of your garments is like that of Lebanon.
12 You are a garden locked up, my sister, my bride;
you are a spring enclosed, a sealed fountain.
13 Your plants are an orchard of pomegranates
with choice fruits,
with henna and nard,
14 nard and saffron,
calamus and cinnamon,
with every kind of incense tree,
with myrrh and aloes
and all the finest spices.

h4 The meaning of the Hebrew for this word is uncertain.

9 ק באחת

גַּנִּים בְּאֵר מַיִם חַיִּים וְנֹזְלִים מִן־ לְבָנוֹן׃
Lebanon from even-ones-streaming-down flowing-ones waters well-of gardens

עוּרִי צָפוֹן וּבוֹאִי תֵימָן הָפִיחִי גַנִּי
garden-of-me blow-on! south-wind and-come! north-wind awake! (16)

יִזְּלוּ בְשָׂמָיו יָבֹא דוֹדִי
lover-of-me let-him-come fragrances-of-him that-they-may-spread

לְגַנּוֹ וְיֹאכַל פְּרִי מְגָדָיו׃ בָּאתִי
I-came (5:1) choice-ones-of-him fruit-of and-let-him-taste into-garden-of-him

לְגַנִּי אֲחֹתִי כַלָּה אָרִיתִי מוֹרִי עִם־ בְּשָׂמִי
spice-of-me with myrrh-of-me I-gathered bride sister-of-me into-garden-of-me

אָכַלְתִּי יַעְרִי עִם־ דִּבְשִׁי שָׁתִיתִי יֵינִי עִם־ חֲלָבִי
milk-of-me and wine-of-me I-drank honey-of-me and honeycomb-of-me I-ate

אִכְלוּ רֵעִים שְׁתוּ וְשִׁכְרוּ דּוֹדִים׃ אֲנִי יְשֵׁנָה וְלִבִּי
but-heart-of-me asleep I (2) lovers and-drink-fill! drink! friends eat!

עֵר קוֹל ׀ דּוֹדִי דוֹפֵק פִּתְחִי־ לִי אֲחֹתִי
sister-of-me to-me open! knocking lover-of-me sound-of being-awake

רַעְיָתִי יוֹנָתִי תַמָּתִי שֶׁרֹּאשִׁי נִמְלָא־
being-drenched for-head-of-me flawless-one-of-me dove-of-me darling-of-me

טָל קְוֻצּוֹתַי רְסִיסֵי לָיְלָה׃ פָּשַׁטְתִּי אֶת־ כֻּתָּנְתִּי אֵיכָכָה
indeed? robe-of-me *** I-took-off (3) night dampnesses-of hairs-of-me dew

אֶלְבָּשֶׁנָּה רָחַצְתִּי אֶת־ רַגְלַי אֵיכָכָה אֲטַנְּפֵם׃
must-I-soil-them indeed? feet-of-me *** I-washed must-I-put-on-her

דּוֹדִי שָׁלַח יָדוֹ מִן־ הַחֹר וּמֵעַי
and-hearts-of-me the-latch-opening through hand-of-him he-thrust lover-of-me (4)

הָמוּ עָלָיו׃ קַמְתִּי אֲנִי לִפְתֹּחַ לְדוֹדִי וְיָדַי
and-hands-of-me for-lover-of-me to-open I I-arose (5) for-him they-pounded

נָטְפוּ־ מוֹר וְאֶצְבְּעֹתַי מוֹר עֹבֵר עַל כַּפּוֹת הַמַּנְעוּל׃
the-lock handles-of on flowing myrrh and-fingers-of-me myrrh they-dripped

פָּתַחְתִּי אֲנִי לְדוֹדִי וְדוֹדִי חָמַק עָבָר נַפְשִׁי
heart-of-me he-went he-left but-lover-of-me for-lover-of-me I I-opened (6)

יָצְאָה בְדַבְּרוֹ בִּקַּשְׁתִּיהוּ וְלֹא מְצָאתִיהוּ
I-found-him but-not I-looked-for-him when-to-speak-him she-went-out

קְרָאתִיו וְלֹא עָנָנִי׃ מְצָאֻנִי הַשֹּׁמְרִים
the-men-watching they-found-me (7) he-answered-me but-not I-called-him

הַסֹּבְבִים בָּעִיר הִכּוּנִי פְצָעוּנִי נָשְׂאוּ
they-took they-bruised-me they-beat-me in-the-city the-ones-going-around

אֶת־ רְדִידִי מֵעָלַי שֹׁמְרֵי הַחֹמוֹת׃ הִשְׁבַּעְתִּי אֶתְכֶם
you I-charge (8) the-walls ones-watching-of from-on-me cloak-of-me ***

[15]You are[i] a garden fountain,
a well of flowing water
streaming down from
Lebanon.

*Beloved*

[16]Awake, north wind,
and come, south wind!
Blow on my garden,
that its fragrance may
spread abroad.
Let my lover come into his
garden
and taste its choice fruits.

*Lover*

5 I have come into my garden,
my sister, my bride;
I have gathered my myrrh
with my spice.
I have eaten my honeycomb
and my honey;
I have drunk my wine and
my milk.

*Friends*

Eat, O friends, and drink;
drink your fill, O lovers.

*Beloved*

[2]I slept but my heart was
awake.
Listen! My lover is
knocking:
"Open to me, my sister, my
darling,
my dove, my flawless one.
My head is drenched with
dew,
my hair with the dampness
of the night."
[3]I have taken off my robe—
must I put it on again?
I have washed my feet—
must I soil them again?
[4]My lover thrust his hand
through the
latch-opening;
my heart began to pound
for him.
[5]I arose to open for my lover,
and my hands dripped with
myrrh,
my fingers with flowing
myrrh,
on the handles of the lock.
[6]I opened for my lover,
but my lover had left; he
was gone.
My heart had gone out to
him when he spoke.
I looked for him but did not
find him.
I called him but he did not
answer.
[7]The watchmen found me
as they made their rounds
in the city.
They beat me, they bruised
me;
they took away my cloak,
those watchmen of the
walls!

[i]15 Or *I am* (spoken by the *Beloved*)

*2 Most mss have no *dagesh* in the *vav* (קוֻ).

בְּנוֹת יְרוּשָׁלָ͏ִם אִם־תִּמְצְאוּ אֶת־ דּוֹדִי מַה־ תַּגִּידוּ לוֹ
to-him will-you-tell what? lover-of-me *** you-find if Jerusalem daughters-of

שֶׁחוֹלַת אַהֲבָה אָנִי׃ מַה־ דּוֹדֵךְ מִדּוֹד
better-than-beloved beloved-of-you how? (9) I love that-one-being-faint-of

הַיָּפָה בַּנָּשִׁים מַה־ דּוֹדֵךְ מִדּוֹד
better-than-beloved beloved-of-you how? among-the-women the-beautiful-one

שֶׁכָּכָה הִשְׁבַּעְתָּנוּ׃ דּוֹדִי צַח וְאָדוֹם דָּגוּל
being-outstanding and-ruddy radiant lover-of-me (10) you-charge-us that-so

מֵרְבָבָה׃ רֹאשׁוֹ כֶּתֶם פָּז קְוּצּוֹתָיו* תַּלְתַּלִּים
wavy-ones hairs-of-him purest-gold gold head-of-him (11) among-ten-thousand

שְׁחֹרוֹת כָּעוֹרֵב׃ עֵינָיו כְּיוֹנִים עַל־ אֲפִיקֵי מָיִם
waters streams-of by like-doves eyes-of-him (12) as-the-raven black-ones

רֹחֲצוֹת בֶּחָלָב יֹשְׁבוֹת עַל־מִלֵּאת׃ לְחָיָו
cheeks-of-him (13) jewel like ones-being-mounted in-the-milk ones-being-washed

כַּעֲרוּגַת הַבֹּשֶׂם מִגְדְּלוֹת† מֶרְקָחִים שִׂפְתוֹתָיו שׁוֹשַׁנִּים נֹטְפוֹת
ones-dripping lilies lips-of-him perfumes †towers-of the-spice like-bed-of

מוֹר עֹבֵר׃ יָדָיו גְּלִילֵי זָהָב מְמֻלָּאִים בַּתַּרְשִׁישׁ
with-the-chrysolite ones-being-set gold rods-of arms-of-him (14) flowing myrrh

מֵעָיו עֶשֶׁת שֵׁן מְעֻלֶּפֶת סַפִּירִים׃
sapphires one-being-decorated ivory polished-work-of bodies-of-him

שׁוֹקָיו עַמּוּדֵי שֵׁשׁ מְיֻסָּדִים עַל־ אַדְנֵי־ פָז
pure-gold bases-of on ones-being-set marble pillars-of legs-of-him (15)

מַרְאֵהוּ כַּלְּבָנוֹן בָּחוּר כָּאֲרָזִים׃
as-the-cedars one-being-choice like-the-Lebanon appearance-of-him

חִכּוֹ מַמְתַקִּים וְכֻלּוֹ מַחֲמַדִּים זֶה דוֹדִי
lover-of-me this lovely-ones and-all-of-him sweetnesses mouth-of-him (16)

וְזֶה רֵעִי בְּנוֹת יְרוּשָׁלָ͏ִם׃ אָנָה הָלַךְ
he-went to-where? (6:1) Jerusalem daughters-of friend-of-me and-this

דּוֹדֵךְ הַיָּפָה בַּנָּשִׁים אָנָה פָּנָה דוֹדֵךְ
lover-of-you he-turned to-where? among-the-women the-beautiful-one lover-of-you

וּנְבַקְשֶׁנּוּ עִמָּךְ׃ דּוֹדִי יָרַד לְגַנּוֹ
to-garden-of-him he-went-down lover-of-me (2) with-you that-we-may-look-for-him

לַעֲרוּגוֹת הַבֹּשֶׂם לִרְעוֹת בַּגַּנִּים וְלִלְקֹט שׁוֹשַׁנִּים׃ אֲנִי
I (3) lilies and-to-gather in-the-gardens to-browse the-spice to-beds-of

לְדוֹדִי וְדוֹדִי לִי הָרֹעֶה בַּשּׁוֹשַׁנִּים׃
among-the-lilies the-one-browsing to-me and-lover-of-me to-lover-of-me

יָפָה אַתְּ רַעְיָתִי כְּתִרְצָה נָאוָה כִּירוּשָׁלָ͏ִם אֲיֻמָּה
majestic as-Jerusalem lovely as-Tirzah darling-of-me you beautiful (4)

*11 Most mss have no *dagesh* in and have *shureq* under the *vav* (קֻ).

†13 The NIV repoints this word as (מְגַדְּ), *ones-yielding*.

8 O daughters of Jerusalem, I charge you—
if you find my lover,
what will you tell him?
Tell him I am faint with love.

*Friends*

9 How is your beloved better than others,
most beautiful of women?
How is your beloved better than others,
that you charge us so?

*Beloved*

10 My lover is radiant and ruddy,
outstanding among ten thousand.
11 His head is purest gold;
his hair is wavy
and black as a raven.
12 His eyes are like doves
by the water streams,
washed in milk,
mounted like jewels.
13 His cheeks are like beds of spice
yielding perfume.
His lips are like lilies
dripping with myrrh.
14 His arms are rods of gold
set with chrysolite.
His body is like polished ivory
decorated with sapphires.[j]
15 His legs are pillars of marble
set on bases of pure gold.
His appearance is like Lebanon,
choice as its cedars.
16 His mouth is sweetness itself;
he is altogether lovely.
This is my lover, this my friend,
O daughters of Jerusalem.

*Friends*

6 Where has your lover gone,
most beautiful of women?
Which way did your lover turn,
that we may look for him with you?

*Beloved*

2 My lover has gone down to his garden,
to the beds of spices,
to browse in the gardens
and to gather lilies.
3 I am my lover's and my lover is mine;
he browses among the lilies.

*Lover*

4 You are beautiful, my darling,
as Tirzah,
lovely as Jerusalem,

j14 *Or lapis lazuli*

כַּנִּדְגָּלוֹת׃ (5) הָסֵבִּי עֵינַיִךְ מִנֶּגְדִּי שֶׁהֵם
for-they from-before-me eyes-of-you turn! (5) as-the-ones-having-banners

הִרְהִיבֻנִי שַׂעְרֵךְ כְּעֵדֶר הָעִזִּים שֶׁגָּלְשׁוּ מִן־
from that-they-descend the-goats like-flock-of hair-of-you they-overwhelm-me

הַגִּלְעָד׃ (6) שִׁנַּיִךְ כְּעֵדֶר הָרְחֵלִים שֶׁעָלוּ מִן־
from that-they-come-up the-sheeps like-flock-of teeth-of-you (6) the-Gilead

הָרַחְצָה שֶׁכֻּלָּם מַתְאִימוֹת וְשַׁכֻּלָה אֵין
there-is-not and-alone ones-having-twins that-each-of-them the-washing

בָּהֶם׃ (7) כְּפֶלַח הָרִמּוֹן רַקָּתֵךְ מִבַּעַד
at-behind temple-of-you the-pomegranate like-half-of (7) of-them

לְצַמָּתֵךְ׃ (8) שִׁשִּׁים הֵמָּה מְּלָכוֹת† וּשְׁמֹנִים פִּילַגְשִׁים וַעֲלָמוֹת
and-virgins concubines and-eighty queens they sixty (8) to-veil-of-you

אֵין מִסְפָּר׃ (9) אַחַת הִיא יוֹנָתִי תַמָּתִי אַחַת הִיא
she only perfect-one-of-me dove-of-me she unique (9) number there-is-no

לְאִמָּהּ בָּרָה הִיא לְיוֹלַדְתָּהּ רָאוּהָ בָנוֹת
maidens they-saw-her of-one-bearing-her she favorite to-mother-of-her

וַיְאַשְּׁרוּהָ מְלָכוֹת וּפִילַגְשִׁים וַיְהַלְלוּהָ׃
also-they-praised-her and-concubines queens and-they-called-blessed-her

(10) מִי־ זֹאת הַנִּשְׁקָפָה כְּמוֹ־ שָׁחַר יָפָה כַלְּבָנָה בָּרָה כַּחַמָּה
as-the-sun bright as-the-moon fair dawn like the-one-appearing this who? (10)

אֲיֻמָּה כַּנִּדְגָּלוֹת׃ (11) אֶל־ גִּנַּת אֱגוֹז יָרַדְתִּי לִרְאוֹת
to-look I-went-down nut-tree grove-of to (11) as-the-ones-proceeding majestic

בְּאִבֵּי הַנָּחַל לִרְאוֹת הֲפָרְחָה הַגֶּפֶן הֵנֵצוּ
they-bloomed the-vine if-she-budded to-see the-valley at-new-growths-of

הָרִמֹּנִים׃ (12) לֹא יָדַעְתִּי נַפְשִׁי שָׂמַתְנִי מַרְכְּבוֹת
chariots-of she-set-me desire-of-me I-realized not (12) the-pomegranates

עַמִּי־ נָדִיב׃ *(7:1) שׁוּבִי שׁוּבִי הַשּׁוּלַמִּית שׁוּבִי
come-back! the-Shulammite come-back! come-back! *(7:1) royal people-of-me

שׁוּבִי וְנֶחֱזֶה־ בָּךְ מַה־ תֶּחֱזוּ בַּשּׁוּלַמִּית
on-the-Shulammite would-you-gaze why? on-you that-we-may-gaze come-back!

כִּמְחֹלַת הַמַּחֲנָיִם׃ (2) מַה־ יָּפוּ פְעָמַיִךְ
feet-of-you they-are-beautiful how! (2) the-Mahanaim as-dance-of

בַּנְּעָלִים בַּת־ נָדִיב חַמּוּקֵי יְרֵכַיִךְ כְּמוֹ חֲלָאִים
jewels like legs-of-you graceful-ones-of prince daughter-of in-the-sandals

מַעֲשֵׂה יְדֵי אָמָּן׃ (3) שָׁרְרֵךְ אַגַּן הַסַּהַר אַל־
never the-roundness goblet-of navel-of-you (3) craftsman hands-of work-of

יֶחְסַר הַמָּזֶג בִּטְנֵךְ עֲרֵמַת חִטִּים סוּגָה
being-encircled wheats mound-of waist-of-you the-blended-wine he-lacks

majestic as troops with banners.
5 Turn your eyes from me;
they overwhelm me.
Your hair is like a flock of goats
descending from Gilead.
6 Your teeth are like a flock of sheep
coming up from the washing.
Each has its twin,
not one of them is alone.
7 Your temples behind your veil
are like the halves of a pomegranate.
8 Sixty queens there may be,
and eighty concubines,
and virgins beyond number;
9 but my dove, my perfect one, is unique,
the only daughter of her mother,
the favorite of the one who bore her.
The maidens saw her and called her blessed;
the queens and concubines praised her.

10 Who is this that appears like the dawn,
fair as the moon, bright as the sun,
majestic as the stars in procession?
11 I went down to the grove of nut trees
to look at the new growth in the valley,
to see if the vines had budded
or the pomegranates were in bloom.
12 Before I realized it,
my desire set me among the royal chariots of my people.[k]

*Friends*

13 Come back, come back, O Shulammite;
come back, come back, that we may gaze on you!

*Lover*

Why would you gaze on the Shulammite
as on the dance of Mahanaim?

7 How beautiful your sandaled feet,
O prince's daughter!
Your graceful legs are like jewels,
the work of a craftsman's hands.
2 Your navel is a rounded goblet
that never lacks blended wine.
Your waist is a mound of wheat

k12 Or *among the chariots of Amminadab;* or *among the chariots of the people of the prince*

***1 The Hebrew numeration of chapter 7 begins with verse 13 of chapter 6 in English; thus, there is a one-verse discrepancy throughout chapter 7.**

**†8 Most mss have no *dagesh* in the *mem* (מְ).**

בַּשּׁוֹשַׁנִּים׃ (4) שְׁנֵי שָׁדַיִךְ כִּשְׁנֵי עֳפָרִים תָּאֳמֵי צְבִיָּה׃
by-the-lilies (4) two-of breasts-of-you like-two-of fawns twins-of gazelle

(5) צַוָּארֵךְ כְּמִגְדַּל הַשֵּׁן עֵינַיִךְ בְּרֵכוֹת בְּחֶשְׁבּוֹן עַל־
(5) neck-of-you like-tower-of the-ivory eyes-of-you pools of-Heshbon by

שַׁעַר בַּת־ רַבִּים אַפֵּךְ כְּמִגְדַּל הַלְּבָנוֹן צוֹפֶה פְּנֵי
gate-of Bath Rabbim nose-of-you like-tower-of the-Lebanon looking faces-of

דַמָּשֶׂק׃ (6) רֹאשֵׁךְ עָלַיִךְ כַּכַּרְמֶל וְדַלַּת רֹאשֵׁךְ
Damascus (6) head-of-you upon-you like-the-Carmel and-hair-of head-of-you

כָּאַרְגָּמָן מֶלֶךְ אָסוּר בָּרְהָטִים׃ (7) מַה־
like-the-tapestry king being-held-captive by-the-tresses (7) how!

יָּפִית וּמַה־ נָּעַמְתְּ אַהֲבָה בַּתַּעֲנוּגִים׃ (8) זֹאת
you-are-beautiful and-how! you-are-pleasing love with-the-delights (8) this

קוֹמָתֵךְ דָּמְתָה לְתָמָר וְשָׁדַיִךְ לְאַשְׁכֹּלוֹת׃
stature-of-you she-is-like to-palm and-breasts-of-you to-clusters-of-fruit

(9) אָמַרְתִּי אֶעֱלֶה בְתָמָר אֹחֲזָה בְּסַנְסִנָּיו
(9) I-said I-will-climb on-palm-tree I-will-take-hold of-fruits-of-him

וְיִהְיוּ־ נָא שָׁדַיִךְ כְּאֶשְׁכְּלוֹת הַגֶּפֶן וְרֵיחַ
and-may-they-be now! breasts-of-you like-clusters-of the-vine and-fragrance-of

אַפֵּךְ כַּתַּפּוּחִים׃ (10) וְחִכֵּךְ כְּיֵין הַטּוֹב
breath-of-you like-the-apples (10) and-mouth-of-you like-wine-of the-best

הוֹלֵךְ לְדוֹדִי לְמֵישָׁרִים דּוֹבֵב שִׂפְתֵי יְשֵׁנִים׃ (11) אֲנִי
going to-lover-of-me as-straight-ones flowing-gently lips-of sleepers (11) I

לְדוֹדִי וְעָלַי תְּשׁוּקָתוֹ׃ (12) לְכָה דוֹדִי נֵצֵא
to-lover-of-me and-for-me desire-of-him (12) come! lover-of-me let-us-go

הַשָּׂדֶה נָלִינָה בַּכְּפָרִים׃ (13) נַשְׁכִּימָה
the-countryside let-us-spend-night in-the-villages (13) let-us-go-early

לַכְּרָמִים נִרְאֶה אִם פָּרְחָה הַגֶּפֶן פִּתַּח הַסְּמָדַר
to-the-vineyards let-us-see if she-budded the-vine he-opened the-blossom

הֵנֵצוּ הָרִמּוֹנִים שָׁם אֶתֵּן אֶת־ דֹּדַי לָךְ׃
they-bloomed the-pomegranates there I-will-give *** loves-of-me to-you

(14) הַדּוּדָאִים נָתְנוּ־ רֵיחַ וְעַל־ פְּתָחֵינוּ כָּל־
(14) the-mandrakes they-send-out fragrance and-at doors-of-us all-of

מְגָדִים חֲדָשִׁים גַּם־ יְשָׁנִים דּוֹדִי צָפַנְתִּי לָךְ׃ (8:1) מִי
delicacies new-ones and old-ones lover-of-me I-stored-up for-you (8:1) who?

יִתֶּנְךָ כְּאָח לִי יוֹנֵק שְׁדֵי אִמִּי
he-could-make-you like-brother of-me one-nursing breasts-of mother-of-me

אֶמְצָאֲךָ בַחוּץ אֶשָּׁקְךָ גַּם לֹא־ יָבוּזוּ
should-I-find-you at-the-outside I-would-kiss-you then not they-would-despise

encircled by lilies.
3 Your breasts are like two fawns,
twins of a gazelle.
4 Your neck is like an ivory tower.
Your eyes are the pools of Heshbon
by the gate of Bath Rabbim.
Your nose is like the tower of Lebanon
looking toward Damascus.
5 Your head crowns you like Mount Carmel.
Your hair is like royal tapestry;
the king is held captive by its tresses.
6 How beautiful you are and how pleasing,
O love, with your delights!
7 Your stature is like that of the palm,
and your breasts like clusters of fruit.
8 I said, "I will climb the palm tree;
I will take hold of its fruit."
May your breasts be like the clusters of the vine,
the fragrance of your breath like apples,
and your mouth like the best wine.

*Beloved*

May the wine go straight to my lover,
flowing gently over lips and teeth.[l]
10 I belong to my lover,
and his desire is for me.
11 Come, my lover, let us go to the countryside,
let us spend the night in the villages.[m]
12 Let us go early to the vineyards
to see if the vines have budded,
if their blossoms have opened,
and if the pomegranates are in bloom—
there I will give you my love.
13 The mandrakes send out their fragrance,
and at our door is every delicacy,
both new and old,
that I have stored up for you, my lover.

8 If only you were to me like a brother,
who was nursed at my mother's breasts!
Then, if I found you outside,
I would kiss you,
and no one would despise

[l] 9 Septuagint, Aquila, Vulgate and Syriac; Hebrew *lips of sleepers*
[m] 11 Or *henna bushes*

*See the note on page 598.

לִי׃ אֶנְהָגֲךָ אֲבִיאֲךָ אֶל־ בֵּית אִמִּי
mother-of-me house-of to I-would-bring-you I-would-lead-you (2) to-me

תְּלַמְּדֵנִי אַשְׁקְךָ מִיַּיִן הָרֶקַח מֵעֲסִיס
from-nectar-of the-spice from-wine I-would-give-to-drink-you she-taught-me

רִמֹּנִי׃ שְׂמֹאלוֹ תַּחַת רֹאשִׁי וִימִינוֹ
and-right-arm-of-him head-of-me under left-arm-of-him (3) pomegranate-of-me

תְּחַבְּקֵנִי׃ הִשְׁבַּעְתִּי אֶתְכֶם בְּנוֹת יְרוּשָׁלִָם מַה־ תָּעִירוּ ׀
you-arouse not Jerusalem daughters-of you I-charge (4) she-embraces-me

וּמַה־ תְּעֹרְרוּ אֶת־ הָאַהֲבָה עַד שֶׁתֶּחְפָּץ׃ מִי זֹאת
this who? (5) that-she-desires until the-love *** you-awaken and-not

עֹלָה מִן־ הַמִּדְבָּר מִתְרַפֶּקֶת עַל־ דּוֹדָהּ תַּחַת הַתַּפּוּחַ
the-apple-tree under lover-of-her on leaning the-desert from coming-up

עוֹרַרְתִּיךָ שָׁמָּה חִבְּלַתְךָ אִמֶּךָ שָׁמָּה
at-there mother-of-you she-conceived-you at-there I-roused-you

חִבְּלָה יְלָדַתְךָ׃ שִׂימֵנִי כַחוֹתָם עַל־ לִבֶּךָ
heart-of-you over like-the-seal place-me! (6) she-bore-you she-was-in-labor

כַּחוֹתָם עַל־ זְרוֹעֶךָ כִּי־ עַזָּה כַמָּוֶת אַהֲבָה קָשָׁה כִשְׁאוֹל
as-Sheol unyielding love as-the-death strong for arm-of-you on like-the-seal

קִנְאָה רְשָׁפֶיהָ רִשְׁפֵּי אֵשׁ שַׁלְהֶבֶתְיָה׃ מַיִם רַבִּים
many-ones waters (7) flame-of-Yahweh fire blazes-of blazes-of-her jealousy

לֹא יוּכְלוּ לְכַבּוֹת אֶת־הָאַהֲבָה וּנְהָרוֹת לֹא יִשְׁטְפוּהָ אִם־
if they-can-wash-away-her not and-rivers the-love *** to-quench they-can not

יִתֵּן אִישׁ אֶת־ כָּל־ הוֹן בֵּיתוֹ בָּאַהֲבָה בּוֹז
to-scorn for-the-love house-of-him wealth-of all-of *** one he-gave

יָבוּזוּ לוֹ׃ אָחוֹת לָנוּ קְטַנָּה וְשָׁדַיִם אֵין לָהּ מַה־
what? to-her not and-breasts young to-us sister (8) at-him they-would-scorn

נַּעֲשֶׂה לַאֲחֹתֵנוּ בַּיּוֹם שֶׁיְּדֻבַּר־ בָּהּ׃ אִם־
if (9) for-her that-he-is-spoken for-the-day for-sister-of-us shall-we-do

חוֹמָה הִיא נִבְנֶה עָלֶיהָ טִירַת כָּסֶף וְאִם־ דֶּלֶת הִיא נָצוּר
we-will-enclose she door and-if silver tower-of on-her we-will-build she wall

עָלֶיהָ לוּחַ אָרֶז׃ אֲנִי חוֹמָה וְשָׁדַי כַּמִּגְדָּלוֹת אָז
thus like-the-towers and-breasts-of-me wall I (10) cedar panel-of to-her

הָיִיתִי בְעֵינָיו כְּמוֹצְאֵת שָׁלוֹם׃ כֶּרֶם הָיָה
he-was vineyard (11) contentment like-one-bringing in-eyes-of-him I-became

לִשְׁלֹמֹה בְּבַעַל הָמוֹן נָתַן אֶת־ הַכֶּרֶם לַנֹּטְרִים
to-the-ones-being-tenants the-vineyard *** he-let-out Hamon in-Baal to-Solomon

אִישׁ יָבִא בְּפִרְיוֹ אֶלֶף כָּסֶף׃ כַּרְמִי
vineyard-of-me (12) silver thousand-of for-fruit-of-him he-would-bring each

me.
2I would lead you
and bring you to my
mother's house—
she who has taught me.
I would give you spiced wine
to drink,
the nectar of my
pomegranates.
3His left arm is under my head
and his right arm embraces
me.
4Daughters of Jerusalem, I
charge you:
Do not arouse or awaken
love
until it so desires.

*Friends*

5Who is this coming up from
the desert
leaning on her lover?

*Beloved*

Under the apple tree I roused
you;
there your mother conceived
you,
there she who was in labor
gave you birth.
6Place me like a seal over your
heart,
like a seal over your arm;
for love is as strong as death,
its jealousy[n] unyielding as
the grave.[o]
It burns like blazing fire,
like a mighty flame.[p]
7Many waters cannot quench
love;
rivers cannot wash it away.
If one were to give
all the wealth of his house
for love,
it[q] would be utterly scorned.

*Friends*

8We have a young sister,
and her breasts are not yet
grown.
What shall we do for our sister
for the day she is spoken
for?
9If she is a wall,
we will build towers of
silver on her.
If she is a door,
we will enclose her with
panels of cedar.

*Beloved*

10I am a wall,
and my breasts are like
towers.
Thus I have become in his
eyes
like one bringing
contentment.
11Solomon had a vineyard in
Baal Hamon;
he let out his vineyard to
tenants.
Each was to bring for its fruit
a thousand shekels[r] of
silver.

n6 Or *ardor* o6 Hebrew *Sheol*
p6 Or / *like the very flame of the* LORD
q7 Or *he*
r11 That is, about 25 pounds (about 11.5 kilograms); also in verse 12

| וּמָאתַ֖יִם | שְׁלֹמֹ֔ה | לְךָ֣ | הָאֶ֣לֶף | לְפָנַ֖י | שֶׁלִּי |
|---|---|---|---|---|---|
| and-two-hundreds | Solomon | for-you | the-thousand | before-me | that-to-me |

| בַּגַּנִּ֗ים | הַיּוֹשֶׁ֣בֶת | (13) | פִּרְיֽוֹ׃ | אֶת־ | לְנֹטְרִ֥ים |
|---|---|---|---|---|---|
| in-the-gardens | the-one-dwelling | | fruit-of-him | *** | for-ones-tending |

| בְּרַח ׀ | (14) | הַשְׁמִיעִֽינִי׃ | לְקוֹלֵ֖ךְ | מַקְשִׁיבִ֥ים | חֲבֵרִ֛ים |
|---|---|---|---|---|---|
| come-away! | | let-hear-me! | to-voice-of-you | ones-attending | friends |

| לְעֹ֣פֶר | א֚וֹ | לִצְבִי֙ | לְךָ֤ | וּֽדְמֵה־ | דּוֹדִ֗י |
|---|---|---|---|---|---|
| to-young-deer-of | or | to-gazelle | to-you | and-be-like! | lover-of-me |

| בְשָׂמִֽים׃ | הָרֵ֥י | עַ֖ל | הָאַיָּלִ֔ים |
|---|---|---|---|
| spices | mountains-of | on | the-stags |

[12]But my own vineyard is mine
to give;
the thousand shekels are for
you, O Solomon,
and two hundred[s] are for
those who tend its fruit.

*Lover*

[13]You who dwell in the gardens
with friends in attendance,
let me hear your voice!

*Beloved*

[14]Come away, my lover,
and be like a gazelle
or like a young stag
on the spice-laden
mountains.

[s]*12 That is, about 5 pounds (about 2.3 kilograms)

The NIV

# Interlinear Hebrew-English Old Testament

## Volume Four
## Isaiah–Malachi

חֲזוֹן יְשַׁעְיָהוּ בֶן־ אָמוֹץ אֲשֶׁר חָזָה עַל־ יְהוּדָה
Judah concerning he-saw that Amoz son-of Isaiah vision-of (1:1)

וִירוּשָׁלָ͏ִם בִּימֵי עֻזִּיָּהוּ יוֹתָם אָחָז יְחִזְקִיָּהוּ מַלְכֵי יְהוּדָה׃
Judah kings-of Hezekiah Ahaz Jotham Uzziah during-days-of and-Jerusalem

שִׁמְעוּ שָׁמַיִם וְהַאֲזִינִי אֶרֶץ כִּי יְהוָה דִּבֵּר בָּנִים גִּדַּלְתִּי
I-reared children he-spoke Yahweh for earth and-listen! heavens hear! (2)

וְרוֹמַמְתִּי וְהֵם פָּשְׁעוּ בִי׃ יָדַע שׁוֹר
ox he-knows (3) against-me they-rebelled but-they and-I-brought-up

קֹנֵהוּ וַחֲמוֹר אֵבוּס בְּעָלָיו יִשְׂרָאֵל לֹא
not Israel owners-of-him manger-of and-donkey one-being-master-of-him

יָדַע עַמִּי לֹא הִתְבּוֹנָן׃ הוֹי גּוֹי חֹטֵא עַם
people one-sinning nation ah! (4) he-understands not people-of-me he-knows

כֶּבֶד עָוֺן זֶרַע מְרֵעִים בָּנִים מַשְׁחִיתִים
ones-being-corrupt children ones-doing-evil brood-of guilt loaded-of

עָזְבוּ אֶת־ יְהוָה נִאֲצוּ אֶת־ קְדוֹשׁ יִשְׂרָאֵל נָזֹרוּ
they-turned Israel Holy-One-of *** they-spurned Yahweh *** they-forsook

אָחוֹר׃ עַל מֶה תֻכּוּ עוֹד תּוֹסִיפוּ סָרָה
rebellion you-persist anymore should-you-be-beaten why? for (5) back

כָּל־ רֹאשׁ לָחֳלִי וְכָל־ לֵבָב דַּוָּי׃ מִכַּף־ רֶגֶל
foot from-sole-of (6) afflicted heart and-whole-of to-injury head whole-of

וְעַד־ רֹאשׁ אֵין־ בּוֹ מְתֹם פֶּצַע וְחַבּוּרָה וּמַכָּה טְרִיָּה
open and-sore and-welt wound soundness in-him there-is-not head even-to

לֹא־ זֹרוּ וְלֹא חֻבָּשׁוּ וְלֹא רֻכְּכָה
she-is-soothed or-not they-are-bandaged or-not they-are-cleansed not

בַּשָּׁמֶן׃ אַרְצְכֶם שְׁמָמָה עָרֵיכֶם שְׂרֻפוֹת
ones-being-burned-of cities-of-you desolation country-of-you (7) with-the-oil

אֵשׁ אַדְמַתְכֶם לְנֶגְדְּכֶם זָרִים אֹכְלִים אֹתָהּ
her ones-stripping ones-being-foreign at-before-you field-of-you fire

וּשְׁמָמָה כְּמַהְפֵּכַת זָרִים׃ וְנוֹתְרָה
and-she-is-left (8) ones-being-strangers as-overthrown-of and-waste

בַת־ צִיּוֹן כְּסֻכָּה בְכָרֶם כִּמְלוּנָה בְמִקְשָׁה כְּעִיר
like-city in-melon-field like-hut in-vineyard like-shelter Zion Daughter-of

נְצוּרָה׃ לוּלֵי יְהוָה צְבָאוֹת הוֹתִיר לָנוּ שָׂרִיד כִּמְעָט
as-some survivor to-us he-left Hosts Yahweh-of unless (9) being-under-siege

כִּסְדֹם הָיִינוּ לַעֲמֹרָה דָּמִינוּ׃
we-would-have-been-like to-Gomorrah we-would-have-become like-Sodom

שִׁמְעוּ דְבַר־ יְהוָה קְצִינֵי סְדֹם הַאֲזִינוּ תּוֹרַת אֱלֹהֵינוּ עַם
people-of God-of-us law-of listen! Sodom rulers-of Yahweh word-of hear! (10)

1 The vision concerning Judah and Jerusalem that Isaiah son of Amoz saw during the reigns of Uzziah, Jotham, Ahaz and Hezekiah, kings of Judah.

*A Rebellious Nation*

2 Hear, O heavens! Listen, O earth!
For the LORD has spoken:
"I reared children and brought them up,
but they have rebelled against me.
3 The ox knows his master,
the donkey his owner's manger,
but Israel does not know,
my people do not understand."

4 Ah, sinful nation,
a people loaded with guilt,
a brood of evildoers,
children given to corruption!
They have forsaken the LORD;
they have spurned the Holy One of Israel
and turned their backs on him.

5 Why should you be beaten anymore?
Why do you persist in rebellion?
Your whole head is injured,
your whole heart afflicted.
6 From the sole of your foot to the top of your head
there is no soundness—
only wounds and welts
and open sores,
not cleansed or bandaged
or soothed with oil.

7 Your country is desolate,
your cities burned with fire;
your fields are being stripped by foreigners
right before you,
laid waste as when overthrown by strangers.
8 The Daughter of Zion is left
like a shelter in a vineyard,
like a hut in a field of melons,
like a city under siege.
9 Unless the LORD Almighty
had left us some survivors,
we would have become like Sodom,
we would have been like Gomorrah.

10 Hear the word of the LORD,
you rulers of Sodom;
listen to the law of our God,
you people of Gomorrah!

| יְהוָה | יֹאמַר | זִבְחֵיכֶם | רֹב־ | לִּי | לָמָּה־ | | עֲמֹרָה׃ |
|---|---|---|---|---|---|---|---|
| Yahweh | he-says | sacrifices-of-you | multitude-of | to-me | for-what? | (11) | Gomorrah |

| מְרִיאִים | וְחֵלֶב | אֵילִים | עֹלוֹת | שָׂבַעְתִּי |
|---|---|---|---|---|
| fattened-animals | and-fat-of | rams | burnt-offerings-of | I-have-enough |

| כִּי | | חָפָצְתִּי׃ | לֹא | וְעַתּוּדִים | וּכְבָשִׂים | פָּרִים | וְדַם |
|---|---|---|---|---|---|---|---|
| when | (12) | I-have-pleasure | not | and-goats | and-lambs | bulls | and-blood-of |

| רְמֹס | מִיֶּדְכֶם | זֹאת | בִקֵּשׁ | מִי־ | פָּנָי | לֵרָאוֹת | תָבֹאוּ |
|---|---|---|---|---|---|---|---|
| trampling-of | from-hand-of-you | this | he-asked | who? | before-me | to-appear | you-come |

| קְטֹרֶת | שָׁוְא | מִנְחַת־ | הָבִיא | תוֹסִיפוּ | לֹא | | חֲצֵרָי׃ |
|---|---|---|---|---|---|---|---|
| incense | meaninglessness | offering-of | to-bring | you-continue | not | (13) | courts-of-me |

| לֹא־ | מִקְרָא | קְרֹא | וְשַׁבָּת | חֹדֶשׁ | לִי | הִיא | תּוֹעֵבָה |
|---|---|---|---|---|---|---|---|
| not | convocation | to-convoke | and-Sabbath | New-Moon | to-me | she | detestable |

| חָדְשֵׁיכֶם | | וַעֲצָרָה׃ | אָוֶן | אוּכַל |
|---|---|---|---|---|
| New-Moon-festivals-of-you | (14) | and-assembly | evil | I-can-bear |

| לָטֹרַח | עָלַי | הָיוּ | נַפְשִׁי | שָׂנְאָה | וּמוֹעֲדֵיכֶם |
|---|---|---|---|---|---|
| as-burden | to-me | they-become | soul-of-me | she-hates | and-appointed-feasts-of-you |

| אַעְלִים | כַּפֵּיכֶם | וּבְפָרִשְׂכֶם | | נְשֹׂא׃ | נִלְאֵיתִי |
|---|---|---|---|---|---|
| I-will-hide | hands-of-you | and-when-to-spread-you | (15) | to-bear | I-am-weary |

| יְדֵיכֶם | שֹׁמֵעַ | אֵינֶנִּי | תְפִלָּה | תַרְבּוּ | כִּי־ | גַּם | מִכֶּם | עֵינַי |
|---|---|---|---|---|---|---|---|---|
| hands-of-you | listening | not-I | prayer | you-make-many | if | even | from-you | eyes-of-me |

| רֹעַ | הָסִירוּ | הִזַּכּוּ | רַחֲצוּ | | מָלֵאוּ׃ | דָּמִים |
|---|---|---|---|---|---|---|
| evil-of | take! | make-yourselves-clean! | wash! | (16) | they-are-full | bloods |

| לִמְדוּ | | הָרֵעַ׃ | חִדְלוּ | עֵינָי | מִנֶּגֶד | מַעַלְלֵיכֶם |
|---|---|---|---|---|---|---|
| learn! | (17) | to-do-wrong | stop! | eyes-of-me | from-before | deeds-of-you |

| רִיבוּ | יָתוֹם | שִׁפְטוּ | חָמוֹץ | אַשְּׁרוּ | מִשְׁפָּט | דִּרְשׁוּ | הֵיטֵב |
|---|---|---|---|---|---|---|---|
| plead-case! | fatherless | defend! | oppressed | encourage! | justice | seek! | to-do-right |

| אִם־ | יְהוָה | יֹאמַר | וְנִוָּכְחָה | נָא | לְכוּ־ | | אַלְמָנָה׃ |
|---|---|---|---|---|---|---|---|
| though | Yahweh | he-says | and-let-us-reason-together | now! | come! | (18) | widow |

| אִם־ | יַלְבִּינוּ | כַּשֶּׁלֶג | כַּשָּׁנִים | חֲטָאֵיכֶם | יִהְיוּ |
|---|---|---|---|---|---|
| though | they-shall-be-white | as-the-snow | like-the-scarlets | sins-of-you | they-are |

| תֹּאבוּ | אִם־ | | יִהְיוּ׃ | כַּצֶּמֶר | כַתּוֹלָע | יַאְדִּימוּ |
|---|---|---|---|---|---|---|
| you-are-willing | if | (19) | they-shall-be | like-the-wool | as-the-crimson | they-are-red |

| תְּמָאֲנוּ | וְאִם־ | | תֹּאכֵלוּ׃ | הָאָרֶץ | טוּב | וּשְׁמַעְתֶּם |
|---|---|---|---|---|---|---|
| you-resist | but-if | (20) | you-will-eat | the-land | best-of | and-you-obey |

| דִּבֵּר׃ | יְהוָה | פִּי | כִּי | תְּאֻכְּלוּ | חֶרֶב | וּמְרִיתֶם |
|---|---|---|---|---|---|---|
| he-spoke | Yahweh | mouth-of | for | you-will-be-devoured | sword | and-you-rebel |

| מִשְׁפָּט | מְלֵאֲתִי | נֶאֱמָנָה | קִרְיָה | לְזוֹנָה | הָיְתָה | אֵיכָה | |
|---|---|---|---|---|---|---|---|
| justice | full-of | being-faithful | city | as-one-being-harlot | she-became | how! | (21) |

11 "The multitude of your
sacrifices—
what are they to me?" says
the LORD.
"I have more than enough of
burnt offerings,
of rams and the fat of
fattened animals;
I have no pleasure
in the blood of bulls and
lambs and goats.
12 When you come to appear
before me,
who has asked this of you,
this trampling of my courts?
13 Stop bringing meaningless
offerings!
Your incense is detestable to
me.
New Moons, Sabbaths and
convocations—
I cannot bear your evil
assemblies.
14 Your New Moon festivals and
your appointed feasts
my soul hates.
They have become a burden to
me;
I am weary of bearing them.
15 When you spread out your
hands in prayer,
I will hide my eyes from
you;
even if you offer many
prayers,
I will not listen.
Your hands are full of blood;
16 wash and make yourselves
clean.
Take your evil deeds
out of my sight!
Stop doing wrong,
17 learn to do right!
Seek justice,
encourage the oppressed.[a]
Defend the cause of the
fatherless,
plead the case of the widow.

18 "Come now, let us reason
together,"
says the LORD.
"Though your sins are like
scarlet,
they shall be as white as
snow;
though they are red as
crimson,
they shall be like wool.
19 If you are willing and
obedient,
you will eat the best from
the land;
20 but if you resist and rebel,
you will be devoured by the
sword."
For the mouth of the
LORD has spoken.

21 See how the faithful city
has become a harlot!
She once was full of justice;

[a]17 Or / *rebuke the oppressor*

צֶדֶק יָלִין בָּהּ וְעַתָּה מְרַצְּחִים׃ כַּסְפֵּךְ
silver-of-you (22) ones-murdering but-now in-her he-dwelled righteousness

הָיָה לְסִיגִים סָבְאֵךְ מָהוּל בַּמָּיִם׃
with-the-waters being-diluted choice-wine-of-you to-drosses he-became

שָׂרַיִךְ סוֹרְרִים וְחַבְרֵי גַּנָּבִים כֻּלּוֹ
all-of-him thieves and-companions-of ones-rebelling rulers-of-you (23)

אֹהֵב שֹׁחַד וְרֹדֵף שַׁלְמֹנִים יָתוֹם לֹא יִשְׁפֹּטוּ וְרִיב אַלְמָנָה
widow and-case-of they-defend not fatherless gifts and-chasing bribe loving

לֹא־יָבוֹא אֲלֵיהֶם׃ לָכֵן נְאֻם הָאָדוֹן יְהוָה
Yahweh-of the-Lord declaration-of therefore (24) before-them he-comes not

צְבָאוֹת אֲבִיר יִשְׂרָאֵל הוֹי אֶנָּחֵם מִצָּרַי
from-foes-of-me I-will-get-relief ah! Israel Mighty-One-of Hosts

וְאִנָּקְמָה מֵאוֹיְבָי׃ וְאָשִׁיבָה
and-I-will-turn (25) on-ones-being-enemies-of-me and-I-will-avenge-myself

יָדִי עָלַיִךְ וְאֶצְרֹף כַּבֹּר סִיגָיִךְ
drosses-of-you with-the-lye and-I-will-purge against-you hand-of-me

וְאָסִירָה כָּל־בְּדִילָיִךְ׃ וְאָשִׁיבָה
and-I-will-restore (26) impurities-of-you all-of and-I-will-remove

שֹׁפְטַיִךְ כְּבָרִאשֹׁנָה וְיֹעֲצַיִךְ
and-ones-counseling-you as-in-the-time-of-old ones-judging-you

כְּבַתְּחִלָּה אַחֲרֵי־כֵן יִקָּרֵא לָךְ עִיר
City-of to-you he-will-be-called this after as-at-the-beginning

הַצֶּדֶק קִרְיָה נֶאֱמָנָה׃ צִיּוֹן בְּמִשְׁפָּט
with-justice Zion (27) being-Faithful City the-Righteousness

תִּפָּדֶה וְשָׁבֶיהָ בִּצְדָקָה׃
with-righteousness and-penitent-ones-of-her she-will-be-redeemed

וְשֶׁבֶר פֹּשְׁעִים וְחַטָּאִים יַחְדָּו וְעֹזְבֵי
and-ones-forsaking-of together and-sinners ones-rebelling but-broken (28)

יְהוָה יִכְלוּ׃ כִּי יֵבֹשׁוּ מֵאֵילִים
because-of-sacred-oaks they-will-be-ashamed indeed (29) they-will-perish Yahweh

אֲשֶׁר חֲמַדְתֶּם וְתַחְפְּרוּ מֵהַגַּנּוֹת אֲשֶׁר
that because-of-the-gardens and-you-will-be-disgraced you-delighted-in which

בְּחַרְתֶּם׃ כִּי תִהְיוּ כְּאֵלָה נֹבֶלֶת עָלֶהָ
leaf-of-her being-faded-of like-oak you-will-be indeed (30) you-chose

וּכְגַנָּה אֲשֶׁר־מַיִם אֵין לָהּ׃ וְהָיָה
and-he-will-become (31) to-her there-is-not waters that and-like-garden

הֶחָסֹן לִנְעֹרֶת וּפֹעֲלוֹ לְנִיצוֹץ וּבָעֲרוּ
and-they-will-burn to-spark and-work-of-him to-tinder the-mighty-man

righteousness used to dwell
in her—
but now murderers!
22 Your silver has become dross,
your choice wine is diluted
with water.
23 Your rulers are rebels,
companions of thieves;
they all love bribes
and chase after gifts.
They do not defend the cause
of the fatherless;
the widow's case does not
come before them.
24 Therefore the Lord, the LORD
Almighty,
the Mighty One of Israel,
declares:
"Ah, I will get relief from my
foes
and avenge myself on my
enemies.
25 I will turn my hand against
you;
I will thoroughly purge
away your dross
and remove all your impurities.
26 I will restore your judges as in
days of old,
your counselors as at the
beginning.
Afterward you will be called
the City of Righteousness,
the Faithful City."

27 Zion will be redeemed with
justice,
her penitent ones with
righteousness.
28 But rebels and sinners will
both be broken,
and those who forsake the
LORD will perish.

29 "You will be ashamed because
of the sacred oaks
in which you have
delighted;
you will be disgraced because
of the gardens
that you have chosen.
30 You will be like an oak with
fading leaves,
like a garden without water.
31 The mighty man will become
tinder
and his work a spark;

שְׁנֵיהֶם יַחְדָּו וְאֵין מְכַבֶּה׃ הַדָּבָר אֲשֶׁר חָזָה
he-saw that the-matter (2:1) quenching and-no-one together both-of-them

יְשַׁעְיָהוּ בֶּן־ אָמוֹץ עַל־ יְהוּדָה וִירוּשָׁלִָם׃ וְהָיָה
and-he-will-be (2) and-Jerusalem Judah concerning Amoz son-of Isaiah

בְּאַחֲרִית הַיָּמִים נָכוֹן יִהְיֶה הַר בֵּית־
temple-of mountain-of he-will-be being-established the-days in-last-of

יְהוָה בְּרֹאשׁ הֶהָרִים וְנִשָּׂא מִגְּבָעוֹת
above-hills and-he-will-be-raised the-mountains as-chief-of Yahweh

וְנָהֲרוּ אֵלָיו כָּל־ הַגּוֹיִם׃ וְהָלְכוּ
and-they-will-come (3) the-nations all-of to-him and-they-will-stream

עַמִּים רַבִּים וְאָמְרוּ לְכוּ ׀ וְנַעֲלֶה אֶל־ הַר־ יְהוָה
Yahweh mountain-of to and-let-us-go-up come! and-they-will-say many peoples

אֶל־ בֵּית אֱלֹהֵי יַעֲקֹב וְיֹרֵנוּ מִדְּרָכָיו וְנֵלְכָה
so-we-may-walk of-ways-of-him and-he-will-teach-us Jacob God-of house-of to

בְּאֹרְחֹתָיו כִּי מִצִּיּוֹן תֵּצֵא תוֹרָה וּדְבַר־ יְהוָה
Yahweh and-word-of law she-will-go-out from-Zion indeed in-paths-of-him

מִירוּשָׁלִָם׃ וְשָׁפַט בֵּין הַגּוֹיִם
the-nations between and-he-will-judge (4) from-Jerusalem

וְהוֹכִיחַ לְעַמִּים רַבִּים וְכִתְּתוּ חַרְבוֹתָם
swords-of-them and-they-will-beat many for-peoples and-he-will-settle-disputes

לְאִתִּים וַחֲנִיתוֹתֵיהֶם לְמַזְמֵרוֹת לֹא־ יִשָּׂא
he-will-take-up no: into-pruning-hooks and-spears-of-them into-plowshares

גוֹי אֶל־ גּוֹי חֶרֶב וְלֹא־ יִלְמְדוּ עוֹד מִלְחָמָה׃
war anymore they-will-train-for and-not sword nation against nation

בֵּית יַעֲקֹב לְכוּ וְנֵלְכָה בְּאוֹר יְהוָה׃ כִּי
indeed (6) Yahweh in-light-of and-let-us-walk come! Jacob house-of (5)

נָטַשְׁתָּה עַמְּךָ בֵּית יַעֲקֹב כִּי מָלְאוּ מִקֶּדֶם
from-East they-are-full indeed Jacob house-of people-of-you you-abandoned

וְעֹנְנִים כַּפְּלִשְׁתִּים וּבְיַלְדֵי נָכְרִים
pagans and-with-children-of like-the-Philistines and-ones-practicing-divination

יַשְׂפִּיקוּ׃ וַתִּמָּלֵא אַרְצוֹ כֶּסֶף וְזָהָב וְאֵין
and-no and-gold silver land-of-him and-she-is-full (7) they-clasp-hands

קֵצֶה לְאֹצְרֹתָיו וַתִּמָּלֵא אַרְצוֹ סוּסִים וְאֵין קֵצֶה
end and-no horses land-of-him and-she-is-full to-treasures-of-him end

לְמַרְכְּבֹתָיו׃ וַתִּמָּלֵא אַרְצוֹ אֱלִילִים לְמַעֲשֵׂה
to-work-of idols land-of-him and-she-is-full (8) to-chariots-of-him

יָדָיו יִשְׁתַּחֲווּ לַאֲשֶׁר עָשׂוּ אֶצְבְּעֹתָיו׃
fingers-of-him they-made to-what they-bow-down hands-of-him

---

both will burn together,
with no one to quench the fire."

*The Mountain of the LORD*

2 This is what Isaiah son of Amoz saw concerning Judah and Jerusalem:

2 In the last days
the mountain of the LORD's temple will be established
as chief among the mountains;
it will be raised above the hills,
and all nations will stream to it.

3 Many peoples will come and say,
"Come, let us go up to the mountain of the LORD,
to the house of the God of Jacob.
He will teach us his ways,
so that we may walk in his paths."
The law will go out from Zion,
the word of the LORD from Jerusalem.
4 He will judge between the nations
and will settle disputes for many peoples.
They will beat their swords into plowshares
and their spears into pruning hooks.
Nation will not take up sword against nation,
nor will they train for war anymore.

5 Come, O house of Jacob,
let us walk in the light of the LORD.

*The Day of the LORD*

6 You have abandoned your people,
the house of Jacob.
They are full of superstitions from the East;
they practice divination like the Philistines
and clasp hands with pagans.
7 Their land is full of silver and gold;
there is no end to their treasures.
Their land is full of horses;
there is no end to their chariots.
8 Their land is full of idols;
they bow down to the work of their hands,
to what their fingers have made.

(9) וַיִּשַּׁח אָדָם וַיִּשְׁפַּל־ אִישׁ וְאַל־
so-not mankind and-he-will-be-humbled man so-he-will-be-brought-low (9)

תִּשָּׂא לָהֶם׃ (10) בּוֹא בַצּוּר וְהִטָּמֵן בֶּעָפָר מִפְּנֵי
from-before in-the-ground and-hide! into-the-rock go! (10) to-them you-forgive

פַּחַד יְהוָה וּמֵהֲדַר גְּאֹנוֹ׃ (11) עֵינֵי
eyes-of (11) majesty-of-him and-from-splendor-of Yahweh dread-of

גַּבְהוּת אָדָם שָׁפֵל וְשַׁח רוּם אֲנָשִׁים
men pride-of and-he-will-be-brought-low he-will-be-humbled man arrogance-of

וְנִשְׂגַּב יְהוָה לְבַדּוֹ בַּיּוֹם הַהוּא׃ (12) כִּי
indeed (12) the-that in-the-day by-himself Yahweh and-he-will-be-exalted

יוֹם לַיהוָה צְבָאוֹת עַל כָּל־ גֵּאֶה וָרָם וְעַל כָּל־
all-of and-for and-one-being-lofty proud all-of for Hosts to-Yahweh-of day

נִשָּׂא וְשָׁפֵל׃ (13) וְעַל כָּל־ אַרְזֵי
cedars-of all-of and-for (13) and-he-will-be-humbled one-being-exalted

הַלְּבָנוֹן הָרָמִים וְהַנִּשָּׂאִים וְעַל כָּל־
all-of and-for and-the-ones-being-lofty the-ones-being-tall the-Lebanon

אַלּוֹנֵי הַבָּשָׁן׃ (14) וְעַל כָּל־ הֶהָרִים הָרָמִים
the-ones-towering the-mountains all-of and-for (14) the-Bashan oaks-of

וְעַל כָּל־ הַגְּבָעוֹת הַנִּשָּׂאוֹת׃ (15) וְעַל כָּל־ מִגְדָּל
tower every-of and-for (15) the-ones-being-high the-hills all-of and-for

גָּבֹהַּ* וְעַל כָּל־ חוֹמָה בְצוּרָה׃ (16) וְעַל כָּל־ אֳנִיּוֹת
ships-of all-of and-for (16) being-fortified wall every-of and-for lofty

תַּרְשִׁישׁ וְעַל כָּל־ שְׂכִיּוֹת הַחֶמְדָּה׃ (17) וְשַׁח
and-he-will-be-brought-low (17) the-stateliness vessels-of all-of and-for Tarshish

גַּבְהוּת הָאָדָם וְשָׁפֵל רוּם אֲנָשִׁים
men pride-of and-he-will-be-humbled the-man arrogance-of

וְנִשְׂגַּב יְהוָה לְבַדּוֹ בַּיּוֹם הַהוּא׃
the-that in-the-day by-himself Yahweh and-he-will-be-exalted

(18) וְהָאֱלִילִים כָּלִיל יַחֲלֹף׃ (19) וּבָאוּ
and-they-will-flee (19) he-will-disappear totally and-the-idols (18)

בִּמְעָרוֹת צֻרִים וּבִמְחִלּוֹת עָפָר מִפְּנֵי פַּחַד יְהוָה
Yahweh dread-of from-before ground and-to-holes-of rocks to-caves-of

וּמֵהֲדַר גְּאוֹנוֹ בְּקוּמוֹ לַעֲרֹץ הָאָרֶץ׃
the-earth to-shake when-to-rise-him majesty-of-him and-from-splendor-of

(20) בַּיּוֹם הַהוּא יַשְׁלִיךְ הָאָדָם אֵת אֱלִילֵי כַּסְפּוֹ
silver-of-him idols-of *** the-man he-will-throw-away the-that in-the-day (20)

וְאֵת אֱלִילֵי זְהָבוֹ אֲשֶׁר עָשׂוּ־ לוֹ לְהִשְׁתַּחֲוֹת †לַחְפֹּר פֵּרוֹת†
†holes to-dig† to-worship for-him they-made which gold-of-him idols-of and

9 So man will be brought low
and mankind humbled—
do not forgive them.[b]

10 Go into the rocks,
hide in the ground
from dread of the LORD
and the splendor of his majesty!
11 The eyes of the arrogant man will be humbled
and the pride of men brought low;
the LORD alone will be exalted in that day.

12 The LORD Almighty has a day in store
for all the proud and lofty,
for all that is exalted
(and they will be humbled),
13 for all the cedars of Lebanon,
tall and lofty,
and all the oaks of Bashan,
14 for all the towering mountains
and all the high hills,
15 for every lofty tower
and every fortified wall,
16 for every trading ship[c]
and every stately vessel.
17 The arrogance of man will be brought low
and the pride of men humbled;
the LORD alone will be exalted in that day,
18 and the idols will totally disappear.

19 Men will flee to caves in the rocks
and to holes in the ground
from dread of the LORD
and the splendor of his majesty,
when he rises to shake the earth.
20 In that day men will throw away
to the rodents and bats
their idols of silver and idols of gold,
which they made to worship.

[b] 9 Or *not raise them up*
[c] 16 Hebrew *every ship of Tarshish*

*15 Most mss have *mappiq* in the *he* (הּ—).

†20 The NIV reads these two words as one (לַחֲפַרְפָּרוֹת), *to-the-rodents*, with some mss and versions.

וְלָעֲטַלֵּפִים׃ לָבוֹא בְּנִקְרוֹת הַצֻּרִים וּבִסְעִפֵי
and-to-overhangings-of the-rocks to-caverns-of to-flee (21) and-to-the-bats

הַסְּלָעִים מִפְּנֵי פַּחַד יְהוָה וּמֵהֲדַר גְּאוֹנוֹ
majesty-of-him and-from-splendor-of Yahweh dread-of from-before the-crags

בְּקוּמוֹ לַעֲרֹץ הָאָרֶץ׃ חִדְלוּ לָכֶם מִן־ הָאָדָם אֲשֶׁר
who the-man from to-you stop! (22) the-earth to-shake when-to-rise-him

נְשָׁמָה בְּאַפּוֹ כִּי־ בַמֶּה נֶחְשָׁב הוּא׃ כִּי הִנֵּה
see! now (3:1) he being-accounted of-the-what? for in-nostril-of-him breath

הָאָדוֹן יְהוָה צְבָאוֹת מֵסִיר מִירוּשָׁלַ͏ִם וּמִיהוּדָה מַשְׁעֵן
supply and-from-Judah from-Jerusalem one-taking Hosts Yahweh-of the-Lord

וּמַשְׁעֵנָה כֹּל מִשְׁעַן־ לֶחֶם וְכֹל מִשְׁעַן־ מָיִם׃ גִּבּוֹר
hero (2) waters supply-of and-all-of food supply-of all-of and-support

וְאִישׁ מִלְחָמָה שׁוֹפֵט וְנָבִיא וְקֹסֵם וְזָקֵן׃
and-elder and-one-being-soothsayer and-prophet one-judging war and-man-of

שַׂר־ חֲמִשִּׁים וּנְשׂוּא פָנִים וְיוֹעֵץ
and-one-counseling faces and-man-being-lifted-of fifty captain-of (3)

וַחֲכַם חֲרָשִׁים וּנְבוֹן לָחַשׁ׃ וְנָתַתִּי
and-I-will-make (4) enchanting and-one-being-clever-of crafts and-skilled-of

נְעָרִים שָׂרֵיהֶם וְתַעֲלוּלִים יִמְשְׁלוּ־ בָם׃
over-them they-will-govern and-children officials-of-them boys

וְנִגַּשׂ הָעָם אִישׁ בְּאִישׁ וְאִישׁ
and-man against-man man the-people and-he-will-oppress-himself (5)

בְּרֵעֵהוּ יִרְהֲבוּ הַנַּעַר בַּזָּקֵן
against-the-old the-young and-they-will-rise-up against-neighbor-of-him

וְהַנִּקְלֶה בַּנִּכְבָּד׃ כִּי־ יִתְפֹּשׂ
he-will-seize indeed (6) against-the-one-being-honorable and-the-one-being-base

אִישׁ בְּאָחִיו בֵּית אָבִיו שִׂמְלָה לְכָה קָצִין תִּהְיֶה־
you-be leader to-you cloak father-of-him home-of onto-brother-of-him man

לָּנוּ וְהַמַּכְשֵׁלָה הַזֹּאת תַּחַת יָדֶךָ׃ יִשָּׂא בַיּוֹם
in-the-day he-will-cry-out (7) hand-of-you under the-this and-the-ruin for-us

הַהוּא ׀ לֵאמֹר לֹא־ אֶהְיֶה חֹבֵשׁ וּבְבֵיתִי אֵין
there-is-no and-in-house-of-me one-having-remedy I-am not to-say the-that

לֶחֶם וְאֵין שִׂמְלָה לֹא תְשִׂימֻנִי קְצִין עָם׃ כִּי
indeed (8) people leader-of you-make-me not clothing and-there-is-no food

כָשְׁלָה יְרוּשָׁלַ͏ִם וִיהוּדָה נָפָל כִּי־ לְשׁוֹנָם וּמַעַלְלֵיהֶם
and-deeds-of-them word-of-them for he-falls and-Judah Jerusalem she-staggers

אֶל־ יְהוָה לַמְרוֹת עֵנֵי כְבוֹדוֹ׃ הַכָּרַת פְּנֵיהֶם
faces-of-them look-of (9) glory-of-him presences-of to-defy Yahweh against

21 They will flee to caverns in the rocks
and to the overhanging crags
from dread of the LORD
and the splendor of his majesty,
when he rises to shake the earth.

22 Stop trusting in man,
who has but a breath in his nostrils.
Of what account is he?

*Judgment on Jerusalem and Judah*

3 See now, the Lord,
the LORD Almighty,
is about to take from Jerusalem and Judah
both supply and support:
all supplies of food and all supplies of water,
2 the hero and warrior,
the judge and prophet,
the soothsayer and elder,
3 the captain of fifty and man of rank,
the counselor, skilled craftsman and clever enchanter.

4 I will make boys their officials;
mere children will govern them.
5 People will oppress each other—
man against man, neighbor against neighbor.
The young will rise up against the old,
the base against the honorable.

6 A man will seize one of his brothers
at his father's home, and say,
"You have a cloak, you be our leader;
take charge of this heap of ruins!"
7 But in that day he will cry out,
"I have no remedy.
I have no food or clothing in my house;
do not make me the leader of the people."

8 Jerusalem staggers,
Judah is falling;
their words and deeds are against the LORD,
defying his glorious presence.
9 The look on their faces testifies

עֲנְתָה בָּם וְחַטָּאתָם כִּסְדֹם הִגִּידוּ לֹא
she-testifies against-them and-sin-of-them like-Sodom they-parade not

כִחֵדוּ אוֹי לְנַפְשָׁם כִּי־ גָמְלוּ לָהֶם רָעָה׃
they-hide woe! to-self-of-them for they-brought upon-them disaster

(10) אִמְרוּ צַדִּיק כִּי־ טוֹב כִּי־ פְרִי מַעַלְלֵיהֶם יֹאכֵלוּ׃
(10) tell! righteous that good for fruit-of deeds-of-them they-will-enjoy

(11) אוֹי לְרָשָׁע רָע כִּי־ גְמוּל יָדָיו יֵעָשֶׂה
(11) woe! to-wicked disaster for deed-of hands-of-him he-will-be-paid-back

לוֹ׃ (12) עַמִּי נֹגְשָׂיו מְעוֹלֵל וְנָשִׁים
to-him (12) people-of-me ones-oppressing-him one-being-youth and-women

מָשְׁלוּ בוֹ עַמִּי מְאַשְּׁרֶיךָ מַתְעִים
they-rule over-him people-of-me ones-guiding-you ones-leading-astray

וְדֶרֶךְ אֹרְחֹתֶיךָ בִּלֵּעוּ׃ (13) נִצָּב לָרִיב יְהוָה
and-path-of ways-of-you they-turn (13) taking-place to-be-in-court Yahweh

וְעֹמֵד לָדִין עַמִּים׃ (14) יְהוָה בְּמִשְׁפָּט יָבוֹא עִם־
and-rising to-judge peoples (14) Yahweh into-judgment he-enters against

זִקְנֵי עַמּוֹ וְשָׂרָיו וְאַתֶּם בִּעַרְתֶּם הַכֶּרֶם
elders-of people-of-him and-leaders-of-him now-you you-ruined the-vineyard

גְּזֵלַת הֶעָנִי בְּבָתֵּיכֶם׃ (15) מַלָּכֶם תְּדַכְּאוּ
plunder-of the-poor in-houses-of-you (15) what-to-you? you-crush

עַמִּי וּפְנֵי עֲנִיִּים תִּטְחָנוּ נְאֻם־ אֲדֹנָי יְהוִה
people-of-me and-faces-of poor-ones you-grind declaration-of Lord Yahweh-of

צְבָאוֹת׃ (16) וַיֹּאמֶר יְהוָה יַעַן כִּי גָבְהוּ בְּנוֹת צִיּוֹן
Hosts (16) and-he-says Yahweh because that they-are-haughty women-of Zion

וַתֵּלַכְנָה נְטוּוֹת גָּרוֹן וּמְשַׂקְּרוֹת עֵינָיִם
and-they-walk ones-being-outstretched-of neck and-ones-flirting-of eyes

הָלוֹךְ וְטָפֹף תֵּלַכְנָה וּבְרַגְלֵיהֶם תְּעַכַּסְנָה׃
to-walk and-to-trip they-walk and-on-ankles-of-them they-jingle-ornaments

(17) וְשִׂפַּח אֲדֹנָי קָדְקֹד בְּנוֹת צִיּוֹן וַיהוָה
(17) so-he-will-bring-sores Lord head-of women-of Zion and-Yahweh

פָּתְהֵן יְעָרֶה׃ (18) בַּיּוֹם הַהוּא יָסִיר
scalp-of-them he-will-make-bald (18) in-the-day the-that he-will-snatch-away

אֲדֹנָי אֵת תִּפְאֶרֶת הָעֲכָסִים וְהַשְּׁבִיסִים וְהַשַּׂהֲרֹנִים׃
Lord *** finery the-bangles and-the-headbands and-the-crescent-necklaces

(19) הַנְּטִיפוֹת וְהַשֵּׁרוֹת וְהָרְעָלוֹת׃ (20) הַפְּאֵרִים
(19) the-earrings and-the-bracelets and-the-veils (20) the-headdresses

וְהַצְּעָדוֹת וְהַקִּשֻּׁרִים וּבָתֵּי הַנֶּפֶשׁ וְהַלְּחָשִׁים׃
and-the-ankle-chains and-the-sashes and-bottles-of the-perfume and-the-charms

against them;
they parade their sin like
Sodom;
they do not hide it.
Woe to them!
They have brought disaster
upon themselves.
10Tell the righteous it will be
well with them,
for they will enjoy the fruit
of their deeds.
11Woe to the wicked! Disaster
is upon them!
They will be paid back for
what their hands have
done.
12Youths oppress my people,
women rule over them.
O my people, your guides lead
you astray;
they turn you from the path.
13The LORD takes his place in
court;
he rises to judge the people.
14The LORD enters into judgment
against the elders and
leaders of his people:
"It is you who have ruined my
vineyard;
the plunder from the poor is
in your houses.
15What do you mean by
crushing my people
and grinding the faces of
the poor?"
declares the Lord, the
LORD Almighty.
16The LORD says,
"The women of Zion are
haughty,
walking along with
outstretched necks,
flirting with their eyes,
tripping along with mincing
steps,
with ornaments jingling on
their ankles.
17Therefore the Lord will bring
sores on the heads of the
women of Zion;
the LORD will make their
scalps bald."
18In that day the Lord will
snatch away their finery: the ban-
gles and headbands and crescent
necklaces, 19the earrings and
bracelets and veils, 20the head-
dresses and ankle chains and
sashes, the perfume bottles and

°15 ק מה לכם
°16 ק נטויות

הַטַּבָּעוֹת וְנִזְמֵי הָאָף׃ הַמַּחֲלָצוֹת וְהַמַּעֲטָפוֹת
and-the-capes the-fine-robes (22) the-nose and-rings-of the-signet-rings (21)

וְהַמִּטְפָּחוֹת וְהָחֲרִיטִים׃ וְהַגִּלְיֹנִים וְהַסְּדִינִים
and-the-linen-garments and-the-mirrors (23) and-the-purses and-the-cloaks

וְהַצְּנִיפוֹת וְהָרְדִידִים׃ וְהָיָה תַחַת בֹּשֶׂם
fragrance instead-of and-he-will-be (24) and-the-shawls and-the-tiaras

מַק יִהְיֶה וְתַחַת חֲגוֹרָה נִקְפָּה וְתַחַת מַעֲשֶׂה מִקְשֶׁה
well-dressed work and-instead-of rope sash and-instead-of he-will-be stench

קָרְחָה וְתַחַת פְּתִיגִיל מַחֲגֹרֶת שָׂק כִּי־ תַחַת
instead-of branding sackcloth wrapping-of fine-clothing and-instead-of baldness

יֹפִי׃ מְתַיִךְ בַּחֶרֶב יִפֹּלוּ וּגְבוּרָתֵךְ
and-warrior-of-you they-will-fall by-the-sword men-of-you (25) beauty

בַּמִּלְחָמָה׃ וְאָנוּ וְאָבְלוּ פְּתָחֶיהָ
gates-of-her and-they-will-mourn and-they-will-lament (26) in-the-battle

וְנִקָּתָה לָאָרֶץ תֵּשֵׁב׃ וְהֶחֱזִיקוּ
and-they-will-hold (4:1) she-will-sit on-the-ground and-she-will-be-destitute

שֶׁבַע נָשִׁים בְּאִישׁ אֶחָד בַּיּוֹם הַהוּא לֵאמֹר לַחְמֵנוּ נֹאכֵל
we-will-eat food-of-us to-say the-that in-the-day one onto-man women seven

וְשִׂמְלָתֵנוּ נִלְבָּשׁ רַק יִקָּרֵא שִׁמְךָ עָלֵינוּ
to-us name-of-you let-him-be-called only we-will-provide and-clothing-of-us

אֱסֹף חֶרְפָּתֵנוּ׃ בַּיּוֹם הַהוּא יִהְיֶה צֶמַח
Branch-of he-will-be the-that in-the-day (2) disgrace-of-us take-away!

יְהוָה לִצְבִי וּלְכָבוֹד וּפְרִי הָאָרֶץ לְגָאוֹן
as-pride the-land and-fruit-of and-as-glorious as-beautiful Yahweh

וּלְתִפְאֶרֶת לִפְלֵיטַת יִשְׂרָאֵל׃ וְהָיָה הַנִּשְׁאָר
the-one-being-left and-he-will-be (3) Israel of-survivor-of and-as-glory

בְּצִיּוֹן וְהַנּוֹתָר בִּירוּשָׁלִַם קָדוֹשׁ יֵאָמֶר לוֹ
to-him he-will-be-called holy in-Jerusalem and-the-one-remaining in-Zion

כָּל־ הַכָּתוּב לַחַיִּים בִּירוּשָׁלִָם׃ אִם
when (4) in-Jerusalem among-the-living-ones the-one-being-recorded all-of

רָחַץ אֲדֹנָי אֵת צֹאַת בְּנוֹת־ צִיּוֹן וְאֶת־ דְּמֵי יְרוּשָׁלִַם
Jerusalem bloods-of and Zion women-of filth-of *** Lord he-will-wash-away

יָדִיחַ מִקִּרְבָּהּ בְּרוּחַ מִשְׁפָּט וּבְרוּחַ
and-by-spirit-of judgment by-spirit-of from-midst-of-her he-will-cleanse

בָּעֵר׃ וּבָרָא יְהוָה עַל כָּל־ מְכוֹן הַר־ צִיּוֹן
Zion Mount-of place-of all-of over Yahweh then-he-will-create (5) to-burn

וְעַל־ מִקְרָאֶהָ עָנָן יוֹמָם וְעָשָׁן וְנֹגַהּ אֵשׁ לֶהָבָה
flame fire-of and-glow-of and-smoke by-day cloud assembly-of-her and-over

charms, [21]the signet rings and
nose rings, [22]the fine robes and the
capes and cloaks, the purses [23]and
mirrors, and the linen garments
and tiaras and shawls.

[24]Instead of fragrance there will
be a stench;
instead of a sash, a rope;
instead of well-dressed hair,
baldness;
instead of fine clothing,
sackcloth;
instead of beauty, branding.
[25]Your men will fall by the
sword,
your warriors in battle.
[26]The gates of Zion will lament
and mourn;
destitute, she will sit on the
ground.

4 In that day seven women
will take hold of one man
and say, "We will eat our own
food
and provide our own
clothes;
only let us be called by your
name.
Take away our disgrace!"

*The Branch of the* LORD

[2]In that day the Branch of the
LORD will be beautiful and glorious, and the fruit of the land will
be the pride and glory of the survivors in Israel. [3]Those who are left
in Zion, who remain in Jerusalem,
will be called holy, all who are
recorded among the living in
Jerusalem. [4]The Lord will wash
away the filth of the women of
Zion; he will cleanse the blood-
stains from Jerusalem by a spirit[d]
of judgment and a spirit[d] of fire.
[5]Then the LORD will create over all
of Mount Zion and over those
who assemble there a cloud of
smoke by day and a glow of flaming fire by night; over all the glory

[d]4 *Or the Spirit*

לַיְלָה כִּי עַל־ כָּל־ כָּבוֹד חֻפָּה׃ וְסֻכָּה תִּהְיֶה לְצֵל־
as-shade she-will-be and-shelter (6) canopy glory all-of over for night

יוֹמָם מֵחֹרֶב וּלְמַחְסֶה וּלְמִסְתּוֹר מִזֶּרֶם וּמִמָּטָר׃
and-from-rain from-storm and-as-hiding-place and-as-refuge from-heat by-day

אָשִׁירָה נָּא לִידִידִי שִׁירַת דּוֹדִי
beloved-of-me song-of for-loved-one-of-me now! I-will-sing (5:1)

לְכַרְמוֹ כֶּרֶם הָיָה לִידִידִי בְּקֶרֶן בֶּן־
son-of on-hillside to-loved-one-of-me he-was vineyard about-vineyard-of-him

שָׁמֶן׃ וַיְעַזְּקֵהוּ וַיְסַקְּלֵהוּ וַיִּטָּעֵהוּ
and-he-planted-him and-he-cleared-of-stones-him and-he-dug-up-him (2) fertility

שֹׂרֵק וַיִּבֶן מִגְדָּל בְּתוֹכוֹ וְגַם־ יֶקֶב
winepress and-also in-midst-of-him watchtower and-he-built choicest-vine

חָצֵב בּוֹ וַיְקַו לַעֲשׂוֹת עֲנָבִים וַיַּעַשׂ בְּאֻשִׁים׃
bad-fruits but-he-yielded grapes to-yield then-he-looked in-him he-cut-out

וְעַתָּה יוֹשֵׁב יְרוּשָׁלִַם וְאִישׁ יְהוּדָה שִׁפְטוּ־ נָא בֵּינִי
between-me now! judge! Judah and-man-of Jerusalem one-dwelling-of and-now (3)

וּבֵין כַּרְמִי׃ מַה־ לַּעֲשׂוֹת עוֹד לְכַרְמִי וְלֹא
that-not for-vineyard-of-me more to-do what? (4) vineyard-of-me and-between

עָשִׂיתִי בּוֹ מַדּוּעַ קִוֵּיתִי לַעֲשׂוֹת עֲנָבִים וַיַּעַשׂ בְּאֻשִׁים׃
bad-fruits but-he-yielded grapes to-yield I-looked why? for-him I-did

וְעַתָּה אוֹדִיעָה־ נָּא אֶתְכֶם אֵת אֲשֶׁר־ אֲנִי עֹשֶׂה לְכַרְמִי
to-vineyard-of-me doing I what *** you now! I-will-tell and-now (5)

הָסֵר מְשׂוּכָּתוֹ וְהָיָה לְבָעֵר פָּרֹץ
to-break-down to-destroy and-he-will-be hedge-of-him to-take-away

גְּדֵרוֹ וְהָיָה לְמִרְמָס׃ וַאֲשִׁיתֵהוּ בָתָה
wasteland and-I-will-make-him (6) for-trampling and-he-will-be wall-of-him

לֹא יִזָּמֵר וְלֹא יֵעָדֵר וְעָלָה שָׁמִיר
brier and-he-will-grow he-will-be-cultivated and-not he-will-be-pruned not

וָשָׁיִת וְעַל הֶעָבִים אֲצַוֶּה מֵהַמְטִיר עָלָיו מָטָר׃
rain on-him from-to-rain I-will-command the-clouds and-to and-thorn

כִּי כֶרֶם יְהוָה צְבָאוֹת בֵּית יִשְׂרָאֵל וְאִישׁ יְהוּדָה
Judah and-man-of Israel house-of Hosts Yahweh-of vineyard-of now (7)

נְטַע שַׁעֲשׁוּעָיו וַיְקַו לְמִשְׁפָּט וְהִנֵּה מִשְׂפָּח
bloodshed but-see! for-justice and-he-looked delights-of-him garden-of

לִצְדָקָה וְהִנֵּה צְעָקָה׃ הוֹי מַגִּיעֵי בַיִת
house ones-adding-of woe! (8) cry-of-distress but-see! for-righteousness

בְּבַיִת שָׂדֶה בְשָׂדֶה יַקְרִיבוּ עַד אֶפֶס מָקוֹם וְהוּשַׁבְתֶּם לְבַדְּכֶם
by-yourselves and-you-live space no till they-join to-field field to-house

will be a canopy. [6]It will be a shelter and shade from the heat of the day, and a refuge and hiding place from the storm and rain.

*The Song of the Vineyard*

5 I will sing for the one I love
a song about his vineyard:
My loved one had a vineyard
on a fertile hillside.
[2]He dug it up and cleared it of stones
and planted it with the choicest vines.
He built a watchtower in it
and cut out a winepress as well.
Then he looked for a crop of good grapes,
but it yielded only bad fruit.

[3]"Now you dwellers in Jerusalem and men of Judah,
judge between me and my vineyard.
[4]What more could have been done for my vineyard
than I have done for it?
When I looked for good grapes,
why did it yield only bad?
[5]Now I will tell you
what I am going to do to my vineyard:
I will take away its hedge,
and it will be destroyed;
I will break down its wall,
and it will be trampled.
[6]I will make it a wasteland,
neither pruned nor cultivated,
and briers and thorns will grow there.
I will command the clouds
not to rain on it."

[7]The vineyard of the LORD Almighty
is the house of Israel,
and the men of Judah
are the garden of his delight.
And he looked for justice, but saw bloodshed;
for righteousness, but heard cries of distress.

*Woes and Judgments*

[8]Woe to you who add house to house
and join field to field
till no space is left
and you live alone in the

בְּקֶרֶב הָאָרֶץ׃ (9) בְּאָזְנָי יְהוָה צְבָאוֹת אִם־לֹא בָּתִּים
in-midst-of the-land (9) in-ears-of-me Yahweh-of Hosts if not houses

רַבִּים לְשַׁמָּה יִהְיוּ גְּדֹלִים וְטוֹבִים מֵאֵין
great-ones as-desolation they-become fine-ones and-good-ones from-no

יוֹשֵׁב׃ (10) כִּי עֲשֶׂרֶת צִמְדֵּי־כֶרֶם יַעֲשׂוּ בַּת
one-occupying (10) indeed ten-of yokes-of vineyard they-will-produce bath

אֶחָת וְזֶרַע חֹמֶר יַעֲשֶׂה אֵיפָה׃ (11) הוֹי מַשְׁכִּימֵי
one and-seed-of homer he-will-produce ephah (11) woe! ones-rising-early-of

בַבֹּקֶר שֵׁכָר יִרְדֹּפוּ מְאַחֲרֵי בַנֶּשֶׁף יַיִן
in-the-morning drink they-run-after ones-staying-up-late-of at-the-night wine

יַדְלִיקֵם׃ (12) וְהָיָה כִנּוֹר וָנֶבֶל תֹּף וְחָלִיל וָיַיִן
he-inflames-them (12) and-he-is harp and-lyre tambourine and-flute and-wine

מִשְׁתֵּיהֶם וְאֵת פֹּעַל יְהוָה לֹא יַבִּיטוּ וּמַעֲשֵׂה יָדָיו
banquet-of-them but deed-of Yahweh not they-regard and-work-of hands-of-him

לֹא רָאוּ׃ (13) לָכֵן גָּלָה עַמִּי מִבְּלִי־
not they-respect (13) therefore he-will-be-exiled people-of-me for-lack-of

דָעַת וּכְבוֹדוֹ מְתֵי* רָעָב וַהֲמוֹנוֹ צִחֵה
understanding and-rank-of-him *men-of hunger and-mass-of-him parched-of

צָמָא׃ (14) לָכֵן הִרְחִיבָה שְּׁאוֹל נַפְשָׁהּ וּפָעֲרָה
thirst (14) therefore she-enlarges Sheol appetite-of-her and-she-opens

פִיהָ לִבְלִי־חֹק וְיָרַד הֲדָרָהּ וַהֲמוֹנָהּ
mouth-of-her without limit and-he-will-descend nobility-of-her and-mass-of-her

וּשְׁאוֹנָהּ וְעָלֵז בָּהּ׃ (15) וַיִּשַּׁח אָדָם
with-brawling-of-her and-reveler into-her (15) so-he-will-be-brought-low man

וַיִּשְׁפַּל־אִישׁ וְעֵינֵי גְבֹהִים תִּשְׁפַּלְנָה׃
and-he-will-be-humbled mankind and-eyes-of arrogant-ones they-will-be-humbled

(16) וַיִּגְבַּהּ יְהוָה צְבָאוֹת בַּמִּשְׁפָּט וְהָאֵל
(16) but-he-will-be-exalted Yahweh-of Hosts by-the-justice and-the-God

הַקָּדוֹשׁ נִקְדָּשׁ בִּצְדָקָה׃ (17) וְרָעוּ
the-holy-one he-will-show-himself-holy by-righteousness (17) then-they-will-graze

כְבָשִׂים כְּדָבְרָם וְחָרְבוֹת מֵחִים גָּרִים†
sheeps as-pasture-of-them and-ruins-of rich-ones †ones-being-strangers

יֹאכֵלוּ׃ (18) הוֹי מֹשְׁכֵי הֶעָוֹן בְּחַבְלֵי
they-will-eat (18) woe! ones-drawing-along-of the-sin with-cords-of

הַשָּׁוְא וְכַעֲבוֹת הָעֲגָלָה חַטָּאָה׃ (19) הָאֹמְרִים
the-deceit and-as-ropes-of the-cart wickedness (19) the-ones-saying

יְמַהֵר׀ יָחִישָׁה מַעֲשֵׂהוּ לְמַעַן נִרְאֶה
let-him-hurry let-him-hasten work-of-him so-that we-may-see

land.

9 The LORD Almighty has declared in my hearing:

"Surely the great houses will
become desolate,
the fine mansions left
without occupants.
10 A ten-acre[e] vineyard will
produce only a bath[f] of
wine,
a homer[g] of seed only an
ephah[h] of grain."

11 Woe to those who rise early in
the morning
to run after their drinks,
who stay up late at night
till they are inflamed with
wine.
12 They have harps and lyres at
their banquets,
tambourines and flutes and
wine,
but they have no regard for
the deeds of the LORD,
no respect for the work of
his hands.
13 Therefore my people will go
into exile
for lack of understanding;
their men of rank will die of
hunger
and their masses will be
parched with thirst.
14 Therefore the grave[i] enlarges
its appetite
and opens its mouth
without limit;
into it will descend their
nobles and masses
with all their brawlers and
revelers.
15 So man will be brought low
and mankind humbled,
the eyes of the arrogant
humbled.
16 But the LORD Almighty will be
exalted by his justice,
and the holy God will show
himself holy by his
righteousness.
17 Then sheep will graze as in
their own pasture;
lambs will feed[j] among the
ruins of the rich.

18 Woe to those who draw sin
along with cords of
deceit,
and wickedness as with cart
ropes,
19 to those who say, "Let God
hurry,
let him hasten his work
so we may see it.

[e]10 Hebrew *ten-yoke*, that is, the land plowed by 10 yoke of oxen in one day
[f]10 That is, probably about 6 gallons (about 22 liters)
[g]10 That is, probably about 6 bushels (about 220 liters)
[h]10 That is, probably about 3/5 bushel (about 22 liters)
[i]14 Hebrew *Sheol*
[j]17 Septuagint; Hebrew / *strangers will eat*

*13 The NIV reads *tsere* for *sheva* (מְתִי), *ones-dying-of*, with some mss and versions.

†17 The NIV reads *daleth* for *resh* (גְּדָיִם), *lambs*, with the LXX.

וְתִקְרַב וְתָבוֹאָה עֲצַת קְדוֹשׁ יִשְׂרָאֵל
Israel Holy-One-of plan-of and-let-her-come and-let-her-approach

וְנֵדָעָה׃ (20) הוֹי הָאֹמְרִים לָרַע טוֹב וְלַטּוֹב
and-to-the-good good to-the-evil the-ones-calling woe! (20) so-we-may-know

רָע שָׂמִים חֹשֶׁךְ לְאוֹר וְאוֹר לְחֹשֶׁךְ שָׂמִים
ones-putting for-darkness and-light for-light darkness ones-putting evil

מַר לְמָתוֹק וּמָתוֹק לְמָר׃ (21) הוֹי חֲכָמִים בְּעֵינֵיהֶם
in-eyes-of-them ones-wise woe! (21) for-bitter and-sweet for-sweet bitter

וְנֶגֶד פְּנֵיהֶם נְבֹנִים׃ (22) הוֹי גִּבּוֹרִים לִשְׁתּוֹת יָיִן
wine to-drink heroes woe! (22) ones-being-clever faces-of-them and-before

וְאַנְשֵׁי־ חַיִל לִמְסֹךְ שֵׁכָר׃ (23) מַצְדִּיקֵי רָשָׁע עֵקֶב שֹׁחַד
bribe for guilty ones-acquitting (23) drink to-mix champion and-men-of

וְצִדְקַת צַדִּיקִים יָסִירוּ מִמֶּנּוּ׃ (24) לָכֵן כֶּאֱכֹל
as-to-lick-up therefore (24) from-him they-deny innocent-ones but-justice-of

קַשׁ לְשׁוֹן אֵשׁ וַחֲשַׁשׁ לֶהָבָה יִרְפֶּה שָׁרְשָׁם
root-of-them he-sinks-down flame and-dry-grass fire tongue-of straw

כַּמָּק יִהְיֶה וּפִרְחָם כָּאָבָק יַעֲלֶה
he-will-go-away like-the-dust and-flower-of-them he-will-be like-the-decay

כִּי מָאֲסוּ אֵת תּוֹרַת יְהוָה צְבָאוֹת וְאֵת אִמְרַת קְדוֹשׁ־ יִשְׂרָאֵל
Israel Holy-One-of word-of and Hosts Yahweh-of law-of *** they-rejected for

נִאֵצוּ׃ (25) עַל־ כֵּן חָרָה אַף־ יְהוָה בְּעַמּוֹ
against-people-of-him Yahweh anger-of he-burns this for (25) they-spurned

וַיֵּט יָדוֹ עָלָיו וַיַּכֵּהוּ וַיִּרְגְּזוּ
and-they-shake and-he-strikes-down-him against-him hand-of-him and-he-raised

הֶהָרִים וַתְּהִי נִבְלָתָם כַּסּוּחָה בְּקֶרֶב
in-middle-of like-the-refuse dead-body-of-them and-she-is the-mountains

חוּצוֹת בְּכָל־ זֹאת לֹא־ שָׁב אַפּוֹ וְעוֹד יָדוֹ
hand-of-him and-still anger-of-him turning-away not this for-all-of streets

נְטוּיָה׃ (26) וְנָשָׂא־ נֵס לַגּוֹיִם מֵרָחוֹק
at-distance for-the-nations banner and-he-lifts-up (26) being-upraised

וְשָׁרַק לוֹ מִקְצֵה הָאָרֶץ וְהִנֵּה מְהֵרָה קַל יָבוֹא׃
he-comes speedy swift and-see! the-earth at-end-of for-him and-he-whistles

(27) אֵין־ עָיֵף וְאֵין־ כּוֹשֵׁל בּוֹ לֹא יָנוּם
he-slumbers not of-him one-stumbling and-there-is-not tired there-is-not (27)

וְלֹא יִישָׁן וְלֹא נִפְתַּח אֵזוֹר חֲלָצָיו וְלֹא
and-not waists-of-him belt-of he-is-loosened and-not he-sleeps and-not

נִתַּק שְׂרוֹךְ נְעָלָיו׃ (28) אֲשֶׁר חִצָּיו שְׁנוּנִים
ones-being-sharp arrows-of-him that (28) sandals-of-him thong-of he-is-broken

---

Let it approach,
let the plan of the Holy One of Israel come,
so we may know it."

[20]Woe to those who call evil good
and good evil,
who put darkness for light
and light for darkness,
who put bitter for sweet
and sweet for bitter.

[21]Woe to those who are wise in their own eyes
and clever in their own sight.

[22]Woe to those who are heroes at drinking wine
and champions at mixing drinks,
[23]who acquit the guilty for a bribe,
but deny justice to the innocent.
[24]Therefore, as tongues of fire lick up straw
and as dry grass sinks down in the flames,
so their roots will decay
and their flowers blow away like dust;
for they have rejected the law of the LORD Almighty
and spurned the word of the Holy One of Israel.
[25]Therefore the LORD's anger burns against his people;
his hand is raised and he strikes them down.
The mountains shake,
and the dead bodies are like refuse in the streets.

Yet for all this, his anger is not turned away,
his hand is still upraised.

[26]He lifts up a banner for the distant nations,
he whistles for those at the ends of the earth.
Here they come,
swiftly and speedily!
[27]Not one of them grows tired or stumbles,
not one slumbers or sleeps;
not a belt is loosened at the waist,
not a sandal thong is broken.
[28]Their arrows are sharp,

וְכָל־ קַשְּׁתֹתָיו דְּרֻכוֹת פַּרְסוֹת סוּסָיו כַּצַּר
like-the-flint horses-of-him hoofs-of ones-being-strung bows-of-him and-all-of

נֶחְשָׁבוּ וְגַלְגִּלָּיו כַּסּוּפָה׃ שְׁאָגָה לוֹ כַּלָּבִיא
like-the-lion of-him roar (29) like-the-whirlwind and-wheels-of-him they-seem

וְשָׁאַג כַּכְּפִירִים וְיִנְהֹם וְיֹאחֵז טֶרֶף
prey and-he-seizes and-he-growls like-the-young-lions he-roars

וְיַפְלִיט וְאֵין מַצִּיל׃ וְיִנְהֹם
and-he-will-roar (30) one-rescuing and-there-is-no and-he-carries-off

עָלָיו בַּיּוֹם הַהוּא כְּנַהֲמַת־ יָם וְנִבַּט לָאָרֶץ
at-the-land if-he-looks sea like-roar-of the-that in-the-day over-him

וְהִנֵּה־ חֹשֶׁךְ צַר וָאוֹר חָשַׁךְ
he-will-be-darkened even-light distress darkness then-see!

בַּעֲרִיפֶיהָ׃ בִּשְׁנַת־ מוֹת הַמֶּלֶךְ עֻזִּיָּהוּ וָאֶרְאֶה אֶת־
*** then-I-saw Uzziah the-king death-of in-year-of (6:1) by-clouds-of-him

אֲדֹנָי יֹשֵׁב עַל־ כִּסֵּא רָם וְנִשָּׂא וְשׁוּלָיו
and-robes-of-him and-being-exalted being-high throne on sitting Lord

מְלֵאִים אֶת־ הַהֵיכָל׃ שְׂרָפִים עֹמְדִים מִמַּעַל לוֹ שֵׁשׁ
six to-him at-above ones-attending seraphs (2) the-temple *** ones-filling

כְּנָפַיִם שֵׁשׁ כְּנָפַיִם לְאֶחָד בִּשְׁתַּיִם ׀ יְכַסֶּה פָנָיו וּבִשְׁתַּיִם
and-with-two faces-of-him he-covered with-two to-each wings six wings

יְכַסֶּה רַגְלָיו וּבִשְׁתַּיִם יְעוֹפֵף׃ וְקָרָא זֶה אֶל־ זֶה
that to this and-he-called (3) he-flew and-with-two feet-of-him he-covered

וְאָמַר קָדוֹשׁ ׀ קָדוֹשׁ קָדוֹשׁ יְהוָה צְבָאוֹת מְלֹא כָל־ הָאָרֶץ
the-earth whole-of fullness-of Hosts Yahweh-of holy holy holy and-he-said

כְּבוֹדוֹ׃ וַיָּנֻעוּ אַמּוֹת הַסִּפִּים מִקּוֹל
at-sound-of the-thresholds doorposts-of and-they-shook (4) glory-of-him

הַקּוֹרֵא וְהַבַּיִת יִמָּלֵא עָשָׁן׃ וָאֹמַר אוֹי־
woe! and-I-cried (5) smoke he-was-filled and-the-temple the-one-calling

לִי כִי־ נִדְמֵיתִי כִּי אִישׁ טְמֵא־ שְׂפָתַיִם אָנֹכִי וּבְתוֹךְ עַם־
people and-in-among I lips unclean-of man for I-am-ruined for to-me

טְמֵא שְׂפָתַיִם אָנֹכִי יוֹשֵׁב כִּי אֶת־ הַמֶּלֶךְ יְהוָה צְבָאוֹת רָאוּ
they-saw Hosts Yahweh-of the-King *** and living I lips unclean-of

עֵינָי׃ וַיָּעָף אֵלַי אֶחָד מִן־ הַשְּׂרָפִים וּבְיָדוֹ
and-in-hand-of-him the-seraphs from one to-me then-he-flew (6) eyes-of-me

רִצְפָּה בְּמֶלְקַחַיִם לָקַח מֵעַל הַמִּזְבֵּחַ׃ וַיַּגַּע עַל־
to and-he-touched (7) the-altar from-upon he-took with-tongs live-coal

פִּי וַיֹּאמֶר הִנֵּה נָגַע זֶה עַל־ שְׂפָתֶיךָ וְסָר
and-he-is-taken lips-of-you to this he-touched see! and-he-said mouth-of-me

all their bows are strung;
their horses' hoofs seem like flint,
their chariot wheels like a whirlwind.
29 Their roar is like that of the lion,
they roar like young lions;
they growl as they seize their prey
and carry it off with no one to rescue.
30 In that day they will roar over it
like the roaring of the sea.
And if one looks at the land,
he will see darkness and distress;
even the light will be darkened by the clouds.

*Isaiah's Commission*

6 In the year that King Uzziah
died, I saw the Lord seated on
a throne, high and exalted, and
the train of his robe filled the temple. 2 Above him were seraphs,
each with six wings: With two
wings they covered their faces,
with two they covered their feet,
and with two they were flying.
3 And they were calling to one another:

"Holy, holy, holy is the LORD Almighty;
the whole earth is full of his glory."

4 At the sound of their voices the
doorposts and thresholds shook
and the temple was filled with
smoke.
5 "Woe to me!" I cried. "I am
ruined! For I am a man of unclean
lips, and I live among a people of
unclean lips, and my eyes have
seen the King, the LORD Almighty."
6 Then one of the seraphs flew to
me with a live coal in his hand,
which he had taken with tongs
from the altar. 7 With it he touched
my mouth and said, "See, this has
touched your lips; your guilt is

°29 ק ישאג

עֲוֹנֶךָ וְחַטָּאתְךָ תְּכֻפָּר׃ (8) וָאֶשְׁמַע אֶת־ קוֹל
guilt-of-you and-sin-of-you she-is-atoned-for (8) then-I-heard *** voice-of

אֲדֹנָי אֹמֵר אֶת־ מִי אֶשְׁלַח וּמִי יֵלֶךְ־ לָנוּ וָאֹמַר
Lord saying *** whom? shall-I-send and-who? he-will-go for-us and-I-said

הִנְנִי שְׁלָחֵנִי׃ (9) וַיֹּאמֶר לֵךְ וְאָמַרְתָּ לָעָם הַזֶּה
here-I! send-me! (9) and-he-said go! and-you-tell to-the-people the-this

שִׁמְעוּ שָׁמוֹעַ וְאַל־ תָּבִינוּ וּרְאוּ רָאוֹ וְאַל־
hear! to-hear but-never you-understand and-see! to-see but-never

תֵּדָעוּ׃ (10) הַשְׁמֵן לֵב־ הָעָם הַזֶּה וְאָזְנָיו
you-perceive (10) make-calloused! heart-of the-people the-this and-ears-of-him

הַכְבֵּד וְעֵינָיו הָשַׁע פֶּן־ יִרְאֶה בְעֵינָיו
make-dull! and-eyes-of-him close! otherwise he-might-see with-eyes-of-him

וּבְאָזְנָיו יִשְׁמָע וּלְבָבוֹ יָבִין
and-with-ears-of-him he-might-hear and-heart-of-him he-might-understand

וָשָׁב וְרָפָא לוֹ׃ (11) וָאֹמַר עַד־ מָתָי
and-he-might-turn and-he-might-heal to-him (11) then-I-said until when?

אֲדֹנָי וַיֹּאמֶר עַד אֲשֶׁר אִם־ שָׁאוּ עָרִים מֵאֵין
Lord and-he-answered until that when they-lie-ruined cities from-no

יוֹשֵׁב וּבָתִּים מֵאֵין אָדָם וְהָאֲדָמָה תִּשָּׁאֶה
one-inhabiting and-houses from-no person and-the-field she-lies-ruined

שְׁמָמָה׃ (12) וְרִחַק יְהוָה אֶת־ הָאָדָם וְרַבָּה
ravaged (12) and-he-sent-away Yahweh *** the-person and-she-is-great

הָעֲזוּבָה בְּקֶרֶב הָאָרֶץ׃ (13) וְעוֹד בָּהּ עֲשִׂרִיָּה
the-forsakenness in-midst-of the-land (13) though-yet in-her tenth

וְשָׁבָה וְהָיְתָה לְבָעֵר כָּאֵלָה
then-she-will-do-again and-she-will-be to-be-laid-waste as-the-terebinth

וְכָאַלּוֹן אֲשֶׁר בְּשַׁלֶּכֶת מַצֶּבֶת בָּם זֶרַע קֹדֶשׁ
and-as-the-oak that in-cutting-down stump to-them seed-of holiness

מַצַּבְתָּהּ׃ (7:1) וַיְהִי בִּימֵי אָחָז בֶּן־ יוֹתָם בֶּן־ עֻזִּיָּהוּ
stump-of-her (7:1) and-he-was in-days-of Ahaz son-of Jotham son-of Uzziah

מֶלֶךְ יְהוּדָה עָלָה רְצִין מֶלֶךְ־ אֲרָם וּפֶקַח בֶּן־ רְמַלְיָהוּ
king-of Judah he-marched-up Rezin king-of Aram and-Pekah son-of Remaliah

מֶלֶךְ־ יִשְׂרָאֵל יְרוּשָׁלַםִ לַמִּלְחָמָה עָלֶיהָ וְלֹא יָכֹל
king-of Israel Jerusalem to-the-fight against-her but-not he-could

לְהִלָּחֵם עָלֶיהָ׃ (2) וַיֻּגַּד לְבֵית דָּוִד לֵאמֹר נָחָה
to-overpower over-her (2) now-he-was-told to-house-of David to-say she-allied

אֲרָם עַל־ אֶפְרָיִם וַיָּנַע לְבָבוֹ וּלְבַב עַמּוֹ
Aram with Ephraim so-he-was-shaken heart-of-him and-heart-of people-of-him

taken away and your sin atoned for."

8Then I heard the voice of the Lord saying, "Whom shall I send? And who will go for us?"

And I said, "Here am I. Send me!"

9He said, "Go and tell this people:

" 'Be ever hearing, but never understanding;
be ever seeing, but never perceiving.'
10Make the heart of this people calloused;
make their ears dull
and close their eyes.[k]
Otherwise they might see with their eyes,
hear with their ears,
understand with their hearts,
and turn and be healed."

11Then I said, "For how long, O Lord?"

And he answered:

"Until the cities lie ruined
and without inhabitant,
until the houses are left deserted
and the fields ruined and ravaged,
12until the LORD has sent everyone far away
and the land is utterly forsaken.
13And though a tenth remains in the land,
it will again be laid waste.
But as the terebinth and oak
leave stumps when they are cut down,
so the holy seed will be the stump in the land."

*The Sign of Immanuel*

7 When Ahaz son of Jotham, the son of Uzziah, was king of Judah, King Rezin of Aram and Pekah son of Remaliah king of Israel marched up to fight against Jerusalem, but they could not overpower it.

2Now the house of David was told, "Aram has allied itself with[l] Ephraim"; so the hearts of Ahaz and his people were shaken, as the

k9,10 Hebrew; Septuagint *'You will be ever hearing, but never understanding; / you will be ever seeing, but never perceiving.' / 10This people's heart has become calloused; / they hardly hear with their ears, / and they have closed their eyes*

l2 Or *has set up camp in*

כְּנוֹעַ עֲצֵי־ יַעַר מִפְּנֵי־ רוּחַ׃ וַיֹּאמֶר יְהוָה אֶל־
to Yahweh then-he-said (3) wind because-of forest trees-of as-to-shake

יְשַׁעְיָהוּ צֵא־ נָא לִקְרַאת אָחָז אַתָּה וּשְׁאָר יָשׁוּב בְּנֶךָ אֶל־
at son-of-you Jashub and-Shear you Ahaz to-meet now! go-out! Isaiah

קְצֵה תְּעָלַת הַבְּרֵכָה הָעֶלְיוֹנָה אֶל־ מְסִלַּת שְׂדֵה כוֹבֵס׃
One-Washing Field-of road-of on the-Upper the-Pool aqueduct-of end-of

וְאָמַרְתָּ אֵלָיו הִשָּׁמֵר וְהַשְׁקֵט אַל־ תִּירָא
you-fear not and-keep-calm! be-careful! to-him and-you-say (4)

וּלְבָבְךָ אַל־ יֵרַךְ מִשְּׁנֵי זַנְבוֹת הָאוּדִים
the-firewoods stubs-of because-of-two-of let-him-be-weak not and-heart-of-you

הָעֲשֵׁנִים הָאֵלֶּה בָּחֳרִי־ אַף רְצִין וַאֲרָם
and-Aram Rezin anger-of because-of-fierceness-of the-these the-ones-smoldering

וּבֶן־ רְמַלְיָהוּ׃ יַעַן כִּי־ יָעַץ עָלֶיךָ אֲרָם רָעָה
ruin Aram against-you he-plotted that because (5) Remaliah and-son-of

אֶפְרַיִם וּבֶן־ רְמַלְיָהוּ לֵאמֹר׃ נַעֲלֶה בִיהוּדָה
into-Judah let-us-invade (6) to-say Remaliah and-son-of Ephraim

וּנְקִיצֶנָּה וְנַבְקִעֶנָּה אֵלֵינוּ וְנַמְלִיךְ
and-let-us-make-king among-us and-let-us-divide-her and-let-us-tear-apart-her

מֶלֶךְ בְּתוֹכָהּ אֵת בֶּן־ טָבְאַל׃ כֹּה אָמַר אֲדֹנָי יְהוִה
Yahweh Sovereign he-says this (7) Tabeel son-of *** in-midst-of-her king

לֹא תָקוּם וְלֹא תִהְיֶה׃ כִּי רֹאשׁ אֲרָם
Aram head-of for (8) she-will-happen and-not she-will-take-place not

דַּמֶּשֶׂק וְרֹאשׁ דַּמֶּשֶׂק רְצִין וּבְעוֹד שִׁשִּׁים וְחָמֵשׁ שָׁנָה
year and-five sixty and-in-still Rezin Damascus and-head-of Damascus

יֵחַת אֶפְרַיִם מֵעָם׃ וְרֹאשׁ אֶפְרַיִם שֹׁמְרוֹן
Samaria Ephraim and-head-of (9) from-people Ephraim he-will-be-shattered

וְרֹאשׁ שֹׁמְרוֹן בֶּן־ רְמַלְיָהוּ אִם לֹא תַאֲמִינוּ כִּי לֹא
not then you-stand-in-faith not if Remaliah son-of Samaria and-head-of

תֵאָמֵנוּ׃ וַיּוֹסֶף יְהוָה דַּבֵּר אֶל־ אָחָז לֵאמֹר׃
to-say Ahaz to to-speak Yahweh and-he-did-again (10) you-will-stand

שְׁאַל־ לְךָ אוֹת מֵעִם יְהוָה אֱלֹהֶיךָ הַעְמֵק שְׁאָלָה* אוֹ
or *ask! to-make-deep God-of-you Yahweh from-with sign for-you ask! (11)

הַגְבֵּהַּ לְמָעְלָה׃ וַיֹּאמֶר אָחָז לֹא־ אֶשְׁאַל וְלֹא־
and-not I-will-ask not Ahaz but-he-said (12) to-at-above to-make-high

אֲנַסֶּה אֶת־ יְהוָה׃ וַיֹּאמֶר שִׁמְעוּ־ נָא בֵּית דָּוִד הַמְעַט
enough? David house-of now! hear! then-he-said (13) Yahweh *** I-will-test

מִכֶּם הַלְאוֹת אֲנָשִׁים כִּי תַלְאוּ גַּם אֶת־ אֱלֹהָי׃
God-of-me *** also will-you-try-patience indeed men to-try-patience for-you

*11 The NIV repoints this word as שְׁאָלָה, *to-depth (to-Sheol)*.

trees of the forest are shaken by the wind.
[3]Then the LORD said to Isaiah, "Go out, you and your son Shear-Jashub,[m] to meet Ahaz at the end of the aqueduct of the Upper Pool, on the road to the Washerman's Field.
[4]Say to him, 'Be careful, keep calm and don't be afraid. Do not lose heart because of these two smoldering stubs of firewood—because of the fierce anger of Rezin and Aram and of the son of Remaliah.
[5]Aram, Ephraim and Remaliah's son have plotted your ruin, saying,
[6]"Let us invade Judah; let us tear it apart and divide it among ourselves, and make the son of Tabeel king over it."
[7]Yet this is what the Sovereign LORD says:

" 'It will not take place,
it will not happen,
[8]for the head of Aram is Damascus,
and the head of Damascus is only Rezin.
Within sixty-five years
Ephraim will be too shattered to be a people.
[9]The head of Ephraim is Samaria,
and the head of Samaria is only Remaliah's son.
If you do not stand firm in your faith,
you will not stand at all.' "

[10]Again the LORD spoke to Ahaz,
[11]"Ask the LORD your God for a sign, whether in the deepest depths or in the highest heights."
[12]But Ahaz said, "I will not ask; I will not put the LORD to the test."
[13]Then Isaiah said, "Hear now, you house of David! Is it not enough to try the patience of men? Will you try the patience of my

[m]3 *Shear-Jashub* means *a remnant will return.*

לָכֵן יִתֵּן אֲדֹנָי הוּא לָכֶם אוֹת הִנֵּה הָעַלְמָה
*the-virgin see! sign to-you himself Lord he-will-give therefore (14)

הָרָה וְיֹלֶדֶת בֵּן וְקָרָאת שְׁמוֹ עִמָּנוּ אֵל׃
El Immanu name-of-him and-she-will-call son and-one-bearing with-child

חֶמְאָה וּדְבַשׁ יֹאכֵל לְדַעְתּוֹ מָאוֹס בָּרָע
to-the-wrong to-reject to-know-him he-will-eat and-honey curd (15)

וּבָחוֹר בַּטּוֹב׃ כִּי בְּטֶרֶם יֵדַע הַנַּעַר מָאֹס
to-reject the-boy he-knows when-before but (16) to-the-right and-to-choose

בָּרָע וּבָחֹר בַּטּוֹב תֵּעָזֵב הָאֲדָמָה אֲשֶׁר
that the-land she-will-be-laid-waste to-the-right and-to-choose to-the-wrong

אַתָּה קָץ מִפְּנֵי שְׁנֵי מְלָכֶיהָ׃ יָבִיא יְהוָה עָלֶיךָ
on-you Yahweh he-will-bring (17) kings-of-her two-of because-of dreading you

וְעַל־ עַמְּךָ וְעַל־ בֵּית אָבִיךָ יָמִים אֲשֶׁר לֹא־ בָאוּ
they-came not that times father-of-you house-of and-on people-of-you and-on

לְמִיּוֹם סוּר־ אֶפְרַיִם מֵעַל יְהוּדָה אֵת מֶלֶךְ אַשּׁוּר׃
Assyria king-of *** Judah from-with Ephraim to-break-away at-since-time

וְהָיָה ׀ בַּיּוֹם הַהוּא יִשְׁרֹק יְהוָה לַזְּבוּב
for-the-fly Yahweh he-will-whistle the-that in-the-day and-he-will-be (18)

אֲשֶׁר בִּקְצֵה יְאֹרֵי מִצְרָיִם וְלַדְּבוֹרָה אֲשֶׁר בְּאֶרֶץ אַשּׁוּר׃
Assyria in-land-of that and-for-the-bee Egypt streams-of at-end-of that

וּבָאוּ וְנָחוּ כֻלָּם בְּנַחֲלֵי
in-ravines-of all-of-them and-they-will-settle and-they-will-come (19)

הַבַּתּוֹת וּבִנְקִיקֵי הַסְּלָעִים וּבְכֹל הַנַּעֲצוּצִים
the-thornbushes and-on-all-of the-rocks and-in-crevices-of the-steep-ones

וּבְכֹל הַנַּהֲלֹלִים׃ בַּיּוֹם הַהוּא יְגַלַּח אֲדֹנָי
Lord he-will-shave the-that in-the-day (20) the-water-holes and-at-all-of

בְּתַעַר הַשְּׂכִירָה בְּעֶבְרֵי נָהָר בְּמֶלֶךְ אַשּׁוּר
Assyria with-king-of River from-parts-beyond-of the-hired-one with-razor-of

אֶת־ הָרֹאשׁ וְשַׂעַר הָרַגְלָיִם וְגַם אֶת־ הַזָּקָן תִּסְפֶּה׃
she-will-take-off the-beard *** and-also the-legs and-hair-of the-head ***

וְהָיָה בַּיּוֹם הַהוּא יְחַיֶּה־ אִישׁ עֶגְלַת
young-one-of man he-will-keep-alive the-that in-the-day and-he-will-be (21)

בָּקָר וּשְׁתֵּי־ צֹאן׃ וְהָיָה מֵרֹב עֲשׂוֹת חָלָב
milk to-give because-of-abundance-of and-he-will-be (22) goat and-two-of cow

יֹאכַל חֶמְאָה כִּי־ חֶמְאָה וּדְבַשׁ יֹאכֵל כָּל־ הַנּוֹתָר
the-one-remaining all-of he-will-eat and-honey curd indeed curd he-will-eat

בְּקֶרֶב הָאָרֶץ׃ וְהָיָה בַּיּוֹם הַהוּא יִהְיֶה
he-will-be the-that in-the-day and-he-will-be (23) the-land in-midst-of

God also? [14]Therefore the Lord
himself will give you[n] a sign: The
virgin will be with child and will
give birth to a son, and[o] will call
him Immanuel.[p] [15]He will eat
curds and honey when he knows
enough to reject the wrong and
choose the right. [16]But before the
boy knows enough to reject the
wrong and choose the right, the
land of the two kings you dread
will be laid waste. [17]The LORD will
bring on you and on your people
and on the house of your father a
time unlike any since Ephraim
broke away from Judah—he will
bring the king of Assyria."
[18]In that day the LORD will whis-
tle for flies from the distant
streams of Egypt and for bees
from the land of Assyria. [19]They
will all come and settle in the steep
ravines and in the crevices in the
rocks, on all the thornbushes and
at all the water holes. [20]In that day
the Lord will use a razor hired
from beyond the River[q]—the king
of Assyria—to shave your head
and the hair of your legs, and to
take off your beards also. [21]In that
day, a man will keep alive a young
cow and two goats. [22]And because
of the abundance of the milk they
give, he will have curds to eat. All
who remain in the land will eat
curds and honey. [23]In that day, in

[n]14 The Hebrew is plural.
[o]14 Masoretic Text; Dead Sea Scrolls *and he* or *and they*
[p]14 *Immanuel* means *God with us.*
[q]20 That is, the Euphrates

**14* See Introduction, page xi.

כָּל־ מְקוֹם אֲשֶׁר יִהְיֶה־ שָּׁם אֶלֶף גֶּפֶן בְּאֶלֶף כָּסֶף
every-of place that he-was there thousand-of vine for-thousand-of silver

לַשָּׁמִיר וְלַשַּׁיִת יִהְיֶה׃ בַּחִצִּים
for-the-brier and-for-the-thorn he-will-be (24) with-the-arrows

וּבַקֶּשֶׁת יָבוֹא שָׁמָּה כִּי־ שָׁמִיר וָשַׁיִת תִּהְיֶה כָל־
and-with-the-bow he-will-go to-there for brier and-thorn she-will-be all-of

הָאָרֶץ׃ וְכֹל הֶהָרִים אֲשֶׁר בַּמַּעְדֵּר יֵעָדֵרוּן
the-land (25) and-all-of the-hills that by-the-hoe they-were-cultivated

לֹא־ תָבוֹא שָׁמָּה יִרְאַת שָׁמִיר וָשָׁיִת וְהָיָה
not you-will-go to-there fear-of brier and-thorn and-he-will-become

לְמִשְׁלַח שׁוֹר וּלְמִרְמַס שֶׂה׃ וַיֹּאמֶר יְהוָה
for-turning-loose-of cattle and-for-running-of sheep (8:1) and-he-said Yahweh

אֵלַי קַח־ לְךָ גִּלָּיוֹן גָּדוֹל וּכְתֹב עָלָיו בְּחֶרֶט אֱנוֹשׁ
to-me take! for-you scroll large and-write! on-him with-pen-of man

לְמַהֵר שָׁלָל חָשׁ בַּז׃ וְאָעִידָה לִּי עֵדִים
namely-Maher Shalal Hash Baz (2) and-I-will-call for-me witnesses

נֶאֱמָנִים אֵת אוּרִיָּה הַכֹּהֵן וְאֶת־ זְכַרְיָהוּ בֶּן יְבֶרֶכְיָהוּ׃
ones-being-reliable *** Uriah the-priest and Zechariah son-of Jeberekiah

וָאֶקְרַב אֶל־ הַנְּבִיאָה וַתַּהַר וַתֵּלֶד בֵּן
(3) then-I-went to the-prophetess and-she-conceived and-she-bore son

וַיֹּאמֶר יְהוָה אֵלַי קְרָא שְׁמוֹ מַהֵר שָׁלָל חָשׁ בַּז׃ כִּי
and-he-said Yahweh to-me call! name-of-him Maher Shalal Hash Baz (4) for

בְּטֶרֶם יֵדַע הַנַּעַר קְרֹא אָבִי וְאִמִּי
at-before he-knows the-boy to-say father-of-me or-mother-of-me

יִשָּׂא ׀ אֶת־ חֵיל דַּמֶּשֶׂק וְאֵת שְׁלַל שֹׁמְרוֹן לִפְנֵי
he-will-carry-off *** wealth-of Damascus and plunder-of Samaria before

מֶלֶךְ אַשּׁוּר׃ וַיֹּסֶף יְהוָה דַּבֵּר אֵלַי עוֹד לֵאמֹר׃
king-of Assyria (5) and-he-did-again Yahweh to-speak to-me again to-say

יַעַן כִּי מָאַס הָעָם הַזֶּה אֵת מֵי הַשִּׁלֹחַ
(6) because that he-rejected the-people the-this *** waters-of the-Shiloah

הַהֹלְכִים לְאַט וּמְשׂוֹשׂ אֶת־ רְצִין וּבֶן־
the-ones-flowing with-gentleness and-rejoicing-of *** Rezin and-son-of

רְמַלְיָהוּ׃ וְלָכֵן הִנֵּה אֲדֹנָי מַעֲלֶה עֲלֵיהֶם אֶת־ מֵי
Remaliah (7) now-therefore see! Lord bringing against-them *** waters-of

הַנָּהָר הָעֲצוּמִים וְהָרַבִּים אֶת־ מֶלֶךְ אַשּׁוּר וְאֶת־ כָּל־
the-River the-mighty-ones and-the-many-ones *** king-of Assyria and all-of

כְּבוֹדוֹ וְעָלָה עַל־ כָּל־ אֲפִיקָיו וְהָלַךְ
pomp-of-him and-he-will-go-up over all-of channels-of-him and-he-will-run

every place where there were a thousand vines worth a thousand silver shekels,[r] there will be only briers and thorns.
24 Men will go there with bow and arrow, for the land will be covered with briers and thorns.
25 As for all the hills once cultivated by the hoe, you will no longer go there for fear of the briers and thorns; they will become places where cattle are turned loose and where sheep run.

*Assyria, the LORD's Instrument*

8 The LORD said to me, "Take a large scroll and write on it with an ordinary pen: Maher-Shalal-Hash-Baz.[s]
2 And I will call in Uriah the priest and Zechariah son of Jeberekiah as reliable witnesses for me."
3 Then I went to the prophetess, and she conceived and gave birth to a son. And the LORD said to me, "Name him Maher-Shalal-Hash-Baz.
4 Before the boy knows how to say 'My father' or 'My mother,' the wealth of Damascus and the plunder of Samaria will be carried off by the king of Assyria."
5 The LORD spoke to me again:

6 "Because this people has rejected
the gently flowing waters of Shiloah
and rejoices over Rezin
and the son of Remaliah,
7 therefore the Lord is about to bring against them
the mighty floodwaters of the River[t] —
the king of Assyria with all his pomp.
It will overflow all its channels,

[r] 23 That is, about 25 pounds (about 11.5 kilograms)
[s] 1 *Maher-Shalal-Hash-Baz* means *quick to the plunder, swift to the spoil;* also in verse 3.
[t] 7 That is, the Euphrates

עַל־ כָּל־ גְּדוֹתָיו׃ וְחָלַף בִּיהוּדָה שָׁטַף
and-he-will-swirl-over into-Judah and-he-will-sweep (8) banks-of-him all-of over

וְעָבַר עַד־ צַוָּאר יַגִּיעַ וְהָיָה
and-he-will-be he-will-reach neck to and-he-will-pass-through

מֻטּוֹת כְּנָפָיו מְלֹא רֹחַב־ אַרְצְךָ עִמָּנוּ אֵל׃
El Immanu land-of-you breadth-of fullness-of wings-of-him outspreadings-of

רֹעוּ עַמִּים וָחֹתּוּ וְהַאֲזִינוּ כֹּל
all-of and-listen! and-be-shattered! nations raise-war-cry! (9)

מֶרְחַקֵּי־ אָרֶץ הִתְאַזְּרוּ וָחֹתּוּ הִתְאַזְּרוּ
prepare-for-battle! and-be-shattered! prepare-for-battle! land distant-ones-of

וָחֹתּוּ׃ עֻצוּ עֵצָה וְתֻפָר דַּבְּרוּ
propose! but-she-will-be-thwarted strategy devise! (10) and-be-shattered!

דָבָר וְלֹא יָקוּם כִּי עִמָּנוּ אֵל׃ כִּי כֹה אָמַר יְהוָה
Yahweh he-spoke thus indeed (11) God with-us for he-will-stand but-not plan

אֵלַי כְּחֶזְקַת* הַיָּד וְיִסְּרֵנִי מִלֶּכֶת בְּדֶרֶךְ
in-way-of from-to-follow and-he-warned-me the-hand with-strength-of to-me

הָעָם־ הַזֶּה לֵאמֹר׃ לֹא־ תֹאמְרוּן קֶשֶׁר לְכֹל אֲשֶׁר־
that to-everything conspiracy you-call not (12) to-say the-this the-people

יֹאמַר הָעָם הַזֶּה קָשֶׁר וְאֶת־ מוֹרָאוֹ לֹא־ תִירְאוּ וְלֹא
and-not you-fear not fear-of-him and conspiracy the-this the-people he-calls

תַעֲרִיצוּ׃ אֶת־ יְהוָה צְבָאוֹת אֹתוֹ תַקְדִּישׁוּ וְהוּא מוֹרַאֲכֶם
fear-of-you and-he you-regard-as-holy him Hosts Yahweh-of *** (13) you-dread

וְהוּא מַעֲרִצְכֶם׃ וְהָיָה לְמִקְדָּשׁ
as-sanctuary and-he-will-be (14) one-causing-dread-of-you and-he

וּלְאֶבֶן נֶגֶף וּלְצוּר מִכְשׁוֹל לִשְׁנֵי בָתֵּי
houses-of for-both-of falling and-as-rock-of stumbling but-as-stone-of

יִשְׂרָאֵל לְפַח וּלְמוֹקֵשׁ לְיוֹשֵׁב יְרוּשָׁלָםִ׃
Jerusalem for-one-dwelling-of and-as-snare as-trap Israel

וְכָשְׁלוּ בָם רַבִּים וְנָפְלוּ
and-they-will-fall many of-them and-they-will-stumble (15)

וְנִשְׁבָּרוּ וְנוֹקָשׁוּ וְנִלְכָּדוּ׃
and-they-will-be-captured and-they-will-be-snared and-they-will-be-broken

צוֹר תְּעוּדָה חֲתוֹם תּוֹרָה בְּלִמֻּדָי׃
among-disciples-of-me law seal-up! testimony bind-up! (16)

וְחִכִּיתִי לַיהוָה הַמַּסְתִּיר פָּנָיו מִבֵּית
from-house-of faces-of-him the-one-hiding for-Yahweh and-I-will-wait (17)

יַעֲקֹב וְקִוֵּיתִי־ לוֹ׃ הִנֵּה אָנֹכִי וְהַיְלָדִים אֲשֶׁר נָתַן־
he-gave whom and-the-children I here! (18) in-him and-I-will-trust Jacob

run over all its banks
[8]and sweep on into Judah,
swirling over it,
passing through it and
reaching up to the neck.
Its outspread wings will cover
the breadth of your land,
O Immanuel[u]!"

[9]Raise the war cry,[v] you
nations, and be shattered!
Listen, all you distant lands.
Prepare for battle, and be
shattered!
Prepare for battle, and be
shattered!
[10]Devise your strategy, but it
will be thwarted;
propose your plan, but it
will not stand,
for God is with us.[w]

*Fear God*

[11]The LORD spoke to me with his strong hand upon me, warning me not to follow the way of this people. He said:

[12]"Do not call conspiracy
everything that these people
call conspiracy[x];
do not fear what they fear,
and do not dread it.
[13]The LORD Almighty is the one
you are to regard as holy,
he is the one you are to
fear,
he is the one you are to
dread,
[14]and he will be a sanctuary;
but for both houses of Israel
he will be
a stone that causes men to
stumble
and a rock that makes them
fall.
And for the people of
Jerusalem he will be
a trap and a snare.
[15]Many of them will stumble;
they will fall and be broken,
they will be snared and
captured."

[16]Bind up the testimony
and seal up the law among
my disciples.
[17]I will wait for the LORD,
who is hiding his face from
the house of Jacob.
I will put my trust in him.

[18]Here am I, and the children the

*u8 Immanuel* means *God with us.*
*v9* Or *Do your worst*
*w10* Hebrew *Immanuel*
*x12* Or *Do not call for a treaty / every time these people call for a treaty*

*11 Most mss have *beth* instead of *kaph* (בְּ).

לִי יְהוָה לְאֹתוֹת וּלְמוֹפְתִים בְּיִשְׂרָאֵל מֵעִם יְהוָה צְבָאוֹת
Hosts Yahweh-of from-with in-Israel and-as-symbols as-signs Yahweh to-me

הַשֹּׁכֵן בְּהַר צִיּוֹן׃ וְכִי־ יֹאמְרוּ אֲלֵיכֶם דִּרְשׁוּ
consult! to-you they-tell and-when (19) Zion on-Mount-of the-one-dwelling

אֶל־ הָאֹבוֹת וְאֶל־ הַיִּדְּעֹנִים הַמְצַפְצְפִים וְהַמַּהְגִּים
and-the-ones-muttering the-ones-whispering the-spiritists and-to the-mediums to

הֲלוֹא־ עַם אֶל־ אֱלֹהָיו יִדְרֹשׁ בְּעַד הַחַיִּים
the-living-ones on-behalf-of he-should-inquire God-of-him to people not?

אֶל־ הַמֵּתִים׃ לְתוֹרָה וְלִתְעוּדָה אִם־ לֹא יֹאמְרוּ
they-speak not if and-to-testimony to-law (20) the-ones-being-dead to

כַּדָּבָר הַזֶּה אֲשֶׁר אֵין־ לוֹ שָׁחַר׃
light-of-dawn to-him there-is-not that the-this according-to-the-word

וְעָבַר בָּהּ נִקְשֶׁה וְרָעֵב
and-hungry one-being-distressed through-her and-he-will-roam (21)

וְהָיָה כִי־ יִרְעַב וְהִתְקַצַּף
then-he-will-become-enraged he-is-famished when and-he-will-be

וְקִלֵּל בְּמַלְכּוֹ וּבֵאלֹהָיו וּפָנָה
and-he-will-look and-to-God-of-him to-king-of-him and-he-will-curse

לְמָעְלָה׃ וְאֶל־ אֶרֶץ יַבִּיט וְהִנֵּה צָרָה וַחֲשֵׁכָה
and-darkness distress and-see! he-will-look earth then-toward (22) to-upward

מְעוּף צוּקָה וַאֲפֵלָה מְנֻדָּח׃ כִּי לֹא
no nevertheless *(23) one-being-thrust and-utter-darkness fearfulness gloom-of

מוּעָף לַאֲשֶׁר מוּצָק לָהּ כָּעֵת הָרִאשׁוֹן הֵקַל אַרְצָה
to-land-of he-humbled the-past in-the-time to-her distress for-whom gloom

זְבֻלוּן וְאַרְצָה נַפְתָּלִי וְהָאַחֲרוֹן הִכְבִּיד דֶּרֶךְ הַיָּם
the-sea way-of he-will-honor but-the-future Naphtali and-to-land-of Zebulun

עֵבֶר הַיַּרְדֵּן גְּלִיל הַגּוֹיִם׃ הָעָם
the-people (9:1) the-Gentiles Galilee-of the-Jordan along-of

הַהֹלְכִים בַּחֹשֶׁךְ רָאוּ אוֹר גָּדוֹל יֹשְׁבֵי בְּאֶרֶץ
in-land-of ones-living-of great light they-saw in-darkness the-ones-walking

צַלְמָוֶת אוֹר נָגַהּ עֲלֵיהֶם׃ הִרְבִּיתָ הַגּוֹי לֹא°
to-him the-nation you-enlarged (2) on-them he-dawned light darkness

הִגְדַּלְתָּ הַשִּׂמְחָה שָׂמְחוּ לְפָנֶיךָ כְּשִׂמְחַת בַּקָּצִיר
at-the-harvest as-rejoicing-of before-you they-rejoice the-joy you-increased

כַּאֲשֶׁר יָגִילוּ בְּחַלְּקָם שָׁלָל׃ כִּי ׀ אֶת־ עֹל
yoke-of *** for (3) plunder when-to-divide-them they-rejoice as-that

סֻבֳּלוֹ וְאֵת מַטֵּה שִׁכְמוֹ שֵׁבֶט הַנֹּגֵשׂ בּוֹ
to-him the-one-oppressing rod-of shoulder-of-him bar-of and burden-of-him

LORD has given me. We are signs and symbols in Israel from the LORD Almighty, who dwells on Mount Zion.

[19]When men tell you to consult mediums and spiritists, who whisper and mutter, should not a people inquire of their God? Why consult the dead on behalf of the living? [20]To the law and to the testimony! If they do not speak according to this word, they have no light of dawn. [21]Distressed and hungry, they will roam through the land; when they are famished, they will become enraged and, looking upward, will curse their king and their God. [22]Then they will look toward the earth and see only distress and darkness and fearful gloom, and they will be thrust into utter darkness.

*To Us a Child Is Born*

9 Nevertheless, there will be no more gloom for those who were in distress. In the past he humbled the land of Zebulun and the land of Naphtali, but in the future he will honor Galilee of the Gentiles, by the way of the sea, along the Jordan—

[2]The people walking in
 darkness
 have seen a great light;
on those living in the land of
 the shadow of death[y]
 a light has dawned.
[3]You have enlarged the nation
 and increased their joy;
they rejoice before you
 as people rejoice at the
 harvest,
as men rejoice
 when dividing the plunder.
[4]For as in the day of Midian's
 defeat,
 you have shattered
the yoke that burdens them,
 the bar across their
 shoulders,
 the rod of their oppressor.

y2 Or *land of darkness*

*23 The Hebrew numeration of chapter 9 begins with verse 2 in English; thus, there is a one-verse discrepancy throughout the chapter.

°2 ק לו

הַחִתֹּתָ כְּיוֹם מִדְיָן׃ (4) כִּי כָל־ סְאוֹן סֹאֵן בְּרַעַשׁ
you-shattered as-day-of Midian (4) for every-of boot-of one-being-warrior in-battle

וְשִׂמְלָה מְגוֹלָלָה בְדָמִים וְהָיְתָה לִשְׂרֵפָה מַאֲכֹלֶת אֵשׁ׃
and-garment being-rolled in-bloods then-she-will-be for-burning fuel-of fire

(5) כִּי־ יֶלֶד יֻלַּד־ לָנוּ בֵּן נִתַּן־ לָנוּ וַתְּהִי
(5) for child he-is-born to-us son he-is-given to-us and-she-will-be

הַמִּשְׂרָה עַל־ שִׁכְמוֹ וַיִּקְרָא שְׁמוֹ פֶּלֶא
the-government on shoulder-of-him and-he-will-call name-of-him Wonder-of

יוֹעֵץ אֵל גִּבּוֹר אֲבִי־ עַד שַׂר־ שָׁלוֹם׃
One-Counseling God-of Might Father-of Everlasting Prince-of Peace

(6) לְםַרְבֵּה הַמִּשְׂרָה וּלְשָׁלוֹם אֵין־ קֵץ עַל־ כִּסֵּא דָוִד
(6) of-increase-of the-government and-of-peace no end on throne-of David

וְעַל־ מַמְלַכְתּוֹ לְהָכִין אֹתָהּ וּלְסַעֲדָהּ בְּמִשְׁפָּט
and-over kingdom-of-him to-establish her and-to-uphold-her with-justice

וּבִצְדָקָה מֵעַתָּה וְעַד־ עוֹלָם קִנְאַת יְהוָה צְבָאוֹת
and-with-righteousness from-now and-to forever zeal-of Yahweh-of Hosts

תַּעֲשֶׂה־ זֹּאת׃ (7) דָּבָר שָׁלַח אֲדֹנָי בְּיַעֲקֹב
she-will-accomplish this (7) message he-sent Lord against-Jacob

וְנָפַל בְּיִשְׂרָאֵל׃ (8) וְיָדְעוּ הָעָם כֻּלּוֹ
and-he-will-fall on-Israel (8) and-they-will-know the-people all-of-him

אֶפְרַיִם וְיוֹשֵׁב שֹׁמְרוֹן בְּגַאֲוָה וּבְגֹדֶל לֵבָב
Ephraim and-one-inhabiting-of Samaria with-pride and-with-arrogance-of heart

לֵאמֹר׃ (9) לְבֵנִים נָפָלוּ וְגָזִית נִבְנֶה שִׁקְמִים
to-say (9) bricks they-fell but-dressed-stone we-will-rebuild fig-trees

גֻּדָּעוּ וַאֲרָזִים נַחֲלִיף׃ (10) וַיְשַׂגֵּב יְהוָה
they-were-felled but-cedars we-will-replace (10) but-he-strengthened Yahweh

אֶת־ צָרֵי רְצִין עָלָיו וְאֶת־ אֹיְבָיו יְסַכְסֵךְ׃
*** foes-of Rezin against-him and ones-being-enemies-of-him he-spurred-on

(11) אֲרָם מִקֶּדֶם וּפְלִשְׁתִּים מֵאָחוֹר וַיֹּאכְלוּ אֶת־
(11) Aramean from-east and-Philistines from-west indeed-they-devoured ***

יִשְׂרָאֵל בְּכָל־ פֶּה בְּכָל־ זֹאת לֹא־ שָׁב אַפּוֹ
Israel with-whole-of mouth for-all-of this not turning-away anger-of-him

וְעוֹד יָדוֹ נְטוּיָה׃ (12) וְהָעָם לֹא־ שָׁב
and-still hand-of-him being-upraised (12) but-the-people not he-returned

עַד־ הַמַּכֵּהוּ וְאֶת־ יְהוָה צְבָאוֹת לֹא דָרָשׁוּ׃
to the-one-striking-him and Yahweh-of Hosts not they-sought

(13) וַיַּכְרֵת יְהוָה מִיִּשְׂרָאֵל רֹאשׁ וְזָנָב כִּפָּה
(13) so-he-will-cut-off Yahweh from-Israel head and-tail palm-branch

5 Every warrior's boot used in battle
and every garment rolled in blood
will be destined for burning,
will be fuel for the fire.
6 For to us a child is born,
to us a son is given,
and the government will be on his shoulders.
And he will be called
Wonderful Counselor,[z]
Mighty God,
Everlasting Father, Prince of Peace.
7 Of the increase of his government and peace
there will be no end.
He will reign on David's throne
and over his kingdom,
establishing and upholding it
with justice and righteousness
from that time on and forever.
The zeal of the LORD Almighty
will accomplish this.

*The LORD's Anger Against Israel*

8 The Lord has sent a message against Jacob;
it will fall on Israel.
9 All the people will know it—
Ephraim and the inhabitants of Samaria—
who say with pride
and arrogance of heart,
10 "The bricks have fallen down,
but we will rebuild with dressed stone;
the fig trees have been felled,
but we will replace them with cedars."
11 But the LORD has strengthened Rezin's foes against them
and has spurred their enemies on.
12 Arameans from the east and Philistines from the west
have devoured Israel with open mouth.

Yet for all this, his anger is not turned away,
his hand is still upraised.

13 But the people have not returned to him who struck them,
nor have they sought the LORD Almighty.
14 So the LORD will cut off from Israel both head and tail,
both palm branch and reed

z6 Or *Wonderful, Counselor*

*See the note on page 18.

°6 ק למרבה

וְאַגְמוֹן יוֹם אֶחָד׃ (14) זָקֵן וּנְשׂוּא־ פָנִים הוּא הָרֹאשׁ
and-reed day single (14) elder and-one-being-lifted-of faces he the-head

וְנָבִיא מוֹרֶה־ שֶּׁקֶר הוּא הַזָּנָב׃ (15) וַיִּהְיוּ מְאַשְּׁרֵי
and-prophet one-teaching lie he the-tail (15) and-they-are ones-guiding-of

הָעָם־ הַזֶּה מַתְעִים וּמְאֻשָּׁרָיו
the-people the-this ones-misleading and-ones-being-guided-of-him

מְבֻלָּעִים׃ (16) עַל־ כֵּן עַל־ בַּחוּרָיו לֹא־
ones-being-led-astray (16) for this in young-men-of-him not

יִשְׂמַח | אֲדֹנָי וְאֶת־ יְתֹמָיו וְאֶת־ אַלְמְנֹתָיו לֹא
he-will-take-pleasure Lord and fatherless-ones-of-him and widows-of-him not

יְרַחֵם כִּי כֻלּוֹ חָנֵף וּמֵרַע וְכָל־ פֶּה
he-will-pity for all-of-him ungodly and-being-wicked and-every-of mouth

דֹּבֵר נְבָלָה בְּכָל־ זֹאת לֹא־ שָׁב אַפּוֹ וְעוֹד
speaking vileness for-all-of this not turning-away anger-of-him and-still

יָדוֹ נְטוּיָה׃ (17) כִּי־ בָעֲרָה כָאֵשׁ רִשְׁעָה
hand-of-him being-upraised (17) surely she-burns like-fire wickedness

שָׁמִיר וָשַׁיִת תֹּאכֵל וַתִּצַּת בְּסִבְכֵי הַיַּעַר
brier and-thorn she-consumes and-she-sets-ablaze to-thickets-of the-forest

וַיִּתְאַבְּכוּ גֵּאוּת עָשָׁן׃ (18) בְּעֶבְרַת יְהוָה צְבָאוֹת
so-they-roll-upward column-of smoke (18) by-wrath-of Yahweh-of Hosts

נֶעְתַּם אָרֶץ וַיְהִי הָעָם כְּמַאֲכֹלֶת אֵשׁ אִישׁ אֶל־
he-will-be-scorched land and-he-will-be the-people as-fuel-of fire man to

אָחִיו לֹא יַחְמֹלוּ׃ (19) וַיִּגְזֹר עַל־ יָמִין
brother-of-him not he-will-spare (19) and-he-will-devour on right

וְרָעֵב וַיֹּאכַל עַל־ שְׂמֹאול וְלֹא שָׂבֵעוּ
but-he-will-be-hungry and-he-will-eat on left but-not they-will-be-satisfied

אִישׁ בְּשַׂר־ זְרֹעוֹ יֹאכֵלוּ׃ (20) מְנַשֶּׁה אֶת־ אֶפְרַיִם
man flesh-of arm-of-him they-will-feed-on (20) Manasseh *** Ephraim

וְאֶפְרַיִם אֶת־ מְנַשֶּׁה יַחְדָּו הֵמָּה עַל־ יְהוּדָה בְּכָל־ זֹאת לֹא־
and-Ephraim *** Manasseh together they against Judah for-all-of this not

שָׁב אַפּוֹ וְעוֹד יָדוֹ נְטוּיָה׃ (10:1) הוֹי
turning-away anger-of-him and-still hand-of-him being-upraised (10:1) woe!

הַחֹקְקִים חִקְקֵי־ אָוֶן וּמְכַתְּבִים עָמָל כִּתֵּבוּ׃
the-ones-making-laws laws-of injustice and-ones-decreeing oppression they-decree

(2) לְהַטּוֹת מִדִּין דַּלִּים וְלִגְזֹל מִשְׁפַּט עֲנִיֵּי
(2) to-deprive from-right-of poor-ones and-to-withhold justice-of oppressed-ones-of

עַמִּי לִהְיוֹת אַלְמָנוֹת שְׁלָלָם וְאֶת־ יְתוֹמִים יָבֹזּוּ׃
people-of-me to-be widows prey-of-them and fatherless-ones they-rob

in a single day;
15 the elders and prominent men
are the head,
the prophets who teach lies
are the tail.
16 Those who guide this people
mislead them,
and those who are guided
are led astray.
17 Therefore the Lord will take no
pleasure in the young
men,
nor will he pity the
fatherless and widows,
for everyone is ungodly and
wicked,
every mouth speaks
vileness.

Yet for all this, his anger is
not turned away,
his hand is still upraised.

18 Surely wickedness burns like a
fire;
it consumes briers and
thorns,
it sets the forest thickets
ablaze,
so that it rolls upward in a
column of smoke.
19 By the wrath of the LORD
Almighty
the land will be scorched
and the people will be fuel for
the fire;
no one will spare his
brother.
20 On the right they will devour,
but still be hungry;
on the left they will eat,
but not be satisfied.
Each will feed on the flesh of
his own offspring[a]:
21 Manasseh will feed on
Ephraim, and Ephraim on
Manasseh;
together they will turn
against Judah.

Yet for all this, his anger is
not turned away,
his hand is still upraised.

10 Woe to those who make
unjust laws,
to those who issue
oppressive decrees,
2 to deprive the poor of their
rights
and withhold justice from the
oppressed of my people,
making widows their prey
and robbing the fatherless.

[a] 20 Or *arm*

*See the note on page 18.

| מִמֶּרְחָק | וּלְשׁוֹאָה | פְּקֻדָּה | לְיוֹם | תַּעֲשׂוּ | וּמַה־ | |
|---|---|---|---|---|---|---|
| from-afar | and-when-disaster | reckoning | on-day-of | will-you-do | and-what? | (3) |

| תַעַזְבוּ | וְאָנָה | לְעֶזְרָה | תָּנוּסוּ | מִי | עַל־ | תָּבוֹא |
|---|---|---|---|---|---|---|
| will-you-leave | and-where? | for-help | will-you-run | whom? | to | she-comes |

| וְתַחַת | אַסִּיר | תַּחַת | כָרַע | בִּלְתִּי | | כְּבוֹדְכֶם׃ |
|---|---|---|---|---|---|---|
| or-among | captive | among | he-will-cringe | nothing | (4) | richness-of-you |

| שָׁב | לֹא־ | זֹאת | בְּכָל־ | יִפֹּלוּ | הֲרוּגִים |
|---|---|---|---|---|---|
| turning-away | not | this | for-all-of | they-will-fall | ones-being-slain |

| שֵׁבֶט | אַשּׁוּר | הוֹי | | נְטוּיָה׃ | יָדוֹ | וְעוֹד | אַפּוֹ |
|---|---|---|---|---|---|---|---|
| rod-of | Assyrian | woe! | (5) | being-upraised | hand-of-him | and-still | anger-of-him |

| בְּגוֹי | | זַעְמִי׃ | בְיָדָם | הוּא | וּמַטֶּה־ | אַפִּי |
|---|---|---|---|---|---|---|
| against-nation | (6) | wrath-of-me | in-hand-of-them | he | and-club | anger-of-me |

| לִשְׁלֹל | אֲצַוֶּנּוּ | עֶבְרָתִי | עַם | וְעַל־ | אֲשַׁלְּחֶנּוּ | חָנֵף |
|---|---|---|---|---|---|---|
| to-seize | I-dispatch-him | anger-of-me | people-of | and-against | I-send-him | godless |

| כְּחֹמֶר | מִרְמָס | וּלְשִׂימוֹ | בַּז | וְלָבֹז | שָׁלָל |
|---|---|---|---|---|---|
| like-mud-of | trampling-place | and-to-make-him | plunder | and-to-snatch | loot |

| יַחְשֹׁב | כֵן | לֹא־ | וּלְבָבוֹ | יְדַמֶּה | כֵן | לֹא־ | וְהוּא | | חוּצוֹת׃ |
|---|---|---|---|---|---|---|---|---|---|
| he-thinks | what | not | and-mind-of-him | he-intends | what | not | but-this | (7) | streets |

| כִּי | | מְעָט׃ | לֹא | גּוֹיִם | וּלְהַכְרִית | בִּלְבָבוֹ | לְהַשְׁמִיד | כִּי |
|---|---|---|---|---|---|---|---|---|
| indeed | (8) | few | not | nations | and-to-make-end | in-mind-of-him | to-destroy | rather |

| כַּלְנוֹ | כְּכַרְכְּמִישׁ | הֲלֹא | | מְלָכִים׃ | יַחְדָּו | שָׂרַי | הֲלֹא | יֹאמַר |
|---|---|---|---|---|---|---|---|---|
| Calno | like-Carchemish | not? | (9) | kings | together | commanders-of-me | not? | he-says |

| כַּאֲשֶׁר | | שֹׁמְרוֹן׃ | כְדַמֶּשֶׂק | לֹא | אִם־ | חֲמָת | כְאַרְפַּד | לֹא | אִם־ |
|---|---|---|---|---|---|---|---|---|---|
| just-as | (10) | Samaria | like-Damascus | not | or | Hamath | like-Arpad | not | or |

| וּפְסִילֵיהֶם | הָאֱלִיל | לְמַמְלְכֹת | יָדִי | מָצְאָה |
|---|---|---|---|---|
| and-images-of-them | the-idol | to-kingdoms-of | hand-of-me | she-seized |

| עָשִׂיתִי | כַּאֲשֶׁר | הֲלֹא | | וּמִשֹּׁמְרוֹן׃ | מִירוּשָׁלִַם |
|---|---|---|---|---|---|
| I-dealt | just-as | not? | (11) | and-better-than-Samaria | better-than-Jerusalem |

| לִירוּשָׁלִַם | אֶעֱשֶׂה | כֵּן | וְלֶאֱלִילֶיהָ | לְשֹׁמְרוֹן |
|---|---|---|---|---|
| with-Jerusalem | shall-I-deal | so | and-with-idols-of-her | with-Samaria |

| כָּל־ | אֶת־ | אֲדֹנָי | יְבַצַּע | כִּי־ | וְהָיָה | | וְלַעֲצַבֶּיהָ׃ |
|---|---|---|---|---|---|---|---|
| all-of | *** | Lord | he-finishes | when | and-he-will-be | (12) | and-with-images-of-her |

| עַל־ | אֶפְקֹד | וּבִירוּשָׁלִַם | צִיּוֹן | בְּהַר | מַעֲשֵׂהוּ |
|---|---|---|---|---|---|
| for | I-will-punish | and-against-Jerusalem | Zion | against-Mount-of | work-of-him |

| רוּם | תִּפְאֶרֶת | וְעַל־ | אַשּׁוּר | מֶלֶךְ־ | לְבַב | גֹּדֶל | פְּרִי־ |
|---|---|---|---|---|---|---|---|
| haughtiness-of | glory-of | and-for | Assyria | king-of | heart-of | pride-of | fruit-of |

| עָשִׂיתִי | יָדִי | בְּכֹחַ | אָמַר | כִּי | | עֵינָיו׃ |
|---|---|---|---|---|---|---|
| I-did | hand-of-me | by-strength-of | he-says | for | (13) | eyes-of-him |

°6 ק ולשומו

[3]What will you do on the day
of reckoning,
when disaster comes from
afar?
To whom will you run for
help?
Where will you leave your
riches?
[4]Nothing will remain but to
cringe among the captives
or fall among the slain.

Yet for all this, his anger is
not turned away,
his hand is still upraised.

*God's Judgment on Assyria*

[5]"Woe to the Assyrian, the rod
of my anger,
in whose hand is the club of
my wrath!
[6]I send him against a godless
nation,
I dispatch him against a
people who anger me,
to seize loot and snatch
plunder,
and to trample them down
like mud in the streets.
[7]But this is not what he
intends,
this is not what he has in
mind;
his purpose is to destroy,
to put an end to many
nations.
[8]'Are not my commanders all
kings?' he says.
[9] 'Has not Calno fared like
Carchemish?
Is not Hamath like Arpad,
and Samaria like Damascus?
[10]As my hand seized the
kingdoms of the idols,
kingdoms whose images
excelled those of
Jerusalem and Samaria—
[11]shall I not deal with Jerusalem
and her images
as I dealt with Samaria and
her idols?' "

[12]When the Lord has finished all
his work against Mount Zion and
Jerusalem, he will say, "I will punish the king of Assyria for the
willful pride of his heart and the
haughty look in his eyes. [13]For he
says:

" 'By the strength of my hand
I have done this,

וּבְחָכְמָתִי כִּי נְבֻנוֹתִי וְאָסִיר ׀ גְּבוּלֹת
boundaries-of and-I-removed I-have-understanding because and-by-wisdom-of-me

עַמִּים וַעֲתִידֹתֵיהֶם° שׁוֹשֵׂתִי וְאוֹרִיד כַּאבִּיר*
*like-the-mighty-one and-I-subdued I-plundered and-treasures-of-them nations

יוֹשְׁבִים׃ (14) וַתִּמְצָא כַקֵּן ׀ יָדִי
hand-of-me as-the-nest and-she-reaches (14) ones-being-enthroned

לְחֵיל הָעַמִּים וְכֶאֱסֹף בֵּיצִים עֲזֻבוֹת כָּל־
all-of ones-being-abandoned eggs and-as-to-gather the-nations for-wealth-of

הָאָרֶץ אֲנִי אָסָפְתִּי וְלֹא הָיָה נֹדֵד כָּנָף וּפֹצֶה
or-one-opening wing one-flapping he-was and-not I-gathered I the-country

פֶּה וּמְצַפְצֵף׃ (15) הֲיִתְפָּאֵר הַגַּרְזֶן עַל
above the-axe does-he-raise-himself? (15) and-chirping mouth

הַחֹצֵב בּוֹ אִם־ יִתְגַּדֵּל הַמַּשּׂוֹר עַל־ מְנִיפוֹ
one-using-him against the-saw does-he-boast or with-him the-one-cutting

כְּהָנִיף שֵׁבֶט וְאֶת־† מְרִימָיו כְּהָרִים מַטֶּה לֹא־ עֵץ׃
wood not club as-to-brandish ones-lifting-him †also rod as-to-wield

(16) לָכֵן יְשַׁלַּח הָאָדוֹן יְהוָה צְבָאוֹת בְּמִשְׁמַנָּיו
upon-sturdy-ones-of-him Hosts Yahweh-of the-Lord he-will-send therefore (16)

רָזוֹן וְתַחַת כְּבֹדוֹ יֵקַד יְקֹד
fire he-will-be-kindled pomp-of-him and-under wasting-disease

כִּיקוֹד אֵשׁ׃ (17) וְהָיָה אוֹר־ יִשְׂרָאֵל לְאֵשׁ
as-fire Israel Light-of and-he-will-become (17) flame like-blazing-of

וּקְדוֹשׁוֹ לְלֶהָבָה וּבָעֲרָה וְאָכְלָה
and-she-will-consume and-she-will-burn as-flame and-Holy-One-of-him

שִׁיתוֹ וּשְׁמִירוֹ בְּיוֹם אֶחָד׃ (18) וּכְבוֹד יַעְרוֹ
forest-of-him and-splendor-of (18) single in-day and-brier-of-him thorn-of-him

וְכַרְמִלּוֹ מִנֶּפֶשׁ וְעַד־ בָּשָׂר יְכַלֶּה וְהָיָה
and-he-will-be he-will-destroy flesh and-to from-soul and-fertile-field-of-him

כִּמְסֹס נֹסֵס׃ (19) וּשְׁאָר עֵץ יַעְרוֹ
forest-of-him tree-of and-remainder-of (19) one-being-sick as-to-waste-away

מִסְפָּר יִהְיוּ וְנַעַר יִכְתְּבֵם׃ (20) וְהָיָה ׀
and-he-will-be (20) he-could-write-down-them and-child they-will-be few

בַּיּוֹם הַהוּא לֹא־ יוֹסִיף עוֹד שְׁאָר יִשְׂרָאֵל
Israel remnant-of longer he-will-do-again not the-that in-the-day

וּפְלֵיטַת בֵּית־ יַעֲקֹב לְהִשָּׁעֵן עַל־ מַכֵּהוּ
one-striking-down-him on to-rely Jacob house-of and-survivor-of

וְנִשְׁעַן עַל־ יְהוָה קְדוֹשׁ יִשְׂרָאֵל בֶּאֱמֶת׃ (21) שְׁאָר
remnant (21) in-truth Israel Holy-One-of Yahweh on but-he-will-rely

and by my wisdom, because
I have understanding.
I removed the boundaries of
nations,
I plundered their treasures;
like a mighty one I
subdued[b] their kings.
14As one reaches into a nest,
so my hand reached for the
wealth of the nations;
as men gather abandoned
eggs,
so I gathered all the
countries;
not one flapped a wing,
or opened its mouth to
chirp.' "
15Does the ax raise itself above
him who swings it,
or the saw boast against
him who uses it?
As if a rod were to wield him
who lifts it up,
or a club brandish him who
is not wood!
16Therefore, the Lord, the LORD
Almighty,
will send a wasting disease
upon his sturdy warriors;
under his pomp a fire will be
kindled
like a blazing flame.
17The Light of Israel will become
a fire,
their Holy One a flame;
in a single day it will burn
and consume
his thorns and his briers.
18The splendor of his forests and
fertile fields
it will completely destroy,
as when a sick man wastes
away.
19And the remaining trees of his
forests will be so few
that a child could write
them down.

### *The Remnant of Israel*

20In that day the remnant of
Israel,
the survivors of the house of
Jacob,
will no longer rely on him
who struck them down
but will truly rely on the LORD,
the Holy One of Israel.

[b]*13* Or *I subdued the mighty,*

**13* Many mss have as a *Qere* form כביר, *mighty.*

†*15* Most mss omit the *vav* (את [the simple direct object indicator]).

°*13* ק ועתודותיהם

יָשׁוּב שְׁאָר יַעֲקֹב אֶל־ אֵל גִּבּוֹר׃ (22) כִּי אִם־ יִהְיֶה
he-is though for (22) Might God-of to Jacob remnant-of he-will-return

עַמְּךָ יִשְׂרָאֵל כְּחוֹל הַיָּם שְׁאָר יָשׁוּב בּוֹ
of-him he-will-return remnant the-sea like-sand-of Israel people-of-you

כִּלָּיוֹן חָרוּץ שׁוֹטֵף צְדָקָה׃ (23) כִּי כָלָה
destruction for (23) righteousness overwhelming being-decreed destruction

וְנֶחֱרָצָה אֲדֹנָי יְהוִה צְבָאוֹת עֹשֶׂה בְּקֶרֶב
in-midst-of one-carrying-out Hosts Yahweh-of Lord and-one-being-decreed

כָּל־ הָאָרֶץ׃ (24) לָכֵן כֹּה־ אָמַר אֲדֹנָי יְהוִה צְבָאוֹת אַל־
not Hosts Yahweh-of Lord he-says this therefore (24) the-land whole-of

תִּירָא עַמִּי יֹשֵׁב צִיּוֹן מֵאַשּׁוּר בַּשֵּׁבֶט
with-the-rod of-Assyrian Zion one-living-of people-of-me you-be-afraid

יַכֶּכָּה וּמַטֵּהוּ יִשָּׂא־ עָלֶיךָ בְּדֶרֶךְ מִצְרָיִם׃
Egypt as-way-of against-you he-lifts-up and-club-of-him he-beats-you

(25) כִּי־ עוֹד מְעַט מִזְעָר וְכָלָה זַעַם וְאַפִּי עַל־
to and-wrath-of-me anger and-he-will-end little few-of yet for (25)

תַּבְלִיתָם׃ (26) וְעוֹרֵר עָלָיו יְהוָה צְבָאוֹת שׁוֹט
whip Hosts Yahweh-of against-him and-he-will-lash (26) destruction-of-them

כְּמַכַּת מִדְיָן בְּצוּר עוֹרֵב וּמַטֵּהוּ עַל־ הַיָּם
the-water over and-staff-of-him Oreb at-Rock-of Midian as-striking-down-of

וּנְשָׂאוֹ בְּדֶרֶךְ מִצְרָיִם׃ (27) וְהָיָה בַּיּוֹם
in-the-day and-he-will-be (27) Egypt as-way-of also-he-will-raise-him

הַהוּא יָסוּר סֻבֳּלוֹ מֵעַל שִׁכְמֶךָ
shoulder-of-you from-on burden-of-him he-will-be-lifted the-that

וְעֻלּוֹ מֵעַל צַוָּארֶךָ וְחֻבַּל עֹל מִפְּנֵי־
because-of yoke and-he-will-be-broken neck-of-you from-on and-yoke-of-him

שָׁמֶן׃ (28) בָּא עַל־ עַיַּת עָבַר בְּמִגְרוֹן לְמִכְמָשׂ
at-Micmash through-Migron he-passes-through Aiath into he-enters (28) fat

יַפְקִיד כֵּלָיו׃ (29) עָבְרוּ מַעְבָּרָה גֶּבַע מָלוֹן לָנוּ
for-us camp Geba pass they-go-over (29) supplies-of-him he-stores

חָרְדָה הָרָמָה גִּבְעַת שָׁאוּל נָסָה׃ (30) צַהֲלִי קוֹלֵךְ
voice-of-you cry-out! (30) she-flees Saul Gibeah-of the-Ramah she-trembles

בַּת־ גַּלִּים הַקְשִׁיבִי לַיְשָׁה עֲנִיָּה עֲנָתוֹת׃ (31) נָדְדָה מַדְמֵנָה
Madmenah she-flees (31) Anathoth poor Laishah listen! Gallim daughter-of

יֹשְׁבֵי הַגֵּבִים הֵעִיזוּ׃ (32) עוֹד הַיּוֹם בְּנֹב לַעֲמֹד
to-halt at-Nob the-day yet (32) they-take-cover the-Gebim ones-living-of

יְנֹפֵף יָדוֹ הַר בֵּית־ צִיּוֹן גִּבְעַת יְרוּשָׁלִָם׃
Jerusalem hill-of Zion Daughter-of mount-of fist-of-him he-will-shake

[21]A remnant will return,[c] a
remnant of Jacob
will return to the Mighty
God.
[22]Though your people, O Israel,
be like the sand by the
sea,
only a remnant will return.
Destruction has been decreed,
overwhelming and
righteous.
[23]The Lord, the LORD Almighty,
will carry out
the destruction decreed
upon the whole land.

[24]Therefore, this is what the Lord, the LORD Almighty, says:
"O my people who live in
Zion,
do not be afraid of the
Assyrians,
who beat you with a rod
and lift up a club against
you, as Egypt did.
[25]Very soon my anger against
you will end
and my wrath will be
directed to their
destruction."

[26]The LORD Almighty will lash
them with a whip,
as when he struck down
Midian at the rock of
Oreb;
and he will raise his staff over
the waters,
as he did in Egypt.
[27]In that day their burden will
be lifted from your
shoulders,
their yoke from your neck;
the yoke will be broken
because you have grown so
fat.[d]

[28]They enter Aiath;
they pass through Migron;
they store supplies at
Micmash.
[29]They go over the pass, and
say,
"We will camp overnight at
Geba."
Ramah trembles;
Gibeah of Saul flees.
[30]Cry out, O Daughter of Gallim!
Listen, O Laishah!
Poor Anathoth!
[31]Madmenah is in flight;
the people of Gebim take
cover.
[32]This day they will halt at Nob;
they will shake their fist
at the mount of the Daughter
of Zion,
at the hill of Jerusalem.

c21 Hebrew *shear-jashub;* also in verse 22
d27 Hebrew; Septuagint *broken / from your shoulders*

°32 בת ק

הִנֵּה הָאָדוֹן יְהוָה צְבָאוֹת מְסָעֵף פֻּארָה בְּמַעֲרָצָה
with-great-power bough lopping-off Hosts Yahweh-of the-Lord see! (33)

וְרָמֵי הַקּוֹמָה גְּדוּעִים וְהַגְּבֹהִים
and-the-tall-ones ones-being-felled the-height and-ones-being-lofty-of

יִשְׁפָּלוּ׃ וְנִקַּף סִבְכֵי הַיַּעַר
the-forest thickets-of and-he-will-cut-down (34) they-will-be-brought-low

בַּבַּרְזֶל וְהַלְּבָנוֹן בְּאַדִּיר יִפּוֹל׃
he-will-fall before-Mighty-One and-the-Lebanon with-the-ax

וְיָצָא חֹטֶר מִגֵּזַע יִשָׁי וְנֵצֶר
and-branch Jesse from-stump-of shoot and-he-will-come-up (11:1)

מִשָּׁרָשָׁיו יִפְרֶה׃ וְנָחָה עָלָיו רוּחַ
Spirit-of on-him and-she-will-rest (2) he-will-bear-fruit from-roots-of-him

יְהוָה רוּחַ חָכְמָה וּבִינָה רוּחַ עֵצָה וּגְבוּרָה
and-power counsel Spirit-of and-understanding wisdom Spirit-of Yahweh

רוּחַ דַּעַת וְיִרְאַת יְהוָה׃ וַהֲרִיחוֹ בְּיִרְאַת
in-fear-of and-to-delight-him (3) Yahweh and-fear-of knowledge Spirit-of

יְהוָה וְלֹא־ לְמַרְאֵה עֵינָיו יִשְׁפּוֹט וְלֹא־ לְמִשְׁמַע
by-hearing-of and-not he-will-judge eyes-of-him by-seeing-of and-not Yahweh

אָזְנָיו יוֹכִיחַ׃ וְשָׁפַט בְּצֶדֶק
with-righteousness but-he-will-judge (4) he-will-decide ears-of-him

דַּלִּים וְהוֹכִיחַ בְּמִישׁוֹר לְעַנְוֵי־ אָרֶץ
earth for-poor-ones-of with-justice and-he-will-decide needy-ones

וְהִכָּה־ אֶרֶץ בְּשֵׁבֶט פִּיו וּבְרוּחַ
and-with-breath-of mouth-of-him with-rod-of earth and-he-will-strike

שְׂפָתָיו יָמִית רָשָׁע׃ וְהָיָה צֶדֶק אֵזוֹר
belt-of righteousness and-he-will-be (5) wicked he-will-slay lips-of-him

מָתְנָיו וְהָאֱמוּנָה אֵזוֹר חֲלָצָיו׃ וְגָר
and-he-will-live (6) waists-of-him sash-of and-the-faithfulness loins-of-him

זְאֵב עִם־ כֶּבֶשׂ וְנָמֵר עִם־ גְּדִי יִרְבָּץ וְעֵגֶל וּכְפִיר
and-lion and-calf he-will-lie-down goat with and-leopard lamb with wolf

וּמְרִיא יַחְדָּו וְנַעַר קָטֹן נֹהֵג בָּם׃ וּפָרָה וָדֹב
and-bear and-cow (7) to-them leading little and-child together and-yearling

תִּרְעֶינָה יַחְדָּו יִרְבְּצוּ יַלְדֵיהֶן וְאַרְיֵה
and-lion young-ones-of-them they-will-lie-down together they-will-feed

כַּבָּקָר יֹאכַל־ תֶּבֶן׃ וְשִׁעֲשַׁע יוֹנֵק עַל־
near one-being-infant and-he-will-play (8) straw he-will-eat like-the-ox

חֻר פָּתֶן וְעַל מְאוּרַת צִפְעוֹנִי גָּמוּל יָדוֹ
hand-of-him one-being-young-child viper nest-of and-into cobra hole-of

33 See, the Lord, the LORD
Almighty,
will lop off the boughs with
great power.
The lofty trees will be felled,
the tall ones will be brought
low.
34 He will cut down the forest
thickets with an ax;
Lebanon will fall before the
Mighty One.

*The Branch From Jesse*

11 A shoot will come up
from the stump of Jesse;
from his roots a Branch will
bear fruit.
2 The Spirit of the LORD will rest
on him—
the Spirit of wisdom and of
understanding,
the Spirit of counsel and of
power,
the Spirit of knowledge and
of the fear of the LORD—
3 and he will delight in the fear
of the LORD.

He will not judge by what he
sees with his eyes,
or decide by what he hears
with his ears;
4 but with righteousness he will
judge the needy,
with justice he will give
decisions for the poor of
the earth.
He will strike the earth with
the rod of his mouth;
with the breath of his lips
he will slay the wicked.
5 Righteousness will be his belt
and faithfulness the sash
around his waist.

6 The wolf will live with the
lamb,
the leopard will lie down
with the goat,
the calf and the lion and the
yearling[e] together;
and a little child will lead
them.
7 The cow will feed with the
bear,
their young will lie down
together,
and the lion will eat straw
like the ox.
8 The infant will play near the
hole of the cobra,
and the young child put his

[e]6 Hebrew; Septuagint *lion will feed*

הָדָה׃ (9) לֹא־ יָרֵעוּ וְלֹא־ יַשְׁחִיתוּ בְּכָל־
he-will-put (9) not they-will-harm and-not they-will-destroy on-all-of

הַר קָדְשִׁי כִּי־ מָלְאָה הָאָרֶץ דֵּעָה אֶת־
mountain-of holiness-of-me for she-will-be-full the-earth knowledge ***

יְהוָה כַּמַּיִם לַיָּם מְכַסִּים׃ (10) וְהָיָה בַּיּוֹם
Yahweh as-the-waters to-the-sea ones-covering (10) and-he-will-be in-the-day

הַהוּא שֹׁרֶשׁ יִשַׁי אֲשֶׁר עֹמֵד לְנֵס עַמִּים אֵלָיו
the-that Root-of Jesse that one-standing as-banner-of peoples to-him

גּוֹיִם יִדְרֹשׁוּ וְהָיְתָה מְנֻחָתוֹ כָּבוֹד׃
nations they-will-rally and-she-will-be resting-place-of-him glory

(11) וְהָיָה בַּיּוֹם הַהוּא יוֹסִיף אֲדֹנָי שֵׁנִית
(11) and-he-will-be in-the-day the-that he-will-do-again Lord second-time

יָדוֹ לִקְנוֹת אֶת־ שְׁאָר עַמּוֹ אֲשֶׁר יִשָּׁאֵר
hand-of-him to-reclaim *** remnant-of people-of-him that he-is-left

מֵאַשּׁוּר וּמִמִּצְרַיִם וּמִפַּתְרוֹס וּמִכּוּשׁ וּמֵעֵילָם
from-Assyria and-from-Egypt and-from-Pathros and-from-Cush and-from-Elam

וּמִשִּׁנְעָר וּמֵחֲמָת וּמֵאִיֵּי הַיָּם׃
and-from-Shinar and-from-Hamath and-from-islands-of the-sea

(12) וְנָשָׂא נֵס לַגּוֹיִם וְאָסַף
(12) and-he-will-raise banner for-the-nations and-he-will-gather

נִדְחֵי יִשְׂרָאֵל וּנְפֻצוֹת יְהוּדָה יְקַבֵּץ
ones-being-exiled-of Israel and-ones-being-scattered-of Judah he-will-assemble

מֵאַרְבַּע כַּנְפוֹת הָאָרֶץ׃ (13) וְסָרָה קִנְאַת
from-four-of quarters-of the-earth (13) and-she-will-vanish jealousy-of

אֶפְרַיִם וְצֹרְרֵי יְהוּדָה יִכָּרֵתוּ אֶפְרַיִם לֹא־
Ephraim and-ones-being-enemies-of Judah they-will-be-cut-off Ephraim not

יְקַנֵּא אֶת־ יְהוּדָה וִיהוּדָה לֹא־ יָצֹר אֶת־אֶפְרָיִם׃
he-will-be-jealous *** Judah and-Judah not he-will-be-hostile *** Ephraim

(14) וְעָפוּ בְכָתֵף פְּלִשְׁתִּים יָמָּה יַחְדָּו
(14) and-they-will-swoop on-slope-of Philistines to-west together

יָבֹזּוּ אֶת־ בְּנֵי־ קֶדֶם אֱדוֹם וּמוֹאָב מִשְׁלוֹחַ* יָדָם
they-will-plunder *** peoples-of east Edom and-Moab laying-on-of hand-of-them

וּבְנֵי עַמּוֹן מִשְׁמַעְתָּם׃ (15) וְהֶחֱרִים† יְהוָה אֵת
and-peoples-of Ammon subject-of-them (15) †and-he-will-destroy Yahweh ***

לְשׁוֹן יָם־ מִצְרַיִם וְהֵנִיף יָדוֹ עַל־ הַנָּהָר
gulf-of sea-of Egypt and-he-will-sweep hand-of-him over the-River

בַּעְיָם רוּחוֹ וְהִכָּהוּ לְשִׁבְעָה נְחָלִים
with-scorching-of wind-of-him and-he-will-break-him into-seven streams

hand into the viper's
nest.
9They will neither harm nor
destroy
on all my holy mountain,
for the earth will be full of the
knowledge of the LORD
as the waters cover the sea.

10In that day the Root of Jesse will stand as a banner for the peoples; the nations will rally to him, and his place of rest will be glorious. 11In that day the Lord will reach out his hand a second time to reclaim the remnant that is left of his people from Assyria, from Lower Egypt, from Upper Egypt,[f] from Cush,[g] from Elam, from Babylonia,[h] from Hamath and from the islands of the sea.

12He will raise a banner for the
nations
and gather the exiles of
Israel;
he will assemble the scattered
people of Judah
from the four quarters of the
earth.
13Ephraim's jealousy will vanish,
and Judah's enemies[i] will
be cut off;
Ephraim will not be jealous of
Judah,
nor Judah hostile toward
Ephraim.
14They will swoop down on the
slopes of Philistia to the
west;
together they will plunder
the people to the east.
They will lay hands on Edom
and Moab,
and the Ammonites will be
subject to them.
15The LORD will dry up
the gulf of the Egyptian sea;
with a scorching wind he will
sweep his hand
over the Euphrates River.
He will break it up into seven
streams

f11 Hebrew *from Pathros*
g11 That is, the upper Nile region
h11 Hebrew *Shinar* i13 Or *hostility*
j15 Hebrew *the River*

*14 Most mss have *furtive pathah* with the *beth* (חַ־)

†15 The NIV, with many versions, reads *beth* for *mem* (והחריב), *and-he-will-dry-up.*

וְהִדְרִיךְ בַּנְּעָלִים׃ (16) וְהָיְתָה מְסִלָּה לִשְׁאָר
so-he-can-cross in-the-sandals (16) and-she-will-be highway for-remnant-of

עַמּוֹ אֲשֶׁר יִשָּׁאֵר מֵאַשּׁוּר כַּאֲשֶׁר הָיְתָה לְיִשְׂרָאֵל
people-of-him that he-is-left from-Assyria just-as she-was for-Israel

בְּיוֹם עֲלֹתוֹ מֵאֶרֶץ מִצְרָיִם׃ (12:1) וְאָמַרְתָּ בַּיּוֹם
on-day to-come-up-him from-land-of Egypt (12:1) and-you-will-say in-the-day

הַהוּא אוֹדְךָ יְהוָה כִּי אָנַפְתָּ בִּי
the-that I-will-praise-you Yahweh although you-were-angry with-me

יָשֹׁב אַפְּךָ וּתְנַחֲמֵנִי׃ (2) הִנֵּה אֵל
he-turned-away anger-of-you and-you-comforted-me (2) surely! God

יְשׁוּעָתִי אֶבְטַח וְלֹא אֶפְחָד כִּי־ עָזִּי
salvation-of-me I-will-trust and-not I-will-be-afraid for strength-of-me

וְזִמְרָת יָהּ יְהוָה וַיְהִי־ לִי לִישׁוּעָה׃
*and-song-of Yah Yahweh and-he-became for-me as-salvation

(3) וּשְׁאַבְתֶּם־ מַיִם בְּשָׂשׂוֹן מִמַּעַיְנֵי הַיְשׁוּעָה׃
(3) and-you-will-draw waters with-joy from-wells-of the-salvation

(4) וַאֲמַרְתֶּם בַּיּוֹם הַהוּא הוֹדוּ לַיהוָה קִרְאוּ
(4) and-you-will-say in-the-day the-that give-thanks! to-Yahweh call!

בִשְׁמוֹ הוֹדִיעוּ בָעַמִּים עֲלִילֹתָיו הַזְכִּירוּ כִּי
on-name-of-him make-known! among-the-nations deeds-of-him proclaim! that

נִשְׂגָּב שְׁמוֹ׃ (5) זַמְּרוּ יְהוָה כִּי גֵאוּת עָשָׂה
being-exalted name-of-him (5) sing! Yahweh for gloriously he-did

מיּדַעַת זֹאת בְּכָל־ הָאָרֶץ׃ (6) צַהֲלִי וָרֹנִּי
being-known this to-all-of the-world (6) shout! and-sing-for-joy!

יוֹשֶׁבֶת צִיּוֹן כִּי־ גָדוֹל בְּקִרְבֵּךְ קְדוֹשׁ יִשְׂרָאֵל׃
one-dwelling-of Zion for great in-midst-of-you Holy-One-of Israel

(13:1) מַשָּׂא בָּבֶל אֲשֶׁר חָזָה יְשַׁעְיָהוּ בֶּן־ אָמוֹץ׃ (2) עַל הַר־
(13:1) oracle-of Babylon that he-saw Isaiah son-of Amoz (2) on hilltop

נִשְׁפֶּה שְׂאוּ־ נֵס הָרִימוּ קוֹל לָהֶם הָנִיפוּ יָד וְיָבֹאוּ
being-bare raise! banner raise! shout to-them beckon! hand so-they-will-enter

פִּתְחֵי נְדִיבִים׃ (3) אֲנִי צִוֵּיתִי לִמְקֻדָּשָׁי גַּם קָרָאתִי
gates-of nobles (3) I I-commanded to-ones-being-holy-of-me also I-summoned

גִבּוֹרַי לְאַפִּי עַלִּיזֵי גַּאֲוָתִי׃ (4) קוֹל
warriors-of-me for-wrath-of-me rejoicers-of triumph-of-me (4) sound-of

הֲמוֹן בֶּהָרִים דְּמוּת עַם־ רָב קוֹל שְׁאוֹן
noise on-the-mountains likeness-of multitude great sound-of uproar-of

מַמְלְכוֹת גּוֹיִם נֶאֱסָפִים יְהוָה צְבָאוֹת מְפַקֵּד צְבָא
kingdoms nations ones-massing-together Yahweh-of Hosts mustering army-of

so that men can cross over
in sandals.
16There will be a highway for
the remnant of his people
that is left from Assyria,
as there was for Israel
when they came up from
Egypt.

*Songs of Praise*

12 In that day you will say:
"I will praise you, O
LORD.
Although you were angry
with me,
your anger has turned away
and you have comforted me.
2Surely God is my salvation;
I will trust and not be
afraid.
The LORD, the LORD, is my
strength and my song;
he has become my
salvation."
3With joy you will draw water
from the wells of salvation.

4In that day you will say:
"Give thanks to the LORD, call
on his name;
make known among the
nations what he has
done,
and proclaim that his name
is exalted.
5Sing to the LORD, for he has
done glorious things;
let this be known to all the
world.
6Shout aloud and sing for joy,
people of Zion,
for great is the Holy One of
Israel among you."

*A Prophecy Against Babylon*

13 An oracle concerning Babylon that Isaiah son of
Amoz saw:

2Raise a banner on a bare
hilltop,
shout to them;
beckon to them
to enter the gates of the
nobles.
3I have commanded my holy
ones;
I have summoned my
warriors to carry out my
wrath—
those who rejoice in my
triumph.

4Listen, a noise on the
mountains,
like that of a great
multitude!
Listen, an uproar among the
kingdoms,
like nations massing
together!
The LORD Almighty is
mustering
an army for war.

***2 The NIV, with some mss and versions, reads a first person pronominal suffix (תִי), *song-of-me*.**

°5 ק מודעת

מִלְחָמָה׃ בָּאִים מֵאֶרֶץ מֶרְחָק מִקְצֵה הַשָּׁמָיִם יְהוָה
Yahweh the-heavens from-end-of faraway from-land-of ones-coming (5) war

וּכְלֵי זַעְמוֹ לְחַבֵּל כָּל־ הָאָרֶץ׃ הֵילִילוּ
wail! (6) the-country whole-of to-destroy wrath-of-him and-weapons-of

כִּי קָרוֹב יוֹם יְהוָה כְּשֹׁד מִשַּׁדַּי יָבוֹא׃
he-will-come from-Almighty like-destruction Yahweh day-of near for

עַל־ כֵּן כָּל־ יָדַיִם תִּרְפֶּינָה וְכָל־ לְבַב
heart-of and-every-of they-will-go-limp hands all-of this because-of (7)

אֱנוֹשׁ יִמָּס׃ וְנִבְהָלוּ ׀ צִירִים וַחֲבָלִים
and-anguishes pains and-they-will-be-terrified (8) he-will-melt man

יֹאחֵזוּן כַּיּוֹלֵדָה יְחִילוּן אִישׁ אֶל־
to each they-will-writhe like-the-woman-being-in-labor they-will-grip

רֵעֵהוּ יִתְמָהוּ פְּנֵי לְהָבִים פְּנֵיהֶם׃ הִנֵּה
see! (9) faces-of-them flames faces-of they-will-look-aghast other-of-him

יוֹם־ יְהוָה בָּא אַכְזָרִי וְעֶבְרָה וַחֲרוֹן אַף לָשׂוּם
to-make anger and-fierceness-of and-wrath cruel coming Yahweh day-of

הָאָרֶץ לְשַׁמָּה וְחַטָּאֶיהָ יַשְׁמִיד מִמֶּנָּה׃
from-her he-will-destroy and-sinners-of-her to-desolation the-land

כִּי־ כוֹכְבֵי הַשָּׁמַיִם וּכְסִילֵיהֶם לֹא יָהֵלּוּ
they-will-show not and-constellations-of-them the-heavens stars-of indeed (10)

אוֹרָם חָשַׁךְ הַשֶּׁמֶשׁ בְּצֵאתוֹ וְיָרֵחַ לֹא־
not and-moon when-to-rise-him the-sun he-will-be-darkened light-of-them

יַגִּיהַ* אוֹרוֹ׃ וּפָקַדְתִּי עַל־ תֵּבֵל רָעָה וְעַל־
and-to evil world to and-I-will-punish (11) light-of-him he-will-give

רְשָׁעִים עֲוֺנָם וְהִשְׁבַּתִּי גְּאוֹן זֵדִים וְגַאֲוַת
and-pride-of haughty-ones arrogance-of and-I-will-end sin-of-them wicked-ones

עָרִיצִים אַשְׁפִּיל׃ אוֹקִיר אֱנוֹשׁ מִפָּז
more-than-pure-gold man I-will-make-scarce (12) I-will-humble ruthless-ones

וְאָדָם מִכֶּתֶם אוֹפִיר׃ עַל־ כֵּן שָׁמַיִם אַרְגִּיז
I-will-make-tremble heavens this for (13) Ophir more-than-gold-of and-mankind

וְתִרְעַשׁ הָאָרֶץ מִמְּקוֹמָהּ בְּעֶבְרַת יְהוָה צְבָאוֹת
Hosts Yahweh-of at-wrath-of from-place-of-her the-earth and-she-will-shake

וּבְיוֹם חֲרוֹן אַפּוֹ׃ וְהָיָה כִּצְבִי
like-gazelle and-he-will-be (14) anger-of-him burning-of and-in-day-of

מֻדָּח וּכְצֹאן וְאֵין מְקַבֵּץ אִישׁ אֶל־ עַמּוֹ
people-of-him to each one-being-shepherd but-not and-like-sheep being-hunted

יִפְנוּ וְאִישׁ אֶל־ אַרְצוֹ יָנוּסוּ׃ כָּל־
each-of (15) they-will-flee land-of-him to and-each they-will-return

[5]They come from faraway
lands,
from the ends of the
heavens—
the LORD and the weapons of
his wrath—
to destroy the whole
country.

[6]Wail, for the day of the LORD
is near;
it will come like destruction
from the Almighty.[k]
[7]Because of this, all hands will
go limp,
every man's heart will melt.
[8]Terror will seize them,
pain and anguish will grip
them;
they will writhe like a
woman in labor.
They will look aghast at each
other,
their faces aflame.

[9]See, the day of the LORD is
coming
—a cruel day, with wrath
and fierce anger—
to make the land desolate
and destroy the sinners
within it.
[10]The stars of heaven and their
constellations
will not show their light.
The rising sun will be
darkened
and the moon will not give
its light.
[11]I will punish the world for its
evil,
the wicked for their sins.
I will put an end to the
arrogance of the haughty
and will humble the pride of
the ruthless.
[12]I will make man scarcer than
pure gold,
more rare than the gold of
Ophir.
[13]Therefore I will make the
heavens tremble;
and the earth will shake
from its place
at the wrath of the LORD
Almighty,
in the day of his burning
anger.

[14]Like a hunted gazelle,
like sheep without a
shepherd,
each will return to his own
people,
each will flee to his native
land.

k6 Hebrew *Shaddai*

*10 Most mss have *mappiq* in the *he* (הּ).

הַנִּמְצָא יִדָּקֵר וְכָל־
and-each-of he-will-be-thrust-through the-one-being-captured

הַנִּסְפֶּה יִפּוֹל בֶּחָרֶב׃ (16) וְעֹלְלֵיהֶם
and-infants-of-them (16) by-the-sword he-will-fall the-one-being-caught

יְרֻטְּשׁוּ לְעֵינֵיהֶם יִשַּׁסּוּ
they-will-be-looted before-eyes-of-them they-will-be-dashed-to-pieces

בָּתֵּיהֶם וּנְשֵׁיהֶם תִּשָּׁגַלְנָה°*׃ (17) הִנְנִי
see-I! (17) *they-will-be-ravished and-wives-of-them houses-of-them

מֵעִיר עֲלֵיהֶם אֶת־ מָדָי אֲשֶׁר־ כֶּסֶף לֹא יַחְשֹׁבוּ וְזָהָב
and-gold they-care-for not silver who Medes *** against-them stirring-up

לֹא יַחְפְּצוּ־ בוֹ׃ (18) וּקְשָׁתוֹת נְעָרִים תְּרַטַּשְׁנָה
they-will-strike-down young-men and-bows (18) in-him they-delight not

וּפְרִי־ בֶטֶן לֹא יְרַחֵמוּ עַל־ בָּנִים לֹא־
not children on they-will-show-mercy not womb and-fruit-of

תָחוּס עֵינָם׃ (19) וְהָיְתָה בָבֶל צְבִי
jewel-of Babylon and-she-will-be (19) eye-of-them she-will-have-compassion

מַמְלָכוֹת תִּפְאֶרֶת גְּאוֹן כַּשְׂדִּים כְּמַהְפֵּכַת אֱלֹהִים אֶת־ סְדֹם וְאֶת־
and Sodom *** God like-overthrow-of Chaldeans pride-of glory-of kingdoms

עֲמֹרָה׃ (20) לֹא־ תֵשֵׁב לָנֶצַח וְלֹא תִשְׁכֹּן
she-will-be-lived-in and-not to-ever she-will-be-inhabited not (20) Gomorrah

עַד־ דּוֹר וָדוֹר וְלֹא־ יַהֵל שָׁם עֲרָבִי
Arab there he-will-pitch-tent and-not and-generation generation to

וְרֹעִים לֹא־ יַרְבִּצוּ שָׁם׃ (21) וְרָבְצוּ־
but-they-will-lie (21) there they-will-make-rest not and-ones-being-shepherd

שָׁם צִיִּים וּמָלְאוּ בָתֵּיהֶם אֹחִים
jackals houses-of-them and-they-will-fill desert-creatures there

וְשָׁכְנוּ שָׁם בְּנוֹת יַעֲנָה וּשְׂעִירִים יְרַקְּדוּ־
they-will-leap-about and-wild-goats owl daughters-of there and-they-will-dwell

שָׁם׃ (22) וְעָנָה אִיִּים בְּאַלְמְנוֹתָיו† וְתַנִּים
and-jackals in-strongholds-of-him hyenas and-he-will-howl (22) there

בְּהֵיכְלֵי עֹנֶג וְקָרוֹב לָבוֹא עִתָּהּ וְיָמֶיהָ לֹא
not and-days-of-her time-of-her to-come and-at-hand luxury in-palaces-of

יִמָּשֵׁכוּ׃ (14:1) כִּי יְרַחֵם יְהוָה אֶת־
*** Yahweh he-will-have-compassion indeed (14:1) they-will-be-prolonged

יַעֲקֹב וּבָחַר עוֹד בְּיִשְׂרָאֵל וְהִנִּיחָם עַל־
in and-he-will-settle-them to-Israel again and-he-will-choose Jacob

אַדְמָתָם וְנִלְוָה הַגֵּר עֲלֵיהֶם וְנִסְפְּחוּ עַל־
with and-they-will-unite with-them the-alien and-he-will-join land-of-them

15 Whoever is captured will be thrust through;
all who are caught will fall by the sword.
16 Their infants will be dashed to pieces before their eyes;
their houses will be looted and their wives ravished.

17 See, I will stir up against them the Medes,
who do not care for silver and have no delight in gold.
18 Their bows will strike down the young men;
they will have no mercy on infants
nor will they look with compassion on children.
19 Babylon, the jewel of kingdoms,
the glory of the Babylonians'[l] pride,
will be overthrown by God like Sodom and Gomorrah.
20 She will never be inhabited or lived in through all generations;
no Arab will pitch his tent there,
no shepherd will rest his flocks there.
21 But desert creatures will lie there,
jackals will fill her houses;
there the owls will dwell,
and there the wild goats will leap about.
22 Hyenas will howl in her strongholds,
jackals in her luxurious palaces.
Her time is at hand,
and her days will not be prolonged.

14 The LORD will have compassion on Jacob;
once again he will choose Israel
and will settle them in their own land.
Aliens will join them

[l] 19 Or *Chaldeans'*

*16 The *Qere* reading is a less graphic synonym for the *Kethib reading.*

†22 Most mss have *sheva* under the *mem* (באלמְ׳).

°16 ק תשכבנה

בֵּית יַעֲקֹב׃ וּלְקָחוּם עַמִּים וֶהֱבִיאוּם

and-they-will-bring-them nations and-they-will-take-them (2) Jacob house-of

אֶל־ מְקוֹמָם וְהִתְנַחֲלוּם בֵּית־ יִשְׂרָאֵל עַל אַדְמַת

land-of in Israel house-of and-they-will-possess-them place-of-them to

יְהוָה לַעֲבָדִים וְלִשְׁפָחוֹת וְהָיוּ שֹׁבִים

ones-capturing and-they-will-be and-as-maidservants as-menservants Yahweh

לְשֹׁבֵיהֶם וְרָדוּ בְּנֹגְשֵׂיהֶם׃

over-ones-oppressing-them and-they-will-rule of-ones-capturing-of-them

וְהָיָה בְּיוֹם הָנִיחַ יְהוָה לְךָ מֵעָצְבְּךָ

from-suffering-of-you to-you Yahweh to-give-relief on-day and-he-will-be (3)

וּמֵרָגְזֶךָ וּמִן־ הָעֲבֹדָה הַקָּשָׁה אֲשֶׁר עֻבַּד־

he-was-worked which the-cruel the-bondage and-from and-from-turmoil-of-you

בָּךְ׃ וְנָשָׂאתָ הַמָּשָׁל הַזֶּה עַל־ מֶלֶךְ

king-of against the-this the-taunt then-you-will-take-up (4) with-you

בָּבֶל וְאָמָרְתָּ אֵיךְ שָׁבַת נֹגֵשׂ שָׁבְתָה מַדְהֵבָה*׃

*fury she-ended one-oppressing he-ended how! and-you-will-say Babylon

שָׁבַר יְהוָה מַטֵּה רְשָׁעִים שֵׁבֶט מֹשְׁלִים׃

ones-ruling scepter-of wicked-ones rod-of Yahweh he-broke (5)

מַכֶּה עַמִּים בְּעֶבְרָה מַכַּת בִּלְתִּי סָרָה רֹדֶה

one-subduing ceasing not blow-of in-anger peoples one-striking-down (6)

בְאַף גּוֹיִם מֻרְדָּף בְּלִי חָשָׂךְ׃ נָחָה שָׁקְטָה

she-is-at-peace she-is-at-rest (7) he-relents not aggression nations in-fury

כָּל־ הָאָרֶץ פָּצְחוּ רִנָּה׃ גַּם־ בְּרוֹשִׁים שָׂמְחוּ

they-exult pine-trees even (8) singing they-break-out the-land all-of

לְךָ אַרְזֵי לְבָנוֹן מֵאָז שָׁכַבְתָּ לֹא־ יַעֲלֶה

he-comes not you-lay-low from-when Lebanon cedars-of over-you

הַכֹּרֵת עָלֵינוּ׃ שְׁאוֹל מִתַּחַת רָגְזָה לְךָ לִקְרַאת

to-meet for-you she-is-astir at-below Sheol (9) of-us the-one-cutting-down

בּוֹאֶךָ עוֹרֵר לְךָ רְפָאִים כָּל־ עַתּוּדֵי אָרֶץ

world leaders-of all-of spirits-of-departed to-you one-rousing to-come-you

הֵקִים מִכִּסְאוֹתָם כֹּל מַלְכֵי גוֹיִם׃ כֻּלָּם

all-of-them (10) nations kings-of all-of from-thrones-of-them he-makes-rise

יַעֲנוּ וְיֹאמְרוּ אֵלֶיךָ גַּם־ אַתָּה חֻלֵּיתָ כָמוֹנוּ

as-us you-became-weak you also to-you and-they-will-say they-will-respond

אֵלֵינוּ נִמְשָׁלְתָּ׃ הוּרַד שְׁאוֹל גְּאוֹנֶךָ הֶמְיַת

noise-of pomp-of-you Sheol he-was-brought-down (11) you-became-like to-us

נְבָלֶיךָ תַּחְתֶּיךָ יֻצַּע רִמָּה וּמְכַסֶּיךָ תּוֹלֵעָה׃

worm and-ones-covering-of-you maggot he-is-spread-out beneath-you harps-of-you

and unite with the house of
Jacob.
[2]Nations will take them
and bring them to their own
place.
And the house of Israel will
possess the nations
as menservants and
maidservants in the
LORD's land.
They will make captives of
their captors
and rule over their
oppressors.

[3]On the day the LORD gives you
relief from suffering and turmoil
and cruel bondage, [4]you will take
up this taunt against the king of
Babylon:

How the oppressor has come
to an end!
How his fury[m] has ended!
[5]The LORD has broken the rod
of the wicked,
the scepter of the rulers,
[6]which in anger struck down
peoples
with unceasing blows,
and in fury subdued nations
with relentless aggression.
[7]All the lands are at rest and at
peace;
they break into singing.
[8]Even the pine trees and the
cedars of Lebanon
exult over you and say,
"Now that you have been laid
low,
no woodsman comes to cut
us down."

[9]The grave[n] below is all astir
to meet you at your coming;
it rouses the spirits of the
departed to greet you—
all those who were leaders
in the world;
it makes them rise from their
thrones—
all those who were kings
over the nations.
[10]They will all respond,
they will say to you,
"You also have become weak,
as we are;
you have become like us."
[11]All your pomp has been
brought down to the
grave,
along with the noise of your
harps;
maggots are spread out
beneath you
and worms cover you.

[m]4 Dead Sea Scrolls, Septuagint and Syriac; the meaning of the word in the Masoretic Text is uncertain.
[n]9 Hebrew *Sheol*; also in verses 11 and 15

*4 The NIV, with some mss and versions, reads *resh* for *daleth* (מרהבה); see note *m* above.

אֵ֣יךְ נָפַ֣לְתָּ מִשָּׁמַ֔יִם הֵילֵ֖ל בֶּן־שָׁ֑חַר נִגְדַּ֣עְתָּ
you-were-cast-down dawn son-of morning-star from-heavens you-fell how! (12)

לָאָ֔רֶץ חוֹלֵ֖שׁ עַל־גּוֹיִֽם׃ וְאַתָּ֞ה אָמַ֣רְתָּ בִֽלְבָבְךָ֗
in-heart-of-you you-said and-you (13) nations to one-laying-low to-the-earth

הַשָּׁמַ֣יִם אֶֽעֱלֶ֔ה מִמַּ֥עַל לְכֽוֹכְבֵי־אֵ֖ל אָרִ֣ים כִּסְאִ֑י
throne-of-me I-will-raise God to-stars-of at-above I-will-ascend the-heavens

וְאֵשֵׁ֥ב בְּהַר־מוֹעֵ֖ד בְּיַרְכְּתֵ֥י צָפֽוֹן׃
Zaphon on-utmost-heights-of assembly on-mount-of and-I-will-sit

אֶֽעֱלֶ֖ה עַל־בָּ֣מֳתֵי עָ֑ב אֶדַּמֶּ֖ה לְעֶלְיֽוֹן׃
to-Most-High I-will-make-myself-like cloud tops-of above I-will-ascend (14)

אַ֧ךְ אֶל־שְׁא֛וֹל תּוּרָ֖ד אֶל־יַרְכְּתֵי־בֽוֹר׃ רֹאֶ֙יךָ֙
ones-seing-you (16) pit depths-of to you-are-brought-down Sheol to but (15)

אֵלֶ֣יךָ יַשְׁגִּ֔יחוּ אֵלֶ֖יךָ יִתְבּוֹנָ֑נוּ הֲזֶ֤ה הָאִישׁ֙ מַרְגִּ֣יז הָאָ֔רֶץ
the-earth one-shaking the-man this? they-ponder about-you they-stare at-you

מַרְעִ֖ישׁ מַמְלָכֽוֹת׃ שָׂ֥ם תֵּבֵ֛ל כַּמִּדְבָּ֖ר
as-the-desert world one-making (17) kingdoms one-making-tremble

וְעָרָ֣יו הָרָ֑ס אֲסִירָ֖יו לֹא־פָ֥תַח בָּֽיְתָה׃
to-home he-let-go not captives-of-him he-overthrew and-cities-of-him

כָּל־מַלְכֵ֥י גוֹיִ֖ם כֻּלָּ֑ם שָׁכְב֥וּ בְכָב֖וֹד אִ֥ישׁ בְּבֵיתֽוֹ׃
in-tomb-of-him each in-glory they-lie all-of-them nations kings-of all-of (18)

וְאַתָּ֞ה הָשְׁלַ֤כְתָּ מִֽקִּבְרְךָ֙ כְּנֵ֣צֶר נִתְעָ֔ב
being-rejected like-branch of-tomb-of-you you-are-cast-out but-you (19)

לְב֣וּשׁ הֲרֻגִ֔ים מְטֹ֣עֲנֵי חָ֑רֶב יוֹרְדֵ֥י
ones-descending-of sword ones-being-pierced-of ones-being-slain covered-of

אֶל־אַבְנֵי־ב֖וֹר כְּפֶ֥גֶר מוּבָֽס׃ לֹא־תֵחַ֤ד
you-will-join not (20) being-trampled like-corpse pit stones-of to

אִתָּם֙ בִּקְבוּרָ֔ה כִּֽי־אַרְצְךָ֥ שִׁחַ֖תָּ עַמְּךָ֣ הָרָ֑גְתָּ
you-killed people-of-you you-destroyed land-of-you for in-burial with-them

לֹֽא־יִקָּרֵ֥א לְעוֹלָ֖ם זֶ֥רַע מְרֵעִֽים׃
ones-being-wicked offspring-of to-forever he-will-be-mentioned not

הָכִ֧ינוּ לְבָנָ֛יו מַטְבֵּ֖חַ בַּעֲוֺ֣ן אֲבוֹתָ֑ם
forefathers-of-them for-sin-of slaughtering-place for-sons-of-him prepare! (21)

בַּל־יָקֻ֙מוּ֙ וְיָ֣רְשׁוּ אָ֔רֶץ וּמָלְא֥וּ פְנֵֽי־
surfaces-of and-they-will-cover land so-they-will-inherit they-will-rise not

תֵבֵ֖ל עָרִֽים׃ וְקַמְתִּ֣י עֲלֵיהֶ֔ם נְאֻ֖ם יְהוָ֣ה
Yahweh-of declaration-of against-them now-I-will-rise-up (22) cities earth

צְבָא֑וֹת וְהִכְרַתִּ֨י לְבָבֶ֜ל שֵׁ֤ם וּשְׁאָר֙ וְנִ֣ין
and-offspring and-survivor name from-Babylon and-I-will-cut-off Hosts

12 How you have fallen from
heaven,
O morning star, son of the
dawn!
You have been cast down to
the earth,
you who once laid low the
nations!
13 You said in your heart,
"I will ascend to heaven;
I will raise my throne
above the stars of God;
I will sit enthroned on the
mount of assembly,
on the utmost heights of the
sacred mountain.[o]
14 I will ascend above the tops of
the clouds;
I will make myself like the
Most High."
15 But you are brought down to
the grave,
to the depths of the pit.
16 Those who see you stare at
you,
they ponder your fate:
"Is this the man who shook
the earth
and made kingdoms
tremble,
17 the man who made the world
a desert,
who overthrew its cities
and would not let his
captives go home?"
18 All the kings of the nations lie
in state,
each in his own tomb.
19 But you are cast out of your
tomb
like a rejected branch;
you are covered with the slain,
with those pierced by the
sword,
those who descend to the
stones of the pit.
Like a corpse trampled
underfoot,
20 you will not join them in
burial,
for you have destroyed your
land
and killed your people.

The offspring of the wicked
will never be mentioned
again.
21 Prepare a place to slaughter his
sons
for the sins of their
forefathers;
they are not to rise to inherit
the land
and cover the earth with
their cities.
22 "I will rise up against them,"
declares the LORD Almighty.
"I will cut off from Babylon
her name and survivors,
her offspring and

[o]13 Or *the north;* Hebrew *Zaphon*

| | | | | | |
|---|---|---|---|---|---|
| לְמוֹרַשׁ | וְשַׂמְתִּיהָ | | יְהוָה׃ | נְאֻם־ | וָנֶכֶד |
| into-place-of | and-I-will-turn-her | (23) | Yahweh | declaration-of | and-descendant |

| | | | | | |
|---|---|---|---|---|---|
| הַשְׁמֵד | בְּמַטְאֲטֵא | וְטֵאטֵאתִיהָ | מָיִם | וְאַגְמֵי־ | קִפֹּד |
| to-destroy | with-broom-of | and-I-will-sweep-her | waters | and-swamps-of | owl |

| | | | | | | | | | |
|---|---|---|---|---|---|---|---|---|---|
| לֹא | אִם־ | לֵאמֹר | צְבָאוֹת | יְהוָה | נִשְׁבַּע | | צְבָאוֹת׃ | יְהוָה | נְאֻם |
| not | if | to-say | Hosts | Yahweh-of | he-swore | (24) | Hosts | Yahweh-of | declaration-of |

| | | | | | | | |
|---|---|---|---|---|---|---|---|
| תָקוּם׃ | הִיא | יָעַצְתִּי | וְכַאֲשֶׁר | הָיָתָה | כֵּן | דִּמִּיתִי | כַּאֲשֶׁר |
| she-will-stand | that | I-purposed | and-just-as | she-will-be | so | I-planned | just-as |

| | | | | | |
|---|---|---|---|---|---|
| הָרַי | וְעַל־ | בְּאַרְצִי | אַשּׁוּר | לִשְׁבֹּר | |
| mountains-of-me | and-on | in-land-of-me | Assyrian | to-crush | (25) |

| | | | |
|---|---|---|---|
| עֻלּוֹ | מֵעֲלֵיהֶם | וְסָר | אֲבוּסֶנּוּ |
| yoke-of-him | from-upon-them | and-he-will-be-taken | I-will-trample-him |

| | | | | | |
|---|---|---|---|---|---|
| זֹאת | | יָסוּר׃ | שִׁכְמוֹ | מֵעַל | וְסֻבֳּלוֹ |
| this | (26) | he-will-be-removed | shoulder-of-him | from-upon | and-burden-of-him |

| | | | | | | |
|---|---|---|---|---|---|---|
| הַיָּד | וְזֹאת | הָאָרֶץ | כָּל־ | עַל־ | הַיְּעוּצָה | הָעֵצָה |
| the-hand | and-this | the-world | whole-of | for | the-one-being-determined | the-plan |

| | | | | | | | |
|---|---|---|---|---|---|---|---|
| צְבָאוֹת | יְהוָה | כִּי־ | | הַגּוֹיִם׃ | כָּל־ | עַל־ | הַנְּטוּיָה |
| Hosts | Yahweh-of | for | (27) | the-nations | all-of | over | the-one-being-stretched |

| | | | | |
|---|---|---|---|---|
| הַנְּטוּיָה | וְיָדוֹ | יָפֵר | וּמִי | יָעָץ |
| the-one-being-stretched | and-hand-of-him | he-can-thwart | and-who? | he-purposed |

| | | | | | | |
|---|---|---|---|---|---|---|
| אָחָז | הַמֶּלֶךְ | מוֹת | בִּשְׁנַת־ | | יְשִׁיבֶנָּה׃ | וּמִי |
| Ahaz | the-king | death-of | in-year-of | (28) | he-can-turn-back-her | and-who? |

| | | | | | | | | |
|---|---|---|---|---|---|---|---|---|
| כִּי | כֻּלֵּךְ | פְלֶשֶׁת | תִּשְׂמְחִי | אַל־ | | הַזֶּה׃ | הַמַּשָּׂא | הָיָה |
| that | all-of-you | Philistia | you-rejoice | not | (29) | the-this | the-oracle | he-came |

| | | | | | | |
|---|---|---|---|---|---|---|
| יֵצֵא | נָחָשׁ | מִשֹּׁרֶשׁ | כִּי־ | מַכֵּךְ | שֵׁבֶט | נִשְׁבַּר |
| he-will-spring-up | snake | from-root-of | for | striking-of-you | rod-of | he-is-broken |

| | | | | | |
|---|---|---|---|---|---|
| וְרָעוּ | | מְעוֹפֵף׃ | שָׂרָף | וּפִרְיוֹ | צֶפַע |
| and-they-will-find-pasture | (30) | darting | venomous-serpent | and-fruit-of-him | viper |

| | | | | |
|---|---|---|---|---|
| יִרְבָּצוּ | לָבֶטַח | וְאֶבְיוֹנִים | דַלִּים | בְּכוֹרֵי |
| they-will-lie-down | in-safety | and-needy-ones | poor-ones | first-ones-of |

| | | | |
|---|---|---|---|
| וּשְׁאֵרִיתֵךְ | שָׁרְשֵׁךְ | בָרָעָב | וְהֵמַתִּי |
| and-survivor-of-you | root-of-you | by-the-famine | but-I-will-destroy |

| | | | | | | | | |
|---|---|---|---|---|---|---|---|---|
| כֻּלֵּךְ | פְּלֶשֶׁת | נָמוֹג | עִיר | זַעֲקִי־ | שַׁעַר | הֵילִילִי | | יַהֲרֹג׃ |
| all-of-you | Philistia | to-melt-away | city | howl! | gate | wail! | (31) | he-will-slay |

| | | | | | | |
|---|---|---|---|---|---|---|
| בְּמוֹעָדָיו׃ | בּוֹדֵד | וְאֵין | בָּא | עָשָׁן | מִצָּפוֹן | כִּי |
| in-ranks-of-him | one-straggling | and-there-is-not | coming | smoke | from-north | for |

| | | | | | | | |
|---|---|---|---|---|---|---|---|
| יִסַּד | יְהוָה | כִּי | גוֹי | מַלְאֲכֵי־ | יַעֲנֶה | וּמַה־ | |
| he-established | Yahweh | that | nation | envoys-of | shall-he-answer | and-what? | (32) |

descendants,"
declares the LORD.
23 "I will turn her into a place for owls
and into swampland;
I will sweep her with the broom of destruction,"
declares the LORD Almighty.

*A Prophecy Against Assyria*

24 The LORD Almighty has sworn,
"Surely, as I have planned, so it will be,
and as I have purposed, so it will stand.
25 I will crush the Assyrian in my land;
on my mountains I will trample him down.
His yoke will be taken from my people,
and his burden removed from their shoulders."
26 This is the plan determined for the whole world;
this is the hand stretched out over all nations.
27 For the LORD Almighty has purposed, and who can thwart him?
His hand is stretched out, and who can turn it back?

*A Prophecy Against the Philistines*

28 This oracle came in the year King Ahaz died:

29 Do not rejoice, all you Philistines,
that the rod that struck you is broken;
from the root of that snake will spring up a viper,
its fruit will be a darting, venomous serpent.
30 The poorest of the poor will find pasture,
and the needy will lie down in safety.
But your root I will destroy by famine;
it will slay your survivors.
31 Wail, O gate! Howl, O city!
Melt away, all you Philistines!
A cloud of smoke comes from the north,
and there is not a straggler in its ranks.
32 What answer shall be given to the envoys of that nation?
"The LORD has established

| עַמּוֹ׃ | עֲנִיֵּי | יֶחֱסוּ | וּבָהּ | צִיּוֹן |
|---|---|---|---|---|
| people-of-him | afflicted-ones-of | they-will-find-refuge | and-in-her | Zion |

| מוֹאָב | עָר | שֻׁדַּד | בְּלֵיל | כִּי | מוֹאָב | מַשָּׂא | |
|---|---|---|---|---|---|---|---|
| Moab | Ar-of | he-is-destroyed | in-night | indeed | Moab | oracle-of | (15:1) |

| נִדְמָה׃ | מוֹאָב | קִיר־ | שֻׁדַּד | בְּלֵיל | כִּי | נִדְמָה |
|---|---|---|---|---|---|---|
| he-is-ruined | Moab | Kir-of | he-is-destroyed | in-night | indeed | he-is-ruined |

| עַל־ | לְבֶכִי | הַבָּמוֹת | וְדִיבֹן | הַבַּיִת | עָלָה | |
|---|---|---|---|---|---|---|
| over | for-weeping | the-high-places | indeed-Dibon | the-temple | he-goes-up | (2) |

| קָרְחָה | רֹאשָׁיו | בְּכָל־ | יְיֵלִיל | מוֹאָב | מֵידְבָא | וְעַל | נְבוֹ |
|---|---|---|---|---|---|---|---|
| shaving | heads-of-him | on-all-of | he-wails | Moab | Medeba | and-over | Nebo |

| עַל | שָׂק | חָגְרוּ | בְּחוּצֹתָיו | | גְּרוּעָה׃ | זָקָן | כָּל־ |
|---|---|---|---|---|---|---|---|
| on | sackcloth | they-wear | in-streets-of-him | (3) | being-cut-off | beard | every-of |

| יֹרֵד | יְיֵלִיל | כֻּלֹּה | וּבִרְחֹבֹתֶיהָ | גַּגּוֹתֶיהָ |
|---|---|---|---|---|
| being-prostrate | he-wails | all-of-him | and-in-public-squares-of-her | roofs-of-her |

| יָהַץ | עַד־ | וְאֶלְעָלֵה | חֶשְׁבּוֹן | וַתִּזְעַק | | בַּבֶּכִי׃ |
|---|---|---|---|---|---|---|
| Jahaz | as-far-as | and-Elealeh | Heshbon | and-she-cries-out | (4) | with-the-weeping |

| יָרִיעוּ | מוֹאָב | חֲלֻצֵי | כֵּן | עַל־ | קוֹלָם | נִשְׁמַע |
|---|---|---|---|---|---|---|
| they-cry-out | Moab | men-being-armed-of | this | for | voice-of-them | he-is-heard |

| יִזְעָק | לְמוֹאָב | לִבִּי | | לוֹ׃ | יָרְעָה | נַפְשׁוֹ |
|---|---|---|---|---|---|---|
| he-cries-out | over-Moab | heart-of-me | (5) | in-him | she-is-faint | heart-of-him |

| מַעֲלֵה | כִּי | שְׁלִשִׁיָּה | עֶגְלַת | צֹעַר | עַד־ | בְּרִיחֶהָ |
|---|---|---|---|---|---|---|
| way-up-of | indeed | Shelishiyah | Eglath | Zoar | as-far-as | fugitives-of-her |

| חוֹרֹנַיִם | דֶּרֶךְ | כִּי | בוֹ | יַעֲלֶה־ | בִּבְכִי | הַלּוּחִית |
|---|---|---|---|---|---|---|
| Horonaim | road-of | indeed | on-him | he-goes-up | with-weeping | the-Luhith |

| מְשַׁמּוֹת | נִמְרִים | מֵי | כִּי־ | | יְעֹעֵרוּ׃ | שֶׁבֶר | זַעֲקַת־ |
|---|---|---|---|---|---|---|---|
| ones-dried | Nimrim | waters-of | indeed | (6) | they-raise | destruction | lamentation-of |

| הָיָה׃ | לֹא | יֶרֶק | דֶשֶׁא | כָּלָה | חָצִיר | יָבֵשׁ | כִּי־ | יִהְיוּ |
|---|---|---|---|---|---|---|---|---|
| he-is | not | green | vegetation | he-is-gone | grass | he-is-withered | indeed | they-are |

| נַחַל | עַל | וּפְקֻדָּתָם | עָשָׂה | יִתְרָה | כֵּן | עַל־ | |
|---|---|---|---|---|---|---|---|
| Ravine-of | over | and-storage-of-them | he-acquired | wealth | this | for | (7) |

| אֶת־ | הַזְּעָקָה | הִקִּיפָה | כִּי־ | | יִשָּׂאוּם׃ | הָעֲרָבִים |
|---|---|---|---|---|---|---|
| *** | the-outcry | she-echoes | indeed | (8) | they-carry-away-them | the-Poplars |

| אֵילִים | וּבְאֵר | יִלְלָתָהּ | אֶגְלַיִם | עַד־ | מוֹאָב | גְּבוּל |
|---|---|---|---|---|---|---|
| Elim | and-Beer | wailing-of-her | Eglaim | as-far-as | Moab | border-of |

| כִּי־ | דָם | מָלְאוּ | דִימוֹן | מֵי | כִּי | | יִלְלָתָהּ׃ |
|---|---|---|---|---|---|---|---|
| but | blood | they-are-full | Dimon | waters-of | indeed | (9) | lamentation-of-her |

| אַרְיֵה | מוֹאָב | לִפְלֵיטַת | נוֹסָפוֹת | דִּימוֹן | עַל־ | אָשִׁית |
|---|---|---|---|---|---|---|
| lion | Moab | upon-fugitive-of | ones-being-more | Dimon | upon | I-will-bring |

Zion,
and in her his afflicted
people will find refuge."

### *A Prophecy Against Moab*

15 An oracle concerning Moab:

Ar in Moab is ruined,
destroyed in a night!
Kir in Moab is ruined,
destroyed in a night!
2 Dibon goes up to its temple,
to its high places to weep;
Moab wails over Nebo and
Medeba.
Every head is shaved
and every beard cut off.
3 In the streets they wear
sackcloth;
on the roofs and in the
public squares
they all wail,
prostrate with weeping.
4 Heshbon and Elealeh cry out,
their voices are heard all the
way to Jahaz.
Therefore the armed men of
Moab cry out,
and their hearts are faint.

5 My heart cries out over Moab;
her fugitives flee as far as
Zoar,
as far as Eglath Shelishiyah.
They go up the way to Luhith,
weeping as they go;
on the road to Horonaim
they lament their
destruction.
6 The waters of Nimrim are
dried up
and the grass is withered;
the vegetation is gone
and nothing green is left.
7 So the wealth they have
acquired and stored up
they carry away over the
Ravine of the Poplars.
8 Their outcry echoes along the
border of Moab;
their wailing reaches as far
as Eglaim,
their lamentation as far as
Beer Elim.
9 Dimon's[p] waters are full of
blood,
but I will bring still more
upon Dimon[p]—
a lion upon the fugitives of
Moab

[p]9 Masoretic Text; Dead Sea Scrolls, some Septuagint manuscripts and Vulgate *Dibon*

וְלִשְׁאֵרִית אֲדָמָה׃ שִׁלְחוּ־כַר מֹשֵׁל־אֶרֶץ מִסֶּלַע
from-Sela land one-ruling-of lamb send! (16:1) land and-upon-remnant-of

מִדְבָּרָה אֶל־הַר בַּת־צִיּוֹן׃ וְהָיָה כְעוֹף־
like-bird and-he-is (2) Zion Daughter-of mount-of to across-desert

נוֹדֵד קֵן מְשֻׁלָּח תִּהְיֶינָה בְּנוֹת מוֹאָב מַעְבָּרֹת לְאַרְנוֹן׃
of-Arnon fords Moab women-of they-are one-being-pushed-out nest fluttering

הָבִיאוּ עֵצָה עֲשׂוּ פְלִילָה שִׁיתִי כַלַּיִל צִלֵּךְ
shadow-of-you like-the-night make! decision render! counsel give! (3)

בְּתוֹךְ צָהֳרָיִם סַתְּרִי נִדָּחִים נֹדֵד אַל־
not one-being-refugee ones-being-fugitives hide! noon at-midst-of

תְּגַלִּי׃ יָגוּרוּ בָךְ נִדָּחַי* מוֹאָב הֱוִי־
be! Moab *ones-being-fugitives-of-me with-you let-them-stay (4) you-betray

סֵתֶר לָמוֹ מִפְּנֵי שׁוֹדֵד כִּי־ אָפֵס
he-will-come-to-end indeed one-destroying from-before to-them shelter

הַמֵּץ כָּלָה שֹׁד תַּמּוּ רֹמֵס
one-being-aggressor they-will-vanish destruction he-will-cease the-oppressor

מִן־הָאָרֶץ׃ וְהוּכַן בַּחֶסֶד כִּסֵּא
throne in-the-love and-he-will-be-established (5) the-land from

וְיָשַׁב עָלָיו בֶּאֱמֶת בְּאֹהֶל דָּוִד שֹׁפֵט
one-judging David from-tent-of in-faithfulness on-him and-he-will-sit

וְדֹרֵשׁ מִשְׁפָּט וּמְהִר צֶדֶק׃ שָׁמַעְנוּ גְאוֹן־
pride-of we-heard (6) righteousness and-speedy-of justice and-one-seeking

מוֹאָב גֵּא מְאֹד גַּאֲוָתוֹ וּגְאוֹנוֹ וְעֶבְרָתוֹ
and-insolence-of-him and-pride-of-him conceit-of-him overweening pride Moab

לֹא־כֵן בַּדָּיו׃ לָכֵן יְיֵלִיל מוֹאָב לְמוֹאָב כֻּלֹּה יְיֵלִיל
he-wails all-of-him for-Moab Moab he-wails therefore (7) boasts-of-him so not

לַאֲשִׁישֵׁי קִיר־חֲרֶשֶׂת תֶּהְגּוּ אַךְ־נְכָאִים׃ כִּי
indeed (8) ones-grieved indeed you-lament Hareseth Kir for-raisin-cakes-of

שַׁדְמוֹת חֶשְׁבּוֹן אֻמְלַל גֶּפֶן שִׂבְמָה בַּעֲלֵי גוֹיִם הָלְמוּ
they-trampled nations rulers-of Sibmah vine-of he-withers Heshbon fields-of

שְׂרוּקֶּיהָ עַד־יַעְזֵר נָגָעוּ תָּעוּ מִדְבָּר
desert they-spread they-reached Jazer to choicest-vines-of-her

שְׁלֻחוֹתֶיהָ נִטְּשׁוּ עָבְרוּ יָם׃ עַל־כֵּן אֶבְכֶּה בִּבְכִי
as-weeping-of I-weep this for (9) sea they-went they-spread-out shoots-of-her

יַעְזֵר גֶּפֶן שִׂבְמָה אֲרַיָּוֶךְ דִּמְעָתִי חֶשְׁבּוֹן וְאֶלְעָלֵה כִּי עַל־
over for and-Elealeh Heshbon tear-of-me I-drench-you Sibmah vine-of Jazer

קֵיצֵךְ וְעַל־קְצִירֵךְ הֵידָד נָפָל׃
he-is-stilled shout-of-joy harvest-of-you and-over ripened-fruit-of-you

---

and upon those who remain
in the land.

16 Send lambs as tribute
to the ruler of the land,
from Sela, across the desert,
to the mount of the
Daughter of Zion.
2 Like fluttering birds
pushed from the nest,
so are the women of Moab
at the fords of the Arnon.

3 "Give us counsel,
render a decision.
Make your shadow like night—
at high noon.
Hide the fugitives,
do not betray the refugees.
4 Let the Moabite fugitives stay
with you;
be their shelter from the
destroyer."

The oppressor will come to an
end,
and destruction will cease;
the aggressor will vanish
from the land.
5 In love a throne will be
established;
in faithfulness a man will
sit on it—
one from the house[q] of
David—
one who in judging seeks
justice
and speeds the cause of
righteousness.

6 We have heard of Moab's
pride—
her overweening pride and
conceit,
her pride and her insolence—
but her boasts are empty.
7 Therefore the Moabites wail,
they wail together for Moab.
Lament and grieve
for the men[r] of Kir
Hareseth.
8 The fields of Heshbon wither,
the vines of Sibmah also.
The rulers of the nations
have trampled down the
choicest vines,
which once reached Jazer
and spread toward the
desert.
Their shoots spread out
and went as far as the sea.
9 So I weep, as Jazer weeps,
for the vines of Sibmah.
O Heshbon, O Elealeh,
I drench you with tears!
The shouts of joy over your
ripened fruit
and over your harvests have
been stilled.

q5 Hebrew *tent*
r7 Or *"raisin cakes,"* a wordplay

*4 Some mss and versions read *sheva* for *qamets* and *tsere* for *pathah* (נִדְּחֵי), *ones-being-fugitives-of*.

°3 ק הביאי

(10) וְנֶאֱסַף שִׂמְחָה וָגִיל מִן־ הַכַּרְמֶל וּבַכְּרָמִים
and-in-the-vineyards the-orchard from and-gladness joy and-he-is-taken (10)

לֹא־ יְרֻנָּן לֹא יְרֹעָע יַיִן בַּיְקָבִים לֹא־ יִדְרֹךְ
he-treads-out not at-the-presses wine he-shouts not he-sings not

הַדֹּרֵךְ הֵידָד הִשְׁבַּתִּי׃ (11) עַל־ כֵּן מֵעַי לְמוֹאָב
for-Moab hearts-of-me this for (11) I-put-to-end shouting the-one-treading

כַּכִּנּוֹר יֶהֱמוּ וְקִרְבִּי לְקִיר חָרֶשׂ׃
Hareseth for-Kir and-inmost-being-of-me they-lament like-the-harp

(12) וְהָיָה כִי־ נִרְאָה כִּי־ נִלְאָה מוֹאָב עַל־
at Moab he-wears-himself-out when he-appears when and-he-will-be (12)

הַבָּמָה וּבָא אֶל־ מִקְדָּשׁוֹ לְהִתְפַּלֵּל וְלֹא יוּכָל׃
he-avails then-not to-pray shrine-of-him to when-he-goes the-high-place

(13) זֶה הַדָּבָר אֲשֶׁר דִּבֶּר יְהוָה אֶל־ מוֹאָב מֵאָז׃ (14) וְעַתָּה
but-now (14) at-then Moab concerning Yahweh he-spoke that the-word this (13)

דִּבֶּר יְהוָה לֵאמֹר בְּשָׁלֹשׁ שָׁנִים כִּשְׁנֵי שָׂכִיר
contracted-servant as-years-of years within-three to-say Yahweh he-speaks

וְנִקְלָה כְּבוֹד מוֹאָב בְּכֹל הֶהָמוֹן הָרָב
the-many the-people with-all-of Moab splendor-of then-he-will-be-despised

וּשְׁאָר מְעַט מִזְעָר לוֹא כַבִּיר׃ (17:1) מַשָּׂא דַּמָּשֶׂק הִנֵּה
see! Damascus oracle-of (17:1) strong not little few-of and-survivor

דַמֶּשֶׂק מוּסָר מֵעִיר וְהָיְתָה מְעִי מַפָּלָה׃
ruin heap-of but-she-will-become from-city being-removed Damascus

(2) עֲזֻבוֹת עָרֵי עֲרֹעֵר לַעֲדָרִים תִּהְיֶינָה
they-will-be to-flocks Aroer cities-of ones-being-deserted (2)

וְרָבְצוּ וְאֵין מַחֲרִיד׃ (3) וְנִשְׁבַּת
and-he-will-disappear (3) making-afraid and-no-one and-they-will-lie-down

מִבְצָר מֵאֶפְרַיִם וּמַמְלָכָה מִדַּמֶּשֶׂק וּשְׁאָר
and-remnant-of from-Damascus and-royal-power from-Ephraim fortified-city

אֲרָם כִּכְבוֹד בְּנֵי־ יִשְׂרָאֵל יִהְיוּ נְאֻם יְהוָה צְבָאוֹת׃
Hosts Yahweh-of declaration-of they-will-be Israel sons-of like-glory-of Aram

(4) וְהָיָה בַּיּוֹם הַהוּא יִדַּל כְּבוֹד יַעֲקֹב
Jacob glory-of he-will-fade the-that in-the-day and-he-will-be (4)

וּמִשְׁמַן בְּשָׂרוֹ יֵרָזֶה׃ (5) וְהָיָה כֶּאֱסֹף
when-to-gather and-he-will-be (5) he-will-waste-away body-of-him and-fat-of

קָצִיר קָמָה וּזְרֹעוֹ שִׁבֳּלִים יִקְצוֹר וְהָיָה
and-he-will-be he-harvests grains and-arm-of-him standing-grain reaper

כִּמְלַקֵּט שִׁבֳּלִים בְּעֵמֶק רְפָאִים׃ (6) וְנִשְׁאַר־
yet-he-will-remain (6) Rephaim in-Valley-of heads-of-grain as-one-gleaning

10 Joy and gladness are taken
away from the orchards;
no one sings or shouts in
the vineyards;
no one treads out wine at the
presses,
for I have put an end to the
shouting.
11 My heart laments for Moab
like a harp,
my inmost being for Kir
Hareseth.
12 When Moab appears at her
high place,
she only wears herself out;
when she goes to her shrine to
pray,
it is to no avail.

13 This is the word the LORD has
already spoken concerning Moab.
14 But now the LORD says: "Within
three years, as a servant bound by
contract would count them,
Moab's splendor and all her many
people will be despised, and her
survivors will be very few and feeble."

*An Oracle Against Damascus*

17 An oracle concerning Damascus:

"See, Damascus will no longer
be a city
but will become a heap of
ruins.
2 The cities of Aroer will be
deserted
and left to flocks, which will
lie down,
with no one to make them
afraid.
3 The fortified city will
disappear from Ephraim,
and royal power from
Damascus;
the remnant of Aram will be
like the glory of the
Israelites,"
declares the LORD
Almighty.

4 "In that day the glory of Jacob
will fade;
the fat of his body will
waste away.
5 It will be as when a reaper
gathers the standing grain
and harvests the grain with
his arm—
as when a man gleans heads
of grain
in the Valley of Rephaim.

בּוֹ עוֹלֵלֹת כְּנֹקֶף זַיִת שְׁנַיִם שְׁלֹשָׁה גַּרְגְּרִים בְּרֹאשׁ אָמִיר
top on-top-of olives three two olive-tree as-beating-of gleanings in-him

אַרְבָּעָה חֲמִשָּׁה בִּסְעִפֶיהָ פֹּרִיָּה נְאֻם־ יְהוָה אֱלֹהֵי
God-of Yahweh declaration-of one-being-fruitful on-boughs-of-her five four

יִשְׂרָאֵל׃ בַּיּוֹם הַהוּא יִשְׁעֶה הָאָדָם עַל־ עֹשֵׂהוּ
One-Making-him to the-man he-will-look the-that in-the-day (7) Israel

וְעֵינָיו אֶל־ קְדוֹשׁ יִשְׂרָאֵל תִּרְאֶינָה׃ וְלֹא יִשְׁעֶה
he-will-look and-not (8) they-will-see Israel Holy-One-of to and-eyes-of-him

אֶל־הַמִּזְבְּחוֹת מַעֲשֵׂה יָדָיו וַאֲשֶׁר עָשׂוּ אֶצְבְּעֹתָיו לֹא
not fingers-of-him they-made and-what hands-of-him work-of the-altars to

יִרְאֶה וְהָאֲשֵׁרִים וְהַחַמָּנִים׃ בַּיּוֹם
in-the-day (9) and-the-incense-altars indeed-the-Asherah-poles he-will-regard

הַהוּא יִהְיוּ עָרֵי מָעֻזּוֹ כַּעֲזוּבַת הַחֹרֶשׁ
the-thicket like-abandoned-of strength-of-him cities-of they-will-be the-that

וְהָאָמִיר אֲשֶׁר עָזְבוּ מִפְּנֵי בְּנֵי יִשְׂרָאֵל וְהָיְתָה
and-she-will-be Israel sons-of because-of they-left that and-the-undergrowth

שְׁמָמָה׃ כִּי שָׁכַחַתְּ אֱלֹהֵי יִשְׁעֵךְ וְצוּר
and-Rock-of Salvation-of-you God-of you-forgot indeed (10) desolation

מָעֻזֵּךְ לֹא זָכָרְתְּ עַל־ כֵּן תִּטְּעִי נִטְעֵי
plants-of you-may-set-out this for you-remembered not fortress-of-you

נַעֲמָנִים וּזְמֹרַת זָר תִּזְרָעֶנּוּ׃ בְּיוֹם
on-day-of (11) you-may-plant-him one-being-imported and-vine-of finest-ones

נִטְעֵךְ תְּשַׂגְשֵׂגִי וּבַבֹּקֶר זַרְעֵךְ
planting-of-you and-on-the-morning you-may-cause-growth setting-out-of-you

תַּפְרִיחִי נֵד קָצִיר בְּיוֹם נַחֲלָה
one-being-diseased in-day-of harvest nothing you-may-bring-to-bud

וּכְאֵב אָנוּשׁ׃ הוֹי הֲמוֹן עַמִּים רַבִּים כַּהֲמוֹת
like-to-rage many nations raging-of oh! (12) one-being-incurable and-pain-of

יַמִּים יֶהֱמָיוּן וּשְׁאוֹן לְאֻמִּים כִּשְׁאוֹן מַיִם כַּבִּירִים
great-ones waters like-roar-of peoples and-uproar-of they-rage seas

יִשָּׁאוּן׃ לְאֻמִּים כִּשְׁאוֹן מַיִם רַבִּים יִשָּׁאוּן
they-roar surging-ones waters like-roar-of peoples (13) they-roar

וְגָעַר בּוֹ וְנָס מִמֶּרְחָק וְרֻדַּף
and-he-is-driven to-far-away then-he-flees to-him when-he-rebukes

כְּמֹץ הָרִים לִפְנֵי־ רוּחַ וּכְגַלְגַּל לִפְנֵי סוּפָה׃
gale before and-like-tumbleweed wind before hills like-chaff-of

לְעֵת עֶרֶב וְהִנֵּה בַלָּהָה בְּטֶרֶם בֹּקֶר אֵינֶנּוּ זֶה
this not-he morning at-before terror then-see! evening at-time-of (14)

6 Yet some gleanings will
remain,
as when an olive tree is
beaten,
leaving two or three olives on
the topmost branches,
four or five on the fruitful
boughs,"
declares the LORD, the
God of Israel.

7 In that day men will look to
their Maker
and turn their eyes to the
Holy One of Israel.
8 They will not look to the
altars,
the work of their hands,
and they will have no regard
for the Asherah poles[r]
and the incense altars their
fingers have made.

9 In that day their strong cities,
which they left because of the Israelites, will be like places abandoned to thickets and under-
growth. And all will be desolation.

10 You have forgotten God your
Savior;
you have not remembered
the Rock, your fortress.
Therefore, though you set out
the finest plants
and plant imported vines,
11 though on the day you set
them out, you make them
grow,
and on the morning when
you plant them, you
bring them to bud,
yet the harvest will be as
nothing
in the day of disease and
incurable pain.
12 Oh, the raging of many
nations—
they rage like the raging sea!
Oh, the uproar of the
peoples—
they roar like the roaring of
great waters!
13 Although the peoples roar like
the roar of surging
waters,
when he rebukes them they
flee far away,
driven before the wind like
chaff on the hills,
like tumbleweed before a
gale.
14 In the evening, sudden terror!
Before the morning, they are
gone!

[r] 8 That is, symbols of the goddess Asherah

חֵלֶק שׁוֹסֵינוּ וְגוֹרָל לְבֹזְזֵינוּ׃ הוֹי אֶרֶץ
land-of woe! (18:1) of-ones-plundering-us and-lot ones-looting-us portion-of

צִלְצַל כְּנָפָיִם אֲשֶׁר מֵעֵבֶר לְנַהֲרֵי־ כוּשׁ׃ הַשֹּׁלֵחַ
the-one-sending (2) Cush by-rivers-of at-along that wings whirring-of

בַּיָּם צִירִים וּבִכְלֵי־ גֹמֶא עַל־ פְּנֵי־ מַיִם לְכוּ ׀ מַלְאָכִים
messengers go! waters surfaces-of over papyrus and-in-boats-of envoys by-the-sea

קַלִּים אֶל־ גּוֹי מְמֻשָּׁךְ וּמוֹרָט אֶל־ עַם
people to and-one-being-smooth-skinned one-being-tall people to swift-ones

נוֹרָא מִן־ הוּא וָהָלְאָה גּוֹי קַו־ קָו וּמְבוּסָה
and-aggressive line line-of nation and-to-there here from one-being-feared

אֲשֶׁר־ בָּזְאוּ נְהָרִים אַרְצוֹ׃ כָּל־ יֹשְׁבֵי תֵבֵל
world ones-dwelling-of all-of (3) land-of-him rivers they-divide that

וְשֹׁכְנֵי אָרֶץ כִּנְשֹׂא־ נֵס הָרִים תִּרְאוּ
you-will-see mountains banner-of when-to-raise earth and-ones-living-of

וְכִתְקֹעַ שׁוֹפָר תִּשְׁמָעוּ׃ כִּי כֹה אָמַר יְהוָה אֵלַי
to-me Yahweh he-says this for (4) you-will-hear trumpet and-when-to-sound

אֶשְׁקֳוטָה וְאַבִּיטָה בִמְכוֹנִי כְּחֹם צַח
shimmering like-heat from-dwelling-of-me and-I-will-look I-will-remain-quiet

עֲלֵי־ אוֹר כְּעָב טַל בְּחֹם קָצִיר׃ כִּי־ לִפְנֵי קָצִיר
harvest before for (5) harvest in-heat-of dew like-cloud-of sunshine in

כְּתָם־ פֶּרַח וּבֹסֶר גֹּמֵל יִהְיֶה נִצָּה
flower he-becomes ripening and-grape blossom when-to-be-gone

וְכָרַת הַזַּלְזַלִּים בַּמַּזְמֵרוֹת וְאֶת־
and with-the-pruning-knives the-shoots then-he-will-cut-off

הַנְּטִישׁוֹת הֵסִיר הֵתַז׃ יֵעָזְבוּ
they-will-be-left (6) he-will-cut-down he-will-take-away the-spreading-branches

יַחְדָּו לְעֵיט הָרִים וּלְבֶהֱמַת הָאָרֶץ
the-land and-to-animal-of mountains to-bird-of-prey-of together

וְקָץ עָלָיו הָעַיִט וְכָל־ בֶּהֱמַת
animal-of and-all-of the-bird-of-prey on-him and-he-will-spend-summer

הָאָרֶץ עָלָיו תֶּחֱרָף׃ בָּעֵת הַהִיא
the-that at-the-time (7) he-will-spend-winter on-him the-land

יוּבַל־ שַׁי לַיהוָה צְבָאוֹת עַם מְמֻשָּׁךְ
one-being-tall people Hosts to-Yahweh-of gift he-will-be-brought

וּמוֹרָט וּמֵעָם נוֹרָא מִן־ הוּא
here from one-being-feared and-from-people and-one-being-smooth-skinned

וָהָלְאָה גּוֹי ׀ קַו־ קָו וּמְבוּסָה אֲשֶׁר בָּזְאוּ נְהָרִים
rivers they-divide that and-aggressive line line-of nation and-to-there

This is the portion of those
who loot us,
the lot of those who plunder
us.

*A Prophecy Against Cush*

18 Woe to the land of
whirring wings[s]
along the rivers of Cush,[t]
2 which sends envoys by sea
in papyrus boats over the
water.

Go, swift messengers,
to a people tall and
smooth-skinned,
to a people feared far and
wide,
an aggressive nation of strange
speech,
whose land is divided by
rivers.

3 All you people of the world,
you who live on the earth,
when a banner is raised on
the mountains,
you will see it,
and when a trumpet sounds,
you will hear it.
4 This is what the LORD says to
me:
"I will remain quiet and
will look on from my
dwelling place,
like shimmering heat in the
sunshine,
like a cloud of dew in the
heat of harvest."
5 For, before the harvest, when
the blossom is gone
and the flower becomes a
ripening grape,
he will cut off the shoots with
pruning knives,
and cut down and take
away the spreading
branches.
6 They will all be left to the
mountain birds of prey
and to the wild animals;
the birds will feed on them all
summer,
the wild animals all winter.

7 At that time gifts will be
brought to the LORD Almighty

from a people tall and
smooth-skinned,
from a people feared far and
wide,
an aggressive nation of strange
speech,
whose land is divided by
rivers—

[s]1 Or *of locusts*
[t]1 That is, the upper Nile region

°4 ק אשקטה

אַרְצוֹ אֶל־ מְקוֹם שֵׁם־ יְהוָה צְבָאוֹת הַר־ צִיּוֹן׃
Zion Mount-of Hosts Yahweh-of Name-of place-of to land-of-him

מַשָּׂא מִצְרָיִם הִנֵּה יְהוָה רֹכֵב עַל־ עָב קַל וּבָא
and-coming swift cloud on riding Yahweh see! Egypt oracle-of (19:1)

מִצְרַיִם וְנָעוּ אֱלִילֵי מִצְרַיִם מִפָּנָיו וּלְבַב
and-heart-of from-before-him Egypt idols-of and-they-tremble Egypt

מִצְרַיִם יִמַּס בְּקִרְבּוֹ׃ וְסִכְסַכְתִּי מִצְרַיִם
Egyptians and-I-will-stir-up (2) at-within-him he-melts Egyptians

בְּמִצְרַיִם וְנִלְחֲמוּ אִישׁ־ בְּאָחִיו
against-brother-of-him man and-they-will-fight against-Egyptians

וְאִישׁ בְּרֵעֵהוּ עִיר בְּעִיר מַמְלָכָה בְּמַמְלָכָה׃
against-kingdom kingdom against-city city against-neighbor-of-him and-man

וְנָבְקָה רוּחַ־ מִצְרַיִם בְּקִרְבּוֹ
at-within-him Egyptians heart-of and-she-will-be-lost (3)

וַעֲצָתוֹ אֲבַלֵּעַ וְדָרְשׁוּ אֶל־
with and-they-will-consult I-will-bring-to-nothing and-plan-of-him

הָאֱלִילִים וְאֶל־ הָאִטִּים וְאֶל־ הָאֹבוֹת
the-mediums and-with the-spirits-of-the-dead and-with the-idols

וְאֶל־ הַיִּדְּעֹנִים׃ וְסִכַּרְתִּי אֶת־ מִצְרַיִם בְּיַד
to-hand-of Egyptians *** and-I-will-give-over (4) the-spiritists and-with

אֲדֹנִים קָשֶׁה וּמֶלֶךְ עַז יִמְשָׁל־ בָּם נְאֻם
declaration-of over-them he-will-rule fierce and-king cruel masters

הָאָדוֹן יְהוָה צְבָאוֹת׃ וְנִשְּׁתוּ־ מַיִם מֵהַיָּם
of-the-river waters and-they-will-dry-up (5) Hosts Yahweh-of the-Lord

וְנָהָר יֶחֱרַב וְיָבֵשׁ׃ וְהֶאֶזְנִיחוּ
and-they-will-stink (6) and-he-will-be-dry he-will-be-parched and-riverbed

נְהָרוֹת דָּלְלוּ וְחָרְבוּ יְאֹרֵי מָצוֹר קָנֶה
reed Egypt streams-of and-they-will-dry-up they-will-dwindle canals

וָסוּף קָמֵלוּ׃ עָרוֹת עַל־ יְאוֹר עַל־ פִּי יְאוֹר
Nile mouth-of at Nile along plants (7) they-will-wither and-rush

וְכֹל מִזְרַע יְאוֹר יִיבַשׁ נִדַּף
he-will-blow-away he-will-become-parched Nile sown-field-of and-every-of

וְאֵינֶנּוּ׃ וְאָנוּ הַדַּיָּגִים וְאָבְלוּ
and-they-will-lament the-fishermen and-they-will-groan (8) and-no-more-he

כָּל־ מַשְׁלִיכֵי בַיְאוֹר חַכָּה וּפֹרְשֵׂי מִכְמֹרֶת
net and-ones-throwing-of hook into-the-Nile ones-casting-of all-of

עַל־ פְּנֵי־ מַיִם אֻמְלָלוּ׃ וּבֹשׁוּ
and-they-will-despair (9) they-will-pine-away waters surfaces-of on

---

the gifts will be brought to Mount Zion, the place of the Name of the LORD Almighty.

*A Prophecy About Egypt*

19 An oracle concerning Egypt:

See, the LORD rides on a swift cloud
and is coming to Egypt.
The idols of Egypt tremble before him,
and the hearts of the Egyptians melt within them.

2 "I will stir up Egyptian against Egyptian—
brother will fight against brother,
neighbor against neighbor,
city against city,
kingdom against kingdom.
3 The Egyptians will lose heart,
and I will bring their plans to nothing;
they will consult the idols and the spirits of the dead,
the mediums and the spiritists.
4 I will hand the Egyptians over
to the power of a cruel master,
and a fierce king will rule over them,"
declares the Lord, the LORD Almighty.

5 The waters of the river will dry up,
and the riverbed will be parched and dry.
6 The canals will stink;
the streams of Egypt will dwindle and dry up.
The reeds and rushes will wither,
also the plants along the Nile,
at the mouth of the river.
Every sown field along the Nile
will become parched, will blow away and be no more.
8 The fishermen will groan and lament,
all who cast hooks into the Nile;
those who throw nets on the water
will pine away.

עֹבְדֵי פִשְׁתִּים שְׂרִיקוֹת וְאֹרְגִים חוֹרָי׃
fine-linen and-ones-weaving-of combed-ones flaxes ones-working-of

וְהָיוּ שָׁתֹתֶיהָ מְדֻכָּאִים כָּל־
all-of ones-being-dejected workers-of-her and-they-will-be (10)

עֹשֵׂי שֶׂכֶר אַגְמֵי־נָפֶשׁ׃ אַךְ־אֱוִלִים שָׂרֵי
officials-of fools only (11) heart ones-sick-of wage ones-earning-of

צֹעַן חַכְמֵי יֹעֲצֵי פַרְעֹה עֵצָה נִבְעָרָה אֵיךְ
how? being-senseless advice Pharaoh ones-counseling-of wise-ones-of Zoan

תֹּאמְרוּ אֶל־פַּרְעֹה בֶּן־חֲכָמִים אֲנִי בֶּן־מַלְכֵי־קֶדֶם׃
antiquity kings-of son-of I wise-men son-of Pharaoh to can-you-say

אַיָּם אֵפוֹא חֲכָמֶיךָ וְיַגִּידוּ נָא לְךָ
to-you now! and-let-them-show wise-men-of-you now where-they? (12)

וְיֵדְעוּ* מַה־יָּעַץ יְהוָה צְבָאוֹת עַל־מִצְרָיִם׃
Egypt against Hosts Yahweh-of he-planned what *and-let-them-know

נוֹאֲלוּ שָׂרֵי צֹעַן נִשְּׁאוּ שָׂרֵי
leaders-of they-are-deceived Zoan officials-of they-became-fools (13)

נֹף הִתְעוּ אֶת־מִצְרַיִם פִּנַּת שְׁבָטֶיהָ׃ יְהוָה
Yahweh (14) peoples-of-her cornerstone-of Egypt *** they-led-astray Noph

מָסַךְ בְּקִרְבָּהּ רוּחַ עִוְעִים וְהִתְעוּ אֶת־
*** and-they-make-stagger dizzinesses spirit-of into-inside-of-her he-poured

מִצְרַיִם בְּכָל־מַעֲשֵׂהוּ כְּהִתָּעוֹת שִׁכּוֹר בְּקִיאוֹ׃ וְלֹא־
and-not (15) in-vomit-of-him drunkard as-to-stagger deed-of-him in-all-of Egypt

יִהְיֶה לְמִצְרַיִם מַעֲשֶׂה אֲשֶׁר יַעֲשֶׂה רֹאשׁ וְזָנָב כִּפָּה וְאַגְמוֹן׃
or-reed palm-branch or-tail head he-can-do that deed for-Egypt he-is

בַּיּוֹם הַהוּא יִהְיֶה מִצְרַיִם כַּנָּשִׁים וְחָרַד ׀
and-he-will-shudder like-the-women Egyptians he-will-be the-that in-the-day (16)

וּפָחַד מִפְּנֵי תְּנוּפַת יַד־יְהוָה צְבָאוֹת אֲשֶׁר־הוּא מֵנִיף
raising he that Hosts Yahweh-of hand-of uplifting-of at-before and-he-will-fear

עָלָיו׃ וְהָיְתָה אַדְמַת יְהוּדָה לְמִצְרַיִם לְחָגָּא כֹּל
everyone as-terror to-Egyptians Judah land-of and-she-will-be (17) against-him

אֲשֶׁר יַזְכִּיר אֹתָהּ אֵלָיו יִפְחָד מִפְּנֵי עֲצַת יְהוָה
Yahweh-of plan-of because-of he-will-be-terrified to-him her he-mentions whom

צְבָאוֹת אֲשֶׁר־הוּא יוֹעֵץ עָלָיו׃ בַּיּוֹם הַהוּא יִהְיוּ
they-will-be the-that in-the-day (18) against-him planning he that Hosts

חָמֵשׁ עָרִים בְּאֶרֶץ מִצְרַיִם מְדַבְּרוֹת שְׂפַת כְּנַעַן
Canaan language-of ones-speaking-of Egypt in-land-of cities five

וְנִשְׁבָּעוֹת לַיהוָה צְבָאוֹת עִיר הַהֶרֶס†
†the-Destruction City-of Hosts to-Yahweh-of and-ones-swearing-allegiance

9 Those who work with combed flax will despair,
the weavers of fine linen will lose hope.
10 The workers in cloth will be dejected,
and all the wage earners will be sick at heart.

11 The officials of Zoan are nothing but fools;
the wise counselors of Pharaoh give senseless advice.
How can you say to Pharaoh,
"I am one of the wise men,
a disciple of the ancient kings"?

12 Where are your wise men now?
Let them show you and make known
what the LORD Almighty has planned against Egypt.
13 The officials of Zoan have become fools,
the leaders of Memphis[u] are deceived;
the cornerstones of her peoples have led Egypt astray.
14 The LORD has poured into them
a spirit of dizziness;
they make Egypt stagger in all that she does,
as a drunkard staggers around in his vomit.
15 There is nothing Egypt can do—
head or tail, palm branch or reed.

16 In that day the Egyptians will be like women. They will shudder with fear at the uplifted hand that the LORD Almighty raises against them.
17 And the land of Judah will bring terror to the Egyptians; everyone to whom Judah is mentioned will be terrified, because of what the LORD Almighty is planning against them.
18 In that day five cities in Egypt will speak the language of Canaan and swear allegiance to the LORD Almighty. One of them will be called the City of Destruction.[v]

[u] 13 Hebrew *Noph*

[v] 18 Most manuscripts of the Masoretic Text; some manuscripts of the Masoretic Text, Dead Sea Scrolls and Vulgate *City of the Sun* (that is, Heliopolis)

*12 The NIV repoints this word as וְיִדְעוּ, *and-let-them-make-known*.

†18 The mss and versions listed in note *v* above read *beth* for the second *he* (הַחֶרֶס), *the-Sun*.

יֵאָמֵר לְאֶחָת׃ בַּיּוֹם הַהוּא יִהְיֶה מִזְבֵּחַ לַיהוָה
to-Yahweh altar he-will-be the-that in-the-day (19) to-one he-will-be-called

בְּתוֹךְ אֶרֶץ מִצְרָיִם וּמַצֵּבָה אֵצֶל־ גְּבוּלָהּ לַיהוָה׃
to-Yahweh border-of-her at and-monument Egypt land-of in-heart-of

וְהָיָה לְאוֹת וּלְעֵד לַיהוָה צְבָאוֹת בְּאֶרֶץ
in-land-of Hosts to-Yahweh-of and-as-witness as-sign and-he-will-be (20)

מִצְרָיִם כִּי־ יִצְעֲקוּ אֶל־ יְהוָה מִפְּנֵי לֹחֲצִים
ones-oppressing because-of Yahweh to they-cry-out when Egypt

וְיִשְׁלַח לָהֶם מוֹשִׁיעַ וָרָב וְהִצִּילָם׃
and-he-will-rescue-them and-one-defending one-saving to-them then-he-will-send

וְנוֹדַע יְהוָה לְמִצְרַיִם וְיָדְעוּ
and-they-will-acknowledge to-Egyptians Yahweh so-he-will-make-himself-known (21)

מִצְרַיִם אֶת־ יְהוָה בַּיּוֹם הַהוּא וְעָבְדוּ זֶבַח
sacrifice and-they-will-worship the-that in-the-day Yahweh *** Egyptians

וּמִנְחָה וְנָדְרוּ־ נֵדֶר לַיהוָה וְשִׁלֵּמוּ׃
and-they-will-keep to-Yahweh vow and-they-will-vow and-grain-offering

וְנָגַף יְהוָה אֶת־ מִצְרַיִם נָגֹף
to-strike-with-plague Egypt *** Yahweh and-he-will-strike-with-plague (22)

וְרָפוֹא וְשָׁבוּ עַד־ יְהוָה וְנֶעְתַּר
and-he-will-respond-to-plea Yahweh to and-they-will-turn and-to-heal

לָהֶם וּרְפָאָם׃ בַּיּוֹם הַהוּא תִּהְיֶה
she-will-be the-that in-the-day (23) and-he-will-heal-them of-them

מְסִלָּה מִמִּצְרַיִם אַשּׁוּרָה וּבָא־ אַשּׁוּר בְּמִצְרַיִם
to-Egypt Assyrian and-he-will-go to-Assyria from-Egypt highway

וּמִצְרַיִם בְּאַשּׁוּר וְעָבְדוּ מִצְרַיִם אֶת־ אַשּׁוּר׃
Assyrian with Egyptians and-they-will-worship to-Assyria and-Egyptians

בַּיּוֹם הַהוּא יִהְיֶה יִשְׂרָאֵל שְׁלִישִׁיָּה לְמִצְרַיִם וּלְאַשּׁוּר
and-with-Assyria with-Egypt third Israel he-will-be the-that in-the-day (24)

בְּרָכָה בְּקֶרֶב הָאָרֶץ׃ אֲשֶׁר בֵּרְכוֹ יְהוָה צְבָאוֹת
Hosts Yahweh-of he-will-bless-him that (25) the-earth in-midst-of blessing

לֵאמֹר בָּרוּךְ עַמִּי מִצְרַיִם וּמַעֲשֵׂה יָדַי אַשּׁוּר
Assyria hands-of-me and-work-of Egypt people-of-me being-blessed to-say

וְנַחֲלָתִי יִשְׂרָאֵל׃ בִּשְׁנַת בֹּא תַרְתָּן
supreme-commander to-come in-year-of (20:1) Israel and-inheritance-of-me

אַשְׁדּוֹדָה בִּשְׁלֹחַ* אֹתוֹ סַרְגוֹן מֶלֶךְ אַשּׁוּר וַיִּלָּחֶם
then-he-attacked Assyria king-of Sargon him when-to-send to-Ashdod

בְּאַשְׁדּוֹד וַיִּלְכְּדָהּ׃ בָּעֵת הַהִיא דִּבֶּר
he-spoke the-that at-the-time (2) and-he-captured-her against-Ashdod

[19]In that day there will be an altar to the LORD in the heart of Egypt, and a monument to the LORD at its border. [20]It will be a sign and witness to the LORD Almighty in the land of Egypt. When they cry out to the LORD because of their oppressors, he will send them a savior and defender, and he will rescue them. [21]So the LORD will make himself known to the Egyptians, and in that day they will acknowledge the LORD. They will worship with sacrifices and grain offerings; they will make vows to the LORD and keep them. [22]The LORD will strike Egypt with a plague; he will strike them and heal them. They will turn to the LORD, and he will respond to their pleas and heal them.

[23]In that day there will be a highway from Egypt to Assyria. The Assyrians will go to Egypt and the Egyptians to Assyria. The Egyptians and Assyrians will worship together. [24]In that day Israel will be the third, along with Egypt and Assyria, a blessing on the earth. [25]The LORD Almighty will bless them, saying, "Blessed be Egypt my people, Assyria my handiwork, and Israel my inheritance."

*A Prophecy Against Egypt and Cush*

20 In the year that the supreme commander, sent by Sargon king of Assyria, came to Ashdod and attacked and captured it— [2]at that time the LORD

*1 Most mss have *furtive pathah* with the *heth* (לַחַ-).

יְהוָה בְּיַד יְשַׁעְיָהוּ בֶן־אָמוֹץ לֵאמֹר לֵךְ וּפִתַּחְתָּ
and-you-take-off go! to-say Amoz son-of Isaiah through-hand-of Yahweh

הַשַּׂק מֵעַל מָתְנֶיךָ וְנַעַלְךָ תַחֲלֹץ
you-take-off and-sandal-of-you bodies-of-you from-on the-sackcloth

מֵעַל רַגְלֶיךָ וַיַּעַשׂ כֵּן הָלֹךְ עָרוֹם וְיָחֵף׃
and-barefoot stripped and-he-went so and-he-did feet-of-you from-on

(3) וַיֹּאמֶר יְהוָה כַּאֲשֶׁר הָלַךְ עַבְדִּי יְשַׁעְיָהוּ עָרוֹם
stripped Isaiah servant-of-me he-went just-as Yahweh then-he-said (3)

וְיָחֵף שָׁלֹשׁ שָׁנִים אוֹת וּמוֹפֵת עַל־מִצְרַיִם וְעַל־כּוּשׁ׃
Cush and-against Egypt against and-portent sign years three and-barefoot

(4) כֵּן יִנְהַג מֶלֶךְ־אַשּׁוּר אֶת־שְׁבִי מִצְרַיִם וְאֶת־גָּלוּת
exile-of and Egypt captive-of *** Assyria king-of he-will-lead-away so (4)

כּוּשׁ נְעָרִים וּזְקֵנִים עָרוֹם וְיָחֵף וַחֲשׂוּפַי
and-ones-being-bare-of and-barefoot stripped and-old-ones young-ones Cush

שֵׁת עֶרְוַת מִצְרָיִם׃ (5) וְחַתּוּ וָבֹשׁוּ מִכּוּשׁ
of-Cush and-they-will-be-ashamed and-they-will-fear (5) Egypt shame-of buttocks

מַבָּטָם וּמִן־מִצְרַיִם תִּפְאַרְתָּם׃ (6) וְאָמַר יֹשֵׁב
one-living-of and-he-will-say (6) boast-of-them Egypt and-of trust-of-them

הָאִי הַזֶּה בַּיּוֹם הַהוּא הִנֵּה־כֹה מַבָּטֵנוּ אֲשֶׁר־נַסְנוּ
we-fled where reliance-of-us thus see! the-that in-the-day the-this the-coast

שָׁם לְעֶזְרָה לְהִנָּצֵל מִפְּנֵי מֶלֶךְ אַשּׁוּר וְאֵיךְ
then-how? Assyria king-of from-before to-be-delivered for-help there

נִמָּלֵט אֲנָחְנוּ׃ (21:1) מַשָּׂא מִדְבַּר־יָם כְּסוּפוֹת
like-whirlwinds Sea Desert-of oracle-of (21:1) we can-we-escape

בַּנֶּגֶב לַחֲלֹף מִמִּדְבָּר בָּא מֵאֶרֶץ נוֹרָאָה׃
being-terrifying from-land he-comes from-desert to-sweep through-the-southland

(2) חָזוּת קָשָׁה הֻגַּד־לִי הַבּוֹגֵד ׀ בּוֹגֵד
betraying the-one-betraying to-me he-was-shown dire vision (2)

וְהַשּׁוֹדֵד ׀ שׁוֹדֵד עֲלִי עֵילָם צוּרִי מָדַי כָּל־אַנְחָתָה
groaning-of-her all-of Media lay-siege! Elam attack! looting and-the-one-looting

הִשְׁבַּתִּי׃ (3) עַל־כֵּן מָלְאוּ מָתְנַי חַלְחָלָה צִירִים
pangs pain bodies-of-me they-are-racked this at (3) I-will-make-end

אֲחָזוּנִי כְּצִירֵי יוֹלֵדָה נַעֲוֵיתִי מִשְּׁמֹעַ
by-to-hear I-am-staggered woman-being-in-labor like-pangs-of they-seize-me

נִבְהַלְתִּי מֵרְאוֹת׃ (4) תָּעָה לְבָבִי פַּלָּצוּת בִּעֲתָתְנִי
she-makes-tremble-me fear heart-of-me she-falters (4) by-to-see I-am-bewildered

אֶת נֶשֶׁף חִשְׁקִי שָׂם לִי לַחֲרָדָה׃ (5) עָרֹךְ הַשֻּׁלְחָן
the-table to-set (5) as-horror to-me he-became longing-of-me twilight-of ***

spoke through Isaiah son of Amoz. He said to him, "Take off the sackcloth from your body and the sandals from your feet." And he did so, going around stripped and barefoot.

3Then the LORD said, "Just as my servant Isaiah has gone stripped and barefoot for three years, as a sign and portent against Egypt
and Cush,[w] 4so the king of Assyria will lead away stripped and barefoot the Egyptian captives and Cushite exiles, young and old, with buttocks bared—to Egypt's
shame. 5Those who trusted in Cush and boasted in Egypt will be afraid and put to shame.
6In that day the people who live on this coast will say, 'See what has happened to those we relied on, those we fled to for help and deliverance from the king of Assyria! How then can we escape?' "

*A Prophecy Against Babylon*

21 An oracle concerning the Desert by the Sea:

Like whirlwinds sweeping
through the southland,
an invader comes from the
desert,
from a land of terror.

2A dire vision has been shown
to me:
The traitor betrays, the
looter takes loot.
Elam, attack! Media, lay siege!
I will bring to an end all the
groaning she caused.

3At this my body is racked
with pain,
pangs seize me, like those of
a woman in labor;
I am staggered by what I hear,
I am bewildered by what I
see.
4My heart falters,
fear makes me tremble;
the twilight I longed for
has become a horror to me.

5They set the tables,

צָפֹה הַצָּפִית אָכוֹל שָׁתֹה קוּמוּ הַשָּׂרִים מִשְׁחוּ מָגֵן׃
shield oil! the-officers get-up! to-drink to-eat the-rug to-spread

(6) כִּי כֹה אָמַר אֵלַי אֲדֹנָי לֵךְ הַעֲמֵד הַמְצַפֶּה אֲשֶׁר
what the-one-looking-out post! go! Lord to-me he-says this indeed (6)

יִרְאֶה יַגִּיד׃ (7) וְרָאָה רֶכֶב צֶמֶד פָּרָשִׁים רֶכֶב
rider-of horses team-of chariot when-he-sees (7) have-him-report he-sees

חֲמוֹר רֶכֶב גָּמָל וְהִקְשִׁיב קֶשֶׁב רַב־ קָשֶׁב׃
alertness full-of alertness and-let-him-be-alert camel rider-of donkey

(8) וַיִּקְרָא אַרְיֵה* עַל־ מִצְפֶּה | אֲדֹנָי אָנֹכִי עֹמֵד תָּמִיד
always standing I lords-of-me watchtower on *lion and-he-shouted (8)

יוֹמָם וְעַל־ מִשְׁמַרְתִּי אָנֹכִי נִצָּב כָּל־ הַלֵּילוֹת׃ (9) וְהִנֵּה־
and-look! (9) the-nights every-of staying I post-of-me and-at daily

זֶה בָא רֶכֶב אִישׁ צֶמֶד פָּרָשִׁים וַיַּעַן וַיֹּאמֶר
and-he-said and-he-answered horses team-of man chariot-of he-comes this

נָפְלָה נָפְלָה בָּבֶל וְכָל־ פְּסִילֵי אֱלֹהֶיהָ שִׁבַּר
he-shattered gods-of-her images-of and-all-of Babylon she-fell she-fell

לָאָרֶץ׃ (10) מְדֻשָׁתִי וּבֶן־ גָּרְנִי
threshing-floor-of-me and-people-of one-crushed-of-me (10) on-the-ground

אֲשֶׁר שָׁמַעְתִּי מֵאֵת יְהוָה צְבָאוֹת אֱלֹהֵי יִשְׂרָאֵל הִגַּדְתִּי לָכֶם׃
to-you I-tell Israel God-of Hosts Yahweh-of from-with I-heard what

(11) מַשָּׂא דּוּמָה אֵלַי קֹרֵא מִשֵּׂעִיר שֹׁמֵר מַה־
what? one-watching from-Seir one-calling to-me Dumah oracle-of (11)

מִלַּיְלָה שֹׁמֵר מַה־ מִלֵּיל׃ (12) אָמַר שֹׁמֵר
one-watching he-replies (12) of-night what? one-watching of-night

אָתָא בֹקֶר וְגַם־ לָיְלָה אִם־ תִּבְעָיוּן בְּעָיוּ שֻׁבוּ אֵתָיוּ׃
come! come-back! ask! you-would-ask if night but-also morning he-comes

(13) מַשָּׂא בַּעְרָב בַּיַּעַר בַּעְרַב תָּלִינוּ אֹרְחוֹת
caravans-of you-camp of-Arabia in-the-thicket concerning-Arabia oracle (13)

דְּדָנִים׃ (14) לִקְרַאת צָמֵא הֵתָיוּ מָיִם יֹשְׁבֵי אֶרֶץ תֵּימָא
Tema land-of ones-living-of waters bring! thirsty to-meet (14) Dedanites

בְּלַחְמוֹ קִדְּמוּ נֹדֵד׃ (15) כִּי־ מִפְּנֵי חֲרָבוֹת
swords from-before indeed (15) one-being-fugitive you-meet with-food-of-him

נָדָדוּ מִפְּנֵי | חֶרֶב נְטוּשָׁה וּמִפְּנֵי קֶשֶׁת דְּרוּכָה
being-bent bow and-from-before being-drawn sword from-before they-flee

וּמִפְּנֵי כֹּבֶד מִלְחָמָה׃ (16) כִּי־ כֹה אָמַר אֲדֹנָי אֵלַי בְּעוֹד
while-yet to-me Lord he-says this indeed (16) battle heat-of and-from-before

שָׁנָה כִּשְׁנֵי שָׂכִיר וְכָלָה כָּל־ כְּבוֹד קֵדָר׃
Kedar pomp-of all-of then-he-will-end contracted-servant as-years-of year

they spread the rugs,
they eat, they drink!
Get up, you officers,
oil the shields!

6 This is what the Lord says to me:

"Go, post a lookout
and have him report what
he sees.
7 When he sees chariots
with teams of horses,
riders on donkeys
or riders on camels,
let him be alert,
fully alert."

8 And the lookout[x] shouted,

"Day after day, my lord, I
stand on the watchtower;
every night I stay at my
post.
9 Look, here comes a man in a
chariot
with a team of horses.
And he gives back the answer:
'Babylon has fallen, has
fallen!
All the images of its gods
lie shattered on the
ground!' "

10 O my people, crushed on the
threshing floor,
I tell you what I have heard
from the LORD Almighty,
from the God of Israel.

*A Prophecy Against Edom*

11 An oracle concerning Dumah[y]:

Someone calls to me from Seir,
"Watchman, what is left of
the night?
Watchman, what is left of
the night?"
12 The watchman replies,
"Morning is coming, but
also the night.
If you would ask, then ask;
and come back yet again."

*A Prophecy Against Arabia*

13 An oracle concerning Arabia:

You caravans of Dedanites,
who camp in the thickets of
Arabia,
14 bring water for the thirsty;
you who live in Tema,
bring food for the fugitives.
15 They flee from the sword,
from the drawn sword,
from the bent bow
and from the heat of battle.

16 This is what the Lord says to me: "Within one year, as a servant bound by contract would count it, all the pomp of Kedar will come to

*w3* That is, the upper Nile region; also in verse 5
*x8* Dead Sea Scrolls and Syriac; Masoretic Text *A lion*
*y11* *Dumah* means *silence* or *stillness*, a word play on *Edom*.

*8 The NIV, with the mss and versions listed in note *x* above, reads הָרֹאֶה, *the-one-looking-out*.

(17) וּשְׁאָר מִסְפַּר־ קֶשֶׁת גִּבּוֹרֵי בְנֵי־ קֵדָר
Kedar peoples-of warriors-of bowman number-of and-survivor-of (17)

יִמְעָטוּ כִּי יְהוָה אֱלֹהֵי־ יִשְׂרָאֵל דִּבֵּר׃ (22:1) מַשָּׂא
oracle-of (22:1) he-spoke Israel God-of Yahweh indeed they-will-be-few

גֵּיא חִזָּיוֹן מַה־ לָּךְ אֵפוֹא כִּי־ עָלִית כֻּלָּךְ לַגַּגּוֹת׃
on-the-roofs all-of-you you-went-up that now to-you what? Vision Valley-of

(2) תְּשֻׁאוֹת ׀ מְלֵאָה עִיר הוֹמִיָּה קִרְיָה עַלִּיזָה חֲלָלַיִךְ
ones-slain-of-you reveling city being-tumultuous town full commotions (2)

לֹא חַלְלֵי־ חֶרֶב וְלֹא מֵתֵי מִלְחָמָה׃ (3) כָּל־
all-of (3) battle ones-dying-of or-not sword ones-slain-of not

קְצִינַיִךְ נָדְדוּ־ יַחַד מִקֶּשֶׁת אֻסָּרוּ כָּל־
all-of they-were-captured without-bow together they-fled leaders-of-you

נִמְצָאַיִךְ אֻסְּרוּ יַחְדָּו מֵרָחוֹק בָּרָחוּ׃
they-fled at-far-away together they-were-captured ones-being-caught-of-you

(4) עַל־ כֵּן אָמַרְתִּי שְׁעוּ מִנִּי אֲמָרֵר בַּבֶּכִי
in-the-weeping let-me-be-bitter from-me turn-away! I-said this for (4)

אַל־ תָּאִיצוּ לְנַחֲמֵנִי עַל־ שֹׁד בַּת־ עַמִּי׃
people-of-me daughter-of destruction-of over to-console-me you-try not

(5) כִּי יוֹם מְהוּמָה וּמְבוּסָה וּמְבוּכָה לַאדֹנָי יְהוִה
Yahweh-of to-Lord and-terror and-trampling tumult day-of indeed (5)

צְבָאוֹת בְּגֵיא חִזָּיוֹן מְקַרְקַר קִר וְשׁוֹעַ אֶל־
to and-crying-out wall battering-down-of Vision in-Valley-of Hosts

הָהָר׃ (6) וְעֵילָם נָשָׂא אַשְׁפָּה בְּרֶכֶב אָדָם פָּרָשִׁים
horses man with-chariot-of quiver he-takes-up and-Elam (6) the-mountain

וְקִיר עֵרָה מָגֵן׃ (7) וַיְהִי מִבְחַר־ עֲמָקַיִךְ
valleys-of-you choicest-of and-he-is (7) shield he-uncovers and-Kir

מָלְאוּ רָכֶב וְהַפָּרָשִׁים שֹׁת שָׁתוּ
they-are-posted to-be-posted and-the-horsemen chariot they-are-full

הַשָּׁעְרָה׃ (8) וַיְגַל אֵת מָסַךְ יְהוּדָה וַתַּבֵּט
and-you-looked Judah defense-of *** and-he-stripped-away (8) at-the-gate

בַּיּוֹם הַהוּא אֶל־ נֶשֶׁק בֵּית הַיָּעַר׃ (9) וְאֵת בְּקִיעֵי
breaches-of and (9) the-Forest Palace-of weapon-of to the-that in-the-day

עִיר־ דָּוִד רְאִיתֶם כִּי־ רָבּוּ וַתְּקַבְּצוּ אֶת־ מֵי
waters-of *** and-you-stored-up they-were-many that you-saw David City-of

הַבְּרֵכָה הַתַּחְתּוֹנָה׃ (10) וְאֶת־ בָּתֵּי יְרוּשָׁלִַם סְפַרְתֶּם
you-counted Jerusalem buildings-of and (10) the-Lower the-Pool

וַתִּתְצוּ הַבָּתִּים לְבַצֵּר הַחוֹמָה׃ (11) וּמִקְוָה ׀
and-reservoir (11) the-wall to-strengthen the-houses and-you-tore-down

an end. [17]The survivors of the
bowmen, the warriors of Kedar,
will be few." The LORD, the God of
Israel, has spoken.

*A Prophecy About Jerusalem*

22 An oracle concerning the
Valley of Vision:

What troubles you now,
that you have all gone up on the roofs,
[2]O town full of commotion,
O city of tumult and revelry?
Your slain were not killed by the sword,
nor did they die in battle.
[3]All your leaders have fled together;
they have been captured without using the bow.
All you who were caught were taken prisoner together,
having fled while the enemy was still far away.
[4]Therefore I said, "Turn away from me;
let me weep bitterly.
Do not try to console me
over the destruction of my people."

[5]The Lord, the LORD Almighty, has a day
of tumult and trampling and terror
in the Valley of Vision,
a day of battering down walls
and of crying out to the mountains.
[6]Elam takes up the quiver,
with her charioteers and horses;
Kir uncovers the shield.
[7]Your choicest valleys are full of chariots,
and horsemen are posted at the city gates;
[8] the defenses of Judah are stripped away.

And you looked in that day
to the weapons in the Palace of the Forest;
[9]you saw that the City of David
had many breaches in its defenses;
you stored up water
in the Lower Pool.
[10]You counted the buildings in Jerusalem
and tore down houses to strengthen the wall.

עֲשִׂיתֶם בֵּין הַחֹמֹתַיִם לְמֵי הַבְּרֵכָה הַיְשָׁנָה וְלֹא
you-built between the-two-walls for-waters-of the-Pool the-Old but-not

הִבַּטְתֶּם אֶל־ עֹשֶׂיהָ וְיֹצְרָהּ מֵרָחוֹק לֹא
you-looked to One-making-her and-One-planning-her at-long-ago not

רְאִיתֶם׃ (12) וַיִּקְרָא אֲדֹנָי יְהוִה צְבָאוֹת בַּיּוֹם הַהוּא
you-regarded (12) and-he-called Lord Yahweh-of Hosts on-the-day the-that

לִבְכִי וּלְמִסְפֵּד וּלְקָרְחָה וְלַחֲגֹר שָׂק׃
for-weeping and-for-wailing and-for-tearing-out-hair and-to-put-on sackcloth

(13) וְהִנֵּה ׀ שָׂשׂוֹן וְשִׂמְחָה הָרֹג ׀ בָּקָר וְשָׁחֹט צֹאן
(13) but-see! joy and-revelry to-slaughter cattle and-to-kill sheep

אָכֹל בָּשָׂר וְשָׁתוֹת יָיִן אָכוֹל וְשָׁתוֹ כִּי מָחָר נָמוּת׃
to-eat meat and-to-drink wine to-eat and-to-drink for tomorrow we-die

(14) וְנִגְלָה בְאָזְנָי יְהוָה צְבָאוֹת אִם־ יְכֻפַּר
(14) and-he-revealed in-ears-of-me Yahweh-of Hosts not he-will-be-atoned-for

הֶעָוֹן הַזֶּה לָכֶם עַד־ תְּמֻתוּן אָמַר אֲדֹנָי יְהוִה צְבָאוֹת׃ (15) כֹּה
the-sin the-this to-you till you-die he-says Lord Yahweh-of Hosts (15) this

אָמַר אֲדֹנָי יְהוִה צְבָאוֹת לֶךְ־ בֹּא אֶל־ הַסֹּכֵן הַזֶּה עַל־
he-says Lord Yahweh-of Hosts leave! go! to the-one-being-steward the-this to

שֶׁבְנָא אֲשֶׁר עַל־ הַבָּיִת׃ (16) מַה־ לְּךָ פֹה וּמִי לְךָ פֹה
Shebna who over the-palace (16) what? to-you here and-who? to-you here

כִּי־ חָצַבְתָּ לְּךָ פֹּה קָבֶר חֹצְבִי מָרוֹם קִבְרוֹ
that you-cut-out for-you here grave one-hewing-of height grave-of-him

חֹקְקִי בַסֶּלַע מִשְׁכָּן לוֹ׃ (17) הִנֵּה יְהוָה
one-chiseling-of in-the-rock resting-place for-him (17) beware! Yahweh

מְטַלְטֶלְךָ טַלְטֵלָה גָּבֶר וְעֹטְךָ
one-hurling-away-you hurling-away mighty-man and-one-taking-hold-of-you

עָטֹה׃ (18) צָנוֹף יִצְנָפְךָ צְנֵפָה כַּדּוּר אֶל־
to-take-hold (18) to-roll-up he-will-roll-up-you rolling-up ball into

אֶרֶץ רַחֲבַת יָדָיִם שָׁמָּה תָמוּת וְשָׁמָּה מַרְכְּבוֹת
country large-of measures at-there you-will-die and-at-there chariots-of

כְּבוֹדֶךָ קְלוֹן בֵּית אֲדֹנֶיךָ׃ (19) וַהֲדַפְתִּיךָ
splendor-of-you disgrace-of house-of masters-of-you (19) and-I-will-depose-you

מִמַּצָּבֶךָ וּמִמַּעֲמָדְךָ יֶהֶרְסֶךָ׃ (20) וְהָיָה
from-office-of-you and-from-position-of-you he-will-oust-you (20) and-he-will-be

בַּיּוֹם הַהוּא וְקָרָאתִי לְעַבְדִּי לְאֶלְיָקִים
in-the-day the-that then-I-will-summon to-servant-of-me to-Eliakim

בֶּן־ חִלְקִיָּהוּ׃ (21) וְהִלְבַּשְׁתִּיו כֻּתָּנְתֶּךָ וְאַבְנֵטְךָ
son-of Hilkiah (21) and-I-will-clothe-him robe-of-you and-sash-of-you

11 You built a reservoir between
the two walls
for the water of the Old
Pool,
but you did not look to the
One who made it,
or have regard for the One
who planned it long ago.
12 The Lord, the LORD Almighty,
called you on that day
to weep and to wail,
to tear out your hair and put
on sackcloth.
13 But see, there is joy and
revelry,
slaughtering of cattle and
killing of sheep,
eating of meat and drinking
of wine!
"Let us eat and drink," you
say,
"for tomorrow we die!"

14 The LORD Almighty has revealed this in my hearing: "Till your dying day this sin will not be atoned for," says the Lord, the LORD Almighty.

15 This is what the Lord, the LORD Almighty, says:

"Go, say to this steward,
to Shebna, who is in charge
of the palace:
16 What are you doing here and
who gave you permission
to cut out a grave for
yourself here,
hewing your grave on the
height
and chiseling your resting
place in the rock?
17 "Beware, the LORD is about to
take firm hold of you
and hurl you away, O you
mighty man.
18 He will roll you up tightly like
a ball
and throw you into a large
country.
There you will die
and there your splendid
chariots will remain—
you disgrace to your
master's house!
19 I will depose you from your
office,
and you will be ousted from
your position.

20 "In that day I will summon my
servant, Eliakim son of Hilkiah. 21 I
will clothe him with your robe

אֲחַזְּקֶנּוּ וּמֶמְשַׁלְתְּךָ אֶתֵּן בְּיָדוֹ
in-hand-of-him I-will-put and-authority-of-you I-will-fasten-around-him

וְהָיָה לְאָב לְיוֹשֵׁב יְרוּשָׁלַםִ וּלְבֵית יְהוּדָה׃
Judah and-to-house-of Jerusalem to-one-living-of as-father and-he-will-be

וְנָתַתִּי מַפְתֵּחַ בֵּית־ דָּוִד עַל־ שִׁכְמוֹ וּפָתַח
and-he-will-open shoulder-of-him on David house-of key-of and-I-will-place (22)

וְאֵין סֹגֵר וְסָגַר וְאֵין פֹּתֵחַ׃ וּתְקַעְתִּיו
and-I-will-drive-him (23) opening and-no-one and-he-will-shut shutting and-no-one

יָתֵד בְּמָקוֹם נֶאֱמָן וְהָיָה לְכִסֵּא כָבוֹד לְבֵית
for-house-of honor as-seat-of and-he-will-be one-being-firm into-place peg

אָבִיו׃ וְתָלוּ עָלָיו כֹּל ׀ כְּבוֹד בֵּית־
house-of glory-of all-of on-him and-they-will-hang (24) father-of-him

אָבִיו הַצֶּאֱצָאִים וְהַצְּפִעוֹת כֹּל כְּלֵי הַקָּטָן
the-lesser vessels-of all-of and-the-offshoots the-offsprings father-of-him

מִכְּלֵי הָאַגָּנוֹת וְעַד כָּל־ כְּלֵי הַנְּבָלִים׃ בַּיּוֹם הַהוּא
the-that in-the-day (25) the-jars vessels-of all-of and-to the-bowls from-vessels-of

נְאֻם יְהוָה צְבָאוֹת תָּמוּשׁ הַיָּתֵד הַתְּקוּעָה
the-one-being-driven the-peg she-will-give-way Hosts Yahweh-of declaration-of

בְּמָקוֹם נֶאֱמָן וְנִגְדְּעָה וְנָפְלָה
and-she-will-fall and-she-will-be-sheared-off one-being-firm into-place

וְנִכְרַת הַמַּשָּׂא אֲשֶׁר־עָלֶיהָ כִּי יְהוָה דִּבֵּר׃ מַשָּׂא
oracle-of (23:1) he-spoke Yahweh indeed on-her that the-load and-he-will-be-cut-down

צֹר הֵילִילוּ ׀ אֳנִיּוֹת תַּרְשִׁישׁ כִּי־ שֻׁדַּד מִבַּיִת מִבּוֹא
without-to-enter without-house he-is-destroyed for Tarshish ships-of wail! Tyre

מֵאֶרֶץ כִּתִּים נִגְלָה־ לָמוֹ׃ דֹּמּוּ יֹשְׁבֵי
ones-being-people-of be-silent! (2) to-them he-was-revealed Kittim from-land-of

אִי סֹחֵר צִידוֹן עֹבֵר יָם מִלְאוּךְ׃
they-enriched-you sea one-faring-of Sidon one-being-merchant-of island

וּבְמַיִם רַבִּים זֶרַע שִׁחֹר קְצִיר יְאוֹר תְּבוּאָתָהּ
revenue-of-her Nile harvest-of Shihor grain-of great-ones and-on-waters (3)

וַתְּהִי סְחַר גּוֹיִם׃ בּוֹשִׁי צִידוֹן כִּי־ אָמַר יָם
sea he-spoke for Sidon be-ashamed! (4) nations marketplace-of and-she-became

מָעוֹז הַיָּם לֵאמֹר לֹא־ חַלְתִּי וְלֹא־ יָלַדְתִּי וְלֹא גִדַּלְתִּי
I-reared or-not I-gave-birth or-not I-was-in-labor not to-say the-sea fortress

בַחוּרִים רוֹמַמְתִּי בְתוּלוֹת׃ כַּאֲשֶׁר־ שֵׁמַע לְמִצְרָיִם יָחִילוּ
they-will-be-in-anguish to-Egypt word as-when (5) daughters I-brought-up sons

כְּשֵׁמַע צֹר׃ עִבְרוּ תַּרְשִׁישָׁה הֵילִילוּ יֹשְׁבֵי אִי׃
island ones-being-people-of wail! to-Tarshish cross-over! (6) Tyre at-report-of

and fasten your sash around him
and hand your authority over to
him. He will be a father to those
who live in Jerusalem and to the
house of Judah. [22]I will place on his
shoulder the key to the house of
David; what he opens no one can
shut, and what he shuts no one
can open. [23]I will drive him like a
peg into a firm place; he will be a
seat[z] of honor for the house of his
father. [24]All the glory of his family
will hang on him: its offspring
and offshoots—all its lesser vessels, from the bowls to all the jars.

[25]"In that day," declares the
LORD Almighty, "the peg driven
into the firm place will give way;
it will be sheared off and will fall,
and the load hanging on it will be
cut down." The LORD has spoken.

*A Prophecy About Tyre*

23 An oracle concerning Tyre:
Wail, O ships of Tarshish!
For Tyre is destroyed
and left without house or
harbor.
From the land of Cyprus[a]
word has come to them.

[2]Be silent, you people of the
island
and you merchants of
Sidon,
whom the seafarers have
enriched.
[3]On the great waters
came the grain of the
Shihor;
the harvest of the Nile[b] was
the revenue of Tyre,
and she became the
marketplace of the
nations.

[4]Be ashamed, O Sidon, and
you, O fortress of the sea,
for the sea has spoken:
"I have neither been in labor
nor given birth;
I have neither reared sons
nor brought up
daughters."
[5]When word comes to Egypt,
they will be in anguish at
the report from Tyre.

[6]Cross over to Tarshish;
wail, you people of the
island.

[z]23 Or *throne* [a]1 Hebrew *Kittim*
[b]2,3 Masoretic Text; one Dead Sea Scroll *Sidon, / who cross over the sea; / your envoys* [3]*are on the great waters. / The grain of the Shihor, / the harvest of the Nile,*

הֲזֹאת לָכֶם עַלִּיזָה מִֽימֵי־ קֶדֶם קַדְמָתָהּ יֹבִלוּהָ
they-took-her oldness-of-her old from-days-of revelry to-you this? (7)

רַגְלֶיהָ מֵרָחוֹק לָגוּר׃ מִי יָעַץ זֹאת עַל־ צֹר
Tyre against this he-planned who? (8) to-settle to-far-off feet-of-her

הַמַּעֲטִירָה אֲשֶׁר סֹחֲרֶיהָ* שָׂרִים כִּנְעָנֶיהָ
traders-of-her princes ones-being-merchants-of-her who the-one-bestowing-crown

נִכְבַּדֵּי־ אָרֶץ׃ יְהוָה צְבָאוֹת יְעָצָהּ לְחַלֵּל
to-bring-low he-planned-her Hosts Yahweh-of (9) earth ones-being-renowned-of

גְּאוֹן כָּל־ צְבִי לְהָקֵל כָּל־ נִכְבַּדֵּי־ אָרֶץ׃
earth ones-being-renowned-of all-of to-humble glory all-of pride-of

עִבְרִי אַרְצֵךְ כַּיְאֹר בַּת־ תַּרְשִׁישׁ אֵין
there-is-not Tarshish Daughter-of like-the-Nile land-of-you go-through! (10)

מֵזַח עוֹד׃ יָדוֹ נָטָה עַל־ הַיָּם הִרְגִּיז
he-made-tremble the-sea over he-stretched-out hand-of-him (11) longer harbor

מַמְלָכוֹת יְהוָה צִוָּה אֶל־ כְּנַעַן לַשְׁמִד מָעֻזְנֶיהָ׃
fortresses-of-her to-destroy Canaan concerning he-gave-order Yahweh kingdoms

וַיֹּאמֶר לֹא־ תוֹסִיפִי עוֹד לַעְלוֹז הַמְעֻשָּׁקָה בְּתוּלַת
Virgin-of the-one-being-crushed to-revel more you-continue not and-he-said (12)

בַּת־ צִידוֹן כִּתִּים° קוּמִי עֲבֹרִי גַּם־ שָׁם לֹא־ יָנוּחַ
you-will-find-rest not there even cross-over! get-up! Kittim Sidon Daughter-of

לָךְ׃ הֵן ׀ אֶרֶץ כַּשְׂדִּים זֶה הָעָם לֹא הָיָה אַשּׁוּר
Assyrian he-is not the-people this Chaldeans land-of look! (13) for-you

יְסָדָהּ לְצִיִּים הֵקִימוּ בַחִינָיו°
siege-towers-of-him they-raised for-desert-creatures he-made-place-of-her

עֹרְרוּ אַרְמְנוֹתֶיהָ שָׂמָהּ לְמַפֵּלָה׃ הֵילִילוּ
wail! (14) into-ruin he-turned-her fortresses-of-her they-stripped-bare

אֳנִיּוֹת תַּרְשִׁישׁ כִּי שֻׁדַּד מָעֻזְּכֶן׃ וְהָיָה
and-he-will-be (15) fortress-of-you he-is-destroyed for Tarshish ships-of

בַּיּוֹם הַהוּא וְנִשְׁכַּחַת צֹר שִׁבְעִים שָׁנָה כִּימֵי מֶלֶךְ
king as-days-of year seventy Tyre also-one-being-forgotten the-that at-the-day

אֶחָד מִקֵּץ שִׁבְעִים שָׁנָה יִהְיֶה לְצֹר כְּשִׁירַת
as-song-of to-Tyre he-will-happen year seventy at-end-of one

הַזּוֹנָה׃ קְחִי כִנּוֹר סֹבִּי עִיר זוֹנָה
one-being-prostitute city walk-through! harp take-up! (16) the-one-being-prostitute

נִשְׁכָּחָה הֵיטִיבִי נַגֵּן הַרְבִּי־ שִׁיר לְמַעַן תִּזָּכֵרִי׃
you-will-be-remembered so-that song make-many! to-play do-well! one-being-forgotten

וְהָיָה מִקֵּץ ׀ שִׁבְעִים שָׁנָה יִפְקֹד יְהוָה אֶת־ צֹר
Tyre *** Yahweh he-will-deal-with year seventy at-end-of and-he-will-be (17)

7 Is this your city of revelry,
the old, old city,
whose feet have taken her
to settle in far-off lands?
8 Who planned this against
Tyre,
the bestower of crowns,
whose merchants are princes,
whose traders are renowned
in the earth?
9 The LORD Almighty planned it,
to bring low the pride of all
glory
and to humble all who are
renowned on the earth.

10 Till[d] your land as along the
Nile,
O Daughter of Tarshish,
for you no longer have a
harbor.
11 The LORD has stretched out his
hand over the sea
and made its kingdoms
tremble.
He has given an order
concerning Phoenicia[e]
that her fortresses be
destroyed.
12 He said, "No more of your
reveling,
O Virgin Daughter of Sidon,
now crushed!

"Up, cross over to Cyprus[f];
even there you will find no
rest."
13 Look at the land of the
Babylonians,[g]
this people that is now of
no account!
The Assyrians have made it
a place for desert creatures;
they raised up their siege
towers,
they stripped its fortresses
bare
and turned it into a ruin.

14 Wail, you ships of Tarshish;
your fortress is destroyed!

15 At that time Tyre will be forgotten for seventy years, the span of a king's life. But at the end of these seventy years, it will happen to Tyre as in the song of the prostitute:

16 "Take up a harp, walk through
the city,
O prostitute forgotten;
play the harp well, sing many
a song,
so that you will be
remembered."

17 At the end of seventy years, the LORD will deal with Tyre. She

[d] 10 Dead Sea Scrolls and some Septuagint manuscripts; Masoretic Text *Go through*
[e] 11 Hebrew *Canaan*
[f] 12 Hebrew *Kittim*
[g] 13 Or *Chaldeans*

*8 Most mss have *qamets* under the *he* (־הָ).

°12 ק כתים
°13 ק בחוניו

וְשָׁבָה לְאֶתְנַנָּהּ וְזָנְתָה אֶת־ כָּל־
all-of *** and-she-will-be-prostitute to-hire-of-her and-she-will-return

מַמְלְכוֹת הָאָרֶץ עַל־ פְּנֵי הָאֲדָמָה׃ וְהָיָה סַחְרָהּ
profit-of-her yet-he-will-be (18) the-earth faces-of on the-earth kingdoms-of

וְאֶתְנַנָּהּ קֹדֶשׁ לַיהוָה לֹא יֵאָצֵר וְלֹא
and-not he-will-be-stored-up not for-Yahweh set-apart and-earning-of-her

יֵחָסֵן כִּי לַיֹּשְׁבִים לִפְנֵי יְהוָה יִהְיֶה סַחְרָהּ
profit-of-her he-will-be Yahweh before to-the-ones-living for he-will-be-hoarded

לֶאֱכֹל לְשָׂבְעָה וְלִמְכַסֶּה עָתִיק׃ הִנֵּה יְהוָה בּוֹקֵק
laying-waste Yahweh see! (24:1) fine and-for-clothing to-abundance to-eat

הָאָרֶץ וּבוֹלְקָהּ וְעִוָּה פָנֶיהָ וְהֵפִיץ
and-he-will-scatter faces-of-her and-he-will-ruin and-devastating-her the-earth

יֹשְׁבֶיהָ׃ וְהָיָה כָעָם כַּכֹּהֵן
as-for-the-priest as-for-the-people and-he-will-be (2) ones-inhabiting-her

כַּעֶבֶד כַּאדֹנָיו כַּשִּׁפְחָה כַּגְּבִרְתָּהּ
as-for-the-mistress-of-her as-for-the-maid as-for-masters-of-him as-for-the-servant

כַּקּוֹנֶה כַּמּוֹכֵר כַּמַּלְוֶה
as-for-the-one-lending as-for-the-one-selling as-for-the-one-buying

כַּלֹּוֶה כַּנֹּשֶׁה כַּאֲשֶׁר
as-for-whom as-for-the-one-being-creditor as-for-the-one-borrowing

נֹשֶׁא בוֹ׃ הִבּוֹק ׀ תִּבּוֹק הָאָרֶץ
the-earth she-will-be-laid-waste to-be-laid-waste (3) to-him one-being-creditor

וְהִבּוֹז ׀ תִּבּוֹז כִּי יְהוָה דִּבֶּר אֶת־ הַדָּבָר
the-word *** he-spoke Yahweh indeed she-will-be-plundered and-to-be-plundered

הַזֶּה׃ אָבְלָה נָבְלָה הָאָרֶץ אֻמְלְלָה נָבְלָה תֵּבֵל
world she-withers she-languishes the-earth she-withers she-dries-up (4) the-this

אֻמְלָלוּ מְרוֹם עַם־ הָאָרֶץ׃ וְהָאָרֶץ חָנְפָה
she-is-defiled and-the-earth (5) the-earth people-of exalted-of they-languish

תַּחַת יֹשְׁבֶיהָ כִּי־ עָבְרוּ תוֹרֹת חָלְפוּ חֹק
statute they-violated laws they-disobeyed for ones-being-people-of-her by

הֵפֵרוּ בְּרִית עוֹלָם׃ עַל־ כֵּן אָלָה אָכְלָה אֶרֶץ
earth she-consumes curse this for (6) everlasting covenant-of they-broke

וַיֶּאְשְׁמוּ יֹשְׁבֵי בָהּ עַל־ כֵּן חָרוּ
they-are-burned-up this for of-her ones-being-people-of and-they-must-bear-guilt

יֹשְׁבֵי אֶרֶץ וְנִשְׁאַר אֱנוֹשׁ מִזְעָר׃ אָבַל תִּירוֹשׁ
new-wine he-dries-up (7) few man-of and-he-is-left earth ones-inhabiting-of

אֻמְלְלָה־ גָפֶן נֶאֶנְחוּ כָּל־ שִׂמְחֵי־ לֵב׃ שָׁבַת מְשׂוֹשׂ
gaiety-of he-is-stilled (8) heart ones-merry-of all-of they-groan vine she-withers

will return to her hire as a prostitute and will ply her trade with all the kingdoms on the face of the earth. [18]Yet her profit and her earnings will be set apart for the LORD; they will not be stored up or hoarded. Her profits will go to those who live before the LORD, for abundant food and fine clothes.

*The LORD's Devastation of the Earth*

24 See, the LORD is going to lay waste the earth
and devastate it;
he will ruin its face
and scatter its inhabitants—
[2]it will be the same
for priest as for people,
for master as for servant,
for mistress as for maid,
for seller as for buyer,
for borrower as for lender,
for debtor as for creditor.
[3]The earth will be completely laid waste
and totally plundered.
The LORD has spoken this word.

[4]The earth dries up and withers,
the world languishes and withers,
the exalted of the earth languish.
[5]The earth is defiled by its people;
they have disobeyed the laws,
violated the statutes
and broken the everlasting covenant.
[6]Therefore a curse consumes the earth;
its people must bear their guilt.
Therefore earth's inhabitants are burned up,
and very few are left.
[7]The new wine dries up and the vine withers;
all the merrymakers groan.
[8]The gaiety of the tambourines is stilled,

תֻּפִּים חָדַל שְׁאוֹן עַלִּיזִים שָׁבַת מְשׂוֹשׂ כִּנּוֹר׃
harp joy-of he-is-silent revelers noise-of he-stopped tambourines

(9) בַּשִּׁיר לֹא יִשְׁתּוּ־יָיִן יֵמַר שֵׁכָר לְשֹׁתָיו׃
to-ones-drinking-him beer he-is-bitter wine they-drink not with-the-song (9)

(10) נִשְׁבְּרָה קִרְיַת־תֹּהוּ סֻגַּר כָּל־בַּיִת מִבּוֹא׃
from-to-enter house every-of he-is-barred ruin city-of she-lies-desolate (10)

(11) צְוָחָה עַל־הַיַּיִן בַּחוּצוֹת עָרְבָה כָּל־שִׂמְחָה
joy all-of she-turns-to-gloom in-the-streets the-wine for outcry (11)

גָּלָה מְשׂוֹשׂ הָאָרֶץ׃ (12) נִשְׁאַר בָּעִיר שַׁמָּה וּשְׁאִיָּה
and-piece ruin in-the-city he-is-left (12) the-earth gaiety-of he-is-banished

יֻכַּת־שָׁעַר׃ (13) כִּי כֹה יִהְיֶה בְּקֶרֶב הָאָרֶץ בְּתוֹךְ
in-among the-earth in-midst-of he-will-be so indeed (13) gate he-is-battered

הָעַמִּים כְּנֹקֶף זַיִת כְּעוֹלֵלֹת אִם־כָּלָה
he-is-finished when as-gleanings olive-tree as-beating-of the-nations

בָצִיר׃ (14) הֵמָּה יִשְׂאוּ קוֹלָם יָרֹנּוּ
they-shout-for-joy voice-of-them they-raise they (14) grape-harvest

בִּגְאוֹן יְהוָה צָהֲלוּ מִיָּם׃ (15) עַל־כֵּן בָּאֻרִים
in-the-eastern-parts this for (15) from-west they-acclaim Yahweh about-majesty-of

כַּבְּדוּ יְהוָה בְּאִיֵּי הַיָּם שֵׁם יְהוָה אֱלֹהֵי יִשְׂרָאֵל׃
Israel God-of Yahweh name-of the-sea in-islands-of Yahweh give-glory!

(16) מִכְּנַף הָאָרֶץ זְמִרֹת שָׁמַעְנוּ צְבִי לַצַּדִּיק וָאֹמַר
but-I-said to-the-Righteous-One glory we-hear songs the-earth from-end-of (16)

רָזִי־לִי רָזִי־לִי אוֹי לִי בֹּגְדִים
ones-being-treacherous to-me woe! to-me wasting-away to-me wasting-away

בָּגָדוּ וּבֶגֶד בּוֹגְדִים בָּגָדוּ׃ (17) פַּחַד וָפַחַת
and-pit terror (17) they-betray ones-being-treacherous and-treachery they-betray

וָפָח עָלֶיךָ יוֹשֵׁב הָאָרֶץ׃ (18) וְהָיָה
and-he-will-be (18) the-earth one-being-people-of for-you and-snare

הַנָּס מִקּוֹל הַפַּחַד יִפֹּל אֶל־הַפַּחַת
the-pit into he-will-fall the-terror at-sound-of the-one-fleeing

וְהָעוֹלֶה מִתּוֹךְ הַפַּחַת יִלָּכֵד בַּפָּח כִּי־
indeed in-the-snare he-will-be-caught the-pit from-inside-of and-the-one-climbing

אֲרֻבּוֹת מִמָּרוֹם נִפְתָּחוּ וַיִּרְעֲשׁוּ מוֹסְדֵי אָרֶץ׃
earth foundations-of and-they-shake they-are-opened of-heaven floodgates

(19) רֹעָה הִתְרֹעֲעָה הָאָרֶץ פּוֹר
to-be-split-asunder the-earth she-is-broken-up to-be-broken-up (19)

הִתְפּוֹרְרָה אֶרֶץ מוֹט הִתְמוֹטְטָה אָרֶץ׃ (20) נוֹעַ תָּנוּעַ
she-reels to-reel (20) earth she-is-shaken to-be-shaken earth she-is-split-asunder

the noise of the revelers has
stopped,
the joyful harp is silent.
9 No longer do they drink wine
with a song;
the beer is bitter to its
drinkers.
10 The ruined city lies desolate;
the entrance to every house
is barred.
11 In the streets they cry out for
wine;
all joy turns to gloom,
all gaiety is banished from
the earth.
12 The city is left in ruins,
its gate is battered to pieces.
13 So will it be on the earth
and among the nations,
as when an olive tree is
beaten,
or as when gleanings are
left after the grape
harvest.

14 They raise their voices, they
shout for joy;
from the west they acclaim
the LORD's majesty.
15 Therefore in the east give
glory to the LORD;
exalt the name of the LORD,
the God of Israel,
in the islands of the sea.
16 From the ends of the earth we
hear singing:
"Glory to the Righteous
One."

But I said, "I waste away, I
waste away!
Woe to me!
The treacherous betray!
With treachery the
treacherous betray!"
17 Terror and pit and snare await
you,
O people of the earth.
18 Whoever flees at the sound of
terror
will fall into a pit;
whoever climbs out of the pit
will be caught in a snare.

The floodgates of the heavens
are opened,
the foundations of the earth
shake.
19 The earth is broken up,
the earth is split asunder,
the earth is thoroughly
shaken.
20 The earth reels like a

אֶרֶץ כַּשִּׁכּוֹר וְהִתְנוֹדְדָה כַּמְּלוּנָה וְכָבַד עָלֶיהָ
upon-her and-he-is-heavy like-the-hut and-she-sways like-the-drunkard earth

פִּשְׁעָהּ וְנָפְלָה וְלֹא־ תֹסִיף קוּם׃
to-rise she-will-do-again and-never so-she-falls rebellion-of-her

(21) וְהָיָה בַּיּוֹם הַהוּא יִפְקֹד יְהוָה עַל־ צְבָא
power-of to Yahweh he-will-punish the-that in-the-day and-he-will-be (21)

הַמָּרוֹם בַּמָּרוֹם וְעַל־ מַלְכֵי הָאֲדָמָה עַל־ הָאֲדָמָה׃
the-earth on the-earth kings-of and-to in-the-heaven the-heaven

(22) וְאֻסְּפוּ אֲסֵפָה אַסִּיר עַל־ בּוֹר וְסֻגְּרוּ
and-they-will-be-shut-up dungeon in prisoner herd and-they-will-be-herded (22)

עַל־מַסְגֵּר וּמֵרֹב יָמִים יִפָּקֵדוּ׃ (23) וְחָפְרָה
and-she-will-be-abashed (23) they-will-be-punished days and-after-many-of prison in

הַלְּבָנָה וּבוֹשָׁה הַחַמָּה כִּי־ מָלַךְ יְהוָה צְבָאוֹת
Hosts Yahweh-of he-will-reign for the-sun and-she-will-be-ashamed the-moon

בְּהַר צִיּוֹן וּבִירוּשָׁלִַם וְנֶגֶד זְקֵנָיו כָּבוֹד׃
glory elders-of-him and-before and-in-Jerusalem Zion on-Mount-of

(25:1) יְהוָה אֱלֹהַי אַתָּה אֲרוֹמִמְךָ אוֹדֶה שִׁמְךָ כִּי
for name-of-you I-will-praise I-will-exalt-you you God-of-me Yahweh (25:1)

עָשִׂיתָ פֶּלֶא עֵצוֹת מֵרָחוֹק אֱמוּנָה אֹמֶן׃
faithfulness faithfulness from-long-ago plans marvelous-thing you-did

(2) כִּי שַׂמְתָּ מֵעִיר לַגָּל קִרְיָה בְצוּרָה לְמַפֵּלָה
into-ruin one-being-fortified town into-the-heap of-city you-made indeed (2)

אַרְמוֹן זָרִים מֵעִיר לְעוֹלָם לֹא יִבָּנֶה׃
he-will-be-rebuilt not to-ever from-city ones-being-foreign stronghold-of

(3) עַל־ כֵּן יְכַבְּדוּךָ עַם־ עָז קִרְיַת גּוֹיִם עָרִיצִים
ruthless-ones nations city-of strong people they-will-honor-you this for (3)

יִירָאוּךָ׃ (4) כִּי־ הָיִיתָ מָעוֹז לַדָּל מָעוֹז לָאֶבְיוֹן
for-the-needy refuge for-the-poor refuge you-are indeed (4) they-will-revere-you

בַּצַּר־ לוֹ מַחְסֶה מִזֶּרֶם צֵל מֵחֹרֶב כִּי רוּחַ
breath-of for from-heat shade from-storm shelter of-him in-the-distress

עָרִיצִים כְּזֶרֶם קִיר׃ (5) כְּחֹרֶב בְּצָיוֹן שְׁאוֹן
uproar-of of-desert like-heat (5) wall like-storm-of ruthless-ones

זָרִים תַּכְנִיעַ חֹרֶב בְּצֵל עָב זְמִיר עָרִיצִים
ruthless-ones song-of cloud in-shadow-of heat you-silence ones-being-foreign

יַעֲנֶה׃ (6) וְעָשָׂה יְהוָה צְבָאוֹת לְכָל־ הָעַמִּים
the-peoples for-all-of Hosts Yahweh-of and-he-will-prepare (6) he-is-stilled

בָּהָר הַזֶּה מִשְׁתֵּה שְׁמָנִים מִשְׁתֵּה שְׁמָרִים שְׁמָנִים
best-ones aged-wines banquet-of rich-foods feast-of the-this on-the-mountain

drunkard,
it sways like a hut in the wind;
so heavy upon it is the guilt of its rebellion
that it falls—never to rise again.

21 In that day the LORD will punish
the powers in the heavens above
and the kings on the earth below.
22 They will be herded together
like prisoners bound in a dungeon;
they will be shut up in prison
and be punished[h] after many days.
23 The moon will be abashed, the sun ashamed;
for the LORD Almighty will reign
on Mount Zion and in Jerusalem,
and before its elders, gloriously.

*Praise to the LORD*

25 O LORD, you are my God;
I will exalt you and praise your name,
for in perfect faithfulness
you have done marvelous things,
things planned long ago.
2 You have made the city a heap of rubble,
the fortified town a ruin,
the foreigners' stronghold a city no more;
it will never be rebuilt.
3 Therefore strong peoples will honor you;
cities of ruthless nations will revere you.
4 You have been a refuge for the poor,
a refuge for the needy in his distress,
a shelter from the storm
and a shade from the heat.
For the breath of the ruthless
is like a storm driving against a wall
5 and like the heat of the desert.
You silence the uproar of foreigners;
as heat is reduced by the shadow of a cloud,
so the song of the ruthless is stilled.

6 On this mountain the LORD Almighty will prepare
a feast of rich food for all peoples,
a banquet of aged wine—

[h] 22 Or *released*

מְמֻחָיִם שְׁמָרִים מְזֻקָּקִים׃ וּבִלַּע
and-he-will-destroy (7) ones-being-refined finest-wines ones-having-marrow

בָּהָר הַזֶּה פְּנֵי־ הַלּוֹט ׀ הַלּוֹט עַל־ כָּל־
all-of over the-one-enfolding the-shroud surfaces-of the-this on-the-mountain

הָעַמִּים וְהַמַּסֵּכָה הַנְּסוּכָה עַל־ כָּל־ הַגּוֹיִם׃
the-nations all-of over the-one-covering and-the-sheet the-peoples

בִּלַּע הַמָּוֶת לָנֶצַח וּמָחָה אֲדֹנָי יְהוִה דִּמְעָה
tear Yahweh Lord and-he-will-wipe-away to-forever the-death he-will-swallow (8)

מֵעַל כָּל־ פָּנִים וְחֶרְפַּת עַמּוֹ יָסִיר מֵעַל
from-upon he-will-remove people-of-him and-disgrace-of faces all-of from-on

כָּל־ הָאָרֶץ כִּי יְהוָה דִּבֵּר׃ וְאָמַר בַּיּוֹם הַהוּא
the-that in-the-day and-he-will-say (9) he-spoke Yahweh indeed the-earth all-of

הִנֵּה אֱלֹהֵינוּ זֶה קִוִּינוּ לוֹ וְיוֹשִׁיעֵנוּ זֶה יְהוָה קִוִּינוּ
we-trusted Yahweh this and-he-saved-us in-him we-trusted this God-of-us surely!

לוֹ נָגִילָה וְנִשְׂמְחָה בִּישׁוּעָתוֹ׃ כִּי־
indeed (10) in-salvation-of-him and-let-us-be-glad let-us-rejoice in-him

תָּנוּחַ יַד־ יְהוָה בָּהָר הַזֶּה וְנָדוֹשׁ
but-he-will-be-trampled the-this on-the-mountain Yahweh hand-of she-will-rest

מוֹאָב תַּחְתָּיו כְּהִדּוֹשׁ מַתְבֵּן בְּמֹ°י מַדְמֵנָה׃ וּפֵרַשׂ
and-he-will-spread-out (11) manure in straw as-to-be-trampled under-him Moab

יָדָיו בְּקִרְבּוֹ כַּאֲשֶׁר יְפָרֵשׂ הַשֹּׂחֶה לִשְׂחוֹת
to-swim the-one-swimming he-spreads-out just-as in-midst-of-him hands-of-him

וְהִשְׁפִּיל גַּאֲוָתוֹ עִם אָרְבּוֹת יָדָיו׃
hands-of-him clevernesses-of despite pride-of-him and-he-will-bring-down

וּמִבְצַר מִשְׂגַּב חוֹמֹתֶיךָ הֵשַׁח
he-will-bring-down walls-of-you height-of and-fortification-of (12)

הִשְׁפִּיל הִגִּיעַ לָאָרֶץ עַד־ עָפָר׃ בַּיּוֹם
in-the-day (26:1) dust to to-the-ground he-will-bring-down he-will-lay-low

הַהוּא יוּשַׁר הַשִּׁיר־ הַזֶּה בְּאֶרֶץ יְהוּדָה עִיר עָז־ לָנוּ
to-us strong city Judah in-land-of the-this the-song he-will-be-sung the-that

יְשׁוּעָה יָשִׁית חוֹמוֹת וָחֵל׃ פִּתְחוּ שְׁעָרִים וְיָבֹא גוֹי־
nation so-he-may-enter gates open! (2) and-rampart walls he-makes salvation

צַדִּיק שֹׁמֵר אֱמֻנִים׃ יֵצֶר סָמוּךְ תִּצֹּר שָׁלוֹם ׀
peace you-will-keep one-being-steadfast mind (3) faiths one-keeping righteous

שָׁלוֹם כִּי בְךָ בָּטוּחַ׃ בִּטְחוּ בַיהוָה עֲדֵי־ עַד כִּי בְּיָהּ
in-Yahweh for forever to in-Yahweh trust! (4) one-trusting in-you because peace

יְהוָה צוּר עוֹלָמִים׃ כִּי הֵשַׁח יֹשְׁבֵי מָרוֹם קִרְיָה
city height ones-dwelling-of he-humbles indeed (5) eternities Rock-of Yahweh

---

the best of meats and the
finest of wines.
7 On this mountain he will
destroy
the shroud that enfolds all
peoples,
the sheet that covers all
nations;
8 he will swallow up death
forever.
The Sovereign LORD will wipe
away the tears
from all faces;
he will remove the disgrace of
his people
from all the earth.
The LORD has spoken.

9 In that day they will say,

"Surely this is our God;
we trusted in him, and he
saved us.
This is the LORD, we trusted in
him;
let us rejoice and be glad in
his salvation."

10 The hand of the LORD will rest
on this mountain;
but Moab will be trampled
under him
as straw is trampled down
in the manure.
11 They will spread out their
hands in it,
as a swimmer spreads out
his hands to swim.
God will bring down their
pride
despite the cleverness[i] of
their hands.
12 He will bring down your high
fortified walls
and lay them low;
he will bring them down to
the ground,
to the very dust.

*A Song of Praise*

26 In that day this song will be
sung in the land of Judah:

We have a strong city;
God makes salvation
its walls and ramparts.
2 Open the gates
that the righteous nation
may enter,
the nation that keeps faith.
3 You will keep in perfect peace
him whose mind is
steadfast,
because he trusts in you.
4 Trust in the LORD forever,
for the LORD, the LORD, is
the Rock eternal.
5 He humbles those who dwell
on high,

[i] *11* The meaning of the Hebrew for this word is uncertain.

°*10* ק במו

נִשְׂגָּבָה יַשְׁפִּילֶנָּה יַשְׁפִּילָהּ עַד־ אֶרֶץ יַגִּיעֶנָּה עַד־
to he-casts-down-her ground to he-levels-her he-lays-low-her one-being-lofty

עָפָר׃ תִּרְמְסֶנָּה רָגֶל רַגְלֵי עָנִי פַּעֲמֵי דַלִּים׃
poor-ones footsteps-of oppressed feet-of foot she-tramples-down-her (6) dust

אֹרַח לַצַּדִּיק מֵישָׁרִים יָשָׁר מַעְגַּל צַדִּיק תְּפַלֵּס׃
you-make-smooth righteous way-of upright-One level-ones of-the-righteous path (7)

אַף אֹרַח מִשְׁפָּטֶיךָ יְהוָה קִוִּינוּךָ לְשִׁמְךָ
for-name-of-you we-wait-for-you Yahweh laws-of-you way-of yes (8)

וּלְזִכְרְךָ תַּאֲוַת־ נָפֶשׁ׃ נַפְשִׁי אִוִּיתִיךָ בַּלַּיְלָה
in-the-night I-yearn-for-you soul-of-me (9) heart desire-of and-for-renown-of-you

אַף־ רוּחִי בְּקִרְבִּי* אֲשַׁחֲרֶךָּ כִּי כַּאֲשֶׁר מִשְׁפָּטֶיךָ
judgments-of-you just-as when I-long-for-you *at-within-me spirit-of-me also

לָאָרֶץ צֶדֶק לָמְדוּ יֹשְׁבֵי תֵבֵל׃
world ones-being-people-of they-learn righteousness upon-the-earth

יֻחַן רָשָׁע בַּל־ לָמַד צֶדֶק בְּאֶרֶץ נְכֹחוֹת
uprightnesses in-land-of righteousness he-learns not wicked he-is-shown-grace (10)

יְעַוֵּל וּבַל־ יִרְאֶה גֵּאוּת יְהוָה׃ יְהוָה רָמָה
she-is-lifted-high Yahweh (11) Yahweh majesty-of he-regards and-not he-does-evil

יָדְךָ בַּל־ יֶחֱזָיוּן יֶחֱזוּ וְיֵבֹשׁוּ קִנְאַת־ עָם
people zeal-of and-let-them-be-ashamed let-them-see they-see not hand-of-you

אַף־ אֵשׁ צָרֶיךָ תֹאכְלֵם׃ יְהוָה תִּשְׁפֹּת
you-establish Yahweh (12) let-her-consume-them enemies-of-you fire-of also

שָׁלוֹם לָנוּ כִּי גַּם כָּל־ מַעֲשֵׂינוּ פָּעַלְתָּ לָּנוּ׃ יְהוָה
Yahweh (13) for-us you-did accomplishments-of-us all-of also indeed for-us peace

אֱלֹהֵינוּ בְּעָלוּנוּ אֲדֹנִים זוּלָתֶךָ לְבַד־ בְּךָ נַזְכִּיר שְׁמֶךָ׃
name-of-you we-honor to-you alone besides-you lords they-ruled-us God-of-us

מֵתִים בַּל־ יִחְיוּ רְפָאִים בַּל־ יָקֻמוּ לָכֵן
for-thus they-rise not departed-spirits they-live not ones-being-dead (14)

פָּקַדְתָּ וַתַּשְׁמִידֵם וַתְּאַבֵּד כָּל־ זֵכֶר
memory all-of and-you-wiped-out and-you-brought-to-ruin-them you-punished

לָמוֹ׃ יָסַפְתָּ לַגּוֹי יְהוָה יָסַפְתָּ לַגּוֹי
to-the-nation you-enlarged Yahweh to-the-nation you-enlarged (15) of-them

נִכְבָּדְתָּ רִחַקְתָּ כָּל־ קַצְוֵי־ אָרֶץ׃ יְהוָה
Yahweh (16) land borders-of all-of you-extended you-glorified-yourself

בַּצַּר פְּקָדוּךָ צָקוּן לַחַשׁ מוּסָרְךָ לָמוֹ׃
to-them discipline-of-you whisper they-prayed they-came-to-you in-the-distress

כְּמוֹ הָרָה תַּקְרִיב לָלֶדֶת תָּחִיל תִּזְעַק
she-cries-out she-writhes to-give-birth she-is-about woman-with-child as (17)

he lays the lofty city low;
he levels it to the ground
and casts it down to the dust.
6 Feet trample it down—
the feet of the oppressed,
the footsteps of the poor.
7 The path of the righteous is level;
O upright One, you make the way of the righteous smooth.
8 Yes, LORD, walking in the way of your laws,[j]
we wait for you;
your name and renown
are the desire of our hearts.
9 My soul yearns for you in the night;
in the morning my spirit longs for you.
When your judgments come upon the earth,
the people of the world learn righteousness.
10 Though grace is shown to the wicked,
they do not learn righteousness;
even in a land of uprightness
they go on doing evil
and regard not the majesty of the LORD.
11 O LORD, your hand is lifted high,
but they do not see it.
Let them see your zeal for your people and be put to shame;
let the fire reserved for your enemies consume them.
12 LORD, you establish peace for us;
all that we have accomplished you have done for us.
13 O LORD, our God, other lords besides you have ruled over us,
but your name alone do we honor.
14 They are now dead, they live no more;
those departed spirits do not rise.
You punished them and brought them to ruin;
you wiped out all memory of them.
15 You have enlarged the nation, O LORD;
you have enlarged the nation.
You have gained glory for yourself;
you have extended all the borders of the land.
16 LORD, they came to you in their distress;
when you disciplined them,
they could barely whisper a prayer.[k]
17 As a woman with child and about to give birth
writhes and cries out in her pain,

j8 Or *judgments*
k16 The meaning of the Hebrew for this clause is uncertain.

*9 The NIV reads בַּבֹּקֶר, *in-the-morning.*

בְּחֶבְלֶיהָ כֵּן הָיִינוּ מִפָּנֶיךָ יְהוָה׃ (18) הָרִינוּ
we-were-with-child (18) Yahweh in-presences-of-you we-were so in-pains-of-her

חַלְנוּ כְּמוֹ יָלַדְנוּ רוּחַ יְשׁוּעֹת בַּל־ נַעֲשֶׂה אֶרֶץ
earth we-brought not salvations wind we-gave-birth but we-writhed-in-pain

וּבַל־ יִפְּלוּ יֹשְׁבֵי תֵבֵל׃ (19) יִחְיוּ
they-will-live (19) world ones-being-people-of they-were-born and-not

מֵתֶיךָ נְבֵלָתִי* יְקוּמוּן הָקִיצוּ
wake-up! they-will-rise *body-of-me ones-being-dead-of-you

וְרַנְּנוּ שֹׁכְנֵי עָפָר כִּי טַל אוֹרֹת טַלֶּךָ
dew-of-you mornings dew-of indeed dust ones-dwelling-of and-shout-for-joy!

וָאָרֶץ רְפָאִים תַּפִּיל׃ (20) לֵךְ עַמִּי בֹּא
enter! people-of-me go! (20) she-will-give-birth dead-ones and-earth

בַּחֲדָרֶיךָ וּסְגֹר דְּלָתֶיךָ° בַּעֲדֶךָ חֲבִי כִמְעַט־ רֶגַע
while as-little-of hide! behind-you †doors-of-you and-shut! into-rooms-of-you

עַד־ יַעֲבָור־° זָעַם׃ (21) כִּי־ הִנֵּה יְהוָה יֹצֵא מִמְּקוֹמוֹ
from-dwelling-of-him coming Yahweh see! indeed (21) wrath he-passes-by until

לִפְקֹד עֲוֹן יֹשֵׁב־ הָאָרֶץ עָלָיו וְגִלְּתָה
and-she-will-disclose upon-him the-earth ones-being-people-of sin-of to-punish

הָאָרֶץ אֶת־ דָּמֶיהָ וְלֹא־ תְכַסֶּה עוֹד עַל־
over longer she-will-conceal and-not bloods-of-her *** the-earth

הֲרוּגֶיהָ׃ (27:1) בַּיּוֹם הַהוּא יִפְקֹד יְהוָה
Yahweh he-will-punish the-that in-the-day (27:1) ones-being-slain-of-her

בְּחַרְבּוֹ†† הַקָּשָׁה וְהַגְּדוֹלָה וְהַחֲזָקָה עַל לִוְיָתָן
Leviathan against and-the-powerful and-the-great the-fierce with-sword-of-him

נָחָשׁ בָּרִחַ וְעַל לִוְיָתָן נָחָשׁ עֲקַלָּתוֹן וְהָרַג אֶת־
*** and-he-will-slay coiling serpent Leviathan and-against gliding serpent

הַתַּנִּין אֲשֶׁר בַּיָּם׃ (2) בַּיּוֹם הַהוּא כֶּרֶם חֶמֶד
fruitfulness vineyard-of the-that in-the-day (2) in-the-sea that the-monster

עַנּוּ־ לָהּ׃ (3) אֲנִי יְהוָה נֹצְרָהּ לִרְגָעִים אַשְׁקֶנָּה
I-water-her at-continual-times watching-over-her Yahweh I (3) about-her sing!

פֶּן יִפְקֹד עָלֶיהָ לַיְלָה וָיוֹם אֶצֳּרֶנָּה׃ (4) חֵמָה אֵין לִי
to-me not anger (4) I-guard-her and-day night against-her he-harms so-not

מִי־ יִתְּנֵנִי שָׁמִיר שַׁיִת בַּמִּלְחָמָה אֶפְשְׂעָה בָהּ
against-her I-would-march in-the-battle thorn brier he-would-give-me who?

אֲצִיתֶנָּה יָחַד׃ (5) אוֹ יַחֲזֵק בְּמָעוּזִּי
of-refuge-of-me let-him-take-hold or (5) together I-would-set-on-fire-her

יַעֲשֶׂה שָׁלוֹם לִי שָׁלוֹם יַעֲשֶׂה־ לִּי׃ (6) הַבָּאִים
the-ones-coming (6) with-me let-him-make peace with-me peace let-him-make

so were we in your
presence, O LORD.
18 We were with child, we
writhed in pain,
but we gave birth to wind.
We have not brought salvation
to the earth;
we have not given birth to
people of the world.

19 But your dead will live;
their bodies will rise.
You who dwell in the dust,
wake up and shout for joy.
Your dew is like the dew of
the morning;
the earth will give birth to
her dead.

20 Go, my people, enter your
rooms
and shut the doors behind
you;
hide yourselves for a little
while
until his wrath has passed
by.
21 See, the LORD is coming out of
his dwelling
to punish the people of the
earth for their sins.
The earth will disclose the
blood shed upon her;
she will conceal her slain no
longer.

*Deliverance of Israel*

27 In that day,
the LORD will punish with
his sword,
his fierce, great and
powerful sword,
Leviathan the gliding serpent,
Leviathan the coiling
serpent;
he will slay the monster of the
sea.

2 In that day—
"Sing about a fruitful
vineyard:
3 I, the LORD, watch over it;
I water it continually.
I guard it day and night
so that no one may harm it.
4 I am not angry.
If only there were briers and
thorns confronting me!
I would march against them
in battle;
I would set them all on fire.
5 Or else let them come to me
for refuge;
let them make peace with
me,
yes, let them make peace
with me."

*19 The NIV reads נִבְלֹתָם, *bodies-of-them.*

†20 The *Kethib* form should have *segbol* under the *tav* for the translation given. The *Qere* form is singular, *door-of-you,* and probably should be pointed דַּלְתְּךָ.

††1 Most mss have *dagesh* in the second *beth* (־בּוֹ).

°20a ק דלתך

°20b ק יעבר

יַשְׁרֵשׁ יַעֲקֹב יָצִיץ וּפָרַח יִשְׂרָאֵל וּמָלְאוּ
and-they-will-fill Israel and-he-will-blossom he-will-bud Jacob he-will-take-root

פְנֵי־ תֵבֵל תְּנוּבָה׃ הַכְּמַכַּת מַכֵּהוּ הִכָּהוּ
he-struck-him one-striking-him like-striking-of? (7) fruit world surfaces-of

אִם־ כְּהֶרֶג הֲרֻגָיו הֹרָג׃
he-was-killed ones-being-killed-of-him like-killing-of or

בְּסַאסְּאָה בְּשַׁלְחָהּ תְּרִיבֶנָּה הָגָה
he-drives-out you-contend-with-her by-to-exile-her by-to-make-war-on-her (8)

בְּרוּחוֹ הַקָּשָׁה בְּיוֹם קָדִים׃ לָכֵן בְּזֹאת
by-this then (9) east-wind on-day-of the-fierce with-blast-of-him

יְכֻפַּר עֲוֺן־ יַעֲקֹב וְזֶה כָּל־ פְּרִי הָסִר
to-remove fruitage-of all-of and-this Jacob guilt-of he-will-be-atoned-for

חַטָּאתוֹ בְּשׂוּמוֹ ׀ כָּל־ אַבְנֵי מִזְבֵּחַ כְּאַבְנֵי־ גִר
chalk like-stones-of altar stones-of all-of when-to-make-him sin-of-him

מְנֻפָּצוֹת לֹא־ יָקֻמוּ אֲשֵׁרִים וְחַמָּנִים׃
or-incense-altars Asherah-poles they-will-stand not ones-being-crushed

כִּי עִיר בְּצוּרָה בָּדָד נָוֶה מְשֻׁלָּח
one-being-abandoned settlement desolate one-being-fortified city indeed (10)

וְנֶעֱזָב כַּמִּדְבָּר שָׁם יִרְעֶה עֵגֶל וְשָׁם יִרְבָּץ
he-lies-down and-there calf he-grazes there like-the-desert and-one-being-forsaken

וְכִלָּה סְעִפֶיהָ׃ בִּיבֹשׁ קְצִירָהּ
twig-of-her when-to-be-dry (11) branches-of-her and-he-strips-bare

תִּשָּׁבַרְנָה נָשִׁים בָּאוֹת מְאִירוֹת אוֹתָהּ כִּי לֹא עַם־
people-of not for her ones-making-fires ones-coming women they-are-broken-off

בִּינוֹת הוּא עַל־ כֵּן לֹא־ יְרַחֲמֶנּוּ עֹשֵׂהוּ
One-Making-him he-has-compassion-on-him not this for this understandings

וְיֹצְרוֹ לֹא יְחֻנֶּנּוּ׃ וְהָיָה בַּיּוֹם
in-the-day and-he-will-be (12) he-shows-favor-to-him not and-One-Creating-him

הַהוּא יַחְבֹּט יְהוָה מִשִּׁבֹּלֶת הַנָּהָר עַד־ נַחַל מִצְרָיִם
Egypt Wadi-of to the-River from-flowing-stream-of Yahweh he-will-thresh the-that

וְאַתֶּם תְּלֻקְּטוּ לְאַחַד אֶחָד בְּנֵי יִשְׂרָאֵל׃ וְהָיָה ׀
and-he-will-be (13) Israel sons-of one by-one-of you-will-be-gathered-up and-you

בַּיּוֹם הַהוּא יִתָּקַע בְּשׁוֹפָר גָּדוֹל וּבָאוּ
and-they-will-come great on-trumpet he-will-sound the-that in-the-day

הָאֹבְדִים בְּאֶרֶץ אַשּׁוּר וְהַנִּדָּחִים בְּאֶרֶץ מִצְרָיִם
Egypt in-land-of and-ones-being-exiled Assyria in-land-of the-ones-perishing

וְהִשְׁתַּחֲווּ לַיהוָה בְּהַר הַקֹּדֶשׁ בִּירוּשָׁלִָם׃
in-Jerusalem the-holiness on-mountain-of to-Yahweh and-they-will-worship

6 In days to come Jacob will take root,
Israel will bud and blossom
and fill all the world with fruit.

7 Has ⌞the LORD⌟ struck her
as he struck down those who struck her?
Has she been killed
as those were killed who killed her?
8 By warfare[l] and exile you contend with her—
with his fierce blast he drives her out,
as on a day the east wind blows.
9 By this, then, will Jacob's guilt be atoned for,
and this will be the full fruitage of the removal of his sin:
When he makes all the altar stones
to be like chalk stones crushed to pieces,
no Asherah poles[m] or incense altars
will be left standing.
10 The fortified city stands desolate,
an abandoned settlement, forsaken like the desert;
there the calves graze,
there they lie down;
they strip its branches bare.
11 When its twigs are dry, they are broken off
and women come and make fires with them.
For this is a people without understanding;
so their Maker has no compassion on them,
and their Creator shows them no favor.

12 In that day the LORD will thresh from the flowing Euphrates[n] to the Wadi of Egypt, and you, O Israelites, will be gathered up one by one. 13 And in that day a great trumpet will sound. Those who were perishing in Assyria and those who were exiled in Egypt will come and worship the LORD on the holy mountain in Jerusalem.

l8 See Septuagint; the meaning of the Hebrew for this word is uncertain.
m9 That is, symbols of the goddess Asherah
n12 Hebrew *River*

הוֹי עֲטֶרֶת גֵּאוּת שִׁכֹּרֵי אֶפְרַיִם וְצִיץ נֹבֵל צְבִי
beauty-of fading and-flower Ephraim drunkards-of pride-of wreath-of woe! (28:1)

תִּפְאַרְתּוֹ אֲשֶׁר עַל־ רֹאשׁ גֵּיא־ שְׁמָנִים הֲלוּמֵי יָיִן׃
wine ones-being-laid-low-of fertilities valley-of head-of on that glory-of-him

הִנֵּה חָזָק וְאַמִּץ לַאדֹנָי כְּזֶרֶם בָּרָד שַׂעַר קָטֶב
destruction wind-of hail like-storm-of to-Lord and-strong powerful see! (2)

כְּזֶרֶם מַיִם כַּבִּירִים שֹׁטְפִים הִנִּיחַ לָאָרֶץ בְּיָד׃
by-hand to-the-ground he-will-throw ones-flooding mighty-ones rains like-storm-of

בְּרַגְלַיִם תֵּרָמַסְנָה עֲטֶרֶת גֵּאוּת שִׁכּוֹרֵי אֶפְרָיִם׃
Ephraim drunkards-of pride-of wreath-of they-will-be-trampled under-feet (3)

וְהָיְתָה צִיצַת נֹבֵל צְבִי תִפְאַרְתּוֹ אֲשֶׁר עַל־ רֹאשׁ
head-of on that glory-of-him beauty-of fading flower-of and-she-will-be (4)

גֵּיא שְׁמָנִים כְּבִכּוּרָהּ בְּטֶרֶם קַיִץ אֲשֶׁר יִרְאֶה
he-sees when harvest at-before like-ripe-fig-of-her fertilities valley-of

הָרֹאֶה אוֹתָהּ בְּעוֹדָהּ בְּכַפּוֹ יִבְלָעֶנָּה׃ בַּיּוֹם
in-the-day (5) he-swallows-her in-hand-of-him when-yet-she her the-one-seeing

הַהוּא יִהְיֶה יְהוָה צְבָאוֹת לַעֲטֶרֶת צְבִי וְלִצְפִירַת
and-as-wreath-of glory as-crown-of Hosts Yahweh-of he-will-be the-that

תִּפְאָרָה לִשְׁאָר עַמּוֹ׃ וּלְרוּחַ מִשְׁפָּט לַיּוֹשֵׁב
to-the-one-sitting justice and-as-spirit-of (6) people-of-him for-remnant-of beauty

עַל־ הַמִּשְׁפָּט וְלִגְבוּרָה מְשִׁיבֵי מִלְחָמָה שָׁעְרָה׃ וְגַם־
and-also (7) at-gate battle ones-turning-back-of and-as-strength the-judgment in

אֵלֶּה בַּיַּיִן שָׁגוּ וּבַשֵּׁכָר תָּעוּ כֹּהֵן וְנָבִיא
and-prophet priest they-reel and-from-the-beer they-stagger from-the-wine these

שָׁגוּ בַשֵּׁכָר נִבְלְעוּ מִן־ הַיַּיִן תָּעוּ מִן־
from they-reel the-wine with they-are-befuddled from-the-beer they-stagger

הַשֵּׁכָר שָׁגוּ בָּרֹאֶה פָּקוּ פְּלִילִיָּה׃ כִּי כָּל־
all-of indeed (8) decision they-stumble from-the-vision they-stagger the-beer

שֻׁלְחָנוֹת מָלְאוּ קִיא צֹאָה בְּלִי מָקוֹם׃ אֶת־ מִי יוֹרֶה דֵעָה
knowledge he-teaches who? *** (9) spot without filth vomit they-are-covered tables

וְאֶת־ מִי יָבִין שְׁמוּעָה גְּמוּלֵי מֵחָלָב עַתִּיקֵי
ones-taken-of from-milk ones-being-weaned-of message he-explains who? and

מִשָּׁדָיִם׃ כִּי צַו לָצָו צַו לָצָו קַו לָקָו קַו לָקָו זְעֵיר
little on-rule rule on-rule rule to-do! do! to-do! do! for (10) from-breasts

שָׁם זְעֵיר שָׁם׃ כִּי בְּלַעֲגֵי שָׂפָה וּבְלָשׁוֹן אַחֶרֶת
strange and-with-tongue lip with-ones-foreign-of then (11) there little here

יְדַבֵּר אֶל־ הָעָם הַזֶּה׃ אֲשֶׁר אָמַר אֲלֵיהֶם זֹאת
this to-them he-said whom (12) the-this the-people to he-will-speak

*Woe to Ephraim*

28 Woe to that wreath, the
pride of Ephraim's
drunkards,
to the fading flower, his
glorious beauty,
set on the head of a fertile
valley—
to that city, the pride of
those laid low by wine!
2 See, the Lord has one who is
powerful and strong.
Like a hailstorm and a
destructive wind,
like a driving rain and a
flooding downpour,
he will throw it forcefully to
the ground.
3 That wreath, the pride of
Ephraim's drunkards,
will be trampled underfoot.
4 That fading flower, his
glorious beauty,
set on the head of a fertile
valley,
will be like a fig ripe before
harvest—
as soon as someone sees it
and takes it in his hand,
he swallows it.

5 In that day the LORD Almighty
will be a glorious crown,
a beautiful wreath
for the remnant of his
people.
6 He will be a spirit of justice
to him who sits in
judgment,
a source of strength
to those who turn back the
battle at the gate.

7 And these also stagger from
wine
and reel from beer:
Priests and prophets stagger
from beer
and are befuddled with
wine;
they reel from beer,
they stagger when seeing
visions,
they stumble when
rendering decisions.
8 All the tables are covered with
vomit
and there is not a spot
without filth.

9 "Who is it he is trying to
teach?
To whom is he explaining
his message?
To children weaned from their
milk,
to those just taken from the
breast?
10 For it is:
Do and do, do and do,
rule on rule, rule on rule[a];
a little here, a little there."

11 Very well then, with foreign
lips and strange tongues
God will speak to this
people,
12 to whom he said,

[a]10 Hebrew / *sav lasav sav lasav / kav lakav kav lakav* (possibly meaningless sounds; perhaps a mimicking of the prophet's words); also in verse 13

הַמְּנוּחָה הָנִיחוּ לֶעָיֵף וְזֹאת הַמַּרְגֵּעָה וְלֹא
but-not the-place-of-repose and-this for-the-weary rest! the-resting-place

אָבוּא שְׁמוֹעַ׃ וְהָיָה לָהֶם דְּבַר־ יְהוָה צַו לָצָו
to-do! do! Yahweh word-of to-them so-he-will-become (13) to-listen being-willing

צַו לָצָו קַו לָקָו קַו לָקָו זְעֵיר שָׁם זְעֵיר שָׁם לְמַעַן יֵלְכוּ
they-will-go so-that there little here little on-rule rule on-rule rule to-do! do!

וְכָשְׁלוּ אָחוֹר וְנִשְׁבָּרוּ וְנוֹקָשׁוּ
and-they-will-be-snared and-they-will-be-injured backward and-they-will-fall

וְנִלְכָּדוּ׃ לָכֵן שִׁמְעוּ דְבַר־ יְהוָה אַנְשֵׁי לָצוֹן
scoffing men-of Yahweh word-of hear! therefore (14) and-they-will-be-captured

מֹשְׁלֵי הָעָם הַזֶּה אֲשֶׁר בִּירוּשָׁלָם׃ כִּי אֲמַרְתֶּם כָּרַתְנוּ
we-entered you-boast indeed (15) in-Jerusalem who the-this the-people ones-ruling-of

בְרִית אֶת־ מָוֶת וְעִם־ שְׁאוֹל עָשִׂינוּ חֹזֶה שִׁיט שׁוֹטֵף כִּי־
when overwhelming scourge agreement we-made Sheol and-with death with covenant

עֲבַר לֹא יְבוֹאֵנוּ כִּי שַׂמְנוּ כָזָב מַחְסֵנוּ וּבַשֶּׁקֶר
and-in-the-falsehood refuge-of-us lie we-made for he-can-touch-us not he-sweeps-by

נִסְתָּרְנוּ׃ לָכֵן כֹּה אָמַר אֲדֹנָי יְהוִה הִנְנִי יִסַּד* בְּצִיּוֹן אָבֶן
stone in-Zion *he-lays see-I! Yahweh Sovereign he-says this so (16) we-hide

אֶבֶן בֹּחַן פִּנַּת יִקְרַת מוּסָד מוּסָּד הַמַּאֲמִין
the-one-trusting being-founded foundation precious-of cornerstone-of test stone-of

לֹא יָחִישׁ׃ וְשַׂמְתִּי מִשְׁפָּט לְקָו
as-measuring-line justice and-I-will-make (17) he-will-be-dismayed never

וּצְדָקָה לְמִשְׁקָלֶת וְיָעָה בָרָד מַחְסֵה כָזָב
lie refuge-of hail and-he-will-sweep-away as-plumb-line and-righteousness

וְסֵתֶר מַיִם יִשְׁטֹפוּ׃ וְכֻפַּר
and-he-will-be-annulled (18) they-will-overflow waters and-hiding-place

בְּרִיתְכֶם אֶת־ מָוֶת וְחָזוּתְכֶם אֶת־ שְׁאוֹל לֹא תָקוּם
she-will-stand not Sheol with and-agreement-of-you death with covenant-of-you

שׁוֹט שׁוֹטֵף כִּי יַעֲבֹר וִהְיִיתֶם לוֹ לְמִרְמָס׃
as-beaten-down by-him then-you-will-be he-sweeps-by when overwhelming scourge

מִדֵּי עָבְרוֹ יִקַּח אֶתְכֶם כִּי־ בַבֹּקֶר
in-the-morning indeed you he-will-carry-away to-come-him as-often-of (19)

בַּבֹּקֶר יַעֲבֹר בַּיּוֹם וּבַלָּיְלָה וְהָיָה רַק־
only and-he-will-be and-by-the-night by-the-day he-sweeps-through in-the-morning

זְוָעָה הָבִין שְׁמוּעָה׃ כִּי־ קָצַר הַמַּצָּע מֵהִשְׂתָּרֵעַ
than-to-stretch-out the-bed he-is-short indeed (20) message to-understand terror

וְהַמַּסֵּכָה צָרָה כְּהִתְכַּנֵּס׃ כִּי כְהַר־ פְּרָצִים
Perazim as-Mount-of indeed (21) than-to-wrap-around she-is-narrow and-the-blanket

"This is the resting place, let
the weary rest";
and, "This is the place of
repose"—
but they would not listen.
13So then, the word of the LORD
to them will become:
Do and do, do and do,
rule on rule, rule on rule;
a little here, a little there—
so that they will go and fall
backward,
be injured and snared and
captured.
14Therefore hear the word of the
LORD, you scoffers
who rule this people in
Jerusalem.
15You boast, "We have entered
into a covenant with
death,
with the grave[p] we have
made an agreement.
When an overwhelming
scourge sweeps by,
it cannot touch us,
for we have made a lie our
refuge
and falsehood[q] our hiding
place."
16So this is what the Sovereign
LORD says:
"See, I lay a stone in Zion,
a tested stone,
a precious cornerstone for a
sure foundation;
the one who trusts will
never be dismayed.
17I will make justice the
measuring line
and righteousness the plumb
line;
hail will sweep away your
refuge, the lie,
and water will overflow
your hiding place.
18Your covenant with death will
be annulled;
your agreement with the
grave will not stand.
When the overwhelming
scourge sweeps by,
you will be beaten down by
it.
19As often as it comes it will
carry you away;
morning after morning, by
day and by night,
it will sweep through."
The understanding of this
message
will bring sheer terror.
20The bed is too short to stretch
out on,
the blanket too narrow to
wrap around you.
21The LORD will rise up as he did
at Mount Perazim,

p15 Hebrew *Sheol*; also in verse 18
q15 Or *false gods*

*16 The NIV reads with many versions יֹסֵד, *one-laying*.

° 15a ק שׁוֹט
° 15b ק יַעֲבֹר

יָקוּם יְהוָה כְּעֵמֶק בְּגִבְעוֹן יִרְגָּז לַעֲשׂוֹת
to-do he-will-rouse-himself in-Gibeon as-Valley-of Yahweh he-will-rise-up

מַעֲשֵׂהוּ זָר מַעֲשֵׂהוּ וְלַעֲבֹד עֲבֹדָתוֹ נָכְרִיָּה
alien task-of-him and-to-perform work-of-him one-being-strange work-of-him

עֲבֹדָתוֹ׃ וְעַתָּה אַל־תִּתְלוֹצָצוּ פֶּן־יֶחְזְקוּ מוֹסְרֵיכֶם
chains-of-you they-will-become-heavier or you-mock not so-now (22) task-of-him

כִּי־כָלָה וְנֶחֱרָצָה שָׁמַעְתִּי מֵאֵת אֲדֹנָי יְהוִה צְבָאוֹת
Hosts Yahweh-of Lord from-with I-heard and-one-being-decreed destruction for

עַל־כָּל־הָאָרֶץ׃ הַאֲזִינוּ וְשִׁמְעוּ קוֹלִי הַקְשִׁיבוּ
pay-attention! voice-of-me and-hear! listen! (23) the-land whole-of against

וְשִׁמְעוּ אִמְרָתִי׃ הֲכֹל הַיּוֹם יַחֲרֹשׁ הַחֹרֵשׁ לִזְרֹעַ
to-plant the-one-plowing he-plows the-day all-of? (24) saying-of-me and-hear!

יְפַתַּח וִישַׂדֵּד אַדְמָתוֹ׃ הֲלוֹא אִם־שִׁוָּה פָנֶיהָ
surfaces-of-her he-levels when not? (25) soil-of-him and-he-harrows he-breaks-up

וְהֵפִיץ קֶצַח וְכַמֹּן יִזְרֹק וְשָׂם חִטָּה שׂוֹרָה וּשְׂעֹרָה
and-barley place wheat and-he-plants he-scatters and-cummin caraway then-he-sows

נִסְמָן וְכֻסֶּמֶת גְּבֻלָתוֹ׃ וְיִסְּרוֹ לַמִּשְׁפָּט
in-the-right-way and-he-teaches-him (26) field-of-him and-spelt one-being-plotted

אֱלֹהָיו יוֹרֶנּוּ׃ כִּי לֹא בֶחָרוּץ יוּדַשׁ קֶצַח
caraway he-is-threshed with-the-sledge not indeed (27) he-instructs-him God-of-him

וְאוֹפַן עֲגָלָה עַל־כַּמֹּן יוּסָּב כִּי בַמַּטֶּה יֵחָבֶט
he-is-beaten-out with-the-rod but he-is-rolled cummin over cart or-wheel-of

קֶצַח וְכַמֹּן בַּשָּׁבֶט׃ לֶחֶם יוּדָק כִּי לֹא לָנֶצַח
to-forever not so he-must-be-ground grain (28) with-the-stick and-cummin caraway

אָדוֹשׁ יְדוּשֶׁנּוּ וְהָמַם גִּלְגַּל עֶגְלָתוֹ וּפָרָשָׁיו
but-horses-of-him cart-of-him wheel-of though-he-drives he-threshes-him to-thresh

לֹא־יְדֻקֶּנּוּ׃ גַּם־זֹאת מֵעִם יְהוָה צְבָאוֹת יָצָאָה
she-comes Hosts Yahweh-of from-with this also (29) he-grinds-him not

הִפְלִיא עֵצָה הִגְדִּיל תּוּשִׁיָּה׃ הוֹי אֲרִיאֵל אֲרִיאֵל
Ariel Ariel woe! (29:1) wisdom he-makes-magnificent counsel he-makes-wonderful

קִרְיַת חָנָה דָוִד סְפוּ שָׁנָה עַל־שָׁנָה חַגִּים יִנְקֹפוּ׃
let-them-cycle-on festivals year to year add! David he-settled city-of

וַהֲצִיקוֹתִי לַאֲרִיאֵל וְהָיְתָה תַאֲנִיָּה וַאֲנִיָּה
and-lamenting mourning and-she-will-be against-Ariel yet-I-will-besiege (2)

וְהָיְתָה לִּי כַּאֲרִיאֵל׃ וְחָנִיתִי כַדּוּר
like-the-circle and-I-will-encamp (3) as-altar-hearth to-me and-she-will-be

עָלַיִךְ וְצַרְתִּי עָלַיִךְ מֻצָּב וַהֲקִימֹתִי עָלַיִךְ
against-you and-I-will-set-up tower against-you and-I-will-encircle against-you

---

he will rouse himself as in the Valley of Gibeon—
to do his work, his strange work,
and perform his task, his alien task.
[22]Now stop your mocking,
or your chains will become heavier;
the Lord, the LORD Almighty, has told me
of the destruction decreed against the whole land.

[23]Listen and hear my voice;
pay attention and hear what I say.
[24]When a farmer plows for planting, does he plow continually?
Does he keep on breaking up and harrowing the soil?
[25]When he has leveled the surface,
does he not sow caraway and scatter cummin?
Does he not plant wheat in its place,[r]
barley in its plot,[r]
and spelt in its field?
[26]His God instructs him
and teaches him the right way.

[27]Caraway is not threshed with a sledge,
nor is a cartwheel rolled over cummin;
caraway is beaten out with a rod,
and cummin with a stick.
[28]Grain must be ground to make bread;
so one does not go on threshing it forever.
Though he drives the wheels of his threshing cart over it,
his horses do not grind it.
[29]All this also comes from the LORD Almighty,
wonderful in counsel and magnificent in wisdom.

*Woe to David's City*

29 Woe to you, Ariel, Ariel, the city where David settled!
Add year to year
and let your cycle of festivals go on.
[2]Yet I will besiege Ariel;
she will mourn and lament,
she will be to me like an altar hearth.[s]
[3]I will encamp against you all around;
I will encircle you with towers
and set up my siege works against you.

r25 The meaning of the Hebrew for this word is uncertain.
s2 The Hebrew for *hearth* sounds like the Hebrew for *Ariel.*

מְצֻרֹת׃ (4) וְשָׁפַלְתְּ מֵאֶרֶץ תְּדַבֵּרִי וּמֵעָפָר
and-out-of-dust you-will-speak from-ground and-you-will-be-low (4) siege-works

תִּשַּׁח אִמְרָתֵךְ וְהָיָה כְּאוֹב מֵאֶרֶץ קוֹלֵךְ
voice-of-you from-earth like-ghost and-he-will-come speech-of-you she-will-mumble

וּמֵעָפָר אִמְרָתֵךְ תְּצַפְצֵף׃ (5) וְהָיָה כְּאָבָק
like-dust but-he-will-become (5) she-will-whisper speech-of-you and-out-of-dust

דַּק הֲמוֹן זָרָיִךְ וּכְמֹץ עֹבֵר הֲמוֹן
horde-of blowing and-like-chaff ones-being-enemies-of-you many-of fine

עָרִיצִים וְהָיָה לְפֶתַע פִּתְאֹם׃ (6) מֵעִם יְהוָה צְבָאוֹת
Hosts Yahweh-of from-with (6) suddenly in-instant and-he-will-be ruthless-ones

תִּפָּקֵד בְּרַעַם וּבְרַעַשׁ וְקוֹל גָּדוֹל סוּפָה
windstorm great and-noise and-with-earthquake with-thunder you-will-be-visited

וּסְעָרָה וְלַהַב אֵשׁ אוֹכֵלָה׃ (7) וְהָיָה כַּחֲלוֹם
as-dream-of then-he-will-be (7) one-devouring fire and-flame-of and-tempest

חֲזוֹן לַיְלָה הֲמוֹן כָּל־ הַגּוֹיִם הַצֹּבְאִים עַל־אֲרִיאֵל
Ariel against the-ones-fighting the-nations all-of horde-of night vision-of

וְכָל־ צֹבֶיהָ וּמְצֹדָתָהּ וְהַמְּצִיקִים
and-the-ones-besieging and-fortress-of-her ones-attacking-her and-all-of

לָהּ׃ (8) וְהָיָה כַּאֲשֶׁר יַחֲלֹם הָרָעֵב וְהִנֵּה אוֹכֵל
one-eating and-see! the-hungry-man he-dreams as-when and-he-will-be (8) against-her

וְהֵקִיץ וְרֵיקָה נַפְשׁוֹ וְכַאֲשֶׁר יַחֲלֹם הַצָּמֵא
the-thirsty-man he-dreams and-as-when self-of-him and-hungry but-he-awakens

וְהִנֵּה שֹׁתֶה וְהֵקִיץ וְהִנֵּה עָיֵף וְנַפְשׁוֹ שׁוֹקֵקָה
thirsting and-self-of-him faint and-see! but-he-awakens one-drinking and-see!

כֵּן יִהְיֶה הֲמוֹן כָּל־ הַגּוֹיִם הַצֹּבְאִים עַל־ הַר צִיּוֹן׃
Zion Mount-of against the-ones-fighting the-nations all-of horde-of he-will-be so

(9) הִתְמַהְמְהוּ וּתְמָהוּ הִשְׁתַּעַשְׁעוּ וָשֹׁעוּ שָׁכְרוּ
they-are-drunk and-be-sightless! blind-yourselves! and-be-amazed! be-stunned! (9)

וְלֹא־ יַיִן נָעוּ וְלֹא שֵׁכָר׃ (10) כִּי־ נָסַךְ עֲלֵיכֶם יְהוָה
Yahweh over-you he-brought for (10) beer but-not they-stagger wine but-not

רוּחַ תַּרְדֵּמָה וַיְעַצֵּם אֶת־ עֵינֵיכֶם אֶת־ הַנְּבִיאִים וְאֶת־
and the-prophets *** eyes-of-you *** and-he-sealed deep-sleep spirit-of

רָאשֵׁיכֶם הַחֹזִים כִּסָּה׃ (11) וַתְּהִי לָכֶם חָזוּת הַכֹּל
the-whole vision-of to-you for-she-is (11) he-covered the-seers heads-of-you

כְּדִבְרֵי הַסֵּפֶר הֶחָתוּם אֲשֶׁר־ יִתְּנוּ אֹתוֹ אֶל־ יוֹדֵעַ
one-knowing to him they-give which the-one-being-sealed the-scroll as-words-of

הַסֵּפֶר לֵאמֹר קְרָא נָא־ זֶה וְאָמַר לֹא אוּכַל כִּי חָתוּם הוּא׃
he being-sealed for I-can not but-he-answers this please! read! to-say writing

°11 ק ספר

4Brought low, you will speak
from the ground;
your speech will mumble
out of the dust.
Your voice will come ghostlike
from the earth;
out of the dust your speech
will whisper.
5But your many enemies will
become like fine dust,
the ruthless hordes like
blown chaff.
Suddenly, in an instant,
6 the LORD Almighty will come
with thunder and earthquake
and great noise,
with windstorm and
tempest and flames of a
devouring fire.
7Then the hordes of all the
nations that fight against
Ariel,
that attack her and her
fortress and besiege her,
will be as it is with a dream,
with a vision in the night—
8as when a hungry man dreams
that he is eating,
but he awakens, and his
hunger remains;
as when a thirsty man dreams
that he is drinking,
but he awakens faint, with
his thirst unquenched.
So will it be with the hordes
of all the nations
that fight against Mount
Zion.
9Be stunned and amazed,
blind yourselves and be
sightless;
be drunk, but not from wine,
stagger, but not from beer.
10The LORD has brought over
you a deep sleep:
He has sealed your eyes (the
prophets);
he has covered your heads
(the seers).

11For you this whole vision is
nothing but words sealed in a
scroll. And if you give the scroll to
someone who can read, and say to
him, "Read this, please," he will
answer, "I can't; it is sealed." 12Or

וְנִתַּן הַסֵּפֶר עַל אֲשֶׁר לֹא־ יָדַע סֵפֶר לֵאמֹר קְרָא נָא־
please! read! to-say writing he-knows not whom to the-scroll or-he-is-given (12)

זֶה וְאָמַר לֹא יָדַעְתִּי סֵפֶר׃ וַיֹּאמֶר אֲדֹנָי יַעַן כִּי
that because Lord and-he-says (13) writing I-know not but-he-answers this

נִגַּשׁ הָעָם הַזֶּה בְּפִיו וּבִשְׂפָתָיו
and-with-lips-of-him with-mouth-of-him the-this the-people he-comes-near

כִּבְּדוּנִי וְלִבּוֹ רִחַק מִמֶּנִּי וַתְּהִי יִרְאָתָם אֹתִי
me to-worship-them and-she-is from-me he-is-far but-heart-of-him they-honor-me

מִצְוַת אֲנָשִׁים מְלֻמָּדָה׃ לָכֵן הִנְנִי יוֹסִף* לְהַפְלִיא
to-astound *he-will-do-again see-I! therefore (14) one-being-taught men rule-of

אֶת־ הָעָם־ הַזֶּה הַפְלֵא וָפֶלֶא וְאָבְדָה חָכְמַת
wisdom-of and-she-will-perish and-wonder to-bring-wonder the-this the-people ***

חֲכָמָיו וּבִינַת נְבֹנָיו תִּסְתַּתָּר׃
she-will-vanish ones-being-intelligent and-intelligence-of wise-ones-of-him

הוֹי הַמַּעֲמִיקִים מֵיהוָה לַסְתִּר עֵצָה וְהָיָה
and-he-is plan to-hide from-Yahweh the-ones-going-to-depths woe! (15)

בְמַחְשָׁךְ מַעֲשֵׂיהֶם וַיֹּאמְרוּ מִי רֹאֵנוּ וּמִי יוֹדְעֵנוּ׃
knowing-us and-who? seeing-us who? and-they-think works-of-them in-darkness

הַפְכְּכֶם אִם־ כְּחֹמֶר הַיֹּצֵר יֵחָשֵׁב
he-were-thought the-one-being-potter like-clay if turning-upside-down-of-you (16)

כִּי־ יֹאמַר מַעֲשֶׂה לְעֹשֵׂהוּ לֹא עָשָׂנִי וְיֵצֶר
and-pot he-made-me not to-one-forming-him formed-thing shall-he-say indeed

אָמַר לְיוֹצְרוֹ לֹא הֵבִין׃ הֲלוֹא־עוֹד מְעַט מִזְעָר
shortness little-of yet not? (17) he-knows not to-one-making-him can-he-say

וְשָׁב לְבָנוֹן לַכַּרְמֶל וְהַכַּרְמֶל
and-the-fertile-field into-the-fertile-field Lebanon and-he-will-be-turned

לַיַּעַר יֵחָשֵׁב׃ וְשָׁמְעוּ בַיּוֹם־ הַהוּא
the-that in-the-day and-they-will-hear (18) he-will-seem like-the-forest

הַחֵרְשִׁים דִּבְרֵי־ סֵפֶר וּמֵאֹפֶל וּמֵחֹשֶׁךְ עֵינֵי עִוְרִים
blind-ones eyes-of and-from-darkness and-from-gloom scroll words-of the-deaf-ones

תִּרְאֶינָה׃ וְיָסְפוּ עֲנָוִים בַּיהוָה שִׂמְחָה
rejoicing in-Yahweh humble-ones and-they-will-do-again (19) they-will-see

וְאֶבְיוֹנֵי אָדָם בִּקְדוֹשׁ יִשְׂרָאֵל יָגִילוּ׃ כִּי־
indeed (20) they-will-rejoice Israel in-Holy-One-of mankind and-ones-needy-of

אֶפֶס עָרִיץ וְכָלָה לֵץ וְנִכְרְתוּ
and-they-will-be-cut-down one-mocking and-he-will-disappear ruthless he-will-vanish

כָּל־ שֹׁקְדֵי אָוֶן׃ מַחֲטִיאֵי אָדָם בְּדָבָר
with-word man ones-making-guilt-of (21) evil ones-having-eye-of all-of

if you give the scroll to someone who cannot read, and say, "Read this, please," he will answer, "I don't know how to read."

13 The Lord says:

"These people come near to me with their mouth
and honor me with their lips,
but their hearts are far from me.
Their worship of me
is made up only of rules taught by men.[l]
14 Therefore once more I will astound these people
with wonder upon wonder;
the wisdom of the wise will perish,
the intelligence of the intelligent will vanish."
15 Woe to those who go to great depths
to hide their plans from the LORD,
who do their work in darkness and think,
"Who sees us? Who will know?"
16 You turn things upside down,
as if the potter were thought to be like the clay!
Shall what is formed say to him who formed it,
"He did not make me"?
Can the pot say of the potter,
"He knows nothing"?
17 In a very short time, will not Lebanon be turned into a fertile field
and the fertile field seem like a forest?
18 In that day the deaf will hear the words of the scroll,
and out of gloom and darkness
the eyes of the blind will see.
19 Once more the humble will rejoice in the LORD;
the needy will rejoice in the Holy One of Israel.
20 The ruthless will vanish,
the mockers will disappear,
and all who have an eye for evil will be cut down—
21 those who with a word make a man out to be guilty,

[l]13 Hebrew; Septuagint *They worship me in vain; / their teachings are but rules taught by men*

*14 The NIV reads *tsere* for *hireq* (יוֹסֵף), *one-doing-again.*

וְלַמּוֹכִיחַ בַּשַּׁעַר יְקֹשׁוּן וַיַּטּוּ
and-they-deprive they-set-snare in-the-court and-for-the-one-defending

בַתֹּהוּ צַדִּיק׃ לָכֵן כֹּה־ אָמַר יְהוָה אֶל־ בֵּית יַעֲקֹב
Jacob house-of to Yahweh he-says this therefore (22) innocent with-the-falseness

אֲשֶׁר פָּדָה אֶת־אַבְרָהָם לֹא־עַתָּה יֵבוֹשׁ יַעֲקֹב וְלֹא עַתָּה
now and-not Jacob he-will-be-ashamed now not Abraham *** he-redeemed who

פָּנָיו יֶחֱוָרוּ׃ כִּי בִרְאֹתוֹ יְלָדָיו
children-of-him when-to-see-him indeed (23) they-will-grow-pale faces-of-him

מַעֲשֵׂה יָדַי בְּקִרְבּוֹ יַקְדִּישׁוּ שְׁמִי
name-of-me they-will-keep-holy in-among-him hands-of-me work-of

וְהִקְדִּישׁוּ אֶת־ קְדוֹשׁ יַעֲקֹב וְאֶת־ אֱלֹהֵי יִשְׂרָאֵל
Israel God-of and Jacob Holy-One-of *** and-they-will-acknowledge-holiness

יַעֲרִיצוּ׃ וְיָדְעוּ תֹעֵי־ רוּחַ
spirit ones-wayward-of and-they-will-know (24) they-will-stand-in-awe

בִּינָה וְרוֹגְנִים יִלְמְדוּ־ לֶקַח׃ הוֹי
woe! (30:1) instruction they-will-accept and-ones-complaining understanding

בָּנִים סוֹרְרִים נְאֻם־ יְהוָה לַעֲשׂוֹת עֵצָה וְלֹא
but-not plan to-carry-out Yahweh declaration-of ones-being-obstinate children

מִנִּי וְלִנְסֹךְ מַסֵּכָה וְלֹא רוּחִי לְמַעַן סְפוֹת חַטָּאת עַל־
upon sin to-heap so-that Spirit-of-me but-not alliance and-to-form from-me

חַטָּאת׃ הַהֹלְכִים לָרֶדֶת מִצְרַיִם וּפִי לֹא שָׁאָלוּ
they-consulted not and-mouth-of-me Egypt to-go-down the-ones-traveling (2) sin

לָעוֹז בְּמָעוֹז פַּרְעֹה וְלַחְסוֹת בְּצֵל
in-shade-of and-to-seek-refuge Pharaoh in-protection-of to-seek-protection

מִצְרָיִם׃ וְהָיָה לָכֶם מָעוֹז פַּרְעֹה לְבֹשֶׁת וְהֶחָסוּת
and-the-refuge as-shame Pharaoh protection-of to-you but-he-will-be (3) Egypt

בְּצֵל־ מִצְרַיִם לִכְלִמָּה׃ כִּי־ הָיוּ בְצֹעַן שָׂרָיו
officials-of-him in-Zoan they-are though (4) as-disgrace Egypt in-shade-of

וּמַלְאָכָיו חָנֵס יַגִּיעוּ׃ כֹּל הִבְאִישׁ° עַל־
because-of he-will-be-shamed everyone (5) they-arrived Hanes and-envoys-of-him

עַם לֹא־ יוֹעִילוּ לָמוֹ לֹא לְעֵזֶר וְלֹא לְהוֹעִיל כִּי
but to-give-advantage and-not as-help not for-him they-have-use not people

לְבֹשֶׁת וְגַם־ לְחֶרְפָּה׃ מַשָּׂא בַּהֲמוֹת נֶגֶב
Negev concerning-animals-of oracle (6) as-disgrace and-also as-shame

בְּאֶרֶץ צָרָה וְצוּקָה לָבִיא וָלַיִשׁ מֵהֶם אֶפְעֶה וְשָׂרָף
and-snake adder of-them and-lioness lion and-distress hardship through-land-of

מְעוֹפֵף יִשְׂאוּ° עַל־ כֶּתֶף עֲיָרִים חֵילֵהֶם וְעַל־ דַּבֶּשֶׁת גְּמַלִּים
camels hump-of and-on riches-of-them donkeys back-of on they-carry one-darting

who ensnare the defender
in court
and with false testimony
deprive the innocent of
justice.

22 Therefore this is what the LORD, who redeemed Abraham, says to the house of Jacob:

"No longer will Jacob be
ashamed;
no longer will their faces
grow pale.
23 When they see among them
their children,
the work of my hands,
they will keep my name holy;
they will acknowledge the
holiness of the Holy One
of Jacob,
and will stand in awe of the
God of Israel.
24 Those who are wayward in
spirit will gain
understanding;
those who complain will
accept instruction."

*Woe to the Obstinate Nation*

30 "Woe to the obstinate
children,"
declares the LORD,
"to those who carry out plans
that are not mine,
forming an alliance, but not
by my Spirit,
heaping sin upon sin;
2 who go down to Egypt
without consulting me;
who look for help to Pharaoh's
protection,
to Egypt's shade for refuge.
3 But Pharaoh's protection will
be to your shame,
Egypt's shade will bring you
disgrace.
4 Though they have officials in
Zoan
and their envoys have
arrived in Hanes,
5 everyone will be put to shame
because of a people useless
to them,
who bring neither help nor
advantage,
but only shame and
disgrace."

6 An oracle concerning the animals of the Negev:

Through a land of hardship
and distress,
of lions and lionesses,
of adders and darting
snakes,
the envoys carry their riches
on donkeys' backs,
their treasures on the humps
of camels,

°5 ק הביש

אוֹצְרֹתָם עַל־ עַם לֹא יוֹעִילוּ׃ וּמִצְרַיִם הֶבֶל
useless and-Egypt (7) they-bring-profit not nation to treasures-of-them

וָרִיק יַעְזֹרוּ לָכֵן קָרָאתִי לָזֹאת רַהַב הֵם שָׁבֶת׃ עַתָּה
now (8) Do-Nothing they Rahab to-this I-call therefore they-help and-empty

בּוֹא כָתְבָהּ עַל־ לוּחַ אִתָּם וְעַל־ סֵפֶר חֻקָּהּ וּתְהִי
that-she-may-be inscribe-her! scroll and-on for-them tablet on write-her! go!

לְיוֹם אַחֲרוֹן לָעַד* עַד־ עוֹלָם׃ כִּי עַם מְרִי הוּא
this rebellion people-of indeed (9) everlasting to *for-ever coming for-day

בָּנִים כֶּחָשִׁים בָּנִים לֹא־ אָבוּ שְׁמוֹעַ תּוֹרַת
instruction-of to-listen they-are-willing not children deceitful-ones children

יְהוָה׃ אֲשֶׁר אָמְרוּ לָרֹאִים לֹא תִרְאוּ וְלַחֹזִים
and-to-the-prophets you-see-visions not to-the-seers they-say who (10) Yahweh

לֹא תֶחֱזוּ־ לָנוּ נְכֹחוֹת דַּבְּרוּ־ לָנוּ חֲלָקוֹת חֲזוּ
prophesy! pleasant-things to-us tell! right-things to-us you-give-visions not

מַהֲתַלּוֹת׃ סוּרוּ מִנֵּי־ דֶרֶךְ הַטּוּ מִנֵּי־ אֹרַח הַשְׁבִּיתוּ מִפָּנֵינוּ אֶת־
*** from-before-us stop! path from get-off! way from leave! (11) illusions

קְדוֹשׁ יִשְׂרָאֵל׃ לָכֵן כֹּה אָמַר קְדוֹשׁ יִשְׂרָאֵל יַעַן
because Israel Holy-One-of he-says this therefore (12) Israel Holy-One-of

מָאָסְכֶם בַּדָּבָר הַזֶּה וַתִּבְטְחוּ בְּעֹשֶׁק
on-oppression and-you-relied the-this to-the-message to-reject-you

וְנָלוֹז וַתִּשָּׁעֲנוּ עָלָיו׃ לָכֵן יִהְיֶה לָכֶם
for-you he-will-become therefore (13) on-him and-you-depended and-one-deceiving

הֶעָוֺן הַזֶּה כְּפֶרֶץ נֹפֵל נִבְעֶה בְּחוֹמָה נִשְׂגָּבָה
one-being-high in-wall one-bulging one-falling like-crack the-this the-sin

אֲשֶׁר־ פִּתְאֹם לְפֶתַע יָבוֹא שִׁבְרָהּ׃ וּשְׁבָרָהּ
and-he-will-break-her (14) collapse-of-her he-comes in-instant suddenly that

כְּשֵׁבֶר נֵבֶל יוֹצְרִים כָּתוּת לֹא יַחְמֹל
he-shows-mercy not being-shattered ones-making-pottery jar-of like-breaking-of

וְלֹא־ יִמָּצֵא בִמְכִתָּתוֹ חֶרֶשׂ לַחְתּוֹת אֵשׁ
fire to-take fragment among-piece-of-him he-will-be-found and-not

מִיָּקוּד וְלַחְשֹׂף מַיִם מִגֶּבֶא׃ כִּי כֹה־ אָמַר
he-says this indeed (15) from-cistern waters or-to-scoop from-one-being-kindled

אֲדֹנָי יְהוִה קְדוֹשׁ יִשְׂרָאֵל בְּשׁוּבָה וָנַחַת תִּוָּשֵׁעוּן
you-are-saved and-rest in-repentance Israel Holy-One-of Yahweh Sovereign

בְּהַשְׁקֵט וּבְבִטְחָה תִּהְיֶה גְּבוּרַתְכֶם וְלֹא אֲבִיתֶם׃
you-are-willing but-not strength-of-you she-is and-in-trust in-to-be-quiet

וַתֹּאמְרוּ לֹא־ כִי עַל־ סוּס נָנוּס עַל־ כֵּן תְּנוּסוּן
you-will-flee this for we-will-flee horse on so not and-you-said (16)

to that unprofitable nation,
7 to Egypt, whose help is
utterly useless.
Therefore I call her
Rahab the Do-Nothing.

8 Go now, write it on a tablet
for them,
inscribe it on a scroll,
that for the days to come
it may be an everlasting
witness.
9 These are rebellious people,
deceitful children,
children unwilling to listen
to the LORD's instruction.
10 They say to the seers,
"See no more visions!"
and to the prophets,
"Give us no more visions of
what is right!
Tell us pleasant things,
prophesy illusions.
11 Leave this way,
get off this path,
and stop confronting us
with the Holy One of
Israel!"

12 Therefore, this is what the
Holy One of Israel says:

"Because you have rejected
this message,
relied on oppression
and depended on deceit,
13 this sin will become for you
like a high wall, cracked and
bulging,
that collapses suddenly, in
an instant.
14 It will break in pieces like
pottery,
shattered so mercilessly
that among its pieces not a
fragment will be found
for taking coals from a
hearth
or scooping water out of a
cistern."

15 This is what the Sovereign
LORD, the Holy One of Israel, says:

"In repentance and rest is
your salvation,
in quietness and trust is
your strength,
but you would have none of
it.
16 You said, 'No, we will flee on
horses.'
Therefore you will flee!

*8 The NIV reads *sheva* for *qamets* and *tsere* for *pathah* (לְעֵד), *for-witness*.

וְעַל־קַל נִרְכָּב עַל־כֵּן יִקַּלּוּ רֹדְפֵיכֶם׃
and-on swift we-will-ride-off for this they-will-be-swift ones-pursuing-you

אֶלֶף אֶחָד מִפְּנֵי גַּעֲרַת אֶחָד מִפְּנֵי גַּעֲרַת חֲמִשָּׁה
(17) thousand one from-before threat-of one from-before threat-of five

תָּנֻסוּ עַד אִם־נוֹתַרְתֶּם כַּתֹּרֶן עַל־רֹאשׁ הָהָר
you-will-flee till when you-are-left like-the-flagstaff on top-of the-mountain

וְכַנֵּס עַל־הַגִּבְעָה׃ וְלָכֵן יְחַכֶּה יְהוָה לַחֲנַנְכֶם
and-like-the-banner on the-hill (18) and-yet he-longs Yahweh to-be-gracious-to-you

וְלָכֵן יָרוּם לְרַחֶמְכֶם כִּי־אֱלֹהֵי מִשְׁפָּט יְהוָה
and-yet he-rises to-show-compassion-to-you for God-of justice Yahweh

אַשְׁרֵי כָּל־חוֹכֵי לוֹ׃ כִּי־עַם בְּצִיּוֹן יֵשֵׁב
blessednesses-of all-of ones-waiting-of for-him (19) O! people of-Zion he-lives

בִּירוּשָׁלִַם בָּכוֹ לֹא־תִבְכֶּה חָנוֹן יָחְנְךָ
in-Jerusalem to-weep not you-will-weep to-be-gracious he-will-be-gracious-to-you

לְקוֹל זַעֲקֶךָ כְּשָׁמְעָתוֹ עָנָךְ׃ וְנָתַן
at-sound-of to-cry-you when-to-hear-him he-will-answer-you (20) although-he-gives

לָכֶם אֲדֹנָי לֶחֶם צָר וּמַיִם לָחַץ וְלֹא־יִכָּנֵף
to-you Lord bread-of adversity and-waters affliction then-not he-will-be-hidden

עוֹד מוֹרֶיךָ וְהָיוּ עֵינֶיךָ רֹאוֹת אֶת־מוֹרֶיךָ׃
more teachers-of-you but-they-will-be eyes-of-you ones-seeing *** teachers-of-you

וְאָזְנֶיךָ תִּשְׁמַעְנָה דָבָר מֵאַחֲרֶיךָ לֵאמֹר זֶה הַדֶּרֶךְ
(21) and-ears-of-you they-will-hear voice from-behind-you to-say this the-way

לְכוּ בוֹ כִּי תַאֲמִינוּ וְכִי תַשְׂמְאִילוּ׃
walk! in-him whether you-turn-right or-whether you-turn-left

וְטִמֵּאתֶם אֶת־צִפּוּי פְּסִילֵי כַסְפֶּךָ וְאֶת־
(22) then-you-will-defile *** one-overlaid-of idols-of silver-of-you and

אֲפֻדַּת מַסֵּכַת זְהָבֶךָ תִּזְרֵם כְּמוֹ דָוָה
covering-of image-of gold-of-you you-will-throw-away-them like menstrual-cloth

צֵא תֹּאמַר לוֹ׃ וְנָתַן מְטַר זַרְעֲךָ אֲשֶׁר־תִּזְרַע
away! you-will-say to-him (23) and-he-will-send rain-of seed-of-you that you-sow

אֶת־הָאֲדָמָה וְלֶחֶם תְּבוּאַת הָאֲדָמָה וְהָיָה דָשֵׁן וְשָׁמֵן
*** the-ground and-food produce-of the-land and-he-will-be rich and-plentiful

יִרְעֶה מִקְנֶיךָ בַּיּוֹם הַהוּא כַּר נִרְחָב׃
he-will-graze cattle-of-you in-the-day the-that meadow one-being-broad

וְהָאֲלָפִים וְהָעֲיָרִים עֹבְדֵי הָאֲדָמָה בְּלִיל חָמִיץ
(24) and-the-oxen and-the-donkeys ones-working-of the-soil fodder mash

יֹאכֵלוּ אֲשֶׁר־זֹרֶה בָרַחַת וּבַמִּזְרֶה׃
they-will-eat that one-spreading-out with-the-fork and-with-the-shovel

You said, 'We will ride off on swift horses.'
Therefore your pursuers will be swift!
17 A thousand will flee
at the threat of one;
at the threat of five
you will all flee away,
till you are left
like a flagstaff on a mountaintop,
like a banner on a hill."

18 Yet the LORD longs to be gracious to you;
he rises to show you compassion.
For the LORD is a God of justice.
Blessed are all who wait for him!

19 O people of Zion, who live in Jerusalem, you will weep no more. How gracious he will be when you cry for help! As soon as he hears, he will answer you.
20 Although the Lord gives you the bread of adversity and the water of affliction, your teachers will be hidden no more; with your own eyes you will see them.
21 Whether you turn to the right or to the left, your ears will hear a voice behind you, saying, "This is the way; walk in it."
22 Then you will defile your idols overlaid with silver and your images covered with gold; you will throw them away like a menstrual cloth and say to them, "Away with you!"

23 He will also send you rain for the seed you sow in the ground, and the food that comes from the land will be rich and plentiful. In that day your cattle will graze in broad meadows.
24 The oxen and donkeys that work the soil will eat fodder and mash, spread out with fork and shovel.
25 In the day of

(25) וְהָיָה ׀ עַל־ כָּל־ הַר גָּבֹהַ וְעַל כָּל־ גִּבְעָה נִשָּׂאָה
being-lofty hill every-of and-on high mountain every-of on and-he-will-be (25)

פְּלָגִים יִבְלֵי־ מָיִם בְּיוֹם הֶרֶג רָב בִּנְפֹל מִגְדָּלִים׃
towers when-to-fall great slaughter in-day-of waters flows-of streams

(26) וְהָיָה אוֹר־ הַלְּבָנָה כְּאוֹר הַחַמָּה וְאוֹר הַחַמָּה
the-sun and-light-of the-sun like-light-of the-moon light-of and-he-will-be (26)

יִהְיֶה שִׁבְעָתַיִם כְּאוֹר שִׁבְעַת הַיָּמִים בְּיוֹם חֲבֹשׁ יְהוָה
Yahweh to-bind-up on-day-of days seven-of like-light-of seven-times he-will-be

אֶת־ שֶׁבֶר עַמּוֹ וּמַחַץ מַכָּתוֹ יִרְפָּא׃ (27) הִנֵּה
see! (27) he-heals infliction-of-him and-wound-of people-of-him bruise-of ***

שֵׁם־ יְהוָה בָּא מִמֶּרְחָק בֹּעֵר אַפּוֹ וְכֹבֶד מַשָּׂאָה
cloud and-density-of anger-of-him burning from-afar coming Yahweh Name-of

שְׂפָתָיו מָלְאוּ זַעַם וּלְשׁוֹנוֹ כְּאֵשׁ אֹכָלֶת׃
one-consuming like-fire and-tongue-of-him wrath they-are-full lips-of-him

(28) וְרוּחוֹ כְּנַחַל שׁוֹטֵף עַד־צַוָּאר יֶחֱצֶה לַהֲנָפָה גוֹיִם
nations to-shake he-rises neck to rushing like-torrent and-breath-of-him (28)

בְּנָפַת שָׁוְא וְרֶסֶן מַתְעֶה עַל לְחָיֵי עַמִּים׃
peoples jaws-of in one-leading-astray and-bit destruction in-sieve-of

(29) הַשִּׁיר יִהְיֶה לָכֶם כְּלֵיל הִתְקַדֶּשׁ־ חָג וְשִׂמְחַת
and-rejoicing-of festival to-celebrate as-night-of to-you he-will-be the-song (29)

לֵבָב כַּהוֹלֵךְ בֶּחָלִיל לָבוֹא בְהַר־ יְהוָה אֶל־צוּר יִשְׂרָאֵל׃
Israel Rock-of to Yahweh to-mountain-of to-go with-the-flute as-the-one-going heart

(30) וְהִשְׁמִיעַ יְהוָה אֶת־ הוֹד קוֹלוֹ וְנַחַת
and-coming-down-of voice-of-him majesty-of *** Yahweh and-he-will-make-hear (30)

זְרוֹעוֹ יַרְאֶה בְּזַעַף אַף וְלַהַב אֵשׁ אוֹכֵלָה
one-consuming fire and-flame-of anger with-rage-of he-will-make-see arm-of-him

נֶפֶץ וָזֶרֶם וְאֶבֶן בָּרָד׃ (31) כִּי־ מִקּוֹל יְהוָה
Yahweh by-voice-of indeed (31) hail and-stone-of and-thunderstorm cloudburst

יֵחַת אַשּׁוּר בַּשֵּׁבֶט יַכֶּה׃ (32) וְהָיָה
and-he-will-be (32) he-will-strike with-the-scepter Assyria he-will-be-shattered

כֹּל מַעֲבַר מַטֵּה מוּסָדָה* אֲשֶׁר יָנִיחַ יְהוָה עָלָיו בְּתֻפִּים
to-tambourines on-him Yahweh he-lays which *appointment rod-of stroke-of every-of

וּבְכִנֹּרוֹת וּבְמִלְחֲמוֹת תְּנוּפָה נִלְחַם־ בָּהּ׃ (33) כִּי־
indeed (33) against-them he-fights blow-of-arm and-in-battles-of and-to-harps

עָרוּךְ מֵאֶתְמוּל תָּפְתֶּה גַּם־ הִוא לַמֶּלֶךְ הוּכָן
he-was-made-ready for-the-king she also Topheth from-long-ago being-prepared

הֶעְמִיק הִרְחִב מְדֻרָתָהּ אֵשׁ וְעֵצִים הַרְבֵּה נִשְׁמַת
breath-of to-be-abundant and-woods fire fire-pit-of-her he-made-wide he-made-deep

great slaughter, when the towers fall, streams of water will flow on every high mountain and every lofty hill. [26]The moon will shine like the sun, and the sunlight will be seven times brighter, like the light of seven full days, when the Lord binds up the bruises of his people and heals the wounds he inflicted.

[27]See, the Name of the Lord
comes from afar,
with burning anger and
dense clouds of smoke;
his lips are full of wrath,
and his tongue is a
consuming fire.
[28]His breath is like a rushing
torrent,
rising up to the neck.
He shakes the nations in the
sieve of destruction;
he places in the jaws of the
peoples
a bit that leads them astray.
[29]And you will sing
as on the night you
celebrate a holy festival;
your hearts will rejoice
as when people go up with
flutes
to the mountain of the Lord,
to the Rock of Israel.
[30]The Lord will cause men to
hear his majestic voice
and will make them see his
arm coming down
with raging anger and
consuming fire,
with cloudburst,
thunderstorm and hail.
[31]The voice of the Lord will
shatter Assyria;
with his scepter he will
strike them down.
[32]Every stroke the Lord lays on
them
with his punishing rod
will be to the music of
tambourines and harps,
as he fights them in battle
with the blows of his
arm.
[33]Topheth has long been
prepared;
it has been made ready for
the king.
Its fire pit has been made deep
and wide,
with an abundance of fire
and wood;
the breath of the Lord,

*32 The NIV reads with some ancient mss מוּסָרָה, *punishment-of-him*.

°32 ק בם

°33 ק היא

יְהוָה כְּנַחַל גָּפְרִית בֹּעֲרָה בָּהּ׃ הוֹי
woe! (31:1) to-her one-setting-ablaze burning-sulfur like-stream-of Yahweh

הַיֹּרְדִים מִצְרַיִם לְעֶזְרָה עַל־ סוּסִים יִשָּׁעֵנוּ וַיִּבְטְחוּ עַל־
in and-they-trust they-rely horses on for-help Egypt the-ones-going-down

רֶכֶב כִּי רָב וְעַל פָּרָשִׁים כִּי־ עָצְמוּ מְאֹד וְלֹא
but-not greatly they-are-strong because horsemen and-in many because chariot

שָׁעוּ עַל־ קְדוֹשׁ יִשְׂרָאֵל וְאֶת־ יְהוָה לֹא דָרָשׁוּ׃ וְגַם־הוּא חָכָם
wise he yet-too (2) they-seek not Yahweh or Israel Holy-One-of to they-look

וַיָּבֵא רָע וְאֶת־ דְּבָרָיו לֹא הֵסִיר וְקָם
and-he-will-rise he-brings-back not words-of-him and disaster and-he-can-bring

עַל־ בֵּית מְרֵעִים וְעַל־ עֶזְרַת פֹּעֲלֵי אָוֶן׃
evil ones-doing-of helper-of and-against ones-being-wicked house-of against

וּמִצְרַיִם אָדָם וְלֹא־ אֵל וְסוּסֵיהֶם בָּשָׂר וְלֹא־ רוּחַ
spirit and-not flesh and-horses-of-them God and-not man but-Egyptians (3)

וַיהוָה יַטֶּה יָדוֹ וְכָשַׁל עוֹזֵר
one-helping then-he-will-stumble hand-of-him he-stretches-out when-Yahweh

וְנָפַל עָזֻר וְיַחְדָּו כֻּלָּם יִכְלָיוּן׃
they-will-perish all-of-them and-together one-being-helped and-he-will-fall

כִּי כֹה אָמַר־ יְהוָה אֵלַי כַּאֲשֶׁר יֶהְגֶּה הָאַרְיֵה וְהַכְּפִיר
and-the-great-lion the-lion he-growls just-as to-me Yahweh he-says this indeed (4)

עַל־ טַרְפּוֹ אֲשֶׁר יִקָּרֵא עָלָיו מְלֹא
band-of against-him he-is-called-together though prey-of-him over

רֹעִים מִקּוֹלָם לֹא יֵחָת וּמֵהֲמוֹנָם
and-by-clamor-of-them he-is-frightened not by-shout-of-them ones-being-shepherds

לֹא יַעֲנֶה כֵּן יֵרֵד יְהוָה צְבָאוֹת לִצְבֹּא עַל־
on to-do-battle Hosts Yahweh-of he-will-come-down so he-is-disturbed not

הַר־ צִיּוֹן וְעַל־ גִּבְעָתָהּ׃ כְּצִפֳּרִים עָפוֹת כֵּן יָגֵן
he-will-shield so ones-hovering like-birds (5) height-of-her and-on Zion Mount-of

יְהוָה צְבָאוֹת עַל־ יְרוּשָׁלִַם גָּנוֹן וְהִצִּיל פָּסֹחַ
to-pass-over and-he-will-deliver to-shield Jerusalem over Hosts Yahweh-of

וְהִמְלִיט׃ שׁוּבוּ לַאֲשֶׁר הֶעְמִיקוּ סָרָה בְּנֵי יִשְׂרָאֵל׃
Israel sons-of revolt they-made-great to-whom return! (6) and-he-will-rescue

כִּי בַּיּוֹם הַהוּא יִמְאָסוּן אִישׁ אֱלִילֵי כַסְפּוֹ
silver-of-him idols-of every-one they-will-reject the-that in-the-day for (7)

וֶאֱלִילֵי זְהָבוֹ אֲשֶׁר עָשׂוּ לָכֶם יְדֵיכֶם חֵטְא׃
sinful hands-of-you for-you they-made that gold-of-him and-idols-of

וְנָפַל אַשּׁוּר בְּחֶרֶב לֹא־ אִישׁ וְחֶרֶב לֹא־ אָדָם
mortal not and-sword man not by-sword Assyria and-he-will-fall (8)

like a stream of burning
sulfur,
sets it ablaze.

*Woe to Those Who Rely on Egypt*

31 Woe to those who go
down to Egypt for help,
who rely on horses,
who trust in the multitude of
their chariots
and in the great strength of
their horsemen,
but do not look to the Holy
One of Israel,
or seek help from the LORD.
2 Yet he too is wise and can
bring disaster;
he does not take back his
words.
He will rise up against the
house of the wicked,
against those who help
evildoers.
3 But the Egyptians are men and
not God;
their horses are flesh and
not spirit.
When the LORD stretches out
his hand,
he who helps will stumble,
he who is helped will fall;
both will perish together.

4 This is what the LORD says to me:

"As a lion growls,
a great lion over his prey—
and though a whole band of
shepherds
is called together against
him,
he is not frightened by their
shouts
or disturbed by their
clamor—
so the LORD Almighty will
come down
to do battle on Mount Zion
and on its heights.
5 Like birds hovering overhead,
the LORD Almighty will
shield Jerusalem;
he will shield it and deliver it,
he will 'pass over' it and
will rescue it."

6 Return to him you have so greatly revolted against, O Israelites. 7 For in that day every one of you will reject the idols of silver and gold your sinful hands have made.

8 "Assyria will fall by a sword
that is not of man;
a sword, not of mortals, will

תֹּאכְלֶנּוּ וְנָס לוֹ מִפְּנֵי־חֶרֶב
she-will-devour-him | and-he-will-flee | for-him | from-before | sword

וּבַחוּרָיו לָמַס יִהְיוּ׃ (9) וְסַלְעוֹ
and-young-men-of-him | for-forced-labor | they-will-be | (9) | and-stronghold-of-him

מִמָּגוֹר יַעֲבוֹר וְחַתּוּ מִנֵּס
because-of-terror | he-will-fall | and-they-will-panic | because-of-battle-standard

שָׂרָיו נְאֻם־יְהוָה אֲשֶׁר־אוּר לוֹ בְּצִיּוֹן וְתַנּוּר
commanders-of-him | declaration-of | Yahweh | who | fire | of-him | in-Zion | and-furnace

לוֹ בִּירוּשָׁלָםִ׃ (32:1) הֵן לְצֶדֶק יִמְלָךְ־מֶלֶךְ
of-him | in-Jerusalem | (32:1) | see! | in-righteousness | he-will-reign | king

וּלְשָׂרִים לְמִשְׁפָּט יָשֹׂרוּ׃ (2) וְהָיָה־אִישׁ כְּמַחֲבֵא־
and-also-rulers | with-justice | they-will-rule | (2) | and-he-will-be | each | like-shelter-of

רוּחַ וְסֵתֶר זָרֶם כְּפַלְגֵי־מַיִם בְּצָיוֹן כְּצֵל סֶלַע־
wind | and-refuge-of | storm | like-streams-of | waters | in-desert | like-shadow-of | rock

כָּבֵד בְּאֶרֶץ עֲיֵפָה׃ (3) וְלֹא תִשְׁעֶינָה עֵינֵי רֹאִים
great | in-land | thirsty | (3) | then-not | they-will-be-closed | eyes-of | ones-seeing

וְאָזְנֵי שֹׁמְעִים תִּקְשַׁבְנָה׃ (4) וּלְבַב נִמְהָרִים
and-ears-of | ones-hearing | they-will-listen | (4) | and-mind-of | ones-being-rash

יָבִין לָדָעַת וּלְשׁוֹן עִלְּגִים תְּמַהֵר לְדַבֵּר
he-will-understand | to-know | and-tongue-of | stammerers | she-will-be-fluent | to-speak

צָחוֹת׃ (5) לֹא־יִקָּרֵא עוֹד לְנָבָל נָדִיב וּלְכִילַי לֹא
clear-things | (5) | not | he-will-be-called | longer | to-fool | noble | or-to-scoundrel | not

יֵאָמֵר שׁוֹעַ׃ (6) כִּי נָבָל נְבָלָה יְדַבֵּר וְלִבּוֹ
he-will-be-said | respectable | (6) | for | fool | folly | he-speaks | and-mind-of-him

יַעֲשֶׂה־אָוֶן לַעֲשׂוֹת חֹנֶף וּלְדַבֵּר אֶל־יְהוָה תּוֹעָה
he-is-busy | evil | to-practice | ungodliness | and-to-speak | concerning | Yahweh | error

לְהָרִיק נֶפֶשׁ רָעֵב וּמַשְׁקֶה צָמֵא יַחְסִיר׃ (7) וְכֵלַי
to-leave-empty | appetite | hungry | and-watering | thirsty | he-withholds | (7) | and-scoundrel

כֵּלָיו רָעִים הוּא זִמּוֹת יָעָץ לְחַבֵּל עֲנָוִים°
methods-of-him | wicked-ones | he | evil-schemes | he-makes-up | to-destroy | poor-ones

בְּאִמְרֵי־שֶׁקֶר וּבְדַבֵּר אֶבְיוֹן מִשְׁפָּט׃ (8) וְנָדִיב נְדִיבוֹת
with-words-of | lie | even-when-to-plead | needy | justice | (8) | but-noble | noble-things

יָעָץ וְהוּא עַל־נְדִיבוֹת יָקוּם׃ (9) נָשִׁים שַׁאֲנַנּוֹת קֹמְנָה
he-plans | and-he | by | noble-things | he-stands | (9) | women | complacent-ones | rise-up!

שְׁמַעְנָה קוֹלִי בָּנוֹת בֹּטְחוֹת* הַאְזֵנָּה אִמְרָתִי׃ (10) יָמִים
listen! | voice-of-me | daughters | ones-feeling-secure | hear! | saying-of-me | (10) | days

עַל־שָׁנָה תִּרְגַּזְנָה בֹּטְחוֹת כִּי כָּלָה בָצִיר
upon | year | you-will-tremble | ones-feeling-secure | for | he-will-fail | grape-harvest

devour them.
They will flee before the sword
and their young men will be put to forced labor.
9 Their stronghold will fall because of terror;
at sight of the battle standard their commanders will panic,"
declares the LORD,
whose fire is in Zion,
whose furnace is in Jerusalem.

*The Kingdom of Righteousness*

32 See, a king will reign in righteousness
and rulers will rule with justice.
2 Each man will be like a shelter from the wind
and a refuge from the storm,
like streams of water in the desert
and the shadow of a great rock in a thirsty land.

3 Then the eyes of those who see will no longer be closed,
and the ears of those who hear will listen.
4 The mind of the rash will know and understand,
and the stammering tongue will be fluent and clear.
5 No longer will the fool be called noble
nor the scoundrel be highly respected.
6 For the fool speaks folly,
his mind is busy with evil:
He practices ungodliness
and spreads error concerning the LORD;
the hungry he leaves empty
and from the thirsty he withholds water.
7 The scoundrel's methods are wicked,
he makes up evil schemes
to destroy the poor with lies,
even when the plea of the needy is just.
8 But the noble man makes noble plans,
and by noble deeds he stands.

*The Women of Jerusalem*

9 You women who are so complacent,
rise up and listen to me;
you daughters who feel secure,
hear what I have to say!
10 In little more than a year
you who feel secure will tremble;
the grape harvest will fail,

*9 Most mss have *sheva* under the *teth* (בֹּטְ).

°7 ק עניים

אֹסֶף בְּלִי יָבוֹא׃ (11) חִרְדוּ שַׁאֲנַנּוֹת רְגָזָה
shudder! complacent-women tremble! (11) he-will-come not fruit-harvest

בֹּטְחוֹת פְּשֹׁטָה וְעֹרָה וַחֲגוֹרָה עַל־ חֲלָצָיִם׃ (12) עַל־
on (12) waists around and-put-on! and-make-bare! strip-off! ones-being-secure

שָׁדַיִם סֹפְדִים עַל־ שְׂדֵי־ חֶמֶד עַל־ גֶּפֶן פֹּרִיָּה׃
one-being-fruitful vine for pleasantness fields-of for ones-beating breasts

(13) עַל אַדְמַת עַמִּי קוֹץ שָׁמִיר תַּעֲלֶה כִּי עַל־ כָּל־ בָּתֵּי
houses-of all-of for yes she-grows brier thorn people-of-me land-of for (13)

מָשׂוֹשׂ קִרְיָה עַלִּיזָה׃ (14) כִּי־ אַרְמוֹן נֻטָּשׁ הֲמוֹן עִיר
city noise-of he-will-be-abandoned fortress indeed (14) reveling city merriment

עֻזָּב עֹפֶל וָבַחַן הָיָה בְעַד מְעָרוֹת
wastelands for-sake-of he-will-become and-watchtower citadel he-will-be-deserted

עַד־עוֹלָם מְשׂוֹשׂ פְּרָאִים מִרְעֵה עֲדָרִים׃ (15) עַד־ יֵעָרֶה עָלֵינוּ
upon-us he-is-poured till (15) flocks pasture-of donkeys delight-of forever to

רוּחַ מִמָּרוֹם וְהָיָה מִדְבָּר לַכַּרְמֶל
into-the-fertile-field desert and-he-becomes from-on-high Spirit

וְכַרְמֶל° לַיַּעַר יֵחָשֵׁב׃ (16) וְשָׁכַן בַּמִּדְבָּר
in-the-desert and-he-will-dwell (16) he-seems like-the-forest and-the-fertile-field

מִשְׁפָּט וּצְדָקָה בַּכַּרְמֶל תֵּשֵׁב׃ (17) וְהָיָה
and-he-will-be (17) she-will-live in-the-fertile-field and-righteousness justice

מַעֲשֵׂה הַצְּדָקָה שָׁלוֹם וַעֲבֹדַת הַצְּדָקָה הַשְׁקֵט
to-be-quiet the-righteousness and-effect-of peace the-righteousness fruit-of

וָבֶטַח עַד־ עוֹלָם׃ (18) וְיָשַׁב עַמִּי בִּנְוֵה
in-dwelling-of people-of-me and-he-will-live (18) forever to and-confidence

שָׁלוֹם וּבְמִשְׁכְּנוֹת מִבְטַחִים וּבִמְנוּחֹת שַׁאֲנַנּוֹת׃
undisturbed-ones and-in-places-of-rest secure-ones and-in-homes peace

(19) וּבָרַד בְּרֶדֶת הַיָּעַר וּבַשִּׁפְלָה
and-into-the-level-place the-forest when-to-flatten though-he-hails (19)

תִּשְׁפַּל הָעִיר׃ (20) אַשְׁרֵיכֶם זֹרְעֵי עַל־ כָּל־
all-of by ones-sowing-of blessednesses-of-you (20) the-city she-will-be-leveled

מָיִם מְשַׁלְּחֵי רֶגֶל־ הַשּׁוֹר וְהַחֲמוֹר׃ (33:1) הוֹי
woe! (33:1) and-the-donkey the-cattle foot-of ones-letting-free-of streams

שׁוֹדֵד וְאַתָּה לֹא שָׁדוּד וּבוֹגֵד וְלֹא־
but-not and-one-being-traitor being-destroyed not but-you one-destroying

בָגְדוּ בוֹ כַּהֲתִמְךָ שׁוֹדֵד תּוּשַּׁד
you-will-be-destroyed destroying when-to-stop-you to-him they-betrayed

כְּנַלֹּתְךָ לִבְגֹּד יִבְגְּדוּ־ בָךְ׃ (2) יְהוָה חָנֵּנוּ
be-gracious-to-us! Yahweh (2) to-you they-will-betray to-betray when-to-stop-you

and the harvest of fruit will
not come.
11 Tremble, you complacent
women;
shudder, you daughters who
feel secure!
Strip off your clothes,
put sackcloth around your
waists.
12 Beat your breasts for the
pleasant fields,
for the fruitful vines
13 and for the land of my people,
a land overgrown with
thorns and briers—
yes, mourn for all houses of
merriment
and for this city of revelry.
14 The fortress will be
abandoned,
the noisy city deserted;
citadel and watchtower will
become a wasteland
forever,
the delight of donkeys, a
pasture for flocks,
15 till the Spirit is poured upon
us from on high,
and the desert becomes a
fertile field,
and the fertile field seems
like a forest.
16 Justice will dwell in the desert
and righteousness live in
the fertile field.
17 The fruit of righteousness will
be peace;
the effect of righteousness
will be quietness and
confidence forever.
18 My people will live in peaceful
dwelling places,
in secure homes,
in undisturbed places of
rest.
19 Though hail flattens the forest
and the city is leveled
completely,
20 how blessed you will be,
sowing your seed by every
stream,
and letting your cattle and
donkeys range free.

*Distress and Help*

33 Woe to you, O destroyer,
you who have not been
destroyed!
Woe to you, O traitor,
you who have not been
betrayed!
When you stop destroying,
you will be destroyed;
when you stop betraying,
you will be betrayed.
2 O LORD, be gracious to us;

°*15* ק והכרמל

לְךָ קִוִּינוּ הֱיֵה זְרֹעָם לַבְּקָרִים אַף־ יְשׁוּעָתֵנוּ
salvation-of-us also in-the-mornings strength-of-them be! we-long for-you

בְּעֵת צָרָה׃ (3) מִקּוֹל הָמוֹן נָדְדוּ עַמִּים מֵרוֹמְמֻתֶךָ
at-rising-of-you peoples they-flee thunder at-voice-of (3) distress in-time-of

נָפְצוּ גּוֹיִם׃ (4) וְאֻסַּף שְׁלַלְכֶם אֹסֶף
harvesting-of plunder-of-you and-he-is-harvested (4) nations they-scatter

הֶחָסִיל כְּמַשַּׁק גֵּבִים שֹׁקֵק בּוֹ׃ (5) נִשְׂגָּב
being-exalted (5) on-him one-pouncing locusts like-swarm-of the-young-locust

יְהוָה כִּי שֹׁכֵן מָרוֹם מִלֵּא צִיּוֹן מִשְׁפָּט וּצְדָקָה׃
and-righteousness justice Zion he-will-fill height one-dwelling for Yahweh

(6) וְהָיָה אֱמוּנַת עִתֶּיךָ חֹסֶן יְשׁוּעֹת
salvations rich-store-of times-of-you sure-foundation-of and-he-will-be (6)

חָכְמַת וָדָעַת יִרְאַת יְהוָה הִיא אוֹצָרוֹ׃ (7) הֵן
look! (7) treasure-of-him she Yahweh fear-of and-knowledge wisdom-of

אֶרְאֶלָּם צָעֲקוּ חֻצָה מַלְאֲכֵי שָׁלוֹם מַר יִבְכָּיוּן׃
they-weep bitter peace envoys-of in-street they-cry brave-man-of-them

(8) נָשַׁמּוּ מְסִלּוֹת שָׁבַת עֹבֵר אֹרַח הֵפֵר בְּרִית
treaty he-broke road one-traveling-of he-ceases highways they-are-deserted (8)

מָאַס עָרִים* לֹא חָשַׁב אֱנוֹשׁ׃ (9) אָבַל אֻמְלְלָה אֶרֶץ
land she-wastes-away he-mourns (9) anyone he-respects not *cities he-despises

הֶחְפִּיר לְבָנוֹן קָמַל הָיָה הַשָּׁרוֹן כָּעֲרָבָה וְנֹעֵר
and-one-dropping like-the-Arabah the-Sharon he-is he-withers Lebanon he-is-ashamed

בָּשָׁן וְכַרְמֶל׃ (10) עַתָּה אָקוּם יֹאמַר יְהוָה עַתָּה אֵרוֹמָם
I-will-be-exalted now Yahweh he-says I-will-arise now (10) and-Carmel Bashan

עַתָּה אֶנָּשֵׂא׃ (11) תַּהֲרוּ חֲשַׁשׁ תֵּלְדוּ קַשׁ רוּחֲכֶם
breath-of-you straw you-bear chaff you-conceive (11) I-will-be-lifted-up now

אֵשׁ תֹּאכַלְכֶם׃ (12) וְהָיוּ עַמִּים מִשְׂרְפוֹת שִׂיד קוֹצִים
thornbushes lime ones-burned peoples and-they-will-be (12) she-consumes-you fire

כְּסוּחִים בָּאֵשׁ יִצַּתּוּ׃ (13) שִׁמְעוּ רְחוֹקִים אֲשֶׁר
what ones-far-away hear! (13) they-will-set-ablaze with-fire ones-being-cut

עָשִׂיתִי וּדְעוּ קְרוֹבִים גְּבֻרָתִי׃ (14) פָּחֲדוּ בְצִיּוֹן
in-Zion they-are-terrified (14) power-of-me ones-near and-acknowledge! I-did

חַטָּאִים אָחֲזָה רְעָדָה חֲנֵפִים מִי ׀ יָגוּר לָנוּ אֵשׁ
fire of-us he-can-dwell who? godless-ones trembling she-grips sinners

אוֹכֵלָה מִי־ יָגוּר לָנוּ מוֹקְדֵי עוֹלָם׃ (15) הֹלֵךְ
one-walking (15) everlasting burnings-of of-us he-can-dwell who? one-consuming

צְדָקוֹת וְדֹבֵר מֵישָׁרִים מֹאֵס בְּבֶצַע מַעֲשַׁקּוֹת
extortions to-gain-of one-rejecting right-things and-one-speaking righteousnesses

we long for you.
Be our strength every
morning,
our salvation in time of
distress.
3 At the thunder of your voice,
the peoples flee;
when you rise up, the
nations scatter.
4 Your plunder, O nations, is
harvested as by young
locusts;
like a swarm of locusts men
pounce on it.

5 The LORD is exalted, for he
dwells on high;
he will fill Zion with justice
and righteousness.
6 He will be the sure foundation
for your times,
a rich store of salvation and
wisdom and knowledge;
the fear of the LORD is the
key to this treasure.[u]

7 Look, their brave men cry
aloud in the streets;
the envoys of peace weep
bitterly.
8 The highways are deserted,
no travelers are on the
roads.
The treaty is broken,
its witnesses[v] are despised,
no one is respected.
9 The land mourns[w] and wastes
away,
Lebanon is ashamed and
withers;
Sharon is like the Arabah,
and Bashan and Carmel
drop their leaves.

10 "Now will I arise," says the
LORD.
"Now will I be exalted;
now will I be lifted up.
11 You conceive chaff,
you give birth to straw;
your breath is a fire that
consumes you.
12 The peoples will be burned as
if to lime;
like cut thornbushes they
will be set ablaze."

13 You who are far away, hear
what I have done;
you who are near,
acknowledge my power!
14 The sinners in Zion are
terrified;
trembling grips the godless:
"Who of us can dwell with the
consuming fire?
Who of us can dwell with
everlasting burning?"
15 He who walks righteously
and speaks what is right,
who rejects gain from
extortion

[u] 6 Or *is a treasure from him*
[v] 8 Dead Sea Scrolls; Masoretic Text / *the cities*
[w] 9 Or *dries up*

*8 The NIV, with the Dead Sea Scrolls, reads *tsere* for *qamets* and *daleth* for *resh* (עֵדִים), *witnesses.*

נֹעֵר כַּפָּיו מִתְּמֹךְ בַּשֹּׁחַד אֹטֵם אָזְנוֹ
ear-of-him one-stopping to-the-bribe from-to-accept hands-of-him one-keeping

מִשְּׁמֹעַ דָּמִים וְעֹצֵם עֵינָיו מֵרְאוֹת
against-to-contemplate eyes-of-him and-one-shutting bloods against-to-hear

בְּרָע׃ הוּא מְרוֹמִים יִשְׁכֹּן מְצָדוֹת סְלָעִים מִשְׂגַּבּוֹ
refuge-of-him mountains fortresses-of he-will-dwell heights he (16) on-evil

לַחְמוֹ נִתָּן מֵימָיו נֶאֱמָנִים׃ מֶלֶךְ
king (17) ones-not-failing waters-of-him one-being-supplied bread-of-him

בְּיָפְיוֹ תֶּחֱזֶינָה עֵינֶיךָ תִּרְאֶינָה אֶרֶץ מַרְחַקִּים׃
afar-ones land-of they-will-view eyes-of-you they-will-see in-beauty-of-him

לִבְּךָ יֶהְגֶּה אֵימָה אַיֵּה סֹפֵר אַיֵּה
where? one-being-chief-officer where? terror he-will-ponder heart-of-you (18)

שֹׁקֵל אַיֵּה סֹפֵר אֶת־הַמִּגְדָּלִים׃ אֶת־עַם
people *** (19) the-towers *** one-being-chief-officer where? one-taking-revenue

נוֹעָז לֹא תִרְאֶה עַם עִמְקֵי שָׂפָה מִשְּׁמוֹעַ
from-to-hear speech ones-obscure-of people you-will-see not one-being-arrogant

נִלְעַג לָשׁוֹן אֵין בִּינָה׃ חֲזֵה צִיּוֹן קִרְיַת
city-of Zion look-upon! (20) comprehension without tongue one-being-strange-of

מוֹעֲדֵנוּ עֵינֶיךָ תִרְאֶינָה יְרוּשָׁלִַם נָוֶה שַׁאֲנָן אֹהֶל בַּל־
not tent peaceful abode Jerusalem they-will-see eyes-of-you festivals-of-us

יִצְעָן בַּל־ יִסַּע יְתֵדֹתָיו לָנֶצַח וְכָל־ חֲבָלָיו
ropes-of-him or-any-of to-forever stakes-of-him he-will-pull-up not he-will-move

בַּל־ יִנָּתֵקוּ׃ כִּי אִם־ שָׁם אַדִּיר יְהוָה לָנוּ מְקוֹם־
place-of to-us Yahweh Mighty-One there when indeed (21) he-will-be-broken not

נְהָרִים יְאֹרִים רַחֲבֵי יָדָיִם בַּל־ תֵּלֶךְ בּוֹ אֳנִי־ שַׁיִט
oar galley-of on-him she-will-ride not hands ones-broad-of streams rivers

וְצִי אַדִּיר לֹא יַעַבְרֶנּוּ׃ כִּי יְהוָה שֹׁפְטֵנוּ יְהוָה
Yahweh one-judging-us Yahweh for (22) he-will-sail-him not mighty and-ship

מְחֹקְקֵנוּ יְהוָה מַלְכֵּנוּ הוּא יוֹשִׁיעֵנוּ׃ נִטְּשׁוּ
they-hang-loose (23) he-will-save-us he king-of-us Yahweh one-giving-law-to-us

חֲבָלָיִךְ בַּל־ יְחַזְּקוּ כֵן־ תָּרְנָם בַּל־ פָּרְשׂוּ נֵס אָז
then sail they-spread not mast-of-them secure they-hold not riggings-of-you

חֻלַּק עַד־ שָׁלָל מַרְבֶּה פִּסְחִים בָּזְזוּ בַז׃
plunder they-will-plunder lame-ones being-abundant spoil to he-will-be-divided

וּבַל־ יֹאמַר שָׁכֵן חָלִיתִי הָעָם הַיֹּשֵׁב בָּהּ
in-her the-one-dwelling the-people I-am-ill resident he-will-say and-not (24)

נְשֻׂא עָוֹן׃ קִרְבוּ גוֹיִם לִשְׁמֹעַ וּלְאֻמִּים
and-peoples to-listen nations come-near! (34:1) sin being-forgiven-of

and keeps his hand from
accepting bribes,
who stops his ears against
plots of murder
and shuts his eyes against
contemplating evil—
16 this is the man who will dwell
on the heights,
whose refuge will be the
mountain fortress.
His bread will be supplied,
and water will not fail him.

17 Your eyes will see the king in
his beauty
and view a land that
stretches afar.
18 In your thoughts you will
ponder the former terror:
"Where is that chief officer?
Where is the one who took
the revenue?
Where is the officer in
charge of the towers?"
19 You will see those arrogant
people no more,
those people of an obscure
speech,
with their strange,
incomprehensible tongue.

20 Look upon Zion, the city of
our festivals;
your eyes will see Jerusalem,
a peaceful abode, a tent that
will not be moved;
its stakes will never be pulled
up,
nor any of its ropes broken.
21 There the LORD will be our
Mighty One.
It will be like a place of
broad rivers and streams.
No galley with oars will ride
them,
no mighty ship will sail
them.
22 For the LORD is our judge,
the LORD is our lawgiver,
the LORD is our king;
it is he who will save us.

23 Your rigging hangs loose:
The mast is not held secure,
the sail is not spread.
Then an abundance of spoils
will be divided
and even the lame will carry
off plunder.
24 No one living in Zion will say,
"I am ill";
and the sins of those who
dwell there will be
forgiven.

*Judgment Against the Nations*

34 Come near, you nations,
and listen;

הַקְשִׁיבוּ pay-attention! | תִּשְׁמַע let-her-hear | הָאָרֶץ the-earth | וּמְלֹאָהּ and-all-in-her | תֵּבֵל world | וְכָל־ and-all-of

צֶאֱצָאֶיהָ׃ ones-coming-out-of-her | (2) | כִּי indeed | קֶצֶף anger | לַיהוָה to-Yahweh | עַל־ with | כָּל־ all-of | הַגּוֹיִם the-nations

וְחֵמָה and-wrath | עַל־ upon | כָּל־ all-of | צְבָאָם army-of-them | הֶחֱרִימָם he-will-destroy-them | נְתָנָם he-will-give-them

לַטָּבַח׃ to-the-slaughter | (3) | וְחַלְלֵיהֶם and-slain-ones-of-them | יֻשְׁלָכוּ they-will-be-thrown-out

וּפִגְרֵיהֶם and-dead-bodies-of-them | יַעֲלֶה he-will-go-up | בָאְשָׁם stench-of-them | וְנָמַסּוּ and-they-will-be-soaked

הָרִים mountains | מִדָּמָם׃ with-blood-of-them | (4) | וְנָמַקּוּ and-they-will-be-dissolved | כָּל־ all-of | צְבָא star-of

הַשָּׁמַיִם the-heavens | וְנָגֹלּוּ and-they-will-be-rolled-up | כַסֵּפֶר like-the-scroll | הַשָּׁמָיִם the-skies | וְכָל־ and-all-of

צְבָאָם host-of-them | יִבּוֹל he-will-fall | כִּנְבֹל like-to-wither | עָלֶה leaf | מִגֶּפֶן from-vine | וּכְנֹבֶלֶת and-like-one-shriveling

מִתְּאֵנָה׃ from-fig-tree | (5) | כִּי־ indeed | רִוְּתָה she-drank-fill | בַשָּׁמַיִם in-the-heavens | חַרְבִּי sword-of-me | הִנֵּה see! | עַל־ on | אֱדוֹם Edom

תֵּרֵד she-descends | וְעַל־ and-on | עַם people-of | חֶרְמִי destruction-of-me | לְמִשְׁפָּט׃ in-judgment | (6) | חֶרֶב sword | לַיהוָה of-Yahweh

מָלְאָה she-is-bathed-in | דָם blood | הֻדַּשְׁנָה she-is-covered | מֵחֵלֶב with-fat | מִדַּם with-blood-of | כָּרִים lambs | וְעַתּוּדִים and-goats

מֵחֵלֶב with-fat-of | כִּלְיוֹת kidneys-of | אֵילִים rams | כִּי for | זֶבַח sacrifice | לַיהוָה to-Yahweh | בְּבָצְרָה in-Bozrah | וְטֶבַח and-slaughter

גָּדוֹל great | בְּאֶרֶץ in-land-of | אֱדוֹם׃ Edom | (7) | וְיָרְדוּ and-they-will-fall | רְאֵמִים wild-oxen | עִמָּם with-them | וּפָרִים and-bull-calves

עִם־ with | אַבִּירִים great-ones | וְרִוְּתָה and-she-will-be-drenched | אַרְצָם land-of-them | מִדָּם with-blood | וַעֲפָרָם and-dust-of-them

מֵחֵלֶב with-fat | יְדֻשָּׁן׃ he-will-be-soaked | (8) | כִּי for | יוֹם day-of | נָקָם vengeance | לַיהוָה to-Yahweh | שְׁנַת year-of

שִׁלּוּמִים retributions | לְרִיב to-uphold-cause | צִיּוֹן׃ Zion | (9) | וְנֶהֶפְכוּ and-they-will-be-turned | נְחָלֶיהָ streams-of-her

לְזֶפֶת into-pitch | וַעֲפָרָהּ and-dust-of-her | לְגָפְרִית into-burning-sulfur | וְהָיְתָה and-she-will-become | אַרְצָהּ land-of-her

לְזֶפֶת into-pitch | בֹּעֵרָה׃ blazing | (10) | לַיְלָה night | וְיוֹמָם and-by-day | לֹא not | תִכְבֶּה she-will-be-quenched | לְעוֹלָם to-forever

יַעֲלֶה he-will-rise | עֲשָׁנָהּ smoke-of-her | מִדּוֹר from-generation | לָדוֹר to-generation | תֶּחֱרָב she-will-lie-desolate

pay attention, you peoples!
Let the earth hear, and all that is in it,
the world, and all that comes out of it!
2 The LORD is angry with all nations;
his wrath is upon all their armies.
He will totally destroy[x] them,
he will give them over to slaughter.
3 Their slain will be thrown out,
their dead bodies will send up a stench;
the mountains will be soaked with their blood.
4 All the stars of the heavens will be dissolved
and the sky rolled up like a scroll;
all the starry host will fall
like withered leaves from the vine,
like shriveled figs from the fig tree.

5 My sword has drunk its fill in the heavens;
see, it descends in judgment on Edom,
the people I have totally destroyed.
6 The sword of the LORD is bathed in blood,
it is covered with fat—
the blood of lambs and goats,
fat from the kidneys of rams.
For the LORD has a sacrifice in Bozrah
and a great slaughter in Edom.
7 And the wild oxen will fall with them,
the bull calves and the great bulls.
Their land will be drenched with blood,
and the dust will be soaked with fat.

8 For the LORD has a day of vengeance,
a year of retribution, to uphold Zion's cause.
9 Edom's streams will be turned into pitch,
her dust into burning sulfur;
her land will become blazing pitch!
10 It will not be quenched night and day;
its smoke will rise forever.
From generation to generation it will lie desolate;

x2 The Hebrew term refers to the irrevocable giving over of things or persons to the LORD, often by totally destroying them; also in verse 5.

לְנֵצַח נְצָחִים אֵין עֹבֵר בָּהּ׃ וִירֵשׁוּהָ
and-they-will-possess-her (11) through-her one-passing not evers for-ever-of

קָאַת וְקִפּוֹד וְיַנְשׁוֹף וְעֹרֵב יִשְׁכְּנוּ־בָהּ
in-her they-will-nest and-raven and-great-owl and-screech-owl desert-owl

וְנָטָה עָלֶיהָ קַו־תֹהוּ וְאַבְנֵי־
and-plumb-lines-of chaos measuring-line-of over-her and-he-will-stretch

בֹהוּ׃ חֹרֶיהָ וְאֵין־שָׁם מְלוּכָה יִקְרָאוּ וְכָל־
and-all-of they-will-call kingdom there and-nothing nobles-of-her (12) desolation

שָׂרֶיהָ יִהְיוּ אָפֶס׃ וְעָלְתָה אַרְמְנֹתֶיהָ
citadels-of-her and-she-will-overrun (13) vanished they-will-be princes-of-her

סִירִים קִמּוֹשׂ וָחוֹחַ בְּמִבְצָרֶיהָ וְהָיְתָה נְוֵה
haunt-of and-she-will-become over-strongholds-of-her and-bramble nettle thorns

תַנִּים חָצִיר לִבְנוֹת יַעֲנָה׃ וּפָגְשׁוּ צִיִּים אֶת־
with desert-creatures and-they-will-meet (14) owl for-daughters-of home jackals

אִיִּים וְשָׂעִיר עַל־רֵעֵהוּ יִקְרָא אַךְ־שָׁם הִרְגִּיעָה
she-will-repose there also he-will-bleat other-of-him to and-wild-goat hyenas

לִּילִית וּמָצְאָה לָהּ מָנוֹחַ׃ שָׁמָּה
at-there (15) place-of-rest for-her and-she-will-find night-creature

קִנְּנָה קִפּוֹז וַתְּמַלֵּט וּבָקְעָה וְדָגְרָה
and-she-will-care-for-young and-she-will-hatch and-she-will-lay-eggs owl she-will-nest

בְצִלָּהּ אַךְ־שָׁם נִקְבְּצוּ דַיּוֹת אִשָּׁה רְעוּתָהּ׃
mate-of-her each falcons they-will-gather there also under-shadow-of-her

דִּרְשׁוּ מֵעַל־סֵפֶר יְהוָה וּקְרָאוּ אַחַת מֵהֵנָּה לֹא נֶעְדָּרָה
she-will-be-missing not of-these one and-read! Yahweh scroll-of in-upon look! (16)

אִשָּׁה רְעוּתָהּ לֹא פָקָדוּ כִּי־פִי הוּא צִוָּה
he-gave-order he mouth-of-me for they-will-lack not mate-of-her each

וְרוּחוֹ הוּא קִבְּצָן׃ וְהוּא־הִפִּיל לָהֶן גּוֹרָל
portion to-them he-allots and-he (17) he-will-gather-them he and-Spirit-of-him

וְיָדוֹ חִלְּקַתָּה לָהֶם בַּקָּו עַד־עוֹלָם
forever to by-the-measure to-them she-distributes and-hand-of-him

יִירָשׁוּהָ לְדוֹר וָדוֹר יִשְׁכְּנוּ־בָהּ׃
in-her they-will-dwell and-generation for-generation they-will-possess-her

יְשֻׂשׂוּם מִדְבָּר וְצִיָּה וְתָגֵל
and-she-will-rejoice and-parched-land desert they-will-be-glad (35:1)

עֲרָבָה וְתִפְרַח כַּחֲבַצָּלֶת׃ פָּרֹחַ תִּפְרַח
she-will-bloom to-bloom (2) like-crocus and-she-will-blossom wilderness

וְתָגֵל אַף גִּילַת וְרַנֵּן כְּבוֹד הַלְּבָנוֹן
the-Lebanon glory-of and-to-shout rejoicing-of indeed and-she-will-rejoice

no one will ever pass
through it again.
11 The desert owl[y] and screech
owl[y] will possess it;
the great owl[y] and the raven
will nest there.
God will stretch out over Edom
the measuring line of chaos
and the plumb line of
desolation.
12 Her nobles will have nothing
there to be called a
kingdom,
all her princes will vanish
away.
13 Thorns will overrun her
citadels,
nettles and brambles her
strongholds.
She will become a haunt for
jackals,
a home for owls.
14 Desert creatures will meet with
hyenas,
and wild goats will bleat to
each other;
there the night creatures will
also repose
and find for themselves
places of rest.
15 The owl will nest there and lay
eggs,
she will hatch them, and
care for her young under
the shadow of her wings;
there also the falcons will
gather,
each with its mate.

16 Look in the scroll of the LORD
and read:

None of these will be missing,
not one will lack her mate.
For it is his mouth that has
given the order,
and his Spirit will gather
them together.
17 He allots their portions;
his hand distributes them
by measure.
They will possess it forever
and dwell there from
generation to generation.

*Joy of the Redeemed*

35 The desert and the
parched land will be glad;
the wilderness will rejoice
and blossom.
Like the crocus, 2 it will burst
into bloom;
it will rejoice greatly and
shout for joy.
The glory of Lebanon will be

y11 The precise identification of these birds is uncertain.

נִתַּן־ לָהּ הֲדַר הַכַּרְמֶל וְהַשָּׁרוֹן הֵמָּה יִרְאוּ
they-will-see they and-the-Sharon the-Carmel splendor-of to-her he-will-be-given

כְבוֹד־ יְהוָה הֲדַר אֱלֹהֵינוּ׃ חַזְּקוּ יָדַיִם רָפוֹת וּבִרְכַּיִם
and-knees feeble-ones hands strengthen! (3) God-of-us splendor-of Yahweh glory-of

כֹּשְׁלוֹת אַמֵּצוּ׃ אִמְרוּ לְנִמְהֲרֵי־ לֵב חִזְקוּ אַל־
not be-strong! heart to-ones-being-fearful-of say! (4) steady! ones-giving-way

תִּירָאוּ הִנֵּה אֱלֹהֵיכֶם נָקָם יָבוֹא גְּמוּל אֱלֹהִים הוּא
he God retribution-of he-will-come vengeance God-of-you see! you-fear

יָבוֹא וְיֹשַׁעֲכֶם׃ אָז תִּפָּקַחְנָה עֵינֵי עִוְרִים
blind-ones eyes-of they-will-be-opened then (5) and-he-will-save-you he-will-come

וְאָזְנֵי חֵרְשִׁים תִּפָּתַחְנָה׃ אָז יְדַלֵּג כָּאַיָּל
like-the-deer he-will-leap then (6) they-will-be-unstopped deaf-ones and-ears-of

פִּסֵּחַ וְתָרֹן לְשׁוֹן אִלֵּם כִּי־ נִבְקְעוּ
they-will-gush-forth indeed mute tongue-of and-she-will-shout lame

בַמִּדְבָּר מַיִם וּנְחָלִים בָּעֲרָבָה׃ וְהָיָה
and-he-will-become (7) in-the-desert and-streams waters in-the-wilderness

הַשָּׁרָב לַאֲגַם וְצִמָּאוֹן לְמַבּוּעֵי מָיִם בִּנְוֵה
in-haunt-of waters into-springs-of and-thirsty-ground into-pool the-burning-sand

תַנִּים רִבְצָהּ חָצִיר לְקָנֶה וָגֹמֶא׃ וְהָיָה־ שָׁם
there and-he-will-be (8) and-papyrus to-reed grass lying-place-of-her jackals

מַסְלוּל וָדֶרֶךְ וְדֶרֶךְ הַקֹּדֶשׁ יִקָּרֵא לָהּ לֹא־
not to-her he-will-be-called the-Holiness and-Way-of and-way highway

יַעַבְרֶנּוּ טָמֵא וְהוּא־ לָמוֹ הֹלֵךְ דֶּרֶךְ
Way the-one-walking-of for-them but-he unclean he-will-journey-on-him

וֶאֱוִילִים לֹא יִתְעוּ׃ לֹא־ יִהְיֶה שָׁם אַרְיֵה
lion there he-will-be not (9) they-will-go-about not and-wicked-fools

וּפְרִיץ חַיּוֹת בַּל־ יַעֲלֶנָּה לֹא תִמָּצֵא שָׁם
there she-will-be-found not he-will-get-up-on-her not beasts or-ferocious-one-of

וְהָלְכוּ גְּאוּלִים׃ וּפְדוּיֵי יְהוָה
Yahweh and-ones-being-ransomed-of (10) ones-being-redeemed but-they-will-walk

יְשֻׁבוּן וּבָאוּ צִיּוֹן בְּרִנָּה וְשִׂמְחַת עוֹלָם
everlasting and-joy-of with-singing Zion and-they-will-enter they-will-return

עַל־ רֹאשָׁם שָׂשׂוֹן וְשִׂמְחָה יַשִּׂיגוּ וְנָסוּ יָגוֹן
sorrow and-they-will-flee they-will-overtake and-joy gladness head-of-them on

וַאֲנָחָה׃ וַיְהִי בְּאַרְבַּע עֶשְׂרֵה שָׁנָה לַמֶּלֶךְ חִזְקִיָּהוּ
Hezekiah of-the-king year ten in-four-of and-he-was (36:1) and-sighing

עָלָה סַנְחֵרִיב מֶלֶךְ־ אַשּׁוּר עַל כָּל־ עָרֵי יְהוּדָה
Judah cities-of all-of against Assyria king-of Sennacherib he-attacked

given to it,
the splendor of Carmel and Sharon;
they will see the glory of the LORD,
the splendor of our God.

[3]Strengthen the feeble hands,
steady the knees that give way;
[4]say to those with fearful hearts,
"Be strong, do not fear;
your God will come,
he will come with vengeance;
with divine retribution
he will come to save you."

[5]Then will the eyes of the blind be opened
and the ears of the deaf unstopped.
[6]Then will the lame leap like a deer,
and the mute tongue shout for joy.
Water will gush forth in the wilderness
and streams in the desert.
[7]The burning sand will become a pool,
the thirsty ground bubbling springs.
In the haunts where jackals once lay,
grass and reeds and papyrus will grow.

[8]And a highway will be there;
it will be called the Way of Holiness.
The unclean will not journey on it;
it will be for those who walk in that Way;
wicked fools will not go about on it.[z]
[9]No lion will be there,
nor will any ferocious beast get up on it;
they will not be found there.
But only the redeemed will walk there,
10 and the ransomed of the LORD will return.
They will enter Zion with singing;
everlasting joy will crown their heads.
Gladness and joy will overtake them,
and sorrow and sighing will flee away.

*Sennacherib Threatens Jerusalem*

36 In the fourteenth year of King Hezekiah's reign, Sennacherib king of Assyria attacked all the fortified cities of

[z]8 Or / *the simple will not stray from it*

הַבְּצֻרוֹת וַיִּתְפְּשֵׂם׃ וַיִּשְׁלַח מֶלֶךְ־אַשּׁוּר ׀
Assyria king-of then-he-sent (2) and-he-captured-them the-ones-being-fortified

אֶת־רַב־שָׁקֵה מִלָּכִישׁ יְרוּשָׁלַ͏ְמָה אֶל־הַמֶּלֶךְ חִזְקִיָּהוּ
Hezekiah the-king to to-Jerusalem from-Lachish field-commander chief-of ***

בְּחֵיל כָּבֵד וַיַּעֲמֹד בִּתְעָלַת הַבְּרֵכָה הָעֶלְיוֹנָה בִּמְסִלַּת
on-road-of the-Upper the-Pool at-aqueduct-of when-he-stopped large with-army

שְׂדֵה כוֹבֵס׃ וַיֵּצֵא אֵלָיו אֶלְיָקִים בֶּן־חִלְקִיָּהוּ אֲשֶׁר עַל־
over who Hilkiah son-of Eliakim to-him and-he-went-out (3) One-Washing Field-of

הַבָּיִת וְשֶׁבְנָא הַסֹּפֵר וְיוֹאָח בֶּן־אָסָף הַמַּזְכִּיר׃
the-one-recording Asaph son-of and-Joah the-secretary and-Shebna the-palace

וַיֹּאמֶר אֲלֵיהֶם רַב־שָׁקֵה אִמְרוּ־נָא אֶל־חִזְקִיָּהוּ כֹּה־
this Hezekiah to now! tell! field-commander chief-of to-them and-he-said (4)

אָמַר הַמֶּלֶךְ הַגָּדוֹל מֶלֶךְ אַשּׁוּר מָה הַבִּטָּחוֹן הַזֶּה אֲשֶׁר
that the-this the-confidence what? Assyria king-of the-great the-king he-says

בָּטָחְתָּ׃ אָמַרְתִּי אַךְ־דְּבַר־שְׂפָתַיִם עֵצָה וּגְבוּרָה לַמִּלְחָמָה
of-the-military and-strength strategy lips word-of only I-said (5) you-confide

עַתָּה עַל־מִי בָטַחְתָּ כִּי מָרַדְתָּ בִּי׃ הִנֵּה בָטַחְתָּ עַל־
on you-depend look! (6) against-me you-rebel that you-depend whom? on now

מִשְׁעֶנֶת הַקָּנֶה הָרָצוּץ הַזֶּה עַל־מִצְרַיִם אֲשֶׁר יִסָּמֵךְ אִישׁ
man he-leans which Egypt on the-that the-one-being-splintered the-reed staff-of

עָלָיו וּבָא בְכַפּוֹ וּנְקָבָהּ כֵּן פַּרְעֹה מֶלֶךְ־
king-of Pharaoh such and-he-wounds-her through-hand-of-him and-he-pierces on-him

מִצְרַיִם לְכָל־הַבֹּטְחִים עָלָיו׃ וְכִי־תֹאמַר אֵלַי אֶל־יְהוָה
Yahweh on to-me you-say and-if (7) on-him the-ones-depending to-all-of Egypt

אֱלֹהֵינוּ בָּטָחְנוּ הֲלוֹא־הוּא אֲשֶׁר הֵסִיר חִזְקִיָּהוּ אֶת־בָּמֹתָיו וְאֶת־
and high-places-of-him *** Hezekiah he-removed who he not? we-depend God-of-us

מִזְבְּחֹתָיו וַיֹּאמֶר לִיהוּדָה וְלִירוּשָׁלַ͏ִם לִפְנֵי הַמִּזְבֵּחַ הַזֶּה
the-this the-altar before and-to-Jerusalem to-Judah and-he-said altars-of-him

תִּשְׁתַּחֲווּ׃ וְעַתָּה הִתְעָרֶב נָא אֶת־אֲדֹנִי הַמֶּלֶךְ
the-king master-of-me with now! make-bargain! and-now (8) you-must-worship

אַשּׁוּר וְאֶתְּנָה לְךָ אַלְפַּיִם סוּסִים אִם־תּוּכַל לָתֶת לְךָ
of-you to-put you-can if horses two-thousands to-you and-I-will-give Assyria

רֹכְבִים עֲלֵיהֶם׃ וְאֵיךְ תָּשִׁיב אֵת פְּנֵי פַחַת אַחַד
one-of officer-of faces-of *** can-you-repulse then-how? (9) on-them ones-riding

עַבְדֵי אֲדֹנִי הַקְּטַנִּים וַתִּבְטַח לְךָ עַל־מִצְרַיִם
Egypt on for-you though-you-depend the-least-ones master-of-me officials-of

לְרֶכֶב וּלְפָרָשִׁים׃ וְעַתָּה הֲמִבַּלְעֲדֵי יְהוָה עָלִיתִי עַל־
against I-attacked Yahweh from-without? and-further (10) and-for-horsemen for-chariot

Judah and captured them. [2]Then the king of Assyria sent his field commander with a large army from Lachish to King Hezekiah at Jerusalem. When the commander stopped at the aqueduct of the Upper Pool, on the road to the Washerman's Field, [3]Eliakim son of Hilkiah the palace administrator, Shebna the secretary, and Joah son of Asaph the recorder went out to him.

[4]The field commander said to them, "Tell Hezekiah,

"'This is what the great king, the king of Assyria, says: On what are you basing this confidence of yours? [5]You say you have strategy and military strength—but you speak only empty words. On whom are you depending, that you rebel against me? [6]Look now, you are depending on Egypt, that splintered reed of a staff, which pierces a man's hand and wounds him if he leans on it! Such is Pharaoh king of Egypt to all who depend on him. [7]And if you say to me, "We are depending on the LORD our God"—isn't he the one whose high places and altars Hezekiah removed, saying to Judah and Jerusalem, "You must worship before this altar"?

[8]"'Come now, make a bargain with my master, the king of Assyria: I will give you two thousand horses—if you can put riders on them! [9]How then can you repulse one officer of the least of my master's officials, even though you are depending on Egypt for chariots and horsemen? [10]Furthermore, have I come to attack and destroy this land without the

הָאָרֶץ הַזֹּאת לְהַשְׁחִיתָהּ יְהוָה אָמַר אֵלַי עֲלֵה אֶל־הָאָרֶץ
the-country against march! to-me he-told Yahweh to-destroy-her the-this the-land

הַזֹּאת וְהַשְׁחִיתָהּ׃ וַיֹּאמֶר אֶלְיָקִים וְשֶׁבְנָא וְיוֹאָח אֶל־
to and-Joah and-Shebna Eliakim then-he-said (11) and-destroy-her! the-this

רַב־שָׁקֵה דַּבֶּר־נָא אֶל־עֲבָדֶיךָ אֲרָמִית כִּי
since Aramaic servants-of-you to now! speak! field-commander chief-of

שֹׁמְעִים אֲנָחְנוּ וְאַל־תְּדַבֵּר אֵלֵינוּ יְהוּדִית בְּאָזְנֵי הָעָם אֲשֶׁר
who the-people in-ears-of Hebrew to-us you-speak but-not we ones-understanding

עַל־הַחוֹמָה׃ וַיֹּאמֶר רַב־שָׁקֵה הַאֶל אֲדֹנֶיךָ
masters-of-you to? field-commander chief-of but-he-replied (12) the-wall on

וְאֵלֶיךָ שְׁלָחַנִי אֲדֹנִי לְדַבֵּר אֶת־הַדְּבָרִים הָאֵלֶּה הֲלֹא עַל־
to not? the-these the-things *** to-say master-of-me he-sent-me and-to-you

הָאֲנָשִׁים הַיֹּשְׁבִים עַל־הַחוֹמָה לֶאֱכֹל אֶת־חֲרָאֵיהֶם* וְלִשְׁתּוֹת אֶת־
*** and-to-drink *filths-of-them *** to-eat the-wall on the-ones-sitting the-men

שֵׁינֵיהֶם† עִמָּכֶם׃ וַיַּעֲמֹד רַב־שָׁקֵה וַיִּקְרָא
and-he-called field-commander chief-of then-he-stood (13) like-you †urines-of-them

בְקוֹל־גָּדוֹל יְהוּדִית וַיֹּאמֶר שִׁמְעוּ אֶת־דִּבְרֵי הַמֶּלֶךְ הַגָּדוֹל מֶלֶךְ
king-of the-great the-king words-of *** hear! and-he-said Hebrew loud with-voice

אַשּׁוּר׃ כֹּה אָמַר הַמֶּלֶךְ אַל־יַשִּׁא לָכֶם חִזְקִיָּהוּ כִּי לֹא־
not for Hezekiah to-you let-him-deceive not the-king he-says this (14) Assyria

יוּכַל לְהַצִּיל אֶתְכֶם׃ וְאַל־יַבְטַח אֶתְכֶם חִזְקִיָּהוּ אֶל־יְהוָה
Yahweh in Hezekiah you let-him-cause-to-trust and-not (15) you to-deliver he-can

לֵאמֹר הַצֵּל יַצִּילֵנוּ יְהוָה לֹא תִנָּתֵן הָעִיר
the-city she-will-be-given not Yahweh he-will-deliver-us to-deliver to-say

הַזֹּאת בְּיַד מֶלֶךְ אַשּׁוּר׃ אַל־תִּשְׁמְעוּ אֶל־חִזְקִיָּהוּ כִּי כֹה
this for Hezekiah to you-listen not (16) Assyria king-of into-hand-of the-this

אָמַר הַמֶּלֶךְ אַשּׁוּר עֲשׂוּ־אִתִּי בְרָכָה וּצְאוּ אֵלַי וְאִכְלוּ אִישׁ־
each then-eat! to-me and-come-out! peace with-me make! Assyria king-of he-says

גַּפְנוֹ וְאִישׁ תְּאֵנָתוֹ וּשְׁתוּ אִישׁ מֵי־בוֹרוֹ׃
cistern-of-him waters-of each and-drink! fig-tree-of-him and-each vine-of-him

עַד־בֹּאִי וְלָקַחְתִּי אֶתְכֶם אֶל־אֶרֶץ כְּאַרְצְכֶם אֶרֶץ דָּגָן
grain land-of like-land-of-you land to you and-I-take to-come-me until (17)

וְתִירוֹשׁ אֶרֶץ לֶחֶם וּכְרָמִים׃ פֶּן־יַסִּית אֶתְכֶם חִזְקִיָּהוּ
Hezekiah you let-him-mislead not (18) and-vineyards bread land-of and-new-wine

לֵאמֹר יְהוָה יַצִּילֵנוּ הַהִצִּילוּ אֱלֹהֵי הַגּוֹיִם אִישׁ אֶת־
*** any the-nations gods-of did-they-deliver? he-will-deliver-us Yahweh to-say

אַרְצוֹ מִיַּד מֶלֶךְ אַשּׁוּר׃ אַיֵּה אֱלֹהֵי חֲמָת וְאַרְפָּד
and-Arpad Hamath gods-of where? (19) Assyria king-of from-hand-of land-of-him

LORD? The LORD himself told me to march against this country and destroy it.' "

11 Then Eliakim, Shebna and Joah said to the field commander, "Please speak to your servants in Aramaic, since we understand it. Don't speak to us in Hebrew in the hearing of the people on the wall."

12 But the commander replied, "Was it only to your master and you that my master sent me to say these things, and not to the men sitting on the wall—who, like you, will have to eat their own filth and drink their own urine?"

13 Then the commander stood and called out in Hebrew, "Hear the words of the great king, the king of Assyria! 14 This is what the king says: Do not let Hezekiah deceive you. He cannot deliver you! 15 Do not let Hezekiah persuade you to trust in the LORD when he says, 'The LORD will surely deliver us; this city will not be given into the hand of the king of Assyria.'

16 "Do not listen to Hezekiah. This is what the king of Assyria says: Make peace with me and come out to me. Then every one of you will eat from his own vine and fig tree and drink water from his own cistern, 17 until I come and take you to a land like your own—a land of grain and new wine, a land of bread and vineyards.

18 "Do not let Hezekiah mislead you when he says, 'The LORD will deliver us.' Has the god of any nation ever delivered his land from the hand of the king of Assyria? 19 Where are the gods of Hamath

*12a The *Qere*, *outgoing-of-them*, is a less graphic word than the *Kethib*.

†12b The *Qere*, *waters-of feet-of-them*, is a less graphic word than the *Kethib*.

°12a ק צואתם

°12b ק מימי רגליהם

אַיֵּה אֱלֹהֵי סְפַרְוָיִם וְכִי־ הִצִּילוּ אֶת־שֹׁמְרוֹן מִיָּדִי׃
from-hand-of-me Samaria *** they-rescued and-indeed Sepharvaim gods-of where?

(20) מִי בְּכָל־ אֱלֹהֵי הָאֲרָצוֹת הָאֵלֶּה אֲשֶׁר־ הִצִּילוּ אֶת־
*** they-saved who the-these the-countries gods-of of-all-of who? (20)

אַרְצָם מִיָּדִי כִּי־ יַצִּיל יְהוָה אֶת־ יְרוּשָׁלַםִ
Jerusalem *** Yahweh can-he-deliver how? from-hand-of-me lands-of-them

מִיָּדִי׃ (21) וַיַּחֲרִישׁוּ וְלֹא־ עָנוּ אֹתוֹ דָּבָר
thing him they-replied and-not but-they-remained-silent (21) from-hand-of-me

כִּי־ מִצְוַת הַמֶּלֶךְ הִיא לֵאמֹר לֹא תַעֲנֻהוּ׃ (22) וַיָּבֹא
then-he-went (22) you-answer-him not to-say this the-king command-of because

אֶלְיָקִים בֶּן־ חִלְקִיָּהוּ אֲשֶׁר־ עַל־ הַבַּיִת וְשֶׁבְנָא הַסּוֹפֵר וְיוֹאָח
and-Joah the-secretary and-Shebna the-palace over who Hilkiah son-of Eliakim

בֶּן־ אָסָף הַמַּזְכִּיר אֶל־ חִזְקִיָּהוּ קְרוּעֵי בְגָדִים
clothes ones-being-torn-of Hezekiah to the-one-recording Asaph son-of

וַיַּגִּידוּ לוֹ אֵת דִּבְרֵי רַב־ שָׁקֵה׃ (37:1) וַיְהִי
and-he-was (37:1) field-commander chief-of words-of *** to-him and-they-told

כִּשְׁמֹעַ הַמֶּלֶךְ חִזְקִיָּהוּ וַיִּקְרַע אֶת־ בְּגָדָיו וַיִּתְכַּס
and-he-put-on clothes-of-him *** then-he-tore Hezekiah the-king when-to-hear

בַּשָּׂק וַיָּבֹא בֵּית יְהוָה׃ (2) וַיִּשְׁלַח אֶת־
*** and-he-sent (2) Yahweh temple-of and-he-went-into with-the-sackcloth

אֶלְיָקִים אֲשֶׁר־עַל־ הַבַּיִת וְאֵת ׀ שֶׁבְנָא הַסּוֹפֵר וְאֵת זִקְנֵי הַכֹּהֲנִים
the-priests leaders-of and the-secretary Shebna and the-palace over who Eliakim

מִתְכַּסִּים בַּשַּׂקִּים אֶל־ יְשַׁעְיָהוּ בֶן־ אָמוֹץ הַנָּבִיא׃
the-prophet Amoz son-of Isaiah to in-the-sackcloths ones-being-clothed

(3) וַיֹּאמְרוּ אֵלָיו כֹּה אָמַר חִזְקִיָּהוּ יוֹם־ צָרָה וְתוֹכֵחָה
and-rebuke distress day-of Hezekiah he-says this to-him and-they-told (3)

וּנְאָצָה הַיּוֹם הַזֶּה כִּי בָאוּ בָנִים עַד־מַשְׁבֵּר וְכֹחַ
and-strength birth to children they-come as-when the-this the-day and-disgrace

אַיִן לְלֵדָה׃ (4) אוּלַי יִשְׁמַע יְהוָה אֱלֹהֶיךָ אֵת ׀ דִּבְרֵי
words-of *** God-of-you Yahweh he-will-hear maybe (4) to-deliver there-is-not

רַב־ שָׁקֵה אֲשֶׁר שְׁלָחוֹ מֶלֶךְ־ אַשּׁוּר ׀ אֲדֹנָיו
masters-of-him Assyria king-of he-sent-him whom field-commander chief-of

לְחָרֵף אֱלֹהִים חַי וְהוֹכִיחַ בַּדְּבָרִים אֲשֶׁר שָׁמַע יְהוָה
Yahweh he-heard that for-the-words and-he-will-rebuke living God to-ridicule

אֱלֹהֶיךָ וְנָשָׂאתָ תְפִלָּה בְּעַד הַשְּׁאֵרִית הַנִּמְצָאָה׃ (5) וַיָּבֹאוּ
when-they-came (5) the-one-surviving the-remnant for prayer so-you-lift God-of-you

עַבְדֵי הַמֶּלֶךְ חִזְקִיָּהוּ אֶל־יְשַׁעְיָהוּ׃ (6) וַיֹּאמֶר אֲלֵיהֶם יְשַׁעְיָהוּ כֹּה
this Isaiah to-them then-he-said (6) Isaiah to Hezekiah the-king officials-of

and Arpad? Where are the gods of Sepharvaim? Have they rescued Samaria from my hand? [20]Who of all the gods of these countries has been able to save his land from me? How then can the LORD deliver Jerusalem from my hand?"

[21]But the people remained silent and said nothing in reply, because the king had commanded, "Do not answer him."

[22]Then Eliakim son of Hilkiah the palace administrator, Shebna the secretary, and Joah son of Asaph the recorder went to Hezekiah, with their clothes torn, and told him what the field commander had said.

### *Jerusalem's Deliverance Foretold*

37 When King Hezekiah heard this, he tore his clothes and put on sackcloth and went into the temple of the LORD. [2]He sent Eliakim the palace administrator, Shebna the secretary, and the leading priests, all wearing sackcloth, to the prophet Isaiah son of Amoz. [3]They told him, "This is what Hezekiah says: This day is a day of distress and rebuke and disgrace, as when children come to the point of birth and there is no strength to deliver them. [4]It may be that the LORD your God will hear the words of the field commander, whom his master, the king of Assyria, has sent to ridicule the living God, and that he will rebuke him for the words the LORD your God has heard. Therefore pray for the remnant that still survives."

[5]When King Hezekiah's officials came to Isaiah, [6]Isaiah said to

תֹּאמְרוּן אֶל־אֲדֹנֵיכֶם כֹּה אָמַר יְהוָה אַל־תִּירָא מִפְּנֵי
from-before you-be-afraid not Yahweh he-says this masters-of-you to you-tell

הַדְּבָרִים אֲשֶׁר שָׁמַעְתָּ אֲשֶׁר גִּדְּפוּ נַעֲרֵי מֶלֶךְ־אַשּׁוּר אוֹתִי׃
me Assyria king-of underlings-of they-blasphemed which you-heard that the-words

הִנְנִי נוֹתֵן בּוֹ רוּחַ וְשָׁמַע שְׁמוּעָה וְשָׁב אֶל־
to then-he-will-return report when-he-hears spirit in-him putting see-I! (7)

אַרְצוֹ וְהִפַּלְתִּיו בַּחֶרֶב בְּאַרְצוֹ׃
in-country-of-him with-the-sword and-I-will-have-cut-down-him country-of-him

וַיָּשָׁב רַב־שָׁקֵה וַיִּמְצָא אֶת־מֶלֶךְ אַשּׁוּר
Assyria king-of *** and-he-found field-commander chief-of and-he-withdrew (8)

נִלְחָם עַל־לִבְנָה כִּי שָׁמַע כִּי נָסַע מִלָּכִישׁ׃ וַיִּשְׁמַע
now-he-heard (9) from-Lachish he-left that he-heard when Libnah against fighting

עַל־תִּרְהָקָה מֶלֶךְ־כּוּשׁ לֵאמֹר יָצָא לְהִלָּחֵם אִתָּךְ
against-you to-fight he-marched-out to-say Cush king-of Tirhakah about

וַיִּשְׁמַע וַיִּשְׁלַח מַלְאָכִים אֶל־חִזְקִיָּהוּ לֵאמֹר׃ כֹּה תֹאמְרוּן אֶל־
to you-say this (10) to-say Hezekiah to messengers then-he-sent when-he-heard

חִזְקִיָּהוּ מֶלֶךְ־יְהוּדָה לֵאמֹר אַל־יַשִּׁאֲךָ אֱלֹהֶיךָ אֲשֶׁר־אַתָּה בּוֹטֵחַ
depending you whom god-of-you let-him-deceive-you not to-say Judah king-of Hezekiah

בּוֹ לֵאמֹר לֹא תִנָּתֵן יְרוּשָׁלַיִם בְּיַד מֶלֶךְ אַשּׁוּר׃
Assyria king-of into-hand-of Jerusalem she-will-be-given not to-say on-him

הִנֵּה ׀ אַתָּה שָׁמַעְתָּ אֲשֶׁר עָשׂוּ מַלְכֵי אַשּׁוּר לְכָל־הָאֲרָצוֹת
the-countries to-all-of Assyria kings-of they-did what you-heard you see! (11)

לְהַחֲרִימָם וְאַתָּה תִּנָּצֵל׃ הַהִצִּילוּ אוֹתָם אֱלֹהֵי
gods-of them did-they-deliver? (12) will-you-be-delivered and-you to-destroy-them

הַגּוֹיִם אֲשֶׁר הִשְׁחִיתוּ אֲבוֹתַי אֶת־גּוֹזָן וְאֶת־חָרָן וְרֶצֶף
and-Rezeph Haran and Gozan *** forefathers-of-me they-destroyed that the-nations

וּבְנֵי־עֶדֶן אֲשֶׁר בִּתְלַשָּׂר׃ אַיֵּה מֶלֶךְ־חֲמָת וּמֶלֶךְ אַרְפָּד
Arpad and-king-of Hamath king-of where? (13) in-Tel-Assar who Eden and-peoples-of

וּמֶלֶךְ לָעִיר סְפַרְוָיִם הֵנַע וְעִוָּה׃ וַיִּקַּח חִזְקִיָּהוּ אֶת־
*** Hezekiah and-he-received (14) or-Ivvah Hena Sepharvaim of-the-city and-king

הַסְּפָרִים מִיַּד הַמַּלְאָכִים וַיִּקְרָאֵהוּ וַיַּעַל בֵּית
temple-of then-he-went-up and-he-read-him the-messengers from-hand-of the-letters

יְהוָה וַיִּפְרְשֵׂהוּ חִזְקִיָּהוּ לִפְנֵי יְהוָה׃ וַיִּתְפַּלֵּל חִזְקִיָּהוּ
Hezekiah and-he-prayed (15) Yahweh before Hezekiah and-he-spread-out-him Yahweh

אֶל־יְהוָה לֵאמֹר׃ יְהוָה צְבָאוֹת אֱלֹהֵי יִשְׂרָאֵל יֹשֵׁב
one-being-enthroned-of Israel God-of Hosts Yahweh-of (16) to-say Yahweh to

הַכְּרֻבִים אַתָּה־הוּא הָאֱלֹהִים לְבַדְּךָ לְכֹל מַמְלְכוֹת הָאָרֶץ אַתָּה
you the-earth kingdoms-of over-all-of by-yourself the-God he you the-cherubim

them, "Tell your master, 'This is what the LORD says: Do not be afraid of what you have heard—those words with which the underlings of the king of Assyria have blasphemed me. [7]Listen! I am going to put a spirit in him so that when he hears a certain report, he will return to his own country, and there I will have him cut down with the sword.' "

[8]When the field commander heard that the king of Assyria had left Lachish, he withdrew and found the king fighting against Libnah.

[9]Now Sennacherib received a report that Tirhakah, the Cushite[a] king ⌊of Egypt⌋, was marching out to fight against him. When he heard it, he sent messengers to Hezekiah with this word: [10]"Say to Hezekiah king of Judah: Do not let the god you depend on deceive you when he says, 'Jerusalem will not be handed over to the king of Assyria.' [11]Surely you have heard what the kings of Assyria have done to all the countries, destroying them completely. And will you be delivered? [12]Did the gods of the nations that were destroyed by my forefathers deliver them—the gods of Gozan, Haran, Rezeph and the people of Eden who were in Tel Assar? [13]Where is the king of Hamath, the king of Arpad, the king of the city of Sepharvaim, or of Hena or Ivvah?"

*Hezekiah's Prayer*

[14]Hezekiah received the letter from the messengers and read it. Then he went up to the temple of the LORD and spread it out before the LORD. [15]And Hezekiah prayed to the LORD: [16]"O LORD Almighty, God of Israel, enthroned between the cherubim, you alone are God over all the kingdoms of the earth.

[a]9 That is, from the upper Nile region

עָשִׂיתָ אֶת־ הַשָּׁמַיִם וְאֶת־ הָאָרֶץ׃ הַטֵּה יְהוָה ׀ אָזְנְךָ וּשְׁמָע
and-hear! ear-of-you Yahweh give! (17) the-earth and the-heavens *** you-made

פְּקַח יְהוָה עֵינֶךָ וּרְאֵה וּשְׁמַע אֵת כָּל־ דִּבְרֵי סַנְחֵרִיב
Sennacherib words-of all-of *** and-listen! and-see! eyes-of-you Yahweh open!

אֲשֶׁר שָׁלַח לְחָרֵף אֱלֹהִים חָי׃ אָמְנָם יְהוָה הֶחֱרִיבוּ מַלְכֵי
kings-of they-laid-waste Yahweh truly (18) living God to-insult he-sent that

אַשּׁוּר אֶת־ כָּל־ הָאֲרָצוֹת וְאֶת־ אַרְצָם׃ וְנָתֹן אֶת־ אֱלֹהֵיהֶם
gods-of-them *** and-to-throw (19) land-of-them and the-peoples all-of *** Assyria

בָּאֵשׁ כִּי לֹא אֱלֹהִים הֵמָּה כִּי אִם־ מַעֲשֵׂה יְדֵי־ אָדָם עֵץ וָאֶבֶן
and-stone wood human hands-of work-of only but they gods not for into-the-fire

וַיְאַבְּדוּם׃ וְעַתָּה יְהוָה אֱלֹהֵינוּ הוֹשִׁיעֵנוּ מִיָּדוֹ*
from-hand-of-him deliver-us! God-of-us Yahweh so-now (20) and-they-destroyed-them

וְיֵדְעוּ כָּל־ מַמְלְכוֹת הָאָרֶץ כִּי־ אַתָּה יְהוָה לְבַדֶּךָ׃
by-yourself Yahweh you that the-earth kingdoms-of all-of so-they-may-know

וַיִּשְׁלַח יְשַׁעְיָהוּ בֶן־ אָמוֹץ אֶל־חִזְקִיָּהוּ לֵאמֹר כֹּה־ אָמַר יְהוָה אֱלֹהֵי
God-of Yahweh he-says this to-say Hezekiah to Amoz son-of Isaiah then-he-sent (21)

יִשְׂרָאֵל אֲשֶׁר הִתְפַּלַּלְתָּ אֵלַי אֶל־ סַנְחֵרִיב מֶלֶךְ אַשּׁוּר׃ זֶה
this (22) Assyria king-of Sennacherib concerning to-me you-prayed because Israel

הַדָּבָר אֲשֶׁר־ דִּבֶּר יְהוָה עָלָיו בָּזָה לְךָ לָעֲגָה
she-mocks against-you she-despises against-him Yahweh he-spoke that the-word

לְךָ בְּתוּלַת בַּת־ צִיּוֹן אַחֲרֶיךָ רֹאשׁ הֵנִיעָה בַּת יְרוּשָׁלָם׃
Jerusalem Daughter-of she-tosses head after-you Zion Daughter-of Virgin-of at-you

אֶת־ מִי חֵרַפְתָּ וְגִדַּפְתָּ וְעַל־ מִי הֲרִימוֹתָה קּוֹל
voice you-raised whom? and-against and-you-blasphemed you-insulted whom? *** (23)

וַתִּשָּׂא מָרוֹם עֵינֶיךָ אֶל־ קְדוֹשׁ יִשְׂרָאֵל׃ בְּיַד
by-hand-of (24) Israel Holy-One-of against eyes-of-you pride and-you-lifted

עֲבָדֶיךָ חֵרַפְתָּ ׀ אֲדֹנָי וַתֹּאמֶר בְּרֹב רִכְבִּי אֲנִי
I chariot-of-me with-many-of and-you-said Lord you-insulted messengers-of-you

עָלִיתִי מְרוֹם הָרִים יַרְכְּתֵי לְבָנוֹן וְאֶכְרֹת קוֹמַת
tall-one-of and-I-cut-down Lebanon utmost-heights-of mountains height-of I-ascended

אֲרָזָיו מִבְחַר בְּרֹשָׁיו וְאָבוֹא מְרוֹם קִצּוֹ
remoteness-of-him height-of and-I-reached pines-of-him choice-of cedars-of-him

יַעַר כַּרְמִלּוֹ׃ אֲנִי קַרְתִּי וְשָׁתִיתִי מַיִם וְאַחְרִב
and-I-dried-up waters and-I-drank I-dug-well I (25) garden-of-him forest-of

בְּכַף־ פְּעָמַי כֹּל יְאֹרֵי מָצוֹר׃ הֲלוֹא־ שָׁמַעְתָּ
you-heard not? (26) Egypt streams-of all-of feet-of-me with-sole-of

לְמֵרָחוֹק אוֹתָהּ עָשִׂיתִי מִימֵי קֶדֶם וִיצַרְתִּיהָ עַתָּה
now then-I-planned-her old from-days-of I-ordained her at-from-long-ago

You have made heaven and earth.
17 Give ear, O LORD, and hear; open
your eyes, O LORD, and see; listen
to all the words Sennacherib has
sent to insult the living God.
18 "It is true, O LORD, that the Assyrian kings have laid waste all
these peoples and their lands.
19 They have thrown their gods
into the fire and destroyed them,
for they were not gods but only
wood and stone, fashioned by human hands. 20 Now, O LORD our
God, deliver us from his hand, so
that all kingdoms on earth may
know that you alone, O LORD, are
God.[b]"

*Sennacherib's Fall*

21 Then Isaiah son of Amoz sent
a message to Hezekiah: "This is
what the LORD, the God of Israel,
says: Because you have prayed to
me concerning Sennacherib king
of Assyria, 22 this is the word the
LORD has spoken against him:

"The Virgin Daughter of Zion
despises and mocks you.
The Daughter of Jerusalem
tosses her head as you flee.
23 Who is it you have insulted
and blasphemed?
Against whom have you
raised your voice
and lifted your eyes in pride?
Against the Holy One of
Israel!
24 By your messengers
you have heaped insults on
the Lord.
And you have said,
'With my many chariots
I have ascended the heights of
the mountains,
the utmost heights of
Lebanon.
I have cut down its tallest
cedars,
the choicest of its pines.
I have reached its remotest
heights,
the finest of its forests.
25 I have dug wells in foreign
lands[c]
and drunk the water there.
With the soles of my feet
I have dried up all the
streams of Egypt.'

26 "Have you not heard?
Long ago I ordained it.
In days of old I planned it;

[b]20 Dead Sea Scrolls (see also 2 Kings 19:19); Masoretic Text *alone are the LORD*
[c]25 Dead Sea Scrolls (see also 2 Kings 19:24); Masoretic Text does not have *in foreign lands.*

*20 Most mss have *dagesh* in the *yod* (מִי).

הֲבֵאתִיהָ וּתְהִי לְהַשְׁאוֹת גַּלִּים נִצִּים עָרִים
cities ones-being-ruins piles-of-stones to-turn so-you-were I-brought-to-pass-her

בְּצֻרוֹת׃ (27) וְיֹשְׁבֵיהֶן קִצְרֵי־ יָד
power ones-drained-of and-ones-living-of-them (27) ones-being-fortified

חַתּוּ וָבֹשׁוּ הָיוּ עֵשֶׂב שָׂדֶה וִירַק
and-tender-shoot-of field plant-of they-are and-they-are-shamed they-are-dismayed

דֶּשֶׁא חֲצִיר גַּגּוֹת וּשְׁדֵמָה לִפְנֵי קָמָה׃ (28) וְשִׁבְתְּךָ
but-to-stay-you (28) growing-up before and-terraced-field roofs grass-of greenery

וְצֵאתְךָ וּבוֹאֲךָ יָדָעְתִּי וְאֵת הִתְרַגֶּזְךָ אֵלָי׃ (29) יַעַן
because (29) against-me to-rage-you and I-know and-to-come-you and-to-go-you

הִתְרַגֶּזְךָ אֵלַי וְשַׁאֲנַנְךָ עָלָה בְאָזְנָי
to-ears-of-me he-reached and-insolence-of-you against-me to-rage-you

וְשַׂמְתִּי חַחִי בְּאַפֶּךָ וּמִתְגִּי בִּשְׂפָתֶיךָ
in-lips-of-you and-bit-of-me in-nose-of-you hook-of-me then-I-will-put

וַהֲשִׁבֹתִיךָ בַּדֶּרֶךְ אֲשֶׁר־ בָּאתָ בָּהּ׃ (30) וְזֶה־ לְּךָ
to-you and-this (30) on-her you-came that by-the-way and-I-will-make-return-you

הָאוֹת אָכוֹל הַשָּׁנָה סָפִיחַ וּבַשָּׁנָה הַשֵּׁנִית שָׁחִיס
aftergrowth the-second and-in-the-year growth the-year to-eat the-sign

וּבַשָּׁנָה הַשְּׁלִישִׁית זִרְעוּ וְקִצְרוּ וְנִטְעוּ כְרָמִים וְאִכְוֹל°
and-eat! vineyards and-plant! and-reap! sow! the-third but-in-the-year

פִּרְיָם׃ (31) וְיָסְפָה פְּלֵיטַת בֵּית־ יְהוּדָה הַנִּשְׁאָרָה
the-one-remaining Judah house-of remnant-of and-she-will-repeat (31) fruit-of-them

שֹׁרֶשׁ לְמָטָּה וְעָשָׂה פְרִי לְמָעְלָה׃ (32) כִּי מִירוּשָׁלַםִ
out-of-Jerusalem for (32) at-above fruit and-he-will-bear at-below root

תֵּצֵא שְׁאֵרִית וּפְלֵיטָה מֵהַר צִיּוֹן קִנְאַת יְהוָה צְבָאוֹת
Hosts Yahweh-of zeal-of Zion out-of-Mount-of and-survivor remnant she-will-come

תַּעֲשֶׂה־ זֹּאת׃ (33) לָכֵן כֹּה־ אָמַר יְהוָה אֶל־ מֶלֶךְ אַשּׁוּר
Assyria king-of concerning Yahweh he-says this therefore (33) this she-will-accomplish

לֹא יָבוֹא אֶל־ הָעִיר הַזֹּאת וְלֹא־ יוֹרֶה שָׁם חֵץ וְלֹא־
or-not arrow there he-will-shoot or-not the-this the-city into he-will-enter not

יְקַדְּמֶנָּה מָגֵן וְלֹא־ יִשְׁפֹּךְ עָלֶיהָ* סֹלְלָה׃
siege-ramp against-her he-will-build or-not shield he-will-come-before-her

(34) בַּדֶּרֶךְ אֲשֶׁר־ בָּא בָּהּ יָשׁוּב וְאֶל־ הָעִיר הַזֹּאת
the-this the-city and-into he-will-return on-her he-came that by-the-way (34)

לֹא יָבוֹא נְאֻם־ יְהוָה׃ (35) וְגַנּוֹתִי עַל־ הָעִיר
the-city to and-I-will-defend (35) Yahweh declaration-of he-will-enter not

הַזֹּאת לְהוֹשִׁיעָהּ לְמַעֲנִי וּלְמַעַן דָּוִד עַבְדִּי׃
servant-of-me David and-for-sake-of for-sake-of-me to-save-her the-this

now I have brought it to pass,
that you have turned fortified cities
into piles of stone.
27 Their people, drained of power,
are dismayed and put to shame.
They are like plants in the field,
like tender green shoots,
like grass sprouting on the roof,
scorched[d] before it grows up.

28 "But I know where you stay
and when you come and go
and how you rage against me.
29 Because you rage against me
and because your insolence
has reached my ears,
I will put my hook in your nose
and my bit in your mouth,
and I will make you return
by the way you came.

30 "This will be the sign for you, O Hezekiah:

"This year you will eat what grows by itself,
and the second year what springs from that.
But in the third year sow and reap,
plant vineyards and eat their fruit.
31 Once more a remnant of the house of Judah
will take root below and bear fruit above.
32 For out of Jerusalem will come a remnant,
and out of Mount Zion a band of survivors.
The zeal of the LORD Almighty
will accomplish this.

33 "Therefore this is what the LORD says concerning the king of Assyria:

"He will not enter this city
or shoot an arrow here.
He will not come before it
with shield
or build a siege ramp against it.
34 By the way that he came he will return;
he will not enter this city,"
declares the LORD.
35 "I will defend this city and save it,
for my sake and for the sake
of David my servant!"

d27 Some manuscripts of the Masoretic Text, Dead Sea Scrolls and some Septuagint manuscripts (see also 2 Kings 19:26); most manuscripts of the Masoretic Text *housetops / and terraced fields*

*33 Most mss have *qamets* under the *ayin* (עָ).

°30 ק ואכלו

וַיֵּצֵא ׀ מַלְאַךְ יְהוָה וַיַּכֶּה בְּמַחֲנֵה אַשּׁוּר מֵאָה
hundred Assyria in-camp-of and-he-killed Yahweh angel-of then-he-went-out (36)

וּשְׁמֹנִים וַחֲמִשָּׁה אָלֶף וַיַּשְׁכִּימוּ בַבֹּקֶר וְהִנֵּה כֻלָּם
all-of-them then-see! in-the-morning when-they-got-up thousand and-five and-eighty

פְּגָרִים מֵתִים׃ וַיִּסַּע וַיֵּלֶךְ וַיָּשָׁב
and-he-returned and-he-withdrew so-he-broke-camp (37) ones-being-dead bodies

סַנְחֵרִיב מֶלֶךְ־אַשּׁוּר וַיֵּשֶׁב בְּנִינְוֵה׃ וַיְהִי הוּא מִשְׁתַּחֲוֶה
worshiping he and-he-was (38) in-Nineveh and-he-stayed Assyria king-of Sennacherib

בֵּית ׀ נִסְרֹךְ אֱלֹהָיו וְאַדְרַמֶּלֶךְ וְשַׂרְאֶצֶר בָּנָיו
sons-of-him and-Sharezer and-Adrammelech gods-of-him Nisroch temple-of

הִכֻּהוּ בַחֶרֶב וְהֵמָּה נִמְלְטוּ אֶרֶץ אֲרָרָט
Ararat land-of they-escaped and-they with-the-sword they-cut-down-him

וַיִּמְלֹךְ אֵסַר־חַדֹּן בְּנוֹ תַּחְתָּיו׃ בַּיָּמִים
in-the-days (38:1) in-place-of-him son-of-him Haddon Esar and-he-became-king

הָהֵם חָלָה חִזְקִיָּהוּ לָמוּת וַיָּבוֹא אֵלָיו יְשַׁעְיָהוּ בֶן־אָמוֹץ
Amoz son-of Isaiah to-him and-he-went to-die Hezekiah he-became-ill the-those

הַנָּבִיא וַיֹּאמֶר אֵלָיו כֹּה־אָמַר יְהוָה צַו לְבֵיתֶךָ
to-house-of-you put-in-order! Yahweh he-says this to-him and-he-said the-prophet

כִּי מֵת אַתָּה וְלֹא תִחְיֶה׃ וַיַּסֵּב חִזְקִיָּהוּ פָּנָיו
faces-of-him Hezekiah and-he-turned (2) you-will-recover and-not you dying because

אֶל־הַקִּיר וַיִּתְפַּלֵּל אֶל־יְהוָה׃ וַיֹּאמַר אָנָּה יְהוָה זְכָר־נָא
now! remember! Yahweh O! and-he-said (3) Yahweh to and-he-prayed the-wall to

אֵת אֲשֶׁר הִתְהַלַּכְתִּי לְפָנֶיךָ בֶּאֱמֶת וּבְלֵב שָׁלֵם וְהַטּוֹב
and-the-good whole and-with-heart in-faith before-you I-walked how ***

בְּעֵינֶיךָ עָשִׂיתִי וַיֵּבְךְּ חִזְקִיָּהוּ בְּכִי גָדוֹל׃ וַיְהִי דְּבַר־
word-of and-he-came (4) bitter weeping Hezekiah and-he-wept I-did in-eyes-of-you

יְהוָה אֶל־יְשַׁעְיָהוּ לֵאמֹר׃ הָלוֹךְ וְאָמַרְתָּ אֶל־חִזְקִיָּהוּ כֹּה־אָמַר יְהוָה
Yahweh he-says this Hezekiah to and-you-tell to-go (5) to-say Isaiah to Yahweh

אֱלֹהֵי דָּוִד אָבִיךָ שָׁמַעְתִּי אֶת־תְּפִלָּתֶךָ רָאִיתִי אֶת־דִּמְעָתֶךָ
tear-of-you *** I-saw prayer-of-you *** I-heard father-of-you David God-of

הִנְנִי יוֹסִף עַל־יָמֶיךָ חֲמֵשׁ עֶשְׂרֵה שָׁנָה׃ וּמִכַּף מֶלֶךְ־
king-of and-from-hand-of (6) year ten five-of days-of-you to adding see-I!

אַשּׁוּר אַצִּילְךָ וְאֵת הָעִיר הַזֹּאת וְגַנּוֹתִי עַל־הָעִיר
the-city to and-I-will-defend the-this the-city and I-will-deliver-you Assyria

הַזֹּאת׃ וְזֶה־לְּךָ הָאוֹת מֵאֵת יְהוָה אֲשֶׁר יַעֲשֶׂה יְהוָה
Yahweh he-will-do that Yahweh from-with the-sign to-you and-this (7) the-this

אֶת־הַדָּבָר הַזֶּה אֲשֶׁר דִּבֵּר׃ הִנְנִי מֵשִׁיב אֶת־צֵל
shadow-of *** making-go-back see-I! (8) he-promised that the-this the-thing ***

36 Then the angel of the LORD went out and put to death a hundred and eighty-five thousand men in the Assyrian camp. When the people got up the next morning—there were all the dead bodies!
37 So Sennacherib king of Assyria broke camp and withdrew. He returned to Nineveh and stayed there.
38 One day, while he was worshiping in the temple of his god Nisroch, his sons Adrammelech and Sharezer cut him down with the sword, and they escaped to the land of Ararat. And Esarhaddon his son succeeded him as king.

*Hezekiah's Illness*

38 In those days Hezekiah became ill and was at the point of death. The prophet Isaiah son of Amoz went to him and said, "This is what the LORD says: Put your house in order, because you are going to die; you will not recover."
2 Hezekiah turned his face to the wall and prayed to the LORD,
3 "Remember, O LORD, how I have walked before you faithfully and with wholehearted devotion and have done what is good in your eyes." And Hezekiah wept bitterly.
4 Then the word of the LORD came to Isaiah:
5 "Go and tell Hezekiah, 'This is what the LORD, the God of your father David, says: I have heard your prayer and seen your tears; I will add fifteen years to your life.
6 And I will deliver you and this city from the hand of the king of Assyria. I will defend this city.
7 "'This is the LORD's sign to you that the LORD will do what he has promised:
8 I will make the shadow

הַֽמַּעֲלוֹת אֲשֶׁר יָרְדָה בְמַעֲלוֹת אָחָז בַּשֶּׁמֶשׁ אֲחֹרַנִּית עֶשֶׂר מַעֲלוֹת
steps ten backward by-the-sun Ahaz on-steps-of she-went-down that the-steps

וַתָּשָׁב הַשֶּׁמֶשׁ עֶשֶׂר מַעֲלוֹת בַּמַּעֲלוֹת אֲשֶׁר יָרָדָה׃
she-went-down that on-the-steps steps ten the-sunlight so-she-went-back

מִכְתָּב לְחִזְקִיָּהוּ מֶלֶךְ־יְהוּדָה בַּחֲלֹתוֹ וַיְחִי
and-he-recovered when-to-be-ill-him Judah king-of of-Hezekiah writing (9)

מֵחָלְיוֹ׃ אֲנִי אָמַרְתִּי בִּדְמִי יָמַי אֵלֵכָה
must-I-go days-of-me in-prime-of I-said I (10) from-illness-of-him

בְּשַׁעֲרֵי שְׁאוֹל פֻּקַּדְתִּי יֶתֶר שְׁנוֹתָי׃ אָמַרְתִּי לֹא־
not I-said (11) years-of-me rest-of must-I-be-robbed Sheol through-gates-of

אֶרְאֶה יָהּ יָהּ בְּאֶרֶץ הַחַיִּים לֹא־אַבִּיט אָדָם
mankind I-will-look-on not the-living-ones in-land-of Yahweh Yahweh I-will-see

עוֹד עִם־יוֹשְׁבֵי חָדֶל׃ דּוֹרִי
house-of-me (12) *place-of-cessation ones-dwelling-of with longer

נִסַּע וְנִגְלָה מִנִּי כְּאֹהֶל רֹעִי
one-being-shepherd-of-me like-tent-of from-me and-he-was-taken he-was-pulled-down

קִפַּדְתִּי כָאֹרֵג חַיַּי מִדַּלָּה יְבַצְּעֵנִי מִיּוֹם
from-day he-cut-off-me from-loom lives-of-me like-the-one-weaving I-rolled-up

עַד־לַיְלָה תַּשְׁלִימֵנִי׃ שִׁוִּיתִי עַד־בֹּקֶר כָּאֲרִי כֵּן יְשַׁבֵּר
he-broke so like-the-lion dawn till I-waited (13) you-made-an-end-of-me night to

כָּל־עַצְמוֹתָי מִיּוֹם עַד־לַיְלָה תַּשְׁלִימֵנִי׃ כְּסוּס עָגוּר
thrush like-swift (14) you-made-an-end-of-me night to from-day bones-of-me all-of

כֵּן אֲצַפְצֵף אֶהְגֶּה כַּיּוֹנָה דַּלּוּ עֵינַי לַמָּרוֹם אֲדֹנָי
Lord to-the-heaven eyes-of-me they-grew-weak like-the-dove I-moaned I-cried so

עָשְׁקָה־לִּי עָרְבֵנִי׃ מָה־אֲדַבֵּר וְאָמַר־לִי וְהוּא
and-he to-me for-he-spoke can-I-say what? (15) come-to-aid-me! to-me trouble

עָשָׂה אֶדַּדֶּה כָל־שְׁנוֹתַי עַל־מַר נַפְשִׁי׃
soul-of-me anguish-of because-of years-of-me all-of I-will-walk-humbly he-did

אֲדֹנָי עֲלֵיהֶם יִחְיוּ וּלְכָל־בָּהֶן חַיֵּי רוּחִי
spirit-of-me lives-of in-them and-by-all-of they-live by-them Lord (16)

וְתַחֲלִימֵנִי וְהַחֲיֵנִי׃ הִנֵּה לְשָׁלוֹם
for-benefit surely! (17) and-let-live-me! and-you-restored-to-health-me

מַר־לִי מָר וְאַתָּה חָשַׁקְתָּ נַפְשִׁי מִשַּׁחַת
from-pit-of self-of-me you-kept-in-love and-you anguish to-me he-was-anguished

בְּלִי כִּי הִשְׁלַכְתָּ אַחֲרֵי גֵוְךָ כָּל־חֲטָאָי׃ כִּי לֹא
not for (18) sins-of-me all-of back-of-you behind you-put indeed destruction

שְׁאוֹל תּוֹדֶךָּ מָוֶת יְהַלְלֶךָּ לֹא־יְשַׂבְּרוּ
they-can-hope not he-can-sing-praise-to-you death she-can-praise-you Sheol

cast by the sun go back the ten steps it has gone down on the stairway of Ahaz.' " So the sunlight went back the ten steps it had gone down.

[9]A writing of Hezekiah king of Judah after his illness and recovery:

[10]I said, "In the prime of my life
must I go through the gates of death[e]
and be robbed of the rest of my years?"
[11]I said, "I will not again see the LORD,
the LORD, in the land of the living;
no longer will I look on mankind,
or be with those who now dwell in this world.[f]
[12]Like a shepherd's tent my house
has been pulled down and taken from me.
Like a weaver I have rolled up my life,
and he has cut me off from the loom;
day and night you made an end of me.
[13]I waited patiently till dawn,
but like a lion he broke all my bones;
day and night you made an end of me.
[14]I cried like a swift or thrush,
I moaned like a mourning dove.
My eyes grew weak as I looked to the heavens.
I am troubled; O Lord, come to my aid!"

[15]But what can I say?
He has spoken to me, and he himself has done this.
I will walk humbly all my years
because of this anguish of my soul.
[16]Lord, by such things men live;
and my spirit finds life in them too.
You restored me to health
and let me live.
[17]Surely it was for my benefit
that I suffered such anguish.
In your love you kept me
from the pit of destruction;
you have put all my sins
behind your back.
[18]For the grave[g] cannot praise you,
death cannot sing your praise;

[e]10 Hebrew *Sheol*
[f]11 A few Hebrew manuscripts; most Hebrew manuscripts *in the place of cessation*
[g]18 Hebrew *Sheol*

**11* The NIV reverses the *daleth* and *lamed*, with some mss, to read חֶלֶד, *world*.

יוֹרְדֵי־בוֹר אֶל־אֲמִתֶּךָ׃ חַי חַי הוּא
he living living (19) faithfulness-of-you for pit ones-going-down-of

יוֹדֶךָ כָּמוֹנִי הַיּוֹם אָב לְבָנִים יוֹדִיעַ אֶל־אֲמִתֶּךָ׃
faithfulness-of-you about he-tells to-children father the-day as-I he-praises-you

יְהוָה לְהוֹשִׁיעֵנִי וּנְגִנוֹתַי נְנַגֵּן כָּל־יְמֵי
days-of all-of we-will-sing and-stringed-instruments-of-me to-save-me Yahweh (20)

חַיֵּינוּ עַל־בֵּית יְהוָה׃ וַיֹּאמֶר יְשַׁעְיָהוּ יִשְׂאוּ
let-them-prepare Isaiah then-he-said (21) Yahweh temple-of in lives-of-us

דְּבֶלֶת תְּאֵנִים וְיִמְרְחוּ עַל־הַשְּׁחִין וְיֶחִי׃
and-he-will-recover the-boil to and-let-them-apply figs poultice-of

וַיֹּאמֶר חִזְקִיָּהוּ מָה אוֹת כִּי אֶעֱלֶה בֵּית יְהוָה׃
Yahweh temple-of I-will-go-up that sign what? Hezekiah now-he-asked (22)

בָּעֵת הַהִוא* שָׁלַח מְרֹדַךְ בַּלְאֲדָן בֶּן־בַּלְאֲדָן מֶלֶךְ־
king-of Baladan son-of Baladan Merodach he-sent the-that at-the-time (39:1)

בָּבֶל סְפָרִים וּמִנְחָה אֶל־חִזְקִיָּהוּ וַיִּשְׁמַע כִּי חָלָה
he-was-ill that because-he-heard Hezekiah to and-gift letters Babylon

וַיֶּחֱזָק׃ וַיִּשְׂמַח עֲלֵיהֶם חִזְקִיָּהוּ וַיַּרְאֵם אֶת־
*** and-he-showed-them Hezekiah about-them and-he-was-glad (2) and-he-recovered

בֵּית נְכֹתֹה° אֶת־הַכֶּסֶף וְאֶת־הַזָּהָב וְאֶת־הַבְּשָׂמִים ׀ וְאֵת ׀ הַשֶּׁמֶן
the-oil and the-spices and the-gold and the-silver *** store-of-him house-of

הַטּוֹב וְאֵת כָּל־בֵּית כֵּלָיו וְאֵת כָּל־אֲשֶׁר נִמְצָא
he-was-found that everything and arms-of-him house-of all-of and the-fine

בְּאֹצְרֹתָיו לֹא־הָיָה דָבָר אֲשֶׁר לֹא־הֶרְאָם חִזְקִיָּהוּ
Hezekiah he-showed-them not that thing he-was not among-treasures-of-him

בְּבֵיתוֹ וּבְכָל־מֶמְשַׁלְתּוֹ׃ וַיָּבֹא יְשַׁעְיָהוּ הַנָּבִיא
the-prophet Isaiah then-he-went (3) kingdom-of-him or-in-all-of in-palace-of-him

אֶל־הַמֶּלֶךְ חִזְקִיָּהוּ וַיֹּאמֶר אֵלָיו מָה אָמְרוּ ׀ הָאֲנָשִׁים הָאֵלֶּה
the-those the-men they-said what? to-him and-he-asked Hezekiah the-king to

וּמֵאַיִן יָבֹאוּ אֵלֶיךָ וַיֹּאמֶר חִזְקִיָּהוּ מֵאֶרֶץ רְחוֹקָה
distant from-land Hezekiah and-he-replied to-you they-came and-from-where?

בָּאוּ אֵלַי מִבָּבֶל׃ וַיֹּאמֶר מָה רָאוּ בְּבֵיתֶךָ
in-palace-of-you they-saw what? and-he-asked (4) from-Babylon to-me they-came

וַיֹּאמֶר חִזְקִיָּהוּ אֵת כָּל־אֲשֶׁר בְּבֵיתִי רָאוּ לֹא־הָיָה
he-is not they-saw in-palace-of-me that everything *** Hezekiah and-he-said

דָבָר אֲשֶׁר לֹא־הִרְאִיתִים בְּאוֹצְרֹתָי׃ וַיֹּאמֶר יְשַׁעְיָהוּ
Isaiah then-he-said (5) among-treasures-of-me I-showed-them not that thing

אֶל־חִזְקִיָּהוּ שְׁמַע דְּבַר־יְהוָה צְבָאוֹת׃ הִנֵּה יָמִים בָּאִים
ones-coming days surely! (6) Hosts Yahweh-of word-of hear! Hezekiah to

those who go down to the pit
cannot hope for your
faithfulness.
19 The living, the living—they
praise you,
as I am doing today;
fathers tell their children
about your faithfulness.

20 The LORD will save me,
and we will sing with
stringed instruments
all the days of our lives
in the temple of the LORD.

21 Isaiah had said, "Prepare a
poultice of figs and apply it to the
boil, and he will recover."
22 Hezekiah had asked, "What
will be the sign that I will go up to
the temple of the LORD?"

*Envoys From Babylon*

39 At that time Merodach-
Baladan son of Baladan
king of Babylon sent Hezekiah letters and a gift, because he had
heard of his illness and recovery.
2 Hezekiah received the envoys
gladly and showed them what
was in his storehouses—the silver,
the gold, the spices, the fine oil,
his entire armory and everything
found among his treasures. There
was nothing in his palace or in all
his kingdom that Hezekiah did
not show them.
3 Then Isaiah the prophet went
to King Hezekiah and asked,
"What did those men say, and
where did they come from?"
"From a distant land," Hezekiah replied. "They came to me
from Babylon."
4 The prophet asked, "What did
they see in your palace?"
"They saw everything in my
palace," Hezekiah said. "There is
nothing among my treasures that
I did not show them."
5 Then Isaiah said to Hezekiah,
"Hear the word of the LORD Almighty: 6 The time will surely

*1 Most mss have *yod* for *vav* (הַהִיא).
°2 ק נכתו

וְנִשָּׂא ׀ כָּל־אֲשֶׁר בְּבֵיתֶךָ וַאֲשֶׁר אָצְרוּ
they-stored-up and-that in-palace-of-you that all and-he-will-be-carried-off

אֲבֹתֶיךָ עַד־הַיּוֹם הַזֶּה בָּבֶל לֹא־יִוָּתֵר דָּבָר אָמַר
he-says thing he-will-be-left not Babylon the-this the-day until fathers-of-you

יְהוָה׃ וּמִבָּנֶיךָ אֲשֶׁר יֵצְאוּ מִמְּךָ אֲשֶׁר
whom from-you they-will-come who and-from-descendants-of-you (7) Yahweh

תּוֹלִיד יִקָּחוּ וְהָיוּ סָרִיסִים בְּהֵיכַל
in-palace-of eunuchs and-they-will-become they-will-be-taken-away you-will-father

מֶלֶךְ בָּבֶל׃ וַיֹּאמֶר חִזְקִיָּהוּ אֶל־יְשַׁעְיָהוּ טוֹב דְּבַר־יְהוָה אֲשֶׁר
that Yahweh word-of good Isaiah to Hezekiah and-he-replied (8) Babylon king-of

דִּבַּרְתָּ וַיֹּאמֶר כִּי יִהְיֶה שָׁלוֹם וֶאֱמֶת בְּיָמָי׃
in-days-of-me and-security peace he-will-be indeed for-he-thought you-spoke

נַחֲמוּ נַחֲמוּ עַמִּי יֹאמַר אֱלֹהֵיכֶם׃ דַּבְּרוּ עַל־לֵב
heart-of to speak! (2) God-of-you he-says people-of-me comfort! comfort! (40:1)

יְרוּשָׁלִַם וְקִרְאוּ אֵלֶיהָ כִּי מָלְאָה צְבָאָהּ כִּי
that hard-service-of-her she-is-completed that to-her and-proclaim! Jerusalem

נִרְצָה עֲוֺנָהּ כִּי לָקְחָה מִיַּד יְהוָה כִּפְלַיִם בְּכָל־
for-all-of double Yahweh from-hand-of she-received that sin-of-her he-is-paid-for

חַטֹּאתֶיהָ׃ קוֹל קוֹרֵא בַּמִּדְבָּר פַּנּוּ דֶּרֶךְ יְהוָה
Yahweh way-of prepare! in-the-desert one-calling voice-of (3) sins-of-her

יַשְּׁרוּ בָּעֲרָבָה מְסִלָּה לֵאלֹהֵינוּ׃ כָּל־גֶּיא
valley every-of (4) for-God-of-us highway in-the-wilderness make-straight!

יִנָּשֵׂא וְכָל־הַר וְגִבְעָה יִשְׁפָּלוּ
they-shall-be-made-low and-hill mountain and-every-of he-shall-be-raised-up

וְהָיָה הֶעָקֹב לְמִישׁוֹר וְהָרְכָסִים לְבִקְעָה׃
as-plain and-the-rugged-places as-level the-rough-ground and-he-shall-become

וְנִגְלָה כְּבוֹד יְהוָה וְרָאוּ כָל־בָּשָׂר
mankind all-of and-they-will-see Yahweh glory-of and-he-will-be-revealed (5)

יַחְדָּו כִּי פִּי יְהוָה דִּבֵּר׃ קוֹל אֹמֵר קְרָא *וְאָמַר מָה
what? *and-he-said cry-out! saying voice (6) he-spoke Yahweh mouth-of for together

אֶקְרָא כָּל־הַבָּשָׂר חָצִיר וְכָל־חַסְדּוֹ כְּצִיץ
like-flower-of glory-of-him and-all-of grass the-mankind all-of shall-I-cry

הַשָּׂדֶה׃ יָבֵשׁ חָצִיר נָבֵל צִיץ כִּי רוּחַ יְהוָה
Yahweh breath-of because flower he-falls grass he-withers (7) the-field

נָשְׁבָה בּוֹ אָכֵן חָצִיר הָעָם׃ יָבֵשׁ חָצִיר נָבֵל צִיץ
flower he-falls grass he-withers (8) the-people grass surely on-him she-blows

וּדְבַר־אֱלֹהֵינוּ יָקוּם לְעוֹלָם׃ עַל הַר־גָּבֹהַ עֲלִי־לָךְ
for-you go-up! high mountain on (9) to-forever he-stands God-of-us but-word-of

come when everything in your palace, and all that your fathers have stored up until this day, will be carried off to Babylon. Nothing will be left, says the LORD. [7]And some of your descendants, your own flesh and blood who will be born to you, will be taken away, and they will become eunuchs in the palace of the king of Babylon."

[8]"The word of the LORD you have spoken is good," Hezekiah replied. For he thought, "There will be peace and security in my lifetime."

*Comfort for God's People*

**40** Comfort, comfort my people,
says your God.
[2]Speak tenderly to Jerusalem,
and proclaim to her
that her hard service has been completed,
that her sin has been paid for,
that she has received from the LORD's hand
double for all her sins.

[3]A voice of one calling:
"In the desert prepare
the way for the LORD[h];
make straight in the wilderness
a highway for our God.[i]
[4]Every valley shall be raised up,
every mountain and hill made low;
the rough ground shall become level,
the rugged places a plain.
[5]And the glory of the LORD will be revealed,
and all mankind together will see it.
For the mouth of the LORD has spoken."

[6]A voice says, "Cry out."
And I said, "What shall I cry?"

"All men are like grass,
and all their glory is like the flowers of the field.
[7]The grass withers and the flowers fall,
because the breath of the LORD blows on them.
Surely the people are grass.
[8]The grass withers and the flowers fall,
but the word of our God stands forever."

[9]You who bring good tidings to Zion,
go up on a high mountain.

[h]3 Or *A voice of one calling in the desert: / "Prepare the way for the LORD*
[i]3 Hebrew; Septuagint *make straight the paths of our God*

*6 The NIV repoints this word as וָאֹמַר *and-I-said.*

מְבַשֶּׂרֶת צִיּוֹן הָרִימִי בַכֹּחַ קוֹלֵךְ
voice-of-you with-the-shout lift-up! Zion one-bringing-good-tidings-of

מְבַשֶּׂרֶת יְרוּשָׁלַ͏ִם הָרִימִי אַל־ תִּירָאִי אִמְרִי לְעָרֵי
to-towns-of say! you-be-afraid not lift-up! Jerusalem one-bringing-good-tidings-of

יְהוּדָה הִנֵּה אֱלֹהֵיכֶם׃ (10) הִנֵּה אֲדֹנָי יְהוִה בְּחָזָק יָבוֹא
he-comes with-power Yahweh Sovereign see! (10) God-of-you here! Judah

וּזְרֹעוֹ מֹשְׁלָה לוֹ הִנֵּה שְׂכָרוֹ אִתּוֹ וּפְעֻלָּתוֹ
and-recompense-of-him with-him reward-of-him see! for-him ruling and-arm-of-him

לְפָנָיו׃ (11) כְּרֹעֶה עֶדְרוֹ יִרְעֶה בִּזְרֹעוֹ
in-arm-of-him he-tends flock-of-him like-one-shepherding (11) accompanying-him

יְקַבֵּץ טְלָאִים וּבְחֵיקוֹ יִשָּׂא עָלוֹת יְנַהֵל׃
he-leads-gently ones-having-young he-carries and-near-heart-of-him lambs he-gathers

(12) מִי־ מָדַד בְּשָׁעֳלוֹ מַיִם וְשָׁמַיִם
or-heavens waters in-hollow-of-hand-of-him he-measured who? (12)

בַּזֶּרֶת תִּכֵּן וְכָל בַּשָּׁלִשׁ עֲפַר הָאָרֶץ
the-earth dust-of in-the-basket or-he-held he-marked-off with-the-handbreadth

וְשָׁקַל בַּפֶּלֶס הָרִים וּגְבָעוֹת בְּמֹאזְנָיִם׃ (13) מִי־ תִכֵּן
he-understood who? (13) in-balances and-hills mountains on-the-scale or-he-weighed

אֶת־ רוּחַ יְהוָה וְאִישׁ עֲצָתוֹ יוֹדִיעֶנּוּ׃ (14) אֶת־ מִי
whom? *** (14) he-instructed-him counsel-of-him or-man-of Yahweh mind-of ***

נוֹעָץ וַיְבִינֵהוּ וַיְלַמְּדֵהוּ בְּאֹרַח מִשְׁפָּט
right about-way-of and-he-taught-him so-he-enlightened-him he-consulted

וַיְלַמְּדֵהוּ דַעַת וְדֶרֶךְ תְּבוּנוֹת יוֹדִיעֶנּוּ׃ (15) הֵן
surely! (15) he-showed-him understandings or-path-of knowledge and-he-taught-him

גּוֹיִם כְּמַר מִדְּלִי וּכְשַׁחַק מֹאזְנַיִם נֶחְשָׁבוּ הֵן
surely! they-are-regarded scales and-like-dust-of in-bucket like-drop nations

אִיִּים כַּדַּק יִטּוֹל׃ (16) וּלְבָנוֹן אֵין דֵּי
sufficient-of not even-Lebanon (16) he-weighs like-the-fine-dust islands

בָּעֵר וְחַיָּתוֹ אֵין דֵּי עוֹלָה׃ (17) כָּל־
all-of (17) burnt-offering sufficient-of not or-animal-of-him to-make-fire

הַגּוֹיִם כְּאַיִן נֶגְדּוֹ מֵאֶפֶס וָתֹהוּ נֶחְשְׁבוּ־
they-are-regarded and-worthless less-than-nothing before-him as-nothing the-nations

לוֹ׃ (18) וְאֶל־ מִי תְּדַמְּיוּן אֵל וּמַה־ דְּמוּת תַּעַרְכוּ־
will-you-compare image and-what? God will-you-compare whom? then-to (18) by-him

לוֹ׃ (19) הַפֶּסֶל נָסַךְ חָרָשׁ וְצֹרֵף בַּזָּהָב
with-the-gold and-one-being-goldsmith craftsman he-casts the-idol (19) to-him

יְרַקְּעֶנּוּ וּרְתֻקוֹת כֶּסֶף צוֹרֵף׃ (20) הַמְסֻכָּן תְּרוּמָה
offering the-one-being-poor (20) fashioning silver and-chains-of he-overlays-him

You who bring good tidings to
Jerusalem,
lift up your voice with a
shout,
lift it up, do not be afraid;
say to the towns of Judah,
"Here is your God!"
10See, the Sovereign LORD comes
with power,
and his arm rules for him.
See, his reward is with him,
and his recompense
accompanies him.
11He tends his flock like a
shepherd:
He gathers the lambs in his
arms
and carries them close to his
heart;
he gently leads those that
have young.

12Who has measured the waters
in the hollow of his hand,
or with the breadth of his
hand marked off the
heavens?
Who has held the dust of the
earth in a basket,
or weighed the mountains
on the scales
and the hills in a balance?
13Who has understood the mind[k]
of the LORD,
or instructed him as his
counselor?
14Whom did the LORD consult to
enlighten him,
and who taught him the
right way?
Who was it that taught him
knowledge
or showed him the path of
understanding?

15Surely the nations are like a
drop in a bucket;
they are regarded as dust on
the scales;
he weighs the islands as
though they were fine
dust.
16Lebanon is not sufficient for
altar fires,
nor its animals enough for
burnt offerings.
17Before him all the nations are
as nothing;
they are regarded by him as
worthless
and less than nothing.

18To whom, then, will you
compare God?
What image will you
compare him to?
19As for an idol, a craftsman
casts it,
and a goldsmith overlays it
with gold
and fashions silver chains
for it.
20A man too poor to present
such an offering

j9 *Or O Zion, bringer of good tidings, / go up on a high mountain. / O Jerusalem, bringer of good tidings*
k13 *Or Spirit; or spirit*

עֵץ לֹא־יִרְקַב יִבְחָר חָרָשׁ חָכָם יְבַקֶּשׁ־לוֹ לְהָכִין
to-set-up for-him he-looks skilled craftsman he-selects he-will-rot not wood

פֶּסֶל לֹא יִמּוֹט׃ (21) הֲלוֹא תֵדְעוּ הֲלוֹא תִשְׁמָעוּ הֲלוֹא הֻגַּד
he-was-told not? you-heard not? you-know not? (21) he-will-topple not idol

מֵרֹאשׁ לָכֶם הֲלוֹא הֲבִינֹתֶם מוֹסְדוֹת הָאָרֶץ׃
the-earth foundations-of you-understood not? to-you from-beginning

(22) הַיֹּשֵׁב עַל־חוּג הָאָרֶץ וְיֹשְׁבֶיהָ
and-ones-being-people-of-her the-earth circle-of above the-one-sitting (22)

כַּחֲגָבִים הַנּוֹטֶה כַדֹּק שָׁמַיִם וַיִּמְתָּחֵם
and-he-spreads-them heavens like-the-canopy the-one-stretching-out like-grasshoppers

כָּאֹהֶל לָשָׁבֶת׃ (23) הַנּוֹתֵן רוֹזְנִים לְאָיִן
to-naught ones-being-princes the-one-bringing (23) to-live like-the-tent

שֹׁפְטֵי אֶרֶץ כַּתֹּהוּ עָשָׂה׃ (24) אַף בַּל־נִטָּעוּ
they-are-planted not indeed (24) he-reduces like-the-nothing world ones-ruling-of

אַף בַּל־זֹרָעוּ אַף בַּל־שֹׁרֵשׁ בָּאָרֶץ גִּזְעָם
stock-of-them in-the-ground he-takes-root not indeed they-are-sown not indeed

וְגַם־נָשַׁף בָּהֶם וַיִּבָשׁוּ וּסְעָרָה כַּקַּשׁ
like-the-chaff and-whirlwind and-they-wither on-them he-blows and-then

תִּשָּׂאֵם׃ (25) וְאֶל־מִי תְדַמְּיוּנִי וְאֶשְׁוֶה
that-I-am-equal will-you-compare-me whom? now-to (25) she-sweeps-away-them

יֹאמַר קָדוֹשׁ׃ (26) שְׂאוּ־מָרוֹם עֵינֵיכֶם וּרְאוּ מִי־בָרָא אֵלֶּה
these he-created who? and-look! eyes-of-you heaven lift! (26) Holy-One he-says

הַמּוֹצִיא בְמִסְפָּר צְבָאָם לְכֻלָּם בְּשֵׁם יִקְרָא
he-calls by-name to-each-of-them host-of-them by-number the-one-bringing-out

מֵרֹב אוֹנִים וְאַמִּיץ כֹּחַ אִישׁ לֹא נֶעְדָּר׃
he-is-missing not one strength and-might-of powers because-of-greatness-of

(27) לָמָּה תֹאמַר יַעֲקֹב וּתְדַבֵּר יִשְׂרָאֵל נִסְתְּרָה דַרְכִּי
way-of-me she-is-hidden Israel and-you-complain Jacob you-say why? (27)

מֵיְהוָה וּמֵאֱלֹהַי מִשְׁפָּטִי יַעֲבוֹר׃ (28) הֲלוֹא יָדַעְתָּ
you-know not? (28) he-is-disregarded cause-of-me and-by-God-of-me from-Yahweh

אִם־לֹא שָׁמַעְתָּ אֱלֹהֵי עוֹלָם יְהוָה בּוֹרֵא קְצוֹת הָאָרֶץ לֹא
not the-earth ends-of One-Creating Yahweh everlasting God-of you-heard not indeed

יִיעַף וְלֹא יִיגָע אֵין חֵקֶר לִתְבוּנָתוֹ׃
of-understanding-of-him fathoming not he-will-grow-weary or-not he-will-grow-tired

(29) נֹתֵן לַיָּעֵף כֹּחַ וּלְאֵין אוֹנִים עָצְמָה יַרְבֶּה׃
he-increases power mights and-to-without strength to-the-weary one-giving (29)

(30) וְיִעֲפוּ נְעָרִים וְיִגָעוּ וּבַחוּרִים כָּשׁוֹל
to-stumble and-young-men and-they-grow-weary youths even-they-grow-tired (30)

selects wood that will not
rot.
He looks for a skilled
craftsman
to set up an idol that will
not topple.
21 Do you not know?
Have you not heard?
Has it not been told you from
the beginning?
Have you not understood
since the earth was
founded?
22 He sits enthroned above the
circle of the earth,
and its people are like
grasshoppers.
He stretches out the heavens
like a canopy,
and spreads them out like a
tent to live in.
23 He brings princes to naught
and reduces the rulers of
this world to nothing.
24 No sooner are they planted,
no sooner are they sown,
no sooner do they take root
in the ground,
than he blows on them and
they wither,
and a whirlwind sweeps
them away like chaff.

25 "To whom will you compare
me?
Or who is my equal?" says
the Holy One.
26 Lift your eyes and look to the
heavens:
Who created all these?
He who brings out the starry
host one by one,
and calls them each by
name.
Because of his great power and
mighty strength,
not one of them is missing.

27 Why do you say, O Jacob,
and complain, O Israel,
"My way is hidden from the
LORD;
my cause is disregarded by
my God"?
28 Do you not know?
Have you not heard?
The LORD is the everlasting
God,
the Creator of the ends of
the earth.
He will not grow tired or
weary,
and his understanding no
one can fathom.
29 He gives strength to the weary
and increases the power of
the weak.
30 Even youths grow tired and
weary,
and young men stumble and
fall;

יִכָּשֵׁלוּ׃ (31) וְקוֵֹי יְהוָה יַחֲלִיפוּ כֹחַ
strength they-will-renew Yahweh but-ones-hoping-of (31) they-stumble

יַעֲלוּ אֵבֶר כַּנְּשָׁרִים יָרוּצוּ וְלֹא יִיגָעוּ
they-will-grow-weary and-not they-will-run like-the-eagles wing they-will-soar

יֵלְכוּ וְלֹא יִיעָפוּ׃ (41:1) הַחֲרִישׁוּ אֵלַי אִיִּים
islands before-me be-silent! (41:1) they-will-be-faint and-not they-will-walk

וּלְאֻמִּים יַחֲלִיפוּ כֹחַ יִגְּשׁוּ אָז יְדַבֵּרוּ
let-them-speak then let-them-come-forward strength let-them-renew and-nations

יַחְדָּו לַמִּשְׁפָּט נִקְרָבָה׃ (2) מִי הֵעִיר מִמִּזְרָח
from-east he-stirred-up who? (2) let-us-meet at-the-place-of-judgment together

צֶדֶק יִקְרָאֵהוּ לְרַגְלוֹ יִתֵּן לְפָנָיו גּוֹיִם
nations before-him he-hands-over to-foot-of-him he-called-him righteousness

וּמְלָכִים יַרְדְּ יִתֵּן כֶּעָפָר חַרְבּוֹ כְּקַשׁ נִדָּף
being-windblown as-chaff sword-of-him as-the-dust he-makes he-subdues and-kings

קַשְׁתּוֹ׃ (3) יִרְדְּפֵם יַעֲבוֹר שָׁלוֹם אֹרַח בְּרַגְלָיו לֹא
not by-feet-of-him path unscathed he-moves-on he-pursues-them (3) bow-of-him

יָבוֹא׃ (4) מִי־ פָעַל וְעָשָׂה קֹרֵא
one-calling-forth and-he-carried-through he-did who? (4) he-traveled

הַדֹּרוֹת מֵרֹאשׁ אֲנִי יְהוָה רִאשׁוֹן וְאֶת־ אַחֲרֹנִים אֲנִי־הוּא׃
he I last-ones and-with first Yahweh I from-beginning the-generations

(5) רָאוּ אִיִּים וְיִירָאוּ קְצוֹת הָאָרֶץ יֶחֱרָדוּ קָרְבוּ
they-approach they-tremble the-earth ends-of and-they-fear islands they-saw (5)

וַיֶּאֱתָיוּן׃ (6) אִישׁ אֶת־ רֵעֵהוּ יַעְזֹרוּ וּלְאָחִיו
and-to-brother-of-him they-help other-of-him *** each (6) and-they-come-forward

יֹאמַר חֲזָק׃ (7) וַיְחַזֵּק חָרָשׁ אֶת־ צֹרֵף
one-being-goldsmith *** craftsman and-he-encourages (7) be-strong! he-says

מַחֲלִיק פַּטִּישׁ אֶת־ הוֹלֶם פָּעַם אֹמֵר לַדֶּבֶק טוֹב הוּא
he good of-the-welding saying anvil one-striking *** hammer one-making-smooth

וַיְחַזְּקֵהוּ בְמַסְמְרִים לֹא יִמּוֹט׃ (8) וְאַתָּה יִשְׂרָאֵל
Israel but-you (8) he-will-topple not with-nails and-he-fastens-down-him

עַבְדִּי יַעֲקֹב אֲשֶׁר בְּחַרְתִּיךָ זֶרַע אַבְרָהָם אֹהֲבִי׃
one-being-friend-of-me Abraham descendant-of I-chose-you whom Jacob servant-of-me

(9) אֲשֶׁר הֶחֱזַקְתִּיךָ מִקְצוֹת הָאָרֶץ וּמֵאֲצִילֶיהָ
and-from-farthest-corners-of-her the-earth from-ends-of I-took-you whom (9)

קְרָאתִיךָ וָאֹמַר לְךָ עַבְדִּי־ אַתָּה בְּחַרְתִּיךָ וְלֹא
and-not I-chose-you you servant-of-me to-you and-I-said I-called-you

מְאַסְתִּיךָ׃ (10) אַל־ תִּירָא כִּי עִמְּךָ־ אָנִי אַל־ תִּשְׁתָּע כִּי־אֲנִי
I for you-be-dismayed not I with-you for you-fear not (10) I-rejected-you

31 but those who hope in the Lord
will renew their strength.
They will soar on wings like eagles;
they will run and not grow weary,
they will walk and not be faint.

*The Helper of Israel*

41 "Be silent before me, you islands!
Let the nations renew their strength!
Let them come forward and speak;
let us meet together at the place of judgment.

2 "Who has stirred up one from the east,
calling him in righteousness to his service[l]?
He hands nations over to him
and subdues kings before him.
He turns them to dust with his sword,
to windblown chaff with his bow.
3 He pursues them and moves on unscathed,
by a path his feet have not traveled before.
4 Who has done this and carried it through,
calling forth the generations from the beginning?
I, the Lord—with the first of them
and with the last—I am he."

5 The islands have seen it and fear;
the ends of the earth tremble.
They approach and come forward;
6 each helps the other
and says to his brother, "Be strong!"
7 The craftsman encourages the goldsmith,
and he who smooths with the hammer
spurs on him who strikes the anvil.
He says of the welding, "It is good."
He nails down the idol so it will not topple.

8 "But you, O Israel, my servant,
Jacob, whom I have chosen,
you descendants of Abraham my friend,
9 I took you from the ends of the earth,
from its farthest corners I called you.
I said, 'You are my servant';
I have chosen you and have not rejected you.
10 So do not fear, for I am with you;
do not be dismayed, for I

[l]2 Or / *whom victory meets at every step*

אֱלֹהֶיךָ אִמַּצְתִּיךָ אַף־ עֲזַרְתִּיךָ אַף־ תְּמַכְתִּיךָ
I-will-uphold-you indeed I-will-help-you indeed I-will-strengthen-you God-of-you

בִּימִין צִדְקִי׃ (11) הֵן יֵבֹשׁוּ
they-will-be-ashamed surely! (11) righteousness-of-me by-right-hand-of

וְיִכָּלְמוּ כֹּל הַנֶּחֱרִים בָּךְ יִהְיוּ
they-will-be against-you the-ones-raging all-of and-they-will-be-disgraced

כְאַיִן וְיֹאבְדוּ אַנְשֵׁי רִיבֶךָ׃
opposition-of-you men-of and-they-will-perish as-nothing

(12) תְּבַקְשֵׁם וְלֹא תִמְצָאֵם אַנְשֵׁי מַצֻּתֶךָ
enmity-of-you men-of you-will-find-them but-not you-will-search-for-them (12)

יִהְיוּ כְאַיִן וּכְאֶפֶס אַנְשֵׁי מִלְחַמְתֶּךָ׃ (13) כִּי אֲנִי יְהוָה אֱלֹהֶיךָ
God-of-you Yahweh I for (13) war-of-you men-of and-as-nothing as-not they-will-be

מַחֲזִיק יְמִינֶךָ הָאֹמֵר לְךָ אַל־ תִּירָא אֲנִי
I you-fear not to-you the-one-saying right-hand-of-you one-taking-hold

עֲזַרְתִּיךָ׃ (14) אַל־ תִּירְאִי תּוֹלַעַת יַעֲקֹב מְתֵי יִשְׂרָאֵל אֲנִי
I Israel little-ones-of Jacob worm you-be-afraid not (14) I-will-help-you

עֲזַרְתִּיךְ נְאֻם־ יְהוָה וְגֹאֲלֵךְ קְדוֹשׁ יִשְׂרָאֵל׃
Israel Holy-One-of and-One-Redeeming-you Yahweh declaration-of I-will-help-you

(15) הִנֵּה שַׂמְתִּיךְ לְמוֹרַג חָרוּץ חָדָשׁ בַּעַל פִּיפִיּוֹת
teeth owner-of new sharp into-threshing-sledge I-will-make-you see! (15)

תָּדוּשׁ הָרִים וְתָדֹק וּגְבָעוֹת כַּמֹּץ
as-the-chaff and-hills and-you-will-crush mountains you-will-thresh

תָּשִׂים׃ (16) תִּזְרֵם וְרוּחַ תִּשָּׂאֵם
she-will-pick-up-them and-wind you-will-winnow-them (16) you-will-reduce

וּסְעָרָה תָּפִיץ אוֹתָם וְאַתָּה תָּגִיל בַּיהוָה
in-Yahweh you-will-rejoice but-you them she-will-blow-away and-gale

בִּקְדוֹשׁ יִשְׂרָאֵל תִּתְהַלָּל׃ (17) הָעֲנִיִּים וְהָאֶבְיוֹנִים
and-the-needy-ones the-poor-ones (17) you-will-glory Israel in-Holy-One-of

מְבַקְשִׁים מַיִם וָאַיִן לְשׁוֹנָם בַּצָּמָא
with-the-thirst tongue-of-them but-there-is-none waters ones-searching

נָשַׁתָּה אֲנִי יְהוָה אֶעֱנֵם אֱלֹהֵי יִשְׂרָאֵל לֹא אֶעֶזְבֵם׃
I-will-forsake-them not Israel God-of I-will-answer-them Yahweh I she-is-parched

(18) אֶפְתַּח עַל־ שְׁפָיִים נְהָרוֹת וּבְתוֹךְ בְּקָעוֹת מַעְיָנוֹת
springs valleys and-within rivers barren-heights on I-will-make-flow (18)

אָשִׂים מִדְבָּר לַאֲגַם־ מַיִם וְאֶרֶץ צִיָּה לְמוֹצָאֵי
into-ones-producing-of parched and-ground waters into-pool-of desert I-will-turn

מָיִם׃ (19) אֶתֵּן בַּמִּדְבָּר אֶרֶז שִׁטָּה וַהֲדַס וְעֵץ שָׁמֶן
olive-oil and-tree-of and-myrtle acacia cedar in-the-desert I-will-put (19) waters

am your God.
I will strengthen you and help you;
I will uphold you with my righteous right hand.

11 "All who rage against you
will surely be ashamed and disgraced;
those who oppose you
will be as nothing and perish.
12 Though you search for your enemies,
you will not find them.
Those who wage war against you
will be as nothing at all.
13 For I am the LORD, your God,
who takes hold of your right hand
and says to you, Do not fear;
I will help you.
14 Do not be afraid, O worm Jacob,
O little Israel,
for I myself will help you,"
declares the LORD,
your Redeemer, the Holy One of Israel.
15 "See, I will make you into a threshing sledge,
new and sharp, with many teeth.
You will thresh the mountains and crush them,
and reduce the hills to chaff.
16 You will winnow them, the wind will pick them up,
and a gale will blow them away.
But you will rejoice in the LORD
and glory in the Holy One of Israel.

17 "The poor and needy search for water,
but there is none;
their tongues are parched with thirst.
But I the LORD will answer them;
I, the God of Israel, will not forsake them.
18 I will make rivers flow on barren heights,
and springs within the valleys.
I will turn the desert into pools of water,
and the parched ground into springs.
19 I will put in the desert
the cedar and the acacia, the myrtle and the olive.

אָשִׂים בָּעֲרָבָה בְּרוֹשׁ תִּדְהָר וּתְאַשּׁוּר יַחְדָּו׃ לְמַעַן
I-will-set in-the-wasteland pine fir and-cypress together (20) so-that

יִרְאוּ וְיֵדְעוּ וְיָשִׂימוּ וְיַשְׂכִּילוּ
they-may-see and-they-may-know and-they-may-consider and-they-may-understand

יַחְדָּו כִּי יַד־ יְהוָה עָשְׂתָה זֹּאת וּקְדוֹשׁ יִשְׂרָאֵל בְּרָאָהּ׃
together that hand-of Yahweh she-did this and-Holy-One-of Israel he-created-her

קָרְבוּ רִיבְכֶם יֹאמַר יְהוָה הַגִּישׁוּ עֲצֻמוֹתֵיכֶם יֹאמַר
(21) present! case-of-you he-says Yahweh set-forth! arguments-of-you he-says

מֶלֶךְ יַעֲקֹב׃ יַגִּישׁוּ וְיַגִּידוּ לָנוּ אֵת אֲשֶׁר
King-of Jacob (22) let-them-bring-in and-let-them-tell to-us *** what

תִּקְרֶינָה הָרִאשֹׁנוֹת ׀ מָה הֵנָּה הַגִּידוּ וְנָשִׂימָה
they-will-happen the-former-things what? they tell! that-we-may-consider

לִבֵּנוּ וְנֵדְעָה אַחֲרִיתָן אוֹ הַבָּאוֹת
heart-of-us and-we-may-know final-outcome-of-them or the-things-coming

הַשְׁמִיעֻנוּ׃ הַגִּידוּ הָאֹתִיּוֹת לְאָחוֹר וְנֵדְעָה כִּי אֱלֹהִים
declare-to-us! (23) tell! the-things-coming in-future so-we-may-know that gods

אַתֶּם אַף־ תֵּיטִיבוּ וְתָרֵעוּ וְנִשְׁתָּעָה וְנִרְאֶ
you indeed you-do-good or-you-do-bad so-we-will-be-dismayed and-we-will-fear

יַחְדָּו׃ הֵן־ אַתֶּם מֵאַיִן וּפָעָלְכֶם מֵאָפַע
together (24) see! you less-than-nothing and-work-of-you less-than-worthless

תּוֹעֵבָה יִבְחַר בָּכֶם׃ הַעִירוֹתִי מִצָּפוֹן וַיַּאת
detestable-one he-chooses to-you (25) I-stirred-up from-north and-he-comes

מִמִּזְרַח־ שֶׁמֶשׁ יִקְרָא בִשְׁמִי וְיָבֹא סְגָנִים כְּמוֹ־ חֹמֶר
from-rising-of sun he-calls on-name-of-me and-he-treads rulers as mortar

וּכְמוֹ יוֹצֵר יִרְמָס־ טִיט׃ מִי־ הִגִּיד מֵרֹאשׁ
and-as one-being-potter he-treads clay (26) who? he-told from-beginning

וְנֵדָעָה וּמִלְּפָנִים וְנֹאמַר צַדִּיק אַף אֵין מַגִּיד
so-we-could-know or-from-beforehand so-we-could-say right indeed not one-telling

אַף אֵין מַשְׁמִיעַ אַף אֵין שֹׁמֵעַ אִמְרֵיכֶם׃ רִאשׁוֹן לְצִיּוֹן
indeed not one-foretelling indeed not one-hearing words-of-you (27) first to-Zion

הִנֵּה הִנָּם וְלִירוּשָׁלַםִ מְבַשֵּׂר אֶתֵּן׃ וְאֵרֶא
look! look-they! and-to-Jerusalem one-bringing-good-tidings I-gave (28) and-I-look

וְאֵין אִישׁ וּמֵאֵלֶּה וְאֵין יוֹעֵץ וְאֶשְׁאָלֵם
but-no one and-among-these also-no one-counseling when-I-ask-them

וְיָשִׁיבוּ דָבָר׃ הֵן כֻּלָּם אָוֶן אֶפֶס מַעֲשֵׂיהֶם
that-they-should-give answer (19) see! all-of-them false nothing deeds-of-them

רוּחַ וָתֹהוּ נִסְכֵּיהֶם׃ הֵן עַבְדִּי אֶתְמָךְ־ בּוֹ
wind and-confusion images-of-them (42:1) here! servant-of-me I-uphold to-him

I will set pines in the wasteland,
the fir and the cypress together,
20 so that people may see and know,
may consider and understand,
that the hand of the LORD has done this,
that the Holy One of Israel has created it.

21 "Present your case," says the LORD.
"Set forth your arguments," says Jacob's King.
22 "Bring in ⌊your idols⌋ to tell us what is going to happen.
Tell us what the former things were,
so that we may consider them
and know their final outcome.
Or declare to us the things to come,
23 tell us what the future holds,
so we may know that you are gods.
Do something, whether good or bad,
so that we will be dismayed and filled with fear.
24 But you are less than nothing
and your works are utterly worthless;
he who chooses you is detestable.

25 "I have stirred up one from the north, and he comes—
one from the rising sun who calls on my name.
He treads on rulers as if they were mortar,
as if he were a potter treading the clay.
26 Who told of this from the beginning, so we could know,
or beforehand, so we could say, 'He was right'?
No one told of this,
no one foretold it,
no one heard any words from you.
27 I was the first to tell Zion, 'Look, here they are!'
I gave to Jerusalem a messenger of good tidings.
28 I look but there is no one—
no one among them to give counsel,
no one to give answer when I ask them.
29 See, they are all false!
Their deeds amount to nothing;
their images are but wind and confusion.

*The Servant of the LORD*

42 "Here is my servant, whom I uphold,

°23 ק ונראה

בְּחִירִי רָצְתָה נַפְשִׁי נָתַתִּי רוּחִי עָלָיו מִשְׁפָּט
justice on-him Spirit-of-me I-will-put self-of-me she-delights chosen-one-of-me

לַגּוֹיִם יוֹצִיא׃ (2) לֹא יִצְעַק וְלֹא יִשָּׂא וְלֹא־
or-not he-will-cry-out or-not he-will-shout not (2) he-will-bring to-the-nations

יַשְׁמִיעַ בַּחוּץ קוֹלוֹ׃ (3) קָנֶה רָצוּץ לֹא
not being-bruised reed (3) voice-of-him in-the-street he-will-raise-sound

יִשְׁבּוֹר וּפִשְׁתָּה כֵהָה לֹא יְכַבֶּנָּה לֶאֱמֶת
in-faithfulness he-will-snuff-out-her not smoldering and-wick he-will-break

יוֹצִיא מִשְׁפָּט׃ (4) לֹא יִכְהֶה וְלֹא יָרוּץ
he-will-be-discouraged or-not he-will-falter not (4) justice he-will-bring-forth

עַד־ יָשִׂים בָּאָרֶץ מִשְׁפָּט וּלְתוֹרָתוֹ אִיִּים יְיַחֵילוּ׃
they-will-hope islands and-in-law-of-him justice on-the-earth he-establishes till

(5) כֹּה־ אָמַר הָאֵל | יְהוָה בּוֹרֵא הַשָּׁמַיִם וְנוֹטֵיהֶם
and-one-stretching-out-them the-heavens one-creating Yahweh the-God he-says this (5)

רֹקַע הָאָרֶץ וְצֶאֱצָאֶיהָ נֹתֵן נְשָׁמָה
breath one-giving and-things-that-come-out-of-her the-earth one-spreading-out

לָעָם עָלֶיהָ וְרוּחַ לַהֹלְכִים בָּהּ׃ (6) אֲנִי יְהוָה קְרָאתִיךָ
I-called-you Yahweh I (6) on-her to-the-ones-walking and-life on-her to-the-people

בְצֶדֶק וְאַחְזֵק בְּיָדֶךָ וְאֶצָּרְךָ
and-I-will-keep-you of-hand-of-you and-I-will-take-hold in-righteousness

וְאֶתֶּנְךָ לִבְרִית עָם לְאוֹר גּוֹיִם׃ (7) לִפְקֹחַ עֵינַיִם
eyes to-open (7) Gentiles as-light-of people as-covenant-of and-I-will-make-you

עִוְרוֹת לְהוֹצִיא מִמַּסְגֵּר אַסִּיר מִבֵּית כֶּלֶא יֹשְׁבֵי
ones-sitting-of dungeon from-house-of captive from-prison to-free blind-ones

חֹשֶׁךְ׃ (8) אֲנִי יְהוָה הוּא שְׁמִי וּכְבוֹדִי לְאַחֵר לֹא־ אֶתֵּן
I-will-give not to-another and-glory-of-me name-of-me that Yahweh I (8) darkness

וּתְהִלָּתִי לַפְּסִילִים׃ (9) הָרִאשֹׁנוֹת הִנֵּה־ בָאוּ
they-took-place see! the-former-things (9) to-the-idols or-praise-of-me

וַחֲדָשׁוֹת אֲנִי מַגִּיד בְּטֶרֶם תִּצְמַחְנָה אַשְׁמִיעַ* אֶתְכֶם׃
you I-announce they-spring-into-being at-before declaring I and-new-things

(10) שִׁירוּ לַיהוָה שִׁיר חָדָשׁ תְּהִלָּתוֹ מִקְצֵה הָאָרֶץ
the-earth from-end-of praise-of-him new song to-Yahweh sing! (10)

יוֹרְדֵי הַיָּם וּמְלֹאוֹ אִיִּים וְיֹשְׁבֵיהֶם׃
and-ones-living-of-them islands and-all-that-in-him the-sea ones-going-down-of

(11) יִשְׂאוּ מִדְבָּר וְעָרָיו חֲצֵרִים תֵּשֵׁב קֵדָר
Kedar she-lives settlements and-towns-of-him desert let-them-raise (11)

יָרֹנּוּ יֹשְׁבֵי סֶלַע מֵרֹאשׁ הָרִים
mountains from-top-of Sela ones-being-people-of let-them-sing-for-joy

my chosen one in whom I delight;
I will put my Spirit on him
and he will bring justice to the nations.
[2]He will not shout or cry out,
or raise his voice in the streets.
[3]A bruised reed he will not break,
and a smoldering wick he will not snuff out.
In faithfulness he will bring forth justice;
[4]he will not falter or be discouraged
till he establishes justice on earth.
In his law the islands will put their hope."

[5]This is what God the LORD says—
he who created the heavens and stretched them out,
who spread out the earth and all that comes out of it,
who gives breath to its people,
and life to those who walk on it:
[6]"I, the LORD, have called you in righteousness;
I will take hold of your hand.
I will keep you and will make you
to be a covenant for the people
and a light for the Gentiles,
[7]to open eyes that are blind,
to free captives from prison
and to release from the dungeon those who sit in darkness.

[8]"I am the LORD; that is my name!
I will not give my glory to another
or my praise to idols.
[9]See, the former things have taken place,
and new things I declare;
before they spring into being
I announce them to you."

*Song of Praise to the LORD*

[10]Sing to the LORD a new song,
his praise from the ends of the earth,
you who go down to the sea,
and all that is in it,
you islands, and all who live in them.
[11]Let the desert and its towns raise their voices;
let the settlements where Kedar lives rejoice.
Let the people of Sela sing for joy;
let them shout from the mountaintops.

*9 Most mss have *furtive pathah* under the *ayin* (יַעַ).

יִצְוָחוּ׃ (12) יָשִׂימוּ לַיהוָה כָּבוֹד וּתְהִלָּתוֹ בָּאִיִּים
let-them-shout (12) let-them-give to-Yahweh glory and-praise-of-him in-the-islands

יַגִּידוּ׃ (13) יְהוָה כַּגִּבּוֹר יֵצֵא כְּאִישׁ
let-them-proclaim (13) Yahweh like-the-mighty-man he-will-march-out like-man-of

מִלְחָמוֹת יָעִיר קִנְאָה יָרִיעַ אַף־ יַצְרִיחַ עַל־
wars he-will-stir-up zeal he-will-shout also he-will-raise-cry over

אֹיְבָיו יִתְגַּבָּר׃ (14) הֶחֱשֵׁיתִי מֵעוֹלָם
ones-being-enemies-of-him he-will-triumph (14) I-was-silent for-long-time

אַחֲרִישׁ אֶתְאַפָּק כַּיּוֹלֵדָה אֶפְעֶה אֶשֹּׁם
I-was-quiet I-held-myself-back like-the-woman-bearing-child I-cry-out I-gasp

וְאֶשְׁאַף יָחַד׃ (15) אַחֲרִיב הָרִים וּגְבָעוֹת וְכָל־
and-I-pant together (15) I-will-lay-waste mountains and-hills and-all-of

עֶשְׂבָּם אוֹבִישׁ וְשַׂמְתִּי נְהָרוֹת לָאִיִּים
vegetation-of-them I-will-dry-up and-I-will-turn rivers into-the-islands

וַאֲגַמִּים אוֹבִישׁ׃ (16) וְהוֹלַכְתִּי עִוְרִים בְּדֶרֶךְ לֹא יָדָעוּ
and-pools I-will-dry-up (16) and-I-will-lead blind-ones by-way not they-knew

בִּנְתִיבוֹת לֹא־ יָדְעוּ אַדְרִיכֵם אָשִׂים מַחְשָׁךְ לִפְנֵיהֶם
along-paths not they-knew I-will-guide-them I-will-turn darkness before-them

לָאוֹר וּמַעֲקַשִּׁים לְמִישׁוֹר אֵלֶּה הַדְּבָרִים עֲשִׂיתִם וְלֹא
into-light and-rough-places into-smooth these the-things I-will-do and-not

עֲזַבְתִּים׃ (17) נָסֹגוּ אָחוֹר יֵבֹשׁוּ בֹשֶׁת
I-will-forsake-them (17) they-will-be-turned back they-will-be-ashamed shame

הַבֹּטְחִים בַּפָּסֶל הָאֹמְרִים לְמַסֵּכָה אַתֶּם אֱלֹהֵינוּ׃
the-ones-trusting in-the-idol the-ones-saying to-image you gods-of-us

(18) הַחֵרְשִׁים שְׁמָעוּ וְהַעִוְרִים הַבִּיטוּ לִרְאוֹת׃ (19) מִי עִוֵּר כִּי
(18) the-deaf-ones hear! and-the-blind-ones look! to-see (19) who? blind but

אִם־ עַבְדִּי וְחֵרֵשׁ כְּמַלְאָכִי אֶשְׁלָח מִי עִוֵּר
if servant-of-me and-deaf like-messenger-of-me I-send who? blind

כִּמְשֻׁלָּם וְעִוֵּר כְּעֶבֶד יְהוָה׃ (20) רָאִית*
like-one-being-committed indeed-blind like-servant-of Yahweh (20) *to-see

רַבּוֹת וְלֹא תִשְׁמֹר פָּקוֹחַ אָזְנַיִם וְלֹא יִשְׁמָע׃
many-things but-not you-paid-attention to-be-open ears but-not he-hears

(21) יְהוָה חָפֵץ לְמַעַן צִדְקוֹ יַגְדִּיל תּוֹרָה
(21) Yahweh he-was-pleased for-sake-of righteousness-of-him he-made-great law

וְיַאְדִּיר׃ (22) וְהוּא עַם־ בָּזוּז וְשָׁסוּי הָפֵחַ
and-he-made-glorious (22) but-this people being-plundered and-being-looted to-trap

בַּחוּרִים כֻּלָּם וּבְבָתֵּי כְלָאִים הָחְבָּאוּ הָיוּ
in-the-pits all-of-them or-in-houses-of prisons they-are-hidden they-became

12 Let them give glory to the Lord
and proclaim his praise in the islands.
13 The Lord will march out like a mighty man,
like a warrior he will stir up his zeal;
with a shout he will raise the battle cry
and will triumph over his enemies.

14 "For a long time I have kept silent,
I have been quiet and held myself back.
But now, like a woman in childbirth,
I cry out, I gasp and pant.
15 I will lay waste the mountains and hills
and dry up all their vegetation;
I will turn rivers into islands
and dry up the pools.
16 I will lead the blind by ways they have not known,
along unfamiliar paths I will guide them;
I will turn the darkness into light before them
and make the rough places smooth.
These are the things I will do;
I will not forsake them.
17 But those who trust in idols,
who say to images, 'You are our gods,'
will be turned back in utter shame.

*Israel Blind and Deaf*

18 "Hear, you deaf;
look, you blind, and see!
19 Who is blind but my servant,
and deaf like the messenger I send?
Who is blind like the one committed to me,
blind like the servant of the Lord?
20 You have seen many things, but have paid no attention;
your ears are open, but you hear nothing."
21 It pleased the Lord
for the sake of his righteousness
to make his law great and glorious.
22 But this is a people plundered and looted,
all of them trapped in pits
or hidden away in prisons.

*20 The NIV points the *Ketbib* form as רָאִיתָ, *you-saw.*

°20 ק ראות

לבז ואין מציל משסה ואין־אמר השב׃ מי
who? (23) send-back! one-saying and-not loot one-rescuing and-not as-plunder

בכם יאזין זאת יקשב וישמע לאחור׃
in-time-to-come and-he-will-heed he-will-pay-attention this he-will-listen of-you

מי־נתן למשוסה יעקב וישראל לבזזים הלוא יהוה
Yahweh not? to-ones-plundering and-Israel Jacob as-loot he-handed-over who? (24)

זו חטאנו לו ולא־אבו בדרכיו הלוך ולא
and-not to-follow on-ways-of-him they-would for-not against-him we-sinned whom

שמעו בתורתו׃ וישפך עליו חמה אפו
anger-of-him burning on-him so-he-poured-out (25) to-law-of-him they-obeyed

ועזוז מלחמה ותלהטהו מסביב ולא ידע
he-understood but-not at-around and-she-burned-him war and-violence-of

ותבער־בו ולא־ישים על־לב׃ ועתה כה־אמר
he-says this but-now (43:1) heart to he-took but-not to-him and-she-consumed

יהוה בראך יעקב ויצרך ישראל אל־תירא כי
for you-fear not Israel and-one-forming-you Jacob one-creating-you Yahweh

גאלתיך קראתי בשמך לי־אתה׃ כי־תעבר
you-pass when (2) you to-me by-name-of-you I-summoned I-redeemed-you

במים אתך־אני ובנהרות לא ישטפוך
they-will-sweep-over-you not and-through-the-rivers I with-you through-the-waters

כי־תלך במו־אש לא תכוה ולהבה לא תבער־
she-will-set-ablaze not and-flame you-will-be-burned not fire through you-walk when

בך׃ כי אני יהוה אלהיך קדוש ישראל מושיעך נתתי
I-give One-Saving-you Israel Holy-One-of God-of-you Yahweh I for (3) to-you

כפרך מצרים כוש וסבא תחתיך׃ מאשר יקרת
you-are-precious since-that (4) instead-of-you and-Seba Cush Egypt ransom-of-you

בעיני נכבדת ואני אהבתיך ואתן אדם
man then-I-will-give I-love-you and-I you-are-honored in-eyes-of-me

תחתיך ולאמים תחת נפשך׃ אל־תירא
you-be-afraid not (5) life-of-you in-exchange and-peoples in-exchange-for-you

כי אתך־אני ממזרח אביא זרעך וממערב אקבצך׃
I-will-gather-you and-from-west child-of-you I-will-bring from-east I with-you for

אמר לצפון תני ולתימן אל־תכלאי הביאי
bring! you-hold-back not and-to-south give! to-the-north I-will-say (6)

בני מרחוק ובנותי מקצה הארץ׃ כל
every-of (7) the-earth from-end-of and-daughters-of-me from-afar sons-of-me

הנקרא בשמי ולכבודי בראתיו יצרתיו
I-formed-him I-created-him and-for-glory-of-me by-name-of-me the-one-being-called

They have become plunder,
with no one to rescue them;
they have been made loot,
with no one to say, "Send
them back."
23 Which of you will listen to
this
or pay close attention in
time to come?
24 Who handed Jacob over to
become loot,
and Israel to the plunderers?
Was it not the LORD,
against whom we have
sinned?
For they would not follow his
ways;
they did not obey his law.
25 So he poured out on them his
burning anger,
the violence of war.
It enveloped them in flames,
yet they did not
understand;
it consumed them, but they
did not take it to heart.

*Israel's Only Savior*

43 But now, this is what the
LORD says—
he who created you, O
Jacob,
he who formed you, O
Israel:
"Fear not, for I have redeemed
you;
I have summoned you by
name; you are mine.
2 When you pass through the
waters,
I will be with you;
and when you pass through
the rivers,
they will not sweep over
you.
When you walk through the
fire,
you will not be burned;
the flames will not set you
ablaze.
3 For I am the LORD, your God,
the Holy One of Israel, your
Savior;
I give Egypt for your ransom,
Cush[m] and Seba in your
stead.
4 Since you are precious and
honored in my sight,
and because I love you,
I will give men in exchange
for you,
and people in exchange for
your life.
5 Do not be afraid, for I am
with you;
I will bring your children
from the east
and gather you from the
west.
6 I will say to the north, 'Give
them up!'
and to the south, 'Do not
hold them back.'
Bring my sons from afar
and my daughters from the
ends of the earth—
7 everyone who is called by my
name,
whom I created for my
glory,

m3 That is, the upper Nile region

°24 ק למשיסה

אַף־ עֲשִׂיתִיו׃ הוֹצִיא עַם־ עִוֵּר וְעֵינַיִם יֵשׁ וְחֵרְשִׁים
and-deaf-ones there-are but-eyes blind people lead-out! (8) I-made-him also

וְאָזְנַיִם לָמוֹ׃ כָּל־ הַגּוֹיִם נִקְבְּצוּ יַחְדָּו וְיֵאָסְפוּ
and-they-assemble together they-gather the-nations all-of (9) to-them but-ears

לְאֻמִּים מִי בָהֶם יַגִּיד זֹאת וְרִאשֹׁנוֹת יַשְׁמִיעֻנוּ
they-proclaimed-to-us and-former-things this he-foretold of-them who? peoples

יִתְּנוּ עֵדֵיהֶם וְיִצְדָּקוּ וְיִשְׁמְעוּ
so-they-may-hear and-let-them-prove-right witnesses-of-them let-them-bring-in

וְיֹאמְרוּ אֱמֶת׃ אַתֶּם עֵדַי נְאֻם־ יְהוָה
Yahweh declaration-of witnesses-of-me you (10) true and-they-may-say

וְעַבְדִּי אֲשֶׁר בָּחָרְתִּי לְמַעַן תֵּדְעוּ וְתַאֲמִינוּ לִי
in-me and-you-may-believe you-may-know so-that I-chose whom and-servant-of-me

וְתָבִינוּ כִּי־אֲנִי הוּא לְפָנַי לֹא־ נוֹצַר אֵל וְאַחֲרַי לֹא
not or-after-me god he-was-formed not before-me he I that and-you-may-understand

יִהְיֶה׃ אָנֹכִי אָנֹכִי יְהוָה וְאֵין מִבַּלְעָדַי מוֹשִׁיעַ׃ אָנֹכִי
I (12) one-saving at-apart-from-me and-not Yahweh I I (11) he-will-be

הִגַּדְתִּי וְהוֹשַׁעְתִּי וְהִשְׁמַעְתִּי וְאֵין בָּכֶם זָר
one-being-foreign among-you and-not and-I-proclaimed and-I-saved I-revealed

וְאַתֶּם עֵדַי נְאֻם־ יְהוָה וַאֲנִי־ אֵל׃ גַּם־ מִיּוֹם אֲנִי הוּא
he I from-day yes (13) God that-I Yahweh declaration-of witnesses-of-me and-you

וְאֵין מִיָּדִי מַצִּיל אֶפְעַל וּמִי יְשִׁיבֶנָּה׃
he-can-reverse-her and-who? I-act one-delivering from-hand-of-me and-not

כֹּה־ אָמַר יְהוָה גֹּאַלְכֶם קְדוֹשׁ יִשְׂרָאֵל לְמַעַנְכֶם
for-sake-of-you Israel Holy-One-of One-Redeeming-you Yahweh he-says this (14)

שִׁלַּחְתִּי בָבֶלָה וְהוֹרַדְתִּי בָרִיחִים כֻּלָּם וְכַשְׂדִּים
even-Chaldeans all-of-them fugitives and-I-will-bring-down to-Babylon I-will-send

בָּאֳנִיּוֹת רִנָּתָם׃ אֲנִי יְהוָה קְדוֹשְׁכֶם בּוֹרֵא יִשְׂרָאֵל
Israel One-Creating Holy-One-of-you Yahweh I (15) pride-of-them in-ships-of

מַלְכְּכֶם׃ כֹּה אָמַר יְהוָה הַנּוֹתֵן בַּיָּם דָּרֶךְ
way through-the-sea the-one-making Yahweh he-says this (16) King-of-you

וּבְמַיִם עַזִּים נְתִיבָה׃ הַמּוֹצִיא רֶכֶב־ וָסוּס
and-horse chariot the-one-drawing-out (17) path mighty-ones and-through-waters

חַיִל וְעִזּוּז יַחְדָּו יִשְׁכְּבוּ בַּל־ יָקוּמוּ
they-will-rise never they-lay together and-reinforcement army

דָּעֲכוּ כַּפִּשְׁתָּה כָבוּ׃ אַל־ תִּזְכְּרוּ
you-remember not (18) they-were-snuffed-out like-the-wick they-were-extinguished

רִאשֹׁנוֹת וְקַדְמֹנִיּוֹת אַל־ תִּתְבֹּנָנוּ׃ הִנְנִי עֹשֶׂה חֲדָשָׁה עַתָּה
now new-thing doing see-I! (19) you-dwell-on not and-past-things former-things

whom I formed and made."
8 Lead out those who have eyes
but are blind,
who have ears but are deaf.
9 All the nations gather together
and the peoples assemble.
Which of them foretold this
and proclaimed to us the
former things?
Let them bring in their
witnesses to prove they
were right,
so that others may hear and
say, "It is true."
10 "You are my witnesses,"
declares the LORD,
"and my servant whom I
have chosen,
so that you may know and
believe me
and understand that I am
he.
Before me no god was formed,
nor will there be one after
me.
11 I, even I, am the LORD,
and apart from me there is
no savior.
12 I have revealed and saved and
proclaimed—
I, and not some foreign god
among you.
You are my witnesses,"
declares the LORD, "that I
am God.
13 Yes, and from ancient days I
am he.
No one can deliver out of my
hand.
When I act, who can reverse
it?"

*God's Mercy and Israel's Unfaithfulness*

14 This is what the LORD says—
your Redeemer, the Holy
One of Israel:
"For your sake I will send to
Babylon
and bring down as fugitives
all the Babylonians,[n]
in the ships in which they
took pride.
15 I am the LORD, your Holy One,
Israel's Creator, your King."
16 This is what the LORD says—
he who made a way through
the sea,
a path through the mighty
waters,
17 who drew out the chariots and
horses,
the army and
reinforcements together,
and they lay there, never to
rise again,
extinguished, snuffed out
like a wick:
18 "Forget the former things;
do not dwell on the past.
19 See, I am doing a new thing!

[n]14 *Or Chaldeans*

תִצְמָח הֲלוֹא תֵדָעוּהָ אַף אָשִׂים בַּמִּדְבָּר דֶּרֶךְ בִּישִׁמֹן
in-wasteland way in-the-desert I-make also you-perceive-her not? she-springs-up

נְהָרוֹת׃ תְּכַבְּדֵנִי חַיַּת הַשָּׂדֶה תַּנִּים וּבְנוֹת יַעֲנָה
owl and-daughters-of jackals the-wild animal-of she-honors-me (20) streams

כִּי־ נָתַתִּי בַמִּדְבָּר מַיִם נְהָרוֹת בִּישִׁימֹן לְהַשְׁקוֹת
to-give-drink in-wasteland streams waters in-the-desert I-provide because

עַמִּי בְחִירִי׃ עַם־ זוּ יָצַרְתִּי לִי תְּהִלָּתִי
praise-of-me for-me I-formed whom people (21) chosen-of-me people-of-me

יְסַפֵּרוּ׃ וְלֹא־ אֹתִי קָרָאתָ יַעֲקֹב כִּי־ יָגַעְתָּ
you-wearied-yourself or Jacob you-called me yet-not (22) they-may-proclaim

בִּי יִשְׂרָאֵל׃ לֹא־ הֵבֵיאתָ לִּי שֵׂה עֹלֹתֶיךָ
burnt-offerings-of-you sheep-of to-me you-brought not (23) Israel for-me

וּזְבָחֶיךָ לֹא כִבַּדְתָּנִי לֹא הֶעֱבַדְתִּיךָ בְּמִנְחָה
with-grain-offering I-burdened-you not you-honored-me not or-sacrifices-of-you

וְלֹא הוֹגַעְתִּיךָ בִּלְבוֹנָה׃ לֹא־ קָנִיתָ לִּי בַכֶּסֶף
with-the-money for-me you-bought not (24) with-incense I-wearied-you or-not

קָנֶה וְחֵלֶב זְבָחֶיךָ לֹא הִרְוִיתָנִי אַךְ הֶעֱבַדְתַּנִי
you-burdened-me but you-lavished-on-me not sacrifices-of-you or-fat-of calamus

בְּחַטֹּאותֶיךָ הוֹגַעְתַּנִי בַּעֲוֺנֹתֶיךָ׃ אָנֹכִי אָנֹכִי הוּא
he I I (25) with-offenses-of-you you-wearied-me with-sins-of-you

מֹחֶה פְשָׁעֶיךָ לְמַעֲנִי וְחַטֹּאתֶיךָ לֹא
not and-sins-of-you for-sake-of-me transgressions-of-you one-blotting-out

אֶזְכֹּר׃ הַזְכִּירֵנִי נִשָּׁפְטָה יָחַד סַפֵּר אַתָּה לְמַעַן
for-sake-of you state-case! together let-us-argue review-for-me! (26) I-remember

תִּצְדָּק׃ אָבִיךָ הָרִאשׁוֹן חָטָא וּמְלִיצֶיךָ
and-ones-speaking-of-you he-sinned the-first father-of-you (27) you-are-innocent

פָּשְׁעוּ בִי׃ וַאֲחַלֵּל שָׂרֵי קֹדֶשׁ
temple dignitaries-of so-I-will-disgrace (28) against-me they-rebelled

וְאֶתְּנָה לַחֵרֶם יַעֲקֹב וְיִשְׂרָאֵל לְגִדּוּפִים׃ וְעַתָּה
but-now (44:1) to-scorns and-Israel Jacob to-the-destruction and-I-will-consign

שְׁמַע יַעֲקֹב עַבְדִּי וְיִשְׂרָאֵל בָּחַרְתִּי בוֹ׃ כֹּה־ אָמַר יְהוָה
Yahweh he-says this (2) to-him I-chose and-Israel servant-of-me Jacob listen!

עֹשֶׂךָ וְיֹצֶרְךָ מִבֶּטֶן יַעְזְרֶךָּ אַל־ תִּירָא
you-be-afraid not he-will-help-you in-womb and-one-forming-you one-making-you

עַבְדִּי יַעֲקֹב וִישֻׁרוּן בָּחַרְתִּי בוֹ׃ כִּי אֶצָּק־ מַיִם עַל־
on waters I-will-pour for (3) to-him I-chose and-Jeshurun Jacob servant-of-me

צָמֵא וְנֹזְלִים עַל־ יַבָּשָׁה אֶצֹּק רוּחִי עַל־
on Spirit-of-me I-will-pour-out dry-ground on and-ones-streaming thirsty

Now it springs up; do you
not perceive it?
I am making a way in the
desert
and streams in the
wasteland.
20 The wild animals honor me,
the jackals and the owls,
because I provide water in the
desert
and streams in the
wasteland,
to give drink to my people, my
chosen,
21 the people I formed for
myself
that they may proclaim my
praise.
22 "Yet you have not called upon
me, O Jacob,
you have not wearied
yourselves for me, O
Israel.
23 You have not brought me
sheep for burnt offerings,
nor honored me with your
sacrifices.
I have not burdened you with
grain offerings
nor wearied you with
demands for incense.
24 You have not bought any
fragrant calamus for me,
or lavished on me the fat of
your sacrifices.
But you have burdened me
with your sins
and wearied me with your
offenses.
25 "I, even I, am he who blots
out
your transgressions, for my
own sake,
and remembers your sins no
more.
26 Review the past for me,
let us argue the matter
together;
state the case for your
innocence.
27 Your first father sinned;
your spokesmen rebelled
against me.
28 So I will disgrace the
dignitaries of your
temple,
and I will consign Jacob to
destruction°
and Israel to scorn.

*Israel the Chosen*

44 "But now listen, O Jacob,
my servant,
Israel, whom I have chosen.
2 This is what the LORD says—
he who made you, who
formed you in the womb,
and who will help you:
Do not be afraid, O Jacob, my
servant,
Jeshurun, whom I have
chosen.
3 For I will pour water on the
thirsty land,
and streams on the dry
ground;
I will pour out my Spirit on

°28 The Hebrew term refers to the irrevocable giving over of things or persons to the LORD, often by totally destroying them.

זַרְעֶךָ וּבִרְכָתִי עַל־ צֶאֱצָאֶיךָ׃ וְצָמְחוּ

and-they-will-spring-up (4) descendants-of-you on and-blessing-of-me offspring-of-you

בְּבֵין חָצִיר כַּעֲרָבִים עַל־ יִבְלֵי־ מָיִם׃ זֶה יֹאמַר לַיהוָה

to-Yahweh he-will-say one (5) waters streams-of by like-poplars grass at-between

אֲנִי וְזֶה יִקְרָא בְשֵׁם־ יַעֲקֹב וְזֶה יִכְתֹּב יָדוֹ

hand-of-him he-will-write and-another Jacob by-name-of he-will-call and-another I

לַיהוָה וּבְשֵׁם יִשְׂרָאֵל יְכַנֶּה׃ כֹּה־ אָמַר יְהוָה

Yahweh he-says this (6) he-will-take-name Israel and-by-name-of to-Yahweh

מֶלֶךְ־ יִשְׂרָאֵל וְגֹאֲלוֹ יְהוָה צְבָאוֹת אֲנִי רִאשׁוֹן וַאֲנִי אַחֲרוֹן

last and-I first I Hosts Yahweh-of and-One-Redeeming-him Israel King-of

וּמִבַּלְעָדַי אֵין אֱלֹהִים׃ וּמִי־ כָמוֹנִי יִקְרָא

let-him-proclaim like-me then-who? (7) God there-is-no and-at-apart-from-me

וְיַגִּידֶהָ וְיַעְרְכֶהָ לִי מִשּׂוּמִי

since-to-establish-me before-me and-let-him-lay-out-her and-let-him-declare-her

עַם־ עוֹלָם וְאֹתִיּוֹת וַאֲשֶׁר תָּבֹאנָה יַגִּידוּ

let-them-foretell they-will-come and-what and-things-coming ancient people-of

לָמוֹ׃ אַל־ תִּפְחֲדוּ וְאַל־ תִּרְהוּ הֲלֹא מֵאָז

from-long-ago not? you-be-afraid and-not you-tremble not (8) about-them

הִשְׁמַעְתִּיךָ וְהִגַּדְתִּי וְאַתֶּם עֵדָי הֲיֵשׁ אֱלוֹהַּ

God is-there? witnesses-of-me now-you and-I-foretold I-proclaimed-to-you

מִבַּלְעָדַי וְאֵין צוּר בַּל־ יָדָעְתִּי׃ יֹצְרֵי־ פֶסֶל

idol ones-making-of (9) I-know not Rock indeed-there-is-not from-besides-me

כֻּלָּם תֹּהוּ וַחֲמוּדֵיהֶם בַּל־ יוֹעִילוּ

they-have-worth not and-things-being-treasured-of-them nothing all-of-them

וְעֵדֵיהֶם הֵמָּה בַּל־ יִרְאוּ וּבַל־ יֵדְעוּ לְמַעַן יֵבֹשׁוּ׃

they-are-ashamed so-that they-know and-not they-see not they and-witnesses-of-them

מִי־ יָצַר אֵל וּפֶסֶל נָסָךְ לְבִלְתִּי הוֹעִיל׃ הֵן

see! (11) he-can-profit to-nothing he-casts and-idol god he-shapes who? (10)

כָּל־ חֲבֵרָיו יֵבֹשׁוּ וְחָרָשִׁים הֵמָּה מֵאָדָם

only-man they and-craftsmen they-will-be-shamed kinds-of-him all-of

יִתְקַבְּצוּ כֻלָּם יַעֲמֹדוּ יִפְחֲדוּ

they-will-be-terrified let-them-stand all-of-them let-them-come-together

יֵבֹשׁוּ יָחַד׃ חָרַשׁ בַּרְזֶל מַעֲצָד וּפָעַל

and-he-works tool iron craftsman-of (12) together they-will-be-infamous

בַּפֶּחָם וּבַמַּקָּבוֹת יִצְּרֵהוּ וַיִּפְעָלֵהוּ בִּזְרוֹעַ

with-arm-of and-he-forges-him he-shapes-him and-with-the-hammers in-the-coal

כֹּחוֹ גַּם־ רָעֵב וְאֵין כֹּחַ לֹא־ שָׁתָה מָיִם

waters he-drinks not strength and-there-is-no he-gets-hungry and might-of-him

---

your offspring,
and my blessing on your descendants.
4They will spring up like grass in a meadow,
like poplar trees by flowing streams.
5One will say, 'I belong to the LORD';
another will call himself by the name of Jacob;
still another will write on his hand, 'The LORD's,'
and will take the name Israel.

*The LORD, Not Idols*

6"This is what the LORD says—
Israel's King and Redeemer, the LORD Almighty:
I am the first and I am the last;
apart from me there is no God.
7Who then is like me? Let him proclaim it.
Let him declare and lay out before me
what has happened since I established my ancient people,
and what is yet to come—
yes, let him foretell what will come.
8Do not tremble, do not be afraid.
Did I not proclaim this and foretell it long ago?
You are my witnesses. Is there any God besides me?
No, there is no other Rock; I know not one."

9All who make idols are nothing,
and the things they treasure are worthless.
Those who would speak up for them are blind;
they are ignorant, to their own shame.
10Who shapes a god and casts an idol,
which can profit him nothing?
11He and his kind will be put to shame;
craftsmen are nothing but men.
Let them all come together and take their stand;
they will be brought down to terror and infamy.

12The blacksmith takes a tool
and works with it in the coals;
he shapes an idol with hammers,
he forges it with the might of his arm.
He gets hungry and loses his strength;
he drinks no water and

וַיִּעָף׃ חָרַשׁ עֵצִים נָטָה קָו יְתָאֲרֵהוּ
he-outlines-him line he-measures woods craftsman-of (13) and-he-grows-faint

בַּשֶּׂרֶד יַעֲשֵׂהוּ בַּמַּקְצֻעוֹת וּבַמְּחוּגָה
and-with-the-compass with-the-chisels he-roughs-out-him with-the-marker

יְתָאֳרֵהוּ וַיַּעֲשֵׂהוּ כְּתַבְנִית אִישׁ כְּתִפְאֶרֶת אָדָם לָשֶׁבֶת בָּיִת׃
shrine to-dwell man as-glory-of man as-form-of and-he-shapes-him he-marks-him

לִכְרָת־ לוֹ אֲרָזִים וַיִּקַּח תִּרְזָה וְאַלּוֹן וַיְאַמֶּץ־ לוֹ
for-him or-he-let-grow or-oak cypress or-he-took cedars for-him to-cut-down (14)

בַּעֲצֵי־ יָעַר נָטַע אֹרֶן וְגֶשֶׁם יְגַדֵּל׃ וְהָיָה
and-he-is (15) he-made-grow and-rain pine he-planted forest among-trees-of

לְאָדָם לְבָעֵר וַיִּקַּח מֵהֶם וַיָּחָם אַף־ יַשִּׂיק
he-kindles-fire also and-he-warms-himself from-them and-he-takes to-burn for-man

וְאָפָה לָחֶם אַף־ יִפְעַל־ אֵל וַיִּשְׁתָּחוּ עָשָׂהוּ פֶסֶל
idol he-makes-him and-he-worships god he-fashions also bread and-he-bakes

וַיִּסְגָּד־ לָמוֹ׃ חֶצְיוֹ שָׂרַף בְּמוֹ־אֵשׁ עַל־ חֶצְיוֹ בָּשָׂר יֹאכֵל
he-eats meal half-of-him over fire in he-burns half-of-him (16) to-him and-he-bows

יִצְלֶה צָלִי וְיִשְׂבָּע אַף־ יָחֹם וְיֹאמַר הֶאָח
ah! and-he-says he-warms-himself also and-he-eats-fill roast-meat he-roasts

חַמּוֹתִי רָאִיתִי אוּר׃ וּשְׁאֵרִיתוֹ לְאֵל עָשָׂה לְפִסְלוֹ
into-idol-of-him he-makes into-god and-rest-of-him (17) fire I-see I-am-warm

יִסְגָּוד־ לוֹ וְיִשְׁתַּחוּ וְיִתְפַּלֵּל אֵלָיו וְיֹאמַר הַצִּילֵנִי כִּי
for save-me! and-he-says to-him and-he-prays and-he-worships to-him he-bows

אֵלִי אָתָּה׃ לֹא יָדְעוּ וְלֹא יָבִינוּ כִּי טַח
he-is-plastered-over for they-understand and-not they-know not (18) you god-of-me

מֵרְאוֹת עֵינֵיהֶם מֵהַשְׂכִּיל לִבֹּתָם׃ וְלֹא־ יָשִׁיב
he-takes and-not (19) minds-of-them from-to-understand eyes-of-them from-to-see

אֶל־ לִבּוֹ וְלֹא דַעַת וְלֹא־ תְבוּנָה לֵאמֹר חֶצְיוֹ שָׂרַפְתִּי
I-burned half-of-him to-say understanding and-no knowledge and-no mind-of-him to

בְמוֹ־אֵשׁ וְאַף אָפִיתִי עַל־ גֶּחָלָיו לֶחֶם אֶצְלֶה בָשָׂר וְאֹכֵל
and-I-ate meat I-roasted bread coals-of-him over I-baked and-even fire in

וְיִתְרוֹ לְתוֹעֵבָה אֶעֱשֶׂה לְבוּל עֵץ אֶסְגּוֹד׃
shall-I-bow wood to-block-of shall-I-make into-detestable-thing and-left-of-him

רֹעֶה אֵפֶר לֵב הוּתַל הֱטָּהוּ וְלֹא־ יַצִּיל
he-can-save and-not he-misleads-him he-is-deluded heart ash one-feeding-on (20)

אֶת־ נַפְשׁוֹ וְלֹא יֹאמַר הֲלוֹא שֶׁקֶר בִּימִינִי׃ זְכָר־
remember! (21) in-right-hand-of-me lie not? he-can-say or-not self-of-him ***

אֵלֶּה יַעֲקֹב וְיִשְׂרָאֵל כִּי עַבְדִּי־ אָתָּה יְצַרְתִּיךָ עֶבֶד־ לִי אַתָּה יִשְׂרָאֵל
Israel you to-me servant I-made-you you servant-of-me for and-Israel Jacob these

grows faint.
13 The carpenter measures with a line
and makes an outline with a marker;
he roughs it out with chisels
and marks it with compasses.
He shapes it in the form of man,
of man in all his glory,
that it may dwell in a shrine.
14 He cut down cedars,
or perhaps took a cypress or oak.
He let it grow among the trees of the forest,
or planted a pine, and the rain made it grow.
15 It is man's fuel for burning;
some of it he takes and warms himself,
he kindles a fire and bakes bread.
But he also fashions a god and worships it;
he makes an idol and bows down to it.
16 Half of the wood he burns in the fire;
over it he prepares his meal,
he roasts his meat and eats his fill.
He also warms himself and says,
"Ah! I am warm; I see the fire."
17 From the rest he makes a god, his idol;
he bows down to it and worships.
He prays to it and says,
"Save me; you are my god."
18 They know nothing, they understand nothing;
their eyes are plastered over so they cannot see,
and their minds closed so they cannot understand.
19 No one stops to think,
no one has the knowledge or understanding to say,
"Half of it I used for fuel;
I even baked bread over its coals,
I roasted meat and I ate.
Shall I make a detestable thing from what is left?
Shall I bow down to a block of wood?"
20 He feeds on ashes, a deluded heart misleads him;
he cannot save himself, or say,
"Is not this thing in my right hand a lie?"
21 "Remember these things, O Jacob,
for you are my servant, O Israel.
I have made you, you are my servant;

°17 ק יסגד

לֹא תִנָּשֵׁנִי׃ מָחִיתִי כָעָב פְּשָׁעֶיךָ
offenses-of-you like-the-cloud I-swept-away (22) you-will-be-forgotten-by-me not

וְכֶעָנָן חַטֹּאותֶיךָ שׁוּבָה אֵלַי כִּי גְאַלְתִּיךָ׃
I-redeemed-you for to-me return! sins-of-you and-like-the-morning-mist

רָנּוּ שָׁמַיִם כִּי־עָשָׂה יְהוָה הָרִיעוּ תַּחְתִּיּוֹת אֶרֶץ
earth ones-beneath-of shout-aloud! Yahweh he-did for heavens sing-for-joy! (23)

פִּצְחוּ הָרִים רִנָּה יַעַר וְכָל־עֵץ בּוֹ כִּי־גָאַל יְהוָה יַעֲקֹב
Jacob Yahweh he-redeemed for in-him tree and-all-of forest song mountains burst!

וּבְיִשְׂרָאֵל יִתְפָּאָר׃ כֹּה־אָמַר יְהוָה גֹּאֲלֶךָ
One-Redeeming-you Yahweh he-says this (24) he-displays-glory and-in-Israel

וְיֹצֶרְךָ מִבָּטֶן אָנֹכִי יְהוָה עֹשֶׂה כֹּל נֹטֶה שָׁמַיִם
heavens one-stretching-out all one-making Yahweh I in-womb and-one-forming-you

לְבַדִּי רֹקַע הָאָרֶץ מִי °אִתִּי׃* מֵפֵר אֹתוֹת
signs-of one-foiling (25) *with-me who?* the-earth one-spreading-out alone-me

בַּדִּים וְקֹסְמִים יְהוֹלֵל מֵשִׁיב חֲכָמִים אָחוֹר
back wise-ones one-overthrowing he-makes-fool and-ones-divining false-prophets

וְדַעְתָּם יְשַׂכֵּל׃ מֵקִים דְּבַר
word-of one-carrying-out (26) he-makes-nonsense and-learning-of-them

עַבְדּוֹ וַעֲצַת מַלְאָכָיו יַשְׁלִים הָאֹמֵר
the-one-saying he-fulfills messengers-of-him and-prediction-of servant-of-him

לִירוּשָׁלַםִ תּוּשָׁב וּלְעָרֵי יְהוּדָה תִּבָּנֶינָה
they-shall-be-built Judah and-of-towns-of she-shall-be-inhabited of-Jerusalem

וְחָרְבוֹתֶיהָ אֲקוֹמֵם׃ הָאֹמֵר לַצּוּלָה
to-the-watery-deep the-one-saying (27) I-will-restore-them and-ruins-of-her

חֳרָבִי וְנַהֲרֹתַיִךְ אוֹבִישׁ׃ הָאֹמֵר לְכוֹרֶשׁ
of-Cyrus the-one-saying (28) I-will-dry-up and-streams-of-you be-dry!

רֹעִי וְכָל־חֶפְצִי יַשְׁלִם וְלֵאמֹר
and-to-say he-will-accomplish pleasure-of-me and-all-of one-being-shepherd-of-me

לִירוּשָׁלַםִ תִּבָּנֶה וְהֵיכָל תִּוָּסֵד׃ כֹּה־אָמַר
he-says this (45:1) let-her-be-founded and-temple let-her-be-rebuilt to-Jerusalem

יְהוָה לִמְשִׁיחוֹ לְכוֹרֶשׁ אֲשֶׁר־הֶחֱזַקְתִּי בִימִינוֹ
of-right-hand-of-him I-take-hold whom to-Cyrus to-anointed-of-him Yahweh

לְרַד־ לְפָנָיו גּוֹיִם וּמָתְנֵי מְלָכִים אֲפַתֵּחַ לִפְתֹּחַ
to-open I-will-strip-off kings and-armors-of nations before-him to-subdue

לְפָנָיו דְּלָתַיִם וּשְׁעָרִים לֹא יִסָּגֵרוּ׃ אֲנִי לְפָנֶיךָ אֵלֵךְ
I-will-go before-you I (2) they-will-be-shut not so-gates doors before-him

וַהֲדוּרִים† °אֲוַשֵּׁר דַּלְתוֹת נְחוּשָׁה אֲשַׁבֵּר
I-will-break-down bronze gates-of I-will-level †and-ones-being-swollen

O Israel, I will not forget
you.
22I have swept away your
offenses like a cloud,
your sins like the morning
mist.
Return to me,
for I have redeemed you."
23Sing for joy, O heavens, for
the LORD has done this;
shout aloud, O earth
beneath.
Burst into song, you
mountains,
you forests and all your
trees,
for the LORD has redeemed
Jacob,
he displays his glory in
Israel.

*Jerusalem to Be Inhabited*

24"This is what the LORD says—
your Redeemer, who formed
you in the womb:

I am the LORD,
who has made all things,
who alone stretched out the
heavens,
who spread out the earth by
myself,
25who foils the signs of false
prophets
and makes fools of diviners,
who overthrows the learning
of the wise
and turns it into nonsense,
26who carries out the words of
his servants
and fulfills the predictions
of his messengers,

who says of Jerusalem, 'It shall
be inhabited,'
of the towns of Judah, 'They
shall be built,'
and of their ruins, 'I will
restore them,'
27who says to the watery deep,
'Be dry,
and I will dry up your
streams,'
28who says of Cyrus, 'He is my
shepherd
and will accomplish all that
I please;
he will say of Jerusalem,
"Let it be rebuilt,"
and of the temple, "Let its
foundations be laid."' '

45 "This is what the LORD
says to his anointed,
to Cyrus, whose right hand
I take hold of
to subdue nations before him
and to strip kings of their
armor,
to open doors before him
so that gates will not be
shut:
2I will go before you
and will level the
mountains[p];

p2 Dead Sea Scrolls and Septuagint; the meaning of the word in the Masoretic Text is uncertain.

*24 The *Qere* reads *from-with-me*

†2 The NIV, with the ancient texts listed above in footnote *p*, reads this word as והררים, *and-mountains.*

°24 ק מאתי °2 ק אישר

וּבְרִיחֵי בַרְזֶל אֲגַדֵּעַ׃ וְנָתַתִּי לְךָ אוֹצְרוֹת חֹשֶׁךְ
darkness treasures-of to-you and-I-will-give (3) I-will-cut iron and-bars-of

וּמַטְמֻנֵי מִסְתָּרִים לְמַעַן תֵּדַע כִּי־אֲנִי יְהוָה הַקּוֹרֵא
the-one-summoning Yahweh I that you-may-know so-that secret-places and-riches-of

בְשִׁמְךָ אֱלֹהֵי יִשְׂרָאֵל׃ לְמַעַן עַבְדִּי יַעֲקֹב וְיִשְׂרָאֵל
and-Israel Jacob servant-of-me for-sake-of (4) Israel God-of by-name-of-you

בְּחִירִי וָאֶקְרָא לְךָ בִּשְׁמֶךָ אֲכַנְּךָ וְלֹא
though-not I-bestow-title-on-you by-name-of-you to-you and-I-summon chosen-of-me

יְדַעְתָּנִי׃ אֲנִי יְהוָה וְאֵין עוֹד זוּלָתִי אֵין
there-is-no apart-from-me other and-there-is-no Yahweh I (5) you-acknowledge-me

אֱלֹהִים אֲאַזֶּרְךָ וְלֹא יְדַעְתָּנִי׃ לְמַעַן יֵדְעוּ
they-may-know so-that (6) you-acknowledged-me though-not I-will-strengthen-you God

מִמִּזְרַח־ שֶׁמֶשׁ וּמִמַּעֲרָבָהּ כִּי־ אֶפֶס בִּלְעָדָי אֲנִי יְהוָה
Yahweh I besides-me none that and-to-setting-place sun from-rising-of

וְאֵין עוֹד׃ יוֹצֵר אוֹר וּבוֹרֵא חֹשֶׁךְ עֹשֶׂה
one-bringing darkness and-one-creating light one-forming (7) other and-there-is-no

שָׁלוֹם וּבוֹרֵא רָע אֲנִי יְהוָה עֹשֶׂה כָל־ אֵלֶּה׃ הַרְעִיפוּ
rain! (8) these all-of one-doing Yahweh I disaster and-one-creating prosperity

שָׁמַיִם מִמַּעַל וּשְׁחָקִים יִזְּלוּ־ צֶדֶק תִּפְתַּח־ אֶרֶץ
earth let-her-open righteousness let-them-shower and-clouds at-above heavens

וְיִפְרוּ־ יֶשַׁע וּצְדָקָה תַצְמִיחַ יַחַד אֲנִי
I together let-her-grow and-righteousness salvation and-let-them-spring-up

יְהוָה בְּרָאתִיו׃ הוֹי רָב אֶת־ יֹצְרוֹ חֶרֶשׂ אֶת־
among potsherd One-Making-him with one-quarreling woe! (9) I-created-him Yahweh

חַרְשֵׂי אֲדָמָה הֲיֹאמַר חֹמֶר לְיֹצְרוֹ מַה־ תַּעֲשֶׂה
you-make what? to-one-being-potter-of-him clay does-he-say? ground potsherds-of

וּפָעָלְךָ אֵין־ יָדַיִם לוֹ׃ הוֹי אֹמֵר לְאָב מַה־
what? to-father one-saying woe! (10) to-him hands there-are-no or-work-of-you

תּוֹלִיד וּלְאִשָּׁה מַה־ תְּחִילִין׃ כֹּה־ אָמַר יְהוָה קְדוֹשׁ יִשְׂרָאֵל
Israel Holy-One-of Yahweh he-says this (11) you-bore what? or-to-mother you-begot

וְיֹצְרוֹ הָאֹתִיּוֹת שְׁאָלוּנִי עַל־ בָּנַי וְעַל־
or-about children-of-me about question-me! the-things-coming and-One-Making-him

פֹּעַל יָדַי תְּצַוֻּנִי׃ אָנֹכִי עָשִׂיתִי אֶרֶץ וְאָדָם עָלֶיהָ
upon-her and-mankind earth I-made I (12) you-order-me hands-of-me work-of

בָּרָאתִי אֲנִי יָדַי נָטוּ שָׁמַיִם וְכָל־ צְבָאָם
host-of-them and-all-of heavens they-stretched-out hands-of-me I I-created

צִוֵּיתִי׃ אָנֹכִי הַעִירֹתִהוּ בְצֶדֶק וְכָל־ דְּרָכָיו
ways-of-him and-all-of in-righteousness I-will-raise-up-him I (13) I-marshaled

I will break down gates of
bronze
and cut through bars of
iron.
3 I will give you the treasures of
darkness,
riches stored in secret
places,
so that you may know that I
am the LORD,
the God of Israel, who
summons you by name.
4 For the sake of Jacob my
servant,
of Israel my chosen,
I summon you by name
and bestow on you a title of
honor,
though you do not
acknowledge me.
5 I am the LORD, and there is no
other;
apart from me there is no
God.
I will strengthen you,
though you have not
acknowledged me,
6 so that from the rising of the
sun
to the place of its setting
men may know there is none
besides me.
I am the LORD, and there is
no other.
7 I form the light and create
darkness,
I bring prosperity and create
disaster;
I, the LORD, do all these
things.

8 "You heavens above, rain
down righteousness;
let the clouds shower it
down.
Let the earth open wide,
let salvation spring up,
let righteousness grow with it;
I, the LORD, have created it.

9 "Woe to him who quarrels
with his Maker,
to him who is but a
potsherd among the
potsherds on the ground.
Does the clay say to the potter,
'What are you making?'
Does your work say,
'He has no hands'?
10 Woe to him who says to his
father,
'What have you begotten?'
or to his mother,
'What have you brought to
birth?'

11 "This is what the LORD says—
the Holy One of Israel, and
its Maker:
Concerning things to come,
do you question me about
my children,
or give me orders about the
work of my hands?
12 It is I who made the earth
and created mankind upon
it.
My own hands stretched out
the heavens;
I marshaled their starry
hosts.
13 I will raise up Cyrus[q] in my
righteousness:
I will make all his ways

[q]13 Hebrew *him*

אֲיַשֵּׁר הוּא־ יִבְנֶה עִירִי וְגָלוּתִי יְשַׁלֵּחַ
he-will-free and-exile-of-me city-of-me he-will-rebuild he I-will-make-straight

לֹא בִמְחִיר וְלֹא בְשֹׁחַד אָמַר יְהוָה צְבָאוֹת׃ כֹּה אָמַר יְהוָה
Yahweh he-says this (14) Hosts Yahweh-of he-says for-reward or-not for-price not

יְגִיעַ מִצְרַיִם וּסְחַר־ כּוּשׁ וּסְבָאִים אַנְשֵׁי מִדָּה עָלַיִךְ
to-you height men-of and-Sabeans Cush and-merchandise-of Egypt product-of

יַעֲבֹרוּ וְלָךְ יִהְיוּ אַחֲרַיִךְ יֵלֵכוּ
they-will-trudge behind-you they-will-be and-to-you they-will-come-over

בַּזִּקִּים יַעֲבֹרוּ וְאֵלַיִךְ יִשְׁתַּחֲווּ אֵלַיִךְ
and-with-you they-will-bow and-before-you they-will-come-over in-the-chains

יִתְפַּלָּלוּ אַךְ בָּךְ אֵל וְאֵין עוֹד אֶפֶס אֱלֹהִים׃ אָכֵן אַתָּה
you truly (15) god not other and-there-is-no God with-you surely they-will-plead

אֵל מִסְתַּתֵּר אֱלֹהֵי יִשְׂרָאֵל מוֹשִׁיעַ׃ בּוֹשׁוּ וְגַם־
and-also they-will-be-shamed (16) One-Saving Israel God-of one-hiding-himself God

נִכְלְמוּ כֻּלָּם יַחְדָּו הָלְכוּ בַכְּלִמָּה
in-the-disgrace they-will-go-off together all-of-them they-will-be-disgraced

חָרָשֵׁי צִירִים׃ יִשְׂרָאֵל נוֹשַׁע בַּיהוָה תְּשׁוּעַת עוֹלָמִים
everlastings salvation-of by-Yahweh he-will-be-saved Israel (17) idols makers-of

לֹא־ תֵבֹשׁוּ וְלֹא־ תִכָּלְמוּ עַד־ עוֹלְמֵי עַד׃
everlasting ages-of to you-will-be-disgraced or-not you-will-be-shamed not

כִּי כֹה אָמַר־ יְהוָה בּוֹרֵא הַשָּׁמַיִם הוּא הָאֱלֹהִים יֹצֵר
one-fashioning the-God he the-heavens one-creating Yahweh he-says this for (18)

הָאָרֶץ וְעֹשָׂהּ הוּא כוֹנְנָהּ לֹא־ תֹהוּ בְרָאָהּ
he-created-her empty not he-founded-her he and-one-making-her the-earth

לָשֶׁבֶת יְצָרָהּ אֲנִי יְהוָה וְאֵין עוֹד׃ לֹא
not (19) other and-there-is-no Yahweh I he-formed-her to-be-inhabited

בַסֵּתֶר דִּבַּרְתִּי בִּמְקוֹם אֶרֶץ חֹשֶׁךְ לֹא אָמַרְתִּי לְזֶרַע
to-descendant-of I-said not darkness land-of in-place-of I-spoke in-the-secret

יַעֲקֹב תֹּהוּ בַקְּשׁוּנִי אֲנִי יְהוָה דֹּבֵר צֶדֶק מַגִּיד מֵישָׁרִים׃
right-things one-declaring truth one-speaking Yahweh I seek-me! in-vain Jacob

הִקָּבְצוּ וָבֹאוּ הִתְנַגְּשׁוּ יַחְדָּו פְּלִיטֵי הַגּוֹיִם
the-nations fugitives-of together assemble! and-come! gather-together! (20)

לֹא יָדְעוּ הַנֹּשְׂאִים אֶת־ עֵץ פִּסְלָם וּמִתְפַּלְלִים אֶל־ אֵל
god to and-ones-praying idol-of-them wood-of *** the-ones-carrying they-know not

לֹא יוֹשִׁיעַ׃ הַגִּידוּ וְהַגִּישׁוּ אַף יִוָּעֲצוּ יַחְדָּו
together let-them-take-counsel also and-present! declare! (21) he-can-save not

מִי הִשְׁמִיעַ זֹאת מִקֶּדֶם מֵאָז הִגִּידָהּ הֲלוֹא אֲנִי
I not? he-declared-her from-distant-past from-long-ago this he-foretold who?

straight.
He will rebuild my city
and set my exiles free,
but not for a price or reward,
says the LORD Almighty."

14 This is what the LORD says:

"The products of Egypt and
the merchandise of
Cush,[r]
and those tall Sabeans—
they will come over to you
and will be yours;
they will trudge behind you,
coming over to you in
chains.
They will bow down before
you
and plead with you, saying,
'Surely God is with you, and
there is no other;
there is no other god.' "

15 Truly you are a God who hides
himself,
O God and Savior of Israel.
16 All the makers of idols will be
put to shame and
disgraced;
they will go off into disgrace
together.
17 But Israel will be saved by the
LORD
with an everlasting
salvation;
you will never be put to shame
or disgraced,
to ages everlasting.

18 For this is what the LORD
says—
he who created the heavens,
he is God;
he who fashioned and made
the earth,
he founded it;
he did not create it to be
empty,
but formed it to be
inhabited—
he says:
"I am the LORD,
and there is no other.
19 I have not spoken in secret,
from somewhere in a land
of darkness;
I have not said to Jacob's
descendants,
'Seek me in vain.'
I, the LORD, speak the truth;
I declare what is right.

20 "Gather together and come;
assemble, you fugitives from
the nations.
Ignorant are those who carry
about idols of wood,
who pray to gods that
cannot save.
21 Declare what is to be, present
it—
let them take counsel
together.
Who foretold this long ago,
who declared it from the
distant past?
Was it not I, the LORD?

r14 That is, the upper Nile region

יְהוָה וְאֵין־ עוֹד אֱלֹהִים מִבַּלְעָדַי אֵל־ צַדִּיק וּמוֹשִׁיעַ
and-One-Saving righteous God at-apart-from-me God other and-there-is-no Yahweh

אַיִן זוּלָתִי׃ פְּנוּ־ אֵלַי וְהִוָּשְׁעוּ כָּל־ אַפְסֵי־ אָרֶץ כִּי
for earth ends-of all-of and-be-saved! to-me turn! (22) but-me there-is-none

אֲנִי־אֵל וְאֵין עוֹד׃ בִּי נִשְׁבַּעְתִּי יָצָא מִפִּי
from-mouth-of-me he-came-out I-swore by-myself (23) other and-there-is-no God I

צְדָקָה דָּבָר וְלֹא יָשׁוּב כִּי־ לִי תִּכְרַע כָּל־
every-of she-will-bow before-me indeed he-will-be-revoked that-not word integrity

בֶּרֶךְ תִּשָּׁבַע כָּל־ לָשׁוֹן׃ אַךְ בַּיהוָה לִי אָמַר
he-will-say of-me in-Yahweh alone (24) tongue every-of she-will-swear knee

צְדָקוֹת וָעֹז עָדָיו יָבוֹא וְיֵבֹשׁוּ כֹּל
all-of and-they-will-be-shamed he-will-come to-him and-strength righteousnesses

הַנֶּחֱרִים בּוֹ׃ בַּיהוָה יִצְדְּקוּ
they-will-be-found-righteous in-Yahweh (25) against-him the-ones-raging

וְיִתְהַלְלוּ כָּל־ זֶרַע יִשְׂרָאֵל׃ כָּרַע בֵּל
Bel he-bows-down (46:1) Israel descendant-of all-of and-they-will-exult

קֹרֵס נְבוֹ הָיוּ עֲצַבֵּיהֶם לַחַיָּה וְלַבְּהֵמָה
and-on-the-cattle on-the-beast idols-of-them they-are Nebo one-stooping-low

נְשֻׂאֹתֵיכֶם עֲמוּסוֹת מַשָּׂא לַעֲיֵפָה׃
for-the-weary burden ones-being-burdensome ones-being-carried-of-you

קָרְסוּ כָרְעוּ יַחְדָּו לֹא יָכְלוּ מַלֵּט מַשָּׂא
burden to-rescue they-are-able not together they-bow-down they-stoop (2)

וְנַפְשָׁם בַּשְּׁבִי הָלָכָה׃ שִׁמְעוּ אֵלַי בֵּית יַעֲקֹב
Jacob house-of to-me listen! (3) she-goes-off to-the-captivity and-self-of-them

וְכָל־ שְׁאֵרִית בֵּית יִשְׂרָאֵל הַעֲמֻסִים מִנִּי־ בֶטֶן
conception since the-ones-being-upheld Israel house-of remainder-of and-all-of

הַנְּשֻׂאִים מִנִּי־ רָחַם׃ וְעַד־ זִקְנָה אֲנִי הוּא וְעַד־ שֵׂיבָה*
gray-hair and-to he I old-age even-to (4) birth since the-ones-being-carried

אֲנִי אֶסְבֹּל אֲנִי עָשִׂיתִי וַאֲנִי אֶשָּׂא וַאֲנִי אֶסְבֹּל
I-will-sustain and-I I-will-carry and-I I-made I I-will-sustain I

וַאֲמַלֵּט׃ לְמִי תְדַמְּיוּנִי וְתַשְׁווּ
or-will-you-count-equal will-you-compare-me to-whom? (5) and-I-will-rescue

וְתַמְשִׁלוּנִי וְנִדְמֶה׃ הַזָּלִים זָהָב מִכִּיס
from-bag gold the-ones-pouring (6) that-we-may-be-compared or-will-you-liken-me

וְכֶסֶף בַּקָּנֶה יִשְׁקֹלוּ יִשְׂכְּרוּ צוֹרֵף וְיַעֲשֵׂהוּ
and-he-makes-him one-being-goldsmith they-hire they-weigh on-the-scale and-silver

אֵל יִסְגְּדוּ אַף־ יִשְׁתַּחֲווּ׃ יִשָּׂאֻהוּ עַל־ כָּתֵף יִסְבְּלֻהוּ
they-carry-him shoulder on they-lift-him (7) they-worship and they-bow god

And there is no God apart from me,
a righteous God and a Savior;
there is none but me.

22 "Turn to me and be saved,
all you ends of the earth;
for I am God, and there is no other.
23 By myself I have sworn,
my mouth has uttered in all integrity
a word that will not be revoked:
Before me every knee will bow;
by me every tongue will swear.
24 They will say of me, 'In the LORD alone
are righteousness and strength.' "
All who have raged against him
will come to him and be put to shame.
25 But in the LORD all the descendants of Israel
will be found righteous and will exult.

*Gods of Babylon*

46 Bel bows down, Nebo stoops low;
their idols are borne by beasts of burden.[s]
The images that are carried about are burdensome,
a burden for the weary.
2 They stoop and bow down together;
unable to rescue the burden,
they themselves go off into captivity.

3 "Listen to me, O house of Jacob,
all you who remain of the house of Israel,
you whom I have upheld since you were conceived,
and have carried since your birth.
4 Even to your old age and gray hairs
I am he, I am he who will sustain you.
I have made you and I will carry you;
I will sustain you and I will rescue you.

5 "To whom will you compare me or count me equal?
To whom will you liken me that we may be compared?
6 Some pour out gold from their bags
and weigh out silver on the scales;
they hire a goldsmith to make it into a god,
and they bow down and worship it.
7 They lift it to their shoulders
and carry it;

[s]1 *Or are but beasts and cattle*

*4 Most mss point the first letter as *sin* (שׂ).

וְיַנִּחֻהוּ תַחְתָּיו וְיַעֲמֹד מִמְּקוֹמוֹ לֹא יָמִישׁ

he-moves not from-spot-of-him and-he-stands place-of-him and-they-set-up-him

אַף־ יִצְעַק אֵלָיו וְלֹא יַעֲנֶה מִצָּרָתוֹ לֹא

not from-trouble-of-him he-answers but-not to-him he-cries-out though

יוֹשִׁיעֶנּוּ׃ זִכְרוּ־ זֹאת וְהִתְאֹשָׁשׁוּ הָשִׁיבוּ פוֹשְׁעִים עַל־לֵב׃

heart to ones-rebelling take! and-fix-in-mind! this remember! (8) he-can-save-him

זִכְרוּ רִאשֹׁנוֹת מֵעוֹלָם כִּי אָנֹכִי אֵל וְאֵין עוֹד אֱלֹהִים

God other and-there-is-no God I for of-long-ago former-things remember! (9)

וְאֶפֶס כָּמוֹנִי׃ מַגִּיד מֵרֵאשִׁית אַחֲרִית וּמִקֶּדֶם

and-from-ancient-time end from-beginning one-making-known (10) like-me and-none

אֲשֶׁר לֹא־ נַעֲשׂוּ אֹמֵר עֲצָתִי תָקוּם וְכָל־

and-all-of she-will-stand purpose-of-me one-saying they-happened not what

חֶפְצִי אֶעֱשֶׂה׃ קֹרֵא מִמִּזְרָח עַיִט מֵאֶרֶץ

from-land bird-of-prey from-east one-summoning (11) I-will-do pleasure-of-me

מֶרְחָק אִישׁ עֲצָתוֹ° אַף־ דִּבַּרְתִּי אַף־ אֲבִיאֶנָּה

I-will-bring-about-her indeed I-said indeed purpose-of-me man-of far-off

יָצַרְתִּי אַף־ אֶעֱשֶׂנָּה׃ שִׁמְעוּ אֵלַי אַבִּירֵי לֵב

heart ones-stubborn-of to-me listen! (12) I-will-do-her indeed I-planned

הָרְחוֹקִים מִצְּדָקָה׃ קֵרַבְתִּי צִדְקָתִי לֹא תִרְחָק

she-is-far not righteousness-of-me I-bring-near (13) from-righteousness the-ones-far

וּתְשׁוּעָתִי לֹא תְאַחֵר וְנָתַתִּי בְצִיּוֹן תְּשׁוּעָה

salvation to-Zion and-I-will-grant she-will-be-delayed not and-salvation-of-me

לְיִשְׂרָאֵל תִּפְאַרְתִּי׃ רְדִי וּשְׁבִי עַל־עָפָר בְּתוּלַת בַּת־

Daughter-of Virgin-of dust in and-sit! go-down! (47:1) splendor-of-me to-Israel

בָּבֶל שְׁבִי־ לָאָרֶץ אֵין־ כִּסֵּא בַּת־ כַּשְׂדִּים כִּי לֹא

not for Chaldeans Daughter-of throne without on-the-ground sit! Babylon

תוֹסִיפִי יִקְרְאוּ־ לָךְ רַכָּה וַעֲנֻגָּה׃ קְחִי רֵחַיִם

millstones take! (2) or-delicate tender to-you they-will-call you-will-do-again

וְטַחֲנִי קָמַח גַּלִּי צַמָּתֵךְ חֶשְׂפִּי־ שֹׁבֶל גַּלִּי־ שׁוֹק עִבְרִי

wade-through! leg bare! skirt lift-up! veil-of-you take-off! flour and-grind!

נְהָרוֹת׃ תִּגָּל עֶרְוָתֵךְ גַּם תֵּרָאֶה

she-will-be-uncovered and nakedness-of-you she-will-be-exposed (3) streams

חֶרְפָּתֵךְ נָקָם אֶקָּח וְלֹא אֶפְגַּע אָדָם׃ גֹּאֲלֵנוּ

One-Redeeming-us (4) anyone I-will-spare and-not I-will-take vengeance shame-of-you

יְהוָה צְבָאוֹת שְׁמוֹ קְדוֹשׁ יִשְׂרָאֵל׃ שְׁבִי דוּמָם וּבֹאִי

and-go! silence sit! (5) Israel Holy-One-of name-of-him Hosts Yahweh-of

בַחֹשֶׁךְ בַּת־ כַּשְׂדִּים כִּי לֹא תוֹסִיפִי יִקְרְאוּ־

they-will-call you-will-do-again not for Chaldeans Daughter-of into-the-darkness

° 11 ק עצתי

they set it up in its place,
and there it stands.
From that spot it cannot
move.
Though one cries out to it, it
does not answer;
it cannot save him from his
troubles.

8 "Remember this, fix it in
mind,
take it to heart, you rebels.
9 Remember the former things,
those of long ago;
I am God, and there is no
other;
I am God, and there is none
like me.
10 I make known the end from
the beginning,
from ancient times, what is
still to come.
I say: My purpose will stand,
and I will do all that I
please.
11 From the east I summon a bird
of prey;
from a far-off land, a man to
fulfill my purpose.
What I have said, that will I
bring about;
what I have planned, that
will I do.
12 Listen to me, you
stubborn-hearted,
you who are far from
righteousness.
13 I am bringing my
righteousness near,
it is not far away;
and my salvation will not be
delayed.
I will grant salvation to Zion,
my splendor to Israel.

*The Fall of Babylon*

47 "Go down, sit in the dust,
Virgin Daughter of
Babylon;
sit on the ground without a
throne,
Daughter of the
Babylonians.[1]
No more will you be called
tender or delicate.
2 Take millstones and grind
flour;
take off your veil.
Lift up your skirts, bare your
legs,
and wade through the
streams.
3 Your nakedness will be
exposed
and your shame uncovered.
I will take vengeance;
I will spare no one."

4 Our Redeemer—the LORD
Almighty is his name—
is the Holy One of Israel.

5 "Sit in silence, go into
darkness,
Daughter of the
Babylonians;
no more will you be called

[1] 1 Or *Chaldeans;* also in verse 5

לָךְ גְּבֶרֶת מַמְלָכוֹת׃ קָצַפְתִּי עַל־ עַמִּי חִלַּלְתִּי
I-desecrated people-of-me with I-was-angry (6) kingdoms queen-of to-you

נַחֲלָתִי וָאֶתְּנֵם בְּיָדֵךְ לֹא־ שַׂמְתְּ לָהֶם
to-them you-showed not into-hand-of-you and-I-gave-them inheritance-of-me

רַחֲמִים עַל־ זָקֵן הִכְבַּדְתְּ עֻלֵּךְ מְאֹד׃ וַתֹּאמְרִי לְעוֹלָם
to-forever and-you-said (7) very yoke-of-you you-made-heavy aged on mercies

אֶהְיֶה גְבֶרֶת עַד לֹא־ שַׂמְתְּ אֵלֶּה עַל־ לִבֵּךְ לֹא
not heart-of-you to these you-took not eternal queen I-will-continue

זָכַרְתְּ אַחֲרִיתָהּ׃ וְעַתָּה שִׁמְעִי־ זֹאת עֲדִינָה
wanton-creature this listen! then-now (8) happening-of-her you-reflected

הַיּוֹשֶׁבֶת לָבֶטַח הָאֹמְרָה בִּלְבָבָהּ* אֲנִי וְאַפְסִי
and-not-besides-me I to-self-of-her the-one-saying in-security the-one-lounging

עוֹד לֹא אֵשֵׁב אַלְמָנָה וְלֹא אֵדַע שְׁכוֹל׃
loss-of-children I-will-suffer or-not widow I-will-live not other

וְתָבֹאנָה לָּךְ שְׁתֵּי־ אֵלֶּה רֶגַע בְּיוֹם אֶחָד
single on-day moment these both-of to-you but-they-will-overtake (9)

שְׁכוֹל וְאַלְמֹן כְּתֻמָּם בָּאוּ עָלַיִךְ
upon-you they-will-come as-fullness-of-them and-widowhood loss-of-children

בְּרֹב כְּשָׁפַיִךְ בְּעָצְמַת חֲבָרַיִךְ מְאֹד׃
all spells-of-you despite-potency-of sorceries-of-you despite-many-of

וַתִּבְטְחִי בְרָעָתֵךְ אָמַרְתְּ אֵין רֹאָנִי חָכְמָתֵךְ
wisdom-of-you one-seeing-me not you-said in-wickedness-of-you and-you-trusted (10)

וְדַעְתֵּךְ הִיא שׁוֹבְבָתֶךְ וַתֹּאמְרִי בְּלִבֵּךְ אֲנִי
I to-self-of-you when-you-say one-misleading-you this and-knowledge-of-you

וְאַפְסִי עוֹד׃ וּבָא עָלַיִךְ רָעָה לֹא תֵדְעִי
you-will-know not disaster upon-you and-he-will-come (11) other and-not-besides-me

שַׁחְרָהּ וְתִפֹּל עָלַיִךְ הֹוָה לֹא תוּכְלִי כַּפְּרָהּ
to-ransom-her you-can not calamity upon-you and-she-will-fall conjuring-of-her

וְתָבֹא עָלַיִךְ פִּתְאֹם שׁוֹאָה לֹא תֵדָעִי׃ עִמְדִי־
keep-on! (12) you-can-foresee not catastrophe suddenly upon-you and-she-will-come

נָא בַחֲבָרַיִךְ וּבְרֹב כְּשָׁפַיִךְ בַּאֲשֶׁר
at-which sorceries-of-you and-with-many-of with-magic-spells-of-you then!

יָגַעַתְּ מִנְּעוּרַיִךְ אוּלַי תּוּכְלִי הוֹעִיל אוּלַי
perhaps to-succeed you-will-be-able perhaps since-childhoods-of-you you-labored

תַּעֲרוֹצִי׃ נִלְאֵית בְּרֹב עֲצָתָיִךְ
counsels-of-you by-all-of you-are-worn-out (13) you-will-cause-terror

יַעַמְדוּ־ נָא וְיוֹשִׁיעֻךְ הֹבְרוּ° שָׁמַיִם
heavens ones-dividing-of and-let-them-save-you now! let-them-come-forward

queen of kingdoms.
6 I was angry with my people
and desecrated my
inheritance;
I gave them into your hand,
and you showed them no
mercy.
Even on the aged
you laid a very heavy yoke.
7 You said, 'I will continue
forever—
the eternal queen!'
But you did not consider these
things
or reflect on what might
happen.
8 "Now then, listen, you
wanton creature,
lounging in your security
and saying to yourself,
'I am, and there is none
besides me.
I will never be a widow
or suffer the loss of
children.'
9 Both of these will overtake you
in a moment, on a single
day:
loss of children and
widowhood.
They will come upon you in
full measure,
in spite of your many
sorceries
and all your potent spells.
10 You have trusted in your
wickedness
and have said, 'No one sees
me.'
Your wisdom and knowledge
mislead you
when you say to yourself,
'I am, and there is none
besides me.'
11 Disaster will come upon you,
and you will not know how
to conjure it away.
A calamity will fall upon you
that you cannot ward off
with a ransom;
a catastrophe you cannot
foresee
will suddenly come upon
you.
12 "Keep on, then, with your
magic spells
and with your many
sorceries,
which you have labored at
since childhood.
Perhaps you will succeed,
perhaps you will cause
terror.
13 All the counsel you have
received has only worn
you out!
Let your astrologers come
forward,

*8 Most mss have the accent on the last syllable (בָבָהּ—).

°13 ק הברי

הַחֹזִים בַּכּוֹכָבִים מוֹדִיעִם לֶחֳדָשִׁים מֵאֲשֶׁר יָבֹאוּ
they-come from-what by-the-months ones-predicting at-the-stars the-ones-gazing

עָלָיִךְ׃ (14) הִנֵּה הָיוּ כְקַשׁ אֵשׁ שְׂרָפָתַם לֹא־
not she-will-burn-them fire like-stubble they-are surely! (14) upon-you

יַצִּילוּ אֶת־ נַפְשָׁם מִיַּד לֶהָבָה אֵין־ גַּחֶלֶת
coal-of there-is-no flame from-power-of self-of-them *** they-can-save

לַחְמָם* אוּר לָשֶׁבֶת נֶגְדּוֹ׃ (15) כֵּן הָיוּ־ לָךְ אֲשֶׁר יָגָעַתְּ
you-labored which for-you they-are that (15) by-him to-sit fire *bread-of-them

סֹחֲרַיִךְ מִנְּעוּרַיִךְ אִישׁ לְעֶבְרוֹ תָּעוּ
they-err in-going-on-of-him each since-childhoods-of-you ones-trafficking-of-you

אֵין מוֹשִׁיעֵךְ׃ (48:1) שִׁמְעוּ־זֹאת בֵּית־ יַעֲקֹב הַנִּקְרָאִים
the-ones-being-called Jacob house-of this listen! (48:1) one-saving-you there-is-no

בְּשֵׁם יִשְׂרָאֵל וּמִמֵּי יְהוּדָה יָצָאוּ הַנִּשְׁבָּעִים ׀
the-ones-taking-oath they-come Judah and-from-waters-of Israel by-name-of

בְּשֵׁם יְהוָה וּבֵאלֹהֵי יִשְׂרָאֵל יַזְכִּירוּ לֹא בֶאֱמֶת וְלֹא
or-not in-truth not they-invoke Israel and-to-God-of Yahweh by-name-of

בִצְדָקָה׃ (2) כִּי־ מֵעִיר הַקֹּדֶשׁ נִקְרָאוּ וְעַל־
and-on they-call-themselves the-holiness of-city-of indeed (2) in-righteousness

אֱלֹהֵי יִשְׂרָאֵל נִסְמָכוּ יְהוָה צְבָאוֹת שְׁמוֹ׃ (3) הָרִאשֹׁנוֹת
the-former-things (3) name-of-him Hosts Yahweh-of they-rely Israel God-of

מֵאָז הִגַּדְתִּי וּמִפִּי יָצְאוּ וְאַשְׁמִיעֵם
and-I-made-known-them they-came and-from-mouth-of-me I-foretold from-long-ago

פִּתְאֹם עָשִׂיתִי וַתָּבֹאנָה׃ (4) מִדַּעְתִּי כִּי קָשֶׁה אָתָּה
you stubborn that for-to-know-me (4) and-they-came-to-pass I-acted suddenly

וְגִיד בַּרְזֶל עָרְפֶּךָ וּמִצְחֲךָ נְחוּשָׁה׃ (5) וָאַגִּיד לְךָ
to-you so-I-told (5) bronze and-forehead-of-you neck-of-you iron and-sinew-of

מֵאָז בְּטֶרֶם תָּבוֹא הִשְׁמַעְתִּיךָ פֶּן־ תֹּאמַר
you-could-say so-not I-announced-to-you she-happened at-before from-long-ago

עָצְבִּי עָשָׂם וּפִסְלִי וְנִסְכִּי צִוָּם׃
he-ordained-them and-metal-god-of-me and-wooden-image-of-me he-did-them idol-of-me

(6) שָׁמַעְתָּ חֲזֵה כֻּלָּהּ וְאַתֶּם הֲלוֹא תַגִּידוּ הִשְׁמַעְתִּיךָ
I-will-tell-you will-you-admit not? and-you all-of-her look! you-heard (6)

חֲדָשׁוֹת מֵעַתָּה וּנְצֻרוֹת וְלֹא יְדַעְתָּם׃ (7) עַתָּה
now (7) you-know-them that-not and-ones-being-hidden from-now new-things

נִבְרְאוּ וְלֹא מֵאָז וְלִפְנֵי־ יוֹם וְלֹא שְׁמַעְתָּם
you-heard-of-them then-not day and-before at-long-ago and-not they-are-created

פֶּן־ תֹּאמַר הִנֵּה יְדַעְתִּין׃ (8) גַּם לֹא־ שָׁמַעְתָּ גַּם לֹא יָדַעְתָּ
you-understood not or you-heard not and (8) I-knew-them see! you-can-say so-not

those stargazers who make predictions month by month,
let them save you from what is coming upon you.
14Surely they are like stubble;
the fire will burn them up.
They cannot even save themselves
from the power of the flame.
Here are no coals to warm anyone;
here is no fire to sit by.
15That is all they can do for you—
these you have labored with and trafficked with since childhood.
Each of them goes on in his error;
there is not one that can save you.

*Stubborn Israel*

48 "Listen to this, O house of Jacob,
you who are called by the name of Israel
and come from the line of Judah,
you who take oaths in the name of the LORD
and invoke the God of Israel—
but not in truth or righteousness—
2you who call yourselves citizens of the holy city
and rely on the God of Israel—
the LORD Almighty is his name:
3I foretold the former things long ago,
my mouth announced them and I made them known;
then suddenly I acted, and they came to pass.
4For I knew how stubborn you were;
the sinews of your neck were iron,
your forehead was bronze.
5Therefore I told you these things long ago;
before they happened I announced them to you
so that you could not say,
'My idols did them;
my wooden image and metal god ordained them.'
6You have heard these things;
look at them all.
Will you not admit them?

"From now on I will tell you of new things,
of hidden things unknown to you.
7They are created now, and not long ago;
you have not heard of them before today.
So you cannot say,
'Yes, I knew of them.'
8You have neither heard nor understood;

*14 The NIV repoints this word as לְחֻמָּם, *to-warm-them*.

גַּם מֵאָז לֹא־ פִתְּחָה אָזְנֶךָ כִּי יָדַעְתִּי בָּגוֹד
to-be-treacherous I-know indeed ear-of-you she-was-open not from-of-old and

תִּבְגּוֹד וּפֹשֵׁעַ מִבֶּטֶן קֹרָא לָךְ׃ לְמַעַן
for-sake-of (9) to-you he-was-called from-birth and-one-rebelling you-are-treacherous

שְׁמִי אַאֲרִיךְ אַפִּי וּתְהִלָּתִי אֶחֱטָם־ לָךְ לְבִלְתִּי
so-not from-you I-hold-back and-praise-of-me wrath-of-me I-delay name-of-me

הַכְרִיתֶךָ׃ הִנֵּה צְרַפְתִּיךָ וְלֹא בְכָסֶף בְּחַרְתִּיךָ
I-tested-you as-silver though-not I-refined-you see! (10) to-cut-off-you

בְּכוּר עֹנִי׃ לְמַעֲנִי לְמַעֲנִי אֶעֱשֶׂה כִּי אֵיךְ
how? indeed I-do for-sake-of-me for-sake-of-me (11) affliction in-furnace-of

יֵחָל וּכְבוֹדִי לְאַחֵר לֹא־ אֶתֵּן׃ שְׁמַע אֵלַי
to-me listen! (12) I-will-yield not to-another and-glory-of-me can-he-be-defamed

יַעֲקֹב וְיִשְׂרָאֵל מְקֹרָאִי אֲנִי־הוּא אֲנִי רִאשׁוֹן אַף אֲנִי אַחֲרוֹן׃ אַף־
also (13) last I and first I he I one-being-called-of-me and-Israel Jacob

יָדִי יָסְדָה אֶרֶץ וִימִינִי טִפְּחָה שָׁמָיִם
heavens she-spread-out and-right-hand-of-me earth she-founded hand-of-me

קֹרֵא אֲנִי אֲלֵיהֶם יַעַמְדוּ יַחְדָּו׃ הִקָּבְצוּ כֻלְּכֶם
all-of-you come-together! (14) together they-stand to-them I one-summoning

וּשְׁמָעוּ מִי בָהֶם הִגִּיד אֶת־ אֵלֶּה יְהוָה אֲהֵבוֹ
he-chose-as-ally-him Yahweh these *** he-foretold of-them who? and-listen!

יַעֲשֶׂה חֶפְצוֹ בְּבָבֶל וּזְרֹעוֹ כַּשְׂדִּים׃
Chaldeans and-arm-of-him against-Babylon purpose-of-him he-will-carry-out

אֲנִי אֲנִי דִּבַּרְתִּי אַף־ קְרָאתִיו הֲבִיאֹתִיו וְהִצְלִיחַ
and-he-will-make-succeed I-will-bring-him I-called-him also I-spoke I I (15)

דַּרְכּוֹ׃ קִרְבוּ אֵלַי שִׁמְעוּ־זֹאת לֹא מֵרֹאשׁ בַּסֵּתֶר
in-the-secret from-first not this listen! to-me come-near! (16) mission-of-him

דִּבַּרְתִּי מֵעֵת הֱיוֹתָהּ שָׁם אָנִי וְעַתָּה אֲדֹנָי יְהוִה שְׁלָחַנִי
he-sent-me Yahweh Sovereign and-now I there to-happen-her at-time-of I-spoke

וְרוּחוֹ׃ כֹּה־ אָמַר יְהוָה גֹּאַלְךָ קְדוֹשׁ יִשְׂרָאֵל
Israel Holy-One-of One-Redeeming-you Yahweh he-says this (17) with-Spirit-of-him

אֲנִי יְהוָה אֱלֹהֶיךָ מְלַמֶּדְךָ לְהוֹעִיל מַדְרִיכֲךָ בְּדֶרֶךְ
in-way one-directing-you to-be-best one-teaching-you God-of-you Yahweh I

תֵּלֵךְ׃ לוּא הִקְשַׁבְתָּ לְמִצְוֹתָי וַיְהִי
then-he-would-be to-commands-of-me you-paid-attention if-only (18) you-should-go

כַנָּהָר שְׁלוֹמֶךָ וְצִדְקָתְךָ כְּגַלֵּי הַיָּם׃
the-sea like-waves-of and-righteousness-of-you peace-of-you like-the-river

וַיְהִי כַחוֹל זַרְעֶךָ וְצֶאֱצָאֵי מֵעֶיךָ
loins-of-you and-children-of descendant-of-you like-the-sand and-he-would-be (19)

from of old your ear has not
been open.
Well do I know how
treacherous you are;
you were called a rebel from
birth.
9 For my own name's sake I
delay my wrath;
for the sake of my praise I
hold it back from you,
so as not to cut you off.
10 See, I have refined you,
though not as silver;
I have tested you in the
furnace of affliction.
11 For my own sake, for my own
sake, I do this.
How can I let myself be
defamed?
I will not yield my glory to
another.

*Israel Freed*

12 "Listen to me, O Jacob,
Israel, whom I have called:
I am he;
I am the first and I am the
last.
13 My own hand laid the
foundations of the earth,
and my right hand spread
out the heavens;
when I summon them,
they all stand up together.

14 "Come together, all of you,
and listen:
Which of ⌞the idols⌟ has
foretold these things?
The LORD's chosen ally
will carry out his purpose
against Babylon;
his arm will be against the
Babylonians.[u]
15 I, even I, have spoken;
yes, I have called him.
I will bring him,
and he will succeed in his
mission.

16 "Come near me and listen to
this:

"From the first announcement
I have not spoken in
secret;
at the time it happens, I am
there."

And now the Sovereign LORD
has sent me,
with his Spirit.

17 This is what the LORD says—
your Redeemer, the Holy
One of Israel:
"I am the LORD your God,
who teaches you what is
best for you,
who directs you in the way
you should go.
18 If only you had paid attention
to my commands,
your peace would have been
like a river,
your righteousness like the
waves of the sea.
19 Your descendants would have
been like the sand,
your children like its

[u] 14 Or *Chaldeans;* also in verse 20

כִּמְעֹתָיו לֹא־ יִכָּרֵת וְלֹא־ יִשָּׁמֵד
he-would-be-destroyed or-never he-would-be-cut-off never like-grains-of-him

שְׁמוֹ מִלְּפָנָי׃ צְאוּ מִבָּבֶל בִּרְחוּ מִכַּשְׂדִּים
from-Chaldeans flee! from-Babylon leave! (20) from-before-me name-of-him

בְּקוֹל רִנָּה הַגִּידוּ הַשְׁמִיעוּ זֹאת הוֹצִיאוּהָ עַד־ קְצֵה הָאָרֶץ
the-earth end-of to send-out-her! this proclaim! announce! joy with-shout-of

אִמְרוּ גָּאַל יְהוָה עַבְדּוֹ יַעֲקֹב׃ וְלֹא צָמְאוּ
they-thirsted and-not (21) Jacob servant-of-him Yahweh he-redeemed say!

בָּחֳרָבוֹת הוֹלִיכָם מַיִם מִצּוּר הִזִּיל לָמוֹ
for-them he-made-flow from-rock waters he-led-them through-the-deserts

וַיִּבְקַע־ צוּר וַיָּזֻבוּ מָיִם׃ אֵין שָׁלוֹם אָמַר
he-says peace there-is-no (22) waters and-they-gushed-out rock and-he-split

יְהוָה לָרְשָׁעִים׃ שִׁמְעוּ אִיִּים אֵלַי וְהַקְשִׁיבוּ לְאֻמִּים
nations and-hear! to-me islands listen! (49:1) for-the-wicked-ones Yahweh

מֵרָחוֹק יְהוָה מִבֶּטֶן קְרָאָנִי מִמְּעֵי אִמִּי
mother-of-me from-inward-parts-of he-called-me before-birth Yahweh at-distance

הִזְכִּיר שְׁמִי׃ וַיָּשֶׂם פִּי כְּחֶרֶב חַדָּה
sharpened like-sword mouth-of-me and-he-made (2) name-of-me he-mentioned

בְּצֵל יָדוֹ הֶחְבִּיאָנִי וַיְשִׂימֵנִי לְחֵץ בָּרוּר
being-polished into-arrow and-he-made-me he-hid-me hand-of-him in-shadow-of

בְּאַשְׁפָּתוֹ הִסְתִּירָנִי׃ וַיֹּאמֶר לִי עַבְדִּי־ אָתָּה יִשְׂרָאֵל
Israel you servant-of-me to-me and-he-said (3) he-concealed-me in-quiver-of-him

אֲשֶׁר־ בְּךָ אֶתְפָּאָר׃ וַאֲנִי אָמַרְתִּי לְרִיק יָגַעְתִּי
I-labored to-no-purpose I-said but-I (4) I-will-display-splendor in-you whom

לְתֹהוּ וְהֶבֶל כֹּחִי כִלֵּיתִי אָכֵן מִשְׁפָּטִי אֶת־ יְהוָה
Yahweh with due-of-me yet I-spent strength-of-me and-nothing in-vain

וּפְעֻלָּתִי אֶת־ אֱלֹהָי׃ וְעַתָּה אָמַר יְהוָה יֹצְרִי מִבֶּטֶן
in-womb one-forming-me Yahweh he-says and-now (5) God-of-me with and-reward-of-me

לְעֶבֶד לוֹ לְשׁוֹבֵב יַעֲקֹב אֵלָיו וְיִשְׂרָאֵל לֹא° יֵאָסֵף
he-will-be-gathered to-him and-Israel to-him Jacob to-bring-back of-him as-servant

וְאֶכָּבֵד בְּעֵינֵי יְהוָה וֵאלֹהַי הָיָה עֻזִּי׃
strength-of-me he-is and-God-of-me Yahweh in-eyes-of for-I-am-honored

וַיֹּאמֶר נָקֵל מִהְיוֹתְךָ לִי עֶבֶד לְהָקִים אֶת־
*** to-restore servant of-me from-to-be-you he-is-small and-he-says (6)

שִׁבְטֵי יַעֲקֹב וּנְצִירֵי° יִשְׂרָאֵל לְהָשִׁיב וּנְתַתִּיךָ
also-I-will-make-you to-bring-back Israel and-ones-being-kept-of Jacob tribes-of

לְאוֹר גּוֹיִם לִהְיוֹת יְשׁוּעָתִי עַד־ קְצֵה הָאָרֶץ׃ כֹּה
this (7) the-earth end-of to salvation-of-me to-bring Gentiles as-light-of

numberless grains;
their name would never be cut off
nor destroyed from before me."

20 Leave Babylon,
flee from the Babylonians!
Announce this with shouts of joy
and proclaim it.
Send it out to the ends of the earth;
say, "The LORD has redeemed his servant Jacob."
21 They did not thirst when he led them through the deserts;
he made water flow for them from the rock;
he split the rock
and water gushed out.
22 "There is no peace," says the LORD, "for the wicked."

*The Servant of the LORD*

49 Listen to me, you islands;
hear this, you distant nations:
Before I was born the LORD called me;
from my birth he has made mention of my name.
2 He made my mouth like a sharpened sword,
in the shadow of his hand he hid me;
he made me into a polished arrow
and concealed me in his quiver.
3 He said to me, "You are my servant,
Israel, in whom I will display my splendor."
4 But I said, "I have labored to no purpose;
I have spent my strength in vain and for nothing.
Yet what is due me is in the LORD's hand,
and my reward is with my God."

5 And now the LORD says—
he who formed me in the womb to be his servant
to bring Jacob back to him
and gather Israel to himself,
for I am honored in the eyes of the LORD
and my God has been my strength—
6 he says:
"It is too small a thing for you to be my servant
to restore the tribes of Jacob
and bring back those of Israel I have kept.
I will also make you a light for the Gentiles,
that you may bring my salvation to the ends of the earth."

°5 ק לו
°6 ק ונצורי

אָמַר־ יְהוָה גֹּאֵל יִשְׂרָאֵל קְדוֹשׁוֹ לִבְזֹה־ נֶפֶשׁ

self to-despise Holy-One-of-him Israel One-Redeeming Yahweh he-says

לִמְתָעֵב גּוֹי לְעֶבֶד מֹשְׁלִים מְלָכִים יִרְאוּ

they-will-see kings ones-ruling to-servant-of nation to-one-being-abhorred-of

וָקָמוּ שָׂרִים וְיִשְׁתַּחֲווּ לְמַעַן יְהוָה אֲשֶׁר

who Yahweh because-of also-they-will-bow-down princes and-they-will-rise-up

נֶאֱמָן קְדֹשׁ יִשְׂרָאֵל וַיִּבְחָרֶךָּ׃ (8) כֹּה אָמַר יְהוָה

Yahweh he-says this (8) and-he-chose-you Israel Holy-One-of being-faithful

בְּעֵת רָצוֹן עֲנִיתִיךָ וּבְיוֹם יְשׁוּעָה עֲזַרְתִּיךָ

I-will-help-you salvation and-in-day-of I-will-answer-you favor in-time-of

וְאֶצָּרְךָ וְאֶתֶּנְךָ לִבְרִית עָם לְהָקִים אֶרֶץ

land to-restore people as-covenant-of and-I-will-make-you and-I-will-keep-you

לְהַנְחִיל נְחָלוֹת שֹׁמֵמוֹת׃ (9) לֵאמֹר לַאֲסוּרִים

to-ones-being-captives to-say (9) ones-being-desolate inheritances to-reassign

צֵאוּ לַאֲשֶׁר בַּחֹשֶׁךְ הִגָּלוּ עַל־ דְּרָכִים יִרְעוּ

they-will-feed roads beside be-free! in-the-darkness to-whom come-out!

וּבְכָל־ שְׁפָיִים מַרְעִיתָם׃ (10) לֹא יִרְעָבוּ וְלֹא

or-not they-will-hunger not (10) pasture-of-them barren-hills and-on-every-of

יִצְמָאוּ וְלֹא־ יַכֵּם שָׁרָב וָשָׁמֶשׁ כִּי־

indeed or-sun desert-heat he-will-beat-on-them or-not they-will-thirst

מְרַחֲמָם יְנַהֲגֵם וְעַל־ מַבּוּעֵי מַיִם

waters springs-of and-beside he-will-guide-them one-having-compassion-on-them

יְנַהֲלֵם׃ (11) וְשַׂמְתִּי כָל־ הָרַי לַדָּרֶךְ

into-the-road mountains-of-me all-of and-I-will-turn (11) he-will-lead-them

וּמְסִלֹּתַי יְרֻמוּן׃ (12) הִנֵּה־ אֵלֶּה מֵרָחוֹק יָבֹאוּ

they-will-come from-afar these see! (12) they-will-be-raised and-highways-of-me

וְהִנֵּה־ אֵלֶּה מִצָּפוֹן וּמִיָּם וְאֵלֶּה מֵאֶרֶץ סִינִים׃

Sinim from-region-of and-these and-from-west from-north these and-see!

(13) רָנּוּ שָׁמַיִם וְגִילִי אֶרֶץ °יִפְצְחוּ הָרִים רִנָּה כִּי־

for song mountains and-burst! earth and-rejoice! heavens shout-for-joy! (13)

נִחַם יְהוָה עַמּוֹ וַעֲנִיָּו יְרַחֵם׃

he-will-have-compassion and-afflicted-ones-of-him people-of-him Yahweh he-comforts

(14) וַתֹּאמֶר צִיּוֹן עֲזָבַנִי יְהוָה וַאדֹנָי שְׁכֵחָנִי׃

he-forgot-me and-Lord Yahweh he-forsook-me Zion but-she-said (14)

(15) הֲתִשְׁכַּח אִשָּׁה עוּלָהּ מֵרַחֵם בֶּן־

child-of from-to-have-compassion baby-at-breast-of-her mother can-she-forget? (15)

בִּטְנָהּ גַּם־ אֵלֶּה תִשְׁכַּחְנָה וְאָנֹכִי לֹא אֶשְׁכָּחֵךְ׃ (16) הֵן

see! (16) I-will-forget-you not but-I they-may-forget these though womb-of-her

[7]This is what the LORD says—
the Redeemer and Holy One of Israel—
to him who was despised and abhorred by the nation,
to the servant of rulers:
"Kings will see you and rise up,
princes will see and bow down,
because of the LORD, who is faithful,
the Holy One of Israel, who has chosen you."

*Restoration of Israel*

[8]This is what the LORD says:

"In the time of my favor I will answer you,
and in the day of salvation I will help you;
I will keep you and will make you
to be a covenant for the people,
to restore the land
and to reassign its desolate inheritances,
[9]to say to the captives, 'Come out,'
and to those in darkness, 'Be free!'

"They will feed beside the roads
and find pasture on every barren hill.
[10]They will neither hunger nor thirst,
nor will the desert heat or the sun beat upon them.
He who has compassion on them will guide them
and lead them beside springs of water.
[11]I will turn all my mountains into roads,
and my highways will be raised up.
[12]See, they will come from afar—
some from the north, some from the west,
some from the region of Aswan.[v]"

[13]Shout for joy, O heavens;
rejoice, O earth;
burst into song, O mountains!
For the LORD comforts his people
and will have compassion on his afflicted ones.

[14]But Zion said, "The LORD has forsaken me,
the Lord has forgotten me."

[15]"Can a mother forget the baby at her breast
and have no compassion on the child she has borne?
Though she may forget,
I will not forget you!

[v]12 Dead Sea Scrolls; Masoretic Text *Sinim*

°*13* ק ופצחו

עַל־כַּפַּיִם חַקֹּתִיךְ חוֹמֹתַיִךְ נֶגְדִּי תָּמִיד׃ מִהֲרוּ בָּנָיִךְ
sons-of-you they-hasten (17) ever before-me walls-of-you I-engraved-you palms on

מְהָרְסַיִךְ וּמַחֲרִבַיִךְ מִמֵּךְ יֵצֵאוּ׃ שְׂאִי־
lift! (18) they-depart from-you and-ones-laying-waste-you ones-throwing-down-you

סָבִיב עֵינַיִךְ וּרְאִי כֻּלָּם נִקְבְּצוּ בָאוּ־ לָךְ חַי־אָנִי
I alive to-you they-come they-gather all-of-them and-look! eyes-of-you around

נְאֻם־ יְהוָה כִּי כֻלָּם כַּעֲדִי תִלְבָּשִׁי
you-will-wear as-the-ornament all-of-them surely Yahweh declaration-of

וּתְקַשְּׁרִים כַּכַּלָּה׃ כִּי חָרְבֹתַיִךְ
ruins-of-you though (19) like-the-bride and-you-will-put-on-them

וְשֹׁמְמֹתַיִךְ וְאֶרֶץ הֲרִסֻתֵךְ כִּי עַתָּה
now indeed laying-waste-of-you and-land-of and-ones-being-desolate-of-you

תֵּצְרִי מִיּוֹשֵׁב וְרָחֲקוּ מְבַלְּעָיִךְ׃
ones-devouring-you and-they-will-be-far from-one-being-people you-will-be-small

עוֹד יֹאמְרוּ בְאָזְנַיִךְ בְּנֵי שִׁכֻּלָיִךְ צַר־ לִי
for-me small bereavements-of-you children-of in-ears-of-you they-will-say yet (20)

הַמָּקוֹם גְּשָׁה־ לִּי וְאֵשֵׁבָה׃ וְאָמַרְתְּ בִּלְבָבֵךְ
in-heart-of-you then-you-will-say (21) so-I-may-live to-me give-space! the-place

מִי יָלַד־ לִי אֶת־ אֵלֶּה וַאֲנִי שְׁכוּלָה וְגַלְמוּדָה גֹּלָה ׀
one-being-exiled and-barren bereaved for-I these *** to-me he-bore who?

וְסוּרָה וְאֵלֶּה מִי גִדֵּל הֵן אֲנִי נִשְׁאַרְתִּי לְבַדִּי
alone-I I-was-left I see! he-brought-up who? so-these and-one-being-rejected

אֵלֶּה אֵיפֹה הֵם׃ כֹּה־ אָמַר אֲדֹנָי יְהוָה הִנֵּה אֶשָּׂא אֶל־
to I-will-beckon see! Yahweh Sovereign he-says this (22) they where? these

גּוֹיִם יָדִי וְאֶל־ עַמִּים אָרִים נִסִּי וְהֵבִיאוּ
and-they-will-bring banner-of-me I-will-lift peoples and-to hand-of-me Gentiles

בָנַיִךְ בְּחֹצֶן וּבְנֹתַיִךְ עַל־ כָּתֵף תִּנָּשֶׂאנָה׃
they-will-be-carried shoulder on and-daughters-of-you in-arm sons-of-you

וְהָיוּ מְלָכִים אֹמְנַיִךְ וְשָׂרוֹתֵיהֶם
and-queens-of-them ones-being-foster-fathers-of-you kings and-they-will-be (23)

מֵינִיקֹתַיִךְ אַפַּיִם אֶרֶץ יִשְׁתַּחֲווּ לָךְ וַעֲפַר רַגְלַיִךְ
feet-of-you and-dust-of before-you they-will-bow ground faces ones-nursing-you

יְלַחֵכוּ וְיָדַעַתְּ כִּי־אֲנִי יְהוָה אֲשֶׁר לֹא־ יֵבֹשׁוּ
they-will-be-disappointed not that Yahweh I that then-you-will-know they-will-lick

קֹוָי׃ הֲיֻקַּח מִגִּבּוֹר מַלְקוֹחַ וְאִם־ שְׁבִי
captive-of or-if plunder from-warrior can-he-be-taken? (24) ones-hoping-in-me

צַדִּיק* יִמָּלֵט׃ כִּי־כֹה ׀ אָמַר יְהוָה גַּם־ שְׁבִי גִבּוֹר
warrior captive-of yes Yahweh he-says this but (25) can-he-be-rescued *righteous

16 See, I have engraved you on
the palms of my hands;
your walls are ever before
me.
17 Your sons hasten back,
and those who laid you
waste depart from you.
18 Lift up your eyes and look
around;
all your sons gather and
come to you.
As surely as I live," declares
the LORD,
"you will wear them all as
ornaments;
you will put them on, like a
bride.

19 "Though you were ruined and
made desolate
and your land laid waste,
now you will be too small for
your people,
and those who devoured
you will be far away.
20 The children born during your
bereavement
will yet say in your hearing,
'This place is too small for us;
give us more space to live
in.'
21 Then you will say in your
heart,
'Who bore me these?
I was bereaved and barren;
I was exiled and rejected.
Who brought these up?
I was left all alone,
but these—where have they
come from?' "

22 This is what the Sovereign
LORD says:

"See, I will beckon to the
Gentiles,
I will lift up my banner to
the peoples;
they will bring your sons in
their arms
and carry your daughters on
their shoulders.
23 Kings will be your foster
fathers,
and their queens your
nursing mothers.
They will bow down before
you with their faces to
the ground;
they will lick the dust at
your feet.
Then you will know that I am
the LORD;
those who hope in me will
not be disappointed."
24 Can plunder be taken from
warriors,
or captives rescued from the
fierce[w]?
25 But this is what the LORD says:

"Yes, captives will be taken
from warriors,

w24 Dead Sea Scrolls, Vulgate and Syriac (see also Septuagint and verse 25); Masoretic Text *righteous*

*24 The NIV, with the texts listed above in footnote *w*, reads this word as עָרִיץ, *fierce* (cf. v. 25).

יֻקָּח וּמַלְקוֹחַ עָרִיץ יִמָּלֵט וְאֶת־
and-with he-will-be-retrieved fierce and-plunder-of he-will-be-taken

יְרִיבֵךְ אָנֹכִי אָרִיב וְאֶת־ בָּנַיִךְ אָנֹכִי אוֹשִׁיעַ׃
I-will-save I children-of-you and I-will-contend I contender-of-you

וְהַאֲכַלְתִּי אֶת־ מוֹנַיִךְ אֶת־ בְּשָׂרָם וְכֶעָסִיס
and-as-the-wine flesh-of-them *** ones-oppressing-you *** and-I-will-make-eat (26)

דָּמָם יִשְׁכָּרוּן וְיָדְעוּ כָל־ בָּשָׂר כִּי אֲנִי
I that mankind all-of then-they-will-know they-will-be-drunk blood-of-them

יְהוָה מוֹשִׁיעֵךְ וְגֹאֲלֵךְ אֲבִיר יַעֲקֹב׃ כֹּה ׀
this (50:1) Jacob Mighty-One-of and-One-Redeeming-you One-Saving-you Yahweh

אָמַר יְהוָה אֵי זֶה סֵפֶר כְּרִיתוּת אִמְּכֶם אֲשֶׁר
which mother-of-you divorce-of certificate-of this where? Yahweh he-says

שִׁלַּחְתִּיהָ אוֹ מִי מִנּוֹשַׁי אֲשֶׁר־מָכַרְתִּי אֶתְכֶם לוֹ הֵן
see! to-him you I-sold that from-ones-being-creditors-of-me who? or I-sent-away-her

בַּעֲוֺנֹתֵיכֶם נִמְכַּרְתֶּם וּבְפִשְׁעֵיכֶם
and-because-of-transgressions-of-you you-were-sold because-of-sins-of-you

שֻׁלְּחָה אִמְּכֶם׃ מַדּוּעַ בָּאתִי וְאֵין אִישׁ קָרָאתִי
I-called one and-there-was-no I-came why? (2) mother-of-you she-was-sent-away

וְאֵין עוֹנֶה הֲקָצוֹר קָצְרָה יָדִי מִפְּדוּת
from-ransom arm-of-me she-was-short to-be-short? one-answering and-there-was-no

וְאִם־ אֵין־ בִּי כֹחַ לְהַצִּיל הֵן בְּגַעֲרָתִי אַחֲרִיב יָם
sea I-dry-up by-rebuke-of-me see! to-rescue strength in-me there-is-not or-indeed

אָשִׂים נְהָרוֹת מִדְבָּר תִּבְאַשׁ דְּגָתָם מֵאֵין מַיִם
waters because-there-are-not fish-of-them she-rots desert rivers I-turn

וְתָמֹת בַּצָּמָא׃ אַלְבִּישׁ שָׁמַיִם קַדְרוּת וְשַׂק
and-sackcloth darkness skies I-clothe (3) because-of-the-thirst and-she-dies

אָשִׂים כְּסוּתָם׃ אֲדֹנָי יְהוִה נָתַן לִי לְשׁוֹן לִמּוּדִים
instructions tongue-of to-me he-gave Yahweh Sovereign (4) covering-of-them I-make

לָדַעַת לָעוּת אֶת־ יָעֵף דָּבָר יָעִיר ׀ בַּבֹּקֶר בַּבֹּקֶר
in-the-morning in-the-morning he-wakens word weary *** to-sustain to-know

יָעִיר לִי אֹזֶן לִשְׁמֹעַ כַּלִּמּוּדִים׃ אֲדֹנָי יְהוִה פָּתַח־
he-opened Yahweh Sovereign (5) as-the-ones-taught to-listen ear of-me he-wakens

לִי אֹזֶן וְאָנֹכִי לֹא מָרִיתִי אָחוֹר לֹא נְסוּגֹתִי׃ גֵּוִי נָתַתִּי
I-offered back-of-me (6) I-drew-back not back I-was-rebellious not and-I ear of-me

לְמַכִּים וּלְחָיַי לְמֹרְטִים פָּנַי לֹא הִסְתַּרְתִּי
I-hid not faces-of-me to-ones-pulling-out-beard and-cheeks-of-me to-ones-beating

מִכְּלִמּוֹת וָרֹק׃ וַאדֹנָי יְהוִה יַעֲזָר־ לִי עַל־ כֵּן
this for to-me he-helps Yahweh because-Sovereign (7) and-spitting from-mockings

---

and plunder retrieved from
the fierce;
I will contend with those who
contend with you,
and your children I will
save.
[26]I will make your oppressors
eat their own flesh;
they will be drunk on their
own blood, as with wine.
Then all mankind will know
that I, the LORD, am your
Savior,
your Redeemer, the Mighty
One of Jacob."

*Israel's Sin and the Servant's Obedience*

50 This is what the LORD says:
"Where is your mother's
certificate of divorce
with which I sent her away?
Or to which of my creditors
did I sell you?
Because of your sins you were
sold;
because of your
transgressions your
mother was sent away.
[2]When I came, why was there
no one?
When I called, why was
there no one to answer?
Was my arm too short to
ransom you?
Do I lack the strength to
rescue you?
By a mere rebuke I dry up the
sea,
I turn rivers into a desert;
their fish rot for lack of water
and die of thirst.
[3]I clothe the sky with darkness
and make sackcloth its
covering."

[4]The Sovereign LORD has given
me an instructed tongue,
to know the word that
sustains the weary.
He wakens me morning by
morning,
wakens my ear to listen like
one being taught.
[5]The Sovereign LORD has
opened my ears,
and I have not been
rebellious;
I have not drawn back.
[6]I offered my back to those
who beat me,
my cheeks to those who
pulled out my beard;
I did not hide my face
from mocking and spitting.
[7]Because the Sovereign LORD
helps me,

לֹא נִכְלָמְתִּי עַל־כֵּן שַׂמְתִּי פָנַי כַּחַלָּמִישׁ וָאֵדַע
and-I-know like-the-flint faces-of-me I-set this for I-will-be-disgraced not

כִּי־לֹא אֵבוֹשׁ׃ קָרוֹב מַצְדִּיקִי מִי־יָרִיב
he-will-bring-charges who? one-vindicating-me near (8) I-will-be-shamed not that

אִתִּי נַעַמְדָה יָּחַד מִי־בַעַל מִשְׁפָּטִי יִגַּשׁ
let-him-confront accusation-of-me master-of who? together let-us-stand against-me

אֵלָי׃ הֵן אֲדֹנָי יְהוִה יַעֲזָר־לִי מִי־הוּא יַרְשִׁיעֵנִי הֵן
see! he-will-condemn-me he who? to-me he-helps Yahweh Sovereign see! (9) to-me

כֻּלָּם כַּבֶּגֶד יִבְלוּ עָשׁ יֹאכְלֵם׃ מִי
who? (10) he-will-eat-them moth they-will-wear-out like-the-garment all-of-them

בָכֶם יְרֵא יְהוָה שֹׁמֵעַ בְּקוֹל עַבְדּוֹ אֲשֶׁר ׀ הָלַךְ
he-walks who servant-of-him to-word-of one-obeying Yahweh one-fearing-of among-you

חֲשֵׁכִים וְאֵין נֹגַהּ לוֹ יִבְטַח בְּשֵׁם יְהוָה
Yahweh in-name-of let-him-trust for-him light and-there-is-no darknesses

וְיִשָּׁעֵן בֵּאלֹהָיו׃ הֵן כֻּלְּכֶם קֹדְחֵי אֵשׁ
fire ones-lighting-of all-of-you now! (11) on-God-of-him and-let-him-rely

מְאַזְּרֵי זִיקוֹת לְכוּ ׀ בְּאוּר אֶשְׁכֶם וּבְזִיקוֹת
and-of-torches fire-of-you in-light-of walk! flaming-torches ones-providing-of

בִּעַרְתֶּם מִיָּדִי הָיְתָה־זֹּאת לָכֶם לְמַעֲצֵבָה תִּשְׁכָּבוּן׃
you-will-lie in-torment to-you this she-will-come from-hand-of-me you-set-ablaze

שִׁמְעוּ אֵלַי רֹדְפֵי צֶדֶק מְבַקְשֵׁי יְהוָה הַבִּיטוּ
look! Yahweh ones-seeking-of righteousness ones-pursuing-of to-me listen! (51:1)

אֶל־צוּר חֻצַּבְתֶּם וְאֶל־מַקֶּבֶת בּוֹר נֻקַּרְתֶּם׃ הַבִּיטוּ אֶל־אַבְרָהָם
Abraham to look! (2) you-were-hewn pit quarry-of and-to you-were-cut rock to

אֲבִיכֶם וְאֶל־שָׂרָה תְּחוֹלֶלְכֶם כִּי־אֶחָד קְרָאתִיו
I-called-him one when she-gave-birth-to-you Sarah and-to father-of-you

וַאֲבָרְכֵהוּ וְאַרְבֵּהוּ׃ כִּי־נִחַם יְהוָה צִיּוֹן
Zion Yahweh he-will-comfort surely (3) and-I-made-many-him and-I-blessed-him

נִחַם כָּל־חָרְבֹתֶיהָ וַיָּשֶׂם מִדְבָּרָהּ
desert-of-her and-he-will-make ruins-of-her all-of he-will-have-compassion

כְּעֵדֶן וְעַרְבָתָהּ כְּגַן־יְהוָה שָׂשׂוֹן וְשִׂמְחָה
and-gladness joy Yahweh like-garden-of and-wasteland-of-her like-Eden

יִמָּצֵא בָהּ תּוֹדָה וְקוֹל זִמְרָה׃ הַקְשִׁיבוּ אֵלַי
to-me listen! (4) singing and-sound-of thanksgiving in-her he-will-be-found

עַמִּי וּלְאוּמִּי אֵלַי הַאֲזִינוּ כִּי תוֹרָה מֵאִתִּי תֵצֵא
she-will-go-out from-with-me law indeed hear! to-me and-nation-of-me people-of-me

וּמִשְׁפָּטִי לְאוֹר עַמִּים אַרְגִּיעַ׃ קָרוֹב צִדְקִי
righteousness-of-me near (5) I-will-make nations as-light-of and-justice-of-me

I will not be disgraced.
Therefore have I set my face like flint,
and I know I will not be put to shame.
8 He who vindicates me is near.
Who then will bring charges against me?
Let us face each other!
Who is my accuser?
Let him confront me!
9 It is the Sovereign LORD who helps me.
Who is he that will condemn me?
They will all wear out like a garment;
the moths will eat them up.

10 Who among you fears the LORD
and obeys the word of his servant?
Let him who walks in the dark,
who has no light,
trust in the name of the LORD
and rely on his God.
11 But now, all you who light fires
and provide yourselves with flaming torches,
go, walk in the light of your fires
and of the torches you have set ablaze.
This is what you shall receive from my hand:
You will lie down in torment.

*Everlasting Salvation for Zion*

51 "Listen to me, you who pursue righteousness
and who seek the LORD:
Look to the rock from which you were cut
and to the quarry from which you were hewn;
2 look to Abraham, your father,
and to Sarah, who gave you birth.
When I called him he was but one,
and I blessed him and made him many.
3 The LORD will surely comfort Zion
and will look with compassion on all her ruins;
he will make her deserts like Eden,
her wastelands like the garden of the LORD.
Joy and gladness will be found in her,
thanksgiving and the sound of singing.

4 "Listen to me, my people;
hear me, my nation:
The law will go out from me;
my justice will become a light to the nations.
5 My righteousness draws near speedily,

יָצָא יִשְׁעִי וּזְרֹעַי עַמִּים יִשְׁפֹּטוּ
they-will-bring-justice nations and-arms-of-me salvation-of-me he-is-on-way

אֵלַי אִיִּים יְקַוּוּ וְאֶל־ זְרֹעִי יְיַחֵלוּן׃ שְׂאוּ
lift-up! (6) they-wait-in-hope arm-of-me and-for they-will-look islands to-me

לַשָּׁמַיִם עֵינֵיכֶם וְהַבִּיטוּ אֶל־ הָאָרֶץ מִתַּחַת כִּי־ שָׁמַיִם
heavens indeed at-beneath the-earth at and-look! eyes-of-you to-the-heavens

כֶּעָשָׁן נִמְלָחוּ וְהָאָרֶץ כַּבֶּגֶד תִּבְלֶה
she-will-wear-out like-the-garment and-the-earth they-will-vanish like-the-smoke

וְיֹשְׁבֶיהָ כְּמוֹ־ כֵן יְמוּתוּן וִישׁוּעָתִי לְעוֹלָם
to-forever but-salvation-of-me they-will-die fly like and-ones-inhabiting-her

תִּהְיֶה וְצִדְקָתִי לֹא תֵחָת׃ שִׁמְעוּ אֵלַי
to-me listen! (7) she-will-fail never and-righteousness-of-me she-will-last

יֹדְעֵי צֶדֶק עַם תּוֹרָתִי בְלִבָּם אַל־ תִּירְאוּ חֶרְפַּת
reproach-of you-fear not in-heart-of-them law-of-me people right ones-knowing-of

אֱנוֹשׁ וּמִגִּדֻּפֹתָם אַל־ תֵּחָתּוּ׃ כִּי כַבֶּגֶד
like-the-garment for (8) you-be-terrified not or-of-insults-of-them man

יֹאכְלֵם עָשׁ וְכַצֶּמֶר יֹאכְלֵם סָס
worm he-will-devour-them and-like-the-wool moth he-will-eat-up-them

וְצִדְקָתִי לְעוֹלָם תִּהְיֶה וִישׁוּעָתִי
and-salvation-of-me she-will-last to-forever but-righteousness-of-me

לְדוֹר דּוֹרִים׃ עוּרִי עוּרִי לִבְשִׁי־ עֹז זְרוֹעַ
arm-of strength clothe-yourself! awake! awake! (9) generations to-generation-of

יְהוָה עוּרִי כִּימֵי קֶדֶם דֹּרוֹת עוֹלָמִים הֲלוֹא אַתְּ־הִיא
she you not? old-ones generations-of time-gone-by as-days-of awake! Yahweh

הַמַּחְצֶבֶת רַהַב מְחוֹלֶלֶת תַּנִּין׃ הֲלוֹא אַתְּ־ הִיא
she you not? (10) monster one-piercing Rahab the-one-cutting-to-pieces

הַמַּחֲרֶבֶת יָם מֵי תְּהוֹם רַבָּה הַשָּׂמָה מַעֲמַקֵּי־ יָם דֶּרֶךְ
road sea depths-of who-she-made great deep waters-of sea the-one-drying-up

לַעֲבֹר גְּאוּלִים׃ וּפְדוּיֵי יְהוָה
Yahweh and-ones-being-ransomed-of (11) ones-being-redeemed to-cross-over

יְשׁוּבוּן וּבָאוּ צִיּוֹן בְּרִנָּה וְשִׂמְחַת עוֹלָם עַל־
on everlasting and-joy-of with-singing Zion and-they-will-enter they-will-return

רֹאשָׁם שָׂשׂוֹן וְשִׂמְחָה יַשִּׂיגוּן נָסוּ יָגוֹן וַאֲנָחָה׃
and-sighing sorrow they-will-flee they-will-overtake and-joy gladness head-of-them

אָנֹכִי אָנֹכִי הוּא מְנַחֶמְכֶם מִי־ אַתְּ וַתִּירְאִי מֵאֱנוֹשׁ יָמוּת
they-die of-man that-you-fear you who? one-comforting-you he I I (12)

וּמִבֶּן־ אָדָם חָצִיר יִנָּתֵן׃ וַתִּשְׁכַּח יְהוָה עֹשֶׂךָ
One-Making-you Yahweh that-you-forget (13) they-are-made grass man and-of-son-of

my salvation is on the way,
and my arm will bring
justice to the nations.
The islands will look to me
and wait in hope for my
arm.
6 Lift up your eyes to the
heavens,
look at the earth beneath;
the heavens will vanish like
smoke,
the earth will wear out like
a garment
and its inhabitants die like
flies.
But my salvation will last
forever,
my righteousness will never
fail.

7 "Hear me, you who know
what is right,
you people who have my
law in your hearts:
Do not fear the reproach of
men
or be terrified by their
insults.
8 For the moth will eat them up
like a garment;
the worm will devour them
like wool.
But my righteousness will last
forever,
my salvation through all
generations."

9 Awake, awake! Clothe yourself
with strength,
O arm of the LORD;
awake, as in days gone by,
as in generations of old.
Was it not you who cut Rahab
to pieces,
who pierced that monster
through?
10 Was it not you who dried up
the sea,
the waters of the great deep,
who made a road in the
depths of the sea
so that the redeemed might
cross over?
11 The ransomed of the LORD will
return.
They will enter Zion with
singing;
everlasting joy will crown
their heads.
Gladness and joy will overtake
them,
and sorrow and sighing will
flee away.

12 "I, even I, am he who
comforts you.
Who are you that you fear
mortal men,
the sons of men, who are
but grass,
13 that you forget the LORD your
Maker,

| | | | | | |
|---|---|---|---|---|---|
| תָּמִיד | וַתְּפַחֵד | אָרֶץ | וְיֹסֵד | שָׁמַיִם | נוֹטֶה |
| constantly | and-you-are-terrified | earth | and-one-founding | heavens | one-stretching-out |

| | | | | | | |
|---|---|---|---|---|---|---|
| כּוֹנֵן | כַּאֲשֶׁר | הַמֵּצִיק | חֲמַת | מִפְּנֵי | הַיּוֹם | כָּל־ |
| one-being-bent | as-who | the-one-oppressing | wrath-of | because-of | the-day | every-of |

| | | | | | | |
|---|---|---|---|---|---|---|
| צֹעֶה | מִהֵר | | הַמֵּצִיק׃ | חֲמַת | וְאַיֵּה | לְהַשְׁחִית |
| one-cowering | he-will-be-soon | (14) | the-one-oppressing | wrath-of | for-where? | to-destroy |

| | | | | | | |
|---|---|---|---|---|---|---|
| לַחְמוֹ׃ | יֶחְסַר | וְלֹא | לַשַּׁחַת | יָמוּת | וְלֹא־ | לְהִפָּתֵחַ |
| bread-of-him | he-will-lack | or-not | in-the-dungeon | he-will-die | and-not | to-be-set-free |

| | | | | | | | |
|---|---|---|---|---|---|---|---|
| גַּלָּיו | וַיֶּהֱמוּ | הַיָּם | רֹגַע | אֱלֹהֶיךָ | יְהוָה | וְאָנֹכִי | |
| waves-of-him | so-they-roar | the-sea | one-churning-up | God-of-you | Yahweh | for-I | (15) |

| | | | | | | |
|---|---|---|---|---|---|---|
| בְּפִיךָ | דְּבָרַי | וָאָשִׂם | | שְׁמוֹ׃ | צְבָאוֹת | יְהוָה |
| in-mouth-of-you | words-of-me | and-I-put | (16) | name-of-him | Hosts | Yahweh-of |

| | | | | | |
|---|---|---|---|---|---|
| וְלִיסֹד | שָׁמַיִם | לִנְטֹעַ | כִּסִּיתִיךָ | יָדִי | וּבְצֵל |
| and-to-found | heavens | to-set-in-place | I-covered-you | hand-of-me | and-with-shadow-of |

| | | | | | | | | | |
|---|---|---|---|---|---|---|---|---|---|
| יְרוּשָׁלִַם | קוּמִי | הִתְעוֹרְרִי | הִתְעוֹרְרִי | | אָתָּה׃ | עַמִּי־ | לְצִיּוֹן | וְלֵאמֹר | אָרֶץ |
| Jerusalem | rise-up! | awake! | awake! | (17) | you | people-of-me | to-Zion | and-to-say | earth |

| | | | | | | | | | |
|---|---|---|---|---|---|---|---|---|---|
| כּוֹס | קֻבַּעַת | אֶת־ | חֲמָתוֹ | כּוֹס | אֶת־ | יְהוָה | מִיַּד | שָׁתִית | אֲשֶׁר |
| cup-of | goblet-of | *** | wrath-of-him | cup-of | *** | Yahweh | from-hand-of | you-drank | who |

| | | | | | | |
|---|---|---|---|---|---|---|
| לָהּ | מְנַהֵל | אֵין־ | | מָצִית׃ | שָׁתִית | הַתַּרְעֵלָה |
| to-her | one-guiding | there-was-no | (18) | you-drained | you-drank | the-staggering |

| | | | | | | | |
|---|---|---|---|---|---|---|---|
| בָּנִים | מִכָּל־ | בְּיָדָהּ | מַחֲזִיק | וְאֵין | יָלָדָה | בָּנִים | מִכָּל־ |
| sons | of-all-of | by-hand-of-her | one-taking | and-there-was-no | she-bore | sons | of-all-of |

| | | | | | | | |
|---|---|---|---|---|---|---|---|
| לָךְ | יָנוּד | מִי | קֹרְאֹתַיִךְ | הֵנָּה | שְׁתַּיִם | | גִּדֵּלָה׃ |
| to-you | he-can-comfort | who? | ones-coming-upon-you | they | double | (19) | she-reared |

| | | | | | |
|---|---|---|---|---|---|
| אֲנַחֲמֵךְ׃ | מִי | וְהַחֶרֶב | וְהָרָעָב | וְהַשֶּׁבֶר | הַשֹּׁד |
| can-I-console-you | who? | and-the-sword | and-the-famine | and-the-destruction | the-ruin |

| | | | | | | | |
|---|---|---|---|---|---|---|---|
| כְּתוֹא | חוּצוֹת | כָּל־ | בְּרֹאשׁ | שָׁכְבוּ | עֻלְּפוּ | בָּנַיִךְ | |
| like-antelope-of | streets | all-of | at-head-of | they-lie | they-fainted | sons-of-you | (20) |

| | | | | | | | | |
|---|---|---|---|---|---|---|---|---|
| שִׁמְעִי־ | לָכֵן | | אֱלֹהָיִךְ׃ | גַּעֲרַת | יְהוָה | חֲמַת־ | הַמְלֵאִים | מִכְמָר |
| hear! | therefore | (21) | God-of-you | rebuke-of | Yahweh | wrath-of | the-ones-filled | net |

| | | | | | | | | |
|---|---|---|---|---|---|---|---|---|
| אָמַר | כֹּה־ | | מִיָּיִן׃ | וְלֹא | וּשְׁכֻרַת | עֲנִיָּה | זֹאת | נָא |
| he-says | this | (22) | with-wine | but-not | and-one-being-drunk | afflicted-one | this | now! |

| | | | | | | |
|---|---|---|---|---|---|---|
| לָקַחְתִּי | הִנֵּה | עַמּוֹ | יָרִיב | וֵאלֹהַיִךְ | יְהוָה | אֲדֹנַיִךְ |
| I-took | see! | people-of-him | he-defends | and-God-of-you | Yahweh | Sovereign-of-you |

| | | | | | | | | |
|---|---|---|---|---|---|---|---|---|
| לֹא־ | חֲמָתִי | כּוֹס | קֻבַּעַת | אֶת־ | הַתַּרְעֵלָה | כּוֹס | אֶת־ | מִיָּדֵךְ |
| not | wrath-of-me | cup-of | goblet-of | *** | the-staggering | cup-of | *** | from-hand-of-you |

| | | | | | |
|---|---|---|---|---|---|
| בְּיַד־ | וְשַׂמְתִּיהָ | | עוֹד׃ | לִשְׁתּוֹתָהּ | תוֹסִיפִי |
| into-hand-of | and-I-will-put-her | (23) | ever | to-drink-her | you-will-do-again |

who stretched out the
heavens
and laid the foundations of
the earth,
that you live in constant terror
every day
because of the wrath of the
oppressor,
who is bent on destruction?
For where is the wrath of the
oppressor?
14 The cowering prisoners will
soon be set free;
they will not die in their
dungeon,
nor will they lack bread.
15 For I am the LORD your God,
who churns up the sea so
that its waves roar—
the LORD Almighty is his
name.
16 I have put my words in your
mouth
and covered you with the
shadow of my hand—
I who set the heavens in place,
who laid the foundations of
the earth,
and who say to Zion, 'You
are my people.' "

*The Cup of the LORD's Wrath*

17 Awake, awake!
Rise up, O Jerusalem,
you who have drunk from the
hand of the LORD
the cup of his wrath,
you who have drained to its
dregs
the goblet that makes men
stagger.
18 Of all the sons she bore
there was none to guide her;
of all the sons she reared
there was none to take her
by the hand.
19 These double calamities have
come upon you—
who can comfort you?—
ruin and destruction, famine
and sword—
who can[x] console you?
20 Your sons have fainted;
they lie at the head of every
street,
like antelope caught in a
net.
They are filled with the wrath
of the LORD
and the rebuke of your God.
21 Therefore hear this, you
afflicted one,
made drunk, but not with
wine.
22 This is what your Sovereign
LORD says,
your God, who defends his
people:
"See, I have taken out of your
hand
the cup that made you
stagger;
from that cup, the goblet of
my wrath,
you will never drink again.
23 I will put it into the hands of

[x]19 Dead Sea Scrolls, Septuagint, Vulgate and Syriac; Masoretic Text / *how can I*

מוֹגַיִךְ אֲשֶׁר־אָמְרוּ לְנַפְשֵׁךְ שְׁחִי
fall-prostrate! to-self-of-you they-said who ones-tormenting-you

וְנַעֲבֹרָה וַתָּשִׂימִי כָאָרֶץ גֵּוֵךְ וְכַחוּץ
and-like-the-street back-of-you like-the-ground and-you-made so-we-may-walk-over

לַעֹבְרִים׃ (52:1) עוּרִי עוּרִי לִבְשִׁי עֻזֵּךְ
strength-of-you clothe-yourself! awake! awake! (52:1) for-the-ones-walking-over

צִיּוֹן לִבְשִׁי ׀ בִּגְדֵי תִפְאַרְתֵּךְ יְרוּשָׁלַםִ עִיר הַקֹּדֶשׁ כִּי
indeed the-holiness city-of Jerusalem splendor-of-you garments-of put-on! Zion

לֹא יוֹסִיף יָבֹא־בָךְ עוֹד עָרֵל וְטָמֵא׃
and-defiled uncircumcised ever into-you he-will-enter he-will-do-again not

(2) הִתְנַעֲרִי מֵעָפָר קוּמִי שְׁבִי* יְרוּשָׁלָםִ הִתְפַּתְּחוּ°
free-yourself! Jerusalem sit-enthroned! rise-up! from-dust shake-off! (2)

מוֹסְרֵי צַוָּארֵךְ שְׁבִיָּה בַּת־צִיּוֹן׃ (3) כִּי־כֹה אָמַר יְהוָה
Yahweh he-says this for (3) Zion Daughter-of captive neck-of-you chains-of

חִנָּם נִמְכַּרְתֶּם וְלֹא בְכֶסֶף תִּגָּאֵלוּ׃ (4) כִּי כֹה
this for (4) you-will-be-redeemed with-money and-not you-were-sold for-nothing

אָמַר אֲדֹנָי יְהוִה מִצְרַיִם יָרַד־עַמִּי בָרִאשֹׁנָה לָגוּר
to-live at-the-first people-of-me he-went-down Egypt Yahweh Sovereign he-says

שָׁם וְאַשּׁוּר בְּאֶפֶס עֲשָׁקוֹ׃ (5) וְעַתָּה מַה°־לִּי־פֹה
here to-me what? and-now (5) he-oppressed-him at-lately and-Assyria there

נְאֻם־יְהוָה כִּי־לֻקַּח עַמִּי חִנָּם
for-nothing people-of-me he-was-taken-away for Yahweh declaration-of

מֹשְׁלָו° יְהֵילִילוּ† נְאֻם־יְהוָה וְתָמִיד כָּל־הַיּוֹם
the-day all-of and-constantly Yahweh declaration-of †they-wail ones-ruling-him

שְׁמִי מִנֹּאָץ׃ (6) לָכֵן יֵדַע עַמִּי שְׁמִי
name-of-me people-of-me he-will-know therefore (6) being-blasphemed name-of-me

לָכֵן בַּיּוֹם הַהוּא כִּי־אֲנִי־הוּא הַמְדַבֵּר הִנֵּנִי׃ (7) מַה־
how! (7) yes-I! the-one-foretelling he I that the-that in-the-day therefore

נָּאווּ עַל־הֶהָרִים רַגְלֵי מְבַשֵּׂר מַשְׁמִיעַ
one-proclaiming one-bringing-good-news feet-of the-mountains on they-are-beautiful

שָׁלוֹם מְבַשֵּׂר טוֹב מַשְׁמִיעַ יְשׁוּעָה אֹמֵר לְצִיּוֹן
to-Zion one-saying salvation one-proclaiming good one-bringing-good-news peace

מָלַךְ אֱלֹהָיִךְ׃ (8) קוֹל צֹפַיִךְ נָשְׂאוּ קוֹל יַחְדָּו
together voice they-lift men-watching-you voice-of (8) God-of-you he-reigns

יְרַנֵּנוּ כִּי עַיִן בְּעַיִן יִרְאוּ בְּשׁוּב יְהוָה צִיּוֹן׃
Zion Yahweh when-to-return they-will-see to-eye eye for they-shout-for-joy

(9) פִּצְחוּ רַנְּנוּ יַחְדָּו חָרְבוֹת יְרוּשָׁלָםִ כִּי־נִחַם יְהוָה עַמּוֹ
people-of-him Yahweh he-comforted for Jerusalem ruins-of together sing! burst! (9)

your tormentors,
who said to you,
'Fall prostrate that we may
walk over you.'
And you made your back like
the ground,
like a street to be walked
over."

52 Awake, awake, O Zion,
clothe yourself with
strength.
Put on your garments of
splendor,
O Jerusalem, the holy city.
The uncircumcised and defiled
will not enter you again.
2 Shake off your dust;
rise up, sit enthroned, O
Jerusalem.
Free yourself from the chains
on your neck,
O captive Daughter of Zion.
3 For this is what the LORD says:

"You were sold for nothing,
and without money you will
be redeemed."

4 For this is what the Sovereign
LORD says:

"At first my people went
down to Egypt to live;
lately, Assyria has oppressed
them.

5 "And now what do I have
here?" declares the LORD.

"For my people have been
taken away for nothing,
and those who rule them
mock,[y]"
declares the LORD.
"And all day long
my name is constantly
blasphemed.
6 Therefore my people will know
my name;
therefore in that day they
will know
that it is I who foretold it.
Yes, it is I."
7 How beautiful on the
mountains
are the feet of those who
bring good news,
who proclaim peace,
who bring good tidings,
who proclaim salvation,
who say to Zion,
"Your God reigns!"
8 Listen! Your watchmen lift up
their voices;
together they shout for joy.
When the LORD returns to
Zion,
they will see it with their
own eyes.
9 Burst into songs of joy
together,
you ruins of Jerusalem,
for the LORD has comforted his
people,

y5 Dead Sea Scrolls and Vulgate; Masoretic Text *wail*

*2 Most mss have no dagesh in the shin (שׁ).

†5 The NIV, with the versions and texts above in footnote y, repoints this word as יְהוֹלְלוּ, *they-mock*.

°2 ק התפתחי

°5a ק מה לי ; °5b ק משליו

גָּאַל יְרוּשָׁלָֽם׃ חָשַׂף יְהוָה אֶת־זְרוֹעַ קָדְשׁוֹ
holiness-of-him arm-of *** Yahweh he-will-lay-bare (10) Jerusalem he-redeemed

לְעֵינֵי כָּל־הַגּוֹיִם וְרָאוּ כָּל־אַפְסֵי־אָרֶץ
earth ends-of all-of and-they-will-see the-nations all-of before-eyes-of

אֵת יְשׁוּעַת אֱלֹהֵֽינוּ׃ סוּרוּ סוּרוּ צְאוּ מִשָּׁם טָמֵא
unclean-thing from-there go-out! depart! depart! (11) God-of-us salvation-of ***

אַל־תִּגָּעוּ צְאוּ מִתּוֹכָהּ הִבָּרוּ נֹשְׂאֵי כְּלֵי
vessels-of ones-carrying-of and-be-pure! from-inside-her come-out! you-touch not

יְהוָֽה׃ כִּי לֹא בְחִפָּזוֹן תֵּצֵאוּ וּבִמְנוּסָה לֹא תֵלֵכוּן כִּי־
for you-will-go not or-in-flight you-will-leave in-haste not but (12) Yahweh

הֹלֵךְ לִפְנֵיכֶם יְהוָה וּמְאַסִּפְכֶם אֱלֹהֵי יִשְׂרָאֵֽל׃ הִנֵּה
see! (13) Israel God-of and-one-guarding-rear-of-you Yahweh before-you one-going

יַשְׂכִּיל עַבְדִּי יָרוּם וְנִשָּׂא
and-he-will-be-lifted-up he-will-be-raised servant-of-me he-will-act-wisely

וְגָבַהּ מְאֹֽד׃ כַּאֲשֶׁר שָׁמְמוּ עָלֶיךָ רַבִּים
many-ones at-you they-were-appalled just-as (14) highly and-he-will-be-exalted

כֵּן־מִשְׁחַת מֵאִישׁ מַרְאֵהוּ וְתֹאֲרוֹ מִבְּנֵי אָדָֽם׃
human beyond-sons-of and-form-of-him appearance-of-him beyond-man disfigured so

כֵּן יַזֶּה גּוֹיִם רַבִּים עָלָיו יִקְפְּצוּ מְלָכִים
kings they-will-shut because-of-him many-ones nations he-will-sprinkle so (15)

פִּיהֶם כִּי אֲשֶׁר לֹא־סֻפַּר לָהֶם רָאוּ וַאֲשֶׁר לֹא־
not and-what they-will-see to-them he-was-told not what for mouth-of-them

שָׁמְעוּ הִתְבּוֹנָֽנוּ׃ מִי הֶאֱמִין לִשְׁמֻעָתֵנוּ וּזְרוֹעַ
and-arm-of to-message-of-us he-believed who? (53:1) they-will-understand they-heard

יְהוָה עַל־מִי נִגְלָֽתָה׃ וַיַּעַל כַּיּוֹנֵק
like-the-tender-shoot now-he-grew-up (2) she-was-revealed whom? to Yahweh

לְפָנָיו וְכַשֹּׁרֶשׁ מֵאֶרֶץ צִיָּה לֹא־תֹאַר לוֹ וְלֹא
and-no to-him beauty no dryness out-of-ground-of and-like-the-root before-him

הָדָר וְנִרְאֵהוּ וְלֹא־מַרְאֶה וְנֶחְמְדֵֽהוּ׃
so-we-should-desire-him appearance and-no so-we-should-be-attracted-to-him majesty

נִבְזֶה וַחֲדַל אִישִׁים אִישׁ מַכְאֹבוֹת וִידוּעַ
and-one-being-familiar-of sorrows man-of men and-rejected-of he-was-despised (3)

חֹלִי וּכְמַסְתֵּר פָּנִים מִמֶּנּוּ נִבְזֶה וְלֹא
and-not he-was-despised from-him faces and-like-one-hiding suffering

חֲשַׁבְנֻֽהוּ׃ אָכֵן חֳלָיֵנוּ הוּא נָשָׂא וּמַכְאֹבֵינוּ
and-sorrows-of-us he-took-up he infirmities-of-us surely (4) we-esteemed-him

סְבָלָם וַאֲנַחְנוּ חֲשַׁבְנֻהוּ נָגוּעַ מֻכֵּה
one-being-smitten-of one-being-stricken we-considered-him yet-we he-carried-them

he has redeemed Jerusalem.
10 The LORD will lay bare his holy arm
in the sight of all the nations,
and all the ends of the earth will see
the salvation of our God.

11 Depart, depart, go out from there!
Touch no unclean thing!
Come out from it and be pure,
you who carry the vessels of the LORD.
12 But you will not leave in haste
or go in flight;
for the LORD will go before you,
the God of Israel will be your rear guard.

*The Suffering and Glory of the Servant*

13 See, my servant will act wisely[z];
he will be raised and lifted up and highly exalted.
14 Just as there were many who were appalled at him[a]—
his appearance was so disfigured beyond that of any man
and his form marred beyond human likeness—
15 so will he sprinkle many nations,[b]
and kings will shut their mouths because of him.
For what they were not told, they will see,
and what they have not heard, they will understand.

53 Who has believed our message
and to whom has the arm of the LORD been revealed?
2 He grew up before him like a tender shoot,
and like a root out of dry ground.
He had no beauty or majesty to attract us to him,
nothing in his appearance that we should desire him.
3 He was despised and rejected by men,
a man of sorrows, and familiar with suffering.
Like one from whom men hide their faces
he was despised, and we esteemed him not.

4 Surely he took up our infirmities
and carried our sorrows,
yet we considered him stricken by God,
smitten by him, and

[z]13 Or *will prosper* [a]14 Hebrew *you*
[b]15 Hebrew; Septuagint *so will many nations marvel at him*

אֱלֹהִים וּמְעֻנֶּה׃ (5) וְהוּא מְחֹלָל מִפְּשָׁעֵנוּ
for-transgressions-of-us being-pierced but-he (5) and-one-being-afflicted God

מְדֻכָּא מֵעֲוֺנֹתֵינוּ מוּסַר שְׁלוֹמֵנוּ עָלָיו
upon-him peace-of-us punishment-of for-iniquities-of-us being-crushed

וּבַחֲבֻרָתוֹ נִרְפָּא־ לָנוּ׃ (6) כֻּלָּנוּ כַּצֹּאן תָּעִינוּ
we-went-astray like-the-sheep all-of-us (6) to-us he-was-healed and-by-wound-of-him

אִישׁ לְדַרְכּוֹ פָּנִינוּ וַיהוָה הִפְגִּיעַ בּוֹ אֵת עֲוֺן כֻּלָּנוּ׃
all-of-us iniquity-of *** on-him he-laid and-Yahweh we-turned to-way-of-him each

(7) נִגַּשׂ וְהוּא נַעֲנֶה וְלֹא יִפְתַּח־ פִּיו
mouth-of-him he-opened yet-not he-was-afflicted and-he he-was-oppressed (7)

כַּשֶּׂה לַטֶּבַח יוּבָל וּכְרָחֵל לִפְנֵי גֹזְזֶיהָ
ones-shearing-her before and-as-sheep he-was-led to-the-slaughter like-the-lamb

נֶאֱלָמָה וְלֹא יִפְתַּח פִּיו׃ (8) מֵעֹצֶר וּמִמִּשְׁפָּט
and-by-judgment by-oppression (8) mouth-of-him he-opened so-not she-is-silent

לֻקָּח וְאֶת־ דּוֹרוֹ מִי יְשׂוֹחֵחַ כִּי נִגְזַר
he-was-cut-off for he-can-speak who? descendant-of-him and he-was-taken-away

מֵאֶרֶץ חַיִּים מִפֶּשַׁע עַמִּי נֶגַע לָמוֹ׃
to-them stroke people-of-me for-transgression-of living-ones from-land-of

(9) וַיִּתֵּן אֶת־ רְשָׁעִים קִבְרוֹ וְאֶת־ עָשִׁיר בְּמֹתָיו
in-deaths-of-him rich and-with grave-of-him wicked-ones with and-he-assigned (9)

עַל לֹא־ חָמָס עָשָׂה וְלֹא מִרְמָה בְּפִיו׃ (10) וַיהוָה חָפֵץ
he-willed yet-Yahweh (10) in-mouth-of-him deceit or-no he-did violence no though

דַּכְּאוֹ הֶחֱלִי אִם־ תָּשִׂים אָשָׁם נַפְשׁוֹ
life-of-him guilt-offering you-make though he-caused-to-suffer to-crush-him

יִרְאֶה זֶרַע יַאֲרִיךְ יָמִים וְחֵפֶץ יְהוָה בְּיָדוֹ
in-hand-of-him Yahweh and-will-of days he-will-prolong offspring he-will-see

יִצְלָח׃ (11) מֵעֲמַל נַפְשׁוֹ יִרְאֶה [אוֹר*]
*[light] he-will-see soul-of-him after-suffering-of (11) he-will-prosper

יִשְׂבָּע בְּדַעְתּוֹ יַצְדִּיק צַדִּיק עַבְדִּי
servant-of-me righteous he-will-justify by-knowledge-of-him he-will-be-satisfied

לָרַבִּים וַעֲוֺנֹתָם הוּא יִסְבֹּל׃ (12) לָכֵן
therefore (12) he-will-bear he and-iniquities-of-them to-the-many-ones

אֲחַלֶּק־ לוֹ בָרַבִּים וְאֶת־ עֲצוּמִים
numerous-ones and-with among-the-many-ones to-him I-will-give-portion

יְחַלֵּק שָׁלָל תַּחַת אֲשֶׁר הֶעֱרָה לַמָּוֶת נַפְשׁוֹ
life-of-him to-the-death he-poured-out that because spoil he-will-divide

וְאֶת־ פֹּשְׁעִים נִמְנָה וְהוּא חֵטְא־ רַבִּים נָשָׂא
he-bore many-ones sin-of for-he he-was-numbered ones-transgressing and-with

afflicted.
5 But he was pierced for our
transgressions,
he was crushed for our
iniquities;
the punishment that brought
us peace was upon him,
and by his wounds we are
healed.
6 We all, like sheep, have gone
astray,
each of us has turned to his
own way;
and the LORD has laid on him
the iniquity of us all.

7 He was oppressed and
afflicted,
yet he did not open his
mouth;
he was led like a lamb to the
slaughter,
and as a sheep before her
shearers is silent,
so he did not open his
mouth.
8 By oppression[c] and judgment
he was taken away.
And who can speak of his
descendants?
For he was cut off from the
land of the living;
for the transgression of my
people he was stricken.[d]
9 He was assigned a grave with
the wicked,
and with the rich in his
death,
though he had done no
violence,
nor was any deceit in his
mouth.

10 Yet it was the LORD's will to
crush him and cause him
to suffer,
and though the LORD makes[e]
his life a guilt offering,
he will see his offspring and
prolong his days,
and the will of the LORD will
prosper in his hand.
11 After the suffering of his soul,
he will see the light ⌞of life⌟[f]
and be satisfied[g];
by his knowledge[h] my
righteous servant will
justify many,
and he will bear their
iniquities.
12 Therefore I will give him a
portion among the great,[i]
and he will divide the spoils
with the strong,[j]
because he poured out his life
unto death,
and was numbered with the
transgressors.
For he bore the sin of many,

c8 Or *From arrest*
d8 Or *away. / Yet who of his generation considered / that he was cut off from the land of the living / for the transgression of my people, / to whom the blow was due?*
e10 Hebrew *though you make*
f11 Dead Sea Scrolls (see also Septuagint); Masoretic Text does not have *the light ⌞of life⌟*
g11 Or (with Masoretic Text) [11]*He will see the result of the suffering of his soul / and be satisfied*
h11 Or *by knowledge of him*
i12 Or *many*
j12 Or *numerous*

*11 The NIV, with the texts listed above in footnote *f*, inserts אוֹר, *light*.

וְלַפֹּשְׁעִים יַפְגִּיעַ׃ רָנִּי עֲקָרָה
barren-woman sing! (54:1) he-made-intercession and-for-the-ones-transgressing

לֹא יָלָדָה פִּצְחִי רִנָּה וְצַהֲלִי לֹא־ חָלָה
she-was-in-labor never and-shout-for-joy! song burst! she-bore-child never

כִּי־ רַבִּים בְּנֵי־ שׁוֹמֵמָה מִבְּנֵי
more-than-children-of woman-being-desolate children-of many-ones because

בְעוּלָה אָמַר יְהוָה׃ הַרְחִיבִי ׀ מְקוֹם אָהֳלֵךְ
tent-of-you place-of enlarge! (2) Yahweh he-says woman-having-husband

וִירִיעוֹת מִשְׁכְּנוֹתַיִךְ יַטּוּ אַל־ תַּחְשֹׂכִי הַאֲרִיכִי
lengthen! you-hold-back not let-them-stretch-wide tents-of-you and-curtains-of

מֵיתָרַיִךְ וִיתֵדֹתַיִךְ חַזֵּקִי׃ כִּי־ יָמִין וּשְׂמֹאול
and-left right for (3) strengthen! and-stakes-of-you cords-of-you

תִּפְרֹצִי וְזַרְעֵךְ גּוֹיִם יִירָשׁ וְעָרִים
and-cities he-will-dispossess nations and-descendant-of-you you-will-spread-out

נְשַׁמּוֹת יוֹשִׁיבוּ׃ אַל־ תִּירְאִי כִּי־ לֹא
not indeed you-be-afraid not (4) they-will-settle ones-being-desolate

תֵבוֹשִׁי וְאַל־ תִּכָּלְמִי כִּי לֹא תַחְפִּירִי
you-will-be-humiliated not indeed you-fear-disgrace and-not you-will-suffer-shame

כִּי בֹשֶׁת עֲלוּמַיִךְ תִּשְׁכָּחִי וְחֶרְפַּת אַלְמְנוּתַיִךְ
widowhoods-of-you and-reproach-of you-will-forget youths-of-you shame-of indeed

לֹא תִזְכְּרִי־ עוֹד׃ כִּי בֹעֲלַיִךְ עֹשַׂיִךְ
One-Making-you one-being-husband-of-you for (5) more you-will-remember not

יְהוָה צְבָאוֹת שְׁמוֹ וְגֹאֲלֵךְ קְדוֹשׁ יִשְׂרָאֵל אֱלֹהֵי
God-of Israel Holy-One-of and-One-Redeeming-you name-of-him Hosts Yahweh-of

כָל־ הָאָרֶץ יִקָּרֵא׃ כִּי־ כְאִשָּׁה עֲזוּבָה
one-being-deserted as-wife indeed (6) he-is-called the-earth all-of

וַעֲצוּבַת רוּחַ קְרָאָךְ יְהוָה וְאֵשֶׁת נְעוּרִים
youths and-wife-of Yahweh he-will-call-you spirit and-one-being-distressed-of

כִּי תִמָּאֵס אָמַר אֱלֹהָיִךְ׃ בְּרֶגַע קָטֹן עֲזַבְתִּיךְ
I-abandoned-you brief for-moment (7) God-of-you he-says she-was-rejected that

וּבְרַחֲמִים גְּדֹלִים אֲקַבְּצֵךְ׃ בְּשֶׁצֶף קֶצֶף
anger in-surge-of (8) I-will-bring-back-you deep-ones but-with-compassions

הִסְתַּרְתִּי פָנַי רֶגַע מִמֵּךְ וּבְחֶסֶד עוֹלָם
everlasting but-with-kindness-of from-you moment faces-of-me I-hid

רִחַמְתִּיךְ אָמַר גֹּאֲלֵךְ יְהוָה׃ *כִּי־
for* (9) Yahweh One-Redeeming-you he-says I-will-have-compassion-on-you

מֵי־ נֹחַ זֹאת לִי אֲשֶׁר נִשְׁבַּעְתִּי מֵעֲבֹר מֵי־ נֹחַ עוֹד
again Noah waters-of from-to-cover I-swore when to-me this Noah *waters-of

and made intercession for
the transgressors.

*The Future Glory of Zion*

54 "Sing, O barren woman,
you who never bore a child;
burst into song, shout for joy,
you who were never in labor;
because more are the children
of the desolate woman
than of her who has a husband,"
says the LORD.

2 "Enlarge the place of your tent,
stretch your tent curtains wide,
do not hold back;
lengthen your cords,
strengthen your stakes.
3 For you will spread out to the right and to the left;
your descendants will dispossess nations
and settle in their desolate cities.

4 "Do not be afraid; you will not suffer shame.
Do not fear disgrace; you will not be humiliated.
You will forget the shame of your youth
and remember no more the reproach of your widowhood.
5 For your Maker is your husband—
the LORD Almighty is his name—
the Holy One of Israel is your Redeemer;
he is called the God of all the earth.
6 The LORD will call you back
as if you were a wife
deserted and distressed in spirit—
a wife who married young,
only to be rejected," says your God.
7 "For a brief moment I abandoned you,
but with deep compassion I will bring you back.
8 In a surge of anger
I hid my face from you for a moment,
but with everlasting kindness
I will have compassion on you,"
says the LORD your Redeemer.

9 "To me this is like the days of Noah,
when I swore that the waters of Noah would never again cover the

*9 The NIV reads the first two words as כִּימֵי, *like-days-of*.

עַל־הָאָרֶץ כֵּן נִשְׁבַּעְתִּי מִקְּצֹף עָלַיִךְ וּמִגְּעָר־בָּךְ׃
at-you and-from-to-rebuke with-you from-to-be-angry I-swore so the-earth over

(10) כִּי הֶהָרִים יָמוּשׁוּ וְהַגְּבָעוֹת תְּמוּטֶנָה
they-are-removed and-the-hills they-are-shaken the-mountains though (10)

וְחַסְדִּי מֵאִתֵּךְ לֹא־יָמוּשׁ וּבְרִית
or-covenant-of he-will-be-shaken not from-with-you yet-unfailing-love-of-me

שְׁלוֹמִי לֹא תָמוּט אָמַר מְרַחֲמֵךְ יְהוָה׃
Yahweh one-having-compassion-on-you he-says she-will-be-removed not peace-of-me

(11) עֲנִיָּה סֹעֲרָה לֹא נֻחָמָה הִנֵּה אָנֹכִי מַרְבִּיץ
building I see! being-comforted not being-lashed-by-storm afflicted-one (11)

בַּפּוּךְ אֲבָנַיִךְ וִיסַדְתִּיךְ בַּסַּפִּירִים׃
with-the-sapphires and-I-will-build-foundation-of-you stones-of-you with-the-turquoise

(12) וְשַׂמְתִּי כַּדְכֹד שִׁמְשֹׁתַיִךְ וּשְׁעָרַיִךְ לְאַבְנֵי
of-jewels-of and-gates-of-you battlements-of-you ruby and-I-will-make (12)

אֶקְדָּח וְכָל־גְּבוּלֵךְ לְאַבְנֵי־חֵפֶץ׃ (13) וְכָל־בָּנַיִךְ
sons-of-you and-all-of (13) precious of-stones-of wall-of-you and-all-of sparkling

לִמּוּדֵי יְהוָה וְרַב שְׁלוֹם בָּנָיִךְ׃ (14) בִּצְדָקָה
in-righteousness (14) children-of-you peace-of and-great Yahweh ones-taught-of

תִּכּוֹנָנִי רַחֲקִי מֵעֹשֶׁק כִּי־לֹא תִירָאִי
you-will-fear nothing indeed from-tyranny be-far! you-will-be-established

וּמִמְּחִתָּה כִּי לֹא־תִקְרַב אֵלָיִךְ׃ (15) הֵן גּוֹר יָגוּר
he-attacks to-attack if (15) to-you she-will-come-near not indeed and-from-terror

אֶפֶס מֵאוֹתִי מִי־גָר אִתָּךְ עָלַיִךְ יִפּוֹל׃ (16) הִן° אָנֹכִי
I see! (16) he-will-surrender to-you against-you he-attacks who? from-me not

בָּרָאתִי חָרָשׁ נֹפֵחַ בְּאֵשׁ פֶּחָם וּמוֹצִיא כְלִי
weapon and-one-forging coal into-flame one-fanning blacksmith I-created

לְמַעֲשֵׂהוּ וְאָנֹכִי בָּרָאתִי מַשְׁחִית לְחַבֵּל׃ (17) כָּל־
every-of (17) to-work-havoc one-destroying I-created and-I for-work-of-him

כְּלִי יוּצַר עָלַיִךְ לֹא יִצְלָח וְכָל־לָשׁוֹן
tongue and-every-of he-will-prevail not against-you he-is-forged weapon

תָּקוּם־אִתָּךְ לַמִּשְׁפָּט תַּרְשִׁיעִי זֹאת נַחֲלַת
heritage-of this you-will-refute for-the-accusation against-you she-rises

עַבְדֵי יְהוָה וְצִדְקָתָם מֵאִתִּי נְאֻם־יְהוָה׃
Yahweh declaration-of from-with-me and-vindication-of-them Yahweh servants-of

(55:1) הוֹי כָּל־צָמֵא לְכוּ לַמַּיִם וַאֲשֶׁר אֵין־לוֹ כֶּסֶף לְכוּ
come! money to-him not and-who to-the-waters come! thirsty all-of ho! (55:1)

שִׁבְרוּ וֶאֱכֹלוּ וּלְכוּ שִׁבְרוּ בְּלוֹא־כֶסֶף וּבְלוֹא מְחִיר יַיִן וְחָלָב׃
and-milk wine cost and-with-no money with-no buy! and-come! and-eat! buy!

earth.
So now I have sworn not to be angry with you,
never to rebuke you again.
10 Though the mountains be shaken
and the hills be removed,
yet my unfailing love for you will not be shaken
nor my covenant of peace be removed,"
says the LORD, who has compassion on you.

11 "O afflicted city, lashed by storms and not comforted,
I will build you with stones of turquoise,[k]
your foundations with sapphires.[l]
12 I will make your battlements of rubies,
your gates of sparkling jewels,
and all your walls of precious stones.
13 All your sons will be taught by the LORD,
and great will be your children's peace.
14 In righteousness you will be established:
Tyranny will be far from you;
you will have nothing to fear.
Terror will be far removed;
it will not come near you.
15 If anyone does attack you, it will not be my doing;
whoever attacks you will surrender to you.

16 "See, it is I who created the blacksmith
who fans the coals into flame
and forges a weapon fit for its work.
And it is I who have created the destroyer to work havoc;
17 no weapon forged against you will prevail,
and you will refute every tongue that accuses you.
This is the heritage of the servants of the LORD,
and this is their vindication from me,"
declares the LORD.

*Invitation to the Thirsty*

55 "Come, all you who are thirsty,
come to the waters;
and you who have no money,
come, buy and eat!
Come, buy wine and milk
without money and without cost.

[k] 11 The meaning of the Hebrew for this word is uncertain.
[l] 11 Or *lapis lazuli*

°16 ק הנה

לָמָּה תִשְׁקְלוּ־ כֶסֶף בְּלוֹא־ לֶחֶם וִיגִיעֲכֶם בְּלוֹא לְשָׂבְעָה
for-satisfaction on-not and-labor-of-you bread on-not money you-spend why? (2)

שִׁמְעוּ שָׁמוֹעַ אֵלַי וְאִכְלוּ־ טוֹב וְתִתְעַנַּג בַּדֶּשֶׁן
in-the-richness and-she-will-delight good and-eat! to-me to-listen listen!

נַפְשְׁכֶם׃ הַטּוּ אָזְנְכֶם וּלְכוּ אֵלַי שִׁמְעוּ וּתְחִי
that-she-may-live hear! to-me and-come! ear-of-you give! (3) soul-of-you

נַפְשְׁכֶם וְאֶכְרְתָה לָכֶם בְּרִית עוֹלָם חַסְדֵי דָוִד
David loves-of everlasting covenant-of with-you indeed-I-will-make soul-of-you

הַנֶּאֱמָנִים׃ הֵן עֵד לְאוּמִּים נְתַתִּיו נָגִיד
leader I-made-him peoples witness-of see! (4) the-ones-being-faithful

וּמְצַוֵּה לְאֻמִּים׃ הֵן גּוֹי לֹא־ תֵדַע תִּקְרָא
you-will-summon you-know not nation surely! (5) peoples and-one-commanding-of

וְגוֹי לֹא־ יְדָעוּךָ אֵלֶיךָ יָרוּצוּ לְמַעַן יְהוָה אֱלֹהֶיךָ
God-of-you Yahweh because-of they-will-hasten to-you they-know-you not and-nation

וְלִקְדוֹשׁ יִשְׂרָאֵל כִּי פֵאֲרָךְ׃ דִּרְשׁוּ יְהוָה
Yahweh seek! (6) he-endowed-with-splendor-you because Israel and-to-Holy-One-of

בְּהִמָּצְאוֹ קְרָאֻהוּ בִּהְיוֹתוֹ קָרוֹב׃ יַעֲזֹב
let-him-forsake (7) near while-to-be-him call-on-him! while-to-be-found-him

רָשָׁע דַּרְכּוֹ וְאִישׁ אָוֶן מַחְשְׁבֹתָיו וְיָשֹׁב אֶל־ יְהוָה
Yahweh to and-let-him-turn thoughts-of-him evil and-man-of way-of-him wicked

וִירַחֲמֵהוּ וְאֶל־ אֱלֹהֵינוּ כִּי־ יַרְבֶּה לִסְלוֹחַ׃
to-pardon he-will-make-great for God-of-us and-to and-he-will-have-mercy-on-him

כִּי לֹא מַחְשְׁבוֹתַי מַחְשְׁבוֹתֵיכֶם וְלֹא דַרְכֵיכֶם דְּרָכָי
ways-of-me ways-of-you and-neither thoughts-of-you thoughts-of-me not for (8)

נְאֻם יְהוָה׃ כִּי־ גָבְהוּ שָׁמַיִם מֵאָרֶץ כֵּן
so more-than-earth heavens they-are-high for (9) Yahweh declaration-of

גָּבְהוּ דְרָכַי מִדַּרְכֵיכֶם וּמַחְשְׁבֹתַי
and-thoughts-of-me more-than-ways-of-you ways-of-me they-are-high

מִמַּחְשְׁבֹתֵיכֶם׃ כִּי כַּאֲשֶׁר יֵרֵד הַגֶּשֶׁם וְהַשֶּׁלֶג
and-the-snow the-rain he-comes-down just-as for (10) more-than-thoughts-of-you

מִן־ הַשָּׁמַיִם וְשָׁמָּה לֹא יָשׁוּב כִּי אִם־ הִרְוָה אֶת־ הָאָרֶץ
the-earth *** he-waters if but he-returns not and-to-there the-heavens from

וְהוֹלִידָהּ וְהִצְמִיחָהּ וְנָתַן זֶרַע לַזֹּרֵעַ
for-the-one-sowing seed so-he-yields and-he-makes-flourish-her and-he-makes-bud-her

וְלֶחֶם לָאֹכֵל׃ כֵּן יִהְיֶה דְבָרִי אֲשֶׁר יֵצֵא
he-goes-out that word-of-me he-is so (11) for-the-one-eating and-bread

מִפִּי לֹא־ יָשׁוּב אֵלַי רֵיקָם כִּי אִם־ עָשָׂה אֶת־
*** he-will-accomplish if but empty to-me he-will-return not from-mouth-of-me

2 Why spend money on what is
not bread,
and your labor on what
does not satisfy?
Listen, listen to me, and eat
what is good,
and your soul will delight in
the richest of fare.
3 Give ear and come to me;
hear me, that your soul may
live.
I will make an everlasting
covenant with you,
my faithful love promised to
David.
4 See, I have made him a
witness to the peoples,
a leader and commander of
the peoples.
5 Surely you will summon
nations you know not,
and nations that do not
know you will hasten to
you,
because of the LORD your God,
the Holy One of Israel,
for he has endowed you
with splendor."
6 Seek the LORD while he may
be found;
call on him while he is near.
7 Let the wicked forsake his way
and the evil man his
thoughts.
Let him turn to the LORD, and
he will have mercy on
him,
and to our God, for he will
freely pardon.
8 "For my thoughts are not your
thoughts,
neither are your ways my
ways,"
declares the LORD.
9 "As the heavens are higher
than the earth,
so are my ways higher than
your ways
and my thoughts than your
thoughts.
10 As the rain and the snow
come down from heaven,
and do not return to it
without watering the earth
and making it bud and
flourish,
so that it yields seed for the
sower and bread for the
eater,
11 so is my word that goes out
from my mouth:
It will not return to me
empty,
but will accomplish what I

אֲשֶׁר חָפַצְתִּי וְהִצְלִיחַ אֲשֶׁר שְׁלַחְתִּיו׃ כִּי־בְשִׂמְחָה
in-joy indeed (12) I-sent-him which and-he-will-achieve-purpose I-desire what

תֵצֵאוּ וּבְשָׁלוֹם תּוּבָלוּן הֶהָרִים וְהַגְּבָעוֹת
and-the-hills the-mountains you-will-be-led-forth and-in-peace you-will-go-out

יִפְצְחוּ לִפְנֵיכֶם רִנָּה וְכָל־ עֲצֵי הַשָּׂדֶה יִמְחֲאוּ־ כָף׃
hand they-will-clap the-field trees-of and-all-of song before-you they-will-burst

תַּחַת הַנַּעֲצוּץ יַעֲלֶה בְרוֹשׁ תַּחַת הַסִּרְפַּד
the-brier and-instead-of pine he-will-grow the-thornbush instead-of (13)

יַעֲלֶה הֲדַס וְהָיָה לַיהוָה לְשֵׁם לְאוֹת עוֹלָם
everlasting as-sign-of as-renown for-Yahweh and-he-will-be myrtle he-will-grow

לֹא יִכָּרֵת׃ כֹּה אָמַר יְהוָה שִׁמְרוּ מִשְׁפָּט וַעֲשׂוּ
and-do! justice maintain! Yahweh he-says this (56:1) he-will-be-destroyed not

צְדָקָה כִּי־קְרוֹבָה יְשׁוּעָתִי לָבוֹא וְצִדְקָתִי לְהִגָּלוֹת׃
to-be-revealed and-righteousness-of-me to-come salvation-of-me close for right

אַשְׁרֵי אֱנוֹשׁ יַעֲשֶׂה־ זֹּאת וּבֶן־ אָדָם יַחֲזִיק בָּהּ
to-her he-holds-fast man and-son-of this he-does man blessednesses-of (2)

שֹׁמֵר שַׁבָּת מֵחַלְּלוֹ וְשֹׁמֵר יָדוֹ מֵעֲשׂוֹת
from-to-do hand-of-him and-one-keeping without-to-desecrate-her Sabbath one-keeping

כָּל־ רָע׃ וְאַל־ יֹאמַר בֶּן־ הַנֵּכָר הַנִּלְוָה
the-one-binding-himself the-foreigner son-of let-him-say and-not (3) evil any-of

אֶל־יְהוָה לֵאמֹר הַבְדֵּל יַבְדִּילַנִי יְהוָה מֵעַל עַמּוֹ
people-of-him from-among Yahweh he-will-exclude-me to-exclude to-say Yahweh to

וְאַל־ יֹאמַר הַסָּרִיס הֵן אֲנִי עֵץ יָבֵשׁ׃ כִּי־כֹה | אָמַר יְהוָה
Yahweh he-says this for (4) dry tree I see! the-eunuch let-him-complain and-not

לַסָּרִיסִים אֲשֶׁר יִשְׁמְרוּ אֶת־ שַׁבְּתוֹתַי וּבָחֲרוּ בַּאֲשֶׁר
to-what and-they-choose Sabbaths-of-me *** they-keep who to-the-eunuchs

חָפָצְתִּי וּמַחֲזִיקִים בִּבְרִיתִי׃ וְנָתַתִּי לָהֶם
to-them and-I-will-give (5) to-covenant-of-me and-ones-holding-fast I-please

בְּבֵיתִי וּבְחוֹמֹתַי יָד וָשֵׁם טוֹב מִבָּנִים
more-than-sons good and-name memorial and-within-walls-of-me within-temple-of-me

וּמִבָּנוֹת שֵׁם עוֹלָם אֶתֶּן־ לוֹ אֲשֶׁר לֹא
not that to-him I-will-give everlasting name-of and-more-than-daughters

יִכָּרֵת׃ וּבְנֵי הַנֵּכָר הַנִּלְוִים עַל־
to the-ones-binding-themselves the-foreigner and-sons-of (6) he-will-be-cut-off

יְהוָה לְשָׁרְתוֹ וּלְאַהֲבָה אֶת־ שֵׁם יְהוָה לִהְיוֹת לוֹ לַעֲבָדִים
as-worshipers to-him and-to-be Yahweh name-of *** and-to-love to-serve-him Yahweh

כָּל־ שֹׁמֵר שַׁבָּת מֵחַלְּלוֹ וּמַחֲזִיקִים
and-ones-holding-fast without-to-desecrate-her Sabbath one-keeping every-of

desire
and achieve the purpose for
which I sent it.
12 You will go out in joy
and be led forth in peace;
the mountains and hills
will burst into song before
you,
and all the trees of the field
will clap their hands.
13 Instead of the thornbush will
grow the pine tree,
and instead of briers the
myrtle will grow.
This will be for the LORD's
renown,
for an everlasting sign,
which will not be
destroyed."

*Salvation for Others*

56 This is what the LORD says:
"Maintain justice
and do what is right,
for my salvation is close at
hand
and my righteousness will
soon be revealed.
2 Blessed is the man who does
this,
the man who holds it fast,
who keeps the Sabbath
without desecrating it,
and keeps his hand from
doing any evil."

3 Let no foreigner who has
bound himself to the
LORD say,
"The LORD will surely
exclude me from his
people."
And let not any eunuch
complain,
"I am only a dry tree."
4 For this is what the LORD says:
"To the eunuchs who keep my
Sabbaths,
who choose what pleases me
and hold fast to my
covenant—
5 to them I will give within my
temple and its walls
a memorial and a name
better than sons and
daughters;
I will give them an everlasting
name
that will not be cut off.
6 And foreigners who bind
themselves to the LORD
to serve him,
to love the name of the LORD,
and to worship him,
all who keep the Sabbath
without desecrating it
and who hold fast to my

°13 ק ותחת

בִּבְרִיתִי׃ (7) וַהֲבִיאוֹתִים אֶל־ הַר קָדְשִׁי
holiness-of-me mountain-of to and-I-will-bring-them (7) to-covenant-of-me

וְשִׂמַּחְתִּים בְּבֵית תְּפִלָּתִי עוֹלֹתֵיהֶם
burnt-offerings-of-them prayer-of-me in-house-of and-I-will-give-joy-to-them

וְזִבְחֵיהֶם לְרָצוֹן עַל־ מִזְבְּחִי כִּי בֵיתִי בֵּית־
house-of house-of-me for altar-of-me on for-acceptance and-sacrifices-of-them

תְּפִלָּה יִקָּרֵא לְכָל־ הָעַמִּים׃ (8) נְאֻם אֲדֹנָי
Sovereign declaration-of (8) the-nations for-all-of he-will-be-called prayer

יְהוִה מְקַבֵּץ נִדְחֵי יִשְׂרָאֵל עוֹד אֲקַבֵּץ עָלָיו
to-him I-will-gather still Israel ones-being-exiled-of one-gathering Yahweh

לְנִקְבָּצָיו׃ (9) כֹּל חַיְתוֹ שָׂדָי אֵתָיוּ לֶאֱכֹל
to-devour come! field beast-of all-of (9) besides-ones-being-gathered-of-him

כָּל־ חַיְתוֹ בַּיָּעַר׃ (10) צֹפָו עִוְרִים כֻּלָּם לֹא
not all-of-them blind-men men-watching-him (10) in-the-forest beast-of all-of

יָדָעוּ כֻּלָּם כְּלָבִים אִלְּמִים לֹא יוּכְלוּ לִנְבֹּחַ הֹזִים שֹׁכְבִים
ones-lying ones-dreaming to-bark they-can not mute-ones dogs all-of-them they-know

אֹהֲבֵי לָנוּם׃ (11) וְהַכְּלָבִים עַזֵּי־ נֶפֶשׁ לֹא יָדְעוּ
they-know not appetite ones-mighty-of and-the-dogs (11) to-sleep ones-loving

שָׂבְעָה וְהֵמָּה רֹעִים לֹא יָדְעוּ הָבִין כֻּלָּם
all-of-them to-understand they-know not ones-being-shepherds and-they enough

לְדַרְכָּם פָּנוּ אִישׁ לְבִצְעוֹ מִקָּצֵהוּ׃ (12) אֵתָיוּ אֶקְחָה־
let-me-get come! (12) at-end-of-him to-gain-of-him each they-turn to-way-of-them

יַיִן וְנִסְבְּאָה שֵׁכָר וְהָיָה כָזֶה יוֹם מָחָר גָּדוֹל
good tomorrow day like-this and-he-will-be beer and-let-us-drink-fill wine

יֶתֶר מְאֹד׃ (57:1) הַצַּדִּיק אָבָד וְאֵין אִישׁ שָׂם עַל־ לֵב
heart in he-ponders one and-not he-perishes the-righteous (57:1) very exceedingly

וְאַנְשֵׁי־ חֶסֶד נֶאֱסָפִים בְּאֵין מֵבִין כִּי־
that understanding with-no-one ones-being-taken-away devotion and-men-of

מִפְּנֵי הָרָעָה נֶאֱסַף הַצַּדִּיק׃ (2) יָבוֹא שָׁלוֹם
peace he-enters (2) the-righteous he-is-taken-away the-evil from-presences-of

יָנוּחוּ עַל־ מִשְׁכְּבוֹתָם הֹלֵךְ נְכֹחוֹ׃
uprightness-of-him one-walking-of lying-places-of-them in they-find-rest

(3) וְאַתֶּם קִרְבוּ־ הֵנָּה בְּנֵי עֹנְנָה זֶרַע
offspring-of one-being-sorceress sons-of to-here come! but-you (3)

מְנָאֵף וַתִּזְנֶה׃ (4) עַל־ מִי תִּתְעַנָּגוּ עַל־ מִי
whom? at you-mock whom? at (4) and-she-is-prostitute one-commiting-adultery

תַּרְחִיבוּ פֶה תַּאֲרִיכוּ לָשׁוֹן הֲלוֹא־אַתֶּם יִלְדֵי־ פֶשַׁע זֶרַע
offspring-of rebellion broods-of you not? tongue you-stick-out mouth you-sneer

° 10 צפיו ק

covenant—
7 these I will bring to my holy mountain
and give them joy in my house of prayer.
Their burnt offerings and sacrifices
will be accepted on my altar;
for my house will be called
a house of prayer for all nations."
8 The Sovereign LORD declares—
he who gathers the exiles of Israel:
"I will gather still others to them
besides those already gathered."

*God's Accusation Against the Wicked*

9 Come, all you beasts of the field,
come and devour, all you beasts of the forest!
10 Israel's watchmen are blind,
they all lack knowledge;
they are all mute dogs,
they cannot bark;
they lie around and dream,
they love to sleep.
11 They are dogs with mighty appetites;
they never have enough.
They are shepherds who lack understanding;
they all turn to their own way,
each seeks his own gain.
12 "Come," each one cries, "let me get wine!
Let us drink our fill of beer!
And tomorrow will be like today,
or even far better."

57 The righteous perish,
and no one ponders it in his heart;
devout men are taken away,
and no one understands
that the righteous are taken away
to be spared from evil.
2 Those who walk uprightly
enter into peace;
they find rest as they lie in death.

3 "But you—come here, you sons of a sorceress,
you offspring of adulterers and prostitutes!
4 Whom are you mocking?
At whom do you sneer
and stick out your tongue?
Are you not a brood of rebels,

שָׁקֶר׃ הַנֵּחָמִים בָּאֵלִים תַּחַת כָּל־ עֵץ רַעֲנָן
spreading tree every-of under among-the-oaks the-ones-burning-with-lust (5) lie

שֹׁחֲטֵי הַיְלָדִים בַּנְּחָלִים תַּחַת סְעִפֵי הַסְּלָעִים׃
the-crags overhangs-of under in-the-ravines the-children ones-sacrificing-of

(6) בְּחַלְּקֵי־ נַחַל חֶלְקֵךְ הֵם הֵם גּוֹרָלֵךְ גַּם־ לָהֶם
to-them yes lot-of-you they they portion-of-you ravine among-smooth-ones-of (6)

שָׁפַכְתְּ נֶסֶךְ הֶעֱלִית מִנְחָה הַעַל אֵלֶּה
these in-light-of? grain-offering you-offered drink-offering you-poured-out

אֶנָּחֵם׃ (7) עַל הַר־ גָּבֹהַּ וְנִשָּׂא שַׂמְתְּ מִשְׁכָּבֵךְ גַּם־ שָׁם
there also bed-of-you you-made and-being-lofty high hill on (7) should-I-relent

עָלִית לִזְבֹּחַ זָבַח׃ (8) וְאַחַר הַדֶּלֶת וְהַמְּזוּזָה
and-the-doorpost the-door and-behind (8) sacrifice to-sacrifice you-went-up

שַׂמְתְּ זִכְרוֹנֵךְ כִּי מֵאִתִּי גִּלִּית וַתַּעֲלִי
and-you-climbed-in you-uncovered apart-from-me indeed symbol-of-you you-put

הִרְחַבְתְּ מִשְׁכָּבֵךְ וַתִּכְרָת־ לָךְ מֵהֶם אָהַבְתְּ
you-love with-them for-you and-you-made-pact bed-of-you you-opened-wide

מִשְׁכָּבָם יָד חָזִית׃ (9) וַתָּשֻׁרִי לַמֶּלֶךְ בַּשֶּׁמֶן
with-the-olive-oil to-the-king and-you-went (9) you-looked-on hand bed-of-them

וַתַּרְבִּי רִקֻּחָיִךְ וַתְּשַׁלְּחִי צִרַיִךְ עַד־ מֵרָחֹק
at-far-away to ambassadors-of-you and-you-sent perfumes-of-you and-you-increased

וַתַּשְׁפִּילִי עַד־ שְׁאוֹל׃ (10) בְּרֹב דַּרְכֵּךְ יָגַעַתְּ לֹא
not you-were-wearied way-of-you by-all-of (10) Sheol to and-you-descended

אָמַרְתְּ נוֹאָשׁ חַיַּת יָדֵךְ מָצָאת עַל־ כֵּן לֹא
not so for you-found strength-of-you renewal-of he-is-hopeless you-would-say

חָלִית׃ (11) וְאֶת־ מִי דָּאַגְתְּ וַתִּירְאִי כִּי תְכַזֵּבִי
you-were-false that and-you-feared you-dreaded whom? now (11) you-fainted

וְאוֹתִי לֹא זָכַרְתְּ לֹא־ שַׂמְתְּ עַל־ לִבֵּךְ הֲלֹא אֲנִי מַחְשֶׁה
being-silent I not? heart-of-you in you-pondered not you-remembered not and-me

וּמֵעֹלָם וְאוֹתִי לֹא תִירָאִי׃ (12) אֲנִי אַגִּיד צִדְקָתֵךְ
righteousness-of-you I-will-expose I (12) you-fear not that-me indeed-from-long-ago

וְאֶת־ מַעֲשַׂיִךְ וְלֹא־ יוֹעִילוּךְ׃ (13) בְּזַעֲקֵךְ
when-to-cry-for-help-you (13) they-will-benefit-you and-not works-of-you and

יַצִּילֻךְ קִבּוּצַיִךְ וְאֶת־ כֻּלָּם יִשָּׂא־ רוּחַ
wind he-will-carry-off all-of-them indeed collections-of-you let-them-save-you

יִקַּח־ הָבֶל וְהַחוֹסֶה בִי יִנְחַל־ אֶרֶץ
land he-will-inherit in-me but-the-one-taking-refuge breath he-will-take-away

וְיִירַשׁ הַר־ קָדְשִׁי׃ (14) וְאָמַר סֹלּוּ־
build-up! and-he-will-say (14) holiness-of-me mountain-of and-he-will-possess

the offspring of liars?
5 You burn with lust among the oaks
and under every spreading tree;
you sacrifice your children in the ravines
and under the overhanging crags.
6 ⌊The idols⌋ among the smooth stones of the ravines are your portion;
they, they are your lot.
Yes, to them you have poured out drink offerings
and offered grain offerings.
In the light of these things, should I relent?
7 You have made your bed on a high and lofty hill;
there you went up to offer your sacrifices.
8 Behind your doors and your doorposts
you have put your pagan symbols.
Forsaking me, you uncovered your bed,
you climbed into it and opened it wide;
you made a pact with those whose beds you love,
and you looked on their nakedness.
9 You went to Molech[m] with olive oil
and increased your perfumes.
You sent your ambassadors[n] far away;
you descended to the grave[o] itself!
10 You were wearied by all your ways,
but you would not say, 'It is hopeless.'
You found renewal of your strength,
and so you did not faint.

11 "Whom have you so dreaded and feared
that you have been false to me,
and have neither remembered me
nor pondered this in your hearts?
Is it not because I have long been silent
that you do not fear me?
12 I will expose your righteousness and your works,
and they will not benefit you.
13 When you cry out for help,
let your collection ⌊of idols⌋ save you!
The wind will carry all of them off,
a mere breath will blow them away.
But the man who makes me his refuge
will inherit the land
and possess my holy mountain."

*Comfort for the Contrite*

14 And it will be said:

m9 Or *to the king* n9 Or *idols*
o9 Hebrew *Sheol*

סֹלּוּ פַּנּוּ־ דָרֶךְ הָרִימוּ מִכְשׁוֹל מִדֶּרֶךְ עַמִּי׃ כִּי כֹה
this for (15) people-of-me from-way-of obstacle remove! road prepare! build-up!

אָמַר רָם וְנִשָּׂא שֹׁכֵן עַד וְקָדוֹשׁ שְׁמוֹ
name-of-him and-holy forever One-living and-One-being-lofty One-being-high he-says

מָרוֹם וְקָדוֹשׁ אֶשְׁכּוֹן וְאֶת־ דַּכָּא וּשְׁפַל־ רוּחַ לְהַחֲיוֹת רוּחַ
spirit-of to-revive spirit and-lowly-of contrite also-with I-live and-holy high-place

שְׁפָלִים וּלְהַחֲיוֹת לֵב נִדְכָּאִים׃ כִּי לֹא לְעוֹלָם
to-forever not indeed (16) ones-being-contrite heart-of and-to-revive lowly-ones

אָרִיב וְלֹא לָנֶצַח אֶקְּצוֹף כִּי־ רוּחַ מִלְּפָנַי
at-before-me spirit for I-will-be-angry to-always or-not I-will-accuse

יַעֲטוֹף וּנְשָׁמוֹת אֲנִי עָשִׂיתִי׃ בַּעֲוֹן בִּצְעוֹ
greed-of-him by-sin-of (17) I-created I and-breaths he-would-grow-faint

קָצַפְתִּי וְאַכֵּהוּ הַסְתֵּר וְאֶקְצֹף וַיֵּלֶךְ שׁוֹבָב
backwards yet-he-kept-on and-I-was-angry to-hide and-I-punished-him I-was-enraged

בְּדֶרֶךְ לִבּוֹ׃ דְּרָכָיו רָאִיתִי וְאֶרְפָּאֵהוּ וְאַנְחֵהוּ
and-I-will-guide-him but-I-will-heal-him I-saw ways-of-him (18) will-of-him in-way-of

וַאֲשַׁלֵּם נִחֻמִים לוֹ וְלַאֲבֵלָיו׃ בּוֹרֵא נוֹב°
praise-of creating (19) and-to-mourners-of-him to-him comforts and-I-will-restore

שְׂפָתָיִם שָׁלוֹם ׀ שָׁלוֹם לָרָחוֹק וְלַקָּרוֹב אָמַר יְהוָה וּרְפָאתִיו׃
and-I-will-heal-him Yahweh he-says and-to-the-near to-the-far peace peace lips

וְהָרְשָׁעִים כַּיָּם נִגְרָשׁ כִּי הַשְׁקֵט לֹא יוּכָל
he-can not to-rest indeed one-tossing like-the-sea but-the-wicked-ones (20)

וַיִּגְרְשׁוּ מֵימָיו רֶפֶשׁ וָטִיט׃ אֵין שָׁלוֹם אָמַר
he-says peace there-is-no (21) and-mud mire waves-of-him and-they-cast-up

אֱלֹהַי לָרְשָׁעִים׃ קְרָא בְגָרוֹן אַל־ תַּחְשֹׂךְ
you-hold-back not with-throat shout! (58:1) for-the-wicked-ones God-of-me

כַּשּׁוֹפָר הָרֵם קוֹלֶךָ וְהַגֵּד לְעַמִּי פִּשְׁעָם
rebellion-of-them to-people-of-me and-declare! voice-of-you raise! like-the-trumpet

וּלְבֵית יַעֲקֹב חַטֹּאתָם׃ וְאוֹתִי יוֹם ׀ יוֹם יִדְרֹשׁוּן וְדַעַת
and-knowledge-of they-seek day day for-me (2) sins-of-them Jacob and-to-house-of

דְּרָכַי יֶחְפָּצוּן כְּגוֹי אֲשֶׁר־צְדָקָה עָשָׂה וּמִשְׁפַּט אֱלֹהָיו
God-of-him and-command-of he-does right that as-nation they-seem-eager ways-of-me

לֹא עָזָב יִשְׁאָלוּנִי מִשְׁפְּטֵי־ צֶדֶק קִרְבַת אֱלֹהִים יֶחְפָּצוּן׃
they-seem-eager God coming-near-of justice decisions-of they-ask-me he-forsook not

לָמָּה צַּמְנוּ וְלֹא רָאִיתָ עִנִּינוּ נַפְשֵׁנוּ וְלֹא תֵדָע
you-noticed and-not self-of-us we-humbled you-saw and-not we-fasted why? (3)

הֵן בְּיוֹם צֹמְכֶם תִּמְצְאוּ־ חֵפֶץ וְכָל־ עַצְּבֵיכֶם תִּנְגֹּשׂוּ׃
you-exploit workers-of-you and-all-of pleasure you-do fast-of-you on-day-of see!

°19 ק ניב

"Build up, build up, prepare
the road!
Remove the obstacles out of
the way of my people."
15 For this is what the high and
lofty One says—
he who lives forever, whose
name is holy:
"I live in a high and holy
place,
but also with him who is
contrite and lowly in
spirit,
to revive the spirit of the lowly
and to revive the heart of
the contrite.
16 I will not accuse forever,
nor will I always be angry,
for then the spirit of man
would grow faint before
me—
the breath of man that I
have created.
17 I was enraged by his sinful
greed;
I punished him, and hid my
face in anger,
yet he kept on in his willful
ways.
18 I have seen his ways, but I
will heal him;
I will guide him and restore
comfort to him,
19 creating praise on the lips of
the mourners in Israel.
Peace, peace, to those far and
near,"
says the LORD. "And I will
heal them."
20 But the wicked are like the
tossing sea,
which cannot rest,
whose waves cast up mire
and mud.
21 "There is no peace," says my
God, "for the wicked."

*True Fasting*

58 "Shout it aloud, do not
hold back.
Raise your voice like a
trumpet.
Declare to my people their
rebellion
and to the house of Jacob
their sins.
2 For day after day they seek me
out;
they seem eager to know my
ways,
as if they were a nation that
does what is right
and has not forsaken the
commands of its God.
They ask me for just decisions
and seem eager for God to
come near them.
3 'Why have we fasted,' they
say,
'and you have not seen it?
Why have we humbled
ourselves,
and you have not noticed?'

"Yet on the day of your
fasting, you do as you
please
and exploit all your workers.

(4) הֵן לְרִיב וּמַצָּה תָּצוּמוּ וּלְהַכּוֹת בְּאֶגְרֹף רֶשַׁע
(4) see! in-quarrel and-strife you-fast and-to-strike with-fist-of wickedness

לֹא־תָצוּמוּ כַיּוֹם לְהַשְׁמִיעַ בַּמָּרוֹם קוֹלְכֶם׃ (5) הֲכָזֶה
not you-fast as-the-day to-make-hear on-the-height voice-of-you (5) as-this?

יִהְיֶה צוֹם אֶבְחָרֵהוּ יוֹם עַנּוֹת אָדָם נַפְשׁוֹ הֲלָכֹף כְּאַגְמֹן
is-he fast I-chose-him day-of to-humble man self-of-him to-bow? like-reed

רֹאשׁוֹ וְשַׂק וָאֵפֶר יַצִּיעַ הֲלָזֶה תִּקְרָא־צוֹם וְיוֹם
head-of-him and-sackcloth and-ash he-lies-down to-this? you-call fast and-day-of

רָצוֹן לַיהוָה׃ (6) הֲלוֹא זֶה צוֹם אֶבְחָרֵהוּ פַּתֵּחַ חַרְצֻבּוֹת רֶשַׁע
acceptance to-Yahweh (6) not? this fast I-chose-him to-loose chains-of injustice

הַתֵּר אֲגֻדּוֹת מוֹטָה וְשַׁלַּח רְצוּצִים חָפְשִׁים וְכָל־מוֹטָה
to-untie cords-of yoke and-to-set-free ones-being-oppressed free-ones and-every-of yoke

תְּנַתֵּקוּ׃ (7) הֲלוֹא פָרֹס לָרָעֵב לַחְמְךָ וַעֲנִיִּים מְרוּדִים
you-break (7) not? to-share with-the-hungry food-of-you and-poor-ones wanderers

תָּבִיא בָיִת כִּי־תִרְאֶה עָרֹם וְכִסִּיתוֹ וּמִבְּשָׂרְךָ
you-provide shelter when you-see naked then-you-clothe-him and-from-flesh-of-you

לֹא תִתְעַלָּם׃ (8) אָז יִבָּקַע כַּשַּׁחַר אוֹרֶךָ
not you-turn-away (8) then he-will-break-forth like-the-dawn light-of-you

וַאֲרֻכָתְךָ מְהֵרָה תִצְמָח וְהָלַךְ לְפָנֶיךָ
and-healing-of-you quickly she-will-appear then-he-will-go before-you

צִדְקֶךָ כְּבוֹד יְהוָה יַאַסְפֶךָ׃ (9) אָז
righteousness-of-you glory-of Yahweh he-will-guard-rear-of-you (9) then

תִּקְרָא וַיהוָה יַעֲנֶה תְּשַׁוַּע וְיֹאמַר
you-will-call and-Yahweh he-will-answer you-will-cry-for-help and-he-will-say

הִנֵּנִי אִם־תָּסִיר מִתּוֹכְךָ מוֹטָה שְׁלַח אֶצְבַּע וְדַבֶּר־אָוֶן׃
here-I! if you-do-away from-among-you yoke to-point finger and-to-talk malice

(10) וְתָפֵק לָרָעֵב נַפְשֶׁךָ וְנֶפֶשׁ נַעֲנָה
(10) and-you-spend for-the-hungry self-of-you and-self-of one-being-oppressed

תַּשְׂבִּיעַ וְזָרַח בַּחֹשֶׁךְ אוֹרֶךָ וַאֲפֵלָתְךָ
you-satisfy then-he-will-rise in-the-darkness light-of-you and-night-of-you

כַּצָּהֳרָיִם׃ (11) וְנָחֲךָ יְהוָה תָּמִיד וְהִשְׂבִּיעַ
like-the-noonday (11) and-he-will-guide-you Yahweh always and-he-will-satisfy

בְּצַחְצָחוֹת נַפְשֶׁךָ וְעַצְמֹתֶיךָ יַחֲלִיץ
in-scorched-places self-of-you and-frames-of-you he-will-strengthen

וְהָיִיתָ כְּגַן רָוֶה וּכְמוֹצָא מַיִם אֲשֶׁר לֹא־
and-you-will-be like-garden well-watered and-like-spring-of waters that not

יְכַזְּבוּ מֵימָיו׃ (12) וּבָנוּ מִמְּךָ חָרְבוֹת עוֹלָם
they-fail waters-of-him (12) and-they-will-rebuild from-you ruins-of ancient

4 Your fasting ends in
quarreling and strife,
and in striking each other
with wicked fists.
You cannot fast as you do
today
and expect your voice to be
heard on high.
5 Is this the kind of fast I have
chosen,
only a day for a man to
humble himself?
Is it only for bowing one's
head like a reed
and for lying on sackcloth
and ashes?
Is that what you call a fast,
a day acceptable to the
LORD?

6 "Is not this the kind of fasting
I have chosen:
to loose the chains of injustice
and untie the cords of the
yoke,
to set the oppressed free
and break every yoke?
7 Is it not to share your food
with the hungry
and to provide the poor
wanderer with shelter—
when you see the naked, to
clothe him,
and not to turn away from
your own flesh and
blood?
8 Then your light will break
forth like the dawn,
and your healing will
quickly appear;
then your righteousness[p] will
go before you,
and the glory of the LORD
will be your rear guard.
9 Then you will call, and the
LORD will answer;
you will cry for help, and he
will say: Here am I.

"If you do away with the yoke
of oppression,
with the pointing finger and
malicious talk,
10 and if you spend yourselves in
behalf of the hungry
and satisfy the needs of the
oppressed,
then your light will rise in the
darkness,
and your night will become
like the noonday.
11 The LORD will guide you
always;
he will satisfy your needs in
a sun-scorched land
and will strengthen your
frame.
You will be like a well-watered
garden,
like a spring whose waters
never fail.
12 Your people will rebuild the
ancient ruins

p8 Or *your righteous One*

מוֹסְדֵי דוֹר־ וָדוֹר תְּקוֹמֵם וְקֹרָא
and-he-will-be-called they-will-raise-up and-generation generation foundations-of

לְךָ גֹּדֵר פֶּרֶץ מְשֹׁבֵב נְתִיבוֹת לָשָׁבֶת׃ אִם־
if (13) to-Dwell Streets One-Restoring-of Broken-Wall One-Repairing-of to-you

תָּשִׁיב מִשַּׁבָּת רַגְלֶךָ עֲשׂוֹת חֲפָצֶךָ בְּיוֹם קָדְשִׁי
holiness-of-me on-day-of pleasures-of-you to-do foot-of-you from-Sabbath you-keep

וְקָרָאתָ לַשַּׁבָּת עֹנֶג לִקְדוֹשׁ יְהוָה מְכֻבָּד
one-being-honorable Yahweh to-holy-one-of delight to-the-Sabbath if-you-call

וְכִבַּדְתּוֹ מֵעֲשׂוֹת דְּרָכֶיךָ מִמְּצוֹא חֶפְצְךָ וְדַבֵּר
or-to-speak pleasure-of-you from-to-do ways-of-you from-to-go if-you-honor-him

דָּבָר׃ אָז תִּתְעַנַּג עַל־ יְהוָה וְהִרְכַּבְתִּיךָ עַל־ בָּמֳתֵי°
heights-of on and-I-will-make-ride-you Yahweh in you-will-find-joy then (14) word

אָרֶץ וְהַאֲכַלְתִּיךָ נַחֲלַת יַעֲקֹב אָבִיךָ כִּי פִּי
mouth-of indeed father-of-you Jacob inheritance-of and-I-will-make-feast-you land

יְהוָה דִּבֵּר׃ הֵן לֹא־ קָצְרָה יַד־ יְהוָה מֵהוֹשִׁיעַ וְלֹא־
or-not from-to-save Yahweh arm-of she-is-short not surely! (59:1) he-spoke Yahweh

כָבְדָה אָזְנוֹ מִשְּׁמוֹעַ׃ כִּי אִם־ עֲוֺנֹתֵיכֶם הָיוּ
they-are iniquities-of-you rather but (2) from-to-hear ear-of-him she-is-dull

מַבְדִּלִים בֵּינֵכֶם לְבֵין אֱלֹהֵיכֶם וְחַטֹּאותֵיכֶם הִסְתִּירוּ פָנִים
faces they-hid and-sins-of-you God-of-you to-between between-you ones-separating

מִכֶּם מִשְּׁמוֹעַ׃ כִּי כַפֵּיכֶם נְגֹאֲלוּ בַדָּם
with-the-blood they-are-stained hands-of-you for (3) from-to-hear from-you

וְאֶצְבְּעוֹתֵיכֶם בֶּעָוֺן שִׂפְתוֹתֵיכֶם דִּבְּרוּ־ שֶׁקֶר לְשׁוֹנְכֶם
tongue-of-you lie they-spoke lips-of-you with-the-guilt and-fingers-of-you

עַוְלָה תֶהְגֶּה׃ אֵין־ קֹרֵא בְצֶדֶק וְאֵין
and-there-is-no for-justice one-calling there-is-no (4) she-mutters wickedness

נִשְׁפָּט בֶּאֱמוּנָה בָּטוֹחַ עַל־ תֹּהוּ וְדַבֶּר־ שָׁוְא הָרוֹ
to-conceive lie and-to-speak emptiness on to-rely with-integrity one-pleading-case

עָמָל וְהוֹלֵיד אָוֶן׃ בֵּיצֵי צִפְעוֹנִי בִּקֵּעוּ וְקוּרֵי עַכָּבִישׁ יֶאֱרֹגוּ
they-spin spider and-webs-of they-hatch viper eggs-of (5) evil and-to-bear trouble

הָאֹכֵל מִבֵּיצֵיהֶם יָמוּת וְהַזּוּרֶה תִּבָּקַע
she-is-hatched and-the-one-being-broken he-will-die of-eggs-of-them the-one-eating

אֶפְעֶה׃ קוּרֵיהֶם לֹא־ יִהְיוּ לְבֶגֶד וְלֹא יִתְכַּסּוּ
they-can-cover-themselves and-not for-clothing they-are not webs-of-them (6) adder

בְּמַעֲשֵׂיהֶם מַעֲשֵׂיהֶם מַעֲשֵׂי־ אָוֶן וּפֹעַל חָמָס
violence and-act-of evil deeds-of deeds-of-them with-things-made-of-them

בְּכַפֵּיהֶם׃ רַגְלֵיהֶם לָרַע יָרֻצוּ וִימַהֲרוּ לִשְׁפֹּךְ
to-shed and-they-are-swift they-rush to-sin feet-of-them (7) in-hands-of-them

°14 ק במתי

and will raise up the age-old foundations;
you will be called Repairer of Broken Walls,
Restorer of Streets with Dwellings.

13 "If you keep your feet from breaking the Sabbath
and from doing as you please on my holy day,
if you call the Sabbath a delight
and the LORD's holy day honorable,
and if you honor it by not going your own way
and not doing as you please or speaking idle words,
14 then you will find your joy in the LORD,
and I will cause you to ride on the heights of the land
and to feast on the inheritance of your father Jacob."
The mouth of the LORD has spoken.

*Sin, Confession and Redemption*

59 Surely the arm of the LORD is not too short to save,
nor his ear too dull to hear.
2 But your iniquities have separated
you from your God;
your sins have hidden his face from you,
so that he will not hear.
3 For your hands are stained with blood,
your fingers with guilt.
Your lips have spoken lies,
and your tongue mutters wicked things.
4 No one calls for justice;
no one pleads his case with integrity.
They rely on empty arguments and speak lies;
they conceive trouble and give birth to evil.
5 They hatch the eggs of vipers
and spin a spider's web.
Whoever eats their eggs will die,
and when one is broken, an adder is hatched.
6 Their cobwebs are useless for clothing;
they cannot cover themselves with what they make.
Their deeds are evil deeds,
and acts of violence are in their hands.
7 Their feet rush into sin;
they are swift to shed

וָשֶׁבֶר שֹׁד אָוֶן מַחְשְׁבוֹת מַחְשְׁבוֹתֵיהֶם נָקִי דָּם
and-destruction ruin evil thoughts-of thoughts-of-them innocent blood

מִשְׁפָּט וְאֵין יָדָעוּ לֹא שָׁלוֹם דֶּרֶךְ בִּמְסִלּוֹתָם׃
justice and-there-is-no they-know not peace way-of (8) in-ways-of-them

דֹּרֵךְ כֹּל לָהֶם עִקְּשׁוּ נְתִיבוֹתֵיהֶם בְּמַעְגְּלוֹתָם
one-walking every-of to-them they-made-crooked roads-of-them in-paths-of-them

וְלֹא מִמֶּנּוּ מִשְׁפָּט רָחַק כֵּן עַל־ שָׁלוֹם׃ יָדַע לֹא בָּהּ
and-not from-us justice he-is-far this for (9) peace he-will-know not on-her

חֹשֶׁךְ וְהִנֵּה־ לָאוֹר נְקַוֶּה צְדָקָה תַשִּׂיגֵנוּ
darkness but-see! for-the-light we-look righteousness she-reaches-us

כַעִוְרִים נְגַשְׁשָׁה נְהַלֵּךְ׃ בָּאֲפֵלוֹת לִנְגֹהוֹת
like-the-blind-ones we-grope (10) we-walk in-the-deep-shadows for-brightnesses

כַּנֶּשֶׁף בַצָּהֳרַיִם כָּשַׁלְנוּ נְגַשֵּׁשָׁה עֵינַיִם וּכְאֵין קִיר
as-the-twilight at-the-midday we-stumble we-feel-way eyes and-like-without wall

כַדֻּבִּים נֶהֱמֶה כַּמֵּתִים׃ בָּאַשְׁמַנִּים
like-the-bears we-growl (11) like-the-ones-being-dead among-the-strong-ones

לַמִּשְׁפָּט נְקַוֶּה נֶהְגֶּה הָגֹה וְכַיּוֹנִים כֻּלָּנוּ
for-the-justice we-look we-moan to-moan and-like-the-doves all-of-us

רַבּוּ כִּי־ מִמֶּנּוּ׃ רָחֲקָה לִישׁוּעָה וָאַיִן
they-are-many for (12) from-us she-is-far for-deliverance but-there-is-none

כִּי־ בָּנוּ עָנְתָה וְחַטֹּאותֵינוּ נֶגְדֶּךָ פְשָׁעֵינוּ
indeed against-us she-testifies and-sins-of-us before-you offenses-of-us

פָּשֹׁעַ יְדַעֲנוּם׃ וַעֲוֹנֹתֵינוּ אִתָּנוּ פְשָׁעֵינוּ
to-rebel (13) we-acknowledge-them and-iniquities-of-us with-us offenses-of-us

דַּבֶּר־ אֱלֹהֵינוּ מֵאַחַר וְנָסוֹג בַּיהוָה וְכַחֵשׁ
to-foment God-of-us from-after and-to-turn against-Yahweh and-to-be-treacherous

שָׁקֶר׃ דִּבְרֵי־ מִלֵּב וְהֹגוֹ הֹרוֹ וְסָרָה עֹשֶׁק
lie words-of from-heart and-to-utter to-conceive and-revolt oppression

כִּי־ תַּעֲמֹד מֵרָחוֹק וּצְדָקָה מִשְׁפָּט אָחוֹר וְהֻסַּג
indeed she-stands at-distance and-righteousness justice back so-he-is-driven (14)

וַתְּהִי לָבוֹא׃ תוּכַל לֹא־ וּנְכֹחָה אֱמֶת בָרְחוֹב כָשְׁלָה
and-she-is (15) to-enter she-can not and-honesty truth in-the-street she-stumbled

מִשְׁתּוֹלֵל מֵרָע וְסָר נֶעְדֶּרֶת הָאֱמֶת
one-becoming-prey from-evil and-one-shunning one-being-not-found the-truth

אֵין כִּי־ בְּעֵינָיו וַיֵּרַע יְהוָה וַיַּרְא
there-was-no that in-eyes-of-him and-he-was-displeasing Yahweh and-he-looked

אֵין כִּי וַיִּשְׁתּוֹמֵם אִישׁ אֵין כִּי־ וַיַּרְא מִשְׁפָּט׃
there-was-no that and-he-was-appalled one there-was-no that and-he-saw (16) justice

innocent blood.
Their thoughts are evil
thoughts;
ruin and destruction mark
their ways.
8 The way of peace they do not
know;
there is no justice in their
paths.
They have turned them into
crooked roads;
no one who walks in them
will know peace.

9 So justice is far from us,
and righteousness does not
reach us.
We look for light, but all is
darkness;
for brightness, but we walk
in deep shadows.
10 Like the blind we grope along
the wall,
feeling our way like men
without eyes.
At midday we stumble as if it
were twilight;
among the strong, we are
like the dead.
11 We all growl like bears;
we moan mournfully like
doves.
We look for justice, but find
none;
for deliverance, but it is far
away.

12 For our offenses are many in
your sight,
and our sins testify against
us.
Our offenses are ever with us,
and we acknowledge our
iniquities:
13 rebellion and treachery against
the LORD,
turning our backs on our
God,
fomenting oppression and
revolt,
uttering lies our hearts have
conceived.
14 So justice is driven back,
and righteousness stands at
a distance;
truth has stumbled in the
streets,
honesty cannot enter.
15 Truth is nowhere to be found,
and whoever shuns evil
becomes a prey.

The LORD looked and was
displeased
that there was no justice.
16 He saw that there was no one,
he was appalled that there

מַפְגִּיעַ וַתּוֹשַׁע לוֹ זְרֹעוֹ וְצִדְקָתוֹ
and-righteousness-of-him arm-of-him for-him so-she-worked-salvation one-intervening

הִיא סְמָכָתְהוּ׃ (17) וַיִּלְבַּשׁ צְדָקָה כַּשִּׁרְיָן
as-the-breastplate righteousness and-he-put-on (17) she-sustained-him she

וְכוֹבַע יְשׁוּעָה בְּרֹאשׁוֹ וַיִּלְבַּשׁ בִּגְדֵי נָקָם
vengeance garments-of and-he-put-on on-head-of-him salvation and-helmet-of

תִּלְבֹּשֶׁת וַיַּעַט כַּמְעִיל קִנְאָה׃ (18) כְּעַל גְּמֻלוֹת כְּעַל
so-accordingly deeds as-according-to (18) zeal as-the-cloak and-he-wrapped clothing

יְשַׁלֵּם חֵמָה לְצָרָיו גְּמוּל לְאֹיְבָיו
to-ones-being-foes-of-him retribution to-enemies-of-him wrath he-will-repay

לָאִיִּים גְּמוּל יְשַׁלֵּם׃ (19) וְיִירְאוּ מִמַּעֲרָב אֶת־ שֵׁם
name-of *** from-west and-they-will-fear (19) he-will-repay due to-the-islands

יְהוָה וּמִמִּזְרַח־ שֶׁמֶשׁ אֶת־ כְּבוֹדוֹ כִּי־ יָבוֹא כַנָּהָר
like-the-flood he-will-come for glory-of-him *** sun and-from-rising-of Yahweh

צָר רוּחַ יְהוָה נֹסְסָה בוֹ׃ (20) וּבָא לְצִיּוֹן
to-Zion and-he-will-come (20) to-him she-drives-along Yahweh breath-of pent-up

גּוֹאֵל וּלְשָׁבֵי פֶשַׁע בְּיַעֲקֹב נְאֻם יְהוָה׃
Yahweh declaration-of in-Jacob sin and-to-ones-repenting-of One-Redeeming

(21) וַאֲנִי זֹאת בְּרִיתִי אוֹתָם אָמַר יְהוָה רוּחִי אֲשֶׁר עָלֶיךָ
on-you who Spirit-of-me Yahweh he-says *them covenant-of-me this and-I (21)

וּדְבָרַי אֲשֶׁר־ שַׂמְתִּי בְּפִיךָ לֹא־ יָמוּשׁוּ מִפִּיךָ
from-mouth-of-you they-will-depart not in-mouth-of-you I-put that and-words-of-me

וּמִפִּי זַרְעֲךָ וּמִפִּי זֶרַע זַרְעֲךָ אָמַר
he-says child-of-you child-of or-from-mouth-of child-of-you or-from-mouth-of

יְהוָה מֵעַתָּה וְעַד־ עוֹלָם׃ (60:1) קוּמִי אוֹרִי כִּי בָא אוֹרֵךְ
light-of-you he-came for shine! arise! (60:1) forever and-to from-now Yahweh

וּכְבוֹד יְהוָה עָלַיִךְ זָרָח׃ (2) כִּי־ הִנֵּה הַחֹשֶׁךְ יְכַסֶּה־
he-covers the-darkness see! indeed (2) he-rises upon-you Yahweh and-glory-of

אֶרֶץ וַעֲרָפֶל לְאֻמִּים וְעָלַיִךְ יִזְרַח יְהוָה וּכְבוֹדוֹ
and-glory-of-him Yahweh he-rises but-upon-you peoples and-thick-darkness earth

עָלַיִךְ יֵרָאֶה׃ (3) וְהָלְכוּ גוֹיִם לְאוֹרֵךְ וּמְלָכִים
and-kings to-light-of-you nations and-they-will-come (3) he-appears over-you

לְנֹגַהּ זַרְחֵךְ׃ (4) שְׂאִי־ סָבִיב עֵינַיִךְ וּרְאִי כֻּלָּם
all-of-them and-look! eyes-of-you about lift-up! (4) dawn-of-you to-brightness-of

נִקְבְּצוּ בָאוּ־ לָךְ בָּנַיִךְ מֵרָחוֹק יָבֹאוּ וּבְנֹתַיִךְ
and-daughters-of-you they-come from-afar sons-of-you to-you they-come they-assemble

עַל־ צַד תֵּאָמַנָה׃ (5) אָז תִּרְאִי וְנָהַרְתְּ
and-you-will-be-radiant you-will-look then (5) they-are-carried side at

was no one to intervene;
so his own arm worked
salvation for him,
and his own righteousness
sustained him.
17 He put on righteousness as his
breastplate,
and the helmet of salvation
on his head;
he put on the garments of
vengeance
and wrapped himself in zeal
as in a cloak.
18 According to what they have
done,
so will he repay
wrath to his enemies
and retribution to his foes;
he will repay the islands
their due.
19 From the west, men will fear
the name of the LORD,
and from the rising of the
sun, they will revere his
glory.
For he will come like a
pent-up flood
that the breath of the LORD
drives along.[q]
20 "The Redeemer will come to
Zion,
to those in Jacob who repent
of their sins,"
declares the LORD.

21 "As for me, this is my covenant with them," says the LORD. "My Spirit, who is on you, and my words that I have put in your mouth will not depart from your mouth, or from the mouths of your children, or from the mouths of their descendants from this time on and forever," says the LORD.

*The Glory of Zion*

60 "Arise, shine, for your
light has come,
and the glory of the LORD
rises upon you.
2 See, darkness covers the earth
and thick darkness is over
the peoples,
but the LORD rises upon you
and his glory appears over
you.
3 Nations will come to your
light,
and kings to the brightness
of your dawn.

4 "Lift up your eyes and look
about you:
All assemble and come to
you;
your sons come from afar,
and your daughters are
carried on the arm.
5 Then you will look and be
radiant,

q19 Or *When the enemy comes in like a flood, / the Spirit of the LORD will put him to flight*

*21 The NIV, with many ancient versions, repoints this word as אִתָּם, *with-them*.

וּפָחַד וְרָחַב לְבָבֵךְ כִּי־ יֵהָפֵךְ עָלַיִךְ
to-you he-will-be-brought indeed heart-of-you and-he-will-swell and-he-will-throb

הֲמוֹן יָם חֵיל גּוֹיִם יָבֹאוּ לָךְ׃ שִׁפְעַת גְּמַלִּים
camels herd-of (6) to-you they-will-come nations richness-of sea wealth-of

תְּכַסֵּךְ בִּכְרֵי מִדְיָן וְעֵיפָה כֻּלָּם מִשְּׁבָא
from-Sheba all-of-them and-Ephah Midian young-camels-of she-will-cover-you

יָבֹאוּ זָהָב וּלְבוֹנָה יִשָּׂאוּ וּתְהִלֹּת יְהוָה
Yahweh and-praises-of they-will-bear and-incense gold they-will-come

יְבַשֵּׂרוּ׃ כָּל־ צֹאן קֵדָר יִקָּבְצוּ לָךְ אֵילֵי
rams-of to-you they-will-be-gathered Kedar flock-of all-of (7) they-will-proclaim

נְבָיוֹת יְשָׁרְתוּנֶךְ יַעֲלוּ עַל־ רָצוֹן מִזְבְּחִי
altar-of-me acceptance for they-will-offer they-will-serve-you Nebaioth

וּבֵית תִּפְאַרְתִּי אֲפָאֵר׃ מִי־ אֵלֶּה כָּעָב תְּעוּפֶינָה
they-fly like-the-cloud these who? (8) I-will-adorn glory-of-me and-temple-of

וְכַיּוֹנִים אֶל־ אֲרֻבֹּתֵיהֶם׃ כִּי־ לִי ׀ אִיִּים יְקַוּוּ
they-look islands to-me surely (9) nests-of-them to and-like-the-doves

וָאֳנִיּוֹת תַּרְשִׁישׁ בָּרִאשֹׁנָה לְהָבִיא בָנַיִךְ מֵרָחוֹק כַּסְפָּם
silver-of-them from-afar sons-of-you to-bring in-the-lead Tarshish and-ships-of

וּזְהָבָם אִתָּם לְשֵׁם יְהוָה אֱלֹהַיִךְ וְלִקְדוֹשׁ יִשְׂרָאֵל
Israel and-to-Holy-One-of God-of-you Yahweh to-honor-of with-them and-gold-of-them

כִּי פֵאֲרָךְ׃ וּבָנוּ בְנֵי־ נֵכָר
foreigner sons-of and-they-will-rebuild (10) he-endowed-with-splendor-you for

חֹמֹתַיִךְ וּמַלְכֵיהֶם יְשָׁרְתוּנֶךְ כִּי בְקִצְפִּי
in-anger-of-me though they-will-serve-you and-kings-of-them walls-of-you

הִכִּיתִיךְ וּבִרְצוֹנִי רִחַמְתִּיךְ׃
I-will-show-compassion-to-you but-in-favor-of-me I-struck-you

וּפִתְּחוּ שְׁעָרַיִךְ תָּמִיד יוֹמָם וָלַיְלָה לֹא
never or-night by-day always gates-of-you and-they-will-stand-open (11)

יִסָּגֵרוּ לְהָבִיא אֵלַיִךְ חֵיל גּוֹיִם וּמַלְכֵיהֶם נְהוּגִים׃
ones-being-led and-kings-of-them nations wealth-of to-you to-bring they-will-be-shut

כִּי־ הַגּוֹי וְהַמַּמְלָכָה אֲשֶׁר לֹא־ יַעַבְדוּךְ יֹאבֵדוּ
they-will-perish they-will-serve-you not that or-the-kingdom the-nation for (12)

וְהַגּוֹיִם חָרֹב יֶחֱרָבוּ׃ כְּבוֹד הַלְּבָנוֹן אֵלַיִךְ
to-you the-Lebanon glory-of (13) they-will-be-ruined to-be-ruined and-the-nations

יָבוֹא בְּרוֹשׁ תִּדְהָר וּתְאַשּׁוּר יַחְדָּו לְפָאֵר מְקוֹם מִקְדָּשִׁי
sanctuary-of-me place-of to-adorn together and-cypress fir pine he-will-come

וּמְקוֹם רַגְלַי אֲכַבֵּד׃ וְהָלְכוּ אֵלַיִךְ שְׁחוֹחַ
to-bow to-you and-they-will-come (14) I-will-glorify feet-of-me and-place-of

your heart will throb and
swell with joy;
the wealth on the seas will be
brought to you,
to you the riches of the
nations will come.
6 Herds of camels will cover
your land,
young camels of Midian and
Ephah.
And all from Sheba will come,
bearing gold and incense
and proclaiming the praise
of the LORD.
7 All Kedar's flocks will be
gathered to you,
the rams of Nebaioth will
serve you;
they will be accepted as
offerings on my altar,
and I will adorn my glorious
temple.
8 "Who are these that fly along
like clouds,
like doves to their nests?
9 Surely the islands look to me;
in the lead are the ships of
Tarshish,[r]
bringing your sons from afar,
with their silver and gold,
to the honor of the LORD your
God,
the Holy One of Israel,
for he has endowed you
with splendor.

10 "Foreigners will rebuild your
walls,
and their kings will serve
you.
Though in anger I struck you,
in favor I will show you
compassion.
11 Your gates will always stand
open,
they will never be shut, day
or night,
so that men may bring you the
wealth of the nations—
their kings led in triumphal
procession.
12 For the nation or kingdom
that will not serve you
will perish;
it will be utterly ruined.
13 "The glory of Lebanon will
come to you,
the pine, the fir and the
cypress together,
to adorn the place of my
sanctuary;
and I will glorify the place
of my feet.
14 The sons of your oppressors
will come bowing before
you;

[r]9 *Or the trading ships*

בְּנֵי מְעַנַּיִךְ וְהִשְׁתַּחֲווּ עַל־ כַּפּוֹת רַגְלַיִךְ כָּל־
all-of feet-of-you soles-of at and-they-will-bow-down ones-oppressing-you sons-of

מְנַאֲצָיִךְ וְקָרְאוּ לָךְ עִיר יְהוָה צִיּוֹן קְדוֹשׁ
Holy-One-of Zion-of Yahweh City-of to-you and-they-will-call ones-despising-you

יִשְׂרָאֵל׃ (15) תַּחַת הֱיוֹתֵךְ עֲזוּבָה וּשְׂנוּאָה וְאֵין
with-no and-one-being-hated one-being-forsaken to-be-you although (15) Israel

עוֹבֵר וְשַׂמְתִּיךְ לִגְאוֹן עוֹלָם מְשׂוֹשׂ דּוֹר
generation joy-of everlasting as-pride-of but-I-will-make-you one-traveling-through

וָדוֹר׃ (16) וְיָנַקְתְּ חֲלֵב גּוֹיִם וְשֹׁד מְלָכִים
royalties and-breast-of nations milk-of and-you-will-drink (16) and-generation

תִּינָקִי וְיָדַעַתְּ כִּי אֲנִי יְהוָה מוֹשִׁיעֵךְ וְגֹאֲלֵךְ
and-One-Redeeming-you One-Saving-you Yahweh I that then-you-will-know you-will-nurse

אֲבִיר יַעֲקֹב׃ (17) תַּחַת הַנְּחֹשֶׁת אָבִיא זָהָב וְתַחַת
and-instead-of gold I-will-bring the-bronze instead-of (17) Jacob Mighty-One-of

הַבַּרְזֶל אָבִיא כֶסֶף וְתַחַת הָעֵצִים נְחֹשֶׁת וְתַחַת
and-instead-of bronze the-woods and-instead-of silver I-will-bring the-iron

הָאֲבָנִים בַּרְזֶל וְשַׂמְתִּי פְקֻדָּתֵךְ שָׁלוֹם וְנֹגְשַׂיִךְ
and-ones-ruling-you peace governor-of-you and-I-will-make iron the-stones

צְדָקָה׃ (18) לֹא־ יִשָּׁמַע עוֹד חָמָס בְּאַרְצֵךְ שֹׁד
ruin in-land-of-you violence longer he-will-be-heard not (18) righteousness

וָשֶׁבֶר בִּגְבוּלָיִךְ וְקָרָאת יְשׁוּעָה חוֹמֹתַיִךְ
walls-of-you Salvation but-you-will-call within-borders-of-you or-destruction

וּשְׁעָרַיִךְ תְּהִלָּה׃ (19) לֹא־ יִהְיֶה־ לָּךְ עוֹד הַשֶּׁמֶשׁ לְאוֹר יוֹמָם
by-day as-light the-sun more for-you he-will-be not (19) Praise and-gates-of-you

וּלְנֹגַהּ הַיָּרֵחַ לֹא־ יָאִיר לָךְ וְהָיָה־ לָךְ
for-you for-he-will-be on-you he-will-shine not the-moon or-as-brightness-of

יְהוָה לְאוֹר עוֹלָם וֵאלֹהַיִךְ לְתִפְאַרְתֵּךְ׃ (20) לֹא־ יָבוֹא
he-will-set not (20) as-glory-of-you and-God-of-you everlasting as-light-of Yahweh

עוֹד שִׁמְשֵׁךְ וִירֵחֵךְ לֹא יֵאָסֵף כִּי יְהוָה יִהְיֶה־
he-will-be Yahweh for he-will-wane not and-moon-of-you sun-of-you again

לָּךְ לְאוֹר עוֹלָם וְשָׁלְמוּ יְמֵי אֶבְלֵךְ׃
sorrow-of-you days-of and-they-will-end everlasting as-light-of for-you

(21) וְעַמֵּךְ כֻּלָּם צַדִּיקִים לְעוֹלָם יִירְשׁוּ
they-will-possess to-forever righteous-ones all-of-them then-people-of-you (21)

אָרֶץ נֵצֶר מַטָּעַו מַעֲשֵׂה יָדַי לְהִתְפָּאֵר׃ (22) הַקָּטֹן
the-least (22) to-display-splendor hands-of-me work-of planting-of-me shoot-of land

יִהְיֶה לָאֶלֶף וְהַצָּעִיר לְגוֹי עָצוּם אֲנִי יְהוָה
Yahweh I mighty as-nation and-the-smallest as-thousand he-will-become

all who despise you will
bow down at your feet
and will call you The City of
the LORD,
Zion of the Holy One of
Israel.

15"Although you have been
forsaken and hated,
with no one traveling
through,
I will make you the everlasting
pride
and the joy of all
generations.

16You will drink the milk of
nations
and be nursed at royal
breasts.
Then you will know that I, the
LORD, am your Savior,
your Redeemer, the Mighty
One of Jacob.

17Instead of bronze I will bring
you gold,
and silver in place of iron.
Instead of wood I will bring
you bronze,
and iron in place of stones.
I will make peace your
governor
and righteousness your
ruler.

18No longer will violence be
heard in your land,
nor ruin or destruction
within your borders,
but you will call your walls
Salvation
and your gates Praise.

19The sun will no more be your
light by day,
nor will the brightness of
the moon shine on you,
for the LORD will be your
everlasting light,
and your God will be your
glory.

20Your sun will never set again,
and your moon will wane
no more;
the LORD will be your
everlasting light,
and your days of sorrow
will end.

21Then will all your people be
righteous
and they will possess the
land forever.
They are the shoot I have
planted,
the work of my hands,
for the display of my
splendor.

22The least of you will become a
thousand,
the smallest a mighty
nation.
I am the LORD;

°21 ק מטעי

בְּעִתָּהּ אֲחִישֶׁנָּה׃ רוּחַ אֲדֹנָי יְהוִה עָלָי
on-me Yahweh Sovereign Spirit-of (61:1) I-will-do-swiftly-her in-time-of-her

יַעַן מָשַׁח יְהוָה אֹתִי לְבַשֵּׂר עֲנָוִים שְׁלָחַנִי
he-sent-me poor-ones to-preach-good-news me Yahweh he-anointed because

לַחֲבֹשׁ לְנִשְׁבְּרֵי־לֵב לִקְרֹא לִשְׁבוּיִם דְּרוֹר
freedom for-ones-being-captive to-proclaim heart to-ones-being-broken-of to-bind-up

וְלַאֲסוּרִים פְּקַח־קוֹחַ׃ לִקְרֹא שְׁנַת־רָצוֹן לַיהוָה
of-Yahweh favor year-of to-proclaim (2) release and-for-ones-being-imprisoned

וְיוֹם נָקָם לֵאלֹהֵינוּ לְנַחֵם כָּל־אֲבֵלִים׃ לָשׂוּם
to-provide (3) mourners all-of to-comfort of-God-of-us vengeance and-day-of

לַאֲבֵלֵי צִיּוֹן לָתֵת לָהֶם פְּאֵר תַּחַת אֵפֶר שֶׁמֶן שָׂשׂוֹן
gladness oil-of ash instead-of beauty on-them to-bestow Zion for-grievers-of

תַּחַת אֵבֶל מַעֲטֵה תְהִלָּה תַּחַת רוּחַ כֵּהָה וְקֹרָא
and-he-will-be-called despair spirit-of instead-of praise garment-of mourning instead-of

לָהֶם אֵילֵי הַצֶּדֶק מַטַּע יְהוָה לְהִתְפָּאֵר׃
to-display-splendor Yahweh planting-of the-righteousness oaks-of to-them

וּבָנוּ חָרְבוֹת עוֹלָם שֹׁמְמוֹת רִאשֹׁנִים
long-ago-ones ones-being-devasted-of ancient ruins-of and-they-will-rebuild (4)

יְקוֹמֵמוּ וְחִדְּשׁוּ עָרֵי חֹרֶב שֹׁמְמוֹת
ones-being-devasted-of ruin cities-of and-they-will-renew they-will-restore

דּוֹר וָדוֹר׃ וְעָמְדוּ זָרִים
ones-being-alien and-they-will-stand (5) and-generation generation

וְרָעוּ צֹאנְכֶם וּבְנֵי נֵכָר אִכָּרֵיכֶם
field-workers-of-you foreigner and-sons-of flock-of-you and-they-will-shepherd

וְכֹרְמֵיכֶם׃ וְאַתֶּם כֹּהֲנֵי יְהוָה תִּקָּרֵאוּ
you-will-be-called Yahweh priests-of and-you (6) and-ones-working-vineyards-of-you

מְשָׁרְתֵי אֱלֹהֵינוּ יֵאָמֵר לָכֶם חֵיל גּוֹיִם
nations wealth-of to-you he-will-be-named God-of-us ones-ministering-of

תֹּאכֵלוּ וּבִכְבוֹדָם תִּתְיַמָּרוּ׃ תַּחַת
instead-of (7) you-will-boast and-in-richness-of-them you-will-feed-on

בָּשְׁתְּכֶם מִשְׁנֶה וּכְלִמָּה יָרֹנּוּ חֶלְקָם
inheritance-of-them they-will-rejoice and-disgrace double-portion shame-of-them

לָכֵן בְּאַרְצָם מִשְׁנֶה יִירָשׁוּ שִׂמְחַת עוֹלָם תִּהְיֶה
she-will-be everlasting joy-of they-will-inherit double-portion in-land-of-them so

לָהֶם׃ כִּי אֲנִי יְהוָה אֹהֵב מִשְׁפָּט שֹׂנֵא גָזֵל בְּעוֹלָה
in-iniquity robbery hating justice loving Yahweh I for (8) for-them

וְנָתַתִּי פְעֻלָּתָם בֶּאֱמֶת וּבְרִית עוֹלָם
everlasting and-covenant-of in-faithfulness reward-of-them and-I-will-give

in its time I will do this
swiftly."

*The Year of the LORD's Favor*

61 The Spirit of the
Sovereign LORD is on me,
because the LORD has
anointed me
to preach good news to the
poor.
He has sent me to bind up the
brokenhearted,
to proclaim freedom for the
captives
and release from darkness for
the prisoners,[s]
2 to proclaim the year of the
LORD's favor
and the day of vengeance of
our God,
to comfort all who mourn,
3 and provide for those who
grieve in Zion—
to bestow on them a crown of
beauty
instead of ashes,
the oil of gladness
instead of mourning,
and a garment of praise
instead of a spirit of despair.
They will be called oaks of
righteousness,
a planting of the LORD
for the display of his
splendor.

4 They will rebuild the ancient
ruins
and restore the places long
devastated;
they will renew the ruined
cities
that have been devastated
for generations.
5 Aliens will shepherd your
flocks;
foreigners will work your
fields and vineyards.
6 And you will be called priests
of the LORD,
you will be named ministers
of our God.
You will feed on the wealth of
nations,
and in their riches you will
boast.

7 Instead of their shame
my people will receive a
double portion,
and instead of disgrace
they will rejoice in their
inheritance;
and so they will inherit a
double portion in their
land,
and everlasting joy will be
theirs.

8 "For I, the LORD, love justice;
I hate robbery and iniquity.
In my faithfulness I will
reward them
and make an everlasting

[s] 1 Hebrew; Septuagint *the blind*

אֶכְרוֹת לָהֶם׃ וְנוֹדַע בַּגּוֹיִם זַרְעָם
descendant-of-them among-the-nations and-he-will-be-known (9) with-them I-will-make

וְצֶאֱצָאֵיהֶם בְּתוֹךְ הָעַמִּים כָּל־ רֹאֵיהֶם
ones-seeing-them all-of the-peoples among and-offsprings-of-them

יַכִּירוּם כִּי הֵם זֶרַע בֵּרַךְ יְהוָה׃ שׂוֹשׂ
to-delight (10) Yahweh he-blessed people they that they-will-acknowledge-them

אָשִׂישׂ בַּיהוָה תָּגֵל נַפְשִׁי בֵּאלֹהַי כִּי הִלְבִּישַׁנִי
he-clothed-me for in-God-of-me soul-of-me she-rejoices in-Yahweh I-delight

בִּגְדֵי־ יֶשַׁע מְעִיל צְדָקָה יְעָטָנִי כֶּחָתָן
as-the-bridegroom he-arrayed-me righteousness robe-of salvation garments-of

יְכַהֵן פְּאֵר וְכַכַּלָּה תַּעְדֶּה כֵלֶיהָ׃
jewels-of-her she-adorns-herself and-as-the-bride headdress he-is-like-priest

כִּי כָאָרֶץ תּוֹצִיא צִמְחָהּ וּכְגַנָּה זֵרוּעֶיהָ
seeds-of-her and-as-garden sprout-of-her she-makes-come-up as-the-soil for (11)

תַצְמִיחַ כֵּן ׀ אֲדֹנָי יְהוִה יַצְמִיחַ צְדָקָה וּתְהִלָּה
and-praise righteousness he-will-make-spring-up Yahweh Sovereign so she-makes-grow

נֶגֶד כָּל־ הַגּוֹיִם׃ לְמַעַן צִיּוֹן לֹא אֶחֱשֶׁה
I-will-keep-silent not Zion for-sake-of (62:1) the-nations all-of before

וּלְמַעַן יְרוּשָׁלַםִ לֹא אֶשְׁקוֹט עַד־ יֵצֵא כַנֹּגַהּ
like-the-dawn he-comes-out till I-will-remain-quiet not Jerusalem and-for-sake-of

צִדְקָהּ וִישׁוּעָתָהּ כְּלַפִּיד יִבְעָר׃ וְרָאוּ
and-they-will-see (2) he-blazes like-torch and-salvation-of-her righteousness-of-her

גוֹיִם צִדְקֵךְ וְכָל־ מְלָכִים כְּבוֹדֵךְ וְקֹרָא
and-he-will-be-called glory-of-you kings and-all-of righteousness-of-you nations

לָךְ שֵׁם חָדָשׁ אֲשֶׁר פִּי יְהוָה יִקֳּבֶנּוּ׃ וְהָיִיתְ*
and-you-will-be (3) he-will-bestow-him Yahweh mouth-of that new name to-you

עֲטֶרֶת תִּפְאֶרֶת בְּיַד־ יְהוָה וּצְנִוף° מְלוּכָה בְּכַף־ אֱלֹהָיִךְ׃
God-of-you in-hand-of royalty and-diadem-of Yahweh in-hand-of splendor crown-of

לֹא־ יֵאָמֵר לָךְ עוֹד עֲזוּבָה וּלְאַרְצֵךְ לֹא־
not or-to-land-of-you One-Being-Deserted longer to-you he-will-be-called not (4)

יֵאָמֵר עוֹד שְׁמָמָה כִּי לָךְ יִקָּרֵא חֶפְצִי־ בָהּ
Bah Hephzi he-will-be-called to-you but Desolation longer he-will-be-named

וּלְאַרְצֵךְ בְּעוּלָה כִּי־ חָפֵץ יְהוָה בָּךְ וְאַרְצֵךְ
and-land-of-you in-you Yahweh he-will-take-delight for Beulah and-to-land-of-you

תִּבָּעֵל׃ כִּי־ יִבְעַל בָּחוּר בְּתוּלָה יִבְעָלוּךְ
they-will-marry-you maiden young-man he-marries as (5) she-will-be-married

בָּנָיִךְ וּמְשׂוֹשׂ חָתָן עַל־ כַּלָּה יָשִׂישׂ עָלָיִךְ
over-you he-will-rejoice bride over bridegroom and-rejoicing-of sons-of-you

covenant with them.
9 Their descendants will be known among the nations
and their offspring among the peoples.
All who see them will acknowledge
that they are a people the LORD has blessed."

10 I delight greatly in the LORD;
my soul rejoices in my God.
For he has clothed me with garments of salvation
and arrayed me in a robe of righteousness,
as a bridegroom adorns his head like a priest,
and as a bride adorns herself with her jewels.
11 For as the soil makes the sprout come up
and a garden causes seeds to grow,
so the Sovereign LORD will make righteousness and praise
spring up before all nations.

*Zion's New Name*

62 For Zion's sake I will not keep silent,
for Jerusalem's sake I will not remain quiet,
till her righteousness shines out like the dawn,
her salvation like a blazing torch.
2 The nations will see your righteousness,
and all kings your glory;
you will be called by a new name
that the mouth of the LORD will bestow.
3 You will be a crown of splendor in the LORD's hand,
a royal diadem in the hand of your God.
4 No longer will they call you Deserted,
or name your land Desolate.
But you will be called Hephzibah,[u]
and your land Beulah[v];
for the LORD will take delight in you,
and your land will be married.
5 As a young man marries a maiden,
so will your sons[w] marry you;
as a bridegroom rejoices over his bride,
so will your God rejoice over you.

u4 *Hephzibah* means *my delight is in her.*
v4 *Beulah* means *married.*
w5 Or *Builder*

*3 Most mss have no *sheva* under the *tav* (־יית).

°3 ק וצניף

אֱלֹהָיִךְ׃ עַל־ חוֹמֹתַיִךְ יְרוּשָׁלַ͏ִם הִפְקַדְתִּי שֹׁמְרִים כָּל־ הַיּוֹם
the-day all-of men-watching I-posted Jerusalem walls-of-you on (6) God-of-you

וְכָל־ הַלַּיְלָה תָּמִיד לֹא יֶחֱשׁוּ הַמַּזְכִּרִים אֶת־
*** the-ones-calling-on they-will-be-silent not always the-night and-all-of

יְהוָה אַל־ דֳּמִי לָכֶם׃ וְאַל־ תִּתְּנוּ דֳמִי לוֹ עַד־ יְכוֹנֵן
he-establishes till to-him rest you-give and-not (7) to-you rest not Yahweh

וְעַד־ יָשִׂים אֶת־ יְרוּשָׁלַ͏ִם תְּהִלָּה בָּאָרֶץ׃ נִשְׁבַּע יְהוָה
Yahweh he-swore (8) of-the-earth praise Jerusalem *** he-makes and-till

בִּימִינוֹ וּבִזְרוֹעַ עֻזּוֹ אִם־ אֶתֵּן אֶת־ דְּגָנֵךְ
grain-of-you *** I-will-give never might-of-him and-by-arm-of by-right-hand-of-him

עוֹד מַאֲכָל לְאֹיְבַיִךְ וְאִם־ יִשְׁתּוּ בְנֵי־
sons-of they-will-drink and-never for-ones-being-enemies-of-you food again

נֵכָר תִּירוֹשֵׁךְ אֲשֶׁר יָגַעַתְּ בּוֹ׃ כִּי מְאַסְפָיו
ones-harvesting-him but (9) for-him you-toiled which new-wine-of-you foreigner

יֹאכְלֻהוּ וְהִלְלוּ אֶת־ יְהוָה וּמְקַבְּצָיו
and-ones-gathering-him Yahweh *** and-they-will-praise they-will-eat-him

יִשְׁתֻּהוּ בְּחַצְרוֹת קָדְשִׁי׃ עִבְרוּ עִבְרוּ
pass-through! pass-through! (10) sanctuary-of-me in-courts-of they-will-drink-him

בַּשְּׁעָרִים פַּנּוּ דֶּרֶךְ הָעָם סֹלּוּ סֹלּוּ הַמְסִלָּה
the-highway build-up! build-up! the-people way-of prepare! through-the-gates

סַקְּלוּ מֵאֶבֶן הָרִימוּ נֵס עַל־ הָעַמִּים׃ הִנֵּה יְהוָה הִשְׁמִיעַ
he-proclaimed Yahweh see! (11) the-nations for banner raise! from-stone remove!

אֶל־קְצֵה הָאָרֶץ אִמְרוּ לְבַת־ צִיּוֹן הִנֵּה יִשְׁעֵךְ בָּא הִנֵּה
see! coming Salvation-of-you see! Zion to-Daughter-of say! the-earth end-of to

שְׂכָרוֹ אִתּוֹ וּפְעֻלָּתוֹ לְפָנָיו׃ וְקָרְאוּ
and-they-will-call (12) accompanying-him and-recompense-of-him with-him reward-of-him

לָהֶם עַם־ הַקֹּדֶשׁ גְּאוּלֵי יְהוָה וְלָךְ
and-to-you Yahweh Ones-Being-Redeemed-of the-Holiness People-of to-them

יִקָּרֵא דְרוּשָׁה עִיר לֹא נֶעֱזָבָה׃ מִי־ זֶה
this who? (63:1) She-Is-Deserted Not City One-Being-Sought he-will-be-called

בָּא מֵאֱדוֹם חֲמוּץ בְּגָדִים מִבָּצְרָה זֶה הָדוּר
being-splendid this from-Bozrah garments one-being-crimson-of from-Edom coming

בִּלְבוּשׁוֹ צֹעֶה בְּרֹב כֹּחוֹ אֲנִי מְדַבֵּר
speaking I strength-of-him in-greatness-of striding-forward in-robe-of-him

בִּצְדָקָה רַב לְהוֹשִׁיעַ׃ מַדּוּעַ אָדֹם לִלְבוּשֶׁךָ וּבְגָדֶיךָ
and-garments-of-you to-robe-of-you red why? (2) to-save mighty in-righteousness

כְּדֹרֵךְ בְּגַת׃ פּוּרָה ׀ דָּרַכְתִּי לְבַדִּי וּמֵעַמִּים
and-from-nations alone-I I-trod winepress (3) in-winepress like-one-treading

[6]I have posted watchmen on
your walls, O Jerusalem;
they will never be silent day
or night.
You who call on the LORD,
give yourselves no rest,
[7]and give him no rest till he
establishes Jerusalem
and makes her the praise of
the earth.

[8]The LORD has sworn by his
right hand
and by his mighty arm:
"Never again will I give your
grain
as food for your enemies,
and never again will
foreigners drink the new
wine
for which you have toiled;
[9]but those who harvest it will
eat it
and praise the LORD,
and those who gather the
grapes will drink it
in the courts of my
sanctuary."

[10]Pass through, pass through the
gates!
Prepare the way for the
people.
Build up, build up the
highway!
Remove the stones.
Raise a banner for the nations.

[11]The LORD has made
proclamation
to the ends of the earth:
"Say to the Daughter of Zion,
'See, your Savior comes!
See, his reward is with him,
and his recompense
accompanies him.'"
[12]They will be called the Holy
People,
the Redeemed of the LORD;
and you will be called Sought
After,
the City No Longer
Deserted.

*God's Day of Vengeance and Redemption*

63 Who is this coming from
Edom,
from Bozrah, with his
garments stained
crimson?
Who is this, robed in splendor,
striding forward in the
greatness of his strength?

"It is I, speaking in
righteousness,
mighty to save."

[2]Why are your garments red,
like those of one treading
the winepress?

[3]"I have trodden the winepress
alone;

אֵין־ אִישׁ אִתִּי וְאֶדְרְכֵם בְּאַפִּי וְאֶרְמְסֵם
and-I-trod-down-them in-anger-of-me and-I-trampled-them with-me one there-was-no

בַּחֲמָתִי וְיֵז נִצְחָם עַל־ בְּגָדַי וְכָל־
and-all-of garments-of-me on blood-of-them and-he-spattered in-wrath-of-me

מַלְבּוּשַׁי אֶגְאָלְתִּי׃ (4) כִּי יוֹם נָקָם בְּלִבִּי וּשְׁנַת
and-year-of in-heart-of-me vengeance day-of for (4) I-stained clothings-of-me

גְּאוּלַי בָּאָה׃ (5) וְאַבִּיט וְאֵין עֹזֵר
one-helping but-there-was-no and-I-looked (5) she-came redemptions-of-me

וְאֶשְׁתּוֹמֵם וְאֵין סוֹמֵךְ וַתּוֹשַׁע
so-she-worked-salvation one-giving-support that-there-was-no and-I-was-appalled

לִי זְרֹעִי וַחֲמָתִי הִיא סְמָכָתְנִי׃ (6) וְאָבוּס עַמִּים
nations and-I-trampled (6) she-sustained-me she and-wrath-of-me arm-of-me for-me

בְּאַפִּי וַאֲשַׁכְּרֵם בַּחֲמָתִי וְאוֹרִיד לָאָרֶץ
on-the-ground and-I-poured in-wrath-of-me and-I-made-drunk-them in-anger-of-me

נִצְחָם׃ (7) חַסְדֵי יְהוָה | אַזְכִּיר תְּהִלֹּת יְהוָה כְּעַל
according-to Yahweh praises-of I-will-tell Yahweh kindnesses-of (7) blood-of-them

כֹּל אֲשֶׁר־ גְּמָלָנוּ יְהוָה וְרַב־ טוּב לְבֵית יִשְׂרָאֵל אֲשֶׁר־
that Israel for-house-of good-thing and-many-of Yahweh he-did-for-us that all

גְּמָלָם כְּרַחֲמָיו וּכְרֹב
and-according-to-many-of according-to-compassions-of-him he-did-for-them

חֲסָדָיו׃ (8) וַיֹּאמֶר אַךְ־ עַמִּי הֵמָּה בָּנִים לֹא
not sons they people-of-me surely and-he-said (8) kindnesses-of-him

יְשַׁקֵּרוּ וַיְהִי לָהֶם לְמוֹשִׁיעַ׃ (9) בְּכָל־
in-all-of (9) as-One-Saving to-them so-he-became they-will-be-false

צָרָתָם | לֹא צָר וּמַלְאַךְ פָּנָיו הוֹשִׁיעָם
he-saved-them presences-of-him and-angel-of distress to-him distress-of-them

בְּאַהֲבָתוֹ וּבְחֶמְלָתוֹ הוּא גְאָלָם וַיְנַטְּלֵם
and-he-lifted-up-them he-redeemed-them he and-in-mercy-of-him in-love-of-him

וַיְנַשְּׂאֵם כָּל־ יְמֵי עוֹלָם׃ (10) וְהֵמָּה מָרוּ וְעִצְּבוּ
and-they-grieved they-rebelled yet-they (10) old days-of all-of and-he-carried-them

אֶת־ רוּחַ קָדְשׁוֹ וַיֵּהָפֵךְ לָהֶם לְאוֹיֵב הוּא
he as-one-being-enemy against-them so-he-turned Holiness-of-him Spirit-of ***

נִלְחַם־ בָּם׃ (11) וַיִּזְכֹּר יְמֵי־ עוֹלָם מֹשֶׁה עַמּוֹ
people-of-him Moses old days-of then-he-recalled (11) against-them he-fought

אַיֵּה | הַמַּעֲלֵם מִיָּם אֵת רֹעֵי צֹאנוֹ
flock-of-him ones-shepherding-of with through-sea the-one-bringing-them where?

אַיֵּה הַשָּׂם בְּקִרְבּוֹ אֶת־ רוּחַ קָדְשׁוֹ׃ (12) מוֹלִיךְ
one-sending (12) Holiness-of-him Spirit-of *** in-among-him the-one-setting where?

from the nations no one
was with me.
I trampled them in my anger
and trod them down in my
wrath;
their blood spattered my
garments,
and I stained all my
clothing.
4 For the day of vengeance was
in my heart,
and the year of my
redemption has come.
5 I looked, but there was no one
to help,
I was appalled that no one
gave support;
so my own arm worked
salvation for me,
and my own wrath
sustained me.
6 I trampled the nations in my
anger;
in my wrath I made them
drunk
and poured their blood on
the ground."

*Praise and Prayer*

7 I will tell of the kindnesses of
the LORD,
the deeds for which he is to
be praised,
according to all the LORD has
done for us—
yes, the many good things he
has done
for the house of Israel,
according to his compassion
and many kindnesses.
8 He said, "Surely they are my
people,
sons who will not be false to
me";
and so he became their
Savior.
9 In all their distress he too was
distressed,
and the angel of his
presence saved them.
In his love and mercy he
redeemed them;
he lifted them up and
carried them
all the days of old.
10 Yet they rebelled
and grieved his Holy Spirit.
So he turned and became their
enemy
and he himself fought
against them.
11 Then his people recalled[w] the
days of old,
the days of Moses and his
people—
where is he who brought them
through the sea,
with the shepherd of his
flock?
Where is he who set
his Holy Spirit among them,

w11 Or *But may he recall*

ק לו°

לִימִין מֹשֶׁה זְרוֹעַ תִּפְאַרְתּוֹ בּוֹקֵעַ מַיִם מִפְּנֵיהֶם
from-before-them waters one-dividing glory-of-him arm-of Moses at-right-hand-of

לַעֲשׂוֹת לוֹ שֵׁם עוֹלָם׃ (13) מוֹלִיכָם בַּתְּהֹמוֹת
through-the-depths one-leading-them (13) everlasting renown-of for-him to-gain

כַּסּוּס בַּמִּדְבָּר לֹא יִכָּשֵׁלוּ׃ (14) כַּבְּהֵמָה
like-the-cattle (14) they-stumbled not in-the-open-country like-the-horse

בַּבִּקְעָה תֵּרֵד רוּחַ יְהוָה תְּנִיחֶנּוּ כֵּן נִהַגְתָּ
you-guided thus she-gave-rest-to-him Yahweh Spirit-of she-goes-down to-the-plain

עַמְּךָ לַעֲשׂוֹת לְךָ שֵׁם תִּפְאָרֶת׃ (15) הַבֵּט מִשָּׁמַיִם וּרְאֵה
and-see! from-heavens look! (15) glory name-of for-you to-make people-of-you

מִזְּבֻל קָדְשְׁךָ וְתִפְאַרְתֶּךָ אַיֵּה קִנְאָתְךָ
zeal-of-you where? and-glory-of-you holiness-of-you from-lofty-place-of

וּגְבוּרֹתֶךָ הֲמוֹן מֵעֶיךָ וְרַחֲמֶיךָ אֵלַי
from-me and-compassions-of-you tendernesses-of-you abundance-of and-mights-of-you

הִתְאַפָּקוּ׃ (16) כִּי־אַתָּה אָבִינוּ כִּי אַבְרָהָם לֹא יְדָעָנוּ
he-knows-us not Abraham though Father-of-us you but (16) they-are-withheld

וְיִשְׂרָאֵל לֹא יַכִּירָנוּ אַתָּה יְהוָה אָבִינוּ גֹּאֲלֵנוּ
One-Redeeming-us Father-of-us Yahweh you he-acknowledges-us not or-Israel

מֵעוֹלָם שְׁמֶךָ׃ (17) לָמָּה תַתְעֵנוּ יְהוָה מִדְּרָכֶיךָ
from-ways-of-you Yahweh you-make-wander-us why? (17) name-of-you from-of-old

תַּקְשִׁיחַ לִבֵּנוּ מִיִּרְאָתֶךָ שׁוּב לְמַעַן עֲבָדֶיךָ
servants-of-you for-sake-of return! from-reverence-of-you heart-of-us you-harden

שִׁבְטֵי נַחֲלָתֶךָ׃ (18) לַמִּצְעָר יָרְשׁוּ עַם־
people-of they-possessed for-the-little-while (18) inheritance-of-you tribes-of

קָדְשֶׁךָ צָרֵינוּ בּוֹסְסוּ מִקְדָּשֶׁךָ׃ (19) הָיִינוּ
we-are (19) sanctuary-of-you they-trampled-down enemies-of-us holiness-of-you

מֵעוֹלָם לֹא־מָשַׁלְתָּ בָּם לֹא־נִקְרָא שִׁמְךָ עֲלֵיהֶם
to-them name-of-you he-was-called not over-them you-ruled not from-of-old

לוּא־קָרַעְתָּ שָׁמַיִם יָרַדְתָּ מִפָּנֶיךָ
at-before-you you-would-come-down heavens you-would-rend oh-that!

הָרִים נָזֹלּוּ׃ *(64:1) כִּקְדֹחַ אֵשׁ הֲמָסִים מַיִם
waters twigs fire as-to-set-ablaze *(64:1) they-would-tremble mountains

תִּבְעֶה־אֵשׁ לְהוֹדִיעַ שִׁמְךָ לְצָרֶיךָ מִפָּנֶיךָ
at-before-you to-enemies-of-you name-of-you to-make-known fire she-makes-boil

גּוֹיִם יִרְגָּזוּ׃ (2) בַּעֲשׂוֹתְךָ נוֹרָאוֹת לֹא נְקַוֶּה
we-expected not things-being-awesome when-to-do-you (2) they-would-quake nations

יָרַדְתָּ מִפָּנֶיךָ הָרִים נָזֹלּוּ׃ (3) וּמֵעוֹלָם לֹא־
not and-since-ancient-time (3) they-trembled mountains at-before-you you-came-down

12 who sent his glorious arm of power
to be at Moses' right hand,
who divided the waters before them,
to gain for himself everlasting renown,
13 who led them through the depths?
Like a horse in open country,
they did not stumble;
14 like cattle that go down to the plain,
they were given rest by the Spirit of the LORD.
This is how you guided your people
to make for yourself a glorious name.

15 Look down from heaven and see
from your lofty throne, holy and glorious.
Where are your zeal and your might?
Your tenderness and compassion are withheld from us.
16 But you are our Father,
though Abraham does not know us
or Israel acknowledge us;
you, O LORD, are our Father,
our Redeemer from of old is your name.
17 Why, O LORD, do you make us wander from your ways
and harden our hearts so we do not revere you?
Return for the sake of your servants,
the tribes that are your inheritance.
18 For a little while your people possessed your holy place,
but now our enemies have trampled down your sanctuary.
19 We are yours from of old;
but you have not ruled over them,
they have not been called by your name.[x]

64 Oh, that you would rend the heavens and come down,
that the mountains would tremble before you!
2 As when fire sets twigs ablaze
and causes water to boil,
come down to make your name known to your enemies
and cause the nations to quake before you!
3 For when you did awesome things that we did not expect,
you came down, and the mountains trembled before you.
4 Since ancient times no one

x19 Or *We are like those you have never ruled, / like those never called by your name*

*Heading. 1* The English numeration of chapter 64 begins in the middle of verse 19 of chapter 63 in Hebrew; thus, there is a one-verse discrepancy thoughout chapter 64.

שָׁמְעוּ לֹא הֶאֱזִינוּ עַיִן לֹא־ רָאָתָה אֱלֹהִים זוּלָתְךָ יַעֲשֶׂה
he-acts besides-you God she-saw not eye they-perceived not they-heard

לִמְחַכֵּה־ לוֹ: פָּגַעְתָּ אֶת־ שָׂשׂ וְעֹשֵׂה צֶדֶק
right and-one-doing-of one-being-glad *** you-help (4) for-him for-one-waiting-of

בִּדְרָכֶיךָ יִזְכְּרוּךָ הֵן־ אַתָּה קָצַפְתָּ וַנֶּחֱטָא
when-we-sinned you-were-angry you see! they-remember-you in-ways-of-you

בָּהֶם עוֹלָם וְנִוָּשֵׁעַ: וַנְּהִי כַטָּמֵא
like-the-unclean and-we-became (5) then-can-we-be-saved continually against-them

כֻּלָּנוּ וּכְבֶגֶד עִדִּים כָּל־ צִדְקֹתֵינוּ וַנָּבֶל
and-we-shrivel-up righteous-acts-of-us all-of filths and-like-rag-of all-of-us

כֶּעָלֶה כֻּלָּנוּ וַעֲוֹנֵנוּ כָּרוּחַ יִשָּׂאֻנוּ:
they-sweep-away-us like-the-wind and-sins-of-us all-of-us like-the-leaf

וְאֵין־ קוֹרֵא בְשִׁמְךָ מִתְעוֹרֵר לְהַחֲזִיק בָּךְ
of-you to-lay-hold one-striving on-name-of-you one-calling and-there-is-no (6)

כִּי־ הִסְתַּרְתָּ פָנֶיךָ מִמֶּנּוּ וַתְּמוּגֵנוּ בְּיַד־
because-of-power-of and-you-made-waste-away-us from-us faces-of-you you-hid for

עֲוֹנֵנוּ: וְעַתָּה יְהוָה אָבִינוּ אָתָּה אֲנַחְנוּ הַחֹמֶר וְאַתָּה
and-you the-clay we you Father-of-us Yahweh yet-now (7) sins-of-us

יֹצְרֵנוּ וּמַעֲשֵׂה יָדְךָ כֻּלָּנוּ: אַל־ תִּקְצֹף
you-be-angry not (8) all-of-us hand-of-you and-work-of one-being-potter-of-us

יְהוָה עַד־ מְאֹד וְאַל־ לָעַד תִּזְכֹּר עָוֺן הֵן הַבֶּט־ נָא
now! look! see! sin you-remember to-forever and-not excess beyond Yahweh

עַמְּךָ כֻלָּנוּ: עָרֵי קָדְשְׁךָ הָיוּ מִדְבָּר צִיּוֹן
Zion desert they-became sacredness-of-you cities-of (9) all-of-us people-of-you

מִדְבָּר הָיָתָה יְרוּשָׁלַםִ שְׁמָמָה: בֵּית קָדְשֵׁנוּ וְתִפְאַרְתֵּנוּ
and-glory-of-us holiness-of-us temple-of (10) desolation Jerusalem she-is desert

אֲשֶׁר הִלְלוּךָ אֲבֹתֵינוּ הָיָה לִשְׂרֵפַת אֵשׁ וְכָל־
and-all-of fire as-burned-of he-is fathers-of-us they-praised-you where

מַחֲמַדֵּינוּ הָיָה לְחָרְבָּה: הַעַל־ אֵלֶּה תִתְאַפַּק יְהוָה
Yahweh will-you-hold-yourself-back these after? (11) as-ruin he-is treasures-of-us

תֶּחֱשֶׁה וּתְעַנֵּנוּ עַד־ מְאֹד: נִדְרַשְׁתִּי
I-revealed-myself (65:1) excess beyond and-will-you-punish-us will-you-keep-silent

לְלוֹא שָׁאָלוּ נִמְצֵאתִי לְלֹא בִקְשֻׁנִי אָמַרְתִּי הִנֵּנִי הִנֵּנִי אֶל־
to here-I! here-I! I-said they-sought-me by-not I-was-found they-asked to-not

גּוֹי לֹא־ קֹרָא† בִשְׁמִי: פֵּרַשְׂתִּי יָדַי כָּל־ הַיּוֹם
the-day all-of hands-of-me I-held-out (2) by-name-of-me †he-was-called not nation

אֶל־ עַם סוֹרֵר הַהֹלְכִים הַדֶּרֶךְ לֹא־ טוֹב אַחַר
after good not the-way the-ones-walking being-obstinate people to

has heard,
no ear has perceived,
no eye has seen any God
besides you,
who acts on behalf of those
who wait for him.
5 You come to the help of those
who gladly do right,
who remember your ways.
But when we continued to sin
against them,
you were angry.
How then can we be saved?
6 All of us have become like one
who is unclean,
and all our righteous acts
are like filthy rags;
we all shrivel up like a leaf,
and like the wind our sins
sweep us away.
7 No one calls on your name
or strives to lay hold of you;
for you have hidden your face
from us
and made us waste away
because of our sins.

8 Yet, O LORD, you are our
Father.
We are the clay, you are the
potter;
we are all the work of your
hand.
9 Do not be angry beyond
measure, O LORD;
do not remember our sins
forever.
Oh, look upon us, we pray,
for we are all your people.
10 Your sacred cities have become
a desert;
even Zion is a desert,
Jerusalem a desolation.
11 Our holy and glorious temple,
where our fathers praised
you,
has been burned with fire,
and all that we treasured lies
in ruins.
12 After all this, O LORD, will you
hold yourself back?
Will you keep silent and
punish us beyond
measure?

### *Judgment and Salvation*

65 "I revealed myself to
those who did not ask for
me;
I was found by those who
did not seek me.
To a nation that did not call
on my name,
I said, 'Here am I, here am
I.'
2 All day long I have held out
my hands
to an obstinate people,
who walk in ways not good,

* *Heading* See the note on page 127.

† *1* The NIV, with many ancient versions, repoints this word as קֹרָא, *be-called.*

מַחְשְׁבֹתֵיהֶם׃ הָעָם הַמַּכְעִיסִים אוֹתִי עַל־ פָּנַי
faces-of-me to me the-ones-provoking the-people (3) imaginations-of-them

תָּמִיד זֹבְחִים בַּגַּנּוֹת וּמְקַטְּרִים עַל־
on and-ones-burning-incense in-the-gardens ones-offering-sacrifices continually

הַלְּבֵנִים׃ הַיֹּשְׁבִים בַּקְּבָרִים וּבַנְּצוּרִים
and-with-the-ones-keeping-vigil among-the-graves the-ones-sitting (4) the-bricks

יָלִינוּ הָאֹכְלִים בְּשַׂר הַחֲזִיר וּפְרַק פִּגֻּלִים
unclean-meats and-broth-of the-pig flesh-of the-ones-eating they-spend-night

כְּלֵיהֶם׃ הָאֹמְרִים קְרַב אֵלֶיךָ אַל־ תִּגַּשׁ־ בִּי כִּי
for to-me you-come-near not to-you keep-away! the-ones-saying (5) pots-of-them

קְדַשְׁתִּיךָ אֵלֶּה עָשָׁן בְּאַפִּי אֵשׁ יֹקֶדֶת כָּל־ הַיּוֹם׃
the-day all-of burning fire in-nostril-of-me smoke these I-am-sacred-for-you

הִנֵּה כְתוּבָה לְפָנָי לֹא אֶחֱשֶׂה* כִּי אִם־ שִׁלַּמְתִּי
I-will-pay-back rather but I-will-keep-silent not before-me being-written see! (6)

וְשִׁלַּמְתִּי עַל־ חֵיקָם׃ עֲוֹנֹתֵיכֶם וַעֲוֹנֹת אֲבוֹתֵיכֶם
fathers-of-you and-sins-of sins-of-you (7) lap-of-them into and-I-will-pay-back

יַחְדָּו אָמַר יְהוָה אֲשֶׁר קִטְּרוּ עַל־ הֶהָרִים וְעַל־
and-on the-mountains on they-burned-sacrifice because Yahweh he-says both

הַגְּבָעוֹת חֵרְפוּנִי וּמַדֹּתִי פְעֻלָּתָם רִאשֹׁנָה עַל־ חֵיקָם׃
lap-of-them into former deed-of-them and-I-will-measure they-defied-me the-hills

כֹּה אָמַר יְהוָה כַּאֲשֶׁר יִמָּצֵא הַתִּירוֹשׁ בָּאֶשְׁכּוֹל וְאָמַר
and-he-says in-the-cluster the-juice he-is-found as-when Yahweh he-says this (8)

אַל־ תַּשְׁחִיתֵהוּ כִּי בְרָכָה בּוֹ כֵּן אֶעֱשֶׂה לְמַעַן עֲבָדַי לְבִלְתִּי
not servants-of-me in-behalf-of I-will-do so in-him good yet you-destroy-him not

הַשְׁחִית הַכֹּל׃ וְהוֹצֵאתִי מִיַּעֲקֹב זֶרַע וּמִיהוּדָה
and-from-Judah descendant from-Jacob and-I-will-bring-forth (9) the-all to-destroy

יוֹרֵשׁ הָרָי וִירֵשׁוּהָ בְחִירַי
ones-chosen-of-me and-they-will-inherit-her mountains-of-me one-possessing

וַעֲבָדַי יִשְׁכְּנוּ־ שָׁמָּה׃ וְהָיָה הַשָּׁרוֹן
the-Sharon and-he-will-become (10) at-there they-will-live and-servants-of-me

לִנְוֵה־ צֹאן וְעֵמֶק עָכוֹר לְרֵבֶץ בָּקָר לְעַמִּי
for-people-of-me herd as-resting-place-of Achor and-Valley-of flock as-pasture-of

אֲשֶׁר דְּרָשׁוּנִי׃ וְאַתֶּם עֹזְבֵי יְהוָה הַשְּׁכֵחִים אֶת־
*** the-ones-forgetting Yahweh ones-forsaking-of but-you (11) they-seek-me who

הַר קָדְשִׁי הָעֹרְכִים לַגַּד שֻׁלְחָן
table for-the-Fortune the-ones-spreading holiness-of-me mountain-of

וְהַמְמַלְאִים לַמְנִי מִמְסָךְ׃ וּמָנִיתִי אֶתְכֶם
you and-I-will-destine (12) mixed-wine for-the-Destiny and-the-ones-filling

pursuing their own
imaginations—
3a people who continually
provoke me
to my very face,
offering sacrifices in gardens
and burning incense on
altars of brick;
4who sit among the graves
and spend their nights
keeping secret vigil;
who eat the flesh of pigs,
and whose pots hold broth
of unclean meat;
5who say, 'Keep away; don't
come near me,
for I am too sacred for you!'
Such people are smoke in my
nostrils,
a fire that keeps burning all
day.

6"See, it stands written before
me:
I will not keep silent but
will pay back in full;
I will pay it back into their
laps—
7both your sins and the sins of
your fathers,"
says the LORD.
"Because they burned
sacrifices on the
mountains
and defied me on the hills,
I will measure into their laps
the full payment for their
former deeds."

8This is what the LORD says:

"As when juice is still found
in a cluster of grapes
and men say, 'Don't destroy
it,
there is yet some good in it,'
so will I do in behalf of my
servants;
I will not destroy them all.
9I will bring forth descendants
from Jacob,
and from Judah those who
will possess my
mountains;
my chosen people will inherit
them,
and there will my servants
live.
10Sharon will become a pasture
for flocks,
and the Valley of Achor a
resting place for herds,
for my people who seek me.

11"But as for you who forsake
the LORD
and forget my holy
mountain,
who spread a table for Fortune
and fill bowls of mixed wine
for Destiny,
12I will destine you for the

*6 Most mss have *shin* instead of *sin* (שה־).

°4 ק ומרק
°7 ק אל

לַחֶרֶב וְכֻלְּכֶם לַטֶּבַח תִּכְרָעוּ יַעַן קָרָאתִי
I-called for you-will-bend-down for-the-slaughter and-all-of-you for-the-sword

וְלֹא עֲנִיתֶם דִּבַּרְתִּי וְלֹא שְׁמַעְתֶּם וַתַּעֲשׂוּ הָרַע
the-evil and-you-did you-listened but-not I-spoke you-answered but-not

בְּעֵינַי וּבַאֲשֶׁר לֹא־ חָפַצְתִּי בְּחַרְתֶּם׃ לָכֵן כֹּה־ אָמַר ׀
he-says this therefore (13) you-chose I-am-pleased not and-to-what in-eyes-of-me

אֲדֹנָי יְהוִה הִנֵּה עֲבָדַי ׀ יֹאכֵלוּ וְאַתֶּם תִּרְעָבוּ הִנֵּה
see! you-will-go-hungry but-you they-will-eat servants-of-me see! Yahweh Sovereign

עֲבָדַי יִשְׁתּוּ וְאַתֶּם תִּצְמָאוּ הִנֵּה עֲבָדַי
servants-of-me see! you-will-go-thirsty but-you they-will-drink servants-of-me

יִשְׂמָחוּ וְאַתֶּם תֵּבֹשׁוּ׃ הִנֵּה עֲבָדַי
servants-of-me see! (14) you-will-be-shamed but-you they-will-rejoice

יָרֹנּוּ מִטּוּב לֵב וְאַתֶּם תִּצְעֲקוּ מִכְּאֵב לֵב
heart from-anguish-of you-will-cry-out but-you heart out-of-joy-of they-will-sing

וּמִשֵּׁבֶר רוּחַ תְּיֵלִילוּ׃ וְהִנַּחְתֶּם שִׁמְכֶם
name-of-you and-you-will-leave (15) you-will-wail spirit and-in-brokenness-of

לִשְׁבוּעָה לִבְחִירַי וֶהֱמִיתְךָ אֲדֹנָי יְהוִה
Yahweh Sovereign and-he-will-put-to-death-you to-chosen-ones-of-me as-curse

וְלַעֲבָדָיו יִקְרָא שֵׁם אַחֵר׃ אֲשֶׁר הַמִּתְבָּרֵךְ
the-one-invoking-blessing who (16) another name he-will-give but-to-servants-of-him

בָּאָרֶץ יִתְבָּרֵךְ בֵּאלֹהֵי אָמֵן וְהַנִּשְׁבָּע בָּאָרֶץ
in-the-land and-the-one-taking-oath truth by-God-of he-will-bless in-the-land

יִשָּׁבַע בֵּאלֹהֵי אָמֵן כִּי נִשְׁכְּחוּ הַצָּרוֹת
the-troubles they-will-be-forgotten for truth by-God-of he-will-take-oath

הָרִאשֹׁנוֹת וְכִי נִסְתְּרוּ מֵעֵינָי׃ כִּי־ הִנְנִי
behold-I! indeed (17) from-eyes-of-me they-will-be-hidden and-indeed the-past-ones

בוֹרֵא שָׁמַיִם חֲדָשִׁים וָאָרֶץ חֲדָשָׁה וְלֹא תִזָּכַרְנָה
they-will-be-remembered and-not new and-earth new-ones heavens creating

הָרִאשֹׁנוֹת וְלֹא תַעֲלֶינָה עַל־ לֵב׃ כִּי־ אִם־ שִׂישׂוּ
be-glad! rather but (18) mind to they-will-come and-not the-former-things

וְגִילוּ עֲדֵי־ עַד אֲשֶׁר אֲנִי בוֹרֵא כִּי הִנְנִי בוֹרֵא אֶת־ יְרוּשָׁלִַם
Jerusalem *** creating see-I! for creating I what forever forevers-of and-rejoice!

גִּילָה וְעַמָּהּ מָשׂוֹשׂ׃ וְגַלְתִּי בִירוּשָׁלִַם
over-Jerusalem and-I-will-rejoice (19) joy and-people-of-her delight

וְשַׂשְׂתִּי בְעַמִּי וְלֹא־ יִשָּׁמַע בָּהּ עוֹד קוֹל
sound-of more in-her he-will-be-heard and-not in-people-of-me and-I-will-delight

בְּכִי וְקוֹל זְעָקָה׃ לֹא־ יִהְיֶה מִשָּׁם עוֹד עוּל יָמִים
days infant-of again in-there he-will-be never (20) crying and-sound-of weeping

sword,
and you will all bend down
for the slaughter;
for I called but you did not
answer,
I spoke but you did not
listen.
You did evil in my sight
and chose what displeases
me."
13 Therefore this is what the Sovereign LORD says:
"My servants will eat,
but you will go hungry;
my servants will drink,
but you will go thirsty;
my servants will rejoice,
but you will be put to
shame.
14 My servants will sing
out of the joy of their
hearts,
but you will cry out
from anguish of heart
and wail in brokenness of
spirit.
15 You will leave your name
to my chosen ones as a
curse;
the Sovereign LORD will put
you to death,
but to his servants he will
give another name.
16 Whoever invokes a blessing in
the land
will do so by the God of
truth;
he who takes an oath in the
land
will swear by the God of
truth.
For the past troubles will be
forgotten
and hidden from my eyes.

*New Heavens and a New Earth*

17 "Behold, I will create
new heavens and a new
earth.
The former things will not be
remembered,
nor will they come to mind.
18 But be glad and rejoice forever
in what I will create,
for I will create Jerusalem to be
a delight
and its people a joy.
19 I will rejoice over Jerusalem
and take delight in my
people;
the sound of weeping and of
crying
will be heard in it no more.
20 "Never again will there be in
it
an infant who lives but a few
days,

וְזָקֵ֕ן אֲשֶׁ֥ר לֹֽא־ יְמַלֵּ֖א אֶת־ יָמָ֑יו כִּ֣י הַנַּ֗עַר בֶּן־
son-of the-youth indeed days-of-him *** he-lives-out not who or-old-man

מֵאָ֤ה שָׁנָה֙ יָמ֔וּת וְהַ֣חוֹטֶ֔א בֶּן־ מֵאָ֥ה שָׁנָ֖ה
year hundred son-of and-the-one-failing-to-reach he-will-die year hundred

יְקֻלָּֽל׃ (21) וּבָנ֥וּ בָתִּ֖ים וְיָשָׁ֑בוּ
and-they-will-dwell houses and-they-will-build (21) he-will-be-accursed

וְנָטְע֣וּ כְרָמִ֔ים וְאָכְל֖וּ פִּרְיָֽם׃ (22) לֹ֤א
not (22) fruit-of-them and-they-will-eat vineyards and-they-will-plant

יִבְנוּ֙ וְאַחֵ֣ר יֵשֵׁ֔ב לֹ֥א יִטְּע֖וּ וְאַחֵ֣ר
and-another they-will-plant not he-will-live and-another they-will-build

יֹאכֵ֑ל כִּֽי־ כִימֵ֤י הָעֵץ֙ יְמֵ֣י עַמִּ֔י וּמַעֲשֵׂ֥ה יְדֵיהֶ֖ם
hands-of-them and-work-of people-of-me days-of the-tree as-days-of for he-will-eat

יְבַלּ֥וּ בְחִירָֽי׃ (23) לֹ֤א יִֽיגְעוּ֙ לָרִ֔יק וְלֹ֥א
or-not in-vain they-will-toil not (23) chosen-ones-of-me they-will-enjoy

יֵלְד֖וּ לַבֶּהָלָ֑ה כִּ֣י זֶ֜רַע בְּרוּכֵ֤י יְהוָה֙
Yahweh ones-being-blessed-of people for to-the-misfortune they-will-bear-child

הֵ֔מָּה וְצֶאֱצָאֵיהֶ֖ם אִתָּֽם׃ (24) וְהָיָ֥ה טֶֽרֶם־ יִקְרָ֖אוּ וַאֲנִ֣י
then-I they-call before and-he-will-be (24) with-them and-descendants-of-them they

אֶעֱנֶ֑ה ע֛וֹד הֵ֥ם מְדַבְּרִ֖ים וַאֲנִ֥י אֶשְׁמָֽע׃ (25) זְאֵ֨ב וְטָלֶ֜ה
and-lamb wolf (25) I-will-hear then-I ones-speaking they still I-will-answer

יִרְע֣וּ כְאֶחָ֗ד וְאַרְיֵה֙ כַּבָּקָ֣ר יֹֽאכַל־ תֶּ֔בֶן וְנָחָ֖שׁ עָפָ֣ר
dust but-serpent straw he-will-eat like-the-ox and-lion as-one they-will-feed

לַחְמ֑וֹ לֹֽא־ יָרֵ֧עוּ וְלֹֽא־ יַשְׁחִ֛יתוּ בְּכָל־ הַ֥ר
mountain-of on-all-of they-will-destroy or-not they-will-harm not food-of-him

קָדְשִׁ֖י אָמַ֥ר יְהוָֽה׃ (66:1) כֹּ֚ה אָמַ֣ר יְהוָ֔ה הַשָּׁמַ֣יִם כִּסְאִ֔י
throne-of-me the-heavens Yahweh he-says this (66:1) Yahweh he-says holiness-of-me

וְהָאָ֖רֶץ הֲדֹ֣ם רַגְלָ֑י אֵי־ זֶ֥ה בַ֙יִת֙ אֲשֶׁ֣ר תִּבְנוּ־ לִ֔י
for-me you-will-build that house this where? feet-of-me footstool-of and-the-earth

וְאֵי־ זֶ֥ה מָק֖וֹם מְנוּחָתִֽי׃ (2) וְאֶת־ כָּל־ אֵ֙לֶּה֙ יָדִ֣י עָשָׂ֔תָה
she-made hand-of-me these all-of even (2) resting-place-of-me place this and-where?

וַיִּהְי֥וּ כָל־ אֵ֖לֶּה נְאֻם־ יְהוָ֑ה וְאֶל־ זֶ֣ה אַבִּ֔יט אֶל־
to I-esteem this and-to Yahweh declaration-of these all-of so-they-came-into-being

עָנִי֙ וּנְכֵה־ ר֔וּחַ וְחָרֵ֖ד עַל־ דְּבָרִֽי׃ (3) שׁוֹחֵ֨ט
one-sacrificing-of (3) word-of-me at and-trembling spirit and-contrite-of humble

הַשּׁ֜וֹר מַכֵּה־ אִ֗ישׁ זוֹבֵ֤חַ הַשֶּׂה֙ עֹ֣רֵֽף כֶּ֔לֶב
dog one-breaking-neck-of the-lamb one-offering-of man one-killing-of the-bull

מַעֲלֵ֤ה מִנְחָה֙ דַּם־ חֲזִ֔יר מַזְכִּ֥יר לְבֹנָ֖ה
incense one-making-memorial-of pig blood-of grain-offering one-offering-of

or an old man who does not
live out his years;
he who dies at a hundred
will be thought a mere
youth;
he who fails to reach[y] a
hundred
will be considered accursed.
21They will build houses and
dwell in them;
they will plant vineyards
and eat their fruit.
22No longer will they build
houses and others live in
them,
or plant and others eat.
For as the days of a tree,
so will be the days of my
people;
my chosen ones will long
enjoy
the works of their hands.
23They will not toil in vain
or bear children doomed to
misfortune;
for they will be a people
blessed by the LORD,
they and their descendants
with them.
24Before they call I will answer;
while they are still speaking
I will hear.
25The wolf and the lamb will
feed together,
and the lion will eat straw
like the ox,
but dust will be the
serpent's food.
They will neither harm nor
destroy
on all my holy mountain,"
says the LORD.

*Judgment and Hope*

66 This is what the LORD says:
"Heaven is my throne,
and the earth is my
footstool.
Where is the house you will
build for me?
Where will my resting place
be?
2Has not my hand made all
these things,
and so they came into
being?"
declares the LORD.

"This is the one I esteem:
he who is humble and
contrite in spirit,
and trembles at my word.
3But whoever sacrifices a bull
is like one who kills a man,
and whoever offers a lamb,
like one who breaks a dog's
neck;
whoever makes a grain
offering
is like one who presents
pig's blood,
and whoever burns memorial
incense,

[y]20 Or / *the sinner who reaches*

מְבָרֵךְ אָוֶן גַּם־ הֵמָּה בָּחֲרוּ בְּדַרְכֵיהֶם
to-ways-of-them they-chose they also idol one-worshiping-of

וּבְשִׁקּוּצֵיהֶם נַפְשָׁם חָפֵצָה׃ גַּם־ אֲנִי אֶבְחַר
I-will-choose I also (4) she-delights soul-of-them and-in-abominations-of-them

בְּתַעֲלֻלֵיהֶם וּמְגוּרֹתָם אָבִיא לָהֶם יַעַן קָרָאתִי
I-called for upon-them I-will-bring and-dreads-of-them to-harsh-treatments-of-them

וְאֵין עוֹנֶה דִּבַּרְתִּי וְלֹא שָׁמֵעוּ וַיַּעֲשׂוּ
and-they-did they-listened and-not I-spoke one-answering and-there-was-no

הָרַע בְּעֵינַי וּבַאֲשֶׁר לֹא־ חָפַצְתִּי בָּחָרוּ׃ שִׁמְעוּ דְּבַר־
word-of hear! (5) they-chose I-am-pleased not and-to-what in-eyes-of-me the-evil

יְהוָה הַחֲרֵדִים אֶל־ דְּבָרוֹ אָמְרוּ אֲחֵיכֶם שֹׂנְאֵיכֶם
ones-hating-you brothers-of-you they-said word-of-him at the-tremblers Yahweh

מְנַדֵּיכֶם לְמַעַן שְׁמִי יִכְבַּד יְהוָה וְנִרְאֶה
that-we-may-see Yahweh let-him-be-glorified name-of-me because-of ones-excluding-you

בְשִׂמְחַתְכֶם וְהֵם יֵבֹשׁוּ׃ קוֹל שָׁאוֹן מֵעִיר קוֹל
noise from-city uproar noise-of (6) they-will-be-shamed yet-they to-joy-of-you

מֵהֵיכָל קוֹל יְהוָה מְשַׁלֵּם גְּמוּל לְאֹיְבָיו׃
to-ones-being-enemies-of-him desert repaying Yahweh sound-of from-temple

בְּטֶרֶם תָּחִיל יָלָדָה בְּטֶרֶם יָבוֹא חֵבֶל
pain he-comes at-before she-gives-birth she-goes-into-labor at-before (7)

לָהּ וְהִמְלִיטָה זָכָר׃ מִי־ שָׁמַע כָּזֹאת מִי רָאָה
he-saw who? such-as-this he-heard who? (8) son then-she-delivers upon-her

כָּאֵלֶּה הֲיוּחַל אֶרֶץ בְּיוֹם אֶחָד אִם־ יִוָּלֵד גּוֹי
nation can-he-be-brought-forth or one in-day country can-he-be-born? such-as-these

פַּעַם אֶחָת כִּי־ חָלָה גַּם־ יָלְדָה צִיּוֹן אֶת־ בָּנֶיהָ׃
children-of-her *** Zion she-gives-birth then she-is-in-labor yet one moment

הַאֲנִי אַשְׁבִּיר וְלֹא אוֹלִיד יֹאמַר
he-says I-give-delivery and-not do-I-bring-to-moment-of-birth I? (9)

יְהוָה אִם־ אֲנִי הַמּוֹלִיד וְעָצַרְתִּי אָמַר אֱלֹהָיִךְ׃
God-of-you he-says then-do-I-close-up the-one-bringing-delivery I or Yahweh

שִׂמְחוּ אֶת־ יְרוּשָׁלַםִ וְגִילוּ בָהּ כָּל־ אֹהֲבֶיהָ
ones-loving-her all-of for-her and-be-glad! Jerusalem with rejoice! (10)

שִׂישׂוּ אִתָּהּ מָשׂוֹשׂ כָּל־ הַמִּתְאַבְּלִים עָלֶיהָ׃ לְמַעַן
for-that (11) over-her the-ones-mourning all-of rejoicing with-her rejoice!

תִּינְקוּ וּשְׂבַעְתֶּם מִשֹּׁד תַּנְחֻמֶיהָ לְמַעַן
for-that comforts-of-her at-breast-of and-you-will-be-satisfied you-will-nurse

תָּמֹצּוּ וְהִתְעַנַּגְתֶּם מִזִּיז כְּבוֹדָהּ׃
abundance-of-her in-overflow-of and-you-will-delight you-will-drink-deeply

like one who worships an
idol.
They have chosen their own
ways,
and their souls delight in
their abominations;
4so I also will choose harsh
treatment for them
and will bring upon them
what they dread.
For when I called, no one
answered,
when I spoke, no one
listened.
They did evil in my sight
and chose what displeases
me."
5Hear the word of the LORD,
you who tremble at his
word:
"Your brothers who hate you,
and exclude you because of
my name, have said,
'Let the LORD be glorified,
that we may see your joy!'
Yet they will be put to
shame.
6Hear that uproar from the city,
hear that noise from the
temple!
It is the sound of the LORD
repaying his enemies all
they deserve.
7"Before she goes into labor,
she gives birth;
before the pains come upon
her,
she delivers a son.
8Who has ever heard of such a
thing?
Who has ever seen such
things?
Can a country be born in a
day
or a nation be brought forth
in a moment?
Yet no sooner is Zion in labor
than she gives birth to her
children.
9Do I bring to the moment of
birth
and not give delivery?" says
the LORD.
"Do I close up the womb
when I bring to delivery?"
says your God.
10"Rejoice with Jerusalem and
be glad for her,
all you who love her;
rejoice greatly with her,
all you who mourn over her.
11For you will nurse and be
satisfied
at her comforting breasts;
you will drink deeply
and delight in her
overflowing abundance."

כִּי־כֹה ׀ אָמַר יְהוָה הִנְנִי נֹטֶה־אֵלֶיהָ כְּנָהָר שָׁלוֹם
peace like-river to-her extending see-I! Yahweh he-says this for (12)

וּכְנַחַל שׁוֹטֵף כְּבוֹד גּוֹיִם וִינַקְתֶּם עַל־צַד
side at and-you-will-nurse nations wealth-of flooding and-like-stream

תִּנָּשֵׂאוּ וְעַל־בִּרְכַּיִם תְּשָׁעֳשָׁעוּ׃ כְּאִישׁ אֲשֶׁר
who as-child (13) you-will-be-dandled knees and-on you-will-be-carried

אִמּוֹ תְּנַחֲמֶנּוּ כֵּן אָנֹכִי אֲנַחֶמְכֶם וּבִירוּשָׁלַםִ
and-over-Jerusalem I-will-comfort-you I so she-comforts-him mother-of-him

תְּנֻחָמוּ׃ וּרְאִיתֶם וְשָׂשׂ לִבְּכֶם
heart-of-you then-he-will-rejoice when-you-see (14) you-will-be-comforted

וְעַצְמוֹתֵיכֶם כַּדֶּשֶׁא תִפְרַחְנָה וְנוֹדְעָה
and-she-will-be-made-known they-will-flourish like-the-grass and-bones-of-you

יַד־יְהוָה אֶת־עֲבָדָיו וְזָעַם אֶת־
*** but-he-will-show-fury servants-of-him *** Yahweh hand-of

אֹיְבָיו׃ כִּי־הִנֵּה יְהוָה בָּאֵשׁ יָבוֹא
he-comes with-fire Yahweh see! indeed (15) ones-being-foes-of-him

וְכַסּוּפָה מַרְכְּבֹתָיו לְהָשִׁיב בְּחֵמָה אַפּוֹ
anger-of-him with-fury to-bring-down chariots-of-him and-like-the-whirlwind

וְגַעֲרָתוֹ בְּלַהֲבֵי־אֵשׁ׃ כִּי בָאֵשׁ יְהוָה
Yahweh with-fire for (16) fire with-flames-of and-rebuke-of-him

נִשְׁפָּט וּבְחַרְבּוֹ אֶת־כָּל־בָּשָׂר
mankind all-of *** and-with-sword-of-him he-will-execute-judgment

וְרַבּוּ חַלְלֵי יְהוָה׃ הַמִּתְקַדְּשִׁים
and-the-ones-consecrating-themselves (17) Yahweh ones-slain-of and-they-will-be-many

וְהַמִּטַּהֲרִים אֶל־הַגַּנּוֹת אַחַר אַחַד בַּתָּוֶךְ
into-the-midst one following the-gardens for and-the-ones-purifying-themselves

אֹכְלֵי בְּשַׂר הַחֲזִיר וְהַשֶּׁקֶץ וְהָעַכְבָּר יַחְדָּו
together and-the-rat and-the-abomination the-pig flesh-of ones-eating-of

יָסֻפוּ נְאֻם־יְהוָה׃ וְאָנֹכִי מַעֲשֵׂיהֶם
actions-of-them and-I (18) Yahweh declaration-of they-will-meet-end

וּמַחְשְׁבֹתֵיהֶם בָּאָה לְקַבֵּץ אֶת־כָּל־הַגּוֹיִם וְהַלְּשֹׁנוֹת
and-the-tongues the-nations all-of *** to-gather coming and-imaginations-of-them

וּבָאוּ וְרָאוּ אֶת־כְּבוֹדִי׃ וְשַׂמְתִּי בָהֶם
among-them and-I-will-set (19) glory-of-me *** and-they-will-see and-they-will-come

אוֹת וְשִׁלַּחְתִּי מֵהֶם ׀ פְּלֵיטִים אֶל־הַגּוֹיִם תַּרְשִׁישׁ פּוּל וְלוּד
and-Lydia Pul Tarshish the-nations to survivors from-them and-I-will-send sign

מֹשְׁכֵי קֶשֶׁת תֻּבַל וְיָוָן הָאִיִּים הָרְחֹקִים אֲשֶׁר לֹא־
not that the-distant-ones the-islands and-Greece Tubal bow ones-drawing-of

°17 ק אחת

12 For this is what the LORD says:

"I will extend peace to her like a river,
and the wealth of nations like a flooding stream;
you will nurse and be carried on her arm
and dandled on her knees.
13 As a mother comforts her child,
so will I comfort you;
and you will be comforted over Jerusalem."

14 When you see this, your heart will rejoice
and you will flourish like grass;
the hand of the LORD will be made known to his servants,
but his fury will be shown to his foes.
15 See, the LORD is coming with fire,
and his chariots are like a whirlwind;
he will bring down his anger with fury,
and his rebuke with flames of fire.
16 For with fire and with his sword
the LORD will execute judgment upon all men,
and many will be those slain by the LORD.

17 "Those who consecrate and purify themselves to go into the gardens, following the one in the midst of[z] those who eat the flesh of pigs and rats and other abominable things—they will meet their end together," declares the LORD.

18 "And I, because of their actions and their imaginations, am about to come[a] and gather all nations and tongues, and they will come and see my glory.

19 "I will set a sign among them, and I will send some of those who survive to the nations—to Tarshish, to the Libyans[b] and Lydians (famous as archers), to Tubal and Greece, and to the distant islands that have not heard of my

[z]17 Or *gardens behind one of your temples, and*
[a]18 The meaning of the Hebrew for this clause is uncertain.
[b]19 Some Septuagint manuscripts *Put* (Libyans); Hebrew *Pul*

שָׁמְעוּ אֶת־ שִׁמְעִי וְלֹא־ רָאוּ אֶת־ כְּבוֹדִי וְהִגִּידוּ
and-they-will-proclaim glory-of-me *** they-saw and-not fame-of-me *** they-heard

אֶת־ כְּבוֹדִי בַּגּוֹיִם׃ וְהֵבִיאוּ אֶת־ כָּל־
all-of *** and-they-will-bring (20) among-the-nations glory-of-me ***

אֲחֵיכֶם מִכָּל־ הַגּוֹיִם ׀ מִנְחָה ׀ לַיהוָה בַּסּוּסִים
on-the-horses to-Yahweh offering the-nations from-all-of brothers-of-you

וּבָרֶכֶב וּבַצַּבִּים וּבַפְּרָדִים וּבַכִּרְכָּרוֹת עַל
to and-on-the-camels and-on-the-mules and-in-the-wagons and-in-the-chariot

הַר קָדְשִׁי יְרוּשָׁלִַם אָמַר יְהוָה כַּאֲשֶׁר יָבִיאוּ בְנֵי
sons-of they-bring just-as Yahweh he-says Jerusalem holiness-of-me mountain-of

יִשְׂרָאֵל אֶת־ הַמִּנְחָה בִּכְלִי טָהוֹר בֵּית יְהוָה׃ וְגַם־
and-also (21) Yahweh temple-of clean in-vessel the-grain-offering *** Israel

מֵהֶם אֶקַּח לַכֹּהֲנִים לַלְוִיִּם אָמַר יְהוָה׃
Yahweh he-says for-the-Levites for-the-priests I-will-select from-them

כִּי כַאֲשֶׁר הַשָּׁמַיִם הַחֳדָשִׁים* וְהָאָרֶץ הַחֲדָשָׁה אֲשֶׁר אֲנִי
I that the-new and-the-earth the-new-ones the-heavens just-as indeed (22)

עֹשֶׂה עֹמְדִים לְפָנַי נְאֻם־ יְהוָה כֵּן יַעֲמֹד
he-will-endure so Yahweh declaration-of before-me ones-enduring making

זַרְעֲכֶם וְשִׁמְכֶם׃ וְהָיָה מִדֵּי־ חֹדֶשׁ
New-Moon from-fullness-of and-he-will-be (23) and-name-of-you descendant-of-you

בְּחָדְשׁוֹ וּמִדֵּי שַׁבָּת בְּשַׁבַּתּוֹ יָבוֹא
he-will-come to-Sabbath-of-him Sabbath and-from-fullness-of to-New-Moon-of-him

כָל־ בָּשָׂר לְהִשְׁתַּחֲוֹת לְפָנַי אָמַר יְהוָה׃ וְיָצְאוּ
and-they-will-go-out (24) Yahweh he-says before-me to-bow-down mankind all-of

וְרָאוּ בְּפִגְרֵי הָאֲנָשִׁים הַפֹּשְׁעִים
the-ones-rebelling the-men upon-dead-bodies-of and-they-will-look

בִּי כִּי תוֹלַעְתָּם לֹא תָמוּת וְאִשָּׁם לֹא
not and-fire-of-them she-will-die not worm-of-them indeed against-me

תִכְבֶּה וְהָיוּ דֵרָאוֹן לְכָל־ בָּשָׂר׃
mankind to-all-of loathsome and-they-will-be she-will-be-quenched

fame or seen my glory. They will
proclaim my glory among the nations.
20 And they will bring all
your brothers, from all the nations, to my holy mountain in
Jerusalem as an offering to the
LORD—on horses, in chariots and
wagons, and on mules and camels," says the LORD. "They will
bring them, as the Israelites bring
their grain offerings, to the temple
of the LORD in ceremonially clean
vessels.
21 And I will select some of
them also to be priests and Levites," says the LORD.

22 "As the new heavens and the
new earth that I make will endure
before me," declares the LORD, "so
will your name and descendants
endure.
23 From one New Moon to
another and from one Sabbath to
another, all mankind will come
and bow down before me," says
the LORD.
24 "And they will go out
and look upon the dead bodies of
those who rebelled against me;
their worm will not die, nor will
their fire be quenched, and they
will be loathsome to all mankind."

*22 Most mss have *hateph pathah* under the *heth* (חֲ׳).

דִּבְרֵי יִרְמְיָהוּ בֶּן־ חִלְקִיָּהוּ מִן־ הַכֹּהֲנִים אֲשֶׁר בַּעֲנָתוֹת
at-Anathoth who the-priests from Hilkiah son-of Jeremiah words-of (1:1)

בְּאֶרֶץ בִּנְיָמִן׃ אֲשֶׁר הָיָה דְבַר־ יְהוָה אֵלָיו בִּימֵי יֹאשִׁיָּהוּ
Josiah in-days-of to-him Yahweh word-of he-came that (2) Benjamin in-territory-of

בֶן־ אָמוֹן מֶלֶךְ יְהוּדָה בִּשְׁלֹשׁ־ עֶשְׂרֵה שָׁנָה לְמָלְכוֹ׃ וַיְהִי
and-he-was (3) to-reign-him year ten-of in-three-of Judah king-of Amon son-of

בִּימֵי יְהוֹיָקִים בֶּן־ יֹאשִׁיָּהוּ מֶלֶךְ יְהוּדָה עַד־ תֹּם עַשְׁתֵּי
one-of to-be-finished to Judah king-of Josiah son-of Jehoiakim through-days-of

עֶשְׂרֵה שָׁנָה לְצִדְקִיָּהוּ בֶן־ יֹאשִׁיָּהוּ מֶלֶךְ יְהוּדָה עַד־ גְּלוֹת יְרוּשָׁלַםִ
Jerusalem to-be-exiled when Judah king-of Josiah son-of of-Zedekiah year ten-of

בַּחֹדֶשׁ הַחֲמִישִׁי׃ וַיְהִי דְבַר־ יְהוָה אֵלַי לֵאמֹר׃ בְּטֶרֶם
at-before (5) to-say to-me Yahweh word-of and-he-came (4) the-fifth in-the-month

אֶצּוֹרְךָ בַבֶּטֶן יְדַעְתִּיךָ וּבְטֶרֶם תֵּצֵא מֵרֶחֶם
from-womb you-came-out and-at-before I-knew-you in-the-womb I-formed-you

הִקְדַּשְׁתִּיךָ נָבִיא לַגּוֹיִם נְתַתִּיךָ׃ וָאֹמַר אֲהָהּ
ah! and-I-said (6) I-appointed-you to-the-nations prophet I-set-apart-you

אֲדֹנָי יְהוִה הִנֵּה לֹא־ יָדַעְתִּי דַּבֵּר כִּי־ נַעַר אָנֹכִי׃ וַיֹּאמֶר יְהוָה
Yahweh but-he-said (7) I child for to-speak I-know not see! Yahweh Sovereign

אֵלַי אַל־ תֹּאמַר נַעַר אָנֹכִי כִּי עַל־ כָּל־ אֲשֶׁר אֶשְׁלָחֲךָ תֵּלֵךְ
you-must-go I-send-you whom every-of to but I child you-say not to-me

וְאֵת כָּל־ אֲשֶׁר אֲצַוְּךָ תְּדַבֵּר׃ אַל־ תִּירָא מִפְּנֵיהֶם
because-of-them you-be-afraid not (8) you-must-say I-command-you what every-of and

כִּי־ אִתְּךָ אֲנִי לְהַצִּלֶךָ נְאֻם־ יְהוָה׃ וַיִּשְׁלַח יְהוָה
Yahweh then-he-reached-out (9) Yahweh declaration-of to-rescue-you I with-you for

אֶת־ יָדוֹ וַיַּגַּע עַל־ פִּי וַיֹּאמֶר יְהוָה אֵלַי הִנֵּה נָתַתִּי
I-put see! to-me Yahweh and-he-said mouth-of-me to and-he-touched hand-of-him ***

דְבָרַי בְּפִיךָ׃ רְאֵה הִפְקַדְתִּיךָ ׀ הַיּוֹם הַזֶּה עַל־
over the-this the-day I-appoint-you see! (10) in-mouth-of-you words-of-me

הַגּוֹיִם וְעַל־ הַמַּמְלָכוֹת לִנְתוֹשׁ וְלִנְתוֹץ וּלְהַאֲבִיד
and-to-destroy and-to-tear-down to-uproot the-kingdoms and-over the-nations

וְלַהֲרוֹס לִבְנוֹת וְלִנְטוֹעַ׃ וַיְהִי דְבַר־ יְהוָה אֵלַי
to-me Yahweh word-of and-he-came (11) and-to-plant to-build and-to-overthrow

לֵאמֹר מָה־ אַתָּה רֹאֶה יִרְמְיָהוּ וָאֹמַר מַקֵּל שָׁקֵד אֲנִי רֹאֶה׃
seeing I almond-tree branch-of and-I-replied Jeremiah seeing you what? to-say

וַיֹּאמֶר יְהוָה אֵלַי הֵיטַבְתָּ לִרְאוֹת כִּי־ שֹׁקֵד אֲנִי עַל־
over I watching for to-see you-are-correct to-me Yahweh and-he-said (12)

דְּבָרִי לַעֲשֹׂתוֹ׃ וַיְהִי דְבַר־ יְהוָה ׀ אֵלַי שֵׁנִית לֵאמֹר
to-say again to-me Yahweh word-of and-he-came (13) to-fulfill-him word-of-me

1 The words of Jeremiah son of
Hilkiah, one of the priests at
Anathoth in the territory of Benjamin. 2 The word of the LORD came
to him in the thirteenth year of
the reign of Josiah son of Amon
king of Judah, 3 and through the
reign of Jehoiakim son of Josiah
king of Judah, down to the fifth
month of the eleventh year of
Zedekiah son of Josiah king of
Judah, when the people of Jerusalem went into exile.

*The Call of Jeremiah*

4 The word of the LORD came to
me, saying,

5 "Before I formed you in the
womb I knew[a] you,
before you were born I set
you apart;
I appointed you as a
prophet to the nations."

6 "Ah, Sovereign LORD," I said,
"I do not know how to speak; I am
only a child."
7 But the LORD said to me, "Do
not say, 'I am only a child.' You
must go to everyone I send you to
and say whatever I command you.
8 Do not be afraid of them, for I am
with you and will rescue you," declares the LORD.
9 Then the LORD reached out his
hand and touched my mouth and
said to me, "Now, I have put my
words in your mouth. 10 See, today
I appoint you over nations and
kingdoms to uproot and tear
down, to destroy and overthrow,
to build and to plant."
11 The word of the LORD came to
me: "What do you see, Jeremiah?"
"I see the branch of an almond
tree," I replied.
12 The LORD said to me, "You
have seen correctly, for I am
watching[b] to see that my word is
fulfilled."
13 The word of the LORD came to

[a]5 Or *chose*
[b]12 The Hebrew for *watching* sounds like the Hebrew for *almond tree*.

°5 ק אצרך

מָה אַתָּה רֹאֶה וָאֹמַר סִיר נָפוּחַ אֲנִי רֹאֶה וּפָנָיו מִפְּנֵי
from-faces-of and-faces-of-him seeing I boiling pot and-I-answered seeing you what?

צָפוֹנָה׃ וַיֹּאמֶר יְהוָה אֵלָי מִצָּפוֹן תִּפָּתַח
she-will-be-poured-out from-north to-me Yahweh and-he-said (14) to-north

הָרָעָה עַל כָּל־ יֹשְׁבֵי הָאָרֶץ׃ כִּי הִנְנִי קֹרֵא
summoning see-I! indeed (15) the-land ones-living-of all-of on the-disaster

לְכָל־ מִשְׁפְּחוֹת מַמְלְכוֹת צָפוֹנָה נְאֻם־ יְהוָה וּבָאוּ
and-they-will-come Yahweh declaration-of at-north kingdoms-of peoples-of to-all-of

וְנָתְנוּ אִישׁ כִּסְאוֹ פֶּתַח שַׁעֲרֵי יְרוּשָׁלִַם
Jerusalem gates-of entrance-of throne-of-him each and-they-will-set-up

וְעַל כָּל־ חוֹמֹתֶיהָ סָבִיב וְעַל כָּל־ עָרֵי יְהוּדָה׃
Judah towns-of all-of and-against surrounding walls-of-her all-of and-against

וְדִבַּרְתִּי מִשְׁפָּטַי אוֹתָם עַל כָּל־ רָעָתָם
wickedness-of-them all-of because-of them judgments-of-me and-I-will-pronounce (16)

אֲשֶׁר עֲזָבוּנִי וַיְקַטְּרוּ לֵאלֹהִים אֲחֵרִים וַיִּשְׁתַּחֲווּ
and-they-worshiped other-ones to-gods and-they-burned-incense they-forsook-me when

לְמַעֲשֵׂי יְדֵיהֶם׃ וְאַתָּה תֶּאְזֹר מָתְנֶיךָ וְקַמְתָּ
and-you-stand loins-of-you get-ready! now-you (17) hands-of-them to-things-made-of

וְדִבַּרְתָּ אֲלֵיהֶם אֵת כָּל־ אֲשֶׁר אָנֹכִי אֲצַוֶּךָּ אַל־ תֵּחַת
you-be-terrified not I-command-you I that all *** to-them and-you-say

מִפְּנֵיהֶם פֶּן־ אֲחִתְּךָ לִפְנֵיהֶם׃ וַאֲנִי הִנֵּה נְתַתִּיךָ
I-made-you see! and-I (18) before-them I-will-terrify-you or because-of-them

הַיּוֹם לְעִיר מִבְצָר וּלְעַמּוּד בַּרְזֶל וּלְחֹמוֹת נְחֹשֶׁת
bronze and-as-walls-of iron and-as-pillar-of fortification as-city-of the-day

עַל־ כָּל־ הָאָרֶץ לְמַלְכֵי יְהוּדָה לְשָׂרֶיהָ
against-officials-of-her Judah against-kings-of the-land whole-of against

לְכֹהֲנֶיהָ וּלְעַם הָאָרֶץ׃ וְנִלְחֲמוּ
and-they-will-fight (19) the-land and-against-people-of against-priests-of-her

אֵלֶיךָ וְלֹא־ יוּכְלוּ לָךְ כִּי־ אִתְּךָ אֲנִי נְאֻם־
declaration-of I with-you for over-you they-will-overcome but-not against-you

יְהוָה לְהַצִּילֶךָ׃ וַיְהִי דְבַר־ יְהוָה אֵלַי לֵאמֹר׃ הָלֹךְ
to-go (2) to-say to-me Yahweh word-of and-he-came (2:1) to-rescue-you Yahweh

וְקָרָאתָ בְאָזְנֵי יְרוּשָׁלִַם לֵאמֹר כֹּה אָמַר יְהוָה זָכַרְתִּי
I-remember Yahweh he-says this to-say Jerusalem in-ears-of and-you-proclaim

לָךְ חֶסֶד נְעוּרַיִךְ אַהֲבַת כְּלוּלֹתָיִךְ לֶכְתֵּךְ אַחֲרַי
after-me to-follow-you brides-of-you love-of youths-of-you devotion-of of-you

בַּמִּדְבָּר בְּאֶרֶץ לֹא זְרוּעָה׃ קֹדֶשׁ יִשְׂרָאֵל לַיהוָה
to-Yahweh Israel holy (3) one-being-sown not through-land through-the-desert

me again: "What do you see?"
"I see a boiling pot, tilting away from the north," I answered.
14The LORD said to me, "From the north disaster will be poured out on all who live in the land. 15I
am about to summon all the peoples of the northern kingdoms," declares the LORD.

"Their kings will come and set up their thrones
in the entrance of the gates of Jerusalem;
they will come against all her surrounding walls
and against all the towns of Judah.
16I will pronounce my judgments on my people
because of their wickedness in forsaking me,
in burning incense to other gods
and in worshiping what their hands have made.

17"Get yourself ready! Stand up and say to them whatever I command you. Do not be terrified by them, or I will terrify you before them. 18Today I have made you a fortified city, an iron pillar and a bronze wall to stand against the whole land—against the kings of Judah, its officials, its priests and the people of the land. 19They will fight against you but will not overcome you, for I am with you and will rescue you," declares the LORD.

*Israel Forsakes God*

2 The word of the LORD came to me: 2"Go and proclaim in the hearing of Jerusalem:

" 'I remember the devotion of your youth,
how as a bride you loved me
and followed me through the desert,
through a land not sown.
3Israel was holy to the LORD,

רֵאשִׁית תְּבוּאָתֹה כָּל־ אֹכְלָיו יֶאְשָׁמוּ
they-were-held-guilty ones-devouring-him all-of harvest-of-him firstfruit-of

רָעָה תָּבֹא אֲלֵיהֶם נְאֻם־ יְהוָה׃ שִׁמְעוּ דְבַר־ יְהוָה
Yahweh word-of hear! (4) Yahweh declaration-of to-them she-overtook disaster

בֵּית יַעֲקֹב וְכָל־ מִשְׁפְּחוֹת בֵּית יִשְׂרָאֵל׃ כֹּה׀ אָמַר יְהוָה מַה־
what? Yahweh he-says this (5) Israel house-of clans-of and-all-of Jacob house-of

מָּצְאוּ אֲבוֹתֵיכֶם בִּי עָוֶל כִּי רָחֲקוּ מֵעָלָי
from-by-me they-strayed-far that fault in-me fathers-of-you they-found

וַיֵּלְכוּ אַחֲרֵי הַהֶבֶל וַיֶּהְבָּלוּ׃ וְלֹא
and-not (6) and-they-became-worthless the-worthless-idol after and-they-followed

אָמְרוּ אַיֵּה יְהוָה הַמַּעֲלֶה אֹתָנוּ מֵאֶרֶץ מִצְרָיִם הַמּוֹלִיךְ
the-one-leading Egypt from-land-of us the-one-bringing-up Yahweh where? they-asked

אֹתָנוּ בַּמִּדְבָּר בְּאֶרֶץ עֲרָבָה וְשׁוּחָה בְּאֶרֶץ צִיָּה
drought through-land-of and-rift desert through-land-of through-the-wilderness us

וְצַלְמָוֶת בְּאֶרֶץ לֹא־ עָבַר בָּהּ אִישׁ וְלֹא־ יָשַׁב אָדָם
one he-lives and-not one through-her he-travels not through-land and-darkness

שָׁם׃ וָאָבִיא אֶתְכֶם אֶל־ אֶרֶץ הַכַּרְמֶל לֶאֱכֹל פִּרְיָהּ
fruit-of-her to-eat the-fertility land-of into you and-I-brought (7) there

וְטוּבָהּ וַתָּבֹאוּ וַתְּטַמְּאוּ אֶת־ אַרְצִי
land-of-me *** and-you-defiled but-you-came and-richness-of-her

וְנַחֲלָתִי שַׂמְתֶּם לְתוֹעֵבָה׃ הַכֹּהֲנִים לֹא אָמְרוּ אַיֵּה
where? they-asked not the-priests (8) as-detestable you-made and-inheritance-of-me

יְהוָה וְתֹפְשֵׂי הַתּוֹרָה לֹא יְדָעוּנִי וְהָרֹעִים
and-the-ones-leading they-knew-me not the-law and-ones-dealing-of Yahweh

פָּשְׁעוּ בִי וְהַנְּבִיאִים נִבְּאוּ בַבַּעַל וְאַחֲרֵי
and-after by-the-Baal they-prophesied and-the-prophets against-me they-rebelled

לֹא־ יוֹעִלוּ הָלָכוּ׃ לָכֵן עֹד אָרִיב אִתְּכֶם
against-you I-bring-charges again therefore (9) they-followed they-have-worth not

נְאֻם־ יְהוָה וְאֶת־ בְּנֵי בְנֵיכֶם אָרִיב׃
I-will-bring-charges children-of-you children-of and-against Yahweh declaration-of

כִּי עִבְרוּ אִיֵּי כִתִּיִּים וּרְאוּ וְקֵדָר שִׁלְחוּ וְהִתְבּוֹנְנוּ
and-observe! send! and-Kedar and-look! Kittim coasts-of cross-over indeed (10)

מְאֹד וּרְאוּ הֵן הָיְתָה כָּזֹאת׃ הַהֵימִיר גּוֹי אֱלֹהִים וְהֵמָּה
yet-they gods nation he-changed? (11) like-this she-was if and-see! closely

לֹא אֱלֹהִים וְעַמִּי הֵמִיר כְּבוֹדוֹ בְּלוֹא יוֹעִיל׃
he-has-worth for-not Glory-of-him he-changed but-people-of-me gods not

שֹׁמּוּ שָׁמַיִם עַל־ זֹאת וְשַׂעֲרוּ חָרְבוּ מְאֹד נְאֻם־
declaration-of greatly be-horrified! and-shudder! this at heavens be-appalled! (12)

the firstfruits of his harvest;
all who devoured her were
held guilty,
and disaster overtook
them,' "
declares the LORD.

4Hear the word of the LORD, O
house of Jacob,
all you clans of the house of
Israel.

5This is what the LORD says:

"What fault did your fathers
find in me,
that they strayed so far from
me?
They followed worthless idols
and became worthless
themselves.
6They did not ask, 'Where is
the LORD,
who brought us up out of
Egypt
and led us through the barren
wilderness,
through a land of deserts
and rifts,
a land of drought and
darkness,[c]
a land where no one travels
and no one lives?'
7I brought you into a fertile
land
to eat its fruit and rich
produce.
But you came and defiled my
land
and made my inheritance
detestable.
8The priests did not ask,
'Where is the LORD?'
Those who deal with the law
did not know me;
the leaders rebelled against
me.
The prophets prophesied by
Baal,
following worthless idols.

9"Therefore I bring charges
against you again,"
declares the LORD.
"And I will bring charges
against your children's
children.
10Cross over to the coasts of
Kittim[d] and look,
send to Kedar[e] and observe
closely;
see if there has ever been
anything like this:
11Has a nation ever changed its
gods?
(Yet they are not gods at all.)
But my people have exchanged
their[f] Glory
for worthless idols.
12Be appalled at this, O heavens,
and shudder with great
horror,"
declares the LORD.

[c]6 *Or and the shadow of death*
[d]10 That is, Cyprus and western coastlands
[e]10 The home of Bedouin tribes in the Syro-Arabian desert
[f]11 Masoretic Text; an ancient Hebrew scribal tradition *my*

°3 ק תבואתו

יְהוָה׃ כִּֽי־שְׁתַּיִם רָעוֹת עָשָׂה עַמִּי אֹתִי עָזְבוּ מְקוֹר ׀
spring-of they-forsook me people-of-me they-committed sins two indeed (13) Yahweh

מַיִם חַיִּים לַחְצֹב לָהֶם בֹּארוֹת בֹּארֹת נִשְׁבָּרִים אֲשֶׁר לֹא־
not that ones-being-broken cisterns cisterns for-them to-dig living-ones waters

יָכִלוּ הַמָּיִם׃ הַעֶבֶד יִשְׂרָאֵל אִם־יְלִיד בַּיִת הוּא מַדּוּעַ הָיָה
he-became why? he house slave-of or Israel servant? (14) the-waters they-can-hold

לָבַז׃ עָלָיו יִשְׁאֲגוּ כְפִרִים נָתְנוּ קוֹלָם וַיָּשִׁיתוּ
and-they-laid growl-of-them they-raised lions they-roared at-him (15) as-plunder

אַרְצוֹ לְשַׁמָּה עָרָיו נִצְּתָה מִבְּלִי יֹשֵׁב׃
one-inhabiting from-not they-are-burned towns-of-him as-waste land-of-him

גַּם־בְּנֵי־נֹף וְתַחְפַּנְסֶ יִרְעוּךְ קָדְקֹד׃ הֲלוֹא־זֹאת
this not? (17) crown-of-head they-shaved-you and-Tahpanhes Noph men-of also (16)

תַּעֲשֶׂה־לָּךְ עָזְבֵךְ אֶת־יְהוָה אֱלֹהַיִךְ בְּעֵת מוֹלִיכֵךְ
leading-you at-time-of God-of-you Yahweh *** to-forsake-you on-you you-brought

בַּדָּרֶךְ׃ וְעַתָּה מַה־לָּךְ לְדֶרֶךְ מִצְרַיִם לִשְׁתּוֹת מֵי שִׁחוֹר
Shihor waters-of to-drink Egypt to-way-of to-you why? and-now (18) in-the-way

וּמַה־לָּךְ לְדֶרֶךְ אַשּׁוּר לִשְׁתּוֹת מֵי נָהָר׃ תְּיַסְּרֵךְ
she-will-punish-you (19) River waters-of to-drink Assyria to-way-of to-you and-why?

רָעָתֵךְ וּמְשֻׁבוֹתַיִךְ תּוֹכִחֻךְ וּדְעִי
then-consider! they-will-rebuke-you and-backslidings-of-you wickedness-of-you

וּרְאִי כִּי־רַע וָמָר עָזְבֵךְ אֶת־יְהוָה אֱלֹהָיִךְ וְלֹא
and-not God-of-you Yahweh *** to-forsake-you and-bitter evil that and-realize!

פַחְדָּתִי אֵלַיִךְ נְאֻם־אֲדֹנָי יְהוִה צְבָאוֹת׃ כִּי מֵעוֹלָם
at-long-ago indeed (20) Hosts Yahweh-of Lord declaration-of to-you awe-of-me

שָׁבַרְתִּי עֻלֵּךְ נִתַּקְתִּי מוֹסְרֹתַיִךְ וַתֹּאמְרִי לֹא אֶעֱבֹד
I-will-serve not and-you-said bonds-of-you *I-tore-off yoke-of-you *I-broke-off

כִּי עַל־כָּל־גִּבְעָה גְּבֹהָה וְתַחַת כָּל־עֵץ רַעֲנָן אַתְּ צֹעָה
lying-down you spreading tree every-of and-under high hill every-of on indeed

זֹנָה׃ וְאָנֹכִי נְטַעְתִּיךְ שֹׂרֵק כֻּלֹּה זֶרַע
stock-of all-of-him choice-vine I-planted-you and-I (21) being-prostitute

אֱמֶת וְאֵיךְ נֶהְפַּכְתְּ לִי סוּרֵי הַגֶּפֶן נָכְרִיָּה׃
wild the-vine ones-being-corrupt against-me you-turned then-how? reliability

כִּי אִם־תְּכַבְּסִי בַּנֶּתֶר וְתַרְבִּי־לָךְ בֹּרִית
soap for-you and-you-make-abundant with-the-soda you-wash if although (22)

נִכְתָּם עֲוֹנֵךְ לְפָנַי נְאֻם אֲדֹנָי יְהוִה׃
Yahweh Sovereign declaration-of before-me guilt-of-you one-being-stained

אֵיךְ תֹּאמְרִי לֹא נִטְמֵאתִי אַחֲרֵי הַבְּעָלִים לֹא הָלַכְתִּי רְאִי
see! I-ran not the-Baals after I-am-defiled not can-you-say how? (23)

13 "My people have committed
two sins:
They have forsaken me,
the spring of living water,
and have dug their own
cisterns,
broken cisterns that cannot
hold water.
14 Is Israel a servant, a slave by
birth?
Why then has he become
plunder?
15 Lions have roared;
they have growled at him.
They have laid waste his land;
his towns are burned and
deserted.
16 Also, the men of Memphis[f]
and Tahpanhes
have shaved the crown of
your head.[g]
17 Have you not brought this on
yourselves
by forsaking the LORD your
God
when he led you in the way?
18 Now why go to Egypt
to drink water from the
Shihor[h]?
And why go to Assyria
to drink water from the
River[i]?
19 Your wickedness will punish
you;
your backsliding will rebuke
you.
Consider then and realize
how evil and bitter it is for
you
when you forsake the LORD
your God
and have no awe of me,"
declares the Lord, the
LORD Almighty.

20 "Long ago you broke off your
yoke
and tore off your bonds;
you said, 'I will not serve
you!'
Indeed, on every high hill
and under every spreading
tree
you lay down as a
prostitute.
21 I had planted you like a choice
vine
of sound and reliable stock.
How then did you turn against
me
into a corrupt, wild vine?
22 Although you wash yourself
with soda
and use an abundance of
soap,
the stain of your guilt is still
before me,"
declares the Sovereign
LORD.
23 "How can you say, 'I am not
defiled;
I have not run after the
Baals'?

f16 Hebrew *Noph*
g16 Or *have cracked your skull*
h18 That is, a branch of the Nile
i18 That is, the Euphrates

*20 The NIV, with the LXX, reads תִּי־ as the old second person feminine ending *you-broke-off . . . you-tore-off*

°15 ק נצתו
°16 ק ותחפנחס
°20 ק אעבור

דַּרְכֵּךְ בַּגַּיְא דְּעִי מֶה עָשִׂית בִּכְרָה קַלָּה
swift she-camel you-did what consider! in-the-valley behavior-of-you

מְשָׂרֶכֶת דְּרָכֶיהָ׃ פֶּרֶה ׀ לִמֻּד מִדְבָּר בְּאַוַּת
in-craving-of desert accustomed-of wild-donkey (24) ways-of-her running-around

נַפְשׁוֹ° שָׁאֲפָה רוּחַ תַּאֲנָתָהּ מִי יְשִׁיבֶנָּה כָּל־
any-of he-can-restrain-her who? heat-of-her wind she-sniffs self-of-her

מְבַקְשֶׁיהָ לֹא יִיעָפוּ בְּחָדְשָׁהּ יִמְצָאוּנְהָ׃
they-will-find-her at-month-of-her they-become-tired not ones-pursuing-her

מִנְעִי רַגְלֵךְ מִיָּחֵף וּגוֹרֵנֵךְ° מִצִּמְאָה
from-dryness and-throat-of-you from-bareness foot-of-you withhold! (25)

וַתֹּאמְרִי נוֹאָשׁ לוֹא כִּי־ אָהַבְתִּי זָרִים וְאַחֲרֵיהֶם
and-after-them ones-being-foreign I-love indeed not being-useless but-you-said

אֵלֵךְ׃ כְּבֹשֶׁת גַּנָּב כִּי יִמָּצֵא כֵּן הֹבִישׁוּ
they-are-disgraced so he-is-caught when thief as-disgrace-of (26) I-must-go

בֵּית יִשְׂרָאֵל הֵמָּה מַלְכֵיהֶם שָׂרֵיהֶם וְכֹהֲנֵיהֶם
and-priests-of-them officials-of-them kings-of-them they Israel house-of

וּנְבִיאֵיהֶם׃ אֹמְרִים לָעֵץ אָבִי אַתָּה וְלָאֶבֶן
and-to-the-stone you father-of-me to-the-wood ones-saying (27) and-prophets-of-them

אַתְּ יְלִדְתָּנִי° כִּי־ פָנוּ אֵלַי עֹרֶף וְלֹא פָנִים וּבְעֵת
yet-in-time-of faces and-not back to-me they-turned indeed you-bore-us you

רָעָתָם יֹאמְרוּ קוּמָה וְהוֹשִׁיעֵנוּ׃ וְאַיֵּה אֱלֹהֶיךָ אֲשֶׁר
that gods-of-you then-where? (28) and-save-us! come! they-say trouble-of-them

עָשִׂיתָ לָּךְ יָקוּמוּ אִם־ יוֹשִׁיעוּךָ בְּעֵת רָעָתֶךָ
trouble-of-you in-time-of they-can-save-you if let-them-come for-you you-made

כִּי מִסְפַּר עָרֶיךָ הָיוּ אֱלֹהֶיךָ יְהוּדָה׃ לָמָּה תָרִיבוּ
you-bring-charges why? (29) Judah gods-of-you they-are towns-of-you number-of for

אֵלָי כֻּלְּכֶם פְּשַׁעְתֶּם בִּי נְאֻם־ יְהוָה׃
Yahweh declaration-of against-me you-rebelled all-of-you against-me

לַשָּׁוְא הִכֵּיתִי אֶת־ בְּנֵיכֶם מוּסָר לֹא לָקָחוּ
they-responded-to not correction peoples-of-you *** I-punished in-the-vain (30)

אָכְלָה חַרְבְּכֶם נְבִיאֵיכֶם כְּאַרְיֵה מַשְׁחִית׃ הַדּוֹר
the-generation (31) ravening like-lion prophets-of-you sword-of-you she-devoured

אַתֶּם רְאוּ דְבַר־ יְהוָה הֲמִדְבָּר הָיִיתִי לְיִשְׂרָאֵל אִם אֶרֶץ מַאְפֵּלְיָה
great-darkness land-of or to-Israel I-was desert? Yahweh word-of consider! you

מַדּוּעַ אָמְרוּ עַמִּי רַדְנוּ לוֹא־ נָבוֹא עוֹד אֵלֶיךָ׃
to-you more we-will-come not we-can-roam people-of-me they-say why?

הֲתִשְׁכַּח בְּתוּלָה עֶדְיָהּ כַּלָּה קִשֻּׁרֶיהָ
wedding-ornaments-of-her bride jewelry-of-her maiden does-she-forget? (32)

See how you behaved in the valley;
consider what you have done.
You are a swift she-camel
running here and there,
24 a wild donkey accustomed to the desert,
sniffing the wind in her craving—
in her heat who can restrain her?
Any males that pursue her need not tire themselves;
at mating time they will find her.
25 Do not run until your feet are bare
and your throat is dry.
But you said, 'It's no use!
I love foreign gods,
and I must go after them.'

26 "As a thief is disgraced when he is caught,
so the house of Israel is disgraced—
they, their kings and their officials,
their priests and their prophets.
27 They say to wood, 'You are my father,'
and to stone, 'You gave me birth.'
They have turned their backs to me
and not their faces;
yet when they are in trouble, they say,
'Come and save us!'
28 Where then are the gods you made for yourselves?
Let them come if they can save you
when you are in trouble!
For you have as many gods
as you have towns, O Judah.

29 "Why do you bring charges against me?
You have all rebelled against me,"
declares the LORD.
30 "In vain I punished your people;
they did not respond to correction.
Your sword has devoured your prophets
like a ravening lion.

31 "You of this generation, consider the word of the LORD:

"Have I been a desert to Israel
or a land of great darkness?
Why do my people say, 'We are free to roam;
we will come to you no more'?
32 Does a maiden forget her jewelry,
a bride her wedding ornaments?

°24 ק נפשה
°25 ק וגרונך
°27 ק ילדתנו

וְעַמִּי שְׁכֵחוּנִי יָמִים אֵין מִסְפָּר׃ מַה־ תֵּיטִבִי
you-make-skilled how! (33) number without days they-forgot-me yet-people-of-me

דַּרְכֵּךְ לְבַקֵּשׁ אַהֲבָה לָכֵן גַּם אֶת־ הָרָעוֹת °לִמַּדְתִּי אֶת־
*** you-can-teach the-worst-women *** even therefore love to-seek way-of-you

דְּרָכָיִךְ׃ גַּם בִּכְנָפַיִךְ נִמְצְאוּ דַּם נַפְשׁוֹת
lives-of blood-of they-are-found on-clothes-of-you also (34) ways-of-you

אֶבְיוֹנִים נְקִיִּים לֹא־ בַמַּחְתֶּרֶת מְצָאתִים כִּי עַל־
in-spite-of yet you-caught-them in-the-breaking-in not innocent-ones poor-ones

כָּל־ אֵלֶּה׃ וַתֹּאמְרִי כִּי נִקֵּיתִי אַךְ שָׁב אַפּוֹ
anger-of-him he-turned surely! I-am-innocent indeed then-you-say (35) these all-of

מִמֶּנִּי הִנְנִי נִשְׁפָּט אוֹתָךְ עַל־ אָמְרֵךְ לֹא חָטָאתִי׃ מַה־ תֵּזְלִי
you-go-about why? (36) I-sinned not to-say-you because you judging see-I! from-me

מְאֹד לְשַׁנּוֹת אֶת־ דַּרְכֵּךְ גַּם מִמִּצְרַיִם תֵּבֹשִׁי כַּאֲשֶׁר־
just-as you-will-be-disappointed by-Egypt also way-of-you *** to-change much

בֹּשְׁתְּ מֵאַשּׁוּר׃ גַּם מֵאֵת זֶה תֵּצְאִי
you-will-leave that from also (37) by-Assyria you-were-disappointed

וְיָדַיִךְ עַל־ רֹאשֵׁךְ כִּי־ מָאַס יְהוָה בְּמִבְטַחַיִךְ
to-ones-trusted-of-you Yahweh he-rejected for head-of-you on and-hands-of-you

וְלֹא תַצְלִיחִי לָהֶם׃ לֵאמֹר הֵן יְשַׁלַּח אִישׁ אֶת־ אִשְׁתּוֹ
wife-of-him *** man he-divorces if to-say (3:1) by-them you-will-be-helped and-not

וְהָלְכָה מֵאִתּוֹ וְהָיְתָה לְאִישׁ־ אַחֵר הֲיָשׁוּב
should-he-return? another to-man and-she-becomes from-with-him and-she-leaves

אֵלֶיהָ עוֹד הֲלוֹא חָנוֹף תֶּחֱנַף הָאָרֶץ הַהִיא וְאַתְּ
but-you the-that the-land she-would-be-defiled to-be-defiled not? again to-her

זָנִית רֵעִים רַבִּים וְשׁוֹב אֵלַי נְאֻם־ יְהוָה׃
Yahweh declaration-of to-me now-to-return many-ones lovers you-were-prostitute

שְׂאִי־ עֵינַיִךְ עַל־ שְׁפָיִם וּרְאִי אֵיפֹה לֹא °שֻׁגַּלְתְּ*
*you-were-ravished not where? and-see! barren-heights to eyes-of-you lift! (2)

עַל־דְּרָכִים יָשַׁבְתְּ לָהֶם כַּעֲרָבִי בַּמִּדְבָּר וַתַּחֲנִיפִי אֶרֶץ
land and-you-defiled in-the-desert like-nomad for-them you-sat roads by

בִּזְנוּתַיִךְ וּבְרָעָתֵךְ׃ וַיִּמָּנְעוּ
so-they-were-withheld (3) and-with-wickedness-of-you with-prostitutions-of-you

רְבִבִים וּמַלְקוֹשׁ לוֹא הָיָה וּמֵצַח אִשָּׁה זוֹנָה
one-being-prostitute woman yet-forehead-of he-fell not and-spring-rain showers

הָיָה לָךְ מֵאַנְתְּ הִכָּלֵם׃ הֲלוֹא מֵעַתָּה °קָרָאתִי לִי
to-me you-called at-now not? (4) to-blush-with-shame you-refuse to-you he-is

אָבִי אַלּוּף נְעֻרַי אָתָּה׃ הֲיִנְטֹר לְעוֹלָם אִם־
or to-always will-he-be-angry? (5) you youths-of-me friend-of Father-of-me

Yet my people have forgotten
me,
days without number.
33How skilled you are at
pursuing love!
Even the worst of women
can learn from your ways.
34On your clothes men find
the lifeblood of the innocent
poor,
though you did not catch
them breaking in.
Yet in spite of all this
35 you say, 'I am innocent;
he is not angry with me.'
But I will pass judgment on
you
because you say, 'I have not
sinned.'
36Why do you go about so
much,
changing your ways?
You will be disappointed by
Egypt
as you were by Assyria.
37You will also leave that place
with your hands on your
head,
for the LORD has rejected those
you trust;
you will not be helped by
them.

3 "If a man divorces his wife
and she leaves him and
marries another man,
should he return to her again?
Would not the land be
completely defiled?
But you have lived as a
prostitute with many
lovers—
would you now return to
me?"
declares the LORD.
2"Look up to the barren heights
and see.
Is there any place where
you have not been
ravished?
By the roadside you sat
waiting for lovers,
sat like a nomad[j] in the
desert.
You have defiled the land
with your prostitution and
wickedness.
3Therefore the showers have
been withheld,
and no spring rains have
fallen.
Yet you have the brazen look
of a prostitute;
you refuse to blush with
shame.
4Have you not just called to me:
'My Father, my friend from
my youth,
5will you always be angry?

j2 Or *an Arab*

*2 The *Qere* word is a less graphic synonym of the *Kethib*.

°33 ק למדת
°2 ק שכבת
°4 ק קראת

יִשְׁמֹר לָנֶצַח הִנֵּה דִבַּרְתִּי וַתַּעֲשִׂי הָרָעוֹת וַתּוּכָל׃
that-you-can the-evils but-you-do you-talk see! to-forever will-he-continue

וַיֹּאמֶר יְהוָה אֵלַי בִּימֵי יֹאשִׁיָּהוּ הַמֶּלֶךְ הֲרָאִיתָ אֲשֶׁר עָשְׂתָה
she-did what you-saw? the-king Josiah in-days-of to-me Yahweh and-he-said (6)

מְשֻׁבָה יִשְׂרָאֵל הֹלְכָה הִיא עַל־ כָּל־ הַר גָּבֹהַּ וְאֶל־ תַּחַת כָּל־
every-of under and-at high hill every-of on she one-going Israel faithless-one

עֵץ רַעֲנָן וַתִּזְנִי־ שָׁם׃ וָאֹמַר אַחֲרֵי עֲשׂוֹתָהּ
to-do-her after and-I-thought (7) there and-she-committed-adultery spreading tree

אֶת־ כָּל־ אֵלֶּה אֵלַי תָּשׁוּב וְלֹא־ שָׁבָה וַתִּרְאֶה°
and-she-saw she-returned but-not she-would-return to-me these all-of ***

בָּגוֹדָה אֲחוֹתָהּ יְהוּדָה׃ וָאֵרֶא כִּי עַל־ כָּל־ אֹדוֹת
causes all-of because-of that and-I-saw (8) Judah sister-of-her unfaithful-one

אֲשֶׁר נִאֲפָה מְשֻׁבָה יִשְׂרָאֵל שִׁלַּחְתִּיהָ וָאֶתֵּן אֶת־
*** and-I-gave I-sent-away-her Israel faithless-one she-committed-adultery that

סֵפֶר כְּרִיתֻתֶיהָ אֵלֶיהָ וְלֹא יָרְאָה בֹּגֵדָה
one-being-unfaithful she-had-fear yet-not to-her divorces-of-her certificate-of

יְהוּדָה אֲחוֹתָהּ וַתֵּלֶךְ וַתִּזֶן גַּם־ הִיא׃
she also and-she-committed-adultery and-she-went-out sister-of-her Judah

וְהָיָה מִקֹּל זְנוּתָהּ וַתֶּחֱנַף אֶת־
*** that-she-defiled immorality-of-her because-of-littleness-of and-he-was (9)

הָאָרֶץ וַתִּנְאַף אֶת־ הָאֶבֶן וְאֶת־ הָעֵץ׃ וְגַם־
yet-also (10) the-wood and-with the-stone with and-she-committed-adultery the-land

בְּכָל־ זֹאת לֹא־ שָׁבָה אֵלַי בָּגוֹדָה אֲחוֹתָהּ
sister-of-her unfaithful-one to-me she-returned not this in-spite-of-all-of

יְהוּדָה בְּכָל־ לִבָּהּ כִּי אִם־ בְּשֶׁקֶר נְאֻם־ יְהוָה׃
Yahweh declaration-of in-pretence only but heart-of-her with-all-of Judah

וַיֹּאמֶר יְהוָה אֵלַי צִדְּקָה נַפְשָׁהּ מְשֻׁבָה יִשְׂרָאֵל
Israel faithless-one self-of-her she-is-righteous to-me Yahweh and-he-said (11)

מִבֹּגֵדָה יְהוּדָה׃ הָלֹךְ וְקָרָאתָ אֶת־ הַדְּבָרִים
the-messages *** and-you-proclaim to-go (12) Judah more-than-one-being-unfaithful

הָאֵלֶּה צָפוֹנָה וְאָמַרְתָּ שׁוּבָה מְשֻׁבָה יִשְׂרָאֵל נְאֻם־
declaration-of Israel faithless-one return! and-you-say toward-north the-these

יְהוָה לוֹא־ אַפִּיל פָּנַי בָּכֶם כִּי־ חָסִיד אֲנִי נְאֻם־
declaration-of I merciful for on-you faces-of-me I-will-turn-down not Yahweh

יְהוָה לֹא אֶטּוֹר לְעוֹלָם׃ אַךְ דְּעִי עֲוֹנֵךְ כִּי
for guilt-of-you acknowledge! only (13) to-forever I-will-be-angry not Yahweh

בַּיהוָה אֱלֹהַיִךְ פָּשָׁעַתְּ וַתְּפַזְּרִי אֶת־ דְּרָכַיִךְ
favors-of-you *** and-you-scattered you-rebelled God-of-you against-Yahweh

°5 ק דברת
°7 ק ותרא

Will your wrath continue
forever?'
This is how you talk,
but you do all the evil you
can."

*Unfaithful Israel*

6During the reign of King Josiah, the LORD said to me, "Have you seen what faithless Israel has done? She has gone up on every high hill and under every spreading tree and has committed adultery there. 7I thought that after she had done all this she would return to me but she did not, and her unfaithful sister Judah saw it. 8I gave faithless Israel her certificate of divorce and sent her away because of all her adulteries. Yet I saw that her unfaithful sister Judah had no fear; she also went out and committed adultery. 9Because Israel's immorality mattered so little to her, she defiled the land and committed adultery with stone and wood. 10In spite of all this, her unfaithful sister Judah did not return to me with all her heart, but only in pretense," declares the LORD.

11The LORD said to me, "Faithless Israel is more righteous than unfaithful Judah. 12Go, proclaim this message toward the north:

" 'Return, faithless Israel,'
declares the LORD,
'I will frown on you no
longer,
for I am merciful,' declares the
LORD,
'I will not be angry forever.
13Only acknowledge your guilt—
you have rebelled against
the LORD your God,
you have scattered your favors

לַזָּרִים תַּחַת כָּל־ עֵץ רַעֲנָן וּבְקוֹלִי לֹא־
not and-to-voice-of-me spreading tree every-of under to-the-ones-being-foreign

שְׁמַעְתֶּם נְאֻם־ יְהוָה׃ שׁוּבוּ בָנִים שׁוֹבָבִים נְאֻם־
declaration-of faithless-ones peoples return! (14) Yahweh declaration-of you-obeyed

יְהוָה כִּי אָנֹכִי בָּעַלְתִּי בָכֶם וְלָקַחְתִּי אֶתְכֶם אֶחָד מֵעִיר וּשְׁנַיִם
and-two from-town one you and-I-will-choose of-you I-am-husband I for Yahweh

מִמִּשְׁפָּחָה וְהֵבֵאתִי אֶתְכֶם צִיּוֹן׃ וְנָתַתִּי לָכֶם רֹעִים
ones-being-shepherds to-you then-I-will-give (15) Zion you and-I-will-bring from-clan

כְּלִבִּי וְרָעוּ אֶתְכֶם דֵּעָה וְהַשְׂכֵּיל׃
and-to-understand knowledge you and-they-will-lead after-heart-of-me

וְהָיָה כִּי תִרְבּוּ וּפְרִיתֶם בָּאָרֶץ
in-the-land and-you-increase you-become-numerous when and-he-will-be (16)

בַּיָּמִים הָהֵמָּה נְאֻם־ יְהוָה לֹא־ יֹאמְרוּ עוֹד אֲרוֹן
ark-of longer they-will-say not Yahweh declaration-of the-those in-the-days

בְּרִית־ יְהוָה וְלֹא יַעֲלֶה עַל־ לֵב וְלֹא יִזְכְּרוּ־
they-will-remember or-not mind into he-will-enter and-not Yahweh covenant-of

בוֹ וְלֹא יִפְקֹדוּ וְלֹא יֵעָשֶׂה עוֹד׃ בָּעֵת הַהִיא
the-that at-the-time (17) again he-will-be-made or-not they-will-miss or-not to-him

יִקְרְאוּ לִירוּשָׁלִַם כִּסֵּא יְהוָה וְנִקְווּ* אֵלֶיהָ כָל־
all-of in-her and-they-will-gather Yahweh Throne-of to-Jerusalem they-will-call

הַגּוֹיִם לְשֵׁם יְהוָה לִירוּשָׁלִָם וְלֹא־ יֵלְכוּ עוֹד אַחֲרֵי
after longer they-will-follow and-not in-Jerusalem Yahweh for-name-of the-nations

שְׁרִרוּת לִבָּם הָרָע׃ בַּיָּמִים הָהֵמָּה יֵלְכוּ
they-will-join the-those in-the-days (18) the-evil heart-of-them stubbornness-of

בֵית־ יְהוּדָה עַל־ בֵּית יִשְׂרָאֵל וְיָבֹאוּ יַחְדָּו מֵאֶרֶץ צָפוֹן
north from-land-of together and-they-will-come Israel house-of with Judah house-of

עַל־הָאָרֶץ אֲשֶׁר הִנְחַלְתִּי אֶת־ אֲבוֹתֵיכֶם׃ וְאָנֹכִי אָמַרְתִּי אֵיךְ
how! I-said and-I (19) fathers-of-you *** I-gave-as-inheritance that the-land to

אֲשִׁיתֵךְ בַּבָּנִים וְאֶתֶּן־ לָךְ אֶרֶץ חֶמְדָּה
desire land-of to-you and-I-would-give like-the-sons I-would-treat-you

נַחֲלַת צְבִי צִבְאוֹת גּוֹיִם וָאֹמַר אָבִי תִּקְרְאוּ־
you-would-call Father-of-me and-I-thought nations hosts-of beauty-of inheritance-of

לִי וּמֵאַחֲרַי לֹא תָשׁוּבוּ׃ אָכֵן בָּגְדָה אִשָּׁה
woman she-is-unfaithful but (20) you-would-turn not and-from-after-me to-me

מֵרֵעָהּ כֵּן בְּגַדְתֶּם בִּי בֵּית יִשְׂרָאֵל נְאֻם־
declaration-of Israel house-of to-me you-were-unfaithful so to-husband-of-her

יְהוָה׃ קוֹל עַל־ שְׁפָיִים נִשְׁמָע בְּכִי תַחֲנוּנֵי בְּנֵי
peoples-of pleadings-of weeping-of he-is-heard barren-heights on cry (21) Yahweh

to foreign gods
under every spreading tree,
and have not obeyed me,' "
declares the LORD.

14"Return, faithless people," declares the LORD, "for I am your husband. I will choose you—one from a town and two from a clan—and bring you to Zion. 15Then I will give you shepherds after my own heart, who will lead you with knowledge and understanding. 16In those days, when your numbers have increased greatly in the land," declares the LORD, "men will no longer say, 'The ark of the covenant of the LORD.' It will never enter their minds or be remembered; it will not be missed, nor will another one be made. 17At that time they will call Jerusalem The Throne of the LORD, and all nations will gather in Jerusalem to honor the name of the LORD. No longer will they follow the stubbornness of their evil hearts. 18In those days the house of Judah will join the house of Israel, and together they will come from a northern land to the land I gave your forefathers as an inheritance.

19"I myself said,

" 'How gladly would I treat
you like sons
and give you a desirable
land,
the most beautiful
inheritance of any
nation.'
I thought you would call me
'Father'
and not turn away from
following me.
20But like a woman unfaithful to
her husband,
so you have been unfaithful
to me, O house of Israel,"
declares the LORD.

21A cry is heard on the barren
heights,
the weeping and pleading of
the people of Israel,

*17 Most mss have no *dagesh* in the first *vav* (וּ).

°19a ק תקראי

°19b ק תשובי

יִשְׂרָאֵל כִּי הֶעֱווּ* אֶת־ דַּרְכָּם שָׁכְחוּ אֶת־ יְהוָה אֱלֹהֵיהֶם׃
God-of-them Yahweh *** they-forgot way-of-them *** they-perverted because Israel

(22) שׁוּבוּ בָּנִים שׁוֹבָבִים אֶרְפָּה מְשׁוּבֹתֵיכֶם הִנְנוּ
see-we! backslidings-of-you I-will-cure faithless-ones peoples return! (22)

אָתָנוּ לָךְ כִּי אַתָּה יְהוָה אֱלֹהֵינוּ׃ (23) אָכֵן לַשֶּׁקֶר
as-the-deception surely! (23) God-of-us Yahweh you for to-you we-will-come

מִגְּבָעוֹת הָמוֹן הָרִים אָכֵן בַּיהוָה אֱלֹהֵינוּ תְּשׁוּעַת יִשְׂרָאֵל׃
Israel salvation-of God-of-us in-Yahweh surely! mountains commotion from-hills

(24) וְהַבֹּשֶׁת אָכְלָה אֶת־ יְגִיעַ אֲבוֹתֵינוּ מִנְּעוּרֵינוּ
from-youths-of-us fathers-of-us labor-of *** she-consumed indeed-the-shame (24)

אֶת־ צֹאנָם וְאֶת־ בְּקָרָם אֶת־ בְּנֵיהֶם וְאֶת־ בְּנוֹתֵיהֶם׃
daughters-of-them and sons-of-them *** herd-of-them and flock-of-them ***

(25) נִשְׁכְּבָה בְּבָשְׁתֵּנוּ וּתְכַסֵּנוּ כְּלִמָּתֵנוּ כִּי
indeed disgrace-of-us and-let-her-cover-us in-shame-of-us let-us-lie-down (25)

לַיהוָה אֱלֹהֵינוּ חָטָאנוּ אֲנַחְנוּ וַאֲבוֹתֵינוּ מִנְּעוּרֵינוּ וְעַד־
and-till from-youths-of-us and-fathers-of-us we we-sinned God-of-us against-Yahweh

הַיּוֹם הַזֶּה וְלֹא שָׁמַעְנוּ בְּקוֹל יְהוָה אֱלֹהֵינוּ׃ (4:1) אִם־
if (4:1) God-of-us Yahweh to-voice-of we-obeyed and-not the-this the-day

תָּשׁוּב יִשְׂרָאֵל נְאֻם־ יְהוָה אֵלַי תָּשׁוּב וְאִם־ תָּסִיר
you-put-away and-if you-return to-me Yahweh declaration-of Israel you-will-return

שִׁקּוּצֶיךָ מִפָּנַי וְלֹא תָנוּד׃ (2) וְנִשְׁבַּעְתָּ
and-you-swear (2) you-go-astray and-not from-faces-of-me detestable-things-of-you

חַי־ יְהוָה בֶּאֱמֶת בְּמִשְׁפָּט וּבִצְדָקָה וְהִתְבָּרְכוּ
then-they-will-be-blessed and-in-righteousness in-justice in-truth Yahweh alive

בוֹ גּוֹיִם וּבוֹ יִתְהַלָּלוּ׃ (3) כִּי־ כֹה אָמַר יְהוָה לְאִישׁ
to-man-of Yahweh he-says this indeed (3) they-will-glory and-in-him nations by-him

יְהוּדָה וְלִירוּשָׁלַם נִירוּ לָכֶם נִיר וְאַל־ תִּזְרְעוּ אֶל־
among you-sow and-not unplowed-ground of-you break-up! and-to-Jerusalem Judah

קוֹצִים׃ (4) הִמֹּלוּ לַיהוָה וְהָסִרוּ עָרְלוֹת
foreskin-of and-circumcise! to-Yahweh circumcise-yourselves! (4) thorns

לְבַבְכֶם אִישׁ יְהוּדָה וְיֹשְׁבֵי יְרוּשָׁלָם פֶּן־ תֵּצֵא
she-will-break-out or Jerusalem and-ones-being-people-of Judah man-of heart-of-you

כָאֵשׁ חֲמָתִי וּבָעֲרָה וְאֵין מְכַבֶּה מִפְּנֵי
because-of one-quenching and-there-is-no and-she-will-burn wrath-of-me like-fire

רֹעַ מַעַלְלֵיכֶם׃ (5) הַגִּידוּ בִיהוּדָה וּבִירוּשָׁלַם הַשְׁמִיעוּ וְאִמְרוּ
and-say! proclaim! and-in-Jerusalem in-Judah announce! (5) deeds-of-you evil-of

וְתִקְעוּ° שׁוֹפָר בָּאָרֶץ קִרְאוּ מַלְאוּ וְאִמְרוּ הֵאָסְפוּ
gather-together! and-say! make-loud! cry! throughout-the-land trumpet sound!

because they have perverted
their ways
and have forgotten the LORD
their God.
22"Return, faithless people;
I will cure you of
backsliding."
"Yes, we will come to you,
for you are the LORD our
God.
23Surely the ⌊idolatrous⌋
commotion on the hills
and mountains is a
deception;
surely in the LORD our God
is the salvation of Israel.
24From our youth shameful gods
have consumed
the fruits of our fathers'
labor—
their flocks and herds,
their sons and daughters.
25Let us lie down in our shame,
and let our disgrace cover
us.
We have sinned against the
LORD our God,
both we and our fathers;
from our youth till this day
we have not obeyed the
LORD our God."

4 "If you will return, O Israel,
return to me,"
declares the LORD.
"If you put your detestable
idols out of my sight
and no longer go astray,
2and if in a truthful, just and
righteous way
you swear, 'As surely as the
LORD lives,'
then the nations will be
blessed by him
and in him they will glory."

3This is what the LORD says to the men of Judah and to Jerusalem:

"Break up your unplowed
ground
and do not sow among
thorns.
4Circumcise yourselves to the
LORD,
circumcise your hearts,
you men of Judah and
people of Jerusalem,
or my wrath will break out
and burn like fire
because of the evil you have
done—
burn with no one to quench
it.

*Disaster From the North*

5"Announce in Judah and
proclaim in Jerusalem and
say:
'Sound the trumpet
throughout the land!'
Cry aloud and say:
'Gather together!

*21 Most mss have no *dagesh* in the first *vav* (־וּו).

°5 ק תקעו

וְנָבוֹאָה אֶל־ עָרֵי הַמִּבְצָר׃ (6) שְׂאוּ־ נֵס צִיּוֹנָה
to-Zion signal raise! (6) the-fortification cities-of to and-let-us-flee

הָעִיזוּ אַל־ תַּעֲמֹדוּ כִּי רָעָה אָנֹכִי מֵבִיא מִצָּפוֹן וְשֶׁבֶר
even-destruction from-north bringing I disaster for you-delay not flee-for-safety!

גָּדוֹל׃ (7) עָלָה אַרְיֵה מִסֻּבְּכוֹ וּמַשְׁחִית גּוֹיִם
nations and-one-destroying-of from-lair-of-him lion he-came-out (7) terrible

נָסַע יָצָא מִמְּקֹמוֹ לָשׂוּם אַרְצֵךְ לְשַׁמָּה עָרַיִךְ
towns-of-you to-waste land-of-you to-lay from-place-of-him he-left he-set-out

תִּצֶּינָה מֵאֵין יוֹשֵׁב׃ (8) עַל־ זֹאת חִגְרוּ שַׂקִּים
sackcloths put-on! this for (8) one-inhabiting from-no they-will-lie-in-ruins

סִפְדוּ וְהֵילִילוּ כִּי לֹא־ שָׁב חֲרוֹן אַף־ יְהוָה מִמֶּנּוּ׃
from-us Yahweh anger-of fierceness-of he-turned-away not for and-wail! lament!

(9) וְהָיָה בַיּוֹם־ הַהוּא נְאֻם־ יְהוָה יֹאבַד
he-will-be-lost Yahweh declaration-of the-that in-the-day and-he-will-be (9)

לֵב־ הַמֶּלֶךְ וְלֵב הַשָּׂרִים וְנָשַׁמּוּ הַכֹּהֲנִים
the-priests and-they-will-be-horrified the-officials and-heart-of the-king heart-of

וְהַנְּבִיאִים יִתְמָהוּ׃ (10) וָאֹמַר אֲהָהּ ׀ אֲדֹנָי יְהוִה
Yahweh Sovereign ah! then-I-said (10) they-will-be-appalled and-the-prophets

אָכֵן הַשֵּׁא הִשֵּׁאתָ לָעָם הַזֶּה וְלִירוּשָׁלִַם לֵאמֹר שָׁלוֹם
peace to-say and-to-Jerusalem the-this to-the-people you-deceived to-deceive how!

יִהְיֶה לָכֶם וְנָגְעָה חֶרֶב עַד־ הַנָּפֶשׁ׃ (11) בָּעֵת הַהִיא
the-that at-the-time (11) the-throat at sword when-she-is-near to-you he-will-be

יֵאָמֵר לָעָם־ הַזֶּה וְלִירוּשָׁלִַם רוּחַ צַח
scorching wind and-to-Jerusalem the-this to-the-people he-will-be-told

שְׁפָיִים בַּמִּדְבָּר דֶּרֶךְ בַּת־ עַמִּי לוֹא לִזְרוֹת
to-winnow not people-of-me daughter-of direction-of in-the-desert barren-heights

וְלוֹא לְהָבַר׃ (12) רוּחַ מָלֵא מֵאֵלֶּה יָבוֹא לִי עַתָּה גַּם־ אֲנִי
I also now from-me he-comes more-than-these strong wind (12) to-cleanse or-not

אֲדַבֵּר מִשְׁפָּטִים אוֹתָם׃ (13) הִנֵּה ׀ כַּעֲנָנִים יַעֲלֶה
he-advances like-the-clouds look! (13) against-them judgments I-pronounce

וְכַסּוּפָה מַרְכְּבוֹתָיו קַלּוּ מִנְּשָׁרִים סוּסָיו
horses-of-him more-than-eagles they-are-swift chariots-of-him and-like-the-whirlwind

אוֹי לָנוּ כִּי שֻׁדָּדְנוּ׃ (14) כַּבְּסִי מֵרָעָה לִבֵּךְ יְרוּשָׁלִַם לְמַעַן
so-that Jerusalem heart-of-you from-evil wash! (14) we-are-ruined for to-us woe!

תִּוָּשֵׁעִי עַד־ מָתַי תָּלִין בְּקִרְבֵּךְ מַחְשְׁבוֹת
thoughts-of in-midst-of-you will-you-harbor when? until you-may-be-saved

אוֹנֵךְ׃ (15) כִּי קוֹל מַגִּיד מִדָּן וּמַשְׁמִיעַ אָוֶן
disaster and-proclaiming from-Dan announcing voice indeed (15) evil-of-you

Let us flee to the fortified
cities!'
6 Raise the signal to go to Zion!
Flee for safety without
delay!
For I am bringing disaster
from the north,
even terrible destruction."
7 A lion has come out of his lair,
a destroyer of nations has
set out.
He has left his place
to lay waste your land.
Your towns will lie in ruins
without inhabitant.
8 So put on sackcloth,
lament and wail,
for the fierce anger of the LORD
has not turned away from
us.
9 "In that day," declares the
LORD,
"the king and the officials
will lose heart,
the priests will be horrified,
and the prophets will be
appalled."
10 Then I said, "Ah, Sovereign
LORD, how completely you have
deceived this people and Jerusalem by saying, 'You will have
peace,' when the sword is at our
throats."
11 At that time this people and
Jerusalem will be told, "A scorching wind from the barren heights
in the desert blows toward my
people, but not to winnow or
cleanse; 12 a wind too strong for
that comes from me.[k] Now I pronounce my judgments against
them."
13 Look! He advances like the
clouds,
his chariots come like a
whirlwind,
his horses are swifter than
eagles.
Woe to us! We are ruined!
14 O Jerusalem, wash the evil
from your heart and be
saved.
How long will you harbor
wicked thoughts?
15 A voice is announcing from
Dan,
proclaiming disaster from

[k] 12 Or *comes at my command*

מֵהַר אֶפְרָיִם׃ הַזְכִּירוּ לַגּוֹיִם הִנֵּה הַשְׁמִיעוּ עַל־ יְרוּשָׁלִָם
Jerusalem to proclaim! see! to-the-nations tell! (16) Ephraim from-hill-of

נֹצְרִים בָּאִים מֵאֶרֶץ הַמֶּרְחָק וַיִּתְּנוּ עַל־
against and-they-raise the-distance from-land-of ones-coming ones-besieging

עָרֵי יְהוּדָה קוֹלָם׃ כְּשֹׁמְרֵי שָׂדַי הָיוּ עָלֶיהָ
against-her they-are field like-ones-guarding-of (17) cry-of-them Judah cities-of

מִסָּבִיב כִּי־ אֹתִי מָרָתָה נְאֻם־ יְהוָה׃ דַּרְכֵּךְ
conduct-of-you (18) Yahweh declaration-of she-rebelled me because at-around

וּמַעֲלָלַיִךְ עָשׂוֹ אֵלֶּה לָךְ זֹאת רָעָתֵךְ כִּי מָר כִּי
how bitter how punishment-of-you this upon-you these to-bring and-actions-of-you

נָגַע עַד־ לִבֵּךְ׃ מֵעַי ׀ מֵעַי ׀ אָחוּלָה
I-writhe-in-pain anguishes-of-me anguishes-of-me (19) heart-of-you to he-pierces

קִירוֹת לִבִּי הֹמֶה־ לִּי לִבִּי לֹא אַחֲרִישׁ כִּי
for I-can-keep-silent not heart-of-me in-me pounding heart-of-me agonies-of

קוֹל שׁוֹפָר שָׁמַעְתִּי נַפְשִׁי תְּרוּעַת מִלְחָמָה׃ שֶׁבֶר עַל־ שֶׁבֶר
disaster after disaster (20) battle cry-of self-of-me you-heard trumpet sound-of

נִקְרָא כִּי שֻׁדְּדָה כָּל־ הָאָרֶץ פִּתְאֹם שֻׁדְּדוּ
they-are-destroyed instantly the-land whole-of she-lies-in-ruins indeed he-follows

אֹהָלַי רֶגַע יְרִיעֹתָי׃ עַד־ מָתַי אֶרְאֶה־ נֵּס אֶשְׁמְעָה
must-I-hear standard must-I-see when? until (21) shelters-of-me moment tents-of-me

קוֹל שׁוֹפָר׃ כִּי ׀ אֱוִיל עַמִּי אוֹתִי לֹא יָדָעוּ בָּנִים
children they-know not me people-of-me fool indeed (22) trumpet sound-of

סְכָלִים הֵמָּה וְלֹא נְבוֹנִים הֵמָּה חֲכָמִים הֵמָּה לְהָרַע
to-do-evil they ones-skilled they ones-understanding and-not they senseless-ones

וּלְהֵיטִיב לֹא יָדָעוּ׃ רָאִיתִי אֶת־ הָאָרֶץ וְהִנֵּה־ תֹהוּ
formless and-see! the-earth *** I-looked (23) they-know not but-to-do-good

וָבֹהוּ וְאֶל־ הַשָּׁמַיִם וְאֵין אוֹרָם׃ רָאִיתִי
I-looked (24) light-of-them and-there-was-no the-heavens and-at and-empty

הֶהָרִים וְהִנֵּה רֹעֲשִׁים וְכָל־ הַגְּבָעוֹת הִתְקַלְקָלוּ׃ רָאִיתִי
I-looked (25) they-swayed the-hills and-all-of ones-quaking and-see! the-mountains

וְהִנֵּה אֵין הָאָדָם וְכָל־ עוֹף הַשָּׁמַיִם נָדָדוּ׃
they-flew-away the-skies bird-of and-every-of the-person there-was-not and-see!

רָאִיתִי וְהִנֵּה הַכַּרְמֶל הַמִּדְבָּר וְכָל־ עָרָיו
towns-of-him and-all-of the-desert the-fruitful-land and-see! I-looked (26)

נִתְּצוּ מִפְּנֵי יְהוָה מִפְּנֵי* חֲרוֹן אַפּוֹ׃ כִּי־
for (27) anger-of-him fierceness-of at-before Yahweh at-before they-lay-in-ruins

כֹּה אָמַר יְהוָה שְׁמָמָה תִהְיֶה כָּל־ הָאָרֶץ וְכָלָה
though-complete-destruction the-land whole-of she-will-be ruin Yahweh he-says this

the hills of Ephraim.
16"Tell this to the nations,
proclaim it to Jerusalem:
'A besieging army is coming
from a distant land,
raising a war cry against the
cities of Judah.
17They surround her like men
guarding a field,
because she has rebelled
against me,' "
declares the LORD.
18"Your own conduct and
actions
have brought this upon you.
This is your punishment.
How bitter it is!
How it pierces to the heart!"
19Oh, my anguish, my anguish!
I writhe in pain.
Oh, the agony of my heart!
My heart pounds within me,
I cannot keep silent.
For I have heard the sound of
the trumpet;
I have heard the battle cry.
20Disaster follows disaster;
the whole land lies in ruins.
In an instant my tents are
destroyed,
my shelter in a moment.
21How long must I see the battle
standard
and hear the sound of the
trumpet?
22"My people are fools;
they do not know me.
They are senseless children;
they have no understanding.
They are skilled in doing evil;
they know not how to do
good."
23I looked at the earth,
and it was formless and
empty;
and at the heavens,
and their light was gone.
24I looked at the mountains,
and they were quaking;
all the hills were swaying.
25I looked, and there were no
people;
every bird in the sky had
flown away.
26I looked, and the fruitful land
was a desert;
all its towns lay in ruins
before the LORD, before his
fierce anger.
27This is what the LORD says:
"The whole land will be
ruined,

*26 Most mss have *shureq* before the *mem* (וּמ׳), *and-at-before*.

°19a ק אוחילה
°19b ק שמעת

לֹא אֶעֱשֶׂה׃ עַל־ זֹאת תֶּאֱבַל הָאָרֶץ וְקָדְרוּ
and-they-will-grow-dark the-earth she-will-mourn this for (28) I-will-do not

הַשָּׁמַיִם מִמָּעַל עַל כִּי־ דִבַּרְתִּי זַמֹּתִי וְלֹא נִחַמְתִּי וְלֹא־
and-not I-will-relent and-not I-decided I-spoke that because at-above the-heavens

אָשׁוּב מִמֶּנָּה׃ מִקּוֹל פָּרָשׁ וְרֹמֵה קֶשֶׁת
bow and-one-shooting-of horseman at-sound-of (29) from-her I-will-turn-back

בֹּרַחַת כָּל־ הָעִיר בָּאוּ בֶּעָבִים וּבַכֵּפִים
and-among-the-rocks into-the-thickets they-go the-town every-of taking-flight

עָלוּ כָּל־ הָעִיר עֲזוּבָה וְאֵין־ יוֹשֵׁב
one-living and-there-is-not one-being-deserted the-town all-of they-climb-up

בָּהֵן אִישׁ׃ וְאַתְּי שָׁדוּד מַה־ תַּעֲשִׂי כִּי־ תִלְבְּשִׁי
you-dress-in that you-do what? one-being-devastated and-you (30) one in-them

שָׁנִי כִּי־ תַעְדִּי עֲדִי־ זָהָב כִּי־ תִקְרְעִי בַפּוּךְ עֵינַיִךְ
eyes-of-you with-the-paint you-shade that gold jewel-of you-put-on that scarlet

לַשָּׁוְא תִּתְיַפִּי מָאֲסוּ־ בָךְ עֹגְבִים
ones-being-lovers-of-you to-you they-despise you-adorn-yourself in-the-vain

נַפְשֵׁךְ יְבַקֵּשׁוּ׃ כִּי קוֹל כְּחוֹלָה שָׁמַעְתִּי צָרָה
groan I-hear like-woman-being-in-labor cry indeed (31) they-seek life-of-you

כְּמַבְכִּירָה קוֹל בַּת־ צִיּוֹן תִּתְיַפֵּחַ
she-gasps-for-breath Zion Daughter-of cry-of like-one-bearing-first-child

תְּפָרֵשׂ כַּפֶּיהָ אוֹי־ נָא לִי כִּי־ עָיְפָה נַפְשִׁי
life-of-me she-is-faint for to-me now! alas! hands-of-her she-stretches-out

לְהֹרְגִים׃ שׁוֹטְטוּ בְּחוּצוֹת יְרוּשָׁלַםִ וּרְאוּ־ נָא
now! and-look! Jerusalem on-streets-of go-up-and-down! (5:1) to-ones-murdering

וּדְעוּ וּבַקְשׁוּ בִרְחוֹבוֹתֶיהָ אִם־ תִּמְצְאוּ אִישׁ אִם־
if person you-can-find if through-squares-of-her and-search! and-consider!

יֵשׁ עֹשֶׂה מִשְׁפָּט מְבַקֵּשׁ אֱמוּנָה וְאֶסְלַח לָהּ׃
to-her and-I-will-forgive truth one-seeking honesty one-dealing there-is

וְאִם חַי־ יְהוָה יֹאמֵרוּ לָכֵן לַשֶּׁקֶר יִשָּׁבֵעוּ׃
they-swear as-the-falsehood still they-say Yahweh alive and-although (2)

יְהוָה עֵינֶיךָ הֲלוֹא לֶאֱמוּנָה הִכִּיתָה אֹתָם וְלֹא־ חָלוּ
they-felt-pain but-not them you-struck for-truth not? eyes-of-you Yahweh (3)

כִּלִּיתָם מֵאֲנוּ קַחַת מוּסָר חִזְּקוּ פְנֵיהֶם
faces-of-them they-made-hard correction to-accept they-refused you-crushed-them

מִסֶּלַע מֵאֲנוּ לָשׁוּב׃ וַאֲנִי אָמַרְתִּי אַךְ־ דַּלִּים הֵם
they poor-ones only I-thought and-I (4) to-repent they-refused more-than-stone

נוֹאֲלוּ כִּי לֹא יָדְעוּ דֶּרֶךְ יְהוָה מִשְׁפַּט אֱלֹהֵיהֶם׃
God-of-them requirement-of Yahweh way-of they-know not for they-are-foolish

though I will not destroy it
completely.
28 Therefore the earth will mourn
and the heavens above grow
dark,
because I have spoken and
will not relent,
I have decided and will not
turn back."

29 At the sound of horsemen and
archers
every town takes to flight.
Some go into the thickets;
some climb up among the
rocks.
All the towns are deserted;
no one lives in them.

30 What are you doing, O
devastated one?
Why dress yourself in scarlet
and put on jewels of gold?
Why shade your eyes with
paint?
You adorn yourself in vain.
Your lovers despise you;
they seek your life.

31 I hear a cry as of a woman in
labor,
a groan as of one bearing
her first child—
the cry of the Daughter of
Zion gasping for breath,
stretching out her hands
and saying,
"Alas! I am fainting;
my life is given over to
murderers."

*Not One Is Upright*

5 "Go up and down the streets
of Jerusalem,
look around and consider,
search through her squares.
If you can find but one person
who deals honestly and
seeks the truth,
I will forgive this city.
2 Although they say, 'As surely
as the LORD lives,'
still they are swearing
falsely."

3 O LORD, do not your eyes look
for truth?
You struck them, but they
felt no pain;
you crushed them, but they
refused correction.
They made their faces harder
than stone
and refused to repent.
4 I thought, "These are only the
poor;
they are foolish,
for they do not know the way
of the LORD,
the requirements of their
God.

°30 ק ואת

אֵלֲכָה־ לִּי אֶל־ הַגְּדֹלִים וַאֲדַבְּרָה אוֹתָם כִּי הֵמָּה יָדְעוּ
they-know they surely them and-I-will-speak the-leaders to for-me I-will-go (5)

דֶּרֶךְ יְהוָה מִשְׁפַּט אֱלֹהֵיהֶם אַךְ הֵמָּה יַחְדָּו שָׁבְרוּ עֹל
yoke they-broke-off one-accord they but God-of-them requirement-of Yahweh way-of

נִתְּקוּ מוֹסֵרוֹת׃ עַל־ כֵּן הִכָּם אַרְיֵה מִיַּעַר זְאֵב
wolf-of from-forest lion he-will-attack-them this for (6) bonds they-tore-off

עֲרָבוֹת יְשָׁדְדֵם נָמֵר שֹׁקֵד עַל־ עָרֵיהֶם כָּל־
any-of towns-of-them near waiting leopard he-will-ravage-them deserts

הַיּוֹצֵא מֵהֵנָּה יִטָּרֵף כִּי רַבּוּ
they-are-great for he-will-be-torn-to-pieces from-at-there the-one-venturing-out

פִּשְׁעֵיהֶם עָצְמוּ מְשֻׁבוֹתֵיהֶם׃ אֵי לָזֹאת
for-this why? (7) backslidings-of-them they-are-many rebellions-of-them

אֶסְלוֹחַ־ לָךְ בָּנַיִךְ עֲזָבוּנִי וַיִּשָּׁבְעוּ בְּלֹא
by-not and-they-swore they-forsook-me children-of-you to-you should-I-forgive

אֱלֹהִים וָאַשְׂבִּעַ אוֹתָם וַיִּנְאָפוּ וּבֵית
and-house-of yet-they-committed-adultery them and-I-supplied-needs gods

זוֹנָה יִתְגֹּדָדוּ׃ סוּסִים מְיֻזָּנִים
ones-being-well-fed stallions (8) they-thronged-to one-being-prostitute

מַשְׁכִּים הָיוּ אִישׁ אֶל־ אֵשֶׁת רֵעֵהוּ יִצְהָלוּ׃ הַעַל־אֵלֶּה
these for? (9) they-neigh other-of-him wife-of for each they-are ones-being-lusty

לוֹא־ אֶפְקֹד נְאֻם־ יְהוָה וְאִם בְּגוֹי אֲשֶׁר־ כָּזֶה לֹא
not as-this that on-nation and-if Yahweh declaration-of should-I-punish not

תִתְנַקֵּם נַפְשִׁי׃ עֲלוּ בְשָׁרוֹתֶיהָ וְשַׁחֵתוּ
and-ravage! through-vineyards-of-her go! (10) self-of-me should-she-take-vengeance

וְכָלָה אַל־ תַּעֲשׂוּ הָסִירוּ נְטִישׁוֹתֶיהָ כִּי לוֹא לַיהוָה
to-Yahweh not for branches-of-her strip-off! you-do not but-complete-destruction

הֵמָּה׃ כִּי בָגוֹד בָּגְדוּ בִּי בֵּית יִשְׂרָאֵל
Israel house-of to-me they-were-unfaithful to-be-unfaithful indeed (11) these

וּבֵית יְהוּדָה נְאֻם־ יְהוָה׃ כִּחֲשׁוּ בַּיהוָה וַיֹּאמְרוּ
and-they-said about-Yahweh they-lied (12) Yahweh declaration-of Judah and-house-of

לֹא־הוּא וְלֹא־ תָבוֹא עָלֵינוּ רָעָה וְחֶרֶב וְרָעָב לוֹא נִרְאֶה׃
we-will-see never or-famine and-sword harm to-us she-will-come and-not he not

וְהַנְּבִיאִים יִהְיוּ לְרוּחַ וְהַדִּבֵּר אֵין בָּהֶם כֹּה
so in-them not and-the-speaking as-wind they-are and-the-prophets (13)

יֵעָשֶׂה לָהֶם׃ לָכֵן כֹּה־ אָמַר יְהוָה אֱלֹהֵי צְבָאוֹת יַעַן
because Hosts God-of Yahweh he-says this therefore (14) to-them let-him-be-done

דַּבֶּרְכֶם אֶת־ הַדָּבָר הַזֶּה הִנְנִי נֹתֵן דְּבָרַי בְּפִיךָ לְאֵשׁ
as-fire in-mouth-of-you words-of-me making see-I! the-this the-word *** to-speak-you

7° ק אסלח

5So I will go to the leaders
and speak to them;
surely they know the way of the LORD,
the requirements of their God."
But with one accord they too had broken off the yoke
and torn off the bonds.
6Therefore a lion from the forest will attack them,
a wolf from the desert will ravage them,
a leopard will lie in wait near their towns
to tear to pieces any who venture out,
for their rebellion is great
and their backslidings many.

7"Why should I forgive you?
Your children have forsaken me
and sworn by gods that are not gods.
I supplied all their needs,
yet they committed adultery
and thronged to the houses of prostitutes.
8They are well-fed, lusty stallions,
each neighing for another man's wife.
9Should I not punish them for this?"
declares the LORD.
"Should I not avenge myself
on such a nation as this?

10"Go through her vineyards and ravage them,
but do not destroy them completely.
Strip off her branches,
for these people do not belong to the LORD.
11The house of Israel and the house of Judah
have been utterly unfaithful to me,"
declares the LORD.

12They have lied about the LORD;
they said, "He will do nothing!
No harm will come to us;
we will never see sword or famine.
13The prophets are but wind
and the word is not in them;
so let what they say be done to them."

14Therefore this is what the LORD God Almighty says:

"Because the people have spoken these words,
I will make my words in your mouth a fire

וְהָעָם הַזֶּה עֵצִים וַאֲכָלָתַם׃ הִנְנִי מֵבִיא
bringing see-I! (15) that-she-consumes-them woods the-this and-the-people

עֲלֵיכֶם גּוֹי מִמֶּרְחָק בֵּית יִשְׂרָאֵל נְאֻם־ יְהוָה גּוֹי
nation Yahweh declaration-of Israel house-of from-distance nation against-you

אֵיתָן הוּא גּוֹי מֵעוֹלָם הוּא גּוֹי לֹא־ תֵדַע לְשֹׁנוֹ וְלֹא
and-not language-of-him you-know not people he from-ancient nation he enduring

תִשְׁמַע מַה־ יְדַבֵּר׃ אַשְׁפָּתוֹ כְּקֶבֶר פָּתוּחַ
one-being-open like-grave quiver-of-him (16) he-speaks what you-understand

כֻּלָּם גִּבּוֹרִים׃ וְאָכַל קְצִירְךָ וְלַחְמֶךָ
and-food-of-you harvest-of-you and-he-will-devour (17) mighty-warriors all-of-them

יֹאכְלוּ בָּנֶיךָ וּבְנוֹתֶיךָ יֹאכַל
and-he-will-devour and-daughters-of-you sons-of-you and-they-will-devour

צֹאנְךָ וּבְקָרֶךָ יֹאכַל גַּפְנְךָ וּתְאֵנָתֶךָ
and-fig-tree-of-you vine-of-you and-he-will-devour and-herd-of-you flock-of-you

יְרֹשֵׁשׁ עָרֵי מִבְצָרֶיךָ אֲשֶׁר אַתָּה בּוֹטֵחַ בָּהֵנָּה
in-them trusting you which fortifications-of-you cities-of and-he-will-destroy

בֶּחָרֶב׃ וְגַם בַּיָּמִים הָהֵמָּה נְאֻם־ יְהוָה לֹא־
not Yahweh declaration-of the-those in-the-days yet-even (18) with-the-sword

אֶעֱשֶׂה אִתְּכֶם כָּלָה׃ וְהָיָה כִּי תֹאמְרוּ תַּחַת
because-of they-ask when and-he-will-be (19) complete-destruction to-you I-will-do

מֶה עָשָׂה יְהוָה אֱלֹהֵינוּ לָנוּ אֶת־ כָּל־ אֵלֶּה וְאָמַרְתָּ אֲלֵיהֶם
to-them then-you-will-tell these all-of *** to-us God-of-us Yahweh he-did why?

כַּאֲשֶׁר עֲזַבְתֶּם אוֹתִי וַתַּעַבְדוּ אֱלֹהֵי נֵכָר בְּאַרְצְכֶם כֵּן
so in-land-of-you foreignness gods-of and-you-served me you-forsook as-that

תַּעַבְדוּ זָרִים בְּאֶרֶץ לֹא לָכֶם׃ הַגִּידוּ זֹאת
this announce! (20) to-you not in-land ones-being-foreign you-will-serve

בְּבֵית יַעֲקֹב וְהַשְׁמִיעוּהָ בִיהוּדָה לֵאמֹר׃ שִׁמְעוּ־ נָא זֹאת
this now! hear! (21) to-say in-Judah and-proclaim-her! Jacob to-house-of

עַם סָכָל וְאֵין לֵב עֵינַיִם לָהֶם וְלֹא יִרְאוּ אָזְנַיִם לָהֶם
to-them ears they-see but-not to-them eyes sense and-without foolish people

וְלֹא יִשְׁמָעוּ׃ הַאוֹתִי לֹא־ תִירָאוּ נְאֻם־ יְהוָה אִם
or Yahweh declaration-of should-you-fear not me? (22) they-hear but-not

מִפָּנַי לֹא תָחִילוּ אֲשֶׁר־שַׂמְתִּי חוֹל גְּבוּל לַיָּם
for-the-sea boundary sand I-made who should-you-tremble not before-presences-of-me

חָק־ עוֹלָם וְלֹא יַעַבְרֶנְהוּ וַיִּתְגָּעֲשׁוּ וְלֹא
but-not now-they-may-roll he-can-cross-him and-not everlasting barrier-of

יוּכָלוּ וְהָמוּ גַלָּיו וְלֹא יַעַבְרֻנְהוּ׃
they-can-cross-him but-not waves-of-him and-they-may-roar they-can-prevail

and these people the wood
it consumes.
15 O house of Israel," declares the LORD,
"I am bringing a distant
nation against you—
an ancient and enduring
nation,
a people whose language
you do not know,
whose speech you do not
understand.
16 Their quivers are like an open
grave;
all of them are mighty
warriors.
17 They will devour your harvests
and food,
devour your sons and
daughters;
they will devour your flocks
and herds,
devour your vines and fig
trees.
With the sword they will
destroy
the fortified cities in which
you trust.

18 "Yet even in those days," declares the LORD, "I will not destroy
you completely. 19 And when the
people ask, 'Why has the LORD our God done all this to us?' you will
tell them, 'As you have forsaken me and served foreign gods in
your own land, so now you will serve foreigners in a land not your
own.'

20 "Announce this to the house
of Jacob
and proclaim it in Judah:
21 Hear this, you foolish and
senseless people,
who have eyes but do not
see,
who have ears but do not
hear:
22 Should you not fear me?"
declares the LORD.
"Should you not tremble in
my presence?
I made the sand a boundary
for the sea,
an everlasting barrier it
cannot cross.
The waves may roll, but they
cannot prevail;
they may roar, but they
cannot cross it.

(23) וְלָעָם הַזֶּה הָיָה לֵב סוֹרֵר וּמוֹרֶה
and-being-rebellious being-stubborn heart he-is the-this but-to-the-people (23)

סָרוּ וַיֵּלֵכוּ׃ (24) וְלֹא־ אָמְרוּ בִלְבָבָם
to-self-of-them they-say and-not (24) and-they-went-away they-turned-aside

נִירָא נָא אֶת־ יְהוָה אֱלֹהֵינוּ הַנֹּתֵן גֶּשֶׁם וירֶה°
autumn-rain rain the-one-giving God-of-us Yahweh *** now! let-us-fear

וּמַלְקוֹשׁ בְּעִתּוֹ שְׁבֻעֹת חֻקּוֹת קָצִיר יִשְׁמָר־ לָנוּ׃
for-us he-assures harvest regular-ones weeks in-season-of-him and-spring-rain

(25) עֲוֹנוֹתֵיכֶם הִטּוּ־ אֵלֶּה וְחַטֹּאותֵיכֶם מָנְעוּ הַטּוֹב
the-good they-deprived and-sins-of-you these they-kept-away wrongdoings-of-you (25)

מִכֶּם׃ (26) כִּי־ נִמְצְאוּ בְעַמִּי רְשָׁעִים יָשׁוּר
he-waits wicked-men among-people-of-me they-are-found indeed (26) from-you

כְּשַׁךְ יְקוּשִׁים הִצִּיבוּ מַשְׁחִית אֲנָשִׁים יִלְכֹּדוּ׃ (27) כִּכְלוּב
like-cage (27) they-catch men trap they-set men-who-snare-birds like-lying-of

מָלֵא עוֹף כֵּן בָּתֵּיהֶם מְלֵאִים מִרְמָה עַל־ כֵּן גָּדְלוּ
they-became-powerful this for deceit ones-full houses-of-them so bird full

וַיַּעֲשִׁירוּ׃ (28) שָׁמְנוּ עָשְׁתוּ גַּם עָבְרוּ
they-go-beyond also they-grew-sleek they-grew-fat (28) and-they-became-rich

דִבְרֵי־ רָע דִּין לֹא־ דָנוּ דִּין יָתוֹם וְיַצְלִיחוּ וּמִשְׁפַּט
and-right-of that-they-win fatherless case-of they-plead not case evil deeds-of

אֶבְיוֹנִים לֹא שָׁפָטוּ׃ (29) הַעַל־אֵלֶּה לֹא־ אֶפְקֹד נְאֻם־
declaration-of should-I-punish not these for? (29) they-defend not poor-ones

יְהוָה אִם בְּגוֹי אֲשֶׁר־ כָּזֶה לֹא תִתְנַקֵּם נַפְשִׁי׃
self-of-me should-she-take-vengeance not as-this that on-nation or Yahweh

(30) שַׁמָּה וְשַׁעֲרוּרָה נִהְיְתָה בָּאָרֶץ׃ (31) הַנְּבִאִים
the-prophets (31) in-the-land she-happened and-shocking-thing horrible-thing (30)

נִבְּאוּ־ בַשֶּׁקֶר וְהַכֹּהֲנִים יִרְדּוּ עַל־ יְדֵיהֶם
authorities-of-them by they-rule and-the-priests about-the-lie they-prophesy

וְעַמִּי אָהֲבוּ כֵן וּמַה־ תַּעֲשׂוּ לְאַחֲרִיתָהּ׃
in-end-of-her will-you-do but-what? this-way they-love and-people-of-me

(6:1) הָעִזוּ׀ בְּנֵי* בִנְיָמִן מִקֶּרֶב יְרוּשָׁלַםִ וּבִתְקוֹעַ
and-in-Tekoa Jerusalem from-midst-of Benjamin peoples-of flee-for-safety! (6:1)

תִּקְעוּ שׁוֹפָר וְעַל־ בֵּית הַכֶּרֶם שְׂאוּ מַשְׂאֵת כִּי רָעָה נִשְׁקְפָה
she-looms disaster for signal raise! Hakkerem Beth and-over trumpet sound!

מִצָּפוֹן וְשֶׁבֶר גָּדוֹל׃ (2) הַנָּוָה
the-beautiful-one (2) terrible even-destruction out-of-north

וְהַמְּעֻנָּגָה דָּמִיתִי בַּת־ צִיּוֹן׃ (3) אֵלֶיהָ
against-her (3) Zion Daughter-of I-will-destroy and-the-one-being-delicate

23 But these people have
stubborn and rebellious
hearts;
they have turned aside and
gone away.
24 They do not say to themselves,
'Let us fear the LORD our
God,
who gives autumn and spring
rains in season,
who assures us of the
regular weeks of harvest.'
25 Your wrongdoings have kept
these away;
your sins have deprived you
of good.

26 "Among my people are wicked
men
who lie in wait like men
who snare birds
and like those who set traps
to catch men.
27 Like cages full of birds,
their houses are full of
deceit;
they have become rich and
powerful
28 and have grown fat and
sleek.
Their evil deeds have no limit;
they do not plead the case
of the fatherless to win it,
they do not defend the
rights of the poor.
29 Should I not punish them for
this?"
declares the LORD.
"Should I not avenge myself
on such a nation as this?

30 "A horrible and shocking
thing
has happened in the land:
31 The prophets prophesy lies,
the priests rule by their own
authority,
and my people love it this
way.
But what will you do in the
end?

*Jerusalem Under Siege*

6 "Flee for safety, people of
Benjamin!
Flee from Jerusalem!
Sound the trumpet in Tekoa!
Raise the signal over Beth
Hakkerem!
For disaster looms out of the
north,
even terrible destruction.
2 I will destroy the Daughter of
Zion,
so beautiful and delicate.

*1 Most mss have *sheva* under the *nun* (בְּנֵי).

°24 ק יורה

יָבֹאוּ רֹעִים וְעֶדְרֵיהֶם תָּקְעוּ עָלֶיהָ
against-her they-will-pitch with-flocks-of-them ones-being-shepherds they-will-come

אֹהָלִים סָבִיב רָעוּ אִישׁ אֶת־ יָדוֹ׃ (4) קַדְּשׁוּ עָלֶיהָ
against-her prepare! (4) portion-of-him *** each they-will-tend around tents

מִלְחָמָה קוּמוּ וְנַעֲלֶה בַצָּהֳרָיִם אוֹי לָנוּ כִּי־ פָנָה הַיּוֹם כִּי
for the-day he-fades for to-us alas! at-the-noon and-let-us-attack arise! battle

יִנָּטוּ צִלְלֵי־ עָרֶב׃ (5) קוּמוּ וְנַעֲלֶה בַלַּיְלָה
at-the-night and-let-us-attack arise! (5) evening shadows-of they-grow-long

וְנַשְׁחִיתָה אַרְמְנוֹתֶיהָ׃ (6) כִּי כֹה אָמַר יְהוָה צְבָאוֹת
Hosts Yahweh-of he-says this indeed (6) fortresses-of-her and-let-us-destroy

כִּרְתוּ עֵצָה וְשִׁפְכוּ עַל־ יְרוּשָׁלִַם סֹלְלָה הִיא הָעִיר
the-city this siege-ramp Jerusalem against and-build! tree cut-down!

הָפְקַד כֻּלָּהּ עֹשֶׁק בְּקִרְבָּהּ׃ (7) כְּהָקִיר
as-to-pour-out (7) in-midst-of-her oppression all-of-her he-must-be-punished

בּוֹר מֵימֶיהָ כֵּן הֵקֵרָה רָעָתָהּ חָמָס וָשֹׁד
and-destruction violence wickedness-of-her she-pours-out so waters-of-her well

יִשָּׁמַע בָּהּ עַל־ פָּנַי תָּמִיד חֳלִי וּמַכָּה׃ (8) הִוָּסְרִי
take-warning! (8) and-wound sickness ever faces-of-me before in-her they-resound

יְרוּשָׁלִַם פֶּן־ תֵּקַע נַפְשִׁי מִמֵּךְ פֶּן־ אֲשִׂימֵךְ שְׁמָמָה אֶרֶץ
land desolation I-will-make-you or from-you self-of-me she-will-turn or Jerusalem

לוֹא נוֹשָׁבָה׃ (9) כֹּה אָמַר יְהוָה צְבָאוֹת עוֹלֵל יְעוֹלְלוּ
let-them-glean to-glean Hosts Yahweh-of he-says this (9) she-can-be-lived-in not

כַגֶּפֶן שְׁאֵרִית יִשְׂרָאֵל הָשֵׁב יָדְךָ כְּבוֹצֵר עַל־
over like-one-gathering hand-of-you make-pass! Israel remnant-of as-the-vine

סַלְסִלּוֹת׃ (10) עַל־ מִי אֲדַבְּרָה וְאָעִידָה וְיִשְׁמָעוּ הִנֵּה
see! and-they-would-listen and-can-I-warn can-I-speak whom? to (10) branches

עֲרֵלָה אָזְנָם וְלֹא יוּכְלוּ לְהַקְשִׁיב הִנֵּה דְבַר־ יְהוָה הָיָה
he-is Yahweh word-of see! to-hear they-can so-not ear-of-them uncircumcised

לָהֶם לְחֶרְפָּה לֹא יַחְפְּצוּ־ בוֹ׃ (11) וְאֶת חֲמַת יְהוָה ׀
Yahweh wrath-of but (11) in-him they-find-pleasure not as-offense to-them

מָלֵאתִי נִלְאֵיתִי הָכִיל שְׁפֹךְ עַל־ עוֹלָל בַּחוּץ וְעַל
and-on in-the-street child on pour-out! to-hold-in I-am-unable I-am-full

סוֹד בַּחוּרִים יַחְדָּו כִּי־ גַם־ אִישׁ עִם־ אִשָּׁה יִלָּכֵדוּ
they-will-be-caught wife with husband both indeed together young-men gathering-of

זָקֵן עִם־ מְלֵא יָמִים׃ (12) וְנָסַבּוּ בָתֵּיהֶם
houses-of-them and-they-will-be-turned-over (12) days weighed-down-of with old

לַאֲחֵרִים שָׂדוֹת וְנָשִׁים יַחְדָּו כִּי־ אַטֶּה אֶת־ יָדִי עַל־
against hand-of-me *** I-stretch-out when together and-wives fields to-others

[3]Shepherds with their flocks
will come against her;
they will pitch their tents
around her,
each tending his own
portion."
[4]"Prepare for battle against her!
Arise, let us attack at noon!
But, alas, the daylight is
fading,
and the shadows of evening
grow long.
[5]So arise, let us attack at night
and destroy her fortresses!"
[6]This is what the LORD Almighty
says:
"Cut down the trees
and build siege ramps
against Jerusalem.
This city must be punished;
it is filled with oppression.
[7]As a well pours out its water,
so she pours out her
wickedness.
Violence and destruction
resound in her;
her sickness and wounds are
ever before me.
[8]Take warning, O Jerusalem,
or I will turn away from you
and make your land desolate
so no one can live in it."
[9]This is what the LORD Almighty
says:
"Let them glean the remnant
of Israel
as thoroughly as a vine;
pass your hand over the
branches again,
like one gathering grapes."
[10]To whom can I speak and give
warning?
Who will listen to me?
Their ears are closed[l]
so they cannot hear.
The word of the LORD is
offensive to them;
they find no pleasure in it.
[11]But I am full of the wrath of
the LORD,
and I cannot hold it in.
"Pour it out on the children in
the street
and on the young men
gathered together;
both husband and wife will be
caught in it,
and the old, those weighed
down with years.
[12]Their houses will be turned
over to others,
together with their fields
and their wives,
when I stretch out my hand

[l]10 Hebrew *uncircumcised*

°7 ק בּוֹר

יֹשְׁבֵי הָאָרֶץ נְאֻם־ יְהוָה׃ כִּי מִקְּטַנָּם וְעַד־
even-to from-least-of-them indeed (13) Yahweh declaration-of the-land ones-living-of

גְּדוֹלָם כֻּלּוֹ בּוֹצֵעַ בָּצַע וּמִנָּבִיא
and-from-prophet unjust-gain one-being-greedy-of all-of-him to-greatest-of-them

וְעַד־ כֹּהֵן כֻּלּוֹ עֹשֶׂה שָּׁקֶר׃ וַיְרַפְּאוּ אֶת־ שֶׁבֶר
wound-of *** and-they-dress (14) deceit one-practicing all-of-him priest even-to

עַמִּי עַל־ נְקַלָּה לֵאמֹר שָׁלוֹם ׀ שָׁלוֹם וְאֵין
when-there-is-no peace peace to-say one-not-being-serious as-though people-of-me

שָׁלוֹם׃ הֹבִישׁוּ כִּי תוֹעֵבָה עָשׂוּ גַּם־ בּוֹשׁ
to-be-ashamed indeed they-did loathsome-thing that are-they-ashamed (15) peace

לֹא־ יֵבוֹשׁוּ גַּם־ הַכְלִים לֹא יָדָעוּ לָכֵן יִפְּלוּ
they-will-fall so they-know not to-blush even they-are-ashamed not

בַנֹּפְלִים בְּעֵת־ פְּקַדְתִּים יִכָּשְׁלוּ אָמַר
he-says they-will-be-brought-down I-punish-them at-time-of among-the-ones-falling

יְהוָה׃ כֹּה אָמַר יְהוָה עִמְדוּ עַל־ דְּרָכִים וּרְאוּ וְשַׁאֲלוּ ׀
and-ask! and-look! crossroads at stand! Yahweh he-says this (16) Yahweh

לִנְתִבוֹת עוֹלָם אֵי־ זֶה דֶרֶךְ הַטּוֹב וּלְכוּ־ בָהּ וּמִצְאוּ מַרְגּוֹעַ
rest and-find! in-her and-walk! the-good way-of this where? ancient for-paths-of

לְנַפְשְׁכֶם וַיֹּאמְרוּ לֹא נֵלֵךְ׃ וַהֲקִמֹתִי עֲלֵיכֶם
over-you and-I-appointed (17) we-will-walk not but-they-said for-soul-of-you

צֹפִים הַקְשִׁיבוּ לְקוֹל שׁוֹפָר וַיֹּאמְרוּ לֹא נַקְשִׁיב׃
we-will-listen not but-they-said trumpet to-sound-of listen! men-watching

לָכֵן שִׁמְעוּ הַגּוֹיִם וּדְעִי עֵדָה אֶת־אֲשֶׁר־ בָּם׃ שִׁמְעִי
hear! (19) to-them what *** witness and-observe! the-nations hear! therefore (18)

הָאָרֶץ הִנֵּה אָנֹכִי מֵבִיא רָעָה אֶל־ הָעָם הַזֶּה פְּרִי מַחְשְׁבוֹתָם
schemes-of-them fruit-of the-this the-people on disaster bringing I see! the-earth

כִּי עַל־ דְּבָרַי לֹא הִקְשִׁיבוּ וְתוֹרָתִי וַיִּמְאֲסוּ־ בָהּ׃
to-her also-they-rejected and-law-of-me they-listened not words-of-me to because

לָמָּה־ זֶּה לִי לְבוֹנָה מִשְּׁבָא תָבוֹא וְקָנֶה הַטּוֹב
the-sweet or-calamus she-comes from-Sheba incense to-me this for-what? (20)

מֵאֶרֶץ מֶרְחָק עֹלוֹתֵיכֶם לֹא לְרָצוֹן וְזִבְחֵיכֶם
and-sacrifices-of-you for-acceptance not burnt-offerings-of-you distance from-land-of

לֹא־ עָרְבוּ לִי׃ לָכֵן כֹּה אָמַר יְהוָה הִנְנִי נֹתֵן
putting see-I! Yahweh he-says this therefore (21) to-me they-are-pleasing not

אֶל־ הָעָם הַזֶּה מִכְשֹׁלִים וְכָשְׁלוּ בָם אָבוֹת
fathers over-them and-they-will-stumble obstacles the-this the-people before

וּבָנִים יַחְדָּו שָׁכֵן וְרֵעוֹ יֹאבֵדוּ׃ כֹּה אָמַר
he-says this (22) and-they-will-perish and-friend-of-him neighbor alike and-sons

against those who live in
the land,"
declares the LORD.
[13]"From the least to the greatest,
all are greedy for gain;
prophets and priests alike,
all practice deceit.
[14]They dress the wound of my
people
as though it were not
serious.
'Peace, peace,' they say,
when there is no peace.
[15]Are they ashamed of their
loathsome conduct?
No, they have no shame at
all;
they do not even know how
to blush.
So they will fall among the
fallen;
they will be brought down
when I punish them,"
says the LORD.

[16]This is what the LORD says:

"Stand at the crossroads and
look;
ask for the ancient paths,
ask where the good way is,
and walk in it,
and you will find rest for
your souls.
But you said, 'We will not
walk in it.'
[17]I appointed watchmen over
you and said,
'Listen to the sound of the
trumpet!'
But you said, 'We will not
listen.'
[18]Therefore hear, O nations;
observe, O witnesses,
what will happen to them.
[19]Hear, O earth:
I am bringing disaster on this
people,
the fruit of their schemes,
because they have not listened
to my words
and have rejected my law.
[20]What do I care about incense
from Sheba
or sweet calamus from a
distant land?
Your burnt offerings are not
acceptable;
your sacrifices do not please
me."

[21]Therefore this is what the LORD
says:

"I will put obstacles before this
people.
Fathers and sons alike will
stumble over them;
neighbors and friends will
perish."

[22]This is what the LORD says:

°21 ק ואבדו

יְהוָה הִנֵּה עַם בָּא מֵאֶרֶץ צָפוֹן וְגוֹי גָּדוֹל יֵעוֹר
he-is-stirred-up great and-nation north from-land-of coming army look! Yahweh

מִיַּרְכְּתֵי־אָרֶץ׃ קֶשֶׁת וְכִידוֹן יַחֲזִיקוּ אַכְזָרִי הוּא וְלֹא
and-not he cruel they-are-armed and-spear bow (23) earth from-ends-of

יְרַחֵמוּ קוֹלָם כַּיָּם יֶהֱמֶה וְעַל־סוּסִים יִרְכָּבוּ
they-ride horses and-on he-roars like-the-sea sound-of-them they-show-mercy

עָרוּךְ כְּאִישׁ לַמִּלְחָמָה עָלַיִךְ בַּת־צִיּוֹן׃ שָׁמַעְנוּ
we-heard (24) Zion Daughter-of against-you for-the-battle like-man being-formed

אֶת־שָׁמְעוֹ רָפוּ יָדֵינוּ צָרָה הֶחֱזִקַתְנוּ חִיל
pain she-gripped-us anguish hands-of-us they-hang-limp report-of-him ***

כַּיּוֹלֵדָה׃ אַל־תֵּצְאִי° הַשָּׂדֶה וּבַדֶּרֶךְ אַל־
not or-on-the-road the-field you-go-out not (25) like-the-woman-being-in-labor

תֵּלֵכִי° כִּי חֶרֶב לְאֹיֵב מָגוֹר מִסָּבִיב׃ בַּת־
daughter-of (26) on-every-side terror to-one-being-enemy sword for you-walk

עַמִּי חִגְרִי־שָׂק וְהִתְפַּלְּשִׁי בָאֵפֶר אֵבֶל יָחִיד עֲשִׂי
do! only-son mourning-of in-the-ash and-roll! sackcloth put-on! people-of-me

לָךְ מִסְפַּד תַּמְרוּרִים כִּי פִתְאֹם יָבֹא הַשֹּׁדֵד
the-one-destroying he-will-come suddenly for bitternesses wailing-of for-you

עָלֵינוּ׃ בָּחוֹן נְתַתִּיךָ בְעַמִּי מִבְצָר וְתֵדַע
that-you-may-observe ore for-people-of-me I-made-you tester-of-metals (27) upon-us

וּבָחַנְתָּ אֶת־דַּרְכָּם׃ כֻּלָּם סָרֵי סוֹרְרִים
ones-being-hardened ones-rebelling-of all-of-them (28) way-of-them *** and-you-may-test

הֹלְכֵי רָכִיל נְחֹשֶׁת וּבַרְזֶל כֻּלָּם מַשְׁחִיתִים הֵמָּה׃
they ones-acting-corruptly all-of-them and-iron bronze slander ones-going-about

נָחַר מַפֻּחַ מֵאֶשְׁתַּם° עֹפָרֶת לַשָּׁוְא צָרַף
he-refines in-the-vain lead he-is-consumed*with-fire bellows he-blows (29)

צָרוֹף וְרָעִים לֹא נִתָּקוּ׃ כֶּסֶף נִמְאָס
being-rejected silver (30) they-are-purged-out not and-wicked-ones to-refine

קָרְאוּ לָהֶם כִּי־מָאַס יְהוָה בָּהֶם׃ הַדָּבָר אֲשֶׁר הָיָה
he-came that the-word (7:1) to-them Yahweh he-rejected because to-them they-call

אֶל־יִרְמְיָהוּ מֵאֵת יְהוָה לֵאמֹר׃ עֲמֹד בְּשַׁעַר בֵּית יְהוָה
Yahweh house-of at-gate-of stand! (2) to-say Yahweh from-with Jeremiah to

וְקָרָאתָ שָּׁם אֶת־הַדָּבָר הַזֶּה וְאָמַרְתָּ שִׁמְעוּ דְבַר־יְהוָה
Yahweh word-of hear! and-you-say the-this the-message *** there and-you-proclaim

כָּל־יְהוּדָה הַבָּאִים בַּשְּׁעָרִים הָאֵלֶּה לְהִשְׁתַּחֲוֹת לַיהוָה׃
to-Yahweh to-worship the-these through-the-gates the-ones-coming Judah all-of

כֹּה־אָמַר יְהוָה צְבָאוֹת אֱלֹהֵי יִשְׂרָאֵל הֵיטִיבוּ דַרְכֵיכֶם
ways-of-you reform! Israel God-of Hosts Yahweh-of he-says this (3)

"Look, an army is coming
from the land of the north;
a great nation is being stirred
up
from the ends of the earth.
23They are armed with bow and
spear;
they are cruel and show no
mercy.
They sound like the roaring
sea
as they ride on their horses;
they come like men in battle
formation
to attack you, O Daughter of
Zion."
24We have heard reports about
them,
and our hands hang limp.
Anguish has gripped us,
pain like that of a woman
in labor.
25Do not go out to the fields
or walk on the roads,
for the enemy has a sword,
and there is terror on every
side.
26O my people, put on sackcloth
and roll in ashes;
mourn with bitter wailing
as for an only son,
for suddenly the destroyer
will come upon us.
27"I have made you a tester of
metals
and my people the ore,
that you may observe
and test their ways.
28They are all hardened rebels,
going about to slander.
They are bronze and iron;
they all act corruptly.
29The bellows blow fiercely
to burn away the lead with
fire,
but the refining goes on in
vain;
the wicked are not purged
out.
30They are called rejected silver,
because the LORD has
rejected them."

*False Religion Worthless*

7 This is the word that came to
Jeremiah from the LORD:
2"Stand at the gate of the LORD's
house and there proclaim this
message:
" 'Hear the word of the LORD, all
you people of Judah who come
through these gates to worship the
LORD. 3This is what the LORD Almighty, the God of Israel, says:

*29 The *Qere* reads this word as two words.

°25a ק תצאו
°25b ק תלכו
°29 ק מאש תם

וּמַעַלְלֵיכֶם וַאֲשַׁכְּנָה אֶתְכֶם בַּמָּקוֹם הַזֶּה׃ אַל־תִּבְטְחוּ
you-trust not (4) the-this in-the-place you and-I-will-let-live and-actions-of-you

לָכֶם אֶל־דִּבְרֵי הַשֶּׁקֶר לֵאמֹר הֵיכַל יְהוָה הֵיכַל יְהוָה
Yahweh temple-of Yahweh temple-of to-say the-deception words-of in for-you

הֵיכַל יְהוָה הֵמָּה׃ כִּי אִם־הֵיטֵיב תֵּיטִיבוּ אֶת־דַּרְכֵיכֶם וְאֶת־
and ways-of-you *** you-change to-change if indeed (5) they Yahweh temple-of

מַעַלְלֵיכֶם אִם־עָשׂוֹ תַעֲשׂוּ מִשְׁפָּט בֵּין אִישׁ וּבֵין רֵעֵהוּ׃
other-of-him and-with each with justice you-deal to-deal if actions-of-you

גֵּר יָתוֹם וְאַלְמָנָה לֹא תַעֲשֹׁקוּ וְדָם נָקִי אַל־תִּשְׁפְּכוּ
you-shed not innocent and-blood you-oppress not and-widow fatherless alien (6)

בַּמָּקוֹם הַזֶּה וְאַחֲרֵי אֱלֹהִים אֲחֵרִים לֹא תֵלְכוּ לְרַע לָכֶם׃
of-you to-harm you-follow not other-ones gods and-after the-this in-the-place

וְשִׁכַּנְתִּי אֶתְכֶם בַּמָּקוֹם הַזֶּה בָּאָרֶץ אֲשֶׁר נָתַתִּי
I-gave that in-the-land the-this in-the-place you then-I-will-let-live (7)

לַאֲבוֹתֵיכֶם לְמִן־עוֹלָם וְעַד־עוֹלָם׃ הִנֵּה אַתֶּם בֹּטְחִים לָכֶם
for-you ones-trusting you look! (8) ever and-to ever at-from to-forefathers-of-you

עַל־דִּבְרֵי הַשָּׁקֶר לְבִלְתִּי הוֹעִיל׃ הֲגָנֹב ׀ רָצֹחַ
to-murder to-steal? (9) to-have-worth not the-deception words-of in

וְנָאֹף וְהִשָּׁבֵעַ לַשֶּׁקֶר וְקַטֵּר לַבָּעַל
to-the-Baal and-to-burn-incense by-the-falsehood and-to-swear and-to-commit-adultery

וְהָלֹךְ אַחֲרֵי אֱלֹהִים אֲחֵרִים אֲשֶׁר לֹא־יְדַעְתֶּם׃ וּבָאתֶם
then-you-come (10) you-know not that other-ones gods after and-to-follow

וַעֲמַדְתֶּם לְפָנַי בַּבַּיִת הַזֶּה אֲשֶׁר נִקְרָא־שְׁמִי עָלָיו
to-him Name-of-me he-is-called which the-this in-the-house before-me and-you-stand

וַאֲמַרְתֶּם נִצַּלְנוּ לְמַעַן עֲשׂוֹת אֵת כָּל־הַתּוֹעֵבוֹת הָאֵלֶּה׃
the-these the-detestable-things all-of *** to-do in-order we-are-safe and-you-say

הַמְעָרַת פָּרִצִים הָיָה הַבַּיִת הַזֶּה אֲשֶׁר־נִקְרָא־שְׁמִי
Name-of-me he-is-called which the-this the-house he-became robbers den-of? (11)

עָלָיו בְּעֵינֵיכֶם גַּם אָנֹכִי הִנֵּה רָאִיתִי נְאֻם־יְהוָה׃ כִּי לְכוּ־נָא
now! go! so (12) Yahweh declaration-of I-watch see! I but in-eyes-of-you to-him

אֶל־מְקוֹמִי אֲשֶׁר בְּשִׁילוֹ אֲשֶׁר שִׁכַּנְתִּי שְׁמִי שָׁם בָּרִאשׁוֹנָה
at-the-first there Name-of-me I-made-dwell where in-Shiloh that place-of-me to

וּרְאוּ אֵת אֲשֶׁר־עָשִׂיתִי לוֹ מִפְּנֵי רָעַת עַמִּי יִשְׂרָאֵל׃
Israel people-of-me wickedness-of because-of to-him I-did what *** and-see!

וְעַתָּה יַעַן עֲשׂוֹתְכֶם אֶת־כָּל־הַמַּעֲשִׂים הָאֵלֶּה נְאֻם־
declaration-of the-these the-things all-of *** to-do-you because and-now (13)

יְהוָה וָאֲדַבֵּר אֲלֵיכֶם הַשְׁכֵּם וְדַבֵּר וְלֹא שְׁמַעְתֶּם
you-listened but-not and-to-speak to-begin-early to-you and-I-spoke Yahweh

Reform your ways and your actions, and I will let you live in this place. [4]Do not trust in deceptive words and say, "This is the temple of the LORD, the temple of the LORD, the temple of the LORD!" [5]If you really change your ways and your actions and deal with each other justly, [6]if you do not oppress the alien, the fatherless or the widow and do not shed innocent blood in this place, and if you do not follow other gods to your own harm, [7]then I will let you live in this place, in the land I gave your forefathers for ever and ever. [8]But look, you are trusting in deceptive words that are worthless.

[9]" 'Will you steal and murder, commit adultery and perjury,[m] burn incense to Baal and follow other gods you have not known, [10]and then come and stand before me in this house, which bears my Name, and say, "We are safe"—safe to do all these detestable things? [11]Has this house, which bears my Name, become a den of robbers to you? But I have been watching! declares the LORD.

[12]" 'Go now to the place in Shiloh where I first made a dwelling for my Name, and see what I did to it because of the wickedness of my people Israel. [13]While you were doing all these things, declares the LORD, I spoke to you again and again, but you did not listen; I

[m]9 Or *and swear by false gods*

וָאֶקְרָא אֶתְכֶם וְלֹא עֲנִיתֶם׃ וְעָשִׂיתִי לַבַּיִת ׀ אֲשֶׁר
that to-the-house so-I-will-do (14) you-answered but-not you and-I-called

נִקְרָא־ שְׁמִי עָלָיו אֲשֶׁר אַתֶּם בֹּטְחִים בּוֹ וְלַמָּקוֹם אֲשֶׁר־
that even-to-the-place in-him ones-trusting you that to-him Name-of-me he-is-called

נָתַתִּי לָכֶם וְלַאֲבוֹתֵיכֶם כַּאֲשֶׁר עָשִׂיתִי לְשִׁלוֹ׃ וְהִשְׁלַכְתִּי
and-I-will-thrust (15) to-Shiloh I-did as-what and-to-fathers-of-you to-you I-gave

אֶתְכֶם מֵעַל פָּנָי כַּאֲשֶׁר הִשְׁלַכְתִּי אֶת־ כָּל־ אֲחֵיכֶם אֵת
*** brothers-of-you all-of *** I-thrust just-as presences-of-me from-in you

כָּל־ זֶרַע אֶפְרָיִם׃ וְאַתָּה אַל־תִּתְפַּלֵּל ׀ בְּעַד־ הָעָם הַזֶּה
the-this the-people on-behalf-of you-pray not so-you (16) Ephraim people-of all-of

וְאַל־ תִּשָּׂא בַעֲדָם רִנָּה וּתְפִלָּה וְאַל־ תִּפְגַּע־ בִּי
with-me you-plead and-not or-petition plea on-behalf-of-them you-offer or-not

כִּי־ אֵינֶנִּי שֹׁמֵעַ אֹתָךְ׃ הַאֵינְךָ רֹאֶה מָה הֵמָּה עֹשִׂים בְּעָרֵי
in-towns-of ones-doing they what seeing not-you? (17) you listening not-I for

יְהוּדָה וּבְחֻצוֹת יְרוּשָׁלָ‍ִם׃ הַבָּנִים מְלַקְּטִים עֵצִים
woods ones-gathering the-children (18) Jerusalem and-in-streets-of Judah

וְהָאָבוֹת מְבַעֲרִים אֶת־ הָאֵשׁ וְהַנָּשִׁים לָשׁוֹת בָּצֵק
dough ones-kneading and-the-women the-fire *** ones-lighting and-the-fathers

לַעֲשׂוֹת כַּוָּנִים לִמְלֶכֶת הַשָּׁמַיִם וְהַסֵּךְ נְסָכִים לֵאלֹהִים
to-gods drink-offerings and-to-pour-out the-Heavens for-Queen-of cakes to-make

אֲחֵרִים לְמַעַן הַכְעִסֵנִי׃ הַאֹתִי הֵם מַכְעִסִים
ones-provoking-to-anger they me? (19) to-provoke-to-anger-me in-order-to other-ones

נְאֻם־ יְהוָה הֲלוֹא אֹתָם לְמַעַן בֹּשֶׁת פְּנֵיהֶם׃ לָכֵן
therefore (20) faces-of-them shame-of in-order-to them not? Yahweh declaration-of

כֹּה־ אָמַר ׀ אֲדֹנָי יְהוִה הִנֵּה אַפִּי וַחֲמָתִי נִתֶּכֶת
being-poured-out and-wrath-of-me anger-of-me see! Yahweh Sovereign he-says this

אֶל־הַמָּקוֹם הַזֶּה עַל־הָאָדָם וְעַל־ הַבְּהֵמָה וְעַל־ עֵץ הַשָּׂדֶה וְעַל־
and-on the-field tree-of and-on the-beast and-on the-man on the-this the-place on

פְּרִי הָאֲדָמָה וּבָעֲרָה וְלֹא תִכְבֶּה׃ כֹּה
this (21) she-will-be-quenched and-not and-she-will-burn the-ground fruit-of

אָמַר יְהוָה צְבָאוֹת אֱלֹהֵי יִשְׂרָאֵל עֹלוֹתֵיכֶם סְפוּ עַל־
to add! burnt-offerings-of-you Israel God-of Hosts Yahweh-of he-says

זִבְחֵיכֶם וְאִכְלוּ בָשָׂר׃ כִּי לֹא־דִבַּרְתִּי אֶת־ אֲבוֹתֵיכֶם וְלֹא
and-not forefathers-of-you *** I-spoke not for (22) meat and-eat! sacrifices-of-you

צִוִּיתִים בְּיוֹם הוֹצִיאָ° אוֹתָם מֵאֶרֶץ מִצְרָיִם עַל־ דִּבְרֵי
matters-of about Egypt from-land-of them to-bring-me on-day-of I-commanded-them

עוֹלָה וָזָבַח׃ כִּי אִם־ אֶת־ הַדָּבָר הַזֶּה צִוִּיתִי
I-commanded the-this the-thing *** rather but (23) and-sacrifice burnt-offering

called you, but you did not answer. [14]Therefore, what I did to
Shiloh I will now do to the house
that bears my Name, the temple
you trust in, the place I gave to you
and your fathers. [15]I will thrust
you from my presence, just as I
did all your brothers, the people of
Ephraim.'
[16]"So do not pray for this people
nor offer any plea or petition for
them; do not plead with me, for I
will not listen to you. [17]Do you not
see what they are doing in the
towns of Judah and in the streets
of Jerusalem? [18]The children gather wood, the fathers light the fire,
and the women knead the dough
and make cakes of bread for the
Queen of Heaven. They pour out
drink offerings to other gods to
provoke me to anger. [19]But am I
the one they are provoking? declares the LORD. Are they not
rather harming themselves, to
their own shame?
[20]" 'Therefore this is what the
Sovereign LORD says: My anger
and my wrath will be poured out
on this place, on man and beast,
on the trees of the field and on the
fruit of the ground, and it will
burn and not be quenched.
[21]" 'This is what the LORD Almighty, the God of Israel, says: Go
ahead, add your burnt offerings to
your other sacrifices and eat the
meat yourselves! [22]For when I
brought your forefathers out of
Egypt and spoke to them, I did not
just give them commands about
burnt offerings and sacrifices,
[23]but I gave them this command:

°22 ק הוציאי

אוֹתָם לֵאמֹר שִׁמְעוּ בְקוֹלִי וְהָיִיתִי לָכֶם לֵאלֹהִים וְאַתֶּם תִּהְיוּ־
you-will-be and-you as-God to-you and-I-will-be to-voice-of-me obey! to-say them

לִי לְעָם וַהֲלַכְתֶּם בְּכָל־ הַדֶּרֶךְ אֲשֶׁר אֲצַוֶּה אֶתְכֶם לְמַעַן
so-that you I-command that the-way in-all-of and-you-walk as-people to-me

יִיטַב לָכֶם׃ וְלֹא שָׁמְעוּ וְלֹא־ הִטּוּ אֶת־
*** they-paid-attention or-not they-listened but-not (24) with-you he-may-go-well

אָזְנָם וַיֵּלְכוּ בְּמֹעֵצוֹת בִּשְׁרִרוּת לִבָּם
heart-of-them to-stubbornness-of to-inclinations instead-they-followed ear-of-them

הָרָע וַיִּהְיוּ לְאָחוֹר וְלֹא לְפָנִים׃ לְמִן־ הַיּוֹם
the-day at-from (25) toward-fronts and-not toward-back and-they-went the-evil

אֲשֶׁר יָצְאוּ אֲבוֹתֵיכֶם מֵאֶרֶץ מִצְרַיִם עַד הַיּוֹם הַזֶּה
the-this the-day until Egypt from-land-of forefathers-of-you they-left that

וָאֶשְׁלַח אֲלֵיכֶם אֶת־ כָּל־ עֲבָדַי הַנְּבִיאִים יוֹם הַשְׁכֵּם
to-begin-early day the-prophets servants-of-me all-of *** to-you then-I-sent

וְשָׁלֹחַ׃ וְלוֹא שָׁמְעוּ אֵלַי וְלֹא הִטּוּ אֶת־
*** they-paid-attention or-not to-me they-listened but-not (26) and-to-send

אָזְנָם וַיַּקְשׁוּ אֶת־ עָרְפָּם הֵרֵעוּ
they-did-evil neck-of-them *** and-they-made-stiff ear-of-them

מֵאֲבוֹתָם׃ וְדִבַּרְתָּ אֲלֵיהֶם אֶת־ כָּל־ הַדְּבָרִים
the-things all-of *** to-them when-you-tell (27) more-than-fathers-of-them

הָאֵלֶּה וְלֹא יִשְׁמְעוּ אֵלֶיךָ וְקָרָאתָ אֲלֵיהֶם וְלֹא
then-not to-them when-you-call to-you they-will-listen then-not the-these

יַעֲנוּכָה׃ וְאָמַרְתָּ אֲלֵיהֶם זֶה הַגּוֹי אֲשֶׁר לוֹא־ שָׁמְעוּ
they-obeyed not that the-nation this to-them so-you-say (28) they-will-answer-you

בְּקוֹל יְהוָה אֱלֹהָיו וְלֹא לָקְחוּ מוּסָר אָבְדָה
she-perished correction they-responded-to or-not God-of-him Yahweh to-voice-of

הָאֱמוּנָה וְנִכְרְתָה מִפִּיהֶם׃ גָּזִּי נִזְרֵךְ
hair-of-you cut-off! (29) from-mouth-of-them and-she-vanished the-truth

וְהַשְׁלִיכִי וּשְׂאִי עַל־ שְׁפָיִם קִינָה כִּי מָאַס יְהוָה
Yahweh he-rejected for lament barren-heights on and-take-up! and-throw-away!

וַיִּטֹּשׁ אֶת־ דּוֹר עֶבְרָתוֹ׃ כִּי־ עָשׂוּ בְנֵי־
peoples-of they-did indeed (30) wrath-of-him generation-of *** and-he-abandoned

יְהוּדָה הָרַע בְּעֵינַי נְאוּם־* יְהוָה שָׂמוּ שִׁקּוּצֵיהֶם
detestable-idols-of-them they-set Yahweh declaration-of in-eyes-of-me the-evil Judah

בַּבַּיִת אֲשֶׁר־ נִקְרָא־ שְׁמִי עָלָיו לְטַמְּאוֹ׃ וּבָנוּ
and-they-built (31) to-defile-him to-him Name-of-me he-is-called that in-the-house

בָּמוֹת הַתֹּפֶת אֲשֶׁר בְּגֵיא בֶן־ הִנֹּם לִשְׂרֹף אֶת־ בְּנֵיהֶם
sons-of-them *** to-burn Hinnom Ben in-Valley-of that the-Topheth high-places-of

Obey me, and I will be your God and you will be my people. Walk in all the ways I command you, that it may go well with you.
24But they did not listen or pay attention; instead, they followed the stubborn inclinations of their evil hearts. They went backward and not forward.
25From the time your forefathers left Egypt until now, day after day, again and again I sent you my servants the prophets.
26But they did not listen to me or pay attention. They were stiff-necked and did more evil than their forefathers.'

27"When you tell them all this, they will not listen to you; when you call to them, they will not answer.
28Therefore say to them, 'This is the nation that has not obeyed the LORD its God or responded to correction. Truth has perished; it has vanished from their lips.
29Cut off your hair and throw it away; take up a lament on the barren heights, for the LORD has rejected and abandoned this generation that is under his wrath.

*The Valley of Slaughter*

30" 'The people of Judah have done evil in my eyes, declares the LORD. They have set up their detestable idols in the house that bears my Name and have defiled it.
31They have built the high places of Topheth in the Valley of Ben Hinnom to burn their sons

*30 Most mss have *qibbuts* instead of *shureq* (נְאוּם).

וְאֶת־ בְּנֹתֵיהֶם בָּאֵשׁ אֲשֶׁר לֹא צִוִּיתִי וְלֹא עָלְתָה עַל־
into she-entered or-not I-commanded not that in-the-fire daughters-of-them and

לִבִּי׃ לָכֵן הִנֵּה־ יָמִים בָּאִים נְאֻם־ יְהוָה וְלֹא־
when-not Yahweh declaration-of ones-coming days beware! so (32) mind-of-me

יֵאָמֵר עוֹד הַתֹּפֶת וְגֵיא בֶן־ הִנֹּם כִּי אִם־ גֵּיא
Valley-of rather but Hinnom Ben or-Valley-of the-Topheth longer he-will-be-called

הַהֲרֵגָה וְקָבְרוּ בְתֹפֶת מֵאֵין מָקוֹם׃
room until-there-is-no in-Topheth for-they-will-bury the-Slaughter

וְהָיְתָה נִבְלַת הָעָם הַזֶּה לְמַאֲכָל לְעוֹף
for-bird-of as-food the-this the-people carcass-of then-she-will-become (33)

הַשָּׁמַיִם וּלְבֶהֱמַת הָאָרֶץ וְאֵין מַחֲרִיד׃
frightening-away and-no-one the-earth and-for-beast-of the-airs

וְהִשְׁבַּתִּי ׀ מֵעָרֵי יְהוּדָה וּמֵחֻצוֹת יְרוּשָׁלִַם קוֹל
sound-of Jerusalem and-in-streets-of Judah in-towns-of and-I-will-make-end (34)

שָׂשׂוֹן וְקוֹל שִׂמְחָה קוֹל חָתָן וְקוֹל כַּלָּה כִּי לְחָרְבָּה
as-desolation for bride and-voice-of bridegroom voice-of gladness and-sound-of joy

תִּהְיֶה הָאָרֶץ׃ בָּעֵת הַהִיא נְאֻם־ יְהוָה
Yahweh declaration-of the-that at-the-time (8:1) the-land she-will-become

ויציאו° אֶת־ עַצְמוֹת מַלְכֵי־ יְהוּדָה וְאֶת־ עַצְמוֹת־ שָׂרָיו וְאֶת־
and officials-of-him bones-of and Judah kings-of bones-of *** they-will-remove

עַצְמוֹת הַכֹּהֲנִים וְאֵת ׀ עַצְמוֹת הַנְּבִיאִים וְאֵת עַצְמוֹת יוֹשְׁבֵי־
ones-being-people-of bones-of and the-prophets bones-of and the-priests bones-of

יְרוּשָׁלִָם מִקִּבְרֵיהֶם׃ וּשְׁטָחוּם לַשֶּׁמֶשׁ
to-the-sun and-they-will-expose-them (2) from-graves-of-them Jerusalem

וְלַיָּרֵחַ וּלְכֹל ׀ צְבָא הַשָּׁמַיִם אֲשֶׁר אֲהֵבוּם וַאֲשֶׁר
and-which they-loved-them which the-heavens star-of and-to-all-of and-to-the-moon

עֲבָדוּם וַאֲשֶׁר הָלְכוּ אַחֲרֵיהֶם וַאֲשֶׁר דְּרָשׁוּם
they-consulted-them and-which after-them they-followed and-which they-served-them

וַאֲשֶׁר הִשְׁתַּחֲווּ לָהֶם לֹא יֵאָסְפוּ וְלֹא
or-not they-will-be-gathered-up not to-them they-worshiped and-which

יִקָּבֵרוּ לְדֹמֶן עַל־ פְּנֵי הָאֲדָמָה יִהְיוּ׃
they-will-be the-ground surfaces-of on like-refuse they-will-be-buried

וְנִבְחַר מָוֶת מֵחַיִּים לְכֹל הַשְּׁאֵרִית
the-survivor by-all-of to-lives death and-he-will-be-preferred (3)

הַנִּשְׁאָרִים מִן־ הַמִּשְׁפָּחָה הָרָעָה הַזֹּאת בְּכָל־ הַמְּקֹמוֹת
the-places in-all-of the-this the-evil the-nation from the-ones-remaining

הַנִּשְׁאָרִים אֲשֶׁר הִדַּחְתִּים שָׁם נְאֻם יְהוָה צְבָאוֹת׃
Hosts Yahweh-of declaration-of there I-banish-them where the-ones-remaining

and daughters in the fire—something I did not command, nor did it
enter my mind. [32]So beware, the
days are coming, declares the
LORD, when people will no longer
call it Topheth or the Valley of Ben
Hinnom, but the Valley of Slaughter, for they will bury the dead in
Topheth until there is no more
room. [33]Then the carcasses of this
people will become food for the
birds of the air and the beasts of
the earth, and there will be no one
to frighten them away. [34]I will
bring an end to the sounds of joy
and gladness and to the voices of
bride and bridegroom in the
towns of Judah and the streets of
Jerusalem, for the land will
become desolate.
8 " 'At that time, declares the
LORD, the bones of the kings
and officials of Judah, the bones of
the priests and prophets, and the
bones of the people of Jerusalem
will be removed from their graves.
[2]They will be exposed to the sun
and the moon and all the stars of
the heavens, which they have
loved and served and which they
have followed and consulted and
worshiped. They will not be gathered up or buried, but will be like
refuse lying on the ground. [3]Wher-
ever I banish them, all the survivors of this evil nation will prefer
death to life, declares the LORD Almighty.'

°1 ק יוצִיאוּ

וְאָמַרְתָּ אֲלֵיהֶם כֹּה אָמַר יְהוָה הֲיִפְּלוּ וְלֹא יָקוּמוּ אִם־
or they-get-up then-not they-fall? Yahweh he-says this to-them and-you-say (4)

יָשׁוּב וְלֹא יָשׁוּב׃ מַדּוּעַ שׁוֹבְבָה הָעָם הַזֶּה
the-this the-people she-turned-away why? (5) he-returns then-not he-turns-away

יְרוּשָׁלִַם מְשֻׁבָה נִצַּחַת הֶחֱזִיקוּ בַּתַּרְמִית מֵאֲנוּ
they-refuse to-the-deceit they-cling one-doing-always turning-away Jerusalem

לָשׁוּב׃ הִקְשַׁבְתִּי וָאֶשְׁמָע לוֹא־כֵן יְדַבֵּרוּ אֵין
there-is-no they-say right not and-I-listened I-was-attentive (6) to-return

אִישׁ נִחָם עַל־רָעָתוֹ לֵאמֹר מֶה עָשִׂיתִי כֻּלֹּה שָׁב
he-pursues each-of-him I-did what? to-say wickedness-of-him of repenting one

בִּמְרֻצָותָם כְּסוּס שׁוֹטֵף בַּמִּלְחָמָה׃ גַּם־חֲסִידָה בַשָּׁמַיִם
in-the-skies stork even (7) into-the-battle charging like-horse to-course-of-them

יָדְעָה מוֹעֲדֶיהָ וְתֹר וְסוּס וְעָגוּר שָׁמְרוּ אֶת־
*** they-observe and-thrush and-swift and-dove appointed-seasons-of-her she-knows

עֵת בֹּאָנָה וְעַמִּי לֹא יָדְעוּ אֵת מִשְׁפַּט יְהוָה׃
Yahweh requirement-of *** they-know not but-people-of-me to-migrate-them time-of

אֵיכָה תֹאמְרוּ חֲכָמִים אֲנַחְנוּ וְתוֹרַת יְהוָה אִתָּנוּ אָכֵן הִנֵּה לַשֶּׁקֶר
as-the-lie see! when with-us Yahweh for-law-of we wise-ones can-you-say how? (8)

עָשָׂה עֵט שֶׁקֶר סֹפְרִים׃ הֹבִישׁוּ חֲכָמִים
wise-ones they-will-be-shamed (9) scribes lying-of pen-of he-handled

חַתּוּ וַיִּלָּכֵדוּ הִנֵּה בִדְבַר־יְהוָה מָאָסוּ
they-rejected Yahweh to-word-of see! and-they-will-be-trapped they-will-be-dismayed

וְחָכְמַת־מֶה לָהֶם׃ לָכֵן אֶתֵּן אֶת־נְשֵׁיהֶם
wives-of-them *** I-will-give therefore (10) to-them what? and-wisdom-of

לַאֲחֵרִים שְׂדוֹתֵיהֶם לְיוֹרְשִׁים כִּי מִקָּטֹן וְעַד־גָּדוֹל
greatest and-to from-least indeed to-ones-owning fields-of-them to-other-men

כֻּלֹּה בֹּצֵעַ בָּצַע מִנָּבִיא וְעַד־כֹּהֵן כֻּלֹּה עֹשֶׂה
one-practicing all-of-him priest and-to from-prophet gain one-greedy-of all-of-him

שָׁקֶר׃ וַיְרַפּוּ אֶת־שֶׁבֶר בַּת־עַמִּי עַל־
as-though people-of-me daughter-of wound-of *** and-they-dress (11) deceit

נְקַלָּה לֵאמֹר שָׁלוֹם ׀ שָׁלוֹם וְאֵין שָׁלוֹם׃
peace when-there-is-no peace peace to-say one-not-being-serious

הֹבִשׁוּ כִּי תוֹעֵבָה עָשׂוּ גַּם־בּוֹשׁ
to-be-ashamed indeed they-did loathsome-thing that are-they-ashamed (12)

לֹא־יֵבֹשׁוּ וְהִכָּלֵם לֹא יָדָעוּ לָכֵן יִפְּלוּ
they-will-fall so they-know not even-to-blush they-are-ashamed not

בַנֹּפְלִים בְּעֵת פְּקֻדָּתָם יִכָּשְׁלוּ אָמַר
he-says they-will-be-brought-down punishment-of-them at-time-of among-the-ones-falling

°6 ק במרוצתם
°7 ק וסיס

*Sin and Punishment*

4"Say to them, 'This is what the LORD says:

" 'When men fall down, do they not get up?
When a man turns away, does he not return?
5Why then have these people turned away?
Why does Jerusalem always turn away?
They cling to deceit;
they refuse to return.
6I have listened attentively,
but they do not say what is right.
No one repents of his wickedness,
saying, "What have I done?"
Each pursues his own course
like a horse charging into battle.
7Even the stork in the sky
knows her appointed seasons,
and the dove, the swift and the thrush
observe the time of their migration.
But my people do not know
the requirements of the LORD.

8" 'How can you say, "We are wise,
for we have the law of the LORD,"
when actually the lying pen of the scribes
has handled it falsely?
9The wise will be put to shame;
they will be dismayed and trapped.
Since they have rejected the word of the LORD,
what kind of wisdom do they have?
10Therefore I will give their wives to other men
and their fields to new owners.
From the least to the greatest,
all are greedy for gain;
prophets and priests alike,
all practice deceit.
11They dress the wound of my people
as though it were not serious.
"Peace, peace," they say,
when there is no peace.
12Are they ashamed of their loathsome conduct?
No, they have no shame at all;
they do not even know how to blush.
So they will fall among the fallen;
they will be brought down when they are punished,
says the LORD.

יְהוָה׃ אָסֹף אֲסִיפֵם נְאֻם־ יְהוָה אֵין
there-will-be-no Yahweh declaration-of I-will-take-away-them to-take-away (13) Yahweh

עֲנָבִים בַּגֶּפֶן וְאֵין תְּאֵנִים בַּתְּאֵנָה וְהֶעָלֶה
and-the-leaf on-the-fig-tree figs and-there-will-be-no on-the-vine grapes

נָבֵל וָאֶתֵּן לָהֶם יַעַבְרוּם׃ עַל־ מָה אֲנַחְנוּ
we what? for (14) they-will-take-away-them to-them and-I-gave he-will-wither

יֹשְׁבִים הֵאָסְפוּ וְנָבוֹא אֶל־ עָרֵי הַמִּבְצָר
the-fortification cities-of to and-let-us-flee gather-together! ones-sitting

וְנִדְּמָה־ שָּׁם כִּי יְהוָה אֱלֹהֵינוּ הֲדִמָּנוּ
he-made-perish-us God-of-us Yahweh for there and-let-us-perish

וַיַּשְׁקֵנוּ מֵי־ רֹאשׁ כִּי חָטָאנוּ לַיהוָה׃
against-Yahweh we-sinned because poison waters-of and-he-gave-to-drink-us

קַוֵּה לְשָׁלוֹם וְאֵין טוֹב לְעֵת מַרְפֵּה וְהִנֵּה בְעָתָה׃
terror but-see! healing for-time-of good but-there-is-no for-peace to-hope (15)

מִדָּן נִשְׁמַע נַחְרַת סוּסָיו מִקּוֹל מִצְהֲלוֹת
neighings-of at-sound-of horses-of-him snort-of he-is-heard from-Dan (16)

אַבִּירָיו רָעֲשָׁה כָּל־ הָאָרֶץ וַיָּבוֹאוּ וַיֹּאכְלוּ אֶרֶץ
land and-they-devoured and-they-came the-land whole-of she-trembles stallions-of-him

וּמְלוֹאָהּ עִיר וְיֹשְׁבֵי בָהּ׃ כִּי הִנְנִי מְשַׁלֵּחַ
sending see-I! indeed (17) in-her and-ones-living-of city and-everything-in-her

בָּכֶם נְחָשִׁים צִפְעֹנִים אֲשֶׁר אֵין לָהֶם לָחַשׁ וְנִשְּׁכוּ
and-they-will-bite charm for-them there-is-not that vipers snakes among-you

אֶתְכֶם נְאֻם־ יְהוָה׃ מַבְלִיגִיתִי עֲלֵי יָגוֹן עָלַי לִבִּי
heart-of-me within-me sorrow in Comforter-of-me (18) Yahweh declaration-of you

דַוָּי׃ הִנֵּה־ קוֹל שַׁוְעַת בַּת־ עַמִּי מֵאֶרֶץ
from-land-of people-of-me daughter-of cry-of sound-of see! (19) faint

מַרְחַקִּים הַיהוָה אֵין בְּצִיּוֹן אִם־ מַלְכָּהּ אֵין בָּהּ מַדּוּעַ
why? in-her is-he-not King-of-her indeed in-Zion is-he-not Yahweh? places-far-away

הִכְעִסוּנִי בִּפְסִלֵיהֶם בְּהַבְלֵי נֵכָר׃
foreignness with-worthless-ones-of with-images-of-them they-provoked-to-anger-me

עָבַר קָצִיר כָּלָה קָיִץ וַאֲנַחְנוּ לוֹא נוֹשָׁעְנוּ׃ עַל־
since (21) we-are-saved not and-we summer he-ended harvest he-passed (20)

שֶׁבֶר בַּת־ עַמִּי הָשְׁבָּרְתִּי קָדַרְתִּי שַׁמָּה הֶחֱזִקָתְנִי׃
she-grips-me horror I-mourn I-am-crushed people-of-me daughter-of crushing-of

הַצֳרִי אֵין בְּגִלְעָד אִם־ רֹפֵא אֵין
is-there-no one-being-physician indeed in-Gilead is-there-no balm? (22)

שָׁם כִּי מַדּוּעַ לֹא עָלְתָה אֲרֻכַת בַּת־ עַמִּי׃
people-of-me daughter-of healing-of she-comes not why? then there

13"'I will take away their
harvest,
declares the LORD.
There will be no grapes on
the vine.
There will be no figs on the
tree,
and their leaves will wither.
What I have given them
will be taken from them.'" [n]
14"Why are we sitting here?
Gather together!
Let us flee to the fortified
cities
and perish there!
For the LORD our God has
doomed us to perish
and given us poisoned
water to drink,
because we have sinned
against him.
15We hoped for peace
but no good has come,
for a time of healing
but there was only terror.
16The snorting of the enemy's
horses
is heard from Dan;
at the neighing of their
stallions
the whole land trembles.
They have come to devour
the land and everything in
it,
the city and all who live
there."
17"See, I will send venomous
snakes among you,
vipers that cannot be
charmed,
and they will bite you,"
declares the LORD.
18O my Comforter[o] in sorrow,
my heart is faint within me.
19Listen to the cry of my people
from a land far away:
"Is the LORD not in Zion?
Is her King no longer
there?"
"Why have they provoked me
to anger with their
images,
with their worthless foreign
idols?"
20"The harvest is past,
the summer has ended,
and we are not saved."
21Since my people are crushed, I
am crushed;
I mourn, and horror grips
me.
22Is there no balm in Gilead?
Is there no physician there?
Why then is there no healing
for the wound of my
people?

[n]13 The meaning of the Hebrew for this sentence is uncertain.
[o]18 The meaning of the Hebrew for this word is uncertain.

מִי־ יִתֵּן רֹאשִׁי מַיִם וְעֵינִי מְקוֹר דִּמְעָה
tear fountain-of and-eye-of-me waters head-of-me he-would-make who? *(23)

וְאֶבְכֶּה יוֹמָם וָלַיְלָה אֵת חַלְלֵי בַת־ עַמִּי׃
people-of-me daughter-of ones-slain-of *** and-night by-day then-I-would-weep

מִי־ יִתְּנֵנִי בַמִּדְבָּר מְלוֹן אֹרְחִים
ones-traveling lodging-place-of in-the-desert he-would-give-me who? (9:1)

וְאֶעֶזְבָה אֶת־ עַמִּי וְאֵלְכָה מֵאִתָּם כִּי
for from-with-them and-I-might-go-away people-of-me *** so-I-might-leave

כֻּלָּם מְנָאֲפִים עֲצֶרֶת בֹּגְדִים׃
ones-being-unfaithful crowd-of ones-committing-adultery all-of-them

וַיַּדְרְכוּ אֶת־ לְשׁוֹנָם קַשְׁתָּם שֶׁקֶר וְלֹא לֶאֱמוּנָה
by-truth and-not lie bow-of-them tongue-of-them *** and-they-make-ready (2)

גָּבְרוּ בָאָרֶץ כִּי מֵרָעָה אֶל־רָעָה ׀ יָצָאוּ וְאֹתִי לֹא־ יָדָעוּ
they-acknowledge not and-me they-go sin to from-sin indeed in-the-land they-triumph

נְאֻם־ יְהוָה׃ אִישׁ מֵרֵעֵהוּ הִשָּׁמֵרוּ וְעַל־ כָּל־ אָח
brother every-of and-in beware! of-friend-of-him each (3) Yahweh declaration-of

אַל־ תִּבְטָחוּ כִּי כָל־ אָח עָקוֹב יַעְקֹב וְכָל־ רֵעַ
friend and-every-of he-deceives to-deceive brother every-of for you-trust not

רָכִיל יַהֲלֹךְ׃ וְאִישׁ בְּרֵעֵהוּ יְהָתֵלּוּ וֶאֱמֶת לֹא
not and-truth he-deceives to-friend-of-him and-man (4) he-continues slander

יְדַבֵּרוּ לִמְּדוּ לְשׁוֹנָם דַּבֶּר־ שֶׁקֶר הַעֲוֵה נִלְאוּ׃
they-weary-themselves to-sin lie to-speak tongue-of-them they-taught they-speak

שִׁבְתְּךָ בְּתוֹךְ מִרְמָה בְּמִרְמָה מֵאֲנוּ דַעַת־ אוֹתִי
me to-acknowledge they-refuse in-deceit deception in-midst-of to-live-you (5)

נְאֻם־ יְהוָה׃ לָכֵן כֹּה אָמַר יְהוָה צְבָאוֹת הִנְנִי
see-I! Hosts Yahweh-of he-says this therefore (6) Yahweh declaration-of

צוֹרְפָם וּבְחַנְתִּים כִּי־ אֵיךְ אֶעֱשֶׂה מִפְּנֵי בַּת־
daughter-of because-of can-I-do what? for and-I-will-test-them refining-them

עַמִּי׃ חֵץ שׁוֹחֵט לְשׁוֹנָם מִרְמָה דִבֵּר
he-speaks deceit tongue-of-them being-deadly arrow (7) people-of-me

בְּפִיו שָׁלוֹם אֶת־ רֵעֵהוּ יְדַבֵּר וּבְקִרְבּוֹ יָשִׂים
he-sets but-in-heart-of-him he-speaks neighbor-of-him with peace with-mouth-of-him

אָרְבּוֹ׃ הַעַל־אֵלֶּה לֹא־ אֶפְקָד־ בָּם נְאֻם־ יְהוָה אִם
or Yahweh declaration-of to-them should-I-punish not these for? (8) trap-of-him

בְּגוֹי אֲשֶׁר־ כָּזֶה לֹא תִתְנַקֵּם נַפְשִׁי׃ עַל־
for (9) self-of-me should-she-take-vengeance not as-this that on-nation

הֶהָרִים אֶשָּׂא בְכִי וָנֶהִי וְעַל־ נְאוֹת מִדְבָּר
desert pastures-of and-concerning and-wailing weeping I-will-raise the-mountains

9 Oh, that my head were a
spring of water
and my eyes a fountain of
tears!
I would weep day and night
for the slain of my people.
2Oh, that I had in the desert
a lodging place for travelers,
so that I might leave my
people
and go away from them;
for they are all adulterers,
a crowd of unfaithful
people.

3"They make ready their tongue
like a bow, to shoot lies;
it is not by truth
that they triumph[p] in the
land.
They go from one sin to
another;
they do not acknowledge
me,"
declares the LORD.
4"Beware of your friends;
do not trust your brothers.
For every brother is a
deceiver,[q]
and every friend a slanderer.
5Friend deceives friend,
and no one speaks the truth.
They have taught their tongues
to lie;
they weary themselves with
sinning.
6You[r] live in the midst of
deception;
in their deceit they refuse to
acknowledge me,"
declares the LORD.

7Therefore this is what the LORD
Almighty says:

"See, I will refine and test
them,
for what else can I do
because of the sin of my
people?
8Their tongue is a deadly
arrow;
it speaks with deceit.
With his mouth each speaks
cordially to his neighbor,
but in his heart he sets a
trap for him.
9Should I not punish them for
this?"
declares the LORD.
"Should I not avenge myself
on such a nation as this?"

10I will weep and wail for the
mountains
and take up a lament
concerning the desert
pastures.

p3 Or *lies; / they are not valiant for truth*
q4 Or *a deceiving Jacob*
r6 That is, Jeremiah (the Hebrew is singular)

**Heading, 23* The English numeration of chapter 9 begins with verse 23 of chapter 8 in the Hebrew; thus, there is a one-verse discrepancy throughout the chapter.

°7 ק שחוט

קִינָה כִּי נִצְּתוּ מִבְּלִי־אִישׁ עֹבֵר וְלֹא שָׁמְעוּ קוֹל
lowing-of they-hear and-not traveling one without they-are-desolate indeed lament

מִקְנֶה מֵעוֹף הַשָּׁמַיִם וְעַד־בְּהֵמָה נָדְדוּ הָלָכוּ׃ וְנָתַתִּי
and-I-will-make (10) they-went they-fled animal and-to the-airs from-bird-of cattle

אֶת־יְרוּשָׁלִַם לְגַלִּים מְעוֹן תַּנִּים וְאֶת־עָרֵי יְהוּדָה אֶתֵּן
I-will-lay Judah towns-of and jackals haunt-of as-heaps-of-ruins Jerusalem ***

שְׁמָמָה מִבְּלִי יוֹשֵׁב׃ מִי־הָאִישׁ הֶחָכָם וְיָבֵן אֶת־
*** that-he-can-understand the-wise the-man who? (11) one-living without waste

זֹאת וַאֲשֶׁר דִּבֶּר פִּי־יְהוָה אֵלָיו וְיַגִּדָהּ עַל־
for that-he-can-explain-her to-him Yahweh mouth-of he-instructed and-whom this

מָה אָבְדָה הָאָרֶץ נִצְּתָה כַמִּדְבָּר מִבְּלִי עֹבֵר׃
one-crossing without like-the-desert she-is-laid-waste the-land she-is-ruined what?

וַיֹּאמֶר יְהוָה עַל־עָזְבָם אֶת־תּוֹרָתִי אֲשֶׁר נָתַתִּי
I-set which law-of-me *** to-forsake-them because Yahweh and-he-said (12)

לִפְנֵיהֶם וְלֹא־שָׁמְעוּ בְקוֹלִי וְלֹא־הָלְכוּ בָהּ׃
after-her they-followed and-not to-voice-of-me they-obeyed and-not before-them

וַיֵּלְכוּ אַחֲרֵי שְׁרִרוּת לִבָּם וְאַחֲרֵי הַבְּעָלִים
the-Baals and-after heart-of-them stubbornness-of after but-they-followed (13)

אֲשֶׁר לִמְּדוּם אֲבוֹתָם׃ לָכֵן כֹּה־אָמַר יְהוָה צְבָאוֹת
Hosts Yahweh-of he-says this therefore (14) fathers-of-them they-taught-them as

אֱלֹהֵי יִשְׂרָאֵל הִנְנִי מַאֲכִילָם אֶת־הָעָם הַזֶּה לַעֲנָה
bitter-food the-this the-people *** making-eat-them see-I! Israel God-of

וְהִשְׁקִיתִים מֵי־רֹאשׁ׃ וַהֲפִצוֹתִים
and-I-will-scatter-them (15) poison waters-of and-I-will-make-drink-them

בַּגּוֹיִם אֲשֶׁר לֹא יָדְעוּ הֵמָּה וַאֲבוֹתָם וְשִׁלַּחְתִּי
and-I-will-pursue or-fathers-of-them they they-knew not that among-the-nations

אַחֲרֵיהֶם אֶת־הַחֶרֶב עַד כַּלּוֹתִי אוֹתָם׃ כֹּה אָמַר יְהוָה צְבָאוֹת
Hosts Yahweh-of he-says this (16) them to-destroy-me until the-sword with after-them

הִתְבּוֹנְנוּ וְקִרְאוּ לַמְקוֹנְנוֹת וּתְבוֹאֶינָה וְאֶל־הַחֲכָמוֹת
the-skilled-women and-for so-they-come for-the-wailing-women and-call! consider!

שִׁלְחוּ וְתָבוֹאנָה׃ וּתְמַהֵרְנָה וְתִשֶּׂנָה עָלֵינוּ נֶהִי
wailing over-us and-let-them-lift and-let-them-be-quick (17) so-they-come send!

וְתֵרַדְנָה עֵינֵינוּ דִּמְעָה וְעַפְעַפֵּינוּ יִזְּלוּ־מָיִם׃
waters let-them-stream and-eyelids-of-us tear eyes-of-us and-let-them-overflow

כִּי קוֹל נְהִי נִשְׁמַע מִצִּיּוֹן אֵיךְ שֻׁדָּדְנוּ בֹּשְׁנוּ
we-are-shamed we-are-ruined how! from-Zion he-is-heard wailing sound-of indeed (18)

מְאֹד כִּי־עָזַבְנוּ אָרֶץ כִּי הִשְׁלִיכוּ מִשְׁכְּנוֹתֵינוּ׃ כִּי־שְׁמַעְנָה
hear! now (19) houses-of-us they-ruined because land we-must-leave indeed greatly

They are desolate and
untraveled,
and the lowing of cattle is
not heard.
The birds of the air have fled
and the animals are gone.

11"I will make Jerusalem a heap
of ruins,
a haunt of jackals;
and I will lay waste the towns
of Judah
so no one can live there."

12What man is wise enough to
understand this? Who has been
instructed by the LORD and can explain it? Why has the land been
ruined and laid waste like a desert
that no one can cross?
13The LORD said, "It is because
they have forsaken my law, which
I set before them; they have not
obeyed me or followed my law.
14Instead, they have followed the
stubbornness of their hearts; they
have followed the Baals, as their
fathers taught them." 15Therefore,
this is what the LORD Almighty,
the God of Israel, says: "See, I will
make this people eat bitter food
and drink poisoned water. 16I will
scatter them among nations that
neither they nor their fathers have
known, and I will pursue them
with the sword until I have destroyed them."

17This is what the LORD Almighty says:

"Consider now! Call for the
wailing women to come;
send for the most skillful of
them.
18Let them come quickly
and wail over us
till our eyes overflow with
tears
and water streams from our
eyelids.
19The sound of wailing is heard
from Zion:
'How ruined we are!
How great is our shame!
We must leave our land
because our houses are in
ruins.' "

20Now, O women, hear the

**Heading* See the note on page 159.

נָשִׁים דְּבַר־יְהוָה וְתִקַּח אָזְנְכֶם דְּבַר־פִּיו וְלַמֵּדְנָה
and-teach! mouth-of-him word-of ear-of-you and-let-her-be-open Yahweh word-of women

בְנוֹתֵיכֶם נֶהִי וְאִשָּׁה רְעוּתָהּ קִינָה׃ כִּי־עָלָה
he-climbed indeed (20) lament another-of-her and-each wailing daughters-of-you

מָוֶת בְּחַלּוֹנֵינוּ בָּא בְּאַרְמְנוֹתֵינוּ לְהַכְרִית עוֹלָל
child to-cut-off into-fortresses-of-us he-entered through-windows-of-us death

מִחוּץ בַּחוּרִים מֵרְחֹבוֹת׃ דַּבֵּר כֹּה נְאֻם־יְהוָה
Yahweh declaration-of this say! (21) from-public-squares young-men from-street

וְנָפְלָה נִבְלַת הָאָדָם כְּדֹמֶן עַל־פְּנֵי הַשָּׂדֶה
the-field surfaces-of on like-refuse the-man dead-body-of she-will-lie

וּכְעָמִיר מֵאַחֲרֵי הַקֹּצֵר וְאֵין מְאַסֵּף׃ כֹּה׀
this (22) gathering with-no-one the-one-reaping at-behind and-like-cut-grain

אָמַר יְהוָה אַל־יִתְהַלֵּל חָכָם בְּחָכְמָתוֹ וְאַל־יִתְהַלֵּל
let-him-boast or-not of-wisdom-of-him wise-man let-him-boast not Yahweh he-says

הַגִּבּוֹר בִּגְבוּרָתוֹ אַל־יִתְהַלֵּל עָשִׁיר בְּעָשְׁרוֹ׃
of-richness-of-him rich-man let-him-boast not of-strength-of-him the-strong-man

כִּי אִם־בְּזֹאת יִתְהַלֵּל הַמִּתְהַלֵּל הַשְׂכֵּל וְיָדֹעַ
and-to-know to-understand the-one-boasting let-him-boast about-this rather but (23)

אוֹתִי כִּי אֲנִי יְהוָה עֹשֶׂה חֶסֶד מִשְׁפָּט וּצְדָקָה בָּאָרֶץ
on-the-earth and-righteousness justice kindness one-exercising Yahweh I that me

כִּי־בְאֵלֶּה חָפַצְתִּי נְאֻם־יְהוָה׃ הִנֵּה יָמִים בָּאִים
ones-coming days see! (24) Yahweh declaration-of I-delight in-these for

נְאֻם־יְהוָה וּפָקַדְתִּי עַל־כָּל־מוּל
one-being-circumcised all-of to when-I-will-punish Yahweh declaration-of

בְּעָרְלָה׃ עַל־מִצְרַיִם וְעַל־יְהוּדָה וְעַל־אֱדוֹם וְעַל־בְּנֵי עַמּוֹן וְעַל־
and-to Ammon peoples-of and-to Edom and-to Judah and-to Egypt to (25) in-flesh

מוֹאָב וְעַל כָּל־קְצוּצֵי פֵאָה הַיֹּשְׁבִים בַּמִּדְבָּר כִּי
for in-the-desert the-ones-living forehead ones-clipping-of all-of and-to Moab

כָל־הַגּוֹיִם עֲרֵלִים וְכָל־בֵּית יִשְׂרָאֵל
Israel house-of and-whole-of ones-being-uncircumcised the-nations all-of

עַרְלֵי־לֵב׃ שִׁמְעוּ אֶת־הַדָּבָר אֲשֶׁר דִּבֶּר יְהוָה
Yahweh he-says that the-word *** hear! (10:1) heart ones-being-uncircumcised-of

עֲלֵיכֶם בֵּית יִשְׂרָאֵל׃ כֹּה׀ אָמַר יְהוָה אֶל־דֶּרֶךְ הַגּוֹיִם אַל־תִּלְמָדוּ
you-learn not the-nations way-of to Yahweh he-says this (2) Israel house-of to-you

וּמֵאֹתוֹת הַשָּׁמַיִם אַל־תֵּחָתּוּ כִּי־יֵחַתּוּ הַגּוֹיִם
the-nations they-are-terrified though you-be-terrified not the-skies or-by-signs-of

מֵהֵמָּה׃ כִּי־חֻקּוֹת הָעַמִּים הֶבֶל הוּא כִּי־עֵץ מִיַּעַר
from-forest tree indeed he worthless the-peoples customs-of for (3) by-them

word of the LORD;
open your ears to the words
of his mouth.
Teach your daughters how to
wail;
teach one another a lament.
21 Death has climbed in through
our windows
and has entered our
fortresses;
it has cut off the children from
the streets
and the young men from
the public squares.

22 Say, "This is what the LORD declares:

" 'The dead bodies of men will
lie
like refuse on the open field,
like cut grain behind the
reaper,
with no one to gather
them.' "

23 This is what the LORD says:

"Let not the wise man boast of
his wisdom
or the strong man boast of
his strength
or the rich man boast of his
riches,
24 but let him who boasts boast
about this:
that he understands and
knows me,
that I am the LORD, who
exercises kindness,
justice and righteousness on
earth,
for in these I delight,"
declares the LORD.

25 "The days are coming," declares the LORD, "when I will punish all who are circumcised only in the flesh— 26 Egypt, Judah, Edom, Ammon, Moab and all who live in the desert in distant places.[s] For all these nations are really uncircumcised, and even the whole house of Israel is uncircumcised in heart."

*God and Idols*

10 Hear what the LORD says to you, O house of Israel. 2 This is what the LORD says:

"Do not learn the ways of the
nations
or be terrified by signs in
the sky,
though the nations are
terrified by them.
3 For the customs of the peoples
are worthless;
they cut a tree out of the
forest,

[s]26 Or *desert and who clip the hair by their foreheads*

*Heading* See the note on page 159.

כְּרָתוֹ מַעֲשֵׂה יְדֵי־חָרָשׁ בַּמַּעֲצָד׃ בְּכֶסֶף
with-silver (4) with-the-chisel craftsman hands-of work-of he-cuts-him

וּבְזָהָב יְיַפֵּהוּ בְּמַסְמְרוֹת וּבְמַקָּבוֹת יְחַזְּקוּם וְלוֹא
so-not they-fasten-them and-with-hammers with-nails he-adorns-him and-with-gold

יָפִיק׃ כְּתֹמֶר מִקְשָׁה הֵמָּה וְלֹא יְדַבֵּרוּ
they-can-speak and-not they melon-patch like-scarecrow-of (5) he-will-totter

נָשׂוֹא יִנָּשׂוּא כִּי לֹא יִצְעָדוּ אַל־תִּירְאוּ מֵהֶם כִּי־לֹא
not for of-them you-fear not they-can-walk not because they-are-carried to-carry

יָרֵעוּ וְגַם־הֵיטֵיב אֵין אוֹתָם׃ מֵאֵין כָּמוֹךָ
like-you from-no-one (6) with-them there-is-not to-do-good and-also they-can-do-harm

יְהוָה גָּדוֹל אַתָּה וְגָדוֹל שִׁמְךָ בִּגְבוּרָה׃ מִי לֹא יִרָאֲךָ
he-should-revere-you not who? (7) in-power name-of-you and-mighty you great Yahweh

מֶלֶךְ הַגּוֹיִם כִּי לְךָ יָאָתָה כִּי בְכָל־חַכְמֵי
wise-men-of among-all-of indeed she-is-due to-you that the-nations King-of

הַגּוֹיִם וּבְכָל־מַלְכוּתָם מֵאֵין כָּמוֹךָ׃ וּבְאַחַת
and-as-one (8) like-you from-no-one kingdom-of-them and-in-all-of the-nations

יִבְעֲרוּ וְיִכְסָלוּ מוּסַר הֲבָלִים עֵץ הוּא׃ כֶּסֶף
silver (9) he wood worthless-ones taught-of and-they-are-foolish they-are-senseless

מְרֻקָּע מִתַּרְשִׁישׁ יוּבָא וְזָהָב מֵאוּפָז מַעֲשֵׂה חָרָשׁ
craftsman work-of from-Uphaz and-gold he-is-brought from-Tarshish being-hammered

וִידֵי צוֹרֵף תְּכֵלֶת וְאַרְגָּמָן לְבוּשָׁם מַעֲשֵׂה חֲכָמִים
skilled-ones work-of dress-of-them and-purple blue one-being-goldsmith and-hands-of

כֻּלָּם׃ וַיהוָה אֱלֹהִים אֱמֶת הוּא־אֱלֹהִים חַיִּים וּמֶלֶךְ עוֹלָם
eternity and-King-of living-ones God he truth God but-Yahweh (10) all-of-them

מִקִּצְפּוֹ תִּרְעַשׁ הָאָרֶץ וְלֹא־יָכִלוּ גוֹיִם זַעְמוֹ׃
wrath-of-him nations they-can-endure and-not the-earth she-trembles at-anger-of-him

כִּדְנָה תֵּאמְרוּן לְהוֹם אֱלָהַיָּא דִּי־שְׁמַיָּא וְאַרְקָא לָא
not and-the-earth the-heavens who the-gods to-them you-tell as-this (11)

עֲבַדוּ יֵאבַדוּ מֵאַרְעָא וּמִן־תְּחוֹת שְׁמַיָּא אֵלֶּה׃
these the-heavens under and-from from-the-earth they-will-perish they-made

עֹשֵׂה אֶרֶץ בְּכֹחוֹ מֵכִין תֵּבֵל בְּחָכְמָתוֹ
by-wisdom-of-him world one-founding by-power-of-him earth one-making-of (12)

וּבִתְבוּנָתוֹ נָטָה שָׁמָיִם׃ לְקוֹל תִּתּוֹ
to-make-him when-thunder (13) heavens he-stretched-out and-by-understanding-of-him

הֲמוֹן מַיִם בַּשָּׁמַיִם וַיַּעֲלֶה נְשִׂאִים מִקְצֵה אָרֶץ
the-earth from-end-of clouds and-he-makes-rise in-the-heavens waters roar-of

בְּרָקִים לַמָּטָר עָשָׂה וַיּוֹצֵא רוּחַ מֵאֹצְרֹתָיו׃
from-storehouses-of-him wind and-he-brings-out he-sends with-the-rain lightnings

and a craftsman shapes it
with his chisel.
4They adorn it with silver and
gold;
they fasten it with hammer
and nails
so it will not totter.
5Like a scarecrow in a melon
patch,
their idols cannot speak;
they must be carried
because they cannot walk.
Do not fear them;
they can do no harm
nor can they do any good."
6No one is like you, O LORD;
you are great,
and your name is mighty in
power.
7Who should not revere you,
O King of the nations?
This is your due.
Among all the wise men of the
nations
and in all their kingdoms,
there is no one like you.
8They are all senseless and
foolish;
they are taught by worthless
wooden idols.
9Hammered silver is brought
from Tarshish
and gold from Uphaz.
What the craftsman and
goldsmith have made
is then dressed in blue and
purple—
all made by skilled workers.
10But the LORD is the true God;
he is the living God, the
eternal King.
When he is angry, the earth
trembles;
the nations cannot endure
his wrath.

11"Tell them this: 'These gods,
who did not make the heavens
and the earth, will perish from the
earth and from under the heavens.' "†
12But God made the earth by his
power;
he founded the world by his
wisdom
and stretched out the
heavens by his
understanding.
13When he thunders, the waters
in the heavens roar;
he makes clouds rise from
the ends of the earth.
He sends lightning with the
rain
and brings out the wind
from his storehouses.

†11 The text of this verse is in Aramaic.

°13 ק הארץ

נִבְעַר כָּל־ אָדָם מִדַּעַת הֹבִישׁ כָּל־
every-of he-is-shamed without-knowledge one every-of he-is-senseless (14)

צוֹרֵף מִפָּסֶל כִּי שֶׁקֶר נִסְכּוֹ וְלֹא־ רוּחַ בָּם׃
in-them breath and-not image-of-him fraud indeed by-idol one-being-goldsmith

הֶבֶל הֵמָּה מַעֲשֵׂה תַּעְתֻּעִים בְּעֵת פְּקֻדָּתָם
judgment-of-them at-time-of mockeries object-of they worthless (15)

יֹאבֵדוּ׃ לֹא־ כְאֵלֶּה חֵלֶק יַעֲקֹב כִּי־ יוֹצֵר הַכֹּל הוּא
he the-all One-Making for Jacob Portion-of like-these not (16) they-will-perish

וְיִשְׂרָאֵל שֵׁבֶט נַחֲלָתוֹ יְהוָה צְבָאוֹת שְׁמוֹ׃
name-of-him Hosts Yahweh-of inheritance-of-him tribe-of including-Israel

אִסְפִּי מֵאֶרֶץ כִּנְעָתֵךְ יֹשֶׁבְתִּי° בַּמָּצוֹר׃ כִּי־
for (18) under-the-siege one-living belonging-of-you from-land gather-up! (17)

כֹה אָמַר יְהוָה הִנְנִי קוֹלֵעַ אֶת־ יוֹשְׁבֵי הָאָרֶץ בַּפַּעַם
at-the-time the-land ones-living-of *** hurling-out see-I! Yahweh he-says this

הַזֹּאת וַהֲצֵרוֹתִי לָהֶם לְמַעַן יִמְצָאוּ׃ אוֹי לִי
to-me woe! (19) they-may-capture so-that on-them and-I-will-bring-distress the-this

עַל־ שִׁבְרִי נַחְלָה מַכָּתִי וַאֲנִי אָמַרְתִּי אַךְ זֶה
this surely! I-said yet-I wound-of-me being-incurable injury-of-me because-of

חֳלִי וְאֶשָּׂאֶנּוּ׃ אָהֳלִי שֻׁדָּד וְכָל־ מֵיתָרַי
ropes-of-me and-all-of he-is-destroyed tent-of-me (20) and-I-must-endure-him sickness

נִתָּקוּ בָּנַי יְצָאֻנִי וְאֵינָם אֵין־
there-is-no and-no-more-they they-are-gone-from-me sons-of-me they-are-snapped

נֹטֶה עוֹד אָהֳלִי וּמֵקִים יְרִיעוֹתָי׃ כִּי
indeed (21) shelters-of-me or-one-setting-up tent-of-me longer one-pitching

נִבְעֲרוּ הָרֹעִים וְאֶת־ יְהוָה לֹא דָרָשׁוּ עַל־ כֵּן
this for they-inquire not Yahweh and the-ones-being-shepherds they-are-senseless

לֹא הִשְׂכִּילוּ וְכָל־ מַרְעִיתָם נְפוֹצָה׃ קוֹל שְׁמוּעָה
report sound-of (22) being-scattered flock-of-them and-all-of they-prosper not

הִנֵּה בָאָה וְרַעַשׁ גָּדוֹל מֵאֶרֶץ צָפוֹן לָשׂוּם אֶת־ עָרֵי יְהוּדָה
Judah towns-of *** to-make north from-land-of great and-commotion coming see!

שְׁמָמָה מְעוֹן תַּנִּים׃ יָדַעְתִּי יְהוָה כִּי לֹא לָאָדָם דַּרְכּוֹ
life-of-him to-the-man not that Yahweh I-know (23) jackals haunt-of desolation

לֹא־ לְאִישׁ הֹלֵךְ וְהָכִין אֶת־ צַעֲדוֹ׃ יַסְּרֵנִי יְהוָה אַךְ־
only Yahweh correct-me! (24) step-of-him *** and-to-direct walking for-man not

בְּמִשְׁפָּט אַל־ בְּאַפְּךָ פֶּן־ תַּמְעִטֵנִי׃ שְׁפֹךְ
pour-out! (25) you-reduce-to-nothing-me lest in-anger-of-you not with-justice

חֲמָתְךָ עַל־ הַגּוֹיִם אֲשֶׁר לֹא־ יְדָעוּךָ וְעַל מִשְׁפָּחוֹת אֲשֶׁר
who peoples and-on they-acknowledge-you not that the-nations on wrath-of-you

14 Everyone is senseless and
without knowledge;
every goldsmith is shamed
by his idols.
His images are a fraud;
they have no breath in
them.
15 They are worthless, the objects
of mockery;
when their judgment comes,
they will perish.
16 He who is the Portion of Jacob
is not like these,
for he is the Maker of all
things,
including Israel, the tribe of
his inheritance—
the LORD Almighty is his
name.

*Coming Destruction*

17 Gather up your belongings to
leave the land,
you who live under siege.
18 For this is what the LORD says:
"At this time I will hurl out
those who live in this land;
I will bring distress on them
so that they may be
captured."
19 Woe to me because of my
injury!
My wound is incurable!
Yet I said to myself,
"This is my sickness, and I
must endure it."
20 My tent is destroyed;
all its ropes are snapped.
My sons are gone from me
and are no more;
no one is left now to pitch
my tent
or to set up my shelter.
21 The shepherds are senseless
and do not inquire of the
LORD;
so they do not prosper
and all their flock is
scattered.
22 Listen! The report is coming—
a great commotion from the
land of the north!
It will make the towns of
Judah desolate,
a haunt of jackals.

*Jeremiah's Prayer*

23 I know, O LORD, that a man's
life is not his own;
it is not for man to direct
his steps.
24 Correct me, LORD, but only
with justice—
not in your anger,
lest you reduce me to
nothing.
25 Pour out your wrath on the
nations
that do not acknowledge
you,
on the peoples who do not

°17 ק ישבת

בִשְׁמְךָ לֹא קָרָאוּ כִּי־ אָכְלוּ אֶת־יַעֲקֹב וַאֲכָלֻהוּ
and-they-devoured-him Jacob *** they-devoured for they-call not on-name-of-you

וַיְכַלֻּהוּ וְאֶת־ נָוֵהוּ הֵשַׁמּוּ׃ הַדָּבָר אֲשֶׁר
that the-word (11:1) they-destroyed homeland-of-him and and-they-finished-him

הָיָה אֶל־יִרְמְיָהוּ מֵאֵת יְהוָה לֵאמֹר׃ שִׁמְעוּ אֶת־ דִּבְרֵי הַבְּרִית
the-covenant terms-of *** listen! (2) to-say Yahweh from-with Jeremiah to he-came

הַזֹּאת וְדִבַּרְתָּם אֶל־ אִישׁ יְהוּדָה וְעַל־ יֹשְׁבֵי יְרוּשָׁלִָם׃
Jerusalem ones-living-of and-to Judah person-of to and-you-tell-them the-this

וְאָמַרְתָּ אֲלֵיהֶם כֹּה־ אָמַר יְהוָה אֱלֹהֵי יִשְׂרָאֵל אָרוּר הָאִישׁ
the-man being-cursed Israel God-of Yahweh he-says this to-them and-you-tell (3)

אֲשֶׁר לֹא יִשְׁמַע אֶת־ דִּבְרֵי הַבְּרִית הַזֹּאת׃ אֲשֶׁר צִוִּיתִי אֶת־
*** I-commanded that (4) the-this the-covenant terms-of *** he-obeys not who

אֲבוֹתֵיכֶם בְּיוֹם הוֹצִיאִי־ אוֹתָם מֵאֶרֶץ־ מִצְרַיִם מִכּוּר
from-furnace-of Egypt from-land-of them to-bring-me on-day-of forefathers-of-you

הַבַּרְזֶל לֵאמֹר שִׁמְעוּ בְקוֹלִי וַעֲשִׂיתֶם אוֹתָם כְּכֹל אֲשֶׁר־ אֲצַוֶּה
I-command that as-everything them and-you-do to-voice-of-me obey! to-say the-iron

אֶתְכֶם וִהְיִיתֶם לִי לְעָם וְאָנֹכִי אֶהְיֶה לָכֶם לֵאלֹהִים׃ לְמַעַן
so-that (5) as-God to-you I-will-be and-I as-people to-me and-you-will-be you

הָקִים אֶת־הַשְּׁבוּעָה אֲשֶׁר־ נִשְׁבַּעְתִּי לַאֲבוֹתֵיכֶם לָתֵת לָהֶם אֶרֶץ
land to-them to-give to-forefathers-of-you I-swore that the-oath *** to-fulfill

זָבַת חָלָב וּדְבַשׁ כַּיּוֹם הַזֶּה וָאַעַן וָאֹמַר אָמֵן ׀ יְהוָה׃
Yahweh amen and-I-said and-I-answered the-this as-the-day and-honey milk flowing-of

וַיֹּאמֶר יְהוָה אֵלַי קְרָא אֶת־ כָּל־ הַדְּבָרִים הָאֵלֶּה בְּעָרֵי
in-towns-of the-these the-words all-of *** proclaim! to-me Yahweh and-he-said (6)

יְהוּדָה וּבְחֻצוֹת יְרוּשָׁלִַם לֵאמֹר שִׁמְעוּ אֶת־ דִּבְרֵי הַבְּרִית
the-covenant terms-of *** listen! to-say Jerusalem and-in-streets-of Judah

הַזֹּאת וַעֲשִׂיתֶם אוֹתָם׃ כִּי הָעֵד הַעִדֹתִי בַּאֲבוֹתֵיכֶם
to-forefathers-of-you I-warned to-warn indeed (7) them and-you-follow the-this

בְּיוֹם הַעֲלוֹתִי אוֹתָם מֵאֶרֶץ מִצְרַיִם וְעַד־ הַיּוֹם הַזֶּה
the-this the-day and-to Egypt from-land-of them to-bring-up-me from-day-of

הַשְׁכֵּם וְהָעֵד לֵאמֹר שִׁמְעוּ בְּקוֹלִי׃ וְלֹא שָׁמְעוּ
they-listened but-not (8) to-voice-of-me obey! to-say and-to-warn to-begin-early

וְלֹא־ הִטּוּ אֶת־ אָזְנָם וַיֵּלְכוּ אִישׁ בִּשְׁרִירוּת
to-stubbornness-of each but-they-followed ear-of-them *** they-made-attentive or-not

לִבָּם הָרָע וָאָבִיא עֲלֵיהֶם אֶת־ כָּל־ דִּבְרֵי הַבְּרִית־
the-covenant curses-of all-of *** on-them so-I-brought the-evil heart-of-them

הַזֹּאת אֲשֶׁר־ צִוִּיתִי לַעֲשׂוֹת וְלֹא עָשׂוּ׃ וַיֹּאמֶר יְהוָה
Yahweh then-he-said (9) they-kept but-not to-follow I-commanded that the-this

call on your name.
For they have devoured Jacob;
they have devoured him
completely
and destroyed his homeland.

*The Covenant Is Broken*

11 This is the word that came
to Jeremiah from the LORD:
2 "Listen to the terms of this covenant and tell them to the people
of Judah and to those who live in
Jerusalem. 3 Tell them that this is
what the LORD, the God of Israel,
says: 'Cursed is the man who does
not obey the terms of this covenant— 4 the terms I commanded
your forefathers when I brought
them out of Egypt, out of the iron-
smelting furnace.' I said, 'Obey
me and do everything I command
you, and you will be my people,
and I will be your God. 5 Then I
will fulfill the oath I swore to your
forefathers, to give them a land
flowing with milk and
honey'—the land you possess today."
I answered, "Amen, LORD."
6 The LORD said to me, "Proclaim
all these words in the towns of
Judah and in the streets of Jerusalem: 'Listen to the terms of this
covenant and follow them. 7 From
the time I brought your forefathers up from Egypt until today, I
warned them again and again,
saying, "Obey me." 8 But they did
not listen or pay attention; instead, they followed the stubbornness of their evil hearts. So I
brought on them all the curses of
the covenant I had commanded
them to follow but that they did
not keep.' "
9 Then the LORD said to me,

אֵלַי נִמְצָא־ קֶשֶׁר בְּאִישׁ יְהוּדָה וּבְיֹשְׁבֵי
and-among-ones-living-of Judah among-person-of conspiracy he-is-found to-me

יְרוּשָׁלִָם׃ שָׁבוּ עַל־ עֲוֹנֹת אֲבוֹתָם הָרִאשֹׁנִים אֲשֶׁר
who the-former-ones fathers-of-them sins-of to they-returned (10) Jerusalem

מֵאֲנוּ לִשְׁמוֹעַ אֶת־ דְּבָרַי וְהֵמָּה הָלְכוּ אַחֲרֵי אֱלֹהִים אֲחֵרִים
other-ones gods after they-followed but-they words-of-me *** to-listen they-refused

לְעָבְדָם הֵפֵרוּ בֵית־ יִשְׂרָאֵל וּבֵית יְהוּדָה אֶת־ בְּרִיתִי
covenant-of-me *** Judah and-house-of Israel house-of they-broke to-serve-them

אֲשֶׁר כָּרַתִּי אֶת־ אֲבוֹתָם׃ לָכֵן כֹּה אָמַר יְהוָה הִנְנִי
see-I! Yahweh he-says this therefore (11) forefathers-of-them with I-made that

מֵבִיא אֲלֵיהֶם רָעָה אֲשֶׁר לֹא־ יוּכְלוּ לָצֵאת מִמֶּנָּה וְזָעֲקוּ
although-they-cry from-her to-escape they-can not that disaster on-them bringing

אֵלַי וְלֹא אֶשְׁמַע אֲלֵיהֶם׃ וְהָלְכוּ עָרֵי יְהוּדָה
Judah towns-of and-they-will-go (12) to-them I-will-listen then-not to-me

וְיֹשְׁבֵי יְרוּשָׁלִַם וְזָעֲקוּ אֶל־ הָאֱלֹהִים אֲשֶׁר הֵם
they whom the-gods to and-they-will-cry-out Jerusalem and-ones-being-people-of

מְקַטְּרִים לָהֶם וְהוֹשֵׁעַ לֹא־ יוֹשִׁיעוּ לָהֶם בְּעֵת
at-time-of to-them they-will-help not but-to-help to-them ones-burning-incense

רָעָתָם׃ כִּי מִסְפַּר עָרֶיךָ הָיוּ אֱלֹהֶיךָ יְהוּדָה
Judah gods-of-you they-are towns-of-you number-of indeed (13) disaster-of-them

וּמִסְפַּר חֻצוֹת יְרוּשָׁלִַם שַׂמְתֶּם מִזְבְּחוֹת לַבֹּשֶׁת מִזְבְּחוֹת
altars to-the-shameful-one altars you-set-up Jerusalem streets-of and-number-of

לְקַטֵּר לַבָּעַל׃ וְאַתָּה אַל־ תִּתְפַּלֵּל בְּעַד־ הָעָם
the-people on-behalf-of you-pray not but-you (14) to-the-Baal to-burn-incense

הַזֶּה וְאַל־ תִּשָּׂא בַעֲדָם רִנָּה וּתְפִלָּה כִּי אֵינֶנִּי
not-I because or-petition plea on-behalf-of-them you-offer or-not the-this

שֹׁמֵעַ בְּעֵת קָרְאָם אֵלַי בְּעַד רָעָתָם׃ מֶה
what? (15) distress-of-them on-behalf-of to-me to-call-them at-time-of listening

לִידִידִי בְּבֵיתִי עֲשׂוֹתָהּ הַמְזִמָּתָה הָרַבִּים
the-many-ones the-scheme to-work-out-her in-temple-of-me to-beloved-of-me

וּבְשַׂר־ קֹדֶשׁ יַעַבְרוּ מֵעָלָיִךְ כִּי רָעָתֵכִי
wickedness-of-you when from-against-you can-they-avert consecration and-meat-of

אָז תַּעֲלֹזִי׃ זַיִת רַעֲנָן יְפֵה פְרִי־ תֹאַר קָרָא
he-called form fruit-of beautiful-of thriving olive-tree (16) you-rejoice then

יְהוָה שְׁמֵךְ לְקוֹל ׀ הֲמוּלָּה גְדֹלָה הִצִּית אֵשׁ עָלֶיהָ
to-her fire he-will-set mighty storm with-roar-of name-of-you Yahweh

וְרָעוּ דָּלִיּוֹתָיו׃ וַיהוָה צְבָאוֹת הַנּוֹטֵעַ
the-one-planting Hosts and-Yahweh-of (17) branches-of-him and-they-will-be-broken

"There is a conspiracy among the people of Judah and those who live in Jerusalem. [10]They have returned to the sins of their forefathers, who refused to listen to my words. They have followed other gods to serve them. Both the house of Israel and the house of Judah have broken the covenant I made with their forefathers. [11]Therefore this is what the LORD says: 'I will bring on them a disaster they cannot escape. Although they cry out to me, I will not listen to them. [12]The towns of Judah and the people of Jerusalem will go and cry out to the gods to whom they burn incense, but they will not help them at all when disaster strikes. [13]You have as many gods as you have towns, O Judah; and the altars you have set up to burn incense to that shameful god Baal are as many as the streets of Jerusalem.'

[14]"Do not pray for this people nor offer any plea or petition for them, because I will not listen when they call to me in the time of their distress.

[15]"What is my beloved doing in
my temple
as she works out her evil
schemes with many?
Can consecrated meat avert
⌞your punishment⌟?
When you engage in your
wickedness,
then you rejoice."[a]

[16]The LORD called you a thriving
olive tree
with fruit beautiful in form.
But with the roar of a mighty
storm
he will set it on fire,
and its branches will be
broken.

[17]The LORD Almighty, who planted

[a]15 *Or Could consecrated meat avert your punishment? / Then you would rejoice*

אוֹתָךְ דִּבֶּר עָלַיִךְ רָעָה בִּגְלַל רָעַת בֵּית־ יִשְׂרָאֵל וּבֵית
and-house-of Israel house-of evil-of because-of disaster for-you he-decreed you

יְהוּדָה אֲשֶׁר עָשׂוּ לָהֶם לְהַכְעִסֵנִי לְקַטֵּר לַבָּעַל׃
to-the-Baal to-burn-incense to-provoke-to-anger-me for-them they-did that Judah

וַיהוָה הוֹדִיעַנִי וָאֵדָעָה אָז הִרְאִיתַנִי מַעַלְלֵיהֶם׃
deeds-of-them he-showed-me then then-I-knew he-revealed-to-me because-Yahweh (18)

וַאֲנִי כְּכֶבֶשׂ אַלּוּף יוּבַל לִטְבוֹחַ וְלֹא־ יָדַעְתִּי כִּי־
that I-realized and-not to-slaughter he-is-led gentle as-lamb and-I (19)

עָלַי ׀ חָשְׁבוּ מַחֲשָׁבוֹת נַשְׁחִיתָה עֵץ בְּלַחְמוֹ
with-fruit-of-him tree let-us-destroy plots they-plotted against-me

וְנִכְרְתֶנּוּ מֵאֶרֶץ חַיִּים וּשְׁמוֹ לֹא־
not that-name-of-him living-ones from-land-of and-let-us-cut-off-him

יִזָּכֵר עוֹד׃ וַיהוָה צְבָאוֹת שֹׁפֵט צֶדֶק
righteousness one-judging Hosts but-Yahweh-of (20) more he-will-be-remembered

בֹּחֵן כְּלָיוֹת וָלֵב אֶרְאֶה נִקְמָתְךָ מֵהֶם כִּי אֵלֶיךָ
to-you for upon-them vengeance-of-you let-me-see and-heart minds one-testing

גִּלִּיתִי אֶת־ רִיבִי׃ לָכֵן כֹּה־ אָמַר יְהוָה עַל־ אַנְשֵׁי
men-of about Yahweh he-says this therefore (21) cause-of-me *** I-committed

עֲנָתוֹת הַמְבַקְשִׁים אֶת־ נַפְשְׁךָ לֵאמֹר לֹא תִנָּבֵא בְּשֵׁם יְהוָה
Yahweh in-name-of you-prophesy not to-say life-of-you *** the-ones-seeking Anathoth

וְלֹא תָמוּת בְּיָדֵנוּ׃ לָכֵן כֹּה אָמַר יְהוָה צְבָאוֹת
Hosts Yahweh-of he-says this therefore (22) by-hand-of-us you-will-die so-not

הִנְנִי פֹקֵד עֲלֵיהֶם הַבַּחוּרִים יָמֻתוּ בַחֶרֶב בְּנֵיהֶם
sons-of-them by-the-sword they-will-die the-young-men to-them punishing see-I!

וּבְנוֹתֵיהֶם יָמֻתוּ בָּרָעָב׃ וּשְׁאֵרִית לֹא
not even-remnant (23) by-the-famine they-will-die and-daughters-of-them

תִהְיֶה לָהֶם כִּי־ אָבִיא רָעָה אֶל־ אַנְשֵׁי עֲנָתוֹת שְׁנַת
year-of Anathoth men-of on disaster I-will-bring because to-them she-will-be

פְּקֻדָּתָם׃ צַדִּיק אַתָּה יְהוָה כִּי אָרִיב אֵלֶיךָ אַךְ
yet before-you I-bring-case when Yahweh you righteous (12:1) punishment-of-them

מִשְׁפָּטִים אֲדַבֵּר אוֹתָךְ מַדּוּעַ דֶּרֶךְ רְשָׁעִים צָלֵחָה
she-prospers wicked-ones way-of why? with-you I-would-speak justices

שָׁלוּ כָּל־ בֹּגְדֵי בָגֶד׃ נְטַעְתָּם
you-planted-them (2) faithlessness ones-being-faithless-of all-of they-live-at-ease

גַּם־ שֹׁרָשׁוּ יֵלְכוּ גַּם־ עָשׂוּ פֶרִי קָרוֹב אַתָּה בְּפִיהֶם וְרָחוֹק
but-far in-mouth-of-them you near fruit they-bear and they-grow they-took-root and

מִכִּלְיוֹתֵיהֶם׃ וְאַתָּה יְהוָה יְדַעְתָּנִי תִּרְאֵנִי וּבָחַנְתָּ
and-you-test you-see-me you-know-me Yahweh yet-you (3) from-hearts-of-them

you, has decreed disaster for you,
because the house of Israel and the
house of Judah have done evil and
provoked me to anger by burning
incense to Baal.

*Plot Against Jeremiah*

18 Because the LORD revealed
their plot to me, I knew it, for at
that time he showed me what they
were doing. 19 I had been like a
gentle lamb led to the slaughter; I
did not realize that they had plotted against me, saying,

"Let us destroy the tree and its
fruit;
let us cut him off from the
land of the living,
that his name be
remembered no more."
20 But, O LORD Almighty, you
who judge righteously
and test the heart and mind,
let me see your vengeance
upon them,
for to you I have committed
my cause.

21 "Therefore this is what the
LORD says about the men of Anathoth who are seeking your life
and saying, 'Do not prophesy in
the name of the LORD or you will
die by our hands'— 22 therefore this
is what the LORD Almighty says: 'I
will punish them. Their young
men will die by the sword, their
sons and daughters by famine.
23 Not even a remnant will be left to
them, because I will bring disaster
on the men of Anathoth in the
year of their punishment.' "

*Jeremiah's Complaint*

12 You are always righteous,
O LORD,
when I bring a case before
you.
Yet I would speak with you
about your justice:
Why does the way of the
wicked prosper?
Why do all the faithless live
at ease?
2 You have planted them, and
they have taken root;
they grow and bear fruit.
You are always on their lips
but far from their hearts.
3 Yet you know me, O LORD;
you see me and test my

לִבִּי אִתָּךְ הַתִּקֵם כְּצֹאן לְטִבְחָה וְהַקְדִּשֵׁם
and-set-apart-them! to-butchery like-sheep drag-off-them! about-you thought-of-me

לְיוֹם הֲרֵגָה׃ עַד־ מָתַי תֶּאֱבַל הָאָרֶץ וְעֵשֶׂב כָּל־
every-of and-grass-of the-land will-she-be-parched when? until (4) slaughter for-day-of

הַשָּׂדֶה יִיבָשׁ מֵרָעַת יֹשְׁבֵי־ בָהּ
in-her ones-living-of because-of-wickedness-of will-he-be-withered the-field

סָפְתָה בְהֵמוֹת וָעוֹף כִּי אָמְרוּ לֹא יִרְאֶה אֶת־ אַחֲרִיתֵנוּ׃
happening-of-us *** he-will-see not they-say moreover and-bird animals she-perished

כִּי אֶת־ רַגְלִים רַצְתָּה וַיַּלְאוּךָ וְאֵיךְ תְּתַחֲרֶה
can-you-compete then-how? and-they-wore-out-you you-raced men-on-foot with if (5)

אֶת־ הַסּוּסִים וּבְאֶרֶץ שָׁלוֹם אַתָּה בוֹטֵחַ וְאֵיךְ תַּעֲשֶׂה
will-you-manage then-how? trusting you safety if-in-land-of the-horses with

בִּגְאוֹן הַיַּרְדֵּן׃ כִּי גַם־ אַחֶיךָ וּבֵית־
even-house-of brothers-of-you also indeed (6) the-Jordan in-thicket-of

אָבִיךָ גַּם־ הֵמָּה בָּגְדוּ בָךְ גַּם־ הֵמָּה קָרְאוּ אַחֲרֶיךָ
against-you they-cried they even to-you they-betrayed they even father-of-you

מָלֵא אַל־ תַּאֲמֵן בָּם כִּי־ יְדַבְּרוּ אֵלֶיךָ טוֹבוֹת׃
good-things of-you they-speak though in-them you-trust not loudly

עָזַבְתִּי אֶת־ בֵּיתִי נָטַשְׁתִּי אֶת־ נַחֲלָתִי נָתַתִּי
I-will-give inheritance-of-me *** I-will-abandon house-of-me *** I-will-forsake (7)

אֶת־יְדִדוּת נַפְשִׁי בְּכַף אֹיְבֶיהָ׃ הָיְתָה־ לִּי
to-me she-became (8) ones-being-enemies-of-her into-hand-of self-of-me love-of ***

נַחֲלָתִי כְּאַרְיֵה בַיָּעַר נָתְנָה עָלַי בְּקוֹלָהּ עַל־ כֵּן
this for with-roar-of-her to-me she-gives in-the-forest like-lion inheritance-of-me

שְׂנֵאתִיהָ׃ הַעַיִט צָבוּעַ נַחֲלָתִי לִי הַעַיִט
the-bird-of-prey to-me inheritance-of-me speckled the-bird-of-prey (9) I-hate-her

סָבִיב עָלֶיהָ לְכוּ אִסְפוּ כָּל־ חַיַּת הַשָּׂדֶה הֵתָיוּ לְאָכְלָה׃
to-devour bring! the-wild beast-of all-of gather! go! against-her surrounding

רֹעִים רַבִּים שִׁחֲתוּ כַרְמִי בֹּסְסוּ
they-will-trample vineyard-of-me they-will-ruin many-ones ones-being-shepherds (10)

אֶת־ חֶלְקָתִי נָתְנוּ אֶת־ חֶלְקַת חֶמְדָּתִי לְמִדְבַּר
into-wasteland-of pleasure-of-me field-of *** they-will-turn field-of-me ***

שְׁמָמָה׃ שָׂמָהּ לִשְׁמָמָה אָבְלָה עָלַי שְׁמֵמָה
desolation before-me she-will-be-parched into-wasteland he-will-make-her (11) desolation

נָשַׁמָּה כָּל־ הָאָרֶץ כִּי אֵין אִישׁ שָׂם עַל־לֵב׃
heart to taking one there-is-no because the-land whole-of she-will-be-laid-waste

עַל־ כָּל־ שְׁפָיִם בַּמִּדְבָּר בָּאוּ שֹׁדְדִים
ones-destroying they-will-swarm in-the-desert barren-heights all-of over (12)

---

thoughts about you.
Drag them off like sheep to be butchered!
Set them apart for the day of slaughter!
4 How long will the land lie parched[v]
and the grass in every field be withered?
Because those who live in it are wicked,
the animals and birds have perished.
Moreover, the people are saying,
"He will not see what happens to us."

*God's Answer*

5 "If you have raced with men on foot
and they have worn you out,
how can you compete with horses?
If you stumble in safe country,[w]
how will you manage in the thickets by[x] the Jordan?
6 Your brothers, your own family—
even they have betrayed you;
they have raised a loud cry against you.
Do not trust them,
though they speak well of you.

7 "I will forsake my house,
abandon my inheritance;
I will give the one I love
into the hands of her enemies.
8 My inheritance has become to me
like a lion in the forest.
She roars at me;
therefore I hate her.
9 Has not my inheritance become to me
like a speckled bird of prey
that other birds of prey surround and attack?
Go and gather all the wild beasts;
bring them to devour.
10 Many shepherds will ruin my vineyard
and trample down my field;
they will turn my pleasant field
into a desolate wasteland.
11 It will be made a wasteland,
parched and desolate before me;
the whole land will be laid waste
because there is no one who cares.
12 Over all the barren heights in the desert
destroyers will swarm,

v4 Or *land mourn*
w5 Or *If you put your trust in a land of safety*
x5 Or *the flooding of*

כִּי חֶרֶב לַיהוָה אֹכְלָה מִקְצֵה־אֶרֶץ וְעַד־קְצֵה הָאָרֶץ

the-land end-of and-to land from-end-of one-devouring of-Yahweh sword for

אֵין שָׁלוֹם לְכָל־בָּשָׂר׃ זָרְעוּ חִטִּים וְקֹצִים

but-thorns wheats they-will-sow (13) person for-any-of safety there-will-be-no

קָצָרוּ נֶחְלוּ לֹא יוֹעִלוּ וּבֹשׁוּ

so-be-ashamed! they-will-gain not they-will-wear-themselves-out they-will-reap

מִתְּבוּאֹתֵיכֶם מֵחֲרוֹן אַף־יְהוָה׃ כֹּה ׀ אָמַר יְהוָה

Yahweh he-says this (14) Yahweh anger-of because-of-fierceness-of of-harvests-of-you

עַל־כָּל־שְׁכֵנַי הָרָעִים הַנֹּגְעִים בַּנַּחֲלָה

onto-the-inheritance the-ones-seizing the-wicked-ones neighbors-of-me all-of for

אֲשֶׁר־הִנְחַלְתִּי אֶת־עַמִּי אֶת־יִשְׂרָאֵל הִנְנִי נֹתְשָׁם

uprooting-them see-I! Israel *** people-of-me *** I-gave-as-inheritance that

מֵעַל אַדְמָתָם וְאֶת־בֵּית יְהוּדָה אֶתּוֹשׁ מִתּוֹכָם׃

from-among-them I-will-uproot Judah house-of and land-of-them from-on

וְהָיָה אַחֲרֵי נָתְשִׁי אוֹתָם אָשׁוּב

I-will-do-again them to-uproot-me after but-he-will-be (15)

וְרִחַמְתִּים וַהֲשִׁבֹתִים אִישׁ לְנַחֲלָתוֹ

to-inheritance-of-him each and-I-will-bring-back-them and-I-will-have-compassion-on-them

וְאִישׁ לְאַרְצוֹ׃ וְהָיָה אִם־לָמֹד יִלְמְדוּ אֶת־דַּרְכֵי

ways-of *** they-learn to-learn if and-he-will-be (16) to-country-of-him and-each

עַמִּי לְהִשָּׁבֵעַ בִּשְׁמִי חַי־יְהוָה כַּאֲשֶׁר לִמְּדוּ אֶת־

*** they-taught even-as Yahweh alive by-name-of-me to-swear people-of-me

עַמִּי לְהִשָּׁבֵעַ בַּבָּעַל וְנִבְנוּ בְּתוֹךְ עַמִּי׃

people-of-me in-among then-they-will-be-established by-the-Baal to-swear people-of-me

וְאִם לֹא יִשְׁמָעוּ וְנָתַשְׁתִּי אֶת־הַגּוֹי הַהוּא נָתוֹשׁ

to-uproot the-that the-nation *** then-I-will-uproot they-listen not but-if (17)

וְאַבֵּד נְאֻם־יְהוָה׃ כֹּה־אָמַר יְהוָה אֵלַי הָלוֹךְ

to-go to-me Yahweh he-said this (13:1) Yahweh declaration-of and-to-destroy

וְקָנִיתָ לְּךָ אֵזוֹר פִּשְׁתִּים וְשַׂמְתּוֹ עַל־מָתְנֶיךָ

waists-of-you around and-you-put-him linens belt-of for-you and-you-buy

וּבַמַּיִם לֹא תְבִאֵהוּ׃ וָאֶקְנֶה אֶת־הָאֵזוֹר כִּדְבַר

as-direction-of the-belt *** so-I-bought (2) you-put-him not but-in-the-waters

יְהוָה וָאָשִׂם עַל־מָתְנָי׃ וַיְהִי דְבַר־יְהוָה אֵלַי

to-me Yahweh word-of then-he-came (3) waists-of-me around and-I-put Yahweh

שֵׁנִית לֵאמֹר׃ קַח אֶת־הָאֵזוֹר אֲשֶׁר קָנִיתָ אֲשֶׁר עַל־

around that you-bought that the-belt *** take! (4) to-say second-time

מָתְנֶיךָ וְקוּם לֵךְ פְּרָתָה וְטָמְנֵהוּ שָׁם בִּנְקִיק הַסָּלַע׃

the-rock in-crevice-of there and-hide-him! to-Perath go! and-get-up! waists-of-you

for the sword of the LORD will devour
from one end of the land to the other;
no one will be safe.
13They will sow wheat but reap thorns;
they will wear themselves out but gain nothing.
So bear the shame of your harvest
because of the LORD's fierce anger."

14This is what the LORD says: "As for all my wicked neighbors who seize the inheritance I gave my people Israel, I will uproot them from their lands and I will uproot the house of Judah from among them.
15But after I uproot them, I will again have compassion and will bring each of them back to his own inheritance and his own country.
16And if they learn well the ways of my people and swear by my name, 'As surely as the LORD lives'—even as they once taught my people to swear by Baal—then they will be established among my people.
17But if any nation does not listen, I will completely uproot and destroy it," declares the LORD.

*A Linen Belt*

**13** This is what the LORD said to me: "Go and buy a linen belt and put it around your waist, but do not let it touch water."
2So I bought a belt, as the LORD directed, and put it around my waist.
3Then the word of the LORD came to me a second time:
4"Take the belt you bought and are wearing around your waist, and go now to Perath[y] and hide it there in a crevice in the rocks."
5So I went

[y]4 Or possibly *the Euphrates*; also in verses 5-7

וָאֵלֵךְ וָאֶטְמְנֵהוּ בִּפְרָת כַּאֲשֶׁר צִוָּה יְהוָה אוֹתִי׃ וַיְהִי
and-he-was (6) me Yahweh he-told just-as at-Perath and-I-hid-him so-I-went (5)

מִקֵּץ יָמִים רַבִּים וַיֹּאמֶר יְהוָה אֵלַי קוּם לֵךְ פְּרָתָה וְקַח
and-get! to-Perath go! get-up! to-me Yahweh then-he-said many-ones days at-end-of

מִשָּׁם אֶת־הָאֵזוֹר אֲשֶׁר צִוִּיתִיךָ לְטָמְנוֹ־שָׁם׃ וָאֵלֵךְ פְּרָתָה
to-Perath so-I-went (7) there to-hide-him I-told-you that the-belt *** from-there

וָאֶחְפֹּר וָאֶקַּח אֶת־הָאֵזוֹר מִן־הַמָּקוֹם אֲשֶׁר־טְמַנְתִּיו שָׁמָּה
at-there I-hid-him where the-place from the-belt *** and-I-took and-I-dug-up

וְהִנֵּה נִשְׁחַת הָאֵזוֹר לֹא יִצְלַח לַכֹּל׃ וַיְהִי
then-he-came (8) for-the-anything he-was-useful not the-belt he-was-ruined but-see!

דְבַר־יְהוָה אֵלַי לֵאמֹר׃ כֹּה אָמַר יְהוָה כָּכָה אַשְׁחִית אֶת־
*** I-will-ruin same-way Yahweh he-says this (9) to-say to-me Yahweh word-of

גְּאוֹן יְהוּדָה וְאֶת־גְּאוֹן יְרוּשָׁלַםִ הָרָב׃ הָעָם הַזֶּה הָרָע
the-wicked the-this the-people (10) the-great Jerusalem pride-of and Judah pride-of

הַמֵּאֲנִים ׀ לִשְׁמוֹעַ אֶת־דְּבָרַי הַהֹלְכִים בִּשְׁרִרוּת
to-stubbornness-of the-ones-following words-of-me *** to-listen the-ones-refusing

לִבָּם וַיֵּלְכוּ אַחֲרֵי אֱלֹהִים אֲחֵרִים לְעָבְדָם וּלְהִשְׁתַּחֲוֺת
and-to-worship to-serve-them other-ones gods after and-they-go heart-of-them

לָהֶם וִיהִי כָּאֵזוֹר הַזֶּה אֲשֶׁר לֹא־יִצְלַח
he-is-useful not that the-this like-the-belt then-he-will-be to-them

לַכֹּל׃ כִּי כַּאֲשֶׁר יִדְבַּק הָאֵזוֹר אֶל־מָתְנֵי־אִישׁ כֵּן
so man waists-of around the-belt he-is-bound just-as for (11) for-the-anything

הִדְבַּקְתִּי אֵלַי אֶת־כָּל־בֵּית יִשְׂרָאֵל וְאֶת־כָּל־בֵּית יְהוּדָה
Judah house-of whole-of and Israel house-of whole-of *** to-me I-bound

נְאֻם־יְהוָה לִהְיוֹת לִי לְעָם וּלְשֵׁם וְלִתְהִלָּה
and-as-praise and-as-renown as-people to-me to-be Yahweh declaration-of

וּלְתִפְאָרֶת וְלֹא שָׁמֵעוּ׃ וְאָמַרְתָּ אֲלֵיהֶם אֶת־הַדָּבָר הַזֶּה
the-this the-word *** to-them and-you-say (12) they-listened but-not and-as-honor

כֹּה־אָמַר יְהוָה אֱלֹהֵי יִשְׂרָאֵל כָּל־נֵבֶל יִמָּלֵא יָיִן
wine he-should-be-filled wineskin every-of Israel God-of Yahweh he-says this

וְאָמְרוּ אֵלֶיךָ הֲיָדֹעַ לֹא נֵדַע כִּי כָל־נֵבֶל יִמָּלֵא
he-should-be-filled wineskin every-of that we-know not to-know? to-you if-they-say

יָיִן׃ וְאָמַרְתָּ אֲלֵיהֶם כֹּה־אָמַר יְהוָה הִנְנִי מְמַלֵּא אֶת־כָּל־
all-of *** filling see-I! Yahweh he-says this to-them then-you-tell (13) wine

יֹשְׁבֵי הָאָרֶץ הַזֹּאת וְאֶת־הַמְּלָכִים הַיֹּשְׁבִים לְדָוִד
of-David the-ones-sitting the-kings including the-this the-land ones-living-of

עַל־כִּסְאוֹ וְאֶת־הַכֹּהֲנִים וְאֶת־הַנְּבִיאִים וְאֵת כָּל־יֹשְׁבֵי
ones-living-of all-of and the-prophets and the-priests and throne-of-him on

and hid it at Perath, as the LORD told me.

6Many days later the LORD said to me, "Go now to Perath and get the belt I told you to hide there." 7So I went to Perath and dug up the belt and took it from the place where I had hidden it, but now it was ruined and completely useless.

8Then the word of the LORD came to me: 9"This is what the LORD says: 'In the same way I will ruin the pride of Judah and the great pride of Jerusalem. 10These wicked people, who refuse to listen to my words, who follow the stubbornness of their hearts and go after other gods to serve and worship them, will be like this belt—completely useless! 11For as a belt is bound around a man's waist, so I bound the whole house of Israel and the whole house of Judah to me,' declares the LORD, 'to be my people for my renown and praise and honor. But they have not listened.'

*Wineskins*

12"Say to them: 'This is what the LORD, the God of Israel, says: Every wineskin should be filled with wine.' And if they say to you, 'Don't we know that every wineskin should be filled with wine?' 13then tell them, 'This is what the LORD says: I am going to fill with drunkenness all who live in this land, including the kings who sit on David's throne, the priests, the prophets and all those living in

יְרוּשָׁלִָם שִׁכָּרוֹן׃ וְנִפַּצְתִּים° אִישׁ אֶל־ אָחִיו
other-of-him against one and-I-will-smash-them (14) drunkenness Jerusalem

וְהָאָבוֹת וְהַבָּנִים יַחְדָּו נְאֻם־ יְהוָה לֹא־ אֶחְמוֹל
I-will-allow-pity not Yahweh declaration-of alike and-the-sons even-the-fathers

וְלֹא־ אָחוּס וְלֹא אֲרַחֵם מֵהַשְׁחִיתָם׃
from-to-destroy-them I-will-allow-compassion or-not I-will-allow-mercy or-not

שִׁמְעוּ וְהַאֲזִינוּ אַל־ תִּגְבָּהוּ כִּי יְהוָה דִּבֵּר׃ תְּנוּ
give! (16) he-spoke Yahweh for you-be-arrogant not and-pay-attention! hear! (15)

לַיהוָה אֱלֹהֵיכֶם כָּבוֹד בְּטֶרֶם יַחְשִׁךְ וּבְטֶרֶם יִתְנַגְּפוּ
they-stumble and-at-before he-brings-darkness at-before glory God-of-you to-Yahweh

רַגְלֵיכֶם עַל־ הָרֵי נָשֶׁף וְקִוִּיתֶם לְאוֹר וְשָׂמָהּ
but-he-will-turn-her for-light and-you-hope darkness hills-of on feet-of-you

לְצַלְמָוֶת יְשִׁית° לַעֲרָפֶל׃ וְאִם לֹא
not but-if (17) to-deep-gloom and-he-will-change to-thick-darkness

תִּשְׁמָעוּהָ בְּמִסְתָּרִים תִּבְכֶּה־ נַפְשִׁי מִפְּנֵי גֵוָה
pride because-of self-of-me she-will-weep in-secret-places you-listen-to-her

וְדָמֹעַ תִּדְמַע וְתֵרַד עֵינִי דִּמְעָה כִּי
because tear eye-of-me and-she-will-overflow she-will-weep and-to-weep

נִשְׁבָּה עֵדֶר יְהוָה׃ אֱמֹר לַמֶּלֶךְ וְלַגְּבִירָה
and-to-the-queen-mother to-the-king say! (18) Yahweh flock-of she-will-be-captured

הַשְׁפִּילוּ שֵׁבוּ כִּי יָרַד מַרְאֲשׁוֹתֵיכֶם עֲטֶרֶת תִּפְאַרְתְּכֶם׃
glory-of-you crown-of from-heads-of-you he-will-fall for sit! come-down!

עָרֵי הַנֶּגֶב סֻגְּרוּ וְאֵין פֹּתֵחַ
one-opening and-there-will-be-no they-will-be-shut-up the-Negev cities-of (19)

הָגְלָת יְהוּדָה כֻּלָּהּ הָגְלָת שְׁלוֹמִים׃
complete-ones she-is-carried-into-exile all-of-her Judah she-is-carried-into-exile

שְׂאִי° עֵינֵיכֶם וּרְאִי° הַבָּאִים מִצָּפוֹן אַיֵּה הָעֵדֶר
the-flock where? from-north the-ones-coming and-see! eyes-of-you lift-up! (20)

נִתַּן־ לָךְ צֹאן תִּפְאַרְתֵּךְ׃ מַה־ תֹּאמְרִי כִּי־ יִפְקֹד
he-sets when will-you-say what? (21) boast-of-you sheep-of to-you he-was-entrusted

עָלַיִךְ וְאַתְּ לִמַּדְתְּ אֹתָם עָלַיִךְ אַלֻּפִים לְרֹאשׁ הֲלוֹא חֲבָלִים
pains not? at-head allies over-you them you-cultivated and-you over-you

יֹאחֱזוּךְ כְּמוֹ אֵשֶׁת לֵדָה׃ וְכִי תֹאמְרִי בִּלְבָבֵךְ
in-heart-of-you you-ask and-if (22) to-bear woman-of like they-will-grip-you

מַדּוּעַ קְרָאֻנִי אֵלֶּה בְּרֹב עֲוֺנֵךְ נִגְלוּ
they-were-torn-off sin-of-you because-of-many-of these they-happened-to-me why?

שׁוּלַיִךְ נֶחְמְסוּ עֲקֵבָיִךְ׃ הֲיַהֲפֹךְ כּוּשִׁי
Cushite can-he-change? (23) heels-of-you and-they-were-mistreated skirts-of-you

Jerusalem. [14]I will smash them one against the other, fathers and sons alike, declares the LORD. I will allow no pity or mercy or compassion to keep me from destroying them.' "

*Threat of Captivity*

[15]Hear and pay attention,
do not be arrogant,
for the LORD has spoken.
[16]Give glory to the LORD your God
before he brings the darkness,
before your feet stumble
on the darkening hills.
You hope for light,
but he will turn it to thick darkness
and change it to deep gloom.
[17]But if you do not listen,
I will weep in secret
because of your pride;
my eyes will weep bitterly,
overflowing with tears,
because the LORD's flock will be taken captive.

[18]Say to the king and to the queen mother,
"Come down from your thrones,
for your glorious crowns
will fall from your heads."
[19]The cities in the Negev will be shut up,
and there will be no one to open them.
All Judah will be carried into exile,
carried completely away.

[20]Lift up your eyes and see
those who are coming from the north.
Where is the flock that was entrusted to you,
the sheep of which you boasted?
[21]What will you say when ⌞the LORD⌟ sets over you
those you cultivated as your special allies?
Will not pain grip you
like that of a woman in labor?
[22]And if you ask yourself,
"Why has this happened to me?"—
it is because of your many sins
that your skirts have been torn off
and your body mistreated.
[23]Can the Ethiopian[z] change his

[z]23 Hebrew *Cushite* (probably a person from the upper Nile region)

°16 ק ושית
°20a ק שאו
°20b ק וראו

עוֹרוֹ וְנָמֵר חֲבַרְבֻּרֹתָיו גַּם־אַתֶּם תּוּכְלוּ לְהֵיטִיב לִמֻּדֵי
ones-accustomed-of to-do-good you-can you also spots-of-him or-leopard skin-of-him

הָרֵעַ׃ (24) וַאֲפִיצֵם כְּקַשׁ־ עוֹבֵר לְרוּחַ מִדְבָּר׃
desert by-wind-of driving like-chaff-of and-I-will-scatter-them (24) to-do-evil

(25) זֶה גוֹרָלֵךְ מְנָת־ מִדַּיִךְ מֵאִתִּי נְאֻם־ יְהוָה
Yahweh declaration-of from-with-me decrees-of-you portion-of lot-of-you this (25)

אֲשֶׁר שָׁכַחַתְּ אוֹתִי וַתִּבְטְחִי בַּשָּׁקֶר׃ (26) וְגַם־ אֲנִי
I so-also (26) in-the-falsehood and-you-trusted me you-forgot because

חָשַׂפְתִּי שׁוּלַיִךְ עַל־ פָּנָיִךְ וְנִרְאָה קְלוֹנֵךְ׃
shame-of-you that-he-may-be-seen faces-of-you over skirts-of-you I-will-pull-up

(27) נִאֻפַיִךְ וּמִצְהֲלוֹתַיִךְ זִמַּת זְנוּתֵךְ
prostitution-of-you shamelessness-of and-neighings-of-you adulteries-of-you (27)

עַל־גְּבָעוֹת בַּשָּׂדֶה רָאִיתִי שִׁקּוּצָיִךְ אוֹי לָךְ יְרוּשָׁלַםִ לֹא
not Jerusalem to-you woe! detestable-acts-of-you I-saw in-the-field hills on

תִטְהֲרִי אַחֲרֵי מָתַי עֹד׃ (14:1) אֲשֶׁר הָיָה דְבַר־ יְהוָה אֶל־יִרְמְיָהוּ
Jeremiah to Yahweh word-of he-is that (14:1) long how? after you-are-clean

עַל־ דִּבְרֵי הַבַּצָּרוֹת׃ (2) אָבְלָה יְהוּדָה וּשְׁעָרֶיהָ
and-cities-of-her Judah she-mourns (2) the-droughts matters-of concerning

אֻמְלְלוּ קָדְרוּ לָאָרֶץ וְצִוְחַת יְרוּשָׁלַםִ עָלָתָה׃
she-goes-up Jerusalem and-cry-of for-the-land they-wail they-languish

(3) וְאַדִּרֵיהֶם שָׁלְחוּ צְעוֹרֵיהֶם° לַמָּיִם בָּאוּ עַל־
to they-go for-the-waters servants-of-them they-send and-nobles-of-them (3)

גֵּבִים לֹא־ מָצְאוּ מַיִם שָׁבוּ כְלֵיהֶם רֵיקָם בֹּשׁוּ
they-are-dismayed unfilled jars-of-them they-return waters they-find not cisterns

וְהָכְלְמוּ וְחָפוּ רֹאשָׁם׃ (4) בַּעֲבוּר הָאֲדָמָה
the-ground on-account-of (4) head-of-them and-they-cover and-they-despair

חַתָּה כִּי לֹא־ הָיָה גֶשֶׁם בָּאָרֶץ בֹּשׁוּ אִכָּרִים
farmers they-are-dismayed in-the-land rain he-is not because she-is-cracked

חָפוּ רֹאשָׁם׃ (5) כִּי גַם־אַיֶּלֶת בַּשָּׂדֶה יָלְדָה וְעָזוֹב
and-to-desert she-bears in-the-field doe even indeed (5) head-of-them they-cover

כִּי לֹא־ הָיָה דֶּשֶׁא׃ (6) וּפְרָאִים עָמְדוּ עַל־ שְׁפָיִם
barren-heights on they-stand and-wild-donkeys (6) grass he-is not because

שָׁאֲפוּ רוּחַ כַּתַּנִּים כָּלוּ עֵינֵיהֶם כִּי־ אֵין עֵשֶׂב׃
pasture there-is-no for eyes-of-them they-fail like-the-jackals breath they-pant

(7) אִם־ עֲוֹנֵינוּ עָנוּ בָנוּ יְהוָה עֲשֵׂה לְמַעַן שְׁמֶךָ
name-of-you for-sake-of do! Yahweh against-us they-testify sins-of-us although (7)

כִּי־ רַבּוּ מְשׁוּבֹתֵינוּ לְךָ חָטָאנוּ׃ (8) מִקְוֵה יִשְׂרָאֵל
Israel Hope-of (8) we-sinned against-you backslidings-of-us they-are-great for

°3 ק צעיריהם

skin
or the leopard its spots?
Neither can you do good
who are accustomed to
doing evil.
24"I will scatter you like chaff
driven by the desert wind.
25This is your lot,
the portion I have decreed
for you,"
declares the LORD,
"because you have forgotten
me
and trusted in false gods.
26I will pull up your skirts over
your face
that your shame may be
seen—
27your adulteries and lustful
neighings,
your shameless prostitution!
I have seen your detestable
acts
on the hills and in the
fields.
Woe to you, O Jerusalem!
How long will you be
unclean?"

*Drought, Famine, Sword*

14 This is the word of the LORD to Jeremiah concerning the drought:

2"Judah mourns,
her cities languish;
they wail for the land,
and a cry goes up from
Jerusalem.
3The nobles send their servants
for water;
they go to the cisterns
but find no water.
They return with their jars
unfilled;
dismayed and despairing,
they cover their heads.
4The ground is cracked
because there is no rain in
the land;
the farmers are dismayed
and cover their heads.
5Even the doe in the field
deserts her newborn fawn
because there is no grass.
6Wild donkeys stand on the
barren heights
and pant like jackals;
their eyesight fails
for lack of pasture."

7Although our sins testify
against us,
O LORD, do something for
the sake of your name.
For our backsliding is great;
we have sinned against you.
8O Hope of Israel,

מוֹשִׁיעוֹ בְּעֵת צָרָה לָמָּה תִהְיֶה כְּגֵר בָּאָרֶץ
in-the-land like-stranger are-you why? distress in-time-of One-Saving-him

וּכְאֹרֵחַ נָטָה לָלוּן׃ (9) לָמָּה תִהְיֶה כְּאִישׁ
like-man are-you why? (9) to-stay-night he-turns-aside and-like-one-traveling

נִדְהָם כְּגִבּוֹר לֹא־ יוּכַל לְהוֹשִׁיעַ וְאַתָּה בְקִרְבֵּנוּ
in-midst-of-us indeed-you to-save he-has-power not like-warrior he-is-surprised

יְהוָה וְשִׁמְךָ עָלֵינוּ נִקְרָא אַל־ תַּנִּחֵנוּ׃ (10) כֹּה־ אָמַר
he-says this (10) you-forsake-us not he-is-called to-us and-name-of-you Yahweh

יְהוָה לָעָם הַזֶּה כֵּן אָהֲבוּ לָנוּעַ רַגְלֵיהֶם לֹא
not feet-of-them to-wander they-love greatly the-this about-the-people Yahweh

חָשָׂכוּ וַיהוָה לֹא רָצָם עַתָּה יִזְכֹּר עֲוֺנָם
wickedness-of-them he-will-remember now he-accepts-them not so-Yahweh they-restrain

וְיִפְקֹד חַטֹּאתָם׃ (11) וַיֹּאמֶר יְהוָה אֵלַי אַל־ תִּתְפַּלֵּל
you-pray not to-me Yahweh then-he-said (11) sins-of-them and-he-will-punish

בְּעַד־ הָעָם הַזֶּה לְטוֹבָה׃ (12) כִּי יָצֻמוּ אֵינֶנִּי
not-I they-fast although (12) for-well-being the-this the-people on-behalf-of

שֹׁמֵעַ אֶל־ רִנָּתָם וְכִי יַעֲלוּ עֹלָה וּמִנְחָה
and-grain-offering burnt-offering they-offer and-though cry-of-them to listening

אֵינֶנִּי רֹצָם כִּי בַּחֶרֶב וּבָרָעָב וּבַדֶּבֶר
and-with-the-plague and-with-the-famine with-the-sword instead accepting-them not-I

אָנֹכִי מְכַלֶּה אוֹתָם׃ (13) וָאֹמַר אֲהָהּ ׀ אֲדֹנָי יְהוִה הִנֵּה הַנְּבִאִים
the-prophets see! Yahweh Sovereign ah! but-I-said (13) them destroying I

אֹמְרִים לָהֶם לֹא־ תִרְאוּ חֶרֶב וְרָעָב לֹא־ יִהְיֶה לָכֶם כִּי־
indeed to-you he-will-be not or-famine sword you-will-see not to-them ones-telling

שְׁלוֹם אֱמֶת אֶתֵּן לָכֶם בַּמָּקוֹם הַזֶּה׃ (14) וַיֹּאמֶר יְהוָה
Yahweh then-he-said (14) the-this in-the-place to-you I-will-give lasting peace-of

אֵלַי שֶׁקֶר הַנְּבִאִים נִבְּאִים בִּשְׁמִי לֹא שְׁלַחְתִּים וְלֹא
or-not I-sent-them not in-name-of-me ones-prophesying the-prophets lie to-me

צִוִּיתִים וְלֹא דִבַּרְתִּי אֲלֵיהֶם חֲזוֹן שֶׁקֶר וְקֶסֶם
and-divination falsehood vision-of to-them I-spoke or-not I-appointed-them

וֶאֱלוּל° וְתַרְמוּת° לִבָּם הֵמָּה מִתְנַבְּאִים לָכֶם׃
to-you ones-prophesying they mind-of-them and-delusion-of and-worthlessness

(15) לָכֵן כֹּה־ אָמַר יְהוָה עַל־ הַנְּבִאִים הַנִּבְּאִים
the-ones-prophesying the-prophets about Yahweh he-says this therefore (15)

בִּשְׁמִי וַאֲנִי לֹא־ שְׁלַחְתִּים וְהֵמָּה אֹמְרִים חֶרֶב וְרָעָב לֹא
not or-famine sword ones-saying yet-they I-sent-them not but-I in-name-of-me

יִהְיֶה בָּאָרֶץ הַזֹּאת בַּחֶרֶב וּבָרָעָב יִתַּמּוּ
they-will-perish and-by-the-famine by-the-sword the-this in-the-land he-will-be

its Savior in times of distress,
why are you like a stranger in the land,
like a traveler who stays only a night?
9 Why are you like a man taken by surprise,
like a warrior powerless to save?
You are among us, O LORD,
and we bear your name;
do not forsake us!

10 This is what the LORD says about this people:

"They greatly love to wander;
they do not restrain their feet.
So the LORD does not accept them;
he will now remember their wickedness
and punish them for their sins."

11 Then the LORD said to me, "Do
not pray for the well-being of this
people. 12 Although they fast, I will
not listen to their cry; though they
offer burnt offerings and grain offerings, I will not accept them. Instead, I will destroy them with the
sword, famine and plague."
13 But I said, "Ah, Sovereign
LORD, the prophets keep telling
them, 'You will not see the sword
or suffer famine. Indeed, I will
give you lasting peace in this
place.' "
14 Then the LORD said to me,
"The prophets are prophesying
lies in my name. I have not sent
them or appointed them or
spoken to them. They are prophesying to you false visions, divinations, idolatries[a] and the delusions of their own minds. 15 Therefore, this is what the LORD says
about the prophets who are
prophesying in my name: I did
not send them, yet they are saying, 'No sword or famine will
touch this land.' Those same
prophets will perish by sword and

[a] 14 Or *visions, worthless divinations*

°14a ק ואליל
°14b ק ותרמית

הַנְּבִאִים הָהֵמָּה׃ וְהָעָם אֲשֶׁר־הֵמָּה נִבְּאִים לָהֶם
to-them ones-prophesying they whom and-the-people (16) the-those the-prophets

יִהְיוּ מֻשְׁלָכִים בְּחֻצוֹת יְרוּשָׁלַםִ מִפְּנֵי ׀ הָרָעָב
the-famine because-of Jerusalem into-streets-of ones-being-thrown-out they-will-be

וְהַחֶרֶב וְאֵין מְקַבֵּר לָהֵמָּה הֵמָּה נְשֵׁיהֶם
wives-of-them they to-them one-burying and-there-will-be-no and-the-sword

וּבְנֵיהֶם וּבְנֹתֵיהֶם וְשָׁפַכְתִּי עֲלֵיהֶם אֶת־
*** on-them and-I-will-pour-out or-daughters-of-them or-sons-of-them

רָעָתָם׃ וְאָמַרְתָּ אֲלֵיהֶם אֶת־הַדָּבָר הַזֶּה תֵּרַדְנָה
let-them-overflow the-this the-word *** to-them and-you-speak (17) calamity-of-them

עֵינַי דִּמְעָה לַיְלָה וְיוֹמָם וְאַל־ תִּדְמֶינָה כִּי שֶׁבֶר גָּדוֹל
grievous wound for let-them-cease and-not and-by-day night tear eyes-of-me

נִשְׁבְּרָה בְּתוּלַת בַּת־ עַמִּי מַכָּה נַחְלָה מְאֹד׃
very being-crushing blow people-of-me daughter-of virgin-of she-suffered

אִם־יָצָאתִי הַשָּׂדֶה וְהִנֵּה חַלְלֵי־ חֶרֶב וְאִם בָּאתִי הָעִיר
the-city I-go and-if sword ones-slain-of then-see! the-country I-go-out if (18)

וְהִנֵּה תַּחֲלוּאֵי רָעָב כִּי־ גַם־ נָבִיא גַם־ כֹּהֵן סָחֲרוּ אֶל־אֶרֶץ
land to they-went priest and prophet both indeed famine ravages-of then-see!

וְלֹא יָדָעוּ׃ הֲמָאֹס מָאַסְתָּ אֶת־יְהוּדָה אִם־בְּצִיּוֹן גָּעֲלָה
she-despised to-Zion or Judah *** you-rejected to-reject? (19) they-know and-not

נַפְשֶׁךָ מַדּוּעַ הִכִּיתָנוּ וְאֵין לָנוּ מַרְפֵּא קַוֵּה לְשָׁלוֹם
for-peace to-hope healing to-us so-there-is-not you-afflicted-us why? self-of-you

וְאֵין טוֹב וּלְעֵת מַרְפֵּא וְהִנֵּה בְעָתָה׃ יָדַעְנוּ
we-acknowledge (20) terror but-see! healing and-for-time-of good but-there-is-no

יְהוָה רִשְׁעֵנוּ עֲוֹן אֲבוֹתֵינוּ כִּי חָטָאנוּ לָךְ׃
against-you we-sinned indeed fathers-of-us guilt-of wickedness-of-us Yahweh

אַל־ תִּנְאַץ לְמַעַן שִׁמְךָ אַל־ תְּנַבֵּל כִּסֵּא
throne-of you-dishonor not name-of-you for-sake-of you-despise not (21)

כְבוֹדֶךָ זְכֹר אַל־ תָּפֵר בְּרִיתְךָ אִתָּנוּ׃ הֲיֵשׁ
is-there? (22) with-us covenant-of-you you-break not remember! glory-of-you

בְּהַבְלֵי הַגּוֹיִם מַגְשִׁמִים וְאִם־ הַשָּׁמַיִם יִתְּנוּ
they-send the-skies or-rather ones-bringing-rain the-nations among-worthless-ones-of

רְבִבִים הֲלֹא אַתָּה־הוּא יְהוָה אֱלֹהֵינוּ וּנְקַוֶּה־ לָּךְ כִּי־אַתָּה עָשִׂיתָ
you-do you for in-you therefore-we-hope God-of-us Yahweh he you not? showers

אֶת־כָּל־ אֵלֶּה׃ וַיֹּאמֶר יְהוָה אֵלַי אִם־ יַעֲמֹד מֹשֶׁה וּשְׁמוּאֵל
or-Samuel Moses he-stood if to-me Yahweh then-he-said (15:1) these all-of ***

לְפָנַי אֵין נַפְשִׁי אֶל־ הָעָם הַזֶּה שַׁלַּח מֵעַל־
from-before send-away! the-this the-people to heart-of-me not before-me

famine. [16]And the people they are prophesying to will be thrown out into the streets of Jerusalem because of the famine and sword. There will be no one to bury them or their wives, their sons or their daughters. I will pour out on them the calamity they deserve.

[17]"Speak this word to them:

" 'Let my eyes overflow with tears
night and day without ceasing;
for my virgin daughter—my people—
has suffered a grievous wound,
a crushing blow.
[18]If I go into the country,
I see those slain by the sword;
if I go into the city,
I see the ravages of famine.
Both prophet and priest
have gone to a land they know not.' "

[19]Have you rejected Judah completely?
Do you despise Zion?
Why have you afflicted us
so that we cannot be healed?
We hoped for peace
but no good has come,
for a time of healing
but there is only terror.
[20]O LORD, we acknowledge our wickedness
and the guilt of our fathers;
we have indeed sinned against you.
[21]For the sake of your name do not despise us;
do not dishonor your glorious throne.
Remember your covenant with us
and do not break it.
[22]Do any of the worthless idols
of the nations bring rain?
Do the skies themselves
send down showers?
No, it is you, O LORD our God.
Therefore our hope is in you,
for you are the one who does all this.

15 Then the LORD said to me: "Even if Moses and Samuel were to stand before me, my heart would not go out to this people.

פְּנַי וְיֵצֵאוּ׃ וְהָיָה כִּי־ יֹאמְרוּ אֵלֶיךָ אָנָה
to-where? to-you they-ask if and-he-will-be (2) and-let-them-go presences-of-me

נֵצֵא וְאָמַרְתָּ אֲלֵיהֶם כֹּה־ אָמַר יְהוָה אֲשֶׁר לַמָּוֶת
for-the-death who Yahweh he-says this to-them then-you-tell shall-we-go

לַמָּוֶת וַאֲשֶׁר לַחֶרֶב לַחֶרֶב וַאֲשֶׁר לָרָעָב
for-the-starvation and-who to-the-sword for-the-sword and-who to-the-death

לָרָעָב וַאֲשֶׁר לַשְּׁבִי לַשֶּׁבִי׃ וּפָקַדְתִּי
and-I-will-send (3) to-the-captivity for-the-captivity and-who to-the-starvation

עֲלֵיהֶם אַרְבַּע מִשְׁפָּחוֹת נְאֻם־ יְהוָה אֶת־ הַחֶרֶב לַהֲרֹג וְאֶת־
and to-kill the-sword *** Yahweh declaration-of kinds four-of against-them

הַכְּלָבִים לִסְחֹב וְאֶת־ עוֹף הַשָּׁמַיִם וְאֶת־ בֶּהֱמַת הָאָרֶץ לֶאֱכֹל
to-devour the-earth beast-of and the-airs bird-of and to-drag-away the-dogs

וּלְהַשְׁחִית׃ וּנְתַתִּים לְזַוֲעָה° לְכֹל מַמְלְכוֹת
kingdoms-of to-all-of as-abhorrence and-I-will-make-them (4) and-to-destroy

הָאָרֶץ בִּגְלַל מְנַשֶּׁה בֶן־ יְחִזְקִיָּהוּ מֶלֶךְ יְהוּדָה עַל אֲשֶׁר־ עָשָׂה
he-did what for Judah king-of Hezekiah son-of Manasseh because-of the-earth

בִּירוּשָׁלָםִ׃ כִּי מִי־ יַחְמֹל עָלַיִךְ יְרוּשָׁלַםִ וּמִי
and-who? Jerusalem on-you he-will-have-pity who? indeed (5) in-Jerusalem

יָנוּד לָךְ וּמִי יָסוּר לִשְׁאֹל לְשָׁלֹם לָךְ׃ אַתְּ
you (6) of-you about-welfare to-ask he-will-stop and-who? for-you he-will-mourn

נָטַשְׁתְּ אֹתִי נְאֻם־ יְהוָה אָחוֹר תֵּלֵכִי וָאַט אֶת־
*** so-I-will-lay you-keep-on backward Yahweh declaration-of me you-rejected

יָדִי עָלַיִךְ וָאַשְׁחִיתֵךְ נִלְאֵיתִי הִנָּחֵם׃
to-show-compassion I-am-unable and-I-will-destroy-you on-you hand-of-me

וָאֶזְרֵם בְּמִזְרֶה בְּשַׁעֲרֵי הָאָרֶץ
the-land at-city-gates-of with-winnowing-fork and-I-will-winnow-them (7)

שִׁכַּלְתִּי אִבַּדְתִּי אֶת־ עַמִּי מִדַּרְכֵיהֶם לוֹא־ שָׁבוּ׃
they-changed not from-ways-of-them people-of-me *** I-will-destroy I-will-bereave

עָצְמוּ־ לִי אַלְמְנֹתָו° מֵחוֹל יַמִּים הֵבֵאתִי
I-will-bring seas more-than-sand-of widows-of-him for-me they-will-be-numerous (8)

לָהֶם עַל־ אֵם בָּחוּר שֹׁדֵד בַּצָּהֳרָיִם הִפַּלְתִּי
I-will-bring-down at-the-midday one-destroying young-man mother-of against to-them

עָלֶיהָ פִּתְאֹם עִיר וּבֶהָלוֹת׃ אֻמְלְלָה יֹלֶדֶת
one-being-mother-of she-will-grow-faint (9) and-terrors anguish suddenly on-them

הַשִּׁבְעָה נָפְחָה נַפְשָׁהּ בָּאָה° שִׁמְשָׁהּ בְּעֹד
while-still sun-of-her he-will-set life-of-her she-will-breathe-out the-seven

יוֹמָם בּוֹשָׁה וְחָפֵרָה וּשְׁאֵרִיתָם לַחֶרֶב
to-the-sword and-survivor-of-them and-she-will-be-humiliated she-will-be-disgraced day

Send them away from my presence! Let them go! [2]And if they ask
you, 'Where shall we go?' tell them, 'This is what the LORD says:

" 'Those destined for death, to death;
those for the sword, to the sword;
those for starvation, to starvation;
those for captivity, to captivity.'

[3]"I will send four kinds of destroyers against them," declares the LORD, "the sword to kill and the dogs to drag away and the birds of the air and the beasts of the earth to devour and destroy.
[4]I will make them abhorrent to all the kingdoms of the earth because of what Manasseh son of Hezekiah king of Judah did in Jerusalem.

[5]"Who will have pity on you, O Jerusalem?
Who will mourn for you?
Who will stop to ask how you are?
[6]You have rejected me," declares the LORD.
"You keep on backsliding.
So I will lay hands on you and destroy you;
I can no longer show compassion.
[7]I will winnow them with a winnowing fork
at the city gates of the land.
I will bring bereavement and destruction on my people,
for they have not changed their ways.
[8]I will make their widows more numerous
than the sand of the sea.
At midday I will bring a destroyer
against the mothers of their young men;
suddenly I will bring down on them
anguish and terror.
[9]The mother of seven will grow faint
and breathe her last.
Her sun will set while it is still day;
she will be disgraced and humiliated.

°4 ק לזועה
°8 ק אלמנותיו
°9 ק בא

אֶתֵּן לִפְנֵי אֹיְבֵיהֶם נְאֻם־ יְהוָה׃ אוֹי־
alas! (10) Yahweh declaration-of ones-being-enemies-of-them before I-will-put

לִי אִמִּי כִּי יְלִדְתִּנִי אִישׁ רִיב וְאִישׁ מָדוֹן
contention and-man-of strife man-of you-bore-me that mother-of-me to-me

לְכָל־ הָאָרֶץ לֹא־ נָשִׁיתִי וְלֹא־ נָשׁוּ־ בִי כֻּלֹּה מְקַלְלַוְנִי*׃
cursing-me every-of-him to-me they-lent or-not I-lent not the-land with-whole-of

(11) אָמַר יְהוָה אִם־ לֹא °שֵׁרוֹתִךָ לְטוֹב אִם־ לוֹא ׀
indeed surely for-good I-will-deliver-you indeed surely Yahweh he-said (11)

הִפְגַּעְתִּי בְךָ בְּעֵת־ רָעָה וּבְעֵת צָרָה אֶת־
*** distress and-in-time-of disaster in-time-of with-you I-will-make-plead

הָאֹיֵב׃ (12) הֲיָרֹעַ בַּרְזֶל ׀ בַּרְזֶל מִצָּפוֹן וּנְחֹשֶׁת׃
or-bronze from-north iron iron can-he-break? (12) the-one-being-enemy

(13) חֵילְךָ וְאוֹצְרוֹתֶיךָ לָבַז אֶתֵּן לֹא בִּמְחִיר
with-charge not I-will-give as-plunder and-treasures-of-you wealth-of-you (13)

וּבְכָל־ חַטֹּאותֶיךָ וּבְכָל־ גְּבוּלֶיךָ׃
countries-of-you and-through-all-of sins-of-you because-of-all-of

(14) וְהַעֲבַרְתִּי אֶת־ אֹיְבֶיךָ בְּאֶרֶץ לֹא יָדָעְתָּ
you-know not into-land ones-being-enemies-of-you *** and-I-will-make-bring (14)

כִּי־ אֵשׁ קָדְחָה בְאַפִּי עֲלֵיכֶם תּוּקָד׃ (15) אַתָּה
you (15) she-will-burn against-you by-anger-of-me she-will-be-kindled fire for

יָדַעְתָּ יְהוָה זָכְרֵנִי וּפָקְדֵנִי וְהִנָּקֶם לִי
for-me and-avenge! and-care-for-me! remember-me! Yahweh you-understand

מֵרֹדְפַי אַל־ לְאֶרֶךְ אַפְּךָ תִּקָּחֵנִי דַּע
think! you-take-away-me anger-of-you in-length-of not on-ones-persecuting-me

שְׂאֵתִי עָלֶיךָ חֶרְפָּה׃ (16) נִמְצְאוּ דְבָרֶיךָ וָאֹכְלֵם וַיְהִי
and-he-was and-I-ate-them words-of-you they-came (16) reproach for-you to-suffer-me

°דְבָרְיךָ לִי לְשָׂשׂוֹן וּלְשִׂמְחַת לְבָבִי כִּי־ נִקְרָא שִׁמְךָ
name-of-you he-is-called for heart-of-me and-as-delight-of as-joy to-me word-of-you

עָלַי יְהוָה אֱלֹהֵי צְבָאוֹת׃ (17) לֹא־ יָשַׁבְתִּי בְסוֹד־ מְשַׂחֲקִים
ones-reveling in-company-of I-sat never (17) Hosts God-of Yahweh to-me

וָאֶעְלֹז מִפְּנֵי יָדְךָ בָּדָד יָשַׁבְתִּי כִּי־ זַעַם
indignation because I-sat alone hand-of-you because-of and-I-made-merry

מִלֵּאתָנִי׃ (18) לָמָּה הָיָה כְאֵבִי נֶצַח וּמַכָּתִי אֲנוּשָׁה
being-grievous and-wound-of-me unending pain-of-me he-is why? (18) you-filled-me

מֵאֲנָה הֵרָפֵא הָיוֹ תִהְיֶה לִי כְּמוֹ אַכְזָב מַיִם לֹא
not springs deception like to-me will-you-be to-be to-be-cured she-refuses

נֶאֱמָנוּ׃ (19) לָכֵן כֹּה־ אָמַר יְהוָה אִם־ תָּשׁוּב
you-repent if Yahweh he-says this therefore (19) they-are-unfailing

I will put the survivors to the
sword
before their enemies,"
declares the LORD.

10 Alas, my mother, that you
gave me birth,
a man with whom the
whole land strives and
contends!
I have neither lent nor
borrowed,
yet everyone curses me.

11 The LORD said,

"Surely I will deliver you for a
good purpose;
surely I will make your
enemies plead with you
in times of disaster and
times of distress.

12 "Can a man break iron—
iron from the north—or
bronze?
13 Your wealth and your
treasures
I will give as plunder,
without charge,
because of all your sins
throughout your country.
14 I will enslave you to your
enemies
in[b] a land you do not know,
for my anger will kindle a fire
that will burn against you."

15 You understand, O LORD;
remember me and care for
me.
Avenge me on my
persecutors.
You are long-suffering—do not
take me away;
think of how I suffer
reproach for your sake.
16 When your words came, I ate
them;
they were my joy and my
heart's delight,
for I bear your name,
O LORD God Almighty.
17 I never sat in the company of
revelers,
never made merry with
them;
I sat alone because your hand
was on me
and you had filled me with
indignation.
18 Why is my pain unending
and my wound grievous and
incurable?
Will you be to me like a
deceptive brook,
like a spring that fails?

19 Therefore this is what the LORD
says:

[b]14 Some Hebrew manuscripts, Septuagint and Syriac (see also Jer. 17:4); most Hebrew manuscripts *I will cause your enemies to bring you / into*

**10* Most mss eliminate the *vav* in a *Qere* reading (־לְנִי).

°*11* ק שריתיך
°*16* ק דברך

וַאֲשִׁיבְךָ לְפָנַי תַּעֲמֹד וְאִם־ תּוֹצִיא יָקָר
then-I-will-restore-you before-me you-may-serve and-if you-utter worthy

מִזּוֹלֵל כְּפִי תִהְיֶה יָשֻׁבוּ הֵמָּה אֵלֶיךָ
rather-than-one-being-worthless as-mouth-of-me you-will-be let-them-turn they to-you

וְאַתָּה לֹא־ תָשׁוּב אֲלֵיהֶם׃ וּנְתַתִּיךָ לָעָם הַזֶּה
but-you not you-must-turn to-them (20) and-I-will-make-you to-the-people the-this

לְחוֹמַת נְחֹשֶׁת בְּצוּרָה וְנִלְחֲמוּ אֵלֶיךָ וְלֹא־
as-wall-of bronze one-being-fortified and-they-will-fight against-you but-not

יוּכְלוּ לָךְ כִּי־ אִתְּךָ אֲנִי לְהוֹשִׁיעֲךָ וּלְהַצִּילֶךָ
they-will-overcome over-you for with-you I to-rescue-you and-to-save-you

נְאֻם־ יְהוָה׃ וְהִצַּלְתִּיךָ מִיַּד רָעִים
declaration-of Yahweh (21) and-I-will-save-you from-hand-of wicked-ones

וּפְדִתִיךָ מִכַּף עָרִצִים׃ וַיְהִי דְבַר־ יְהוָה
and-I-will-redeem-you from-grasp-of cruel-ones (16:1) then-he-came word-of Yahweh

אֵלַי לֵאמֹר׃ לֹא־ תִקַּח לְךָ אִשָּׁה וְלֹא־ יִהְיוּ לְךָ בָּנִים
to-me to-say (2) not you-must-marry for-you wife and-not let-them-be for-you sons

וּבָנוֹת בַּמָּקוֹם הַזֶּה׃ כִּי־ כֹה אָמַר יְהוָה עַל־ הַבָּנִים
or-daughters in-the-place the-this (3) for this he-says Yahweh about the-sons

וְעַל־ הַבָּנוֹת הַיִּלּוֹדִים בַּמָּקוֹם הַזֶּה וְעַל־ אִמֹּתָם
and-about the-daughters the-ones-born in-the-land the-this and-about mothers-of-them

הַיֹּלְדוֹת אוֹתָם וְעַל־ אֲבוֹתָם הַמּוֹלִדִים אוֹתָם
the-women-bearing them and-about fathers-of-them the-men-fathering them

בָּאָרֶץ הַזֹּאת׃ מְמוֹתֵי תַחֲלֻאִים יָמֻתוּ לֹא יִסָּפְדוּ
in-the-land the-this (4) deaths-of diseases they-will-die not they-will-be-mourned

וְלֹא יִקָּבֵרוּ לְדֹמֶן עַל־ פְּנֵי הָאֲדָמָה יִהְיוּ
and-not they-will-be-buried as-refuse on surfaces-of the-ground they-will-be

וּבַחֶרֶב וּבָרָעָב יִכְלוּ וְהָיְתָה
and-by-the-sword and-by-the-famine they-will-perish and-she-will-become

נִבְלָתָם לְמַאֲכָל לְעוֹף הַשָּׁמַיִם וּלְבֶהֱמַת הָאָרֶץ׃ כִּי־
dead-body-of-them as-food for-bird-of the-airs and-for-beast-of the-earth (5) for

כֹה אָמַר יְהוָה אַל־ תָּבוֹא בֵּית מַרְזֵחַ וְאַל־ תֵּלֵךְ לִסְפּוֹד
this he-says Yahweh not you-enter house-of funeral-meal and-not you-go to-mourn

וְאַל־ תָּנֹד לָהֶם כִּי־ אָסַפְתִּי אֶת־ שְׁלוֹמִי מֵאֵת
or-not you-show-sympathy to-them because I-withdrew *** blessing-of-me from-with

הָעָם־ הַזֶּה נְאֻם־ יְהוָה אֶת־ הַחֶסֶד וְאֶת־הָרַחֲמִים׃
the-people the-this declaration-of Yahweh *** the-love and the-pities

וּמֵתוּ גְדֹלִים וּקְטַנִּים בָּאָרֶץ הַזֹּאת לֹא
(6) and-they-will-die high-ones and-low-ones in-the-land the-this not

"If you repent, I will restore
you
that you may serve me;
if you utter worthy, not
worthless, words,
you will be my spokesman.
Let this people turn to you,
but you must not turn to
them.
20 I will make you a wall to this
people,
a fortified wall of bronze;
they will fight against you
but will not overcome you,
for I am with you
to rescue and save you,"
declares the LORD.
21 "I will save you from the
hands of the wicked
and redeem you from the
grasp of the cruel."

*Day of Disaster*

16 Then the word of the LORD
came to me: 2 "You must not
marry and have sons or daughters
in this place." 3 For this is what the
LORD says about the sons and
daughters born in this land and
about the women who are their
mothers and the men who are
their fathers: 4 "They will die of
deadly diseases. They will not be
mourned or buried but will be like
refuse lying on the ground. They
will perish by sword and famine,
and their dead bodies will become
food for the birds of the air and
the beasts of the earth."
5 For this is what the LORD says:
"Do not enter a house where there
is a funeral meal; do not go to
mourn or show sympathy, because I have withdrawn my
blessing, my love and my pity
from this people," declares the
LORD. 6 "Both high and low will die

יִקָּבְרוּ וְלֹא־ יִסְפְּדוּ לָהֶם וְלֹא יִתְגֹּדַד
he-will-cut-himself and-not for-them they-will-mourn or-not they-will-be-buried

וְלֹא יִקָּרֵחַ לָהֶם׃ וְלֹא־ יִפְרְסוּ לָהֶם עַל־
for to-them they-will-offer-food and-not (7) for-them he-will-shave-bald or-not

אֵבֶל לְנַחֲמוֹ עַל־ מֵת וְלֹא־ יַשְׁקוּ אוֹתָם כּוֹס
cup-of them they-will-give-drink or-not one-being-dead for to-comfort-him mourning

תַּנְחוּמִים עַל־ אָבִיו וְעַל־ אִמּוֹ׃ וּבֵית־ מִשְׁתֶּה
feasting and-house-of (8) mother-of-him or-for father-of-him for consolations

לֹא־ תָבוֹא לָשֶׁבֶת אוֹתָם לֶאֱכֹל וְלִשְׁתּוֹת׃ כִּי כֹה אָמַר יְהוָה
Yahweh-of he-says this for (9) and-to-drink to-eat with-them to-sit you-enter not

צְבָאוֹת אֱלֹהֵי יִשְׂרָאֵל הִנְנִי מַשְׁבִּית מִן־ הַמָּקוֹם הַזֶּה לְעֵינֵיכֶם
before-eyes-of-you the-this the-place in bringing-end see-I! Israel God-of Hosts

וּבִימֵיכֶם קוֹל שָׂשׂוֹן וְקוֹל שִׂמְחָה קוֹל חָתָן וְקוֹל
and-voice-of bridegroom voice-of gladness and-sound-of joy sound-of and-in-days-of-you

כַּלָּה׃ וְהָיָה כִּי תַגִּיד לָעָם הַזֶּה אֵת כָּל־
all-of *** the-this to-the-people you-tell when and-he-will-be (10) bride

הַדְּבָרִים הָאֵלֶּה וְאָמְרוּ אֵלֶיךָ עַל־ מֶה דִבֶּר יְהוָה עָלֵינוּ
against-us Yahweh he-decreed why? for to-you and-they-ask the-these the-words

אֵת כָּל־ הָרָעָה הַגְּדוֹלָה הַזֹּאת וּמֶה עֲוֹנֵנוּ וּמֶה
and-what? wrong-of-us and-what? the-this the-great the-disaster all-of ***

חַטָּאתֵנוּ אֲשֶׁר חָטָאנוּ לַיהוָה אֱלֹהֵינוּ׃ וְאָמַרְתָּ אֲלֵיהֶם
to-them then-you-say (11) God-of-us against-Yahweh we-committed-sin that sin-of-us

עַל אֲשֶׁר־ עָזְבוּ אֲבוֹתֵיכֶם אוֹתִי נְאֻם־ יְהוָה וַיֵּלְכוּ
and-they-followed Yahweh declaration-of me fathers-of-you they-forsook that because

אַחֲרֵי אֱלֹהִים אֲחֵרִים וַיַּעַבְדוּם וַיִּשְׁתַּחֲווּ לָהֶם וְאֹתִי
but-me to-them and-they-worshiped and-they-served-them other-ones gods after

עָזָבוּ וְאֶת־ תּוֹרָתִי לֹא שָׁמָרוּ׃ וְאַתֶּם הֲרֵעֹתֶם לַעֲשׂוֹת
to-behave you-were-wicked but-you (12) they-kept not law-of-me and they-forsook

מֵאֲבוֹתֵיכֶם וְהִנְּכֶם הֹלְכִים אִישׁ אַחֲרֵי שְׁרִרוּת
stubbornness-of after each ones-following and-see-you! more-than-fathers-of-you

לִבּוֹ־ הָרָע לְבִלְתִּי שְׁמֹעַ אֵלָי׃ וְהֵטַלְתִּי אֶתְכֶם מֵעַל הָאָרֶץ
the-land from-in you so-I-will-throw (13) to-me to-obey not the-evil heart-of-him

הַזֹּאת עַל־ הָאָרֶץ אֲשֶׁר לֹא יְדַעְתֶּם אַתֶּם וַאֲבוֹתֵיכֶם וַעֲבַדְתֶּם־
and-you-will-serve or-fathers-of-you you you-know not that the-land into the-this

שָׁם אֶת־ אֱלֹהִים אֲחֵרִים יוֹמָם וָלַיְלָה אֲשֶׁר לֹא־ אֶתֵּן לָכֶם חֲנִינָה׃
favor to-you I-will-show not for and-night by-day other-ones gods *** there

לָכֵן הִנֵּה־ יָמִים בָּאִים נְאֻם־ יְהוָה וְלֹא־ יֵאָמֵר
he-will-be-said when-not Yahweh declaration-of ones-coming days see! however (14)

in this land. They will not be buried or mourned, and no one will cut himself or shave his head for
them. 7No one will offer food to comfort those who mourn for the dead—not even for a father or a mother—nor will anyone give them a drink to console them.
8"And do not enter a house where there is feasting and sit down to eat and drink.
9For this is what the LORD Almighty, the God of Israel, says: Before your eyes and in your days I will bring an end to the sounds of joy and gladness and to the voices of bride and bridegroom in this place.
10"When you tell these people all this and they ask you, 'Why has the LORD decreed such a great disaster against us? What wrong have we done? What sin have we committed against the LORD our God?'
11then say to them, 'It is because your fathers forsook me,' declares the LORD, 'and followed other gods and served and worshiped them. They forsook me and did not keep my law.
12But you have behaved more wickedly than your fathers. See how each of you is following the stubbornness of his evil heart instead of obeying me.
13So I will throw you out of this land into a land neither you nor your fathers have known, and there you will serve other gods day and night, for I will show you no favor.'
14"However, the days are coming," declares the LORD, "when men will no longer say, 'As surely

עוֹד חַי־ יְהוָה אֲשֶׁר הֶעֱלָה אֶת־ בְּנֵי יִשְׂרָאֵל מֵאֶרֶץ מִצְרָיִם׃
Egypt from-land-of Israel sons-of *** he-brought-up who Yahweh alive longer

(15) כִּי אִם־ חַי־ יְהוָה אֲשֶׁר הֶעֱלָה אֶת־ בְּנֵי יִשְׂרָאֵל מֵאֶרֶץ
from-land-of Israel sons-of *** he-brought-up who Yahweh alive rather but (15)

צָפוֹן וּמִכֹּל הָאֲרָצוֹת אֲשֶׁר הִדִּיחָם שָׁמָּה
to-there he-banished-them where the-countries and-from-all-of north

וַהֲשִׁבֹתִים עַל־ אַדְמָתָם אֲשֶׁר נָתַתִּי לַאֲבוֹתָם׃
to-forefathers-of-them I-gave that land-of-them to for-I-will-restore-them

(16) הִנְנִי שֹׁלֵחַ לְדַוָּגִים רַבִּים נְאֻם־ יְהוָה
Yahweh declaration-of many-ones for-fishermen sending see-I! (16)

וְדִיגוּם וְאַחֲרֵי־ כֵן אֶשְׁלַח לְרַבִּים צַיָּדִים
hunters for-many-ones I-will-send that and-after and-they-will-catch-them

וְצָדוּם מֵעַל כָּל־ הַר וּמֵעַל כָּל־גִּבְעָה
hill every-of and-from-on mountain every-of from-on and-they-will-hunt-down-them

וּמִנְּקִיקֵי הַסְּלָעִים׃ (17) כִּי עֵינַי עַל־ כָּל־ דַּרְכֵיהֶם לֹא
not ways-of-them all-of on eyes-of-me for (17) the-rocks and-from-crevices-of

נִסְתְּרוּ מִלְּפָנָי וְלֹא־ נִצְפַּן עֲוֹנָם מִנֶּגֶד
from-before sin-of-them he-is-concealed and-not from-before-me they-are-hidden

עֵינָי׃ (18) וְשִׁלַּמְתִּי רִאשׁוֹנָה מִשְׁנֵה עֲוֹנָם וְחַטָּאתָם
and-sin-of-them wickedness-of-them double-of first and-I-will-repay (18) eyes-of-me

עַל חַלְּלָם אֶת־ אַרְצִי בְּנִבְלַת שִׁקּוּצֵיהֶם
vile-ones-of-them with-lifeless-form-of land-of-me *** to-defile-them because

וְתוֹעֲבוֹתֵיהֶם מָלְאוּ אֶת־ נַחֲלָתִי׃ (19) יְהוָה
Yahweh (19) inheritance-of-me *** they-filled and-detestable-ones-of-them

עֻזִּי וּמָעֻזִּי וּמְנוּסִי בְּיוֹם צָרָה אֵלֶיךָ
to-you distress in-time-of and-refuge-of-me and-fortress-of-me strength-of-me

גּוֹיִם יָבֹאוּ מֵאַפְסֵי־ אָרֶץ וְיֹאמְרוּ אַךְ־ שֶׁקֶר
falsehood only and-they-will-say earth from-ends-of they-will-come nations

נָחֲלוּ אֲבוֹתֵינוּ הֶבֶל וְאֵין־ בָּם מוֹעִיל׃
one-doing-good to-them and-not worthlessness fathers-of-us they-possessed

(20) הֲיַעֲשֶׂה־ לּוֹ אָדָם אֱלֹהִים וְהֵמָּה לֹא אֱלֹהִים׃ (21) לָכֵן הִנְנִי
see-I! therefore (21) gods not but-they gods man for-him does-he-make? (20)

מוֹדִיעָם בַּפַּעַם הַזֹּאת אוֹדִיעֵם אֶת־ יָדִי וְאֶת־
and power-of-me *** I-will-teach-them the-this at-the-time teaching-them

גְּבוּרָתִי וְיָדְעוּ כִּי־ שְׁמִי יְהוָה׃ (17:1) חַטַּאת יְהוּדָה
Judah sin-of (17:1) Yahweh name-of-me that then-they-will-know might-of-me

כְּתוּבָה בְּעֵט בַּרְזֶל בְּצִפֹּרֶן שָׁמִיר חֲרוּשָׁה עַל־ לוּחַ
tablet-of on being-inscribed flint with-point-of iron with-tool-of being-engraved

as the LORD lives, who brought the
Israelites up out of Egypt,' [15]but
they will say, 'As surely as the
LORD lives, who brought the Israelites up out of the land of the
north and out of all the countries
where he had banished them.' For
I will restore them to the land I
gave their forefathers.
[16]"But now I will send for many
fishermen," declares the LORD,
"and they will catch them. After
that I will send for many hunters,
and they will hunt them down on
every mountain and hill and from
the crevices of the rocks. [17]My eyes
are on all their ways; they are not
hidden from me, nor is their sin
concealed from my eyes. [18]I will
repay them double for their
wickedness and their sin, because
they have defiled my land with
the lifeless forms of their vile images and have filled my inheritance with their detestable idols."

[19]O LORD, my strength and my
fortress,
my refuge in time of
distress,
to you the nations will come
from the ends of the earth
and say,
"Our fathers possessed
nothing but false gods,
worthless idols that did
them no good.
[20]Do men make their own gods?
Yes, but they are not gods!"

[21]"Therefore I will teach them—
this time I will teach them
my power and might.
Then they will know
that my name is the LORD.

17 "Judah's sin is engraved
with an iron tool,
inscribed with a flint point,
on the tablets of their hearts

°16 ק לדיגים

לִבָּם וּלְקַרְנוֹת מִזְבְּחוֹתֵיכֶם׃ כִּזְכֹּר בְּנֵיהֶם
children-of-them even-to-remember (2) altars-of-you and-on-horns-of heart-of-them

מִזְבְּחוֹתָם וַאֲשֵׁרֵיהֶם עַל־ עֵץ רַעֲנָן עַל גְּבָעוֹת
hills on spreading tree beside and-Asherah-poles-of-them altars-of-them

הַגְּבֹהוֹת׃ הֲרָרִי בַּשָּׂדֶה חֵילְךָ כָל־ אוֹצְרוֹתֶיךָ
treasures-of-you all-of wealth-of-you in-the-land mountain-of-me (3) the-high-ones

לָבַז אֶתֵּן בָּמֹתֶיךָ בְּחַטָּאת בְּכָל־
through-all-of because-of-sin high-places-of-you I-will-give as-plunder

גְּבוּלֶיךָ׃ וְשָׁמַטְתָּה וּבְךָ מִנַּחֲלָתְךָ
from-inheritance-of-you and-because-of-you and-you-will-lose (4) countries-of-you

אֲשֶׁר נָתַתִּי לָךְ וְהַעֲבַדְתִּיךָ אֶת־ אֹיְבֶיךָ בָּאָרֶץ
in-the-land ones-being-enemies-of-you *** and-I-will-enslave-you to-you I-gave that

אֲשֶׁר לֹא־ יָדָעְתָּ כִּי־ אֵשׁ קְדַחְתֶּם בְּאַפִּי עַד־עוֹלָם תּוּקָד׃
she-will-burn forever to by-anger-of-me you-kindled fire for you-know not that

כֹּה ׀ אָמַר יְהוָה אָרוּר הַגֶּבֶר אֲשֶׁר יִבְטַח בָּאָדָם
in-the-man he-trusts who the-one being-cursed Yahweh he-says this (5)

וְשָׂם בָּשָׂר זְרֹעוֹ וּמִן־ יְהוָה יָסוּר לִבּוֹ׃
heart-of-him he-turns Yahweh and-from strength-of-him flesh and-he-makes

וְהָיָה כְּעַרְעָר בָּעֲרָבָה וְלֹא יִרְאֶה כִּי־ יָבוֹא
he-comes when he-will-see and-not in-the-wasteland like-bush and-he-will-be (6)

טוֹב וְשָׁכַן חֲרֵרִים בַּמִּדְבָּר אֶרֶץ מְלֵחָה וְלֹא
and-not salt land-of of-the-desert parched-places and-he-will-dwell prosperity

תֵשֵׁב׃ בָּרוּךְ הַגֶּבֶר אֲשֶׁר יִבְטַח בַּיהוָה וְהָיָה יְהוָה
Yahweh and-he-is in-Yahweh he-trusts who the-man being-blessed (7) she-is-lived-in

מִבְטַחוֹ׃ וְהָיָה כְּעֵץ ׀ שָׁתוּל עַל־ מַיִם וְעַל־
and-by waters by being-planted like-tree and-he-will-be (8) confidence-of-him

יוּבַל יְשַׁלַּח שָׁרָשָׁיו וְלֹא יִרְאֶ° כִּי־ יָבֹא חֹם וְהָיָה
and-he-is heat he-comes when *he-will-see and-not roots-of-him he-sends-out stream

עָלֵהוּ רַעֲנָן וּבִשְׁנַת בַּצֹּרֶת לֹא יִדְאָג וְלֹא יָמִישׁ
he-fails and-never he-worries not drought and-in-year-of green leaf-of-him

מֵעֲשׂוֹת פֶּרִי׃ עָקֹב הַלֵּב מִכֹּל וְאָנֻשׁ הוּא
he and-being-incurable above-all the-heart to-be-deceitful (9) fruit from-to-bear

מִי יֵדָעֶנּוּ׃ אֲנִי יְהוָה חֹקֵר לֵב בֹּחֵן כְּלָיוֹת
minds examining-of heart searching-of Yahweh I (10) he-can-understand-him who?

וְלָתֵת לְאִישׁ כִּדְרָכָו° כִּפְרִי
according-to-desert-of according-to-conducts-of-him to-man and-to-reward

מַעֲלָלָיו׃ קֹרֵא דָגַר וְלֹא יָלָד עֹשֶׂה עֹשֶׁר
richness one-gaining he-laid that-not he-hatches partridge (11) deeds-of-him

and on the horns of their
altars.
[2]Even their children remember
their altars and Asherah
poles[c]
beside the spreading trees
and on the high hills.
[3]My mountain in the land
and your[d] wealth and all
your treasures
I will give away as plunder,
together with your high
places,
because of sin throughout
your country.
[4]Through your own fault you
will lose
the inheritance I gave you.
I will enslave you to your
enemies
in a land you do not know,
for you have kindled my
anger,
and it will burn forever."

[5]This is what the LORD says:

"Cursed is the one who trusts
in man,
who depends on flesh for
his strength
and whose heart turns away
from the LORD.
[6]He will be like a bush in the
wastelands;
he will not see prosperity
when it comes.
He will dwell in the parched
places of the desert,
in a salt land where no one
lives.

[7]"But blessed is the man who
trusts in the LORD,
whose confidence is in him.
[8]He will be like a tree planted
by the water
that sends out its roots by
the stream.
It does not fear when heat
comes;
its leaves are always green.
It has no worries in a year of
drought
and never fails to bear
fruit."

[9]The heart is deceitful above all
things
and beyond cure.
Who can understand it?

[10]"I the LORD search the heart
and examine the mind,
to reward a man according to
his conduct,
according to what his deeds
deserve."

[11]Like a partridge that hatches
eggs it did not lay
is the man who gains riches

[c]2 That is, symbols of the goddess Asherah
[d]2,3 Or *hills* / [3]*and the mountains of the land.* / *Your*

*8 The NIV, with some ancient versions, repoints the *Kethib* form as יִרְאֶה, *be-will-fear.*

°8 ק יראה
°10 ק כדרכיו

וְלֹא בְמִשְׁפָּט בַּחֲצִי יָמָו° יַעַזְבֶנּוּ וּבְאַחֲרִיתוֹ
and-at-end-of-him he-will-desert-him days-of-him when-half-of by-justice that-not

יִהְיֶה נָבָל׃ כִּסֵּא כָבוֹד מָרוֹם מֵרִאשׁוֹן מְקוֹם
place-of from-beginning exalted glory throne-of (12) fool he-will-be

מִקְדָּשֵׁנוּ׃ מִקְוֵה יִשְׂרָאֵל יְהוָה כָּל־ עֹזְבֶיךָ
ones-forsaking-you all-of Yahweh Israel hope-of (13) sanctuary-of-us

יֵבֹשׁוּ יְסוּרַי° בָּאָרֶץ יִכָּתֵבוּ
they-will-be-written in-the-dust and-ones-turning-away-from-me they-will-be-shamed

כִּי עָזְבוּ מְקוֹר מַיִם־ חַיִּים אֶת־ יְהוָה׃ רְפָאֵנִי יְהוָה
Yahweh heal-me! (14) Yahweh *** living-ones waters spring-of they-forsook because

וְאֵרָפֵא הוֹשִׁיעֵנִי וְאִוָּשֵׁעָה כִּי תְהִלָּתִי אָתָּה׃ הִנֵּה־
see! (15) you praise-of-me for and-I-will-be-saved save-me! and-I-will-be-healed

הֵמָּה אֹמְרִים אֵלָי אַיֵּה דְבַר־ יְהוָה יָבוֹא נָא׃ וַאֲנִי
but-I (16) now! let-him-be-fulfilled Yahweh word-of where? to-me ones-saying they

לֹא־ אַצְתִּי מֵרֹעֶה אַחֲרֶיךָ וְיוֹם אָנוּשׁ לֹא הִתְאַוֵּיתִי
I-desired not despairing and-day-of after-you from-being-shepherd I-ran-away not

אַתָּה יָדָעְתָּ מוֹצָא שְׂפָתַי נֹכַח פָּנֶיךָ הָיָה׃ אַל־ תִּהְיֵה־
you-be not (17) he-is faces-of-you before lips-of-me passing-of you-know you

לִי לִמְחִתָּה מַחֲסִי־ אַתָּה בְּיוֹם רָעָה׃ יֵבֹשׁוּ
let-them-be-shamed (18) disaster in-day-of you refuge-of-me as-terror to-me

רֹדְפַי וְאַל־ אֵבֹשָׁה אָנִי יֵחַתּוּ הֵמָּה וְאַל־
but-not they let-them-be-terrified I let-me-be-shamed but-not ones-persecuting-me

אֵחַתָּה אָנִי הָבִיא עֲלֵיהֶם יוֹם רָעָה וּמִשְׁנֶה שִׁבָּרוֹן
destruction and-double disaster day-of on-them bring! I let-me-be-terrified

שָׁבְרֵם׃ כֹּה־ אָמַר יְהוָה אֵלַי הָלֹךְ וְעָמַדְתָּ בְּשַׁעַר בְּנֵי־
sons-of at-gate-of and-you-stand to-go to-me Yahweh he-said this (19) destroy-them!

עָם° אֲשֶׁר יָבֹאוּ בוֹ מַלְכֵי יְהוּדָה וַאֲשֶׁר יֵצְאוּ
they-go-out and-which Judah kings-of through-him they-go-in which the-people

בוֹ וּבְכֹל שַׁעֲרֵי יְרוּשָׁלִָם׃ וְאָמַרְתָּ אֲלֵיהֶם שִׁמְעוּ
hear! to-them and-you-say (20) Jerusalem gates-of and-at-all-of through-him

דְּבַר־ יְהוָה מַלְכֵי יְהוּדָה וְכָל־ יְהוּדָה וְכֹל יֹשְׁבֵי יְרוּשָׁלִָם
Jerusalem ones-living-of and-all-of Judah and-all-of Judah kings-of Yahweh word-of

הַבָּאִים בַּשְּׁעָרִים הָאֵלֶּה׃ כֹּה אָמַר יְהוָה הִשָּׁמְרוּ
be-careful! Yahweh he-says this (21) the-these through-the-gates the-ones-coming

בְּנַפְשׁוֹתֵיכֶם וְאַל־ תִּשְׂאוּ מַשָּׂא בְּיוֹם הַשַּׁבָּת וַהֲבֵאתֶם
or-you-bring the-Sabbath on-day-of load you-carry that-not of-selves-of-you

בְּשַׁעֲרֵי יְרוּשָׁלִָם׃ וְלֹא־ תוֹצִיאוּ מַשָּׂא מִבָּתֵּיכֶם בְּיוֹם
on-day-of from-houses-of-you load you-bring and-not (22) Jerusalem through-gates-of

by unjust means.
When his life is half gone,
they will desert him,
and in the end he will prove
to be a fool.

12 A glorious throne, exalted from
the beginning,
is the place of our sanctuary.
13 O LORD, the hope of Israel,
all who forsake you will be
put to shame.
Those who turn away from
you will be written in the
dust
because they have forsaken
the LORD,
the spring of living water.

14 Heal me, O LORD, and I will be
healed;
save me and I will be saved,
for you are the one I praise.
15 They keep saying to me,
"Where is the word of the
LORD?
Let it now be fulfilled!"
16 I have not run away from
being your shepherd;
you know I have not desired
the day of despair.
What passes my lips is open
before you.
17 Do not be a terror to me;
you are my refuge in the
day of disaster.
18 Let my persecutors be put to
shame,
but keep me from shame;
let them be terrified,
but keep me from terror.
Bring on them the day of
disaster;
destroy them with double
destruction.

*Keeping the Sabbath Holy*

19 This is what the LORD said to
me: "Go and stand at the gate of
the people, through which the
kings of Judah go in and out;
stand also at all the other gates of
Jerusalem.
20 Say to them, 'Hear the
word of the LORD, O kings of
Judah and all people of Judah and
everyone living in Jerusalem who
come through these gates.
21 This is
what the LORD says: Be careful not
to carry a load on the Sabbath day
or bring it through the gates of
Jerusalem.
22 Do not bring a load
out of your houses or do any work

°*11* ק ימיו
°*13* ק וסורי
°*19* ק העם

הַשַּׁבָּת וְכָל־מְלָאכָה לֹא תַעֲשׂוּ וְקִדַּשְׁתֶּם אֶת־יוֹם הַשַּׁבָּת
the-Sabbath day-of *** but-you-keep-holy you-do not work or-any-of the-Sabbath

כַּאֲשֶׁר צִוִּיתִי אֶת־אֲבוֹתֵיכֶם׃ (23) וְלֹא שָׁמְעוּ וְלֹא
or-not they-listened yet-not (23) forefathers-of-you *** I-commanded just-as

הִטּוּ אֶת־אָזְנָם וַיַּקְשׁוּ אֶת־עָרְפָּם לְבִלְתִּי
not neck-of-them *** but-they-made-stiff ear-of-them *** they-made-attentive

שׁוֹמֵעַ° וּלְבִלְתִּי קַחַת מוּסָר׃ (24) וְהָיָה אִם־שָׁמֹעַ תִּשְׁמְעוּן
you-obey to-obey if but-he-will-be (24) discipline to-respond-to or-not to-listen

אֵלַי נְאֻם־יְהוָה לְבִלְתִּי ׀ הָבִיא מַשָּׂא בְּשַׁעֲרֵי הָעִיר הַזֹּאת
the-this the-city through-gates-of load to-bring not Yahweh declaration-of to-me

בְּיוֹם הַשַּׁבָּת וּלְקַדֵּשׁ אֶת־יוֹם הַשַּׁבָּת לְבִלְתִּי עֲשׂוֹת־בֹּה°
on-him to-do not the-Sabbath day-of *** but-to-keep-holy the-Sabbath on-day-of

כָּל־מְלָאכָה׃ (25) וּבָאוּ בְשַׁעֲרֵי הָעִיר הַזֹּאת מְלָכִים ׀
kings the-this the-city through-gates-of then-they-will-come (25) work any-of

וְשָׂרִים יֹשְׁבִים עַל־כִּסֵּא דָוִד רֹכְבִים ׀ בָּרֶכֶב
in-the-chariot ones-riding David throne-of on ones-sitting and-officials

וּבַסּוּסִים הֵמָּה וְשָׂרֵיהֶם אִישׁ יְהוּדָה וְיֹשְׁבֵי
and-ones-living-of Judah man-of and-officials-of-them they and-on-the-horses

יְרוּשָׁלִָם וְיָשְׁבָה הָעִיר־הַזֹּאת לְעוֹלָם׃
to-forever the-this the-city and-she-will-be-inhabited Jerusalem

(26) וּבָאוּ מֵעָרֵי־יְהוּדָה וּמִסְּבִיבוֹת יְרוּשָׁלִַם
Jerusalem and-from-ones-around Judah from-towns-of and-they-will-come (26)

וּמֵאֶרֶץ בִּנְיָמִן וּמִן־הַשְּׁפֵלָה וּמִן־
and-from the-western-foothill and-from Benjamin and-from-territory-of

הָהָר וּמִן־הַנֶּגֶב מְבִאִים עוֹלָה וָזֶבַח
and-sacrifice burnt-offering ones-bringing the-Negev and-from the-hill-country

וּמִנְחָה וּלְבוֹנָה וּמְבִאֵי תוֹדָה בֵּית יְהוָה׃
Yahweh house-of thank-offering and-ones-bringing-of and-incense and-grain-offering

(27) וְאִם־לֹא תִשְׁמְעוּ אֵלַי לְקַדֵּשׁ אֶת־יוֹם הַשַּׁבָּת וּלְבִלְתִּי ׀ שְׂאֵת
to-carry and-not the-Sabbath day-of *** to-keep-holy to-me you-obey not but-if (27)

מַשָּׂא וּבֹא בְּשַׁעֲרֵי יְרוּשָׁלִָם בְּיוֹם הַשַּׁבָּת וְהִצַּתִּי
then-I-will-kindle the-Sabbath on-day-of Jerusalem through-gates-of and-to-come load

אֵשׁ בִּשְׁעָרֶיהָ וְאָכְלָה אַרְמְנוֹת יְרוּשָׁלִַם וְלֹא
and-not Jerusalem fortresses-of and-she-will-consume in-gates-of-her fire

תִכְבֶּה׃ (18:1) הַדָּבָר אֲשֶׁר הָיָה אֶל־יִרְמְיָהוּ מֵאֵת יְהוָה
Yahweh from-with Jeremiah to he-came that the-word (18:1) she-will-be-quenched

לֵאמֹר׃ (2) קוּם וְיָרַדְתָּ בֵּית הַיּוֹצֵר וְשָׁמָּה
and-at-there the-one-being-potter house-of and-you-go-down get-up! (2) to-say

°23 ק שמוע
°24 ק בו

on the Sabbath, but keep the Sabbath day holy, as I commanded
your forefathers. 23 Yet they did not
listen or pay attention; they were
stiff-necked and would not listen
or respond to discipline. 24 But if
you are careful to obey me, declares the LORD, and bring no load
through the gates of this city on
the Sabbath, but keep the Sabbath
day holy by not doing any work
on it, 25 then kings who sit on David's throne will come through the
gates of this city with their officials. They and their officials will
come riding in chariots and on
horses, accompanied by the men
of Judah and those living in
Jerusalem, and this city will be inhabited forever. 26 People will come
from the towns of Judah and the
villages around Jerusalem, from
the territory of Benjamin and the
western foothills, from the hill
country and the Negev, bringing
burnt offerings and sacrifices,
grain offerings, incense and
thank offerings to the house of the
LORD. 27 But if you do not obey me
to keep the Sabbath day holy by
not carrying any load as you come
through the gates of Jerusalem on
the Sabbath day, then I will kindle
an unquenchable fire in the gates
of Jerusalem that will consume her
fortresses.' "

*At the Potter's House*

18 This is the word that came
to Jeremiah from the LORD:
2 "Go down to the potter's house,

אַשְׁמִיעֲךָ אֶת־ דְּבָרָי׃ וָאֵרֵד בֵּית הַיּוֹצֵר
the-one-being-potter house-of so-I-went-down (3) messages-of-me *** I-will-give-you

וְהִנֵּהוּ עֹשֶׂה מְלָאכָה עַל־הָאָבְנָיִם׃ וְנִשְׁחַת הַכְּלִי אֲשֶׁר הוּא עֹשֶׂה
shaping he that the-pot but-he-was-marred (4) the-wheels at work doing and-see-he!

בַּחֹמֶר* בְּיַד הַיּוֹצֵר וְשָׁב וַיַּעֲשֵׂהוּ
and-he-formed-him so-he-did-again the-one-being-potter in-hand-of from-the-clay

כְּלִי אַחֵר כַּאֲשֶׁר יָשַׁר בְּעֵינֵי הַיּוֹצֵר לַעֲשׂוֹת׃
to-shape the-one-being-potter in-eyes-of he-was-best just-as another pot

וַיְהִי דְבַר־ יְהוָה אֵלַי לֵאמוֹר׃ הֲכַיּוֹצֵר הַזֶּה
the-this as-the-one-being-potter? (6) to-say to-me Yahweh word-of then-he-came (5)

לֹא־אוּכַל לַעֲשׂוֹת לָכֶם בֵּית יִשְׂרָאֵל נְאֻם־ יְהוָה הִנֵּה כַחֹמֶר
like-the-clay see! Yahweh declaration-of Israel house-of with-you to-do I-can not

בְּיַד הַיּוֹצֵר כֵּן־אַתֶּם בְּיָדִי בֵּית יִשְׂרָאֵל׃ רֶגַע
any-time (7) Israel house-of in-hand-of-me you so the-one-being-potter in-hand-of

אֲדַבֵּר עַל־ גּוֹי וְעַל־ מַמְלָכָה לִנְתוֹשׁ וְלִנְתוֹץ וּלְהַאֲבִיד׃
and-to-destroy and-to-tear-down to-uproot kingdom or-about nation about I-announce

וְשָׁב הַגּוֹי הַהוּא מֵרָעָתוֹ אֲשֶׁר דִּבַּרְתִּי עָלָיו
about-him I-warned that of-evil-of-him the-that the-nation and-he-repents (8)

וְנִחַמְתִּי עַל־ הָרָעָה אֲשֶׁר חָשַׁבְתִּי לַעֲשׂוֹת לוֹ׃
on-him to-inflict I-planned that the-disaster concerning then-I-will-relent

וְרֶגַע אֲדַבֵּר עַל־ גּוֹי וְעַל־ מַמְלָכָה לִבְנֹת
to-build-up kingdom or-about nation about I-announce and-another-time (9)

וְלִנְטֹעַ׃ וְעָשָׂה הָרָעָה בְּעֵינַי לְבִלְתִּי שְׁמֹעַ בְּקוֹלִי
to-voice-of-me to-obey not in-eyes-of-me the-evil and-he-does (10) and-to-plant

וְנִחַמְתִּי עַל־ הַטּוֹבָה אֲשֶׁר אָמַרְתִּי לְהֵיטִיב אוֹתוֹ׃
him to-do-good I-intended that the-good concerning then-I-will-reconsider

וְעַתָּה אֱמָר־ נָא אֶל־ אִישׁ־ יְהוּדָה וְעַל־ יוֹשְׁבֵי יְרוּשָׁלַםִ
Jerusalem ones-living-of and-to Judah person-of to now! say! therefore-now (11)

לֵאמֹר כֹּה אָמַר יְהוָה הִנֵּה אָנֹכִי יוֹצֵר עֲלֵיכֶם רָעָה וְחֹשֵׁב
and-devising disaster for-you preparing I look! Yahweh he-says this to-say

עֲלֵיכֶם מַחֲשָׁבָה שׁוּבוּ נָא אִישׁ מִדַּרְכּוֹ הָרָעָה וְהֵיטִיבוּ דַרְכֵיכֶם
ways-of-you and-reform! the-evil from-way-of-him each now! turn! plan against-you

וּמַעַלְלֵיכֶם׃ וְאָמְרוּ נוֹאָשׁ כִּי־אַחֲרֵי מַחְשְׁבוֹתֵינוּ
plans-of-us with indeed being-no-use but-they-will-reply (12) and-actions-of-you

נֵלֵךְ וְאִישׁ שְׁרִרוּת לִבּוֹ־ הָרָע נַעֲשֶׂה׃
we-will-follow the-evil heart-of-him stubbornness-of and-each we-will-continue

לָכֵן כֹּה אָמַר יְהוָה שַׁאֲלוּ־ נָא בַּגּוֹיִם מִי שָׁמַע
he-heard who? among-the-nations now! inquire! Yahweh he-says this therefore (13)

and there I will give you my message." [3]So I went down to the potter's house, and I saw him working at the wheel. [4]But the pot he
was shaping from the clay was
marred in his hands; so the potter
formed it into another pot, shaping it as seemed best to him.

[5]Then the word of the LORD
came to me: [6]"O house of Israel,
can I not do with you as this potter
does?" declares the LORD. "Like
clay in the hand of the potter, so
are you in my hand, O house of
Israel. [7]If at any time I announce
that a nation or kingdom is to be
uprooted, torn down and destroyed, [8]and if that nation I
warned repents of its evil, then I
will relent and not inflict on it the
disaster I had planned. [9]And if at
another time I announce that a
nation or kingdom is to be built
up and planted, [10]and if it does evil
in my sight and does not obey me,
then I will reconsider the good I
had intended to do for it.

[11]"Now therefore say to the
people of Judah and those living
in Jerusalem, 'This is what the
LORD says: Look! I am preparing a
disaster for you and devising a
plan against you. So turn from
your evil ways, each one of you,
and reform your ways and your
actions.' [12]But they will reply, 'It's
no use. We will continue with our
own plans; each of us will follow
the stubbornness of his evil
heart.' "

[13]Therefore this is what the LORD
says:

"Inquire among the nations:
Who has ever heard

*4 Most mss have *kaph* for *beth* (כַּ).

°3 ק והנה הוא

°10 ק הרע

כָּאֵלֶּה שַׁעֲרֻרִת עָשְׂתָה מְאֹד בְּתוּלַת יִשְׂרָאֵל׃ הֲיַעֲזֹב
does-he-vanish? (14) Israel Virgin-of most she-did horrible-thing like-these

מִצּוּר שָׂדַי שֶׁלֶג לְבָנוֹן אִם־ יִנָּתְשׁוּ מַיִם זָרִים
ones-being-distant waters do-they-cease or Lebanon snow-of slope from-rock-of

קָרִים נוֹזְלִים׃ כִּי־ שְׁכֵחֻנִי עַמִּי לַשָּׁוְא
to-the-worthless-one people-of-me they-forgot-me yet (15) ones-flowing cool-ones

יְקַטֵּרוּ וַיַּכְשִׁלוּם בְּדַרְכֵיהֶם שְׁבִילֵי עוֹלָם
ancient paths-of in-ways-of-them and-they-make-stumble-them they-burn-incense

לָלֶכֶת נְתִיבוֹת דֶּרֶךְ לֹא סְלוּלָה׃ לָשׂוּם אַרְצָם לְשַׁמָּה
to-waste land-of-them to-lay (16) being-built-up not road bypaths to-walk

שְׁרוּקֹת° עוֹלָם כֹּל עוֹבֵר עָלֶיהָ יִשֹּׁם
he-will-be-appalled by-her one-passing all-of lasting objects-of-scorns-of

וְיָנִיד בְּרֹאשׁוֹ׃ כְּרוּחַ־ קָדִים אֲפִיצֵם
I-will-scatter-them east like-wind-of (17) with-head-of-him and-he-will-shake

לִפְנֵי אוֹיֵב עֹרֶף וְלֹא־ פָנִים אַרְאֵם בְּיוֹם
in-day-of I-will-show-them faces and-not back one-being-enemy before

אֵידָם׃ וַיֹּאמְרוּ לְכוּ וְנַחְשְׁבָה עַל־ יִרְמְיָהוּ
Jeremiah against and-let-us-make-plans come! and-they-said (18) disaster-of-them

מַחֲשָׁבוֹת כִּי לֹא־ תֹאבַד תּוֹרָה מִכֹּהֵן וְעֵצָה מֵחָכָם וְדָבָר
or-word from-wise or-counsel by-priest law she-will-be-lost not for plans

מִנָּבִיא לְכוּ וְנַכֵּהוּ בַלָּשׁוֹן וְאַל־ נַקְשִׁיבָה
let-us-pay-attention and-not with-the-tongue and-let-us-attack-him come! from-prophet

אֶל־ כָּל־ דְּבָרָיו׃ הַקְשִׁיבָה יְהוָה אֵלַי וּשְׁמַע לְקוֹל
to-saying-of and-hear! to-me Yahweh listen! (19) sayings-of-him any-of to

יְרִיבָי׃ הַיְשֻׁלַּם תַּחַת־טוֹבָה רָעָה כִּי־ כָרוּ שׁוּחָה°
pit they-dug yet evil good for should-he-be-repaid? (20) accusers-of-me

לְנַפְשִׁי זְכֹר ׀ עָמְדִי לְפָנֶיךָ לְדַבֵּר עֲלֵיהֶם טוֹבָה לְהָשִׁיב
to-turn good for-them to-speak before-you to-stand-me remember! for-life-of-me

אֶת־ חֲמָתְךָ מֵהֶם׃ לָכֵן תֵּן אֶת־ בְּנֵיהֶם לָרָעָב
to-the-famine children-of-them *** give! so (21) from-them wrath-of-you ***

וְהַגִּרֵם עַל־ יְדֵי־ חֶרֶב וְתִהְיֶנָה נְשֵׁיהֶם
wives-of-them and-let-them-become sword powers-of to and-hand-over-them!

שַׁכֻּלוֹת וְאַלְמָנוֹת וְאַנְשֵׁיהֶם יִהְיוּ הֲרֻגֵי מָוֶת
death ones-being-killed-of let-them-be and-men-of-them and-widows childless-ones

בַּחוּרֵיהֶם מֻכֵּי־ חֶרֶב בַּמִּלְחָמָה׃ תִּשָּׁמַע זְעָקָה
cry let-her-be-heard (22) in-the-battle sword ones-being-slain-of young-men-of-them

מִבָּתֵּיהֶם כִּי־ תָבִיא עֲלֵיהֶם גְּדוּד פִּתְאֹם כִּי־ כָרוּ שִׁיחָה
pit they-dug for suddenly invader against-them you-bring when from-houses-of-them

anything like this?
A most horrible thing has been done
by Virgin Israel.
14 Does the snow of Lebanon
ever vanish from its rocky slopes?
Do its cool waters from distant sources
ever cease to flow?[c]
15 Yet my people have forgotten me;
they burn incense to worthless idols,
which made them stumble in their ways
and in the ancient paths.
They made them walk in bypaths
and on roads not built up.
16 Their land will be laid waste,
an object of lasting scorn;
all who pass by will be appalled
and will shake their heads.
17 Like a wind from the east,
I will scatter them before their enemies;
I will show them my back and not my face
in the day of their disaster."

18 They said, "Come, let's make plans against Jeremiah; for the teaching of the law by the priest will not be lost, nor will counsel from the wise, nor the word from the prophets. So come, let's attack him with our tongues and pay no attention to anything he says."

19 Listen to me, O LORD;
hear what my accusers are saying!
20 Should good be repaid with evil?
Yet they have dug a pit for me.
Remember that I stood before you
and spoke in their behalf
to turn your wrath away from them.
21 So give their children over to famine;
hand them over to the power of the sword.
Let their wives be made childless and widows;
let their men be put to death,
their young men slain by the sword in battle.
22 Let a cry be heard from their houses
when you suddenly bring invaders against them,
for they have dug a pit to

c14 The meaning of the Hebrew for this sentence is uncertain.

°16 ק שריקת
°22 ק שוחה

לְלָכְדֵ֔נִי וּפַחִ֖ים טָמְנ֥וּ לְרַגְלָֽי׃ וְאַתָּ֣ה יְהוָ֗ה יָדַ֙עְתָּ֙
you-know Yahweh but-you (23) for-feet-of-me they-hid and-snares to-capture-me

אֶֽת־כָּל־עֲצָתָ֤ם עָלַי֙ לַמָּ֔וֶת אַל־תְּכַפֵּר֙ עַל־עֲוֺנָ֔ם
crime-of-them to you-forgive not for-the-death against-me plot-of-them all-of ***

וְחַטָּאתָ֖ם מִלְּפָנֶ֣יךָ אַל־תֶּ֑מְחִי וְהָי֤וּ מֻכְשָׁלִים֙
ones-being-overthrown and-let-them-be you-blot-out not from-before-you or-sin-of-them

לְפָנֶ֔יךָ בְּעֵ֥ת אַפְּךָ֖ עֲשֵׂ֥ה בָהֶֽם׃ כֹּ֚ה אָמַ֣ר יְהוָ֔ה
Yahweh he-says this (19:1) with-them deal! anger-of-you in-time-of before-you

הָל֥וֹךְ וְקָנִ֛יתָ בַקְבֻּ֥ק יוֹצֵ֖ר חָ֑רֶשׂ וּמִזִּקְנֵ֣י הָעָ֔ם
the-people and-from-elders-of clay one-being-potter jar-of and-you-buy to-go

וּמִזִּקְנֵ֖י הַכֹּהֲנִֽים׃ וְיָצָ֙אתָ֙ אֶל־גֵּ֣יא בֶן־הִנֹּ֔ם אֲשֶׁ֕ר
that Hinnom Ben Valley-of to and-you-go-out (2) the-priests and-from-elders-of

פֶּ֖תַח שַׁ֣עַר הַחַרְס֑וּת וְקָרָ֣אתָ שָּׁ֔ם אֶת־הַדְּבָרִ֖ים אֲשֶׁר־אֲדַבֵּ֥ר
I-tell that the-words *** there and-you-proclaim the-Potsherd Gate-of entrance-of

אֵלֶֽיךָ׃ וְאָמַרְתָּ֙ שִׁמְע֣וּ דְבַר־יְהוָ֔ה מַלְכֵ֣י יְהוּדָ֔ה וְיֹשְׁבֵ֖י
and-ones-being-people-of Judah kings-of Yahweh word-of hear! and-you-say (3) to-you

יְרוּשָׁלִָ֑ם כֹּֽה־אָמַ֞ר יְהוָ֤ה צְבָאוֹת֙ אֱלֹהֵ֣י יִשְׂרָאֵ֔ל הִנְנִ֨י מֵבִ֤יא רָעָה֙ עַל־
on disaster bringing see-I! Israel God-of Hosts Yahweh-of he-says this Jerusalem

הַמָּק֣וֹם הַזֶּ֔ה אֲשֶׁ֥ר כָּל־שֹׁמְעָ֖הּ תִּצַּ֥לְנָה אָזְנָֽיו׃
ears-of-him they-will-tingle one-hearing-her every-of that the-this the-place

יַ֣עַן ׀ אֲשֶׁ֣ר עֲזָבֻ֗נִי וַיְנַכְּר֞וּ אֶת־הַמָּק֤וֹם הַזֶּה֙
the-this the-place *** and-they-made-foreign they-forsook-me that because (4)

וַיְקַטְּרוּ־ב֙וֹ֙ לֵאלֹהִ֣ים אֲחֵרִ֔ים אֲשֶׁ֧ר לֹא־יְדָע֛וּם הֵ֥מָּה
they they-knew not that other-ones to-gods in-him and-they-burned-sacrifices

וַאֲבוֹתֵיהֶ֖ם וּמַלְכֵ֣י יְהוּדָ֑ה וּמָלְא֛וּ אֶת־הַמָּק֥וֹם הַזֶּ֖ה
the-this the-place *** and-they-filled Judah or-kings-of or-fathers-of-them

דַּ֥ם נְקִיִֽם׃ וּבָנ֞וּ אֶת־בָּמ֣וֹת הַבַּ֗עַל לִשְׂרֹ֧ף אֶת־
*** to-burn the-Baal high-places-of *** and-they-built (5) innocent-ones blood-of

בְּנֵיהֶ֛ם בָּאֵ֖שׁ עֹל֣וֹת לַבָּ֑עַל אֲשֶׁ֣ר לֹא־צִוִּ֗יתִי וְלֹ֣א
or-not I-commanded not that to-the-Baal burnt-offerings in-the-fire sons-of-them

דִבַּ֔רְתִּי וְלֹ֥א עָלְתָ֖ה עַל־לִבִּֽי׃ לָכֵ֞ן הִנֵּֽה־יָמִ֣ים בָּאִ֗ים
ones-coming days see! so (6) mind-of-me into she-entered or-not I-mentioned

נְאֻם־יְהוָ֔ה וְלֹא־יִקָּרֵא֩ לַמָּק֨וֹם הַזֶּ֥ה ע֛וֹד
longer the-this to-the-place he-will-be-called when-not Yahweh declaration-of

הַתֹּ֖פֶת וְגֵ֣יא בֶן־הִנֹּ֑ם כִּ֥י אִם־גֵּ֖יא הַהֲרֵגָֽה׃
the-Slaughter Valley-of rather but Hinnom Ben or-Valley-of the-Topheth

וּ֠בַקֹּתִי אֶת־עֲצַ֨ת יְהוּדָ֜ה וִירוּשָׁלִַ֗ם בַּמָּק֣וֹם הַזֶּ֔ה
the-this in-the-place and-Jerusalem Judah plan-of *** and-I-will-ruin (7)

capture me
and have hidden snares for
my feet.
23 But you know, O LORD,
all their plots to kill me.
Do not forgive their crimes
or blot out their sins from
your sight.
Let them be overthrown before
you;
deal with them in the time
of your anger.

19 This is what the LORD says:
"Go and buy a clay jar from
a potter. Take along some of the
elders of the people and of the
priests 2 and go out to the Valley of
Ben Hinnom, near the entrance of
the Potsherd Gate. There proclaim
the words I tell you, 3 and say,
'Hear the word of the LORD, O
kings of Judah and people of
Jerusalem. This is what the LORD
Almighty, the God of Israel, says:
Listen! I am going to bring a disaster on this place that will make the
ears of everyone who hears of it
tingle. 4 For they have forsaken me
and made this a place of foreign
gods; they have burned sacrifices
in it to gods that neither they nor
their fathers nor the kings of
Judah ever knew, and they have
filled this place with the blood of
the innocent. 5 They have built the
high places of Baal to burn their
sons in the fire as offerings to
Baal—something I did not command or mention, nor did it enter
my mind. 6 So beware, the days are
coming, declares the LORD, when
people will no longer call this
place Topheth or the Valley of Ben
Hinnom, but the Valley of Slaughter.
7 "'In this place I will ruin[f] the
plans of Judah and Jerusalem. I

f7 The Hebrew for *ruin* sounds like the Hebrew for *jar* (see verses 1 and 10).

°23 ק ויהיו
°2 ק החרסית

וְהִפַּלְתִּים בַּחֶרֶב לִפְנֵי אֹיְבֵיהֶם
ones-being-enemies-of-them before by-the-sword and-I-will-make-fall-them

וּבְיַד מְבַקְשֵׁי נַפְשָׁם וְנָתַתִּי אֶת־ נִבְלָתָם
carcass-of-them *** and-I-will-give life-of-them ones-seeking-of and-at-hand-of

לְמַאֲכָל לְעוֹף הַשָּׁמַיִם וּלְבֶהֱמַת הָאָרֶץ׃ וְשַׂמְתִּי אֶת־
*** and-I-will-make (8) the-earth and-to-beast-of the-airs to-bird-of as-food

הָעִיר הַזֹּאת לְשַׁמָּה וְלִשְׁרֵקָה כֹּל עֹבֵר
one-passing all-of and-as-object-of-scorn as-devastation the-this the-city

עָלֶיהָ יִשֹּׁם וְיִשְׁרֹק עַל־ כָּל־ מַכֹּתֶהָ׃
wounds-of-her all-of because-of and-he-will-scoff he-will-be-appalled by-her

וְהַאֲכַלְתִּים אֶת־ בְּשַׂר בְּנֵיהֶם וְאֵת בְּשַׂר בְּנֹתֵיהֶם
daughters-of-them flesh-of and sons-of-them flesh-of *** and-I-will-make-eat-them (9)

וְאִישׁ בְּשַׂר־ רֵעֵהוּ יֹאכֵלוּ בְּמָצוֹר וּבְמָצוֹק אֲשֶׁר
that and-during-siege during-stress they-will-eat another-of-him flesh-of and-one

יָצִיקוּ לָהֶם אֹיְבֵיהֶם וּמְבַקְשֵׁי נַפְשָׁם׃
life-of-them and-ones-seeking-of ones-being-enemies-of-them on-them they-will-impose

וְשָׁבַרְתָּ הַבַּקְבֻּק לְעֵינֵי הָאֲנָשִׁים הַהֹלְכִים אוֹתָךְ׃
with-you the-ones-going the-men before-eyes-of the-jar then-you-break (10)

וְאָמַרְתָּ אֲלֵיהֶם כֹּה־ אָמַר ׀ יְהוָה צְבָאוֹת כָּכָה אֶשְׁבֹּר אֶת־
*** I-will-smash so Hosts Yahweh-of he-says this to-them and-you-say (11)

הָעָם הַזֶּה וְאֶת־ הָעִיר הַזֹּאת כַּאֲשֶׁר יִשְׁבֹּר אֶת־ כְּלִי
jar-of *** he-smashed just-as the-this the-city and the-this the-nation

הַיּוֹצֵר אֲשֶׁר לֹא־ יוּכַל לְהֵרָפֵה עוֹד וּבְתֹפֶת
and-in-Topheth again to-be-repaired he-can not that the-one-being-potter

יִקְבְּרוּ מֵאֵין מָקוֹם לִקְבּוֹר׃ כֵּן־ אֶעֱשֶׂה לַמָּקוֹם
to-the-place I-will-do this (12) to-bury room until-there-is-no they-will-bury

הַזֶּה נְאֻם־ יְהוָה וּלְיוֹשְׁבָיו וְלָתֵת אֶת־ הָעִיר
the-city *** and-to-make and-to-ones-living-in-him Yahweh declaration-of the-this

הַזֹּאת כְּתֹפֶת׃ וְהָיוּ בָּתֵּי יְרוּשָׁלִַם וּבָתֵּי
and-houses-of Jerusalem houses-of and-they-will-be (13) like-Topheth the-this

מַלְכֵי יְהוּדָה כִּמְקוֹם הַתֹּפֶת הַטְּמֵאִים לְכֹל הַבָּתִּים אֲשֶׁר
that the-houses to-all-of the-defiled-ones the-Topheth like-place-of Judah kings-of

קִטְּרוּ עַל־ גַּגֹּתֵיהֶם לְכֹל צְבָא הַשָּׁמַיִם וְהַסֵּךְ
and-to-pour-out the-heavens host-of to-all-of roofs-of-them on they-burned-incense

נְסָכִים לֵאלֹהִים אֲחֵרִים׃ וַיָּבֹא יִרְמְיָהוּ מֵהַתֹּפֶת
from-the-Topheth Jeremiah then-he-returned (14) other-ones to-gods drink-offerings

אֲשֶׁר שְׁלָחוֹ יְהוָה שָׁם לְהִנָּבֵא וַיַּעֲמֹד בַּחֲצַר בֵּית־
temple-of in-court-of and-he-stood to-prophesy there Yahweh he-sent-him where

will make them fall by the sword before their enemies, at the hands of those who seek their lives, and I will give their carcasses as food to the birds of the air and the beasts of the earth. [8]I will devastate this city and make it an object of scorn; all who pass by will be appalled and will scoff because of all its wounds. [9]I will make them eat the flesh of their sons and daughters, and they will eat one another's flesh during the stress of the siege imposed on them by the enemies who seek their lives.'

[10]"Then break the jar while those who go with you are watching, [11]and say to them, 'This is what the LORD Almighty says: I will smash this nation and this city just as this potter's jar is smashed and cannot be repaired. They will bury the dead in Topheth until there is no more room. [12]This is what I will do to this place and to those who live here, declares the LORD. I will make this city like Topheth. [13]The houses in Jerusalem and those of the kings of Judah will be defiled like this place, Topheth—all the houses where they burned incense on the roofs to all the starry hosts and poured out drink offerings to other gods.' "

[14]Jeremiah then returned from Topheth, where the LORD had sent him to prophesy, and stood in the court of the LORD's temple and

יְהוָ֔ה וַיֹּ֖אמֶר אֶל־כָּל־הָעָֽם׃ כֹּה־אָמַ֨ר יְהוָ֤ה צְבָאוֹת֙ אֱלֹהֵ֣י
God-of Hosts Yahweh-of he-says this (15) the-people all-of to and-he-said Yahweh

יִשְׂרָאֵ֔ל הִנְנִ֨י מֵבִ֜י אֶל־הָעִ֤יר הַזֹּאת֙ וְעַל־כָּל־עָרֶ֔יהָ אֵ֚ת
*** villages-of-her all-of and-on the-this the-city on bringing see-I! Israel

כָּל־הָ֣רָעָ֔ה אֲשֶׁ֥ר דִּבַּ֖רְתִּי עָלֶ֑יהָ כִּ֤י הִקְשׁוּ֙ אֶת־
*** they-made-stiff because against-her I-pronounced that the-disaster every-of

עָרְפָּ֔ם לְבִלְתִּ֖י שְׁמ֥וֹעַ אֶת־דְּבָרָֽי׃ וַיִּשְׁמַע֙ פַּשְׁח֣וּר בֶּן־
son-of Pashhur when-he-heard (20:1) words-of-me *** to-listen not neck-of-them

אִמֵּ֣ר הַכֹּהֵ֔ן וְהוּא־פָקִ֥יד נָגִ֖יד בְּבֵ֣ית יְהוָ֑ה אֶֽת־יִרְמְיָ֔הוּ נִבָּ֖א
prophesying Jeremiah *** Yahweh in-temple-of chief officer now-he the-priest Immer

אֶת־הַדְּבָרִ֥ים הָאֵֽלֶּה׃ וַיַּכֶּה֙ פַּשְׁח֔וּר אֵ֖ת יִרְמְיָ֣הוּ הַנָּבִ֑יא
the-prophet Jeremiah *** Pashhur then-he-had-beaten (2) the-these the-things ***

וַיִּתֵּ֨ן אֹת֜וֹ עַל־הַמַּהְפֶּ֗כֶת אֲשֶׁר֙ בְּשַׁ֤עַר בִּנְיָמִן֙ הָֽעֶלְי֔וֹן אֲשֶׁ֖ר בְּבֵ֥ית
at-temple-of that the-Upper Benjamin at-Gate-of that the-stock in him and-he-put

יְהוָֽה׃ וַֽיְהִי֙ מִֽמָּחֳרָ֔ת וַיֹּצֵ֥א פַשְׁח֛וּר אֶֽת־יִרְמְיָ֖הוּ מִן־
from Jeremiah *** Pashhur when-he-released on-next-day and-he-was (3) Yahweh

הַמַּהְפָּ֑כֶת וַיֹּ֨אמֶר אֵלָ֜יו יִרְמְיָ֗הוּ לֹ֤א פַשְׁחוּר֙ קָרָ֤א יְהוָה֙ שְׁמֶ֔ךָ כִּ֖י
but name-of-you Yahweh he-calls Pashhur not Jeremiah to-him then-he-said the-stock

אִם־מָג֥וֹר מִסָּבִֽיב׃ כִּ֣י כֹ֣ה אָמַ֣ר יְהוָ֗ה הִנְנִ֨י נֹתֶנְךָ֜ לְמָג֗וֹר
as-terror making-you see-I! Yahweh he-says this for (4) Missabib Magor rather

לְךָ֙ וּֽלְכָל־אֹ֣הֲבֶ֔יךָ וְנָ֛פְלוּ בְּחֶ֥רֶב
by-sword-of and-they-will-fall ones-being-friends-of-you and-to-all-of to-you

אֹיְבֵיהֶ֖ם וְעֵינֶ֣יךָ רֹא֑וֹת וְאֶת־כָּל־יְהוּדָ֗ה אֶתֵּן֙
I-will-give Judah all-of and ones-seeing and-eyes-of-you ones-being-enemies-of-them

בְּיַד֙ מֶֽלֶךְ־בָּבֶ֔ל וְהִגְלָ֥ם בָּבֶ֖לָה וְהִכָּ֥ם
or-he-will-put-them to-Babylon and-he-will-carry-them Babylon king-of into-hand-of

בֶּחָֽרֶב׃ וְנָתַתִּ֗י אֶת־כָּל־חֹ֙סֶן֙ הָעִ֣יר הַזֹּ֔את וְאֶת־
and the-this the-city wealth-of all-of *** and-I-will-hand-over (5) to-the-sword

כָּל־יְגִיעָ֖הּ וְאֶת־כָּל־יְקָרָ֑הּ וְאֵ֨ת כָּל־אוֹצְר֜וֹת מַלְכֵ֣י
kings-of treasures-of all-of and valuable-of-her all-of and product-of-her all-of

יְהוּדָ֗ה אֶתֵּן֙ בְּיַ֣ד אֹֽיְבֵיהֶ֔ם וּבְזָזוּם֙
and-they-will-plunder-them ones-being-enemies-of-them into-hand-of I-will-give Judah

וּלְקָח֔וּם וֶהֱבִיא֖וּם בָּבֶֽלָה׃ וְאַתָּ֣ה פַשְׁח֗וּר
Pashhur and-you (6) to-Babylon and-they-will-carry-them and-they-will-take-them

וְכֹל֙ יֹשְׁבֵ֣י בֵיתֶ֔ךָ תֵּלְכ֖וּ בַּשֶּׁ֑בִי וּבָבֶ֣ל
and-Babylon into-the-exile you-will-go house-of-you ones-living-of and-all-of

תָּב֗וֹא וְשָׁ֤ם תָּמוּת֙ וְשָׁ֣ם תִּקָּבֵ֔ר אַתָּה֙ וְכָל־
and-all-of you you-will-be-buried and-there you-will-die and-there you-will-go

said to all the people, [15]"This is what the LORD Almighty, the God of Israel, says: 'Listen! I am going to bring on this city and the villages around it every disaster I pronounced against them, because they were stiff-necked and would not listen to my words.' "

*Jeremiah and Pashhur*

**20** When the priest Pashhur son of Immer, the chief officer in the temple of the LORD, heard Jeremiah prophesying these things, [2]he had Jeremiah the prophet beaten and put in the stocks at the Upper Gate of Benjamin at the LORD's temple. [3]The next day, when Pashhur released him from the stocks, Jeremiah said to him, "The LORD's name for you is not Pashhur, but Magor-Missabib.[g] [4]For this is what the LORD says: 'I will make you a terror to yourself and to all your friends; with your own eyes you will see them fall by the sword of their enemies. I will hand all Judah over to the king of Babylon, who will carry them away to Babylon or put them to the sword. [5]I will hand over to their enemies all the wealth of this city—all its products, all its valuables and all the treasures of the kings of Judah. They will take it away as plunder and carry it off to Babylon. [6]And you, Pashhur, and all who live in your house will go into exile to Babylon. There you will die and be buried, you and all your friends

g3 Magor-Missabib means *terror on every side.*

°15 ק מביא

אֹהֲבֶ֔יךָ אֲשֶׁר־ נִבֵּ֥אתָ לָהֶ֖ם בַּשָּֽׁקֶר׃

about-the-lie to-them you-prophesied whom ones-being-friends-of-you

(7) פִּתִּיתַ֤נִי יְהוָה֙ וָאֶפָּ֔ת חֲזַקְתַּ֖נִי וַתּוּכָ֑ל

and-you-prevailed you-overpowered-me and-I-was-deceived Yahweh you-deceived-me (7)

הָיִ֤יתִי לִשְׂחוֹק֙ כָּל־ הַיּ֔וֹם כֻּלֹּ֖ה לֹעֵ֥ג לִֽי׃ (8) כִּֽי־ מִדֵּ֤י

as-often-of when (8) at-me mocking every-of-him the-day all-of for-ridicule I-am

אֲדַבֵּר֙ אֶזְעָ֔ק חָמָ֥ס וָשֹׁ֖ד אֶקְרָ֑א כִּֽי־ הָיָה֩ דְבַר־ יְהוָ֥ה

Yahweh word-of he-came so I-proclaim and-destruction violence I-cry-out I-speak

לִ֛י לְחֶרְפָּ֥ה וּלְקֶ֖לֶס כָּל־ הַיּֽוֹם׃ (9) וְאָמַרְתִּ֣י לֹא־ אֶזְכְּרֶ֗נּוּ

I-will-mention-him not if-I-say (9) the-day all-of and-for-reproach for-insult to-me

וְלֹֽא־ אֲדַבֵּ֥ר עוֹד֙ בִּשְׁמ֔וֹ וְהָיָ֤ה בְלִבִּי֙ כְּאֵ֣שׁ בֹּעֶ֔רֶת

burning like-fire in-heart-of-me then-he-is in-name-of-him more I-will-speak or-not

עָצֻ֖ר בְּעַצְמֹתָ֑י וְנִלְאֵ֥יתִי כַּלְכֵ֖ל וְלֹ֥א אוּכָֽל׃ (10) כִּ֣י

indeed (10) I-can indeed-not to-hold-in and-I-am-weary in-bones-of-me being-shut-up

שָׁמַ֜עְתִּי דִּבַּ֣ת רַבִּ֗ים מָג֣וֹר מִסָּבִ֔יב הַגִּ֙ידוּ֙ וְנַגִּידֶ֔נּוּ

now-let-us-report-him report! on-every-side terror many-ones whispering-of I-hear

כֹּ֚ל אֱנ֣וֹשׁ שְׁלוֹמִ֔י שֹׁמְרֵ֖י צַלְעִ֑י אוּלַ֤י יְפֻתֶּה֙

he-will-be-deceived perhaps slip-of-me ones-waiting-of peace-of-me man-of all-of

וְנ֣וּכְלָה ל֔וֹ וְנִקְחָ֥ה נִקְמָתֵ֖נוּ מִמֶּֽנּוּ׃ (11) וַיהוָ֤ה

but-Yahweh (11) on-him revenge-of-us and-we-will-take over-him then-we-will-prevail

אוֹתִי֙ כְּגִבּ֣וֹר עָרִ֔יץ עַל־כֵּ֛ן רֹדְפַ֥י יִכָּשְׁל֖וּ וְלֹ֣א

and-not they-will-stumble ones-persecuting-me this for mighty like-warrior with-me

יֻכָ֑לוּ בֹּ֤שׁוּ מְאֹד֙ כִּֽי־ לֹ֣א הִשְׂכִּ֔ילוּ

they-will-succeed not for thoroughly they-will-be-disgraced they-will-prevail

כְּלִמַּ֥ת עוֹלָ֖ם לֹ֥א תִשָּׁכֵֽחַ׃ (12) וַיהוָ֣ה צְבָא֗וֹת

Hosts and-Yahweh-of (12) she-will-be-forgotten never eternity dishonor-of

בֹּחֵ֣ן צַדִּ֔יק רֹאֶ֥ה כְלָי֖וֹת וָלֵ֑ב אֶרְאֶ֤ה נִקְמָֽתְךָ֙

vengeance-of-you let-me-see and-mind hearts one-probing righteous one-examining-of

מֵהֶ֔ם כִּ֥י אֵלֶ֖יךָ גִּלִּ֥יתִי אֶת־ רִיבִֽי׃ (13) שִׁ֚ירוּ לַֽיהוָ֔ה הַֽלְל֖וּ

give-praise! to-Yahweh sing! (13) cause-of-me *** I-committed to-you for on-them

אֶת־ יְהוָ֑ה כִּ֣י הִצִּ֛יל אֶת־ נֶ֥פֶשׁ אֶבְי֖וֹן מִיַּ֥ד מְרֵעִֽים׃

ones-being-wicked from-hand-of needy life-of *** he-rescues for Yahweh ***

(14) אָר֣וּר הַיּ֔וֹם אֲשֶׁ֥ר יֻלַּ֖דְתִּי בּ֑וֹ י֛וֹם אֲשֶׁר־ יְלָדַ֥תְנִי אִמִּ֖י

mother-of-me she-bore-me that day on-him I-was-born that the-day being-cursed (14)

אַל־ יְהִ֥י בָרֽוּךְ׃ (15) אָר֣וּר הָאִ֗ישׁ אֲשֶׁ֨ר בִּשַּׂ֤ר אֶת־

*** he-brought-news who the-man being-cursed (15) being-blessed may-he-be not

אָבִי֙ לֵאמֹ֔ר יֻלַּד־ לְךָ֖ בֵּ֣ן זָכָ֑ר שַׂמֵּ֖חַ שִׂמְּחָֽהוּ׃

he-made-glad-him to-make-glad son child to-you he-is-born to-say father-of-me

to whom you have prophesied lies.' "

*Jeremiah's Complaint*

7 O LORD, you deceived[h] me,
and I was deceived[h];
you overpowered me and prevailed.
I am ridiculed all day long;
everyone mocks me.
8 Whenever I speak, I cry out
proclaiming violence and destruction.
So the word of the LORD has brought me
insult and reproach all day long.
9 But if I say, "I will not mention him
or speak any more in his name,"
his word is in my heart like a fire,
a fire shut up in my bones.
I am weary of holding it in;
indeed, I cannot.
10 I hear many whispering,
"Terror on every side!
Report him! Let's report him!"
All my friends
are waiting for me to slip,
saying,
"Perhaps he will be deceived;
then we will prevail over him
and take our revenge on him."

11 But the LORD is with me like a mighty warrior;
so my persecutors will stumble and not prevail.
They will fail and be thoroughly disgraced;
their dishonor will never be forgotten.
12 O LORD Almighty, you who examine the righteous
and probe the heart and mind,
let me see your vengeance upon them,
for to you I have committed my cause.

13 Sing to the LORD!
Give praise to the LORD!
He rescues the life of the needy
from the hands of the wicked.

14 Cursed be the day I was born!
May the day my mother bore me not be blessed!
15 Cursed be the man who brought my father the news,
who made him very glad, saying,
"A child is born to you—a son!"

[h]7 Or *persuaded*

וְהָיָה הָאִישׁ הַהוּא כֶּעָרִים אֲשֶׁר־הָפַךְ יְהוָה וְלֹא

and-not Yahweh he-overthrew that like-the-towns the-that the-man and-may-he-be (16)

נִחָם וְשָׁמַע זְעָקָה בַּבֹּקֶר וּתְרוּעָה בְּעֵת

at-time-of and-battle-cry in-the-morning wailing and-may-he-hear he-had-pity

צָהֳרָיִם׃ אֲשֶׁר לֹא־מוֹתְתַנִי מֵרָחֶם וַתְּהִי־לִי אִמִּי קִבְרִי

grave-of-me mother-of-me to-me so-she-was in-womb he-killed-me not for (17) noon

וְרַחְמָה הֲרַת עוֹלָם׃ לָמָּה זֶּה מֵרֶחֶם יָצָאתִי לִרְאוֹת

to-see I-came-out from-womb this why? (18) forever enlarged-of and-womb-of-her

עָמָל וְיָגוֹן וַיִּכְלוּ בְּבֹשֶׁת יָמָי׃ הַדָּבָר אֲשֶׁר־

that the-word (21:1) days-of-me in-shame so-they-would-end and-sorrow trouble

הָיָה אֶל־יִרְמְיָהוּ מֵאֵת יְהוָה בִּשְׁלֹחַ אֵלָיו הַמֶּלֶךְ צִדְקִיָּהוּ אֶת־

*** Zedekiah the-king to-him when-to-send Yahweh from-with Jeremiah to he-came

פַּשְׁחוּר בֶּן־מַלְכִּיָּה וְאֶת־צְפַנְיָה בֶן־מַעֲשֵׂיָה הַכֹּהֵן לֵאמֹר׃

to-say the-priest Maaseiah son-of Zephaniah and Malkijah son-of Passhur

דְּרָשׁ־נָא בַעֲדֵנוּ אֶת־יְהוָה כִּי נְבוּכַדְרֶאצַּר מֶלֶךְ־

king-of Nebuchadrezzar because Yahweh *** on-behalf-of-us now! inquire! (2)

בָּבֶל נִלְחָם עָלֵינוּ אוּלַי יַעֲשֶׂה יְהוָה אוֹתָנוּ כְּכָל־

as-all-of for-us Yahweh he-will-perform perhaps against-us attacking Babylon

נִפְלְאֹתָיו וְיַעֲלֶה מֵעָלֵינוּ׃ וַיֹּאמֶר

but-he-answered (3) from-against-us so-he-will-withdraw things-being-wonderful-of-him

יִרְמְיָהוּ אֲלֵיהֶם כֹּה תֹאמְרֻן אֶל־צִדְקִיָּהוּ׃ כֹּה־אָמַר יְהוָה אֱלֹהֵי יִשְׂרָאֵל

Israel God-of Yahweh he-says this (4) Zedekiah to you-tell this to-them Jeremiah

הִנְנִי מֵסֵב אֶת־כְּלֵי הַמִּלְחָמָה אֲשֶׁר בְּיֶדְכֶם אֲשֶׁר אַתֶּם נִלְחָמִים

ones-fighting you that in-hand-of-you that the-war weapons-of *** turning see-I!

בָּם אֶת־מֶלֶךְ בָּבֶל וְאֶת־הַכַּשְׂדִּים הַצָּרִים עֲלֵיכֶם

against-you the-ones-besieging the-Chaldeans and Babylon king-of *** with-them

מִחוּץ לַחוֹמָה וְאָסַפְתִּי אוֹתָם אֶל־תּוֹךְ הָעִיר הַזֹּאת׃

the-this the-city inside-of to them and-I-will-gather to-the-wall from-outside

וְנִלְחַמְתִּי אֲנִי אִתְּכֶם בְּיָד נְטוּיָה וּבִזְרוֹעַ חֲזָקָה

mighty and-with-arm being-outstretched with-hand against-you I and-I-will-fight (5)

וּבְאַף וּבְחֵמָה וּבְקֶצֶף גָּדוֹל׃ וְהִכֵּיתִי אֶת־

*** and-I-will-strike-down (6) great and-in-wrath and-in-fury and-in-anger

יוֹשְׁבֵי הָעִיר הַזֹּאת וְאֶת־הָאָדָם וְאֶת־הַבְּהֵמָה בְּדֶבֶר גָּדוֹל

terrible by-plague the-animal and the-man both the-this the-city ones-living-of

יָמֻתוּ׃ וְאַחֲרֵי־כֵן נְאֻם־יְהוָה אֶתֵּן אֶת־צִדְקִיָּהוּ

Zedekiah *** I-will-give Yahweh declaration-of that and-after (7) they-will-die

מֶלֶךְ־יְהוּדָה וְאֶת־עֲבָדָיו ׀ וְאֶת־הָעָם וְאֶת־הַנִּשְׁאָרִים בָּעִיר

in-the-city the-ones-surviving and the-people and officials-of-him and Judah king-of

16 May that man be like the towns
the LORD overthrew without pity.
May he hear wailing in the morning,
a battle cry at noon.
17 For he did not kill me in the womb,
with my mother as my grave,
her womb enlarged forever.
18 Why did I ever come out of the womb
to see trouble and sorrow
and to end my days in shame?

*God Rejects Zedekiah's Request*

21 The word came to Jeremiah from the LORD when King Zedekiah sent to him Pashhur son of Malkijah and the priest Zephaniah son of Maaseiah. They said: 2 "Inquire now of the LORD for us because Nebuchadnezzar[i] king of Babylon is attacking us. Perhaps the LORD will perform wonders for us as in times past so that he will withdraw from us."

3 But Jeremiah answered them, "Tell Zedekiah, 4 'This is what the LORD, the God of Israel, says: I am about to turn against you the weapons of war that are in your hands, which you are using to fight the king of Babylon and the Babylonians[j] who are outside the wall besieging you. And I will gather them inside this city. 5 I myself will fight against you with an outstretched hand and a mighty arm in anger and fury and great wrath. 6 I will strike down those who live in this city—both men and animals—and they will die of a terrible plague. 7 After that, declares the LORD, I will hand over Zedekiah king of Judah, his officials and the people in this city

i2 Hebrew *Nebuchadrezzar,* of which *Nebuchadnezzar* is a variant; here and often in Jeremiah and Ezekiel

j4 Or *Chaldeans;* also in verse 9

הַזֹּאת מִן־ הַדֶּבֶר ׀ מִן־ הַחֶרֶב וּמִן־ הָרָעָב בְּיַד נְבוּכַדְרֶאצַּר
Nebuchadrezzar into-hand-of the-famine and-from the-sword from the-plague from the-this

מֶלֶךְ־ בָּבֶל וּבְיַד אֹיְבֵיהֶם וּבְיַד
and-into-hand-of ones-being-enemies-of-them and-into-hand-of Babylon king-of

מְבַקְשֵׁי נַפְשָׁם וְהִכָּם לְפִי־ חֶרֶב לֹא־
not sword to-edge-of and-he-will-put-them life-of-them ones-seeking-of

יָחוּס עֲלֵיהֶם וְלֹא יַחְמֹל וְלֹא יְרַחֵם׃
he-will-show-compassion or-not he-will-show-pity or-not to-them he-will-show-mercy

(8) וְאֶל־ הָעָם הַזֶּה תֹּאמַר כֹּה אָמַר יְהוָה הִנְנִי
see-I! Yahweh he-says this you-tell the-this the-people furthermore-to (8)

נֹתֵן לִפְנֵיכֶם אֶת־ דֶּרֶךְ הַחַיִּים וְאֶת־ דֶּרֶךְ הַמָּוֶת׃ (9) הַיֹּשֵׁב
the-one-staying (9) the-death way-of and the-lives way-of *** before-you setting

בָּעִיר הַזֹּאת יָמוּת בַּחֶרֶב וּבָרָעָב וּבַדָּבֶר
or-by-the-plague or-by-the-famine by-the-sword he-will-die the-this in-the-city

וְהַיּוֹצֵא וְנָפַל עַל־ הַכַּשְׂדִּים הַצָּרִים
the-ones-besieging the-Chaldeans to and-he-surrenders but-the-one-going-out

עֲלֵיכֶם יִחְיֶה° וְהָיְתָה־ לוֹ נַפְשׁוֹ לְשָׁלָל׃
as-plunder life-of-him to-him and-she-will-be then-he-will-live against-you

(10) כִּי שַׂמְתִּי פָנַי בָּעִיר הַזֹּאת לְרָעָה וְלֹא לְטוֹבָה
for-good and-not for-harm the-this against-the-city faces-of-me I-set indeed (10)

נְאֻם־ יְהוָה בְּיַד־ מֶלֶךְ בָּבֶל תִּנָּתֵן
she-will-be-given Babylon king-of into-hand-of Yahweh declaration-of

וּשְׂרָפָהּ בָּאֵשׁ׃ (11) וּלְבֵית מֶלֶךְ יְהוּדָה שִׁמְעוּ
hear! Judah royalty-of moreover-to-house-of (11) with-fire and-he-will-destroy-her

דְּבַר־ יְהוָה׃ (12) בֵּית דָּוִד כֹּה אָמַר יְהוָה דִּינוּ לַבֹּקֶר
in-the-morning administer! Yahweh he-says this David house-of (12) Yahweh word-of

מִשְׁפָּט וְהַצִּילוּ גָזוּל מִיַּד עוֹשֵׁק פֶּן־
or one-oppressing from-hand-of one-being-robbed and-rescue! justice

תֵּצֵא כָאֵשׁ חֲמָתִי וּבָעֲרָה וְאֵין מְכַבֶּה
one-quenching and-no and-she-will-burn wrath-of-me like-fire she-will-break-out

מִפְּנֵי רֹעַ מַעַלְלֵיהֶם° ׃ (13) הִנְנִי אֵלַיִךְ יֹשֶׁבֶת הָעֵמֶק
the-valley one-living-of against-you see-I! (13) deeds-of-you evil-of because-of

צוּר הַמִּישֹׁר נְאֻם־ יְהוָה הָאֹמְרִים מִי־ יֵחַת
he-can-come who? the-ones-saying Yahweh declaration-of the-plateau rock-of

עָלֵינוּ וּמִי יָבוֹא בִּמְעוֹנוֹתֵינוּ׃ (14) וּפָקַדְתִּי
and-I-will-punish (14) into-refuges-of-us he-can-enter and-who? against-us

עֲלֵיכֶם כִּפְרִי מַעַלְלֵיכֶם נְאֻם־ יְהוָה וְהִצַּתִּי אֵשׁ
fire and-I-will-kindle Yahweh declaration-of deeds-of-you as-desert-of to-you

who survive the plague, sword and famine, to Nebuchadnezzar king of Babylon and to their enemies who seek their lives. He will put them to the sword; he will show them no mercy or pity or compassion.'

[8]"Furthermore, tell the people, 'This is what the LORD says: See, I am setting before you the way of life and the way of death. [9]Whoever stays in this city will die by the sword, famine or plague. But whoever goes out and surrenders to the Babylonians who are besieging you will live; he will escape with his life. [10]I have determined to do this city harm and not good, declares the LORD. It will be given into the hands of the king of Babylon, and he will destroy it with fire.'

[11]"Moreover, say to the royal house of Judah, 'Hear the word of the LORD; [12]O house of David, this is what the LORD says:

" 'Administer justice every morning;
rescue from the hand of his oppressor
the one who has been robbed,
or my wrath will break out and burn like fire
because of the evil you have done—
burn with no one to quench it.
[13]I am against you, Jerusalem,
you who live above this valley
on the rocky plateau,
declares the LORD—
you who say, "Who can come against us?
Who can enter our refuge?"
[14]I will punish you as your deeds deserve,
declares the LORD.
I will kindle a fire in your

°9 ק וחיה
°12 ק מעלליכם

בְּיַעְרָהּ וְאָכְלָה כָּל־ סְבִיבֶיהָ׃ כֹּה אָמַר
he-says this (22:1) ones-around-her all-of and-she-will-consume in-forest-of-her

יְהוָה רֵד בֵּית־ מֶלֶךְ יְהוּדָה וְדִבַּרְתָּ שָּׁם אֶת־ הַדָּבָר
the-message *** there and-you-proclaim Judah king-of palace-of go-down! Yahweh

הַזֶּה׃ וְאָמַרְתָּ שְׁמַע דְּבַר־ יְהוָה מֶלֶךְ יְהוּדָה הַיֹּשֵׁב עַל־
on the-one-sitting Judah king-of Yahweh word-of hear! and-you-say (2) the-this

כִּסֵּא דָוִד אַתָּה וַעֲבָדֶיךָ וְעַמְּךָ הַבָּאִים
the-ones-coming and-people-of-you and-officials-of-you you David throne-of

בַּשְּׁעָרִים הָאֵלֶּה׃ כֹּה ׀ אָמַר יְהוָה עֲשׂוּ מִשְׁפָּט וּצְדָקָה
and-right justice do! Yahweh he-says this (3) the-these through-the-gates

וְהַצִּילוּ גָזוּל מִיַּד עָשׁוֹק וְגֵר יָתוֹם וְאַלְמָנָה
or-widow fatherless and-alien oppressor from-hand-of one-being-robbed and-rescue!

אַל־ תֹּנוּ אַל־ תַּחְמֹסוּ וְדָם נָקִי אַל־ תִּשְׁפְּכוּ בַּמָּקוֹם
in-the-place you-shed not innocent and-blood you-do-violence not you-wrong not

הַזֶּה׃ כִּי אִם־ עָשׂוֹ תַּעֲשׂוּ אֶת־ הַדָּבָר הַזֶּה
the-this the-command *** you-carry-out to-carry-out if for (4) the-this

וּבָאוּ בְשַׁעֲרֵי הַבַּיִת הַזֶּה מְלָכִים יֹשְׁבִים
ones-sitting kings the-this the-palace through-gates-of then-they-will-come

לְדָוִד עַל־ כִּסְאוֹ רֹכְבִים בָּרֶכֶב וּבַסּוּסִים הוּא
he and-on-the-horses in-the-chariot ones-riding throne-of-him on of-David

וַעֲבָדָו וְעַמּוֹ׃ וְאִם לֹא תִשְׁמְעוּ אֶת־ הַדְּבָרִים
the-commands *** you-obey not but-if (5) and-people-of-him and-officials-of-him

הָאֵלֶּה בִּי נִשְׁבַּעְתִּי נְאֻם־ יְהוָה כִּי־ לְחָרְבָּה יִהְיֶה
he-will-become as-ruin that Yahweh declaration-of I-swear by-myself the-these

הַבַּיִת הַזֶּה׃ כִּי־ כֹה ׀ אָמַר יְהוָה עַל־ בֵּית מֶלֶךְ יְהוּדָה
Judah king-of palace-of about Yahweh he-says this for (6) the-this the-palace

גִּלְעָד אַתָּה לִי רֹאשׁ הַלְּבָנוֹן אִם־ לֹא אֲשִׁיתְךָ מִדְבָּר עָרִים
towns desert I-will-make-you surely indeed the-Lebanon summit-of to-me you Gilead

לֹא נוֹשָׁבָה׃ וְקִדַּשְׁתִּי עָלֶיךָ מַשְׁחִתִים אִישׁ
man ones-destroying against-you and-I-will-send (7) they-are-inhabited not

וְכֵלָיו וְכָרְתוּ מִבְחַר אֲרָזֶיךָ
cedar-beams-of-you finest-of and-they-will-cut-up with-weapons-of-him

וְהִפִּילוּ עַל־ הָאֵשׁ׃ וְעָבְרוּ גּוֹיִם רַבִּים עַל
by many-ones nations and-they-will-pass (8) the-fire into and-they-will-throw

הָעִיר הַזֹּאת וְאָמְרוּ אִישׁ אֶל־ רֵעֵהוּ עַל־ מֶה עָשָׂה יְהוָה
Yahweh he-did why? for another-of-him to each and-they-will-ask the-this the-city

כָּכָה לָעִיר הַגְּדוֹלָה הַזֹּאת׃ וְאָמְרוּ עַל אֲשֶׁר
that because and-they-will-answer (9) the-this the-great to-the-city such

forests
that will consume
everything around you.' "

*Judgment Against Evil Kings*

22 This is what the LORD says:
"Go down to the palace of
the king of Judah and proclaim
this message there: 2 "Hear the
word of the LORD, O king of Judah,
you who sit on David's throne—
you, your officials and your
people who come through these
gates. 3 This is what the LORD says:
Do what is just and right. Rescue
from the hand of his oppressor the
one who has been robbed. Do no
wrong or violence to the alien, the
fatherless or the widow, and do
not shed innocent blood in this
place. 4 For if you are careful to carry out these commands, then
kings who sit on David's throne
will come through the gates of this
palace, riding in chariots and on
horses, accompanied by their officials and their people. 5 But if you
do not obey these commands, declares the LORD, I swear by myself
that this palace will become a
ruin.' "
6 For this is what the LORD says
about the palace of the king of
Judah:

"Though you are like Gilead to
me,
like the summit of Lebanon,
I will surely make you like a
desert,
like towns not inhabited.
7 I will send destroyers against
you,
each man with his weapons,
and they will cut up your fine
cedar beams
and throw them into the
fire.

8 "People from many nations
will pass by this city and will ask
one another, 'Why has the LORD
done such a thing to this great
city?' 9 And the answer will be: 'Because they have forsaken the covenant of the LORD their God and

°4 ק ועבדיו
°6 ק נושבו

עָזְבוּ אֶת־ בְּרִית יְהוָה אֱלֹהֵיהֶם וַיִּשְׁתַּחֲווּ לֵאלֹהִים
to-gods and-they-worshiped God-of-them Yahweh covenant-of *** they-forsook

אֲחֵרִים וַיַּעַבְדוּם׃ אַל־ תִּבְכּוּ לְמֵת וְאַל־
or-not for-one-being-dead you-weep not (10) and-they-served-them other-ones

תָּנֻדוּ לוֹ בְּכוּ בָכוֹ לַהֹלֵךְ כִּי לֹא
never because for-the-one-being-exiled to-weep weep! for-him you-mourn

יָשׁוּב עוֹד וְרָאָה אֶת־ אֶרֶץ מוֹלַדְתּוֹ׃ כִּי כֹה
this for (11) native-one-of-him land-of *** or-he-will-see again he-will-return

אָמַר־ יְהוָה אֶל־ שַׁלֻּם בֶּן־ יֹאשִׁיָּהוּ מֶלֶךְ יְהוּדָה הַמֹּלֵךְ
the-one-becoming-king Judah king-of Josiah son-of Shallum about Yahweh he-says

תַּחַת יֹאשִׁיָּהוּ אָבִיו אֲשֶׁר יָצָא מִן־ הַמָּקוֹם הַזֶּה לֹא־
never the-this the-place from he-went who father-of-him Josiah in-place-of

יָשׁוּב שָׁם עוֹד׃ כִּי בִּמְקוֹם אֲשֶׁר־ הִגְלוּ אֹתוֹ שָׁם
there him they-led-captive where in-place-of but (12) again there he-will-return

יָמוּת וְאֶת־ הָאָרֶץ הַזֹּאת לֹא־ יִרְאֶה עוֹד׃ הוֹי בֹּנֶה
one-building woe! (13) again he-will-see not the-this the-land and he-will-die

בֵיתוֹ בְּלֹא־ צֶדֶק וַעֲלִיּוֹתָיו בְּלֹא מִשְׁפָּט
justice by-not and-upper-rooms-of-him righteous by-not palace-of-him

בְּרֵעֵהוּ יַעֲבֹד חִנָּם וּפֹעֲלוֹ לֹא יִתֶּן־ לוֹ׃
to-him he-pays not and-labor-of-him for-nothing he-works with-countryman-of-him

הָאֹמֵר אֶבְנֶה־ לִּי בֵּית מִדּוֹת וַעֲלִיּוֹת
and-upper-rooms greatnesses palace-of for-myself I-will-build the-one-saying (14)

מְרֻוָּחִים וְקָרַע לוֹ חַלּוֹנָי וְסָפוּן
and-being-panelled windows for-him and-he-makes-large ones-being-spacious

בָּאָרֶז וּמָשׁוֹחַ בַּשָּׁשַׁר׃ הֲתִמְלֹךְ כִּי אַתָּה
you because are-you-king? (15) with-the-red and-to-decorate with-the-cedar

מְתַחֲרֶה בָאָרֶז אָבִיךָ הֲלוֹא אָכַל וְשָׁתָה וְעָשָׂה מִשְׁפָּט
justice and-he-did and-he-drank he-ate not? father-of-you of-the-cedar having-much

וּצְדָקָה אָז טוֹב לוֹ׃ דָּן דִּין־ עָנִי וְאֶבְיוֹן אָז טוֹב הֲלוֹא־
not? well so and-needy poor cause-of he-defended (16) to-him well so and-right

הִיא הַדַּעַת אֹתִי נְאֻם־ יְהוָה׃ כִּי אֵין עֵינֶיךָ
eyes-of-you not but (17) Yahweh declaration-of of-me the-knowledge that

וְלִבְּךָ כִּי אִם־ עַל־ בִּצְעֶךָ וְעַל דַּם־ הַנָּקִי
the-innocent blood-of and-on dishonest-gain-of-you on only but and-heart-of-you

לִשְׁפּוֹךְ וְעַל־ הָעֹשֶׁק וְעַל־ הַמְּרוּצָה לַעֲשׂוֹת׃ לָכֵן כֹּה־
this therefore (18) to-do the-extortion and-on the-oppression and-on to-shed

אָמַר יְהוָה אֶל־ יְהוֹיָקִים בֶּן־ יֹאשִׁיָּהוּ מֶלֶךְ יְהוּדָה לֹא־ יִסְפְּדוּ
they-will-mourn not Judah king-of Josiah son-of Jehoiakim about Yahweh he-says

have worshiped and served other gods.' "

10 Do not weep for the dead ⌞king⌟ or mourn his loss;
rather, weep bitterly for him who is exiled,
because he will never return
nor see his native land again.

11 For this is what the LORD says about Shallum[k] son of Josiah, who succeeded his father as king of Judah but has gone from this place: "He will never return.
12 He will die in the place where they have led him captive; he will not see this land again."

13 "Woe to him who builds his palace by unrighteousness,
his upper rooms by injustice,
making his countrymen work for nothing,
not paying them for their labor.
14 He says, 'I will build myself a great palace
with spacious upper rooms.'
So he makes large windows in it,
panels it with cedar
and decorates it in red.

15 "Does it make you a king
to have more and more cedar?
Did not your father have food and drink?
He did what was right and just,
so all went well with him.
16 He defended the cause of the poor and needy,
and so all went well.
Is that not what it means to know me?"
declares the LORD.
17 "But your eyes and your heart
are set only on dishonest gain,
on shedding innocent blood
and on oppression and extortion."

18 Therefore this is what the LORD says about Jehoiakim son of Josiah king of Judah:

"They will not mourn for him:

k 11 Also called *Jehoahaz*

לוֹ הוֹי אָחִי וְהוֹי אָחוֹת לֹא־ יִסְפְּדוּ לוֹ הוֹי
for-him alas! brother-of-me and-alas! sister not they-will-mourn for-him alas!

אָדוֹן וְהוֹי הֹדֹה׃ (19) קְבוּרַת חֲמוֹר יִקָּבֵר סָחוֹב
master and-alas! splendor-of-him (19) burial-of donkey he-will-be-buried to-drag

וְהַשְׁלֵךְ מֵהָלְאָה לְשַׁעֲרֵי יְרוּשָׁלִָם׃ (20) עֲלִי הַלְּבָנוֹן וּצְעָקִי
and-to-throw to-outside of-gates-of Jerusalem (20) go-up! the-Lebanon and-cry-out!

וּבַבָּשָׁן תְּנִי קוֹלֵךְ וְצַעֲקִי מֵעֲבָרִים כִּי נִשְׁבְּרוּ
and-in-the-Bashan raise! voice-of-you and-cry-out! from-Abarim for they-are-crushed

כָּל־ מְאַהֲבָיִךְ׃ (21) דִּבַּרְתִּי אֵלַיִךְ בְּשַׁלְוֹתַיִךְ אָמַרְתְּ
all-of ones-being-allies-of-you (21) I-warned to-you in-securities-of-you you-said

לֹא אֶשְׁמָע זֶה דַרְכֵּךְ מִנְּעוּרַיִךְ כִּי לֹא־ שָׁמַעַתְּ
not I-will-listen this way-of-you from-youths-of-you indeed not you-obeyed

בְּקוֹלִי׃ (22) כָּל־ רֹעַיִךְ תִּרְעֶה־ רוּחַ
to-voice-of-me (22) all-of ones-being-shepherds-of-you she-will-drive-away wind

וּמְאַהֲבַיִךְ בַּשְּׁבִי יֵלֵכוּ כִּי אָז
and-ones-being-allies-of-you into-the-exile they-will-go indeed then

תֵּבֹשִׁי וְנִכְלַמְתְּ מִכֹּל רָעָתֵךְ׃
you-will-be-ashamed and-you-will-be-disgraced because-of-all-of wickedness-of-you

(23) יֹשַׁבְתְּ° בַּלְּבָנוֹן מְקֻנַּנְתְּ° בָּאֲרָזִים מַה־
(23) one-living in-the-Lebanon one-being-nestled in-the-cedars how!

נֵּחַנְתְּ* בְּבֹא־ לָךְ חֲבָלִים חִיל כַּיֹּלֵדָה׃
you-will-groan when-to-come upon-you pangs pain like-the-woman-being-in-labor

(24) חַי־ אָנִי נְאֻם־ יְהוָה כִּי אִם־ יִהְיֶה כָּנְיָהוּ בֶּן־ יְהוֹיָקִים
(24) alive I declaration-of Yahweh even if he-were Coniah son-of Jehoiakim

מֶלֶךְ יְהוּדָה חוֹתָם עַל־ יַד יְמִינִי כִּי מִשָּׁם
king-of Judah signet-ring on hand-of right-of-me indeed from-there

אֶתְּקֶנְךָּ׃ (25) וּנְתַתִּיךָ בְּיַד מְבַקְשֵׁי
I-would-pull-off-you (25) and-I-will-give-you into-hand-of ones-seeking-of

נַפְשֶׁךָ וּבְיַד אֲשֶׁר־ אַתָּה יָגוֹר מִפְּנֵיהֶם וּבְיַד
life-of-you and-into-hand-of whom you fearing because-of-them and-into-hand-of

נְבוּכַדְרֶאצַּר מֶלֶךְ־ בָּבֶל וּבְיַד הַכַּשְׂדִּים׃ (26) וְהֵטַלְתִּי
Nebuchadrezzar king-of Babylon and-into-hand-of the-Chaldeans (26) and-I-will-hurl

אֹתְךָ וְאֶת־ אִמְּךָ אֲשֶׁר יְלָדַתְךָ עַל הָאָרֶץ אַחֶרֶת אֲשֶׁר לֹא־
you and mother-of-you who she-bore-you into the-country another where not

יֻלַּדְתֶּם שָׁם וְשָׁם תָּמוּתוּ׃ (27) וְעַל־ הָאָרֶץ אֲשֶׁר־ הֵם
you-were-born there and-there you-will-die (27) and-to the-land where they

מְנַשְּׂאִים אֶת־ נַפְשָׁם לָשׁוּב שָׁם שָׁמָּה לֹא יָשׁוּבוּ׃
ones-longing *** self-of-them to-return there to-there never you-will-return

'Alas, my brother! Alas, my sister!'
They will not mourn for him:
'Alas, my master! Alas, his splendor!'
19 He will have the burial of a donkey—
dragged away and thrown
outside the gates of Jerusalem."

20 "Go up to Lebanon and cry out,
let your voice be heard in Bashan,
cry out from Abarim,
for all your allies are crushed.
21 I warned you when you felt secure,
but you said, 'I will not listen!'
This has been your way from your youth;
you have not obeyed me.
22 The wind will drive all your shepherds away,
and your allies will go into exile.
Then you will be ashamed and disgraced
because of all your wickedness.
23 You who live in 'Lebanon,'[l]
who are nestled in cedar buildings,
how you will groan when pangs come upon you,
pain like that of a woman in labor!

24 "As surely as I live," declares the LORD, "even if you, Jehoiachin[m] son of Jehoiakim king of Judah, were a signet ring on my right hand, I would still pull you off. 25 I will hand you over to those who seek your life, those you fear—to Nebuchadnezzar king of Babylon and to the Babylonians.[n] 26 I will hurl you and the mother who gave you birth into another country, where neither of you was born, and there you both will die. 27 You will never come back to the land you long to return to."

[l] 23 That is, the palace in Jerusalem (see 1 Kings 7:2)
[m] 24 Hebrew *Coniah*, a variant of *Jehoiachin*; also in verse 28
[n] 25 Or *Chaldeans*

*23 Most mss duplicate the accent *pashta* over the penultimate syllable (נֵחַנְתְּ).

°18 ק הדו
°23a ק ישבת
°23b ק מקננת

הַעֶ֫צֶב נִבְזֶה נָפוּץ הָאִישׁ הַזֶּה כָּנְיָהוּ אִם־כְּלִי אֵין
there-is-no object or Coniah the-this the-man being-broken being-despised pot? (28)

חֵפֶץ בּוֹ מַדּוּעַ הוּטְלוּ הוּא וְזַרְעוֹ וְהֻשְׁלְכוּ
and-they-will-be-cast and-child-of-him he will-they-be-hurled why? for-him wanting

עַל־הָאָרֶץ אֲשֶׁר לֹא־יָדָעוּ׃ אֶרֶץ אֶרֶץ אָרֶץ שִׁמְעִי דְּבַר־יְהוָה׃ כֹּה ׀
this (30) Yahweh word-of hear! land land land (29) they-know not that the-land into

אָמַר יְהוָה כִּתְבוּ אֶת־הָאִישׁ הַזֶּה עֲרִירִי גֶּבֶר לֹא־יִצְלַח
he-will-prosper not man childless the-this the-man *** record! Yahweh he-says

בְּיָמָיו כִּי לֹא יִצְלַח מִזַּרְעוֹ אִישׁ יֹשֵׁב עַל־
on sitting one from-offspring-of-him he-will-prosper not for in-days-of-him

כִּסֵּא דָוִד וּמֹשֵׁל עוֹד בִּיהוּדָה׃ הוֹי רֹעִים
ones-being-shepherds woe! (23:1) in-Judah anymore or-ruling David throne-of

מְאַבְּדִים וּמְפִצִים אֶת־צֹאן מַרְעִיתִי נְאֻם־
declaration-of pasture-of-me sheep-of *** and-ones-scattering ones-destroying

יְהוָה׃ לָכֵן כֹּה־אָמַר יְהוָה אֱלֹהֵי יִשְׂרָאֵל עַל־הָרֹעִים
the-ones-being-shepherds to Israel God-of Yahweh he-says this therefore (2) Yahweh

הָרֹעִים אֶת־עַמִּי אַתֶּם הֲפִצֹתֶם אֶת־צֹאנִי
flock-of-me *** you-scattered you people-of-me *** the-ones-shepherding

וַתַּדִּחוּם וְלֹא פְקַדְתֶּם אֹתָם הִנְנִי פֹקֵד עֲלֵיכֶם אֶת־
*** on-you punishing see-I! them you-cared-for and-not and-you-drove-away-them

רֹעַ מַעַלְלֵיכֶם נְאֻם־יְהוָה׃ וַאֲנִי אֲקַבֵּץ אֶת־שְׁאֵרִית
remnant-of *** I-will-gather so-I (3) Yahweh declaration-of deeds-of-you evil-of

צֹאנִי מִכֹּל הָאֲרָצוֹת אֲשֶׁר־הִדַּחְתִּי אֹתָם שָׁם וַהֲשִׁבֹתִי
and-I-will-bring-back there them I-drove where the-countries from-all-of flock-of-me

אֶתְהֶן עַל־נְוֵהֶן וּפָרוּ וְרָבוּ׃
and-they-will-increase and-they-will-be-fruitful pasture-of-them to them

וַהֲקִמֹתִי עֲלֵיהֶם רֹעִים וְרָעוּם
and-they-will-shepherd-them ones-being-shepherds over-them and-I-will-place (4)

וְלֹא־יִירְאוּ עוֹד וְלֹא־יֵחַתּוּ וְלֹא
or-not they-will-be-terrified or-not longer they-will-be-afraid and-not

יִפָּקֵדוּ נְאֻם־יְהוָה׃ הִנֵּה יָמִים בָּאִים נְאֻם־
declaration-of ones-coming days see! (5) Yahweh declaration-of they-will-be-missing

יְהוָה וַהֲקִמֹתִי לְדָוִד צֶמַח צַדִּיק וּמָלַךְ מֶלֶךְ
King and-he-will-reign righteous Branch to-David when-I-will-raise-up Yahweh

וְהִשְׂכִּיל וְעָשָׂה מִשְׁפָּט וּצְדָקָה בָּאָרֶץ׃ בְּיָמָיו
in-days-of-him (6) in-the-land and-right justice and-he-will-do and-he-will-be-wise

תִּוָּשַׁע יְהוּדָה וְיִשְׂרָאֵל יִשְׁכֹּן לָבֶטַח וְזֶה־שְּׁמוֹ
name-of-him and-this in-safety he-will-live and-Israel Judah she-will-be-saved

[28]Is this man Jehoiachin a
despised, broken pot,
an object no one wants?
Why will he and his children
be hurled out,
cast into a land they do not
know?
[29]O land, land, land,
hear the word of the LORD!
[30]This is what the LORD says:
"Record this man as if
childless,
a man who will not prosper
in his lifetime,
for none of his offspring will
prosper,
none will sit on the throne
of David
or rule anymore in Judah."

*The Righteous Branch*

23 "Woe to the shepherds who are destroying and scattering the sheep of my pasture!" declares the LORD. [2]Therefore this is what the LORD, the God of Israel, says to the shepherds who tend my people: "Because you have scattered my flock and driven them away and have not bestowed care on them, I will bestow punishment on you for the evil you have done," declares the LORD. [3]"I myself will gather the remnant of my flock out of all the countries where I have driven them and will bring them back to their pasture, where they will be fruitful and increase in number. [4]I will place shepherds over them who will tend them, and they will no longer be afraid or terrified, nor will any be missing," declares the LORD.

[5]"The days are coming,"
declares the LORD,
"when I will raise up to
David[e] a righteous
Branch,
a King who will reign wisely
and do what is just and
right in the land.
[6]In his days Judah will be
saved
and Israel will live in safety.
This is the name by which he

[e]5 *Or up from David's line*

אֲשֶׁר־ יִקְרְאוֹ יְהוָה׀ צִדְקֵנוּ׃ לָכֵן הִנֵּה־יָמִים בָּאִים
ones-coming days see! so (7) Righteousness-of-Us Yahweh he-will-call-him that

נְאֻם־ יְהוָה וְלֹא־ יֹאמְרוּ עוֹד חַי־ יְהוָה אֲשֶׁר הֶעֱלָה
he-brought-up who Yahweh alive longer they-will-say when-not Yahweh declaration-of

אֶת־בְּנֵי יִשְׂרָאֵל מֵאֶרֶץ מִצְרָיִם׃ כִּי אִם־ חַי־ יְהוָה אֲשֶׁר הֶעֱלָה
he-brought-up who Yahweh alive rather but (8) Egypt from-land-of Israel sons-of ***

וַאֲשֶׁר הֵבִיא אֶת־ זֶרַע בֵּית יִשְׂרָאֵל מֵאֶרֶץ צָפוֹנָה
at-north from-land-of Israel house-of descendant-of *** he-brought-back and-who

וּמִכֹּל הָאֲרָצוֹת אֲשֶׁר הִדַּחְתִּים שָׁם וְיָשְׁבוּ עַל־
in then-they-will-live there he-banished-them where the-countries and-from-all-of

אַדְמָתָם׃ לַנְּבִאִים נִשְׁבַּר לִבִּי בְקִרְבִּי
at-within-me heart-of-me he-is-broken concerning-the-prophets (9) land-of-them

רָחֲפוּ כָּל־ עַצְמוֹתַי הָיִיתִי כְּאִישׁ שִׁכּוֹר וּכְגֶבֶר עֲבָרוֹ
he-overcame-him and-like-man drunken like-man I-am bones-of-me all-of they-tremble

יָיִן מִפְּנֵי יְהוָה וּמִפְּנֵי דִּבְרֵי קָדְשׁוֹ׃ כִּי
indeed (10) holiness-of-him words-of and-because-of Yahweh because-of wine

מְנָאֲפִים מָלְאָה הָאָרֶץ כִּי־ מִפְּנֵי אָלָה אָבְלָה
she-is-parched curse because-of indeed the-land she-is-full ones-committing-adultery

הָאָרֶץ יָבְשׁוּ נְאוֹת מִדְבָּר וַתְּהִי מְרוּצָתָם רָעָה
evil course-of-them and-she-is desert pastures-of they-are-withered the-land

וּגְבוּרָתָם לֹא־כֵן׃ כִּי־ גַם־ נָבִיא גַם־ כֹּהֵן חָנֵפוּ
they-are-godless priest and prophet both indeed (11) just not and-power-of-them

גַּם־ בְּבֵיתִי מָצָאתִי רָעָתָם נְאֻם־ יְהוָה׃ לָכֵן
therefore (12) Yahweh declaration-of wickedness-of-them I-find in-temple-of-me even

יִהְיֶה דַרְכָּם לָהֶם כַּחֲלַקְלַקּוֹת בָּאֲפֵלָה
to-the-darkness as-slippery-ones to-them path-of-them he-will-become

יִדַּחוּ וְנָפְלוּ בָהּ כִּי־ אָבִיא עֲלֵיהֶם
on-them I-will-bring indeed in-her and-they-will-fall they-will-be-banished

רָעָה שְׁנַת פְּקֻדָּתָם נְאֻם־ יְהוָה׃ וּבִנְבִיאֵי
and-among-prophets-of (13) Yahweh declaration-of punishment-of-them year-of disaster

שֹׁמְרוֹן רָאִיתִי תִפְלָה הִנַּבְּאוּ בַבַּעַל וַיַּתְעוּ אֶת־
*** and-they-led-astray by-the-Baal they-prophesied repulsive-thing I-saw Samaria

עַמִּי אֶת־יִשְׂרָאֵל׃ וּבִנְבִאֵי יְרוּשָׁלִַם רָאִיתִי שַׁעֲרוּרָה
horrible-thing I-saw Jerusalem and-among-prophets-of (14) Israel *** people-of-me

נָאוֹף וְהָלֹךְ בַּשֶּׁקֶר וְחִזְּקוּ יְדֵי
hands-of and-they-strengthen by-the-lie and-to-live to-commit-adultery

מְרֵעִים לְבִלְתִּי־שָׁבוּ אִישׁ מֵרָעָתוֹ הָיוּ־ לִי כֻלָּם
all-of-them to-me they-are from-wickedness-of-him one they-turn not ones-doing-evil

will be called:
The LORD Our
Righteousness.

7 "So then, the days are coming," declares the LORD, "when people will no longer say, 'As surely as the LORD lives, who brought the Israelites up out of Egypt,' 8 but they will say, 'As surely as the LORD lives, who brought the descendants of Israel up out of the land of the north and out of all the countries where he had banished them.' Then they will live in their own land."

*Lying Prophets*

9 Concerning the prophets:

My heart is broken within me;
all my bones tremble.
I am like a drunken man,
like a man overcome by wine,
because of the LORD
and his holy words.
10 The land is full of adulterers;
because of the curse[p] the land lies parched[q]
and the pastures in the desert are withered.
The ⌊prophets⌋ follow an evil course
and use their power unjustly.

11 "Both prophet and priest are godless;
even in my temple I find their wickedness,"
declares the LORD.
12 "Therefore their path will become slippery;
they will be banished to darkness
and there they will fall.
I will bring disaster on them
in the year they are punished,"
declares the LORD.

13 "Among the prophets of Samaria
I saw this repulsive thing:
They prophesied by Baal
and led my people Israel astray.
14 And among the prophets of Jerusalem
I have seen something horrible:
They commit adultery and live a lie.
They strengthen the hands of evildoers,
so that no one turns from his wickedness.

[p] 10 Or *because of these things*
[q] 10 Or *land mours*

כִּסְדֹם וְיֹשְׁבֶיהָ כַּעֲמֹרָה׃ לָכֵן כֹּה־ אָמַר
he-says this therefore (15) like-Gomorrah and-ones-being-people-of-her like-Sodom

יְהוָה צְבָאוֹת עַל־ הַנְּבִאִים הִנְנִי מַאֲכִיל אוֹתָם לַעֲנָה
bitter-food them making-eat see-I! the-prophets concerning Hosts Yahweh-of

וְהִשְׁקִתִים מֵי־ רֹאשׁ כִּי מֵאֵת נְבִיאֵי יְרוּשָׁלִַם
Jerusalem prophets-of from-with because poison waters-of and-I-will-make-drink-them

יָצְאָה חֲנֻפָּה לְכָל־ הָאָרֶץ׃ כֹּה־ אָמַר יְהוָה צְבָאוֹת
Hosts Yahweh-of he-says this (16) the-land through-all-of ungodliness she-spread

אַל־ תִּשְׁמְעוּ עַל־ דִּבְרֵי הַנְּבִאִים הַנִּבְּאִים לָכֶם
to-you the-ones-prophesying the-prophets words-of to you-listen not

מַהְבִּלִים הֵמָּה אֶתְכֶם חֲזוֹן לִבָּם יְדַבֵּרוּ לֹא
not they-speak mind-of-them vision-of you they ones-giving-false-hopes

מִפִּי יְהוָה׃ אֹמְרִים אָמוֹר לִמְנַאֲצַי דִּבֶּר יְהוָה
Yahweh he-says to-ones-despising-me to-say ones-saying (17) Yahweh from-mouth-of

שָׁלוֹם יִהְיֶה לָכֶם וְכֹל הֹלֵךְ בִּשְׁרִרוּת לִבּוֹ
heart-of-him to-stubbornness-of one-following and-all-of to-you he-will-be peace

אָמְרוּ לֹא־ תָבוֹא עֲלֵיכֶם רָעָה׃ כִּי מִי עָמַד בְּסוֹד יְהוָה
Yahweh in-council-of he-stood who? but (18) harm to-you she-will-come not they-say

וְיֵרֶא וְיִשְׁמַע אֶת־ דְּבָרוֹ מִי־ הִקְשִׁיב דְּבָרִי וַיִּשְׁמָע׃
and-he-heard word-of-him he-listened who? word-of-him *** and-he-heard and-he-saw

הִנֵּה ׀ סַעֲרַת יְהוָה חֵמָה יָצְאָה וְסַעַר מִתְחוֹלֵל עַל
on swirling-down and-whirlwind she-will-burst-out wrath Yahweh storm-of see! (19)

רֹאשׁ רְשָׁעִים יָחוּל׃ לֹא יָשׁוּב אַף־ יְהוָה
Yahweh anger-of he-will-turn-back not (20) he-swirls-down wicked-ones head-of

עַד־ עֲשֹׂתוֹ וְעַד־ הֲקִימוֹ מְזִמּוֹת לִבּוֹ
heart-of-him purposes-of to-complete-him and-until to-accomplish-him until

בְּאַחֲרִית הַיָּמִים תִּתְבּוֹנְנוּ בָהּ בִּינָה׃ לֹא־שָׁלַחְתִּי אֶת־
*** I-sent not (21) understanding to-her you-will-understand the-days in-coming-of

הַנְּבִאִים וְהֵם רָצוּ לֹא־ דִבַּרְתִּי אֲלֵיהֶם וְהֵם נִבָּאוּ׃
they-prophesied yet-they to-them I-spoke not they-ran yet-they the-prophets

וְאִם־ עָמְדוּ בְּסוֹדִי וְיַשְׁמִעוּ דְבָרַי
words-of-me then-they-would-have-proclaimed in-council-of-me they-stood but-if (22)

אֶת־ עַמִּי וִישִׁבוּם מִדַּרְכָּם הָרָע
the-evil from-way-of-them and-they-would-have-turned-them people-of-me ***

וּמֵרֹעַ מַעַלְלֵיהֶם׃ הַאֱלֹהֵי מִקָּרֹב אָנִי נְאֻם־ יְהוָה וְלֹא
and-not Yahweh declaration-of I at-nearby God-of? (23) deeds-of-them and-from-evil-of

אֱלֹהֵי מֵרָחֹק׃ אִם־ יִסָּתֵר אִישׁ בַּמִּסְתָּרִים וַאֲנִי לֹא־
not so-I in-the-secret-places anyone can-he-hide or (24) at-far-away God-of

They are all like Sodom to me;
the people of Jerusalem are like Gomorrah."

[15]Therefore, this is what the LORD Almighty says concerning the prophets:

"I will make them eat bitter food
and drink poisoned water,
because from the prophets of Jerusalem
ungodliness has spread throughout the land."

[16]This is what the LORD Almighty says:

"Do not listen to what the prophets are prophesying to you;
they fill you with false hopes.
They speak visions from their own minds,
not from the mouth of the LORD.
[17]They keep saying to those who despise me,
'The LORD says: You will have peace.'
And to all who follow the stubbornness of their hearts
they say, 'No harm will come to you.'
[18]But which of them has stood in the council of the LORD
to see or to hear his word?
Who has listened and heard his word?
[19]See, the storm of the LORD will burst out in wrath,
a whirlwind swirling down on the heads of the wicked.
[20]The anger of the LORD will not turn back
until he fully accomplishes the purposes of his heart.
In days to come
you will understand it clearly.
[21]I did not send these prophets,
yet they have run with their message;
I did not speak to them,
yet they have prophesied.
[22]But if they had stood in my council,
they would have proclaimed my words to my people
and would have turned them from their evil ways
and from their evil deeds.

[23]"Am I only a God nearby,"
declares the LORD,
"and not a God far away?
[24]Can anyone hide in secret places

°18 ק דברו

אֶרְאֶנּוּ נְאֻם־ יְהוָה הֲלוֹא אֶת־ הַשָּׁמַיִם וְאֶת־ הָאָרֶץ אֲנִי מָלֵא
filling I the-earth and the-heavens *** not? Yahweh declaration-of I-can-see-him

נְאֻם־ יְהוָה׃ (25) שָׁמַעְתִּי אֵת אֲשֶׁר־אָמְרוּ הַנְּבִאִים הַנִּבְּאִים
the-ones-prophesying the-prophets they-say what *** I-heard (25) Yahweh declaration-of

בִּשְׁמִי שֶׁקֶר לֵאמֹר חָלַמְתִּי חָלָמְתִּי׃ (26) עַד־ מָתַי הֲיֵשׁ בְּלֵב
in-heart-of is-there? when? until (26) I-dreamed I-dreamed to-say lie in-name-of-me

הַנְּבִאִים נִבְּאֵי הַשָּׁקֶר וּנְבִיאֵי תַּרְמִת לִבָּם׃
mind-of-them delusion-of and-prophets-of the-lie ones-prophesying-of the-prophets

(27) הַחֹשְׁבִים לְהַשְׁכִּיחַ אֶת־ עַמִּי שְׁמִי בַּחֲלוֹמֹתָם
by-dreams-of-them name-of-me people-of-me *** to-make-forget the-ones-thinking (27)

אֲשֶׁר יְסַפְּרוּ אִישׁ לְרֵעֵהוּ כַּאֲשֶׁר שָׁכְחוּ אֲבוֹתָם אֶת־
*** fathers-of-them they-forgot just-as to-another-of-him each they-tell that

שְׁמִי בַּבָּעַל׃ (28) הַנָּבִיא אֲשֶׁר־ אִתּוֹ חֲלוֹם יְסַפֵּר חֲלוֹם
dream let-him-tell dream to-him who the-prophet (28) through-the-Baal name-of-me

וַאֲשֶׁר דְּבָרִי אִתּוֹ יְדַבֵּר דְּבָרִי אֱמֶת מַה־ לַתֶּבֶן
to-the-straw what? faithfulness word-of-me let-him-speak to-him word-of-me but-who

אֶת־ הַבָּר נְאֻם־ יְהוָה׃ (29) הֲלוֹא כֹה דְבָרִי כָּאֵשׁ
like-fire word-of-me this not? (29) Yahweh declaration-of the-grain with

נְאֻם־ יְהוָה וּכְפַטִּישׁ יְפֹצֵץ סָלַע׃ (30) לָכֵן הִנְנִי
see-I! therefore (30) rock he-breaks-to-pieces and-like-hammer Yahweh declaration-of

עַל־ הַנְּבִאִים נְאֻם־ יְהוָה מְגַנְּבֵי דְבָרַי אִישׁ
each words-of-me ones-stealing-of Yahweh declaration-of the-prophets against

מֵאֵת רֵעֵהוּ׃ (31) הִנְנִי עַל־ הַנְּבִיאִם נְאֻם־ יְהוָה
Yahweh declaration-of the-prophets against see-I! (31) another-of-him from-with

הַלֹּקְחִים לְשׁוֹנָם וַיִּנְאֲמוּ נְאֻם׃ (32) הִנְנִי עַל־
against see-I! (32) declaration-of yet-they-declare tongue-of-them ones-wagging

נִבְּאֵי חֲלֹמוֹת שֶׁקֶר נְאֻם־ יְהוָה וַיְסַפְּרוּם
and-they-tell-them Yahweh declaration-of falsehood dreams-ot ones-prophesying-of

וַיַּתְעוּ אֶת־ עַמִּי בְּשִׁקְרֵיהֶם וּבְפַחֲזוּתָם
and-with-recklessness-of-them with-lies-of-them people-of-me *** and-they-lead-astray

וְאָנֹכִי לֹא־ שְׁלַחְתִּים וְלֹא צִוִּיתִים וְהוֹעֵיל לֹא־ יוֹעִילוּ
they-benefit not and-to-benefit I-appointed-them or-not I-sent-them not yet-I

לָעָם־ הַזֶּה נְאֻם־ יְהוָה׃ (33) וְכִי־ יִשְׁאָלְךָ הָעָם
the-people he-asks-you and-when (33) Yahweh declaration-of the-this to-the-people

הַזֶּה אוֹ־ הַנָּבִיא אוֹ־ כֹהֵן לֵאמֹר מַה־ מַשָּׂא יְהוָה וְאָמַרְתָּ
then-you-say Yahweh oracle-of what? to-say priest or the-prophet or the-this

אֲלֵיהֶם אֶת־ מַה־ מַשָּׂא וְנָטַשְׁתִּי אֶתְכֶם נְאֻם־ יְהוָה׃
Yahweh declaration-of you indeed-I-will-forsake oracle what? *** to-them

so that I cannot see him?"
declares the LORD.
"Do not I fill heaven and earth?"
declares the LORD.

[25]"I have heard what the prophets say who prophesy lies in my name. They say, 'I had a dream! I had a dream!'
[26]How long will this continue in the hearts of these lying prophets, who prophesy the delusions of their own minds?
[27]They think the dreams they tell one another will make my people forget my name, just as their fathers forgot my name through Baal worship.
[28]Let the prophet who has a dream tell his dream, but let the one who has my word speak it faithfully. For what has straw to do with grain?" declares the LORD.
[29]"Is not my word like fire," declares the LORD, "and like a hammer that breaks a rock in pieces?

[30]"Therefore," declares the LORD, "I am against the prophets who steal from one another words supposedly from me.
[31]"Yes," declares the LORD, "I am against the prophets who wag their own tongues and yet declare, 'The LORD declares.'
[32]Indeed, I am against those who prophesy false dreams," declares the LORD. "They tell them and lead my people astray with their reckless lies, yet I did not send or appoint them. They do not benefit these people in the least," declares the LORD.

*False Oracles and False Prophets*

[33]"When these people, or a prophet or a priest, ask you, 'What is the oracle[q] of the LORD?' say to them, 'What oracle?'[r] I will forsake you, declares the LORD.'
[34]If a

[q]33 Or *burden* (see Septuagint and Vulgate)
[r]33 Hebrew; Septuagint and Vulgate *'You are the burden.* (The Hebrew for *oracle* and *burden* is the same.)

וְהַנָּבִיא וְהַכֹּהֵן וְהָעָם אֲשֶׁר יֹאמַר מַשָּׂא יְהוָה
Yahweh oracle-of he-claims who or-the-person or-the-priest and-the-prophet (34)

וּפָקַדְתִּי עַל־הָאִישׁ הַהוּא וְעַל־בֵּיתוֹ׃ כֹּה תֹאמְרוּ
you-say this (35) household-of-him and-to the-that the-man to then-I-will-punish

אִישׁ עַל־רֵעֵהוּ וְאִישׁ אֶל־אָחִיו מֶה־עָנָה יְהוָה וּמַה־
or-what? Yahweh he-answers what? relative-of-him to or-each friend-of-him to each

דִּבֶּר יְהוָה׃ וּמַשָּׂא יְהוָה לֹא תִזְכְּרוּ־עוֹד כִּי
because again you-must-mention not Yahweh but-oracle-of (36) Yahweh he-spoke

הַמַּשָּׂא יִהְיֶה לְאִישׁ דְּבָרוֹ וַהֲפַכְתֶּם אֶת־דִּבְרֵי אֱלֹהִים
God words-of *** so-you-distort word-of-him to-everyone he-becomes the-oracle

חַיִּים יְהוָה צְבָאוֹת אֱלֹהֵינוּ׃ כֹּה תֹאמַר אֶל־הַנָּבִיא מֶה־
what? the-prophet to you-say this (37) God-of-us Hosts Yahweh-of living-ones

עָנָךְ יְהוָה וּמַה־דִּבֶּר יְהוָה׃ וְאִם־מַשָּׂא יְהוָה
Yahweh oracle-of and-although (38) Yahweh he-spoke and-what? Yahweh he-answered-you

תֹּאמֵרוּ לָכֵן כֹּה אָמַר יְהוָה יַעַן אֲמָרְכֶם אֶת־הַדָּבָר הַזֶּה
the-this the-word *** you-said because Yahweh he-says this therefore you-claim

מַשָּׂא יְהוָה וָאֶשְׁלַח אֲלֵיכֶם לֵאמֹר לֹא תֹאמְרוּ מַשָּׂא יְהוָה׃
Yahweh oracle-of you-must-claim not to-say to-you though-I-told Yahweh oracle-of

לָכֵן הִנְנִי וְנָשִׁיתִי אֶתְכֶם נָשֹׁא וְנָטַשְׁתִּי אֶתְכֶם וְאֶת־
and you and-I-will-cast to-forget you I-will-forget see-I! therefore (39)

הָעִיר אֲשֶׁר נָתַתִּי לָכֶם וְלַאֲבוֹתֵיכֶם מֵעַל פָּנָי׃
presences-of-me from-in and-to-fathers-of-you to-you I-gave that the-city

וְנָתַתִּי עֲלֵיכֶם חֶרְפַּת עוֹלָם וּכְלִמּוּת עוֹלָם
everlasting and-shame-of everlasting disgrace-of upon-you and-I-will-bring (40)

אֲשֶׁר לֹא תִשָּׁכֵחַ׃ הִרְאַנִי יְהוָה וְהִנֵּה שְׁנֵי
two-of and-see! Yahweh and-he-showed-me (24:1) she-will-be-forgotten not that

דּוּדָאֵי תְאֵנִים מוּעָדִים לִפְנֵי הֵיכַל יְהוָה אַחֲרֵי הַגְלוֹת
to-exile after Yahweh temple-of in-front-of ones-being-placed figs baskets-of

נְבוּכַדְרֶאצַּר מֶלֶךְ־בָּבֶל אֶת־יְכָנְיָהוּ בֶן־יְהוֹיָקִים מֶלֶךְ־יְהוּדָה וְאֶת־
and Judah king-of Jehoiakim son-of Jeconiah *** Babylon king-of Nebuchadrezzar

שָׂרֵי יְהוּדָה וְאֶת־הֶחָרָשׁ וְאֶת־הַמַּסְגֵּר מִירוּשָׁלַםִ
from-Jerusalem the-artisan and the-craftsman and Judah officials-of

וַיְבִאֵם בָּבֶל׃ הַדּוּד אֶחָד תְּאֵנִים טֹבוֹת מְאֹד כִּתְאֵנֵי
like-figs-of very good-ones figs one the-basket (2) Babylon and-he-carried-them

הַבַּכֻּרוֹת וְהַדּוּד אֶחָד תְּאֵנִים רָעוֹת מְאֹד אֲשֶׁר לֹא־
not that very poor-ones figs other and-the-basket the-early-ripening-ones

תֵאָכַלְנָה מֵרֹעַ׃ וַיֹּאמֶר יְהוָה אֵלַי מָה־אַתָּה רֹאֶה
seeing you what? to-me Yahweh then-he-asked (3) from-badness they-could-be-eaten

prophet or a priest or anyone else
claims, 'This is the oracle of the
LORD,' I will punish that man and
his household. [35]This is what each
of you keeps on saying to his
friend or relative: 'What is the
LORD's answer?' or 'What has the
LORD spoken?' [36]But you must not
mention 'the oracle of the LORD'
again, because every man's own
word becomes his oracle and so
you distort the words of the living
God, the LORD Almighty, our God.
[37]This is what you keep saying to
a prophet: 'What is the LORD's answer to you?' or 'What has the
LORD spoken?' [38]Although you
claim, 'This is the oracle of the
LORD,' this is what the LORD says:
You used the words, 'This is the
oracle of the LORD,' even though I
told you that you must not claim,
'This is the oracle of the LORD.'
[39]Therefore, I will surely forget you
and cast you out of my presence
along with the city I gave to you
and your fathers. [40]I will bring
upon you everlasting disgrace—
everlasting shame that will not be
forgotten."

*Two Baskets of Figs*

24 After Jehoiachin[s] son of
Jehoiakim king of Judah
and the officials, the craftsmen
and the artisans of Judah were
carried into exile from Jerusalem
to Babylon by Nebuchadnezzar
king of Babylon, the LORD showed
me two baskets of figs placed in
front of the temple of the LORD.
[2]One basket had very good figs,
like those that ripen early; the other basket had very poor figs, so
bad they could not be eaten.
[3]Then the LORD asked me,
"What do you see, Jeremiah?"

[s]1 Hebrew *Jeconiah*, a variant of *Jehoiachin*

יִרְמְיָ֑הוּ וָאֹמַר֙ תְּאֵנִ֔ים הַתְּאֵנִ֤ים הַטֹּבוֹת֙ טֹב֣וֹת מְאֹ֔ד וְהָרָעוֹת֙
but-the-poor-ones very good-ones the-good-ones the-figs figs and-I-answered Jeremiah

רָע֣וֹת מְאֹ֔ד אֲשֶׁ֥ר לֹא־ תֵאָכַ֖לְנָה מֵרֹֽעַ׃ וַיְהִ֥י דְבַר־
word-of then-he-came (4) from-badness they-can-be-eaten not that very poor-ones

יְהוָ֖ה אֵלַ֥י לֵאמֹֽר׃ כֹּה־ אָמַ֤ר יְהוָה֙ אֱלֹהֵ֣י יִשְׂרָאֵ֔ל כַּתְּאֵנִ֥ים
like-the-figs Israel God-of Yahweh he-says this (5) to-say to-me Yahweh

הַטֹּב֖וֹת הָאֵ֑לֶּה כֵּֽן־ אַכִּ֞יר אֶת־ גָּל֣וּת יְהוּדָ֗ה אֲשֶׁ֨ר שִׁלַּ֜חְתִּי מִן־ הַמָּק֥וֹם
the-place from I-sent whom Judah exile-of *** I-regard so the-these the-good-ones

הַזֶּ֛ה אֶ֥רֶץ כַּשְׂדִּ֖ים לְטוֹבָֽה׃ וְשַׂמְתִּ֨י עֵינִ֤י עֲלֵיהֶם֙ לְטוֹבָ֔ה
for-good over-them eye-of-me and-I-will-set (6) as-good Chaldeans land-of the-this

וַהֲשִׁבֹתִ֖ים עַל־ הָאָ֣רֶץ הַזֹּ֑את וּבְנִיתִים֙ וְלֹ֣א
and-not and-I-will-build-them the-this the-land to and-I-will-bring-back-them

אֶהֱרֹ֔ס וּנְטַעְתִּ֖ים וְלֹ֥א אֶתּֽוֹשׁ׃ וְנָתַתִּ֨י
and-I-will-give (7) I-will-uproot and-not and-I-will-plant-them I-will-tear-down

לָהֶ֥ם לֵב֙ לָדַ֣עַת אֹתִ֔י כִּ֖י אֲנִ֣י יְהוָ֑ה וְהָיוּ־ לִ֣י לְעָ֔ם וְאָ֣נֹכִ֔י
and-I as-people to-me and-they-will-be Yahweh I that me to-know heart to-them

אֶהְיֶ֥ה לָהֶ֖ם לֵאלֹהִ֑ים כִּֽי־ יָשֻׁ֥בוּ אֵלַ֖י בְּכָל־ לִבָּֽם׃
heart-of-them with-all-of to-me they-will-return for as-God to-them I-will-be

וְכַתְּאֵנִים֙ הָֽרָע֔וֹת אֲשֶׁ֥ר לֹא־ תֵאָכַ֖לְנָה מֵרֹ֑עַ
from-badness they-can-be-eaten not which the-poor-ones but-like-the-figs (8)

כִּי־ כֹ֣ה ׀ אָמַ֣ר יְהוָ֗ה כֵּ֣ן אֶ֠תֵּן אֶת־ צִדְקִיָּ֨הוּ מֶֽלֶךְ־ יְהוּדָ֜ה וְאֶת־
and-with Judah king-of Zedekiah with I-will-deal so Yahweh he-says this indeed

שָׂרָ֗יו וְאֵ֣ת ׀ שְׁאֵרִ֣ית יְרוּשָׁלִַ֗ם הַנִּשְׁאָרִים֙ בָּאָ֣רֶץ
in-the-land the-ones-remaining Jerusalem survivor-of and-with officials-of-him

הַזֹּ֔את וְהַיֹּשְׁבִ֖ים בְּאֶ֥רֶץ מִצְרָֽיִם׃ וּנְתַתִּים֙ לְזַוָעָ֔ה
as-abhorrence and-I-will-make-them (9) Egypt in-land-of or-the-ones-living the-this

לְרָעָ֔ה לְכֹ֖ל מַמְלְכ֣וֹת הָאָ֑רֶץ לְחֶרְפָּ֤ה וּלְמָשָׁל֙
and-as-byword as-reproach the-earth kingdoms-of to-all-of as-offense

לִשְׁנִינָ֣ה וְלִקְלָלָ֔ה בְּכָל־ הַמְּקֹמ֖וֹת אֲשֶׁר־ אַדִּיחֵ֥ם שָֽׁם׃
there I-banish-them where the-places in-every-of and-as-curse as-object-of-ridicule

וְשִׁלַּ֣חְתִּי בָ֔ם אֶת־ הַחֶ֖רֶב אֶת־ הָרָעָ֣ב וְאֶת־ הַדָּ֑בֶר עַד־
until the-plague and the-famine *** the-sword *** against-them and-I-will-send (10)

תֻּמָּם֙ מֵעַ֣ל הָאֲדָמָ֔ה אֲשֶׁר־ נָתַ֥תִּי לָהֶ֖ם וְלַאֲבוֹתֵיהֶֽם׃
and-to-fathers-of-them to-them I-gave that the-land from-on to-be-destroyed-them

הַדָּבָ֞ר אֲשֶׁר־ הָיָ֣ה עַל־ יִרְמְיָ֗הוּ עַל־ כָּל־ עַ֣ם יְהוּדָ֔ה
Judah people-of all-of concerning Jeremiah to he-came that the-word (25:1)

בַּשָּׁנָה֙ הָרְבִעִ֔ית לִיהוֹיָקִ֥ים בֶּן־ יֹאשִׁיָּ֖הוּ מֶ֣לֶךְ יְהוּדָ֑ה הִ֗יא הַשָּׁנָה֙
the-year this Judah king-of Josiah son-of of-Jehoiakim the-fourth in-the-year

"Figs," I answered. "The good
ones are very good, but the poor
ones are so bad they cannot be
eaten."
4Then the word of the LORD
came to me: 5"This is what the
LORD, the God of Israel, says: 'Like
these good figs, I regard as good
the exiles from Judah, whom I
sent away from this place to the
land of the Babylonians.[a] 6My
eyes will watch over them for
their good, and I will bring them
back to this land. I will build them
up and not tear them down; I will
plant them and not uproot them. 7I
will give them a heart to know me,
that I am the LORD. They will be
my people, and I will be their God,
for they will return to me with all
their heart.
8" 'But like the poor figs, which
are so bad they cannot be eaten,'
says the LORD, 'so will I deal with
Zedekiah king of Judah, his officials and the survivors from
Jerusalem, whether they remain
in this land or live in Egypt. 9I will
make them abhorrent and an offense to all the kingdoms of the
earth, a reproach and a byword,
an object of ridicule and cursing,
wherever I banish them. 10I will
send the sword, famine and
plague against them until they are
destroyed from the land I gave to
them and their fathers.' "

*Seventy Years of Captivity*

25 The word came to Jeremiah
concerning all the people of
Judah in the fourth year of Jehoiakim son of Josiah king of Judah,

[a]5 Or *Chaldeans*

°9 ק לזועה

הָרִאשֹׁנִית לִנְבוּכַדְרֶאצַּר מֶלֶךְ בָּבֶל׃ אֲשֶׁר דִּבֶּר יִרְמְיָהוּ הַנָּבִיא
the-prophet Jeremiah he-said that (2) Babylon king-of of-Nebuchadrezzar the-first

עַל־כָּל־ עַם יְהוּדָה וְאֶל כָּל־ יֹשְׁבֵי יְרוּשָׁלַםִ לֵאמֹר׃ מִן־
from (3) to-say Jerusalem ones-living-of all-of and-to Judah people-of all-of to

שְׁלֹשׁ עֶשְׂרֵה שָׁנָה לְיֹאשִׁיָּהוּ בֶן־ אָמוֹן מֶלֶךְ יְהוּדָה וְעַד ׀ הַיּוֹם הַזֶּה
the-this the-day and-until Judah king-of Amon son-of of-Josiah year ten three-of

זֶה שָׁלֹשׁ וְעֶשְׂרִים שָׁנָה הָיָה דְבַר־ יְהוָה אֵלָי וָאֲדַבֵּר אֲלֵיכֶם
to-you and-I-spoke to-me Yahweh word-of he-came year and-twenty three this

אַשְׁכֵּים וְדַבֵּר וְלֹא שְׁמַעְתֶּם׃ וְשָׁלַח יְהוָה אֲלֵיכֶם אֶת־
*** to-you Yahweh and-he-sent (4) you-listened but-not and-to-speak to-begin-early

כָּל־ עֲבָדָיו הַנְּבִאִים הַשְׁכֵּם וְשָׁלֹחַ וְלֹא שְׁמַעְתֶּם
you-listened but-not and-to-send to-begin-early the-prophets servants-of-him all-of

וְלֹא־ הִטִּיתֶם אֶת־ אָזְנְכֶם לִשְׁמֹעַ׃ לֵאמֹר שׁוּבוּ־ נָא אִישׁ
each now! turn! to-say (5) to-listen ear-of-you *** you-made-attentive or-not

מִדַּרְכּוֹ הָרָעָה וּמֵרֹעַ מַעַלְלֵיכֶם וּשְׁבוּ עַל־הָאֲדָמָה
the-land in and-stay! practices-of-you and-from-evil-of the-evil from-way-of-him

אֲשֶׁר נָתַן יְהוָה לָכֶם וְלַאֲבוֹתֵיכֶם לְמִן־ עוֹלָם וְעַד־ עוֹלָם׃
forever and-to forever at-from and-to-fathers-of-you to-you Yahweh he-gave that

וְאַל־ תֵּלְכוּ אַחֲרֵי אֱלֹהִים אֲחֵרִים לְעָבְדָם וּלְהִשְׁתַּחֲוֺת לָהֶם
to-them and-to-worship to-serve-them other-ones gods after you-follow and-not (6)

וְלֹא־ תַכְעִיסוּ אוֹתִי בְּמַעֲשֵׂה יְדֵיכֶם וְלֹא אָרַע
I-will-harm then-not hands-of-you with-making-of me you-provoke-to-anger and-not

לָכֶם׃ וְלֹא־ שְׁמַעְתֶּם אֵלַי נְאֻם־ יְהוָה לְמַעַן
so-that Yahweh declaration-of to-me you-listened but-not (7) to-you

הַכְעִסוּנִי בְּמַעֲשֵׂה יְדֵיכֶם לְרַע לָכֶם׃ לָכֵן
therefore (8) of-you to-harm hands-of-you with-making-of you-provoked-to-anger-me

כֹּה אָמַר יְהוָה צְבָאוֹת יַעַן אֲשֶׁר לֹא־ שְׁמַעְתֶּם אֶת־ דְּבָרָי׃
words-of-me *** you-listened not that because Hosts Yahweh-of he-says this

הִנְנִי שֹׁלֵחַ וְלָקַחְתִּי אֶת־ כָּל־ מִשְׁפְּחוֹת צָפוֹן נְאֻם־
declaration-of north peoples-of all-of *** and-I-will-take summoning see-I! (9)

יְהוָה וְאֶל־ נְבוּכַדְרֶאצַּר מֶלֶךְ־ בָּבֶל עַבְדִּי וַהֲבִאֹתִים
and-I-will-bring-them servant-of-me Babylon king-of Nebuchadrezzar and-to Yahweh

עַל־ הָאָרֶץ הַזֹּאת וְעַל־ יֹשְׁבֶיהָ וְעַל כָּל־
all-of and-against ones-inhabiting-her and-against the-this the-land against

הַגּוֹיִם הָאֵלֶּה סָבִיב וְהַחֲרַמְתִּים וְשַׂמְתִּים
and-I-will-make-them and-I-will-destroy-them surrounding the-these the-nations

לְשַׁמָּה וְלִשְׁרֵקָה וּלְחָרְבוֹת עוֹלָם׃
everlasting and-as-ruins-of and-as-object-of-scorn as-object-of-horror

°7 ק הכעיסני

which was the first year of Nebuchadnezzar king of Babylon. [2]So Jeremiah the prophet said to all the people of Judah and to all those living in Jerusalem: [3]For twenty-three years—from the thirteenth year of Josiah son of Amon king of Judah until this very day—the word of the LORD has come to me and I have spoken to you again and again, but you have not listened.

[4]And though the LORD has sent all his servants the prophets to you again and again, you have not listened or paid any attention. [5]They said, "Turn now, each of you, from your evil ways and your evil practices, and you can stay in the land the LORD gave to you and your fathers for ever and ever. [6]Do not follow other gods to serve and worship them; do not provoke me to anger with what your hands have made. Then I will not harm you."

[7]"But you did not listen to me," declares the LORD, "and you have provoked me with what your hands have made, and you have brought harm to yourselves."

[8]Therefore the LORD Almighty says this: "Because you have not listened to my words, [9]I will summon all the peoples of the north and my servant Nebuchadnezzar king of Babylon," declares the LORD, "and I will bring them against this land and its inhabitants and against all the surrounding nations. I will completely destroy[u] them and make them an object of horror and scorn, and an everlasting ruin. [10]I will banish

[u]9 The Hebrew term refers to the irrevocable giving over of things or persons to the LORD, often by totally destroying them.

(10) וְהַאֲבַדְתִּי מֵהֶם קוֹל שָׂשׂוֹן וְקוֹל שִׂמְחָה קוֹל
voice-of gladness and-sound-of joy sound-of from-them and-I-will-banish (10)

חָתָן וְקוֹל כַּלָּה קוֹל רֵחַיִם וְאוֹר נֵר׃
lamp and-light-of millstones sound-of bride and-voice-of bridegroom

(11) וְהָיְתָה כָּל־הָאָרֶץ הַזֹּאת לְחָרְבָּה לְשַׁמָּה
as-desolation as-wasteland the-this the-country whole-of and-she-will-become (11)

וְעָבְדוּ הַגּוֹיִם הָאֵלֶּה אֶת־מֶלֶךְ בָּבֶל שִׁבְעִים שָׁנָה׃
year seventy Babylon king-of *** the-these the-nations and-they-will-serve

(12) וְהָיָה כִמְלֹאות שִׁבְעִים שָׁנָה אֶפְקֹד עַל־מֶלֶךְ־
king-of to I-will-punish year seventy when-to-be-fulfilled and-he-will-be (12)

בָּבֶל וְעַל־הַגּוֹי הַהוּא נְאֻם־יְהוָה אֶת־עֲוֺנָם
guilt-of-them *** Yahweh declaration-of the-that the-nation and-to Babylon

וְעַל־אֶרֶץ כַּשְׂדִּים וְשַׂמְתִּי אֹתוֹ לְשִׁמְמוֹת עוֹלָם׃
forever as-desolations-of him and-I-will-make Chaldeans land-of even-on

(13) וְהֵבֵאתִי עַל־הָאָרֶץ הַהִיא אֶת־כָּל־דְּבָרַי אֲשֶׁר־דִּבַּרְתִּי
I-spoke that words-of-me all-of *** the-that the-land upon and-I-will-bring (13)

עָלֶיהָ אֵת כָּל־הַכָּתוּב בַּסֵּפֶר הַזֶּה אֲשֶׁר־נִבָּא
he-prophesied that the-this in-the-book the-one-being-written all-of *** against-her

יִרְמְיָהוּ עַל־כָּל־הַגּוֹיִם׃ (14) כִּי עָבְדוּ־בָם
by-them they-will-be-enslaved indeed (14) the-nations all-of against Jeremiah

גַּם־הֵמָּה גּוֹיִם רַבִּים וּמְלָכִים גְּדוֹלִים וְשִׁלַּמְתִּי לָהֶם
to-them and-I-will-repay great-ones and-kings many-ones nations they also

כְּפָעֳלָם וּכְמַעֲשֵׂה יְדֵיהֶם׃ (15) כִּי כֹה
this indeed (15) hands-of-them and-according-to-work-of according-to-deed-of-them

אָמַר יְהוָה אֱלֹהֵי יִשְׂרָאֵל אֵלַי קַח אֶת־כּוֹס הַיַּיִן הַחֵמָה הַזֹּאת
the-this the-wrath the-wine cup-of *** take! to-me Israel God-of Yahweh he-said

מִיָּדִי וְהִשְׁקִיתָה אֹתוֹ אֶת־כָּל־הַגּוֹיִם אֲשֶׁר אָנֹכִי שֹׁלֵחַ אוֹתְךָ
you sending I whom the-nations all-of *** him and-you-make-drink from-hand-of-me

אֲלֵיהֶם׃ (16) וְשָׁתוּ וְהִתְגֹּעֲשׁוּ וְהִתְהֹלָלוּ מִפְּנֵי
because-of and-they-will-go-mad then-they-will-stagger when-they-drink (16) to-them

הַחֶרֶב אֲשֶׁר אָנֹכִי שֹׁלֵחַ בֵּינֹתָם׃ (17) וָאֶקַּח אֶת־הַכּוֹס מִיַּד יְהוָה
Yahweh from-hand-of the-cup *** so-I-took (17) among-them sending I that the-sword

וָאַשְׁקֶה אֶת־כָּל־הַגּוֹיִם אֲשֶׁר־שְׁלָחַנִי יְהוָה אֲלֵיהֶם׃ (18) אֶת־
*** (18) to-them Yahweh he-sent-me whom the-nations all-of *** and-I-made-drink

יְרוּשָׁלִַם וְאֶת־עָרֵי יְהוּדָה וְאֶת־מְלָכֶיהָ אֶת־שָׂרֶיהָ לָתֵת אֹתָם
them to-make officials-of-her *** kings-of-her and Judah towns-of and Jerusalem

לְחָרְבָּה לְשַׁמָּה לִשְׁרֵקָה וְלִקְלָלָה כַּיּוֹם הַזֶּה׃
the-this as-the-day and-as-curse as-object-of-scorn as-object-of-horror as-ruin

°7 ק והבאתי

from them the sounds of joy and
gladness, the voices of bride and
bridegroom, the sound of millstones and the light of the lamp.
11 This whole country will become
a desolate wasteland, and these
nations will serve the king of Babylon seventy years.
12 "But when the seventy years
are fulfilled, I will punish the king
of Babylon and his nation, the
land of the Babylonians,[v] for their
guilt," declares the LORD, "and
will make it desolate forever. 13 I
will bring upon that land all the
things I have spoken against it, all
that are written in this book and
prophesied by Jeremiah against
all the nations. 14 They themselves
will be enslaved by many nations
and great kings; I will repay them
according to their deeds and the
work of their hands."

*The Cup of God's Wrath*

15 This is what the LORD, the God
of Israel, said to me: "Take from
my hand this cup filled with the
wine of my wrath and make all
the nations to whom I send you
drink it. 16 When they drink it, they
will stagger and go mad because of
the sword I will send among
them."
17 So I took the cup from the
LORD's hand and made all the nations to whom he sent me drink it:
18 Jerusalem and the towns of
Judah, its kings and officials, to
make them a ruin and an object of
horror and scorn and cursing, as

[v] 12 Or *Chaldeans*

אֶת־פַּרְעֹה מֶלֶךְ־מִצְרַיִם וְאֶת־עֲבָדָיו וְאֶת־שָׂרָיו וְאֶת־

and officials-of-him and attendants-of-him and Egypt king-of Pharaoh *** (19)

כָּל־עַמּוֹ׃ וְאֵת כָּל־הָעֶרֶב וְאֵת כָּל־מַלְכֵי אֶרֶץ

land-of kings-of all-of and the-foreigner all-of and (20) people-of-him all-of

הָעוּץ וְאֵת כָּל־מַלְכֵי אֶרֶץ פְּלִשְׁתִּים וְאֶת־אַשְׁקְלוֹן וְאֶת־עַזָּה וְאֶת־עֶקְרוֹן

Ekron and Gaza and Ashkelon even Philistines land-of kings-of all-of and the-Uz

וְאֵת שְׁאֵרִית אַשְׁדּוֹד׃ אֶת־אֱדוֹם וְאֶת־מוֹאָב וְאֶת־בְּנֵי עַמּוֹן׃ וְאֵת כָּל־

all-of and (22) Ammon sons-of and Moab and Edom *** (21) Ashdod remnant-of and

מַלְכֵי־צֹר וְאֵת כָּל־מַלְכֵי צִידוֹן וְאֵת מַלְכֵי הָאִי אֲשֶׁר בְּעֵבֶר

at-across that the-coastland kings-of and Sidon kings-of all-of and Tyre kings-of

הַיָּם׃ וְאֶת־דְּדָן וְאֶת־תֵּימָא וְאֶת־בּוּז וְאֵת כָּל־קְצוּצֵי פֵאָה׃

forehead ones-clipping-of all-of and Buz and Tema and Dedan and (23) the-sea

וְאֵת כָּל־מַלְכֵי עֲרָב וְאֵת כָּל־מַלְכֵי הָעֶרֶב הַשֹּׁכְנִים

the-ones-living the-foreigner kings-of all-of and Arabia kings-of all-of and (24)

בַּמִּדְבָּר׃ וְאֵת ׀ כָּל־מַלְכֵי זִמְרִי וְאֵת כָּל־מַלְכֵי עֵילָם וְאֵת כָּל־

all-of and Elam kings-of all-of and Zimri kings-of all-of and (25) in-the-desert

מַלְכֵי מָדָי׃ וְאֵת ׀ כָּל־מַלְכֵי הַצָּפוֹן הַקְּרֹבִים וְהָרְחֹקִים

and-the-ones-far the-ones-near the-north kings-of all-of and (26) Media kings-of

אִישׁ אֶל־אָחִיו וְאֵת כָּל־הַמַּמְלְכוֹת הָאָרֶץ אֲשֶׁר עַל־פְּנֵי הָאֲדָמָה

the-earth faces-of on that the-earth kingdoms-of all-of and other-of-him after one

וּמֶלֶךְ שֵׁשַׁךְ יִשְׁתֶּה אַחֲרֵיהֶם׃ וְאָמַרְתָּ אֲלֵיהֶם כֹּה־

this to-them then-you-tell (27) after-them he-will-drink Sheshach and-king-of

אָמַר יְהוָה צְבָאוֹת אֱלֹהֵי יִשְׂרָאֵל שְׁתוּ וְשִׁכְרוּ וּקְיוּ וּנְפְלוּ

and-fall! and-vomit! and-get-drunk! drink! Israel God-of Hosts Yahweh-of he-says

וְלֹא תָקוּמוּ מִפְּנֵי הַחֶרֶב אֲשֶׁר אָנֹכִי שֹׁלֵחַ בֵּינֵיכֶם׃ וְהָיָה

but-he-will-be (28) among-you sending I that the-sword because-of you-rise and-not

כִּי יְמָאֲנוּ לָקַחַת־הַכּוֹס מִיָּדְךָ לִשְׁתּוֹת וְאָמַרְתָּ אֲלֵיהֶם

to-them then-you-tell to-drink from-hand-of-you the-cup to-take they-refuse if

כֹּה אָמַר יְהוָה צְבָאוֹת שָׁתוֹ תִּשְׁתּוּ׃ כִּי הִנֵּה בָעִיר אֲשֶׁר

that on-the-city see! indeed (29) you-drink to-drink Hosts Yahweh-of he-says this

נִקְרָא־שְׁמִי עָלֶיהָ אָנֹכִי מֵחֵל לְהָרַע וְאַתֶּם

and-you to-bring-disaster beginning I to-her Name-of-me he-is-called

הִנָּקֵה תִנָּקוּ לֹא תִנָּקוּ כִּי חֶרֶב אֲנִי

I sword for you-will-go-unpunished not will-you-go-unpunished to-go-unpunished

קֹרֵא עַל־כָּל־יֹשְׁבֵי הָאָרֶץ נְאֻם יְהוָה צְבָאוֹת׃

Hosts Yahweh-of declaration-of the-earth ones-living-of all-of on calling

וְאַתָּה תִּנָּבֵא אֲלֵיהֶם אֵת כָּל־הַדְּבָרִים הָאֵלֶּה וְאָמַרְתָּ

and-you-say the-these the-words all-of *** against-them you-prophesy now-you (30)

they are today; [19]Pharaoh king of
Egypt, his attendants, his officials
and all his people, [20]and all the foreign people there; all the kings of
Uz; all the kings of the Philistines
(those of Ashkelon, Gaza, Ekron,
and the people left at Ashdod);
[21]Edom, Moab and Ammon; [22]all
the kings of Tyre and Sidon; the
kings of the coastlands across the
sea; [23]Dedan, Tema, Buz and all
who are in distant places[w]; [24]all the
kings of Arabia and all the kings
of the foreign people who live in
the desert; [25]all the kings of Zimri,
Elam and Media; [26]and all the
kings of the north, near and far,
one after the other—all the kingdoms on the face of the earth. And
after all of them, the king of Sheshach[x] will drink it too.

[27]"Then tell them, 'This is what
the LORD Almighty, the God of Israel, says: Drink, get drunk and
vomit, and fall to rise no more because of the sword I will send
among you.' [28]But if they refuse to
take the cup from your hand and
drink, tell them, 'This is what the
LORD Almighty says: You must
drink it! [29]See, I am beginning to
bring disaster on the city that
bears my Name, and will you indeed go unpunished? You will not
go unpunished, for I am calling
down a sword upon all who live
on the earth, declares the LORD Almighty.'

[30]"Now prophesy all these
words against them and say to
them:

[w]23 Or *who clip the hair by their foreheads*
[x]26 *Sheshach* is a cryptogram for Babylon.

אֲלֵיהֶם יְהוָה מִמָּרוֹם יִשְׁאָג וּמִמְּעוֹן קָדְשׁוֹ
holiness-of-him and-from-dwelling-of he-will-roar from-on-high Yahweh to-them

יִתֵּן קוֹלוֹ שָׁאֹג יִשְׁאַג עַל־ נָוֵהוּ הֵידָד
shout land-of-him against he-will-roar to-roar thunder-of-him he-will-give

כְּדֹרְכִים יַעֲנֶה אֶל כָּל־ יֹשְׁבֵי הָאָרֶץ׃
the-earth ones-living-of all-of against he-will-cry like-ones-treading

בָּא שָׁאוֹן עַד־ קְצֵה הָאָרֶץ כִּי רִיב לַיהוָה
to-Yahweh charge for the-earth end-of to tumult he-will-resound (31)

בַּגּוֹיִם נִשְׁפָּט הוּא לְכָל־ בָּשָׂר הָרְשָׁעִים נְתָנָם
he-will-put-them the-wicked-ones mankind to-all-of he judging against-the-nations

לַחֶרֶב נְאֻם־ יְהוָה׃ כֹּה אָמַר יְהוָה צְבָאוֹת הִנֵּה רָעָה
disaster look! Hosts Yahweh-of he-says this (32) Yahweh declaration-of to-the-sword

יֹצֵאת מִגּוֹי אֶל־ גּוֹי וְסַעַר גָּדוֹל יֵעוֹר מִיַּרְכְּתֵי־ אָרֶץ׃
earth from-ends-of he-rises mighty and-storm nation to from-nation spreading

וְהָיוּ חַלְלֵי יְהוָה בַּיּוֹם הַהוּא מִקְצֵה הָאָרֶץ
the-earth from-end-of the-that at-the-day Yahweh ones-slain-of and-they-will-be (33)

וְעַד־ קְצֵה הָאָרֶץ לֹא יִסָּפְדוּ וְלֹא יֵאָסְפוּ
they-will-be-gathered or-not they-will-be-mourned not the-earth end-of and-to

וְלֹא יִקָּבֵרוּ לְדֹמֶן עַל־ פְּנֵי הָאֲדָמָה יִהְיוּ׃
they-will-be the-ground surfaces-of on like-refuse they-will-be-buried or-not

הֵילִילוּ הָרֹעִים וְזַעֲקוּ וְהִתְפַּלְּשׁוּ אַדִּירֵי הַצֹּאן
the-flock leaders-of and-roll-in-dust! and-wail! the-ones-being-shepherds weep! (34)

כִּי־ מָלְאוּ יְמֵיכֶם לִטְבוֹחַ וּתְפוֹצוֹתִיכֶם וּנְפַלְתֶּם
and-you-will-fall and-shatterings-of-you to-slaughter days-of-you they-came for

כִּכְלִי חֶמְדָּה׃ וְאָבַד מָנוֹס מִן־ הָרֹעִים
the-ones-being-shepherds from flight and-he-will-go (35) fineness like-pottery-of

וּפְלֵיטָה מֵאַדִּירֵי הַצֹּאן׃ קוֹל צַעֲקַת הָרֹעִים
the-ones-being-shepherds cry-of sound-of (36) the-flock from-leaders-of and-escape

וִילְלַת* אַדִּירֵי הַצֹּאן כִּי־ שֹׁדֵד יְהוָה אֶת־ מַרְעִיתָם׃
pasture-of-them *** Yahweh destroying for the-flock leaders-of and-wailing-of

וְנָדַמּוּ נְאוֹת הַשָּׁלוֹם מִפְּנֵי חֲרוֹן
fierceness-of because-of the-peace meadows-of and-they-will-be-laid-waste (37)

אַף־ יְהוָה׃ עָזַב כַּכְּפִיר סֻכּוֹ כִּי־ הָיְתָה
she-will-become indeed lair-of-him like-the-lion he-will-leave (38) Yahweh anger-of

אַרְצָם לְשַׁמָּה מִפְּנֵי חֲרוֹן הַיּוֹנָה וּמִפְּנֵי
and-because-of the-one-oppressing anger-of because-of as-desolation land-of-them

חֲרוֹן אַפּוֹ׃ בְּרֵאשִׁית מַמְלְכוּת יְהוֹיָקִים בֶּן־ יֹאשִׁיָּהוּ
Josiah son-of Jehoiakim reign-of in-early-part-of (26:1) anger-of-him fierceness-of

" 'The LORD will roar from on high;
he will thunder from his holy dwelling
and roar mightily against his land.
He will shout like those who tread the grapes,
shout against all who live on the earth.
31 The tumult will resound to the ends of the earth,
for the LORD will bring charges against the nations;
he will bring judgment on all mankind
and put the wicked to the sword,' "
declares the LORD.

32 This is what the LORD Almighty says:

"Look! Disaster is spreading from nation to nation;
a mighty storm is rising from the ends of the earth."

33 At that time those slain by the LORD will be everywhere—from one end of the earth to the other. They will not be mourned or gathered up or buried, but will be like refuse lying on the ground.

34 Weep and wail, you shepherds;
roll in the dust, you leaders of the flock.
For your time to be slaughtered has come;
you will fall and be shattered like fine pottery.
35 The shepherds will have nowhere to flee,
the leaders of the flock no place to escape.
36 Hear the cry of the shepherds,
the wailing of the leaders of the flock,
for the LORD is destroying their pasture.
37 The peaceful meadows will be laid waste
because of the fierce anger of the LORD.
38 Like a lion he will leave his lair,
and their land will become desolate
because of the sword[v] of the oppressor
and because of the LORD's fierce anger.

### *Jeremiah Threatened With Death*

26 Early in the reign of Jehoiakim son of Josiah king of

v38 Some Hebrew manuscripts and Septuagint (see also Jer. 46:16 and 50:16); most Hebrew manuscripts *anger*

*36 Most mss point this word as וִילֵל.

מֶלֶךְ יְהוּדָה הָיָה הַדָּבָר הַזֶּה מֵאֵת יְהוָה לֵאמֹר׃ כֹּה ׀ אָמַר

he-says this (2) to-say Yahweh from-with the-this the-word he-came Judah king-of

יְהוָה עֲמֹד בַּחֲצַר בֵּית־ יְהוָה וְדִבַּרְתָּ עַל־ כָּל־ עָרֵי

towns-of all-of to and-you-speak Yahweh house-of in-courtyard-of stand! Yahweh

יְהוּדָה הַבָּאִים לְהִשְׁתַּחֲוֺת בֵּית־ יְהוָה אֵת כָּל־ הַדְּבָרִים אֲשֶׁר

that the-words all-of *** Yahweh house-of to-worship the-ones-coming Judah

צִוִּיתִיךָ לְדַבֵּר אֲלֵיהֶם אַל־ תִּגְרַע דָּבָר׃ אוּלַי יִשְׁמְעוּ

they-will-listen perhaps (3) word you-omit not to-them to-tell I-command-you

וְיָשֻׁבוּ אִישׁ מִדַּרְכּוֹ הָרָעָה וְנִחַמְתִּי אֶל־

concerning then-I-will-relent the-evil from-way-of-him each and-they-will-turn

הָרָעָה אֲשֶׁר אָנֹכִי חֹשֵׁב לַעֲשׂוֹת לָהֶם מִפְּנֵי רֹעַ מַעַלְלֵיהֶם׃

deeds-of-them evil-of because-of on-them to-bring planning I that the-disaster

וְאָמַרְתָּ אֲלֵיהֶם כֹּה אָמַר יְהוָה אִם־לֹא תִשְׁמְעוּ אֵלַי לָלֶכֶת

to-follow to-me you-listen not if Yahweh he-says this to-them and-you-say (4)

בְּתוֹרָתִי אֲשֶׁר נָתַתִּי לִפְנֵיכֶם׃ לִשְׁמֹעַ עַל־ דִּבְרֵי עֲבָדַי

servants-of-me words-of to to-listen (5) before-you I-set which to-law-of-me

הַנְּבִאִים אֲשֶׁר אָנֹכִי שֹׁלֵחַ אֲלֵיכֶם וְהַשְׁכֵּם וְשָׁלֹחַ וְלֹא

though-not and-to-send even-to-begin-early to-you sending I whom the-prophets

שְׁמַעְתֶּם׃ וְנָתַתִּי אֶת־ הַבַּיִת הַזֶּה כְּשִׁלֹה וְאֶת־ הָעִיר

the-city and like-Shiloh the-this the-house *** then-I-will-make (6) you-listened

הַזֹּאתָה אֶתֵּן לִקְלָלָה לְכֹל גּוֹיֵי הָאָרֶץ׃

the-earth nations-of among-all-of as-object-of-cursing I-will-make the-this

וַיִּשְׁמְעוּ הַכֹּהֲנִים וְהַנְּבִאִים וְכָל־ הָעָם אֶת־ יִרְמְיָהוּ

Jeremiah *** the-people and-all-of and-the-prophets the-priests and-they-heard (7)

מְדַבֵּר אֶת־הַדְּבָרִים הָאֵלֶּה בְּבֵית יְהוָה׃ וַיְהִי ׀ כְּכַלּוֹת

as-to-finish but-he-was (8) Yahweh in-house-of the-these the-words *** speaking

יִרְמְיָהוּ לְדַבֵּר אֵת כָּל־אֲשֶׁר־ צִוָּה יְהוָה לְדַבֵּר אֶל־ כָּל־ הָעָם

the-people all-of to to-say Yahweh he-commanded that all *** to-tell Jeremiah

וַיִּתְפְּשׂוּ אֹתוֹ הַכֹּהֲנִים וְהַנְּבִאִים וְכָל־ הָעָם לֵאמֹר

to-say the-people and-all-of and-the-prophets the-priests him then-they-seized

מוֹת תָּמוּת׃ מַדּוּעַ נִבֵּיתָ בְשֵׁם־ יְהוָה לֵאמֹר כְּשִׁלוֹ

like-Shiloh to-say Yahweh in-name-of you-prophesy why? (9) you-must-die to-die

יִהְיֶה הַבַּיִת הַזֶּה וְהָעִיר הַזֹּאת תֶּחֱרַב מֵאֵין

with-no she-will-be-desolate the-this and-the-city the-this the-house he-will-be

יוֹשֵׁב וַיִּקָּהֵל כָּל־ הָעָם אֶל־ יִרְמְיָהוּ בְּבֵית יְהוָה׃

Yahweh in-house-of Jeremiah around the-people all-of and-they-crowded one-living

וַיִּשְׁמְעוּ ׀ שָׂרֵי יְהוּדָה אֵת הַדְּבָרִים הָאֵלֶּה וַיַּעֲלוּ

then-they-went-up the-these the-things *** Judah officials-of when-they-heard (10)

°6 ק הזאת

Judah, this word came from the
LORD: 2"This is what the LORD
says: Stand in the courtyard of the
LORD's house and speak to all the
people of the towns of Judah who
come to worship in the house of
the LORD. Tell them everything I
command you; do not omit a
word. 3Perhaps they will listen
and each will turn from his evil
way. Then I will relent and not
bring on them the disaster I was
planning because of the evil they
have done. 4Say to them, 'This is
what the LORD says: If you do not
listen to me and follow my law,
which I have set before you, 5and
if you do not listen to the words of
my servants the prophets, whom I
have sent to you again and again
(though you have not listened),
6then I will make this house like
Shiloh and this city an object of
cursing among all the nations of
the earth.' "

7The priests, the prophets and
all the people heard Jeremiah
speak these words in the house of
the LORD. 8But as soon as Jeremiah
finished telling all the people
everything the LORD had commanded him to say, the priests,
the prophets and all the people
seized him and said, "You must
die! 9Why do you prophesy in the
LORD's name that this house will
be like Shiloh and this city will be
desolate and deserted?" And all
the people crowded around Jeremiah in the house of the LORD.

10When the officials of Judah
heard about these things, they

מִבֵּית־ הַמֶּלֶךְ בֵּית יְהוָה וַיֵּשְׁבוּ בְּפֶתַח
at-entrance-of and-they-took-places Yahweh house-of the-royalty from-palace-of

שַׁעַר־ יְהוָה הֶחָדָשׁ׃ וַיֹּאמְרוּ הַכֹּהֲנִים וְהַנְּבִאִים אֶל־
to and-the-prophets the-priests then-they-said (11) the-New Yahweh Gate-of

הַשָּׂרִים וְאֶל־ כָּל־ הָעָם לֵאמֹר מִשְׁפַּט־ מָוֶת לָאִישׁ הַזֶּה
the-this to-the-man death sentence-of to-say the-people all-of and-to the-officials

כִּי נִבָּא אֶל־ הָעִיר הַזֹּאת כַּאֲשֶׁר שְׁמַעְתֶּם בְּאָזְנֵיכֶם׃
with-ears-of-you you-heard just-as the-this the-city against he-prophesied because

וַיֹּאמֶר יִרְמְיָהוּ אֶל־ כָּל־ הַשָּׂרִים וְאֶל־ כָּל־ הָעָם לֵאמֹר
to-say the-people all-of and-to the-officials all-of to Jeremiah then-he-said (12)

יְהוָה שְׁלָחַנִי לְהִנָּבֵא אֶל־ הַבַּיִת הַזֶּה וְאֶל־ הָעִיר
the-city and-against the-this the-house against to-prophesy he-sent-me Yahweh

הַזֹּאת אֵת כָּל־ הַדְּבָרִים אֲשֶׁר שְׁמַעְתֶּם׃ וְעַתָּה הֵיטִיבוּ דַרְכֵיכֶם
ways-of-you reform! and-now (13) you-heard that the-things all-of *** the-this

וּמַעַלְלֵיכֶם וְשִׁמְעוּ בְּקוֹל יְהוָה אֱלֹהֵיכֶם וְיִנָּחֵם
then-he-will-relent God-of-you Yahweh to-voice-of and-obey! and-actions-of-you

יְהוָה אֶל־ הָרָעָה אֲשֶׁר דִּבֶּר עֲלֵיכֶם׃ וַאֲנִי הִנְנִי
see-I! and-I (14) against-you he-pronounced that the-disaster concerning Yahweh

בְיֶדְכֶם עֲשׂוּ־ לִי כַּטּוֹב וְכַיָּשָׁר בְּעֵינֵיכֶם׃ אַךְ ׀
however (15) in-eyes-of-you and-as-the-right as-the-good with-me do! in-hand-of-you

יָדֹעַ תֵּדְעוּ כִּי אִם־ מְמִתִים אַתֶּם אֹתִי כִּי־ דָם
blood that me you ones-putting-to-death if that you-be-assured to-be-assured

נָקִי אַתֶּם נֹתְנִים עֲלֵיכֶם וְאֶל־ הָעִיר הַזֹּאת וְאֶל־ יֹשְׁבֶיהָ
ones-living-of-her and-on the-this the-city and-on on-you ones-bringing you innocent

כִּי בֶאֱמֶת שְׁלָחַנִי יְהוָה עֲלֵיכֶם לְדַבֵּר בְּאָזְנֵיכֶם אֵת כָּל־ הַדְּבָרִים
the-words all-of *** in-ears-of-you to-speak to-you Yahweh he-sent-me in-truth for

הָאֵלֶּה׃ וַיֹּאמְרוּ הַשָּׂרִים וְכָל־ הָעָם אֶל־ הַכֹּהֲנִים
the-priests to the-people and-all-of the-officials then-they-said (16) the-these

וְאֶל־ הַנְּבִיאִים אֵין־ לָאִישׁ הַזֶּה מִשְׁפַּט־ מָוֶת כִּי בְּשֵׁם
in-name-of indeed death sentence-of the-this to-the-man not the-prophets and-to

יְהוָה אֱלֹהֵינוּ דִּבֶּר אֵלֵינוּ׃ וַיָּקֻמוּ אֲנָשִׁים מִזִּקְנֵי
from-elders-of men then-they-stepped-forward (17) to-us he-spoke God-of-us Yahweh

הָאָרֶץ וַיֹּאמְרוּ אֶל־ כָּל־ קְהַל הָעָם לֵאמֹר׃ מִיכָיה°
Micah (18) to-say the-people assembly-of entire-of to and-they-said the-land

הַמּוֹרַשְׁתִּי הָיָה נִבָּא בִּימֵי חִזְקִיָּהוּ מֶלֶךְ־ יְהוּדָה וַיֹּאמֶר
and-he-told Judah king-of Hezekiah in-days-of prophesying he-was the-Moreshethite

אֶל־ כָּל־ עַם יְהוּדָה לֵאמֹר כֹּה־ אָמַר ׀ יְהוָה צְבָאוֹת צִיּוֹן שָׂדֶה
field Zion Hosts Yahweh-of he-says this to-say Judah people-of all-of to

°18 ק מיכה

went up from the royal palace to the house of the LORD and took their places at the entrance of the New Gate of the LORD's house. [11]Then the priests and the prophets said to the officials and all the people, "This man should be sentenced to death because he has prophesied against this city. You have heard it with your own ears!"

[12]Then Jeremiah said to all the officials and all the people: "The LORD sent me to prophesy against this house and this city all the things you have heard. [13]Now reform your ways and your actions and obey the LORD your God. Then the LORD will relent and not bring the disaster he has pronounced against you. [14]As for me, I am in your hands; do with me whatever you think is good and right. [15]Be assured, however, that if you put me to death, you will bring the guilt of innocent blood on yourselves and on this city and on those who live in it, for in truth the LORD has sent me to you to speak all these words in your hearing."

[16]Then the officials and all the people said to the priests and the prophets, "This man should not be sentenced to death! He has spoken to us in the name of the LORD our God."

[17]Some of the elders of the land stepped forward and said to the entire assembly of people, [18]"Micah of Moresheth prophesied in the days of Hezekiah king of Judah. He told all the people of Judah, 'This is what the LORD Almighty says:

תֵחָרֵשׁ וִירוּשָׁלַיִם עִיִּים תִּהְיֶה וְהַר
and-hill-of she-will-become heaps-of-rubble and-Jerusalem she-will-be-plowed

הַבַּיִת לְבָמוֹת יָעַר׃ הֶהָמֵת הֱמִתֻהוּ
did-they-put-to-death-him to-put-to-death? (19) thicket as-mounds-of the-temple

חִזְקִיָּהוּ מֶלֶךְ־יְהוּדָה וְכָל־יְהוּדָה הֲלֹא יָרֵא אֶת־יְהוָה וַיְחַל אֶת־
*** and-he-sought Yahweh *** he-feared not? Judah or-any-of Judah king-of Hezekiah

פְּנֵי יְהוָה וַיִּנָּחֶם יְהוָה אֶל־הָרָעָה אֲשֶׁר־דִּבֶּר
he-pronounced that the-disaster concerning Yahweh and-he-relented Yahweh faces-of

עֲלֵיהֶם וַאֲנַחְנוּ עֹשִׂים רָעָה גְדוֹלָה עַל־נַפְשׁוֹתֵינוּ׃ וְגַם־
now-also (20) selves-of-us on terrible disaster ones-bringing now-we against-them

אִישׁ הָיָה מִתְנַבֵּא בְּשֵׁם יְהוָה אוּרִיָּהוּ בֶּן־שְׁמַעְיָהוּ מִקִּרְיַת
from-Kiriath-of Shemaiah son-of Uriah Yahweh in-name-of one-prophesying he-was man

הַיְּעָרִים וַיִּנָּבֵא עַל־הָעִיר הַזֹּאת וְעַל־הָאָרֶץ
the-land and-against the-this the-city against and-he-prophesied the-Jearim

הַזֹּאת כְּכֹל דִּבְרֵי יִרְמְיָהוּ׃ וַיִּשְׁמַע הַמֶּלֶךְ־יְהוֹיָקִים
Jehoiakim the-king when-he-heard (21) Jeremiah words-of as-all-of the-this

וְכָל־גִּבּוֹרָיו וְכָל־הַשָּׂרִים אֶת־דְּבָרָיו וַיְבַקֵּשׁ
then-he-sought words-of-him *** the-officials and-all-of officers-of-him and-all-of

הַמֶּלֶךְ הֲמִיתוֹ וַיִּשְׁמַע אוּרִיָּהוּ וַיִּרָא וַיִּבְרַח
and-he-fled and-he-feared Uriah but-he-heard to-put-to-death-him the-king

וַיָּבֹא מִצְרָיִם׃ וַיִּשְׁלַח הַמֶּלֶךְ יְהוֹיָקִים אֲנָשִׁים מִצְרָיִם אֵת אֶלְנָתָן
Elnathan *** Egypt men Jehoiakim the-king but-he-sent (22) Egypt and-he-went

בֶּן־עַכְבּוֹר וַאֲנָשִׁים אִתּוֹ אֶל־מִצְרָיִם׃ וַיּוֹצִיאוּ אֶת־אוּרִיָּהוּ
Uriah *** and-they-brought-out (23) Egypt to with-him and-men Acbor son-of

מִמִּצְרַיִם וַיְבִאֻהוּ אֶל־הַמֶּלֶךְ יְהוֹיָקִים וַיַּכֵּהוּ
and-he-had-struck-him Jehoiakim the-king to and-they-took-him from-Egypt

בֶּחָרֶב וַיַּשְׁלֵךְ אֶת־נִבְלָתוֹ אֶל־קִבְרֵי בְּנֵי הָעָם׃
the-people sons-of burial-places-of into body-of-him *** and-he-threw with-the-sword

אַךְ יַד אֲחִיקָם בֶּן־שָׁפָן הָיְתָה אֶת־יִרְמְיָהוּ לְבִלְתִּי תֵּת־
to-give not Jeremiah with she-was Shaphan son-of Ahikam hand-of furthermore (24)

אֹתוֹ בְיַד־הָעָם לַהֲמִיתוֹ׃ בְּרֵאשִׁית מַמְלֶכֶת
reign-of in-early-part-of (27:1) to-put-to-death-him the-people into-hand-of him

יְהוֹיָקִם בֶּן־יֹאושִׁיָּהוּ מֶלֶךְ יְהוּדָה הָיָה הַדָּבָר הַזֶּה אֶל־יִרְמְיָה
Jeremiah to the-this the-word he-came Judah king-of Josiah son-of Jehoiakim

מֵאֵת יְהוָה לֵאמֹר׃ כֹּה־אָמַר יְהוָה אֵלַי עֲשֵׂה לְךָ מוֹסֵרוֹת
straps for-you make! to-me Yahweh he-said this (2) to-say Yahweh from-with

וּמֹטוֹת וּנְתַתָּם עַל־צַוָּארֶךָ׃ וְשִׁלַּחְתָּם אֶל־מֶלֶךְ
king-of to then-you-send-them (3) neck-of-you on and-you-put-them and-crossbars

" 'Zion will be plowed like a
field,
Jerusalem will become a
heap of rubble,
the temple hill a mound
overgrown with
thickets.'[z]

[19]"Did Hezekiah king of Judah or
anyone else in Judah put him to
death? Did not Hezekiah fear the
LORD and seek his favor? And did
not the LORD relent, so that he did
not bring the disaster he pronounced against them? We are
about to bring a terrible disaster
on ourselves!"

[20](Now Uriah son of Shemaiah
from Kiriath Jearim was another
man who prophesied in the name
of the LORD; he prophesied the
same things against this city and
this land as Jeremiah did. [21]When
King Jehoiakim and all his officers
and officials heard his words, the
king sought to put him to death.
But Uriah heard of it and fled in
fear to Egypt. [22]King Jehoiakim,
however, sent Elnathan son of Acbor to Egypt, along with some other men. [23]They brought Uriah out
of Egypt and took him to King
Jehoiakim, who had him struck
down with a sword and his body
thrown into the burial place of the
common people.)

[24]Furthermore, Ahikam son of
Shaphan supported Jeremiah, and
so he was not handed over to the
people to be put to death.

*Judah to Serve Nebuchadnezzar*

27 Early in the reign of Zedekiah[a] son of Josiah king of
Judah, this word came to Jeremiah
from the LORD: [2]This is what the
LORD said to me: "Make a yoke out
of straps and crossbars and put it
on your neck. [3]Then send word to

[z]*18* Micah 3:12

[a]*1* A few Hebrew manuscripts and Syriac (see also Jer. 27:3, 12 and 28:1); most Hebrew manuscripts *Jehoiakim* (Most Septuagint manuscripts do not have this verse.)

אֱדוֹם וְאֶל־ מֶלֶךְ מוֹאָב וְאֶל־ מֶלֶךְ בְּנֵי עַמּוֹן וְאֶל־ מֶלֶךְ צֹר וְאֶל־
and-to Tyre king-of and-to Ammon sons-of king-of and-to Moab king-of and-to Edom

מֶלֶךְ צִידוֹן בְּיַד מַלְאָכִים הַבָּאִים יְרוּשָׁלַםִ אֶל־צִדְקִיָּהוּ מֶלֶךְ יְהוּדָה׃
Judah king-of Zedekiah to Jerusalem the-ones-coming envoys by-hand-of Sidon king-of

וְצִוִּיתָ אֹתָם אֶל־ אֲדֹנֵיהֶם לֵאמֹר כֹּה־ אָמַר יְהוָה צְבָאוֹת
Hosts Yahweh-of he-says this to-say masters-of-them for them and-you-command (4)

אֱלֹהֵי יִשְׂרָאֵל כֹּה תֹאמְרוּ אֶל־ אֲדֹנֵיכֶם׃ אָנֹכִי עָשִׂיתִי אֶת־ הָאָרֶץ אֶת־
*** the-earth *** I-made I (5) masters-of-you to you-tell this Israel God-of

הָאָדָם וְאֶת־הַבְּהֵמָה אֲשֶׁר עַל־ פְּנֵי הָאָרֶץ בְּכֹחִי הַגָּדוֹל
the-great with-power-of-me the-earth surfaces-of on that the-animal and the-person

וּבִזְרוֹעִי הַנְּטוּיָה וּנְתַתִּיהָ לַאֲשֶׁר יָשַׁר
he-is-pleasing to-whom and-I-give-her the-one-being-outstretched and-with-arm-of-me

בְּעֵינָי׃ וְעַתָּה אָנֹכִי נָתַתִּי אֶת־ כָּל־ הָאֲרָצוֹת הָאֵלֶּה
the-these the-countries all-of *** I-will-give I and-now (6) in-eyes-of-me

בְּיַד נְבוּכַדְנֶאצַּר מֶלֶךְ־ בָּבֶל עַבְדִּי וְגַם אֶת־ חַיַּת
animal-of *** and-even servant-of-me Babylon king-of Nebuchadnezzar into-hand-of

הַשָּׂדֶה נָתַתִּי לוֹ לְעָבְדוֹ׃ וְעָבְדוּ אֹתוֹ
him and-they-will-serve (7) to-be-subject-to-him to-him I-will-give the-wild

כָּל־ הַגּוֹיִם וְאֶת־ בְּנוֹ וְאֶת־ בֶּן־ בְּנוֹ עַד בֹּא־ עֵת
time-of to-come until son-of-him son-of and son-of-him and the-nations all-of

אַרְצוֹ גַּם־הוּא וְעָבְדוּ בוֹ גּוֹיִם רַבִּים וּמְלָכִים
and-kings many-ones nations to-him then-they-will-subjugate he also land-of-him

גְּדֹלִים׃ וְהָיָה הַגּוֹי וְהַמַּמְלָכָה אֲשֶׁר לֹא־ יַעַבְדוּ
they-will-serve not that or-the-kingdom the-nation and-he-will-be (8) great-ones

אֹתוֹ אֶת־ נְבוּכַדְנֶאצַּר מֶלֶךְ־ בָּבֶל וְאֵת אֲשֶׁר לֹא־ יִתֵּן אֶת־ צַוָּארוֹ
neck-of-him *** he-will-bow not that or Babylon king-of Nebuchadnezzar *** him

בְּעֹל מֶלֶךְ בָּבֶל בַּחֶרֶב וּבָרָעָב וּבַדֶּבֶר
and-with-the-plague and-with-the-famine with-the-sword Babylon king-of under-yoke-of

אֶפְקֹד עַל־ הַגּוֹי הַהוּא נְאֻם־ יְהוָה עַד־ תֻּמִּי
to-destroy-me until Yahweh declaration-of the-that the-nation to I-will-punish

אֹתָם בְּיָדוֹ׃ וְאַתֶּם אַל־ תִּשְׁמְעוּ אֶל־ נְבִיאֵיכֶם וְאֶל־
or-to prophets-of-you to you-listen not so-you (9) by-hand-of-him them

קֹסְמֵיכֶם וְאֶל חֲלֹמֹתֵיכֶם וְאֶל־ עֹנְנֵיכֶם
ones-being-mediums-of-you or-to dreams-of-you or-to ones-practicing-divination-of-you

וְאֶל־ כַּשָּׁפֵיכֶם אֲשֶׁר־הֵם אֹמְרִים אֲלֵיכֶם לֵאמֹר לֹא תַעַבְדוּ אֶת־
*** you-will-serve not to-say to-you ones-telling they who sorcerers-of-you or-to

מֶלֶךְ בָּבֶל׃ כִּי שֶׁקֶר הֵם נִבְּאִים לָכֶם לְמַעַן הַרְחִיק
to-remove-far so-that to-you ones-prophesying they lie indeed (10) Babylon king-of

the kings of Edom, Moab, Ammon, Tyre and Sidon through the envoys who have come to Jerusalem to Zedekiah king of Judah. 4 Give them a message for their masters and say, 'This is what the LORD Almighty, the God of Israel, says: "Tell this to your masters: 5 With my great power and outstretched arm I made the earth and its people and the animals that are on it, and I give it to anyone I please. 6 Now I will hand all your countries over to my servant Nebuchadnezzar king of Babylon; I will make even the wild animals subject to him. 7 All nations will serve him and his son and his grandson until the time for his land comes; then many nations and great kings will subjugate him.

8 " ' "If, however, any nation or kingdom will not serve Nebuchadnezzar king of Babylon or bow its neck under his yoke, I will punish that nation with the sword, famine and plague, declares the LORD, until I destroy it by his hand. 9 So do not listen to your prophets, your diviners, your interpreters of dreams, your mediums or your sorcerers who tell you, 'You will not serve the king of Babylon.' 10 They prophesy lies to you that will only serve to

אֶתְכֶם מֵעַל אַדְמַתְכֶם וְהִדַּחְתִּי אֶתְכֶם וַאֲבַדְתֶּם׃ וְהַגּוֹי
but-the-nation (11) and-you-will-perish you and-I-will-banish land-of-you from-on you

אֲשֶׁר יָבִיא אֶת־ צַוָּארוֹ בְּעֹל מֶלֶךְ־ בָּבֶל וַעֲבָדוֹ
and-he-will-serve-him Babylon king-of under-yoke-of neck-of-him *** he-will-bow that

וְהִנַּחְתִּיו עַל־ אַדְמָתוֹ נְאֻם־ יְהוָה וַעֲבָדָהּ
and-he-will-till-her Yahweh declaration-of land-of-him in then-I-will-let-remain-him

וְיָשַׁב בָּהּ׃ וְאֶל־ צִדְקִיָּה מֶלֶךְ־ יְהוּדָה דִּבַּרְתִּי כְּכָל־
as-all-of I-spoke Judah king-of Zedekiah and-to (12) on-her and-he-will-live

הַדְּבָרִים הָאֵלֶּה לֵאמֹר הָבִיאוּ אֶת־ צַוְּארֵיכֶם בְּעֹל מֶלֶךְ־ בָּבֶל
Babylon king-of under-yoke-of necks-of-you *** bow! to-say the-these the-messages

וְעִבְדוּ אֹתוֹ וְעַמּוֹ וִחְיוּ׃ לָמָּה תָמוּתוּ אַתָּה
you will-you-die why? (13) and-live! and-people-of-him him and-serve!

וְעַמֶּךָ בַּחֶרֶב בָּרָעָב וּבַדֶּבֶר כַּאֲשֶׁר דִּבֶּר
he-threatened just-as and-by-the-plague by-the-famine by-the-sword and-people-of-you

יְהוָה אֶל־ הַגּוֹי אֲשֶׁר לֹא־ יַעֲבֹד אֶת־ מֶלֶךְ בָּבֶל׃ וְאַל־
so-not (14) Babylon king-of *** he-will-serve not that the-nation to Yahweh

תִּשְׁמְעוּ אֶל־ דִּבְרֵי הַנְּבִאִים הָאֹמְרִים אֲלֵיכֶם לֵאמֹר לֹא
not to-say to-you the-ones-saying the-prophets words-of to you-listen

תַעַבְדוּ אֶת־ מֶלֶךְ בָּבֶל כִּי שֶׁקֶר הֵם נִבְּאִים לָכֶם׃ כִּי
indeed (15) to-you ones-prophesying they lie for Babylon king-of *** you-will-serve

לֹא שְׁלַחְתִּים נְאֻם־ יְהוָה וְהֵם נִבְּאִים בִּשְׁמִי
in-name-of-me ones-prophesying and-they Yahweh declaration-of I-sent-them not

לַשָּׁקֶר לְמַעַן הַדִּיחִי אֶתְכֶם וַאֲבַדְתֶּם אַתֶּם
you and-you-will-perish you to-banish-me therefore about-the-lie

וְהַנְּבִאִים הַנִּבְּאִים לָכֶם׃ וְאֶל־ הַכֹּהֲנִים וְאֶל־ כָּל־
all-of and-to the-priests then-to (16) to-you the-ones-prophesying and-the-prophets

הָעָם הַזֶּה דִּבַּרְתִּי לֵאמֹר כֹּה אָמַר יְהוָה אַל־ תִּשְׁמְעוּ אֶל־ דִּבְרֵי
words-of to you-listen not Yahweh he-says this to-say I-spoke the-this the-people

נְבִיאֵיכֶם הַנִּבְּאִים לָכֶם לֵאמֹר הִנֵּה כְלֵי בֵית־ יְהוָה
Yahweh house-of articles-of see! to-say to-you the-ones-prophesying prophets-of-you

מוּשָׁבִים מִבָּבֶלָה עַתָּה מְהֵרָה כִּי שֶׁקֶר הֵמָּה נִבְּאִים
ones-prophesying they lie for soon now from-at-Babylon ones-being-brought-back

לָכֶם׃ אַל־ תִּשְׁמְעוּ אֲלֵיהֶם עִבְדוּ אֶת־ מֶלֶךְ־ בָּבֶל וִחְיוּ לָמָּה
why? and-live! Babylon king-of *** serve! to-them you-listen not (17) to-you

תִהְיֶה הָעִיר הַזֹּאת חָרְבָּה׃ וְאִם־ נְבִאִים הֵם וְאִם־
and-if they prophets indeed-if (18) ruin the-this the-city should-she-become

יֵשׁ דְּבַר־ יְהוָה אִתָּם יִפְגְּעוּ־ נָא בַּיהוָה צְבָאוֹת לְבִלְתִּי־
not Hosts with-Yahweh-of now! let-them-plead with-them Yahweh word-of there-is

remove you far from your lands; I
will banish you and you will perish. 11 But if any nation will bow its
neck under the yoke of the king of
Babylon and serve him, I will let
that nation remain in its own land
to till it and to live there, declares
the LORD.'" '"

12 I gave the same message to
Zedekiah king of Judah. I said,
"Bow your neck under the yoke of
the king of Babylon; serve him
and his people, and you will live.
13 Why will you and your people
die by the sword, famine and
plague with which the LORD has
threatened any nation that will
not serve the king of Babylon?
14 Do not listen to the words of the
prophets who say to you, 'You will
not serve the king of Babylon,'
for they are prophesying lies to
you. 15 'I have not sent them,' declares the LORD. 'They are prophesying lies in my name. Therefore,
I will banish you and you will perish, both you and the prophets
who prophesy to you.'"

16 Then I said to the priests and
all these people, "This is what the
LORD says: Do not listen to the
prophets who say, 'Very soon
now the articles from the LORD's
house will be brought back from
Babylon.' They are prophesying
lies to you. 17 Do not listen to them.
Serve the king of Babylon, and
you will live. Why should this city
become a ruin? 18 If they are prophets and have the word of the LORD,

בֹּאוּ הַכֵּלִים ׀ הַנּוֹתָרִים בְּבֵית־ יְהוָה וּבֵית
and-palace-of Yahweh in-house-of the-ones-remaining the-furnishings they-might-go

מֶלֶךְ יְהוּדָה וּבִירוּשָׁלִַם בָּבֶלָה׃ כִּי כֹה אָמַר יְהוָה צְבָאוֹת
Hosts Yahweh-of he-says this for (19) to-Babylon and-in-Jerusalem Judah king-of

אֶל־ הָעַמֻּדִים וְעַל־ הַיָּם וְעַל־ הַמְּכֹנוֹת וְעַל יֶתֶר
other-of and-about the-movable-stands and-about the-Sea and-about the-pillars about

הַכֵּלִים הַנּוֹתָרִים בָּעִיר הַזֹּאת׃ אֲשֶׁר לֹא־ לְקָחָם
he-took-them not which (20) the-this in-the-city the-ones-being-left the-furnishings

נְבוּכַדְנֶאצַּר מֶלֶךְ בָּבֶל בַּגְלוֹתוֹ אֶת־ יְכוֹנְיָה בֶן־ יְהוֹיָקִים
Jehoiakim son-of Jeconiah *** when-to-exile-him Babylon king-of Nebuchadnezzar

מֶלֶךְ־ יְהוּדָה מִירוּשָׁלִַם בָּבֶלָה וְאֵת כָּל־ חֹרֵי יְהוּדָה וִירוּשָׁלִָם׃
and-Jerusalem Judah nobles-of all-of with to-Babylon from-Jerusalem Judah king-of

כִּי כֹה אָמַר יְהוָה צְבָאוֹת אֱלֹהֵי יִשְׂרָאֵל עַל־ הַכֵּלִים
the-things about Israel God-of Hosts Yahweh-of he-says this yes (21)

הַנּוֹתָרִים בֵּית יְהוָה וּבֵית מֶלֶךְ־ יְהוּדָה וִירוּשָׁלִָם׃
and-Jerusalem Judah king-of and-palace-of Yahweh house-of the-ones-being-left

בָּבֶלָה יוּבָאוּ וְשָׁמָּה יִהְיוּ עַד יוֹם
day-of until they-will-remain and-at-there they-will-be-taken to-Babylon (22)

פָּקְדִי אֹתָם נְאֻם־ יְהוָה וְהַעֲלִיתִים
then-I-will-bring-back-them Yahweh declaration-of for-them to-come-me

וַהֲשִׁבֹתִים אֶל־ הַמָּקוֹם הַזֶּה׃ וַיְהִי ׀ בַּשָּׁנָה הַהִיא
the-same in-the-year and-he-was (28:1) the-this the-place to and-I-will-restore-them

בְּרֵאשִׁית מַמְלֶכֶת צִדְקִיָּה מֶלֶךְ־ יְהוּדָה בִּשְׁנַת הָרְבִעִית בַּחֹדֶשׁ
in-the-month the-fourth in-the-year Judah king-of Zedekiah reign-of in-early-part-of

הַחֲמִישִׁי אָמַר אֵלַי חֲנַנְיָה בֶן־ עַזּוּר הַנָּבִיא אֲשֶׁר מִגִּבְעוֹן
from-Gibeon who the-prophet Azzur son-of Hananiah to-me he-said the-fifth

בְּבֵית יְהוָה לְעֵינֵי הַכֹּהֲנִים וְכָל־ הָעָם לֵאמֹר׃ כֹּה־
this (2) to-say the-people and-all-of the-priests before-eyes-of Yahweh in-house-of

אָמַר יְהוָה צְבָאוֹת אֱלֹהֵי יִשְׂרָאֵל לֵאמֹר שָׁבַרְתִּי אֶת־ עֹל מֶלֶךְ
king-of yoke-of *** I-will-break to-say Israel God-of Hosts Yahweh-of he-says

בָּבֶל׃ בְּעוֹד ׀ שְׁנָתַיִם יָמִים אֲנִי מֵשִׁיב אֶל־ הַמָּקוֹם הַזֶּה אֶת־
*** the-this the-place to bringing-back I days two-years while-yet (3) Babylon

כָּל־ כְּלֵי בֵּית יְהוָה אֲשֶׁר לָקַח נְבוּכַדְנֶאצַּר מֶלֶךְ־ בָּבֶל
Babylon king-of Nebuchadnezzar he-removed that Yahweh house-of articles-of all-of

מִן־ הַמָּקוֹם הַזֶּה וַיְבִיאֵם בָּבֶל׃ וְאֶת־ יְכָנְיָה בֶן־ יְהוֹיָקִים
Jehoiakim son-of Jeconiah and (4) Babylon and-he-took-them the-this the-place from

מֶלֶךְ־ יְהוּדָה וְאֶת־ כָּל־ גָּלוּת יְהוּדָה הַבָּאִים בָּבֶלָה אֲנִי מֵשִׁיב
bringing-back I to-Babylon the-ones-going Judah exile-of all-of and Judah king-of

let them plead with the LORD Almighty that the furnishings remaining in the house of the LORD and in the palace of the king of Judah and in Jerusalem not be taken to Babylon.
19For this is what the LORD Almighty says about the pillars, the Sea, the movable stands and the other furnishings that are left in this city,
20which Nebuchadnezzar king of Babylon did not take away when he carried Jehoiachin[c] son of Jehoiakim king of Judah into exile from Jerusalem to Babylon, along with all the nobles of Judah and Jerusalem—
21yes, this is what the LORD Almighty, the God of Israel, says about the things that are left in the house of the LORD and in the palace of the king of Judah and in Jerusalem:
22'They will be taken to Babylon and there they will remain until the day I come for them,' declares the LORD. 'Then I will bring them back and restore them to this place.'"

*The False Prophet Hananiah*

28 In the fifth month of that same year, the fourth year, early in the reign of Zedekiah king of Judah, the prophet Hananiah son of Azzur, who was from Gibeon, said to me in the house of the LORD in the presence of the priests and all the people:
2"This is what the LORD Almighty, the God of Israel, says: 'I will break the yoke of the king of Babylon.
3Within two years I will bring back to this place all the articles of the LORD's house that Nebuchadnezzar king of Babylon removed from here and took to Babylon.
4I will also bring back to this place Jehoiachin[c] son of Jehoiakim king of Judah and all the other exiles from Judah who went to Babylon,' declares the

[c]20,4 Hebrew *Jeconiah*, a variant of *Jehoiachin*

*3 Most mss have *sheva* under the *daleth* (קְדִי־).

° 1 ק בשנה

אֶל־הַמָּקוֹם הַזֶּה נְאֻם־ יְהוָה כִּי אֶשְׁבֹּר אֶת־ עֹל מֶלֶךְ
king-of yoke-of *** I-will-break for Yahweh declaration-of the-this the-place to

בָּבֶל׃ וַיֹּאמֶר יִרְמְיָה הַנָּבִיא אֶל־ חֲנַנְיָה הַנָּבִיא
the-prophet Hananiah to the-prophet Jeremiah then-he-replied (5) Babylon

לְעֵינֵי הַכֹּהֲנִים וּלְעֵינֵי כָּל־ הָעָם הָעֹמְדִים
the-ones-standing the-people all-of and-before-eyes-of the-priests before-eyes-of

בְּבֵית יְהוָה׃ וַיֹּאמֶר יִרְמְיָה הַנָּבִיא אָמֵן כֵּן יַעֲשֶׂה יְהוָה
Yahweh may-he-do so amen the-prophet Jeremiah and-he-said (6) Yahweh in-house-of

יָקֵם יְהוָה אֶת־ דְּבָרֶיךָ אֲשֶׁר נִבֵּאתָ לְהָשִׁיב כְּלֵי
articles-of to-bring-back you-prophesied that words-of-you *** Yahweh may-he-fulfill

בֵית־ יְהוָה וְכָל־ הַגּוֹלָה מִבָּבֶל אֶל־ הַמָּקוֹם הַזֶּה׃
the-this the-place to from-Babylon the-exile and-all-of Yahweh house-of

אַךְ־ שְׁמַע־ נָא הַדָּבָר הַזֶּה אֲשֶׁר אָנֹכִי דֹּבֵר בְּאָזְנֶיךָ
in-ears-of-you saying I that the-this the-word now! listen! nevertheless (7)

וּבְאָזְנֵי כָּל־ הָעָם׃ הַנְּבִיאִים אֲשֶׁר הָיוּ לְפָנַי
preceding-me they-were who the-prophets (8) the-people all-of and-in-ears-of

וּלְפָנֶיךָ מִן־ הָעוֹלָם וַיִּנָּבְאוּ אֶל־ אֲרָצוֹת
countries against and-they-prophesied the-early-time from and-preceding-you

רַבּוֹת וְעַל־ מַמְלָכוֹת גְּדֹלוֹת לְמִלְחָמָה וּלְרָעָה
and-about-disaster about-war great-ones kingdoms and-against many-ones

וּלְדָבֶר׃ הַנָּבִיא אֲשֶׁר יִנָּבֵא לְשָׁלוֹם בְּבֹא
when-to-come-true about-peace he-prophesies who the-prophet (9) and-about-plague

דְּבַר הַנָּבִיא יִוָּדַע הַנָּבִיא אֲשֶׁר־ שְׁלָחוֹ יְהוָה
Yahweh he-sent-him that the-prophet he-will-be-recognized the-prophet prediction-of

בֶּאֱמֶת׃ וַיִּקַּח חֲנַנְיָה הַנָּבִיא אֶת־ הַמּוֹטָה מֵעַל צַוַּאר
neck-of from-on the-yoke *** the-prophet Hananiah then-he-took (10) in-truth

יִרְמְיָה הַנָּבִיא וַיִּשְׁבְּרֵהוּ׃ וַיֹּאמֶר חֲנַנְיָה לְעֵינֵי
before-eyes-of Hananiah and-he-said (11) and-he-broke-him the-prophet Jeremiah

כָל־ הָעָם לֵאמֹר כֹּה אָמַר יְהוָה כָּכָה אֶשְׁבֹּר אֶת־ עֹל
yoke-of *** I-will-break same-way Yahweh he-says this to-say the-people all-of

נְבֻכַדְנֶאצַּר מֶלֶךְ־ בָּבֶל בְּעוֹד שְׁנָתַיִם יָמִים מֵעַל־ צַוַּאר כָּל־
all-of neck-of from-on days two-years while-yet Babylon king-of Nebuchadnezzar

הַגּוֹיִם וַיֵּלֶךְ יִרְמְיָה הַנָּבִיא לְדַרְכּוֹ׃ וַיְהִי
and-he-came (12) on-way-of-him the-prophet Jeremiah then-he-went the-nations

דְבַר־ יְהוָה אֶל־יִרְמְיָה אַחֲרֵי שְׁבוֹר חֲנַנְיָה הַנָּבִיא אֶת־הַמּוֹטָה
the-yoke *** the-prophet Hananiah to-break-off after Jeremiah to Yahweh word-of

מֵעַל צַוַּאר יִרְמְיָה הַנָּבִיא לֵאמֹר׃ הָלוֹךְ וְאָמַרְתָּ אֶל־ חֲנַנְיָה
Hananiah to and-you-tell to-go (13) to-say the-prophet Jeremiah neck-of from-on

LORD, 'for I will break the yoke of
the king of Babylon.' "
[5]Then the prophet Jeremiah replied to the prophet Hananiah before the priests and all the people
who were standing in the house
of the LORD. [6]He said, "Amen! May
the LORD do so! May the LORD fulfill the words you have prophesied by bringing the articles of the
LORD's house and all the exiles
back to this place from Babylon.
[7]Nevertheless, listen to what I
have to say in your hearing and in
the hearing of all the people:
[8]From early times the prophets
who preceded you and me have
prophesied war, disaster and
plague against many countries
and great kingdoms. [9]But the
prophet who prophesies peace
will be recognized as one truly
sent by the LORD only if his pre-
diction comes true."
[10]Then the prophet Hananiah
took the yoke off the neck of the
prophet Jeremiah and broke it,
[11]and he said before all the people,
"This is what the LORD says: 'In
the same way will I break the yoke
of Nebuchadnezzar king of Babylon off the neck of all the nations
within two years.' " At this, the
prophet Jeremiah went on his
way.
[12]Shortly after the prophet
Hananiah had broken the yoke off
the neck of the prophet Jeremiah,
the word of the LORD came to Jeremiah: [13]"Go and tell Hananiah,

לֵאמֹר כֹּה אָמַר יְהוָה מוֹטֹת עֵץ שָׁבָרְתָּ וְעָשִׂיתָ
but-you-will-get you-broke wood yokes-of Yahweh he-says this to-say

תַחְתֵּיהֶן מֹטוֹת בַּרְזֶל׃ כִּי כֹה־ אָמַר יְהוָה צְבָאוֹת אֱלֹהֵי יִשְׂרָאֵל
Israel God-of Hosts Yahweh-of he-says this for (14) iron yokes-of in-place-of-them

עֹל בַּרְזֶל נָתַתִּי עַל־ צַוַּאר כָּל־ הַגּוֹיִם הָאֵלֶּה לַעֲבֹד אֶת־
*** to-serve the-these the-nations all-of neck-of on I-will-put iron yoke-of

נְבֻכַדְנֶאצַּר מֶלֶךְ־ בָּבֶל וַעֲבָדֻהוּ וְגַם אֶת־ חַיַּת
animal-of *** and-even and-they-will-serve-him Babylon king-of Nebuchadnezzar

הַשָּׂדֶה נָתַתִּי לוֹ׃ וַיֹּאמֶר יִרְמְיָה הַנָּבִיא אֶל־ חֲנַנְיָה
Hananiah to the-prophet Jeremiah then-he-said (15) to-him I-will-give the-wild

הַנָּבִיא שְׁמַע־ נָא חֲנַנְיָה לֹא־ שְׁלָחֲךָ יְהוָה וְאַתָּה הִבְטַחְתָּ
you-made-trust yet-you Yahweh he-sent-you not Hananiah now! listen! the-prophet

אֶת־ הָעָם הַזֶּה עַל־ שָׁקֶר׃ לָכֵן כֹּה אָמַר יְהוָה הִנְנִי
see-I! Yahweh he-says this therefore (16) lie in the-this the-nation ***

מְשַׁלֵּחֲךָ מֵעַל פְּנֵי הָאֲדָמָה הַשָּׁנָה אַתָּה מֵת כִּי־ סָרָה
rebellion because dying you the-year the-earth faces-of from-on removing-you

דִבַּרְתָּ אֶל־ יְהוָה׃ וַיָּמָת חֲנַנְיָה הַנָּבִיא בַּשָּׁנָה
in-the-year the-prophet Hananiah and-he-died (17) Yahweh against you-preached

הַהִיא בַּחֹדֶשׁ הַשְּׁבִיעִי׃ וְאֵלֶּה דִּבְרֵי הַסֵּפֶר אֲשֶׁר
that the-letter texts-of and-these (29:1) the-seventh in-the-month the-that

שָׁלַח יִרְמְיָה הַנָּבִיא מִירוּשָׁלָיִם אֶל־ יֶתֶר זִקְנֵי הַגּוֹלָה
the-exile elders-of survivor-of to from-Jerusalem the-prophet Jeremiah he-sent

וְאֶל־ הַכֹּהֲנִים וְאֶל־ הַנְּבִיאִים וְאֶל־ כָּל־ הָעָם אֲשֶׁר הֶגְלָה
he-exiled whom the-people all-of and-to the-prophets and-to the-priests and-to

נְבוּכַדְנֶאצַּר מִירוּשָׁלַיִם בָּבֶלָה׃ אַחֲרֵי צֵאת יְכָנְיָה־ הַמֶּלֶךְ
the-king Jeconiah to-go after (2) to-Babylon from-Jerusalem Nebuchadnezzar

וְהַגְּבִירָה וְהַסָּרִיסִים שָׂרֵי יְהוּדָה וִירוּשָׁלַיִם
and-Jerusalem Judah leaders-of and-the-court-officials and-the-queen-mother

וְהֶחָרָשׁ וְהַמַּסְגֵּר מִירוּשָׁלָיִם׃ בְּיַד אֶלְעָשָׂה בֶן־
son-of Elasah by-hand-of (3) from-Jerusalem and-the-artisan and-the-craftsman

שָׁפָן וּגְמַרְיָה בֶּן־ חִלְקִיָּה אֲשֶׁר שָׁלַח צִדְקִיָּה מֶלֶךְ־ יְהוּדָה אֶל־
to Judah king-of Zedekiah he-sent whom Hilkiah son-of and-Gemariah Shaphan

נְבוּכַדְנֶאצַּר מֶלֶךְ בָּבֶל בָּבֶלָה לֵאמֹר׃ כֹּה אָמַר יְהוָה צְבָאוֹת
Hosts Yahweh-of he-says this (4) to-say in-Babylon Babylon king-of Nebuchadnezzar

אֱלֹהֵי יִשְׂרָאֵל לְכָל־ הַגּוֹלָה אֲשֶׁר־ הִגְלֵיתִי מִירוּשָׁלַיִם בָּבֶלָה׃
to-Babylon from-Jerusalem I-exiled whom the-exile to-all-of Israel God-of

בְּנוּ בָתִּים וְשֵׁבוּ וְנִטְעוּ גַנּוֹת וְאִכְלוּ אֶת־ פִּרְיָן׃
produce-of-them *** and-eat! gardens and-plant! and-settle-down! houses build! (5)

'This is what the LORD says: You have broken a wooden yoke, but in its place you will get a yoke of iron. [14]This is what the LORD Almighty, the God of Israel, says: I will put an iron yoke on the necks of all these nations to make them serve Nebuchadnezzar king of Babylon, and they will serve him. I will even give him control over the wild animals.' "

[15]Then the prophet Jeremiah said to Hananiah the prophet, "Listen, Hananiah! The LORD has not sent you, yet you have persuaded this nation to trust in lies. [16]Therefore, this is what the LORD says: 'I am about to remove you from the face of the earth. This very year you are going to die, because you have preached rebellion against the LORD.' "

[17]In the seventh month of that same year, Hananiah the prophet died.

*A Letter to the Exiles*

**29** This is the text of the letter that the prophet Jeremiah sent from Jerusalem to the surviving elders among the exiles and to the priests, the prophets and all the other people Nebuchadnezzar had carried into exile from Jerusalem to Babylon. [2](This was after King Jehoiachin[d] and the queen mother, the court officials and the leaders of Judah and Jerusalem, the craftsmen and the artisans had gone into exile from Jerusalem.) [3]He entrusted the letter to Elasah son of Shaphan and to Gemariah son of Hilkiah, whom Zedekiah king of Judah sent to King Nebuchadnezzar in Babylon. It said:

[4]This is what the LORD Almighty, the God of Israel, says to all those I carried into exile from Jerusalem to Babylon: [5]"Build houses and settle down; plant gardens and eat

[d]2 Hebrew *Jeconiah*, a variant of *Jehoiachin*

קְחוּ נָשִׁים וְהוֹלִידוּ בָּנִים וּבָנוֹת וּקְחוּ לִבְנֵיכֶם נָשִׁים
wives for-sons-of-you and-find! and-daughters sons and-have! wives marry! (6)

וְאֶת־ בְּנוֹתֵיכֶם תְּנוּ לַאֲנָשִׁים וְתֵלַדְנָה בָּנִים וּבָנוֹת
and-daughters sons so-they-may-have to-husbands give! daughters-of-you and

וּרְבוּ־ שָׁם וְאַל־ תִּמְעָטוּ׃ וְדִרְשׁוּ אֶת־ שְׁלוֹם הָעִיר
the-city prosperity-of *** also-seek! (7) you-decrease and-not there and-increase!

אֲשֶׁר הִגְלֵיתִי אֶתְכֶם שָׁמָּה וְהִתְפַּלְלוּ בַעֲדָהּ אֶל־ יְהוָה כִּי
because Yahweh to on-behalf-of-her and-pray! to-there you I-exiled which

בִשְׁלוֹמָהּ יִהְיֶה לָכֶם שָׁלוֹם׃ כִּי כֹה אָמַר יְהוָה
Yahweh-of he-says this yes (8) prosperity to-you he-will-be in-prosperity-of-her

צְבָאוֹת אֱלֹהֵי יִשְׂרָאֵל אַל־ יַשִּׁיאוּ לָכֶם נְבִיאֵיכֶם אֲשֶׁר־ בְּקִרְבְּכֶם
in-among-you that prophets-of-you to-you let-them-deceive not Israel God-of Hosts

וְקֹסְמֵיכֶם וְאַל־ תִּשְׁמְעוּ אֶל־ חֲלֹמֹתֵיכֶם אֲשֶׁר אַתֶּם
you that dreams-of-you to you-listen and-not and-ones-practicing-divination-of-you

מַחְלְמִים׃ כִּי בְשֶׁקֶר הֵם נִבְּאִים לָכֶם בִּשְׁמִי לֹא
not in-name-of-me to-you ones-prophesying they about-lie for (9) ones-making-dream

שְׁלַחְתִּים נְאֻם־ יְהוָה׃ כִּי־ כֹה אָמַר יְהוָה כִּי
when Yahweh he-says this indeed (10) Yahweh declaration-of I-sent-them

לְפִי מְלֹאת לְבָבֶל שִׁבְעִים שָׁנָה אֶפְקֹד אֶתְכֶם
to-you I-will-come year seventy for-Babylon to-be-completed by-mouth-of-me

וַהֲקִמֹתִי עֲלֵיכֶם אֶת־ דְּבָרִי הַטּוֹב לְהָשִׁיב אֶתְכֶם אֶל־
to you to-bring-back the-gracious promise-of-me *** for-you and-I-will-fulfill

הַמָּקוֹם הַזֶּה׃ כִּי אָנֹכִי יָדַעְתִּי אֶת־הַמַּחֲשָׁבֹת אֲשֶׁר אָנֹכִי חֹשֵׁב עֲלֵיכֶם
for-you planning I that the-plans *** I-know I for (11) the-this the-place

נְאֻם־ יְהוָה מַחְשְׁבוֹת שָׁלוֹם וְלֹא לְרָעָה לָתֵת לָכֶם אַחֲרִית
future to-you to-give for-harm and-not prosperity plans-of Yahweh declaration-of

וְתִקְוָה׃ וּקְרָאתֶם אֹתִי וַהֲלַכְתֶּם וְהִתְפַּלַּלְתֶּם אֵלָי
to-me and-you-will-pray and-you-will-come me then-you-will-call-upon (12) and-hope

וְשָׁמַעְתִּי אֲלֵיכֶם׃ וּבִקַּשְׁתֶּם אֹתִי וּמְצָאתֶם כִּי
when and-you-will-find me and-you-will-seek (13) to-you and-I-will-listen

תִדְרְשֻׁנִי בְּכָל־ לְבַבְכֶם׃ וְנִמְצֵאתִי לָכֶם נְאֻם־
declaration-of by-you and-I-will-be-found (14) heart-of-you with-all-of you-seek-me

יְהוָה וְשַׁבְתִּי אֶת־ שְׁבִיתְכֶם וְקִבַּצְתִּי אֶתְכֶם מִכָּל־
from-all-of you and-I-will-gather captivity-of-you *** and-I-will-bring-back Yahweh

הַגּוֹיִם וּמִכָּל־ הַמְּקוֹמוֹת אֲשֶׁר הִדַּחְתִּי אֶתְכֶם שָׁם נְאֻם־
declaration-of there you I-banished where the-places and-from-all-of the-nations

יְהוָה וַהֲשִׁבֹתִי אֶתְכֶם אֶל־ הַמָּקוֹם אֲשֶׁר־הִגְלֵיתִי אֶתְכֶם מִשָּׁם׃
from-there you I-exiled which the-place to you and-I-will-bring-back Yahweh

°14 ק שבותכם

what they produce. 6Marry and
have sons and daughters; find
wives for your sons and give
your daughters in marriage, so
that they too may have sons
and daughters. Increase in
number there; do not decrease.
7Also, seek the peace and prosperity of the city to which I
have carried you into exile.
Pray to the LORD for it, because
if it prospers, you too will prosper." 8Yes, this is what the
LORD Almighty, the God of Israel, says: "Do not let the
prophets and diviners among
you deceive you. Do not listen
to the dreams you encourage
them to have. 9They are
prophesying lies to you in my
name. I have not sent them,"
declares the LORD.
10This is what the LORD says:
"When seventy years are completed for Babylon, I will come
to you and fulfill my gracious
promise to bring you back to
this place. 11For I know the
plans I have for you," declares
the LORD, "plans to prosper
you and not to harm you, plans
to give you hope and a future.
12Then you will call upon me
and come and pray to me, and
I will listen to you. 13You will
seek me and find me when you
seek me with all your heart. 14I
will be found by you," declares
the LORD, "and will bring you
back from captivity.[e] I will
gather you from all the nations
and places where I have banished you," declares the LORD,
"and will bring you back to the
place from which I carried you
into exile."

[e]14 Or *will restore your fortunes*

כִּי אֲמַרְתֶּם הֵקִים לָנוּ יְהוָה נְבִאִים בָּבֶלָה׃ כִּי־
but (16) in-Babylon prophets Yahweh for-us he-raised-up you-may-say indeed (15)

כֹה ׀ אָמַר יְהוָה אֶל־הַמֶּלֶךְ הַיּוֹשֵׁב אֶל־כִּסֵּא דָוִד וְאֶל־כָּל־
all-of and-about David throne-of on the-one-sitting the-king about Yahweh he-says this

הָעָם הַיּוֹשֵׁב בָּעִיר הַזֹּאת אֲחֵיכֶם אֲשֶׁר לֹא־
not who countrymen-of-you the-this in-the-city the-one-remaining the-people

יָצְאוּ אִתְּכֶם בַּגּוֹלָה׃ כֹּה אָמַר יְהוָה צְבָאוֹת הִנְנִי מְשַׁלֵּחַ
sending see-I! Hosts Yahweh-of he-says this (17) into-the-exile with-you they-went

בָּם אֶת־הַחֶרֶב אֶת־הָרָעָב וְאֶת־הַדָּבֶר וְנָתַתִּי אוֹתָם
them and-I-will-make the-plague and the-famine *** the-sword *** against-them

כַּתְּאֵנִים הַשֹּׁעָרִים אֲשֶׁר לֹא־ תֵאָכַלְנָה מֵרֹעַ׃
from-badness they-can-be-eaten not that the-poor-ones like-the-figs

וְרָדַפְתִּי אַחֲרֵיהֶם בַּחֶרֶב בָּרָעָב וּבַדָּבֶר
and-with-the-plague with-the-famine with-the-sword after-them and-I-will-pursue (18)

וּנְתַתִּים לְזַוָעָה לְכֹל ׀ מַמְלְכוֹת הָאָרֶץ לְאָלָה
as-curse the-earth kingdoms-of to-all-of as-abhorrence and-I-will-make-them

וּלְשַׁמָּה וְלִשְׁרֵקָה וּלְחֶרְפָּה בְּכָל־ הַגּוֹיִם אֲשֶׁר־
where the-nations among-all-of and-as-reproach and-as-scorn and-as-horror

הִדַּחְתִּים שָׁם׃ תַּחַת אֲשֶׁר־לֹא־ שָׁמְעוּ אֶל־ דְּבָרַי נְאֻם־
declaration-of words-of-me to they-listened not that for (19) there I-drive-them

יְהוָה אֲשֶׁר שָׁלַחְתִּי אֲלֵיהֶם אֶת־ עֲבָדַי הַנְּבִאִים הַשְׁכֵּם וְשָׁלֹחַ
and-to-send to-begin-early the-prophets servants-of-me by to-them I-sent that Yahweh

וְלֹא שְׁמַעְתֶּם נְאֻם־ יְהוָה׃ וְאַתֶּם שִׁמְעוּ דְבַר־ יְהוָה
Yahweh word-of hear! therefore-you (20) Yahweh declaration-of you-listened and-not

כָּל־ הַגּוֹלָה אֲשֶׁר־ שִׁלַּחְתִּי מִירוּשָׁלַםִ בָּבֶלָה׃ כֹּה־ אָמַר
he-says this (21) to-Babylon from-Jerusalem I-sent-away whom the-exile all-of

יְהוָה צְבָאוֹת אֱלֹהֵי יִשְׂרָאֵל אֶל־אַחְאָב בֶּן־ קוֹלָיָה וְאֶל־ צִדְקִיָּהוּ בֶן־
son-of Zedekiah and-about Kolaiah son-of Ahab about Israel God-of Hosts Yahweh-of

מַעֲשֵׂיָה הַנִּבְּאִים לָכֶם בִּשְׁמִי שָׁקֶר הִנְנִי ׀ נֹתֵן אֹתָם
them giving see-I! lie in-name-of-me to-you the-ones-prophesying Maaseiah

בְּיַד נְבוּכַדְרֶאצַּר מֶלֶךְ־ בָּבֶל וְהִכָּם
and-he-will-put-to-death-them Babylon king-of Nebuchadrezzar into-hand-of

לְעֵינֵיכֶם׃ וְלֻקַּח מֵהֶם קְלָלָה לְכֹל גָּלוּת
exile-of by-all-of curse because-of-them and-he-will-be-used (22) before-eyes-of-you

יְהוּדָה אֲשֶׁר בְּבָבֶל לֵאמֹר יְשִׂמְךָ יְהוָה כְּצִדְקִיָּהוּ וּכְאֶחָב
and-like-Ahab like-Zedekiah Yahweh may-he-treat-you to-say in-Babylon who Judah

אֲשֶׁר־ קָלָם מֶלֶךְ־ בָּבֶל בָּאֵשׁ׃ יַעַן אֲשֶׁר עָשׂוּ
they-did that for (23) in-the-fire Babylon king-of he-burned-them whom

[15]You may say, "The LORD has raised up prophets for us in Babylon," [16]but this is what the LORD says about the king who sits on David's throne and all the people who remain in this city, your countrymen who did not go with you into exile— [17]yes, this is what the LORD Almighty says: "I will send the sword, famine and plague against them and I will make them like poor figs that are so bad they cannot be eaten. [18]I will pursue them with the sword, famine and plague and will make them abhorrent to all the kingdoms of the earth and an object of cursing and horror, of scorn and reproach, among all the nations where I drive them. [19]For they have not listened to my words," declares the LORD, "words that I sent to them again and again by my servants the prophets. And you exiles have not listened either," declares the LORD.

[20]Therefore, hear the word of the LORD, all you exiles whom I have sent away from Jerusalem to Babylon. [21]This is what the LORD Almighty, the God of Israel, says about Ahab son of Kolaiah and Zedekiah son of Maaseiah, who are prophesying lies to you in my name: "I will hand them over to Nebuchadnezzar king of Babylon, and he will put them to death before your very eyes. [22]Because of them, all the exiles from Judah who are in Babylon will use this curse: 'The LORD treat you like Zedekiah and Ahab, whom the king of Babylon burned in the fire.' [23]For

°18 ק לזועה

נְבָלָה בְּיִשְׂרָאֵל וַיְנַאֲפוּ אֶת־ נְשֵׁי רֵעֵיהֶם
neighbors-of-them wives-of with and-they-committed-adultery in-Israel outrage

וַיְדַבְּרוּ דָבָר בִּשְׁמִי שֶׁקֶר אֲשֶׁר לוֹא צִוִּיתָם וְאָנֹכִי
and-I I-commanded-them not which lie in-name-of-me word and-they-spoke

הַוּיֹדֵעַ° וָעֵד נְאֻם־ יְהוָה׃ וְאֶל־ שְׁמַעְיָהוּ
Shemaiah and-to (24) Yahweh declaration-of and-witness the-one-knowing

הַנֶּחֱלָמִי תֹּאמַר לֵאמֹר׃ כֹּה־ אָמַר יְהוָה צְבָאוֹת אֱלֹהֵי יִשְׂרָאֵל
Israel God-of Hosts Yahweh-of he-says this (25) to-say you-tell the-Nehelamite

לֵאמֹר יַעַן אֲשֶׁר אַתָּה שָׁלַחְתָּ בְשִׁמְכָה סְפָרִים אֶל־ כָּל־ הָעָם
the-people all-of to letters in-name-of-you you-sent you that because to-say

אֲשֶׁר בִּירוּשָׁלִַם וְאֶל־ צְפַנְיָה בֶן־ מַעֲשֵׂיָה הַכֹּהֵן וְאֶל כָּל־
all-of and-to the-priest Maaseiah son-of Zephaniah and-to in-Jerusalem that

הַכֹּהֲנִים לֵאמֹר׃ יְהוָה נְתָנְךָ כֹהֵן תַּחַת יְהוֹיָדָע
Jehoiada in-place-of priest he-appointed-you Yahweh (26) to-say the-priests

הַכֹּהֵן לִהְיוֹת פְּקִדִים בֵּית יְהוָה לְכָל־ אִישׁ מְשֻׁגָּע
being-mad man to-any-of Yahweh house-of ones-in-charge to-be the-priest

וּמִתְנַבֵּא וְנָתַתָּה אֹתוֹ אֶל־הַמַּהְפֶּכֶת וְאֶל־ הַצִּינֹק׃
the-neck-iron and-into the-stock into him then-you-should-put and-acting-like-prophet

וְעַתָּה לָמָּה לֹא גָעַרְתָּ בְּיִרְמְיָהוּ הָעֲנְּתֹתִי*
the-Anathothite to-Jeremiah you-reprimanded not why? so-now (27)

הַמִּתְנַבֵּא לָכֶם׃ כִּי עַל־ כֵּן שָׁלַח אֵלֵינוּ בָּבֶל
in-Babylon to-us he-sent this as indeed (28) among-you the-one-posing-as-prophet

לֵאמֹר אֲרֻכָּה הִיא בְּנוּ בָתִּים וְשֵׁבוּ וְנִטְעוּ גַנּוֹת וְאִכְלוּ אֶת־
*** and-eat! gardens and-plant! and-settle-down! houses build! she long to-say

פְּרִיהֶן׃ וַיִּקְרָא צְפַנְיָה הַכֹּהֵן אֶת־ הַסֵּפֶר הַזֶּה
the-this the-letter *** the-priest Zephaniah however-he-read (29) produce-of-them

בְּאָזְנֵי יִרְמְיָהוּ הַנָּבִיא׃ וַיְהִי דְּבַר־ יְהוָה אֶל־יִרְמְיָהוּ
Jeremiah to Yahweh word-of then-he-came (30) the-prophet Jeremiah in-ears-of

לֵאמֹר׃ שְׁלַח עַל־ כָּל־ הַגּוֹלָה לֵאמֹר כֹּה אָמַר יְהוָה אֶל־ שְׁמַעְיָה
Shemaiah about Yahweh he-says this to-say the-exile all-of to send! (31) to-say

הַנֶּחֱלָמִי יַעַן אֲשֶׁר נִבָּא לָכֶם שְׁמַעְיָה וַאֲנִי לֹא שְׁלַחְתִּיו
I-sent-him not though-I Shemaiah to-you he-prophesied that because the-Nehelamite

וַיַּבְטַח אֶתְכֶם עַל־שָׁקֶר׃ לָכֵן כֹּה־ אָמַר יְהוָה הִנְנִי פֹקֵד
punishing see-I! Yahweh he-says this therefore (32) lie in you and-he-made-trust

עַל־שְׁמַעְיָה הַנֶּחֱלָמִי וְעַל־ זַרְעוֹ לֹא־ יִהְיֶה לוֹ אִישׁ ׀
one to-him he-will-be not descendant-of-him and-to the-Nehelamite Shemaiah to

יוֹשֵׁב ׀ בְּתוֹךְ־ הָעָם הַזֶּה וְלֹא־ יִרְאֶה בַטּוֹב אֲשֶׁר־אֲנִי עֹשֶׂה־
doing I that to-the-good he-will-see or-not the-this the-people in-among living

they have done outrageous things in Israel; they have committed adultery with their neighbors' wives and in my name have spoken lies, which I did not tell them to do. I know it and am a witness to it," declares the LORD.

*Message to Shemaiah*

[24]Tell Shemaiah the Nehelamite, [25]"This is what the LORD Almighty, the God of Israel, says: You sent letters in your own name to all the people in Jerusalem, to Zephaniah son of Maaseiah the priest, and to all the other priests. You said to Zephaniah, [26]'The LORD has appointed you priest in place of Jehoiada to be in charge of the house of the LORD; you should put any madman who acts like a prophet into the stocks and neck-irons. [27]So why have you not reprimanded Jeremiah from Anathoth, who poses as a prophet among you? [28]He has sent this message to us in Babylon: It will be a long time. Therefore build houses and settle down; plant gardens and eat what they produce.' "

[29]Zephaniah the priest, however, read the letter to Jeremiah the prophet. [30]Then the word of the LORD came to Jeremiah: [31]"Send this message to all the exiles: 'This is what the LORD says about Shemaiah the Nehelamite: Because Shemaiah has prophesied to you, even though I did not send him, and has led you to believe a lie, [32]this is what the LORD says: I will surely punish Shemaiah the Nehelamite and his descendants. He will have no one left among this people, nor will he see the good things I will do for my

*27 Most mss have *pathah* under the *ayin* (הָעַ).

°23 ק היודע

לְעַמִּי נְאֻם־יְהוָה כִּי־סָרָה דִבֶּר עַל־יְהוָה׃
Yahweh against he-preached rebellion because Yahweh declaration-of for-people-of-me

הַדָּבָר אֲשֶׁר הָיָה אֶל־יִרְמְיָהוּ מֵאֵת יְהוָה לֵאמֹר׃ כֹּה־
this (2) to-say Yahweh from-with Jeremiah to he-came that the-word (30:1)

אָמַר יְהוָה אֱלֹהֵי יִשְׂרָאֵל לֵאמֹר כְּתָב־לְךָ אֵת כָּל־הַדְּבָרִים אֲשֶׁר־
that the-words all-of *** for-you write! to-say Israel God-of Yahweh he-says

דִּבַּרְתִּי אֵלֶיךָ אֶל־סֵפֶר׃ כִּי הִנֵּה יָמִים בָּאִים נְאֻם־יְהוָה
Yahweh declaration-of ones-coming days see! indeed (3) book in to-you I-spoke

וְשַׁבְתִּי אֶת־שְׁבוּת עַמִּי יִשְׂרָאֵל וִיהוּדָה אָמַר
he-says and-Judah Israel people-of-me captivity-of *** when-I-will-bring-back

יְהוָה וַהֲשִׁבֹתִים אֶל־הָאָרֶץ אֲשֶׁר־נָתַתִּי לַאֲבוֹתָם
to-forefathers-of-them I-gave that the-land to and-I-will-restore-them Yahweh

וִירֵשׁוּהָ׃ וְאֵלֶּה הַדְּבָרִים אֲשֶׁר דִּבֶּר יְהוָה אֶל־יִשְׂרָאֵל
Israel concerning Yahweh he-spoke that the-words and-these (4) that-they-might-possess-her

וְאֶל־יְהוּדָה׃ כִּי־כֹה אָמַר יְהוָה קוֹל חֲרָדָה שָׁמָעְנוּ פַּחַד וְאֵין
and-not terror we-hear fear cry-of Yahweh he-says this indeed (5) Judah and-concerning

שָׁלוֹם׃ שַׁאֲלוּ־נָא וּרְאוּ אִם־יֹלֵד זָכָר מַדּוּעַ רָאִיתִי כָל־
every-of I-see why? man one-bearing-children if and-see! now! ask! (6) peace

גֶּבֶר יָדָיו עַל־חֲלָצָיו כַּיּוֹלֵדָה
like-the-woman-being-in-labor stomachs-of-him on hands-of-him strong-man

וְנֶהֶפְכוּ כָל־פָּנִים לְיֵרָקוֹן׃ הוֹי כִּי גָדוֹל הַיּוֹם הַהוּא
the-that the-day awful how woe! (7) to-deadly-pale faces every-of and-they-turned

מֵאַיִן כָּמֹהוּ וְעֵת־צָרָה הִיא לְיַעֲקֹב וּמִמֶּנָּה
but-out-of-her for-Jacob she trouble and-time-of like-him with-none

יִוָּשֵׁעַ׃ וְהָיָה בַיּוֹם הַהוּא נְאֻם ׀ יְהוָה
Yahweh-of declaration-of the-that in-the-day and-he-will-be (8) he-will-be-saved

צְבָאוֹת אֶשְׁבֹּר עֻלּוֹ מֵעַל צַוָּארֶךָ וּמוֹסְרוֹתֶיךָ
and-bonds-of-you neck-of-you from-on yoke-of-him I-will-break-off Hosts

אֲנַתֵּק וְלֹא־יַעַבְדוּ־בוֹ עוֹד זָרִים׃
ones-being-foreign longer to-him they-will-enslave and-not I-will-tear-off

וְעָבְדוּ אֵת יְהוָה אֱלֹהֵיהֶם וְאֵת דָּוִד מַלְכָּם אֲשֶׁר
whom king-of-them David and God-of-them Yahweh *** instead-they-will-serve (9)

אָקִים לָהֶם׃ וְאַתָּה אַל־תִּירָא עַבְדִּי יַעֲקֹב נְאֻם־
declaration-of Jacob servant-of-me you-fear not so-you (10) for-them I-will-raise

יְהוָה וְאַל־תֵּחַת יִשְׂרָאֵל כִּי הִנְנִי מוֹשִׁיעֲךָ מֵרָחוֹק
from-distant-place saving-you see-I! surely Israel you-be-dismayed and-not Yahweh

וְאֶת־זַרְעֲךָ מֵאֶרֶץ שִׁבְיָם וְשָׁב יַעֲקֹב
Jacob and-he-will-do-again exile-of-them from-land-of descendant-of-you and

people, declares the LORD, because he has preached rebellion against me.' "

*Restoration of Israel*

30 This is the word that came to Jeremiah from the LORD:
2"This is what the LORD, the God of Israel, says: 'Write in a book all the words I have spoken to you.
3The days are coming,' declares the LORD, 'when I will bring my people Israel and Judah back from captivity[f] and restore them to the land I gave their forefathers to possess,' says the LORD."
4These are the words the LORD spoke concerning Israel and Judah: 5"This is what the LORD says:

" 'Cries of fear are heard—
terror, not peace.
6Ask and see:
Can a man bear children?
Then why do I see every strong man
with his hands on his stomach like a woman in labor,
every face turned deathly pale?
7How awful that day will be!
None will be like it.
It will be a time of trouble for Jacob,
but he will be saved out of it.

8" 'In that day,' declares the LORD Almighty,
'I will break the yoke off their necks
and will tear off their bonds;
no longer will foreigners enslave them.
9Instead, they will serve the LORD their God
and David their king,
whom I will raise up for them.

10" 'So do not fear, O Jacob my servant;
do not be dismayed, O Israel,'
declares the LORD.
'I will surely save you out of a distant place,
your descendants from the land of their exile.

f3 Or *will restore the fortunes of my people Israel and Judah*

וְשָׁקַט וְשַׁאֲנַן וְאֵין מַחֲרִיד׃
making-afraid and-no-one and-he-will-have-security and-he-will-have-peace

כִּי־אִתְּךָ אֲנִי נְאֻם־יְהוָה לְהוֹשִׁיעֶךָ כִּי אֶעֱשֶׂה כָלָה
destruction I-do though to-save-you Yahweh declaration-of I with-you indeed (11)

בְּכָל־הַגּוֹיִם ׀ אֲשֶׁר הֲפִצוֹתִיךָ שָּׁם אַךְ אֹתְךָ לֹא־אֶעֱשֶׂה
I-will-do not you however there I-scatter-you which the-nations of-all-of

כָלָה וְיִסַּרְתִּיךָ לַמִּשְׁפָּט וְנַקֵּה לֹא
not and-to-let-go-unpunished with-the-justice but-I-will-discipline-you destruction

אֲנַקֶּךָּ׃ כִּי כֹה אָמַר יְהוָה אָנוּשׁ
being-incurable Yahweh he-says this indeed (12) I-will-let-go-unpunished-you

לְשִׁבְרֵךְ נַחְלָה מַכָּתֵךְ׃ אֵין־דָּן
one-pleading there-is-no (13) injury-of-you being-beyond-healing to-wound-of-you

דִּינֵךְ לְמָזוֹר רְפֻאוֹת תְּעָלָה אֵין לָךְ׃ כָּל־
all-of (14) for-you there-is-no healing remedies for-sore cause-of-you

מְאַהֲבַיִךְ שְׁכֵחוּךְ אוֹתָךְ לֹא יִדְרֹשׁוּ כִּי מַכַּת
striking-of indeed they-care-for not you they-forgot-you ones-being-allies-of-you

אוֹיֵב הִכִּיתִיךְ מוּסַר אַכְזָרִי עַל רֹב עֲוֺנֵךְ
guilt-of-you greatness-of because-of cruel discipline-of I-struck-you one-being-enemy

עָצְמוּ חַטֹּאתָיִךְ׃ מַה־תִּזְעַק עַל־שִׁבְרֵךְ אָנוּשׁ
being-incurable wound-of-you over you-cry-out why? (15) sins-of-you they-are-many

מַכְאֹבֵךְ עַל ׀ רֹב עֲוֺנֵךְ עָצְמוּ חַטֹּאתַיִךְ עָשִׂיתִי
I-did sins-of-you they-are-many guilt-of-you greatness-of because-of pain-of-you

אֵלֶּה לָךְ׃ לָכֵן כָּל־אֹכְלַיִךְ יֵאָכֵלוּ וְכָל־
and-all-of they-will-be-devoured ones-devouring-you all-of but (16) to-you these

צָרַיִךְ כֻּלָּם בַּשְּׁבִי יֵלֵכוּ וְהָיוּ
and-they-will-be they-will-go into-the-exile all-of-them enemies-of-you

שֹׁאסַיִךְ לִמְשִׁסָּה וְכָל־בֹּזְזַיִךְ אֶתֵּן
I-will-make ones-making-spoil-of-you and-all-of as-plunder ones-plundering-you

לָבַז׃ כִּי אַעֲלֶה אֲרֻכָה לָךְ וּמִמַּכּוֹתַיִךְ
and-from-wounds-of-you to-you health I-will-restore but (17) as-spoil

אֶרְפָּאֵךְ נְאֻם־יְהוָה כִּי נִדָּחָה קָרְאוּ לָךְ
to-you they-call one-being-outcast because Yahweh declaration-of I-will-heal-you

צִיּוֹן הִיא דֹּרֵשׁ אֵין לָהּ׃ כֹּה ׀ אָמַר יְהוָה הִנְנִי־
see-I! Yahweh he-says this (18) for-her there-is-not one-caring she Zion

שָׁב שְׁבוּת אָהֳלֵי יַעֲקוֹב וּמִשְׁכְּנֹתָיו אֲרַחֵם
I-will-have-compassion and-dwellings-of-him Jacob tents-of fortune-of restoring

וְנִבְנְתָה עִיר עַל־תִּלָּהּ וְאַרְמוֹן עַל־מִשְׁפָּטוֹ
proper-place-of-him in and-palace ruin-of-her on city and-she-will-be-rebuilt

Jacob will again have peace
and security,
and no one will make him
afraid.
11 I am with you and will save
you,'
declares the LORD.
'Though I completely destroy
all the nations
among which I scatter you,
I will not completely destroy
you.
I will discipline you but only
with justice;
I will not let you go entirely
unpunished.'

12 "This is what the LORD says:

" 'Your wound is incurable,
your injury beyond healing.
13 There is no one to plead your
cause,
no remedy for your sore,
no healing for you.
14 All your allies have forgotten
you;
they care nothing for you.
I have struck you as an enemy
would
and punished you as would
the cruel,
because your guilt is so great
and your sins so many.
15 Why do you cry out over your
wound,
your pain that has no cure?
Because of your great guilt and
many sins
I have done these things to
you.

16 " 'But all who devour you will
be devoured;
all your enemies will go into
exile.
Those who plunder you will be
plundered;
all who make spoil of you I
will despoil.
17 But I will restore you to health
and heal your wounds,'
declares the LORD,
'because you are called an
outcast,
Zion for whom no one
cares.'

18 "This is what the LORD says:

" 'I will restore the fortunes of
Jacob's tents
and have compassion on his
dwellings;
the city will be rebuilt on her
ruins,
and the palace will stand in
its proper place.

יֵשֵׁב׃ (19) וְיָצָא מֵהֶם תּוֹדָה וְקוֹל
and-sound-of song-of-thanksgiving from-them and-he-will-come (19) he-will-stand

מְשַׂחֲקִים וְהִרְבִּתִים וְלֹא יִמְעָטוּ
they-will-decrease and-not and-I-will-add-to-number-of-them ones-rejoicing

וְהִכְבַּדְתִּים וְלֹא יִצְעָרוּ׃ (20) וְהָיוּ
and-they-will-be (20) they-will-be-disdained and-not and-I-will-honor-them

בָנָיו כְּקֶדֶם וַעֲדָתוֹ לְפָנַי תִּכּוֹן
she-will-be-established before-me and-community-of-him as-of-old children-of-him

וּפָקַדְתִּי עַל כָּל־ לֹחֲצָיו׃ (21) וְהָיָה אַדִּירוֹ
leader-of-him and-he-will-be (21) ones-oppressing-him all-of to and-I-will-punish

מִמֶּנּוּ וּמֹשְׁלוֹ מִקִּרְבּוֹ יֵצֵא וְהִקְרַבְתִּיו
and-I-will-bring-near-him he-will-arise from-among-him and-one-ruling-him from-him

וְנִגַּשׁ אֵלָי כִּי מִי הוּא־ זֶה עָרַב אֶת־ לִבּוֹ
self-of-him *** he-will-devote this he who? for to-me and-he-will-come-close

לָגֶשֶׁת אֵלַי נְאֻם־ יְהוָה׃ (22) וִהְיִיתֶם לִי לְעָם וְאָנֹכִי
and-I as-people to-me so-you-will-be (22) Yahweh declaration-of to-me to-be-close

אֶהְיֶה לָכֶם לֵאלֹהִים׃ (23) הִנֵּה ׀ סַעֲרַת יְהוָה חֵמָה יָצְאָה סַעַר
wind she-will-burst-out wrath Yahweh storm-of see! (23) as-God to-you I-will-be

מִתְגּוֹרֵר עַל רֹאשׁ רְשָׁעִים יָחוּל׃ (24) לֹא יָשׁוּב
he-will-turn-back not (24) he-will-swirl-down wicked-ones head-of on driving

חֲרוֹן אַף־ יְהוָה עַד־ עֲשֹׂתוֹ וְעַד־ הֲקִימוֹ
to-complete-him and-until to-accomplish-him until Yahweh anger-of fierceness-of

מְזִמּוֹת לִבּוֹ בְּאַחֲרִית הַיָּמִים תִּתְבּוֹנְנוּ בָהּ׃
to-her you-will-understand the-days in-coming-of heart-of-him purposes-of

(31:1) בָּעֵת הַהִיא נְאֻם־ יְהוָה אֶהְיֶה לֵאלֹהִים לְכֹל
of-all-of as-God I-will-be Yahweh declaration-of the-that at-the-time (31:1)

מִשְׁפְּחוֹת יִשְׂרָאֵל וְהֵמָּה יִהְיוּ־ לִי לְעָם׃ (2) כֹּה אָמַר יְהוָה
Yahweh he-says this (2) as-people to-me they-will-be and-they Israel clans-of

מָצָא חֵן בַּמִּדְבָּר עַם שְׂרִידֵי חָרֶב הָלוֹךְ לְהַרְגִּיעוֹ
to-give-rest-him to-come sword survivors-of people in-the-desert favor he-will-find

יִשְׂרָאֵל׃ (3) מֵרָחוֹק יְהוָה נִרְאָה לִי וְאַהֲבַת עוֹלָם
everlasting indeed-love-of to-me he-appeared Yahweh in-past (3) Israel

אֲהַבְתִּיךְ עַל־ כֵּן מְשַׁכְתִּיךְ חָסֶד׃ (4) עוֹד אֶבְנֵךְ
I-will-build-up-you again (4) loving-kindness I-drew-you this for I-loved-you

וְנִבְנֵית בְּתוּלַת יִשְׂרָאֵל עוֹד תַּעְדִּי תֻפַּיִךְ
tambourines-of-you you-will-take-up again Israel Virgin-of and-you-will-be-rebuilt

וְיָצָאת בִּמְחוֹל מְשַׂחֲקִים׃ (5) עוֹד תִּטְּעִי כְרָמִים
vineyards you-will-plant again (5) ones-being-joyful to-dance-of and-you-will-go-out

19 From them will come songs of
thanksgiving
and the sound of rejoicing.
I will add to their numbers,
and they will not be
decreased;
I will bring them honor,
and they will not be
disdained.
20 Their children will be as in
days of old,
and their community will be
established before me;
I will punish all who
oppress them.
21 Their leader will be one of
their own;
their ruler will arise from
among them.
I will bring him near and he
will come close to me,
for who is he who will
devote himself
to be close to me?'
declares the LORD.
22 "'So you will be my people,
and I will be your God.'"
23 See, the storm of the LORD
will burst out in wrath,
a driving wind swirling down
on the heads of the wicked.
24 The fierce anger of the LORD
will not turn back
until he fully accomplishes
the purposes of his heart.
In days to come
you will understand this.

31 "At that time," declares the
LORD, "I will be the God of
all the clans of Israel, and they will
be my people."
2 This is what the LORD says:

"The people who survive the
sword
will find favor in the desert;
I will come to give rest to
Israel."

3 The LORD appeared to us in the
past,[g] saying:

"I have loved you with an
everlasting love;
I have drawn you with
loving-kindness.
4 I will build you up again
and you will be rebuilt, O
Virgin Israel.
Again you will take up your
tambourines
and go out to dance with
the joyful.
5 Again you will plant vineyards

*g3 Or LORD has appeared to us from afar*

בְּהָרֵי שֹׁמְרוֹן נָטְעוּ נֹטְעִים וְחִלֵּלוּ׃
and-they-will-enjoy-fruit ones-planting they-will-plant Samaria on-hills-of

כִּי יֶשׁ־יוֹם קָרְאוּ נֹצְרִים בְּהַר אֶפְרָיִם
Ephraim on-hill-of men-watching they-will-cry-out day there-will-be indeed (6)

קוּמוּ וְנַעֲלֶה צִיּוֹן אֶל־יְהוָה אֱלֹהֵינוּ׃ כִּי־כֹה ׀ אָמַר יְהוָה רָנּוּ
sing! Yahweh he-says this indeed (7) God-of-us Yahweh to Zion and-let-us-go come!

לְיַעֲקֹב שִׂמְחָה וְצַהֲלוּ בְּרֹאשׁ הַגּוֹיִם הַשְׁמִיעוּ הַלְלוּ וְאִמְרוּ
and-say! praise! make-heard! the-nations for-foremost-of and-shout! joy for-Jacob

הוֹשַׁע יְהוָה אֶת־עַמְּךָ אֵת שְׁאֵרִית יִשְׂרָאֵל׃ הִנְנִי מֵבִיא אוֹתָם
them bringing see-I! (8) Israel remnant-of *** people-of-you *** Yahweh save!

מֵאֶרֶץ צָפוֹן וְקִבַּצְתִּים מִיַּרְכְּתֵי־אָרֶץ בָּם עִוֵּר
blind among-them earth from-ends-of and-I-will-gather-them north from-land-of

וּפִסֵּחַ הָרָה וְיֹלֶדֶת יַחְדָּו קָהָל גָּדוֹל
great throng together and-woman-being-in-labor expectant-mother and-lame

יָשׁוּבוּ הֵנָּה׃ בִּבְכִי יָבֹאוּ וּבְתַחֲנוּנִים
and-with-prayers they-will-come with-weeping (9) to-here they-will-return

אוֹבִילֵם אוֹלִיכֵם אֶל־נַחֲלֵי מַיִם בְּדֶרֶךְ יָשָׁר
level on-path waters streams-of beside I-will-lead-them I-will-bring-back-them

לֹא יִכָּשְׁלוּ בָּהּ כִּי־הָיִיתִי לְיִשְׂרָאֵל לְאָב וְאֶפְרַיִם
and-Ephraim as-father to-Israel I-am because on-her they-will-stumble not

בְּכֹרִי הוּא׃ שִׁמְעוּ דְבַר־יְהוָה גּוֹיִם וְהַגִּידוּ בָאִיִּים
in-the-coastlands and-proclaim! nations Yahweh word-of hear! (10) he firstborn-of-me

מִמֶּרְחָק וְאִמְרוּ מְזָרֵה יִשְׂרָאֵל יְקַבְּצֶנּוּ וּשְׁמָרוֹ
and-he-will-watch-him he-will-gather-him Israel one-scattering-of and-say! at-distance

כְּרֹעֶה עֶדְרוֹ׃ כִּי־פָדָה יְהוָה אֶת־יַעֲקֹב
Jacob *** Yahweh he-will-ransom for (11) flock-of-him like-one-being-shepherd

וּגְאָלוֹ מִיַּד חָזָק מִמֶּנּוּ׃ וּבָאוּ
and-they-will-come (12) more-than-him strong-one from-hand-of and-he-will-redeem-him

וְרִנְּנוּ בִמְרוֹם־צִיּוֹן וְנָהֲרוּ אֶל־טוּב יְהוָה
Yahweh bounty-of in and-they-will-rejoice Zion on-height-of and-they-will-shout

עַל־דָּגָן וְעַל־תִּירֹשׁ וְעַל־יִצְהָר וְעַל־בְּנֵי־צֹאן וּבָקָר
and-herd flock young-ones-of and-in oil and-in new-wine and-in grain in

וְהָיְתָה נַפְשָׁם כְּגַן רָוֶה וְלֹא־יוֹסִיפוּ
they-will-do-again and-not well-watered like-garden self-of-them and-she-will-be

לְדַאֲבָה עוֹד׃ אָז תִּשְׂמַח בְּתוּלָה בְּמָחוֹל וּבַחֻרִים וּזְקֵנִים
and-old-men and-young-men in-dance maiden she-will-be-glad then (13) more to-sorrow

יַחְדָּו וְהָפַכְתִּי אֶבְלָם לְשָׂשׂוֹן וְנִחַמְתִּים
and-I-will-comfort-them into-gladness mourning-of-them and-I-will-turn together

on the hills of Samaria;
the farmers will plant them
and enjoy their fruit.
6There will be a day when watchmen cry out
on the hills of Ephraim,
'Come, let us go up to Zion,
to the LORD our God.' "

7This is what the LORD says:

"Sing with joy for Jacob;
shout for the foremost of the nations.
Make your praises heard, and say,
'O LORD, save your people,
the remnant of Israel.'
8See, I will bring them from the land of the north
and gather them from the ends of the earth.
Among them will be the blind and the lame,
expectant mothers and women in labor;
a great throng will return.
9They will come with weeping;
they will pray as I bring them back.
I will lead them beside streams of water
on a level path where they will not stumble,
because I am Israel's father,
and Ephraim is my firstborn son.

10"Hear the word of the LORD, O nations;
proclaim it in distant coastlands:
'He who scattered Israel will gather them
and will watch over his flock like a shepherd.'
11For the LORD will ransom Jacob
and redeem them from the hand of those stronger than they.
12They will come and shout for joy on the heights of Zion;
they will rejoice in the bounty of the LORD—
the grain, the new wine and the oil,
the young of the flocks and herds.
They will be like a well-watered garden,
and they will sorrow no more.
13Then maidens will dance and be glad,
young men and old as well.
I will turn their mourning into gladness;
I will give them comfort and

וְשִׂמַּחְתִּים מִיגוֹנָם ׃ וְרִוֵּיתִי נֶפֶשׁ
self-of and-I-will-satisfy (14) instead-of-sorrow-of-them and-I-will-give-joy-to-them

הַכֹּהֲנִים דָּשֶׁן וְעַמִּי אֶת־ טוּבִי יִשְׂבָּעוּ
they-will-be-filled bounty-of-me *** and-people-of-me abundance the-priests

נְאֻם־ יְהוָה׃ כֹּה׀ אָמַר יְהוָה קוֹל בְּרָמָה נִשְׁמָע נְהִי
mourning he-is-heard in-Ramah voice Yahweh he-says this (15) Yahweh declaration-of

בְּכִי תַמְרוּרִים רָחֵל מְבַכָּה עַל־ בָּנֶיהָ מֵאֲנָה לְהִנָּחֵם
to-be-comforted she-refuses children-of-her for weeping Rachel great-ones weeping

עַל־ בָּנֶיהָ כִּי אֵינֶנּוּ ׃ כֹּה׀ אָמַר יְהוָה מִנְעִי
restrain! Yahweh he-says this (16) no-more-he because children-of-her about

קוֹלֵךְ מִבֶּכִי וְעֵינַיִךְ מִדִּמְעָה כִּי יֵשׁ שָׂכָר
reward there-will-be for from-tear and-eyes-of-you from-weeping voice-of-you

לִפְעֻלָּתֵךְ נְאֻם־ יְהוָה וְשָׁבוּ מֵאֶרֶץ
from-land-of and-they-will-return Yahweh declaration-of for-work-of-you

אוֹיֵב׃ וְיֵשׁ־ תִּקְוָה לְאַחֲרִיתֵךְ נְאֻם־ יְהוָה
Yahweh declaration-of for-future-of-you hope so-there-is (17) one-being-enemy

וְשָׁבוּ בָנִים לִגְבוּלָם׃ שָׁמוֹעַ שָׁמַעְתִּי אֶפְרַיִם מִתְנוֹדֵד
moaning Ephraim I-heard to-hear (18) to-land-of-them children and-they-will-return

יִסַּרְתַּנִי וָאִוָּסֵר כְּעֵגֶל לֹא לֻמָּד הֲשִׁבֵנִי
restore-me! he-was-trained not like-calf and-I-was-disciplined you-disciplined-me

וְאָשׁוּבָה כִּי אַתָּה יְהוָה אֱלֹהָי׃ כִּי־ אַחֲרֵי שׁוּבִי
to-stray-me after indeed (19) God-of-me Yahweh you because and-I-will-return

נִחַמְתִּי וְאַחֲרֵי הִוָּדְעִי סָפַקְתִּי עַל־ יָרֵךְ בֹּשְׁתִּי וְגַם־
and-also I-was-ashamed breast on I-beat to-understand-me and-after I-repented

נִכְלַמְתִּי כִּי נָשָׂאתִי חֶרְפַּת נְעוּרָי׃ הֲבֵן יַקִּיר לִי
to-me dear son? (20) youths-of-me disgrace-of I-bore because I-was-humiliated

אֶפְרַיִם אִם יֶלֶד שַׁעֲשֻׁעִים כִּי־ מִדֵּי דַבְּרִי בּוֹ
against-him to-speak-me as-often-of though delights child-of or Ephraim

זָכֹר אֶזְכְּרֶנּוּ עוֹד עַל־ כֵּן הָמוּ מֵעַי לוֹ
for-him hearts-of-me they-yearn this for still I-remember-him to-remember

רַחֵם אֲרַחֲמֶנּוּ נְאֻם־ יְהוָה׃ הַצִּיבִי
set-up! (21) Yahweh declaration-of I-have-compassion-for-him to-have-compassion

לָךְ צִיֻּנִים שִׂמִי לָךְ תַּמְרוּרִים שִׁתִי לִבֵּךְ לַמְסִלָּה
about-the-highway heart-of-you put! guideposts for-you put-up! road-signs for-you

דֶּרֶךְ הָלָכְתִּי שׁוּבִי בְּתוּלַת יִשְׂרָאֵל שֻׁבִי אֶל־ עָרַיִךְ אֵלֶּה׃ עַד־
until (22) these towns-of-you to return! Israel Virgin-of return! you-take road

מָתַי תִּתְחַמָּקִין הַבַּת הַשּׁוֹבֵבָה כִּי־ בָרָא יְהוָה
Yahweh he-will-create indeed the-unfaithful the-daughter will-you-wander when?

joy instead of sorrow.
14 I will satisfy the priests with abundance,
and my people will be filled with my bounty,"
declares the LORD.

15 This is what the LORD says:

"A voice is heard in Ramah,
mourning and great weeping,
Rachel weeping for her children
and refusing to be comforted,
because her children are no more."

16 This is what the LORD says:

"Restrain your voice from weeping
and your eyes from tears,
for your work will be rewarded,"
declares the LORD.
"They will return from the land of the enemy.
17 So there is hope for your future,"
declares the LORD.
"Your children will return to their own land.

18 "I have surely heard Ephraim's moaning:
'You disciplined me like an unruly calf,
and I have been disciplined.
Restore me, and I will return,
because you are the LORD my God.
19 After I strayed,
I repented;
after I came to understand,
I beat my breast.
I was ashamed and humiliated
because I bore the disgrace of my youth.'
20 Is not Ephraim my dear son,
the child in whom I delight?
Though I often speak against him,
I still remember him.
Therefore my heart yearns for him;
I have great compassion for him,"
declares the LORD.

21 "Set up road signs;
put up guideposts.
Take note of the highway,
the road that you take.
Return, O Virgin Israel,
return to your towns.
22 How long will you wander,
O unfaithful daughter?
The LORD will create a new

°21 ק הלכת

חֲדָשָׁה֙ בָּאָ֔רֶץ נְקֵבָ֖ה תְּסֹ֣ובֵב גֶּ֑בֶר : כֹּֽה־ אָמַ֨ר יְהוָ֤ה

Yahweh-of  he-says  this  (23)  man  she-will-surround  woman  on-the-earth  new-thing

צְבָאֹות֙ אֱלֹהֵ֣י יִשְׂרָאֵ֔ל עֹ֚וד יֹאמְר֣וּ אֶת־ הַדָּבָ֣ר הַזֶּ֔ה בְּאֶ֖רֶץ יְהוּדָ֑ה

Judah  in-land-of  the-this  the-word  ***  they-will-say  again  Israel  God-of  Hosts

וּבְעָרָ֑יו בְּשׁוּבִ֖י אֶת־ שְׁבוּתָ֑ם יְבָרֶכְךָ֧

may-he-bless-you  captivity-of-them  ***  when-to-bring-back-me  and-in-towns-of-him

יְהוָ֛ה נְוֵה־ צֶ֖דֶק הַ֥ר הַקֹּֽדֶשׁ : (24) וְיָ֥שְׁבוּ

and-they-will-live  (24)  the-sacredness  mountain-of  righteousness  dwelling-of  Yahweh

בָ֛הּ יְהוּדָ֥ה וְכָל־ עָרָ֖יו יַחְדָּ֑ו אִכָּרִ֖ים וְנָסְע֥וּ

and-they-will-move-about  farmers  together  towns-of-him  and-all-of  Judah  in-her

בַּעֵֽדֶר : כִּ֥י הִרְוֵ֖יתִי נֶ֣פֶשׁ עֲיֵפָ֑ה וְכָל־ נֶ֥פֶשׁ דָּאֲבָ֖ה

she-is-faint  soul  and-every-of  weary  soul  I-will-refresh  indeed  (25)  with-the-flock

מִלֵּֽאתִי : (26) עַל־ זֹ֣את הֱקִיצֹ֗תִי וָאֶרְאֶ֑ה וּשְׁנָתִ֖י

and-sleep-of-me  and-I-looked-around  I-awoke  this  at  (26)  I-will-satisfy

עָ֥רְבָה לִּֽי : (27) הִנֵּ֛ה יָמִ֥ים בָּאִ֖ים נְאֻם־ יְהוָ֑ה

Yahweh  declaration-of  ones-coming  days  see!  (27)  to-me  she-was-pleasant

וְזָרַעְתִּ֗י אֶת־ בֵּ֤ית יִשְׂרָאֵל֙ וְאֶת־ בֵּ֣ית יְהוּדָ֔ה זֶ֥רַע אָדָ֖ם

man  offspring-of  Judah  house-of  and  Israel  house-of  ***  when-I-will-plant

וְזֶ֥רַע בְּהֵמָֽה : (28) וְהָיָ֞ה כַּאֲשֶׁ֧ר שָׁקַ֣דְתִּי עֲלֵיהֶ֗ם לִנְתֹ֧ושׁ

to-uproot  over-them  I-watched  just-as  and-he-will-be  (28)  animal  and-offspring-of

וְלִנְתֹ֛וץ וְלַהֲרֹ֖ס וּלְהַאֲבִ֣יד וּלְהָרֵ֑עַ כֵּ֣ן

so  and-to-bring-disaster  and-to-destroy  and-to-overthrow  and-to-tear-down

אֶשְׁקֹ֧ד עֲלֵיהֶ֛ם לִבְנֹ֥ות וְלִנְטֹ֖ועַ נְאֻם־ יְהוָֽה : (29) בַּיָּמִ֣ים

in-the-days  (29)  Yahweh  declaration-of  and-to-plant  to-build  over-them  I-will-watch

הָהֵ֔ם לֹא־ יֹאמְר֖וּ עֹ֑וד אָבֹ֣ות אָ֣כְלוּ בֹ֔סֶר וְשִׁנֵּ֥י בָנִ֖ים

children  and-teeth-of  sour-grape  they-ate  fathers  longer  they-will-say  not  the-those

תִּקְהֶֽינָה : (30) כִּ֛י אִם־ אִ֥ישׁ בַּעֲוֹנֹ֖ו יָמ֑וּת כָּל־

every-of  he-will-die  for-sin-of-him  each  instead  but  (30)  they-are-set-on-edge

הָֽאָדָ֛ם הָאֹכֵ֥ל הַבֹּ֖סֶר תִּקְהֶ֥ינָה שִׁנָּֽיו :

teeth-of-him  they-will-be-set-on-edge  the-sour-grape  the-one-eating  the-person

הִנֵּ֛ה יָמִ֥ים בָּאִ֖ים נְאֻם־ יְהוָ֑ה וְכָרַתִּ֗י אֶת־ בֵּ֤ית

house-of  with  when-I-will-make  Yahweh  declaration-of  ones-coming  days  see!  (31)

יִשְׂרָאֵ֛ל וְאֶת־ בֵּ֥ית יְהוּדָ֖ה בְּרִ֥ית חֲדָשָֽׁה : (32) לֹ֣א כַבְּרִ֗ית אֲשֶׁ֤ר כָּרַ֨תִּי֙

I-made  that  like-the-covenant  not  (32)  new  covenant  Judah  house-of  and-with  Israel

אֶת־ אֲבֹותָ֔ם בְּיֹום֙ הֶחֱזִיקִ֣י בְיָדָ֔ם לְהֹוצִיאָ֖ם מֵאֶ֣רֶץ

from-land-of  to-lead-out-them  by-hand-of-them  I-took  on-day  forefathers-of-them  with

מִצְרָ֑יִם אֲשֶׁר־הֵ֜מָּה הֵפֵ֣רוּ אֶת־ בְּרִיתִ֗י וְאָנֹכִ֛י בָּעַ֥לְתִּי בָ֖ם

to-them  I-was-husband  though-I  covenant-of-me  ***  they-broke  they  because  Egypt

thing on earth—
a woman will surround[h] a
man."

[23]This is what the LORD Almighty, the God of Israel, says: "When I bring them back from captivity,[i] the people in the land of Judah and in its towns will once again use these words: 'The LORD bless you, O righteous dwelling, O sacred mountain.' [24]People will live together in Judah and all its towns—farmers and those who move about with their flocks. [25]I will refresh the weary and satisfy the faint."

[26]At this I awoke and looked around. My sleep had been pleasant to me.

[27]"The days are coming," declares the LORD, "when I will plant the house of Israel and the house of Judah with the offspring of men and of animals. [28]Just as I watched over them to uproot and tear down, and to overthrow, destroy and bring disaster, so I will watch over them to build and to plant," declares the LORD. [29]"In those days people will no longer say,

'The fathers have eaten sour grapes,
and the children's teeth are set on edge.'

[30]Instead, everyone will die for his own sin; whoever eats sour grapes—his own teeth will be set on edge.

[31]"The time is coming," declares the LORD,
"when I will make a new covenant
with the house of Israel
and with the house of
Judah.
[32]It will not be like the covenant
I made with their
forefathers
when I took them by the hand
to lead them out of Egypt,
because they broke my
covenant,
though I was a husband to[j]
them,[k]"

h22 Or will go about seeking; or will protect
i23 Or I restore their fortunes
j32 Hebrew; Septuagint and Syriac / and I turned away from
k32 Or was their master

נְאֻם־ יְהוָה׃ כִּי זֹאת הַבְּרִית אֲשֶׁר אֶכְרֹת אֶת־ בֵּית
house-of with I-will-make that the-covenant this but (33) Yahweh declaration-of

יִשְׂרָאֵל אַחֲרֵי הַיָּמִים הָהֵם נְאֻם־ יְהוָה נָתַתִּי אֶת־ תּוֹרָתִי
law-of-me *** I-will-put Yahweh declaration-of the-those the-days after Israel

בְּקִרְבָּם וְעַל־ לִבָּם אֶכְתֲּבֶנָּה וְהָיִיתִי לָהֶם לֵאלֹהִים
as-God to-them and-I-will-be I-will-write-her heart-of-them and-on in-mind-of-them

וְהֵמָּה יִהְיוּ־ לִי לְעָם׃ וְלֹא יְלַמְּדוּ עוֹד אִישׁ אֶת־
*** man longer they-will-teach and-not (34) as-people to-me they-will-be and-they

רֵעֵהוּ וְאִישׁ אֶת־ אָחִיו לֵאמֹר דְּעוּ אֶת־ יְהוָה כִּי־
because Yahweh *** know! to-say brother-of-him *** or-man neighbor-of-him

כוּלָּם יֵדְעוּ אוֹתִי לְמִקְּטַנָּם וְעַד־ גְּדוֹלָם
greatest-of-them and-to from-least-of-them me they-will-know all-of-them

נְאֻם־ יְהוָה כִּי אֶסְלַח לַעֲוֺנָם וּלְחַטָּאתָם
and-to-sin-of-them to-wickedness-of-them I-will-forgive for Yahweh declaration-of

לֹא אֶזְכָּר־ עוֹד׃ כֹּה ׀ אָמַר יְהוָה נֹתֵן שֶׁמֶשׁ לְאוֹר
as-light-of sun one-appointing Yahweh he-says this (35) more I-will-remember not

יוֹמָם חֻקֹּת יָרֵחַ וְכוֹכָבִים לְאוֹר לָיְלָה רֹגַע הַיָּם
the-sea one-stirring-up-of night as-light-of and-stars moon decrees-of by-day

וַיֶּהֱמוּ גַלָּיו יְהוָה צְבָאוֹת שְׁמוֹ׃ אִם־ יָמֻשׁוּ
they-vanish if (36) name-of-him Hosts Yahweh-of waves-of-him so-they-roar

הַחֻקִּים הָאֵלֶּה מִלְּפָנַי נְאֻם־ יְהוָה גַּם זֶרַע יִשְׂרָאֵל
Israel descendant-of then Yahweh declaration-of from-before-me the-these the-decrees

יִשְׁבְּתוּ מִהְיוֹת גּוֹי לְפָנַי כָּל־ הַיָּמִים׃ כֹּה ׀ אָמַר
he-says this (37) the-days all-of before-me nation from-to-be they-will-cease

יְהוָה אִם־ יִמַּדּוּ שָׁמַיִם מִלְמַעְלָה וְיֵחָקְרוּ
and-they-can-be-searched-out at-above heavens they-can-be-measured if Yahweh

מוֹסְדֵי־ אֶרֶץ לְמָטָּה גַּם־ אֲנִי אֶמְאַס בְּכָל־ זֶרַע יִשְׂרָאֵל
Israel descendant-of to-all-of I-will-reject I then at-below earth foundations-of

עַל־ כָּל־ אֲשֶׁר עָשׂוּ נְאֻם־ יְהוָה׃ הִנֵּה יָמִים °*
*ones-coming days see! (38) Yahweh declaration-of they-did that all because-of

נְאֻם־ יְהוָה וְנִבְנְתָה הָעִיר לַיהוָה מִמִּגְדַּל
from-Tower-of for-Yahweh the-city when-she-will-be-rebuilt Yahweh declaration-of

חֲנַנְאֵל שַׁעַר הַפִּנָּה׃ וְיָצָא עוֹד קָוֶה הַמִּדָּה
the-measure line-of yet and-he-will-stretch-out (39) the-Corner Gate-of Hananel

נֶגְדּוֹ עַל גִּבְעַת גָּרֵב וְנָסַב גֹּעָתָה׃ וְכָל־ הָעֵמֶק
the-valley and-whole-of (40) to-Goah and-he-will-turn Gareb hill-of to before-him

הַפְּגָרִים ׀ וְהַדֶּשֶׁן וְכָל־ הַשְּׁרֵמוֹת עַד־ נַחַל קִדְרוֹן עַד־
as-far-as Kidron Valley-of to the-terraces and-all-of and-the-ash the-dead-bodies

declares the LORD.
33"This is the covenant I will make with the house of Israel
after that time," declares the LORD.
"I will put my law in their minds
and write it on their hearts.
I will be their God,
and they will be my people.
34No longer will a man teach his neighbor,
or a man his brother,
saying, 'Know the LORD,'
because they will all know me,
from the least of them to the greatest,"
declares the LORD.
"For I will forgive their wickedness
and will remember their sins no more."

35This is what the LORD says,

he who appoints the sun
to shine by day,
who decrees the moon and stars
to shine by night,
who stirs up the sea
so that its waves roar—
the LORD Almighty is his name:
36"Only if these decrees vanish from my sight,"
declares the LORD,
"will the descendants of Israel ever cease
to be a nation before me."

37This is what the LORD says:

"Only if the heavens above can be measured
and the foundations of the earth below be searched out
will I reject all the descendants of Israel
because of all they have done,"
declares the LORD.

38"The days are coming," declares the LORD, "when this city will be rebuilt for me from the Tower of Hananel to the Corner Gate. 39The measuring line will stretch from there straight to the hill of Gareb and then turn to Goah. 40The whole valley where dead bodies and ashes are thrown, and all the terraces out to the Kidron Valley on the east as far as

*38 Many ancient mss and versions include the *Qere* form in the text.

°38 ק באים
°39 ק קו
°40 ק השדמות

פִּנַּת שַׁעַר הַסּוּסִים מִזְרָחָה קֹדֶשׁ לַיהוָה לֹא־ יִנָּתֵשׁ וְלֹא־
or-not he-will-be-uprooted not to-Yahweh holy on-east the-Horses Gate-of corner-of

יֵהָרֵס עוֹד לְעוֹלָם׃ הַדָּבָר אֲשֶׁר־ הָיָה אֶל־יִרְמְיָהוּ
Jeremiah to he-came that the-word (32:1) to-forever again he-will-be-demolished

מֵאֵת יְהוָה בַּשְּׁנַת° הָעֲשִׂרִית לְצִדְקִיָּהוּ מֶלֶךְ יְהוּדָה הִיא הַשָּׁנָה
the-year this Judah king-of of-Zedekiah the-tenth in-the-year Yahweh from-with

שְׁמֹנֶה־עֶשְׂרֵה שָׁנָה לִנְבוּכַדְרֶאצַּר׃ וְאָז חֵיל מֶלֶךְ בָּבֶל
Babylon king-of army-of and-then (2) of-Nebuchadrezzar year ten eight

צָרִים עַל־ יְרוּשָׁלִָם וְיִרְמְיָהוּ הַנָּבִיא הָיָה כָלוּא
being-confined he-was the-prophet and-Jeremiah Jerusalem against ones-besieging

בַּחֲצַר הַמַּטָּרָה אֲשֶׁר בֵּית־ מֶלֶךְ יְהוּדָה׃ אֲשֶׁר כְּלָאוֹ
to-imprison-him that (3) Judah royalty-of palace-of that the-guard in-courtyard-of

צִדְקִיָּהוּ מֶלֶךְ־ יְהוּדָה לֵאמֹר מַדּוּעַ אַתָּה נִבָּא לֵאמֹר כֹּה אָמַר
he-says this to-say prophesying you why? to-say Judah king-of Zedekiah

יְהוָה הִנְנִי נֹתֵן אֶת־ הָעִיר הַזֹּאת בְּיַד מֶלֶךְ־ בָּבֶל
Babylon king-of into-hand-of the-this the-city *** giving see-I! Yahweh

וּלְכָדָהּ׃ וְצִדְקִיָּהוּ מֶלֶךְ יְהוּדָה לֹא יִמָּלֵט
he-will-escape not Judah king-of and-Zedekiah (4) and-he-will-capture-her

מִיַּד הַכַּשְׂדִּים כִּי הִנָּתֹן יִנָּתֵן בְּיַד מֶלֶךְ־
king-of into-hand-of he-will-be-given to-be-given but the-Chaldeans from-hand-of

בָּבֶל וְדִבֶּר־ פִּיו עִם־ פִּיו וְעֵינָיו אֶת־
*** and-eyes-of-him mouth-of-him with mouth-of-him and-he-will-speak Babylon

עֵינָו° תִּרְאֶינָה׃ וּבָבֶל יוֹלִךְ אֶת־ צִדְקִיָּהוּ וְשָׁם
and-there Zedekiah *** he-will-take and-Babylon (5) they-will-see eyes-of-him

יִהְיֶה עַד־ פָּקְדִי אֹתוֹ נְאֻם־ יְהוָה כִּי תִלָּחֲמוּ אֶת־
against you-fight if Yahweh declaration-of with-him to-deal-me until he-will-remain

הַכַּשְׂדִּים לֹא תַצְלִיחוּ׃ וַיֹּאמֶר יִרְמְיָהוּ הָיָה דְּבַר־ יְהוָה
Yahweh word-of he-came Jeremiah and-he-said (6) you-will-succeed not the-Chaldeans

אֵלַי לֵאמֹר׃ הִנֵּה חֲנַמְאֵל בֶּן־ שַׁלֻּם דֹּדְךָ בָּא אֵלֶיךָ לֵאמֹר
to-say to-you coming uncle-of-you Shallum son-of Hanamel see! (7) to-say to-me

קְנֵה לְךָ אֶת־ שָׂדִי אֲשֶׁר בַּעֲנָתוֹת כִּי לְךָ מִשְׁפַּט
right-of to-you because at-Anathoth that field-of-me *** for-you buy!

הַגְּאֻלָּה לִקְנוֹת׃ וַיָּבֹא אֵלַי חֲנַמְאֵל בֶּן־ דֹּדִי
uncle-of-me son-of Hanamel to-me then-he-came (8) to-buy the-duty-of-nearest-relative

כִּדְבַר יְהוָה אֶל־ חֲצַר הַמַּטָּרָה וַיֹּאמֶר אֵלַי קְנֵה נָא אֶת־
*** now! buy! to-me and-he-said the-guard courtyard-of in Yahweh as-saying-of

שָׂדִי אֲשֶׁר־בַּעֲנָתוֹת אֲשֶׁר בְּאֶרֶץ בִּנְיָמִין כִּי־ לְךָ מִשְׁפַּט
right-of to-you since Benjamin in-territory-of that at-Anathoth that field-of-me

°1 ק בשנה
°4 ק עיניו

the corner of the Horse Gate, will be holy to the LORD. The city will never again be uprooted or demolished."

*Jeremiah Buys a Field*

32 This is the word that came to Jeremiah from the LORD
in the tenth year of Zedekiah king of Judah, which was the eighteenth year of Nebuchadnezzar.
2 The army of the king of Babylon was then besieging Jerusalem, and Jeremiah the prophet was confined in the courtyard of the guard in the royal palace of Judah.
3 Now Zedekiah king of Judah had imprisoned him there, saying, "Why do you prophesy as you do? You say, 'This is what the LORD says: I am about to hand this city over to the king of Babylon, and he will capture it.
4 Zedekiah king of Judah will not escape out of the hands of the Babylonians[l] but will certainly be handed over to the king of Babylon, and will speak with him face to face and see him with his own eyes.
5 He will take Zedekiah to Babylon, where he will remain until I deal with him, declares the LORD. If you fight against the Babylonians, you will not succeed.' "
6 Jeremiah said, "The word of the LORD came to me:
7 Hanamel son of Shallum your uncle is going to come to you and say, 'Buy my field at Anathoth, because as nearest relative it is your right and duty to buy it.'
8 "Then, just as the LORD had said, my cousin Hanamel came to me in the courtyard of the guard and said, 'Buy my field at Anathoth in the territory of Benjamin. Since it is your right to redeem it

l4 Or *Chaldeans;* also in verses 5, 24, 25, 28, 29 and 43

הַיְרֻשָּׁה וּלְךָ הַגְּאֻלָּה קְנֵה־לָךְ וָאֵדַע כִּי דְבַר־
word-of that and-I-knew for-you buy! the-redemption and-to-you the-possession

יְהוָה הוּא׃ וָאֶקְנֶה אֶת־הַשָּׂדֶה מֵאֵת חֲנַמְאֵל בֶּן־דֹּדִי
uncle-of-me son-of Hanamel from-with the-field *** so-I-bought (9) this Yahweh

אֲשֶׁר בַּעֲנָתוֹת וָאֶשְׁקֲלָה־לּוֹ אֶת־הַכֶּסֶף שִׁבְעָה שְׁקָלִים וַעֲשָׂרָה
and-ten shekels seven the-silver *** for-him and-I-weighed-out at-Anathoth that

הַכָּסֶף׃ וָאֶכְתֹּב בַּסֵּפֶר וָאֶחְתֹּם וָאָעֵד עֵדִים
witnesses and-I-had-witness and-I-sealed on-the-deed and-I-signed (10) the-silver

וָאֶשְׁקֹל הַכֶּסֶף בְּמֹאזְנָיִם׃ וָאֶקַּח אֶת־סֵפֶר הַמִּקְנָה
the-purchase deed-of *** and-I-took (11) on-scales the-silver and-I-weighed-out

אֶת־הֶחָתוּם הַמִּצְוָה וְהַחֻקִּים וְאֶת־הַגָּלוּי׃
the-one-being-unsealed and and-the-conditions the-term the-one-being-sealed ***

וָאֶתֵּן אֶת־הַסֵּפֶר הַמִּקְנָה אֶל־בָּרוּךְ בֶּן־נֵרִיָּה בֶּן־מַחְסֵיָה
Mahseiah son-of Neriah son-of Baruch to the-purchase the-deed *** and-I-gave (12)

לְעֵינֵי חֲנַמְאֵל דֹּדִי וּלְעֵינֵי הָעֵדִים
the-witnesses and-before-eyes-of cousin-of-me Hanamel before-eyes-of

הַכֹּתְבִים בְּסֵפֶר הַמִּקְנָה לְעֵינֵי כָּל־הַיְּהוּדִים
the-Jews all-of before-eyes-of the-purchase on-deed-of the-ones-signing

הַיֹּשְׁבִים בַּחֲצַר הַמַּטָּרָה׃ וָאֲצַוֶּה אֶת *בָּרוּךְ
Baruch *** and-I-instructed (13) the-guard in-courtyard-of the-ones-sitting

לְעֵינֵיהֶם לֵאמֹר׃ כֹּה־אָמַר יְהוָה צְבָאוֹת אֱלֹהֵי יִשְׂרָאֵל לָקוֹחַ
to-take Israel God-of Hosts Yahweh-of he-says this (14) to-say before-eyes-of-them

אֶת־הַסְּפָרִים הָאֵלֶּה אֵת סֵפֶר הַמִּקְנָה הַזֶּה וְאֵת
and the-this the-purchase deed-of *** the-these the-documents ***

הֶחָתוּם וְאֵת סֵפֶר הַגָּלוּי הַזֶּה וּנְתַתָּם
and-you-put-them the-this the-one-being-unsealed deed-of and the-one-being-sealed

בִּכְלִי־חָרֶשׂ לְמַעַן יַעַמְדוּ יָמִים רַבִּים׃ כִּי כֹה אָמַר יְהוָה
Yahweh-of he-says this for (15) many days they-will-last so-that clay in-jar-of

צְבָאוֹת אֱלֹהֵי יִשְׂרָאֵל עוֹד יִקָּנוּ בָתִּים וְשָׂדוֹת וּכְרָמִים
and-vineyards and-fields houses they-will-be-bought again Israel God-of Hosts

בָּאָרֶץ הַזֹּאת׃ וָאֶתְפַּלֵּל אֶל־יְהוָה אַחֲרֵי תִתִּי אֶת־סֵפֶר
deed-of *** to-give-me after Yahweh to and-I-prayed (16) the-this in-the-land

הַמִּקְנָה אֶל־בָּרוּךְ בֶּן־נֵרִיָּה לֵאמֹר׃ אֲהָהּ אֲדֹנָי יְהוִה הִנֵּה ׀ אַתָּה
you see! Yahweh Sovereign ah! (17) to-say Neriah son-of Baruch to the-purchase

עָשִׂיתָ אֶת־הַשָּׁמַיִם וְאֶת־הָאָרֶץ בְּכֹחֲךָ הַגָּדוֹל וּבִזְרֹעֲךָ
and-by-arm-of-you the-great by-power-of-you the-earth and the-heavens *** you-made

הַנְּטוּיָה לֹא־יִפָּלֵא מִמְּךָ כָּל־דָּבָר׃ עֹשֶׂה
one-showing (18) thing any-of for-you he-is-too-hard not the-one-being-outstretched

and possess it, buy it for yourself.'

"I knew that this was the word of the LORD; 9so I bought the field at Anathoth from my cousin Hanamel and weighed out for him seventeen shekels[m] of silver. 10I signed and sealed the deed, had it witnessed, and weighed out the silver on the scales. 11I took the deed of purchase—the sealed copy containing the terms and conditions, as well as the unsealed copy— 12and I gave this deed to Baruch son of Neriah, the son of Mahseiah, in the presence of my cousin Hanamel and of the witnesses who had signed the deed and of all the Jews sitting in the courtyard of the guard.

13"In their presence I gave Baruch these instructions: 14'This is what the LORD Almighty, the God of Israel, says: Take these documents, both the sealed and unsealed copies of the deed of purchase, and put them in a clay jar so they will last a long time. 15For this is what the LORD Almighty, the God of Israel, says: Houses, fields and vineyards will again be bought in this land.'

16"After I had given the deed of purchase to Baruch son of Neriah, I prayed to the LORD:

17"Ah, Sovereign LORD, you have made the heavens and the earth by your great power and outstretched arm. Nothing is too hard for you. 18You show

m9 That is, about 7 ounces (about 200 grams)

*13 Most mss connect these words with *maqqeph* (אֶת־בָּ).

חֶסֶד לַאֲלָפִים וּמְשַׁלֵּם עֲוֹן אָבוֹת אֶל־חֵיק בְּנֵיהֶם
children-of-them lap-of into fathers sin-of but-punishing to-thousands love

אַחֲרֵיהֶם הָאֵל הַגָּדוֹל הַגִּבּוֹר יְהוָה צְבָאוֹת שְׁמוֹ׃ גְּדֹל
great-of (19) name-of-him Hosts Yahweh-of the-powerful the-great the-God after-them

הָעֵצָה וְרַב הָעֲלִילִיָּה אֲשֶׁר־עֵינֶיךָ פְּקֻחוֹת עַל־כָּל־דַּרְכֵי
ways-of all-of to ones-being-open eyes-of-you who the-deed and-mighty-of the-purpose

בְּנֵי אָדָם לָתֵת לְאִישׁ כִּדְרָכָיו וְכִפְרִי
and-according-to-desert-of according-to-conducts-of-him to-each to-reward man sons-of

מַעֲלָלָיו׃ אֲשֶׁר־שַׂמְתָּ אֹתוֹת וּמֹפְתִים בְּאֶרֶץ־מִצְרַיִם
Egypt in-land-of and-wonders miraculous-signs you-performed who (20) deeds-of-him

עַד־הַיּוֹם הַזֶּה וּבְיִשְׂרָאֵל וּבָאָדָם וַתַּעֲשֶׂה־לְּךָ
for-you and-you-gained and-among-the-mankind both-in-Israel the-this the-day to

שֵׁם כַּיּוֹם הַזֶּה׃ וַתֹּצֵא אֶת־עַמְּךָ אֶת־יִשְׂרָאֵל
Israel *** people-of-you *** and-you-brought-out (21) the-this as-the-day renown

מֵאֶרֶץ מִצְרָיִם בְּאֹתוֹת וּבְמוֹפְתִים וּבְיָד חֲזָקָה וּבְאֶזְרוֹעַ
and-by-arm mighty and-by-hand and-with-wonders with-signs Egypt from-land-of

נְטוּיָה וּבְמוֹרָא גָּדוֹל׃ וַתִּתֵּן לָהֶם אֶת־הָאָרֶץ
the-land *** to-them and-you-gave (22) great and-with-terror one-being-outstretched

הַזֹּאת אֲשֶׁר־נִשְׁבַּעְתָּ לַאֲבוֹתָם לָתֵת לָהֶם אֶרֶץ זָבַת
flowing-of land to-them to-give to-forefathers-of-them you-swore that the-this

חָלָב וּדְבָשׁ׃ וַיָּבֹאוּ וַיִּרְשׁוּ אֹתָהּ וְלֹא־שָׁמְעוּ
they-obeyed but-not her and-they-possessed and-they-came-in (23) and-honey milk

בְקוֹלֶךָ וּבְתֹרוֹתְךָ° לֹא־הָלָכוּ אֵת כָּל־אֲשֶׁר צִוִּיתָה
you-commanded that all *** they-followed not or-to-law-of-you to-voice-of-you

לָהֶם לַעֲשׂוֹת לֹא עָשׂוּ וַתַּקְרֵא אֹתָם אֵת כָּל־הָרָעָה
the-disaster all-of *** upon-them so-you-brought they-did not to-do to-them

הַזֹּאת׃ הִנֵּה הַסֹּלְלוֹת בָּאוּ הָעִיר לְלָכְדָהּ וְהָעִיר
and-the-city to-take-her the-city they-come the-siege-ramps see! (24) the-this

נִתְּנָה בְּיַד הַכַּשְׂדִּים הַנִּלְחָמִים עָלֶיהָ
against-her the-ones-attacking the-Chaldeans into-hand-of she-will-be-given

מִפְּנֵי הַחֶרֶב וְהָרָעָב וְהַדָּבֶר וַאֲשֶׁר דִּבַּרְתָּ הָיָה
he-happened you-said and-what and-the-plague and-the-famine the-sword because-of

וְהִנְּךָ רֹאֶה׃ וְאַתָּה אָמַרְתָּ אֵלַי אֲדֹנָי יְהוִה קְנֵה־
buy! Yahweh Sovereign to-me you-say and-you (25) one-seeing and-see-you!

לְךָ הַשָּׂדֶה בַּכֶּסֶף וְהָעֵד עֵדִים וְהָעִיר
though-the-city witnesses and-have-witness! with-the-silver the-field for-you

נִתְּנָה בְּיַד הַכַּשְׂדִּים׃ וַיְהִי דְּבַר־יְהוָה אֶל־
to Yahweh word-of then-he-came (26) the-Chaldeans into-hand-of she-will-be-given

love to thousands but bring the punishment for the fathers' sins into the laps of their children after them. O great and powerful God, whose name is the LORD Almighty, [19]great are your purposes and mighty are your deeds. Your eyes are open to all the ways of men; you reward everyone according to his conduct and as his deeds deserve. [20]You performed miraculous signs and wonders in Egypt and have continued them to this day, both in Israel and among all mankind, and have gained the renown that is still yours. [21]You brought your people Israel out of Egypt with signs and wonders, by a mighty hand and an outstretched arm and with great terror. [22]You gave them this land you had sworn to give their forefathers, a land flowing with milk and honey. [23]They came in and took possession of it, but they did not obey you or follow your law; they did not do what you commanded them to do. So you brought all this disaster upon them.

[24]"See how the siege ramps are built up to take the city. Because of the sword, famine and plague, the city will be handed over to the Babylonians who are attacking it. What you said has happened, as you now see. [25]And though the city will be handed over to the Babylonians, you, O Sovereign LORD, say to me, 'Buy the field with silver and have the transaction witnessed.' "

[26]Then the word of the LORD

°23 ק ובתורתך

יִרְמְיָהוּ לֵאמֹר׃ הִנֵּה אֲנִי יְהוָה אֱלֹהֵי כָּל־ בָּשָׂר הֲמִמֶּנִּי יִפָּלֵא
is-he-too-hard for-me? mankind all-of God-of Yahweh I see! (27) to-say Jeremiah

כָּל־ דָּבָר׃ לָכֵן כֹּה אָמַר יְהוָה הִנְנִי נֹתֵן אֶת־ הָעִיר הַזֹּאת
the-this the-city *** giving see-I! Yahweh he-says this therefore (28) thing any-of

בְּיַד הַכַּשְׂדִּים וּבְיַד נְבוּכַדְרֶאצַּר מֶלֶךְ־ בָּבֶל
Babylon king-of Nebuchadrezzar and-into-hand-of the-Chaldeans into-hand-of

וּלְכָדָהּ׃ וּבָאוּ הַכַּשְׂדִּים הַנִּלְחָמִים
the-ones-attacking the-Chaldeans and-they-will-come (29) and-he-will-capture-her

עַל־ הָעִיר הַזֹּאת וְהִצִּיתוּ אֶת־ הָעִיר הַזֹּאת בָּאֵשׁ
with-fire the-this the-city *** and-they-will-set-on-fire the-this the-city against

וּשְׂרָפוּהָ וְאֵת הַבָּתִּים אֲשֶׁר קִטְּרוּ עַל־ גַּגּוֹתֵיהֶם
roofs-of-them on they-burned-incense where the-houses and and-they-will-burn-down-her

לַבַּעַל וְהִסִּכוּ נְסָכִים לֵאלֹהִים אֲחֵרִים לְמַעַן
so-that other-ones to-gods drink-offerings and-they-poured-out to-the-Baal

הַכְעִסֵנִי׃ כִּי־ הָיוּ בְנֵי־ יִשְׂרָאֵל וּבְנֵי
and-peoples-of Israel peoples-of they-were indeed (30) to-provoke-to-anger-me

יְהוּדָה אַךְ עֹשִׂים הָרַע בְּעֵינַי מִנְּעֻרֹתֵיהֶם כִּי
indeed from-youths-of-them in-eyes-of-me the-evil ones-doing nothing-but Judah

בְנֵי־ יִשְׂרָאֵל אַךְ מַכְעִסִים אֹתִי בְּמַעֲשֵׂה יְדֵיהֶם
hands-of-them with-making-of me ones-provoking-to-anger nothing-but Israel peoples-of

נְאֻם־ יְהוָה׃ כִּי עַל־ אַפִּי וְעַל־ חֲמָתִי הָיְתָה
she-aroused wrath-of-me and-to anger-of-me to indeed (31) Yahweh declaration-of

לִּי הָעִיר הַזֹּאת לְמִן־ הַיּוֹם אֲשֶׁר בָּנוּ אוֹתָהּ וְעַד הַיּוֹם
the-day and-until her they-built that the-day at-from the-this the-city to-me

הַזֶּה לַהֲסִירָהּ מֵעַל פָּנָי׃ עַל כָּל־ רָעַת בְּנֵי־
peoples-of evil-of all-of by (32) faces-of-me from-before to-remove-her the-this

יִשְׂרָאֵל וּבְנֵי יְהוּדָה אֲשֶׁר עָשׂוּ לְהַכְעִסֵנִי הֵמָּה מַלְכֵיהֶם
kings-of-them they to-provoke-to-anger-me they-did that Judah and-peoples-of Israel

שָׂרֵיהֶם כֹּהֲנֵיהֶם וּנְבִיאֵיהֶם וְאִישׁ יְהוּדָה
Judah and-man-of and-prophets-of-them priests-of-them officials-of-them

וְיֹשְׁבֵי יְרוּשָׁלִָם׃ וַיִּפְנוּ אֵלַי עֹרֶף וְלֹא פָנִים
faces and-not back to-me and-they-turned (33) Jerusalem and-ones-being-people-of

וְלַמֵּד אֹתָם הַשְׁכֵּם וְלַמֵּד וְאֵינָם שֹׁמְעִים
ones-listening but-not-they and-to-teach to-begin-early them though-to-teach

לָקַחַת מוּסָר׃ וַיָּשִׂימוּ שִׁקּוּצֵיהֶם בַּבַּיִת
in-the-house abominations-of-them and-they-set-up (34) discipline to-respond-to

אֲשֶׁר־ נִקְרָא־ שְׁמִי עָלָיו לְטַמְּאוֹ׃ וַיִּבְנוּ אֶת־
*** and-they-built (35) to-defile-him to-him Name-of-me he-is-called that

came to Jeremiah: [27]"I am the
LORD, the God of all mankind. Is
anything too hard for me? [28]There-
fore, this is what the LORD says: I
am about to hand this city over to
the Babylonians and to Nebuchadnezzar king of Babylon, who
will capture it. [29]The Babylonians
who are attacking this city will
come in and set it on fire; they will
burn it down, along with the
houses where the people provoked me to anger by burning incense on the roofs to Baal and by
pouring out drink offerings to other gods.
[30]"The people of Israel and
Judah have done nothing but evil
in my sight from their youth; indeed, the people of Israel have
done nothing but provoke me
with what their hands have made,
declares the LORD. [31]From the day
it was built until now, this city has
so aroused my anger and wrath
that I must remove it from my
sight. [32]The people of Israel and
Judah have provoked me by all the
evil they have done—they, their
kings and officials, their priests
and prophets, the men of Judah
and the people of Jerusalem.
[33]They turned their backs to me
and not their faces; though I
taught them again and again, they
would not listen or respond to discipline. [34]They set up their abominable idols in the house that bears
my Name and defiled it. [35]They

בָּמוֹת הַבַּעַל אֲשֶׁר ׀ בְּגֵיא בֶן־ הִנֹּם לְהַעֲבִיר אֶת־ בְּנֵיהֶם
sons-of-them *** to-sacrifice Hinnom Ben in-Valley-of that the-Baal high-places

וְאֶת־ בְּנוֹתֵיהֶם לַמֹּלֶךְ אֲשֶׁר לֹא־ צִוִּיתִים וְלֹא
or-not I-commanded-them never though to-the-Molech daughters-of-them and

עָלְתָה עַל־ לִבִּי לַעֲשׂוֹת הַתּוֹעֵבָה הַזֹּאת לְמַעַן הַחֲטִי
to-make-sin so-that the-this the-detestable-thing to-do mind-of-me into she-entered

אֶת־יְהוּדָה׃ וְעַתָּה לָכֵן כֹּה־ אָמַר יְהוָה אֱלֹהֵי יִשְׂרָאֵל אֶל־ הָעִיר
the-city about Israel God-of Yahweh he-says this therefore but-now (36) Judah ***

הַזֹּאת אֲשֶׁר ׀ אַתֶּם אֹמְרִים נִתְּנָה בְּיַד מֶלֶךְ־ בָּבֶל
Babylon king-of into-hand-of she-will-be-given ones-saying you though the-this

בַּחֶרֶב וּבָרָעָב וּבַדָּבֶר׃ הִנְנִי מְקַבְּצָם
gathering-them see-I! (37) and-by-the-plague and-by-the-famine by-the-sword

מִכָּל־ הָאֲרָצוֹת אֲשֶׁר הִדַּחְתִּים שָׁם בְּאַפִּי וּבַחֲמָתִי
and-in-anger-of-me in-fury-of-me there I-banish-them where the-lands from-all-of

וּבְקֶצֶף גָּדוֹל וַהֲשִׁבֹתִים אֶל־ הַמָּקוֹם הַזֶּה
the-this the-place to and-I-will-bring-back-them great and-in-wrath

וְהֹשַׁבְתִּים לָבֶטַח׃ וְהָיוּ לִי לְעָם וַאֲנִי
and-I as-people to-me and-they-will-be (38) in-safety and-I-will-let-live-them

אֶהְיֶה לָהֶם לֵאלֹהִים׃ וְנָתַתִּי לָהֶם לֵב אֶחָד וְדֶרֶךְ אֶחָד
single and-way single heart to-them and-I-will-give (39) as-God to-them I-will-be

לְיִרְאָה אוֹתִי כָּל־ הַיָּמִים לְטוֹב לָהֶם וְלִבְנֵיהֶם אַחֲרֵיהֶם׃
after-them and-for-children-of-them for-them for-good the-days all-of me to-fear

וְכָרַתִּי לָהֶם בְּרִית עוֹלָם אֲשֶׁר לֹא־ אָשׁוּב
I-will-stop never that everlasting covenant-of with-them and-I-will-make (40)

מֵאַחֲרֵיהֶם לְהֵיטִיבִי אוֹתָם וְאֶת־ יִרְאָתִי אֶתֵּן בִּלְבָבָם
in-heart-of-them I-will-put fear-of-me and to-them to-do-good-me from-after-them

לְבִלְתִּי סוּר מֵעָלָי׃ וְשַׂשְׂתִּי עֲלֵיהֶם לְהֵטִיב אוֹתָם
to-them to-do-good over-them and-I-will-rejoice (41) from-with-me to-turn not

וּנְטַעְתִּים בָּאָרֶץ הַזֹּאת בֶּאֱמֶת בְּכָל־ לִבִּי
heart-of-me with-all-of with-assurance the-this in-the-land and-I-will-plant-them

וּבְכָל־ נַפְשִׁי׃ כִּי־ כֹה אָמַר יְהוָה כַּאֲשֶׁר הֵבֵאתִי אֶל־
on I-brought just-as Yahweh he-says this indeed (42) soul-of-me and-with-all-of

הָעָם הַזֶּה אֵת כָּל־ הָרָעָה הַגְּדוֹלָה הַזֹּאת כֵּן אָנֹכִי מֵבִיא עֲלֵיהֶם
to-them giving I so the-this the-great the-calamity all-of *** the-this the-people

אֶת־ כָּל־ הַטּוֹבָה אֲשֶׁר אָנֹכִי דֹּבֵר עֲלֵיהֶם׃ וְנִקְנָה
and-he-will-be-bought (43) to-them promising I that the-prosperity all-of ***

הַשָּׂדֶה בָּאָרֶץ הַזֹּאת אֲשֶׁר ׀ אַתֶּם אֹמְרִים שְׁמָמָה הִיא מֵאֵין אָדָם
man with-no she desolation ones-saying you which the-this in-the-land the-field

built high places for Baal in the
Valley of Ben Hinnom to sacrifice
their sons and daughters[n] to Molech, though I never commanded,
nor did it enter my mind, that
they should do such a detestable
thing and so make Judah sin.
36 "You are saying about this
city, 'By the sword, famine and
plague it will be handed over to
the king of Babylon'; but this is
what the LORD, the God of Israel,
says: 37 I will surely gather them
from all the lands where I banish
them in my furious anger and
great wrath; I will bring them
back to this place and let them live
in safety. 38 They will be my
people, and I will be their God. 39 I
will give them singleness of heart
and action, so that they will always fear me for their own good
and the good of their children after them. 40 I will make an everlasting covenant with them: I will
never stop doing good to them,
and I will inspire them to fear me,
so that they will never turn away
from me. 41 I will rejoice in doing
them good and will assuredly
plant them in this land with all
my heart and soul.
42 "This is what the LORD says: As
I have brought all this great
calamity on this people, so I will
give them all the prosperity I have
promised them. 43 Once more
fields will be bought in this land
of which you say, 'It is a desolate
waste, without men or animals,

[n]35 *Or to make their sons and daughters pass through ⌊the fire⌋*

°35 ק החטיא

וּבְהֵמָ֔ה נִתְּנָ֖ה בְּיַ֥ד הַכַּשְׂדִּֽים׃ שָׂד֞וֹת בַּכֶּ֣סֶף
for-the-silver fields (44) the-Chaldeans into-hand-of she-was-given or-animal

יִקְנ֗וּ וְכָת֨וֹב בַּסֵּ֥פֶר ׀ וְחָת֗וֹם וְהָעֵ֤ד עֵדִים֙
witnesses and-to-have-witness and-to-seal on-the-deed and-to-sign they-will-buy

בְּאֶ֨רֶץ בִּנְיָמִ֜ן וּבִסְבִיבֵ֣י יְרוּשָׁלִַ֗ם וּבְעָרֵ֤י יְהוּדָה֙
Judah and-in-towns-of Jerusalem and-in-ones-around-of Benjamin in-territory-of

וּבְעָרֵ֣י הָהָ֔ר וּבְעָרֵ֥י הַשְּׁפֵלָ֖ה וּבְעָרֵ֣י
and-in-towns-of the-western-foothill and-in-towns-of the-hill-country and-in-towns-of

הַנֶּ֑גֶב כִּֽי־ אָשִׁ֥יב אֶת־ שְׁבוּתָ֖ם נְאֻם־ יְהוָֽה׃
Yahweh declaration-of fortune-of-them *** I-will-restore because the-Negev

וַיְהִ֧י דְבַר־ יְהוָ֛ה אֶֽל־ יִרְמְיָ֖הוּ שֵׁנִ֑ית וְהוּא֙ עוֹדֶ֣נּוּ
still-he and-he second-time Jeremiah to Yahweh word-of and-he-came (33:1)

עָצ֔וּר בַּחֲצַ֥ר הַמַּטָּרָ֖ה לֵאמֹֽר׃ כֹּֽה־ אָמַ֤ר יְהוָה֙
Yahweh he-says this (2) to-say the-guard in-courtyard-of being-confined

עֹשָׂ֔הּ יְהוָ֗ה יוֹצֵ֥ר אוֹתָ֛הּ לַהֲכִינָ֖הּ יְהוָ֥ה שְׁמֽוֹ׃
name-of-him Yahweh to-establish-her her one-forming Yahweh one-making-her

קְרָ֣א אֵלַ֔י וְאֶעֱנֶ֑ךָּ וְאַגִּ֨ידָה לְּךָ֜ גְּדֹל֤וֹת
great-things to-you and-I-will-tell and-I-will-answer-you to-me call! (3)

וּבְצֻר֔וֹת לֹ֖א יְדַעְתָּֽם׃ כִּי֩ כֹ֨ה אָמַ֤ר יְהוָה֙ אֱלֹהֵ֣י
God-of Yahweh he-says this for (4) you-know-them not and-things-being-unsearchable

יִשְׂרָאֵ֔ל עַל־ בָּתֵּי֙ הָעִ֣יר הַזֹּ֔את וְעַל־ בָּתֵּ֖י מַלְכֵ֣י יְהוּדָ֑ה
Judah royalties-of palaces-of and-about the-this the-city houses-of about Israel

הַנְּתֻצִ֔ים אֶל־ הַסֹּלְל֖וֹת וְאֶל־ הֶחָֽרֶב׃
the-sword and-against the-siege-ramps against the-ones-being-torn-down

בָּאִ֗ים לְהִלָּחֵם֙ אֶת־ הַכַּשְׂדִּ֔ים וּלְמַלְאָם֙ אֶת־ פִּגְרֵ֣י
dead-bodies-of with and-to-be-filled-them the-Chaldeans *** to-fight ones-coming (5)

הָאָדָ֔ם אֲשֶׁר־ הִכֵּ֥יתִי בְאַפִּ֖י וּבַחֲמָתִ֑י וַאֲשֶׁ֨ר הִסְתַּ֤רְתִּי
I-will-hide and-that and-in-wrath-of-me in-anger-of-me I-will-slay whom the-man

פָנַי֙ מֵהָעִ֣יר הַזֹּ֔את עַ֖ל כָּל־ רָעָתָֽם׃ הִנְנִ֧י
see-I! (6) wickedness-of-them all-of because-of the-this from-the-city faces-of-me

מַעֲלֶה־ לָּ֛הּ אֲרֻכָ֥ה וּמַרְפֵּ֖א וּרְפָאתִ֑ים וְגִלֵּיתִ֣י
and-I-will-let-enjoy and-I-will-heal-them and-healing health to-her bringing

לָהֶ֔ם עֲתֶ֥רֶת שָׁל֖וֹם וֶאֱמֶֽת׃ וַהֲשִׁבֹתִי֙ אֶת־ שְׁב֣וּת
captivity-of *** and-I-will-bring-back (7) and-security peace abundance-of to-them

יְהוּדָ֔ה וְאֵ֖ת שְׁב֣וּת יִשְׂרָאֵ֑ל וּבְנִתִ֖ים כְּבָרִאשֹׁנָֽה׃
as-at-the-before and-I-will-rebuild-them Israel captivity-of and Judah

וְטִ֣הַרְתִּ֔ים מִכָּל־ עֲוֺנָ֖ם אֲשֶׁ֣ר חָֽטְאוּ־
they-committed-sin that sin-of-them from-all-of and-I-will-cleanse-them (8)

for it has been handed over to the Babylonians.' 44 "Fields will be bought for silver, and deeds will be signed, sealed and witnessed in the territory of Benjamin, in the villages around Jerusalem, in the towns of Judah and in the towns of the hill country, of the western foothills and of the Negev, because I will restore their fortunes,[o] declares the LORD."

*Promise of Restoration*

33 While Jeremiah was still confined in the courtyard of the guard, the word of the LORD came to him a second time: 2 "This is what the LORD says, he who made the earth, the LORD who formed it and established it—the LORD is his name: 3 'Call to me and I will answer you and tell you great and unsearchable things you do not know.' 4 For this is what the LORD, the God of Israel, says about the houses in this city and the royal palaces of Judah that have been torn down to be used against the siege ramps and the sword 5 in the fight with the Babylonians[p]: 'They will be filled with the dead bodies of the men I will slay in my anger and wrath. I will hide my face from this city because of all its wickedness.

6 " 'Nevertheless, I will bring health and healing to it; I will heal my people and will let them enjoy abundant peace and security. 7 I will bring Judah and Israel back from captivity[q] and will rebuild them as they were before. 8 I will cleanse them from all the sin they have committed against me and

o44 Or *will bring them back from captivity*
p5 Or *Chaldeans*
q7 Or *will restore the fortunes of Judah and Israel*

לִ֔י וְסָלַחְתִּ֗י לְכָל־ עֲוֺנֽוֹתֵיהֶם֙ אֲשֶׁ֣ר חָֽטְאוּ־
they-committed-sin that sins-of-them to-all-of and-I-will-forgive against-me

לִ֔י וַאֲשֶׁ֥ר פָּ֖שְׁעוּ בִֽי׃ וְהָ֣יְתָה לִּ֡י לְשֵׁ֣ם
as-renown to-me and-she-will-be (9) against-me they-rebelled and-that against-me

שָׂשׂוֹן֩ לִתְהִלָּ֨ה וּלְתִפְאֶ֔רֶת לְכֹ֖ל גּוֹיֵ֣י הָאָ֑רֶץ אֲשֶׁ֨ר יִשְׁמְע֜וּ אֶת־
*** they-hear that the-earth nations-of before-all-of and-as-honor as-praise joy

כָּל־הַטּוֹבָ֗ה אֲשֶׁ֤ר אָנֹכִי֙ עֹשֶׂ֣ה אֹתָ֔ם וּפָחֲד֣וּ וְרָגְז֗וּ
and-they-will-tremble and-they-will-be-in-awe for-them doing I that the-good all-of

עַ֤ל כָּל־ הַטּוֹבָה֙ וְעַ֣ל כָּל־ הַשָּׁל֔וֹם אֲשֶׁ֥ר
that the-peace abundance-of and-at the-prosperity abundance-of at

אָנֹכִ֖י עֹ֥שֶׂה לָּֽהּ׃ כֹּ֣ה ׀ אָמַ֣ר יְהוָ֗ה ע֣וֹד יִשָּׁמַ֣ע
he-will-be-heard once-more Yahweh he-says this (10) for-her providing I

בַּמָּקוֹם־ הַזֶּה֒ אֲשֶׁ֣ר אַתֶּם֩ אֹֽמְרִ֨ים חָרֵ֜ב ה֗וּא מֵאֵ֥ין אָדָ֖ם
man with-no he desolate-waste ones-saying you that the-this in-the-place

וּמֵאֵ֣ין בְּהֵמָ֑ה בְּעָרֵ֤י יְהוּדָה֙ וּבְחֻצ֣וֹת יְרֽוּשָׁלִַ֔ם
Jerusalem and-in-streets-of Judah in-towns-of animal and-with-no

הַנְשַׁמּ֗וֹת מֵאֵ֥ין אָדָ֛ם וּמֵאֵ֥ין יוֹשֵׁ֖ב וּמֵאֵ֥ין בְּהֵמָֽה׃
animal and-with-no one-inhabiting even-with-no man with-no the-ones-being-deserted

ק֣וֹל שָׂשׂ֞וֹן וְק֣וֹל שִׂמְחָ֗ה ק֣וֹל חָתָן֮ וְק֣וֹל כַּלָּה֒
bride and-voice-of bridegroom voice-of gladness and-sound-of joy sound-of (11)

ק֣וֹל אֹמְרִ֡ים הוֹדוּ֩ אֶת־ יְהוָ֨ה צְבָא֜וֹת כִּֽי־ ט֣וֹב יְהוָ֗ה כִּֽי־
for Yahweh good for Hosts Yahweh-of *** give-thanks! ones-saying voice-of

לְעוֹלָ֣ם חַסְדּ֔וֹ מְבִאִ֥ים תּוֹדָ֖ה בֵּ֣ית יְהוָ֑ה כִּֽי־
for Yahweh house-of thank-offering ones-bringing love-of-him to-forever

אָשִׁ֧יב אֶת־ שְׁבוּת־ הָאָ֛רֶץ כְּבָרִאשֹׁנָ֖ה אָמַ֥ר יְהוָֽה׃ כֹּֽה־
this (12) Yahweh he-says as-at-the-before the-land fortune-of *** I-will-restore

אָמַר֮ יְהוָ֣ה צְבָאוֹת֒ ע֣וֹד יִהְיֶ֣ה ׀ בַּמָּק֣וֹם הַזֶּ֗ה הֶחָרֵ֛ב
the-desolate the-this in-the-place he-will-be again Hosts Yahweh-of he-says

מֵֽאֵין־ אָדָ֥ם וְעַד־ בְּהֵמָ֖ה וּבְכָל־ עָרָ֑יו נְוֵ֣ה רֹעִ֔ים
ones-being-shepherds pasture-of towns-of-him in-all-of animal or-to man with-no

מַרְבִּצִ֖ים צֹֽאן׃ בְּעָרֵ֨י הָהָ֜ר בְּעָרֵ֤י
in-towns-of the-hill-country in-towns-of (13) flock ones-giving-rest

הַשְּׁפֵלָה֙ וּבְעָרֵ֣י הַנֶּ֔גֶב וּבְאֶ֥רֶץ בִּנְיָמִ֖ן
Benjamin and-in-territory-of the-Negev and-in-towns-of the-western-foothill

וּבִסְבִיבֵ֥י יְרוּשָׁלִַ֖ם וּבְעָרֵ֣י יְהוּדָ֑ה עֹ֣ד תַּעֲבֹ֧רְנָה
they-will-pass again Judah and-in-towns-of Jerusalem and-in-ones-around-of

הַצֹּ֛אן עַל־ יְדֵ֥י מוֹנֶ֖ה אָמַ֥ר יְהוָֽה׃ הִנֵּ֛ה יָמִ֥ים בָּאִ֖ים
ones-coming days see! (14) Yahweh he-says one-counting hands-of under the-flock

8° ק לכל

will forgive all their sins of rebellion against me. [9]Then this city will bring me renown, joy, praise and honor before all nations on earth that hear of all the good things I do for it; and they will be in awe and will tremble at the abundant prosperity and peace I provide for it.'

[10]"This is what the LORD says: 'You say about this place, "It is a desolate waste, without men or animals." Yet in the towns of Judah and the streets of Jerusalem that are deserted, inhabited by neither men nor animals, there will be heard once more [11]the sounds of joy and gladness, the voices of bride and bridegroom, and the voices of those who bring thank offerings to the house of the LORD, saying,

"Give thanks to the LORD Almighty,
for the LORD is good;
his love endures forever."

For I will restore the fortunes of the land as they were before,' says the LORD.

[12]"This is what the LORD Almighty says: 'In this place, desolate and without men or animals—in all its towns there will again be pastures for shepherds to rest their flocks. [13]In the towns of the hill country, of the western foothills and of the Negev, in the territory of Benjamin, in the villages around Jerusalem and in the towns of Judah, flocks will again pass under the hand of the one who counts them,' says the LORD.

נְאֻם־ יְהוָה וַהֲקִמֹתִי אֶת־ הַדָּבָר הַטּוֹב אֲשֶׁר
that the-gracious the-promise *** when-I-will-fulfill Yahweh declaration-of

דִּבַּרְתִּי אֶל־ בֵּית יִשְׂרָאֵל וְעַל־ בֵּית יְהוּדָה׃ בַּיָּמִים הָהֵם
the-those in-the-days (15) Judah house-of and-to Israel house-of to I-promised

וּבָעֵת הַהִיא אַצְמִיחַ לְדָוִד צֶמַח צְדָקָה
righteous Branch from-David I-will-make-sprout the-that and-at-the-time

וְעָשָׂה מִשְׁפָּט וּצְדָקָה בָּאָרֶץ׃ בַּיָּמִים הָהֵם
the-those in-the-days (16) in-the-land and-right justice and-he-will-do

תִּוָּשַׁע יְהוּדָה וִירוּשָׁלַם תִּשְׁכּוֹן לָבֶטַח וְזֶה אֲשֶׁר־
which and-this in-safety she-will-live and-Jerusalem Judah she-will-be-saved

יִקְרָא־ לָהּ יְהוָה ׀ צִדְקֵנוּ׃ כִּי־ כֹה אָמַר יְהוָה
Yahweh he-says this for (17) Righteousness-of-Us Yahweh to-her he-will-call

לֹא־ יִכָּרֵת לְדָוִד אִישׁ יֹשֵׁב עַל־ כִּסֵּא בֵית־יִשְׂרָאֵל׃
Israel house-of throne-of on one-sitting man to-David he-will-fail never

וְלַכֹּהֲנִים הַלְוִיִּם לֹא־ יִכָּרֵת אִישׁ מִלְּפָנָי מַעֲלֶה
one-offering at-before-me man he-will-fail never the-Levites or-to-the-priests (18)

עוֹלָה וּמַקְטִיר מִנְחָה וְעֹשֶׂה זֶּבַח כָּל־ הַיָּמִים׃
the-days all-of sacrifice and-presenting grain-offering and-burning burnt-offering

וַיְהִי דְּבַר־ יְהוָה אֶל־יִרְמְיָהוּ לֵאמוֹר׃ כֹּה אָמַר יְהוָה אִם־
if Yahweh he-says this (20) to-say Jeremiah to Yahweh word-of and-he-came (19)

תָּפֵרוּ אֶת־ בְּרִיתִי הַיּוֹם וְאֶת־ בְּרִיתִי הַלַּיְלָה וּלְבִלְתִּי
so-not the-night covenant-of-me and the-day covenant-of-me *** you-can-break

הֱיוֹת יוֹמָם־וָלַיְלָה בְּעִתָּם׃ גַּם־ בְּרִיתִי תֻפַר
she-can-be-broken covenant-of-me then (21) at-time-of-them and-night by-day to-come

אֶת־ דָּוִד עַבְדִּי מִהְיוֹת־ לוֹ בֵן מֹלֵךְ עַל־ כִּסְאוֹ
throne-of-him on reigning descendant to-him from-to-be servant-of-me David with

וְאֶת־ הַלְוִיִּם הַכֹּהֲנִים מְשָׁרְתָי׃ אֲשֶׁר לֹא־
not that (22) ones-ministering-of-me the-priests the-Levites and-with

יִסָּפֵר צְבָא הַשָּׁמַיִם וְלֹא יִמַּד חוֹל הַיָּם
the-sea sand-of he-can-be-measured and-not the-skies star-of he-can-be-counted

כֵּן אַרְבֶּה אֶת־ זֶרַע דָּוִד עַבְדִּי וְאֶת־ הַלְוִיִּם
the-Levites and servant-of-me David descendant-of *** I-will-make-many so

מְשָׁרְתֵי אֹתִי׃ וַיְהִי דְּבַר־ יְהוָה אֶל־יִרְמְיָהוּ לֵאמֹר׃ הֲלוֹא
not? (24) to-say Jeremiah to Yahweh word-of and-he-came (23) me ones-ministering-of

רָאִיתָ מָה־ הָעָם הַזֶּה דִּבְּרוּ לֵאמֹר שְׁתֵּי הַמִּשְׁפָּחוֹת אֲשֶׁר
that the-kingdoms two-of to-say they-say the-this the-people what? you-noticed

בָּחַר יְהוָה בָּהֶם וַיִּמְאָסֵם וְאֶת־ עַמִּי יִנְאָצוּן
they-despise people-of-me so now-he-rejected-them to-them Yahweh he-chose

[14]" 'The days are coming,' declares the LORD, 'when I will fulfill the gracious promise I made to the house of Israel and to the house of Judah.

[15]" 'In those days and at that time
I will make a righteous Branch sprout from David's line;
he will do what is just and right in the land.
[16]In those days Judah will be saved
and Jerusalem will live in safety.
This is the name by which it[r] will be called:
The LORD Our Righteousness.'

[17]For this is what the LORD says: 'David will never fail to have a man to sit on the throne of the house of Israel, [18]nor will the priests, who are Levites, ever fail to have a man to stand before me continually to offer burnt offerings, to burn grain offerings and to present sacrifices.' "

[19]The word of the LORD came to Jeremiah: [20]"This is what the LORD says: 'If you can break my covenant with the day and my covenant with the night, so that day and night no longer come at their appointed time, [21]then my covenant with David my servant—and my covenant with the Levites who are priests ministering before me—can be broken and David will no longer have a descendant to reign on his throne. [22]I will make the descendants of David my servant and the Levites who minister before me as countless as the stars of the sky and as measureless as the sand on the seashore.' "

[23]The word of the LORD came to Jeremiah: [24]"Have you not noticed that these people are saying, 'The LORD has rejected the two kingdoms[s] he chose'? So they despise

[r]16 Or *he*
[s]24 Or *families*

*22 Most mss have *soph pasuq* at the end of the verse (:).

מִהְיוֹת עוֹד גּוֹי לִפְנֵיהֶם׃ כֹּה אָמַר יְהוָה אִם־לֹא בְרִיתִי
covenant-of-me not if Yahweh he-says this (25) before-them nation longer from-to-be

יוֹמָם וָלָיְלָה חֻקּוֹת שָׁמַיִם וָאָרֶץ לֹא־שָׂמְתִּי׃ גַּם־
then (26) I-established not and-earth heavens fixed-laws-of and-night by-day

זֶרַע יַעֲקוֹב וְדָוִד עַבְדִּי אֶמְאַס מִקַּחַת
from-to-choose I-will-reject servant-of-me and-David Jacob descendant-of

מִזַּרְעוֹ מֹשְׁלִים אֶל־זֶרַע אַבְרָהָם יִשְׂחָק וְיַעֲקֹב כִּי־
for and-Jacob Isaac Abraham descendant-of over ones-ruling from-son-of-him

אָשׁוּב אֶת־שְׁבוּתָם וְרִחַמְתִּים׃ הַדָּבָר
the-word (34:1) and-I-will-have-compassion-on-them fortune-of-them *** I-will-restore

אֲשֶׁר־הָיָה אֶל־יִרְמְיָהוּ מֵאֵת יְהוָה וּנְבוּכַדְרֶאצַּר מֶלֶךְ־בָּבֶל ׀
Babylon king-of while-Nebuchadrezzar Yahweh from-with Jeremiah to he-came that

וְכָל־חֵילוֹ וְכָל־מַמְלְכוֹת אֶרֶץ מֶמְשֶׁלֶת יָדוֹ
hand-of-him rule-of empire-of kingdoms-of and-all-of army-of-him and-all-of

וְכָל־הָעַמִּים נִלְחָמִים עַל־יְרוּשָׁלִַם וְעַל־כָּל־
all-of and-against Jerusalem against ones-fighting the-peoples and-all-of

עָרֶיהָ לֵאמֹר׃ כֹּה־אָמַר יְהוָה אֱלֹהֵי יִשְׂרָאֵל הָלֹךְ וְאָמַרְתָּ אֶל־
to and-you-tell to-go Israel God-of Yahweh he-says this (2) to-say towns-of-her

צִדְקִיָּהוּ מֶלֶךְ יְהוּדָה וְאָמַרְתָּ אֵלָיו כֹּה אָמַר יְהוָה הִנְנִי נֹתֵן אֶת־
*** giving see-I! Yahweh he-says this to-him and-you-say Judah king-of Zedekiah

הָעִיר הַזֹּאת בְּיַד מֶלֶךְ־בָּבֶל וּשְׂרָפָהּ בָּאֵשׁ׃
with-fire and-he-will-burn-down-her Babylon king-of into-hand-of the-this the-city

וְאַתָּה לֹא תִמָּלֵט מִיָּדוֹ כִּי תָּפֹשׂ תִּתָּפֵשׂ
you-will-be-captured to-capture but from-grasp-of-him you-will-escape not and-you (3)

וּבְיָדוֹ תִּנָּתֵן וְעֵינֶיךָ אֶת־עֵינֵי מֶלֶךְ־בָּבֶל
Babylon king-of eyes-of *** and-eyes-of-you you-will-be-given and-into-hand-of-him

תִּרְאֶינָה וּפִיהוּ אֶת־פִּיךָ יְדַבֵּר וּבָבֶל
and-Babylon he-will-speak mouth-of-you *** and-mouth-of-him they-will-see

תָּבוֹא׃ אַךְ שְׁמַע דְּבַר־יְהוָה צִדְקִיָּהוּ מֶלֶךְ יְהוּדָה כֹּה־אָמַר
he-says this Judah king-of Zedekiah Yahweh promise-of hear! yet (4) you-will-go

יְהוָה עָלֶיךָ לֹא תָמוּת בֶּחָרֶב׃ בְּשָׁלוֹם תָּמוּת
you-will-die in-peace (5) by-the-sword you-will-die not concerning-you Yahweh

וּכְמִשְׂרְפוֹת אֲבוֹתֶיךָ הַמְּלָכִים הָרִאשֹׁנִים אֲשֶׁר־הָיוּ
they-came who the-former-ones the-kings fathers-of-you and-as-funeral-fires-of

לְפָנֶיךָ כֵּן יִשְׂרְפוּ־לָךְ וְהוֹי אָדוֹן יִסְפְּדוּ־
they-will-lament master and-alas! for-you they-will-make-fire so before-you

לָךְ כִּי־דָבָר אֲנִי־דִבַּרְתִּי נְאֻם־יְהוָה׃ וַיְדַבֵּר יִרְמְיָהוּ
Jeremiah then-he-told (6) Yahweh declaration-of I-promise I promise for for-you

my people and no longer regard them as a nation. [25]This is what the LORD says: 'If I have not established my covenant with day and night and the fixed laws of heaven and earth, [26]then I will reject the descendants of Jacob and David my servant and will not choose one of his sons to rule over the descendants of Abraham, Isaac and Jacob. For I will restore their fortunes[†] and have compassion on them.' "

*Warning to Zedekiah*

34 While Nebuchadnezzar king of Babylon and all his army and all the kingdoms and peoples in the empire he ruled were fighting against Jerusalem and all its surrounding towns, this word came to Jeremiah from the LORD: [2]"This is what the LORD, the God of Israel, says: Go to Zedekiah king of Judah and tell him, 'This is what the LORD says: I am about to hand this city over to the king of Babylon, and he will burn it down. [3]You will not escape from his grasp but will surely be captured and handed over to him. You will see the king of Babylon with your own eyes, and he will speak with you face to face. And you will go to Babylon.

[4]" 'Yet hear the promise of the LORD, O Zedekiah king of Judah. This is what the LORD says concerning you: You will not die by the sword; [5]you will die peacefully. As people made a funeral fire in honor of your fathers, the former kings who preceded you, so they will make a fire in your honor and lament, "Alas, O master!" I myself make this promise, declares the LORD.' "

[6]Then Jeremiah the prophet told

[†]26 Or *will bring them back from captivity*

°26 ק אשיב

הַנָּבִיא אֶל־צִדְקִיָּהוּ מֶלֶךְ יְהוּדָה אֵת כָּל־הַדְּבָרִים הָאֵלֶּה בִּירוּשָׁלִָם׃
in-Jerusalem the-these the-words all-of *** Judah king-of Zedekiah to the-prophet

וְחֵיל מֶלֶךְ־בָּבֶל נִלְחָמִים עַל־יְרוּשָׁלִַם וְעַל כָּל־
all-of and-against Jerusalem against ones-fighting Babylon king-of while-army-of (7)

עָרֵי יְהוּדָה הַנּוֹתָרוֹת אֶל־לָכִישׁ וְאֶל־עֲזֵקָה כִּי הֵנָּה
these now Azekah and-against Lachish against the-ones-holding-out Judah cities-of

נִשְׁאֲרוּ בְּעָרֵי יְהוּדָה עָרֵי מִבְצָר׃ הַדָּבָר אֲשֶׁר־
that the-word (8) fortification cities-of Judah of-cities-of they-were-left

הָיָה אֶל־יִרְמְיָהוּ מֵאֵת יְהוָה אַחֲרֵי כְּרֹת הַמֶּלֶךְ צִדְקִיָּהוּ בְּרִית
covenant Zedekiah the-king to-make after Yahweh from-with Jeremiah to he-came

אֶת־כָּל־הָעָם אֲשֶׁר בִּירוּשָׁלִַם לִקְרֹא לָהֶם דְּרוֹר׃
freedom-from-slavery for-them to-proclaim in-Jerusalem who the-people all-of with

לְשַׁלַּח אִישׁ אֶת־עַבְדּוֹ וְאִישׁ אֶת־שִׁפְחָתוֹ
female-slave-of-him *** and-each male-slave-of-him *** each to-free (9)

הָעִבְרִי וְהָעִבְרִיָּה חָפְשִׁים לְבִלְתִּי עֲבָד־בָּם
to-them to-hold-in-bondage not free-ones and-the-Hebrew-woman the-Hebrew-man

בִּיהוּדִי אָחִיהוּ אִישׁ׃ וַיִּשְׁמְעוּ כָל־הַשָּׂרִים וְכָל־
and-all-of the-officials all-of so-they-agreed (10) anyone fellow-of-him to-Jew

הָעָם אֲשֶׁר־בָּאוּ בַבְּרִית לְשַׁלַּח אִישׁ אֶת־עַבְדּוֹ
male-slave-of-him *** each to-free into-the-covenant they-entered who the-people

וְאִישׁ אֶת־שִׁפְחָתוֹ חָפְשִׁים לְבִלְתִּי עֲבָד־בָּם עוֹד
longer to-them to-hold-in-bondage not free-ones female-slave-of-him *** and-each

וַיִּשְׁמְעוּ וַיְשַׁלֵּחוּ׃ וַיָּשׁוּבוּ אַחֲרֵי־כֵן
this after but-they-changed-minds (11) and-they-set-free and-they-agreed

וַיָּשִׁבוּ אֶת־הָעֲבָדִים וְאֶת־הַשְּׁפָחוֹת אֲשֶׁר שִׁלְּחוּ
they-freed that the-female-slaves and the-male-slaves *** and-they-took-back

חָפְשִׁים °וַיִּכְבִּישׁוּם לַעֲבָדִים וְלִשְׁפָחוֹת׃ וַיְהִי
and-he-came (12) and-as-female-slaves as-male-slaves and-they-enslaved-them free-ones

דְבַר־יְהוָה אֶל־יִרְמְיָהוּ מֵאֵת יְהוָה לֵאמֹר׃ כֹּה־אָמַר יְהוָה אֱלֹהֵי
God-of Yahweh he-says this (13) to-say Yahweh from-with Jeremiah to Yahweh word-of

יִשְׂרָאֵל אָנֹכִי כָּרַתִּי בְרִית אֶת־אֲבוֹתֵיכֶם בְּיוֹם הוֹצִאִי אוֹתָם
them to-bring-me on-day-of forefathers-of-you with covenant I-made I Israel

מֵאֶרֶץ מִצְרַיִם מִבֵּית עֲבָדִים לֵאמֹר׃ מִקֵּץ שֶׁבַע שָׁנִים
years seven at-end-of (14) to-say slaveries from-house-of Egypt from-land-of

תְּשַׁלְּחוּ אִישׁ אֶת־אָחִיו הָעִבְרִי אֲשֶׁר־יִמָּכֵר לְךָ
to-you he-sold-himself who the-Hebrew fellow-of-him *** each you-must-free

וַעֲבָדְךָ שֵׁשׁ שָׁנִים וְשִׁלַּחְתּוֹ חָפְשִׁי מֵעִמָּךְ וְלֹא־
but-not from-with-you free then-you-must-let-go-him years six after-he-served-you

°11 ק ויכבשום

all this to Zedekiah king of Judah,
in Jerusalem, 7 while the army of
the king of Babylon was fighting
against Jerusalem and the other
cities of Judah that were still holding out—Lachish and Azekah.
These were the only fortified cities
left in Judah.

*Freedom for Slaves*

8 The word came to Jeremiah
from the LORD after King Zedekiah had made a covenant with all
the people in Jerusalem to proclaim freedom for the slaves.
9 Everyone was to free his Hebrew
slaves, both male and female; no
one was to hold a fellow Jew in
bondage. 10 So all the officials and
people who entered into this covenant agreed that they would free
their male and female slaves and
no longer hold them in bondage.
They agreed, and set them free.
11 But afterward they changed their
minds and took back the slaves
they had freed and enslaved them
again.
12 Then the word of the LORD
came to Jeremiah: 13 "This is what
the LORD, the God of Israel, says: I
made a covenant with your forefathers when I brought them out of
Egypt, out of the land of slavery. I
said, 14 'Every seventh year each of
you must free any fellow Hebrew
who has sold himself to you. After
he has served you six years, you
must let him go free.'[u] Your fathers,

[u]14 Deut. 15:12

שָׁמְעוּ אֲבוֹתֵיכֶם אֵלַי וְלֹא הִטּוּ אֶת־אָזְנָם׃
ear-of-them *** they-made-attentive or-not to-me fathers-of-you they-listened

וַתָּשֻׁבוּ אַתֶּם הַיּוֹם וַתַּעֲשׂוּ אֶת־הַיָּשָׁר בְּעֵינַי
in-eyes-of-me the-right *** and-you-did the-day you and-you-repented (15)

לִקְרֹא דְרוֹר אִישׁ לְרֵעֵהוּ וַתִּכְרְתוּ בְרִית לְפָנַי
before-me covenant even-you-made to-countryman-of-you each freedom to-proclaim

בַּבַּיִת אֲשֶׁר־נִקְרָא שְׁמִי עָלָיו׃ וַתָּשֻׁבוּ וַתְּחַלְּלוּ
and-you-profaned but-you-turned (16) to-him Name-of-me he-is-called that in-the-house

אֶת־שְׁמִי וַתָּשִׁבוּ אִישׁ אֶת־עַבְדּוֹ וְאִישׁ אֶת־
*** and-each male-slave-of-him *** each and-you-took-back name-of-me ***

שִׁפְחָתוֹ אֲשֶׁר־שִׁלַּחְתֶּם חָפְשִׁים לְנַפְשָׁם וַתִּכְבְּשׁוּ
and-you-forced by-desire-of-them free-ones you-set-free whom female-slave-of-him

אֹתָם לִהְיוֹת לָכֶם לַעֲבָדִים וְלִשְׁפָחוֹת׃ לָכֵן כֹּה־אָמַר
he-says this therefore (17) and-as-female-slaves as-male-slaves for-you to-be them

יְהוָה אַתֶּם לֹא־שְׁמַעְתֶּם אֵלַי לִקְרֹא דְרוֹר אִישׁ לְאָחִיו וְאִישׁ
and-each for-fellow-of-him each freedom to-proclaim to-me you-obeyed not you Yahweh

לְרֵעֵהוּ הִנְנִי קֹרֵא לָכֶם דְּרוֹר נְאֻם־יְהוָה אֶל־
to Yahweh declaration-of freedom for-you proclaiming see-I! for-countryman-of-him

הַחֶרֶב אֶל־הַדֶּבֶר וְאֶל־הָרָעָב וְנָתַתִּי אֶתְכֶם לְזַוְעָה
as-abhorrence you and-I-will-make the-famine and-to the-plague to the-sword

לְכֹל מַמְלְכוֹת הָאָרֶץ׃ וְנָתַתִּי אֶת־הָאֲנָשִׁים הָעֹבְרִים
the-ones-violating the-men *** and-I-will-treat (18) the-earth kingdoms-of to-all-of

אֶת־בְּרִתִי אֲשֶׁר לֹא־הֵקִימוּ אֶת־דִּבְרֵי הַבְּרִית אֲשֶׁר כָּרְתוּ
they-made that the-covenant terms-of *** they-fulfilled not who covenant-of-me ***

לְפָנָי הָעֵגֶל אֲשֶׁר כָּרְתוּ לִשְׁנַיִם וַיַּעַבְרוּ בֵּין בְּתָרָיו׃
pieces-of-him between and-they-walked in-two they-cut that the-calf before-me

שָׂרֵי יְהוּדָה וְשָׂרֵי יְרוּשָׁלַםִ הַסָּרִסִים וְהַכֹּהֲנִים
and-the-priests the-court-officials Jerusalem and-leaders-of Judah leaders-of (19)

וְכֹל עַם הָאָרֶץ הָעֹבְרִים בֵּין בִּתְרֵי הָעֵגֶל׃
the-calf pieces-of between the-ones-walking the-land people-of and-all-of

וְנָתַתִּי אוֹתָם בְּיַד אֹיְבֵיהֶם וּבְיַד
even-into-hand-of ones-being-enemies-of-them into-hand-of them and-I-will-give (20)

מְבַקְשֵׁי נַפְשָׁם וְהָיְתָה נִבְלָתָם לְמַאֲכָל
as-food dead-body-of-them and-she-will-become life-of-them ones-seeking-of

לְעוֹף הַשָּׁמַיִם וּלְבֶהֱמַת הָאָרֶץ׃ וְאֶת־צִדְקִיָּהוּ מֶלֶךְ־יְהוּדָה
Judah king-of Zedekiah and (21) the-earth and-for-beast-of the-airs for-bird-of

וְאֶת־שָׂרָיו אֶתֵּן בְּיַד אֹיְבֵיהֶם
ones-being-enemies-of-them into-hand-of I-will-give officials-of-him and

however, did not listen to me or pay attention to me. [15]Recently you repented and did what is right in my sight: Each of you proclaimed freedom to his countrymen. You even made a covenant before me in the house that bears my Name. [16]But now you have turned around and profaned my name; each of you has taken back the male and female slaves you had set free to go where they wished. You have forced them to become your slaves again.

[17]"Therefore, this is what the LORD says: You have not obeyed me; you have not proclaimed freedom for your fellow countrymen. So I now proclaim 'freedom' for you, declares the LORD—'freedom' to fall by the sword, plague and famine. I will make you abhorrent to all the kingdoms of the earth. [18]The men who have violated my covenant and have not fulfilled the terms of the covenant they made before me, I will treat like the calf they cut in two and then walked between its pieces. [19]The leaders of Judah and Jerusalem, the court officials, the priests and all the people of the land who walked between the pieces of the calf, [20]I will hand over to their enemies who seek their lives. Their dead bodies will become food for the birds of the air and the beasts of the earth.

[21]"I will hand Zedekiah king of Judah and his officials over to their enemies who seek their

°17 ק לזועה

וּבְיַד מְבַקְשֵׁי נַפְשָׁם וּבְיַד חֵיל מֶלֶךְ
king-of army-of and-into-hand-of life-of-them ones-seeking-of even-into-hand-of

בָּבֶל הָעֹלִים מֵעֲלֵיכֶם׃ הִנְנִי מְצַוֶּה נְאֻם־
declaration-of ordering see-I! (22) from-against-you the-ones-withdrawing Babylon

יְהוָה וַהֲשִׁבֹתִים אֶל־ הָעִיר הַזֹּאת וְנִלְחֲמוּ
and-they-will-fight the-this the-city to and-I-will-bring-back-them Yahweh

עָלֶיהָ וּלְכָדוּהָ וּשְׂרָפֻהָ בָאֵשׁ וְאֶת־
and with-fire and-they-will-burn-down-her and-they-will-take-her against-her

עָרֵי יְהוּדָה אֶתֵּן שְׁמָמָה מֵאֵין יֹשֵׁב׃ הַדָּבָר אֲשֶׁר־ הָיָה אֶל־
to he-came that the-word (35:1) one-living with-no waste I-will-lay Judah towns-of

יִרְמְיָהוּ מֵאֵת יְהוָה בִּימֵי יְהוֹיָקִים בֶּן־ יֹאשִׁיָּהוּ מֶלֶךְ יְהוּדָה לֵאמֹר׃
to-say Judah king-of Josiah son-of Jehoiakim in-days-of Yahweh from-with Jeremiah

הָלוֹךְ אֶל־ בֵּית הָרֵכָבִים וְדִבַּרְתָּ אוֹתָם וַהֲבִאוֹתָם בֵּית
house-of and-you-bring-them them and-you-invite the-Recabites family-of to to-go (2)

יְהוָה אֶל־ אַחַת הַלְּשָׁכוֹת וְהִשְׁקִיתָ אוֹתָם יָיִן׃ וָאֶקַּח אֶת־
*** so-I-got (3) wine them and-you-give-drink the-side-rooms one-of to Yahweh

יַאֲזַנְיָה בֶן־ יִרְמְיָהוּ בֶּן־ חֲבַצִּנְיָה וְאֶת־ אֶחָיו וְאֶת־ כָּל־
all-of and brothers-of-him and Habazziniah son-of Jeremiah son-of Jaazaniah

בָּנָיו וְאֵת כָּל־ בֵּית הָרֵכָבִים׃ וָאָבִא אֹתָם בֵּית
house-of them and-I-brought (4) the-Recabites family-of whole-of and sons-of-him

יְהוָה אֶל־ לִשְׁכַּת בְּנֵי חָנָן בֶּן־ יִגְדַּלְיָהוּ אִישׁ הָאֱלֹהִים אֲשֶׁר־ אֵצֶל
next-to that the-God man-of Igdaliah son-of Hanan sons-of room-of into Yahweh

לִשְׁכַּת הַשָּׂרִים אֲשֶׁר מִמַּעַל לְלִשְׁכַּת מַעֲשֵׂיָהוּ בֶן־ שַׁלֻּם שֹׁמֵר
one-keeping Shallum son-of Maaseiah to-room-of at-over which the-officials room-of

הַסַּף׃ וָאֶתֵּן לִפְנֵי׀ בְּנֵי בֵית־ הָרֵכָבִים גְּבִעִים מְלֵאִים יַיִן
wine full-ones bowls the-Recabites family-of men-of before then-I-set (5) the-door

וְכֹסוֹת וָאֹמַר אֲלֵיהֶם שְׁתוּ־ יָיִן׃ וַיֹּאמְרוּ לֹא נִשְׁתֶּה־ יָּיִן
wine we-drink not but-they-replied (6) wine drink! to-them and-I-said and-cups

כִּי יוֹנָדָב בֶּן־ רֵכָב אָבִינוּ צִוָּה עָלֵינוּ לֵאמֹר לֹא
never to-say to-us he-commanded forefather-of-us Recab son-of Jonadab because

תִשְׁתּוּ־ יַיִן אַתֶּם וּבְנֵיכֶם עַד־ עוֹלָם׃ וּבַיִת לֹא־
never also-house (7) forever to or-descendants-of-you you wine you-must-drink

תִבְנוּ וְזֶרַע לֹא־ תִזְרָעוּ וְכֶרֶם לֹא־ תִטָּעוּ וְלֹא
indeed-never you-must-plant not or-vineyard you-must-sow not or-seed you-must-build

יִהְיֶה לָכֶם כִּי בָּאֳהָלִים תֵּשְׁבוּ כָּל־ יְמֵיכֶם לְמַעַן
so-that days-of-you all-of you-must-live in-tents but to-you he-must-be

תִּחְיוּ יָמִים רַבִּים עַל־ פְּנֵי הָאֲדָמָה אֲשֶׁר אַתֶּם גָּרִים שָׁם׃
there ones-being-nomads you that the-land faces-of on many-ones days you-will-live

lives, to the army of the king of Babylon, which has withdrawn
from you. [22]I am going to give the
order, declares the LORD, and I will bring them back to this city. They will fight against it, take it and burn it down. And I will lay waste the towns of Judah so no one can live there."

*The Recabites*

35 This is the word that came to Jeremiah from the LORD during the reign of Jehoiakim son of Josiah king of Judah:
[2]"Go to the Recabite family and invite them to come to one of the side rooms of the house of the LORD and give them wine to drink."
[3]So I went to get Jaazaniah son of Jeremiah, the son of Habazziniah, and his brothers and all his sons—the whole family of the Recabites.
[4]I brought them into the house of the LORD, into the room of the sons of Hanan son of Igdaliah the man of God. It was next to the room of the officials, which was over that of Maaseiah son of Shallum the doorkeeper.
[5]Then I set bowls full of wine and some cups before the men of the Recabite family and said to them, "Drink some wine."
[6]But they replied, "We do not drink wine, because our forefather Jonadab son of Recab gave us this command: 'Neither you nor your descendants must ever drink wine.
[7]Also you must never build houses, sow seed or plant vineyards; you must never have any of these things, but must always live in tents. Then you will live a long time in the land where you are

וַנִּשְׁמַע בְּקוֹל יְהוֹנָדָב בֶּן־ רֵכָב אָבִינוּ לְכֹל אֲשֶׁר
that to-every forefather-of-us Recab son-of Jonadab to-voice-of and-we-obeyed (8)

צִוָּנוּ לְבִלְתִּי שְׁתוֹת־ יַיִן כָּל־ יָמֵינוּ אֲנַחְנוּ נָשֵׁינוּ בָּנֵינוּ
sons-of-us wives-of-us we days-of-us all-of wine to-drink not he-commanded-us

וּבְנֹתֵינוּ׃ וּלְבִלְתִּי בְּנוֹת בָּתִּים לְשִׁבְתֵּנוּ וְכֶרֶם וְשָׂדֶה
or-field or-vineyard to-live-us houses to-build or-not (9) or-daughters-of-us

וָזֶרַע לֹא יִהְיֶה־ לָּנוּ׃ וַנֵּשֶׁב בָּאֳהָלִים וַנִּשְׁמַע וַנַּעַשׂ
and-we-did and-we-obeyed in-tents but-we-lived (10) to-us he-is not or-crop

כְּכֹל אֲשֶׁר־ צִוָּנוּ יוֹנָדָב אָבִינוּ׃ וַיְהִי
but-he-was (11) forefather-of-us Jonadab he-commanded-us that as-everything

בַּעֲלוֹת נְבוּכַדְרֶאצַּר מֶלֶךְ־ בָּבֶל אֶל־הָאָרֶץ וַנֹּאמֶר בֹּאוּ
come! then-we-said the-land into Babylon king-of Nebuchadrezzar when-to-invade

וְנָבוֹא יְרוּשָׁלִַם מִפְּנֵי חֵיל הַכַּשְׂדִּים וּמִפְּנֵי חֵיל
army-of and-because-of the-Chaldeans army-of because-of Jerusalem for-we-must-go

אֲרָם וַנֵּשֶׁב בִּירוּשָׁלִָם׃ וַיְהִי דְּבַר־יְהוָה אֶל־יִרְמְיָהוּ לֵאמֹר׃
to-say Jeremiah to Yahweh word-of and-he-came (12) in-Jerusalem so-we-remained Aram

כֹּה־ אָמַר יְהוָה צְבָאוֹת אֱלֹהֵי יִשְׂרָאֵל הָלֹךְ וְאָמַרְתָּ לְאִישׁ יְהוּדָה
Judah to-man-of and-you-tell to-go Israel God-of Hosts Yahweh-of he-says this (13)

וּלְיוֹשְׁבֵי יְרוּשָׁלִָם הֲלוֹא תִקְחוּ מוּסָר לִשְׁמֹעַ אֶל־
to to-obey lesson will-you-learn not? Jerusalem and-to-ones-being-people-of

דְּבָרַי נְאֻם־ יְהוָה׃ הוּקַם אֶת־ דִּבְרֵי יְהוֹנָדָב בֶּן־
son-of Jonadab commands-of *** he-was-kept (14) Yahweh declaration-of words-of-me

רֵכָב אֲשֶׁר־ צִוָּה אֶת־ בָּנָיו לְבִלְתִּי שְׁתוֹת־ יַיִן וְלֹא שָׁתוּ עַד־
to they-drink and-not wine to-drink not sons-of-him *** he-ordered who Recab

הַיּוֹם הַזֶּה כִּי שָׁמְעוּ אֵת מִצְוַת אֲבִיהֶם וְאָנֹכִי דִּבַּרְתִּי
I-spoke but-I forefather-of-them command-of *** they-obey because the-this the-day

אֲלֵיכֶם הַשְׁכֵּם וְדַבֵּר וְלֹא שְׁמַעְתֶּם אֵלָי׃ וָאֶשְׁלַח אֲלֵיכֶם
to-you and-I-sent (15) to-me you-obeyed yet-not and-to-speak to-begin-early to-you

אֶת־ כָּל־ עֲבָדַי הַנְּבִאִים ׀ הַשְׁכֵּים וְשָׁלֹחַ ׀ לֵאמֹר שֻׁבוּ־
turn! to-say and-to-send to-begin-early the-prophets servants-of-me all-of ***

נָא אִישׁ מִדַּרְכּוֹ הָרָעָה וְהֵיטִיבוּ מַעַלְלֵיכֶם וְאַל־ תֵּלְכוּ
you-follow and-not actions-of-you and-reform! the-wicked from-way-of-him each now!

אַחֲרֵי אֱלֹהִים אֲחֵרִים לְעָבְדָם וּשְׁבוּ אֶל־ הָאֲדָמָה אֲשֶׁר־נָתַתִּי לָכֶם
to-you I-gave that the-land in then-live! to-serve-them other-ones gods after

וְלַאֲבֹתֵיכֶם וְלֹא הִטִּיתֶם אֶת־ אָזְנְכֶם וְלֹא שְׁמַעְתֶּם
you-listened or-not ear-of-you *** you-made-attentive but-not and-to-fathers-of-you

אֵלָי׃ כִּי הֵקִימוּ בְּנֵי יְהוֹנָדָב בֶּן־ רֵכָב אֶת־
*** Recab son-of Jonadab descendants-of they-carried-out indeed (16) to-me

nomads.’ [8]We have obeyed everything our forefather Jonadab son
of Recab commanded us. Neither
we nor our wives nor our sons and
daughters have ever drunk wine
[9]or built houses to live in or had
vineyards, fields or crops. [10]We
have lived in tents and have fully
obeyed everything our forefather
Jonadab commanded us. [11]But
when Nebuchadnezzar king of
Babylon invaded this land, we
said, ‘Come, we must go to Jerusalem to escape the Babylonian[a] and
Aramean armies.’ So we have remained in Jerusalem.”
[12]Then the word of the LORD
came to Jeremiah, saying: [13]“This
is what the LORD Almighty, the
God of Israel, says: Go and tell the
men of Judah and the people of
Jerusalem, ‘Will you not learn a
lesson and obey my words?’ declares the LORD. [14]‘Jonadab son of
Recab ordered his sons not to
drink wine and this command has
been kept. To this day they do not
drink wine, because they obey
their forefather’s command. But I
have spoken to you again and
again, yet you have not obeyed
me. [15]Again and again I sent all my
servants the prophets to you. They
said, “Each of you must turn from
your wicked ways and reform
your actions; do not follow other
gods to serve them. Then you will
live in the land I have given to you
and your fathers.” But you have
not paid attention or listened to
me. [16]The descendants of Jonadab
son of Recab have carried out the

[a]11 Or *Chaldean*

מִצְוַת אֲבִיהֶם אֲשֶׁר צִוָּם וְהָעָם הַזֶּה לֹא
not the-this but-the-people he-commanded-them that forefather-of-them command-of

שָׁמְעוּ אֵלָי׃ לָכֵן כֹּה־אָמַר יְהוָה אֱלֹהֵי צְבָאוֹת אֱלֹהֵי יִשְׂרָאֵל
Israel God-of Hosts God-of Yahweh he-says this therefore (17) to-me they-obeyed

הִנְנִי מֵבִיא אֶל־יְהוּדָה וְאֶל כָּל־יוֹשְׁבֵי יְרוּשָׁלִַם אֵת
*** Jerusalem ones-living-of every-of and-on Judah on bringing see-I!

כָּל־הָרָעָה אֲשֶׁר דִּבַּרְתִּי עֲלֵיהֶם יַעַן דִּבַּרְתִּי אֲלֵיהֶם וְלֹא
but-not to-them I-spoke because against-them I-pronounced that the-disaster every-of

שָׁמֵעוּ וָאֶקְרָא לָהֶם וְלֹא עָנוּ׃ וּלְבֵית
then-to-family-of (18) they-answered but-not to-them and-I-called they-listened

הָרֵכָבִים אָמַר יִרְמְיָהוּ כֹּה־אָמַר יְהוָה צְבָאוֹת אֱלֹהֵי יִשְׂרָאֵל יַעַן
because Israel God-of Hosts Yahweh-of he-says this Jeremiah he-said the-Recabites

אֲשֶׁר שְׁמַעְתֶּם עַל־מִצְוַת יְהוֹנָדָב אֲבִיכֶם וַתִּשְׁמְרוּ אֶת־כָּל־
all-of *** and-you-followed forefather-of-you Jonadab command-of to you-obeyed that

מִצְוֺתָיו וַתַּעֲשׂוּ כְּכֹל אֲשֶׁר־צִוָּה אֶתְכֶם׃ לָכֵן
therefore (19) you he-ordered that as-everything and-you-did instructions-of-him

כֹּה אָמַר יְהוָה צְבָאוֹת אֱלֹהֵי יִשְׂרָאֵל לֹא־יִכָּרֵת אִישׁ לְיוֹנָדָב בֶּן־
son-of of-Jonadab man he-will-fail never Israel God-of Hosts Yahweh-of he-says this

רֵכָב עֹמֵד לְפָנַי כָּל־הַיָּמִים׃ וַיְהִי בַּשָּׁנָה הָרְבִיעִת
the-fourth in-the-year and-he-was (36:1) the-days all-of before-me serving Recab

לִיהוֹיָקִים בֶּן־יֹאשִׁיָּהוּ מֶלֶךְ יְהוּדָה הָיָה הַדָּבָר הַזֶּה אֶל־יִרְמְיָהוּ
Jeremiah to the-this the-word he-came Judah king-of Josiah son-of of-Jehoiakim

מֵאֵת יְהוָה לֵאמֹר׃ קַח־לְךָ מְגִלַּת־סֵפֶר וְכָתַבְתָּ אֵלֶיהָ
on-her and-you-write writing scroll-of for-you take! (2) to-say Yahweh from-with

אֵת כָּל־הַדְּבָרִים אֲשֶׁר־דִּבַּרְתִּי אֵלֶיךָ עַל־יִשְׂרָאֵל וְעַל־יְהוּדָה
Judah and-concerning Israel concerning to-you I-spoke that the-words all-of ***

וְעַל־כָּל־הַגּוֹיִם מִיּוֹם דִּבַּרְתִּי אֵלֶיךָ מִימֵי יֹאשִׁיָּהוּ
Josiah in-days-of to-you I-spoke from-day the-nations all-of and-concerning

וְעַד הַיּוֹם הַזֶּה׃ אוּלַי יִשְׁמְעוּ בֵּית יְהוּדָה אֵת כָּל־
every-of *** Judah people-of they-will-hear perhaps (3) the-this the-day and-till

הָרָעָה אֲשֶׁר אָנֹכִי חֹשֵׁב לַעֲשׂוֹת לָהֶם לְמַעַן יָשׁוּבוּ אִישׁ
each they-will-turn so-that on-them to-inflict planning I that the-disaster

מִדַּרְכּוֹ הָרָעָה וְסָלַחְתִּי לַעֲוֺנָם וּלְחַטָּאתָם׃
and-to-sin-of-them to-wickedness-of-them then-I-will-forgive the-wicked from-way-of-him

וַיִּקְרָא יִרְמְיָהוּ אֶת־בָּרוּךְ בֶּן־נֵרִיָּה וַיִּכְתֹּב בָּרוּךְ
Baruch and-he-wrote Neriah son-of Baruch *** Jeremiah so-he-called (4)

מִפִּי יִרְמְיָהוּ אֵת כָּל־דִּבְרֵי יְהוָה אֲשֶׁר־דִּבֶּר אֵלָיו עַל־
on to-him he-spoke that Yahweh words-of all-of *** Jeremiah at-dictation-of

command their forefather gave them, but these people have not obeyed me.'

17 "Therefore, this is what the LORD God Almighty, the God of Israel, says: 'Listen! I am going to bring on Judah and on everyone living in Jerusalem every disaster I pronounced against them. I spoke to them, but they did not listen; I called to them, but they did not answer.' "

18 Then Jeremiah said to the family of the Recabites, "This is what the LORD Almighty, the God of Israel, says: 'You have obeyed the command of your forefather Jonadab and have followed all his instructions and have done everything he ordered.'
19 Therefore, this is what the LORD Almighty, the God of Israel, says: 'Jonadab son of Recab will never fail to have a man to serve me.' "

*Jehoiakim Burns Jeremiah's Scroll*

36 In the fourth year of Jehoiakim son of Josiah king of Judah, this word came to Jeremiah from the LORD:
2 "Take a scroll and write on it all the words I have spoken to you concerning Israel, Judah and all the other nations from the time I began speaking to you in the reign of Josiah till now.
3 Perhaps when the people of Judah hear about every disaster I plan to inflict on them, each of them will turn from his wicked way; then I will forgive their wickedness and their sin."

4 So Jeremiah called Baruch son of Neriah, and while Jeremiah dictated all the words the LORD had spoken to him, Baruch wrote

מְגִלַּת־ סֵפֶר׃ וַיְצַוֶּה יִרְמְיָהוּ אֶת־ בָּרוּךְ לֵאמֹר אֲנִי עָצוּר
being-restricted I to-say Baruch *** Jeremiah then-he-told (5) writing scroll-of

לֹא אוּכַל לָבוֹא בֵּית יְהוָה׃ וּבָאתָ אַתָּה וְקָרָאתָ בַמְּגִלָּה
from-the-scroll and-you-read you so-you-go (6) Yahweh temple-of to-go I-can not

אֲשֶׁר־ כָּתַבְתָּ־ מִפִּי אֶת־ דִּבְרֵי יְהוָה בְּאָזְנֵי הָעָם
the-people in-ears-of Yahweh words-of *** from-dictation-of-me you-wrote that

בֵּית יְהוָה בְּיוֹם צוֹם וְגַם בְּאָזְנֵי כָל־יְהוּדָה הַבָּאִים
the-ones-coming Judah all-of in-ears-of and-also fasting on-day-of Yahweh house-of

מֵעָרֵיהֶם תִּקְרָאֵם׃ אוּלַי תִּפֹּל תְּחִנָּתָם
petition-of-them she-will-come perhaps (7) you-read-them from-towns-of-them

לִפְנֵי יְהוָה וְיָשֻׁבוּ אִישׁ מִדַּרְכּוֹ הָרָעָה כִּי־גָדוֹל הָאַף
the-anger great for the-wicked from-way-of-him each and-they-will-turn Yahweh before

וְהַחֵמָה אֲשֶׁר־ דִּבֶּר יְהוָה אֶל־ הָעָם הַזֶּה׃ וַיַּעַשׂ
and-he-did (8) the-this the-people against Yahweh he-pronounced that and-the-wrath

בָּרוּךְ בֶּן־ נֵרִיָּה כְּכֹל אֲשֶׁר־ צִוָּהוּ יִרְמְיָהוּ הַנָּבִיא לִקְרֹא
to-read the-prophet Jeremiah he-told-him that as-everything Neriah son-of Baruch

בַסֵּפֶר דִּבְרֵי יְהוָה בֵּית יְהוָה׃ וַיְהִי בַשָּׁנָה
in-the-year and-he-was (9) Yahweh temple-of Yahweh words-of from-the-scroll

הַחֲמִשִׁית לִיהוֹיָקִים בֶּן־ יֹאשִׁיָּהוּ מֶלֶךְ־ יְהוּדָה בַּחֹדֶשׁ הַתְּשִׁעִי
the-ninth in-the-month Judah king-of Josiah son-of of-Jehoiakim the-fifth

קָרְאוּ צוֹם לִפְנֵי יְהוָה כָּל־ הָעָם בִּירוּשָׁלָםִ וְכָל־
and-all-of in-Jerusalem the-people all-of Yahweh before fast they-proclaimed

הָעָם הַבָּאִים מֵעָרֵי יְהוּדָה בִּירוּשָׁלָםִ׃ וַיִּקְרָא בָרוּךְ
Baruch and-he-read (10) to-Jerusalem Judah from-towns-of the-ones-coming the-people

בַּסֵּפֶר אֶת־ דִּבְרֵי יִרְמְיָהוּ בֵּית יְהוָה בְּלִשְׁכַּת גְּמַרְיָהוּ בֶן־
son-of Gemariah from-room-of Yahweh temple-of Jeremiah words-of *** from-the-scroll

שָׁפָן הַסֹּפֵר בֶּחָצֵר הָעֶלְיוֹן פֶּתַח שַׁעַר בֵּית־
temple-of Gate-of entrance-of the-upper in-the-courtyard the-secretary Shaphan

יְהוָה הֶחָדָשׁ בְּאָזְנֵי כָּל־ הָעָם׃ וַיִּשְׁמַע מִכָיְהוּ בֶן־
son-of Micaiah when-he-heard (11) the-people all-of in-ears-of the-New Yahweh

גְּמַרְיָהוּ בֶן־ שָׁפָן אֶת־ כָּל־ דִּבְרֵי יְהוָה מֵעַל הַסֵּפֶר׃
the-scroll from-on Yahweh words-of all-of *** Shaphan son-of Gemariah

וַיֵּרֶד בֵּית־ הַמֶּלֶךְ עַל־ לִשְׁכַּת הַסֹּפֵר וְהִנֵּה־ שָׁם
there and-see! the-secretary room-of to the-royalty palace-of then-he-went-down (12)

כָּל־ הַשָּׂרִים יוֹשְׁבִים אֱלִישָׁמָע הַסֹּפֵר וּדְלָיָהוּ בֶן־ שְׁמַעְיָהוּ
Shemaiah son-of and-Delaiah the-secretary Elishama ones-sitting the-officials all-of

וְאֶלְנָתָן בֶּן־ עַכְבּוֹר וּגְמַרְיָהוּ בֶן־ שָׁפָן וְצִדְקִיָּהוּ בֶן־ חֲנַנְיָהוּ
Hananiah son-of and-Zedekiah Shaphan son-of and-Gemariah Acbor son-of and-Elnathan

them on the scroll. [5]Then Jeremiah
told Baruch, "I am restricted; I
cannot go to the LORD's temple. [6]So
you go to the house of the LORD on
a day of fasting and read to the
people from the scroll the words of
the LORD that you wrote as I dictated. Read them to all the people
of Judah who come in from their
towns. [7]Perhaps they will bring
their petition before the LORD, and
each will turn from his wicked
ways, for the anger and wrath
pronounced against this people by
the LORD are great."

[8]Baruch son of Neriah did
everything Jeremiah the prophet
told him to do; at the LORD's temple he read the words of the LORD
from the scroll. [9]In the ninth
month of the fifth year of Jehoiakim son of Josiah king of Judah, a
time of fasting before the LORD
was proclaimed for all the people
in Jerusalem and those who had
come from the towns of Judah.
[10]From the room of Gemariah son
of Shaphan the secretary, which
was in the upper courtyard at the
entrance of the New Gate of the
temple, Baruch read to all the
people at the LORD's temple the
words of Jeremiah from the scroll.

[11]When Micaiah son of Gemariah, the son of Shaphan, heard all
the words of the LORD from the
scroll, [12]he went down to the secretary's room in the royal palace,
where all the officials were sitting:
Elishama the secretary, Delaiah
son of Shemaiah, Elnathan son of
Acbor, Gemariah son of Shaphan,
Zedekiah son of Hananiah, and

וְכָל־ הַשָּׂרִים׃ וַיַּגֵּד לָהֶם מִכָיְהוּ אֵת כָּל־ הַדְּבָרִים
the-things every-of *** Micaiah to-them after-he-told (13) the-officials and-all-of

אֲשֶׁר שָׁמֵעַ בִּקְרֹא בָרוּךְ בַּסֵּפֶר בְּאָזְנֵי הָעָם׃
the-people in-ears-of from-the-scroll Baruch when-to-read he-heard that

וַיִּשְׁלְחוּ כָל־ הַשָּׂרִים אֶל־ בָּרוּךְ אֶת־ יְהוּדִי בֶּן־ נְתַנְיָהוּ
Nethaniah son-of Jehudi *** Baruch to the-officials all-of then-they-sent (14)

בֶּן־ שֶׁלֶמְיָהוּ בֶן־ כּוּשִׁי לֵאמֹר הַמְּגִלָּה אֲשֶׁר קָרָאתָ בָּהּ בְּאָזְנֵי
in-ears-of from-her you-read that the-scroll to-say Cushi son-of Shelemiah son-of

הָעָם קָחֶנָּה בְיָדְךָ וָלֵךְ וַיִּקַּח בָּרוּךְ בֶּן־ נֵרִיָּהוּ
Neriah son-of Baruch so-he-brought and-come! in-hand-of-you bring-her! the-people

אֶת־ הַמְּגִלָּה בְּיָדוֹ וַיָּבֹא אֲלֵיהֶם׃ וַיֹּאמְרוּ אֵלָיו
to-him and-they-said (15) to-them and-he-went in-hand-of-him the-scroll ***

שֵׁב נָא וּקְרָאֶנָּה בְּאָזְנֵינוּ וַיִּקְרָא בָרוּךְ בְּאָזְנֵיהֶם׃
in-ears-of-them Baruch so-he-read in-ears-of-us and-read-her! now! sit-down!

וַיְהִי כְּשָׁמְעָם אֶת־ כָּל־ הַדְּבָרִים פָּחֲדוּ אִישׁ אֶל־
to each they-were-afraid the-words all-of *** when-to-hear-them and-he-was (16)

רֵעֵהוּ וַיֹּאמְרוּ אֶל־ בָּרוּךְ הַגֵּיד נַגִּיד לַמֶּלֶךְ אֵת
*** to-the-king we-must-report to-report Baruch to and-they-said other-of-him

כָּל־ הַדְּבָרִים הָאֵלֶּה׃ וְאֶת־ בָּרוּךְ שָׁאֲלוּ לֵאמֹר הַגֶּד־ נָא לָנוּ אֵיךְ
how? to-us now! tell! to-say they-asked Baruch then (17) the-these the-words all-of

כָּתַבְתָּ אֶת־ כָּל־ הַדְּבָרִים הָאֵלֶּה מִפִּיו׃ וַיֹּאמֶר
and-he-replied (18) from-dictation-of-him the-these the-words all-of *** you-wrote

לָהֶם בָּרוּךְ מִפִּיו יִקְרָא אֵלַי אֵת כָּל־ הַדְּבָרִים הָאֵלֶּה
the-these the-words all-of *** to-me he-spoke from-dictation-of-him Baruch to-them

וַאֲנִי כֹּתֵב עַל־ הַסֵּפֶר בַּדְּיוֹ׃ וַיֹּאמְרוּ הַשָּׂרִים אֶל־
to the-officials then-they-said (19) in-the-ink the-scroll on writing and-I

בָּרוּךְ לֵךְ הִסָּתֵר אַתָּה וְיִרְמְיָהוּ וְאִישׁ אַל־ יֵדַע אֵיפֹה אַתֶּם׃
you where? let-him-know not and-anyone and-Jeremiah you hide! go! Baruch

וַיָּבֹאוּ אֶל־ הַמֶּלֶךְ חָצֵרָה וְאֶת־ הַמְּגִלָּה הִפְקִדוּ בְּלִשְׁכַּת
in-room-of they-put the-scroll and in-courtyard the-king to and-they-went (20)

אֱלִישָׁמָע הַסֹּפֵר וַיַּגִּידוּ בְּאָזְנֵי הַמֶּלֶךְ אֵת כָּל־הַדְּבָרִים׃
the-things every-of *** the-king in-ears-of and-they-reported the-secretary Elishama

וַיִּשְׁלַח הַמֶּלֶךְ אֶת־ יְהוּדִי לָקַחַת אֶת־ הַמְּגִלָּה וַיִּקָּחֶהָ
and-he-brought-her the-scroll *** to-get Jehudi *** the-king and-he-sent (21)

מִלִּשְׁכַּת אֱלִישָׁמָע הַסֹּפֵר וַיִּקְרָאֶהָ יְהוּדִי בְּאָזְנֵי הַמֶּלֶךְ
the-king in-ears-of Jehudi and-he-read-her the-secretary Elishama from-room-of

וּבְאָזְנֵי כָּל־ הַשָּׂרִים הָעֹמְדִים מֵעַל הַמֶּלֶךְ׃
the-king at-beside the-ones-standing the-officials all-of and-in-ears-of

all the other officials.
13After Micaiah told them everything he had heard Baruch read to the people from the scroll,
14all the officials sent Jehudi son of Nethaniah, the son of Shelemiah, the son of Cushi, to say to Baruch, "Bring the scroll from which you have read to the people and come." So Baruch son of Neriah went to them with the scroll in his hand.
15They said to him, "Sit down, please, and read it to us."

So Baruch read it to them.
16When they heard all these words, they looked at each other in fear and said to Baruch, "We must report all these words to the king."
17Then they asked Baruch, "Tell us, how did you come to write all this? Did Jeremiah dictate it?"

18"Yes," Baruch replied, "he dictated all these words to me, and I wrote them in ink on the scroll."

19Then the officials said to Baruch, "You and Jeremiah, go and hide. Don't let anyone know where you are."

20After they put the scroll in the room of Elishama the secretary, they went to the king in the courtyard and reported everything to him.
21The king sent Jehudi to get the scroll, and Jehudi brought it from the room of Elishama the secretary and read it to the king and all the officials standing beside him.
22It was the ninth month

וְהַמֶּ֣לֶךְ  יוֹשֵׁב֮  בֵּ֣ית  הַחֹ֒רֶף֒  בַּחֹ֣דֶשׁ  הַתְּשִׁיעִ֑י  וְאֶת־
and  the-ninth  in-the-month  the-winter  apartment-of  sitting  now-the-king  (22)

הָאָ֖ח  לְפָנָ֥יו  מְבֹעָֽרֶת:  וַיְהִ֣י ׀  כִּקְר֣וֹא  יְהוּדִ֗י  שָׁלֹ֤שׁ
three  Jehudi  when-to-read  and-he-was  (23)  burning  in-front-of-him  the-firepot

דְּלָתוֹת֙  וְאַרְבָּעָ֔ה  יִֽקְרָעֶ֙הָ֙  בְּתַ֣עַר  הַסֹּפֵ֔ר  וְהַשְׁלֵ֖ךְ  אֶל־
into  and-to-throw  the-scribe  with-knife-of  then-he-cut-off-her  or-four  columns

הָאֵ֖שׁ  אֲשֶׁ֣ר  אֶל־  הָאָ֑ח  עַ֚ד  תֹּם֙  כָּל־  הַמְּגִלָּ֔ה  עַל־
in  the-scroll  entire-of  to-be-consumed  until  the-firepot  in  that  the-fire

הָאֵ֖שׁ  אֲשֶׁ֥ר  עַל־  הָאָֽח:  וְלֹ֣א  פָחֲד֔וּ  וְלֹ֥א  קָרְע֖וּ  אֶת־
***  they-tore  or-not  they-showed-fear  and-not  (24)  the-firepot  in  that  the-fire

בִּגְדֵיהֶ֑ם  הַמֶּ֙לֶךְ֙  וְכָל־  עֲבָדָ֔יו  הַשֹּׁמְעִ֕ים  אֵ֖ת  כָּל־
all-of  ***  the-ones-hearing  attendants-of-him  and-all-of  the-king  clothes-of-them

הַדְּבָרִ֖ים  הָאֵֽלֶּה:  וְגַ֡ם  אֶלְנָתָן֩  וּדְלָיָ֨הוּ  וּגְמַרְיָ֜הוּ  הִפְגִּ֣עוּ
they-urged  and-Gemariah  and-Delaiah  Elnathan  even-though  (25)  the-these  the-words

בַמֶּ֗לֶךְ  לְבִלְתִּ֛י  שְׂרֹ֥ף  אֶת־  הַמְּגִלָּ֖ה  וְלֹ֥א  שָׁמַ֖ע  אֲלֵיהֶֽם:
to-them  he-would-listen  but-not  the-scroll  ***  to-burn  not  to-the-king

וַיְצַוֶּ֣ה  הַמֶּ֡לֶךְ  אֶת־יְרַחְמְאֵ֣ל  בֶּן־  הַמֶּ֡לֶךְ  וְאֶת־שְׂרָיָ֣הוּ  בֶן־
son-of  Seraiah  and-the-king  son-of  Jerahmeel  ***  the-king  instead-he-commanded  (26)

עַזְרִיאֵ֗ל  וְאֶת־שֶׁלֶמְיָ֙הוּ֙  בֶּן־  עַבְדְּאֵ֔ל  לָקַ֙חַת֙  אֶת־  בָּר֣וּךְ  הַסֹּפֵ֔ר  וְאֵ֖ת  יִרְמְיָ֣הוּ
Jeremiah  and-the-scribe  Baruch  ***  to-arrest  Abdeel  son-of  Shelemiah  and  Azriel

הַנָּבִ֑יא  וַיַּסְתִּרֵ֖ם  יְהֹוָֽה:  וַיְהִ֣י  דְבַר־  יְהֹוָ֔ה  אֶל־יִרְמְיָ֖הוּ
Jeremiah  to  Yahweh  word-of  and-he-came  (27)  Yahweh  but-he-hid-them  the-prophet

אַחֲרֵ֣י ׀  שְׂרֹ֣ף  הַמֶּ֗לֶךְ  אֶת־  הַמְּגִלָּה֙  וְאֶת־  הַדְּבָרִ֔ים  אֲשֶׁ֥ר  כָּתַ֖ב  בָּר֑וּךְ
Baruch  he-wrote  that  the-words  and  the-scroll  ***  the-king  to-burn  after

מִפִּ֣י  יִרְמְיָ֖הוּ  לֵאמֹֽר:  שׁ֣וּב  קַח־  לְךָ֗  מְגִלָּ֣ה  אַחֶ֔רֶת  וּכְתֹ֣ב
and-write!  another  scroll  for-you  take!  return!  (28)  to-say  Jeremiah  at-dictation-of

עָלֶ֔יהָ  אֵ֚ת  כָּל־  הַדְּבָרִים֙  הָרִ֣אשֹׁנִ֔ים  אֲשֶׁ֣ר  הָי֗וּ  עַל־הַמְּגִלָּה֙  הָרִ֣אשֹׁנָ֔ה
the-first  the-scroll  on  they-were  that  the-first-ones  the-words  all-of  ***  on-her

אֲשֶׁ֥ר  שָׂרַ֖ף  יְהוֹיָקִ֣ים  מֶֽלֶךְ־יְהוּדָֽה:  וְעַל־  יְהוֹיָקִ֤ים  מֶֽלֶךְ־יְהוּדָה֙  תֹּאמַ֔ר
you-tell  Judah  king-of  Jehoiakim  and-to  (29)  Judah  king-of  Jehoiakim  he-burned  which

כֹּ֣ה  אָמַ֣ר  יְהֹוָ֔ה  אַתָּ֣ה  שָׂרַ֗פְתָּ  אֶת־  הַמְּגִלָּ֤ה  הַזֹּאת֙  לֵאמֹ֔ר  מַדּוּעַ֩  כָּתַ֨בְתָּ
you-wrote  why?  to-say  the-that  the-scroll  ***  you-burned  you  Yahweh  he-says  this

עָלֶ֜יהָ  לֵאמֹ֗ר  בֹּֽא־  יָב֤וֹא  מֶֽלֶךְ־  בָּבֶל֙  וְהִשְׁחִ֣ית  אֶת־הָאָ֔רֶץ
the-land  ***  and-he-will-destroy  Babylon  king-of  he-will-come  to-come  to-say  on-her

הַזֹּ֔את  וְהִשְׁבִּ֥ית  מִמֶּ֖נָּה  אָדָ֥ם  וּבְהֵמָֽה:  לָכֵ֗ן  כֹּֽה־  אָמַ֣ר
he-says  this  therefore  (30)  and-animal  man  from-her  and-he-will-cut-off  the-this

יְהֹוָ֗ה  עַל־  יְהוֹיָקִים֙  מֶ֣לֶךְ  יְהוּדָ֔ה  לֹא־  יִֽהְיֶה־  לּ֔וֹ  יוֹשֵׁ֖ב  עַל־  כִּסֵּ֣א
throne-of  on  one-sitting  to-him  he-will-be  not  Judah  king-of  Jehoiakim  about  Yahweh

and the king was sitting in the winter apartment, with a fire burning in the firepot in front of him. [23]Whenever Jehudi had read three or four columns of the scroll, the king cut them off with a scribe's knife and threw them into the firepot, until the entire scroll was burned in the fire. [24]The king and all his attendants who heard all these words showed no fear, nor did they tear their clothes. [25]Even though Elnathan, Delaiah and Gemariah urged the king not to burn the scroll, he would not listen to them. [26]Instead, the king commanded Jerahmeel, a son of the king, Seraiah son of Azriel and Shelemiah son of Abdeel to arrest Baruch the scribe and Jeremiah the prophet. But the LORD had hidden them.

[27]After the king burned the scroll containing the words that Baruch had written at Jeremiah's dictation, the word of the LORD came to Jeremiah: [28]"Take another scroll and write on it all the words that were on the first scroll, which Jehoiakim king of Judah burned up. [29]Also tell Jehoiakim king of Judah, 'This is what the LORD says: You burned that scroll and said, "Why did you write on it that the king of Babylon would certainly come and destroy this land and cut off both men and animals from it?" [30]Therefore, this is what the LORD says about Jehoiakim king of Judah: He will have no one to sit on the throne of David; his

דָוִד וְנִבְלָתוֹ תִּהְיֶה מֻשְׁלֶכֶת לַחֹרֶב בַּיּוֹם
by-the-day to-the-heat one-being-thrown-out she-will-be and-body-of-him David

וְלַקֶּרַח בַּלָּיְלָה׃ וּפָקַדְתִּי עָלָיו וְעַל־ זַרְעוֹ
child-of-him and-to to-him and-I-will-punish (31) by-the-night and-to-the-frost

וְעַל־ עֲבָדָיו אֶת־ עֲוֺנָם וְהֵבֵאתִי עֲלֵיהֶם וְעַל־
and-on on-them and-I-will-bring wickedness-of-them *** attendants-of-him and-to

יֹשְׁבֵי יְרוּשָׁלִַם וְאֶל־ אִישׁ יְהוּדָה אֵת כָּל־ הָרָעָה אֲשֶׁר־
that the-disaster every-of *** Judah person-of and-on Jerusalem ones-living-of

דִּבַּרְתִּי אֲלֵיהֶם וְלֹא שָׁמֵעוּ׃ וְיִרְמְיָהוּ לָקַח ׀ מְגִלָּה
scroll he-took so-Jeremiah (32) they-listened because-not against-them I-pronounced

אַחֶרֶת וַיִּתְּנָהּ אֶל־ בָּרוּךְ בֶּן־ נֵרִיָּהוּ הַסֹּפֵר וַיִּכְתֹּב עָלֶיהָ
on-her and-he-wrote the-scribe Neriah son-of Baruch to and-he-gave-her another

מִפִּי יִרְמְיָהוּ אֵת כָּל־ דִּבְרֵי הַסֵּפֶר אֲשֶׁר שָׂרַף יְהוֹיָקִים
Jehoiakim he-burned that the-scroll words-of all-of *** Jeremiah at-dictation-of

מֶלֶךְ־יְהוּדָה בָּאֵשׁ וְעוֹד נוֹסַף עֲלֵיהֶם דְּבָרִים רַבִּים כָּהֵמָּה׃
like-them many-ones words to-them he-was-added and-more in-the-fire Judah king-of

וַיִּמְלָךְ־ מֶלֶךְ צִדְקִיָּהוּ בֶּן־ יֹאשִׁיָּהוּ תַּחַת כָּנְיָהוּ בֶּן־
son-of Coniah in-place-of Josiah son-of Zedekiah king and-he-reigned (37:1)

יְהוֹיָקִים אֲשֶׁר הִמְלִיךְ נְבוּכַדְרֶאצַּר מֶלֶךְ־ בָּבֶל בְּאֶרֶץ יְהוּדָה׃
Judah over-land-of Babylon king-of Nebuchadrezzar he-made-king whom Jehoiakim

וְלֹא שָׁמַע הוּא וַעֲבָדָיו וְעַם הָאָרֶץ אֶל־
to the-land or-people-of or-attendants-of-him he he-paid-attention and-not (2)

דִּבְרֵי יְהוָה אֲשֶׁר דִּבֶּר בְּיַד יִרְמְיָהוּ הַנָּבִיא׃ וַיִּשְׁלַח
however-he-sent (3) the-prophet Jeremiah by-hand-of he-spoke that Yahweh words-of

הַמֶּלֶךְ צִדְקִיָּהוּ אֶת־יְהוּכַל בֶּן־ שֶׁלֶמְיָה וְאֶת־ צְפַנְיָהוּ בֶן־ מַעֲשֵׂיָה
Maaseiah son-of Zephaniah with Shelemiah son-of Jehucal *** Zedekiah the-king

הַכֹּהֵן אֶל־יִרְמְיָהוּ הַנָּבִיא לֵאמֹר הִתְפַּלֶּל־נָא בַּעֲדֵנוּ אֶל־ יְהוָה
Yahweh to on-behalf-of-us now! pray! to-say the-prophet Jeremiah to the-priest

אֱלֹהֵינוּ׃ וְיִרְמְיָהוּ בָּא וְיֹצֵא בְּתוֹךְ הָעָם וְלֹא־ נָתְנוּ
they-put for-not the-people in-among and-going coming now-Jeremiah (4) God-of-us

אֹתוֹ בֵּית הַכְּלִיא׃ וְחֵיל פַּרְעֹה יָצָא מִמִּצְרָיִם
from-Egypt he-marched-out Pharaoh and-army-of (5) the-prison house-of him

וַיִּשְׁמְעוּ הַכַּשְׂדִּים הַצָּרִים עַל־ יְרוּשָׁלִַם אֶת־
*** Jerusalem against the-ones-besieging the-Chaldeans when-they-heard

שִׁמְעָם וַיֵּעָלוּ מֵעַל יְרוּשָׁלִָם׃ וַיְהִי דְּבַר־
word-of then-he-came (6) Jerusalem from-against then-they-withdrew report-of-them

יְהוָה אֶל־יִרְמְיָהוּ הַנָּבִיא לֵאמֹר׃ כֹּה־ אָמַר יְהוָה אֱלֹהֵי יִשְׂרָאֵל כֹּה
this Israel God-of Yahweh he-says this (7) to-say the-prophet Jeremiah to Yahweh

body will be thrown out and exposed to the heat by day and the frost by night. [31]I will punish him and his children and his attendants for their wickedness; I will bring on them and those living in Jerusalem and the people of Judah every disaster I pronounced against them, because they have not listened.' "

[32]So Jeremiah took another scroll and gave it to the scribe Baruch son of Neriah, and as Jeremiah dictated, Baruch wrote on it all the words of the scroll that Jehoiakim king of Judah had burned in the fire. And many similar words were added to them.

*Jeremiah in Prison*

37 Zedekiah son of Josiah was made king of Judah by Nebuchadnezzar king of Babylon; he reigned in place of Jehoiachin[v] son of Jehoiakim. [2]Neither he nor his attendants nor the people of the land paid any attention to the words the LORD had spoken through Jeremiah the prophet.

[3]King Zedekiah, however, sent Jehucal son of Shelemiah with the priest Zephaniah son of Maaseiah to Jeremiah the prophet with this message: "Please pray to the LORD our God for us."

[4]Now Jeremiah was free to come and go among the people, for he had not yet been put in prison. [5]Pharaoh's army had marched out of Egypt, and when the Babylonians[w] who were besieging Jerusalem heard the report about them, they withdrew from Jerusalem.

[6]Then the word of the LORD came to Jeremiah the prophet: [7]"This is what the LORD, the God

v1 Hebrew *Coniah,* a variant of *Jehoiachin*
w5 Or *Chaldeans;* also in verses 8, 9, 13 and 14

°4 ק הכלוא

תֹאמְרוּ אֶל־מֶלֶךְ יְהוּדָה הַשֹּׁלֵחַ אֶתְכֶם אֵלַי לְדָרְשֵׁנִי הִנֵּה ׀ חֵיל
army-of see! to-inquire-of-me to-me you the-one-sending Judah king-of to you-tell

פַּרְעֹה הַיֹּצֵא לָכֶם לְעֶזְרָה שָׁב לְאַרְצוֹ
to-land-of-him he-will-go-back for-support to-you the-one-marching-out Pharaoh

מִצְרָיִם: וְשָׁבוּ הַכַּשְׂדִּים וְנִלְחֲמוּ עַל־ הָעִיר
the-city against and-they-will-attack the-Chaldeans then-they-will-return (8) Egypt

הַזֹּאת וּלְכָדֻהָ וּשְׂרָפֻהָ בָאֵשׁ: כֹּה ׀
this (9) with-fire and-they-will-burn-down-her and-they-will-capture-her the-this

אָמַר יְהוָה אַל־ תַּשִּׁאוּ נַפְשֹׁתֵיכֶם לֵאמֹר הָלֹךְ יֵלְכוּ
they-will-leave to-leave to-think selves-of-you you-deceive not Yahweh he-says

מֵעָלֵינוּ הַכַּשְׂדִּים כִּי־ לֹא יֵלֵכוּ: כִּי אִם־ הִכִּיתֶם
you-defeated if even (10) they-will-leave not for the-Chaldeans from-against-us

כָּל־ חֵיל כַּשְׂדִּים הַנִּלְחָמִים אִתְּכֶם וְנִשְׁאֲרוּ
and-they-were-left against-you the-ones-attacking Chaldeans army-of entire-of

בָם אֲנָשִׁים מְדֻקָּרִים אִישׁ בְּאָהֳלוֹ יָקוּמוּ
they-would-come-out in-tent-of-him man ones-being-wounded men of-them

וְשָׂרְפוּ אֶת־הָעִיר הַזֹּאת בָּאֵשׁ: וְהָיָה בְּהֵעָלוֹת
after-to-withdraw and-he-was (11) with-fire the-this the-city *** and-they-would-burn

חֵיל הַכַּשְׂדִּים מֵעַל יְרוּשָׁלִָם מִפְּנֵי חֵיל פַּרְעֹה:
Pharaoh army-of because-of Jerusalem from-against the-Chaldeans army-of

וַיֵּצֵא יִרְמְיָהוּ מִירוּשָׁלִַם לָלֶכֶת אֶרֶץ בִּנְיָמִן לַחֲלִק
to-get-share Benjamin territory-of to-go from-Jerusalem Jeremiah then-he-left (12)

מִשָּׁם בְּתוֹךְ הָעָם: וַיְהִי־ הוּא בְּשַׁעַר בִּנְיָמִן וְשָׁם
and-there Benjamin at-Gate-of he but-he-was (13) the-people in-among from-there

בַּעַל פְּקִדֻת וּשְׁמוֹ יִרְאִיָּיה בֶּן־ שֶׁלֶמְיָה בֶּן־ חֲנַנְיָה
Hananiah son-of Shelemiah son-of Irijah and-name-of-him guard captain-of

וַיִּתְפֹּשׂ אֶת־ יִרְמְיָהוּ הַנָּבִיא לֵאמֹר אֶל־ הַכַּשְׂדִּים אַתָּה נֹפֵל:
deserting you the-Chaldeans to to-say the-prophet Jeremiah *** and-he-arrested

וַיֹּאמֶר יִרְמְיָהוּ שֶׁקֶר אֵינֶנִּי נֹפֵל עַל־ הַכַּשְׂדִּים וְלֹא
but-not the-Chaldeans to deserting not-I not-true Jeremiah and-he-said (14)

שָׁמַע אֵלָיו וַיִּתְפֹּשׂ יִרְאִיָּיה בְּיִרְמְיָהוּ וַיְבִאֵהוּ אֶל־
to and-he-brought-him to-Jeremiah Irijah and-he-arrested to-him he-would-listen

הַשָּׂרִים: וַיִּקְצְפוּ הַשָּׂרִים עַל־ יִרְמְיָהוּ
Jeremiah with the-officials and-they-were-angry (15) the-officials

וְהִכּוּ אֹתוֹ וְנָתְנוּ אוֹתוֹ בֵּית הָאֵסוּר בֵּית יְהוֹנָתָן
Jonathan house-of the-prison house-of him and-they-put him and-they-had-beaten

הַסֹּפֵר כִּי־אֹתוֹ עָשׂוּ לְבֵית הַכֶּלֶא: כִּי בָא יִרְמְיָהוּ
Jeremiah he-went so (16) the-prison into-house-of they-made him for the-secretary

of Israel, says: Tell the king of
Judah, who sent you to inquire of
me, 'Pharaoh's army, which has
marched out to support you, will
go back to its own land, to Egypt.
[8]Then the Babylonians will return
and attack this city; they will capture it and burn it down.'
[9]"This is what the LORD says: Do
not deceive yourselves, thinking,
'The Babylonians will surely leave
us.' They will not! [10]Even if you
were to defeat the entire Babylonian[x] army that is attacking you
and only wounded men were left
in their tents, they would come
out and burn this city down."
[11]After the Babylonian army had
withdrawn from Jerusalem because of Pharaoh's army, [12]Jere-
miah started to leave the city to go
to the territory of Benjamin to get
his share of the property among
the people there. [13]But when he
reached the Benjamin Gate, the
captain of the guard, whose name
was Irijah son of Shelemiah, the
son of Hananiah, arrested him
and said, "You are deserting to the
Babylonians!"
[14]"That's not true!" Jeremiah
said. "I am not deserting to the
Babylonians." But Irijah would
not listen to him; instead, he arrested Jeremiah and brought him
to the officials. [15]They were angry
with Jeremiah and had him beat-
en and imprisoned in the house of
Jonathan the secretary, which
they had made into a prison.

[x]10 Or *Chaldean;* also in verse 11

אֶל־ בֵּית הַבּוֹר וְאֶל־ הַחֲנֻיוֹת וַיֵּשֶׁב־ שָׁם
there and-he-remained the-vaulted-cells indeed-into the-dungeon house-of into

יִרְמְיָהוּ יָמִים רַבִּים׃ וַיִּשְׁלַח הַמֶּלֶךְ צִדְקִיָּהוּ וַיִּקָּחֵהוּ
and-he-brought-him Zedekiah the-king then-he-sent (17) many-ones days Jeremiah

וַיִּשְׁאָלֵהוּ הַמֶּלֶךְ בְּבֵיתוֹ בַּסֵּתֶר וַיֹּאמֶר הֲיֵשׁ
is-there? and-he-said in-the-private in-palace-of-him the-king and-he-asked-him

דָּבָר מֵאֵת יְהוָה וַיֹּאמֶר יִרְמְיָהוּ יֵשׁ וַיֹּאמֶר בְּיַד
into-hand-of and-he-said there-is Jeremiah and-he-replied Yahweh from-with word

מֶלֶךְ־ בָּבֶל תִּנָּתֵן׃ וַיֹּאמֶר יִרְמְיָהוּ אֶל־ הַמֶּלֶךְ
the-king to Jeremiah then-he-said (18) you-will-be-given Babylon king-of

צִדְקִיָּהוּ מֶה חָטָאתִי לְךָ וְלַעֲבָדֶיךָ
or-against-officials-of-you against-you I-committed-crime what? Zedekiah

וְלָעָם הַזֶּה כִּי־ נְתַתֶּם אוֹתִי אֶל־ בֵּית הַכֶּלֶא׃
the-prison house-of in me you-put that the-this or-against-the-people

וְאַיֵּו נְבִיאֵיכֶם אֲשֶׁר־ נִבְּאוּ לָכֶם לֵאמֹר לֹא־ יָבֹא
he-will-attack not to-say to-you they-prophesied who prophets-of-you and-where? (19)

מֶלֶךְ־ בָּבֶל עֲלֵיכֶם וְעַל הָאָרֶץ הַזֹּאת׃ וְעַתָּה שְׁמַע־
listen! but-now (20) the-this the-land or-against against-you Babylon king-of

נָא אֲדֹנִי הַמֶּלֶךְ תִּפָּל־ נָא תְחִנָּתִי לְפָנֶיךָ וְאַל־
not before-you petition-of-me now! let-her-come the-king lord-of-me now!

תְּשִׁבֵנִי בֵּית יְהוֹנָתָן הַסֹּפֵר וְלֹא אָמוּת שָׁם׃
there I-will-die so-not the-secretary Jonathan house-of you-send-back-me

וַיְצַוֶּה הַמֶּלֶךְ צִדְקִיָּהוּ וַיַּפְקִדוּ אֶת־יִרְמְיָהוּ בַּחֲצַר
in-courtyard-of Jeremiah *** and-they-placed Zedekiah the-king then-he-ordered (21)

הַמַּטָּרָה וְנָתֹן לוֹ כִכַּר־לֶחֶם לַיּוֹם מִחוּץ הָאֹפִים
the-ones-baking from-street-of on-the-day bread loaf-of to-him and-to-give the-guard

עַד־ תֹּם כָּל־ הַלֶּחֶם מִן־ הָעִיר וַיֵּשֶׁב יִרְמְיָהוּ
Jeremiah so-he-remained the-city from the-bread all-of to-be-gone until

בַּחֲצַר הַמַּטָּרָה׃ וַיִּשְׁמַע שְׁפַטְיָה בֶן־ מַתָּן וּגְדַלְיָהוּ
and-Gedaliah Mattan son-of Shephatiah and-he-heard (38:1) the-guard in-courtyard-of

בֶּן־ פַּשְׁחוּר וְיוּכַל בֶּן־ שֶׁלֶמְיָהוּ וּפַשְׁחוּר בֶּן־מַלְכִּיָּה אֶת־ הַדְּבָרִים
the-words *** Malkijah son-of and-Pashhur Shelemiah son-of and-Jucal Pashhur son-of

אֲשֶׁר יִרְמְיָהוּ מְדַבֵּר אֶל־ כָּל־ הָעָם לֵאמֹר׃ כֹּה אָמַר יְהוָה
Yahweh he-says this (2) to-say the-people all-of to telling Jeremiah that

הַיֹּשֵׁב בָּעִיר הַזֹּאת יָמוּת בַּחֶרֶב בָּרָעָב
by-the-famine by-the-sword he-will-die the-this in-the-city the-one-staying

וּבַדָּבֶר וְהַיֹּצֵא אֶל־ הַכַּשְׂדִּים יְחְיֶה וְהָיְתָה־
and-she-will-be he-will-live the-Chaldeans to but-the-one-going-over or-by-the-plague

[16]Jeremiah was put into a vaulted cell in a dungeon, where he remained a long time. [17]Then King Zedekiah sent for him and had him brought to the palace, where he asked him privately, "Is there any word from the LORD?"

"Yes," Jeremiah replied, "you will be handed over to the king of Babylon."

[18]Then Jeremiah said to King Zedekiah, "What crime have I committed against you or your officials or this people, that you have put me in prison? [19]Where are your prophets who prophesied to you, 'The king of Babylon will not attack you or this land'? [20]But now, my lord the king, please listen. Let me bring my petition before you: Do not send me back to the house of Jonathan the secretary, or I will die there."

[21]King Zedekiah then gave orders for Jeremiah to be placed in the courtyard of the guard and given bread from the street of the bakers each day until all the bread in the city was gone. So Jeremiah remained in the courtyard of the guard.

*Jeremiah Thrown Into a Cistern*

38 Shephatiah son of Mattan, Gedaliah son of Pashhur, Jehucal[y] son of Shelemiah, and Pashhur son of Malkijah heard what Jeremiah was telling all the people when he said, [2]"This is what the LORD says: 'Whoever stays in this city will die by the sword, famine or plague, but whoever goes over to the Babylonians[z] will live. He will escape with his

y1 Hebrew *Jucal*, a variant of *Jehucal*
z2 Or *Chaldeans*; also in verses 18, 19 and 23

°19 ק ואיה
°2 ק וחיה

לוֹ נַפְשׁוֹ לְשָׁלָל וָחָי׃ כֹּה אָמַר יְהוָה הִנָּתֹן
to-be-given Yahweh he-says this (3) and-he-will-live as-plunder life-of-him to-him

תִּנָּתֵן הָעִיר הַזֹּאת בְּיַד חֵיל מֶלֶךְ־בָּבֶל
Babylon king-of army-of into-hand-of the-this the-city she-will-be-given

וּלְכָדָהּ׃ וַיֹּאמְרוּ הַשָּׂרִים אֶל־הַמֶּלֶךְ
the-king to the-officials then-they-said (4) and-he-will-capture-her

יוּמַת נָא אֶת־הָאִישׁ הַזֶּה כִּי־עַל־כֵּן הוּא־מְרַפֵּא אֶת־
*** discouraging he this because for the-this the-man *** now! he-should-be-killed

יְדֵי אַנְשֵׁי הַמִּלְחָמָה הַנִּשְׁאָרִים ׀ בָּעִיר הַזֹּאת וְאֵת יְדֵי
hands-of and the-this in-the-city the-ones-being-left the-army men-of hands-of

כָל־הָעָם לְדַבֵּר אֲלֵיהֶם כַּדְּבָרִים הָאֵלֶּה כִּי ׀ הָאִישׁ הַזֶּה
the-this the-man indeed the-these by-the-things to-them to-say the-people all-of

אֵינֶנּוּ דֹרֵשׁ לְשָׁלוֹם לָעָם הַזֶּה כִּי אִם־לְרָעָה׃ וַיֹּאמֶר
and-he-answered (5) for-ruin rather but the-this of-the-people for-good seeking not-he

הַמֶּלֶךְ צִדְקִיָּהוּ הִנֵּה־הוּא בְּיֶדְכֶם כִּי־אֵין הַמֶּלֶךְ יוּכַל אֶתְכֶם
against-you he-can-do the-king not indeed in-hand-of-you he see! Zedekiah the-king

דָּבָר׃ וַיִּקְחוּ אֶת־יִרְמְיָהוּ וַיַּשְׁלִכוּ אֹתוֹ אֶל־הַבּוֹר ׀ מַלְכִּיָּהוּ
Malkijah the-cistern into him and-they-put Jeremiah *** so-they-took (6) anything

בֶן־הַמֶּלֶךְ אֲשֶׁר בַּחֲצַר הַמַּטָּרָה וַיְשַׁלְּחוּ אֶת־יִרְמְיָהוּ
Jeremiah *** and-they-lowered the-guard in-courtyard-of which the-king son-of

בַּחֲבָלִים וּבַבּוֹר אֵין־מַיִם כִּי אִם־טִיט וַיִּטְבַּע יִרְמְיָהוּ
Jeremiah and-he-sank mud only but waters there-were-no now-in-the-cistern by-ropes

בַּטִּיט׃ וַיִּשְׁמַע עֶבֶד־מֶלֶךְ הַכּוּשִׁי אִישׁ סָרִיס וְהוּא
and-he official man the-Cushite Melech Ebed but-he-heard (7) into-the-mud

בְּבֵית הַמֶּלֶךְ כִּי־נָתְנוּ אֶת־יִרְמְיָהוּ אֶל־הַבּוֹר וְהַמֶּלֶךְ
while-the-king the-cistern into Jeremiah *** they-put that the-royalty in-palace-of

יוֹשֵׁב בְּשַׁעַר בִּנְיָמִן׃ וַיֵּצֵא עֶבֶד־מֶלֶךְ מִבֵּית
from-palace-of Melech Ebed and-he-went-out (8) Benjamin in-Gate-of sitting

הַמֶּלֶךְ וַיְדַבֵּר אֶל־הַמֶּלֶךְ לֵאמֹר׃ אֲדֹנִי הַמֶּלֶךְ
the-king lord-of-me (9) to-say the-king to and-he-said the-royalty

הֵרֵעוּ הָאֲנָשִׁים הָאֵלֶּה אֵת כָּל־אֲשֶׁר עָשׂוּ לְיִרְמְיָהוּ הַנָּבִיא
the-prophet to-Jeremiah they-did that all *** the-these the-men they-acted-wickedly

אֵת אֲשֶׁר־הִשְׁלִיכוּ אֶל־הַבּוֹר וַיָּמָת תַּחְתָּיו מִפְּנֵי הָרָעָב
the-starvation because-of in-him and-he-will-die the-cistern into they-threw whom ***

כִּי אֵין הַלֶּחֶם עוֹד בָּעִיר׃ וַיְצַוֶּה הַמֶּלֶךְ אֵת
*** the-king then-he-commanded (10) in-the-city longer the-bread there-is-not when

עֶבֶד־מֶלֶךְ הַכּוּשִׁי לֵאמֹר קַח בְּיָדְךָ מִזֶּה שְׁלֹשִׁים אֲנָשִׁים
men thirty from-this under-hand-of-you take! to-say the-Cushite Melech Ebed

life; he will live.' 3And this is what the LORD says: 'This city will certainly be handed over to the army of the king of Babylon, who will capture it.' "

4Then the officials said to the king, "This man should be put to death. He is discouraging the soldiers who are left in this city, as well as all the people, by the things he is saying to them. This man is not seeking the good of these people but their ruin."

5"He is in your hands," King Zedekiah answered. "The king can do nothing to oppose you."

6So they took Jeremiah and put him into the cistern of Malkijah, the king's son, which was in the courtyard of the guard. They lowered Jeremiah by ropes into the cistern; it had no water in it, only mud, and Jeremiah sank down into the mud.

7But Ebed-Melech, a Cushite,[a] an official[b] in the royal palace, heard that they had put Jeremiah into the cistern. While the king was sitting in the Benjamin Gate, 8Ebed-Melech went out of the palace and said to him, 9"My lord the king, these men have acted wickedly in all they have done to Jeremiah the prophet. They have thrown him into a cistern, where he will starve to death when there is no longer any bread in the city."

10Then the king commanded Ebed-Melech the Cushite, "Take thirty men from here with you

a7 Probably from the upper Nile region
b7 Or *a eunuch*

וְהַעֲלִיתָ אֶת־ יִרְמְיָהוּ הַנָּבִיא מִן־ הַבּוֹר בְּטֶרֶם יָמוּת׃
he-dies at-before the-cistern from the-prophet Jeremiah *** and-you-lift

(11) וַיִּקַּח | עֶבֶד־ מֶלֶךְ אֶת־הָאֲנָשִׁים בְּיָדוֹ וַיָּבֹא בֵית־
palace-of and-he-went under-hand-of-him the-men *** Melech Ebed so-he-took (11)

הַמֶּלֶךְ אֶל־תַּחַת הָאוֹצָר וַיִּקַּח מִשָּׁם בְּלוֹיֵ° הַסְחָבוֹת
rags worn-out-ones-of from-there and-he-took the-treasury under to the-royalty

וּבְלוֹיֵ מְלָחִים וַיְשַׁלְּחֵם אֶל־ יִרְמְיָהוּ אֶל־ הַבּוֹר
the-cistern in Jeremiah to and-he-let-down-them clothes and-worn-out-ones-of

בַּחֲבָלִים׃ (12) וַיֹּאמֶר עֶבֶד־ מֶלֶךְ הַכּוּשִׁי אֶל־יִרְמְיָהוּ שִׂים נָא
now! put! Jeremiah to the-Cushite Melech Ebed and-he-said (12) with-ropes

בְּלוֹאֵי הַסְּחָבוֹת וְהַמְּלָחִים תַּחַת אַצִּלוֹת יָדֶיךָ מִתַּחַת
at-under arms-of-you joints-of under and-the-clothes the-rags worn-out-ones-of

לַחֲבָלִים וַיַּעַשׂ יִרְמְיָהוּ כֵּן׃ (13) וַיִּמְשְׁכוּ אֶת־ יִרְמְיָהוּ בַּחֲבָלִים
with-ropes Jeremiah *** and-they-pulled-up (13) so Jeremiah and-he-did to-ropes

וַיַּעֲלוּ אֹתוֹ מִן־ הַבּוֹר וַיֵּשֶׁב יִרְמְיָהוּ בַּחֲצַר
in-courtyard-of Jeremiah and-he-remained the-cistern from him and-they-lifted

הַמַּטָּרָה׃ (14) וַיִּשְׁלַח הַמֶּלֶךְ צִדְקִיָּהוּ וַיִּקַּח אֶת־ יִרְמְיָהוּ
Jeremiah *** and-he-brought Zedekiah the-king then-he-sent (14) the-guard

הַנָּבִיא אֵלָיו אֶל־ מָבוֹא הַשְּׁלִישִׁי אֲשֶׁר בְּבֵית יְהוָה וַיֹּאמֶר
and-he-said Yahweh to-temple-of that the-third entrance to to-him the-prophet

הַמֶּלֶךְ אֶל־יִרְמְיָהוּ שֹׁאֵל אֲנִי אֹתְךָ דָּבָר אַל־ תְּכַחֵד מִמֶּנִּי דָּבָר׃
anything from-me you-hide not something you I asking Jeremiah to the-king

(15) וַיֹּאמֶר יִרְמְיָהוּ אֶל־ צִדְקִיָּהוּ כִּי אַגִּיד לְךָ הֲלוֹא הָמֵת
to-kill not? to-you I-answer if Zedekiah to Jeremiah and-he-said (15)

תְּמִיתֵנִי וְכִי אִיעָצְךָ לֹא תִשְׁמַע אֵלָי׃
to-me you-would-listen not I-give-counsel-to-you even-if will-you-kill-me

(16) וַיִּשָּׁבַע הַמֶּלֶךְ צִדְקִיָּהוּ אֶל־יִרְמְיָהוּ בַּסֵּתֶר לֵאמֹר חַי־
alive to-say in-the-secret Jeremiah to Zedekiah the-king but-he-swore-oath (16)

יְהוָה את* אֲשֶׁר עָשָׂה־ לָנוּ אֶת־ הַנֶּפֶשׁ הַזֹּאת אִם־ אֲמִיתֶךָ וְאִם־
or-not I-will-kill-you not the-this the-breath *** to-us he-gave who *** Yahweh

אֶתֶּנְךָ בְּיַד הָאֲנָשִׁים הָאֵלֶּה אֲשֶׁר מְבַקְשִׁים אֶת־ נַפְשֶׁךָ׃
life-of-you *** ones-seeking who the-those the-men into-hand-of I-will-give-you

(17) וַיֹּאמֶר יִרְמְיָהוּ אֶל־צִדְקִיָּהוּ כֹּה־ אָמַר יְהוָה אֱלֹהֵי צְבָאוֹת אֱלֹהֵי
God-of Hosts God-of Yahweh he-says this Zedekiah to Jeremiah then-he-said (17)

יִשְׂרָאֵל אִם־ יָצֹא תֵצֵא אֶל־ שָׂרֵי מֶלֶךְ־ בָּבֶל
Babylon king-of officers-of to you-surrender to-surrender if Israel

וְחָיְתָה נַפְשֶׁךָ וְהָעִיר הַזֹּאת לֹא תִשָּׂרֵף
she-will-be-burned-down not the-this and-the-city life-of-you then-she-will-be-spared

and lift Jeremiah the prophet out of the cistern before he dies."

[11]So Ebed-Melech took the men with him and went to a room under the treasury in the palace. He took some old rags and worn-out clothes from there and let them down with ropes to Jeremiah in the cistern. [12]Ebed-Melech the Cushite said to Jeremiah, "Put these old rags and worn-out clothes under your arms to pad the ropes." Jeremiah did so, [13]and they pulled him up with the ropes and lifted him out of the cistern. And Jeremiah remained in the courtyard of the guard.

*Zedekiah Questions Jeremiah Again*

[14]Then King Zedekiah sent for Jeremiah the prophet and had him brought to the third entrance to the temple of the LORD. "I am going to ask you something," the king said to Jeremiah. "Do not hide anything from me."

[15]Jeremiah said to Zedekiah, "If I give you an answer, will you not kill me? Even if I did give you counsel, you would not listen to me."

[16]But King Zedekiah swore this oath secretly to Jeremiah: "As surely as the LORD lives, who has given us breath, I will neither kill you nor hand you over to those who are seeking your life."

[17]Then Jeremiah said to Zedekiah, "This is what the LORD God Almighty, the God of Israel, says: 'If you surrender to the officers of the king of Babylon, your life will be spared and this city will not be burned down; you and your

**16* Most mss have no *Qere* form for this unpointed word.

°*11* ק סחבות

בָּאֵשׁ וְחָיִתָה אַתָּה וּבֵיתֶךָ׃ וְאִם לֹא־ תֵצֵא
you-will-surrender not but-if (18) and-family-of-you you and-you-will-live with-fire

אֶל־ שָׂרֵי מֶלֶךְ בָּבֶל וְנִתְּנָה הָעִיר הַזֹּאת בְּיַד
into-hand-of the-this the-city then-she-will-be-given Babylon king-of officers-of to

הַכַּשְׂדִּים וּשְׂרָפוּהָ בָּאֵשׁ וְאַתָּה לֹא־ תִמָּלֵט
you-will-escape not and-you with-fire and-they-will-burn-down-her the-Chaldeans

מִיָּדָם׃ וַיֹּאמֶר הַמֶּלֶךְ צִדְקִיָּהוּ אֶל־יִרְמְיָהוּ אֲנִי דֹאֵג אֶת־
*** fearing I Jeremiah to Zedekiah the-king and-he-said (19) from-hand-of-them

הַיְּהוּדִים אֲשֶׁר נָפְלוּ אֶל־ הַכַּשְׂדִּים פֶּן־ יִתְּנוּ אֹתִי בְּיָדָם
into-hand-of-them me they-give lest the-Chaldeans to they-went-over who the-Jews

וְהִתְעַלְּלוּ־ בִי׃ וַיֹּאמֶר יִרְמְיָהוּ לֹא יִתֵּנוּ שְׁמַע־
obey! they-will-hand-over not Jeremiah and-he-replied (20) to-me and-they-mistreat

נָא ׀ בְּקוֹל יְהוָה לַאֲשֶׁר אֲנִי דֹּבֵר אֵלֶיךָ וְיִיטַב לְךָ
with-you and-he-will-go-well to-you telling I to-what Yahweh to-voice-of now!

וּתְחִי נַפְשֶׁךָ׃ וְאִם־ מָאֵן אַתָּה לָצֵאת זֶה הַדָּבָר
the-word this to-surrender you refusing but-if (21) life-of-you and-she-will-be-spared

אֲשֶׁר הִרְאַנִי יְהוָה׃ וְהִנֵּה כָל־ הַנָּשִׁים אֲשֶׁר נִשְׁאֲרוּ
they-are-left who the-women all-of and-see! (22) Yahweh he-revealed-to-me that

בְּבֵית מֶלֶךְ־ יְהוּדָה מוּצָאוֹת אֶל־ שָׂרֵי מֶלֶךְ בָּבֶל
Babylon king-of officials-of to ones-being-brought-out Judah king-of in-palace-of

וְהֵנָּה אֹמְרוֹת הִסִּיתוּךָ וְיָכְלוּ לְךָ אַנְשֵׁי
friends-of over-you and-they-overcame they-misled-you ones-saying and-they

שְׁלֹמֶךָ הָטְבְּעוּ בַבֹּץ רַגְלֶךָ נָסֹגוּ אָחוֹר׃ וְאֶת־
and (23) backwards they-deserted feet-of-you in-the-mud they-are-sunk trust-of-you

כָּל־ נָשֶׁיךָ וְאֶת־ בָּנֶיךָ מוֹצִאִים אֶל־ הַכַּשְׂדִּים
the-Chaldeans to ones-bringing-out children-of-you and wives-of-you all-of

וְאַתָּה לֹא־ תִמָּלֵט מִיָּדָם כִּי בְיַד מֶלֶךְ־ בָּבֶל
Babylon king-of by-hand-of but from-hand-of-them you-will-escape not and-you

תִּתָּפֵשׂ וְאֶת־ הָעִיר הַזֹּאת תִּשְׂרֹף בָּאֵשׁ׃
with-fire you-will-burn-down the-this the-city and you-will-be-captured

וַיֹּאמֶר צִדְקִיָּהוּ אֶל־יִרְמְיָהוּ אִישׁ אַל־ יֵדַע בַּדְּבָרִים־
about-the-words let-him-know not anyone Jeremiah to Zedekiah then-he-said (24)

הָאֵלֶּה וְלֹא תָמוּת׃ וְכִי־ יִשְׁמְעוּ הַשָּׂרִים כִּי־ דִבַּרְתִּי
I-talked that the-officials they-hear and-if (25) you-will-die so-not the-these

אִתָּךְ וּבָאוּ אֵלֶיךָ וְאָמְרוּ אֵלֶיךָ הַגִּידָה־נָּא לָנוּ מַה־ דִּבַּרְתָּ
you-said what? to-us now! tell! to-you and-they-say to-you and-they-come with-you

אֶל־הַמֶּלֶךְ אַל־ תְּכַחֵד מִמֶּנּוּ וְלֹא נְמִיתֶךָ וּמַה־ דִּבֶּר אֵלֶיךָ
to-you he-said and-what? we-kill-you so-not from-us you-hide not the-king to

family will live. [18]But if you will not surrender to the officers of the king of Babylon, this city will be handed over to the Babylonians and they will burn it down; you yourself will not escape from their hands.' "

[19]King Zedekiah said to Jeremiah, "I am afraid of the Jews who have gone over to the Babylonians, for the Babylonians may hand me over to them and they will mistreat me."

[20]"They will not hand you over," Jeremiah replied. "Obey the LORD by doing what I tell you. Then it will go well with you, and your life will be spared. [21]But if you refuse to surrender, this is what the LORD has revealed to me: [22]All the women left in the palace of the king of Judah will be brought out to the officials of the king of Babylon. Those women will say to you:

" 'They misled you and
overcame you—
those trusted friends of
yours.
Your feet are sunk in the mud;
your friends have deserted
you.'

[23]"All your wives and children will be brought out to the Babylonians. You yourself will not escape from their hands but will be captured by the king of Babylon; and this city will[c] be burned down."

[24]Then Zedekiah said to Jeremiah, "Do not let anyone know about this conversation, or you may die. [25]If the officials hear that I talked with you, and they come to you and say, 'Tell us what you said to the king and what the king said to you; do not hide it from us or we will kill you,' [26]then tell

[c]23 Or *and you will cause this city to*

הַמֶּלֶךְ׃ וְאָמַרְתָּ אֲלֵיהֶם מַפִּיל־אֲנִי תְחִנָּתִי לִפְנֵי הַמֶּלֶךְ לְבִלְתִּי
not the-king before plea-of-me I bringing to-them then-you-tell (26) the-king

הֲשִׁיבֵנִי בֵּית יְהוֹנָתָן לָמוּת שָׁם׃ וַיָּבֹאוּ כָל־
all-of and-they-came (27) there to-die Jonathan house-of to-send-back-me

הַשָּׂרִים אֶל־יִרְמְיָהוּ וַיִּשְׁאֲלוּ אֹתוֹ וַיַּגֵּד לָהֶם כְּכָל־
as-every-of to-them and-he-told him and-they-questioned Jeremiah to the-officials

הַדְּבָרִים הָאֵלֶּה אֲשֶׁר צִוָּה הַמֶּלֶךְ וַיַּחֲרִשׁוּ מִמֶּנּוּ כִּי לֹא־
not for to-him so-they-said-no-more the-king he-ordered that the-these the-things

נִשְׁמַע הַדָּבָר׃ וַיֵּשֶׁב יִרְמְיָהוּ בַּחֲצַר
in-courtyard-of Jeremiah and-he-remained (28) the-conversation he-was-heard

הַמַּטָּרָה עַד־יוֹם אֲשֶׁר־נִלְכְּדָה יְרוּשָׁלִָם וְהָיָה כַּאֲשֶׁר נִלְכְּדָה
she-was-taken as-how and-he-was Jerusalem she-was-captured that day until the-guard

יְרוּשָׁלִָם׃ בַּשָּׁנָה הַתְּשִׁעִית לְצִדְקִיָּהוּ מֶלֶךְ־יְהוּדָה בַּחֹדֶשׁ
in-the-month Judah king-of of-Zedekiah the-ninth in-the-year (39:1) Jerusalem

הָעֲשִׂרִי בָּא נְבוּכַדְרֶאצַּר מֶלֶךְ־בָּבֶל וְכָל־חֵילוֹ
army-of-him with-whole-of Babylon king-of Nebuchadrezzar he-marched the-tenth

אֶל־יְרוּשָׁלִַם וַיָּצֻרוּ עָלֶיהָ׃ בְּעַשְׁתֵּי־עֶשְׂרֵה שָׁנָה לְצִדְקִיָּהוּ
of-Zedekiah year ten in-one-of (2) to-her and-they-laid-siege Jerusalem against

בַּחֹדֶשׁ הָרְבִיעִי בְּתִשְׁעָה לַחֹדֶשׁ הָבְקְעָה הָעִיר׃
the-wall she-was-broken-through of-the-month on-nine the-fourth in-the-month

וַיָּבֹאוּ כֹּל שָׂרֵי מֶלֶךְ־בָּבֶל וַיֵּשְׁבוּ
and-they-took-seats Babylon king-of officials-of all-of then-they-came (3)

בְּשַׁעַר הַתָּוֶךְ נֵרְגַל שַׂר־אֶצֶר סַמְגַּר־נְבוּ שַׂר־סְכִים רַב־סָרִיס
officer chief-of Sekim Sar Nebo Samgar Ezer Shar Nergal the-Middle in-Gate-of

נֵרְגַל שַׂר־אֶצֶר רַב־מָג וְכָל־שְׁאֵרִית שָׂרֵי מֶלֶךְ
king-of officials-of other-of and-all-of official high-one-of Ezer Shar Nergal

בָּבֶל׃ וַיְהִי כַּאֲשֶׁר רָאָם צִדְקִיָּהוּ מֶלֶךְ־יְהוּדָה וְכֹל ׀
and-all-of Judah king-of Zedekiah he-saw-them as-when and-he-was (4) Babylon

אַנְשֵׁי הַמִּלְחָמָה וַיִּבְרְחוּ וַיֵּצְאוּ לַיְלָה מִן־הָעִיר דֶּרֶךְ גַּן
garden-of way-of the-city from night and-they-left then-they-fled the-army men-of

הַמֶּלֶךְ בְּשַׁעַר בֵּין הַחֹמֹתַיִם וַיֵּצֵא דֶּרֶךְ הָעֲרָבָה׃
the-Arabah way-of and-he-headed the-two-walls between through-gate the-king

וַיִּרְדְּפוּ חֵיל־כַּשְׂדִּים אַחֲרֵיהֶם וַיַּשִּׂגוּ אֶת־צִדְקִיָּהוּ
Zedekiah *** and-they-overtook after-them Chaldeans army-of but-they-pursued (5)

בְּעַרְבוֹת יְרֵחוֹ וַיִּקְחוּ אֹתוֹ וַיַּעֲלֻהוּ אֶל־נְבוּכַדְרֶאצַּר
Nebuchadrezzar to and-they-took-him him and-they-captured Jericho in-plains-of

מֶלֶךְ־בָּבֶל רִבְלָתָה בְּאֶרֶץ חֲמָת וַיְדַבֵּר אִתּוֹ מִשְׁפָּטִים׃
sentences on-him and-he-pronounced Hamath in-land-of at-Riblah Babylon king-of

them, 'I was pleading with the king not to send me back to Jonathan's house to die there.' "

27 All the officials did come to Jeremiah and question him, and he told them everything the king had ordered him to say. So they said no more to him, for no one had heard his conversation with the king.

28 And Jeremiah remained in the courtyard of the guard until the day Jerusalem was captured.

*The Fall of Jerusalem*

**39** This is how Jerusalem was taken: 1 In the ninth year of Zedekiah king of Judah, in the tenth month, Nebuchadnezzar king of Babylon marched against Jerusalem with his whole army and laid siege to it. 2 And on the ninth day of the fourth month of Zedekiah's eleventh year, the city wall was broken through. 3 Then all the officials of the king of Babylon came and took seats in the Middle Gate: Nergal-Sharezer of Samgar, Nebo-Sarsekim[d] a chief officer, Nergal-Sharezer a high official and all the other officials of the king of Babylon. 4 When Zedekiah king of Judah and all the soldiers saw them, they fled; they left the city at night by way of the king's garden, through the gate between the two walls, and headed toward the Arabah.[e]

5 But the Babylonian[f] army pursued them and overtook Zedekiah in the plains of Jericho. They captured him and took him to Nebuchadnezzar king of Babylon at Riblah in the land of Hamath, where he pronounced sentence on

[d]3 Or *Nergal-Sharezer, Samgar-Nebo, Sarsekim*
[e]4 Or *the Jordan Valley*
[f]5 Or *Chaldean*

וַיִּשְׁחַט מֶלֶךְ בָּבֶל אֶת־ בְּנֵי צִדְקִיָּהוּ בְּרִבְלָה
at-Riblah Zedekiah sons-of *** Babylon king-of and-he-slaughtered (6)

לְעֵינָיו וְאֵת כָּל־ חֹרֵי יְהוּדָה שָׁחַט מֶלֶךְ בָּבֶל׃
Babylon king-of he-slaughtered Judah nobles-of all-of also before-eyes-of-him

וְאֶת־ עֵינֵי צִדְקִיָּהוּ עִוֵּר וַיַּאַסְרֵהוּ בַּנְחֻשְׁתַּיִם
with-the-bronze-shackles and-he-bound-him he-put-out Zedekiah eyes-of then (7)

לָבִיא אֹתוֹ בָּבֶלָה׃ וְאֶת־ בֵּית הַמֶּלֶךְ וְאֶת־ בֵּית הָעָם
the-people house-of and the-royalty palace-of and (8) to-Babylon him to-take

שָׂרְפוּ הַכַּשְׂדִּים בָּאֵשׁ וְאֶת־חֹמוֹת יְרוּשָׁלִַם נָתָצוּ׃ וְאֵת
and (9) they-broke-down Jerusalem walls-of and with-fire the-Chaldeans they-burned

יֶתֶר הָעָם הַנִּשְׁאָרִים בָּעִיר וְאֶת־ הַנֹּפְלִים אֲשֶׁר
that the-ones-going-over and in-the-city the-ones-remaining the-people rest-of

נָפְלוּ עָלָיו וְאֵת יֶתֶר הָעָם הַנִּשְׁאָרִים הֶגְלָה נְבוּזַר־
Nebuzar he-exiled the-ones-remaining the-people rest-of and to-him they-went-over

אֲדָן רַב־ טַבָּחִים בָּבֶל׃ וּמִן־ הָעָם הַדַּלִּים
the-poor-ones the-people but-from (10) Babylon imperial-guards commander-of Adan

אֲשֶׁר אֵין־ לָהֶם מְאוּמָה הִשְׁאִיר נְבוּזַרְאֲדָן רַב־ טַבָּחִים
imperial-guards commander-of Nebuzaradan he-left-behind anything to-them not who

בְּאֶרֶץ יְהוּדָה וַיִּתֵּן לָהֶם כְּרָמִים וִיגֵבִים בַּיּוֹם הַהוּא׃
the-that on-the-day and-fields vineyards to-them and-he-gave Judah in-land-of

וַיְצַו נְבוּכַדְרֶאצַּר מֶלֶךְ־ בָּבֶל עַל־ יִרְמְיָהוּ בְּיַד
by-hand-of Jeremiah about Babylon king-of Nebuchadrezzar now-he-ordered (11)

נְבוּזַרְאֲדָן רַב־ טַבָּחִים לֵאמֹר׃ קָחֶנּוּ וְעֵינֶיךָ
and-eyes-of-you take-him! (12) to-say imperial-guards commander-of Nebuzaradan

שִׂים עָלָיו וְאַל־ תַּעַשׂ לוֹ מְאוּמָה רָּע* כִּי אם† כַּאֲשֶׁר יְדַבֵּר אֵלֶיךָ
to-you he-asks just-as *** but harm anything to-him you-do and-not on-him keep!

כֵּן עֲשֵׂה עִמּוֹ׃ וַיִּשְׁלַח נְבוּזַרְאֲדָן רַב־ טַבָּחִים
imperial-guards commander-of Nebuzaradan so-he-sent (13) for-him do! so

וּנְבוּשַׁזְבָּן רַב־ סָרִיס וְנֵרְגַל שַׂר־ אֶצֶר רַב־ מָג
official high-one-of Ezer Shar and-Nergal officer chief-of and-Nebushazban

וְכֹל רַבֵּי מֶלֶךְ־ בָּבֶל׃ וַיִּשְׁלְחוּ וַיִּקְחוּ אֶת־יִרְמְיָהוּ
Jeremiah *** and-they-took and-they-sent (14) Babylon king-of officers-of and-all-of

מֵחֲצַר הַמַּטָּרָה וַיִּתְּנוּ אֹתוֹ אֶל־גְּדַלְיָהוּ בֶּן־ אֲחִיקָם
Ahikam son-of Gedaliah to him and-they-handed-over the-guard from-courtyard-of

בֶּן־ שָׁפָן לְהוֹצִאֵהוּ אֶל־ הַבָּיִת וַיֵּשֶׁב בְּתוֹךְ הָעָם׃
the-people in-among so-he-remained the-home to to-take-back-him Shaphan son-of

וְאֶל־ יִרְמְיָהוּ הָיָה דְבַר־ יְהוָה בִּהְיֹתוֹ עָצוּר
being-confined while-to-be-him Yahweh word-of he-came Jeremiah now-to (15)

him. [6]There at Riblah the king of
Babylon slaughtered the sons of
Zedekiah before his eyes and also
killed all the nobles of Judah.
[7]Then he put out Zedekiah's eyes
and bound him with bronze
shackles to take him to Babylon.
[8]The Babylonians[g] set fire to the
royal palace and the houses of the
people and broke down the walls
of Jerusalem. [9]Nebuzaradan commander of the imperial guard carried into exile to Babylon the
people who remained in the city,
along with those who had gone
over to him, and the rest of the
people. [10]But Nebuzaradan the
commander of the guard left behind in the land of Judah some of
the poor people, who owned nothing; and at that time he gave them
vineyards and fields.
[11]Now Nebuchadnezzar king of
Babylon had given these orders
about Jeremiah through Nebuzaradan commander of the imperial
guard: [12]"Take him and look after
him; don't harm him but do for
him whatever he asks." [13]So Nebuzaradan the commander of the
guard, Nebushazban a chief officer, Nergal-Sharezer a high official and all the other officers of the
king of Babylon [14]sent and had
Jeremiah taken out of the courtyard of the guard. They turned
him over to Gedaliah son of Ahikam, the son of Shaphan, to take
him back to his home. So he remained among his own people.
[15]While Jeremiah had been confined in the courtyard of the
guard, the word of the LORD came

g8 Or *Chaldeans*

*12a Most mss have no *dagesh* in the *resh* (רָע).

†12b Most mss have no *Qere* form for this unpointed word.

בַּחֲצַר הַמַּטָּרָה לֵאמֹר׃ הָלוֹךְ וְאָמַרְתָּ לְעֶבֶד־מֶלֶךְ הַכּוּשִׁי
the-Cushite Melech to-Ebed and-you-tell to-go (16) to-say the-guard in-courtyard-of

לֵאמֹר כֹּה־אָמַר יְהוָה צְבָאוֹת אֱלֹהֵי יִשְׂרָאֵל הִנְנִי מֵבִי אֶת־
*** fulfilling see-I! Israel God-of Hosts Yahweh-of he-says this to-say

דְּבָרַי אֶל־הָעִיר הַזֹּאת לְרָעָה וְלֹא לְטוֹבָה
through-prosperity and-not through-disaster the-this the-city against words-of-me

וְהָיוּ לְפָנֶיךָ בַּיּוֹם הַהוּא׃ וְהִצַּלְתִּיךָ
but-I-will-rescue-you (17) the-that on-the-day before-you and-they-will-be

בַיּוֹם־הַהוּא נְאֻם־יְהוָה וְלֹא תִנָּתֵן בְּיַד
into-hand-of you-will-be-given and-not Yahweh declaration-of the-that on-the-day

הָאֲנָשִׁים אֲשֶׁר־אַתָּה יָגוֹר מִפְּנֵיהֶם׃ כִּי מַלֵּט אֲמַלֶּטְךָ
I-will-save-you to-save indeed (18) because-of-them fearful you whom the-men

וּבַחֶרֶב לֹא תִפֹּל וְהָיְתָה לְךָ נַפְשְׁךָ לְשָׁלָל
as-plunder life-of-you to-you but-she-will-be you-will-fall not and-by-the-sword

כִּי־בָטַחְתָּ בִּי נְאֻם־יְהוָה׃ הַדָּבָר אֲשֶׁר־הָיָה אֶל־
to he-came that the-word (40:1) Yahweh declaration-of in-me you-trust because

יִרְמְיָהוּ מֵאֵת יְהוָה אַחַר ׀ שַׁלַּח אֹתוֹ נְבוּזַרְאֲדָן רַב־
commander-of Nebuzaradan him to-release after Yahweh from-with Jeremiah

טַבָּחִים מִן־הָרָמָה בְּקַחְתּוֹ אֹתוֹ וְהוּא־אָסוּר בָּאזִקִּים
in-the-chains being-bound then-he him when-to-find-him the-Ramah at imperial-guards

בְּתוֹךְ כָּל־גָּלוּת יְרוּשָׁלַםִ וִיהוּדָה הַמֻּגְלִים בָּבֶלָה׃
to-Babylon the-ones-being-exiled and-Judah Jerusalem captive-of all-of in-among

וַיִּקַּח רַב־טַבָּחִים לְיִרְמְיָהוּ וַיֹּאמֶר אֵלָיו
to-him then-he-said to-Jeremiah imperial-guards commander-of when-he-found (2)

יְהוָה אֱלֹהֶיךָ דִּבֶּר אֶת־הָרָעָה הַזֹּאת אֶל־הַמָּקוֹם הַזֶּה׃
the-this the-place for the-this the-disaster *** he-decreed God-of-you Yahweh

וַיָּבֵא וַיַּעַשׂ יְהוָה כַּאֲשֶׁר דִּבֵּר כִּי־חֲטָאתֶם
you-sinned because he-said just-as Yahweh and-he-did now-he-brought-about (3)

לַיהוָה וְלֹא־שְׁמַעְתֶּם בְּקוֹלוֹ וְהָיָה לָכֶם דָּבָר
the-thing to-you so-he-happened to-voice-of-him you-obeyed and-not against-Yahweh

הַזֶּה׃ וְעַתָּה הִנֵּה פִתַּחְתִּיךָ הַיּוֹם מִן־הָאזִקִּים אֲשֶׁר עַל־יָדֶךָ
wrist-of-you on that the-chains from the-day I-free-you see! but-now (4) the-this

אִם־טוֹב בְּעֵינֶיךָ לָבוֹא אִתִּי בָבֶל בֹּא וְאָשִׂים אֶת־עֵינִי
eye-of-me *** and-I-will-set come! Babylon with-me to-come in-eyes-of-you good if

עָלֶיךָ וְאִם־רַע בְּעֵינֶיךָ לָבוֹא־אִתִּי בָבֶל חֲדָל רְאֵה
look! do-not-come! Babylon with-me to-come in-eyes-of-you bad but-if on-you

כָּל־הָאָרֶץ לְפָנֶיךָ אֶל־טוֹב וְאֶל־הַיָּשָׁר בְּעֵינֶיךָ לָלֶכֶת
to-go in-eyes-of-you the-right and-to good to before-you the-country whole-of

to him: [16]"Go and tell Ebed-Melech the Cushite, 'This is what the LORD Almighty, the God of Israel, says: I am about to fulfill my words against this city through disaster, not prosperity. At that time they will be fulfilled before your eyes. [17]But I will rescue you on that day, declares the LORD; you will not be handed over to those you fear. [18]I will save you; you will not fall by the sword but will escape with your life, because you trust in me, declares the LORD.' "

*Jeremiah Freed*

40 The word came to Jeremiah from the LORD after Nebuzaradan commander of the imperial guard had released him at Ramah. He had found Jeremiah bound in chains among all the captives from Jerusalem and Judah who were being carried into exile to Babylon. [2]When the commander of the guard found Jeremiah, he said to him, "The LORD your God decreed this disaster for this place. [3]And now the LORD has brought it about; he has done just as he said he would. All this happened because you people sinned against the LORD and did not obey him. [4]But today I am freeing you from the chains on your wrists. Come with me to Babylon, if you like, and I will look after you; but if you do not want to, then don't come. Look, the whole country lies before you; go

°*16* ק מביא
°*4* ק הדבר

שָׁמָּה לֵךְ : וְעוֹדֶנּוּ לֹא־יָשׁוּב וְשֻׁבָה אֶל־גְּדַלְיָה בֶן־
son-of Gedaliah to and-go-back! he-went not however-still-he (5) go! to-there

אֲחִיקָם בֶּן־שָׁפָן אֲשֶׁר הִפְקִיד מֶלֶךְ־בָּבֶל בְּעָרֵי יְהוּדָה
Judah over-towns-of Babylon king-of he-appointed whom Shaphan son-of Ahikam

וְשֵׁב אִתּוֹ בְּתוֹךְ הָעָם אוֹ אֶל־כָּל־הַיָּשָׁר בְּעֵינֶיךָ
in-eyes-of-you the-right any-of to or the-people in-among with-him and-live!

לָלֶכֶת לֵךְ וַיִּתֶּן־לוֹ רַב־טַבָּחִים אֲרֻחָה וּמַשְׂאֵת
and-present provision imperial-guards commander-of to-him then-he-gave go! to-go

וַיְשַׁלְּחֵהוּ : וַיָּבֹא יִרְמְיָהוּ אֶל־גְּדַלְיָה בֶן־אֲחִיקָם הַמִּצְפָּתָה
at-the-Mizpah Ahikam son-of Gedaliah to Jeremiah so-he-went (6) and-he-let-go-him

וַיֵּשֶׁב אִתּוֹ בְּתוֹךְ הָעָם הַנִּשְׁאָרִים בָּאָרֶץ :
in-the-land the-ones-being-left the-people in-among with-him and-he-stayed

וַיִּשְׁמְעוּ כָל־שָׂרֵי הַחֲיָלִים אֲשֶׁר בַּשָּׂדֶה הֵמָּה
they in-the-open-country who the-armies officers-of all-of when-they-heard (7)

וְאַנְשֵׁיהֶם כִּי־הִפְקִיד מֶלֶךְ־בָּבֶל אֶת־גְּדַלְיָהוּ בֶן־אֲחִיקָם
Ahikam son-of Gedaliah *** Babylon king-of he-appointed that and-men-of-them

בָּאָרֶץ וְכִי הִפְקִיד אִתּוֹ אֲנָשִׁים וְנָשִׁים וָטָף וּמִדַּלַּת
from-poor-of and-child and-women men to-him he-put-in-charge and-that over-the-land

הָאָרֶץ מֵאֲשֶׁר לֹא־הֶגְלוּ בָּבֶלָה : וַיָּבֹאוּ אֶל־גְּדַלְיָה
Gedaliah to then-they-came (6) to-Babylon they-were-exiled not from-whom the-land

הַמִּצְפָּתָה וְיִשְׁמָעֵאל בֶּן־נְתַנְיָהוּ וְיוֹחָנָן וְיוֹנָתָן בְּנֵי־
sons-of and-Jonathan and-Johanan Nethaniah son-of indeed-Ishmael at-the-Mizpah

קָרֵחַ וּשְׂרָיָה בֶן־תַּנְחֻמֶת וּבְנֵי עוֹפַי הַנְּטֹפָתִי וְיֵזַנְיָהוּ
and-Jezaniah the-Netophathite Ephai and-sons-of Tanhumeth son-of and-Seraiah Kareah

בֶּן־הַמַּעֲכָתִי הֵמָּה וְאַנְשֵׁיהֶם : וַיִּשָּׁבַע לָהֶם גְּדַלְיָהוּ
Gedaliah for-them and-he-took-oath (9) and-men-of-them they the-Maacathite son-of

בֶּן־אֲחִיקָם בֶּן־שָׁפָן וּלְאַנְשֵׁיהֶם לֵאמֹר אַל־תִּירְאוּ
you-be-afraid not to-say and-for-men-of-them Shaphan son-of Ahikam son-of

מֵעֲבוֹד הַכַּשְׂדִּים שְׁבוּ בָאָרֶץ וְעִבְדוּ אֶת־מֶלֶךְ בָּבֶל
Babylon king-of *** and-serve! in-the-land settle-down! the-Chaldeans from-to-serve

וְיִטַב לָכֶם : וַאֲנִי הִנְנִי יֹשֵׁב בַּמִּצְפָּה לַעֲמֹד
to-represent at-the-Mizpah staying see-I! and-I (10) with-you and-he-will-go-well

לִפְנֵי הַכַּשְׂדִּים אֲשֶׁר יָבֹאוּ אֵלֵינוּ וְאַתֶּם אִסְפוּ יַיִן וָקַיִץ
and-summer-fruit wine harvest! but-you to-us they-come who the-Chaldeans before

וְשֶׁמֶן וְשִׂמוּ בִּכְלֵיכֶם וּשְׁבוּ בְּעָרֵיכֶם אֲשֶׁר תְּפַשְׂתֶּם :
you-took-over that in-towns-of-you and-live! in-jars-of-you and-put! and-oil

וְגַם כָּל־הַיְּהוּדִים אֲשֶׁר־בְּמוֹאָב וּבִבְנֵי־עַמּוֹן וּבֶאֱדוֹם
and-in-Edom Ammon and-among-sons-of in-Moab who the-Jews all-of when-also (11)

---

wherever you please." [5]However, before Jeremiah turned to go,[h] Nebuzaradan added, "Go back to Gedaliah son of Ahikam, the son of Shaphan, whom the king of Babylon has appointed over the towns of Judah, and live with him among the people, or go anywhere else you please."

Then the commander gave him provisions and a present and let him go. [6]So Jeremiah went to Gedaliah son of Ahikam at Mizpah and stayed with him among the people who were left behind in the land.

*Gedaliah Assassinated*

[7]When all the army officers and their men who were still in the open country heard that the king of Babylon had appointed Gedaliah son of Ahikam as governor over the land and had put him in charge of the men, women and children who were the poorest in the land and who had not been carried into exile to Babylon, [8]they came to Gedaliah at Mizpah—Ishmael son of Nethaniah, Johanan and Jonathan the sons of Kareah, Seraiah son of Tanhumeth, the sons of Ephai the Netophathite, and Jaazaniah[i] the son of the Maacathite, and their men. [9]Gedaliah son of Ahikam, the son of Shaphan, took an oath to reassure them and their men. "Do not be afraid to serve the Babylonians,[j]" he said. "Settle down in the land and serve the king of Babylon, and it will go well with you. [10]I myself will stay at Mizpah to represent you before the Babylonians who come to us, but you are to harvest the wine, summer fruit and oil, and put them in your storage jars, and live in the towns you have taken over."

[11]When all the Jews in Moab, Ammon, Edom and all the other

[h]5 Or *Jeremiah answered*
[i]8 Hebrew *Jezaniah*, a variant of *Jaazaniah*
[j]9 Or *Chaldeans*; also in verse 10

°8 עיפי ק

וַאֲשֶׁר בְּכָל־ הָאֲרָצוֹת שָׁמְעוּ כִּי־ נָתַן מֶלֶךְ־ בָּבֶל שְׁאֵרִית
remnant Babylon king-of he-left that they-heard the-countries in-all-of and-who

לִיהוּדָה וְכִי הִפְקִיד עֲלֵיהֶם אֶת־גְּדַלְיָהוּ בֶּן־ אֲחִיקָם בֶּן־
son-of Ahikam son-of Gedaliah *** over-them he-appointed and-that in-Judah

שָׁפָן׃ וַיָּשֻׁבוּ כָל־ הַיְּהוּדִים מִכָּל־ הַמְּקֹמוֹת אֲשֶׁר
where the-countries from-all-of the-Jews all-of then-they-returned (12) Shaphan

נִדְּחוּ־ שָׁם וַיָּבֹאוּ אֶרֶץ־ יְהוּדָה אֶל־גְּדַלְיָהוּ הַמִּצְפָּתָה
at-the-Mizpah Gedaliah to Judah land-of and-they-came there they-were-scattered

וַיַּאַסְפוּ יַיִן וָקַיִץ הַרְבֵּה מְאֹד׃ וְיוֹחָנָן בֶּן־
son-of and-Johanan (13) very to-be-abundant and-summer-fruit wine and-they-harvested

קָרֵחַ וְכָל־ שָׂרֵי הַחֲיָלִים אֲשֶׁר בַּשָּׂדֶה בָּאוּ אֶל־
to they-came in-the-open-country who the-armies officers-of and-all-of Kareah

גְּדַלְיָהוּ הַמִּצְפָּתָה׃ וַיֹּאמְרוּ אֵלָיו הֲיָדֹעַ תֵּדַע כִּי בַּעֲלִיס ׀
Baalis that you-know to-know? to-him and-they-said (14) at-the-Mizpah Gedaliah

מֶלֶךְ בְּנֵי־ עַמּוֹן שָׁלַח אֶת־יִשְׁמָעֵאל בֶּן־ נְתַנְיָה לְהַכֹּתְךָ נֶפֶשׁ וְלֹא־
but-not life to-kill-you Nethaniah son-of Ishmael *** he-sent Ammon sons-of king-of

הֶאֱמִין לָהֶם גְּדַלְיָהוּ בֶּן־ אֲחִיקָם׃ וְיוֹחָנָן בֶּן־ קָרֵחַ אָמַר
he-said Kareah son-of then-Johanan (15) Ahikam son-of Gedaliah to-them he-believed

אֶל־גְּדַלְיָהוּ בַסֵּתֶר בַּמִּצְפָּה לֵאמֹר אֵלְכָה נָּא וְאַכֶּה
and-I-will-kill now! let-me-go to-say in-the-Mizpah in-the-private Gedaliah to

אֶת־יִשְׁמָעֵאל בֶּן־ נְתַנְיָה וְאִישׁ לֹא יֵדָע לָמָּה יַכֶּכָּה
should-he-kill-you for-why? he-will-know not and-anyone Nethaniah son-of Ishmael ***

נֶּפֶשׁ וְנָפֹצוּ כָּל־ יְהוּדָה הַנִּקְבָּצִים אֵלֶיךָ
around-you the-ones-being-gathered Judah all-of so-they-would-be-scattered life

וְאָבְדָה שְׁאֵרִית יְהוּדָה׃ וַיֹּאמֶר גְּדַלְיָהוּ בֶן־אֲחִיקָם אֶל־
to Ahikam son-of Gedaliah but-he-said (16) Judah remnant-of and-she-would-perish

יוֹחָנָן בֶּן־ קָרֵחַ אַל־ תַּעַשׂ° אֶת־ הַדָּבָר הַזֶּה כִּי־ שֶׁקֶר אַתָּה דֹבֵר
saying you not-true indeed the-this the-thing *** you-do not Kareah son-of Johanan

אֶל־יִשְׁמָעֵאל׃ וַיְהִי ׀ בַּחֹדֶשׁ הַשְּׁבִיעִי בָּא יִשְׁמָעֵאל בֶּן־
son-of Ishmael he-came the-seventh in-the-month and-he-was (41:1) Ishmael about

נְתַנְיָה בֶּן־ אֱלִישָׁמָע מִזֶּרַע הַמְּלוּכָה וְרַבֵּי הַמֶּלֶךְ
the-king and-officers-of the-royalty from-descendant-of Elishama son-of Nethaniah

וַעֲשָׂרָה אֲנָשִׁים אִתּוֹ אֶל־גְּדַלְיָהוּ בֶּן־ אֲחִיקָם הַמִּצְפָּתָה וַיֹּאכְלוּ שָׁם
there while-they-ate at-the-Mizpah Ahikam son-of Gedaliah to with-him men and-ten

לֶחֶם יַחְדָּו בַּמִּצְפָּה׃ וַיָּקָם יִשְׁמָעֵאל בֶּן־ נְתַנְיָה וַעֲשֶׂרֶת
and-ten-of Nethaniah son-of Ishmael and-he-got-up (2) at-the-Mizpah together food

הָאֲנָשִׁים ׀ אֲשֶׁר־הָיוּ אִתּוֹ וַיַּכּוּ אֶת־גְּדַלְיָהוּ בֶּן־ אֲחִיקָם
Ahikam son-of Gedaliah *** and-they-struck-down with-him they-were who the-men

countries heard that the king of Babylon had left a remnant in Judah and had appointed Gedaliah son of Ahikam, the son of Shaphan, as governor over them, [12]they all came back to the land of Judah, to Gedaliah at Mizpah, from all the countries where they had been scattered. And they harvested an abundance of wine and summer fruit.

[13]Johanan son of Kareah and all the army officers still in the open country came to Gedaliah at Mizpah [14]and said to him, "Don't you know that Baalis king of the Ammonites has sent Ishmael son of Nethaniah to take your life?" But Gedaliah son of Ahikam did not believe them.

[15]Then Johanan son of Kareah said privately to Gedaliah in Mizpah, "Let me go and kill Ishmael son of Nethaniah, and no one will know it. Why should he take your life and cause all the Jews who are gathered around you to be scattered and the remnant of Judah to perish?"

[16]But Gedaliah son of Ahikam said to Johanan son of Kareah, "Don't do such a thing! What you are saying about Ishmael is not true."

**41** In the seventh month Ishmael son of Nethaniah, the son of Elishama, who was of royal blood and had been one of the king's officers, came with ten men to Gedaliah son of Ahikam at Mizpah. While they were eating together there, [2]Ishmael son of Nethaniah and the ten men who were with him got up and struck down Gedaliah son of Ahikam,

°16 ק תעשה

בֶּן־ שָׁפָן בַּחֶרֶב וַיָּמֶת אֹתוֹ אֲשֶׁר־ הִפְקִיד מֶלֶךְ־
king-of he-appointed whom him and-they-killed with-the-sword Shaphan son-of

בָּבֶל בָּאָרֶץ׃ וְאֵת כָּל־הַיְּהוּדִים אֲשֶׁר־ הָיוּ אִתּוֹ אֶת־גְּדַלְיָהוּ
Gedaliah with with-him they-were who the-Jews all-of also (3) over-the-land Babylon

בַּמִּצְפָּה וְאֶת־ הַכַּשְׂדִּים אֲשֶׁר נִמְצְאוּ־ שָׁם אֵת אַנְשֵׁי הַמִּלְחָמָה
the-army men-of *** there they-were-found who the-Chaldeans and at-the-Mizpah

הִכָּה יִשְׁמָעֵאל׃ וַיְהִי בַּיּוֹם הַשֵּׁנִי לְהָמִית אֶת־
*** to-assassinate the-second on-the-day and-he-was (4) Ishmael he-killed

גְּדַלְיָהוּ וְאִישׁ לֹא יָדָע׃ וַיָּבֹאוּ אֲנָשִׁים מִשְּׁכֶם מִשִּׁלוֹ
from-Shiloh from-Shechem men then-they-came (5) he-knew not and-anyone Gedaliah

וּמִשֹּׁמְרוֹן שְׁמֹנִים אִישׁ מְגֻלְּחֵי זָקָן וּקְרֻעֵי
and-ones-being-torn-of beard ones-being-shaved-of man eighty and-from-Samaria

בְגָדִים וּמִתְגֹּדְדִים וּמִנְחָה וּלְבוֹנָה בְּיָדָם
in-hand-of-them and-incense and-grain-offering and-ones-cutting-themselves clothes

לְהָבִיא בֵּית יְהוָה׃ וַיֵּצֵא יִשְׁמָעֵאל בֶּן־ נְתַנְיָה לִקְרָאתָם
to-meet-them Nethaniah son-of Ishmael and-he-went-out (6) Yahweh house-of to-bring

מִן־ הַמִּצְפָּה הֹלֵךְ הָלֹךְ וּבֹכֶה וַיְהִי כִּפְגֹשׁ אֹתָם וַיֹּאמֶר
then-he-said them when-to-meet and-he-was and-weeping to-go going the-Mizpah from

אֲלֵיהֶם בֹּאוּ אֶל־גְּדַלְיָהוּ בֶן־ אֲחִיקָם׃ וַיְהִי כְּבוֹאָם אֶל־
into when-to-go-them and-he-was (7) Ahikam son-of Gedaliah to come! to-them

תּוֹךְ הָעִיר וַיִּשְׁחָטֵם יִשְׁמָעֵאל בֶּן־ נְתַנְיָה אֶל־ תּוֹךְ
inside-of into Nethaniah son-of Ishmael then-he-slaughtered-them the-city inside-of

הַבּוֹר הוּא וְהָאֲנָשִׁים אֲשֶׁר־ אִתּוֹ׃ וַעֲשָׂרָה אֲנָשִׁים נִמְצְאוּ־ בָם
among-them they-were-found men but-ten (8) with-him who and-the-men he the-cistern

וַיֹּאמְרוּ אֶל־יִשְׁמָעֵאל אַל־ תְּמִתֵנוּ כִּי־ יֶשׁ־ לָנוּ מַטְמֹנִים בַּשָּׂדֶה
in-the-field ones-hidden to-us there-is for you-kill-us not Ishmael to and-they-said

חִטִּים וּשְׂעֹרִים וְשֶׁמֶן וּדְבָשׁ וַיֶּחְדַּל וְלֹא הֱמִיתָם
he-killed-them and-not so-he-let-alone and-honey and-oil and-barleys wheats

בְּתוֹךְ אֲחֵיהֶם׃ וְהַבּוֹר אֲשֶׁר הִשְׁלִיךְ שָׁם יִשְׁמָעֵאל אֵת ׀ כָּל־
all-of *** Ishmael there he-threw where now-the-cistern (9) others-of-them in-among

פִּגְרֵי הָאֲנָשִׁים אֲשֶׁר הִכָּה בְּיַד־ גְּדַלְיָהוּ הוּא אֲשֶׁר עָשָׂה הַמֶּלֶךְ אָסָא
Asa the-king he-made that one Gedaliah at-side-of he-killed whom the-men bodies-of

מִפְּנֵי בַּעְשָׁא מֶלֶךְ־יִשְׂרָאֵל אֹתוֹ מִלֵּא יִשְׁמָעֵאל בֶּן־ נְתַנְיָהוּ חֲלָלִים׃
dead-ones Nethaniah son-of Ishmael he-filled him Israel king-of Baasha because-of

וַיִּשְׁבְּ ׀ יִשְׁמָעֵאל אֶת־ כָּל־ שְׁאֵרִית הָעָם אֲשֶׁר בַּמִּצְפָּה
in-the-Mizpah who the-people rest-of all-of *** Ishmael and-he-made-captive (10)

אֶת־ בְּנוֹת הַמֶּלֶךְ וְאֶת־ כָּל־ הָעָם הַנִּשְׁאָרִים בַּמִּצְפָּה
in-the-Mizpah the-ones-being-left the-people all-of and the-king daughters-of ***

the son of Shaphan, with the sword, killing the one whom the king of Babylon had appointed as governor over the land. 3Ishmael also killed all the Jews who were with Gedaliah at Mizpah, as well as the Babylonian[k] soldiers who were there.

4The day after Gedaliah's assassination, before anyone knew about it, 5eighty men who had shaved off their beards, torn their clothes and cut themselves came from Shechem, Shiloh and Samaria, bringing grain offerings and incense with them to the house of the LORD. 6Ishmael son of Nethaniah went out from Mizpah to meet them, weeping as he went. When he met them, he said, "Come to Gedaliah son of Ahikam." 7When they went into the city, Ishmael son of Nethaniah and the men who were with him slaughtered them and threw them into a cistern. 8But ten of them said to Ishmael, "Don't kill us! We have wheat and barley, oil and honey, hidden in a field." So he let them alone and did not kill them with the others. 9Now the cistern where he threw all the bodies of the men he had killed along with Gedaliah was the one King Asa had made as part of his defense against Baasha king of Israel. Ishmael son of Nethaniah filled it with the dead.

10Ishmael made captives of all the rest of the people who were in Mizpah—the king's daughters along with all the others who were

k3 Or *Chaldean*

אֲשֶׁר הִפְקִיד נְבוּזַרְאֲדָן רַב־ טַבָּחִים אֶת־גְּדַלְיָהוּ בֶּן־
son-of Gedaliah *** imperial-guards commander-of Nebuzaradan he-appointed whom

אֲחִיקָם וַיִּשְׁבֵּם יִשְׁמָעֵאל בֶּן־ נְתַנְיָה וַיֵּלֶךְ
and-he-set-out Nethaniah son-of Ishmael and-he-took-captive-them Ahikam

לַעֲבֹר אֶל־ בְּנֵי עַמּוֹן׃ וַיִּשְׁמַע יוֹחָנָן בֶּן־ קָרֵחַ וְכָל־
and-all-of Kareah son-of Johanan when-he-heard (11) Ammon sons-of to to-cross-over

שָׂרֵי הַחֲיָלִים אֲשֶׁר אִתּוֹ אֵת כָּל־ הָרָעָה אֲשֶׁר עָשָׂה יִשְׁמָעֵאל בֶּן־
son-of Ishmael he-did that the-crime all-of *** with-him who the-armies officers-of

נְתַנְיָה׃ וַיִּקְחוּ אֶת־ כָּל־ הָאֲנָשִׁים וַיֵּלְכוּ לְהִלָּחֵם עִם־
against to-fight and-they-went the-men all-of *** then-they-took (12) Nethaniah

יִשְׁמָעֵאל בֶּן־ נְתַנְיָה וַיִּמְצְאוּ אֹתוֹ אֶל־מַיִם רַבִּים אֲשֶׁר בְּגִבְעוֹן׃
in-Gibeon that great-ones pools near him and-they-found Nethaniah son-of Ishmael

וַיְהִי כִּרְאוֹת כָּל־ הָעָם אֲשֶׁר אֶת־יִשְׁמָעֵאל אֶת־יוֹחָנָן בֶּן־
son-of Johanan *** Ishmael with who the-people all-of when-to-see and-he-was (13)

קָרֵחַ וְאֵת כָּל־ שָׂרֵי הַחֲיָלִים אֲשֶׁר אִתּוֹ וַיִּשְׂמָחוּ׃
then-they-were-glad with-him who the-armies officers-of all-of and Kareah

וַיָּסֹבּוּ כָּל־ הָעָם אֲשֶׁר־ שָׁבָה יִשְׁמָעֵאל מִן־הַמִּצְפָּה
the-Mizpah at Ishmael he-took-captive whom the-people all-of and-they-turned (14)

וַיָּשֻׁבוּ וַיֵּלְכוּ אֶל־ יוֹחָנָן בֶּן־ קָרֵחַ׃ וְיִשְׁמָעֵאל בֶּן־
son-of but-Ishmael (15) Kareah son-of Johanan to and-they-went-over and-they-turned

נְתַנְיָה נִמְלַט בִּשְׁמֹנָה אֲנָשִׁים מִפְּנֵי יוֹחָנָן וַיֵּלֶךְ אֶל־ בְּנֵי
sons-of to and-he-fled Johanan from-before men with-eight he-escaped Nethaniah

עַמּוֹן׃ וַיִּקַּח יוֹחָנָן בֶּן־ קָרֵחַ וְכָל־ שָׂרֵי הַחֲיָלִים
the-armies officers-of and-all-of Kareah son-of Johanan then-he-led-away (16) Ammon

אֲשֶׁר־ אִתּוֹ אֵת כָּל־ שְׁאֵרִית הָעָם אֲשֶׁר הֵשִׁיב מֵאֵת יִשְׁמָעֵאל
Ishmael from-with he-recovered whom the-people survivor-of all-of *** with-him who

בֶּן־ נְתַנְיָה מִן־ הַמִּצְפָּה אַחַר הִכָּה אֶת־ גְּדַלְיָה בֶּן־ אֲחִיקָם
Ahikam son-of Gedaliah *** he-assassinated after the-Mizpah from Nethaniah son-of

גְּבָרִים אַנְשֵׁי הַמִּלְחָמָה וְנָשִׁים וָטַף וְסָרִסִים אֲשֶׁר הֵשִׁיב
he-brought whom and-court-officials and-child and-women the-army men-of soldiers

מִגִּבְעוֹן׃ וַיֵּלְכוּ וַיֵּשְׁבוּ בְּגֵרוּת כִּמוֹהָם אֲשֶׁר־אֵצֶל
near that Kimham at-Geruth and-they-stopped and-they-went-on (17) from-Gibeon

בֵּית לֶחֶם לָלֶכֶת לָבוֹא מִצְרָיִם׃ מִפְּנֵי הַכַּשְׂדִּים כִּי יָרְאוּ
they-were-afraid for the-Chaldeans because-of (18) Egypt to-go to-go-on Lehem Beth

מִפְּנֵיהֶם כִּי־ הִכָּה יִשְׁמָעֵאל בֶּן־ נְתַנְיָה אֶת־גְּדַלְיָהוּ בֶּן־ אֲחִיקָם
Ahikam son-of Gedaliah *** Nethaniah son-of Ishmael he-killed because because-of-them

אֲשֶׁר־ הִפְקִיד מֶלֶךְ־ בָּבֶל בָּאָרֶץ׃ וַיִּגְּשׁוּ כָּל־
all-of and-they-approached (42:1) over-the-land Babylon king-of he-appointed whom

left there, over whom Nebuzaradan commander of the imperial guard had appointed Gedaliah son of Ahikam. Ishmael son of Nethaniah took them captive and set out to cross over to the Ammonites.

[11]When Johanan son of Kareah and all the army officers who were with him heard about all the crimes Ishmael son of Nethaniah had committed, [12]they took all their men and went to fight Ishmael son of Nethaniah. They caught up with him near the great pool in Gibeon. [13]When all the people Ishmael had with him saw Johanan son of Kareah and the army officers who were with him, they were glad. [14]All the people Ishmael had taken captive at Mizpah turned and went over to Johanan son of Kareah. [15]But Ishmael son of Nethaniah and eight of his men escaped from Johanan and fled to the Ammonites.

*Flight to Egypt*

[16]Then Johanan son of Kareah and all the army officers who were with him led away all the survivors from Mizpah whom he had recovered from Ishmael son of Nethaniah after he had assassinated Gedaliah son of Ahikam: the soldiers, women, children and court officials he had brought from Gibeon. [17]And they went on, stopping at Geruth Kimham near Bethlehem on their way to Egypt [18]to escape the Babylonians.[l] They were afraid of them because Ishmael son of Nethaniah had killed Gedaliah son of Ahikam, whom the king of Babylon had appointed as governor over the land.

[l]18 Or *Chaldeans*

17 ק כמהם

שָׂרֵי הַחֲיָלִים וְיוֹחָנָן בֶּן־ קָרֵחַ וִיזַנְיָה בֶּן־ הוֹשַׁעְיָה

Hoshaiah son-of and-Jezaniah Kareah son-of and-Johanan the-armies officers-of

וְכָל־ הָעָם מִקָּטֹן וְעַד־ גָּדוֹל׃ וַיֹּאמְרוּ אֶל־ יִרְמְיָהוּ

Jeremiah to and-they-said (2) great and-to from-least the-people and-all-of

הַנָּבִיא תִּפָּל־ נָא תְחִנָּתֵנוּ לְפָנֶיךָ וְהִתְפַּלֵּל בַּעֲדֵנוּ

on-behalf-of-us and-pray! before-you petition-of-us now! let-her-come the-prophet

אֶל־יְהוָה אֱלֹהֶיךָ בְּעַד כָּל־ הַשְּׁאֵרִית הַזֹּאת כִּי־ נִשְׁאַרְנוּ

we-are-left for the-this the-remnant entire-of on-behalf-of God-of-you Yahweh to

מְעַט מֵהַרְבֵּה כַּאֲשֶׁר עֵינֶיךָ רֹאוֹת אֹתָנוּ׃ וְיַגֶּד־ לָנוּ

to-us so-he-will-tell (3) us ones-seeing eyes-of-you just-as from-to-be-many few

יְהוָה אֱלֹהֶיךָ אֶת־ הַדֶּרֶךְ אֲשֶׁר נֵלֶךְ־ בָּהּ וְאֶת־ הַדָּבָר אֲשֶׁר

that the-thing and on-her we-should-go that the-way *** God-of-you Yahweh

נַעֲשֶׂה׃ וַיֹּאמֶר אֲלֵיהֶם יִרְמְיָהוּ הַנָּבִיא שָׁמַעְתִּי הִנְנִי מִתְפַּלֵּל

praying see-I! I-heard the-prophet Jeremiah to-them and-he-replied (4) we-should-do

אֶל־ יְהוָה אֱלֹהֵיכֶם כְּדִבְרֵיכֶם וְהָיָה כָּל־ הַדָּבָר אֲשֶׁר־

that the-thing every-of and-he-will-be as-requests-of-you God-of-you Yahweh to

יַעֲנֶה יְהוָה אֶתְכֶם אַגִּיד לָכֶם לֹא־ אֶמְנַע מִכֶּם דָּבָר׃

anything from-you I-will-keep-back not to-you I-will-tell to-you Yahweh he-says

וְהֵמָּה אָמְרוּ אֶל־יִרְמְיָהוּ יְהִי יְהוָה בָּנוּ לְעֵד אֱמֶת

true as-witness against-us Yahweh may-he-be Jeremiah to they-said then-they (5)

וְנֶאֱמָן אִם־לֹא כְּכָל־ הַדָּבָר אֲשֶׁר יִשְׁלָחֲךָ

he-sends-you that the-thing according-to-every-of not if and-one-being-faithful

יְהוָה אֱלֹהֶיךָ אֵלֵינוּ כֵּן נַעֲשֶׂה׃ אִם־ טוֹב וְאִם־ רָע

unfavorable or-whether favorable whether (6) we-act so to-us God-of-you Yahweh

בְּקוֹל ׀ יְהוָה אֱלֹהֵינוּ אֲשֶׁר אֲנוּ שֹׁלְחִים אֹתְךָ אֵלָיו נִשְׁמָע לְמַעַן

so-that we-will-obey to-him you ones-sending we whom God-of-us Yahweh to-voice-of

אֲשֶׁר יִיטַב־ לָנוּ כִּי נִשְׁמַע בְּקוֹל יְהוָה אֱלֹהֵינוּ׃

God-of-us Yahweh to-voice-of we-will-obey for for-us he-will-go-well that

וַיְהִי מִקֵּץ עֲשֶׂרֶת יָמִים וַיְהִי דְבַר־ יְהוָה אֶל־יִרְמְיָהוּ׃

Jeremiah to Yahweh word-of then-he-came days ten-of at-end-of and-he-was (7)

וַיִּקְרָא אֶל־ יוֹחָנָן בֶּן־ קָרֵחַ וְאֵל כָּל־ שָׂרֵי הַחֲיָלִים

the-armies officers-of all-of and-to Kareah son-of Johanan to so-he-called (8)

אֲשֶׁר אִתּוֹ וּלְכָל־ הָעָם לְמִקָּטֹן וְעַד־ גָּדוֹל׃ וַיֹּאמֶר

and-he-said (9) great and-to to-from-least the-people and-to-all-of with-him who

אֲלֵיהֶם כֹּה־ אָמַר יְהוָה אֱלֹהֵי יִשְׂרָאֵל אֲשֶׁר שְׁלַחְתֶּם אֹתִי אֵלָיו לְהַפִּיל

to-present to-him me you-sent whom Israel God-of Yahweh he-says this to-them

תְּחִנַּתְכֶם לְפָנָיו׃ אִם־ שׁוֹב תֵּשְׁבוּ בָּאָרֶץ הַזֹּאת

the-this in-the-land you-stay to-stay if (10) before-him petition-of-you

°6 ק אנחנו

42 Then all the army officers,
including Johanan son of
Kareah and Jezaniah[m] son of Hoshaiah, and all the people from the
least to the greatest approached
2Jeremiah the prophet and said to
him, "Please hear our petition and
pray to the LORD your God for this
entire remnant. For as you now
see, though we were once many,
now only a few are left. 3Pray that
the LORD your God will tell us
where we should go and what we
should do."
4"I have heard you," replied
Jeremiah the prophet. "I will certainly pray to the LORD your God
as you have requested; I will tell
you everything the LORD says and
will keep nothing back from you."
5Then they said to Jeremiah,
"May the LORD be a true and faithful witness against us if we do not
act in accordance with everything
the LORD your God sends you to
tell us. 6Whether it is favorable or
unfavorable, we will obey the
LORD our God, to whom we are
sending you, so that it will go well
with us, for we will obey the LORD
our God."
7Ten days later the word of the
LORD came to Jeremiah. 8So he
called together Johanan son of Kareah and all the army officers who
were with him and all the people
from the least to the greatest. 9He
said to them, "This is what the
LORD, the God of Israel, to whom
you sent me to present your petition, says: 10'If you stay in this

[m] 1 Hebrew; Septuagint (see also 43:2) *Azariah*

וּבָנִיתִי אֶתְכֶם וְלֹא אֶהֱרֹס וְנָטַעְתִּי אֶתְכֶם וְלֹא
and-not you and-I-will-plant I-will-tear-down and-not you then-I-will-build-up

אֶתּוֹשׁ כִּי נִחַמְתִּי אֶל־ הָרָעָה אֲשֶׁר עָשִׂיתִי לָכֶם׃ אַל־
not (11) on-you I-inflicted that the-disaster over I-am-grieved for I-will-uproot

תִּירְאוּ מִפְּנֵי מֶלֶךְ בָּבֶל אֲשֶׁר־אַתֶּם יְרֵאִים מִפָּנָיו
because-of-him ones-fearing you whom Babylon king-of because-of you-be-afraid

אַל־ תִּירְאוּ מִמֶּנּוּ נְאֻם־ יְהוָה כִּי־אִתְּכֶם אֲנִי לְהוֹשִׁיעַ אֶתְכֶם
you to-save I with-you for Yahweh declaration-of of-him you-be-afraid not

וּלְהַצִּיל אֶתְכֶם מִיָּדוֹ׃ וְאֶתֵּן לָכֶם רַחֲמִים
compassions to-you and-I-will-show (12) from-hand-of-him you and-to-deliver

וְרִחַם אֶתְכֶם וְהֵשִׁיב אֶתְכֶם אֶל־ אַדְמַתְכֶם׃
land-of-you to you and-he-will-restore on-you so-he-will-have-compassion

וְאִם־ אֹמְרִים אַתֶּם לֹא נֵשֵׁב בָּאָרֶץ הַזֹּאת לְבִלְתִּי שְׁמֹעַ
to-obey not the-this in-the-land we-will-stay not you ones-saying however-if (13)

בְּקוֹל יְהוָה אֱלֹהֵיכֶם׃ לֵאמֹר לֹא כִּי אֶרֶץ מִצְרַיִם נָבוֹא אֲשֶׁר
where we-will-go Egypt land-of but no to-say (14) God-of-you Yahweh to-voice-of

לֹא־ נִרְאֶה מִלְחָמָה וְקוֹל שׁוֹפָר לֹא נִשְׁמָע וְלַלֶּחֶם לֹא־
not or-for-the-bread we-will-hear not trumpet or-sound-of war we-will-see not

נִרְעָב וְשָׁם נֵשֵׁב׃ וְעַתָּה לָכֵן שִׁמְעוּ דְבַר־
word-of hear! therefore then-now (15) we-will-live and-there we-will-be-hungry

יְהוָה שְׁאֵרִית יְהוּדָה כֹּה־ אָמַר יְהוָה צְבָאוֹת אֱלֹהֵי יִשְׂרָאֵל אִם־אַתֶּם
you if Israel God-of Hosts Yahweh-of he-says this Judah remnant-of Yahweh

שׂוֹם תְּשִׂמוּן פְּנֵיכֶם לָבֹא מִצְרַיִם וּבָאתֶם לָגוּר שָׁם׃
there to-settle and-you-go Egypt to-go faces-of-you you-determine to-determine

וְהָיְתָה הַחֶרֶב אֲשֶׁר אַתֶּם יְרֵאִים מִמֶּנָּה שָׁם תַּשִּׂיג
she-will-overtake there of-her ones-fearing you that the-sword then-she-will-be (16)

אֶתְכֶם בְּאֶרֶץ מִצְרָיִם וְהָרָעָב אֲשֶׁר־אַתֶּם דֹּאֲגִים מִמֶּנּוּ שָׁם
there of-him ones-dreading you that and-the-famine Egypt in-land-of you

יִדְבַּק אַחֲרֵיכֶם מִצְרַיִם וְשָׁם תָּמֻתוּ׃ וְיִהְיוּ
indeed-they-will-be (17) you-will-die and-there Egypt after-you he-will-follow

כָל־ הָאֲנָשִׁים אֲשֶׁר־ שָׂמוּ אֶת־ פְּנֵיהֶם לָבוֹא מִצְרַיִם לָגוּר שָׁם
there to-settle Egypt to-go faces-of-them *** they-determined who the-men all-of

יָמוּתוּ בַּחֶרֶב בָּרָעָב וּבַדָּבֶר וְלֹא־ יִהְיֶה
he-will-be and-not and-by-the-plague by-the-famine by-the-sword they-will-die

לָהֶם שָׂרִיד וּפָלִיט מִפְּנֵי הָרָעָה אֲשֶׁר אֲנִי מֵבִיא עֲלֵיהֶם׃
on-them bringing I that the-disaster from-before or-escapee survivor of-them

כִּי כֹה אָמַר יְהוָה צְבָאוֹת אֱלֹהֵי יִשְׂרָאֵל כַּאֲשֶׁר נִתַּךְ
he-was-poured-out just-as Israel God-of Hosts Yahweh-of he-says this indeed (18)

land, I will build you up and not
tear you down; I will plant you
and not uproot you, for I am
grieved over the disaster I have
inflicted on you. [11]Do not be afraid
of the king of Babylon, whom you
now fear. Do not be afraid of him,
declares the LORD, for I am with
you and will save you and deliver
you from his hands. [12]I will show
you compassion so that he will
have compassion on you and restore you to your land.'
[13]"However, if you say, 'We will
not stay in this land,' and so disobey the LORD your God, [14]and if
you say, 'No, we will go and live
in Egypt, where we will not see
war or hear the trumpet or be hungry for bread,' [15]then hear the
word of the LORD, O remnant of
Judah. This is what the LORD Almighty, the God of Israel, says: 'If
you are determined to go to Egypt
and you do go to settle there,
[16]then the sword you fear will
overtake you there, and the famine you dread will follow you into
Egypt, and there you will die. [17]In-
deed, all who are determined to go
to Egypt to settle there will die by
the sword, famine and plague; not
one of them will survive or escape
the disaster I will bring on them.'
[18]This is what the LORD Almighty,
the God of Israel, says: 'As my anger and wrath have been poured

אַפִּי֙ וַחֲמָתִ֔י עַל־ יֹשְׁבֵי֙ יְרוּשָׁלַ֔͏ִם כֵּ֤ן תִּתַּךְ֙

she-will-be-poured-out so Jerusalem ones-living-of on and-wrath-of-me anger-of-me

חֲמָתִי֙ עֲלֵיכֶ֔ם בְּבֹאֲכֶ֖ם מִצְרָ֑יִם וִהְיִיתֶ֞ם לְאָלָ֤ה וּלְשַׁמָּה֙

and-as-horror as-curse and-you-will-become Egypt when-to-go-you on-you wrath-of-me

וְלִקְלָלָ֣ה וּלְחֶרְפָּ֔ה וְלֹֽא־ תִרְא֣וּ ע֔וֹד אֶת־ הַמָּק֖וֹם

the-place *** again you-will-see and-never and-as-reproach and-as-condemnation

הַזֶּֽה׃ דִּבֶּ֨ר יְהוָ֤ה עֲלֵיכֶם֙ שְׁאֵרִ֣ית יְהוּדָ֔ה אַל־ תָּבֹ֖אוּ מִצְרָ֑יִם יָדֹ֙עַ֙ (19)

the-this to-be-sure Egypt you-go not Judah remnant-of to-you Yahweh he-told (19) the-this

תֵּֽדְע֔וּ כִּי־ הַעִידֹ֥תִי בָכֶ֖ם הַיּֽוֹם׃ כִּ֣י הִתְעֵתֶם֮ בְּנַפְשֽׁוֹתֵיכֶם֒ כִּֽי־

when in-hearts-of-you you-erred that (20) the-day to-you I-warn that you-be-sure

אַתֶּ֞ם שְׁלַחְתֶּ֣ם אֹתִ֗י אֶל־ יְהוָ֤ה אֱלֹֽהֵיכֶם֙ לֵאמֹ֔ר הִתְפַּלֵּ֥ל בַּעֲדֵ֖נוּ אֶל־ יְהוָ֣ה

Yahweh to on-behalf-of-us pray! to-say God-of-you Yahweh to me you-sent you

אֱלֹהֵ֑ינוּ וּכְכֹל֙ אֲשֶׁ֨ר יֹאמַ֜ר יְהוָ֧ה אֱלֹהֵ֛ינוּ כֵּ֥ן הַגֶּד־ לָ֖נוּ

to-us tell! so God-of-us Yahweh he-says that and-as-everything God-of-us

וְעָשִֽׂינוּ׃ וָאַגִּ֥ד לָכֶ֖ם הַיּ֑וֹם וְלֹ֣א שְׁמַעְתֶּ֗ם בְּק֛וֹל יְהוָ֥ה (21)

Yahweh to-voice-of you-obeyed but-not the-day to-you and-I-told (21) and-we-will-do

אֱלֹֽהֵיכֶ֖ם וּלְכֹ֥ל אֲשֶׁר־ שְׁלָחַ֣נִי אֲלֵיכֶֽם׃ וְעַתָּה֙ יָדֹ֣עַ תֵּֽדְע֔וּ (22)

you-be-sure to-be-sure so-now (22) to-you he-sent-me that and-in-all God-of-you

כִּ֗י בַּחֶ֛רֶב בָּרָעָ֥ב וּבַדֶּ֖בֶר תָּמ֑וּתוּ בַּמָּקוֹם֙ אֲשֶׁ֣ר

where in-the-place you-will-die and-by-the-plague by-the-famine by-the-sword that

חֲפַצְתֶּ֔ם לָב֖וֹא לָג֥וּר שָֽׁם׃ וַיְהִי֙ (43:1) כְּכַלּ֣וֹת יִרְמְיָ֔הוּ לְדַבֵּ֣ר

to-tell Jeremiah when-to-finish and-he-was (43:1) there to-settle to-go you-want

אֶל־ כָּל־ הָעָ֑ם אֶת־ כָּל־ דִּבְרֵי֙ יְהוָ֣ה אֱלֹֽהֵיהֶ֔ם אֲשֶׁ֥ר שְׁלָח֛וֹ

he-sent-him that God-of-them Yahweh words-of all-of *** the-people all-of to

יְהוָ֥ה אֱלֹהֵיהֶ֖ם אֲלֵיהֶ֑ם אֵ֥ת כָּל־ הַדְּבָרִ֖ים הָאֵֽלֶּה׃ וַיֹּ֨אמֶר (2) עֲזַרְיָ֤ה

Azariah then-he-said (2) the-these the-things all-of *** to-them God-of-them Yahweh

בֶן־ הוֹשַֽׁעְיָה֙ וְיוֹחָנָ֣ן בֶּן־ קָרֵ֔חַ וְכָל־ הָאֲנָשִׁ֖ים הַזֵּדִ֑ים

the-arrogant-ones the-men and-all-of Kareah son-of and-Johanan Hoshaiah son-of

אֹמְרִ֣ים אֶֽל־ יִרְמְיָ֗הוּ שֶׁ֣קֶר אַתָּ֣ה מְדַבֵּ֔ר לֹ֤א שְׁלָחֲךָ֙ יְהוָ֣ה אֱלֹהֵ֔ינוּ לֵאמֹ֔ר

to-say God-of-us Yahweh he-sent-you not speaking you lie Jeremiah to ones-saying

לֹֽא־ תָבֹ֥אוּ מִצְרַ֖יִם לָג֥וּר שָֽׁם׃ כִּ֣י (3) בָּר֗וּךְ בֶּן־ נֵֽרִיָּה֙ מַסִּ֤ית אֹֽתְךָ֙

you inciting Neriah son-of Baruch but (3) there to-settle Egypt you-must-go not

בָּ֔נוּ לְמַ֛עַן תֵּ֥ת אֹתָ֖נוּ בְיַד־ הַכַּשְׂדִּ֗ים לְהָמִ֤ית אֹתָ֙נוּ֙ וּלְהַגְל֥וֹת

or-to-exile us to-kill the-Chaldeans into-hand-of us to-give in-order-to against-us

אֹתָ֖נוּ בָּבֶֽל׃ וְלֹֽא־ (4) שָׁמַ֞ע יוֹחָנָ֤ן בֶּן־ קָרֵ֙חַ֙ וְכָל־ שָׂרֵ֣י

officers-of and-all-of Kareah son-of Johanan he-obeyed so-not (4) Babylon us

הַחֲיָלִ֗ים וְכָל־ הָעָ֛ם בְּק֥וֹל יְהוָ֖ה לָשֶׁ֥בֶת בְּאֶ֥רֶץ יְהוּדָֽה׃

Judah in-land-of to-stay Yahweh to-voice-of the-people and-all-of the-armies

---

out on those who lived in Jerusalem, so will my wrath be poured out on you when you go to Egypt. You will be an object of cursing and horror, of condemnation and reproach; you will never see this place again.'

[19]"O remnant of Judah, the LORD has told you, 'Do not go to Egypt.' Be sure of this: I warn you today [20]that you made a fatal mistake[n] when you sent me to the LORD your God and said, 'Pray to the LORD our God for us; tell us everything he says and we will do it.' [21]I have told you today, but you still have not obeyed the LORD your God in all he sent me to tell you. [22]So now, be sure of this: You will die by the sword, famine and plague in the place where you want to go to settle."

**43** When Jeremiah finished telling the people all the words of the LORD their God—everything the LORD had sent him to tell them— [2]Azariah son of Hoshaiah and Johanan son of Kareah and all the arrogant men said to Jeremiah, "You are lying! The LORD our God has not sent you to say, 'You must not go to Egypt to settle there.' [3]But Baruch son of Neriah is inciting you against us to hand us over to the Babylonians,[o] so they may kill us or carry us into exile to Babylon."

[4]So Johanan son of Kareah and all the army officers and all the people disobeyed the LORD's command to stay in the land of Judah.

---

[n]20 Or you erred in your hearts
[o]3 Or Chaldeans

ק התעיתם 20°

וַיִּקַּח יוֹחָנָן בֶּן־ קָרֵחַ וְכָל־ שָׂרֵי הַחֲיָלִים

the-armies officers-of and-all-of Kareah son-of Johanan instead-he-led-away (5)

אֵת כָּל־ שְׁאֵרִית יְהוּדָה אֲשֶׁר־ שָׁבוּ מִכָּל־ הַגּוֹיִם אֲשֶׁר

where the-nations from-all-of they-came-back who Judah remnant-of all-of ***

נִדְּחוּ־ שָׁם לָגוּר בְּאֶרֶץ יְהוּדָה׃ אֶת־הַגְּבָרִים וְאֶת־ הַנָּשִׁים

the-women and the-men *** (6) Judah in-land-of to-live there they-were-scattered

וְאֶת־ הַטַּף וְאֶת־ בְּנוֹת הַמֶּלֶךְ וְאֵת כָּל־ הַנֶּפֶשׁ אֲשֶׁר הִנִּיחַ

he-left whom the-person all-of and the-king daughters-of and the-child and

נְבוּזַרְאֲדָן רַב־ טַבָּחִים אֶת־גְּדַלְיָהוּ בֶּן־ אֲחִיקָם בֶּן־ שָׁפָן

Shaphan son-of Ahikam son-of Gedaliah with imperial-guards commander-of Nebuzaradan

וְאֵת יִרְמְיָהוּ הַנָּבִיא וְאֶת־ בָּרוּךְ בֶּן־ נֵרִיָּהוּ׃ וַיָּבֹאוּ

so-they-entered (7) Neriah son-of Baruch and the-prophet Jeremiah and

אֶרֶץ מִצְרַיִם כִּי לֹא שָׁמְעוּ בְּקוֹל יְהוָה וַיָּבֹאוּ עַד־

as-far-as and-they-went Yahweh to-voice-of they-obeyed not but Egypt land-of

תַּחְפַּנְחֵס׃ וַיְהִי דְבַר־ יְהוָה אֶל־יִרְמְיָהוּ בְּתַחְפַּנְחֵס לֵאמֹר׃ קַח

take! (8) to-say in-Tahpanhes Jeremiah to Yahweh word-of and-he-came (8) Tahpanhes

בְּיָדְךָ אֲבָנִים גְּדֹלוֹת וּטְמַנְתָּם בַּמֶּלֶט בַּמַּלְבֵּן

in-the-brick-pavement in-the-clay and-you-bury-them large-ones stones in-hand-of-you

אֲשֶׁר בְּפֶתַח בֵּית־ פַּרְעֹה בְּתַחְפַּנְחֵס לְעֵינֵי אֲנָשִׁים יְהוּדִים׃

Jews men before-eyes-of in-Tahpanhes Pharaoh palace-of at-entrance-of that

וְאָמַרְתָּ אֲלֵיהֶם כֹּה־ אָמַר יְהוָה צְבָאוֹת אֱלֹהֵי יִשְׂרָאֵל הִנְנִי

see-I! Israel God-of Hosts Yahweh-of he-says this to-them then-you-say (10)

שֹׁלֵחַ וְלָקַחְתִּי אֶת־ נְבוּכַדְרֶאצַּר מֶלֶךְ־ בָּבֶל עַבְדִּי

servant-of-me Babylon king-of Nebuchadrezzar *** and-I-will-get sending

וְשַׂמְתִּי כִסְאוֹ מִמַּעַל לָאֲבָנִים הָאֵלֶּה אֲשֶׁר טָמָנְתִּי

I-buried that the-these to-the-stones at-over throne-of-him and-I-will-set

וְנָטָה אֶת־ °שַׁפְרוּרוֹ עֲלֵיהֶם׃ °וּבָאה

and-he-will-come (11) above-them canopy-of-him *** and-he-will-spread

וְהִכָּה אֶת־ אֶרֶץ מִצְרַיִם אֲשֶׁר לַמָּוֶת לַמָּוֶת וַאֲשֶׁר

and-whom with-the-death for-the-death whom Egypt land-of *** and-he-will-attack

לַשְּׁבִי לַשֶּׁבִי וַאֲשֶׁר לַחֶרֶב לֶחָרֶב׃

with-the-sword for-the-sword and-whom with-the-captivity for-the-captivity

וְהִצַּתִּי אֵשׁ בְּבָתֵּי אֱלֹהֵי מִצְרַיִם וּשְׂרָפָם

and-he-will-burn-them Egypt gods-of to-temples-of fire and-I-will-set (12)

וְשָׁבָם וְעָטָה אֶת־ אֶרֶץ מִצְרַיִם כַּאֲשֶׁר־

just-as Egypt land-of with and-he-will-wrap-himself and-he-will-take-captive-them

יַעְטֶה* הָרֹעֶה אֶת־ בִּגְדוֹ וְיָצָא

and-he-will-depart garment-of-him with the-one-being-shepherd he-wraps-himself

5Instead, Johanan son of Kareah and all the army officers led away all the remnant of Judah who had come back to live in the land of Judah from all the nations where they had been scattered. 6They also led away all the men, women and children and the king's daughters whom Nebuzaradan commander of the imperial guard had left with Gedaliah son of Ahikam, the son of Shaphan, and Jeremiah the prophet and Baruch son of Neriah. 7So they entered Egypt in disobedience to the LORD and went as far as Tahpanhes.

8In Tahpanhes the word of the LORD came to Jeremiah: 9"While the Jews are watching, take some large stones with you and bury them in clay in the brick pavement at the entrance to Pharaoh's palace in Tahpanhes. 10Then say to them, 'This is what the LORD Almighty, the God of Israel, says: I will send for my servant Nebuchadnezzar king of Babylon, and I will set his throne over these stones I have buried here; he will spread his royal canopy above them. 11He will come and attack Egypt, bringing death to those destined for death, captivity to those destined for captivity, and the sword to those destined for the sword. 12He[p] will set fire to the temples of the gods of Egypt; he will burn their temples and take their gods captive. As a shepherd wraps his garment around him, so

[p]12 Or I

*13 Most mss have *hateph pathah* under the *ayin* (יַעֲטֶה).

°10 ק שפרירו

°11 ק ובא

מִשָּׁם בְּשָׁלוֹם׃ וְשִׁבַּר אֶת־ מַצְּבוֹת בֵּית
temple-of sacred-pillars-of *** and-he-will-demolish (13) as-unscathed from-there

שֶׁמֶשׁ אֲשֶׁר בְּאֶרֶץ מִצְרָיִם וְאֶת־ בָּתֵּי אֱלֹהֵי־מִצְרַיִם יִשְׂרֹף בָּאֵשׁ׃
with-fire he-will-burn Egypt gods-of temples-of and Egypt in-land-of that sun

הַדָּבָר אֲשֶׁר הָיָה אֶל־יִרְמְיָהוּ אֶל כָּל־הַיְּהוּדִים הַיֹּשְׁבִים
the-ones-living the-Jews all-of concerning Jeremiah to he-came that the-word (44:1)

בְּאֶרֶץ מִצְרַיִם הַיֹּשְׁבִים בְּמִגְדֹּל וּבְתַחְפַּנְחֵס וּבְנֹף
and-in-Noph and-in-Tahpanhes in-Migdol the-ones-living Egypt in-land-of

וּבְאֶרֶץ פַּתְרוֹס לֵאמֹר׃ כֹּה־ אָמַר יְהוָה צְבָאוֹת אֱלֹהֵי יִשְׂרָאֵל אַתֶּם
you Israel God-of Hosts Yahweh-of he-says this (2) to-say Pathros and-in-land-of

רְאִיתֶם אֵת כָּל־ הָרָעָה אֲשֶׁר הֵבֵאתִי עַל־יְרוּשָׁלִַם וְעַל כָּל־ עָרֵי
towns-of all-of and-on Jerusalem on I-brought that the-disaster all-of *** you-saw

יְהוּדָה וְהִנָּם חָרְבָּה הַיּוֹם הַזֶּה וְאֵין בָּהֶם יוֹשֵׁב׃ מִפְּנֵי
because-of (3) one-living in-them and-not the-this the-day ruin and-see-they! Judah

רָעָתָם אֲשֶׁר עָשׂוּ לְהַכְעִסֵנִי לָלֶכֶת לְקַטֵּר לַעֲבֹד
to-worship to-burn-incense to-go to-provoke-to-anger-me they-did that evil-of-them

לֵאלֹהִים אֲחֵרִים אֲשֶׁר לֹא יְדָעוּם הֵמָּה אַתֶּם וַאֲבֹתֵיכֶם׃ וָאֶשְׁלַח
and-I-sent (4) or-fathers-of-you you they they-knew-them not that other-ones to-gods

אֲלֵיכֶם אֶת־ כָּל־ עֲבָדַי הַנְּבִיאִים הַשְׁכֵּים וְשָׁלֹחַ לֵאמֹר
to-say and-to-send to-begin-early the-prophets servants-of-me all-of *** to-you

אַל־ נָא תַעֲשׂוּ אֵת דְּבַר־ הַתֹּעֵבָה הַזֹּאת אֲשֶׁר שָׂנֵאתִי׃
I-hate that the-this the-detestable-one thing-of *** you-do now! not

וְלֹא שָׁמְעוּ וְלֹא־ הִטּוּ אֶת־ אָזְנָם לָשׁוּב
to-turn ear-of-them *** they-made-attentive or-not they-listened but-not (5)

מֵרָעָתָם לְבִלְתִּי קַטֵּר לֵאלֹהִים אֲחֵרִים׃ וַתִּתַּךְ
so-she-was-poured-out (6) other-ones to-gods to-burn-incense not from-wickedness-of-them

חֲמָתִי וְאַפִּי וַתִּבְעַר בְּעָרֵי יְהוּדָה
Judah against-towns-of and-she-raged and-anger-of-me fierceness-of-me

וּבְחֻצוֹת יְרוּשָׁלִַם וַתִּהְיֶינָה לְחָרְבָּה לִשְׁמָמָה כַּיּוֹם
as-the-day as-desolation as-ruin so-they-became Jerusalem and-against-streets-of

הַזֶּה׃ וְעַתָּה כֹּה־ אָמַר יְהוָה אֱלֹהֵי צְבָאוֹת אֱלֹהֵי יִשְׂרָאֵל לָמָה אַתֶּם
you for-why? Israel God-of Hosts God-of Yahweh he-says this and-now (7) the-this

עֹשִׂים רָעָה גְדוֹלָה אֶל־ נַפְשֹׁתֵכֶם לְהַכְרִית לָכֶם אִישׁ־ וְאִשָּׁה
and-woman man of-you to-cut-off selves-of-you on great disaster ones-bringing

עוֹלֵל וְיוֹנֵק מִתּוֹךְ יְהוּדָה לְבִלְתִּי הוֹתִיר לָכֶם שְׁאֵרִית׃
remnant to-you to-leave not Judah from-midst-of and-one-being-infant child

לְהַכְעִסֵנִי בְּמַעֲשֵׂי יְדֵיכֶם לְקַטֵּר לֵאלֹהִים
to-gods to-burn-incense hands-of-you with-things-made-of to-provoke-to-anger-me (8)

will he wrap Egypt around himself and depart from there unscathed. 13There in the temple of the sun[q] in Egypt he will demolish the sacred pillars and will burn down the temples of the gods of Egypt.' "

*Disaster Because of Idolatry*

44 This word came to Jeremiah concerning all the Jews living in Lower Egypt—in Migdol, Tahpanhes and Memphis[r]—and in Upper Egypt[s]: 2"This is what the LORD Almighty, the God of Israel, says: You saw the great disaster I brought on Jerusalem and on all the towns of Judah. Today they lie deserted and in ruins 3because of the evil they have done. They provoked me to anger by burning incense and by worshiping other gods that neither they nor you nor your fathers ever knew. 4Again and again I sent my servants the prophets, who said, 'Do not do this detestable thing that I hate!' 5But they did not listen or pay attention; they did not turn from their wickedness or stop burning incense to other gods. 6Therefore, my fierce anger was poured out; it raged against the towns of Judah and the streets of Jerusalem and made them the desolate ruins they are today.

7"Now this is what the LORD God Almighty, the God of Israel, says: Why bring such great disaster on yourselves by cutting off from Judah the men and women, the children and infants, and so leave yourselves without a remnant? 8Why provoke me to anger with what your hands have made, burning incense to other gods in

q13 Or *in Heliopolis*
r1 Hebrew *Noph*
s1 Hebrew *in Pathros*

אֲחֵרִים֙ בְּאֶ֣רֶץ מִצְרַ֔יִם אֲשֶׁר־אַתֶּ֥ם בָּאִ֖ים לָג֣וּר שָׁ֑ם לְמַ֙עַן֙ הַכְרִ֣ית
to-destroy   so-that   there   to-live   ones-coming   you   where   Egypt   in-land-of   other-ones

לָכֶ֔ם וּלְמַ֗עַן הֱיֽוֹתְכֶ֤ם לִקְלָלָה֙ וּלְחֶרְפָּ֔ה בְּכֹ֖ל גּוֹיֵ֥י
nations-of   among-all-of   and-as-reproach   as-curse   to-become-you   and-so-that   to-you

הָאָֽרֶץ׃ הַשְׁכַחְתֶּ֞ם אֶת־ רָע֣וֹת אֲבֽוֹתֵיכֶ֗ם וְאֶת־ רָעוֹת֣ ׀
wickednesses-of   and   fathers-of-you   wickednesses-of   ***   you-forgot?   (9)   the-earth

מַלְכֵ֤י יְהוּדָה֙ וְאֵת֙ רָע֣וֹת נָשָׁ֔יו וְאֵת֙ רָעֹֽתֵכֶ֔ם וְאֵ֖ת
and   wickednesses-of-you   and   wives-of-him   wickednesses-of   and   Judah   kings-of

רָעֹ֖ת נְשֵׁיכֶ֑ם אֲשֶׁ֤ר עָשׂוּ֙ בְּאֶ֣רֶץ יְהוּדָ֔ה וּבְחֻצ֖וֹת
and-in-streets-of   Judah   in-land-of   they-committed   that   wives-of-you   wickednesses-of

יְרוּשָׁלָֽ͏ִם׃ לֹ֣א דֻכְּא֔וּ עַ֖ד הַיּ֣וֹם הַזֶּ֑ה וְלֹ֣א
or-not   the-this   the-day   to   they-humbled-themselves   not   (10)   Jerusalem

יָרְא֗וּ וְלֹֽא־ הָלְכ֤וּ בְתוֹרָתִי֙ וּבְחֻקֹּתַ֔י אֲשֶׁר־
that   and-to-decrees-of-me   to-law-of-me   they-followed   or-not   they-showed-reverence

נָתַ֥תִּי לִפְנֵיכֶ֖ם וְלִפְנֵ֣י אֲבֽוֹתֵיכֶֽם׃ לָכֵ֗ן כֹּֽה־ אָמַ֞ר יְהוָ֤ה
Yahweh-of   he-says   this   therefore   (11)   fathers-of-you   and-before   before-you   I-set

צְבָאוֹת֙ אֱלֹהֵ֣י יִשְׂרָאֵ֔ל הִנְנִ֨י שָׂ֥ם פָּנַ֛י בָּכֶ֖ם לְרָעָ֑ה
for-disaster   against-you   faces-of-me   determining   see-I!   Israel   God-of   Hosts

וּלְהַכְרִ֖ית אֶת־ כָּל־ יְהוּדָֽה׃ וְלָקַחְתִּ֞י אֶת־ שְׁאֵרִ֣ית יְהוּדָ֗ה
Judah   remnant-of   ***   and-I-will-take-away   (12)   Judah   all-of   ***   and-to-destroy

אֲשֶׁר־ שָׂ֣מוּ פְנֵיהֶ֗ם לָב֞וֹא אֶ֤רֶץ מִצְרַ֙יִם֙ לָג֣וּר שָׁ֔ם
there   to-settle   Egypt   land-of   to-go   faces-of-them   they-determined   who

וְתַ֙מּוּ֙ כֹ֣ל בְּאֶ֣רֶץ מִצְרַ֔יִם יִפֹּ֕לוּ בַּחֶ֖רֶב בָּרָעָ֣ב
by-the-famine   by-the-sword   they-will-fall   Egypt   in-land-of   all   and-they-will-perish

יִתַּ֜מּוּ מִקָּטֹן֙ וְעַד־ גָּד֔וֹל בַּחֶ֥רֶב וּבָרָעָ֖ב יָמֻ֑תוּ
they-will-die   or-by-the-famine   by-the-sword   greatest   and-to   from-least   they-will-die

וְהָיוּ֙ לְאָלָ֣ה לְשַׁמָּ֔ה וְלִקְלָלָ֖ה וּלְחֶרְפָּֽה׃
and-as-reproach   and-as-condemnation   as-horror   as-curse   and-they-will-become

וּפָקַדְתִּ֗י עַ֤ל הַיּֽוֹשְׁבִים֙ בְּאֶ֣רֶץ מִצְרַ֔יִם כַּאֲשֶׁ֥ר פָּקַ֖דְתִּי עַל־
to   I-punished   just-as   Egypt   in-land-of   the-ones-living   to   and-I-will-punish   (13)

יְרוּשָׁלָ֑͏ִם בַּחֶ֥רֶב בָּרָעָ֖ב וּבַדָּֽבֶר׃ וְלֹ֤א יִהְיֶה֙
he-will-be   and-not   (14)   and-with-the-plague   with-the-famine   with-the-sword   Jerusalem

פָּלִ֣יט וְשָׂרִ֔יד לִשְׁאֵרִ֣ית יְהוּדָ֔ה הַבָּאִ֛ים לָג֥וּר שָׁ֖ם בָּאֶ֣רֶץ
in-land-of   there   to-live   the-ones-going   Judah   of-remnant-of   or-survivor   escapee

מִצְרָ֑יִם וְלָשׁ֣וּב ׀ אֶ֣רֶץ יְהוּדָ֗ה אֲשֶׁר־ הֵ֜מָּה מְנַשְּׂאִ֤ים אֶת־ נַפְשָׁם֙ לָשׁוּב֙
to-return   self-of-them   ***   ones-longing   they   which   Judah   land-of   or-to-return   Egypt

לָשֶׁ֣בֶת שָׁ֔ם כִּ֥י לֹֽא־ יָשׁ֖וּבוּ כִּ֥י אִם־ פְּלֵטִֽים׃ וַיַּעֲנ֣וּ
then-they-answered   (15)   fugitives   only   except   they-will-return   not   for   there   to-live

Egypt, where you have come to
live? You will destroy yourselves
and make yourselves an object of
cursing and reproach among all
the nations on earth. [9]Have you
forgotten the wickedness committed by your fathers and by the
kings and queens of Judah and the
wickedness committed by you
and your wives in the land of
Judah and the streets of Jerusalem? [10]To this day they have not
humbled themselves or shown
reverence, nor have they followed
my law and the decrees I set before you and your fathers.

[11]"Therefore, this is what the
Lord Almighty, the God of Israel,
says: I am determined to bring
disaster on you and to destroy all
Judah. [12]I will take away the remnant of Judah who were determined to go to Egypt to settle
there. They will all perish in
Egypt; they will fall by the sword
or die from famine. From the least
to the greatest, they will die by
sword or famine. They will
become an object of cursing and
horror, of condemnation and reproach. [13]I will punish those who
live in Egypt with the sword, famine and plague, as I punished
Jerusalem. [14]None of the remnant
of Judah who have gone to live in
Egypt will escape or survive to return to the land of Judah, to which
they long to return and live; none
will return except a few fugitives."

אֶת־יִרְמְיָהוּ כָּל־הָאֲנָשִׁים הַיֹּדְעִים כִּי־ מְקַטְּרוֹת נְשֵׁיהֶם
wives-of-them ones-burning-incense that the-ones-knowing the-men all-of Jeremiah ***

לֵאלֹהִים אֲחֵרִים וְכָל־ הַנָּשִׁים הָעֹמְדוֹת קָהָל
assembly the-ones-being-present the-women with-all-of other-ones to-gods

גָּדוֹל וְכָל־ הָעָם הַיֹּשְׁבִים בְּאֶרֶץ־ מִצְרַיִם בְּפַתְרוֹס לֵאמֹר׃
to-say in-Pathros Egypt in-land-of the-ones-living the-people and-all-of large

הַדָּבָר אֲשֶׁר־דִּבַּרְתָּ אֵלֵינוּ בְּשֵׁם יְהוָה אֵינֶנּוּ שֹׁמְעִים אֵלֶיךָ׃
to-you ones-listening not-we Yahweh in-name-of to-us you-spoke that the-message (16)

כִּי עָשֹׂה נַעֲשֶׂה אֶת־ כָּל־ הַדָּבָר ׀ אֲשֶׁר־ יָצָא מִפִּינוּ
from-mouth-of-us he-came that the-thing every-of *** we-will-do to-do indeed (17)

לְקַטֵּר לִמְלֶכֶת הַשָּׁמַיִם וְהַסֵּיךְ־ לָהּ נְסָכִים
drink-offerings to-her and-to-pour-out the-Heavens to-Queen-of to-burn-incense

כַּאֲשֶׁר עָשִׂינוּ אֲנַחְנוּ וַאֲבֹתֵינוּ מְלָכֵינוּ וְשָׂרֵינוּ בְּעָרֵי
in-towns-of and-officials-of-us kings-of-us and-fathers-of-us we we-did just-as

יְהוּדָה וּבְחֻצוֹת יְרוּשָׁלִָם וַנִּשְׂבַּע־ לֶחֶם וַנִּהְיֶה טוֹבִים
ones-well-off and-we-were food and-we-had-plenty Jerusalem and-in-streets-of Judah

וְרָעָה לֹא רָאִינוּ׃ וּמִן־ אָז חָדַלְנוּ לְקַטֵּר לִמְלֶכֶת
to-Queen-of to-burn-incense we-stopped then but-since (18) we-saw not and-harm

הַשָּׁמַיִם וְהַסֵּךְ־ לָהּ נְסָכִים חָסַרְנוּ כֹל
everything we-lacked drink-offerings to-her and-to-pour-out the-Heavens

וּבַחֶרֶב וּבָרָעָב תָּמְנוּ׃ וְכִי־אֲנַחְנוּ מְקַטְּרִים
ones-burning-incense we and-when (19) we-perish and-by-the-famine and-by-the-sword

לִמְלֶכֶת הַשָּׁמַיִם וּלְהַסֵּךְ לָהּ נְסָכִים הֲמִבַּלְעָדֵי
at-apart-from? drink-offerings to-her and-to-pour-out the-Heavens to-Queen-of

אֲנָשֵׁינוּ עָשִׂינוּ לָהּ כַּוָּנִים לְהַעֲצִבָה וְהַסֵּךְ לָהּ
to-her and-to-pour-out to-make-image-of-her cakes for-her we-made husbands-of-us

נְסָכִים׃ וַיֹּאמֶר יִרְמְיָהוּ אֶל־כָּל־ הָעָם עַל־הַגְּבָרִים וְעַל־
and-to the-men to the-people all-of to Jeremiah then-he-said (20) drink-offerings

הַנָּשִׁים וְעַל־ כָּל־ הָעָם הָעֹנִים אֹתוֹ דָּבָר לֵאמֹר׃ הֲלוֹא אֶת־
*** not? (21) to-say word him the-ones-answering the-people all-of and-to the-women

הַקִּטֵּר אֲשֶׁר קִטַּרְתֶּם בְּעָרֵי יְהוּדָה וּבְחֻצוֹת יְרוּשָׁלִַם אַתֶּם
you Jerusalem and-in-streets-of Judah in-towns-of you-burned that the-incense

וַאֲבוֹתֵיכֶם מַלְכֵיכֶם וְשָׂרֵיכֶם וְעַם הָאָרֶץ אֹתָם
them the-land and-people-of and-officials-of-you kings-of-you and-fathers-of-you

זָכַר יְהוָה וַתַּעֲלֶה עַל־ לִבּוֹ׃ וְלֹא־ יוּכַל
he-could when-not (22) mind-of-him into and-she-entered Yahweh he-remembered

יְהוָה עוֹד לָשֵׂאת מִפְּנֵי רֹעַ מַעַלְלֵיכֶם מִפְּנֵי
because-of actions-of-you wickedness-of because-of to-endure longer Yahweh

[15]Then all the men who knew that their wives were burning incense to other gods, along with all the women who were present—a large assembly—and all the people living in Lower and Upper Egypt,[f] said to Jeremiah, [16]"We will not listen to the message you have spoken to us in the name of the LORD! [17]We will certainly do everything we said we would: We will burn incense to the Queen of Heaven and will pour out drink offerings to her just as we and our fathers, our kings and our officials did in the towns of Judah and in the streets of Jerusalem. At that time we had plenty of food and were well off and suffered no harm. [18]But ever since we stopped burning incense to the Queen of Heaven and pouring out drink offerings to her, we have had nothing and have been perishing by sword and famine."

[19]The women added, "When we burned incense to the Queen of Heaven and poured out drink offerings to her, did not our husbands know that we were making cakes like her image and pouring out drink offerings to her?"

[20]Then Jeremiah said to all the people, both men and women, who were answering him, [21]"Did not the LORD remember and think about the incense burned in the towns of Judah and the streets of Jerusalem by you and your fathers, your kings and your officials and the people of the land? [22]When the LORD could no longer endure your wicked actions and

[f]15 Hebrew *in Egypt and Pathros*

הַתּוֹעֵבֹת אֲשֶׁר עֲשִׂיתֶם וַתְּהִי אַרְצְכֶם לְחָרְבָּה
as-desolation land-of-you then-she-became you-did that the-detestable-things

וּלְשַׁמָּה וְלִקְלָלָה מֵאֵין יוֹשֵׁב כְּהַיּוֹם הַזֶּה׃ מִפְּנֵי
because-of (23) the-this as-the-day one-inhabiting with-no and-as-curse and-as-waste

אֲשֶׁר קִטַּרְתֶּם וַאֲשֶׁר חֲטָאתֶם לַיהוָה וְלֹא שְׁמַעְתֶּם
you-obeyed and-not against-Yahweh you-sinned and-that you-burned-incense that

בְּקוֹל יְהוָה וּבְתֹרָתוֹ וּבְחֻקֹּתָיו וּבְעֵדְוֹתָיו
or-to-stipulations-of-him or-to-decrees-of-him or-to-law-of-him Yahweh to-voice-of

לֹא הֲלַכְתֶּם עַל־כֵּן קָרָאת אֶתְכֶם הָרָעָה הַזֹּאת כַּיּוֹם
as-the-day the-this the-disaster you she-came-upon this for you-followed not

הַזֶּה׃ וַיֹּאמֶר יִרְמְיָהוּ אֶל־כָּל־הָעָם וְאֶל כָּל־הַנָּשִׁים
the-women all-of and-to the-people all-of to Jeremiah then-he-said (24) the-this

שִׁמְעוּ דְּבַר־יְהוָה כָּל־יְהוּדָה אֲשֶׁר בְּאֶרֶץ מִצְרָיִם׃ כֹּה־אָמַר יְהוָה־
Yahweh-of he-says this (25) Egypt in-land-of who Judah all-of Yahweh word-of hear!

צְבָאוֹת אֱלֹהֵי יִשְׂרָאֵל לֵאמֹר אַתֶּם וּנְשֵׁיכֶם וַתְּדַבֵּרְנָה בְּפִיכֶם
by-mouth-of-you and-you-promised and-wives-of-you you to-say Israel God-of Hosts

וּבִידֵיכֶם מִלֵּאתֶם ׀ לֵאמֹר עָשֹׂה נַעֲשֶׂה אֶת־נְדָרֵינוּ
vows-of-you *** we-will-carry-out to-carry-out to-say you-showed and-by-hands-of-you

אֲשֶׁר נָדַרְנוּ לְקַטֵּר לִמְלֶכֶת הַשָּׁמַיִם וּלְהַסֵּךְ לָהּ
to-her and-to-pour-out the-Heavens to-Queen-of to-burn-incense we-vowed that

נְסָכִים הָקֵים תָּקִימְנָה אֶת־נִדְרֵיכֶם וְעָשֹׂה תַעֲשֶׂינָה אֶת־נִדְרֵיכֶם׃
vows-of-us *** you-keep and-to-keep vows-of-you *** you-do to-do drink-offerings

לָכֵן שִׁמְעוּ דְבַר־יְהוָה כָּל־יְהוּדָה הַיֹּשְׁבִים בְּאֶרֶץ מִצְרָיִם הִנְנִי
see-I! Egypt in-land-of the-ones-living Judah all-of Yahweh word-of hear! but (26)

נִשְׁבַּעְתִּי בִּשְׁמִי הַגָּדוֹל אָמַר יְהוָה אִם־יִהְיֶה עוֹד שְׁמִי
name-of-me again he-will-be not Yahweh he-says the-great by-name-of-me I-swear

נִקְרָא ׀ בְּפִי ׀ כָּל־אִישׁ יְהוּדָה אֹמֵר חַי־אֲדֹנָי יְהוִה
Yahweh Sovereign alive swearing Judah person-of any-of by-mouth-of being-invoked

בְּכָל־אֶרֶץ מִצְרָיִם׃ הִנְנִי שֹׁקֵד עֲלֵיהֶם לְרָעָה וְלֹא לְטוֹבָה
for-good and-not for-harm over-them watching see-I! (27) Egypt land-of in-any-of

וְתַמּוּ כָל־אִישׁ יְהוּדָה אֲשֶׁר בְּאֶרֶץ־מִצְרַיִם בַּחֶרֶב
by-the-sword Egypt in-land-of who Judah person-of every-of and-they-will-perish

וּבָרָעָב עַד־כְּלוֹתָם׃ וּפְלִיטֵי חֶרֶב
sword and-escapees-of (28) to-be-destroyed-them until and-by-the-famine

יְשֻׁבוּן מִן־אֶרֶץ מִצְרַיִם אֶרֶץ יְהוּדָה מְתֵי מִסְפָּר וְיָדְעוּ
then-they-will-know number men-of Judah land-of Egypt land-of from they-will-return

כָּל־שְׁאֵרִית יְהוּדָה הַבָּאִים לְאֶרֶץ־מִצְרַיִם לָגוּר שָׁם דְּבַר־
word-of there to-live Egypt to-land-of the-ones-coming Judah remnant-of whole-of

the detestable things you did,
your land became an object of
cursing and a desolate waste without inhabitants, as it is today. 23Be-
cause you have burned incense
and have sinned against the LORD
and have not obeyed him or followed his law or his decrees or his
stipulations, this disaster has
come upon you, as you now see."
24Then Jeremiah said to all the
people, including the women,
"Hear the word of the LORD, all
you people of Judah in Egypt.
25This is what the LORD Almighty,
the God of Israel, says: You and
your wives have shown by your
actions what you promised when
you said, 'We will certainly carry
out the vows we made to burn incense and pour out drink offerings
to the Queen of Heaven.'

"Go ahead then, do what you
promised! Keep your vows! 26But
hear the word of the LORD, all Jews
living in Egypt: 'I swear by my
great name,' says the LORD, 'that
no one from Judah living anywhere in Egypt will ever again invoke my name or swear, "As surely as the Sovereign LORD lives."
27For I am watching over them for
harm, not for good; the Jews in
Egypt will perish by sword and
famine until they are all destroyed. 28Those who escape the
sword and return to the land of
Judah from Egypt will be very few.
Then the whole remnant of Judah
who came to live in Egypt will
know whose word will stand—

מִי יָקוּם מִמֶּנִּי וּמֵהֶם׃ וְזֹאת־לָכֶם הָאוֹת נְאֻם־
declaration-of the-sign to-you and-this (29) or-of-them of-me he-will-stand who?

יְהוָה כִּי־פֹקֵד אֲנִי עֲלֵיכֶם בַּמָּקוֹם הַזֶּה לְמַעַן תֵּדְעוּ כִּי
that you-will-know so-that the-this in-the-place to-you I punishing that Yahweh

קוֹם יָקוּמוּ דְבָרַי עֲלֵיכֶם לְרָעָה׃ כֹּה ׀ אָמַר יְהוָה
Yahweh he-says this (30) of-harm against-you threats-of-me they-will-stand to-stand

הִנְנִי נֹתֵן אֶת־פַּרְעֹה חָפְרַע מֶלֶךְ־מִצְרַיִם בְּיַד אֹיְבָיו
ones-being-enemies-of-him into-hand-of Egypt king-of Hophra Pharaoh *** giving see-I!

וּבְיַד מְבַקְשֵׁי נַפְשׁוֹ כַּאֲשֶׁר נָתַתִּי אֶת־צִדְקִיָּהוּ מֶלֶךְ־
king-of Zedekiah *** I-gave just-as life-of-him ones-seeking-of even-into-hand-of

יְהוּדָה בְּיַד נְבוּכַדְרֶאצַּר מֶלֶךְ־בָּבֶל אֹיְבוֹ
one-being-enemy-of-him Babylon king-of Nebuchadrezzar into-hand-of Judah

וּמְבַקֵּשׁ נַפְשׁוֹ׃ הַדָּבָר אֲשֶׁר דִּבֶּר יִרְמְיָהוּ הַנָּבִיא
the-prophet Jeremiah he-told that the-word (45:1) life-of-him even-one-seeking-of

אֶל־בָּרוּךְ בֶּן־נֵרִיָּה בְּכָתְבוֹ אֶת־הַדְּבָרִים הָאֵלֶּה עַל־סֵפֶר
scroll on the-these the-words *** after-to-write-him Neriah son-of Baruch to

מִפִּי יִרְמְיָהוּ בַּשָּׁנָה הָרְבִעִית לִיהוֹיָקִים בֶּן־יֹאשִׁיָּהוּ מֶלֶךְ
king-of Josiah son-of of-Jehoiakim the-fourth in-the-year Jeremiah at-dictation-of

יְהוּדָה לֵאמֹר׃ כֹּה־אָמַר יְהוָה אֱלֹהֵי יִשְׂרָאֵל עָלֶיךָ בָּרוּךְ׃ אָמַרְתָּ
you-said (3) Baruch to-you Israel God-of Yahweh he-says this (2) to-say Judah

אוֹי־נָא לִי כִּי־יָסַף יְהוָה יָגוֹן עַל־מַכְאֹבִי יָגַעְתִּי
I-am-worn-out pain-of-me to sorrow Yahweh he-added indeed to-me now! woe!

בְּאַנְחָתִי וּמְנוּחָה לֹא מָצָאתִי׃ כֹּה ׀ תֹּאמַר אֵלָיו כֹּה אָמַר יְהוָה
Yahweh he-says this to-him you-say this (4) I-find not and-rest with-groaning-of-me

הִנֵּה אֲשֶׁר־בָּנִיתִי אֲנִי הֹרֵס וְאֵת אֲשֶׁר־נָטַעְתִּי אֲנִי נֹתֵשׁ וְאֶת־כָּל־
all-of indeed uprooting I I-planted what and overthrowing I I-built what see!

הָאָרֶץ הִיא׃ וְאַתָּה תְּבַקֶּשׁ־לְךָ גְדֹלוֹת אַל־תְּבַקֵּשׁ כִּי
for you-seek not great-things for-you should-you-seek and-you (5) this the-land

הִנְנִי מֵבִיא רָעָה עַל־כָּל־בָּשָׂר נְאֻם־יְהוָה וְנָתַתִּי
but-I-will-give Yahweh declaration-of people all-of on disaster bringing see-I!

לְךָ אֶת־נַפְשְׁךָ לְשָׁלָל עַל כָּל־הַמְּקֹמוֹת אֲשֶׁר תֵּלֶךְ־שָׁם׃
there you-go where the-places all-of in as-plunder life-of-you *** to-you

אֲשֶׁר הָיָה דְבַר־יְהוָה אֶל־יִרְמְיָהוּ הַנָּבִיא עַל־הַגּוֹיִם׃
the-nations concerning the-prophet Jeremiah to Yahweh word-of he-came that (46:1)

לְמִצְרַיִם עַל־חֵיל פַּרְעֹה נְכוֹ מֶלֶךְ מִצְרַיִם אֲשֶׁר־הָיָה עַל־
to he-went which Egypt king-of Neco Pharaoh army-of against concerning-Egypt (2)

נְהַר־פְּרָת בְּכַרְכְּמִשׁ אֲשֶׁר הִכָּה נְבוּכַדְרֶאצַּר מֶלֶךְ בָּבֶל
Babylon king-of Nebuchadrezzar he-defeated which at-Carchemish Euphrates River-of

mine or theirs.

29 " 'This will be the sign to you that I will punish you in this place,' declares the LORD, 'so that you will know that my threats of harm against you will surely stand.' 30 This is what the LORD says: 'I am going to hand Pharaoh Hophra king of Egypt over to his enemies who seek his life, just as I handed Zedekiah king of Judah over to Nebuchadnezzar king of Babylon, the enemy who was seeking his life.' "

*A Message to Baruch*

45 This is what Jeremiah the prophet told Baruch son of Neriah in the fourth year of Jehoiakim son of Josiah king of Judah, after Baruch had written on a scroll the words Jeremiah was then dictating: 2 "This is what the LORD, the God of Israel, says to you, Baruch: 3 You said, 'Woe to me! The LORD has added sorrow to my pain; I am worn out with groaning and find no rest.' "

4 ⌞The LORD said,⌟ "Say this to him: 'This is what the LORD says: I will overthrow what I have built and uproot what I have planted, throughout the land. 5 Should you then seek great things for yourself? Seek them not. For I will bring disaster on all people, declares the LORD, but wherever you go I will let you escape with your life.' "

*A Message About Egypt*

46 This is the word of the LORD that came to Jeremiah the prophet concerning the nations:

2 Concerning Egypt:

This is the message against the army of Pharaoh Neco king of Egypt, which was defeated at Carchemish on the Euphrates River

בִּשְׁנַת הָרְבִיעִית לִיהוֹיָקִים בֶּן־ יֹאשִׁיָּהוּ מֶלֶךְ יְהוּדָה׃ עִרְכוּ
prepare! (3) Judah king-of Josiah son-of of-Jehoiakim the-fourth in-year-of

מָגֵן וְצִנָּה וּגְשׁוּ לַמִּלְחָמָה׃ אִסְרוּ הַסּוּסִים
the-horses harness! (4) for-the-battle and-march-out! and-large-shield small-shield

וַעֲלוּ הַפָּרָשִׁים וְהִתְיַצְּבוּ בְּכוֹבָעִים מִרְקוּ הָרְמָחִים
the-spears polish! in-helmets and-take-positions! the-steeds and-mount!

לִבְשׁוּ הַסִּרְיֹנֹת׃ מַדּוּעַ רָאִיתִי הֵמָּה חַתִּים נְסֹגִים אָחוֹר
back ones-retreating terrified-ones they I-see what? (5) the-armors put-on!

וְגִבּוֹרֵיהֶם יֻכַּתּוּ וּמָנוֹס נָסוּ וְלֹא הִפְנוּ
they-look-back and-not they-flee and-flight they-are-defeated and-warriors-of-them

מָגוֹר מִסָּבִיב נְאֻם־ יְהוָה׃ אַל־ יָנוּס הַקַּל וְאַל־
or-not the-swift he-can-flee not (6) Yahweh declaration-of on-every-side terror

יִמָּלֵט הַגִּבּוֹר צָפוֹנָה עַל־ יַד־ נְהַר־ פְּרָת כָּשְׁלוּ
they-stumble Euphrates River-of side-of by in-north the-strong he-can-escape

וְנָפָלוּ׃ מִי־ זֶה כַּיְאֹר יַעֲלֶה כַּנְּהָרוֹת יִתְגָּעֲשׁוּ
they-surge like-the-rivers he-rises like-the-Nile this who? (7) and-they-fall

מֵימָיו׃ מִצְרַיִם כַּיְאֹר יַעֲלֶה וְכַנְּהָרוֹת יִתְגֹּעֲשׁוּ
they-surge and-like-the-rivers he-rises like-the-Nile Egypt (8) waters-of-him

מַיִם וַיֹּאמֶר אַעֲלֶה אֲכַסֶּה־ אֶרֶץ אֹבִידָה עִיר
city I-will-destroy earth and-I-will-cover I-will-rise and-he-says waters

וְיֹשְׁבֵי בָהּ׃ עֲלוּ הַסּוּסִים וְהִתְהֹלְלוּ
and-drive-furiously! the-horses charge! (9) in-her and-ones-being-people-of

הָרֶכֶב וְיֵצְאוּ הַגִּבּוֹרִים כּוּשׁ וּפוּט תֹּפְשֵׂי
ones-carrying-of and-Put Cush the-warriors and-let-them-march-on the-charioteer

מָגֵן וְלוּדִים תֹּפְשֵׂי דֹּרְכֵי קָשֶׁת׃ וְהַיּוֹם הַהוּא
the-that but-the-day (10) bow ones-drawing-of ones-carrying-of and-Lydians shield

לַאדֹנָי יְהוִה צְבָאוֹת יוֹם נְקָמָה לְהִנָּקֵם מִצָּרָיו
on-foes-of-him to-get-vengeance vengeance day-of Hosts Yahweh-of to-Lord

וְאָכְלָה חֶרֶב וְשָׂבְעָה וְרָוְתָה
till-she-will-quench-thirst till-she-will-be-satisfied sword and-she-will-devour

מִדָּמָם כִּי זֶבַח לַאדֹנָי יְהוִה צְבָאוֹת בְּאֶרֶץ צָפוֹן אֶל־
by north in-land-of Hosts Yahweh-of to-Lord sacrifice for with-blood-of-them

נְהַר־ פְּרָת׃ עֲלִי גִלְעָד וּקְחִי צֳרִי בְּתוּלַת בַּת־ מִצְרָיִם
Egypt Daughter-of Virgin-of balm and-get! Gilead go-up! (11) Euphrates River-of

לַשָּׁוְא הִרְבֵּיתִי רְפֻאוֹת תְּעָלָה אֵין לָךְ׃ שָׁמְעוּ גוֹיִם
nations they-will-hear (12) for-you not healing remedies you-multiply in-the-vain

קְלוֹנֵךְ וְצִוְחָתֵךְ מָלְאָה הָאָרֶץ כִּי־ גִבּוֹר בְּגִבּוֹר
over-warrior warrior indeed the-earth she-will-fill and-cry-of-you shame-of-you

by Nebuchadnezzar king of Babylon in the fourth year of Jehoiakim son of Josiah king of Judah:

3 "Prepare your shields, both
large and small,
and march out for battle!
4 Harness the horses,
mount the steeds!
Take your positions
with helmets on!
Polish your spears,
put on your armor!
5 What do I see?
They are terrified,
they are retreating,
their warriors are defeated.
They flee in haste
without looking back,
and there is terror on every side,"
declares the LORD.
6 "The swift cannot flee
nor the strong escape.
In the north by the River Euphrates
they stumble and fall.
7 "Who is this that rises like the Nile,
like rivers of surging waters?
8 Egypt rises like the Nile,
like rivers of surging waters.
She says, 'I will rise and cover the earth;
I will destroy cities and their people.'
9 Charge, O horses!
Drive furiously, O charioteers!
March on, O warriors—
men of Cush[a] and Put who carry shields,
men of Lydia who draw the bow.
10 But that day belongs to the Lord, the LORD Almighty—
a day of vengeance, for vengeance on his foes.
The sword will devour till it is satisfied,
till it has quenched its thirst with blood.
For the Lord, the LORD Almighty, will offer sacrifice
in the land of the north by the River Euphrates.

11 "Go up to Gilead and get balm,
O Virgin Daughter of Egypt.
But you multiply remedies in vain;
there is no healing for you.
12 The nations will hear of your shame;
your cries will fill the earth.
One warrior will stumble over another;

a9 That is, the upper Nile region

°11 ק הרבית

כָּשָׁלוּ יַחְדָּיו נָפְלוּ שְׁנֵיהֶם׃ הַדָּבָר אֲשֶׁר

that the-message (13) both-of-them they-will-fall together they-will-stumble

דִּבֶּר יְהוָה אֶל־יִרְמְיָהוּ הַנָּבִיא לָבוֹא נְבוּכַדְרֶאצַּר מֶלֶךְ בָּבֶל

Babylon king-of Nebuchadrezzar to-come the-prophet Jeremiah to Yahweh he-spoke

לְהַכּוֹת אֶת־אֶרֶץ מִצְרָיִם׃ הַגִּידוּ בְמִצְרַיִם וְהַשְׁמִיעוּ בְמִגְדּוֹל

in-Migdol and-proclaim! in-Egypt announce! (14) Egypt land-of *** to-attack

וְהַשְׁמִיעוּ בְנֹף וּבְתַחְפַּנְחֵס אִמְרוּ הִתְיַצֵּב וְהָכֵן

and-get-ready! take-position! say! and-in-Tahpanhes in-Noph also-proclaim!

לָךְ כִּי־אָכְלָה חֶרֶב סְבִיבֶיךָ׃ מַדּוּעַ נִסְחַף

he-will-be-laid-low why? (15) ones-around-you sword she-devours for for-you

אַבִּירֶיךָ לֹא עָמַד כִּי יְהוָה הֲדָפוֹ׃ הִרְבָּה

he-repeats (16) he-will-push-down-him Yahweh for he-can-stand not warriors-of-you

כּוֹשֵׁל גַּם־נָפַל אִישׁ אֶל־רֵעֵהוּ וַיֹּאמְרוּ קוּמָה ׀

get-up! and-they-will-say other-of-him over each he-falls also stumbling

וְנָשֻׁבָה אֶל־עַמֵּנוּ וְאֶל־אֶרֶץ מוֹלַדְתֵּנוּ מִפְּנֵי

from-before native-one-of-us land-of and-to people-of-us to and-let-us-go-back

חֶרֶב הַיּוֹנָה׃ קָרְאוּ שָׁם פַּרְעֹה מֶלֶךְ־מִצְרַיִם

Egypt king-of Pharaoh there they-will-exclaim (17) the-one-oppressing sword-of

שָׁאוֹן הֶעֱבִיר הַמּוֹעֵד׃ חַי־אָנִי נְאֻם־הַמֶּלֶךְ

the-King declaration-of I alive (18) the-opportunity he-missed loud-noise

יְהוָה צְבָאוֹת שְׁמוֹ כִּי כְּתָבוֹר בֶּהָרִים וּכְכַרְמֶל

and-like-Carmel among-the-mountains like-Tabor indeed name-of-him Hosts Yahweh-of

בַּיָּם יָבוֹא׃ כְּלֵי גוֹלָה עֲשִׂי לָךְ יוֹשֶׁבֶת

one-living-of for-you pack! exile belongings-of (19) he-will-come by-the-sea

בַּת־מִצְרָיִם כִּי־נֹף לְשַׁמָּה תִהְיֶה וְנִצְּתָה מֵאֵין

with-no and-she-will-be-ruined she-will-be as-waste Noph for Egypt Daughter-of

יוֹשֵׁב׃ עֶגְלָה יְפֵה־פִיָּה מִצְרָיִם קֶרֶץ מִצָּפוֹן בָּא בָא׃*

*he-comes he-comes from-north gadfly Egypt beautiful heifer (20) one-inhabiting

גַּם־שְׂכִרֶיהָ בְקִרְבָּהּ כְּעֶגְלֵי מַרְבֵּק כִּי־גַם־

too indeed stall like-calves-of in-rank-of-her mercenaries-of-her also (21)

הֵמָּה הִפְנוּ נָסוּ יַחְדָּיו לֹא עָמָדוּ כִּי יוֹם

day-of for they-will-stand not together they-will-flee they-will-turn they

אֵידָם בָּא עֲלֵיהֶם עֵת פְּקֻדָּתָם׃ קוֹלָהּ

sound-of-her (22) punishment-of-them time-of upon-them he-comes disaster-of-them

כַּנָּחָשׁ יֵלֵךְ כִּי־בְחַיִל יֵלֵכוּ וּבְקַרְדֻּמּוֹת בָּאוּ

they-will-come and-with-axes they-advance in-force as he-flees like-the-serpent

לָהּ כְּחֹטְבֵי עֵצִים׃ כָּרְתוּ יַעְרָהּ

forest-of-her they-will-chop-down (23) trees like-men-cutting-down-of against-her

---

both will fall down
together."

13 This is the message the LORD spoke to Jeremiah the prophet about the coming of Nebuchadnezzar king of Babylon to attack Egypt:

14 "Announce this in Egypt, and
proclaim it in Migdol;
proclaim it also in
Memphis[p] and
Tahpanhes:
'Take your positions and get
ready,
for the sword devours those
around you.'
15 Why will your warriors be laid
low?
They cannot stand, for the
LORD will push them
down.
16 They will stumble repeatedly;
they will fall over each
other.
They will say, 'Get up, let us
go back
to our own people and our
native lands,
away from the sword of the
oppressor.'
17 There they will exclaim,
'Pharaoh king of Egypt is
only a loud noise;
he has missed his
opportunity.'

18 "As surely as I live," declares
the King,
whose name is the LORD
Almighty,
"one will come who is like
Tabor among the
mountains,
like Carmel by the sea.
19 Pack your belongings for exile,
you who live in Egypt,
for Memphis will be laid waste
and lie in ruins without
inhabitant.

20 "Egypt is a beautiful heifer,
but a gadfly is coming
against her from the north.
21 The mercenaries in her ranks
are like fattened calves.
They too will turn and flee
together,
they will not stand their
ground,
for the day of disaster is
coming upon them,
the time for them to be
punished.
22 Egypt will hiss like a fleeing
serpent
as the enemy advances in
force;
they will come against her
with axes,
like men who cut down
trees.
23 They will chop down her
forest,"

p14 Hebrew *Noph*; also in verse 19

*20 The NIV, with many ancient versions, reads *be* for *aleph* (בָּה), *against-her*.

נְאֻם־ יְהוָה כִּי לֹא יֵחָקֵר כִּי רַבּוּ
they-are-numerous indeed he-can-be-searched-out not though Yahweh declaration-of

מֵאַרְבֶּה וְאֵין לָהֶם מִסְפָּר׃ הֹבִישָׁה בַּת־ מִצְרָיִם
Egypt Daughter-of she-will-be-shamed (24) count to-them that-not more-than-locust

נִתְּנָה בְּיַד עַם־ צָפוֹן׃ אָמַר יְהוָה צְבָאוֹת אֱלֹהֵי
God-of Hosts Yahweh-of he-says (25) north people-of into-hand-of she-will-be-given

יִשְׂרָאֵל הִנְנִי פוֹקֵד אֶל־אָמוֹן מִנֹּא וְעַל־ פַּרְעֹה וְעַל־מִצְרַיִם וְעַל־
and-on Egypt and-on Pharaoh and-on of-No Amon on punishing see-I! Israel

אֱלֹהֶיהָ וְעַל־ מְלָכֶיהָ וְעַל־ פַּרְעֹה וְעַל הַבֹּטְחִים בּוֹ׃
on-him the-ones-relying and-on Pharaoh and-on kings-of-her and-on gods-of-her

וּנְתַתִּים בְּיַד מְבַקְשֵׁי נַפְשָׁם וּבְיַד
and-into-hand-of life-of-them ones-seeking-of into-hand-of and-I-will-give-them (26)

נְבוּכַדְרֶאצַּר מֶלֶךְ־ בָּבֶל וּבְיַד־ עֲבָדָיו וְאַחֲרֵי־ כֵן
this however-after officers-of-him and-into-hand-of Babylon king-of Nebuchadrezzar

תִּשְׁכֹּן כִּימֵי־ קֶדֶם נְאֻם־ יְהוָה׃ וְאַתָּה אַל־
not but-you (27) Yahweh declaration-of past as-days-of she-will-be-inhabited

תִּירָא עַבְדִּי יַעֲקֹב וְאַל־ תֵּחַת יִשְׂרָאֵל כִּי הִנְנִי
see-I! surely Israel you-be-dismayed and-not Jacob servant-of-me you-fear

מוֹשִׁעֲךָ מֵרָחוֹק וְאֶת־ זַרְעֲךָ מֵאֶרֶץ שִׁבְיָם
exile-of-them from-land-of descendant-of-you and from-distant-place saving-you

וְשָׁב יַעֲקוֹב וְשָׁקַט וְשַׁאֲנַן וְאֵין
and-not and-he-will-have-security and-he-will-have-peace Jacob and-he-will-do-again

מַחֲרִיד׃ אַתָּה אַל־ תִּירָא עַבְדִּי יַעֲקֹב נְאֻם־ יְהוָה
Yahweh declaration-of Jacob servant-of-me you-fear not you (28) one-making-afraid

כִּי אִתְּךָ אָנִי כִּי אֶעֱשֶׂה כָלָה בְּכָל־ הַגּוֹיִם ׀ אֲשֶׁר
which the-nations of-all-of complete-destruction I-make though I with-you for

הִדַּחְתִּיךָ שָׁמָּה וְאֹתְךָ לֹא־ אֶעֱשֶׂה כָלָה
complete-destruction I-will-make not but-you to-there I-scatter-you

וְיִסַּרְתִּיךָ לַמִּשְׁפָּט וְנַקֵּה לֹא
not and-to-let-go-unpunished with-the-justice only-I-will-discipline-you

אֲנַקֶּךָּ׃ אֲשֶׁר הָיָה דְבַר־ יְהוָה אֶל־ יִרְמְיָהוּ
Jeremiah to Yahweh word-of he-came that (47:1) I-will-let-go-unpunished-you

הַנָּבִיא אֶל־ פְּלִשְׁתִּים בְּטֶרֶם יַכֶּה פַּרְעֹה אֶת־עַזָּה׃ כֹּה ׀
this (2) Gaza *** Pharaoh he-attacked at-before Philistines concerning the-prophet

אָמַר יְהוָה הִנֵּה־ מַיִם עֹלִים מִצָּפוֹן וְהָיוּ לְנַחַל
as-torrent and-they-will-become in-north ones-rising waters see! Yahweh he-says

שׁוֹטֵף וְיִשְׁטְפוּ אֶרֶץ וּמְלוֹאָהּ עִיר וְיֹשְׁבֵי
and-ones-living-of town and-everything-in-her land and-they-will-overflow overflowing

declares the LORD,
"dense though it be.
They are more numerous than
locusts,
they cannot be counted.
24 The Daughter of Egypt will be
put to shame,
handed over to the people of
the north."

25 The LORD Almighty, the God of Israel, says: "I am about to bring punishment on Amon god of Thebes,[w] on Pharaoh, on Egypt and her gods and her kings, and on those who rely on Pharaoh.
26 I will hand them over to those who seek their lives, to Nebuchadnezzar king of Babylon and his officers. Later, however, Egypt will be inhabited as in times past," declares the LORD.

27 "Do not fear, O Jacob my
servant;
do not be dismayed, O
Israel.
I will surely save you out of a
distant place,
your descendants from the
land of their exile.
Jacob will again have peace
and security,
and no one will make him
afraid.
28 Do not fear, O Jacob my
servant,
for I am with you," declares
the LORD.
"Though I completely destroy
all the nations
among which I scatter you,
I will not completely destroy
you.
I will discipline you but only
with justice;
I will not let you go entirely
unpunished."

*A Message About the Philistines*

47 This is the word of the LORD that came to Jeremiah the prophet concerning the Philistines before Pharaoh attacked Gaza:

2 This is what the LORD says:

"See how the waters are rising
in the north;
they will become an
overflowing torrent.
They will overflow the land
and everything in it,
the towns and those who
live in them.

[w]25 Hebrew *No*

בָּהּ וְזָעֲקוּ הָאָדָם וְהֵילִל כֹּל יוֹשֵׁב
one-dwelling-of all-of and-he-will-wail the-people and-they-will-cry-out in-her

הָאָרֶץ׃ מִקּוֹל שַׁעֲטַת פַּרְסוֹת אַבִּירָיו מֵרַעַשׁ
at-noise mighty-ones-of-him hoofs-of galloping-of at-sound-of (3) the-land

לְרִכְבּוֹ הֲמוֹן גַּלְגִּלָּיו לֹא־ הִפְנוּ אָבוֹת אֶל־ בָּנִים
children to fathers they-will-turn not wheels-of-him rumble-of of-chariot-of-him

מֵרִפְיוֹן יָדָיִם׃ עַל־ הַיּוֹם הַבָּא לִשְׁדוֹד אֶת־ כָּל־
all-of *** to-destroy the-one-coming the-day for (4) hands from-limpness-of

פְּלִשְׁתִּים לְהַכְרִית לְצֹר וּלְצִידוֹן כֹּל שָׂרִיד עֹזֵר כִּי־
indeed one-helping survivor all-of and-of-Sidon of-Tyre to-cut-off Philistines

שֹׁדֵד יְהוָה אֶת־פְּלִשְׁתִּים שְׁאֵרִית אִי כַפְתּוֹר׃ בָּאָה
she-will-come (5) Caphtor coast-of remnant-of Philistines *** Yahweh one-destroying

קָרְחָה אֶל־עַזָּה נִדְמְתָה אַשְׁקְלוֹן שְׁאֵרִית עִמְקָם עַד־
until plain-of-them remnant-of Ashkelon she-will-be-silenced Gaza to shaved-head

מָתַי תִּתְגּוֹדָדִי׃ הוֹי חֶרֶב לַיהוָה עַד־ אָנָה לֹא
not at-where? until of-Yahweh sword ah! (6) will-you-cut-yourself when?

תִשְׁקֹטִי הֵאָסְפִי אֶל*־ תַּעְרֵךְ הֵרָגְעִי וָדֹמִּי׃ אֵיךְ תִּשְׁקֹטִי
can-you-rest how? (7) and-be-still! cease! scabbard-of-you to return! will-you-rest

וַיהוָה צִוָּה־ לָהּ אֶל־ אַשְׁקְלוֹן וְאֶל־ חוֹף הַיָּם שָׁם
there the-sea coast-of and-against Ashkelon against to-her he-commanded when-Yahweh

יְעָדָהּ׃ לְמוֹאָב כֹּה־ אָמַר יְהוָה צְבָאוֹת אֱלֹהֵי יִשְׂרָאֵל
Israel God-of Hosts Yahweh-of he-says this concerning-Moab (48:1) he-ordered-her

הוֹי אֶל־ נְבוֹ כִּי שֻׁדָּדָה הֹבִישָׁה נִלְכְּדָה
she-will-be-captured she-will-be-disgraced she-will-be-ruined for Nebo to woe!

קִרְיָתָיִם הֹבִישָׁה הַמִּשְׂגָּב וָחָתָּה׃ אֵין
no (2) and-she-will-be-shattered the-stronghold she-will-be-disgraced Kiriathaim

עוֹד תְּהִלַּת מוֹאָב בְּחֶשְׁבּוֹן חָשְׁבוּ עָלֶיהָ רָעָה לְכוּ
come! downfall against-her they-will-plot in-Heshbon Moab praise-of more

וְנַכְרִיתֶנָּה מִגּוֹי גַּם־ מַדְמֵן תִּדֹּמִּי אַחֲרַיִךְ
after-you you-will-be-silenced Madmen too from-nation and-let-us-put-end-to-her

תֵּלֶךְ חָרֶב׃ קוֹל צְעָקָה מֵחֹרוֹנַיִם שֹׁד וָשֶׁבֶר גָּדוֹל׃
great and-destruction havoc from-Horonaim cry sound-of (3) sword she-will-pursue

נִשְׁבְּרָה מוֹאָב הִשְׁמִיעוּ זְּעָקָה צְעוֹרֶיהָ׃ כִּי
indeed (5) little-ones-of-her cry they-will-make-heard Moab she-will-be-broken (4)

מַעֲלֵה הַלֻּחוֹת בִּבְכִי יַעֲלֶה־ בֶּכִי כִּי בְּמוֹרַד
on-going-down-of indeed weeping he-goes-up with-weeping the-Luhith one-going-up-of

חוֹרֹנַיִם צָרֵי צַעֲקַת־ שֶׁבֶר שָׁמֵעוּ׃ נֻסוּ מַלְּטוּ
run-away! flee! (6) they-hear destruction cry-of anguished-ones-of Horonaim

The people will cry out;
all who dwell in the land will wail
3 at the sound of the hoofs of galloping steeds,
at the noise of enemy chariots
and the rumble of their wheels.
Fathers will not turn to help their children;
their hands will hang limp.
4 For the day has come
to destroy all the Philistines
and to cut off all survivors
who could help Tyre and Sidon.
The LORD is about to destroy the Philistines,
the remnant from the coasts of Caphtor.[w]
5 Gaza will shave her head in mourning;
Ashkelon will be silenced.
O remnant on the plain,
how long will you cut yourselves?

6 "'Ah, sword of the LORD,' ⌞you cry,⌟
'how long till you rest?
Return to your scabbard;
cease and be still.'
7 But how can it rest
when the LORD has commanded it,
when he has ordered it
to attack Ashkelon and the coast?"

*A Message About Moab*

48 Concerning Moab:
This is what the LORD Almighty, the God of Israel, says:

"Woe to Nebo, for it will be ruined.
Kiriathaim will be disgraced and captured;
the stronghold[x] will be disgraced and shattered.
2 Moab will be praised no more;
in Heshbon[y] men will plot her downfall:
'Come, let us put an end to that nation.'
You too, O Madmen,[z] will be silenced;
the sword will pursue you.
3 Listen to the cries from Horonaim,
cries of great havoc and destruction.
4 Moab will be broken;
her little ones will cry out.[a]
5 They go up the way to Luhith,
weeping bitterly as they go;
on the road down to Horonaim
anguished cries over the destruction are heard.
6 Flee! Run for your lives;

w4 That is, Crete x1 Or / *Misgab*
y2 The Hebrew for *Heshbon* sounds like the Hebrew for *plot*.
z2 The name of the Moabite town Madmen sounds like the Hebrew for *be silenced*.
a4 Hebrew; Septuagint / *proclaim it to Zoar*

*6 Most mss have *segol* for *pathah* (אֶל).

°4 ק צעיריה
°5 ק הלחית

נַפְשְׁכֶם וְתִהְיֶינָה כַּעֲרוֹעֵר בַּמִּדְבָּר׃ כִּי יַעַן בִּטְחֵךְ
trust-of-you because since (7) in-the-desert like-Aroer and-you-become life-of-you

בְּמַעֲשַׂיִךְ וּבְאוֹצְרוֹתַיִךְ גַּם־ אַתְּ תִּלָּכֵדִי וְיָצָא
and-he-will-go you-will-be-captured you too and-in-riches-of-you in-deeds-of-you

כְמוֹשׁ בַּגּוֹלָה כֹּהֲנָיו וְשָׂרָיו יַחְדָּו׃
together and-officials-of-him priests-of-him into-the-exile Chemosh

וְיָבֹא שֹׁדֵד אֶל־ כָּל־ עִיר וְעִיר לֹא
not and-town town every-of against one-destroying and-he-will-come (8)

תִמָּלֵט וְאָבַד הָעֵמֶק וְנִשְׁמַד הַמִּישֹׁר
the-plateau and-he-will-be-destroyed the-valley and-he-will-be-ruined she-will-escape

אֲשֶׁר אָמַר יְהוָה׃ תְּנוּ־ צִיץ לְמוֹאָב כִּי נָצֹא תֵּצֵא
she-will-go-away to-fly for to-Moab wing give! (9) Yahweh he-spoke because

וְעָרֶיהָ לְשַׁמָּה תִהְיֶינָה מֵאֵין יוֹשֵׁב בָּהֵן׃
in-them one-living with-no they-will-become as-desolation and-towns-of-her

אָרוּר עֹשֶׂה מְלֶאכֶת יְהוָה רְמִיָּה וְאָרוּר מֹנֵעַ
one-keeping-back and-being-cursed laxity Yahweh work-of one-doing being-cursed (10)

חַרְבּוֹ מִדָּם׃ שַׁאֲנַן מוֹאָב מִנְּעוּרָיו
from-youths-of-him Moab he-has-been-at-rest (11) from-blood sword-of-him

וְשֹׁקֵט הוּא אֶל־ שְׁמָרָיו וְלֹא־ הוּרַק מִכְּלִי אֶל־כֶּלִי
jar to from-jar he-was-poured and-not dregs-of-him on he and-one-being-left

וּבַגּוֹלָה לֹא הָלָךְ עַל־ כֵּן עָמַד טַעְמוֹ בּוֹ
in-him taste-of-him he-remains so for he-went not and-into-the-exile

וְרֵיחוֹ לֹא נָמָר׃ לָכֵן הִנֵּה־יָמִים בָּאִים נְאֻם־
declaration-of ones-coming days see! but (12) he-is-changed not and-aroma-of-him

יְהוָה וְשִׁלַּחְתִּי־ לוֹ צֹעִים וְצֵעֻהוּ
and-they-will-pour-out-him men-pouring-out to-him when-I-will-send Yahweh

וְכֵלָיו יָרִיקוּ וְנִבְלֵיהֶם יְנַפֵּצוּ׃
they-will-smash and-jugs-of-them they-will-empty and-jars-of-him

וּבֹשׁ מוֹאָב מִכְּמוֹשׁ כַּאֲשֶׁר־ בֹּשׁוּ בֵּית
house-of they-were-ashamed just-as of-Chemosh Moab and-he-will-be-ashamed (13)

יִשְׂרָאֵל מִבֵּית אֵל מִבְטֶחָם׃ אֵיךְ תֹּאמְרוּ גִּבּוֹרִים אֲנָחְנוּ וְאַנְשֵׁי־ חַיִל
valor and-men-of we warriors can-you-say how? (14) trust-of-them El of-Beth Israel

לַמִּלְחָמָה׃ שֻׁדַּד מוֹאָב וְעָרֶיהָ עָלָה
he-will-invade and-towns-of-her Moab he-will-be-destroyed (15) in-the-battle

וּמִבְחַר בַּחוּרָיו יָרְדוּ לַטָּבַח נְאֻם־
declaration-of in-the-slaughter they-will-go-down young-men-of-her and-finest-of

הַמֶּלֶךְ יְהוָה צְבָאוֹת שְׁמוֹ׃ קָרוֹב אֵיד־ מוֹאָב לָבוֹא
to-come Moab fall-of near (16) name-of-him Hosts Yahweh-of the-King

become like a bush[b] in the desert.
7 Since you trust in your deeds and riches,
you too will be taken captive,
and Chemosh will go into exile,
together with his priests and officials.
8 The destroyer will come against every town,
and not a town will escape.
The valley will be ruined
and the plateau destroyed,
because the LORD has spoken.
9 Put salt on Moab,
for she will be laid waste[c];
her towns will become desolate,
with no one to live in them.

10 "A curse on him who is lax in doing the LORD's work!
A curse on him who keeps his sword from bloodshed!

11 "Moab has been at rest from youth,
like wine left on its dregs,
not poured from one jar to another—
she has not gone into exile.
So she tastes as she did,
and her aroma is unchanged.
12 But days are coming,"
declares the LORD,
"when I will send men who pour from jars,
and they will pour her out;
they will empty her jars
and smash her jugs.
13 Then Moab will be ashamed of Chemosh,
as the house of Israel was ashamed
when they trusted in Bethel.

14 "How can you say, 'We are warriors,
men valiant in battle'?
15 Moab will be destroyed and her towns invaded;
her finest young men will go down in the slaughter,"
declares the King, whose name is the LORD Almighty.
16 "The fall of Moab is at hand;

b6 *Or like Aroer*
c9 *Or Give wings to Moab, / for she will fly away*

°7a ק כמוש
°7b ק יחדיו

וְרָעָתוֹ מִהֲרָה מְאֹד׃ נֻדוּ לוֹ כָּל־
all-of for-him mourn! (17) very she-will-come-quickly and-calamity-of-him

סְבִיבָיו וְכֹל יֹדְעֵי שְׁמוֹ אִמְרוּ אֵיכָה נִשְׁבַּר
he-is-broken how! say! fame-of-him ones-knowing-of and-all-of ones-around-him

מַטֵּה־ עֹז מַקֵּל תִּפְאָרָה׃ רְדִי מִכָּבוֹד יֹשְׁבִי
and-sit! from-glory come-down! (18) glory staff-of might scepter-of

בַצָּמָא יֹשֶׁבֶת בַּת־ דִּיבוֹן כִּי־ שֹׁדֵד מוֹאָב
Moab one-destroying for Dibon Daughter-of one-inhabiting-of on-the-parched-ground

עָלָה בָךְ שִׁחֵת מִבְצָרָיִךְ׃ אֶל־דֶּרֶךְ עִמְדִי
stand! road by (19) fortifications-of-you he-will-ruin against-you he-will-come-up

וְצַפִּי יוֹשֶׁבֶת עֲרוֹעֵר שַׁאֲלִי־ נָס וְנִמְלָטָה אִמְרִי מַה־
what? ask! and-woman-escaping man-fleeing ask! Aroer one-living-of and-watch!

נִּהְיָתָה׃ הֹבִישׁ מוֹאָב כִּי־ חַתָּה הֵילִילִי וּזְעָקִי
and-cry-out! wail! she-is-shattered for Moab he-is-disgraced (20) she-happened

הַגִּידוּ בְּאַרְנוֹן כִּי שֻׁדַּד מוֹאָב׃ וּמִשְׁפָּט בָּא אֶל־אֶרֶץ
land-of to he-came and-judgment (21) Moab he-is-destroyed that by-Arnon announce!

הַמִּישֹׁר אֶל־חֹלוֹן וְאֶל־ יַהְצָה וְעַל־ מוֹפָעַת׃ וְעַל־ דִּיבוֹן וְעַל־ נְבוֹ
Nebo and-to Dibon and-to (22) Mephaath and-to Jahzah and-to Holon to the-plateau

וְעַל־בֵּית דִּבְלָתָיִם׃ וְעַל קִרְיָתַיִם וְעַל־ בֵּית גָּמוּל וְעַל־בֵּית מְעוֹן׃
Meon Beth and-to Gamul Beth and-to Kiriathaim and-to (23) Diblathaim Beth and-to

וְעַל־ קְרִיּוֹת וְעַל־בָּצְרָה וְעַל כָּל־ עָרֵי אֶרֶץ מוֹאָב הָרְחֹקוֹת
the-far-ones Moab land-of towns-of all-of and-to Bozrah and-to Kerioth and-to (24)

וְהַקְּרֹבוֹת׃ נִגְדְּעָה קֶרֶן מוֹאָב וּזְרֹעוֹ נִשְׁבָּרָה
she-is-broken and-arm-of-him Moab horn-of and-she-is-cut-off (25) and-the-near-ones

נְאֻם יְהוָה׃ הַשְׁכִּירֻהוּ כִּי עַל־ יְהוָה הִגְדִּיל
he-defied Yahweh against for make-drunk-him! (26) Yahweh declaration-of

וְסָפַק מוֹאָב בְּקִיאוֹ וְהָיָה לִשְׂחֹק גַּם־הוּא׃
he also for-ridicule and-let-him-be in-vomit-of-him Moab and-let-him-wallow

וְאִם ׀ לוֹא הַשְּׂחֹק הָיָה לְךָ יִשְׂרָאֵל אִם־
indeed Israel for-you he-was the-object-of-ridicule not and-indeed (27)

בְּגַנָּבִים נִמְצָאָה כִּי־ מִדֵּי דְבָרֶיךָ בּוֹ תִּתְנוֹדָד׃
you-shake-head about-him words-of-you as-often-of that he-was-caught among-thieves

עִזְבוּ עָרִים וְשִׁכְנוּ בַּסֶּלַע יֹשְׁבֵי מוֹאָב וִהְיוּ כְיוֹנָה
like-dove and-be! Moab ones-living-of among-the-rock and-dwell! towns! abandon! (28)

תְּקַנֵּן בְּעֶבְרֵי פִי־ פָחַת׃ שָׁמַעְנוּ גְאוֹן־ מוֹאָב גֵּאֶה
pride Moab pride-of we-heard (29) cave mouth-of at-ones-across-of she-makes-nest

מְאֹד גָּבְהוֹ וּגְאוֹנוֹ וְגַאֲוָתוֹ וְרֻם
and-haughtiness-of and-arrogance-of-him and-pride-of-him conceit-of-him overweening

her calamity will come
quickly.
17Mourn for her, all who live
around her,
all who know her fame;
say, 'How broken is the
mighty scepter,
how broken the glorious
staff!'
18"Come down from your glory
and sit on the parched
ground,
O inhabitants of the
Daughter of Dibon,
for he who destroys Moab
will come up against you
and ruin your fortified
cities.
19Stand by the road and watch,
you who live in Aroer.
Ask the man fleeing and the
woman escaping,
ask them, 'What has
happened?'
20Moab is disgraced, for she is
shattered.
Wail and cry out!
Announce by the Arnon
that Moab is destroyed.
21Judgment has come to the
plateau—
to Holon, Jahzah and
Mephaath,
22 to Dibon, Nebo and Beth
Diblathaim,
23 to Kiriathaim, Beth Gamul
and Beth Meon,
24 to Kerioth and Bozrah—
to all the towns of Moab, far
and near.
25Moab's horn[d] is cut off;
her arm is broken,"
declares the LORD.
26"Make her drunk,
for she has defied the LORD.
Let Moab wallow in her vomit;
let her be an object of
ridicule.
27Was not Israel the object of
your ridicule?
Was she caught among
thieves,
that you shake your head in
scorn
whenever you speak of her?
28Abandon your towns and
dwell among the rocks,
you who live in Moab.
Be like a dove that makes its
nest
at the mouth of a cave.
29"We have heard of Moab's
pride—
her overweening pride and
conceit,
her pride and arrogance
and the haughtiness of her

d25 *Horn* here symbolizes strength.

°18 ק ושבי
°20a ק הילילו; °20b ק וזעקו
°21 ק מיפעת; °27 ק נמצא

לִבּוֹ׃ אֲנִי יָדַעְתִּי נְאֻם־ יְהוָה עֶבְרָתוֹ וְלֹא־ כֵן
so but-not insolence-of-him Yahweh declaration-of I-know I (30) heart-of-him

בַּדָּיו לֹא־ כֵן עָשׂוּ׃ עַל־כֵּן עַל־מוֹאָב אֲיֵלִיל וּלְמוֹאָב
and-for-Moab I-wail Moab over this for (31) they-accomplish right not boasts-of-him

כֻּלֹּה אֶזְעָק אֶל־ אַנְשֵׁי קִיר־ חֶרֶשׂ יֶהְגֶּה׃ מִבְּכִי יַעְזֵר
Jazer as-weeping-of (32) he-moans Hareseth Kir men-of for I-cry-out all-of-him

אֶבְכֶּה־ לָּךְ הַגֶּפֶן שִׂבְמָה נְטִישֹׁתַיִךְ עָבְרוּ יָם עַד יָם
sea-of as-far-as sea they-spread branches-of-you Sibmah the-vine for-you I-weep

יַעְזֵר נָגָעוּ עַל־ קֵיצֵךְ וְעַל־ בְּצִירֵךְ שֹׁדֵד
one-destroying grape-of-you and-on ripened-fruit-of-you on they-reached Jazer

נָפָל׃ וְנֶאֶסְפָה שִׂמְחָה וָגִיל מִכַּרְמֶל וּמֵאֶרֶץ מוֹאָב
Moab and-from-field-of from-orchard and-gladness joy and-she-is-gone (33) he-fell

וְיַיִן מִיקָבִים הִשְׁבַּתִּי לֹא־ יִדְרֹךְ הֵידָד הֵידָד לֹא הֵידָד׃ מִזַּעֲקַת
from-cry-of (34) shout not shout shout he-treads not I-stopped from-presses and-wine

חֶשְׁבּוֹן עַד־אֶלְעָלֵה עַד־יַהַץ נָתְנוּ קוֹלָם מִצֹּעַר עַד־ חֹרֹנַיִם
Horonaim as-far-as from-Zoar sound-of-them they-raise Jahaz to Elealeh to Heshbon

עֶגְלַת שְׁלִשִׁיָּה כִּי גַם־ מֵי נִמְרִים לִמְשַׁמּוֹת יִהְיוּ׃
they-are as-ones-dried-up Nimrim waters-of even for Shelishiyah Eglath

וְהִשְׁבַּתִּי לְמוֹאָב נְאֻם־ יְהוָה מַעֲלֶה בָמָה
high-place one-offering Yahweh declaration-of in-Moab and-I-will-make-end (35)

וּמַקְטִיר לֵאלֹהָיו׃ עַל־ כֵּן לִבִּי לְמוֹאָב
for-Moab heart-of-me this for (36) to-gods-of-him and-one-burning-incense

כַּחֲלִלִים יֶהֱמֶה וְלִבִּי אֶל־ אַנְשֵׁי קִיר־ חֶרֶשׂ כַּחֲלִילִים
like-flutes Hareseth Kir men-of for and-heart-of-me he-laments like-flutes

יֶהֱמֶה עַל־ כֵּן יִתְרַת עָשָׂה אָבָדוּ׃ כִּי כָל־ רֹאשׁ
head every-of indeed (37) they-are-gone he-acquired wealth-of this for he-laments

קָרְחָה וְכָל־ זָקָן גְּרֻעָה עַל כָּל־ יָדַיִם גְּדֻדֹת וְעַל־
and-on ones-slashed hands every-of to being-cut-off beard and-every-of shaved

מָתְנַיִם שָׂק׃ עַל כָּל־ גַּגּוֹת מוֹאָב וּבִרְחֹבֹתֶיהָ כֻּלֹּה
all-of-him and-in-public-squares-of-her Moab roofs-of all-of on (38) sackcloth waists

מִסְפֵּד כִּי־ שָׁבַרְתִּי אֶת־מוֹאָב כִּכְלִי אֵין חֵפֶץ בּוֹ נְאֻם־
declaration-of for-him want there-is-no like-jar Moab *** I-broke for mourning

יְהוָה׃ אֵיךְ חַתָּה הֵילִילוּ אֵיךְ הִפְנָה־עֹרֶף מוֹאָב בּוֹשׁ
he-is-ashamed Moab back he-turns how! they-wail she-is-shattered how! (39) Yahweh

וְהָיָה מוֹאָב לִשְׂחֹק וְלִמְחִתָּה לְכָל־ סְבִיבָיו׃
ones-around-him to-all-of and-as-horror as-object-of-ridicule Moab and-he-became

כִּי־ כֹה אָמַר יְהוָה הִנֵּה כַנֶּשֶׁר יִדְאֶה וּפָרַשׂ
and-he-spreads he-swoops-down like-the-eagle look! Yahweh he-says this indeed (40)

heart.
30 I know her insolence but it is futile,"
declares the LORD,
"and her boasts accomplish nothing.
31 Therefore I wail over Moab,
for all Moab I cry out,
I moan for the men of Kir Hareseth.
32 I weep for you, as Jazer weeps,
O vines of Sibmah.
Your branches spread as far as the sea;
they reached as far as the sea of Jazer.
The destroyer has fallen
on your ripened fruit and grapes.
33 Joy and gladness are gone
from the orchards and fields of Moab.
I have stopped the flow of wine from the presses;
no one treads them with shouts of joy.
Although there are shouts,
they are not shouts of joy.
34 "The sound of their cry rises
from Heshbon to Elealeh and Jahaz,
from Zoar as far as Horonaim and Eglath Shelishiyah,
for even the waters of Nimrim are dried up.
35 In Moab I will put an end
to those who make offerings on the high places
and burn incense to their gods,"
declares the LORD.
36 "So my heart laments for Moab like a flute;
it laments like a flute for the men of Kir Hareseth.
The wealth they acquired is gone.
37 Every head is shaved
and every beard cut off;
every hand is slashed
and every waist is covered with sackcloth.
38 On all the roofs in Moab
and in the public squares
there is nothing but mourning,
for I have broken Moab
like a jar that no one wants,"
declares the LORD.
39 "How shattered she is! How they wail!
How Moab turns her back in shame!
Moab has become an object of ridicule,
an object of horror to all those around her."
40 This is what the LORD says:
"Look! An eagle is swooping down,

כְּנָפָיו אֶל־מוֹאָב׃ נִלְכְּדָה הַקְּרִיּוֹת וְהַמְּצָדוֹת
and-the-strongholds the-Kerioth she-will-be-captured (41) Moab over wings-of-him

נִתְפָּשָׂה וְהָיָה לֵב גִּבּוֹרֵי מוֹאָב בַּיּוֹם הַהוּא
the-that in-the-day Moab warriors-of heart-of and-he-will-be she-will-be-taken

כְּלֵב אִשָּׁה מְצֵרָה׃ וְנִשְׁמַד מוֹאָב מֵעָם כִּי
for as-nation Moab and-he-will-be-destroyed (42) being-in-labor woman like-heart-of

עַל־יְהוָה הִגְדִּיל׃ פַּחַד וָפַחַת וָפָח עָלֶיךָ יוֹשֵׁב
one-being-people-of for-you and-snare and-pit terror (43) he-defied Yahweh because

מוֹאָב נְאֻם־יְהוָה׃ הַנִּיס מִפְּנֵי הַפַּחַד יִפֹּל
he-will-fall the-terror from-before the-one-fleeing (44) Yahweh declaration-of Moab

אֶל־הַפַּחַת וְהָעֹלֶה מִן־הַפַּחַת יִלָּכֵד בַּפָּח
in-the-snare he-will-be-caught the-pit from and-the-one-climbing-out the-pit into

כִּי־אָבִיא אֵלֶיהָ אֶל־מוֹאָב שְׁנַת פְּקֻדָּתָם נְאֻם־יְהוָה׃
Yahweh declaration-of punishment-of-her year-of Moab upon upon-her I-will-bring for

בְּצֵל חֶשְׁבּוֹן עָמְדוּ מִכֹּחַ נָסִים כִּי־אֵשׁ
fire for ones-being-fugitives without-strength they-stand Heshbon in-shadow-of (45)

יָצָא מֵחֶשְׁבּוֹן וְלֶהָבָה מִבֵּין סִיחוֹן וַתֹּאכַל פְּאַת
forehead-of and-she-burns Sihon from-midst-of and-blaze from-Heshbon he-went-out

מוֹאָב וְקָדְקֹד בְּנֵי שָׁאוֹן׃ אוֹי־לְךָ מוֹאָב אָבַד עַם־
people-of he-is-destroyed Moab to-you woe! (46) noisy-boast men-of and-skull-of Moab

כְּמוֹשׁ כִּי־לֻקְּחוּ בָנֶיךָ בַּשֶּׁבִי וּבְנֹתֶיךָ
and-daughters-of-you into-the-exile sons-of-you they-are-taken indeed Chemosh

בַּשִּׁבְיָה׃ וְשַׁבְתִּי שְׁבוּת־מוֹאָב בְּאַחֲרִית הַיָּמִים
the-days in-coming-of Moab fortune-of yet-I-will-restore (47) into-the-captivity

נְאֻם־יְהוָה עַד־הֵנָּה מִשְׁפַּט מוֹאָב׃ לִבְנֵי עַמּוֹן
Ammon concerning-sons-of (49:1) Moab judgment-of at-here to Yahweh declaration-of

כֹּה אָמַר יְהוָה הֲבָנִים אֵין לְיִשְׂרָאֵל אִם־יוֹרֵשׁ אֵין
there-is-not one-being-heir or to-Israel there-are-no sons? Yahweh he-says this

לוֹ מַדּוּעַ יָרַשׁ מַלְכָּם אֶת־גָּד וְעַמּוֹ בְּעָרָיו
in-towns-of-him and-people-of-him Gad *** Molech he-took-possession why? to-him

יָשָׁב׃ לָכֵן הִנֵּה יָמִים בָּאִים נְאֻם־יְהוָה וְהִשְׁמַעְתִּי
when-I-will-sound Yahweh declaration-of ones-coming days see! but (2) he-lives

אֶל־רַבַּת בְּנֵי־עַמּוֹן תְּרוּעַת מִלְחָמָה וְהָיְתָה לְתֵל שְׁמָמָה
ruin as-mound-of and-she-will-become battle cry-of Ammon sons-of Rabbah-of against

וּבְנֹתֶיהָ בָּאֵשׁ תִּצַּתְנָה וְיָרַשׁ יִשְׂרָאֵל
Israel then-he-will-drive-out they-will-be-set-on-fire with-fire and-daughters-of-her

אֶת־יֹרְשָׁיו אָמַר יְהוָה׃ הֵילִילִי חֶשְׁבּוֹן כִּי שֻׁדְּדָה־עַי
Ai she-is-destroyed for Heshbon wail! (3) Yahweh he-says ones-driving-out-him ***

spreading its wings over
Moab.
41 Kerioth[d] will be captured
and the strongholds taken.
In that day the hearts of
Moab's warriors
will be like the heart of a
woman in labor.
42 Moab will be destroyed as a
nation
because she defied the LORD.
43 Terror and pit and snare await
you,
O people of Moab,"
declares the LORD.
44 "Whoever flees from the terror
will fall into a pit,
whoever climbs out of the pit
will be caught in a snare;
for I will bring upon Moab
the year of her
punishment,"
declares the LORD.

45 "In the shadow of Heshbon
the fugitives stand helpless,
for a fire has gone out from
Heshbon,
a blaze from the midst of
Sihon;
it burns the foreheads of
Moab,
the skulls of the noisy
boasters.
46 Woe to you, O Moab!
The people of Chemosh are
destroyed;
your sons are taken into exile
and your daughters into
captivity.

47 "Yet I will restore the fortunes
of Moab
in days to come,"
declares the LORD.

Here ends the judgment on Moab.

*A Message About Ammon*

49 Concerning the Ammonites:

This is what the LORD says:

"Has Israel no sons?
Has she no heirs?
Why then has Molech[e] taken
possession of Gad?
Why do his people live in
its towns?
2 But the days are coming,"
declares the LORD,
"when I will sound the battle
cry
against Rabbah of the
Ammonites;
it will become a mound of
ruins,
and its surrounding villages
will be set on fire.
Then Israel will drive out
those who drove her out,"
says the LORD.
3 "Wail, O Heshbon, for Ai is
destroyed!

[d] 41 Or *The cities*
[e] 1 Or *their king;* Hebrew *malcam;* also in verse 3

°44 ק הנס

צְעַקְנָה בְּנוֹת רַבָּה חֲגֹרְנָה שַׂקִּים סְפֹדְנָה וְהִתְשׁוֹטַטְנָה
and-rush-here-and-there! mourn! sackcloths put-on! Rabbah inhabitants-of cry-out!

בַּגְּדֵרוֹת כִּי מַלְכָּם בַּגּוֹלָה יֵלֵךְ כֹּהֲנָיו
priests-of-him he-will-go into-the-exile Molech for inside-the-walls

וְשָׂרָיו יַחְדָּיו׃ מַה־תִּתְהַלְלִי בָּעֲמָקִים זָב
one-being-fruitful of-the-valleys you-boast why? (4) together and-officials-of-him

עִמְקֵךְ הַבַּת הַשּׁוֹבֵבָה הַבֹּטְחָה בְּאֹצְרֹתֶיהָ מִי
who? in-riches-of-her the-one-trusting the-unfaithful the-daughter valley-of-you

יָבוֹא אֵלָי׃ הִנְנִי מֵבִיא עָלַיִךְ פַּחַד נְאֻם־אֲדֹנָי
Lord declaration-of terror on-you bringing see-I! (5) against-me he-will-attack

יְהוִה צְבָאוֹת מִכָּל־סְבִיבָיִךְ וְנִדַּחְתֶּם אִישׁ
everyone and-you-will-be-driven-away ones-around-you from-all-of Hosts Yahweh-of

לְפָנָיו וְאֵין מְקַבֵּץ לַנֹּדֵד׃ וְאַחֲרֵי־כֵן
this yet-after (6) to-the-one-being-fugitive one-gathering and-no before-him

אָשִׁיב אֶת־שְׁבוּת בְּנֵי־עַמּוֹן נְאֻם־יְהוָה׃ לֶאֱדוֹם
concerning-Edom (7) Yahweh declaration-of Ammon sons-of fortune-of *** I-will-restore

כֹּה אָמַר יְהוָה צְבָאוֹת הַאֵין עוֹד חָכְמָה בְּתֵימָן אָבְדָה עֵצָה
counsel she-perished in-Teman wisdom longer no? Hosts Yahweh-of he-says this

מִבָּנִים נִסְרְחָה חָכְמָתָם׃ נֻסוּ הָפְנוּ הֶעְמִיקוּ
make-deep! turn! flee! (8) wisdom-of-them she-decayed from-ones-being-prudent

לָשֶׁבֶת יֹשְׁבֵי דְּדָן כִּי אֵיד עֵשָׂו הֵבֵאתִי עָלָיו עֵת
time-of on-him I-will-bring Esau disaster-of for Dedan ones-living-of to-hide

פְּקַדְתִּיו׃ אִם־בֹּצְרִים בָּאוּ לָךְ לֹא יַשְׁאִרוּ
they-would-leave not to-you they-came ones-picking-grapes if (9) I-punish-him

עוֹלֵלוֹת אִם־גַּנָּבִים בַּלַּיְלָה הִשְׁחִיתוּ דַיָּם׃ כִּי־אֲנִי
I but (10) want-of-them they-would-steal during-the-night thieves if gleanings

חָשַׂפְתִּי אֶת־עֵשָׂו גִּלֵּיתִי אֶת־מִסְתָּרָיו
hiding-places-of-him *** I-will-uncover Esau *** I-will-strip-bare

וְנֶחְבָּה לֹא יוּכָל שֻׁדַּד זַרְעוֹ
child-of-him he-will-perish he-will-be-able not so-he-will-conceal-himself

וְאֶחָיו וּשְׁכֵנָיו וְאֵינֶנּוּ׃ עָזְבָה יְתֹמֶיךָ
orphans-of-you leave! (11) and-no-more-he and-neighbors-of-him and-relatives-of-him

אֲנִי אֲחַיֶּה וְאַלְמְנוֹתֶיךָ עָלַי תִּבְטָחוּ׃ כִּי־כֹה ׀
this indeed (12) you-can-trust in-me and-widows-of-you I-will-protect-life I

אָמַר יְהוָה הִנֵּה אֲשֶׁר־אֵין מִשְׁפָּטָם לִשְׁתּוֹת הַכּוֹס שָׁתוֹ יִשְׁתּוּ
they-drink to-drink the-cup to-drink desert-of-them not who see! Yahweh he-says

וְאַתָּה הוּא נָקֹה תִּנָּקֶה לֹא תִנָּקֶה כִּי
but you-will-go-unpunished not should-you-go-unpunished to-go-unpunished he and-you

Cry out, O inhabitants of Rabbah!
Put on sackcloth and mourn;
rush here and there inside the walls,
for Molech will go into exile,
together with his priests and officials.
4 Why do you boast of your valleys,
boast of your valleys so fruitful?
O unfaithful daughter,
you trust in your riches and say,
'Who will attack me?'
5 I will bring terror on you
from all those around you,"
declares the Lord, the LORD Almighty.
"Every one of you will be driven away,
and no one will gather the fugitives.

6 "Yet afterward, I will restore the fortunes of the Ammonites,"
declares the LORD.

*A Message About Edom*

7 Concerning Edom:

This is what the LORD Almighty says:

"Is there no longer wisdom in Teman?
Has counsel perished from the prudent?
Has their wisdom decayed?
8 Turn and flee, hide in deep caves,
you who live in Dedan,
for I will bring disaster on Esau
at the time I punish him.
9 If grape pickers came to you,
would they not leave a few grapes?
If thieves came during the night,
would they not steal only as much as they wanted?
10 But I will strip Esau bare;
I will uncover his hiding places,
so that he cannot conceal himself.
His children, relatives and neighbors will perish,
and he will be no more.
11 Leave your orphans; I will protect their lives.
Your widows too can trust in me."

12 This is what the LORD says: "If those who do not deserve to drink the cup must drink it, why should you go unpunished? You will not

שָׁתֹה תִּשְׁתֶּה׃ כִּי בִי נִשְׁבַּעְתִּי נְאֻם־ יְהוָה כִּי־
that Yahweh declaration-of I-swear by-myself indeed (13) you-must-drink to-drink

לְשַׁמָּה לְחֶרְפָּה לְחֹרֶב וְלִקְלָלָה תִּהְיֶה בָצְרָה וְכָל־
and-all-of Bozrah she-will-become and-as-curse as-reproach as-horror as-ruin

עָרֶיהָ תִהְיֶינָה לְחָרְבוֹת עוֹלָם׃ שְׁמוּעָה שָׁמַעְתִּי מֵאֵת יְהוָה
Yahweh from-with I-heard message (14) forever as-ruins they-will-become towns-of-her

וְצִיר בַּגּוֹיִם שָׁלוּחַ הִתְקַבְּצוּ וּבֹאוּ עָלֶיהָ
against-her and-attack! assemble-yourselves! being-sent to-the-nations indeed-envoy

וְקוּמוּ לַמִּלְחָמָה׃ כִּי־ הִנֵּה קָטֹן נְתַתִּיךָ בַּגּוֹיִם
among-the-nations I-will-make-you small see! now (15) for-the-battle and-rise-up!

בָּזוּי בָּאָדָם׃ תִּפְלַצְתְּךָ הִשִּׁיא אֹתָךְ זְדוֹן
pride-of you he-deceived terror-of-you (16) among-the-man one-being-despised

לִבֶּךָ שֹׁכְנִי בְּחַגְוֵי הַסֶּלַע תֹּפְשִׂי מְרוֹם גִּבְעָה
hill height-of one-occupying the-rock in-clefts-of one-living heart-of-you

כִּי־ תַגְבִּיהַ* כַּנֶּשֶׁר קִנֶּךָ מִשָּׁם אוֹרִידְךָ
I-will-bring-down-you from-there nest-of-you like-the-eagle you-make-high though

נְאֻם־ יְהוָה׃ וְהָיְתָה אֱדוֹם לְשַׁמָּה כֹּל עֹבֵר
one-passing all-of as-horror Edom and-she-will-become (17) Yahweh declaration-of

עָלֶיהָ יִשֹּׁם וְיִשְׁרֹק עַל־ כָּל־ מַכּוֹתֶהָ׃
wounds-of-her all-of because-of and-he-will-scoff he-will-be-appalled by-her

כְּמַהְפֵּכַת סְדֹם וַעֲמֹרָה וּשְׁכֵנֶיהָ אָמַר יְהוָה לֹא־
not Yahweh he-says and-neighbors-of-her and-Gomorrah Sodom as-overthrow-of (18)

יֵשֵׁב שָׁם אִישׁ וְלֹא־ יָגוּר בָּהּ בֶּן־ אָדָם׃ הִנֵּה
see! (19) man son-of in-her he-will-dwell and-not one there he-will-live

כְּאַרְיֵה יַעֲלֶה מִגְּאוֹן הַיַּרְדֵּן אֶל־ נְוֵה אֵיתָן כִּי־
indeed rich pastureland-of to the-Jordan from-thicket-of he-comes-up like-lion

אַרְגִּיעָה אֲרִיצֶנּוּ מֵעָלֶיהָ וּמִי בָחוּר אֵלֶיהָ
for-her one-being-chosen and-who? from-upon-her I-will-chase-him I-will-do-instantly

אֶפְקֹד כִּי מִי כָמוֹנִי וּמִי יְעִידֶנִּי וּמִי־ זֶה
this and-who? he-can-challenge-me and-who? like-me who? indeed I-will-appoint

רֹעֶה אֲשֶׁר יַעֲמֹד לְפָנָי׃ לָכֵן שִׁמְעוּ עֲצַת־ יְהוָה
Yahweh plan-of hear! therefore (20) against-me he-can-stand who one-being-shepherd

אֲשֶׁר יָעַץ אֶל־ אֱדוֹם וּמַחְשְׁבוֹתָיו אֲשֶׁר חָשַׁב אֶל־
against he-purposed that and-purposes-of-him Edom against he-planned that

יֹשְׁבֵי תֵימָן אִם־ לֹא יִסְחָבוּם צְעִירֵי הַצֹּאן
the-flock young-ones-of they-will-drag-away-them indeed that Teman ones-living-of

אִם־ לֹא יַשִּׁים עֲלֵיהֶם נְוֵהֶם׃ מִקּוֹל
at-sound-of (21) pasture-of-them because-of-them he-will-destroy indeed that

go unpunished, but must drink it. [13]I swear by myself," declares the LORD, "that Bozrah will become a ruin and an object of horror, of reproach and of cursing; and all its towns will be in ruins forever."

[14]I have heard a message from the LORD:
An envoy was sent to the nations to say,
"Assemble yourselves to attack it!
Rise up for battle!"

[15]"Now I will make you small among the nations,
despised among men.
[16]The terror you inspire
and the pride of your heart have deceived you,
you who live in the clefts of the rocks,
who occupy the heights of the hill.
Though you build your nest as high as the eagle's,
from there I will bring you down,"
declares the LORD.
[17]"Edom will become an object of horror;
all who pass by will be appalled and will scoff
because of all its wounds.
[18]As Sodom and Gomorrah were overthrown,
along with their neighboring towns,"
says the LORD,
"so no one will live there;
no man will dwell in it.

[19]"Like a lion coming up from Jordan's thickets
to a rich pastureland,
I will chase Edom from its land in an instant.
Who is the chosen one I will appoint for this?
Who is like me and who can challenge me?
And what shepherd can stand against me?"
[20]Therefore, hear what the LORD has planned against Edom,
what he has purposed against those who live in Teman:
The young of the flock will be dragged away;
he will completely destroy their pasture because of them.

*16 Most mss have *mappiq* in the *he* (הּ־).

נִפְלָם רָעֲשָׁה הָאָרֶץ צְעָקָה בְּיַם־ סוּף נִשְׁמַע
he-will-be-heard Reed to-Sea-of cry the-earth she-will-tremble to-fall-them

קוֹלָהּ׃ (22) הִנֵּה כַנֶּשֶׁר יַעֲלֶה וְיִדְאֶה
and-he-will-swoop-down he-will-soar like-the-eagle look! (22) sound-of-her

וְיִפְרֹשׂ כְּנָפָיו עַל־ בָּצְרָה וְהָיָה לֵב גִּבּוֹרֵי
warriors-of heart-of and-he-will-be Bozrah over wings-of-him and-he-will-spread

אֱדוֹם בַּיּוֹם הַהוּא כְּלֵב אִשָּׁה מְצֵרָה׃ (23) לְדַמֶּשֶׂק
concerning-Damascus (23) being-in-labor woman like-heart-of the-that in-the-day Edom

בּוֹשָׁה חֲמָת וְאַרְפָּד כִּי־ שְׁמֻעָה רָעָה שָׁמְעוּ נָמֹגוּ
they-are-troubled they-heard bad news for and-Arpad Hamath she-is-dismayed

בַּיָּם דְּאָגָה הַשְׁקֵט לֹא יוּכָל׃ (24) רָפְתָה דַמֶּשֶׂק
Damascus she-became-feeble (24) he-can not to-be-calm restlessness by-the-sea

הִפְנְתָה לָנוּס וְרֶטֶט ׀ הֶחֱזִיקָה צָרָה וַחֲבָלִים אֲחָזַתָּה
she-seized-her and-pains anguish he-gripped-her and-panic to-flee she-turned

כַּיּוֹלֵדָה׃ (25) אֵיךְ לֹא־ עֻזְּבָה עִיר תְּהִלָּה קִרְיַת
town-of renown city-of she-was-abandoned not why? (25) like-the-woman-being-in-labor

מְשׂוֹשִׂי׃ (26) לָכֵן יִפְּלוּ בַחוּרֶיהָ בִּרְחֹבֹתֶיהָ
in-streets-of-her young-men-of-her they-will-fall surely (26) delight-of-me

וְכָל־ אַנְשֵׁי הַמִּלְחָמָה יִדַּמּוּ בַּיּוֹם הַהוּא נְאֻם
declaration-of the-that in-the-day they-will-be-silenced the-army men-of and-all-of

יְהוָה צְבָאוֹת׃ (27) וְהִצַּתִּי אֵשׁ בְּחוֹמַת דַּמָּשֶׂק וְאָכְלָה
and-she-will-consume Damascus to-wall-of fire and-I-will-set (27) Hosts Yahweh-of

אַרְמְנוֹת בֶּן־ הֲדָד׃ (28) לְקֵדָר ׀ וּלְמַמְלְכוֹת חָצוֹר אֲשֶׁר
which Hazor and-concerning-kingdoms-of concerning-Kedar (28) Hadad Ben fortresses-of

הִכָּה נְבוּכַדְרֶאצּוֹר מֶלֶךְ־ בָּבֶל כֹּה אָמַר יְהוָה קוּמוּ עֲלוּ
attack! arise! Yahweh he-says this Babylon king-of Nebuchadrezzar he-attacked

אֶל־ קֵדָר וְשָׁדְדוּ אֶת־ בְּנֵי־ קֶדֶם׃ (29) אָהֳלֵיהֶם וְצֹאנָם
and-flock-of-them tents-of-them (29) East peoples-of *** and-destroy! Kedar against

יִקָּחוּ יְרִיעוֹתֵיהֶם וְכָל־ כְּלֵיהֶם וּגְמַלֵּיהֶם
and-camels-of-them goods-of-them with-all-of shelters-of-them they-will-be-taken

יִשְׂאוּ לָהֶם וְקָרְאוּ עֲלֵיהֶם מָגוֹר מִסָּבִיב׃
on-every-side terror to-them and-they-will-shout for-them they-will-carry-off

(30) נֻסוּ נֻּדוּ מְאֹד הֶעְמִיקוּ לָשֶׁבֶת יֹשְׁבֵי חָצוֹר נְאֻם־
declaration-of Hazor ones-living-of to-stay make-deep! quickly go-away! flee! (30)

יְהוָה כִּי־ יָעַץ עֲלֵיכֶם נְבוּכַדְרֶאצַּר מֶלֶךְ־ בָּבֶל עֵצָה
plot Babylon king-of Nebuchadrezzar against-you he-plotted indeed Yahweh

וְחָשַׁב עֲלֵיהֶם מַחֲשָׁבָה׃ (31) קוּמוּ עֲלוּ אֶל־ גּוֹי שְׁלֵיו
at-ease nation against attack! arise! (31) plan against-you and-he-devised

21 At the sound of their fall the
earth will tremble;
their cry will resound to the
Red Sea.[f]
22 Look! An eagle will soar and
swoop down,
spreading its wings over
Bozrah.
In that day the hearts of
Edom's warriors
will be like the heart of a
woman in labor.

*A Message About Damascus*

23 Concerning Damascus:

"Hamath and Arpad are
dismayed,
for they have heard bad
news.
They are disheartened,
troubled like[g] the restless
sea.
24 Damascus has become feeble,
she has turned to flee
and panic has gripped her;
anguish and pain have seized
her,
pain like that of a woman
in labor.
25 Why has the city of renown
not been abandoned,
the town in which I delight?
26 Surely, her young men will fall
in the streets;
all her soldiers will be
silenced in that day,"
declares the LORD
Almighty.
27 "I will set fire to the walls of
Damascus;
it will consume the
fortresses of Ben-Hadad."

*A Message About Kedar and Hazor*

28 Concerning Kedar and the kingdoms of Hazor, which Nebuchadnezzar king of Babylon attacked:

This is what the LORD says:

"Arise, and attack Kedar
and destroy the people of
the East.
29 Their tents and their flocks
will be taken;
their shelters will be carried
off
with all their goods and
camels.
Men will shout to them,
'Terror on every side!'
30 "Flee quickly away!
Stay in deep caves, you who
live in Hazor,"
declares the LORD.
"Nebuchadnezzar king of
Babylon has plotted
against you;
he has devised a plan
against you.
31 "Arise and attack a nation at
ease,

f21 Hebrew *Yam Suph;* that is, Sea of Reeds
g23 Hebrew *on* or *by*

°25 ק תהלת
°28 ק נבוכדראצר
°30 ק עליכם

יוֹשֵׁב לָבֶטַח נְאֻם־ יְהוָה לֹא־דְלָתַיִם וְלֹא־בְרִיחַ לוֹ בָּדָד
alone to-him bar or-not gates not Yahweh declaration-of in-confidence one-living

יִשְׁכֹּנוּ׃ וְהָיוּ גְמַלֵּיהֶם לָבַז וַהֲמוֹן
and-largeness-of as-plunder camels-of-them and-they-will-become (32) they-live

מִקְנֵיהֶם לְשָׁלָל וְזֵרִתִים לְכָל־ רוּחַ קְצוּצֵי
ones-being-clipped-of wind to-all-of and-I-will-scatter-them as-booty herds-of-them

פֵאָה וּמִכָּל־ עֲבָרָיו אָבִיא אֶת־ אֵידָם
disaster-of-them *** I-will-bring sides-of-him and-from-every-of forehead

נְאֻם־ יְהוָה׃ וְהָיְתָה חָצוֹר לִמְעוֹן תַּנִּים
jackals as-haunt-of Hazor and-she-will-become (33) Yahweh declaration-of

שְׁמָמָה עַד־עוֹלָם לֹא־ יֵשֵׁב שָׁם אִישׁ וְלֹא־ יָגוּר בָּהּ
in-her he-will-dwell and-not one there he-will-live not forever to desolate-place

בֶּן־ אָדָם׃ אֲשֶׁר הָיָה דְבַר־ יְהוָה אֶל־יִרְמְיָהוּ הַנָּבִיא אֶל־
concerning the-prophet Jeremiah to Yahweh word-of he-came that (34) man son-of

עֵילָם בְּרֵאשִׁית מַלְכוּת צִדְקִיָּה מֶלֶךְ־ יְהוּדָה לֵאמֹר׃ כֹּה אָמַר
he-says this (35) to-say Judah king-of Zedekiah reign-of in-early-part-of Elam

יְהוָה צְבָאוֹת הִנְנִי שֹׁבֵר אֶת־ קֶשֶׁת עֵילָם רֵאשִׁית גְּבוּרָתָם׃
might-of-them mainstay-of Elam bow-of *** breaking see-I! Hosts Yahweh-of

וְהֵבֵאתִי אֶל־עֵילָם אַרְבַּע רוּחוֹת מֵאַרְבַּע קְצוֹת הַשָּׁמַיִם
the-heavens quarters-of from-four-of winds four-of Elam against and-I-will-bring (36)

וְזֵרִתִים לְכֹל הָרֻחוֹת הָאֵלֶּה וְלֹא־ יִהְיֶה הַגּוֹי
the-nation he-will-be and-not the-these the-winds to-all-of and-I-will-scatter-them

אֲשֶׁר לֹא־ יָבוֹא שָׁם נִדְּחֵי עוֹלָם׃ וְהַחְתַּתִּי אֶת־
*** and-I-will-shatter (37) Elam ones-being-exiled-of there he-goes not where

עֵילָם לִפְנֵי אֹיְבֵיהֶם וְלִפְנֵי מְבַקְשֵׁי נַפְשָׁם
life-of-them ones-seeking-of and-before ones-being-foes-of-them before Elam

וְהֵבֵאתִי עֲלֵיהֶם רָעָה אֶת־ חֲרוֹן אַפִּי נְאֻם־
declaration-of anger-of-me fierceness-of *** disaster upon-them and-I-will-bring

יְהוָה וְשִׁלַּחְתִּי אַחֲרֵיהֶם אֶת־ הַחֶרֶב עַד כַּלּוֹתִי אוֹתָם׃
them to-make-end-me until the-sword with after-them and-I-will-pursue Yahweh

וְשַׂמְתִּי כִסְאִי בְּעֵילָם וְהַאֲבַדְתִּי מִשָּׁם מֶלֶךְ
king from-there and-I-will-destroy in-Elam throne-of-me and-I-will-set (38)

וְשָׂרִים נְאֻם־ יְהוָה׃ וְהָיָה בְּאַחֲרִית הַיָּמִים
the-days in-coming-of yet-he-will-be (39) Yahweh declaration-of and-officials

אָשׁוּב אֶת־ שְׁבִית עֵילָם נְאֻם־ יְהוָה׃ הַדָּבָר אֲשֶׁר
that the-word (50:1) Yahweh declaration-of Elam fortune-of *** I-will-restore

דִּבֶּר יְהוָה אֶל־ בָּבֶל אֶל־ אֶרֶץ כַּשְׂדִּים בְּיַד
by-hand-of Chaldeans land-of concerning Babylon concerning Yahweh he-spoke

which lives in confidence,"
declares the LORD,
"a nation that has neither
gates nor bars;
its people live alone.
32 Their camels will become
plunder,
and their large herds will be
booty.
I will scatter to the winds
those who are in distant
places[h]
and will bring disaster on
them from every side,"
declares the LORD.
33 "Hazor will become a haunt of
jackals,
a desolate place forever.
No one will live there;
no man will dwell in it."

*A Message About Elam*

34 This is the word of the LORD
that came to Jeremiah the prophet
concerning Elam, early in the
reign of Zedekiah king of Judah:

35 This is what the LORD Almighty says:

"See, I will break the bow of
Elam,
the mainstay of their might.
36 I will bring against Elam the
four winds
from the four quarters of the
heavens;
I will scatter them to the four
winds,
and there will not be a
nation
where Elam's exiles do not
go.
37 I will shatter Elam before their
foes,
before those who seek their
lives;
I will bring disaster upon
them,
even my fierce anger,"
declares the LORD.
"I will pursue them with the
sword
until I have made an end of
them.
38 I will set my throne in Elam
and destroy her king and
officials,"
declares the LORD.

39 "Yet I will restore the fortunes
of Elam
in days to come,"
declares the LORD.

*A Message About Babylon*

50 This is the word the LORD
spoke through Jeremiah
the prophet concerning Babylon
and the land of the Babylonians[i]:

h32 Or *who clip the hair by their foreheads*
i1 Or *Chaldeans*; also in verses 8, 25, 35 and 45

°36 ק עילם
°39a ק אשיב
°39b ק שבות

יִרְמְיָהוּ הַנָּבִיא׃ הַגִּידוּ בַגּוֹיִם וְהַשְׁמִיעוּ וּשְׂאוּ־נֵס
banner and-lift! and-proclaim! among-the-nations announce! (2) the-prophet Jeremiah

הַשְׁמִיעוּ אַל־תְּכַחֵדוּ אִמְרוּ נִלְכְּדָה בָבֶל הֹבִישׁ בֵּל
Bel he-will-be-shamed Babylon she-will-be-captured say! you-keep-back not proclaim!

חַת מְרֹדָךְ הֹבִישׁוּ עֲצַבֶּיהָ חַתּוּ
they-will-be-terrified images-of-her they-will-be-shamed Marduk he-will-be-terrified

גִּלּוּלֶיהָ׃ כִּי עָלָה עָלֶיהָ גּוֹי מִצָּפוֹן הוּא־יָשִׁית
he-will-lay he from-north nation against-her he-will-attack indeed (3) idols-of-her

אֶת־אַרְצָהּ לְשַׁמָּה וְלֹא־יִהְיֶה יוֹשֵׁב בָּהּ מֵאָדָם וְעַד־
and-to from-man in-her one-living he-will-be and-not to-waste land-of-her ***

בְּהֵמָה נָדוּ הָלָכוּ׃ בַּיָּמִים הָהֵמָּה וּבָעֵת
and-at-the-time the-those in-the-days (4) they-will-go they-will-flee animal

הַהִיא נְאֻם־יְהוָה יָבֹאוּ בְנֵי־יִשְׂרָאֵל הֵמָּה וּבְנֵי־
and-peoples-of they Israel peoples-of they-will-go Yahweh declaration-of the-that

יְהוּדָה יַחְדָּו הָלוֹךְ וּבָכוֹ יֵלֵכוּ וְאֶת־יְהוָה אֱלֹהֵיהֶם יְבַקֵּשׁוּ׃
they-will-seek God-of-them Yahweh and they-will-go and-to-weep to-go together Judah

צִיּוֹן יִשְׁאָלוּ דֶּרֶךְ הֵנָּה פְנֵיהֶם בֹּאוּ
they-will-come faces-of-them toward-there way they-will-ask Zion (5)

וְנִלְווּ אֶל־יְהוָה בְּרִית עוֹלָם לֹא תִשָּׁכֵחַ׃
she-will-be-forgotten not everlasting covenant-of Yahweh to and-they-will-bind-selves

צֹאן אֹבְדוֹת הָיוּ° עַמִּי רֹעֵיהֶם
ones-being-shepherds-of-them people-of-me they-were ones-being-lost sheep (6)

הִתְעוּם הָרִים שׁוֹבְבִים° מֵהַר אֶל־גִּבְעָה הָלָכוּ
they-wandered hill to from-mountain they-made-roam-them mountains they-led-astray-them

שָׁכְחוּ רִבְצָם׃ כָּל־מוֹצְאֵיהֶם אֲכָלוּם
they-devoured-them ones-finding-them all-of (7) resting-place-of-them they-forgot

וְצָרֵיהֶם אָמְרוּ לֹא נֶאְשָׁם תַּחַת אֲשֶׁר חָטְאוּ לַיהוָה
against-Yahweh they-sinned that for we-are-guilty not they-said and-enemies-of-them

נְוֵה־צֶדֶק וּמִקְוֵה אֲבוֹתֵיהֶם יְהוָה׃ נֻדוּ מִתּוֹךְ בָּבֶל
Babylon from-inside-of flee! (8) Yahweh fathers-of-them and-hope-of truth pasture-of

וּמֵאֶרֶץ כַּשְׂדִּים יֵצֵאוּ° וִהְיוּ כְּעַתּוּדִים לִפְנֵי־צֹאן׃ כִּי הִנֵּה אָנֹכִי
I see! for (9) flock before like-goats and-be! leave! Chaldeans and-from-land-of

מֵעִיר וּמַעֲלֶה עַל־בָּבֶל קְהַל־גּוֹיִם גְּדֹלִים מֵאֶרֶץ
from-land-of great-ones nations alliance-of Babylon against and-bringing stirring-up

צָפוֹן וְעָרְכוּ לָהּ מִשָּׁם תִּלָּכֵד
she-will-be-captured from-there against-her and-they-will-take-positions north

חִצָּיו כְּגִבּוֹר מַשְׁכִּיל* לֹא יָשׁוּב רֵיקָם׃
empty-handed he-returns not *one-bereaving like-warrior arrows-of-him

2"Announce and proclaim
among the nations,
lift up a banner and
proclaim it;
keep nothing back, but say,
'Babylon will be captured;
Bel will be put to shame,
Marduk filled with terror.
Her images will be put to
shame
and her idols filled with
terror.'
3A nation from the north will
attack her
and lay waste her land.
No one will live in it;
both men and animals will
flee away.
4"In those days, at that time,"
declares the LORD,
"the people of Israel and the
people of Judah together
will go in tears to seek the
LORD their God.
5They will ask the way to Zion
and turn their faces toward
it.
They will come and bind
themselves to the LORD
in an everlasting covenant
that will not be forgotten.
6"My people have been lost
sheep;
their shepherds have led
them astray
and caused them to roam on
the mountains.
They wandered over mountain
and hill
and forgot their own resting
place.
7Whoever found them devoured
them;
their enemies said, 'We are
not guilty,
for they sinned against the
LORD, their true pasture,
the LORD, the hope of their
fathers.'
8"Flee out of Babylon;
leave the land of the
Babylonians,
and be like the goats that
lead the flock.
9For I will stir up and bring
against Babylon
an alliance of great nations
from the land of the
north.
They will take up their
positions against her,
and from the north she will
be captured.
Their arrows will be like
skilled warriors
who do not return
empty-handed.

*9 The NIV, with many mss and versions, reads *sin* for *shin* (מַשְׂ), *being-skilled*.

°6a ק היו
°6b ק שובבים
°8 ק צאו

וְהָיְתָה כַשְׂדִּים לְשָׁלָל כָּל־ שֹׁלְלֶיהָ יִשְׂבָּעוּ
they-will-have-fill ones-plundering-her all-of as-plunder Chaldea so-she-will-be (10)

נְאֻם־ יְהוָה׃ כִּי תִשְׂמְחִי° כִּי תַעֲלְזִי°* שֹׁסֵי
ones-pillaging-of you-are-glad because you-rejoice because (11) Yahweh declaration-of

נַחֲלָתִי כִּי תָפוּשִׁי° כְּעֶגְלָה דָשָׁה וְתִצְהֲלִי°
and-you-neigh threshing like-heifer you-frolic because inheritance-of-me

כָּאַבִּרִים׃† בּוֹשָׁה אִמְּכֶם מְאֹד
greatly mother-of-you she-will-be-ashamed (12) like-the-mighty-ones

חָפְרָה יוֹלַדְתְּכֶם הִנֵּה אַחֲרִית גּוֹיִם מִדְבָּר צִיָּה
dry-land wilderness nations least-of see! one-bearing-you she-will-be-disgraced

וַעֲרָבָה׃ מִקֶּצֶף יְהוָה לֹא תֵשֵׁב וְהָיְתָה
but-she-will-be she-will-be-inhabited not Yahweh because-of-anger-of (13) and-desert

שְׁמָמָה כֻּלָּהּ כֹּל עֹבֵר עַל־ בָּבֶל יִשֹּׁם
he-will-be-horrified Babylon by one-passing all-of all-of-her desolation

וְיִשְׁרֹק עַל־ כָּל־ מַכּוֹתֶיהָ׃ עִרְכוּ עַל־
against take-up-positions! (14) wounds-of-her all-of because-of and-he-will-scoff

בָּבֶל ׀ סָבִיב כָּל־ דֹּרְכֵי קֶשֶׁת יְדוּ אֵלֶיהָ אַל־ תַּחְמְלוּ אֶל־ חֵץ
arrow to you-spare not at-her shoot! bow ones-drawing-of all-of around Babylon

כִּי לַיהוָה חָטָאָה׃ הָרִיעוּ עָלֶיהָ סָבִיב נָתְנָה
she-surrenders every-side against-her shout! (15) she-sinned against-Yahweh for

יָדָהּ נָפְלוּ אָשְׁיוֹתֶיהָ° נֶהֶרְסוּ חוֹמוֹתֶיהָ כִּי
since walls-of-her they-are-torn-down towers-of-her they-fall hand-of-her

נִקְמַת יְהוָה הִיא הִנָּקְמוּ בָהּ כַּאֲשֶׁר עָשְׂתָה עֲשׂוּ־ לָהּ׃
to-her do! she-did just-as on-her take-vengeance! this Yahweh vengeance-of

כִּרְתוּ זוֹרֵעַ מִבָּבֶל וְתֹפֵשׂ מַגָּל בְּעֵת קָצִיר
harvest at-time-of sickle and-one-reaping from-Babylon one-sowing cut-off! (16)

מִפְּנֵי חֶרֶב הַיּוֹנָה אִישׁ אֶל־ עַמּוֹ יִפְנוּ
let-them-return people-of-him to everyone the-one-oppressing sword-of because-of

וְאִישׁ לְאַרְצוֹ יָנֻסוּ׃ שֶׂה פְזוּרָה יִשְׂרָאֵל אֲרָיוֹת
lions Israel being-scattered flock (17) let-them-flee to-land-of-him and-everyone

הִדִּיחוּ הָרִאשׁוֹן אֲכָלוֹ מֶלֶךְ אַשּׁוּר וְזֶה הָאַחֲרוֹן
the-last and-this Assyria king-of he-devoured-him the-first they-chased-away

עִצְּמוֹ נְבוּכַדְרֶאצַּר מֶלֶךְ בָּבֶל׃ לָכֵן כֹּה־ אָמַר
he-says this therefore (18) Babylon king-of Nebuchadrezzar he-crushed-bones-of-him

יְהוָה צְבָאוֹת אֱלֹהֵי יִשְׂרָאֵל הִנְנִי פֹקֵד אֶל־ מֶלֶךְ בָּבֶל וְאֶל־ אַרְצוֹ
land-of-him and-to Babylon king-of to punishing see-I! Israel God-of Hosts Yahweh-of

כַּאֲשֶׁר פָּקַדְתִּי אֶל־ מֶלֶךְ אַשּׁוּר׃ וְשֹׁבַבְתִּי אֶת־ יִשְׂרָאֵל אֶל־
to Israel *** but-I-will-bring-back (19) Assyria king-of to I-punished just-as

10So Babylonia[i] will be plundered;
all who plunder her will have their fill,"
declares the LORD.

11"Because you rejoice and are glad,
you who pillage my inheritance,
because you frolic like a heifer threshing grain
and neigh like stallions,
12your mother will be greatly ashamed;
she who gave you birth will be disgraced.
She will be the least of the nations—
a wilderness, a dry land, a desert.
13Because of the LORD's anger she will not be inhabited
but will be completely desolate.
All who pass Babylon will be horrified and scoff
because of all her wounds.

14"Take up your positions around Babylon,
all you who draw the bow.
Shoot at her! Spare no arrows,
for she has sinned against the LORD.
15Shout against her on every side!
She surrenders, her towers fall,
her walls are torn down.
Since this is the vengeance of the LORD,
take vengeance on her;
do to her as she has done to others.
16Cut off from Babylon the sower,
and the reaper with his sickle at harvest.
Because of the sword of the oppressor
let everyone return to his own people,
let everyone flee to his own land.

17"Israel is a scattered flock
that lions have chased away.
The first to devour him
was the king of Assyria;
the last to crush his bones
was Nebuchadnezzar king of Babylon."

18Therefore this is what the LORD Almighty, the God of Israel, says:
"I will punish the king of Babylon and his land
as I punished the king of Assyria.
19But I will bring Israel back to

i10 Or *Chaldea*

*11a Most mss have *pathah* under the *ayin* (תַּעַל־).
†11b Most mss have *pathah* under the *aleph* (כָּאַ־).

°11a ק תשמחו; °11b ק תעלזו
°11c ק תפושו; °11d ק ותצהלו
°15 ק אשיותיה

נָוֵהוּ וְרָעָה הַכַּרְמֶל וְהַבָּשָׁן וּבְהַר אֶפְרַיִם
Ephraim and-on-hill-of and-the-Bashan the-Carmel and-he-will-graze pasture-of-him

וְהַגִּלְעָד תִּשְׂבַּע נַפְשׁוֹ׃ בַּיָּמִים הָהֵם
the-those in-the-days (20) appetite-of-him she-will-be-satisfied and-the-Gilead

וּבָעֵת הַהִיא נְאֻם־ יְהוָה יְבֻקַּשׁ אֶת־ עֲוֺן יִשְׂרָאֵל
Israel guilt-of *** he-will-be-searched Yahweh declaration-of the-that and-at-the-time

וְאֵינֶנּוּ וְאֶת־חַטֹּאת יְהוּדָה וְלֹא תִמָּצֶאינָה כִּי אֶסְלַח לַאֲשֶׁר
to-whom I-will-forgive for they-will-be-found but-not Judah sins-of and but-not-he

אַשְׁאִיר׃ עַל־ הָאָרֶץ מְרָתַיִם עֲלֵה עָלֶיהָ וְאֶל־
and-against against-her attack! Merathaim the-land against (21) I-spare

יוֹשְׁבֵי פְּקוֹד חֲרֹב וְהַחֲרֵם אַחֲרֵיהֶם נְאֻם־ יְהוָה וַעֲשֵׂה
and-do! Yahweh declaration-of after-them and-destroy! kill! Pekod ones-living-of

כְּכֹל אֲשֶׁר צִוִּיתִיךָ׃ קוֹל מִלְחָמָה בָּאָרֶץ וְשֶׁבֶר
and-destruction in-the-land battle noise-of (22) I-commanded-you that as-everything

גָּדוֹל׃ אֵיךְ נִגְדַּע וַיִּשָּׁבֵר פַּטִּישׁ כָּל־ הָאָרֶץ אֵיךְ
how! the-earth whole-of hammer-of and-he-is-shattered he-is-broken how! (23) great

הָיְתָה לְשַׁמָּה בָּבֶל בַּגּוֹיִם׃ יָקֹשְׁתִּי לָךְ וְגַם־
and-also for-you I-set-trap (24) among-the-nations Babylon as-desolation she-is

נִלְכַּדְתְּ בָּבֶל וְאַתְּ לֹא יָדָעַתְּ נִמְצֵאת וְגַם־
and-also you-were-found you-knew not when-you Babylon you-were-caught

נִתְפַּשְׂתְּ כִּי בַיהוָה הִתְגָּרִית׃ פָּתַח יְהוָה אֶת־
*** Yahweh he-opened (25) you-opposed against-Yahweh because you-were-captured

אוֹצָרוֹ וַיּוֹצֵא אֶת־ כְּלֵי זַעְמוֹ כִּי־מְלָאכָה הִיא
she work for wrath-of-him weapons-of *** and-he-brought-out arsenal-of-him

לַאדֹנָי יְהוִה צְבָאוֹת בְּאֶרֶץ כַּשְׂדִּים׃ בֹּאוּ־ לָהּ מִקֵּץ
from-afar against-her come! (26) Chaldeans in-land-of Hosts Yahweh-of to-Sovereign

פִּתְחוּ מַאֲבֻסֶיהָ סָלּוּהָ כְמוֹ־ עֲרֵמִים וְהַחֲרִימוּהָ אַל־
not and-destroy-her! heaps-of-grain like pile-up-her! granaries-of-her break-open!

תְּהִי־ לָהּ שְׁאֵרִית׃ חִרְבוּ כָּל־ פָּרֶיהָ יֵרְדוּ
let-them-go-down young-bulls-of-her all-of kill! (27) remnant to-her let-her-be

לַטָּבַח הוֹי עֲלֵיהֶם כִּי־ בָא יוֹמָם עֵת פְּקֻדָּתָם׃
punishment-of-them time-of day-of-them he-came for to-them woe! to-the-slaughter

קוֹל נָסִים וּפְלֵטִים מֵאֶרֶץ בָּבֶל לְהַגִּיד
to-declare Babylon from-land-of and-refugees ones-being-fugitives sound-of (28)

בְּצִיּוֹן אֶת־ נִקְמַת יְהוָה אֱלֹהֵינוּ נִקְמַת הֵיכָלוֹ׃ הַשְׁמִיעוּ
summon! (29) temple-of-him vengeance-of God-of-us Yahweh vengeance-of *** in-Zion

אֶל־ בָּבֶל ׀ רַבִּים כָּל־ דֹּרְכֵי קֶשֶׁת חֲנוּ עָלֶיהָ סָבִיב אַל־
not around against-her encamp! bow ones-drawing-of all-of archers Babylon against

his own pasture
and he will graze on Carmel
and Bashan;
his appetite will be satisfied
on the hills of Ephraim and
Gilead.
20 In those days, at that time,"
declares the LORD,
"search will be made for
Israel's guilt,
but there will be none,
and for the sins of Judah,
but none will be found,
for I will forgive the
remnant I spare.

21 "Attack the land of Merathaim
and those who live in
Pekod.
Pursue, kill and completely
destroy[k] them,"
declares the LORD.
"Do everything I have
commanded you.
22 The noise of battle is in the
land,
the noise of great
destruction!
23 How broken and shattered
is the hammer of the whole
earth!
How desolate is Babylon
among the nations!
24 I set a trap for you, O Babylon,
and you were caught before
you knew it;
you were found and captured
because you opposed the
LORD.
25 The LORD has opened his
arsenal
and brought out the
weapons of his wrath,
for the Sovereign LORD
Almighty has work to do
in the land of the
Babylonians.
26 Come against her from afar.
Break open her granaries;
pile her up like heaps of
grain.
Completely destroy her
and leave her no remnant.
27 Kill all her young bulls;
let them go down to the
slaughter!
Woe to them! For their day has
come,
the time for them to be
punished.
28 Listen to the fugitives and
refugees from Babylon
declaring in Zion
how the LORD our God has
taken vengeance,
vengeance for his temple.

29 "Summon archers against
Babylon,
all those who draw the bow.
Encamp all around her;

[k]21 The Hebrew term refers to the irrevocable giving over of things or persons to the LORD, often by totally destroying them; also in verse 26.

יהי־ °* פלטה שלמו־ לה כפעלה ככל אשר עשתה עשו־
do! she-did that as-all as-deed-of-her to-her repay! escapee *of-her let-him-be

לה כי אל־ יהוה זדה אל־ קדוש ישראל׃ לכן
therefore (30) Israel Holy-One-of against she-defied Yahweh against for to-her

יפלו בחוריה ברחבתיה וכל־ אנשי מלחמתה
army-of-her men-of and-all-of in-streets-of-her young-men-of-her they-will-fall

ידמו ביום ההוא נאם־ יהוה׃ הנני
see-I! (31) Yahweh declaration-of the-that in-the-day they-will-be-silenced

אליך זדון נאם־ אדני יהוה צבאות כי בא יומך
day-of-you he-came for Hosts Yahweh-of Lord declaration-of arrogant-one against-you

עת פקדתיך׃ וכשל זדון ונפל
and-he-will-fall arrogant-one and-he-will-stumble (32) I-punish-you time-of

ואין לו מקים והצתי אש בעריו
in-towns-of-him fire and-I-will-kindle one-helping-up for-him and-not

ואכלה כל־ סביבתיו׃ כה אמר יהוה צבאות
Hosts Yahweh-of he-says this (33) ones-around-him all-of and-she-will-consume

עשוקים בני־ ישראל ובני־ יהודה יחדו וכל־
and-all-of as-well Judah and-peoples-of Israel peoples-of ones-being-oppressed

שביהם החזיקו בם מאנו שלחם׃
to-let-go-them they-refuse to-them they-hold-fast ones-capturing-them

גאלם ׀ חזק יהוה צבאות שמו ריב יריב
he-will-defend to-defend name-of-him Hosts Yahweh-of strong One-Redeeming-them (34)

את־ ריבם למען הרגיע את־ הארץ והרגיז
but-he-may-bring-unrest the-land *** he-may-bring-rest so-that cause-of-them ***

לישבי בבל׃ חרב על־ כשדים נאם־ יהוה
Yahweh declaration-of Chaldeans against sword (35) Babylon to-ones-living-of

ואל־ ישבי בבל ואל־ שריה ואל־
and-against officials-of-her and-against Babylon ones-living-of and-against

חכמיה׃ חרב אל־ הבדים ונאלו
and-they-will-become-fools the-false-prophets against sword (36) wise-men-of-her

חרב אל־ גבוריה וחתו׃ חרב אל־
against sword (37) and-they-will-be-terrified warriors-of-her against sword

סוסיו ואל־ רכבו ואל־ כל־ הערב אשר
who the-foreigner all-of and-against chariot-of-him and-against horses-of-him

בתוכה והיו לנשים חרב אל־ אוצרתיה
treasures-of-her against sword as-women and-they-will-become in-rank-of-her

ובזזו׃ חרב אל־ מימיה ויבשו
and-they-will-dry-up waters-of-her on drought (38) and-they-will-be-plundered

let no one escape.
Repay her for her deeds;
do to her as she has done.
For she has defied the LORD,
the Holy One of Israel.
30 Therefore, her young men will
fall in the streets;
all her soldiers will be
silenced in that day,"
declares the LORD.
31 "See, I am against you, O
arrogant one,"
declares the Lord, the LORD
Almighty,
"for your day has come,
the time for you to be
punished.
32 The arrogant one will stumble
and fall
and no one will help her up;
I will kindle a fire in her
towns
that will consume all who
are around her."
33 This is what the LORD Almighty says:
"The people of Israel are
oppressed,
and the people of Judah as
well.
All their captors hold them
fast,
refusing to let them go.
34 Yet their Redeemer is strong;
the LORD Almighty is his
name.
He will vigorously defend
their cause
so that he may bring rest to
their land,
but unrest to those who live
in Babylon.
35 "A sword against the
Babylonians!"
declares the LORD—
"against those who live in
Babylon
and against her officials and
wise men!
36 A sword against her false
prophets!
They will become fools.
A sword against her warriors!
They will be filled with
terror.
37 A sword against her horses
and chariots
and all the foreigners in her
ranks!
They will become women.
A sword against her treasures!
They will be plundered.
38 A drought on[l] her waters!
They will dry up.

[l]38 Or *A sword against*

*29 Many mss do not have a *Kethib* form for the *Qere* reading.

°29 ק לה

כִּי אֶרֶץ פְּסִלִים הִיא וּבָאֵימִים יִתְהֹלָלוּ׃ לָכֵן יֵשְׁבוּ
they-will-live so (39) they-go-mad and-with-the-terrors she idols land-of for

צִיִּים אֶת־אִיִּים וְיָשְׁבוּ בָהּ בְּנוֹת יַעֲנָה וְלֹא־
and-not owl daughters-of in-her and-they-will-dwell hyenas with desert-creatures

תֵשֵׁב עוֹד לָנֶצַח וְלֹא תִשְׁכּוֹן עַד־דּוֹר
generation to she-will-be-lived-in or-not to-forever again she-will-be-inhabited

וָדוֹר׃ כְּמַהְפֵּכַת אֱלֹהִים אֶת־סְדֹם וְאֶת־עֲמֹרָה וְאֶת־שְׁכֵנֶיהָ
neighbors-of-them and Gomorrah and Sodom *** God as-overthrow-of (40) and-generation

נְאֻם־יְהוָה לֹא־יֵשֵׁב שָׁם אִישׁ וְלֹא־יָגוּר בָּהּ בֶּן־
son-of in-her he-will-dwell and-not one there he-will-live not Yahweh declaration-of

אָדָם׃ הִנֵּה עַם בָּא מִצָּפוֹן וְגוֹי גָּדוֹל וּמְלָכִים רַבִּים
many-ones and-kings great and-nation from-north coming army look! (41) man

יֵעֹרוּ מִיַּרְכְּתֵי־אָרֶץ׃ קֶשֶׁת וְכִידֹן יַחֲזִיקוּ אַכְזָרִי הֵמָּה
they cruel they-are-armed and-spear bow (42) earth from-ends-of they-are-stirred-up

וְלֹא יְרַחֵמוּ קוֹלָם כַּיָּם יֶהֱמֶה וְעַל־סוּסִים יִרְכָּבוּ
they-ride horses and-on he-roars like-the-sea sound-of-them they-have-mercy and-not

עָרוּךְ כְּאִישׁ לַמִּלְחָמָה עָלַיִךְ בַּת־בָּבֶל׃ שָׁמַע
he-heard (43) Babylon Daughter-of against-you for-the-battle like-man being-formed

מֶלֶךְ־בָּבֶל אֶת־שִׁמְעָם וְרָפוּ יָדָיו צָרָה
anguish hands-of-him and-they-hang-limp report-of-them *** Babylon king-of

הֶחֱזִיקַתְהוּ חִיל כַּיּוֹלֵדָה׃ הִנֵּה כְּאַרְיֵה יַעֲלֶה
he-comes-up like-lion see! (44) like-the-woman-being-in-labor pain she-gripped-him

מִגְּאוֹן הַיַּרְדֵּן אֶל־נְוֵה אֵיתָן כִּי־אַרְגִּעָה
I-will-do-instantly indeed rich pastureland-of to the-Jordan from-thicket-of

אֲרוֹצֵם מֵעָלֶיהָ וּמִי בָחוּר אֵלֶיהָ אֶפְקֹד
I-will-appoint for-her one-being-chosen and-who? from-upon-her I-will-chase-them

כִּי מִי כָמוֹנִי וּמִי יוֹעִדֶנִּי וּמִי־זֶה רֹעֶה
one-being-shepherd this and-who? he-can-challenge-me and-who? like-me who? indeed

אֲשֶׁר יַעֲמֹד לְפָנָי׃ לָכֵן שִׁמְעוּ עֲצַת־יְהוָה אֲשֶׁר יָעַץ
he-planned that Yahweh plan-of hear! therefore (45) against-me he-can-stand who

אֶל־בָּבֶל וּמַחְשְׁבוֹתָיו אֲשֶׁר חָשַׁב אֶל־אֶרֶץ כַּשְׂדִּים אִם־
that Chaldeans land-of against he-purposed that and-purposes-of-him Babylon against

לֹא יִסְחָבוּם צְעִירֵי הַצֹּאן אִם־לֹא יַשִּׁים
he-will-destroy indeed that the-flock young-ones-of they-will-drag-away-them indeed

עֲלֵיהֶם נָוֶה׃ מִקּוֹל נִתְפְּשָׂה בָבֶל נִרְעֲשָׁה
she-will-tremble Babylon she-is-captured at-sound-of (21) pasture because-of-them

הָאָרֶץ וּזְעָקָה בַּגּוֹיִם נִשְׁמָע׃ כֹּה אָמַר יְהוָה
Yahweh he-says this (51:1) he-will-be-heard among-the-nations and-cry the-earth

For it is a land of idols,
idols that will go mad with terror.

39 "So desert creatures and hyenas will live there,
and there the owl will dwell.
It will never again be inhabited
or lived in from generation to generation.
40 As God overthrew Sodom and Gomorrah
along with their neighboring towns,"
declares the LORD,
"so no one will live there;
no man will dwell in it.

41 "Look! An army is coming from the north;
a great nation and many kings
are being stirred up from the ends of the earth.
42 They are armed with bows and spears;
they are cruel and without mercy.
They sound like the roaring sea
as they ride on their horses;
they come like men in battle formation
to attack you, O Daughter of Babylon.
43 The king of Babylon has heard reports about them,
and his hands hang limp.
Anguish has gripped him,
pain like that of a woman in labor.
44 Like a lion coming up from Jordan's thickets
to a rich pastureland,
I will chase Babylon from its land in an instant.
Who is the chosen one I will appoint for this?
Who is like me and who can challenge me?
And what shepherd can stand against me?"
45 Therefore, hear what the LORD has planned against Babylon,
what he has purposed against the land of the Babylonians:
The young of the flock will be dragged away;
he will completely destroy their pasture because of them.
46 At the sound of Babylon's capture the earth will tremble;
its cry will resound among the nations.

51 This is what the LORD says:
"See, I will stir up the

°44 ק אריצם

הִנְנִי מֵעִיר עַל־ בָּבֶל וְאֶל־ יֹשְׁבֵי לֵב קָמָי
Kamai Leb ones-being-people-of and-against Babylon against stirring-up see-I!

רוּחַ מַשְׁחִית׃ (2) וְשִׁלַּחְתִּי לְבָבֶל ׀ זָרִים
ones-being-foreign to-Babylon and-I-will-send (2) one-destroying spirit-of

וְזֵרוּהָ וִיבֹקְקוּ אֶת־ אַרְצָהּ כִּי־ הָיוּ
they-will-be indeed land-of-her *** and-they-will-devastate and-they-will-winnow-her

עָלֶיהָ מִסָּבִיב בְּיוֹם רָעָה׃ (3) אֶל־ יִדְרֹךְ ידרך†
†*** let-him-string *to (3) disaster in-day-of on-every-side opposite-her

הַדֹּרֵךְ קַשְׁתּוֹ וְאֶל־†† יִתְעַל בְּסִרְיֹנוֹ וְאַל־
and-not to-armor-of-him let-him-put-on ††or-to bow-of-him the-one-being-archer

תַּחְמְלוּ אֶל־ בַּחֻרֶיהָ הַחֲרִימוּ כָּל־ צְבָאָהּ׃ (4) וְנָפְלוּ
and-they-will-fall (4) army-of-her all-of destroy! young-men-of-her to you-spare

חֲלָלִים בְּאֶרֶץ כַּשְׂדִּים וּמְדֻקָּרִים בְּחוּצוֹתֶיהָ׃
in-streets-of-her and-ones-being-fatally-wounded Chaldea in-land-of slain-ones

(5) כִּי לֹא־ אַלְמָן יִשְׂרָאֵל וִיהוּדָה מֵאֱלֹהָיו מֵיְהוָה צְבָאוֹת כִּי
though Hosts by-Yahweh-of by-God-of-him and-Judah Israel forsaken not for (5)

אַרְצָם מָלְאָה אָשָׁם מִקְּדוֹשׁ יִשְׂרָאֵל׃ (6) נֻסוּ ׀ מִתּוֹךְ
from-inside-of flee! (6) Israel before-Holy-One-of guilt she-is-full land-of-them

בָּבֶל וּמַלְּטוּ אִישׁ נַפְשׁוֹ אַל־ תִּדַּמּוּ בַּעֲוֺנָהּ כִּי
indeed because-of-sin-of-her you-be-destroyed not life-of-him each and-run! Babylon

עֵת נְקָמָה הִיא לַיהוָה גְּמוּל הוּא מְשַׁלֵּם לָהּ׃ (7) כּוֹס־ זָהָב בָּבֶל
Babylon gold cup-of (7) to-her paying he desert for-Yahweh she vengeance time-of

בְּיַד־ יְהוָה מְשַׁכֶּרֶת כָּל־ הָאָרֶץ מִיֵּינָהּ שָׁתוּ
they-drank from-wine-of-her the-earth whole-of one-making-drunk Yahweh in-hand-of

גוֹיִם עַל־ כֵּן יִתְהֹלְלוּ גוֹיִם׃ (8) פִּתְאֹם נָפְלָה בָבֶל
Babylon she-will-fall suddenly (8) nations they-went-mad this for nations

וַתִּשָּׁבֵר הֵילִילוּ עָלֶיהָ קְחוּ צֳרִי לְמַכְאוֹבָהּ אוּלַי
perhaps for-pain-of-her balm get! over-her wail! and-she-will-be-broken

תֵּרָפֵא׃ (9) רִפִּאנוּ אֶת־ בָּבֶל וְלֹא נִרְפָּתָה
she-can-be-healed but-not Babylon *** we-would-have-healed (9) she-can-be-healed

עִזְבוּהָ וְנֵלֵךְ אִישׁ לְאַרְצוֹ כִּי־ נָגַע אֶל־ הַשָּׁמַיִם
the-skies to he-reaches for to-land-of-him each and-let-us-go leave-her!

מִשְׁפָּטָהּ וְנִשָּׂא עַד־ שְׁחָקִים׃ (10) הוֹצִיא יְהוָה אֶת־ צִדְקֹתֵינוּ
vindications-of-us *** Yahweh he-brought (10) clouds to and-he-rises judgment-of-her

בֹּאוּ וּנְסַפְּרָה בְצִיּוֹן אֶת־ מַעֲשֵׂה יְהוָה אֱלֹהֵינוּ׃ (11) הָבֵרוּ הַחִצִּים
the-arrows sharpen! (11) God-of-us Yahweh deed-of *** in-Zion and-let-us-tell come!

מִלְאוּ הַשְּׁלָטִים הֵעִיר יְהוָה אֶת־ רוּחַ מַלְכֵי מָדַי כִּי־
because Medes kings-of spirit-of *** Yahweh he-stirred-up the-shields take-up!

spirit of a destroyer
against Babylon and the
people of Leb Kamai.[m]
2 I will send foreigners to
Babylon
to winnow her and to
devastate her land;
they will oppose her on every
side
in the day of her disaster.
3 Let not the archer string his
bow,
nor let him put on his
armor.
Do not spare her young men;
completely destroy[n] her
army.
4 They will fall down slain in
Babylon,[o]
fatally wounded in her
streets.
5 For Israel and Judah have not
been forsaken
by their God, the LORD
Almighty,
though their land[p] is full of
guilt
before the Holy One of
Israel.
6 "Flee from Babylon!
Run for your lives!
Do not be destroyed because
of her sins.
It is time for the LORD's
vengeance;
he will pay her what she
deserves.
7 Babylon was a gold cup in the
LORD's hand;
she made the whole earth
drunk.
The nations drank her wine;
therefore they have now
gone mad.
8 Babylon will suddenly fall and
be broken.
Wail over her!
Get balm for her pain;
perhaps she can be healed.
9 " 'We would have healed
Babylon,
but she cannot be healed;
let us leave her and each go to
his own land,
for her judgment reaches to
the skies,
it rises as high as the
clouds.'
10 " 'The LORD has vindicated us;
come, let us tell in Zion
what the LORD our God has
done.'
11 "Sharpen the arrows,
take up the shields!
The LORD has stirred up the
kings of the Medes,

m1 *Leb Kamai* is a cryptogram for Chaldea, that is, Babylonia.
n3 The Hebrew term refers to the irrevocable giving over of things or persons to the LORD, often by totally destroying them.
o4 Or *Chaldea*
p5 Or / *and the land* ⌞*of the Babylonians*⌟

*3a Most mss have *pathah* under the *aleph* (אַל), *not*.

†3b Most mss do not have a *Qere* reading for the *Ketbib* form; some point it like the preceding word.

††3b Most mss have *pathah* under the *aleph* (וְאַל), *and-not*.

q9 ק רפינו

עַל־ בָּבֶל מְזִמָּתוֹ לְהַשְׁחִיתָהּ כִּי־ נִקְמַת יְהוָה הִיא
she Yahweh vengeance-of indeed to-destroy-her purpose-of-him Babylon against

נִקְמַת הֵיכָלוֹ׃ אֶל־ חוֹמֹת בָּבֶל שְׂאוּ־ נֵס הַחֲזִיקוּ
reinforce! banner lift-up! Babylon walls-of against (12) temple-of-him vengeance-of

הַמִּשְׁמָר הָקִימוּ שֹׁמְרִים הָכִינוּ הָאֹרְבִים כִּי גַם־ זָמַם
he-purposed also for the-ones-ambushing prepare! men-watching station! the-guard

יְהוָה גַּם־ עָשָׂה אֵת אֲשֶׁר־ דִּבֶּר אֶל־ יֹשְׁבֵי
ones-being-people-of against he-decreed what *** he-will-carry-out also Yahweh

בָבֶל׃ שֹׁכַנְתְּי° עַל־ מַיִם רַבִּים רַבַּת אוֹצָרֹת בָּא קִצֵּךְ
end-of-you he-came treasures rich-of many-ones waters by one-living (13) Babylon

אַמַּת בִּצְעֵךְ׃ נִשְׁבַּע יְהוָה צְבָאוֹת בְּנַפְשׁוֹ כִּי
indeed by-self-of-him Hosts Yahweh-of he-swore (14) cutting-off-of-you time-of

אִם־ מִלֵּאתִיךְ אָדָם כַּיֶּלֶק וְעָנוּ עָלַיִךְ הֵידָד׃
shout over-you and-they-will-shout as-the-locust man I-will-fill-you surely

עֹשֵׂה אֶרֶץ בְּכֹחוֹ מֵכִין תֵּבֵל בְּחָכְמָתוֹ
by-wisdom-of-him world one-founding-of by-power-of-him earth one-making-of (15)

וּבִתְבוּנָתוֹ נָטָה שָׁמָיִם׃ לְקוֹל תִּתּוֹ
to-give-him when-thunder (16) heavens he-stretched-out and-by-understanding-of-him

הֲמוֹן מַיִם בַּשָּׁמַיִם וַיַּעַל נְשִׂאִים מִקְצֵה־ אָרֶץ
earth from-end-of clouds and-he-makes-rise in-the-heavens waters roar-of

בְּרָקִים לַמָּטָר עָשָׂה וַיֹּצֵא רוּחַ מֵאֹצְרֹתָיו׃
from-storehouses-of-him wind and-he-brings-out he-sends with-the-rain lightnings

נִבְעַר כָּל־ אָדָם מִדַּעַת הֹבִישׁ כָּל־
every-of he-is-shamed without-knowledge man every-of he-is-senseless (17)

צֹרֵף מִפָּסֶל כִּי שֶׁקֶר נִסְכּוֹ וְלֹא־ רוּחַ בָּם׃
in-them breath and-no image-of-him fraud indeed by-idol one-being-goldsmith

הֶבֶל הֵמָּה מַעֲשֵׂה תַּעְתֻּעִים בְּעֵת פְּקֻדָּתָם יֹאבֵדוּ׃
they-will-perish judgment-of-them at-time-of mockeries object-of they worthless (18)

לֹא־ כְאֵלֶּה חֵלֶק יַעֲקוֹב כִּי־ יוֹצֵר הַכֹּל הוּא וְשֵׁבֶט
including-tribe-of he the-all One-Making for Jacob Portion-of like-these not (19)

נַחֲלָתוֹ יְהוָה צְבָאוֹת שְׁמוֹ׃ מַפֵּץ־אַתָּה לִי כְּלֵי
weapons-of to-me you war-club (20) name-of-him Hosts Yahweh-of inheritance-of-him

מִלְחָמָה וְנִפַּצְתִּי בְךָ גוֹיִם וְהִשְׁחַתִּי בְךָ מַמְלָכוֹת׃
kingdoms with-you and-I-will-destroy nations with-you and-I-will-shatter battle

וְנִפַּצְתִּי בְךָ סוּס וְרֹכְבוֹ וְנִפַּצְתִּי בְךָ
with-you and-I-will-shatter and-one-riding-him horse with-you and-I-will-shatter (21)

רֶכֶב וְרֹכְבוֹ׃ וְנִפַּצְתִּי בְךָ אִישׁ וְאִשָּׁה
and-woman man with-you and-I-will-shatter (22) and-one-driving-him chariot

because his purpose is to
destroy Babylon.
The LORD will take vengeance,
vengeance for his temple.
12 Lift up a banner against the
walls of Babylon!
Reinforce the guard,
station the watchmen,
prepare an ambush!
The LORD will carry out his
purpose,
his decree against the people
of Babylon.
13 You who live by many waters
and are rich in treasures,
your end has come,
the time for you to be cut
off.
14 The LORD Almighty has sworn
by himself:
I will surely fill you with
men, as with a swarm of
locusts,
and they will shout in
triumph over you.

15 "He made the earth by his
power;
he founded the world by his
wisdom
and stretched out the
heavens by his
understanding.
16 When he thunders, the waters
in the heavens roar;
he makes clouds rise from
the ends of the earth.
He sends lightning with the
rain
and brings out the wind
from his storehouses.

17 "Every man is senseless and
without knowledge;
every goldsmith is shamed
by his idols.
His images are a fraud;
they have no breath in
them.
18 They are worthless, the objects
of mockery;
when their judgment comes,
they will perish.
19 He who is the Portion of Jacob
is not like these,
for he is the Maker of all
things,
including the tribe of his
inheritance—
the LORD Almighty is his
name.

20 "You are my war club,
my weapon for battle—
with you I shatter nations,
with you I destroy
kingdoms,
21 with you I shatter horse and
rider,
with you I shatter chariot
and driver,
22 with you I shatter man and
woman,

°13 ק שכנת

וְנִפַּצְתִּי בְךָ זָקֵן וָנָעַר וְנִפַּצְתִּי בְךָ בָּחוּר
young-man with-you and-I-will-shatter and-youth old-man with-you and-I-will-shatter

וּבְתוּלָה׃ (23) וְנִפַּצְתִּי בְךָ רֹעֶה וְעֶדְרוֹ
and-flock-of-him one-being-shepherd with-you and-I-will-shatter (23) and-maiden

וְנִפַּצְתִּי בְךָ אִכָּר וְצִמְדּוֹ וְנִפַּצְתִּי בְךָ
with-you and-I-will-shatter and-oxen-of-him farmer with-you and-I-will-shatter

פַּחוֹת וּסְגָנִים׃ (24) וְשִׁלַּמְתִּי לְבָבֶל וּלְכֹל יוֹשְׁבֵי
ones-living-of and-to-all-of to-Babylon and-I-will-repay (24) and-officials governors

כַשְׂדִּים אֵת כָּל־ רָעָתָם אֲשֶׁר־ עָשׂוּ בְצִיּוֹן לְעֵינֵיכֶם
before-eyes-of-you in-Zion they-did that wrong-of-them all-of *** Chaldea

נְאֻם יְהוָה׃ (25) הִנְנִי אֵלֶיךָ הַר הַמַּשְׁחִית
the-one-destroying mountain-of against-you see-I! (25) Yahweh declaration-of

נְאֻם־ יְהוָה הַמַּשְׁחִית אֶת־ כָּל־ הָאָרֶץ וְנָטִיתִי
and-I-will-stretch the-earth whole-of *** the-one-destroying Yahweh declaration-of

אֶת־ יָדִי עָלֶיךָ וְגִלְגַּלְתִּיךָ מִן־ הַסְּלָעִים וּנְתַתִּיךָ
and-I-will-make-you the-cliffs from and-I-will-roll-you against-you hand-of-me ***

לְהַר שְׂרֵפָה׃ (26) וְלֹא־ יִקְחוּ מִמְּךָ אֶבֶן לְפִנָּה
for-corner rock from-you they-will-take and-not (26) burned-out into-mountain

וְאֶבֶן לְמוֹסָדוֹת כִּי־ שִׁמְמוֹת עוֹלָם תִּהְיֶה נְאֻם־
declaration-of you-will-be forever desolations-of for for-foundations or-stone

יְהוָה׃ (27) שְׂאוּ־ נֵס בָּאָרֶץ תִּקְעוּ שׁוֹפָר בַּגּוֹיִם קַדְּשׁוּ
prepare! among-the-nations trumpet blow! in-the-land banner lift-up! (27) Yahweh

עָלֶיהָ גּוֹיִם הַשְׁמִיעוּ עָלֶיהָ מַמְלְכוֹת אֲרָרַט מִנִּי וְאַשְׁכְּנָז פִּקְדוּ
appoint! and-Ashkenaz Minni Ararat kingdoms against-her summon! nations against-her

עָלֶיהָ טִפְסָר הַעֲלוּ־ סוּס כְּיֶלֶק סָמָר׃ (28) קַדְּשׁוּ עָלֶיהָ
against-her prepare! (28) swarming like-locust horse send-up! commander against-her

גוֹיִם אֶת־ מַלְכֵי מָדַי אֶת־ פַּחוֹתֶיהָ וְאֶת־ כָּל־ סְגָנֶיהָ וְאֵת
and officials-of-her all-of and governors-of-her *** Medes kings-of *** nations

כָּל־ אֶרֶץ מֶמְשַׁלְתּוֹ׃ (29) וַתִּרְעַשׁ הָאָרֶץ וַתָּחֹל כִּי
for and-she-writhes the-land and-she-trembles (29) rule-of-him country-of all-of

קָמָה עַל־ בָּבֶל מַחְשְׁבוֹת יְהוָה לָשׂוּם אֶת־ אֶרֶץ בָּבֶל
Babylon land-of *** to-lay Yahweh purposes-of Babylon against she-stands

לְשַׁמָּה מֵאֵין יוֹשֵׁב׃ (30) חָדְלוּ גִבּוֹרֵי בָבֶל לְהִלָּחֵם
to-fight Babylon warriors-of they-stopped (30) one-living with-no to-waste

יָשְׁבוּ בַּמְּצָדוֹת נָשְׁתָה גְבוּרָתָם הָיוּ
they-became strength-of-them she-is-exhausted in-the-strongholds they-remain

לְנָשִׁים הִצִּיתוּ מִשְׁכְּנֹתֶיהָ נִשְׁבְּרוּ בְרִיחֶיהָ׃
bars-of-her they-are-broken dwellings-of-her they-set-on-fire like-women

with you I shatter old man
and youth,
with you I shatter young
man and maiden,
23 with you I shatter shepherd
and flock,
with you I shatter farmer
and oxen,
with you I shatter governors
and officials.

24 "Before your eyes I will repay
Babylon and all who live in Babylonia[a] for all the wrong they have
done in Zion," declares the LORD.

25 "I am against you, O
destroying mountain,
you who destroy the whole
earth,"
declares the LORD.
"I will stretch out my hand
against you,
roll you off the cliffs,
and make you a burned-out
mountain.
26 No rock will be taken from
you for a cornerstone,
nor any stone for a
foundation,
for you will be desolate
forever,"
declares the LORD.

27 "Lift up a banner in the land!
Blow the trumpet among the
nations!
Prepare the nations for battle
against her;
summon against her these
kingdoms:
Ararat, Minni and
Ashkenaz.
Appoint a commander against
her;
send up horses like a swarm
of locusts.
28 Prepare the nations for battle
against her—
the kings of the Medes,
their governors and all their
officials,
and all the countries they
rule.
29 The land trembles and writhes,
for the LORD's purposes
against Babylon stand—
to lay waste the land of
Babylon
so that no one will live
there.
30 Babylon's warriors have
stopped fighting;
they remain in their
strongholds.
Their strength is exhausted;
they have become like
women.
Her dwellings are set on fire;
the bars of her gates are
broken.

a24 Or *Chaldea;* also in verse 35

רָץ לִקְרַאת־ רָץ יָרוּץ וּמַגִּיד
and-one-being-messenger he-runs one-being-courier to-follow one-being-courier (31)

לִקְרַאת מַגִּיד לְהַגִּיד לְמֶלֶךְ בָּבֶל כִּי־ נִלְכְּדָה
she-is-captured that Babylon to-king-of to-announce one-being-messenger to-follow

עִירוֹ מִקָּצֶה׃ וְהַמַּעְבָּרוֹת נִתְפָּשׂוּ וְאֶת־ הָאֲגַמִּים
the-marshes and they-are-seized and-the-river-crossings (32) to-entirety city-of-him

שָׂרְפוּ בָאֵשׁ וְאַנְשֵׁי הַמִּלְחָמָה נִבְהָלוּ׃ כִּי כֹה
this for (33) they-are-terrified the-battle and-men-of on-fire they-set

אָמַר יְהוָה צְבָאוֹת אֱלֹהֵי יִשְׂרָאֵל בַּת־ בָּבֶל כְּגֹרֶן
like-threshing-floor Babylon Daughter-of Israel God-of Hosts Yahweh-of he-says

עֵת הִדְרִיכָהּ עוֹד מְעַט וּבָאָה עֵת־ הַקָּצִיר לָהּ׃
to-her the-harvest time-of and-she-will-come soon yet he-tramples-her time-of

אֲכָלַנוּ הֲמָמַנוּ נְבוּכַדְרֶאצַּר מֶלֶךְ בָּבֶל הִצִּיגַנוּ כְּלִי
jar he-made-me Babylon king-of Nebuchadrezzar he-confused-me he-devoured-me (34)

רִיק בְּלָעַנוּ כַּתַּנִּין מִלָּא כְרֵשׂוֹ מֵעֲדָנָי
with-delicacies-of-me stomach-of-him he-filled like-the-serpent he-swallowed-me empty

הֱדִיחָנוּ׃ חֲמָסִי וּשְׁאֵרִי עַל־ בָּבֶל תֹּאמַר
she-says Babylon upon and-flesh-of-me violence-of-me (35) he-spewed-out-me

יֹשֶׁבֶת צִיּוֹן וְדָמִי אֶל־ יֹשְׁבֵי כַשְׂדִּים תֹּאמַר
she-says Chaldea ones-living-of on and-blood-of-me Zion one-inhabiting-of

יְרוּשָׁלִָם׃ לָכֵן כֹּה אָמַר יְהוָה הִנְנִי־ רָב אֶת־ רִיבֵךְ
cause-of-you *** defending see-I! Yahweh he-says this therefore (36) Jerusalem

וְנִקַּמְתִּי אֶת־ נִקְמָתֵךְ וְהַחֲרַבְתִּי אֶת־ יַמָּהּ
sea-of-her *** and-I-will-dry-up vengeance-of-you *** and-I-will-avenge

וְהֹבַשְׁתִּי אֶת־ מְקוֹרָהּ׃ וְהָיְתָה בָבֶל ׀ לְגַלִּים ׀
as-heap-of-ruins Babylon and-she-will-be (37) spring-of-her *** and-I-will-make-dry

מְעוֹן־ תַּנִּים שַׁמָּה וּשְׁרֵקָה מֵאֵין יוֹשֵׁב׃
one-living with-no and-object-of-scorn object-of-horror jackals haunt-of

יַחְדָּו כַּכְּפִרִים יִשְׁאָגוּ נָעֲרוּ כְּגוֹרֵי אֲרָיוֹת׃
lions like-cubs-of they-growl they-roar like-the-young-lions together (38)

בְּחֻמָּם אָשִׁית אֶת־ מִשְׁתֵּיהֶם
feast-of-them *** I-will-set-out while-to-be-aroused-them (39)

וְהִשְׁכַּרְתִּים לְמַעַן יַעֲלֹזוּ וְיָשְׁנוּ שְׁנַת־ עוֹלָם
forever sleep-of and-they-sleep they-laugh so-that and-I-will-make-drunk-them

וְלֹא יָקִיצוּ נְאֻם יְהוָה׃ אוֹרִידֵם
I-will-bring-down-them (40) Yahweh declaration-of they-will-awake and-not

כְּכָרִים לִטְבוֹחַ כְּאֵילִים עִם־ עַתּוּדִים׃ אֵיךְ נִלְכְּדָה שֵׁשַׁךְ
Sheshach she-will-be-captured how! (41) goats and like-rams to-slaughter like-lambs

°34a ק אכלני; °34b ק הממני
°34c ק הציגני; °34d ק בלעני
°34e ק הדיחני

31 One courier follows another
and messenger follows messenger
to announce to the king of Babylon
that his entire city is captured,
32 the river crossings seized,
the marshes set on fire,
and the soldiers terrified."

33 This is what the LORD Almighty, the God of Israel, says:

"The Daughter of Babylon is like a threshing floor
at the time it is trampled;
the time to harvest her will soon come."

34 "Nebuchadnezzar king of Babylon has devoured us,
he has thrown us into confusion,
he has made us an empty jar.
Like a serpent he has swallowed us
and filled his stomach with our delicacies,
and then has spewed us out.
35 May the violence done to our flesh[r] be upon Babylon,"
say the inhabitants of Zion.
"May our blood be on those who live in Babylonia,"
says Jerusalem.

36 Therefore, this is what the LORD says:

"See, I will defend your cause
and avenge you;
I will dry up her sea
and make her springs dry.
37 Babylon will be a heap of ruins,
a haunt of jackals,
an object of horror and scorn,
a place where no one lives.
38 Her people all roar like young lions,
they growl like lion cubs.
39 But while they are aroused,
I will set out a feast for them
and make them drunk,
so that they shout with laughter—
then sleep forever and not awake,"
declares the LORD.
40 "I will bring them down
like lambs to the slaughter,
like rams and goats.

41 "How Sheshach[s] will be captured,

[r] 35 Or *done to us and to our children*
[s] 41 *Sheshach* is a cryptogram for Babylon.

וַתִּתָּפֵשׂ תְּהִלַּת כָּל־ הָאָרֶץ אֵיךְ הָיְתָה לְשַׁמָּה
as-horror she-will-be what! the-earth whole-of boast-of and-she-will-be-seized

בָּבֶל בַּגּוֹיִם׃ עָלָה עַל־ בָּבֶל הַיָּם בַּהֲמוֹן
with-roar-of the-sea Babylon over he-will-rise (42) among-the-nations Babylon

גַּלָּיו נִכְסָתָה׃ הָיוּ עָרֶיהָ לְשַׁמָּה אֶרֶץ
land-of as-desolation towns-of-her they-will-be (43) she-will-be-covered waves-of-him

צִיָּה וַעֲרָבָה אֶרֶץ לֹא־ יֵשֵׁב בָּהֵן כָּל־ אִישׁ וְלֹא־ יַעֲבֹר בָּהֵן
through-them he-travels and-not one any-of in-them he-lives not land and-desert dryness

בֶּן־ אָדָם׃ וּפָקַדְתִּי עַל־ בֵּל בְּבָבֶל וְהֹצֵאתִי אֶת־
*** and-I-will-make-spew-out in-Babylon Bel to and-I-will-punish (44) man son-of

בִּלְעוֹ מִפִּיו וְלֹא־ יִנְהֲרוּ אֵלָיו עוֹד
longer to-him they-will-stream and-not from-mouth-of-him thing-swallowed-of-him

גּוֹיִם גַּם־ חוֹמַת בָּבֶל נָפָלָה׃ צְאוּ מִתּוֹכָהּ
from-inside-of-her come-out! (45) she-will-fall Babylon wall-of and nations

עַמִּי וּמַלְּטוּ אִישׁ אֶת־ נַפְשׁוֹ מֵחֲרוֹן אַף־ יְהוָה׃
Yahweh anger-of from-fierceness-of life-of-him *** each and-run! people-of-me

וּפֶן־ יֵרַךְ לְבַבְכֶם וְתִירְאוּ בַּשְּׁמוּעָה
when-the-rumor or-you-be-afraid heart-of-you let-him-be-lost and-not (46)

הַנִּשְׁמַעַת בָּאָרֶץ וּבָא בַשָּׁנָה הַשְּׁמוּעָה וְאַחֲרָיו
and-after-him the-rumor in-the-year for-he-comes in-the-land the-one-being-heard

בַּשָּׁנָה הַשְּׁמוּעָה וְחָמָס בָּאָרֶץ וּמֹשֵׁל עַל־ מֹשֵׁל׃
one-ruling against and-one-ruling in-the-land indeed-violence the-rumor in-the-year

לָכֵן הִנֵּה יָמִים בָּאִים וּפָקַדְתִּי עַל־פְּסִילֵי בָבֶל וְכָל־
and-whole-of Babylon idols-of to when-I-will-punish ones-coming days see! for (47)

אַרְצָהּ תֵּבוֹשׁ וְכָל־ חֲלָלֶיהָ יִפְּלוּ
they-will-lie ones-slain-of-her and-all-of she-will-be-disgraced land-of-her

בְּתוֹכָהּ׃ וְרִנְּנוּ עַל־ בָּבֶל שָׁמַיִם וָאָרֶץ וְכֹל אֲשֶׁר
that and-all and-earth heavens Babylon over then-they-will-shout (48) at-within-her

בָּהֶם כִּי מִצָּפוֹן יָבוֹא־ לָהּ הַשּׁוֹדְדִים נְאֻם־
declaration-of the-ones-destroying against-her he-will-attack from-north for in-them

יְהוָה׃ גַּם־ בָּבֶל לִנְפֹּל חַלְלֵי יִשְׂרָאֵל גַּם־ לְבָבֶל
because-of-Babylon indeed Israel ones-slain-of to-fall Babylon indeed (49) Yahweh

נָפְלוּ חַלְלֵי כָל־ הָאָרֶץ׃ פְּלֵטִים מֵחֶרֶב הִלְכוּ אַל־
not leave! from-sword escapees (50) the-earth all-of ones-slain-of they-fell

תַּעֲמֹדוּ זִכְרוּ מֵרָחוֹק אֶת־ יְהוָה וִירוּשָׁלַםִ תַּעֲלֶה עַל־
into you-take and-Jerusalem Yahweh *** in-distant-land remember! you-linger

לְבַבְכֶם׃ בֹּשְׁנוּ כִּי־ שָׁמַעְנוּ חֶרְפָּה כִּסְּתָה כְלִמָּה פָּנֵינוּ
faces-of-us shame she-covers insult we-heard for we-are-disgraced (51) heart-of-you

the boast of the whole earth
seized!
What a horror Babylon will be
among the nations!
42 The sea will rise over Babylon;
its roaring waves will cover
her.
43 Her towns will be desolate,
a dry and desert land,
a land where no one lives,
through which no man
travels.
44 I will punish Bel in Babylon
and make him spew out
what he has swallowed.
The nations will no longer
stream to him.
And the wall of Babylon
will fall.

45 "Come out of her, my people!
Run for your lives!
Run from the fierce anger of
the LORD.
46 Do not lose heart or be afraid
when rumors are heard in
the land;
one rumor comes this year,
another the next,
rumors of violence in the
land
and of ruler against ruler.
47 For the time will surely come
when I will punish the idols
of Babylon;
her whole land will be
disgraced
and her slain will all lie
fallen within her.
48 Then heaven and earth and all
that is in them
will shout for joy over
Babylon,
for out of the north
destroyers will attack her,"
declares the LORD.

49 "Babylon must fall because of
Israel's slain,
just as the slain in all the
earth
have fallen because of
Babylon.
50 You who have escaped the
sword,
leave and do not linger!
Remember the LORD in a
distant land,
and think on Jerusalem."

51 "We are disgraced,
for we have been insulted
and shame covers our faces,

כִּי בָּאוּ זָרִים עַל־ מִקְדְּשֵׁי בֵּית יְהוָה׃
Yahweh house-of holy-places-of into ones-being-foreign they-entered because

לָכֵן הִנֵּה־יָמִים בָּאִים נְאֻם־ יְהוָה וּפָקַדְתִּי עַל־
to when-I-will-punish Yahweh declaration-of ones-coming days see! but (52)

פְּסִילֶיהָ וּבְכָל־ אַרְצָהּ יֶאֱנֹק חָלָל׃ כִּי־
if (53) wounded he-will-groan land-of-her and-through-all-of idols-of-her

תַעֲלֶה בָבֶל הַשָּׁמַיִם וְכִי תְבַצֵּר מְרוֹם עֻזָּהּ
stronghold-of-her loftiness-of she-fortifies and-if the-skies Babylon she-reaches

מֵאִתִּי יָבֹאוּ שֹׁדְדִים לָהּ נְאֻם־ יְהוָה׃
Yahweh declaration-of against-her ones-destroying they-will-come from-with-me

קוֹל זְעָקָה מִבָּבֶל וְשֶׁבֶר גָּדוֹל מֵאֶרֶץ כַּשְׂדִּים׃
Chaldeans from-land-of great and-destruction from-Babylon cry sound-of (54)

כִּי־ שֹׁדֵד יְהוָה אֶת־ בָּבֶל וְאִבַּד מִמֶּנָּה קוֹל גָּדוֹל
great noise from-her and-he-will-silence Babylon *** Yahweh destroying indeed (55)

וְהָמוּ גַלֵּיהֶם כְּמַיִם רַבִּים נִתַּן שְׁאוֹן
roar-of he-will-resound great-ones like-waters waves-of-them and-they-will-rage

קוֹלָם׃ כִּי בָא עָלֶיהָ עַל־ בָּבֶל שׁוֹדֵד
one-destroying Babylon against against-her he-will-come indeed (56) voice-of-them

וְנִלְכְּדוּ גִּבּוֹרֶיהָ חִתְּתָה קַשְּׁתוֹתָם
bows-of-them she-will-be-broken warriors-of-her and-they-will-be-captured

כִּי אֵל גְּמֻלוֹת יְהוָה שַׁלֵּם יְשַׁלֵּם׃ וְהִשְׁכַּרְתִּי
and-I-will-make-drunk (57) he-will-repay to-repay Yahweh retributions God-of for

שָׂרֶיהָ וַחֲכָמֶיהָ פַּחוֹתֶיהָ וּסְגָנֶיהָ
and-officers-of-her governors-of-her and-wise-men-of-her officials-of-her

וְגִבּוֹרֶיהָ וְיָשְׁנוּ שְׁנַת־ עוֹלָם וְלֹא יָקִיצוּ
they-will-awake and-not forever sleep-of and-they-will-sleep and-warriors-of-her

נְאֻם־ הַמֶּלֶךְ יְהוָה צְבָאוֹת שְׁמוֹ׃ כֹּה־ אָמַר יְהוָה
Yahweh-of he-says this (58) name-of-him Hosts Yahweh-of the-King declaration-of

צְבָאוֹת חֹמוֹת בָּבֶל הָרְחָבָה עַרְעֵר תִּתְעַרְעָר וּשְׁעָרֶיהָ
and-gates-of-her she-will-be-leveled to-level the-thick Babylon walls-of Hosts

הַגְּבֹהִים בָּאֵשׁ יִצַּתּוּ וְיִגְעוּ עַמִּים בְּדֵי־
for-sake-of peoples and-they-exhaust-themselves they-will-set on-fire the-high-ones

רִיק וּלְאֻמִּים בְּדֵי־ אֵשׁ וְיָעֵפוּ׃ הַדָּבָר אֲשֶׁר־ צִוָּה ׀
he-gave that the-message (59) also-they-labor flame for-sake-of and-nations nothing

יִרְמְיָהוּ הַנָּבִיא אֶת־ שְׂרָיָה בֶן־ נֵרִיָּה בֶּן־ מַחְסֵיָה בְּלֶכְתּוֹ אֶת־
with when-to-go-him Mahseiah son-of Neriah son-of Seraiah *** the-prophet Jeremiah

צִדְקִיָּהוּ מֶלֶךְ־ יְהוּדָה בָּבֶל בִּשְׁנַת הָרְבִעִית לְמָלְכוֹ וּשְׂרָיָה
now-Seraiah to-reign-him the-fourth in-year-of Babylon Judah king-of Zedekiah

because foreigners have
entered
the holy places of the LORD's
house."

52"But days are coming,"
declares the LORD,
"when I will punish her
idols,
and throughout her land
the wounded will groan.
53Even if Babylon reaches the
sky
and fortifies her lofty
stronghold,
I will send destroyers
against her,"
declares the LORD.

54"The sound of a cry comes
from Babylon,
the sound of great
destruction
from the land of the
Babylonians.[i]
55The LORD will destroy Babylon;
he will silence her noisy
din.
Waves ⌊of enemies⌋ will rage
like great waters;
the roar of their voices will
resound.
56A destroyer will come against
Babylon;
her warriors will be
captured,
and their bows will be
broken.
For the LORD is a God of
retribution;
he will repay in full.
57I will make her officials and
wise men drunk,
her governors, officers and
warriors as well;
they will sleep forever and not
awake,"
declares the King, whose
name is the LORD
Almighty.

58This is what the LORD Almighty says:

"Babylon's thick wall will be
leveled
and her high gates set on
fire;
the peoples exhaust themselves
for nothing,
the nations' labor is only
fuel for the flames."

59This is the message Jeremiah gave to the staff officer Seraiah son of Neriah, the son of Mahseiah, when he went to Babylon with Zedekiah king of Judah in

[i]54 Or *Chaldeans*

שַׂר מְנוּחָה׃ וַיִּכְתֹּב יִרְמְיָהוּ אֵת כָּל־ הָרָעָה
the-disaster all-of *** Jeremiah now-he-wrote (60) resting-place officer-of

אֲשֶׁר־ תָּבוֹא אֶל־ בָּבֶל אֶל־סֵפֶר אֶחָד אֵת כָּל־ הַדְּבָרִים הָאֵלֶּה
the-these the-things all-of *** one scroll on Babylon upon she-would-come that

הַכְּתֻבִים אֶל־ בָּבֶל׃ וַיֹּאמֶר יִרְמְיָהוּ אֶל־שְׂרָיָה
Seraiah to Jeremiah and-he-said (61) Babylon concerning the-ones-being-recorded

כְּבֹאֲךָ בָבֶל וְרָאִיתָ וְקָרָאתָ אֵת כָּל־ הַדְּבָרִים הָאֵלֶּה׃
the-these the-words all-of *** that-you-read then-you-see Babylon when-to-get-to-you

וְאָמַרְתָּ יְהוָה אַתָּה דִבַּרְתָּ אֶל־ הַמָּקוֹם הַזֶּה לְהַכְרִיתוֹ
to-destroy-him the-this the-place concerning you-said you Yahweh then-you-say (62)

לְבִלְתִּי הֱיוֹת־בּוֹ יוֹשֵׁב לְמֵאָדָם וְעַד־בְּהֵמָה כִּי־ שִׁמְמוֹת עוֹלָם
forever desolations-of but animal or-to either-of-man one-living in-him to-be not

תִּהְיֶה׃ וְהָיָה כְּכַלֹּתְךָ לִקְרֹא אֶת־ הַסֵּפֶר הַזֶּה
the-this the-scroll *** to-read when-to-finish-you and-he-will-be (63) she-will-be

תִּקְשֹׁר עָלָיו אֶבֶן וְהִשְׁלַכְתּוֹ אֶל־ תּוֹךְ פְּרָת׃ וְאָמַרְתָּ
then-you-say (64) Euphrates middle-of into and-you-throw-him stone on-him you-tie

כָּכָה תִּשְׁקַע בָּבֶל וְלֹא־ תָקוּם מִפְּנֵי הָרָעָה אֲשֶׁר אָנֹכִי
I that the-disaster because-of she-will-rise and-not Babylon she-will-sink so

מֵבִיא עָלֶיהָ וְיָעֵפוּ עַד־ הֵנָּה דִּבְרֵי יִרְמְיָהוּ׃ בֶּן־
son-of (52:1) Jeremiah words-of at-here end and-they-will-fall upon-her bringing

עֶשְׂרִים וְאַחַת שָׁנָה צִדְקִיָּהוּ בְּמָלְכוֹ וְאַחַת עֶשְׂרֵה שָׁנָה מָלַךְ
he-reigned year ten and-one-of when-to-become-king-him Zedekiah year and-one-of twenty

בִּירוּשָׁלִָם וְשֵׁם אִמּוֹ חֲמִיטַל° בַּת־ יִרְמְיָהוּ מִלִּבְנָה׃
from-Libnah Jeremiah daughter-of Hamutal mother-of-him and-name-of in-Jerusalem

וַיַּעַשׂ הָרַע בְּעֵינֵי יְהוָה כְּכֹל אֲשֶׁר־עָשָׂה יְהוֹיָקִים׃ כִּי ׀
indeed (3) Jehoiakim he-did that as-all Yahweh in-eyes-of the-evil and-he-did (2)

עַל־ אַף יְהוָה הָיְתָה בִּירוּשָׁלִַם וִיהוּדָה עַד־
until and-to-Judah to-Jerusalem she-happened Yahweh anger-of because-of

הִשְׁלִיכוֹ אוֹתָם מֵעַל פָּנָיו וַיִּמְרֹד צִדְקִיָּהוּ בְּמֶלֶךְ
against-king-of Zedekiah now-he-rebelled presences-of-him from-in them he-thrust-him

בָּבֶל׃ וַיְהִי בַשָּׁנָה הַתְּשִׁעִית לְמָלְכוֹ בַּחֹדֶשׁ הָעֲשִׂירִי
the-tenth in-the-month to-reign-him the-ninth in-the-year so-he-was (4) Babylon

בֶּעָשׂוֹר לַחֹדֶשׁ בָּא נְבוּכַדְרֶאצַּר מֶלֶךְ־ בָּבֶל הוּא וְכָל־
and-whole-of he Babylon king-of Nebuchadrezzar he-marched of-the-month on-the-ten

חֵילוֹ עַל־ יְרוּשָׁלִַם וַיַּחֲנוּ עָלֶיהָ וַיִּבְנוּ עָלֶיהָ
against-her and-they-built outside-her and-they-camped Jerusalem against army-of-him

דָּיֵק סָבִיב׃ וַתָּבֹא הָעִיר בַּמָּצוֹר עַד עַשְׁתֵּי עֶשְׂרֵה
ten one-of until under-the-siege the-city and-she-went (5) around siege-work

°1 ק חמוטל

the fourth year of his reign. [60]Jeremiah had written on a scroll about all the disasters that would come upon Babylon—all that had been recorded concerning Babylon. [61]He said to Seraiah, "When you get to Babylon, see that you read all these words aloud. [62]Then say, 'O LORD, you have said you will destroy this place, so that neither man nor animal will live in it; it will be desolate forever.' [63]When you finish reading this scroll, tie a stone to it and throw it into the Euphrates. [64]Then say, 'So will Babylon sink to rise no more because of the disaster I will bring upon her. And her people will fall.' "

The words of Jeremiah end here.

*The Fall of Jerusalem*

52 Zedekiah was twenty-one years old when he became king, and he reigned in Jerusalem eleven years. His mother's name was Hamutal daughter of Jeremiah; she was from Libnah. [2]He did evil in the eyes of the LORD, just as Jehoiakim had done. [3]It was because of the LORD's anger that all this happened to Jerusalem and Judah, and in the end he thrust them from his presence.

Now Zedekiah rebelled against the king of Babylon.

[4]So in the ninth year of Zedekiah's reign, on the tenth day of the tenth month, Nebuchadnezzar king of Babylon marched against Jerusalem with his whole army. They camped outside the city and built siege works all around it. [5]The city was kept under siege until the eleventh year of

שָׁנָה לַמֶּלֶךְ צִדְקִיָּהוּ׃ בַּחֹדֶשׁ הָרְבִיעִי בְּתִשְׁעָה לַחֹדֶשׁ
of-the-month on-nine the-fourth by-the-month (6) Zedekiah of-the-king year

וַיֶּחֱזַק הָרָעָב בָּעִיר וְלֹא־ הָיָה לֶחֶם לְעַם
for-people-of food he-was so-not in-the-city the-famine then-he-became-severe

הָאָרֶץ׃ וַתִּבָּקַע הָעִיר וְכָל־ אַנְשֵׁי הַמִּלְחָמָה
the-army men-of and-all-of the-city then-she-was-broken-through (7) the-land

יִבְרְחוּ וַיֵּצְאוּ מֵהָעִיר לַיְלָה דֶּרֶךְ שַׁעַר בֵּין הַחֹמֹתַיִם
the-two-walls between gate way-of night from-the-city and-they-left they-fled

אֲשֶׁר עַל־ גַּן הַמֶּלֶךְ וְכַשְׂדִּים עַל־ הָעִיר סָבִיב
surrounding the-city against though-Chaldeans the-king garden-of near that

וַיֵּלְכוּ דֶּרֶךְ הָעֲרָבָה׃ וַיִּרְדְּפוּ חֵיל־ כַּשְׂדִּים אַחֲרֵי
after Chaldeans army-of but-they-pursued (8) the-Arabah way-of and-they-fled

הַמֶּלֶךְ וַיַּשִּׂיגוּ אֶת־ צִדְקִיָּהוּ בְּעַרְבֹת יְרֵחוֹ וְכָל־
and-all-of Jericho in-plains-of Zedekiah *** and-they-overtook the-king

חֵילוֹ נָפֹצוּ מֵעָלָיו׃ וַיִּתְפְּשׂוּ אֶת־ הַמֶּלֶךְ
the-king *** and-they-captured (9) from-with-him they-were-scattered soldier-of-him

וַיַּעֲלוּ אֹתוֹ אֶל־ מֶלֶךְ בָּבֶל רִבְלָתָה בְּאֶרֶץ חֲמָת וַיְדַבֵּר
and-he-pronounced Hamath in-land-of at-Riblah Babylon king-of to him and-they-took

אִתּוֹ מִשְׁפָּטִים׃ וַיִּשְׁחַט מֶלֶךְ־ בָּבֶל אֶת־ בְּנֵי צִדְקִיָּהוּ
Zedekiah sons-of *** Babylon king-of and-he-slaughtered (10) sentences on-him

לְעֵינָיו וְגַם אֶת־ כָּל־ שָׂרֵי יְהוּדָה שָׁחַט בְּרִבְלָתָה׃
in-at-Riblah he-slaughtered Judah officials-of all-of *** and-also before-eyes-of-him

וְאֶת־ עֵינֵי צִדְקִיָּהוּ עִוֵּר וַיַּאַסְרֵהוּ בַנְחֻשְׁתַּיִם
with-the-bronze-shackles and-he-bound-him he-put-out Zedekiah eyes-of then (11)

וַיְבִאֵהוּ מֶלֶךְ־ בָּבֶל בָּבֶלָה וַיִּתְּנֵהוּ בְבֵית־ הַפְּקֻדֹּת
the-prisons in-house-of and-he-put-him to-Babylon Babylon king-of and-he-took-him

עַד־ יוֹם מוֹתוֹ׃ וּבַחֹדֶשׁ הַחֲמִישִׁי בֶּעָשׂוֹר לַחֹדֶשׁ
of-the-month on-the-ten the-fifth and-in-the-month (12) death-of-him day-of till

הִיא שְׁנַת תְּשַׁע־עֶשְׂרֵה שָׁנָה לַמֶּלֶךְ נְבוּכַדְרֶאצַּר מֶלֶךְ־ בָּבֶל בָּא
he-came Babylon king-of Nebuchadrezzar of-the-king year ten nine-of year-of she

נְבוּזַרְאֲדָן רַב־ טַבָּחִים עָמַד לִפְנֵי מֶלֶךְ־ בָּבֶל
Babylon king-of before he-served imperial-guards commander-of Nebuzaradan

בִּירוּשָׁלִָם׃ וַיִּשְׂרֹף אֶת־ בֵּית־ יְהוָה וְאֶת־ בֵּית הַמֶּלֶךְ
the-royalty palace-of and Yahweh temple-of *** and-he-set-fire (13) to-Jerusalem

וְאֵת כָּל־ בָּתֵּי יְרוּשָׁלִַם וְאֶת־ כָּל־ בֵּית הַגָּדוֹל שָׂרַף
he-burned the-important building-of every-of and Jerusalem houses-of all-of and

בָּאֵשׁ׃ וְאֶת־כָּל־ חֹמוֹת יְרוּשָׁלִַם סָבִיב נָתְצוּ כָּל־ חֵיל
army-of whole-of they-broke-down around Jerusalem walls-of all-of and (14) with-fire

King Zedekiah.
6 By the ninth day of the fourth month the famine in the city had become so severe that there was no food for the people to eat. 7 Then the city wall was broken through, and the whole army fled. They left the city at night through the gate between the two walls near the king's garden, though the Babylonians[u] were surrounding the city. They fled toward the Arabah,[v] 8 but the Babylonian[w] army pursued King Zedekiah and overtook him in the plains of Jericho. All his soldiers were separated from him and scattered, 9 and he was captured.

He was taken to the king of Babylon at Riblah in the land of Hamath, where he pronounced sentence on him. 10 There at Riblah the king of Babylon slaughtered the sons of Zedekiah before his eyes; he also killed all the officials of Judah. 11 Then he put out Zedekiah's eyes, bound him with bronze shackles and took him to Babylon, where he put him in prison till the day of his death.

12 On the tenth day of the fifth month, in the nineteenth year of Nebuchadnezzar king of Babylon, Nebuzaradan commander of the imperial guard, who served the king of Babylon, came to Jerusalem. 13 He set fire to the temple of the LORD, the royal palace and all the houses of Jerusalem. Every important building he burned down. 14 The whole Babylonian army under the commander of the imperial guard broke down all the walls

u7 Or *Chaldeans;* also in verse 17
v7 Or *the Jordan Valley*
w8 Or *Chaldean;* also in verse 14

°11 ק בית

כַּשְׂדִּים אֲשֶׁר אֶת־ רַב־ טַבָּחִים׃ וּמִדַּלּוֹת הָעָם
the-people and-of-poor-ones-of (15) imperial-guards commander-of under who Chaldeans

וְאֶת־יֶתֶר הָעָם הַנִּשְׁאָרִים בָּעִיר וְאֶת־ הַנֹּפְלִים אֲשֶׁר
who the-ones-going-over and in-the-city the-ones-remaining the-people rest-of and

נָפְלוּ אֶל־ מֶלֶךְ בָּבֶל וְאֵת יֶתֶר הָאָמוֹן הֶגְלָה נְבוּזַרְאֲדָן
Nebuzaradan he-exiled the-craftsman rest-of and Babylon king-of to they-went-over

רַב־ טַבָּחִים׃ וּמִדַּלּוֹת הָאָרֶץ הִשְׁאִיר
he-left-behind the-land but-of-poor-ones-of (16) imperial-guards commander-of

נְבוּזַרְאֲדָן רַב־ טַבָּחִים לְכֹרְמִים
as-ones-working-vineyards imperial-guards commander-of Nebuzaradan

וּלְיֹגְבִים׃ וְאֶת־ עַמּוּדֵי הַנְּחֹשֶׁת אֲשֶׁר לְבֵית־ יְהוָה
Yahweh at-temple-of that the-bronze pillars-of and (17) and-as-ones-working-fields

וְאֶת־ הַמְּכֹנוֹת וְאֶת־ יָם הַנְּחֹשֶׁת אֲשֶׁר בְּבֵית־ יְהוָה שִׁבְּרוּ
they-broke-up Yahweh at-temple-of that the-bronze Sea-of and the-movable-stands and

כַשְׂדִּים וַיִּשְׂאוּ אֶת־ כָּל־ נְחֻשְׁתָּם בָּבֶלָה׃ וְאֶת־הַסִּרוֹת
the-pots and (18) to-Babylon bronze-of-them all-of *** and-they-carried Chaldeans

וְאֶת־ הַיָּעִים וְאֶת־ הַמְזַמְּרוֹת וְאֶת־ הַמִּזְרָקֹת וְאֶת־ הַכַּפּוֹת וְאֵת
and the-dishes and the-sprinkling-bowls and the-wick-trimmers and the-shovels and

כָּל־ כְּלֵי הַנְּחֹשֶׁת אֲשֶׁר־ יְשָׁרְתוּ בָהֶם לָקָחוּ׃ וְאֶת־
and (19) they-took-away with-them they-served that the-bronze articles-of all-of

הַסִּפִּים וְאֶת־הַמַּחְתּוֹת וְאֶת־ הַמִּזְרָקוֹת וְאֶת־ הַסִּירוֹת וְאֶת־ הַמְּנֹרוֹת
the-lampstands and the-pots and the-sprinkling-bowls and the-censers and the-basins

וְאֶת־ הַכַּפּוֹת וְאֶת־ הַמְּנַקִּיּוֹת* אֲשֶׁר זָהָב זָהָב וַאֲשֶׁר־ כֶּסֶף
silver or-that gold gold that the-bowls-for-drink-offerings and the-dishes and

כֶּסֶף לָקַח רַב־ טַבָּחִים׃ הָעַמּוּדִים שְׁנַיִם הַיָּם אֶחָד
one the-Sea two the-pillars (20) imperial-guards commander-of he-took-away silver

וְהַבָּקָר שְׁנֵים־עָשָׂר נְחֹשֶׁת אֲשֶׁר־תַּחַת הַמְּכֹנוֹת אֲשֶׁר עָשָׂה הַמֶּלֶךְ
the-king he-made which the-movable-stands under that bronze ten two and-the-bull

שְׁלֹמֹה לְבֵית יְהוָה לֹא־ הָיָה מִשְׁקָל לִנְחֻשְׁתָּם כָּל־
all-of for-bronze-of-them weight he-was not Yahweh for-temple-of Solomon

הַכֵּלִים הָאֵלֶּה׃ וְהָעַמּוּדִים שְׁמֹנֶה עֶשְׂרֵה אַמָּה קוֹמָה° הָעַמֻּד
the-pillar height-of cubit ten eight now-the-pillars (21) the-these the-articles

הָאֶחָד וְחוּט שְׁתֵּים־עֶשְׂרֵה אַמָּה יְסֻבֶּנּוּ וְעָבְיוֹ אַרְבַּע
four and-thickness-of-him he-went-around-him cubit ten two and-measure-of the-each

אֶצְבָּעוֹת† נָבוּב׃ וְכֹתֶרֶת עָלָיו נְחֹשֶׁת וְקוֹמַת הַכֹּתֶרֶת
the-capital and-height-of bronze on-him and-capital (22) being-hollow fingers

הָאַחַת חָמֵשׁ אַמּוֹת וּשְׂבָכָה וְרִמּוֹנִים עַל־הַכּוֹתֶרֶת סָבִיב הַכֹּל
the-all around the-capital on and-pomegranates and-network cubits five the-each

around Jerusalem. [15]Nebuzaradan the commander of the guard carried into exile some of the poorest people and those who remained in the city, along with the rest of the craftsmen[x] and those who had gone over to the king of Babylon. [16]But Nebuzaradan left behind the rest of the poorest people of the land to work the vineyards and fields.

[17]The Babylonians broke up the bronze pillars, the movable stands and the bronze Sea that were at the temple of the LORD and they carried all the bronze to Babylon. [18]They also took away the pots, shovels, wick trimmers, sprinkling bowls, dishes and all the bronze articles used in the temple service. [19]The commander of the imperial guard took away the basins, censers, sprinkling bowls, pots, lampstands, dishes and bowls used for drink offerings—all that were made of pure gold or silver.

[20]The bronze from the two pillars, the Sea and the twelve bronze bulls under it, and the movable stands, which King Solomon had made for the temple of the LORD, was more than could be weighed. [21]Each of the pillars was eighteen cubits high and twelve cubits in circumference[y]; each was four fingers thick, and hollow. [22]The bronze capital on top of the one pillar was five cubits[z] high and was decorated with a network and pomegranates of bronze all

[x]15 Or *populace*
[y]21 That is, about 27 feet (about 8.1 meters) high and 18 feet (about 5.4 meters) in circumference
[z]22 That is, about 7 1/2 feet (about 2.3 meters)

*19 Most mss have no *dagesh* in the *mem*, but do in the *qoph* and *yod* (הַמְּנַקִּיּוֹת).

†21 Most mss have *segbol* under the *aleph* (אֶצְ).

°21 ק קומת

נְחֹשֶׁת וְכָאֵלֶּה לָעַמּוּד הַשֵּׁנִי וְרִמּוֹנִים ׃
with-pomegranates the-other to-the-pillar and-similar-to-these bronze

(23) וַיִּהְיוּ הָרִמֹּנִים תִּשְׁעִים וְשִׁשָּׁה רוּחָה כָּל־ הָרִמּוֹנִים
the-pomegranates total-of on-side and-six ninety the-pomegranates and-they-were (23)

מֵאָה עַל־ הַשְּׂבָכָה סָבִיב׃ (24) וַיִּקַּח רַב־
commander-of and-he-took-prisoner (24) surrounding the-network above hundred

טַבָּחִים אֶת־ שְׂרָיָה כֹּהֵן הָרֹאשׁ וְאֶת־ צְפַנְיָה כֹּהֵן הַמִּשְׁנֶה
the-next priest-of Zephaniah and the-chief priest-of Seraiah *** imperial-guards

וְאֶת־שְׁלֹשֶׁת שֹׁמְרֵי הַסַּף׃ (25) וּמִן־ הָעִיר לָקַח סָרִיס אֶחָד
one officer he-took the-city and-from (25) the-door ones-keeping-of three-of and

אֲשֶׁר־הָיָה פָקִיד ׀ עַל־אַנְשֵׁי הַמִּלְחָמָה וְשִׁבְעָה אֲנָשִׁים מֵרֹאֵי
from-ones-seeing-of men and-seven the-fight men-of over officer-in-charge he-was who

פְנֵי־ הַמֶּלֶךְ אֲשֶׁר נִמְצְאוּ בָעִיר וְאֵת סֹפֵר שַׂר
chief-officer-of secretary and in-the-city they-were-found who the-king faces-of

הַצָּבָא הַמַּצְבִּא אֶת־ עַם הָאָרֶץ וְשִׁשִּׁים אִישׁ
man and-sixty the-land people-of *** the-one-conscripting the-conscription

מֵעַם הָאָרֶץ הַנִּמְצְאִים בְּתוֹךְ הָעִיר׃ (26) וַיִּקַּח
and-he-took (26) the-city at-inside-of the-ones-being-found the-land from-people-of

אוֹתָם נְבוּזַרְאֲדָן רַב־ טַבָּחִים וַיֹּלֶךְ אוֹתָם אֶל־ מֶלֶךְ
king-of to them and-he-brought imperial-guards commander-of Nebuzaradan them

בָּבֶל רִבְלָתָה׃ (27) וַיַּכֶּה אוֹתָם מֶלֶךְ בָּבֶל וַיְמִתֵם
and-he-executed-them Babylon king-of them and-he-struck (27) at-Riblah Babylon

בְּרִבְלָה בְּאֶרֶץ חֲמָת וַיִּגֶל יְהוּדָה מֵעַל אַדְמָתוֹ׃
land-of-him from-on Judah so-he-went-into-captivity Hamath in-land-of at-Riblah

(28) זֶה הָעָם אֲשֶׁר הֶגְלָה נְבוּכַדְרֶאצַּר בִּשְׁנַת־שֶׁבַע יְהוּדִים שְׁלֹשֶׁת
three-of Jews seven in-year-of Nebuchadrezzar he-exiled whom the-people this (28)

אֲלָפִים וְעֶשְׂרִים וּשְׁלֹשָׁה׃ (29) בִּשְׁנַת שְׁמוֹנֶה עֶשְׂרֵה לִנְבוּכַדְרֶאצַּר
of-Nebuchadrezzar ten eight in-year-of (29) and-three and-twenty thousands

מִירוּשָׁלַםִ נֶפֶשׁ שְׁמֹנֶה מֵאוֹת שְׁלֹשִׁים וּשְׁנָיִם׃ (30) בִּשְׁנַת שָׁלֹשׁ וְעֶשְׂרִים
and-twenty three in-year-of (30) and-two thirty hundreds eight person from-Jerusalem

לִנְבוּכַדְרֶאצַּר הֶגְלָה נְבוּזַרְאֲדָן רַב־ טַבָּחִים יְהוּדִים נֶפֶשׁ
person Jews imperial-guards commander-of Nebuzaradan he-exiled of-Nebuchadrezzar

שְׁבַע מֵאוֹת אַרְבָּעִים וַחֲמִשָּׁה כָּל־ נֶפֶשׁ אַרְבַּעַת אֲלָפִים וְשֵׁשׁ מֵאוֹת׃
hundreds and-six-of thousands four-of person all-of and-five forty hundreds seven-of

(31) וַיְהִי בִשְׁלֹשִׁים וָשֶׁבַע שָׁנָה לְגָלוּת יְהוֹיָכִן מֶלֶךְ־יְהוּדָה
Judah king-of Jehoiachin of-exile-of year and-seven in-thirty and-he-was (31)

בִּשְׁנֵים עָשָׂר חֹדֶשׁ בְּעֶשְׂרִים וַחֲמִשָּׁה לַחֹדֶשׁ נָשָׂא אֱוִיל מְרֹדַךְ
Merodach Evil he-lifted of-the-month and-five on-twenty month ten in-two

around. The other pillar, with its pomegranates, was similar.
[23] There were ninety-six pomegranates on the sides; the total number of pomegranates above the surrounding network was a hundred.

[24] The commander of the guard took as prisoners Seraiah the chief priest, Zephaniah the priest next in rank and the three doorkeepers.
[25] Of those still in the city, he took the officer in charge of the fighting men, and seven royal advisers. He also took the secretary who was chief officer in charge of conscripting the people of the land and sixty of his men who were found in the city.
[26] Nebuzaradan the commander took them all and brought them to the king of Babylon at Riblah.
[27] There at Riblah, in the land of Hamath, the king had them executed.

So Judah went into captivity, away from her land.
[28] This is the number of the people Nebuchadnezzar carried into exile:

in the seventh year, 3,023 Jews;
[29] in Nebuchadnezzar's eighteenth year,
832 people from Jerusalem;
[30] in his twenty-third year,
745 Jews taken into exile by Nebuzaradan
the commander of the imperial guard.
There were 4,600 people in all.

*Jehoiachin Released*

[31] In the thirty-seventh year of the exile of Jehoiachin king of Judah, in the year Evil-Merodach[a]

[a] 31 Also called *Amel-Marduk*

מֶלֶךְ בָּבֶל בִּשְׁנַת מַלְכֻתוֹ אֶת־ רֹאשׁ יְהוֹיָכִין מֶלֶךְ־יְהוּדָה

Judah king-of Jehoiachin head-of *** kingship-of-him in-year-of Babylon king-of

וַיֹּצֵא אוֹתוֹ מִבֵּית הַכְּלִיא° ׃ וַיְדַבֵּר אִתּוֹ טֹבוֹת

kind-things to-him and-he-spoke (32) the-prison from-house-of him and-he-freed

וַיִּתֵּן אֶת־ כִּסְאוֹ מִמַּעַל לְכִסֵּא מְלָכִים° אֲשֶׁר אִתּוֹ בְּבָבֶל׃

in-Babylon with-him who the-kings to-seat-of at-above seat-of-him *** and-he-gave

וְשִׁנָּה אֵת בִּגְדֵי כִלְאוֹ וְאָכַל לֶחֶם לְפָנָיו

before-him food and-he-ate imprisonment-of-him clothes-of *** so-he-put-aside (33)

תָּמִיד כָּל־ יְמֵי חַיָּו ׃ וַאֲרֻחָתוֹ אֲרֻחַת

allowance-of and-allowance-of-him (34) lives-of-him days-of all-of regularly

תָּמִיד נִתְּנָה־ לּוֹ מֵאֵת מֶלֶךְ־ בָּבֶל דְּבַר־ יוֹם

day matter-of Babylon king-of from-with to-him she-was-given regular

בְּיוֹמוֹ עַד־ יוֹם מוֹתוֹ כֹּל יְמֵי חַיָּיו ׃

lives-of-him days-of all-of death-of-him day-of till by-day-of-him

became king of Babylon, he released Jehoiachin king of Judah and freed him from prison on the twenty-fifth day of the twelfth month. [32]He spoke kindly to him and gave him a seat of honor higher than those of the other kings who were with him in Babylon. [33]So Jehoiachin put aside his prison clothes and for the rest of his life ate regularly at the king's table. [34]Day by day the king of Babylon gave Jehoiachin a regular allowance as long as he lived, till the day of his death.

°31 ק הכלוא
°32 ק המלכים

אֵיכָה ׀ יָשְׁבָה בָדָד הָעִיר רַבָּתִי עָם הָיְתָה כְּאַלְמָנָה רַבָּתִי
great-of like-widow she-is people full-of the-city deserted she-lies how! (1:1)

בַגּוֹיִם שָׂרָתִי בַּמְּדִינוֹת הָיְתָה לָמַס׃ בָּכוֹ
to-weep (2) as-slave she-became among-the-provinces queen-of among-the-nations

תִבְכֶּה בַּלַּיְלָה וְדִמְעָתָהּ עַל לֶחֱיָהּ אֵין־לָהּ מְנַחֵם
one-comforting to-her not cheek-of-her upon and-tear-of-her at-the-night she-weeps

מִכָּל־אֹהֲבֶיהָ כָּל־רֵעֶיהָ בָּגְדוּ בָהּ הָיוּ
they-became to-her they-betrayed friends-of-her all-of ones-loving-her among-all-of

לָהּ לְאֹיְבִים׃ גָּלְתָה יְהוּדָה מֵעֹנִי
after-affliction Judah she-went-into-exile (3) as-ones-being-enemies to-her

וּמֵרֹב עֲבֹדָה הִיא יָשְׁבָה בַגּוֹיִם לֹא מָצְאָה
she-finds not among-the-nations she-dwells she labor and-after-harshness-of

מָנוֹחַ כָּל־רֹדְפֶיהָ הִשִּׂיגוּהָ בֵּין הַמְּצָרִים׃
the-distresses in-midst-of they-overtook-her ones-pursuing-her all-of resting-place

דַּרְכֵי צִיּוֹן אֲבֵלוֹת מִבְּלִי בָּאֵי מוֹעֵד כָּל־
all-of appointed-feast ones-coming-of from-without mourners Zion roads-of (4)

שְׁעָרֶיהָ שׁוֹמֵמִין כֹּהֲנֶיהָ נֶאֱנָחִים בְּתוּלֹתֶיהָ
maidens-of-her ones-groaning priests-of-her ones-being-desolate gateways-of-her

נּוּגוֹת וְהִיא מַר־לָהּ׃ הָיוּ צָרֶיהָ לְרֹאשׁ
as-master foes-of-her they-became (5) to-her bitter-anguish and-she ones-grieving

אֹיְבֶיהָ שָׁלוּ כִּי־יְהוָה הוֹגָהּ
he-brought-grief-to-her Yahweh indeed they-are-at-ease ones-being-enemies-of-her

עַל רֹב־פְּשָׁעֶיהָ עוֹלָלֶיהָ הָלְכוּ שְׁבִי לִפְנֵי־צָר׃
foe before exile they-went children-of-her sins-of-her many-of because-of

וַיֵּצֵא °מִן־ בַּת־ צִיּוֹן כָּל־ הֲדָרָהּ הָיוּ
they-are splendor-of-her all-of Zion *Daughter-of from* and-he-departed (6)

שָׂרֶיהָ כְּאַיָּלִים לֹא־מָצְאוּ מִרְעֶה וַיֵּלְכוּ בְלֹא־כֹחַ
strength with-no and-they-fled pasture they-find not like-deers princes-of-her

לִפְנֵי רוֹדֵף׃ זָכְרָה יְרוּשָׁלִַם יְמֵי עָנְיָהּ
affliction-of-her days-of Jerusalem she-remembers (7) one-pursuing before

וּמְרוּדֶיהָ כֹּל מַחֲמֻדֶיהָ אֲשֶׁר הָיוּ מִימֵי קֶדֶם
old in-days-of they-were that treasures-of-her all-of and-wanderings-of-her

בִּנְפֹל עַמָּהּ בְּיַד־צָר וְאֵין עוֹזֵר לָהּ
to-her helping and-no-one enemy into-hand-of people-of-her before-to-fall

רָאוּהָ צָרִים שָׂחֲקוּ עַל מִשְׁבַּתֶּהָ׃ חֵטְא חָטְאָה
she-sinned sin (8) destruction-of-her at they-laughed enemies they-looked-at-her

יְרוּשָׁלִַם עַל־כֵּן לְנִידָה הָיָתָה כָּל־מְכַבְּדֶיהָ הִזִּילוּהָ
they-despise-her ones-honoring-her all-of she-became as-unclean this for Jerusalem

1[a] How deserted lies the city,
once so full of people!
How like a widow is she,
who once was great among the nations!
She who was queen among the provinces
has now become a slave.

2 Bitterly she weeps at night,
tears are upon her cheeks.
Among all her lovers
there is none to comfort her.
All her friends have betrayed her;
they have become her enemies.

3 After affliction and harsh labor,
Judah has gone into exile.
She dwells among the nations;
she finds no resting place.
All who pursue her have overtaken her
in the midst of her distress.

4 The roads to Zion mourn,
for no one comes to her appointed feasts.
All her gateways are desolate,
her priests groan,
her maidens grieve,
and she is in bitter anguish.

5 Her foes have become her masters;
her enemies are at ease.
The LORD has brought her grief
because of her many sins.
Her children have gone into exile,
captive before the foe.

6 All the splendor has departed
from the Daughter of Zion.
Her princes are like deer
that find no pasture;
in weakness they have fled
before the pursuer.

7 In the days of her affliction and wandering
Jerusalem remembers all the treasures
that were hers in days of old.
When her people fell into enemy hands,
there was no one to help her.
Her enemies looked at her
and laughed at her destruction.

8 Jerusalem has sinned greatly
and so has become unclean.
All who honored her despise her,

[a] This chapter is an acrostic poem, the verses of which begin with the successive letters of the Hebrew alphabet.

*6 The *Qere* reads these two words as one.

°6 ק מבת

כִּי־ רָאוּהָ עֶרְוָתָהּ גַּם־ הִיא נֶאֶנְחָה וַתָּשָׁב אָחוֹר׃
away and-she-turns she-groans she and nakedness-of-her they-saw for

(9) טֻמְאָתָהּ בְּשׁוּלֶיהָ לֹא זָכְרָה אַחֲרִיתָהּ וַתֵּרֶד
and-she-fell future-of-her she-considered not on-skirts-of-her filthiness-of-her (9)

פְּלָאִים אֵין מְנַחֵם לָהּ רְאֵה יְהוָה אֶת־ עָנְיִי כִּי
for affliction-of-me *** Yahweh look! to-her comforting no-one astounding-ones

הִגְדִּיל אוֹיֵב׃ (10) יָדוֹ פָּרַשׂ צָר עַל כָּל־
all-of on enemy he-laid hand-of-him (10) one-being-enemy he-triumphed

מַחֲמַדֶּיהָ כִּי־ רָאֲתָה גוֹיִם בָּאוּ מִקְדָּשָׁהּ אֲשֶׁר
that sanctuary-of-her they-entered nations she-saw indeed treasures-of-her

צִוִּיתָה לֹא־ יָבֹאוּ בַקָּהָל לָךְ׃ (11) כָּל־ עַמָּהּ
people-of-her all-of (11) of-you into-the-assembly they-enter not you-commanded

נֶאֱנָחִים מְבַקְּשִׁים לֶחֶם נָתְנוּ מַחֲמוּדֵיהֶם בְּאֹכֶל לְהָשִׁיב
to-keep for-food treasures-of-them they-barter bread ones-searching ones-groaning

נֶפֶשׁ רְאֵה יְהוָה וְהַבִּיטָה כִּי הָיִיתִי זוֹלֵלָה׃ (12) לוֹא אֲלֵיכֶם
to-you nothing (12) one-being-despised I-am for and-consider! Yahweh look! life

כָּל־ עֹבְרֵי דֶרֶךְ הַבִּיטוּ וּרְאוּ אִם־ יֵשׁ מַכְאוֹב
suffering there-is if and-see! look-around! road ones-passing-by-of all-of

כְּמַכְאֹבִי אֲשֶׁר עוֹלַל לִי אֲשֶׁר הוֹגָה יְהוָה בְּיוֹם
in-day-of Yahweh he-brought that on-me he-was-inflicted that like-suffering-of-me

חֲרוֹן אַפּוֹ׃ (13) מִמָּרוֹם שָׁלַח־ אֵשׁ בְּעַצְמֹתַי
into-bones-of-me fire he-sent from-on-high (13) anger-of-him fierceness-of

וַיִּרְדֶּנָּה פָּרַשׂ רֶשֶׁת לְרַגְלַי הֱשִׁיבַנִי אָחוֹר נְתָנַנִי
he-made-me back he-turned-me for-feet-of-me net he-spread and-he-sent-down-her

שֹׁמֵמָה כָּל־ הַיּוֹם דָּוָה׃ (14) נִשְׂקַד עֹל פְּשָׁעַי
sins-of-me yoke he-was-bound (14) faint the-day all-of one-being-desolate

בְּיָדוֹ יִשְׂתָּרְגוּ עָלוּ עַל־ צַוָּארִי הִכְשִׁיל
he-sapped neck-of-me upon they-came they-were-woven-together by-hand-of-him

כֹּחִי נְתָנַנִי אֲדֹנָי בִּידֵי לֹא־אוּכַל קוּם׃ (15) סִלָּה
he-rejected (15) to-withstand I-can not into-hands-of Lord he-gave-me strength-of-me

כָל־ אַבִּירַי | אֲדֹנָי בְּקִרְבִּי קָרָא עָלַי מוֹעֵד לִשְׁבֹּר
to-crush army against-me he-summoned in-midst-of-me Lord warriors-of-me all-of

בַּחוּרָי גַּת דָּרַךְ אֲדֹנָי לִבְתוּלַת בַּת־ יְהוּדָה׃
Judah Daughter-of to-Virgin-of Lord he-trampled winepress young-men-of-me

(16) עַל־אֵלֶּה | אֲנִי בוֹכִיָּה עֵינִי | עֵינִי יֹרְדָה מַּיִם כִּי־ רָחַק
he-is-distant indeed tears overflowing eye-of-me eye-of-me weeping I these for (16)

מִמֶּנִּי מְנַחֵם מֵשִׁיב נַפְשִׁי הָיוּ בָנַי
children-of-me they-are spirit-of-me one-restoring one-comforting from-me

°11 ק מחמדיהם

for they have seen her
nakedness;
she herself groans
and turns away.
9 Her filthiness clung to her
skirts;
she did not consider her
future.
Her fall was astounding;
there was none to comfort
her.
"Look, O LORD, on my
affliction,
for the enemy has
triumphed."
10 The enemy laid hands
on all her treasures;
she saw pagan nations
enter her sanctuary—
those you had forbidden
to enter your assembly.
11 All her people groan
as they search for bread;
they barter their treasures for
food
to keep themselves alive.
"Look, O LORD, and consider,
for I am despised."
12 "Is it nothing to you, all you
who pass by?
Look around and see.
Is any suffering like my
suffering
that was inflicted on me,
that the LORD brought on me
in the day of his fierce
anger?
13 "From on high he sent fire,
sent it down into my bones.
He spread a net for my feet
and turned me back.
He made me desolate,
faint all the day long.
14 "My sins have been bound
into a yoke[b];
by his hands they were
woven together.
They have come upon my
neck
and the Lord has sapped my
strength.
He has handed me over
to those I cannot withstand.
15 "The Lord has rejected
all the warriors in my midst;
he has summoned an army
against me
to[c] crush my young men.
In his winepress the Lord has
trampled
the Virgin Daughter of
Judah.
16 "This is why I weep
and my eyes overflow with
tears.
No one is near to comfort me,
no one to restore my spirit.
My children are destitute

[b]14 Most Hebrew manuscripts; Septuagint *He kept watch over my sins*
[c]15 Or *has set a time for me / when he will*

שֹׁומְמִים כִּי גָבַר אֹויֵב׃ פֵּרְשָׂה
she-stretches-out (17) one-being-enemy he-prevailed because ones-being-destitute

צִיּוֹן בְּיָדֶיהָ אֵין מְנַחֵם לָהּ צִוָּה יְהוָה לְיַעֲקֹב
for-Jacob Yahweh he-decreed to-her comforting no-one with-hands-of-her Zion

סְבִיבָיו צָרָיו הָיְתָה יְרוּשָׁלַ͏ִם לְנִדָּה בֵּינֵיהֶם׃
among-them as-unclean-thing Jerusalem she-became foes-of-him ones-around-him

צַדִּיק הוּא יְהוָה כִּי פִיהוּ מָרִיתִי שִׁמְעוּ־נָא כָל־
all-of now! listen! I-rebelled command-of-him yet Yahweh he righteous (18)

עַמִּים וּרְאוּ מַכְאֹבִי בְּתוּלֹתַי וּבַחוּרַי
and-young-men-of-me maidens-of-me suffering-of-me and-look-upon! the-peoples

הָלְכוּ בַשֶּׁבִי׃ קָרָאתִי לַמְאַהֲבַי הֵמָּה
they to-the-ones-being-allies-of-me I-called (19) into-the-exile they-went

רִמּוּנִי כֹּהֲנַי וּזְקֵנַי בָּעִיר גָּוָעוּ כִּי־
while they-perished in-the-city and-elders-of-me priests-of-me they-betrayed-me

בִקְשׁוּ אֹכֶל לָמוֹ וְיָשִׁיבוּ אֶת־נַפְשָׁם׃ רְאֵה יְהוָה
Yahweh see! (20) life-of-them *** so-they-could-keep for-them food they-searched

כִּי־צַר־לִי מֵעַי חֳמַרְמָרוּ נֶהְפַּךְ לִבִּי
heart-of-me he-is-disturbed they-are-in-torment insides-of-me to-me distress that

בְּקִרְבִּי כִּי מָרוֹ מָרִיתִי מִחוּץ שִׁכְּלָה־חֶרֶב
sword she-bereaves at-outside I-was-rebellious to-be-rebellious for at-within-me

בַּבַּיִת כַּמָּוֶת׃ שָׁמְעוּ כִּי נֶאֱנָחָה אָנִי אֵין מְנַחֵם
comforting no-one I one-groaning that they-heard (21) only-the-death in-the-house

לִי כָּל־אֹיְבַי שָׁמְעוּ רָעָתִי שָׂשׂוּ
they-rejoice distress-of-me they-heard ones-being-enemies-of-me all-of to-me

כִּי אַתָּה עָשִׂיתָ הֵבֵאתָ יוֹם־קָרָאתָ וְיִהְיוּ כָמוֹנִי׃
like-me so-they-may-become you-announced day may-you-bring you-did you because

תָּבֹא כָל־רָעָתָם לְפָנֶיךָ וְעוֹלֵל לָמוֹ כַּאֲשֶׁר
just-as with-them and-deal! before-you wickedness-of-them all-of let-her-come (22)

עוֹלַלְתָּ לִי עַל כָּל־פְּשָׁעָי כִּי־רַבּוֹת אַנְחֹתַי
groans-of-me many-ones indeed sins-of-me all-of because-of with-me you-dealt

וְלִבִּי דַוָּי׃ אֵיכָה יָעִיב בְּאַפּוֹ׀ אֲדֹנָי אֶת־
*** Lord in-anger-of-him he-covered-with-cloud how! (2:1) faint and-heart-of-me

בַּת־צִיּוֹן הִשְׁלִיךְ מִשָּׁמַיִם אֶרֶץ תִּפְאֶרֶת יִשְׂרָאֵל וְלֹא־
and-not Israel splendor-of earth from-heavens he-hurled Zion Daughter-of

זָכַר הֲדֹם־רַגְלָיו בְּיוֹם אַפּוֹ׃ בִּלַּע
he-swallowed (2) anger-of-him in-day-of feet-of-him footstool-of he-remembered

אֲדֹנָי לֹא חָמַל אֵת כָּל־נְאוֹת יַעֲקֹב הָרַס בְּעֶבְרָתוֹ
in-wrath-of-him he-tore-down Jacob dwellings-of all-of *** he-pitied and-not Lord

because the enemy has
prevailed."

17 Zion stretches out her hands,
but there is no one to
comfort her.
The LORD has decreed for Jacob
that his neighbors become
his foes;
Jerusalem has become
an unclean thing among
them.

18 "The LORD is righteous,
yet I rebelled against his
command.
Listen, all you peoples;
look upon my suffering.
My young men and maidens
have gone into exile.

19 "I called to my allies
but they betrayed me.
My priests and my elders
perished in the city
while they searched for food
to keep themselves alive.

20 "See, O LORD, how distressed I
am!
I am in torment within,
and in my heart I am
disturbed,
for I have been most
rebellious.
Outside, the sword bereaves;
inside, there is only death.

21 "People have heard my
groaning,
but there is no one to
comfort me.
All my enemies have heard of
my distress;
they rejoice at what you
have done.
May you bring the day you
have announced
so they may become like
me.

22 "Let all their wickedness come
before you;
deal with them
as you have dealt with me
because of all my sins.
My groans are many
and my heart is faint."

2 [d] How the Lord has covered
the Daughter of Zion
with the cloud of his anger[e]!
He has hurled down the
splendor of Israel
from heaven to earth;
he has not remembered his
footstool
in the day of his anger.

2 Without pity the Lord has
swallowed up
all the dwellings of Jacob;
in his wrath he has torn down

[d] This chapter is an acrostic poem, the verses of which begin with the successive letters of the Hebrew alphabet.
[e] 1 Or *How the Lord in his anger / has treated the Daughter of Zion with contempt*

°18 ק העמים; °2 ק ולא

מִבְצְרֵי בַת־יְהוּדָה הִגִּיעַ לָאָרֶץ חִלֵּל
he-dishonored to-the-ground he-brought-down Judah Daughter-of strongholds-of

מַמְלָכָה וְשָׂרֶיהָ׃ גָּדַע בָּחֳרִי־אַף כֹּל
every-of anger in-fierceness-of he-cut-off (3) and-princes-of-her kingdom

קֶרֶן יִשְׂרָאֵל הֵשִׁיב אָחוֹר יְמִינוֹ מִפְּנֵי
at-presences-of right-hand-of-him back he-withdrew Israel horn-of

אוֹיֵב וַיִּבְעַר בְּיַעֲקֹב כְּאֵשׁ לֶהָבָה אָכְלָה סָבִיב׃
around she-consumes flame like-fire-of in-Jacob and-he-burned one-being-enemy

דָּרַךְ קַשְׁתּוֹ כְּאוֹיֵב נִצָּב יְמִינוֹ
right-hand-of-him being-ready like-one-being-enemy bow-of-him he-strung (4)

כְּצָר וַיַּהֲרֹג כֹּל מַחֲמַדֵּי־עָיִן בְּאֹהֶל בַּת־צִיּוֹן
Zion Daughter-of on-tent-of eye ones-pleasing-of all-of also-he-slew like-foe

שָׁפַךְ כָּאֵשׁ חֲמָתוֹ׃ הָיָה אֲדֹנָי ׀ כְּאוֹיֵב
like-one-being-enemy Lord he-is (5) wrath-of-him like-fire he-poured-out

בִּלַּע יִשְׂרָאֵל בִּלַּע כָּל־אַרְמְנוֹתֶיהָ שִׁחֵת
he-destroyed palaces-of-her all-of he-swallowed-up Israel he-swallowed-up

מִבְצָרָיו וַיֶּרֶב בְּבַת־יְהוּדָה תַּאֲנִיָּה
mourning Judah for-Daughter-of and-he-multiplied strongholds-of-him

וַאֲנִיָּה׃ וַיַּחְמֹס כַּגַּן שֻׂכּוֹ שִׁחֵת
he-destroyed dwelling-of-him like-the-garden and-he-laid-waste (6) and-lamentation

מוֹעֲדוֹ שִׁכַּח יְהוָה ׀ בְּצִיּוֹן מוֹעֵד וְשַׁבָּת
and-Sabbath appointed-feast to-Zion Yahweh he-made-forget meeting-place-of-him

וַיִּנְאַץ בְּזַעַם־אַפּוֹ מֶלֶךְ וְכֹהֵן׃ זָנַח
he-rejected (7) and-priest king anger-of-him in-fierceness-of and-he-spurned

אֲדֹנָי ׀ מִזְבְּחוֹ נִאֵר מִקְדָּשׁוֹ הִסְגִּיר בְּיַד־
into-hand-of he-gave sanctuary-of-him he-abandoned altar-of-him Lord

אוֹיֵב חוֹמֹת אַרְמְנוֹתֶיהָ קוֹל נָתְנוּ בְּבֵית־יְהוָה
Yahweh in-house-of they-raised shout palaces-of-her walls-of one-being-enemy

כְּיוֹם מוֹעֵד׃ חָשַׁב יְהוָה ׀ לְהַשְׁחִית חוֹמַת
wall-of to-tear-down Yahweh he-determined (8) appointed-feast as-day-of

בַּת־צִיּוֹן נָטָה קָו לֹא־הֵשִׁיב יָדוֹ
hand-of-him he-withheld not measuring-line he-stretched-out Zion Daughter-of

מִבַּלֵּעַ וַיַּאֲבֶל־חֵל וְחוֹמָה יַחְדָּו אֻמְלָלוּ׃
they-wasted-away together and-wall rampart and-he-made-lament from-to-destroy

טָבְעוּ בָאָרֶץ שְׁעָרֶיהָ אִבַּד וְשִׁבַּר בְּרִיחֶיהָ
bars-of-her and-he-destroyed he-broke gates-of-her into-the-ground they-sank (9)

מַלְכָּהּ וְשָׂרֶיהָ בַגּוֹיִם אֵין תּוֹרָה גַּם־נְבִיאֶיהָ
prophets-of-her and law no-more among-the-nations and-princes-of-her king-of-her

the strongholds of the
Daughter of Judah.
He has brought her kingdom
and its princes
down to the ground in
dishonor.

3In fierce anger he has cut off
every horn[f] of Israel.
He has withdrawn his right
hand
at the approach of the
enemy.
He has burned in Jacob like a
flaming fire
that consumes everything
around it.

4Like an enemy he has strung
his bow;
his right hand is ready.
Like a foe he has slain
all who were pleasing to the
eye;
he has poured out his wrath
like fire
on the tent of the Daughter
of Zion.

5The Lord is like an enemy;
he has swallowed up Israel.
He has swallowed up all her
palaces
and destroyed her
strongholds.
He has multiplied mourning
and lamentation
for the Daughter of Judah.

6He has laid waste his dwelling
like a garden;
he has destroyed his place
of meeting.
The LORD has made Zion
forget
her appointed feasts and her
Sabbaths;
in his fierce anger he has
spurned
both king and priest.

7The Lord has rejected his altar
and abandoned his
sanctuary.
He has handed over to the
enemy
the walls of her palaces;
they have raised a shout in the
house of the LORD
as on the day of an
appointed feast.

8The LORD determined to tear
down
the wall around the
Daughter of Zion.
He stretched out a measuring
line
and did not withhold his
hand from destroying.
He made ramparts and walls
lament;
together they wasted away.

9Her gates have sunk into the
ground;
their bars he has broken
and destroyed.
Her king and her princes are
exiled among the nations,
the law is no more,
and her prophets no longer

f3 Or *all the strength;* or *every king; horn* here symbolizes strength.

לֹא־ מָצְאוּ חָזוֹן מֵיְהוָה׃ יֵשְׁבוּ לָאָרֶץ יִדְּמוּ
they-are-silent on-the-ground they-sit (10) from-Yahweh vision they-find not

זִקְנֵי בַת־ צִיּוֹן הֶעֱלוּ עָפָר עַל־ רֹאשָׁם חָגְרוּ
they-put-on head-of-them on dust they-sprinkled Zion Daughter-of elders-of

שַׂקִּים הוֹרִידוּ לָאָרֶץ רֹאשָׁן בְּתוּלֹת יְרוּשָׁלָםִ׃
Jerusalem young-women-of head-of-them to-the-ground they-bowed sackcloths

כָּלוּ בַדְּמָעוֹת עֵינַי חֳמַרְמְרוּ מֵעַי
insides-of-me they-are-in-torment eyes-of-me from-the-weepings they-fail (11)

נִשְׁפַּךְ לָאָרֶץ כְּבֵדִי עַל־ שֶׁבֶר בַּת־
daughter-of destruction-of because-of heart-of-me on-the-ground he-is-poured-out

עַמִּי בֵּעָטֵף עוֹלֵל וְיוֹנֵק בִּרְחֹבוֹת קִרְיָה׃
city in-streets-of and-one-being-infant child because-to-faint people-of-me

לְאִמֹּתָם יֹאמְרוּ אַיֵּה דָּגָן וָיָיִן בְּהִתְעַטְּפָם
as-to-faint-them and-wine bread where? they-say to-mothers-of-them (12)

כֶּחָלָל בִּרְחֹבוֹת עִיר בְּהִשְׁתַּפֵּךְ נַפְשָׁם אֶל־ חֵיק
arm-of in life-of-them as-to-ebb-away city in-streets-of like-the-wounded

אִמֹּתָם׃ מָה־ אֲעִידֵךְ מָה אֲדַמֶּה־ לָּךְ
with-you can-I-compare what? can-I-say-for-you what? (13) mothers-of-them

הַבַּת יְרוּשָׁלַםִ מָה אַשְׁוֶה־ לָּךְ וַאֲנַחֲמֵךְ
that-I-may-comfort-you to-you can-I-liken what? Jerusalem the-Daughter

בְּתוּלַת בַּת־ צִיּוֹן כִּי־ גָדוֹל כַּיָּם שִׁבְרֵךְ מִי יִרְפָּא־
can-he-heal who? wound-of-you as-the-sea deep indeed Zion Daughter-of Virgin-of

לָךְ׃ נְבִיאַיִךְ חָזוּ לָךְ שָׁוְא וְתָפֵל
and-worthless falseness for-you they-saw-visions prophets-of-you (14) to-you

וְלֹא־ גִלּוּ עַל־ עֲוֹנֵךְ לְהָשִׁיב °שְׁבִיתֵךְ וַיֶּחֱזוּ
and-they-saw captivity-of-you to-ward-off sin-of-you to they-exposed and-not

לָךְ מַשְׂאוֹת שָׁוְא וּמַדּוּחִים׃ סָפְקוּ עָלַיִךְ כַּפַּיִם כָּל־
all-of hands at-you they-clap (15) and-misleading-ones falseness oracles for-you

עֹבְרֵי דֶרֶךְ שָׁרְקוּ וַיָּנִעוּ רֹאשָׁם עַל־ בַּת
Daughter-of at head-of-them and-they-shake they-scoff way ones-passing-of

יְרוּשָׁלָםִ הֲזֹאת הָעִיר שֶׁיֹּאמְרוּ כְּלִילַת יֹפִי מָשׂוֹשׂ לְכָל־
of-whole-of joy beauty perfection-of that-they-called the-city this? Jerusalem

הָאָרֶץ׃ פָּצוּ עָלַיִךְ פִּיהֶם כָּל־ אוֹיְבָיִךְ
ones-being-enemies-of-you all-of mouth-of-them against-you they-open (16) the-earth

שָׁרְקוּ וַיַּחַרְקוּ־ שֵׁן אָמְרוּ בִּלָּעְנוּ אַךְ זֶה הַיּוֹם
the-day this indeed we-swallowed-up they-say tooth and-they-gnash they-scoff

שֶׁקִּוִּינֻהוּ מָצָאנוּ רָאִינוּ׃ עָשָׂה יְהוָה אֲשֶׁר זָמָם
he-planned what Yahweh he-did (17) we-saw we-lived that-we-waited-for-him

find
visions from the LORD.

10 The elders of the Daughter of Zion
sit on the ground in silence;
they have sprinkled dust on their heads
and put on sackcloth.
The young women of Jerusalem
have bowed their heads to the ground.

11 My eyes fail from weeping,
I am in torment within,
my heart is poured out on the ground
because my people are destroyed,
because children and infants faint
in the streets of the city.

12 They say to their mothers,
"Where is bread and wine?"
as they faint like wounded men
in the streets of the city,
as their lives ebb away
in their mothers' arms.

13 What can I say for you?
With what can I compare you,
O Daughter of Jerusalem?
To what can I liken you,
that I may comfort you,
O Virgin Daughter of Zion?
Your wound is as deep as the sea.
Who can heal you?

14 The visions of your prophets
were false and worthless;
they did not expose your sin
to ward off your captivity.
The oracles they gave you
were false and misleading.

15 All who pass your way
clap their hands at you;
they scoff and shake their heads
at the Daughter of Jerusalem:
"Is this the city that was called
the perfection of beauty,
the joy of the whole earth?"

16 All your enemies open their mouths
wide against you;
they scoff and gnash their teeth
and say, "We have swallowed her up.
This is the day we have waited for;
we have lived to see it."

17 The LORD has done what he planned;

°14 שבותך ק

בִּצַּע אֶמְרָתוֹ אֲשֶׁר צִוָּה מִימֵי־ קֶדֶם הָרַס וְלֹא
and-not he-overthrew old from-days-of he-decreed which word-of-him he-fulfilled

חָמָל וַיְשַׂמַּח עָלַיִךְ אוֹיֵב הֵרִים קֶרֶן
horn-of he-exalted one-being-enemy over-you and-he-let-gloat he-showed-pity

צָרָיִךְ׃ צָעַק לִבָּם אֶל־ אֲדֹנָי חוֹמַת בַּת־ צִיּוֹן
Zion Daughter-of wall-of Lord to heart-of-them he-cries-out (18) foes-of-you

הוֹרִידִי כַנַּחַל דִּמְעָה יוֹמָם וָלַיְלָה אַל־ תִּתְּנִי פוּגַת לָךְ
to-yourself relief-of you-give not and-night by-day tear like-the-river make-flow!

אַל־ תִּדֹּם בַּת־ עֵינֵךְ׃ קוּמִי ׀ רֹנִּי בַלַּיִל°
in-the-night cry-out! arise! (19) eye-of-you daughter-of you-give-rest not

לְרֹאשׁ אַשְׁמֻרוֹת שִׁפְכִי כַמַּיִם לִבֵּךְ נֹכַח
in-front-of heart-of-you like-the-waters pour-out! night-watches at-beginning-of

פְּנֵי אֲדֹנָי שְׂאִי אֵלָיו כַּפַּיִךְ עַל־ נֶפֶשׁ עוֹלָלַיִךְ
children-of-you life-of for hands-of-you to-him lift-up! Lord presences-of

הָעֲטוּפִים בְּרָעָב בְּרֹאשׁ כָּל־ חוּצוֹת׃ רְאֵה יְהוָה
Yahweh look! (20) streets every-of at-head-of from-hunger the-ones-fainting

וְהַבִּיטָה לְמִי עוֹלַלְתָּ כֹּה אִם־ תֹּאכַלְנָה נָשִׁים
women should-they-eat indeed like-this you-treated to-whom? and-consider!

פִּרְיָם עֹלְלֵי טִפֻּחִים אִם־ יֵהָרֵג בְּמִקְדַּשׁ
in-sanctuary-of should-he-be-killed indeed carings children-of offspring-of-them

אֲדֹנָי כֹּהֵן וְנָבִיא׃ שָׁכְבוּ לָאָרֶץ חוּצוֹת נַעַר וְזָקֵן
and-old young streets in-the-dust they-lie (21) and-prophet priest Lord

בְּתוּלֹתַי וּבַחוּרַי נָפְלוּ בֶחָרֶב הָרַגְתָּ בְּיוֹם
in-day-of you-slew by-the-sword they-fell and-young-men-of-me maidens-of-me

אַפֶּךָ טָבַחְתָּ לֹא חָמָלְתָּ׃ תִּקְרָא כְיוֹם מוֹעֵד
feast as-day-of you-summon (22) you-showed-pity not you-slaughtered anger-of-you

מְגוּרַי מִסָּבִיב וְלֹא הָיָה בְּיוֹם אַף־ יְהוָה פָּלִיט
escapee Yahweh anger-of in-day-of he-was and-not on-every-side terrors-of-me

וְשָׂרִיד אֲשֶׁר־ טִפַּחְתִּי וְרִבִּיתִי אֹיְבִי כִלָּם׃
he-destroyed-them one-being-enemy-of-me and-I-reared I-cared-for whom or-survivor

אֲנִי הַגֶּבֶר רָאָה עֳנִי בְּשֵׁבֶט עֶבְרָתוֹ׃ אוֹתִי נָהַג
he-drove-away me (2) wrath-of-him by-rod-of affliction he-saw the-man I (3:1)

וַיֹּלַךְ חֹשֶׁךְ וְלֹא־ אוֹר׃ אַךְ בִּי יָשֻׁב
he-did-again against-me indeed (3) light and-not darkness and-he-made-walk

יַהֲפֹךְ יָדוֹ כָּל־ הַיּוֹם׃ בִּלָּה בְשָׂרִי וְעוֹרִי
and-skin-of-me flesh-of-me he-made-old (4) the-day all-of hand-of-him he-turned

שִׁבַּר עַצְמוֹתָי׃ בָּנָה עָלַי וַיַּקַּף רֹאשׁ
bitterness and-he-surrounded against-me he-besieged (5) bones-of-me he-broke

he has fulfilled his word,
which he decreed long ago.
He has overthrown you
without pity,
he has let the enemy gloat
over you,
he has exalted the horn[g] of
your foes.
18 The hearts of the people
cry out to the Lord.
O wall of the Daughter of
Zion,
let your tears flow like a
river
day and night;
give yourself no relief,
your eyes no rest.
19 Arise, cry out in the night,
as the watches of the night
begin;
pour out your heart like water
in the presence of the Lord.
Lift up your hands to him
for the lives of your
children,
who faint from hunger
at the head of every street.
20 "Look, O LORD, and consider:
Whom have you ever treated
like this?
Should women eat their
offspring,
the children they have cared
for?
Should priest and prophet be
killed
in the sanctuary of the
Lord?
21 "Young and old lie together
in the dust of the streets;
my young men and maidens
have fallen by the sword.
You have slain them in the
day of your anger;
you have slaughtered them
without pity.
22 "As you summon to a feast
day,
so you summoned against
me terrors on every side.
In the day of the LORD's anger
no one escaped or survived;
those I cared for and reared,
my enemy has destroyed."

3[h] I am the man who has seen
affliction
by the rod of his wrath.
2 He has driven me away and
made me walk
in darkness rather than
light;
3 indeed, he has turned his
hand against me
again and again, all day
long.
4 He has made my skin and my
flesh grow old
and has broken my bones.
5 He has besieged me and
surrounded me
with bitterness and

[g]17 *Horn* here symbolizes strength.
[h]This chapter is an acrostic poem; the verses of each stanza begin with the successive letters of the Hebrew alphabet, and the verses within each stanza begin with the same letter.

°19 ק בלילה

וּתְלָאָה׃ בְּמַחֲשַׁכִּים הוֹשִׁיבַנִי כְּמֵתֵי עוֹלָם׃
long-time like-ones-being-dead-of he-made-dwell-me in-darknesses (6) and-hardship

גָּדַר בַּעֲדִי וְלֹא אֵצֵא הִכְבִּיד נְחָשְׁתִּי׃
chains-of-me he-weighed-down I-can-escape and-not against-me he-walled-in (7)

גַּם כִּי אֶזְעַק וַאֲשַׁוֵּעַ שָׂתַם תְּפִלָּתִי׃
prayer-of-me he-shuts-out or-I-cry-for-help I-call-out when even (8)

גָּדַר דְּרָכַי בְּגָזִית נְתִיבֹתַי עִוָּה׃ דֹּב
bear (10) he-made-crooked paths-of-me with-stone-block ways-of-me he-barred (9)

אֹרֵב הוּא לִי אֲרִיה בְּמִסְתָּרִים׃ דְּרָכַי סוֹרֵר
dragging-away paths-of-me (11) in-hiding-places lion to-me he lying-in-wait

וַיְפַשְּׁחֵנִי שָׂמַנִי שֹׁמֵם׃ דָּרַךְ קַשְׁתּוֹ
bow-of-him he-drew (12) one-being-without-help he-left-me and-he-mangled-me

וַיַּצִּיבֵנִי כַּמַּטָּרָא לַחֵץ׃ הֵבִיא בְּכִלְיוֹתָי
into-hearts-of-me he-pierced (13) for-the-arrow as-the-target and-he-made-me

בְּנֵי אַשְׁפָּתוֹ׃ הָיִיתִי שְּׂחֹק לְכָל־ עַמִּי
people-of-me of-all-of laughingstock I-became (14) quiver-of-him sons-of

נְגִינָתָם כָּל־ הַיּוֹם׃ הִשְׂבִּיעַנִי בַמְּרוֹרִים הִרְוַנִי
he-sated-me with-the-bitter-herbs he-filled-me (15) the-day all-of song-of-them

לַעֲנָה׃ וַיַּגְרֵס בֶּחָצָץ שִׁנָּי הִכְפִּישַׁנִי בָּאֵפֶר׃
in-the-dust he-trampled-me tooth-of-me with-the-gravel and-he-broke (16) gall

וַתִּזְנַח מִשָּׁלוֹם נַפְשִׁי נָשִׁיתִי טוֹבָה׃
prosperity I-forgot self-of-me of-peace and-she-was-deprived (17)

וָאֹמַר אָבַד נִצְחִי וְתוֹחַלְתִּי מֵיְהוָה׃ זְכָר־
remember! (19) from-Yahweh and-hope-of-me splendor-of-me he-is-gone so-I-say (18)

עָנְיִי וּמְרוּדִי לַעֲנָה וָרֹאשׁ׃ זָכוֹר
to-remember (20) and-bitterness gall and-wandering-of-me affliction-of-me

תִּזְכּוֹר וְתָשִׁיחַ עָלַי נַפְשִׁי׃ זֹאת אָשִׁיב אֶל־
to I-call this (21) soul-of-me within-me and-she-is-downcast she-remembers

לִבִּי עַל־ כֵּן אוֹחִיל׃ חַסְדֵי יְהוָה כִּי לֹא־
not that Yahweh great-loves-of (22) I-have-hope this for mind-of-me

תָמְנוּ כִּי לֹא־ כָלוּ רַחֲמָיו׃ חֲדָשִׁים
new-ones (23) compassions-of-him they-fail never for we-are-consumed

לַבְּקָרִים רַבָּה אֱמוּנָתֶךָ׃ חֶלְקִי יְהוָה אָמְרָה
she-says Yahweh portion-of-me (24) faithfulness-of-you great in-the-mornings

נַפְשִׁי עַל־ כֵּן אוֹחִיל לוֹ׃ טוֹב יְהוָה לְקֹוָו
to-ones-hoping-in-him Yahweh good (25) for-him I-will-wait this for self-of-me

לְנֶפֶשׁ תִּדְרְשֶׁנּוּ׃ טוֹב וְיָחִיל וְדוּמָם לִתְשׁוּעַת יְהוָה׃
Yahweh for-salvation-of and-quietness also-waiting good (26) she-seeks-him to-one

hardship.
6 He has made me dwell in
darkness
like those long dead.
7 He has walled me in so I
cannot escape;
he has weighed me down
with chains.
8 Even when I call out or cry for
help,
he shuts out my prayer.
9 He has barred my way with
blocks of stone;
he has made my paths
crooked.
10 Like a bear lying in wait,
like a lion in hiding,
11 he dragged me from the path
and mangled me
and left me without help.
12 He drew his bow
and made me the target for
his arrows.
13 He pierced my heart
with arrows from his quiver.
14 I became the laughingstock of
all my people;
they mock me in song all
day long.
15 He has filled me with bitter
herbs
and sated me with gall.
16 He has broken my teeth with
gravel;
he has trampled me in the
dust.
17 I have been deprived of peace;
I have forgotten what
prosperity is.
18 So I say, "My splendor is gone
and all that I had hoped
from the LORD."
19 I remember my affliction and
my wandering,
the bitterness and the gall.
20 I well remember them,
and my soul is downcast
within me.
21 Yet this I call to mind
and therefore I have hope:
22 Because of the LORD's great
love we are not
consumed,
for his compassions never
fail.
23 They are new every morning;
great is your faithfulness.
24 I say to myself, "The LORD is
my portion;
therefore I will wait for
him."
25 The LORD is good to those
whose hope is in him,
to the one who seeks him;
26 it is good to wait quietly
for the salvation of the
LORD.

°10 ק ארי ;°20 ק ותשוח
°25 ק לקויו

טוֹב לַגֶּבֶר כִּי־ יִשָּׂא עֹל בִּנְעוּרָיו׃ יֵשֵׁב
let-him-sit (28) in-youths-of-him yoke he-should-bear that for-the-man good (27)

בָּדָד וְיִדֹּם כִּי נָטַל עָלָיו׃ יִתֵּן בֶּעָפָר
in-the-dust let-him-bury (29) on-him he-laid for and-let-him-be-silent alone

פִּיהוּ אוּלַי יֵשׁ תִּקְוָה׃ יִתֵּן לְמַכֵּהוּ לֶחִי
cheek to-one-striking-him let-him-offer (30) hope there-is maybe face-of-him

יִשְׂבַּע בְּחֶרְפָּה׃ כִּי לֹא יִזְנַח לְעוֹלָם אֲדֹנָי׃
Lord to-forever he-casts-off not for (31) with-disgrace let-him-be-filled

כִּי אִם־ הוֹגָה וְרִחַם כְּרֹב
as-greatness-of so-he-will-show-compassion he-brings-grief though even (32)

חֲסָדָו׃ כִּי לֹא עִנָּה מִלִּבּוֹ
from-heart-of-him he-brings-affliction not for (33) unfailing-loves-of-him

וַיַּגֶּה בְּנֵי־ אִישׁ׃ לְדַכֵּא תַּחַת רַגְלָיו כֹּל
all-of feet-of-him under to-crush (34) man children-of or-he-brings-grief

אֲסִירֵי אָרֶץ׃ לְהַטּוֹת מִשְׁפַּט־ גָּבֶר נֶגֶד פְּנֵי עֶלְיוֹן׃
Most-High faces-of before man right-of to-deny (35) land prisoners-of

לְעַוֵּת אָדָם בְּרִיבוֹ אֲדֹנָי לֹא רָאָה׃ מִי זֶה
this who? (37) would-he-see not Lord of-justice-of-him man to-deprive (36)

אָמַר וַתֶּהִי אֲדֹנָי לֹא צִוָּה׃ מִפִּי
from-mouth-of (38) he-decreed not Lord and-she-will-happen he-can-speak

עֶלְיוֹן לֹא תֵצֵא הָרָעוֹת וְהַטּוֹב׃ מַה־ יִּתְאוֹנֵן
should-he-complain why? (39) and-the-good the-calamities she-comes not Most-High

אָדָם חָי גֶּבֶר עַל־ חֲטָאוֹ׃ נַחְפְּשָׂה דְרָכֵינוּ וְנַחְקֹרָה
and-let-us-test ways-of-us let-us-examine (40) sins-of-him for man living man

וְנָשׁוּבָה עַד־ יְהוָה׃ נִשָּׂא לְבָבֵנוּ אֶל־ כַּפַּיִם אֶל־ אֵל
God to hands with heart-of-us let-us-lift (41) Yahweh to and-let-us-return

בַּשָּׁמָיִם׃ נַחְנוּ פָשַׁעְנוּ וּמָרִינוּ אַתָּה לֹא סָלָחְתָּ׃
you-forgave not you and-we-rebelled we-sinned we (42) in-the-heavens

סַכֹּתָה בָאַף וַתִּרְדְּפֵנוּ הָרַגְתָּ לֹא
not you-slew and-you-pursued-us with-the-anger you-covered-yourself (43)

חָמָלְתָּ׃ סַכּוֹתָה בֶעָנָן לָךְ
to-yourself with-the-cloud you-covered-yourself (44) you-showed-pity

מֵעֲבוֹר תְּפִלָּה׃ סְחִי וּמָאוֹס תְּשִׂימֵנוּ בְּקֶרֶב הָעַמִּים׃
the-nations in-among you-made-us and-refuse scum (45) prayer from-to-get-through

פָּצוּ עָלֵינוּ פִּיהֶם כָּל־ אֹיְבֵינוּ׃
ones-being-enemies-of-us all-of mouth-of-them against-us they-opened-wide (46)

פַּחַד וָפַחַת הָיָה לָנוּ הַשֵּׁאת וְהַשָּׁבֶר׃
and-the-destruction the-ruin to-us he-happened and-pitfall terror (47)

27 It is good for a man to bear
the yoke
while he is young.

28 Let him sit alone in silence,
for the LORD has laid it on
him.

29 Let him bury his face in the
dust—
there may yet be hope.

30 Let him offer his cheek to one
who would strike him,
and let him be filled with
disgrace.

31 For men are not cast off
by the Lord forever.

32 Though he brings grief, he will
show compassion,
so great is his unfailing
love.

33 For he does not willingly bring
affliction
or grief to the children of
men.

34 To crush underfoot
all prisoners in the land,

35 to deny a man his rights
before the Most High,

36 to deprive a man of justice—
would not the Lord see such
things?

37 Who can speak and have it
happen
if the Lord has not decreed
it?

38 Is it not from the mouth of the
Most High
that both calamities and
good things come?

39 Why should any living man
complain
when punished for his sins?

40 Let us examine our ways and
test them,
and let us return to the
LORD.

41 Let us lift up our hearts and
our hands
to God in heaven, and say:

42 "We have sinned and rebelled
and you have not forgiven.

43 "You have covered yourself
with anger and pursued
us;
you have slain without pity.

44 You have covered yourself
with a cloud
so that no prayer can get
through.

45 You have made us scum and
refuse
among the nations.

46 "All our enemies have opened
their mouths
wide against us.

47 We have suffered terror and
pitfalls,
ruin and destruction."

°32 ק חסדיו; °39 ק חטאיו

(48) פַּלְגֵי־ מַיִם תֵּרַד עֵינִי עַל־ שֶׁבֶר
destruction-of because-of eye-of-me she-flows-down tears streams-of (48)

בַּת־ עַמִּי׃ (49) עֵינִי נִגְּרָה וְלֹא תִדְמֶה
she-will-cease and-not she-will-flow eye-of-me (49) people-of-me daughter-of

מֵאֵין הֲפֻגוֹת׃ (50) עַד־ יַשְׁקִיף וְיֵרֶא יְהוָה מִשָּׁמָיִם׃
from-heavens Yahweh and-he-sees he-looks-down until (50) reliefs with-no

(51) עֵינִי עוֹלְלָה לְנַפְשִׁי מִכֹּל בְּנוֹת
women-of because-of-all-of to-soul-of-me she-brings-grief eye-of-me (51)

עִירִי׃ (52) צוֹד צָדוּנִי כַּצִּפּוֹר אֹיְבַי
ones-being-enemies-of-me like-the-bird they-hunted-me to-hunt (52) city-of-me

חִנָּם׃ (53) צָמְתוּ בַבּוֹר חַיָּי וַיַּדּוּ־ אֶבֶן
stone and-they-threw lives-of-me in-the-pit they-tried-to-end (53) without-cause

בִּי׃ (54) צָפוּ־ מַיִם עַל־ רֹאשִׁי אָמַרְתִּי נִגְזָרְתִּי׃
I-would-be-cut-off I-thought head-of-me over waters they-closed (54) at-me

(55) קָרָאתִי שִׁמְךָ יְהוָה מִבּוֹר תַּחְתִּיּוֹת׃ (56) קוֹלִי שָׁמָעְתָּ
you-heard plea-of-me (56) depths from-pit-of Yahweh name-of-you I-called-on (55)

אַל־ תַּעְלֵם אָזְנְךָ לְרַוְחָתִי לְשַׁוְעָתִי׃ (57) קָרַבְתָּ בְּיוֹם
on-day you-came-near (57) to-cry-of-me to-relief-of-me ear-of-you you-close not

אֶקְרָאֶךָּ אָמַרְתָּ אַל־ תִּירָא׃ (58) רַבְתָּ אֲדֹנָי רִיבֵי
cases-of Lord you-took-up-case (58) you-fear not you-said I-called-you

נַפְשִׁי גָּאַלְתָּ חַיָּי׃ (59) רָאִיתָה יְהוָה עַוָּתָתִי שָׁפְטָה
uphold! wrong-of-me Yahweh you-saw (59) lives-of-me you-redeemed self-of-me

מִשְׁפָּטִי׃ (60) רָאִיתָה כָּל־ נִקְמָתָם כָּל־ מַחְשְׁבֹתָם
plots-of-them all-of vengeance-of-them all-of you-saw (60) cause-of-me

לִי׃ (61) שָׁמַעְתָּ חֶרְפָּתָם יְהוָה כָּל־ מַחְשְׁבֹתָם עָלָי׃
against-me plots-of-them all-of Yahweh insult-of-them you-heard (61) against-me

(62) שִׂפְתֵי קָמַי וְהֶגְיוֹנָם עָלַי
against-me and-muttering-of-them ones-being-enemies-of-me whisperings-of (62)

כָּל־ הַיּוֹם׃ (63) שִׁבְתָּם וְקִימָתָם הַבִּיטָה אֲנִי מַנְגִּינָתָם׃
song-of-them I look! or-standing-of-them to-sit-them (63) the-day all-of

(64) תָּשִׁיב לָהֶם גְּמוּל יְהוָה כְּמַעֲשֵׂה יְדֵיהֶם׃ (65) תִּתֵּן
you-put (65) hands-of-them as-deed-of Yahweh desert to-them you-pay-back (64)

לָהֶם מְגִנַּת־ לֵב תַּאֲלָתְךָ לָהֶם׃ (66) תִּרְדֹּף בְּאַף
in-anger you-pursue (66) on-them curse-of-you heart veil-of over-them

וְתַשְׁמִידֵם מִתַּחַת שְׁמֵי יְהוָה׃ (4:1) אֵיכָה יוּעַם
he-lost-luster how! (4:1) Yahweh heavens-of from-under and-you-destroy-them

זָהָב יוּעַם יִשְׁנֶא הַכֶּתֶם הַטּוֹב תִּשְׁתַּפֵּכְנָה אַבְנֵי־ קֹדֶשׁ
sacredness gems-of they-are-scattered the-fine the-gold he-became-dull gold

48Streams of tears flow from my eyes
because my people are destroyed.
49My eyes will flow unceasingly, without relief,
50until the LORD looks down from heaven and sees.
51What I see brings grief to my soul
because of all the women of my city.

52Those who were my enemies without cause
hunted me like a bird.
53They tried to end my life in a pit
and threw stones at me;
54the waters closed over my head,
and I thought I was about to be cut off.

55I called on your name, O LORD,
from the depths of the pit.
56You heard my plea: "Do not close your ears
to my cry for relief."
57You came near when I called you,
and you said, "Do not fear."

58O Lord, you took up my case;
you redeemed my life.
59You have seen, O LORD, the wrong done to me.
Uphold my cause!
60You have seen the depth of their vengeance,
all their plots against me.

61O LORD, you have heard their insults,
all their plots against me—
62what my enemies whisper and mutter
against me all day long.
63Look at them! Sitting or standing,
they mock me in their songs.

64Pay them back what they deserve, O LORD,
for what their hands have done.
65Put a veil over their hearts,
and may your curse be on them!
66Pursue them in anger and destroy them
from under the heavens of the LORD.

4 How the gold has lost its luster,
the fine gold become dull!
The sacred gems are scattered

[f]This chapter is an acrostic poem, the verses of which begin with the successive letters of the Hebrew alphabet.

בְּרֹאשׁ כָּל־ חוּצוֹת׃ (2) בְּנֵי צִיּוֹן הַיְקָרִים
at-head-of every-of streets (2) sons-of Zion the-precious-ones

הַמְסֻלָּאִים בַּפָּז אֵיכָה נֶחְשְׁבוּ לְנִבְלֵי־ חֶרֶשׂ
the-ones-being-weighed with-the-gold how! they-are-considered as-pots-of clay

מַעֲשֵׂה יְדֵי יוֹצֵר׃ (3) גַּם־ °תַּנִּין חָלְצוּ שַׁד הֵינִיקוּ
work-of hands-of one-being-potter (3) even jackals they-offer breast they-nurse

גּוּרֵיהֶן בַּת־ עַמִּי לְאַכְזָר °כִּי עֵנִים
young-ones-of-them daughter-of people-of-me as-heartless like-ostriches

בַּמִּדְבָּר׃ (4) דָּבַק לְשׁוֹן יוֹנֵק אֶל־ חִכּוֹ
in-the-desert (4) he-sticks tongue-of one-being-infant to roof-of-mouth-of-him

בַּצָּמָא עוֹלָלִים שָׁאֲלוּ לֶחֶם פֹּרֵשׂ אֵין לָהֶם׃
because-of-the-thirst children they-beg bread one-giving there-is-not to-them

(5) הָאֹכְלִים לְמַעֲדַנִּים נָשַׁמּוּ בַּחוּצוֹת
(5) the-ones-eating of-delicacies they-are-destitute in-the-streets

הָאֱמֻנִים עֲלֵי תוֹלָע חִבְּקוּ אַשְׁפַּתּוֹת׃ (6) וַיִּגְדַּל
the-ones-being-nurtured in purple they-lie-on ash-heaps (6) and-he-is-great

עֲוֹן בַּת־ עַמִּי מֵחַטַּאת סְדֹם
punishment-of daughter-of people-of-me more-than-punishment-of Sodom

הַהֲפוּכָה כְמוֹ־ רָגַע וְלֹא־ חָלוּ בָהּ יָדָיִם׃
the-one-being-overthrown in moment and-not they-helped to-her hands

(7) זַכּוּ נְזִירֶיהָ מִשֶּׁלֶג צַחוּ מֵחָלָב
(7) they-were-bright princes-of-her more-than-snow they-were-white more-than-milk

אָדְמוּ עֶצֶם מִפְּנִינִים סַפִּיר גִּזְרָתָם׃
they-were-ruddy body more-than-rubies sapphire appearance-of-them

(8) חָשַׁךְ מִשְּׁחוֹר תָּאֳרָם לֹא נִכְּרוּ
(8) he-is-black more-than-soot form-of-them not they-are-recognized

בַּחוּצוֹת צָפַד עוֹרָם עַל־ עַצְמָם יָבֵשׁ
in-the-streets he-shriveled skin-of-them on bone-of-them he-dried-up

הָיָה כָעֵץ׃ (9) טוֹבִים הָיוּ חַלְלֵי־ חֶרֶב
he-became as-the-stick (9) better-ones they-are ones-killed-of sword

מֵחַלְלֵי רָעָב שֶׁהֵם יָזוּבוּ מְדֻקָּרִים
more-than-ones-killed-of famine who-they they-waste-away ones-being-pierced

מִתְּנוּבֹת שָׂדָי׃ (10) יְדֵי נָשִׁים רַחֲמָנִיּוֹת בִּשְּׁלוּ
without-foods-of field (10) hands-of women compassionate-ones they-cooked

יַלְדֵיהֶן הָיוּ לְבָרוֹת לָמוֹ בְּשֶׁבֶר בַּת־
children-of-them they-became to-be-food for-them in-destruction-of daughter-of

עַמִּי׃ (11) כִּלָּה יְהוָה אֶת־ חֲמָתוֹ שָׁפַךְ
people-of-me (11) he-made-full Yahweh *** wrath-of-him he-poured-out

at the head of every street.

2How the precious sons of Zion,
once worth their weight in gold,
are now considered as pots of clay,
the work of a potter's hands!

3Even jackals offer their breasts
to nurse their young,
but my people have become heartless
like ostriches in the desert.

4Because of thirst the infant's tongue
sticks to the roof of its mouth;
the children beg for bread,
but no one gives it to them.

5Those who once ate delicacies
are destitute in the streets.
Those nurtured in purple
now lie on ash heaps.

6The punishment of my people
is greater than that of Sodom,
which was overthrown in a moment
without a hand turned to help her.

7Their princes were brighter than snow
and whiter than milk,
their bodies more ruddy than rubies,
their appearance like sapphires.[j]

8But now they are blacker than soot;
they are not recognized in the streets.
Their skin has shriveled on their bones;
it has become as dry as a stick.

9Those killed by the sword are better off
than those who die of famine;
racked with hunger, they waste away
for lack of food from the field.

10With their own hands compassionate women
have cooked their own children,
who became their food
when my people were destroyed.

11The LORD has given full vent
to his wrath;

j7 Or *lapis lazuli*

°3a ק כיענים; °3b ק תנים

חֲרוֹן אַפּוֹ וַיַּצֶּת־ אֵשׁ בְּצִיּוֹן וַתֹּאכַל
and-she-consumed in-Zion fire and-he-kindled anger-of-him fierceness-of

יְסוֹדֹתֶיהָ׃ (12) לֹא הֶאֱמִינוּ מַלְכֵי־ אֶרֶץ וְכֹל
any-of earth kings-of they-believed not (12) foundations-of-her

יֹשְׁבֵי תֵבֵל כִּי יָבֹא צַר וְאוֹיֵב
and-one-being-enemy foe he-could-enter that world ones-being-people-of

בְּשַׁעֲרֵי יְרוּשָׁלִָם׃ (13) מֵחַטֹּאת נְבִיאֶיהָ
prophets-of-her because-of-sins-of (13) Jerusalem through-gates-of

עֲוֹנוֹת כֹּהֲנֶיהָ הַשֹּׁפְכִים בְּקִרְבָּהּ דַּם
blood-of at-within-her the-ones-shedding priests-of-her iniquities-of

צַדִּיקִים׃ (14) נָעוּ עִוְרִים בַּחוּצוֹת נְגֹאֲלוּ
they-are-defiled through-the-streets blind-men they-grope (14) righteous-ones

בַּדָּם בְּלֹא יוּכְלוּ יִגְּעוּ בִּלְבֻשֵׁיהֶם׃ (15) סוּרוּ
go-away! (15) to-garments-of-them they-touch they-dare that-not with-the-blood

טָמֵא קָרְאוּ לָמוֹ סוּרוּ סוּרוּ אַל־ תִּגָּעוּ כִּי נָצוּ גַּם־
and they-flee when you-touch not go-away! go-away! to-them they-cry unclean

נָעוּ אָמְרוּ בַּגּוֹיִם לֹא יוֹסִיפוּ לָגוּר׃
to-stay they-can-do-longer not among-the-nations they-say they-wander

(16) פְּנֵי יְהוָה חִלְּקָם לֹא יוֹסִיף לְהַבִּיטָם
to-watch-them he-does-longer not he-scattered-them Yahweh faces-of (16)

פְּנֵי כֹהֲנִים לֹא נָשָׂאוּ זְקֵנִים לֹא חָנָנוּ׃ (17) עוֹדֵינָה
moreover-we (17) they-show-favor not and-elders they-honor not priests faces-of

תִּכְלֶינָה עֵינֵינוּ אֶל־ עֶזְרָתֵנוּ הָבֶל בְּצִפִּיָּתֵנוּ צִפִּינוּ אֶל־
for we-watched from-tower-of-us in-vain help-of-us to eyes-of-us they-failed

גּוֹי לֹא יוֹשִׁעַ׃ (18) צָדוּ צְעָדֵינוּ מִלֶּכֶת בִּרְחֹבֹתֵינוּ
in-streets-of-us from-to-walk steps-of-us they-stalked (18) he-could-save not nation

קָרַב קִצֵּנוּ מָלְאוּ יָמֵינוּ כִּי־ בָא קִצֵּנוּ׃
end-of-us he-came for days-of-us they-were-numbered end-of-us he-was-near

(19) קַלִּים הָיוּ רֹדְפֵינוּ מִנִּשְׁרֵי שָׁמָיִם
skies more-than-eagles-of ones-pursuing-us they-were swift-ones (19)

עַל־ הֶהָרִים דְּלָקֻנוּ בַּמִּדְבָּר אָרְבוּ לָנוּ׃
for-us they-lay-in-wait in-the-desert they-chased-us the-mountains over

(20) רוּחַ אַפֵּינוּ מְשִׁיחַ יְהוָה נִלְכַּד בִּשְׁחִיתוֹתָם
in-traps-of-them he-was-caught Yahweh anointed-of nostrils-of-us breath-of (20)

אֲשֶׁר אָמַרְנוּ בְּצִלּוֹ נִחְיֶה בַגּוֹיִם׃
among-the-nations we-would-live under-shadow-of-him we-thought whom

(21) שִׂישִׂי וְשִׂמְחִי בַּת־ אֱדוֹם יוֹשֶׁבֶתִי בְּאֶרֶץ עוּץ גַּם־
also Uz in-land-of one-living Edom Daughter-of and-be-glad! rejoice! (21)

he has poured out his fierce
anger.
He kindled a fire in Zion
that consumed her
foundations.

12 The kings of the earth did not
believe,
nor did any of the world's
people,
that enemies and foes could
enter
the gates of Jerusalem.

13 But it happened because of the
sins of her prophets
and the iniquities of her
priests,
who shed within her
the blood of the righteous.

14 Now they grope through the
streets
like men who are blind.
They are so defiled with blood
that no one dares to touch
their garments.

15 "Go away! You are unclean!"
men cry to them.
"Away! Away! Don't touch
us!"
When they flee and wander
about,
people among the nations
say,
"They can stay here no
longer."

16 The Lord himself has scattered
them;
he no longer watches over
them.
The priests are shown no
honor,
the elders no favor.

17 Moreover, our eyes failed,
looking in vain for help;
from our towers we watched
for a nation that could not
save us.

18 Men stalked us at every step,
so we could not walk in our
streets.
Our end was near, our days
were numbered,
for our end had come.

19 Our pursuers were swifter
than eagles in the sky;
they chased us over the
mountains
and lay in wait for us in the
desert.

20 The Lord's anointed, our very
life breath,
was caught in their traps.
We thought that under his
shadow
we would live among the
nations.

21 Rejoice and be glad, O
Daughter of Edom,
you who live in the land of
Uz.

°12 ק כל; °16 ק וזקנים
°17 ק עודינו; °21 ק יושבת

עָלַיִךְ תַּעֲבָר־ כּוֹס תִּשְׁכְּרִי וְתִתְעָרִי׃
to-you she-will-pass cup you-will-be-drunk and-you-will-be-stripped-naked

(22) תַּם־ עֲוֺנֵךְ בַּת־ צִיּוֹן לֹא יוֹסִיף
(22) he-will-end punishment-of-you Daughter-of Zion not he-will-prolong

לְהַגְלוֹתֵךְ פָּקַד עֲוֺנֵךְ בַּת־ אֱדוֹם גִּלָּה עַל־
to-exile-you he-will-punish sin-of-you Daughter-of Edom he-will-expose to

חַטֹּאתָיִךְ׃ (5:1) זְכֹר יְהוָה מֶה־ הָיָה לָנוּ הַבִּיט
wickednesses-of-you (5:1) remember! Yahweh what! he-happened to-us look!

וּרְאֵה אֶת־ חֶרְפָּתֵנוּ׃ (2) נַחֲלָתֵנוּ נֶהֶפְכָה
and-see! *** disgrace-of-us (2) inheritance-of-us she-was-turned-over

לְזָרִים בָּתֵּינוּ לְנָכְרִים׃ (3) יְתוֹמִים הָיִינוּ
to-ones-being-aliens homes-of-us to-foreigners (3) orphans we-became

אֵין אָב אִמֹּתֵינוּ כְּאַלְמָנוֹת׃ (4) מֵימֵינוּ בְּכֶסֶף
and-without father mothers-of-us like-widows (4) waters-of-us with-silver

שָׁתִינוּ עֵצֵינוּ בִּמְחִיר יָבֹאוּ׃ (5) עַל צַוָּארֵנוּ נִרְדָּפְנוּ
we-drink woods-of-us for-price they-come (5) at neck-of-us we-are-pursued

יָגַעְנוּ לֹא הוּנַח־ לָנוּ׃ (6) מִצְרַיִם נָתַנּוּ יָד
we-are-weary and-not he-is-given-rest for-us (6) Egypt we-submitted hand

אַשּׁוּר לִשְׂבֹּעַ לָחֶם׃ (7) אֲבֹתֵינוּ חָטְאוּ אֵינָם
Assyria to-get-enough bread (7) fathers-of-us they-sinned and-no-more-they

אֲנַחְנוּ עֲוֺנֹתֵיהֶם סָבָלְנוּ׃ (8) עֲבָדִים מָשְׁלוּ בָנוּ פֹּרֵק
and-we punishments-of-them we-bear (8) slaves they-rule over-us one-freeing

אֵין מִיָּדָם׃ (9) בְּנַפְשֵׁנוּ נָבִיא לַחְמֵנוּ
there-is-not from-hand-of-them (9) with-life-of-us we-get bread-of-us

מִפְּנֵי חֶרֶב הַמִּדְבָּר׃ (10) עוֹרֵנוּ כְּתַנּוּר נִכְמָרוּ
because-of sword-of the-desert (10) skin-of-us like-oven they-are-hot

מִפְּנֵי זַלְעֲפוֹת רָעָב׃ (11) נָשִׁים בְּצִיּוֹן עִנּוּ בְּתֻלֹת
because-of fevers-of hunger (11) women in-Zion they-ravished virgins

בְּעָרֵי יְהוּדָה׃ (12) שָׂרִים בְּיָדָם נִתְלוּ פְּנֵי
in-towns-of Judah (12) princes by-hand-of-them they-were-hung-up faces-of

זְקֵנִים לֹא נֶהְדָּרוּ׃ (13) בַּחוּרִים טְחוֹן נָשָׂאוּ
elders not they-are-shown-respect (13) young-men millstone they-toil

וּנְעָרִים בָּעֵץ כָּשָׁלוּ׃ (14) זְקֵנִים מִשַּׁעַר שָׁבָתוּ
and-boys under-wood they-stagger (14) elders from-city-gate they-are-gone

בַּחוּרִים מִנְּגִינָתָם׃ (15) שָׁבַת מְשׂוֹשׂ לִבֵּנוּ נֶהְפַּךְ
young-men from-music-of-them (15) he-is-gone joy-of heart-of-us he-was-turned

לְאֵבֶל מְחֹלֵנוּ׃ (16) נָפְלָה עֲטֶרֶת רֹאשֵׁנוּ אוֹי־ נָא
into-mourning dancing-of-us (16) she-fell-off crown-of head-of-us woe! now!

But to you also the cup will be passed;
you will be drunk and stripped naked.
22 O Daughter of Zion, your punishment will end;
he will not prolong your exile.
But, O Daughter of Edom, he will punish your sin
and expose your wickedness.

5 Remember, O LORD, what has happened to us;
look, and see our disgrace.
2 Our inheritance has been turned over to aliens,
our homes to foreigners.
3 We have become orphans and fatherless,
our mothers like widows.
4 We must buy the water we drink;
our wood can be had only at a price.
5 Those who pursue us are at our heels;
we are weary and find no rest.
6 We submitted to Egypt and Assyria
to get enough bread.
7 Our fathers sinned and are no more,
and we bear their punishment.
8 Slaves rule over us,
and there is none to free us from their hands.
9 We get our bread at the risk of our lives
because of the sword in the desert.
10 Our skin is hot as an oven,
feverish from hunger.
11 Women have been ravished in Zion,
and virgins in the towns of Judah.
12 Princes have been hung up by their hands;
elders are shown no respect.
13 Young men toil at the millstones;
boys stagger under loads of wood.
14 The elders are gone from the city gate;
the young men have stopped their music.
15 Joy is gone from our hearts;
our dancing has turned to mourning.
16 The crown has fallen from our head.

°1 ק הביטה; °3 ק ואין
°5 ק ולא; °7a ק ואינם
°7b ק ואנחנו

לָנוּ כִּי חָטָאנוּ׃ (17) עַל־ זֶה הָיָה דָוֶה לִבֵּנוּ
heart-of-us faint he-is this because-of (17) we-sinned for to-us

עַל־ אֵלֶּה חָשְׁכוּ עֵינֵינוּ׃ (18) עַל הַר־ צִיּוֹן
Zion Mount-of for (18) eyes-of-us they-grow-dim these because-of

שֶׁשָּׁמֵם שׁוּעָלִים הִלְּכוּ־ בוֹ׃ (19) אַתָּה יְהוָה לְעוֹלָם
to-forever Yahweh you (19) over-him they-prowl jackals which-he-is-desolate

תֵּשֵׁב כִּסְאֲךָ לְדֹר וָדוֹר׃ (20) לָמָּה לָנֶצַח
to-always why? (20) and-generation to-generation throne-of-you you-reign

תִּשְׁכָּחֵנוּ תַּעַזְבֵנוּ לְאֹרֶךְ יָמִים׃ (21) הֲשִׁיבֵנוּ יְהוָה ׀
Yahweh restore-us! (21) days for-length-of you-forsake-us you-forget-us

אֵלֶיךָ וְנָשׁ°וֹב חַדֵּשׁ יָמֵינוּ כְּקֶדֶם׃ (22) כִּי
unless (22) as-of-old days-of-us renew! that-we-may-return to-yourself

אִם־ מָאֹס מְאַסְתָּנוּ קָצַפְתָּ עָלֵינוּ עַד־ מְאֹד׃
beyond-measure to with-us you-are-angry you-rejected-us to-reject if

Woe to us, for we have
sinned!
[17]Because of this our hearts are
faint,
because of these things our
eyes grow dim
[18]for Mount Zion, which lies
desolate,
with jackals prowling over
it.
[19]You, O LORD, reign forever;
your throne endures from
generation to generation.
[20]Why do you always forget us?
Why do you forsake us so
long?
[21]Restore us to yourself, O LORD,
that we may return;
renew our days as of old
[22]unless you have utterly
rejected us
and are angry with us
beyond measure.

ק ונשובה 21°

וַיְהִי ׀ בִּשְׁלֹשִׁים שָׁנָה בָּרְבִיעִי בַּחֲמִשָּׁה לַחֹדֶשׁ וַאֲנִי בְתוֹךְ־
in-among while-I of-the-month on-five in-the-fourth year in-thirty and-he-was (1:1)

הַגּוֹלָה עַל־ נְהַר־ כְּבָר נִפְתְּחוּ הַשָּׁמַיִם וָאֶרְאֶה מַרְאוֹת אֱלֹהִים׃
God visions-of and-I-saw the-heavens they-were-opened Kebar River-of by the-exile

בַּחֲמִשָּׁה לַחֹדֶשׁ הִיא הַשָּׁנָה הַחֲמִישִׁית לְגָלוּת הַמֶּלֶךְ יוֹיָכִין׃
Jehoiachin the-king of-exile-of the-fifth the-year she of-the-month on-five (2)

הָיֹה הָיָה דְבַר־ יְהוָה אֶל־יְחֶזְקֵאל בֶּן־ בּוּזִי הַכֹּהֵן בְּאֶרֶץ
in-land-of the-priest Buzi son-of Ezekiel to Yahweh word-of he-came to-come (3)

כַּשְׂדִּים עַל־ נְהַר־ כְּבָר וַתְּהִי עָלָיו שָׁם יַד־ יְהוָה׃
Yahweh hand-of there upon-him and-she-was Kebar River-of by Chaldeans

וָאֵרֶא וְהִנֵּה רוּחַ סְעָרָה בָּאָה מִן־ הַצָּפוֹן עָנָן גָּדוֹל
immense cloud the-north from coming storm wind-of and-see! and-I-looked (4)

וְאֵשׁ מִתְלַקַּחַת וְנֹגַהּ לוֹ סָבִיב וּמִתּוֹכָהּ
and-at-center-of-her surrounding to-him and-brilliant-light flashing and-lightning

כְּעֵין הַחַשְׁמַל מִתּוֹךְ הָאֵשׁ׃ וּמִתּוֹכָהּ
and-at-center-of-her (5) the-fire at-center-of the-glowing-metal like-appearance-of

דְּמוּת אַרְבַּע חַיּוֹת וְזֶה מַרְאֵיהֶן דְּמוּת אָדָם לָהֵנָּה׃
to-them man form-of appearances-of-them and-this living-creatures four form-of

וְאַרְבָּעָה פָנִים לְאֶחָת וְאַרְבַּע כְּנָפַיִם לְאַחַת לָהֶם׃ וְרַגְלֵיהֶם
and-legs-of-them (7) to-them to-each wings and-four to-each faces but-four (6)

רֶגֶל יְשָׁרָה וְכַף רַגְלֵיהֶם כְּכַף רֶגֶל עֵגֶל וְנֹצְצִים
and-ones-gleaming calf leg-of like-foot-of legs-of-them and-foot-of straight leg

כְּעֵין נְחֹשֶׁת קָלָל׃ וִידֵו אָדָם מִתַּחַת כַּנְפֵיהֶם
wings-of-them at-under man and-hands-of (8) burnished bronze like-appearance-of

עַל אַרְבַּעַת רִבְעֵיהֶם וּפְנֵיהֶם וְכַנְפֵיהֶם לְאַרְבַּעְתָּם׃
to-four-of-them and-wings-of-them and-faces-of-them sides-of-them four-of on

חֹבְרֹת אִשָּׁה אֶל־ אֲחוֹתָהּ כַּנְפֵיהֶם לֹא־ יִסַּבּוּ בְלֶכְתָּן
as-to-move-them they-turned not wings-of-them other-of-her to each ones-touching (9)

אִישׁ אֶל־עֵבֶר פָּנָיו יֵלֵכוּ׃ וּדְמוּת פְּנֵיהֶם פְּנֵי
faces-of faces-of-them and-likeness-of (10) they-went faces-of-him ahead to each

אָדָם וּפְנֵי אַרְיֵה אֶל־ הַיָּמִין לְאַרְבַּעְתָּם וּפְנֵי־ שׁוֹר מֵהַשְּׂמֹאול
on-the-left ox and-faces-of to-four-of-them the-right on lion also-faces-of man

לְאַרְבַּעְתָּן וּפְנֵי־ נֶשֶׁר לְאַרְבַּעְתָּן׃ וּפְנֵיהֶם
so-faces-of-them (11) to-four-of-them eagle and-faces-of to-four-of-them

וְכַנְפֵיהֶם פְּרֻדוֹת מִלְמָעְלָה לְאִישׁ שְׁתַּיִם חֹבְרוֹת אִישׁ
other ones-touching two to-each to-at-upward ones-spreading and-wings-of-them

וּשְׁתַּיִם מְכַסּוֹת אֵת גְּוִיֹתֵיהֶנָה׃* וְאִישׁ אֶל־עֵבֶר פָּנָיו
faces-of-him ahead to and-each (12) bodies-of-them *** ones-covering and-two

### *The Living Creatures and the Glory of the* Lord

1 In the[a] thirtieth year, in the
fourth month on the fifth day,
while I was among the exiles by
the Kebar River, the heavens were
opened and I saw visions of God.
2On the fifth of the month—it
was the fifth year of the exile of
King Jehoiachin— 3the word of
the Lord came to Ezekiel the
priest, the son of Buzi,[b] by the Kebar River in the land of the Babylonians.[c] There the hand of the
Lord was upon him.
4I looked, and I saw a windstorm coming out of the north—an
immense cloud with flashing
lightning and surrounded by brilliant light. The center of the fire
looked like glowing metal, 5and in
the fire was what looked like four
living creatures. In appearance
their form was that of a man, 6but
each of them had four faces and
four wings. 7Their legs were
straight; their feet were like those
of a calf and gleamed like burnished bronze. 8Under their wings
on their four sides they had the
hands of a man. All four of them
had faces and wings, 9and their
wings touched one another. Each
one went straight ahead; they did
not turn as they moved.
10Their faces looked like this:
Each of the four had the face of a
man, and on the right side each
had the face of a lion, and on the
left the face of an ox; each also had
the face of an eagle. 11Such were
their faces. Their wings were
spread out upward; each had two
wings, one touching the wing of
another creature on either side,
and two wings covering its body.
12Each one went straight ahead.

[a]1 Or ⌞my⌟
[b]3 Or *Ezekiel son of Buzi the priest*
[c]3 Or *Chaldeans*

*11 Most mss have *dagesh* in the *yod* (גוי״)

°8 ק וידי

יֵלֵכוּ אֶל אֲשֶׁר יִהְיֶה־ שָׁמָּה הָרוּחַ לָלֶכֶת יֵלֵכוּ לֹא יִסַּבּוּ
they-turned not they-would-go to-go the-spirit to-there he-was where to they-went

בְּלֶכְתָּן׃ וּדְמוּת הַחַיּוֹת מַרְאֵיהֶם
appearances-of-them the-living-creatures and-likeness-of (13) as-to-go-them

כְּגַחֲלֵי־ אֵשׁ בֹּעֲרוֹת כְּמַרְאֵה הַלַּפִּדִים הִיא
she the-torches like-appearance-of ones-burning fire like-coals-of

מִתְהַלֶּכֶת בֵּין הַחַיּוֹת וְנֹגַהּ לָאֵשׁ וּמִן־
and-from to-the-fire and-brightness the-living-creatures among moving-back-and-forth

הָאֵשׁ יוֹצֵא בָרָק׃ וְהַחַיּוֹת רָצוֹא
to-speed-forth and-the-living-creatures (14) lightning flashing-out the-fire

וָשׁוֹב כְּמַרְאֵה הַבָּזָק׃ וָאֵרֶא
and-I-looked-at (15) the-lightning like-appearance-of and-to-come-back

הַחַיּוֹת וְהִנֵּה אוֹפַן אֶחָד בָּאָרֶץ אֵצֶל הַחַיּוֹת
the-living-creatures beside on-the-ground one wheel and-see! the-living-creatures

לְאַרְבַּעַת פָּנָיו׃ מַרְאֵה הָאוֹפַנִּים וּמַעֲשֵׂיהֶם
and-structures-of-them the-wheels appearance-of (16) faces-of-him with-four-of

כְּעֵין תַּרְשִׁישׁ וּדְמוּת אֶחָד לְאַרְבַּעְתָּן וּמַרְאֵיהֶם
and-appearances-of-them to-four-of-them one and-look chrysolite like-appearance-of

וּמַעֲשֵׂיהֶם כַּאֲשֶׁר יִהְיֶה הָאוֹפַן בְּתוֹךְ הָאוֹפָן׃ עַל־
to (17) the-wheel at-intersecting-of the-wheel he-was like-that and-makings-of-them

אַרְבַּעַת רִבְעֵיהֶן בְּלֶכְתָּם יֵלֵכוּ לֹא יִסַּבּוּ בְּלֶכְתָּן׃
as-to-go-them they-turned not they-would-go when-to-move-them faces-of-them four-of

וְגַבֵּיהֶן וְגֹבַהּ לָהֶם וְיִרְאָה לָהֶם וְגַבֹּתָם
and-rims-of-them to-them and-awesomeness to-them also-height and-rims-of-them (18)

מְלֵאֹת עֵינַיִם סָבִיב לְאַרְבַּעְתָּן׃ וּבְלֶכֶת הַחַיּוֹת
the-living-creatures and-when-to-move (19) to-four-of-them around eyes ones-full-of

יֵלְכוּ הָאוֹפַנִּים אֶצְלָם וּבְהִנָּשֵׂא הַחַיּוֹת מֵעַל
from-on the-living-creatures and-when-to-rise beside-them the-wheels they-moved

הָאָרֶץ יִנָּשְׂאוּ הָאוֹפַנִּים׃ עַל אֲשֶׁר יִהְיֶה־ שָּׁם הָרוּחַ לָלֶכֶת
to-go the-spirit there he-was where to (20) the-wheels they-rose the-ground

יֵלֵכוּ שָׁמָּה הָרוּחַ לָלֶכֶת וְהָאוֹפַנִּים יִנָּשְׂאוּ לְעֻמָּתָם
at-with-them they-would-rise and-the-wheels to-go the-spirit to-there they-would-go

כִּי רוּחַ הַחַיָּה בָּאוֹפַנִּים׃ בְּלֶכְתָּם
when-to-move-them (21) in-the-wheels the-living-creatures spirit-of because

יֵלֵכוּ וּבְעָמְדָם יַעֲמֹדוּ וּבְהִנָּשְׂאָם
and-when-to-rise-them they-stood-still and-when-to-stand-still-them they-moved

מֵעַל הָאָרֶץ יִנָּשְׂאוּ הָאוֹפַנִּים לְעֻמָּתָם כִּי רוּחַ
spirit-of because at-with-them the-wheels they-rose the-ground from-on

Wherever the spirit would go,
they would go, without turning as
they went. 13The appearance of the
living creatures was like burning
coals of fire or like torches. Fire
moved back and forth among the
creatures; it was bright, and lightning flashed out of it. 14The creatures sped back and forth like
flashes of lightning.
15As I looked at the living creatures, I saw a wheel on the ground
beside each creature with its four
faces. 16This was the appearance
and structure of the wheels: They
sparkled like chrysolite, and all
four looked alike. Each appeared
to be made like a wheel intersecting a wheel. 17As they moved, they
would go in any one of the four
directions the creatures faced; the
wheels did not turn about[d] as the
creatures went. 18Their rims were
high and awesome, and all four
rims were full of eyes all around.
19When the living creatures
moved, the wheels beside them
moved; and when the living creatures rose from the ground, the
wheels also rose. 20Wherever the
spirit would go, they would go,
and the wheels would rise along
with them, because the spirit of
the living creatures was in the
wheels. 21When the creatures
moved, they also moved; when
the creatures stood still, they also
stood still; and when the creatures
rose from the ground, the wheels
rose along with them, because the

[d]17 Or *aside*

הַחַיָּה בָּאוֹפַנִּים׃ וּדְמוּת עַל־ רָאשֵׁי הַחַיָּה
the-living-creature heads-of above and-form (22) in-the-wheels the-living-creatures

רָקִיעַ כְּעֵין הַקֶּרַח הַנּוֹרָא נָטוּי
one-being-spread-out the-one-being-awesome the-ice like-appearance-of expanse

עַל־ רָאשֵׁיהֶם מִלְמָעְלָה׃ וְתַחַת הָרָקִיעַ כַּנְפֵיהֶם
wings-of-them the-expanse and-under (23) to-at-upward heads-of-them above

יְשָׁרוֹת אִשָּׁה אֶל־ אֲחוֹתָהּ לְאִישׁ שְׁתַּיִם מְכַסּוֹת לָהֵנָּה
to-them ones-covering two to-each other-of-her toward each ones-stretched-out

וּלְאִישׁ שְׁתַּיִם מְכַסּוֹת לָהֵנָּה אֵת גְּוִיֹּתֵיהֶם׃ וָאֶשְׁמַע אֶת־
*** and-I-heard (24) bodies-of-them *** to-them ones-covering two and-to-each

קוֹל כַּנְפֵיהֶם כְּקוֹל[e] מַיִם רַבִּים כְּקוֹל־ שַׁדַּי
Shaddai like-voice-of many-ones waters like-roar-of wings-of-them sound-of

בְּלֶכְתָּם קוֹל הֲמֻלָּה כְּקוֹל מַחֲנֶה בְּעָמְדָם
and-when-to-stand-still-them army like-sound-of tumult sound-of when-to-move-them

תְּרַפֶּינָה כַנְפֵיהֶן׃ וַיְהִי־ קוֹל מֵעַל לָרָקִיעַ אֲשֶׁר
that to-the-expanse from-above voice then-he-came (25) wings-of-them they-lowered

עַל־ רֹאשָׁם בְּעָמְדָם תְּרַפֶּינָה כַנְפֵיהֶן׃ וּמִמַּעַל
and-at-above (26) wings-of-them they-lowered as-to-stand-them head-of-them over

לָרָקִיעַ אֲשֶׁר עַל־ רֹאשָׁם כְּמַרְאֵה אֶבֶן־ סַפִּיר
sapphire stone-of like-appearance-of head-of-them over that to-the-expanse

דְּמוּת כִּסֵּא וְעַל דְּמוּת הַכִּסֵּא דְּמוּת כְּמַרְאֵה אָדָם
man like-appearance-of figure the-throne likeness-of and-above throne likeness-of

עָלָיו מִלְמָעְלָה׃ וָאֵרֶא ׀ כְּעֵין חַשְׁמַל כְּמַרְאֵה־
like-appearance-of glowing-metal like-look-of and-I-saw (27) to-at-upward on-him

אֵשׁ בֵּית־ לָהּ סָבִיב מִמַּרְאֵה מָתְנָיו וּלְמָעְלָה
and-to-upward waists-of-him from-appearance-of around to-her encasing-of fire

וּמִמַּרְאֵה מָתְנָיו וּלְמַטָּה רָאִיתִי כְּמַרְאֵה־ אֵשׁ
fire like-appearance-of I-saw and-to-downward waists-of-him and-from-appearance-of

וְנֹגַהּ לוֹ סָבִיב׃ כְּמַרְאֵה הַקֶּשֶׁת אֲשֶׁר
that the-rainbow like-appearance-of (28) surrounding to-him and-brilliant-light

יִהְיֶה בֶעָנָן בְּיוֹם הַגֶּשֶׁם כֵּן מַרְאֵה הַנֹּגַהּ סָבִיב הוּא
this around the-radiance appearance-of so the-rain on-day-of in-the-cloud he-is

מַרְאֵה דְּמוּת כְּבוֹד־ יְהוָה וָאֶרְאֶה וָאֶפֹּל עַל־ פָּנַי
faces-of-me on then-I-fell when-I-saw Yahweh glory-of likeness-of appearance-of

וָאֶשְׁמַע קוֹל מְדַבֵּר׃ וַיֹּאמֶר אֵלָי בֶּן־ אָדָם עֲמֹד
stand-up! man son-of to-me and-he-said (2:1) one-speaking voice-of and-I-heard

עַל־ רַגְלֶיךָ וַאֲדַבֵּר אֹתָךְ׃ וַתָּבֹא בִי רוּחַ כַּאֲשֶׁר
just-as Spirit into-me and-she-came (2) to-you and-I-will-speak feet-of-you on

spirit of the living creatures was in the wheels.

22 Spread out above the heads of the living creatures was what looked like an expanse, sparkling like ice, and awesome. 23 Under the expanse their wings were stretched out one toward the other, and each had two wings covering its body. 24 When the creatures moved, I heard the sound of their wings, like the roar of rushing waters, like the voice of the Almighty,[e] like the tumult of an army. When they stood still, they lowered their wings.

25 Then there came a voice from above the expanse over their heads as they stood with lowered wings. 26 Above the expanse over their heads was what looked like a throne of sapphire,[f] and high above on the throne was a figure like that of a man. 27 I saw that from what appeared to be his waist up he looked like glowing metal, as if full of fire, and that from there down he looked like fire; and brilliant light surrounded him. 28 Like the appearance of a rainbow in the clouds on a rainy day, so was the radiance around him.

This was the appearance of the likeness of the glory of the LORD. When I saw it, I fell facedown, and I heard the voice of one speaking.

*Ezekiel's Call*

2 He said to me, "Son of man, stand up on your feet and I will speak to you." 2 As he spoke, the Spirit came into me and raised

[e] 24 Hebrew *Shaddai*
[f] 26 Or *lapis lazuli*

דַּבֵּר אֵלַי וַתַּעֲמִדֵנִי עַל־רַגְלָי וָאֶשְׁמַע אֵת מִדַּבֵּר אֵלָי׃
to-me one-speaking *** and-I-heard feet-of-me to and-she-raised-me to-me he-spoke

(3) וַיֹּאמֶר אֵלַי בֶּן־אָדָם שׁוֹלֵחַ אֲנִי אוֹתְךָ אֶל־בְּנֵי יִשְׂרָאֵל אֶל־גּוֹיִם
nations to Israel sons-of to you I sending man son-of to-me and-he-said (3)

הַמּוֹרְדִים אֲשֶׁר מָרְדוּ־בִי הֵמָּה וַאֲבוֹתָם
and-fathers-of-them they against-me they-rebelled that the-ones-being-rebellious

פָּשְׁעוּ בִי עַד־עֶצֶם הַיּוֹם הַזֶּה׃ (4) וְהַבָּנִים
and-the-peoples (4) the-this the-day very-of to against-me they-revolted

קְשֵׁי פָנִים וְחִזְקֵי־לֵב אֲנִי שׁוֹלֵחַ אוֹתְךָ אֲלֵיהֶם
to-them you sending I heart and-ones-stubborn-of faces ones-obstinate-of

וְאָמַרְתָּ אֲלֵיהֶם כֹּה אָמַר אֲדֹנָי יְהוִה׃ (5) וְהֵמָּה אִם־יִשְׁמְעוּ
they-listen whether and-they (5) Yahweh Sovereign he-says this to-them and-you-say

וְאִם־יֶחְדָּלוּ כִּי בֵּית מְרִי הֵמָּה וְיָדְעוּ כִּי
that yet-they-will-know they rebellion house-of for they-fail-to-listen or-whether

נָבִיא הָיָה בְתוֹכָם׃ (6) וְאַתָּה בֶן־אָדָם אַל־תִּירָא מֵהֶם
of-them you-be-afraid not man son-of and-you (6) in-among-them he-was prophet

וּמִדִּבְרֵיהֶם אַל־תִּירָא כִּי סָרָבִים וְסַלּוֹנִים אוֹתָךְ וְאֶל־
and-among around-you and-thorns briers though you-be-afraid not or-of-words-of-them

עַקְרַבִּים אַתָּה יוֹשֵׁב מִדִּבְרֵיהֶם אַל־תִּירָא וּמִפְּנֵיהֶם אַל־
not and-because-of-them you-be-afraid not of-words-of-them living you scorpions

תֵּחָת כִּי בֵּית מְרִי הֵמָּה׃ (7) וְדִבַּרְתָּ אֶת־
*** and-you-must-speak (7) they rebellion house-of though you-be-terrified

דְּבָרַי אֲלֵיהֶם אִם־יִשְׁמְעוּ וְאִם־יֶחְדָּלוּ כִּי
for they-fail-to-listen or-whether they-listen whether to-them words-of-me

מְרִי הֵמָּה׃ (8) וְאַתָּה בֶן־אָדָם שְׁמַע אֵת אֲשֶׁר־אֲנִי מְדַבֵּר אֵלֶיךָ אַל־תְּהִי־
you-be not to-you saying I what *** listen! man son-of but-you (8) they rebellion

מֶרִי כְּבֵית הַמֶּרִי פְּצֵה פִיךָ וֶאֱכֹל אֵת אֲשֶׁר־אֲנִי נֹתֵן
giving I what *** and-eat! mouth-of-you open! the-rebellion like-house-of rebel

אֵלֶיךָ׃ (9) וָאֶרְאֶה וְהִנֵּה־יָד שְׁלוּחָה אֵלָי וְהִנֵּה־בוֹ
in-him and-see! to-me being-stretched-out hand and-see! then-I-looked (9) to-you

מְגִלַּת־סֵפֶר׃ (10) וַיִּפְרֹשׂ אוֹתָהּ לְפָנַי וְהִיא כְתוּבָה פָּנִים
fronts one-being-written and-she before-me her and-he-unrolled (10) book scroll-of

וְאָחוֹר וְכָתוּב אֵלֶיהָ קִנִים וָהֶגֶה וָהִי׃ (3:1) וַיֹּאמֶר
and-he-said (3:1) and-woe and-mourning laments on-her and-being-written and-back

אֵלַי בֶּן־אָדָם אֵת אֲשֶׁר־תִּמְצָא אֱכוֹל אֱכוֹל אֶת־הַמְּגִלָּה הַזֹּאת וְלֵךְ
then-go! the-this the-scroll *** eat! eat! you-find what *** man son-of to-me

דַּבֵּר אֶל־בֵּית יִשְׂרָאֵל׃ (2) וָאֶפְתַּח אֶת־פִּי וַיַּאֲכִלֵנִי
and-he-gave-to-eat-me mouth-of-me *** so-I-opened (2) Israel house-of to speak!

me to my feet, and I heard him
speaking to me.
3 He said: "Son of man, I am
sending you to the Israelites, to a
rebellious nation that has rebelled
against me; they and their fathers
have been in revolt against me to
this very day. 4 The people to
whom I am sending you are obstinate and stubborn. Say to them,
'This is what the Sovereign LORD
says.' 5 And whether they listen or
fail to listen—for they are a rebellious house—they will know that a
prophet has been among them.
6 And you, son of man, do not be
afraid of them or their words. Do
not be afraid, though briers and
thorns are all around you and you
live among scorpions. Do not be
afraid of what they say or terrified
by them, though they are a rebellious house. 7 You must speak my
words to them, whether they listen or fail to listen, for they are
rebellious. 8 But you, son of man,
listen to what I say to you. Do not
rebel like that rebellious house;
open your mouth and eat what I
give you."
9 Then I looked, and I saw a hand
stretched out to me. In it was a
scroll, 10 which he unrolled before
me. On both sides of it were written words of lament and mourning and woe.
3 And he said to me, "Son of
man, eat what is before you,
eat this scroll; then go and speak
to the house of Israel." 2 So I
opened my mouth, and he gave
me the scroll to eat.

אֶת־ הַמְּגִלָּ֖ה הַזֹּ֑את ׃ וַיֹּ֣אמֶר אֵלַ֗י בֶּן־ אָדָם֙ בִּטְנְךָ֤ תַאֲכֵ֔ל
you-make-eat  belly-of-you  man  son-of  to-me  then-he-said  (3)  the-this  the-scroll  ***

וּמֵעֶ֣יךָ תְמַלֵּ֔א אֵ֚ת הַמְּגִלָּ֣ה הַזֹּ֔את אֲשֶׁ֥ר אֲנִ֖י נֹתֵ֣ן אֵלֶ֑יךָ וָאֹ֣כְלָ֔ה
so-I-ate  to-you  giving  I  that  the-this  the-scroll  ***  you-fill  and-stomachs-of-you

וַתְּהִ֣י בְּפִ֔י כִּדְבַ֖שׁ לְמָתֽוֹק ׃ וַיֹּ֖אמֶר אֵלָ֑י בֶּן־ אָדָ֗ם
man  son-of  to-me  then-he-said  (4)  in-sweetness  as-honey  in-mouth-of-me  and-she-was

לֶךְ־ בֹּא֙ אֶל־ בֵּ֣ית יִשְׂרָאֵ֔ל וְדִבַּרְתָּ֥ בִדְבָרַ֖י אֲלֵיהֶֽם ׃ כִּ֣י לֹ֤א
not  indeed  (5)  to-them  with-words-of-me  and-you-speak  Israel  house-of  to  go!  walk!

אֶל־ עַ֛ם עִמְקֵ֥י שָׂפָ֖ה וְכִבְדֵ֣י לָשׁ֑וֹן אַתָּ֖ה שָׁל֑וּחַ
being-sent  you  language  and-ones-difficult-of  speech  ones-obscure-of  people  to

אֶל־ בֵּ֣ית יִשְׂרָאֵֽל ׃ לֹ֣א ׀ אֶל־ עַמִּ֣ים רַבִּ֗ים עִמְקֵ֥י שָׂפָ֖ה
speech  ones-obscure-of  many-ones  peoples  to  not  (6)  Israel  house-of  to

וְכִבְדֵ֣י לָשׁ֔וֹן אֲשֶׁ֥ר לֹא־ תִשְׁמַ֖ע דִּבְרֵיהֶ֑ם אִם־ לֹ֤א
surely  if  words-of-them  you-can-understand  not  whom  language  and-ones-difficult-of

אֲלֵיהֶ֣ם שְׁלַחְתִּ֔יךָ הֵ֖מָּה יִשְׁמְע֥וּ אֵלֶֽיךָ ׃ וּבֵ֣ית יִשְׂרָאֵ֗ל
Israel  but-house-of  (7)  to-you  they-would-have-listened  they  I-sent-you  to-them

לֹ֤א יֹאב֙וּ לִשְׁמֹ֣עַ אֵלֶ֔יךָ כִּֽי־ אֵינָ֥ם אֹבִ֖ים לִשְׁמֹ֣עַ
to-listen  ones-willing  not-they  because  to-you  to-listen  they-are-willing  not

אֵלַ֔י כִּ֖י כָּל־ בֵּ֣ית יִשְׂרָאֵ֗ל חִזְקֵי־ מֵ֖צַח וּקְשֵׁי־
and-ones-obstinate-of  forehead  ones-hard-of  Israel  house-of  whole-of  for  to-me

לֵ֖ב הֵֽמָּה ׃ הִנֵּ֨ה נָתַ֧תִּי אֶת־ פָּנֶ֛יךָ חֲזָקִ֖ים לְעֻמַּ֣ת
like-against-of  unyielding-ones  faces-of-you  ***  I-will-make  see!  (8)  they  heart

פְּנֵיהֶ֑ם וְאֶת־ מִצְחֲךָ֖ חָזָ֥ק לְעֻמַּ֥ת מִצְחָֽם ׃
forehead-of-them  like-against-of  hard  forehead-of-you  and  faces-of-them

כְּשָׁמִ֥יר חָזָ֛ק מִצֹּ֖ר נָתַ֣תִּי מִצְחֶ֑ךָ לֹא־
not  forehead-of-you  I-will-make  more-than-flint  hard  like-hardest-stone  (9)

תִירָ֤א אוֹתָם֙ וְלֹא־ תֵחַ֣ת מִפְּנֵיהֶ֔ם כִּ֛י בֵּֽית־
house-of  though  because-of-them  you-be-terrified  and-not  of-them  you-be-afraid

מְרִ֖י הֵֽמָּה ׃ וַיֹּ֖אמֶר אֵלָ֑י בֶּן־ אָדָ֗ם אֶת־ כָּל־ דְּבָרַ֛י אֲשֶׁ֥ר
that  words-of-me  all-of  ***  man  son-of  to-me  and-he-said  (10)  they  rebellion

אֲדַבֵּ֥ר אֵלֶ֖יךָ קַ֣ח בִּלְבָבְךָ֑ וּבְאָזְנֶ֖יךָ שְׁמָֽע ׃ וְלֵ֥ךְ
now-walk!  (11)  listen!  and-with-ears-of-you  to-heart-of-you  take!  to-you  I-speak

בֹ֤א אֶל־ הַגּוֹלָה֙ אֶל־ בְּנֵ֣י עַמֶּ֔ךָ וְדִבַּרְתָּ֤ אֲלֵיהֶם֙
to-them  and-you-speak  people-of-you  countrymen-of  to  the-exile  to  go!

וְאָמַרְתָּ֣ אֲלֵיהֶ֔ם כֹּ֥ה אָמַ֖ר אֲדֹנָ֣י יְהוִ֑ה אִֽם־ יִשְׁמְע֖וּ וְאִם־
or-whether  they-listen  whether  Yahweh  Sovereign  he-says  this  to-them  and-you-say

יֶחְדָּֽלוּ ׃ וַתִּשָּׂאֵ֣נִי ר֔וּחַ וָאֶשְׁמַ֣ע אַחֲרַ֔י ק֖וֹל
sound-of  behind-me  and-I-heard  Spirit  then-she-lifted-me  (12)  they-fail-to-listen

<sup></sup>
[3]Then he said to me, "Son of man, eat this scroll I am giving you and fill your stomach with it." So I ate it, and it tasted as sweet as honey in my mouth.

[4]He then said to me: "Son of man, go now to the house of Israel and speak my words to them. [5]You are not being sent to a people of obscure speech and difficult language, but to the house of Israel— [6]not to many peoples of obscure speech and difficult language, whose words you cannot understand. Surely if I had sent you to them, they would have listened to you. [7]But the house of Israel is not willing to listen to you because they are not willing to listen to me, for the whole house of Israel is hardened and obstinate. [8]But I will make you as unyielding and hardened as they are. [9]I will make your forehead like the hardest stone, harder than flint. Do not be afraid of them or terrified by them, though they are a rebellious house."

[10]And he said to me, "Son of man, listen carefully and take to heart all the words I speak to you. [11]Go now to your countrymen in exile and speak to them. Say to them, 'This is what the Sovereign LORD says,' whether they listen or fail to listen."

[12]Then the Spirit lifted me up, and I heard behind me a loud

רַעַשׁ גָּדוֹל בָּרוּךְ כְּבוֹד־ יְהוָה מִמְּקוֹמוֹ׃ וְקוֹל ׀
and-sound-of (13) in-dwelling-of-him Yahweh glory-of being-praised loud rumbling

כַּנְפֵי הַחַיּוֹת מַשִּׁיקוֹת אִשָּׁה אֶל־ אֲחוֹתָהּ וְקוֹל
and-sound-of other-of-her against each ones-brushing the-living-creatures wings-of

הָאוֹפַנִּים לְעֻמָּתָם וְקוֹל רַעַשׁ גָּדוֹל׃ וְרוּחַ
then-the-Spirit (14) loud rumbling and-sound-of at-beside-them the-wheels

נְשָׂאַתְנִי וַתִּקָּחֵנִי וָאֵלֵךְ מַר בַּחֲמַת רוּחִי
spirit-of-me in-anger-of bitter and-I-went and-she-took-away-me she-lifted-up-me

וְיַד־ יְהוָה עָלַי חָזָקָה׃ וָאָבוֹא אֶל־ הַגּוֹלָה תֵּל אָבִיב
Abib Tel the-exile to and-I-came (15) strong upon-me Yahweh with-hand-of

הַיֹּשְׁבִים אֶל־ נְהַר־ כְּבָר וָאֵשֵׁר הֵמָּה יוֹשְׁבִים שָׁם וָאֵשֵׁב
and-I-sat there ones-living they and-I-sat Kebar River-of near the-ones-living

שָׁם שִׁבְעַת יָמִים מַשְׁמִים בְּתוֹכָם׃ וַיְהִי מִקְצֵה
at-end-of and-he-was (16) in-among-them ones-being-overwhelmed days seven-of there

שִׁבְעַת יָמִים וַיְהִי דְבַר־ יְהוָה אֵלַי לֵאמֹר׃ בֶּן־ אָדָם צֹפֶה
man-watching man son-of (17) to-say to-me Yahweh word-of then-he-came days seven-of

נְתַתִּיךָ לְבֵית יִשְׂרָאֵל וְשָׁמַעְתָּ מִפִּי דָּבָר וְהִזְהַרְתָּ
and-you-warn word from-mouth-of-me so-you-hear Israel for-house-of I-made-you

אוֹתָם מִמֶּנִּי׃ בְּאָמְרִי לָרָשָׁע מוֹת תָּמוּת וְלֹא
and-not you-will-die to-die to-the-wicked-man when-to-say-me (18) from-me them

הִזְהַרְתּוֹ וְלֹא דִבַּרְתָּ לְהַזְהִיר רָשָׁע מִדַּרְכּוֹ הָרְשָׁעָה
the-evil from-way-of-him wicked-man to-dissuade you-speak or-not you-warn-him

לְחַיֹּתוֹ הוּא רָשָׁע בַּעֲוֹנוֹ יָמוּת וְדָמוֹ
and-blood-of-him he-will-die for-sin-of-him wicked-man that to-save-life-of-him

מִיָּדְךָ אֲבַקֵּשׁ׃ וְאַתָּה כִּי־ הִזְהַרְתָּ רָשָׁע וְלֹא־
and-not wicked-man you-warn if but-you (19) I-will-ask-account from-hand-of-you

שָׁב מֵרִשְׁעוֹ וּמִדַּרְכּוֹ הָרְשָׁעָה הוּא בַּעֲוֹנוֹ
for-sin-of-him he the-evil or-from-way-of-him from-wickedness-of-him he-turns

יָמוּת וְאַתָּה אֶת־ נַפְשְׁךָ הִצַּלְתָּ׃ וּבְשׁוּב
again-when-to-turn (20) you-will-save self-of-you *** but-you he-will-die

צַדִּיק מִצִּדְקוֹ וְעָשָׂה עָוֶל וְנָתַתִּי
and-I-put evil and-he-does from-righteousness-of-him righteous-man

מִכְשׁוֹל לְפָנָיו הוּא יָמוּת כִּי לֹא הִזְהַרְתּוֹ בְּחַטָּאתוֹ
for-sin-of-him you-warned-him not since he-will-die he before-him stumbling-block

יָמוּת וְלֹא תִזָּכַרְןָ צִדְקָתוֹ אֲשֶׁר עָשָׂה
he-did that righteous-things-of-him they-will-be-remembered and-not he-will-die

וְדָמוֹ מִיָּדְךָ אֲבַקֵּשׁ׃ וְאַתָּה כִּי הִזְהַרְתּוֹ
you-warn-him if but-you (21) I-will-ask-account from-hand-of-you and-blood-of-him

°15 ק ואשב
°20 ק צדקתיו

rumbling sound—May the glory of the LORD be praised in his dwelling place!— [13]the sound of the wings of the living creatures brushing against each other and the sound of the wheels beside them, a loud rumbling sound. [14]The Spirit then lifted me up and took me away, and I went in bitterness and in the anger of my spirit, with the strong hand of the LORD upon me. [15]I came to the exiles who lived at Tel Abib near the Kebar River. And there, where they were living, I sat among them for seven days—overwhelmed.

*Warning to Israel*

[16]At the end of seven days the word of the LORD came to me: [17]"Son of man, I have made you a watchman for the house of Israel; so hear the word I speak and give them warning from me. [18]When I say to a wicked man, 'You will surely die,' and you do not warn him or speak out to dissuade him from his evil ways in order to save his life, that wicked man will die for[g] his sin, and I will hold you accountable for his blood. [19]But if you do warn the wicked man and he does not turn from his wickedness or from his evil ways, he will die for his sin; but you will have saved yourself.

[20]"Again, when a righteous man turns from his righteousness and does evil, and I put a stumbling block before him, he will die. Since you did not warn him, he will die for his sin. The righteous things he did will not be remembered, and I will hold you accountable for his blood. [21]But if you do warn the righteous man

g18 Or *in*; also in verses 19 and 20

צַדִּיק לְבִלְתִּי חֲטֹא צַדִּיק וְהוּא לֹא־ חָטָא חָיוֹ יִחְיֶה

he-will-live to-live he-sins not and-he righteous-man to-sin not righteous-man

כִּי נִזְהָר וְאַתָּה אֶת־ נַפְשְׁךָ הִצַּלְתָּ׃ וַתְּהִי

and-she-was (22) you-will-save self-of-you *** and-you he-took-warning because

עָלַי שָׁם יַד־ יְהוָה וַיֹּאמֶר אֵלַי קוּם צֵא אֶל־הַבִּקְעָה

the-plain to go-out! get-up! to-me and-he-said Yahweh hand-of there upon-me

וְשָׁם אֲדַבֵּר אוֹתָךְ׃ וָאָקוּם וָאֵצֵא אֶל־הַבִּקְעָה וְהִנֵּה־

and-see! the-plain to and-I-went-out so-I-got-up (23) to-you I-will-speak and-there

שָׁם כְּבוֹד־ יְהוָה עֹמֵד כַּכָּבוֹד אֲשֶׁר רָאִיתִי עַל־ נְהַר־ כְּבָר

Kebar River-of by I-saw that like-the-glory standing Yahweh glory-of there

וָאֶפֹּל עַל־ פָּנָי׃ וַתָּבֹא־ בִי רוּחַ וַתַּעֲמִדֵנִי עַל־

to and-she-raised-me Spirit into-me then-she-came (24) faces-of-me on and-I-fell

רַגְלָי וַיְדַבֵּר אֹתִי וַיֹּאמֶר אֵלַי בֹּא הִסָּגֵר בְּתוֹךְ

inside-of shut-yourself! go! to-me and-he-said to-me and-he-spoke feet-of-me

בֵּיתֶךָ׃ וְאַתָּה בֶן־ אָדָם הִנֵּה נָתְנוּ עָלֶיךָ עֲבוֹתִים

ropes on-you they-will-tie see! man son-of and-you (25) house-of-you

וַאֲסָרוּךָ בָּהֶם וְלֹא תֵצֵא בְּתוֹכָם׃

in-among-them you-can-go-out so-not with-them and-they-will-bind-you

וּלְשׁוֹנְךָ אַדְבִּיק אֶל־ חִכֶּךָ וְנֶאֱלַמְתָּ

so-you-will-be-silent roof-of-mouth-of-you to I-will-make-stick and-tongue-of-you (26)

וְלֹא־ תִהְיֶה לָהֶם לְאִישׁ מוֹכִיחַ כִּי בֵּית מְרִי הֵמָּה׃

they rebellion house-of though one-rebuking as-man to-them you-can-be so-not

וּבְדַבְּרִי אוֹתְךָ אֶפְתַּח אֶת־ פִּיךָ וְאָמַרְתָּ

and-you-shall-say mouth-of-you *** I-will-open to-you but-when-to-speak-me (27)

אֲלֵיהֶם כֹּה אָמַר אֲדֹנָי יְהוִה הַשֹּׁמֵעַ ׀ יִשְׁמָע וְהֶחָדֵל ׀

and-the-refuser let-him-listen the-one-listening Yahweh Sovereign he-says this to-them

יֶחְדָּל כִּי בֵּית מְרִי הֵמָּה׃ וְאַתָּה בֶן־ אָדָם קַח־ לְךָ

for-you take! man son-of now-you (4:1) they rebellion house-of for let-him-refuse

לְבֵנָה וְנָתַתָּה אוֹתָהּ לְפָנֶיךָ וְחַקּוֹתָ עָלֶיהָ עִיר אֶת־יְרוּשָׁלִָם׃

Jerusalem *** city on-her and-you-draw in-front-of-you her and-you-put clay-tablet

וְנָתַתָּה עָלֶיהָ מָצוֹר וּבָנִיתָ עָלֶיהָ דָּיֵק

siege-work against-her and-you-erect siege against-her then-you-lay (2)

וְשָׁפַכְתָּ עָלֶיהָ סֹלְלָה וְנָתַתָּה עָלֶיהָ מַחֲנוֹת וְשִׂים־ עָלֶיהָ

against-her and-put! camps against-her and-you-set-up ramp to-her and-you-build

כָּרִים סָבִיב׃ וְאַתָּה קַח־ לְךָ מַחֲבַת בַּרְזֶל וְנָתַתָּה אוֹתָהּ

her and-you-place iron pan-of for-you take! then-you (3) around battering-rams

קִיר בַּרְזֶל בֵּינְךָ וּבֵין הָעִיר וַהֲכִינֹתָה אֶת־ פָּנֶיךָ

faces-of-you *** and-you-turn the-city and-between between-you iron wall-of

not to sin and he does not sin, he
will surely live because he took
warning, and you will have saved
yourself."
22 The hand of the LORD was
upon me there, and he said to me,
"Get up and go out to the plain,
and there I will speak to you." 23 So
I got up and went out to the plain.
And the glory of the LORD was
standing there, like the glory I had
seen by the Kebar River, and I fell
facedown.
24 Then the Spirit came into me
and raised me to my feet. He
spoke to me and said: "Go, shut
yourself inside your house. 25 And
you, son of man, they will tie with
ropes; you will be bound so that
you cannot go out among the
people. 26 I will make your tongue
stick to the roof of your mouth so
that you will be silent and unable
to rebuke them, though they are a
rebellious house. 27 But when I
speak to you, I will open your
mouth and you shall say to them,
'This is what the Sovereign LORD
says.' Whoever will listen let him
listen, and whoever will refuse let
him refuse; for they are a rebellious house.

*Siege of Jerusalem Symbolized*

4 "Now, son of man, take a clay
tablet, put it in front of you
and draw the city of Jerusalem on
it. 2 Then lay siege to it: Erect siege
works against it, build a ramp up
to it, set up camps against it and
put battering rams around it.
3 Then take an iron pan, place it as
an iron wall between you and the
city and turn your face toward it.

אֵלֶיהָ וְהָיְתָה בַמָּצוֹר וְצַרְתָּ עָלֶיהָ אוֹת

sign against-her and-you-shall-besiege under-the-siege and-she-will-be toward-her

הִיא לְבֵית יִשְׂרָאֵל׃ וְאַתָּה שְׁכַב עַל־ צִדְּךָ הַשְּׂמָאלִי וְשַׂמְתָּ

and-you-put the-left side-of-you on lie! then-you (4) Israel to-house-of this

אֶת־ עֲוֹן בֵּית־ יִשְׂרָאֵל עָלָיו מִסְפַּר הַיָּמִים אֲשֶׁר תִּשְׁכַּב עָלָיו

on-him you-lie that the-days number-of upon-him Israel house-of sin-of ***

תִּשָּׂא אֶת־ עֲוֹנָם׃ וַאֲנִי נָתַתִּי לְךָ אֶת־ שְׁנֵי עֲוֹנָם

sin-of-them years-of *** to-you I-assigned and-I (5) sin-of-them *** you-will-bear

לְמִסְפַּר יָמִים שְׁלֹשׁ־ מֵאוֹת וְתִשְׁעִים יוֹם וְנָשָׂאתָ עֲוֹן בֵּית־

house-of sin-of so-you-will-bear day and-ninety hundreds three-of days as-number-of

יִשְׂרָאֵל׃ וְכִלִּיתָ אֶת־אֵלֶּה וְשָׁכַבְתָּ עַל־ צִדְּךָ הַיְמָונִי שֵׁנִית

again the-right side-of-you on then-you-lie these *** after-you-finish (6) Israel

וְנָשָׂאתָ אֶת־ עֲוֹן בֵּית־יְהוּדָה אַרְבָּעִים יוֹם יוֹם לַשָּׁנָה יוֹם לַשָּׁנָה

for-the-year day for-the-year day day forty Judah house-of sin-of *** and-you-bear

נְתַתִּיו לָךְ׃ וְאֶל־ מְצוֹר יְרוּשָׁלִַם תָּכִין פָּנֶיךָ

faces-of-you you-turn Jerusalem siege-of and-toward (7) to-you I-assigned-him

וּזְרֹעֲךָ חֲשׂוּפָה וְנִבֵּאתָ עָלֶיהָ׃ וְהִנֵּה נָתַתִּי

I-will-tie and-see! (8) against-her and-you-prophesy being-bared and-arm-of-you

עָלֶיךָ עֲבוֹתִים וְלֹא־ תֵהָפֵךְ מִצִּדְּךָ אֶל־ צִדֶּךָ עַד־ כַּלּוֹתְךָ

to-finish-you until side-of-you to from-side-of-you you-can-turn so-not ropes on-you

יְמֵי מְצוּרֶךָ׃ וְאַתָּה קַח־ לְךָ חִטִּין וּשְׂעֹרִים וּפוֹל

and-bean and-barleys wheats for-you take! and-you (9) siege-of-you days-of

וַעֲדָשִׁים וְדֹחַן וְכֻסְּמִים וְנָתַתָּה אוֹתָם בִּכְלִי אֶחָד וְעָשִׂיתָ

and-you-make one in-storage-jar them and-you-put and-spelts and-millet and-lentils

אוֹתָם לְךָ לְלָחֶם מִסְפַּר הַיָּמִים אֲשֶׁר־אַתָּה ׀ שׁוֹכֵב עַל־ צִדְּךָ שְׁלֹשׁ־

three-of side-of-you on lying you that the-days number-of for-bread for-you them

מֵאוֹת וְתִשְׁעִים יוֹם תֹּאכְלֶנּוּ׃ וּמַאֲכָלְךָ אֲשֶׁר תֹּאכְלֶנּוּ בְּמִשְׁקוֹל

by-weight you-eat-him that and-food-of-you (10) you-eat-him day and-ninety hundreds

עֶשְׂרִים שֶׁקֶל לַיּוֹם מֵעֵת עַד־עֵת תֹּאכְלֶנּוּ׃ וּמַיִם בִּמְשׂוּרָה

by-measure also-waters (11) you-eat-him time to from-time for-the-day shekel twenty

תִשְׁתֶּה שִׁשִּׁית הַהִין מֵעֵת עַד־עֵת תִּשְׁתֶּה׃ וְעֻגַת שְׂעֹרִים

barleys and-cake-of (12) you-drink time to from-time the-hin sixth-of you-drink

תֹּאכֲלֶנָּה וְהִיא בְּגֶלְלֵי צֵאַת הָאָדָם תְּעֻגֶנָה

you-bake-her the-human coming-out-of with-excrements-of and-she you-eat-her

לְעֵינֵיהֶם׃ וַיֹּאמֶר יְהוָה כָּכָה יֹאכְלוּ בְנֵי־

peoples-of they-will-eat this-way Yahweh and-he-said (13) before-eyes-of-them

יִשְׂרָאֵל אֶת־ לַחְמָם טָמֵא בַּגּוֹיִם אֲשֶׁר אַדִּיחֵם שָׁם׃

there I-will-drive-them where among-the-nations defiled food-of-them *** Israel

°6 ק הימני

It will be under siege, and you
shall besiege it. This will be a sign
to the house of Israel.
4"Then lie on your left side and
put the sin of the house of Israel
upon yourself.[h] You are to bear
their sin for the number of days
you lie on your side. 5I have assigned you the same number of
days as the years of their sin. So
for 390 days you will bear the sin
of the house of Israel.
6"After you have finished this,
lie down again, this time on your
right side, and bear the sin of the
house of Judah. I have assigned
you 40 days, a day for each year.
7Turn your face toward the siege of
Jerusalem and with bared arm
prophesy against her. 8I will tie
you up with ropes so that you cannot turn from one side to the other
until you have finished the days
of your siege.
9"Take wheat and barley, beans
and lentils, millet and spelt; put
them in a storage jar and use them
to make bread for yourself. You
are to eat it during the 390 days
you lie on your side. 10Weigh out
twenty shekels[i] of food to eat each
day and eat it at set times. 11Also
measure out a sixth of a hin[j] of
water and drink it at set times.
12Eat the food as you would a barley cake; bake it in the sight of the
people, using human excrement
for fuel." 13The LORD said, "In this
way the people of Israel will eat
defiled food among the nations
where I will drive them."

h4 Or *your side*
i10 That is, about 8 ounces (about 0.2 kilogram)
j11 That is, about 2/3 quart (about 0.6 liter)

וָאֹמַר אֲהָהּ אֲדֹנָי יְהוִה הִנֵּה נַפְשִׁי לֹא מְטֻמָּאָה
being-defiled never self-of-me see! Yahweh Sovereign not-so! then-I-said (14)

וּנְבֵלָה וּטְרֵפָה לֹא־אָכַלְתִּי מִנְּעוּרַי וְעַד־
and-until from-youths-of-me I-ate never or-thing-torn-by-animal and-dead-thing

עַתָּה וְלֹא־בָא בְּפִי בְּשַׂר פִּגּוּל׃ וַיֹּאמֶר אֵלַי
to-me and-he-said (15) uncleanness meat-of into-mouth-of-me he-entered and-not now

רְאֵה נָתַתִּי לְךָ אֶת־צְפִועֵי הַבָּקָר תַּחַת גֶּלְלֵי הָאָדָם
the-human excrements-of instead-of the-cow manures-of *** to-you I-will-give see!

וְעָשִׂיתָ אֶת־לַחְמְךָ עֲלֵיהֶם׃ וַיֹּאמֶר אֵלַי בֶּן־אָדָם
man son-of to-me then-he-said (16) over-them bread-of-you *** and-you-can-make

הִנְנִי שֹׁבֵר מַטֵּה־לֶחֶם בִּירוּשָׁלִַם וְאָכְלוּ־לֶחֶם בְּמִשְׁקָל
by-ration food and-they-will-eat in-Jerusalem food supply-of cutting-off see-I!

וּבִדְאָגָה וּמַיִם בִּמְשׂוּרָה וּבְשִׁמָּמוֹן יִשְׁתּוּ׃ לְמַעַן
for-that (17) they-will-drink and-in-despair by-ration and-waters and-in-anxiety

יַחְסְרוּ לֶחֶם וָמָיִם וְנָשַׁמּוּ אִישׁ וְאָחִיו
and-other-of-him each and-they-will-be-appalled and-waters food they-will-be-scarce

וְנָמַקּוּ בַּעֲוֺנָם׃ וְאַתָּה בֶן־אָדָם קַח־
take! man son-of now-you (5:1) because-of-sin-of-them and-they-will-waste-away

לְךָ ׀ חֶרֶב חַדָּה תַּעַר הַגַּלָּבִים תִּקָּחֶנָּה לָּךְ וְהַעֲבַרְתָּ עַל־
on and-you-shave for-you you-use-her the-barbers razor-of sharp sword for-you

רֹאשְׁךָ וְעַל־זְקָנֶךָ וְלָקַחְתָּ לְךָ מֹאזְנֵי מִשְׁקָל
weight set-of-scales-of for-you then-you-take beard-of-you and-on head-of-you

וְחִלַּקְתָּם׃ שְׁלִשִׁית בָּאוּר תַּבְעִיר בְּתוֹךְ הָעִיר
the-city at-inside-of you-burn with-the-fire third (2) and-you-divide-them

כִּמְלֹאת יְמֵי הַמָּצוֹר וְלָקַחְתָּ אֶת־הַשְּׁלִשִׁית תַּכֶּה בַחֶרֶב
with-the-sword you-strike the-third *** and-you-take the-siege days-of when-to-end

סְבִיבוֹתֶיהָ וְהַשְּׁלִשִׁית תִּזְרֶה לָרוּחַ וְחֶרֶב אָרִיק
I-will-draw for-sword to-the-wind you-scatter and-the-third ones-around-her

אַחֲרֵיהֶם׃ וְלָקַחְתָּ מִשָּׁם מְעַט בְּמִסְפָּר וְצַרְתָּ אוֹתָם
them and-you-tuck in-number few from-there but-you-take (3) after-them

בִּכְנָפֶיךָ׃ וּמֵהֶם עוֹד תִּקָּח וְהִשְׁלַכְתָּ אוֹתָם
them and-you-throw you-take again and-from-them (4) into-folds-of-garments-of-you

אֶל־תּוֹךְ הָאֵשׁ וְשָׂרַפְתָּ אֹתָם בָּאֵשׁ מִמֶּנּוּ תֵצֵא־
she-will-spread from-him in-the-fire them and-you-burn the-fire midst-of into

אֵשׁ אֶל־כָּל־בֵּית יִשְׂרָאֵל׃ כֹּה אָמַר אֲדֹנָי יְהוִה זֹאת
this Yahweh Sovereign he-says this (5) Israel house-of whole-of to fire

יְרוּשָׁלִַם בְּתוֹךְ הַגּוֹיִם שַׂמְתִּיהָ וּסְבִיבוֹתֶיהָ אֲרָצוֹת׃
countries with-ones-around-her I-set-her the-nations in-center-of Jerusalem

c15 ק צפיעי

[14]Then I said, "Not so, Sovereign LORD! I have never defiled myself. From my youth until now I have never eaten anything found dead or torn by wild animals. No unclean meat has ever entered my mouth."

[15]"Very well," he said, "I will let you bake your bread over cow manure instead of human excrement."

[16]He then said to me: "Son of man, I will cut off the supply of food in Jerusalem. The people will eat rationed food in anxiety and drink rationed water in despair, [17]for food and water will be scarce. They will be appalled at the sight of each other and will waste away because of[k] their sin.

5 "Now, son of man, take a sharp sword and use it as a barber's razor to shave your head and your beard. Then take a set of scales and divide up the hair. [2]When the days of your siege come to an end, burn a third of the hair with fire inside the city. Take a third and strike it with the sword all around the city. And scatter a third to the wind. For I will pursue them with drawn sword. [3]But take a few strands of hair and tuck them away in the folds of your garment. [4]Again, take a few of these and throw them into the fire and burn them up. A fire will spread from there to the whole house of Israel.

[5]"This is what the Sovereign LORD says: This is Jerusalem, which I have set in the center of the nations, with countries all

k17 Or *away in*

וַתֶּמֶר אֶת־ מִשְׁפָּטַי לְרִשְׁעָה מִן־ הַגּוֹיִם וְאֶת־
and the-nations more-than in-wickedness laws-of-me against yet-she-rebelled (6)

חֻקּוֹתַי מִן־ הָאֲרָצוֹת אֲשֶׁר סְבִיבוֹתֶיהָ כִּי בְמִשְׁפָּטַי
to-laws-of-me indeed ones-around-her that the-countries more-than decrees-of-me

מָאָסוּ וְחֻקּוֹתַי לֹא־ הָלְכוּ בָהֶם׃ לָכֵן כֹּה־ אָמַר ׀
he-says this therefore (7) to-them they-followed not and-decrees-of-me they-rejected

אֲדֹנָי יְהוִה יַעַן הֲמָנְכֶם מִן־ הַגּוֹיִם אֲשֶׁר סְבִיבוֹתֵיכֶם
ones-around-you that the-nations more-than to-be-unruly-you because Yahweh Sovereign

בְּחֻקּוֹתַי לֹא הֲלַכְתֶּם וְאֶת־ מִשְׁפָּטַי לֹא עֲשִׂיתֶם וּכְמִשְׁפְּטֵי
even-as-standards-of you-kept not laws-of-me or you-followed not to-decrees-of-me

הַגּוֹיִם אֲשֶׁר סְבִיבוֹתֵיכֶם לֹא עֲשִׂיתֶם׃ לָכֵן כֹּה אָמַר
he-says this therefore (8) you-conformed-to not ones-around-you that the-nations

אֲדֹנָי יְהוִה הִנְנִי עָלַיִךְ גַּם־ אָנִי וְעָשִׂיתִי בְתוֹכֵךְ
in-midst-of-you and-I-will-inflict I even against-you see-I! Yahweh Sovereign

מִשְׁפָּטִים לְעֵינֵי הַגּוֹיִם׃ וְעָשִׂיתִי בָךְ אֵת אֲשֶׁר לֹא־עָשִׂיתִי
I-did never what *** to-you and-I-will-do (9) the-nations before-eyes-of punishments

וְאֵת אֲשֶׁר־ לֹא־ אֶעֱשֶׂה כָמֹהוּ עוֹד יַעַן כָּל־ תּוֹעֲבֹתָיִךְ׃
detestable-ones-of-you all-of because-of again like-him I-will-do never what and

לָכֵן אָבוֹת יֹאכְלוּ בָנִים בְּתוֹכֵךְ וּבָנִים
and-children in-midst-of-you children they-will-eat fathers therefore (10)

יֹאכְלוּ אֲבוֹתָם וְעָשִׂיתִי בָךְ שְׁפָטִים וְזֵרִיתִי
and-I-will-scatter punishments on-you and-I-will-inflict fathers they-will-eat

אֶת־ כָּל־ שְׁאֵרִיתֵךְ לְכָל־ רוּחַ׃ לָכֵן חַי־ אָנִי נְאֻם
declaration-of I alive therefore (11) wind to-all-of survivor-of-you all-of ***

אֲדֹנָי יְהוִה אִם־ לֹא יַעַן אֶת־ מִקְדָּשִׁי טִמֵּאת בְּכָל־
with-all-of you-defiled sanctuary-of-me *** because surely indeed Yahweh Sovereign

שִׁקּוּצַיִךְ וּבְכָל־ תּוֹעֲבֹתַיִךְ וְגַם־ אֲנִי
I then-also detestable-practices-of-you and-with-all-of vile-ones-of-you

אֶגְרַע וְלֹא־ תָחוֹס עֵינִי וְגַם־ אֲנִי לֹא אֶחְמוֹל׃
I-will-spare not I and-also eye-of-me she-will-show-pity and-not I-will-withdraw

שְׁלִשִׁתַיִךְ בַּדֶּבֶר יָמוּתוּ וּבָרָעָב יִכְלוּ
they-will-perish or-by-the-famine they-will-die of-the-plague third-of-you (12)

בְתוֹכֵךְ וְהַשְּׁלִשִׁית בַּחֶרֶב יִפְּלוּ סְבִיבוֹתָיִךְ
ones-around-you they-will-fall by-the-sword and-the-third at-inside-of-you

וְהַשְּׁלִישִׁית לְכָל־ רוּחַ אֱזָרֶה וְחֶרֶב אָרִיק אַחֲרֵיהֶם׃
after-them I-will-draw and-sword I-will-scatter wind to-all-of and-the-third

וְכָלָה אַפִּי וַהֲנִחוֹתִי חֲמָתִי בָּם
against-them wrath-of-me and-I-will-make-subside anger-of-me then-he-will-cease (13)

around her. 6Yet in her wickedness she has rebelled against my
laws and decrees more than the
nations and countries around her.
She has rejected my laws and has
not followed my decrees.
7"Therefore this is what the
Sovereign LORD says: You have
been more unruly than the nations around you and have not
followed my decrees or kept my
laws. You have not even[l] conformed to the standards of the nations around you.
8"Therefore this is what the
Sovereign LORD says: I myself am
against you, Jerusalem, and I will
inflict punishment on you in the
sight of the nations. 9Because of all
your detestable idols, I will do to
you what I have never done before and will never do again.
10Therefore in your midst fathers
will eat their children, and children will eat their fathers. I will
inflict punishment on you and
will scatter all your survivors to
the winds. 11Therefore as surely as
I live, declares the Sovereign
LORD, because you have defiled
my sanctuary with all your vile
images and detestable practices, I
myself will withdraw my favor; I
will not look on you with pity or
spare you. 12A third of your people
will die of the plague or perish by
famine inside you; a third will fall
by the sword outside your walls;
and a third I will scatter to the
winds and pursue with drawn
sword.
13"Then my anger will cease and
my wrath against them will subside, and I will be avenged. And

l7 Most Hebrew manuscripts; some Hebrew manuscripts and Syriac *You have*

וְהִנֶּחָמְתִּי וְיָדְעוּ כִּי־אֲנִי יְהוָה דִּבַּרְתִּי בְּקִנְאָתִי
in-zeal-of-me I-spoke Yahweh I that then-they-will-know and-I-will-be-avenged

בְּכַלּוֹתִי חֲמָתִי בָּם׃ וְאֶתְּנֵךְ לְחָרְבָּה
as-ruin and-I-will-make-you (14) upon-them wrath-of-me when-to-spend-me

וּלְחֶרְפָּה בַּגּוֹיִם אֲשֶׁר סְבִיבוֹתָיִךְ לְעֵינֵי כָּל־
all-of before-eyes-of ones-around-you that among-the-nations and-as-reproach

עוֹבֵר׃ וְהָיְתָה חֶרְפָּה וּגְדוּפָה מוּסָר וּמְשַׁמָּה
and-object-of-horror warning and-taunt reproach and-she-will-be (15) one-passing-by

לַגּוֹיִם אֲשֶׁר סְבִיבוֹתָיִךְ בַּעֲשׂוֹתִי בָךְ שְׁפָטִים בְּאַף
in-anger punishments on-you when-to-inflict-me ones-around-you that to-the-nations

וּבְחֵמָה וּבְתֹכְחוֹת חֵמָה אֲנִי יְהוָה דִּבַּרְתִּי׃ בְּשַׁלְּחִי אֶת־
*** when-to-shoot-me (16) I-spoke Yahweh I wrath and-with-rebukes-of and-in-wrath

חִצֵּי הָרָעָב הָרָעִים בָּהֶם אֲשֶׁר הָיוּ לְמַשְׁחִית
for-destruction they-are that with-them the-deadly-ones the-famine arrows-of

אֲשֶׁר־אֲשַׁלַּח אוֹתָם לְשַׁחֶתְכֶם וְרָעָב אֹסֵף עֲלֵיכֶם
upon-you I-will-bring-more and-famine to-destroy-you them I-will-shoot that

וְשָׁבַרְתִּי לָכֶם מַטֵּה־לָחֶם׃ וְשִׁלַּחְתִּי עֲלֵיכֶם רָעָב
famine against-you and-I-will-send (17) food supply-of of-you and-I-will-cut-off

וְחַיָּה רָעָה וְשִׁכְּלֻךְ וְדֶבֶר וָדָם
and-bloodshed and-plague and-they-will-leave-childless-you wild and-beast

יַעֲבָר־בָּךְ וְחֶרֶב אָבִיא עָלַיִךְ אֲנִי יְהוָה דִּבַּרְתִּי׃
I-spoke Yahweh I against-you I-will-bring and-sword through-you he-will-sweep

וַיְהִי דְבַר־יְהוָה אֵלַי לֵאמֹר׃ בֶּן־אָדָם שִׂים פָּנֶיךָ
faces-of-you set! man son-of (2) to-say to-me Yahweh word-of and-he-came (6:1)

אֶל־הָרֵי יִשְׂרָאֵל וְהִנָּבֵא אֲלֵיהֶם׃ וְאָמַרְתָּ
and-you-say (3) against-them and-prophesy! Israel mountains-of against

הָרֵי יִשְׂרָאֵל שִׁמְעוּ דְּבַר־אֲדֹנָי יְהוִה כֹּה־אָמַר אֲדֹנָי יְהוִה
Yahweh Sovereign he-says this Yahweh Sovereign word-of hear! Israel mountains-of

לֶהָרִים וְלַגְּבָעוֹת לָאֲפִיקִים וְלַגֵּאָיֹת הִנְנִי
see-I! and-to-the-valleys to-the-ravines and-to-the-hills to-the-mountains

אֲנִי מֵבִיא עֲלֵיכֶם חֶרֶב וְאִבַּדְתִּי בָּמוֹתֵיכֶם׃
high-places-of-you and-I-will-destroy sword against-you bringing I

וְנָשַׁמּוּ מִזְבְּחוֹתֵיכֶם וְנִשְׁבְּרוּ
and-they-will-be-smashed altars-of-you and-they-will-be-demolished (4)

חַמָּנֵיכֶם וְהִפַּלְתִּי חַלְלֵיכֶם לִפְנֵי גִּלּוּלֵיכֶם׃
idols-of-you in-front-of slain-ones-of-you and-I-will-make-fall incense-altars-of-you

וְנָתַתִּי אֶת־פִּגְרֵי בְּנֵי יִשְׂרָאֵל לִפְנֵי גִּלּוּלֵיהֶם
idols-of-them in-front-of Israel sons-of dead-bodies-of *** and-I-will-lay (5)

[3] ק ולגאיות

when I have spent my wrath upon them, they will know that I the LORD have spoken in my zeal.
14 "I will make you a ruin and a reproach among the nations around you, in the sight of all who pass by.
15 You will be a reproach and a taunt, a warning and an object of horror to the nations around you when I inflict punishment on you in anger and in wrath and with stinging rebuke. I the LORD have spoken.
16 When I shoot at you with my deadly and destructive arrows of famine, I will shoot to destroy you. I will bring more and more famine upon you and cut off your supply of food.
17 I will send famine and wild beasts against you, and they will leave you childless. Plague and bloodshed will sweep through you, and I will bring the sword against you. I the LORD have spoken."

### *A Prophecy Against the Mountains of Israel*

6 The word of the LORD came to me:
2 "Son of man, set your face against the mountains of Israel; prophesy against them
3 and say: 'O mountains of Israel, hear the word of the Sovereign LORD. This is what the Sovereign LORD says to the mountains and hills, to the ravines and valleys: I am about to bring a sword against you, and I will destroy your high places.
4 Your altars will be demolished and your incense altars will be smashed; and I will slay your people in front of your idols.
5 I will lay the dead bodies of the Israelites in front of their idols, and I

וְזֵרִיתִי֙ אֶת־ עַצְמֽוֹתֵיכֶ֔ם סְבִיב֖וֹת מִזְבְּחוֹתֵיכֶֽם׃ בְּכֹל֙
in-every-of (6) altars-of-you ones-around bones-of-you *** and-I-will-scatter

מֽוֹשְׁבֽוֹתֵיכֶ֔ם הֶעָרִ֖ים תֶּחֱרַ֑בְנָה וְהַבָּמ֖וֹת
and-the-high-places they-will-be-laid-waste the-towns living-places-of-you

תִּישָׁ֑מְנָה לְמַ֨עַן יֶחֶרְב֜וּ וְיֶאְשְׁמ֗וּ
and-they-will-be-devastated they-will-be-laid-waste so-that they-will-be-demolished

מִזְבְּחוֹתֵיכֶ֔ם וְנִשְׁבְּר֣וּ וְנִשְׁבְּת֔וּ גִּלּ֣וּלֵיכֶ֔ם
idols-of-you and-they-will-be-ruined and-they-will-be-smashed altars-of-you

וְנִגְדְּעוּ֙ חַמָּ֣נֵיכֶ֔ם וְנִמְח֖וּ
and-they-will-be-wiped-out incense-altars-of-you and-they-will-be-broken-down

מַעֲשֵׂיכֶֽם׃ וְנָפַ֥ל חָלָ֖ל בְּתוֹכְכֶ֑ם וִֽידַעְתֶּ֖ם כִּֽי־
that and-you-will-know in-among-you slain and-he-will-fall (7) things-made-of-you

אֲנִ֥י יְהוָֽה׃ וְהוֹתַרְתִּ֗י בִּֽהְי֥וֹת לָכֶ֛ם פְּלִיטֵ֥י חֶ֖רֶב בַּגּוֹיִ֑ם
among-the-nations sword escapees-of of-you for-to-be but-I-will-spare (8) Yahweh I

בְּהִזָּרֽוֹתֵיכֶ֖ם בָּאֲרָצֽוֹת׃ וְזָכְר֨וּ פְלִיטֵיכֶ֜ם
escapees-of-you then-they-will-remember (9) among-the-lands when-to-be-scattered-you

אוֹתִ֗י בַּגּוֹיִם֮ אֲשֶׁ֣ר נִשְׁבּוּ־ שָׁם֒ אֲשֶׁ֣ר נִשְׁבַּ֡רְתִּי אֶת־
*** I-was-grieved how there they-were-carried-captive where in-the-nations me

לִבָּ֣ם הַזּוֹנֶה֩ אֲשֶׁר־ סָ֨ר מֵעָלַ֜י וְאֵ֣ת
and from-with-me they-turned which the-one-being-adulterous heart-of-them

עֵ֣ינֵיהֶ֔ם הַזֹּנ֖וֹת אַחֲרֵ֣י גִּלּוּלֵיהֶ֑ם וְנָקֹ֙טּוּ֙
and-they-will-loathe idols-of-them after the-ones-lusting eyes-of-them

בִּפְנֵיהֶ֔ם אֶל־ הָֽרָעוֹת֙ אֲשֶׁ֣ר עָשׂ֔וּ לְכֹ֖ל תּוֹעֲבֹתֵיהֶֽם׃
detestable-practices-of-them for-all-of they-did that the-evils for to-faces-of-them

וְיָדְע֖וּ כִּֽי־ אֲנִ֣י יְהוָ֑ה לֹ֤א אֶל־ חִנָּם֙ דִּבַּ֔רְתִּי לַעֲשׂ֥וֹת לָהֶ֖ם
on-them to-bring I-threatened vain in not Yahweh I that and-they-will-know (10)

הָרָעָ֥ה הַזֹּֽאת׃ כֹּֽה־ אָמַ֞ר אֲדֹנָ֣י יְהוִ֗ה הַכֵּ֨ה בְכַפְּךָ֜
with-hand-of-you strike! Yahweh Sovereign he-says this (11) the-this the-calamity

וּרְקַ֤ע בְּרַגְלְךָ֙ וֶאֱמָר־ אָ֔ח אֶ֛ל כָּל־ תּוֹעֲב֥וֹת
detestable-practices-of all-of because-of alas! and-cry! with-foot-of-you and-stamp!

רָע֖וֹת בֵּ֣ית יִשְׂרָאֵ֑ל אֲשֶׁ֗ר בַּחֶ֛רֶב בָּרָעָ֥ב וּבַדֶּ֖בֶר
and-by-the-plague by-the-famine by-the-sword that Israel house-of wicked-ones-of

יִפֹּֽלוּ׃ הָרָח֞וֹק בַּדֶּ֣בֶר יָמ֗וּת וְהַקָּרוֹב֙
and-the-one-near he-will-die by-the-plague the-one-far-away (12) they-will-fall

בַּחֶ֣רֶב יִפּ֔וֹל וְהַנִּשְׁאָר֙ וְהַנָּצ֔וּר בָּרָעָ֖ב
of-the-famine and-the-one-being-spared and-the-one-surviving he-will-fall by-the-sword

יָמ֑וּת וְכִלֵּיתִ֥י חֲמָתִ֖י בָּֽם׃ וִֽידַעְתֶּם֙ כִּֽי־
that and-they-will-know (13) upon-them wrath-of-me so-I-will-spend he-will-die

will scatter your bones around
your altars. 6Wherever you live,
the towns will be laid waste and
the high places demolished, so
that your altars will be laid waste
and devastated, your idols
smashed and ruined, your incense
altars broken down, and what you
have made wiped out. 7Your
people will fall slain among you,
and you will know that I am the
LORD.

8" 'But I will spare some, for
some of you will escape the sword
when you are scattered among the
lands and nations. 9Then in the
nations where they have been carried captive, those who escape
will remember me—how I have
been grieved by their adulterous
hearts, which have turned away
from me, and by their eyes, which
have lusted after their idols. They
will loathe themselves for the evil
they have done and for all their
detestable practices. 10And they
will know that I am the LORD; I did
not threaten in vain to bring this
calamity on them.

11" 'This is what the Sovereign
LORD says: Strike your hands together and stamp your feet and
cry out "Alas!" because of all the
wicked and detestable practices of
the house of Israel, for they will
fall by the sword, famine and
plague. 12He that is far away will
die of the plague, and he that is
near will fall by the sword, and he
that survives and is spared will die
of famine. So will I spend my
wrath upon them. 13And they will

אֲנִי יְהוָה בִּהְיוֹת חַלְלֵיהֶם בְּתוֹךְ גִּלּוּלֵיהֶם סְבִיבוֹת
ones-around idols-of-them in-among slain-ones-of-them when-to-be Yahweh I

מִזְבְּחוֹתֵיהֶם אֶל כָּל־ גִּבְעָה רָמָה בְּכֹל | רָאשֵׁי הֶהָרִים
the-mountains tops-of on-all-of one-being-high hill every-of on altars-of-them

וְתַחַת כָּל־ עֵץ רַעֲנָן וְתַחַת כָּל־ אֵלָה עֲבֻתָּה מְקוֹם אֲשֶׁר
where place-of leafy oak every-of and-under spreading tree every-of and-under

נָתְנוּ־ שָׁם רֵיחַ נִיחֹחַ לְכֹל גִּלּוּלֵיהֶם׃
idols-of-them to-all-of soothing-incense fragrance-of there they-offered

(14) וְנָטִיתִי אֶת־ יָדִי עֲלֵיהֶם וְנָתַתִּי אֶת־ הָאָרֶץ
the-land *** and-I-will-make against-them hand-of-me *** and-I-will-stretch-out (14)

שְׁמָמָה וּמְשַׁמָּה מִמִּדְבַּר דִּבְלָתָה בְּכֹל מוֹשְׁבוֹתֵיהֶם
living-places-of-them in-every-of to-Diblah from-desert-of and-waste desolation

וְיָדְעוּ כִּי־אֲנִי יְהוָה׃ (7:1) וַיְהִי דְבַר־ יְהוָה אֵלַי לֵאמֹר׃
to-say to-me Yahweh word-of and-he-came (7:1) Yahweh I that then-they-will-know

(2) וְאַתָּה בֶן־אָדָם כֹּה־ אָמַר אֲדֹנָי יְהוִה לְאַדְמַת יִשְׂרָאֵל קֵץ בָּא
he-came end Israel to-land-of Yahweh Sovereign he-says this man son-of now-you (2)

הַקֵּץ עַל־אַרְבַּעַת כַּנְפוֹת הָאָרֶץ׃ (3) עַתָּה הַקֵּץ עָלַיִךְ וְשִׁלַּחְתִּי
and-I-will-unleash upon-you the-end now (3) the-land corners-of four-of upon the-end

אַפִּי בָּךְ וּשְׁפַטְתִּיךְ כִּדְרָכָיִךְ וְנָתַתִּי
and-I-will-repay according-to-conducts-of-you and-I-will-judge-you against-you anger-of-me

עָלַיִךְ אֵת כָּל־ תּוֹעֲבֹתָיִךְ׃ (4) וְלֹא־ תָחוֹס
she-will-have-pity and-not (4) detestable-practices-of-you all-of *** to-you

עֵינִי עָלַיִךְ וְלֹא אֶחְמוֹל כִּי דְרָכַיִךְ עָלַיִךְ אֶתֵּן
I-will-repay to-you conducts-of-you for I-will-spare or-not on-you eye-of-me

וְתוֹעֲבוֹתַיִךְ בְּתוֹכֵךְ תִּהְיֶיןָ וִידַעְתֶּם כִּי־
that then-you-will-know they-will-be in-among-you and-detestable-practices-of-you

אֲנִי יְהוָה׃ (5) כֹּה אָמַר אֲדֹנָי יְהוִה רָעָה אַחַת רָעָה הִנֵּה
see! disaster unheard-of disaster Yahweh Sovereign he-says this (5) Yahweh I

בָּאָה׃ (6) קֵץ בָּא בָּא הַקֵּץ הֵקִיץ אֵלָיִךְ הִנֵּה בָּאָה׃
coming see! against-you he-roused-himself the-end he-came he-came end (6) coming

(7) בָּאָה הַצְּפִירָה אֵלֶיךָ יוֹשֵׁב הָאָרֶץ בָּא הָעֵת קָרוֹב
near the-time he-came the-land one-dwelling-of upon-you the-doom she-came (7)

הַיּוֹם מְהוּמָה וְלֹא־ הֵד הָרִים׃ (8) עַתָּה מִקָּרוֹב אֶשְׁפּוֹךְ חֲמָתִי
wrath-of-me I-will-pour-out at-near now (8) mountains joy-of and-not panic the-day

עָלַיִךְ וְכִלֵּיתִי אַפִּי בָּךְ וּשְׁפַטְתִּיךְ
and-I-will-judge-you against-you anger-of-me and-I-will-spend on-you

כִּדְרָכָיִךְ וְנָתַתִּי עָלַיִךְ אֵת כָּל־
all-of *** to-you and-I-will-repay according-to-conducts-of-you

°2 ק ארבע

know that I am the LORD, when their people lie slain among their idols around their altars, on every high hill and on all the mountaintops, under every spreading tree and every leafy oak—places where they offered fragrant incense to all their idols. [14]And I will stretch out my hand against them and make the land a desolate waste from the desert to Diblah[m]—wherever they live. Then they will know that I am the LORD.' "

*The End Has Come*

7 The word of the LORD came to me: [2]"Son of man, this is what the Sovereign LORD says to the land of Israel: The end! The end has come upon the four corners of the land. [3]The end is now upon you and I will unleash my anger against you. I will judge you according to your conduct and repay you for all your detestable practices. [4]I will not look on you with pity or spare you; I will surely repay you for your conduct and the detestable practices among you. Then you will know that I am the LORD.

[5]"This is what the Sovereign LORD says: Disaster! An unheard-of[n] disaster is coming. [6]The end has come! The end has come! It has roused itself against you. It has come! [7]Doom has come upon you—you who dwell in the land. The time has come, the day is near; there is panic, not joy, upon the mountains. [8]I am about to pour out my wrath on you and spend my anger against you; I will

[m]14 Most Hebrew manuscripts; a few Hebrew manuscripts *Riblah*
[n]5 Most Hebrew manuscripts; some Hebrew manuscripts and Syriac *Disaster after*

תּוֹעֲבוֹתַיִךְ׃ וְלֹא־ תָחוֹס עֵינִי וְלֹא אֶחְמוֹל
I-will-spare or-not eye-of-me she-will-pity and-not (9) detestable-practices-of-you

כִּדְרָכַיִךְ עָלַיִךְ אֶתֵּן וְתוֹעֲבוֹתַיִךְ
and-detestable-practices-of-you I-will-repay to-you according-to-conducts-of-you

בְּתוֹכֵךְ תִּהְיֶיןָ וִידַעְתֶּם כִּי אֲנִי יְהוָה מַכֶּה׃
one-striking-blow Yahweh I that then-you-will-know they-will-be in-among-you

הִנֵּה הַיּוֹם הִנֵּה בָאָה יָצְאָה הַצְּפִרָה צָץ הַמַּטֶּה
the-rod he-budded the-doom she-burst-forth coming see! the-day see! (10)

פָּרַח הַזָּדוֹן׃ הֶחָמָס׀ קָם לְמַטֵּה־ רֶשַׁע לֹא־
none wickedness into-rod-of he-grew the-violence (11) the-arrogance he-blossomed

מֵהֶם וְלֹא מֵהֲמוֹנָם וְלֹא מֶהֱמֵהֶם* וְלֹא־ נֹהַּ
valuable and-nothing of-wealth-of-them and-none of-crowd-of-them and-none of-them

בָּהֶם׃ בָּא הָעֵת הִגִּיעַ הַיּוֹם הַקּוֹנֶה אַל־ יִשְׂמָח
let-him-rejoice not the-one-buying the-day he-arrived the-time he-came (12) of-them

וְהַמּוֹכֵר אַל־ יִתְאַבָּל כִּי חָרוֹן אֶל־ כָּל־ הֲמוֹנָהּ׃
crowd-of-her whole-of upon wrath for let-him-grieve not or-the-one-selling

כִּי הַמּוֹכֵר אֶל־ הַמִּמְכָּר לֹא יָשׁוּב וְעוֹד
even-as-long-as he-will-recover not the-thing-sold to the-one-selling indeed (13)

בַּחַיִּים חַיָּתָם כִּי־ חָזוֹן אֶל־ כָּל־ הֲמוֹנָהּ לֹא
not crowd-of-her whole-of concerning vision for life-of-them while-the-lives

יָשׁוּב וְאִישׁ בַּעֲוֹנוֹ חַיָּתוֹ לֹא יִתְחַזָּקוּ׃
they-will-preserve not life-of-him because-of-sin-of-him and-each he-will-be-reversed

תָּקְעוּ בַתָּקוֹעַ וְהָכִין הַכֹּל וְאֵין הֹלֵךְ
going but-no-one the-everything and-to-get-ready on-the-trumpet they-blow (14)

לַמִּלְחָמָה כִּי חֲרוֹנִי אֶל־ כָּל־ הֲמוֹנָהּ׃ הַחֶרֶב
the-sword (15) crowd-of-her whole-of upon wrath-of-me for into-the-battle

בַּחוּץ וְהַדֶּבֶר וְהָרָעָב מִבָּיִת אֲשֶׁר בַּשָּׂדֶה
in-the-country who inside-house and-the-famine and-the-plague at-the-outside

בַּחֶרֶב יָמוּת וַאֲשֶׁר בָּעִיר רָעָב וָדֶבֶר יֹאכְלֶנּוּ׃
he-will-devour-him and-plague famine in-the-city and-who he-will-die by-the-sword

וּפָלְטוּ פְּלִיטֵיהֶם וְהָיוּ אֶל־ הֶהָרִים
the-mountains in and-they-will-be escapees-of-them and-they-will-escape (16)

כְּיוֹנֵי הַגֵּאָיוֹת כֻּלָּם הֹמוֹת אִישׁ בַּעֲוֹנוֹ׃
because-of-sin-of-him each ones-moaning all-of-them the-valleys like-doves-of

כָּל־ הַיָּדַיִם תִּרְפֶּינָה וְכָל־ בִּרְכַּיִם תֵּלַכְנָה מָּיִם׃
waters they-will-become knees and-every-of they-will-go-limp the-hands every-of (17)

וְחָגְרוּ שַׂקִּים וְכִסְּתָה אוֹתָם פַּלָּצוּת וְאֶל כָּל־
all-of and-on terror them and-she-will-clothe sackcloths and-they-will-put-on (18)

judge you according to your conduct and repay you for all your detestable practices. 9 I will not look
on you with pity or spare you; I
will repay you in accordance with
your conduct and the detestable
practices among you. Then you
will know that it is I the LORD who
strikes the blow.
10 "The day is here! It has come!
Doom has burst forth, the rod has
budded, arrogance has blossomed!
11 Violence has grown into[o] a rod
to punish wickedness; none of the
people will be left, none of that
crowd—no wealth, nothing of value. 12 The time has come, the day
has arrived. Let not the buyer rejoice nor the seller grieve, for
wrath is upon the whole crowd.
13 The seller will not recover the
land he has sold as long as both of
them live, for the vision concerning the whole crowd will not be
reversed. Because of their sins, not
one of them will preserve his life.
14 Though they blow the trumpet
and get everything ready, no one
will go into battle, for my wrath is
upon the whole crowd.
15 "Outside is the sword, inside
are plague and famine; those in
the country will die by the sword,
and those in the city will be devoured by famine and plague. 16 All
who survive and escape will be in
the mountains, moaning like
doves of the valleys, each because
of his sins. 17 Every hand will go
limp, and every knee will become
as weak as water. 18 They will put
on sackcloth and be clothed with

[o] 11 Or *The violent one has become*

*11 Most mss have *tsere* under the *mem* (מֵ).

פָּנִים בּוּשָׁה וּבְכָל־ רָאשֵׁיהֶם קָרְחָה׃ כַּסְפָּם בַּחוּצוֹת
into-the-streets silver-of-them (19) shaved-bald heads-of-them and-on-all-of shame faces

יַשְׁלִיכוּ וּזְהָבָם לְנִדָּה יִהְיֶה כַּסְפָּם
silver-of-them he-will-be as-unclean-thing and-gold-of-them they-will-throw

וּזְהָבָם לֹא־ יוּכַל לְהַצִּילָם בְּיוֹם עֶבְרַת יְהוָה
Yahweh wrath-of in-day-of to-save-them he-will-be-able not and-gold-of-them

נַפְשָׁם לֹא יְשַׂבֵּעוּ וּמְעֵיהֶם לֹא יְמַלֵּאוּ כִּי־
for they-will-fill not and-stomachs-of-them they-will-satisfy not hunger-of-them

מִכְשׁוֹל עֲוֺנָם הָיָה׃ וּצְבִי עֶדְיוֹ לְגָאוֹן
as-pride jewelry-of-him and-beauty-of (20) he-was sin-of-them stumbling-block

שָׂמָהוּ וְצַלְמֵי תוֹעֲבֹתָם שִׁקּוּצֵיהֶם עָשׂוּ
they-made vile-ones-of-them detestable-ones-of-them and-images-of he-made-him

בוֹ עַל־כֵּן נְתַתִּיו לָהֶם לְנִדָּה׃ וּנְתַתִּיו
and-I-will-give-him (21) into-unclean-thing for-them I-will-turn-him this for with-him

בְּיַד־ הַזָּרִים לָבַז וּלְרִשְׁעֵי הָאָרֶץ
the-earth and-to-wicked-ones-of as-plunder the-ones-being-foreign into-hand-of

לְשָׁלָל וְחִלְּלֻהָ׃ וַהֲסִבּוֹתִי פָנַי מֵהֶם
from-them faces-of-me and-I-will-turn (22) and-they-will-defile-him as-loot

וְחִלְּלוּ אֶת־ צְפוּנִי וּבָאוּ־ בָהּ
into-her and-they-will-enter one-being-treasured-of-me *** and-they-will-desecrate

פָּרִיצִים וְחִלְּלוּהָ׃ עֲשֵׂה הָרַתּוֹק כִּי הָאָרֶץ
the-land because the-chain prepare! (23) and-they-will-desecrate-her robbers

מָלְאָה מִשְׁפַּט דָּמִים וְהָעִיר מָלְאָה חָמָס׃
violence she-is-full and-the-city bloodsheds judgment-of she-is-full

וְהֵבֵאתִי רָעֵי גוֹיִם וְיָרְשׁוּ אֶת־ בָּתֵּיהֶם
houses-of-them *** and-they-will-possess nations wicked-ones-of and-I-will-bring (24)

וְהִשְׁבַּתִּי גְּאוֹן עַזִּים וְנִחֲלוּ מְקַדְשֵׁיהֶם׃
sanctuaries-of-them and-they-will-be-desecrated mighty-ones pride-of and-I-will-end

קְפָדָה־ בָא וּבִקְשׁוּ שָׁלוֹם וָאָיִן׃ הֹוָה
calamity (26) but-there-will-be-none peace and-they-will-seek he-comes terror (25)

עַל־ הֹוָה תָּבוֹא וּשְׁמֻעָה אֶל־שְׁמוּעָה תִּהְיֶה וּבִקְשׁוּ
and-they-will-seek she-will-be rumor upon and-rumor she-will-come calamity upon

חָזוֹן מִנָּבִיא וְתוֹרָה תֹּאבַד מִכֹּהֵן וְעֵצָה מִזְּקֵנִים׃
by-elders and-counsel by-priest she-will-be-lost and-law from-prophet vision

הַמֶּלֶךְ יִתְאַבָּל וְנָשִׂיא יִלְבַּשׁ שְׁמָמָה וִידֵי
and-hands-of despair he-will-be-clothed and-prince he-will-mourn the-king (27)

עַם־ הָאָרֶץ תִּבָּהַלְנָה מִדַּרְכָּם אֶעֱשֶׂה
I-will-deal according-to-conduct-of-them they-will-tremble the-land people-of

terror. Their faces will be covered with shame and their heads will be shaved. 19They will throw their silver into the streets, and their gold will be an unclean thing. Their silver and gold will not be able to save them in the day of the LORD's wrath. They will not satisfy their hunger or fill their stomachs with it, for it has made them stumble into sin. 20They were proud of their beautiful jewelry and used it to make their detestable idols and vile images. Therefore I will turn these into an unclean thing for them. 21I will hand it all over as plunder to foreigners and as loot to the wicked of the earth, and they will defile it. 22I will turn my face away from them, and they will desecrate my treasured place; robbers will enter it and desecrate it.

23"Prepare chains, because the land is full of bloodshed and the city is full of violence. 24I will bring the most wicked of the nations to take possession of their houses; I will put an end to the pride of the mighty, and their sanctuaries will be desecrated. 25When terror comes, they will seek peace, but there will be none. 26Calamity upon calamity will come, and rumor upon rumor. They will try to get a vision from the prophet; the teaching of the law by the priest will be lost, as will the counsel of the elders. 27The king will mourn, the prince will be clothed with despair, and the hands of the people of the land will tremble. I will deal

°21 ק וחללוהו

אוֹתָם וּבְמִשְׁפְּטֵיהֶם אֶשְׁפְּטֵם וְיָדְעוּ כִּי־אֲנִי
I that then-they-will-know I-will-judge-them and-by-standards-of-them with-them

יְהוָה׃ וַיְהִי ׀ בַּשָּׁנָה הַשִּׁשִּׁית בַּשִּׁשִּׁי בַּחֲמִשָּׁה לַחֹדֶשׁ
of-the-month on-five in-the-sixth the-sixth in-the-year and-he-was (8:1) Yahweh

אֲנִי יוֹשֵׁב בְּבֵיתִי וְזִקְנֵי יְהוּדָה יוֹשְׁבִים לְפָנָי וַתִּפֹּל
and-she-came before-me ones-sitting Judah and-elders-of in-house-of-me sitting I

עָלַי שָׁם יַד אֲדֹנָי יְהוִה׃ וָאֶרְאֶה וְהִנֵּה דְמוּת
figure and-see! and-I-looked (2) Yahweh Sovereign hand-of there upon-me

כְּמַרְאֵה־אֵשׁ מִמַּרְאֵה מָתְנָיו וּלְמַטָּה אֵשׁ
fire and-to-downward waists-of-him from-appearance-of fire as-likeness-of

וּמִמָּתְנָיו וּלְמַעְלָה כְּמַרְאֵה־זֹהַר כְּעֵין
like-look-of brightness like-appearance-of and-to-upward and-from-waists-of-him

הַחַשְׁמַלָה׃ וַיִּשְׁלַח תַּבְנִית יָד וַיִּקָּחֵנִי בְּצִיצִת
by-hair-of and-he-took-me hand look-of and-he-stretched-out (3) to-the-glowing-metal

רֹאשִׁי וַתִּשָּׂא אֹתִי רוּחַ ׀ בֵּין־הָאָרֶץ וּבֵין הַשָּׁמַיִם
the-heavens and-between the-earth between Spirit me and-she-lifted head-of-me

וַתָּבֵא אֹתִי יְרוּשָׁלַמָה בְּמַרְאוֹת אֱלֹהִים אֶל־פֶּתַח שַׁעַר הַפְּנִימִית
the-inner-one gate-of entrance-of to God in-visions-of to-Jerusalem me and-she-took

הַפּוֹנֶה צָפוֹנָה אֲשֶׁר־שָׁם מוֹשַׁב סֵמֶל הַקִּנְאָה
the-jealousy idol-of standing-place-of there where to-north the-one-facing

הַמַּקְנֶה׃ וְהִנֵּה־שָׁם כְּבוֹד אֱלֹהֵי יִשְׂרָאֵל כַּמַּרְאֶה
as-the-vision Israel God-of glory-of there and-see! (4) the-one-provoking-jealousy

אֲשֶׁר רָאִיתִי בַּבִּקְעָה׃ וַיֹּאמֶר אֵלַי בֶּן־אָדָם שָׂא־נָא עֵינֶיךָ
eyes-of-you now! lift! man son-of to-me then-he-said (5) in-the-plain I-saw that

דֶּרֶךְ צָפוֹנָה וָאֶשָּׂא עֵינַי דֶּרֶךְ צָפוֹנָה וְהִנֵּה מִצָּפוֹן לְשַׁעַר
of-gate-of at-north and-see! to-north toward eyes-of-me so-I-lifted to-north toward

הַמִּזְבֵּחַ סֵמֶל הַקִּנְאָה הַזֶּה בַּבִּאָה׃ וַיֹּאמֶר אֵלַי
to-me and-he-said (6) in-the-entrance the-this the-jealousy idol-of the-altar

בֶּן־אָדָם הֲרֹאֶה אַתָּה מֵהֵם עֹשִׂים תּוֹעֵבוֹת גְּדֹלוֹת אֲשֶׁר
that utter-ones detestable-things ones-doing they*what? you seeing? man son-of

בֵּית־יִשְׂרָאֵל ׀ עֹשִׂים פֹּה לְרָחֳקָה מֵעַל מִקְדָּשִׁי וְעוֹד
but-more sanctuary-of-me from-in to-drive-far here ones-doing Israel house-of

תָּשׁוּב תִּרְאֶה תּוֹעֵבוֹת גְּדֹלוֹת׃ וַיָּבֵא
then-he-brought (7) utter-ones detestable-things you-will-see you-will-do-again

אֹתִי אֶל־פֶּתַח הֶחָצֵר וָאֶרְאֶה וְהִנֵּה חֹר־אֶחָד בַּקִּיר׃
in-the-wall one hole and-see! and-I-looked the-court entrance-of to me

וַיֹּאמֶר אֵלַי בֶּן־אָדָם חֲתָר־נָא בַקִּיר וָאֶחְתֹּר בַּקִּיר
into-the-wall so-I-dug into-the-wall now! dig! man son-of to-me and-he-said (8)

with them according to their conduct, and by their own standards I will judge them. Then they will know that I am the LORD."

*Idolatry in the Temple*

8 In the sixth year, in the sixth month on the fifth day, while I was sitting in my house and the elders of Judah were sitting before me, the hand of the Sovereign LORD came upon me there. [2]I looked, and I saw a figure like that of a man.[p] From what appeared to be his waist down he was like fire, and from there up his appearance was as bright as glowing metal. [3]He stretched out what looked like a hand and took me by the hair of my head. The Spirit lifted me up between earth and heaven and in visions of God he took me to Jerusalem, to the entrance to the north gate of the inner court, where the idol that provokes to jealousy stood. [4]And there before me was the glory of the God of Israel, as in the vision I had seen in the plain.

[5]Then he said to me, "Son of man, look toward the north." So I looked, and in the entrance north of the gate of the altar I saw this idol of jealousy.

[6]And he said to me, "Son of man, do you see what they are doing—the utterly detestable things the house of Israel is doing here, things that will drive me far from my sanctuary? But you will see things that are even more detestable."

[7]Then he brought me to the entrance to the court. I looked, and I saw a hole in the wall. [8]He said to me, "Son of man, now dig into the wall." So I dug into the wall and

p2 Or *saw a fiery figure*

*6 The *Qere* reads this form as two words.

°6 ק מה הם

וְהִנֵּה פֶּתַח אֶחָד׃ וַיֹּאמֶר אֵלַי בֹּא וּרְאֵה אֶת־ הַתּוֹעֵבוֹת
the-detestable-things *** and-see! go-in! to-me and-he-said (9) one doorway and-see!

הָרָעוֹת אֲשֶׁר הֵם עֹשִׂים פֹּה׃ וָאָבוֹא וָאֶרְאֶה וְהִנֵּה
and-see! and-I-looked so-I-went-in (10) here ones-doing they that the-wicked-ones

כָל־ תַּבְנִית רֶמֶשׂ וּבְהֵמָה שֶׁקֶץ וְכָל־ גִּלּוּלֵי בֵּית
house-of idols-of and-all-of detestable and-animal crawling-thing kind-of all-of

יִשְׂרָאֵל מְחֻקֶּה עַל־ הַקִּיר סָבִיב ׀ סָבִיב׃ וְשִׁבְעִים אִישׁ
man and-seventy (11) all-over all-over the-wall on being-portrayed Israel

מִזִּקְנֵי בֵית־ יִשְׂרָאֵל וְיַאֲזַנְיָהוּ בֶן־ שָׁפָן עֹמֵד בְּתוֹכָם
in-among-them standing Shaphan son-of and-Jaazaniah Israel house-of from-elders-of

עֹמְדִים לִפְנֵיהֶם וְאִישׁ מִקְטַרְתּוֹ בְּיָדוֹ
in-hand-of-him censer-of-him and-each in-front-of-them ones-standing

וַעֲתַר עֲנַן־ הַקְּטֹרֶת עֹלֶה׃ וַיֹּאמֶר אֵלַי הֲרָאִיתָ בֶן־אָדָם
man son-of you-see? to-me and-he-said (12) rising the-incense cloud-of and-fragrance-of

אֲשֶׁר זִקְנֵי בֵית־ יִשְׂרָאֵל עֹשִׂים בַּחֹשֶׁךְ אִישׁ בְּחַדְרֵי
at-shrines-of each in-the-darkness ones-doing Israel house-of elders-of what

מַשְׂכִּיתוֹ כִּי אֹמְרִים אֵין יְהוָה רֹאֶה אֹתָנוּ עָזַב יְהוָה אֶת־הָאָרֶץ׃
the-land *** Yahweh he-forsook us seeing Yahweh not ones-saying indeed idol-of-him

וַיֹּאמֶר אֵלָי עוֹד תָּשׁוּב תִּרְאֶה תּוֹעֵבוֹת
detestable-things you-will-see you-will-do-again again to-me and-he-said (13)

גְּדֹלוֹת אֲשֶׁר־הֵמָּה עֹשִׂים׃ וַיָּבֵא אֹתִי אֶל־ פֶּתַח שַׁעַר
gate-of entrance-of to me then-he-brought (14) ones-doing they that great-ones

בֵּית־ יְהוָה אֲשֶׁר אֶל־ הַצָּפוֹנָה וְהִנֵּה־ שָׁם הַנָּשִׁים יֹשְׁבוֹת
ones-sitting the-women there and-see! to-the-north at that Yahweh house-of

מְבַכּוֹת אֶת־ הַתַּמּוּז׃ וַיֹּאמֶר אֵלַי הֲרָאִיתָ בֶן־ אָדָם עוֹד
more man son-of you-see? to-me and-he-said (15) the-Tammuz *** ones-mourning

תָּשׁוּב תִּרְאֶה תּוֹעֵבוֹת גְּדֹלוֹת מֵאֵלֶּה׃
more-than-these great-ones detestable-things you-will-see you-will-do-again

וַיָּבֵא אֹתִי אֶל־חֲצַר בֵּית־ יְהוָה הַפְּנִימִית וְהִנֵּה־ פֶתַח
entrance-of and-see! the-inner Yahweh house-of court-of into me then-he-brought (16)

הֵיכַל יְהוָה בֵּין הָאוּלָם וּבֵין הַמִּזְבֵּחַ כְּעֶשְׂרִים וַחֲמִשָּׁה
and-five about-twenty the-altar and-between the-portico between Yahweh temple-of

אִישׁ אֲחֹרֵיהֶם אֶל־ הֵיכַל יְהוָה וּפְנֵיהֶם קֵדְמָה וְהֵמָּה
and-they toward-east and-faces-of-them Yahweh temple-of toward backs-of-them man

מִשְׁתַּחֲוִיתֶם קֵדְמָה לַשָּׁמֶשׁ׃ וַיֹּאמֶר אֵלַי הֲרָאִיתָ בֶן־ אָדָם
man son-of you-see? to-me and-he-said (17) to-the-sun in-the-east ones-bowing-down

הֲנָקֵל לְבֵית יְהוּדָה מֵעֲשׂוֹת אֶת־ הַתּוֹעֵבוֹת אֲשֶׁר
that the-detestable-things *** from-to-do Judah for-house-of is-he-trivial?

saw a doorway there.
9And he said to me, "Go in and
see the wicked and detestable
things they are doing here." 10So I
went in and looked, and I saw
portrayed all over the walls all
kinds of crawling things and detestable animals and all the idols
of the house of Israel. 11In front of
them stood seventy elders of the
house of Israel, and Jaazaniah son
of Shaphan was standing among
them. Each had a censer in his
hand, and a fragrant cloud of incense was rising.
12He said to me, "Son of man,
have you seen what the elders of
the house of Israel are doing in the
darkness, each at the shrine of his
own idol? They say, 'The LORD
does not see us; the LORD has forsaken the land.' " 13Again, he said,
"You will see them doing things
that are even more detestable."
14Then he brought me to the entrance to the north gate of the
house of the LORD, and I saw
women sitting there, mourning
for Tammuz. 15He said to me, "Do
you see this, son of man? You will
see things that are even more detestable than this."
16He then brought me into the
inner court of the house of the
LORD, and there at the entrance to
the temple, between the portico
and the altar, were about twenty-
five men. With their backs toward
the temple of the LORD and their
faces toward the east, they were
bowing down to the sun in the
east.
17He said to me, "Have you seen
this, son of man? Is it a trivial matter for the house of Judah to do the
detestable things they are doing

עָשׂוּ־ פֹה כִּי־ מָלְאוּ אֶת־ הָאָרֶץ חָמָס וַיָּשֻׁבוּ
and-must-they-continue violence the-land *** must-they-fill indeed here they-do

לְהַכְעִיסֵנִי וְהִנָּם שֹׁלְחִים אֶת־ הַזְּמוֹרָה אֶל־ אַפָּם׃
nose-of-them to the-branch *** ones-putting now-look-at-them! to-provoke-to-anger-me

(18) וְגַם־ אֲנִי אֶעֱשֶׂה בְחֵמָה לֹא־ תָחוֹס עֵינִי וְלֹא
or-not eye-of-me she-will-show-pity not in-anger I-will-deal I and-therefore (18)

אֶחְמֹל וְקָרְאוּ בְאָזְנַי קוֹל גָּדוֹל וְלֹא אֶשְׁמַע אוֹתָם׃
them I-will-listen then-not loud shout in-ears-of-me though-they-cry I-will-spare

(9:1) וַיִּקְרָא בְאָזְנַי קוֹל גָּדוֹל לֵאמֹר קָרְבוּ פְּקֻדּוֹת הָעִיר
the-city guards-of bring! to-say loud voice in-ears-of-me then-he-called-out (9:1)

וְאִישׁ כְּלִי מַשְׁחֵתוֹ בְּיָדוֹ׃ (2) וְהִנֵּה שִׁשָּׁה אֲנָשִׁים
men six and-see! (2) in-hand-of-him destruction-of-him weapon-of and-each

בָּאִים ׀ מִדֶּרֶךְ־ שַׁעַר הָעֶלְיוֹן אֲשֶׁר ׀ מָפְנֶה צָפוֹנָה וְאִישׁ
and-each to-north one-facing that the-upper gate-of from-direction-of ones-coming

כְּלִי מַפָּצוֹ בְּיָדוֹ וְאִישׁ־ אֶחָד בְּתוֹכָם לָבֻשׁ
being-clothed at-with-them one and-man in-hand-of-him deadliness-of-him weapon-of

בַּדִּים וְקֶסֶת הַסֹּפֵר בְּמָתְנָיו וַיָּבֹאוּ וַיַּעַמְדוּ
and-they-stood and-they-came-in at-sides-of-him the-scroll and-writing-kit-of linens

אֵצֶל מִזְבַּח הַנְּחֹשֶׁת׃ (3) וּכְבוֹד ׀ אֱלֹהֵי יִשְׂרָאֵל נַעֲלָה מֵעַל
from-above he-went-up Israel God-of now-glory-of (3) the-bronze altar-of beside

הַכְּרוּב אֲשֶׁר הָיָה עָלָיו אֶל מִפְתַּן הַבָּיִת וַיִּקְרָא אֶל־
to then-he-called the-temple threshold-of to above-him he-was where the-cherub

הָאִישׁ הַלָּבֻשׁ הַבַּדִּים אֲשֶׁר קֶסֶת הַסֹּפֵר
the-scroll writing-kit-of who the-linens the-one-being-clothed the-man

בְּמָתְנָיו׃ (4) וַיֹּאמֶר יְהוָה אֵלָו° עֲבֹר בְּתוֹךְ הָעִיר
the-city through-midst-of go! to-him Yahweh and-he-said (4) at-sides-of-him

בְּתוֹךְ יְרוּשָׁלָםִ וְהִתְוִיתָ תָּו עַל־ מִצְחוֹת הָאֲנָשִׁים
the-men foreheads-of on mark and-you-put Jerusalem through-midst-of

הַנֶּאֱנָחִים וְהַנֶּאֱנָקִים עַל כָּל־ הַתּוֹעֵבוֹת
the-detestable-things all-of over and-the-ones-lamenting the-ones-grieving

הַנַּעֲשׂוֹת בְּתוֹכָהּ׃ (5) וּלְאֵלֶּה אָמַר בְּאָזְנַי עִבְרוּ
follow! in-ears-of-me he-said and-to-these (5) in-midst-of-her the-ones-being-done

בָעִיר אַחֲרָיו וְהַכּוּ עַל°־ תָּחֹס עֵינֵיכֶם° וְאַל־
or-not eye-of-you let-her-show-pity not and-kill! after-him through-the-city

תַּחְמֹלוּ׃ (6) זָקֵן בָּחוּר וּבְתוּלָה וְטַף וְנָשִׁים
and-women and-child and-maiden young-man old-man (6) you-show-compassion

תַּהַרְגוּ לְמַשְׁחִית וְעַל־ כָּל־ אִישׁ אֲשֶׁר־ עָלָיו הַתָּו אַל־ תִּגַּשׁוּ
you-touch not the-mark on-him who one any-of but-on to-destroy you-slaughter

here? Must they also fill the land with violence and continually provoke me to anger? Look at them putting the branch to their nose! [18]Therefore I will deal with them in anger; I will not look on them with pity or spare them. Although they shout in my ears, I will not listen to them."

*Idolaters Killed*

9 Then I heard him call out in a loud voice, "Bring the guards of the city here, each with a weapon in his hand." [2]And I saw six men coming from the direction of the upper gate, which faces north, each with a deadly weapon in his hand. With them was a man clothed in linen who had a writing kit at his side. They came in and stood beside the bronze altar.

[3]Now the glory of the God of Israel went up from above the cherubim, where it had been, and moved to the threshold of the temple. Then the LORD called to the man clothed in linen who had the writing kit at his side [4]and said to him, "Go throughout the city of Jerusalem and put a mark on the foreheads of those who grieve and lament over all the detestable things that are done in it."

[5]As I listened, he said to the others, "Follow him through the city and kill, without showing pity or compassion. [6]Slaughter old men, young men and maidens, women and children, but do not touch anyone who has the mark.

°4 ק אליו
°5a ק אל
°5b ק עינכם

וּמִמִּקְדָּשִׁי תָּחֵלּוּ וַיָּחֵלּוּ בָּאֲנָשִׁים הַזְּקֵנִים אֲשֶׁר
who the-elders with-the-men so-they-began you-begin and-at-sanctuary-of-me

לִפְנֵי הַבָּיִת׃ וַיֹּאמֶר אֲלֵיהֶם טַמְּאוּ אֶת־ הַבַּיִת וּמַלְאוּ
and-fill! the-temple *** defile! to-them then-he-said (7) the-temple in-front-of

אֶת־ הַחֲצֵרוֹת חֲלָלִים צֵאוּ וְיָצְאוּ וְהִכּוּ בָעִיר׃
throughout-the-city and-they-killed so-they-went go! slain-ones the-courts ***

וַיְהִי כְּהַכּוֹתָם וְנֵאשֲׁאַר* אֲנִי וָאֶפְּלָה עַל־ פָּנַי
faces-of-me on and-I-fell I and-being-left-alone while-to-kill-them and-he-was (8)

וָאֶזְעַק וָאֹמַר אֲהָהּ אֲדֹנָי יְהוִה הֲמַשְׁחִית אַתָּה אֵת כָּל־
entire-of *** you destroying? Yahweh Sovereign ah! and-I-said and-I-cried-out

שְׁאֵרִית יִשְׂרָאֵל בְּשָׁפְכְּךָ אֶת־ חֲמָתְךָ עַל־ יְרוּשָׁלִָם׃
Jerusalem on wrath-of-you *** when-to-pour-out-you Israel remnant-of

וַיֹּאמֶר אֵלַי עֲוֹן בֵּית־ יִשְׂרָאֵל וִיהוּדָה גָּדוֹל בִּמְאֹד
to-exceedingly great and-Judah Israel house-of sin-of to-me and-he-answered (9)

מְאֹד וַתִּמָּלֵא הָאָרֶץ דָּמִים וְהָעִיר מָלְאָה
she-is-full and-the-city bloodsheds the-land and-she-is-full exceedingly

מֻטֶּה כִּי אָמְרוּ עָזַב יְהוָה אֶת־ הָאָרֶץ וְאֵין יְהוָה רֹאֶה׃
seeing Yahweh and-not the-land *** Yahweh he-forsook they-say indeed injustice

וְגַם־ אֲנִי לֹא־ תָחוֹס עֵינִי וְלֹא אֶחְמֹל דַּרְכָּם
doing-of-them I-will-spare or-not eye-of-me she-will-show-pity not I so-also (10)

בְּרֹאשָׁם נָתָתִּי׃ וְהִנֵּה הָאִישׁ ׀ לְבֻשׁ הַבַּדִּים
the-linens one-being-clothed-of the-man and-see! (11) I-will-bring on-head-of-them

אֲשֶׁר הַקֶּסֶת בְּמָתְנָיו מֵשִׁיב דָּבָר לֵאמֹר עָשִׂיתִי כַּאֲשֶׁר
†as-what I-did to-say word bringing-back at-sides-of-him the-writing-kit who

צִוִּיתָנִי׃ וָאֶרְאֶה וְהִנֵּה אֶל־ הָרָקִיעַ אֲשֶׁר עַל־ רֹאשׁ
head-of over that the-expanse above and-see! and-I-looked (10:1) you-commanded-me

הַכְּרֻבִים כְּאֶבֶן סַפִּיר כְּמַרְאֵה דְּמוּת כִּסֵּא נִרְאָה
appearing throne likeness-of like-appearance-of sapphire like-stone-of the-cherubim

עֲלֵיהֶם׃ וַיֹּאמֶר אֶל־ הָאִישׁ ׀ לְבֻשׁ הַבַּדִּים וַיֹּאמֶר
and-he-said the-linens one-being-clothed-of the-man to and-he-said (2) over-them

בֹּא אֶל־ בֵּינוֹת לַגַּלְגַּל אֶל־ תַּחַת לַכְּרוּב וּמַלֵּא חָפְנֶיךָ
hands-of-you and-fill! to-the-cherub beneath at to-the-wheel ones-among in go!

גַחֲלֵי־ אֵשׁ מִבֵּינוֹת לַכְּרֻבִים וּזְרֹק עַל־ הָעִיר וַיָּבֹא
and-he-went-in the-city over and-scatter! to-the-cherubim from-ones-among fire coals-of

לְעֵינָי׃ וְהַכְּרֻבִים עֹמְדִים מִימִין לַבַּיִת
of-the-temple on-south ones-standing now-the-cherubim (3) before-eyes-of-me

בְּבֹאוֹ הָאִישׁ וְהֶעָנָן מָלֵא אֶת־ הֶחָצֵר הַפְּנִימִית׃
the-inner the-court *** he-filled and-the-cloud the-man when-to-go-in-him

Begin at my sanctuary." So they
began with the elders who were in
front of the temple.
7Then he said to them, "Defile
the temple and fill the courts with
the slain. Go!" So they went out
and began killing throughout the
city. 8While they were killing and
I was left alone, I fell facedown,
crying out, "Ah, Sovereign LORD!
Are you going to destroy the entire remnant of Israel in this out-
pouring of your wrath on Jerusalem?"
9He answered me, "The sin of
the house of Israel and Judah is
exceedingly great; the land is full
of bloodshed and the city is full of
injustice. They say, 'The LORD has
forsaken the land; the LORD does
not see.' 10So I will not look on
them with pity or spare them, but
I will bring down on their own
heads what they have done."
11Then the man in linen with
the writing kit at his side brought
back word, saying, "I have done
as you commanded."

*The Glory Departs From the Temple*

10 I looked, and I saw the likeness of a throne of sap-
phire[q] above the expanse that was
over the heads of the cherubim.
2The LORD said to the man clothed
in linen, "Go in among the wheels
beneath the cherubim. Fill your
hands with burning coals from
among the cherubim and scatter
them over the city." And as I
watched, he went in.
3Now the cherubim were standing on the south side of the temple
when the man went in, and a
cloud filled the inner court. 4Then

q1 Or *lapis lazuli*

*8 This form appears to be a combination of the participle וְנִשְׁאָר, *and-being-left-alone*, and the first person preterite וָאֶשָּׁאֵר, *and-I-was-left-alone.*

†11 The *Qere* reads this as two words, *as-all that.*

°11 ק ככל אשר

וַיָּרָם כְּבוֹד־ יְהוָה מֵעַל הַכְּרוּב עַל מִפְתַּן הַבָּיִת
the-temple threshold-of to the-cherub from-above Yahweh glory-of then-he-rose (4)

וַיִּמָּלֵא הַבַּיִת אֶת־ הֶעָנָן וְהֶחָצֵר מָלְאָה אֶת־
*** she-was-full and-the-court the-cloud *** the-temple and-he-was-filled

נֹגַהּ כְּבוֹד יְהוָה׃ וְקוֹל כַּנְפֵי הַכְּרוּבִים נִשְׁמַע
he-was-heard the-cherubim wings-of and-sound-of (5) Yahweh glory-of radiance-of

עַד־ הֶחָצֵר הַחִיצֹנָה כְּקוֹל אֵל־ שַׁדַּי בְּדַבְּרוֹ׃
when-to-speak-him Shaddai El like-voice-of the-outer the-court as-far-as

וַיְהִי בְּצַוֺּתוֹ אֶת־ הָאִישׁ לְבֻשׁ־ הַבַּדִּים
the-linens one-being-clothed-of the-man *** when-to-command-him and-he-was (6)

לֵאמֹר קַח אֵשׁ מִבֵּינוֹת לַגַּלְגַּל מִבֵּינוֹת לַכְּרוּבִים
to-the-cherubim from-ones-among to-the-wheel from-ones-among fire take! to-say

וַיָּבֹא וַיַּעֲמֹד אֵצֶל הָאוֹפָן׃ וַיִּשְׁלַח הַכְּרוּב
the-cherub then-he-reached-out (7) the-wheel beside and-he-stood then-he-went-in

אֶת־ יָדוֹ מִבֵּינוֹת לַכְּרוּבִים אֶל־ הָאֵשׁ אֲשֶׁר בֵּינוֹת
ones-among that the-fire to to-the-cherubim from-ones-among hand-of-him ***

הַכְּרֻבִים וַיִּשָּׂא וַיִּתֵּן אֶל־ חָפְנֵי לְבֻשׁ
one-being-clothed-of hands-of into and-he-put and-he-took-up the-cherubim

הַבַּדִּים וַיִּקַּח וַיֵּצֵא׃ וַיֵּרָא לַכְּרֻבִים תַּבְנִית
look-of on-the-cherubim and-he-could-be-seen (8) and-he-went-out and-he-took the-linens

יַד־ אָדָם תַּחַת כַּנְפֵיהֶם׃ וָאֶרְאֶה וְהִנֵּה אַרְבָּעָה אוֹפַנִּים אֵצֶל
beside wheels four and-see! and-I-looked (9) wings-of-them under man hand-of

הַכְּרוּבִים אוֹפַן אֶחָד אֵצֶל הַכְּרוּב אֶחָד וְאוֹפַן אֶחָד אֵצֶל הַכְּרוּב
the-cherub beside one and-wheel one the-cherub beside one wheel the-cherubim

אֶחָד וּמַרְאֵה הָאוֹפַנִּים כְּעֵין אֶבֶן תַּרְשִׁישׁ׃
chrysolite stone-of like-look-of the-wheels and-appearance-of one

וּמַרְאֵיהֶם דְּמוּת אֶחָד לְאַרְבַּעְתָּם כַּאֲשֶׁר יִהְיֶה הָאוֹפַן
the-wheel he-was like-that to-four-of-them one look and-appearance-of-them (10)

בְּתוֹךְ הָאוֹפָן׃ בְּלֶכְתָּם אֶל־ אַרְבַּעַת רִבְעֵיהֶם
directions-of-them four-of in as-to-move-them (11) the-wheel at-intersecting-of

יֵלֵכוּ לֹא יִסַּבּוּ בְּלֶכְתָּם כִּי הַמָּקוֹם אֲשֶׁר־ יִפְנֶה
he-faced that the-direction indeed as-to-go-them they-turned not they-would-go

הָרֹאשׁ אַחֲרָיו יֵלֵכוּ לֹא יִסַּבּוּ בְּלֶכְתָּם׃ וְכָל־
and-entire-of (12) as-to-go-them they-turned not they-went after-him the-head

בְּשָׂרָם וְגַבֵּהֶם וִידֵיהֶם וְכַנְפֵיהֶם וְהָאוֹפַנִּים
and-the-wheels and-wings-of-them and-hands-of-them and-back-of-them body-of-them

מְלֵאִים עֵינַיִם סָבִיב לְאַרְבַּעְתָּם אוֹפַנֵּיהֶם׃ לָאוֹפַנִּים
to-the-wheels (13) wheels-of-them to-four-of-them completely eyes ones-full

the glory of the LORD rose from above the cherubim and moved to the threshold of the temple. The cloud filled the temple, and the court was full of the radiance of the glory of the LORD. [5]The sound of the wings of the cherubim could be heard as far away as the outer court, like the voice of God Almighty[r] when he speaks.

[6]When the LORD commanded the man in linen, "Take fire from among the wheels, from among the cherubim," the man went in and stood beside a wheel. [7]Then one of the cherubim reached out his hand to the fire that was among them. He took up some of it and put it into the hands of the man in linen, who took it and went out. [8](Under the wings of the cherubim could be seen what looked like the hands of a man.)

[9]I looked, and I saw beside the cherubim four wheels, one beside each of the cherubim; the wheels sparkled like chrysolite. [10]As for their appearance, the four of them looked alike; each was like a wheel intersecting a wheel. [11]As they moved, they would go in any one of the four directions the cherubim faced; the wheels did not turn about[s] as the cherubim went. The cherubim went in whatever direction the head faced, without turning as they went. [12]Their entire bodies, including their backs, their hands and their wings, were completely full of eyes, as were their four wheels. [13]I heard the

[r]5 Hebrew *El-Shaddai*
[s]11 Or *aside*

לָהֶ֖ם קוֹרָ֣א הַגַּלְגַּ֑ל בְּאָזְנָֽי׃ וְאַרְבָּעָ֧ה פָנִ֛ים לְאֶחָ֖ד
to-them    he-was-called    the-whirling-wheel    in-ears-of-me    (14)    and-four    faces    to-each

פְּנֵ֤י הָֽאֶחָד֙ פְּנֵ֣י הַכְּר֔וּב וּפְנֵ֥י הַשֵּׁנִ֖י פְּנֵ֣י אָדָ֑ם
faces-of    the-one    faces-of    the-cherub    and-faces-of    the-second    faces-of    man

וְהַשְּׁלִישִׁי֙ פְּנֵ֣י אַרְיֵ֔ה וְהָרְבִיעִ֖י פְּנֵי־נָֽשֶׁר׃ וַיֵּרֹ֖מּוּ
and-the-third    faces-of    lion    and-the-fourth    faces-of    eagle    (15)    then-they-rose-up

הַכְּרוּבִ֑ים הִ֣יא הַֽחַיָּ֔ה אֲשֶׁ֥ר רָאִ֖יתִי בִּֽנְהַר־כְּבָֽר׃
the-cherubim    this    the-living-creature    that    I-saw    by-River-of    Kebar

וּבְלֶ֙כֶת֙ הַכְּרוּבִ֔ים יֵלְכ֥וּ הָאוֹפַנִּ֖ים אֶצְלָ֑ם
and-when-to-move    (16)    the-cherubim    they-moved    the-wheels    beside-them

וּבִשְׂאֵ֨ת הַכְּרוּבִ֜ים אֶת־כַּנְפֵיהֶ֗ם לָר֙וּם֙ מֵעַ֣ל הָאָ֔רֶץ לֹא־
and-when-to-spread    the-cherubim    ***    wings-of-them    to-rise    from-on    the-ground    not

יִסַּ֧בּוּ הָאוֹפַנִּ֛ים גַּם־הֵ֖ם מֵאֶצְלָֽם׃ בְּעָמְדָ֣ם
they-left    the-wheels    also    they    from-beside-them    (17)    when-to-stand-still-them

יַעֲמֹ֔דוּ וּבְרוֹמָ֖ם יֵר֣וֹמּוּ אוֹתָ֑ם כִּ֛י ר֥וּחַ
they-stood-still    and-when-to-rise-them    they-rose    with-them    because    spirit-of

הַחַיָּ֖ה בָּהֶֽם׃ וַיֵּצֵא֙ כְּב֣וֹד יְהוָ֔ה מֵעַ֖ל
the-living-creature    in-them    (18)    then-he-departed    glory-of    Yahweh    from-over

מִפְתַּ֣ן הַבָּ֑יִת וַֽיַּעֲמֹ֖ד עַל־הַכְּרוּבִֽים׃ וַיִּשְׂא֣וּ
threshold-of    the-temple    and-he-stopped    above    the-cherubim    (19)    and-they-spread

הַכְּרוּבִ֣ים אֶת־כַּנְפֵיהֶ֗ם וַיֵּר֙וֹמּוּ֙ מִן־הָאָ֜רֶץ לְעֵינַ֗י
the-cherubim    ***    wings-of-them    and-they-rose    from    the-ground    before-eyes-of-me

בְּצֵאתָ֔ם וְהָאוֹפַנִּ֖ים לְעֻמָּתָ֑ם וַֽיַּעֲמֹ֗ד פֶּ֜תַח שַׁ֤עַר
as-to-go-them    and-the-wheels    at-with-them    and-he-stopped    entrance-of    gate-of

בֵּית־יְהוָה֙ הַקַּדְמוֹנִ֔י וּכְב֥וֹד אֱלֹהֵֽי־יִשְׂרָאֵ֖ל עֲלֵיהֶ֥ם מִלְמָֽעְלָה׃
house-of    Yahweh    the-eastern    and-glory-of    God-of    Israel    over-them    at-to-above

הִ֣יא הַֽחַיָּ֔ה אֲשֶׁ֣ר רָאִ֗יתִי תַּ֛חַת אֱלֹהֵֽי־יִשְׂרָאֵ֖ל בִּֽנְהַר־כְּבָ֑ר
this    the-living-creature    that    I-saw    beneath    God-of    Israel    by-River-of    Kebar

וָאֵדַ֕ע כִּ֥י כְרוּבִ֖ים הֵֽמָּה׃ אַרְבָּעָ֨ה אַרְבָּעָ֤ה פָנִים֙ לְאֶחָ֔ד וְאַרְבַּ֥ע כְּנָפַ֖יִם
and-I-realized    that    cherubim    they    (21)    four    four    faces    to-each    and-four    wings

לְאֶחָ֑ד וּדְמוּת֙ יְדֵ֣י אָדָ֔ם תַּ֖חַת כַּנְפֵיהֶֽם׃ וּדְמ֣וּת
to-each    and-look-of    hands-of    man    under    wings-of-them    (22)    and-appearance-of

פְּנֵיהֶ֔ם הֵ֣מָּה הַפָּנִ֗ים אֲשֶׁ֤ר רָאִ֙יתִי֙ עַל־נְהַר־כְּבָ֔ר מַרְאֵיהֶ֖ם
faces-of-them    they    the-faces    that    I-saw    by    River-of    Kebar    appearance-of-them

וְאוֹתָ֑ם אִ֛ישׁ אֶל־עֵ֥בֶר פָּנָ֖יו יֵלֵֽכוּ׃ וַתִּשָּׂ֣א אֹתִ֗י
and-them    each    to    straight-ahead    faces-of-him    they-went    (11:1)    then-she-lifted    me

ר֙וּחַ֙ וַתָּבֵ֣א אֹתִ֗י אֶל־שַׁ֤עַר בֵּית־יְהוָה֙ הַקַּדְמוֹנִ֔י הַפּוֹנֶ֖ה
Spirit    and-she-brought    me    to    gate-of    house-of    Yahweh    the-eastern    the-one-facing

---

wheels being called "the whirling wheels." [14]Each of the cherubim had four faces: One face was that of a cherub, the second the face of a man, the third the face of a lion, and the fourth the face of an eagle.

[15]Then the cherubim rose upward. These were the living creatures I had seen by the Kebar River. [16]When the cherubim moved, the wheels beside them moved; and when the cherubim spread their wings to rise from the ground, the wheels did not leave their side. [17]When the cherubim stood still, they also stood still; and when the cherubim rose, they rose with them, because the spirit of the living creatures was in them.

[18]Then the glory of the LORD departed from over the threshold of the temple and stopped above the cherubim. [19]While I watched, the cherubim spread their wings and rose from the ground, and as they went, the wheels went with them. They stopped at the entrance to the east gate of the LORD's house, and the glory of the God of Israel was above them.

[20]These were the living creatures I had seen beneath the God of Israel by the Kebar River, and I realized that they were cherubim. [21]Each had four faces and four wings, and under their wings was what looked like the hands of a man. [22]Their faces had the same appearance as those I had seen by the Kebar River. Each one went straight ahead.

*Judgment on Israel's Leaders*

**11** Then the Spirit lifted me up and brought me to the gate of the house of the LORD that faces

קָדִימָה וְהִנֵּה בְּפֶתַח הַשַּׁעַר עֶשְׂרִים וַחֲמִשָּׁה אִישׁ וָאֶרְאֶה
and-I-saw man and-five twenty the-gate at-entrance-of and-see! to-east

בְתוֹכָם אֶת־יַאֲזַנְיָה בֶן־עַזֻּר וְאֶת־פְּלַטְיָהוּ בֶן־בְּנָיָהוּ שָׂרֵי
leaders-of Benaiah son-of Pelatiah and Azzur son-of Jaazaniah *** in-among-them

הָעָם׃ וַיֹּאמֶר אֵלָי בֶּן־אָדָם אֵלֶּה הָאֲנָשִׁים הַחֹשְׁבִים אָוֶן
evil the-ones-plotting the-men these man son-of to-me and-he-said (2) the-people

וְהַיֹּעֲצִים עֲצַת־רָע בָּעִיר הַזֹּאת׃ הָאֹמְרִים
the-ones-saying (3) the-this in-the-city wickedness advice-of and-the-ones-giving-advice

לֹא בְקָרוֹב בְּנוֹת בָּתִּים הִיא הַסִּיר וַאֲנַחְנוּ הַבָּשָׂר׃ לָכֵן
therefore (4) the-meat and-we the-cooking-pot this houses to-build at-soon not

הִנָּבֵא עֲלֵיהֶם הִנָּבֵא בֶּן־אָדָם׃ וַתִּפֹּל עָלַי רוּחַ
Spirit-of upon-me then-she-came (5) man son-of prophesy! against-them prophesy!

יְהוָה וַיֹּאמֶר אֵלַי אֱמֹר כֹּה־אָמַר יְהוָה כֵּן אֲמַרְתֶּם בֵּית יִשְׂרָאֵל
Israel house-of you-say that Yahweh he-says this say! to-me and-he-told Yahweh

וּמַעֲלוֹת רוּחֲכֶם אֲנִי יְדַעְתִּיהָ׃ הִרְבֵּיתֶם חַלְלֵיכֶם
ones-killed-of-you you-made-many (6) I-know-her I mind-of-you but-goings-through-of

בָּעִיר הַזֹּאת וּמִלֵּאתֶם חוּצֹתֶיהָ חָלָל׃ לָכֵן כֹּה־אָמַר
he-says this therefore (7) dead streets-of-her and-you-filled the-this in-the-city

אֲדֹנָי יְהוִה חַלְלֵיכֶם אֲשֶׁר שַׂמְתֶּם בְּתוֹכָהּ הֵמָּה הַבָּשָׂר
the-meat they in-midst-of-her you-threw that bodies-of-you Yahweh Sovereign

וְהִיא הַסִּיר וְאֶתְכֶם הוֹצִיא מִתּוֹכָהּ׃ חֶרֶב יְרֵאתֶם
you-fear sword (8) from-midst-of-her he-will-drive but-you the-pot and-this

וְחֶרֶב אָבִיא עֲלֵיכֶם נְאֻם אֲדֹנָי יְהוִה׃
Yahweh Sovereign declaration-of against-you I-will-bring and-sword

וְהוֹצֵאתִי אֶתְכֶם מִתּוֹכָהּ וְנָתַתִּי אֶתְכֶם בְּיַד־
into-hand-of you and-I-will-give from-midst-of-her you and-I-will-drive (9)

זָרִים וְעָשִׂיתִי בָכֶם שְׁפָטִים׃ בַּחֶרֶב
by-the-sword (10) punishments on-you and-I-will-inflict ones-being-foreign

תִּפֹּלוּ עַל־גְּבוּל יִשְׂרָאֵל אֶשְׁפּוֹט אֶתְכֶם וִידַעְתֶּם כִּי־אֲנִי יְהוָה׃
Yahweh I that then-you-will-know you I-will-judge Israel border-of at you-will-fall

הִיא לֹא־תִהְיֶה לָכֶם לְסִיר וְאַתֶּם תִּהְיוּ בְתוֹכָהּ לְבָשָׂר
as-meat in-midst-of-her you-will-be or-you as-pot for-you she-will-be not this (11)

אֶל־גְּבוּל יִשְׂרָאֵל אֶשְׁפֹּט אֶתְכֶם׃ וִידַעְתֶּם כִּי־אֲנִי יְהוָה
Yahweh I that and-you-will-know (12) you I-will-judge Israel border-of at

אֲשֶׁר בְּחֻקַּי לֹא הֲלַכְתֶּם וּמִשְׁפָּטַי לֹא עֲשִׂיתֶם וּכְמִשְׁפְּטֵי
but-as-standards-of you-kept not or-laws-of-me you-followed not to-decrees-of-me for

הַגּוֹיִם אֲשֶׁר סְבִיבוֹתֵיכֶם עֲשִׂיתֶם׃ וַיְהִי כְּהִנָּבְאִי
as-to-prophesy-me now-he-was (13) you-conformed-to ones-around-you that the-nations

east. There at the entrance to the
gate were twenty-five men, and I
saw among them Jaazaniah son of
Azzur and Pelatiah son of Benaiah, leaders of the people. [2]The
LORD said to me, "Son of man,
these are the men who are plotting
evil and giving wicked advice in
this city. [3]They say, 'Will it not
soon be time to build houses?'
This city is a cooking pot, and we
are the meat.' [4]Therefore prophesy
against them; prophesy, son of
man."
[5]Then the Spirit of the LORD
came upon me, and he told me to
say: "This is what the LORD says:
That is what you are saying, O
house of Israel, but I know what is
going through your mind. [6]You
have killed many people in this
city and filled its streets with the
dead.
[7]"Therefore this is what the
Sovereign LORD says: The bodies
you have thrown there are the
meat and this city is the pot, but I
will drive you out of it. [8]You fear
the sword, and the sword is what
I will bring against you, declares
the Sovereign LORD. [9]I will drive
you out of the city and hand you
over to foreigners and inflict punishment on you. [10]You will fall by
the sword, and I will execute judgment on you at the borders of Israel. Then you will know that I am
the LORD. [11]This city will not be a
pot for you, nor will you be the
meat in it; I will execute judgment
on you at the borders of Israel.
[12]And you will know that I am the
LORD, for you have not followed
my decrees or kept my laws but
have conformed to the standards
of the nations around you."
[13]Now as I was prophesying,

†3 Or *This is not the time to build houses.*

וּפְלַטְיָהוּ בֶן־ בְּנָיָה מֵת וָאֶפֹּל עַל־ פָּנַי וָאֶזְעַק
and-I-cried-out faces-of-me on then-I-fell he-died Benaiah son-of then-Pelatiah

קוֹל־גָּדוֹל וָאֹמַר אֲהָהּ אֲדֹנָי יְהוִה כָּלָה אַתָּה עֹשֶׂה אֵת
*** making you complete-destruction Yahweh Sovereign ah! and-I-said loud voice

שְׁאֵרִית יִשְׂרָאֵל׃ וַיְהִי דְבַר־ יְהוָה אֵלַי לֵאמֹר׃ בֶּן־ אָדָם
man son-of (15) to-say to-me Yahweh word-of and-he-came (14) Israel remnant-of

אַחֶיךָ אַחֶיךָ אַנְשֵׁי גְאֻלָּתֶךָ וְכָל־ בֵּית
house-of and-whole-of blood-relative-of-you men-of brothers-of-you brothers-of-you

יִשְׂרָאֵל כֻּלֹּה אֲשֶׁר אָמְרוּ לָהֶם יֹשְׁבֵי יְרוּשָׁלַםִ
Jerusalem ones-being-people-of of-them they-say whom whole-of-him Israel

רַחֲקוּ מֵעַל יְהוָה לָנוּ הִיא נִתְּנָה הָאָרֶץ לְמוֹרָשָׁה׃
as-possession the-land she-was-given this to-us Yahweh from-with they-are-far

לָכֵן אֱמֹר כֹּה־ אָמַר אֲדֹנָי יְהוִה כִּי הִרְחַקְתִּים
I-sent-far-away-them although Yahweh Sovereign he-says this say! therefore (16)

בַּגּוֹיִם וְכִי הֲפִיצוֹתִים בָּאֲרָצוֹת וָאֱהִי
yet-I-have-been among-the-countries I-scattered-them and-although among-the-nations

לָהֶם לְמִקְדָּשׁ מְעַט בָּאֲרָצוֹת אֲשֶׁר־ בָּאוּ שָׁם׃
there they-went where in-the-countries little-while as-sanctuary for-them

לָכֵן אֱמֹר כֹּה־ אָמַר אֲדֹנָי יְהוִה וְקִבַּצְתִּי אֶתְכֶם מִן־
from you indeed-I-will-gather Yahweh Sovereign he-says this say! therefore (17)

הָעַמִּים וְאָסַפְתִּי אֶתְכֶם מִן־ הָאֲרָצוֹת אֲשֶׁר נְפֹצוֹתֶם
you-were-scattered where the-countries from you and-I-will-bring-back the-nations

בָּהֶם וְנָתַתִּי לָכֶם אֶת־ אַדְמַת יִשְׂרָאֵל׃ וּבָאוּ
and-they-will-return (18) Israel land-of *** to-you and-I-will-give-back among-them

שָׁמָּה וְהֵסִירוּ אֶת־ כָּל־ שִׁקּוּצֶיהָ וְאֶת־ כָּל־
all-of and vile-ones-of-her all-of *** and-they-will-remove to-there

תּוֹעֲבוֹתֶיהָ מִמֶּנָּה׃ וְנָתַתִּי לָהֶם לֵב אֶחָד
undivided heart to-them and-I-will-give (19) from-her detestable-ones-of-her

וְרוּחַ חֲדָשָׁה אֶתֵּן בְּקִרְבְּכֶם וַהֲסִרֹתִי לֵב הָאֶבֶן
the-stone heart-of and-I-will-remove at-inside-of-you I-will-put new and-spirit

מִבְּשָׂרָם וְנָתַתִּי לָהֶם לֵב בָּשָׂר׃ לְמַעַן
so-that (20) flesh heart-of to-them and-I-will-give from-flesh-of-them

בְּחֻקֹּתַי יֵלֵכוּ וְאֶת־ מִשְׁפָּטַי יִשְׁמְרוּ
they-will-be-careful laws-of-me and they-will-follow to-decrees-of-me

וְעָשׂוּ אֹתָם וְהָיוּ־ לִי לְעָם וַאֲנִי אֶהְיֶה לָהֶם
to-them I-will-be and-I as-people to-me and-they-will-be them and-they-will-keep

לֵאלֹהִים׃ וְאֶל־ לֵב שִׁקּוּצֵיהֶם וְתוֹעֲבוֹתֵיהֶם
and-detestable-ones-of-them vile-ones-of-them heart-of but-to (21) as-God

Pelatiah son of Benaiah died. Then I fell facedown and cried out in a loud voice, "Ah, Sovereign LORD! Will you completely destroy the remnant of Israel?"
14 The word of the LORD came to me:
15 "Son of man, your brothers—your brothers who are your blood relatives[u] and the whole house of Israel—are those of whom the people of Jerusalem have said, 'They are[v] far away from the LORD; this land was given to us as our possession.'

*Promised Return of Israel*

16 "Therefore say: 'This is what the Sovereign LORD says: Although I sent them far away among the nations and scattered them among the countries, yet for a little while I have been a sanctuary for them in the countries where they have gone.'
17 "Therefore say: 'This is what the Sovereign LORD says: I will gather you from the nations and bring you back from the countries where you have been scattered, and I will give you back the land of Israel again.'
18 "They will return to it and remove all its vile images and detestable idols.
19 I will give them an undivided heart and put a new spirit in them; I will remove from them their heart of stone and give them a heart of flesh.
20 Then they will follow my decrees and be careful to keep my laws. They will be my people, and I will be their God.
21 But as for those whose hearts are devoted to their vile images and detestable idols, I will

[u]15 Or *are in exile with you* (see Septuagint and Syriac)
[v]15 Or *those to whom the people of Jerusalem have said, 'Stay*

לִבָּם הֹלֵךְ דַּרְכָּם בְּרֹאשָׁם נָתַתִּי

I-will-bring-down on-head-of-them doing-of-them being-devoted heart-of-them

נְאֻם אֲדֹנָי יְהוִה׃ וַיִּשְׂאוּ הַכְּרוּבִים אֶת־ כַּנְפֵיהֶם

wings-of-them *** the-cherubim then-they-spread (22) Yahweh Sovereign declaration-of

וְהָאוֹפַנִּים לְעֻמָּתָם וּכְבוֹד אֱלֹהֵי־יִשְׂרָאֵל עֲלֵיהֶם מִלְמָעְלָה׃

at-to-above over-them Israel God-of and-glory-of at-beside-them with-the-wheels

וַיַּעַל כְּבוֹד יְהוָה מֵעַל תּוֹךְ הָעִיר וַיַּעֲמֹד

and-he-stopped the-city inside-of from-within Yahweh glory-of and-he-went-up (23)

עַל־ הָהָר אֲשֶׁר מִקֶּדֶם לָעִיר׃ וְרוּחַ נְשָׂאַתְנִי

she-lifted-me and-the-Spirit (24) of-the-city at-east that the-mountain above

וַתְּבִיאֵנִי כַשְׂדִּימָה אֶל־ הַגּוֹלָה בַּמַּרְאֶה בְּרוּחַ אֱלֹהִים

God by-Spirit-of in-the-vision the-exile to to-Chaldea and-she-brought-me

וַיַּעַל מֵעָלַי הַמַּרְאֶה אֲשֶׁר רָאִיתִי׃ וָאֲדַבֵּר אֶל־ הַגּוֹלָה

the-exile to and-I-told (25) I-saw that the-vision from-with-me then-he-went-up

אֵת כָּל־ דִּבְרֵי יְהוָה אֲשֶׁר הֶרְאָנִי׃ וַיְהִי דְבַר־ יְהוָה

Yahweh word-of and-he-came (12:1) he-showed-me that Yahweh things-of every-of ***

אֵלַי לֵאמֹר׃ בֶּן־ אָדָם בְּתוֹךְ בֵּית־ הַמֶּרִי אַתָּה יֹשֵׁב אֲשֶׁר

that living you the-rebellion house-of in-among man son-of (2) to-say to-me

עֵינַיִם לָהֶם לִרְאוֹת וְלֹא רָאוּ אָזְנַיִם לָהֶם לִשְׁמֹעַ וְלֹא שָׁמֵעוּ כִּי

for they-hear but-not to-hear to-them ears they-see but-not to-see to-them eyes

בֵּית מְרִי הֵם׃ וְאַתָּה בֶן־ אָדָם עֲשֵׂה לְךָ כְּלֵי

belongings-of for-you pack! man son-of therefore-you (3) they rebellion house-of

גוֹלָה וּגְלֵה יוֹמָם לְעֵינֵיהֶם וְגָלִיתָ מִמְּקוֹמְךָ אֶל־

to from-place-of-you and-you-go before-eyes-of-them by-day and-set-out! exile

מָקוֹם אַחֵר לְעֵינֵיהֶם אוּלַי יִרְאוּ כִּי בֵּית

house-of though they-will-understand perhaps before-eyes-of-them another place

מְרִי הֵמָּה׃ וְהוֹצֵאתָ כֵלֶיךָ כִּכְלֵי גוֹלָה

exile as-belongings-of belongings-of-you and-you-bring-out (4) they rebellion

יוֹמָם לְעֵינֵיהֶם וְאַתָּה תֵּצֵא בָעֶרֶב לְעֵינֵיהֶם

before-eyes-of-them in-the-evening you-go-out then-you before-eyes-of-them during-day

כְּמוֹצָאֵי גוֹלָה׃ לְעֵינֵיהֶם חֲתָר־ לְךָ בַקִּיר

through-the-wall for-you dig! before-eyes-of-them (5) exile like-goings-out-of

וְהוֹצֵאתָ בּוֹ׃ לְעֵינֵיהֶם עַל־ כָּתֵף תִּשָּׂא בָּעֲלָטָה

at-the-dusk you-put shoulder on before-eyes-of-them (6) through-him and-you-take

תוֹצִיא פָּנֶיךָ תְכַסֶּה וְלֹא תִרְאֶה אֶת־ הָאָרֶץ כִּי־ מוֹפֵת

sign for the-land *** you-can-see so-not you-cover faces-of-you you-carry-out

נְתַתִּיךָ לְבֵית יִשְׂרָאֵל׃ וָאַעַשׂ כֵּן כַּאֲשֶׁר צֻוֵּיתִי כֵּלַי

things-of-me I-was-commanded just-as so so-I-did (7) Israel to-house-of I-made-you

bring down on their own heads what they have done, declares the Sovereign LORD."

[22]Then the cherubim, with the wheels beside them, spread their wings, and the glory of the God of Israel was above them. [23]The glory of the LORD went up from within the city and stopped above the mountain east of it. [24]The Spirit lifted me up and brought me to the exiles in Babylonia[w] in the vision given by the Spirit of God.

Then the vision I had seen went up from me, [25]and I told the exiles everything the LORD had shown me.

*The Exile Symbolized*

12 The word of the LORD came to me: [2]"Son of man, you are living among a rebellious people. They have eyes to see but do not see and ears to hear but do not hear, for they are a rebellious people.

[3]"Therefore, son of man, pack your belongings for exile and in the daytime, as they watch, set out and go from where you are to another place. Perhaps they will understand, though they are a rebellious house. [4]During the daytime, while they watch, bring out your belongings packed for exile. Then in the evening, while they are watching, go out like those who go into exile. [5]While they watch, dig through the wall and take your belongings out through it. [6]Put them on your shoulder as they are watching and carry them out at dusk. Cover your face so that you cannot see the land, for I have made you a sign to the house of Israel."

[7]So I did as I was commanded.

w24 Or *Chaldea*

הוֹצֵאתִי כִּכְלֵי גוֹלָה יוֹמָם וּבָעֶרֶב חָתַרְתִּי־לִי

for-me I-dug then-in-the-evening during-day exile as-things-of I-brought-out

בַקִּיר בְּיָד בָּעֲלָטָה הוֹצֵאתִי עַל־כָּתֵף נָשָׂאתִי

I-carried shoulder on I-took-out at-the-dusk with-hand through-the-wall

לְעֵינֵיהֶם׃ וַיְהִי דְבַר־יְהוָה אֵלַי בַּבֹּקֶר לֵאמֹר׃

to-say in-the-morning to-me Yahweh word-of and-he-came (8) before-eyes-of-them

בֶּן־אָדָם הֲלֹא אָמְרוּ אֵלֶיךָ בֵּית יִשְׂרָאֵל בֵּית הַמֶּרִי

the-rebellion house-of Israel house-of to-you they-asked not? man son-of (9)

מָה אַתָּה עֹשֶׂה׃ אֱמֹר אֲלֵיהֶם כֹּה אָמַר אֲדֹנָי יְהוִה הַנָּשִׂיא

the-prince Yahweh Sovereign he-says this to-them say! (10) doing you what?

הַמַּשָּׂא הַזֶּה בִּירוּשָׁלַם* וְכָל־בֵּית יִשְׂרָאֵל אֲשֶׁר־הֵמָּה

they who Israel house-of and-whole-of in-Jerusalem the-this the-oracle

בתוכם׃ אֱמֹר אֲנִי מוֹפֶתְכֶם כַּאֲשֶׁר עָשִׂיתִי כֵּן יֵעָשֶׂה לָהֶם

to-them he-will-be-done so I-did just-as sign-of-you I say! (11) in-midst-of-them

בַּגּוֹלָה בַשְּׁבִי יֵלֵכוּ׃ וְהַנָּשִׂיא אֲשֶׁר־בְּתוֹכָם אֶל־

on in-among-them who and-the-prince (12) they-will-go as-the-captive into-the-exile

כָּתֵף יִשָּׂא בָּעֲלָטָה וְיֵצֵא בַּקִּיר יַחְתְּרוּ

they-will-dig in-the-wall and-he-will-leave at-the-dusk he-will-put shoulder

לְהוֹצִיא בוֹ פָּנָיו יְכַסֶּה יַעַן אֲשֶׁר לֹא־יִרְאֶה

he-can-see not that so he-will-cover faces-of-him through-him to-bring-out

לַעַיִן הוּא אֶת־הָאָרֶץ׃ וּפָרַשְׂתִּי אֶת־רִשְׁתִּי עָלָיו

for-him net-of-me *** and-I-will-spread (13) the-land *** he with-the-eye

וְנִתְפַּשׂ בִּמְצוּדָתִי וְהֵבֵאתִי אֹתוֹ בָבֶלָה אֶרֶץ

land-of to-Babylonia him and-I-will-bring in-snare-of-me and-he-will-be-caught

כַּשְׂדִּים וְאוֹתָהּ לֹא־יִרְאֶה וְשָׁם יָמוּת׃ וְכֹל° אֲשֶׁר

who and-all (14) he-will-die and-there he-will-see not but-her Chaldeans

סְבִיבֹתָיו עֶזְרֹה וְכָל־אֲגַפָּיו אֱזָרֶה לְכָל־רוּחַ

wind to-all-of I-will-scatter troops-of-him and-all-of staff-of-him ones-around-him

וְחֶרֶב אָרִיק אַחֲרֵיהֶם׃ וְיָדְעוּ כִּי־אֲנִי יְהוָה

Yahweh I that and-they-will-know (15) after-them I-will-draw and-sword

בַּהֲפִיצִי אוֹתָם בַּגּוֹיִם וְזֵרִיתִי אוֹתָם בָּאֲרָצוֹת׃

through-the-countries them and-I-scatter among-the-nations them when-to-disperse-me

וְהוֹתַרְתִּי מֵהֶם אַנְשֵׁי מִסְפָּר מֵחֶרֶב מֵרָעָב וּמִדָּבֶר

and-from-plague from-famine from-sword number men-of of-them but-I-will-spare (16)

לְמַעַן יְסַפְּרוּ אֶת־כָּל־תּוֹעֲבוֹתֵיהֶם בַּגּוֹיִם

in-the-nations detestable-practices-of-them all-of *** they-may-acknowledge so-that

אֲשֶׁר־בָּאוּ שָׁם וְיָדְעוּ כִּי־אֲנִי יְהוָה׃ וַיְהִי דְבַר־

word-of and-he-came (17) Yahweh I that then-they-will-know there they-go where

During the day I brought out my things packed for exile. Then in the evening I dug through the wall with my hands. I took my belongings out at dusk, carrying them on my shoulders while they watched.
8In the morning the word of the LORD came to me: 9"Son of man, did not that rebellious house of Israel ask you, 'What are you doing?'
10"Say to them, 'This is what the Sovereign LORD says: This oracle concerns the prince in Jerusalem and the whole house of Israel who are there.' 11Say to them, 'I am a sign to you.'
"As I have done, so it will be done to them. They will go into exile as captives.
12"The prince among them will put his things on his shoulder at dusk and leave, and a hole will be dug in the wall for him to go through. He will cover his face so that he cannot see the land. 13I will spread my net for him, and he will be caught in my snare; I will bring him to Babylonia, the land of the Chaldeans, but he will not see it, and there he will die. 14I will scatter to the winds all those around him—his staff and all his troops—and I will pursue them with drawn sword.
15"They will know that I am the LORD, when I disperse them among the nations and scatter them through the countries. 16But I will spare a few of them from the sword, famine and plague, so that in the nations where they go they may acknowledge all their detestable practices. Then they will know that I am the LORD."
17The word of the LORD came to

*10 Most mss include *bireq* under the *lamed* (לַ‍ִם).

°14 ק עזרו

יְהוָה אֵלַי לֵאמֹר׃ בֶּן־ אָדָם לַחְמְךָ בְּרַעַשׁ תֹּאכֵל
you-eat with-trembling food-of-you man son-of (18) to-say to-me Yahweh

וּמֵימֶיךָ בְּרָגְזָה וּבִדְאָגָה תִּשְׁתֶּה׃ וְאָמַרְתָּ אֶל־
to and-you-say (19) you-drink and-with-fear with-shuddering and-waters-of-you

עַם הָאָרֶץ כֹּה־ אָמַר אֲדֹנָי יְהוִה לְיוֹשְׁבֵי יְרוּשָׁלִַם
Jerusalem about-ones-living-of Yahweh Sovereign he-says this the-land people-of

אֶל־אַדְמַת יִשְׂרָאֵל לַחְמָם בִּדְאָגָה יֹאכֵלוּ וּמֵימֵיהֶם
and-waters-of-them they-will-eat in-anxiety bread-of-them Israel land-of in

בְּשִׁמָּמוֹן יִשְׁתּוּ לְמַעַן תֵּשַׁם אַרְצָהּ
land-of-her she-will-be-stripped because-that they-will-drink in-despair

מִמְּלֹאָהּ מֵחֲמַס כָּל־ הַיֹּשְׁבִים בָּהּ׃
in-her the-ones-living all-of because-of-violence-of of-everything-of-her

וְהֶעָרִים הַנּוֹשָׁבוֹת תֶּחֱרַבְנָה וְהָאָרֶץ
and-the-land they-will-be-laid-waste the-ones-being-inhabited and-the-towns (20)

שְׁמָמָה תִהְיֶה וִידַעְתֶּם כִּי־אֲנִי יְהוָה׃ וַיְהִי דְבַר־
word-of and-he-came (21) Yahweh I that then-you-will-know she-will-be desolation

יְהוָה אֵלַי לֵאמֹר׃ בֶּן־ אָדָם מָה־ הַמָּשָׁל הַזֶּה לָכֶם עַל־אַדְמַת
land-of in to-you the-this the-proverb what? man son-of (22) to-say to-me Yahweh

יִשְׂרָאֵל לֵאמֹר יַאַרְכוּ הַיָּמִים וְאָבַד כָּל־ חָזוֹן׃
vision every-of and-he-comes-to-nothing the-days they-go-by to-say Israel

לָכֵן אֱמֹר אֲלֵיהֶם כֹּה־ אָמַר אֲדֹנָי יְהוִה הִשְׁבַּתִּי אֶת־
*** I-will-put-to-end Yahweh Sovereign he-says this to-them say! therefore (23)

הַמָּשָׁל הַזֶּה וְלֹא־ יִמְשְׁלוּ אֹתוֹ עוֹד בְּיִשְׂרָאֵל כִּי אִם־
also indeed in-Israel longer him they-will-quote and-not the-this the-proverb

דַּבֵּר אֲלֵיהֶם קָרְבוּ הַיָּמִים וּדְבַר כָּל־ חָזוֹן׃ כִּי
for (24) vision every-of and-fulfillment-of the-days they-are-near to-them say!

לֹא יִהְיֶה עוֹד כָּל־ חֲזוֹן שָׁוְא וּמִקְסַם חָלָק
flattery or-divination-of falsehood vision-of any-of more he-will-be not

בְּתוֹךְ בֵּית יִשְׂרָאֵל׃ כִּי ׀ אֲנִי יְהוָה אֲדַבֵּר אֵת אֲשֶׁר אֲדַבֵּר דָּבָר
word I-will-speak what *** I-will-speak Yahweh I but (25) Israel house-of in-among

וְיֵעָשֶׂה לֹא תִמָּשֵׁךְ עוֹד כִּי בִימֵיכֶם בֵּית
house-of in-days-of-you for again she-will-be-delayed not and-he-shall-be-fulfilled

הַמֶּרִי אֲדַבֵּר דָּבָר וַעֲשִׂיתִיו נְאֻם אֲדֹנָי יְהוִה׃
Yahweh Sovereign declaration-of and-I-will-fulfill-him word I-will-say the-rebellion

וַיְהִי דְבַר־ יְהוָה אֵלַי לֵאמֹר׃ בֶּן־אָדָם הִנֵּה בֵית־יִשְׂרָאֵל
Israel house-of see! man son-of (27) to-say to-me Yahweh word-of and-he-came (26)

אֹמְרִים הֶחָזוֹן אֲשֶׁר־ הוּא חֹזֶה לְיָמִים רַבִּים וּלְעִתִּים
and-about-futures many-ones for-days seeing he that the-vision ones-saying

me: 18"Son of man, tremble as you
eat your food, and shudder in fear
as you drink your water. 19Say to
the people of the land: 'This is
what the Sovereign LORD says
about those living in Jerusalem
and in the land of Israel: They will
eat their food in anxiety and drink
their water in despair, for their
land will be stripped of everything
in it because of the violence of all
who live there. 20The inhabited
towns will be laid waste and the
land will be desolate. Then you
will know that I am the LORD.' "
21The word of the LORD came to
me: 22"Son of man, what is this
proverb you have in the land of
Israel: 'The days go by and every
vision comes to nothing'? 23Say to
them, 'This is what the Sovereign
LORD says: I am going to put an
end to this proverb, and they will
no longer quote it in Israel.' Say to
them, 'The days are near when
every vision will be fulfilled. 24For
there will be no more false visions
or flattering divinations among
the people of Israel. 25But I the
LORD will speak what I will, and it
shall be fulfilled without delay.
For in your days, you rebellious
house, I will fulfill whatever I say,
declares the Sovereign LORD.' "
26The word of the LORD came to
me: 27"Son of man, the house of
Israel is saying, 'The vision he
sees is for many years from now,

רְחוֹקוֹת הוּא נִבָּא׃ לָכֵן אֱמֹר אֲלֵיהֶם כֹּה אָמַר אֲדֹנָי
Sovereign he-says this to-them say! therefore (28) prophesying he distant-ones

יְהוִה לֹא־ תִמָּשֵׁךְ עוֹד כָּל־ דְּבָרָי אֲשֶׁר אֲדַבֵּר דָּבָר
word I-say what words-of-me any-of longer she-will-be-delayed not Yahweh

וְיֵעָשֶׂה נְאֻם אֲדֹנָי יְהוִה׃ וַיְהִי
and-he-came (13:1) Yahweh Sovereign declaration-of then-he-will-be-fulfilled

דְבַר־ יְהוָה אֵלַי לֵאמֹר׃ בֶּן־ אָדָם הִנָּבֵא אֶל־ נְבִיאֵי יִשְׂרָאֵל
Israel prophets-of against prophesy! man son-of (2) to-say to-me Yahweh word-of

הַנִּבָּאִים וְאָמַרְתָּ לִנְבִיאֵי מִלִּבָּם שִׁמְעוּ
hear! from-imagination-of-them to-prophets-of and-you-say the-ones-prophesying

דְּבַר־ יְהוָה׃ כֹּה אָמַר אֲדֹנָי יְהוִה הוֹי עַל־ הַנְּבִיאִים
the-prophets to woe! Yahweh Sovereign he-says this (3) Yahweh word-of

הַנְּבָלִים אֲשֶׁר הֹלְכִים אַחַר רוּחָם וּלְבִלְתִּי רָאוּ׃
they-saw and-to-nothing spirit-of-them after ones-following who the-foolish-ones

כְּשֻׁעָלִים בֶּחֳרָבוֹת נְבִיאֶיךָ יִשְׂרָאֵל הָיוּ׃ לֹא
not (5) they-are Israel prophets-of-you among-the-ruins like-jackals (4)

עֲלִיתֶם בַּפְּרָצוֹת וַתִּגְדְּרוּ גָדֵר עַל־ בֵּית יִשְׂרָאֵל לַעֲמֹד
to-stand-firm Israel house-of for wall so-you-repaired to-the-breaks you-went-up

בַּמִּלְחָמָה בְּיוֹם יְהוָה׃ חָזוּ שָׁוְא וְקֶסֶם כָּזָב
lie and-divination-of falsehood they-saw-vision (6) Yahweh on-day-of in-the-battle

הָאֹמְרִים נְאֻם־ יְהוָה וַיהוָה לֹא שְׁלָחָם וְיִחֲלוּ
yet-they-expect he-sent-them not when-Yahweh Yahweh declaration-of the-ones-saying

לְקַיֵּם דָּבָר׃ הֲלוֹא מַחֲזֵה־ שָׁוְא חֲזִיתֶם וּמִקְסַם כָּזָב
lie and-divination-of you-saw falsehood vision-of not? (7) word to-fulfill

אֲמַרְתֶּם וְאֹמְרִים נְאֻם־ יְהוָה וַאֲנִי לֹא דִבַּרְתִּי׃ לָכֵן
therefore (8) I-spoke not though-I Yahweh declaration-of when-ones-saying you-uttered

כֹּה אָמַר אֲדֹנָי יְהוִה יַעַן דַּבֶּרְכֶם שָׁוְא וַחֲזִיתֶם
and-you-saw-vision falsehood to-speak-you because Yahweh Sovereign he-says this

כָּזָב לָכֵן הִנְנִי אֲלֵיכֶם נְאֻם אֲדֹנָי יְהוִה׃
Yahweh Sovereign declaration-of against-you see-I! therefore lie

וְהָיְתָה יָדִי אֶל־ הַנְּבִאִים הַחֹזִים שָׁוְא
falsehood the-ones-seeing-vision the-prophets against hand-of-me and-she-will-be (9)

וְהַקֹּסְמִים כָּזָב בְּסוֹד עַמִּי לֹא־ יִהְיוּ
they-will-be not people-of-me in-council-of lie and-the-ones-uttering-divination

וּבִכְתָב בֵּית־ יִשְׂרָאֵל לֹא יִכָּתֵבוּ וְאֶל־ אַדְמַת יִשְׂרָאֵל
Israel land-of or-into they-will-be-listed not Israel house-of or-in-record-of

לֹא יָבֹאוּ וִידַעְתֶּם כִּי אֲנִי אֲדֹנָי יְהוִה׃ יַעַן
because (10) Yahweh Sovereign I that then-you-will-know they-will-enter not

and he prophesies about the distant future.'

28"Therefore say to them, 'This is what the Sovereign LORD says: None of my words will be delayed any longer; whatever I say will be fulfilled, declares the Sovereign LORD.' "

*False Prophets Condemned*

13 The word of the LORD came to me: 2"Son of man, prophesy against the prophets of Israel who are now prophesying. Say to those who prophesy out of their own imagination: 'Hear the word of the LORD! 3This is what the Sovereign LORD says: Woe to the foolish[x] prophets who follow their own spirit and have seen nothing! 4Your prophets, O Israel, are like jackals among ruins. 5You have not gone up to the breaks in the wall to repair it for the house of Israel so that it will stand firm in the battle on the day of the LORD. 6Their visions are false and their divinations a lie. They say, "The LORD declares," when the LORD has not sent them; yet they expect their words to be fulfilled. 7Have you not seen false visions and uttered lying divinations when you say, "The LORD declares," though I have not spoken?

8" 'Therefore this is what the Sovereign LORD says: Because of your false words and lying visions, I am against you, declares the Sovereign LORD. 9My hand will be against the prophets who see false visions and utter lying divinations. They will not belong to the council of my people or be listed in the records of the house of Israel, nor will they enter the land of Israel. Then you will know that I am the Sovereign LORD.

x3 Or *wicked*

וּבְיַ֡עַן הִטְע֤וּ אֶת־ עַמִּי֙ לֵאמֹ֣ר שָׁל֔וֹם וְאֵ֖ין
when-there-is-no peace to-say people-of-me *** they-lead-astray and-for-because

שָׁל֑וֹם וְהוּא֙ בֹּ֣נֶה חַ֔יִץ וְהִנָּ֖ם טָחִ֥ים אֹת֖וֹ תָּפֵֽל׃
whitewash him ones-covering and-see-they! flimsy-wall building when-he peace

אֱמֹ֛ר אֶל־ טָחֵ֥י תָפֵ֖ל וְיִפֹּ֑ל הָיָ֣ה ׀ גֶּ֣שֶׁם
rain he-will-come that-he-will-fall whitewash ones-covering-of to tell! (11)

שׁוֹטֵ֗ף וְאַתֵּ֨נָה אַבְנֵ֤י אֶלְגָּבִישׁ֙ תִּפֹּ֔לְנָה וְר֥וּחַ
and-wind-of they-will-hurtle-down hail stones-of and-I-will-send one-being-torrent

סְעָר֖וֹת תְּבַקֵּֽעַ׃ וְהִנֵּ֖ה נָפַ֣ל הַקִּ֑יר הֲל֨וֹא
not? the-wall he-collapses when-see! (12) she-will-burst-forth violent-storms

יֵאָמֵ֤ר אֲלֵיכֶם֙ אַיֵּ֔ה הַטִּ֖יחַ אֲשֶׁ֥ר טַחְתֶּֽם׃ לָכֵ֗ן
therefore (13) you-covered that the-whitewash where? to-you he-will-be-asked

כֹּ֤ה אָמַר֙ אֲדֹנָ֣י יְהֹוִ֔ה וּבִקַּעְתִּ֥י רֽוּחַ־ סְעָר֖וֹת
violent-storms wind-of indeed-I-will-unleash Yahweh Sovereign he-says this

בַּחֲמָתִ֑י וְגֶ֤שֶׁם שֹׁטֵף֙ בְּאַפִּ֣י יִהְיֶ֔ה
he-will-fall in-anger-of-me one-being-torrent and-rain in-wrath-of-me

וְאַבְנֵ֥י אֶלְגָּבִ֛ישׁ בְּחֵמָ֖ה לְכָלָֽה׃ וְהָרַסְתִּ֣י אֶת־ הַקִּ֞יר
the-wall *** and-I-will-tear-down (14) to-destruction with-fury hail and-stones-of

אֲשֶׁר־ טַחְתֶּ֣ם תָּפֵ֗ל וְהִגַּעְתִּ֙יהוּ֙ אֶל־ הָאָ֔רֶץ וְנִגְלָ֖ה
so-he-will-be-laid-bare the-ground to and-I-will-level-him whitewash you-covered that

יְסֹד֑וֹ וְנָֽפְלָ֗ה וּכְלִיתֶם֙ בְּתוֹכָ֔הּ
at-within-her then-you-will-be-destroyed when-she-falls foundation-of-him

וִֽידַעְתֶּ֖ם כִּֽי־ אֲנִ֥י יְהֹוָֽה׃ וְכִלֵּיתִ֤י אֶת־ חֲמָתִי֙ בַּקִּ֔יר
against-the-wall wrath-of-me *** so-I-will-spend (15) Yahweh I that and-you-will-know

וּבַטָּחִ֥ים אֹת֖וֹ תָּפֵ֑ל וְאֹמַ֣ר לָכֶ֗ם אֵ֚ין הַקִּ֔יר
the-wall gone to-you and-I-will-say whitewash him and-against-the-ones-covering

וְאֵ֖ין הַטָּחִ֥ים אֹתֽוֹ׃ נְבִיאֵ֣י יִשְׂרָאֵ֔ל הַֽנִּבְּאִים֙* אֶל־
to the-ones-prophesying Israel prophets-of (16) him the-ones-whitewashing and-gone

יְר֣וּשָׁלִַ֔ם וְהַחֹזִ֥ים לָ֖הּ חֲז֣וֹן שָׁלֹ֑ם וְאֵ֣ין שָׁלֹ֔ם
peace when-there-was-no peace vision-of for-her and-the-ones-seeing-vision Jerusalem

נְאֻ֖ם אֲדֹנָ֥י יְהֹוִֽה׃ וְאַתָּ֣ה בֶן־ אָדָ֗ם שִׂ֤ים פָּנֶ֙יךָ֙ אֶל־
against faces-of-you set! man son-of now-you (17) Yahweh Sovereign declaration-of

בְּנ֣וֹת עַמְּךָ֔ הַמִּֽתְנַבְּא֖וֹת מִלִּבְּהֶ֑ן וְהִנָּבֵ֖א
and-prophesy! from-imagination-of-them the-ones-prophesying people-of-me daughters-of

עֲלֵיהֶֽן׃ וְאָמַרְתָּ֞ כֹּֽה־ אָמַ֣ר ׀ אֲדֹנָ֣י יְהֹוִ֗ה ה֣וֹי לִֽמְתַפְּר֨וֹת
to-ones-sewing woe! Yahweh Sovereign he-says this and-you-say (18) against-them

כְּסָת֜וֹת עַ֣ל ׀ כָּל־ אַצִּילֵ֣י יָדַ֗י וְעֹשׂ֧וֹת הַמִּסְפָּח֛וֹת עַל־ רֹ֥אשׁ
head for the-veils and-ones-making hands-of-me wrists-of all-of on magic-charms

---

10" 'Because they lead my people astray, saying, "Peace," when there is no peace, and because, when a flimsy wall is built, they cover it with whitewash, 11therefore tell those who cover it with whitewash that it is going to fall. Rain will come in torrents, and I will send hailstones hurtling down, and violent winds will burst forth. 12When the wall collapses, will people not ask you, "Where is the whitewash you covered it with?"

13" 'Therefore this is what the Sovereign LORD says: In my wrath I will unleash a violent wind, and in my anger hailstones and torrents of rain will fall with destructive fury. 14I will tear down the wall you have covered with whitewash and will level it to the ground so that its foundation will be laid bare. When it[y] falls, you will be destroyed in it; and you will know that I am the LORD. 15So I will spend my wrath against the wall and against those who covered it with whitewash. I will say to you, "The wall is gone and so are those who whitewashed it, 16those prophets of Israel who prophesied to Jerusalem and saw visions of peace for her when there was no peace, declares the Sovereign LORD." '

17"Now, son of man, set your face against the daughters of your people who prophesy out of their own imagination. Prophesy against them 18and say, 'This is what the Sovereign LORD says: Woe to the women who sew magic charms on all their wrists and make veils of various lengths for

y14 Or *the city*

*16 Most mss have *dagesh* in the *nun* (הַנִּ).

כָּל־ קוֹמָה לְצוֹדֵד נְפָשׁוֹת הַנְּפָשׁוֹת תְּצוֹדֵדְנָה לְעַמִּי
of-people-of-me will-you-ensnare the-lives lives to-ensnare length every-of

וּנְפָשׁוֹת לָכֶנָה תְחַיֶּינָה׃ וַתְּחַלֶּלְנָה אֹתִי אֶל־ עַמִּי
people-of-me among me now-you-profaned (19) will-you-preserve of-you but-lives

בְּשַׁעֲלֵי שְׂעֹרִים וּבִפְתוֹתֵי לֶחֶם לְהָמִית נְפָשׁוֹת אֲשֶׁר לֹא־
not who lives to-kill bread and-for-scraps-of barleys for-handfuls-of

תְמוּתֶנָה וּלְחַיּוֹת נְפָשׁוֹת אֲשֶׁר לֹא־ תִחְיֶינָה בְּכַזֶּבְכֶם
by-to-lie-you they-should-live not who lives and-to-spare they-should-die

לְעַמִּי שֹׁמְעֵי כָזָב׃ לָכֵן כֹּה־ אָמַר ׀ אֲדֹנָי יְהוִה
Yahweh Sovereign he-says this therefore (20) lie ones-listening-of to-people-of-me

הִנְנִי אֶל־ כִּסְּתוֹתֵיכֶנָה אֲשֶׁר אַתֵּנָה מְצֹדְדוֹת שָׁם אֶת־ הַנְּפָשׁוֹת
the-peoples *** there ones-ensnaring you which magic-charms-of-you against see-I!

לְפֹרְחוֹת וְקָרַעְתִּי אֹתָם מֵעַל זְרוֹעֹתֵיכֶם וְשִׁלַּחְתִּי
and-I-will-set-free arms-of-you from-on them and-I-will-tear like-ones-flying

אֶת־ הַנְּפָשׁוֹת אֲשֶׁר אַתֶּם מְצֹדְדוֹת אֶת־ נְפָשִׁים לְפֹרְחֹת׃
like-ones-flying peoples *** ones-ensnaring you that the-peoples ***

וְקָרַעְתִּי אֶת־ מִסְפְּחֹתֵיכֶם וְהִצַּלְתִּי אֶת־ עַמִּי
people-of-me *** and-I-will-save veils-of-you *** and-I-will-tear-off (21)

מִיֶּדְכֶן וְלֹא־ יִהְיוּ עוֹד בְּיֶדְכֶן לִמְצוּדָה
as-prey in-power-of-you longer they-will-be and-not from-hand-of-you

וִידַעְתֶּן כִּי־ אֲנִי יְהוָה׃ יַעַן הַכְאוֹת לֵב־ צַדִּיק שֶׁקֶר
lie righteous heart-of to-dishearten because (22) Yahweh I that then-you-will-know

וַאֲנִי לֹא הִכְאַבְתִּיו וּלְחַזֵּק יְדֵי רָשָׁע לְבִלְתִּי־ שׁוּב
to-turn not wicked hands-of and-to-encourage I-brought-grief-him not when-I

מִדַּרְכּוֹ הָרָע לְהַחֲיֹתוֹ׃ לָכֵן שָׁוְא לֹא
not falsehood therefore (23) to-save-life-of-him the-evil from-way-of-him

תֶחֱזֶינָה וְקֶסֶם לֹא־ תִקְסַמְנָה עוֹד
longer you-will-practice-divination not and-divination you-will-see-vision

וְהִצַּלְתִּי אֶת־ עַמִּי מִיֶּדְכֶן וִידַעְתֶּן כִּי־ אֲנִי יְהוָה׃
Yahweh I that then-you-will-know from-hand-of-you people-of-me *** and-I-will-save

וַיָּבוֹא אֵלַי אֲנָשִׁים מִזִּקְנֵי יִשְׂרָאֵל וַיֵּשְׁבוּ לְפָנָי׃
in-front-of-me and-they-sat Israel from-elders-of men to-me and-he-came (14:1)

וַיְהִי דְבַר־ יְהוָה אֵלַי לֵאמֹר׃ בֶּן־ אָדָם הָאֲנָשִׁים הָאֵלֶּה
the-these the-men man son-of (3) to-say to-me Yahweh word-of then-he-came (2)

הֶעֱלוּ גִלּוּלֵיהֶם עַל־ לִבָּם וּמִכְשׁוֹל עֲוֺנָם
wickedness-of-them and-stumbling-block-of heart-of-them in idols-of-them they-set-up

נָתְנוּ נֹכַח פְּנֵיהֶם הַאִדָּרֹשׁ אִדָּרֵשׁ לָהֶם׃
by-them should-I-be-inquired to-be-inquired? faces-of-them before they-put

their heads in order to ensnare people. Will you ensnare the lives of my people but preserve your own? [19]You have profaned me among my people for a few handfuls of barley and scraps of bread. By lying to my people, who listen to lies, you have killed those who should not have died and have spared those who should not live.

[20]" 'Therefore this is what the Sovereign LORD says: I am against your magic charms with which you ensnare people like birds and I will tear them from your arms; I will set free the people that you ensnare like birds. [21]I will tear off your veils and save my people from your hands, and they will no longer fall prey to your power. Then you will know that I am the LORD. [22]Because you disheartened the righteous with your lies, when I had brought them no grief, and because you encouraged the wicked not to turn from their evil ways and so save their lives, [23]therefore you will no longer see false visions or practice divination. I will save my people from your hands. And then you will know that I am the LORD.' "

*Idolaters Condemned*

14 Some of the elders of Israel came to me and sat down in front of me. [2]Then the word of the LORD came to me: [3]"Son of man, these men have set up idols in their hearts and put wicked stumbling blocks before their faces. Should I let them inquire of

לָכֵן דַּבֵּר־אוֹתָם וְאָמַרְתָּ אֲלֵיהֶם כֹּה־אָמַר ׀ אֲדֹנָי יְהוִה
Yahweh Sovereign he-says this to-them and-you-tell to-them speak! therefore (4)

אִישׁ אִישׁ מִבֵּית יִשְׂרָאֵל אֲשֶׁר יַעֲלֶה אֶת־גִּלּוּלָיו אֶל־לִבּוֹ
heart-of-him in idols-of-him *** he-sets-up when Israel of-house-of anyone anyone

וּמִכְשׁוֹל עֲוֺנוֹ יָשִׂים נֹכַח פָּנָיו וּבָא
then-he-goes faces-of-him before he-puts wickedness-of-him and-stumbling-block-of

אֶל־הַנָּבִיא אֲנִי יְהוָה נַעֲנֵיתִי לוֹ בָה° בְּרֹב גִּלּוּלָיו׃
idols-of-him with-greatness-of coming to-him I-will-answer Yahweh I the-prophet to

לְמַעַן תְּפֹשׂ אֶת־בֵּית־יִשְׂרָאֵל בְּלִבָּם אֲשֶׁר נָזֹרוּ
they-deserted who to-heart-of-them Israel house-of *** to-recapture so-that (5)

מֵעָלַי בְּגִלּוּלֵיהֶם כֻּלָּם׃ לָכֵן אֱמֹר ׀ אֶל־בֵּית יִשְׂרָאֵל
Israel house-of to say! therefore (6) all-of-them for-idols-of-them from-with-me

כֹּה אָמַר אֲדֹנָי יְהוִה שׁוּבוּ וְהָשִׁיבוּ מֵעַל גִּלּוּלֵיכֶם וּמֵעַל
and-from-with idols-of-you from-with and-turn! repent! Yahweh Sovereign he-says this

כָּל־תּוֹעֲבֹתֵיכֶם הָשִׁיבוּ פְנֵיכֶם׃ כִּי אִישׁ אִישׁ
anyone anyone when (7) faces-of-you turn! detestable-practices-of-you all-of

מִבֵּית יִשְׂרָאֵל וּמֵהַגֵּר אֲשֶׁר־יָגוּר בְּיִשְׂרָאֵל וְיִנָּזֵר
when-he-separates-himself in-Israel he-lives who or-of-the-alien Israel of-house-of

מֵאַחֲרַי וְיַעַל גִּלּוּלָיו אֶל־לִבּוֹ וּמִכְשׁוֹל
and-stumbling-block-of heart-of-him in idols-of-him and-he-sets-up from-after-me

עֲוֺנוֹ יָשִׂים נֹכַח פָּנָיו וּבָא אֶל־הַנָּבִיא לִדְרָשׁ־
to-inquire the-prophet to then-he-goes faces-of-him before he-puts wickedness-of-him

לוֹ בִי אֲנִי יְהוָה נַעֲנֶה־לּוֹ בִּי׃ וְנָתַתִּי
and-I-will-set (8) by-myself to-him I-will-answer Yahweh I of-me through-him

פָּנַי בָּאִישׁ הַהוּא וַהֲשִׂמֹתִיהוּ לְאוֹת וְלִמְשָׁלִים
and-as-bywords as-example and-I-will-make-him the-that against-the-man faces-of-me

וְהִכְרַתִּיו מִתּוֹךְ עַמִּי וִידַעְתֶּם כִּי־אֲנִי יְהוָה׃
Yahweh I that then-you-will-know people-of-me from-midst-of and-I-will-cut-off-him

וְהַנָּבִיא כִי־יְפֻתֶּה וְדִבֶּר דָּבָר אֲנִי יְהוָה פִּתֵּיתִי
I-enticed Yahweh I prophecy and-he-utters he-is-enticed if and-the-prophet (9)

אֵת הַנָּבִיא הַהוּא וְנָטִיתִי אֶת־יָדִי עָלָיו
against-him hand-of-me *** and-I-will-stretch-out the-that the-prophet ***

וְהִשְׁמַדְתִּיו מִתּוֹךְ עַמִּי יִשְׂרָאֵל׃ וְנָשְׂאוּ
and-they-will-bear (10) Israel people-of-me from-among and-I-will-destroy-him

עֲוֺנָם כַּעֲוֺן הַדֹּרֵשׁ כַּעֲוֺן הַנָּבִיא יִהְיֶה׃
he-will-be the-prophet so-guilt-of the-one-consulting as-guilt-of guilt-of-them

לְמַעַן לֹא־יִתְעוּ עוֹד בֵּית־יִשְׂרָאֵל מֵאַחֲרַי וְלֹא־
or-not from-after-me Israel house-of longer they-will-stray not so-that (11)

me at all? [4]Therefore speak to them and tell them, 'This is what the Sovereign LORD says: When any Israelite sets up idols in his heart and puts a wicked stumbling block before his face and then goes to a prophet, I the LORD will answer him myself in keeping with his great idolatry. [5]I will do this to recapture the hearts of the people of Israel, who have all deserted me for their idols.'

[6]"Therefore say to the house of Israel, 'This is what the Sovereign LORD says: Repent! Turn from your idols and renounce all your detestable practices!

[7]" 'When any Israelite or any alien living in Israel separates himself from me and sets up idols in his heart and puts a wicked stumbling block before his face and then goes to a prophet to inquire of me, I the LORD will answer him myself. [8]I will set my face against that man and make him an example and a byword. I will cut him off from my people. Then you will know that I am the LORD.

[9]" 'And if the prophet is enticed to utter a prophecy, I the LORD have enticed that prophet, and I will stretch out my hand against him and destroy him from among my people Israel. [10]They will bear their guilt—the prophet will be as guilty as the one who consults him. [11]Then the people of Israel will no longer stray from me, nor will they defile

°4 ק בא

יִטַּמְּאוּ עוֹד בְּכָל־ פִּשְׁעֵיהֶם וְהָיוּ לִי
to-me and-they-will-be sins-of-them with-all-of anymore they-will-defile-themselves

לְעָם וַאֲנִי אֶהְיֶה לָהֶם לֵאלֹהִים נְאֻם אֲדֹנָי יְהוִה׃
Yahweh Sovereign declaration-of as-God to-them I-will-be and-I as-people

וַיְהִי דְבַר־ יְהוָה אֵלַי לֵאמֹר׃ בֶּן־אָדָם אֶרֶץ כִּי תֶחֱטָא־
she-sins if country man son-of (13) to-say to-me Yahweh word-of and-he-came (12)

לִי לִמְעָל־ מַעַל וְנָטִיתִי יָדִי עָלֶיהָ
against-her hand-of-me and-I-stretch-out unfaithfulness to-be-unfaithful against-me

וְשָׁבַרְתִּי לָהּ מַטֵּה־לָחֶם וְהִשְׁלַחְתִּי־ בָהּ רָעָב וְהִכְרַתִּי מִמֶּנָּה
of-her and-I-kill famine upon-her and-I-send food supply-of of-her and-I-cut-off

אָדָם וּבְהֵמָה׃ וְהָיוּ שְׁלֹשֶׁת הָאֲנָשִׁים הָאֵלֶּה בְּתוֹכָהּ נֹחַ
Noah in-midst-of-her the-these the-men three-of if-they-were (14) and-animal man

דָּנִאֵל° וְאִיּוֹב הֵמָּה בְצִדְקָתָם יְנַצְּלוּ נַפְשָׁם
self-of-them they-could-save by-righteousness-of-them they and-Job Daniel

נְאֻם אֲדֹנָי יְהוִה׃ לוּ־חַיָּה רָעָה אַעֲבִיר בָּאָרֶץ
through-the-country I-send wild beast if (15) Yahweh Sovereign declaration-of

וְשִׁכְּלָתָּה וְהָיְתָה שְׁמָמָה מִבְּלִי עוֹבֵר
one-passing-through with-no desolation and-she-becomes and-she-leaves-childless-her

מִפְּנֵי הַחַיָּה׃ שְׁלֹשֶׁת הָאֲנָשִׁים הָאֵלֶּה בְּתוֹכָהּ חַי־אָנִי
I alive in-midst-of-her the-these the-men three-of (16) the-beast because-of

נְאֻם אֲדֹנָי יְהוִה אִם־בָּנִים וְאִם־ בָּנוֹת יַצִּילוּ הֵמָּה
they they-could-save daughters or-not sons not Yahweh Sovereign declaration-of

לְבַדָּם יִנָּצֵלוּ וְהָאָרֶץ תִּהְיֶה שְׁמָמָה׃ אוֹ חֶרֶב
sword or (17) desolation she-would-be but-the-land they-would-be-saved alone-they

אָבִיא עַל־ הָאָרֶץ הַהִיא וְאָמַרְתִּי חֶרֶב תַּעֲבֹר בָּאָרֶץ
through-the-land let-her-pass sword and-I-say the-that the-country against I-bring

וְהִכְרַתִּי מִמֶּנָּה אָדָם וּבְהֵמָה׃ וּשְׁלֹשֶׁת הָאֲנָשִׁים הָאֵלֶּה בְּתוֹכָהּ
in-midst-of-her the-these the-men if-three-of (18) and-animal man of-her and-I-kill

חַי־אָנִי נְאֻם אֲדֹנָי יְהוִה לֹא יַצִּילוּ בָּנִים וּבָנוֹת כִּי
but or-daughters sons they-could-save not Yahweh Sovereign declaration-of I alive

הֵם לְבַדָּם יִנָּצֵלוּ׃ אוֹ דֶּבֶר אֲשַׁלַּח אֶל־ הָאָרֶץ הַהִיא
the-that the-land into I-send plague or (19) they-would-be-saved alone-they they

וְשָׁפַכְתִּי חֲמָתִי עָלֶיהָ בְּדָם לְהַכְרִית מִמֶּנָּה אָדָם וּבְהֵמָה׃
and-animal man of-her to-kill through-bloodshed upon-her wrath-of-me and-I-pour-out

וְנֹחַ דָּנִאֵל° וְאִיּוֹב בְּתוֹכָהּ חַי־אָנִי נְאֻם אֲדֹנָי
Sovereign declaration-of I alive in-midst-of-her and-Job Daniel even-Noah (20)

יְהוִה אִם־ בֵּן אִם־ בַּת יַצִּילוּ הֵמָּה בְצִדְקָתָם
by-righteousness-of-them they they-could-save daughter nor son neither Yahweh

°14 ק דניאל
°20 ק דניאל

themselves anymore with all their sins. They will be my people, and I will be their God, declares the Sovereign LORD.' "

*Judgment Inescapable*

[12]The word of the LORD came to me: [13]"Son of man, if a country sins against me by being unfaithful and I stretch out my hand against it to cut off its food supply and send famine upon it and kill its men and their animals, [14]even if these three men—Noah, Daniel[a] and Job—were in it, they could save only themselves by their righteousness, declares the Sovereign LORD.

[15]"Or if I send wild beasts through that country and they leave it childless and it becomes desolate so that no one can pass through it because of the beasts, [16]as surely as I live, declares the Sovereign LORD, even if these three men were in it, they could not save their own sons or daughters. They alone would be saved, but the land would be desolate.

[17]"Or if I bring a sword against that country and say, 'Let the sword pass throughout the land,' and I kill its men and their animals, [18]as surely as I live, declares the Sovereign LORD, even if these three men were in it, they could not save their own sons or daughters. They alone would be saved.

[19]"Or if I send a plague into that land and pour out my wrath upon it through bloodshed, killing its men and their animals, [20]as surely as I live, declares the Sovereign LORD, even if Noah, Daniel and Job were in it, they could save neither son nor daughter. They

[a]14 Or *Danel;* the Hebrew spelling may suggest a person other than the prophet Daniel; also in verse 20.

יַצִּ֥ילוּ נַפְשָֽׁם׃ כִּי֩ כֹ֨ה אָמַ֜ר אֲדֹנָ֣י יְהוִ֗ה אַף֩ כִּֽי־
indeed how! Yahweh Sovereign he-says this for (21) self-of-them they-could-save

אַרְבַּ֨עַת שְׁפָטַ֜י ׀ הָרָעִ֗ים חֶ֠רֶב וְרָעָ֞ב וְחַיָּ֤ה רָעָה֙
wild and-beast and-famine sword the-dreadful-ones judgments-of-me four-of

וָדֶ֔בֶר שִׁלַּ֖חְתִּי אֶל־יְרוּשָׁלִָ֑ם לְהַכְרִ֥ית מִמֶּ֖נָּה אָדָ֥ם וּבְהֵמָֽה׃ וְהִנֵּ֨ה
yet-see! (22) and-animal man of-her to-kill Jerusalem against I-send and-plague

נֽוֹתְרָה־ בָּ֜הּ פְּלֵטָ֗ה הַֽמּוּצָאִים֙ בָּנִ֣ים וּבָנ֔וֹת
and-daughters sons the-ones-being-brought-out survivor in-her she-will-remain

הִנָּ֤ם יוֹצְאִים֙ אֲלֵיכֶ֔ם וּרְאִיתֶ֥ם אֶת־ דַּרְכָּ֖ם וְאֶת־ עֲלִילוֹתָ֑ם
actions-of-them and conduct-of-them *** when-you-see to-you ones-coming see-they!

וְנִחַמְתֶּ֗ם עַל־ הָֽרָעָה֙ אֲשֶׁ֤ר הֵבֵ֙אתִי֙ עַל־ יְר֣וּשָׁלִַ֔ם אֵ֛ת
*** Jerusalem upon I-brought that the-disaster regarding then-you-will-be-consoled

כָּל־ אֲשֶׁ֥ר הֵבֵ֖אתִי עָלֶֽיהָ׃ וְנִחֲמ֣וּ אֶתְכֶ֔ם כִּֽי־ תִרְא֥וּ אֶת־
*** you-see when you and-they-will-console (23) upon-her I-brought that all

דַּרְכָּ֖ם וְאֶת־ עֲלִילוֹתָ֑ם וִֽידַעְתֶּ֗ם כִּי֩ לֹ֨א חִנָּ֜ם עָשִׂ֗יתִי
I-did without-cause not that for-you-will-know actions-of-them and conduct-of-them

אֵ֛ת כָּל־אֲשֶׁר־עָשִׂ֥יתִי בָ֖הּ נְאֻ֖ם אֲדֹנָ֥י יְהוִֽה׃ וַיְהִ֥י דְבַר־
word-of and-he-came (15:1) Yahweh Sovereign declaration-of in-her I-did that all ***

יְהוָ֖ה אֵלַ֥י לֵאמֹֽר׃ בֶּן־ אָדָ֕ם מַה־יִּהְיֶ֥ה עֵֽץ־ הַגֶּ֖פֶן מִכָּל־
better-than-any-of the-vine wood-of he-is how? man son-of (2) to-say to-me Yahweh

עֵ֑ץ הַזְּמוֹרָ֕ה אֲשֶׁ֥ר הָיָ֖ה בַּעֲצֵ֥י הַיָּֽעַר׃ הֲיֻקַּ֤ח מִמֶּ֙נּוּ֙ עֵ֔ץ
wood from-him is-he-taken? (3) the-forest on-trees-of he-is that the-branch wood

לַעֲשׂ֖וֹת לִמְלָאכָ֑ה אִם־ יִקְח֤וּ מִמֶּ֙נּוּ֙ יָתֵ֔ד לִתְל֥וֹת עָלָ֖יו כָּל־ כֶּֽלִי׃
thing any-of on-him to-hang peg from-him they-take or into-anything to-make

הִנֵּ֥ה לָאֵ֖שׁ נִתַּ֣ן לְאָכְלָ֑ה אֵ֣ת שְׁנֵ֣י קְצוֹתָ֞יו אָכְלָ֤ה
she-burns ends-of-him both-of *** as-fuel he-is-thrown on-the-fire see! (4)

הָאֵשׁ֙ וְתוֹכ֣וֹ נָחָ֔ר הֲיִצְלַ֖ח לִמְלָאכָֽה׃ הִנֵּ֗ה
see! (5) for-anything is-he-useful? he-is-charred and-middle-of-him the-fire

בִּֽהְיוֹתוֹ֙ תָמִ֔ים לֹ֥א יֵעָשֶׂ֖ה לִמְלָאכָ֑ה אַ֞ף כִּֽי־ אֵ֤שׁ אֲכָלַ֙תְהוּ֙
she-burned-him fire when how! for-anything he-was-useful not whole when-to-be-him

וַיֵּחָ֔ר וְנַעֲשָׂ֥ה ע֖וֹד לִמְלָאכָֽה׃ לָכֵ֗ן
therefore (6) into-something again then-how-can-he-be-made and-he-is-charred

כֹּ֤ה אָמַר֙ אֲדֹנָ֣י יְהוִ֔ה כַּאֲשֶׁ֨ר עֵֽץ־ הַגֶּ֜פֶן בְּעֵ֣ץ הַיַּ֔עַר
the-forest among-tree-of the-vine wood-of just-as Yahweh Sovereign he-says this

אֲשֶׁר־ נְתַתִּ֥יו לָאֵ֖שׁ לְאָכְלָ֑ה כֵּ֣ן נָתַ֔תִּי אֶת־ יֹשְׁבֵ֖י יְרוּשָׁלִָֽם׃
Jerusalem ones-living-of *** I-will-treat so as-fuel for-the-fire I-gave-him that

וְנָתַתִּ֣י אֶת־ פָּנַי֮ בָּהֶם֒ מֵהָאֵ֣שׁ יָצָ֔אוּ
they-came-out from-the-fire against-them faces-of-me *** and-I-will-set (7)

would save only themselves by their righteousness.

[21] "For this is what the Sovereign LORD says: How much worse will it be when I send against Jerusalem my four dreadful judgments—sword and famine and wild beasts and plague—to kill its men and their animals! [22] Yet there will be some survivors—sons and daughters who will be brought out of it. They will come to you, and when you see their conduct and their actions, you will be consoled regarding the disaster I have brought upon Jerusalem—every disaster I have brought upon it. [23] You will be consoled when you see their conduct and their actions, for you will know that I have done nothing in it without cause, declares the Sovereign LORD."

*Jerusalem, A Useless Vine*

15 The word of the LORD came to me: [2] "Son of man, how is the wood of a vine better than that of a branch on any of the trees in the forest? [3] Is wood ever taken from it to make anything useful? Do they make pegs from it to hang things on? [4] And after it is thrown on the fire as fuel and the fire burns both ends and chars the middle, is it then useful for anything? [5] If it was not useful for anything when it was whole, how much less can it be made into something useful when the fire has burned it and it is charred?

[6] "Therefore this is what the Sovereign LORD says: As I have given the wood of the vine among the trees of the forest as fuel for the fire, so will I treat the people living in Jerusalem. [7] I will set my face against them. Although they have come out of the fire, the fire

וְהָאֵשׁ תֹּאכְלֵם וִידַעְתֶּם כִּי־אֲנִי יְהוָה בְּשׂוּמִי

when-to-set-me Yahweh I that and-you-will-know she-will-consume-them yet-the-fire

אֶת־פָּנַי בָּהֶם׃ וְנָתַתִּי אֶת־הָאָרֶץ שְׁמָמָה יַעַן

because desolation the-land *** and-I-will-make (8) against-them faces-of-me ***

מָעֲלוּ מַעַל נְאֻם אֲדֹנָי יְהוִה׃ וַיְהִי

and-he-came (16:1) Yahweh Sovereign declaration-of unfaithfulness they-were-unfaithful

דְבַר־יְהוָה אֵלַי לֵאמֹר׃ בֶּן־אָדָם הוֹדַע אֶת־יְרוּשָׁלִַם אֶת־

with Jerusalem *** confront! man son-of (2) to-say to-me Yahweh word-of

תּוֹעֲבֹתֶיהָ׃ וְאָמַרְתָּ כֹּה־אָמַר אֲדֹנָי יְהוִה לִירוּשָׁלִַם

to-Jerusalem Yahweh Sovereign he-says this and-you-say (3) detestable-practices-of-her

מְכֹרֹתַיִךְ וּמֹלְדֹתַיִךְ מֵאֶרֶץ הַכְּנַעֲנִי אָבִיךְ הָאֱמֹרִי

the-Amorite father-of-you the-Canaanite in-land-of and-births-of-you ancestries-of-you

וְאִמֵּךְ חִתִּית׃ וּמוֹלְדוֹתַיִךְ בְּיוֹם הוּלֶּדֶת אֹתָךְ

you to-be-born on-day-of and-births-of-you (4) the-Hittite and-mother-of-you

לֹא־כָרַּת שָׁרֵּךְ וּבְמַיִם לֹא־רֻחַצְתְּ לְמִשְׁעִי

for-cleaning you-were-washed not or-with-waters cord-of-you he-was-cut not

וְהָמְלֵחַ לֹא הֻמְלַחַתְּ וְהָחְתֵּל לֹא

not or-to-be-wrapped you-were-rubbed-with-salt not or-to-be-rubbed-with-salt

חֻתָּלְתְּ׃ לֹא־חָסָה עָלַיִךְ עַיִן לַעֲשׂוֹת לָךְ אַחַת מֵאֵלֶּה

of-these one for-you to-do eye to-you she-pitied not (5) you-were-wrapped

לְחֻמְלָה עָלָיִךְ וַתֻּשְׁלְכִי אֶל־פְּנֵי הַשָּׂדֶה

the-field open-parts-of into rather-you-were-thrown on-you to-have-compassion

בְּגֹעַל נַפְשֵׁךְ בְּיוֹם הֻלֶּדֶת אֹתָךְ׃ וָאֶעֱבֹר עָלַיִךְ

by-you then-I-passed (6) you to-be-born on-day-of self-of-you for-despising-of

וָאֶרְאֵךְ מִתְבּוֹסֶסֶת בְּדָמָיִךְ וָאֹמַר לָךְ בְּדָמַיִךְ חֲיִי

live! in-bloods-of-you to-you and-I-said in-bloods-of-you kicking and-I-saw-you

וָאֹמַר לָךְ בְּדָמַיִךְ חֲיִי׃ רְבָבָה כְּצֶמַח הַשָּׂדֶה

the-field like-plant-of multitude (7) live! in-bloods-of-you to-you and-I-said

נְתַתִּיךְ וַתִּרְבִּי וַתִּגְדְּלִי וַתָּבֹאִי בַּעֲדִי עֲדָיִים

jewels into-jewel-of and-you-became and-you-developed and-you-grew-up I-made-you

שָׁדַיִם נָכֹנוּ וּשְׂעָרֵךְ צִמֵּחַ וְאַתְּ עֵרֹם וְעֶרְיָה׃

and-bareness nakedness even-you he-grew and-hair-of-you they-were-formed breasts-of-you

וָאֶעֱבֹר עָלַיִךְ וָאֶרְאֵךְ וְהִנֵּה עִתֵּךְ עֵת דֹּדִים

loves time-of time-of-you and-see! and-I-looked-at-you by-you then-I-passed (8)

וָאֶפְרֹשׂ כְּנָפִי עָלַיִךְ וָאֲכַסֶּה עֶרְוָתֵךְ

nakedness-of-you and-I-covered over-you corner-of-garment-of-me so-I-spread

וָאֶשָּׁבַע לָךְ וָאָבוֹא בִבְרִית אֹתָךְ נְאֻם אֲדֹנָי

Sovereign declaration-of with-you into-covenant and-I-entered to-you and-I-gave-oath

will yet consume them. And when I set my face against them, you will know that I am the LORD. [8]I will make the land desolate because they have been unfaithful, declares the Sovereign LORD."

*An Allegory of Unfaithful Jerusalem*

16 The word of the LORD came to me: [2]"Son of man, confront Jerusalem with her detestable practices [3]and say, 'This is what the Sovereign LORD says to Jerusalem: Your ancestry and birth were in the land of the Canaanites; your father was an Amorite and your mother a Hittite. [4]On the day you were born your cord was not cut, nor were you washed with water to make you clean, nor were you rubbed with salt or wrapped in cloths. [5]No one looked on you with pity or had compassion enough to do any of these things for you. Rather, you were thrown out into the open field, for on the day you were born you were despised.

[6]" 'Then I passed by and saw you kicking about in your blood, and as you lay there in your blood I said to you, "Live!"[b] [7]I made you grow like a plant of the field. You grew up and developed and became the most beautiful of jewels.[c] Your breasts were formed and your hair grew, you who were naked and bare.

[8]" 'Later I passed by, and when I looked at you and saw that you were old enough for love, I spread the corner of my garment over you and covered your nakedness. I gave you my solemn oath and entered into a covenant with you, declares the Sovereign LORD, and

[b]6 A few Hebrew manuscripts, Septuagint and Syriac; most Hebrew manuscripts *"Live!" And as you lay there in your blood I said to you, "Live!"*

[c]7 Or *became mature*

יְהוָה *וַתִּהְיִי לִי׃ וָאֶרְחָצֵךְ בַּמַּיִם וָאֶשְׁטֹף
and-I-washed with-the-waters and-I-bathed-you (9) to-me and-you-became Yahweh

דָּמַיִךְ מֵעָלָיִךְ וָאֲסֻכֵךְ בַּשָּׁמֶן׃ וָאַלְבִּישֵׁךְ
and-I-clothed-you (10) with-the-ointment and-I-put-on-you from-on-you bloods-of-you

רִקְמָה וָאֶנְעֲלֵךְ תָּחַשׁ וָאֶחְבְּשֵׁךְ
and-I-dressed-you leather and-I-put-sandals-on-you embroidered-dress

בַּשֵּׁשׁ וַאֲכַסֵּךְ מֶשִׁי׃ וָאֶעְדֵּךְ עֶדִי
jewelry and-I-adorned-you (11) costly-garment and-I-covered-you in-the-fine-linen

וָאֶתְּנָה צְמִידִים עַל־ יָדַיִךְ וְרָבִיד עַל־ גְּרוֹנֵךְ׃ וָאֶתֵּן
and-I-put (12) neck-of-you around and-necklace arms-of-you on bracelets and-I-put

נֶזֶם עַל־ אַפֵּךְ וַעֲגִילִים עַל־ אָזְנָיִךְ וַעֲטֶרֶת תִּפְאֶרֶת בְּרֹאשֵׁךְ׃
on-head-of-you beauty and-crown-of ears-of-you on and-earrings nose-of-you on ring

וַתַּעְדִּי זָהָב וָכֶסֶף וּמַלְבּוּשֵׁךְ °שֵׁשִׁי
fine-linen and-clothing-of-you and-silver gold so-you-were-adorned-with (13)

וָמֶשִׁי וְרִקְמָה סֹלֶת וּדְבַשׁ וָשֶׁמֶן °אָכָלְתִּי
you-ate and-olive-oil and-honey fine-flour and-embroidered-cloth and-costly-fabric

וַתִּיפִי בִּמְאֹד מְאֹד וַתִּצְלְחִי לִמְלוּכָה׃ וַיֵּצֵא
and-he-spread (14) to-queenship and-you-rose very to-very and-you-became-beautiful

לָךְ שֵׁם בַּגּוֹיִם בְּיָפְיֵךְ כִּי כָּלִיל הוּא
he perfect because on-account-of-beauty-of-you among-the-nations fame of-you

בַּהֲדָרִי אֲשֶׁר־ שַׂמְתִּי עָלַיִךְ נְאֻם אֲדֹנָי יְהוָה׃
Yahweh Sovereign declaration-of to-you I-gave that because-of-splendor-of-me

וַתִּבְטְחִי בְיָפְיֵךְ וַתִּזְנִי עַל־ שְׁמֵךְ
fame-of-you by and-you-became-prositItute in-beauty-of-you but-you-trusted (15)

וַתִּשְׁפְּכִי אֶת־ תַּזְנוּתַיִךְ עַל־ כָּל־ עוֹבֵר לוֹ־ יֶהִי׃
he-became to-him one-passing-by any-of on favors-of-you *** and-you-lavished

וַתִּקְחִי מִבְּגָדַיִךְ וַתַּעֲשִׂי־ לָךְ בָּמוֹת
high-places for-you and-you-made from-garments-of-you and-you-took (16)

טְלֻאוֹת וַתִּזְנִי עֲלֵיהֶם לֹא בָאוֹת וְלֹא
or-not ones-happening not on-them and-you-carried-on-prosititution ones-being-gaudy

יִהְיֶה׃ וַתִּקְחִי כְּלֵי תִפְאַרְתֵּךְ מִזְּהָבִי
of-gold-of-me finery-of-you jewels-of also-you-took (17) he-should-occur

וּמִכַּסְפִּי אֲשֶׁר נָתַתִּי לָךְ וַתַּעֲשִׂי־ לָךְ צַלְמֵי זָכָר
male idols-of for-you and-you-made to-you I-gave that and-of-silver-of-me

וַתִּזְנִי־ בָם׃ וַתִּקְחִי אֶת־ בִּגְדֵי
clothes-of *** and-you-took (18) with-them and-you-engaged-in-prosititution

רִקְמָתֵךְ וַתְּכַסִּים וְשַׁמְנִי וּקְטָרְתִּי °נָתַתְּי
you-offered and-incense-of-me and-oil-of-me and-you-put-on-them embroidery-of-you

you became mine.

9 " 'I bathed[d] you with water and washed the blood from you and put ointments on you. 10 I clothed you with an embroidered dress and put leather sandals on you. I dressed you in fine linen and covered you with costly garments. 11 I adorned you with jewelry: I put bracelets on your arms and a necklace around your neck, 12 and I put a ring on your nose, earrings on your ears and a beautiful crown on your head. 13 So you were adorned with gold and silver; your clothes were of fine linen and costly fabric and embroidered cloth. Your food was fine flour, honey and olive oil. You became very beautiful and rose to be a queen. 14 And your fame spread among the nations on account of your beauty, because the splendor I had given you made your beauty perfect, declares the Sovereign LORD.

15 " 'But you trusted in your beauty and used your fame to become a prostitute. You lavished your favors on anyone who passed by and your beauty became his.[e] 16 You took some of your garments to make gaudy high places, where you carried on your prostitution. Such things should not happen, nor should they ever occur. 17 You also took the fine jewelry I gave you, the jewelry made of my gold and silver, and you made for yourself male idols and engaged in prostitution with them. 18 And you took your embroidered clothes to put on them,

[d]9 Or *I had bathed*
[e]15 Most Hebrew manuscripts; one Hebrew manuscript (see some Septuagint manuscripts) *by. Such a thing should not happen*

*8 Most mss bind these words with *maqqeph* (ותהיי־לי).

°*13a* ק שש
°*13b* ק אכלת
°*18* ק נתת

לִפְנֵיהֶם׃ וְלַחְמִי אֲשֶׁר־נָתַתִּי לָךְ סֹלֶת וָשֶׁמֶן
and-olive-oil fine-flour for-you I-provided that also-food-of-me (19) before-them

וּדְבַשׁ הֶאֱכַלְתִּיךְ וּנְתַתִּיהוּ לִפְנֵיהֶם לְרֵיחַ
as-fragrance-of before-them also-you-offered-him I-gave-to-eat-you and-honey

נִיחֹחַ וַיֶּהִי נְאֻם אֲדֹנָי יְהוִה׃ וַתִּקְחִי
and-you-took (20) Yahweh Sovereign declaration-of and-he-happened soothing-incense

אֶת־בָּנַיִךְ וְאֶת־בְּנוֹתַיִךְ אֲשֶׁר יָלַדְתְּ לִי וַתִּזְבָּחִים
and-you-sacrificed-them to-me you-bore whom daughters-of-you and sons-of-you ***

לָהֶם לֶאֱכוֹל הַמְעַט מִתַּזְנֻתֵךְ׃ וַתִּשְׁחֲטִי
and-you-slaughtered (21) from-prostitutions-of-you not-enough? to-be-food to-them

אֶת־בָּנַי וַתִּתְּנִים בְּהַעֲבִיר אוֹתָם לָהֶם׃ וְאֵת
and (22) to-them them to-make-pass-through and-you-gave-them children-of-me ***

כָּל־תּוֹעֲבֹתַיִךְ וְתַזְנֻתַיִךְ לֹא זָכַרְתִּי אֶת־
*** you-remembered not and-prostitutions-of-you detestable-practices-of-you all-of

יְמֵי נְעוּרָיִךְ בִּהְיוֹתֵךְ עֵרֹם וְעֶרְיָה מִתְבּוֹסֶסֶת בְּדָמֵךְ
in-blood-of-you kicking-about and-bareness nakedness when-to-be-you youths-of-you days-of

הָיִית׃ וַיְהִי אַחֲרֵי כָּל־רָעָתֵךְ אוֹי אוֹי לָךְ
to-you woe! woe! wickedness-of-you all-of in-addition-of and-he-was (23) you-were

נְאֻם אֲדֹנָי יְהוִה׃ וַתִּבְנִי־לָךְ גֶּב* וַתַּעֲשִׂי־
and-you-made mound for-you then-you-built (24) Yahweh Sovereign declaration-of

לָךְ רָמָה בְּכָל־רְחוֹב׃ אֶל־כָּל־רֹאשׁ דֶּרֶךְ
street head-of every-of at (25) public-square in-every-of lofty-shrine for-you

בָּנִית רָמָתֵךְ וַתְּתַעֲבִי אֶת־יָפְיֵךְ וַתְּפַשְּׂקִי
and-you-spread-wide beauty-of-you *** and-you-degraded lofty-shrine-of-you you-built

אֶת־רַגְלַיִךְ לְכָל־עוֹבֵר וַתַּרְבִּי אֶת־תַּזְנֻתֵךְ׃
promiscuities-of-you *** and-you-increased one-passing-by to-any-of feet-of-you ***

וַתִּזְנִי אֶל־בְּנֵי־מִצְרַיִם שְׁכֵנַיִךְ
neighbors-of-you Egypt sons-of with and-you-engaged-in-prosititution (26)

גִּדְלֵי בָשָׂר וַתַּרְבִּי אֶת־תַּזְנֻתֵךְ לְהַכְעִיסֵנִי׃
to-provoke-to-anger-me promiscuities-of-you *** and-you-increased lust ones-great-of

וְהִנֵּה נָטִיתִי יָדִי עָלַיִךְ וָאֶגְרַע חֻקֵּךְ
territory-of-you and-I-reduced against-you hand-of-me I-stretched-out so-see! (27)

וָאֶתְּנֵךְ בְּנֶפֶשׁ שֹׂנְאוֹתַיִךְ בְּנוֹת פְּלִשְׁתִּים
Philistines daughters-of ones-being-enemies-of-you to-greed-of and-I-gave-over-you

הַנִּכְלָמוֹת מִדַּרְכֵּךְ זִמָּה׃ וַתִּזְנִי
also-you-engaged-in-prosititution (28) lewdness by-conduct-of-you the-ones-being-shocked

אֶל־בְּנֵי אַשּׁוּר מִבִּלְתִּי שָׂבְעָתֵךְ וַתִּזְנִים
also-you-engaged-in-prosititution-them satiation-of-you because-no Assyria sons-of with

and you offered my oil and incense before them. 19 Also the food
I provided for you—the fine flour,
olive oil and honey I gave you to
eat—you offered as fragrant incense before them. That is what
happened, declares the Sovereign
LORD.
20 " 'And you took your sons and
daughters whom you bore to me
and sacrificed them as food to the
idols. Was your prostitution not
enough? 21 You slaughtered my
children and sacrificed them[f] to
the idols. 22 In all your detestable
practices and your prostitution
you did not remember the days of
your youth, when you were naked
and bare, kicking about in your
blood.
23 " 'Woe! Woe to you, declares
the Sovereign LORD. In addition to
all your other wickedness, 24 you
built a mound for yourself and
made a lofty shrine in every public square. 25 At the head of every
street you built your lofty shrines
and degraded your beauty, offering your body with increasing
promiscuity to anyone who
passed by. 26 You engaged in prostitution with the Egyptians, your
lustful neighbors, and provoked
me to anger with your increasing
promiscuity. 27 So I stretched out
my hand against you and reduced
your territory; I gave you over to
the greed of your enemies, the
daughters of the Philistines, who
were shocked by your lewd conduct. 28 You engaged in prostitution with the Assyrians too, because you were insatiable; and

f21 Or *and made them pass through ⌊the fire⌋*

*24 Most mss have *qamets* under the *gimel* (גָּב).

°20 ק מתזנותיך ; °22 ק זכרת

°25 ק תזנותיך

וְגַם לֹא שָׂבָעַתְּ׃ וַתַּרְבִּי אֶת־ תַּזְנוּתֵךְ
promiscuity-of-you *** then-you-increased (29) you-were-satisfied not even-then

אֶל־אֶרֶץ כְּנַעַן כַּשְׂדִּימָה וְגַם־ בְּזֹאת לֹא שָׂבָעַתְּ׃ מָה
how! (30) you-were-satisfied not with-this but-even to-Chaldea merchant land-of to

אֲמֻלָה לִבָּתֵךְ נְאֻם אֲדֹנָי יְהוִה בַּעֲשׂוֹתֵךְ אֶת־ כָּל־
all-of *** when-to-do-you Yahweh Sovereign declaration-of will-of-you being-weak

אֵלֶּה מַעֲשֵׂה אִשָּׁה־ זוֹנָה שַׁלָּטֶת׃ בִּבְנוֹתַיִךְ גַּבֵּךְ
mound-of-you when-to-build-you (31) brazen one-being-prostitute woman act-of these

בְּרֹאשׁ כָּל־ דֶּרֶךְ וְרָמָתֵךְ עָשִׂיתִי בְּכָל־ רְחוֹב
public-square in-every-of you-made and-lofty-shrine-of-you street every-of at-head-of

וְלֹא־ הָיִיתִי כַּזּוֹנָה לְקַלֵּס אֶתְנָן׃ הָאִשָּׁה
the-wife (32) payment to-scorn like-the-one-being-prostitute you-were then-not

הַמְנָאֶפֶת תַּחַת אִישָׁהּ תִּקַּח אֶת־ זָרִים׃
ones-being-strangers *** you-prefer husband-of-you instead-of the-one-being-adulterous

לְכָל־ זֹנוֹת יִתְּנוּ־ נֵדֶה וְאַתְּ נָתַתְּ אֶת־
*** you-give but-you gift they-give ones-being-prostitutes to-every-of (33)

נְדָנַיִךְ לְכָל־ מְאַהֲבַיִךְ וַתִּשְׁחֳדִי אוֹתָם לָבוֹא אֵלַיִךְ
to-you to-come them and-you-bribe ones-loving-you to-all-of gifts-of-you

מִסָּבִיב בְּתַזְנוּתָיִךְ׃ וַיְהִי־ בָךְ הֵפֶךְ מִן־
from opposite with-you and-he-is (34) for-illicit-favors-of-you from-everywhere

הַנָּשִׁים בְּתַזְנוּתַיִךְ וְאַחֲרַיִךְ לֹא זוּנָּה
favor-was-sought not and-after-you in-prostitutions-of-you the-women

וּבְתִתֵּךְ אֶתְנָן וְאֶתְנַן לֹא נִתַּן־ לָךְ וַתְּהִי לְהֶפֶךְ׃
as-opposite so-you-are to-you he-is-given not and-payment payment and-for-to-give-you

לָכֵן זוֹנָה שִׁמְעִי דְּבַר־ יְהוָה׃ כֹּה־ אָמַר אֲדֹנָי
Sovereign he-says this (36) Yahweh word-of hear! one-being-prostitute therefore (35)

יְהוִה יַעַן הִשָּׁפֵךְ נְחֻשְׁתֵּךְ וַתִּגָּלֶה עֶרְוָתֵךְ
nakedness-of-you and-you-exposed wealth-of-you to-be-poured-out because Yahweh

בְּתַזְנוּתַיִךְ עַל־ מְאַהֲבָיִךְ וְעַל כָּל־ גִּלּוּלֵי
idols-of all-of and-because-of ones-loving-you with in-promiscuities-of-you

תוֹעֲבוֹתַיִךְ וְכִדְמֵי בָנַיִךְ אֲשֶׁר נָתַתְּ לָהֶם׃
to-them you-gave that children-of-you and-because-of-bloods-of detestable-ones-of-you

לָכֵן הִנְנִי מְקַבֵּץ אֶת־ כָּל־ מְאַהֲבַיִךְ אֲשֶׁר עָרַבְתְּ
you-found-pleasure whom ones-loving-you all-of *** gathering see-I! therefore (37)

עֲלֵיהֶם וְאֵת כָּל־ אֲשֶׁר אָהַבְתְּ עַל כָּל־ אֲשֶׁר שָׂנֵאת וְקִבַּצְתִּי
and-I-will-gather you-hated whom all as-well-as you-loved whom all indeed with-them

אֹתָם עָלַיִךְ מִסָּבִיב וְגִלֵּיתִי עֶרְוָתֵךְ אֲלֵהֶם
in-front-of-them nakedness-of-you and-I-will-strip from-all-around against-you them

°31a ק עשית
°31b ק היית

even after that, you still were not satisfied. [29]Then you increased your promiscuity to include Babylonia,[g] a land of merchants, but even with this you were not satisfied.

[30]" 'How weak-willed you are, declares the Sovereign LORD, when you do all these things, acting like a brazen prostitute! [31]When you built your mounds at the head of every street and made your lofty shrines in every public square, you were unlike a prostitute, because you scorned payment.

[32]" 'You adulterous wife! You prefer strangers to your own husband! [33]Every prostitute receives a fee, but you give gifts to all your lovers, bribing them to come to you from everywhere for your illicit favors. [34]So in your prostitution you are the opposite of others; no one runs after you for your favors. You are the very opposite, for you give payment and none is given to you.

[35]" 'Therefore, you prostitute, hear the word of the LORD! [36]This is what the Sovereign LORD says: Because you poured out your wealth[h] and exposed your nakedness in your promiscuity with your lovers, and because of all your detestable idols, and because you gave them your children's blood, [37]therefore I am going to gather all your lovers, with whom you found pleasure, those you loved as well as those you hated. I will gather them against you from all around and will strip you in front

[g]29 Or *Chaldea*
[h]36 Or *lust*

וְרָאוּ אֶת־ כָּל־ עֶרְוָתֵךְ׃ וּשְׁפַטְתִּיךְ
and-I-will-sentence-you (38) nakedness-of-you all-of *** and-they-will-see

מִשְׁפְּטֵי נֹאֲפוֹת וְשֹׁפְכֹת דָּם
blood and-ones-shedding-of women-committing-adultery punishments-of

וּנְתַתִּיךְ דַּם חֵמָה וְקִנְאָה׃ וְנָתַתִּי
then-I-will-give (39) and-jealous-anger wrath blood-of and-I-will-bring-upon-you

אוֹתָךְ בְּיָדָם וְהָרְסוּ גַבֵּךְ וְנִתְּצוּ
and-they-will-destroy mound-of-you and-they-will-tear-down into-hand-of-them you

רָמֹתַיִךְ וְהִפְשִׁיטוּ אוֹתָךְ בְּגָדַיִךְ וְלָקְחוּ כְּלֵי
jewels-of and-they-will-take clothes-of-you you and-they-will-strip-off lofty-shrines-of-you

תִפְאַרְתֵּךְ וְהִנִּיחוּךְ עֵירֹם וְעֶרְיָה׃ וְהֶעֱלוּ
and-they-will-bring (40) and-bareness nakedness and-they-will-leave-you finery-of-you

עָלַיִךְ קָהָל וְרָגְמוּ אוֹתָךְ בָּאֶבֶן וּבִתְּקוּךְ
and-they-will-hack-to-pieces-you with-the-stone you and-they-will-stone mob against-you

בְּחַרְבוֹתָם׃ וְשָׂרְפוּ בָתַּיִךְ בָּאֵשׁ
with-fire houses-of-you and-they-will-burn-down (41) with-swords-of-them

וְעָשׂוּ־ בָךְ שְׁפָטִים לְעֵינֵי נָשִׁים רַבּוֹת
many-ones women before-eyes-of punishments on-you and-they-will-inflict

וְהִשְׁבַּתִּיךְ מִזּוֹנָה וְגַם־ אֶתְנַן לֹא תִתְּנִי־ עוֹד׃
longer you-will-pay not payment and-also from-being-prostitute and-I-will-stop-you

וַהֲנִחֹתִי חֲמָתִי בָּךְ וְסָרָה
and-she-will-turn-away against-you wrath-of-me then-I-will-make-subside (42)

קִנְאָתִי מִמֵּךְ וְשָׁקַטְתִּי וְלֹא אֶכְעַס עוֹד׃
longer I-will-be-angry and-not and-I-will-be-calm from-you jealous-anger-of-me

יַעַן אֲשֶׁר לֹא־ °זָכַרְתִּי אֶת־ יְמֵי נְעוּרַיִךְ וַתִּרְגְּזִי־
and-you-enraged youths-of-you days-of *** you-remembered not that because (43)

לִי בְּכָל־ אֵלֶּה וְגַם־ אֲנִי הֵא דַּרְכֵּךְ׀ בְּרֹאשׁ נָתַתִּי
I-will-bring on-head doing-of-you surely! I and-also these with-all-of to-me

נְאֻם אֲדֹנָי יְהוִה וְלֹא °עָשִׂיתִי אֶת־ הַזִּמָּה עַל כָּל־
all-of to the-lewdness *** you-added and-not Yahweh Sovereign declaration-of

תּוֹעֲבֹתָיִךְ׃ הִנֵּה כָּל־ הַמֹּשֵׁל עָלַיִךְ
about-you the-one-quoting-proverb every-of see! (44) detestable-practices-of-you

יִמְשֹׁל לֵאמֹר כְּאִמָּה בִּתָּהּ׃ בַּת־
daughter-of (45) daughter-of-her like-mother to-say he-will-quote-proverb

אִמֵּךְ אַתְּ גֹּעֶלֶת אִישָׁהּ וּבָנֶיהָ וַאֲחוֹת
and-sister-of and-children-of-her husband-of-her one-despising you mother-of-you

אֲחוֹתֵךְ אַתְּ אֲשֶׁר גָּעֲלוּ* אַנְשֵׁיהֶן וּבְנֵיהֶן
and-children-of-them husbands-of-them they-despised who you sister-of-you

of them, and they will see all your
nakedness. [38]I will sentence you to
the punishment of women who
commit adultery and who shed
blood; I will bring upon you the
blood vengeance of my wrath and
jealous anger. [39]Then I will hand
you over to your lovers, and they
will tear down your mounds and
destroy your lofty shrines. They
will strip you of your clothes and
take your fine jewelry and leave
you naked and bare. [40]They will
bring a mob against you, who will
stone you and hack you to pieces
with their swords. [41]They will
burn down your houses and inflict punishment on you in the
sight of many women. I will put a
stop to your prostitution, and you
will no longer pay your lovers.
[42]Then my wrath against you will
subside and my jealous anger will
turn away from you; I will be calm
and no longer angry.

[43]" 'Because you did not remember the days of your youth but enraged me with all these things, I
will surely bring down on your
head what you have done, declares the Sovereign LORD. Did
you not add lewdness to all your
other detestable practices?

[44]" 'Everyone who quotes proverbs will quote this proverb about
you: "Like mother, like daughter."
[45]You are a true daughter of your
mother, who despised her husband and her children; and you
are a true sister of your sisters,
who despised their husbands and

*45 Most mss accent the final syllable (געלוֹ).

°43a זכרת ק; °43b עשית ק

אִמְּכֶן חִתִּית וַאֲבִיכֶן אֱמֹרִי׃ וַאֲחוֹתֵךְ הַגְּדוֹלָה
the-older and-sister-of-you (46) Amorite and-father-of-you Hittite mother-of-you

שֹׁמְרוֹן הִיא וּבְנוֹתֶיהָ הַיּוֹשֶׁבֶת עַל־ שְׂמֹאולֵךְ וַאֲחוֹתֵךְ
and-sister-of-you north-of-you to the-one-living with-daughters-of-her she Samaria

הַקְּטַנָּה מִמֵּךְ הַיּוֹשֶׁבֶת מִימִינֵךְ סְדֹם וּבְנוֹתֶיהָ׃
with-daughters-of-her Sodom to-south-of-you the-one-living than-you the-younger

וְלֹא בְדַרְכֵיהֶן הָלַכְתְּ וּבְתוֹעֲבוֹתֵיהֶן עָשִׂיתִי
you-copied and-to-detestable-practices-of-them you-walked in-ways-of-them only-not (47)

כִּמְעַט קָט וַתַּשְׁחִתִי מֵהֵן בְּכָל־ דְּרָכָיִךְ׃
ways-of-you in-all-of more-than-they but-you-became-depraved very as-soon

חַי־ אָנִי נְאֻם אֲדֹנָי יְהוִה אִם־ עָשְׂתָה סְדֹם אֲחוֹתֵךְ
sister-of-you Sodom she-did never Yahweh Sovereign declaration-of I alive (48)

הִיא וּבְנוֹתֶיהָ כַּאֲשֶׁר עָשִׂית אַתְּ וּבְנוֹתָיִךְ׃ הִנֵּה־ זֶה
this see! (49) and-daughters-of-you you you-did as-what and-daughters-of-her she

הָיָה עֲוֹן סְדֹם אֲחוֹתֵךְ גָּאוֹן שִׂבְעַת־ לֶחֶם וְשַׁלְוַת
and-unconcerned-of food overfed-of arrogance sister-of-you Sodom sin-of he-was

הַשְׁקֵט הָיָה לָהּ וְלִבְנוֹתֶיהָ וְיַד־ עָנִי וְאֶבְיוֹן
and-needy poor and-hand-of and-to-daughters-of-her to-her he-was to-be-unconcerned

לֹא הֶחֱזִיקָה׃ וַתִּגְבְּהֶינָה וַתַּעֲשֶׂינָה תוֹעֵבָה לְפָנָי
before-me detestable-thing and-they-did and-they-were-haughty (50) she-helped not

וָאָסִיר אֶתְהֶן כַּאֲשֶׁר רָאִיתִי׃ וְשֹׁמְרוֹן כַּחֲצִי חַטֹּאתַיִךְ
sins-of-you as-half-of and-Samaria (51) *you-saw just-as with-them so-I-did-away

לֹא חָטָאָה וַתַּרְבִּי אֶת־ תּוֹעֲבוֹתַיִךְ מֵהֵנָּה
more-than-they detestable-things-of-you *** and-you-made-more she-committed-sin not

וַתְּצַדְּקִי אֶת־ אֲחוֹתֵךְ בְּכָל־ תּוֹעֲבוֹתַיִךְ אֲשֶׁר
that detestable-things-of-you by-all-of sisters-of-you *** and-you-made-righteous

עָשִׂיתִי׃ גַּם־ אַתְּ שְׂאִי כְלִמָּתֵךְ אֲשֶׁר פִּלַּלְתְּ
you-furnished-justification for disgrace-of-you bear! you now (52) you-did

לַאֲחוֹתֵךְ בְּחַטֹּאתַיִךְ אֲשֶׁר־ הִתְעַבְתְּ מֵהֵן
more-than-they you-made-vile that because-of-sins-of-you for-sisters-of-you

תִּצְדַּקְנָה מִמֵּךְ וְגַם־ אַתְּ בּוֹשִׁי וּשְׂאִי כְלִמָּתֵךְ
disgrace-of-you and-bear! be-ashamed! you so-then more-than-you they-appear-righteous

בְּצַדֶּקְתֵּךְ אַחְיוֹתֵךְ׃ וְשַׁבְתִּי
however-I-will-restore (53) sisters-of-you for-to-make-appear-righteous-you

אֶת־ שְׁבִיתְהֶן אֶת־ שְׁבִית סְדֹם וּבְנוֹתֶיהָ וְאֶת־ שְׁבִית
fortune-of and and-daughters-of-her Sodom fortune-of *** fortune-of-them ***

שֹׁמְרוֹן וּבְנוֹתֶיהָ וּשְׁבִית שְׁבִיתַיִךְ בְּתוֹכֲהֶנָה׃
with-among-them fortunes-of-you and-fortune-of and-daughters-of-her Samaria

their children. Your mother was a Hittite and your father an Amorite. [46]Your older sister was Samaria, who lived to the north of you with her daughters; and your younger sister, who lived to the south of you with her daughters, was Sodom. [47]You not only walked in their ways and copied their detestable practices, but in all your ways you soon became more depraved than they. [48]As surely as I live, declares the Sovereign LORD, your sister Sodom and her daughters never did what you and your daughters have done.

[49]" 'Now this was the sin of your sister Sodom: She and her daughters were arrogant, overfed and unconcerned; they did not help the poor and needy. [50]They were haughty and did detestable things before me. Therefore I did away with them as you have seen. [51]Samaria did not commit half the sins you did. You have done more detestable things than they, and have made your sisters seem righteous by all these things you have done. [52]Bear your disgrace, for you have furnished some justification for your sisters. Because your sins were more vile than theirs, they appear more righteous than you. So then, be ashamed and bear your disgrace, for you have made your sisters appear righteous.

[53]" 'However, I will restore the fortunes of Sodom and her daughters and of Samaria and her daughters, and your fortunes

*50 The NIV reads this as the archaic second person feminine singular ending.

°47 עשית ק; °51a אחותיך ק
°51b עשית ק; °53a,b,c שבות ק

לְמַעַן תִּשְׂאִי כְלִמָּתֵךְ וְנִכְלַמְתְּ מִכֹּל אֲשֶׁר עָשִׂית
you-did that of-all and-you-may-be-ashamed disgrace-of-you you-may-bear so-that (54)

בְּנַחֲמֵךְ אֹתָן׃ וַאֲחוֹתַיִךְ סְדֹם וּבְנוֹתֶיהָ
with-daughters-of-her Sodom and-sisters-of-you (55) them when-to-comfort-you

תָּשֹׁבְןָ לְקַדְמָתָן וְשֹׁמְרוֹן וּבְנוֹתֶיהָ
with-daughters-of-her and-Samaria to-former-state-of-them they-will-return

תָּשֹׁבְןָ לְקַדְמָתָן וְאַתְּ וּבְנוֹתַיִךְ תְּשֻׁבֶינָה
you-will-return and-daughters-of-you and-you to-former-state-of-them they-will-return

לְקַדְמַתְכֶן׃ וְלוֹא הָיְתָה סְדֹם אֲחוֹתֵךְ לִשְׁמוּעָה
as-one-mentioned sister-of-you Sodom she-would-be and-not (56) to-former-state-of-you

בְּפִיךְ בְּיוֹם גְּאוֹנָיִךְ׃ בְּטֶרֶם תִּגָּלֶה
she-was-uncovered at-before (57) prides-of-you in-day-of by-mouth-of-you

רָעָתֵךְ כְּמוֹ עֵת חֶרְפַּת בְּנוֹת־ אֲרָם וְכָל־ סְבִיבוֹתֶיהָ
ones-around-her and-all-of Aram daughters-of scorn-of time-of so wickedness-of-you

בְּנוֹת פְּלִשְׁתִּים הַשָּׁאטוֹת אוֹתָךְ מִסָּבִיב׃ אֶת־ זִמָּתֵךְ
lewdness-of-you *** (58) at-around you the-ones-despising Philistines daughters-of

וְאֶת־ תּוֹעֲבוֹתַיִךְ אַתְּ נְשָׂאתִים נְאֻם יְהוָה׃
Yahweh declaration-of you-will-bear-them you detestable-practices-of-you and

כִּי כֹה אָמַר אֲדֹנָי יְהוִה וְעָשִׂית אוֹתָךְ כַּאֲשֶׁר
just-as with-you indeed-I-will-deal Yahweh Sovereign he-says this indeed (59)

עָשִׂית אֲשֶׁר־ בָּזִית אָלָה לְהָפֵר בְּרִית׃ וְזָכַרְתִּי
yet-I-will-remember (60) covenant to-break oath you-despised because you-deserve

אֲנִי אֶת־ בְּרִיתִי אוֹתָךְ בִּימֵי נְעוּרָיִךְ וַהֲקִמוֹתִי
and-I-will-establish youths-of-you in-days-of with-you covenant-of-me *** I

לָךְ בְּרִית עוֹלָם׃ וְזָכַרְתְּ אֶת־ דְּרָכַיִךְ
ways-of-you *** then-you-will-remember (61) everlasting covenant-of with-you

וְנִכְלַמְתְּ בְּקַחְתֵּךְ אֶת־ אֲחוֹתַיִךְ הַגְּדֹלוֹת
the-ones-older sisters-of-you *** when-to-receive-you and-you-will-be-ashamed

מִמֵּךְ אֶל־ הַקְּטַנּוֹת מִמֵּךְ וְנָתַתִּי אֶתְהֶן לָךְ לְבָנוֹת
as-daughters to-you them and-I-will-give than-you the-ones-younger with than-you

וְלֹא מִבְּרִיתֵךְ׃ וַהֲקִימוֹתִי אֲנִי אֶת־ בְּרִיתִי
covenant-of-me *** I so-I-will-establish (62) on-basis-of-covenant-of-you but-not

אִתָּךְ וְיָדַעַתְּ כִּי־ אֲנִי יְהוָה׃ לְמַעַן תִּזְכְּרִי
you-will-remember so-that (63) Yahweh I that and-you-will-know with-you

וָבֹשְׁתְּ וְלֹא יִהְיֶה־ לָּךְ עוֹד פִּתְחוֹן פֶּה
mouth opening-of again of-you he-will-be and-never and-you-will-be-ashamed

מִפְּנֵי כְּלִמָּתֵךְ בְּכַפְּרִי־ לָךְ לְכָל־ אֲשֶׁר עָשִׂית
you-did that for-all for-you when-to-make-atonement-me humiliation-of-you because-of

along with them, [54]so that you
may bear your disgrace and be
ashamed of all you have done in
giving them comfort. [55]And your
sisters, Sodom with her daughters
and Samaria with her daughters,
will return to what they were before; and you and your daughters
will return to what you were before. [56]You would not even mention your sister Sodom in the day
of your pride, [57]before your
wickedness was uncovered. Even
so, you are now scorned by the
daughters of Edom[i] and all her
neighbors and the daughters of
the Philistines—all those around
you who despise you. [58]You will
bear the consequences of your
lewdness and your detestable
practices, declares the LORD.

[59]" 'This is what the Sovereign
LORD says: I will deal with you as
you deserve, because you have despised my oath by breaking the
covenant. [60]Yet I will remember
the covenant I made with you in
the days of your youth, and I will
establish an everlasting covenant
with you. [61]Then you will remember your ways and be ashamed
when you receive your sisters,
both those who are older than you
and those who are younger. I will
give them to you as daughters, but
not on the basis of my covenant
with you. [62]So I will establish my
covenant with you, and you will
know that I am the LORD. [63]Then,
when I make atonement for you
for all you have done, you will
remember and be ashamed and
never again open your mouth because of your humiliation, declares the Sovereign LORD.' "

[i]57 Many Hebrew manuscripts and Syriac; most Hebrew manuscripts, Septuagint and Vulgate *Aram*

°59 ק ועשיתי

נְאֻם אֲדֹנָי יְהוִה׃ וַיְהִי דְבַר־ יְהוָה אֵלַי לֵאמֹר׃
to-say to-me Yahweh word-of and-he-came (17:1) Yahweh Sovereign declaration-of

בֶּן־ אָדָם חוּד חִידָה וּמְשֹׁל מָשָׁל אֶל־ בֵּית
house-of to parable and-tell-parable! allegory set-forth-allegory! man son-of (2)

יִשְׂרָאֵל׃ וְאָמַרְתָּ כֹּה־ אָמַר ׀ אֲדֹנָי יְהוִה הַנֶּשֶׁר הַגָּדוֹל גְּדוֹל
powerful-of the-great the-eagle Yahweh Sovereign he-says this and-you-say (3) Israel

הַכְּנָפַיִם אֶרֶךְ הָאֵבֶר מָלֵא הַנּוֹצָה אֲשֶׁר־ לוֹ הָרִקְמָה
the-varied-color to-him that the-plumage full the-feather long-of the-wings

בָּא אֶל־ הַלְּבָנוֹן וַיִּקַּח אֶת־צַמֶּרֶת הָאָרֶז׃ אֶת רֹאשׁ
topmost-of *** (4) the-cedar top-of *** and-he-took-hold the-Lebanon to he-came

יְנִיקוֹתָיו קָטָף וַיְבִיאֵהוּ אֶל־ אֶרֶץ כְּנַעַן בְּעִיר
in-city-of merchant land-of to and-he-carried-away-him he-broke-off shoots-of-him

רֹכְלִים שָׂמוֹ׃ וַיִּקַּח מִזֶּרַע הָאָרֶץ וַיִּתְּנֵהוּ
and-he-put-him the-land from-seed-of and-he-took (5) he-planted-him ones-trading

בִּשְׂדֵה־ זָרַע קָח עַל־ מַיִם רַבִּים צַפְצָפָה שָׂמוֹ׃
he-planted-him willow abundant-ones waters by he-took fertility in-soil-of

וַיִּצְמַח וַיְהִי לְגֶפֶן סֹרַחַת שִׁפְלַת קוֹמָה לִפְנוֹת
to-turn height low-of one-spreading as-vine and-he-became and-he-sprouted (6)

דָּלִיּוֹתָיו אֵלָיו וְשָׁרָשָׁיו תַּחְתָּיו יִהְיוּ וַתְּהִי
so-she-became they-remained under-him but-roots-of-him toward-him branches-of-him

לְגֶפֶן וַתַּעַשׂ בַּדִּים וַתְּשַׁלַּח פֹּארוֹת׃ וַיְהִי
but-he-was (7) leafy-boughs and-she-put-out branches and-she-produced as-vine

נֶשֶׁר־אֶחָד גָּדוֹל גְּדוֹל כְּנָפַיִם וְרַב־ נוֹצָה וְהִנֵּה הַגֶּפֶן הַזֹּאת
the-this the-vine now-see! plumage and-full-of wings powerful-of great one eagle

כָּפְנָה שָׁרָשֶׁיהָ* עָלָיו וְדָלִיּוֹתָיו שִׁלְחָה־ לוֹ
to-him she-stretched-out and-branches-of-him toward-him roots-of-her she-sent-out

לְהַשְׁקוֹת אוֹתָהּ מֵעֲרֻגוֹת מַטָּעָהּ׃ אֶל־שָׂדֶה טּוֹב אֶל־ מַיִם
waters by good soil in (8) planting-of-her from-plots-of her to-get-water

רַבִּים הִיא שְׁתוּלָה לַעֲשׂוֹת עָנָף וְלָשֵׂאת פֶּרִי לִהְיוֹת לְגֶפֶן
as-vine to-become fruit to-bear branch to-produce being-planted she abundant-ones

אַדָּרֶת׃ אֱמֹר כֹּה אָמַר אֲדֹנָי יְהוִה תִּצְלָח ׀ הֲלוֹא אֶת־
*** not? will-she-thrive Yahweh Sovereign he-says this say! (9) splendid

שָׁרָשֶׁיהָ יְנַתֵּק וְאֶת־ פִּרְיָהּ ׀ יְקוֹסֵס וְיָבֵשׁ כָּל־
all-of so-he-withers he-will-strip-off fruit-of-her and he-will-uproot roots-of-her

טַרְפֵּי צִמְחָהּ תִּיבָשׁ וְלֹא־ בִזְרֹעַ גְּדוֹלָה וּבְעַם־ רָב
many or-by-people strong by-arm and-not she-will-wither growth-of-her new-ones-of

לְמַשְׂאוֹת אוֹתָהּ מִשָּׁרָשֶׁיהָ׃ וְהִנֵּה שְׁתוּלָה הֲתִצְלָח
will-she-thrive? being-transplanted but-see! (10) by-roots-of-her her to-pull-up

*Two Eagles and a Vine*

17 The word of the LORD came
to me: [2]"Son of man, set
forth an allegory and tell the house
of Israel a parable. [3]Say to them,
'This is what the Sovereign LORD
says: A great eagle with powerful
wings, long feathers and full
plumage of varied colors came to
Lebanon. Taking hold of the top of
a cedar, [4]he broke off its topmost
shoot and carried it away to a land
of merchants, where he planted it
in a city of traders.
[5]" 'He took some of the seed of
your land and put it in fertile soil.
He planted it like a willow by
abundant water, [6]and it sprouted
and became a low, spreading vine.
Its branches turned toward him,
but its roots remained under it. So
it became a vine and produced
branches and put out leafy
boughs.
[7]" 'But there was another great
eagle with powerful wings and
full plumage. The vine now sent
out its roots toward him from the
plot where it was planted and
stretched out its branches to him
for water. [8]It had been planted in
good soil by abundant water so
that it would produce branches,
bear fruit and become a splendid
vine.'
[9]"Say to them, 'This is what the
Sovereign LORD says: Will it
thrive? Will it not be uprooted and
stripped of its fruit so that it withers? All its new growth will wither. It will not take a strong arm or
many people to pull it up by the
roots. [10]Even if it is transplanted,

*7 Most mss have *qamets* under the *resh* (שָׁרָ).

הֲלוֹא כְגַעַת בָּהּ רוּחַ הַקָּדִים תִּיבַשׁ יָבֹשׁ
to-wither she-will-wither the-east-wind wind-of against-her when-to-strike not?

עַל־עֲרֻגֹת צִמְחָהּ תִּיבָשׁ׃ וַיְהִי דְבַר־יְהוָה אֵלַי
to-me Yahweh word-of and-he-came (11) she-will-wither growth-of-her plots-of in

לֵאמֹר׃ אֱמָר־נָא לְבֵית הַמֶּרִי הֲלֹא יְדַעְתֶּם מָה־אֵלֶּה אֱמֹר
say! these what? you-know not? the-rebellion to-house-of now! say! (12) to-say

הִנֵּה־בָא מֶלֶךְ־בָּבֶל יְרוּשָׁלַםִ וַיִּקַּח אֶת־מַלְכָּהּ וְאֶת־
and king-of-her *** and-he-carried-off Jerusalem Babylon king-of he-went see!

שָׂרֶיהָ וַיָּבֵא אוֹתָם אֵלָיו בָּבֶלָה׃ וַיִּקַּח
then-he-took (13) to-Babylon with-him them and-he-brought nobles-of-her

מִזֶּרַע הַמְּלוּכָה וַיִּכְרֹת אִתּוֹ בְּרִית וַיָּבֵא אֹתוֹ בְּאָלָה
under-oath him and-he-put treaty with-him and-he-made the-royalty from-family-of

וְאֶת־אֵילֵי הָאָרֶץ לָקָח׃ לִהְיוֹת מַמְלָכָה שְׁפָלָה לְבִלְתִּי
not low kingdom to-be (14) he-carried-away the-land leading-men-of also

הִתְנַשֵּׂא לִשְׁמֹר אֶת־בְּרִיתוֹ לְעָמְדָהּ׃ וַיִּמְרָד־בּוֹ
against-him but-he-rebelled (15) to-survive-her treaty-of-him *** to-keep to-rise

לִשְׁלֹחַ מַלְאָכָיו מִצְרַיִם לָתֶת־לוֹ סוּסִים וְעַם־רָב הֲיִצְלָח
will-he-succeed? large and-army horses for-him to-get Egypt envoys-of-him to-send

הֲיִמָּלֵט הָעֹשֵׂה אֵלֶּה וְהֵפֵר בְּרִית וְנִמְלָט׃
yet-will-he-escape treaty and-will-he-break these the-one-doing-of will-he-escape?

חַי־אָנִי נְאֻם אֲדֹנָי יְהוִה אִם־לֹא בִּמְקוֹם הַמֶּלֶךְ
the-king in-land-of indeed surely Yahweh Sovereign declaration-of I alive (16)

הַמַּמְלִיךְ אֹתוֹ אֲשֶׁר בָּזָה אֶת־אָלָתוֹ וַאֲשֶׁר הֵפֵר אֶת־
*** he-broke and-whom oath-of-him *** he-despised whom him the-one-making-king

בְּרִיתוֹ אִתּוֹ בְתוֹךְ־בָּבֶל יָמוּת׃ וְלֹא בְחַיִל
with-army and-not (17) he-shall-die Babylon in-midst-of with-him treaty-of-him

גָּדוֹל וּבְקָהָל רָב יַעֲשֶׂה אוֹתוֹ פַרְעֹה בַּמִּלְחָמָה בִּשְׁפֹּךְ
when-to-build in-the-war Pharaoh him he-will-help great and-with-horde mighty

סֹלְלָה וּבִבְנוֹת דָּיֵק לְהַכְרִית נְפָשׁוֹת רַבּוֹת׃ וּבָזָה
and-he-despised (18) many-ones lives to-destroy siege-work and-when-to-erect ramp

אָלָה לְהָפֵר בְּרִית וְהִנֵּה נָתַן יָדוֹ וְכָל־אֵלֶּה עָשָׂה
he-did these yet-all-of hand-of-him he-gave because-see! covenant to-break oath

לֹא יִמָּלֵט׃ לָכֵן כֹּה־אָמַר אֲדֹנָי יְהוִה חַי־אָנִי
I alive Yahweh Sovereign he-says this therefore (19) he-shall-escape not

אִם־לֹא אָלָתִי אֲשֶׁר בָּזָה וּבְרִיתִי אֲשֶׁר הֵפִיר
he-broke that and-covenant-of-me he-despised that oath-of-me indeed surely

וּנְתַתִּיו בְּרֹאשׁוֹ׃ וּפָרַשְׂתִּי עָלָיו רִשְׁתִּי
net-of-me for-him and-I-will-spread (20) on-head-of-him I-will-bring-down-on-him

will it thrive? Will it not wither
completely when the east wind
strikes it—wither away in the plot
where it grew?' "
11Then the word of the LORD
came to me: 12"Say to this rebellious house, 'Do you not know
what these things mean?' Say to
them: 'The king of Babylon went
to Jerusalem and carried off her
king and her nobles, bringing
them back with him to Babylon.
13Then he took a member of the
royal family and made a treaty
with him, putting him under
oath. He also carried away the
leading men of the land, 14so that
the kingdom would be brought
low, unable to rise again, surviving only by keeping his treaty.
15But the king rebelled against him
by sending his envoys to Egypt to
get horses and a large army. Will
he succeed? Will he who does such
things escape? Will he break the
treaty and yet escape?
16" 'As surely as I live, declares
the Sovereign LORD, he shall die in
Babylon, in the land of the king
who put him on the throne,
whose oath he despised and
whose treaty he broke. 17Pharaoh
with his mighty army and great
horde will be of no help to him in
war, when ramps are built and
siege works erected to destroy
many lives. 18He despised the oath
by breaking the covenant. Because he had given his hand in
pledge and yet did all these things,
he shall not escape.
19" 'Therefore this is what the
Sovereign LORD says: As surely as
I live, I will bring down on his
head my oath that he despised
and my covenant that he broke. 20I
will spread my net for him, and he

וְנִתְפַּשׂ בִּמְצוּדָתִי וַהֲבִיאוֹתִיהוּ בָבֶלָה וְנִשְׁפַּטְתִּי
and-I-will-judge to-Babylon and-I-will-bring-him in-snare-of-me and-he-will-be-caught

אִתּוֹ שָׁם מַעֲלוֹ אֲשֶׁר מָעַל־ בִּי׃ וְאֵת
and (21) to-me he-was-unfaithful because unfaithfulness-of-him there upon-him

כָּל־ °מִבְרָחָו בְּכָל־ אֲגַפָּיו בַּחֶרֶב יִפֹּלוּ
they-will-fall by-the-sword troops-of-him with-all-of ones-who-flee-of-him all-of

וְהַנִּשְׁאָרִים לְכָל־ רוּחַ יִפָּרֵשׂוּ וִידַעְתֶּם
then-you-will-know they-will-be-scattered wind to-every-of and-the-ones-surviving

כִּי אֲנִי יְהוָה דִּבַּרְתִּי׃ כֹּה אָמַר אֲדֹנָי יְהוִה וְלָקַחְתִּי אָנִי
I indeed-I-will-take Yahweh Sovereign he-says this (22) I-spoke Yahweh I that

מִצַּמֶּרֶת הָאֶרֶז הָרָמָה וְנָתָתִּי מֵרֹאשׁ
from-topmost-of and-I-will-plant the-one-being-top the-cedar from-shoot-of

יֹנְקוֹתָיו רַךְ אֶקְטֹף וְשָׁתַלְתִּי אָנִי עַל הַר־ גָּבֹהַּ*
high mountain on I and-I-will-plant I-will-break-off tender-sprig shoots-of-him

וְתָלוּל׃ בְּהַר מְרוֹם יִשְׂרָאֵל אֶשְׁתֳּלֶנּוּ וְנָשָׂא
and-he-will-produce I-will-plant-him Israel height-of on-mountain-of (23) and-lofty

עָנָף וְעָשָׂה פֶרִי וְהָיָה לְאֶרֶז אַדִּיר וְשָׁכְנוּ
and-they-will-nest splendid as-cedar and-he-will-become fruit and-he-will-bear branch

תַחְתָּיו כֹּל צִפּוֹר כָּל־ כָּנָף בְּצֵל דָּלִיּוֹתָיו תִּשְׁכֹּנָּה׃
they-will-find-shelter branches-of-him in-shade-of wing every-of bird all-of in-him

וְיָדְעוּ כָּל־ עֲצֵי הַשָּׂדֶה כִּי אֲנִי יְהוָה הִשְׁפַּלְתִּי ׀
I-bring-down Yahweh I that the-field trees-of all-of and-they-will-know (24)

עֵץ גָּבֹהַּ* הִגְבַּהְתִּי עֵץ שָׁפָל הוֹבַשְׁתִּי עֵץ לָח וְהִפְרַחְתִּי
and-I-make-flourish green tree I-dry-up low tree and-I-make-grow-tall tall tree

עֵץ יָבֵשׁ אֲנִי יְהוָה דִּבַּרְתִּי וְעָשִׂיתִי׃ וַיְהִי דְבַר־ יְהוָה אֵלַי
to-me Yahweh word-of and-he-came (18:1) and-I-will-do I-spoke Yahweh I dry tree

לֵאמֹר׃ מַה־ לָּכֶם אַתֶּם מֹשְׁלִים אֶת־ הַמָּשָׁל הַזֶּה עַל־
about the-this the-proverb *** ones-quoting-proverb you to-you what? (2) to-say

אַדְמַת יִשְׂרָאֵל לֵאמֹר אָבוֹת יֹאכְלוּ בֹסֶר וְשִׁנֵּי הַבָּנִים
the-children and-teeth-of sour-grape they-eat fathers to-say Israel land-of

תִּקְהֶינָה׃ חַי־ אָנִי נְאֻם אֲדֹנָי יְהוִה אִם־ יִהְיֶה
he-will-be not Yahweh Sovereign declaration-of I alive (3) they-are-set-on-edge

לָכֶם עוֹד מְשֹׁל הַמָּשָׁל הַזֶּה בְּיִשְׂרָאֵל׃ הֵן כָּל־
every-of see! (4) in-Israel the-this the-proverb to-quote-proverb longer to-you

הַנְּפָשׁוֹת לִי הֵנָּה כְּנֶפֶשׁ הָאָב וּכְנֶפֶשׁ הַבֵּן
the-son and-alike-soul-of the-father alike-soul-of they to-me the-living-souls

לִי־ הֵנָּה הַנֶּפֶשׁ הַחֹטֵאת הִיא תָמוּת׃ וְאִישׁ כִּי־יִהְיֶה צַדִּיק
righteous he-is if now-man (5) she-will-die she the-one-sinning the-soul they to-me

will be caught in my snare. I will bring him to Babylon and execute judgment upon him there because he was unfaithful to me.
21All his fleeing troops will fall by the sword, and the survivors will be scattered to the winds. Then you will know that I the LORD have spoken.
22" 'This is what the Sovereign LORD says: I myself will take a shoot from the very top of a cedar and plant it; I will break off a tender sprig from its topmost shoots and plant it on a high and lofty mountain.
23On the mountain heights of Israel I will plant it; it will produce branches and bear fruit and become a splendid cedar. Birds of every kind will nest in it; they will find shelter in the shade of its branches.
24All the trees of the field will know that I the LORD bring down the tall tree and make the low tree grow tall. I dry up the green tree and make the dry tree flourish.

" 'I the LORD have spoken, and I will do it.' "

### *The Soul Who Sins Will Die*

18 The word of the LORD came to me:
2"What do you people mean by quoting this proverb about the land of Israel:

" 'The fathers eat sour grapes,
and the children's teeth are set on edge'?

3"As surely as I live, declares the Sovereign LORD, you will no longer quote this proverb in Israel.
4For every living soul belongs to me, the father as well as the son—both alike belong to me. The soul who sins is the one who will die.

5"Suppose there is a righteous man

*22, 24 Most mss have *mappiq* in the *he* (הּ־).

°21 ק מברחיו

וְעָשָׂה מִשְׁפָּט וּצְדָקָה׃ אֶל־הֶהָרִים לֹא אָכָל וְעֵינָיו לֹא
not or-eyes-of-him he-eats not the-mountains at (6) and-right justice and-he-does

נָשָׂא אֶל־גִּלּוּלֵי בֵּית יִשְׂרָאֵל וְאֶת־אֵשֶׁת רֵעֵהוּ לֹא טִמֵּה
he-defiles not neighbor-of-him wife-of or Israel house-of idols-of to he-lifts

וְאֶל־אִשָּׁה נִדָּה לֹא יִקְרָב׃ וְאִישׁ לֹא יוֹנֶה
he-oppresses not and-anyone (7) he-lies not time-of-period woman or-with

חֲבֹלָתוֹ חוֹב יָשִׁיב גְּזֵלָה לֹא יִגְזֹל לַחְמוֹ לְרָעֵב
to-hungry food-of-him he-commits-robbery not robbery he-returns loan pledge-of-him

יִתֵּן וְעֵירֹם יְכַסֶּה־בָּגֶד׃ בַּנֶּשֶׁךְ לֹא־יִתֵּן וְתַרְבִּית
or-interest he-lends not at-the-usury (8) clothing he-provides and-naked he-gives

לֹא יִקָּח מֵעָוֶל יָשִׁיב יָדוֹ מִשְׁפַּט אֱמֶת יַעֲשֶׂה
he-makes fairness judgment-of hand-of-him he-withholds from-wrong he-takes not

בֵּין אִישׁ לְאִישׁ׃ בְּחֻקּוֹתַי יְהַלֵּךְ וּמִשְׁפָּטַי שָׁמַר
he-is-careful and-laws-of-me he-follows to-decrees-of-me (9) to-man man between

לַעֲשׂוֹת אֱמֶת צַדִּיק הוּא חָיֹה יִחְיֶה נְאֻם אֲדֹנָי
Sovereign declaration-of he-will-live to-live he righteous faithfulness to-keep

יְהוִה׃ וְהוֹלִיד בֵּן־פָּרִיץ שֹׁפֵךְ דָּם וְעָשָׂה אָח
brother or-he-does blood one-shedding violent son if-he-fathers (10) Yahweh

מֵאַחַד מֵאֵלֶּה׃ וְהוּא אֶת־כָּל־אֵלֶּה לֹא עָשָׂה כִּי גַם אֶל־
at also if he-did not these any-of *** though-he (11) of-these from-one

הֶהָרִים אָכַל וְאֶת־אֵשֶׁת רֵעֵהוּ טִמֵּא׃ עָנִי וְאֶבְיוֹן
and-needy poor (12) he-defiles neighbor-of-him wife-of or he-eats the-mountains

הוֹנָה גְּזֵלוֹת גָּזָל חֲבֹל לֹא יָשִׁיב וְאֶל־הַגִּלּוּלִים
the-idols or-to he-returns not pledge he-commits-robbery robberies he-oppresses

נָשָׂא עֵינָיו תּוֹעֵבָה עָשָׂה׃ בַּנֶּשֶׁךְ נָתַן וְתַרְבִּית
and-interest he-lends at-the-usury (13) he-does detestable-thing eyes-of-him he-lifts

לָקַח וָחָי לֹא יִחְיֶה אֵת כָּל־הַתּוֹעֵבוֹת הָאֵלֶּה
the-these the-detestable-things all-of *** he-will-live not so-will-he-live he-takes

עָשָׂה מוֹת יוּמָת דָּמָיו בּוֹ יִהְיֶה׃ וְהִנֵּה
but-see! (14) he-will-be on-him bloods-of-him he-will-be-put-to-death to-die he-did

הוֹלִיד בֵּן וַיַּרְא אֶת־כָּל־חַטֹּאת אָבִיו אֲשֶׁר עָשָׂה
he-commits that father-of-him sins-of all-of *** and-he-sees son he-fathers

וַיִּרְאֶה וְלֹא יַעֲשֶׂה כָּהֵן׃ עַל־הֶהָרִים לֹא אָכָל
he-eats not the-mountains at (15) such-as-them he-does but-not and-he-sees

וְעֵינָיו לֹא נָשָׂא אֶל־גִּלּוּלֵי בֵּית יִשְׂרָאֵל אֶת־אֵשֶׁת רֵעֵהוּ
neighbor-of-him wife-of *** Israel house-of idols-of to he-lifts not or-eyes-of-him

לֹא טִמֵּא׃ וְאִישׁ לֹא הוֹנָה חֲבֹל לֹא חָבָל
he-requires-pledge not pledge he-oppresses not or-anyone (16) he-defiles not

who does what is just and
right.
6He does not eat at the
mountain shrines
or look to the idols of the
house of Israel.
He does not defile his
neighbor's wife
or lie with a woman during
her period.
7He does not oppress anyone,
but returns what he took in
pledge for a loan.
He does not commit robbery
but gives his food to the
hungry
and provides clothing for
the naked.
8He does not lend at usury
or take excessive interest.[j]
He withholds his hand from
doing wrong
and judges fairly between
man and man.
9He follows my decrees
and faithfully keeps my
laws.
That man is righteous;
he will surely live,
declares the Sovereign
LORD.

10"Suppose he has a violent son,
who sheds blood or does any of
these other things[k] 11(though the
father has done none of them):

"He eats at the mountain
shrines.
He defiles his neighbor's wife.
12He oppresses the poor and
needy.
He commits robbery.
He does not return what he
took in pledge.
He looks to the idols.
He does detestable things.
13He lends at usury and takes
excessive interest.

Will such a man live? He will not! Because he has done all these detestable things, he will surely be put to death and his blood will be on his own head.

14"But suppose this son has a son who sees all the sins his father commits, and though he sees them, he does not do such things:

15"He does not eat at the
mountain shrines
or look to the idols of the
house of Israel.
He does not defile his
neighbor's wife.
16He does not oppress anyone
or require a pledge for a
loan.

j8 Or *take interest;* similarly in verses 13 and 17
k10 Or *things to a brother*

וּגְזֵלָה לֹא גָזָל לַחְמוֹ לְרָעֵב נָתָן וְעֵרוֹם
and-naked he-gives to-hungry food-of-him he-commits-robbery not or-robbery

כִּסָּה־ בָגֶד׃ (17) מֵעָנִי הֵשִׁיב יָדוֹ נֶשֶׁךְ וְתַרְבִּית
or-interest usury hand-of-him he-withholds from-poor (17) clothing he-provides

לֹא לָקָח מִשְׁפָּטַי עָשָׂה בְּחֻקּוֹתַי הָלָךְ הוּא לֹא יָמוּת
he-will-die not he he-follows to-decrees-of-me he-keeps laws-of-me he-takes not

בַּעֲוֹן אָבִיו חָיֹה יִחְיֶה׃ (18) אָבִיו כִּי־ עָשַׁק
he-extorted because father-of-him (18) he-will-live to-live father-of-him for-sin-of

עֹשֶׁק גָּזַל גֵּזֶל אָח וַאֲשֶׁר לֹא־ טוֹב עָשָׂה בְּתוֹךְ
in-among he-did good not and-what brother robbery-of he-robbed extortion

עַמָּיו וְהִנֵּה־ מֵת בַּעֲוֹנוֹ׃ (19) וַאֲמַרְתֶּם מַדֻּעַ לֹא־
not why? yet-you-ask (19) for-sin-of-him he-will-die so-see! peoples-of-him

נָשָׂא הַבֵּן בַּעֲוֹן הָאָב וְהַבֵּן מִשְׁפָּט וּצְדָקָה עָשָׂה אֵת
*** he-did and-right justice since-the-son the-father in-guilt-of the-son he-shares

כָּל־ חֻקּוֹתַי שָׁמַר וַיַּעֲשֶׂה אֹתָם חָיֹה יִחְיֶה׃
he-will-live to-live them and-he-kept he-was-careful decrees-of-me all-of

(20) הַנֶּפֶשׁ הַחֹטֵאת הִיא תָמוּת בֵּן לֹא־ יִשָּׂא ׀ בַּעֲוֹן
in-guilt-of he-will-share not son she-will-die she the-one-sinning the-soul (20)

הָאָב וְאָב לֹא יִשָּׂא בַּעֲוֹן הַבֵּן צִדְקַת
righteousness-of the-son in-guilt-of he-will-share not and-father the-father

הַצַּדִּיק עָלָיו תִּהְיֶה וְרִשְׁעַת רָשָׁע עָלָיו
against-him the-wicked-man and-wickedness-of she-will-be to-him the-righteous-man

תִּהְיֶה׃ (21) וְהָרָשָׁע כִּי יָשׁוּב מִכָּל־ חַטֹּאתָו אֲשֶׁר
that sins-of-him from-all-of he-turns-away if but-the-wicked-man (21) she-will-be

עָשָׂה וְשָׁמַר אֶת־כָּל־ חֻקּוֹתַי וְעָשָׂה מִשְׁפָּט וּצְדָקָה חָיֹה
to-live and-right justice and-he-does decrees-of-me all-of *** and-he-keeps he-committed

יִחְיֶה לֹא יָמוּת׃ (22) כָּל־ פְּשָׁעָיו אֲשֶׁר עָשָׂה לֹא
not he-committed that offenses-of-him all-of (22) he-will-die not he-will-live

יִזָּכְרוּ לוֹ בְּצִדְקָתוֹ אֲשֶׁר־ עָשָׂה
he-did that because-of-righteous-thing-of-him against-him they-will-be-remembered

יִחְיֶה׃ (23) הֶחָפֹץ אֶחְפֹּץ מוֹת רָשָׁע נְאֻם
declaration-of wicked death-of do-I-take-pleasure to-take-pleasure? (23) he-will-live

אֲדֹנָי יְהוִה הֲלוֹא בְּשׁוּבוֹ מִדְּרָכָיו וְחָיָה׃
and-he-lives from-ways-of-him when-to-turn-him not? Yahweh Sovereign

(24) וּבְשׁוּב צַדִּיק מִצִּדְקָתוֹ וְעָשָׂה עָוֶל
sin and-he-commits from-righteousness-of-him righteous-man but-if-to-turn (24)

כְּכֹל הַתּוֹעֵבוֹת אֲשֶׁר־ עָשָׂה הָרָשָׁע יַעֲשֶׂה וָחָי
then-will-he-live he-does the-wicked-man he-does that the-detestable-things as-all-of

He does not commit robbery
but gives his food to the hungry
and provides clothing for the naked.
17 He withholds his hand from sin[l]
and takes no usury or excessive interest.
He keeps my laws and follows my decrees.

He will not die for his father's sin; he will surely live. 18 But his father will die for his own sin, because he practiced extortion, robbed his brother and did what was wrong among his people.

19 "Yet you ask, 'Why does the son not share the guilt of his father?' Since the son has done what is just and right and has been careful to keep all my decrees, he will surely live. 20 The soul who sins is the one who will die. The son will not share the guilt of the father, nor will the father share the guilt of the son. The righteousness of the righteous man will be credited to him, and the wickedness of the wicked will be charged against him.

21 "But if a wicked man turns away from all the sins he has committed and keeps all my decrees and does what is just and right, he will surely live; he will not die. 22 None of the offenses he has committed will be remembered against him. Because of the righteous things he has done, he will live. 23 Do I take any pleasure in the death of the wicked? declares the Sovereign LORD. Rather, am I not pleased when they turn from their ways and live?

24 "But if a righteous man turns from his righteousness and commits sin and does the same detestable things the wicked man does,

[l]17 Septuagint (see also verse 8); Hebrew *from the poor*

°20 ק הרשע
°21 ק חטאתיו

כָּל־ צִדְקֹתָו אֲשֶׁר־ עָשָׂה לֹא תִזָּכַרְנָה
they-will-be-remembered not he-did that righteous-things-of-him all-of

בְּמַעֲלוֹ אֲשֶׁר־ מָעַל וּבְחַטָּאתוֹ אֲשֶׁר־
that and-because-of-sin-of-him he-was-unfaithful that because-of-unfaithfulness-of-him

חָטָא בָּם יָמוּת׃ וַאֲמַרְתֶּם לֹא יִתָּכֵן דֶּרֶךְ אֲדֹנָי
Lord way-of he-is-just not yet-you-say (25) he-will-die for-them he-committed-sin

שִׁמְעוּ־נָא בֵּית יִשְׂרָאֵל הֲדַרְכִּי לֹא יִתָּכֵן הֲלֹא דַרְכֵיכֶם לֹא
not ways-of-you not? is-he-just not way-of-me? Israel house-of now! hear!

יִתָּכֵנוּ׃ בְּשׁוּב־ צַדִּיק מִצִּדְקָתוֹ וְעָשָׂה
and-he-commits from-righteousness-of-him righteous-man if-to-turn (26) they-are-just

עָוֶל וּמֵת עֲלֵיהֶם בְּעַוְלוֹ אֲשֶׁר־ עָשָׂה יָמוּת׃
he-will-die he-committed that because-of-sin-of-him for-them then-he-will-die sin

וּבְשׁוּב רָשָׁע מֵרִשְׁעָתוֹ אֲשֶׁר עָשָׂה
he-committed that from-wickedness-of-him wicked-man but-if-to-turn-away (27)

וַיַּעַשׂ מִשְׁפָּט וּצְדָקָה הוּא אֶת־ נַפְשׁוֹ יְחַיֶּה׃ וַיִּרְאֶה
because-he-considers (28) he-will-save life-of-him *** he and-right justice and-he-does

וַיָּשׁוֹב מִכָּל־ פְּשָׁעָיו אֲשֶׁר עָשָׂה חָיוֹ יִחְיֶה
he-will-live to-live he-committed that offenses-of-him from-all-of and-he-turns-away

לֹא יָמוּת׃ וְאָמְרוּ בֵּית יִשְׂרָאֵל לֹא יִתָּכֵן דֶּרֶךְ אֲדֹנָי
Lord way-of he-is-just not Israel house-of yet-they-say (29) he-will-die not

הַדְּרָכַי* לֹא יִתָּכְּנוּ† בֵּית יִשְׂרָאֵל הֲלֹא דַרְכֵיכֶם לֹא יִתָּכֵן׃
he-is-just not ways-of-you not? Israel house-of are-they-just not ways-of-me?

לָכֵן אִישׁ כִּדְרָכָיו אֶשְׁפֹּט אֶתְכֶם בֵּית יִשְׂרָאֵל
Israel house-of you I-will-judge according-to-ways-of-him each therefore (30)

נְאֻם אֲדֹנָי יְהוִה שׁוּבוּ וְהָשִׁיבוּ מִכָּל־ פִּשְׁעֵיכֶם
offenses-of-you from-all-of and-turn-away! repent! Yahweh Sovereign declaration-of

וְלֹא־ יִהְיֶה לָכֶם לְמִכְשׁוֹל עָוֺן׃ הַשְׁלִיכוּ מֵעֲלֵיכֶם אֶת־ כָּל־
all-of *** from-with-you rid! (31) sin as-downfall to-you he-will-be then-not

פִּשְׁעֵיכֶם אֲשֶׁר פְּשַׁעְתֶּם בָּם וַעֲשׂוּ לָכֶם לֵב חָדָשׁ
new heart for-you and-get! by-them you-committed-offense that offenses-of-you

וְרוּחַ חֲדָשָׁה וְלָמָּה תָמֻתוּ בֵּית יִשְׂרָאֵל׃ כִּי לֹא אֶחְפֹּץ
I-take-pleasure not for (32) Israel house-of will-you-die now-why? new and-spirit

בְּמוֹת הַמֵּת נְאֻם אֲדֹנָי יְהוִה וְהָשִׁיבוּ וִחְיוּ׃
and-live! so-repent! Yahweh Sovereign declaration-of the-one-dying in-death-of

וְאַתָּה שָׂא קִינָה אֶל־ נְשִׂיאֵי יִשְׂרָאֵל׃ וְאָמַרְתָּ מָה
what! and-you-say (2) Israel princes-of concerning lament take-up! now-you (19:1)

אִמְּךָ לְבִיָּא בֵּין אֲרָיוֹת רָבָצָה בְּתוֹךְ כְּפִרִים רִבְּתָה
she-reared young-lions in-among she-lay-down lions among lioness mother-of-you

will he live? None of the righteous things he has done will be remembered. Because of the unfaithfulness he is guilty of and because of the sins he has committed, he will die.

25 "Yet you say, 'The way of the Lord is not just.' Hear, O house of Israel: Is my way unjust? Is it not your ways that are unjust? 26 If a righteous man turns from his righteousness and commits sin, he will die for it; because of the sin he has committed he will die. 27 But if a wicked man turns away from the wickedness he has committed and does what is just and right, he will save his life. 28 Because he considers all the offenses he has committed and turns away from them, he will surely live; he will not die. 29 Yet the house of Israel says, 'The way of the Lord is not just.' Are my ways unjust, O house of Israel? Is it not your ways that are unjust?

30 "Therefore, O house of Israel, I will judge you, each one according to his ways, declares the Sovereign LORD. Repent! Turn away from all your offenses; then sin will not be your downfall. 31 Rid yourselves of all the offenses you have committed, and get a new heart and a new spirit. Why will you die, O house of Israel? 32 For I take no pleasure in the death of anyone, declares the Sovereign LORD. Repent and live!

### *A Lament for Israel's Princes*

19 "Take up a lament concerning the princes of Israel
2 and say:

" 'What a lioness was your mother
among the lions!
She lay down among the young lions

*29a Some mss have no *dagesh* in the *daleth* (הַדְּ).

†29b Most mss have no *dagesh* in the *nun* (־נּוּ).

°24 ק צדקתיו; °28 ק וישב

גּוּרֶיהָ׃ וַתַּעַל אֶחָד מִגֻּרֶיהָ כְּפִיר הָיָה
he-became strong-lion from-cubs-of-her one and-she-brought-up (3) cubs-of-her

וַיִּלְמַד לִטְרָף־טֶרֶף אָדָם אָכָל׃ וַיִּשְׁמְעוּ אֵלָיו גּוֹיִם
nations about-him and-they-heard (4) he-devoured man prey to-tear and-he-learned

בְּשַׁחְתָּם נִתְפָּשׂ וַיְבִאֻהוּ בַחַחִים אֶל־אֶרֶץ מִצְרָיִם׃
Egypt land-of to with-the-hooks and-they-led-him he-was-trapped in-pit-of-them

וַתֵּרֶא כִּי נוֹחֲלָה אָבְדָה תִּקְוָתָהּ
expectation-of-her she-was-gone she-was-unfulfilled that when-she-saw (5)

וַתִּקַּח אֶחָד מִגֻּרֶיהָ כְּפִיר שָׂמָתְהוּ׃ וַיִּתְהַלֵּךְ
and-he-prowled (6) she-made-him strong-lion from-cubs-of-her one then-she-took

בְּתוֹךְ־אֲרָיוֹת כְּפִיר הָיָה וַיִּלְמַד לִטְרָף־טֶרֶף אָדָם אָכָל׃
he-devoured man prey to-tear and-he-learned he-was strong-lion lions in-among

וַיֵּדַע אַלְמְנוֹתָיו וְעָרֵיהֶם הֶחֱרִיב
he-devastated and-towns-of-them strongholds-of-him and-he-knew (7)

וַתֵּשַׁם אֶרֶץ וּמְלֹאָהּ מִקּוֹל שַׁאֲגָתוֹ׃ וַיִּתְּנוּ
then-they-came (8) roar-of-him at-sound-of and-all-in-her land and-she-was-terrified

עָלָיו גּוֹיִם סָבִיב מִמְּדִינוֹת וַיִּפְרְשׂוּ עָלָיו רִשְׁתָּם
net-of-them for-him and-they-spread from-regions round-about nations against-him

בְּשַׁחְתָּם נִתְפָּשׂ׃ וַיִּתְּנֻהוּ בַסּוּגַר בַּחַחִים
with-the-hooks into-the-cage and-they-pulled-him (9) he-was-trapped in-pit-of-them

וַיְבִאֻהוּ אֶל־מֶלֶךְ בָּבֶל יְבִאֻהוּ בַּמְּצֹדוֹת לְמַעַן
so-that into-the-prisons and-they-put-him Babylon king-of to and-they-brought-him

לֹא־יִשָּׁמַע קוֹלוֹ עוֹד אֶל־הָרֵי יִשְׂרָאֵל׃ אִמְּךָ
mother-of-you (10) Israel mountains-of on longer roar-of-him he-was-heard not

כַגֶּפֶן בְּדָמְךָ עַל־מַיִם שְׁתוּלָה פֹּרִיָּה
being-fruitful being-planted waters by in-blood-of-you like-the-vine

וַעֲנֵפָה הָיְתָה מִמַּיִם רַבִּים׃ וַיִּהְיוּ־
and-they-were (11) abundant-ones because-of-waters she-was and-full-of-branches

לָהּ מַטּוֹת עֹז אֶל־שִׁבְטֵי מֹשְׁלִים וַתִּגְבַּהּ קוֹמָתוֹ
height-of-him and-she-towered ones-ruling scepters-of for strength branches-of to-her

עַל־בֵּין עֲבֹתִים וַיֵּרָא בְגָבְהוֹ בְּרֹב
for-many-of for-height-of-him and-he-was-conspicuous thick-foliages among above

דָּלִיֹּתָיו׃ וַתֻּתַּשׁ בְּחֵמָה לָאָרֶץ הֻשְׁלָכָה
she-was-thrown to-the-ground in-fury but-she-was-uprooted (12) branches-of-him

וְרוּחַ הַקָּדִים הוֹבִישׁ פִּרְיָהּ הִתְפָּרְקוּ
they-were-stripped fruit-of-her he-made-shrivel the-east-wind and-wind-of

וְיָבֵשׁוּ מַטֵּה עֻזָּהּ אֵשׁ אֲכָלָתְהוּ׃ וְעַתָּה
and-now (13) she-consumed-him fire strength-of-her branch-of and-they-withered

and reared her cubs.
3She brought up one of her cubs,
and he became a strong lion.
He learned to tear the prey
and he devoured men.
4The nations heard about him,
and he was trapped in their pit.
They led him with hooks
to the land of Egypt.

5" 'When she saw her hope unfulfilled,
her expectation gone,
she took another of her cubs
and made him a strong lion.
6He prowled among the lions,
for he was now a strong lion.
He learned to tear the prey
and he devoured men.
7He broke down[m] their strongholds
and devastated their towns.
The land and all who were in it
were terrified by his roaring.
8Then the nations came against him,
those from regions round about.
They spread their net for him,
and he was trapped in their pit.
9With hooks they pulled him into a cage
and brought him to the king of Babylon.
They put him in prison,
so his roar was heard no longer
on the mountains of Israel.

10" 'Your mother was like a vine in your vineyard[n]
planted by the water;
it was fruitful and full of branches
because of abundant water.
11Its branches were strong,
fit for a ruler's scepter.
It towered high
above the thick foliage,
conspicuous for its height
and for its many branches.
12But it was uprooted in fury
and thrown to the ground.
The east wind made it shrivel,
it was stripped of its fruit;
its strong branches withered
and fire consumed them.

m7 Targum (see Septuagint); Hebrew *He knew*
n10 Two Hebrew manuscripts; most Hebrew manuscripts *your blood*

שְׁתוּלָה בַמִּדְבָּר בְּאֶרֶץ צִיָּה וְצָמָא׃ וַתֵּצֵא אֵשׁ
being-planted in-the-desert in-land-of dryness and-thirst (14) and-she-spread fire

מִמַּטֵּה בַדֶּיהָ פִּרְיָהּ אָכָלָה וְלֹא־הָיָה בָהּ
from-branch-of branches-of-her fruit-of-her she-consumed so-not he-is on-her

מַטֵּה־עֹז שֵׁבֶט לִמְשׁוֹל קִינָה הִיא וַתְּהִי לְקִינָה׃
branch-of strength scepter to-rule lament this and-she-is for-lament

(20:1) וַיְהִי ׀ בַּשָּׁנָה הַשְּׁבִיעִית בַּחֲמִשִׁי בֶּעָשׂוֹר לַחֹדֶשׁ
(20:1) and-he-was in-the-year the-seventh in-the-fifth on-the-ten of-the-month

בָּאוּ אֲנָשִׁים מִזִּקְנֵי יִשְׂרָאֵל לִדְרֹשׁ אֶת־יְהוָה וַיֵּשְׁבוּ
they-came men from-elders-of Israel to-inquire *** Yahweh and-they-sat-down

לְפָנָי׃ וַיְהִי דְבַר־יְהוָה אֵלַי לֵאמֹר׃ בֶּן־אָדָם דַּבֵּר
in-front-of-me (2) then-he-came word-of Yahweh to-me to-say (3) son-of man speak!

אֶת־זִקְנֵי יִשְׂרָאֵל וְאָמַרְתָּ אֲלֵהֶם כֹּה אָמַר אֲדֹנָי יְהוִה הֲלִדְרֹשׁ
*** elders-of Israel and-you-say to-them this he-says Sovereign Yahweh to-inquire?

אֹתִי אַתֶּם בָּאִים חַי־אָנִי אִם־אִדָּרֵשׁ לָכֶם נְאֻם
me you ones-coming alive I not I-will-let-inquire to-you declaration-of

אֲדֹנָי יְהוִה׃ הֲתִשְׁפֹּט אֹתָם הֲתִשְׁפּוֹט בֶּן־אָדָם אֶת־
Sovereign Yahweh (4) will-you-judge? them will-you-judge? son-of man with

תּוֹעֲבֹת אֲבוֹתָם הוֹדִיעֵם׃ וְאָמַרְתָּ אֲלֵיהֶם
detestable-practices-of fathers-of-them confront-them! (5) and-you-say to-them

כֹּה־אָמַר אֲדֹנָי יְהוִה בְּיוֹם בָּחֳרִי בְיִשְׂרָאֵל וָאֶשָּׂא
this he-says Sovereign Yahweh on-day-of to-choose-me to-Israel then-I-lifted

יָדִי לְזֶרַע בֵּית יַעֲקֹב וָאִוָּדַע לָהֶם בְּאֶרֶץ
hand-of-me to-descendant-of house-of Jacob and-I-revealed-myself to-them in-land-of

מִצְרָיִם וָאֶשָּׂא יָדִי לָהֶם לֵאמֹר אֲנִי יְהוָה אֱלֹהֵיכֶם׃ בַּיּוֹם
Egypt and-I-lifted hand-of-me to-them to-say I Yahweh God-of-you (6) on-the-day

הַהוּא נָשָׂאתִי יָדִי לָהֶם לְהוֹצִיאָם מֵאֶרֶץ מִצְרָיִם אֶל־אֶרֶץ
the-that I-lifted hand-of-me to-them to-bring-out-them from-land-of Egypt into land

אֲשֶׁר־תַּרְתִּי לָהֶם זָבַת חָלָב וּדְבַשׁ צְבִי הִיא לְכָל־
that I-searched-out for-them flowing-of milk and-honey beautiful she of-all-of

הָאֲרָצוֹת׃ וָאֹמַר אֲלֵהֶם אִישׁ שִׁקּוּצֵי עֵינָיו הַשְׁלִיכוּ
the-lands (7) and-I-said to-them each vile-ones-of eyes-of-him get-rid!

וּבְגִלּוּלֵי מִצְרַיִם אַל־ תִּטַּמָּאוּ אֲנִי יְהוָה אֱלֹהֵיכֶם׃
and-with-idols-of Egypt not you-defile-yourselves I Yahweh God-of-you

וַיַּמְרוּ־ בִי וְלֹא אָבוּ לִשְׁמֹעַ אֵלַי אִישׁ אֶת־
(8) but-they-rebelled against-me and-not they-would to-listen to-me each ***

שִׁקּוּצֵי עֵינֵיהֶם לֹא הִשְׁלִיכוּ וְאֶת־גִּלּוּלֵי מִצְרַיִם לֹא עָזָבוּ
vile-ones-of eyes-of-them not they-got-rid or idols-of Egypt not they-forsook

13 Now it is planted in the
desert,
in a dry and thirsty land.
14 Fire spread from one of its
main[o] branches
and consumed its fruit.
No strong branch is left on it
fit for a ruler's scepter.'

This is a lament and is to be used as a lament."

*Rebellious Israel*

20 In the seventh year, in the fifth month on the tenth day, some of the elders of Israel came to inquire of the LORD, and they sat down in front of me.

2 Then the word of the LORD came to me: 3 "Son of man, speak to the elders of Israel and say to them, 'This is what the Sovereign LORD says: Have you come to inquire of me? As surely as I live, I will not let you inquire of me, declares the Sovereign LORD.'

4 "Will you judge them? Will you judge them, son of man? Then confront them with the detestable practices of their fathers 5 and say to them: 'This is what the Sovereign LORD says: On the day I chose Israel, I swore with uplifted hand to the descendants of the house of Jacob and revealed myself to them in Egypt. With uplifted hand I said to them, "I am the LORD your God." 6 On that day I swore to them that I would bring them out of Egypt into a land I had searched out for them, a land flowing with milk and honey, the most beautiful of all lands. 7 And I said to them, "Each of you, get rid of the vile images you have set your eyes on, and do not defile yourselves with the idols of Egypt. I am the LORD your God."

8 " 'But they rebelled against me and would not listen to me; they did not get rid of the vile images they had set their eyes on, nor did they forsake the idols of Egypt. So

[o]14 Or *from under its*

וָאֹמַר לִשְׁפֹּךְ חֲמָתִי עֲלֵיהֶם לְכַלּוֹת אַפִּי בָּהֶם
against-them anger-of-me to-spend on-them wrath-of-me to-pour-out so-I-said

בְּתוֹךְ אֶרֶץ מִצְרָיִם׃ וָאַעַשׂ לְמַעַן שְׁמִי לְבִלְתִּי הֵחֵל
to-be-profaned not name-of-me for-sake-of but-I-did (9) Egypt land-of in-midst-of

לְעֵינֵי הַגּוֹיִם אֲשֶׁר־הֵמָּה בְתוֹכָם אֲשֶׁר נוֹדַעְתִּי אֲלֵיהֶם
to-them I-revealed-myself whom in-among-them they that the-nations before-eyes-of

לְעֵינֵיהֶם לְהוֹצִיאָם מֵאֶרֶץ מִצְרָיִם׃ וָאוֹצִיאֵם
so-I-led-them (10) Egypt from-land-of to-bring-out-them before-eyes-of-them

מֵאֶרֶץ מִצְרָיִם וָאֲבִאֵם אֶל־ הַמִּדְבָּר׃ וָאֶתֵּן לָהֶם
to-them and-I-gave (11) the-desert into and-I-brought-them Egypt from-land-of

אֶת־ חֻקּוֹתַי וְאֶת־ מִשְׁפָּטַי הוֹדַעְתִּי אוֹתָם אֲשֶׁר יַעֲשֶׂה אוֹתָם הָאָדָם
the-man them he-obeys who them I-made-known laws-of-me and decrees-of-me ***

וָחַי בָּהֶם׃ וְגַם אֶת־ שַׁבְּתוֹתַי נָתַתִּי לָהֶם לִהְיוֹת
to-be to-them I-gave Sabbaths-of-me *** and-also (12) by-them then-he-will-live

לְאוֹת בֵּינִי וּבֵינֵיהֶם לָדַעַת כִּי אֲנִי יְהוָה מְקַדְּשָׁם׃
making-holy-them Yahweh I that to-know and-between-them between-me as-sign

וַיַּמְרוּ־ בִי בֵית־ יִשְׂרָאֵל בַּמִּדְבָּר בְּחֻקּוֹתַי
to-decrees-of-me in-the-desert Israel house-of against-me yet-they-rebelled (13)

לֹא־ הָלָכוּ וְאֶת־ מִשְׁפָּטַי מָאָסוּ אֲשֶׁר יַעֲשֶׂה אֹתָם הָאָדָם
the-man them he-obeys who they-rejected laws-of-me and they-followed not

וָחַי בָּהֶם וְאֶת־ שַׁבְּתֹתַי חִלְּלוּ מְאֹד וָאֹמַר
so-I-said utterly they-desecrated Sabbaths-of-me and by-them then-he-will-live

לִשְׁפֹּךְ חֲמָתִי עֲלֵיהֶם בַּמִּדְבָּר לְכַלּוֹתָם׃ וָאֶעֱשֶׂה
but-I-did (14) to-destroy-them in-the-desert on-them wrath-of-me to-pour-out

לְמַעַן שְׁמִי לְבִלְתִּי הֵחֵל לְעֵינֵי הַגּוֹיִם אֲשֶׁר
whom the-nations before-eyes-of to-profane not name-of-me for-sake-of

הוֹצֵאתִים לְעֵינֵיהֶם׃ וְגַם־ אֲנִי נָשָׂאתִי יָדִי לָהֶם
to-them hand-of-me I-lifted I and-also (15) before-eyes-of-them I-brought-out-them

בַּמִּדְבָּר לְבִלְתִּי הָבִיא אוֹתָם אֶל־הָאָרֶץ אֲשֶׁר־נָתַתִּי זָבַת חָלָב וּדְבַשׁ
and-honey milk flowing-of I-gave that the-land into them to-bring not in-the-desert

צְבִי הִיא לְכָל־ הָאֲרָצוֹת׃ יַעַן בְּמִשְׁפָּטַי מָאָסוּ וְאֶת־
and they-rejected to-laws-of-me because (16) the-lands of-all-of she beautiful

חֻקּוֹתַי לֹא־ הָלְכוּ בָהֶם וְאֶת־ שַׁבְּתוֹתַי חִלֵּלוּ כִּי
for they-desecrated Sabbaths-of-me and to-them they-followed not decrees-of-me

אַחֲרֵי גִלּוּלֵיהֶם לִבָּם הֹלֵךְ׃ וַתָּחָס עֵינִי
eye-of-me yet-she-had-pity (17) being-devoted heart-of-them idols-of-them after

עֲלֵיהֶם מִשַּׁחֲתָם וְלֹא־עָשִׂיתִי אוֹתָם כָּלָה בַּמִּדְבָּר׃ וָאֹמַר
and-I-said (18) in-the-desert end them I-made or-not from-to-destroy-them on-them

I said I would pour out my wrath on them and spend my anger against them in Egypt. [9]But for the sake of my name I did what would keep it from being profaned in the eyes of the nations they lived among and in whose sight I had revealed myself to the Israelites by bringing them out of Egypt. [10]Therefore I led them out of Egypt and brought them into the desert. [11]I gave them my decrees and made known to them my laws, for the man who obeys them will live by them. [12]Also I gave them my Sabbaths as a sign between us, so they would know that I the LORD made them holy.

[13]" 'Yet the people of Israel rebelled against me in the desert. They did not follow my decrees but rejected my laws—although the man who obeys them will live by them—and they utterly desecrated my Sabbaths. So I said I would pour out my wrath on them and destroy them in the desert. [14]But for the sake of my name I did what would keep it from being profaned in the eyes of the nations in whose sight I had brought them out. [15]Also with uplifted hand I swore to them in the desert that I would not bring them into the land I had given them—a land flowing with milk and honey, most beautiful of all lands— [16]because they rejected my laws and did not follow my decrees and desecrated my Sabbaths. For their hearts were devoted to their idols. [17]Yet I looked on them with pity and did not destroy them or put an end to them in the desert. [18]I

אֶל־ בְּנֵיהֶם בַּמִּדְבָּר בְּחוּקֵּי אֲבוֹתֵיכֶם אַל־ תֵּלֵכוּ
you-follow not fathers-of-you to-statutes-of in-the-desert children-of-them to

וְאֶת־מִשְׁפְּטֵיהֶם אַל־ תִּשְׁמֹרוּ וּבְגִלּוּלֵיהֶם אַל־ תִּטַּמָּאוּ׃
you-defile-yourselves not or-with-idols-of-them you-keep not laws-of-them or

אֲנִי יְהוָה אֱלֹהֵיכֶם בְּחֻקּוֹתַי לֵכוּ וְאֶת־ מִשְׁפָּטַי שִׁמְרוּ
be-careful! laws-of-me and follow! to-decrees-of-me God-of-you Yahweh I (19)

וַעֲשׂוּ אוֹתָם׃ וְאֶת־ שַׁבְּתוֹתַי קַדֵּשׁוּ וְהָיוּ לְאוֹת
as-sign that-they-may-be keep-holy! Sabbaths-of-me and (20) them and-keep!

בֵּינִי וּבֵינֵיכֶם לָדַעַת כִּי אֲנִי יְהוָה אֱלֹהֵיכֶם׃ וַיַּמְרוּ־
but-they-rebelled (21) God-of-you Yahweh I that to-know and-between-you between-me

בִי הַבָּנִים בְּחֻקּוֹתַי לֹא־ הָלָכוּ וְאֶת־ מִשְׁפָּטַי לֹא־
not laws-of-me and they-followed not to-decrees-of-me the-children against-me

שָׁמְרוּ לַעֲשׂוֹת אוֹתָם אֲשֶׁר יַעֲשֶׂה אוֹתָם הָאָדָם וָחַי בָּהֶם
by-them then-he-will-live the-man them he-obeys who them to-keep they-were-careful

אֶת־ שַׁבְּתוֹתַי חִלֵּלוּ וָאֹמַר לִשְׁפֹּךְ חֲמָתִי עֲלֵיהֶם
on-them wrath-of-me to-pour-out so-I-said they-desecrated Sabbaths-of-me ***

לְכַלּוֹת אַפִּי בָּם בַּמִּדְבָּר׃ וַהֲשִׁבֹתִי אֶת־ יָדִי
hand-of-me *** but-I-withheld (22) in-the-desert against-them anger-of-me to-spend

וָאַעַשׂ לְמַעַן שְׁמִי לְבִלְתִּי הֵחֵל לְעֵינֵי הַגּוֹיִם
the-nations before-eyes-of to-profane not name-of-me for-sake-of and-I-did

אֲשֶׁר־ הוֹצֵאתִי אוֹתָם לְעֵינֵיהֶם׃ גַּם־אֲנִי נָשָׂאתִי אֶת־ יָדִי
hand-of-me *** I-lifted I also (23) before-eyes-of-them them I-brought-out whom

לָהֶם בַּמִּדְבָּר לְהָפִיץ אֹתָם בַּגּוֹיִם וּלְזָרוֹת אוֹתָם
them and-to-scatter among-the-nations them to-disperse in-the-desert to-them

בָּאֲרָצוֹת׃ יַעַן מִשְׁפָּטַי לֹא־ עָשׂוּ וְחֻקּוֹתַי
but-decrees-of-me they-obeyed not laws-of-me because (24) through-the-countries

מָאָסוּ וְאֶת־ שַׁבְּתוֹתַי חִלֵּלוּ וְאַחֲרֵי גִּלּוּלֵי אֲבוֹתָם
fathers-of-them idols-of and-after they-desecrated Sabbaths-of-me and they-rejected

הָיוּ עֵינֵיהֶם׃ וְגַם־ אֲנִי נָתַתִּי לָהֶם חֻקִּים לֹא טוֹבִים
good-ones not statutes to-them I-gave-over I and-also (25) eyes-of-them they-were

וּמִשְׁפָּטִים לֹא יִחְיוּ בָּהֶם׃ וָאֲטַמֵּא אוֹתָם
them and-I-let-become-defiled (26) by-them they-could-live not and-laws

בְּמַתְּנוֹתָם בְּהַעֲבִיר כָּל־ פֶּטֶר רֶחֶם לְמַעַן
so-that womb firstborn-of every-of when-to-make-pass-through through-gifts-of-them

אֲשִׁמֵּם לְמַעַן אֲשֶׁר יֵדְעוּ אֲשֶׁר אֲנִי יְהוָה׃ לָכֵן
therefore (27) Yahweh I that they-would-know that so-that I-might-horrify-them

דַּבֵּר אֶל־ בֵּית יִשְׂרָאֵל בֶּן־ אָדָם וְאָמַרְתָּ אֲלֵיהֶם כֹּה אָמַר אֲדֹנָי
Sovereign he-says this to-them and-you-say man son-of Israel house-of to speak!

said to their children in the desert,
"Do not follow the statutes of your
fathers or keep their laws or defile
yourselves with their idols. [19]I am
the LORD your God; follow my decrees and be careful to keep my
laws. [20]Keep my Sabbaths holy,
that they may be a sign between
us. Then you will know that I am
the LORD your God."
[21]" 'But the children rebelled
against me: They did not follow
my decrees, they were not careful
to keep my laws—although the
man who obeys them will live by
them—and they desecrated my
Sabbaths. So I said I would pour
out my wrath on them and spend
my anger against them in the
desert. [22]But I withheld my hand,
and for the sake of my name I did
what would keep it from being
profaned in the eyes of the nations in whose sight I had brought
them out. [23]Also with uplifted
hand I swore to them in the desert
that I would disperse them among
the nations and scatter them
through the countries, [24]because
they had not obeyed my laws but
had rejected my decrees and desecrated my Sabbaths, and their
eyes ⌊lusted⌋ after their fathers'
idols. [25]I also gave them over to
statutes that were not good and
laws they could not live by; [26]I let
them become defiled through
their gifts—the sacrifice of every
firstborn[p]—that I might fill them
with horror so they would know
that I am the LORD.'
[27]"Therefore, son of man, speak
to the people of Israel and say to
them, 'This is what the Sovereign

[p]26 Or *—making every firstborn pass through ⌊the fire⌋*

יְהוִה עוֹד זֹאת גִּדְּפוּ אוֹתִי אֲבוֹתֵיכֶם בְּמַעֲלָם בִּי
to-me by-to-forsake-them fathers-of-you me they-blasphemed this also Yahweh

מָעַל׃ וָאֲבִיאֵם אֶל־הָאָרֶץ אֲשֶׁר נָשָׂאתִי אֶת־יָדִי
hand-of-me *** I-raised that the-land into when-I-brought-them (28) forsaking

לָתֵת אוֹתָהּ לָהֶם וַיִּרְאוּ כָל־גִּבְעָה רָמָה וְכָל־עֵץ עָבֹת
leaf tree-of or-any-of being-high hill any-of and-they-saw to-them her to-give

וַיִּזְבְּחוּ־שָׁם אֶת־זִבְחֵיהֶם וַיִּתְּנוּ־שָׁם
there and-they-made sacrifices-of-them *** there then-they-sacrificed

כַּעַס קָרְבָּנָם וַיָּשִׂימוּ שָׁם רֵיחַ
fragrance-of there and-they-presented offering-of-them anger-provocation-of

נִיחוֹחֵיהֶם וַיַּסִּיכוּ שָׁם אֶת־נִסְכֵּיהֶם׃
drink-offerings-of-them *** there and-they-poured-out soothing-incenses-of-them

וָאֹמַר אֲלֵהֶם מָה הַבָּמָה אֲשֶׁר־אַתֶּם הַבָּאִים שָׁם
there the-ones-going you that the-high-place what? to-them then-I-said (29)

וַיִּקָּרֵא שְׁמָהּ בָּמָה עַד הַיּוֹם הַזֶּה׃ לָכֵן אֱמֹר ׀ אֶל־
to say! therefore (30) the-this the-day to Bamah name-of-her and-he-is-called

בֵּית יִשְׂרָאֵל כֹּה אָמַר אֲדֹנָי יְהוִה הַבְדֶרֶךְ אֲבוֹתֵיכֶם אַתֶּם
you fathers-of-you in-way-of? Yahweh Sovereign he-says this Israel house-of

נִטְמְאִים וְאַחֲרֵי שִׁקּוּצֵיהֶם אַתֶּם זֹנִים׃
ones-lusting you vile-ones-of-them and-after ones-defiling-yourselves

וּבִשְׂאֵת מַתְּנֹתֵיכֶם בְּהַעֲבִיר בְּנֵיכֶם בָּאֵשׁ
through-the-fire sons-of-you when-to-make-pass gifts-of-you and-when-to-offer (31)

אַתֶּם נִטְמְאִים לְכָל־גִּלּוּלֵיכֶם עַד־הַיּוֹם וַאֲנִי
and-I the-day to idols-of-you with-all-of ones-defiling-yourselves you

אִדָּרֵשׁ לָכֶם בֵּית יִשְׂרָאֵל חַי־אָנִי נְאֻם אֲדֹנָי יְהוִה
Yahweh Sovereign declaration-of I alive Israel house-of to-you should-I-let-inquire

אִם־אִדָּרֵשׁ לָכֶם׃ וְהָעֹלָה עַל־רוּחֲכֶם הָיוֹ לֹא
not to-happen mind-of-you into but-the-one-coming (32) to-you I-will-let-inquire not

תִהְיֶה אֲשֶׁר ׀ אַתֶּם אֹמְרִים נִהְיֶה כַגּוֹיִם כְּמִשְׁפְּחוֹת
like-peoples-of like-the-nations we-would-be ones-saying you that she-will-happen

הָאֲרָצוֹת לְשָׁרֵת עֵץ וָאָבֶן׃ חַי־אָנִי נְאֻם אֲדֹנָי יְהוִה
Yahweh Sovereign declaration-of I alive (33) and-stone wood to-serve the-worlds

אִם־לֹא בְּיָד חֲזָקָה וּבִזְרוֹעַ נְטוּיָה וּבְחֵמָה
and-with-wrath being-outstretched and-with-arm mighty with-hand indeed surely

שְׁפוּכָה אֶמְלוֹךְ עֲלֵיכֶם׃ וְהוֹצֵאתִי אֶתְכֶם מִן־הָעַמִּים
the-nations from you and-I-will-bring (34) over-you I-will-rule being-outpoured

וְקִבַּצְתִּי אֶתְכֶם מִן־הָאֲרָצוֹת אֲשֶׁר נְפוֹצֹתֶם בָּם
among-them you-were-scattered where the-countries from you and-I-will-gather

LORD says: In this also your fathers
blasphemed me by forsaking me:
[28]When I brought them into the
land I had sworn to give them and
they saw any high hill or any leafy
tree, there they offered their sacrifices, made offerings that provoked me to anger, presented
their fragrant incense and poured
out their drink offerings. [29]Then I
said to them: What is this high
place you go to?' " (It is called
Bamah[q] to this day.)

*Judgment and Restoration*

[30]"Therefore say to the house of
Israel: 'This is what the Sovereign
LORD says: Will you defile yourselves the way your fathers did
and lust after their vile images?
[31]When you offer your gifts—the
sacrifice of your sons in[r] the fire—
you continue to defile yourselves
with all your idols to this day. Am
I to let you inquire of me, O house
of Israel? As surely as I live, declares the Sovereign LORD, I will
not let you inquire of me.
[32]" 'You say, "We want to be like
the nations, like the peoples of the
world, who serve wood and
stone." But what you have in
mind will never happen. [33]As
surely as I live, declares the Sovereign LORD, I will rule over you
with a mighty hand and an outstretched arm and with outpoured
wrath. [34]I will bring you from the
nations and gather you from the
countries where you have been

q29 *Bamah* means *high place.*
r31 Or *—making your sons pass through*

בְּיָד חֲזָקָה֙ וּבִזְר֣וֹעַ נְטוּיָ֔ה וּבְחֵמָ֖ה שְׁפוּכָֽה׃
being-outpoured and-with-wrath being-outstretched and-with-arm mighty with-hand

(35) וְהֵבֵאתִ֣י אֶתְכֶ֔ם אֶל־מִדְבַּ֖ר הָֽעַמִּ֑ים וְנִשְׁפַּטְתִּ֤י אִתְּכֶם֙ שָׁ֔ם
there on-you and-I-will-judge the-nations desert-of into you and-I-will-bring (35)

פָּנִ֖ים אֶל־פָּנִֽים׃ (36) כַּאֲשֶׁ֤ר נִשְׁפַּ֙טְתִּי֙ אֶת־אֲב֣וֹתֵיכֶ֔ם בְּמִדְבַּ֖ר אֶ֣רֶץ מִצְרָ֑יִם
Egypt land-of in-desert-of fathers-of-you on I-judged just-as (36) faces to faces

כֵּ֚ן אִשָּׁפֵ֣ט אִתְּכֶ֔ם נְאֻ֖ם אֲדֹנָ֥י יְהוִֽה׃ (37) וְהַעֲבַרְתִּ֥י אֶתְכֶ֖ם
you and-I-will-make-pass (37) Yahweh Sovereign declaration-of on-you I-will-judge so

תַּ֣חַת הַשָּׁ֑בֶט וְהֵבֵאתִ֥י אֶתְכֶ֖ם בְּמָסֹ֥רֶת הַבְּרִֽית׃ (38) וּבָרוֹתִ֨י
and-I-will-purge (38) the-covenant into-bond-of you and-I-will-bring the-rod under

מִכֶּ֜ם הַמֹּרְדִ֗ים וְהַפּֽוֹשְׁעִים֙ בִּ֔י מֵאֶ֤רֶץ
from-land-of against-me and-the-ones-rebelling the-ones-revolting from-you

מְגֽוּרֵיהֶם֙ אוֹצִ֣יא אוֹתָ֔ם וְאֶל־אַדְמַ֥ת יִשְׂרָאֵ֖ל לֹ֣א
not Israel land-of yet-into them I-will-bring-out living-places-of-them

יָב֑וֹא וִֽידַעְתֶּ֖ם כִּֽי־אֲנִ֥י יְהוָֽה׃ (39) וְאַתֶּ֣ם בֵּֽית־יִשְׂרָאֵ֗ל כֹּֽה־
this Israel house-of and-you (39) Yahweh I that then-you-will-know he-will-enter

אָמַ֣ר ׀ אֲדֹנָ֣י יְהוִ֗ה אִ֤ישׁ גִּלּוּלָיו֙ לְכ֣וּ עֲבֹ֔דוּ וְאַחַ֕ר אִם־
indeed but-afterward serve! go! idols-of-him everyone Yahweh Sovereign he-says

אֵינְכֶ֖ם שֹׁמְעִ֣ים אֵלָ֑י וְאֶת־שֵׁ֤ם קָדְשִׁי֙ לֹ֣א תְחַלְּלוּ־
you-will-profane not holiness-of-me name-of and to-me ones-listening surely-you

ע֔וֹד בְּמַתְּנוֹתֵיכֶ֖ם וּבְגִלּוּלֵיכֶֽם׃ (40) כִּ֣י בְהַר־קָדְשִׁ֞י
holiness-of-me on-mountain-of for (40) and-with-idols-of-you with-gifts-of-you longer

בְּהַ֣ר ׀ מְר֣וֹם יִשְׂרָאֵ֗ל נְאֻם֙ אֲדֹנָ֣י יְהוִ֔ה שָׁ֣ם
there Yahweh Sovereign declaration-of Israel height-of on-mountain-of

יַֽעַבְדֻ֜נִי כָּל־בֵּ֧ית יִשְׂרָאֵ֛ל כֻּלֹּ֖ה בָּאָ֑רֶץ שָׁ֣ם
there in-the-land all-of-him Israel house-of entire-of they-will-serve-me

אֶרְצֵ֗ם וְשָׁ֨ם אֶדְר֤וֹשׁ אֶת־תְּרוּמֹֽתֵיכֶם֙ וְאֶת־רֵאשִׁ֣ית
first-of and offerings-of-you *** I-will-require and-there I-will-accept-them

מַשְׂאוֹתֵיכֶ֔ם בְּכָל־קָדְשֵׁיכֶֽם׃ (41) בְּרֵ֣יחַ נִיחֹ֞חַ
soothing-incense as-fragrance-of (41) holy-ones-of-you with-all-of gifts-of-you

אֶרְצֶ֣ה אֶתְכֶ֗ם בְּהוֹצִיאִ֤י אֶתְכֶם֙ מִן־הָ֣עַמִּ֔ים וְקִבַּצְתִּ֣י אֶתְכֶ֔ם מִן־
from you and-I-gather the-nations from you when-to-bring-out-me you I-will-accept

הָ֣אֲרָצ֔וֹת אֲשֶׁ֥ר נְפֹצֹתֶ֖ם בָּ֑ם וְנִקְדַּשְׁתִּ֥י
and-I-will-show-myself-holy among-them you-were-scattered where the-countries

בָכֶ֖ם לְעֵינֵ֥י הַגּוֹיִֽם׃ (42) וִֽידַעְתֶּם֙ כִּֽי־אֲנִ֣י יְהוָ֔ה
Yahweh I that then-you-will-know (42) the-nations before-eyes-of among-you

בַּהֲבִיאִ֤י אֶתְכֶם֙ אֶל־אַדְמַ֣ת יִשְׂרָאֵ֔ל אֶל־הָאָ֗רֶץ אֲשֶׁ֤ר נָשָׂ֙אתִי֙ אֶת־יָדִ֔י
hand-of-me *** I-lifted that the-land into Israel land-of into you when-to-bring-me

scattered—with a mighty hand
and an outstretched arm and with
outpoured wrath. 35 I will bring
you into the desert of the nations
and there, face to face, I will execute judgment upon you. 36 As I
judged your fathers in the desert
of the land of Egypt, so I will judge
you, declares the Sovereign LORD.
37 I will take note of you as you pass
under my rod, and I will bring
you into the bond of the covenant.
38 I will purge you of those who revolt and rebel against me. Although I will bring them out of the
land where they are living, yet
they will not enter the land of Israel. Then you will know that I am
the LORD.

39 "'As for you, O house of Israel,
this is what the Sovereign LORD
says: Go and serve your idols,
every one of you! But afterward
you will surely listen to me and no
longer profane my holy name
with your gifts and idols. 40 For on
my holy mountain, the high
mountain of Israel, declares the
Sovereign LORD, there in the land
the entire house of Israel will
serve me, and there I will accept
them. There I will require your offerings and your choice gifts,[s]
along with all your holy sacrifices.
41 I will accept you as fragrant incense when I bring you out from
the nations and gather you from
the countries where you have
been scattered, and I will show
myself holy among you in the
sight of the nations. 42 Then you
will know that I am the LORD,
when I bring you into the land of
Israel, the land I had sworn with

[s] 40 Or *and the gifts of your firstfruits*

לָתֵת אוֹתָהּ לַאֲבוֹתֵיכֶם׃ וּזְכַרְתֶּם־ שָׁם אֶת־ דַּרְכֵיכֶם
conducts-of-you *** there and-you-will-remember (43) to-fathers-of-you her to-give

וְאֵת כָּל־ עֲלִילוֹתֵיכֶם אֲשֶׁר נִטְמֵאתֶם בָּם וּנְקֹטֹתֶם
and-you-will-loathe by-them you-defiled-yourselves which actions-of-you all-of and

בִּפְנֵיכֶם בְּכָל־ רָעוֹתֵיכֶם אֲשֶׁר עֲשִׂיתֶם׃ וִידַעְתֶּם כִּי־
that then-you-will-know (44) you-did that evils-of-you for-all-of to-faces-of-you

אֲנִי יְהוָה בַּעֲשׂוֹתִי אִתְּכֶם לְמַעַן שְׁמִי לֹא כְדַרְכֵיכֶם
according-to-ways-of-you not name-of-me for-sake-of with-you when-to-deal-me Yahweh I

הָרָעִים וְכַעֲלִילוֹתֵיכֶם הַנִּשְׁחָתוֹת בֵּית יִשְׂרָאֵל
Israel house-of the-ones-being-corrupt and-according-to-practices-of-you the-evil-ones

נְאֻם אֲדֹנָי יְהוִה׃ וַיְהִי דְבַר־יְהוָה אֵלַי לֵאמֹר׃
to-say to-me Yahweh word-of and-he-came *(21:1[20:45]) Yahweh Sovereign declaration-of

בֶּן־ אָדָם שִׂים פָּנֶיךָ דֶּרֶךְ תֵּימָנָה וְהַטֵּף אֶל־
against and-preach! to-south toward faces-of-you set! man son-of (2[46])

דָּרוֹם וְהִנָּבֵא אֶל־ יַעַר הַשָּׂדֶה נֶגֶב׃ וְאָמַרְתָּ
and-you-say (3[47]) southland the-land forest-of against and-prophesy! south

לְיַעַר הַנֶּגֶב שְׁמַע דְּבַר־ יְהוָה כֹּה־ אָמַר אֲדֹנָי יְהוִה הִנְנִי
see-I! Yahweh Sovereign he-says this Yahweh word-of hear! the-southland to-forest-of

מַצִּית־ בְּךָ | אֵשׁ וְאָכְלָה בְךָ כָל־ עֵץ־ לַח וְכָל־
and-all-of green tree all-of of-you and-she-will-consume fire to-you setting-fire

עֵץ יָבֵשׁ לֹא־ תִכְבֶּה לַהֶבֶת שַׁלְהֶבֶת וְנִצְרְבוּ־ בָהּ
by-her and-they-will-be-scorched blaze flame-of she-will-be-quenched not dry tree

כָּל־ פָּנִים מִנֶּגֶב צָפוֹנָה׃ וְרָאוּ כָּל־ בָּשָׂר כִּי אֲנִי
I that person every-of and-they-will-see (4[48]) to-north from-south faces every-of

יְהוָה בִּעַרְתִּיהָ לֹא תִּכְבֶּה׃ וָאֹמַר אֲהָהּ אֲדֹנָי
Sovereign ah! then-I-said (5[49]) she-will-be-quenched not I-kindled-her Yahweh

יְהוִה הֵמָּה אֹמְרִים לִי הֲלֹא מְמַשֵּׁל מְשָׁלִים הוּא׃ וַיְהִי
and-he-came (6[21:1]) he parables one-telling not? of-me ones-saying they Yahweh

דְבַר־ יְהוָה אֵלַי לֵאמֹר׃ בֶּן־ אָדָם שִׂים פָּנֶיךָ אֶל־
against faces-of-you set! man son-of (7[2]) to-say to-me Yahweh word-of

יְרוּשָׁלִַם וְהַטֵּף אֶל־ מִקְדָּשִׁים וְהִנָּבֵא אֶל־ אַדְמַת יִשְׂרָאֵל׃
Israel land-of against and-prophesy! sanctuaries against and-preach! Jerusalem

וְאָמַרְתָּ לְאַדְמַת יִשְׂרָאֵל כֹּה אָמַר יְהוָה הִנְנִי אֵלַיִךְ
against-you see-I! Yahweh he-says this Israel to-land-of and-you-say (8[3])

וְהוֹצֵאתִי חַרְבִּי מִתַּעְרָהּ וְהִכְרַתִּי מִמֵּךְ
from-you and-I-will-cut-off from-scabbard-of-her sword-of-me and-I-will-draw

צַדִּיק וְרָשָׁע׃ יַעַן אֲשֶׁר־ הִכְרַתִּי מִמֵּךְ צַדִּיק וְרָשָׁע
and-wicked righteous from-you I-will-cut-off that because (9[4]) and-wicked righteous

uplifted hand to give to your fathers. [43]There you will remember your conduct and all the actions by which you have defiled yourselves, and you will loathe yourselves for all the evil you have done. [44]You will know that I am the LORD, when I deal with you for my name's sake and not according to your evil ways and your corrupt practices, O house of Israel, declares the Sovereign LORD.' "

*Prophecy Against the South*

[45]The word of the LORD came to me: [46]"Son of man, set your face toward the south; preach against the south and prophesy against the forest of the southland. [47]Say to the southern forest: 'Hear the word of the LORD. This is what the Sovereign LORD says: I am about to set fire to you, and it will consume all your trees, both green and dry. The blazing flame will not be quenched, and every face from south to north will be scorched by it. [48]Everyone will see that I the LORD have kindled it; it will not be quenched.' "

[49]Then I said, "Ah, Sovereign LORD! They are saying of me, 'Isn't he just telling parables?' "

*Babylon, God's Sword of Judgment*

21 The word of the LORD came to me: [2]"Son of man, set your face against Jerusalem and preach against the sanctuary. Prophesy against the land of Israel [3]and say to her: 'This is what the LORD says: I am against you. I will draw my sword from its scabbard and cut off from you both the righteous and the wicked. [4]Because I am going to cut off the righteous and the wicked, my

******Heading, 45* **The English numeration of chapter 21 begins with verse 6 of the Hebrew; the number in brackets indicates the English numeration.**

לָכֵן תֵּצֵא חַרְבִּי מִתַּעְרָהּ אֶל־כָּל־בָּשָׂר
person every-of against from-sheath-of-her sword-of-me she-will-come-out therefore

מִנֶּגֶב צָפוֹן׃ וְיָדְעוּ כָּל־בָּשָׂר כִּי אֲנִי יְהוָה הוֹצֵאתִי
I-drew Yahweh I that people all-of then-they-will-know (10[5]) north from-south

חַרְבִּי מִתַּעְרָהּ לֹא תָשׁוּב עוֹד׃ וְאַתָּה
therefore-you (11[6]) again she-will-return not from-scabbard-of-her sword-of-me

בֶן־אָדָם הֵאָנַח בְּשִׁבְרוֹן מָתְנַיִם וּבִמְרִירוּת תֵּאָנַח
you-groan and-with-bitter-grief hearts with-breaking-of groan! man son-of

לְעֵינֵיהֶם׃ וְהָיָה כִּי־יֹאמְרוּ אֵלֶיךָ עַל־מָה אַתָּה נֶאֱנָח
groaning you why? for to-you they-ask when and-he-will-be (12[7]) before-eyes-of-them

וְאָמַרְתָּ אֶל־שְׁמוּעָה כִי־בָאָה וְנָמֵס כָּל־לֵב
heart every-of and-he-will-melt coming that news because-of then-you-shall-say

וְרָפוּ כָל־יָדַיִם וְכִהֲתָה כָל־רוּחַ
spirit every-of and-she-will-become-faint hands every-of and-they-will-go-limp

וְכָל־בִּרְכַּיִם תֵּלַכְנָה מַּיִם הִנֵּה בָאָה וְנִהְיָתָה
and-she-will-take-place coming see! waters they-will-become knees and-every-of

נְאֻם אֲדֹנָי יְהוִה׃ וַיְהִי דְבַר־יְהוָה אֵלַי לֵאמֹר׃
to-say to-me Yahweh word-of and-he-came (13[8]) Yahweh Sovereign declaration-of

בֶּן־אָדָם הִנָּבֵא וְאָמַרְתָּ כֹּה אָמַר אֲדֹנָי אֱמֹר חֶרֶב חֶרֶב
sword sword say! Lord he-says this and-you-say prophesy! man son-of (14[9])

הוּחַדָּה וְגַם־מְרוּטָה׃ לְמַעַן טְבֹחַ טֶבַח
slaughter to-slaughter so-that (15[10]) being-polished and-also she-is-sharpened

הוּחַדָּה לְמַעַן־הֱיֵה־לָהּ בָּרָק מֹרָטָּה אוֹ נָשִׂישׂ
shall-we-rejoice but she-is-polished lightning to-her to-be so-that she-is-sharpened

שֵׁבֶט בְּנִי מֹאֶסֶת כָּל־עֵץ׃ וַיִּתֵּן אֹתָהּ
her and-he-appointed (16[11]) stick every-of one-despising son-of-me scepter-of

לְמָרְטָה לִתְפֹּשׂ בַּכָּף הִיא־הוּחַדָּה חֶרֶב וְהִיא מֹרָטָּה
she-is-polished and-she sword she-is-sharpened she with-the-hand to-grasp to-polish

לָתֵת אוֹתָהּ בְּיַד־הוֹרֵג׃ זְעַק וְהֵילֵל בֶּן־אָדָם
man son-of and-wail! cry-out! (17[12]) one-slaying for-hand-of her to-make-ready

כִּי־הִיא הָיְתָה† בְעַמִּי הִיא בְּכָל־נְשִׂיאֵי יִשְׂרָאֵל
Israel princes-of against-all-of she against-people-of-me she-is she for

מְגוּרֵי אֶל־חֶרֶב הָיוּ אֶת־עַמִּי לָכֵן סְפֹק אֶל־
on beat! therefore people-of-me with they-are sword to ones-being-thrown-of

יָרֵךְ׃ כִּי בֹחַן וּמָה אִם־גַּם־שֵׁבֶט מֹאֶסֶת לֹא
not one-despising scepter also if and-what? testing surely (18[13]) breast

יִהְיֶה נְאֻם אֲדֹנָי יְהוִה׃ וְאַתָּה בֶן־אָדָם הִנָּבֵא
prophesy! man son-of so-you (19[14]) Yahweh Sovereign declaration-of he-continues

sword will be unsheathed against everyone from south to north. [5]Then all people will know that I the LORD have drawn my sword from its scabbard; it will not return again.'

[6]"Therefore groan, son of man! Groan before them with broken heart and bitter grief. [7]And when they ask you, 'Why are you groaning?' you shall say, 'Because of the news that is coming. Every heart will melt and every hand go limp; every spirit will become faint and every knee become as weak as water.' It is coming! It will surely take place, declares the Sovereign LORD."

[8]The word of the LORD came to me: [9]"Son of man, prophesy and say, 'This is what the Lord says:

" 'A sword, a sword,
sharpened and polished—
[10]sharpened for the slaughter,
polished to flash like
lightning!

" 'Shall we rejoice in the scepter of my son ⌞Judah⌟? The sword despises every such stick.

[11]" 'The sword is appointed to
be polished,
to be grasped with the
hand;
it is sharpened and polished,
made ready for the hand of
the slayer.
[12]Cry out and wail, son of man,
for it is against my people;
it is against all the princes
of Israel.
They are thrown to the sword
along with my people.
Therefore beat your breast.

[13]" 'Testing will surely come. And what if the scepter ⌞of Judah⌟, which the sword despises, does not continue? declares the Sovereign LORD.'

[14]"So then, son of man,
prophesy

**Heading* See the note on page 352.

†17 Most mss have *sheva* under the *yod* (הָיְ).

וְהַךְ כַּף אֶל־כָּף וְתִכָּפֵל חֶרֶב שְׁלִישִׁתָה חֶרֶב
sword-of third-time sword and-let-her-strike-twice hand against hand and-strike!

חֲלָלִים הִיא חֶרֶב חָלָל הַגָּדוֹל הַחֹדֶרֶת לָהֶם׃
to-them the-one-surrounding the-great slaughter sword-of she slaughters

לְמַעַן לָמוּג לֵב וְהַרְבֵּה הַמִּכְשֹׁלִים עַל כָּל־שַׁעֲרֵיהֶם
gates-of-them all-of at the-fallen-ones and-to-be-many heart to-melt so-that (20[15])

נָתַתִּי אִבְחַת־חָרֶב אָח עֲשׂוּיָה לְבָרָק מְעֻטָּה
one-being-grasped like-lightning one-being-made oh! sword slaughter-of I-stationed

לְטָבַח׃ הִתְאַחֲדִי הֵימִנִי הָשִׂימִי הַשְׂמִילִי אָנָה פָּנַיִךְ
faces-of-you to-where go-left! turn! go-right! slash! (21[16]) for-slaughter

מֻעָדוֹת׃ וְגַם־אֲנִי אַכֶּה כַפִּי אֶל־כַּפִּי
hand-of-me against hand-of-me I-will-strike I and-too (22[17]) ones-being-turned

וַהֲנִחֹתִי חֲמָתִי אֲנִי יְהוָה דִּבַּרְתִּי׃ וַיְהִי דְבַר־
word-of and-he-came (23[18]) I-spoke Yahweh I wrath-of-me and-I-will-make-subside

יְהוָה אֵלַי לֵאמֹר׃ וְאַתָּה בֶן־אָדָם שִׂים־לְךָ שְׁנַיִם דְּרָכִים
roads two for-you mark-out! man son-of now-you (24[19]) to-say to-me Yahweh

לָבוֹא חֶרֶב מֶלֶךְ־בָּבֶל מֵאֶרֶץ אֶחָד יֵצְאוּ שְׁנֵיהֶם
both-of-them let-them-start-out same from-country Babylon king-of sword-of to-come

וְיָד בָּרֵא בְּרֹאשׁ דֶּרֶךְ־עִיר בָּרֵא׃ דֶּרֶךְ תָּשִׂים
you-mark-out road (25[20]) to-make city road-of at-branch-of to-make and-signpost

לָבוֹא חֶרֶב אֵת רַבַּת בְּנֵי־עַמּוֹן וְאֶת־יְהוּדָה בִירוּשָׁלַםִ
against-Jerusalem Judah and-against Ammon sons-of Rabbah-of against sword to-take

בְּצוּרָה׃ כִּי־עָמַד מֶלֶךְ־בָּבֶל אֶל־אֵם הַדֶּרֶךְ
the-road fork-of at Babylon king-of he-will-stop for (26[21]) one-being-fortified

בְּרֹאשׁ שְׁנֵי הַדְּרָכִים לִקְסָם־קָסֶם קִלְקַל
he-will-cast-lots omen to-seek-omen the-roads two-of at-junction-of

בַּחִצִּים שָׁאַל בַּתְּרָפִים רָאָה בַּכָּבֵד׃
to-the-liver he-will-examine with-the-idols he-will-consult with-the-arrows

בִּימִינוֹ הָיָה הַקֶּסֶם יְרוּשָׁלַםִ לָשׂוּם
to-set-up Jerusalem the-lot he-will-come into-right-hand-of-him (27[22])

כָּרִים לִפְתֹּחַ פֶּה בְּרֶצַח לְהָרִים קוֹל בִּתְרוּעָה לָשׂוּם
to-set-up of-battle-cry sound to-raise for-slaughter mouth to-open battering-rams

כָּרִים עַל־שְׁעָרִים לִשְׁפֹּךְ סֹלְלָה לִבְנוֹת דָּיֵק׃ וְהָיָה
and-he-will-be (28[23]) siege-work to-erect ramp to-build gates against battering-rams

לָהֶם כִּקְסָום־שָׁוְא בְּעֵינֵיהֶם שְׁבֻעֵי שְׁבֻעוֹת לָהֶם
to-them allegiances ones-being-sworn-of in-eyes-of-them falsehood like-omen-of to-them

וְהוּא־מַזְכִּיר עָוֺן לְהִתָּפֵשׂ׃ לָכֵן כֹּה־אָמַר אֲדֹנָי
Sovereign he-says this therefore (29[24]) to-be-captured guilt one-reminding but-he

and strike your hands
together.
Let the sword strike twice,
even three times.
It is a sword for slaughter—
a sword for great slaughter,
closing in on them from
every side.
[15]So that hearts may melt
and the fallen be many,
I have stationed the sword for
slaughter[a]
at all their gates.
Oh! It is made to flash like
lightning,
it is grasped for slaughter.
[16]O sword, slash to the right,
then to the left,
wherever your blade is
turned.
[17]I too will strike my hands
together,
and my wrath will subside.
I the LORD have spoken."

[18]The word of the LORD came to
me: [19]"Son of man, mark out two
roads for the sword of the king of
Babylon to take, both starting
from the same country. Make a
signpost where the road branches
off to the city. [20]Mark out one road
for the sword to come against
Rabbah of the Ammonites and
another against Judah and fortified Jerusalem. [21]For the king of
Babylon will stop at the fork in the
road, at the junction of the two
roads, to seek an omen: He will
cast lots with arrows, he will consult his idols, he will examine the
liver. [22]Into his right hand will
come the lot for Jerusalem, where
he is to set up battering rams, to
give the command to slaughter, to
sound the battle cry, to set battering rams against the gates, to
build a ramp and to erect siege
works. [23]It will seem like a false
omen to those who have sworn
allegiance to him, but he will remind them of their guilt and take
them captive.
[24]"Therefore this is what the
Sovereign LORD says: 'Because you

[a]*15* Septuagint; the meaning of the Hebrew for this word is uncertain.

**Heading* See the note on page 352.

°28 ק כקסם

יְהוִה יַעַן הַזְכַּרְכֶם עֲוֺנְכֶם בְּהִגָּלוֹת פִּשְׁעֵיכֶם
rebellions-of-you by-to-be-open guilt-of-you to-bring-to-mind-you because Yahweh

לְהֵרָאוֹת חַטֹּאותֵיכֶם בְּכֹל עֲלִילוֹתֵיכֶם יַעַן הִזָּכֶרְכֶם בַּכַּף
by-the-hand to-be-reminded-you because doings-of-you in-all-of sins-of-you to-reveal

תִּתָּפֵשׂוּ׃ וְאַתָּה חָלָל רָשָׁע נְשִׂיא יִשְׂרָאֵל אֲשֶׁר־בָּא
he-came who Israel prince-of wicked profane and-you (30[25]) you-will-be-captured

יוֹמוֹ בְּעֵת עֲוֺן קֵץ׃ כֹּה אָמַר אֲדֹנָי יְהוִה
Yahweh Sovereign he-says this (31[26]) climax punishment-of at-time-of day-of-him

הָסִיר הַמִּצְנֶפֶת וְהָרִים הָעֲטָרָה זֹאת לֹא־זֹאת הַשָּׁפָלָה הַגְבֵּהַ†
to-exalt the-lowly this not this the-crown and-remove! the-turban take-off!

וְהַגָּבֹהַּ הַשְׁפִּיל׃ עַוָּה עַוָּה עַוָּה אֲשִׂימֶנָּה גַּם־זֹאת
this also I-will-make-her ruin ruin ruin (32[27]) to-bring-low and-the-exalted

לֹא הָיָה עַד־בֹּא אֲשֶׁר־לוֹ הַמִּשְׁפָּט וּנְתַתִּיו׃
and-I-will-give-to-him the-right to-him whom to-come until he-will-be not

וְאַתָּה בֶן־אָדָם הִנָּבֵא וְאָמַרְתָּ כֹּה אָמַר אֲדֹנָי יְהוִה
Yahweh Sovereign he-says this and-you-say prophesy! man son-of and-you (33[28])

אֶל־בְּנֵי עַמּוֹן וְאֶל־חֶרְפָּתָם וְאָמַרְתָּ חֶרֶב חֶרֶב
sword sword and-you-say insult-of-them and-about Ammon sons-of about

פְּתוּחָה לְטֶבַח מְרוּטָה לְהָכִיל לְמַעַן בָּרָק׃
lightning so-that to-consume being-polished for-slaughter being-drawn

בַּחֲזוֹת לָךְ שָׁוְא בִּקְסָם־לָךְ
about-you despite-to-divine falsehood concerning-you despite-to-see-vision (34[29])

כָּזָב לָתֵת אוֹתָךְ אֶל־צַוְּארֵי חַלְלֵי רְשָׁעִים אֲשֶׁר־בָּא יוֹמָם
day-of-them he-came who wicked-ones ones-slain-of necks-of on you to-lay lie

בְּעֵת עֲוֺן קֵץ׃ הָשַׁב אֶל־תַּעְרָהּ בִּמְקוֹם
in-place-of scabbard-of-her to return! (35[30]) climax punishment-of at-time-of

אֲשֶׁר־נִבְרֵאת בְּאֶרֶץ מְכֻרוֹתַיִךְ אֶשְׁפֹּט אֹתָךְ׃
you I-will-judge ancestries-of-you in-land-of you-were-created where

וְשָׁפַכְתִּי עָלַיִךְ זַעְמִי בְּאֵשׁ עֶבְרָתִי
anger-of-me with-fire-of wrath-of-me on-you and-I-will-pour-out (36[31])

אָפִיחַ עָלַיִךְ וּנְתַתִּיךְ בְּיַד אֲנָשִׁים בֹּעֲרִים
ones-being-brutal men into-hand-of and-I-will-give-you against-you I-will-breathe-out

חָרָשֵׁי מַשְׁחִית׃ לָאֵשׁ תִּהְיֶה לְאָכְלָה דָּמֵךְ
blood-of-you as-fuel you-will-be for-the-fire (37[32]) destruction ones-skilled-of

יִהְיֶה בְּתוֹךְ הָאָרֶץ לֹא תִזָּכֵרִי כִּי אֲנִי יְהוָה דִּבַּרְתִּי׃
I-spoke Yahweh I for you-will-be-remembered not the-land in-midst-of he-will-be

וַיְהִי דְבַר־יְהוָה אֵלַי לֵאמֹר׃ וְאַתָּה בֶן־אָדָם הֲתִשְׁפֹּט
will-you-judge? man son-of now-you (2) to-say to-me Yahweh word-of and-he-came (22:1)

people have brought to mind your guilt by your open rebellion, revealing your sins in all that you do—because you have done this, you will be taken captive.
25 "'O profane and wicked prince of Israel, whose day has come, whose time of punishment has reached its climax,
26 this is what the Sovereign LORD says: Take off the turban, remove the crown. It will not be as it was: The lowly will be exalted and the exalted will be brought low.
27 A ruin! A ruin! I will make it a ruin! It will not be restored until he comes to whom it rightfully belongs; to him I will give it.'
28 "And you, son of man, prophesy and say, 'This is what the Sovereign LORD says about the Ammonites and their insults:

"'A sword, a sword,
drawn for the slaughter,
polished to consume
and to flash like lightning!
29 Despite false visions
concerning you
and lying divinations about
you,
it will be laid on the necks
of the wicked who are to be
slain,
whose day has come,
whose time of punishment
has reached its climax.
30 Return the sword to its
scabbard.
In the place where you were
created,
in the land of your ancestry,
I will judge you.
31 I will pour out my wrath upon
you
and breathe out my fiery
anger against you;
I will hand you over to brutal
men,
men skilled in destruction.
32 You will be fuel for the fire,
your blood will be shed in
your land,
you will be remembered no
more;
for I the LORD have
spoken.'"

*Jerusalem's Sins*

22 The word of the LORD came to me:
2 "Son of man, will

**Heading* See the note on page 352.

†*31* Most mss have *mappiq* in the *he* (ה־).

הֲתִשְׁפֹּט אֶת־ עִיר הַדָּמִים וְהוֹדַעְתָּהּ אֵת כָּל־
all-of with then-you-confront-her the-bloodsheds city-of *** will-you-judge?

תּוֹעֲבוֹתֶיהָ׃ וְאָמַרְתָּ כֹּה אָמַר אֲדֹנָי יְהוִה עִיר
city Yahweh Sovereign he-says this and-you-say (3) detestable-practices-of-her

שֹׁפֶכֶת דָּם בְּתוֹכָהּ לָבוֹא עִתָּהּ וְעָשְׂתָה גִלּוּלִים עָלֶיהָ
for-her idols and-she-makes doom-of-her to-come in-midst-of-her blood shedding

לְטָמְאָה׃ בְּדָמֵךְ אֲשֶׁר־ שָׁפַכְתְּ אָשַׁמְתְּ
you-became-guilty you-shed that because-of-blood-of-you (4) to-be-defiled

וּבְגִלּוּלַיִךְ אֲשֶׁר־ עָשִׂית טָמֵאת וַתַּקְרִיבִי
and-you-brought-to-close you-became-defiled you-made that and-by-idols-of-you

יָמַיִךְ וַתָּבוֹא עַד־* שְׁנוֹתָיִךְ עַל־ כֵּן נְתַתִּיךְ חֶרְפָּה
object-of-scorn I-will-make-you this for years-of-you *to and-she-came days-of-you

לַגּוֹיִם וְקַלָּסָה לְכָל־ הָאֲרָצוֹת׃ הַקְּרֹבוֹת
the-near-ones (5) the-countries to-all-of and-laughingstock to-the-nations

וְהָרְחֹקוֹת מִמֵּךְ יִתְקַלְּסוּ־ בָךְ טְמֵאַת הַשֵּׁם רַבַּת
full-of the-name unclean-of at-you they-will-mock from-you and-the-far-away-ones

הַמְּהוּמָה׃ הִנֵּה נְשִׂיאֵי יִשְׂרָאֵל אִישׁ לִזְרֹעוֹ הָיוּ בָךְ לְמַעַן
so-that in-you they-are by-power-of-him each Israel princes-of see! (6) the-turmoil

שְׁפָךְ־ דָּם׃ אָב וָאֵם הֵקַלּוּ בָךְ לַגֵּר
to-the-alien in-you they-treated-with-contempt and-mother father (7) blood to-shed

עָשׂוּ בַעֹשֶׁק בְּתוֹכֵךְ יָתוֹם וְאַלְמָנָה הוֹנוּ
they-mistreated and-widow fatherless in-midst-of-you with-the-oppression they-treated

בָךְ׃ קָדָשַׁי בָּזִית וְאֶת־ שַׁבְּתֹתַי חִלָּלְתְּ׃
you-desecrated Sabbaths-of-me and you-despised holy-things-of-me (8) in-you

אַנְשֵׁי רָכִיל הָיוּ בָךְ לְמַעַן שְׁפָךְ־ דָּם וְאֶל־ הֶהָרִים
the-mountains and-at blood to-shed so-that in-you they-are slander men-of (9)

אָכְלוּ בָךְ זִמָּה עָשׂוּ בְתוֹכֵךְ׃ עֶרְוַת־ אָב
father nakedness-of (10) in-midst-of-you they-commit lewd-act in-you they-eat

גִּלָּה־ בָךְ טְמֵאַת הַנִּדָּה עִנּוּ־ בָךְ׃ וְאִישׁ ׀
and-man (11) in-you they-violate the-period uncleanness-of in-you he-dishonors

אֶת־ אֵשֶׁת רֵעֵהוּ עָשָׂה תּוֹעֵבָה וְאִישׁ אֶת־
*** and-man detestable-offense he-commits neighbor-of-him wife-of with

כַּלָּתוֹ טִמֵּא בְזִמָּה וְאִישׁ אֶת־ אֲחֹתוֹ בַת־
daughter-of sister-of-him *** and-man in-shame he-defiles daughter-in-law-of-him

אָבִיו עִנָּה־ בָךְ׃ שֹׁחַד לָקְחוּ־ בָךְ לְמַעַן שְׁפָךְ־
to-shed so-that in-you they-accept bribe (12) in-you he-violates father-of-him

דָּם נֶשֶׁךְ וְתַרְבִּית לָקַחַתְּ וַתְּבַצְּעִי רֵעַיִךְ
neighbors-of-you and-you-make-unjust-gain you-take and-interest usury blood

you judge her? Will you judge this city of bloodshed? Then confront her with all her detestable practices [3]and say: 'This is what the Sovereign LORD says: O city that brings on herself doom by shedding blood in her midst and defiles herself by making idols, [4]you have become guilty because of the blood you have shed and have become defiled by the idols you have made. You have brought your days to a close, and the end of your years has come. Therefore I will make you an object of scorn to the nations and a laughingstock to all the countries. [5]Those who are near and those who are far away will mock you, O infamous city, full of turmoil.

[6]" 'See how each of the princes of Israel who are in you uses his power to shed blood. [7]In you they have treated father and mother with contempt; in you they have oppressed the alien and mistreated the fatherless and the widow. [8]You have despised my holy things and desecrated my Sabbaths. [9]In you are slanderous men bent on shedding blood; in you are those who eat at the mountain shrines and commit lewd acts. [10]In you are those who dishonor their fathers' bed; in you are those who violate women during their period, when they are ceremonially unclean. [11]In you one man commits a detestable offense with his neighbor's wife, another shamefully defiles his daughter-in-law, and another violates his sister, his own father's daughter. [12]In you men accept bribes to shed blood; you take usury and excessive interest[v] and make unjust gain from

[v]12 Or *usury and interest*

*4 The NIV, with some ancient mss and versions, reads עַד as עֵת, *end-of*

בַּעֹ֫שֶׁק וְאֹתִי שָׁכַחַתְּ נְאֻם אֲדֹנָי יְהוִה׃ וְהִנֵּה
and-surely! (13) Yahweh Sovereign declaration-of you-forgot and-me by-the-extortion

הִכֵּיתִי כַפִּי אֶל־ בִּצְעֵךְ אֲשֶׁר עָשִׂית וְעַל־ דָּמֵךְ
blood-of-you and-at you-made that unjust-gain-of-you at hand-of-me I-will-strike

אֲשֶׁר הָיוּ בְּתוֹכֵךְ׃ הֲיַעֲמֹד לִבֵּךְ אִם־
or courage-of-you will-he-endure? (14) in-midst-of-you they-are that

תֶּחֱזַקְנָה יָדַיִךְ לַיָּמִים אֲשֶׁר אֲנִי עֹשֶׂה אוֹתָךְ אֲנִי יְהוָה
Yahweh I with-you dealing I that in-the-days hands-of-you will-they-be-strong

דִּבַּרְתִּי וְעָשִׂיתִי׃ וַהֲפִיצוֹתִי אוֹתָךְ בַּגּוֹיִם
among-the-nations you and-I-will-disperse (15) and-I-will-do I-spoke

וְזֵרִיתִיךְ בָּאֲרָצוֹת וַהֲתִמֹּתִי טֻמְאָתֵךְ
uncleanness-of-you and-I-will-put-to-end through-the-countries and-I-will-scatter-you

מִמֵּךְ׃ וְנִחַלְתְּ בָּךְ לְעֵינֵי גוֹיִם וְיָדַעַתְּ
then-you-will-know nations before-eyes-of to-you when-you-are-defiled (16) from-you

כִּי־אֲנִי יְהוָה׃ וַיְהִי דְבַר־ יְהוָה אֵלַי לֵאמֹר׃ בֶּן־ אָדָם
man son-of (18) to-say to-me Yahweh word-of then-he-came (17) Yahweh I that

הָיוּ־ לִי בֵית־ יִשְׂרָאֵל לְסוּג° כֻּלָּם נְחֹשֶׁת וּבְדִיל וּבַרְזֶל
and-iron and-tin copper all-of-them into-dross Israel house-of to-me they-became

וְעוֹפֶרֶת בְּתוֹךְ כּוּר סִגִים כֶּסֶף הָיוּ׃ לָכֵן כֹּה אָמַר
he-says this therefore (19) they-are silver drosses furnace at-inside-of and-lead

אֲדֹנָי יְהוִה יַעַן הֱיוֹת כֻּלְּכֶם לְסִגִים לָכֵן הִנְנִי
see-I! therefore into-drosses all-of-you to-become because Yahweh Sovereign

קֹבֵץ אֶתְכֶם אֶל־ תּוֹךְ יְרוּשָׁלִָם׃ קְבֻצַת כֶּסֶף וּנְחֹשֶׁת וּבַרְזֶל
and-iron and-copper silver gathering-of (20) Jerusalem midst-of into you gathering

וְעוֹפֶרֶת וּבְדִיל אֶל־ תּוֹךְ כּוּר לָפַחַת־ עָלָיו אֵשׁ לְהַנְתִּיךְ כֵּן
so to-melt fire on-him to-blast furnace midst-of into and-tin and-lead

אֶקְבֹּץ בְּאַפִּי וּבַחֲמָתִי וְהִנַּחְתִּי וְהִתַּכְתִּי אֶתְכֶם׃
you and-I-will-melt and-I-will-put and-in-wrath-of-me in-anger-of-me I-will-gather

וְכִנַּסְתִּי אֶתְכֶם וְנָפַחְתִּי עֲלֵיכֶם בְּאֵשׁ עֶבְרָתִי
wrath-of-me with-fire-of on-you and-I-will-blow you and-I-will-gather (21)

וְנִתַּכְתֶּם בְּתוֹכָהּ׃ כְּהִתּוּךְ כֶּסֶף בְּתוֹךְ כּוּר
furnace at-inside-of silver as-melting-of (22) at-inside-her and-you-will-be-melted

כֵּן תֻּתְּכוּ בְּתוֹכָהּ וִידַעְתֶּם כִּי־אֲנִי יְהוָה שָׁפַכְתִּי
I-poured-out Yahweh I that and-you-will-know at-inside-her you-will-be-melted so

חֲמָתִי עֲלֵיכֶם׃ וַיְהִי דְבַר־ יְהוָה אֵלַי לֵאמֹר׃ בֶּן־אָדָם
man son-of (24) to-say to-me Yahweh word-of and-he-came (23) upon-you wrath-of-me

אֱמָר־לָהּ אַתְּ אֶרֶץ לֹא מְטֹהָרָה הִיא לֹא גֻשְׁמָהּ בְּיוֹם זָעַם׃
wrath in-day-of he-was-rained-on-her not she being-cleansed not land you to-her say!

°18 ק לסיג

your neighbors by extortion. And you have forgotten me, declares the Sovereign LORD.

[13]" 'I will surely strike my hands together at the unjust gain you have made and at the blood you have shed in your midst. [14]Will your courage endure or your hands be strong in the day I deal with you? I the LORD have spoken, and I will do it. [15]I will disperse you among the nations and scatter you through the countries; and I will put an end to your uncleanness. [16]When you have been defiled[w] in the eyes of the nations, you will know that I am the LORD.' "

[17]Then the word of the LORD came to me: [18]"Son of man, the house of Israel has become dross to me; all of them are the copper, tin, iron and lead left inside a furnace. They are but the dross of silver. [19]Therefore this is what the Sovereign LORD says: 'Because you have all become dross, I will gather you into Jerusalem. [20]As men gather silver, copper, iron, lead and tin into a furnace to melt it with a fiery blast, so will I gather you in my anger and my wrath and put you inside the city and melt you. [21]I will gather you and I will blow on you with my fiery wrath, and you will be melted inside her. [22]As silver is melted in a furnace, so you will be melted inside her, and you will know that I the LORD have poured out my wrath upon you.' "

[23]Again the word of the LORD came to me: [24]"Son of man, say to the land, 'You are a land that has had no rain or showers[x] in the day

[w]16 Or *When I have allotted you your inheritance*
[x]24 Septuagint; Hebrew *has not been cleansed or rained on*

טָרֶף טֹרֵף שׁוֹאֵג כַּאֲרִי בְּתוֹכָהּ נְבִיאֶיהָ קֶשֶׁר
prey tearing roaring like-lion at-within-her prophets-of-her conspiracy-of (25)

הִרְבּוּ אַלְמְנוֹתֶיהָ יִקָּחוּ וִיקָר חֹסֶן אָכָלוּ נֶפֶשׁ
they-make-many widows-of-her they-take and-precious-thing treasure they-devour people

וַיְחַלְּלוּ תוֹרָתִי חָמְסוּ כֹּהֲנֶיהָ בְּתוֹכָהּ׃
and-they-profane law-of-me they-do-violence priests-of-her (26) at-within-her

וּבֵין־ הִבְדִּילוּ לֹא לְחֹל קֹדֶשׁ בֵּין־ קָדָשַׁי
and-between they-distinguish not to-common holy between holy-things-of-me

עֵינֵיהֶם הֶעְלִימוּ וּמִשַּׁבְּתוֹתַי* הוֹדִיעוּ לֹא לְטָהוֹר הַטָּמֵא
eyes-of-them they-shut and-to-Sabbaths-of-me they-teach not to-clean the-unclean

כִּזְאֵבִים בְקִרְבָּהּ שָׂרֶיהָ בְּתוֹכָם׃ וָאֵחַל
like-wolves at-within-her officials-of-her (27) in-among-them so-I-am-profaned

בָּצַע לְמַעַן נְפָשׁוֹת לְאַבֵּד דָּם לִשְׁפָּךְ־ טָרֶף טֹרְפֵי
to-gain-unjustly so-that peoples to-kill blood to-shed prey ones-tearing-of

חֹזִים תָּפֵל לָהֶם טָחוּ וּנְבִיאֶיהָ בָּצַע׃
ones-seeing-visions whitewash for-them they-cover and-prophets-of-her (28) unjust-gain

יְהוִה אֲדֹנָי אָמַר כֹּה אֹמְרִים כָּזָב לָהֶם וְקֹסְמִים שָׁוְא
Yahweh Sovereign he-says this ones-saying lie for-them and-ones-divining falsehood

וְגָזְלוּ עֹשֶׁק עָשְׁקוּ הָאָרֶץ עַם דִבֵּר׃ לֹא וַיהוָה
and-they-rob extortion they-extort the-land people-of (29) he-spoke not when-Yahweh

מִשְׁפָּט׃ בְּלֹא עָשְׁקוּ הַגֵּר וְאֶת־ הוֹנוּ וְאֶבְיוֹן וְעָנִי גָּזֵל
justice with-no they-mistreat the-alien and they-oppress and-needy and-poor robbery

וְעֹמֵד גָדֵר גֹּדֵר־ אִישׁ מֵהֶם וָאֲבַקֵּשׁ
and-one-standing wall one-building man among-them and-I-looked-for (30)

מָצָאתִי׃ וְלֹא שַׁחֲתָהּ לְבִלְתִּי הָאָרֶץ בְּעַד לְפָנַי בַּפֶּרֶץ
I-found but-not to-destroy-her not the-land on-behalf-of before-me in-the-gap

עֶבְרָתִי בְּאֵשׁ זַעְמִי עֲלֵיהֶם וָאֶשְׁפֹּךְ
anger-of-me with-fire-of wrath-of-me on-them so-I-will-pour-out (31)

נְאֻם נָתַתִּי בְּרֹאשָׁם דַּרְכָּם כִּלִּיתִים
declaration-of I-will-bring on-head-of-them deed-of-them I-will-consume-them

בֶּן־אָדָם לֵאמֹר׃ אֵלַי יְהוָה דְבַר־ וַיְהִי יְהוִה׃ אֲדֹנָי
man son-of (2) to-say to-me Yahweh word-of and-he-came (23:1) Yahweh Sovereign

בְמִצְרַיִם וַתִּזְנֶינָה הָיוּ׃ אַחַת אֵם־ בְּנוֹת נָשִׁים שְׁתַּיִם
in-Egypt and-they-became-prostitutes (3) they-were same mother daughters-of women two

מֹעֲכוּ שָׁמָּה זָנוּ בִּנְעוּרֵיהֶן
they-were-fondled at-there they-engaged-in-prostitution from-youths-of-them

בְּתוּלֵיהֶן׃ דַּדֵּי עִשּׂוּ וְשָׁם שְׁדֵיהֶן
virginities-of-them bosoms-of they-caressed and-there breasts-of-them

of wrath.' 25There is a conspiracy
of her princes[y] within her like a
roaring lion tearing its prey; they
devour people, take treasures and
precious things and make many
widows within her. 26Her priests
do violence to my law and profane
my holy things; they do not distinguish between the holy and the
common; they teach that there is
no difference between the unclean and the clean; and they shut
their eyes to the keeping of my
Sabbaths, so that I am profaned
among them. 27Her officials within her are like wolves tearing their
prey; they shed blood and kill
people to make unjust gain. 28Her
prophets whitewash these deeds
for them by false visions and lying
divinations. They say, 'This is
what the Sovereign LORD
says'—when the LORD has not
spoken. 29The people of the land
practice extortion and commit
robbery; they oppress the poor
and needy and mistreat the alien,
denying them justice.
30"I looked for a man among
them who would build up the wall
and stand before me in the gap on
behalf of the land so I would not
have to destroy it, but I found
none. 31So I will pour out my
wrath on them and consume them
with my fiery anger, bringing
down on their own heads all they
have done, declares the Sovereign
LORD."

*Two Adulterous Sisters*

23 The word of the LORD came
to me: 2"Son of man, there
were two women, daughters of
the same mother. 3They became
prostitutes in Egypt, engaging in
prostitution from their youth. In
that land their breasts were fondled and their virgin bosoms caressed. 4The older was named

y25 Septuagint; Hebrew *prophets*

*26 Most mss have *dagesh* in the *shin* (ומשׁ׳).

וּשְׁמוֹתָן אָהֳלָה הַגְּדוֹלָה וְאָהֳלִיבָה אֲחוֹתָהּ וַתִּהְיֶינָה
and-they-were sister-of-her and-Oholibah the-older Oholah and-names-of-them (4)

לִי וַתֵּלַדְנָה בָּנִים וּבָנוֹת וּשְׁמוֹתָן שֹׁמְרוֹן אָהֳלָה
Oholah Samaria and-names-of-them and-daughters sons and-they-bore to-me

וִירוּשָׁלִַם אָהֳלִיבָה׃ וַתִּזֶן אָהֳלָה תַּחְתָּי
still-to-me Oholah and-she-engaged-in-prostitution (5) Oholibah and-Jerusalem

וַתַּעְגַּב עַל־ מְאַהֲבֶיהָ אֶל־ אַשּׁוּר קְרוֹבִים׃ לְבֻשֵׁי
ones-being-clothed-of (6) warriors Assyria after ones-loving-her after and-she-lusted

תְכֵלֶת פַּחוֹת וּסְגָנִים בַּחוּרֵי חֶמֶד כֻּלָּם פָּרָשִׁים
horsemen all-of-them handsomeness young-men-of and-commanders governors blue

רֹכְבֵי סוּסִים׃ וַתִּתֵּן תַּזְנוּתֶיהָ עֲלֵיהֶם מִבְחַר
elite-of to-them prostitutions-of-her and-she-gave (7) horses ones-mounting-of

בְּנֵי־ אַשּׁוּר כֻּלָּם וּבְכֹל אֲשֶׁר־ עָגְבָה בְּכָל־
with-all-of she-lusted-after whom and-to-everyone all-of-them Assyria sons-of

גִּלּוּלֵיהֶם נִטְמָאָה׃ וְאֶת־ תַּזְנוּתֶיהָ מִמִּצְרַיִם לֹא
not from-Egypt prostitutions-of-her and (8) she-defiled-herself idols-of-them

עָזָבָה כִּי אוֹתָהּ שָׁכְבוּ בִנְעוּרֶיהָ וְהֵמָּה עִשּׂוּ
they-caressed and-they during-youths-of-her they-slept with-her when she-gave-up

דַּדֵּי בְּתוּלֶיהָ וַיִּשְׁפְּכוּ תַזְנוּתָם עָלֶיהָ׃ לָכֵן
therefore (9) on-her lust-of-them and-they-poured-out virginities-of-her bosoms-of

נְתַתִּיהָ בְּיַד־ מְאַהֲבֶיהָ בְּיַד בְּנֵי אַשּׁוּר אֲשֶׁר עָגְבָה
she-lusted whom Assyria men-of into-hand-of ones-loving-her into-hand-of I-gave-her

עֲלֵיהֶם׃ הֵמָּה גִּלּוּ עֶרְוָתָהּ בָּנֶיהָ וּבְנוֹתֶיהָ
and-daughters-of-her sons-of-her nakedness-of-her they-stripped they (10) for-them

לָקָחוּ וְאוֹתָהּ בַּחֶרֶב הָרָגוּ וַתְּהִי־ שֵׁם לַנָּשִׁים
among-the-women byword and-she-became they-killed with-the-sword and-her they-took

וּשְׁפוּטִים עָשׂוּ בָהּ׃ וַתֵּרֶא אֲחוֹתָהּ אָהֳלִיבָה
Oholibah sister-of-her and-she-saw (11) on-her they-inflicted and-punishments

וַתַּשְׁחֵת עַגְבָתָהּ מִמֶּנָּה וְאֶת־ תַּזְנוּתֶיהָ
prostitutions-of-her and more-than-her lust-of-her yet-she-made-depraved

מִזְּנוּנֵי אֲחוֹתָהּ׃ אֶל־ בְּנֵי אַשּׁוּר עָגָבָה
she-lusted Assyria men-of after (12) sister-of-her more-than-prostitutions-of

פַּחוֹת וּסְגָנִים קְרֹבִים לְבֻשֵׁי מִכְלוֹל פָּרָשִׁים
horsemen fullness ones-being-dressed-of warriors and-commanders governors

רֹכְבֵי סוּסִים בַּחוּרֵי חֶמֶד כֻּלָּם׃ וָאֵרֶא כִּי
that and-I-saw (13) all-of-them handsomeness young-men-of horses ones-mounting-of

נִטְמָאָה דֶּרֶךְ אֶחָד לִשְׁתֵּיהֶן׃ וַתּוֹסֶף אֶל־
to but-she-carried-further (14) to-both-of-them same way she-defiled-herself

Oholah, and her sister was Oholibah. They were mine and gave birth to sons and daughters. Oholah is Samaria, and Oholibah is Jerusalem.

5"Oholah engaged in prostitution while she was still mine; and she lusted after her lovers, the Assyrians—warriors 6clothed in blue, governors and commanders, all of them handsome young men, and mounted horsemen. 7She gave herself as a prostitute to all the elite of the Assyrians and defiled herself with all the idols of everyone she lusted after. 8She did not give up the prostitution she began in Egypt, when during her youth men slept with her, caressed her virgin bosom and poured out their lust upon her.

9"Therefore I handed her over to her lovers, the Assyrians, for whom she lusted. 10They stripped her naked, took away her sons and daughters and killed her with the sword. She became a byword among women, and punishment was inflicted on her.

11"Her sister Oholibah saw this, yet in her lust and prostitution she was more depraved than her sister. 12She too lusted after the Assyrians—governors and commanders, warriors in full dress, mounted horsemen, all handsome young men. 13I saw that she too defiled herself; both of them went the same way.

תַּזְנוּתֶיהָ וַתֵּרֶא אַנְשֵׁי מְחֻקֶּה עַל־ הַקִּיר צַלְמֵי
figures-of the-wall on being-portrayed men-of and-she-saw prostitutions-of-her

כשדיים° חֲקֻקִים בַּשָּׁשַׁר׃ חֲגוֹרֵי אֵזוֹר
belt ones-wrapped-of (15) in-the-red ones-being-portrayed Chaldeans

בְּמָתְנֵיהֶם סְרוּחֵי טְבוּלִים בְּרָאשֵׁיהֶם מַרְאֵה
look-of on-heads-of-them turbans ones-flowing-of around-waists-of-them

שָׁלִשִׁים כֻּלָּם דְּמוּת בְּנֵי־ בָבֶל כַּשְׂדִּים אֶרֶץ
land-of Chaldea Babylon men-of appearance-of all-of-them chariot-officers

מוֹלַדְתָּם׃ ותעגב° עֲלֵיהֶם לְמַרְאֵה עֵינֶיהָ וַתִּשְׁלַח
and-she-sent eyes-of-her at-sight-of after-them and-she-lusted (16) birth-of-them

מַלְאָכִים אֲלֵיהֶם כַּשְׂדִּימָה׃ וַיָּבֹאוּ אֵלֶיהָ בְנֵי־ בָבֶל לְמִשְׁכַּב
to-bed-of Babylon men-of to-her then-they-came (17) in-Chaldea to-them messengers

דֹּדִים וַיְטַמְּאוּ אוֹתָהּ בְּתַזְנוּתָם וַתִּטְמָא־ בָם
by-them after-she-was-defiled in-lust-of-them her and-they-defiled loves

וַתֵּקַע נַפְשָׁהּ מֵהֶם׃ וַתְּגַל תַּזְנוּתֶיהָ
prostitutions-of-her when-she-made-open (18) from-them self-of-her then-she-turned

וַתְּגַל אֶת־ עֶרְוָתָהּ וַתֵּקַע נַפְשִׁי מֵעָלֶיהָ
from-with-her self-of-me then-she-turned nakedness-of-her *** and-she-exposed

כַּאֲשֶׁר נָקְעָה נַפְשִׁי מֵעַל אֲחוֹתָהּ׃ וַתַּרְבֶּה אֶת־
*** yet-she-made-more (19) sister-of-her from-with self-of-me she-turned just-as

תַּזְנוּתֶיהָ לִזְכֹּר אֶת־ יְמֵי נְעוּרֶיהָ אֲשֶׁר זָנְתָה
she-was-prostitute when youths-of-her days-of *** to-recall promiscuities-of-her

בְּאֶרֶץ מִצְרָיִם׃ וַתַּעְגְּבָה עַל פִּלַגְשֵׁיהֶם אֲשֶׁר בְּשַׂר־ חֲמוֹרִים
donkeys genital-of who lovers-of-her after and-she-lusted (20) Egypt in-land-of

בְּשָׂרָם וְזִרְמַת סוּסִים זִרְמָתָם׃ וַתִּפְקְדִי
so-you-longed-for (21) emission-of-them horses and-emission-of genital-of-them

אֵת זִמַּת נְעוּרָיִךְ בַּעְשׂוֹת מִמִּצְרַיִם דַּדַּיִךְ לְמַעַן
because-of bosoms-of-you in-Egypt when-to-caress youths-of-you lewdness-of ***

שְׁדֵי נְעוּרָיִךְ׃ לָכֵן אָהֳלִיבָה כֹּה־ אָמַר אֲדֹנָי יְהוִה
Yahweh Sovereign he-says this Oholibah therefore (22) youths-of-you breasts-of

הִנְנִי מֵעִיר אֶת־ מְאַהֲבַיִךְ עָלַיִךְ אֵת אֲשֶׁר־ נָקְעָה נַפְשֵׁךְ
self-of-you she-turned whom *** against-you ones-loving-you *** stirring-up see-I!

מֵהֶם וַהֲבֵאתִים עָלַיִךְ מִסָּבִיב׃ בְּנֵי בָבֶל
Babylon men-of (23) from-every-side against-you and-I-will-bring-them from-them

וְכָל־ כַּשְׂדִּים פְּקוֹד וְשׁוֹעַ וְקוֹעַ כָּל־ בְּנֵי אַשּׁוּר אוֹתָם
with-them Assyria men-of all-of and-Koa and-Shoa Pekod Chaldeans and-all-of

בַּחוּרֵי חֶמֶד פַּחוֹת וּסְגָנִים כֻּלָּם שָׁלִשִׁים
chariot-officers all-of-them and-commanders governors handsomeness young-men-of

°14 ק כשדים
°16 ק ותעגבה

14"But she carried her prostitution still further. She saw men
portrayed on a wall, figures of
Chaldeans[z] portrayed in red,
15with belts around their waists
and flowing turbans on their
heads; all of them looked like Babylonian chariot officers, natives of
Chaldea.[a] 16As soon as she saw
them, she lusted after them and
sent messengers to them in Chaldea. 17Then the Babylonians came
to her, to the bed of love, and in
their lust they defiled her. After
she had been defiled by them, she
turned away from them in disgust. 18When she carried on her
prostitution openly and exposed
her nakedness, I turned away
from her in disgust, just as I had
turned away from her sister. 19Yet
she became more and more promiscuous as she recalled the days
of her youth, when she was a
prostitute in Egypt. 20There she
lusted after her lovers, whose
genitals were like those of donkeys and whose emission was like
that of horses. 21So you longed for
the lewdness of your youth, when
in Egypt your bosom was caressed
and your young breasts fondled.[b]
22"Therefore, Oholibah, this is
what the Sovereign LORD says: I
will stir up your lovers against
you, those you turned away from
in disgust, and I will bring them
against you from every side— 23the
Babylonians and all the Chaldeans, the men of Pekod and Shoa
and Koa, and all the Assyrians
with them, handsome young
men, all of them governors and
commanders, chariot officers and

z14 Or *Babylonians*
a15 Or *Babylonia*; also in verse 16
b21 Syriac (see also verse 3); Hebrew *caressed because of your young breasts*

וּקְרוּאִים רֹכְבֵי סוּסִים כֻּלָּם׃ וּבָאוּ
and-they-will-come (24) all-of-them horses ones-mounting-of and-men-being-called

עָלַיִךְ הֹצֶן רֶכֶב וְגַלְגַּל וּבִקְהַל עַמִּים צִנָּה
large-shield peoples and-with-throng-of and-wagon chariot weapon against-you

וּמָגֵן וְקוֹבַע יָשִׂימוּ עָלַיִךְ סָבִיב
every-side against-you they-will-take-positions and-helmet and-small-shield

וְנָתַתִּי לִפְנֵיהֶם מִשְׁפָּט וּשְׁפָטוּךְ
and-they-will-punish-you punishment before-them and-I-will-turn-over

בְּמִשְׁפְּטֵיהֶם׃ וְנָתַתִּי קִנְאָתִי בָּךְ
against-you jealous-anger-of-me and-I-will-direct (25) according-to-standards-of-them

וְעָשׂוּ אוֹתָךְ בְּחֵמָה אַפֵּךְ וְאָזְנַיִךְ יָסִירוּ
they-will-cut-off and-ears-of-you nose-of-you in-fury with-you and-they-will-deal

וְאַחֲרִיתֵךְ בַּחֶרֶב תִּפּוֹל הֵמָּה בָּנַיִךְ וּבְנוֹתַיִךְ
and-daughters-of-you sons-of-you they she-will-fall by-the-sword and-one-left-of-you

יִקָּחוּ וְאַחֲרִיתֵךְ תֵּאָכֵל בָּאֵשׁ׃
by-fire she-will-be-consumed and-one-left-of-you they-will-take-away

וְהִפְשִׁיטוּךְ אֶת־ בְּגָדַיִךְ וְלָקְחוּ כְּלֵי
jewels-of and-they-will-take clothes-of-you *** also-they-will-strip-off-you (26)

תִפְאַרְתֵּךְ׃ וְהִשְׁבַּתִּי זִמָּתֵךְ מִמֵּךְ וְאֶת־ זְנוּתֵךְ
prostitution-of-you and from-you lewdness-of-you so-I-will-stop (27) finery-of-you

מֵאֶרֶץ מִצְרָיִם וְלֹא־ תִשְׂאִי עֵינַיִךְ אֲלֵיהֶם וּמִצְרַיִם לֹא
not or-Egypt on-them eyes-of-you you-will-lift and-not Egypt from-land-of

תִזְכְּרִי־ עוֹד׃ כִּי כֹה אָמַר אֲדֹנָי יְהוִה הִנְנִי נֹתְנָךְ
giving-you see-I! Yahweh Sovereign he-says this for (28) anymore you-will-remember

בְּיַד אֲשֶׁר שָׂנֵאת בְּיַד אֲשֶׁר־ נָקְעָה נַפְשֵׁךְ מֵהֶם׃
from-them self-of-you she-turned whom into-hand-of you-hate whom into-hand-of

וְעָשׂוּ אוֹתָךְ בְּשִׂנְאָה וְלָקְחוּ כָּל־
all-of and-they-will-take-away in-hatred with-you and-they-will-deal (29)

יְגִיעֵךְ וַעֲזָבוּךְ עֵירֹם וְעֶרְיָה וְנִגְלָה עֶרְוַת
shame-of and-he-will-be-exposed and-bare naked and-they-will-leave-you work-of-you

זְנוּנַיִךְ וְזִמָּתֵךְ וְתַזְנוּתָיִךְ׃ עָשֹׂה
to-bring (30) and-promiscuities-of-you and-lewdness-of-you prostitutions-of-you

אֵלֶּה לָךְ בִּזְנוֹתֵךְ אַחֲרֵי גוֹיִם עַל אֲשֶׁר־ נִטְמֵאת
you-defiled-yourself that because nations after because-to-lust-you upon-you these

בְּגִלּוּלֵיהֶם׃ בְּדֶרֶךְ אֲחוֹתֵךְ הָלָכְתְּ וְנָתַתִּי כוֹסָהּ
cup-of-her so-I-will-put you-went sister-of-you on-way-of (31) with-idols-of-them

בְּיָדֵךְ׃ כֹּה אָמַר אֲדֹנָי יְהוִה כּוֹס אֲחוֹתֵךְ
sister-of-you cup-of Yahweh Sovereign he-says this (32) into-hand-of-you

men of high rank, all mounted on horses. [24]They will come against you with weapons,[c] chariots and wagons and with a throng of people; they will take up positions against you on every side with large and small shields and with helmets. I will turn you over to them for punishment, and they will punish you according to their standards. [25]I will direct my jealous anger against you, and they will deal with you in fury. They will cut off your noses and your ears, and those of you who are left will fall by the sword. They will take away your sons and daughters, and those of you who are left will be consumed by fire. [26]They will also strip you of your clothes and take your fine jewelry. [27]So I will put a stop to the lewdness and prostitution you began in Egypt. You will not look on these things with longing or remember Egypt anymore.

[28]"For this is what the Sovereign LORD says: I am about to hand you over to those you hate, to those you turned away from in disgust. [29]They will deal with you in hatred and take away everything you have worked for. They will leave you naked and bare, and the shame of your prostitution will be exposed. Your lewdness and promiscuity [30]have brought this upon you, because you lusted after the nations and defiled yourself with their idols. [31]You have gone the way of your sister; so I will put her cup into your hand.

[32]"This is what the Sovereign LORD says:

"You will drink your sister's
cup,

c24 The meaning of the Hebrew for this word is uncertain.

תִּשְׁתִּי הָעֲמֻקָּה וְהָרְחָבָה תִּהְיֶה לִצְחֹק וּלְלַעַג
and-for-derision for-scorn she-will-be and-the-large-one the-deep-one you-will-drink

מִרְבָּה לְהָכִיל׃ שִׁכָּרוֹן וְיָגוֹן תִּמָּלֵאִי כּוֹס שַׁמָּה
ruin cup-of you-will-be-filled and-sorrow drunkenness (33) to-hold much

וּשְׁמָמָה כּוֹס אֲחוֹתֵךְ שֹׁמְרוֹן׃ וְשָׁתִית אוֹתָהּ
her and-you-will-drink (34) Samaria sister-of-you cup-of and-desolation

וּמָצִית וְאֶת־ חֲרָשֶׂיהָ תְּגָרֵמִי וְשָׁדַיִךְ
and-breasts-of-you you-will-dash pieces-of-her and and-you-will-drain-dry

תְּנַתֵּקִי כִּי אֲנִי דִבַּרְתִּי נְאֻם אֲדֹנָי יְהוִה׃ לָכֵן כֹּה
this therefore (35) Yahweh Sovereign declaration-of I-spoke I for you-will-tear

אָמַר אֲדֹנָי יְהוִה יַעַן שָׁכַחַתְּ אוֹתִי וַתַּשְׁלִיכִי אוֹתִי אַחֲרֵי גַוֵּךְ
back-of-you behind me and-you-thrust me you-forgot since Yahweh Sovereign he-says

וְגַם־ אַתְּ שְׂאִי זִמָּתֵךְ וְאֶת־ תַּזְנוּתָיִךְ׃ וַיֹּאמֶר יְהוָה
Yahweh and-he-said (36) prostitutions-of-you and lewdness-of-you bear! you so-also

אֵלַי בֶּן־ אָדָם הֲתִשְׁפּוֹט אֶת־ אָהֳלָה וְאֶת־ אָהֳלִיבָה וְהַגֵּד לָהֶן
to-them then-confront! Oholibah and Oholah *** will-you-judge? man son-of to-me

אֵת תּוֹעֲבוֹתֵיהֶן׃ כִּי נִאֵפוּ וְדָם
and-blood they-committed-adultery for (37) detestable-practices-of-them with

בִּידֵיהֶן וְאֶת־ גִּלּוּלֵיהֶן נִאֵפוּ וְגַם אֶת־
*** and-even they-committed-adultery idols-of-them and-with on-hands-of-them

בְּנֵיהֶן אֲשֶׁר יָלְדוּ־ לִי הֶעֱבִירוּ לָהֶם לְאָכְלָה׃
as-food to-them they-made-pass-through to-me they-bore whom children-of-them

עוֹד זֹאת עָשׂוּ לִי טִמְּאוּ אֶת־ מִקְדָּשִׁי בַּיּוֹם
at-the-day sanctuary-of-me *** they-defiled to-me they-did this also (38)

הַהוּא וְאֶת־ שַׁבְּתוֹתַי חִלֵּלוּ׃ וּבְשַׁחֲטָם אֶת־
*** and-when-to-sacrifice-them (39) they-desecrated Sabbaths-of-me and the-that

בְּנֵיהֶם לְגִלּוּלֵיהֶם וַיָּבֹאוּ אֶל־ מִקְדָּשִׁי בַּיּוֹם
on-the-day sanctuary-of-me into then-they-entered to-idols-of-them children-of-them

הַהוּא לְחַלְּלוֹ וְהִנֵּה־ כֹה עָשׂוּ בְּתוֹךְ בֵּיתִי׃
house-of-me at-inside-of they-did that so-see! to-desecrate-him the-that

וְאַף כִּי תִשְׁלַחְנָה לַאֲנָשִׁים בָּאִים מִמֶּרְחָק אֲשֶׁר מַלְאָךְ
messenger who from-far-away ones-coming for-men they-sent indeed and-even (40)

שָׁלוּחַ אֲלֵיהֶם וְהִנֵּה־ בָאוּ לַאֲשֶׁר רָחַצְתְּ כָּחַלְתְּ עֵינַיִךְ
eyes-of-you you-painted you-bathed at-when they-arrived and-see! to-them being-sent

וְעָדִית* עֶדִי׃ וְיָשַׁבְתְּ עַל־ מִטָּה כְבוּדָּה וְשֻׁלְחָן
with-table elegant couch on and-you-sat (41) jewelry and-you-put-on-jewelry

עָרוּךְ לְפָנֶיהָ וּקְטָרְתִּי וְשַׁמְנִי שַׂמְתְּ עָלֶיהָ׃
on-her you-placed and-oil-of-me and-incense-of-me before-her being-spread

a cup large and deep;
it will bring scorn and
derision,
for it holds so much.
33 You will be filled with
drunkenness and sorrow,
the cup of ruin and
desolation,
the cup of your sister
Samaria.
34 You will drink it and drain it
dry;
you will dash it to pieces
and tear your breasts.

I have spoken, declares the Sovereign LORD.

35 "Therefore this is what the Sovereign LORD says: Since you have forgotten me and thrust me behind your back, you must bear the consequences of your lewdness and prostitution."

36 The LORD said to me: "Son of man, will you judge Oholah and Oholibah? Then confront them with their detestable practices,
37 for they have committed adultery and blood is on their hands. They committed adultery with their idols; they even sacrificed their children, whom they bore to me,[d] as food for them.
38 They have also done this to me: At that same time they defiled my sanctuary and desecrated my Sabbaths.
39 On the very day they sacrificed their children to their idols, they entered my sanctuary and desecrated it. That is what they did in my house.

40 "They even sent messengers for men who came from far away, and when they arrived you bathed yourself for them, painted your eyes and put on your jewelry.
41 You sat on an elegant couch, with a table spread before it on which you had placed the incense and oil that belonged to me.

[d]37 Or *even made the children they bore to me pass through ⌊the fire⌋*

*40 Most mss have the accent on the final syllable (וְעָדִית).

וְקוֹל הָמוֹן שָׁלֵו בָהּ וְאֶל־אֲנָשִׁים מֵרֹב אָדָם
man from-rabble-of men and-with around-her carefree crowd and-noise-of (42)

מוּבָאִים סוֹבָאִים מִמִּדְבָּר וַיִּתְּנוּ צְמִידִים אֶל־יְדֵיהֶן
arms-of-them on bracelets and-they-put from-desert Sabeans ones-being-brought

וַעֲטֶרֶת תִּפְאֶרֶת עַל־רָאשֵׁיהֶן׃ וָאֹמַר לַבָּלָה
about-the-one-worn-out then-I-said (43) heads-of-them on beauty and-crown-of

נִאוּפִים עַתְּ יִזְנֶה תַזְנוּתֶהָ וָהִיא׃
for-she prostitution-of-her let-them-use-as-prostitute now adulteries

וַיָּבוֹא אֵלֶיהָ כְּבוֹא אֶל־אִשָּׁה זוֹנָה כֵּן בָּאוּ
they-went so one-being-prostitute woman into as-to-go into-her and-they-went (44)

אֶל־אָהֳלָה וְאֶל־אָהֳלִיבָה אִשֹּׁת הַזִּמָּה׃ וַאֲנָשִׁים צַדִּיקִם
righteous-ones but-men (45) the-lewdness women-of Oholibah and-into Oholah into

הֵמָּה יִשְׁפְּטוּ אוֹתְהֶם מִשְׁפַּט נֹאֲפוֹת וּמִשְׁפַּט
and-judgment-of women-committing-adultery judgment-of them they-will-sentence they

שֹׁפְכוֹת דָּם כִּי נֹאֲפֹת הֵנָּה וְדָם בִּידֵיהֶן׃
on-hands-of-them and-blood they women-committing-adultery because blood women-shedding

כִּי כֹה אָמַר אֲדֹנָי יְהוִה הַעֲלֵה עֲלֵיהֶם קָהָל וְנָתֹן
and-to-give-over mob against-them bring! Yahweh Sovereign he-says this for (46)

אֶתְהֶן לַזַעֲוָה וְלָבַז׃ וְרָגְמוּ עֲלֵיהֶן אֶבֶן קָהָל
mob stone on-them and-they-will-stone (47) and-to-plunder to-terror them

וּבָרֵא אוֹתְהֶן בְּחַרְבוֹתָם בְּנֵיהֶם וּבְנוֹתֵיהֶם
and-daughters-of-them sons-of-them with-swords-of-them them and-to-cut-down

יַהֲרֹגוּ וּבָתֵּיהֶן בָּאֵשׁ יִשְׂרֹפוּ׃ וְהִשְׁבַּתִּי
so-I-will-end (48) they-will-burn-down with-fire and-houses-of-them they-will-kill

זִמָּה מִן־הָאָרֶץ וְנִוַּסְּרוּ כָּל־הַנָּשִׁים וְלֹא תַעֲשֶׂינָה
they-may-do and-not the-women all-of that-they-may-take-warning the-land in lewdness

כְּזִמַּתְכֶנָה׃ וְנָתְנוּ זִמַּתְכֶנָה עֲלֵיכֶן וַחֲטָאֵי
and-sins-of upon-you lewdness-of-you and-they-will-put (49) as-lewdness-of-you

גִלּוּלֵיכֶן תִּשֶּׂאינָה וִידַעְתֶּם כִּי אֲנִי אֲדֹנָי יְהוִה׃
Yahweh Sovereign I that then-you-will-know you-will-bear idols-of-you

וַיְהִי דְבַר־יְהוָה אֵלַי בַּשָּׁנָה הַתְּשִׁיעִית בַּחֹדֶשׁ הָעֲשִׂירִי
the-tenth in-the-month the-ninth in-the-year to-me Yahweh word-of and-he-came (24:1)

בֶּעָשׂוֹר לַחֹדֶשׁ לֵאמֹר׃ בֶּן־אָדָם כְּתָוב־לְךָ אֶת־שֵׁם הַיּוֹם
the-day name-of *** for-you record! man son-of (2) to-say of-the-month on-the-ten

אֶת־עֶצֶם הַיּוֹם הַזֶּה סָמַךְ מֶלֶךְ־בָּבֶל אֶל־יְרוּשָׁלַםִ בְּעֶצֶם
on-very-of Jerusalem to Babylon king-of he-laid-siege the-this the-day very-of ***

הַיּוֹם הַזֶּה׃ וּמְשֹׁל אֶל־בֵּית־הַמֶּרִי מָשָׁל וְאָמַרְתָּ
and-you-say parable the-rebellion house-of to and-tell-parable! (3) the-this the-day

42"The noise of a carefree crowd was around her; Sabeans[e] were brought from the desert along with men from the rabble, and they put bracelets on the arms of the woman and her sister and beautiful crowns on their heads. 43Then I said about the one worn out by adultery, 'Now let them use her as a prostitute, for that is all she is.' 44And they slept with her. As men sleep with a prostitute, so they slept with those lewd women, Oholah and Oholibah. 45But righteous men will sentence them to the punishment of women who commit adultery and shed blood, because they are adulterous and blood is on their hands.

46"This is what the Sovereign LORD says: Bring a mob against them and give them over to terror and plunder. 47The mob will stone them and cut them down with their swords; they will kill their sons and daughters and burn down their houses.

48"So I will put an end to lewdness in the land, that all women may take warning and not imitate you. 49You will suffer the penalty for your lewdness and bear the consequences of your sins of idolatry. Then you will know that I am the Sovereign LORD."

*The Cooking Pot*

24 In the ninth year, in the tenth month on the tenth day, the word of the LORD came to me: 2"Son of man, record this date, this very date, because the king of Babylon has laid siege to Jerusalem this very day. 3Tell this rebellious house a parable and say to

e42 Or *drunkards*

°42 ק סבאים ;°43a ק עתה
°43b ק יזנו ;°2 ק כתב

אֲלֵיהֶם כֹּה אָמַר אֲדֹנָי יְהוִה שְׁפֹת הַסִּיר שְׁפֹת וְגַם־
and-also put-on! the-cooking-pot put-on! Yahweh Sovereign he-says this to-them

יְצֹק בּוֹ מָיִם׃ אֱסֹף נְתָחֶיהָ אֵלֶיהָ כָּל־ נֵתַח
piece-of-meat all-of into-her pieces-of-meat-of-her put! (4) waters into-him pour!

טוֹב יָרֵךְ וְכָתֵף מִבְחַר עֲצָמִים מַלֵּא׃ מִבְחַר הַצֹּאן לָקוֹחַ וְגַם
and-also to-take the-flock pick-of (5) fill! bones best-of and-shoulder leg choice

דּוּר הָעֲצָמִים תַּחְתֶּיהָ רַתַּח רְתָחֶיהָ גַּם־ בָּשְׁלוּ
let-them-cook and boilings-of-her bring-to-boil! beneath-her the-bones pile!

עֲצָמֶיהָ בְּתוֹכָהּ׃ לָכֵן כֹּה־ אָמַר ׀ אֲדֹנָי יְהוִה אוֹי עִיר
city-of woe! Yahweh Sovereign he-says this for (6) in-midst-of-her bones-of-her

הַדָּמִים סִיר אֲשֶׁר חֶלְאָתָה בָהּ וְחֶלְאָתָהּ לֹא יָצְאָה
she-will-go-away not and-deposit-of-her on-her crust-of-her that pot the-bloodsheds

מִמֶּנָּה לִנְתָחֶיהָ לִנְתָחֶיהָ הוֹצִיאָהּ לֹא־ נָפַל עָלֶיהָ גּוֹרָל׃
lot for-her let-him-cast not empty-her! by-pieces-of-her by-pieces-of-her from-her

כִּי דָמָהּ בְּתוֹכָהּ הָיָה עַל־ צְחִיחַ סֶלַע שָׂמָתְהוּ
she-poured-him rock bare-part-of on he-is in-midst-of-her blood-of-her for (7)

לֹא שְׁפָכַתְהוּ עַל־ הָאָרֶץ לְכַסּוֹת עָלָיו עָפָר׃ לְהַעֲלוֹת חֵמָה
wrath to-stir-up (8) dust over-him to-cover the-ground on she-poured-him not

לִנְקֹם נָקָם נָתַתִּי אֶת־ דָּמָהּ עַל־ צְחִיחַ סָלַע לְבִלְתִּי
so-not rock bare-part-of on blood-of-her *** I-put revenge to-take-revenge

הִכָּסוֹת׃ לָכֵן כֹּה אָמַר אֲדֹנָי יְהוִה אוֹי עִיר הַדָּמִים
the-bloodsheds city-of woe! Yahweh Sovereign he-says this therefore (9) to-be-covered

גַּם־ אֲנִי אַגְדִּיל הַמְּדוּרָה׃ הַרְבֵּה הָעֵצִים הַדְלֵק הָאֵשׁ הָתֵם
cook-well! the-fire kindle! the-woods heap! (10) the-pile I-will-make-high I too

הַבָּשָׂר וְהַרְקַח הַמֶּרְקָחָה וְהָעֲצָמוֹת יֵחָרוּ׃ וְהַעֲמִידֶהָ
then-set-her! (11) let-them-be-charred and-the-bones the-spice and-mix-in! the-meat

עַל־ גֶּחָלֶיהָ רֵקָה לְמַעַן תֵּחַם וְחָרָה נְחֻשְׁתָּהּ
copper-of-her and-she-glows she-becomes-hot so-that empty-one coals-of-her on

וְנִתְּכָה בְתוֹכָהּ טֻמְאָתָהּ תִּתֹּם
she-may-be-burned-away impurity-of-her at-within-her so-she-may-be-melted

חֶלְאָתָהּ׃ תְּאֻנִים הֶלְאָת וְלֹא־ תֵצֵא מִמֶּנָּה
from-her she-was-removed and-not she-frustrated efforts (12) deposit-of-her

רַבַּת חֶלְאָתָהּ בְּאֵשׁ חֶלְאָתָהּ׃ בְּטֻמְאָתֵךְ זִמָּה
lewdness to-impurity-of-you (13) deposit-of-her by-fire deposit-of-her heaviness-of

יַעַן טִהַרְתִּיךְ וְלֹא טָהַרְתְּ מִטֻּמְאָתֵךְ
from-impurity-of-you you-would-be-cleansed but-not I-tried-to-cleanse-you because

לֹא תִטְהֲרִי־ עוֹד עַד־ הֲנִיחִי אֶת־ חֲמָתִי בָּךְ׃
against-you wrath-of-me *** to-make-subside-me until again you-will-be-clean not

them: 'This is what the Sovereign
LORD says:
" 'Put on the cooking pot; put
it on
and pour water into it.
4 Put into it the pieces of meat,
all the choice pieces—the leg
and the shoulder.
Fill it with the best of these
bones;
5 take the pick of the flock.
Pile wood beneath it for the
bones;
bring it to a boil
and cook the bones in it.

6 " 'For this is what the Sovereign
LORD says:
" 'Woe to the city of
bloodshed,
to the pot now encrusted,
whose deposit will not go
away!
Empty it piece by piece
without casting lots for
them.

7 " 'For the blood she shed is in
her midst:
She poured it on the bare
rock;
she did not pour it on the
ground,
where the dust would cover
it.
8 To stir up wrath and take
revenge
I put her blood on the bare
rock,
so that it would not be
covered.

9 " 'Therefore this is what the Sovereign LORD says:
" 'Woe to the city of
bloodshed!
I, too, will pile the wood
high.
10 So heap on the wood
and kindle the fire.
Cook the meat well,
mixing in the spices;
and let the bones be
charred.
11 Then set the empty pot on the
coals
till it becomes hot and its
copper glows
so its impurities may be
melted
and its deposit burned
away.
12 It has frustrated all efforts;
its heavy deposit has not
been removed,
not even by fire.

13 " 'Now your impurity is lewdness. Because I tried to cleanse you but you would not be cleansed from your impurity, you will not be clean again until my wrath against you has subsided.

אֲנִי יְהוָה דִּבַּרְתִּי בָּאָה וְעָשִׂיתִי לֹא־ אֶפְרַע וְלֹא־ אָחוּס
I-will-pity or-not I-will-hold-back not and-I-will-act coming I-spoke Yahweh I (14)

וְלֹא אֶנָּחֵם כִּדְרָכַיִךְ וְכַעֲלִילוֹתַיִךְ
and-according-to-actions-of-you according-to-conducts-of-you I-will-relent or-not

שְׁפָטוּךְ נְאֻם אֲדֹנָי יְהוִה׃ וַיְהִי דְבַר־ יְהוָה
Yahweh word-of and-he-came (15) Yahweh Sovereign declaration-of they-will-judge-you

אֵלַי לֵאמֹר׃ בֶּן־ אָדָם הִנְנִי לֹקֵחַ מִמְּךָ אֶת־ מַחְמַד עֵינֶיךָ
eyes-of-you delight-of *** from-you taking see-I! man son-of (16) to-say to-me

בְּמַגֵּפָה וְלֹא תִסְפֹּד וְלֹא תִבְכֶּה וְלוֹא תָבוֹא דִּמְעָתֶךָ׃
tear-of-you let-her-come or-not you-weep or-not you-lament yet-not with-blow

הֵאָנֵק ׀ דֹּם מֵתִים אֵבֶל לֹא־תַעֲשֶׂה פְאֵרְךָ* חֲבוֹשׁ
keep-fastened! turban-of-you you-do not mourning ones-being-dead be-quiet! groan! (17)

עָלֶיךָ וּנְעָלֶיךָ תָּשִׂים בְּרַגְלֶיךָ וְלֹא תַעְטֶה עַל־
over you-cover not on-feet-of-you you-keep and-sandals-of-you on-you

שָׂפָם וְלֶחֶם אֲנָשִׁים לֹא תֹאכֵל׃ וָאֲדַבֵּר אֶל־ הָעָם
the-people to so-I-spoke (18) you-eat not men or-food-of lower-part-of-face

בַּבֹּקֶר וַתָּמָת אִשְׁתִּי בָּעָרֶב וָאַעַשׂ בַּבֹּקֶר
in-the-morning and-I-did in-the-evening wife-of-me and-she-died in-the-morning

כַּאֲשֶׁר צֻוֵּיתִי׃ וַיֹּאמְרוּ אֵלַי הָעָם הֲלֹא־ תַגִּיד
will-you-tell not? the-people to-me then-they-asked (19) I-was-commanded just-as

לָנוּ מָה־ אֵלֶּה לָּנוּ כִּי אַתָּה עֹשֶׂה׃ וָאֹמַר אֲלֵיהֶם דְּבַר־ יְהוָה הָיָה
he-came Yahweh word-of to-them so-I-said (20) doing you that to-us these what? to-us

אֵלַי לֵאמֹר׃ אֱמֹר ׀ לְבֵית יִשְׂרָאֵל כֹּה־ אָמַר אֲדֹנָי יְהוִה הִנְנִי
see-I! Yahweh Sovereign he-says this Israel to-house-of say! (21) to-say to-me

מְחַלֵּל אֶת־ מִקְדָּשִׁי גְּאוֹן עֻזְּכֶם מַחְמַד עֵינֵיכֶם
eyes-of-you delight-of stronghold-of-you pride-of sanctuary-of-me *** desecrating

וּמַחְמַל נַפְשְׁכֶם וּבְנֵיכֶם וּבְנוֹתֵיכֶם אֲשֶׁר
whom and-daughters-of-you and-sons-of-you self-of-you and-object-of-affection-of

עֲזַבְתֶּם בַּחֶרֶב יִפֹּלוּ׃ וַעֲשִׂיתֶם כַּאֲשֶׁר עָשִׂיתִי עַל־
over I-did just-as and-you-will-do (22) they-will-fall by-the-sword you-left-behind

שָׂפָם לֹא תַעְטוּ וְלֶחֶם אֲנָשִׁים לֹא תֹאכֵלוּ׃
you-will-eat not men or-food-of you-will-cover not lower-part-of-face

וּפְאֵרְכֶם עַל־ רָאשֵׁיכֶם וְנַעֲלֵיכֶם בְּרַגְלֵיכֶם לֹא
not on-feet-of-you and-sandals-of-you heads-of-you on and-turban-of-you (23)

תִסְפְּדוּ וְלֹא תִבְכּוּ וּנְמַקֹּתֶם בַּעֲוֹנֹתֵיכֶם
because-of-sins-of-you but-you-will-waste-away you-will-weep or-not you-will-mourn

וּנְהַמְתֶּם אִישׁ אֶל־ אָחִיו׃ וְהָיָה יְחֶזְקֵאל לָכֶם לְמוֹפֵת
for-sign to-you Ezekiel and-he-will-be (24) other-of-him to each and-you-will-groan

14" 'I the LORD have spoken. The
time has come for me to act. I will
not hold back; I will not have pity,
nor will I relent. You will be
judged according to your conduct
and your actions, declares the
Sovereign LORD.' "

*Ezekiel's Wife Dies*

15The word of the LORD came to
me: 16"Son of man, with one blow
I am about to take away from you
the delight of your eyes. Yet do not
lament or weep or shed any tears.
17Groan quietly; do not mourn for
the dead. Keep your turban fastened and your sandals on your
feet; do not cover the lower part of
your face or eat the customary
food ⌊of mourners⌋."
18So I spoke to the people in the
morning, and in the evening my
wife died. The next morning I did
as I had been commanded.
19Then the people asked me,
"Won't you tell us what these
things have to do with us?"
20So I said to them, "The word of
the LORD came to me: 21Say to the
house of Israel, 'This is what the
Sovereign LORD says: I am about to
desecrate my sanctuary—the
stronghold in which you take
pride, the delight of your eyes, the
object of your affection. The sons
and daughters you left behind will
fall by the sword. 22And you will
do as I have done. You will not
cover the lower part of your face or
eat the customary food ⌊of mourn-
ers⌋. 23You will keep your turbans
on your heads and your sandals
on your feet. You will not mourn
or weep but will waste away because of[f] your sins and groan
among yourselves. 24Ezekiel will
be a sign to you; you will do just as

f23 Or *away in*

*17 Most mss have *dagesh* in the *pe* (פּ).

כְּכֹל אֲשֶׁר־עָשָׂה תַּעֲשׂוּ בְּבֹאָהּ וִידַעְתֶּם כִּי אֲנִי
I that then-you-will-know when-to-happen-her you-will-do he-did that as-all

אֲדֹנָי יְהוִה׃ וְאַתָּה בֶן־אָדָם הֲלוֹא בְּיוֹם קַחְתִּי מֵהֶם אֶת־
*** from-them I-take-away on-day not? man son-of and-you (25) Yahweh Sovereign

מָעוּזָּם מְשׂוֹשׂ תִּפְאַרְתָּם אֶת־מַחְמַד עֵינֵיהֶם וְאֶת־מַשָּׂא
desire-of and eyes-of-them delight-of *** glory-of-them joy-of stronghold-of-them

נַפְשָׁם בְּנֵיהֶם וּבְנוֹתֵיהֶם׃ בַּיּוֹם הַהוּא יָבוֹא
he-will-come the-that on-the-day (26) and-daughters-of-them sons-of-them heart-of-them

הַפָּלִיט אֵלֶיךָ לְהַשְׁמָעוּת אָזְנָיִם׃ בַּיּוֹם הַהוּא יִפָּתַח
he-will-be-opened the-that at-the-time (27) ears with-news-of to-you the-fugitive

פִּיךָ אֶת־הַפָּלִיט וּתְדַבֵּר וְלֹא תֵאָלֵם עוֹד
longer you-will-be-silent and-not also-you-will-speak the-fugitive with mouth-of-you

וְהָיִיתָ לָהֶם לְמוֹפֵת וְיָדְעוּ כִּי־אֲנִי יְהוָה׃ וַיְהִי
and-he-came (25:1) Yahweh I that and-they-will-know for-sign to-them so-you-will-be

דְבַר־יְהוָה אֵלַי לֵאמֹר׃ בֶּן־אָדָם שִׂים פָּנֶיךָ אֶל־בְּנֵי עַמּוֹן
Ammon sons-of against faces-of-you set! man son-of (2) to-say to-me Yahweh word-of

וְהִנָּבֵא עֲלֵיהֶם׃ וְאָמַרְתָּ לִבְנֵי עַמּוֹן שִׁמְעוּ דְּבַר־אֲדֹנָי
Sovereign word-of hear! Ammon to-sons-of and-you-say (3) against-them and-prophesy!

יְהוִה כֹּה־אָמַר אֲדֹנָי יְהוִה יַעַן אָמְרֵךְ הֶאָח אֶל־מִקְדָּשִׁי
sanctuary-of-me over aha! to-say-you because Yahweh Sovereign he-says this Yahweh

כִי־נִחָל וְאֶל־אַדְמַת יִשְׂרָאֵל כִּי נָשַׁמָּה וְאֶל־
and-over she-was-laid-waste when Israel land-of and-over he-was-desecrated when

בֵּית יְהוּדָה כִּי הָלְכוּ בַּגּוֹלָה׃ לָכֵן הִנְנִי נֹתְנָךְ
giving-you see-I! therefore (4) into-the-exile they-went when Judah house-of

לִבְנֵי־קֶדֶם לְמוֹרָשָׁה וְיִשְּׁבוּ טִירוֹתֵיהֶם בָּךְ
among-you camps-of-them and-they-will-set-up as-possession East to-peoples-of

וְנָתְנוּ בָךְ מִשְׁכְּנֵיהֶם הֵמָּה יֹאכְלוּ פִרְיֵךְ
fruit-of-you they-will-eat they tents-of-them among-you and-they-will-pitch

וְהֵמָּה יִשְׁתּוּ חֲלָבֵךְ׃ וְנָתַתִּי אֶת־רַבָּה לִנְוֵה
into-pasture-of Rabbah *** and-I-will-turn (5) milk-of-you they-will-drink and-they

גְמַלִּים וְאֶת־בְּנֵי עַמּוֹן לְמִרְבַּץ־צֹאן וִידַעְתֶּם כִּי־אֲנִי
I that then-you-will-know sheep into-resting-place-of Ammon sons-of and camels

יְהוָה׃ כִּי כֹה אָמַר אֲדֹנָי יְהוִה יַעַן מַחְאֲךָ יָד וְרַקְעֲךָ
and-to-stamp-you hand to-clap-you because Yahweh Sovereign he-says this for (6) Yahweh

בְּרֶגֶל וַתִּשְׂמַח בְּכָל־שָׁאטְךָ בְּנֶפֶשׁ אֶל־אַדְמַת יִשְׂרָאֵל׃
Israel land-of against in-heart malice-of-you with-all-of and-you-rejoiced with-foot

לָכֵן הִנְנִי נָטִיתִי אֶת־יָדִי עָלֶיךָ וּנְתַתִּיךָ־*
and-I-will-give-you against-you hand-of-me *** I-will-stretch-out see-I! therefore (7)

he has done. When this happens,
you will know that I am the Sovereign LORD.'
25 "And you, son of man, on the
day I take away their stronghold,
their joy and glory, the delight of
their eyes, their heart's desire, and
their sons and daughters as well—
26 on that day a fugitive will come
to tell you the news. 27 At that time
your mouth will be opened; you
will speak with him and will no
longer be silent. So you will be a
sign to them, and they will know
that I am the LORD."

*A Prophecy Against Ammon*

25 The word of the LORD came
to me: 2 "Son of man, set
your face against the Ammonites
and prophesy against them. 3 Say
to them, 'Hear the word of the
Sovereign LORD. This is what the
Sovereign LORD says: Because you
said "Aha!" over my sanctuary
when it was desecrated and over
the land of Israel when it was laid
waste and over the people of
Judah when they went into exile,
4 therefore I am going to give you
to the people of the East as a
possession. They will set up their
camps and pitch their tents
among you; they will eat your
fruit and drink your milk. 5 I will
turn Rabbah into a pasture for
camels and Ammon into a resting
place for sheep. Then you will
know that I am the LORD. 6 For this
is what the Sovereign LORD says:
Because you have clapped your
hands and stamped your feet, rejoicing with all the malice of your
heart against the land of Israel,
7 therefore I will stretch out my
hand against you and give you as

*7 Most mss have no *maqqeph* (־), binding this word with the next.

לְבַג לַגּוֹיִם וְהִכְרַתִּיךָ מִן־ הָעַמִּים
the-nations from and-I-will-cut-off-you to-the-nations as-plunder

וְהַאֲבַדְתִּיךָ מִן־ הָאֲרָצוֹת אַשְׁמִידְךָ וְיָדַעְתָּ
and-you-will-know I-will-destroy-you the-countries from and-I-will-exterminate-you

כִּי־ אֲנִי יְהוָה׃ כֹּה אָמַר אֲדֹנָי יְהוִה יַעַן אֲמֹר מוֹאָב וְשֵׂעִיר
and-Seir Moab to-say because Yahweh Sovereign he-says this (8) Yahweh I that

הִנֵּה כְּכָל־ הַגּוֹיִם בֵּית יְהוּדָה׃ לָכֵן הִנְנִי פֹתֵחַ אֶת־
*** exposing see-I! therefore (9) Judah house-of the-nations like-all-of look!

כֶּתֶף מוֹאָב מֵהֶעָרִים מֵעָרָיו מִקָּצֵהוּ צְבִי אֶרֶץ
land-of glory-of at-frontier-of-him from-towns-of-him from-the-towns Moab flank-of

בֵּית הַיְשִׁימֹת בַּעַל מְעוֹן וְקִרְיָתָמָה׃ לִבְנֵי־ קֶדֶם עַל־
with East to-peoples-of (10) and-to-Kiriathaim Meon Baal the-Jeshimoth Beth

בְּנֵי עַמּוֹן וּנְתַתִּיהָ לְמוֹרָשָׁה לְמַעַן לֹא־ תִזָּכֵר
she-will-be-remembered not so-that as-possession also-I-will-give-her Ammon sons-of

בְּנֵי־ עַמּוֹן בַּגּוֹיִם׃ וּבְמוֹאָב אֶעֱשֶׂה שְׁפָטִים
punishments I-will-inflict and-on-Moab (11) among-the-nations Ammon sons-of

וְיָדְעוּ כִּי־ אֲנִי יְהוָה׃ כֹּה אָמַר אֲדֹנָי יְהוִה יַעַן עֲשׂוֹת
to-do because Yahweh Sovereign he-says this (12) Yahweh I that then-they-will-know

אֱדוֹם בִּנְקֹם נָקָם לְבֵית יְהוּדָה וַיֶּאְשְׁמוּ אָשׁוֹם
to-be-guilty and-they-became-guilty Judah on-house-of revenge to-take-revenge Edom

וְנִקְּמוּ בָהֶם׃ לָכֵן כֹּה אָמַר אֲדֹנָי יְהוִה
Yahweh Sovereign he-says this therefore (13) on-them when-they-took-revenge

וְנָטִתִי יָדִי עַל־ אֱדוֹם וְהִכְרַתִּי מִמֶּנָּה אָדָם
man from-her and-I-will-cut-off Edom against hand-of-me indeed-I-will-stretch-out

וּבְהֵמָה וּנְתַתִּיהָ חָרְבָּה מִתֵּימָן וּדְדָנֶה בַּחֶרֶב
by-the-sword and-to-Dedan from-Teman waste and-I-will-lay-her and-animal

יִפֹּלוּ׃ וְנָתַתִּי אֶת־ נִקְמָתִי בֶּאֱדוֹם בְּיַד
by-hand-of on-Edom vengeance-of-me *** and-I-will-take (14) they-will-fall

עַמִּי יִשְׂרָאֵל וְעָשׂוּ בֶאֱדוֹם כְּאַפִּי
according-to-anger-of-me with-Edom and-they-will-deal Israel people-of-me

וְכַחֲמָתִי וְיָדְעוּ אֶת־ נִקְמָתִי נְאֻם
declaration-of vengeance-of-me *** and-they-will-know and-according-to-wrath-of-me

אֲדֹנָי יְהוִה׃ כֹּה אָמַר אֲדֹנָי יְהוִה יַעַן עֲשׂוֹת פְּלִשְׁתִּים
Philistines to-act because Yahweh Sovereign he-says this (15) Yahweh Sovereign

בִּנְקָמָה וַיִּנָּקְמוּ נָקָם בִּשְׁאָט בְּנֶפֶשׁ
in-heart with-malice revenge and-they-took-revenge in-vengeance

לְמַשְׁחִית אֵיבַת עוֹלָם׃ לָכֵן כֹּה אָמַר אֲדֹנָי יְהוִה
Yahweh Sovereign he-says this therefore (16) ancient hostility-of with-destruction-of

---

plunder to the nations. I will cut you off from the nations and exterminate you from the countries. I will destroy you, and you will know that I am the LORD.' "

*A Prophecy Against Moab*

8"This is what the Sovereign LORD says: 'Because Moab and Seir said, "Look, the house of Judah has become like all the other nations," 9therefore I will expose the flank of Moab, beginning at its frontier towns—Beth Jeshimoth, Baal Meon and Kiriathaim—the glory of that land. 10I will give Moab along with the Ammonites to the people of the East as a possession, so that the Ammonites will not be remembered among the nations; 11and I will inflict punishment on Moab. Then they will know that I am the LORD.' "

*A Prophecy Against Edom*

12"This is what the Sovereign LORD says: 'Because Edom took revenge on the house of Judah and became very guilty by doing so, 13therefore this is what the Sovereign LORD says: I will stretch out my hand against Edom and kill its men and their animals. I will lay it waste, and from Teman to Dedan they will fall by the sword. 14I will take vengeance on Edom by the hand of my people Israel, and they will deal with Edom in accordance with my anger and my wrath; they will know my vengeance, declares the Sovereign LORD.' "

*A Prophecy Against Philistia*

15"This is what the Sovereign LORD says: 'Because the Philistines acted in vengeance and took revenge with malice in their hearts, and with ancient hostility sought to destroy Judah, 16therefore this is what the Sovereign LORD says: I

°7 ק לבז
°9 ק וקריתימה

הִנְנִי נוֹטֶה יָדִי עַל־ פְּלִשְׁתִּים וְהִכְרַתִּי אֶת־ כְּרֵתִים
Kerethites *** and-I-will-cut-off Philistines against hand-of-me stretching see-I!

וְהַאֲבַדְתִּי אֶת־ שְׁאֵרִית חוֹף הַיָּם׃ וְעָשִׂיתִי
and-I-will-carry-out (17) the-sea coast-of remainder-of *** and-I-will-destroy

בָם נְקָמוֹת גְּדֹלוֹת בְּתוֹכְחוֹת חֵמָה וְיָדְעוּ כִּי־
that then-they-will-know wrath with-punishments-of great-ones vengeances on-them

אֲנִי יְהוָה בְּתִתִּי אֶת־ נִקְמָתִי בָּם׃ וַיְהִי בְּעַשְׁתֵּי־
in-one-of and-he-was (26:1) on-them vengeance-of-me *** when-to-take-me Yahweh I

עֶשְׂרֵה שָׁנָה בְּאֶחָד לַחֹדֶשׁ הָיָה דְבַר־ יְהוָה אֵלַי לֵאמֹר׃ בֶּן־ אָדָם
man son-of (2) to-say to-me Yahweh word-of he-came of-the-month on-one year ten

יַעַן אֲשֶׁר־ אָמְרָה צֹּר עַל־ יְרוּשָׁלַםִ הֶאָח נִשְׁבְּרָה דַּלְתוֹת הָעַמִּים
the-nations gates-of she-is-broken aha! Jerusalem of Tyre she-said that because

נָסֵבָּה אֵלַי אִמָּלְאָה הָחֳרָבָה׃ לָכֵן כֹּה אָמַר
he-says this therefore (3) she-lies-in-ruins I-will-prosper to-me she-swung-open

אֲדֹנָי יְהוִה הִנְנִי עָלַיִךְ צֹר וְהַעֲלֵיתִי עָלַיִךְ גּוֹיִם
nations against-you and-I-will-bring Tyre against-you see-I! Yahweh Sovereign

רַבִּים כְּהַעֲלוֹת הַיָּם לְגַלָּיו׃ וְשִׁחֲתוּ חֹמוֹת
walls-of and-they-will-destroy (4) to-waves-of-him the-sea like-to-cast-up many-ones

צֹר וְהָרְסוּ מִגְדָּלֶיהָ וְסִחֵיתִי עֲפָרָהּ
rubble-of-her and-I-will-scrape-away towers-of-her and-they-will-pull-down Tyre

מִמֶּנָּה וְנָתַתִּי אוֹתָהּ לִצְחִיחַ סָלַע׃ מִשְׁטַח חֲרָמִים
nets spreading-place-of (5) rock into-bareness-of her and-I-will-make from-her

תִּהְיֶה בְּתוֹךְ הַיָּם כִּי אֲנִי דִבַּרְתִּי נְאֻם אֲדֹנָי יְהוִה
Yahweh Sovereign declaration-of I-spoke I for the-sea in-middle-of she-will-become

וְהָיְתָה לְבַז לַגּוֹיִם׃ וּבְנוֹתֶיהָ אֲשֶׁר
that and-settlements-of-her (6) for-the-nations as-plunder and-she-will-become

בַּשָּׂדֶה בַּחֶרֶב תֵּהָרַגְנָה וְיָדְעוּ כִּי־ אֲנִי
I that then-they-will-know they-will-be-ravaged by-the-sword on-the-mainland

יְהוָה׃ כִּי כֹה אָמַר אֲדֹנָי יְהוִה הִנְנִי מֵבִיא אֶל־ צֹר
Tyre against bringing see-I! Yahweh Sovereign he-says this for (7) Yahweh

נְבוּכַדְרֶאצַּר מֶלֶךְ־ בָּבֶל מִצָּפוֹן מֶלֶךְ מְלָכִים בְּסוּס וּבְרֶכֶב
and-with-chariot with-horse kings king-of from-north Babylon king-of Nebuchadrezzar

וּבְפָרָשִׁים וְקָהָל וְעַם־ רָב׃ בְּנוֹתַיִךְ בַּשָּׂדֶה
on-the-mainland settlements-of-you (8) great and-people and-army and-with-horsemen

בַּחֶרֶב יַהֲרֹג וְנָתַן עָלַיִךְ דָּיֵק
siege-work against-you and-he-will-set-up he-will-ravage with-the-sword

וְשָׁפַךְ עָלַיִךְ סֹלְלָה וְהֵקִים עָלַיִךְ צִנָּה׃
shield against-you and-he-will-raise ramp against-you and-he-will-build

am about to stretch out my hand
against the Philistines, and I will
cut off the Kerethites and destroy
those remaining along the coast. 17I
will carry out great vengeance on
them and punish them in my
wrath. Then they will know that I
am the LORD, when I take vengeance on them.' "

*A Prophecy Against Tyre*

26 In the eleventh year, on the
first day of the month, the
word of the LORD came to me:
2"Son of man, because Tyre has
said of Jerusalem, 'Aha! The gate
to the nations is broken, and its
doors have swung open to me;
now that she lies in ruins I will
prosper,' 3therefore this is what
the Sovereign LORD says: I am
against you, O Tyre, and I will
bring many nations against you,
like the sea casting up its waves.
4They will destroy the walls of
Tyre and pull down her towers; I
will scrape away her rubble and
make her a bare rock. 5Out in the
sea she will become a place to
spread fishnets, for I have spoken,
declares the Sovereign LORD. She
will become plunder for the nations, 6and her settlements on the
mainland will be ravaged by the
sword. Then they will know that I
am the LORD.
7"For this is what the Sovereign
LORD says: From the north I am
going to bring against Tyre Nebuchadnezzar[g] king of Babylon, king
of kings, with horses and chariots,
with horsemen and a great army.
8He will ravage your settlements
on the mainland with the sword;
he will set up siege works against
you, build a ramp up to your walls
and raise his shields against you.

g7 Hebrew *Nebuchadrezzar,* of which *Nebuchadnezzar* is a variant; here and often in Ezekiel and Jeremiah

וּמְחִי קָבָלּוֹ יִתֵּן בְּחֹמוֹתַיִךְ
against-walls-of-you he-will-direct battering-ram-of-him and-blow-of (9)

וּמִגְדְּלֹתַיִךְ יִתֹּץ בְּחַרְבוֹתָיו׃ מִשִּׁפְעַת סוּסָיו
horses-of-him by-many-of (10) with-weapons-of-him he-will-demolish and-towers-of-you

יְכַסֵּךְ אֲבָקָם מִקּוֹל פָּרָשׁ וְגַלְגַּל וָרֶכֶב
and-chariot and-wagon war-horse at-noise-of dust-of-them he-will-cover-you

תִּרְעַשְׁנָה חוֹמוֹתַיִךְ בְּבֹאוֹ בִּשְׁעָרַיִךְ כִּמְבוֹאֵי
as-entrances-of through-gates-of-you when-to-enter-him walls-of-you they-will-tremble

עִיר מְבֻקָּעָה׃ בְּפַרְסוֹת סוּסָיו יִרְמֹס אֶת־
*** he-will-trample horses-of-him by-hoofs-of (11) being-broken-through city

כָּל־ חוּצוֹתָיִךְ עַמֵּךְ בַּחֶרֶב יַהֲרֹג וּמַצְּבוֹת
and-pillars-of he-will-kill with-the-sword people-of-you streets-of-you all-of

עֻזֵּךְ לָאָרֶץ תֵּרֵד׃ וְשָׁלְלוּ חֵילֵךְ
wealth-of-you and-they-will-plunder (12) she-will-fall to-the-ground strength-of-you

וּבָזְזוּ רְכֻלָּתֵךְ וְהָרְסוּ חוֹמוֹתַיִךְ
walls-of-you and-they-will-break-down merchandise-of-you and-they-will-loot

וּבָתֵּי חֶמְדָּתֵךְ יִתֹּצוּ וַאֲבָנַיִךְ וְעֵצַיִךְ
and-timbers-of-you and-stones-of-you they-will-demolish fineness-of-you and-houses-of

וַעֲפָרֵךְ בְּתוֹךְ מַיִם יָשִׂימוּ׃ וְהִשְׁבַּתִּי
and-I-will-end (13) they-will-throw seas into-midst-of and-rubble-of-you

הֲמוֹן שִׁירָיִךְ וְקוֹל כִּנּוֹרַיִךְ לֹא יִשָּׁמַע עוֹד׃
more he-will-be-heard not harps-of-you and-music-of songs-of-you noise-of

וּנְתַתִּיךְ לִצְחִיחַ סֶלַע מִשְׁטַח חֲרָמִים
fishnets spreading-place-of rock into-bareness-of and-I-will-make-you (14)

תִּהְיֶה לֹא תִבָּנֶה עוֹד כִּי אֲנִי יְהוָה דִּבַּרְתִּי נְאֻם
declaration-of I-spoke Yahweh I for ever you-will-be-rebuilt not you-will-become

אֲדֹנָי יְהוִה׃ כֹּה אָמַר אֲדֹנָי יְהוִה לְצוֹר הֲלֹא מִקּוֹל
at-sound-of not? to-Tyre Yahweh Sovereign he-says this (15) Yahweh Sovereign

מַפַּלְתֵּךְ בֶּאֱנֹק חָלָל בֵּהָרֵג הֶרֶג בְּתוֹכֵךְ
in-midst-of-you slaughter when-to-slaughter wounded when-to-groan fall-of-you

יִרְעֲשׁוּ הָאִיִּים׃ וְיָרְדוּ מֵעַל כִּסְאוֹתָם
thrones-of-them from-on then-they-will-step-down (16) the-coastlands they-will-tremble

כֹּל נְשִׂיאֵי הַיָּם וְהֵסִירוּ אֶת־ מְעִילֵיהֶם וְאֶת־
and robes-of-them *** and-they-will-lay-aside the-coast princes-of all-of

בִּגְדֵי רִקְמָתָם יִפְשֹׁטוּ חֲרָדוֹת ׀ יִלְבָּשׁוּ עַל־
on they-will-be-clothed terrors they-will-take-off embroidery-of-them garments-of

הָאָרֶץ יֵשֵׁבוּ וְחָרְדוּ לִרְגָעִים וְשָׁמְמוּ
and-they-will-be-appalled at-moments and-they-will-tremble they-will-sit the-ground

[9]He will direct the blows of his battering rams against your walls and demolish your towers with his weapons. [10]His horses will be so many that they will cover you with dust. Your walls will tremble at the noise of the war horses, wagons and chariots when he enters your gates as men enter a city whose walls have been broken through. [11]The hoofs of his horses will trample all your streets; he will kill your people with the sword, and your strong pillars will fall to the ground. [12]They will plunder your wealth and loot your merchandise; they will break down your walls and demolish your fine houses and throw your stones, timber and rubble into the sea. [13]I will put an end to your noisy songs, and the music of your harps will be heard no more. [14]I will make you a bare rock, and you will become a place to spread fishnets. You will never be rebuilt, for I the LORD have spoken, declares the Sovereign LORD.

[15]"This is what the Sovereign LORD says to Tyre: Will not the coastlands tremble at the sound of your fall, when the wounded groan and the slaughter takes place in you? [16]Then all the princes of the coast will step down from their thrones and lay aside their robes and take off their embroidered garments. Clothed with terror, they will sit on the ground,

עָלָיִךְ׃ וְנָשְׂאוּ עָלַיִךְ קִינָה וְאָמְרוּ לָךְ
to-you and-they-will-say lament concerning-you then-they-will-take-up (17) at-you

אֵיךְ אָבַדְתְּ נוֹשֶׁבֶת מִיַּמִּים הָעִיר הַהֻלָּלָה
that-she-was-renowned the-city from-seas one-being-peopled you-are-destroyed how!

אֲשֶׁר הָיְתָה חֲזָקָה בַיָּם הִיא וְיֹשְׁבֶיהָ אֲשֶׁר־נָתְנוּ
they-put that and-ones-living-of-her she on-the-sea power you-were that

חִתִּיתָם לְכָל־יוֹשְׁבֶיהָ׃ עַתָּה יֶחֶרְדוּ הָאִין
the-coastlands they-tremble now (18) ones-living-of-her on-all-of terror-of-them

יוֹם מַפַּלְתֵּךְ וְנִבְהֲלוּ הָאִיִּים אֲשֶׁר־בַּיָּם
in-the-sea that the-islands and-they-are-terrified fall-of-you day-of

מִצֵּאתֵךְ׃ כִּי כֹה אָמַר אֲדֹנָי יְהוִה בְּתִתִּי אֹתָךְ
you when-to-make-me Yahweh Sovereign he-says this indeed (19) at-to-collapse-you

עִיר נֶחֱרֶבֶת כֶּעָרִים אֲשֶׁר לֹא־נוֹשָׁבוּ בְּהַעֲלוֹת
when-to-bring they-are-inhabited not that like-the-cities being-desolate city

עָלַיִךְ אֶת־תְּהוֹם וְכִסּוּךְ הַמַּיִם הָרַבִּים׃
the-vast-ones the-waters and-they-cover-you ocean-depth *** over-you

וְהוֹרַדְתִּיךְ אֶת־יוֹרְדֵי בוֹר אֶל־עַם עוֹלָם
long-ago people-of to pit ones-going-down-of with then-I-will-bring-down-you (20)

וְהוֹשַׁבְתִּיךְ בְּאֶרֶץ תַּחְתִּיּוֹת כָּחֳרָבוֹת מֵעוֹלָם אֶת־
with of-ancient as-ruins parts-below in-earth-of and-I-will-make-dwell-you

יוֹרְדֵי בוֹר לְמַעַן לֹא תֵשֵׁבִי וְנָתַתִּי צְבִי בְּאֶרֶץ
in-land-of glory and-I-will-give you-will-return not so-that pit ones-going-down-of

חַיִּים׃ בַּלָּהוֹת אֶתְּנֵךְ וְאֵינֵךְ וּתְבֻקְשִׁי
and-you-will-be-sought and-no-more-you I-will-bring-you horrible-ends (21) living-ones

וְלֹא־תִמָּצְאִי עוֹד לְעוֹלָם נְאֻם אֲדֹנָי יְהוִה׃
Yahweh Sovereign declaration-of to-ever again you-will-be-found but-not

וַיְהִי דְבַר־יְהוָה אֵלַי לֵאמֹר׃ וְאַתָּה בֶן־אָדָם שָׂא
take-up! man son-of now-you (2) to-say to-me Yahweh word-of and-he-came (27:1)

עַל־צֹר קִינָה׃ וְאָמַרְתָּ לְצוֹר הַיֹּשֶׁבֶתִי עַל־מְבוֹאֹת יָם
sea gateways-of at the-one-being-situated to-Tyre and-you-say (3) lament Tyre for

רֹכֶלֶת הָעַמִּים אֶל־אִיִּים רַבִּים כֹּה אָמַר אֲדֹנָי יְהוִה
Yahweh Sovereign he-says this many-ones coasts on the-peoples one-being-merchant-of

צוֹר אַתְּ אָמַרְתְּ אֲנִי כְּלִילַת יֹפִי׃ בְּלֵב יַמִּים גְּבוּלָיִךְ
domains-of-you seas in-heart-of (4) beauty perfect-of I you-say you Tyre

בֹּנַיִךְ כָּלְלוּ יָפְיֵךְ׃ בְּרוֹשִׁים מִשְּׂנִיר בָּנוּ לָךְ
for-you they-made from-Senir pines (5) beauty-of-you they-perfected ones-building-you

אֵת כָּל־לֻחֹתָיִם אֶרֶז מִלְּבָנוֹן לָקָחוּ לַעֲשׂוֹת תֹּרֶן עָלָיִךְ׃ אַלּוֹנִים
oaks (6) for-you mast to-make they-took from-Lebanon cedar timbers all-of ***

°3 ק הישבת

trembling every moment, appalled at you. [17]Then they will take up a lament concerning you and say to you:

"'How you are destroyed, O
city of renown,
peopled by men of the sea!
You were a power on the seas,
you and your citizens;
you put your terror
on all who lived there.
[18]Now the coastlands tremble
on the day of your fall;
the islands in the sea
are terrified at your
collapse.'

[19]"This is what the Sovereign LORD says: When I make you a desolate city, like cities no longer inhabited, and when I bring the ocean depths over you and its vast waters cover you, [20]then I will bring you down with those who go down to the pit, to the people of long ago. I will make you dwell in the earth below, as in ancient ruins, with those who go down to the pit, and you will not return or take your place[h] in the land of the living. [21]I will bring you to a horrible end and you will be no more. You will be sought, but you will never again be found, declares the Sovereign LORD."

*A Lament for Tyre*

27 The word of the LORD came to me: [2]"Son of man, take up a lament concerning Tyre. [3]Say to Tyre, situated at the gateway to the sea, merchant of peoples on many coasts, 'This is what the Sovereign LORD says:

"'You say, O Tyre,
"I am perfect in beauty."
[4]Your domain was on the high
seas;
your builders brought your
beauty to perfection.
[5]They made all your timbers
of pine trees from Senir[i];
they took a cedar from
Lebanon
to make a mast for you.

[h]20 Septuagint; Hebrew *return, and I will give glory*
[i]5 That is, Hermon

מִבָּשָׁן עָשׂוּ מִשּׁוֹטָיִךְ קַרְשֵׁךְ עָשׂוּ־ שֵׁן בַּת־ אֲשֻׁרִים
cypresses daughter-of ivory they-made deck-of-you oars-of-you they-made from-Bashan

מֵאִיֵּי כִּתִּים׃ שֵׁשׁ־ בְּרִקְמָה מִמִּצְרַיִם הָיָה מִפְרָשֵׂךְ
sail-of-you he-was from-Egypt with-embroidery fine-linen (7) Kittim from-coasts-of

לִהְיוֹת לָךְ לְנֵס תְּכֵלֶת וְאַרְגָּמָן מֵאִיֵּי אֱלִישָׁה הָיָה
he-was Elishah from-coasts-of and-purple blue as-banner for-you to-serve

מְכַסֵּךְ׃ יֹשְׁבֵי צִידוֹן וְאַרְוַד הָיוּ שָׁטִים
ones-being-oarsmen they-were and-Arvad Sidon ones-being-men-of (8) awning-of-you

לָךְ חֲכָמַיִךְ צוֹר הָיוּ בָךְ הֵמָּה חֹבְלָיִךְ׃ זִקְנֵי
veterans-of (9) seamen-of-you they on-you they-were Tyre skilled-men-of-you of-you

גְבַל וַחֲכָמֶיהָ הָיוּ בָךְ מַחֲזִיקֵי בִּדְקֵךְ כָּל־
all-of seam-of-you ones-caulking-of on-you they-were even-craftsmen-of-her Gebal

אֳנִיּוֹת הַיָּם וּמַלָּחֵיהֶם הָיוּ בָךְ לַעֲרֹב מַעֲרָבֵךְ׃
ware-of-you to-trade-for on-you they-were and-sailors-of-them the-sea ships-of

פָּרַס וְלוּד וּפוּט הָיוּ בְחֵילֵךְ אַנְשֵׁי מִלְחַמְתֵּךְ
battle-of-you men-of in-army-of-you they-served and-Put and-Lydia Persia (10)

מָגֵן וְכוֹבַע תִּלּוּ־ בָךְ הֵמָּה נָתְנוּ הֲדָרֵךְ׃ בְּנֵי
men-of (11) splendor-of-you they-brought they on-you they-hung and-helmet shield

אַרְוַד וְחֵילֵךְ עַל־ חוֹמוֹתַיִךְ סָבִיב וְגַמָּדִים בְּמִגְדְּלוֹתַיִךְ הָיוּ
they-were in-towers-of-you and-Gammadites every-side walls-of-you on and-Helech Arvad

שִׁלְטֵיהֶם תִּלּוּ עַל־ חוֹמוֹתַיִךְ סָבִיב הֵמָּה כָּלְלוּ יָפְיֵךְ׃
beauty-of-you they-perfected they around walls-of-you on they-hung shields-of-them

תַּרְשִׁישׁ סֹחַרְתֵּךְ מֵרֹב כָּל־ הוֹן
wealth all-of because-of-greatness-of doing-business-with-you Tarshish (12)

בְּכֶסֶף בַּרְזֶל בְּדִיל וְעוֹפֶרֶת נָתְנוּ עִזְבוֹנָיִךְ׃ יָוָן
Greece (13) merchandises-of-you they-exchanged-for and-lead tin iron with-silver

תֻּבַל וָמֶשֶׁךְ הֵמָּה רֹכְלָיִךְ בְּנֶפֶשׁ אָדָם וּכְלֵי
and-articles-of human with-life-of ones-trading-with-you they and-Meshech Tubal

נְחֹשֶׁת נָתְנוּ מַעֲרָבֵךְ׃ מִבֵּית תּוֹגַרְמָה סוּסִים
work-horses Togarmah from-Beth (14) ware-of-you they-exchanged-for bronze

וּפָרָשִׁים וּפְרָדִים נָתְנוּ עִזְבוֹנָיִךְ׃ בְּנֵי דְדָן
Dedan men-of (15) merchandises-of-you they-exchanged-for and-mules and-war-horses

רֹכְלַיִךְ אִיִּים רַבִּים סְחֹרַת יָדֵךְ קַרְנוֹת
tusks-of hand-of-you merchandise-of many-ones coastlands ones-trading-with-you

שֵׁן וְהָובְנִים הֵשִׁיבוּ אֶשְׁכָּרֵךְ׃ אֲרָם סֹחַרְתֵּךְ
doing-business-with-you Aram (16) pay-of-you they-gave and-ebony-woods ivory

מֵרֹב מַעֲשָׂיִךְ בְּנֹפֶךְ אַרְגָּמָן וְרִקְמָה וּבוּץ
and-fine-linen and-embroidery purple with-turqoise products-of-you because-of-many-of

°6 ק כתיים
°15 ק והבנים

6 Of oaks from Bashan
they made your oars;
of cypress wood[j] from the
coasts of Cyprus[k]
they made your deck, inlaid
with ivory.
7 Fine embroidered linen from
Egypt was your sail
and served as your banner;
your awnings were of blue
and purple
from the coasts of Elishah.
8 Men of Sidon and Arvad were
your oarsmen;
your skilled men, O Tyre,
were aboard as your
seamen.
9 Veteran craftsmen of Gebal[l]
were on board
as shipwrights to caulk your
seams.
All the ships of the sea and
their sailors
came alongside to trade for
your wares.

10 "'Men of Persia, Lydia and
Put
served as soldiers in your
army.
They hung their shields and
helmets on your walls,
bringing you splendor.
11 Men of Arvad and Helech
manned your walls on every
side;
men of Gammad
were in your towers.
They hung their shields
around your walls;
they brought your beauty to
perfection.

12 "'Tarshish did business with you because of your great wealth of goods; they exchanged silver, iron, tin and lead for your merchandise.

13 "'Greece, Tubal and Meshech traded with you; they exchanged slaves and articles of bronze for your wares.

14 "'Men of Beth Togarmah exchanged work horses, war horses and mules for your merchandise.

15 "'The men of Rhodes[m] traded with you, and many coastlands were your customers; they paid you with ivory tusks and ebony.

16 "'Aram[n] did business with you because of your many products; they exchanged turquoise, purple fabric, embroidered work,

j6 Targum; the Masoretic Text has a different division of the consonants.
k6 Hebrew *Kittim*
l9 That is, Byblos
m15 Septuagint; Hebrew *Dedan*
n16 Most Hebrew manuscripts; some Hebrew manuscripts and Syriac *Edom*

וְרָאמֹת וְכַדְכֹּד נָתְנוּ בְּעִזְבוֹנָיִךְ׃ יְהוּדָה וְאֶרֶץ
and-land-of Judah (17) for-merchandises-of-you they-exchanged and-ruby and-corals

יִשְׂרָאֵל הֵמָּה רֹכְלָיִךְ בְּחִטֵּי מִנִּית וּפַנַּג וּדְבַשׁ
and-honey and-confection Minnith with-wheats-of ones-trading-with-you they Israel

וָשֶׁמֶן וָצֹרִי נָתְנוּ מַעֲרָבֵךְ׃ דַּמֶּשֶׂק סֹחַרְתֵּךְ
doing-business-with-you Damascus (18) ware-of-you they-exchanged-for and-balm and-oil

בְּרֹב מַעֲשַׂיִךְ מֵרֹב כָּל־הוֹן בְּיֵין
in-wine-of wealth all-of because-of-greatness-of products-of-you because-of-many-of

חֶלְבּוֹן וְצֶמֶר צָחַר׃ וְדָן וְיָוָן מְאוּזָּל בְּעִזְבוֹנַיִךְ
to-merchandises-of-you from-Uzal and-Greece and-Dan (19) Zahar and-wool-of Helbon

נָתָנּוּ בַּרְזֶל עָשׁוֹת קִדָּה וְקָנֶה בְּמַעֲרָבֵךְ הָיָה׃
he-exchanged for-ware-of-you and-calamus cassia to-be-wrought iron they-bought

דְּדָן רֹכַלְתֵּךְ בְּבִגְדֵי־* חֹפֶשׁ לְרִכְבָּה׃ עֲרַב
Arabia (21) for-riding saddle-blanket in-cloths-of one-trading-with-you Dedan (20)

וְכָל־נְשִׂיאֵי קֵדָר הֵמָּה סֹחֲרֵי יָדֵךְ בְּכָרִים
in-lambs hand-of-you ones-being-customers-of they Kedar princes-of and-all-of

וְאֵילִים וְעַתּוּדִים בָּם סֹחֲרָיִךְ׃ רֹכְלֵי
ones-being-merchants-of (22) ones-doing-business-with-you in-them and-goats and-rams

שְׁבָא וְרַעְמָה הֵמָּה רֹכְלָיִךְ בְּרֹאשׁ כָּל־בֹּשֶׂם
spice all-of with-finest-of ones-trading-with-you they and-Raamah Sheba

וּבְכָל־אֶבֶן יְקָרָה וְזָהָב נָתְנוּ עִזְבוֹנָיִךְ׃
merchandises-of-you they-exchanged-for and-gold precious stone and-with-all-of

חָרָן וְכַנֵּה וָעֶדֶן רֹכְלֵי שְׁבָא אַשּׁוּר כִּלְמַד
Kilmad Asshur Sheba ones-being-merchants-of and-Eden and-Canneh Haran (23)

רֹכַלְתֵּךְ׃ הֵמָּה רֹכְלַיִךְ בְמַכְלֻלִים
with-beautiful-garments ones-trading-with-you they (24) trading-with-you

בִּגְלוֹמֵי תְּכֵלֶת וְרִקְמָה וּבְגִנְזֵי בְּרֹמִים בַּחֲבָלִים
with-cords multicolored-ones and-with-rugs-of and-embroidery blue with-fabrics-of

חֲבֻשִׁים וַאֲרֻזִים בְּמַרְכֻלְתֵּךְ׃ אֳנִיּוֹת
ships-of (25) in-marketplace-of-you and-ones-being-tightly-knotted ones-being-twisted

תַּרְשִׁישׁ שָׁרוֹתַיִךְ מַעֲרָבֵךְ וַתִּמָּלְאִי וַתִּכְבְּדִי מְאֹד
very and-you-are-heavy and-you-are-filled ware-of-you ones-carrying-of-you Tarshish

בְּלֵב יַמִּים׃ בְּמַיִם רַבִּים הֱבִיאוּךְ הַשָּׁטִים אֹתָךְ
you the-ones-being-oarsmen they-take-you high-ones on-seas (26) seas in-heart-of

רוּחַ הַקָּדִים שְׁבָרֵךְ בְּלֵב יַמִּים׃ הוֹנֵךְ
wealth-of-you (27) seas in-heart-of he-will-break-to-pieces-you the-east-wind wind-of

וְעִזְבוֹנַיִךְ מַעֲרָבֵךְ מַלָּחַיִךְ וְחֹבְלָיִךְ מַחֲזִיקֵי
ones-caulking-of and-seamen-of-you mariners-of-you ware-of-you and-merchandises-of-you

fine linen, coral and rubies for your merchandise.
17 'Judah and Israel traded with you; they exchanged wheat from Minnith and confections,° honey, oil and balm for your wares.
18 'Damascus, because of your many products and great wealth of goods, did business with you in wine from Helbon and wool from Zahar.
19 'Danites and Greeks from Uzal bought your merchandise; they exchanged wrought iron, cassia and calamus for your wares.
20 'Dedan traded in saddle blankets with you.
21 'Arabia and all the princes of Kedar were your customers; they did business with you in lambs, rams and goats.
22 'The merchants of Sheba and Raamah traded with you; for your merchandise they exchanged the finest of all kinds of spices and precious stones, and gold.
23 'Haran, Canneh and Eden and merchants of Sheba, Asshur and Kilmad traded with you.
24 In your marketplace they traded with you beautiful garments, blue fabric, embroidered work and multicolored rugs with cords twisted and tightly knotted.

25 'The ships of Tarshish serve
as carriers for your wares.
You are filled with heavy
cargo
in the heart of the sea.
26 Your oarsmen take you
out to the high seas.
But the east wind will break
you to pieces
in the heart of the sea.
27 Your wealth, merchandise and
wares,
your mariners, seamen and

°17 The meaning of the Hebrew for this word is uncertain.

*20 Most mss have *dagesh* in the first *beth* (בּב').

בִּדְקֵךְ* וְעֹרְבֵי מַעֲרָבֵךְ וְכָל־ אַנְשֵׁי מִלְחַמְתֵּךְ
battle-of-you men-of and-all-of ware-of-you and-ones-being-merchants-of seam-of-you

אֲשֶׁר־ בָּךְ וּבְכָל־ קְהָלֵךְ אֲשֶׁר בְּתוֹכֵךְ יִפְּלוּ
they-will-sink in-midst-of-you who crowd-of-you and-with-all-of on-you who

בְּלֵב יַמִּים בְּיוֹם מַפַּלְתֵּךְ׃ (28) לְקוֹל זַעֲקַת חֹבְלָיִךְ
seamen-of-you cry-of at-sound-of (28) wreck-of-you on-day-of seas into-heart-of

יִרְעֲשׁוּ מִגְרֹשׁוֹת׃ (29) וְיָרְדוּ מֵאֳנִיּוֹתֵיהֶם† כֹּל
all-of from-ships-of-them and-they-will-abandon (29) shorelands they-will-quake

תֹּפְשֵׂי מָשׁוֹט מַלָּחִים כֹּל חֹבְלֵי הַיָּם אֶל־ הָאָרֶץ יַעֲמֹדוּ׃
they-will-stand the-shore on the-sea seamen-of all-of mariners oar ones-handling-of

(30) וְהִשְׁמִיעוּ עָלַיִךְ בְּקוֹלָם וְיִזְעֲקוּ מָרָה
bitterness and-they-will-cry with-voice-of-them over-you and-they-will-raise-cry (30)

וְיַעֲלוּ עָפָר עַל־ רָאשֵׁיהֶם בָּאֵפֶר יִתְפַּלָּשׁוּ׃
they-will-roll in-the-ash heads-of-them on dust and-they-will-sprinkle

(31) וְהִקְרִיחוּ אֵלַיִךְ קָרְחָה וְחָגְרוּ
and-they-will-put-on baldness because-of-you and-they-will-shave-bald (31)

שַׂקִּים וּבָכוּ אֵלַיִךְ בְּמַר־ נֶפֶשׁ מִסְפֵּד מָר׃
bitter mourning soul with-anguish-of over-you and-they-will-weep sackcloths

(32) וְנָשְׂאוּ אֵלַיִךְ בְּנִיהֶם קִינָה וְקוֹנְנוּ
and-they-will-lament mourning with-wailing-of-them over-you and-they-will-raise (32)

עָלָיִךְ מִי כְצוֹר כְּדֻמָה בְּתוֹךְ הַיָּם׃ (33) בְּצֵאת
when-to-go-out (33) the-sea in-midst-of like-one-silenced like-Tyre who? concerning-you

עִזְבוֹנַיִךְ מִיַּמִּים הִשְׂבַּעַתְּ עַמִּים רַבִּים בְּרֹב
with-greatness-of many-ones nations you-satisfied on-seas merchandises-of-you

הוֹנַיִךְ וּמַעֲרָבַיִךְ הֶעֱשַׁרְתְּ מַלְכֵי־ אָרֶץ׃ (34) עֵת נִשְׁבֶּרֶת
being-shattered now (34) earth kings-of you-enriched and-wares-of-you wealths-of-you

מִיַּמִּים בְּמַעֲמַקֵּי־ מָיִם מַעֲרָבֵךְ וְכָל־ קְהָלֵךְ בְּתוֹכֵךְ
in-midst-of-you company-of-you and-all-of ware-of-you waters in-depths-of by-seas

נָפָלוּ׃ (35) כֹּל יֹשְׁבֵי הָאִיִּים שָׁמְמוּ
they-are-appalled the-coastlands ones-living-of all-of (35) they-went-down

עָלָיִךְ וּמַלְכֵיהֶם שָׂעֲרוּ שַׂעַר רָעֲמוּ פָּנִים׃
faces they-are-distorted shudder they-shudder and-kings-of-them at-you

(36) סֹחֲרִים בָּעַמִּים שָׁרְקוּ עָלָיִךְ בַּלָּהוֹת הָיִית
you-came horrible-ends at-you they-hiss among-the-nations ones-being-merchants (36)

וְאֵינֵךְ עַד־ עוֹלָם׃ (28:1) וַיְהִי דְבַר־ יְהוָה אֵלַי לֵאמֹר׃
to-say to-me Yahweh word-of and-he-came (28:1) forever to and-no-more-you

(2) בֶּן־ אָדָם אֱמֹר לִנְגִיד צֹר כֹּה־ אָמַר ׀ אֲדֹנָי יְהוִה יַעַן
because Yahweh Sovereign he-says this Tyre to-ruler-of say! man son-of (2)

shipwrights,
your merchants and all your soldiers,
and everyone else on board
will sink into the heart of the sea
on the day of your shipwreck.
28 The shorelands will quake
when your seamen cry out.
29 All who handle the oars
will abandon their ships;
the mariners and all the seamen
will stand on the shore.
30 They will raise their voice
and cry bitterly over you;
they will sprinkle dust on their heads
and roll in ashes.
31 They will shave their heads because of you
and will put on sackcloth.
They will weep over you with anguish of soul
and with bitter mourning.
32 As they wail and mourn over you,
they will take up a lament concerning you:
"Who was ever silenced like Tyre,
surrounded by the sea?"
33 When your merchandise went out on the seas,
you satisfied many nations;
with your great wealth and your wares
you enriched the kings of the earth.
34 Now you are shattered by the sea
in the depths of the waters;
your wares and all your company
have gone down with you.
35 All who live in the coastlands
are appalled at you;
their kings shudder with horror
and their faces are distorted with fear.
36 The merchants among the nations hiss at you;
you have come to a horrible end
and will be no more.' "

### *A Prophecy Against the King of Tyre*

**28** The word of the LORD came to me: 2 "Son of man, say to the ruler of Tyre, 'This is what the Sovereign LORD says:

*27 Most mss have *sheva* in the *kaph* (ךְ).

†29 Most mss have *hateph qamets* under the *aleph* ('מֳא).

גָּבַהּ לִבְּךָ וַתֹּאמֶר אֵל אָנִי מוֹשַׁב אֱלֹהִים יָשַׁבְתִּי בְּלֵב

in-heart-of I-sit gods throne-of I god and-you-say heart-of-you he-is-proud

יַמִּים וְאַתָּה אָדָם וְלֹא־אֵל וַתִּתֵּן לִבְּךָ כְּלֵב אֱלֹהִים׃

gods as-mind-of mind-of-you though-you-think god and-not man but-you seas

הִנֵּה חָכָם אַתָּה מִדָּנִאֵל כָּל־סָתוּם לֹא עֲמָמוּךָ׃

they-hid-from-you not one-being-secret any-of more-than-Daniel you wise see! (3)

בְּחָכְמָתְךָ וּבִתְבוּנָתְךָ עָשִׂיתָ לְּךָ חָיִל

wealth for-yourself you-gained and-by-understanding-of-you by-wisdom-of-you (4)

וַתַּעַשׂ זָהָב וָכֶסֶף בְּאוֹצְרוֹתֶיךָ׃ בְּרֹב חָכְמָתְךָ

skill-of-you by-greatness-of (5) in-treasuries-of-you and-silver gold and-you-amassed

בִּרְכֻלָּתְךָ הִרְבִּיתָ חֵילֶךָ וַיִּגְבַּהּ לְבָבְךָ

heart-of-you and-he-grew-proud wealth-of-you you-increased in-trading-of-you

בְּחֵילֶךָ׃ לָכֵן כֹּה אָמַר אֲדֹנָי יְהוִה יַעַן

because Yahweh Sovereign he-says this therefore (6) because-of-wealth-of-you

תִּתְּךָ אֶת־לְבָבְךָ כְּלֵב אֱלֹהִים׃ לָכֵן הִנְנִי מֵבִיא עָלֶיךָ

against-you bringing see-I! therefore (7) gods as-mind-of mind-of-you *** to-think-you

זָרִים עָרִיצֵי גּוֹיִם וְהֵרִיקוּ חַרְבוֹתָם עַל־

against swords-of-them and-they-will-draw nations ones-ruthless-of ones-being-foreign

יְפִי חָכְמָתֶךָ וְחִלְּלוּ יִפְעָתֶךָ׃ לַשַּׁחַת

to-the-pit (8) splendor-of-you and-they-will-pierce wisdom-of-you beauty-of

יוֹרִדוּךָ וָמַתָּה מְמוֹתֵי חָלָל בְּלֵב יַמִּים׃

seas in-heart-of violence deaths-of and-you-will-die they-will-bring-down-you

הֶאָמֹר תֹּאמַר אֱלֹהִים אָנִי לִפְנֵי הֹרְגֶךָ וְאַתָּה אָדָם וְלֹא־

and-not man and-you one-killing-you in-presences-of I gods will-you-say to-say? (9)

אֵל בְּיַד מְחַלְלֶיךָ׃ מוֹתֵי עֲרֵלִים תָּמוּת

you-will-die uncircumcised-ones deaths-of (10) ones-slaying-you in-hand-of god

בְּיַד־זָרִים כִּי אֲנִי דִבַּרְתִּי נְאֻם אֲדֹנָי יְהוִה׃

Yahweh Sovereign declaration-of I-spoke I for ones-being-foreign at-hand-of

וַיְהִי דְבַר־יְהוָה אֵלַי לֵאמֹר׃ בֶּן־אָדָם שָׂא קִינָה

lament take-up! man son-of (12) to-say to-me Yahweh word-of and-he-came (11)

עַל־מֶלֶךְ צוֹר וְאָמַרְתָּ לּוֹ כֹּה אָמַר אֲדֹנָי יְהוִה אַתָּה

you Yahweh Sovereign he-says this to-him and-you-say Tyre king-of concerning

חוֹתֵם תָּכְנִית מָלֵא חָכְמָה וּכְלִיל יֹפִי׃ בְּעֵדֶן גַּן־אֱלֹהִים

God garden-of in-Eden (13) beauty and-perfect-of wisdom full perfection model-of

הָיִיתָ כָּל־אֶבֶן יְקָרָה מְסֻכָתֶךָ אֹדֶם פִּטְדָה וְיָהֲלֹם תַּרְשִׁישׁ

chrysolite and-emerald topaz ruby adornment-of-you precious stone every-of you-were

שֹׁהַם וְיָשְׁפֵה סַפִּיר נֹפֶךְ וּבָרְקַת וְזָהָב מְלֶאכֶת תֻּפֶּיךָ

settings-of-you work-of and-gold and-beryl turquoise sapphire and-jasper onyx

" 'In the pride of your heart
you say, "I am a god;
I sit on the throne of a god
in the heart of the seas."
But you are a man and not a god,
though you think you are as wise as a god.
3 Are you wiser than Daniel[p]?
Is no secret hidden from you?
4 By your wisdom and understanding
you have gained wealth for yourself
and amassed gold and silver
in your treasuries.
5 By your great skill in trading
you have increased your wealth,
and because of your wealth
your heart has grown proud.

6 " 'Therefore this is what the Sovereign LORD says:

" 'Because you think you are wise,
as wise as a god,
7 I am going to bring foreigners against you,
the most ruthless of nations;
they will draw their swords
against your beauty and wisdom
and pierce your shining splendor.
8 They will bring you down to the pit,
and you will die a violent death
in the heart of the seas.
9 Will you then say, "I am a god,"
in the presence of those who kill you?
You will be but a man, not a god,
in the hands of those who slay you.
10 You will die the death of the uncircumcised
at the hands of foreigners.

I have spoken, declares the Sovereign LORD.' "

11 The word of the LORD came to me: 12 "Son of man, take up a lament concerning the king of Tyre and say to him: 'This is what the Sovereign LORD says:

" 'You were the model of perfection,
full of wisdom and perfect in beauty.
13 You were in Eden,
the garden of God;
every precious stone adorned you:
ruby, topaz and emerald,
chrysolite, onyx and jasper,
sapphire,[q] turquoise and beryl.[r]
Your settings and mountings[s]
were made of gold;

p3 Or *Danel*; the Hebrew spelling may suggest a person other than the prophet Daniel.
q13 Or *lapis lazuli*
r13 The precise identification of some of these precious stones is uncertain.
s13 The meaning of the Hebrew for this phrase is uncertain.

°3 ק מדניאל

וּנְקָבֶיךָ בָּךְ בְּיוֹם הִבָּרַאֲךָ כּוֹנָנוּ׃
they-were-prepared to-be-created-you on-day-of in-you and-mountings-of-you

(14) אַתְּ־ כְּרוּב מִמְשַׁח הַסּוֹכֵךְ וּנְתַתִּיךָ בְּהַר
on-mount-of so-I-ordained-you the-one-guarding anointed-of cherub you (14)

קֹדֶשׁ אֱלֹהִים הָיִיתָ בְּתוֹךְ אַבְנֵי־ אֵשׁ הִתְהַלָּכְתָּ׃ (15) תָּמִים אַתָּה
you blameless (15) you-walked fire stones-of in-among you-were God holiness-of

בִּדְרָכֶיךָ מִיּוֹם הִבָּרְאָךְ עַד־ נִמְצָא עַוְלָתָה בָּךְ׃
in-you wickedness he-was-found till to-be-created-you from-day-of in-ways-of-you

(16) בְּרֹב רְכֻלָּתְךָ מָלוּ תוֹכְךָ חָמָס
violence inside-of-you they-were-filled trade-of-you through-wideness-of (16)

וַתֶּחֱטָא וָאֲחַלֶּלְךָ* מֵהַר אֱלֹהִים וָאַבֶּדְךָ
and-I-expelled-you God from-mount-of so-I-drove-in-disgrace-you and-you-sinned

כְּרוּב הַסֹּכֵךְ מִתּוֹךְ אַבְנֵי־ אֵשׁ׃ (17) גָּבַהּ לִבְּךָ
heart-of-you he-became-proud (17) fire stones-of from-among the-one-guarding cherub-of

בְּיָפְיֶךָ שִׁחַתָּ חָכְמָתְךָ עַל־ יִפְעָתֶךָ
splendor-of-you because-of wisdom-of-you you-corrupted on-account-of-beauty-of-you

עַל־ אֶרֶץ הִשְׁלַכְתִּיךָ לִפְנֵי מְלָכִים נְתַתִּיךָ לְרַאֲוָה בָךְ׃ (18) מֵרֹב
by-many-of (18) at-you to-look I-made-you kings before I-threw-you earth to

עֲוֹנֶיךָ בְּעֶוֶל רְכֻלָּתְךָ חִלַּלְתָּ מִקְדָּשֶׁיךָ
sanctuaries-of-you you-desecrated trade-of-you by-dishonesty-of sins-of-you

וָאוֹצִא־ אֵשׁ מִתּוֹכְךָ הִיא אֲכָלַתְךָ וָאֶתֶּנְךָ
and-I-reduced-you she-consumed-you she from-midst-of-you fire so-I-made-come-out

לְאֵפֶר עַל־ הָאָרֶץ לְעֵינֵי כָּל־ רֹאֶיךָ׃ (19) כָּל־
all-of (19) ones-watching-you all-of before-eyes-of the-ground on to-ash

יוֹדְעֶיךָ בָּעַמִּים שָׁמְמוּ עָלֶיךָ בַּלָּהוֹת הָיִיתָ
you-came horrible-ends at-you they-are-appalled among-the-nations ones-knowing-you

וְאֵינְךָ עַד־ עוֹלָם׃ (20) וַיְהִי דְבַר־ יְהוָה אֵלַי לֵאמֹר׃
to-say to-me Yahweh word-of and-he-came (20) forever to and-no-more-you

(21) בֶּן־ אָדָם שִׂים פָּנֶיךָ אֶל־ צִידוֹן וְהִנָּבֵא עָלֶיהָ׃
against-her and-prophesy! Sidon against faces-of-you set! man son-of (21)

(22) וְאָמַרְתָּ כֹּה אָמַר אֲדֹנָי יְהוִה הִנְנִי עָלַיִךְ צִידוֹן
Sidon against-you see-I! Yahweh Sovereign he-says this and-you-say (22)

וְנִכְבַּדְתִּי בְּתוֹכֵךְ וְיָדְעוּ כִּי־ אֲנִי יְהוָה בַּעֲשׂוֹתִי
when-to-inflict-me Yahweh I that and-they-will-know at-within-you and-I-will-gain-glory

בָהּ שְׁפָטִים וְנִקְדַּשְׁתִּי בָהּ׃ (23) וְשִׁלַּחְתִּי־
and-I-will-send (23) within-her and-I-will-show-myself-holy punishments on-her

בָהּ דֶּבֶר וָדָם בְּחוּצוֹתֶיהָ וְנִפְלַל חָלָל בְּתוֹכָהּ
at-within-her slain and-he-will-fall in-streets-of-her and-blood plague upon-her

on the day you were created
they were prepared.
14 You were anointed as a guardian cherub,
for so I ordained you.
You were on the holy mount of God;
you walked among the fiery stones.
15 You were blameless in your ways
from the day you were created
till wickedness was found in you.
16 Through your widespread trade
you were filled with violence,
and you sinned.
So I drove you in disgrace from the mount of God,
and I expelled you, O guardian cherub,
from among the fiery stones.
17 Your heart became proud
on account of your beauty,
and you corrupted your wisdom
because of your splendor.
So I threw you to the earth;
I made a spectacle of you before kings.
18 By your many sins and dishonest trade
you have desecrated your sanctuaries.
So I made a fire come out from you,
and it consumed you,
and I reduced you to ashes on the ground
in the sight of all who were watching.
19 All the nations who knew you
are appalled at you;
you have come to a horrible end
and will be no more.' "

*A Prophecy Against Sidon*

20 The word of the LORD came to
me: 21 "Son of man, set your face
against Sidon; prophesy against
her 22 and say: 'This is what the
Sovereign LORD says:

" 'I am against you, O Sidon,
and I will gain glory within you.
They will know that I am the LORD,
when I inflict punishment on her
and show myself holy within her.
23 I will send a plague upon her
and make blood flow in her streets.
The slain will fall within her,

*16 Most mss have *hateph pathah* under the *aleph* (אֲ).

בְּחֶרֶב עָלֶיהָ מִסָּבִיב וְיָדְעוּ כִּי־אֲנִי יְהוָה׃ וְלֹא־
and-not (24) Yahweh I that then-they-will-know on-every-side against-her with-sword

יִהְיֶה עוֹד לְבֵית יִשְׂרָאֵל סִלּוֹן מַמְאִיר וְקוֹץ מַכְאִב
causing-pain and-thorn causing-pain brier Israel to-house-of longer he-will-be

מִכֹּל סְבִיבֹתָם הַשָּׁאטִים אוֹתָם וְיָדְעוּ
then-they-will-know them the-ones-treating-with-malice neighbors-of-them from-all-of

כִּי אֲנִי אֲדֹנָי יְהוִה׃ כֹּה־אָמַר אֲדֹנָי יְהוִה בְּקַבְּצִי ׀
when-to-gather-me Yahweh Sovereign he-says this (25) Yahweh Sovereign I that

אֶת־בֵּית יִשְׂרָאֵל מִן־הָעַמִּים אֲשֶׁר נָפֹצוּ בָם
among-them they-were-scattered where the-nations from Israel house-of ***

וְנִקְדַּשְׁתִּי בָם לְעֵינֵי הַגּוֹיִם וְיָשְׁבוּ
then-they-will-live the-nations before-eyes-of among-them then-I-will-show-myself-holy

עַל־אַדְמָתָם אֲשֶׁר נָתַתִּי לְעַבְדִּי לְיַעֲקֹב׃ וְיָשְׁבוּ
and-they-will-live (26) to-Jacob to-servant-of-me I-gave which land-of-them in

עָלֶיהָ לָבֶטַח וּבָנוּ בָתִּים וְנָטְעוּ כְרָמִים
vineyards and-they-will-plant houses and-they-will-build in-safety in-her

וְיָשְׁבוּ לָבֶטַח בַּעֲשׂוֹתִי שְׁפָטִים בְּכֹל
on-all-of punishments when-to-inflict-me in-safety and-they-will-live

הַשָּׁאטִים אֹתָם מִסְּבִיבוֹתָם וְיָדְעוּ כִּי אֲנִי יְהוָה
Yahweh I that then-they-will-know from-neighbors-of-them them the-ones-maligning

אֱלֹהֵיהֶם׃ בַּשָּׁנָה הָעֲשִׂרִית בָּעֲשִׂרִי בִּשְׁנֵים עָשָׂר לַחֹדֶשׁ
of-the-month ten on-two in-the-tenth the-tenth in-the-year (29:1) God-of-them

הָיָה דְבַר־יְהוָה אֵלַי לֵאמֹר׃ בֶּן־אָדָם שִׂים פָּנֶיךָ עַל־
against faces-of-you set! man son-of (2) to-say to-me Yahweh word-of he-came

פַּרְעֹה מֶלֶךְ מִצְרָיִם וְהִנָּבֵא עָלָיו וְעַל־מִצְרַיִם כֻּלָּהּ׃
all-of-her Egypt and-against against-him and-prophesy! Egypt king-of Pharaoh

דַּבֵּר וְאָמַרְתָּ כֹּה־אָמַר ׀ אֲדֹנָי יְהוִה הִנְנִי עָלֶיךָ פַּרְעֹה
Pharaoh against-you see-I! Yahweh Sovereign he-says this and-you-say speak! (3)

מֶלֶךְ־מִצְרַיִם הַתַּנִּים הַגָּדוֹל הָרֹבֵץ בְּתוֹךְ יְאֹרָיו אֲשֶׁר
who streams-of-him in-among the-one-lying the-great the-monster Egypt king-of

אָמַר לִי יְאֹרִי וַאֲנִי עֲשִׂיתִנִי׃ וְנָתַתִּי חַחִיִּים בִּלְחָיֶיךָ
in-jaws-of-you hooks but-I-will-put (4) I-made-for-me and-I Nile-of-me to-me he-says

וְהִדְבַּקְתִּי דְגַת־יְאֹרֶיךָ בְּקַשְׂקְשֹׂתֶיךָ וְהַעֲלִיתִיךָ
and-I-will-pull-out-you to-scales-of-you streams-of-you fish-of and-I-will-make-stick

מִתּוֹךְ יְאֹרֶיךָ וְאֵת כָּל־דְּגַת יְאֹרֶיךָ בְּקַשְׂקְשֹׂתֶיךָ
to-scales-of-you streams-of-you fish-of all-of and streams-of-you from-among

תִּדְבָּק׃ וּנְטַשְׁתִּיךָ הַמִּדְבָּרָה אוֹתְךָ וְאֵת כָּל־דְּגַת
fish-of all-of and you in-the-desert and-I-will-leave-you (5) she-will-stick

with the sword against her
on every side.
Then they will know that I am
the LORD.

24 " 'No longer will the people of Israel have malicious neighbors who are painful briers and sharp thorns. Then they will know that I am the Sovereign LORD.

25 " 'This is what the Sovereign LORD says: When I gather the people of Israel from the nations where they have been scattered, I will show myself holy among them in the sight of the nations. Then they will live in their own land, which I gave to my servant Jacob. 26 They will live there in safety and will build houses and plant vineyards; they will live in safety when I inflict punishment on all their neighbors who maligned them. Then they will know that I am the LORD their God.' "

*A Prophecy Against Egypt*

29 In the tenth year, in the tenth month on the twelfth day, the word of the LORD came to me: 2 "Son of man, set your face against Pharaoh king of Egypt and prophesy against him and against all Egypt. 3 Speak to him and say: 'This is what the Sovereign LORD says:

" 'I am against you, Pharaoh
king of Egypt,
you great monster lying
among your streams.
You say, "The Nile is mine;
I made it for myself."
4 But I will put hooks in your
jaws
and make the fish of your
streams stick to your
scales.
I will pull you out from among
your streams,
with all the fish sticking to
your scales.
5 I will leave you in the desert,
you and all the fish of your

°4 ק חחים

יְאֹרֶיךָ עַל־ פְּנֵי הַשָּׂדֶה תִּפּוֹל לֹא תֵאָסֵף
you-will-be-gathered not you-will-fall the-field open-parts-of on streams-of-you

וְלֹא תִקָּבֵץ לְחַיַּת הָאָרֶץ וּלְעוֹף הַשָּׁמַיִם
the-airs and-to-bird-of the-earth to-beast-of you-will-be-picked-up or-not

נְתַתִּיךָ לְאָכְלָה׃ וְיָדְעוּ כָּל־ יֹשְׁבֵי מִצְרַיִם כִּי
that Egypt ones-living-of all-of then-they-will-know (6) as-food I-will-give-you

אֲנִי יְהוָה יַעַן הֱיוֹתָם מִשְׁעֶנֶת קָנֶה לְבֵית יִשְׂרָאֵל׃ בְּתָפְשָׂם
when-to-grasp-them (7) Israel for-house-of reed staff-of to-be-them because Yahweh I

בְךָ בַכַּפְּךָ תֵּרוֹץ וּבָקַעְתָּ לָהֶם כָּל־ כָּתֵף
shoulder every-of of-them and-you-tore-open you-splintered with-the-hand onto-you

וּבְהִשָּׁעֲנָם עָלֶיךָ תִּשָּׁבֵר וְהַעֲמַדְתָּ לָהֶם כָּל־ מָתְנָיִם׃
backs all-of of-them and-you-caused-to-stand you-broke on-you and-when-to-lean-them

לָכֵן כֹּה אָמַר אֲדֹנָי יְהוִה הִנְנִי מֵבִיא עָלַיִךְ חָרֶב
sword against-you bringing see-I! Yahweh Sovereign he-says this therefore (8)

וְהִכְרַתִּי מִמֵּךְ אָדָם וּבְהֵמָה׃ וְהָיְתָה אֶרֶץ־ מִצְרַיִם
Egypt land-of and-she-will-become (9) and-animal man from-you and-I-will-kill

לִשְׁמָמָה וְחָרְבָּה וְיָדְעוּ כִּי־ אֲנִי יְהוָה יַעַן
because Yahweh I that then-they-will-know and-into-wasteland into-desolation

אָמַר יְאֹר לִי וַאֲנִי עָשִׂיתִי׃ לָכֵן הִנְנִי אֵלֶיךָ וְאֶל־
and-against against-you see-I! therefore (10) I-made and-I to-me Nile he-said

יְאֹרֶיךָ וְנָתַתִּי אֶת־ אֶרֶץ מִצְרַיִם לְחָרְבוֹת חֹרֶב שְׁמָמָה
desolation wasteland-of into-ruins Egypt land-of *** and-I-will-make streams-of-you

מִמִּגְדֹּל סְוֵנֵה וְעַד־ גְּבוּל כּוּשׁ׃ לֹא תַעֲבָר־ בָּהּ
through-her she-will-pass not (11) Cush border-of and-as-far-as Aswan from-Migdol

רֶגֶל אָדָם וְרֶגֶל בְּהֵמָה לֹא תַעֲבָר־ בָּהּ וְלֹא
and-not through-her she-will-pass not animal or-foot-of man foot-of

תֵשֵׁב אַרְבָּעִים שָׁנָה׃ וְנָתַתִּי אֶת־ אֶרֶץ מִצְרַיִם שְׁמָמָה
desolation Egypt land-of *** and-I-will-make (12) year forty she-will-be-lived-in

בְּתוֹךְ ׀ אֲרָצוֹת נְשַׁמּוֹת וְעָרֶיהָ בְּתוֹךְ עָרִים
cities in-among and-cities-of-her ones-being-devastated lands in-among

מָחֳרָבוֹת תִּהְיֶיןָ שְׁמָמָה אַרְבָּעִים שָׁנָה וַהֲפִצֹתִי אֶת־
*** and-I-will-disperse year forty desolation they-will-lie ones-being-ruined

מִצְרַיִם בַּגּוֹיִם וְזֵרִיתִים בָּאֲרָצוֹת׃ כִּי
yet (13) through-the-countries and-I-will-scatter-them among-the-nations Egyptians

כֹּה אָמַר אֲדֹנָי יְהוִה מִקֵּץ אַרְבָּעִים שָׁנָה אֲקַבֵּץ אֶת־ מִצְרַיִם מִן־
from Egyptians *** I-will-gather year forty at-end-of Yahweh Sovereign he-says this

הָעַמִּים אֲשֶׁר־ נָפֹצוּ שָׁמָּה׃ וְשַׁבְתִּי אֶת־
*** and-I-will-bring-back (14) to-there they-were-scattered where the-nations

°7 ק בכף

streams.
You will fall on the open field
and not be gathered or
picked up.
I will give you as food
to the beasts of the earth
and the birds of the air.

6 Then all who live in Egypt will know that I am the LORD.

" 'You have been a staff of reed for the house of Israel. 7 When they grasped you with their hands, you splintered and you tore open their shoulders; when they leaned on you, you broke and their backs were wrenched.[j]

8 " 'Therefore this is what the Sovereign LORD says: I will bring a sword against you and kill your men and their animals. 9 Egypt will become a desolate wasteland. Then they will know that I am the LORD.

" 'Because you said, "The Nile is mine; I made it," 10 therefore I am against you and against your streams, and I will make the land of Egypt a ruin and a desolate waste from Migdol to Aswan, as far as the border of Cush.[k] 11 No foot of man or animal will pass through it; no one will live there for forty years. 12 I will make the land of Egypt desolate among devastated lands, and her cities will lie desolate forty years among ruined cities. And I will disperse the Egyptians among the nations and scatter them through the countries.

13 " 'Yet this is what the Sovereign LORD says: At the end of forty years I will gather the Egyptians from the nations where they were scattered. 14 I will bring them back

j7 Syriac (see also Septuagint and Vulgate); Hebrew *and you caused their backs to stand*
k10 That is, the upper Nile region

שְׁבוּת מִצְרַיִם וַהֲשִׁבֹתִי אֹתָם אֶרֶץ פַּתְרוֹס עַל־אֶרֶץ מְכוּרָתָם
ancestry-of-them land-of to Pathros land-of them and-I-will-return Egypt captivity-of

וְהָיוּ שָׁם מַמְלָכָה שְׁפָלָה׃ מִן־הַמַּמְלָכוֹת תִּהְיֶה שְׁפָלָה
lowly she-will-be the-kingdoms more-than (15) lowly kingdom there and-they-will-be

וְלֹא־תִתְנַשֵּׂא עוֹד עַל־הַגּוֹיִם וְהִמְעַטְתִּים
and-I-will-make-weak-them the-nations above again she-will-exalt-herself and-never

לְבִלְתִּי רְדוֹת בַּגּוֹיִם׃ וְלֹא יִהְיֶה־עוֹד לְבֵית
for-house-of longer he-will-be and-not (16) over-the-nations to-rule never

יִשְׂרָאֵל לְמִבְטָח מַזְכִּיר עָוֺן בִּפְנוֹתָם אַחֲרֵיהֶם
to-them in-to-turn-them sin one-reminding-of as-source-of-confidence Israel

וְיָדְעוּ כִּי אֲנִי אֲדֹנָי יְהוִה׃ וַיְהִי בְּעֶשְׂרִים וָשֶׁבַע
and-seven in-twenty and-he-was (17) Yahweh Sovereign I that then-they-will-know

שָׁנָה בָּרִאשׁוֹן בְּאֶחָד לַחֹדֶשׁ הָיָה דְבַר־יְהוָה אֵלַי לֵאמֹר׃
to-say to-me Yahweh word-of he-came of-the-month on-one in-the-first year

בֶּן־אָדָם נְבוּכַדְרֶאצַּר מֶלֶךְ־בָּבֶל הֶעֱבִיד אֶת־חֵילוֹ עֲבֹדָה
campaign army-of-him *** he-drove Babylon king-of Nebuchadrezzar man son-of (18)

גְדֹלָה אֶל־צֹר כָּל־רֹאשׁ מֻקְרָח וְכָל־כָּתֵף
shoulder and-every-of being-rubbed-bare head every-of Tyre against hard

מְרוּטָה וְשָׂכָר לֹא־הָיָה לוֹ וּלְחֵילוֹ מִצֹּר עַל־
from from-Tyre and-for-army-of-him for-him he-was not yet-reward being-made-raw

הָעֲבֹדָה אֲשֶׁר־עָבַד עָלֶיהָ׃ לָכֵן כֹּה אָמַר אֲדֹנָי
Sovereign he-says this therefore (19) against-her he-led that the-campaign

יְהוִה הִנְנִי נֹתֵן לִנְבוּכַדְרֶאצַּר מֶלֶךְ־בָּבֶל אֶת־אֶרֶץ מִצְרָיִם
Egypt land-of *** Babylon king-of to-Nebuchadrezzar giving see-I! Yahweh

וְנָשָׂא הֲמֹנָהּ וְשָׁלַל שְׁלָלָהּ וּבָזַז
and-he-will-plunder loot-of-her and-he-will-loot wealth-of-her and-he-will-carry-off

בִּזָּהּ וְהָיְתָה שָׂכָר לְחֵילוֹ׃ פְּעֻלָּתוֹ אֲשֶׁר־
that effort-of-him (20) for-army-of-him pay and-she-will-be plunder-of-her

עָבַד בָּהּ נָתַתִּי לוֹ אֶת־אֶרֶץ מִצְרַיִם אֲשֶׁר עָשׂוּ לִי
for-me they-did because Egypt land-of *** to-him I-gave against-her he-worked

נְאֻם אֲדֹנָי יְהוִה׃ בַּיּוֹם הַהוּא אַצְמִיחַ קֶרֶן
horn I-will-make-grow the-that on-the-day (21) Yahweh Sovereign declaration-of

לְבֵית יִשְׂרָאֵל וּלְךָ אֶתֵּן פִּתְחוֹן־פֶּה בְּתוֹכָם
in-among-them mouth opening-of I-will-give and-to-you Israel for-house-of

וְיָדְעוּ כִּי־אֲנִי יְהוָה׃ וַיְהִי דְבַר־יְהוָה אֵלַי לֵאמֹר׃
to-say to-me Yahweh word-of and-he-came (30:1) Yahweh I that then-they-will-know

בֶּן־אָדָם הִנָּבֵא וְאָמַרְתָּ כֹּה אָמַר אֲדֹנָי יְהוִה הֵילִילוּ הָהּ
alas! wail! Yahweh Sovereign he-says this and-you-say prophesy! man son-of (2)

from captivity and return them to Upper Egypt,[u] the land of their ancestry. There they will be a lowly kingdom. 15It will be the lowliest of kingdoms and will never again exalt itself above the other nations. I will make it so weak that it will never again rule over the nations. 16Egypt will no longer be a source of confidence for the people of Israel but will be a reminder of their sin in turning to her for help. Then they will know that I am the Sovereign LORD.' "

17In the twenty-seventh year, in the first month on the first day, the word of the LORD came to me: 18"Son of man, Nebuchadnezzar king of Babylon drove his army in a hard campaign against Tyre; every head was rubbed bare and every shoulder made raw. Yet he and his army got no reward from the campaign he led against Tyre. 19Therefore this is what the Sovereign LORD says: I am going to give Egypt to Nebuchadnezzar king of Babylon, and he will carry off its wealth. He will loot and plunder the land as pay for his army. 20I have given him Egypt as a reward for his efforts because he and his army did it for me, declares the Sovereign LORD.

21"On that day I will make a horn[v] grow for the house of Israel, and I will open your mouth among them. Then they will know that I am the LORD."

### *A Lament for Egypt*

30 The word of the LORD came to me: 2"Son of man, prophesy and say: 'This is what the Sovereign LORD says:

" 'Wail and say,

u14 Hebrew *to Pathros*
v21 *Horn* here symbolizes strength.

לַיּוֹם׃ כִּי־קָרוֹב יוֹם וְקָרוֹב יוֹם לַיהוָה יוֹם עָנָן עֵת
time-of cloud day-of of-Yahweh day indeed-near day near for (3) for-the-day

גּוֹיִם יִהְיֶה׃ וּבָאָה חֶרֶב בְּמִצְרַיִם וְהָיְתָה חַלְחָלָה
anguish and-she-will-come against-Egypt sword and-coming (4) he-is nations

בְּכוּשׁ בִּנְפֹל חָלָל בְּמִצְרָיִם וְלָקְחוּ הֲמוֹנָהּ
wealth-of-her then-they-will-carry-away in-Egypt slain when-to-fall upon-Cush

וְנֶהֶרְסוּ יְסוֹדֹתֶיהָ׃ כּוּשׁ וּפוּט וְלוּד וְכָל־
and-all-of and-Lydia and-Put Cush (5) foundations-of-her and-they-will-be-torn-down

הָעֶרֶב וְכוּב וּבְנֵי אֶרֶץ הַבְּרִית אִתָּם בַּחֶרֶב
by-the-sword with-them the-covenant land-of and-peoples-of and-Cub the-Arabia

יִפֹּלוּ׃ כֹּה אָמַר יְהוָה וְנָפְלוּ סֹמְכֵי
ones-being-allies-of indeed-they-will-fall Yahweh he-says this (6) they-will-fall

מִצְרַיִם וְיָרַד גְּאוֹן עֻזָּהּ מִמִּגְדֹּל סְוֵנֵה בַּחֶרֶב
by-the-sword Aswan from-Migdol strength-of-her pride-of and-he-will-fail Egypt

יִפְּלוּ־ בָהּ נְאֻם אֲדֹנָי יְהוִה׃ וְנָשַׁמּוּ
and-they-will-be-desolate (7) Yahweh Sovereign declaration-of within-her they-will-fall

בְּתוֹךְ אֲרָצוֹת נְשַׁמּוֹת וְעָרָיו בְּתוֹךְ־ עָרִים נַחֲרָבוֹת
ones-being-ruined cities in-among and-cities-of-him ones-being-desolate lands in-among

תִּהְיֶינָה׃ וְיָדְעוּ כִּי־ אֲנִי יְהוָה בְּתִתִּי־ אֵשׁ בְּמִצְרַיִם
to-Egypt fire when-to-set-me Yahweh I that then-they-will-know (8) they-will-lie

וְנִשְׁבְּרוּ כָּל־ עֹזְרֶיהָ׃ בַּיּוֹם הַהוּא יֵצְאוּ
they-will-go-out the-that on-the-day (9) ones-helping-her all-of and-they-are-crushed

מַלְאָכִים מִלְּפָנַי בַּצִּים לְהַחֲרִיד אֶת־ כּוּשׁ בֶּטַח
complacency Cush *** to-frighten in-the-ships from-before-me messengers

וְהָיְתָה חַלְחָלָה בָהֶם בְּיוֹם מִצְרַיִם כִּי הִנֵּה בָּאָה׃ כֹּה אָמַר
he-says this (10) coming surely! for Egypt on-day-of to-them anguish and-she-will-come

אֲדֹנָי יְהוִה וְהִשְׁבַּתִּי אֶת־ הֲמוֹן מִצְרַיִם בְּיַד נְבוּכַדְרֶאצַּר
Nebuchadrezzar by-hand-of Egypt horde-of *** indeed-I-will-end Yahweh Sovereign

מֶלֶךְ־ בָּבֶל׃ הוּא וְעַמּוֹ אִתּוֹ עָרִיצֵי גּוֹיִם
nations ruthless-ones-of with-him and-army-of-him he (11) Babylon king-of

מוּבָאִים לְשַׁחֵת הָאָרֶץ וְהֵרִיקוּ חַרְבוֹתָם עַל־
against swords-of-them and-they-will-draw the-land to-destroy ones-being-brought-in

מִצְרַיִם וּמָלְאוּ אֶת־ הָאָרֶץ חָלָל׃ וְנָתַתִּי יְאֹרִים חָרָבָה
dryness streams and-I-will-make (12) slain the-land *** and-they-will-fill Egypt

וּמָכַרְתִּי אֶת־ הָאָרֶץ בְּיַד־ רָעִים וַהֲשִׁמֹּתִי אֶרֶץ
land and-I-will-lay-waste evil-men to-hand-of the-land *** and-I-will-sell

וּמְלֹאָהּ בְּיַד־ זָרִים אֲנִי יְהוָה דִּבַּרְתִּי׃
I-spoke Yahweh I ones-being-foreign by-hand-of and-everything-in-her

"Alas for that day!"
3For the day is near,
the day of the LORD is
near—
a day of clouds,
a time of doom for the
nations.
4A sword will come against
Egypt,
and anguish will come upon
Cush.[w]
When the slain fall in Egypt,
her wealth will be carried
away
and her foundations torn
down.

5Cush and Put, Lydia and all
Arabia, Libya[x] and the people of
the covenant land will fall by the
sword along with Egypt.
6" 'This is what the LORD says:

" 'The allies of Egypt will fall
and her proud strength will
fail.
From Migdol to Aswan
they will fall by the sword
within her,
declares the Sovereign
LORD.
7" 'They will be desolate
among desolate lands,
and their cities will lie
among ruined cities.
8Then they will know that I am
the LORD,
when I set fire to Egypt
and all her helpers are
crushed.

9" 'On that day messengers will
go out from me in ships to fright-
en Cush out of her complacency.
Anguish will take hold of them on
the day of Egypt's doom, for it is
sure to come.

10" 'This is what the Sovereign
LORD says:

" 'I will put an end to the
hordes of Egypt
by the hand of
Nebuchadnezzar king of
Babylon.
11He and his army—the most
ruthless of nations—
will be brought in to destroy
the land.
They will draw their swords
against Egypt
and fill the land with the
slain.
12I will dry up the streams of
the Nile
and sell the land to evil
men;
by the hand of foreigners
I will lay waste the land and
everything in it.
I the LORD have spoken.

w4 That is, the upper Nile region; also in verses 5 and 9
x5 Hebrew *Cub*

כֹּה־אָמַר אֲדֹנָי יְהוִה וְהַאֲבַדְתִּי גִלּוּלִים וְהִשְׁבַּתִּי
and-I-will-end idols indeed-I-will-destroy Yahweh Sovereign he-says this (13)

אֱלִילִים מִנֹּף וְנָשִׂיא מֵאֶרֶץ־מִצְרַיִם לֹא יִהְיֶה־עוֹד וְנָתַתִּי
and-I-will-spread longer he-will-be not Egypt in-land-of and-prince in-Noph images

יִרְאָה בְּאֶרֶץ מִצְרָיִם׃ וַהֲשִׁמֹּתִי אֶת־פַּתְרוֹס וְנָתַתִּי
and-I-will-set Pathros *** and-I-will-lay-waste (14) Egypt throughout-land-of fear

אֵשׁ בְּצֹעַן וְעָשִׂיתִי שְׁפָטִים בְּנֹא׃ וְשָׁפַכְתִּי
and-I-will-pour-out (15) on-No punishments and-I-will-inflict to-Zoan fire

חֲמָתִי עַל־סִין מָעוֹז מִצְרָיִם וְהִכְרַתִּי אֶת־הֲמוֹן נֹא׃
No horde-of *** and-I-will-cut-off Egypt stronghold-of Sin on wrath-of-me

וְנָתַתִּי אֵשׁ בְּמִצְרַיִם חוּל תָּחִיל סִין וְנֹא תִּהְיֶה
she-will-be and-No Sin she-will-writhe to-writhe to-Egypt fire and-I-will-set (16)

לְהִבָּקֵעַ וְנֹף צָרֵי יוֹמָם׃ בַּחוּרֵי אָוֶן וּפִי־
and-Pi Awen young-men-of (17) constant distresses-of and-Noph to-be-taken-by-storm

בֶסֶת בַּחֶרֶב יִפֹּלוּ וְהֵנָּה בַּשְּׁבִי תֵלַכְנָה׃
they-will-go into-the-captivity and-they they-will-fall by-the-sword Beseth

וּבִתְחַפְנְחֵס חָשַׁךְ הַיּוֹם בְּשִׁבְרִי־שָׁם אֶת־מֹטוֹת
yokes-of *** there when-to-break-me the-day he-will-be-dark and-at-Tahpanhes (18)

מִצְרַיִם וְנִשְׁבַּת־בָּהּ גְּאוֹן עֻזָּהּ הִיא עָנָן יְכַסֶּנָּה
he-will-cover-her cloud she strength-of-her pride-of in-her and-he-will-end Egypt

וּבְנוֹתֶיהָ בַּשְּׁבִי תֵלַכְנָה׃ וְעָשִׂיתִי שְׁפָטִים
punishments so-I-will-inflict (19) they-will-go into-the-captivity and-villages-of-her

בְּמִצְרָיִם וְיָדְעוּ כִּי־אֲנִי יְהוָה׃ וַיְהִי בְּאַחַת עֶשְׂרֵה שָׁנָה
year ten in-one-of and-he-was (20) Yahweh I that and-they-will-know on-Egypt

בָּרִאשׁוֹן בְּשִׁבְעָה לַחֹדֶשׁ הָיָה דְבַר־יְהוָה אֵלַי לֵאמֹר׃ בֶּן־
son-of (21) to-say to-me Yahweh word-of he-came of-the-month on-seven in-the-first

אָדָם אֶת־זְרוֹעַ פַּרְעֹה מֶלֶךְ־מִצְרַיִם שָׁבַרְתִּי וְהִנֵּה לֹא־חֻבְּשָׁה לָתֵת
to-bring she-was-bound not and-see! I-broke Egypt king-of Pharaoh arm-of *** man

רְפֻאוֹת לָשׂוּם חִתּוּל לְחָבְשָׁהּ לְחָזְקָהּ לִתְפֹּשׂ בֶּחָרֶב׃
onto-the-sword to-hold to-become-strong-her to-bind-her splint to-put healings

לָכֵן כֹּה־אָמַר׀ אֲדֹנָי יְהוִה הִנְנִי אֶל־פַּרְעֹה מֶלֶךְ־מִצְרַיִם
Egypt king-of Pharaoh against see-I! Yahweh Sovereign he-says this therefore (22)

וְשָׁבַרְתִּי אֶת־זְרֹעֹתָיו אֶת־הַחֲזָקָה וְאֶת־הַנִּשְׁבָּרֶת
the-one-being-broken as-well-as the-good *** arms-of-him *** and-I-will-break

וְהִפַּלְתִּי אֶת־הַחֶרֶב מִיָּדוֹ׃ וַהֲפִצוֹתִי אֶת־
*** and-I-will-disperse (23) from-hand-of-him the-sword *** and-I-will-make-fall

מִצְרַיִם בַּגּוֹיִם וְזֵרִיתִם בָּאֲרָצוֹת׃
through-the-countries and-I-will-scatter-them among-the-nations Egyptians

13"'This is what the Sovereign
LORD says:

"'I will destroy the idols
and put an end to the
images in Memphis.[x]
No longer will there be a
prince in Egypt,
and I will spread fear
throughout the land.
14I will lay waste Upper Egypt,[y]
set fire to Zoan
and inflict punishment on
Thebes.[z]
15I will pour out my wrath on
Pelusium,[a]
the stronghold of Egypt,
and cut off the hordes of
Thebes.
16I will set fire to Egypt;
Pelusium will writhe in
agony.
Thebes will be taken by storm;
Memphis will be in constant
distress.
17The young men of Heliopolis[b]
and Bubastis[c]
will fall by the sword,
and the cities themselves
will go into captivity.
18Dark will be the day at
Tahpanhes
when I break the yoke of
Egypt;
there her proud strength will
come to an end.
She will be covered with
clouds,
and her villages will go into
captivity.
19So I will inflict punishment on
Egypt,
and they will know that I
am the LORD.'"

20In the eleventh year, in the
first month on the seventh day,
the word of the LORD came to me:
21"Son of man, I have broken the
arm of Pharaoh king of Egypt. It
has not been bound up for healing
or put in a splint so as to become
strong enough to hold a sword.
22Therefore this is what the Sovereign LORD says: I am against Pharaoh king of Egypt. I will break
both his arms, the good arm as
well as the broken one, and make
the sword fall from his hand. 23I
will disperse the Egyptians among
the nations and scatter them
through the countries. 24I will

x13 Hebrew *Noph;* also in verse 16
y14 Hebrew *waste Pathros*
z14 Hebrew *No;* also in verses 15 and 16
a15 Hebrew *Sin;* also in verse 16
b17 Hebrew *Awen* (or *On*)
c17 Hebrew *Pi Beseth*

°16 ק תחול

וְחִזַּקְתִּי אֶת־ זְרֹעוֹת מֶלֶךְ בָּבֶל וְנָתַתִּי אֶת־
*** and-I-will-put Babylon king-of arms-of *** and-I-will-strengthen (24)

חַרְבִּי בְּיָדוֹ וְשָׁבַרְתִּי אֶת־זְרֹעוֹת פַּרְעֹה וְנָאַק
and-he-will-groan Pharaoh arms-of *** but-I-will-break in-hand-of-him sword-of-me

נַאֲקוֹת חָלָל לְפָנָיו׃ וְהַחֲזַקְתִּי אֶת־זְרֹעוֹת מֶלֶךְ
king-of arms-of *** and-I-will-strengthen (25) before-him wounded-man groans-of

בָּבֶל וּזְרֹעוֹת פַּרְעֹה תִּפֹּלְנָה וְיָדְעוּ כִּי־אֲנִי יְהוָה
Yahweh I that then-they-will-know they-will-fall-limp Pharaoh but-arms-of Babylon

בְּתִתִּי חַרְבִּי בְּיַד מֶלֶךְ־ בָּבֶל וְנָטָה אוֹתָהּ
her and-he-brandishes Babylon king-of into-hand-of sword-of-me when-to-put-me

אֶל־ אֶרֶץ מִצְרָיִם׃ וַהֲפִצוֹתִי אֶת־ מִצְרַיִם בַּגּוֹיִם
among-the-nations Egyptians *** and-I-will-disperse (26) Egypt land-of against

וְזֵרִיתִי אוֹתָם בָּאֲרָצוֹת וְיָדְעוּ כִּי־אֲנִי יְהוָה׃
Yahweh I that then-they-will-know through-the-countries them and-I-will-scatter

וַיְהִי בְּאַחַת עֶשְׂרֵה שָׁנָה בַּשְּׁלִישִׁי בְּאֶחָד לַחֹדֶשׁ הָיָה
he-came of-the-month on-one in-the-third year ten in-one-of and-he-was (31:1)

דְבַר־ יְהוָה אֵלַי לֵאמֹר׃ בֶּן־אָדָם אֱמֹר אֶל־פַּרְעֹה מֶלֶךְ־מִצְרַיִם וְאֶל־
and-to Egypt king-of Pharaoh to say! man son-of (2) to-say to-me Yahweh word-of

הֲמוֹנוֹ אֶל־ מִי דָּמִיתָ בְגָדְלֶךָ׃ הִנֵּה אַשּׁוּר
Assyria consider! (3) in-majesty-of-you can-you-be-compared whom? with horde-of-him

אֶרֶז בַּלְּבָנוֹן יְפֵה עָנָף וְחֹרֶשׁ מֵצַל וּגְבַהּ
and-towering-of overshadowing and-forest-of branch beautiful-of in-the-Lebanon cedar

קוֹמָה וּבֵין עֲבֹתִים הָיְתָה צַמַּרְתּוֹ׃ מַיִם גִּדְּלוּהוּ
they-nourished-him waters (4) top-of-him she-was thick-foliages and-above height

תְּהוֹם רֹמְמָתְהוּ אֶת־ נַהֲרֹתֶיהָ הֹלֵךְ סְבִיבוֹת מַטָּעָהּ
base-of-her ones-around flowing streams-of-her *** she-made-grow-tall-him deep-spring

וְאֶת־ תְּעָלֹתֶיהָ שִׁלְחָה אֶל כָּל־ עֲצֵי הַשָּׂדֶה׃ עַל־כֵּן גָּבְהָא
she-towered so for (5) the-field trees-of all-of to she-sent channels-of-her and

קֹמָתוֹ מִכֹּל עֲצֵי הַשָּׂדֶה וַתִּרְבֶּינָה סַרְעַפֹּתָיו
boughs-of-him and-they-increased the-field trees-of more-than-all-of height-of-him

וַתֶּאֱרַכְנָה פֹארֹתָו מִמַּיִם רַבִּים בְּשַׁלְּחוֹ׃
when-to-spread-him abundant-ones because-of-waters branches-of-him and-they-grew-long

בִּסְעַפֹּתָיו קִנְנוּ כָּל־ עוֹף הַשָּׁמַיִם וְתַחַת פֹּארֹתָיו
branches-of-him and-under the-airs bird-of all-of they-nested in-boughs-of-him (6)

יָלְדוּ כֹּל חַיַּת הַשָּׂדֶה וּבְצִלּוֹ יֵשְׁבוּ כֹּל
all-of they-lived and-in-shade-of-him the-field beast-of all-of they-gave-birth

גּוֹיִם רַבִּים׃ וַיִּיף בְּגָדְלוֹ בְּאֹרֶךְ
with-spreading-of in-majesty-of-him and-he-was-beautiful (7) great-ones nations

°5 ק פארתיו

strengthen the arms of the king of Babylon and put my sword in his hand, but I will break the arms of Pharaoh, and he will groan before him like a mortally wounded man. [25]I will strengthen the arms of the king of Babylon, but the arms of Pharaoh will fall limp. Then they will know that I am the LORD, when I put my sword into the hand of the king of Babylon and he brandishes it against Egypt. [26]I will disperse the Egyptians among the nations and scatter them through the countries. Then they will know that I am the LORD."

*A Cedar in Lebanon*

31 In the eleventh year, in the third month on the first day, the word of the LORD came to me: [2]"Son of man, say to Pharaoh king of Egypt and to his hordes:

" 'Who can be compared with
you in majesty?
[3]Consider Assyria, once a cedar
in Lebanon,
with beautiful branches
overshadowing the forest;
it towered on high,
its top above the thick
foliage.
[4]The waters nourished it,
deep springs made it grow
tall;
their streams flowed
all around its base
and sent their channels
to all the trees of the field.
[5]So it towered higher
than all the trees of the
field;
its boughs increased
and its branches grew long,
spreading because of
abundant waters.
[6]All the birds of the air
nested in its boughs,
all the beasts of the field
gave birth under its
branches;
all the great nations
lived in its shade.
[7]It was majestic in beauty,
with its spreading boughs,

דָּלִיּוֹתָיו כִּי־ הָיָה שָׁרְשׁוֹ אֶל־ מַיִם רַבִּים׃ אֲרָזִים לֹא־

not cedars (8) abundant-ones waters to root-of-him he-went for boughs-of-him

עֲמָמֻהוּ בְּגַן־ אֱלֹהִים בְּרוֹשִׁים לֹא דָמוּ אֶל־ סְעַפֹּתָיו

boughs-of-him to they-could-equal not pines God in-garden-of they-could-rival-him

וְעַרְמֹנִים לֹא־ הָיוּ כְּפֹארֹתָיו כָּל־ עֵץ בְּגַן־ אֱלֹהִים

God in-garden-of tree any-of like-branches-of-him they-could-be not or-plane-trees

לֹא־ דָמָה אֵלָיו בְּיָפְיוֹ׃ יָפֶה עֲשִׂיתִיו בְּרֹב

with-abundance-of I-made-him beautiful (9) in-beauty-of-him to-him he-could-match not

דָּלִיּוֹתָיו וַיְקַנְאֻהוּ כָּל־ עֲצֵי־ עֵדֶן אֲשֶׁר בְּגַן הָאֱלֹהִים׃

the-God in-garden-of that Eden trees-of all-of and-they-envied-him branches-of-him

לָכֵן כֹּה אָמַר אֲדֹנָי יְהוִה יַעַן אֲשֶׁר גָּבַהְתָּ בְּקוֹמָה

on-height you-towered that because Yahweh Sovereign he-says this therefore (10)

וַיִּתֵּן צַמַּרְתּוֹ אֶל־ בֵּין עֲבוֹתִים וְרָם לְבָבוֹ

heart-of-him and-he-was-proud thick-foliages above to top-of-him and-he-lifted

בְּגָבְהוֹ׃ וְאֶתְּנֵהוּ בְּיַד אֵיל גּוֹיִם עָשׂוֹ

to-deal nations ruler-of into-hand-of so-I-gave-him (11) of-height-of-him

יַעֲשֶׂה לוֹ כְּרִשְׁעוֹ גֵּרַשְׁתִּהוּ׃

I-cast-aside-him according-to-wickedness-of-him with-him he-would-deal

וַיִּכְרְתֻהוּ זָרִים עָרִיצֵי גוֹיִם

nations ruthless-ones-of ones-being-foreign and-they-cut-down-him (12)

וַיִּטְּשֻׁהוּ אֶל־ הֶהָרִים וּבְכָל־ גֵּאָיוֹת נָפְלוּ דָלִיּוֹתָיו

boughs-of-him they-fell valleys and-in-all-of the-mountains on and-they-left-him

וַתִּשָּׁבַרְנָה פֹארֹתָיו בְּכֹל אֲפִיקֵי הָאָרֶץ וַיֵּרְדוּ

and-they-came-out the-land ravines-of in-all-of branches-of-him and-they-lay-broken

מִצִּלּוֹ כָּל־ עַמֵּי הָאָרֶץ וַיִּטְּשֻׁהוּ׃ עַל־

on (13) and-they-left-him the-earth nations-of all-of from-shade-of-him

מַפַּלְתּוֹ יִשְׁכְּנוּ כָּל־ עוֹף הַשָּׁמַיִם וְאֶל־ פֹּארֹתָיו

branches-of-him and-among the-airs bird-of all-of they-settled fallen-one-of-him

הָיוּ כֹּל חַיַּת הַשָּׂדֶה׃ לְמַעַן אֲשֶׁר לֹא־ יִגְבְּהוּ

they-may-tower not that therefore (14) the-field beast-of all-of they-were

בְקוֹמָתָם כָּל־ עֲצֵי־ מַיִם וְלֹא־ יִתְּנוּ אֶת־ צַמַּרְתָּם אֶל־

to top-of-them *** they-may-lift and-not waters trees-of any-of on-height-of-them

בֵּין עֲבֹתִים וְלֹא־ יַעַמְדוּ אֲלֵיהֶם בְּגָבְהָם כָּל־

any-of to-height-of-them to-them they-may-reach and-not thick-foliages above

שֹׁתֵי מַיִם כִּי־ כֻלָּם נִתְּנוּ לַמָּוֶת אֶל־

for for-the-death they-are-destined all-of-them for waters ones-drinking-of

אֶרֶץ תַּחְתִּית בְּתוֹךְ בְּנֵי אָדָם אֶל־ יוֹרְדֵי בוֹר׃

pit ones-going-down-of with mortality men-of in-among part-below earth-of

for its roots went down
to abundant waters.
8 The cedars in the garden of
God
could not rival it,
nor could the pine trees
equal its boughs,
nor could the plane trees
compare with its branches—
no tree in the garden of God
could match its beauty.
9 I made it beautiful
with abundant branches,
the envy of all the trees of
Eden
in the garden of God.

10 "'Therefore this is what the
Sovereign LORD says: Because it
towered on high, lifting its top
above the thick foliage, and because it was proud of its height, 11 I
handed it over to the ruler of the
nations, for him to deal with according to its wickedness. I cast it
aside, 12 and the most ruthless of
foreign nations cut it down and
left it. Its boughs fell on the mountains and in all the valleys; its
branches lay broken in all the ravines of the land. All the nations
of the earth came out from under
its shade and left it. 13 All the birds
of the air settled on the fallen tree,
and all the beasts of the field were
among its branches. 14 Therefore
no other trees by the waters are
ever to tower proudly on high, lifting their tops above the thick foliage. No other trees so well-
watered are ever to reach such a
height; they are all destined for
death, for the earth below, among
mortal men, with those who go
down to the pit.

כֹּה־ אָמַר אֲדֹנָי יְהוִה בְּיוֹם רִדְתּוֹ שְׁאֹלָה
to-Sheol to-go-down-him on-day-of Yahweh Sovereign he-says this (15)

הֶאֱבַלְתִּי כִּסֵּתִי עָלָיו אֶת־ תְּהוֹם וָאֶמְנַע נַהֲרוֹתֶיהָ
streams-of-her and-I-held-back deep-spring *** for-him I-covered I-made-mourn

וַיִּכָּלְאוּ מַיִם רַבִּים וָאַקְדִּר עָלָיו
because-of-him and-I-clothed-with-gloom abundant-ones waters and-they-were-restrained

לְבָנוֹן וְכָל־ עֲצֵי הַשָּׂדֶה עָלָיו עֻלְפֶּה׃ מִקּוֹל
at-sound-of (16) withered-away because-of-him the-field trees-of and-all-of Lebanon

מַפַּלְתּוֹ הִרְעַשְׁתִּי גוֹיִם בְּהוֹרִדִי אֹתוֹ שְׁאוֹלָה אֶת־
with to-Sheol him when-to-bring-down-me nations I-made-tremble fall-of-him

יוֹרְדֵי בוֹר וַיִּנָּחֲמוּ בְּאֶרֶץ תַּחְתִּית כָּל־ עֲצֵי־
trees-of all-of part-below in-earth-of then-they-were-consoled pit ones-going-down-of

עֵדֶן מִבְחַר וְטוֹב־ לְבָנוֹן כָּל־ שֹׁתֵי מָיִם׃ גַּם־ הֵם
they also (17) waters ones-drinking-of all-of Lebanon and-best-of choicest-of Eden

אִתּוֹ יָרְדוּ שְׁאוֹלָה אֶל־ חַלְלֵי־ חָרֶב וּזְרֹעוֹ יָשְׁבוּ
they-lived and-ally-of-him sword ones-killed-of to to-Sheol they-went-down with-him

בְצִלּוֹ בְּתוֹךְ גּוֹיִם׃ אֶל־ מִי דָמִיתָ כָּכָה בְּכָבוֹד
in-splendor so can-you-be-compared whom? with (18) nations in-among in-shade-of-him

וּבְגֹדֶל בַּעֲצֵי־ עֵדֶן וְהוּרַדְתָּ אֶת־ עֲצֵי־ עֵדֶן
Eden trees-of with yet-you-will-be-brought-down Eden among-trees-of and-in-majesty

אֶל־ אֶרֶץ תַּחְתִּית בְּתוֹךְ עֲרֵלִים תִּשְׁכַּב אֶת־ חַלְלֵי־
ones-killed-of with you-will-lie uncircumcised-ones in-among part-below earth-of to

חֶרֶב הוּא פַרְעֹה וְכָל־ הֲמוֹנֹה נְאֻם אֲדֹנָי יְהוִה׃
Yahweh Sovereign declaration-of horde-of-him and-all-of Pharaoh this sword

וַיְהִי בִּשְׁתֵּי עֶשְׂרֵה שָׁנָה בִּשְׁנֵי עָשָׂר חֹדֶשׁ בְּאֶחָד לַחֹדֶשׁ
of-the-month on-one month ten in-two-of year ten in-two-of and-he-was (32:1)

הָיָה דְבַר־ יְהוָה אֵלַי לֵאמֹר׃ בֶּן־ אָדָם שָׂא קִינָה עַל־
concerning lament take-up! man son-of (2) to-say to-me Yahweh word-of he-came

פַּרְעֹה מֶלֶךְ־מִצְרַיִם וְאָמַרְתָּ אֵלָיו כְּפִיר גּוֹיִם נִדְמֵיתָ וְאַתָּה
and-you you-are-like nations lion-of to-him and-you-say Egypt king-of Pharaoh

כַּתַּנִּים בַּיַּמִּים וַתָּגַח בְּנַהֲרוֹתֶיךָ וַתִּדְלַח־
and-you-churned in-streams-of-you and-you-thrashed-about in-the-seas like-the-monster

מַיִם בְּרַגְלֶיךָ וַתִּרְפֹּס נַהֲרוֹתָם׃ כֹּה אָמַר אֲדֹנָי
Sovereign he-says this (3) streams-of-them and-you-muddied with-feet-of-you waters

יְהוִה וּפָרַשְׂתִּי עָלֶיךָ אֶת־ רִשְׁתִּי בִּקְהַל עַמִּים רַבִּים
great-ones peoples with-throng-of net-of-me *** over-you indeed-I-will-cast Yahweh

וְהֶעֱלוּךָ בְּחֶרְמִי׃ וּנְטַשְׁתִּיךָ בָאָרֶץ עַל־
on on-the-land and-I-will-throw-you (4) in-net-of-me and-they-will-haul-up-you

[15] " 'This is what the Sovereign LORD says: On the day it was brought down to the grave[d] I covered the deep springs with mourning for it; I held back its streams, and its abundant waters were restrained. Because of it I clothed Lebanon with gloom, and all the trees of the field withered away. [16] I made the nations tremble at the sound of its fall when I brought it down to the grave with those who go down to the pit. Then all the trees of Eden, the choicest and best of Lebanon, all the trees that were well-watered, were consoled in the earth below. [17] Those who lived in its shade, its allies among the nations, had also gone down to the grave with it, joining those killed by the sword.

[18] " 'Which of the trees of Eden can be compared with you in splendor and majesty? Yet you, too, will be brought down with the trees of Eden to the earth below; you will lie among the uncircumcised, with those killed by the sword.

" 'This is Pharaoh and all his hordes, declares the Sovereign LORD.' "

*A Lament for Pharaoh*

32 In the twelfth year, in the twelfth month on the first day, the word of the LORD came to me: [2] "Son of man, take up a lament concerning Pharaoh king of Egypt and say to him:

" 'You are like a lion among
the nations;
you are like a monster in
the seas
thrashing about in your
streams,
churning the water with
your feet
and muddying the streams.

[3] " 'This is what the Sovereign LORD says:

" 'With a great throng of
people
I will cast my net over you,
and they will haul you up in
my net.
[4] I will throw you on the land

[d]15 Hebrew *Sheol;* also in verses 16 and 17

°18 ק המונו

פְּנֵי הַשָּׂדֶה אֲטִילֶךָ וְהִשְׁכַּנְתִּי עָלֶיךָ כָּל־ עוֹף
bird-of all-of on-you and-I-will-let-settle I-will-hurl-you the-field open-parts-of

הַשָּׁמַיִם וְהִשְׂבַּעְתִּי מִמְּךָ חַיַּת כָּל־ הָאָרֶץ׃ וְנָתַתִּי
and-I-will-spread (5) the-earth all-of beast-of on-you and-I-will-let-gorge the-airs

אֶת־ בְּשָׂרְךָ עַל־ הֶהָרִים וּמִלֵּאתִי הַגֵּאָיוֹת רָמוּתֶךָ׃
remainder-of-you the-valleys and-I-will-fill the-mountains on flesh-of-you ***

וְהִשְׁקֵיתִי אֶרֶץ צָפָתְךָ מִדָּמְךָ אֶל־ הֶהָרִים וַאֲפִקִים
and-ravines the-mountains to of-blood-of-you flow-of-you land and-I-will-drench (6)

יִמָּלְאוּן מִמֶּךָּ׃ וְכִסֵּיתִי בְכַבּוֹתְךָ שָׁמַיִם
heavens when-to-snuff-out-you and-I-will-cover (7) with-you they-will-be-filled

וְהִקְדַּרְתִּי אֶת־ כֹּכְבֵיהֶם שֶׁמֶשׁ בֶּעָנָן אֲכַסֶּנּוּ וְיָרֵחַ
and-moon I-will-cover-him with-the-cloud sun stars-of-them *** and-I-will-darken

לֹא־ יָאִיר אוֹרוֹ׃ כָּל־ מְאוֹרֵי אוֹר בַּשָּׁמַיִם
in-the-heavens light shining-ones-of all-of (8) light-of-him he-will-give-light not

אַקְדִּירֵם עָלֶיךָ וְנָתַתִּי חֹשֶׁךְ עַל־ אַרְצְךָ
land-of-you over darkness and-I-will-bring over-you I-will-darken-them

נְאֻם אֲדֹנָי יְהוִה׃ וְהִכְעַסְתִּי לֵב עַמִּים רַבִּים
many-ones peoples heart-of and-I-will-trouble (9) Yahweh Sovereign declaration-of

בַּהֲבִיאִי שִׁבְרְךָ בַּגּוֹיִם עַל־ אֲרָצוֹת אֲשֶׁר לֹא־
not that lands among among-the-nations destruction-of-you when-to-bring-me

יְדַעְתָּם׃ וַהֲשִׁמּוֹתִי עָלֶיךָ עַמִּים רַבִּים
many-ones peoples at-you and-I-will-make-appalled (10) you-know-them

וּמַלְכֵיהֶם יִשְׂעֲרוּ עָלֶיךָ שַׂעַר בְּעוֹפְפִי
when-to-brandish-me shuddering because-of-you they-will-shudder and-kings-of-them

חַרְבִּי עַל־ פְּנֵיהֶם וְחָרְדוּ לִרְגָעִים אִישׁ לְנַפְשׁוֹ
for-life-of-him each at-moments and-they-will-tremble faces-of-them before sword-of-me

בְּיוֹם מַפַּלְתֶּךָ׃ כִּי כֹּה אָמַר אֲדֹנָי יְהוִה חֶרֶב מֶלֶךְ־
king-of sword-of Yahweh Sovereign he-says this for (11) downfall-of-you on-day-of

בָּבֶל תְּבוֹאֶךָּ׃ בְּחַרְבוֹת גִּבּוֹרִים אַפִּיל
I-will-make-fall mighty-men by-swords-of (12) she-will-come-against-you Babylon

הֲמוֹנֶךָ עָרִיצֵי גוֹיִם כֻּלָּם וְשָׁדְדוּ אֶת־ גְּאוֹן
pride-of *** and-they-will-shatter all-of-them nations ruthless-ones-of horde-of-you

מִצְרַיִם וְנִשְׁמַד כָּל־ הֲמוֹנָהּ׃ וְהַאֲבַדְתִּי אֶת־ כָּל־
all-of *** and-I-will-destroy (13) horde-of-her all-of and-he-will-be-overthrown Egypt

בְּהֶמְתָּהּ מֵעַל מַיִם רַבִּים וְלֹא תִדְלָחֵם רֶגֶל־
foot-of she-will-stir-them and-not abundant-ones waters from-beside cattle-of-her

אָדָם עוֹד וּפַרְסוֹת בְּהֵמָה לֹא תִדְלָחֵם׃ אָז אַשְׁקִיעַ
I-will-let-settle then (14) she-will-muddy-them not cattle or-hoofs-of longer man

and hurl you on the open
field.
I will let all the birds of the air
settle on you
and all the beasts of the
earth gorge themselves on
you.
5 I will spread your flesh on the
mountains
and fill the valleys with
your remains.
6 I will drench the land with
your flowing blood
all the way to the
mountains,
and the ravines will be filled
with your flesh.
7 When I snuff you out, I will
cover the heavens
and darken their stars;
I will cover the sun with a
cloud,
and the moon will not give
its light.
8 All the shining lights in the
heavens
I will darken over you;
I will bring darkness over
your land,
declares the Sovereign
LORD.
9 I will trouble the hearts of
many peoples
when I bring about your
destruction among the
nations,
among[e] lands you have not
known.
10 I will cause many peoples to
be appalled at you,
and their kings will shudder
with horror because of
you
when I brandish my sword
before them.
On the day of your downfall
each of them will tremble
every moment for his life.
11 " 'For this is what the Sovereign LORD says:
" 'The sword of the king of
Babylon
will come against you.
12 I will cause your hordes to fall
by the swords of mighty
men—
the most ruthless of all
nations.
They will shatter the pride of
Egypt,
and all her hordes will be
overthrown.
13 I will destroy all her cattle
from beside abundant
waters
no longer to be stirred by the
foot of man
or muddied by the hoofs of
cattle.
14 Then I will let her waters settle

[e]9 Hebrew; Septuagint *bring you into captivity among the nations, / to*

מֵימֵיהֶם וְנַהֲרוֹתָם כַּשֶּׁמֶן אוֹלִיךְ נְאֻם
declaration-of I-will-make-flow like-the-oil and-streams-of-them waters-of-them

אֲדֹנָי יְהוִה׃ בְּתִתִּי אֶת־אֶרֶץ מִצְרַיִם שְׁמָמָה וּנְשַׁמָּה
and-being-stripped desolation Egypt land-of *** when-to-make-me (15) Yahweh Sovereign

אֶרֶץ מִמְּלֹאָהּ בְּהַכּוֹתִי אֶת־כָּל־יוֹשְׁבֵי בָהּ
in-her ones-living-of all-of *** when-to-strike-down-me of-everything-of-her land

וְיָדְעוּ כִּי־אֲנִי יְהוָה׃ קִינָה הִיא וְקוֹנְנוּהָ
and-they-will-chant-for-her this lament (16) Yahweh I that then-they-will-know

בְּנוֹת הַגּוֹיִם תְּקוֹנֵנָּה אוֹתָהּ עַל־מִצְרַיִם וְעַל־כָּל־הֲמוֹנָהּ
horde-of-her all-of and-for Egypt for her they-will-chant the-nations daughters-of

תְּקוֹנֵנָּה אוֹתָהּ נְאֻם אֲדֹנָי יְהוִה׃ וַיְהִי בִּשְׁתֵּי עֶשְׂרֵה
ten in-two-of and-he-was (17) Yahweh Sovereign declaration-of her they-will-chant

שָׁנָה בַּחֲמִשָּׁה עָשָׂר לַחֹדֶשׁ הָיָה דְבַר־יְהוָה אֵלַי לֵאמֹר׃ בֶּן־אָדָם
man son-of (18) to-say to-me Yahweh word-of he-came of-the-month ten on-five year

נְהֵה עַל־הֲמוֹן מִצְרַיִם וְהוֹרִדֵהוּ אוֹתָהּ וּבְנוֹת גּוֹיִם
nations and-daughters-of her and-consign-below-him! Egypt horde-of for wail!

אַדִּרִם אֶל־אֶרֶץ תַּחְתִּיּוֹת אֶת־יוֹרְדֵי בוֹר׃ מִמִּי
more-than-whom? (19) pit ones-going-down-of with parts-below earth-of to mighty-ones

נָעָמְתָּ רְדָה וְהָשְׁכְּבָה אֶת־עֲרֵלִים׃ בְּתוֹךְ
in-among (20) uncircumcised-ones among and-be-laid! go-down! are-you-favored

חַלְלֵי־חֶרֶב יִפֹּלוּ חֶרֶב נִתָּנָה מָשְׁכוּ אוֹתָהּ וְכָל־
with-all-of her drag-off! she-is-drawn sword they-will-fall sword ones-killed-of

הֲמוֹנֶיהָ׃ יְדַבְּרוּ־לוֹ אֵלֵי גִבּוֹרִים מִתּוֹךְ שְׁאוֹל
Sheol from-within mighty-ones leaders-of of-him they-will-say (21) hordes-of-her

אֶת־עֹזְרָיו יָרְדוּ שָׁכְבוּ הָעֲרֵלִים
the-uncircumcised-ones they-lie they-came-down ones-being-allies-of-him with

חַלְלֵי־חָרֶב׃ שָׁם אַשּׁוּר וְכָל־קְהָלָהּ סְבִיבוֹתָיו
ones-surrounding-him army-of-her with-whole-of Assyria there (22) sword ones-killed-of

קִבְרֹתָיו כֻּלָּם חֲלָלִים הַנֹּפְלִים בֶּחָרֶב׃ אֲשֶׁר
that (23) by-the-sword the-ones-falling ones-slain all-of-them graves-of-him

נִתְּנוּ קִבְרֹתֶיהָ בְּיַרְכְּתֵי־בוֹר וַיְהִי קְהָלָהּ סְבִיבֹת
ones-around army-of-her and-he-lies pit in-depths-of graves-of-her they-are-put

קְבֻרָתָהּ כֻּלָּם חֲלָלִים נֹפְלִים בַּחֶרֶב אֲשֶׁר־נָתְנוּ
they-spread who by-the-sword ones-falling ones-slain all-of-them grave-of-her

חִתִּית בְּאֶרֶץ חַיִּים׃ שָׁם עֵילָם וְכָל־הֲמוֹנָהּ סְבִיבוֹת
ones-around horde-of-her with-whole-of Elam there (24) living-ones in-land-of terror

קְבֻרָתָהּ כֻּלָּם חֲלָלִים הַנֹּפְלִים בַּחֶרֶב אֲשֶׁר־יָרְדוּ
they-went-down who by-the-sword the-ones-falling ones-slain all-of-them grave-of-her

and make her streams flow
like oil,
declares the Sovereign
LORD.
15 When I make Egypt desolate
and strip the land of
everything in it,
when I strike down all who
live there,
then they will know that I
am the LORD.'

16 "This is the lament they will
chant for her. The daughters of the
nations will chant it; for Egypt
and all her hordes they will chant
it, declares the Sovereign LORD."

17 In the twelfth year, on the fifteenth day of the month, the word
of the LORD came to me: 18 "Son of
man, wail for the hordes of Egypt
and consign to the earth below
both her and the daughters of
mighty nations, with those who
go down to the pit. 19 Say to them,
'Are you more favored than
others? Go down and be laid
among the uncircumcised.' 20 They
will fall among those killed by the
sword. The sword is drawn; let her
be dragged off with all her hordes.
21 From within the grave[f] the
mighty leaders will say of Egypt
and her allies, 'They have come
down and they lie with the uncircumcised, with those killed by the
sword.'
22 "Assyria is there with her
whole army; she is surrounded by
the graves of all her slain, all who
have fallen by the sword. 23 Their
graves are in the depths of the pit
and her army lies around her
grave. All who had spread terror
in the land of the living are slain,
fallen by the sword.
24 "Elam is there, with all her
hordes around her grave. All of
them are slain, fallen by the

f21 Hebrew *Sheol;* also in verse 27

עֲרֵלִים׀ אֶל־אֶרֶץ תַּחְתִּיּוֹת אֲשֶׁר נָתְנוּ חִתִּיתָם בְּאֶרֶץ
in-land-of terror-of-them they-spread who parts-below earth-of to uncircumcised-ones

חַיִּים וַיִּשְׂאוּ כְלִמָּתָם אֶת־יוֹרְדֵי בוֹר׃ בְּתוֹךְ
in-among (25) pit ones-going-down-of with shame-of-them and-they-bear living-ones

חֲלָלִים נָתְנוּ מִשְׁכָּב לָהּ בְּכָל־הֲמוֹנָהּ סְבִיבוֹתָיו
ones-around-him horde-of-her with-all-of for-her bed they-made ones-slain

קִבְרֹתֶהָ כֻּלָּם עֲרֵלִים חַלְלֵי־חֶרֶב כִּי־
because sword ones-killed-of uncircumcised-ones all-of-them graves-of-her

נִתַּן חִתִּיתָם בְּאֶרֶץ חַיִּים וַיִּשְׂאוּ כְלִמָּתָם
shame-of-them and-they-bear living-ones in-land-of terror-of-them he-was-spread

אֶת־יוֹרְדֵי בוֹר בְּתוֹךְ חֲלָלִים נִתָּן׃ שָׁם מֶשֶׁךְ תֻּבַל
Tubal Meshech there (26) he-is-laid ones-slain in-among pit ones-going-down-of with

וְכָל־הֲמוֹנָהּ סְבִיבוֹתָיו קִבְרוֹתֶיהָ כֻּלָּם עֲרֵלִים
uncircumcised-ones all-of-them graves-of-her ones-around-him horde-of-her with-all-of

מְחֻלְלֵי חֶרֶב כִּי־נָתְנוּ חִתִּיתָם בְּאֶרֶץ חַיִּים׃
living-ones in-land-of terror-of-them they-spread because sword ones-being-killed-of

וְלֹא יִשְׁכְּבוּ אֶת־גִּבּוֹרִים נֹפְלִים מֵעֲרֵלִים אֲשֶׁר
who from-uncircumcised-ones ones-falling warriors with they-lie and-not (27)

יָרְדוּ־שְׁאוֹל בִּכְלֵי־מִלְחַמְתָּם וַיִּתְּנוּ אֶת־חַרְבוֹתָם
swords-of-them *** and-they-placed war-of-them with-weapons-of Sheol they-went-down

תַּחַת רָאשֵׁיהֶם וַתְּהִי עֲוֺנֹתָם עַל־עַצְמוֹתָם
bones-of-them on punishments-for-sins-of-them and-she-rested heads-of-them under

כִּי־חִתִּית גִּבּוֹרִים בְּאֶרֶץ חַיִּים׃ וְאַתָּה בְּתוֹךְ
in-among too-you (28) living-ones through-land-of warriors terror-of though

עֲרֵלִים תִּשָּׁבַר וְתִשְׁכַּב אֶת־חַלְלֵי־חָרֶב׃
sword ones-killed-of with and-you-will-lie you-will-be-broken uncircumcised-ones

שָׁמָּה אֱדוֹם מְלָכֶיהָ וְכָל־נְשִׂיאֶיהָ אֲשֶׁר־נִתְּנוּ
they-are-laid who princes-of-her and-all-of kings-of-her Edom at-there (29)

בִגְבוּרָתָם אֶת־חַלְלֵי־חֶרֶב הֵמָּה אֶת־עֲרֵלִים יִשְׁכָּבוּ
they-lie uncircumcised-ones with they sword ones-killed-of with despite-power-of-them

וְאֶת־יֹרְדֵי בוֹר׃ שָׁמָּה נְסִיכֵי צָפוֹן כֻּלָּם וְכָל־
and-all-of all-of-them north princes-of at-there (30) pit ones-going-down-of and-with

צִדֹנִי אֲשֶׁר־יָרְדוּ אֶת־חֲלָלִים בְּחִתִּיתָם מִגְּבוּרָתָם
by-power-of-them despite-terror-of-them ones-slain with they-went-down who Sidonian

בּוֹשִׁים וַיִּשְׁכְּבוּ עֲרֵלִים אֶת־חַלְלֵי־חֶרֶב
sword ones-killed-of with uncircumcised-ones and-they-lie ones-being-disgraced

וַיִּשְׂאוּ כְלִמָּתָם אֶת־יוֹרְדֵי בוֹר׃ אוֹתָם יִרְאֶה
he-will-see them (31) pit ones-going-down-of with shame-of-them and-they-bear

sword. All who had spread terror
in the land of the living went
down uncircumcised to the earth
below. They bear their shame
with those who go down to the
pit. 25A bed is made for her among
the slain, with all her hordes
around her grave. All of them are
uncircumcised, killed by the
sword. Because their terror had
spread in the land of the living,
they bear their shame with those
who go down to the pit; they are
laid among the slain.
26"Meshech and Tubal are there,
with all their hordes around their
graves. All of them are uncircumcised, killed by the sword because
they spread their terror in the land
of the living. 27Do they not lie with
the other uncircumcised warriors
who have fallen, who went down
to the grave with their weapons of
war, whose swords were placed
under their heads? The punishment for their sins rested on their
bones, though the terror of these
warriors had stalked through the
land of the living.
28"You too, O Pharaoh, will be
broken and will lie among the uncircumcised, with those killed by
the sword.
29"Edom is there, her kings and
all her princes; despite their
power, they are laid with those
killed by the sword. They lie with
the uncircumcised, with those
who go down to the pit.
30"All the princes of the north
and all the Sidonians are there;
they went down with the slain in
disgrace despite the terror caused
by their power. They lie uncircumcised with those killed by the
sword and bear their shame with
those who go down to the pit.

פַּרְעֹה וְנִחַם עַל־ כָּל־ הֲמוֹנֹה חַלְלֵי־ חֶרֶב

sword ones-killed-of horde-of-him all-of for and-he-will-be-consoled Pharaoh

פַּרְעֹה וְכָל־ חֵילוֹ נְאֻם אֲדֹנָי יְהוִה׃ כִּי־

although (32) Yahweh Sovereign declaration-of army-of-him and-all-of Pharaoh

נָתַתִּי אֶת־ חִתִּיתוֹ בְּאֶרֶץ חַיִּים וְהֻשְׁכַּב בְּתוֹךְ

in-among yet-he-will-be-laid living-ones in-land-of terror-of-him *** I-spread

עֲרֵלִים אֶת־ חַלְלֵי־ חֶרֶב פַּרְעֹה וְכָל־ הֲמוֹנֹה

horde-of-him and-all-of Pharaoh sword ones-killed-of with uncircumcised-ones

נְאֻם אֲדֹנָי יְהוִה׃ וַיְהִי דְבַר־ יְהוָה אֵלַי לֵאמֹר׃

to-say to-me Yahweh word-of and-he-came (33:1) Yahweh Sovereign declaration-of

בֶּן־ אָדָם דַּבֵּר אֶל־ בְּנֵי־ עַמְּךָ וְאָמַרְתָּ אֲלֵיהֶם אֶרֶץ

land to-them and-you-say countryman-of-you peoples-of to speak! man son-of (2)

כִּי־ אָבִיא עָלֶיהָ חָרֶב וְלָקְחוּ עַם־ הָאָרֶץ אִישׁ אֶחָד

one man the-land people-of and-they-choose sword against-her I-bring when

מִקְצֵיהֶם וְנָתְנוּ אֹתוֹ לָהֶם לְצֹפֶה׃ וְרָאָה אֶת־

*** and-he-sees (3) into-man-watching for-them him and-they-make from-ends-of-them

הַחֶרֶב בָּאָה עַל־ הָאָרֶץ וְתָקַע בַּשּׁוֹפָר וְהִזְהִיר אֶת־

*** and-he-warns on-the-trumpet and-he-blows the-land against coming the-sword

הָעָם׃ וְשָׁמַע הַשֹּׁמֵעַ אֶת־ קוֹל הַשּׁוֹפָר וְלֹא

but-not the-trumpet sound-of *** the-one-hearing if-he-hears (4) the-people

נִזְהָר וַתָּבוֹא חֶרֶב וַתִּקָּחֵהוּ דָּמוֹ בְרֹאשׁוֹ

on-head-of-him blood-of-him and-she-takes-him sword and-she-comes he-takes-warning

יִהְיֶה׃ אֵת קוֹל הַשּׁוֹפָר שָׁמַע וְלֹא נִזְהָר דָּמוֹ

blood-of-him he-took-warning but-not he-heard the-trumpet sound-of *** (5) he-will-be

בּוֹ יִהְיֶה וְהוּא נִזְהָר נַפְשׁוֹ מִלֵּט׃

he-would-have-saved self-of-him he-took-warning if-he he-will-be on-him

וְהַצֹּפֶה כִּי־ יִרְאֶה אֶת־ הַחֶרֶב בָּאָה וְלֹא־ תָקַע

he-blows and-not coming the-sword *** he-sees if but-the-man-watching (6)

בַּשּׁוֹפָר וְהָעָם לֹא־ נִזְהָר וַתָּבוֹא חֶרֶב וַתִּקַּח

and-she-takes sword and-she-comes he-is-warned not and-the-people on-the-trumpet

מֵהֶם נֶפֶשׁ הוּא בַּעֲוֹנוֹ נִלְקָח וְדָמוֹ

but-blood-of-him he-will-be-taken-away because-of-sin-of-him he life from-them

מִיַּד־ הַצֹּפֶה אֶדְרֹשׁ׃ וְאַתָּה בֶן־ אָדָם

man son-of now-you (7) I-will-require-account the-man-watching from-hand-of

צֹפֶה נְתַתִּיךָ לְבֵית יִשְׂרָאֵל וְשָׁמַעְתָּ מִפִּי דָּבָר

word from-mouth-of-me so-you-hear Israel for-house-of I-made-you man-watching

וְהִזְהַרְתָּ אֹתָם מִמֶּנִּי׃ בְּאָמְרִי לָרָשָׁע רָשָׁע

wicked-man to-the-wicked-man when-to-say-me (8) from-me them and-you-give-warning

31 "Pharaoh—he and all his
army—will see them and he will
be consoled for all his hordes that
were killed by the sword, declares
the Sovereign LORD. 32 Although I
had him spread terror in the land
of the living, Pharaoh and all his
hordes will be laid among the uncircumcised, with those killed by
the sword, declares the Sovereign
LORD."

*Ezekiel a Watchman*

33 The word of the LORD came
to me: 2 "Son of man, speak
to your countrymen and say to
them: 'When I bring the sword
against a land, and the people of
the land choose one of their men
and make him their watchman,
3 and he sees the sword coming
against the land and blows the
trumpet to warn the people, 4 then
if anyone hears the trumpet but
does not take warning and the
sword comes and takes his life, his
blood will be on his own head.
5 Since he heard the sound of the
trumpet but did not take warning,
his blood will be on his own head.
If he had taken warning, he would
have saved himself. 6 But if the
watchman sees the sword coming
and does not blow the trumpet to
warn the people and the sword
comes and takes the life of one of
them, that man will be taken away
because of his sin, but I will hold
the watchman accountable for his
blood.'
7 "Son of man, I have made you
a watchman for the house of Israel; so hear the word I speak and
give them warning from me.
8 When I say to the wicked, 'O

°31 ק חתיתי; °32a ק המונו
°32b ק המונו

מוֹת תָּמוּת וְלֹא דִבַּרְתָּ לְהַזְהִיר רָשָׁע מִדַּרְכּוֹ
from-way-of-him wicked-man to-dissuade you-speak-out and-not you-will-die to-die

הוּא רָשָׁע בַּעֲוֺנוֹ יָמוּת וְדָמוֹ מִיָּדְךָ
from-hand-of-you and-blood-of-him he-will-die for-sin-of-him wicked-man that

אֲבַקֵּשׁ׃ וְאַתָּה כִּי־הִזְהַרְתָּ רָשָׁע מִדַּרְכּוֹ לָשׁוּב
to-turn from-way-of-him wicked-man you-warn if but-you (9) I-will-require-account

מִמֶּנָּה וְלֹא־שָׁב מִדַּרְכּוֹ הוּא בַּעֲוֺנוֹ יָמוּת וְאַתָּה
but-you he-will-die for-sin-of-him he from-way-of-him he-turns and-not from-her

נַפְשְׁךָ הִצַּלְתָּ׃ וְאַתָּה בֶן־אָדָם אֱמֹר אֶל־בֵּית יִשְׂרָאֵל
Israel house-of to say! man son-of now-you (10) you-will-have-saved self-of-you

כֵּן אֲמַרְתֶּם לֵאמֹר כִּי־פְשָׁעֵינוּ וְחַטֹּאתֵינוּ עָלֵינוּ וּבָם
and-because-of-them upon-us and-sins-of-us offenses-of-us indeed to-say you-say this

אֲנַחְנוּ נְמַקִּים וְאֵיךְ נִחְיֶה׃ אֱמֹר אֲלֵיהֶם חַי־אָנִי ׀ נְאֻם ׀
declaration-of I alive to-them say! (11) can-we-live then-how? ones-wasting-away we

אֲדֹנָי יְהוִה אִם־אֶחְפֹּץ בְּמוֹת הָרָשָׁע כִּי אִם־בְּשׁוּב
when-to-turn rather but the-wicked in-death-of I-take-pleasure not Yahweh Sovereign

רָשָׁע מִדַּרְכּוֹ וְחָיָה שׁוּבוּ שׁוּבוּ מִדַּרְכֵיכֶם הָרָעִים
the-evil-ones from-ways-of-you turn! turn! so-he-lives from-way-of-him wicked

וְלָמָּה תָמוּתוּ בֵּית יִשְׂרָאֵל׃ וְאַתָּה בֶן־אָדָם
man son-of therefore-you (12) Israel house-of will-you-die now-for-why?

אֱמֹר אֶל־בְּנֵי־עַמְּךָ צִדְקַת הַצַּדִּיק לֹא
not the-righteous-man righteousness-of countryman-of-you peoples-of to say!

תַצִּילֶנּוּ בְּיוֹם פִּשְׁעוֹ וְרִשְׁעַת הָרָשָׁע לֹא־
not the-wicked-man and-wickedness-of disobedience-of-him on-day-of she-will-save-him

יִכָּשֶׁל בָּהּ בְּיוֹם שׁוּבוֹ מֵרִשְׁעוֹ
from-wickedness-of-him to-turn-him on-day-of by-her he-will-be-caused-to-fall

וְצַדִּיק לֹא יוּכַל לִחְיוֹת בָּהּ בְּיוֹם חֲטֹאתוֹ׃
to-sin-him on-day-of because-of-her to-live he-will-be-allowed not and-righteous-man

בְּאָמְרִי לַצַּדִּיק חָיֹה יִחְיֶה וְהוּא־בָטַח
he-trusts but-he he-will-live to-live to-the-righteous-man if-to-tell-me (13)

עַל־צִדְקָתוֹ וְעָשָׂה עָוֶל כָּל־°צִדְקֹתָו לֹא
not righteousnesses-of-him all-of evil and-he-does righteousness-of-him in

תִזָּכַרְנָה וּבְעַוְלוֹ אֲשֶׁר־עָשָׂה בּוֹ יָמוּת׃
he-will-die for-him he-did that and-for-evil-of-him they-will-be-remembered

וּבְאָמְרִי לָרָשָׁע מוֹת תָּמוּת וְשָׁב
but-he-turns-away you-will-die to-die to-the-wicked-man and-if-to-say-me (14)

מֵחַטָּאתוֹ וְעָשָׂה מִשְׁפָּט וּצְדָקָה׃ חֲבֹל יָשִׁיב רָשָׁע
wicked-man he-gives-back pledge (15) and-right justice and-he-does from-sin-of-him

wicked man, you will surely die,'
and you do not speak out to dissuade him from his ways, that
wicked man will die for[g] his sin,
and I will hold you accountable
for his blood. [9]But if you do warn
the wicked man to turn from his
ways and he does not do so, he
will die for his sin, but you will
have saved yourself.
[10]"Son of man, say to the house
of Israel, 'This is what you are saying: "Our offenses and sins weigh
us down, and we are wasting
away because of[h] them. How then
can we live?"' [11]Say to them, 'As
surely as I live, declares the Sovereign LORD, I take no pleasure in
the death of the wicked, but rather
that they turn from their ways and
live. Turn! Turn from your evil
ways! Why will you die, O house
of Israel?'
[12]"Therefore, son of man, say to
your countrymen, 'The righteousness of the righteous man will not
save him when he disobeys, and
the wickedness of the wicked man
will not cause him to fall when he
turns from it. The righteous man,
if he sins, will not be allowed to
live because of his former righteousness.' [13]If I tell the righteous
man that he will surely live, but
then he trusts in his righteousness
and does evil, none of the righteous things he has done will be
remembered; he will die for the
evil he has done. [14]And if I say to
the wicked man, 'You will surely
die,' but he then turns away from
his sin and does what is just and
right— [15]if he gives back what he

[g]8 Or *in*; also in verse 9 [h]10 Or *away in*

°13 ק צדקתיו

גְּזֵלָה יְשַׁלֵּם בְּחֻקּוֹת הַחַיִּים הָלַךְ לְבִלְתִּי עֲשׂוֹת עָוֶל
evil to-do not he-follows the-lives to-decrees-of he-returns stolen-thing

חָיוֹ יִחְיֶה לֹא יָמוּת׃ כָּל־ חַטֹּאתוֹ° אֲשֶׁר חָטָא
he-committed-sin that sins-of-him all-of (16) he-will-die not he-will-live to-live

לֹא תִזָּכַרְנָה לוֹ מִשְׁפָּט וּצְדָקָה עָשָׂה חָיוֹ יִחְיֶה׃
he-will-live to-live he-did and-right justice against-him they-will-be-remembered not

וְאָמְרוּ בְּנֵי עַמְּךָ לֹא יִתָּכֵן דֶּרֶךְ אֲדֹנָי וְהֵמָּה
but-they Lord way-of he-is-just not countryman-of-you peoples-of yet-they-say (17)

דַּרְכָּם לֹא־ יִתָּכֵן׃ בְּשׁוּב־ צַדִּיק מִצִּדְקָתוֹ
from-righteousness-of-him righteous-man if-to-turn (18) he-is-just not way-of-them

וְעָשָׂה עָוֶל וּמֵת בָּהֶם׃ וּבְשׁוּב רָשָׁע
wicked-man and-if-to-turn-away (19) for-them then-he-will-die evil and-he-does

מֵרִשְׁעָתוֹ וְעָשָׂה מִשְׁפָּט וּצְדָקָה עֲלֵיהֶם הוּא יִחְיֶה׃
he-will-live he by-them and-right justice and-he-does from-wickedness-of-him

וַאֲמַרְתֶּם לֹא יִתָּכֵן דֶּרֶךְ אֲדֹנָי אִישׁ כִּדְרָכָיו אֶשְׁפּוֹט
I-will-judge according-to-ways-of-him each Lord way-of he-is-just not yet-you-say (20)

אֶתְכֶם בֵּית יִשְׂרָאֵל׃ וַיְהִי בִּשְׁתֵּי עֶשְׂרֵה שָׁנָה בָּעֲשִׂרִי בַּחֲמִשָּׁה
on-five in-the-tenth year ten in-two-of and-he-was (21) Israel house-of you

לַחֹדֶשׁ לְגָלוּתֵנוּ בָּא־ אֵלַי הַפָּלִיט מִירוּשָׁלַםִ לֵאמֹר הֻכְּתָה
she-fell to-say from-Jerusalem the-escapee to-me he-came of-exile-of-us of-the-month

הָעִיר׃ וְיַד־ יְהוָה הָיְתָה אֵלַי בָּעֶרֶב לִפְנֵי בּוֹא
to-arrive before in-the-evening upon-me she-was Yahweh now-hand-of (22) the-city

הַפָּלִיט וַיִּפְתַּח אֶת־ פִּי עַד־ בּוֹא אֵלַי בַּבֹּקֶר
in-the-morning to-me to-come before mouth-of-me *** and-he-opened the-escapee

וַיִּפָּתַח פִּי וְלֹא נֶאֱלַמְתִּי עוֹד׃ וַיְהִי דְבַר־
word-of then-he-came (23) longer I-was-silent and-not mouth-of-me so-he-was-opened

יְהוָה אֵלַי לֵאמֹר׃ בֶּן־ אָדָם יֹשְׁבֵי הֶחֳרָבוֹת הָאֵלֶּה עַל־ אַדְמַת
land-of in the-those the-ruins ones-living-of man son-of (24) to-say to-me Yahweh

יִשְׂרָאֵל אֹמְרִים לֵאמֹר אֶחָד הָיָה אַבְרָהָם וַיִּירַשׁ אֶת־ הָאָרֶץ וַאֲנַחְנוּ
but-we the-land *** yet-he-possessed Abraham he-was one to-say ones-saying Israel

רַבִּים לָנוּ נִתְּנָה הָאָרֶץ לְמוֹרָשָׁה׃ לָכֵן אֱמֹר אֲלֵיהֶם
to-them say! therefore (25) as-possession the-land she-was-given to-us many-ones

כֹּה־ אָמַר ׀ אֲדֹנָי יְהוִה עַל־ הַדָּם ׀ תֹּאכֵלוּ וְעֵינֵכֶם תִּשְׂאוּ אֶל־
to you-lift and-eye-of-you you-eat the-blood since Yahweh Sovereign he-says this

גִּלּוּלֵיכֶם וְדָם תִּשְׁפֹּכוּ וְהָאָרֶץ תִּירָשׁוּ׃ עֲמַדְתֶּם
you-rely (26) should-you-possess then-the-land you-shed and-blood idols-of-you

עַל־ חַרְבְּכֶם עֲשִׂיתֶן תּוֹעֵבָה וְאִישׁ אֶת־ אֵשֶׁת רֵעֵהוּ
neighbor-of-him wife-of *** and-each detestable-thing you-do sword-of-you on

took in pledge for a loan, returns
what he has stolen, follows the decrees that give life, and does no
evil, he will surely live; he will not
die. 16None of the sins he has committed will be remembered
against him. He has done what is
just and right; he will surely live.
17"Yet your countrymen say,
'The way of the Lord is not just.'
But it is their way that is not just.
18If a righteous man turns from his
righteousness and does evil, he
will die for it. 19And if a wicked
man turns away from his wickedness and does what is just and
right, he will live by doing so.
20Yet, O house of Israel, you say,
'The way of the Lord is not just.'
But I will judge each of you according to his own ways."

*Jerusalem's Fall Explained*

21In the twelfth year of our exile,
in the tenth month on the fifth
day, a man who had escaped from
Jerusalem came to me and said,
"The city has fallen!" 22Now the
evening before the man arrived,
the hand of the LORD was upon
me, and he opened my mouth before the man came to me in the
morning. So my mouth was
opened and I was no longer silent.
23Then the word of the LORD
came to me: 24"Son of man, the
people living in those ruins in the
land of Israel are saying, 'Abraham was only one man, yet he
possessed the land. But we are
many; surely the land has been
given to us as our possession.'
25Therefore say to them, 'This is
what the Sovereign LORD says:
Since you eat meat with the blood
still in it and look to your idols and
shed blood, should you then possess the land? 26You rely on your
sword, you do detestable things,

°16 ק חטאתיו

טִמֵּאתֶם וְהָאָרֶץ תִּירָשׁוּ׃ כֹּה־ תֹאמַר אֲלֵהֶם כֹּה־ אָמַר
he-says this to-them you-say this (27) should-you-possess then-the-land you-defile

אֲדֹנָי יְהוִה חַי־ אָנִי אִם־ לֹא אֲשֶׁר בֶּחֳרָבוֹת בַּחֶרֶב יִפֹּלוּ
they-will-fall by-the-sword in-the-ruins who indeed surely I alive Yahweh Sovereign

וַאֲשֶׁר עַל־ פְּנֵי הַשָּׂדֶה לַחַיָּה נְתַתִּיו לְאָכְלוֹ
to-devour-him I-will-give-him to-the-wild-animal the-country open-parts-of in and-who

וַאֲשֶׁר בַּמְּצָדוֹת וּבַמְּעָרוֹת בַּדֶּבֶר יָמוּתוּ׃
they-will-die of-the-plague and-in-the-caves in-the-strongholds and-who

וְנָתַתִּי אֶת־ הָאָרֶץ שְׁמָמָה וּמְשַׁמָּה וְנִשְׁבַּת גְּאוֹן
pride-of and-he-will-end and-waste desolation the-land *** and-I-will-make (28)

עֻזָּהּ וְשָׁמְמוּ הָרֵי יִשְׂרָאֵל מֵאֵין עוֹבֵר׃
one-crossing with-no Israel mountains-of and-they-will-become-desolate strength-of-her

וְיָדְעוּ כִּי־ אֲנִי יְהוָה בְּתִתִּי אֶת־ הָאָרֶץ שְׁמָמָה
desolation the-land *** when-to-make-me Yahweh I that then-they-will-know (29)

וּמְשַׁמָּה עַל כָּל־ תּוֹעֲבֹתָם אֲשֶׁר עָשׂוּ׃ וְאַתָּה
and-you (30) they-did that detestable-things-of-them all-of because-of and-waste

בֶן־ אָדָם בְּנֵי עַמְּךָ הַנִּדְבָּרִים בְּךָ אֵצֶל
by about-you the-ones-talking-together countryman-of-you peoples-of man son-of

הַקִּירוֹת וּבְפִתְחֵי הַבָּתִּים וְדִבֶּר־ חַד אֶת־ אַחַד אִישׁ אֶת־ אָחִיו
other-of-him to each one to one and-he-says the-houses and-at-doors-of the-walls

לֵאמֹר בֹּאוּ־ נָא וְשִׁמְעוּ מָה הַדָּבָר הַיּוֹצֵא מֵאֵת יְהוָה׃
Yahweh from-with the-one-coming the-message what and-hear! now! come! to-say

וְיָבוֹאוּ אֵלֶיךָ כִּמְבוֹא־ עָם וְיֵשְׁבוּ לְפָנֶיךָ עַמִּי
people-of-me before-you and-they-sit people as-coming-of to-you and-they-come (31)

וְשָׁמְעוּ אֶת־ דְּבָרֶיךָ וְאוֹתָם לֹא יַעֲשׂוּ כִּי־ עֲגָבִים
devotions indeed they-practice not but-them words-of-you *** and-they-listen-to

בְּפִיהֶם הֵמָּה עֹשִׂים אַחֲרֵי בִּצְעָם לִבָּם הֹלֵךְ׃
pursuing heart-of-them unjust-gain-of-them for ones-expressing they with-mouth-of-them

וְהִנְּךָ לָהֶם כְּשִׁיר עֲגָבִים יְפֵה קוֹל וּמֵטִב
and-doing-well voice beautiful-of loves as-song-of to-them indeed-see-you! (32)

נַגֵּן וְשָׁמְעוּ אֶת־ דְּבָרֶיךָ וְעֹשִׂים אֵינָם אוֹתָם׃
them not-they but-ones-practicing words-of-you *** for-they-hear to-play

וּבְבֹאָהּ הִנֵּה בָאָה וְיָדְעוּ כִּי נָבִיא הָיָה
he-was prophet that then-they-will-know coming surely! and-when-to-come-her (33)

בְתוֹכָם׃ וַיְהִי דְבַר־ יְהוָה אֵלַי לֵאמֹר׃ בֶּן־ אָדָם
man son-of (2) to-say to-me Yahweh word-of and-he-came (34:1) in-among-them

הִנָּבֵא עַל־ רוֹעֵי יִשְׂרָאֵל הִנָּבֵא וְאָמַרְתָּ אֲלֵיהֶם
to-them and-you-say prophesy! Israel ones-being-shepherds-of against prophesy!

and each of you defiles his neighbor's wife. Should you then possess the land?'

27"Say this to them: 'This is what the Sovereign LORD says: As surely as I live, those who are left in the ruins will fall by the sword, those out in the country I will give to the wild animals to be devoured, and those in strongholds and caves will die of a plague. 28I will make the land a desolate waste, and her proud strength will come to an end, and the mountains of Israel will become desolate so that no one will cross them. 29Then they will know that I am the LORD, when I have made the land a desolate waste because of all the detestable things they have done.'

30"As for you, son of man, your countrymen are talking together about you by the walls and at the doors of the houses, saying to each other, 'Come and hear the message that has come from the LORD.' 31My people come to you, as they usually do, and sit before you to listen to your words, but they do not put them into practice. With their mouths they express devotion, but their hearts are greedy for unjust gain. 32Indeed, to them you are nothing more than one who sings love songs with a beautiful voice and plays an instrument well, for they hear your words but do not put them into practice.

33"When all this comes true—and it surely will—then they will know that a prophet has been among them."

*Shepherds and Sheep*

34 The word of the LORD came to me: 2"Son of man, prophesy against the shepherds of Israel; prophesy and say to them:

לָרֹעִים כֹּה אָמַר ׀ אֲדֹנָי יְהוִה הוֹי רֹעֵי־

ones-being-shepherds-of woe! Yahweh Sovereign he-says this to-the-ones-being-shepherds

יִשְׂרָאֵל אֲשֶׁר הָיוּ רֹעִים אוֹתָם הֲלוֹא הַצֹּאן יִרְעוּ

should-they-shepherd the-flock not? themselves ones-shepherding they-are who Israel

הָרֹעִים׃ אֶת־הַחֵלֶב תֹּאכֵלוּ וְאֶת־הַצֶּמֶר תִּלְבָּשׁוּ

you-clothe-yourself the-wool and you-eat the-curd *** (3) the-ones-being-shepherds

הַבְּרִיאָה תִּזְבָּחוּ הַצֹּאן לֹא תִרְעוּ׃ אֶת־הַנַּחְלוֹת

the-ones-being-weak *** (4) you-shepherd not the-flock you-slaughter the-choice-animal

לֹא חִזַּקְתֶּם וְאֶת־הַחוֹלָה לֹא־רִפֵּאתֶם וְלַנִּשְׁבֶּרֶת

or-to-the-one-being-injured you-healed not the-one-being-sick or you-strengthened not

לֹא חֲבַשְׁתֶּם וְאֶת־הַנִּדַּחַת לֹא הֲשֵׁבֹתֶם וְאֶת־הָאֹבֶדֶת

the-one-being-lost or you-brought-back not the-one-straying and you-bound-up not

לֹא בִקַּשְׁתֶּם וּבְחָזְקָה רְדִיתֶם אֹתָם וּבְפָרֶךְ׃

and-with-brutality them you-ruled but-with-harshness you-searched-for not

וַתְּפוּצֶינָה מִבְּלִי רֹעֶה וַתִּהְיֶינָה לְאָכְלָה

for-food and-they-became one-being-shepherd because-no so-they-were-scattered (5)

לְכָל־חַיַּת הַשָּׂדֶה וַתְּפוּצֶינָה׃ יִשְׁגּוּ

they-wandered (6) when-they-were-scattered the-field wild-animal-of for-all-of

צֹאנִי בְּכָל־הֶהָרִים וְעַל כָּל־גִּבְעָה רָמָה וְעַל

and-over being-high hill every-of and-on the-mountains over-all-of sheep-of-me

כָּל־פְּנֵי הָאָרֶץ נָפֹצוּ צֹאנִי וְאֵין דּוֹרֵשׁ

searching and-no-one flock-of-me they-were-scattered the-earth surfaces-of whole-of

וְאֵין מְבַקֵּשׁ׃ לָכֵן רֹעִים שִׁמְעוּ אֶת־דְּבַר יְהוָה׃

Yahweh word-of *** hear! ones-being-shepherds therefore (7) looking-for and-no-one

חַי־אָנִי נְאֻם ׀ אֲדֹנָי יְהוִה אִם־לֹא יַעַן הֱיוֹת־צֹאנִי ׀

flock-of-me to-be because indeed surely Yahweh Sovereign declaration-of I alive (8)

לָבַז וַתִּהְיֶינָה צֹאנִי לְאָכְלָה לְכָל־חַיַּת הַשָּׂדֶה

the-field wild-animal-of for-all-of for-food flock-of-me and-they-became for-plunder

מֵאֵין רֹעֶה וְלֹא־דָרְשׁוּ רֹעַי

ones-being-shepherds-of-me they-searched-for because-not one-being-shepherd because-no

אֶת־צֹאנִי וַיִּרְעוּ הָרֹעִים אוֹתָם וְאֶת־צֹאנִי

flock-of-me and themselves the-ones-being-shepherds but-they-shepherd flock-of-me ***

לֹא רָעוּ׃ לָכֵן הָרֹעִים שִׁמְעוּ דְּבַר־יְהוָה׃

Yahweh word-of hear! the-ones-being-shepherds therefore (9) they-shepherd not

כֹּה־אָמַר אֲדֹנָי יְהוִה הִנְנִי אֶל־הָרֹעִים

the-ones-being-shepherds against see-I! Yahweh Sovereign he-says this (10)

וְדָרַשְׁתִּי אֶת־צֹאנִי מִיָּדָם וְהִשְׁבַּתִּים

and-I-will-remove-them from-hand-of-them flock-of-me for and-I-will-require-account

'This is what the Sovereign LORD says: Woe to the shepherds of Israel who only take care of themselves! Should not shepherds take care of the flock? 3You eat the curds, clothe yourselves with the wool and slaughter the choice animals, but you do not take care of the flock. 4You have not strengthened the weak or healed the sick or bound up the injured. You have not brought back the strays or searched for the lost. You have ruled them harshly and brutally. 5So they were scattered because there was no shepherd, and when they were scattered they became food for all the wild animals. 6My sheep wandered over all the mountains and on every high hill. They were scattered over the whole earth, and no one searched or looked for them.

7" 'Therefore, you shepherds, hear the word of the LORD: 8As surely as I live, declares the Sovereign LORD, because my flock lacks a shepherd and so has been plundered and has become food for all the wild animals, and because my shepherds did not search for my flock but cared for themselves rather than for my flock, 9therefore, O shepherds, hear the word of the LORD: 10This is what the Sovereign LORD says: I am against the shepherds and will hold them accountable for my flock. I will remove them from tending the

מֵרְעוֹת צֹאן וְלֹא־ יִרְעוּ עוֹד הָרֹעִים
the-ones-being-shepherds longer they-can-shepherd so-not flock from-to-shepherd

אוֹתָם וְהִצַּלְתִּי צֹאנִי מִפִּיהֶם וְלֹא־ תִהְיֶיןָ
they-will-be and-not from-mouth-of-them sheep-of-me and-I-will-rescue themselves

לָהֶם לְאָכְלָה׃ כִּי כֹּה אָמַר אֲדֹנָי יְהוִה הִנְנִי־ אָנִי וְדָרַשְׁתִּי
indeed-I-will-search I see-I! Yahweh Sovereign he-says this for (11) for-food for-them

אֶת־ צֹאנִי וּבִקַּרְתִּים׃ כְּבַקָּרַת רֹעֶה
one-being-shepherd as-looking-after-of (12) and-I-will-look-after-them flock-of-me for

עֶדְרוֹ בְּיוֹם־ הֱיוֹתוֹ בְתוֹךְ־ צֹאנוֹ נִפְרָשׁוֹת
ones-being-scattered flock-of-him in-among to-be-him on-day-of flock-of-him

כֵּן אֲבַקֵּר אֶת־ צֹאנִי וְהִצַּלְתִּי אֶתְהֶם מִכָּל־
from-all-of them and-I-will-rescue sheep-of-me *** I-will-look-after so

הַמְּקוֹמֹת אֲשֶׁר נָפֹצוּ שָׁם בְּיוֹם עָנָן וַעֲרָפֶל׃
and-darkness cloud on-day-of there they-were-scattered where the-places

וְהוֹצֵאתִים מִן־ הָעַמִּים וְקִבַּצְתִּים מִן־
from and-I-will-gather-them the-nations from and-I-will-bring-out-them (13)

הָאֲרָצוֹת וַהֲבִיאֹתִים אֶל־ אַדְמָתָם וּרְעִיתִים אֶל־
on and-I-will-shepherd-them land-of-them into and-I-will-bring-them the-countries

הָרֵי יִשְׂרָאֵל בָּאֲפִיקִים וּבְכֹל מוֹשְׁבֵי הָאָרֶץ׃
the-land settlements-of and-in-all-of in-the-ravines Israel mountains-of

בְּמִרְעֶה־ טּוֹב אֶרְעֶה אֹתָם וּבְהָרֵי מְרוֹם־ יִשְׂרָאֵל
Israel height-of and-on-mountains-of them I-will-shepherd good in-pasture (14)

יִהְיֶה נְוֵהֶם שָׁם תִּרְבַּצְנָה בְּנָוֶה טוֹב
good in-grazing-land they-will-lie-down there grazing-land-of-them he-will-be

וּמִרְעֶה שָׁמֵן תִּרְעֶינָה אֶל־ הָרֵי יִשְׂרָאֵל׃ אֲנִי אֶרְעֶה
I-will-shepherd I (15) Israel mountains-of on they-will-feed rich and-in-pasture

צֹאנִי וַאֲנִי אַרְבִּיצֵם נְאֻם אֲדֹנָי יְהוִה׃ אֶת־
*** (16) Yahweh Sovereign declaration-of I-will-have-lie-down-them and-I sheep-of-me

הָאֹבֶדֶת אֲבַקֵּשׁ וְאֶת־ הַנִּדַּחַת אָשִׁיב
I-will-bring-back the-one-straying and I-will-search-for the-one-being-lost

וְלַנִּשְׁבֶּרֶת אֶחֱבֹשׁ וְאֶת־ הַחוֹלָה אֲחַזֵּק
I-will-strengthen the-one-being-weak and I-will-bind-up and-to-the-one-being-injured

וְאֶת־ הַשְּׁמֵנָה וְאֶת־ הַחֲזָקָה אַשְׁמִיד אֶרְעֶנָּה בְמִשְׁפָּט׃
with-justice I-will-shepherd-her I-will-destroy the-strong and the-sleek but

וְאַתֵּנָה צֹאנִי כֹּה אָמַר אֲדֹנָי יְהוִה הִנְנִי שֹׁפֵט בֵּין־
between judging see-I! Yahweh Sovereign he-says this flock-of-me and-you (17)

שֶׂה לָשֶׂה לָאֵילִים וְלָעַתּוּדִים׃ הַמְעַט מִכֶּם
for-you not-enough? (18) and-between-the-goats between-the-rams to-sheep sheep

flock so that the shepherds can no
longer feed themselves. I will rescue my flock from their mouths,
and it will no longer be food for
them.
11 'For this is what the Sovereign LORD says: I myself will
search for my sheep and look after
them. 12 As a shepherd looks after
his scattered flock when he is with
them, so will I look after my sheep.
I will rescue them from all the
places where they were scattered
on a day of clouds and darkness.
13 I will bring them out from the
nations and gather them from the
countries, and I will bring them
into their own land. I will pasture
them on the mountains of Israel,
in the ravines and in all the settlements in the land. 14 I will tend
them in a good pasture, and the
mountain heights of Israel will be
their grazing land. There they will
lie down in good grazing land,
and there they will feed in a rich
pasture on the mountains of Israel. 15 I myself will tend my sheep
and have them lie down, declares
the Sovereign LORD. 16 I will search
for the lost and bring back the
strays. I will bind up the injured
and strengthen the weak, but the
sleek and the strong I will destroy.
I will shepherd the flock with
justice.
17 'As for you, my flock, this is
what the Sovereign LORD says: I
will judge between one sheep and
another, and between rams and
goats. 18 Is it not enough for you to

הַמִּרְעֶה הַטּוֹב תִּרְעוּ וְיֶתֶר מִרְעֵיכֶם תִּרְמְסוּ

must-you-trample pastures-of-you but-rest-of you-feed-on the-good the-pasture

בְּרַגְלֵיכֶם וּמִשְׁקַע־ מַיִם תִּשְׁתּוּ וְאֵת הַנּוֹתָרִים

the-ones-remaining but you-drink waters and-clearness-of with-feet-of-you

בְּרַגְלֵיכֶם תִּרְפֹּשׂוּן׃ (19) וְצֹאנִי מִרְמַס רַגְלֵיכֶם

feet-of-you thing-trampled-of so-flock-of-me (19) must-you-muddy with-feet-of-you

תִּרְעֶינָה וּמִרְפַּשׂ רַגְלֵיכֶם תִּשְׁתֶּינָה׃ (20) לָכֵן

therefore (20) must-they-drink feet-of-you and-thing-muddied-of must-they-feed-on

כֹּה אָמַר אֲדֹנָי יְהוִה אֲלֵיהֶם הִנְנִי־ אָנִי וְשָׁפַטְתִּי בֵּין־ שֶׂה

sheep between indeed-I-will-judge I see-I! to-them Yahweh Sovereign he-says this

בִרְיָה וּבֵין שֶׂה רָזָה׃ (21) יַעַן בְּצַד וּבְכָתֵף תֶּהְדֹּפוּ

you-shove and-with-shoulder with-flank because (21) lean sheep and-between fat

וּבְקַרְנֵיכֶם תְּנַגְּחוּ כָּל־ הַנַּחְלוֹת עַד אֲשֶׁר הֲפִיצוֹתֶם

you-drive-away when until the-ones-being-weak all-of you-butt and-with-horns-of-you

אוֹתָנָה אֶל־ הַחוּצָה׃ (22) וְהוֹשַׁעְתִּי לְצֹאנִי וְלֹא־ תִהְיֶינָה

they-will-be and-not to-flock-of-me so-I-will-save (22) to-the-outside to them

עוֹד לָבַז וְשָׁפַטְתִּי בֵּין שֶׂה לָשֶׂה׃ (23) וַהֲקִמֹתִי

and-I-will-place (23) to-sheep sheep between and-I-will-judge for-plunder longer

עֲלֵיהֶם רֹעֶה אֶחָד וְרָעָה אֶתְהֶן אֵת עַבְדִּי דָוִיד

David servant-of-me *** them and-he-will-shepherd one one-being-shepherd over-them

הוּא יִרְעֶה אֹתָם וְהוּא־ יִהְיֶה לָהֶן לְרֹעֶה׃

as-one-being-shepherd to-them he-will-be and-he them he-will-shepherd he

(24) וַאֲנִי יְהוָה אֶהְיֶה לָהֶם לֵאלֹהִים וְעַבְדִּי דָוִד נָשִׂיא

prince David and-servant-of-me as-God to-them I-will-be Yahweh and-I (24)

בְתוֹכָם אֲנִי יְהוָה דִּבַּרְתִּי׃ (25) וְכָרַתִּי לָהֶם בְּרִית שָׁלוֹם

peace covenant-of with-them and-I-will-make (25) I-spoke Yahweh I in-among-them

וְהִשְׁבַּתִּי חַיָּה־ רָעָה מִן־ הָאָרֶץ וְיָשְׁבוּ בַמִּדְבָּר לָבֶטַח

in-safety in-the-desert so-they-may-live the-land from wild beast and-I-will-rid

וְיָשְׁנוּ בַּיְּעָרִים׃ (26) וְנָתַתִּי אוֹתָם וּסְבִיבוֹת

and-places-surrounding them and-I-will-give (26) in-the-forests and-they-may-sleep

גִּבְעָתִי בְּרָכָה וְהוֹרַדְתִּי הַגֶּשֶׁם בְּעִתּוֹ גִּשְׁמֵי

showers-of in-season-of-him the-shower and-I-will-send-down blessing hill-of-me

בְרָכָה יִהְיוּ׃ (27) וְנָתַן עֵץ הַשָּׂדֶה אֶת־ פִּרְיוֹ

fruit-of-him *** the-field tree-of and-he-will-yield (27) they-will-be blessing

וְהָאָרֶץ תִּתֵּן יְבוּלָהּ וְהָיוּ עַל־ אַדְמָתָם לָבֶטַח

in-security land-of-them in and-they-will-be crop-of-her she-will-yield and-the-ground

וְיָדְעוּ כִּי־ אֲנִי יְהוָה בְּשִׁבְרִי אֶת־ מֹטוֹת עֻלָּם

yoke-of-them bars-of *** when-to-break-me Yahweh I that and-they-will-know

feed on the good pasture? Must
you also trample the rest of your
pasture with your feet? Is it not
enough for you to drink clear
water? Must you also muddy the
rest with your feet? [19]Must my
flock feed on what you have trampled and drink what you have
muddied with your feet?
[20]"'Therefore this is what the
Sovereign LORD says to them: See,
I myself will judge between the fat
sheep and the lean sheep. [21]Be-
cause you shove with flank and
shoulder, butting all the weak
sheep with your horns until you
have driven them away, [22]I will
save my flock, and they will no
longer be plundered. I will judge
between one sheep and another.
[23]I will place over them one shepherd, my servant David, and he
will tend them; he will tend them
and be their shepherd. [24]I the LORD
will be their God, and my servant
David will be prince among them.
I the LORD have spoken.
[25]"'I will make a covenant of
peace with them and rid the land
of wild beasts so that they may
live in the desert and sleep in the
forests in safety. [26]I will bless them
and the places surrounding my
hill.[i] I will send down showers in
season; there will be showers of
blessing. [27]The trees of the field
will yield their fruit and the
ground will yield its crops; the
people will be secure in their land.
They will know that I am the
LORD, when I break the bars of

[i]26 Or *I will make them and the places surrounding my hill a blessing*

וְהִצַּלְתִּים מִיַּד הָעֹבְדִים בָּהֶם׃ וְלֹא־ יִהְיוּ
they-will-be and-not (28) to-them the-ones-enslaving from-hand-of and-I-rescue-them

עוֹד בַּז לַגּוֹיִם וְחַיַּת הָאָרֶץ לֹא תֹאכְלֵם
she-will-devour-them not the-land or-wild-animal-of for-the-nations plunder longer

וְיָשְׁבוּ לָבֶטַח וְאֵין מַחֲרִיד׃ וַהֲקִמֹתִי
and-I-will-provide (29) making-afraid and-no-one in-safety and-they-will-live

לָהֶם מַטָּע לְשֵׁם וְלֹא־ יִהְיוּ עוֹד אֲסֻפֵי
ones-being-victims-of longer they-will-be and-not of-renown land-of-crop for-them

רָעָב בָּאָרֶץ וְלֹא־ יִשְׂאוּ עוֹד כְּלִמַּת הַגּוֹיִם׃
the-nations scorn-of longer they-will-bear or-not in-the-land famine

וְיָדְעוּ כִּי אֲנִי יְהוָה אֱלֹהֵיהֶם אִתָּם וְהֵמָּה עַמִּי
people-of-me and-they with-them God-of-them Yahweh I that then-they-will-know (30)

בֵּית יִשְׂרָאֵל נְאֻם אֲדֹנָי יְהוִה׃ וְאַתֵּן צֹאנִי
sheep-of-me and-you (31) Yahweh Sovereign declaration-of Israel house-of

צֹאן מַרְעִיתִי אָדָם אַתֶּם אֲנִי אֱלֹהֵיכֶם נְאֻם אֲדֹנָי יְהוִה׃
Yahweh Sovereign declaration-of God-of-you I you people pasture-of-me sheep-of

וַיְהִי דְבַר־ יְהוָה אֵלַי לֵאמֹר׃ בֶּן־ אָדָם שִׂים פָּנֶיךָ
faces-of-you set! man son-of (2) to-say to-me Yahweh word-of and-he-came (35:1)

עַל־ הַר שֵׂעִיר וְהִנָּבֵא עָלָיו׃ וְאָמַרְתָּ לּוֹ כֹּה אָמַר
he-says this to-him and-you-say (3) against-him and-prophesy! Seir Mount-of against

אֲדֹנָי יְהוִה הִנְנִי אֵלֶיךָ הַר־ שֵׂעִיר וְנָטִיתִי יָדִי
hand-of-me and-I-will-stretch-out Seir Mount-of against-you see-I! Yahweh Sovereign

עָלֶיךָ וּנְתַתִּיךָ שְׁמָמָה וּמְשַׁמָּה׃ עָרֶיךָ חָרְבָּה
ruin towns-of-you (4) and-waste desolation and-I-will-make-you against-you

אָשִׂים וְאַתָּה שְׁמָמָה תִהְיֶה וְיָדַעְתָּ כִּי־ אֲנִי יְהוָה׃
Yahweh I that then-you-will-know you-will-be desolation and-you I-will-turn-into

יַעַן הֱיוֹת לְךָ אֵיבַת עוֹלָם וַתַּגֵּר אֶת־ בְּנֵי־ יִשְׂרָאֵל
Israel sons-of *** and-you-delivered ancient hostility-of to-you to-be because (5)

עַל־ יְדֵי־ חָרֶב בְּעֵת אֵידָם בְּעֵת עֲוֹן קֵץ׃
climax punishment-of at-time-of calamity-of-them at-time-of sword edges-of to

לָכֵן חַי־ אָנִי נְאֻם אֲדֹנָי יְהוִה כִּי־ לְדָם
to-bloodshed surely Yahweh Sovereign declaration-of I alive therefore (6)

אֶעֶשְׂךָ וְדָם יִרְדֲּפֶךָ אִם־ לֹא דָם שָׂנֵאתָ
you-hated bloodshed not since he-will-pursue-you and-bloodshed I-will-give-you

וְדָם יִרְדֲּפֶךָ׃ וְנָתַתִּי אֶת־ הַר שֵׂעִיר
Seir Mount-of *** and-I-will-make (7) he-will-pursue-you then-bloodshed

לְשִׁמְמָה וּשְׁמָמָה וְהִכְרַתִּי מִמֶּנּוּ עֹבֵר וָשָׁב׃
and-one-coming one-going from-him and-I-will-cut-off and-waste into-desolation

their yoke and rescue them from
the hands of those who enslaved
them. [28]They will no longer be
plundered by the nations, nor will
wild animals devour them. They
will live in safety, and no one will
make them afraid. [29]I will provide
for them a land renowned for its
crops, and they will no longer be
victims of famine in the land or
bear the scorn of the nations.
[30]Then they will know that I, the
LORD their God, am with them and
that they, the house of Israel, are
my people, declares the Sovereign
LORD. [31]You my sheep, the sheep of
my pasture, are people, and I am
your God, declares the Sovereign
LORD.' "

*A Prophecy Against Edom*

35 The word of the LORD came
to me: [2]"Son of man, set
your face against Mount Seir;
prophesy against it [3]and say: 'This
is what the Sovereign LORD says: I
am against you, Mount Seir, and I
will stretch out my hand against
you and make you a desolate
waste. [4]I will turn your towns into
ruins and you will be desolate.
Then you will know that I am the
LORD.

[5]" 'Because you harbored an ancient hostility and delivered the
Israelites over to the sword at the
time of their calamity, the time
their punishment reached its climax, [6]therefore as surely as I live,
declares the Sovereign LORD, I will
give you over to bloodshed and it
will pursue you. Since you did not
hate bloodshed, bloodshed will
pursue you. [7]I will make Mount
Seir a desolate waste and cut off

וּמִלֵּאתִי אֶת־הָרָיו חֲלָלָיו גִּבְעוֹתֶיךָ
hills-of-you ones-slain-of-him mountains-of-him *** and-I-will-fill (8)

וְגֵאוֹתֶיךָ וְכָל־אֲפִיקֶיךָ חַלְלֵי־חֶרֶב יִפְּלוּ
they-will-fall sword ones-killed-of ravines-of-you and-all-of and-valleys-of-you

בָהֶם׃ שִׁמְמוֹת עוֹלָם אֶתֶּנְךָ וְעָרֶיךָ לֹא
not and-towns-of-you I-will-make-you forever desolations-of (9) in-them

תִּישַׁבְנָה וִידַעְתֶּם כִּי־אֲנִי יְהוָה׃ יַעַן
because (10) Yahweh I that then-you-will-know they-will-be-inhabited

אֲמָרְךָ אֶת־שְׁנֵי הַגּוֹיִם וְאֶת־שְׁתֵּי הָאֲרָצוֹת לִי תִהְיֶינָה
they-will-be to-me the-countries two-of and the-nations two-of *** to-say-you

וִירַשְׁנוּהָ וַיהוָה שָׁם הָיָה׃ לָכֵן חַי־אָנִי
I alive therefore (11) he-was there though-Yahweh and-we-will-possess-her

נְאֻם אֲדֹנָי יְהוִה וְעָשִׂיתִי כְּאַפְּךָ
according-to-anger-of-you so-I-will-treat Yahweh Sovereign declaration-of

וּכְקִנְאָתְךָ אֲשֶׁר עָשִׂיתָה מִשִּׂנְאָתֶיךָ בָּם
of-them in-hatreds-of-you you-showed that and-according-to-jealousy-of-you

וְנוֹדַעְתִּי בָם כַּאֲשֶׁר אֶשְׁפְּטֶךָ׃ וְיָדַעְתָּ
then-you-will-know (12) I-judge-you as-when among-them and-I-will-make-myself-known

כִּי־אֲנִי יְהוָה שָׁמַעְתִּי ׀ אֶת־כָּל־נָאָצוֹתֶיךָ אֲשֶׁר אָמַרְתָּ עַל־
against you-said that contemptible-things-of-you all-of *** I-heard Yahweh I that

הָרֵי יִשְׂרָאֵל לֵאמֹר ׀ שְׁמֵמָה לָנוּ נִתְּנוּ לְאָכְלָה׃
for-food they-were-given to-us they-were-laid-waste to-say Israel mountains-of

וַתַּגְדִּילוּ עָלַי בְּפִיכֶם וְהַעְתַּרְתֶּם עָלַי
against-me you-made-unrestrained with-mouth-of-you against-me and-you-boasted (13)

דִּבְרֵיכֶם אֲנִי שָׁמָעְתִּי׃ כֹּה אָמַר אֲדֹנָי יְהוִה כִּשְׂמֹחַ
while-to-rejoice Yahweh Sovereign he-says this (14) I-heard I words-of-you

כָּל־הָאָרֶץ שְׁמָמָה אֶעֱשֶׂה־לָּךְ׃ כְּשִׂמְחָתְךָ
because-rejoicing-of-you (15) of-you I-will-make desolation the-earth whole-of

לְנַחֲלַת בֵּית־יִשְׂרָאֵל עַל אֲשֶׁר־שָׁמֵמָה כֵּן אֶעֱשֶׂה־
I-will-treat so she-became-desolate when at Israel house-of about-inheritance-of

לָּךְ שְׁמָמָה תִהְיֶה הַר־שֵׂעִיר וְכָל־אֱדוֹם כֻּלָּהּ
all-of-her Edom and-all-of Seir Mount-of you-will-be desolation to-you

וְיָדְעוּ כִּי־אֲנִי יְהוָה׃ וְאַתָּה בֶן־אָדָם הִנָּבֵא אֶל־הָרֵי
mountains-of to prophesy! man son-of now-you (36:1) Yahweh I that then-they-will-know

יִשְׂרָאֵל וְאָמַרְתָּ הָרֵי יִשְׂרָאֵל שִׁמְעוּ דְּבַר־יְהוָה׃ כֹּה אָמַר
he-says this (2) Yahweh word-of hear! Israel mountains-of and-you-say Israel

אֲדֹנָי יְהוִה יַעַן אָמַר הָאוֹיֵב עֲלֵיכֶם הֶאָח וּבָמוֹת
and-heights-of aha! of-you the-one-being-enemy he-said because Yahweh Sovereign

°9 ק תשבנה
°12 ק שממו

from it all who come and go. [8]I will
fill your mountains with the slain;
those killed by the sword will fall
on your hills and in your valleys
and in all your ravines. [9]I will
make you desolate forever; your
towns will not be inhabited. Then
you will know that I am the LORD.
[10]" 'Because you have said,
"These two nations and countries
will be ours and we will take
possession of them," even though
I the LORD was there, [11]therefore as
surely as I live, declares the Sovereign LORD, I will treat you in
accordance with the anger and
jealousy you showed in your hatred of them and I will make myself known among them when I
judge you. [12]Then you will know
that I the LORD have heard all the
contemptible things you have said
against the mountains of Israel.
You said, "They have been laid
waste and have been given over to
us to devour." [13]You boasted
against me and spoke against me
without restraint, and I heard it.
[14]This is what the Sovereign LORD
says: While the whole earth rejoices, I will make you desolate.
[15]Because you rejoiced when the
inheritance of the house of Israel
became desolate, that is how I will
treat you. You will be desolate, O
Mount Seir, you and all of Edom.
Then they will know that I am the
LORD.' "

### *A Prophecy to the Mountains of Israel*

36 "Son of man, prophesy to
the mountains of Israel and
say, 'O mountains of Israel, hear
the word of the LORD. [2]This is what
the Sovereign LORD says: The enemy said of you, "Aha! The ancient

עוֹלָם לְמוֹרָשָׁה הָיְתָה לָּנוּ׃ לָכֵן הִנָּבֵא וְאָמַרְתָּ כֹּה

this and-you-say prophesy! therefore (3) to-us she-became as-possession ancient

אָמַר אֲדֹנָי יְהוִה יַעַן בְּיַעַן שַׁמּוֹת וְשָׁאֹף אֶתְכֶם

you and-to-hound to-ravage indeed-because because Yahweh Sovereign he-says

מִסָּבִיב לִהְיוֹתְכֶם מוֹרָשָׁה לִשְׁאֵרִית הַגּוֹיִם וַתַּעֲלוּ עַל־

on and-you-went-up the-nations of-rest-of possession to-become-you from-every-side

שְׂפַת לָשׁוֹן וְדִבַּת־ עָם׃ לָכֵן הָרֵי יִשְׂרָאֵל שִׁמְעוּ דְּבַר־

word-of hear! Israel mountains-of therefore (4) people and-slander-of speech lip-of

אֲדֹנָי יְהוִה כֹּה־ אָמַר אֲדֹנָי יְהוִה לֶהָרִים וְלַגְּבָעוֹת

and-to-the-hills to-the-mountains Yahweh Sovereign he-says this Yahweh Sovereign

לָאֲפִיקִים וְלַגֵּאָיוֹת וְלֶחֳרָבוֹת הַשֹּׁמְמוֹת

the-ones-being-desolate and-to-the-ruins and-to-the-valleys to-the-ravines

וְלֶעָרִים הַנֶּעֱזָבוֹת אֲשֶׁר הָיוּ לְבַז וּלְלַעַג

and-for-ridicule for-plunder they-were that the-ones-being-deserted and-to-the-towns

לִשְׁאֵרִית הַגּוֹיִם אֲשֶׁר מִסָּבִיב׃ לָכֵן כֹּה־ אָמַר אֲדֹנָי יְהוִה

Yahweh Sovereign he-says this therefore (5) at-around that the-nations by-rest-of

אִם־ לֹא בְּאֵשׁ קִנְאָתִי דִבַּרְתִּי עַל־ שְׁאֵרִית הַגּוֹיִם

the-nations rest-of against I-spoke zeal-of-me in-burning-of indeed surely

וְעַל־ אֱדוֹם כֻּלָּא אֲשֶׁר נָתְנוּ־ אֶת־ אַרְצִי ׀ לָהֶם לְמוֹרָשָׁה

as-possession for-them land-of-me *** they-made for all-of-her Edom and-against

בְּשִׂמְחַת כָּל־ לֵבָב בִּשְׁאָט נֶפֶשׁ לְמַעַן מִגְרָשָׁהּ לָבַז׃

for-plunder pastureland-of-her so-that soul with-malice-of heart all-of with-glee-of

לָכֵן הִנָּבֵא עַל־ אַדְמַת יִשְׂרָאֵל וְאָמַרְתָּ לֶהָרִים

to-the-mountains and-you-say Israel land-of concerning prophesy! therefore (6)

וְלַגְּבָעוֹת לָאֲפִיקִים וְלַגֵּאָיוֹת כֹּה־ אָמַר ׀ אֲדֹנָי יְהוִה

Yahweh Sovereign he-says this and-to-the-valleys to-the-ravines and-to-the-hills

הִנְנִי בְקִנְאָתִי וּבַחֲמָתִי דִּבַּרְתִּי יַעַן כְּלִמַּת גּוֹיִם

nations scorn-of because I-speak and-in-wrath-of-me in-jealousy-of-me see-I!

נְשָׂאתֶם׃ לָכֵן כֹּה אָמַר אֲדֹנָי יְהוִה אֲנִי נָשָׂאתִי אֶת־ יָדִי

hand-of-me *** I-lift I Yahweh Sovereign he-says this therefore (7) you-suffered

אִם־ לֹא הַגּוֹיִם אֲשֶׁר לָכֶם מִסָּבִיב הֵמָּה כְּלִמָּתָם יִשָּׂאוּ׃

they-will-suffer scorn-of-them they at-around by-you that the-nations indeed surely

וְאַתֶּם הָרֵי יִשְׂרָאֵל עַנְפְּכֶם תִּתֵּנוּ וּפֶרְיְכֶם

and-fruit-of-you you-will-produce branch-of-you Israel mountains-of but-you (8)

תִּשְׂאוּ לְעַמִּי יִשְׂרָאֵל כִּי קֵרְבוּ לָבוֹא׃ כִּי הִנְנִי

see-I! for (9) to-come they-are-near for Israel for-people-of-me you-will-bear

אֲלֵיכֶם וּפָנִיתִי אֲלֵיכֶם וְנֶעֱבַדְתֶּם וְנִזְרַעְתֶּם׃

and-you-will-be-sown and-you-will-be-plowed on-you and-I-will-look for-you

heights have become our possession." ' 3Therefore prophesy and
say, 'This is what the Sovereign
LORD says: Because they ravaged
and hounded you from every side
so that you became the possession
of the rest of the nations and the
object of people's malicious talk
and slander, 4therefore, O mountains of Israel, hear the word of
the Sovereign LORD: This is what
the Sovereign LORD says to the
mountains and hills, to the ravines and valleys, to the desolate
ruins and the deserted towns that
have been plundered and ridiculed by the rest of the nations
around you— 5this is what the
Sovereign LORD says: In my burning zeal I have spoken against the
rest of the nations, and against all
Edom, for with glee and with malice in their hearts they made my
land their own possession so that
they might plunder its pastureland.' 6Therefore prophesy concerning the land of Israel and say
to the mountains and hills, to the
ravines and valleys: 'This is what
the Sovereign LORD says: I speak
in my jealous wrath because you
have suffered the scorn of the nations. 7Therefore this is what the
Sovereign LORD says: I swear with
uplifted hand that the nations
around you will also suffer scorn.
8" 'But you, O mountains of Israel, will produce branches and
fruit for my people Israel, for they
will soon come home. 9I am concerned for you and will look on
you with favor; you will be
plowed and sown, 10and I will

וְהִרְבֵּיתִי עֲלֵיכֶם אָדָם כָּל־ בֵּית יִשְׂרָאֵל כֻּלֹּה
all-of-him Israel house-of whole-of people upon-you and-I-will-multiply-number (10)

וְנֹשְׁבוּ הֶעָרִים וְהֶחֳרָבוֹת תִּבָּנֶינָה׃
they-will-be-rebuilt and-the-ruins the-towns and-they-will-be-inhabited

וְהִרְבֵּיתִי עֲלֵיכֶם אָדָם וּבְהֵמָה וְרָבוּ
and-they-will-be-fruitful and-animal man upon-you and-I-will-increase-number (11)

וּפָרוּ וְהוֹשַׁבְתִּי אֶתְכֶם כְּקַדְמוֹתֵיכֶם
as-times-past-of-you you and-I-will-settle and-they-will-become-numerous

וְהֵטִבֹתִי מֵרִאשֹׁתֵיכֶם וִידַעְתֶּם כִּי־ אֲנִי
I that then-you-will-know more-than-times-before-of-you and-I-will-make-prosper

יְהוָה׃ וְהוֹלַכְתִּי עֲלֵיכֶם אָדָם אֶת־ עַמִּי יִשְׂרָאֵל
Israel people-of-me *** people on-you and-I-will-make-walk (12) Yahweh

וִירֵשׁוּךָ וְהָיִיתָ לָהֶם לְנַחֲלָה וְלֹא־
and-never for-inheritance to-them and-you-will-be and-they-will-possess-you

תוֹסִף עוֹד לְשַׁכְּלָם׃ כֹּה אָמַר אֲדֹנָי יְהוִה
Yahweh Sovereign he-says this (13) to-deprive-of-children-them again you-will-do-again

יַעַן אֹמְרִים לָכֶם אֹכֶלֶת אָדָם אָתִּי וּמְשַׁכֶּלֶת
and-one-depriving-of-children you man one-devouring to-you ones-saying because

גּוֹיִךְ הָיִית׃ לָכֵן אָדָם לֹא־ תֹאכְלִי עוֹד וְגוֹיִךְ
or-nation-of-you longer you-will-devour not man therefore (14) you-are nation-of-you

לֹא תְכַשְּׁלִי־ עוֹד נְאֻם אֲדֹנָי יְהוִה׃ וְלֹא־
and-not (15) Yahweh Sovereign declaration-of longer you-will-make-childless not

אַשְׁמִיעַ אֵלַיִךְ עוֹד כְּלִמַּת הַגּוֹיִם וְחֶרְפַּת עַמִּים לֹא
not peoples and-scorn-of the-nations taunt-of longer to-you I-will-make-hear

תִשְׂאִי־ עוֹד וְגוֹיִךְ לֹא־ תְכַשְׁלִי עוֹד נְאֻם
declaration-of longer you-will-make-fall not or-nation-of-you longer you-will-suffer

אֲדֹנָי יְהוִה׃ וַיְהִי דְבַר־ יְהוָה אֵלַי לֵאמֹר׃ בֶּן־ אָדָם
man son-of (17) to-say to-me Yahweh word-of and-he-came (16) Yahweh Sovereign

בֵּית יִשְׂרָאֵל יֹשְׁבִים עַל־ אַדְמָתָם וַיְטַמְּאוּ אוֹתָהּ בְּדַרְכָּם
by-conduct-of-them her and-they-defiled land-of-them in ones-living Israel house-of

וּבַעֲלִילוֹתָם כְּטֻמְאַת הַנִּדָּה הָיְתָה דַרְכָּם
conduct-of-them she-was the-monthly-period like-uncleanness-of and-by-actions-of-them

לְפָנָי׃ וָאֶשְׁפֹּךְ חֲמָתִי עֲלֵיהֶם עַל־ הַדָּם אֲשֶׁר־
that the-blood because-of on-them wrath-of-me so-I-poured-out (18) before-me

שָׁפְכוּ עַל־ הָאָרֶץ וּבְגִלּוּלֵיהֶם טִמְּאוּהָ׃ וָאָפִיץ
and-I-dispersed (19) they-defiled-her and-with-idols-of-them the-land in they-shed

אֹתָם בַּגּוֹיִם וַיִּזָּרוּ בָּאֲרָצוֹת
through-the-countries and-they-were-scattered among-the-nations them

multiply the number of people
upon you, even the whole house
of Israel. The towns will be inhabited and the ruins rebuilt. [11]I will
increase the number of men and
animals upon you, and they will
be fruitful and become numerous.
I will settle people on you as in the
past and will make you prosper
more than before. Then you will
know that I am the LORD. [12]I will
cause people, my people Israel, to
walk upon you. They will possess
you, and you will be their inheritance; you will never again deprive them of their children.
[13]" 'This is what the Sovereign
LORD says: Because people say to
you, "You devour men and deprive your nation of its children,"
[14]therefore you will no longer devour men or make your nation
childless, declares the Sovereign
LORD. [15]No longer will I make you
hear the taunts of the nations, and
no longer will you suffer the scorn
of the peoples or cause your nation to fall, declares the Sovereign
LORD.' "
[16]Again the word of the LORD
came to me: [17]"Son of man, when
the people of Israel were living in
their own land, they defiled it by
their conduct and their actions.
Their conduct was like a woman's
monthly uncleanness in my sight.
[18]So I poured out my wrath on
them because they had shed blood
in the land and because they had
defiled it with their idols. [19]I dispersed them among the nations,
and they were scattered through

°13a ק את ;°13b ק גויך
°14a ק וגויך ;°14b ק תשכלי
°15 ק וגויך

כְּדַרְכָּם וְכַעֲלִילוֹתָם שְׁפַטְתִּים׃
I-judged-them and-according-to-actions-of-them according-to-conduct-of-them

(20) וַיָּבוֹא אֶל־ הַגּוֹיִם אֲשֶׁר־ בָּאוּ שָׁם וַיְחַלְּלוּ
then-they-profaned there they-went wherever the-nations among when-he-went (20)

אֶת־ שֵׁם קָדְשִׁי בֶּאֱמֹר לָהֶם עַם־ יְהוָה אֵלֶּה
these Yahweh people-of of-them for-to-say holiness-of-me name-of ***

וּמֵאַרְצוֹ יָצָאוּ׃ (21) וָאֶחְמֹל עַל־ שֵׁם קָדְשִׁי
holiness-of-me name-of for and-I-had-concern (21) they-left yet-from-land-of-him

אֲשֶׁר חִלְּלֻהוּ בֵּית יִשְׂרָאֵל בַּגּוֹיִם אֲשֶׁר־ בָּאוּ שָׁמָּה׃
to-there they-went where among-the-nations Israel house-of they-profaned-him which

(22) לָכֵן אֱמֹר לְבֵית־ יִשְׂרָאֵל כֹּה אָמַר אֲדֹנָי יְהוִה לֹא
not Yahweh Sovereign he-says this Israel to-house-of say! therefore (22)

לְמַעַנְכֶם אֲנִי עֹשֶׂה בֵּית יִשְׂרָאֵל כִּי אִם־ לְשֵׁם־ קָדְשִׁי
holiness-of-me for-name-of rather but Israel house-of doing I for-sake-of-you

אֲשֶׁר חִלַּלְתֶּם בַּגּוֹיִם אֲשֶׁר־ בָּאתֶם שָׁם׃ (23) וְקִדַּשְׁתִּי
and-I-will-show-holy (23) there you-went where among-the-nations you-profaned which

אֶת־ שְׁמִי הַגָּדוֹל הַמְחֻלָּל בַּגּוֹיִם אֲשֶׁר חִלַּלְתֶּם
you-profaned which among-the-nations the-one-being-profaned the-great name-of-me ***

בְּתוֹכָם וְיָדְעוּ הַגּוֹיִם כִּי־אֲנִי יְהוָה נְאֻם אֲדֹנָי
Sovereign declaration-of Yahweh I that the-nations then-they-will-know in-among-them

יְהוִה בְּהִקָּדְשִׁי בָכֶם לְעֵינֵיהֶם׃ (24) וְלָקַחְתִּי
for-I-will-take (24) before-eyes-of-them through-you when-to-show-holy-myself Yahweh

אֶתְכֶם מִן־ הַגּוֹיִם וְקִבַּצְתִּי אֶתְכֶם מִכָּל־ הָאֲרָצוֹת
the-countries from-all-of you and-I-will-gather the-nations out-of you

וְהֵבֵאתִי אֶתְכֶם אֶל־ אַדְמַתְכֶם׃ (25) וְזָרַקְתִּי עֲלֵיכֶם מַיִם
waters on-you and-I-will-sprinkle (25) land-of-you into you and-I-will-bring-back

טְהוֹרִים וּטְהַרְתֶּם מִכֹּל טֻמְאוֹתֵיכֶם וּמִכָּל־
and-from-all-of impurities-of-you from-all-of and-you-will-be-clean clean-ones

גִּלּוּלֵיכֶם אֲטַהֵר אֶתְכֶם׃ (26) וְנָתַתִּי לָכֶם לֵב חָדָשׁ וְרוּחַ
and-spirit new heart to-you and-I-will-give (26) you I-will-cleanse idols-of-you

חֲדָשָׁה אֶתֵּן בְּקִרְבְּכֶם וַהֲסִרֹתִי אֶת־ לֵב הָאֶבֶן
the-stone heart-of *** and-I-will-remove at-inside-of-you I-will-put new

מִבְּשַׂרְכֶם וְנָתַתִּי לָכֶם לֵב בָּשָׂר׃ (27) וְאֶת־ רוּחִי
Spirit-of-me and (27) flesh heart-of to-you and-I-will-give from-flesh-of-you

אֶתֵּן בְּקִרְבְּכֶם וְעָשִׂיתִי אֵת אֲשֶׁר־ בְּחֻקַּי תֵּלֵכוּ
you-will-follow in-decrees-of-me what *** and-I-will-move at-inside-of-you I-will-put

וּמִשְׁפָּטַי תִּשְׁמְרוּ וַעֲשִׂיתֶם׃ (28) וִישַׁבְתֶּם
and-you-will-live (28) and-you-will-keep you-will-be-careful and-laws-of-me

the countries; I judged them according to their conduct and their
actions. 20 And wherever they
went among the nations they profaned my holy name, for it was said of them, 'These are the LORD's people, and yet they had to leave
his land.' 21 I had concern for my
holy name, which the house of Israel profaned among the nations where they had gone.

22 "Therefore say to the house of Israel, 'This is what the Sovereign LORD says: It is not for your sake, O house of Israel, that I am going to do these things, but for the sake of my holy name, which you have profaned among the nations where you have gone.
23 I will
show the holiness of my great name, which has been profaned among the nations, the name you have profaned among them. Then the nations will know that I am the LORD, declares the Sovereign LORD, when I show myself holy through you before their eyes.

24 " 'For I will take you out of the nations; I will gather you from all the countries and bring you back into your own land.
25 I will sprinkle clean water on you, and you will be clean; I will cleanse you from all your impurities and from all your idols.
26 I will give you a
new heart and put a new spirit in you; I will remove from you your heart of stone and give you a heart of flesh.
27 And I will put my Spirit
in you and move you to follow my decrees and be careful to keep my
laws.
28 You will live in the land I

בָּאָרֶץ אֲשֶׁר נָתַתִּי לַאֲבֹתֵיכֶם וִהְיִיתֶם לִי לְעָם
as-people to-me and-you-will-be to-forefathers-of-you I-gave that in-the-land

וְאָנֹכִי אֶהְיֶה לָכֶם לֵאלֹהִים׃ וְהוֹשַׁעְתִּי אֶתְכֶם מִכֹּל
from-all-of you and-I-will-save (29) as-God to-you I-will-be and-I

טֻמְאוֹתֵיכֶם וְקָרָאתִי אֶל־ הַדָּגָן וְהִרְבֵּיתִי אֹתוֹ
him and-I-will-make-plentiful the-grain for and-I-will-call uncleannesses-of-you

וְלֹא־ אֶתֵּן עֲלֵיכֶם רָעָב׃ וְהִרְבֵּיתִי אֶת־ פְּרִי הָעֵץ
the-tree fruit-of *** and-I-will-increase (30) famine on-you I-will-bring and-not

וּתְנוּבַת הַשָּׂדֶה לְמַעַן אֲשֶׁר לֹא תִקְחוּ עוֹד חֶרְפַּת רָעָב
famine disgrace-of longer you-will-suffer not that so-that the-field and-crop-of

בַּגּוֹיִם׃ וּזְכַרְתֶּם אֶת־ דַּרְכֵיכֶם הָרָעִים
the-evil-ones ways-of-you *** then-you-will-remember (31) among-the-nations

וּמַעַלְלֵיכֶם אֲשֶׁר לֹא־ טוֹבִים וּנְקֹטֹתֶם בִּפְנֵיכֶם עַל
for to-selves-of-you and-you-will-loathe good-ones not that and-deeds-of-you

עֲוֹנֹתֵיכֶם וְעַל תּוֹעֲבוֹתֵיכֶם׃ לֹא לְמַעַנְכֶם אֲנִי־ עֹשֶׂה
doing I for-sake-of-you not (32) detestable-practices-of-you and-for sins-of-you

נְאֻם אֲדֹנָי יְהוִה יִוָּדַע לָכֶם בּוֹשׁוּ וְהִכָּלְמוּ
and-be-disgraced! be-ashamed! to-you he-must-be-known Yahweh Sovereign declaration-of

מִדַּרְכֵיכֶם בֵּית יִשְׂרָאֵל׃ כֹּה אָמַר אֲדֹנָי יְהוִה בְּיוֹם
on-day-of Yahweh Sovereign he-says this (33) Israel house-of for-conducts-of-you

טַהֲרִי אֶתְכֶם מִכֹּל עֲוֹנוֹתֵיכֶם וְהוֹשַׁבְתִּי אֶת־ הֶעָרִים
the-towns *** then-I-will-resettle sins-of-you from-all-of you to-cleanse-me

וְנִבְנוּ הֶחֳרָבוֹת׃ וְהָאָרֶץ הַנְּשַׁמָּה
the-one-being-desolate and-the-land (34) the-ruins and-they-will-be-rebuilt

תֵּעָבֵד תַּחַת אֲשֶׁר הָיְתָה שְׁמָמָה לְעֵינֵי כָּל־
all-of before-eyes-of desolation she-lies that instead-of she-will-be-cultivated

עוֹבֵר׃ וְאָמְרוּ הָאָרֶץ הַלֵּזוּ הַנְּשַׁמָּה
the-one-being-laid-waste this the-land and-they-will-say (35) one-passing-through

הָיְתָה כְּגַן־ עֵדֶן וְהֶעָרִים הֶחֳרֵבוֹת וְהַנְשַׁמּוֹת
and-the-ones-being-desolate the-ruins and-the-cities Eden like-garden-of she-became

וְהַנֶּהֱרָסוֹת בְּצוּרוֹת יָשָׁבוּ׃
they-are-inhabited ones-being-fortified and-the-ones-being-destroyed

וְיָדְעוּ הַגּוֹיִם אֲשֶׁר יִשָּׁאֲרוּ סְבִיבוֹתֵיכֶם כִּי ׀ אֲנִי
I that ones-around-you they-remain that the-nations then-they-will-know (36)

יְהוָה בָּנִיתִי הַנֶּהֱרָסוֹת נָטַעְתִּי הַנְּשַׁמָּה
the-one-being-desolate I-replanted the-ones-being-destroyed I-rebuilt Yahweh

אֲנִי יְהוָה דִּבַּרְתִּי וְעָשִׂיתִי׃ כֹּה אָמַר אֲדֹנָי יְהוִה עוֹד זֹאת
this again Yahweh Sovereign he-says this (37) and-I-will-do I-spoke Yahweh I

gave your forefathers; you will be
my people, and I will be your God.
29 I will save you from all your uncleanness. I will call for the grain
and make it plentiful and will not
bring famine upon you. 30 I will increase the fruit of the trees and the
crops of the field, so that you will
no longer suffer disgrace among
the nations because of famine.
31 Then you will remember your
evil ways and wicked deeds, and
you will loathe yourselves for your
sins and detestable practices. 32 I
want you to know that I am not
doing this for your sake, declares
the Sovereign LORD. Be ashamed
and disgraced for your conduct, O
house of Israel!

33 " 'This is what the Sovereign
LORD says: On the day I cleanse
you from all your sins, I will resettle your towns, and the ruins will
be rebuilt. 34 The desolate land will
be cultivated instead of lying
desolate in the sight of all who
pass through it. 35 They will say,
"This land that was laid waste has
become like the garden of Eden;
the cities that were lying in ruins,
desolate and destroyed, are now
fortified and inhabited." 36 Then
the nations around you that remain will know that I the LORD
have rebuilt what was destroyed
and have replanted what was
desolate. I the LORD have spoken,
and I will do it.'

37 "This is what the Sovereign
LORD says: Once again I will yield

אִדָּרֵשׁ לְבֵית־ יִשְׂרָאֵל לַעֲשׂוֹת לָהֶם אַרְבֶּה

I-will-make-numerous for-them to-do Israel of-house-of I-will-yield-to-plea

אֹתָם כַּצֹּאן אָדָם׃ כְּצֹאן קָדָשִׁים כְּצֹאן יְרוּשָׁלִַם

Jerusalem as-flock-of offerings as-flock-of (38) people as-the-sheep them

בְּמוֹעֲדֶיהָ כֵּן תִּהְיֶינָה הֶעָרִים הֶחֳרֵבוֹת מְלֵאוֹת

ones-filled the-ruined-ones the-cities they-will-be so during-appointed-feasts-of-her

צֹאן אָדָם וְיָדְעוּ כִּי־ אֲנִי יְהוָה׃ הָיְתָה עָלַי יַד־

hand-of upon-me she-was (37:1) Yahweh I that then-they-will-know people flock-of

יְהוָה וַיּוֹצִאֵנִי בְרוּחַ יְהוָה וַיְנִיחֵנִי בְּתוֹךְ

in-middle-of and-he-set-me Yahweh by-Spirit-of and-he-brought-out-me Yahweh

הַבִּקְעָה וְהִיא מְלֵאָה עֲצָמוֹת׃ וְהֶעֱבִירַנִי עֲלֵיהֶם סָבִיב ׀ סָבִיב

forth back among-them and-he-led-me (2) bones full and-she the-valley

וְהִנֵּה רַבּוֹת מְאֹד עַל־ פְּנֵי הַבִּקְעָה וְהִנֵּה יְבֵשׁוֹת מְאֹד׃

very dry-ones and-see! the-valley floors-of on great many-ones and-see!

וַיֹּאמֶר אֵלַי בֶּן־ אָדָם הֲתִחְיֶינָה הָעֲצָמוֹת הָאֵלֶּה וָאֹמַר

and-I-said the-these the-bones can-they-live? man son-of to-me and-he-asked (3)

אֲדֹנָי יְהוִה אַתָּה יָדָעְתָּ׃ וַיֹּאמֶר אֵלַי הִנָּבֵא עַל־הָעֲצָמוֹת הָאֵלֶּה

the-these the-bones to prophesy! to-me and-he-said (4) you-know you Yahweh Sovereign

וְאָמַרְתָּ אֲלֵיהֶם הָעֲצָמוֹת הַיְבֵשׁוֹת שִׁמְעוּ דְּבַר־ יְהוָה׃ כֹּה אָמַר

he-says this (5) Yahweh word-of hear! the-dry-ones the-bones to-them and-you-say

אֲדֹנָי יְהוִה לָעֲצָמוֹת הָאֵלֶּה הִנֵּה אֲנִי מֵבִיא בָכֶם רוּחַ

breath into-you making-enter I see! the-these to-the-bones Yahweh Sovereign

וִחְיִיתֶם׃ וְנָתַתִּי עֲלֵיכֶם גִּדִים וְהַעֲלֵתִי

and-I-will-make-come tendons to-you and-I-will-attach (6) and-you-will-come-to-life

עֲלֵיכֶם בָּשָׂר וְקָרַמְתִּי עֲלֵיכֶם עוֹר וְנָתַתִּי בָכֶם רוּחַ

breath in-you and-I-will-put skin on-you and-I-will-cover flesh upon-you

וִחְיִיתֶם וִידַעְתֶּם כִּי־ אֲנִי יְהוָה׃ וְנִבֵּאתִי

so-I-prophesied (7) Yahweh I that then-you-will-know and-you-will-come-to-life

כַּאֲשֶׁר צֻוֵּיתִי וַיְהִי־ קוֹל כְּהִנָּבְאִי וְהִנֵּה־ רַעַשׁ

rattling and-see! as-to-prophesy-me noise and-he-was I-was-commanded as-what

וַתִּקְרְבוּ עֲצָמוֹת עֶצֶם אֶל־ עַצְמוֹ׃ וְרָאִיתִי וְהִנֵּה־ עֲלֵיהֶם

on-them and-see! and-I-looked (8) bone-of-him to bone bones and-they-came-together

גִּדִים וּבָשָׂר עָלָה וַיִּקְרַם עֲלֵיהֶם עוֹר מִלְמָעְלָה וְרוּחַ

but-breath to-at-above skin on-them and-he-covered he-appeared and-flesh tendons

אֵין בָּהֶם׃ וַיֹּאמֶר אֵלַי הִנָּבֵא אֶל־ הָרוּחַ הִנָּבֵא

prophesy! the-breath to prophesy! to-me then-he-said (9) in-them there-was-not

בֶּן־ אָדָם וְאָמַרְתָּ אֶל־ הָרוּחַ כֹּה־ אָמַר ׀ אֲדֹנָי יְהוִה מֵאַרְבַּע

from-four-of Yahweh Sovereign he-says this the-breath to and-you-say man son-of

to the plea of the house of Israel
and do this for them: I will make
their people as numerous as
sheep, [38]as numerous as the flocks
for offerings at Jerusalem during
her appointed feasts. So will the
ruined cities be filled with flocks
of people. Then they will know
that I am the LORD."

*The Valley of Dry Bones*

37 The hand of the LORD was
upon me, and he brought
me out by the Spirit of the LORD
and set me in the middle of a valley; it was full of bones. [2]He led me
back and forth among them, and I
saw a great many bones on the
floor of the valley, bones that were
very dry. [3]He asked me, "Son of
man, can these bones live?"

I said, "O Sovereign LORD, you
alone know."

[4]Then he said to me, "Prophesy
to these bones and say to them,
'Dry bones, hear the word of the
LORD! [5]This is what the Sovereign
LORD says to these bones: I will
make breath[j] enter you, and you
will come to life. [6]I will attach tendons to you and make flesh come
upon you and cover you with
skin; I will put breath in you, and
you will come to life. Then you
will know that I am the LORD.' "

[7]So I prophesied as I was commanded. And as I was prophesying, there was a noise, a rattling
sound, and the bones came together, bone to bone. [8]I looked,
and tendons and flesh appeared
on them and skin covered them,
but there was no breath in them.

[9]Then he said to me, "Prophesy
to the breath; prophesy, son of
man, and say to it, 'This is what
the Sovereign LORD says: Come
from the four winds, O breath,

j5 The Hebrew for this word can also mean *wind* or *spirit* (see verses 6-14).

רוּחוֹת בֹּאִי הָרוּחַ וּפְחִי בַּהֲרוּגִים הָאֵלֶּה וְיִחְיוּ׃
that-they-may-live the-these into-the-ones-slain and-breathe! the-breath come! winds

וְהִנַּבֵּאתִי כַּאֲשֶׁר צִוָּנִי וַתָּבוֹא בָהֶם הָרוּחַ
the-breath into-them and-she-entered he-commanded-me as-what so-I-prophesied (10)

וַיִּחְיוּ וַיַּעַמְדוּ עַל־רַגְלֵיהֶם חַיִל גָּדוֹל מְאֹד־מְאֹד׃
very very vast army feet-of-them on and-they-stood-up and-they-came-to-life

וַיֹּאמֶר אֵלַי בֶּן־אָדָם הָעֲצָמוֹת הָאֵלֶּה כָּל־בֵּית יִשְׂרָאֵל
Israel house-of whole-of the-these the-bones man son-of to-me then-he-said (11)

הֵמָּה הִנֵּה אֹמְרִים יָבְשׁוּ עַצְמוֹתֵינוּ וְאָבְדָה תִקְוָתֵנוּ
hope-of-us and-she-is-gone bones-of-us they-are-dried-up ones-saying see! they

נִגְזַרְנוּ לָנוּ׃ לָכֵן הִנָּבֵא וְאָמַרְתָּ אֲלֵיהֶם כֹּה־אָמַר
he-says this to-them and-you-say prophesy! therefore (12) to-us and-we-are-cut-off

אֲדֹנָי יְהוִה הִנֵּה אֲנִי פֹתֵחַ אֶת־קִבְרוֹתֵיכֶם וְהַעֲלֵיתִי אֶתְכֶם
you and-I-will-bring-up graves-of-you *** opening I see! Yahweh Sovereign

מִקִּבְרוֹתֵיכֶם עַמִּי וְהֵבֵאתִי אֶתְכֶם אֶל־אַדְמַת יִשְׂרָאֵל׃
Israel land-of to you and-I-will-bring-back people-of-me from-graves-of-you

וִידַעְתֶּם כִּי־אֲנִי יְהוָה בְּפִתְחִי אֶת־קִבְרוֹתֵיכֶם
graves-of-you *** when-to-open-me Yahweh I that then-you-will-know (13)

וּבְהַעֲלוֹתִי אֶתְכֶם מִקִּבְרוֹתֵיכֶם עַמִּי׃ וְנָתַתִּי
and-I-will-put (14) people-of-me from-graves-of-you you and-when-to-bring-up-me

רוּחִי בָכֶם וִחְיִיתֶם וְהִנַּחְתִּי אֶתְכֶם עַל־אַדְמַתְכֶם
land-of-you in you and-I-will-settle and-you-will-live in-you Spirit-of-me

וִידַעְתֶּם כִּי־אֲנִי יְהוָה דִּבַּרְתִּי וְעָשִׂיתִי נְאֻם־יְהוָה׃
Yahweh declaration-of and-I-did I-spoke Yahweh I that then-you-will-know

וַיְהִי דְבַר־יְהוָה אֵלַי לֵאמֹר׃ וְאַתָּה בֶן־אָדָם קַח־לְךָ
for-you take! man son-of now-you (16) to-say to-me Yahweh word-of and-he-came (15)

עֵץ אֶחָד וּכְתֹב עָלָיו לִיהוּדָה וְלִבְנֵי יִשְׂרָאֵל חֲבֵרָו
associates-of-him Israel and-to-sons-of to-Judah on-him and-write! one stick

וּלְקַח עֵץ אֶחָד וּכְתוֹב עָלָיו לְיוֹסֵף עֵץ אֶפְרַיִם וְכָל־
and-all-of Ephraim stick-of to-Joseph on-him and-write! another stick then-take!

בֵּית יִשְׂרָאֵל חֲבֵרָו׃ וְקָרַב אֹתָם אֶחָד אֶל־אֶחָד לְךָ לְעֵץ
into-stick for-you other to one them and-join! (17) associates-of-him Israel house-of

אֶחָד וְהָיוּ לַאֲחָדִים בְּיָדֶךָ׃ וְכַאֲשֶׁר יֹאמְרוּ אֵלֶיךָ
to-you they-ask and-as-when (18) in-hand-of-you into-ones so-they-will-become one

בְּנֵי עַמְּךָ לֵאמֹר הֲלוֹא־תַגִּיד לָנוּ מָה־אֵלֶּה לָּךְ׃
to-you these what? to-us you-will-tell not? to-say countryman-of-you peoples-of

דַּבֵּר אֲלֵהֶם כֹּה־אָמַר אֲדֹנָי יְהוִה הִנֵּה אֲנִי לֹקֵחַ אֶת־עֵץ יוֹסֵף
Joseph stick-of *** taking I see! Yahweh Sovereign he-says this to-them say! (19)

and breathe into these slain, that
they may live.' " [10]So I prophesied
as he commanded me, and breath
entered them; they came to life
and stood up on their feet—a vast
army.

[11]Then he said to me: "Son of
man, these bones are the whole
house of Israel. They say, 'Our
bones are dried up and our hope is
gone; we are cut off.' [12]Therefore
prophesy and say to them: 'This is
what the Sovereign LORD says: O
my people, I am going to open
your graves and bring you up
from them; I will bring you back
to the land of Israel. [13]Then you,
my people, will know that I am
the LORD, when I open your graves
and bring you up from them. [14]I
will put my Spirit in you and you
will live, and I will settle you in
your own land. Then you will
know that I the LORD have spoken,
and I have done it, declares the
LORD.' "

*One Nation Under One King*

[15]The word of the LORD came to
me: [16]"Son of man, take a stick of
wood and write on it, 'Belonging
to Judah and the Israelites associated with him.' Then take another stick of wood, and write on
it, 'Ephraim's stick, belonging to
Joseph and all the house of Israel
associated with him.' [17]Join them
together into one stick so that they
will become one in your hand.

[18]"When your countrymen ask
you, 'Won't you tell us what you
mean by this?' [19]say to them, 'This
is what the Sovereign LORD says: I
am going to take the stick of Joseph—which is in Ephraim's

°*16a,b* ק חבריו

אֲשֶׁר בְּיַד־אֶפְרַיִם וְשִׁבְטֵי יִשְׂרָאֵל חֲבֵרָו° וְנָתַתִּי אוֹתָם
**them and-I-will-join associates-of-him Israel and-tribes-of Ephraim in-hand-of which**

עָלָיו אֶת־עֵץ יְהוּדָה וַעֲשִׂיתִם לְעֵץ אֶחָד וְהָיוּ
**and-they-will-become single into-stick and-I-will-make-them Judah stick-of *** to-him**

אֶחָד בְּיָדִי׃ וְהָיוּ הָעֵצִים אֲשֶׁר־תִּכְתֹּב עֲלֵיהֶם
**on-them you-wrote that the-sticks and-they-shall-be (20) in-hand-of-me one**

בְּיָדְךָ לְעֵינֵיהֶם׃ וְדַבֵּר אֲלֵיהֶם כֹּה־אָמַר אֲדֹנָי
**Sovereign he-says this to-them and-say! (21) before-eyes-of-them in-hand-of-you**

יְהוִה הִנֵּה אֲנִי לֹקֵחַ אֶת־בְּנֵי יִשְׂרָאֵל מִבֵּין הַגּוֹיִם אֲשֶׁר הָלְכוּ־
**they-went where the-nations out-of-among Israel sons-of *** taking I see! Yahweh**

שָׁם וְקִבַּצְתִּי אֹתָם מִסָּבִיב וְהֵבֵאתִי אוֹתָם אֶל־
**into them and-I-will-bring-back from-all-around them and-I-will-gather there**

אַדְמָתָם׃ וְעָשִׂיתִי אֹתָם לְגוֹי אֶחָד בָּאָרֶץ בְּהָרֵי
**on-mountains-of in-the-land one into-nation them and-I-will-make (22) land-of-them**

יִשְׂרָאֵל וּמֶלֶךְ אֶחָד יִהְיֶה לְכֻלָּם לְמֶלֶךְ וְלֹא יִהְיֶה°־
**they-will-be and-never as-king over-all-of-them he-will-be one and-king Israel**

עוֹד לִשְׁנֵי גוֹיִם וְלֹא יֵחָצוּ עוֹד לִשְׁתֵּי מַמְלָכוֹת
**kingdoms into-two-of again they-will-be-divided and-never nations into-two-of again**

עוֹד׃ וְלֹא יִטַמְּאוּ* עוֹד בְּגִלּוּלֵיהֶם
**with-idols-of-them longer they-will-defile-themselves and-not (23) again**

וּבְשִׁקּוּצֵיהֶם וּבְכֹל פִּשְׁעֵיהֶם וְהוֹשַׁעְתִּי אֹתָם
**them for-I-will-save offenses-of-them or-with-any-of and-with-vile-images-of-them**

מִכֹּל מוֹשְׁבֹתֵיהֶם אֲשֶׁר חָטְאוּ בָהֶם וְטִהַרְתִּי
**and-I-will-cleanse in-them they-sinned where dwelling-places-of-them from-all-of**

אוֹתָם וְהָיוּ־לִי לְעָם וַאֲנִי אֶהְיֶה לָהֶם לֵאלֹהִים׃
**as-God to-them I-will-be and-I as-people to-me and-they-will-be them**

וְעַבְדִּי דָוִד מֶלֶךְ עֲלֵיהֶם וְרוֹעֶה אֶחָד
**one and-one-being-shepherd over-them king David and-servant-of-me (24)**

יִהְיֶה לְכֻלָּם וּבְמִשְׁפָּטַי יֵלֵכוּ וְחֻקֹּתַי
**and-decrees-of-me they-will-follow and-to-laws-of-me for-all-of-them he-will-be**

יִשְׁמְרוּ וְעָשׂוּ אוֹתָם׃ וְיָשְׁבוּ עַל־הָאָרֶץ
**the-land in and-they-will-live (25) them and-they-will-keep they-will-be-careful**

אֲשֶׁר נָתַתִּי לְעַבְדִּי לְיַעֲקֹב אֲשֶׁר יָשְׁבוּ־בָהּ אֲבוֹתֵיכֶם
**fathers-of-you in-her they-lived where to-Jacob to-servant-of-me I-gave that**

וְיָשְׁבוּ עָלֶיהָ הֵמָּה וּבְנֵיהֶם וּבְנֵי בְנֵיהֶם
**children-of-them and-children-of and-children-of-them they in-her and-they-will-live**

עַד־עוֹלָם וְדָוִד עַבְדִּי נָשִׂיא לָהֶם לְעוֹלָם׃ וְכָרַתִּי
**and-I-will-make (26) to-forever of-them prince servant-of-me and-David forever to**

hand—and of the Israelite tribes associated with him, and join it to Judah's stick, making them a single stick of wood, and they will become one in my hand.' [20]Hold before their eyes the sticks you have written on [21]and say to them, 'This is what the Sovereign LORD says: I will take the Israelites out of the nations where they have gone. I will gather them from all around and bring them back into their own land. [22]I will make them one nation in the land, on the mountains of Israel. There will be one king over all of them and they will never again be two nations or be divided into two kingdoms. [23]They will no longer defile themselves with their idols and vile images or with any of their offenses, for I will save them from all their sinful backsliding,[k] and I will cleanse them. They will be my people, and I will be their God.

[24]"'My servant David will be king over them, and they will all have one shepherd. They will follow my laws and be careful to keep my decrees. [25]They will live in the land I gave to my servant Jacob, the land where your fathers lived. They and their children and their children's children will live there forever, and David my servant will be their prince forever. [26]I will make a covenant of peace

k23 Many Hebrew manuscripts (see also Septuagint); most Hebrew manuscripts *all their dwelling places where they sinned*

*23 Most mss have *dagesh* in the *teth* (יטּ־).

°19 ק חבריו

°22 ק יהיו

לָהֶם בְּרִית שָׁלוֹם בְּרִית עוֹלָם יִהְיֶה אוֹתָם
with-them he-will-be everlasting covenant-of peace covenant-of with-them

וּנְתַתִּים וְהִרְבֵּיתִי אוֹתָם וְנָתַתִּי אֶת־
*** and-I-will-put them and-I-will-increase-in-number and-I-will-establish-them

מִקְדָּשִׁי בְּתוֹכָם לְעוֹלָם׃ וְהָיָה מִשְׁכָּנִי
dwelling-place-of-me and-he-will-be (27) to-forever in-among-them sanctuary-of-me

עֲלֵיהֶם וְהָיִיתִי לָהֶם לֵאלֹהִים וְהֵמָּה יִהְיוּ־ לִי לְעָם׃
as-people to-me they-will-be and-they as-God to-them and-I-will-be with-them

וְיָדְעוּ הַגּוֹיִם כִּי אֲנִי יְהוָה מְקַדֵּשׁ אֶת־יִשְׂרָאֵל
Israel *** making-holy Yahweh I that the-nations then-they-will-know (28)

בִּהְיוֹת מִקְדָּשִׁי בְּתוֹכָם לְעוֹלָם׃ וַיְהִי דְבַר־
word-of and-he-came (38:1) to-forever in-among-them sanctuary-of-me when-to-be

יְהוָה אֵלַי לֵאמֹר׃ בֶּן־אָדָם שִׂים פָּנֶיךָ אֶל־ גּוֹג אֶרֶץ הַמָּגוֹג
the-Magog land-of Gog against faces-of-you set! man son-of (2) to-say to-me Yahweh

נְשִׂיא רֹאשׁ מֶשֶׁךְ וְתֻבָל וְהִנָּבֵא עָלָיו׃ וְאָמַרְתָּ
and-you-say (3) against-him and-prophesy! and-Tubal Meshech chief-of prince-of

כֹּה אָמַר אֲדֹנָי יְהוָה הִנְנִי אֵלֶיךָ גּוֹג נְשִׂיא רֹאשׁ מֶשֶׁךְ
Meshech chief-of prince-of Gog against-you see-I! Yahweh Sovereign he-says this

וְתֻבָל׃ וְשׁוֹבַבְתִּיךָ וְנָתַתִּי חַחִים בִּלְחָיֶיךָ
in-jaws-of-you hooks and-I-will-put and-I-will-turn-around-you (4) and-Tubal

וְהוֹצֵאתִי אוֹתְךָ וְאֶת־ כָּל־ חֵילֶךָ סוּסִים וּפָרָשִׁים
and-horsemen horses army-of-you whole-of with you and-I-will-bring-out

לְבֻשֵׁי מִכְלוֹל כֻּלָּם קָהָל רָב צִנָּה וּמָגֵן
and-small-shield large-shield great horde all-of-them fullness ones-being-armed-of

תֹּפְשֵׂי חֲרָבוֹת כֻּלָּם׃ פָּרַס כּוּשׁ וּפוּט אִתָּם כֻּלָּם
all-of-them with-them and-Put Cush Persia (5) all-of-them swords ones-brandishing-of

מָגֵן וְכוֹבָע׃ גֹּמֶר וְכָל־ אֲגַפֶּיהָ בֵּית תּוֹגַרְמָה יַרְכְּתֵי
far-parts-of Togarmah Beth troops-of-her with-all-of Gomer (6) and-helmet shield

צָפוֹן וְאֶת־ כָּל־ אֲגַפָּיו עַמִּים רַבִּים אִתָּךְ׃ הִכֹּן
get-ready! (7) with-you many-ones nations troops-of-him all-of with north

וְהָכֵן לְךָ אַתָּה וְכָל־ קְהָלֶךָ הַנִּקְהָלִים
the-ones-being-gathered horde-of-you and-all-of you for-you and-be-prepared!

עָלֶיךָ וְהָיִיתָ לָהֶם לְמִשְׁמָר׃ מִיָּמִים רַבִּים
many-ones after-days (8) as-commander to-them and-you-will-be about-you

תִּפָּקֵד בְּאַחֲרִית הַשָּׁנִים תָּבוֹא ׀ אֶל־אֶרֶץ ׀
land into you-will-invade the-years in-future-of you-will-be-called-to-arms

מְשׁוֹבֶבֶת מֵחֶרֶב מְקֻבֶּצֶת מֵעַמִּים רַבִּים עַל
to many-ones from-nations one-being-gathered from-sword one-being-recovered

with them; it will be an everlasting covenant. I will establish them and increase their numbers, and I will put my sanctuary among them forever.
27 My dwelling place will be with them; I will be their God, and they will be my people.
28 Then the nations will know that I the LORD make Israel holy, when my sanctuary is among them forever.' "

*A Prophecy Against Gog*

38 The word of the LORD came to me:
2 "Son of man, set your face against Gog, of the land of Magog, the chief prince of[l] Meshech and Tubal; prophesy against him
3 and say: 'This is what the Sovereign LORD says: I am against you, O Gog, chief prince of[m] Meshech and Tubal.
4 I will turn you around, put hooks in your jaws and bring you out with your whole army—your horses, your horsemen fully armed, and a great horde with large and small shields, all of them brandishing their swords.
5 Persia, Cush[n] and Put will be with them, all with shields and helmets,
6 also Gomer with all its troops, and Beth Togarmah from the far north with all its troops—the many nations with you.

7 " 'Get ready; be prepared, you and all the hordes gathered about you, and take command of them.
8 After many days you will be called to arms. In future years you will invade a land that has recovered from war, whose people were gathered from many nations to

[l] 2 Or *the prince of Rosh,*
[m] 3 Or *Gog, prince of Rosh,*
[n] 5 That is, the upper Nile region

הָרֵי יִשְׂרָאֵל אֲשֶׁר־הָיוּ לְחָרְבָּה תָּמִיד וְהִיא מֵעַמִּים
from-nations and-she long-time as-desolation they-were which Israel mountains-of

הוּצָאָה וְיָשְׁבוּ לָבֶטַח כֻּלָּם׃ וְעָלִיתָ
and-you-will-go-up (9) all-of-them in-safety and-they-live she-was-brought

כַּשֹּׁאָה תָבוֹא כֶּעָנָן לְכַסּוֹת הָאָרֶץ תִּהְיֶה אַתָּה
you you-will-be the-land to-cover like-the-cloud you-will-advance like-the-storm

וְכָל־אֲגַפֶּיךָ וְעַמִּים רַבִּים אוֹתָךְ׃ כֹּה אָמַר אֲדֹנָי
Sovereign he-says this (10) with-you many-ones and-nations troops-of-you and-all-of

יְהוִה וְהָיָה׀ בַּיּוֹם הַהוּא יַעֲלוּ דְבָרִים עַל־לְבָבֶךָ
mind-of-you into thoughts they-will-come the-that on-the-day and-he-will-be Yahweh

וְחָשַׁבְתָּ מַחֲשֶׁבֶת רָעָה׃ וְאָמַרְתָּ אֶעֱלֶה עַל־אֶרֶץ
land-of into I-will-invade and-you-will-say (11) evil scheme and-you-will-devise

פְּרָזוֹת אָבוֹא הַשֹּׁקְטִים יֹשְׁבֵי לָבֶטַח
in-security ones-living-of the-ones-being-peaceful I-will-attack unwalled-villages

כֻּלָּם יֹשְׁבִים בְּאֵין חוֹמָה וּבְרִיחַ וּדְלָתַיִם אֵין לָהֶם׃
to-them there-are-not and-gates and-bar wall with-no ones-living all-of-them

לִשְׁלֹל שָׁלָל וְלָבֹז בַּז לְהָשִׁיב יָדְךָ עַל־חֳרָבוֹת
ruins against hand-of-you and-to-turn loot and-to-loot plunder to-plunder (12)

נוֹשָׁבֹת וְאֶל־עַם מְאֻסָּף מִגּוֹיִם עֹשֶׂה
being-rich from-nations being-gathered people and-against ones-being-resettled

מִקְנֶה וְקִנְיָן יֹשְׁבֵי עַל־טַבּוּר הָאָרֶץ׃ שְׁבָא וּדְדָן
and-Dedan Sheba (13) the-land center-of in ones-living-of and-goods livestock

וְסֹחֲרֵי תַרְשִׁישׁ וְכָל־כְּפִרֶיהָ יֹאמְרוּ לְךָ
to-you they-will-say villages-of-her and-all-of Tarshish and-ones-being-merchants-of

הֲלִשְׁלֹל שָׁלָל אַתָּה בָא הֲלָבֹז בַּז הִקְהַלְתָּ קְהָלֶךָ לָשֵׂאת׀
to-carry-off horde-of-you you-gathered loot to-loot? coming you plunder to-plunder?

כֶּסֶף וְזָהָב לָקַחַת מִקְנֶה וְקִנְיָן לִשְׁלֹל שָׁלָל גָּדוֹל׃
much plunder to-plunder and-goods livestock to-take-away and-gold silver

לָכֵן הִנָּבֵא בֶן־אָדָם וְאָמַרְתָּ לְגוֹג כֹּה אָמַר אֲדֹנָי
Sovereign he-says this to-Gog and-you-say man son-of prophesy! therefore (14)

יְהוִה הֲלוֹא׀ בַּיּוֹם הַהוּא בְּשֶׁבֶת עַמִּי יִשְׂרָאֵל לָבֶטַח
in-safety Israel people-of-me when-to-live the-that in-the-day not? Yahweh

תֵּדָע׃ וּבָאתָ מִמְּקוֹמְךָ מִיַּרְכְּתֵי צָפוֹן
north from-far-parts-of from-place-of-you and-you-will-come (15) will-you-take-notice

אַתָּה וְעַמִּים רַבִּים אִתָּךְ רֹכְבֵי סוּסִים כֻּלָּם קָהָל גָּדוֹל
great horde all-of-them horses ones-riding-of with-you many-ones and-nations you

וְחַיִל רָב׃ וְעָלִיתָ עַל־עַמִּי יִשְׂרָאֵל כֶּעָנָן
like-the-cloud Israel people-of-me against and-you-will-advance (16) mighty and-army

the mountains of Israel, which had long been desolate. They had been brought out from the nations, and now all of them live in safety. [9]You and all your troops and the many nations with you will go up, advancing like a storm; you will be like a cloud covering the land.

[10]" 'This is what the Sovereign LORD says: On that day thoughts will come into your mind and you will devise an evil scheme. [11]You will say, "I will invade a land of unwalled villages; I will attack a peaceful and unsuspecting people—all of them living without walls and without gates and bars. [12]I will plunder and loot and turn my hand against the resettled ruins and the people gathered from the nations, rich in livestock and goods, living at the center of the land." [13]Sheba and Dedan and the merchants of Tarshish and all her villages[o] will say to you, "Have you come to plunder? Have you gathered your hordes to loot, to carry off silver and gold, to take away livestock and goods and to seize much plunder?" '

[14]"Therefore, son of man, prophesy and say to Gog: 'This is what the Sovereign LORD says: In that day, when my people Israel are living in safety, will you not take notice of it? [15]You will come from your place in the far north, you and many nations with you, all of them riding on horses, a great horde, a mighty army. [16]You will advance against my people Israel like a cloud that covers the

[o]13 Or *her strong lions*

לְכַסּוֹת הָאָרֶץ בְּאַחֲרִית הַיָּמִים תִּהְיֶה וַהֲבִאוֹתִיךָ עַל־
against and-I-will-bring-you she-will-come the-days at-end-of the-land to-cover

אַרְצִי לְמַעַן דַּעַת הַגּוֹיִם אֹתִי בְּהִקָּדְשִׁי בְךָ
through-you when-to-show-holy-myself me the-nations to-know so-that land-of-me

לְעֵינֵיהֶם גּוֹג׃ כֹּה־אָמַר אֲדֹנָי יְהוִה הַאַתָּה־הוּא אֲשֶׁר־דִּבַּרְתִּי
I-spoke whom he you? Yahweh Sovereign he-says this (17) Gog before-eyes-of-them

בְּיָמִים קַדְמוֹנִים בְּיַד עֲבָדַי נְבִיאֵי יִשְׂרָאֵל הַנִּבְּאִים
the-ones-prophesying Israel prophets-of servants-of-me by-hand-of former-ones in-days

בַּיָּמִים הָהֵם שָׁנִים לְהָבִיא אֹתְךָ עֲלֵיהֶם׃ וְהָיָה ׀
and-he-will-happen (18) against-them you to-bring years the-those in-the-days

בַּיּוֹם הַהוּא בְּיוֹם בּוֹא גוֹג עַל־אַדְמַת יִשְׂרָאֵל נְאֻם
declaration-of Israel land-of against Gog to-attack on-day-of the-that in-the-day

אֲדֹנָי יְהוִה תַּעֲלֶה חֲמָתִי בְּאַפִּי׃ וּבְקִנְאָתִי
and-in-zeal-of-me (19) in-heat-of-me anger-of-me she-will-be-aroused Yahweh Sovereign

בְאֵשׁ־עֶבְרָתִי דִּבַּרְתִּי אִם־לֹא ׀ בַּיּוֹם הַהוּא יִהְיֶה
he-shall-be the-that at-the-day indeed surely I-declare wrath-of-me in-fire-of

רַעַשׁ גָּדוֹל עַל אַדְמַת יִשְׂרָאֵל׃ וְרָעֲשׁוּ מִפָּנַי
at-presences-of-me and-they-will-tremble (20) Israel land-of in great earthquake

דְּגֵי הַיָּם וְעוֹף הַשָּׁמַיִם וְחַיַּת הַשָּׂדֶה וְכָל־הָרֶמֶשׂ
the-creature and-all-of the-field and-beast-of the-airs and-bird-of the-sea fishes-of

הָרֹמֵשׂ עַל־הָאֲדָמָה וְכֹל הָאָדָם אֲשֶׁר עַל־פְּנֵי הָאֲדָמָה
the-earth faces-of on that the-people and-all-of the-ground along the-creature-moving

וְנֶהֶרְסוּ הֶהָרִים וְנָפְלוּ הַמַּדְרֵגוֹת וְכָל־
and-every-of the-cliffs and-they-will-crumble the-mountains and-they-will-be-overturned

חוֹמָה לָאָרֶץ תִּפּוֹל׃ וְקָרָאתִי עָלָיו לְכָל־
on-all-of against-him and-I-will-summon (21) she-will-fall to-the-ground wall

הָרַי חֶרֶב נְאֻם אֲדֹנָי יְהוִה חֶרֶב אִישׁ
man sword-of Yahweh Sovereign declaration-of sword mountains-of-me

בְּאָחִיו תִּהְיֶה׃ וְנִשְׁפַּטְתִּי אִתּוֹ בְּדֶבֶר
with-plague upon-him and-I-will-judge (22) she-will-be against-brother-of-him

וּבְדָם וְגֶשֶׁם שׁוֹטֵף וְאַבְנֵי אֶלְגָּבִישׁ אֵשׁ וְגָפְרִית
and-sulfur burning hail and-stones-of being-torrent and-rain and-with-bloodshed

אַמְטִיר עָלָיו וְעַל־אֲגַפָּיו וְעַל־עַמִּים רַבִּים אֲשֶׁר אִתּוֹ׃
with-him that many-ones nations and-on troops-of-him and-on on-him I-will-pour-down

וְהִתְגַּדִּלְתִּי וְהִתְקַדִּשְׁתִּי וְנוֹדַעְתִּי
and-I-will-make-myself-known and-I-will-show-myself-holy and-I-will-show-myself-great (23)

לְעֵינֵי גּוֹיִם רַבִּים וְיָדְעוּ כִּי־אֲנִי יְהוָה׃
Yahweh I that then-they-will-know many-ones nations before-eyes-of

land. In days to come, O Gog, I
will bring you against my land, so
that the nations may know me
when I show myself holy through
you before their eyes.
17 'This is what the Sovereign
LORD says: Are you not the one I
spoke of in former days by my servants the prophets of Israel? At
that time they prophesied for
years that I would bring you
against them. 18 This is what will
happen in that day: When Gog attacks the land of Israel, my hot anger will be aroused, declares the
Sovereign LORD. 19 In my zeal and
fiery wrath I declare that at that
time there shall be a great earthquake in the land of Israel. 20 The
fish of the sea, the birds of the air,
the beasts of the field, every creature that moves along the ground,
and all the people on the face of
the earth will tremble at my presence. The mountains will be overturned, the cliffs will crumble and
every wall will fall to the ground.
21 I will summon a sword against
Gog on all my mountains, declares
the Sovereign LORD. Every man's
sword will be against his brother.
22 I will execute judgment upon
him with plague and bloodshed; I
will pour down torrents of rain,
hailstones and burning sulfur on
him and on his troops and on the
many nations with him. 23 And so
I will show my greatness and my
holiness, and I will make myself
known in the sight of many nations. Then they will know that I
am the LORD.'

וְאַתָּה בֶן־ אָדָם הִנָּבֵא עַל־ גּוֹג וְאָמַרְתָּ כֹּה אָמַר
he-says this and-you-say Gog against prophesy! man son-of now-you (39:1)

אֲדֹנָי יְהוִה הִנְנִי אֵלֶיךָ גּוֹג נְשִׂיא רֹאשׁ מֶשֶׁךְ וְתֻבָל׃
and-Tubal Meshech chief-of prince-of Gog against-you see-I! Yahweh Sovereign

וְשֹׁבַבְתִּיךָ וְשִׁשֵּׁאתִיךָ וְהַעֲלִיתִיךָ
and-I-will-bring-you and-I-will-drag-along-you and-I-will-turn-around-you (2)

מִיַּרְכְּתֵי צָפוֹן וַהֲבֵאוֹתִךָ עַל־ הָרֵי יִשְׂרָאֵל׃
Israel mountains-of against and-I-will-send-you north from-far-parts-of

וְהִכֵּיתִי קַשְׁתְּךָ מִיַּד שְׂמֹאולֶךָ וְחִצֶּיךָ
and-arrows-of-you left-of-you from-hand-of bow-of-you then-I-will-strike (3)

מִיַּד יְמִינְךָ אַפִּיל׃ עַל־ הָרֵי יִשְׂרָאֵל תִּפּוֹל
you-will-fall Israel mountains-of on (4) I-will-make-drop right-of-you from-hand-of

אַתָּה וְכָל־ אֲגַפֶּיךָ וְעַמִּים אֲשֶׁר אִתָּךְ לְעֵיט צִפּוֹר
bird to-carrion-bird-of with-you that and-nations troops-of-you and-all-of you

כָּל־ כָּנָף וְחַיַּת הַשָּׂדֶה נְתַתִּיךָ לְאָכְלָה׃ עַל־
in (5) as-food I-will-give-you the-field and-wild-animal-of bird every-of

פְּנֵי הַשָּׂדֶה תִּפּוֹל כִּי אֲנִי דִבַּרְתִּי נְאֻם אֲדֹנָי יְהוִה׃
Yahweh Sovereign declaration-of I-spoke I for you-will-fall the-field open-parts-of

וְשִׁלַּחְתִּי־ אֵשׁ בְּמָגוֹג וּבְיֹשְׁבֵי הָאִיִּים לָבֶטַח
in-safety the-coastlands and-on-ones-living-of on-Magog fire and-I-will-send (6)

וְיָדְעוּ כִּי־ אֲנִי יְהוָה׃ וְאֶת־ שֵׁם קָדְשִׁי אוֹדִיעַ
I-will-make-known holiness-of-me name-of and (7) Yahweh I that and-they-will-know

בְּתוֹךְ עַמִּי יִשְׂרָאֵל וְלֹא־ אַחֵל אֶת־ שֵׁם־ קָדְשִׁי
holiness-of-me name-of *** I-will-let-be-profaned and-not Israel people-of-me in-among

עוֹד וְיָדְעוּ הַגּוֹיִם כִּי־ אֲנִי יְהוָה קָדוֹשׁ בְּיִשְׂרָאֵל׃ הִנֵּה
see! (8) in-Israel Holy-One Yahweh I that the-nations and-they-will-know longer

בָאָה וְנִהְיָתָה נְאֻם אֲדֹנָי יְהוִה הוּא הַיּוֹם
the-day this Yahweh Sovereign declaration-of and-she-will-take-place coming

אֲשֶׁר דִּבַּרְתִּי׃ וְיָצְאוּ יֹשְׁבֵי ׀ עָרֵי יִשְׂרָאֵל
Israel towns-of ones-living-of then-they-will-go-out (9) I-spoke that

וּבִעֲרוּ וְהִשִּׂיקוּ בְּנֶשֶׁק וּמָגֵן
even-small-shield to-weapon and-they-will-burn-up and-they-will-use-for-fuel

וְצִנָּה בְּקֶשֶׁת וּבְחִצִּים וּבְמַקֵּל יָד וּבְרֹמַח
and-to-spear hand and-to-war-club-of and-to-arrows to-bow and-large-shield

וּבִעֲרוּ בָהֶם אֵשׁ שֶׁבַע שָׁנִים׃ וְלֹא־ יִשְׂאוּ
they-will-gather and-not (10) years seven fire to-them and-they-will-use-for-fuel

עֵצִים מִן־ הַשָּׂדֶה וְלֹא יַחְטְבוּ מִן־ הַיְּעָרִים כִּי בַנֶּשֶׁק
to-the-weapon because the-forests from they-will-cut or-not the-field from woods

39 "Son of man, prophesy
against Gog and say: 'This
is what the Sovereign LORD says: I
am against you, O Gog, chief
prince of[p] Meshech and Tubal. 2 I
will turn you around and drag you
along. I will bring you from the far
north and send you against the
mountains of Israel. 3 Then I will
strike your bow from your left
hand and make your arrows drop
from your right hand. 4 On the
mountains of Israel you will fall,
you and all your troops and the
nations with you. I will give you
as food to all kinds of carrion birds
and to the wild animals. 5 You will
fall in the open field, for I have
spoken, declares the Sovereign
LORD. 6 I will send fire on Magog
and on those who live in safety in
the coastlands, and they will
know that I am the LORD.
7 " 'I will make known my holy
name among my people Israel. I
will no longer let my holy name be
profaned, and the nations will
know that I the LORD am the Holy
One in Israel. 8 It is coming! It will
surely take place, declares the Sovereign LORD. This is the day I have
spoken of.
9 " 'Then those who live in the
towns of Israel will go out and use
the weapons for fuel and burn
them up—the small and large
shields, the bows and arrows, the
war clubs and spears. For seven
years they will use them for fuel.
10 They will not need to gather
wood from the fields or cut it from
the forests, because they will use

p1 Or *Gog, prince of Rosh,*

יְבַעֲרוּ־ אֵשׁ וְשָׁלְלוּ אֶת־ שֹׁלְלֵיהֶם
ones-plundering-them *** and-they-will-plunder fire they-will-use-for-fuel

וּבָזְזוּ אֶת־ בֹּזְזֵיהֶם נְאֻם אֲדֹנָי יְהוִה׃
Yahweh Sovereign declaration-of ones-looting-them *** and-they-will-loot

וְהָיָה בַיּוֹם הַהוּא אֶתֵּן לְגוֹג מְקוֹם־ שָׁם קֶבֶר
burial there place-of to-Gog I-will-give the-that on-the-day and-he-will-be (11)

בִּישְׂרָאֵל גֵּי הָעֹבְרִים קִדְמַת הַיָּם וְחֹסֶמֶת הִיא אֶת־
*** she and-one-blocking the-sea east-of the-ones-traveling valley-of in-Israel

הָעֹבְרִים וְקָבְרוּ שָׁם אֶת־ גּוֹג וְאֶת־ כָּל־ הֲמוֹנֹה
horde-of-him all-of and Gog *** there because-they-will-bury the-ones-traveling

וְקָרְאוּ גֵּיא הֲמוֹן גּוֹג׃ וּקְבָרוּם בֵּית יִשְׂרָאֵל
Israel house-of and-they-will-bury-them (12) Gog Hamon Valley-of so-they-will-call

לְמַעַן טַהֵר אֶת־ הָאָרֶץ שִׁבְעָה חֳדָשִׁים׃ וְקָבְרוּ כָּל־
all-of and-they-will-bury (13) months seven the-land *** to-cleanse in-order-to

עַם הָאָרֶץ וְהָיָה לָהֶם לְשֵׁם יוֹם הִכָּבְדִי
to-be-glorified-me day-of as-memorable for-them and-he-will-be the-land people-of

נְאֻם אֲדֹנָי יְהוִה׃ וְאַנְשֵׁי תָמִיד יַבְדִּילוּ עֹבְרִים
ones-going they-will-employ regular and-men-of (14) Yahweh Sovereign declaration-of

בָּאָרֶץ מְקַבְּרִים אֶת־ הָעֹבְרִים אֶת־ הַנּוֹתָרִים עַל־
on the-ones-remaining *** the-ones-going with ones-burying throughout-the-land

פְּנֵי הָאָרֶץ לְטַהֲרָהּ מִקְצֵה שִׁבְעָה־חֳדָשִׁים יַחְקֹרוּ׃
they-will-search months seven at-end-of to-cleanse-her the-ground surfaces-of

וְעָבְרוּ הָעֹבְרִים בָּאָרֶץ וְרָאָה עֶצֶם אָדָם
human bone-of when-he-sees through-the-land the-ones-going and-they-will-go (15)

וּבָנָה אֶצְלוֹ צִיּוּן עַד קָבְרוּ אֹתוֹ הַמְקַבְּרִים
the-ones-digging-graves him they-bury until marker beside-him then-he-will-set-up

אֶל־ גֵּיא הֲמוֹן גּוֹג׃ וְגַם שֶׁם־ עִיר הֲמוֹנָה וְטִהֲרוּ
so-they-will-cleanse Hamonah town name-of and-also (16) Gog Hamon Valley-of in

הָאָרֶץ׃ וְאַתָּה בֶן־ אָדָם כֹּה־ אָמַר אֲדֹנָי יְהוִה אֱמֹר לְצִפּוֹר
to-bird call-out! Yahweh Sovereign he-says this man son-of now-you (17) the-land

כָּל־ כָּנָף וּלְכֹל חַיַּת הַשָּׂדֶה הִקָּבְצוּ וָבֹאוּ
and-come! assemble! the-field wild-animal-of and-to-all-of bird every-of

הֵאָסְפוּ מִסָּבִיב עַל־ זִבְחִי אֲשֶׁר אֲנִי זֹבֵחַ
preparing-sacrifice I that sacrifice-of-me to from-all-around come-together!

לָכֶם זֶבַח גָּדוֹל עַל הָרֵי יִשְׂרָאֵל וַאֲכַלְתֶּם בָּשָׂר
flesh and-you-will-eat Israel mountains-of on great sacrifice for-you

וּשְׁתִיתֶם דָּם׃ בְּשַׂר גִּבּוֹרִים תֹּאכֵלוּ וְדַם־
and-blood-of you-will-eat mighty-men flesh-of (18) blood and-you-will-drink

the weapons for fuel. And they will plunder those who plundered them and loot those who looted them, declares the Sovereign LORD.

11"'On that day I will give Gog a burial place in Israel, in the valley of those who travel east toward[q] the Sea.[r] It will block the way of travelers, because Gog and all his hordes will be buried there. So it will be called the Valley of Hamon Gog.[s]

12"'For seven months the house of Israel will be burying them in order to cleanse the land. 13All the people of the land will bury them, and the day I am glorified will be a memorable day for them, declares the Sovereign LORD.

14"'Men will be regularly employed to cleanse the land. Some will go throughout the land and, in addition to them, others will bury those that remain on the ground. At the end of the seven months they will begin their search. 15As they go through the land and one of them sees a human bone, he will set up a marker beside it until the gravediggers have buried it in the Valley of Hamon Gog. 16(Also a town called Hamonah[t] will be there.) And so they will cleanse the land.'

17"Son of man, this is what the Sovereign LORD says: Call out to every kind of bird and all the wild animals: 'Assemble and come together from all around to the sacrifice I am preparing for you, the great sacrifice on the mountains of Israel. There you will eat flesh and drink blood. 18You will eat the flesh of mighty men and drink the

q11 Or *of* r11 That is, the Dead Sea
s11 *Hamon Gog* means *hordes of Gog*.

°11 ק המונו

נְשִׂיאֵי הָאָרֶץ תִּשְׁתּוּ אֵילִים כָּרִים וְעַתּוּדִים פָּרִים מְרִיאֵי
fattened-animals-of bulls and-goats lambs rams you-will-drink the-earth princes-of

בָשָׁן כֻּלָּם׃ וַאֲכַלְתֶּם־ חֵלֶב לְשָׂבְעָה וּשְׁתִיתֶם
and-you-will-drink till-glutting fat and-you-will-eat (19) all-of-them Bashan

דָּם לְשִׁכָּרוֹן מִזִּבְחִי אֲשֶׁר־ זָבַחְתִּי לָכֶם׃
for-you I-prepare-sacrifice that at-sacrifice-of-me till-drunkenness blood

וּשְׂבַעְתֶּם עַל־ שֻׁלְחָנִי סוּס וָרֶכֶב גִּבּוֹר וְכָל־
and-every-of mighty-man and-rider horse table-of-me at and-you-will-eat-fill (20)

אִישׁ מִלְחָמָה נְאֻם אֲדֹנָי יְהוִה׃ וְנָתַתִּי אֶת־ כְּבוֹדִי
glory-of-me *** and-I-will-display (21) Yahweh Sovereign declaration-of war man-of

בַּגּוֹיִם וְרָאוּ כָל־ הַגּוֹיִם אֶת־ מִשְׁפָּטִי אֲשֶׁר
that punishment-of-me *** the-nations all-of and-they-will-see among-the-nations

עָשִׂיתִי וְאֶת־ יָדִי אֲשֶׁר־ שַׂמְתִּי בָהֶם׃ וְיָדְעוּ בֵּית יִשְׂרָאֵל
Israel house-of and-they-will-know (22) on-them I-lay that hand-of-me and I-inflict

כִּי אֲנִי יְהוָה אֱלֹהֵיהֶם מִן־ הַיּוֹם הַהוּא וָהָלְאָה׃ וְיָדְעוּ
and-they-will-know (23) and-forward the-that the-day from God-of-them Yahweh I that

הַגּוֹיִם כִּי בַעֲוֺנָם גָּלוּ בֵית־ יִשְׂרָאֵל עַל
because Israel house-of they-went-into-exile for-sin-of-them that the-nations

אֲשֶׁר מָעֲלוּ־ בִי וָאַסְתִּר פָּנַי מֵהֶם וָאֶתְּנֵם
and-I-gave-them from-them faces-of-me so-I-hid to-me they-were-unfaithful that

בְּיַד צָרֵיהֶם וַיִּפְּלוּ בַחֶרֶב כֻּלָּם׃
all-of-them by-the-sword and-they-fell enemies-of-them into-hand-of

כְּטֻמְאָתָם וּכְפִשְׁעֵיהֶם עָשִׂיתִי
I-dealt-with and-according-to-offenses-of-them according-to-uncleanness-of-them (24)

אֹתָם וָאַסְתִּר פָּנַי מֵהֶם׃ לָכֵן כֹּה אָמַר אֲדֹנָי יְהוִה
Yahweh Sovereign he-says this therefore (25) from-them faces-of-me and-I-hid them

עַתָּה אָשִׁיב אֶת־ שְׁבִית יַעֲקֹב וְרִחַמְתִּי
and-I-will-have-compassion Jacob captivity-of *** I-will-bring-back now

כָּל־ בֵּית יִשְׂרָאֵל וְקִנֵּאתִי לְשֵׁם קָדְשִׁי׃
holiness-of-me for-name-of and-I-will-be-jealous Israel house-of all-of

וְנָשׂוּ אֶת־ כְּלִמָּתָם וְאֶת־ כָּל־ מַעֲלָם אֲשֶׁר
that unfaithfulness-of-them all-of and shame-of-them *** and-they-will-forget (26)

מָעֲלוּ־ בִי בְּשִׁבְתָּם עַל־ אַדְמָתָם לָבֶטַח
in-safety land-of-them in when-to-live-them toward-me they-showed-unfaithfulness

וְאֵין מַחֲרִיד׃ בְּשׁוֹבְבִי אוֹתָם מִן־ הָעַמִּים וְקִבַּצְתִּי
and-I-gather the-nations from them when-to-bring-back-me (27) making-afraid and-no-one

אֹתָם מֵאַרְצוֹת אֹיְבֵיהֶם וְנִקְדַּשְׁתִּי
then-I-will-show-myself-holy ones-being-enemies-of-them from-countries-of them

°25 ק שבות

blood of the princes of the earth as
if they were rams and lambs, goats
and bulls—all of them fattened
animals from Bashan. [19]At the sacrifice I am preparing for you, you
will eat fat till you are glutted and
drink blood till you are drunk. [20]At
my table you will eat your fill of
horses and riders, mighty men
and soldiers of every kind,' declares the Sovereign LORD.
[21]"I will display my glory among
the nations, and all the nations
will see the punishment I inflict
and the hand I lay upon them.
[22]From that day forward the house
of Israel will know that I am the
LORD their God. [23]And the nations
will know that the people of Israel
went into exile for their sin, because they were unfaithful to me.
So I hid my face from them and
handed them over to their enemies, and they all fell by the
sword. [24]I dealt with them according to their uncleanness and their
offenses, and I hid my face from
them.
[25]"Therefore this is what the
Sovereign LORD says: I will now
bring Jacob back from captivity[u]
and will have compassion on all
the people of Israel, and I will be
zealous for my holy name. [26]They
will forget their shame and all the
unfaithfulness they showed
toward me when they lived in
safety in their land with no one to
make them afraid. [27]When I have
brought them back from the nations and have gathered them
from the countries of their enemies, I will show myself holy

[t]16 *Hamonah* means *horde*.
[u]25 *Or now restore the fortunes of Jacob*

בָּם לְעֵינֵי הַגּוֹיִם רַבִּים׃ וְיָדְעוּ כִּי אֲנִי
**I that then-they-will-know (28) many-ones the-nations before-eyes-of through-them**

יְהוָה אֱלֹהֵיהֶם בְּהַגְלוֹתִי אֹתָם אֶל־ הַגּוֹיִם וְכִנַּסְתִּים
**yet-I-will-gather-them the-nations among them though-to-exile-me God-of-them Yahweh**

עַל־ אַדְמָתָם וְלֹא־ אוֹתִיר עוֹד מֵהֶם שָׁם׃ וְלֹא־
**and-not (29) there of-them any I-will-leave-behind and-not land-of-them to**

אַסְתִּיר עוֹד פָּנַי מֵהֶם אֲשֶׁר שָׁפַכְתִּי אֶת־ רוּחִי עַל־
**on Spirit-of-me *** I-will-pour-out for from-them faces-of-me longer I-will-hide**

בֵּית יִשְׂרָאֵל נְאֻם אֲדֹנָי יְהוִה׃ בְּעֶשְׂרִים וְחָמֵשׁ שָׁנָה
**year and-five in-twenty (40:1) Yahweh Sovereign declaration-of Israel house-of**

לְגָלוּתֵנוּ בְּרֹאשׁ הַשָּׁנָה בֶּעָשׂוֹר לַחֹדֶשׁ בְּאַרְבַּע עֶשְׂרֵה
**ten in-four-of of-the-month on-the-ten the-year at-beginning-of of-exile-of-us**

שָׁנָה אַחַר אֲשֶׁר הֻכְּתָה הָעִיר בְּעֶצֶם ׀ הַיּוֹם הַזֶּה הָיְתָה
**she-was the-this the-day on-very-of the-city she-was-made-to-fall when after year**

עָלַי יַד־ יְהוָה וַיָּבֵא אֹתִי שָׁמָּה׃ בְּמַרְאוֹת אֱלֹהִים הֱבִיאַנִי אֶל־
**to he-took-me God in-visions-of (2) to-there me and-he-took Yahweh hand-of upon-me**

אֶרֶץ יִשְׂרָאֵל וַיְנִיחֵנִי אֶל־ הַר גָּבֹהַּ מְאֹד וְעָלָיו כְּמִבְנֵה־ עִיר
**city like-building-of and-on-him very high mountain on and-he-set-me Israel land-of**

מִנֶּגֶב׃ וַיָּבִיא אוֹתִי שָׁמָּה וְהִנֵּה־ אִישׁ מַרְאֵהוּ כְּמַרְאֵה
**like-appearance-of appearance-of-him man and-see! to-there me and-he-took (3) on-south**

נְחֹשֶׁת וּפְתִיל־ פִּשְׁתִּים בְּיָדוֹ וּקְנֵה הַמִּדָּה וְהוּא עֹמֵד
**standing and-he the-measure and-rod-of in-hand-of-him linens and-cord-of bronze**

בַּשָּׁעַר׃ וַיְדַבֵּר אֵלַי הָאִישׁ בֶּן־ אָדָם רְאֵה בְעֵינֶיךָ
**with-eyes-of-you look! man son-of the-man to-me and-he-said (4) in-the-gateway**

וּבְאָזְנֶיךָ שְּׁמָע וְשִׂים לִבְּךָ לְכֹל אֲשֶׁר־ אֲנִי
**I that to-everything heart-of-you and-make-attend! hear! and-with-ears-of-you**

מַרְאֶה אוֹתָךְ כִּי לְמַעַן הַרְאוֹתְכָה הֻבָאתָה הֵנָּה הַגֵּד אֶת־
***** tell! to-here you-were-brought to-show-you in-order-to for you showing**

כָּל־ אֲשֶׁר־ אַתָּה רֹאֶה לְבֵית יִשְׂרָאֵל׃ וְהִנֵּה חוֹמָה מִחוּץ
**at-outside wall and-see! (5) Israel to-house-of seeing you that everything**

לַבַּיִת סָבִיב ׀ סָבִיב וּבְיַד הָאִישׁ קְנֵה הַמִּדָּה
**the-measure rod-of the-man and-in-hand-of surrounding surrounding of-the-temple**

שֵׁשׁ־ אַמּוֹת בָּאַמָּה וָטֹפַח וַיָּמָד אֶת־ רֹחַב הַבִּנְיָן
**the-wall thickness-of *** and-he-measured and-handbreadth by-the-cubit cubits six**

קָנֶה אֶחָד וְקוֹמָה קָנֶה אֶחָד׃ וַיָּבוֹא אֶל־ שַׁעַר אֲשֶׁר פָּנָיו דֶּרֶךְ
**direction-of faces-of-him that gate to and-he-went (6) one rod and-height one rod**

הַקָּדִימָה וַיַּעַל בְּמַעֲלוֹתָו וַיָּמָד ׀ אֶת־ סַף הַשַּׁעַר
**the-gate threshold-of *** and-he-measured on-steps-of-him and-he-climbed to-the-east**

°6 ק במעלותיו

through them in the sight of many nations. [28]Then they will know that I am the LORD their God, for though I sent them into exile among the nations, I will gather them to their own land, not leaving any behind. [29]I will no longer hide my face from them, for I will pour out my Spirit on the house of Israel, declares the Sovereign LORD."

*The New Temple Area*

40 In the twenty-fifth year of our exile, at the beginning of the year, on the tenth of the month, in the fourteenth year after the fall of the city—on that very day the hand of the LORD was upon me and he took me there. [2]In visions of God he took me to the land of Israel and set me on a very high mountain, on whose south side were some buildings that looked like a city. [3]He took me there, and I saw a man whose appearance was like bronze; he was standing in the gateway with a linen cord and a measuring rod in his hand. [4]The man said to me, "Son of man, look with your eyes and hear with your ears and pay attention to everything I am going to show you, for that is why you have been brought here. Tell the house of Israel everything you see."

*The East Gate to the Outer Court*

[5]I saw a wall completely surrounding the temple area. The length of the measuring rod in the man's hand was six long cubits, each of which was a cubit[v] and a handbreadth.[w] He measured the wall; it was one measuring rod thick and one rod high.

[6]Then he went to the gate facing east. He climbed its steps and measured the threshold of the

[v]5 The common cubit was about 1 1/2 feet (about 0.5 meter).
[w]5 That is, about 3 inches (about 8 centimeters)

קָנֶה אֶחָד רֹחַב וְאֵת סַף אֶחָד קָנֶה אֶחָד רֹחַב׃ וְהַתָּא קָנֶה אֶחָד
one rod and-the-alcove (7) depth one rod one threshold and depth one rod

אֹרֶךְ וְקָנֶה אֶחָד רֹחַב וּבֵין הַתָּאִים חָמֵשׁ אַמּוֹת וְסַף
and-threshold-of cubits five the-alcoves and-between width one and-rod length

הַשַּׁעַר מֵאֵצֶל אוּלָם הַשַּׁעַר מֵהַבַּיִת קָנֶה אֶחָד׃ וַיָּמָד
then-he-measured (8) one rod facing-the-temple the-gate portico-of at-next-to the-gate

אֶת־אֻלָם הַשַּׁעַר מֵהַבַּיִת קָנֶה אֶחָד׃ וַיָּמָד אֶת־
*** then-he-measured (9) one rod facing-the-temple the-gateway portico-of ***

אֻלָם הַשַּׁעַר שְׁמֹנֶה אַמּוֹת וְאֵילָו שְׁתַּיִם אַמּוֹת וְאֻלָם
indeed-portico-of cubits two and-jambs-of-him cubits eight the-gateway portico-of

הַשַּׁעַר מֵהַבָּיִת׃ וְתָאֵי הַשַּׁעַר דֶּרֶךְ הַקָּדִים
the-east direction-of the-gateway and-alcoves-of (10) facing-the-temple the-gateway

שְׁלֹשָׁה מִפֹּה וּשְׁלֹשָׁה מִפֹּה מִדָּה אַחַת לִשְׁלָשְׁתָּם וּמִדָּה
and-measurement for-three-of-them same measurement on-side and-three on-side three

אַחַת לָאֵילִם מִפֹּה וּמִפּוֹ׃ וַיָּמָד אֶת־רֹחַב
width-of *** then-he-measured (11) and-on-side on-side for-the-projecting-walls same

פֶּתַח־הַשַּׁעַר עֶשֶׂר אַמּוֹת אֹרֶךְ הַשַּׁעַר שְׁלוֹשׁ עֶשְׂרֵה אַמּוֹת׃
cubits ten three-of the-gateway length-of cubits ten the-gateway entrance-of

וּגְבוּל לִפְנֵי הַתָּאוֹת אַמָּה אֶחָת וְאַמָּה־אַחַת גְּבוּל מִפֹּה
on-side wall one and-cubit one cubit the-alcoves in-front-of and-wall (12)

וְהַתָּא שֵׁשׁ־אַמּוֹת מִפּוֹ וְשֵׁשׁ אַמּוֹת מִפּוֹ׃ וַיָּמָד
then-he-measured (13) on-side cubits and-six on-side cubits six and-the-alcove

אֶת־הַשַּׁעַר מִגַּג הַתָּא לְגַגּוֹ רֹחַב עֶשְׂרִים וְחָמֵשׁ
and-five twenty distance to-top-of-him the-alcove from-top-of the-gateway ***

אַמּוֹת פֶּתַח נֶגֶד פָּתַח׃ וַיַּעַשׂ אֶת־אֵילִים שִׁשִּׁים
sixty projecting-walls *** and-he-measured (14) opening opposite opening cubits

אַמָּה וְאֶל־אֵיל הֶחָצֵר הַשַּׁעַר סָבִיב ׀ סָבִיב׃
around around the-gateway the-courtyard projecting-wall-of and-to cubit

וְעַל פְּנֵי הַשַּׁעַר הָיאתוֹן עַל־לִפְנֵי אֻלָם הַשַּׁעַר
the-gateway portico-of faces-of to the-entrance the-gateway faces-of and-from (15)

הַפְּנִימִי חֲמִשִּׁים אַמָּה׃ וְחַלֹּנוֹת אֲטֻמוֹת אֶל־הַתָּאִים
the-alcoves to ones-being-narrow and-openings (16) cubit fifty the-far-end

וְאֶל אֵלֵיהֵמָה לִפְנִימָה לַשַּׁעַר סָבִיב ׀ סָבִיב וְכֵן
and-so around around of-the-gateway at-inside projecting-walls-of-them and-to

לָאֵלַמּוֹת וְחַלּוֹנוֹת סָבִיב ׀ סָבִיב לִפְנִימָה וְאֶל־אַיִל
projecting-wall and-on to-inward around around and-openings for-the-porticos

תִּמֹרִים׃ וַיְבִיאֵנִי אֶל־הֶחָצֵר הַחִיצוֹנָה וְהִנֵּה לְשָׁכוֹת
rooms and-see! the-outer the-court into then-he-brought-me (17) palm-trees

gate; it was one rod deep.[x] [7]The alcoves for the guards were one rod long and one rod wide, and the projecting walls between the alcoves were five cubits thick. And the threshold of the gate next to the portico facing the temple was one rod deep.

[8]Then he measured the portico of the gateway; [9]it[y] was eight cubits deep and its jambs were two cubits thick. The portico of the gateway faced the temple.

[10]Inside the east gate were three alcoves on each side; the three had the same measurements, and the faces of the projecting walls on each side had the same measurements. [11]Then he measured the width of the entrance to the gateway; it was ten cubits and its length was thirteen cubits. [12]In front of each alcove was a wall one cubit high, and the alcoves were six cubits square. [13]Then he measured the gateway from the top of the rear wall of one alcove to the top of the opposite one; the distance was twenty-five cubits from one parapet opening to the opposite one. [14]He measured along the faces of the projecting walls all around the inside of the gateway—sixty cubits. The measurement was up to the portico[z] facing the courtyard.[a] [15]The distance from the entrance of the gateway to the far end of its portico was fifty cubits. [16]The alcoves and the projecting walls inside the gateway were surmounted by narrow parapet openings all around, as was the portico; the openings all around faced inward. The faces of the projecting walls were decorated with palm trees.

*The Outer Court*

[17]Then he brought me into the outer court. There I saw some

x6 Septuagint; Hebrew *deep, the first threshold, one rod deep*
y8,9 Many Hebrew manuscripts, Septuagint, Vulgate and Syriac; most Hebrew manuscripts *gateway facing the temple; it was one rod deep. [9]Then he measured the portico of the gateway; it*
z14 Septuagint; Hebrew *projecting wall*
a14 The meaning of the Hebrew for this verse is uncertain.

°9 ק ואיליו
°15 ק האיתון

וְרִֽצְפָ֔ה עָשׂ֥וּי לֶחָצֵ֖ר סָבִ֣יב ׀ סָבִ֑יב שְׁלֹשִׁ֥ים לְשָׁכ֖וֹת אֶל־
along rooms thirty around around for-the-court being-constructed and-pavement

הָֽרִצְפָֽה׃ וְהָֽרִצְפָה֙ אֶל־כֶּ֣תֶף הַשְּׁעָרִ֔ים לְעֻמַּ֖ת אֹ֣רֶךְ
length-of as-same-as the-gateways side-of at and-the-pavement (18) the-pavement

הַשְּׁעָרִ֑ים הָרִֽצְפָ֖ה הַתַּחְתּוֹנָֽה׃ וַיָּ֣מָד רֹ֡חַב מִלִּפְנֵי֩
from-faces-of distance then-he-measured (19) the-lower the-pavement the-gateways

הַשַּׁ֨עַר הַתַּחְתּוֹנָ֜ה לִפְנֵ֨י הֶחָצֵ֧ר הַפְּנִימִ֛י מִח֖וּץ מֵאָ֣ה אַמָּ֑ה
cubit hundred at-outside the-inner the-court to-faces-of the-lower the-gateway

הַקָּדִ֖ים וְהַצָּפֽוֹן׃ וְהַשַּׁ֗עַר אֲשֶׁ֤ר פָּנָיו֙ דֶּ֣רֶךְ
direction-of faces-of-him that then-the-gate (20) and-the-north the-east

הַצָּפ֔וֹן לֶחָצֵ֖ר הַחִֽיצוֹנָ֑ה מָדַ֥ד אָרְכּ֖וֹ וְרָחְבּֽוֹ׃
and-width-of-him length-of-him he-measured the-outer into-the-court the-north

וְתָאָ֗ו שְׁלוֹשָׁ֤ה מִפּוֹ֙ וּשְׁלֹשָׁ֣ה מִפּ֔וֹ וְאֵלָ֤ו
and-projecting-walls-of-him on-side and-three on-side three and-alcoves-of-him (21)

וְאֵֽלַמָּו֙ הָיָ֔ה כְּמִדַּ֖ת הַשַּׁ֣עַר הָרִאשׁ֑וֹן חֲמִשִּׁ֤ים אַמָּה֙
cubit fifty the-first the-gateway as-measurement-of he-was and-portico-of-him

אָרְכּ֔וֹ וְרֹ֕חַב חָמֵ֥שׁ וְעֶשְׂרִ֖ים בָּאַמָּֽה׃ וְחַלּוֹנָ֤ו
and-openings-of-him (22) by-the-cubit and-twenty five and-width length-of-him

וְאֵֽלַמָּו֙ וְתִֽמֹרָ֔ו כְּמִדַּ֣ת הַשַּׁ֔עַר אֲשֶׁ֥ר פָּנָ֖יו
faces-of-him that the-gate as-measurement-of and-palm-trees-of-him and-portico-of-him

דֶּ֣רֶךְ הַקָּדִ֑ים וּבְמַעֲל֤וֹת שֶׁ֙בַע֙ יַֽעֲלוּ־ב֔וֹ וְאֵילַמָּ֖ו
with-portico-of-him to-him they-went-up seven and-on-steps the-east direction-of

לִפְנֵיהֶֽם׃ וְשַׁ֙עַר֙ לֶחָצֵ֣ר הַפְּנִימִ֔י נֶ֥גֶד הַשַּׁ֖עַר לַצָּפ֣וֹן
on-the-north the-gate facing the-inner to-the-court and-gate (23) opposite-them

וְלַקָּדִ֑ים וַיָּ֧מָד מִשַּׁ֛עַר אֶל־שַׁ֖עַר מֵאָ֥ה אַמָּֽה׃ וַיּוֹלִכֵ֙נִי֙
then-he-led-me (24) cubit hundred gate to from-gate and-he-measured and-on-the-east

דֶּ֣רֶךְ הַדָּר֔וֹם וְהִנֵּה־שַׁ֖עַר דֶּ֣רֶךְ הַדָּר֑וֹם וּמָדַ֤ד
and-he-measured the-south direction-of gate and-see! the-south direction-of

אֵילָו֙ וְאֵֽילַמָּ֔ו כַּמִּדּ֖וֹת הָאֵֽלֶּה׃ וְחַלּוֹנִ֨ים ל֤וֹ
to-him and-openings (25) the-these as-the-measurements and-portico-of-him jambs-of-him

וּלְאֵילַמָּו֙ סָבִ֣יב ׀ סָבִ֔יב כְּהַחַלֹּנ֖וֹת* הָאֵ֑לֶּה חֲמִשִּׁ֤ים אַמָּה֙ אֹ֔רֶךְ
length cubit fifty the-these like-the-openings around around and-to-portico-of-him

וְרֹ֕חַב חָמֵ֥שׁ וְעֶשְׂרִ֖ים אַמָּֽה׃ וּמַעֲל֤וֹת שִׁבְעָה֙ עֹלוֹתָ֔ו
ones-leading-up-to-him seven and-steps (26) cubit and-twenty five and-width

וְאֵלַמָּ֖ו לִפְנֵיהֶ֑ם וְתִמֹרִ֣ים ל֔וֹ אֶחָ֥ד מִפּ֖וֹ וְאֶחָ֥ד מִפּ֖וֹ
on-side and-one on-side one on-him and-palm-trees opposite-them with-portico-of-him

אֶל־אֵילָֽו׃ וְשַׁ֛עַר לֶחָצֵ֥ר הַפְּנִימִ֖י דֶּ֣רֶךְ
direction-of the-inner to-the-court and-gate (27) projecting-walls-of-him on

rooms and a pavement that had been constructed all around the court; there were thirty rooms along the pavement. [18]It abutted the sides of the gateways and was as wide as they were long; this was the lower pavement. [19]Then he measured the distance from the inside of the lower gateway to the outside of the inner court; it was a hundred cubits on the east side as well as on the north.

*The North Gate*

[20]Then he measured the length and width of the gate facing north, leading into the outer court. [21]Its alcoves—three on each side—its projecting walls and its portico had the same measurements as those of the first gateway. It was fifty cubits long and twenty-five cubits wide. [22]Its openings, its portico and its palm tree decorations had the same measurements as those of the gate facing east. Seven steps led up to it, with its portico opposite them. [23]There was a gate to the inner court facing the north gate, just as there was on the east. He measured from one gate to the opposite one; it was a hundred cubits.

*The South Gate*

[24]Then he led me to the south side and I saw a gate facing south. He measured its jambs and its portico, and they had the same measurements as the others. [25]The gateway and its portico had narrow openings all around, like the openings of the others. It was fifty cubits long and twenty-five cubits wide. [26]Seven steps led up to it, with its portico opposite them; it had palm tree decorations on the faces of the projecting walls on each side. [27]The inner court also had a gate facing south, and he

*25 Most mss have *pathah* under the *beth* (כהח־).

°21a ק ותאיו; °21b ק ואיליו
°21c ק ואלמיו; °22a ק וחלוניו
°22b ק ואלמיו; °22c ק ותמריו
°22d ק ואילמיו; °24a ק איליו
°24b ק ואילמיו; °25 ק ולאילמיו
°26a ק עלותיו; °26b ק ואלמיו
°26c ק איליו

הַדָּרוֹם וַיָּמָד מִשַּׁעַר אֶל־הַשַּׁעַר דֶּרֶךְ הַדָּרוֹם מֵאָה
hundred the-south direction-of the-gate to from-gate and-he-measured the-south

אַמּוֹת׃ וַיְבִיאֵנִי אֶל־חָצֵר הַפְּנִימִי בְּשַׁעַר הַדָּרוֹם
the-south through-gate-of the-inner court into then-he-brought-me (28) cubits

וַיָּמָד אֶת־הַשַּׁעַר הַדָּרוֹם כַּמִּדּוֹת הָאֵלֶּה׃
the-these as-the-measurements the-south the-gate *** and-he-measured

וְתָאָו וְאֵלָו וְאֵלַמָּו
and-portico-of-him and-projecting-walls-of-him and-alcoves-of-him (29)

כַּמִּדּוֹת הָאֵלֶּה וְחַלּוֹנוֹת לוֹ וּלְאֵלַמָּו סָבִיב ׀
around and-to-portico-of-him to-him and-openings the-these as-the-measurements

סָבִיב חֲמִשִּׁים אַמָּה אֹרֶךְ וְרֹחַב עֶשְׂרִים וְחָמֵשׁ אַמּוֹת׃ וְאֵלַמּוֹת סָבִיב ׀
around and-porticoes (30) cubits and-five twenty and-width length cubit fifty around

סָבִיב אֹרֶךְ חָמֵשׁ וְעֶשְׂרִים אַמָּה וְרֹחַב חָמֵשׁ אַמּוֹת׃ וְאֵלַמָּו
and-portico-of-him (31) cubits fifty and-depth cubit and-twenty five width around

אֶל־חָצֵר הַחִצֹנָה וְתִמֹרִים אֶל־אֵלָו וּמַעֲלוֹת שְׁמוֹנֶה
eight and-steps jambs-of-him on and-palm-trees the-outer court facing

מַעֲלוֹ׃ וַיְבִיאֵנִי אֶל־הֶחָצֵר הַפְּנִימִי דֶּרֶךְ
direction-of the-inner the-court to then-he-brought-me (32) ones-leading-up-to-him

הַקָּדִים וַיָּמָד אֶת־הַשַּׁעַר כַּמִּדּוֹת הָאֵלֶּה׃
the-these as-the-measurements the-gateway *** and-he-measured the-east

וְתָאָו וְאֵלָו וְאֵלַמָּו
and-portico-of-him and-projecting-walls-of-him and-alcoves-of-him (33)

כַּמִּדּוֹת הָאֵלֶּה וְחַלּוֹנוֹת לוֹ וּלְאֵלַמָּו סָבִיב ׀
around and-to-portico-of-him to-him and-openings the-these as-the-measurements

סָבִיב אֹרֶךְ חֲמִשִּׁים אַמָּה וְרֹחַב חָמֵשׁ וְעֶשְׂרִים אַמָּה׃ וְאֵלַמָּו
and-portico-of-him (34) cubit and-twenty five and-width cubit fifty length around

לֶחָצֵר הַחִיצוֹנָה וְתִמֹרִים אֶל־אֵלָו מִפּוֹ וּמִפּוֹ
and-on-side on-side jambs-of-him on and-palm-trees the-outer facing-the-court

וּשְׁמֹנֶה מַעֲלוֹת מַעֲלוֹ׃ וַיְבִיאֵנִי אֶל־שַׁעַר
gate-of to then-he-brought-me (35) ones-leading-up-to-him steps and-eight

הַצָּפוֹן וּמָדַד כַּמִּדּוֹת הָאֵלֶּה׃ תָּאָו
alcoves-of-him (36) the-these as-the-measurements and-he-measured the-north

אֵלָו וְאֵלַמָּו וְחַלּוֹנוֹת לוֹ סָבִיב ׀ סָבִיב
around around to-him and-openings and-portico-of-him projecting-walls-of-him

אֹרֶךְ חֲמִשִּׁים אַמָּה וְרֹחַב חָמֵשׁ וְעֶשְׂרִים אַמָּה׃ וְאֵילָו
and-jambs-of-him (37) cubit and-twenty five and-width cubit fifty length

לֶחָצֵר הַחִיצוֹנָה וְתִמֹרִים אֶל־אֵילָו מִפּוֹ וּמִפּוֹ
and-on-side on-side jambs-of-him on and-palm-trees the-outer facing-the-court

measured from this gate to the outer gate on the south side; it was a hundred cubits.

*Gates to the Inner Court*

[28]Then he brought me into the inner court through the south gate, and he measured the south gate; it had the same measurements as the others. [29]Its alcoves, its projecting walls and its portico had the same measurements as the others. The gateway and its portico had openings all around. It was fifty cubits long and twenty-five cubits wide. [30](The porticoes of the gateways around the inner court were twenty-five cubits wide and five cubits deep.) [31]Its portico faced the outer court; palm trees decorated its jambs, and eight steps led up to it.

[32]Then he brought me to the inner court on the east side, and he measured the gateway; it had the same measurements as the others. [33]Its alcoves, its projecting walls and its portico had the same measurements as the others. The gateway and its portico had openings all around. It was fifty cubits long and twenty-five cubits wide. [34]Its portico faced the outer court; palm trees decorated the jambs on either side, and eight steps led up to it.

[35]Then he brought me to the north gate and measured it. It had the same measurements as the others, [36]as did its alcoves, its projecting walls and its portico, and it had openings all around. It was fifty cubits long and twenty-five cubits wide. [37]Its portico[b] faced the outer court; palm trees decorated the jambs on either side, and eight

[b]37 Septuagint (see also verses 31 and 34); Hebrew *jambs*

°29a ק ותאיו; °29b ק ואיליו
°29c ק ואלמיו; °29d ק ולאלמיו
°31a ק ואלמיו; °31b ק איליו
°31c ק מעליו; °33a ק ותאיו
°33b ק ואליו; °33c ק ואלמיו
°33d ק ולאלמיו; °34a ק ואלמיו
°34b ק אליו; °34c ק מעליו
°36a ק תאיו; °36b ק אליו
°36c ק ואלמיו; °37a ק ואיליו
°37b ק איליו

וּשְׁמֹנֶה מַעֲלוֹת מַעֲלָו׃ וְלִשְׁכָּה וּפִתְחָהּ בְּאֵילִים
by-porticoes with-doorway-of-her and-room (38) ones-leading-up-to-him steps and-eight

הַשְּׁעָרִים שָׁם יָדִיחוּ אֶת־ הָעֹלָה׃ וּבְאֻלָם
and-in-portico-of (39) the-burnt-offering *** they-washed there the-gateways

הַשַּׁעַר שְׁנַיִם שֻׁלְחָנוֹת מִפּוֹ וּשְׁנַיִם שֻׁלְחָנוֹת מִפֹּה לִשְׁחוֹט אֲלֵיהֶם
on-them to-slaughter on-side tables and-two on-side tables two the-gateway

הָעוֹלָה וְהַחַטָּאת וְהָאָשָׁם׃ וְאֶל־ הַכָּתֵף
the-side and-by (40) and-the-guilt-offering and-the-sin-offering the-burnt-offering

מִחוּצָה לָעוֹלֶה לְפֶתַח הַשַּׁעַר הַצָּפוֹנָה שְׁנַיִם
two to-the-north the-gateway at-entrance-of near-the-one-going-up at-outside

שֻׁלְחָנוֹת וְאֶל־הַכָּתֵף הָאַחֶרֶת אֲשֶׁר לְאֻלָם הַשַּׁעַר שְׁנַיִם שֻׁלְחָנוֹת׃
tables two the-gateway to-portico-of that the-other the-side and-on tables

אַרְבָּעָה שֻׁלְחָנוֹת מִפֹּה וְאַרְבָּעָה שֻׁלְחָנוֹת מִפֹּה לְכֶתֶף הַשַּׁעַר שְׁמוֹנָה
eight the-gateway at-side-of on-side tables and-four on-side tables four (41)

שֻׁלְחָנוֹת אֲלֵיהֶם יִשְׁחָטוּ׃ וְאַרְבָּעָה שֻׁלְחָנוֹת לָעוֹלָה
for-the-burnt-offering tables and-four (42) they-slaughtered on-them tables

אַבְנֵי גָזִית אֹרֶךְ אַמָּה אַחַת וָחֵצִי וְרֹחַב אַמָּה אַחַת וָחֵצִי
and-half one cubit and-width and-half one cubit length one-dressed stones-of

וְגֹבַהּ אַמָּה אֶחָת אֲלֵיהֶם וְיַנִּיחוּ אֶת־ הַכֵּלִים אֲשֶׁר יִשְׁחֲטוּ
they-slaughtered that the-utensils *** and-they-placed on-them one cubit and-height

אֶת־ הָעוֹלָה בָּם וְהַזָּבַח׃ וְהַשְׁפַתַּיִם
and-the-double-pronged-hooks (43) and-the-sacrifice with-them the-burnt-offering ***

טֹפַח אֶחָד מוּכָנִים בַּבַּיִת סָבִיב ׀ סָבִיב וְאֶל־הַשֻּׁלְחָנוֹת
the-tables and-on around around to-the-wall ones-being-attached one handbreadth

בְּשַׂר הַקָּרְבָּן׃ וּמִחוּצָה לַשַּׁעַר הַפְּנִימִי לִשְׁכוֹת שָׁרִים
ones-singing rooms-of the-inner of-the-gate and-at-outside (44) the-offering flesh-of

בֶּחָצֵר הַפְּנִימִי אֲשֶׁר אֶל־כֶּתֶף שַׁעַר הַצָּפוֹן וּפְנֵיהֶם
and-faces-of-them the-north gate-of side-of at which the-inner within-the-court

דֶּרֶךְ הַדָּרוֹם אֶחָד אֶל־כֶּתֶף שַׁעַר הַקָּדִים פְּנֵי דֶּרֶךְ
direction-of faces-of the-east gate-of side-of at one the-south direction-of

הַצָּפֹן׃ וַיְדַבֵּר אֵלַי זֹה הַלִּשְׁכָּה אֲשֶׁר פָּנֶיהָ דֶּרֶךְ
direction-of faces-of-her that the-room this to-me and-he-said (45) the-north

הַדָּרוֹם לַכֹּהֲנִים שֹׁמְרֵי מִשְׁמֶרֶת הַבָּיִת׃
the-temple charge-of ones-being-in-charge-of for-the-priests the-south

וְהַלִּשְׁכָּה אֲשֶׁר פָּנֶיהָ דֶּרֶךְ הַצָּפוֹן לַכֹּהֲנִים
for-the-priests the-north direction-of faces-of-her that and-the-room (46)

שֹׁמְרֵי מִשְׁמֶרֶת הַמִּזְבֵּחַ הֵמָּה בְנֵי־ צָדוֹק הַקְּרֵבִים
the-ones-drawing-near Zadok sons-of these the-altar charge-of ones-being-in-charge-of

steps led up to it.

*The Rooms for Preparing Sacrifices*

[38]A room with a doorway was by the portico in each of the inner gateways, where the burnt offerings were washed. [39]In the portico of the gateway were two tables on each side, on which the burnt offerings, sin offerings and guilt offerings were slaughtered. [40]By the outside wall of the portico of the gateway, near the steps at the entrance to the north gateway were two tables, and on the other side of the steps were two tables. [41]So there were four tables on one side of the gateway and four on the other—eight tables in all—on which the sacrifices were slaughtered. [42]There were also four tables of dressed stone for the burnt offerings, each a cubit and a half long, a cubit and a half wide and a cubit high. On them were placed the utensils for slaughtering the burnt offerings and the other sacrifices. [43]And double-pronged hooks, each a handbreadth long, were attached to the wall all around. The tables were for the flesh of the offerings.

*Rooms for the Priests*

[44]Outside the inner gate, within the inner court, were two rooms, one[c] at the side of the north gate and facing south, and another at the side of the south[d] gate and facing north. [45]He said to me, "The room facing south is for the priests who have charge of the temple, [46]and the room facing north is for the priests who have charge of the altar. These are the sons of Zadok,

[c]44 Septuagint; Hebrew *were rooms for singers, which were*
[d]44 Septuagint; Hebrew *east*

°37 ק מעליו

מִבְּנֵי־ לֵוִי אֶל־יְהוָה לְשָׁרְתוֹ׃ וַיָּמָד אֶת־ הֶחָצֵר
the-court *** then-he-measured (47) to-minister-before-him Yahweh to Levi of-sons-of

אֹרֶךְ ׀ מֵאָה אַמָּה וְרֹחַב מֵאָה אַמָּה מְרֻבָּעַת וְהַמִּזְבֵּחַ לִפְנֵי
in-front-of and-the-altar being-square cubit hundred and-width cubit hundred length

הַבָּיִת׃ וַיְבִאֵנִי אֶל־ אֻלָם הַבַּיִת וַיָּמָד אֵל
jamb-of and-he-measured the-temple portico-of to and-he-brought-me (48) the-temple

אֻלָם חָמֵשׁ אַמּוֹת מִפֹּה וְחָמֵשׁ אַמּוֹת מִפֹּה וְרֹחַב הַשַּׁעַר
the-entrance and-width-of on-side cubits and-five on-side cubits five the-portico

שָׁלֹשׁ אַמּוֹת מִפּוֹ וְשָׁלֹשׁ אַמּוֹת מִפּוֹ׃ אֹרֶךְ הָאֻלָם עֶשְׂרִים אַמָּה
cubit twenty the-portico width-of (49) on-side cubits and-three on-side cubits three

וְרֹחַב עַשְׁתֵּי עֶשְׂרֵה אַמָּה וּבַמַּעֲלוֹת אֲשֶׁר יַעֲלוּ אֵלָיו וְעַמֻּדִים
and-pillars to-him they-reached that and-on-the-stairs cubit ten one-of and-length

אֶל־ הָאֵילִים אֶחָד מִפֹּה וְאֶחָד מִפֹּה׃ וַיְבִיאֵנִי אֶל־
to then-he-brought-me (41:1) on-side and-one on-side one the-jambs beside

הַהֵיכָל וַיָּמָד אֶת־ הָאֵילִים שֵׁשׁ־ אַמּוֹת רֹחַב־ מִפּוֹ
on-side width cubits six the-jambs *** and-he-measured the-outer-sanctuary

וְשֵׁשׁ־ אַמּוֹת־רֹחַב מִפּוֹ רֹחַב הָאֹהֶל׃ וְרֹחַב הַפֶּתַח עֶשֶׂר
ten the-entrance and-width-of (2) the-tent width-of on-side width cubits and-six

אַמּוֹת וְכִתְפוֹת הַפֶּתַח חָמֵשׁ אַמּוֹת מִפּוֹ וְחָמֵשׁ אַמּוֹת
cubits and-five on-side cubits five the-entrance and-projecting-walls-of cubits

מִפּוֹ וַיָּמָד אָרְכּוֹ אַרְבָּעִים אַמָּה וְרֹחַב עֶשְׂרִים אַמָּה׃
cubit twenty and-width cubit forty length-of-him also-he-measured on-side

וּבָא לִפְנִימָה וַיָּמָד אֵיל־ הַפֶּתַח שְׁתַּיִם
two the-entrance jamb-of and-he-measured into-inner-sanctuary then-he-went (3)

אַמּוֹת וְהַפֶּתַח שֵׁשׁ אַמּוֹת וְרֹחַב הַפֶּתַח שֶׁבַע אַמּוֹת׃
cubits seven the-entrance and-width-of cubits six and-the-entrance cubits

וַיָּמָד אֶת־ אָרְכּוֹ עֶשְׂרִים אַמָּה וְרֹחַב עֶשְׂרִים אַמָּה אֶל־
across cubit twenty and-width cubit twenty length-of-him *** and-he-measured (4)

פְּנֵי הַהֵיכָל וַיֹּאמֶר אֵלַי זֶה קֹדֶשׁ הַקֳּדָשִׁים׃
the-Holy-Places Holy-Place-of this to-me and-he-said the-outer-sanctuary ends-of

וַיָּמָד קִיר־ הַבַּיִת שֵׁשׁ אַמּוֹת וְרֹחַב הַצֵּלָע אַרְבַּע
four the-side-room and-width-of cubits six the-temple wall-of then-he-measured (5)

אַמּוֹת סָבִיב ׀ סָבִיב לַבַּיִת סָבִיב׃ וְהַצְּלָעוֹת צֵלָע אֶל־
above side-room and-the-side-rooms (6) around to-the-temple around around cubits

צֵלָע שָׁלוֹשׁ וּשְׁלֹשִׁים פְּעָמִים וּבָאוֹת בַּקִּיר אֲשֶׁר־ לַבַּיִת
of-the-temple that on-the-wall and-ones-going units and-thirty three side-room

לַצְּלָעוֹת סָבִיב ׀ סָבִיב לִהְיוֹת אֲחוּזִים וְלֹא־ יִהְיוּ
they-were so-not ones-being-supported to-serve around around for-the-side-rooms

who are the only Levites who may draw near to the LORD to minister before him."

47 Then he measured the court: It was square—a hundred cubits long and a hundred cubits wide. And the altar was in front of the temple.

*The Temple*

48 He brought me to the portico of the temple and measured the jambs of the portico; they were five cubits wide on either side. The width of the entrance was fourteen cubits and its projecting walls were[e] three cubits wide on either side. 49 The portico was twenty cubits wide, and twelve[f] cubits from front to back. It was reached by a flight of stairs,[g] and there were pillars on each side of the jambs.

**41** Then the man brought me to the outer sanctuary and measured the jambs; the width of the jambs was six cubits[h] on each side.[i] 2 The entrance was ten cubits wide, and the projecting walls on each side of it were five cubits wide. He also measured the outer sanctuary; it was forty cubits long and twenty cubits wide.

3 Then he went into the inner sanctuary and measured the jambs of the entrance; each was two cubits wide. The entrance was six cubits wide, and the projecting walls on each side of it were seven cubits wide. 4 And he measured the length of the inner sanctuary; it was twenty cubits, and its width was twenty cubits across the end of the outer sanctuary. He said to me, "This is the Most Holy Place."

5 Then he measured the wall of the temple; it was six cubits thick, and each side room around the temple was four cubits wide. 6 The side rooms were on three levels, one above another, thirty on each level. There were ledges all around the wall of the temple to serve as supports for the side rooms, so

[e] 48 Septuagint; Hebrew *entrance was*
[f] 49 Septuagint; Hebrew *eleven*
[g] 49 Hebrew; Septuagint *Ten steps led up to it*
[h] 1 The common cubit was about 1 1/2 feet (about 0.5 meter).
[i] 1 One Hebrew manuscript and Septuagint; most Hebrew manuscripts *side, the width of the tent*

אֲחוּזִים בְּקִיר הַבָּיִת׃ וְרָחֲבָה וְנָסְבָה
and-she-went-around and-she-was-wide (7) the-temple into-wall-of ones-being-supported

לְמַעְלָה לְמַעְלָה לַצְּלָעוֹת כִּי מוּסַב־ הַבַּיִת לְמַעְלָה
to-upward the-temple surrounding indeed to-the-side-rooms to-upward to-upward

לְמַעְלָה סָבִיב ׀ סָבִיב לַבַּיִת עַל־ כֵּן רֹחַב־ לַבַּיִת לְמַעְלָה וְכֵן
and-so to-upward to-the-temple width this for to-the-temple around around to-upward

הַתַּחְתּוֹנָה יַעֲלֶה עַל־ הָעֶלְיוֹנָה לַתִּיכוֹנָה׃ וְרָאִיתִי לַבַּיִת
to-the-temple and-I-saw (8) through-the-middle the-top to he-went-up the-low

גֹּבַהּ סָבִיב ׀ סָבִיב מיסדות הַצְּלָעוֹת מְלוֹ הַקָּנֶה
the-rod length-of the-side-rooms foundations-of around around raised-base

שֵׁשׁ אַמּוֹת אַצִּילָה׃ רֹחַב הַקִּיר אֲשֶׁר־ לַצֵּלָע אֶל־ הַחוּץ
the-outside at of-the-side-room that the-wall thickness-of (9) to-length cubits six

חָמֵשׁ אַמּוֹת וַאֲשֶׁר מֻנָּח בֵּית צְלָעוֹת אֲשֶׁר לַבָּיִת׃
of-the-temple that side-rooms between area-being-open and-that cubits five

וּבֵין הַלְּשָׁכוֹת רֹחַב עֶשְׂרִים אַמָּה סָבִיב לַבַּיִת סָבִיב ׀
around to-the-temple around cubit twenty width the-rooms and-between (10)

סָבִיב׃ וּפֶתַח הַצֵּלָע לַמֻּנָּח פֶּתַח אֶחָד
one entrance from-the-area-being-open the-side-room and-entrance-of (11) around

דֶּרֶךְ הַצָּפוֹן וּפֶתַח אֶחָד לַדָּרוֹם וְרֹחַב מְקוֹם
base-of and-width-of on-the-south one and-entrance the-north direction-of

הַמֻּנָּח חָמֵשׁ אַמּוֹת סָבִיב ׀ סָבִיב׃ וְהַבִּנְיָן אֲשֶׁר אֶל־ פְּנֵי
faces-of to that and-the-building (12) around around cubits five the-area-being-open

הַגִּזְרָה פְּאַת דֶּרֶךְ־ הַיָּם רֹחַב שִׁבְעִים אַמָּה וְקִיר
and-wall-of cubit seventy width the-west direction-of corner-of the-temple-courtyard

הַבִּנְיָן חֲמֵשׁ־ אַמּוֹת רֹחַב סָבִיב ׀ סָבִיב וְאָרְכּוֹ תִּשְׁעִים אַמָּה׃
cubit ninety and-length-of-him around around thickness cubits five the-building

וּמָדַד אֶת־ הַבַּיִת אֹרֶךְ מֵאָה אַמָּה וְהַגִּזְרָה
and-the-temple-courtyard cubit hundred length the-temple *** then-he-measured (13)

וְהַבִּנְיָה וְקִירוֹתֶיהָ אֹרֶךְ מֵאָה אַמָּה׃ וְרֹחַב פְּנֵי
faces-of and-width-of (14) cubit hundred length with-walls-of-her and-the-building

הַבַּיִת וְהַגִּזְרָה לַקָּדִים מֵאָה אַמָּה׃ וּמָדַד
then-he-measured (15) cubit hundred on-the-east and-the-temple-courtyard the-temple

אֹרֶךְ־ הַבִּנְיָן אֶל־ פְּנֵי הַגִּזְרָה אֲשֶׁר עַל־ אַחֲרֶיהָ
rears-of-her at that the-temple-courtyard faces-of to the-building length-of

וְאַתּוּקֶיהָא מִפּוֹ וּמִפּוֹ מֵאָה אַמָּה וְהַהֵיכָל
and-the-outer-sanctuary cubit hundred and-on-side* on-side and-galleries-of-her

הַפְּנִימִי וְאֻלַמֵּי הֶחָצֵר׃ הַסִּפִּים וְהַחַלּוֹנִים
and-the-windows the-thresholds (16) the-court and-porticoes-of the-inner

°8 ק מוסדות
°15 ק ואתיקיהא

that the supports were not inserted into the wall of the temple. [7]The side rooms all around the temple were wider at each successive level. The structure surrounding the temple was built in ascending stages, so that the rooms widened as one went upward. A stairway went up from the lowest floor to the top floor through the middle floor.

[8]I saw that the temple had a raised base all around it, forming the foundation of the side rooms. It was the length of the rod, six long cubits. [9]The outer wall of the side rooms was five cubits thick. The open area between the side rooms of the temple [10]and the ⌊priests'⌋ rooms was twenty cubits wide all around the temple. [11]There were entrances to the side rooms from the open area, one on the north and another on the south; and the base adjoining the open area was five cubits wide all around.

[12]The building facing the temple courtyard on the west side was seventy cubits wide. The wall of the building was five cubits thick all around, and its length was ninety cubits.

[13]Then he measured the temple; it was a hundred cubits long, and the temple courtyard and the building with its walls were also a hundred cubits long. [14]The width of the temple courtyard on the east, including the front of the temple, was a hundred cubits.

[15]Then he measured the length of the building facing the courtyard at the rear of the temple, including its galleries on each side; it was a hundred cubits.

The outer sanctuary, the inner sanctuary and the portico facing the court, [16]as well as the thresholds and the narrow windows and

הָאֲטֻמוֹת וְהָאַתִּיקִים ׀ סָבִיב לִשְׁלָשְׁתָּם נֶגֶד הַסַּף
the-threshold beyond to-three-of-them around and-the-galleries the-ones-being-narrow

שְׂחִיף עֵץ סָבִיב ׀ סָבִיב וְהָאָרֶץ עַד־ הַחַלֹּנוֹת וְהַחַלֹּנוֹת
and-the-windows the-windows up-to and-the-floor around around wood covering-of

מְכֻסּוֹת׃ עַל־ מֵעַל הַפֶּתַח וְעַד־ הַבַּיִת הַפְּנִימִי
the-inner the-sanctuary and-to the-entrance at-above in (17) ones-being-covered

וְלַחוּץ וְאֶל־ כָּל־ הַקִּיר סָבִיב ׀ סָבִיב בַּפְּנִימִי וּבַחִיצוֹן
and-on-the-outer on-the-inner around around the-wall all-of and-on and-at-outside

מִדּוֹת׃ וְעָשׂוּי כְּרוּבִים וְתִמֹּרִים וְתִמֹּרָה
and-palm-tree and-palm-trees cherubim and-one-being-carved (18) regular-intervals

בֵּין־ כְּרוּב לִכְרוּב וּשְׁנַיִם פָּנִים לַכְּרוּב׃ וּפְנֵי אָדָם אֶל־
toward man and-faces-of (19) to-the-cherub faces and-two to-cherub cherub between

הַתִּמֹּרָה מִפּוֹ וּפְנֵי־ כְפִיר אֶל־ הַתִּמֹּרָה מִפּוֹ עָשׂוּי
being-carved on-side the-palm-tree toward lion and-faces-of on-side the-palm-tree

אֶל־ כָּל־ הַבַּיִת סָבִיב ׀ סָבִיב׃ מֵהָאָרֶץ עַד־ מֵעַל הַפֶּתַח
the-entrance at-above to from-the-floor (20) around around the-temple whole-of on

הַכְּרוּבִים וְהַתִּמֹּרִים עֲשׂוּיִם וְקִיר הַהֵיכָל׃
the-outer-sancturary and-wall-of ones-being-carved and-the-palm-trees the-cherubim

הַהֵיכָל מְזוּזַת רְבֻעָה וּפְנֵי
and-fronts-of being-rectangular doorframe-of and-the-outer-sanctuary (21)

הַקֹּדֶשׁ הַמַּרְאֶה כַּמַּרְאֶה׃ הַמִּזְבֵּחַ עֵץ
wooden and-the-altar (22) similar-to-the-appearance the-appearance the-Holy-Place

שָׁלוֹשׁ אַמּוֹת גָּבֹהַּ וְאָרְכּוֹ שְׁתַּיִם־ אַמּוֹת וּמִקְצֹעוֹתָיו לוֹ
to-him and-corners-of-him cubits two and-length-of-him height cubits three

וְאָרְכּוֹ וְקִירֹתָיו עֵץ וַיְדַבֵּר אֵלַי זֶה הַשֻּׁלְחָן אֲשֶׁר לִפְנֵי
before that the-table this to-me and-he-said wood and-sides-of-him and-length-of-him

יְהוָה׃ וּשְׁתַּיִם דְּלָתוֹת לַהֵיכָל וְלַקֹּדֶשׁ׃
and-to-the-Holy-Place to-the-outer-sanctuary doors and-double (23) Yahweh

וּשְׁתַּיִם דְּלָתוֹת לַדְּלָתוֹת שְׁתַּיִם מוּסַבּוֹת דְּלָתוֹת שְׁתַּיִם לְדֶלֶת
for-door two leaves ones-being-hinged two to-the-doors leaves and-double (24)

אֶחָת וּשְׁתֵּי דְלָתוֹת לָאַחֶרֶת׃ וַעֲשׂוּיָה אֲלֵיהֶן אֶל־ דַּלְתוֹת
doors-of on on-them and-being-carved (25) for-the-other leaves and-two-of one

הַהֵיכָל כְּרוּבִים וְתִמֹּרִים כַּאֲשֶׁר עֲשׂוּיִם לַקִּירוֹת
on-the-walls ones-being-carved like-that and-palm-trees cherubim the-outer-sanctuary

וְעָב עֵץ אֶל־ פְּנֵי הָאוּלָם מֵהַחוּץ׃ וְחַלּוֹנִים
and-the-windows (26) at-the-outside the-portico fronts-of on wood and-overhang-of

אֲטֻמוֹת וְתִמֹּרִים מִפּוֹ וּמִפּוֹ אֶל־ כִּתְפוֹת הָאוּלָם
the-portico sidewalls-of on and-on-side on-side with-palm-trees ones-being-narrow

galleries around the three of them—everything beyond and including the threshold was covered with wood. The floor, the wall up to the windows, and the windows were covered. [17]In the space above the outside of the entrance to the inner sanctuary and on the walls at regular intervals all around the inner and outer sanctuary [18]were carved cherubim and palm trees. Palm trees alternated with cherubim. Each cherub had two faces: [19]the face of a man toward the palm tree on one side and the face of a lion toward the palm tree on the other. They were carved all around the whole temple. [20]From the floor to the area above the entrance, cherubim and palm trees were carved on the wall of the outer sanctuary.

[21]The outer sanctuary had a rectangular doorframe, and the one at the front of the Most Holy Place was similar. [22]There was a wooden altar three cubits high and two cubits square[k]; its corners, its base[l] and its sides were of wood. The man said to me, "This is the table that is before the LORD." [23]Both the outer sanctuary and the Most Holy Place had double doors. [24]Each door had two leaves—two hinged leaves for each door. [25]And on the doors of the outer sanctuary were carved cherubim and palm trees like those carved on the walls, and there was a wooden overhang on the front of the portico. [26]On the sidewalls of the portico were narrow windows with palm trees carved on each side.

[k]22 Septuagint; Hebrew *long*
[l]22 Septuagint; Hebrew *length*

וְצַלְעוֹת הַבַּיִת וְהָעֻבִּים׃ וַיּוֹצִאֵנִי אֶל־הֶחָצֵר
the-court into then-he-led-me (42:1) also-the-overhangs the-temple and-side-rooms-of

הַחִיצוֹנָה הַדֶּרֶךְ דֶּרֶךְ הַצָּפוֹן וַיְבִאֵנִי אֶל־הַלִּשְׁכָּה אֲשֶׁר
that the-room to and-he-brought-me the-north direction-of the-direction the-outer

נֶגֶד הַגִּזְרָה וַאֲשֶׁר־נֶגֶד הַבִּנְיָן אֶל־הַצָּפוֹן׃
the-north on the-outer-wall opposite and-that the-temple-courtyard opposite

אֶל־פְּנֵי־אֹרֶךְ אַמּוֹת הַמֵּאָה פֶּתַח הַצָּפוֹן וְהָרֹחַב חֲמִשִּׁים
fifty and-the-width the-north door-of the-hundred cubits-of length faces-of to (2)

אַמּוֹת׃ נֶגֶד הָעֶשְׂרִים אֲשֶׁר לֶחָצֵר הַפְּנִימִי וְנֶגֶד רִצְפָה
pavement and-opposite the-inner to-the-court that the-twenty opposite (3) cubits

אֲשֶׁר לֶחָצֵר הַחִיצוֹנָה אַתִּיק אֶל־פְּנֵי־אַתִּיק בַּשְּׁלִשִׁים׃
at-the-three-levels gallery faces-of to gallery the-outer to-the-court that

וְלִפְנֵי הַלְּשָׁכוֹת מַהֲלַךְ עֶשֶׂר אַמּוֹת רֹחַב אֶל־הַפְּנִימִית דֶּרֶךְ
length the-inner at width cubits ten passageway the-rooms and-in-fronts-of (4)

אַמָּה אֶחָת וּפִתְחֵיהֶם לַצָּפוֹן׃ וְהַלְּשָׁכוֹת הָעֶלְיוֹנֹת
the-upper-ones now-the-rooms (5) on-the-north and-doors-of-them one cubit

קְצֻרוֹת כִּי־יוֹכְלוּ אַתִּיקִים מֵהֵנָּה* מֵהַתַּחְתֹּנוֹת
more-than-the-lower-ones from-them galleries they-took-space for ones-being-narrow

וּמֵהַתִּכֹנוֹת בִּנְיָן׃ כִּי מְשֻׁלָּשׁוֹת הֵנָּה וְאֵין
and-there-were-not they ones-being-third for (6) building and-more-than-the-middle-ones

לָהֶן עַמּוּדִים כְּעַמּוּדֵי הַחֲצֵרוֹת עַל־כֵּן נֶאֱצַל מֵהַתַּחְתּוֹנוֹת
more-than-the-lower-ones he-was-small this for the-courts as-pillars-of pillars to-them

וּמֵהַתִּיכֹנוֹת מֵהָאָרֶץ׃ וְגָדֵר אֲשֶׁר־לַחוּץ
to-the-outside that and-wall (7) in-the-floor-space and-more-the-than-middle-ones

לְעֻמַּת הַלְּשָׁכוֹת דֶּרֶךְ הֶחָצֵר הַחִצוֹנָה אֶל־פְּנֵי הַלְּשָׁכוֹת
the-rooms fronts-of to the-outer the-court direction-of the-rooms at-parallel-of

אָרְכּוֹ חֲמִשִּׁים אַמָּה׃ כִּי־אֹרֶךְ הַלְּשָׁכוֹת אֲשֶׁר לֶחָצֵר
by-the-court that the-rooms length-of while (8) cubit fifty extension-of-him

הַחִצוֹנָה חֲמִשִּׁים אַמָּה וְהִנֵּה עַל־פְּנֵי הַהֵיכָל מֵאָה אַמָּה׃
cubit hundred the-outer-sanctuary faces-of at then-see! cubit fifty the-outer

וּמִתַּחַתה ˚לְשָׁכוֹת הָאֵלֶּה הַמֵּבִוֹא מֵהַקָּדִים בְּבֹאוֹ לָהֵנָּה
to-them as-to-enter-him on-the-east the-entrance the-these the-rooms and-at-below (9)

מֵהֶחָצֵר הַחִצֹנָה׃ בְּרֹחַב ׀ גֶּדֶר הֶחָצֵר דֶּרֶךְ
direction-of the-court wall-of along-length-of (10) the-outer from-the-court

הַקָּדִים אֶל־פְּנֵי הַגִּזְרָה וְאֶל־פְּנֵי הַבִּנְיָן לְשָׁכוֹת׃
rooms the-outer-wall faces-of and-at the-temple-courtyard faces-of at the-east

וְדֶרֶךְ לִפְנֵיהֶם כְּמַרְאֵה הַלְּשָׁכוֹת אֲשֶׁר
that the-rooms like-appearance-of in-fronts-of-them and-passageway (11)

The side rooms of the temple also had overhangs.

*Rooms for the Priests*

42 Then the man led me northward into the outer court and brought me to the rooms opposite the temple courtyard and opposite the outer wall on the north side. [2]The building whose door faced north was a hundred cubits[m] long and fifty cubits wide. [3]Both in the section twenty cubits from the inner court and in the section opposite the pavement of the outer court, gallery faced gallery at the three levels. [4]In front of the rooms was an inner passageway ten cubits wide and a hundred cubits[n] long. Their doors were on the north. [5]Now the upper rooms were narrower, for the galleries took more space from them than from the rooms on the lower and middle floors of the building. [6]The rooms on the third floor had no pillars, as the courts had; so they were smaller in floor space than those on the lower and middle floors. [7]There was an outer wall parallel to the rooms and the outer court; it extended in front of the rooms for fifty cubits. [8]While the row of rooms on the side next to the outer court was fifty cubits long, the row on the side nearest the sanctuary was a hundred cubits long. [9]The lower rooms had an entrance on the east side as one enters them from the outer court.

[10]On the south side[o] along the length of the wall of the outer court, adjoining the temple courtyard and opposite the outer wall, were rooms [11]with a passageway in front of them. These were like

[m]2 The common cubit was about 1 1/2 feet (about 0.5 meter).
[n]4 Septuagint and Syriac; Hebrew *and one cubit*
[o]10 Septuagint; Hebrew *Eastward*

*5 Most mss have *dagesh* in the *nun* (־נה).

°9a ק ומתחת הלשכות
°9b ק המביא

דֶּרֶךְ הַצָּפוֹן כְּאָרְכָּן כֵּן רָחְבָּן וְכֹל
with-all-of width-of-them same-as same-as-length-of-them the-north direction-of

מוֹצָאֵיהֶן וּכְמִשְׁפְּטֵיהֶן וּכְפִתְחֵיהֶן׃
and-similar-to-doorways-of-them and-similar-to-dimensions-of-them exits-of-them

וּכְפִתְחֵי הַלְּשָׁכוֹת אֲשֶׁר דֶּרֶךְ הַדָּרוֹם פֶּתַח
doorway the-south direction-of that the-rooms and-similar-to-doorways-of (12)

בְּרֹאשׁ דָּרֶךְ דֶּרֶךְ בִּפְנֵי הַגְּדֶרֶת הֲגִינָה דֶּרֶךְ
extension-of corresponding the-wall to-faces-of passageway passageway at-beginning-of

הַקָּדִים בְּבוֹאָן׃ וַיֹּאמֶר אֵלַי לִשְׁכוֹת הַצָּפוֹן לִשְׁכוֹת
rooms-of the-north rooms-of to-me then-he-said (13) by-to-enter-them the-east

הַדָּרוֹם אֲשֶׁר אֶל־פְּנֵי הַגִּזְרָה הֵנָּה ׀ לִשְׁכוֹת הַקֹּדֶשׁ אֲשֶׁר יֹאכְלוּ־
they-eat where the-holiness rooms-of they the-temple-courtyard faces-of to that the-south

שָׁם הַכֹּהֲנִים אֲשֶׁר־קְרוֹבִים לַיהוָה קָדְשֵׁי הַקֳּדָשִׁים שָׁם
there the-holy-ones holy-ones-of to-Yahweh ones-who-approach who the-priests there

יַנִּיחוּ ׀ קָדְשֵׁי הַקֳּדָשִׁים וְהַמִּנְחָה וְהַחַטָּאת
and-the-sin-offering namely-the-grain-offering the-holy-ones holy-ones-of they-will-put

וְהָאָשָׁם כִּי הַמָּקוֹם קָדֹשׁ׃ בְּבֹאָם הַכֹּהֲנִים וְלֹא־
then-not the-priests when-to-enter-them (14) holy the-place for and-the-guilt-offering

יֵצְאוּ מֵהַקֹּדֶשׁ אֶל־הֶחָצֵר הַחִיצוֹנָה וְשָׁם יַנִּיחוּ
they-must-leave but-there the-outer the-court into from-the-holy-precinct they-must-go

בִגְדֵיהֶם אֲשֶׁר־יְשָׁרְתוּ בָהֶן כִּי־קֹדֶשׁ הֵנָּה יִלְבְּשׁוּ
and-they-must-put-on these holiness for in-them they-minister which garments-of-them

בְּגָדִים אֲחֵרִים וְקָרְבוּ אֶל־אֲשֶׁר לָעָם׃ וְכִלָּה
when-he-finished (15) for-the-people where to then-they-may-go-near other-ones clothes

אֶת־מִדּוֹת הַבַּיִת הַפְּנִימִי וְהוֹצִיאַנִי דֶּרֶךְ הַשַּׁעַר
the-gate direction-of then-he-led-out-me the-inner the-temple measurements-of ***

אֲשֶׁר פָּנָיו דֶּרֶךְ הַקָּדִים וּמְדָדוֹ סָבִיב ׀ סָבִיב׃
around around and-he-measured-him the-east direction-of faces-of-him that

מָדַד רוּחַ הַקָּדִים בִּקְנֵה הַמִּדָּה חֲמֵשׁ־אֲמוֹת קָנִים
rods hundreds five-of the-measure with-rod-of the-east side-of he-measured (16)

בִּקְנֵה הַמִּדָּה סָבִיב׃ מָדַד רוּחַ הַצָּפוֹן חֲמֵשׁ־מֵאוֹת
hundreds five-of the-north side-of he-measured (17) around the-measure by-rod-of

קָנִים בִּקְנֵה הַמִּדָּה סָבִיב׃ אֵת רוּחַ הַדָּרוֹם מָדַד חֲמֵשׁ־
five-of he-measured the-south side-of *** (18) around the-measure by-rod-of rods

מֵאוֹת קָנִים בִּקְנֵה הַמִּדָּה׃ סָבַב אֶל־רוּחַ הַיָּם מָדַד
he-measured the-west side-of to he-turned (19) the-measure by-rod-of rods hundreds

חֲמֵשׁ־מֵאוֹת קָנִים בִּקְנֵה הַמִּדָּה׃ לְאַרְבַּע רוּחוֹת מְדָדוֹ
he-measured-him sides to-four-of (20) the-measure by-rod-of rods hundreds five-of

◦14 ק ולבשו
◦16 ק מאות

the rooms on the north; they had the same length and width, with similar exits and dimensions. Similar to the doorways on the north [12]were the doorways of the rooms on the south. There was a doorway at the beginning of the passageway that was parallel to the corresponding wall extending eastward, by which one enters the rooms.

[13]Then he said to me, "The north and south rooms facing the temple courtyard are the priests' rooms, where the priests who approach the LORD will eat the most holy offerings. There they will put the most holy offerings—the grain offerings, the sin offerings and the guilt offerings—for the place is holy. [14]Once the priests enter the holy precincts, they are not to go into the outer court until they leave behind the garments in which they minister, for these are holy. They are to put on other clothes before they go near the places that are for the people."

[15]When he had finished measuring what was inside the temple area, he led me out by the east gate and measured the area all around: [16]He measured the east side with the measuring rod; it was five hundred cubits.[p] [17]He measured the north side; it was five hundred cubits[q] by the measuring rod. [18]He measured the south side; it was five hundred cubits by the measuring rod. [19]Then he turned to the west side and measured; it was five hundred cubits by the measuring rod. [20]So he measured the area on all four sides. It had a wall

[p]16 See Septuagint of verse 17; Hebrew *rods;* also in verses 18 and 19.
[q]17 Septuagint; Hebrew *rods*

חוֹמָה לוֹ סָבִיב ׀ סָבִיב אֹרֶךְ חֲמֵשׁ מֵאוֹת וְרֹחַב חֲמֵשׁ מֵאוֹת
hundreds five-of and-width hundreds five-of length around around to-him wall

לְהַבְדִּיל בֵּין הַקֹּדֶשׁ לְחֹל׃ וַיּוֹלִכֵנִי אֶל־הַשָּׁעַר שַׁעַר
gate the-gate to then-he-brought-me (43:1) from-common the-holiness between to-separate

אֲשֶׁר פֹּנֶה דֶּרֶךְ הַקָּדִים׃ וְהִנֵּה כְּבוֹד אֱלֹהֵי יִשְׂרָאֵל בָּא
coming Israel God-of glory-of and-see! (2) the-east direction-of facing that

מִדֶּרֶךְ הַקָּדִים וְקוֹלוֹ כְּקוֹל מַיִם רַבִּים
rushing-ones waters like-roar-of and-voice-of-him the-east from-direction-of

וְהָאָרֶץ הֵאִירָה מִכְּבֹדוֹ׃ וּכְמַרְאֵה הַמַּרְאֶה
the-vision and-like-vision-of (3) with-glory-of-him she-was-radiant and-the-land

אֲשֶׁר רָאִיתִי כַּמַּרְאֶה אֲשֶׁר־רָאִיתִי בְּבֹאִי לְשַׁחֵת אֶת־הָעִיר
the-city *** to-destroy when-to-come-me I-saw that like-the-vision I-saw that

וּמַרְאוֹת כַּמַּרְאֶה אֲשֶׁר רָאִיתִי אֶל־נְהַר־כְּבָר וָאֶפֹּל אֶל־פָּנָי׃
faces-of-me to and-I-fell Kebar River-of by I-saw that like-the-vision and-visions

וּכְבוֹד יְהוָה בָּא אֶל־הַבָּיִת דֶּרֶךְ שַׁעַר אֲשֶׁר פָּנָיו
faces-of-him that gate through the-temple into he-entered Yahweh and-glory-of (4)

דֶּרֶךְ הַקָּדִים׃ וַתִּשָּׂאֵנִי רוּחַ וַתְּבִיאֵנִי אֶל־הֶחָצֵר
the-court into and-she-brought-me Spirit then-she-lifted-me (5) the-east direction-of

הַפְּנִימִי וְהִנֵּה מָלֵא כְבוֹד־יְהוָה הַבָּיִת׃ וָאֶשְׁמַע מִדַּבֵּר
one-speaking and-I-heard (6) the-temple Yahweh glory-of he-filled and-see! the-inner

אֵלַי מֵהַבָּיִת וְאִישׁ הָיָה עֹמֵד אֶצְלִי׃ וַיֹּאמֶר אֵלַי
to-me and-he-said (7) beside-me standing he-was while-man from-the-temple to-me

בֶּן־אָדָם אֶת־מְקוֹם כִּסְאִי וְאֶת־מְקוֹם כַּפּוֹת רַגְלַי אֲשֶׁר
where feet-of-me soles-of place-of and throne-of-me place-of *** man son-of

אֶשְׁכָּן־שָׁם בְּתוֹךְ בְּנֵי־יִשְׂרָאֵל לְעוֹלָם וְלֹא יְטַמְּאוּ עוֹד
again will-they-defile and-never to-forever Israel sons-of in-among there I-will-live

בֵית־יִשְׂרָאֵל שֵׁם קָדְשִׁי הֵמָּה וּמַלְכֵיהֶם בִּזְנוּתָם
by-prostitution-of-them or-kings-of-them they holiness-of-me name-of Israel house-of

וּבְפִגְרֵי מַלְכֵיהֶם בָּמוֹתָם׃ בְּתִתָּם
when-to-place-them (8) high-places-of-them kings-of-them and-by-corpses-of

סִפָּם אֶת־סִפִּי וּמְזוּזָתָם אֵצֶל מְזוּזָתִי
doorpost-of-me beside and-doorpost-of-them threshold-of-me next-to threshold-of-them

וְהַקִּיר בֵּינִי וּבֵינֵיהֶם וְטִמְּאוּ ׀ אֶת־שֵׁם קָדְשִׁי
holiness-of-me name-of *** then-they-defiled and-between-them between-me with-the-wall

בְּתוֹעֲבוֹתָם אֲשֶׁר עָשׂוּ וָאֲכַל אֹתָם בְּאַפִּי׃
in-anger-of-me them so-I-destroyed they-did that by-detestable-practices-of-them

עַתָּה יְרַחֲקוּ אֶת־זְנוּתָם וּפִגְרֵי מַלְכֵיהֶם
kings-of-them and-corpses-of prostitution-of-them *** let-them-put-away now (9)

around it, five hundred cubits long and five hundred cubits wide, to separate the holy from the common.

*The Glory Returns to the Temple*

**43** Then the man brought me
to the gate facing east, [2]and
I saw the glory of the God of Israel
coming from the east. His voice
was like the roar of rushing waters,
and the land was radiant
with his glory. [3]The vision I saw
was like the vision I had seen
when he[r] came to destroy the city
and like the visions I had seen by
the Kebar River, and I fell face-down.
[4]The glory of the LORD entered
the temple through the gate
facing east. [5]Then the Spirit lifted
me up and brought me into the
inner court, and the glory of the
LORD filled the temple.
[6]While the man was standing
beside me, I heard someone
speaking to me from inside the
temple. [7]He said: "Son of man,
this is the place of my throne and
the place for the soles of my feet.
This is where I will live among the
Israelites forever. The house of Israel
will never again defile my
holy name—neither they nor their
kings—by their prostitution[s] and
the lifeless idols[t] of their kings at
their high places. [8]When they
placed their threshold next to my
threshold and their doorposts beside
my doorposts, with only a
wall between me and them, they
defiled my holy name by their detestable
practices. So I destroyed
them in my anger. [9]Now let them
put away from me their prostitution
and the lifeless idols of their

[r]3 Some Hebrew manuscripts and Vulgate; most Hebrew manuscripts *I*
[s]7 Or *their spiritual adultery;* also in verse 9
[t]7 Or *the corpses;* also in verse 9

מִמֶּנִּי וְשָׁכַנְתִּי בְתוֹכָם לְעוֹלָם׃ אַתָּה בֶן־אָדָם הַגֵּד
describe! man son-of you (10) to-forever in-among-them and-I-will-live from-me

אֶת־בֵּית־יִשְׂרָאֵל אֶת־הַבַּיִת וְיִכָּלְמוּ מֵעֲוֺנוֹתֵיהֶם
of-sins-of-them that-they-may-be-ashamed the-temple *** Israel house-of to

וּמָדְדוּ אֶת־תָּכְנִית׃ וְאִם־נִכְלְמוּ מִכֹּל אֲשֶׁר־עָשׂוּ
they-did that of-all they-are-ashamed and-if (11) plan *** and-let-them-consider

צוּרַת הַבַּיִת וּתְכוּנָתוֹ וּמוֹצָאָיו וּמוֹבָאָיו
and-entrances-of-him and-exits-of-him even-arrangement-of-him the-temple design-of

וְכָל־צוּרֹתָו וְאֵת כָּל־חֻקֹּתָיו וְכָל־צוּרֹתָי
design-of-him and-whole-of regulations-of-him all-of and design-of-him even-whole-of

וְכָל־תּוֹרֹתָו הוֹדַע אוֹתָם וּכְתֹב לְעֵינֵיהֶם
before-eyes-of-them and-write! them make-known! laws-of-him and-all-of

וְיִשְׁמְרוּ אֶת־כָּל־צוּרָתוֹ וְאֶת־כָּל־חֻקֹּתָיו
regulations-of-him all-of and design-of-him whole-of *** that-they-may-be-faithful

וְעָשׂוּ אוֹתָם׃ זֹאת תּוֹרַת הַבָּיִת עַל־רֹאשׁ הָהָר כָּל־
all-of the-mountain top-of on the-temple law-of this (12) them that-they-may-follow

גְּבֻלוֹ סָבִיב ׀ סָבִיב קֹדֶשׁ קָדָשִׁים הִנֵּה־זֹאת תּוֹרַת הַבָּיִת׃
the-temple law-of such see! holy-ones holy-of surrounding surrounding area-of-him

וְאֵלֶּה מִדּוֹת הַמִּזְבֵּחַ בָּאַמּוֹת אַמָּה אַמָּה וָטֹפַח
and-handbreadth cubit cubit in-the-cubits the-altar measurements-of now-these (13)

וְחֵיק הָאַמָּה וְאַמָּה־רֹחַב וּגְבוּלָהּ אֶל־שְׂפָתָהּ סָבִיב זֶרֶת
span-of around edge-of-her at with-rim-of-her width and-cubit the-cubit now-gutter

הָאֶחָד וְזֶה גַּב הַמִּזְבֵּחַ׃ וּמֵחֵיק הָאָרֶץ עַד־
up-to the-ground and-from-gutter-of (14) the-altar height-of and-this the-one

הָעֲזָרָה הַתַּחְתּוֹנָה שְׁתַּיִם אַמּוֹת וְרֹחַב אַמָּה אֶחָת וּמֵהָעֲזָרָה* הַקְּטַנָּה
the-smaller and-from-the-ledge one cubit and-width cubits two the-lower the-ledge

עַד־הָעֲזָרָה הַגְּדוֹלָה אַרְבַּע אַמּוֹת וְרֹחַב הָאַמָּה׃ וְהַהַרְאֵל
and-the-altar-hearth (15) the-cubit and-height cubits four the-larger the-ledge up-to

אַרְבַּע אַמּוֹת וּמֵהָאֲרִאֵיל וּלְמַעְלָה הַקְּרָנוֹת אַרְבַּע׃ וְהָאֲרִאֵיל
and-the-altar-hearth (16) four the-horns and-to-upward and-from-the-hearth cubits four

שְׁתֵּים עֶשְׂרֵה אֹרֶךְ בִּשְׁתֵּים עֶשְׂרֵה רֹחַב רָבוּעַ אֶל אַרְבַּעַת רְבָעָיו׃
fourths-of-her four-of on being-square width ten by-two length ten two

וְהָעֲזָרָה אַרְבַּע עֶשְׂרֵה אֹרֶךְ בְּאַרְבַּע עֶשְׂרֵה רֹחַב אֶל אַרְבַּעַת רְבָעֶיהָ
fourths-of-him four-of on width ten by-four length ten four and-the-ledge (17)

וְהַגְּבוּל† סָבִיב אוֹתָהּ חֲצִי הָאַמָּה וְהַחֵיק־לָהּ אַמָּה סָבִיב
around cubit to-her and-the-gutter the-cubit half-of her around with-the-rim

וּמַעֲלֹתֵהוּ פְּנוֹת קָדִים׃ וַיֹּאמֶר אֵלַי בֶּן־אָדָם כֹּה אָמַר
he-says this man son-of to-me then-he-said (18) east to-face and-steps-of-him

kings, and I will live among them
forever.
[10]"Son of man, describe the temple to the people of Israel, that
they may be ashamed of their
sins. Let them consider the plan,
[11]and if they are ashamed of all
they have done, make known to
them the design of the temple—its
arrangement, its exits and entrances—its whole design and all
its regulations[u] and laws. Write
these down before them so that
they may be faithful to its design
and follow all its regulations.
[12]"This is the law of the temple:
All the surrounding area on top of
the mountain will be most holy.
Such is the law of the temple.

### *The Altar*

[13]"These are the measurements
of the altar in long cubits, that cubit being a cubit[v] and a handbreadth[w]: Its gutter is a cubit deep
and a cubit wide, with a rim of
one span[x] around the edge. And
this is the height of the altar:
[14]From the gutter on the ground up
to the lower ledge it is two cubits
high and a cubit wide, and from
the smaller ledge up to the larger
ledge it is four cubits high and a
cubit wide. [15]The altar hearth is
four cubits high, and four horns
project upward from the hearth.
[16]The altar hearth is square, twelve
cubits long and twelve cubits
wide. [17]The upper ledge also is
square, fourteen cubits long and
fourteen cubits wide, with a rim
of half a cubit and a gutter of a
cubit all around. The steps of the
altar face east."
[18]Then he said to me, "Son of
man, this is what the Sovereign

[u]*11* Some Hebrew manuscripts and Septuagint; most Hebrew manuscripts *regulations and its whole design*
[v]*13* The common cubit was about 1 1/2 feet (about 0.5 meter).
[w]*13* That is, about 3 inches (about 8 centimeters)
[x]*13* That is, about 9 inches (about 22 centimeters)

**14* Most mss have *qamets* under the *he* (וּמֵהָ').
†*17* Most mss have the accent *telisha parvum* on the final syllable (־בוּל֩).

°*11a* ק צוּרֹתָיו; °*11b* ק צוּרֹתָיו
°*11c* ק תּוֹרֹתָיו; °*15* ק וּמֵהָאֲרִיאֵל
°*16* ק וְהָאֲרִיאֵל

אֲדֹנָי יְהֹוִה אֵלֶּה חֻקּוֹת הַמִּזְבֵּחַ בְּיוֹם הֵעָשׂוֹתוֹ לְהַעֲלוֹת
to-sacrifice to-be-built-him on-day-of the-altar regulations-of these Yahweh Sovereign

עָלָיו עוֹלָה וְלִזְרֹק עָלָיו דָּם׃ וְנָתַתָּה אֶל־
to and-you-must-give (19) blood upon-him and-to-sprinkle burnt-offering upon-him

הַכֹּהֲנִים הַלְוִיִּם אֲשֶׁר הֵם מִזֶּרַע צָדוֹק הַקְּרֹבִים אֵלַי
to-me the-ones-who-come-near Zadok from-family-of they who the-Levites the-priests

נְאֻם אֲדֹנָי יְהֹוִה לְשָׁרְתֵנִי פַּר בֶּן־ בָּקָר
herd young-one-of bull to-minister-before-me Yahweh Sovereign declaration-of

לְחַטָּאת׃ וְלָקַחְתָּ מִדָּמוֹ וְנָתַתָּה עַל־
on and-you-must-put from-blood-of-him and-you-must-take (20) as-sin-offering

אַרְבַּע קַרְנֹתָיו וְאֶל־ אַרְבַּע פִּנּוֹת הָעֲזָרָה וְאֶל־ הַגְּבוּל סָבִיב
around the-rim and-on the-ledge corners-of four-of and-on horns-of-him four-of

וְחִטֵּאתָ אוֹתוֹ וְכִפַּרְתָּהוּ׃ וְלָקַחְתָּ אֵת
*** and-you-must-take (21) and-you-must-make-atonement-for-him him so-you-must-purify

הַפָּר הַחַטָּאת וּשְׂרָפוֹ בְּמִפְקַד הַבַּיִת
the-temple at-designated-part-of and-he-must-burn-him the-sin-offering the-bull

מִחוּץ לַמִּקְדָּשׁ׃ וּבַיּוֹם הַשֵּׁנִי תַּקְרִיב שְׂעִיר־
male-goat-of you-must-offer the-second and-on-the-day (22) of-the-sanctuary at-outside

עִזִּים תָּמִים לְחַטָּאת וְחִטְּאוּ אֶת־ הַמִּזְבֵּחַ כַּאֲשֶׁר
as-that the-altar *** and-they-must-purify for-sin-offering without-defect goats

חִטְּאוּ בַּפָּר׃ בְּכַלּוֹתְךָ מֵחַטֵּא תַּקְרִיב
you-must-offer from-to-purify when-to-finish-you (23) with-the-bull they-purified

פַּר בֶּן־ בָּקָר תָּמִים וְאַיִל מִן־ הַצֹּאן תָּמִים׃
without-defect the-flock from and-ram without-defect herd young-one-of bull

וְהִקְרַבְתָּם לִפְנֵי יְהֹוָה וְהִשְׁלִיכוּ הַכֹּהֲנִים עֲלֵיהֶם
on-them the-priests and-they-must-sprinkle Yahweh before and-you-must-offer-them (24)

מֶלַח וְהֶעֱלוּ אוֹתָם עֹלָה לַיהֹוָה׃ שִׁבְעַת יָמִים
days seven-of (25) to-Yahweh burnt-offering them and-they-must-sacrifice salt

תַּעֲשֶׂה שְׂעִיר־ חַטָּאת לַיּוֹם וּפַר בֶּן־ בָּקָר
herd young-one-of and-bull for-the-day sin-offering male-goat-of you-must-provide

וְאַיִל מִן־ הַצֹּאן תְּמִימִים יַעֲשׂוּ׃ שִׁבְעַת יָמִים
days seven-of (26) they-must-provide ones-without-defect the-flock from and-ram

יְכַפְּרוּ אֶת־ הַמִּזְבֵּחַ וְטִהֲרוּ אֹתוֹ וּמִלְאוּ
so-they-will-dedicate him and-they-must-cleanse the-altar for they-must-make-atonement

יָדָו׃ וִיכַלּוּ אֶת־ הַיָּמִים וְהָיָה בַיּוֹם הַשְּׁמִינִי
the-eighth on-the-day then-he-will-be the-days *** when-they-end (27) hands-of-him

וָהָלְאָה יַעֲשׂוּ הַכֹּהֲנִים עַל־ הַמִּזְבֵּחַ אֶת־ עוֹלוֹתֵיכֶם
burnt-offerings-of-you *** the-altar on the-priests they-must-present and-onwards

LORD says: These will be the regulations for sacrificing burnt offerings and sprinkling blood upon the altar when it is built: [19]You are to give a young bull as a sin offering to the priests, who are Levites, of the family of Zadok, who come near to minister before me, declares the Sovereign LORD. [20]You are to take some of its blood and put it on the four horns of the altar and on the four corners of the upper ledge and all around the rim, and so purify the altar and make atonement for it. [21]You are to take the bull for the sin offering and burn it in the designated part of the temple area outside the sanctuary.

[22]"On the second day you are to offer a male goat without defect for a sin offering, and the altar is to be purified as it was purified with the bull. [23]When you have finished purifying it, you are to offer a young bull and a ram from the flock, both without defect. [24]You are to offer them before the LORD, and the priests are to sprinkle salt on them and sacrifice them as a burnt offering to the LORD.

[25]"For seven days you are to provide a male goat daily for a sin offering; you are also to provide a young bull and a ram from the flock, both without defect. [26]For seven days they are to make atonement for the altar and cleanse it; thus they will dedicate it. [27]At the end of these days, from the eighth day on, the priests are to present your burnt offerings

°26 ק ידיו

וְאֶת־ שַׁלְמֵיכֶם וְרָצֵאתִי אֶתְכֶם נְאֻם אֲדֹנָי יְהוִה׃
Yahweh Sovereign declaration-of you then-I-will-accept fellowship-offerings-of-you and

וַיָּשֶׁב אֹתִי דֶּרֶךְ שַׁעַר הַמִּקְדָּשׁ הַחִיצוֹן הַפֹּנֶה
the-one-facing the-outer the-sanctuary gate-of direction-of me then-he-brought (44:1)

קָדִים וְהוּא סָגוּר׃ וַיֹּאמֶר אֵלַי יְהוָה הַשַּׁעַר הַזֶּה סָגוּר
being-shut the-this the-gate Yahweh to-me and-he-said (2) being-shut and-he east

יִהְיֶה לֹא יִפָּתֵחַ וְאִישׁ לֹא־ יָבֹא בוֹ כִּי
because through-him he-may-enter not and-anyone he-must-be-opened not he-must-remain

יְהוָה אֱלֹהֵי־יִשְׂרָאֵל בָּא בוֹ וְהָיָה סָגוּר׃ אֶת־
*** (3) being-shut so-he-must-remain through-him he-entered Israel God-of Yahweh

הַנָּשִׂיא נָשִׂיא הוּא יֵשֶׁב־ בּוֹ לֶאֱכוֹל־לֶחֶם לִפְנֵי יְהוָה
Yahweh in-presences-of food to-eat inside-him he-may-sit he prince the-prince

מִדֶּרֶךְ אֻלָם הַשַּׁעַר יָבוֹא וּמִדַּרְכּוֹ יֵצֵא׃
he-must-go-out and-by-way-of-him he-must-enter the-gateway portico-of by-way-of

וַיְבִיאֵנִי דֶּרֶךְ־ שַׁעַר הַצָּפוֹן אֶל־ פְּנֵי הַבַּיִת וָאֵרֶא
and-I-looked the-temple fronts-of to the-north gate-of way-of then-he-brought-me (4)

וְהִנֵּה מָלֵא כְבוֹד־ יְהוָה אֶת־ בֵּית יְהוָה וָאֶפֹּל אֶל־ פָּנָי׃
faces-of-me to and-I-fell Yahweh temple-of *** Yahweh glory-of he-filled and-see!

וַיֹּאמֶר אֵלַי יְהוָה בֶּן־ אָדָם שִׂים לִבְּךָ וּרְאֵה
and-look! heart-of-you make-attentive! man son-of Yahweh to-me and-he-said (5)

בְעֵינֶיךָ וּבְאָזְנֶיךָ שְׁמָע אֵת כָּל־ אֲשֶׁר אֲנִי מְדַבֵּר אֹתָךְ
you telling I that everything *** listen! and-with-ears-of-you with-eyes-of-you

לְכָל־ חֻקּוֹת בֵּית־ יְהוָה וּלְכָל־ תּוֹרֹתָו
laws-of-him and-concerning-all-of Yahweh temple-of regulations-of concerning-all-of

וְשַׂמְתָּ לִבְּךָ לִמְבוֹא הַבַּיִת בְּכֹל מוֹצָאֵי
exits-of to-all-of the-temple to-entrance-of heart-of-you so-you-make-attentive

הַמִּקְדָּשׁ׃ וְאָמַרְתָּ אֶל־ מֶרִי אֶל־ בֵּית יִשְׂרָאֵל כֹּה אָמַר
he-says this Israel house-of to rebellious to and-you-say (6) the-sanctuary

אֲדֹנָי יְהוִה רַב־ לָכֶם מִכָּל־ תּוֹעֲבוֹתֵיכֶם בֵּית
house-of detestable-practices-of-you of-all-of to-you enough Yahweh Sovereign

יִשְׂרָאֵל׃ בַּהֲבִיאֲכֶם בְּנֵי־ נֵכָר עַרְלֵי־ לֵב
heart ones-uncircumcised-of foreigner sons-of because-to-bring-you (7) Israel

וְעַרְלֵי בָשָׂר לִהְיוֹת בְּמִקְדָּשִׁי לְחַלְּלוֹ אֶת־
*** to-desecrate-him in-sanctuary-of-me to-be flesh and-ones-uncircumcised-of

בֵּיתִי בְּהַקְרִיבְכֶם אֶת־ לַחְמִי חֵלֶב וָדָם וַיָּפֵרוּ אֶת־
*** and-they-broke and-blood fat food-of-me *** while-to-offer-you temple-of-me

בְּרִיתִי אֶל כָּל־ תּוֹעֲבוֹתֵיכֶם׃ וְלֹא שְׁמַרְתֶּם
you-carried-out and-not (8) detestable-practices-of-you all-of by covenant-of-me

and fellowship offerings[y] on the altar. Then I will accept you, declares the Sovereign LORD."

*The Prince, the Levites, the Priests*

44 Then the man brought me back to the outer gate of the sanctuary, the one facing east, and
it was shut. 2The LORD said to me,
"This gate is to remain shut. It must not be opened; no one may enter through it. It is to remain shut because the LORD, the God of
Israel, has entered through it. 3The
prince himself is the only one who may sit inside the gateway to eat in the presence of the LORD. He is to enter by way of the portico of the gateway and go out the same way."
4Then the man brought me by way of the north gate to the front of the temple. I looked and saw the glory of the LORD filling the temple of the LORD, and I fell facedown.
5The LORD said to me, "Son of man, look carefully, listen closely and give attention to everything I tell you concerning all the regulations regarding the temple of the LORD. Give attention to the entrance of the temple and all the exits of the sanctuary. 6Say to the
rebellious house of Israel, 'This is what the Sovereign LORD says: Enough of your detestable practices, O house of Israel! 7In addi-
tion to all your other detestable practices, you brought foreigners uncircumcised in heart and flesh into my sanctuary, desecrating my temple while you offered me food, fat and blood, and you broke
my covenant. 8Instead of carrying

y27 Traditionally *peace offerings*

°3 ק לאכל
°5 ק תורתיו

מִשְׁמֶרֶת קָדָשַׁי וַתְּשִׂימוּן לְשֹׁמְרֵי מִשְׁמַרְתִּי
duty-of-me as-ones-being-in-charge-of but-you-put holy-things-of-me duty-of

בְּמִקְדָּשִׁי לָכֶם׃ כֹּה־אָמַר אֲדֹנָי יְהוִה כָּל־בֶּן־
son-of any-of Yahweh Sovereign he-says this (9) for-you over-sanctuary-of-me

נֵכָר עֶרֶל לֵב וְעֶרֶל בָּשָׂר לֹא יָבוֹא אֶל־
into he-may-enter not flesh and-uncircumcised-of heart uncircumcised-of foreigner

מִקְדָּשִׁי לְכָל־בֶּן־נֵכָר אֲשֶׁר בְּתוֹךְ בְּנֵי יִשְׂרָאֵל׃ כִּי
indeed (10) Israel sons-of in-among who foreigner son-of even-any-of sanctuary-of-me

אִם־הַלְוִיִּם אֲשֶׁר רָחֲקוּ מֵעָלַי בִּתְעוֹת יִשְׂרָאֵל אֲשֶׁר
who Israel when-to-go-astray from-with-me they-went-far who the-Levites even

תָּעוּ מֵעָלַי אַחֲרֵי גִּלּוּלֵיהֶם וְנָשְׂאוּ עֲוֺנָם׃
sin-of-them now-they-must-bear idols-of-them after from-with-me they-wandered

וְהָיוּ בְמִקְדָּשִׁי מְשָׁרְתִים פְּקֻדּוֹת אֶל־
of ones-who-have-charge ones-serving in-sanctuary-of-me and-they-may-be (11)

שַׁעֲרֵי הַבַּיִת וּמְשָׁרְתִים אֶת־הַבַּיִת הֵמָּה יִשְׁחֲטוּ אֶת־
*** they-may-slaughter they the-temple in and-ones-serving the-temple gates-of

הָעֹלָה וְאֶת־הַזֶּבַח לָעָם וְהֵמָּה יַעַמְדוּ
they-may-stand and-they for-the-people the-sacrifice and the-burnt-offering

לִפְנֵיהֶם לְשָׁרְתָם׃ יַעַן אֲשֶׁר יְשָׁרְתוּ אוֹתָם לִפְנֵי
in-presences-of them they-served that because (12) to-serve-them before-them

גִלּוּלֵיהֶם וְהָיוּ לְבֵית־יִשְׂרָאֵל לְמִכְשׁוֹל עָוֺן
sin as-one-who-makes-fall-into Israel to-house-of and-they-were idols-of-them

עַל־כֵּן נָשָׂאתִי יָדִי עֲלֵיהֶם נְאֻם אֲדֹנָי יְהוִה
Yahweh Sovereign declaration-of against-them hand-of-me I-lifted this for

וְנָשְׂאוּ עֲוֺנָם׃ וְלֹא־יִגְּשׁוּ אֵלַי
to-me they-must-come-near and-not (13) sin-of-them that-they-must-bear

לְכַהֵן לִי וְלָגֶשֶׁת עַל־כָּל־קָדָשַׁי אֶל־קָדְשֵׁי
holy-ones-of to holy-things-of-me any-of to or-to-come-near to-me to-serve-as-priest

הַקְּדָשִׁים וְנָשְׂאוּ כְּלִמָּתָם וְתוֹעֲבוֹתָם אֲשֶׁר
that and-detestable-practices-of-them shame-of-them but-they-must-bear the-holy-ones

עָשׂוּ׃ וְנָתַתִּי אוֹתָם שֹׁמְרֵי מִשְׁמֶרֶת הַבָּיִת
the-temple duty-of ones-being-in-charge-of them yet-I-will-put (14) they-did

לְכֹל עֲבֹדָתוֹ וּלְכֹל אֲשֶׁר יֵעָשֶׂה בּוֹ׃ וְהַכֹּהֲנִים
but-the-priests (15) in-him he-must-be-done that and-of-all work-of-him of-all-of

הַלְוִיִּם בְּנֵי צָדוֹק אֲשֶׁר שָׁמְרוּ אֶת־מִשְׁמֶרֶת מִקְדָּשִׁי
sanctuary-of-me duty-of *** they-carried-out who Zadok descendants-of the-Levites

בִּתְעוֹת בְּנֵי־יִשְׂרָאֵל מֵעָלַי הֵמָּה יִקְרְבוּ אֵלַי
to-me they-must-come-near they from-with-me Israel sons-of when-to-go-astray

out your duty in regard to my holy things, you put others in charge of my sanctuary. 9This is what the Sovereign LORD says: No foreigner uncircumcised in heart and flesh is to enter my sanctuary, not even the foreigners who live among the Israelites.

10" 'The Levites who went far from me when Israel went astray and who wandered from me after their idols must bear the consequences of their sin. 11They may serve in my sanctuary, having charge of the gates of the temple and serving in it; they may slaughter the burnt offerings and sacrifices for the people and stand before the people and serve them. 12But because they served them in the presence of their idols and made the house of Israel fall into sin, therefore I have sworn with uplifted hand that they must bear the consequences of their sin, declares the Sovereign LORD. 13They are not to come near to serve me as priests or come near any of my holy things or my most holy offerings; they must bear the shame of their detestable practices. 14Yet I will put them in charge of the duties of the temple and all the work that is to be done in it.

15" 'But the priests, who are Levites and descendants of Zadok and who faithfully carried out the duties of my sanctuary when the Israelites went astray from me, are to come near to minister before

לְשָׁרְתֵנִי וְעָמְדוּ לְפָנַי לְהַקְרִיב לִי חֵלֶב

fat to-me to-offer-sacrifice before-me and-they-must-stand to-minister-before-me

וָדָם נְאֻם אֲדֹנָי יְהוִה׃ הֵמָּה יָבֹאוּ אֶל־

into they-may-enter they (16) Yahweh Sovereign declaration-of and-blood

מִקְדָּשִׁי וְהֵמָּה יִקְרְבוּ אֶל־ שֻׁלְחָנִי לְשָׁרְתֵנִי

to-minister-before-me table-of-me to they-may-come-near and-they sanctuary-of-me

וְשָׁמְרוּ אֶת־ מִשְׁמַרְתִּי׃ וְהָיָה בְּבוֹאָם אֶל־

into when-to-enter-them and-he-will-be (17) service-of-me *** and-they-may-perform

שַׁעֲרֵי הֶחָצֵר הַפְּנִימִית בִּגְדֵי פִשְׁתִּים יִלְבָּשׁוּ וְלֹא־ יַעֲלֶה

he-may-put and-not they-must-wear linens clothes-of the-inner the-court gates-of

עֲלֵיהֶם צֶמֶר בְּשָׁרְתָם בְּשַׁעֲרֵי הֶחָצֵר הַפְּנִימִית וָבָיְתָה׃

or-inside-temple the-inner the-court at-gates-of while-to-minister-them wool on-them

פַּאֲרֵי פִשְׁתִּים יִהְיוּ עַל־ רֹאשָׁם וּמִכְנְסֵי פִשְׁתִּים

linens and-undergarments-of head-of-them on they-must-be linens turbans-of (18)

יִהְיוּ עַל־ מָתְנֵיהֶם לֹא יַחְגְּרוּ בַּיָּזַע׃

to-the-perspiration they-must-wear not waists-of-them around they-must-be

וּבְצֵאתָם אֶל־ הֶחָצֵר הַחִיצוֹנָה אֶל־ הֶחָצֵר הַחִיצוֹנָה

the-outer the-court into the-outer the-court into and-when-to-go-out-them (19)

אֶל־ הָעָם יִפְשְׁטוּ אֶת־ בִּגְדֵיהֶם אֲשֶׁר־הֵמָּה מְשָׁרְתִם

ones-ministering they that clothes-of-them *** they-must-take-off the-people to

בָּם וְהִנִּיחוּ אוֹתָם בְּלִשְׁכֹת הַקֹּדֶשׁ וְלָבְשׁוּ

and-they-must-put-on the-sacredness in-rooms-of them and-they-must-leave in-them

בְּגָדִים אֲחֵרִים וְלֹא־ יְקַדְּשׁוּ אֶת־ הָעָם בְּבִגְדֵיהֶם׃

by-garments-of-them the-people *** they-consecrate so-not other-ones clothes

וְרֹאשָׁם לֹא יְגַלֵּחוּ וּפֶרַע לֹא יְשַׁלֵּחוּ כָּסוֹם

to-trim they-must-let-grow not or-long-hair they-must-shave not and-head-of-them (20)

יִכְסְמוּ אֶת־ רָאשֵׁיהֶם׃ וְיַיִן לֹא־ יִשְׁתּוּ כָּל־ כֹּהֵן

priest any-of they-must-drink not and-wine (21) heads-of-them *** they-must-trim

בְּבוֹאָם אֶל־ הֶחָצֵר הַפְּנִימִית׃ וְאַלְמָנָה וּגְרוּשָׁה

or-one-being-divorced and-widow (22) the-inner the-court into when-to-enter-them

לֹא־ יִקְחוּ לָהֶם לְנָשִׁים כִּי אִם־בְּתוּלֹת מִזֶּרַע בֵּית

house-of from-descendant-of virgins only but as-wives for-them they-must-marry not

יִשְׂרָאֵל וְהָאַלְמָנָה אֲשֶׁר תִּהְיֶה אַלְמָנָה מִכֹּהֵן יִקָּחוּ׃ וְאֶת־ עַמִּי

people-of-me and (23) they-may-marry of-priest widow she-is who or-the-widow Israel

יוֹרוּ בֵּין קֹדֶשׁ לְחֹל וּבֵין־ טָמֵא לְטָהוֹר

from-clean unclean and-between from-common holiness between they-must-teach

יוֹדִעֻם׃ וְעַל־ רִיב הֵמָּה יַעַמְדוּ

they-must-serve they dispute and-in (24) they-must-show-distinguishing-to-them

me; they are to stand before me to offer sacrifices of fat and blood, declares the Sovereign LORD.
16 They alone are to enter my sanctuary; they alone are to come near my table to minister before me and perform my service.

17 "'When they enter the gates of the inner court, they are to wear linen clothes; they must not wear any woolen garment while ministering at the gates of the inner court or inside the temple.
18 They are to wear linen turbans on their heads and linen undergarments around their waists. They must not wear anything that makes them perspire.
19 When they go out into the outer court where the people are, they are to take off the clothes they have been ministering in and are to leave them in the sacred rooms, and put on other clothes, so that they do not consecrate the people by means of their garments.

20 "'They must not shave their heads or let their hair grow long, but they are to keep the hair of their heads trimmed.
21 No priest is to drink wine when he enters the inner court.
22 They must not marry widows or divorced women; they may marry only virgins of Israelite descent or widows of priests.
23 They are to teach my people the difference between the holy and the common and show them how to distinguish between the unclean and the clean.

24 "'In any dispute, the priests

לִשְׁפֹּט בְּמִשְׁפָּטַי וּשְׁפָטֻהוּ וְאֶת־ תּוֹרֹתַי וְאֶת־
and laws-of-me and they-must-decide-him according-to-ordinances-of-me for-judgment

חֻקֹּתַי בְּכָל־ מוֹעֲדַי יִשְׁמֹרוּ וְאֶת־ שַׁבְּתוֹתַי
Sabbaths-of-me and they-must-keep appointed-feasts-of-me for-all-of decrees-of-me

יְקַדֵּשׁוּ׃ וְאֶל־ מֵת אָדָם לֹא יָבוֹא לְטָמְאָה
to-be-defiled he-must-go not person one-being-dead and-near (25) they-must-keep-holy

כִּי אִם־ לְאָב וּלְאֵם וּלְבֵן וּלְבַת לְאָח וּלְאָחוֹת
or-by-sister by-brother or-by-daughter or-by-son or-by-mother by-father if however

אֲשֶׁר־לֹא־הָיְתָה לְאִישׁ יִטַּמָּאוּ׃ וְאַחֲרֵי טָהֳרָתוֹ
cleansing-of-him and-after (26) they-may-defile-themselves to-husband she-was not who

שִׁבְעַת יָמִים יִסְפְּרוּ־ לוֹ׃ וּבְיוֹם בֹּאוֹ אֶל־
into to-go-him and-on-day-of (27) for-him they-must-count days seven-of

הַקֹּדֶשׁ אֶל־ הֶחָצֵר הַפְּנִימִית לְשָׁרֵת בַּקֹּדֶשׁ יַקְרִיב
he-must-offer in-the-sanctuary to-minister the-inner the-court into the-sanctuary

חַטָּאתוֹ נְאֻם אֲדֹנָי יְהוִה׃ וְהָיְתָה לָהֶם
to-them and-she-will-be (28) Yahweh Sovereign declaration-of sin-offering-of-him

לְנַחֲלָה אֲנִי נַחֲלָתָם וַאֲחֻזָּה לֹא־ תִתְּנוּ לָהֶם
to-them you-must-give not and-possession inheritance-of-them I for-inheritance

בְּיִשְׂרָאֵל אֲנִי אֲחֻזָּתָם׃ הַמִּנְחָה וְהַחַטָּאת
and-the-sin-offering the-grain-offering (29) possession-of-them I in-Israel

וְהָאָשָׁם הֵמָּה יֹאכְלוּם וְכָל־ חֵרֶם בְּיִשְׂרָאֵל
in-Israel devoted-thing and-every-of they-will-eat-them they and-the-guilt-offering

לָהֶם יִהְיֶה׃ וְרֵאשִׁית כָּל־ בִּכּוּרֵי כֹל וְכָל־
and-all-of all firstfruits-of all-of and-best-of (30) he-will-be to-them

תְּרוּמַת כֹּל מִכֹּל תְּרוּמוֹתֵיכֶם לַכֹּהֲנִים יִהְיֶה
he-will-be to-the-priests special-gifts-of-you from-all-of all special-gift-of

וְרֵאשִׁית עֲרִסוֹתֵיכֶם תִּתְּנוּ לַכֹּהֵן לְהָנִיחַ בְּרָכָה
blessing to-make-rest to-the-priest you-must-give ground-meals-of-you and-first-of

אֶל־ בֵּיתֶךָ׃ כָּל־ נְבֵלָה וּטְרֵפָה מִן־ הָעוֹף וּמִן־
or-from the-bird from or-torn-animal dead-animal any-of (31) household-of-you on

הַבְּהֵמָה לֹא יֹאכְלוּ הַכֹּהֲנִים׃ וּבְהַפִּילְכֶם אֶת־הָאָרֶץ
the-land *** and-when-to-allot-you (45:1) the-priests they-must-eat not the-animal

בְּנַחֲלָה תָּרִימוּ תְרוּמָה לַיהוָה ׀ קֹדֶשׁ מִן־ הָאָרֶץ
the-land from sacred-district to-Yahweh portion you-must-present as-inheritance

אֹרֶךְ חֲמִשָּׁה וְעֶשְׂרִים אֶלֶף אֹרֶךְ וְרֹחַב עֲשָׂרָה אֶלֶף קֹדֶשׁ־הוּא בְּכָל־
in-entire-of he holy thousand ten and-width length thousand and-twenty five length

גְּבוּלָהּ סָבִיב׃ יִהְיֶה מִזֶּה אֶל־ הַקֹּדֶשׁ חֲמֵשׁ מֵאוֹת
hundreds five-of the-sanctuary for of-this he-must-be (2) around area-of-her

°24a ק למשפט
°24b ק ישפטהו

are to serve as judges and decide it according to my ordinances. They are to keep my laws and my decrees for all my appointed feasts, and they are to keep my Sabbaths holy.

25" 'A priest must not defile himself by going near a dead person; however, if the dead person was his father or mother, son or daughter, brother or unmarried sister, then he may defile himself. 26After he is cleansed, he must wait seven days. 27On the day he goes into the inner court of the sanctuary to minister in the sanctuary, he is to offer a sin offering for himself, declares the Sovereign LORD.

28" 'I am to be the only inheritance the priests have. You are to give them no possession in Israel; I will be their possession. 29They will eat the grain offerings, the sin offerings and the guilt offerings; and everything in Israel devoted[z] to the LORD will belong to them. 30The best of all the firstfruits and of all your special gifts will belong to the priests. You are to give them the first portion of your ground meal so that a blessing may rest on your household. 31The priests must not eat anything, bird or animal, found dead or torn by wild animals.

*Division of the Land*

45 " 'When you allot the land as an inheritance, you are to present to the LORD a portion of the land as a sacred district, 25,000 cubits long and 20,000[a] cubits wide; the entire area will be holy. 2Of this, a section 500 cubits square is to be for the sanctuary,

z29 The Hebrew term refers to the irrevocable giving over of things or persons to the LORD.
a1 Septuagint (see also verses 3 and 5 and 48:9); Hebrew *10,000*

בַּחֲמֵשׁ מֵאוֹת מְרֻבָּע סָבִיב וַחֲמִשִּׁים אַמָּה מִגְרָשׁ לוֹ סָבִיב׃
around for-him open-land cubit with-fifty around being-square hundreds by-five-of

(3) וּמִן־ הַמִּדָּה הַזֹּאת תָּמוֹד אֹרֶךְ חֲמֵשׁ וְעֶשְׂרִים אֶלֶף
thousand and-twenty five length you-measure-off the-this the-district and-in (3)

וְרֹחַב עֲשֶׂרֶת אֲלָפִים וּבוֹ־ יִהְיֶה הַמִּקְדָּשׁ קֹדֶשׁ
Holy-Place-of the-sanctuary he-will-be and-in-him thousands ten-of and-width

קָדָשִׁים׃ (4) קֹדֶשׁ מִן־ הָאָרֶץ הוּא לַכֹּהֲנִים מְשָׁרְתֵי
ones-ministering-of for-the-priests he the-land from sacred-portion (4) Holy-Places

הַמִּקְדָּשׁ יִהְיֶה הַקְּרֵבִים לְשָׁרֵת אֶת־ יְהוָה
Yahweh before to-minister the-ones-who-draw-near he-will-be the-sanctuary

וְהָיָה לָהֶם מָקוֹם לְבָתִּים וּמִקְדָּשׁ לַמִּקְדָּשׁ׃ (5) וַחֲמִשָּׁה
and-five (5) for-the-sanctuary and-holy-place for-houses place for-them and-he-will-be

וְעֶשְׂרִים אֶלֶף אֹרֶךְ וַעֲשֶׂרֶת אֲלָפִים רֹחַב יִהְיֶה לַלְוִיִּם
to-the-Levites and-he-will-be width thousands and-ten-of length thousand and-twenty

מְשָׁרְתֵי הַבַּיִת לָהֶם לַאֲחֻזָּה עֶשְׂרִים לְשָׁכֹת׃ (6) וַאֲחֻזַּת
and-property-of (6) rooms twenty as-possession for-them the-temple ones-serving-of

הָעִיר תִּתְּנוּ חֲמֵשֶׁת אֲלָפִים רֹחַב וְאֹרֶךְ חֲמִשָּׁה וְעֶשְׂרִים אֶלֶף
thousand and-twenty five and-length width thousands five-of you-must-give the-city

לְעֻמַּת תְּרוּמַת הַקֹּדֶשׁ לְכָל־ בֵּית יִשְׂרָאֵל יִהְיֶה׃
he-will-be Israel house-of to-whole-of the-sacredness portion-of at-adjoining-of

(7) וְלַנָּשִׂיא מִזֶּה וּמִזֶּה לִתְרוּמַת הַקֹּדֶשׁ
the-sacredness of-district-of and-on-side on-side and-to-the-prince (7)

וְלַאֲחֻזַּת הָעִיר אֶל־ פְּנֵי תְרוּמַת־ הַקֹּדֶשׁ וְאֶל־ פְּנֵי
faces-of and-to the-sacredness district-of faces-of to the-city and-of-property-of

אֲחֻזַּת הָעִיר מִפְּאַת־ יָם יָמָּה וּמִפְּאַת־ קֵדְמָה קָדִימָה
eastward eastward and-from-side-of westward west from-side-of the-city property-of

וְאֹרֶךְ לְעֻמּוֹת אַחַד הַחֲלָקִים מִגְּבוּל יָם אֶל־
to west from-border-of the-tribal-portions one-of at-parallels-of and-length

גְּבוּל קָדִימָה׃ (8) לָאָרֶץ יִהְיֶה־ לּוֹ לַאֲחֻזָּה בְּיִשְׂרָאֵל
in-Israel for-possession for-him he-will-be to-the-land (8) to-east border-of

וְלֹא־ יוֹנוּ עוֹד נְשִׂיאַי אֶת־ עַמִּי וְהָאָרֶץ
but-the-land people-of-me *** princes-of-me longer they-will-oppress and-not

יִתְּנוּ לְבֵית־ יִשְׂרָאֵל לְשִׁבְטֵיהֶם׃ (9) כֹּה־ אָמַר
he-says this (9) according-to-tribes-of-them Israel to-house-of they-will-allow

אֲדֹנָי יְהוִה רַב־ לָכֶם נְשִׂיאֵי יִשְׂרָאֵל חָמָס וָשֹׁד הָסִירוּ
give-up! and-oppression violence Israel princes-of to-you enough Yahweh Sovereign

וּמִשְׁפָּט וּצְדָקָה עֲשׂוּ הָרִימוּ גְרֻשֹׁתֵיכֶם מֵעַל עַמִּי
people-of-me from-against dispossessions-of-you stop! do! and-right and-justice

with 50 cubits around it for open land. 3In the sacred district, measure off a section 25,000 cubits[b] long and 10,000 cubits[c] wide. In it will be the sanctuary, the Most Holy Place. 4It will be the sacred portion of the land for the priests, who minister in the sanctuary and who draw near to minister before the LORD. It will be a place for their houses as well as a holy place for the sanctuary. 5An area 25,000 cubits long and 10,000 cubits wide will belong to the Levites, who serve in the temple, as their possession for towns to live in.[d]

6"'You are to give the city as its property an area 5,000 cubits wide and 25,000 cubits long, adjoining the sacred portion; it will belong to the whole house of Israel.

7"'The prince will have the land bordering each side of the area formed by the sacred district and the property of the city. It will extend westward from the west side and eastward from the east side, running lengthwise from the western to the eastern border parallel to one of the tribal portions. 8This land will be his possession in Israel. And my princes will no longer oppress my people but will allow the house of Israel to possess the land according to their tribes.

9"'This is what the Sovereign LORD says: You have gone far enough, O princes of Israel! Give up your violence and oppression and do what is just and right. Stop dispossessing my people, declares

b3 That is, about 7 miles (about 12 kilometers)
c3 That is, about 3 miles (about 5 kilometers)
d5 Septuagint; Hebrew *temple; they will have as their possession 20 rooms*

°3 ק חמשה
°5 ק והיה

נְאֻם אֲדֹנָי יְהוִה׃ מֹאזְנֵי־ צֶדֶק וְאֵיפַת־ צֶדֶק
accuracy and-ephah-of accuracy scales-of (10) Yahweh Sovereign declaration-of

וּבַת־ צֶדֶק יְהִי לָכֶם׃ הָאֵיפָה וְהַבַּת תֹּכֶן אֶחָד
same size and-the-bath the-ephah (11) to-you he-must-be accuracy and-bath-of

יִהְיֶה לָשֵׂאת מַעְשַׂר הַחֹמֶר הַבָּת וַעֲשִׂירִת הַחֹמֶר הָאֵיפָה
the-ephah the-homer and-tenth-of the-bath the-homer tenth-of to-contain he-must-be

אֶל־ הַחֹמֶר יִהְיֶה מַתְכֻּנְתּוֹ׃ וְהַשֶּׁקֶל עֶשְׂרִים גֵּרָה עֶשְׂרִים
twenty gerah twenty and-the-shekel (12) standard-of-him he-must-be the-homer by

שְׁקָלִים חֲמִשָּׁה וְעֶשְׂרִים שְׁקָלִים עֲשָׂרָה וַחֲמִשָּׁה שֶׁקֶל הַמָּנֶה יִהְיֶה לָכֶם׃
to-you he-must-be the-mina shekel and-five ten shekels and-twenty five shekels

זֹאת הַתְּרוּמָה אֲשֶׁר תָּרִימוּ שִׁשִּׁית הָאֵיפָה מֵחֹמֶר
from-homer-of the-ephah sixth-of you-must-offer that the-special-gift this (13)

הַחִטִּים וְשִׁשִּׁיתֶם הָאֵיפָה מֵחֹמֶר הַשְּׂעֹרִים׃
the-barleys from-homer-of the-ephah and-you-must-take-sixth the-wheats

וְחֹק הַשֶּׁמֶן הַבַּת הַשֶּׁמֶן מַעְשַׂר הַבַּת מִן־
from the-bath tenth-of the-oil the-bath the-oil and-prescribed-portion-of (14)

הַכֹּר עֲשֶׂרֶת הַבַּתִּים חֹמֶר כִּי־ עֲשֶׂרֶת הַבַּתִּים חֹמֶר׃ וְשֶׂה־ אַחַת
one also-sheep (15) homer the-baths ten-of for homer the-baths ten-of the-cor

מִן־ הַצֹּאן מִן־ הַמָּאתַיִם מִמַּשְׁקֵה יִשְׂרָאֵל
Israel from-well-watered-pasture-of the-two-hundreds of the-flock from

לְמִנְחָה וּלְעוֹלָה וְלִשְׁלָמִים
and-for-fellowship-offerings and-for-burnt-offering for-grain-offering

לְכַפֵּר עֲלֵיהֶם נְאֻם אֲדֹנָי יְהוִה׃ כֹּל הָעָם
the-people all-of (16) Yahweh Sovereign declaration-of for-them to-make-atonement

הָאָרֶץ יִהְיוּ אֶל־ הַתְּרוּמָה הַזֹּאת לַנָּשִׂיא בְּיִשְׂרָאֵל׃
in-Israel for-the-prince the-this the-special-gift in they-will-participate the-land

וְעַל־ הַנָּשִׂיא יִהְיֶה הָעוֹלוֹת וְהַמִּנְחָה
and-the-grain-offering the-burnt-offerings he-will-be the-prince and-upon (17)

וְהַנֵּסֶךְ בַּחַגִּים וּבֶחֳדָשִׁים וּבַשַּׁבָּתוֹת
and-at-the-Sabbaths and-at-the-New-Moons at-the-festivals and-the-drink-offering

בְּכָל־ מוֹעֲדֵי בֵּית יִשְׂרָאֵל הוּא־ יַעֲשֶׂה אֶת־ הַחַטָּאת
the-sin-offering *** he-will-provide he Israel house-of appointed-feasts-of at-all-of

וְאֶת־ הַמִּנְחָה וְאֶת־ הָעוֹלָה וְאֶת־ הַשְּׁלָמִים
the-fellowship-offerings and the-burnt-offering and the-grain-offering and

לְכַפֵּר בְּעַד בֵּית־ יִשְׂרָאֵל׃ כֹּה־ אָמַר אֲדֹנָי יְהוִה
Yahweh Sovereign he-says this (18) Israel house-of on-behalf-of to-make-atonement

בָּרִאשׁוֹן בְּאֶחָד לַחֹדֶשׁ תִּקַּח פַּר־ בֶּן־ בָּקָר תָּמִים
without-defect herd young-one-of bull you-must-take of-the-month on-one in-the-first

the Sovereign LORD. 10 You are to use accurate scales, an accurate ephah[e] and an accurate bath.[f] 11 The ephah and the bath are to be the same size, the bath containing a tenth of a homer[g] and the ephah a tenth of a homer; the homer is to be the standard measure for both. 12 The shekel[h] is to consist of twenty gerahs. Twenty shekels plus twenty-five shekels plus fifteen shekels equal one mina.[i]

*Offerings and Holy Days*

13 "'This is the special gift you are to offer: a sixth of an ephah from each homer of wheat and a sixth of an ephah from each homer of barley. 14 The prescribed portion of oil, measured by the bath, is a tenth of a bath from each cor (which consists of ten baths or one homer, for ten baths are equivalent to a homer). 15 Also one sheep is to be taken from every flock of two hundred from the well-watered pastures of Israel. These will be used for the grain offerings, burnt offerings and fellowship offerings[j] to make atonement for the people, declares the Sovereign LORD. 16 All the people of the land will participate in this special gift for the use of the prince in Israel. 17 It will be the duty of the prince to provide the burnt offerings, grain offerings and drink offerings at the festivals, the New Moons and the Sabbaths—at all the appointed feasts of the house of Israel. He will provide the sin offerings, grain offerings, burnt offerings and fellowship offerings to make atonement for the house of Israel.

18 "'This is what the Sovereign LORD says: In the first month on the first day you are to take a young bull without defect and

e10 An ephah was a dry measure.
f10 A bath was a liquid measure.
g11 A homer was a dry measure.
h12 A shekel weighed about 2/5 ounce (about 11.5 grams).
i12 That is, 60 shekels; the common mina was 50 shekels.
j15 Traditionally *peace offerings;* also in verse 17

וְחִטֵּאתָ אֶת־ הַמִּקְדָּשׁ׃ וְלָקַח הַכֹּהֵן מִדַּם
from-blood-of the-priest and-he-must-take (19) the-sanctuary *** and-you-must-purify

הַחַטָּאת וְנָתַן אֶל־ מְזוּזַת הַבַּיִת וְאֶל־אַרְבַּע פִּנּוֹת
corners-of four-of and-on the-temple doorpost-of on and-he-must-put the-sin-offering

הָעֲזָרָה לַמִּזְבֵּחַ וְעַל־ מְזוּזַת שַׁעַר הֶחָצֵר הַפְּנִימִית׃ וְכֵן
and-same (20) the-inner the-court gate-of post-of and-on of-the-altar the-ledge

תַּעֲשֶׂה בְּשִׁבְעָה בַחֹדֶשׁ מֵאִישׁ שֹׁגֶה
sinning-unintentionally for-anyone of-the-month on-seven you-must-do

וּמִפֶּתִי וְכִפַּרְתֶּם אֶת־ הַבָּיִת׃ בָּרִאשׁוֹן
in-the-first (21) the-temple for so-you-must-make-atonement or-through-ignorance

בָּאַרְבָּעָה עָשָׂר יוֹם לַחֹדֶשׁ יִהְיֶה לָכֶם הַפָּסַח חָג שְׁבֻעוֹת יָמִים
days sevens-of feast the-Passover for-you he-must-be of-the-month day ten on-four

מַצּוֹת יֵאָכֵל׃ וְעָשָׂה הַנָּשִׂיא בַּיּוֹם
on-the-day the-prince and-he-must-provide (22) he-must-be-eaten breads-without-yeast

הַהוּא בַּעֲדוֹ וּבְעַד כָּל־ עַם הָאָרֶץ פַּר
bull-of the-land people-of all-of and-on-behalf-of on-behalf-of-him the-that

חַטָּאת׃ וְשִׁבְעַת יְמֵי־ הֶחָג יַעֲשֶׂה עוֹלָה
burnt-offering he-must-provide the-Feast days-of and-seven-of (23) sin-offering

לַיהוָה שִׁבְעַת פָּרִים וְשִׁבְעַת אֵילִים תְּמִימִם לַיּוֹם שִׁבְעַת
seven-of for-the-day ones-without-defect rams and-seven-of bulls seven-of to-Yahweh

הַיָּמִים וְחַטָּאת שְׂעִיר עִזִּים לַיּוֹם׃ וּמִנְחָה
and-grain-offering (24) for-the-day goats male-goat-of and-sin-offering the-days

אֵיפָה לַפָּר וְאֵיפָה לָאַיִל יַעֲשֶׂה וְשֶׁמֶן הִין לָאֵיפָה׃
for-the-ephah hin with-oil he-must-provide for-the-ram and-ephah for-the-bull ephah

בַּשְּׁבִיעִי בַּחֲמִשָּׁה עָשָׂר יוֹם לַחֹדֶשׁ בֶּחָג יַעֲשֶׂה
he-must-provide during-the-Feast of-the-month day ten on-five in-the-seventh (25)

כָּאֵלֶּה שִׁבְעַת הַיָּמִים כַּחַטָּאת כָּעֹלָה
for-the-burnt-offering for-the-sin-offering the-days seven-of like-these

וְכַמִּנְחָה וְכַשָּׁמֶן׃ כֹּה־ אָמַר אֲדֹנָי יְהוִה
Yahweh Sovereign he-says this (46:1) and-for-the-oil and-for-the-grain-offering

שַׁעַר הֶחָצֵר הַפְּנִימִית הַפֹּנָה קָדִים יִהְיֶה סָגוּר שֵׁשֶׁת
six-of being-shut he-must-be east the-one-facing the-inner the-court gate-of

יְמֵי הַמַּעֲשֶׂה וּבְיוֹם הַשַּׁבָּת יִפָּתֵחַ וּבְיוֹם
and-on-day-of he-must-be-opened the-Sabbath but-on-day-of the-work days-of

הַחֹדֶשׁ יִפָּתֵחַ׃ וּבָא הַנָּשִׂיא דֶּרֶךְ אוּלָם
portico-of way-of the-prince and-he-must-enter (2) he-must-be-opened the-New-Moon

הַשַּׁעַר מִחוּץ וְעָמַד עַל־מְזוּזַת הַשַּׁעַר וְעָשׂוּ
and-they-must-sacrifice the-gate post-of by and-he-must-stand from-outside the-gateway

purify the sanctuary. [19]The priest is to take some of the blood of the sin offering and put it on the doorposts of the temple, on the four corners of the upper ledge of the altar and on the gateposts of the inner court. [20]You are to do the same on the seventh day of the month for anyone who sins unintentionally or through ignorance; so you are to make atonement for the temple.

[21]" 'In the first month on the fourteenth day you are to observe the Passover, a feast lasting seven days, during which you shall eat bread made without yeast. [22]On that day the prince is to provide a bull as a sin offering for himself and for all the people of the land. [23]Every day during the seven days of the Feast he is to provide seven bulls and seven rams without defect as a burnt offering to the LORD, and a male goat for a sin offering. [24]He is to provide as a grain offering an ephah for each bull and an ephah for each ram, along with a hin[k] of oil for each ephah.

[25]" 'During the seven days of the Feast, which begins in the seventh month on the fifteenth day, he is to make the same provision for sin offerings, burnt offerings, grain offerings and oil.

46 " 'This is what the Sovereign LORD says: The gate of the inner court facing east is to be shut on the six working days, but on the Sabbath day and on the day of the New Moon it is to be opened. [2]The prince is to enter from the outside through the portico of the gateway and stand by

[k]24,5 That is, probably about 4 quarts (about 4 liters)

הַכֹּהֲנִים אֶת־ עוֹלָתוֹ וְאֶת־ שְׁלָמָיו
fellowship-offerings-of-him and burnt-offering-of-him *** the-priests

וְהִשְׁתַּחֲוָה עַל־ מִפְתַּן הַשַּׁעַר וְיָצָא וְהַשַּׁעַר לֹא־
not but-the-gate then-he-must-go-out the-gateway threshold-of at and-he-must-worship

יִסָּגֵר עַד־ הָעָרֶב׃ וְהִשְׁתַּחֲווּ עַם־ הָאָרֶץ
the-land people-of and-they-must-worship (3) the-evening until he-will-be-shut

פֶּתַח הַשַּׁעַר הַהוּא בַּשַּׁבָּתוֹת וּבֶחֳדָשִׁים לִפְנֵי
in-presences-of and-on-the-New-Moons on-the-Sabbaths the-that the-gateway entrance-of

יְהוָה׃ וְהָעֹלָה אֲשֶׁר־ יַקְרִב הַנָּשִׂיא לַיהוָה בְּיוֹם
on-day-of to-Yahweh the-prince he-brings that and-the-burnt-offering (4) Yahweh

הַשַּׁבָּת שִׁשָּׁה כְבָשִׂים תְּמִימִם וְאַיִל תָּמִים׃
without-defect and-ram ones-without-defect male-lambs six the-Sabbath

וּמִנְחָה אֵיפָה לָאַיִל וְלַכְּבָשִׂים מִנְחָה
grain-offering and-with-the-lambs with-the-ram ephah and-grain-offering (5)

מַתַּת יָדוֹ וְשֶׁמֶן הִין לָאֵיפָה׃ וּבְיוֹם הַחֹדֶשׁ פַּר
bull the-New-Moon and-on-day-of (6) for-the-ephah hin with-oil hand-of-him gift-of

בֶּן־ בָּקָר תְּמִימִם וְשֵׁשֶׁת כְּבָשִׂם וָאַיִל תְּמִימִם
ones-without-defect and-ram lambs and-six-of ones-without-defect herd young-one-of

יִהְיוּ׃ וְאֵיפָה לַפָּר וְאֵיפָה לָאַיִל יַעֲשֶׂה
he-must-provide with-the-ram and-ephah with-the-bull and-ephah (7) they-must-be

מִנְחָה וְלַכְּבָשִׂים כַּאֲשֶׁר תַּשִּׂיג יָדוֹ וְשֶׁמֶן הִין
hin with-oil hand-of-him she-would-give as-that and-with-the-lambs grain-offering

לָאֵיפָה׃ וּבְבוֹא הַנָּשִׂיא דֶּרֶךְ אוּלָם הַשַּׁעַר
the-gateway portico-of way-of the-prince and-when-to-enter (8) for-the-ephah

יָבוֹא וּבְדַרְכּוֹ יֵצֵא׃ וּבְבוֹא עַם־
people-of and-when-to-come (9) he-must-come-out and-through-way-of-him he-must-go-in

הָאָרֶץ לִפְנֵי יְהוָה בַּמּוֹעֲדִים הַבָּא דֶּרֶךְ־ שַׁעַר צָפוֹן
north gate-of way-of the-one-entering at-the-appointed-feasts Yahweh before the-land

לְהִשְׁתַּחֲוֹת יֵצֵא דֶּרֶךְ־ שַׁעַר נֶגֶב וְהַבָּא דֶּרֶךְ־ שַׁעַר
gate-of way-of and-the-one-entering south gate-of way-of he-must-go-out to-worship

נֶגֶב יֵצֵא דֶּרֶךְ־ שַׁעַר צָפוֹנָה לֹא יָשׁוּב דֶּרֶךְ הַשַּׁעַר
the-gate through he-must-return not to-north gate-of way-of he-must-go-out south

אֲשֶׁר־ בָּא בוֹ כִּי נִכְחוֹ יֵצֵאו׃ וְהַנָּשִׂיא
and-the-prince (10) he-must-go-out opposite-of-him but through-him he-entered which

בְּתוֹכָם בְּבוֹאָם יָבוֹא וּבְצֵאתָם יֵצֵאוּ׃
he-must-go-out and-when-to-go-out-them he-must-go-in when-to-go-in-them in-among-them

וּבַחַגִּים וּבַמּוֹעֲדִים תִּהְיֶה הַמִּנְחָה
the-grain-offering she-must-be and-at-the-appointed-feasts and-at-the-festivals (11)

ק יצא °9

the gatepost. The priests are to sacrifice his burnt offering and his fellowship offerings.[l] He is to worship at the threshold of the gateway and then go out, but the gate will not be shut until evening. 3 On the Sabbaths and New Moons the people of the land are to worship in the presence of the LORD at the entrance to that gateway. 4 The burnt offering the prince brings to the LORD on the Sabbath day is to be six male lambs and a ram, all without defect. 5 The grain offering given with the ram is to be an ephah,[m] and the grain offering with the lambs is to be as much as he pleases, along with a hin of oil for each ephah. 6 On the day of the New Moon he is to offer a young bull, six lambs and a ram, all without defect. 7 He is to provide as a grain offering one ephah with the bull, one ephah with the ram, and with the lambs as much as he wants to give, along with a hin of oil with each ephah. 8 When the prince enters, he is to go in through the portico of the gateway, and he is to come out the same way.

9 "'When the people of the land come before the LORD at the appointed feasts, whoever enters by the north gate to worship is to go out the south gate; and whoever enters by the south gate is to go out the north gate. No one is to return through the gate by which he entered, but each is to go out the opposite gate. 10 The prince is to be among them, going in when they go in and going out when they go out.

11 "'At the festivals and the appointed feasts, the grain offering

[l]2 Traditionally *peace offerings*; also in verse 12

[m]5 That is, probably about 3/5 bushel (about 22 liters)

אֵיפָה לַפָּר וְאֵיפָה לָאַיִל וְלַכְּבָשִׂים מַתַּת יָדוֹ
hand-of-him gift-of and-with-the-lambs with-the-ram and-ephah with-the-bull ephah

וְשֶׁמֶן הִין לָאֵיפָה׃ וְכִי־ יַעֲשֶׂה הַנָּשִׂיא נְדָבָה
freewill-offering the-prince he-provides and-when (12) for-the-ephah hin with-oil

עוֹלָה אוֹ־ שְׁלָמִים נְדָבָה לַיהוָה וּפָתַח
then-he-must-open to-Yahweh freewill-offering fellowship-offerings or burnt-offering

לוֹ אֶת* הַשַּׁעַר הַפֹּנֶה קָדִים וְעָשָׂה אֶת־ עֹלָתוֹ
burnt-offering-of-him *** and-he-shall-offer east the-one-facing the-gate *** for-him

וְאֶת־ שְׁלָמָיו כַּאֲשֶׁר יַעֲשֶׂה בְּיוֹם הַשַּׁבָּת
the-Sabbath on-day-of he-offers as-that fellowship-offerings-of-him or

וְיָצָא וְסָגַר אֶת־ הַשַּׁעַר אַחֲרֵי צֵאתוֹ׃ וְכֶבֶשׂ
and-lamb (13) to-go-out-him after the-gate *** and-he-will-shut then-he-shall-go-out

בֶּן־ שְׁנָתוֹ תָּמִים תַּעֲשֶׂה עוֹלָה לַיּוֹם
for-the-day burnt-offering you-must-provide without-defect year-of-him son-of

לַיהוָה בַּבֹּקֶר בַּבֹּקֶר תַּעֲשֶׂה אֹתוֹ׃ וּמִנְחָה
also-grain-offering (14) him you-shall-provide in-the-morning in-the-morning to-Yahweh

תַעֲשֶׂה עָלָיו בַּבֹּקֶר בַּבֹּקֶר שִׁשִּׁית הָאֵיפָה וְשֶׁמֶן
with-oil the-ephah sixth-of in-the-morning in-the-morning with-him you-must-provide

שְׁלִישִׁית הַהִין לָרֹס אֶת־ הַסֹּלֶת מִנְחָה לַיהוָה חֻקּוֹת
ordinances-of to-Yahweh grain-offering the-flour *** to-moisten the-hin third-of

עוֹלָם תָּמִיד׃ °וַעֲשׂוּ אֶת־ הַכֶּבֶשׂ וְאֶת־ הַמִּנְחָה וְאֶת־
and the-grain-offering and the-lamb *** they-shall-provide (15) regular lasting

הַשֶּׁמֶן בַּבֹּקֶר בַּבֹּקֶר עוֹלַת תָּמִיד׃ כֹּה־ אָמַר
he-says this (16) regular burnt-offering-of in-the-morning in-the-morning the-oil

אֲדֹנָי יְהוִה כִּי־ יִתֵּן הַנָּשִׂיא מַתָּנָה לְאִישׁ מִבָּנָיו נַחֲלָתוֹ
inheritance-of-him of-sons-of-him to-one gift the-prince he-makes if Yahweh Sovereign

הִיא לְבָנָיו תִּהְיֶה אֲחֻזָּתָם הִיא בְּנַחֲלָה׃
by-inheritance she property-of-them she-will-be for-descendants-of-him she

וְכִי־ יִתֵּן מַתָּנָה מִנַּחֲלָתוֹ לְאַחַד מֵעֲבָדָיו
of-servants-of-him to-one from-inheritance-of-him gift he-makes however-if (17)

וְהָיְתָה לּוֹ עַד־ שְׁנַת הַדְּרוֹר וְשָׁבַת לַנָּשִׂיא
to-the-prince then-he-will-revert the-freedom year-of until to-him then-she-may-be

אַךְ נַחֲלָתוֹ בָּנָיו לָהֶם תִּהְיֶה׃ וְלֹא־ יִקַּח
he-must-take and-not (18) she-is to-them sons-of-him inheritance-of-him only

הַנָּשִׂיא מִנַּחֲלַת הָעָם לְהוֹנֹתָם מֵאֲחֻזָּתָם
from-property-of-them to-drive-off-them the-people from-inheritance-of the-prince

מֵאֲחֻזָּתוֹ יַנְחִל אֶת־ בָּנָיו לְמַעַן אֲשֶׁר לֹא־
not that so-that sons-of-him *** he-must-give-inheritance from-property-of-him

is to be an ephah with a bull, an
ephah with a ram, and with the
lambs as much as one pleases,
along with a hin of oil for each
ephah. [12]When the prince provides a freewill offering to the
LORD—whether a burnt offering or
fellowship offerings—the gate facing east is to be opened for him.
He shall offer his burnt offering or
his fellowship offerings as he does
on the Sabbath day. Then he shall
go out, and after he has gone out,
the gate will be shut.

[13]" 'Every day you are to provide
a year-old lamb without defect for
a burnt offering to the LORD;
morning by morning you shall
provide it. [14]You are also to provide with it morning by morning
a grain offering, consisting of a
sixth of an ephah with a third of a
hin of oil to moisten the flour. The
presenting of this grain offering to
the LORD is a lasting ordinance.
[15]So the lamb and the grain offering and the oil shall be provided
morning by morning for a regular
burnt offering.

[16]" 'This is what the Sovereign
LORD says: If the prince makes a
gift from his inheritance to one of
his sons, it will also belong to his
descendants; it is to be their property by inheritance. [17]If, however,
he makes a gift from his inheritance to one of his servants, the
servant may keep it until the year
of freedom; then it will revert to
the prince. His inheritance belongs to his sons only; it is theirs.
[18]The prince must not take any of
the inheritance of the people,
driving them off their property.
He is to give his sons their inheritance out of his own property, so

*12 Most mss have *maqqeph* (־) binding this word to the next.

°15 ק יעשו

יָפֻצוּ עַמִּי אִישׁ מֵאֲחֻזָּתוֹ׃ וַיְבִיאֵנִי
then-he-brought-me (19) from-property-of-him anyone people-of-me they-will-be-separated

בַמָּבוֹא אֲשֶׁר עַל־כֶּתֶף הַשַּׁעַר אֶל־הַלְּשָׁכוֹת הַקֹּדֶשׁ אֶל־הַכֹּהֲנִים
the-priests to the-sacred the-rooms to the-gate side-of at that through-the-entrance

הַפֹּנוֹת צָפוֹנָה וְהִנֵּה־ שָׁם מָקוֹם בַּיַּרְכָתָם יָמָּה׃ וַיֹּאמֶר
and-he-said (20) to-west at-the-ends place there and-see! to-north the-ones-facing

אֵלַי זֶה הַמָּקוֹם אֲשֶׁר יְבַשְּׁלוּ־ שָׁם הַכֹּהֲנִים אֶת־ הָאָשָׁם
the-guilt-offering *** the-priests there they-will-cook where the-place this to-me

וְאֶת־ הַחַטָּאת אֲשֶׁר יֹאפוּ אֶת־ הַמִּנְחָה לְבִלְתִּי הוֹצִיא אֶל־
into to-bring not the-grain-offering *** they-will-bake where the-sin-offering and

הֶחָצֵר הַחִיצוֹנָה לְקַדֵּשׁ אֶת־ הָעָם׃ וַיּוֹצִיאֵנִי אֶל־
to then-he-brought-me (21) the-people *** to-consecrate the-outer the-court

הֶחָצֵר הַחִיצֹנָה וַיַּעֲבִירֵנִי אֶל־אַרְבַּעַת מִקְצוֹעֵי הֶחָצֵר וְהִנֵּה
and-see! the-court corners-of four-of to and-he-led-around-me the-outer the-court

חָצֵר בְּמִקְצֹעַ הֶחָצֵר חָצֵר בְּמִקְצֹעַ הֶחָצֵר׃ בְּאַרְבַּעַת
in-four-of (22) the-court in-corner-of court the-court in-corner-of court

מִקְצֹעוֹת הֶחָצֵר חֲצֵרוֹת קְטֻרוֹת אַרְבָּעִים אֹרֶךְ וּשְׁלֹשִׁים רֹחַב
width and-thirty length forty ones-being-enclosed courts the-court corners-of

מִדָּה אַחַת לְאַרְבַּעְתָּם מְהֻקְצָעוֹת׃ וְטוּר סָבִיב בָּהֶם
inside-them around and-ledge (23) ones-being-in-corners to-four-of-them same size

סָבִיב לְאַרְבַּעְתָּם וּמְבַשְּׁלוֹת עָשׂוּי מִתַּחַת הַטִּירוֹת סָבִיב׃
around the-ledges at-under being-built with-fire-places to-four-of-them around

וַיֹּאמֶר אֵלַי אֵלֶּה בֵּית הַמְבַשְּׁלִים אֲשֶׁר יְבַשְּׁלוּ־
they-will-cook where the-ones-cooking kitchen-of these to-me and-he-said (24)

שָׁם מְשָׁרְתֵי הַבַּיִת אֶת־ זֶבַח הָעָם׃
the-people sacrifice-of *** the-temple ones-ministering-of there

וַיְשִׁבֵנִי אֶל־ פֶּתַח הַבַּיִת וְהִנֵּה־ מַיִם
waters and-see! the-temple entrance-of to and-he-brought-back-me (47:1)

יֹצְאִים מִתַּחַת מִפְתַּן הַבַּיִת קָדִימָה כִּי־ פְנֵי
faces-of for toward-east the-temple threshold-of from-under ones-coming-out

הַבַּיִת קָדִים וְהַמַּיִם יֹרְדִים מִתַּחַת מִכֶּתֶף הַבַּיִת
the-temple from-side-of from-under ones-coming-down and-the-waters east the-temple

הַיְמָנִית מִנֶּגֶב לַמִּזְבֵּחַ׃ וַיּוֹצִאֵנִי דֶּרֶךְ־ שַׁעַר צָפוֹנָה
to-north gate-of through then-he-brought-out-me (2) of-the-altar from-south the-south

וַיְסִבֵּנִי דֶּרֶךְ חוּץ אֶל־ שַׁעַר הַחוּץ דֶּרֶךְ הַפּוֹנֶה
the-one-facing way-of the-outer gate-of to outside way-of and-he-led-around-me

קָדִים וְהִנֵּה־ מַיִם מְפַכִּים מִן־ הַכָּתֵף הַיְמָנִית׃ בְּצֵאת־ הָאִישׁ
the-man as-to-go (3) the-south the-side from ones-flowing waters and-see! east

that none of my people will be separated from his property.' "

[19]Then the man brought me through the entrance at the side of the gate to the sacred rooms facing north, which belonged to the priests, and showed me a place at the western end. [20]He said to me, "This is the place where the priests will cook the guilt offering and the sin offering and bake the grain offering, to avoid bringing them into the outer court and consecrating the people."

[21]He then brought me to the outer court and led me around to its four corners, and I saw in each corner another court. [22]In the four corners of the outer court were enclosed[n] courts, forty cubits long and thirty cubits wide; each of the courts in the four corners was the same size. [23]Around the inside of each of the four courts was a ledge of stone, with places for fire built all around under the ledge. [24]He said to me, "These are the kitchens where those who minister at the temple will cook the sacrifices of the people."

*The River From the Temple*

**47** The man brought me back to the entrance of the temple, and I saw water coming out from under the threshold of the temple toward the east (for the temple faced east). The water was coming down from under the south side of the temple, south of the altar. [2]He then brought me out through the north gate and led me around the outside to the outer gate facing east, and the water was flowing from the south side.

[3]As the man went eastward

[n]22 The meaning of the Hebrew for this word is uncertain.

ק בירכתים °19

קָדִים וְקָו בְּיָדוֹ וַיָּמָד אֶלֶף בָּאַמָּה
by-the-cubit thousand then-he-measured-off in-hand-of-him with-measuring-line east

וַיַּעֲבִרֵנִי בַמַּיִם מֵי אָפְסָיִם׃ וַיָּמָד אֶלֶף
thousand and-he-measured-off (4) ankles waters-of through-the-waters then-he-led-me

וַיַּעֲבִרֵנִי בַמַּיִם מַיִם בִּרְכָּיִם וַיָּמָד אֶלֶף
thousand and-he-measured-off knees waters through-the-waters and-he-led-me

וַיַּעֲבִרֵנִי מֵי מָתְנָיִם׃ וַיָּמָד אֶלֶף נַחַל אֲשֶׁר לֹא־
not that river thousand and-he-measured-off (5) waists waters-of and-he-led-me

אוּכַל לַעֲבֹר כִּי־ גָאוּ הַמַּיִם מֵי שָׂחוּ נַחַל אֲשֶׁר לֹא־
not that river swimming waters-of the-waters they-rose because to-cross I-could

יֵעָבֵר׃ וַיֹּאמֶר אֵלַי הֲרָאִיתָ בֶן־ אָדָם וַיּוֹלִכֵנִי
then-he-led-me man son-of you-see? to-me and-he-asked (6) he-could-be-crossed

וַיְשִׁבֵנִי שְׂפַת הַנָּחַל׃ בְּשׁוּבֵנִי וְהִנֵּה אֶל־ שְׂפַת
bank-of on then-see! when-to-arrive-me (7) the-river bank-of and-he-brought-back-me

הַנַּחַל עֵץ רַב מְאֹד מִזֶּה וּמִזֶּה׃ וַיֹּאמֶר אֵלַי הַמַּיִם
the-waters to-me and-he-said (8) and-on-side on-side great numerous tree the-river

הָאֵלֶּה יוֹצְאִים אֶל־ הַגְּלִילָה הַקַּדְמוֹנָה וְיָרְדוּ עַל־
into and-they-go-down the-eastern the-region toward ones-flowing the-these

הָעֲרָבָה וּבָאוּ הַיָּמָּה אֶל־ הַיָּמָּה הַמּוּצָאִים
the-ones-emptying into-the-Sea into into-the-Sea and-they-enter the-Arabah

וְנִרְפְּאוּ הַמָּיִם׃ וְהָיָה כָל־ נֶפֶשׁ חַיָּה ׀
creature living-one-of all-of and-he-will-be (9) the-waters then-they-become-fresh

אֲשֶׁר־ יִשְׁרֹץ אֶל כָּל־ אֲשֶׁר יָבוֹא שָׁם נַחֲלַיִם יִחְיֶה וְהָיָה
and-he-will-be he-will-live rivers there he-flows that everywhere in he-swarms that

הַדָּגָה רַבָּה מְאֹד כִּי בָאוּ שָׁמָּה הַמַּיִם הָאֵלֶּה
the-these the-waters to-there they-flow because large numerous the-fish

וְיֵרָפְאוּ וָחָי כֹּל אֲשֶׁר־ יָבוֹא שָׁמָּה הַנָּחַל׃
the-river to-there he-flows that everything so-he-will-live and-they-are-made-fresh

וְהָיָה יעמדו עָלָיו דַּוָּגִים מֵעֵין גֶּדִי וְעַד־ עֵין
En and-to Gedi from-En fishermen along-him they-will-stand and-he-will-be (10)

עֶגְלַיִם מִשְׁטוֹחַ לַחֲרָמִים יִהְיוּ לְמִינָה תִּהְיֶה דְגָתָם
fish-of-them she-will-be of-kind-of-her they-will-be for-nets spreading-place Eglaim

כִּדְגַת הַיָּם הַגָּדוֹל רַבָּה מְאֹד׃ בִּצֹּאתָו וּגְבָאָיו
and-marshes-of-him swamps-of-him (11) very many the-Great the-Sea like-fish-of

וְלֹא יֵרָפְאוּ לְמֶלַח נִתָּנוּ׃ וְעַל־ הַנַּחַל
the-river and-by (12) they-will-be-left for-salt they-will-become-fresh but-not

יַעֲלֶה עַל־ שְׂפָתוֹ מִזֶּה ׀ וּמִזֶּה ׀ כָּל־ עֵץ־ מַאֲכָל לֹא־
not fruit tree-of every-of and-on-side on-side bank-of-him on he-will-grow

with a measuring line in his hand,
he measured off a thousand cubits[o] and then led me through
water that was ankle-deep. [4]He
measured off another thousand
cubits and led me through water
that was knee-deep. He measured
off another thousand and led me
through water that was up to the
waist. [5]He measured off another
thousand, but now it was a river
that I could not cross, because the
water had risen and was deep
enough to swim in—a river that
no one could cross. [6]He asked me,
"Son of man, do you see this?"

Then he led me back to the bank
of the river. [7]When I arrived there,
I saw a great number of trees on
each side of the river. [8]He said to
me, "This water flows toward the
eastern region and goes down
into the Arabah,[p] where it enters
the Sea.[q] When it empties into the
Sea,[q] the water there becomes
fresh. [9]Swarms of living creatures
will live wherever the river flows.
There will be large numbers of
fish, because this water flows
there and makes the salt water
fresh; so where the river flows
everything will live. [10]Fishermen
will stand along the shore; from
En Gedi to En Eglaim there will be
places for spreading nets. The fish
will be of many kinds—like the
fish of the Great Sea.[r] [11]But the
swamps and marshes will not
become fresh; they will be left for
salt. [12]Fruit trees of all kinds will
grow on both banks of the river.

[o]3 That is, about 1,500 feet (about 450 meters)
[p]8 Or *the Jordan Valley*
[q]8 That is, the Dead Sea
[r]10 That is, the Mediterranean; also in verses 15, 19 and 20

°8 ק ונרפו; °10 ק עמדו
°11 ק בצאתיו

יַבּוֹל עָלֵהוּ וְלֹא־ יִתֹּם פִּרְיוֹ לָחֳדָשָׁיו
in-months-of-him fruit-of-him he-will-fail or-not leaf-of-him he-will-wither

יְבַכֵּר כִּי מֵימָיו מִן־ הַמִּקְדָּשׁ הֵמָּה יוֹצְאִים
ones-flowing they the-sanctuary from waters-of-him because he-will-bear

וְהָיָו° פִּרְיוֹ לְמַאֲכָל וְעָלֵהוּ לִתְרוּפָה׃ כֹּה אָמַר
he-says this (13) for-healing and-leaf-of-him for-food fruit-of-him and-he-will-serve

אֲדֹנָי יְהוִה גֵּה גְּבוּל אֲשֶׁר תִּתְנַחֲלוּ אֶת־ הָאָרֶץ
the-land *** you-must-divide-as-inheritance which boundary this Yahweh Sovereign

לִשְׁנֵי עָשָׂר שִׁבְטֵי יִשְׂרָאֵל יוֹסֵף חֲבָלִים׃ וּנְחַלְתֶּם אוֹתָהּ
her and-you-must-divide (14) portions Joseph Israel tribes-of ten among-two-of

אִישׁ כְּאָחִיו אֲשֶׁר נָשָׂאתִי אֶת־ יָדִי לְתִתָּהּ
to-give-her hand-of-me *** I-lifted because equal-to-brother-of-him each

לַאֲבֹתֵיכֶם וְנָפְלָה הָאָרֶץ הַזֹּאת לָכֶם בְּנַחֲלָה׃
for-inheritance to-you the-this the-land and-she-will-become to-forefathers-of-you

וְזֶה גְּבוּל הָאָרֶץ לִפְאַת צָפוֹנָה מִן־ הַיָּם הַגָּדוֹל
the-Great the-Sea from to-north on-side-of the-land boundary-of and-this (15)

הַדֶּרֶךְ חֶתְלֹן לְבוֹא צְדָדָה׃ חֲמָת | בֵּרוֹתָה סִבְרַיִם אֲשֶׁר בֵּין־
between which Sibraim Berothah Hamath (16) into-Zedad to-go Hethlon the-road

גְּבוּל דַּמֶּשֶׂק וּבֵין גְּבוּל חֲמָת חָצֵר הַתִּיכוֹן אֲשֶׁר אֶל־ גְּבוּל
border-of on which Hatticon Hazer Hamath border-of and-between Damascus border-of

חַוְרָן׃ וְהָיָה גְבוּל מִן־ הַיָּם חֲצַר עֵינוֹן גְּבוּל דַּמֶּשֶׂק
Damascus border-of Enan Hazer the-sea from boundary and-he-will-extend (17) Hauran

וְצָפוֹן | צָפוֹנָה וּגְבוּל חֲמָת וְאֵת פְּאַת צָפוֹן׃ וּפְאַת
and-side-of (18) north boundary-of indeed Hamath with-border-of to-north and-north

קָדִים מִבֵּין חַוְרָן וּמִבֵּין־ דַּמֶּשֶׂק וּמִבֵּין הַגִּלְעָד
the-Gilead and-from-between Damascus and-from-between Hauran from-between east

וּמִבֵּין אֶרֶץ יִשְׂרָאֵל הַיַּרְדֵּן מִגְּבוּל עַל־ הַיָּם הַקַּדְמוֹנִי
the-eastern the-sea to from-boundary the-Jordan Israel land-of and-from-between

תָּמֹדּוּ וְאֵת פְּאַת קָדִימָה׃ וּפְאַת נֶגֶב תֵּימָנָה מִתָּמָר
from-Tamar to-south south and-side-of (19) to-east boundary-of indeed you-will-measure

עַד־ מֵי מְרִיבוֹת קָדֵשׁ נַחֲלָה אֶל־ הַיָּם הַגָּדוֹל וְאֵת פְּאַת־ תֵּימָנָה
to-south boundary-of indeed the-Great the-Sea to Wadi Kadesh Meribah waters-of to

נֶגְבָּה׃ וּפְאַת־ יָם הַיָּם הַגָּדוֹל מִגְּבוּל עַד־ נֹכַח לְבוֹא חֲמָת
Hamath Lebo opposite to as-boundary the-Great the-Sea west and-side-of (20) to-south

זֹאת פְּאַת־ יָם׃ וְחִלַּקְתֶּם אֶת־ הָאָרֶץ הַזֹּאת לָכֶם
among-you the-this the-land *** and-you-must-distribute (21) west boundary-of this

לְשִׁבְטֵי יִשְׂרָאֵל׃ וְהָיָה תַּפִּלוּ אוֹתָהּ בְּנַחֲלָה
as-inheritance her you-must-allot and-he-will-be (22) Israel according-to-tribes-of

°12 ק והיה

Their leaves will not wither, nor will their fruit fail. Every month they will bear, because the water from the sanctuary flows to them. Their fruit will serve for food and their leaves for healing."

*The Boundaries of the Land*

13 This is what the Sovereign LORD says: "These are the boundaries by which you are to divide the land for an inheritance among the twelve tribes of Israel, with two portions for Joseph. 14 You are to divide it equally among them. Because I swore with uplifted hand to give it to your forefathers, this land will become your inheritance.

15 "This is to be the boundary of the land:

"On the north side it will run from the Great Sea by the Hethlon road past Lebo[s] Hamath to Zedad, 16 Berothah[t] and Sibraim (which lies on the border between Damascus and Hamath), as far as Hazer Hatticon, which is on the border of Hauran. 17 The boundary will extend from the sea to Hazar Enan,[u] along the northern border of Damascus, with the border of Hamath to the north. This will be the north boundary.

18 "On the east side the boundary will run between Hauran and Damascus, along the Jordan between Gilead and the land of Israel, to the eastern sea and as far as Tamar.[v] This will be the east boundary.

19 "On the south side it will run from Tamar as far as the waters of Meribah Kadesh, then along the Wadi ⌞of Egypt⌟ to the Great Sea. This will be the south boundary.

20 "On the west side, the Great Sea will be the boundary to a point opposite Lebo[w] Hamath. This will be the west boundary.

21 "You are to distribute this land among yourselves according to the tribes of Israel. 22 You are to allot it as an inheritance for yourselves and for the aliens who have

s15 Or *past the entrance to*
t15,16 See Septuagint and Ezekiel 48:1; Hebrew *road to go into Zedad, 16 Hamath, Berothah*
u17 Hebrew *Enon,* a variant of *Enan*
v18 Septuagint and Syriac; Hebrew *Israel. You will measure to the eastern sea*
w20 Or *opposite the entrance to*

לָכֶם וּלְהַגֵּרִים הַגָּרִים בְּתוֹכְכֶם אֲשֶׁר־הוֹלִדוּ בָנִים
children they-bore who in-among-you the-ones-settling and-for-the-aliens for-you

בְּתוֹכְכֶם וְהָיוּ לָכֶם כְּאֶזְרָח בִּבְנֵי יִשְׂרָאֵל אִתְּכֶם
with-you Israel of-sons-of as-native-born to-you and-they-must-be in-among-you

יִפְּלוּ בְנַחֲלָה בְּתוֹךְ שִׁבְטֵי יִשְׂרָאֵל׃ וְהָיָה
and-he-will-be (23) Israel tribes-of in-among as-inheritance they-must-allot

בַשֵּׁבֶט אֲשֶׁר־גָּר הַגֵּר אִתּוֹ שָׁם תִּתְּנוּ נַחֲלָתוֹ
inheritance-of-him you-must-give there in-him the-alien he-settles that in-the-tribe

נְאֻם אֲדֹנָי יְהוִה׃ וְאֵלֶּה שְׁמוֹת הַשְּׁבָטִים מִקְצֵה
at-frontier-of the-tribes names-of and-these (48:1) Yahweh Sovereign declaration-of

צָפוֹנָה אֶל־יַד דֶּרֶךְ־חֶתְלֹן לְבוֹא־חֲמָת חֲצַר עֵינָן גְּבוּל דַּמֶּשֶׂק
Damascus border-of Enan Hazar Hamath Lebo Hethlon road-of side-of along to-north

צָפוֹנָה אֶל־יַד חֲמָת וְהָיוּ־לוֹ פְאַת־קָדִים הַיָּם
the-west east border-of to-him and-they-will-be Hamath side-of next-to to-north

דָּן אֶחָד׃ וְעַל גְּבוּל דָּן מִפְּאַת קָדִים עַד־פְּאַת־יָמָּה
to-west border-of to east from-border-of Dan territory-of and-along (2) one Dan

אָשֵׁר אֶחָד׃ וְעַל גְּבוּל אָשֵׁר מִפְּאַת קָדִימָה וְעַד־פְּאַת־
border-of and-to to-east from-border-of Asher territory-of and-along (3) one Asher

יָמָּה נַפְתָּלִי אֶחָד׃ וְעַל גְּבוּל נַפְתָּלִי מִפְּאַת קָדְמָה עַד־
to to-east from-border-of Naphtali territory-of and-along (4) one Naphtali to-west

פְּאַת־יָמָּה מְנַשֶּׁה אֶחָד׃ וְעַל גְּבוּל מְנַשֶּׁה מִפְּאַת
from-border-of Manasseh territory-of and-along (5) one Manasseh to-west border-of

קָדְמָה עַד־פְּאַת־יָמָּה אֶפְרַיִם אֶחָד׃ וְעַל גְּבוּל אֶפְרַיִם
Ephraim territory-of and-along (6) one Ephraim to-west border-of to to-east

מִפְּאַת קָדִים וְעַד־פְּאַת־יָמָּה רְאוּבֵן אֶחָד׃ וְעַל גְּבוּל
territory-of and-along (7) one Reuben to-west border-of and-to east from-border-of

רְאוּבֵן מִפְּאַת קָדִים עַד־פְּאַת־יָמָּה יְהוּדָה אֶחָד׃ וְעַל גְּבוּל
territory-of and-along (8) one Judah to-west border-of to east from-border-of Reuben

יְהוּדָה מִפְּאַת קָדִים עַד־פְּאַת־יָמָּה תִּהְיֶה הַתְּרוּמָה
the-special-gift she-will-be to-west border-of to east from-border-of Judah

אֲשֶׁר־תָּרִימוּ חֲמִשָּׁה וְעֶשְׂרִים אֶלֶף רֹחַב וְאֹרֶךְ כְּאַחַד
as-one-of and-length width thousand and-twenty five you-must-present that

הַחֲלָקִים מִפְּאַת קָדִימָה עַד־פְּאַת־יָמָּה וְהָיָה
and-he-will-be to-west border-of to to-east from-border-of the-tribal-portions

הַמִּקְדָּשׁ בְּתוֹכוֹ׃ הַתְּרוּמָה אֲשֶׁר תָּרִימוּ
you-must-offer that the-special-portion (9) in-center-of-him the-sanctuary

לַיהוָה אֹרֶךְ חֲמִשָּׁה וְעֶשְׂרִים אֶלֶף וְרֹחַב עֲשֶׂרֶת אֲלָפִים׃
thousands ten-of and-width thousand and-twenty five length to-Yahweh

settled among you and who have children. You are to consider them as native-born Israelites; along with you they are to be allotted an inheritance among the tribes of Israel. [23]In whatever tribe the alien settles, there you are to give him his inheritance," declares the Sovereign LORD.

*The Division of the Land*

**48** "These are the tribes, listed by name: At the northern frontier, Dan will have one portion; it will follow the Hethlon road to Lebo[x] Hamath; Hazar Enan and the northern border of Damascus next to Hamath will be part of its border from the east side to the west side.

[2]"Asher will have one portion; it will border the territory of Dan from east to west.

[3]"Naphtali will have one portion; it will border the territory of Asher from east to west.

[4]"Manasseh will have one portion; it will border the territory of Naphtali from east to west.

[5]"Ephraim will have one portion; it will border the territory of Manasseh from east to west.

[6]"Reuben will have one portion; it will border the territory of Ephraim from east to west.

[7]"Judah will have one portion; it will border the territory of Reuben from east to west.

[8]"Bordering the territory of Judah from east to west will be the portion you are to present as a special gift. It will be 25,000 cubits[y] wide, and its length from east to west will equal one of the tribal portions; the sanctuary will be in the center of it.

[9]"The special portion you are to offer to the LORD will be 25,000 cubits long and 10,000 cubits[z]

x1 Or *to the entrance to*
y8 That is, about 7 miles (about 12 kilometers)
z9 That is, about 3 miles (about 5 kilometers)

וּלְאֵלֶּה תִּהְיֶה תְרוּמַת־ הַקֹּדֶשׁ לַכֹּהֲנִים צָפוֹנָה חֲמִשָּׁה
five on-north for-the-priests the-sacredness portion-of she-will-be and-to-these (10)

וְעֶשְׂרִים אֶלֶף וְיָמָּה רֹחַב עֲשֶׂרֶת אֲלָפִים וְקָדִימָה רֹחַב עֲשֶׂרֶת
ten-of width and-on-east thousands ten-of width and-on-west thousand and-twenty

אֲלָפִים וְנֶגְבָּה אֹרֶךְ חֲמִשָּׁה וְעֶשְׂרִים אָלֶף וְהָיָה מִקְדַּשׁ־
sanctuary-of and-he-will-be thousand and-twenty five length and-on-south thousands

יְהוָה בְּתוֹכוֹ׃ לַכֹּהֲנִים הַמְקֻדָּשׁ מִבְּנֵי
from-sons-of the-ones-being-consecrated for-the-priests (11) in-center-of-him Yahweh

צָדוֹק אֲשֶׁר שָׁמְרוּ מִשְׁמַרְתִּי אֲשֶׁר לֹא־ תָעוּ בִּתְעוֹת
when-to-go-astray they-went-astray not who service-of-me they-were-faithful who Zadok

בְּנֵי יִשְׂרָאֵל כַּאֲשֶׁר תָּעוּ הַלְוִיִּם׃ וְהָיְתָה לָהֶם
to-them and-she-will-be (12) the-Levites they-went-astray as-that Israel sons-of

תְּרוּמִיָּה מִתְּרוּמַת הָאָרֶץ קֹדֶשׁ קָדָשִׁים אֶל־ גְּבוּל
territory-of along holy-ones holy-of the-land from-portion-of special-gift

הַלְוִיִּם׃ וְהַלְוִיִּם לְעֻמַּת גְּבוּל הַכֹּהֲנִים חֲמִשָּׁה
five the-priests territory-of at-alongside-of and-the-Levites (13) the-Levites

וְעֶשְׂרִים אֶלֶף אֹרֶךְ וְרֹחַב עֲשֶׂרֶת אֲלָפִים כָּל־ אֹרֶךְ חֲמִשָּׁה וְעֶשְׂרִים
and-twenty five length total-of thousands ten-of and-width length thousand and-twenty

אֶלֶף וְרֹחַב עֲשֶׂרֶת אֲלָפִים׃ וְלֹא־ יִמְכְּרוּ מִמֶּנּוּ וְלֹא
or-not from-him they-must-sell and-not (14) thousands ten-of and-width thousand

יָמֵר וְלֹא °יַעֲבוֹר רֵאשִׁית הָאָרֶץ כִּי־ קֹדֶשׁ לַיהוָה׃
to-Yahweh holiness because the-land best-of he-must-pass and-not he-must-exchange

וַחֲמֵשֶׁת אֲלָפִים הַנּוֹתָר בָּרֹחַב עַל־ פְּנֵי חֲמִשָּׁה וְעֶשְׂרִים
and-twenty five faces-of to in-the-width the-one-remaining thousands and-five-of (15)

אֶלֶף חֹל־ הוּא לָעִיר לְמוֹשָׁב וּלְמִגְרָשׁ וְהָיְתָה הָעִיר
the-city and-she-will-be and-for-pasture for-house for-the-city he common thousand

°בְּתוֹכֹה׃ וְאֵלֶּה מִדּוֹתֶיהָ פְּאַת צָפוֹן חֲמֵשׁ מֵאוֹת
hundreds five-of north side-of measurements-of-her and-these (16) in-center-of-him

וְאַרְבַּעַת אֲלָפִים וּפְאַת־ נֶגֶב חֲמֵשׁ *חמש מֵאוֹת וְאַרְבַּעַת אֲלָפִים
thousands and-four-of hundreds *** five-of south and-side-of thousands and-four-of

וּמִפְּאַת קָדִים חֲמֵשׁ מֵאוֹת וְאַרְבַּעַת אֲלָפִים וּפְאַת־ יָמָּה
to-west and-side-of thousands and-four-of hundreds five-of east and-on-side-of

חֲמֵשׁ מֵאוֹת וְאַרְבַּעַת אֲלָפִים׃ וְהָיָה מִגְרָשׁ לָעִיר
for-the-city pastureland and-he-will-be (17) thousands and-four-of hundreds five-of

צָפוֹנָה חֲמִשִּׁים וּמָאתַיִם וְנֶגְבָּה חֲמִשִּׁים וּמָאתַיִם וְקָדִימָה
and-on-east and-two-hundreds fifty and-on-south and-two-hundreds fifty on-north

חֲמִשִּׁים וּמָאתַיִם וְיָמָּה חֲמִשִּׁים וּמָאתָיִם׃ וְהַנּוֹתָר
and-the-one-remaining (18) and-two-hundreds fifty and-on-west and-two-hundreds fifty

wide. 10 This will be the sacred portion for the priests. It will be 25,000 cubits long on the north side, 10,000 cubits wide on the west side, 10,000 cubits wide on the east side and 25,000 cubits long on the south side. In the center of it will be the sanctuary of the LORD. 11 This will be for the consecrated priests, the Zadokites, who were faithful in serving me and did not go astray as the Levites did when the Israelites went astray. 12 It will be a special gift to them from the sacred portion of the land, a most holy portion, bordering the territory of the Levites.

13 "Alongside the territory of the priests, the Levites will have an allotment 25,000 cubits long and 10,000 cubits wide. Its total length will be 25,000 cubits and its width 10,000 cubits. 14 They must not sell or exchange any of it. This is the best of the land and must not pass into other hands, because it is holy to the LORD.

15 "The remaining area, 5,000 cubits wide and 25,000 cubits long, will be for the common use of the city, for houses and for pastureland. The city will be in the center of it 16 and will have these measurements: the north side 4,500 cubits, the south side 4,500 cubits, the east side 4,500 cubits, and the west side 4,500 cubits. 17 The pastureland for the city will be 250 cubits on the north, 250 cubits on the south, 250 cubits on the east, and 250 cubits on the west. 18 What

*16 Most mss have no *Qere* form.

°14 ק יעביר

°15 ק בתוכו

בָּאֹרֶךְ לְעֻמַּת ׀ תְּרוּמַת הַקֹּדֶשׁ עֲשֶׂרֶת אֲלָפִים קָדִימָה
on-east thousands ten-of the-sacredness portion-of on-border-of along-the-length

וַעֲשֶׂרֶת אֲלָפִים יָמָּה וְהָיָה לְעֻמַּת תְּרוּמַת הַקֹּדֶשׁ
the-sacredness portion-of on-border-of and-he-will-be on-west thousands and-ten-of

וְהָיְתָה תְבוּאָתֹה° לְלֶחֶם לְעֹבְדֵי הָעִיר׃
the-city for-ones-working-of for-food produce-of-him and-she-will-be

(19) וְהָעֹבֵד הָעִיר יַעַבְדוּהוּ מִכֹּל שִׁבְטֵי יִשְׂרָאֵל׃
Israel tribes-of from-all-of they-will-farm-him the-city and-the-one-working (19)

(20) כָּל־הַתְּרוּמָה חֲמִשָּׁה וְעֶשְׂרִים אֶלֶף בַּחֲמִשָּׁה וְעֶשְׂרִים אָלֶף
thousand and-twenty by-five thousand and-twenty five the-portion entire-of (20)

רְבִיעִית תָּרִימוּ אֶת־תְּרוּמַת הַקֹּדֶשׁ אֶל־אֲחֻזַּת הָעִיר׃
the-city property-of with the-sacredness portion-of *** you-will-set-aside square

(21) וְהַנּוֹתָר לַנָּשִׂיא מִזֶּה ׀ וּמִזֶּה ׀ לִתְרוּמַת־הַקֹּדֶשׁ
the-sacredness of-portion-of and-on-side on-side to-the-prince and-the-one-remaining (21)

וְלַאֲחֻזַּת הָעִיר אֶל־פְּנֵי חֲמִשָּׁה וְעֶשְׂרִים אֶלֶף ׀ תְּרוּמָה
portion thousand and-twenty five faces-of from the-city and-of-property-of

עַד־גְּבוּל קָדִימָה וְיָמָּה עַל־פְּנֵי חֲמִשָּׁה וְעֶשְׂרִים אֶלֶף עַל־גְּבוּל
border-of to thousand and-twenty five faces-of to and-westward to-east border-of to

יָמָּה לְעֻמַּת חֲלָקִים לַנָּשִׂיא וְהָיְתָה תְּרוּמַת
portion-of and-she-will-be to-the-prince tribal-portions along-length-of to-west

הַקֹּדֶשׁ וּמִקְדַּשׁ הַבַּיִת בְּתוֹכֹה°׃ (22) וּמֵאֲחֻזַּת
so-from-property-of (22) in-center-of-him the-temple with-sanctuary-of the-sacredness

הַלְוִיִּם וּמֵאֲחֻזַּת הָעִיר בְּתוֹךְ אֲשֶׁר לַנָּשִׂיא יִהְיֶה
he-will-lie to-the-prince what in-center-of the-city and-from-property-of the-Levites

בֵּין ׀ גְּבוּל יְהוּדָה וּבֵין גְּבוּל בִּנְיָמִן לַנָּשִׂיא יִהְיֶה׃
he-will-lie to-the-prince Benjamin border-of and-between Judah border-of between

(23) וְיֶתֶר הַשְּׁבָטִים מִפְּאַת קָדִימָה עַד־פְּאַת־יָמָּה בִּנְיָמִן אֶחָד׃
one Benjamin to-west side-of to to-east from-side-of the-tribes and-rest-of (23)

(24) וְעַל ׀ גְּבוּל בִּנְיָמִן מִפְּאַת קָדִימָה עַד־פְּאַת־יָמָּה
to-west border-of to to-east from-border-of Benjamin territory-of and-along (24)

שִׁמְעוֹן אֶחָד׃ (25) וְעַל ׀ גְּבוּל שִׁמְעוֹן מִפְּאַת קָדִימָה עַד־פְּאַת־
border-of to to-east from-border-of Simeon territory-of and-along (25) one Simeon

יָמָּה יִשָּׂשכָר* אֶחָד׃ (26) וְעַל ׀ גְּבוּל יִשָּׂשכָר* מִפְּאַת קָדִימָה
to-east from-border-of Issachar territory-of and-along (26) one Issachar to-west

עַד־פְּאַת־יָמָּה זְבוּלֻן אֶחָד׃ (27) וְעַל ׀ גְּבוּל זְבוּלֻן מִפְּאַת
from-border-of Zebulun territory-of and-along (27) one Zebulun to-west border-of to

קָדִמָה עַד־פְּאַת־יָמָּה גָּד אֶחָד׃ (28) וְעַל גְּבוּל גָּד אֶל־פְּאַת
boundary-of to Gad territory-of and-along (28) one Gad to-west border-of to to-east

remains of the area, bordering on the sacred portion and running the length of it, will be 10,000 cubits on the east side and 10,000 cubits on the west side. Its produce will supply food for the workers of the city. [19]The workers from the city who farm it will come from all the tribes of Israel. [20]The entire portion will be a square, 25,000 cubits on each side. As a special gift you will set aside the sacred portion, along with the property of the city.

[21]"What remains on both sides of the area formed by the sacred portion and the city property will belong to the prince. It will extend eastward from the 25,000 cubits of the sacred portion to the eastern border, and westward from the 25,000 cubits to the western border. Both these areas running the length of the tribal portions will belong to the prince, and the sacred portion with the temple sanctuary will be in the center of them. [22]So the property of the Levites and the property of the city will lie in the center of the area that belongs to the prince. The area belonging to the prince will lie between the border of Judah and the border of Benjamin.

[23]"As for the rest of the tribes: Benjamin will have one portion; it will extend from the east side to the west side.

[24]"Simeon will have one portion; it will border the territory of Benjamin from east to west.

[25]"Issachar will have one portion; it will border the territory of Simeon from east to west.

[26]"Zebulun will have one portion; it will border the territory of Issachar from east to west.

[27]"Gad will have one portion; it will border the territory of Zebulun from east to west.

[28]"The southern boundary of Gad will run south from Tamar to

*25, 26 Most mss have *dagesh* in the *sin* (יִשּׂ).

°18 ק תבואתו

°21 ק בתוכו

נֶגֶב תֵּימָנָה וְהָיָה גְבוּל מִתָּמָר מֵי מְרִיבַת קָדֵשׁ נַחֲלָה
Wadi Kadesh Meribah waters-of from-Tamar boundary and-he-will-run to-south south

עַל־הַיָּם הַגָּדוֹל׃ זֹאת הָאָרֶץ אֲשֶׁר־תַּפִּילוּ מִנַּחֲלָה
as-inheritance you-must-allot that the-land this (29) the-Great the-Sea to

לְשִׁבְטֵי יִשְׂרָאֵל וְאֵלֶּה מַחְלְקוֹתָם נְאֻם אֲדֹנָי יְהוִה׃
Yahweh Sovereign declaration-of portions-of-them and-these Israel to-tribes-of

וְאֵלֶּה תּוֹצְאֹת הָעִיר מִפְּאַת צָפוֹן חֲמֵשׁ מֵאוֹת וְאַרְבַּעַת
and-four-of hundreds five-of north on-side-of the-city exits-of and-these (30)

אֲלָפִים מִדָּה׃ וְשַׁעֲרֵי הָעִיר עַל־שְׁמוֹת שִׁבְטֵי יִשְׂרָאֵל
Israel tribes-of names-of after the-city indeed-gates-of (31) length thousands

שְׁעָרִים שְׁלוֹשָׁה צָפוֹנָה שַׁעַר רְאוּבֵן אֶחָד שַׁעַר יְהוּדָה אֶחָד שַׁעַר לֵוִי אֶחָד׃
one Levi gate-of one Judah gate-of one Reuben gate-of on-north three gates

וְאֶל־פְּאַת קָדִימָה חֲמֵשׁ מֵאוֹת וְאַרְבַּעַת אֲלָפִים וּשְׁעָרִים
also-gates thousands and-four-of hundreds five-of to-east side-of and-on (32)

שְׁלֹשָׁה וְשַׁעַר יוֹסֵף אֶחָד שַׁעַר בִּנְיָמִן אֶחָד שַׁעַר דָּן אֶחָד׃
one Dan gate-of one Benjamin gate-of one Joseph indeed-gate-of three

וּפְאַת־נֶגְבָּה חֲמֵשׁ מֵאוֹת וְאַרְבַּעַת אֲלָפִים מִדָּה
measure thousands and-four-of hundreds five-of to-south and-side-of (33)

וּשְׁעָרִים שְׁלֹשָׁה שַׁעַר שִׁמְעוֹן אֶחָד שַׁעַר יִשָּׂשכָר אֶחָד שַׁעַר זְבוּלֻן אֶחָד׃
one Zebulun gate-of one Issachar gate-of one Simeon gate-of three also-gates

פְּאַת־יָמָּה חֲמֵשׁ מֵאוֹת וְאַרְבַּעַת אֲלָפִים שַׁעֲרֵיהֶם
gates-of-them thousands and-four-of hundreds five-of to-west side-of (34)

שְׁלֹשָׁה שַׁעַר גָּד אֶחָד שַׁעַר אָשֵׁר אֶחָד שַׁעַר נַפְתָּלִי אֶחָד׃
one Naphtali gate-of one Asher gate-of one Gad gate-of three

סָבִיב שְׁמֹנָה עָשָׂר אָלֶף וְשֵׁם־הָעִיר מִיּוֹם יְהוָה שָׁמָּה׃
at-there Yahweh from-day the-city and-name-of thousand ten eight around (35)

the waters of Meribah Kadesh, then along the Wadi ⌞of Egypt⌟ to the Great Sea.[a]

29 "This is the land you are to allot as an inheritance to the tribes of Israel, and these will be their portions," declares the Sovereign LORD.

*The Gates of the City*

30 "These will be the exits of the city: Beginning on the north side, which is 4,500 cubits long, 31 the gates of the city will be named after the tribes of Israel. The three gates on the north side will be the gate of Reuben, the gate of Judah and the gate of Levi.

32 "On the east side, which is 4,500 cubits long, will be three gates: the gate of Joseph, the gate of Benjamin and the gate of Dan.

33 "On the south side, which measures 4,500 cubits, will be three gates: the gate of Simeon, the gate of Issachar and the gate of Zebulun.

34 "On the west side, which is 4,500 cubits long, will be three gates: the gate of Gad, the gate of Asher and the gate of Naphtali.

35 "The distance all around will be 18,000 cubits.

"And the name of the city from that time on will be:

THE LORD IS THERE."

[a] 28 That is, the Mediterranean

בִּשְׁנַת שָׁלוֹשׁ לְמַלְכוּת יְהוֹיָקִים מֶלֶךְ־יְהוּדָה בָּא נְבוּכַדְנֶאצַּר
Nebuchadnezzar he-came Judah king-of Jehoiakim of-reign-of three in-year-of (1:1)

מֶלֶךְ־בָּבֶל יְרוּשָׁלַם וַיָּצַר עָלֶיהָ׃ וַיִּתֵּן אֲדֹנָי
Lord and-he-delivered (2) against-her and-he-besieged Jerusalem Babylon king-of

בְּיָדוֹ אֶת־יְהוֹיָקִים מֶלֶךְ־יְהוּדָה וּמִקְצָת כְּלֵי בֵית־
temple-of articles-of and-from-end-of Judah king-of Jehoiakim *** into-hand-of-him

הָאֱלֹהִים וַיְבִיאֵם אֶרֶץ־שִׁנְעָר בֵּית אֱלֹהָיו וְאֶת־הַכֵּלִים
the-articles and gods-of-him temple-of Shinar land-of and-he-carried-off-them the-God

הֵבִיא בֵּית אוֹצַר אֱלֹהָיו׃ וַיֹּאמֶר הַמֶּלֶךְ לְאַשְׁפְּנַז
to-Ashpenaz the-king then-he-ordered (3) gods-of-him treasury-of house-of he-put

רַב סָרִיסָיו לְהָבִיא מִבְּנֵי יִשְׂרָאֵל וּמִזֶּרַע
even-from-family-of Israel from-sons-of to-bring court-officials-of-him chief-of

הַמְּלוּכָה וּמִן־הַפַּרְתְּמִים׃ יְלָדִים אֲשֶׁר אֵין בָּהֶם כָּל־
any-of to-them there-is-not who young-men (4) the-nobles and-from the-royalty

מְאוּם וְטוֹבֵי מַרְאֶה וּמַשְׂכִּילִים בְּכָל־
for-all-of and-ones-having-aptitude appearance and-ones-handsome-of physical-defect

חָכְמָה וְיֹדְעֵי דַעַת וּמְבִינֵי מַדָּע
knowledge and-ones-understanding-of information and-ones-being-informed-of learning

וַאֲשֶׁר כֹּחַ בָּהֶם לַעֲמֹד בְּהֵיכַל הַמֶּלֶךְ וּלְלַמְּדָם
and-to-teach-them the-king in-palace-of to-serve to-them qualification and-who

סֵפֶר וּלְשׁוֹן כַּשְׂדִּים׃ וַיְמַן לָהֶם הַמֶּלֶךְ
the-king to-them and-he-assigned (5) Chaldeans and-language-of literature

דְּבַר־יוֹם בְּיוֹמוֹ מִפַּת־בַּג הַמֶּלֶךְ וּמִיֵּין מִשְׁתָּיו
drinking-of-him and-from-wine-of the-king from-food-of for-day-of-him day amount-of

וּלְגַדְּלָם שָׁנִים שָׁלוֹשׁ וּמִקְצָתָם יַעַמְדוּ לִפְנֵי הַמֶּלֶךְ׃
the-king before they-would-serve and-at-end-of-them three years and-to-train-them

וַיְהִי בָהֶם מִבְּנֵי יְהוּדָה דָּנִיֵּאל חֲנַנְיָה מִישָׁאֵל וַעֲזַרְיָה׃
and-Azariah Mishael Hananiah Daniel Judah from-sons-of among-them and-he-was (6)

וַיָּשֶׂם לָהֶם שַׂר הַסָּרִיסִים שֵׁמוֹת וַיָּשֶׂם לְדָנִיֵּאל
to-Daniel and-he-gave names the-officials chief-of to-them and-he-gave (7)

בֵּלְטְשַׁאצַּר וְלַחֲנַנְיָה שַׁדְרַךְ וּלְמִישָׁאֵל מֵישַׁךְ וְלַעֲזַרְיָה
and-to-Azariah Meshach and-to-Mishael Shadrach and-to-Hananiah Belteshazzar

עֲבֵד נְגוֹ׃ וַיָּשֶׂם דָּנִיֵּאל עַל־לִבּוֹ אֲשֶׁר לֹא־יִתְגָּאַל
he-would-defile-himself not that heart-of-him in Daniel but-he-resolved (8) Nego Abed

בְּפַתְבַּג הַמֶּלֶךְ וּבְיֵין מִשְׁתָּיו וַיְבַקֵּשׁ
and-he-asked-permission drinking-of-him and-with-wine-of the-royalty with-food-of

מִשַּׂר הַסָּרִיסִים אֲשֶׁר לֹא יִתְגָּאָל׃ וַיִּתֵּן
now-he-gave (9) he-would-defile-himself not that the-officials from-chief-of

°4 ק מום

*Daniel's Training in Babylon*

1 In the third year of the reign of Jehoiakim king of Judah, Nebuchadnezzar king of Babylon came to Jerusalem and besieged it. 2And the Lord delivered Jehoiakim king of Judah into his hand, along with some of the articles from the temple of God. These he carried off to the temple of his god in Babylonia[a] and put in the treasure house of his god.

3Then the king ordered Ashpenaz, chief of his court officials, to bring in some of the Israelites from the royal family and the nobility— 4young men without any physical defect, handsome, showing aptitude for every kind of learning, well informed, quick to understand, and qualified to serve in the king's palace. He was to teach them the language and literature of the Babylonians.[b] 5The king assigned them a daily amount of food and wine from the king's table. They were to be trained for three years, and after that they were to enter the king's service.

6Among these were some from Judah: Daniel, Hananiah, Mishael and Azariah. 7The chief official gave them new names: to Daniel, the name Belteshazzar; to Hananiah, Shadrach; to Mishael, Meshach; and to Azariah, Abednego.

8But Daniel resolved not to defile himself with the royal food and wine, and he asked the chief official for permission not to defile himself this way. 9Now God

a2 Hebrew *Shinar* b4 Or *Chaldeans*

הָאֱלֹהִים אֶת־דָּנִיֵּאל לְחֶסֶד וּלְרַחֲמִים לִפְנֵי שַׂר הַסָּרִיסִים׃
the-officials chief-of before and-for-sympathies for-favor Daniel *** the-God

וַיֹּאמֶר שַׂר הַסָּרִיסִים לְדָנִיֵּאל יָרֵא אֲנִי אֶת־אֲדֹנִי הַמֶּלֶךְ
the-king lord-of-me *** I fearing to-Daniel the-officials chief-of but-he-told (10)

אֲשֶׁר מִנָּה אֶת־מַאֲכַלְכֶם וְאֶת־מִשְׁתֵּיכֶם אֲשֶׁר לָמָּה יִרְאֶה
should-he-see for-why? because drink-of-you and food-of-you *** he-assigned who

אֶת־פְּנֵיכֶם זֹעֲפִים מִן־הַיְלָדִים אֲשֶׁר כְּגִילְכֶם
as-age-of-you who the-young-men more-than ones-being-bad faces-of-you ***

וְחִיַּבְתֶּם אֶת־רֹאשִׁי לַמֶּלֶךְ׃ וַיֹּאמֶר דָּנִיֵּאל
Daniel then-he-said (11) to-the-king head-of-me *** then-you-would-be-responsible

אֶל־הַמֶּלְצַר אֲשֶׁר מִנָּה שַׂר הַסָּרִיסִים עַל־דָּנִיֵּאל חֲנַנְיָה מִישָׁאֵל
Mishael Hananiah Daniel over the-officials chief-of he-appointed whom the-guard to

וַעֲזַרְיָה׃ נַס־נָא אֶת־עֲבָדֶיךָ יָמִים עֲשָׂרָה וְיִתְּנוּ־
and-let-them-give ten days servants-of-you *** now! test! (12) and-Azariah

לָנוּ מִן־הַזֵּרֹעִים וְנֹאכְלָה וּמַיִם וְנִשְׁתֶּה׃
also-let-us-drink and-waters and-let-us-eat the-vegetables from to-us

וְיֵרָאוּ לְפָנֶיךָ מַרְאֵינוּ וּמַרְאֵה
with-appearance-of appearance-of-us before-you then-let-them-compare (13)

הַיְלָדִים הָאֹכְלִים אֵת פַּתְבַּג הַמֶּלֶךְ וְכַאֲשֶׁר תִּרְאֵה
you-see and-according-to-what the-royalty food-of *** the-ones-eating the-young-men

עֲשֵׂה עִם־עֲבָדֶיךָ׃ וַיִּשְׁמַע לָהֶם לַדָּבָר הַזֶּה
the-this to-the-thing with-them so-he-agreed (14) servants-of-you to treat!

וַיְנַסֵּם יָמִים עֲשָׂרָה׃ וּמִקְצָת יָמִים עֲשָׂרָה נִרְאָה מַרְאֵיהֶם
appearance-of-them he-looked ten days and-at-end-of (15) ten days and-he-tested-them

טוֹב וּבְרִיאֵי בָּשָׂר מִן־כָּל־הַיְלָדִים הָאֹכְלִים
the-ones-eating the-young-men any-of more-than body and-ones-nourished-of healthy

אֵת פַּתְבַּג הַמֶּלֶךְ׃ וַיְהִי הַמֶּלְצַר נֹשֵׂא אֶת־פַּתְבָּגָם
choice-food-of-them *** taking-away the-guard so-he-was (16) the-royalty food-of ***

וְיֵין מִשְׁתֵּיהֶם וְנֹתֵן לָהֶם זֵרְעֹנִים׃ וְהַיְלָדִים
and-the-young-men (17) vegetables to-them and-giving drinking-of-them and-wine-of

הָאֵלֶּה אַרְבַּעְתָּם נָתַן לָהֶם הָאֱלֹהִים מַדָּע וְהַשְׂכֵּל בְּכָל־
to-all-of and-to-understand knowledge the-God to-them he-gave four-of-them the-these

סֵפֶר וְחָכְמָה וְדָנִיֵּאל הֵבִין בְּכָל־חָזוֹן וַחֲלֹמוֹת׃
and-dreams vision to-all-of he-understood and-Daniel and-learning literature

וּלְמִקְצָת הַיָּמִים אֲשֶׁר־אָמַר הַמֶּלֶךְ לַהֲבִיאָם וַיְבִיאֵם
then-he-presented-them to-bring-them the-king he-set that the-days and-at-end-of (18)

שַׂר הַסָּרִיסִים לִפְנֵי נְבֻכַדְנֶצַּר׃ וַיְדַבֵּר אִתָּם הַמֶּלֶךְ
the-king with-them and-he-talked (19) Nebuchadnezzar before the-officials chief-of

had caused the official to show favor and sympathy to Daniel, [10]but the official told Daniel, "I am afraid of my lord the king, who has assigned your[c] food and drink. Why should he see you looking worse than the other young men your age? The king would then have my head because of you."

[11]Daniel then said to the guard whom the chief official had appointed over Daniel, Hananiah, Mishael and Azariah, [12]"Please test your servants for ten days: Give us nothing but vegetables to eat and water to drink. [13]Then compare our appearance with that of the young men who eat the royal food, and treat your servants in accordance with what you see." [14]So he agreed to this and tested them for ten days.

[15]At the end of the ten days they looked healthier and better nourished than any of the young men who ate the royal food. [16]So the guard took away their choice food and the wine they were to drink and gave them vegetables instead.

[17]To these four young men God gave knowledge and understanding of all kinds of literature and learning. And Daniel could understand visions and dreams of all kinds.

[18]At the end of the time set by the king to bring them in, the chief official presented them to Nebuchadnezzar. [19]The king talked with them, and he found

c10 The Hebrew for *your* and *you* in this verse is plural.

וְלֹא נִמְצָא מִכֻּלָּם כְּדָנִיֵּאל חֲנַנְיָה מִישָׁאֵל וַעֲזַרְיָה
and-Azariah Mishael Hananiah equal-to-Daniel among-all-of-them he-was-found and-not

וַיַּעַמְדוּ לִפְנֵי הַמֶּלֶךְ׃ וְכֹל דְּבַר חָכְמַת בִּינָה
understanding wisdom-of matter-of and-every-of (20) the-king before so-they-served

אֲשֶׁר־בִּקֵּשׁ מֵהֶם הַמֶּלֶךְ וַיִּמְצָאֵם עֶשֶׂר יָדוֹת עַל כָּל־
all-of over times ten then-he-found-them the-king from-them he-questioned which

הַחַרְטֻמִּים הָאַשָּׁפִים אֲשֶׁר בְּכָל־ מַלְכוּתוֹ׃ וַיְהִי
and-he-remained (21) kingdom-of-him in-whole-of who the-enchanters the-magicians

דָּנִיֵּאל עַד־ שְׁנַת אַחַת לְכוֹרֶשׁ הַמֶּלֶךְ׃ וּבִשְׁנַת שְׁתַּיִם לְמַלְכוּת
of-reign-of two and-in-year-of (2:1) the-king of-Cyrus one year-of until Daniel

נְבֻכַדְנֶצַּר חָלַם נְבֻכַדְנֶצַּר חֲלֹמוֹת וַתִּתְפָּעֶם רוּחוֹ
mind-of-him and-she-was-troubled dreams Nebuchadnezzar he-dreamed Nebuchadnezzar

וּשְׁנָתוֹ נִהְיְתָה עָלָיו׃ וַיֹּאמֶר הַמֶּלֶךְ לִקְרֹא
to-summon the-king so-he-ordered (2) upon-him she-was-finished and-sleep-of-him

לַחַרְטֻמִּים וְלָאַשָּׁפִים וְלַמְכַשְּׁפִים
and-to-the-ones-practicing-sorcery and-to-the-enchanters to-the-magicians

וְלַכַּשְׂדִּים לְהַגִּיד לַמֶּלֶךְ חֲלֹמֹתָיו וַיָּבֹאוּ
when-they-came-in dreams-of-him to-the-king to-tell and-to-the-Chaldeans

וַיַּעַמְדוּ לִפְנֵי הַמֶּלֶךְ׃ וַיֹּאמֶר לָהֶם הַמֶּלֶךְ חֲלוֹם חָלָמְתִּי
I-dreamed dream the-king to-them then-he-said (3) the-king before and-they-stood

וַתִּפָּעֶם רוּחִי לָדַעַת אֶת־ הַחֲלוֹם׃ וַיְדַבְּרוּ
then-they-answered (4) the-dream *** to-know mind-of-me and-she-is-troubled

הַכַּשְׂדִּים לַמֶּלֶךְ אֲרָמִית מַלְכָּא לְעָלְמִין חֱיִי אֱמַר חֶלְמָא
the-dream tell! live! to-forevers O-king Aramaic to-the-king the-Chaldeans

לְעַבְדָךְ° וּפִשְׁרָא נְחַוֵּא׃ עָנֵה מַלְכָּא
the-king replying (5) we-will-tell and-the-interpretation to-servants-of-you

וְאָמַר לְכַשְׂדָּיֵא° מִלְּתָא מִנִּי אַזְדָּא הֵן לָא תְהוֹדְעוּנַּנִי חֶלְמָא
the-dream you-tell-me not if firm from-me the-decision to-the-Chaldeans and-saying

וּפִשְׁרֵהּ הַדָּמִין תִּתְעַבְדוּן וּבָתֵּיכוֹן נְוָלִי
pile-of-rubble and-houses-of-you you-will-be-cut pieces and-interpretation-of-him

יִתְּשָׂמוּן׃ וְהֵן חֶלְמָא וּפִשְׁרֵהּ תְּהַחֲוֺן
you-tell and-explanation-of-him the-dream but-if (6) they-will-be-turned-into

מַתְּנָן וּנְבִזְבָּה וִיקָר שַׂגִּיא תְּקַבְּלוּן מִן־ קֳדָמָי לָהֵן חֶלְמָא
the-dream so before-me from you-will-receive great and-honor and-reward gifts

וּפִשְׁרֵהּ הַחֲוֺנִי׃ עֲנוֹ תִנְיָנוּת וְאָמְרִין
and-ones-saying once-more they-replied (7) tell-me! and-interpretation-of-him

מַלְכָּא חֶלְמָא יֵאמַר לְעַבְדוֹהִי וּפִשְׁרָה
and-interpretation-of-him to-servants-of-him let-him-tell the-dream the-king

°4 ק לעבדך
°5 ק לכשדאי

none equal to Daniel, Hananiah, Mishael and Azariah; so they entered the king's service. [20]In every matter of wisdom and understanding about which the king questioned them, he found them ten times better than all the magicians and enchanters in his whole kingdom.

[21]And Daniel remained there until the first year of King Cyrus.

*Nebuchadnezzar's Dream*

2 In the second year of his reign, Nebuchadnezzar had dreams; his mind was troubled and he could not sleep. [2]So the king summoned the magicians, enchanters, sorcerers and astrologers[d] to tell him what he had dreamed. When they came in and stood before the king, [3]he said to them, "I have had a dream that troubles me and I want to know what it means.[e]"

[4]Then the astrologers answered the king in Aramaic,[f] "O king, live forever! Tell your servants the dream, and we will interpret it."

[5]The king replied to the astrologers, "This is what I have firmly decided: If you do not tell me what my dream was and interpret it, I will have you cut into pieces and your houses turned into piles of rubble. [6]But if you tell me the dream and explain it, you will receive from me gifts and rewards and great honor. So tell me the dream and interpret it for me."

[7]Once more they replied, "Let the king tell his servants the dream, and we will interpret it."

d2 Or *Chaldeans*; also in verses 4, 5 and 10
e3 Or *was*
f4 The text from here through chapter 7 is in Aramaic.

נְהַחֲוֵה׃ עָנֵה מַלְכָּא וְאָמַר מִן־יַצִּיב יָדַע אֲנָה דִּי
that I knowing certainty from and-saying the-king answering (8) we-will-tell

עִדָּנָא אַנְתּוּן זָבְנִין כָּל־קֳבֵל דִּי חֲזֵיתוֹן* דִּי אַזְדָּא מִנִּי
from-me firm that you-realize that because all-of ones-trying-to-gain you the-time

מִלְּתָא׃ דִּי הֵן־חֶלְמָא לָא תְהוֹדְעֻנַּנִי חֲדָה־הִיא דָתְכוֹן
penalty-of-you she one you-tell-me not the-dream if that (9) the-decision

וּמִלָּה כִדְבָה וּשְׁחִיתָה הִזְמִנְתּוּן° לְמֵאמַר קָדָמַי עַד דִּי
that until before-me to-tell you-conspired and-being-wicked misleading and-thing

עִדָּנָא יִשְׁתַּנֵּא לָהֵן חֶלְמָא אֱמַרוּ לִי וְאִנְדַּע דִּי
that and-I-will-know to-me tell! the-dream so he-will-change the-situation

פִּשְׁרֵהּ תְּהַחֲוֻנַּנִי׃ עֲנוֹ כַשְׂדָּיֵא° קֳדָם־מַלְכָּא
the-king before the-Chaldeans they-answered (10) you-can-tell-me interpretation-of-him

וְאָמְרִין לָא־אִיתַי אֱנָשׁ† עַל־יַבֶּשְׁתָּא דִּי מִלַּת מַלְכָּא יוּכַל
he-can the-king request-of who the-earth on man there-is not and-ones-saying

לְהַחֲוָיָה כָּל־קֳבֵל דִּי כָּל־מֶלֶךְ רַב וְשַׁלִּיט מִלָּה כִדְנָה לָא
not such-as-this request or-mighty great king any-of that because all-of to-answer

שְׁאֵל לְכָל־חַרְטֹּם וְאָשַׁף וְכַשְׂדָּי׃ וּמִלְּתָא דִּי־
that and-the-request (11) or-Chaldean or-enchanter magician of-any-of he-asked

מַלְכָּה שָׁאֵל יַקִּירָה וְאָחֳרָן לָא אִיתַי דִּי יְחַוִּנַּהּ קֳדָם
before he-can-reveal-her who there-is not and-another difficult asking the-king

מַלְכָּא לָהֵן אֱלָהִין דִּי מְדָרְהוֹן עִם־בִּשְׂרָא לָא אִיתוֹהִי׃
there-is-him not the-man among living-place-of-them who gods except the-king

כָּל־קֳבֵל דְּנָה מַלְכָּא בְּנַס וּקְצַף שַׂגִּיא
very and-he-became-furious he-became-angry the-king this because-of all-of (12)

וַאֲמַר לְהוֹבָדָה לְכֹל חַכִּימֵי בָבֶל׃ וְדָתָא
so-the-decree (13) Babylon wise-men-of to-all-of to-execute that-he-ordered

נֶפְקַת וְחַכִּימַיָּא מִתְקַטְּלִין וּבְעוֹ דָּנִיֵּאל
Daniel and-they-looked-for ones-being-put-to-death that-the-wise-men she-was-issued

וְחַבְרוֹהִי לְהִתְקְטָלָה׃ בֵּאדַיִן דָּנִיֵּאל הֲתִיב עֵטָא
wisdom he-spoke Daniel when-then (14) to-be-put-to-death and-friends-of-him

וּטְעֵם לְאַרְיוֹךְ רַב־טַבָּחַיָּא דִּי מַלְכָּא דִּי נְפַק
he-went-out who the-king who-of the-guards commander-of to-Arioch and-tact

לְקַטָּלָה לְחַכִּימֵי בָּבֶל׃ עָנֵה וְאָמַר לְאַרְיוֹךְ שַׁלִּיטָא
the-officer to-Arioch and-saying asking (15) Babylon to-wise-men-of to-put-to-death

דִּי־מַלְכָּא עַל־מָה דָתָא מְהַחְצְפָה מִן־קֳדָם מַלְכָּא אֱדַיִן
then the-king before from being-harsh the-decree what? for the-king who-of

מִלְּתָא הוֹדַע אַרְיוֹךְ לְדָנִיֵּאל׃ וְדָנִיֵּאל עַל וּבְעָה
and-he-asked he-went-in and-Daniel (16) to-Daniel Arioch he-explained the-matter

[8]Then the king answered, "I am certain that you are trying to gain time, because you realize that this is what I have firmly decided: [9]If you do not tell me the dream, there is just one penalty for you. You have conspired to tell me misleading and wicked things, hoping the situation will change. So then, tell me the dream, and I will know that you can interpret it for me."

[10]The astrologers answered the king, "There is not a man on earth who can do what the king asks! No king, however great and mighty, has ever asked such a thing of any magician or enchanter or astrologer. [11]What the king asks is too difficult. No one can reveal it to the king except the gods, and they do not live among men."

[12]This made the king so angry and furious that he ordered the execution of all the wise men of Babylon. [13]So the decree was issued to put the wise men to death, and men were sent to look for Daniel and his friends to put them to death.

[14]When Arioch, the commander of the king's guard, had gone out to put to death the wise men of Babylon, Daniel spoke to him with wisdom and tact. [15]He asked the king's officer, "Why did the king issue such a harsh decree?" Arioch then explained the matter to Daniel. [16]At this, Daniel went in

*8 Most mss have *shureq* instead of *holem vav* (־תון).

†10 Most mss have *hateph segol* under the *aleph* (אֱ).

°8 ק הזדמנתון

°10 ק כשדאי

מִן־ מַלְכָּא דִּי זְמָן יִנְתֵּן־ לֵהּ וּפִשְׁרָא לְהַחֲוָיָה
to-tell so-the-interpretation to-him he-would-give time that the-king from

לְמַלְכָּא׃ (17) אֱדַיִן דָּנִיֵּאל לְבַיְתֵהּ אֲזַל וְלַחֲנַנְיָה מִישָׁאֵל
Mishael and-to-Hananiah he-returned to-house-of-him Daniel then (17) to-the-king

וַעֲזַרְיָה חַבְרוֹהִי מִלְּתָא הוֹדַע׃ (18) וְרַחֲמִין לְמִבְעֵא
to-plead-for and-merices (18) he-explained the-matter friends-of-him and-Azariah

מִן־ קֳדָם אֱלָהּ שְׁמַיָּא עַל־ רָזָה דְּנָה דִּי לָא
not that this the-mystery concerning the-heavens God-of before from

יְהֹבְדוּן דָּנִיֵּאל וְחַבְרוֹהִי עִם־ שְׁאָר חַכִּימֵי בָבֶל׃
Babylon wise-men-of rest-of with and-friends-of-him Daniel they-might-execute

(19) אֱדַיִן לְדָנִיֵּאל בְּחֶזְוָא דִּי־ לֵילְיָא רָזָה גֲלִי
he-was-revealed the-mystery the-night that-of in-the-vision to-Daniel then (19)

אֱדַיִן דָּנִיֵּאל בָּרִךְ לֶאֱלָהּ שְׁמַיָּא׃ (20) עָנֵה דָנִיֵּאל וְאָמַר
and-saying Daniel speaking (20) the-heavens to-God-of he-praised Daniel then

לֶהֱוֵא שְׁמֵהּ דִּי־ אֱלָהָא מְבָרַךְ מִן־ עָלְמָא וְעַד־
and-to the-forever from being-praised the-God that-to name-of-him let-him-be

עָלְמָא דִּי חָכְמְתָא וּגְבוּרְתָא דִּי לֵהּ־ הִיא׃ (21) וְהוּא מְהַשְׁנֵא
changing indeed-he (21) she to-him that and-the-power the-wisdom who the-forever

עִדָּנַיָּא וְזִמְנַיָּא מְהַעְדֵּה מַלְכִין וּמְהָקֵים מַלְכִין יָהֵב חָכְמְתָא
the-wisdom giving kings and-setting-up kings deposing and-the-seasons the-times

לְחַכִּימִין וּמַנְדְּעָא לְיָדְעֵי בִינָה׃ (22) הוּא גָּלֵא
revealing he (22) discernment to-ones-knowing-of and-the-knowledge to-wise-men

עַמִּיקָתָא וּמְסַתְּרָתָא יָדַע מָה בַחֲשׁוֹכָא וּנְהִירָא
and-the-light in-the-darkness what knowing and-things-being-hidden deep-things

עִמֵּהּ שְׁרֵא׃ (23) לָךְ ׀ אֱלָהּ אֲבָהָתִי מְהוֹדֵא וּמְשַׁבַּח אֲנָה
I and-praising thanking fathers-of-me God-of to-you (23) dwelling with-him

דִּי חָכְמְתָא וּגְבוּרְתָא יְהַבְתְּ לִי וּכְעַן הוֹדַעְתַּנִי דִּי־
what you-made-known-to-me and-now to-me you-gave and-the-power the-wisdom who

בְּעֵינָא מִנָּךְ דִּי־ מִלַּת מַלְכָּא הוֹדַעְתֶּנָא׃ (24) כָּל־ קֳבֵל
because-of all-of (24) you-made-known-to-us the-king dream-of what of-you we-asked

דְּנָה דָּנִיֵּאל עַל עַל־ אַרְיוֹךְ דִּי מַנִּי מַלְכָּא לְהוֹבָדָה לְחַכִּימֵי
to-wise-men-of to-execute the-king he-appointed whom Arioch to he-went Daniel this

בָבֶל אֲזַל ׀ וְכֵן אֲמַר־ לֵהּ לְחַכִּימֵי בָבֶל אַל־ תְּהוֹבֵד
you-execute not Babylon to-wise-men-of to-him he-said and-this he-went Babylon

הַעֵלְנִי קֳדָם מַלְכָּא וּפִשְׁרָא לְמַלְכָּא אֲחַוֵּא׃ (25) אֱדַיִן
then (25) I-will-tell to-the-king and-the-interpretation the-king before take-me!

אַרְיוֹךְ בְּהִתְבְּהָלָה הַנְעֵל לְדָנִיֵּאל קֳדָם מַלְכָּא וְכֵן אֲמַר־ לֵהּ
to-him he-said and-this the-king before to-Daniel he-took in-to-hurry Arioch

°22 ק ונהורא

to the king and asked for time, so that he might interpret the dream for him.

[17]Then Daniel returned to his house and explained the matter to his friends Hananiah, Mishael and Azariah. [18]He urged them to plead for mercy from the God of heaven concerning this mystery, so that he and his friends might not be executed with the rest of the wise men of Babylon. [19]During the night the mystery was revealed to Daniel in a vision. Then Daniel praised the God of heaven [20]and said:

"Praise be to the name of God
for ever and ever;
wisdom and power are his.
[21]He changes times and seasons;
he sets up kings and
deposes them.
He gives wisdom to the wise
and knowledge to the
discerning.
[22]He reveals deep and hidden
things;
he knows what lies in
darkness,
and light dwells with him.
[23]I thank and praise you, O God
of my fathers:
You have given me wisdom
and power,
you have made known to me
what we asked of you,
you have made known to us
the dream of the king."

*Daniel Interprets the Dream*

[24]Then Daniel went to Arioch, whom the king had appointed to execute the wise men of Babylon, and said to him, "Do not execute the wise men of Babylon. Take me to the king, and I will interpret his dream for him."

[25]Arioch took Daniel to the king at once and said, "I have found a

דִּֽי־הַשְׁכַּחַת גְּבַר מִן־בְּנֵי גָלוּתָא דִּי יְהוּד דִּי פִשְׁרָא
the-interpretation who Judah who-of the-exile sons-of from man I-found that

לְמַלְכָּא יְהוֹדַע׃ עָנֵה מַלְכָּא וְאָמַר לְדָנִיֵּאל דִּי שְׁמֵהּ
name-of-him who to-Daniel and-saying the-king asking (26) he-can-tell to-the-king

בֵּלְטְשַׁאצַּר הַאִיתָךְ כָּהֵל לְהוֹדָעֻתַנִי חֶלְמָא דִּֽי־חֲזֵית
I-saw that the-dream to-tell-me being-able is-there-to-you? Belteshazzar

וּפִשְׁרֵהּ׃ עָנֵה דָנִיֵּאל קֳדָם מַלְכָּא וְאָמַר רָזָה
the-mystery and-saying the-king before Daniel replying (27) and-interpretation-of-him

דִּֽי־מַלְכָּא שָׁאֵל לָא חַכִּימִין אָשְׁפִין חַרְטֻמִּין גָּזְרִין
ones-divining magicians enchanters wise-men no asking-about the-king that

יָכְלִין לְהַחֲוָיָה לְמַלְכָּא׃ בְּרַם אִיתַי אֱלָהּ בִּשְׁמַיָּא
in-the-heavens God there-is but (28) to-the-king to-explain ones-being-able

גָּלֵא רָזִין וְהוֹדַע לְמַלְכָּא נְבוּכַדְנֶצַּר מָה דִּי לֶהֱוֵא
he-will-happen that what Nebuchadnezzar to-the-king and-he-showed mysteries revealing

בְּאַחֲרִית יוֹמַיָּא חֶלְמָךְ וְחֶזְוֵי רֵאשָׁךְ עַל־מִשְׁכְּבָךְ דְּנָה הוּא׃
he this bed-of-you on mind-of-you and-visions-of dream-of-you the-days in-coming-of

אַנְתְּה מַלְכָּא רַעְיוֹנָךְ עַל־מִשְׁכְּבָךְ סְלִקוּ מָה דִּי לֶהֱוֵא
he-will-come that what they-turned-to bed-of-you on minds-of-you O-king you (29)

אַחֲרֵי דְנָה וְגָלֵא רָזַיָּא הוֹדְעָךְ מָה־דִּי לֶהֱוֵא׃
he-will-happen that what he-showed-you the-mysteries and-one-revealing this after

וַאֲנָה לָא בְחָכְמָה דִּי־אִיתַי בִּי מִן־כָּל־חַיַּיָּא
the-living-men all-of more-than to-me there-is that because-of-wisdom not and-I (30)

רָזָא דְנָה גֱּלִי לִי לָהֵן עַל־דִּבְרַת דִּי פִשְׁרָא
the-interpretation that reason-of for so to-me he-was-revealed this the-mystery

לְמַלְכָּא יְהוֹדְעוּן וְרַעְיוֹנֵי לִבְבָךְ תִּנְדַּע׃
you-might-understand mind-of-you and-thoughts-of they-might-make-known to-the-king

אַנְתְּה מַלְכָּא חָזֵה הֲוַיְתָ וַאֲלוּ צְלֵם חַד שַׂגִּיא צַלְמָא דִּכֵּן רַב
enormous that the-statue large a statue and-see! you-were looking O-king you (31)

וְזִיוֵהּ יַתִּיר קָאֵם לְקָבְלָךְ וְרֵוֵהּ דְּחִיל׃
being-awesome and-appearance-of-him at-before-you standing great and-dazzling-of-him

הוּא צַלְמָא רֵאשֵׁהּ דִּי־דְהַב טָב חֲדוֹהִי וּדְרָעוֹהִי
and-arms-of-him and-chests-of-him pure gold of head-of-him the-statue that (32)

דִּי כְסַף מְעוֹהִי וְיַרְכָתֵהּ דִּי נְחָשׁ׃ שָׁקוֹהִי דִּי פַרְזֶל
iron of legs-of-him (33) bronze of and-thighs-of-him bellies-of-him silver of

רַגְלוֹהִי מִנְּהוֹן דִּי פַרְזֶל וּמִנְּהוֹן דִּי חֲסַף׃ חָזֵה הֲוַיְתָ
you-were watching (34) baked-clay of and-of-them iron of of-them feet-of-him

עַד דִּי הִתְגְּזֶרֶת אֶבֶן דִּי־לָא בִידַיִן וּמְחָת לְצַלְמָא
on-the-statue and-she-struck by-hands not that rock she-was-cut-out that while

man among the exiles from Judah who can tell the king what his dream means."

26The king asked Daniel (also called Belteshazzar), "Are you able to tell me what I saw in my dream and interpret it?"

27Daniel replied, "No wise man, enchanter, magician or diviner can explain to the king the mystery he has asked about, 28but there is a God in heaven who reveals mysteries. He has shown King Nebuchadnezzar what will happen in days to come. Your dream and the visions that passed through your mind as you lay on your bed are these:

29"As you were lying there, O king, your mind turned to things to come, and the revealer of mysteries showed you what is going to happen. 30As for me, this mystery has been revealed to me, not because I have greater wisdom than other living men, but so that you, O king, may know the interpretation and that you may understand what went through your mind.

31"You looked, O king, and there before you stood a large statue—an enormous, dazzling statue, awesome in appearance. 32The head of the statue was made of pure gold, its chest and arms of silver, its belly and thighs of bronze, 33its legs of iron, its feet partly of iron and partly of baked clay. 34While you were watching, a rock was cut out, but not by human hands. It struck

°26 ק האיתך
°29 ק אנת ;°31 ק אנת
°33a ק ומנהין ;°33b ק מנהין

באדין המון׃ והדקת וחספא פרזלא די על־רגלוהי
at-then (35) them and-she-smashed and-the-clay the-iron of feet-of-him on

כספא נחשא חספא פרזלא כחדה דקו
the-silver the-bronze the-clay the-iron as-same they-were-broken-to-pieces

קיט אדרי־ מן־ כעור והוו ודהבא
summer threshing-floors-of on like-chaff and-they-became and-the-gold

להון השתכח לא־ אתר וכל־ רוחא המון ונשא
of-them he-was-found not trace and-any-of the-wind them and-he-swept-away

רב לטור הות לצלמא מחת די־ ואבנא ׀
huge into-mountain she-became on-the-statue she-struck that but-the-rock

ופשרה חלמא דנה ארעא׃ כל־ ומלת
now-interpretation-of-him the-dream this (36) the-earth whole-of and-she-filled

אלה די מלכיא מלך מלכא אנתה מלכא׃ קדם־ נאמר
God-of whom the-kings king-of O-king you (37) the-king before we-will-tell

לך׃ יהב־ ויקרא ותקפא חסנא מלכותא שמיא
to-you he-gave and-the-glory and-the-might the-power the-dominion the-heavens

ברא חיות אנשא בני־ דארין די ובכל־
the-field beast-of the-mankind children-of ones-living that and-in-everywhere (38)

בכלהון והשלטך בידך יהב שמיא ועוף־
over-all-of-them and-he-made-ruler-you in-hand-of-you he-placed the-airs and-bird-of

אחרי מלכו תקום ובתרך דהבא׃ די ראשה אנתה־הוא
another kingdom she-will-rise and-after-you (39) the-gold of the-head that you

תשלט די נחשא די אחרי תליתיא ומלכו מנך ארעא
she-will-rule that bronze of another third next-kingdom more-than-you earthward

כפרזלא תקיפה תהוא רביעיה ומלכו ארעא׃ בכל־
as-the-iron strong she-will-be fourth finally-kingdom (40) the-earth over-whole-of

די־ וכפרזלא כלא וחשל מהדק פרזלא די כל־קבל
that and-as-the-iron the-everything and-smashing breaking the-iron that for all-of

ודי־ ותרע׃ תדק אלין כל־ מרעע
and-that (41) and-she-will-break she-will-crush these all-of breaking-to-pieces

פרזל ומנהון פחר די־ חסף מנהון ואצבעתא רגליא חזיתה
iron and-of-them potter of baked-clay of-them and-the-toes the-feet you-saw

להוא־ פרזלא די נצבתא ומן־ תהוה פליגה מלכו
he-will-be the-iron of the-strength yet-of she-will-be being-divided kingdom

טינא׃ בחסף מערב פרזלא חזיתה די קבל כל־ בה
the-clay with-clay-of being-mixed the-iron you-saw that because all-of in-her

מלכותא קצת מן־ חסף ומנהון פרזל מנהון רגליא ואצבעת
the-kingdom part-of of clay and-of-them iron of-them the-feet and-toes-of (42)

the statue on its feet of iron and
clay and smashed them. [35]Then
the iron, the clay, the bronze, the
silver and the gold were broken to
pieces at the same time and
became like chaff on a threshing
floor in the summer. The wind
swept them away without leaving
a trace. But the rock that struck the
statue became a huge mountain
and filled the whole earth.
[36]"This was the dream, and now
we will interpret it to the king.
[37]You, O king, are the king of
kings. The God of heaven has giv-
en you dominion and power and
might and glory; [38]in your hands
he has placed mankind and the
beasts of the field and the birds of
the air. Wherever they live, he has
made you ruler over them all. You
are that head of gold.
[39]"After you, another kingdom
will rise, inferior to yours. Next, a
third kingdom, one of bronze, will
rule over the whole earth. [40]Fi-
nally, there will be a fourth kingdom, strong as iron—for iron
breaks and smashes everything—
and as iron breaks things to
pieces, so it will crush and break
all the others. [41]Just as you saw that
the feet and toes were partly of
baked clay and partly of iron, so
this will be a divided kingdom;
yet it will have some of the
strength of iron in it, even as you
saw iron mixed with clay. [42]As the
toes were partly iron and partly

°37 ק אנת
°38a ק דירין; °38b ק אנת
°39 ק תליתאה; °40 ק רביעאה
°41a ק מנהין; °41b ק ומנהין
°42a ק מנהין; °42b ק ומנהין

תֶּהֱוֵה תַקִּיפָה וּמִנַּהּ תֶּהֱוֵה תְבִירָה׃ דִּי° חֲזַיְתָ

you-saw and-that (43) being-brittle she-will-be and-of-her strong she-will-be

פַּרְזְלָא מְעָרַב בַּחֲסַף טִינָא מִתְעָרְבִין לֶהֱוֺן

they-will-be ones-being-mixture the-clay with-baked-clay-of being-mixed the-iron

בִּזְרַע אֲנָשָׁא וְלָא־ לֶהֱוֺן דָּבְקִין דְּנָה עִם־

with this ones-being-united they-will-remain and-not the-people of-descendant-of

דְּנָה הֵא־ כְדִי פַּרְזְלָא לָא מִתְעָרַב עִם־ חַסְפָּא׃ וּבְיוֹמֵיהוֹן

and-in-days-of-them (44) the-clay with mixing not the-iron like-that see! that

דִּי מַלְכַיָּא אִנּוּן יְקִים אֱלָהּ שְׁמַיָּא מַלְכוּ דִּי לְעָלְמִין

to-forevers that kingdom the-heavens God-of he-will-set-up those the-kings that-of

לָא תִתְחַבַּל וּמַלְכוּתָה לְעַם אָחֳרָן לָא תִשְׁתְּבִק

she-will-be-left not another to-people or-the-kingdom she-will-be-destroyed not

תַּדִּק וְתָסֵיף כָּל־ אִלֵּין מַלְכְוָתָא וְהִיא

but-she the-kingdoms those all-of and-she-will-bring-to-end she-will-crush

תְּקוּם לְעָלְמַיָּא׃ כָּל־ קֳבֵל דִּי־ חֲזַיְתָ דִּי

that you-saw-vision that because all-of (45) to-the-forevers she-will-endure

מִטּוּרָא אִתְגְּזֶרֶת אֶבֶן דִּי־ לָא בִידַיִן וְהַדֶּקֶת

and-she-broke-to-pieces by-hands not that rock she-was-cut-out from-the-mountain

פַּרְזְלָא נְחָשָׁא חַסְפָּא כַּסְפָּא וְדַהֲבָא אֱלָהּ רַב הוֹדַע לְמַלְכָּא

to-the-king he-showed great God and-the-gold the-silver the-clay the-bronze the-iron

מָה דִּי לֶהֱוֵא אַחֲרֵי דְנָה וְיַצִּיב חֶלְמָא וּמְהֵימַן

and-being-trustworthy the-dream and-true this after he-will-take-place that what

פִּשְׁרֵהּ׃ בֵּאדַיִן מַלְכָּא נְבוּכַדְנֶצַּר נְפַל עַל־ אַנְפּוֹהִי

faces-of-him to he-fell Nebuchadnezzar the-king at-then (46) interpretation-of-him

וּלְדָנִיֵּאל סְגִד וּמִנְחָה וְנִיחֹחִין אֲמַר לְנַסָּכָה לֵהּ׃

to-him to-present he-ordered and-incenses and-offering he-paid-honor and-to-Daniel

עָנֵה מַלְכָּא לְדָנִיֵּאל וְאָמַר מִן־ קְשֹׁט דִּי אֱלָהֲכוֹן הוּא אֱלָהּ

God-of he God-of-you that surety of and-saying to-Daniel the-king speaking (47)

אֱלָהִין וּמָרֵא מַלְכִין וְגָלֵה רָזִין דִּי יְכֵלְתָּ לְמִגְלֵא

to-reveal you-were-able that mysteries and-one-revealing kings and-Lord-of gods

רָזָה דְנָה׃ אֱדַיִן מַלְכָּא לְדָנִיֵּאל רַבִּי וּמַתְּנָן

and-gifts he-placed-in-high-position to-Daniel the-king then (48) this the-mystery

רַבְרְבָן שַׂגִּיאָן יְהַב־ לֵהּ וְהַשְׁלְטֵהּ עַל כָּל־

entire-of over and-he-made-ruler-him on-him he-lavished great-ones many-ones

מְדִינַת בָּבֶל וְרַב־ סִגְנִין עַל כָּל־ חַכִּימֵי בָבֶל׃

Babylon wise-men-of all-of over ones-in-charge and-chief-of Babylon province-of

וְדָנִיֵּאל בְּעָא מִן־ מַלְכָּא וּמַנִּי עַל

over and-he-appointed the-king from he-requested moreover-Daniel (49)

°43 ק ודי

clay, so this kingdom will be partly strong and partly brittle. [43]And just as you saw the iron mixed with baked clay, so the people will be a mixture and will not remain united, any more than iron mixes with clay.

[44]"In the time of those kings, the God of heaven will set up a kingdom that will never be destroyed, nor will it be left to another people. It will crush all those kingdoms and bring them to an end, but it will itself endure forever. [45]This is the meaning of the vision of the rock cut out of a mountain, but not by human hands—a rock that broke the iron, the bronze, the clay, the silver and the gold to pieces.

"The great God has shown the king what will take place in the future. The dream is true and the interpretation is trustworthy."

[46]Then King Nebuchadnezzar fell prostrate before Daniel and paid him honor and ordered that an offering and incense be presented to him. [47]The king said to Daniel, "Surely your God is the God of gods and the Lord of kings and a revealer of mysteries, for you were able to reveal this mystery."

[48]Then the king placed Daniel in a high position and lavished many gifts on him. He made him ruler over the entire province of Babylon and placed him in charge of all its wise men. [49]Moreover, at Daniel's request the king appointed Shadrach, Meshach and Abednego administrators over the

עֲבִידְתָּא דִּי מְדִינַת בָּבֶל לְשַׁדְרַךְ מֵישַׁךְ וַעֲבֵד נְגוֹ
Nego and-Abed Meshach to-Shadrach Babylon province-of of the-administration

וְדָנִיֵּאל בִּתְרַע מַלְכָּא׃ נְבוּכַדְנֶצַּר מַלְכָּא עֲבַד
he-made the-king Nebuchadnezzar (3:1) the-royalty at-court-of while-Daniel

צְלֵם דִּי־דְהַב רוּמֵהּ אַמִּין שִׁתִּין פְּתָיֵהּ אַמִּין שִׁת אֲקִימֵהּ
he-set-up -him six cubits width-of-him sixty cubits height-of-him gold of image

בְּבִקְעַת דּוּרָא בִּמְדִינַת בָּבֶל׃ וּנְבוּכַדְנֶצַּר מַלְכָּא שְׁלַח
he-summoned the-king then-Nebuchadnezzar (2) Babylon in-province-of Dura on-plain-of

לְמִכְנַשׁ ׀ לַאֲחַשְׁדַּרְפְּנַיָּא סִגְנַיָּא וּפַחֲוָתָא אֲדַרְגָּזְרַיָּא גְדָבְרַיָּא
the-treasurers the-advisers and-the-governors the-prefects to-the-satraps to-gather

דְּתָבְרַיָּא תִּפְתָּיֵא וְכֹל שִׁלְטֹנֵי מְדִינָתָא לְמֵתֵא
to-come the-provinces officials-of and-all-of the-magistrates the-judges

לַחֲנֻכַּת צַלְמָא דִּי הֲקֵים נְבוּכַדְנֶצַּר מַלְכָּא׃ בֵּאדַיִן
so-then (3) the-king Nebuchadnezzar he-set-up that the-image to-dedication-of

מִתְכַּנְּשִׁין אֲחַשְׁדַּרְפְּנַיָּא סִגְנַיָּא וּפַחֲוָתָא אֲדַרְגָּזְרַיָּא גְדָבְרַיָּא
the-treasurers the-advisers and-the-governors the-prefects the-satraps ones-assembling

דְּתָבְרַיָּא תִּפְתָּיֵא וְכֹל שִׁלְטֹנֵי מְדִינָתָא לַחֲנֻכַּת
for-dedication-of the-provinces officials-of and-all-of the-magistrates the-judges

צַלְמָא דִּי הֲקֵים נְבוּכַדְנֶצַּר מַלְכָּא וְקָאֲמִין לָקֳבֵל
at-before and-ones-standing the-king Nebuchadnezzar he-set-up that the-image

צַלְמָא דִּי הֲקֵים נְבוּכַדְנֶצַּר׃ וְכָרוֹזָא קָרֵא בְחָיִל
with-loudness proclaiming and-the-herald (4) Nebuchadnezzar he-set-up that the-image

לְכוֹן אָמְרִין עַמְמַיָּא אֻמַּיָּא וְלִשָּׁנַיָּא׃ בְּעִדָּנָא דִּי־
that at-the-time (5) and-O-languages O-nations O-peoples ones-commanding to-you

תִשְׁמְעוּן קָל קַרְנָא מַשְׁרוֹקִיתָא קִיתָרוֹס סַבְּכָא פְּסַנְתֵּרִין סוּמְפֹּנְיָה וְכֹל
and-all-of pipe harp lyre zither the-flute the-horn sound-of you-hear

זְנֵי זְמָרָא תִּפְּלוּן וְתִסְגְּדוּן לְצֶלֶם דַּהֲבָא
the-gold to-image-of and-you-must-worship you-must-fall-down the-music kinds-of

דִּי הֲקֵים נְבוּכַדְנֶצַּר מַלְכָּא׃ וּמַן־ דִּי־ לָא יִפֵּל
he-falls-down not that and-who (6) the-king Nebuchadnezzar he-set-up that

וְיִסְגֻּד בַּהּ־ שַׁעֲתָא יִתְרְמֵא לְגוֹא־ אַתּוּן
furnace-of into-inside-of he-will-be-thrown the-moment in-her and-he-worships

נוּרָא יָקִדְתָּא׃ כָּל־ קֳבֵל דְּנָה בֵּהּ־ זִמְנָא כְּדִי
as-that the-time to-him this for all-of (7) the-one-blazing the-fire

שָׁמְעִין כָּל־ עַמְמַיָּא קָל קַרְנָא מַשְׁרוֹקִיתָא קִיתָרֹס שַׂבְּכָא פְּסַנְטֵרִין
harp lyre zither the-flute the-horn sound-of the-peoples all-of ones-hearing

וְכֹל זְנֵי זְמָרָא נָפְלִין כָּל־ עַמְמַיָּא אֻמַּיָּא
the-nations the-peoples all-of ones-falling-down the-music kinds-of and-all-of

°3 ק ויקמין
°5, 7 ק קתרוס

province of Babylon, while Daniel himself remained at the royal court.

*The Image of Gold and the Fiery Furnace*

3 King Nebuchadnezzar made an image of gold, ninety feet high and nine feet[s] wide, and set it up on the plain of Dura in the province of Babylon. [2]He then summoned the satraps, prefects, governors, advisers, treasurers, judges, magistrates and all the other provincial officials to come to the dedication of the image he had set up. [3]So the satraps, prefects, governors, advisers, treasurers, judges, magistrates and all the other provincial officials assembled for the dedication of the image that King Nebuchadnezzar had set up, and they stood before it.

[4]Then the herald loudly proclaimed, "This is what you are commanded to do, O peoples, nations and men of every language: [5]As soon as you hear the sound of the horn, flute, zither, lyre, harp, pipes and all kinds of music, you must fall down and worship the image of gold that King Nebuchadnezzar has set up. [6]Whoever does not fall down and worship will immediately be thrown into a blazing furnace."

[7]Therefore, as soon as they heard the sound of the horn, flute, zither, lyre, harp and all kinds of music, all the peoples, nations and

s1 Aramaic *sixty cubits high and six cubits wide* (about 27 meters high and 2.7 meters wide)

וְלִשָּׁנַיָּא סָגְדִין לְצֶלֶם דַּהֲבָא דִּי הֲקֵים נְבוּכַדְנֶצַּר

Nebuchadnezzar he-set-up that the-gold to-image-of ones-worshiping and-the-languages

מַלְכָּא׃ כָּל־קֳבֵל דְּנָה בֵּהּ־זִמְנָא קְרִבוּ גֻּבְרִין כַּשְׂדָּאִין

Chaldeans men they-came-forward the-time to-him this for all-of (8) the-king

וַאֲכַלוּ קַרְצֵיהוֹן דִּי יְהוּדָיֵא׃ עֲנוֹ וְאָמְרִין

and-ones-saying they-spoke (9) the-Jews of pieces-of-them and-they-chewed-up

לִנְבוּכַדְנֶצַּר מַלְכָּא מַלְכָּא לְעָלְמִין חֱיִי׃ אַנְתָּה מַלְכָּא שָׂמְתָּ

you-issued O-king you (10) live! to-forevers O-king the-king to-Nebuchadnezzar

טְּעֵם* דִּי כָל־אֱנָשׁ דִּי־יִשְׁמַע קָל קַרְנָא מַשְׁרֹקִיתָא קִיתְרֹס

zither the-flute the-horn sound-of he-hears who person every-of that decree

שַׂבְּכָא פְסַנְתֵּרִין וְסִיפֹּנְיָה וְכֹל זְנֵי זְמָרָא יִפֵּל

he-must-fall-down the-music kinds-of and-all-of and-pipe harp lyre

וְיִסְגֻּד לְצֶלֶם דַּהֲבָא׃ וּמַן־דִּי־לָא יִפֵּל

he-falls-down not that and-who (11) the-gold to-image-of and-he-must-worship

וְיִסְגֻּד יִתְרְמֵא לְגוֹא־אַתּוּן נוּרָא יָקִדְתָּא׃

the-one-blazing the-fire furnace-of into-inside-of he-will-be-thrown and-he-worships

אִיתַי גֻּבְרִין יְהוּדָאִין דִּי־מַנִּיתָ יָתְהוֹן עַל־עֲבִידַת מְדִינַת בָּבֶל

Babylon province-of affair-of over them you-set whom Jews men there-are (12)

שַׁדְרַךְ מֵישַׁךְ וַעֲבֵד נְגוֹ גֻּבְרַיָּא אִלֵּךְ לָא־שָׂמוּ עֲלָיךְ מַלְכָּא

O-king to-you they-pay-attention not these the-men Nego and-Abed Meshach Shadrach

טְעֵם לֵאלָהָיךְ לָא פָלְחִין וּלְצֶלֶם דַּהֲבָא דִּי הֲקֵימְתָּ לָא

not you-set-up that the-gold or-to-image-of ones-serving not to-gods-of-you attention

סָגְדִין׃ בֵּאדַיִן נְבוּכַדְנֶצַּר בִּרְגַז וַחֲמָה אֲמַר לְהַיְתָיָה

to-bring he-summoned and-rage in-fury Nebuchadnezzar at-then (13) ones-worshiping

לְשַׁדְרַךְ מֵישַׁךְ וַעֲבֵד נְגוֹ בֵּאדַיִן גֻּבְרַיָּא אִלֵּךְ הֵיתָיוּ קֳדָם

before they-were-brought these the-men at-then Nego and-Abed Meshach to-Shadrach

מַלְכָּא׃ עָנֵה נְבֻכַדְנֶצַּר וְאָמַר לְהוֹן הַצְדָּא שַׁדְרַךְ מֵישַׁךְ

Meshach Shadrach true? to-them and-saying Nebuchadnezzar speaking (14) the-king

וַעֲבֵד נְגוֹ לֵאלָהַי לָא אִיתֵיכוֹן פָּלְחִין וּלְצֶלֶם דַּהֲבָא

the-gold or-to-image-of ones-serving there-are-you not to-gods-of-me Nego and-Abed

דִּי הֲקֵימֶת לָא סָגְדִין׃ כְּעַן הֵן אִיתֵיכוֹן עֲתִידִין דִּי

that ones-ready there-are-you if now (15) ones-worshiping not I-set-up that

בְעִדָּנָא דִּי־תִשְׁמְעוּן קָל קַרְנָא מַשְׁרוֹקִיתָא קִיתְרֹס שַׂבְּכָא פְּסַנְתֵּרִין

harp lyre zither the-flute the-horn sound-of you-hear that at-the-time

וְסוּמְפֹּנְיָה וְכֹל ׀ זְנֵי זְמָרָא תִּפְּלוּן וְתִסְגְּדוּן לְצַלְמָא

to-the-image and-you-worship you-fall-down the-music kinds-of and-all-of and-pipe

דִּי־עַבְדֵת וְהֵן לָא תִסְגְּדוּן בַּהּ־שַׁעֲתָה תִתְרְמוֹן

you-will-be-thrown the-moment in-her you-worship not but-if I-made that

men of every language fell down and worshiped the image of gold that King Nebuchadnezzar had set up.

8 At this time some astrologers[h] came forward and denounced the Jews. 9 They said to King Nebuchadnezzar, "O king, live forever! 10 You have issued a decree, O king, that everyone who hears the sound of the horn, flute, zither, lyre, harp, pipes and all kinds of music must fall down and worship the image of gold, 11 and that whoever does not fall down and worship will be thrown into a blazing furnace. 12 But there are some Jews whom you have set over the affairs of the province of Babylon—Shadrach, Meshach and Abednego—who pay no attention to you, O king. They neither serve your gods nor worship the image of gold you have set up."

13 Furious with rage, Nebuchadnezzar summoned Shadrach, Meshach and Abednego. So these men were brought before the king, 14 and Nebuchadnezzar said to them, "Is it true, Shadrach, Meshach and Abednego, that you do not serve my gods or worship the image of gold I have set up? 15 Now when you hear the sound of the horn, flute, zither, lyre, harp, pipes and all kinds of music, if you are ready to fall down and worship the image I made, very good. But if you do not worship it, you will be thrown immediately into a

[h] 8 Or *Chaldeans*

*10 Most mss have no *dagesh* in the *teth* (טְ).

°10a ק אנת; °10b ק קתרוס

°10c ק וסופניה; °12a ק עלך

°12c ק לאלהך; °15 ק קתרוס

לְגוֹא־ אַתּוּן נוּרָא יָקִדְתָּא וּמַן־ הוּא אֱלָהּ דִּי*
who god he then-who? the-one-blazing the-fire furnace-of into-inside-of

יְשֵׁיזְבִנְכוֹן מִן־ יְדָי׃ עֲנוֹ שַׁדְרַךְ מֵישַׁךְ וַעֲבֵד נְגוֹ
Nego and-Abed Meshach Shadrach they-replied (16) hands-of-me from he-can-save-you

וְאָמְרִין לְמַלְכָּא נְבוּכַדְנֶצַּר לָא־ חַשְׁחִין אֲנַחְנָה עַל־דְּנָה פִּתְגָם
defense this in we ones-needing not Nebuchadnezzar to-the-king and-ones-saying

לַהֲתָבוּתָךְ׃ הֵן אִיתַי אֱלָהַנָא† דִּי־אֲנַחְנָא פָלְחִין יָכִל
one-being-able ones-serving we who God-of-us there-is if (17) to-return-to-you

לְשֵׁיזָבוּתַנָא מִן־ אַתּוּן נוּרָא יָקִדְתָּא וּמִן־ יְדָךְ מַלְכָּא
O-king hand-of-you and-from the-one-blazing the-fire furnace-of from to-save-us

יְשֵׁיזִב׃ וְהֵן לָא יְדִיעַ לֶהֱוֵא־ לָךְ מַלְכָּא דִּי
that O-king to-you let-him-be being-known not but-if (18) he-will-rescue

לֵאלָהָיךְ לָא־ אִיתַנָא° פָלְחִין וּלְצֶלֶם דַּהֲבָא דִּי
that the-gold or-to-image-of ones-serving there-will-be-us not to-gods-of-you

הֲקֵימְתָּ לָא נִסְגֻּד׃ בֵּאדַיִן נְבוּכַדְנֶצַּר הִתְמְלִי חֱמָא
fury he-was-filled Nebuchadnezzar at-then (19) we-will-worship not you-set-up

וּצְלֵם אַנְפּוֹהִי אֶשְׁתַּנּוֹ° עַל־ שַׁדְרַךְ מֵישַׁךְ וַעֲבֵד נְגוֹ
Nego and-Abed Meshach Shadrach toward he-changed faces-of-him and-attitude-of

עָנֵה וְאָמַר לְמֵזֵא לְאַתּוּנָא חַד־שִׁבְעָה עַל דִּי חֲזֵה
he-was-usual that over seven one to-the-furnace to-heat and-saying ordering

לְמֵזְיֵהּ׃ וּלְגֻבְרִין גִּבָּרֵי־ חַיִל דִּי בְחַיְלֵהּ אֲמַר
he-commanded in-army-of-him who strength men-of and-to-soldiers (20) to-heat-him

לְכַפָּתָה לְשַׁדְרַךְ מֵישַׁךְ וַעֲבֵד נְגוֹ לְמִרְמֵא לְאַתּוּן נוּרָא
the-fire into-furnace-of to-throw Nego and-Abed Meshach to-Shadrach to-tie-up

יָקִדְתָּא׃ בֵּאדַיִן גֻּבְרַיָּא אִלֵּךְ כְּפִתוּ בְּסַרְבָּלֵיהוֹן פַּטְּשֵׁיהוֹן°
trousers-of-them in-robes-of-them they-bound these the-men at-then (21) the-one-blazing

וְכַרְבְּלָתְהוֹן וּלְבֻשֵׁיהוֹן וּרְמִיו לְגוֹא־ אַתּוּן
furnace-of into-inside-of and-they-were-thrown and-clothes-of-them and-turbans-of-them

נוּרָא יָקִדְתָּא׃ כָּל־קֳבֵל דְּנָה מִן־ דִּי מִלַּת מַלְכָּא
the-king command-of that from this for all-of (22) the-one-blazing the-fire

מַחְצְפָה וְאַתּוּנָא אֵזֵה יַתִּירָא גֻּבְרַיָּא אִלֵּךְ דִּי הַסִּקוּ
they-took-up who these the-soldiers the-very being-hot and-the-furnace being-urgent

לְשַׁדְרַךְ מֵישַׁךְ וַעֲבֵד נְגוֹ קַטִּל הִמּוֹן שְׁבִיבָא דִּי נוּרָא׃
the-fire of the-flame them he-killed Nego and-Abed Meshach to-Shadrach

וְגֻבְרַיָּא אִלֵּךְ תְּלָתֵּהוֹן שַׁדְרַךְ מֵישַׁךְ וַעֲבֵד נְגוֹ נְפַלוּ
they-fell Nego and-Abed Meshach Shadrach three-of-them these and-the-men (23)

לְגוֹא־ אַתּוּן־ נוּרָא יָקִדְתָּא מְכַפְּתִין׃
ones-being-firmly-tied the-one-blazing the-fire furnace-of into-inside-of

blazing furnace. Then what god will be able to rescue you from my hand?"

16 Shadrach, Meshach and Abednego replied to the king, "O Nebuchadnezzar, we do not need to defend ourselves before you in this matter. 17 If we are thrown into the blazing furnace, the God we serve is able to save us from it, and he will rescue us from your hand, O king. 18 But even if he does not, we want you to know, O king, that we will not serve your gods or worship the image of gold you have set up."

19 Then Nebuchadnezzar was furious with Shadrach, Meshach and Abednego, and his attitude toward them changed. He ordered the furnace heated seven times hotter than usual 20 and commanded some of the strongest soldiers in his army to tie up Shadrach, Meshach and Abednego and throw them into the blazing furnace. 21 So these men, wearing their robes, trousers, turbans and other clothes, were bound and thrown into the blazing furnace. 22 The king's command was so urgent and the furnace so hot that the flames of the fire killed the soldiers who took up Shadrach, Meshach and Abednego, 23 and these three men, firmly tied, fell into the blazing furnace.

*15 Most mss have *hireq* under the *daleth* (דִּי).

†17 Most mss have *qamets* under the *he* (־הָנָא).

°18 קְ איתנא; °19 קְ אשתני

°21 קְ פטשיהון

אֱדַיִן נְבוּכַדְנֶצַּר מַלְכָּא תְּוַהּ וְקָם בְּהִתְבְּהָלָה
in-to-be-amazed and-he-leaped-up he-was-startled the-king Nebuchadnezzar then (24)

עָנֵה וְאָמַר לְהַדָּבְרוֹהִי הֲלָא גֻבְרִין תְּלָתָא רְמֵינָא לְגוֹא־
into-inside-of we-threw three men not? to-advisers-of-him and-saying asking

נוּרָא מְכַפְּתִין עָנַיִן וְאָמְרִין לְמַלְכָּא יַצִּיבָא
the-certainty to-the-king and-ones-saying ones-replying ones-being-tied the-fire

מַלְכָּא׃ עָנֵה וְאָמַר הָא־אֲנָה חָזֵה גֻּבְרִין אַרְבְּעָה שְׁרַיִן
ones-being-unbound four men seeing I look! and-saying speaking (25) O-king

מַהְלְכִין בְּגוֹא־ נוּרָא וַחֲבָל לָא־ אִיתַי בְּהוֹן
to-them there-is not and-harm the-fire at-inside-of ones-walking-around

וְרֵוֵהּ דִּי רְבִיעָיָא דָּמֵה לְבַר־ אֱלָהִין׃ בֵּאדַיִן
at-then (26) gods like-son-of looking-like the-fourth who and-appearance-of-him

קְרֵב נְבוּכַדְנֶצַּר לִתְרַע אַתּוּן נוּרָא יָקִדְתָּא
the-one-blazing the-fire furnace-of to-opening-of Nebuchadnezzar he-approached

עָנֵה וְאָמַר שַׁדְרַךְ מֵישַׁךְ וַעֲבֵד־ נְגוֹ עַבְדוֹהִי דִּי־ אֱלָהָא
the-God who servants-of-him Nego and-Abed Meshach Shadrach and-saying shouting

עִלָּיָא פֻּקוּ וֶאֱתוֹ בֵּאדַיִן נָפְקִין שַׁדְרַךְ מֵישַׁךְ
Meshach Shadrach ones-coming-out at-then and-come-here! come-out! the-Most-High

וַעֲבֵד נְגוֹ מִן־ גּוֹא נוּרָא׃ וּמִתְכַּנְּשִׁין אֲחַשְׁדַּרְפְּנַיָּא
the-satraps and-ones-crowding-around (27) the-fire inside-of from Nego and-Abed

סִגְנַיָּא וּפַחֲוָתָא וְהַדָּבְרֵי מַלְכָּא חָזַיִן לְגֻבְרַיָּא
to-the-men ones-seeing the-royalty and-advisers-of and-the-governors the-prefects

אִלֵּךְ דִּי לָא־ שְׁלֵט נוּרָא בְּגֶשְׁמְהוֹן וּשְׂעַר רֵאשְׁהוֹן לָא
not head-of-them or-hair-of to-body-of-them the-fire he-harmed not that these

הִתְחָרַךְ וְסָרְבָּלֵיהוֹן לָא שְׁנוֹ וְרֵיחַ נוּר לָא
not fire and-smell-of they-were-scorched not or-robes-of-them he-was-singed

עֲדָּת בְּהוֹן׃ עָנֵה נְבוּכַדְנֶצַּר וְאָמַר בְּרִיךְ אֱלָהֲהוֹן
God-of-them being-praised and-saying Nebuchadnezzar speaking (28) onto-them she-went

דִּי־ שַׁדְרַךְ מֵישַׁךְ וַעֲבֵד נְגוֹ דִּי־ שְׁלַח מַלְאֲכֵהּ וְשֵׁיזִב
and-he-rescued angel-of-him he-sent who Nego and-Abed Meshach Shadrach of

לְעַבְדוֹהִי דִּי הִתְרְחִצוּ עֲלוֹהִי וּמִלַּת מַלְכָּא שַׁנִּיו
they-defied the-king and-command-of in-him they-trusted who to-servants-of-him

וִיהַבוּ גֶשְׁמֵיהוֹן דִּי לָא־ יִפְלְחוּן וְלָא־ יִסְגְּדוּן
they-would-worship or-not they-would-serve not that body-of-them and-they-gave-up

לְכָל־ אֱלָהּ לָהֵן לֵאלָהֲהוֹן׃ וּמִנִּי שִׂים טְעֵם
decree he-is-issued therefore-from-me (29) to-God-of-them except God to-any-of

דִּי כָל־ עַם אֻמָּה וְלִשָּׁן דִּי־ יֵאמַר שָׁלָה עַל אֱלָהֲהוֹן
God-of-them against anything he-says who or-language nation people-of any-of that

24 Then King Nebuchadnezzar
leaped to his feet in amazement
and asked his advisers, "Weren't
there three men that we tied up and
threw into the fire?"
They replied, "Certainly, O
king."
25 He said, "Look! I see four men
walking around in the fire, un-
bound and unharmed, and the
fourth looks like a son of the
gods."
26 Nebuchadnezzar then approached the opening of the blazing furnace and shouted, "Shadrach, Meshach and Abednego,
servants of the Most High God,
come out! Come here!"
So Shadrach, Meshach and
Abednego came out of the fire,
27 and the satraps, prefects, governors and royal advisers crowded
around them. They saw that the
fire had not harmed their bodies,
nor was a hair of their heads
singed; their robes were not
scorched, and there was no smell
of fire on them.
28 Then Nebuchadnezzar said,
"Praise be to the God of Shadrach,
Meshach and Abednego, who has
sent his angel and rescued his servants! They trusted in him and defied the king's command and
were willing to give up their lives
rather than serve or worship any
god except their own God. 29 Therefore I decree that the people of any
nation or language who say anything against the God of Shadrach, Meshach and Abednego be

°25 ק רביעאה
°26 ק עלאה
°28 ק גשמהין
°29 ק שלו

דִּי־שַׁדְרַךְ מֵישַׁךְ וַעֲבֵד נְגוֹא הַדָּמִין יִתְעֲבֵד וּבַיְתֵהּ
and-house-of-him he-will-be-cut-into pieces Nego and-Abed Meshach Shadrach of

נְוָלִי יִשְׁתַּוֵּה כָּל־קֳבֵל דִּי לָא אִיתַי אֱלָהּ אָחֳרָן דִּי־
who other god there-is not that for all-of he-will-be-turned-into pile-of-rubble

יָכִל לְהַצָּלָה כִּדְנָה׃ בֵּאדַיִן מַלְכָּא הַצְלַח לְשַׁדְרַךְ מֵישַׁךְ
Meshach to-Shadrach he-promoted the-king at-then (30) like-this to-save he-can

וַעֲבֵד נְגוֹ בִּמְדִינַת בָּבֶל׃ נְבוּכַדְנֶצַּר מַלְכָּא לְכָל־
to-all-of the-king Nebuchadnezzar *(31[4:1]) Babylon in-province-of Nego and-Abed

עַמְמַיָּא אֻמַיָּא וְלִשָּׁנַיָּא דִּי־דָאְרִין בְּכָל־אַרְעָא
the-world in-all-of ones-living who and-the-languages the-nations the-peoples

שְׁלָמְכוֹן יִשְׂגֵּא׃ אָתַיָּא וְתִמְהַיָּא דִּי עֲבַד
he-performed that and-the-wonders the-signs (32[2]) may-he-be-great prosperity-of-you

עִמִּי אֱלָהָא עִלָּיָא שְׁפַר קָדָמַי לְהַחֲוָיָה׃ אָתוֹהִי כְּמָה
as-how! signs-of-him (33[3]) to-tell to-me he-pleases the-Most-High the-God for-me

רַבְרְבִין וְתִמְהוֹהִי כְּמָה תַקִּיפִין מַלְכוּתֵהּ מַלְכוּת עָלַם
eternity kingdom-of kingdom-of-him mighty-ones as-how! and-wonders-of-him great-ones

וְשָׁלְטָנֵהּ עִם־דָּר וְדָר׃ אֲנָה נְבוּכַדְנֶצַּר
Nebuchadnezzar I (4:1[4]) and-generation generation with and-dominion-of-him

שְׁלֵה הֲוֵית בְּבֵיתִי וְרַעְנַן בְּהֵיכְלִי׃ חֵלֶם חֲזֵית
I-saw dream (2[5]) in-palace-of-me and-prosperous in-home-of-me I-was contented

וִידַחֲלִנַּנִי וְהַרְהֹרִין עַל־מִשְׁכְּבִי וְחֶזְוֵי רֵאשִׁי
mind-of-me and-visions-of bed-of-me in and-images and-he-made-afraid-me

יְבַהֲלֻנַּנִי׃ וּמִנִּי שִׂים טְעֵם לְהַנְעָלָה קֳדָמַי
before-me to-bring command he-was-issued so-from-me (3[6]) they-terrified-me

לְכֹל חַכִּימֵי בָבֶל דִּי־פְשַׁר חֶלְמָא יְהוֹדְעֻנַּנִי׃
they-might-tell-me the-dream interpretation-of that Babylon wise-men-of to-all-of

בֵּאדַיִן עָלְלִין חַרְטֻמַיָּא אָשְׁפַיָּא כַּשְׂדָּיֵא
the-Chaldeans the-enchanters the-magicians ones-coming at-then (4[7])

וְגָזְרַיָּא וְחֶלְמָא אָמַר אֲנָה קֳדָמֵיהוֹן וּפִשְׁרֵהּ
but-interpretation-of-him before-them I telling and-the-dream and-the-ones-divining

לָא־מְהוֹדְעִין לִי׃ וְעַד אָחֳרֵין עַל קָדָמַי דָּנִיֵּאל דִּי־
who Daniel presence-of-me into finally and-until (5[8]) to-me ones-telling not

שְׁמֵהּ בֵּלְטְשַׁאצַּר כְּשֻׁם אֱלָהִי וְדִי רוּחַ־אֱלָהִין קַדִּישִׁין
holy-ones gods spirit-of and-who god-of-me after-name-of Belteshazzar name-of-him

בֵּהּ וְחֶלְמָא קָדָמוֹהִי אַמְרֵת׃ בֵּלְטְשַׁאצַּר רַב חַרְטֻמַיָּא
the-magicians chief-of Belteshazzar (6[9]) I-told before-him and-the-dream in-him

דִּי ׀ אֲנָה יִדְעֵת דִּי רוּחַ אֱלָהִין קַדִּישִׁין בָּךְ וְכָל־רָז לָא־
not mystery and-any-of in-you holy-ones gods spirit-of that I-know I whom

cut into pieces and their houses be turned into piles of rubble, for no other god can save in this way."
30 Then the king promoted Shadrach, Meshach and Abednego in the province of Babylon.

*Nebuchadnezzar's Dream of a Tree*

4 King Nebuchadnezzar,
To the peoples, nations and men of every language, who live in all the world:

May you prosper greatly!

2 It is my pleasure to tell you about the miraculous signs and wonders that the Most High God has performed for me.

3 How great are his signs,
how mighty his wonders!
His kingdom is an eternal kingdom;
his dominion endures from generation to generation.

4 I, Nebuchadnezzar, was at home in my palace, contented and prosperous. 5 I had a dream that made me afraid. As I was lying in my bed, the images and visions that passed through my mind terrified me. 6 So I commanded that all the wise men of Babylon be brought before me to interpret the dream for me. 7 When the magicians, enchanters, astrologers[i] and diviners came, I told them the dream, but they could not interpret it for me. 8 Finally, Daniel came into my presence and I told him the dream. (He is called Belteshazzar, after the name of my god, and the spirit of the holy gods is in him.)
9 I said, "Belteshazzar, chief of the magicians, I know that the spirit of the holy gods is in you, and no mystery is too difficult for you. Here is my

i7 Or *Chaldeans*

**Heading, 31* The Hebrew numeration of chapter 4 begins with verse 4 of the English. The number in brackets indicates the English numeration.

† Most mss have *mappiq* in the *he* (אֱלָהּ).

°*31* קְ דָּיְרִין; °*32* קְ עִלָּאָה
°*4a* קְ עָלִּין; °*4b* קְ כַּשְׂדָּאֵי

אנס לך חזוי חלמי די־חזית ופשרה
and-interpretation-of-him I-saw that dream-of-me visions-of for-you being-difficult

אמר׃ וחזוי ראשי על־משכבי חזה הוית ואלו אילן
tree and-see! I-was looking bed-of-me in mind-of-me indeed-visions-of (7[10]) tell!

בגוא ארעא ורומה שגיא׃ רבה אילנא
the-tree he-grew-large (8[11]) enormous and-height-of-him the-land in-middle-of

ותקף ורומה ימטא לשמיא וחזותה
and-visibility-of-him to-the-skies he-touched and-top-of-him and-he-grew-strong

לסוף כל־ארעא׃ עפיה שפיר ואנבה שגיא
abundant and-fruit-of-him beautiful leaf-of-him (9[12]) the-earth all-of to-end-of

ומזון לכלא־בה תחתוהי תטלל | חיות ברא
the-field beast-of she-found-shelter under-him on-him for-the-all and-food

ובענפוהי ידרון צפרי שמיא ומנה יתזין כל־
every-of he-was-fed and-from-him the-airs birds-of they-lived and-in-branches-of-him

בשרא׃ חזה הוית בחזוי ראשי על־משכבי ואלו
and-look! bed-of-me in mind-of-me in-visions-of I-was seeing (10[13]) the-creature

עיר וקדיש מן־שמיא נחת׃ קרא בחיל
with-loudness calling (11[14]) coming-down the-heavens from indeed-holy-one messenger

וכן אמר גדו אילנא וקצצו ענפוהי אתרו
strip-off! branches-of-him and-trim-off! the-tree cut-down! saying and-this

עפיה ובדרו אנבה תנד חיותא מן־תחתוהי
under-him from the-animal let-her-flee fruit-of-him and-scatter! leaf-of-him

וצפריא מן־ענפוהי׃ ברם עקר שרשוהי בארעא
in-the-ground roots-of-him stump-of but (12[15]) branches-of-him from and-the-birds

שבקו ובאסור די־פרזל ונחש בדתאא די ברא
the-field of in-the-grass and-bronze iron of but-in-binding let-remain!

ובטל שמיא יצטבע ועם־חיותא חלקה
living-place-of-him the-animal and-with let-him-be-drenched the-heavens and-with-dew-of

בעשב ארעא׃ לבבה מן־אנושא ישנון
let-them-change the-man from mind-of-him (13[16]) the-earth among-plant-of

ולבב חיוה יתיהב לה ושבעה עדנין יחלפון עלוהי׃
for-him they-pass-by times till-seven to-him let-him-be-given animal and-mind-of

בגזרת עירין פתגמא ומאמר קדישין
holy-ones and-declaration-of the-decision messengers by-announcement-of (14[17])

שאלתא עד־דברת די ינדעון חייא די־שליט
sovereign that the-living-ones they-may-know that reason-of for the-verdict

עליא במלכות אנושא ולמן־די יצבא יתננה
he-gives-her he-wishes that and-to-whom the-man over-kingdom-of the-Most-High

dream; interpret it for me. [10]These are the visions I saw while lying in my bed: I looked, and there before me stood a tree in the middle of the land. Its height was enormous. [11]The tree grew large and strong and its top touched the sky; it was visible to the ends of the earth. [12]Its leaves were beautiful, its fruit abundant, and on it was food for all. Under it the beasts of the field found shelter, and the birds of the air lived in its branches; from it every creature was fed.

[13]"In the visions I saw while lying in my bed, I looked, and there before me was a messenger,[j] a holy one, coming down from heaven. [14]He called in a loud voice: 'Cut down the tree and trim off its branches; strip off its leaves and scatter its fruit. Let the animals flee from under it and the birds from its branches. [15]But let the stump and its roots, bound with iron and bronze, remain in the ground, in the grass of the field.

" 'Let him be drenched with the dew of heaven, and let him live with the animals among the plants of the earth. [16]Let his mind be changed from that of a man and let him be given the mind of an animal, till seven times[k] pass by for him.

[17]" 'The decision is announced by messengers, the holy ones declare the verdict, so that the living may know that the Most High is sovereign over the kingdoms of men and gives them to anyone he

j13 Or *watchman;* also in verses 17 and 23
k16 Or *years;* also in verses 23, 25 and 32

**Heading* See the note on page 450.

°9 ק ידורן; °13 ק אנשא
°14a ק עלאה; °14b ק אנשא

וּשְׁפַל אֲנָשִׁים יְקִים עֲלַיהּ׃ דְּנָה חֶלְמָא חֲזֵית אֲנָה מַלְכָּא
the-king I I-saw the-dream this (15[18]) over-her he-sets men and-lowly-of

נְבוּכַדְנֶצַּר וְאַנְתְּה בֵּלְטְשַׁאצַּר פִּשְׁרֵא° אֱמַר כָּל־קֳבֵל דִּי°
that for all-of tell! †meaning-of-him Belteshazzar now-you Nebuchadnezzar

כָּל־ חַכִּימֵי מַלְכוּתִי לָא־ יָכְלִין פִּשְׁרָא לְהוֹדָעֻתַנִי
to-tell-me the-interpretation ones-being-able not kingdom-of-me wise-men-of all-of

וְאַנְתְּה כָּהֵל דִּי רוּחַ־ אֱלָהִין קַדִּישִׁין בָּךְ׃ אֱדַיִן דָּנִיֵּאל
Daniel then (16[19]) in-you holy-ones gods spirit-of because being-able but-you

דִּי־ שְׁמֵהּ בֵּלְטְשַׁאצַּר אֶשְׁתּוֹמַם כְּשָׁעָה חֲדָה וְרַעְיֹנֹהִי
and-thoughts-of-him a for-time he-was-perplexed Belteshazzar name-of-him who

יְבַהֲלֻנֵּהּ עָנֵה מַלְכָּא וְאָמַר בֵּלְטְשַׁאצַּר חֶלְמָא
the-dream Belteshazzar and-saying the-king speaking they-terrified-him

וּפִשְׁרֵא° אַל־ יְבַהֲלָךְ עָנֵה בֵלְטְשַׁאצַּר וְאָמַר מָרִאי°
lord-of-me and-saying Belteshazzar answering let-him-alarm-you not †or-meaning-of-him

חֶלְמָא לְשָׂנְאָךְ° וּפִשְׁרֵהּ לְעָרָךְ°
to-adversaries-of-you and-meaning-of-him to-ones-being-enemies-of-you the-dream

אִילָנָא דִּי חֲזַיְתָ דִּי רְבָה וּתְקִף וְרוּמֵהּ
with-top-of-him and-he-grew-strong he-grew-large which you-saw that the-tree (17[20])

יִמְטֵא לִשְׁמַיָּא וַחֲזוֹתֵהּ לְכָל־ אַרְעָא׃
the-earth to-whole-of and-visibility-of-him to-the-skies he-touched

וְעָפְיֵהּ שַׁפִּיר וְאִנְבֵּהּ שַׂגִּיא וּמָזוֹן לְכֹלָּא־
for-the-all and-food abundant and-fruit-of-him beautiful with-leaf-of-him (18[21])

בֵּהּ תְּחֹתוֹהִי תְּטַלֵּל חֵיוַת בָּרָא וּבְעַנְפוֹהִי
and-in-branches-of-him the-field beast-of she-found-shelter under-him on-him

יִשְׁכְּנָן צִפֲּרֵי שְׁמַיָּא׃ אַנְתְּה־הוּא מַלְכָּא דִּי רְבַיְת
you-became-great who O-king that you (19[22]) the-airs birds-of they-had-nests

וּתְקִפְתְּ וּרְבוּתָךְ רְבָת וּמְטָת לִשְׁמַיָּא
to-the-skies until-she-reached she-grew and-greatness-of-you and-you-became-strong

וְשָׁלְטָנָךְ לְסוֹף אַרְעָא׃ וְדִי חֲזָה מַלְכָּא
O-king he-saw and-that (20[23]) the-earth to-distant-part-of and-dominion-of-you

עִיר וְקַדִּישׁ נָחִת מִן־ שְׁמַיָּא וְאָמַר גֹּדּוּ אִילָנָא
the-tree cut-down! and-saying the-heavens from coming-down indeed-holy-one messenger

וְחַבְּלוּהִי בְּרַם עִקַּר שָׁרְשׁוֹהִי בְּאַרְעָא שְׁבֻקוּ וּבֶאֱסוּר
but-in-binding leave! in-the-ground roots-of-him stump-of but and-destroy-him!

דִּי־ פַרְזֶל וּנְחָשׁ בְּדִתְאָא דִּי בָרָא וּבְטַל שְׁמַיָּא
the-heavens and-with-dew-of the-field of in-the-grass and-bronze iron of

יִצְטַבַּע וְעִם־ חֵיוַת בָּרָא חֲלָקֵהּ עַד דִּי־
that until living-place-of-him the-field animal-of and-with let-him-be-drenched

wishes and sets over them the
lowliest of men.'
18"This is the dream that I,
King Nebuchadnezzar, had.
Now, Belteshazzar, tell me
what it means, for none of the
wise men in my kingdom can
interpret it for me. But you can,
because the spirit of the holy
gods is in you."

*Daniel Interprets the Dream*

19Then Daniel (also called
Belteshazzar) was greatly per-
plexed for a time, and his
thoughts terrified him. So the
king said, "Belteshazzar, do
not let the dream or its meaning alarm you."
Belteshazzar answered, "My
lord, if only the dream applied
to your enemies and its meaning to your adversaries! 20The
tree you saw, which grew large
and strong, with its top touching the sky, visible to the
whole earth, 21with beautiful
leaves and abundant fruit, providing food for all, giving shelter to the beasts of the field,
and having nesting places in
its branches for the birds of the
air— 22you, O king, are that
tree! You have become great
and strong; your greatness has
grown until it reaches the sky,
and your dominion extends to
distant parts of the earth.
23"You, O king, saw a messenger, a holy one, coming
down from heaven and say-
ing, 'Cut down the tree and destroy it, but leave the stump,
bound with iron and bronze,
in the grass of the field, while
its roots remain in the ground.
Let him be drenched with the
dew of heaven; let him live like
the wild animals, until seven

*Heading* See the note on page 450.

†15, 16 Many mss have as a Qere form the third masculine singular pronoun (־ֵהּ).

°14 ק עלה; °15a,b ק ואנת
°16a ק מרי; °16b ק לשנאך
°16c ק לערך; °19 ק אנת

שִׁבְעָה עִדָּנִין יַחְלְפוּן עֲלוֹהִי׃ דְּנָה פִשְׁרָא מַלְכָּא וּגְזֵרַת
and-decree-of O-king the-interpretation this (21[24]) for-him they-pass-by times seven

עִלָּיָא הִיא דִּי מְטָת עַל־ מָרְאִי מַלְכָּא׃ וְלָךְ
and-to-you (22[25]) the-king lord-of-me against she-was-issued that this the-Most-High

טָרְדִין מִן־ אֲנָשָׁא וְעִם־ חֵיוַת בָּרָא לֶהֱוֵה
he-will-be the-field wild-animal-of and-with the-people from ones-driving-away

מְדֹרָךְ וְעִשְׂבָּא כְתוֹרִין ׀ לָךְ יְטַעֲמוּן
they-will-make-eat to-you like-cattles and-the-grass living-place-of-you

וּמִטַּל שְׁמַיָּא לָךְ מְצַבְּעִין וְשִׁבְעָה עִדָּנִין יַחְלְפוּן
they-will-pass-by times and-seven ones-drenching to-you the-heavens and-with-dew-of

עֲלַיִךְ עַד דִּי־ תִנְדַּע דִּי־ שַׁלִּיט עִלָּיָא בְּמַלְכוּת
over-kingdom-of the-Most-High sovereign that you-acknowledge that until for-you

אֲנָשָׁא וּלְמַן־ דִּי יִצְבֵּא יִתְּנִנַּהּ׃ וְדִי אֲמַרוּ
they-command and-that (23[26]) he-gives-her he-wishes that and-to-whom the-man

לְמִשְׁבַּק עִקַּר שָׁרְשׁוֹהִי דִּי אִילָנָא מַלְכוּתָךְ לָךְ קַיָּמָה מִן־ דִּי
that when restored to-you kingdom-of-you the-tree of roots-of-him stump-of to-leave

תִנְדַּע דִּי שַׁלִּטִן שְׁמַיָּא׃ לָהֵן מַלְכָּא מִלְכִּי
advice-of-me O-king therefore (24[27]) the-Heavens ruling that you-acknowledge

יִשְׁפַּר עֲלַיִךְ וַחֲטָיָךְ בְּצִדְקָה פְרֻק וַעֲוָיָתָךְ
and-wickednesses-of-you renounce! by-right and-sins-of-you to-you may-he-be-pleasing

בְּמִחַן עֲנָיִן הֵן תֶּהֱוֵא אַרְכָה לִשְׁלֵוְתָךְ׃
to-prosperity-of-you continuation she-will-be maybe oppressed-ones by-to-be-kind

כֹּלָּא מְטָא‡ עַל־ נְבוּכַדְנֶצַּר מַלְכָּא׃ לִקְצָת יַרְחִין
months at-end-of (26[29]) the-king Nebuchadnezzar to he-happened the-all (25[28])

תְּרֵי־עֲשַׂר עַל־ הֵיכַל מַלְכוּתָא דִּי בָבֶל מְהַלֵּךְ הֲוָה׃ עָנֵה
speaking (27[30]) he-was walking Babylon in the-royalty palace-of on ten two-of

מַלְכָּא וְאָמַר הֲלָא דָא־ הִיא בָּבֶל רַבְּתָא דִּי־ אֲנָה בֱנַיְתַהּ
I-built-her I that the-great Babylon she this not? and-saying the-king

לְבֵית מַלְכוּ בִּתְקַף חִסְנִי וְלִיקָר הַדְרִי׃
majesty-of-me and-for-glory-of might-of-me by-power-of royalty as-residence-of

עוֹד מִלְּתָא בְּפֻם מַלְכָּא קָל מִן־ שְׁמַיָּא נְפַל לָךְ
for-you he-came the-heavens from voice the-king in-mouth-of the-word still (28[31])

אָמְרִין נְבוּכַדְנֶצַּר מַלְכָּא מַלְכוּתָה עֲדָת מִנָּךְ׃
from-you she-passed the-royal-authority the-king Nebuchadnezzar ones-decreeing

וּמִן־ אֲנָשָׁא לָךְ טָרְדִין וְעִם־ חֵיוַת
wild-animal-of and-with ones-driving-away to-you the-people and-from (29[32])

בָּרָא מְדֹרָךְ עִשְׂבָּא כְתוֹרִין לָךְ יְטַעֲמוּן
they-will-make-eat to-you like-cattles the-grass living-place-of-you the-field

times pass by for him.'
24 "This is the interpretation, O king, and this is the decree the Most High has issued against my lord the king:
25 You will be driven away from people and will live with the wild animals; you will eat grass like cattle and be drenched with the dew of heaven. Seven times will pass by for you until you acknowledge that the Most High is sovereign over the kingdoms of men and gives them to anyone he wishes.
26 The command to leave the stump of the tree with its roots means that your kingdom will be restored to you when you acknowledge that Heaven rules.
27 Therefore, O king, be pleased to accept my advice: Renounce your sins by doing what is right, and your wickedness by being kind to the oppressed. It may be that then your prosperity will continue."

*The Dream Is Fulfilled*

28 All this happened to King Nebuchadnezzar.
29 Twelve months later, as the king was walking on the roof of the royal palace of Babylon,
30 he said, "Is not this the great Babylon I have built as the royal residence, by my mighty power and for the glory of my majesty?"
31 The words were still on his lips when a voice came from heaven, "This is what is decreed for you, King Nebuchadnezzar: Your royal authority has been taken from you.
32 You will be driven away from people and will live with the wild animals; you will eat grass

**Heading* See the note on page 450.

‡25 Most mss have no *dagesh* in the *mem* (מְ).

°*21a* ק עלאה; °*21b* ק מרי
°*22a* ק עלאה; °*22b* ק עלך
°*24a* ק עלך; °*24b* ק וחטאך

ושבעה עדנין יחלפון עליך עד די תנדע די
that you-acknowledge that until for-you they-will-pass-by times and-seven

שליט עליא במלכות אנשא ולמן די יצבא
he-wishes that and-to-whom the-man over-kingdom-of the-Most-High sovereign

יתננה׃ בה שעתא מלתא ספת על
about she-was-fulfilled the-saying the-moment in-her (30[33]) he-gives-her

נבוכדנצר ומן אנשא טריד ועשבא כתורין יאכל
he-ate like-cattles and-the-grass being-driven-away the-people and-from Nebuchadnezzar

ומטל שמיא גשמה יצטבע עד די שערה
hair-of-him that until he-was-drenched body-of-him the-heavens and-from-dew-of

כנשרין רבה וטפרוהי כצפרין׃ ולקצת יומיה אנה
I the-days at-end-of (31[34]) like-birds and-nails-of-him he-grew like-eagles

נבוכדנצר עיני | לשמיא נטלת ומנדעי עלי
to-me and-sanity-of-me I-raised toward-the-heavens eyes-of-me Nebuchadnezzar

יתוב ולעליא ברכת ולחי עלמא
the-forever and-to-one-living-of I-praised then-to-the-Most-High he-returned

שבחת והדרת די שלטנה שלטן עלם ומלכותה
and-kingdom-of-him eternity dominion-of dominion-of-him who and-I-glorified I-honored

עם דר ודר׃ וכל דארי ארעא
the-earth ones-being-peoples-of and-all-of (32[35]) and-generation generation with

כלה חשיבין וכמצביה עבד בחיל שמיא
the-heavens with-power-of doing and-as-to-please-him ones-regarding as-nothing

ודארי ארעא ולא איתי די ימחא
he-can-hold-back who there-is and-not the-earth and-ones-being-peoples-of

בידה ויאמר לה מה עבדת׃ בה זמנא
the-time in-him (33[36]) you-did what? to-him or-he-can-say to-hand-of-him

מנדעי | יתוב עלי וליקר מלכותי הדרי
honor-of-me kingdom-of-me also-for-glory-of to-me he-returned sanity-of-me

וזיוי יתוב עלי ולי הדברי ורברבני
and-nobles-of-me advisers-of-me and-to-me to-me he-returned and-splendor-of-me

יבעון ועל מלכותי התקנת ורבו יתירה
the-exceeding and-greatness she-was-restored throne-of-me and-to they-sought-out

הוספת לי׃ כען אנה נבוכדנצר משבח ומרומם ומהדר
and-glorifying and-exalting praising Nebuchadnezzar I now (34[37]) to-me she-was-added

למלך שמיא די כל מעבדוהי קשט וארחתה דין
justice and-ways-of-him right deeds-of-him every-of because the-heavens to-King-of

ודי מהלכין בגוה יכל להשפלה׃ בלשאצר מלכא עבד
he-gave the-king Belshazzar (5:1) to-humble being-able in-pride ones-walking and-who

like cattle. Seven times will pass by for you until you acknowledge that the Most High is sovereign over the kingdoms of men and gives them to anyone he wishes."

[33]Immediately what had been said about Nebuchadnezzar was fulfilled. He was driven away from people and ate grass like cattle. His body was drenched with the dew of heaven until his hair grew like the feathers of an eagle and his nails like the claws of a bird.

[34]At the end of that time, I, Nebuchadnezzar, raised my eyes toward heaven, and my sanity was restored. Then I praised the Most High; I honored and glorified him who lives forever.

His dominion is an eternal dominion;
his kingdom endures from generation to generation.
[35]All the peoples of the earth are regarded as nothing.
He does as he pleases with the powers of heaven and the peoples of the earth.
No one can hold back his hand or say to him: "What have you done?"

[36]At the same time that my sanity was restored, my honor and splendor were returned to me for the glory of my kingdom. My advisers and nobles sought me out, and I was restored to my throne and became even greater than before. [37]Now I, Nebuchadnezzar, praise and exalt and glorify the King of heaven, because everything he does is right and all his ways are just. And those who walk in pride he is able to humble.

*Heading See the note on page 450.

°29a ק עלאה; °29b ק עלך
°31 ק ולעלאה; °32a ק דירי
°32b ק ודירי

לְחֶם רַב לְרַבְרְבָנוֹהִי אֲלַף וְלָקֳבֵל אַלְפָּא חַמְרָא שָׁתֵה׃
drinking the-wine the-thousand and-in-among thousand for-nobles-of-him great banquet

בֵּלְשַׁאצַּר אֲמַר ׀ בִּטְעֵם חַמְרָא לְהַיְתָיָה לְמָאנֵי
to-goblets-of to-bring-in the-wine while-drinking-of he-ordered Belshazzar (2)

דַּהֲבָא וְכַסְפָּא דִּי הַנְפֵּק נְבוּכַדְנֶצַּר אֲבוּהִי מִן־הֵיכְלָא
the-temple from father-of-him Nebuchadnezzar he-took that and-the-silver the-gold

דִּי בִירוּשְׁלֶם וְיִשְׁתּוֹן בְּהוֹן מַלְכָּא וְרַבְרְבָנוֹהִי
and-nobles-of-him the-king from-them so-they-might-drink in-Jerusalem that

שֵׁגְלָתֵהּ וּלְחֵנָתֵהּ׃ בֵּאדַיִן הַיְתִיו מָאנֵי דַהֲבָא
the-gold goblets-of they-brought-in at-then (3) and-concubines-of-him wives-of-him

דִּי הַנְפִּקוּ מִן־הֵיכְלָא דִּי־בֵית אֱלָהָא דִּי בִירוּשְׁלֶם
in-Jerusalem that the-God house-of that the-temple from they-took that

וְאִשְׁתִּיו בְּהוֹן מַלְכָּא וְרַבְרְבָנוֹהִי שֵׁגְלָתֵהּ וּלְחֵנָתֵהּ׃
and-concubines-of-him wives-of-him and-nobles-of-him the-king from-them and-they-drank

אִשְׁתִּיו חַמְרָא וְשַׁבַּחוּ לֵאלָהֵי דַּהֲבָא וְכַסְפָּא
and-the-silver the-gold to-gods-of and-they-praised the-wine they-drank (4)

נְחָשָׁא פַרְזְלָא אָעָא וְאַבְנָא׃ בַּהּ־שַׁעֲתָה נְפַקוּ
they-appeared the-moment in-her (5) and-the-stone the-wood the-iron the-bronze

אֶצְבְּעָן דִּי יַד־אֱנָשׁ וְכָתְבָן לָקֳבֵל נֶבְרַשְׁתָּא עַל־גִּירָא
the-plaster on the-lampstand at-near and-ones-writing human hand-of of fingers

דִּי־כְתַל הֵיכְלָא דִּי מַלְכָּא וּמַלְכָּא חָזֵה פַּס יְדָה דִּי
that the-hand palm-of watching and-the-king the-royalty of the-palace wall-of of

כָתְבָה׃ אֱדַיִן מַלְכָּא זִיוֺהִי שַׁנּוֹהִי וְרַעְיֹנֹהִי*
and-thoughts-of-him they-changed-him faces-of-him the-king then (6) writing

יְבַהֲלוּנֵּהּ וְקִטְרֵי חַרְצֵהּ מִשְׁתָּרַיִן וְאַרְכֻבָּתֵהּ
and-knees-of-him ones-giving-way leg-of-him and-joints-of they-frightened-him

דָּא לְדָא נָקְשָׁן׃ קָרֵא מַלְכָּא בְּחַיִל לְהֶעָלָה
to-bring with-loudness the-king calling-out (7) ones-knocking to-that this

לְאָשְׁפַיָּא כַּשְׂדָּיֵא וְגָזְרַיָּא עָנֵה מַלְכָּא וְאָמַר ׀
and-saying the-king speaking and-the-ones-divining the-Chaldeans to-the-enchanters

לְחַכִּימֵי בָבֶל דִּי כָל־אֱנָשׁ דִּי־יִקְרֵה כְּתָבָה דְנָה
this the-writing he-reads who man any-of whoever Babylon to-wise-men-of

וּפִשְׁרֵהּ יְחַוִּנַּנִי אַרְגְּוָנָא יִלְבַּשׁ וְהַמְוֹנְכָא דִי־דַהֲבָא
the-gold of and-the-chain he-will-be-clothed-in the-purple he-tells-me and-meaning-of-him

עַל־צַוְּארֵהּ וְתַלְתִּי בְמַלְכוּתָא יִשְׁלַט׃ אֱדַיִן עָלִּלִין
ones-coming-in then (8) he-will-be-ruler in-the-kingdom and-third neck-of-him around

כֹּל חַכִּימֵי מַלְכָּא וְלָא־כָהֲלִין כְּתָבָא לְמִקְרֵא
to-read the-writing ones-being-able but-not the-king wise-men-of all-of

### *The Writing on the Wall*

5 King Belshazzar gave a great
banquet for a thousand of his
nobles and drank wine with
them. [2]While Belshazzar was
drinking his wine, he gave orders
to bring in the gold and silver goblets that Nebuchadnezzar his father[l] had taken from the temple in
Jerusalem, so that the king and his
nobles, his wives and his concubines might drink from them. [3]So
they brought in the gold goblets
that had been taken from the temple of God in Jerusalem, and the
king and his nobles, his wives and
his concubines drank from them.
[4]As they drank the wine, they
praised the gods of gold and silver,
of bronze, iron, wood and stone.
[5]Suddenly the fingers of a human hand appeared and wrote on
the plaster of the wall, near the
lampstand in the royal palace. The
king watched the hand as it wrote.
[6]His face turned pale and he was
so frightened that his knees
knocked together and his legs
gave way.
[7]The king called out for the enchanters, astrologers[m] and diviners to be brought and said to these
wise men of Babylon, "Whoever
reads this writing and tells me
what it means will be clothed in
purple and have a gold chain
placed around his neck, and he
will be made the third highest ruler in the kingdom."
[8]Then all the king's wise men
came in, but they could not read

[l]2 Or *ancestor;* or *predecessor;* also in verses 11, 13 and 18
[m]7 Or *Chaldeans;* also in verse 11

*6 Most mss have *sheva* under the *ayin* (עְ־).

°5 ק נפקה; °7a ק כשדאי
°7b ק והמניכא; °8 ק עלין

וּפִשְׁרָא לְהוֹדָעָה לְמַלְכָּא׃ אֱדַיִן מַלְכָּא בֵלְשַׁאצַּר שַׂגִּיא
more Belshazzar the-king so (9) to-the-king to-tell or-meaning-of-him

מִתְבָּהַל וְזִיוֺהִי שָׁנַיִן עֲלוֹהִי וְרַבְרְבָנוֹהִי
and-nobles-of-him to-him ones-changing and-faces-of-him being-terrified

מִשְׁתַּבְּשִׁין׃ מַלְכְּתָא לָקֳבֵל מִלֵּי מַלְכָּא וְרַבְרְבָנוֹהִי
and-nobles-of-him the-king voices-of at-because-of the-queen (10) ones-being-baffled

לְבֵית מִשְׁתְּיָא עַלַּלַת עֲנָת מַלְכְּתָא וַאֲמֶרֶת מַלְכָּא
O-king and-she-said the-queen she-spoke she-came the-banquet into-hall-of

לְעָלְמִין חֱיִי אַל־ יְבַהֲלוּךְ רַעְיוֹנָךְ וְזִיוָיךְ אַל־
not and-faces-of-you thoughts-of-you let-them-alarm-you not live! to-forevers

יִשְׁתַּנּוֹ׃ אִיתַי גְּבַר בְּמַלְכוּתָךְ דִּי רוּחַ אֱלָהִין קַדִּישִׁין
holy-ones gods spirit-of who in-kingdom-of-you man there-is (11) let-them-change

בֵּהּ וּבְיוֹמֵי אֲבוּךְ נַהִירוּ וְשָׂכְלְתָנוּ וְחָכְמָה
and-wisdom and-intelligence insight father-of-you and-in-days-of in-him

כְּחָכְמַת־ אֱלָהִין הִשְׁתְּכַחַת בֵּהּ וּמַלְכָּא נְבֻכַדְנֶצַּר אֲבוּךְ
father-of-you Nebuchadnezzar and-the-king in-him she-was-found gods like-wisdom-of

רַב חַרְטֻמִּין אָשְׁפִין כַּשְׂדָּאִין גָּזְרִין הֲקִימֵהּ אֲבוּךְ
father-of-you he-appointed-him ones-divining Chaldeans enchanters magicians chief-of

מַלְכָּא׃ כָּל־קֳבֵל דִּי רוּחַ ׀ יַתִּירָה וּמַנְדַּע וְשָׂכְלְתָנוּ מְפַשַּׁר
interpreting and-understanding and-knowledge keen mind that for all-of (12) the-king

חֶלְמִין וַאֲחֲוָיַת* אֲחִידָן וּמְשָׁרֵא קִטְרִין הִשְׁתְּכַחַת בֵּהּ
in-him she-was-found difficult-problems and-solving riddles and-to-explain dreams

בְּדָנִיֵּאל דִּי־ מַלְכָּא שָׂם־ שְׁמֵהּ בֵּלְטְשַׁאצַּר כְּעַן דָּנִיֵּאל יִתְקְרֵי
let-him-be-called Daniel now Belteshazzar name-of-him he-made the-king whom in-Daniel

וּפִשְׁרָה יְהַחֲוֵה׃ בֵּאדַיִן דָּנִיֵּאל הֻעַל קֳדָם מַלְכָּא
the-king before he-was-brought Daniel at-then (13) he-will-tell and-the-meaning

עָנֵה מַלְכָּא וְאָמַר לְדָנִיֵּאל אַנְתְּה־הוּא דָנִיֵּאל דִּי־ מִן־ בְּנֵי
peoples-of from who Daniel he you to-Daniel and-saying the-king speaking

גָלוּתָא דִּי יְהוּד דִּי הַיְתִי מַלְכָּא אַבִי מִן־ יְהוּד׃ וְשִׁמְעֵת
now-I-heard (14) Judah from father-of-me the-king he-brought whom Judah of the-exile

עֲלָיִךְ דִּי רוּחַ אֱלָהִין בָּךְ וְנַהִירוּ וְשָׂכְלְתָנוּ וְחָכְמָה
and-wisdom and-intelligence and-insight in-you gods spirit-of that about-you

יַתִּירָה הִשְׁתְּכַחַת בָּךְ׃ וּכְעַן הֻעַלּוּ קֳדָמַי
before-me they-were-brought-in and-now (15) in-you she-is-found outstanding

חַכִּימַיָּא אָשְׁפַיָּא דִּי־ כְתָבָה דְנָה יִקְרוֹן וּפִשְׁרֵהּ
and-meaning-of-him they-might-read this the-writing that the-enchanters the-wise-men

לְהוֹדָעֻתַנִי וְלָא־ כָהֲלִין פְּשַׁר־ מִלְּתָא לְהַחֲוָיָה׃ וַאֲנָה
now-I (16) to-tell the-thing explanation-of ones-being-able but-not to-tell-me

the writing or tell the king what it meant. [9]So King Belshazzar became even more terrified and his face grew more pale. His nobles were baffled.

[10]The queen,[n] hearing the voices of the king and his nobles, came into the banquet hall. "O king, live forever!" she said. "Don't be alarmed! Don't look so pale! [11]There is a man in your kingdom who has the spirit of the holy gods in him. In the time of your father he was found to have insight and intelligence and wisdom like that of the gods. King Nebuchadnezzar your father—your father the king, I say—appointed him chief of the magicians, enchanters, astrologers and diviners. [12]This man Daniel, whom the king called Belteshazzar, was found to have a keen mind and knowledge and understanding, and also the ability to interpret dreams, explain riddles and solve difficult problems. Call for Daniel, and he will tell you what the writing means."

[13]So Daniel was brought before the king, and the king said to him, "Are you Daniel, one of the exiles my father the king brought from Judah? [14]I have heard that the spirit of the gods is in you and that you have insight, intelligence and outstanding wisdom. [15]The wise men and enchanters were brought before me to read this writing and tell me what it means, but they could not explain it. [16]Now I have

[n]10 Or *queen mother*

*12 Most mss have *sheva* under the *vav* (וְ).

°8 ק ופשרה ;°10 ק עלת
°13 ק אנת ;°14 ק עלך

שִׁמְעֵת עֲלָיִךְ דִּי־ תוּכַל פִּשְׁרִין לְמִפְשַׁר
to-give-interpretation interpretations you-are-able that about-you I-heard

וְקִטְרִין לְמִשְׁרֵא כְּעַן הֵן תוּכֻל כְּתָבָא לְמִקְרֵא
to-read the-writing you-are-able if now to-solve and-difficult-problems

וּפִשְׁרֵהּ לְהוֹדָעֻתַנִי אַרְגְּוָנָא תִלְבַּשׁ וְהַמְוֹנְכָא דִי־
of and-the-chain you-will-be-clothed-in the-purple to-tell-me and-meaning-of-him

דַהֲבָא עַל־ צַוְּארָךְ וְתַלְתָּא בְמַלְכוּתָא תִּשְׁלַט׃
you-will-be-ruler in-the-kingdom and-the-third neck-of-you around the-gold

(17) בֵּאדַיִן עָנֵה דָנִיֵּאל וְאָמַר קֳדָם מַלְכָּא מַתְּנָתָךְ לָךְ
for-you gifts-of-you the-king before and-saying Daniel answering at-then (17)

לֶהֶוְיָן וּנְבָזְבְּיָתָךְ לְאָחֳרָן הַב בְּרַם כְּתָבָא
the-writing nevertheless give! to-someone-else and-rewards-of-you let-them-be

אֶקְרֵא לְמַלְכָּא וּפִשְׁרָא אֲהוֹדְעִנֵּהּ׃ (18) אַנְתָּה מַלְכָּא אֱלָהָא
the-God O-king you (18) I-will-tell-him and-the-meaning for-the-king I-will-read

עִלָּיָא מַלְכוּתָא וּרְבוּתָא וִיקָרָא וְהַדְרָה
and-the-splendor and-the-glory and-the-greatness the-sovereignty the-Most-High

יְהַב לִנְבֻכַדְנֶצַּר אֲבוּךְ׃ (19) וּמִן־ רְבוּתָא דִּי
that the-high-position and-because-of (19) father-of-you to-Nebuchadnezzar he-gave

יְהַב־ לֵהּ כֹּל עַמְמַיָּא אֻמַיָּא וְלִשָּׁנַיָּא הֲוֺו
they-were and-the-languages the-nations the-peoples all-of to-him he-gave

זָאְעִין וְדָחֲלִין מִן־ קֳדָמוֹהִי דִּי־ הֲוָה צָבֵא הֲוָא
he-was wanting-to he-was whom before-him at and-ones-fearing ones-dreading

קָטֵל וְדִי־ הֲוָה צָבֵא הֲוָה מַחֵא וְדִי־ הֲוָה צָבֵא
wanting-to he-was and-whom sparing he-was wanting-to he-was and-whom putting-to-death

הֲוָה מָרִים וְדִי־ הֲוָה צָבֵא הֲוָה מַשְׁפִּיל׃ (20) וּכְדִי
but-as-when (20) humbling he-was wanting-to he-was and-whom promoting he-was

רִם לִבְבֵהּ וְרוּחֵהּ תִּקְפַת לַהֲזָדָה
to-be-proud she-became-hardened and-spirit-of-him heart-of-him he-became-arrogant

הָנְחַת מִן־ כָּרְסֵא מַלְכוּתֵהּ וִיקָרָה הֶעְדִּיו מִנֵּהּ׃
from-him they-stripped and-the-glory royalty-of-him throne-of from he-was-deposed

(21) וּמִן־ בְּנֵי אֲנָשָׁא טְרִיד וְלִבְבֵהּ׀ עִם־
like and-mind-of-him he-was-driven-away the-people sons-of and-from (21)

חֵיוְתָא שַׁוִּי וְעִם־ עֲרָדַיָּא מְדוֹרֵהּ עִשְׂבָּא
the-grass living-place-of-him with-wild-donkeys and-with he-was-made the-animal

כְּתוֹרִין יְטַעֲמוּנֵּהּ וּמִטַּל שְׁמַיָּא גִּשְׁמֵהּ יִצְטַבַּע
he-was-drenched body-of-him the-heavens and-with-dew-of they-made-eat-him like-cattles

עַד דִּי־ יְדַע דִּי־ שַׁלִּיט אֱלָהָא עִלָּיָא בְּמַלְכוּת
over-kingdom-of the-Most-High the-God sovereign that he-acknowledged that until

heard that you are able to give interpretations and to solve difficult
problems. If you can read this
writing and tell me what it means,
you will be clothed in purple and
have a gold chain placed around
your neck, and you will be made
the third highest ruler in the kingdom."
17Then Daniel answered the
king, "You may keep your gifts for
yourself and give your rewards to
someone else. Nevertheless, I will
read the writing for the king and
tell him what it means.
18"O king, the Most High God
gave your father Nebuchadnezzar
sovereignty and greatness and
glory and splendor. 19Because of
the high position he gave him, all
the peoples and nations and men
of every language dreaded and
feared him. Those the king wanted to put to death, he put to death;
those he wanted to spare, he
spared; those he wanted to promote, he promoted; and those he
wanted to humble, he humbled.
20But when his heart became arrogant and hardened with pride, he
was deposed from his royal throne
and stripped of his glory. 21He was
driven away from people and giv-
en the mind of an animal; he lived
with the wild donkeys and ate
grass like cattle; and his body was
drenched with the dew of heaven,
until he acknowledged that the
Most High God is sovereign over
the kingdoms of men and sets

°16a ק עלך ;°16b ק תכול
°16c ק תכול ;°16d ק והמניכא
°18a ק אנת ;°18b ק עלאה
°19 ק זיעין ;°21a ק שויו
°21b ק עלאה

אנשא ולמן די יצבה יהקים עליה ואנתה ברה
son-of-him but-you (22) over-her he-sets he-wishes that and-to-whom the-man

בלשאצר לא השפלת לבבך כל קבל די כל דנה ידעת:
you-knew this all-of that though all-of heart-of-you you-humbled not Belshazzar

ועל מרא שמיא ׀ התרוממת ולמאניא
and-to-the-goblets you-set-yourself-up the-heavens Lord-of instead-against (23)

די ביתה היתיו קדמיך ואנתה ורברבניך שגלתך
wives-of-you and-nobles-of-you and-you before-you they-brought temple-of-him of

ולחנתך חמרא שתין בהון ולאלהי כספא
the-silver and-to-gods-of from-them ones-drinking the-wine and-concubines-of-you

ודהבא נחשא פרזלא אעא ואבנא די לא חזין ולא
or-not ones-seeing not which and-the-stone the-wood the-iron the-bronze and-the-gold

שמעין ולא ידעין שבחת ולאלהא די נשמתך
life-of-you who but-to-the-God you-praised ones-understanding or-not ones-hearing

בידה וכל ארחתך לה לא הדרת: באדין מן
from for-then (24) you-honored not to-him ways-of-you and-all-of in-hand-of-him

קדמוהי שליח† פסא די ידא וכתבא דנה רשים:
he-was-written this and-the-inscription the-hand of the-palm he-was-sent before-him

ודנה כתבא די רשים מנא מנא תקל ופרסין:
uparsin tekel mene mene he-was-written that the-inscription and-this (25)

דנה פשר מלתא מנא מנה אלהא מלכותך
reign-of-you the-God he-numbered mene the-word meaning-of this (26)

והשלמה: תקל תקילתה במאזניא והשתכחת
and-you-were-found on-the-scales you-were-weighed tekel (27) and-he-brought-to-end-her

חסיר: פרס פריסת מלכותך ויהיבת למדי ופרס:
and-Persian to-Mede and-she-is-given kingdom-of-you she-is-divided peres (28) wanting

באדין ׀ אמר בלשאצר והלבשו לדניאל ארגונא והמונכא
and-the-chain the-purple to-Daniel and-they-clothed Belshazzar he-commanded at-then (29)

די דהבא על צוארה והכרזו עלוהי די להוא שליט
ruler he-was that about-him and-they-proclaimed neck-of-him around the-gold of

תלתא במלכותא: בה בליליא קטיל בלאשצר מלכא
the-king Belshazzar he-was-slain in-the-night in-him (30) in-the-kingdom the-third

כשדיא: ודריוש מדיא קבל מלכותא כבר
as-son-of the-kingdom he-took-over the-Mede and-Darius *(6:1[31]) the-Chaldeans

שנין שתין ותרתין: שפר קדם דריוש והקים על
over and-he-appointed Darius before he-was-pleasing (2) and-two sixty years

מלכותא לאחשדרפניא מאה ועשרין די להון בכל
through-all-of they-were who and-twenty hundred to-the-satraps the-kingdom

over them anyone he wishes.
22"But you his son,[o] O Belshazzar, have not humbled yourself, though you knew all this. 23Instead, you have set yourself up against the Lord of heaven. You had the goblets from his temple brought to you, and you and your nobles, your wives and your concubines drank wine from them. You praised the gods of silver and gold, of bronze, iron, wood and stone, which cannot see or hear or understand. But you did not honor the God who holds in his hand your life and all your ways. 24Therefore he sent the hand that wrote the inscription.
25"This is the inscription that was written:

MENE, MENE, TEKEL, PARSIN[p]

26"This is what these words mean:

*Mene*[q]: God has numbered the days of your reign and brought it to an end.
27*Tekel*[r]: You have been weighed on the scales and found wanting.
28*Peres*[s]: Your kingdom is divided and given to the Medes and Persians."

29Then at Belshazzar's command, Daniel was clothed in purple, a gold chain was placed around his neck, and he was proclaimed the third highest ruler in the kingdom.
30That very night Belshazzar, king of the Babylonians,[t] was slain, 31and Darius the Mede took over the kingdom, at the age of sixty-two.

*Daniel in the Den of Lions*

6 It pleased Darius to appoint 120 satraps to rule throughout

o22 Or *descendant;* or *successor*
p25 Aramaic *UPARSIN* (that is, *AND PARSIN*)
q26 *Mene* can mean *numbered* or *mina* (a unit of money).
r27 *Tekel* can mean *weighed* or *shekel.*
s28 *Peres* (the singular of *Parsin*) can mean *divided* or *Persia* or *a half mina* or *a half shekel.*
t30 Or *Chaldeans*

**Heading, 1* The Hebrew numeration of chapter 6 begins with the final verse of chapter five in English; thus, there is a one-verse discrepancy throughout the chapter.

†24 Most mss have no *pathah* under the *yod* (שליח).

°21 ק עלה; °22 ק ואנת
°23a ק קדמך; °23b ק ואנת
°23c ק ורברבנך; °29 ק והמניכא
°30 ק כשדאה; °1 ק מדאה

מַלְכוּתָא׃ וְעֵלָּא מִנְּהוֹן סָרְכִין תְּלָתָא דִּי דָנִיֵּאל חַד־ מִנְּהוֹן
of-them one Daniel who three administrators from-them and-over (3) the-kingdom

דִּי־ לֶהֱוֺן אֲחַשְׁדַּרְפְּנַיָּא אִלֵּין יָהֲבִין לְהוֹן טַעְמָא וּמַלְכָּא לָא־
not so-the-king the-account to-them ones-giving these the-satraps they-were who

לֶהֱוֵא נָזִק׃ אֱדַיִן דָּנִיֵּאל דְּנָה הֲוָא מִתְנַצַּח
distinguishing-himself he-was this Daniel now (4) one-suffering-loss he-might-be

עַל־ סָרְכַיָּא וַאֲחַשְׁדַּרְפְּנַיָּא כָּל־ קֳבֵל דִּי רוּחַ יַתִּירָא
exceptional spirit that for all-of and-the-satraps the-administrators among

בֵּהּ וּמַלְכָּא עֲשִׁית לַהֲקָמוּתֵהּ עַל־ כָּל־ מַלְכוּתָא׃ אֱדַיִן
then (5) the-kingdom whole-of over to-set-him he-planned that-the-king in-him

סָרְכַיָּא וַאֲחַשְׁדַּרְפְּנַיָּא הֲווֹ בָעַיִן עִלָּה לְהַשְׁכָּחָה לְדָנִיֵּאל
against-Daniel to-find charge ones-trying they-were and-the-satraps the-administrators

מִצַּד מַלְכוּתָא וְכָל־ עִלָּה וּשְׁחִיתָה לָא־
not or-thing-being-corrupt charge but-any-of the-government in-affair-of

יָכְלִין לְהַשְׁכָּחָה כָּל־ קֳבֵל דִּי־ מְהֵימַן הוּא וְכָל־
and-any-of he being-trustworthy that because all-of to-find ones-being-able

שָׁלוּ וּשְׁחִיתָה לָא הִשְׁתְּכַחַת עֲלוֹהִי׃ אֱדַיִן גֻּבְרַיָּא
the-men finally (6) against-him she-was-found not or-thing-being-corrupt negligence

אִלֵּךְ אָמְרִין דִּי לָא נְהַשְׁכַּח לְדָנִיֵּאל דְּנָה כָּל־ עִלָּא לָהֵן
unless charge any-of this against-Daniel we-will-find never that ones-saying these

הַשְׁכַּחְנָה עֲלוֹהִי בְּדָת אֱלָהֵהּ׃ אֱדַיִן סָרְכַיָּא וַאֲחַשְׁדַּרְפְּנַיָּא
and-the-satraps the-administrators so (7) God-of-him in-law-of against-him we-find

אִלֵּן הַרְגִּשׁוּ עַל־ מַלְכָּא וְכֵן אָמְרִין לֵהּ דָּרְיָוֶשׁ מַלְכָּא
O-king Darius to-him ones-saying and-this the-king to they-went-as-group these

לְעָלְמִין חֱיִי׃ אִתְיָעַטוּ כֹּל ׀ סָרְכֵי מַלְכוּתָא סִגְנַיָּא
the-prefects the-royalty administrators-of all-of they-agreed (8) live! to-forevers

וַאֲחַשְׁדַּרְפְּנַיָּא הַדָּבְרַיָּא וּפַחֲוָתָא לְקַיָּמָה קְיָם מַלְכָּא וּלְתַקָּפָה
and-to-enforce the-king edict to-issue and-the-governors the-advisers and-the-satraps

אֱסָר דִּי כָל־ דִּי־ יִבְעֵה בָעוּ מִן־ כָּל־ אֱלָהּ וֶאֱנָשׁ עַד־ יוֹמִין
days during or-man god any-of to prayer he-prays who any-of that decree

תְּלָתִין לָהֵן מִנָּךְ מַלְכָּא יִתְרְמֵא לְגֹב אַרְיָוָתָא׃ כְּעַן
now (9) the-lions into-den-of he-shall-be-thrown O-king to-you except thirty

מַלְכָּא תְּקִים אֱסָרָא וְתִרְשֻׁם כְּתָבָא דִּי לָא לְהַשְׁנָיָה
to-alter not that the-writing and-you-inscribe the-decree you-issue O-king

כְּדָת־ מָדַי וּפָרַס דִּי־ לָא תֶעְדֵּא׃ כָּל־
all-of (10) she-can-be-repealed not which and-Persian Mede according-to-law-of

קֳבֵל דְּנָה מַלְכָּא דָּרְיָוֶשׁ רְשַׁם כְּתָבָא וֶאֱסָרָא׃ וְדָנִיֵּאל
now-Daniel (11) and-the-decree the-writing he-inscribed Darius the-king this for

the kingdom, [2]with three administrators over them, one of whom
was Daniel. The satraps were
made accountable to them so that
the king might not suffer loss.
[3]Now Daniel so distinguished
himself among the administrators
and the satraps by his exceptional
qualities that the king planned to
set him over the whole kingdom.
[4]At this, the administrators and
the satraps tried to find grounds
for charges against Daniel in his
conduct of government affairs,
but they were unable to do so.
They could find no corruption in
him, because he was trustworthy
and neither corrupt nor negligent.
[5]Finally these men said, "We will
never find any basis for charges
against this man Daniel unless it
has something to do with the law
of his God."
[6]So the administrators and the
satraps went as a group to the king
and said: "O King Darius, live forever! [7]The royal administrators,
prefects, satraps, advisers and
governors have all agreed that the
king should issue an edict and en-
force the decree that anyone who
prays to any god or man during
the next thirty days, except to you,
O king, shall be thrown into the
lions' den. [8]Now, O king, issue the
decree and put it in writing so that
it cannot be altered—in accordance with the laws of the Medes
and Persians, which cannot be repealed." [9]So King Darius put the
decree in writing.
[10]Now when Daniel learned that

**Heading* See the note on page 458.

כְּדִי יְדַע דִּי־ רְשִׁים כְּתָבָא עַל לְבַיְתֵהּ
o-home-of-him he-went the-decree he-was-published that he-learned as-when

וְכַוִּין פְּתִיחָן לֵהּ בְּעִלִּיתֵהּ נֶגֶד יְרוּשְׁלֶם
Jerusalem toward in-upstairs-room-of-him to-him ones-being-open and-windows

וְזִמְנִין תְּלָתָה בְּיוֹמָא הוּא | בָּרֵךְ עַל־ בִּרְכוֹהִי וּמְצַלֵּא וּמוֹדֵא
and-giving-thanks and-praying knees-of-him on kneeling he in-the-day three and-times

קֳדָם אֱלָהֵהּ כָּל־קֳבֵל דִּי־ הֲוָא עָבֵד מִן־ קַדְמַת דְּנָה׃ אֱדַיִן
then (12) this before-of from doing he-was that for all-of God-of-him before

גֻּבְרַיָּא אִלֵּךְ הַרְגִּשׁוּ וְהַשְׁכַּחוּ לְדָנִיֵּאל בָּעֵא וּמִתְחַנַּן
and-asking-for-help praying to-Daniel and-they-found they-went-as-group these the-men

קֳדָם אֱלָהֵהּ׃ בֵּאדַיִן קְרִיבוּ וְאָמְרִין קֳדָם־ מַלְכָּא עַל־
about the-king before and-ones-saying they-went at-then (13) God-of-him before

אֱסָר מַלְכָּא הֲלָא אֱסָר רְשַׁמְתָּ דִּי כָל־ אֱנָשׁ דִּי־ יִבְעֵה מִן־
to he-prays who one any-of that you-published decree not? the-royalty decree-of

כָּל־ אֱלָהּ וֶאֱנָשׁ עַד־יוֹמִין תְּלָתִין לָהֵן מִנָּךְ מַלְכָּא יִתְרְמֵא
he-would-be-thrown O-king to-you except thirty days during or-man god any-of

לְגוֹב אַרְיָוָתָא‡ עָנֵה מַלְכָּא וְאָמַר יַצִּיבָא מִלְּתָא
the-decree standing and-saying the-king answering the-lions into-den-of

כְּדָת־ מָדַי וּפָרַס דִּי־ לָא תֶעְדֵּא׃ בֵּאדַיִן
at-then (14) she-can-be-repealed not which and-Persian Mede according-to-law-of

עֲנוֹ וְאָמְרִין קֳדָם מַלְכָּא דִּי דָנִיֵּאל דִּי מִן־ בְּנֵי גָלוּתָא
the-exile peoples-of from who Daniel that the-king before and-ones-saying they-spoke

דִּי יְהוּד לָא־ שָׂם עֲלָיךְ° מַלְכָּא טְעֵם וְעַל־ אֱסָרָא דִּי
that the-decree or-to attention O-king to-you he-pays-attention not Judah of

רְשַׁמְתָּ וְזִמְנִין תְּלָתָה בְּיוֹמָא בָּעֵא בָּעוּתֵהּ׃ אֱדַיִן
then (15) prayer-of-him praying in-the-day three still-times you-put-in-writing

מַלְכָּא כְּדִי מִלְּתָא שְׁמַע שַׂגִּיא בְּאֵשׁ עֲלוֹהִי וְעַל
and-concerning to-him he-was-distressing greatly he-heard the-word as-when the-king

דָּנִיֵּאל שָׂם בָּל לְשֵׁיזָבוּתֵהּ וְעַד מֶעָלֵי שִׁמְשָׁא הֲוָא
he-was the-sun goings-down-of and-until to-rescue-him mind he-determined Daniel

מִשְׁתַּדַּר לְהַצָּלוּתֵהּ׃ בֵּאדַיִן גֻּבְרַיָּא אִלֵּךְ הַרְגִּשׁוּ
they-went-as-group these the-men at-then (16) to-save-him making-every-effort

עַל־מַלְכָּא וְאָמְרִין לְמַלְכָּא דַּע מַלְכָּא דִּי־ דָת לְמָדַי
of-Mede law that O-king remember! to-the-king and-ones-saying the-king to

וּפָרַס דִּי־ כָל־ אֱסָר וּקְיָם דִּי־ מַלְכָּא יְהָקֵים לָא לְהַשְׁנָיָה׃
to-change not he-issues the-king that or-edict decree any-of that and-Persian

(17) בֵּאדַיִן מַלְכָּא אֲמַר וְהַיְתִיו לְדָנִיֵּאל וּרְמוֹ
and-they-threw to-Daniel and-they-brought he-ordered the-king at-then (17)

the decree had been published, he
went home to his upstairs room
where the windows opened
toward Jerusalem. Three times a
day he got down on his knees and
prayed, giving thanks to his God,
just as he had done before. [11]Then
these men went as a group and
found Daniel praying and asking
God for help. [12]So they went to the
king and spoke to him about his
royal decree: "Did you not publish
a decree that during the next
thirty days anyone who prays to
any god or man except to you, O
king, would be thrown into the
lions' den?"

The king answered, "The decree
stands—in accordance with the
laws of the Medes and Persians,
which cannot be repealed."

[13]Then they said to the king,
"Daniel, who is one of the exiles
from Judah, pays no attention to
you, O king, or to the decree you
put in writing. He still prays three
times a day." [14]When the king
heard this, he was greatly distressed; he was determined to rescue Daniel and made every effort
until sundown to save him.

[15]Then the men went as a group
to the king and said to him,
"Remember, O king, that according to the law of the Medes and
Persians no decree or edict that
the king issues can be changed."

[16]So the king gave the order, and
they brought Daniel and threw

*Heading See the note on page 458.

‡13 Most mss have *qamets* under the *vav* (וָ).

°14 ק עלך

לְגֻבָּא דִּי אַרְיָוָתָא עָנֵה מַלְכָּא וְאָמַר לְדָנִיֵּאל אֱלָהָךְ דִּי
whom God-of-you to-Daniel and-saying the-king speaking the-lions of into-the-den

אַנְתָּה פָּלַח־לֵהּ בִּתְדִירָא הוּא יְשֵׁיזְבִנָּךְ׃ וְהֵיתָיִת
and-she-was-brought (18) may-he-rescue-you he at-continually to-him serving you

אֶבֶן חֲדָה וְשֻׂמַת עַל־פֻּם גֻּבָּא וְחַתְמַהּ מַלְכָּא
the-king and-he-sealed-her the-den mouth-of over and-she-was-placed a stone

בְּעִזְקְתֵהּ וּבְעִזְקָת רַבְרְבָנוֹהִי דִּי לָא־
not that nobles-of-him and-with-signet-rings-of with-signet-ring-of-him

תִשְׁנֵא צְבוּ בְּדָנִיֵּאל׃ אֱדַיִן אֲזַל מַלְכָּא לְהֵיכְלֵהּ
to-palace-of-him the-king he-returned then (19) of-Daniel situation she-might-change

וּבָת טְוָת וְדַחֲוָן לָא־הַנְעֵל קֳדָמוֹהִי
before-him he-brought not and-entertainments without-eating and-he-spent-night

וְשִׁנְתֵּהּ נַדַּת עֲלוֹהִי׃ בֵּאדַיִן מַלְכָּא בִּשְׁפַרְפָּרָא יְקוּם
he-got-up at-the-dawn the-king at-then (20) from-him she-fled and-sleep-of-him

בְּנָגְהָא וּבְהִתְבְּהָלָה לְגֻבָּא דִּי־אַרְיָוָתָא אֲזַל׃
he-went the-lions of to-the-den and-in-to-hurry at-the-light

וּכְמִקְרְבֵהּ לְגֻבָּא לְדָנִיֵּאל בְּקָל עֲצִיב
being-anguished in-voice to-Daniel to-the-den and-when-to-come-near-him (21)

זְעִק עָנֵה מַלְכָּא וְאָמַר לְדָנִיֵּאל דָּנִיֵּאל עֲבֵד אֱלָהָא
the-God servant-of Daniel to-Daniel and-saying the-king speaking he-called

חַיָּא אֱלָהָךְ דִּי אַנְתָּה פָּלַח־לֵהּ בִּתְדִירָא הֲיָכִל
was-he-able? at-continually to-him serving you whom God-of-you the-living

לְשֵׁיזָבוּתָךְ מִן־אַרְיָוָתָא׃ אֱדַיִן דָּנִיֵּאל עִם־מַלְכָּא מַלִּל מַלְכָּא
O-king he-answered the-king to Daniel then (22) the-lions from to-rescue-you

לְעָלְמִין חֱיִי׃ אֱלָהִי שְׁלַח מַלְאֲכֵהּ וּסֲגַר פֻּם
mouth-of and-he-shut angel-of-him he-sent God-of-me (23) live! to-forevers

אַרְיָוָתָא וְלָא חַבְּלוּנִי כָּל־קֳבֵל דִּי קָדָמוֹהִי זָכוּ הִשְׁתְּכַחַת
she-was-found innocence before-him that because all-of they-hurt-me and-not the-lions

לִי וְאַף קָדָמַיךְ מַלְכָּא חֲבוּלָה לָא עַבְדֵת׃ בֵּאדַיִן מַלְכָּא שַׂגִּיא
greatly the-king at-then (24) I-did never wrong O-king before-you and-also to-me

טְאֵב עֲלוֹהִי וּלְדָנִיֵּאל אֲמַר לְהַנְסָקָה מִן־גֻּבָּא
the-den from to-lift-out he-ordered and-concerning-Daniel to-him he-was-joyous

וְהֻסַּק דָּנִיֵּאל מִן־גֻּבָּא וְכָל־חֲבָל לָא־הִשְׁתְּכַח בֵּהּ
on-him he-was-found not wound then-any-of the-den from Daniel when-he-was-lifted

דִּי הֵימִן בֵּאלָהֵהּ׃ וַאֲמַר מַלְכָּא וְהַיְתִיו
and-they-brought the-king then-he-commanded (25) in-God-of-him he-trusted because

גֻּבְרַיָּא אִלֵּךְ דִּי־אֲכַלוּ קַרְצוֹהִי דִּי דָנִיֵּאל וּלְגֹב אַרְיָוָתָא
the-lions and-into-den-of Daniel of pieces-of-him they-chewed-up who these the-men

him into the lions' den. The king
said to Daniel, "May your God,
whom you serve continually, rescue you!"
[17]A stone was brought and
placed over the mouth of the den,
and the king sealed it with his
own signet ring and with the
rings of his nobles, so that Daniel's situation might not be
changed. [18]Then the king returned
to his palace and spent the night
without eating and without any
entertainment being brought to
him. And he could not sleep.
[19]At the first light of dawn, the
king got up and hurried to the
lions' den. [20]When he came near
the den, he called to Daniel in an
anguished voice, "Daniel, servant
of the living God, has your God,
whom you serve continually,
been able to rescue you from the
lions?"
[21]Daniel answered, "O king, live
forever! [22]My God sent his angel,
and he shut the mouths of the
lions. They have not hurt me, because I was found innocent in his
sight. Nor have I ever done any
wrong before you, O king."
[23]The king was overjoyed and
gave orders to lift Daniel out of the
den. And when Daniel was lifted
from the den, no wound was
found on him, because he had
trusted in his God.
[24]At the king's command, the
men who had falsely accused
Daniel were brought in and
thrown into the lions' den, along

*Heading* See the note on page 458.

*22* Most mss have *tsere* under the *yod* (‑ֵ‑).

°*17, 21* ק אנת; °*23* ק קדמך

רְמוֹ אִנּוּן בְּנֵיהוֹן וּנְשֵׁיהוֹן וְלָא־מְטוֹ לְאַרְעִית
to-floor-of they-reached and-not and-wives-of-them children-of-them they they-threw

גֻּבָּא עַד דִּי־שְׁלִטוּ בְהוֹן אַרְיָוָתָא וְכָל־גַּרְמֵיהוֹן
bones-of-them and-all-of the-lions over-them they-overpowered that until the-den

הַדִּקוּ׃ בֵּאדַיִן דָּרְיָוֶשׁ מַלְכָּא כְּתַב לְכָל־עַמְמַיָּא אֻמַיָּא
the-nations the-peoples to-all-of he-wrote the-king Darius at-then (26) they-crushed

וְלִשָּׁנַיָּא דִּי־דָאְרִין° בְּכָל־אַרְעָא שְׁלָמְכוֹן
prosperity-of-you the-land through-all-of ones-living who and-the-languages

יִשְׂגֵּא׃ מִן־קֳדָמַי שִׂים טְעֵם דִּי׀ בְּכָל־שָׁלְטָן
part-of in-every-of that decree he-is-issued before-me from (27) may-he-be-great

מַלְכוּתִי לֶהֱוֺן זָאְעִין° וְדָחֲלִין מִן־קֳדָם אֱלָהֵהּ
the-God before at and-ones-reverencing ones-fearing they-must-be kingdom-of-me

דִּי־דָנִיֵּאל דִּי־הוּא׀ אֱלָהָא חַיָּא וְקַיָּם לְעָלְמִין וּמַלְכוּתֵהּ
and-kingdom-of-him to-forevers and-enduring the-living the-God he for Daniel of

דִּי־לָא תִתְחַבַּל וְשָׁלְטָנֵהּ עַד־סוֹפָא׃
the-never-ending to and-dominion-of-him she-will-be-destroyed not that

מְשֵׁיזִב וּמַצִּל וְעָבֵד אָתִין וְתִמְהִין בִּשְׁמַיָּא
in-the-heavens and-wonders signs and-one-performing and-one-saving one-rescuing (28)

וּבְאַרְעָא דִּי שֵׁיזִיב לְדָנִיֵּאל מִן־יַד אַרְיָוָתָא׃ וְדָנִיֵּאל
so-Daniel (29) the-lions power-of from to-Daniel he-rescued who and-on-the-earth

דְּנָה הַצְלַח בְּמַלְכוּת דָּרְיָוֶשׁ וּבְמַלְכוּת כּוֹרֶשׁ פָּרְסָאָה°׃
the-Persian Cyrus and-during-reign-of Darius during-reign-of he-prospered this

בִּשְׁנַת חֲדָה לְבֵלְאשַׁצַּר מֶלֶךְ בָּבֶל דָּנִיֵּאל חֵלֶם חֲזָה
he-saw dream Daniel Babylon king-of of-Belshazzar one in-year-of (7:1)

וְחֶזְוֵי רֵאשֵׁהּ עַל־מִשְׁכְּבֵהּ בֵּאדַיִן חֶלְמָא כְתַב
he-wrote-down the-dream at-then bed-of-him on mind-of-him and-visions-of

רֵאשׁ מִלִּין אֲמַר׃ עָנֵה דָנִיֵּאל וְאָמַר חָזֵה הֲוֵית
I-was looking and-saying Daniel speaking (2) he-told things substance-of

בְּחֶזְוִי עִם־לֵילְיָא וַאֲרוּ אַרְבַּע רוּחֵי שְׁמַיָּא מְגִיחָן
ones-churning-up the-heavens winds-of four and-see! the-night at in-vision-of-me

לְיַמָּא רַבָּא׃ וְאַרְבַּע חֵיוָן רַבְרְבָן סָלְקָן מִן־יַמָּא
the-sea from ones-coming-up great-ones beasts and-four (3) the-great to-the-sea

שָׁנְיָן דָּא מִן־דָּא׃ קַדְמָיְתָא כְאַרְיֵה וְגַפִּין דִּי־נְשַׁר
eagle of and-wings like-lion the-first (4) other from each ones-being-different

לַהּ חָזֵה הֲוֵית עַד דִּי־מְּרִיטוּ גַפַּיהּ וּנְטִילַת
and-she-was-lifted wings-of-her they-were-torn-off that until I-was watching to-her

מִן־אַרְעָא וְעַל־רַגְלַיִן כֶּאֱנָשׁ הֳקִימַת וּלְבַב אֱנָשׁ יְהִיב
he-was-given man and-heart-of she-was-stood like-man two-feet and-on the-ground from

with their wives and children. And before they reached the floor of the den, the lions overpowered them and crushed all their bones.

[25]Then King Darius wrote to all the peoples, nations and men of every language throughout the land:

"May you prosper greatly!

[26]"I issue a decree that in every part of my kingdom people must fear and reverence the God of Daniel.

"For he is the living God
and he endures forever;
his kingdom will not be
destroyed,
his dominion will never
end.
[27]He rescues and he saves;
he performs signs and
wonders
in the heavens and on the
earth.
He has rescued Daniel
from the power of the
lions."

[28]So Daniel prospered during the reign of Darius and the reign of Cyrus[u] the Persian.

*Daniel's Dream of Four Beasts*

7 In the first year of Belshazzar king of Babylon, Daniel had a dream, and visions passed through his mind as he was lying on his bed. He wrote down the substance of his dream.

[2]Daniel said: "In my vision at night I looked, and there before me were the four winds of heaven churning up the great sea. [3]Four great beasts, each different from the others, came up out of the sea.

[4]"The first was like a lion, and it had the wings of an eagle. I watched until its wings were torn off and it was lifted from the ground so that it stood on two feet like a man, and the heart of a man was given to it.

[u]28 Or *Darius, that is, the reign of Cyrus*

*Heading See the note on page 458.

†29 Most mss have *pathah* under the *pe* (פַּ).

°26 ק דירין; °27 ק זיעין

°29 ק פרסאה

לַהּ׃ (5) וַאֲרוּ חֵיוָה אׇחֳרִי תִנְיָנָה דָּמְיָה לְדֹב וְלִשְׂטַר־חַד
one and-on-side to-bear looking-like second another beast and-see! (5) to-her

הֳקִמַת וּתְלָת עִלְעִין בְּפֻמַּהּ בֵּין שִׁנַּיהּ וְכֵן
and-this teeth-of-her between in-mouth-of-her ribs and-three she-was-raised-up

אָמְרִין לַהּ קוּמִי אֲכֻלִי בְּשַׂר שַׂגִּיא׃ (6) בָּאתַר דְּנָה חָזֵה הֲוֵית
I-was looking that at-after (6) much flesh eat! get-up! to-her ones-saying

וַאֲרוּ אׇחֳרִי כִּנְמַר וְלַהּ גַּפִּין אַרְבַּע דִּי־עוֹף עַל־גַּבַּיהּ
backs-of-her on bird of four wings and-on-her like-leopard another and-see!

וְאַרְבְּעָה רֵאשִׁין לְחֵיוְתָא וְשָׁלְטָן יְהִיב לַהּ׃ (7) בָּאתַר דְּנָה
that at-after (7) to-her he-was-given and-authority to-the-beast heads and-four

חָזֵה הֲוֵית בְּחֶזְוֵי לֵילְיָא וַאֲרוּ חֵיוָה רְבִיעָיָה דְּחִילָה
being-terrifying fourth beast and-see! the-night in-visions-of I-was looking

וְאֵימְתָנִי וְתַקִּיפָא יַתִּירָא וְשִׁנַּיִן דִּי־פַרְזֶל לַהּ רַבְרְבָן אָכְלָה
devouring large-ones to-her iron of and-teeth very and-powerful and-frightening

וּמַדֱּקָה וּשְׁאָרָא בְּרַגְלַיהּ רָפְסָה וְהִיא מְשַׁנְּיָה
being-different and-she trampling under-feet-of-her and-the-one-left and-crushing

מִן־כָּל־חֵיוָתָא דִּי קָדָמַיהּ וְקַרְנַיִן עֲשַׂר לַהּ׃ (8) מִשְׂתַּכַּל הֲוֵית
I-was thinking (8) to-her ten and-horns before-her that the-beasts all-of from

בְּקַרְנַיָּא וַאֲלוּ קֶרֶן אׇחֳרִי זְעֵירָה סִלְקָת בֵּינֵיהֵן וּתְלָת
and-three among-them she-came-up little another horn and-see! about-the-horns

מִן־קַרְנַיָּא קַדְמָיָתָא אֶתְעֲקַרוּ מִן־קֳדָמַיהּ וַאֲלוּ עַיְנִין
eyes and-see! before-her from they-were-uprooted the-first-ones the-horns from

כְּעַיְנֵי אֲנָשָׁא בְּקַרְנָא־דָא וּפֻם מְמַלִּל רַבְרְבָן׃
boastful-things speaking and-mouth this to-the-horn the-man like-eyes-of

(9) חָזֵה הֲוֵית עַד דִּי כׇרְסָוָן רְמִיו וְעַתִּיק יוֹמִין
Days and-Ancient-of they-were-set-in-place thrones that until I-was looking (9)

יְתִב לְבוּשֵׁהּ׀ כִּתְלַג חִוָּר וּשְׂעַר רֵאשֵׁהּ כַּעֲמַר נְקֵא
white like-wool head-of-him and-hair-of white as-snow clothing-of-him he-took-seat

כׇּרְסְיֵהּ שְׁבִיבִין דִּי־נוּר גַּלְגִּלּוֹהִי נוּר דָּלִק׃ (10) נְהַר דִּי־נוּר
fire of river (10) blazing fire wheels-of-him fire of flames throne-of-him

נָגֵד וְנָפֵק מִן־קֳדָמוֹהִי אֶלֶף אַלְפִים יְשַׁמְּשׁוּנֵּהּ
they-attended-him thousands thousand-of before-him from and-coming-out flowing

וְרִבּוֹ רִבְּוָן קׇדָמוֹהִי יְקוּמוּן דִּינָא יְתִב
he-was-seated the-court they-stood before-him ten-thousands and-ten-thousand-of

וְסִפְרִין פְּתִיחוּ׃ (11) חָזֵה הֲוֵית בֵּאדַיִן מִן־קָל מִלַּיָּא
the-words sound-of because-of at-then I-was watching (11) they-were-opened and-books

רַבְרְבָתָא דִּי קַרְנָא מְמַלֱּלָה חָזֵה הֲוֵית עַד דִּי קְטִילַת
she-was-slain that until I-was looking speaking the-horn that the-boastful-ones

5 "And there before me was a second beast, which looked like a bear. It was raised up on one of its sides, and it had three ribs in its mouth between its teeth. It was told, 'Get up and eat your fill of flesh!'

6 "After that, I looked, and there before me was another beast, one that looked like a leopard. And on its back it had four wings like those of a bird. This beast had four heads, and it was given authority to rule.

7 "After that, in my vision at night I looked, and there before me was a fourth beast—terrifying and frightening and very powerful. It had large iron teeth; it crushed and devoured its victims and trampled underfoot whatever was left. It was different from all the former beasts, and it had ten horns.

8 "While I was thinking about the horns, there before me was another horn, a little one, which came up among them; and three of the first horns were uprooted before it. This horn had eyes like the eyes of a man and a mouth that spoke boastfully.

9 "As I looked,

"thrones were set in place,
and the Ancient of Days
took his seat.
His clothing was as white as snow;
the hair of his head was white like wool.
His throne was flaming with fire,
and its wheels were all ablaze.
10 A river of fire was flowing,
coming out from before him.
Thousands upon thousands attended him;
ten thousand times ten thousand stood before him.
The court was seated,
and the books were opened.

11 "Then I continued to watch because of the boastful words the horn was speaking. I kept looking until the beast was slain and its

°5 ק שנה ;°6 ק גבה
°7a ק רביעאה ;°7b ק ברגלה
°8a ק ביניהן ;°8b ק אתעקרה
°8c ק קדמה ;°10a ק אלפין
°10b ק רבבן

חֵיוְתָא וְהוּבַד גִּשְׁמַהּ וִיהִיבַת לִיקֵדַת
into-blaze-of and-she-was-thrown body-of-her and-he-was-destroyed the-beast

אֶשָּׁא׃ (12) וּשְׁאָר חֵיוָתָא הֶעְדִּיו שָׁלְטָנְהוֹן וְאַרְכָה
but-length authority-of-them they-stripped the-beasts and-other-of (12) the-fire

בְחַיִּין יְהִיבַת לְהוֹן עַד־ זְמַן וְעִדָּן׃ (13) חָזֵה הֲוֵית
I-was looking (13) and-time period for to-them she-was-allowed of-lives

בְּחֶזְוֵי לֵילְיָא וַאֲרוּ עִם־ עֲנָנֵי שְׁמַיָּא כְּבַר אֱנָשׁ אָתֵה
coming man like-son-of the-heavens clouds-of with and-see! the-night in-visions-of

הֲוָה וְעַד־ עַתִּיק יוֹמַיָּא מְטָה וּקְדָמוֹהִי הַקְרְבוּהִי׃
they-led-him and-presences-of-him he-approached the-Days Ancient-of and-to he-was

(14) וְלֵהּ יְהִיב שָׁלְטָן וִיקָר וּמַלְכוּ וְכֹל
and-all-of and-sovereign-power and-glory authority he-was-given and-to-him (14)

עַמְמַיָּא אֻמַיָּא וְלִשָּׁנַיָּא לֵהּ יִפְלְחוּן שָׁלְטָנֵהּ
dominion-of-him they-worshiped to-him and-the-languages the-nations the-peoples

שָׁלְטָן עָלַם דִּי־ לָא יֶעְדֵּה וּמַלְכוּתֵהּ דִּי־ לָא
never that and-kingdom-of-him he-will-pass-away not that everlasting dominion-of

תִתְחַבַּל׃ (15) אֶתְכְּרִיַּת רוּחִי אֲנָה דָנִיֵּאל בְּגוֹא נִדְנֶה
body at-inside-of Daniel I spirit-of-me she-was-troubled (15) she-will-be-destroyed

וְחֶזְוֵי רֵאשִׁי יְבַהֲלֻנַּנִי׃ (16) קִרְבֵת עַל־ חַד מִן־
from one to I-approached (16) they-disturbed-me mind-of-me and-visions-of

קָאֲמַיָּא וְיַצִּיבָא אֶבְעֵא־ מִנֵּהּ עַל־ כָּל־ דְּנָה
this all-of concerning from-him I-asked and-true-meaning the-ones-standing

וַאֲמַר־ לִי וּפְשַׁר מִלַּיָּא יְהוֹדְעִנַּנִי׃ (17) אִלֵּין חֵיוָתָא
the-beasts these (17) he-gave-me the-things and-interpretation-of to-me so-he-told

רַבְרְבָתָא דִּי אִנִּין אַרְבַּע אַרְבְּעָה מַלְכִין יְקוּמוּן מִן־ אַרְעָא׃
the-earth from they-will-rise kingdoms four four they that the-great-ones

(18) וִיקַבְּלוּן מַלְכוּתָא קַדִּישֵׁי עֶלְיוֹנִין וְיַחְסְנוּן
and-they-will-possess Most-High-Ones saints-of the-kingdom but-they-will-receive (18)

מַלְכוּתָא עַד־ עָלְמָא וְעַד עָלַם עָלְמַיָּא׃ (19) אֱדַיִן צְבִית
I-wanted then (19) the-forevers forever-of yes-to the-forever to the-kingdom

לְיַצָּבָא עַל־ חֵיוְתָא רְבִיעָיְתָא דִּי־ הֲוָת שָׁנְיָה
being-different she-was which the-fourth the-beast concerning to-know-true-meaning

מִן־ כָּלְהֹון° דְּחִילָה יַתִּירָה שִׁנַּיַּהּ° דִּי־פַרְזֶל וְטִפְרַיַּהּ דִּי־
of and-claws-of-her iron of teeth-of-her most being-terrifying all-of-them from

נְחָשׁ אָכְלָה מַדֲּקָה וּשְׁאָרָא בְּרַגְלַיַּהּ רָפְסָה׃ (20) וְעַל־
and-about (20) trampling under-feet-of-her and-the-one-left crushing devouring bronze

קַרְנַיָּא עֲשַׂר דִּי בְרֵאשַׁהּ וְאָחֳרִי דִּי סִלְקַת וּנְפַלוּ°
and-they-fell she-came-up that and-other on-head-of-her that ten the-horns

body destroyed and thrown into
the blazing fire. [12](The other beasts
had been stripped of their authority, but were allowed to live for a
period of time.)
[13]"In my vision at night I
looked, and there before me was
one like a son of man, coming
with the clouds of heaven. He approached the Ancient of Days and
was led into his presence. [14]He
was given authority, glory and
sovereign power; all peoples, nations and men of every language
worshiped him. His dominion is
an everlasting dominion that will
not pass away, and his kingdom is
one that will never be destroyed.

*The Interpretation of the Dream*

[15]"I, Daniel, was troubled in
spirit, and the visions that passed
through my mind disturbed me.
[16]I approached one of those standing there and asked him the true
meaning of all this.

"So he told me and gave me the
interpretation of these things:
[17]'The four great beasts are four
kingdoms that will rise from the
earth. [18]But the saints of the Most
High will receive the kingdom
and will possess it forever—yes,
for ever and ever.'

[19]"Then I wanted to know the
true meaning of the fourth beast,
which was different from all the
others and most terrifying, with
its iron teeth and bronze claws—
the beast that crushed and devoured its victims and trampled
underfoot whatever was left. [20]I
also wanted to know about the ten
horns on its head and about the
other horn that came up, before

°19a ק כלהין; °19b ק שנה
°20 ק ונפלה

מִן־קֳדָמַיהּ תְּלָת וְקַרְנָא דִכֵּן וְעַיְנִין לַהּ וּפֶם* מְמַלִּל
speaking and-mouth to-her also-eyes that and-the-horn three before-her at

רַבְרְבָן וְחֶזְוַהּ רַב מִן־חַבְרָתַהּ׃ חָזֵה הֲוֵית
I-was watching (21) others-of-her than more and-look-of-her boastful-things

וְקַרְנָא דִכֵּן עָבְדָה קְרָב עִם־קַדִּישִׁין וְיָכְלָה לְהוֹן׃ עַד
until (22) to-them and-defeating saints against war waging this and-the-horn

דִּי אֲתָה עַתִּיק יוֹמַיָּא וְדִינָא יְהִב לְקַדִּישֵׁי
for-saints-of he-was-pronounced and-the-judgment the-Days Ancient-of he-came that

עֶלְיוֹנִין וְזִמְנָא מְטָה וּמַלְכוּתָא הֶחֱסִנוּ קַדִּישִׁין׃
saints they-possessed when-the-kingdom he-came and-the-time Most-High-Ones

כֵּן אֲמַר חֵיוְתָא רְבִיעָיְתָא מַלְכוּ רְבִיעָיָא תֶּהֱוֵא
she-will-appear fourth kingdom the-fourth the-beast he-explained this (23)

בְּאַרְעָא דִּי תִשְׁנֵא מִן־כָּל־מַלְכְוָתָא וְתֵאכֻל
and-she-will-devour the-kingdoms all-of from she-will-be-different that on-the-earth

כָּל־אַרְעָא וּתְדוּשִׁנַּהּ וְתַדְּקִנַּהּ׃ וְקַרְנַיָּא
and-the-horns (24) and-she-will-crush-her and-she-will-trample-her the-earth whole-of

עֲשַׂר מִנַּהּ מַלְכוּתָה עַשְׂרָה מַלְכִין יְקֻמוּן וְאָחֳרָן יְקוּם
he-will-arise and-another they-will-come kings ten the-kingdom from-her ten

אַחֲרֵיהוֹן וְהוּא יִשְׁנֵא מִן־קַדְמָיֵא וּתְלָתָה מַלְכִין
kings and-three the-earlier-ones from he-will-be-different and-he after-them

יְהַשְׁפִּל׃ וּמִלִּין לְצַד עִלָּיָא יְמַלִּל
he-will-speak the-Most-High against-side-of and-words (25) he-will-subdue

וּלְקַדִּישֵׁי עֶלְיוֹנִין יְבַלֵּא וְיִסְבַּר לְהַשְׁנָיָה זִמְנִין
set-times to-change and-he-will-try he-will-oppress Most-High-Ones and-to-saints-of

וְדָת וְיִתְיַהֲבוּן בִּידֵהּ עַד־עִדָּן וְעִדָּנִין וּפְלַג עִדָּן׃
time and-half-of and-times time for into-hand-of-him and-they-will-be-given and-law

וְדִינָא יִתִּב וְשָׁלְטָנֵהּ יְהַעְדּוֹן לְהַשְׁמָדָה
to-destroy they-will-take-away and-power-of-him he-will-sit but-the-court (26)

וּלְהוֹבָדָה עַד־ סוֹפָא׃ וּמַלְכוּתָה וְשָׁלְטָנָא
and-the-power then-the-sovereignty (27) the-forever to and-to-destroy

וּרְבוּתָא דִּי מַלְכְוָת תְּחוֹת כָּל־ שְׁמַיָּא יְהִיבַת
she-will-be-handed-over the-heavens whole-of under kingdoms-of of and-the-greatness

לְעַם קַדִּישֵׁי עֶלְיוֹנִין מַלְכוּתֵהּ מַלְכוּת עָלַם
everlasting kingdom-of kingdom-of-him Most-High-Ones saints-of to-people-of

וְכֹל שָׁלְטָנַיָּא לֵהּ יִפְלְחוּן וְיִשְׁתַּמְּעוּן׃ עַד־ כָּה
here to (28) and-they-will-obey they-will-worship to-him the-rulers and-all-of

סוֹפָא דִּי־ מִלְּתָא אֲנָה דָנִיֵּאל שַׂגִּיא ׀ רַעְיוֹנַי יְבַהֲלֻנַּנִי
they-troubled-me thoughts-of-me deeply Daniel I the-matter of the-end

which three of them fell—the horn
that looked more imposing than
the others and that had eyes and a
mouth that spoke boastfully. 21 As I
watched, this horn was waging
war against the saints and defeating them, 22 until the Ancient of
Days came and pronounced judgment in favor of the saints of the
Most High, and the time came
when they possessed the kingdom.

23 "He gave me this explanation:
'The fourth beast is a fourth kingdom that will appear on earth. It
will be different from all the other
kingdoms and will devour the
whole earth, trampling it down
and crushing it. 24 The ten horns
are ten kings who will come from
this kingdom. After them another
king will arise, different from the
earlier ones; he will subdue three
kings. 25 He will speak against the
Most High and oppress his saints
and try to change the set times
and the laws. The saints will be
handed over to him for a time,
times and half a time.[v]

26 " 'But the court will sit, and his
power will be taken away and
completely destroyed forever.
27 Then the sovereignty, power and
greatness of the kingdoms under
the whole heaven will be handed
over to the saints, the people of
the Most High. His kingdom will
be an everlasting kingdom, and all
rulers will worship and obey him.'

28 "This is the end of the matter.
I, Daniel, was deeply troubled by

v25 *Or for a year, two years and half a year*

*20 Most mss have *shureq* before the *pe* (וּפֻם).

°20 ק קדמה ;°23 ק רביעאה
°25 ק עלאה

וְדִיוַי֙   יִשְׁתַּנּ֣וֹן   עֲלַ֔י   וּמִלְּתָ֖א   בְּלִבִּ֥י   נִטְרֵֽת:
and-faces-of-me   they-were-changed   on-me   but-the-matter   in-self-of-me   I-kept

(8:1)   בִּשְׁנַ֣ת   שָׁל֔וֹשׁ   לְמַלְכ֖וּת   בֵּלְאשַׁצַּ֣ר   הַמֶּ֑לֶךְ   חָז֞וֹן   נִרְאָ֤ה   אֵלַי֙
in-year-of   three   of-reign-of   Belshazzar   the-king   vision   he-appeared   to-me

אֲנִ֣י   דָֽנִיֵּ֔אל   אַחֲרֵ֛י   הַנִּרְאָ֥ה   אֵלַ֖י   בַּתְּחִלָּֽה:   (2)   וָֽאֶרְאֶה֙   בֶּֽחָז֔וֹן
I   Daniel   after   the-one-appearing   to-me   at-the-first   and-I-saw   in-the-vision

וַיְהִי֙   בִּרְאֹתִ֔י   וַאֲנִי֙   בְּשׁוּשַׁ֣ן   הַבִּירָ֔ה   אֲשֶׁ֖ר   בְּעֵילָ֣ם   הַמְּדִינָ֑ה
and-he-was   when-to-see-me   then-I   in-Susa   the-citadel   that   in-Elam   the-province

וָֽאֶרְאֶה֙   בֶּֽחָז֔וֹן   וַאֲנִ֥י   הָיִ֖יתִי   עַל־   אוּבַ֣ל   אוּלָֽי:   (3)   וָאֶשָּׂ֤א
and-I-saw   in-the-vision   that-I   I-was   beside   Canal-of   Ulai   and-I-lifted

עֵינַי֙   וָאֶרְאֶ֔ה   וְהִנֵּ֣ה ׀   אַ֣יִל   אֶחָ֗ד   עֹמֵ֛ד   לִפְנֵ֥י   הָאֻבָ֖ל   וְל֣וֹ
eyes-of-me   and-I-looked   and-see!   ram   one   standing   beside   the-canal   and-to-him

קְרָנָ֑יִם   וְהַקְּרָנַ֣יִם   גְּבֹה֗וֹת   וְהָֽאַחַת֙   גְּבֹהָ֣ה   מִן־   הַשֵּׁנִ֔ית
two-horns   and-the-two-horns   long-ones   and-the-one   long   more-than   the-other

וְהַ֨גְּבֹהָ֔ה   עֹלָ֖ה   בָּאַחֲרֹנָֽה:   (4)   רָאִ֣יתִי   אֶת־   הָאַ֗יִל   מְנַגֵּ֧חַ
but-the-long-one   growing-up   at-the-later-time   I-watched   ***   the-ram   charging

יָ֠מָּה   וְצָפ֨וֹנָה   וָנֶ֜גְבָּה   וְכָל־   חַיּ֗וֹת   לֹֽא־   יַֽעַמְד֣וּ   לְפָנָ֔יו
to-west   and-to-north   and-to-south   and-any-of   animals   not   they-could-stand   against-him

וְאֵ֥ין   מַצִּ֖יל   מִיָּד֑וֹ   וְעָשָׂ֥ה   כִרְצֹנ֖וֹ
and-there-was-no   one-rescuing   from-power-of-him   and-he-did   as-pleasure-of-him

וְהִגְדִּֽיל:   (5)   וַאֲנִ֣י ׀   הָיִ֣יתִי   מֵבִ֗ין   וְהִנֵּ֤ה   צְפִיר־   הָֽעִזִּים֙   בָּ֤א
and-he-became-great   and-I   I-was   thinking   and-see!   male-goat-of   the-goats   coming

מִן־   הַֽמַּעֲרָב֙   עַל־   פְּנֵ֣י   כָל־   הָאָ֔רֶץ   וְאֵ֥ין   נוֹגֵ֖עַ
from   the-west   across   surfaces-of   whole-of   the-earth   and-there-was-not   one-touching

בָּאָ֑רֶץ   וְהַ֨צָּפִ֔יר   קֶ֥רֶן   חָז֖וּת   בֵּ֥ין   עֵינָֽיו:   (6)   וַיָּבֹ֗א
to-the-ground   and-the-goat   horn-of   prominence   between   eyes-of-him   and-he-came

עַד־   הָאַ֙יִל֙   בַּ֣עַל   הַקְּרָנַ֔יִם   אֲשֶׁ֣ר   רָאִ֔יתִי   עֹמֵ֖ד   לִפְנֵ֣י   הָאֻבָ֑ל
toward   the-ram   owner-of   the-two-horns   that   I-saw   standing   beside   the-canal

וַיָּ֤רָץ   אֵלָיו֙   בַּחֲמַ֣ת   כֹּח֔וֹ:   (7)   וּרְאִיתִ֞יו   מַגִּ֣יעַ ׀   אֵ֣צֶל
and-he-charged   at-him   in-rage-of   greatness-of-him   and-I-saw-him   attacking   against

הָאַ֗יִל   וַיִּתְמַרְמַ֤ר   אֵלָיו֙   וַיַּ֣ךְ   אֶת־   הָאַ֔יִל   וַיְשַׁבֵּר֙
the-ram   and-he-was-furious   against-him   and-he-struck   ***   the-ram   and-he-shattered

אֶת־   שְׁתֵּ֣י   קְרָנָ֔יו   וְלֹא־   הָ֥יָה   כֹ֛חַ   בָּאַ֖יִל   לַעֲמֹ֣ד   לְפָנָ֑יו
***   two-of   horns-of-him   and-not   he-was   power   in-the-ram   to-stand   against-him

וַיַּשְׁלִיכֵ֤הוּ   אַ֙רְצָה֙   וַֽיִּרְמְסֵ֔הוּ   וְלֹא־   הָיָ֥ה   מַצִּ֖יל
and-he-knocked-him   to-ground   and-he-trampled-on-him   and-not   he-was   one-rescuing

לָאַ֖יִל   מִיָּדֽוֹ:   (8)   וּצְפִ֥יר   הָעִזִּ֖ים   הִגְדִּ֣יל   עַד־מְאֹ֑ד
to-the-ram   from-power-of-him   and-male-goat-of   the-goats   he-became-great   very

---

my thoughts, and my face turned pale, but I kept the matter to myself."

### Daniel's Vision of a Ram and a Goat

8 In the third year of King Belshazzar's reign, I, Daniel, had a vision, after the one that had already appeared to me. [2] In my vision I saw myself in the citadel of Susa in the province of Elam; in the vision I was beside the Ulai Canal. [3] I looked up, and there before me was a ram with two horns, standing beside the canal, and the horns were long. One of the horns was longer than the other but grew up later. [4] I watched the ram as he charged toward the west and the north and the south. No animal could stand against him, and none could rescue from his power. He did as he pleased and became great.

[5] As I was thinking about this, suddenly a goat with a prominent horn between his eyes came from the west, crossing the whole earth without touching the ground. [6] He came toward the two-horned ram I had seen standing beside the canal and charged at him in great rage. [7] I saw him attack the ram furiously, striking the ram and shattering his two horns. The ram was powerless to stand against him; the goat knocked him to the ground and trampled on him, and none could rescue the ram from his power. [8] The goat became very

וּכְעָצְמוֹ נִשְׁבְּרָה הַקֶּרֶן הַגְּדוֹלָה וַתַּעֲלֶנָה
and-they-grew-up the-large the-horn she-was-broken-off but-at-to-be-powerful-him

חָזוּת אַרְבַּע תַּחְתֶּיהָ לְאַרְבַּע רוּחוֹת הַשָּׁמָיִם׃ וּמִן־
and-out-of (9) the-heavens winds-of toward-four-of in-place-of-her four prominence

הָאַחַת מֵהֶם יָצָא קֶרֶן־ אַחַת מִצְּעִירָה וַתִּגְדַּל־ יֶתֶר אֶל־
to greatly but-she-grew from-smallness another horn he-came-out of-them the-one

הַנֶּגֶב וְאֶל־ הַמִּזְרָח וְאֶל־ הַצֶּבִי׃ וַתִּגְדַּל עַד־
until and-she-grew (10) the-Beautiful-One and-toward the-east and-to the-south

צְבָא הַשָּׁמָיִם וַתַּפֵּל אַרְצָה מִן־ הַצָּבָא וּמִן־ הַכּוֹכָבִים
the-stars and-from the-host from to-earth and-she-threw-down the-heavens host-of

וַתִּרְמְסֵם׃ וְעַד שַׂר־ הַצָּבָא הִגְדִּיל וּמִמֶּנּוּ
and-from-him he-set-greatness the-host Prince-of and-to (11) and-she-trampled-on-them

הֵרִים הַתָּמִיד וְהֻשְׁלַךְ מְכוֹן מִקְדָּשׁוֹ׃
sanctuary-of-him place-of and-he-was-brought-low the-daily-sacrifice he-was-taken

וְצָבָא תִּנָּתֵן עַל־ הַתָּמִיד בְּפָשַׁע
because-of-rebellion the-daily-sacrifice with she-was-given and-host (12)

וְתַשְׁלֵךְ אֱמֶת אַרְצָה וְעָשְׂתָה וְהִצְלִיחָה׃ וָאֶשְׁמְעָה אֶחָד־
one then-I-heard (13) and-she-prospered and-she-did to-ground truth and-she-threw

קָדוֹשׁ מְדַבֵּר וַיֹּאמֶר אֶחָד קָדוֹשׁ לַפַּלְמוֹנִי הַמְדַבֵּר עַד־
until the-one-speaking to-the-other holy-one another and-he-said speaking holy-one

מָתַי הֶחָזוֹן הַתָּמִיד וְהַפֶּשַׁע שֹׁמֵם
one-causing-desolation and-the-rebellion the-daily-sacrifice the-vision when?

תֵּת וְקֹדֶשׁ וְצָבָא מִרְמָס׃ וַיֹּאמֶר אֵלַי עַד עֶרֶב
evening until to-me and-he-said (14) trampling and-host also-sanctuary to-surrender

בֹּקֶר אַלְפַּיִם וּשְׁלֹשׁ מֵאוֹת וְנִצְדַּק קֹדֶשׁ׃
sanctuary then-he-will-be-reconsecrated hundreds and-three-of two-thousands morning

וַיְהִי בִּרְאֹתִי אֲנִי דָנִיֵּאל אֶת־ הֶחָזוֹן וָאֲבַקְשָׁה
and-I-tried-to-find the-vision *** Daniel I while-to-watch-me and-he-was (15)

בִינָה וְהִנֵּה עֹמֵד לְנֶגְדִּי כְּמַרְאֵה־ גָבֶר׃ וָאֶשְׁמַע
and-I-heard (16) man like-look-of at-before-me standing then-see! understanding

קוֹל־ אָדָם בֵּין אוּלָי וַיִּקְרָא וַיֹּאמַר גַּבְרִיאֵל הָבֵן לְהַלָּז
to-this-one tell-meaning! Gabriel and-he-said and-he-called Ulai from man voice-of

אֶת־ הַמַּרְאֶה׃ וַיָּבֹא אֵצֶל עָמְדִי וּבְבֹאוֹ נִבְעַתִּי
I-was-terrified and-as-to-come-him to-stand-me near and-he-came (17) the-vision ***

וָאֶפְּלָה עַל־ פָּנָי וַיֹּאמֶר אֵלַי הָבֵן בֶּן־ אָדָם כִּי
that man son-of understand! to-me and-he-said faces-of-me to and-I-fell

לְעֶת־ קֵץ הֶחָזוֹן׃ וּבְדַבְּרוֹ עִמִּי נִרְדַּמְתִּי
I-was-in-deep-sleep to-me and-while-to-speak-him (18) the-vision end concerning-time-of

great, but at the height of his
power his large horn was broken
off, and in its place four prominent horns grew up toward the
four winds of heaven.
9 Out of one of them came another horn, which started small
but grew in power to the south
and to the east and toward the
Beautiful Land. 10 It grew until it
reached the host of the heavens,
and it threw some of the starry
host down to the earth and trampled on them. 11 It set itself up to be
as great as the Prince of the host;
it took away the daily sacrifice
from him, and the place of his
sanctuary was brought low. 12 Because of rebellion, the host of the
saints[w] and the daily sacrifice
were given over to it. It prospered
in everything it did, and truth was
thrown to the ground.
13 Then I heard a holy one
speaking, and another holy one
said to him, "How long will it take
for the vision to be fulfilled—the
vision concerning the daily sacrifice, the rebellion that causes
desolation, and the surrender of
the sanctuary and of the host that
will be trampled underfoot?"
14 He said to me, "It will take 2,-
300 evenings and mornings; then
the sanctuary will be reconsecrat-
ed."

*The Interpretation of the Vision*

15 While I, Daniel, was watching
the vision and trying to understand it, there before me stood one
who looked like a man. 16 And I
heard a man's voice from the Ulai
calling, "Gabriel, tell this man the
meaning of the vision."
17 As he came near the place
where I was standing, I was terrified and fell prostrate. "Son of
man," he said to me, "understand
that the vision concerns the time
of the end."
18 While he was speaking to me,
I was in a deep sleep, with my face

w12 Or *rebellion, the armies*

°11 ק הורם

עַל־ פָּנַי אָרְצָה וַיִּגַּע־ בִּי וַיַּעֲמִידֵנִי עַל־ עָמְדִי׃
to-stand-me to and-he-raised-me to-me then-he-touched to-ground faces-of-me with

וַיֹּאמֶר הִנְנִי מוֹדִיעֲךָ אֵת אֲשֶׁר־ יִהְיֶה בְּאַחֲרִית
in-later-time-of he-will-happen what *** telling-you see-I! and-he-said (19)

הַזָּעַם כִּי לְמוֹעֵד קֵץ׃ הָאַיִל אֲשֶׁר־ רָאִיתָ
you-saw that the-ram (20) end concerning-appointed-time-of because the-wrath

בַּעַל הַקְּרָנָיִם מַלְכֵי מָדַי וּפָרָס׃ וְהַצָּפִיר הַשָּׂעִיר
the-shaggy-goat and-the-goat (21) and-Persia Media kings-of the-two-horns owner-of

מֶלֶךְ יָוָן וְהַקֶּרֶן הַגְּדוֹלָה אֲשֶׁר בֵּין־ עֵינָיו הוּא הַמֶּלֶךְ
the-king he eyes-of-him between that the-large and-the-horn Greece king-of

הָרִאשׁוֹן׃ וְהַנִּשְׁבֶּרֶת וַתַּעֲמֹדְנָה אַרְבַּע תַּחְתֶּיהָ
in-place-of-her four and-they-grew-up and-the-one-being-broken-off (22) the-first

אַרְבַּע מַלְכֻיוֹת* מִגּוֹי יַעֲמֹדְנָה וְלֹא בְכֹחוֹ׃
with-power-of-him but-not they-will-emerge from-nation kingdoms four-of

וּבְאַחֲרִית מַלְכוּתָם כְּהָתֵם הַפֹּשְׁעִים
the-ones-rebelling when-to-become-complete reign-of-them and-in-latter-part-of (23)

יַעֲמֹד מֶלֶךְ עַז־ פָּנִים וּמֵבִין חִידוֹת׃
intrigues and-one-mastering-of faces stern-of king he-will-arise

וְעָצַם כֹּחוֹ וְלֹא בְכֹחוֹ
by-power-of-him but-not strength-of-him and-he-will-become-great (24)

וְנִפְלָאוֹת יַשְׁחִית וְהִצְלִיחַ וְעָשָׂה
and-he-will-do and-he-will-succeed he-will-cause-devastation and-ones-being-astounding

וְהִשְׁחִית עֲצוּמִים וְעַם־ קְדֹשִׁים׃ וְעַל־ שִׂכְלוֹ
cunning-of-him and-by (25) holy-ones and-people-of mighty-men and-he-will-destroy

וְהִצְלִיחַ מִרְמָה בְּיָדוֹ וּבִלְבָבוֹ
and-in-self-of-him by-hand-of-him deceit also-he-will-cause-to-prosper

יַגְדִּיל וּבְשַׁלְוָה יַשְׁחִית רַבִּים וְעַל־
and-against many-ones he-will-destroy and-when-security he-will-be-superior

שַׂר־ שָׂרִים יַעֲמֹד וּבְאֶפֶס יָד יִשָּׁבֵר׃
he-will-be-destroyed human-power yet-by-not he-will-take-stand princes Prince-of

וּמַרְאֵה הָעֶרֶב וְהַבֹּקֶר אֲשֶׁר נֶאֱמַר אֱמֶת הוּא וְאַתָּה
but-you he truth he-was-given that and-the-morning the-evening and-vision-of (26)

סְתֹם הֶחָזוֹן כִּי לְיָמִים רַבִּים׃ וַאֲנִי דָנִיֵּאל נִהְיֵיתִי
I-was-exhausted Daniel and-I (27) distant-ones concerning-days for the-vision seal-up!

וְנֶחֱלֵיתִי יָמִים וָאָקוּם וָאֶעֱשֶׂה אֶת־ מְלֶאכֶת הַמֶּלֶךְ
the-king business-of *** and-I-went-about then-I-got-up days and-I-lay-ill

וָאֶשְׁתּוֹמֵם עַל־הַמַּרְאֶה וְאֵין מֵבִין׃ בִּשְׁנַת אַחַת
one in-year-of (9:1) one-understanding and-there-was-no the-vision by and-I-was-appalled

to the ground. Then he touched me and raised me to my feet.

[19]He said: "I am going to tell you what will happen later in the time of wrath, because the vision concerns the appointed time of the end.[x] [20]The two-horned ram that you saw represents the kings of Media and Persia. [21]The shaggy goat is the king of Greece, and the large horn between his eyes is the first king. [22]The four horns that replaced the one that was broken off represent four kingdoms that will emerge from his nation but will not have the same power.

[23]"In the latter part of their reign, when rebels have become completely wicked, a stern-faced king, a master of intrigue, will arise. [24]He will become very strong, but not by his own power. He will cause astounding devastation and will succeed in whatever he does. He will destroy the mighty men and the holy people. [25]He will cause deceit to prosper, and he will consider himself superior. When they feel secure, he will destroy many and take his stand against the Prince of princes. Yet he will be destroyed, but not by human power.

[26]"The vision of the evenings and mornings that has been given you is true, but seal up the vision, for it concerns the distant future."

[27]I, Daniel, was exhausted and lay ill for several days. Then I got up and went about the king's business. I was appalled by the vision; it was beyond understanding.

[x]19 Or *because the end will be at the appointed time*

*22 Most mss have *dagesh* in the *yod* (־כּיּוֹת).

לְדָרְיָוֶשׁ בֶּן־אֲחַשְׁוֵרוֹשׁ מִזֶּרַע מָדָי אֲשֶׁר הָמְלַךְ עַל
over he-was-made-ruler who Mede from-descendant-of Ahasuerus son-of of-Darius

מַלְכוּת כַּשְׂדִּים׃ בִּשְׁנַת אַחַת לְמָלְכוֹ אֲנִי דָּנִיֵּאל בִּינֹתִי
I-understood Daniel I to-reign-him one in-year-of (2) Chaldeans kingdom-of

בַּסְּפָרִים מִסְפַּר הַשָּׁנִים אֲשֶׁר הָיָה דְבַר־יְהוָה אֶל־יִרְמִיָה*
Jeremiah to Yahweh word-of he-gave that years number-of from-the-Scriptures

הַנָּבִיא לְמַלֹּאות לְחָרְבוֹת יְרוּשָׁלִָם שִׁבְעִים שָׁנָה׃ וָאֶתְּנָה אֶת־
*** so-I-turned (3) year seventy Jerusalem for-desolations-of to-last the-prophet

פָּנַי אֶל־אֲדֹנָי הָאֱלֹהִים לְבַקֵּשׁ תְּפִלָּה וְתַחֲנוּנִים בְּצוֹם וְשַׂק
and-sackcloth in-fasting and-petitions prayer to-plead the-God Lord to faces-of-me

וָאֵפֶר׃ וָאֶתְפַּלְלָה לַיהוָה אֱלֹהַי וָאֶתְוַדֶּה וָאֹמְרָה אָנָּא אֲדֹנָי
Lord O! and-I-said and-I-confessed God-of-me to-Yahweh and-I-prayed (4) and-ash

הָאֵל הַגָּדוֹל וְהַנּוֹרָא שֹׁמֵר הַבְּרִית וְהַחֶסֶד
and-the-love the-covenant one-keeping and-the-one-being-awesome the-great the-God

לְאֹהֲבָיו וּלְשֹׁמְרֵי מִצְוֹתָיו׃ חָטָאנוּ
we-sinned (5) commands-of-him and-with-ones-obeying-of with-ones-loving-him

וְעָוִינוּ וְהִרְשַׁעְנוּ° וּמָרָדְנוּ וְסוֹר מִמִּצְוֹתֶךָ
from-commands-of-you and-to-turn-away and-we-rebelled we-were-wicked and-we-did-wrong

וּמִמִּשְׁפָּטֶיךָ׃ וְלֹא שָׁמַעְנוּ אֶל־עֲבָדֶיךָ הַנְּבִיאִים אֲשֶׁר
who the-prophets servants-of-you to we-listened and-not (6) and-from-laws-of-you

דִּבְּרוּ בְּשִׁמְךָ אֶל־מְלָכֵינוּ שָׂרֵינוּ וַאֲבֹתֵינוּ וְאֶל
and-to and-fathers-of-us princes-of-us kings-of-us to in-name-of-you they-spoke

כָּל־עַם הָאָרֶץ׃ לְךָ אֲדֹנָי הַצְּדָקָה וְלָנוּ בֹּשֶׁת
shame-of but-to-us the-righteousness Lord to-you (7) the-land people-of all-of

הַפָּנִים כַּיּוֹם הַזֶּה לְאִישׁ יְהוּדָה וּלְיוֹשְׁבֵי יְרוּשָׁלִַם
Jerusalem and-to-ones-being-people-of Judah to-man-of the-this as-the-day the-faces

וּלְכָל־יִשְׂרָאֵל הַקְּרֹבִים וְהָרְחֹקִים בְּכָל־הָאֲרָצוֹת אֲשֶׁר
where the-countries in-all-of and-the-far-ones the-near-ones Israel and-to-all-of

הִדַּחְתָּם שָׁם בְּמַעֲלָם אֲשֶׁר מָעֲלוּ־
they-were-unfaithful that because-of-unfaithfulness-of-them there you-scattered-them

בָךְ׃ יְהוָה לָנוּ בֹּשֶׁת הַפָּנִים לִמְלָכֵינוּ לְשָׂרֵינוּ
to-princes-of-us to-kings-of-us the-faces shame-of to-us Yahweh (8) to-you

וְלַאֲבֹתֵינוּ אֲשֶׁר חָטָאנוּ לָךְ׃ לַאדֹנָי אֱלֹהֵינוּ הָרַחֲמִים
the-mercies God-of-us to-Lord (9) against-you we-sinned because and-to-fathers-of-us

וְהַסְּלִחוֹת כִּי מָרַדְנוּ בּוֹ׃ וְלֹא שָׁמַעְנוּ בְּקוֹל
to-voice-of we-obeyed not (10) against-him we-rebelled though and-the-forgivenesses

יְהוָה אֱלֹהֵינוּ לָלֶכֶת בְּתוֹרֹתָיו אֲשֶׁר נָתַן לְפָנֵינוּ בְּיַד עֲבָדָיו
servants-of-him by-hand-of to-us he-gave that to-laws-of-him to-keep God-of-us Yahweh

*Daniel's Prayer*

9 In the first year of Darius son of Xerxes[y] (a Mede by descent), who was made ruler over the Babylonian[z] kingdom— [2]in the first year of his reign, I, Daniel, understood from the Scriptures, according to the word of the LORD given to Jeremiah the prophet, that the desolation of Jerusalem would last seventy years. [3]So I turned to the Lord God and pleaded with him in prayer and petition, in fasting, and in sackcloth and ashes.

[4]I prayed to the LORD my God and confessed:

"O Lord, the great and awesome God, who keeps his covenant of love with all who love him and obey his commands, [5]we have sinned and done wrong. We have been wicked and have rebelled; we have turned away from your commands and laws. [6]We have not listened to your servants the prophets, who spoke in your name to our kings, our princes and our fathers, and to all the people of the land.

[7]"Lord, you are righteous, but this day we are covered with shame—the men of Judah and people of Jerusalem and all Israel, both near and far, in all the countries where you have scattered us because of our unfaithfulness to you. [8]O LORD, we and our kings, our princes and our fathers are covered with shame because we have sinned against you. [9]The Lord our God is merciful and forgiving, even though we have rebelled against him; [10]we have not obeyed the LORD our God or kept the laws he gave us through his servants the

y1 Hebrew *Ahasuerus* z1 Or *Chaldean*

*2 Most mss have *sheva* under the *mem* (־מְ).

°5 ק הרשענו

הַנְּבִיאִים׃ וְכָל־ יִשְׂרָאֵל עָבְרוּ אֶת־ תּוֹרָתֶךָ וְסוֹר
and-to-turn-away law-of-you *** they-transgressed Israel and-all-of (11) the-prophets

לְבִלְתִּי שְׁמוֹעַ בְּקֹלֶךָ וַתִּתַּךְ עָלֵינוּ הָאָלָה
the-curse on-us therefore-you-poured-out to-voice-of-you to-obey not

וְהַשְּׁבֻעָה אֲשֶׁר כְּתוּבָה בְּתוֹרַת מֹשֶׁה עֶבֶד־ הָאֱלֹהִים כִּי
because the-God servant-of Moses in-Law-of being-written that and-the-sworn-judgment

חָטָאנוּ לוֹ׃ וַיָּקֶם אֶת־ דְּבָרָיו | אֲשֶׁר־ דִּבֶּר עָלֵינוּ
against-us he-spoke that word-of-him *** and-he-fulfilled (12) against-him we-sinned

וְעַל שֹׁפְטֵינוּ אֲשֶׁר שְׁפָטוּנוּ לְהָבִיא עָלֵינוּ רָעָה גְדֹלָה אֲשֶׁר
that great disaster upon-us to-bring they-ruled-us who ones-ruling-us and-against

לֹא־ נֶעֶשְׂתָה תַּחַת כָּל־ הַשָּׁמַיִם כַּאֲשֶׁר נֶעֶשְׂתָה בִּירוּשָׁלִָם׃
to-Jerusalem she-was-done like-what the-heavens whole-of under she-was-done never

כַּאֲשֶׁר כָּתוּב בְּתוֹרַת מֹשֶׁה אֵת כָּל־ הָרָעָה הַזֹּאת בָּאָה
she-came the-this the-disaster all-of *** Moses in-Law-of being-written just-as (13)

עָלֵינוּ וְלֹא־ חִלִּינוּ אֶת־ פְּנֵי | יְהוָה אֱלֹהֵינוּ לָשׁוּב מֵעֲוֺנֵנוּ
from-sin-of-us to-turn God-of-us Yahweh faces-of *** we-sought yet-not upon-us

וּלְהַשְׂכִּיל בַּאֲמִתֶּךָ׃ וַיִּשְׁקֹד יְהוָה עַל־
concerning Yahweh and-he-did-not-hesitate (14) to-truth-of-you and-to-give-attention

הָרָעָה וַיְבִיאֶהָ עָלֵינוּ כִּי־ צַדִּיק יְהוָה אֱלֹהֵינוּ עַל־ כָּל־
every-of in God-of-us Yahweh righteous for upon-us and-he-brought-her the-disaster

מַעֲשָׂיו אֲשֶׁר עָשָׂה וְלֹא שָׁמַעְנוּ בְּקֹלוֹ׃ וְעַתָּה | אֲדֹנָי
Lord and-now (15) to-voice-of-him we-obeyed yet-not he-does that deeds-of-him

אֱלֹהֵינוּ אֲשֶׁר הוֹצֵאתָ אֶת־ עַמְּךָ מֵאֶרֶץ מִצְרַיִם בְּיָד חֲזָקָה
mighty with-hand Egypt from-land-of people-of-you *** you-brought who God-of-us

וַתַּעַשׂ־ לְךָ שֵׁם כַּיּוֹם הַזֶּה חָטָאנוּ רָשָׁעְנוּ׃ אֲדֹנָי
Lord (16) we-did-wrong we-sinned the-this as-the-day name for-yourself and-you-made

כְּכָל־ צִדְקֹתֶךָ יָשָׁב־ נָא אַפְּךָ וַחֲמָתְךָ
and-wrath-of-you anger-of-you now! let-him-turn righteous-acts-of-you as-all-of

מֵעִירְךָ יְרוּשָׁלִַם הַר־ קָדְשֶׁךָ כִּי בַחֲטָאֵינוּ
because-of-sins-of-us indeed holiness-of-you hill-of Jerusalem from-city-of-you

וּבַעֲוֺנוֹת אֲבֹתֵינוּ יְרוּשָׁלִַם וְעַמְּךָ
and-people-of-you Jerusalem fathers-of-us and-because-of-iniquities-of

לְחֶרְפָּה לְכָל־ סְבִיבֹתֵינוּ׃ וְעַתָּה | שְׁמַע אֱלֹהֵינוּ אֶל־ תְּפִלַּת
prayer-of to God-of-us hear! and-now (17) ones-around-us to-all-of as-object-of-scorn

עַבְדְּךָ וְאֶל־ תַּחֲנוּנָיו וְהָאֵר פָּנֶיךָ עַל־
on faces-of-you and-look-with-favor! petitions-of-him and-to servant-of-you

מִקְדָּשְׁךָ הַשָּׁמֵם לְמַעַן אֲדֹנָי׃ הַטֵּה אֱלֹהַי | אָזְנְךָ
ear-of-you God-of-me give! (18) Lord for-sake-of the-desolate sanctuary-of-you

prophets. 11 All Israel has trans-
gressed your law and turned
away, refusing to obey you.
"Therefore the curses and
sworn judgments written in
the Law of Moses, the servant
of God, have been poured out
on us, because we have sinned
against you. 12 You have fulfilled the words spoken against
us and against our rulers by
bringing upon us great disaster. Under the whole heaven
nothing has ever been done
like what has been done to
Jerusalem. 13 Just as it is written
in the Law of Moses, all this
disaster has come upon us, yet
we have not sought the favor
of the LORD our God by turning
from our sins and giving attention to your truth. 14 The LORD
did not hesitate to bring the
disaster upon us, for the LORD
our God is righteous in everything he does; yet we have not
obeyed him.
15 "Now, O Lord our God,
who brought your people out
of Egypt with a mighty hand
and who made for yourself a
name that endures to this day,
we have sinned, we have done
wrong. 16 O Lord, in keeping
with all your righteous acts,
turn away your anger and your
wrath from Jerusalem, your
city, your holy hill. Our sins
and the iniquities of our fathers have made Jerusalem and
your people an object of scorn
to all those around us.
17 "Now, our God, hear the
prayers and petitions of your
servant. For your sake, O Lord,
look with favor on your desolate sanctuary. 18 Give ear, O

°12 ק דברו

וּשְׁמָע פִּקְחָה עֵינֶיךָ וּרְאֵה שֹׁמְמֹתֵינוּ וְהָעִיר אֲשֶׁר־

that and-the-city ones-being-desolate-of-us and-see! eyes-of-you open! and-hear!

נִקְרָא שִׁמְךָ עָלֶיהָ כִּי ׀ לֹא עַל־ צִדְקֹתֵינוּ אֲנַחְנוּ

we righteousnesses-of-us because-of not indeed to-her Name-of-you he-is-called

מַפִּילִים תַּחֲנוּנֵינוּ לְפָנֶיךָ כִּי עַל־ רַחֲמֶיךָ הָרַבִּים׃

the-great-ones mercies-of-you because-of but before-you requests-of-us ones-making

אֲדֹנָי ׀ שְׁמָעָה אֲדֹנָי ׀ סְלָחָה אֲדֹנָי הַקְשִׁיבָה וַעֲשֵׂה אַל־ תְּאַחַר לְמַעַנְךָ*

for-sake-of-you you-delay not and-act! hear! Lord forgive! Lord listen! Lord (19)

אֱלֹהַי כִּי־ שִׁמְךָ נִקְרָא עַל־ עִירְךָ וְעַל־ עַמֶּךָ׃

people-of-you and-to city-of-you to he-is-called Name-of-you because God-of-me

וְעוֹד אֲנִי מְדַבֵּר וּמִתְפַּלֵּל וּמִתְוַדֶּה חַטָּאתִי וְחַטַּאת

and-sin-of sin-of-me and-confessing and-praying speaking I and-while (20)

עַמִּי יִשְׂרָאֵל וּמַפִּיל תְּחִנָּתִי לִפְנֵי יְהוָה אֱלֹהַי עַל הַר־

hill-of for God-of-me Yahweh before request-of-me and-making Israel people-of-me

קֹדֶשׁ אֱלֹהָי׃ וְעוֹד אֲנִי מְדַבֵּר בַּתְּפִלָּה וְהָאִישׁ גַּבְרִיאֵל

Gabriel then-the-man in-the-prayer speaking I and-while (21) God-of-me holiness-of

אֲשֶׁר רָאִיתִי בֶחָזוֹן בַּתְּחִלָּה מֻעָף בִּיעָף נֹגֵעַ

coming in-flight flying at-the-earlier-time in-the-vision I-saw whom

אֵלַי כְּעֵת מִנְחַת־ עָרֶב׃ וַיָּבֶן וַיְדַבֵּר

and-he-spoke and-he-instructed (22) evening sacrifice-of about-time-of to-me

עִמִּי וַיֹּאמַר דָּנִיֵּאל עַתָּה יָצָאתִי לְהַשְׂכִּילְךָ בִינָה׃

understanding to-give-insight-to-you I-came now Daniel and-he-said to-me

בִּתְחִלַּת תַּחֲנוּנֶיךָ יָצָא דָבָר וַאֲנִי בָּאתִי לְהַגִּיד כִּי

for to-tell I-came and-I answer he-came prayers-of-you at-beginning-of (23)

חֲמוּדוֹת אָתָּה וּבִין בַּדָּבָר וְהָבֵן

and-understand! to-the-message therefore-consider! you ones-highly-esteemed

בַּמַּרְאֶה׃ שָׁבֻעִים שִׁבְעִים נֶחְתַּךְ עַל־ עַמְּךָ ׀ וְעַל־ עִיר

city-of and-for people-of-you for he-is-decreed seventy sevens (24) to-the-vision

קָדְשֶׁךָ לְכַלֵּא הַפֶּשַׁע וּלְחָתֹם חַטָּאוֹת וּלְכַפֵּר

and-to-atone-for sin and-to-put-end-to the-transgression to-finish holiness-of-you

עָוֹן וּלְהָבִיא צֶדֶק עֹלָמִים וְלַחְתֹּם חָזוֹן

vision and-to-seal-up everlasting-ones righteousness-of and-to-bring-in wickedness

וְנָבִיא וְלִמְשֹׁחַ קֹדֶשׁ קָדָשִׁים׃ וְתֵדַע וְתַשְׂכֵּל

and-you-understand so-you-know (25) holy-ones holy-of and-to-anoint and-prophet

מִן־ מֹצָא דָבָר לְהָשִׁיב וְלִבְנוֹת יְרוּשָׁלַםִ עַד־ מָשִׁיחַ נָגִיד

ruler anointed-one until Jerusalem and-to-rebuild to-restore decree issuing-of from

שָׁבֻעִים שִׁבְעָה וְשָׁבֻעִים שִׁשִּׁים וּשְׁנַיִם תָּשׁוּב וְנִבְנְתָה רְחוֹב

street and-she-will-be-rebuilt she-will-return and-two sixty and-sevens seven sevens

God, and hear; open your eyes and see the desolation of the city that bears your Name. We do not make requests of you because we are righteous, but because of your great mercy.
[19]O Lord, listen! O Lord, forgive! O Lord, hear and act! For your sake, O my God, do not delay, because your city and your people bear your Name."

*The Seventy "Sevens"*

[20]While I was speaking and praying, confessing my sin and the sin of my people Israel and making my request to the LORD my God for his holy hill— [21]while I was still in prayer, Gabriel, the man I had seen in the earlier vision, came to me in swift flight about the time of the evening sacrifice. [22]He instructed me and said to me, "Daniel, I have now come to give you insight and understanding. [23]As soon as you began to pray, an answer was given, which I have come to tell you, for you are highly esteemed. Therefore, consider the message and understand the vision:

[24]"Seventy 'sevens'[a] are decreed for your people and your holy city to finish[b] transgression, to put an end to sin, to atone for wickedness, to bring in everlasting righteousness, to seal up vision and prophecy and to anoint the most holy.[c]

[25]"Know and understand this: From the issuing of the decree[d] to restore and rebuild Jerusalem until the Anointed One,[e] the ruler, comes, there will be seven 'sevens,' and sixty-two 'sevens.' It will be rebuilt with streets and a

[a]24 Or *'weeks'*; also in verses 25 and 26
[b]24 Or *restrain*
[c]24 Or *Most Holy Place; or most holy One*
[d]25 Or *word*
[e]25 Or *an anointed one;* also in verse 26

*19 Most mss have *pathah* under the *ayin* (עַ־)

°*18* ק פקח; °*24a* ק ולחתם
°*24b* ק חטאת

וְחָרוּץ וּבְצוֹק הָעִתִּים׃ וְאַחֲרֵי הַשָּׁבֻעִים שִׁשִּׁים וּשְׁנַיִם
and-two sixty the-sevens and-after (26) the-times but-in-trouble-of and-trench

יִכָּרֵת מָשִׁיחַ וְאֵין לוֹ וְהָעִיר
and-the-city to-him and-there-will-be-nothing anointed-one he-will-be-cut-off

וְהַקֹּדֶשׁ יַשְׁחִית עַם נָגִיד הַבָּא וְקִצּוֹ
and-end-of-him the-one-coming ruler people-of he-will-destroy and-the-sanctuary

בַשֶּׁטֶף וְעַד קֵץ מִלְחָמָה נֶחֱרֶצֶת שֹׁמֵמוֹת׃
ones-being-desolate being-decreed war end until-to like-the-flood

וְהִגְבִּיר בְּרִית לָרַבִּים שָׁבוּעַ אֶחָד וַחֲצִי
but-middle-of one seven with-the-many-ones covenant and-he-will-confirm (27)

הַשָּׁבוּעַ יַשְׁבִּית ׀ זֶבַח וּמִנְחָה וְעַל כְּנַף
pinnacle-of and-on and-offering sacrifice he-will-put-end-to the-seven

שִׁקּוּצִים מְשֹׁמֵם וְעַד־ כָּלָה וְנֶחֱרָצָה
even-one-being-decreed end and-until one-causing-desolation abominable-ones

תִּתַּךְ עַל־ שֹׁמֵם׃ בִּשְׁנַת שָׁלוֹשׁ לְכוֹרֶשׁ מֶלֶךְ
king-of of-Cyrus three in-year-of (10:1) one-being-desolated on she-is-poured-out

פָּרַס דָּבָר נִגְלָה לְדָנִיֵּאל אֲשֶׁר־ נִקְרָא שְׁמוֹ בֵּלְטְשַׁאצַּר
Belteshazzar name-of-him he-was-called who to-Daniel he-was-given revelation Persia

וֶאֱמֶת הַדָּבָר וְצָבָא גָדוֹל וּבִין אֶת־ הַדָּבָר
the-message *** and-he-understood great and-war the-message and-truth

וּבִינָה לוֹ בַּמַּרְאֶה׃ בַּיָּמִים הָהֵם אֲנִי דָנִיֵּאל הָיִיתִי
I-was Daniel I the-those at-the-days (2) in-the-vision to-him and-understanding

מִתְאַבֵּל שְׁלֹשָׁה שָׁבֻעִים יָמִים׃ לֶחֶם חֲמֻדוֹת לֹא אָכַלְתִּי וּבָשָׂר וָיַיִן לֹא־
not or-wine and-meat I-ate not choice-ones food-of (3) days weeks three mourning

בָא אֶל־ פִּי וְסוֹךְ לֹא־ סָכְתִּי עַד־ מְלֹאת
to-be-over until I-used-lotion not and-to-use-lotion mouth-of-me to he-touched

שְׁלֹשֶׁת שָׁבֻעִים יָמִים׃ וּבְיוֹם עֶשְׂרִים וְאַרְבָּעָה לַחֹדֶשׁ הָרִאשׁוֹן וַאֲנִי
as-I the-first of-the-month and-four twenty and-on-day-of (4) days weeks three-of

הָיִיתִי עַל יַד הַנָּהָר הַגָּדוֹל הוּא חִדָּקֶל׃ וָאֶשָּׂא אֶת־ עֵינַי
eyes-of-me *** then-I-lifted (5) Tigris that the-great the-river bank-of on I-was

וָאֵרֶא וְהִנֵּה אִישׁ־ אֶחָד לָבוּשׁ בַּדִּים וּמָתְנָיו
with-waists-of-him linens being-dressed-in one man and-see! and-I-looked

חֲגֻרִים בְּכֶתֶם אוּפָז׃ וּגְוִיָּתוֹ כְתַרְשִׁישׁ
like-chrysolite and-body-of-him (6) Uphaz of-finest-gold-of ones-wearing-belt

וּפָנָיו כְּמַרְאֵה בָרָק וְעֵינָיו כְּלַפִּידֵי אֵשׁ
flame like-torches-of and-eyes-of-him lightning like-appearance-of and-faces-of-him

וּזְרֹעֹתָיו וּמַרְגְּלֹתָיו כְּעֵין נְחֹשֶׁת קָלָל וְקוֹל
and-sound-of burnished bronze like-gleam-of and-legs-of-him and-arms-of-him

trench, but in times of trouble. [26]After the sixty-two 'sevens,' the Anointed One will be cut off and will have nothing.[f] The people of the ruler who will come will destroy the city and the sanctuary. The end will come like a flood: War will continue until the end, and desolations have been decreed. [27]He will confirm a covenant with many for one 'seven.'[g] In the middle of the 'seven,'[g] he will put an end to sacrifice and offering. And on a wing ⌊of the temple⌋ he will set up an abomination that causes desolation, until the end that is decreed is poured out on him.[h][i]

*Daniel's Vision of a Man*

10 In the third year of Cyrus king of Persia, a revelation was given to Daniel (who was called Belteshazzar). Its message was true and it concerned a great war.[i] The understanding of the message came to him in a vision.

[2]At that time I, Daniel, mourned for three weeks. [3]I ate no choice food; no meat or wine touched my lips; and I used no lotions at all until the three weeks were over.

[4]On the twenty-fourth day of the first month, as I was standing on the bank of the great river, the Tigris, [5]I looked up and there before me was a man dressed in linen, with a belt of the finest gold around his waist. [6]His body was like chrysolite, his face like lightning, his eyes like flaming torches, his arms and legs like the gleam of burnished bronze, and

f26 Or *off and will have no one;* or *off, but not for himself*
g27 Or *'week'* h27 Or *it*
i27 Or *And one who causes desolation will come upon the pinnacle of the abominable ⌊temple⌋, until the end that is decreed is poured out on the desolated ⌊city⌋*
i1 Or *true and burdensome*

דְּבָרָיו כְּקוֹל הָמוֹן׃ וְרָאִיתִי אֲנִי דָנִיֵּאל לְבַדִּי אֶת־הַמַּרְאָה
the-vision *** only-I Daniel I and-I-saw (7) multitude like-sound-of words-of-him

וְהָאֲנָשִׁים אֲשֶׁר הָיוּ עִמִּי לֹא רָאוּ אֶת־הַמַּרְאָה אֲבָל חֲרָדָה גְדֹלָה
such terror but the-vision *** they-saw not with-me they-were who and-the-men

נָפְלָה עֲלֵיהֶם וַיִּבְרְחוּ בְּהֵחָבֵא׃ וַאֲנִי נִשְׁאַרְתִּי
I-was-left so-I (8) for-to-hide-self that-they-fled over-them she-overwhelmed

לְבַדִּי וָאֶרְאֶה אֶת־הַמַּרְאָה הַגְּדֹלָה הַזֹּאת וְלֹא נִשְׁאַר־
he-was-left and-not the-this the-great the-vision *** and-I-gazed-at alone-I

בִּי כֹחַ וְהוֹדִי נֶהְפַּךְ עָלַי לְמַשְׁחִית וְלֹא עָצַרְתִּי כֹּחַ׃
strength I-retained and-not to-death to-me he-turned and-face-of-me strength in-me

וָאֶשְׁמַע אֶת־קוֹל דְּבָרָיו וּכְשָׁמְעִי אֶת־קוֹל
sound-of *** and-as-to-listen-me speakings-of-him sound-of *** then-I-heard (9)

דְּבָרָיו וַאֲנִי הָיִיתִי נִרְדָּם עַל־פָּנַי וּפָנַי
and-faces-of-me faces-of-me on one-sleeping-deeply I-became then-I speakings-of-him

אָרְצָה׃ וְהִנֵּה־יָד נָגְעָה בִּי וַתְּנִיעֵנִי עַל־בִּרְכַּי
knees-of-me on and-she-set-trembling-me to-me she-touched hand and-see! (10) to-ground

וְכַפּוֹת יָדָי׃ וַיֹּאמֶר אֵלַי דָּנִיֵּאל אִישׁ־חֲמֻדוֹת
ones-highly-esteemed man-of Daniel to-me and-he-said (11) hands-of-me and-palms-of

הָבֵן בַּדְּבָרִים אֲשֶׁר אָנֹכִי דֹּבֵר אֵלֶיךָ וַעֲמֹד עַל־
on and-stand-up! to-you speaking I that to-the-words consider-carefully!

עָמְדֶךָ כִּי עַתָּה שֻׁלַּחְתִּי אֵלֶיךָ וּבְדַבְּרוֹ עִמִּי אֶת־
*** to-me and-when-to-say-him to-you I-was-sent now for standing-place-of-you

הַדָּבָר הַזֶּה עָמַדְתִּי מַרְעִיד׃ וַיֹּאמֶר אֵלַי אַל־תִּירָא
you-be-afraid not to-me then-he-said (12) trembling I-stood-up the-this the-word

דָנִיֵּאל כִּי ׀ מִן־הַיּוֹם הָרִאשׁוֹן אֲשֶׁר נָתַתָּ אֶת־לִבְּךָ לְהָבִין
to-gain-understanding mind-of-you *** you-set that the-first the-day since for Daniel

וּלְהִתְעַנּוֹת לִפְנֵי אֱלֹהֶיךָ נִשְׁמְעוּ דְבָרֶיךָ וַאֲנִי־בָאתִי
I-came and-I words-of-you they-were-heard God-of-you before and-to-humble-yourself

בִּדְבָרֶיךָ׃ וְשַׂר ׀ מַלְכוּת פָּרַס עֹמֵד
resisting Persia kingdom-of but-prince-of (13) in-response-to-words-of-you

לְנֶגְדִּי עֶשְׂרִים וְאֶחָד יוֹם וְהִנֵּה מִיכָאֵל אַחַד הַשָּׂרִים הָרִאשֹׁנִים
the-chief-ones the-princes one-of Michael then-see! day and-one twenty at-against-me

בָּא לְעָזְרֵנִי וַאֲנִי נוֹתַרְתִּי שָׁם אֵצֶל מַלְכֵי פָרָס׃
Persia kings-of with there I-was-detained because-I to-help-me he-came

וּבָאתִי לַהֲבִינְךָ אֵת אֲשֶׁר־יִקְרָה לְעַמְּךָ
to-people-of-you he-will-happen what *** to-explain-to-you now-I-came (14)

בְּאַחֲרִית הַיָּמִים כִּי־עוֹד חָזוֹן לַיָּמִים׃ וּבְדַבְּרוֹ
and-while-to-say-him (15) concerning-the-days vision yet for the-days in-future-of

his voice like the sound of a multitude.

7 I, Daniel, was the only one who saw the vision; the men with me did not see it, but such terror overwhelmed them that they fled and hid themselves. 8 So I was left alone, gazing at this great vision; I had no strength left, my face turned deathly pale and I was helpless. 9 Then I heard him speaking, and as I listened to him, I fell into a deep sleep, my face to the ground.

10 A hand touched me and set me trembling on my hands and knees. 11 He said, "Daniel, you who are highly esteemed, consider carefully the words I am about to speak to you, and stand up, for I have now been sent to you." And when he said this to me, I stood up trembling.

12 Then he continued, "Do not be afraid, Daniel. Since the first day that you set your mind to gain understanding and to humble yourself before your God, your words were heard, and I have come in response to them. 13 But the prince of the Persian kingdom resisted me twenty-one days. Then Michael, one of the chief princes, came to help me, because I was detained there with the king of Persia. 14 Now I have come to explain to you what will happen to your people in the future, for the vision concerns a time yet to come."

15 While he was saying this to

עִמִּי כַּדְּבָרִים הָאֵלֶּה נָתַתִּי פָנַי אַרְצָה וְנֶאֱלָמְתִּי׃
and-I-was-speechless to-ground faces-of-me I-bowed the-these as-the-words to-me

וְהִנֵּה כִּדְמוּת בְּנֵי אָדָם נֹגֵעַ עַל־ שְׂפָתָי וָאֶפְתַּח־
and-I-opened lips-of-me to touching man sons-of like-look-of then-see! (16)

פִּי וָאֲדַבְּרָה וָאֹמְרָה אֶל־ הָעֹמֵד לְנֶגְדִּי אֲדֹנִי
lord-of-me at-before-me the-one-standing to and-I-said and-I-spoke mouth-of-me

בַּמַּרְאָה נֶהֶפְכוּ צִירַי עָלַי וְלֹא עָצַרְתִּי כֹּחַ׃
strength I-retain and-not over-me anguishes-of-me they-overcome because-of-the-vision

וְהֵיךְ יוּכַל עֶבֶד אֲדֹנִי זֶה לְדַבֵּר עִם־ אֲדֹנִי זֶה
this lord-of-me with to-talk this lord-of-me servant-of can-he and-how? (17)

וַאֲנִי מֵעַתָּה לֹא־ יַעֲמָד־ בִּי כֹחַ וּנְשָׁמָה לֹא נִשְׁאֲרָה־ בִי׃
in-me she-is-left not and-breath strength in-me he-stands not from-now for-I

וַיֹּסֶף וַיִּגַּע־ בִּי כְּמַרְאֵה אָדָם וַיְחַזְּקֵנִי׃
and-he-gave-strength-to-me man like-look-of to-me and-he-touched and-he-did-again (18)

וַיֹּאמֶר אַל־ תִּירָא אִישׁ־ חֲמֻדוֹת שָׁלוֹם לָךְ
to-you peace ones-highly-esteemed man-of you-be-afraid not and-he-said (19)

חֲזַק וַחֲזָק וּכְדַבְּרוֹ עִמִּי הִתְחַזַּקְתִּי וָאֹמְרָה
and-I-said I-was-strengthened to-me and-when-to-speak-him now-be-strong! be-strong!

יְדַבֵּר אֲדֹנִי כִּי חִזַּקְתָּנִי׃ וַיֹּאמֶר הֲיָדַעְתָּ
do-you-know? so-he-said (20) you-gave-strength-to-me since lord-of-me let-him-speak

לָמָּה־ בָּאתִי אֵלֶיךָ וְעַתָּה אָשׁוּב לְהִלָּחֵם עִם־ שַׂר פָּרָס
Persia prince-of against to-fight I-will-return and-soon to-you I-came for-why?

וַאֲנִי יוֹצֵא וְהִנֵּה שַׂר־ יָוָן בָּא׃ אֲבָל אַגִּיד לְךָ
to-you I-will-tell but (21) he-will-come Greece prince-of then-see! going when-I

אֶת־ הָרָשׁוּם בִּכְתָב אֱמֶת וְאֵין אֶחָד מִתְחַזֵּק עִמִּי
to-me supporting one and-there-is-no Truth in-Book-of the-one-being-written ***

עַל־ אֵלֶּה כִּי אִם־ מִיכָאֵל שַׂרְכֶם׃ וַאֲנִי בִּשְׁנַת אַחַת
one in-year-of and-I (11:1) prince-of-you Michael only except these against

לְדָרְיָוֶשׁ הַמָּדִי עָמְדִי לְמַחֲזִיק וּלְמָעוֹז לוֹ׃ וְעַתָּה
then-now (2) to-him for-protection to-support to-stand-me the-Mede of-Darius

אֱמֶת אַגִּיד לָךְ הִנֵּה־ עוֹד שְׁלֹשָׁה מְלָכִים עֹמְדִים לְפָרַס
in-Persia ones-appearing kings three more see! to-you I-tell truth

וְהָרְבִיעִי יַעֲשִׁיר עֹשֶׁר־ גָּדוֹל מִכֹּל וּכְחֶזְקָתוֹ
and-when-to-gain-power-him more-than-all great richness he-will-be-rich then-the-fourth

בְעָשְׁרוֹ יָעִיר הַכֹּל אֵת מַלְכוּת יָוָן׃
Greece kingdom-of against the-everyone he-will-stir-up by-wealth-of-him

וְעָמַד מֶלֶךְ גִּבּוֹר וּמָשַׁל מִמְשָׁל רַב וְעָשָׂה
and-he-will-do great power and-he-will-rule mighty king then-he-will-appear (3)

me, I bowed with my face toward the ground and was speechless. [16]Then one who looked like a man[i] touched my lips, and I opened my mouth and began to speak. I said to the one standing before me, "I am overcome with anguish because of the vision, my lord, and I am helpless. [17]How can I, your servant, talk with you, my lord? My strength is gone and I can hardly breathe."

[18]Again the one who looked like a man touched me and gave me strength. [19]"Do not be afraid, O man highly esteemed," he said. "Peace! Be strong now; be strong."

When he spoke to me, I was strengthened and said, "Speak, my lord, since you have given me strength."

[20]So he said, "Do you know why I have come to you? Soon I will return to fight against the prince of Persia, and when I go, the prince of Greece will come; [21]but first I will tell you what is written in the Book of Truth. (No one supports me against them except Michael, your prince. 11 [1]And in the first year of Darius the Mede, I took my stand to support and protect him.)

*The Kings of the South and the North*

[2]"Now then, I tell you the truth: Three more kings will appear in Persia, and then a fourth, who will be far richer than all the others. When he has gained power by his wealth, he will stir up everyone against the kingdom of Greece. [3]Then a mighty king will appear, who will rule with great power

i16 Most manuscripts of the Masoretic Text; one manuscript of the Masoretic Text, Dead Sea Scrolls and Septuagint *Then something that looked like a man's hand*

כִּרְצוֹנוֹ׃ וּכְעָמְדוֹ תִּשָּׁבֵר מַלְכוּתוֹ
empire-of-him she-will-be-broken-up and-after-to-appear-him (4) as-pleasure-of-him

וְתֵחָץ לְאַרְבַּע רוּחוֹת הַשָּׁמָיִם וְלֹא
and-not the-heavens winds-of to-four-of and-she-will-be-parceled-out

לְאַחֲרִיתוֹ וְלֹא כְמָשְׁלוֹ אֲשֶׁר מָשָׁל כִּי
because he-exercised-power that as-power-of-him or-not to-descendant-of-him

תִנָּתֵשׁ מַלְכוּתוֹ וְלַאֲחֵרִים מִלְּבַד־ אֵלֶּה׃
these than-besides and-to-others empire-of-him she-will-be-uprooted

וְיֶחֱזַק מֶלֶךְ־ הַנֶּגֶב וּמִן־ שָׂרָיו
commanders-of-him but-from the-South king-of and-he-will-become-strong (5)

וְיֶחֱזַק עָלָיו וּמָשָׁל מִמְשָׁל רַב מֶמְשַׁלְתּוֹ׃
kingdom-of-him great kingdom and-he-will-rule more-then-he he-will-become-strong

וּלְקֵץ שָׁנִים יִתְחַבָּרוּ וּבַת מֶלֶךְ־ הַנֶּגֶב
the-South king-of and-daughter-of they-will-become-allies years and-at-end-of (6)

תָּבוֹא אֶל־ מֶלֶךְ הַצָּפוֹן לַעֲשׂוֹת מֵישָׁרִים וְלֹא־ תַעְצֹר כּוֹחַ
power-of she-will-retain but-not alliances to-make the-North king-of to she-will-go

הַזְּרוֹעַ וְלֹא יַעֲמֹד וּזְרֹעוֹ וְתִנָּתֵן הִיא
she and-she-will-be-handed-over and-power-of-him he-will-last and-not the-arm

וּמְבִיאֶיהָ וְהַיֹּלְדָהּ וּמַחֲזִקָהּ בָּעִתִּים׃
in-the-days and-one-supporting-her and-the-one-fathering-her with-ones-escorting-her

וְעָמַד מִנֵּצֶר שָׁרָשֶׁיהָ כַּנּוֹ וְיָבֹא
and-he-will-attack place-of-him families-of-her from-line-of and-he-will-arise (7)

אֶל־ הַחַיִל וְיָבֹא בְּמָעוֹז מֶלֶךְ הַצָּפוֹן
the-North king-of into-fortress-of and-he-will-enter the-force against

וְעָשָׂה בָהֶם וְהֶחֱזִיק׃ וְגַם אֱלֹהֵיהֶם
gods-of-them and-also (8) and-he-will-be-victorious against-them and-he-will-fight

עִם־ נְסִכֵיהֶם עִם־ כְּלֵי חֶמְדָּתָם כֶּסֶף וְזָהָב בַּשְּׁבִי
to-the-exile and-gold silver value-of-them articles-of with metal-images-of-them with

יָבִא מִצְרָיִם וְהוּא שָׁנִים יַעֲמֹד מִמֶּלֶךְ הַצָּפוֹן׃
the-North to-king-of he-will-leave-alone years then-he Egypt he-will-carry-off

וּבָא בְּמַלְכוּת מֶלֶךְ הַנֶּגֶב וְשָׁב אֶל־
to but-he-will-retreat the-South king-of into-realm-of then-he-will-invade (9)

אַדְמָתוֹ׃ וּבְנָו יִתְגָּרוּ וְאָסְפוּ
and-they-will-assemble they-will-prepare-for-war and-sons-of-him (10) country-of-him

הֲמוֹן חֲיָלִים רַבִּים וּבָא בוֹא וְשָׁטַף
and-he-will-flood to-sweep-on and-he-will-sweep-on great-ones soldiers army-of

וְעָבַר וְיָשֹׁב וְיִתְגָּרוּ עַד־
as-far-as and-he-will-do-battle and-he-will-carry-on and-he-will-pass-through

°10a ק׳ ובניו
°10b ק׳ ויתגרה

and do as he pleases. [4]After he has appeared, his empire will be broken up and parceled out toward the four winds of heaven. It will not go to his descendants, nor will it have the power he exercised, because his empire will be uprooted and given to others.

[5]"The king of the South will become strong, but one of his commanders will become even stronger than he and will rule his own kingdom with great power. [6]After some years, they will become allies. The daughter of the king of the South will go to the king of the North to make an alliance, but she will not retain her power, and he and his power[k] will not last. In those days she will be handed over, together with her royal escort and her father[l] and the one who supported her.

[7]"One from her family line will arise to take her place. He will attack the forces of the king of the North and enter his fortress; he will fight against them and be victorious. [8]He will also seize their gods, their metal images and their valuable articles of silver and gold and carry them off to Egypt. For some years he will leave the king of the North alone. [9]Then the king of the North will invade the realm of the king of the South but will retreat to his own country. [10]His sons will prepare for war and assemble a great army, which will sweep on like an irresistible flood and carry the battle as far as his

[k]6 Or *offspring*
[l]6 Or *child* (see Vulgate and Syriac)

מָעֻזּֽוֹ׃ (11) וְיִתְמַרְמַר מֶלֶךְ הַנֶּגֶב וְיָצָא
fortress-of-him (11) then-he-will-be-enraged king-of the-South and-he-will-march-out

וְנִלְחַם עִמּוֹ עִם־ מֶלֶךְ הַצָּפוֹן וְהֶעֱמִיד הָמוֹן רָב
and-he-will-fight against-him against king-of the-North and-he-will-raise army large

וְנִתַּן הֶהָמוֹן בְּיָדֽוֹ׃ (12) וְנִשָּׂא הֶהָמוֹן
but-he-will-be-given the-army into-hand-of-him (12) when-he-is-carried-off the-army

יָרוּם לְבָבוֹ וְהִפִּיל רִבֹּאוֹת וְלֹא
he-will-be-proud heart-of-him and-he-will-slaughter many-thousands yet-not

יָעֽוֹז׃ (13) וְשָׁב מֶלֶךְ הַצָּפוֹן
he-will-remain-triumphant (13) for-he-will-do-again king-of the-North

וְהֶעֱמִיד הָמוֹן רַב מִן־ הָרִאשׁוֹן וּלְקֵץ הָעִתִּים שָׁנִים
and-he-will-muster army large more-than the-first and-at-end-of the-times years

יָבוֹא בוֹא בְּחַיִל גָּדוֹל וּבִרְכוּשׁ רָֽב׃ (14) וּבָעִתִּים
he-will-advance to-advance with-army huge and-with-equipment full (14) and-in-the-times

הָהֵם רַבִּים יַֽעַמְדוּ עַל־ מֶלֶךְ הַנֶּגֶב וּבְנֵי | פָּרִיצֵי
the-those many-ones they-will-rise against king-of the-South and-men-of violent-ones-of

עַמְּךָ יִנַּשְּׂאוּ לְהַעֲמִיד חָזוֹן וְנִכְשָֽׁלוּ׃
people-of-you they-will-rebel to-fulfill vision but-they-will-not-succeed

(15) וְיָבֹא מֶלֶךְ הַצָּפוֹן וְיִשְׁפֹּךְ סֽוֹלְלָה
(15) then-he-will-come king-of the-North and-he-will-build siege-ramp

וְלָכַד עִיר מִבְצָרוֹת וּזְרֹעוֹת הַנֶּגֶב לֹא יַֽעֲמֹדוּ
and-he-will-capture city-of fortifications and-forces-of the-South not they-will-resist

וְעַם מִבְחָרָיו וְאֵין כֹּחַ לַעֲמֹֽד׃
even-troop-of best-ones-of-him then-there-will-be-no strength to-stand

(16) וְיַעַשׂ הַבָּא אֵלָיו כִּרְצוֹנוֹ וְאֵין
(16) and-he-will-do the-one-invading to-him as-pleasure-of-him and-there-will-be-no

עוֹמֵד לְפָנָיו וַיַּעֲמֹד בְּאֶֽרֶץ־ הַצְּבִי
one-standing against-him and-he-will-establish in-Land-of the-Beautiful-One

וְכָלָה בְיָדֽוֹ׃ (17) וְיָשֵׂם | פָּנָיו לָבוֹא
with-destructive-power in-hand-of-him (17) and-he-will-determine faces-of-him to-come

בְּתֹקֶף כָּל־ מַלְכוּתוֹ וִישָׁרִים עִמּוֹ וְעָשָׂה
with-might-of entire-of kingdom-of-him and-alliances with-him also-he-will-make

וּבַת הַנָּשִׁים יִתֶּן־ לוֹ לְהַשְׁחִיתָהּ וְלֹא
and-daughter-of the-women he-will-give to-him to-overthrow-her but-not

תַעֲמֹד וְלֹא־ לוֹ תִהְיֶֽה׃ (18) וְיָשֵׁב | פָּנָיו
she-will-succeed or-not to-him she-will-be (18) then-he-will-turn faces-of-him

לְאִיִּים וְלָכַד רַבִּים וְהִשְׁבִּית קָצִין
to-coastlands and-he-will-take many-ones but-he-will-put-end-to commander

°10 ק מעוז; °12 ק ורם
°18 ק וישם

fortress.
11"Then the king of the South
will march out in a rage and fight
against the king of the North, who
will raise a large army, but it will
be defeated. 12When the army is
carried off, the king of the South
will be filled with pride and will
slaughter many thousands, yet he
will not remain triumphant. 13For
the king of the North will muster
another army, larger than the
first; and after several years, he
will advance with a huge army
fully equipped.
14"In those times many will rise
against the king of the South. The
violent men among your own
people will rebel in fulfillment of
the vision, but without success.
15Then the king of the North will
come and build up siege ramps
and will capture a fortified city.
The forces of the South will be
powerless to resist; even their best
troops will not have the strength
to stand. 16The invader will do as
he pleases; no one will be able to
stand against him. He will establish himself in the Beautiful Land
and will have the power to destroy
it. 17He will determine to come
with the might of his entire kingdom and will make an alliance
with the king of the South. And he
will give him a daughter in marriage in order to overthrow the
kingdom, but his plans[m] will not
succeed or help him. 18Then he
will turn his attention to the coastlands and will take many of them,
but a commander will put an end

[m]17 Or *but she*

חֶרְפָּתוֹ לוֹ בִּלְתִּי חֶרְפָּתוֹ יָשִׁיב לוֹ׃

upon-him he-will-turn-back insolence-of-him without to-him insolence-of-him

וְיָשֵׁב פָּנָיו לְמָעוּזֵּי אַרְצוֹ

country-of-him toward-fortresses-of faces-of-him then-he-will-turn-back (19)

וְנִכְשַׁל וְנָפַל וְלֹא יִמָּצֵא׃ וְעָמַד

and-he-will-succeed (20) he-will-be-seen and-not and-he-will-fall but-he-will-stumble

עַל־ כַּנּוֹ מַעֲבִיר נוֹגֵשׂ הֶדֶר מַלְכוּת

royalty splendor-of one-collecting-tax one-sending-out place-of-him to

וּבְיָמִים אֲחָדִים יִשָּׁבֵר וְלֹא בְאַפַּיִם וְלֹא בְמִלְחָמָה׃

in-battle or-not in-angers yet-not he-will-be-destroyed few-ones but-in-days

וְעָמַד עַל־ כַּנּוֹ נִבְזֶה וְלֹא־ נָתְנוּ

they-gave and-not one-being-contemptible place-of-him to and-he-will-succeed (21)

עָלָיו הוֹד מַלְכוּת וּבָא בְשַׁלְוָה וְהֶחֱזִיק מַלְכוּת

kingdom and-he-will-seize when-security and-he-will-invade royalty honor-of to-him

בַּחֲלַקְלַקּוֹת׃ וּזְרֹעוֹת הַשֶּׁטֶף יִשָּׁטְפוּ

they-will-be-swept-away the-overwhelmer then-armies-of (22) through-intrigues

מִלְּפָנָיו וְיִשָּׁבֵרוּ וְגַם נְגִיד בְּרִית׃

covenant prince-of and-also and-they-will-be-destroyed from-before-him

וּמִן־ הִתְחַבְּרוּת אֵלָיו יַעֲשֶׂה מִרְמָה וְעָלָה

and-he-will-rise deceit he-will-act with-him to-come-to-agreement and-after (23)

וְעָצַם בִּמְעַט־ גּוֹי׃ בְּשַׁלְוָה וּבְמִשְׁמַנֵּי

even-in-rich-ones-of when-security (24) people with-few-of and-he-will-be-powerful

מְדִינָה יָבוֹא וְעָשָׂה אֲשֶׁר לֹא־ עָשׂוּ אֲבֹתָיו

fathers-of-him they-achieved not what and-he-will-achieve he-will-invade province

וַאֲבוֹת אֲבֹתָיו בִּזָּה וְשָׁלָל וּרְכוּשׁ לָהֶם יִבְזוֹר

he-will-distribute among-them and-wealth and-loot plunder fathers-of-him or-fathers-of

וְעַל מִבְצָרִים יְחַשֵּׁב מַחְשְׁבֹתָיו וְעַד־ עֵת׃

time but-for overthrows-of-them he-will-plot fortresses and-against

וְיָעֵר כֹּחוֹ וּלְבָבוֹ עַל־ מֶלֶךְ הַנֶּגֶב

the-South king-of against and-courage-of-him strength-of-him and-he-will-stir-up (25)

בְּחַיִל גָּדוֹל וּמֶלֶךְ הַנֶּגֶב יִתְגָּרֶה לַמִּלְחָמָה בְּחַיִל־ גָּדוֹל

large with-army in-the-war he-will-wage-war the-South and-king-of large with-army

וְעָצוּם עַד־מְאֹד וְלֹא יַעֲמֹד כִּי־ יַחְשְׁבוּ עָלָיו מַחֲשָׁבוֹת׃

plots against-him they-devised because he-will-stand but-not very to and-powerful

וְאֹכְלֵי פַת־בָּגוֹ יְשַׁבְּרוּהוּ וְחֵילוֹ

and-army-of-him they-will-try-to-destroy-him provision-of-him and-ones-eating-of (26)

יִשְׁטוֹף וְנָפְלוּ חֲלָלִים רַבִּים׃ וּשְׁנֵיהֶם

and-two-of-them (27) many-ones ones-slain and-they-will-fall he-will-sweep-away

to his insolence and will turn his insolence back upon him. [19]After this, he will turn back toward the fortresses of his own country but will stumble and fall, to be seen no more.

[20]"His successor will send out a tax collector to maintain the royal splendor. In a few years, however, he will be destroyed, yet not in anger or in battle.

[21]"He will be succeeded by a contemptible person who has not been given the honor of royalty. He will invade the kingdom when its people feel secure, and he will seize it through intrigue. [22]Then an overwhelming army will be swept away before him; both it and a prince of the covenant will be destroyed. [23]After coming to an agreement with him, he will act deceitfully, and with only a few people he will rise to power. [24]When the richest provinces feel secure, he will invade them and will achieve what neither his fathers nor his forefathers did. He will distribute plunder, loot and wealth among his followers. He will plot the overthrow of fortresses—but only for a time.

[25]"With a large army he will stir up his strength and courage against the king of the South. The king of the South will wage war with a large and very powerful army, but he will not be able to stand because of the plots devised against him. [26]Those who eat from the king's provisions will try to destroy him; his army will be swept away, and many will fall in battle. [27]The two kings, with their

הַמְּלָכִים לְבָבָם לְמֵרָע וְעַל־שֻׁלְחָן אֶחָד כָּזָב יְדַבֵּרוּ וְלֹא
but-not they-will-speak lie same table and-at to-doing-evil heart-of-them the-kings

תִצְלָח כִּי־ עוֹד קֵץ לַמּוֹעֵד׃ וְיָשֹׁב
and-he-will-return (28) at-the-appointed-time end still because she-will-avail

אַרְצוֹ בִּרְכוּשׁ גָּדוֹל וּלְבָבוֹ עַל־ בְּרִית קֹדֶשׁ
holiness covenant-of against but-heart-of-him great with-wealth country-of-him

וְעָשָׂה וְשָׁב לְאַרְצוֹ׃ לַמּוֹעֵד
at-the-appointed-time (29) to-country-of-him then-he-will-return and-he-will-act

יָשׁוּב וּבָא בַנֶּגֶב וְלֹא־ תִהְיֶה
she-will-be but-not into-the-South and-he-will-invade he-will-do-again

כָרִאשֹׁנָה וְכָאַחֲרֹנָה׃ וּבָאוּ בוֹ צִיִּים
ships against-him and-they-will-oppose (30) and-as-the-outcome as-the-time-before

כִּתִּים וְנִכְאָה וְשָׁב וְזָעַם עַל־
against and-he-will-vent-fury then-he-will-turn-back and-he-will-lose-heart Kittim

בְּרִית־ קוֹדֶשׁ וְעָשָׂה וְשָׁב וְיָבֵן עַל־
to and-he-will-show-favor and-he-will-return and-he-will-act holiness covenant-of

עֹזְבֵי בְּרִית קֹדֶשׁ׃ וּזְרֹעִים מִמֶּנּוּ יַעֲמֹדוּ
they-will-rise-up of-him and-armed-forces (31) holiness covenant-of ones-forsaking-of

וְחִלְּלוּ הַמִּקְדָּשׁ הַמָּעוֹז וְהֵסִירוּ
and-they-will-abolish the-fortress the-temple and-they-will-desecrate

הַתָּמִיד וְנָתְנוּ הַשִּׁקּוּץ מְשׁוֹמֵם׃
one-causing-desolation the-abomination then-they-will-set-up the-daily-sacrifice

וּמַרְשִׁיעֵי בְרִית יַחֲנִיף בַּחֲלַקּוֹת וְעַם
but-people with-flatteries he-will-corrupt covenant and-ones-violating-of (32)

יֹדְעֵי אֱלֹהָיו יַחֲזִקוּ וְעָשׂוּ׃
and-they-will-resist they-will-be-strong God-of-him ones-knowing-of

וּמַשְׂכִּילֵי עָם יָבִינוּ לָרַבִּים
to-the-many-ones they-will-instruct people and-ones-being-wise-of (33)

וְנִכְשְׁלוּ בְּחֶרֶב וּבְלֶהָבָה בִּשְׁבִי וּבְבִזָּה יָמִים׃
days or-by-plunder by-captivity or-by-burning by-sword though-they-will-fall

וּבְהִכָּשְׁלָם יֵעָזְרוּ עֵזֶר מְעָט וְנִלְווּ
and-they-will-join little help they-will-receive-help and-when-to-fall-them (34)

עֲלֵיהֶם רַבִּים בַּחֲלַקְלַקּוֹת׃ וּמִן־ הַמַּשְׂכִּילִים
the-ones-being-wise and-from (35) with-insincereties many-ones with-them

יִכָּשְׁלוּ לִצְרוֹף בָּהֶם וּלְבָרֵר וְלַלְבֵּן עַד־ עֵת
time-of until and-to-make-spotless and-to-purify to-them to-refine they-will-stumble

קֵץ כִּי־עוֹד לַמּוֹעֵד׃ וְעָשָׂה כִרְצוֹנוֹ הַמֶּלֶךְ
the-king as-pleasure-of-him and-he-will-do (36) at-the-appointed-time still for end

hearts bent on evil, will sit at the same table and lie to each other, but to no avail, because an end will still come at the appointed time. 28The King of the North will return to his own country with great wealth, but his heart will be set against the holy covenant. He will take action against it and then return to his own country.

29"At the appointed time he will invade the South again, but this time the outcome will be different from what it was before. 30Ships of the western coastlands[n] will oppose him, and he will lose heart. Then he will turn back and vent his fury against the holy covenant. He will return and show favor to those who forsake the holy covenant.

31"His armed forces will rise up to desecrate the temple fortress and will abolish the daily sacrifice. Then they will set up the abomination that causes desolation. 32With flattery he will corrupt those who have violated the covenant, but the people who know their God will firmly resist him.

33"Those who are wise will instruct many, though for a time they will fall by the sword or be burned or captured or plundered. 34When they fall, they will receive a little help, and many who are not sincere will join them. 35Some of the wise will stumble, so that they may be refined, purified and made spotless until the time of the end, for it will still come at the appointed time.

*The King Who Exalts Himself*

36"The king will do as he pleases.

n30 Hebrew *of Kittim*

וְיִתְרוֹמֵם וְיִתְגַּדֵּל עַל־ כָּל־ אֵל וְעַל
and-against god every-of above and-he-will-magnify-himself and-he-will-exalt-himself

אֵל אֵלִים יְדַבֵּר נִפְלָאוֹת וְהִצְלִיחַ עַד־
until and-he-will-succeed things-being-unheard-of he-will-say gods God-of

כָּלָה זַעַם כִּי נֶחֱרָצָה נֶעֱשָׂתָה׃ וְעַל־
and-for (37) she-must-take-place one-being-determined for wrath he-is-completed

אֱלֹהֵי אֲבֹתָיו לֹא יָבִין וְעַל־ חֶמְדַּת נָשִׁים וְעַל־ כָּל־
any-of or-for women desire-of or-for he-will-show-regard not fathers-of-him gods-of

אֱלוֹהַּ לֹא יָבִין כִּי עַל־ כֹּל יִתְגַּדָּל׃ וְלֶאֱלֹהַּ
and-to-god-of (38) he-will-exalt-himself all above but he-will-show-regard not god

מָעֻזִּים עַל־ כַּנּוֹ יְכַבֵּד וְלֶאֱלוֹהַּ אֲשֶׁר לֹא־ יְדָעֻהוּ
they-knew-him not that even-to-god he-will-honor stead-of-him in fortresses

אֲבֹתָיו יְכַבֵּד בְּזָהָב וּבְכֶסֶף וּבְאֶבֶן יְקָרָה
precious and-with-stone and-with-silver with-gold he-will-honor fathers-of-him

וּבַחֲמֻדוֹת׃ וְעָשָׂה לְמִבְצְרֵי מָעֻזִּים
fortresses against-mighty-ones-of and-he-will-attack (39) and-with-costly-gifts

עִם־ אֱלוֹהַּ נֵכָר אֲשֶׁר הִכִּיר יַרְבֶּה כָבוֹד
honor he-will-make-great he-acknowledges who foreignness god-of with

וְהִמְשִׁילָם בָּרַבִּים וַאֲדָמָה יְחַלֵּק בִּמְחִיר׃
at-price also-to-distribute and-land over-the-many-ones and-he-will-make-rule-them

וּבְעֵת קֵץ יִתְנַגַּח עִמּוֹ מֶלֶךְ הַנֶּגֶב
the-South king-of with-him he-will-engage-in-battle end and-at-time-of (40)

וְיִשְׂתָּעֵר עָלָיו מֶלֶךְ הַצָּפוֹן בְּרֶכֶב וּבְפָרָשִׁים
and-with-cavalries with-chariot the-North king-of against-him and-he-will-storm-out

וּבָאֳנִיּוֹת רַבּוֹת וּבָא בַאֲרָצוֹת וְשָׁטַף
and-he-will-flood into-countries and-he-will-invade many-ones and-with-ships

וְעָבָר׃ וּבָא בְּאֶרֶץ הַצְּבִי
the-Beautiful-One into-Land-of also-he-will-invade (41) and-he-will-sweep-through

וְרַבּוֹת יִכָּשֵׁלוּ וְאֵלֶּה יִמָּלְטוּ מִיָּדוֹ
from-hand-of-him they-will-be-delivered but-these they-will-fall and-many-ones

אֱדוֹם וּמוֹאָב וְרֵאשִׁית בְּנֵי עַמּוֹן׃ וְיִשְׁלַח יָדוֹ
power-of-him and-he-will-extend (42) Ammon sons-of and-leader-of and-Moab Edom

בַּאֲרָצוֹת וְאֶרֶץ מִצְרַיִם לֹא תִהְיֶה לִפְלֵיטָה׃ וּמָשַׁל
and-he-will-control (43) for-escape she-will-be not Egypt and-land-of over-countries

בְּמִכְמַנֵּי הַזָּהָב וְהַכֶּסֶף וּבְכֹל חֲמֻדוֹת מִצְרָיִם וְלֻבִים
with-Lybians Egypt riches-of and-over-all-of and-the-silver the-gold over-treasures-of

וְכֻשִׁים בְּמִצְעָדָיו׃ וּשְׁמֻעוֹת יְבַהֲלֻהוּ מִמִּזְרָח
from-east they-will-alarm-him but-reports (44) at-feet-of-him and-Nubians

He will exalt and magnify himself above every god and will say unheard-of things against the God of gods. He will be successful until the time of wrath is completed, for what has been determined must take place. [37]He will show no regard for the gods of his fathers or for the one desired by women, nor will he regard any god, but will exalt himself above them all. [38]Instead of them, he will honor a god of fortresses; a god unknown to his fathers he will honor with gold and silver, with precious stones and costly gifts. [39]He will attack the mightiest fortresses with the help of a foreign god and will greatly honor those who acknowledge him. He will make them rulers over many people and will distribute the land at a price.[o]

[40]"At the time of the end the king of the South will engage him in battle, and the king of the North will storm out against him with chariots and cavalry and a great fleet of ships. He will invade many countries and sweep through them like a flood. [41]He will also invade the Beautiful Land. Many countries will fall, but Edom, Moab and the leaders of Ammon will be delivered from his hand. [42]He will extend his power over many countries; Egypt will not escape. [43]He will gain control of the treasures of gold and silver and all the riches of Egypt, with the Libyans and Nubians in submission. [44]But reports from the east and the north will alarm him,

o39 Or *land for a reward*

°39 ק יכיר

וּמִצָּפוֹן וְיָצָא בְּחֵמָא גְדֹלָה לְהַשְׁמִיד וּלְהַחֲרִים
and-to-annihilate to-destroy great in-rage and-he-will-set-out and-from-north

רַבִּים׃ (45) וְיִטַּע אָהֳלֵי* אַפַּדְנוֹ בֵּין יַמִּים לְהַר־
at-mountain-of seas between royalty-of-him tents-of and-he-will-pitch (45) many-ones

צְבִי־ קֹדֶשׁ וּבָא עַד־ קִצּוֹ וְאֵין עוֹזֵר
one-helping and-there-will-be-no end-of-him to yet-he-will-come holiness beauty-of

לוֹ׃ (12:1) וּבָעֵת הַהִיא יַעֲמֹד מִיכָאֵל הַשַּׂר הַגָּדוֹל
the-great the-prince Michael he-will-arise the-that and-at-the-time (12:1) to-him

הָעֹמֵד עַל־ בְּנֵי עַמֶּךָ וְהָיְתָה עֵת צָרָה
distress time-of and-she-will-be people-of-you sons-of over the-one-protecting

אֲשֶׁר לֹא־ נִהְיְתָה מִהְיוֹת גּוֹי עַד הָעֵת הַהִיא וּבָעֵת
but-at-the-time the-that the-time until nation from-to-begin she-happened not that

הַהִיא יִמָּלֵט עַמְּךָ כָּל־ הַנִּמְצָא כָּתוּב
being-written the-one-being-found every-of people-of-you he-will-be-delivered the-that

בַּסֵּפֶר׃ (2) וְרַבִּים מִיְּשֵׁנֵי אַדְמַת־ עָפָר יָקִיצוּ
they-will-awake dust earth-of of-sleepers-of and-multitudes (2) in-the-book

אֵלֶּה לְחַיֵּי עוֹלָם וְאֵלֶּה לַחֲרָפוֹת לְדִרְאוֹן עוֹלָם׃
everlasting to-contempt-of to-shames and-these everlasting to-lives-of these

(3) וְהַמַּשְׂכִּלִים יַזְהִרוּ כְּזֹהַר הָרָקִיעַ
the-heaven like-brightness-of they-will-shine and-the-ones-being-wise (3)

וּמַצְדִּיקֵי הָרַבִּים כַּכּוֹכָבִים לְעוֹלָם וָעֶד׃
and-ever to-forever like-the-stars the-many-ones and-ones-leading-to-righteousness-of

(4) וְאַתָּה דָנִיֵּאל סְתֹם הַדְּבָרִים וַחֲתֹם הַסֵּפֶר עַד־ עֵת קֵץ
end time-of until the-scroll and-seal! the-words close-up! Daniel but-you (4)

יְשֹׁטְטוּ רַבִּים וְתִרְבֶּה הַדָּעַת׃
the-knowledge and-she-will-increase many-ones they-will-go-here-and-there

(5) וְרָאִיתִי אֲנִי דָנִיֵּאל וְהִנֵּה שְׁנַיִם אֲחֵרִים עֹמְדִים אֶחָד הֵנָּה
at-here one ones-standing others two and-see! Daniel I then-I-looked (5)

לִשְׂפַת הַיְאֹר וְאֶחָד הֵנָּה לִשְׂפַת הַיְאֹר׃ (6) וַיֹּאמֶר לָאִישׁ
to-the-man and-he-said (6) the-river on-bank-of at-there one the-river on-bank-of

לְבוּשׁ הַבַּדִּים אֲשֶׁר מִמַּעַל לְמֵימֵי הַיְאֹר עַד־ מָתַי
when? until the-river to-waters-of at-above who the-linens being-clothed-of

קֵץ הַפְּלָאוֹת׃ (7) וָאֶשְׁמַע אֶת־ הָאִישׁ ׀
the-man *** and-I-heard (7) the-things-being-astonishing fulfillment-of

לְבוּשׁ הַבַּדִּים אֲשֶׁר מִמַּעַל לְמֵימֵי הַיְאֹר וַיָּרֶם
and-he-lifted the-river to-waters-of at-above who the-linens being-clothed-of

יְמִינוֹ וּשְׂמֹאלוֹ אֶל־ הַשָּׁמַיִם וַיִּשָּׁבַע בְּחֵי
by-one-alive-of and-he-swore the-heavens to and-left-hand-of-him right-hand-of-him

and he will set out in a great rage to destroy and annihilate many. 45He will pitch his royal tents between the seas at[p] the beautiful holy mountain. Yet he will come to his end, and no one will help him.

*The End Times*

12 "At that time Michael, the great prince who protects your people, will arise. There will be a time of distress such as has not happened from the beginning of nations until then. But at that time your people—everyone whose name is found written in the book—will be delivered. 2Multitudes who sleep in the dust of the earth will awake: some to everlasting life, others to shame and everlasting contempt. 3Those who are wise[q] will shine like the brightness of the heavens, and those who lead many to righteousness, like the stars for ever and ever. 4But you, Daniel, close up and seal the words of the scroll until the time of the end. Many will go here and there to increase knowledge."

5Then I, Daniel, looked, and there before me stood two others, one on this bank of the river and one on the opposite bank. 6One of them said to the man clothed in linen, who was above the waters of the river, "How long will it be before these astonishing things are fulfilled?"

7The man clothed in linen, who was above the waters of the river, lifted his right hand and his left hand toward heaven, and I heard

p45 Or *the sea and*
q3 Or *who impart wisdom*

*45 Most mss have *tsere* under the *lamed* (־לֵי)

הָעוֹלָם כִּי לְמוֹעֵד מוֹעֲדִים וָחֵצִי וּכְכַלּוֹת נַפֵּץ יַד־
power-of to-break and-when-to-be-final and-half times for-time that the-forever

עַם־ קֹדֶשׁ תִּכְלֶינָה כָל־ אֵלֶּה׃ וַאֲנִי שָׁמַעְתִּי וְלֹא
but-not I-heard and-I (8) these all-of they-will-be-completed holiness people-of

אָבִין וָאֹמְרָה אֲדֹנִי מָה אַחֲרִית אֵלֶּה׃ וַיֹּאמֶר לֵךְ
go! and-he-replied (9) these outcome-of what? lord-of-me so-I-asked I-understood

דָּנִיֵּאל כִּי־ סְתֻמִים וַחֲתֻמִים הַדְּבָרִים עַד־
until the-words and-ones-being-sealed ones-being-closed-up because Daniel

עֵת קֵץ׃ יִתְבָּרְרוּ וְיִתְלַבְּנוּ
and-they-will-be-made-spotless they-will-be-purified (10) end time-of

וְיִצָּרְפוּ רַבִּים וְהִרְשִׁיעוּ רְשָׁעִים וְלֹא
and-not wicked-ones but-they-will-be-wicked many-ones and-they-will-be-refined

יָבִינוּ כָּל־ רְשָׁעִים וְהַמַּשְׂכִּלִים יָבִינוּ׃
they-will-understand but-the-ones-being-wise wicked-ones any-of they-will-understand

וּמֵעֵת הוּסַר הַתָּמִיד וְלָתֵת שִׁקּוּץ
abomination and-to-set-up the-daily-sacrifice he-is-abolished and-from-time-of (11)

שֹׁמֵם יָמִים אֶלֶף מָאתַיִם וְתִשְׁעִים׃ אַשְׁרֵי
blessednesses-of (12) and-ninety two-hundreds thousand days one-causing-desolation

הַמְחַכֶּה וְיַגִּיעַ לְיָמִים אֶלֶף שְׁלֹשׁ מֵאוֹת
hundreds three-of thousand to-days and-he-reaches the-one-waiting-for

שְׁלֹשִׁים וַחֲמִשָּׁה׃ וְאַתָּה לֵךְ לַקֵּץ וְתָנוּחַ
and-you-will-rest till-the-end go! and-you (13) and-five thirty

וְתַעֲמֹד לְגֹרָלְךָ לְקֵץ הַיָּמִין׃
the-days at-end-of to-allotted-inheritance-of-you and-you-will-rise

him swear by him who lives forever, saying, "It will be for a time, times and half a time.' When the power of the holy people has been finally broken, all these things will be completed."

8 I heard, but I did not understand. So I asked, "My lord, what will the outcome of all this be?"

9 He replied, "Go your way, Daniel, because the words are closed up and sealed until the time of the end. 10 Many will be purified, made spotless and refined, but the wicked will continue to be wicked. None of the wicked will understand, but those who are wise will understand.

11 "From the time that the daily sacrifice is abolished and the abomination that causes desolation is set up, there will be 1,290 days. 12 Blessed is the one who waits for and reaches the end of the 1,335 days.

13 "As for you, go your way till the end. You will rest, and then at the end of the days you will rise to receive your allotted inheritance."

[r]7 Or *a year, two years and half a year*

דְּבַר־יְהוָה אֲשֶׁר הָיָה אֶל־הוֹשֵׁעַ בֶּן־בְּאֵרִי בִּימֵי עֻזִּיָּה יוֹתָם
Jotham Uzziah during-days-of Beeri son-of Hosea to he-came that Yahweh word-of (1:1)

אָחָז יְחִזְקִיָּה מַלְכֵי יְהוּדָה וּבִימֵי יָרָבְעָם בֶּן־יוֹאָשׁ מֶלֶךְ
king-of Joash son-of Jeroboam and-during-days-of Judah kings-of Hezekiah Ahaz

יִשְׂרָאֵל׃ תְּחִלַּת דִּבֶּר־יְהוָה בְּהוֹשֵׁעַ וַיֹּאמֶר יְהוָה אֶל־הוֹשֵׁעַ
Hosea to Yahweh and-he-said through-Hosea Yahweh he-spoke beginning-of (2) Israel

לֵךְ קַח־לְךָ אֵשֶׁת זְנוּנִים וְיַלְדֵי זְנוּנִים כִּי־
because unfaithfulnesses and-children-of adulteries wife-of to-yourself take! go!

זָנֹה תִזְנֶה הָאָרֶץ מֵאַחֲרֵי יְהוָה׃
Yahweh from-after the-land she-is-guilty-of-adultery to-be-guilty-of-adultery

וַיֵּלֶךְ וַיִּקַּח אֶת־גֹּמֶר בַּת־דִּבְלָיִם וַתַּהַר
and-she-conceived Diblaim daughter-of Gomer *** and-he-married so-he-went (3)

וַתֵּלֶד־לוֹ בֵּן׃ וַיֹּאמֶר יְהוָה אֵלָיו קְרָא שְׁמוֹ יִזְרְעֶאל
Jezreel name-of-him call! to-him Yahweh then-he-said (4) son to-him and-she-bore

כִּי־עוֹד מְעַט וּפָקַדְתִּי אֶת־דְּמֵי יִזְרְעֶאל עַל־בֵּית יֵהוּא
Jehu house-of on Jezreel bloods-of *** and-I-will-punish soon yet because

וְהִשְׁבַּתִּי מַמְלְכוּת בֵּית יִשְׂרָאֵל׃ וְהָיָה בַּיּוֹם
in-the-day and-he-will-be (5) Israel house-of kingdom-of and-I-will-put-to-end

הַהוּא וְשָׁבַרְתִּי אֶת־קֶשֶׁת יִשְׂרָאֵל בְּעֵמֶק יִזְרְעֶאל׃
Jezreel in-Valley-of Israel bow-of *** then-I-will-break the-that

וַתַּהַר עוֹד וַתֵּלֶד בַּת וַיֹּאמֶר לוֹ קְרָא
call! to-him then-he-said daughter and-she-bore again and-she-conceived (6)

שְׁמָהּ לֹא רֻחָמָה כִּי לֹא אוֹסִיף עוֹד אֲרַחֵם אֶת־
*** I-will-show-love longer I-will-continue not for Ruhamah Lo name-of-her

בֵּית יִשְׂרָאֵל כִּי־נָשֹׂא אֶשָּׂא לָהֶם׃ וְאֶת־בֵּית יְהוּדָה
Judah house-of yet (7) to-them I-should-forgive to-forgive that Israel house-of

אֲרַחֵם וְהוֹשַׁעְתִּים בַּיהוָה אֱלֹהֵיהֶם וְלֹא אוֹשִׁיעֵם
I-will-save-them but-not God-of-them by-Yahweh and-I-will-save-them I-will-show-love

בְּקֶשֶׁת וּבְחֶרֶב וּבְמִלְחָמָה בְּסוּסִים וּבְפָרָשִׁים׃ וַתִּגְמֹל אֶת־
*** after-she-weaned (8) and-by-horsemen by-horses or-by-battle or-by-sword by-bow

לֹא רֻחָמָה וַתַּהַר וַתֵּלֶד בֵּן׃ וַיֹּאמֶר קְרָא שְׁמוֹ
name-of-him call! then-he-said (9) son and-she-bore then-she-conceived Ruhamah Lo

לֹא עַמִּי כִּי אַתֶּם לֹא עַמִּי וְאָנֹכִי לֹא־אֶהְיֶה לָכֶם׃ וְהָיָה
yet-he-will-be *(2:1[10]) to-you I-am not and-I people-of-me not you for Ammi Lo

מִסְפַּר בְּנֵי־יִשְׂרָאֵל כְּחוֹל הַיָּם אֲשֶׁר לֹא־יִמַּד
he-can-be-measured not which the-sea like-sand-of Israel sons-of number-of

וְלֹא יִסָּפֵר וְהָיָה בִּמְקוֹם אֲשֶׁר־יֵאָמֵר לָהֶם
to-them he-was-said where in-place-of and-he-will-be he-can-be-counted or-not

1 The word of the LORD that came to Hosea son of Beeri during the reigns of Uzziah, Jotham, Ahaz and Hezekiah, kings of Judah, and during the reign of Jeroboam son of Jehoash[a] king of Israel:

*Hosea's Wife and Children*

2 When the LORD began to speak through Hosea, the LORD said to him, "Go, take to yourself an adulterous wife and children of unfaithfulness, because the land is guilty of the vilest adultery in departing from the LORD."
3 So he married Gomer daughter of Diblaim, and she conceived and bore him a son.

4 Then the LORD said to Hosea, "Call him Jezreel, because I will soon punish the house of Jehu for the massacre at Jezreel, and I will put an end to the kingdom of Israel.
5 In that day I will break Israel's bow in the Valley of Jezreel."

6 Gomer conceived again and gave birth to a daughter. Then the LORD said to Hosea, "Call her Lo-Ruhamah,[b] for I will no longer show love to the house of Israel, that I should at all forgive them.
7 Yet I will show love to the house of Judah; and I will save them—not by bow, sword or battle, or by horses and horsemen, but by the LORD their God."

8 After she had weaned Lo-Ruhamah, Gomer had another son.
9 Then the LORD said, "Call him Lo-Ammi,[c] for you are not my people, and I am not your God.

10 "Yet the Israelites will be like the sand on the seashore, which cannot be measured or counted. In the place where it was said to

[a]1 Hebrew *Joash*, a variant of *Jehoash*
[b]6 *Lo-Ruhamah* means *not loved.*
[c]9 *Lo-Ammi* means *not my people.*

**Heading, 1* The Hebrew numeration of chapter 2 begins with verse 10 of chapter 1 in English; the number in brackets indicates the English numeration.

לֹא־ עַמִּי אַתֶּם יֵאָמֵר לָהֶם בְּנֵי אֵל־ חָי׃

living-one God sons-of to-them he-will-be-called you people-of-me not

וְנִקְבְּצוּ בְּנֵי־ יְהוּדָה וּבְנֵי־ יִשְׂרָאֵל יַחְדָּו

together Israel and-peoples-of Judah peoples-of and-they-will-be-reunited (2[11])

וְשָׂמוּ לָהֶם רֹאשׁ אֶחָד וְעָלוּ מִן־ הָאָרֶץ

the-land out-of and-they-will-come-up one leader for-them and-they-will-appoint

כִּי גָדוֹל יוֹם יִזְרְעֶאל׃ אִמְרוּ לַאֲחֵיכֶם עַמִּי

people-of-me of-brothers-of-you say! (3[2:1]) Jezreel day-of great for

וְלַאֲחוֹתֵיכֶם רֻחָמָה׃ רִיבוּ בְאִמְּכֶם רִיבוּ כִּי־

for rebuke! to-mother-of-you rebuke! (4[2]) she-is-loved and-of-sisters-of-you

הִיא לֹא אִשְׁתִּי וְאָנֹכִי לֹא אִישָׁהּ וְתָסֵר זְנוּנֶיהָ

adulteries-of-her and-let-her-remove husband-of-her not and-I wife-of-me not she

מִפָּנֶיהָ† וְנַאֲפוּפֶיהָ מִבֵּין שָׁדֶיהָ׃

breasts-of-her from-between and-unfaithfulnesses-of-her from-faces-of-her

פֶּן־ אַפְשִׁיטֶנָּה עֲרֻמָּה וְהִצַּגְתִּיהָ כְּיוֹם הִוָּלְדָהּ

to-be-born-her as-day-of and-I-will-make-bare-her naked I-will-strip-her otherwise (5[3])

וְשַׂמְתִּיהָ כַמִּדְבָּר וְשַׁתִּהָ כְּאֶרֶץ צִיָּה

parched-one into-land-of and-I-will-turn-her like-the-desert and-I-will-make-her

וַהֲמִתִּיהָ בַּצָּמָא׃ וְאֶת־ בָּנֶיהָ לֹא אֲרַחֵם

I-will-show-love not children-of-her and (6[4]) with-the-thirst and-I-will-slay-her

כִּי־ בְנֵי זְנוּנִים הֵמָּה׃ כִּי זָנְתָה אִמָּם

mother-of-them she-was-unfaithful indeed (7[5]) they adulteries children-of because

הֹבִישָׁה הוֹרָתָם כִּי אָמְרָה אֵלְכָה אַחֲרֵי מְאַהֲבַי

ones-loving-me after I-will-go she-said indeed conceiving-of-them she-made-disgraceful

נֹתְנֵי לַחְמִי וּמֵימַי צַמְרִי וּפִשְׁתִּי שַׁמְנִי

oil-of-me and-linen-of-me wool-of-me and-waters-of-me food-of-me ones-giving-of

וְשִׁקּוּיָי׃ לָכֵן הִנְנִי־ שָׂךְ אֶת־ דַּרְכֵּךְ בַּסִּירִים

with-the-thornbushes path-of-her *** blocking see-I! therefore (8[6]) and-drinks-of-me

וְגָדַרְתִּי אֶת־ גְּדֵרָהּ וּנְתִיבוֹתֶיהָ לֹא תִמְצָא׃

she-can-find not so-ways-of-her wall-of-her *** and-I-will-wall-in

וְרִדְּפָה אֶת־ מְאַהֲבֶיהָ וְלֹא־ תַשִּׂיג אֹתָם

them she-will-catch but-not ones-loving-her *** and-she-will-chase (9[7])

וּבִקְשָׁתַם וְלֹא תִמְצָא וְאָמְרָה אֵלְכָה

I-will-go then-she-will-say she-will-find but-not indeed-she-will-look-for-them

וְאָשׁוּבָה אֶל־ אִישִׁי הָרִאשׁוֹן כִּי טוֹב לִי אָז מֵעָתָּה׃

more-than-now then for-me good for the-first husband-of-me to and-I-will-go-back

וְהִיא לֹא יָדְעָה כִּי אָנֹכִי נָתַתִּי לָהּ הַדָּגָן וְהַתִּירוֹשׁ

and-the-new-wine the-grain to-her I-gave I that she-acknowledged not and-she (10[8])

them, 'You are not my people,' they will be called 'sons of the living God.' [11]The people of Judah and the people of Israel will be reunited, and they will appoint one leader and will come up out of the land, for great will be the day of Jezreel.

2 "Say of your brothers, 'My people,' and of your sisters, 'My loved one.'

*Israel Punished and Restored*

[2]"Rebuke your mother, rebuke her,
for she is not my wife,
and I am not her husband.
Let her remove the adulterous look from her face
and the unfaithfulness from between her breasts.
[3]Otherwise I will strip her naked
and make her as bare as on the day she was born;
I will make her like a desert,
turn her into a parched land,
and slay her with thirst.
[4]I will not show my love to her children,
because they are the children of adultery.
[5]Their mother has been unfaithful
and has conceived them in disgrace.
She said, 'I will go after my lovers,
who give me my food and my water,
my wool and my linen, my oil and my drink.'
[6]Therefore I will block her path with thornbushes;
I will wall her in so that she cannot find her way.
[7]She will chase after her lovers
but not catch them;
she will look for them but not find them.
Then she will say,
'I will go back to my husband as at first,
for then I was better off than now.'
[8]She has not acknowledged that I was the one
who gave her the grain, the new wine and oil,

**Heading* See the note on page 482.

†4 Most mss have *qamets* under the *he* (ה־).

וְהַיִּצְהָר וְכֶסֶף הִרְבֵּיתִי לָהּ וְזָהָב עָשׂוּ לַבָּעַל׃
for-the-Baal they-used and-gold on-her I-lavished and-silver and-the-oil

לָכֵן אָשׁוּב וְלָקַחְתִּי דְגָנִי בְּעִתּוֹ
when-time-of-him grain-of-me and-I-will-take-away I-will-turn therefore (11[9])

וְתִירוֹשִׁי בְּמוֹעֲדוֹ וְהִצַּלְתִּי צַמְרִי
wool-of-me and-I-will-take-back when-readiness-of-him and-new-wine-of-me

וּפִשְׁתִּי לְכַסּוֹת אֶת־ עֶרְוָתָהּ׃ וְעַתָּה אֲגַלֶּה אֶת־
*** I-will-expose so-now (12[10]) nakedness-of-her *** to-cover and-linen-of-me

נַבְלֻתָהּ לְעֵינֵי מְאַהֲבֶיהָ וְאִישׁ לֹא־ יַצִּילֶנָּה
he-will-take-her not and-anyone ones-loving-her before-eyes-of lewdness-of-her

מִיָּדִי׃ וְהִשְׁבַּתִּי כָּל־ מְשׂוֹשָׂהּ
celebration-of-her all-of and-I-will-stop (13[11]) from-hand-of-me

חַגָּהּ חָדְשָׁהּ וְשַׁבַּתָּהּ וְכֹל
even-all-of and-Sabbath-day-of-her New-Moon-of-her yearly-festival-of-her

מוֹעֲדָהּ׃ וַהֲשִׁמֹּתִי גַּפְנָהּ וּתְאֵנָתָהּ אֲשֶׁר
which and-fig-tree-of-her vine-of-her and-I-will-ruin (14[12]) appointed-feast-of-her

אָמְרָה אֶתְנָה הֵמָּה לִי אֲשֶׁר נָתְנוּ־ לִי מְאַהֲבָי וְשַׂמְתִּים
and-I-will-make-them ones-loving-me to-me they-gave that to-me they pay she-said

לְיַעַר וַאֲכָלָתַם חַיַּת הַשָּׂדֶה׃ וּפָקַדְתִּי
and-I-will-punish (15[13]) the-wild animal-of and-she-will-devour-them into-thicket

עָלֶיהָ אֶת־ יְמֵי הַבְּעָלִים אֲשֶׁר תַּקְטִיר לָהֶם וַתַּעַד
and-she-decked-herself to-them she-burned-incense when the-Baals days-of *** to-her

נִזְמָהּ וְחֶלְיָתָהּ וַתֵּלֶךְ אַחֲרֵי מְאַהֲבֶיהָ וְאֹתִי שָׁכְחָה
she-forgot but-me ones-loving-her after and-she-went and-jewelry-of-her ring-of-her

נְאֻם־ יְהוָה׃ לָכֵן הִנֵּה אָנֹכִי מְפַתֶּיהָ וְהֹלַכְתִּיהָ
and-I-will-lead-her alluring-her I see! therefore (16[14]) Yahweh declaration-of

הַמִּדְבָּר וְדִבַּרְתִּי עַל־ לִבָּהּ׃ וְנָתַתִּי לָהּ אֶת־
*** to-her and-I-will-give-back (17[15]) heart-of-her to and-I-will-speak the-desert

כְּרָמֶיהָ מִשָּׁם וְאֶת־ עֵמֶק עָכוֹר לְפֶתַח תִּקְוָה וְעָנְתָה
and-she-will-respond hope into-door-of Achor Valley-of and at-there vineyards-of-her

שָׁמָּה כִּימֵי נְעוּרֶיהָ וּכְיוֹם† עֲלֹתָהּ מֵאֶרֶץ־מִצְרָיִם׃
Egypt from-land-of to-come-up-her and-as-day-of youths-of-her as-days-of at-there

וְהָיָה בַיּוֹם־ הַהוּא נְאֻם־ יְהוָה תִּקְרְאִי
you-will-call Yahweh declaration-of the-that in-the-day and-he-will-be (18[16])

אִישִׁי וְלֹא־ תִקְרְאִי־ לִי עוֹד בַּעְלִי׃
master-of-me longer to-me you-will-call and-not husband-of-me

וַהֲסִרֹתִי אֶת־ שְׁמוֹת הַבְּעָלִים מִפִּיהָ וְלֹא־
and-not from-mouth-of-her the-Baals names-of *** and-I-will-remove (19[17])

who lavished on her the silver
and gold—
which they used for Baal.

9"Therefore I will take away
my grain when it ripens,
and my new wine when it
is ready.
I will take back my wool and
my linen,
intended to cover her
nakedness.
10So now I will expose her
lewdness
before the eyes of her lovers;
no one will take her out of
my hands.
11I will stop all her celebrations:
her yearly festivals, her New
Moons,
her Sabbath days—all her
appointed feasts.
12I will ruin her vines and her
fig trees,
which she said were her pay
from her lovers;
I will make them a thicket,
and wild animals will
devour them.
13I will punish her for the days
she burned incense to the
Baals;
she decked herself with rings
and jewelry,
and went after her lovers,
but me she forgot,"
declares the LORD.

14"Therefore I am now going to
allure her;
I will lead her into the
desert
and speak tenderly to her.
15There I will give her back her
vineyards,
and will make the Valley of
Achor[d] a door of hope.
There she will sing[e] as in the
days of her youth,
as in the day she came up
out of Egypt.

16"In that day," declares the
LORD,
"you will call me 'my
husband';
you will no longer call me
'my master.[f]'
17I will remove the names of the
Baals from her lips;

[d]15 *Achor* means *trouble.* [e]15 Or *respond*
[f]16 Hebrew *baal*

**Heading* See the note on page 482.

†17 Most mss have no *hireq* under the *shureq* (וּכ׳).

יִזָּכְרוּ עוֹד בִּשְׁמָם׃ וְכָרַתִּי לָהֶם
for-them and-I-will-make (20[18]) by-name-of-them longer they-will-be-invoked

בְּרִית בַּיּוֹם הַהוּא עִם־ חַיַּת הַשָּׂדֶה וְעִם־ עוֹף הַשָּׁמַיִם
the-airs bird-of and-with the-field beast-of with the-that in-the-day covenant

וְרֶמֶשׂ הָאֲדָמָה וְקֶשֶׁת וְחֶרֶב וּמִלְחָמָה אֶשְׁבּוֹר מִן־ הָאָרֶץ
the-land from I-will-abolish and-battle and-sword and-bow the-ground and-creature-of

וְהִשְׁכַּבְתִּים לָבֶטַח׃ וְאֵרַשְׂתִּיךְ לִי לְעוֹלָם
to-forever to-me and-I-will-betroth-you (21[19]) in-safety so-I-may-make-lie-down-them

וְאֵרַשְׂתִּיךְ לִי בְּצֶדֶק וּבְמִשְׁפָּט וּבְחֶסֶד
and-in-love and-in-justice in-righteousness to-me and-I-will-betroth-you

וּבְרַחֲמִים׃ וְאֵרַשְׂתִּיךְ לִי בֶּאֱמוּנָה
in-faithfulness to-me and-I-will-betroth-you (22[20]) and-in-compassions

וְיָדַעַתְּ אֶת־ יְהוָה׃ וְהָיָה׀ בַּיּוֹם הַהוּא
the-that in-the-day and-he-will-be (23[21]) Yahweh *** and-you-will-acknowledge

אֶעֱנֶה נְאֻם־ יְהוָה אֶעֱנֶה אֶת־ הַשָּׁמָיִם וְהֵם
and-they the-skies to I-will-respond Yahweh declaration-of I-will-respond

יַעֲנוּ אֶת־ הָאָרֶץ׃ וְהָאָרֶץ תַּעֲנֶה אֶת־ הַדָּגָן
the-grain to she-will-respond and-the-earth (24[22]) the-earth to they-will-respond

וְאֶת־ הַתִּירוֹשׁ וְאֶת־ הַיִּצְהָר וְהֵם יַעֲנוּ אֶת־יִזְרְעֶאל׃
Jezreel to they-will-respond and-they the-oil and-to the-new-wine and-to

וּזְרַעְתִּיהָ לִּי בָּאָרֶץ וְרִחַמְתִּי אֶת־
to and-I-will-show-love in-the-land for-myself and-I-will-plant-her (25[23])

לֹא רֻחָמָה וְאָמַרְתִּי לְלֹא־ עַמִּי עַמִּי־ אַתָּה וְהוּא
and-he you people-of-me people-of-me to-not and-I-will-say she-is-loved not

יֹאמַר אֱלֹהָי׃ וַיֹּאמֶר יְהוָה אֵלַי עוֹד לֵךְ אֱהַב־ אִשָּׁה
wife show-love! go! again to-me Yahweh and-he-said (3:1) God-of-me he-will-say

אֲהֻבַת רֵעַ וּמְנָאָפֶת כְּאַהֲבַת יְהוָה אֶת־ בְּנֵי
sons-of *** Yahweh as-to-love and-one-being-adulteress another one-being-loved-of

יִשְׂרָאֵל וְהֵם פֹּנִים אֶל־אֱלֹהִים אֲחֵרִים וְאֹהֲבֵי אֲשִׁישֵׁי
raisin-cakes-of and-ones-loving-of other-ones gods to ones-turning though-they Israel

עֲנָבִים׃ וָאֶכְּרֶהָ לִּי בַּחֲמִשָּׁה עָשָׂר כָּסֶף וְחֹמֶר שְׂעֹרִים
barleys and-homer-of silver ten for-five for-me so-I-bought-her (2) raisins

וְלֶתֶךְ שְׂעֹרִים׃ וָאֹמַר אֵלֶיהָ יָמִים רַבִּים תֵּשְׁבִי לִי
with-me you-must-live many-ones days to-her then-I-told (3) barleys and-lethek-of

לֹא תִזְנִי וְלֹא תִהְיִי לְאִישׁ וְגַם־ אֲנִי אֵלָיִךְ׃
with-you I and-also with-man you-must-be and-not you-must-be-prostitute not

כִּי׀ יָמִים רַבִּים יֵשְׁבוּ בְּנֵי יִשְׂרָאֵל אֵין מֶלֶךְ וְאֵין שָׂר
prince or-without king without Israel sons-of they-will-live many-ones days for (4)

no longer will their names
be invoked.
18 In that day I will make a
covenant for them
with the beasts of the field
and the birds of the air
and the creatures that move
along the ground.
Bow and sword and battle
I will abolish from the land,
so that all may lie down in
safety.
19 I will betroth you to me
forever;
I will betroth you in[g]
righteousness and justice,
in[h] love and compassion.
20 I will betroth you in
faithfulness,
and you will acknowledge
the LORD.

21 "In that day I will respond,"
declares the LORD—
"I will respond to the skies,
and they will respond to the
earth;
22 and the earth will respond to
the grain,
the new wine and oil,
and they will respond to
Jezreel.[i]
23 I will plant her for myself in
the land;
I will show my love to the
one I called 'Not my
loved one.[j]'
I will say to those called 'Not
my people,[k]' 'You are my
people';
and they will say, 'You are
my God.'"

*Hosea's Reconciliation With His Wife*

3 The LORD said to me, "Go, show your love to your wife again, though she is loved by another and is an adulteress. Love her as the LORD loves the Israelites, though they turn to other gods and love the sacred raisin cakes."
2 So I bought her for fifteen shekels[l] of silver and about a homer and a lethek[m] of barley.
3 Then I told her, "You are to live with[n] me many days; you must not be a prostitute or be intimate with any man, and I will live with[n] you."
4 For the Israelites will live many days without king or prince, without sacrifice or sacred stones,

[g] 19 Or *with*; also in verse 20
[h] 19 Or *with*
[i] 22 *Jezreel* means *God plants.*
[j] 23 Hebrew *Lo-Ruhamah*
[k] 23 Hebrew *Lo-Ammi*
[l] 2 That is, about 6 ounces (about 170 grams)
[m] 2 That is, probably about 10 bushels (about 330 liters)
[n] 3 Or *wait for*

**Heading* See the note on page 482.

וְאֵין זֶבַח וְאֵין מַצֵּבָה וְאֵין אֵפוֹד וּתְרָפִים׃ אַחַר
afterward (5) or-idols ephod or-without sacred-stone or-without sacrifice or-without

יָשֻׁבוּ בְּנֵי יִשְׂרָאֵל וּבִקְשׁוּ אֶת־ יְהוָה אֱלֹהֵיהֶם וְאֵת
and God-of-them Yahweh *** and-they-will-seek Israel sons-of they-will-return

דָּוִד מַלְכָּם וּפָחֲדוּ אֶל־ יְהוָה וְאֶל־ טוּבוֹ
blessing-of-him and-to Yahweh to and-they-will-come-trembling king-of-them David

בְּאַחֲרִית הַיָּמִים׃ שִׁמְעוּ דְבַר־ יְהוָה בְּנֵי יִשְׂרָאֵל כִּי רִיב
charge because Israel sons-of Yahweh word-of hear! (4:1) the-days in-last-one-of

לַיהוָה עִם־ יוֹשְׁבֵי הָאָרֶץ כִּי אֵין־ אֱמֶת
faithfulness there-is-no indeed the-land ones-living-of against to-Yahweh

וְאֵין־ חֶסֶד וְאֵין־ דַּעַת אֱלֹהִים בָּאָרֶץ׃ אָלֹה
to-curse (2) in-the-land God acknowledgement-of and-there-is-no love and-there-is-no

וְכַחֵשׁ וְרָצֹחַ וְגָנֹב וְנָאֹף פָּרָצוּ
they-break-bounds and-to-commit-adultery and-to-steal and-to-murder and-to-lie

וְדָמִים בְּדָמִים נָגָעוּ׃ עַל־ כֵּן תֶּאֱבַל הָאָרֶץ
the-land she-mourns this because-of (3) they-follow to-bloodsheds and-bloodsheds

וְאֻמְלַל כָּל־ יוֹשֵׁב בָּהּ בְּחַיַּת הַשָּׂדֶה וּבְעוֹף
and-even-bird-of the-field even-beast-of in-her one-living all-of and-he-wastes-away

הַשָּׁמַיִם וְגַם־ דְּגֵי הַיָּם יֵאָסֵפוּ׃ אַךְ אִישׁ אַל־ יָרֵב
let-him-bring-charge not man but (4) they-die the-sea fishes-of and-also the-airs

וְאַל־ יוֹכַח אִישׁ וְעַמְּךָ כִּמְרִיבֵי כֹהֵן׃
priest like-ones-bringing-charges-of for-people-of-you man let-him-accuse and-not

וְכָשַׁלְתָּ הַיּוֹם וְכָשַׁל גַּם־ נָבִיא עִמְּךָ לָיְלָה
night with-you prophet also and-he-stumbles the-day indeed-you-stumble (5)

וְדָמִיתִי אִמֶּךָ׃ נִדְמוּ עַמִּי מִבְּלִי
from-lack-of people-of-me they-are-destroyed (6) mother-of-you so-I-will-destroy

הַדָּעַת כִּי־ אַתָּה הַדַּעַת מָאַסְתָּ וְאֶמְאָסְאךָ מִכַּהֵן
from-to-be-priest so-I-reject-you you-rejected the-knowledge you because the-knowledge

לִי וַתִּשְׁכַּח תּוֹרַת אֱלֹהֶיךָ אֶשְׁכַּח בָּנֶיךָ גַּם־אָנִי׃
I also children-of-you I-will-ignore God-of-you law-of because-you-ignored to-me

כְּרֻבָּם כֵּן חָטְאוּ־ לִי כְּבוֹדָם בְּקָלוֹן
for-disgraceful-thing Glory-of-them against-me they-sinned so as-to-increase-them (7)

אָמִיר׃ חַטַּאת עַמִּי יֹאכֵלוּ וְאֶל־ עֲוֺנָם
wickedness-of-them and-on they-feed-on people-of-me sin-of (8) I-will-exchange

יִשְׂאוּ נַפְשׁוֹ׃ וְהָיָה כָעָם כַּכֹּהֵן
like-the-priest like-the-people and-he-will-be (9) self-of-him they-relish

וּפָקַדְתִּי עָלָיו דְּרָכָיו וּמַעֲלָלָיו אָשִׁיב לוֹ׃
to-him I-will-repay and-deeds-of-him ways-of-him to-him and-I-will-punish

without ephod or idol. 5Afterward the Israelites will return and seek the LORD their God and David their king. They will come trembling to the LORD and to his blessings in the last days.

*The Charge Against Israel*

4 Hear the word of the LORD,
you Israelites,
because the LORD has a
charge to bring
against you who live in the
land:
"There is no faithfulness, no
love,
no acknowledgment of God
in the land.
2There is only cursing,[o] lying
and murder,
stealing and adultery;
they break all bounds,
and bloodshed follows
bloodshed.
3Because of this the land
mourns,[p]
and all who live in it waste
away;
the beasts of the field and the
birds of the air
and the fish of the sea are
dying.
4"But let no man bring a
charge,
let no man accuse another,
for your people are like those
who bring charges against a
priest.
5You stumble day and night,
and the prophets stumble
with you.
So I will destroy your mother—
6 my people are destroyed
from lack of knowledge.

"Because you have rejected
knowledge,
I also reject you as my
priests;
because you have ignored the
law of your God,
I also will ignore your
children.
7The more the priests increased,
the more they sinned
against me;
they exchanged[q] their[r] Glory
for something disgraceful.
8They feed on the sins of my
people
and relish their wickedness.
9And it will be: Like people,
like priests.
I will punish both of them
for their ways
and repay them for their
deeds.

o2 That is, to pronounce a curse upon
p3 Or *dries up*
q7 Syriac and an ancient Hebrew scribal tradition; Masoretic Text *I will exchange*
r7 Masoretic Text; an ancient Hebrew scribal tradition *my*

וְאָכְלוּ וְלֹא יִשְׂבָּעוּ הִזְנוּ
they-will-engage-in-prostitution they-will-have-enough but-not and-they-will-eat (10)

וְלֹא יִפְרֹצוּ כִּי־ אֶת־ יְהוָה עָזְבוּ לִשְׁמֹר׃
to-give-to they-deserted Yahweh *** because they-will-increase but-not

זְנוּת וְיַיִן וְתִירוֹשׁ יִקַּח־ לֵב׃
understanding he-takes-away and-new-wine and-old-wine prostitution (11)

עַמִּי בְּעֵצוֹ יִשְׁאָל וּמַקְלוֹ
and-stick-of-wood-of-him he-consults to-wooden-idol-of-him people-of-me (12)

יַגִּיד לוֹ כִּי רוּחַ זְנוּנִים הִתְעָה
he-leads-astray prostitutions spirit-of indeed to-him he-answers

וַיִּזְנוּ מִתַּחַת אֱלֹהֵיהֶם׃ עַל־ רָאשֵׁי הֶהָרִים
the-mountains tops-of on (13) God-of-them from-after and-they-are-unfaithful

יְזַבֵּחוּ וְעַל־ הַגְּבָעוֹת יְקַטֵּרוּ תַּחַת אַלּוֹן וְלִבְנֶה וְאֵלָה
and-terebinth and-poplar oak under they-burn-offerings the-hills and-on they-sacrifice

כִּי טוֹב צִלָּהּ עַל־ כֵּן תִּזְנֶינָה בְּנוֹתֵיכֶם
daughters-of-you they-turn-to-prostitution this for shade-of-her pleasant for

וְכַלּוֹתֵיכֶם תְּנָאַפְנָה׃ לֹא־ אֶפְקוֹד עַל־
to I-will-punish not (14) they-turn-to-adultery and-daughters-in-law-of-you

בְּנוֹתֵיכֶם כִּי תִזְנֶינָה וְעַל־ כַּלּוֹתֵיכֶם
daughters-in-law-of-you or-to they-turn-to-prostitution when daughters-of-you

כִּי תְנָאַפְנָה כִּי־ הֵם עִם־ הַזֹּנוֹת יְפָרֵדוּ
they-consort the-ones-being-harlots with they because they-commit-adultery when

וְעִם־ הַקְּדֵשׁוֹת יְזַבֵּחוּ וְעָם לֹא־ יָבִין
he-understands not indeed-people they-sacrifice the-shrine-prostitutes and-with

יִלָּבֵט׃ אִם־ זֹנֶה אַתָּה יִשְׂרָאֵל אַל־
not Israel you committing-adultery though (15) he-will-come-to-ruin

יֶאְשַׁם יְהוּדָה וְאַל־ תָּבֹאוּ הַגִּלְגָּל וְאַל־ תַּעֲלוּ בֵּית אָוֶן
Aven Beth you-go-up and-not the-Gilgal you-go and-not Judah let-him-become-guilty

וְאַל־ תִּשָּׁבְעוּ חַי־ יְהוָה׃ כִּי כְּפָרָה סֹרֵרָה
being-stubborn like-heifer indeed (16) Yahweh alive you-swear and-not

סֹרֵר יִשְׂרָאֵל עַתָּה יִרְעֵם יְהוָה כְּכֶבֶשׂ בַּמֶּרְחָב׃
in-the-meadow like-lamb Yahweh can-he-pasture-them then Israel he-is-stubborn

חֲבוּר עֲצַבִּים אֶפְרָיִם הַנַּח־ לוֹ׃ סָר
he-is-gone (18) to-him leave-alone! Ephraim idols one-being-joined-of (17)

סָבְאָם הַזְנֵה הִזְנוּ אָהֲבוּ הֵבוּ
love! they-love they-commit-prostitution to-commit-prostitution drink-of-them

קָלוֹן מָגִנֶּיהָ׃ צָרַר רוּחַ אוֹתָהּ בִּכְנָפֶיהָ
with-wings-of-her her whirlwind he-will-sweep-away (19) rulers-of-her shameful-way

10 "They will eat but not have
enough;
they will engage in
prostitution but not
increase,
because they have deserted the
LORD
to give themselves
11 to
prostitution,
to old wine and new,
which take away the
understanding
12 of my
people.
They consult a wooden idol
and are answered by a stick
of wood.
A spirit of prostitution leads
them astray;
they are unfaithful to their
God.
13 They sacrifice on the
mountaintops
and burn offerings on the
hills,
under oak, poplar and
terebinth,
where the shade is pleasant.
Therefore your daughters turn
to prostitution
and your daughters-in-law
to adultery.
14 "I will not punish your
daughters
when they turn to
prostitution,
nor your daughters-in-law
when they commit adultery,
because the men themselves
consort with harlots
and sacrifice with shrine
prostitutes—
a people without
understanding will come
to ruin!
15 "Though you commit adultery,
O Israel,
let not Judah become guilty.
"Do not go to Gilgal;
do not go up to Beth Aven.[s]
And do not swear, 'As
surely as the LORD lives!'
16 The Israelites are stubborn,
like a stubborn heifer.
How then can the LORD
pasture them
like lambs in a meadow?
17 Ephraim is joined to idols;
leave him alone!
18 Even when their drinks are
gone,
they continue their
prostitution;
their rulers dearly love
shameful ways.
19 A whirlwind will sweep them
away,

[s] 15 *Beth Aven* means *house of wickedness* (a name for Bethel, which means *house of God*)

וְיֵבֹשׁוּ מִזִּבְחוֹתָם ׃ שִׁמְעוּ־ זֹאת הַכֹּהֲנִים

the-priests this hear! (5:1) altars-of-them and-they-will-bring-shame

וְהַקְשִׁיבוּ ׀ בֵּית יִשְׂרָאֵל וּבֵית הַמֶּלֶךְ הַאֲזִינוּ כִּי לָכֶם

against-you indeed listen! the-royalty and-house-of Israel house-of and-pay-attention!

הַמִּשְׁפָּט כִּי־ פַח הֱיִיתֶם לְמִצְפָּה וְרֶשֶׁת פְּרוּשָׂה עַל־ תָּבוֹר׃

Tabor on being-spread-out and-net at-Mizpah you-were snare indeed the-judgment

וְשַׁחֲטָה שֵׂטִים הֶעְמִיקוּ וַאֲנִי מוּסָר לְכֻלָּם ׃ אֲנִי יָדַעְתִּי

I-know I (3) to-all-of-them discipline and-I they-are-deep rebels and-slaughter (2)

אֶפְרַיִם וְיִשְׂרָאֵל לֹא־ נִכְחַד מִמֶּנִּי כִּי עַתָּה הִזְנֵיתָ

you-turned-to-prostitution now indeed from-me he-is-hidden not and-Israel Ephraim

אֶפְרַיִם נִטְמָא יִשְׂרָאֵל׃ לֹא יִתְּנוּ מַעַלְלֵיהֶם לָשׁוּב אֶל־

to to-return deeds-of-them they-permit not (4) Israel he-is-corrupt Ephraim

אֱלֹהֵיהֶם כִּי רוּחַ זְנוּנִים בְּקִרְבָּם וְאֶת־ יְהוָה לֹא

not Yahweh and in-heart-of-them prostitutions spirit-of indeed God-of-them

יָדָעוּ׃ וְעָנָה גְאוֹן־ יִשְׂרָאֵל בְּפָנָיו

against-faces-of-him Israel arrogance-of and-he-testifies (5) they-acknowledge

וְיִשְׂרָאֵל וְאֶפְרַיִם יִכָּשְׁלוּ בַּעֲוֺנָם כָּשַׁל גַּם־יְהוּדָה עִמָּם ׃

with-them Judah also he-stumbles in-sin-of-them they-stumble even-Ephraim and-Israel

בְּצֹאנָם וּבִבְקָרָם יֵלְכוּ לְבַקֵּשׁ אֶת־ יְהוָה וְלֹא

but-not Yahweh *** to-seek they-go and-with-herd-of-them with-flock-of-them (6)

יִמְצָאוּ חָלַץ מֵהֶם׃ בַּיהוָה בָּגָדוּ כִּי־ בָנִים

children indeed they-are-unfaithful to-Yahweh (7) from-them he-withdrew they-will-find

זָרִים יָלָדוּ עַתָּה יֹאכְלֵם חֹדֶשׁ

New-Moon-festival he-will-devour-them now they-give-birth ones-being-illegitimate

אֶת ־ חֶלְקֵיהֶם׃ תִּקְעוּ שׁוֹפָר בַּגִּבְעָה חֲצֹצְרָה בָּרָמָה

in-the-Ramah horn in-the-Gibeah trumpet sound! (8) fields-of-them with

הָרִיעוּ בֵּית אָוֶן אַחֲרֶיךָ בִּנְיָמִין׃ אֶפְרַיִם לְשַׁמָּה תִהְיֶה

she-will-be to-waste Ephraim (9) Benjamin after-you Aven Beth raise-battle-cry!

בְּיוֹם תּוֹכֵחָה בְּשִׁבְטֵי יִשְׂרָאֵל הוֹדַעְתִּי נֶאֱמָנָה׃ הָיוּ

they-are (10) one-being-certain I-proclaim Israel among-tribes-of reckoning on-day-of

שָׂרֵי יְהוּדָה כְּמַסִּיגֵי גְּבוּל עֲלֵיהֶם אֶשְׁפּוֹךְ

I-will-pour-out on-them boundary-stone like-ones-moving-of Judah leaders-of

כַּמַּיִם עֶבְרָתִי׃ עָשׁוּק אֶפְרַיִם רְצוּץ מִשְׁפָּט

judgment being-trampled-of Ephraim being-oppressed (11) wrath-of-me like-the-waters

כִּי הוֹאִיל הָלַךְ אַחֲרֵי־ צָו ׃ וַאֲנִי כָעָשׁ לְאֶפְרָיִם

to-Ephraim like-the-moth and-I (12) idol after he-pursues he-is-intent indeed

וְכָרָקָב לְבֵית יְהוּדָה׃ וַיַּרְא אֶפְרַיִם אֶת־ חָלְיוֹ

sickness-of-him *** Ephraim when-he-saw (13) Judah to-house-of and-like-the-rot

and their sacrifices will
bring them shame.

*Judgment Against Israel*

5 "Hear this, you priests!
Pay attention, you Israelites!
Listen, O royal house!
This judgment is against
you:
You have been a snare at
Mizpah,
a net spread out on Tabor.
2 The rebels are deep in
slaughter.
I will discipline all of them.
3 I know all about Ephraim;
Israel is not hidden from
me.
Ephraim, you have now
turned to prostitution;
Israel is corrupt.
4 "Their deeds do not permit
them
to return to their God.
A spirit of prostitution is in
their heart;
they do not acknowledge the
LORD.
5 Israel's arrogance testifies
against them;
the Israelites, even Ephraim,
stumble in their sin;
Judah also stumbles with
them.
6 When they go with their flocks
and herds
to seek the LORD,
they will not find him;
he has withdrawn himself
from them.
7 They are unfaithful to the
LORD;
they give birth to
illegitimate children.
Now their New Moon festivals
will devour them and their
fields.
8 "Sound the trumpet in Gibeah,
the horn in Ramah.
Raise the battle cry in Beth
Aven[t];
lead on, O Benjamin.
9 Ephraim will be laid waste
on the day of reckoning.
Among the tribes of Israel
I proclaim what is certain.
10 Judah's leaders are like those
who move boundary stones.
I will pour out my wrath on
them
like a flood of water.
11 Ephraim is oppressed,
trampled in judgment,
intent on pursuing idols.[u]
12 I am like a moth to Ephraim,
like rot to the people of
Judah.
13 "When Ephraim saw his
sickness,

[t]8 *Beth Aven* means *house of wickedness* (a name for Bethel, which means *house of God*).
[u]11 The meaning of the Hebrew for this word is uncertain.

וִיהוּדָה אֶת־ מְזֹרוֹ וַיֵּלֶךְ אֶפְרַיִם אֶל־ אַשּׁוּר וַיִּשְׁלַח אֶל־ מֶלֶךְ
king to and-he-sent Assyria to Ephraim then-he-turned sore-of-him *** and-Judah

יָרֵב וְהוּא לֹא יוּכַל לִרְפֹּא לָכֶם וְלֹא־ יִגְהֶה מִכֶּם מָזוֹר׃
sore of-you he-can-heal and-not to-you to-cure he-is-able not but-he great

כִּי אָנֹכִי כַשַּׁחַל לְאֶפְרַיִם וְכַכְּפִיר לְבֵית יְהוּדָה
Judah to-house-of and-like-the-great-lion to-Ephraim like-the-lion I for (14)

אֲנִי אֲנִי אֶטְרֹף וְאֵלֵךְ אֶשָּׂא וְאֵין
and-there-will-be-no I-will-carry-off and-I-will-go-away I-will-tear-to-pieces I I

מַצִּיל׃ אֵלֵךְ אָשׁוּבָה אֶל־ מְקוֹמִי עַד אֲשֶׁר־ יֶאְשְׁמוּ
they-admit-guilt when until place-of-me to I-will-go-back I-will-go (15) one-rescuing

וּבִקְשׁוּ פָנָי בַּצַּר לָהֶם יְשַׁחֲרֻנְנִי׃
they-will-earnestly-seek-me of-them in-the-misery faces-of-me and-they-will-seek

לְכוּ וְנָשׁוּבָה אֶל־ יְהוָה כִּי הוּא טָרָף וְיִרְפָּאֵנוּ
but-he-will-heal-us he-tore-to-pieces he for Yahweh to and-let-us-return come! (6:1)

יַךְ וְיַחְבְּשֵׁנוּ׃ יְחַיֵּנוּ מִיֹּמָיִם
after-two-days he-will-revive-us (2) but-he-will-bind-wounds-of-us he-injured

בַּיּוֹם הַשְּׁלִישִׁי יְקִמֵנוּ וְנִחְיֶה לְפָנָיו׃
in-presences-of-him that-we-may-live he-will-retore-us the-third on-the-day

וְנֵדְעָה נִרְדְּפָה לָדַעַת אֶת־ יְהוָה כְּשַׁחַר
as-sunrise Yahweh *** to-acknowledge let-us-press-on so-let-us-acknowledge (3)

נָכוֹן מוֹצָאוֹ וְיָבוֹא כַגֶּשֶׁם לָנוּ
to-us like-the-winter-rain and-he-will-come coming-of-him he-will-appear

כְּמַלְקוֹשׁ יוֹרֶה אָרֶץ׃ מָה אֶעֱשֶׂה־ לְּךָ אֶפְרַיִם מָה
what? Ephraim with-you can-I-do what? (4) earth he-waters like-spring-rain

אֶעֱשֶׂה־ לְּךָ יְהוּדָה וְחַסְדְּכֶם כַּעֲנַן־ בֹּקֶר וְכַטַּל
and-like-the-dew morning like-mist-of indeed-love-of-you Judah with-you can-I-do

מַשְׁכִּים הֹלֵךְ׃ עַל־ כֵּן חָצַבְתִּי בַּנְּבִיאִים
with-the-prophets I-cut-to-pieces this for (5) one-disappearing one-being-early

הֲרַגְתִּים בְּאִמְרֵי־ פִי וּמִשְׁפָּטֶיךָ אוֹר
lightning and-judgments-of-you mouth-of-me with-words-of I-killed-them

יֵצֵא׃ כִּי חֶסֶד חָפַצְתִּי וְלֹא־ זָבַח וְדַעַת אֱלֹהִים
God and-acknowledgment-of sacrifice and-not I-desire mercy for (6) he-flashed

מֵעֹלוֹת׃ וְהֵמָּה כְּאָדָם עָבְרוּ בְרִית שָׁם
there covenant they-broke like-Adam but-they (7) rather-than-burnt-offerings

בָּגְדוּ בִי׃ גִּלְעָד קִרְיַת פֹּעֲלֵי אָוֶן
wickedness men-doing-of city-of Gilead (8) to-me they-were-unfaithful

עֲקֻבָּה מִדָּם׃ וּכְחַכֵּי אִישׁ גְּדוּדִים
marauders man and-as-ones-lying-in-ambush-of (9) of-blood stained-with-footprint

and Judah his sores,
then Ephraim turned to
Assyria,
and sent to the great king
for help.
But he is not able to cure you,
not able to heal your sores.
14For I will be like a lion to
Ephraim,
like a great lion to Judah.
I will tear them to pieces and
go away;
I will carry them off, with
no one to rescue them.
15Then I will go back to my
place
until they admit their guilt.
And they will seek my face;
in their misery they will
earnestly seek me."

*Israel Unrepentant*

6 "Come, let us return to the
LORD.
He has torn us to pieces
but he will heal us;
he has injured us
but he will bind up our
wounds.
2After two days he will revive
us;
on the third day he will
restore us,
that we may live in his
presence.
3Let us acknowledge the LORD;
let us press on to
acknowledge him.
As surely as the sun rises,
he will appear;
he will come to us like the
winter rains,
like the spring rains that
water the earth."
4"What can I do with you,
Ephraim?
What can I do with you,
Judah?
Your love is like the morning
mist,
like the early dew that
disappears.
5Therefore I cut you in pieces
with my prophets,
I killed you with the words
of my mouth;
my judgments flashed like
lightning upon you.
6For I desire mercy, not
sacrifice,
and acknowledgment of God
rather than burnt
offerings.
7Like Adam,[v] they have broken
the covenant—
they were unfaithful to me
there.
8Gilead is a city of wicked men,
stained with footprints of
blood.
9As marauders lie in ambush
for a man,

[v]7 Or *As at Adam;* or *Like men*

חֶבֶר כֹּהֲנִים דֶּרֶךְ יְרַצְּחוּ־ שֶׁכְמָה כִּי זִמָּה עָשׂוּ׃
they-commit shameful-crime indeed to-Shechem they-murder road priests band-of

(10) בְּבֵית יִשְׂרָאֵל רָאִיתִי שַׁעֲרִירִיָּה° שָׁם זְנוּת לְאֶפְרַיִם
to-Ephraim prostitution there horrible-thing I-saw Israel in-house-of (10)

נִטְמָא יִשְׂרָאֵל׃ (11) גַּם־יְהוּדָה שָׁת קָצִיר לָךְ בְּשׁוּבִי
when-to-restore-me for-you harvest he-appointed Judah also (11) Israel he-is-defiled

שְׁבוּת עַמִּי׃ (7:1) כְּרָפְאִי לְיִשְׂרָאֵל וְנִגְלָה עֲוֹן
sin-of then-he-is-exposed to-Israel when-to-heal-me (7:1) people-of-me fortune-of

אֶפְרַיִם וְרָעוֹת שֹׁמְרוֹן כִּי פָעֲלוּ שָׁקֶר וְגַנָּב יָבוֹא
he-breaks-in and-thief deceit they-practice indeed Samaria and-crimes-of Ephraim

פָּשַׁט גְּדוּד בַּחוּץ׃ (2) וּבַל־ יֹאמְרוּ לִלְבָבָם כָּל־
all-of in-heart-of-them they-realize but-not (2) in-the-street bandit he-robs

רָעָתָם זָכָרְתִּי עַתָּה סְבָבוּם מַעַלְלֵיהֶם נֶגֶד פָּנַי הָיוּ׃
they-are faces-of-me before sins-of-them they-engulf-them now I-remember evil-of-them

(3) בְּרָעָתָם יְשַׂמְּחוּ־ מֶלֶךְ וּבְכַחֲשֵׁיהֶם שָׂרִים׃
princes and-with-lies-of-them king they-delight with-wickedness-of-them (3)

(4) כֻּלָּם מְנָאֲפִים כְּמוֹ תַנּוּר בֹּעֵרָה מֵאֹפֶה יִשְׁבּוֹת
he-stops from-one-baking burning oven like ones-committing-adultery all-of-them (4)

מֵעִיר מִלּוּשׁ בָּצֵק עַד־ חֻמְצָתוֹ׃ (5) יוֹם מַלְכֵּנוּ
king-of-us day-of (5) to-rise-him till dough from-to-knead from-to-stir

הֶחֱלוּ שָׂרִים חֲמַת מִיָּיִן מָשַׁךְ יָדוֹ אֶת־ לֹצְצִים׃
ones-mocking with hand-of-him he-joins from-wine heat-of princes they-become-inflamed

(6) כִּי־ קֵרְבוּ כַתַּנּוּר לִבָּם בְּאָרְבָּם כָּל־
all-of with-intrigue-of-them heart-of-them like-the-oven they-approach indeed (6)

הַלַּיְלָה יָשֵׁן אֹפֵהֶם* בֹּקֶר הוּא בֹעֵר כְּאֵשׁ לֶהָבָה׃
flame like-fire-of blazing he morning *one-baking-of-them smoldering the-night

(7) כֻּלָּם יֵחַמּוּ כַּתַּנּוּר וְאָכְלוּ אֶת־ שֹׁפְטֵיהֶם
ones-ruling-them *** and-they-devour as-the-oven they-are-hot all-of-them (7)

כָּל־ מַלְכֵיהֶם נָפָלוּ אֵין־ קֹרֵא בָהֶם אֵלָי׃ (8) אֶפְרַיִם
Ephraim (8) on-me of-them one-calling there-is-no they-fall kings-of-them all-of

בָּעַמִּים הוּא יִתְבּוֹלָל אֶפְרַיִם הָיָה עֻגָה בְּלִי הֲפוּכָה׃
being-turned-over not flat-cake he-is Ephraim he-mixes he with-the-nations

(9) אָכְלוּ זָרִים כֹּחוֹ וְהוּא לֹא יָדָע גַּם־ שֵׂיבָה
gray-hair and he-realizes not but-he strength-of-him ones-being-foreign they-sap (9)

זָרְקָה בּוֹ וְהוּא לֹא יָדָע׃ (10) וְעָנָה גְאוֹן־
arrogance-of and-he-testifies (10) he-notices not but-he on-him she-is-sprinkled

יִשְׂרָאֵל בְּפָנָיו וְלֹא־ שָׁבוּ אֶל־ יְהוָה אֱלֹהֵיהֶם וְלֹא
or-not God-of-them Yahweh to they-return but-not against-faces-of-him Israel

so do bands of priests;
they murder on the road to Shechem,
committing shameful crimes.
10 I have seen a horrible thing
in the house of Israel.
There Ephraim is given to prostitution
and Israel is defiled.
11 "Also for you, Judah,
a harvest is appointed.
"Whenever I would restore
the fortunes of my people,
7 whenever I would heal Israel,
the sins of Ephraim are exposed
and the crimes of Samaria revealed.
They practice deceit,
thieves break into houses,
bandits rob in the streets;
2 but they do not realize
that I remember all their evil deeds.
Their sins engulf them;
they are always before me.
3 "They delight the king with their wickedness,
the princes with their lies.
4 They are all adulterers,
burning like an oven
whose fire the baker need not stir
from the kneading of the dough till it rises.
5 On the day of the festival of our king
the princes become inflamed with wine,
and he joins hands with the mockers.
6 Their hearts are like an oven;
they approach him with intrigue.
Their passion smolders all night;
in the morning it blazes like a flaming fire.
7 All of them are hot as an oven;
they devour their rulers.
All their kings fall,
and none of them calls on me.
8 "Ephraim mixes with the nations;
Ephraim is a flat cake not turned over.
9 Foreigners sap his strength,
but he does not realize it.
His hair is sprinkled with gray,
but he does not notice.
10 Israel's arrogance testifies against him,
but despite all this
he does not return to the LORD his God

*6 The NIV, with some ancient versions, repoints this word as אַפְּהֶם, *passion (anger)-of-them.*

°10 ק שערוריה

בִקְשֻׁהוּ בְּכָל־ זֹאת׃ וַיְהִי אֶפְרַיִם כְּיוֹנָה
like-dove Ephraim and-he-is (11) this despite-all-of they-search-for-him

פוֹתָה אֵין לֵב מִצְרַיִם קָרָאוּ אַשּׁוּר הָלָכוּ׃
they-turn-to Assyria they-call-to Egypt sense without being-easily-deceived

כַּאֲשֶׁר יֵלֵכוּ אֶפְרוֹשׂ עֲלֵיהֶם רִשְׁתִּי כְּעוֹף הַשָּׁמַיִם
the-airs like-bird-of net-of-me over-them I-will-throw they-go as-when (12)

אוֹרִידֵם אַיְסִרֵם כְּשֵׁמַע לַעֲדָתָם׃
of-flocking-together-of-them at-hearing I-will-catch-them I-will-pull-down-them

אוֹי לָהֶם כִּי־ נָדְדוּ מִמֶּנִּי שֹׁד לָהֶם כִּי־
because to-them destruction from-me they-strayed because to-them woe! (13)

פָּשְׁעוּ בִי וְאָנֹכִי אֶפְדֵּם וְהֵמָּה דִּבְּרוּ עָלַי כְּזָבִים׃
lies against-me they-speak but-they I-would-redeem-them and-I against-me they-rebelled

וְלֹא־ זָעֲקוּ אֵלַי בְּלִבָּם כִּי יְיֵלִילוּ עַל־ מִשְׁכְּבוֹתָם
beds-of-them on they-wail but from-heart-of-them to-me they-cry-out and-not (14)

עַל־ דָּגָן וְתִירוֹשׁ יִתְגּוֹרָרוּ יָסוּרוּ בִי׃ וַאֲנִי
and-I (15) from-me they-turn-away they-gather-together and-new-wine grain for

יִסַּרְתִּי חִזַּקְתִּי זְרוֹעֹתָם וְאֵלַי יְחַשְּׁבוּ־ רָע׃ יָשׁוּבוּ
they-turn (16) evil they-plot but-against-me arms-of-them I-strengthened I-trained

לֹא עָל הָיוּ כְּקֶשֶׁת רְמִיָּה יִפְּלוּ בַחֶרֶב
by-the-sword they-will-fall faultiness like-bow-of they-are Most-High not

שָׂרֵיהֶם מִזַּעַם לְשׁוֹנָם זוֹ לַעְגָּם בְּאֶרֶץ
in-land-of ridicule-of-them this tongue-of-them because-of-insolence-of leaders-of-them

מִצְרָיִם׃ אֶל־ חִכְּךָ שֹׁפָר כַּנֶּשֶׁר עַל־ בֵּית יְהוָה יַעַן
because Yahweh house-of over like-the-eagle trumpet lip-of-you to (8:1) Egypt

עָבְרוּ בְרִיתִי וְעַל־ תּוֹרָתִי פָּשָׁעוּ׃ לִי יִזְעָקוּ
they-cry-out to-me (2) they-rebelled law-of-me and-against covenant-of-me they-broke

אֱלֹהַי יְדַעֲנוּךָ יִשְׂרָאֵל׃ זָנַח יִשְׂרָאֵל טוֹב אוֹיֵב
one-being-enemy good Israel he-rejected (3) Israel we-acknowledge-you God-of-me

יִרְדְּפוֹ*׃ הֵם הִמְלִיכוּ† וְלֹא מִמֶּנִּי הֵשִׂירוּ
they-choose-princes from-me but-not they-set-up-kings they (4) he-will-pursue-him

וְלֹא יָדָעְתִּי כַּסְפָּם וּזְהָבָם עָשׂוּ לָהֶם עֲצַבִּים לְמַעַן
so-that idols for-them they-make and-gold-of-them silver-of-them I-approve but-not

יִכָּרֵת׃ זָנַח עֶגְלֵךְ שֹׁמְרוֹן חָרָה אַפִּי
anger-of-me he-burns Samaria calf-idol let-him-throw-out (5) he-might-be-destroyed

בָּם עַד־ מָתַי לֹא יוּכְלוּ נִקָּיֹן׃ כִּי מִיִּשְׂרָאֵל
from-Israel indeed (6) purity they-will-be-capable not when? until against-them

וְהוּא חָרָשׁ עָשָׂהוּ וְלֹא אֱלֹהִים הוּא כִּי־ שְׁבָבִים יִהְיֶה עֵגֶל
calf-idol-of he-will-be pieces indeed he God and-not he-made-him craftsman and-he

or search for him.
11 "Ephraim is like a dove,
easily deceived and senseless—
now calling to Egypt,
now turning to Assyria.
12 When they go, I will throw my net over them;
I will pull them down like birds of the air.
When I hear them flocking together,
I will catch them.
13 Woe to them,
because they have strayed from me!
Destruction to them,
because they have rebelled against me!
I long to redeem them
but they speak lies against me.
14 They do not cry out to me from their hearts
but wail upon their beds.
They gather together[w] for grain and new wine
but turn away from me.
15 I trained them and strengthened them,
but they plot evil against me.
16 They do not turn to the Most High;
they are like a faulty bow.
Their leaders will fall by the sword
because of their insolent words.
For this they will be ridiculed
in the land of Egypt.

### *Israel to Reap the Whirlwind*

8 "Put the trumpet to your lips!
An eagle is over the house of the LORD
because the people have broken my covenant
and rebelled against my law.
2 Israel cries out to me,
'O our God, we acknowledge you!'
3 But Israel has rejected what is good;
an enemy will pursue him.
4 They set up kings without my consent;
they choose princes without my approval.
With their silver and gold
they make idols for themselves
to their own destruction.
5 Throw out your calf-idol, O Samaria!
My anger burns against them.
How long will they be incapable of purity?
6 They are from Israel!
This calf—a craftsman has made it;
it is not God.
It will be broken in pieces,
that calf of Samaria.

w14 Most Hebrew manuscripts; some Hebrew manuscripts and Septuagint *They slash themselves*

***3 Most mss have the accent on the final syllable (יִרְדְּפוֹ).**

**†4 Most mss accent the pentultimate syllable (הִמְלִיכוּ).**

שֹׁמְרוֹן׃ כִּי רוּחַ יִזְרָעוּ וְסוּפָתָה יִקְצֹרוּ קָמָה אֵין־
there-is-not stalk they-reap and-to-whirlwind they-sow wind indeed (7) Samaria

לוֹ צֶמַח בְּלִי יַעֲשֶׂה־ קֶּמַח אוּלַי יַעֲשֶׂה זָרִים
ones-being-foreign he-would-yield if flour he-will-produce not head to-him

יִבְלָעֻהוּ׃ נִבְלַע יִשְׂרָאֵל עַתָּה הָיוּ בַגּוֹיִם
among-the-nations they-are now Israel he-is-swallowed-up (8) they-would-swallow-him

כִּכְלִי אֵין־ חֵפֶץ בּוֹ׃ כִּי־הֵמָּה עָלוּ אַשּׁוּר פֶּרֶא
wild-donkey Assyria they-went-up they for (9) to-him worth there-is-no like-thing

בּוֹדֵד לוֹ אֶפְרַיִם הִתְנוּ אֲהָבִים׃ גַּם כִּי־
although but (10) lovers they-sold-themselves Ephraim for-him wandering-alone

יִתְנוּ בַגּוֹיִם עַתָּה אֲקַבְּצֵם וַיָּחֵלּוּ
and-they-will-begin I-will-gather-them now among-the-nations they-sold-themselves

מְּעָט מִמַּשָּׂא מֶלֶךְ שָׂרִים׃ כִּי־ הִרְבָּה
he-built-many though (11) mighty-ones king-of under-oppression-of wasting-away

אֶפְרַיִם מִזְבְּחֹת לַחֲטֹא הָיוּ־ לוֹ מִזְבְּחוֹת לַחֲטֹא׃ אֶכְתּוֹב־ לוֹ
for-him I-wrote (12) to-sin altars for-him they-became to-sin altars Ephraim

רֻבּוֹ תּוֹרָתִי כְּמוֹ־ זָר נֶחְשָׁבוּ׃ זִבְחֵי
sacrifices-of (13) they-were-regarded one-being-alien as law-of-me many-things-of

הַבְהָבַי יִזְבְּחוּ בָשָׂר וַיֹּאכֵלוּ יְהוָה לֹא רָצָם
he-is-pleased-with-them not Yahweh and-they-eat meat they-offer-sacrifices gifts-of-me

עַתָּה יִזְכֹּר עֲוֺנָם וְיִפְקֹד חַטֹּאותָם הֵמָּה מִצְרַיִם
Egypt they sins-of-them and-he-will-punish wickedness-of-them he-will-remember now

יָשׁוּבוּ׃ וַיִּשְׁכַּח יִשְׂרָאֵל אֶת־ עֹשֵׂהוּ וַיִּבֶן הֵיכָלוֹת
palaces and-he-built One-Making-him *** Israel and-he-forgot (14) they-will-return

וִיהוּדָה הִרְבָּה עָרִים בְּצֻרוֹת וְשִׁלַּחְתִּי־ אֵשׁ
fire but-I-will-send ones-being-fortified towns he-made-many and-Judah

בְּעָרָיו וְאָכְלָה אַרְמְנֹתֶיהָ׃ אַל־ תִּשְׂמַח יִשְׂרָאֵל
Israel you-rejoice not (9:1) fortresses-of-her and-she-will-consume upon-cities-of-him

אֶל־ גִּיל כָּעַמִּים כִּי זָנִיתָ מֵעַל אֱלֹהֶיךָ
God-of-you from-with you-were-unfaithful for like-the-nations jubilation to

אָהַבְתָּ אֶתְנָן עַל כָּל־ גָּרְנוֹת דָּגָן׃ גֹּרֶן
threshing-floor (2) grain threshing-floors-of every-of at wage-of-prostitute you-love

וָיֶקֶב לֹא יִרְעֵם וְתִירוֹשׁ יְכַחֶשׁ בָּהּ׃ לֹא
not (3) to-her he-will-fail and-new-wine he-will-feed-them not and-winepress

יֵשְׁבוּ בְּאֶרֶץ יְהוָה וְשָׁב אֶפְרַיִם מִצְרַיִם וּבְאַשּׁוּר
and-in-Assyria Egypt Ephraim and-he-will-return Yahweh in-land-of they-will-remain

טָמֵא יֹאכֵלוּ׃ לֹא־ יִסְּכוּ לַיהוָה יַיִן וְלֹא
or-not wine to-Yahweh they-will-pour-out not (4) they-will-eat unclean

°12a ק אכתב
°12b ק רבי

7 "They sow the wind
and reap the whirlwind.
The stalk has no head;
it will produce no flour.
Were it to yield grain,
foreigners would swallow it up.
8 Israel is swallowed up;
now she is among the nations
like a worthless thing.
9 For they have gone up to Assyria
like a wild donkey wandering alone.
Ephraim has sold herself to lovers.
10 Although they have sold themselves among the nations,
I will now gather them together.
They will begin to waste away
under the oppression of the mighty king.
11 "Though Ephraim built many altars for sin offerings,
these have become altars for sinning.
12 I wrote for them the many things of my law,
but they regarded them as something alien.
13 They offer sacrifices given to me
and they eat the meat,
but the LORD is not pleased with them.
Now he will remember their wickedness
and punish their sins:
They will return to Egypt.
14 Israel has forgotten his Maker
and built palaces;
Judah has fortified many towns.
But I will send fire upon their cities
that will consume their fortresses."

*Punishment for Israel*

9 Do not rejoice, O Israel;
do not be jubilant like the other nations.
For you have been unfaithful to your God;
you love the wages of a prostitute
at every threshing floor.
2 Threshing floors and winepresses will not feed the people;
the new wine will fail them.
3 They will not remain in the LORD's land;
Ephraim will return to Egypt
and eat unclean[x] food in Assyria.
4 They will not pour out wine offerings to the LORD,

x3 That is, ceremonially unclean

יֶעֶרְבוּ־ לוֹ זִבְחֵיהֶם כְּלֶחֶם אוֹנִים לָהֶם

to-them mourners like-bread-of sacrifices-of-them to-him they-will-be-pleasing

כָּל־ אֹכְלָיו יִטַמָּאוּ* כִּי־ לַחְמָם לְנַפְשָׁם

for-self-of-them food-of-them indeed they-will-be-unclean ones-eating-him all-of

לֹא יָבוֹא בֵּית יְהוָה׃ מַה־ תַּעֲשׂוּ לְיוֹם מוֹעֵד

appointed-feast on-day-of will-you-do what? (5) Yahweh temple-of he-will-come-into not

וּלְיוֹם חַג־ יְהוָה׃ כִּי־ הִנֵּה הָלְכוּ מִשֹּׁד מִצְרַיִם

Egypt from-destruction they-escape see! if (6) Yahweh festival-of and-on-day-of

תְּקַבְּצֵם מֹף תְּקַבְּרֵם מַחְמַד לְכַסְפָּם קִמּוֹשׂ

brier of-silver-of-them treasure she-will-bury-them Memphis she-will-gather-them

יִירָשֵׁם חוֹחַ בְּאָהֳלֵיהֶם׃ בָּאוּ יְמֵי הַפְּקֻדָּה

the-punishment days-of they-come (7) in-tents-of-them thorn he-will-take-over-them

בָּאוּ יְמֵי הַשִׁלֻּם† יֵדְעוּ יִשְׂרָאֵל אֱוִיל הַנָּבִיא

the-prophet foolish Israel let-them-know the-reckoning days-of they-come

מְשֻׁגָּע אִישׁ הָרוּחַ עַל רֹב עֲוֹנְךָ וְרַבָּה

and-great sin-of-you many-of because-of the-inspiration man-of one-being-maniac

מַשְׂטֵמָה׃ צֹפֶה אֶפְרַיִם עִם־ אֱלֹהָי נָבִיא פַּח יָקוֹשׁ

fowler snare-of prophet God-of-me with Ephraim man-watching-over (8) hostility

עַל־ כָּל־ דְּרָכָיו מַשְׂטֵמָה בְּבֵית אֱלֹהָיו׃ הֶעְמִיקוּ־

they-sank-deep (9) God-of-him in-house-of hostility paths-of-him all-of on

שִׁחֵתוּ כִּימֵי הַגִּבְעָה יִזְכּוֹר עֲוֹנָם

wickedness-of-them he-will-remember the-Gibeah as-days-of they-became-corrupt

יִפְקוֹד חַטֹּאותָם׃ כַּעֲנָבִים בַּמִּדְבָּר מָצָאתִי יִשְׂרָאֵל

Israel I-found in-the-desert like-grapes (10) sins-of-them he-will-punish

כְּבִכּוּרָה בִתְאֵנָה בְּרֵאשִׁיתָהּ רָאִיתִי אֲבוֹתֵיכֶם הֵמָּה בָּאוּ

they-came they fathers-of-you I-saw at-beginning-of-her on-fig-tree like-early-fruit

בַעַל־ פְּעוֹר וַיִּנָּזְרוּ לַבֹּשֶׁת וַיִּהְיוּ

and-they-became to-the-shameful-thing and-they-consecrated-themselves Peor Baal

שִׁקּוּצִים כְּאָהֳבָם׃ אֶפְרַיִם כָּעוֹף יִתְעוֹפֵף

he-will-fly-away like-the-bird Ephraim (11) as-thing-loved-of-them viles-ones

כְּבוֹדָם מִלֵּדָה וּמִבֶּטֶן וּמֵהֵרָיוֹן׃ כִּי אִם־

if even (12) and-from-conception and-from-pregnancy from-to-bear glory-of-them

יְגַדְּלוּ אֶת־ בְּנֵיהֶם וְשִׁכַּלְתִּים מֵאָדָם כִּי־ גַם־

also indeed of-everyone then-I-will-bereave-them children-of-them *** they-rear

אוֹי לָהֶם בְּשׂוּרִי מֵהֶם׃ אֶפְרַיִם כַּאֲשֶׁר־ רָאִיתִי לְצוֹר

to-Tyre I-saw like-that Ephraim (13) from-them when-to-turn-away-me to-them woe!

שְׁתוּלָה בְנָוֶה וְאֶפְרַיִם לְהוֹצִיא אֶל־ הֹרֵג

one-slaying to to-bring-out but-Ephraim in-pleasant-place one-being-planted

nor will their sacrifices
please him.
Such sacrifices will be to them
like the bread of
mourners;
all who eat them will be
unclean.
This food will be for
themselves;
it will not come into the
temple of the LORD.

[5]What will you do on the day
of your appointed feasts,
on the festival days of the
LORD?

[6]Even if they escape from
destruction,
Egypt will gather them,
and Memphis will bury
them.
Their treasures of silver will be
taken over by briers,
and thorns will overrun
their tents.

[7]The days of punishment are
coming,
the days of reckoning are at
hand.
Let Israel know this.
Because your sins are so many
and your hostility so great,
the prophet is considered a
fool,
the inspired man a maniac.

[8]The prophet, along with my
God,
is the watchman over
Ephraim,[y]
yet snares await him on all his
paths,
and hostility in the house of
his God.

[9]They have sunk deep into
corruption,
as in the days of Gibeah.
God will remember their
wickedness
and punish them for their
sins.

[10]"When I found Israel,
it was like finding grapes in
the desert;
when I saw your fathers,
it was like seeing the early
fruit on the fig tree.
But when they came to Baal
Peor,
they consecrated themselves
to that shameful idol
and became as vile as the
thing they loved.

[11]Ephraim's glory will fly away
like a bird—
no birth, no pregnancy, no
conception.

[12]Even if they rear children,
I will bereave them of every
one.
Woe to them
when I turn away from
them!

[13]I have seen Ephraim, like
Tyre,
planted in a pleasant place.
But Ephraim will bring out
their children to the slayer."

y8 Or *The prophet is the watchman over Ephraim, / the people of my God*

*4 Most mss have *dagesh* in the *teth* (טּ).

†7 Most mss have *dagesh* in the *shin* (שּׁ).

בָּנָיו׃ תֵּן־ לָהֶם יְהוָה מַה־ תִּתֵּן תֵּן־ לָהֶם
to-them give! will-you-give what? Yahweh to-them give! (14) children-of-him

רֶחֶם מַשְׁכִּיל וְשָׁדַיִם צֹמְקִים׃ כָּל־ רָעָתָם
wickedness-of-them all-of (15) ones-being-dry and-breasts one-miscarrying womb

בַּגִּלְגָּל כִּי־ שָׁם שְׂנֵאתִים עַל רֹעַ מַעַלְלֵיהֶם
deeds-of-them sinfulness-of because-of I-hated-them there indeed in-the-Gilgal

מִבֵּיתִי אֲגָרְשֵׁם לֹא אוֹסֵף אַהֲבָתָם כָּל־
all-of to-love-them I-will-do-longer not I-will-drive-them from-house-of-me

שָׂרֵיהֶם* סֹרְרִים׃ הֻכָּה אֶפְרַיִם שָׁרְשָׁם
root-of-them Ephraim he-is-blighted (16) ones-being-rebellious leaders-of-them

יָבֵשׁ פְּרִי בְּלִי־ יַעֲשׂוּן גַּם כִּי יֵלֵדוּן וְהֵמַתִּי
then-I-will-slay they-bear-children if even they-yield not fruit he-is-withered

מַחֲמַדֵּי בִטְנָם׃ יִמְאָסֵם אֱלֹהַי כִּי לֹא
not because God-of-me he-will-reject-them (17) womb-of-them cherished-ones-of

שָׁמְעוּ לוֹ וְיִהְיוּ נֹדְדִים בַּגּוֹיִם׃ גֶּפֶן
vine (10:1) among-the-nations ones-wandering and-they-will-be to-him they-obeyed

בּוֹקֵק יִשְׂרָאֵל פְּרִי יְשַׁוֶּה־ לּוֹ כְּרֹב לְפִרְיוֹ
to-fruit-of-him as-to-increase for-himself he-brought-forth fruit Israel spreading

הִרְבָּה לַמִּזְבְּחוֹת כְּטוֹב לְאַרְצוֹ הֵיטִיבוּ מַצֵּבוֹת׃
sacred-stones they-adorned to-land-of-him as-to-prosper to-the-altars he-built-more

חָלַק לִבָּם עַתָּה יֶאְשָׁמוּ הוּא יַעֲרֹף
he-will-demolish he they-must-bear-guilt now heart-of-them he-is-deceitful (2)

מִזְבְּחוֹתָם יְשֹׁדֵד מַצֵּבוֹתָם׃ כִּי עַתָּה יֹאמְרוּ
they-will-say then indeed (3) sacred-stones-of-them he-will-destory altars-of-them

אֵין מֶלֶךְ לָנוּ כִּי לֹא יָרֵאנוּ אֶת־ יְהוָה וְהַמֶּלֶךְ מַה־
what? but-the-king Yahweh *** we-revered not because to-us king there-is-no

יַּעֲשֶׂה־ לָּנוּ׃ דִּבְּרוּ דְבָרִים אָלוֹת שָׁוְא כָּרֹת
to-make falsehood to-take-oath promises they-promise (4) for-us could-he-do

בְּרִית וּפָרַח כָּרֹאשׁ מִשְׁפָּט עַל תַּלְמֵי שָׂדָי׃
field plowed-parts-of in lawsuit like-the-poison so-he-springs-up agreement

לְעֶגְלוֹת בֵּית אָוֶן יָגוּרוּ שְׁכַן שֹׁמְרוֹן כִּי־ אָבַל
he-mourns indeed Samaria people-of they-fear Aven Beth for-calf-idols-of (5)

עָלָיו עַמּוֹ וּכְמָרָיו עָלָיו יָגִילוּ עַל־
over they-rejoiced over-him and-idolatrous-priests-of-him people-of-him over-him

כְּבוֹדוֹ כִּי־ גָלָה מִמֶּנּוּ׃ גַּם־ אוֹתוֹ לְאַשּׁוּר
to-Assyria him also (6) from-him he-is-taken-into-exile because splendor-of-him

יוּבָל מִנְחָה לְמֶלֶךְ יָרֵב בָּשְׁנָה אֶפְרַיִם יִקָּח
he-will-take Ephraim disgrace great for-king tribute he-will-be-carried

14 Give them, O LORD—
what will you give them?
Give them wombs that miscarry
and breasts that are dry.

15 "Because of all their wickedness in Gilgal,
I hated them there.
Because of their sinful deeds,
I will drive them out of my house.
I will no longer love them;
all their leaders are rebellious.

16 Ephraim is blighted,
their root is withered,
they yield no fruit.
Even if they bear children,
I will slay their cherished offspring."

17 My God will reject them
because they have not obeyed him;
they will be wanderers
among the nations.

10 Israel was a spreading vine;
he brought forth fruit for himself.
As his fruit increased,
he built more altars;
as his land prospered,
he adorned his sacred stones.

2 Their heart is deceitful,
and now they must bear their guilt.
The LORD will demolish their altars
and destroy their sacred stones.

3 Then they will say, "We have no king
because we did not revere the LORD.
But even if we had a king,
what could he do for us?"

4 They make many promises,
take false oaths
and make agreements;
therefore lawsuits spring up
like poisonous weeds in a plowed field.

5 The people who live in Samaria fear
for the calf-idol of Beth Aven.[z]
Its people will mourn over it,
and so will its idolatrous priests,
those who had rejoiced over its splendor,
because it is taken from them into exile.

6 It will be carried to Assyria
as tribute for the great king.
Ephraim will be disgraced;

[z] 5 *Beth Aven* means *house of wickedness* (a name for Bethel, which means *house of God*).

*15 Most mss have *qamets* under the *sin* (שָׂ).

°16 ק בל

וְיֵבוֹשׁ יִשְׂרָאֵל מֵעֲצָתוֹ׃ נִדְמֶה שֹׁמְרוֹן
Samaria he-will-float-away (7) of-counsel-of-him Israel and-he-will-be-ashamed

מַלְכָּהּ כְּקֶצֶף עַל־ פְּנֵי־ מָיִם׃ וְנִשְׁמְדוּ
and-they-will-be-destroyed (8) waters surfaces-of on like-twig king-of-her

בָּמוֹת אָוֶן חַטַּאת יִשְׂרָאֵל קוֹץ וְדַרְדַּר יַעֲלֶה עַל־
over he-will-grow-up and-thistle thorn Israel sin-of wickedness high-places-of

מִזְבְּחוֹתָם וְאָמְרוּ לֶהָרִים כַּסּוּנוּ וְלַגְּבָעוֹת נִפְלוּ
fall! and-to-the-hills cover-us! to-the-mountains then-they-will-say altars-of-them

עָלֵינוּ׃ מִימֵי הַגִּבְעָה חָטָאתָ יִשְׂרָאֵל שָׁם עָמָדוּ לֹא־
not they-remained there Israel you-sinned the-Gibeah since-days-of (9) on-us

תַשִּׂיגֵם בַגִּבְעָה מִלְחָמָה עַל־ בְּנֵי עַלְוָה׃ בְּאַוָּתִי
when-to-please-me (10) evil peoples-of to war in-the-Gibeah she-overtook-them

וְאֶסֳּרֵם וְאֻסְּפוּ עֲלֵיהֶם עַמִּים
nations against-them and-they-will-be-gathered then-I-will-punish-them

בְּאָסְרָם לִשְׁתֵּי עֵינֹתָם׃ וְאֶפְרַיִם עֶגְלָה מְלֻמָּדָה
one-being-trained heifer now-Ephraim (11) sins-of-them for-double-of when-to-bind-them

אֹהַבְתִּי לָדוּשׁ וַאֲנִי עָבַרְתִּי עַל־ טוּב צַוָּארָהּ אַרְכִּיב
I-will-drive neck-of-her fairness-of on I-will-put-yoke so-I to-thresh one-loving-of

אֶפְרַיִם יַחֲרוֹשׁ יְהוּדָה יְשַׂדֶּד־ לוֹ יַעֲקֹב׃ זִרְעוּ
sow! (12) Jacob for-him he-must-break-up-ground Judah he-must-plow Ephraim

לָכֶם לִצְדָקָה קִצְרוּ לְפִי־* חֶסֶד נִירוּ לָכֶם
of-you break-up! unfailing-love *to-mouth-of reap! to-righteousness for-yourselves

נִיר וְעֵת לִדְרוֹשׁ אֶת־ יְהוָה עַד־ יָבוֹא וְיֹרֶה
and-he-showers he-comes until Yahweh *** to-seek for-time-of unplowed-ground

צֶדֶק לָכֶם׃ חֲרַשְׁתֶּם־ רֶשַׁע עַוְלָתָה קְצַרְתֶּם אֲכַלְתֶּם
you-ate you-reaped to-evil wickedness you-planted (13) on-you righteousness

פְּרִי־ כָחַשׁ כִּי־ בָטַחְתָּ בְדַרְכְּךָ בְּרֹב גִּבּוֹרֶיךָ׃
warriors-of-you on-many-of on-strength-of-you you-depended because deception fruit-of

וְקָאם שָׁאוֹן בְּעַמֶּךָ וְכָל־ מִבְצָרֶיךָ
fortresses-of-you and-all-of against-people-of-you battle-roar and-he-will-rise (14)

יוּשַּׁד כְּשֹׁד שַׁלְמַן בֵּית אַרְבֵאל בְּיוֹם מִלְחָמָה אֵם
mother battle on-day-of Arbel Beth Shalman as-to-devastate he-will-be-devastated

עַל־ בָּנִים רֻטָּשָׁה׃ כָּכָה עָשָׂה לָכֶם בֵּית־אֵל
El Beth to-you he-will-happen thus (15) she-was-dashed-to-ground children with

מִפְּנֵי רָעַת רָעַתְכֶם בַּשַּׁחַר נִדְמֹה
to-be-destroyed when-the-dawn wickedness-of-you wickedness-of because-of

נִדְמָה מֶלֶךְ יִשְׂרָאֵל׃ כִּי נַעַר יִשְׂרָאֵל וָאֹהֲבֵהוּ
then-I-loved-him Israel child when (11:1) Israel king-of he-will-be-destroyed

Israel will be ashamed of its
wooden idols.[a]
7Samaria and its king will float
away
like a twig on the surface of
the waters.
8The high places of
wickedness[b] will be
destroyed—
it is the sin of Israel.
Thorns and thistles will grow
up
and cover their altars.
Then they will say to the
mountains, "Cover us!"
and to the hills, "Fall on
us!"
9"Since the days of Gibeah, you
have sinned, O Israel,
and there you have
remained.[c]
Did not war overtake
the evildoers in Gibeah?
10When I please, I will punish
them;
nations will be gathered
against them
to put them in bonds for
their double sin.
11Ephraim is a trained heifer
that loves to thresh;
so I will put a yoke
on her fair neck.
I will drive Ephraim,
Judah must plow,
and Jacob must break up the
ground.
12Sow for yourselves
righteousness,
reap the fruit of unfailing
love,
and break up your unplowed
ground;
for it is time to seek the
LORD,
until he comes
and showers righteousness
on you.
13But you have planted
wickedness,
you have reaped evil,
you have eaten the fruit of
deception.
Because you have depended on
your own strength
and on your many warriors,
14the roar of battle will rise
against your people,
so that all your fortresses
will be devastated—
as Shalman devastated Beth
Arbel on the day of
battle,
when mothers were dashed
to the ground with their
children.
15Thus will it happen to you, O
Bethel,
because your wickedness is
great.
When that day dawns,
the king of Israel will be
completely destroyed.

a6 Or *its counsel*
b8 Hebrew *aven*, a reference to Beth Aven (a derogatory name for Bethel)
c9 Or *there a stand was taken*

***12 The NIV, with some ancient versions, reads this word as לִפְרִי, *to-fruit-of*.**

°10 ק עונתם

וּמִמִּצְרַיִם קָרָאתִי לִבְנִי׃ קָרְאוּ לָהֶם כֵּן הָלְכוּ
and-from-Egypt I-called to-son-of-me (2) they-called to-them so they-went

מִפְּנֵיהֶם לַבְּעָלִים יְזַבֵּחוּ וְלַפְּסִלִים יְקַטֵּרוּן׃
from-before-them to-the-Baals they-sacrificed and-to-the-images they-burned-incense

(3) וְאָנֹכִי תִרְגַּלְתִּי לְאֶפְרַיִם קָחָם עַל־זְרוֹעֹתָיו וְלֹא
(3) indeed-I I-taught-to-walk to-Ephraim to-take-them by arms-of-him but-not

יָדְעוּ כִּי רְפָאתִים׃ (4) בְּחַבְלֵי אָדָם אֶמְשְׁכֵם בַּעֲבֹתוֹת אַהֲבָה
they-realized that I-healed-them (4) with-cords-of human I-led-them with-ties-of love

וָאֶהְיֶה לָהֶם כִּמְרִימֵי עֹל עַל לְחֵיהֶם וְאַט אֵלָיו
and-I-was to-them as-ones-lifting-of yoke on necks-of-them and-I-bent-down to-him

אוֹכִיל׃ (5) לֹא יָשׁוּב אֶל־אֶרֶץ מִצְרַיִם וְאַשּׁוּר הוּא מַלְכּוֹ
I-fed (5) not he-will-return to land-of Egypt and-Assyria he ruler-of-him

כִּי מֵאֲנוּ לָשׁוּב׃ (6) וְחָלָה חֶרֶב בְּעָרָיו
because they-refused to-repent (6) and-she-will-flash sword in-cities-of-him

וְכִלְּתָה בַדָּיו וְאָכָלָה מִמֹּעֲצוֹתֵיהֶם׃
and-she-will-destroy gate-bars-of-him and-she-will-put-end to-plans-of-them

(7) וְעַמִּי תְלוּאִים לִמְשׁוּבָתִי וְאֶל־עַל
(7) and-people-of-me ones-being-determined to-turning-away-from-me if-to Most-High

יִקְרָאֻהוּ יַחַד לֹא יְרוֹמֵם׃ (8) אֵיךְ אֶתֶּנְךָ אֶפְרַיִם
they-call-to-him altogether not he-will-exalt-them (8) how? can-I-give-up-you Ephraim

אֲמַגֶּנְךָ יִשְׂרָאֵל אֵיךְ אֶתֶּנְךָ כְאַדְמָה אֲשִׂימְךָ כִּצְבֹאיִם
can-I-hand-over-you Israel how? can-I-treat-you like-Admah can-I-make-you like-Zeboiim

נֶהְפַּךְ עָלַי לִבִּי יַחַד נִכְמְרוּ נִחוּמָי׃
he-is-changed within-me heart-of-me altogether they-are-aroused compassions-of-me

(9) לֹא אֶעֱשֶׂה חֲרוֹן אַפִּי לֹא אָשׁוּב לְשַׁחֵת
(9) not I-will-carry-out fierceness-of anger-of-me not I-will-turn to-devastate

אֶפְרָיִם כִּי אֵל אָנֹכִי וְלֹא־אִישׁ בְּקִרְבְּךָ קָדוֹשׁ וְלֹא אָבוֹא
Ephraim for God I and-not man in-among-you Holy-One and-not I-will-come

בְּעִיר׃ (10) אַחֲרֵי יְהוָה יֵלְכוּ כְּאַרְיֵה יִשְׁאָג כִּי־הוּא יִשְׁאַג
in-wrath (10) after Yahweh they-will-follow like-lion he-will-roar when he he-roars

וְיֶחֶרְדוּ בָנִים מִיָּם׃ (11) יֶחֶרְדוּ
then-they-will-come-trembling children from-west (11) they-will-come-trembling

כְצִפּוֹר מִמִּצְרַיִם וּכְיוֹנָה מֵאֶרֶץ אַשּׁוּר וְהוֹשַׁבְתִּים
like-bird from-Egypt and-like-dove from-land-of Assyria and-I-will-settle-them

עַל־בָּתֵּיהֶם נְאֻם־יְהוָה׃ *(12:1) סְבָבֻנִי בְכַחַשׁ אֶפְרַיִם
in homes-of-them declaration-of Yahweh *(12:1) they-surrounded-me with-lie Ephraim

וּבְמִרְמָה בֵּית יִשְׂרָאֵל וִיהוּדָה עֹד רָד עִם־אֵל
and-with-deceit house-of Israel and-Judah still he-is-unruly against God

*God's Love for Israel*

11 "When Israel was a child,
I loved him,
and out of Egypt I called my
son.
2 But the more I[d] called Israel,
the further they went from
me.[e]
They sacrificed to the Baals
and they burned incense to
images.
3 It was I who taught Ephraim
to walk,
taking them by the arms;
but they did not realize
it was I who healed them.
4 I led them with cords of
human kindness,
with ties of love;
I lifted the yoke from their
neck
and bent down to feed them.
5 "Will they not return to Egypt
and will not Assyria rule
over them
because they refuse to
repent?
6 Swords will flash in their
cities,
will destroy the bars of their
gates
and put an end to their
plans.
7 My people are determined to
turn from me.
Even if they call to the Most
High,
he will by no means exalt
them.
8 "How can I give you up,
Ephraim?
How can I hand you over,
Israel?
How can I treat you like
Admah?
How can I make you like
Zeboiim?
My heart is changed within me;
all my compassion is
aroused.
9 I will not carry out my fierce
anger,
nor will I turn and devastate
Ephraim.
For I am God, and not man—
the Holy One among you.
I will not come in wrath.
10 They will follow the LORD;
he will roar like a lion.
When he roars,
his children will come
trembling from the west.
11 They will come trembling
like birds from Egypt,
like doves from Assyria.
I will settle them in their
homes,"
declares the LORD.

*Israel's Sin*

12 Ephraim has surrounded me
with lies,
the house of Israel with
deceit.
And Judah is unruly against
God,

d2 Some Septuagint manuscripts; Hebrew *they* e2 Septuagint; Hebrew *them*
f9 Or *come against any city*

***Heading**, 1* The Hebrew numeration of chapter 12 begins with the final verse of chapter 11 in English; thus, there is a one-verse descrepancy throughout chapter 12.

וְעִם־ קְדוֹשִׁים נֶאֱמָן׃ אֶפְרַיִם רֹעֶה רוּחַ וְרֹדֵף
and-pursuing wind feeding-on Ephraim (2) one-being-faithful Holy-Ones even-against

קָדִים כָּל־ הַיּוֹם כָּזָב וָשֹׁד יַרְבֶּה וּבְרִית עִם־ אַשּׁוּר
Assyria with and-treaty he-multiplies and-violence lie the-day all-of east-wind

יִכְרֹתוּ וְשֶׁמֶן לְמִצְרַיִם יוּבָל׃ וְרִיב לַיהוָה עִם־ יְהוּדָה
Judah against to-Yahweh indeed-charge (3) he-is-sent to-Egypt and-oil they-make

וְלִפְקֹד עַל־ יַעֲקֹב כִּדְרָכָיו כְּמַעֲלָלָיו יָשִׁיב
he-will-repay according-to-deeds-of-him according-to-ways-of-him Jacob to and-to-punish

לוֹ׃ בַּבֶּטֶן עָקַב אֶת־ אָחִיו וּבְאוֹנוֹ
and-in-manhood-of-him brother-of-him *** he-grasped-heel in-the-womb (4) to-him

שָׂרָה אֶת־אֱלֹהִים׃ וַיָּשַׂר אֶל־ מַלְאָךְ וַיֻּכָל בָּכָה
he-wept and-he-overcame angel with and-he-struggled (5) God with he-struggled

וַיִּתְחַנֶּן־ לוֹ בֵּית־אֵל יִמְצָאֶנּוּ וְשָׁם יְדַבֵּר עִמָּנוּ׃
with-him he-talked and-there he-found-him El Beth of-him and-he-begged-favor

וַיהוָה אֱלֹהֵי הַצְּבָאוֹת יְהוָה זִכְרוֹ׃ וְאַתָּה
but-you (7) name-of-renown-of-him Yahweh the-Hosts God-of indeed-Yahweh (6)

בֵּאלֹהֶיךָ תָשׁוּב חֶסֶד וּמִשְׁפָּט שְׁמֹר וְקַוֵּה אֶל־ אֱלֹהֶיךָ
God-of-you for and-wait! maintain! and-justice love you-must-return to-God-of-you

תָּמִיד׃ כְּנַעַן בְּיָדוֹ מֹאזְנֵי מִרְמָה לַעֲשֹׁק אָהֵב׃
he-loves to-defraud dishonesty scales-of in-hand-of-him merchant (8) always

וַיֹּאמֶר אֶפְרַיִם אַךְ עָשַׁרְתִּי מָצָאתִי אוֹן לִי כָּל־
all-of for-myself wealth I-found I-am-rich very Ephraim and-he-boasts (9)

יְגִיעַי לֹא יִמְצְאוּ־ לִי עָוֺן אֲשֶׁר־חֵטְא׃ וְאָנֹכִי יְהוָה
Yahweh indeed-I (10) sin that iniquity in-me they-will-find not wealths-of-me

אֱלֹהֶיךָ מֵאֶרֶץ מִצְרָיִם עֹד אוֹשִׁיבְךָ בָאֳהָלִים כִּימֵי
as-days-of in-tents I-will-make-live-you again Egypt from-land-of God-of-you

מוֹעֵד׃ וְדִבַּרְתִּי עַל־ הַנְּבִיאִים וְאָנֹכִי חָזוֹן הִרְבֵּיתִי
I-gave-many vision and-I the-prophets to and-I-spoke (11) appointed-feast

וּבְיַד הַנְּבִיאִים אֲדַמֶּה׃ אִם־ גִּלְעָד אָוֶן אַךְ־
surely wickedness Gilead if (12) I-told-parables the-prophets and-through-hand-of

שָׁוְא הָיוּ בַּגִּלְגָּל שְׁוָרִים זִבֵּחוּ גַּם מִזְבְּחוֹתָם
altars-of-them also they-sacrifice bulls in-the-Gilgal they-are worthlessness

כְּגַלִּים עַל תַּלְמֵי שָׂדָי׃ וַיִּבְרַח יַעֲקֹב שְׂדֵה אֲרָם
Aram country-of Jacob and-he-fled (13) field plowed-parts-of on like-piles-of-stones

וַיַּעֲבֹד יִשְׂרָאֵל בְּאִשָּׁה וּבְאִשָּׁה שָׁמָר׃ וּבְנָבִיא הֶעֱלָה
he-brought-up and-by-prophet (14) he-tended and-for-wife for-wife Israel and-he-served

יְהוָה אֶת־יִשְׂרָאֵל מִמִּצְרָיִם וּבְנָבִיא נִשְׁמָר׃ הִכְעִיס
he-provoked-to-anger (15) he-took-care and-by-prophet from-Egypt Israel *** Yahweh

---

even against the faithful
Holy One.

12 Ephraim feeds on the
wind;
he pursues the east wind all
day
and multiplies lies and
violence.
He makes a treaty with
Assyria
and sends olive oil to Egypt.
2 The LORD has a charge to bring
against Judah;
he will punish Jacob[g]
according to his ways
and repay him according to
his deeds.
3 In the womb he grasped his
brother's heel;
as a man he struggled with
God.
4 He struggled with the angel
and overcame him;
he wept and begged for his
favor.
He found him at Bethel
and talked with him there—
5 the LORD God Almighty,
the LORD is his name of
renown!
6 But you must return to your
God;
maintain love and justice,
and wait for your God
always.

7 The merchant uses dishonest
scales;
he loves to defraud.
8 Ephraim boasts,
"I am very rich; I have
become wealthy.
With all my wealth they will
not find in me
any iniquity or sin."

9 "I am the LORD your God,
⌊who brought you⌋ out of[h]
Egypt;
I will make you live in tents
again,
as in the days of your
appointed feasts.
10 I spoke to the prophets,
gave them many visions
and told parables through
them."
11 Is Gilead wicked?
Its people are worthless!
Do they sacrifice bulls in
Gilgal?
Their altars will be like piles
of stones
on a plowed field.
12 Jacob fled to the country of
Aram[i];
Israel served to get a wife,
and to pay for her he tended
sheep.
13 The LORD used a prophet to
bring Israel up from
Egypt,
by a prophet he cared for
him.

g2 *Jacob* means *he grasps the heel* (figuratively, *he deceives*).
h9 Or *God / ever since you were in*
i12 That is, Northwest Mesopotamia

**Heading* See the note on page 496.

אֶפְרַיִם תַּמְרוּרִים וְדָמָיו עָלָיו יִטּוֹשׁ וְחֶרְפָּתוֹ
and-contempt-of-him he-will-leave upon-him and-bloods-of-him bitternesses Ephraim

יָשִׁיב לוֹ אֲדֹנָיו׃ כְּדַבֵּר אֶפְרַיִם רְתֵת נָשָׂא
he-was-exalted trembling Ephraim when-to-speak (13:1) Lord-of-him to-him he-will-repay

הוּא בְּיִשְׂרָאֵל וַיֶּאְשַׁם בַּבַּעַל וַיָּמֹת׃ וְעַתָּה
and-now (2) and-he-died concerning-the-Baal but-he-became-guilty in-Israel he

יוֹסִפוּ לַחֲטֹא וַיַּעֲשׂוּ לָהֶם מַסֵּכָה מִכַּסְפָּם
from-silver-of-them idol for-themselves and-they-make to-sin they-do-more

כִּתְבוּנָם עֲצַבִּים מַעֲשֵׂה חָרָשִׁים כֻּלֹּה לָהֶם הֵם
they of-them all-of-him craftsmen work-of images according-to-cleverness-of-them

אֹמְרִים זֹבְחֵי אָדָם עֲגָלִים יִשָּׁקוּן׃ לָכֵן
therefore (3) they-kiss calf-idols human ones-offering-sacrifice-of ones-saying

יִהְיוּ כַּעֲנַן־ בֹּקֶר וְכַטַּל מַשְׁכִּים הֹלֵךְ
one-disappearing one-being-early and-like-the-dew morning like-mist-of they-will-be

כְּמֹץ יְסֹעֵר מִגֹּרֶן וּכְעָשָׁן מֵאֲרֻבָּה׃ וְאָנֹכִי
but-I (4) through-window and-like-smoke from-threshing-floor he-swirls like-chaff

יְהוָה אֱלֹהֶיךָ מֵאֶרֶץ מִצְרָיִם וֵאלֹהִים זוּלָתִי לֹא תֵדָע
you-shall-acknowledge not but-me and-God Egypt from-land-of God-of-you Yahweh

וּמוֹשִׁיעַ אַיִן בִּלְתִּי׃ אֲנִי יְדַעְתִּיךָ בַּמִּדְבָּר בְּאֶרֶץ
in-land-of in-the-desert I-cared-for-you I (5) except-me there-is-no and-One-Saving

תַּלְאֻבוֹת׃ כְּמַרְעִיתָם וַיִּשְׂבָּעוּ שָׂבְעוּ
they-were-satisfied then-they-were-satisfied when-feeding-of-them (6) burning-heats

וַיָּרָם לִבָּם עַל־ כֵּן שְׁכֵחוּנִי׃ וָאֱהִי
so-I-will-come (7) they-forgot-me this for heart-of-them then-he-became-proud

לָהֶם כְּמוֹ־שָׁחַל כְּנָמֵר עַל־דֶּרֶךְ אָשׁוּר׃ אֶפְגְּשֵׁם כְּדֹב
like-bear I-will-attack-them (8) I-will-lurk path by like-leopard lion like upon-them

שַׁכּוּל וְאֶקְרַע סְגוֹר לִבָּם וְאֹכְלֵם
and-I-will-devour-them heart-of-them enclosure-of and-I-will-rip-open robbed-of-cubs

שָׁם כְּלָבִיא חַיַּת הַשָּׂדֶה תְּבַקְּעֵם׃ שִׁחֶתְךָ
he-will-destroy-you (9) she-will-tear-apart-them the-wild animal-of like-lion there

יִשְׂרָאֵל כִּי־ בִי בְעֶזְרֶךָ׃ אֱהִי מַלְכְּךָ אֵפוֹא
then? king-of-you where? (10) against-help-of-you against-me because Israel

וְיוֹשִׁיעֲךָ בְּכָל־ עָרֶיךָ וְשֹׁפְטֶיךָ אֲשֶׁר אָמַרְתָּ
you-said whom and-ones-ruling-you towns-of-you in-all-of that-he-may-save-you

תְּנָה־ לִּי מֶלֶךְ וְשָׂרִים׃ אֶתֶּן־ לְךָ מֶלֶךְ בְּאַפִּי וְאֶקַּח
and-I-took-away in-anger-of-me king to-you I-gave (11) and-princes king to-me give!

בְּעֶבְרָתִי׃ צָרוּר עֲוֹן אֶפְרָיִם צְפוּנָה חַטָּאתוֹ׃
sin-of-him being-recorded Ephraim guilt-of being-stored-up (12) in-wrath-of-me

14 But Ephraim has bitterly
provoked him to anger;
his Lord will leave upon
him the guilt of his
bloodshed
and will repay him for his
contempt.

*The LORD's Anger Against Israel*

13 When Ephraim spoke,
men trembled;
he was exalted in Israel.
But he became guilty of Baal
worship and died.
2 Now they sin more and more;
they make idols for
themselves from their
silver,
cleverly fashioned images,
all of them the work of
craftsmen.
It is said of these people,
"They offer human sacrifice
and kiss[j] the calf-idols."
3 Therefore they will be like the
morning mist,
like the early dew that
disappears,
like chaff swirling from a
threshing floor,
like smoke escaping through
a window.
4 "But I am the LORD your God,
⌊who brought you⌋ out of[k]
Egypt.
You shall acknowledge no God
but me,
no Savior except me.
5 I cared for you in the desert,
in the land of burning heat.
6 When I fed them, they were
satisfied;
when they were satisfied,
they became proud;
then they forgot me.
7 So I will come upon them like
a lion,
like a leopard I will lurk by
the path.
8 Like a bear robbed of her cubs,
I will attack them and rip
them open.
Like a lion I will devour them;
a wild animal will tear them
apart.
9 "You are destroyed, O Israel,
because you are against me,
against your helper.
10 Where is your king, that he
may save you?
Where are your rulers in all
your towns,
of whom you said,
'Give me a king and
princes'?
11 So in my anger I gave you a
king,
and in my wrath I took him
away.
12 The guilt of Ephraim is stored
up,
his sins are kept on record.

j2 Or *"Men who sacrifice / kiss*
k4 Or *God / ever since you were in*

****Heading*** See the note on page 496.

חֶבְלֵי יוֹלֵדָה יָבֹאוּ לוֹ הוּא־בֵן לֹא חָכָם כִּי־עֵת
time when wise not child he to-him they-come woman-bearing-child pains-of (13)

לֹא־יַעֲמֹד בְּמִשְׁבַּר בָּנִים׃ מִיַּד שְׁאוֹל אֶפְדֵּם
I-will-ransom-them Sheol from-power-of (14) children to-opening-of-womb-of he-comes not

מִמָּוֶת אֶגְאָלֵם אֱהִי דְבָרֶיךָ מָוֶת אֱהִי קָטָבְךָ
destruction-of-you where? death plagues-of-you where? I-will-redeem-them from-death

שְׁאוֹל נֹחַם יִסָּתֵר מֵעֵינָי׃ כִּי הוּא בֵּן אַחִים
brothers among he though (15) from-eyes-of-me he-will-be-hidden compassion Sheol

יַפְרִיא יָבוֹא קָדִים רוּחַ יְהוָה מִמִּדְבָּר עֹלֶה
blowing-in from-desert Yahweh wind-of east-wind he-will-come he-thrives

וְיֵבוֹשׁ מְקוֹרוֹ וְיֶחֱרַב מַעְיָנוֹ הוּא יִשְׁסֶה
he-will-plunder he well-of-him and-he-will-dry-up spring-of-him and-he-will-fail

אוֹצַר כָּל־ כְּלִי חֶמְדָּה׃ תֶּאְשַׁם שֹׁמְרוֹן כִּי
because Samaria she-must-bear-guilt *(14:1) treasure article-of all-of storehouse

מָרְתָה בֵּאלֹהֶיהָ בַּחֶרֶב יִפְּלוּ עֹלְלֵיהֶם
little-ones-of-them they-will-fall by-the-sword against-God-of-her she-rebelled

יְרֻטָּשׁוּ וְהָרִיּוֹתָיו יְבֻקָּעוּ׃
they-will-be-ripped-open and-pregnant-women-of-him they-will-be-dashed-to-the-ground

שׁוּבָה יִשְׂרָאֵל עַד יְהוָה אֱלֹהֶיךָ כִּי כָשַׁלְתָּ בַּעֲוֺנֶךָ׃
because-of-sin-of-you you-fell-down indeed God-of-you Yahweh to Israel return! (2)

קְחוּ עִמָּכֶם דְּבָרִים וְשׁוּבוּ אֶל־ יְהוָה אִמְרוּ אֵלָיו כָּל־ תִּשָּׂא
you-forgive all-of to-him say! Yahweh to and-return! words with-you take! (3)

עָוֺן וְקַח־ טוֹב וּנְשַׁלְּמָה פָרִים שְׂפָתֵינוּ׃ אַשּׁוּר ׀ לֹא
not Assyria (4) lips-of-us bulls that-we-may-offer graciously and-receive! sin

יוֹשִׁיעֵנוּ עַל־ סוּס לֹא נִרְכָּב וְלֹא־ נֹאמַר עוֹד אֱלֹהֵינוּ
gods-of-us again we-will-say and-never we-will-mount not horse on he-can-save-us

לְמַעֲשֵׂה יָדֵינוּ אֲשֶׁר־ בְּךָ יְרֻחַם יָתוֹם׃ אֶרְפָּא
I-will-heal (5) fatherless he-finds-compassion in-you for hands-of-us to-thing-made-of

מְשׁוּבָתָם אֹהֲבֵם נְדָבָה כִּי שָׁב אַפִּי
anger-of-me he-turned-away for freedom I-will-love-them waywardness-of-them

מִמֶּנּוּ׃ אֶהְיֶה כַטַּל לְיִשְׂרָאֵל יִפְרַח כַּשּׁוֹשַׁנָּה
like-the-lily he-will-blossom to-Israel like-the-dew I-will-be (6) from-him

וְיַךְ שָׁרָשָׁיו כַּלְּבָנוֹן׃ יֵלְכוּ
they-will-grow (7) like-the-Lebanon roots-of-him and-he-will-send-down

יֹנְקוֹתָיו וִיהִי כַזַּיִת הוֹדוֹ
splendor-of-him like-the-olive-tree and-he-will-be young-shoots-of-him

וְרֵיחַ לוֹ כַּלְּבָנוֹן׃ יָשֻׁבוּ יֹשְׁבֵי
men-dwelling-of they-will-dwell (8) like-the-Lebanon of-him and-fragrance

13 Pains as of a woman in
childbirth come to him,
but he is a child without
wisdom;
when the time arrives,
he does not come to the
opening of the womb.
14 "I will ransom them from the
power of the grave[l];
I will redeem them from
death.
Where, O death, are your
plagues?
Where, O grave,[m] is your
destruction?
"I will have no compassion,
15 even though he thrives
among his brothers.
An east wind from the LORD
will come,
blowing in from the desert;
his spring will fail
and his well dry up.
His storehouse will be
plundered
of all its treasures.
16 The people of Samaria must
bear their guilt,
because they have rebelled
against their God.
They will fall by the sword;
their little ones will be
dashed to the ground,
their pregnant women
ripped open."

*Repentance to Bring Blessing*

14 Return, O Israel, to the
LORD your God.
Your sins have been your
downfall!
2 Take words with you
and return to the LORD.
Say to him:
"Forgive all our sins
and receive us graciously,
that we may offer the fruit
of our lips.[n]
3 Assyria cannot save us;
we will not mount
war-horses.
We will never again say 'Our
gods'
to what our own hands
have made,
for in you the fatherless find
compassion."
4 "I will heal their waywardness
and love them freely,
for my anger has turned
away from them.
5 I will be like the dew to Israel;
he will blossom like a lily.
Like a cedar of Lebanon
he will send down his roots;
6 his young shoots will grow.
His splendor will be like an
olive tree,
his fragrance like a cedar of
Lebanon.
7 Men will dwell again in his

[l] 14 Hebrew *Sheol*
[m] 14 Hebrew *Sheol*
[n] 2 Or *offer our lips as sacrifices of bulls*

***Heading, 1*** **The Hebrew numeration of chapter 14 begins with the final verse of chapter 13 in English; thus, there is a one-verse discrepancy throughout chapter 14.**

**†7 Most mss have no accent under the *beth* (וְרֵיחַ).**

| בְצִלּוֹ | יְחַיּוּ | דָגָן | וְיִפְרְחוּ | כַגָּפֶן |
|---|---|---|---|---|
| in-shade-of-him | they-will-flourish | grain | and-they-will-blossom | like-the-vine |

| זִכְרוֹ | כְּיֵין | לְבָנוֹן׃ | | אֶפְרַיִם | מַה־ | לִּי | עוֹד | לָעֲצַבִּים |
|---|---|---|---|---|---|---|---|---|
| fame-of-him | like-wine-of | Lebanon | (9) | Ephraim | what? | to-me | more | with-the-idols |

| אֲנִי | עָנִיתִי | וַאֲשׁוּרֶנּוּ | אֲנִי | כִּבְרוֹשׁ | רַעֲנָן |
|---|---|---|---|---|---|
| I | I-will-answer | and-I-will-take-care-of-him | I | like-pine-tree | green |

| מִמֶּנִּי | פֶּרְיְךָ | נִמְצָא׃ | | מִי | חָכָם | וְיָבֵן |
|---|---|---|---|---|---|---|
| from-me | fruitfulness-of-you | he-is-found | (10) | who? | wise | indeed-he-will-realize |

| אֵלֶּה | נָבוֹן | וְיֵדָעֵם |
|---|---|---|
| these | one-being-discerning | indeed-he-will-understand-them |

| כִּי־ | יְשָׁרִים | דַּרְכֵי | יְהוָה | וְצַדִּקִים |
|---|---|---|---|---|
| indeed | right-ones | ways-of | Yahweh | and-righteous-ones |

| יֵלְכוּ | בָם | וּפֹשְׁעִים | יִכָּשְׁלוּ | בָם׃ |
|---|---|---|---|---|
| they-walk | in-them | but-ones-being-rebellious | they-stumble | in-them |

shade.
He will flourish like the grain.
He will blossom like a vine,
and his fame will be like the wine from Lebanon.
8 O Ephraim, what more have I[c] to do with idols?
I will answer him and care for him.
I am like a green pine tree;
your fruitfulness comes from me."

9 Who is wise? He will realize these things.
Who is discerning? He will understand them.
The ways of the LORD are right;
the righteous walk in them,
but the rebellious stumble in them.

c8 Or *What more has Ephraim*

**Heading* See the note on page 499.

דְּבַר־ יְהוָה אֲשֶׁר הָיָה אֶל־יוֹאֵל בֶּן־ פְּתוּאֵל׃ שִׁמְעוּ־זֹאת
this hear! (2) Pethuel son-of Joel to he-came that Yahweh word-of (1:1)

הַזְּקֵנִים וְהַאֲזִינוּ כֹּל יוֹשְׁבֵי הָאָרֶץ הֶהָיְתָה זֹּאת
this has-she-happened? the-land ones-living-of all-of and-listen! the-elders

בִּימֵיכֶם וְאִם בִּימֵי אֲבֹתֵיכֶם׃ עָלֶיהָ לִבְנֵיכֶם
to-children-of-you about-her (3) forefathers-of-you in-days-of or-indeed in-days-of-you

סַפֵּרוּ וּבְנֵיכֶם לִבְנֵיהֶם וּבְנֵיהֶם לְדוֹר אַחֵר׃
next to-generation and-children-of-them to-children-of-them and-children-of-you tell!

יֶתֶר הַגָּזָם אָכַל הָאַרְבֶּה וְיֶתֶר
and-left-over-of the-great-locust he-ate the-locust-swarm left-over-of (4)

הָאַרְבֶּה אָכַל הַיָּלֶק וְיֶתֶר הַיֶּלֶק אָכַל
he-ate the-young-locust and-left-over-of the-young-locust he-ate the-great-locust

הֶחָסִיל׃ הָקִיצוּ שִׁכּוֹרִים וּבְכוּ וְהֵילִלוּ כָּל־ שֹׁתֵי יָיִן
wine ones-drinking-of all-of and-wail! and-weep! drunkards wake-up! (5) the-locust

עַל־ עָסִיס כִּי נִכְרַת מִפִּיכֶם׃ כִּי־ גוֹי עָלָה
he-invaded nation indeed (6) from-lip-of-you he-was-snatched for new-wine because-of

עַל־ אַרְצִי עָצוּם וְאֵין מִסְפָּר שִׁנָּיו שִׁנֵּי אַרְיֵה וּמְתַלְּעוֹת
and-fangs-of lion teeth-of teeth-of-him number and-without powerful land-of-me into

לָבִיא לוֹ׃ שָׂם גַּפְנִי לְשַׁמָּה וּתְאֵנָתִי לִקְצָפָה
to-ruin and-fig-tree-of-me to-waste vine-of-me he-laid (7) to-him lioness

חָשֹׂף חֲשָׂפָהּ וְהִשְׁלִיךְ הִלְבִּינוּ שָׂרִיגֶיהָ׃
branches-of-her they-left-white and-he-threw-away he-stripped-off-her to-strip-off

אֱלִי כִּבְתוּלָה חֲגֻרַת־ שַׂק עַל־ בַּעַל נְעוּרֶיהָ׃
youths-of-her husband-of for sackcloth one-being-dressed-of like-virgin mourn! (8)

הָכְרַת מִנְחָה וָנֶסֶךְ מִבֵּית יְהוָה אָבְלוּ
they-mourn Yahweh from-house-of and-drink-offering grain-offering he-is-cut-off (9)

הַכֹּהֲנִים מְשָׁרְתֵי יְהוָה׃ שֻׁדַּד שָׂדֶה אָבְלָה
she-is-dried-up field he-is-ruined (10) Yahweh ones-ministering-of the-priests

אֲדָמָה כִּי שֻׁדַּד דָּגָן הוֹבִישׁ תִּירוֹשׁ אֻמְלַל יִצְהָר׃
oil he-fails new-wine he-is-dried-up grain he-is-destroyed indeed ground

הֹבִישׁוּ אִכָּרִים הֵילִילוּ כֹּרְמִים עַל־ חִטָּה וְעַל־ שְׂעֹרָה כִּי
because barley and-for wheat for ones-growing-vines wail! farmers despair! (11)

אָבַד קְצִיר שָׂדֶה׃ הַגֶּפֶן הוֹבִישָׁה וְהַתְּאֵנָה
and-the-fig-tree she-is-dried-up the-vine (12) field harvest-of he-is-destroyed

אֻמְלָלָה רִמּוֹן גַּם־ תָּמָר וְתַפּוּחַ כָּל־ עֲצֵי הַשָּׂדֶה
the-field trees-of all-of and-apple-tree palm and pomegranate she-is-withered

יָבֵשׁוּ כִּי־ הֹבִישׁ שָׂשׂוֹן מִן־ בְּנֵי אָדָם׃
mankind children-of from joy he-is-withered-away surely they-are-dried-up

1 The word of the LORD that came to Joel son of Pethuel.

*An Invasion of Locusts*

2 Hear this, you elders;
listen, all who live in the land.
Has anything like this ever happened in your days
or in the days of your forefathers?
3 Tell it to your children,
and let your children tell it to their children,
and their children to the next generation.
4 What the locust swarm has left
the great locusts have eaten;
what the great locusts have left
the young locusts have eaten;
what the young locusts have left
other locusts[a] have eaten.

5 Wake up, you drunkards, and weep!
Wail, all you drinkers of wine;
wail because of the new wine,
for it has been snatched from your lips.
6 A nation has invaded my land,
powerful and without number;
it has the teeth of a lion,
the fangs of a lioness.
7 It has laid waste my vines
and ruined my fig trees.
It has stripped off their bark
and thrown it away,
leaving their branches white.

8 Mourn like a virgin[b] in sackcloth
grieving for the husband[c] of her youth.
9 Grain offerings and drink offerings
are cut off from the house of the LORD.
The priests are in mourning,
those who minister before the LORD.
10 The fields are ruined,
the ground is dried up[d];
the grain is destroyed,
the new wine is dried up,
the oil fails.
11 Despair, you farmers,
wail, you vine growers;
grieve for the wheat and the barley,
because the harvest of the field is destroyed.
12 The vine is dried up
and the fig tree is withered;
the pomegranate, the palm and the apple tree—
all the trees of the field—are dried up.
Surely the joy of mankind
is withered away.

[a]4 The precise meaning of the four Hebrew words used here for locusts is uncertain.
[b]8 Or *young woman* [c]8 Or *betrothed*
[d]10 Or *ground mourns*

חִגְרוּ וְסִפְדוּ הַכֹּהֲנִים הֵילִילוּ מְשָׁרְתֵי מִזְבֵּחַ
altar ones-ministering-of wail! the-priests and-mourn! put-on-sackcloth! (13)

בֹּאוּ לִינוּ בַשַּׂקִּים מְשָׁרְתֵי אֱלֹהָי כִּי נִמְנַע
he-is-withheld for God-of-me ones-ministering-of in-the-sackcloths spend-night! come!

מִבֵּית אֱלֹהֵיכֶם מִנְחָה וָנָסֶךְ׃ קַדְּשׁוּ־צוֹם
fast declare-holy! (14) and-drink-offering grain-offering God-of-you from-house-of

קִרְאוּ עֲצָרָה אִסְפוּ זְקֵנִים כֹּל יֹשְׁבֵי הָאָרֶץ בֵּית יְהוָה
Yahweh house-of the-land ones-living-of all-of elders summon! sacred-assembly call!

אֱלֹהֵיכֶם וְזַעֲקוּ אֶל־יְהוָה׃ אֲהָהּ לַיּוֹם כִּי קָרוֹב יוֹם יְהוָה
Yahweh day-of near for for-the-day alas! (15) Yahweh to and-cry-out! God-of-you

וּכְשֹׁד מִשַּׁדַּי* יָבוֹא׃ הֲלוֹא נֶגֶד עֵינֵינוּ אֹכֶל
food eyes-of-us before not? (16) he-will-come from-Shaddai and-like-destruction

נִכְרָת מִבֵּית אֱלֹהֵינוּ שִׂמְחָה וָגִיל׃ עָבְשׁוּ
they-are-shriveled (17) and-gladness joy God-of-us from-house-of he-was-cut-off

פְרֻדוֹת תַּחַת מֶגְרְפֹתֵיהֶם נָשַׁמּוּ אֹצָרוֹת נֶהֶרְסוּ
they-are-broken-down storehouses they-are-in-ruins clods-of-them beneath seeds

מַמְּגֻרוֹת כִּי הֹבִישׁ דָּגָן׃ מַה־נֶּאֶנְחָה בְהֵמָה נָבֹכוּ עֶדְרֵי
herds-of they-mill-about cattle she-moans how! (18) grain he-dried-up for granaries

בָקָר כִּי אֵין מִרְעֶה לָהֶם גַּם־עֶדְרֵי הַצֹּאן נֶאְשָׁמוּ׃
they-suffer the-sheep flocks-of even for-them pasture there-is-no because livestock

אֵלֶיךָ יְהוָה אֶקְרָא כִּי אֵשׁ אָכְלָה נְאוֹת מִדְבָּר וְלֶהָבָה
and-flame open-field pastures-of she-devoured fire for I-call Yahweh to-you (19)

לִהֲטָה כָּל־עֲצֵי הַשָּׂדֶה׃ גַּם־בַּהֲמוֹת שָׂדֶה תַּעֲרוֹג אֵלֶיךָ
for-you she-pants wild animals-of even (20) the-field trees-of all-of she-burned-up

כִּי יָבְשׁוּ אֲפִיקֵי מָיִם וְאֵשׁ אָכְלָה נְאוֹת הַמִּדְבָּר׃
the-open-field pastures-of she-devoured and-fire waters streams-of they-dried-up for

תִּקְעוּ שׁוֹפָר בְּצִיּוֹן וְהָרִיעוּ בְּהַר קָדְשִׁי
holiness-of-me on-hill-of and-sound-alarm! in-Zion trumpet blow! (2:1)

יִרְגְּזוּ כֹּל יֹשְׁבֵי הָאָרֶץ כִּי־בָא יוֹם־יְהוָה כִּי
indeed Yahweh day-of he-comes for the-land ones-living-of all-of let-them-tremble

קָרוֹב׃ יוֹם חֹשֶׁךְ וַאֲפֵלָה יוֹם עָנָן וַעֲרָפֶל כְּשַׁחַר
like-dawn and-blackness cloud day-of and-gloom darkness day-of (2) close-at-hand

פָּרֻשׂ עַל־הֶהָרִים עַם רַב וְעָצוּם כָּמֹהוּ לֹא נִהְיָה
he-was never such-as-him and-mighty large army the-mountains across spreading

מִן־הָעוֹלָם וְאַחֲרָיו לֹא יוֹסֵף עַד־שְׁנֵי דּוֹר
generation ages-of to he-will-be-again never or-after-him the-old-time from

וָדוֹר׃ לְפָנָיו אָכְלָה אֵשׁ וְאַחֲרָיו תְּלַהֵט לֶהָבָה
flame she-blazes and-behind-him fire she-devours before-him (3) and-generation

*A Call to Repentance*

13 Put on sackcloth, O priests,
and mourn;
wail, you who minister
before the altar.
Come, spend the night in
sackcloth,
you who minister before my
God;
for the grain offerings and
drink offerings
are withheld from the house
of your God.
14 Declare a holy fast;
call a sacred assembly.
Summon the elders
and all who live in the land
to the house of the LORD your
God,
and cry out to the LORD.

15 Alas for that day!
For the day of the LORD is
near;
it will come like destruction
from the Almighty.[e]

16 Has not the food been cut off
before our very eyes—
joy and gladness
from the house of our God?
17 The seeds are shriveled
beneath the clods.[f]
The storehouses are in ruins,
the granaries have been
broken down,
for the grain has dried up.
18 How the cattle moan!
The herds mill about
because they have no pasture;
even the flocks of sheep are
suffering.

19 To you, O LORD, I call,
for fire has devoured the
open pastures
and flames have burned up
all the trees of the field.
20 Even the wild animals pant for
you;
the streams of water have
dried up
and fire has devoured the
open pastures.

*An Army of Locusts*

2 Blow the trumpet in Zion;
sound the alarm on my holy
hill.
Let all who live in the land
tremble,
for the day of the LORD is
coming.
It is close at hand—
2 a day of darkness and
gloom,
a day of clouds and
blackness.
Like dawn spreading across
the mountains
a large and mighty army
comes,
such as never was of old
nor ever will be in ages to
come.
3 Before them fire devours,
behind them a flame blazes.

e15 Hebrew *Shaddai*
f17 The meaning of the Hebrew for this word is uncertain.

***15** **Most mss have *dagesh* in the *shin* (משׁ').**

כְּגַן־ עֵדֶן הָאָרֶץ לְפָנָיו וְאַחֲרָיו מִדְבַּר שְׁמָמָה וְגַם־
and-also waste desert-of and-behind-him before-him the-land Eden like-garden-of

פְּלֵיטָה לֹא־ הָיְתָה לּוֹ׃ כְּמַרְאֵה סוּסִים מַרְאֵהוּ
appearance-of-him horses like-appearance-of (4) from-him she-is not escapee

וּכְפָרָשִׁים כֵּן יְרוּצוּן׃ כְּקוֹל מַרְכָּבוֹת עַל־ רָאשֵׁי
tops-of over chariots like-noise-of (5) they-gallop so and-like-cavalries

הֶהָרִים יְרַקֵּדוּן כְּקוֹל לַהַב אֵשׁ אֹכְלָה קָשׁ כְּעַם
like-army stubble consuming fire flame-of like-noise-of they-leap the-mountains

עָצוּם עֱרוּךְ מִלְחָמָה׃ מִפָּנָיו יָחִילוּ עַמִּים
nations they-are-in-anguish at-faces-of-them (6) battle being-drawn-up-of mighty

כָּל־ פָּנִים קִבְּצוּ פָארוּר׃ כְּגִבּוֹרִים יְרֻצוּן כְּאַנְשֵׁי מִלְחָמָה
war like-men-of they-charge like-warriors (7) pale they-turn faces every-of

יַעֲלוּ חוֹמָה וְאִישׁ בִּדְרָכָיו יֵלֵכוּן וְלֹא יְעַבְּטוּן
they-swerve-from and-not they-march in-lines-of-him and-each wall they-scale

אֹרְחוֹתָם׃ וְאִישׁ אָחִיו לֹא יִדְחָקוּן גֶּבֶר בִּמְסִלָּתוֹ
on-straight-road-of-him each they-jostle not other-of-him and-each (8) courses-of-them

יֵלֵכוּן וּבְעַד הַשֶּׁלַח יִפֹּלוּ לֹא יִבְצָעוּ׃ בָּעִיר
upon-the-city (9) they-break-ranks not they-plunge the-defense and-through they-march

יָשֹׁקּוּ בַּחוֹמָה יְרֻצוּן בַּבָּתִּים יַעֲלוּ בְּעַד הַחַלּוֹנִים
the-windows through they-climb into-the-houses they-run along-the-wall they-rush

יָבֹאוּ כַּגַּנָּב׃ לְפָנָיו רָגְזָה אֶרֶץ רָעֲשׁוּ שָׁמָיִם
skies they-tremble earth she-shakes before-him (10) like-the-thief they-enter

שֶׁמֶשׁ וְיָרֵחַ קָדָרוּ וְכוֹכָבִים אָסְפוּ נָגְהָם׃
shining-of-them they-hold-back and-stars they-are-darkened and-moon sun

וַיהוָה נָתַן קוֹלוֹ לִפְנֵי חֵילוֹ כִּי רַב מְאֹד
very great indeed army-of-him at-heads-of thunder-of-him he-gives and-Yahweh (11)

מַחֲנֵהוּ כִּי עָצוּם עֹשֵׂה דְבָרוֹ כִּי־ גָדוֹל יוֹם־ יְהוָה
Yahweh day-of great indeed command-of-him one-obeying mighty indeed force-of-him

וְנוֹרָא מְאֹד וּמִי יְכִילֶנּוּ׃ וְגַם־ עַתָּה נְאֻם־
declaration-of now and-even (12) he-can-endure-him and-who? very and-being-dreadful

יְהוָה שֻׁבוּ עָדַי בְּכָל־ לְבַבְכֶם וּבְצוֹם וּבִבְכִי*
and-with-weeping and-with-fasting heart-of-you with-all-of to-me return! Yahweh

וּבְמִסְפֵּד׃ וְקִרְעוּ לְבַבְכֶם וְאַל־ בִּגְדֵיכֶם וְשׁוּבוּ
and-return! garments-of-you and-not heart-of-you now-rend! (13) and-with-mourning

אֶל־ יְהוָה אֱלֹהֵיכֶם כִּי־ חַנּוּן וְרַחוּם הוּא אֶרֶךְ אַפַּיִם
angers slow-of he and-compassionate gracious for God-of-you Yahweh to

וְרַב־ חֶסֶד וְנִחָם עַל־ הָרָעָה׃ מִי יוֹדֵעַ יָשׁוּב
he-may-turn knowing who? (14) the-calamity from and-he-relents love and-abundant-of

Before them the land is like
the garden of Eden,
behind them, a desert
waste—
nothing escapes them.
4They have the appearance of
horses;
they gallop along like
cavalry.
5With a noise like that of
chariots
they leap over the
mountaintops,
like a crackling fire consuming
stubble,
like a mighty army drawn
up for battle.

6At the sight of them, nations
are in anguish;
every face turns pale.
7They charge like warriors;
they scale walls like soldiers.
They all march in line,
not swerving from their
course.
8They do not jostle each other;
each marches straight ahead.
They plunge through defenses
without breaking ranks.
9They rush upon the city;
they run along the wall.
They climb into the houses;
like thieves they enter
through the windows.

10Before them the earth shakes,
the sky trembles,
the sun and moon are
darkened,
and the stars no longer
shine.
11The LORD thunders
at the head of his army;
his forces are beyond number,
and mighty are those who
obey his command.
The day of the LORD is great;
it is dreadful.
Who can endure it?

*Rend Your Heart*

12"Even now," declares the
LORD,
"return to me with all your
heart,
with fasting and weeping
and mourning."

13Rend your heart
and not your garments.
Return to the LORD your God,
for he is gracious and
compassionate,
slow to anger and abounding
in love,
and he relents from sending
calamity.
14Who knows? He may turn and

*12 Most mss have *bireq* under the first *beth* (וּבִבְ).

וְנִחָם וְהִשְׁאִיר אַחֲרָיו בְּרָכָה מִנְחָה
grain-offering blessing behind-him and-he-may-leave and-he-may-have-pity

וָנֶסֶךְ לַיהוָה אֱלֹהֵיכֶם׃ תִּקְעוּ שׁוֹפָר בְּצִיּוֹן קַדְּשׁוּ־
declare-holy! in-Zion trumpet blow! (15) God-of-you for-Yahweh and-drink-offering

צוֹם קִרְאוּ עֲצָרָה׃ אִסְפוּ־ עָם קַדְּשׁוּ קָהָל קִבְצוּ
bring-together! assembly consecrate! people gather! (16) sacred-assembly call! fast

זְקֵנִים אִסְפוּ עוֹלָלִים וְיֹנְקֵי שָׁדָיִם יֵצֵא חָתָן
bridegroom let-him-leave breasts even-ones-nursing-of children gather! elders

מֵחֶדְרוֹ וְכַלָּה מֵחֻפָּתָהּ׃ בֵּין הָאוּלָם
the-temple-porch between (17) from-chamber-of-her and-bride from-room-of-him

וְלַמִּזְבֵּחַ יִבְכּוּ הַכֹּהֲנִים מְשָׁרְתֵי יְהוָה וְיֹאמְרוּ
and-let-them-say Yahweh ones-ministering-of the-priests let-them-weep and-to-the-altar

חוּסָה יְהוָה עַל־ עַמֶּךָ וְאַל־ תִּתֵּן נַחֲלָתְךָ לְחֶרְפָּה
to-object-of-scorn inheritance-of-you you-make and-not people-of-you to Yahweh spare!

לִמְשָׁל־ בָּם גּוֹיִם לָמָּה יֹאמְרוּ בָעַמִּים אַיֵּה
where? among-the-peoples should-they-say why? nations among-them to-be-byword

אֱלֹהֵיהֶם׃ וַיְקַנֵּא יְהוָה לְאַרְצוֹ וַיַּחְמֹל
and-he-will-take-pity for-land-of-him Yahweh then-he-will-be-jealous (18) God-of-them

עַל־ עַמּוֹ׃ וַיַּעַן יְהוָה וַיֹּאמֶר לְעַמּוֹ הִנְנִי
see-I! to-people-of-him and-he-will-say Yahweh and-he-will-reply (19) people-of-him on

שֹׁלֵחַ לָכֶם אֶת־ הַדָּגָן וְהַתִּירוֹשׁ וְהַיִּצְהָר וּשְׂבַעְתֶּם
and-you-will-be-satisfied and-the-oil and-the-new-wine the-grain *** to-you sending

אֹתוֹ וְלֹא־ אֶתֵּן אֶתְכֶם עוֹד חֶרְפָּה בַּגּוֹיִם׃ וְאֶת־
and (20) among-the-nations object-of-scorn again you I-will-make and-never by-him

הַצְּפוֹנִי אַרְחִיק מֵעֲלֵיכֶם וְהִדַּחְתִּיו אֶל־ אֶרֶץ
land-of into and-I-will-push-him from-upon-you I-will-drive-far the-northern-one

צִיָּה וּשְׁמָמָה אֶת־ פָּנָיו אֶל־ הַיָּם הַקַּדְמֹנִי וְסֹפוֹ
and-rear-of-him the-eastern the-sea into fronts-of-him *** and-barrenness parchedness

אֶל־ הַיָּם הָאַחֲרוֹן וְעָלָה בָאְשׁוֹ וְתַעַל
and-she-will-rise stench-of-him and-he-will-go-up the-western the-sea into

צַחֲנָתוֹ כִּי הִגְדִּיל לַעֲשׂוֹת׃ אַל־ תִּירְאִי אֲדָמָה גִּילִי
be-glad! land you-be-afraid not (21) to-do he-made-great surely smell-of-him

וּשְׂמָחִי כִּי־ הִגְדִּיל יְהוָה לַעֲשׂוֹת׃ אַל־ תִּירְאוּ בַּהֲמוֹת
animals-of you-be-afraid not (22) to-do Yahweh he-made-great surely and-rejoice!

שָׂדַי כִּי דָשְׁאוּ נְאוֹת מִדְבָּר כִּי־ עֵץ נָשָׂא פִרְיוֹ
fruit-of-him he-bears tree for open-field pastures-of they-become-green for wild

תְּאֵנָה וָגֶפֶן נָתְנוּ חֵילָם׃ וּבְנֵי צִיּוֹן גִּילוּ
be-glad! Zion and-peoples-of (23) richness-of-them they-yield and-vine fig-tree

have pity
and leave behind a blessing—
grain offerings and drink offerings
for the LORD your God.

15 Blow the trumpet in Zion,
declare a holy fast,
call a sacred assembly.
16 Gather the people,
consecrate the assembly;
bring together the elders,
gather the children,
those nursing at the breast.
Let the bridegroom leave his room
and the bride her chamber.
17 Let the priests, who minister before the LORD,
weep between the temple porch and the altar.
Let them say, "Spare your people, O LORD.
Do not make your inheritance an object of scorn,
a byword among the nations.
Why should they say among the peoples,
'Where is their God?' "

*The LORD's Answer*

18 Then the LORD will be jealous for his land
and take pity on his people.
19 The LORD will reply[g] to them:
"I am sending you grain, new wine and oil,
enough to satisfy you fully;
never again will I make you an object of scorn to the nations.

20 "I will drive the northern army far from you,
pushing it into a parched and barren land,
with its front columns going into the eastern sea[h]
and those in the rear into the western sea.[i]
And its stench will go up;
its smell will rise."
Surely he has done great things.[j]

21 Be not afraid, O land;
be glad and rejoice.
Surely the LORD has done great things.
22 Be not afraid, O wild animals,
for the open pastures are becoming green.
The trees are bearing their fruit;
the fig tree and the vine yield their riches.
23 Be glad, O people of Zion,

g18,19 Or LORD *was jealous . . . / and took pity . . . / [19]The* LORD *replied*
h20 That is, the Dead Sea
i20 That is, the Mediterranean
j20 Or *rise. / Surely it has done great things."*

וְשִׂמְחוּ֙ בַּיהוָ֣ה אֱלֹהֵיכֶ֔ם כִּֽי־ נָתַ֥ן לָכֶ֛ם אֶת־ הַמּוֹרֶ֖ה
the-autumn-rain *** to-you he-gave for God-of-you in-Yahweh and-rejoice!

לִצְדָקָ֑ה וַיּ֣וֹרֶד לָ֠כֶם גֶּ֣שֶׁם מוֹרֶ֧ה וּמַלְק֛וֹשׁ
and-spring-rain autumn-rain shower to-you and-he-sends-down in-righteousness

בָּרִאשֽׁוֹן׃ וּמָלְא֥וּ הַגֳּרָנ֖וֹת בָּ֑ר
grain the-threshing-floors and-they-will-be-filled (24) at-the-time-before

וְהֵשִׁ֥יקוּ הַיְקָבִ֖ים תִּיר֥וֹשׁ וְיִצְהָֽר׃ וְשִׁלַּמְתִּ֤י לָכֶם֙ אֶת־
*** to-you and-I-will-repay (25) and-oil new-wine the-vats and-they-will-overflow

הַשָּׁנִ֔ים אֲשֶׁר֙ אָכַ֣ל הָֽאַרְבֶּ֔ה הַיֶּ֖לֶק וְהֶחָסִ֣יל
and-the-other-locust the-young-locust the-great-locust he-ate that the-years

וְהַגָּזָ֑ם חֵילִי֙ הַגָּד֔וֹל אֲשֶׁ֥ר שִׁלַּ֖חְתִּי בָּכֶֽם׃ וַאֲכַלְתֶּ֤ם
and-you-will-eat (26) among-you I-sent that the-great army-of-me and-the-locust-swarm

אָכוֹל֙ וְשָׂב֔וֹעַ וְהִלַּלְתֶּ֗ם אֶת־ שֵׁ֤ם יְהוָה֙ אֱלֹהֵיכֶ֔ם אֲשֶׁר־
who God-of-you Yahweh name-of *** and-you-will-praise and-to-be-full to-eat

עָשָׂ֥ה עִמָּכֶ֖ם לְהַפְלִ֑יא וְלֹא־ יֵבֹ֥שׁוּ עַמִּ֖י לְעוֹלָֽם׃
to-forever people-of-me they-will-be-shamed and-never to-do-wonders for-you he-worked

וִֽידַעְתֶּ֗ם כִּ֣י בְקֶ֤רֶב יִשְׂרָאֵל֙ אָ֔נִי וַאֲנִ֛י יְהוָ֥ה אֱלֹהֵיכֶ֖ם
God-of-you Yahweh that-I I Israel in-midst-of that then-you-will-know (27)

וְאֵ֣ין ע֑וֹד וְלֹֽא־ יֵבֹ֥שׁוּ עַמִּ֖י לְעוֹלָֽם׃
to-forever people-of-me they-will-be-shamed and-never other and-there-is-no

וְהָיָ֣ה אַחֲרֵי־ כֵ֗ן אֶשְׁפּ֤וֹךְ אֶת־ רוּחִי֙ עַל־ כָּל־ בָּשָׂ֔ר
people all-of on spirit-of-me *** I-will-pour-out this after and-he-will-be *(3:1[28])

וְנִבְּא֖וּ בְּנֵיכֶ֣ם וּבְנֽוֹתֵיכֶ֑ם זִקְנֵיכֶם֙ חֲלֹמ֣וֹת
dreams old-men-of-you and-daughters-of-you sons-of-you and-they-will-prophesy

יַחֲלֹמ֔וּן בַּח֣וּרֵיכֶ֔ם חֶזְיֹנ֖וֹת יִרְאֽוּ׃ וְגַ֥ם עַל־
on and-even (2[29]) they-will-see visions young-men-of-you they-will-dream

הָֽעֲבָדִ֖ים וְעַל־ הַשְּׁפָח֑וֹת בַּיָּמִ֣ים הָהֵ֔מָּה אֶשְׁפּ֖וֹךְ אֶת־
*** I-will-pour-out the-those in-the-days the-women-servants and-on the-men-servants

רוּחִֽי׃ וְנָתַתִּי֙ מֽוֹפְתִ֔ים בַּשָּׁמַ֖יִם וּבָאָ֑רֶץ דָּ֣ם
blood and-on-the-earth in-the-heavens wonders and-I-will-show (3[30]) spirit-of-me

וָאֵ֔שׁ וְתִֽימְר֖וֹת עָשָֽׁן׃ הַשֶּׁ֙מֶשׁ֙ יֵהָפֵ֣ךְ לְחֹ֔שֶׁךְ
to-darkness he-will-be-turned the-sun (4[31]) smoke and-billows-of and-fire

וְהַיָּרֵ֖חַ לְדָ֑ם לִפְנֵ֗י בּ֚וֹא י֣וֹם יְהוָ֔ה הַגָּד֖וֹל וְהַנּוֹרָֽא׃
and-the-one-being-dreadful the-great Yahweh day-of to-come before to-blood and-the-moon

וְהָיָ֗ה כֹּ֧ל אֲשֶׁר־ יִקְרָ֛א בְּשֵׁ֥ם יְהוָ֖ה יִמָּלֵ֑ט
he-will-be-saved Yahweh on-name-of he-calls who every-one and-he-will-be (5[32])

כִּ֠י בְּהַר־ צִיּ֨וֹן וּבִירוּשָׁלִַ֜ם תִּהְיֶ֣ה פְלֵיטָ֗ה כַּאֲשֶׁר֙ אָמַ֣ר יְהוָ֔ה
Yahweh he-said as-what delivered-one she-will-be and-in-Jerusalem Zion on-Mount-of for

rejoice in the LORD your God,
for he has given you
the autumn rains in
righteousness.[k]
He sends you abundant
showers,
both autumn and spring
rains, as before.
24 The threshing floors will be
filled with grain;
the vats will overflow with
new wine and oil.

25 "I will repay you for the years
the locusts have eaten—
the great locust and the
young locust,
the other locusts and the
locust swarm[l]—
my great army that I sent
among you.
26 You will have plenty to eat,
until you are full,
and you will praise the
name of the LORD your
God,
who has worked wonders
for you;
never again will my people be
shamed.
27 Then you will know that I am
in Israel,
that I am the LORD your
God,
and that there is no other;
never again will my people be
shamed.

*The Day of the LORD*

28 "And afterward,
I will pour out my Spirit on
all people.
Your sons and daughters will
prophesy,
your old men will dream
dreams,
your young men will see
visions.
29 Even on my servants, both
men and women,
I will pour out my Spirit in
those days.
30 I will show wonders in the
heavens
and on the earth,
blood and fire and billows
of smoke.
31 The sun will be turned to
darkness
and the moon to blood
before the coming of the
great and dreadful day of
the LORD.
32 And everyone who calls
on the name of the LORD
will be saved;
for on Mount Zion and in
Jerusalem
there will be deliverance,
as the LORD has said,

[k] 23 Or / *the teacher for righteousness:*
[l] 25 The precise meaning of the four Hebrew words used here for locusts is uncertain.

***Heading, 1** The Hebrew numeration of 3:1-5 corresponds to 2:28-32 in English; the number in brackets indicates the English numeration.*

וּבַשְּׂרִידִים אֲשֶׁר יְהוָה קֹרֵא׃ כִּי הִנֵּה בַּיָּמִים
in-the-days see! indeed †(4[3]:1) calling Yahweh whom even-among-the-survivors

הָהֵמָּה וּבָעֵת הַהִיא אֲשֶׁר אָשׁוּב אֶת־ שְׁבוּת יְהוּדָה וִירוּשָׁלִָם׃
and-Jerusalem Judah fortune-of *** I-restore when the-that and-at-the-time the-those

וְקִבַּצְתִּי אֶת־ כָּל־ הַגּוֹיִם וְהוֹרַדְתִּים אֶל־ עֵמֶק
Valley-of to and-I-will-bring-down-them the-nations all-of *** then-I-will-gather (2)

יְהוֹשָׁפָט וְנִשְׁפַּטְתִּי עִמָּם שָׁם עַל־ עַמִּי
people-of-me concerning there against-them and-I-will-enter-into-judgment Jehoshaphat

וְנַחֲלָתִי יִשְׂרָאֵל אֲשֶׁר פִּזְּרוּ בַגּוֹיִם וְאֶת־ אַרְצִי
land-of-me and among-the-nations they-scattered for Israel and-inheritance-of-me

חִלֵּקוּ׃ וְאֶל־ עַמִּי יַדּוּ גוֹרָל וַיִּתְּנוּ הַיֶּלֶד
the-boy and-they-traded lot they-cast people-of-me and-for (3) they-divided-up

בַּזּוֹנָה וְהַיַּלְדָּה מָכְרוּ בַיַּיִן וַיִּשְׁתּוּ׃
that-they-might-drink for-the-wine they-sold and-the-girl for-the-one-being-prostitute

וְגַם מָה־ אַתֶּם לִי צֹר וְצִידוֹן וְכֹל גְּלִילוֹת פְּלָשֶׁת
Philistia regions-of and-all-of and-Sidon Tyre against-me you what? and-now (4)

הַגְּמוּל אַתֶּם מְשַׁלְּמִים עָלָי וְאִם־ גֹּמְלִים אַתֶּם עָלַי קַל מְהֵרָה
speedy swift to-me you ones-paying-back and-if to-me ones-repaying you the-deed

אָשִׁיב גְּמֻלְכֶם בְּרֹאשְׁכֶם׃ אֲשֶׁר־ כַּסְפִּי וּזְהָבִי לְקַחְתֶּם
you-took and-gold-of-me silver-of-me for (5) on-head-of-you deed-of-you I-will-return

וּמַחֲמַדַּי הַטֹּבִים הֲבֵאתֶם לְהֵיכְלֵיכֶם׃ וּבְנֵי
and-peoples-of (6) to-temples-of-you you-carried-off the-fine-ones and-treasures-of-me

יְהוּדָה וּבְנֵי יְרוּשָׁלִַם מְכַרְתֶּם לִבְנֵי הַיְּוָנִים לְמַעַן הַרְחִיקָם
to-send-far-them that the-Greeks to-peoples-of you-sold Jerusalem and-peoples-of Judah

מֵעַל גְּבוּלָם׃ הִנְנִי מְעִירָם מִן־ הַמָּקוֹם אֲשֶׁר־ מְכַרְתֶּם
you-sold which the-place from rousing-them see-I! (7) homeland-of-them from-on

אֹתָם שָׁמָּה וַהֲשִׁבֹתִי גְמֻלְכֶם בְּרֹאשְׁכֶם׃ וּמָכַרְתִּי אֶת־
*** and-I-will-sell (8) on-head-of-you deed-of-you and-I-will-return to-there them

בְּנֵיכֶם וְאֶת־ בְּנוֹתֵיכֶם בְּיַד בְּנֵי יְהוּדָה וּמְכָרוּם
and-they-will-sell-them Judah peoples-of to-hand-of daughters-of-you and sons-of-you

לִשְׁבָאיִם אֶל־ גּוֹי רָחוֹק כִּי יְהוָה דִּבֵּר׃ קִרְאוּ־ זֹאת
this proclaim! (9) he-spoke Yahweh indeed far-away nation-of to to-Sabeans

בַּגּוֹיִם קַדְּשׁוּ מִלְחָמָה הָעִירוּ הַגִּבּוֹרִים יִגְּשׁוּ יַעֲלוּ
let-them-attack let-them-draw-near the-warriors rouse! war prepare! among-the-nations

כָּל אַנְשֵׁי הַמִּלְחָמָה׃ כֹּתּוּ אִתֵּיכֶם לַחֲרָבוֹת וּמַזְמְרֹתֵיכֶם
and-pruning-hooks-of-you into-swords plowshares-of-you beat! (10) the-fight men-of all-of

לִרְמָחִים הַחַלָּשׁ יֹאמַר גִּבּוֹר אָנִי׃ עוּשׁוּ וָבֹאוּ כָל־
all-of and-come! come-help! (11) I strong let-him-say the-weakling into-spears

among the survivors
whom the LORD calls.

*The Nations Judged*

3 "In those days and at that
time,
when I restore the fortunes
of Judah and Jerusalem,
2 I will gather all nations
and bring them down to the
Valley of Jehoshaphat.[m]
There I will enter into
judgment against them
concerning my inheritance,
my people Israel,
for they scattered my people
among the nations
and divided up my land.
3 They cast lots for my people
and traded boys for
prostitutes;
they sold girls for wine
that they might drink.

4 "Now what have you against
me, O Tyre and Sidon and all you
regions of Philistia? Are you
repaying me for something I have
done? If you are paying me back,
I will swiftly and speedily return
on your own heads what you have
done. 5 For you took my silver and
my gold and carried off my finest
treasures to your temples. 6 You
sold the people of Judah and
Jerusalem to the Greeks, that you
might send them far from their
homeland.
7 "See, I am going to rouse them
out of the places to which you sold
them, and I will return on your
own heads what you have done. 8 I
will sell your sons and daughters
to the people of Judah, and they
will sell them to the Sabeans, a nation far away." The LORD has
spoken.

9 Proclaim this among the
nations:
Prepare for war!
Rouse the warriors!
Let all the fighting men
draw near and attack.
10 Beat your plowshares into
swords
and your pruning hooks
into spears.
Let the weakling say,
"I am strong!"
11 Come quickly, all you nations

[m]2 *Jehoshaphat* means *the LORD judges;* also in verse 12.

**Heading* See the note on page 505.

†*Heading, 1* The Hebrew numeration of chapter 4 corresponds to the English numeration of chapter 3; thus, there is a one-chapter discrepancy.

°1 ק אשיב

הַגּוֹיִם מִסָּבִיב וְנִקְבָּצוּ שָׁמָּה הַנְחַת יְהוָה

Yahweh bring-down! at-there and-let-them-assemble from-every-side the-nations

גִּבּוֹרֶיךָ׃ יֵעוֹרוּ וְיַעֲלוּ הַגּוֹיִם אֶל־

into the-nations and-let-them-advance let-them-be-roused (12) warriors-of-you

עֵמֶק יְהוֹשָׁפָט כִּי שָׁם אֵשֵׁב לִשְׁפֹּט אֶת־ כָּל־ הַגּוֹיִם

the-nations all-of *** to-judge I-will-sit there for Jehoshaphat Valley-of

מִסָּבִיב׃ שִׁלְחוּ מַגָּל כִּי בָשַׁל קָצִיר בֹּאוּ רְדוּ כִּי־ מָלְאָה

she-is-full for trample! come! harvest he-is-ripe for sickle swing! (13) on-every-side

גַּת הֵשִׁיקוּ הַיְקָבִים כִּי רַבָּה רָעָתָם׃ הֲמוֹנִים הֲמוֹנִים

multitudes multitudes (14) wickedness-of-them great so the-vats they-overflow winepress

בְּעֵמֶק הֶחָרוּץ כִּי קָרוֹב יוֹם יְהוָה בְּעֵמֶק הֶחָרוּץ׃ שֶׁמֶשׁ

sun (15) the-decision in-valley-of Yahweh day-of near for the-decision in-valley-of

וְיָרֵחַ קָדָרוּ וְכוֹכָבִים אָסְפוּ נָגְהָם׃

shining-of-them they-will-hold-back and-stars they-will-be-darkened and-moon

וַיהוָה מִצִּיּוֹן יִשְׁאָג וּמִירוּשָׁלַםִ יִתֵּן קוֹלוֹ

thunder-of-him he-will-give and-from-Jerusalem he-will-roar from-Zion and-Yahweh (16)

וְרָעֲשׁוּ שָׁמַיִם וָאָרֶץ וַיהוָה מַחֲסֶה לְעַמּוֹ

for-people-of-him refuge but-Yahweh and-earth skies and-they-will-tremble

וּמָעוֹז לִבְנֵי יִשְׂרָאֵל׃ וִידַעְתֶּם כִּי אֲנִי יְהוָה

Yahweh I that then-you-will-know (17) Israel for-peoples-of and-stronghold

אֱלֹהֵיכֶם שֹׁכֵן בְּצִיּוֹן הַר־ קָדְשִׁי וְהָיְתָה יְרוּשָׁלַםִ קֹדֶשׁ

holiness Jerusalem and-she-will-be holiness-of-me hill-of in-Zion dwelling God-of-you

וְזָרִים לֹא־ יַעַבְרוּ־ בָהּ עוֹד׃ וְהָיָה בַיּוֹם

in-the-day and-he-will-be (18) again to-her they-will-invade never and-ones-being-foreign

הַהוּא יִטְּפוּ הֶהָרִים עָסִיס וְהַגְּבָעוֹת תֵּלַכְנָה חָלָב

milk they-will-flow and-the-hills new-wine the-mountains they-will-drip the-that

וְכָל־ אֲפִיקֵי יְהוּדָה יֵלְכוּ מָיִם וּמַעְיָן מִבֵּית יְהוָה

Yahweh from-house-of and-fountain waters they-will-run Judah ravines-of and-all-of

יֵצֵא וְהִשְׁקָה אֶת־ נַחַל הַשִּׁטִּים׃ מִצְרַיִם לִשְׁמָמָה

to-desolation Egypt (19) the-acacias valley-of *** and-he-will-water he-will-flow

תִהְיֶה וֶאֱדוֹם לְמִדְבַּר שְׁמָמָה תִּהְיֶה מֵחֲמַס בְּנֵי

peoples-of because-of-violence-of she-will-be waste to-desert-of and-Edom she-will-be

יְהוּדָה אֲשֶׁר־ שָׁפְכוּ דָם־ נָקִיא בְּאַרְצָם׃ וִיהוּדָה לְעוֹלָם

to-forever and-Judah (20) in-land-of-them innocent blood they-shed whom Judah

תֵּשֵׁב וִירוּשָׁלַםִ לְדוֹר וָדוֹר׃

and-generation through-generation and-Jerusalem she-will-be-inhabited

וְנִקֵּיתִי דָּמָם לֹא־ נִקֵּיתִי וַיהוָה שֹׁכֵן בְּצִיּוֹן׃

in-Zion dwelling indeed-Yahweh I-pardoned not bloodguilt-of-them and-I-will-pardon (21)

from every side,
and assemble there.

Bring down your warriors, O
LORD!

12"Let the nations be roused;
let them advance into the
Valley of Jehoshaphat,
for there I will sit
to judge all the nations on
every side.
13Swing the sickle,
for the harvest is ripe.
Come, trample the grapes,
for the winepress is full
and the vats overflow—
so great is their wickedness!"

14Multitudes, multitudes
in the valley of decision!
For the day of the LORD is near
in the valley of decision.
15The sun and moon will be
darkened,
and the stars no longer
shine.
16The LORD will roar from Zion
and thunder from Jerusalem;
the earth and the sky will
tremble.
But the LORD will be a refuge
for his people,
a stronghold for the people
of Israel.

*Blessings for God's People*

17"Then you will know that I,
the LORD your God,
dwell in Zion, my holy hill.
Jerusalem will be holy;
never again will foreigners
invade her.

18"In that day the mountains
will drip new wine,
and the hills will flow with
milk;
all the ravines of Judah will
run with water.
A fountain will flow out of the
LORD's house
and will water the valley of
acacias.[n]
19But Egypt will be desolate,
Edom a desert waste,
because of violence done to
the people of Judah,
in whose land they shed
innocent blood.
20Judah will be inhabited forever
and Jerusalem through all
generations.
21Their bloodguilt, which I have
not pardoned,
I will pardon."

The LORD dwells in Zion!

[n]18 Or *Valley of Shittim*

**Heading* See the second note on page 506.

דִּבְרֵי עָמוֹס אֲשֶׁר־הָיָה בַנֹּקְדִים מִתְּקוֹעַ אֲשֶׁר חָזָה עַל־
concerning he-saw what of-Tekoa of-the-shepherds he-was who Amos words-of (1:1)

יִשְׂרָאֵל בִּימֵי׀ עֻזִיָּה מֶלֶךְ־יְהוּדָה וּבִימֵי יָרָבְעָם בֶּן־יוֹאָשׁ
Joash son-of Jeroboam and-in-days-of Judah king-of Uzziah in-days-of Israel

מֶלֶךְ יִשְׂרָאֵל שְׁנָתַיִם לִפְנֵי הָרָעַשׁ׃ וַיֹּאמַר׀ יְהוָה מִצִּיּוֹן
from-Zion Yahweh and-he-said (2) the-earthquake before two-years Israel king-of

יִשְׁאָג וּמִירוּשָׁלִַם יִתֵּן קוֹלוֹ וְאָבְלוּ נְאוֹת
pastures-of and-they-dry-up thunder-of-him he-gives and-from-Jerusalem he-roars

הָרֹעִים וְיָבֵשׁ רֹאשׁ הַכַּרְמֶל׃ כֹּה אָמַר יְהוָה
Yahweh he-says this (3) the-Carmel top-of and-he-withers the-ones-being-shepherds

עַל־שְׁלֹשָׁה פִּשְׁעֵי דַמֶּשֶׂק וְעַל־אַרְבָּעָה לֹא אֲשִׁיבֶנּוּ עַל־
because I-will-turn-back-him not four even-for Damascus sins-of three for

דּוּשָׁם בַּחֲרֻצוֹת הַבַּרְזֶל אֶת־הַגִּלְעָד׃ וְשִׁלַּחְתִּי
so-I-will-send (4) the-Gilead *** the-iron with-sledges-of to-thresh-them

אֵשׁ בְּבֵית חֲזָאֵל וְאָכְלָה אַרְמְנוֹת בֶּן־הֲדָד׃
Hadad Ben fortresses-of that-she-will-consume Hazael on-house-of fire

וְשָׁבַרְתִּי בְּרִיחַ דַּמֶּשֶׂק וְהִכְרַתִּי יוֹשֵׁב
one-inhabiting and-I-will-destroy Damascus gate-of and-I-will-break-down (5)

מִבִּקְעַת־אָוֶן וְתוֹמֵךְ שֵׁבֶט מִבֵּית עֶדֶן וְגָלוּ
and-they-will-go-into-exile Eden in-Beth scepter and-one-holding Aven in-Valley-of

עַם־אֲרָם קִירָה אָמַר יְהוָה׃ כֹּה אָמַר יְהוָה עַל־שְׁלֹשָׁה פִּשְׁעֵי
sins-of three for Yahweh he-says this (6) Yahweh he-says to-Kir Aram people-of

עַזָּה וְעַל־אַרְבָּעָה לֹא אֲשִׁיבֶנּוּ עַל־הַגְלוֹתָם
to-take-captive-them because I-will-turn-back-him not four even-for Gaza

גָּלוּת שְׁלֵמָה לְהַסְגִּיר לֶאֱדוֹם׃ וְשִׁלַּחְתִּי אֵשׁ בְּחוֹמַת עַזָּה
Gaza upon-wall-of fire so-I-will-send (7) to-Edom to-sell whole community

וְאָכְלָה אַרְמְנֹתֶיהָ׃ וְהִכְרַתִּי יוֹשֵׁב
one-inhabiting and-I-will-destroy (8) fortresses-of-her that-she-will-consume

מֵאַשְׁדּוֹד וְתוֹמֵךְ שֵׁבֶט מֵאַשְׁקְלוֹן וַהֲשִׁיבוֹתִי יָדִי עַל־
against hand-of-me and-I-will-turn in-Ashkelon scepter and-one-holding in-Ashdod

עֶקְרוֹן וְאָבְדוּ שְׁאֵרִית פְּלִשְׁתִּים אָמַר אֲדֹנָי יְהוִה׃ כֹּה
this (9) Yahweh Sovereign he-says Philistines last-of till-they-are-dead Ekron

אָמַר יְהוָה עַל־שְׁלֹשָׁה פִּשְׁעֵי־ צֹר וְעַל־אַרְבָּעָה לֹא אֲשִׁיבֶנּוּ
I-will-turn-back-him not four even-for Tyre sins-of three for Yahweh he-says

עַל־הַסְגִּירָם גָּלוּת שְׁלֵמָה לֶאֱדוֹם וְלֹא זָכְרוּ בְּרִית
treaty-of they-regarded and-not to-Edom whole community to-sell-them because

אַחִים׃ וְשִׁלַּחְתִּי אֵשׁ בְּחוֹמַת צֹר וְאָכְלָה
that-she-will-consume Tyre upon-wall-of fire so-I-will-send (10) brotherhoods

1 The words of Amos, one of the shepherds of Tekoa—what he saw concerning Israel two years before the earthquake, when Uzziah was king of Judah and Jeroboam son of Jehoash[a] was king of Israel.

2 He said:

"The LORD roars from Zion
and thunders from Jerusalem;
the pastures of the shepherds dry up,[b]
and the top of Carmel withers."

*Judgment on Israel's Neighbors*

3 This is what the LORD says:

"For three sins of Damascus,
even for four, I will not turn back ⌊my wrath⌋.
Because she threshed Gilead
with sledges having iron teeth,
4 I will send fire upon the house of Hazael
that will consume the fortresses of Ben-Hadad.
5 I will break down the gate of Damascus;
I will destroy the king who is in[c] the Valley of Aven[d]
and the one who holds the scepter in Beth Eden.
The people of Aram will go into exile to Kir,"
says the LORD.

6 This is what the LORD says:

"For three sins of Gaza,
even for four, I will not turn back ⌊my wrath⌋.
Because she took captive whole communities
and sold them to Edom,
7 I will send fire upon the walls of Gaza
that will consume her fortresses.
8 I will destroy the king[e] of Ashdod
and the one who holds the scepter in Ashkelon.
I will turn my hand against Ekron,
till the last of the Philistines is dead,"
says the Sovereign LORD.

9 This is what the LORD says:

"For three sins of Tyre,
even for four, I will not turn back ⌊my wrath⌋.
Because she sold whole communities of captives
to Edom,
disregarding a treaty of brotherhood,
10 I will send fire upon the walls of Tyre
that will consume her

a1 Hebrew *Joash*, a variant of *Jehoash*
b2 Or *shepherds mourn*
c5 Or *the inhabitants of*
d5 *Aven* means *wickedness.*
e8 Or *inhabitants*

אַרְמְנֹתֶיהָ׃ כֹּה אָמַר יְהוָה עַל־שְׁלֹשָׁה פִּשְׁעֵי אֱדוֹם וְעַל־
even-for Edom sins-of three for Yahweh he-says this (11) fortresses-of-her

אַרְבָּעָה לֹא אֲשִׁיבֶנּוּ עַל־ רָדְפוֹ בַחֶרֶב אָחִיו
brother-of-him with-the-sword to-pursue-him because I-will-turn-back-him not four

וְשִׁחֵת רַחֲמָיו וַיִּטְרֹף לָעַד אַפּוֹ
anger-of-him to-continuance because-he-raged compassions-of-him and-he-stifled

וְעֶבְרָתוֹ שְׁמָרָה נֶצַח׃ וְשִׁלַּחְתִּי אֵשׁ בְּתֵימָן
upon-Teman fire so-I-will-send (12) unchecked he-kept-her and-fury-of-him

וְאָכְלָה אַרְמְנוֹת בָּצְרָה׃ כֹּה אָמַר יְהוָה עַל־שְׁלֹשָׁה
three for Yahweh he-says this (13) Bozrah fortresses-of that-she-will-consume

פִּשְׁעֵי בְנֵי־ עַמּוֹן וְעַל־אַרְבָּעָה לֹא אֲשִׁיבֶנּוּ עַל־ בִּקְעָם
to-rip-open-them because I-will-turn-back-him not four even-for Ammon sons-of sins-of

הָרוֹת הַגִּלְעָד לְמַעַן הַרְחִיב אֶת־ גְּבוּלָם׃
border-of-them *** to-extend in-order-to the-Gilead pregnant-women-of

וְהִצַּתִּי אֵשׁ בְּחוֹמַת רַבָּה וְאָכְלָה אַרְמְנוֹתֶיהָ
fortresses-of-her that-she-will-consume Rabbah to-wall-of fire so-I-will-set (14)

בִּתְרוּעָה בְּיוֹם מִלְחָמָה בְּסַעַר בְּיוֹם סוּפָה׃ וְהָלַךְ
and-he-will-go (15) storm on-day-of amid-violent-wind battle on-day-of amid-war-cry

מַלְכָּם בַּגּוֹלָה הוּא וְשָׂרָיו יַחְדָּו אָמַר יְהוָה׃
Yahweh he-says together and-officials-of-him he into-the-exile king-of-them

כֹּה אָמַר יְהוָה עַל־שְׁלֹשָׁה פִּשְׁעֵי מוֹאָב וְעַל־אַרְבָּעָה לֹא
not four even-for Moab sins-of three for Yahweh he-says this (2:1)

אֲשִׁיבֶנּוּ עַל־ שָׂרְפוֹ עַצְמוֹת מֶלֶךְ־ אֱדוֹם לַשִּׂיד׃
to-the-lime Edom king-of bones-of to-burn-him because I-will-turn-back-him

וְשִׁלַּחְתִּי־ אֵשׁ בְּמוֹאָב וְאָכְלָה אַרְמְנוֹת הַקְּרִיּוֹת
the-Kerioth fortresses-of that-she-will-consume upon-Moab fire so-I-will-send (2)

וּמֵת בְּשָׁאוֹן מוֹאָב בִּתְרוּעָה בְּקוֹל שׁוֹפָר׃
trumpet with-blast-of amid-war-cry Moab in-tumult and-he-will-go-down

וְהִכְרַתִּי שׁוֹפֵט מִקִּרְבָּהּ וְכָל־ שָׂרֶיהָ
officials-of-her and-all-of from-midst-of-her one-ruling and-I-will-destroy (3)

אֶהֱרוֹג עִמּוֹ אָמַר יְהוָה׃ כֹּה אָמַר יְהוָה עַל־שְׁלֹשָׁה פִּשְׁעֵי יְהוּדָה
Judah sins-of three for Yahweh he-says this (4) Yahweh he-says with-him I-will-kill

וְעַל־ אַרְבָּעָה לֹא אֲשִׁיבֶנּוּ עַל־ מָאֳסָם אֶת־ תּוֹרַת יְהוָה
Yahweh law-of *** to-reject-them because I-will-turn-back-him not four even-for

וְחֻקָּיו לֹא שָׁמָרוּ וַיַּתְעוּם כִּזְבֵיהֶם
false-ones-of-them because-they-led-astray-them they-kept not and-decrees-of-him

אֲשֶׁר־ הָלְכוּ אֲבוֹתָם אַחֲרֵיהֶם׃ וְשִׁלַּחְתִּי אֵשׁ בִּיהוּדָה
upon-Judah fire so-I-will-send (5) after-them ancestors-of-them they-followed that

fortresses."

11 This is what the LORD says:

"For three sins of Edom,
even for four, I will not turn back ⌊my wrath⌋.
Because he pursued his brother with a sword,
stifling all compassion,[f]
because his anger raged continually
and his fury flamed unchecked,
12 I will send fire upon Teman
that will consume the fortresses of Bozrah."

13 This is what the LORD says:

"For three sins of Ammon,
even for four, I will not turn back ⌊my wrath⌋.
Because he ripped open the pregnant women of Gilead
in order to extend his borders,
14 I will set fire to the walls of Rabbah
that will consume her fortresses
amid war cries on the day of battle,
amid violent winds on a stormy day.
15 Her king[g] will go into exile,
he and his officials together,"
says the LORD.

2 This is what the LORD says:
"For three sins of Moab,
even for four, I will not turn back ⌊my wrath⌋.
Because he burned, as if to lime,
the bones of Edom's king,
2 I will send fire upon Moab
that will consume the fortresses of Kerioth.[h]
Moab will go down in great tumult
amid war cries and the blast of the trumpet.
3 I will destroy her ruler
and kill all her officials with him,"
says the LORD.

4 This is what the LORD says:

"For three sins of Judah,
even for four, I will not turn back ⌊my wrath⌋.
Because they have rejected the law of the LORD
and have not kept his decrees,
because they have been led astray by false gods,[i]
the gods[j] their ancestors followed,
5 I will send fire upon Judah

f11 Or *sword / and destroyed his allies*
g15 Or / *Molech;* Hebrew *malcam*
h2 Or *of her cities*
i4 Or *by lies*
j4 Or *lies*

וְאָכְלָה אַרְמְנוֹת יְרוּשָׁלִָם׃ כֹּה אָמַר יְהוָה עַל־שְׁלֹשָׁה
three for Yahweh he-says this (6) Jerusalem fortresses-of that-she-will-consume

פִּשְׁעֵי יִשְׂרָאֵל וְעַל־אַרְבָּעָה לֹא אֲשִׁיבֶנּוּ עַל־מִכְרָם
to-sell-them because I-will-turn-back-him not four even-for Israel sins-of

בַּכֶּסֶף צַדִּיק וְאֶבְיוֹן בַּעֲבוּר נַעֲלָיִם׃ הַשֹּׁאֲפִים
the-ones-trampling (7) pair-of-sandals for-sake-of and-needy righteous for-the-silver

עַל־עֲפַר־אֶרֶץ בְּרֹאשׁ דַּלִּים וְדֶרֶךְ עֲנָוִים יַטּוּ
they-deny oppressed-ones and-justice-of poor-ones on-head-of ground dust-of upon

וְאִישׁ וְאָבִיו יֵלְכוּ אֶל־הַנַּעֲרָה לְמַעַן חַלֵּל אֶת־שֵׁם
name-of *** to-profane so-that the-girl to they-use and-father-of-him and-son

קָדְשִׁי׃ וְעַל־בְּגָדִים חֲבֻלִים יַטּוּ אֵצֶל
beside they-lie-down ones-taken-in-pledge garments and-on (8) holiness-of-me

כָּל־מִזְבֵּחַ וְיֵין עֲנוּשִׁים יִשְׁתּוּ בֵּית אֱלֹהֵיהֶם׃
gods-of-them house-of they-drink ones-being-fined and-wine-of altar every-of

וְאָנֹכִי הִשְׁמַדְתִּי אֶת־הָאֱמֹרִי מִפְּנֵיהֶם אֲשֶׁר כְּגֹבַהּ אֲרָזִים
cedars as-tallness-of though at-before-them the-Amorite *** I-destroyed now-I (9)

גָּבְהוֹ וְחָסֹן הוּא כָּאַלּוֹנִים וָאַשְׁמִיד פִּרְיוֹ מִמַּעַל
at-above fruit-of-him indeed-I-destroyed as-the-oaks he and-strong tallness-of-him

וְשָׁרָשָׁיו מִתָּחַת׃ וְאָנֹכִי הֶעֱלֵיתִי אֶתְכֶם מֵאֶרֶץ מִצְרַיִם וָאוֹלֵךְ
and-I-led Egypt from-land-of you I-brought-up and-I (10) at-below and-roots-of-him

אֶתְכֶם בַּמִּדְבָּר אַרְבָּעִים שָׁנָה לָרֶשֶׁת אֶת־אֶרֶץ הָאֱמֹרִי׃ וָאָקִים
also-I-raised (11) the-Amorite land-of *** to-possess year forty in-the-desert you

מִבְּנֵיכֶם לִנְבִיאִים וּמִבַּחוּרֵיכֶם לִנְזִרִים הַאַף
indeed? to-Nazirites and-from-young-men-of-you to-prophets from-sons-of-you

אֵין־זֹאת בְּנֵי יִשְׂרָאֵל נְאֻם־יְהוָה׃ וַתַּשְׁקוּ אֶת־
*** but-you-made-drink (12) Yahweh declaration-of Israel peoples-of this not

הַנְּזִרִים יָיִן וְעַל־הַנְּבִיאִים צִוִּיתֶם לֵאמֹר לֹא תִּנָּבְאוּ׃
you-prophesy not to-say you-commanded the-prophets and-to wine the-Nazirites

הִנֵּה אָנֹכִי מֵעִיק תַּחְתֵּיכֶם כַּאֲשֶׁר תָּעִיק הָעֲגָלָה הַמְלֵאָה
the-one-loaded the-cart she-crushes as-that to-you crushing I see! (13)

לָהּ עָמִיר׃ וְאָבַד מָנוֹס מִקָּל וְחָזָק לֹא־
not and-strong from-swift escape and-he-will-be-destroyed (14) grain on-her

יְאַמֵּץ כֹּחוֹ וְגִבּוֹר לֹא־יְמַלֵּט נַפְשׁוֹ׃
life-of-him he-will-save not and-warrior strength-of-him he-will-muster

וְתֹפֵשׂ הַקֶּשֶׁת לֹא יַעֲמֹד וְקַל בְּרַגְלָיו לֹא
not of-feet-of-him and-one-fleet he-will-stand not the-bow and-one-holding (15)

יְמַלֵּט וְרֹכֵב הַסּוּס לֹא יְמַלֵּט נַפְשׁוֹ׃
life-of-him he-will-save not the-horse and-man-riding he-will-get-away

that will consume the
fortresses of Jerusalem."

*Judgment on Israel*

6 This is what the LORD says:

"For three sins of Israel,
even for four, I will not turn
back ⌞my wrath⌟.
They sell the righteous for
silver,
and the needy for a pair of
sandals.
7 They trample on the heads of
the poor
as upon the dust of the
ground
and deny justice to the
oppressed.
Father and son use the same
girl
and so profane my holy
name.
8 They lie down beside every
altar
on garments taken in
pledge.
In the house of their god
they drink wine taken as
fines.

9 "I destroyed the Amorite
before them,
though he was tall as the
cedars
and strong as the oaks.
I destroyed his fruit above
and his roots below.

10 "I brought you up out of
Egypt,
and I led you forty years in
the desert
to give you the land of the
Amorites.
11 I also raised up prophets from
among your sons
and Nazirites from among
your young men.
Is this not true, people of
Israel?"
declares the LORD.
12 "But you made the Nazirites
drink wine
and commanded the
prophets not to prophesy.

13 "Now then, I will crush you
as a cart crushes when
loaded with grain.
14 The swift will not escape,
the strong will not muster
their strength,
and the warrior will not
save his life.
15 The archer will not stand his
ground,
the fleet-footed soldier will
not get away,
and the horseman will not
save his life.

וְאַמִּיץ לִבּוֹ בַּגִּבּוֹרִים עָרוֹם יָנוּס בַּיּוֹם־
on-the-day he-will-flee naked among-the-warriors heart-of-him even-one-brave-of (16)

הַהוּא נְאֻם־ יְהוָה׃ שִׁמְעוּ אֶת־הַדָּבָר הַזֶּה אֲשֶׁר דִּבֶּר יְהוָה
Yahweh he-spoke that the-this the-word *** hear! (3:1) Yahweh declaration-of the-that

עֲלֵיכֶם בְּנֵי יִשְׂרָאֵל עַל כָּל־ הַמִּשְׁפָּחָה אֲשֶׁר הֶעֱלֵיתִי
I-brought-up that the-family whole-of against Israel peoples-of against-you

מֵאֶרֶץ מִצְרַיִם לֵאמֹר׃ רַק אֶתְכֶם יָדַעְתִּי מִכֹּל מִשְׁפְּחוֹת הָאֲדָמָה
the-earth families-of from-all-of I-chose you only (2) to-say Egypt from-land-of

עַל־ כֵּן אֶפְקֹד עֲלֵיכֶם אֵת כָּל־ עֲוֺנֹתֵיכֶם׃ הֲיֵלְכוּ שְׁנַיִם
two do-they-walk? (3) sins-of-you all-of *** to-you I-will-punish this for

יַחְדָּו בִּלְתִּי אִם־ נוֹעָדוּ׃ הֲיִשְׁאַג אַרְיֵה בַּיַּעַר וְטֶרֶף
when-prey in-the-thicket lion does-he-roar? (4) they-are-agreed if unless together

אֵין לוֹ הֲיִתֵּן כְּפִיר קוֹלוֹ מִמְּעֹנָתוֹ בִּלְתִּי אִם־ לָכָד׃
he-caught if unless in-den-of-him growl-of-him lion does-he-give? to-him there-is-not

הֲתִפֹּל צִפּוֹר עַל־ פַּח הָאָרֶץ וּמוֹקֵשׁ אֵין לָהּ
for-her there-is-not when-snare the-ground trap-of into bird does-she-fall? (5)

הֲיַעֲלֶה־ פַּח מִן־ הָאֲדָמָה וְלָכוֹד לֹא יִלְכּוֹד׃ אִם
when (6) he-catches not when-to-catch the-earth from trap does-he-spring-up?

יִתָּקַע שׁוֹפָר בְּעִיר וְעָם לֹא יֶחֱרָדוּ אִם־ תִּהְיֶה רָעָה
disaster she-comes when they-tremble not then-people in-city trumpet he-is-sounded

בְּעִיר וַיהוָה לֹא עָשָׂה׃ כִּי לֹא יַעֲשֶׂה אֲדֹנָי יְהוִה דָּבָר
anything Yahweh Sovereign he-does not surely (7) he-caused not then-Yahweh to-city

כִּי אִם־ גָּלָה סוֹדוֹ אֶל־ עֲבָדָיו הַנְּבִיאִים׃ אַרְיֵה שָׁאָג
he-roared lion (8) the-prophets servants-of-him to plan-of-him he-reveals if except

מִי לֹא יִירָא אֲדֹנָי יְהוִה דִּבֶּר מִי לֹא יִנָּבֵא׃
he-will-prophesy not who? he-spoke Yahweh Sovereign he-will-fear not who?

הַשְׁמִיעוּ עַל־אַרְמְנוֹת בְּאַשְׁדּוֹד וְעַל־ אַרְמְנוֹת בְּאֶרֶץ מִצְרַיִם וְאִמְרוּ
and-say! Egypt of-land-of fortresses and-to of-Ashdod fortresses to proclaim! (9)

הֵאָסְפוּ עַל־ הָרֵי שֹׁמְרוֹן וּרְאוּ מְהוּמֹת רַבּוֹת בְּתוֹכָהּ
within-her great-ones unrests and-see! Samaria mountains-of on assemble-yourselves!

וַעֲשׁוּקִים בְּקִרְבָּהּ׃ וְלֹא־ יָדְעוּ עֲשׂוֹת־נְכֹחָה נְאֻם־
declaration-of right to-do they-know indeed-not (10) in-among-her and-oppressions

יְהוָה הָאוֹצְרִים חָמָס וָשֹׁד בְּאַרְמְנוֹתֵיהֶם׃ לָכֵן כֹּה
this therefore (11) in-fortresses-of-them and-loot plunder the-ones-hoarding Yahweh

אָמַר אֲדֹנָי יְהוִה צַר וּסְבִיב הָאָרֶץ וְהוֹרִד
and-he-will-pull-down the-land and-overrunning-of enemy Yahweh Sovereign he-says

מִמֵּךְ עֻזֵּךְ וְנָבֹזּוּ אַרְמְנוֹתָיִךְ׃ כֹּה
this (12) fortresses-of-you and-they-will-be-plundered stronghold-of-you of-you

16 Even the bravest warriors
will flee naked on that day,"
declares the LORD.

*Witnesses Summoned Against Israel*

3 Hear this word the LORD has spoken against you, O people of Israel—against the whole family I brought up out of Egypt:

2 "You only have I chosen
of all the families of the earth;
therefore I will punish you
for all your sins."

3 Do two walk together
unless they have agreed to do so?
4 Does a lion roar in the thicket
when he has no prey?
Does he growl in his den
when he has caught nothing?
5 Does a bird fall into a trap on the ground
where no snare has been set?
Does a trap spring up from the earth
when there is nothing to catch?
6 When a trumpet sounds in a city,
do not the people tremble?
When disaster comes to a city,
has not the LORD caused it?

7 Surely the Sovereign LORD does nothing
without revealing his plan
to his servants the prophets.

8 The lion has roared—
who will not fear?
The Sovereign LORD has spoken—
who can but prophesy?

9 Proclaim to the fortresses of Ashdod
and to the fortresses of Egypt:
"Assemble yourselves on the mountains of Samaria;
see the great unrest within her
and the oppression among her people."

10 "They do not know how to do right," declares the LORD,
"who hoard plunder and loot in their fortresses."

11 Therefore this is what the Sovereign LORD says:

"An enemy will overrun the land;
he will pull down your strongholds
and plunder your fortresses."

אָמַר יְהוָה כַּאֲשֶׁר יַצִּיל הָרֹעֶה מִפִּי הָאֲרִי
the-lion from-mouth-of the-one-being-shepherd he-saves as-that Yahweh he-says

שְׁתֵּי כְרָעַיִם אוֹ בְדַל־ אֹזֶן כֵּן יִנָּצְלוּ בְּנֵי יִשְׂרָאֵל
Israel peoples-of they-will-be-saved so ear piece-of or leg-bones two-of

הַיֹּשְׁבִים בְּשֹׁמְרוֹן בִּפְאַת מִטָּה וּבִדְמֶשֶׁק עָרֶשׂ׃ שִׁמְעוּ
hear! (13) couch and-in-Damascus bed on-edge-of in-Samaria the-ones-sitting

וְהָעִידוּ בְּבֵית יַעֲקֹב נְאֻם־ אֲדֹנָי יְהוִה אֱלֹהֵי הַצְּבָאוֹת׃
the-Hosts God-of Yahweh Sovereign declaration-of Jacob against-house-of and-testify!

כִּי בְּיוֹם פָּקְדִי פִשְׁעֵי־יִשְׂרָאֵל עָלָיו וּפָקַדְתִּי עַל־
to then-I-will-destroy on-him Israel sins-of to-punish-me on-day-of indeed (14)

מִזְבְּחוֹת בֵּית־ אֵל וְנִגְדְּעוּ קַרְנוֹת הַמִּזְבֵּחַ וְנָפְלוּ
and-they-will-fall the-altar horns-of and-they-will-be-cut-off El Beth altars-of

לָאָרֶץ׃ וְהִכֵּיתִי בֵית־ הַחֹרֶף עַל־ בֵּית הַקָּיִץ
the-summer house-of with the-winter house-of and-I-will-tear-down (15) to-the-ground

וְאָבְדוּ בָּתֵּי הַשֵּׁן וְסָפוּ בָּתִּים
houses and-they-will-be-demolished the-ivory houses-of and-they-will-be-destroyed

רַבִּים נְאֻם־ יְהוָה׃ שִׁמְעוּ הַדָּבָר הַזֶּה פָּרוֹת הַבָּשָׁן
the-Bashan cows-of the-this the-word hear! (4:1) Yahweh declaration-of great-ones

אֲשֶׁר בְּהַר שֹׁמְרוֹן הָעֹשְׁקוֹת דַּלִּים הָרֹצְצוֹת אֶבְיוֹנִים
needy-ones the-women-crushing poor-ones the-women-oppressing Samaria on-Mount-of who

הָאֹמְרֹת לַאֲדֹנֵיהֶם הָבִיאָה וְנִשְׁתֶּה׃ נִשְׁבַּע אֲדֹנָי
Sovereign he-swore (2) so-we-may-drink bring! to-husbands-of-them the-women-saying

יְהוִה בְּקָדְשׁוֹ כִּי הִנֵּה יָמִים בָּאִים עֲלֵיכֶם וְנִשָּׂא
when-he-will-take-away upon-you ones-coming days see! surely by-holiness-of-him Yahweh

אֶתְכֶם בְּצִנּוֹת וְאַחֲרִיתְכֶן בְּסִירוֹת דּוּגָה׃ וּפְרָצִים
and-breaks-in-wall (3) fishing with-hooks-of and-last-of-you with-hooks you

תֵּצֶאנָה אִשָּׁה נֶגְדָּהּ וְהִשְׁלַכְתֶּנָה הַהַרְמוֹנָה
toward-the-Harmon and-you-will-cast-out straight-ahead-of-her each you-will-go-out

נְאֻם־ יְהוָה׃ בֹּאוּ בֵית־ אֵל וּפִשְׁעוּ הַגִּלְגָּל הַרְבּוּ לִפְשֹׁעַ
to-sin do-more! the-Gilgal and-sin! El Beth go! (4) Yahweh declaration-of

וְהָבִיאוּ לַבֹּקֶר זִבְחֵיכֶם לִשְׁלֹשֶׁת יָמִים מַעְשְׂרֹתֵיכֶם׃
tithes-of-you days on-three-of sacrifices-of-you for-the-morning and-bring!

וְקַטֵּר מֵחָמֵץ תּוֹדָה וְקִרְאוּ נְדָבוֹת
freewill-offerings and-brag-about thank-offering of-leavened-bread and-burn! (5)

הַשְׁמִיעוּ כִּי כֵן אֲהַבְתֶּם בְּנֵי יִשְׂרָאֵל נְאֻם אֲדֹנָי יְהוִה׃
Yahweh Sovereign declaration-of Israel peoples-of you-love this for boast!

וְגַם־ אֲנִי נָתַתִּי לָכֶם נִקְיוֹן שִׁנַּיִם בְּכָל־ עָרֵיכֶם
cities-of-you in-every-of teeth cleanness-of to-you I-gave I and-also (6)

12 This is what the LORD says:

"As a shepherd saves from the
lion's mouth
only two leg bones or a
piece of an ear,
so will the Israelites be
saved,
those who sit in Samaria
on the edge of their beds
and in Damascus on their
couches.[j]"

13 "Hear this and testify against the house of Jacob," declares the Lord, the LORD God Almighty.

14 "On the day I punish Israel
for her sins,
I will destroy the altars of
Bethel;
the horns of the altar will be
cut off
and fall to the ground.
15 I will tear down the winter
house
along with the summer
house;
the houses adorned with ivory
will be destroyed
and the mansions will be
demolished,"
declares the LORD.

*Israel Has Not Returned to God*

4 Hear this word, you cows of
Bashan on Mount Samaria,
you women who oppress
the poor and crush the
needy
and say to your husbands,
"Bring us some drinks!"
2 The Sovereign LORD has sworn
by his holiness:
"The time will surely come
when you will be taken away
with hooks,
the last of you with
fishhooks.
3 You will each go straight out
through breaks in the wall,
and you will be cast out
toward Harmon,[k]"
declares the LORD.
4 "Go to Bethel and sin;
go to Gilgal and sin yet
more.
Bring your sacrifices every
morning,
your tithes every three
years.[l]
5 Burn leavened bread as a
thank offering
and brag about your freewill
offerings—
boast about them, you
Israelites,
for this is what you love to
do,"
declares the Sovereign
LORD.

6 "I gave you empty stomachs[m]
in every city

j12 The meaning of the Hebrew for this line is uncertain.
k3 Masoretic Text; with a different word division of the Hebrew (see Septuagint) *out, O mountain of oppression*
l4 Or *tithes on the third day*
m6 Hebrew *you cleanness of teeth*

וְחֹסֶר לֶחֶם בְּכֹל מְקוֹמֹתֵיכֶם וְלֹא־ שַׁבְתֶּם עָדַי נְאֻם־
declaration-of to-me you-returned yet-not towns-of-you in-every-of bread and-lack-of

יְהוָה׃ וְגַם אָנֹכִי מָנַעְתִּי מִכֶּם אֶת־ הַגֶּשֶׁם בְּעוֹד שְׁלֹשָׁה חֳדָשִׁים
months three when-still the-rain *** from-you I-withheld I and-also (7) Yahweh

לַקָּצִיר וְהִמְטַרְתִּי עַל־ עִיר אֶחָת וְעַל־ עִיר אַחַת לֹא אַמְטִיר
I-sent-rain not another town but-on one town on and-I-sent-rain to-the-harvest

חֶלְקָה אַחַת תִּמָּטֵר וְחֶלְקָה אֲשֶׁר־ לֹא־ תַמְטִיר עָלֶיהָ תִּיבָשׁ׃
she-dried-up on-her she-rained not that but-field she-had-rain one field

וְנָעוּ שְׁתַּיִם שָׁלֹשׁ עָרִים אֶל־ עִיר אַחַת לִשְׁתּוֹת מַיִם וְלֹא
but-not waters to-drink one town to towns three two and-they-staggered (8)

יִשְׂבָּעוּ וְלֹא־ שַׁבְתֶּם עָדַי נְאֻם־ יְהוָה׃ הִכֵּיתִי
I-struck (9) Yahweh declaration-of to-me you-returned yet-not they-got-enough

אֶתְכֶם בַּשִּׁדָּפוֹן וּבַיֵּרָקוֹן הַרְבּוֹת גַּנּוֹתֵיכֶם
gardens-of-you to-do-many-times and-with-the-mildew with-the-blight you

וְכַרְמֵיכֶם וּתְאֵנֵיכֶם וְזֵיתֵיכֶם יֹאכַל
he-devoured and-olive-trees-of-you and-fig-trees-of-you and-vineyards-of-you

הַגָּזָם וְלֹא־ שַׁבְתֶּם עָדַי נְאֻם־ יְהוָה׃ שִׁלַּחְתִּי בָכֶם
among-you I-sent (10) Yahweh declaration-of to-me you-returned yet-not the-locust

דֶּבֶר בְּדֶרֶךְ מִצְרַיִם הָרַגְתִּי בַחֶרֶב בַּחוּרֵיכֶם עִם שְׁבִי
captivity-of with young-men-of-you with-the-sword I-killed Egypt as-way-of plague

סוּסֵיכֶם וָאַעֲלֶה בְּאֹשׁ מַחֲנֵיכֶם וּבְאַפְּכֶם וְלֹא־
yet-not also-into-nostril-of-you camps-of-you stench-of and-I-filled horses-of-you

שַׁבְתֶּם עָדַי נְאֻם־ יְהוָה׃ הָפַכְתִּי בָכֶם כְּמַהְפֵּכַת
as-overthrow-of of-you I-overthrew (11) Yahweh declaration-of to-me you-returned

אֱלֹהִים אֶת־סְדֹם וְאֶת־ עֲמֹרָה וַתִּהְיוּ כְּאוּד מֻצָּל
being-snatched like-burning-stick and-you-were Gomorrah and Sodom *** God

מִשְּׂרֵפָה וְלֹא־ שַׁבְתֶּם עָדַי נְאֻם־ יְהוָה׃ לָכֵן כֹּה
this therefore (12) Yahweh declaration-of to-me you-returned yet-not from-fire

אֶעֱשֶׂה־ לְּךָ יִשְׂרָאֵל עֵקֶב כִּי־ זֹאת אֶעֱשֶׂה־ לָּךְ הִכּוֹן לִקְרַאת־
to-meet prepare! to-you I-will-do this that because Israel to-you I-will-do

אֱלֹהֶיךָ יִשְׂרָאֵל׃ כִּי הִנֵּה יוֹצֵר הָרִים וּבֹרֵא רוּחַ
wind and-one-creating mountains one-forming see! indeed (13) Israel God-of-you

וּמַגִּיד לְאָדָם מַה־ שֵּׂחוֹ עֹשֵׂה שַׁחַר עֵיפָה
darkness dawn one-turning-of thought-of-him what to-man and-one-revealing

וְדֹרֵךְ עַל־ בָּמֳתֵי אָרֶץ יְהוָה אֱלֹהֵי־ צְבָאוֹת שְׁמוֹ׃
name-of-him Hosts God-of Yahweh earth high-places-of on and-one-treading

שִׁמְעוּ אֶת־ הַדָּבָר הַזֶּה אֲשֶׁר אָנֹכִי נֹשֵׂא עֲלֵיכֶם קִינָה בֵּית
house-of lament concerning-you taking-up I that the-this the-word *** hear! (5:1)

and lack of bread in every town,
yet you have not returned to me,"
declares the LORD.

7 "I also withheld rain from you
when the harvest was still three months away.
I sent rain on one town,
but withheld it from another.
One field had rain;
another had none and dried up.
8 People staggered from town to town for water
but did not get enough to drink,
yet you have not returned to me,"
declares the LORD.

9 "Many times I struck your gardens and vineyards,
I struck them with blight and mildew.
Locusts devoured your fig and olive trees,
yet you have not returned to me,"
declares the LORD.

10 "I sent plagues among you
as I did to Egypt.
I killed your young men with the sword,
along with your captured horses.
I filled your nostrils with the stench of your camps,
yet you have not returned to me,"
declares the LORD.

11 "I overthrew some of you
as I[n] overthrew Sodom and Gomorrah.
You were like a burning stick snatched from the fire,
yet you have not returned to me,"
declares the LORD.

12 "Therefore this is what I will do to you, Israel,
and because I will do this to you,
prepare to meet your God, O Israel."

13 He who forms the mountains,
creates the wind,
and reveals his thoughts to man,
he who turns dawn to darkness,
and treads the high places of the earth—
the LORD God Almighty is his name.

*A Lament and Call to Repentance*

5 Hear this word, O house of Israel, this lament I take up concerning you:

[n]11 Hebrew *God*

יִשְׂרָאֵל׃ (2) נָפְלָה לֹא־ תוֹסִיף קוּם בְּתוּלַת יִשְׂרָאֵל
Israel Virgin-of to-rise she-will-do-again never she-is-fallen (2) Israel

נִטְּשָׁה עַל־ אַדְמָתָהּ אֵין מְקִימָהּ׃ (3) כִּי כֹה
this indeed (3) one-lifting-up-her there-is-no land-of-her in she-is-deserted

אָמַר אֲדֹנָי יְהוִה הָעִיר הַיֹּצֵאת אֶלֶף תַּשְׁאִיר
she-will-have-left thousand the-one-marching-out the-city Yahweh Sovereign he-says

מֵאָה וְהַיּוֹצֵאת מֵאָה תַּשְׁאִיר עֲשָׂרָה לְבֵית
for-house-of ten she-will-have-left hundred and-the-one-marching-out hundred

יִשְׂרָאֵל׃ (4) כִּי כֹה אָמַר יְהוָה לְבֵית יִשְׂרָאֵל דִּרְשׁוּנִי וִחְיוּ׃
and-live! seek-me! Israel to-house-of Yahweh he-says this indeed (4) Israel

(5) וְאַל־ תִּדְרְשׁוּ בֵּית־ אֵל וְהַגִּלְגָּל לֹא תָבֹאוּ וּבְאֵר שֶׁבַע לֹא
not Sheba and-Beer you-go not and-the-Gilgal El Beth you-seek and-not (5)

תַעֲבֹרוּ כִּי הַגִּלְגָּל גָּלֹה יִגְלֶה וּבֵית־ אֵל
El and-Beth he-will-go-into-exile to-go-into-exile the-Gilgal for you-journey

יִהְיֶה לְאָוֶן׃ (6) דִּרְשׁוּ אֶת־ יְהוָה וִחְיוּ פֶּן־ יִצְלַח
he-will-sweep-through or and-live! Yahweh *** seek! (6) to-nothing he-will-be

כָּאֵשׁ בֵּית יוֹסֵף וְאָכְלָה וְאֵין־ מְכַבֶּה
one-quenching and-there-will-be-no and-she-will-devour Joseph house-of like-fire

לְבֵית־ אֵל׃ (7) הַהֹפְכִים לְלַעֲנָה מִשְׁפָּט וּצְדָקָה לָאָרֶץ
to-the-ground and-righteousness justice to-bitterness the-ones-turning (7) El to-Beth

הִנִּיחוּ׃ (8) עֹשֵׂה כִימָה וּכְסִיל וְהֹפֵךְ לַבֹּקֶר
into-the-dawn and-one-turning and-Orion Pleiades one-making-of (8) they-cast

צַלְמָוֶת וְיוֹם לַיְלָה הֶחְשִׁיךְ הַקּוֹרֵא לְמֵי־ הַיָּם
the-sea for-waters-of the-one-calling he-darkens night and-day blackness

וַיִּשְׁפְּכֵם עַל־ פְּנֵי הָאָרֶץ יְהוָה שְׁמוֹ׃ (9) הַמַּבְלִיג
the-one-flashing (9) name-of-him Yahweh the-land faces-of over and-he-pours-out-them

שֹׁד עַל־ עָז וְשֹׁד עַל־ מִבְצָר יָבוֹא׃ (10) שָׂנְאוּ
they-hate (10) he-brings fortified-city to and-destruction stronghold on destruction

בַשַּׁעַר מוֹכִיחַ וְדֹבֵר תָּמִים יְתָעֵבוּ׃ (11) לָכֵן יַעַן
because therefore (11) they-despise truth and-one-telling one-reproving in-the-court

בּוֹשַׁסְכֶם עַל־ דָּל וּמַשְׂאַת־ בַּר תִּקְחוּ מִמֶּנּוּ בָּתֵּי גָזִית
stone mansions-of from-him you-take grain and-portion-of poor on to-trample-you

בְּנִיתֶם וְלֹא־ תֵשְׁבוּ בָם כַּרְמֵי־ חֶמֶד נְטַעְתֶּם וְלֹא
but-not you-planted lushness vineyards-of in-them you-will-live but-not you-built

תִשְׁתּוּ אֶת־ יֵינָם׃ (12) כִּי יָדַעְתִּי רַבִּים פִּשְׁעֵיכֶם
offenses-of-you many-ones I-know for (12) wine-of-them *** you-will-drink

וַעֲצֻמִים חַטֹּאתֵיכֶם צֹרְרֵי צַדִּיק לֹקְחֵי כֹפֶר
bribe ones-taking-of righteous ones-oppressing-of sins-of-you and-great-ones

2 "Fallen is Virgin Israel,
never to rise again,
deserted in her own land,
with no one to lift her up."

3 This is what the Sovereign
LORD says:
"The city that marches out a
thousand strong for Israel
will have only a hundred
left;
the town that marches out a
hundred strong
will have only ten left."

4 This is what the LORD says to
the house of Israel:
"Seek me and live;
5 do not seek Bethel,
do not go to Gilgal,
do not journey to Beersheba.
For Gilgal will surely go into
exile,
and Bethel will be reduced
to nothing.[o]"
6 Seek the LORD and live,
or he will sweep through
the house of Joseph like a
fire;
it will devour,
and Bethel will have no one
to quench it.
7 You who turn justice into
bitterness
and cast righteousness to
the ground
8 (he who made the Pleiades
and Orion,
who turns blackness into
dawn
and darkens day into night,
who calls for the waters of the
sea
and pours them out over the
face of the land—
the LORD is his name—
9 he flashes destruction on the
stronghold
and brings the fortified city
to ruin),
10 you hate the one who reproves
in court
and despise him who tells
the truth.
11 You trample on the poor
and force him to give you
grain.
Therefore, though you have
built stone mansions,
you will not live in them;
though you have planted lush
vineyards,
you will not drink their
wine.
12 For I know how many are
your offenses
and how great your sins.

You oppress the righteous and
take bribes

o5 Or *grief*; or *wickedness*; Hebrew *aven*, a reference to Beth Aven (a derogatory name for Bethel)

וְאֶבְיוֹנִים בַּשַּׁעַר הִטּוּ׃ לָכֵן הַמַּשְׂכִּיל

the-man-being-prudent therefore (13) they-deprive-justice in-the-court and-poor-ones

בָּעֵת הַהִיא יִדֹּם כִּי עֵת רָעָה הִיא׃ דִּרְשׁוּ־טוֹב וְאַל־

and-not good seek! (14) this evil time for he-keeps-quiet the-this in-the-time

רָע לְמַעַן תִּחְיוּ וִיהִי־כֵן יְהוָה אֱלֹהֵי־צְבָאוֹת אִתְּכֶם

with-you Hosts God-of Yahweh so then-he-will-be you-may-live so-that evil

כַּאֲשֶׁר אֲמַרְתֶּם׃ שִׂנְאוּ־רָע וְאֶהֱבוּ טוֹב וְהַצִּיגוּ בַשַּׁעַר מִשְׁפָּט

justice in-the-court and-maintain! good and-love! evil hate! (15) you-say just-as

אוּלַי יֶחֱנַן יְהוָה אֱלֹהֵי־צְבָאוֹת שְׁאֵרִית יוֹסֵף׃ לָכֵן

therefore (16) Joseph remnant-of Hosts God-of Yahweh he-will-have-mercy perhaps

כֹּה־אָמַר יְהוָה אֱלֹהֵי צְבָאוֹת אֲדֹנָי בְּכָל־רְחֹבוֹת מִסְפֵּד וּבְכָל־

and-in-every-of wailing streets in-all-of Lord Hosts God-of Yahweh he-says this

חוּצוֹת יֹאמְרוּ הוֹ־הוֹ וְקָרְאוּ אִכָּר אֶל־אֵבֶל

weeping for farmer and-they-will-summon Oh! Oh! they-cry public-squares

וּמִסְפֵּד אֶל־יוֹדְעֵי נֶהִי׃ וּבְכָל־כְּרָמִים מִסְפֵּד כִּי־

for wailing vineyards and-in-all-of (17) mourning ones-knowing-of to and-wailing

אֶעֱבֹר בְּקִרְבְּךָ אָמַר יְהוָה׃ הוֹי הַמִּתְאַוִּים אֶת־

*** the-ones-longing-for woe! (18) Yahweh he-says through-midst-of-you I-will-pass

יוֹם יְהוָה לָמָּה־זֶּה לָכֶם יוֹם יְהוָה הוּא־חֹשֶׁךְ וְלֹא־אוֹר׃

light and-not darkness that Yahweh day-of to-you this for-why? Yahweh day-of

כַּאֲשֶׁר יָנוּס אִישׁ מִפְּנֵי הָאֲרִי וּפְגָעוֹ הַדֹּב

the-bear and-he-met-him the-lion from-before man he-fled as-though (19)

וּבָא הַבַּיִת וְסָמַךְ יָדוֹ עַל־הַקִּיר וּנְשָׁכוֹ

and-he-bit-him the-wall on hand-of-him and-he-rested the-house though-he-entered

הַנָּחָשׁ׃ הֲלֹא־חֹשֶׁךְ יוֹם יְהוָה וְלֹא־אוֹר וְאָפֵל וְלֹא־

and-no even-pitch-dark light and-not Yahweh day-of darkness not? (20) the-snake

נֹגַהּ לוֹ׃ שָׂנֵאתִי מָאַסְתִּי חַגֵּיכֶם וְלֹא אָרִיחַ

I-can-stand and-not [illegible]ious-feasts-of-you I-despise I-hate (21) to-him brightness

בְּעַצְּרֹתֵיכֶם׃ כִּי אִם־תַּעֲל[illegible] עֹלוֹת

burnt-offerings [illegible] you-bring though even (22) to-assemblies-of-you

וּמִנְחֹתֵיכֶם לֹא אֶרְצֶה וְשֶׁלֶם [illegible]רִיאֵיכֶם

choice-one[illegible] [illegible]nd-fellowship-offering-of I-will-accept not and-grain-offerings

לֹא אַבִּיט׃ הָסֵר מֵעָלַי הֲמוֹן שִׁרֶי[illegible] [illegible]ְרַת

and-mu[illegible] [illegible]ngs-of-you noise-of from-with-me turn-away! (23) I-will-have-regard not

נְבָלֶיךָ לֹא אֶשְׁמָע׃ וְיִגַּל כַּמַּיִם מִשְׁפָּט

justice like-the-rivers but-let-him-roll-on (24) I-will-listen not harps-of-you

וּצְדָקָה כְּנַחַל אֵיתָן׃ הַזְּבָחִים וּמִנְחָה

and-grain-offering the-sacrifices (25) never-failing like-stream and-righteousness

---

and you deprive the poor of
justice in the courts.
[13]Therefore the prudent man
keeps quiet in such times,
for the times are evil.

[14]Seek good, not evil,
that you may live.
Then the LORD God Almighty
will be with you,
just as you say he is.
[15]Hate evil, love good;
maintain justice in the
courts.
Perhaps the LORD God
Almighty will have mercy
on the remnant of Joseph.

[16]Therefore this is what the Lord, the LORD God Almighty, says:

"There will be wailing in all
the streets
and cries of anguish in
every public square.
The farmers will be summoned
to weep
and the mourners to wail.
[17]There will be wailing in all the
vineyards,
for I will pass through your
midst,"
says the LORD.

### *The Day of the LORD*

[18]Woe to you who long
for the day of the LORD!
Why do you long for the day
of the LORD?
That day will be darkness,
not light.
[19]It will be as though a man fled
from a lion
only to meet a bear,
as though he entered his
house
and rested his hand on the
wall
only to have a snake bite
him.
[20]Will not the day of the LORD
be darkness, not light—
pitch-dark, without a ray of
brightness?

[21]"I hate, I despise your
religious feasts;
I cannot stand your
assemblies.
[22]Even though you bring me
burnt offerings and grain
offerings,
I will not accept them.
Though you bring choice
fellowship offerings,[p]
I will have no regard for
them.
[23]Away with the noise of your
songs!
I will not listen to the music
of your harps.
[24]But let justice roll on like a
river,
righteousness like a
never-failing stream!

[25]"Did you bring me sacrifices
and offerings

[p]22 Traditionally *peace offerings*

הִגַּשְׁתֶּם־ לִי בַמִּדְבָּר אַרְבָּעִים שָׁנָה בֵּית יִשְׂרָאֵל׃ וּנְשָׂאתֶם
and-you-lifted-up (26) Israel house-of year forty in-the-desert to-me did-you-bring

אֵת סִכּוּת מַלְכְּכֶם וְאֵת כִּיּוּן צַלְמֵיכֶם כּוֹכַב אֱלֹהֵיכֶם אֲשֶׁר
which gods-of-you star-of idols-of-you pedestal-of and king-of-you shrine-of ***

עֲשִׂיתֶם לָכֶם׃ וְהִגְלֵיתִי אֶתְכֶם מֵהָלְאָה לְדַמָּשֶׂק
to-Damascus to-beyond you therefore-I-will-exile (27) for-yourselves you-made

אָמַר יְהוָה אֱלֹהֵי־צְבָאוֹת שְׁמוֹ׃ הוֹי הַשַּׁאֲנַנִּים בְּצִיּוֹן
in-Zion the-complacent-ones woe! (6:1) name-of-him Hosts God-of Yahweh he-says

וְהַבֹּטְחִים בְּהַר שֹׁמְרוֹן נְקֻבֵי רֵאשִׁית
foremost-of men-being-notable-of Samaria on-Mount-of and-the-ones-feeling-secure

הַגּוֹיִם וּבָאוּ לָהֶם בֵּית יִשְׂרָאֵל׃ עִבְרוּ כַלְנֵה וּרְאוּ
and-look! Calneh go-to! (2) Israel house-of to-them and-they-come the-nations

וּלְכוּ מִשָּׁם חֲמַת רַבָּה וּרְדוּ גַת־ פְּלִשְׁתִּים* הֲטוֹבִים
good-ones? Philistines Gath-of then-go-down! great Hamath from-there and-go!

מִן־ הַמַּמְלָכוֹת הָאֵלֶּה אִם־ רַב גְּבוּלָם מִגְּבֻלְכֶם׃
more-than-land-of-you land-of-them large or the-these the-kingdoms more-than

הַמְנַדִּים לְיוֹם רָע וַתַּגִּישׁוּן שֶׁבֶת חָמָס׃
terror reign-of and-you-bring-near evil to-day-of the-ones-putting-off (3)

הַשֹּׁכְבִים עַל־ מִטּוֹת שֵׁן וּסְרֻחִים עַל־ עַרְשׂוֹתָם
couches-of-them on and-ones-lounging ivory beds-of on the-ones-lying (4)

וְאֹכְלִים כָּרִים מִצֹּאן וַעֲגָלִים מִתּוֹךְ מַרְבֵּק׃
fattening-stall from-inside-of and-calves from-flock lambs and-ones-dining-on

הַפֹּרְטִים עַל־ פִּי הַנָּבֶל כְּדָוִיד חָשְׁבוּ לָהֶם
for-them they-improvise like-David the-harp string-of on the-ones-strumming (5)

כְּלֵי־ שִׁיר׃ הַשֹּׁתִים בְּמִזְרְקֵי יַיִן וְרֵאשִׁית שְׁמָנִים
lotions and-finest-of wine by-bowls-of the-ones-drinking (6) music instruments-of

יִמְשָׁחוּ וְלֹא נֶחְלוּ עַל־ שֵׁבֶר יוֹסֵף׃ לָכֵן עַתָּה
now therefore (7) Joseph ruin-of over they-grieve but-not they-use-lotion

יִגְלוּ בְּרֹאשׁ גֹּלִים וְסָר מִרְזַח
feast-of and-he-will-end ones-going-into-exile among-first-of they-will-go-into-exile

סְרוּחִים׃ נִשְׁבַּע אֲדֹנָי יְהוִה בְּנַפְשׁוֹ נְאֻם־ יְהוָה
Yahweh declaration-of by-self-of-him Yahweh Sovereign he-swore (8) ones-lounging

אֱלֹהֵי צְבָאוֹת מְתָאֵב אָנֹכִי אֶת־ גְּאוֹן יַעֲקֹב וְאַרְמְנֹתָיו שָׂנֵאתִי
I-detest and-fortresses-of-him Jacob pride-of *** I abhorring Hosts God-of

וְהִסְגַּרְתִּי עִיר וּמְלֹאָהּ׃ וְהָיָה אִם־
if and-he-will-be (9) and-everything-in-her city indeed-I-will-deliver-up

יִוָּתְרוּ עֲשָׂרָה אֲנָשִׁים בְּבַיִת אֶחָד וָמֵתוּ׃ וּנְשָׂאוֹ
and-he-carries-him (10) too-they-will-die one in-house men ten they-are-left

forty years in the desert, O
house of Israel?
26 You have lifted up the shrine
of your king,
the pedestal of your idols,
the star of your god[a]—
which you made for
yourselves.
27 Therefore I will send you into
exile beyond Damascus,"
says the LORD, whose name
is God Almighty.

*Woe to the Complacent*

6 Woe to you who are
complacent in Zion,
and to you who feel secure
on Mount Samaria,
you notable men of the
foremost nation,
to whom the people of Israel
come!
2 Go to Calneh and look at it;
go from there to great
Hamath,
and then go down to Gath
in Philistia.
Are they better off than your
two kingdoms?
Is their land larger than
yours?
3 You put off the evil day
and bring near a reign of
terror.
4 You lie on beds inlaid with
ivory
and lounge on your couches.
You dine on choice lambs
and fattened calves.
5 You strum away on your harps
like David
and improvise on musical
instruments.
6 You drink wine by the bowlful
and use the finest lotions,
but you do not grieve over
the ruin of Joseph.
7 Therefore you will be among
the first to go into exile;
your feasting and lounging
will end.

*The LORD Abhors the Pride of Israel*

8 The Sovereign LORD has sworn
by himself—the LORD God Almighty declares:

"I abhor the pride of Jacob
and detest his fortresses;
I will deliver up the city
and everything in it."

9 If ten men are left in one house,
they too will die. 10 And if a relative

a26 Or *lifted up Sakkuth your king / and Kaiwan your idols, / your star-gods;* Septuagint *lifted up the shrine of Molech / and the star of your god Rephan, / their idols*

*2 Most mss have *bireq* under the *tav* (תִּים).

דּוֹדוֹ וּמְסָרְפוֹ לְהוֹצִיא עֲצָמִים מִן־ הַבַּיִת וְאָמַר
and-he-asks the-house from bodies to-bring-out even-one-burning-him relative-of-him

לַאֲשֶׁר בְּיַרְכְּתֵי הַבַּיִת הַעוֹד עִמָּךְ וְאָמַר אָפֶס וְאָמַר
then-he-will-say no and-he-says with-you still? the-house in-insides-of to-anyone

הָס כִּי לֹא לְהַזְכִּיר בְּשֵׁם יְהוָה׃ כִּי־הִנֵּה יְהוָה מְצַוֶּה
commanding Yahweh see! for (11) Yahweh name-of to-mention not indeed hush!

וְהִכָּה הַבַּיִת הַגָּדוֹל רְסִיסִים וְהַבַּיִת הַקָּטֹן בְּקִעִים׃
bits the-small and-the-house pieces the-great the-house and-he-will-smash

הַיְרֻצוּן בַּסֶּלַע סוּסִים אִם־ יַחֲרוֹשׁ בַּבְּקָרִים כִּי־
but with-the-oxen does-he-plow or horses on-the-rocky-crag do-they-run? (12)

הֲפַכְתֶּם לְרֹאשׁ מִשְׁפָּט וּפְרִי צְדָקָה לְלַעֲנָה׃
into-bitterness righteousness and-fruit-of justice into-poison you-turned

הַשְּׂמֵחִים לְלֹא דָבָר הָאֹמְרִים הֲלוֹא בְחָזְקֵנוּ לָקַחְנוּ
we-took by-strength-of-us not? the-ones-saying Debar in-Lo the-rejoicers (13)

לָנוּ קַרְנָיִם׃ כִּי הִנְנִי מֵקִים עֲלֵיכֶם בֵּית יִשְׂרָאֵל
Israel house-of against-you stirring-up see-I! for (14) Karnaim for-us

נְאֻם־ יְהוָה אֱלֹהֵי הַצְּבָאוֹת גּוֹי וְלָחֲצוּ אֶתְכֶם מִלְּבוֹא
from-Lebo you that-they-will-oppress nation the-Hosts God-of Yahweh declaration-of

חֲמָת עַד־ נַחַל הָעֲרָבָה׃ כֹּה הִרְאַנִי אֲדֹנָי יְהוִה וְהִנֵּה
and-see! Yahweh Sovereign he-showed-me this (7:1) the-Arabah valley-of to Hamath

יוֹצֵר גֹּבַי בִּתְחִלַּת עֲלוֹת הַלָּקֶשׁ וְהִנֵּה־
and-see! the-second-crop to-come-up at-beginning-of swarm-of-locusts preparing

לֶקֶשׁ אַחַר גִּזֵּי הַמֶּלֶךְ׃ וְהָיָה אִם־ כִּלָּה לֶאֱכוֹל
to-strip-clean he-finished when and-he-was (2) the-king harvests-of after second-crop

אֶת־ עֵשֶׂב הָאָרֶץ וָאֹמַר אֲדֹנָי יְהוִה סְלַח־ נָא מִי
how? now! forgive! Yahweh Sovereign then-I-cried-out the-land vegetation-of ***

יָקוּם יַעֲקֹב כִּי קָטֹן הוּא׃ נִחַם יְהוָה עַל־זֹאת לֹא תִהְיֶה
she-will-happen not this at Yahweh he-relented (3) he small so Jacob can-he-survive

אָמַר יְהוָה׃ כֹּה הִרְאַנִי אֲדֹנָי יְהוִה וְהִנֵּה קֹרֵא לָרִב
to-judge calling and-see! Yahweh Sovereign he-showed-me this (4) Yahweh he-said

בָּאֵשׁ אֲדֹנָי יְהוִה וַתֹּאכַל אֶת־תְּהוֹם רַבָּה וְאָכְלָה אֶת־
*** and-she-devoured great deep *** and-she-dried-up Yahweh Sovereign by-fire

הַחֵלֶק׃ וָאֹמַר אֲדֹנָי יְהוִה חֲדַל־ נָא מִי יָקוּם
can-he-survive how? now! stop! Yahweh Sovereign then-I-cried-out (5) the-land

יַעֲקֹב כִּי קָטֹן הוּא׃ נִחַם יְהוָה עַל־זֹאת גַּם־ הִיא לֹא תִהְיֶה
she-will-happen not this either this at Yahweh he-relented (6) he small so Jacob

אָמַר אֲדֹנָי יְהוִה׃ כֹּה הִרְאַנִי וְהִנֵּה אֲדֹנָי נִצָּב עַל־ חוֹמַת
wall-of by standing Lord and-see! he-showed-me this (7) Yahweh Sovereign he-said

who is to burn the bodies comes to carry them out of the house and asks anyone still hiding there, "Is anyone with you?" and he says, "No," then he will say, "Hush! We must not mention the name of the LORD."

11 For the LORD has given the command,
and he will smash the great house into pieces
and the small house into bits.

12 Do horses run on the rocky crags?
Does one plow there with oxen?
But you have turned justice into poison
and the fruit of righteousness into bitterness—
13 you who rejoice in the conquest of Lo Debar[r]
and say, "Did we not take Karnaim[s] by our own strength?"

14 For the LORD God Almighty declares,
"I will stir up a nation against you, O house of Israel,
that will oppress you all the way
from Lebo[t] Hamath to the valley of the Arabah."

*Locusts, Fire and a Plumb Line*

7 This is what the Sovereign LORD showed me: He was preparing swarms of locusts after the king's share had been harvested and just as the second crop was coming up. 2 When they had stripped the land clean, I cried out, "Sovereign LORD, forgive! How can Jacob survive? He is so small!"
3 So the LORD relented.
"This will not happen," the LORD said.
4 This is what the Sovereign LORD showed me: The Sovereign LORD was calling for judgment by fire; it dried up the great deep and devoured the land. 5 Then I cried out, "Sovereign LORD, I beg you, stop! How can Jacob survive? He is so small!"
6 So the LORD relented.
"This will not happen either," the Sovereign LORD said.

7 This is what he showed me: The Lord was standing by a wall

[r] 13 *Lo Debar* means *nothing.*
[s] 13 *Karnaim* means *horns; horn* here symbolizes strength.
[t] 14 Or *from the entrance to*

אֲנָךְ וּבְיָדוֹ אֲנָךְ׃ וַיֹּאמֶר יְהוָה אֵלַי מָה־אַתָּה

you what? to-me Yahweh and-he-asked (8) plumb-line and-in-hand-of-him plumb-line

רֹאֶה עָמוֹס וָאֹמַר אֲנָךְ וַיֹּאמֶר אֲדֹנָי הִנְנִי שָׂם אֲנָךְ

plumb-line setting look-I! Lord then-he-said plumb-line and-I-replied Amos seeing

בְּקֶרֶב עַמִּי יִשְׂרָאֵל לֹא־ אוֹסִיף עוֹד עֲבוֹר לוֹ׃

to-him to-spare longer I-will-do-again not Israel people-of-me in-among

וְנָשַׁמּוּ בָּמוֹת יִשְׂחָק וּמִקְדְּשֵׁי יִשְׂרָאֵל

Israel and-sanctuaries-of Isaac high-places-of and-they-will-be-destroyed (9)

יֶחֱרָבוּ וְקַמְתִּי עַל־ בֵּית יָרָבְעָם בֶּחָרֶב׃

with-the-sword Jeroboam house-of against and-I-will-rise they-will-be-ruined

וַיִּשְׁלַח אֲמַצְיָה כֹּהֵן בֵּית־אֵל אֶל־יָרָבְעָם מֶלֶךְ־יִשְׂרָאֵל לֵאמֹר

to-say Israel king-of Jeroboam to El Beth priest-of Amaziah then-he-sent (10)

קָשַׁר עָלֶיךָ עָמוֹס בְּקֶרֶב בֵּית יִשְׂרָאֵל לֹא־ תוּכַל

she-can not Israel house-of in-heart-of Amos against-you he-raises-conspiracy

הָאָרֶץ לְהָכִיל אֶת־ כָּל־ דְּבָרָיו׃ כִּי־ כֹה אָמַר עָמוֹס בַּחֶרֶב

by-the-sword Amos he-says this for (11) words-of-him all-of *** to-bear the-land

יָמוּת יָרָבְעָם וְיִשְׂרָאֵל גָּלֹה יִגְלֶה מֵעַל

from-on he-will-go-into-exile to-go-into-exile and-Israel Jeroboam he-will-die

אַדְמָתוֹ׃ וַיֹּאמֶר אֲמַצְיָה אֶל־עָמוֹס חֹזֶה לֵךְ בְּרַח־ לְךָ אֶל־

to for-you go-back! get-out! seer Amos to Amaziah then-he-said (12) land-of-him

אֶרֶץ יְהוּדָה וֶאֱכָל־ שָׁם לֶחֶם וְשָׁם תִּנָּבֵא׃ וּבֵית־ אֵל לֹא־

not El but-Beth (13) you-prophesy and-there bread there and-eat! Judah land-of

תוֹסִיף עוֹד לְהִנָּבֵא כִּי מִקְדַּשׁ־ מֶלֶךְ הוּא וּבֵית

and-temple-of this king sanctuary-of because to-prophesy anymore you-do-again

מַמְלָכָה הוּא׃ וַיַּעַן עָמוֹס וַיֹּאמֶר אֶל־אֲמַצְיָה לֹא־ נָבִיא

prophet not Amaziah to and-he-said Amos and-he-answered (14) this kingdom

אָנֹכִי וְלֹא בֶן־ נָבִיא אָנֹכִי כִּי־ בוֹקֵר אָנֹכִי וּבוֹלֵס

and-one-taking-care-of I shepherd but I prophet son-of or-not I

שִׁקְמִים׃ וַיִּקָּחֵנִי יְהוָה מֵאַחֲרֵי הַצֹּאן וַיֹּאמֶר

and-he-said the-flock from-after Yahweh but-he-took-me (15) sycamore-fig-trees

אֵלַי יְהוָה לֵךְ הִנָּבֵא אֶל־ עַמִּי יִשְׂרָאֵל׃ וְעַתָּה שְׁמַע דְּבַר־

word-of hear! then-now (16) Israel people-of-me to prophesy! go! Yahweh to-me

יְהוָה אַתָּה אֹמֵר לֹא תִנָּבֵא עַל־ יִשְׂרָאֵל וְלֹא תַטִּיף עַל־

against you-preach and-not Israel against you-prophesy not saying you Yahweh

בֵּית יִשְׂחָק׃ לָכֵן כֹּה־ אָמַר יְהוָה אִשְׁתְּךָ בָּעִיר

in-the-city wife-of-you Yahweh he-says this therefore (17) Isaac house-of

תִּזְנֶה וּבָנֶיךָ וּבְנֹתֶיךָ בַּחֶרֶב

by-the-sword and-daughters-of-you and-sons-of-you she-will-become-prostitute

that had been built true to plumb, with a plumb line in his hand. [8]And the LORD asked me, "What do you see, Amos?"

"A plumb line," I replied.

Then the Lord said, "Look, I am setting a plumb line among my people Israel; I will spare them no longer.

[9]"The high places of Isaac will be destroyed
and the sanctuaries of Israel will be ruined;
with my sword I will rise against the house of Jeroboam."

*Amos and Amaziah*

[10]Then Amaziah the priest of Bethel sent a message to Jeroboam king of Israel: "Amos is raising a conspiracy against you in the very heart of Israel. The land cannot bear all his words. [11]For this is what Amos is saying:

" 'Jeroboam will die by the sword,
and Israel will surely go into exile,
away from their native land.' "

[12]Then Amaziah said to Amos, "Get out, you seer! Go back to the land of Judah. Earn your bread there and do your prophesying there. [13]Don't prophesy anymore at Bethel, because this is the king's sanctuary and the temple of the kingdom."

[14]Amos answered Amaziah, "I was neither a prophet nor a prophet's son, but I was a shepherd, and I also took care of sycamore-fig trees. [15]But the LORD took me from tending the flock and said to me, 'Go, prophesy to my people Israel.' [16]Now then, hear the word of the LORD. You say,

" 'Do not prophesy against Israel,
and stop preaching against the house of Isaac.'

[17]"Therefore this is what the LORD says:

" 'Your wife will become a prostitute in the city,
and your sons and daughters will fall by the sword.

יִפֹּלוּ וְאַדְמָתְךָ בַּחֶבֶל תְּחֻלָּק וְאַתָּה
they-will-fall and-land-of-you by-the-measure she-will-be-divided-up and-you

עַל־אֲדָמָה טְמֵאָה תָּמוּת וְיִשְׂרָאֵל גָּלֹה יִגְלֶה
in land unclean you-will-die and-Israel to-go-into-exile he-will-go-into-exile

מֵעַל אַדְמָתוֹ׃ כֹּה הִרְאַנִי אֲדֹנָי יְהוִה וְהִנֵּה כְּלוּב
from-on land-of-him (8:1) this he-showed-me Sovereign Yahweh and-see! basket-of

קָיִץ׃ וַיֹּאמֶר מָה־אַתָּה רֹאֶה עָמוֹס וָאֹמַר כְּלוּב קָיִץ
ripe-fruit (2) and-he-asked what? you seeing Amos and-I-answered basket-of ripe-fruit

וַיֹּאמֶר יְהוָה אֵלַי בָּא הַקֵּץ אֶל־עַמִּי יִשְׂרָאֵל לֹא־
then-he-said Yahweh to-me he-came the-ripe-time for people-of-me Israel not

אוֹסִיף עוֹד עֲבוֹר לוֹ׃ וְהֵילִילוּ שִׁירוֹת
I-will-do-again longer to-spare to-him (3) and-they-will-turn-to-wailing songs-of

הֵיכָל בַּיּוֹם הַהוּא נְאֻם אֲדֹנָי יְהוִה רַב הַפֶּגֶר
temple in-the-day the-that declaration-of Sovereign Yahweh many-of the-body

בְּכָל־מָקוֹם הִשְׁלִיךְ הָס׃ שִׁמְעוּ־זֹאת הַשֹּׁאֲפִים אֶבְיוֹן
in-every-of place he-will-fling silence! (4) hear! this the-ones-trampling needy

וְלַשְׁבִּית עֲנִוֵּי־אָרֶץ׃ לֵאמֹר מָתַי יַעֲבֹר הַחֹדֶשׁ
and-to-do-away-with poor-ones-of land (5) to-say when? will-he-be-over the-New-Moon

וְנַשְׁבִּירָה שֶּׁבֶר וְהַשַּׁבָּת וְנִפְתְּחָה־בָּר לְהַקְטִין אֵיפָה
that-we-may-sell grain and-the-Sabbath that-we-may-market wheat to-skimp measure

וּלְהַגְדִּיל שֶׁקֶל וּלְעַוֵּת מֹאזְנֵי מִרְמָה׃ לִקְנוֹת בַּכֶּסֶף
and-to-boost price and-to-cheat with-scales-of dishonesty (6) to-buy with-the-silver

דַּלִּים וְאֶבְיוֹן בַּעֲבוּר נַעֲלָיִם וּמַפַּל בַּר נַשְׁבִּיר׃
poor-ones and-needy for-sake-of pair-of-sandals even-sweeping-of wheat we-sell

נִשְׁבַּע יְהוָה בִּגְאוֹן יַעֲקֹב אִם־אֶשְׁכַּח לָנֶצַח כָּל־
(7) he-swore Yahweh by-Pride-of Jacob not I-will-forget to-forever any-of

מַעֲשֵׂיהֶם׃ הַעַל זֹאת לֹא־תִרְגַּז הָאָרֶץ וְאָבַל
deeds-of-them (8) for? this not will-she-tremble the-land and-he-will-mourn

כָּל־יוֹשֵׁב בָּהּ וְעָלְתָה כָאֹר כֻּלָּהּ
all-of one-living in-her and-she-will-rise like-the-Nile whole-of-her

וְנִגְרְשָׁה וְנִשְׁקְהָ כִּיאוֹר מִצְרָיִם׃ וְהָיָה
and-she-will-be-stirred-up then-she-will-sink like-river-of Egypt (9) and-he-will-be

בַּיּוֹם הַהוּא נְאֻם אֲדֹנָי יְהוִה וְהֵבֵאתִי הַשֶּׁמֶשׁ
in-the-day the-that declaration-of Sovereign Yahweh then-I-will-make-go-down the-sun

בַּצָּהֳרָיִם וְהַחֲשַׁכְתִּי לָאָרֶץ בְּיוֹם אוֹר׃ וְהָפַכְתִּי
at-the-noons and-I-will-darken to-the-earth in-day-of light (10) and-I-will-turn

חַגֵּיכֶם לְאֵבֶל וְכָל־שִׁירֵיכֶם לְקִינָה
religious-feasts-of-you into-mourning and-all-of songs-of-you into-weeping

Your land will be measured and divided up,
and you yourself will die in a pagan[u] country.
And Israel will certainly go into exile,
away from their native land.' "

*A Basket of Ripe Fruit*

8 This is what the Sovereign
LORD showed me: a basket of
ripe fruit. 2"What do you see,
Amos?" he asked.
"A basket of ripe fruit," I answered.
Then the LORD said to me, "The
time is ripe for my people Israel; I
will spare them no longer.
3"In that day," declares the Sovereign LORD, "the songs in the
temple will turn to wailing.[v]
Many, many bodies—flung everywhere! Silence!"

4Hear this, you who trample the needy
and do away with the poor of the land,

5saying,

"When will the New Moon be over
that we may sell grain,
and the Sabbath be ended
that we may market wheat?"—
skimping the measure,
boosting the price
and cheating with dishonest scales,
6buying the poor with silver
and the needy for a pair of sandals,
selling even the sweepings with the wheat.

7The LORD has sworn by the
Pride of Jacob: "I will never forget
anything they have done.

8"Will not the land tremble for this,
and all who live in it mourn?
The whole land will rise like the Nile;
it will be stirred up and then sink
like the river of Egypt.

9"In that day," declares the Sovereign LORD,

"I will make the sun go down at noon
and darken the earth in broad daylight.
10I will turn your religious feasts into mourning
and all your singing into weeping.

[u]17 Hebrew *an unclean*
[v]3 Or *"the temple singers will wail*

°4 ק עניי
°8 ק ונשקעה

וְהַעֲלֵיתִי עַל־ כָּל־ מָתְנַיִם שָׂק וְעַל־ כָּל־ רֹאשׁ קָרְחָה
shaving head every-of and-to sackcloth bodies all-of on and-I-will-make-wear

וְשַׂמְתִּיהָ כְּאֵבֶל יָחִיד וְאַחֲרִיתָהּ כְּיוֹם מָר׃
bitter like-day and-end-of-her only-son like-mourning-of and-I-will-make-her

הִנֵּה ׀ יָמִים בָּאִים נְאֻם אֲדֹנָי יְהוִה וְהִשְׁלַחְתִּי רָעָב
famine when-I-will-send Yahweh Sovereign declaration-of ones-coming days see! (11)

בָּאָרֶץ לֹא־ רָעָב לַלֶּחֶם וְלֹא־ צָמָא לַמַּיִם כִּי אִם־
rather but for-the-waters thirst or-not of-the-food famine not through-the-land

לִשְׁמֹעַ אֵת דִּבְרֵי יְהוָה׃ וְנָעוּ מִיָּם עַד־ יָם וּמִצָּפוֹן
and-from-north sea to from-sea and-they-will-stagger (12) Yahweh words-of *** to-hear

וְעַד־ מִזְרָח יְשׁוֹטְטוּ לְבַקֵּשׁ אֶת־ דְּבַר־ יְהוָה וְלֹא יִמְצָאוּ׃
they-will-find but-not Yahweh word-of *** to-search-for they-will-wander east and-to

בַּיּוֹם הַהוּא תִּתְעַלַּפְנָה הַבְּתוּלֹת הַיָּפוֹת
the-lovely-ones the-young-women they-will-faint the-that in-the-day (13)

וְהַבַּחוּרִים בַּצָּמָא׃ הַנִּשְׁבָּעִים בְּאַשְׁמַת שֹׁמְרוֹן
Samaria by-shame-of the-ones-swearing (14) because-of-the-thirst and-the-young-men

וְאָמְרוּ חֵי אֱלֹהֶיךָ דָּן וְחֵי דֶּרֶךְ בְּאֵר־ שָׁבַע וְנָפְלוּ
indeed-they-will-fall Sheba Beer power-of or-alive Dan gods-of-you alive or-they-say

וְלֹא־ יָקוּמוּ עוֹד׃ רָאִיתִי אֶת־ אֲדֹנָי נִצָּב עַל־ הַמִּזְבֵּחַ וַיֹּאמֶר
and-he-said the-altar by standing Lord *** I-saw (9:1) again they-will-rise and-never

הַךְ הַכַּפְתּוֹר וְיִרְעֲשׁוּ הַסִּפִּים וּבְצַעַם
and-bring-down-them! the-thresholds so-they-shake the-top-of-the-pillar strike!

בְּרֹאשׁ כֻּלָּם וְאַחֲרִיתָם בַּחֶרֶב אֶהֱרֹג לֹא־
not I-will-kill with-the-sword and-one-left-of-them all-of-them on-head-of

יָנוּס לָהֶם נָס וְלֹא־ יִמָּלֵט לָהֶם פָּלִיט׃
escapee of-them he-will-escape and-not one-getting-away of-them he-will-get-away

אִם־ יַחְתְּרוּ בִשְׁאוֹל מִשָּׁם יָדִי תִקָּחֵם וְאִם־
and-though she-will-take-them hand-of-me from-there to-Sheol they-dig-down though (2)

יַעֲלוּ הַשָּׁמַיִם מִשָּׁם אוֹרִידֵם׃ וְאִם־
and-though (3) I-will-bring-down-them from-there the-heavens they-climb-up

יֵחָבְאוּ בְּרֹאשׁ הַכַּרְמֶל מִשָּׁם אֲחַפֵּשׂ וּלְקַחְתִּים
and-I-will-seize-them I-will-hunt at-there the-Carmel on-top-of they-hide-themselves

וְאִם־ יִסָּתְרוּ מִנֶּגֶד עֵינַי בְּקַרְקַע הַיָּם מִשָּׁם
at-there the-sea at-bottom-of eyes-of-me from-before they-hide-themselves and-though

אֲצַוֶּה אֶת־ הַנָּחָשׁ וּנְשָׁכָם׃ וְאִם־ יֵלְכוּ
they-are-driven and-though (4) so-he-will-bite-them the-serpent *** I-will-command

בַשְּׁבִי לִפְנֵי אֹיְבֵיהֶם* מִשָּׁם אֲצַוֶּה אֶת־ הַחֶרֶב
the-sword *** I-will-command at-there ones-being-enemies-of-them before into-the-exile

I will make all of you wear
sackcloth
and shave your heads.
I will make that time like
mourning for an only son
and the end of it like a
bitter day.

11"The days are coming,"
declares the Sovereign
LORD,
"when I will send a famine
through the land—
not a famine of food or a
thirst for water,
but a famine of hearing the
words of the LORD.
12Men will stagger from sea to
sea
and wander from north to
east,
searching for the word of the
LORD,
but they will not find it.

13"In that day
"the lovely young women and
strong young men
will faint because of thirst.
14They who swear by the
shame[w] of Samaria,
or say, 'As surely as your
god lives, O Dan,'
or, 'As surely as the god[x] of
Beersheba lives'—
they will fall,
never to rise again."

*Israel to Be Destroyed*

9 I saw the Lord standing by the
altar, and he said:

"Strike the tops of the pillars
so that the thresholds shake.
Bring them down on the
heads of all the people;
those who are left I will kill
with the sword.
Not one will get away,
none will escape.
2Though they dig down to the
depths of the grave,[y]
from there my hand will
take them.
Though they climb up to the
heavens,
from there I will bring them
down.
3Though they hide themselves
on the top of Carmel,
there I will hunt them down
and seize them.
Though they hide from me at
the bottom of the sea,
there I will command the
serpent to bite them.
4Though they are driven into
exile by their enemies,
there I will command the
sword to slay them.

w14 Or *by Ashima*; or *by the idol*
x14 Or *power*
y2 Hebrew *to Sheol*

***4 Most mss have *sheva* under the first *yodh* (אֹיְ).**

וַהֲרָגָתַם וְשַׂמְתִּי עֵינִי עֲלֵיהֶם לְרָעָה וְלֹא לְטוֹבָה׃
for-good and-not for-evil upon-them eye-of-me and-I-will-fix so-she-will-slay-them

(5) וַאדֹנָי יְהוִה הַצְּבָאוֹת הַנּוֹגֵעַ בָּאָרֶץ וַתָּמוֹג
and-she-melts to-the-earth the-one-touching the-Hosts Yahweh-of indeed-Lord (5)

וְאָבְלוּ כָּל־ יוֹשְׁבֵי בָהּ וְעָלְתָה כַיְאֹר כֻּלָּהּ
whole-of-her like-the-Nile and-she-rises in-her ones-living-of all-of and-they-mourn

וְשָׁקְעָה כִּיאֹר מִצְרָיִם׃ (6) הַבּוֹנֶה בַשָּׁמַיִם
in-the-heavens the-one-building (6) Egypt like-river-of then-she-sinks

מַעֲלוֹתָו וַאֲגֻדָּתוֹ עַל־ אֶרֶץ יְסָדָהּ הַקֹּרֵא
the-one-calling he-sets-her earth on and-foundation-of-him lofty-palaces-of-him

לְמֵי־ הַיָּם וַיִּשְׁפְּכֵם עַל־ פְּנֵי הָאָרֶץ יְהוָה שְׁמוֹ׃
name-of-him Yahweh the-land faces-of over and-he-pours-out-them the-sea for-waters-of

(7) הֲלוֹא כִבְנֵי כֻשִׁיִּים אַתֶּם לִי בְּנֵי יִשְׂרָאֵל נְאֻם־ יְהוָה
Yahweh declaration-of Israel peoples-of to-me you Cushites as-peoples-of not? (7)

הֲלוֹא אֶת־יִשְׂרָאֵל הֶעֱלֵיתִי מֵאֶרֶץ מִצְרַיִם וּפְלִשְׁתִּיִּים מִכַּפְתּוֹר
from-Caphtor and-Philistines Egypt from-land-of I-brought-up Israel *** not?

וַאֲרָם מִקִּיר׃ (8) הִנֵּה עֵינֵי ׀ אֲדֹנָי יְהוִה בַּמַּמְלָכָה הַחַטָּאָה
the-sinful on-the-kingdom Yahweh Sovereign eyes-of surely! (8) from-Kir and-Aram

וְהִשְׁמַדְתִּי אֹתָהּ מֵעַל פְּנֵי הָאֲדָמָה אֶפֶס כִּי לֹא הַשְׁמֵיד
to-destroy not indeed yet the-earth faces-of from-upon her and-I-will-destroy

אַשְׁמִיד אֶת־ בֵּית יַעֲקֹב נְאֻם־ יְהוָה׃ (9) כִּי־הִנֵּה אָנֹכִי
I see! for (9) Yahweh declaration-of Jacob house-of *** I-will-destroy

מְצַוֶּה וַהֲנִעוֹתִי בְכָל־ הַגּוֹיִם אֶת־ בֵּית יִשְׂרָאֵל כַּאֲשֶׁר
as-that Israel house-of *** the-nations among-all-of and-I-will-shake commanding

יִנּוֹעַ בַּכְּבָרָה וְלֹא־ יִפּוֹל צְרוֹר אָרֶץ׃ (10) בַּחֶרֶב
by-the-sword (10) ground pebble he-will-reach but-not in-the-sieve he-is-shaken

יָמוּתוּ כֹּל חַטָּאֵי עַמִּי הָאֹמְרִים לֹא־ תַגִּישׁ
she-will-overtake not the-ones-saying people-of-me sinners-of all-of they-will-die

וְתַקְדִּים בַּעֲדֵינוּ הָרָעָה׃ (11) בַּיּוֹם הַהוּא אָקִים אֶת־
*** I-will-restore the-that in-the-day (11) the-disaster to-us or-she-will-meet

סֻכַּת דָּוִיד הַנֹּפֶלֶת וְגָדַרְתִּי אֶת־ פִּרְצֵיהֶן
broken-places-of-them *** and-I-will-repair the-one-having-fallen David tent-of

וַהֲרִסֹתָיו אָקִים וּבְנִיתִיהָ כִּימֵי עוֹלָם׃
former-time as-days-of and-I-will-build-her I-will-restore and-ruins-of-him

(12) לְמַעַן יִירְשׁוּ אֶת־ שְׁאֵרִית אֱדוֹם וְכָל־ הַגּוֹיִם
the-nations and-all-of Edom remnant-of *** they-may-possess so-that (12)

אֲשֶׁר־ נִקְרָא שְׁמִי עֲלֵיהֶם נְאֻם־ יְהוָה עֹשֶׂה זֹּאת׃
this the-one-doing Yahweh declaration-of to-them name-of-me he-is-called that

°8 ק מעלותיו

I will fix my eyes upon them
for evil and not for good."

5 The Lord, the LORD Almighty,
he who touches the earth
and it melts,
and all who live in it
mourn—
the whole land rises like the
Nile,
then sinks like the river of
Egypt—
6 he who builds his lofty palace[y]
in the heavens
and sets its foundation[z] on
the earth,
who calls for the waters of the
sea
and pours them out over the
face of the land—
the LORD is his name.

7 "Are not you Israelites
the same to me as the
Cushites[a]?"
declares the LORD.
"Did I not bring Israel up
from Egypt,
the Philistines from
Caphtor[b]
and the Arameans from Kir?

8 "Surely the eyes of the
Sovereign LORD
are on the sinful kingdom.
I will destroy it
from the face of the earth—
yet I will not totally destroy
the house of Jacob,"
declares the LORD.
9 "For I will give the command,
and I will shake the house
of Israel
among all the nations
as grain is shaken in a sieve,
but not a pebble will reach to
the ground.
10 All the sinners among my
people
will die by the sword,
all those who say,
'Disaster will not overtake or
meet us.'

*Israel's Restoration*

11 "In that day I will restore
David's fallen tent.
I will repair its broken places,
restore its ruins,
and build it as it used to be,
12 so that they may possess the
remnant of Edom
and all the nations that bear
my name,[c]"
declares the LORD, who
will do these things.

[y]6 The meaning of the Hebrew for this phrase is uncertain.
[z]6 The meaning of the Hebrew for this word is uncertain
[a]7 That is, people from the upper Nile region
[b]7 That is, Crete
[c]12 Hebrew; Septuagint *so that the remnant of men / and all the nations that bear my name may seek ⌊the Lord⌋*

(13) הִנֵּה יָמִים בָּאִים נְאֻם־ יְהוָה וְנִגַּשׁ
see! days ones-coming declaration-of Yahweh when-he-will-be-overtaken

חוֹרֵשׁ בַּקֹּצֵר וְדֹרֵךְ עֲנָבִים בְּמֹשֵׁךְ
one-reaping by-the-man-plowing and-one-treading-of grapes by-one-planting-of

הַזָּרַע וְהִטִּיפוּ הֶהָרִים עָסִיס וְכָל־ הַגְּבָעוֹת
the-seed and-they-will-drip the-mountains new-wine and-all-of the-hills

תִּתְמוֹגַגְנָה׃ (14) וְשַׁבְתִּי אֶת־ שְׁבוּת עַמִּי יִשְׂרָאֵל
they-will-flow (14) and-I-will-bring-back *** exile-of people-of-me Israel

וּבָנוּ עָרִים נְשַׁמּוֹת וְיָשָׁבוּ
and-they-will-rebuild cities ones-being-ruined and-they-will-live-in

וְנָטְעוּ כְרָמִים וְשָׁתוּ אֶת־ יֵינָם
and-they-will-plant vineyards and-they-will-drink *** wine-of-them

וְעָשׂוּ גַנּוֹת וְאָכְלוּ אֶת־ פְּרִיהֶם׃
and-they-will-make gardens and-they-will-eat *** fruit-of-them

(15) וּנְטַעְתִּים עַל־ אַדְמָתָם וְלֹא יִנָּתְשׁוּ
(15) and-I-will-plant-them in land-of-them and-never they-will-be-uprooted

עוֹד מֵעַל אַדְמָתָם אֲשֶׁר נָתַתִּי לָהֶם אָמַר יְהוָה אֱלֹהֶיךָ׃
again from-on land-of-them that I-gave to-them he-says Yahweh God-of-you

13 "The days are coming," declares the LORD,

"when the reaper will be overtaken by the plowman
and the planter by the one treading grapes.
New wine will drip from the mountains
and flow from all the hills.
14 I will bring back my exiled[d] people Israel;
they will rebuild the ruined cities and live in them.
They will plant vineyards and drink their wine;
they will make gardens and eat their fruit.
15 I will plant Israel in their own land,
never again to be uprooted
from the land I have given them,"
says the LORD your God.

[d] 14 Or *will restore the fortunes of my*

חֲזוֹן עֹבַדְיָה כֹּה־ אָמַר אֲדֹנָי יְהוִה לֶאֱדוֹם שְׁמוּעָה שָׁמַעְנוּ
we-heard message about-Edom Yahweh Sovereign he-says this Obadiah vision-of (1)

מֵאֵת יְהוָה וְצִיר בַּגּוֹיִם שֻׁלָּח קוּמוּ וְנָקוּמָה
and-let-us-go rise! he-was-sent to-the-nations indeed-envoy Yahweh from-with

עָלֶיהָ לַמִּלְחָמָה׃ הִנֵּה קָטֹן נְתַתִּיךָ בַּגּוֹיִם
among-the-nations I-will-make-you small see! (2) for-the-battle against-her

בָּזוּי אַתָּה מְאֹד׃ זְדוֹן לִבְּךָ הִשִּׁיאֶךָ
he-deceived-you heart-of-you pride-of (3) utterly you one-being-despised

שֹׁכְנִי בְחַגְוֵי־ סֶלַע מְרוֹם שִׁבְתּוֹ אֹמֵר בְּלִבּוֹ מִי
who? to-self-of-you one-saying home-of-you height-of rock in-clefts-of one-living

יוֹרִדֵנִי אָרֶץ׃ אִם־ תַּגְבִּיהַּ כַּנֶּשֶׁר וְאִם־ בֵּין
among and-though like-the-eagle you-soar-high though (4) ground he-can-bring-down-me

כּוֹכָבִים שִׂים קִנֶּךָ מִשָּׁם אוֹרִידְךָ נְאֻם־ יְהוָה׃
Yahweh declaration-of I-will-bring-down-you from-there nest-of-you he-makes stars

אִם־גַּנָּבִים בָּאוּ־ לְךָ אִם־ שׁוֹדְדֵי לַיְלָה אֵיךְ נִדְמֵיתָה
you-will-meet-disaster Oh! night ones-robbing-of if to-you they-came thieves if (5)

הֲלוֹא יִגְנְבוּ דַּיָּם אִם־ בֹּצְרִים בָּאוּ לָךְ הֲלוֹא
not? to-you they-came ones-picking-grapes if want-of-them they-would-steal not?

יַשְׁאִירוּ עֹלֵלוֹת׃ אֵיךְ נֶחְפְּשׂוּ עֵשָׂו
Esau they-will-be-ransacked how! (6) gleanings-of-grapes they-would-leave

נִבְעוּ מַצְפֻּנָיו׃ עַד־ הַגְּבוּל שִׁלְּחוּךָ
they-will-force-you the-border to (7) hidden-treasures-of-him they-will-be-pillaged

כֹּל אַנְשֵׁי בְרִיתֶךָ הִשִּׁיאוּךָ יָכְלוּ לְךָ
over-you they-will-overpower they-will-deceive-you alliance-of-you men-of all-of

אַנְשֵׁי שְׁלֹמֶךָ לַחְמְךָ יָשִׂימוּ מָזוֹר תַּחְתֶּיךָ אֵין
there-will-be-no for-you trap they-will-set bread-of-you friendship-of-you men-of

תְּבוּנָה בּוֹ׃ הֲלוֹא בַּיּוֹם הַהוּא נְאֻם־ יְהוָה
Yahweh declaration-of the-that in-the-day not? (8) of-him detection

וְהַאֲבַדְתִּי חֲכָמִים מֵאֱדוֹם וּתְבוּנָה מֵהַר עֵשָׂו׃
Esau from-mountain-of and-understanding from-Edom wise-men indeed-will-I-destroy

וְחַתּוּ גִבּוֹרֶיךָ תֵּימָן לְמַעַן יִכָּרֶת־
he-will-be-cut-down so-that Teman warriors-of-you and-they-will-be-terrified (9)

אִישׁ מֵהַר עֵשָׂו מִקָּטֶל׃ מֵחֲמַס אָחִיךָ
brother-of-you because-of-violence-of (10) in-slaughter Esau in-mountain-of everyone

יַעֲקֹב תְּכַסְּךָ בוּשָׁה וְנִכְרַתָּ לְעוֹלָם׃ בְּיוֹם
on-day-of (11) to-forever and-you-will-be-destroyed shame she-will-cover-you Jacob

עֲמָדְךָ מִנֶּגֶד בְּיוֹם שְׁבוֹת זָרִים חֵילוֹ
wealth-of-him ones-being-strangers to-carry-off on-day-of in-aloofness to-stand-you

1 The vision of Obadiah.

This is what the Sovereign LORD says about Edom—

We have heard a message from the LORD:
An envoy was sent to the nations to say,
"Rise, and let us go against her for battle"—

2 "See, I will make you small among the nations;
you will be utterly despised.
3 The pride of your heart has deceived you,
you who live in the clefts of the rocks[a]
and make your home on the heights,
you who say to yourself,
'Who can bring me down to the ground?'
4 Though you soar like the eagle
and make your nest among the stars,
from there I will bring you down,"
declares the LORD.
5 "If thieves came to you,
if robbers in the night—
Oh, what a disaster awaits you—
would they not steal only as much as they wanted?
If grape pickers came to you,
would they not leave a few grapes?
6 But how Esau will be ransacked,
his hidden treasures pillaged!
7 All your allies will force you to the border;
your friends will deceive and overpower you;
those who eat your bread will set a trap for you,[b]
but you will not detect it.

8 "In that day," declares the LORD,
"will I not destroy the wise men of Edom,
men of understanding in the mountains of Esau?
9 Your warriors, O Teman, will be terrified,
and everyone in Esau's mountains
will be cut down in the slaughter.
10 Because of the violence against your brother Jacob,
you will be covered with shame;
you will be destroyed forever.
11 On the day you stood aloof
while strangers carried off his wealth

[a] 3 Or *of Sela*
[b] 7 The meaning of the Hebrew for this clause is uncertain.

וְנָכְרִים בָּאוּ שְׁעָרָו וְעַל־ יְרוּשָׁלַםִ יַדּוּ גוֹרָל גַּם־
also lot they-cast Jerusalem and-for gates-of-him they-entered and-foreigners

אַתָּה כְּאַחַד מֵהֶם׃ וְאַל־ תֵּרֶא בְיוֹם־ אָחִיךָ
brother-of-you on-day-of you-should-look-down and-not (12) of-them like-one you

בְּיוֹם נָכְרוֹ וְאַל־ תִּשְׂמַח לִבְנֵי־ יְהוּדָה
Judah over-peoples-of you-should-rejoice or-not misfortune-of-him in-day-of

בְּיוֹם אָבְדָם וְאַל־ תַּגְדֵּל פִּיךָ בְּיוֹם
in-day-of mouth-of-you she-should-boast-much or-not to-be-destroyed-them in-day-of

צָרָה׃ אַל־ תָּבוֹא בְשַׁעַר־ עַמִּי בְּיוֹם
in-day-of people-of-me through-gate-of you-should-march not (13) trouble

אֵידָם אַל־ תֵּרֶא גַם־ אַתָּה בְּרָעָתוֹ בְּיוֹם
in-day-of on-calamity-of-him you also you-should-look-down not disaster-of-them

אֵידוֹ וְאַל־ תִּשְׁלַחְנָה בְחֵילוֹ בְּיוֹם אֵידוֹ׃
disaster-of-him in-day-of to-wealth-of-him you-should-seize or-not disaster-of-him

וְאַל־ תַּעֲמֹד עַל־ הַפֶּרֶק לְהַכְרִית אֶת־ פְּלִיטָיו
fugitives-of-him *** to-cut-down the-crossroad at you-should-wait and-not (14)

וְאַל־ תַּסְגֵּר שְׂרִידָיו בְּיוֹם צָרָה׃ כִּי־
indeed (15) trouble in-day-of survivors-of-him you-should-hand-over or-not

קָרוֹב יוֹם־ יְהוָה עַל־ כָּל־ הַגּוֹיִם כַּאֲשֶׁר עָשִׂיתָ יֵעָשֶׂה
he-will-be-done you-did as-that the-nations all-of for Yahweh day-of near

לָּךְ גְּמֻלְךָ יָשׁוּב בְּרֹאשֶׁךָ׃ כִּי כַּאֲשֶׁר שְׁתִיתֶם
you-drank just-as for (16) upon-head-of-you he-will-return deed-of-you to-you

עַל־ הַר קָדְשִׁי יִשְׁתּוּ כָל־ הַגּוֹיִם תָּמִיד
continually the-nations all-of they-will-drink holiness-of-me hill-of on

וְשָׁתוּ וְלָעוּ וְהָיוּ כְּלוֹא הָיוּ׃
they-were as-never and-they-will-be and-they-will-drink and-they-will-drink

וּבְהַר צִיּוֹן תִּהְיֶה פְלֵיטָה וְהָיָה קֹדֶשׁ
holiness and-he-will-be delivered-one she-will-be Zion but-on-Mount-of (17)

וְיָרְשׁוּ בֵּית יַעֲקֹב אֵת מוֹרָשֵׁיהֶם׃ וְהָיָה
and-he-will-be (18) inheritances-of-them *** Jacob house-of and-they-will-possess

בֵית־ יַעֲקֹב אֵשׁ וּבֵית יוֹסֵף לֶהָבָה וּבֵית עֵשָׂו לְקַשׁ
to-stubble Esau and-house-of flame Joseph and-house-of fire Jacob house-of

וְדָלְקוּ בָהֶם וַאֲכָלוּם וְלֹא־ יִהְיֶה
he-will-be and-not and-they-will-consume-them to-them and-they-will-set-fire

שָׂרִיד לְבֵית עֵשָׂו כִּי יְהוָה דִּבֵּר׃ וְיָרְשׁוּ
and-they-will-occupy (19) he-spoke Yahweh indeed Esau from-house-of survivor

הַנֶּגֶב אֶת־ הַר עֵשָׂו וְהַשְּׁפֵלָה אֶת־ פְּלִשְׁתִּים וְיָרְשׁוּ
and-they-will-occupy Philistines *** and-the-foothill Esau mountain-of *** the-Negev

and foreigners entered his gates
and cast lots for Jerusalem,
you were like one of them.
12 You should not look down on your brother
in the day of his misfortune,
nor rejoice over the people of Judah
in the day of their destruction,
nor boast so much
in the day of their trouble.
13 You should not march through the gates of my people
in the day of their disaster,
nor look down on them in their calamity
in the day of their disaster,
nor seize their wealth
in the day of their disaster.
14 You should not wait at the crossroads
to cut down their fugitives,
nor hand over their survivors
in the day of their trouble.

15 "The day of the LORD is near
for all nations.
As you have done, it will be done to you;
your deeds will return upon your own head.
16 Just as you drank on my holy hill,
so all the nations will drink continually;
they will drink and drink
and be as if they had never been.
17 But on Mount Zion will be deliverance;
it will be holy,
and the house of Jacob
will possess its inheritance.
18 The house of Jacob will be a fire
and the house of Joseph a flame;
the house of Esau will be stubble,
and they will set it on fire
and consume it.
There will be no survivors
from the house of Esau."
The LORD has spoken.

19 People from the Negev will occupy
the mountains of Esau,
and people from the foothills will possess
the land of the Philistines.

°11 ק שעריו

אֶת־ שְׂדֵה אֶפְרַיִם וְאֵת שְׂדֵה שֹׁמְרוֹן וּבִנְיָמִן אֶת־ הַגִּלְעָד׃
the-Gilead *** and-Benjamin Samaria field-of and Ephraim field-of ***

וְגָלֻת הַחֵל־ הַזֶּה לִבְנֵי יִשְׂרָאֵל אֲשֶׁר־ כְּנַעֲנִים
Canaanites who Israel of-peoples-of the-this the-company and-exile-of (20)

עַד־ צָרְפַת וְגָלֻת יְרוּשָׁלַםִ אֲשֶׁר בִּסְפָרַד יִרְשׁוּ
they-will-possess in-Sepharad who Jerusalem and-exile-of Zarephath as-far-as

אֵת עָרֵי הַנֶּגֶב׃ וְעָלוּ מֹשִׁעִים בְּהַר צִיּוֹן
Zion on-Mount-of ones-delivering and-they-will-go-up (21) the-Negev towns-of ***

לִשְׁפֹּט אֶת־ הַר עֵשָׂו וְהָיְתָה לַיהוָה הַמְּלוּכָה׃
the-kingdom to-Yahweh and-she-will-be Esau mountain-of *** to-govern

They will occupy the fields of
Ephraim and Samaria,
and Benjamin will possess
Gilead.
[20]This company of Israelite
exiles who are in Canaan
will possess ⌞the land⌟ as far
as Zarephath;
the exiles from Jerusalem who
are in Sepharad
will possess the towns of the
Negev.
[21]Deliverers will go up on[c]
Mount Zion
to govern the mountains of
Esau.
And the kingdom will be
the LORD's.

[c]21 Or *from*

וַיְהִי֙ דְּבַר־ יְהוָ֔ה אֶל־ יוֹנָ֥ה בֶן־ אֲמִתַּ֖י לֵאמֹֽר׃ ק֠וּם לֵ֧ךְ
go! get-up! (2) to-say Amittai son-of Jonah to Yahweh word-of now-he-came (1:1)

אֶל־ נִֽינְוֵ֛ה הָעִ֥יר הַגְּדוֹלָ֖ה וּקְרָ֣א עָלֶ֑יהָ כִּֽי־ עָלְתָ֥ה
she-came-up because against-her and-preach! the-great the-city Nineveh to

רָעָתָ֖ם לְפָנָֽי׃ וַיָּ֤קָם יוֹנָה֙ לִבְרֹ֣חַ תַּרְשִׁ֔ישָׁה
to-Tarshish to-run-away Jonah but-he-got-up (3) before-me wickedness-of-them

מִלִּפְנֵ֖י יְהוָ֑ה וַיֵּ֨רֶד יָפ֜וֹ וַיִּמְצָ֥א אָנִיָּ֣ה ׀ בָּאָ֣ה תַרְשִׁ֗ישׁ
Tarshish being-bound ship and-he-found Joppa and-he-went-down Yahweh from-before

וַיִּתֵּ֨ן שְׂכָרָ֜הּ וַיֵּ֣רֶד בָּ֗הּ לָב֤וֹא עִמָּהֶם֙ תַּרְשִׁ֔ישָׁה
for-Tarshish with-them to-sail aboard-her and-he-went fare-of-her and-he-paid

מִלִּפְנֵ֖י יְהוָֽה׃ וַֽיהוָ֗ה הֵטִ֤יל רֽוּחַ־גְּדוֹלָה֙ אֶל־הַיָּ֔ם וַֽיְהִ֥י סַֽעַר־
storm and-he-arose the-sea on great wind he-sent then-Yahweh (4) Yahweh from-before

גָּד֖וֹל בַּיָּ֑ם וְהָ֣אֲנִיָּ֔ה חִשְּׁבָ֖ה לְהִשָּׁבֵֽר׃ וַיִּֽירְא֣וּ
and-they-were-afraid (5) to-break-up she-threatened that-the-ship on-the-sea violent

הַמַּלָּחִ֗ים וַֽיִּזְעֲקוּ֮ אִ֣ישׁ אֶל־ אֱלֹהָיו֒ וַיָּטִ֨לוּ אֶת־ הַכֵּלִ֜ים
the-cargoes *** and-they-threw gods-of-him to each and-they-cried-out the-sailors

אֲשֶׁ֤ר בָּֽאֳנִיָּה֙ אֶל־ הַיָּ֔ם לְהָקֵ֖ל מֵעֲלֵיהֶ֑ם וְיוֹנָ֗ה יָרַד֙ אֶל־
to he-had-gone-down but-Jonah from-on-her to-lighten the-sea into in-the-ship that

יַרְכְּתֵ֣י הַסְּפִינָ֔ה וַיִּשְׁכַּ֖ב וַיֵּרָדַֽם׃ וַיִּקְרַ֤ב
and-he-went (6) and-he-fell-deeply-asleep and-he-lay-down the-ship lower-parts-of

אֵלָיו֙ רַ֣ב הַחֹבֵ֔ל וַיֹּ֥אמֶר ל֖וֹ מַה־ לְּךָ֣ נִרְדָּ֑ם ק֚וּם קְרָ֣א
call! get-up! sleeping to-you how? to-him and-he-said the-sailor captain-of to-him

אֶל־ אֱלֹהֶ֔יךָ אוּלַ֞י יִתְעַשֵּׁ֧ת הָאֱלֹהִ֛ים לָ֖נוּ וְלֹ֥א נֹאבֵֽד׃
we-will-perish and-not of-us the-gods he-will-take-notice maybe gods-of-you on

וַיֹּאמְר֞וּ אִ֣ישׁ אֶל־ רֵעֵ֗הוּ לְכוּ֙ וְנַפִּ֣ילָה גוֹרָל֔וֹת וְנֵ֣דְעָ֔ה
and-let-us-find-out lots and-let-us-cast come! other-of-him to each then-they-said (7)

בְּשֶׁלְּמִ֛י הָרָעָ֥ה הַזֹּ֖את לָ֑נוּ וַיַּפִּ֙לוּ֙ גּֽוֹרָל֔וֹת וַיִּפֹּ֥ל הַגּוֹרָ֖ל
the-lot and-he-fell lots and-they-cast to-us the-this the-calamity on-account-of-whom

עַל־ יוֹנָֽה׃ וַיֹּאמְר֣וּ אֵלָ֔יו הַגִּֽידָה־נָּ֣א לָ֔נוּ בַּאֲשֶׁ֛ר לְמִי־
of-whom on-account-of-that to-us now! tell! to-him so-they-asked (8) Jonah on

הָרָעָ֥ה הַזֹּ֖את לָ֑נוּ מַה־ מְּלַאכְתְּךָ֙ וּמֵאַ֣יִן תָּב֔וֹא מָ֣ה
what? you-come and-from-where? occupation-of-you what? to-us the-this the-trouble

אַרְצֶ֔ךָ וְאֵֽי־ מִזֶּ֥ה עַ֖ם אָֽתָּה׃ וַיֹּ֥אמֶר אֲלֵיהֶ֖ם עִבְרִ֣י
Hebrew to-them and-he-answered (9) you people from-this and-where? country-of-you

אָנֹ֑כִי וְאֶת־ יְהוָ֞ה אֱלֹהֵ֤י הַשָּׁמַ֙יִם֙ אֲנִ֣י יָרֵ֔א אֲשֶׁר־ עָשָׂ֥ה אֶת־ הַיָּ֖ם וְאֶת־
and the-sea *** he-made who worshiping I the-heavens God-of Yahweh and I

הַיַּבָּשָֽׁה׃ וַיִּֽירְא֤וּ הָֽאֲנָשִׁים֙ יִרְאָ֣ה גְדוֹלָ֔ה וַיֹּאמְר֥וּ אֵלָ֖יו
to-him and-they-asked great terror the-men and-they-were-terrified (10) the-land

*Jonah Flees From the Lord*

1 The word of the LORD came to
Jonah son of Amittai: [2]"Go to
the great city of Nineveh and
preach against it, because its
wickedness has come up before
me."
[3]But Jonah ran away from the
LORD and headed for Tarshish. He
went down to Joppa, where he
found a ship bound for that port.
After paying the fare, he went
aboard and sailed for Tarshish to
flee from the LORD.
[4]Then the LORD sent a great
wind on the sea, and such a violent storm arose that the ship
threatened to break up. [5]All the
sailors were afraid and each cried
out to his own god. And they
threw the cargo into the sea to
lighten the ship.
But Jonah had gone below deck,
where he lay down and fell into a
deep sleep. [6]The captain went to
him and said, "How can you
sleep? Get up and call on your god!
Maybe he will take notice of us,
and we will not perish."
[7]Then the sailors said to each
other, "Come, let us cast lots to
find out who is responsible for
this calamity." They cast lots and
the lot fell on Jonah.
[8]So they asked him, "Tell us,
who is responsible for making all
this trouble for us? What do you
do? Where do you come from?
What is your country? From what
people are you?"
[9]He answered, "I am a Hebrew
and I worship the LORD, the God
of heaven, who made the sea and
the land."
[10]This terrified them and they

*3 Most mss have *hateph qamets* under the *aleph* (אֳנִיָּה).

מַה־זֹּאת עָשִׂיתָ כִּֽי־יָדְעוּ הָאֲנָשִׁים כִּֽי־מִלִּפְנֵי יְהוָה הוּא בֹרֵחַ
running-away he Yahweh from-before that the-men they-knew now you-did this what?

כִּי הִגִּיד לָהֶם׃ וַיֹּאמְרוּ אֵלָיו מַה־נַּעֲשֶׂה לָּךְ
to-you should-we-do what? to-him so-they-asked (11) to-them he-had-told because

וְיִשְׁתֹּק הַיָּם מֵעָלֵינוּ כִּי הַיָּם הוֹלֵךְ וְסֹעֵר׃
and-being-rough continuing the-sea for from-against-us the-sea so-he-will-be-calm

וַיֹּאמֶר אֲלֵיהֶם שָׂאוּנִי וַהֲטִילֻנִי אֶל־הַיָּם
the-sea into and-throw-me! pick-up-me! to-them and-he-replied (12)

וְיִשְׁתֹּק הַיָּם מֵעֲלֵיכֶם כִּי יוֹדֵעַ אָנִי כִּי בְשֶׁלִּי
on-account-of-me that I knowing for from-against-you the-sea and-he-will-become-calm

הַסַּעַר הַגָּדוֹל הַזֶּה עֲלֵיכֶם׃ וַיַּחְתְּרוּ הָאֲנָשִׁים לְהָשִׁיב
to-bring-back the-men instead-they-rowed (13) upon-you the-this the-great the-storm

אֶל־הַיַּבָּשָׁה וְלֹא יָכֹלוּ כִּי הַיָּם הוֹלֵךְ וְסֹעֵר עֲלֵיהֶם׃
against-them and-growing-wild continuing the-sea for they-could but-not the-land to

וַיִּקְרְאוּ אֶל־יְהוָה וַיֹּאמְרוּ אָנָּה יְהוָה אַל־נָא נֹאבְדָה
let-us-die please! not Yahweh O! and-they-said Yahweh to then-they-cried (14)

בְּנֶפֶשׁ הָאִישׁ הַזֶּה וְאַל־תִּתֵּן עָלֵינוּ דָּם נָקִיא כִּֽי־אַתָּה
you for innocent blood against-us you-hold and-not the-this the-man for-life-of

יְהוָה כַּאֲשֶׁר חָפַצְתָּ עָשִׂיתָ׃ וַיִּשְׂאוּ אֶת־יוֹנָה וַיְטִלֻהוּ
and-they-threw-him Jonah *** then-they-took (15) you-did you-pleased just-as Yahweh

אֶל־הַיָּם וַיַּעֲמֹד הַיָּם מִזַּעְפּוֹ׃ וַיִּירְאוּ
and-they-feared (16) from-raging-of-him the-sea and-he-grew-calm the-sea into

הָאֲנָשִׁים יִרְאָה גְדוֹלָה אֶת־יְהוָה וַיִּזְבְּחוּ־זֶבַח לַיהוָה
to-Yahweh sacrifice and-they-sacrificed Yahweh *** great fear the-men

וַיִּדְּרוּ נְדָרִים׃ וַיְמַן יְהוָה דָּג גָּדוֹל לִבְלֹעַ אֶת־יוֹנָה
Jonah *** to-swallow great fish Yahweh but-he-provided *(2:1) vows and-they-vowed

וַיְהִי יוֹנָה בִּמְעֵי הַדָּג שְׁלֹשָׁה יָמִים וּשְׁלֹשָׁה לֵילוֹת׃
nights and-three days three the-fish in-insides-of Jonah and-he-was

וַיִּתְפַּלֵּל יוֹנָה אֶל־יְהוָה אֱלֹהָיו מִמְּעֵי הַדָּגָה׃
the-fish from-insides-of God-of-him Yahweh to Jonah and-he-prayed (2)

וַיֹּאמֶר קָרָאתִי מִצָּרָה לִי אֶל־יְהוָה וַיַּעֲנֵנִי
and-he-answered-me Yahweh to of-me in-distress I-called and-he-said (3)

מִבֶּטֶן שְׁאוֹל שִׁוַּעְתִּי שָׁמַעְתָּ קוֹלִי׃ וַתַּשְׁלִיכֵנִי
and-you-hurled-me (4) cry-of-me you-heard I-called-for-help Sheol from-depth-of

מְצוּלָה בִּלְבַב יַמִּים וְנָהָר יְסֹבְבֵנִי כָּל־מִשְׁבָּרֶיךָ
breakers-of-you all-of he-swirled-about-me and-current seas into-heart-of deep

וְגַלֶּיךָ עָלַי עָבָרוּ׃ וַאֲנִי אָמַרְתִּי נִגְרַשְׁתִּי מִנֶּגֶד
from-before I-was-banished I-said and-I (5) they-swept over-me and-waves-of-you

asked, "What have you done?" (They knew he was running away from the LORD, because he had already told them so.)
11 The sea was getting rougher and rougher. So they asked him, "What should we do to you to make the sea calm down for us?"
12 "Pick me up and throw me into the sea," he replied, "and it will become calm. I know that it is my fault that this great storm has come upon you."
13 Instead, the men did their best to row back to land. But they could not, for the sea grew even wilder
than before. 14 Then they cried to
the LORD, "O LORD, please do not let us die for taking this man's life. Do not hold us accountable for killing an innocent man, for you, O LORD, have done as you
pleased." 15 Then they took Jonah and threw him overboard, and the
raging sea grew calm. 16 At this the men greatly feared the LORD, and they offered a sacrifice to the LORD and made vows to him.
17 But the LORD provided a great fish to swallow Jonah, and Jonah was inside the fish three days and three nights.

*Jonah's Prayer*

2 From inside the fish Jonah prayed to the LORD his God.
2 He said:

"In my distress I called to the LORD,
and he answered me.
From the depths of the grave[a]
I called for help,
and you listened to my cry.
3 You hurled me into the deep,
into the very heart of the seas,
and the currents swirled about me;
all your waves and breakers
swept over me.
4 I said, 'I have been banished

[a] 2 Hebrew *Sheol*

***Heading, 1* The Hebrew numeration of chapter 2 begins with the final verse of chapter 1 in English; thus, there is a one-verse discrepancy throughout chapter 2.**

עֵינֶיךָ אַךְ אוֹסִיף לְהַבִּיט אֶל־הֵיכַל קָדְשֶׁךָ׃
holiness-of-you temple-of toward to-look I-will-do-again yet eyes-of-you

אֲפָפוּנִי מַיִם עַד־נֶפֶשׁ תְּהוֹם יְסֹבְבֵנִי סוּף חָבוּשׁ
being-wrapped seaweed he-surrounded-me deep throat at waters they-engulfed-me (6)

לְרֹאשִׁי׃ לְקִצְבֵי הָרִים יָרַדְתִּי הָאָרֶץ בְּרִחֶיהָ
bars-of-her the-earth I-sank-down mountains to-roots-of (7) around-head-of-me

בַעֲדִי לְעוֹלָם וַתַּעַל מִשַּׁחַת חַיַּי יְהוָה אֱלֹהָי׃
God-of-me Yahweh lives-of-me from-pit but-you-brought-up to-forever about-me

בְּהִתְעַטֵּף עָלַי נַפְשִׁי אֶת־יְהוָה זָכָרְתִּי וַתָּבוֹא אֵלֶיךָ
to-you and-she-rose I-remembered Yahweh *** life-of-me from-me when-to-ebb-away (8)

תְּפִלָּתִי אֶל־הֵיכַל קָדְשֶׁךָ׃ מְשַׁמְּרִים הַבְלֵי־
worthless-ones-of ones-clinging-to (9) holiness-of-you temple-of to prayer-of-me

שָׁוְא חַסְדָּם יַעֲזֹבוּ׃ וַאֲנִי בְּקוֹל תּוֹדָה
thanksgiving with-song-of but-I (10) they-forfeit grace-of-them emptiness

אֶזְבְּחָה־לָּךְ אֲשֶׁר נָדַרְתִּי אֲשַׁלֵּמָה יְשׁוּעָתָה לַיהוָה׃
from-Yahweh salvation I-will-make-good I-vowed what to-you I-will-sacrifice

וַיֹּאמֶר יְהוָה לַדָּג וַיָּקֵא אֶת־יוֹנָה אֶל־הַיַּבָּשָׁה׃
the-dry-land on Jonah *** and-he-vomited to-the-fish Yahweh and-he-commanded (11)

וַיְהִי דְבַר־יְהוָה אֶל־יוֹנָה שֵׁנִית לֵאמֹר׃ קוּם לֵךְ
go! get-up! (2) to-say second-time Jonah to Yahweh word-of then-he-came (3:1)

אֶל־נִינְוֵה הָעִיר הַגְּדוֹלָה וּקְרָא† אֵלֶיהָ אֶת־הַקְּרִיאָה אֲשֶׁר אָנֹכִי
I that the-message *** to-her and-proclaim! the-great the-city Nineveh to

דֹּבֵר אֵלֶיךָ׃ וַיָּקָם יוֹנָה וַיֵּלֶךְ אֶל־נִינְוֵה†† כִּדְבַר יְהוָה
Yahweh as-word-of Nineveh to and-he-went Jonah and-he-got-up (3) to-you giving

וְנִינְוֵה הָיְתָה עִיר־גְּדוֹלָה לֵאלֹהִים מַהֲלַךְ שְׁלֹשֶׁת יָמִים׃ וַיָּחֶל
and-he-started (4) days three-of visit-of to-God important city she-was now-Nineveh

יוֹנָה לָבוֹא בָעִיר מַהֲלַךְ יוֹם אֶחָד וַיִּקְרָא וַיֹּאמַר עוֹד
more and-he-said and-he-proclaimed one day journey-of into-the-city to-go Jonah

אַרְבָּעִים יוֹם וְנִינְוֵה נֶהְפָּכֶת׃ וַיַּאֲמִינוּ אַנְשֵׁי נִינְוֵה
Nineveh men-of and-they-believed (5) being-overturned and-Nineveh day forty

בֵּאלֹהִים וַיִּקְרְאוּ־צוֹם וַיִּלְבְּשׁוּ שַׂקִּים מִגְּדוֹלָם
from-greatest-of-them sackcloths and-they-put-on fast and-they-declared in-God

וְעַד־קְטַנָּם׃ וַיִּגַּע הַדָּבָר אֶל־מֶלֶךְ‡ נִינְוֵה
Nineveh king-of to the-news when-he-reached (6) least-of-them and-to

וַיָּקָם מִכִּסְאוֹ וַיַּעֲבֵר אַדַּרְתּוֹ מֵעָלָיו
from-upon-him royal-robe-of-him and-he-took-off from-throne-of-him then-he-rose

וַיְכַס שַׂק וַיֵּשֶׁב עַל־הָאֵפֶר׃ וַיַּזְעֵק
then-he-proclaimed (7) the-dust in and-he-sat-down sackcloth and-he-covered-himself

from your sight;
yet I will look again
toward your holy temple.'
5The engulfing waters
threatened me,[b]
the deep surrounded me;
seaweed was wrapped
around my head.
6To the roots of the mountains
I sank down;
the earth beneath barred me
in forever.
But you brought my life up
from the pit,
O LORD my God.
7"When my life was ebbing
away,
I remembered you, LORD,
and my prayer rose to you,
to your holy temple.
8"Those who cling to worthless
idols
forfeit the grace that could
be theirs.
9But I, with a song of
thanksgiving,
will sacrifice to you.
What I have vowed I will
make good.
Salvation comes from the
LORD."

10And the LORD commanded the
fish, and it vomited Jonah onto
dry land.

*Jonah Goes to Nineveh*

3 Then the word of the LORD
came to Jonah a second time:
2"Go to the great city of Nineveh
and proclaim to it the message I
give you."
3Jonah obeyed the word of the
LORD and went to Nineveh. Now
Nineveh was a very important city
—a visit required three days. 4On
the first day, Jonah started into the
city. He proclaimed: "Forty more
days and Nineveh will be overturned." 5The Ninevites believed
God. They declared a fast, and all
of them, from the greatest to the
least, put on sackcloth.
6When the news reached the
king of Nineveh, he rose from his
throne, took off his royal robes,
covered himself with sackcloth
and sat down in the dust. 7Then he

b5 Or *waters were at my throat*

***Heading** See the note on page 527.

†2 Most mss have no *hireq* under the *vav* (וּק).

††3 Most mss have *tsere* under the *vav* (־וֵה).

‡6 Most mss have *sheva* under the *kaph* (־ךְ).

וַיֹּאמֶר בְּנִינְוֵה מִטַּעַם הַמֶּלֶךְ וּגְדֹלָיו לֵאמֹר הָאָדָם
the-man to-say and-nobles-of-him the-king by-decree-of in-Nineveh and-he-said

וְהַבְּהֵמָה הַבָּקָר וְהַצֹּאן אַל־ יִטְעֲמוּ מְאוּמָה אַל־ יִרְעוּ
let-them-eat not anything let-them-taste not or-the-flock the-herd or-the-beast

וּמַיִם אַל־ יִשְׁתּוּ׃ וְיִתְכַּסּוּ שַׂקִּים הָאָדָם
the-man sackcloths but-let-them-be-covered (8) let-them-drink not or-waters

וְהַבְּהֵמָה וְיִקְרְאוּ אֶל־אֱלֹהִים בְּחָזְקָה וְיָשֻׁבוּ אִישׁ
each and-let-them-give-up with-urgency God on and-let-them-call and-the-beast

מִדַּרְכּוֹ הָרָעָה וּמִן־ הֶחָמָס אֲשֶׁר בְּכַפֵּיהֶם׃ מִי־
who? (9) in-hands-of-them that the-violence and-from the-evil from-way-of-him

יוֹדֵעַ יָשׁוּב וְנִחַם הָאֱלֹהִים וְשָׁב
and-he-may-turn the-God and-he-may-have-compassion he-may-relent knowing

מֵחֲרוֹן אַפּוֹ וְלֹא נֹאבֵד׃ וַיַּרְא הָאֱלֹהִים
the-God when-he-saw (10) we-will-perish so-not anger-of-him from-fierceness-of

אֶת־ מַעֲשֵׂיהֶם כִּי־ שָׁבוּ מִדַּרְכָּם הָרָעָה וַיִּנָּחֶם
then-he-had-compassion the-evil from-way-of-them they-turned how deeds-of-them ***

הָאֱלֹהִים עַל־ הָרָעָה אֲשֶׁר־ דִּבֶּר לַעֲשׂוֹת־ לָהֶם
upon-them to-bring he-threatened that the-destruction concerning the-God

וְלֹא עָשָׂה׃ וַיֵּרַע אֶל־ יוֹנָה רָעָה גְדוֹלָה
great displeasure Jonah to but-he-was-displeasing (4:1) he-brought and-not

וַיִּחַר לוֹ׃ וַיִּתְפַּלֵּל אֶל־ יְהוָה וַיֹּאמַר אָנָּה יְהוָה הֲלוֹא־
not? Yahweh O! and-he-said Yahweh to and-he-prayed (2) to-him and-he-angered

זֶה דְבָרִי עַד־ הֱיוֹתִי עַל־ אַדְמָתִי עַל־ כֵּן קִדַּמְתִּי לִבְרֹחַ
to-flee I-was-quick this for home-of-me at to-be-me still saying-of-me this

תַּרְשִׁישָׁה כִּי יָדַעְתִּי כִּי אַתָּה אֵל־ חַנּוּן וְרַחוּם אֶרֶךְ אַפַּיִם
angers slow-of and-compassionate gracious God you that I-knew indeed to-Tarshish

וְרַב־ חֶסֶד וְנִחָם עַל־ הָרָעָה׃ וְעַתָּה יְהוָה
Yahweh and-now (3) the-calamity concerning and-relenting love and-abundant-of

קַח־ נָא אֶת־ נַפְשִׁי מִמֶּנִּי כִּי טוֹב מוֹתִי מֵחַיָּי׃
more-than-lives-of-me death-of-me good for from-me life-of-me *** now! take-away!

וַיֹּאמֶר יְהוָה הַהֵיטֵב חָרָה לָךְ׃ וַיֵּצֵא
and-he-went-out (5) to-you he-angers is-he-right? Yahweh but-he-replied (4)

יוֹנָה מִן־ הָעִיר וַיֵּשֶׁב מִקֶּדֶם לָעִיר וַיַּעַשׂ לוֹ
for-himself and-he-made of-the-city at-east and-he-sat-down the-city from Jonah

שָׁם סֻכָּה וַיֵּשֶׁב תַּחְתֶּיהָ בַּצֵּל עַד אֲשֶׁר יִרְאֶה
he-would-see that until in-the-shade under-her and-he-sat shelter there

מַה־ יִּהְיֶה בָּעִיר׃ וַיְמַן יְהוָה־אֱלֹהִים קִיקָיוֹן
vine God Yahweh then-he-provided (6) to-the-city he-would-happen what

issued a proclamation in Nineveh:

"By the decree of the king and his nobles:

Do not let any man or beast, herd or flock, taste anything; do not let them eat or drink. [8]But let man and beast be covered with sackcloth. Let everyone call urgently on God. Let them give up their evil ways and their violence. [9]Who knows? God may yet relent and with compassion turn from his fierce anger so that we will not perish."

[10]When God saw what they did and how they turned from their evil ways, he had compassion and did not bring upon them the destruction he had threatened.

*Jonah's Anger at the LORD's Compassion*

4 But Jonah was greatly displeased and became angry. [2]He prayed to the LORD, "O LORD, is this not what I said when I was still at home? That is why I was so quick to flee to Tarshish. I knew that you are a gracious and compassionate God, slow to anger and abounding in love, a God who relents from sending calamity. [3]Now, O LORD, take away my life, for it is better for me to die than to live."

[4]But the LORD replied, "Have you any right to be angry?"

[5]Jonah went out and sat down at a place east of the city. There he made himself a shelter, sat in its shade and waited to see what would happen to the city. [6]Then the LORD God provided a vine and

וַיַּעַל מֵעַל לְיוֹנָה לִהְיוֹת צֵל עַל־ רֹאשׁוֹ לְהַצִּיל
and-to-ease head-of-him for shade to-give to-Jonah at-over and-he-made-grow

לוֹ מֵרָעָתוֹ וַיִּשְׂמַח יוֹנָה עַל־ הַקִּיקָיוֹן שִׂמְחָה
happiness the-vine about Jonah and-he-was-happy from-discomfort-of-him to-him

גְדוֹלָה׃ וַיְמַן הָאֱלֹהִים תּוֹלַעַת בַּעֲלוֹת הַשַּׁחַר לַמָּחֳרָת
on-the-next-day the-dawn when-to-come worm the-God but-he-provided (7) great

וַתַּךְ אֶת־ הַקִּיקָיוֹן וַיִּיבָשׁ׃ וַיְהִי כִּזְרֹחַ הַשֶּׁמֶשׁ
the-sun when-to-rise and-he-was (8) so-he-withered the-vine *** and-she-chewed

וַיְמַן אֱלֹהִים רוּחַ קָדִים חֲרִישִׁית וַתַּךְ הַשֶּׁמֶשׁ עַל־ רֹאשׁ
head-of on the-sun and-she-blazed scorching east wind-of God then-he-provided

יוֹנָה וַיִּתְעַלָּף וַיִּשְׁאַל אֶת־ נַפְשׁוֹ לָמוּת וַיֹּאמֶר טוֹב
good and-he-said to-die self-of-him *** and-he-asked so-he-grew-faint Jonah

מוֹתִי מֵחַיָּי׃ וַיֹּאמֶר אֱלֹהִים אֶל־יוֹנָה הַהֵיטֵב
is-he-right? Jonah to God but-he-said (9) more-than-lives-of-me death-of-me

חָרָה־ לְךָ עַל־ הַקִּיקָיוֹן וַיֹּאמֶר הֵיטֵב חָרָה־ לִי עַד־ מָוֶת׃
death to to-me he-angers he-is-right and-he-said the-vine about to-you he-angers

וַיֹּאמֶר יְהוָה אַתָּה חַסְתָּ עַל־ הַקִּיקָיוֹן אֲשֶׁר לֹא־
not though the-vine about you-were-concerned you Yahweh but-he-said (10)

עָמַלְתָּ בּוֹ וְלֹא גִדַּלְתּוֹ שֶׁבִּן־ לַיְלָה הָיָה וּבִן־
and-son-of he-was night that-son-of you-made-grow-him or-not to-him you-tended

לַיְלָה אָבָד׃ וַאֲנִי לֹא אָחוּס עַל־ נִינְוֵה הָעִיר הַגְּדוֹלָה
the-great the-city Nineveh about should-I-be-concerned not but-I (11) he-died night

אֲשֶׁר יֶשׁ־ בָּהּ הַרְבֵּה מִשְׁתֵּים־ עֶשְׂרֵה רִבּוֹ אָדָם אֲשֶׁר לֹא־
not who people ten-thousand ten-of more-than-two to-be-many in-her there-are that

יָדַע בֵּין־ יְמִינוֹ לִשְׂמֹאלוֹ וּבְהֵמָה רַבָּה׃
many and-cattle from-left-hand-of-him right-hand-of-him between he-can-tell

made it grow up over Jonah to give shade for his head to ease his discomfort, and Jonah was very happy about the vine. [7]But at dawn the next day God provided a worm, which chewed the vine so that it withered. [8]When the sun rose, God provided a scorching east wind, and the sun blazed on Jonah's head so that he grew faint. He wanted to die, and said, "It would be better for me to die than to live."

[9]But God said to Jonah, "Do you have a right to be angry about the vine?"

"I do," he said. "I am angry enough to die."

[10]But the LORD said, "You have been concerned about this vine, though you did not tend it or make it grow. It sprang up overnight and died overnight. [11]But Nineveh has more than a hundred and twenty thousand people who cannot tell their right hand from their left, and many cattle as well. Should I not be concerned about that great city?"

דְּבַר־יְהוָה׀ אֲשֶׁר הָיָה אֶל־מִיכָה הַמֹּרַשְׁתִּי בִּימֵי יוֹתָם
Jotham during-days-of the-Moreshethite Micah to he-came that Yahweh word-of (1:1)

אָחָז יְחִזְקִיָּה מַלְכֵי יְהוּדָה אֲשֶׁר־חָזָה עַל־שֹׁמְרוֹן וִירוּשָׁלִָם׃
and-Jerusalem Samaria concerning he-saw that Judah kings-of Hezekiah Ahaz

שִׁמְעוּ עַמִּים כֻּלָּם הַקְשִׁיבִי אֶרֶץ וּמְלֹאָהּ וִיהִי אֲדֹנָי
Sovereign that-he-may-be and-all-in-her earth listen! all-of-them peoples hear! (2)

יְהוִה בָּכֶם לְעֵד אֲדֹנָי מֵהֵיכַל קָדְשׁוֹ׃ כִּי־
indeed (3) holiness-of-him from-temple-of Lord for-witness against-you Yahweh

הִנֵּה יְהוָה יֹצֵא מִמְּקוֹמוֹ וְיָרַד וְדָרַךְ עַל־
on and-he-treads and-he-comes-down from-dwelling-place-of-him coming Yahweh look!

בָּמֳותֵי אָרֶץ׃ וְנָמַסּוּ הֶהָרִים תַּחְתָּיו וְהָעֲמָקִים
and-the-valleys beneath-him the-mountains and-they-melt (4) earth high-places-of

יִתְבַּקָּעוּ כַּדּוֹנַג מִפְּנֵי הָאֵשׁ כְּמַיִם מֻגָּרִים
ones-rushing-down like-waters the-fire at-before like-the-wax they-split-apart

בְּמוֹרָד׃ בְּפֶשַׁע יַעֲקֹב כָּל־זֹאת וּבְחַטֹּאות
and-because-of-sins-of this all-of Jacob because-of-transgression-of (5) on-slope

בֵּית יִשְׂרָאֵל מִי־פֶשַׁע יַעֲקֹב הֲלוֹא שֹׁמְרוֹן וּמִי בָּמוֹת
high-places-of and-what? Samaria not? Jacob transgression-of what? Israel house-of

יְהוּדָה הֲלוֹא יְרוּשָׁלִָם׃ וְשַׂמְתִּי שֹׁמְרוֹן לְעִי הַשָּׂדֶה
the-field into-rubble-heap-of Samaria therefore-I-will-make (6) Jerusalem not? Judah

לְמַטָּעֵי כָרֶם וְהִגַּרְתִּי לַגַּי אֲבָנֶיהָ
stones-of-her into-the-valley and-I-will-pour vineyard into-places-of-planting-of

וִיסֹדֶיהָ אֲגַלֶּה׃ וְכָל־פְּסִילֶיהָ
idols-of-her and-all-of (7) I-will-lay-bare and-foundations-of-her

יֻכַּתּוּ וְכָל־אֶתְנַנֶּיהָ יִשָּׂרְפוּ
they-will-be-burned temple-gifts-of-her and-all-of they-will-be-broken-to-pieces

בָאֵשׁ וְכָל־עֲצַבֶּיהָ אָשִׂים שְׁמָמָה כִּי מֵאֶתְנַן
from-wage-of since destruction I-will-make images-of-her and-all-of with-fire

זוֹנָה קִבָּצָה וְעַד־אֶתְנַן זוֹנָה
one-being-prostitute wage-of then-as she-gathered one-being-prostitute

יָשׁוּבוּ׃ עַל־זֹאת אֶסְפְּדָה וְאֵילִילָה
and-I-will-wail I-will-weep this because-of (8) they-will-be-used-again

אֵילְכָה שֵׁילָל וְעָרוֹם אֶעֱשֶׂה מִסְפֵּד כַּתַּנִּים וְאֵבֶל
and-moan like-the-jackals howl I-will-make and-naked barefoot I-will-go-about

כִּבְנוֹת יַעֲנָה׃ כִּי אֲנוּשָׁה מַכּוֹתֶיהָ כִּי־בָאָה עַד־
to she-came indeed wounds-of-her being-incurable for (9) owl like-daughters-of

יְהוּדָה נָגַע עַד־שַׁעַר עַמִּי עַד־יְרוּשָׁלִָם׃ בְּגַת אַל־תַּגִּידוּ
you-tell not in-Gath (10) Jerusalem to people-of-me gate-of to he-reached Judah

°3 ק במתי
°8 ק שולל

1 The word of the LORD that came to Micah of Moresheth during the reigns of Jotham, Ahaz and Hezekiah, kings of Judah—the vision he saw concerning Samaria and Jerusalem.

2 Hear, O peoples, all of you,
listen, O earth and all who are in it,
that the Sovereign LORD may witness against you,
the Lord from his holy temple.

*Judgment Against Samaria and Jerusalem*

3 Look! The LORD is coming from his dwelling place;
he comes down and treads the high places of the earth.
4 The mountains melt beneath him
and the valleys split apart,
like wax before the fire,
like water rushing down a slope.
5 All this is because of Jacob's transgression,
because of the sins of the house of Israel.
What is Jacob's transgression?
Is it not Samaria?
What is Judah's high place?
Is it not Jerusalem?

6 "Therefore I will make Samaria a heap of rubble,
a place for planting vineyards.
I will pour her stones into the valley
and lay bare her foundations.
7 All her idols will be broken to pieces;
all her temple gifts will be burned with fire;
I will destroy all her images.
Since she gathered her gifts from the wages of prostitutes,
as the wages of prostitutes they will again be used."

*Weeping and Mourning*

8 Because of this I will weep and wail;
I will go about barefoot and naked.
I will howl like a jackal
and moan like an owl.
9 For her wound is incurable;
it has come to Judah.
It[a] has reached the very gate of my people,
even to Jerusalem itself.
10 Tell it not in Gath[b];

[a] 9 *Or He*
[b] 10 *Gath* sounds like the Hebrew for *tell*.

בָּכוֹ אַל־תִּבְכּוּ בְּבֵית לְעַפְרָה עָפָר הִתְפַּלָּשְׁתִּי° ׃ עִבְרִי לָכֶם

for-you pass-on! (11) roll! dust of-Ophrah in-Beth you-weep not to-weep

יוֹשֶׁבֶת שָׁפִיר עֶרְיָה־בֹשֶׁת לֹא יָצְאָה יוֹשֶׁבֶת צַאֲנָן

Zaanan one-living-of she-will-come-out not shame nakedness Shaphir ones-living-of

מִסְפַּד בֵּית הָאֵצֶל יִקַּח מִכֶּם עֶמְדָּתוֹ ׃ כִּי־

indeed (12) protection-of-him from-you he-took the-Ezel Beth mourning-of

חָלָה לְטוֹב יוֹשֶׁבֶת מָרוֹת כִּי־ יָרַד רָע מֵאֵת

from-with disaster he-came because Maroth one-living-of for-relief she-writhes-in-pain

יְהוָה לְשַׁעַר יְרוּשָׁלִָם ׃ רְתֹם הַמֶּרְכָּבָה לָרֶכֶשׁ יוֹשֶׁבֶת

one-living-of to-the-team the-chariot harness! (13) Jerusalem to-gate-of Yahweh

לָכִישׁ רֵאשִׁית חַטָּאת הִיא לְבַת־ צִיּוֹן כִּי־ בָךְ נִמְצְאוּ

they-were-found in-you for Zion to-Daughter-of she sin beginning-of Lachish

פִּשְׁעֵי יִשְׂרָאֵל ׃ לָכֵן תִּתְּנִי שִׁלּוּחִים עַל מוֹרֶשֶׁת גַּת

Gath Moresheth to parting-gifts you-will-give therefore (14) Israel transgressions-of

בָּתֵּי אַכְזִיב לְאַכְזָב לְמַלְכֵי יִשְׂרָאֵל ׃ עֹד הַיֹּרֵשׁ

the-one-conquering yet (15) Israel to-kings-of to-deception Aczib towns-of

אָבִי לָךְ יוֹשֶׁבֶת מָרֵשָׁה עַד־ עֲדֻלָּם יָבוֹא כְּבוֹד

glory-of he-will-come Adullam to Mareshah one-living-of against-you I-will-bring

יִשְׂרָאֵל ׃ קָרְחִי וָגֹזִּי עַל־ בְּנֵי תַּעֲנוּגָיִךְ הַרְחִבִי

enlarge! delights-of-you children-of for and-shear! shave-head! (16) Israel

קָרְחָתֵךְ כַּנֶּשֶׁר כִּי גָלוּ מִמֵּךְ ׃ הוֹי

woe! (2:1) from-you they-will-go-into-exile for as-the-vulture baldness-of-you

חֹשְׁבֵי־ אָוֶן וּפֹעֲלֵי רָע עַל־ מִשְׁכְּבוֹתָם בְּאוֹר

at-light-of beds-of-them on evil and-ones-plotting-of iniquity ones-planning-of

הַבֹּקֶר יַעֲשׂוּהָ כִּי יֶשׁ־ לְאֵל יָדָם ׃

hand-of-them in-power-of there-is because they-carry-out-her the-morning

וְחָמְדוּ שָׂדוֹת וְגָזָלוּ וּבָתִּים וְנָשָׂאוּ וְעָשְׁקוּ

and-they-defraud and-they-take and-houses and-they-seize fields and-they-covet (2)

גֶּבֶר וּבֵיתוֹ וְאִישׁ וְנַחֲלָתוֹ ׃ לָכֵן כֹּה אָמַר

he-says this therefore (3) and-inheritance-of-him and-fellowman and-home-of-him man

יְהוָה הִנְנִי חֹשֵׁב עַל־ הַמִּשְׁפָּחָה הַזֹּאת רָעָה אֲשֶׁר לֹא־ תָמִישׁוּ

you-can-save not which disaster the-this the-people against planning see-I! Yahweh

מִשָּׁם צַוְּארֹתֵיכֶם וְלֹא תֵלְכוּ רוֹמָה כִּי עֵת רָעָה הִיא ׃

she calamity time-of for pride you-will-walk and-not necks-of-you from-there

בַּיּוֹם הַהוּא יִשָּׂא עֲלֵיכֶם מָשָׁל וְנָהָה נְהִי

taunt and-he-will-taunt ridicule against-you he-will-bring the-that in-the-day (4)

נִהְיָה אָמַר שָׁדוֹד נְשַׁדֻּנוּ חֵלֶק עַמִּי

people-of-me possession-of we-are-ruined to-be-ruined he-will-say he-will-be

weep not at all.[c]
In Beth Ophrah[d]
roll in the dust.
11 Pass on in nakedness and shame,
you who live in Shaphir.[e]
Those who live in Zaanan[f]
will not come out.
Beth Ezel is in mourning;
its protection is taken from you.
12 Those who live in Maroth[g]
writhe in pain,
waiting for relief,
because disaster has come
from the LORD,
even to the gate of Jerusalem.
13 You who live in Lachish,[h]
harness the team to the chariot.
You were the beginning of sin
to the Daughter of Zion,
for the transgressions of Israel
were found in you.
14 Therefore you will give parting gifts
to Moresheth Gath.
The town of Aczib[i] will prove deceptive
to the kings of Israel.
15 I will bring a conqueror
against you
who live in Mareshah.[j]
He who is the glory of Israel
will come to Adullam.
16 Shave your heads in mourning
for the children in whom
you delight;
make yourselves as bald as the vulture,
for they will go from you
into exile.

*Man's Plans and God's*

2 Woe to those who plan iniquity,
to those who plot evil on their beds!
At morning's light they carry it out
because it is in their power
to do it.
2 They covet fields and seize them,
and houses, and take them.
They defraud a man of his home,
a fellowman of his inheritance.

3 Therefore, the LORD says:

"I am planning disaster
against this people,
from which you cannot save
yourselves.
You will no longer walk
proudly,
for it will be a time of
calamity.
4 In that day men will ridicule
you;

c10 Hebrew; Septuagint may suggest *not in Acco.* The Hebrew for *in Acco* sounds like the Hebrew for *weep.*
d10 *Beth Ophrah* means *house of dust.*
e11 *Shaphir* means *pleasant.*
f11 *Zaanan* sounds like the Hebrew for *come out.*
g12 *Maroth* sounds like the Hebrew for *bitter.*
h13 *Lachish* sounds like the Hebrew for *team.*
i14 *Aczib* means *deception.*
j15 *Mareshah* sounds like the Hebrew for *conqueror.*

°10 ק התפלשי

יָמִיר אֵיךְ יָמִישׁ לִי לְשׁוֹבֵב שָׂדֵינוּ יְחַלֵּק׃

he-assigns fields-of-us to-traitor from-me he-takes indeed! he-is-divided-up

(5) לָכֵן לֹא־ יִהְיֶה לְךָ מַשְׁלִיךְ חֶבֶל בְּגוֹרָל בִּקְהַל

in-assembly-of by-lot land one-dividing-of to-you he-will-be not therefore (5)

יְהוָה׃ (6) אַל־ תַּטִּפוּ יַטִּיפוּן לֹא־ יַטִּפוּ לָאֵלֶּה

about-these let-them-prophesy not they-prophesy you-prophesy not (6) Yahweh

לֹא יִסַּג כְּלִמּוֹת׃ (7) הֶאָמוּר בֵּית־ יַעֲקֹב הֲקָצַר

is-he-angry? Jacob house-of being-said? (7) disgraces he-will-be-overtaken not

רוּחַ יְהוָה אִם־ אֵלֶּה מַעֲלָלָיו הֲלוֹא דְבָרַי יֵיטִיבוּ עִם

to they-do-good words-of-me not? deeds-of-him these or Yahweh Spirit-of

הַיָּשָׁר הוֹלֵךְ׃ (8) וְאֶתְמוּל עַמִּי לְאוֹיֵב

like-one-being-enemy people-of-me but-lately (8) one-walking the-upright-one

יְקוֹמֵם מִמּוּל שַׂלְמָה אֶדֶר תַּפְשִׁטוּן מֵעֹבְרִים

from-ones-passing-by you-strip-off rich-robe garment in-front-of he-rose-up

בֶּטַח שׁוּבֵי מִלְחָמָה׃ (9) נְשֵׁי עַמִּי תְּגָרְשׁוּן

you-drive-away people-of-me women-of (9) battle men-returning-of without-care

מִבֵּית תַּעֲנֻגֶיהָ מֵעַל עֹלָלֶיהָ תִּקְחוּ

you-take-away children-of-her from-with pleasantnesses-of-her from-home-of

הֲדָרִי לְעוֹלָם׃ (10) קוּמוּ וּלְכוּ כִּי לֹא־ זֹאת הַמְּנוּחָה

the-resting-place this not for and-go-away! get-up! (10) to-forever blessing-of-me

בַּעֲבוּר טָמְאָה תְּחַבֵּל וְחֶבֶל נִמְרָץ׃ (11) לוּ־ אִישׁ הֹלֵךְ

coming man if (11) he-is-sick and-beyond-remedy she-is-ruined defiling because-of

רוּחַ וָשֶׁקֶר כִּזֵּב אַטִּף לְךָ לַיַּיִן וְלַשֵּׁכָר

and-about-the-beer about-the-wine for-you I-will-prophesy he-lies and-deceit wind

וְהָיָה מַטִּיף הָעָם הַזֶּה׃ (12) אָסֹף אֶאֱסֹף

I-will-gather to-gather (12) the-this the-people one-prophesying-of then-he-would-be

יַעֲקֹב כֻּלָּךְ קַבֵּץ אֲקַבֵּץ שְׁאֵרִית יִשְׂרָאֵל יַחַד

together Israel remnant-of I-will-bring-together to-bring-together all-of-you Jacob

אֲשִׂימֶנּוּ כְּצֹאן בָּצְרָה כְּעֵדֶר בְּתוֹךְ הַדָּבְרוֹ

the-pasture-of-him at-inside-of like-flock pen like-sheep-of I-will-bring-him

תְּהִימֶנָה מֵאָדָם׃ (13) עָלָה הַפֹּרֵץ לִפְנֵיהֶם

before-them the-one-breaking-open he-will-go-up (13) with-people they-will-throng

פָּרְצוּ וַיַּעֲבֹרוּ שַׁעַר וַיֵּצְאוּ בוֹ

through-him and-they-will-go-out gate and-they-will-go-through they-will-break-open

וַיַּעֲבֹר מַלְכָּם לִפְנֵיהֶם וַיהוָה בְּרֹאשָׁם׃

at-head-of-them and-Yahweh before-them king-of-them and-he-will-pass-through

(3:1) וָאֹמַר שִׁמְעוּ־ נָא רָאשֵׁי יַעֲקֹב וּקְצִינֵי בֵּית יִשְׂרָאֵל

Israel house-of and-rulers-of Jacob leaders-of now! listen! then-I-said (3:1)

they will taunt you with
this mournful song:
'We are utterly ruined;
my people's possession is
divided up.
He takes it from me!
He assigns our fields to
traitors.' "

5 Therefore you will have no
one in the assembly of
the LORD
to divide the land by lot.

*False Prophets*

6 "Do not prophesy," their
prophets say.
"Do not prophesy about
these things;
disgrace will not overtake
us."
7 Should it be said, O house of
Jacob:
"Is the Spirit of the LORD
angry?
Does he do such things?"

"Do not my words do good
to him whose ways are
upright?
8 Lately my people have risen
up
like an enemy.
You strip off the rich robe
from those who pass by
without a care,
like men returning from
battle.
9 You drive the women of my
people
from their pleasant homes.
You take away my blessing
from their children forever.
10 Get up, go away!
For this is not your resting
place,
because it is defiled,
it is ruined, beyond all
remedy.
11 If a liar and deceiver comes
and says,
'I will prophesy for you
plenty of wine and beer,'
he would be just the prophet
for this people!

*Deliverance Promised*

12 "I will surely gather all of you,
O Jacob;
I will surely bring together
the remnant of Israel.
I will bring them together like
sheep in a pen,
like a flock in its pasture;
the place will throng with
people.
13 One who breaks open the way
will go up before them;
they will break through the
gate and go out.
Their king will pass through
before them,
the LORD at their head."

*Leaders and Prophets Rebuked*

3 Then I said,
"Listen, you leaders of Jacob,
you rulers of the house of
Israel.

הֲלוֹא לָכֶם לָדַעַת אֶת־הַמִּשְׁפָּט׃ שֹׂנְאֵי טוֹב וְאֹהֲבֵי רָעָה
evil and-ones-loving-of good ones-hating-of (2) the-justice *** to-know to-you not?

גֹּזְלֵי עוֹרָם מֵעֲלֵיהֶם וּשְׁאֵרָם מֵעַל עַצְמוֹתָם׃
bones-of-them from-upon and-flesh-of-them from-upon-them skin-of-them ones-tearing-of

וַאֲשֶׁר אָכְלוּ שְׁאֵר עַמִּי וְעוֹרָם מֵעֲלֵיהֶם
from-upon-them and-skin-of-them people-of-me flesh-of they-eat and-who (3)

הִפְשִׁיטוּ וְאֶת־עַצְמֹתֵיהֶם פִּצֵּחוּ וּפָרְשׂוּ כַּאֲשֶׁר
like-that and-they-chop-up they-break-in-pieces bones-of-them and they-strip-off

בַּסִּיר וּכְבָשָׂר בְּתוֹךְ קַלָּחַת׃ אָז יִזְעֲקוּ אֶל־יְהוָה
Yahweh to they-will-cry-out then (4) pot for-inside-of and-like-flesh for-the-pan

וְלֹא יַעֲנֶה אוֹתָם וְיַסְתֵּר פָּנָיו מֵהֶם בָּעֵת
at-the-time from-them faces-of-him and-he-will-hide them he-will-answer but-not

הַהִיא כַּאֲשֶׁר הֵרֵעוּ מַעַלְלֵיהֶם׃ כֹּה אָמַר יְהוָה עַל־
for Yahweh he-says this (5) deeds-of-them they-made-evil because-that the-that

הַנְּבִיאִים הַמַּתְעִים אֶת־ עַמִּי הַנֹּשְׁכִים
the-ones-feeding people-of-me *** the-ones-leading-astray the-prophets

בְּשִׁנֵּיהֶם וְקָרְאוּ שָׁלוֹם וַאֲשֶׁר לֹא־ יִתֵּן עַל־ פִּיהֶם
mouth-of-them for he-provides not but-if peace and-they-proclaim with-teeth-of-them

וְקִדְּשׁוּ עָלָיו מִלְחָמָה׃ לָכֵן לַיְלָה לָכֶם מֵחָזוֹן
without-vision to-you night therefore (6) war against-him then-they-prepare

וְחָשְׁכָה לָכֶם מִקְּסֹם וּבָאָה הַשֶּׁמֶשׁ עַל־
for the-sun and-she-will-set without-to-divine to-you and-darkness

הַנְּבִיאִים וְקָדַר עֲלֵיהֶם הַיּוֹם׃ וּבֹשׁוּ
and-they-will-be-ashamed (7) the-day for-them and-he-will-go-dark the-prophets

הַחֹזִים וְחָפְרוּ הַקֹּסְמִים וְעָטוּ עַל־
over and-they-will-cover the-ones-divining and-they-will-be-disgraced the-seers

שָׂפָם כֻּלָּם כִּי אֵין מַעֲנֵה אֱלֹהִים׃ וְאוּלָם אָנֹכִי
I but-however (8) God answer-of there-is-no because all-of-them face-of-them

מָלֵאתִי כֹחַ אֶת־ רוּחַ יְהוָה וּמִשְׁפָּט וּגְבוּרָה לְהַגִּיד לְיַעֲקֹב
to-Jacob to-declare and-might and-justice Yahweh Spirit-of with power I-am-filled

פִּשְׁעוֹ וּלְיִשְׂרָאֵל חַטָּאתוֹ׃ שִׁמְעוּ־נָא זֹאת רָאשֵׁי בֵּית
house-of leaders-of this now! hear! (9) sin-of-him and-to-Israel transgression-of-him

יַעֲקֹב וּקְצִינֵי בֵּית יִשְׂרָאֵל הַמְתַעֲבִים מִשְׁפָּט וְאֶת כָּל־ הַיְשָׁרָה
the-right all-of and justice the-ones-despising Israel house-of and-rulers-of Jacob

יְעַקֵּשׁוּ׃ בֹּנֶה צִיּוֹן בְּדָמִים וִירוּשָׁלַםִ בְּעַוְלָה׃
with-wickedness and-Jerusalem with-bloodsheds Zion one-building (10) they-distort

רָאשֶׁיהָ ׀ בְּשֹׁחַד יִשְׁפֹּטוּ וְכֹהֲנֶיהָ בִּמְחִיר יוֹרוּ
they-teach for-price and-priests-of-her they-judge for-bribe leaders-of-her (11)

Should you not know justice,
2 you who hate good and love evil;
who tear the skin from my people
and the flesh from their bones;
3 who eat my people's flesh,
strip off their skin
and break their bones in pieces;
who chop them up like meat for the pan,
like flesh for the pot?"
4 Then they will cry out to the LORD,
but he will not answer them.
At that time he will hide his face from them
because of the evil they have done.
5 This is what the LORD says:
"As for the prophets
who lead my people astray,
if one feeds them,
they proclaim 'peace';
if he does not,
they prepare to wage war against him.
6 Therefore night will come over you, without visions,
and darkness, without divination.
The sun will set for the prophets,
and the day will go dark for them.
7 The seers will be ashamed
and the diviners disgraced.
They will all cover their faces
because there is no answer from God."
8 But as for me, I am filled with power,
with the Spirit of the LORD,
and with justice and might,
to declare to Jacob his transgression,
to Israel his sin.
9 Hear this, you leaders of the house of Jacob,
you rulers of the house of Israel,
who despise justice
and distort all that is right;
10 who build Zion with bloodshed,
and Jerusalem with wickedness.
11 Her leaders judge for a bribe,
her priests teach for a price,

וּנְבִיאֶיהָ בְּכֶסֶף יִקְסֹמוּ וְעַל־ יְהוָה יִשָּׁעֵנוּ לֵאמֹר
to-say they-lean Yahweh yet-upon they-tell-fortunes for-money and-prophets-of-her

הֲלוֹא יְהוָה בְּקִרְבֵּנוּ לֹא־ תָבוֹא עָלֵינוּ רָעָה׃ לָכֵן
therefore (12) disaster upon-us she-will-come not in-among-us Yahweh not?

בִּגְלַלְכֶם צִיּוֹן שָׂדֶה תֵחָרֵשׁ וִירוּשָׁלַםִ עִיִּין
heaps-of-rubble and-Jerusalem she-will-be-plowed field Zion because-of-you

תִּהְיֶה וְהַר הַבַּיִת לְבָמוֹת יָעַר׃ וְהָיָה׀
and-he-will-be (4:1) thicket to-mounds-of the-temple and-hill-of she-will-become

בְּאַחֲרִית הַיָּמִים יִהְיֶה הַר בֵּית־ יְהוָה נָכוֹן
being-established Yahweh temple-of mountain-of he-will-be the-days in-last-of

בְּרֹאשׁ הֶהָרִים וְנִשָּׂא הוּא מִגְּבָעוֹת וְנָהֲרוּ
and-they-will-stream above-hills he and-he-will-be-raised the-mountains as-chief-of

עָלָיו עַמִּים וְהָלְכוּ גּוֹיִם רַבִּים וְאָמְרוּ לְכוּ׀
come! and-they-will-say many-ones nations and-they-will-come (2) peoples to-him

וְנַעֲלֶה אֶל־ הַר־ יְהוָה וְאֶל־ בֵּית אֱלֹהֵי יַעֲקֹב וְיוֹרֵנוּ
and-he-will-teach-us Jacob God-of house-of and-to Yahweh mountain-of to and-let-us-go

מִדְּרָכָיו וְנֵלְכָה בְּאֹרְחֹתָיו כִּי מִצִּיּוֹן תֵּצֵא תוֹרָה
law she-will-go-out from-Zion indeed in-paths-of-him so-we-may-walk of-ways-of-him

וּדְבַר־ יְהוָה מִירוּשָׁלָםִ׃ וְשָׁפַט בֵּין עַמִּים רַבִּים
many-ones peoples between and-he-will-judge (3) from-Jerusalem Yahweh and-word-of

וְהוֹכִיחַ לְגוֹיִם עֲצֻמִים עַד־ רָחוֹק וְכִתְּתוּ
and-they-will-beat far to strong-ones for-nations and-he-will-settle-disputes

חַרְבֹתֵיהֶם לְאִתִּים וַחֲנִיתֹתֵיהֶם לְמַזְמֵרוֹת לֹא־
not into-pruning-hooks and-spears-of-them into-plowshares swords-of-them

יִשְׂאוּ גּוֹי אֶל־ גּוֹי חֶרֶב וְלֹא־ יִלְמְדוּן עוֹד מִלְחָמָה׃
war anymore they-will-train or-not sword nation against nation they-will-take-up

וְיָשְׁבוּ אִישׁ תַּחַת גַּפְנוֹ וְתַחַת תְּאֵנָתוֹ
fig-tree-of-him and-under vine-of-him under every-man and-they-will-sit (4)

וְאֵין מַחֲרִיד כִּי־ פִי יְהוָה צְבָאוֹת דִּבֵּר׃
he-spoke Hosts Yahweh-of mouth-of for one-making-afraid and-there-will-be-no

כִּי כָּל־ הָעַמִּים יֵלְכוּ אִישׁ בְּשֵׁם אֱלֹהָיו וַאֲנַחְנוּ
but-we gods-of-him in-name-of each they-may-walk the-nations all-of indeed (5)

נֵלֵךְ בְּשֵׁם־ יְהוָה אֱלֹהֵינוּ לְעוֹלָם וָעֶד׃ בַּיּוֹם הַהוּא
the-that in-the-day (6) and-ever to-forever God-of-us Yahweh in-name-of we-will-walk

נְאֻם־ יְהוָה אֹסְפָה הַצֹּלֵעָה וְהַנִּדָּחָה
and-the-one-being-exiled the-one-being-lame I-will-gather Yahweh declaration-of

אֲקַבֵּצָה וַאֲשֶׁר הֲרֵעֹתִי׃ וְשַׂמְתִּי אֶת־ הַצֹּלֵעָה
the-one-being-lame *** and-I-will-make (7) I-brought-to-grief and-whom I-will-assemble

---

and her prophets tell
fortunes for money.
Yet they lean upon the LORD
and say,
"Is not the LORD among us?
No disaster will come upon
us."
[12]Therefore because of you,
Zion will be plowed like a
field,
Jerusalem will become a heap
of rubble,
the temple hill a mound
overgrown with thickets.

*The Mountain of the LORD*

4 In the last days
the mountain of the LORD's
temple will be established
as chief among the
mountains;
it will be raised above the
hills,
and peoples will stream to
it.

[2]Many nations will come and say,

"Come, let us go up to the
mountain of the LORD,
to the house of the God of
Jacob.
He will teach us his ways,
so that we may walk in his
paths."
The law will go out from Zion,
the word of the LORD from
Jerusalem.
[3]He will judge between many
peoples
and will settle disputes for
strong nations far and
wide.
They will beat their swords
into plowshares
and their spears into
pruning hooks.
Nation will not take up sword
against nation,
nor will they train for war
anymore.
[4]Every man will sit under his
own vine
and under his own fig tree,
and no one will make them
afraid,
for the LORD Almighty has
spoken.
[5]All the nations may walk
in the name of their gods;
we will walk in the name of
the LORD
our God for ever and ever.

*The LORD's Plan*

[6]"In that day," declares the LORD,

"I will gather the lame;
I will assemble the exiles
and those I have brought to
grief.
[7]I will make the lame a

לִשְׁאֵרִית וְהַנַּהֲלָאָה לְגוֹי עָצוּם וּמָלַךְ יְהוָה
Yahweh and-he-will-rule strong into-nation and-the-one-being-driven-away into-remnant

עֲלֵיהֶם בְּהַר צִיּוֹן מֵעַתָּה וְעַד־ עוֹלָם׃ וְאַתָּה מִגְדַּל־ עֵדֶר
flock watchtower-of and-you (8) forever and-to from-now Zion in-Mount-of over-them

עֹפֶל בַּת־ צִיּוֹן עָדֶיךָ תֵּאתֶה וּבָאָה
and-she-will-come she-will-be-restored to-you Zion Daughter-of stronghold-of

הַמֶּמְשָׁלָה הָרִאשֹׁנָה מַמְלֶכֶת לְבַת־ יְרוּשָׁלִָם׃ עַתָּה לָמָּה
for-why? now (9) Jerusalem to-Daughter-of kingship the-former the-dominion

תָרִיעִי רֵעַ הֲמֶלֶךְ אֵין־ בָּךְ אִם־ יוֹעֲצֵךְ אָבָד
has-he-perished one-counseling-you or to-you there-is-not king? cry you-cry-aloud

כִּי־ הֶחֱזִיקֵךְ חִיל כַּיּוֹלֵדָה׃ חוּלִי וָגֹחִי
and-be-in-agony! writhe! (10) like-the-woman-being-in-labor pain he-seizes-you that

בַּת־ צִיּוֹן כַּיּוֹלֵדָה כִּי־עַתָּה תֵצְאִי מִקִּרְיָה
from-city you-must-leave now for like-the-woman-being-in-labor Zion Daughter-of

וְשָׁכַנְתְּ בַּשָּׂדֶה וּבָאת עַד־ בָּבֶל שָׁם תִּנָּצֵלִי
you-will-be-rescued there Babylon to and-you-will-go in-the-field and-you-must-camp

שָׁם יִגְאָלֵךְ יְהוָה מִכַּף אֹיְבָיִךְ׃ וְעַתָּה
but-now (11) ones-being-enemies-of-you from-hand-of Yahweh he-will-redeem-you there

נֶאֶסְפוּ עָלַיִךְ גּוֹיִם רַבִּים הָאֹמְרִים תֶּחֱנָף
let-her-be-defiled the-ones-saying many-ones nations against-you they-are-gathered

וְתַחַז בְּצִיּוֹן עֵינֵינוּ׃ וְהֵמָּה לֹא יָדְעוּ מַחְשְׁבוֹת
thoughts-of they-know not but-they (12) eyes-of-us over-Zion and-let-her-gloat

יְהוָה וְלֹא הֵבִינוּ עֲצָתוֹ כִּי קִבְּצָם כֶּעָמִיר
like-the-sheaf he-gathers-them indeed plan-of-him they-understand and-not Yahweh

גֹּרְנָה׃ קוּמִי וָדוֹשִׁי בַת־ צִיּוֹן כִּי־ קַרְנֵךְ
horn-of-you for Zion Daughter-of and-thresh! rise! (13) to-threshing-floor

אָשִׂים בַּרְזֶל וּפַרְסֹתַיִךְ אָשִׂים נְחוּשָׁה וַהֲדִקּוֹת
and-you-will-break-to-pieces bronze I-will-give and-hoofs-of-you iron I-will-give

עַמִּים רַבִּים וְהַחֲרַמְתִּי†† לַיהוָה בִּצְעָם
ill-gotten-gain-of-them to-Yahweh ††and-you-will-devote many-ones nations

וְחֵילָם לַאֲדוֹן כָּל־ הָאָרֶץ׃ עַתָּה תִּתְגֹּדְדִי
you-marshall-troops now *(14) the-earth all-of to-Lord-of and-wealth-of-them

בַּת־ גְּדוּד מָצוֹר שָׂם עָלֵינוּ בַּשֵּׁבֶט יַכּוּ עַל־
on they-will-strike with-the-rod against-us he-is-laid siege troop city-of

הַלְּחִי אֶת שֹׁפֵט יִשְׂרָאֵל׃ וְאַתָּה בֵּית־ לֶחֶם אֶפְרָתָה צָעִיר לִהְיוֹת
to-be small Ephrathah Lehem Beth but-you (5:1) Israel one-ruling-of *** the-cheek

בְּאַלְפֵי יְהוּדָה מִמְּךָ לִי יֵצֵא לִהְיוֹת מוֹשֵׁל בְּיִשְׂרָאֵל
over-Israel one-ruling to-be he-will-come-out for-me from-you Judah among-clans-of

remnant,
those driven away a strong nation.
The LORD will rule over them in Mount Zion
from that day and forever.
8 As for you, O watchtower of the flock,
O stronghold[k] of the Daughter of Zion,
the former dominion will be restored to you;
kingship will come to the Daughter of Jerusalem."

9 Why do you now cry aloud—
have you no king?
Has your counselor perished,
that pain seizes you like that of a woman in labor?
10 Writhe in agony, O Daughter of Zion,
like a woman in labor,
for now you must leave the city
to camp in the open field.
You will go to Babylon;
there you will be rescued.
There the LORD will redeem you
out of the hand of your enemies.

11 But now many nations
are gathered against you.
They say, "Let her be defiled,
let our eyes gloat over Zion!"
12 But they do not know
the thoughts of the LORD;
they do not understand his plan,
he who gathers them like sheaves to the threshing floor.

13 "Rise and thresh, O Daughter of Zion,
for I will give you horns of iron;
I will give you hoofs of bronze
and you will break to pieces many nations."

You will devote their ill-gotten gains to the LORD,
their wealth to the Lord of all the earth.

*A Promised Ruler From Bethlehem*

5 Marshal your troops, O city of troops,[l]
for a siege is laid against us.
They will strike Israel's ruler
on the cheek with a rod.

2 "But you, Bethlehem Ephrathah,
though you are small among the clans[m] of Judah,
out of you will come for me
one who will be ruler over Israel,

k8 Or *hill*
l1 Or *Strengthen your walls, O walled city*
m2 Or *rulers*

***Heading, 14*** **The Hebrew numeration of chapter 5 begins with verse 2 in English; thus, there is a one-verse discrepancy throughout the chapter.**

**†8 Most mss have no *dagesh* in the first *tav* (תָ).**

**††*13* The NIV reads this ending, normally understood as first person singular (*I-*), as the archaic second feminine singular ending.**

וּמוֹצָאֹתָיו מִקֶּדֶם מִימֵי עוֹלָם׃ לָכֵן
therefore (2) ancient-time from-days-of from-of-old and-goings-out-of-him

יִתְּנֵם עַד־ עֵת יוֹלֵדָה יָלָדָה וְיֶתֶר
and-rest-of she-gives-birth one-being-in-labor time-of until he-will-abandon-them

אֶחָיו יְשׁוּבוּן עַל־ בְּנֵי יִשְׂרָאֵל׃ וְעָמַד
and-he-will-stand (3) Israel peoples-of to they-will-return brothers-of-him

וְרָעָה בְּעֹז יְהוָה בִּגְאוֹן שֵׁם יְהוָה אֱלֹהָיו
God-of-him Yahweh name-of in-majesty-of Yahweh in-strength-of and-he-will-shepherd

וְיָשָׁבוּ כִּי־ עַתָּה יִגְדַּל עַד־ אַפְסֵי־ אָרֶץ׃ וְהָיָה
and-he-will-be (4) earth ends-of to he-will-be-great then for and-they-will-live

זֶה שָׁלוֹם אַשּׁוּר׀ כִּי־ יָבוֹא בְאַרְצֵנוּ וְכִי יִדְרֹךְ
he-marches and-when into-land-of-us he-invades when Assyria peace this

בְּאַרְמְנֹתֵינוּ וַהֲקֵמֹנוּ עָלָיו שִׁבְעָה רֹעִים
ones-being-shepherds seven against-him then-we-will-raise through-fortresses-of-us

וּשְׁמֹנָה נְסִיכֵי אָדָם׃ וְרָעוּ אֶת־ אֶרֶץ אַשּׁוּר בַּחֶרֶב
with-the-sword Assyria land-of *** and-they-will-rule (5) man leaders-of even-eight

וְאֶת־ אֶרֶץ נִמְרֹד בִּפְתָחֶיהָ וְהִצִּיל מֵאַשּׁוּר כִּי־
when from-Assyrian and-he-will-deliver with-drawn-swords-of-her Nimrod land-of even

יָבוֹא בְאַרְצֵנוּ וְכִי יִדְרֹךְ בִּגְבוּלֵנוּ׃ וְהָיָה׀
and-he-will-be (6) into-border-of-us he-marches and-when into-land-of-us he-invades

שְׁאֵרִית יַעֲקֹב בְּקֶרֶב עַמִּים רַבִּים כְּטַל מֵאֵת יְהוָה
Yahweh from-with like-dew many-ones peoples in-midst-of Jacob remnant-of

כִּרְבִיבִים עֲלֵי־עֵשֶׂב אֲשֶׁר לֹא־ יְקַוֶּה לְאִישׁ וְלֹא יְיַחֵל לִבְנֵי
for-sons-of he-lingers or-not for-man he-waits not which grass on like-showers

אָדָם׃ וְהָיָה שְׁאֵרִית יַעֲקֹב בַּגּוֹיִם בְּקֶרֶב עַמִּים
peoples in-midst-of among-the-nations Jacob remnant-of and-he-will-be (7) mankind

רַבִּים כְּאַרְיֵה בְּבַהֲמוֹת יַעַר כִּכְפִיר בְּעֶדְרֵי־ צֹאן
sheep among-flocks-of like-young-lion forest among-beasts-of like-lion many-ones

אֲשֶׁר אִם† עָבַר וְרָמַס וְטָרַף וְאֵין מַצִּיל׃
one-rescuing and-there-is-no and-he-mangles then-he-mauls he-goes as which

תָּרֹם יָדְךָ עַל־ צָרֶיךָ וְכָל־
and-all-of enemies-of-you over hand-of-you she-will-be-lifted-up (8)

אֹיְבֶיךָ יִכָּרֵתוּ׃ וְהָיָה בַיּוֹם־
in-the-day and-he-will-be (9) they-will-be-destroyed ones-being-foes-of-you

הַהוּא נְאֻם־ יְהוָה וְהִכְרַתִּי סוּסֶיךָ מִקִּרְבֶּךָ
from-among-you horses-of-you then-I-will-destroy Yahweh declaration-of the-that

וְהַאֲבַדְתִּי מַרְכְּבֹתֶיךָ׃ וְהִכְרַתִּי עָרֵי אַרְצֶךָ
land-of-you cities-of and-I-will-destroy (10) chariots-of-you and-I-will-demolish

whose origins[n] are from of old,
from ancient times.[o]"
3 Therefore Israel will be
abandoned
until the time when she
who is in labor gives
birth
and the rest of his brothers
return
to join the Israelites.
4 He will stand and shepherd
his flock
in the strength of the LORD,
in the majesty of the name
of the LORD his God.
And they will live securely, for
then his greatness
will reach to the ends of the
earth.
5 And he will be their peace.

*Deliverance and Destruction*

When the Assyrian invades
our land
and marches through our
fortresses,
we will raise against him
seven shepherds,
even eight leaders of men.
6 They will rule[p] the land of
Assyria with the sword,
the land of Nimrod with
drawn sword.[q]
He will deliver us from the
Assyrian
when he invades our land
and marches into our
borders.
7 The remnant of Jacob will be
in the midst of many
peoples
like dew from the LORD,
like showers on the grass,
which do not wait for man
or linger for mankind.
8 The remnant of Jacob will be
among the nations,
in the midst of many
peoples,
like a lion among the beasts of
the forest,
like a young lion among
flocks of sheep,
which mauls and mangles as it
goes,
and no one can rescue.
9 Your hand will be lifted up in
triumph over your
enemies,
and all your foes will be
destroyed.
10 "In that day," declares the
LORD,
"I will destroy your horses
from among you
and demolish your chariots.
11 I will destroy the cities of your
land

n2 Hebrew *goings out*
o2 Or *from days of eternity*
p6 Or *crush* q6 Or *Nimrod in its gates*

***Heading*** **See the first note on page 536.**

**†7 Most mss connect this word to the following with *maqqeph* (אִם־).**

וְהָרַסְתִּי כָּל־ מִבְצָרֶיךָ׃ וְהִכְרַתִּי
and-I-will-destroy (11) strongholds-of-you all-of and-I-will-tear-down

כְשָׁפִים מִיָּדֶךָ וּמְעוֹנְנִים לֹא יִהְיוּ־ לָךְ׃
to-you they-will-be not and-ones-casting-spells from-hand-of-you witchcrafts

וְהִכְרַתִּי פְסִילֶיךָ וּמַצֵּבוֹתֶיךָ מִקִּרְבֶּךָ
from-among-you and-sacred-stones-of-you carved-images-of-you and-I-will-destroy (12)

וְלֹא־ תִשְׁתַּחֲוֶה עוֹד לְמַעֲשֵׂה יָדֶיךָ׃ וְנָתַשְׁתִּי
and-I-will-uproot (13) hands-of-you to-work-of longer you-will-bow-down and-not

אֲשֵׁירֶיךָ מִקִּרְבֶּךָ וְהִשְׁמַדְתִּי עָרֶיךָ׃
cities-of-you and-I-will-demolish from-among-you Asherah-poles-of-you

וְעָשִׂיתִי בְּאַף וּבְחֵמָה נָקָם אֶת־ הַגּוֹיִם אֲשֶׁר לֹא
not that the-nations upon vengeance and-in-wrath in-anger and-I-will-take (14)

שָׁמֵעוּ׃ שִׁמְעוּ־ נָא אֵת אֲשֶׁר־ יְהוָה אֹמֵר קוּם רִיב
plead-case! stand-up! saying Yahweh what *** now! listen! (6:1) they-obeyed

אֶת־ הֶהָרִים וְתִשְׁמַעְנָה הַגְּבָעוֹת קוֹלֶךָ׃ שִׁמְעוּ הָרִים
mountains hear! (2) saying-of-you the-hills and-let-them-hear the-mountains before

אֶת־ רִיב יְהוָה וְהָאֵתָנִים מֹסְדֵי אָרֶץ כִּי רִיב
case for earth foundations-of and-the-everlasting-ones Yahweh accusation-of ***

לַיהוָה עִם־ עַמּוֹ וְעִם־ יִשְׂרָאֵל יִתְוַכָּח׃ עַמִּי
people-of-me (3) he-lodges-charge Israel and-against people-of-him against to-Yahweh

מֶה־ עָשִׂיתִי לְךָ וּמָה הֶלְאֵתִיךָ עֲנֵה בִי׃ כִּי
indeed (4) to-me answer! I-burdened-you and-how? to-you I-did what?

הֶעֱלִתִיךָ מֵאֶרֶץ מִצְרַיִם וּמִבֵּית עֲבָדִים פְּדִיתִיךָ
I-redeemed-you slaves and-from-house-of Egypt from-land-of I-brought-up-you

וָאֶשְׁלַח לְפָנֶיךָ אֶת־ מֹשֶׁה אַהֲרֹן וּמִרְיָם׃ עַמִּי זְכָר־ נָא
now! remember! people-of-me (5) and-Miriam Aaron Moses *** before-you and-I-sent

מַה־ יָּעַץ בָּלָק מֶלֶךְ מוֹאָב וּמֶה־ עָנָה אֹתוֹ בִּלְעָם בֶּן־
son-of Balaam him he-answered and-what Moab king-of Balak he-counseled what

בְּעוֹר מִן־ הַשִּׁטִּים עַד־ הַגִּלְגָּל לְמַעַן דַּעַת צִדְקוֹת יְהוָה׃
Yahweh righteous-acts-of to-know so-that the-Gilgal to the-Shittim from Beor

בַּמָּה אֲקַדֵּם יְהוָה אִכַּף לֵאלֹהֵי מָרוֹם
exaltation before-God-of shall-I-bow-down Yahweh shall-I-come-before with-what? (6)

הַאֲקַדְּמֶנּוּ בְעוֹלוֹת בַּעֲגָלִים בְּנֵי שָׁנָה׃
year sons-of with-calves with-burnt-offerings shall-I-come-before-him?

הֲיִרְצֶה יְהוָה בְּאַלְפֵי אֵילִים בְּרִבְבוֹת
with-tens-of-thousands-of rams with-thousands-of Yahweh will-he-be-pleased? (7)

נַחֲלֵי־ שָׁמֶן הַאֶתֵּן בְּכוֹרִי פִּשְׁעִי פְּרִי בִטְנִי
body-of-me fruit-of transgression-of-me firstborn-of-me shall-I-offer? oil rivers-of

and tear down all your
strongholds.
12 I will destroy your witchcraft
and you will no longer cast
spells.
13 I will destroy your carved
images
and your sacred stones from
among you;
you will no longer bow down
to the work of your hands.
14 I will uproot from among you
your Asherah poles[r]
and demolish your cities.
15 I will take vengeance in anger
and wrath
upon the nations that have
not obeyed me."

*The LORD's Case Against Israel*

6 Listen to what the LORD says:
"Stand up, plead your case
before the mountains;
let the hills hear what you
have to say.
2 Hear, O mountains, the LORD's
accusation;
listen, you everlasting
foundations of the earth.
For the LORD has a case
against his people;
he is lodging a charge
against Israel.

3 "My people, what have I done
to you?
How have I burdened you?
Answer me.
4 I brought you up out of Egypt
and redeemed you from the
land of slavery.
I sent Moses to lead you,
also Aaron and Miriam.
5 My people, remember
what Balak king of Moab
counseled
and what Balaam son of
Beor answered.
Remember ⌊your journey⌋ from
Shittim to Gilgal,
that you may know the
righteous acts of the
LORD."

6 With what shall I come before
the LORD
and bow down before the
exalted God?
Shall I come before him with
burnt offerings,
with calves a year old?
7 Will the LORD be pleased with
thousands of rams,
with ten thousand rivers of
oil?
Shall I offer my firstborn for
my transgression,
the fruit of my body for the

[r] 14 That is, symbols of the goddess Asherah

**Heading* See the first note on page 536.

חַטַּאת נַפְשִׁי׃ הִגִּיד לְךָ אָדָם מַה־טּוֹב וּמָה־יְהוָה דּוֹרֵשׁ
requiring Yahweh and-what? good what man to-you he-showed (8) soul-of-me sin-of

מִמְּךָ כִּי אִם־עֲשׂוֹת מִשְׁפָּט וְאַהֲבַת חֶסֶד וְהַצְנֵעַ לֶכֶת
to-walk and-to-make-humble mercy and-to-love justice to-act indeed surely of-you

עִם־אֱלֹהֶיךָ׃ קוֹל יְהוָה לָעִיר יִקְרָא וְתוּשִׁיָּה יִרְאֶה*
*he-sees and-wisdom he-calls to-the-city Yahweh voice-of (9) God-of-you with

שְׁמֶךָ שִׁמְעוּ מַטֶּה וּמִי יְעָדָהּ׃ עוֹד הַאִשׁ† בֵּית
house-of †is-there? still (10) he-appointed-her and-who rod heed! name-of-you

רָשָׁע אֹצְרוֹת רֶשַׁע וְאֵיפַת רָזוֹן זְעוּמָה׃
one-being-accursed shortness and-ephah-of wickedness treasures-of wickedness

הַאֶזְכֶּה בְּמֹאזְנֵי רֶשַׁע וּבְכִיס אַבְנֵי מִרְמָה׃
falseness weights-of and-to-bag-of dishonesty to-scales-of shall-I-acquit? (11)

אֲשֶׁר עֲשִׁירֶיהָ מָלְאוּ חָמָס וְיֹשְׁבֶיהָ
and-ones-being-peoples-of-her violence they-are-filled rich-men-of-her that (12)

דִּבְּרוּ־שָׁקֶר וּלְשׁוֹנָם רְמִיָּה בְּפִיהֶם׃ וְגַם־אֲנִי
I so-therefore (13) in-speech-of-them deceit and-tongue-of-them lie they-speak

הֶחֱלֵיתִי†† הַכּוֹתֶךָ הַשְׁמֵם עַל־חַטֹּאתֶךָ׃ אַתָּה תֹאכַל
you-will-eat you (14) sins-of-you because-of to-ruin to-destroy-you ††I-made-sick

וְלֹא תִשְׂבָּע וְיֶשְׁחֲךָ בְּקִרְבֶּךָ
in-stomach-of-you and-emptiness-of-you you-will-be-satisfied but-not

וְתַסֵּג וְלֹא תַפְלִיט וַאֲשֶׁר תְּפַלֵּט לַחֶרֶב
to-the-sword you-save because-what you-will-save but-not and-you-will-store-up

אֶתֵּן׃ אַתָּה תִזְרַע וְלֹא תִקְצוֹר אַתָּה תִדְרֹךְ־
you-will-press you you-will-harvest but-not you-will-plant you (15) I-will-give

זַיִת וְלֹא־תָסוּךְ שֶׁמֶן וְתִירוֹשׁ וְלֹא תִשְׁתֶּה־יָּיִן׃
wine you-will-drink but-not and-crushed-grape oil you-will-use but-not olive

וְיִשְׁתַּמֵּר חֻקּוֹת עָמְרִי וְכֹל מַעֲשֵׂה בֵית־אַחְאָב
Ahab house-of practice-of and-all-of Omri statutes-of for-he-observed (16)

וַתֵּלְכוּ בְּמֹעֲצוֹתָם לְמַעַן תִּתִּי אֹתְךָ לְשַׁמָּה
to-ruin you to-give-over-me therefore to-traditions-of-them and-you-followed

וְיֹשְׁבֶיהָ לִשְׁרֵקָה וְחֶרְפַּת עַמִּי תִּשָּׂאוּ׃
you-will-bear people-of-me and-scorn-of to-derision and-ones-being-peoples-of-her

אַלְלַי לִי כִּי הָיִיתִי כְּאָסְפֵּי־ קַיִץ כְּעֹלְלֹת
at-gleanings-of summer-fruit like-gatherings-of I-am indeed to-me misery! (7:1)

בָּצִיר אֵין־ אֶשְׁכּוֹל לֶאֱכוֹל בִּכּוּרָה אִוְּתָה נַפְשִׁי׃
self-of-me she-craves early-fig to-eat cluster-of-grapes there-is-no vineyard

אָבַד חָסִיד מִן־הָאָרֶץ וְיָשָׁר בָּאָדָם אַיִן
there-is-not among-the-man and-upright-one the-land from godly he-was-swept (2)

sin of my soul?
8He has showed you, O man,
what is good.
And what does the LORD
require of you?
To act justly and to love mercy
and to walk humbly with
your God.

*Israel's Guilt and Punishment*

9Listen! The LORD is calling to
the city—
and to fear your name is
wisdom—
"Heed the rod and the One
who appointed it.[s]
10Am I still to forget, O wicked
house,
your ill-gotten treasures
and the short ephah,[t] which
is accursed?
11Shall I acquit a man with
dishonest scales,
with a bag of false weights?
12Her rich men are violent;
her people are liars
and their tongues speak
deceitfully.
13Therefore, I have begun to
destroy you,
to ruin you because of your
sins.
14You will eat but not be
satisfied;
your stomach will still be
empty.[u]
You will store up but save
nothing,
because what you save I will
give to the sword.
15You will plant but not harvest;
you will press olives but not
use the oil on yourselves,
you will crush grapes but
not drink the wine.
16You have observed the statutes
of Omri
and all the practices of
Ahab's house,
and you have followed their
traditions.
Therefore I will give you over
to ruin
and your people to derision;
you will bear the scorn of
the nations.[v]"

*Israel's Misery*

7 What misery is mine!
I am like one who gathers
summer fruit
at the gleaning of the
vineyard;
there is no cluster of grapes to
eat,
none of the early figs that I
crave.
2The godly have been swept
from the land;
not one upright man
remains.

*s9* The meaning of the Hebrew for this line is uncertain.
*t10* An ephah was a dry measure.
*u14* The meaning of the Hebrew for this word is uncertain.
*v16* Septuagint; Hebrew *scorn due my people*

***9 The NIV, with the Septuagint, repoints this word as יִרְאָה, *to-fear*.**

**†10 The NIV reads this word as הַאֶשָּׁה, *shall-I-forget?***

**††13 The NIV, with many ancient versions, repoints this word as הַחִלּוֹתִי, *I-have-begun*.**

כֻּלָּם לְדָמִים יֶאֱרֹבוּ אִישׁ אֶת־ אָחִיהוּ יָצוּדוּ חֵרֶם׃
net they-hunt brother-of-him *** each they-lie-in-wait for-bloods all-of-them

עַל־ הָרַע כַּפַּיִם לְהֵיטִיב הַשַּׂר שֹׁאֵל וְהַשֹּׁפֵט
and-the-one-judging demanding the-ruler to-be-skilled both-hands the-evil in (3)

בַּשִּׁלּוּם וְהַגָּדוֹל דֹּבֵר הַוַּת נַפְשׁוֹ הוּא
he self-of-him desire-of dictating and-the-powerful for-the-bribe

וַיְעַבְּתוּהָ׃ טוֹבָם כְּחֵדֶק יָשָׁר מִמְּסוּכָה
worse-than-thorn-hedge upright like-brier best-of-them (4) and-they-conspire-about-her

יוֹם מְצַפֶּיךָ פְּקֻדָּתְךָ בָּאָה עַתָּה תִהְיֶה מְבוּכָתָם׃
confusion-of-them she-is now she-came visitation-of-you men-watching-you day-of

אַל־ תַּאֲמִינוּ בְרֵעַ אַל־ תִּבְטְחוּ בְּאַלּוּף מִשֹּׁכֶבֶת
with-woman-lying-of in-friend you-put-confidence not in-neighbor you-trust not (5)

חֵיקֶךָ שְׁמֹר פִּתְחֵי־ פִיךָ׃ כִּי־ בֵן מְנַבֵּל אָב
father dishonoring son for (6) mouth-of-you words-of be-careful! embrace-of-you

בַּת קָמָה בְאִמָּהּ כַּלָּה בַּחֲמֹתָהּ
against-mother-in-law-of-her daughter-in-law against-mother-of-her rising-up daughter

אֹיְבֵי אִישׁ אַנְשֵׁי בֵיתוֹ׃ וַאֲנִי בַּיהוָה
for-Yahweh but-I (7) household-of-him members-of man ones-being-enemies-of

אֲצַפֶּה אוֹחִילָה לֵאלֹהֵי יִשְׁעִי יִשְׁמָעֵנִי אֱלֹהָי׃ אַל־
not (8) God-of-me he-will-hear-me salvation-of-me for-God-of I-wait I-watch-in-hope

תִּשְׂמְחִי אֹיַבְתִּי לִי כִּי נָפַלְתִּי קָמְתִּי כִּי־ אֵשֵׁב
I-sit though I-will-rise I-fell though over-me one-being-enemy-of-me you-gloat

בַּחֹשֶׁךְ יְהוָה אוֹר לִי׃ זַעַף יְהוָה אֶשָּׂא כִּי חָטָאתִי
I-sinned because I-will-bear Yahweh wrath-of (9) to-me light Yahweh in-the-darkness

לוֹ עַד אֲשֶׁר יָרִיב רִיבִי וְעָשָׂה מִשְׁפָּטִי
right-of-me and-he-establishes case-of-me he-pleads when until against-him

יוֹצִיאֵנִי לָאוֹר אֶרְאֶה בְּצִדְקָתוֹ׃
to-righteousness-of-him I-will-see into-the-light and-he-will-bring-out-me

וְתֵרֶא אֹיַבְתִּי וּתְכַסֶּהָ בוּשָׁה
shame and-she-will-cover-her one-being-enemy-of-me then-she-will-see (10)

הָאֹמְרָה אֵלַי אַיּוֹ יְהוָה אֱלֹהָיִךְ עֵינַי תִּרְאֶינָּה בָּהּ
to-her they-will-see eyes-of-me God-of-you Yahweh where-he? to-me the-one-saying

עַתָּה תִּהְיֶה לְמִרְמָס כְּטִיט חוּצוֹת׃ יוֹם לִבְנוֹת גְּדֵרָיִךְ
walls-of-you to-build day (11) streets like-mire-of for-trampling she-will-be now

יוֹם הַהוּא יִרְחַק־ חֹק׃ יוֹם הוּא וְעָדֶיךָ יָבוֹא לְמִנִּי
at-from he-will-come and-to-you that day (12) boundary he-will-extend the-that day-of

אַשּׁוּר וְעָרֵי מָצוֹר וּלְמִנִּי מָצוֹר וְעַד־ נָהָר וְיָם מִיָּם
from-sea and-sea Euphrates and-to Egypt even-at-from Egypt and-cities-of Assyria

All men lie in wait to shed
blood;
each hunts his brother with
a net.
3Both hands are skilled in
doing evil;
the ruler demands gifts,
the judge accepts bribes,
the powerful dictate what
they desire—
they all conspire together.
4The best of them is like a
brier,
the most upright worse than
a thorn hedge.
The day of your watchmen has
come,
the day God visits you.
Now is the time of their
confusion.
5Do not trust a neighbor;
put no confidence in a
friend.
Even with her who lies in
your embrace
be careful of your words.
6For a son dishonors his father,
a daughter rises up against
her mother,
a daughter-in-law against her
mother-in-law—
a man's enemies are the
members of his own
household.

7But as for me, I watch in hope
for the LORD,
I wait for God my Savior;
my God will hear me.

*Israel Will Rise*

8Do not gloat over me, my
enemy!
Though I have fallen, I will
rise.
Though I sit in darkness,
the LORD will be my light.
9Because I have sinned against
him,
I will bear the LORD's wrath,
until he pleads my case
and establishes my right.
He will bring me out into the
light;
I will see his righteousness.
10Then my enemy will see it
and will be covered with
shame,
she who said to me,
"Where is the LORD your
God?"
My eyes will see her downfall;
even now she will be
trampled underfoot
like mire in the streets.

11The day for building your
walls will come,
the day for extending your
boundaries.
12In that day people will come
to you
from Assyria and the cities
of Egypt,
even from Egypt to the
Euphrates
and from sea to sea

וְהַר הָהָר׃ וְהָיְתָה הָאָרֶץ לִשְׁמָמָה
into-desolation the-earth and-she-will-become (13) the-mountain and-mountain-of

עַל־ יֹשְׁבֶיהָ מִפְּרִי מַעַלְלֵיהֶם׃ רְעֵה
shepherd! (14) deeds-of-them as-result-of ones-inhabiting-her because-of

עַמְּךָ בְשִׁבְטֶךָ צֹאן נַחֲלָתֶךָ שֹׁכְנִי
one-living inheritance-of-you flock-of with-staff-of-you people-of-you

לְבָדָד יַעַר בְּתוֹךְ כַּרְמֶל יִרְעוּ בָשָׁן וְגִלְעָד
and-Gilead Bashan let-them-feed fertile-pastureland in-midst-of forest by-self

כִּימֵי עוֹלָם׃ כִּימֵי צֵאתְךָ מֵאֶרֶץ מִצְרָיִם
Egypt from-land-of to-come-out-you as-days-of (15) long-ago as-days-of

אַרְאֶנּוּ נִפְלָאוֹת׃ יִרְאוּ גוֹיִם
nations they-will-see (16) things-being-wonderful I-will-show-him

וְיֵבֹשׁוּ מִכֹּל גְּבוּרָתָם יָשִׂימוּ יָד עַל־ פֶּה
mouth on hand they-will-lay power-of-them of-all-of and-they-will-be-ashamed

אָזְנֵיהֶם תֶּחֱרַשְׁנָה׃ יְלַחֲכוּ עָפָר כַּנָּחָשׁ
like-the-snake dust they-will-lick (17) they-will-become-deaf ears-of-them

כְּזֹחֲלֵי אֶרֶץ יִרְגְּזוּ מִמִּסְגְּרֹתֵיהֶם
from-dens-of-them they-will-come-trembling ground like-ones-crawling-of

אֶל־ יְהוָה אֱלֹהֵינוּ יִפְחָדוּ וְיִרְאוּ מִמֶּךָּ׃
of-you and-they-will-be-afraid they-will-turn-in-fear God-of-us Yahweh to

מִי־ אֵל כָּמוֹךָ נֹשֵׂא עָוֹן וְעֹבֵר עַל־ פֶּשַׁע
transgression to and-one-forgiving sin one-pardoning like-you God who? (18)

לִשְׁאֵרִית נַחֲלָתוֹ לֹא־ הֶחֱזִיק לָעַד אַפּוֹ
anger-of-him to-forever he-will-make-stay not inheritance-of-him of-remnant-of

כִּי־ חָפֵץ חֶסֶד הוּא׃ יָשׁוּב יְרַחֲמֵנוּ
he-will-have-compassion-on-us he-will-do-again (19) he mercy he-delights-in but

יִכְבֹּשׁ עֲוֹנֹתֵינוּ וְתַשְׁלִיךְ בִּמְצֻלוֹת יָם
sea into-depths-of and-you-will-hurl sins-of-us he-will-tread-underfoot

כָּל־ חַטֹּאותָם׃ תִּתֵּן אֱמֶת לְיַעֲקֹב חֶסֶד
mercy to-Jacob truth you-will-give (20) iniquities-of-them all-of

לְאַבְרָהָם אֲשֶׁר־ נִשְׁבַּעְתָּ לַאֲבֹתֵינוּ מִימֵי קֶדֶם׃
long-ago in-days-of to-fathers-of-us you-pledged-on-oath as to-Abraham

and from mountain to
mountain.
13 The earth will become desolate
because of its inhabitants,
as the result of their deeds.

*Prayer and Praise*

14 Shepherd your people with
your staff,
the flock of your
inheritance,
which lives by itself in a
forest,
in fertile pasturelands.[w]
Let them feed in Bashan and
Gilead
as in days long ago.

15 "As in the days when you
came out of Egypt,
I will show them my
wonders."

16 Nations will see and be
ashamed,
deprived of all their power.
They will lay their hands on
their mouths
and their ears will become
deaf.
17 They will lick dust like a
snake,
like creatures that crawl on
the ground.
They will come trembling out
of their dens;
they will turn in fear to the
LORD our God
and will be afraid of you.
18 Who is a God like you,
who pardons sin and
forgives the transgression
of the remnant of his
inheritance?
You do not stay angry forever
but delight to show mercy.
19 You will again have
compassion on us;
you will tread our sins
underfoot
and hurl all our iniquities
into the depths of the sea.
20 You will be true to Jacob,
and show mercy to
Abraham,
as you pledged on oath to our
fathers
in days long ago.

[w]14 Or *in the middle of Carmel*

מַשָּׂא נִֽינְוֵה סֵפֶר חֲזוֹן נַחוּם הָאֶלְקֹשִׁי׃ אֵל קַנּוֹא
jealous God (2) the-Elkoshite Nahum vision-of book-of Nineveh oracle-of (1:1)

וְנֹקֵם יְהוָה נֹקֵם יְהוָה וּבַעַל חֵמָה נֹקֵם
taking-vengeance wrath and-one-filled-of Yahweh taking-vengeance Yahweh and-avenging

יְהוָה לְצָרָיו וְנוֹטֵר הוּא לְאֹיְבָיו׃
against-ones-being-enemies-of-him he and-maintaining-wrath on-foes-of-him Yahweh

יְהוָה אֶרֶךְ אַפַּיִם וּגְדָול־ כֹּחַ וְנַקֵּה לֹא
not and-to-leave-guilty-unpunished power and-great-of angers slow-of Yahweh (3)

יְנַקֶּה יְהוָה בְּסוּפָה וּבִשְׂעָרָה דַּרְכּוֹ וְעָנָן
and-cloud way-of-him and-in-storm in-whirlwind Yahweh he-will-leave-guilty-unpunished

אֲבַק רַגְלָיו׃ גּוֹעֵר בַּיָּם וַיַּבְּשֵׁהוּ וְכָל־
and-all-of and-he-dries-up-him to-the-sea one-rebuking (4) feet-of-him dust-of

הַנְּהָרוֹת הֶחֱרִיב אֻמְלַל בָּשָׁן וְכַרְמֶל וּפֶרַח לְבָנוֹן
Lebanon and-blossom-of and-Carmel Bashan he-is-withered he-makes-run-dry the-rivers

אֻמְלָל׃ הָרִים רָעֲשׁוּ מִמֶּנּוּ וְהַגְּבָעוֹת הִתְמֹגָגוּ
they-melt-away and-the-hills before-him they-quake mountains (5) he-is-faded

וַתִּשָּׂא הָאָרֶץ מִפָּנָיו וְתֵבֵל וְכָל־ יֹשְׁבֵי
ones-living-of and-all-of and-world at-presences-of-him the-earth and-she-trembles

בָהּ׃ לִפְנֵי זַעְמוֹ מִי יַעֲמוֹד וּמִי יָקוּם
he-can-endure and-who? he-can-withstand who? indignation-of-him before (6) in-her

בַּחֲרוֹן אַפּוֹ חֲמָתוֹ נִתְּכָה כָאֵשׁ וְהַצֻּרִים
and-the-rocks like-fire she-is-poured-out wrath-of-him anger-of-him to-fierceness-of

נִתְּצוּ מִמֶּנּוּ׃ טוֹב יְהוָה לְמָעוֹז בְּיוֹם צָרָה
trouble in-day-of for-refuge Yahweh good (7) before-him they-are-shattered

וְיֹדֵעַ חֹסֵי בוֹ׃ וּבְשֶׁטֶף עֹבֵר כָּלָה
end one-overwhelming but-with-flood (8) in-him ones-trusting-of and-one-caring-for

יַעֲשֶׂה מְקוֹמָהּ וְאֹיְבָיו יְרַדֶּף־ חֹשֶׁךְ׃
darkness he-will-pursue and-ones-being-foes-of-him place-of-her he-will-make

מַה־ תְּחַשְּׁבוּן אֶל־ יְהוָה כָּלָה הוּא עֹשֶׂה לֹא־ תָקוּם פַּעֲמַיִם
second-time she-will-come not bringing-to he end Yahweh against you-plot what? (9)

צָרָה׃ כִּי עַד־ סִירִים סְבֻכִים וּכְסָבְאָם
and-from-wine-of-them ones-being-entangled thorns among indeed (10) trouble

סְבוּאִים אֻכְּלוּ כְּקַשׁ יָבֵשׁ מָלֵא׃ מִמֵּךְ
from-you (11) fully dry like-stubble they-will-be-consumed ones-being-drunk

יָצָא חֹשֵׁב עַל־ יְהוָה רָעָה יֹעֵץ בְּלִיָּעַל׃
wickedness one-counseling evil Yahweh against one-plotting he-came-forth

כֹּה ׀ אָמַר יְהוָה אִם־ שְׁלֵמִים וְכֵן רַבִּים וְכֵן
yet-so numerous-ones and-so allied-ones although Yahweh he-says this (12)

**1** An oracle concerning Nineveh. The book of the vision of Nahum the Elkoshite.

*The LORD's Anger Against Nineveh*

[2]The LORD is a jealous and avenging God;
the LORD takes vengeance and is filled with wrath.
The LORD takes vengeance on his foes
and maintains his wrath against his enemies.
[3]The LORD is slow to anger and great in power;
the LORD will not leave the guilty unpunished.
His way is in the whirlwind and the storm,
and clouds are the dust of his feet.
[4]He rebukes the sea and dries it up;
he makes all the rivers run dry.
Bashan and Carmel wither
and the blossoms of Lebanon fade.
[5]The mountains quake before him
and the hills melt away.
The earth trembles at his presence,
the world and all who live in it.
[6]Who can withstand his indignation?
Who can endure his fierce anger?
His wrath is poured out like fire;
the rocks are shattered before him.

[7]The LORD is good,
a refuge in times of trouble.
He cares for those who trust in him,
[8] but with an overwhelming flood
he will make an end of ⌊Nineveh⌋;
he will pursue his foes into darkness.

[9]Whatever they plot against the LORD
he[a] will bring to an end;
trouble will not come a second time.
[10]They will be entangled among thorns
and drunk from their wine;
they will be consumed like dry stubble.[b]
[11]From you, ⌊O Nineveh,⌋ has one come forth
who plots evil against the LORD
and counsels wickedness.

[12]This is what the LORD says:

"Although they have allies and are numerous,
they will be cut off and pass away.

[a]9 Or *What do you foes plot against the LORD? / He*
[b]10 The meaning of the Hebrew for this verse is uncertain.

°3 ק וגדל

נָגֹזּוּ וְעָבָר וְעִנִּתִךְ לֹא
not although-I-afflicted-you and-he-will-pass-away they-will-be-cut-off

אֲעַנֵּךְ עוֹד׃ וְעַתָּה אֶשְׁבֹּר מֹטֵהוּ מֵעָלָיִךְ
from-upon-you yoke-of-him I-will-break and-now (13) more I-will-afflict-you

וּמוֹסְרֹתַיִךְ אֲנַתֵּק׃ וְצִוָּה עָלֶיךָ יְהוָה לֹא־
not Yahweh concerning-you now-he-commanded (14) I-will-tear-away and-shackles-of-you

יִזָּרַע מִשִּׁמְךָ עוֹד מִבֵּית אֱלֹהֶיךָ אַכְרִית
I-will-destroy gods-of-you in-temple-of more for-name-of-you he-will-be-descendant

פֶּסֶל וּמַסֵּכָה אָשִׂים קִבְרֶךָ כִּי קַלּוֹתָ׃
you-are-vile for grave-of-you I-will-prepare and-cast-idol carved-image

הִנֵּה עַל־ הֶהָרִים רַגְלֵי מְבַשֵּׂר מַשְׁמִיעַ שָׁלוֹם
peace one-proclaiming one-bringing-good-news feet-of the-mountains on look! *(2:1)

חָגִּי יְהוּדָה חַגַּיִךְ שַׁלְּמִי נְדָרָיִךְ כִּי לֹא יוֹסִיף
he-will-repeat not indeed vows-of-you fulfill! festivals-of-you Judah celebrate!

עוֹד לַעֲבָור־ בָּךְ בְּלִיַּעַל כֻּלֹּה נִכְרָת׃ עָלָה
he-advances (2) he-will-be-destroyed all-of-him wicked into-you to-invade more

מֵפִיץ עַל־ פָּנַיִךְ נָצוֹר מְצֻרָה צַפֵּה־ דֶרֶךְ חַזֵּק מָתְנַיִם
loins brace! road watch! fortress to-guard faces-of-you against attacker

אַמֵּץ כֹּחַ מְאֹד׃ כִּי שָׁב יְהוָה אֶת־ גְּאוֹן יַעֲקֹב
Jacob splendor-of *** Yahweh he-will-restore indeed (3) all strength marshal!

כִּגְאוֹן יִשְׂרָאֵל כִּי בְקָקוּם בֹּקְקִים וּזְמֹרֵיהֶם
and-vines-of-them ones-destroying they-destroyed-them though Israel like-splendor-of

שִׁחֵתוּ׃ מָגֵן גִּבֹּרֵיהוּ מְאָדָּם אַנְשֵׁי־ חַיִל מְתֻלָּעִים
ones-wearing-scarlet war men-of being-red soldiers-of-him shield-of (4) they-ruined

בְּאֵשׁ־ פְּלָדוֹת הָרֶכֶב בְּיוֹם הֲכִינוֹ וְהַבְּרֹשִׁים
and-the-pine-spears to-make-ready-him on-day-of the-chariot metals-of with-flash-of

הָרְעָלוּ׃ בַּחוּצוֹת יִתְהוֹלְלוּ הָרֶכֶב
the-chariot they-storm through-the-streets (5) they-are-brandished

יִשְׁתַּקְשְׁקוּן בָּרְחֹבוֹת מַרְאֵיהֶן כַּלַּפִּידִם
like-the-flaming-torches looks-of-them through-the-squares they-rush-back-and-forth

כַּבְּרָקִים יְרוֹצֵצוּ׃ יִזְכֹּר אַדִּירָיו יִכָּשְׁלוּ
they-stumble picked-troops-of-him he-summons (6) they-dart-about like-the-lightnings

בַּהֲלִכוֹתָם יְמַהֲרוּ חוֹמָתָהּ וְהֻכַן הַסֹּכֵךְ׃
the-protective-shield and-he-is-put-in-place city-wall-of-her they-dash on-way-of-them

שַׁעֲרֵי הַנְּהָרוֹת נִפְתָּחוּ וְהַהֵיכָל נָמוֹג׃
he-collapses and-the-palace they-are-thrown-open the-rivers gates-of (7)

וְהֻצַּב גֻּלְּתָה הֹעֲלָתָה וְאַמְהֹתֶיהָ
and-slave-girls-of-her she-is-carried-away she-is-exiled and-he-is-decreed (8)

Although I have afflicted you,
⌞O Judah,⌟
I will afflict you no more.
13Now I will break their yoke
from your neck
and tear your shackles
away."
14The LORD has given a
command concerning
you, ⌞Nineveh⌟:
"You will have no
descendants to bear your
name.
I will destroy the carved
images and cast idols
that are in the temple of
your gods.
I will prepare your grave,
for you are vile."
15Look, there on the mountains,
the feet of one who brings
good news,
who proclaims peace!
Celebrate your festivals, O
Judah,
and fulfill your vows.
No more will the wicked
invade you;
they will be completely
destroyed.

*Nineveh to Fall*

2 An attacker advances against
you, ⌞Nineveh⌟.
Guard the fortress,
watch the road,
brace yourselves,
marshal all your strength!
2The LORD will restore the
splendor of Jacob
like the splendor of Israel,
though destroyers have laid
them waste
and have ruined their vines.
3The shields of his soldiers are
red;
the warriors are clad in
scarlet.
The metal on the chariots
flashes
on the day they are made
ready;
the spears of pine are
brandished.[c]
4The chariots storm through the
streets,
rushing back and forth
through the squares.
They look like flaming torches;
they dart about like
lightning.
5He summons his picked
troops,
yet they stumble on their
way.
They dash to the city wall;
the protective shield is put
in place.
6The river gates are thrown
open
and the palace collapses.
7It is decreed[d] that ⌞the city⌟
be exiled and carried away.

[c]3 Hebrew; Septuagint and Syriac / *the horsemen rush to and fro*
[d]7 The meaning of the Hebrew for this word is uncertain.

***Heading, 1* The Hebrew numeration of chapter 2 begins with the final verse of chapter 1 in English; thus, there is a one-verse discrepancy throughout chapter 2.**

°1 ק לעבר; °6 ק בהליכתם

מְנַהֲגוֹת כְּקוֹל יוֹנִים מְתֹפְפֹת עַל־ לִבְבֵהֶן׃ וְנִינְוֵה
and-Nineveh (9) breast-of-them on ones-beating doves like-sound-of ones-moaning

כִבְרֵכַת־ מַיִם מִימֵי הִיא וְהֵמָּה נָסִים עִמְדוּ עֲמֹדוּ
stop! stop! ones-draining-away and-they she waters-of waters like-pool-of

וְאֵין מַפְנֶה׃ בֹּזּוּ כֶסֶף בֹּזּוּ זָהָב וְאֵין
and-there-is-no gold plunder! silver plunder! (10) one-turning-back but-there-is-no

קֵצֶה לַתְּכוּנָה כָּבֹד מִכֹּל כְּלִי חֶמְדָּה׃ בּוּקָה וּמְבוּקָה
and-plundered pillaged (11) treasure article-of from-all-of wealth to-the-supply end

וּמְבֻלָּקָה וְלֵב נָמֵס וּפַק בִּרְכַּיִם וְחַלְחָלָה בְּכָל־
in-all-of and-trembling knees and-giving-way-of melting and-heart and-being-stripped

מָתְנַיִם וּפְנֵי כֻלָּם קִבְּצוּ פָארוּר׃ אַיֵּה מְעוֹן אֲרָיוֹת
lions den-of where? (12) paleness they-grow every-of-them and-faces-of bodies

וּמִרְעֶה הוּא לַכְּפִרִים אֲשֶׁר הָלַךְ אַרְיֵה לָבִיא שָׁם
there lioness lion he-went where for-the-young-lions he indeed-feeding-place

גּוּר אַרְיֵה וְאֵין מַחֲרִיד׃ אַרְיֵה טֹרֵף בְּדֵי
for-enough-of killing lion (13) one-making-afraid and-there-was-no lion cub-of

גֹרוֹתָיו וּמְחַנֵּק לְלִבְאֹתָיו וַיְמַלֵּא־ טֶרֶף חֹרָיו
lairs-of-him kill and-he-filled for-mates-of-him and-strangling cubs-of-him

וּמְעֹנֹתָיו טְרֵפָה׃ הִנְנִי אֵלַיִךְ נְאֻם יְהוָה צְבָאוֹת
Hosts Yahweh-of declaration-of against-you see-I! (14) prey and-dens-of-him

וְהִבְעַרְתִּי בֶעָשָׁן רִכְבָּהּ וּכְפִירַיִךְ תֹּאכַל
she-will-devour and-young-lions-of-you chariot-of-you in-the-smoke and-I-will-burn-up

חָרֶב וְהִכְרַתִּי מֵאֶרֶץ טַרְפֵּךְ וְלֹא־ יִשָּׁמַע עוֹד
longer he-will-be-heard and-not prey-of-you from-earth and-I-will-cut-off sword

קוֹל מַלְאָכֵכֵה׃ הוֹי עִיר דָּמִים כֻּלָּהּ כַּחַשׁ פֶּרֶק
plunder lie fullness-of-her bloods city-of woe! (3:1) messenger-of-you voice-of

מְלֵאָה לֹא יָמִישׁ טָרֶף׃ קוֹל שׁוֹט וְקוֹל רַעַשׁ אוֹפָן
wheel clatter-of and-sound-of whip crack-of (2) victim he-is-without never full

וְסוּס דֹּהֵר וּמֶרְכָּבָה מְרַקֵּדָה׃ פָּרָשׁ מַעֲלֶה וְלַהַב חֶרֶב
sword and-flash-of charging cavalry (3) jolting and-chariot galloping and-horse

וּבְרַק חֲנִית וְרֹב חָלָל וְכֹבֶד פָּגֶר וְאֵין קֵצֶה
number and-there-is-no dead and-pile-of casualty and-many-of spear and-glitter-of

לַגְּוִיָּה יִכְשְׁלוּ בִּגְוִיָּתָם׃ מֵרֹב זְנוּנֵי
lusts-of because-of-all-of (4) over-corpse-of-them and-they-stumble to-the-body

זוֹנָה טוֹבַת חֵן בַּעֲלַת כְּשָׁפִים הַמֹּכֶרֶת
the-one-enslaving sorceries mistress-of alluringness good-of one-being-harlot

גּוֹיִם בִּזְנוּנֶיהָ וּמִשְׁפָּחוֹת בִּכְשָׁפֶיהָ׃ הִנְנִי
see-I! (5) by-witchcrafts-of-her and-peoples by-prostitutions-of-her nations

Its slave girls moan like doves
and beat upon their breasts.
8Nineveh is like a pool,
and its water is draining away.
"Stop! Stop!" they cry,
but no one turns back.
9Plunder the silver!
Plunder the gold!
The supply is endless,
the wealth from all its treasures!
10She is pillaged, plundered, stripped!
Hearts melt, knees give way,
bodies tremble, every face grows pale.

11Where now is the lions' den,
the place where they fed their young,
where the lion and lioness went,
and the cubs, with nothing to fear?
12The lion killed enough for his cubs
and strangled the prey for his mate,
filling his lairs with the kill
and his dens with the prey.

13"I am against you,"
declares the LORD Almighty.
"I will burn up your chariots in smoke,
and the sword will devour your young lions.
I will leave you no prey on the earth.
The voices of your messengers
will no longer be heard."

*Woe to Nineveh*

3 Woe to the city of blood,
full of lies,
full of plunder,
never without victims!
2The crack of whips,
the clatter of wheels,
galloping horses
and jolting chariots!
3Charging cavalry,
flashing swords
and glittering spears!
Many casualties,
piles of dead,
bodies without number,
people stumbling over the corpses—
4all because of the wanton lust of a harlot,
alluring, the mistress of sorceries,
who enslaved nations by her prostitution
and peoples by her witchcraft.

***Heading** See the note on page 543.

°3 וכשלו ק

אֵלַיִךְ נְאֻם יְהוָה צְבָאוֹת וְגִלֵּיתִי שׁוּלַיִךְ עַל־
over skirts-of-you and-I-will-lift Hosts Yahweh-of declaration-of against-you

פָּנָיִךְ וְהַרְאֵיתִי גוֹיִם מַעְרֵךְ וּמַמְלָכוֹת קְלוֹנֵךְ׃
shame-of-you and-kingdoms nakedness-of-you nations and-I-will-show faces-of-you

וְהִשְׁלַכְתִּי עָלַיִךְ שִׁקֻּצִים וְנִבַּלְתִּיךְ וְשַׂמְתִּיךְ
and-I-will-make-you and-I-will-treat-with-contempt-you filths on-you and-I-will-pelt (6)

כְּרֹאִי׃ וְהָיָה כָל־ רֹאַיִךְ יִדּוֹד מִמֵּךְ
from-you he-will-flee ones-seeing-you all-of and-he-will-be (7) as-spectacle

וְאָמַר שָׁדְּדָה נִינְוֵה מִי יָנוּד לָהּ מֵאַיִן
from-where? for-her he-will-mourn who? Nineveh she-is-in-ruins and-he-will-say

אֲבַקֵּשׁ מְנַחֲמִים לָךְ׃ הֲתֵיטְבִי מִנֹּא אָמוֹן
Amon than-No are-you-better? (8) to-you ones-comforting can-I-find

הַיֹּשְׁבָה בַּיְאֹרִים מַיִם סָבִיב לָהּ אֲשֶׁר־ חֵיל יָם
river defense-of that to-her around waters on-the-Niles the-one-being-situated

מִיָּם* חוֹמָתָהּ׃ כּוּשׁ עָצְמָה וּמִצְרַיִם וְאֵין קֵצֶה פּוּט
Put boundary and-there-is-no and-Egypt strength Cush (9) wall-of-her *from-river

וְלוּבִים הָיוּ בְּעֶזְרָתֵךְ׃ גַּם־ הִיא לַגֹּלָה הָלְכָה
she-went to-the-captivity she yet (10) among-ally-of-you they-were and-Libya

בַשֶּׁבִי גַּם עֹלָלֶיהָ יְרֻטְּשׁוּ בְּרֹאשׁ כָּל־
every-of at-head-of they-were-dashed-to-pieces infants-of-her and into-the-exile

חוּצוֹת וְעַל־ נִכְבַּדֶּיהָ יַדּוּ גוֹרָל וְכָל־ גְּדוֹלֶיהָ
great-men-of-her and-all-of lot they-cast ones-being-nobles-of-her and-for streets

רֻתְּקוּ בַזִּקִּים׃ גַּם־ אַתְּ תִּשְׁכְּרִי תְּהִי נַעֲלָמָה
one-hiding you-will-be you-will-become-drunk you too (11) in-the-chains they-were-put

גַּם־ אַתְּ תְּבַקְשִׁי מָעוֹז מֵאוֹיֵב׃ כָּל־ מִבְצָרַיִךְ
fortresses-of-you all-of (12) from-one-being-enemy refuge you-will-seek you and

תְּאֵנִים עִם־ בִּכּוּרִים אִם־ יִנּוֹעוּ וְנָפְלוּ עַל־ פִּי
mouth-of into then-they-fall they-are-shaken when first-ripe-fruits with fig-trees

אוֹכֵל׃ הִנֵּה עַמֵּךְ נָשִׁים בְּקִרְבֵּךְ לְאֹיְבַיִךְ
to-ones-being-enemies-of-you in-midst-of-you women troop-of-you look! (13) one-eating

פָּתוֹחַ נִפְתְּחוּ שַׁעֲרֵי אַרְצֵךְ אָכְלָה אֵשׁ בְּרִיחָיִךְ†׃
bars-of-you fire she-consumed land-of-you gates-of they-are-opened to-be-open

מֵי מָצוֹר שַׁאֲבִי־ לָךְ חַזְּקִי מִבְצָרָיִךְ בֹּאִי בַטִּיט
in-the-clay work! defenses-of-you strengthen! for-you draw! siege waters-of (14)

וְרִמְסִי בַחֹמֶר הַחֲזִיקִי מַלְבֵּן׃ שָׁם תֹּאכְלֵךְ אֵשׁ
fire she-will-devour-you there (15) brickwork repair! in-the-mortar and-tread!

תַּכְרִיתֵךְ חֶרֶב תֹּאכְלֵךְ כַּיֶּלֶק הִתְכַּבֵּד
multiply! like-the-grasshopper she-will-consume-you sword she-will-cut-down-you

5 "I am against you," declares
the LORD Almighty.
"I will lift your skirts over
your face.
I will show the nations your
nakedness
and the kingdoms your
shame.
6 I will pelt you with filth,
I will treat you with
contempt
and make you a spectacle.
7 All who see you will flee from
you and say,
'Nineveh is in ruins—who
will mourn for her?'
Where can I find anyone to
comfort you?"
8 Are you better than Thebes,[e]
situated on the Nile,
with water around her?
The river was her defense,
the waters her wall.
9 Cush[f] and Egypt were her
boundless strength;
Put and Libya were among
her allies.
10 Yet she was taken captive
and went into exile.
Her infants were dashed to
pieces
at the head of every street.
Lots were cast for her nobles,
and all her great men were
put in chains.
11 You too will become drunk;
you will go into hiding
and seek refuge from the
enemy.
12 All your fortresses are like fig
trees
with their first ripe fruit;
when they are shaken,
the figs fall into the mouth
of the eater.
13 Look at your troops—
they are all women!
The gates of your land
are wide open to your
enemies;
fire has consumed their
bars.
14 Draw water for the siege,
strengthen your defenses!
Work the clay,
tread the mortar,
repair the brickwork!
15 There the fire will devour you;
the sword will cut you down
and, like grasshoppers,
consume you.

e8 Hebrew *No Amon*
f9 That is, the upper Nile region

*8 The NIV, with many ancient versions, repoints this word as מַיִם, *waters*.

†13 Most mss have *sheva* in the *kaph* (ךְ).

כַּיֶּלֶק הִתְכַּבְּדִי כָּאַרְבֶּה׃ הִרְבֵּית

you-increased (16) like-the-locust multiply! like-the-grasshopper

רֹכְלַיִךְ מִכּוֹכְבֵי הַשָּׁמָיִם יֶלֶק פָּשַׁט

he-strips locust the-skies more-than-stars-of ones-being-merchants-of-you

וַיָּעֹף׃ מִנְּזָרַיִךְ כָּאַרְבֶּה וְטַפְסְרַיִךְ

and-officials-of-you like-the-locust guards-of-you (17) then-he-flies-away

כְּגוֹב גֹּבָי הַחוֹנִים בַּגְּדֵרוֹת בְּיוֹם קָרָה

coldness on-day-of in-the-walls the-ones-settling locust like-locust-swarm-of

שֶׁמֶשׁ זָרְחָה וְנוֹדַד וְלֹא־ נוֹדַע מְקוֹמוֹ

place-of-him he-is-known and-not and-he-flies-away she-appears sun

אַיָּם׃ נָמוּ רֹעֶיךָ מֶלֶךְ אַשּׁוּר

Assyria king-of ones-being-shepherds-of-you they-slumber (18) where-they?

יִשְׁכְּנוּ אַדִּירֶיךָ נָפֹשׁוּ עַמְּךָ עַל־ הֶהָרִים

the-mountains on people-of-you they-are-scattered nobles-of-you they-lie-down

וְאֵין מְקַבֵּץ׃ אֵין־ כֵּהָה לְשִׁבְרֶךָ

for-wound-of-you healing there-is-no (19) one-gathering and-there-is-no

נַחְלָה מַכָּתֶךָ כֹּל שֹׁמְעֵי שִׁמְעֲךָ תָּקְעוּ

they-will-clap news-of-you ones-hearing-of every-of injury-of-you being-fatal

כַף עָלֶיךָ כִּי עַל־ מִי לֹא־ עָבְרָה רָעָתְךָ תָּמִיד׃

endless cruelty-of-you she-came not whom? to for at-you hand

Multiply like grasshoppers,
multiply like locusts!
16 You have increased the number of your merchants
till they are more than the stars of the sky,
but like locusts they strip the land
and then fly away.
17 Your guards are like locusts,
your officials like swarms of locusts
that settle in the walls on a cold day—
but when the sun appears they fly away,
and no one knows where.

18 O king of Assyria, your shepherds[g] slumber;
your nobles lie down to rest.
Your people are scattered on the mountains
with no one to gather them.
19 Nothing can heal your wound;
your injury is fatal.
Everyone who hears the news about you
claps his hands at your fall,
for who has not felt
your endless cruelty?

g18 Or *rulers*

הַמַּשָּׂא אֲשֶׁר חָזָה חֲבַקּוּק הַנָּבִיא׃ עַד־אָנָה יְהוָה
Yahweh when? until (2) the-prophet Habakkuk he-received that the-oracle (1:1)

שִׁוַּעְתִּי וְלֹא תִשְׁמָע אֶזְעַק אֵלֶיךָ חָמָס וְלֹא
but-not violence to-you must-I-cry-out you-listen but-not must-I-call-for-help

תוֹשִׁיעַ׃ לָמָּה תַרְאֵנִי אָוֶן וְעָמָל תַּבִּיט
you-tolerate and-wrong injustice you-make-look-at-me for-why? (3) you-save

וְשֹׁד וְחָמָס לְנֶגְדִּי וַיְהִי רִיב וּמָדוֹן יִשָּׂא׃
he-abounds and-conflict strife and-he-is at-before-me and-violence indeed-destruction

עַל־כֵּן תָּפוּג תּוֹרָה וְלֹא־יֵצֵא לָנֶצַח מִשְׁפָּט כִּי
indeed justice to-ever he-prevails and-not law she-is-paralyzed this for (4)

רָשָׁע מַכְתִּיר אֶת־הַצַּדִּיק עַל־כֵּן יֵצֵא מִשְׁפָּט מְעֻקָּל׃
being-perverted justice he-goes-out that so the-righteous *** hemming-in wicked

רְאוּ בַגּוֹיִם וְהַבִּיטוּ וְהִתַּמְּהוּ תְּמָהוּ כִּי־פֹעַל פֹּעֵל
doing something for be-amazed! and-be-amazed! and-watch! at-the-nations look! (5)

בִּימֵיכֶם לֹא תַאֲמִינוּ כִּי יְסֻפָּר׃ כִּי־הִנְנִי מֵקִים אֶת־
*** raising-up see-I! indeed (6) he-was-told if you-would-believe not in-days-of-you

הַכַּשְׂדִּים הַגּוֹי הַמַּר וְהַנִּמְהָר הַהוֹלֵךְ
the-one-sweeping and-the-one-being-impetuous the-ruthless the-people the-Chaldeans

לְמֶרְחֲבֵי־אֶרֶץ לָרֶשֶׁת מִשְׁכָּנוֹת לֹּא־לוֹ׃ אָיֹם
feared (7) to-him not dwelling-places to-seize earth across-whole-parts-of

וְנוֹרָא הוּא מִמֶּנּוּ מִשְׁפָּטוֹ וּשְׂאֵתוֹ יֵצֵא׃
he-promotes and-honor-of-him law-of-him to-himself he and-one-being-dreaded

וְקַלּוּ מִנְּמֵרִים סוּסָיו וְחַדּוּ
and-they-are-fierce horses-of-him more-than-leopards and-they-are-swift (8)

מִזְּאֵבֵי עֶרֶב וּפָשׁוּ פָּרָשָׁיו וּפָרָשָׁיו
and-cavalries-of-him cavalries-of-him and-they-gallop dusk more-than-wolves-of

מֵרָחוֹק יָבֹאוּ יָעֻפוּ כְּנֶשֶׁר חָשׁ לֶאֱכוֹל׃ כֻּלֹּה
all-of-him (9) to-devour swooping like-vulture they-fly they-come from-afar

לְחָמָס יָבוֹא מְגַמַּת פְּנֵיהֶם קָדִימָה וַיֶּאֱסֹף כַּחוֹל
like-the-sand and-he-gathers to-desert faces-of-them horde-of he-comes for-violence

שֶׁבִי׃ וְהוּא בַּמְּלָכִים יִתְקַלָּס וְרֹזְנִים מִשְׂחָק לוֹ הוּא
he to-him scoff and-ones-ruling he-derides to-the-kings and-he (10) prisoner

לְכָל־מִבְצָר יִשְׂחָק וַיִּצְבֹּר עָפָר וַיִּלְכְּדָהּ׃
and-he-captures-her earthen-ramp and-he-builds he-laughs fortified-city at-all-of

אָז חָלַף רוּחַ וַיַּעֲבֹר וְאָשֵׁם זוּ כֹחוֹ
strength-of-him who indeed-he-is-guilty and-he-goes-on wind he-sweeps-past then (11)

לֵאלֹהוֹ׃ הֲלוֹא אַתָּה מִקֶּדֶם יְהוָה אֱלֹהַי קְדֹשִׁי
Holy-One-of-me God-of-me Yahweh from-everlasting you not? (12) as-god-of-him

**1** The oracle that Habakkuk the prophet received.

*Habakkuk's Complaint*

2 How long, O LORD, must I call for help,
but you do not listen?
Or cry out to you, "Violence!"
but you do not save?
3 Why do you make me look at injustice?
Why do you tolerate wrong?
Destruction and violence are before me;
there is strife, and conflict abounds.
4 Therefore the law is paralyzed,
and justice never prevails.
The wicked hem in the righteous,
so that justice is perverted.

*The LORD's Answer*

5 "Look at the nations and watch—
and be utterly amazed.
For I am going to do something in your days
that you would not believe,
even if you were told.
6 I am raising up the Babylonians,[a]
that ruthless and impetuous people,
who sweep across the whole earth
to seize dwelling places not their own.
7 They are a feared and dreaded people;
they are a law to themselves
and promote their own honor.
8 Their horses are swifter than leopards,
fiercer than wolves at dusk.
Their cavalry gallops headlong;
their horsemen come from afar.
They fly like a vulture swooping to devour;
9 they all come bent on violence.
Their hordes[b] advance like a desert wind
and gather prisoners like sand.
10 They deride kings
and scoff at rulers.
They laugh at all fortified cities;
they build earthen ramps and capture them.
11 Then they sweep past like the wind and go on—
guilty men, whose own strength is their god."

*Habakkuk's Second Complaint*

12 O LORD, are you not from everlasting?
My God, my Holy One, we

[a] 6 Or *Chaldeans*
[b] 9 The meaning of the Hebrew for this word is uncertain.

לֹא נָמוּת יְהוָה לְמִשְׁפָּט שַׂמְתּוֹ וְצוּר לְהוֹכִיחַ
to-punish and-Rock you-appointed-him for-judgment Yahweh we-will-die not

יְסַדְתּוֹ׃ טְהוֹר עֵינַיִם מֵרְאוֹת רָע וְהַבִּיט אֶל־
to and-to-tolerate evil than-to-look-on eyes pureness-of (13) you-ordained-him

עָמָל לֹא תוּכָל לָמָּה תַבִּיט בּוֹגְדִים תַּחֲרִישׁ
are-you-silent ones-being-treacherous you-tolerate for-why? you-can not wrong

בְּבַלַּע רָשָׁע צַדִּיק מִמֶּנּוּ׃ וַתַּעֲשֶׂה אָדָם כִּדְגֵי
like-fishes-of man and-you-made (14) more-than-him righteous wicked while-to-swallow

הַיָּם כְּרֶמֶשׂ לֹא־ מֹשֵׁל בּוֹ׃ כֻּלֹּה בְּחַכָּה הֵעֲלָה
he-pulls-up with-hook all-of-him (15) over-him one-ruling not like-creature the-sea

יְגֹרֵהוּ בְחֶרְמוֹ וְיַאַסְפֵהוּ בְּמִכְמַרְתּוֹ עַל־ כֵּן
so for in-dragnet-of-him and-he-gathers-up-him in-net-of-him he-catches-him

יִשְׂמַח וְיָגִיל׃ עַל־ כֵּן יְזַבֵּחַ לְחֶרְמוֹ
to-net-of-him he-sacrifices this for (16) and-he-is-glad he-rejoices

וִיקַטֵּר לְמִכְמַרְתּוֹ כִּי בָהֵמָּה שָׁמֵן חֶלְקוֹ
life-of-him luxurious by-those for to-dragnet-of-him and-he-burns-incense

וּמַאֲכָלוֹ בְּרִאָה׃ הַעַל כֵּן יָרִיק חֶרְמוֹ וְתָמִיד
and-continually net-of-him will-he-empty this for? (17) choice and-food-of-him

לַהֲרֹג גּוֹיִם לֹא יַחְמוֹל׃ עַל־ מִשְׁמַרְתִּי אֶעֱמֹדָה
I-will-stand watch-of-me at (2:1) he-will-show-mercy not nations to-destroy

וְאֶתְיַצְּבָה עַל־ מָצוֹר וַאֲצַפֶּה לִרְאוֹת מַה־ יְדַבֶּר־ בִּי
to-me he-will-say what to-see and-I-will-look rampart on and-I-will-station-myself

וּמָה אָשִׁיב עַל־ תּוֹכַחְתִּי׃ וַיַּעֲנֵנִי יְהוָה
Yahweh then-he-replied-to-me (2) complaint-of-me to I-shall-answer and-what

וַיֹּאמֶר כְּתוֹב חָזוֹן וּבָאֵר עַל־ הַלֻּחוֹת לְמַעַן יָרוּץ
he-may-run so-that the-tablets on and-make-plain! revelation write-down! and-he-said

קוֹרֵא בוֹ׃ כִּי עוֹד חָזוֹן לַמּוֹעֵד וְיָפֵחַ
and-he-speaks for-the-appointed-time revelation yet for (3) with-him one-being-herald

לַקֵּץ וְלֹא יְכַזֵּב אִם־ יִתְמַהְמָהּ חַכֵּה־ לוֹ כִּי־ בֹא
to-come for for-him wait! he-linger though he-will-prove-false and-not of-the-end

יָבֹא לֹא יְאַחֵר׃ הִנֵּה עֻפְּלָה לֹא־ יָשְׁרָה
she-is-upright not she-is-puffed-up see! (4) he-will-delay not he-will-come

נַפְשׁוֹ בּוֹ וְצַדִּיק בֶּאֱמוּנָתוֹ יִחְיֶה׃ וְאַף כִּי־
indeed and-also (5) he-will-live by-faith-of-him but-righteous in-him desire-of-him

הַיַּיִן בּוֹגֵד גֶּבֶר יָהִיר וְלֹא יִנְוֶה אֲשֶׁר הִרְחִיב
he-makes-large because he-is-at-rest and-never arrogant man betraying the-wine

כִּשְׁאוֹל נַפְשׁוֹ וְהוּא כַמָּוֶת וְלֹא יִשְׂבָּע וַיֶּאֱסֹף
and-he-gathers he-is-satisfied that-never like-the-death and-he greed-of-him like-Sheol

---

will not die.
O LORD, you have appointed them to execute judgment;
O Rock, you have ordained them to punish.
13 Your eyes are too pure to look on evil;
you cannot tolerate wrong.
Why then do you tolerate the treacherous?
Why are you silent while the wicked
swallow up those more righteous than themselves?
14 You have made men like fish in the sea,
like sea creatures that have no ruler.
15 The wicked foe pulls all of them up with hooks,
he catches them in his net,
he gathers them up in his dragnet;
and so he rejoices and is glad.
16 Therefore he sacrifices to his net
and burns incense to his dragnet,
for by his net he lives in luxury
and enjoys the choicest food.
17 Is he to keep on emptying his net,
destroying nations without mercy?

2 I will stand at my watch
and station myself on the ramparts;
I will look to see what he will say to me,
and what answer I am to give to this complaint.[c]

*The LORD's Answer*

2 Then the LORD replied:

"Write down the revelation
and make it plain on tablets
so that a herald[d] may run with it.
3 For the revelation awaits an appointed time;
it speaks of the end
and will not prove false.
Though it linger, wait for it;
it[e] will certainly come and will not delay.

4 "See, he is puffed up;
his desires are not upright—
but the righteous will live by his faith[f]—
5 indeed, wine betrays him;
he is arrogant and never at rest.
Because he is as greedy as the grave[g]
and like death is never satisfied,

[c]1 Or *and what to answer when I am rebuked*
[d]2 Or *so that whoever reads it*
[e]3 Or *Though he linger, wait for him; / he*
[f]4 Or *faithfulness*
[g]5 Hebrew *Sheol*

אֵלָיו כָּל־הַגּוֹיִם וַיִּקְבֹּץ אֵלָיו כָּל־הָעַמִּים׃
the-peoples all-of to-himself and-he-takes-captive the-nations all-of to-himself

הֲלוֹא־אֵלֶּה כֻלָּם עָלָיו מָשָׁל יִשָּׂאוּ וּמְלִיצָה
with-ridicule they-will-take-up taunt against-him all-of-them these not? (6)

חִידוֹת לוֹ וְיֹאמַר הוֹי הַמַּרְבֶּה לֹּא־לוֹ עַד־מָתַי
when? until to-him not the-one-piling-up woe! and-he-will-say to-him scorns

וּמַכְבִּיד עָלָיו עַבְטִיט׃ הֲלוֹא פֶתַע יָקוּמוּ
will-they-rise suddenly not? (7) extortion to-him and-one-making-wealthy

נֹשְׁכֶיךָ וְיִקְצוּ מְזַעְזְעֶיךָ
ones-making-tremble-you and-will-they-wake-up ones-being-debtors-of-you

וְהָיִיתָ לִמְשִׁסּוֹת לָמוֹ׃ כִּי אַתָּה שַׁלּוֹתָ גּוֹיִם רַבִּים
many-ones nations you-plundered you because (8) to-them to-victim then-you-will-become

יְשָׁלּוּךָ כָּל־יֶתֶר עַמִּים מִדְּמֵי אָדָם וַחֲמַס־
and-destruction-of man for-bloods-of peoples one-left-of all-of they-will-plunder-you

אֶרֶץ קִרְיָה וְכָל־יֹשְׁבֵי בָהּ׃ הוֹי בֹּצֵעַ בֶּצַע רָע
unjust gain one-gaining woe! (9) in-her ones-being-peoples-of and-all-of city land

לְבֵיתוֹ לָשׂוּם בַּמָּרוֹם קִנּוֹ לְהִנָּצֵל מִכַּף־רָע׃
ruin from-clutch-of to-escape nest-of-him on-the-height to-set for-realm-of-him

יָעַצְתָּ בֹּשֶׁת לְבֵיתֶךָ קְצוֹת־עַמִּים רַבִּים וְחוֹטֵא
thus-forfeiting many-ones peoples ruins-of of-house-of-you shame you-plotted (10)

נַפְשֶׁךָ׃ כִּי־אֶבֶן מִקִּיר תִּזְעָק וְכָפִיס מֵעֵץ
of-woodwork and-beam she-will-cry-out of-wall stone indeed (11) life-of-you

יַעֲנֶנָּה׃ הוֹי בֹּנֶה עִיר בְּדָמִים וְכוֹנֵן
and-establishing with-bloodsheds city one-building woe! (12) he-will-echo-her

קִרְיָה בְּעַוְלָה׃ הֲלוֹא הִנֵּה מֵאֵת יְהוָה צְבָאוֹת וְיִיגְעוּ עַמִּים
peoples that-they-labor Hosts Yahweh-of from-with see! not? (13) by-crime town

בְּדֵי־אֵשׁ וּלְאֻמִּים בְּדֵי־רִיק יִעָפוּ׃
they-exhaust-themselves nothing for-sufficiency-of that-nations fire for-sufficiency-of

כִּי תִּמָּלֵא הָאָרֶץ לָדַעַת אֶת־כְּבוֹד יְהוָה כַּמַּיִם
as-the-waters Yahweh glory-of *** to-know the-earth she-will-be-filled for (14)

יְכַסּוּ עַל־יָם׃ הוֹי מַשְׁקֵה רֵעֵהוּ מְסַפֵּחַ
pouring neighbor-of-him one-giving-drink-of woe! (15) sea over they-cover

חֲמָתְךָ וְאַף שַׁכֵּר לְמַעַן הַבִּיט עַל־מְעוֹרֵיהֶם׃
naked-bodies-of-them on to-gaze so-that to-be-drunk even-till inflaming-wine-of-you

שָׂבַעְתָּ קָלוֹן מִכָּבוֹד שְׁתֵה גַם־אַתָּה וְהֵעָרֵל
and-be-exposed! you also drink! instead-of-glory shame you-will-be-filled (16)

תִּסּוֹב עָלֶיךָ כּוֹס יְמִין יְהוָה וְקִיקָלוֹן עַל־כְּבוֹדֶךָ׃
glory-of-you over and-disgrace Yahweh right-hand-of cup-of to-you she-comes-around

he gathers to himself all the nations
and takes captive all the peoples.

6 "Will not all of them taunt him with ridicule and scorn, saying,

" 'Woe to him who piles up stolen goods
and makes himself wealthy by extortion!
How long must this go on?'
7 Will not your debtors[h] suddenly arise?
Will they not wake up and make you tremble?
Then you will become their victim.
8 Because you have plundered many nations,
the peoples who are left will plunder you.
For you have shed man's blood;
you have destroyed lands and cities and everyone in them.

9 "Woe to him who builds his realm by unjust gain
to set his nest on high,
to escape the clutches of ruin!
10 You have plotted the ruin of many peoples,
shaming your own house and forfeiting your life.
11 The stones of the wall will cry out,
and the beams of the woodwork will echo it.

12 "Woe to him who builds a city with bloodshed
and establishes a town by crime!
13 Has not the LORD Almighty determined
that the people's labor is only fuel for the fire,
that the nations exhaust themselves for nothing?
14 For the earth will be filled with the knowledge of the glory of the LORD,
as the waters cover the sea.

15 "Woe to him who gives drink to his neighbors,
pouring it from the wineskin till they are drunk,
so that he can gaze on their naked bodies.
16 You will be filled with shame instead of glory.
Now it is your turn! Drink and be exposed[i]!
The cup from the LORD's right hand is coming around to you,
and disgrace will cover your glory.

[h] 7 Or *creditors*
[i] 16 Masoretic Text; Dead Sea Scrolls, Aquila, Vulgate and Syriac (see also Septuagint) *and stagger*

כִּי חֲמַס לְבָנוֹן֙ יְכַסֶּ֔ךָּ וְשֹׁ֥ד בְּהֵמ֖וֹת

animals and-destruction-of he-will-overwhelm-you Lebanon violence-of indeed (17)

יְחִיתַ֑ן מִדְּמֵ֤י אָדָם֙ וַחֲמַס־ אֶ֔רֶץ קִרְיָ֖ה וְכָל־

and-every-of city land and-destruction-of man for-bloods-of he-will-terrify-them

יֹ֥שְׁבֵי בָֽהּ׃ מָה־ הוֹעִ֣יל פֶּ֗סֶל כִּ֤י פְסָלוֹ֙

he-carved-him since idol he-has-value what? (18) in-her ones-living-of

יֹֽצְר֔וֹ מַסֵּכָ֖ה וּמ֣וֹרֶה שָּׁ֑קֶר כִּ֣י בָטַ֞ח יֹצֵ֤ר יִצְרוֹ֙

creation-of-him one-forming he-trusts for lie even-one-teaching image one-forming-him

עָלָ֔יו לַעֲשׂ֖וֹת אֱלִילִ֥ים אִלְּמִֽים׃ ה֣וֹי אֹמֵ֤ר לָעֵץ֙

to-the-wood one-saying woe! (19) ones-without-speech idols to-make in-him

הָקִ֔יצָה ע֖וּרִי לְאֶ֣בֶן דּוּמָ֑ם ה֣וּא יוֹרֶ֔ה הִנֵּה־ה֗וּא

he see! can-he-give-guidance he lifelessness to-stone-of wake-up! come-to-life!

תָּפ֛וּשׂ זָהָ֥ב וָכֶ֖סֶף וְכָל־ ר֖וּחַ אֵ֥ין בְּקִרְבּֽוֹ׃

in-inside-of-him there-is-not breath and-any-of and-silver gold being-covered

וַֽיהוָ֖ה בְּהֵיכַ֣ל קָדְשׁ֑וֹ הַ֥ס מִפָּנָ֖יו כָּל־ הָאָֽרֶץ׃

the-earth all-of at-before-him silence! holiness-of-him in-temple-of but-Yahweh (20)

תְּפִלָּ֖ה לַחֲבַקּ֣וּק הַנָּבִ֑יא עַ֖ל שִׁגְיֹנֽוֹת׃ יְהוָ֗ה שָׁמַ֣עְתִּי שִׁמְעֲךָ֮

fame-of-you I-heard Yahweh (2) shigionoth on the-prophet of-Habakkuk prayer (3:1)

יָרֵאתִי֒ יְהוָ֗ה פָּֽעָלְךָ֙ בְּקֶ֤רֶב שָׁנִים֙ חַיֵּ֔יהוּ בְּקֶ֥רֶב שָׁנִ֖ים

years in-midst-of renew-him! years in-midst-of deed-of-you Yahweh I-stand-in-awe

תּוֹדִ֑יעַ בְּרֹ֖גֶז רַחֵ֥ם תִּזְכּֽוֹר׃ אֱל֙וֹהַ֙* מִתֵּימָ֣ן יָב֔וֹא וְקָד֥וֹשׁ

even-Holy-One he-came from-Teman God (3) you-remember mercy in-wrath you-make-known

מֵֽהַר־ פָּארָ֖ן סֶ֑לָה כִּסָּ֤ה שָׁמַ֙יִם֙ הוֹד֔וֹ וּתְהִלָּת֖וֹ מָלְאָ֥ה

she-filled and-praise-of-him glory-of-him heavens he-covered selah Paran from-Mount-of

הָאָֽרֶץ׃ וְנֹ֙גַהּ֙ כָּא֣וֹר תִּֽהְיֶ֔ה קַרְנַ֥יִם מִיָּד֖וֹ ל֑וֹ

to-him from-hand-of-him rays she-was like-the-sunrise and-splendor (4) the-earth

וְשָׁ֖ם חֶבְי֥וֹן עֻזֹּֽה°׃ לְפָנָ֖יו יֵ֣לֶךְ דָּ֑בֶר וְיֵצֵ֥א

and-he-followed plague he-went before-him (5) power-of-him hiding-place-of and-there

רֶ֖שֶׁף לְרַגְלָֽיו׃ עָמַ֣ד ׀ וַיְמֹ֣דֶד אֶ֗רֶץ רָאָה֙

he-looked earth and-he-shook he-stood (6) to-steps-of-him pestilence

וַיַּתֵּ֣ר גּוֹיִ֔ם וַיִּתְפֹּֽצְצוּ֙ הַרְרֵי־ עַ֔ד שַׁח֖וּ

they-collapsed ancient-time mountains-of and-they-crumbled nations and-he-made-tremble

גִּבְע֣וֹת עוֹלָ֑ם הֲלִיכ֥וֹת עוֹלָ֖ם לֽוֹ׃ תַּ֣חַת אָ֔וֶן רָאִ֖יתִי אָהֳלֵ֣י כוּשָׁ֑ן

Cushan tents-of I-saw distress in (7) to-him eternity ways-of age-old-time hills-of

יִרְגְּז֕וּן יְרִיע֖וֹת אֶ֥רֶץ מִדְיָֽן׃ הֲבִנְהָרִים֙ חָרָ֣ה יְהוָ֔ה

Yahweh was-he-angry with-rivers? (8) Midian land-of dwellings-of they-were-in-anguish

אִ֤ם בַּנְּהָרִים֙ אַפֶּ֔ךָ אִם־ בַּיָּ֖ם עֶבְרָתֶ֑ךָ כִּ֤י תִרְכַּב֙

you-rode when rage-of-you against-the-sea or wrath-of-you against-the-streams or

17 The violence you have done to
Lebanon will overwhelm
you,
and your destruction of
animals will terrify you.
For you have shed man's
blood;
you have destroyed lands
and cities and everyone
in them.

18 "Of what value is an idol,
since a man has carved
it?
Or an image that teaches
lies?
For he who makes it trusts in
his own creation;
he makes idols that cannot
speak.
19 Woe to him who says to wood,
'Come to life!'
Or to lifeless stone, 'Wake
up!'
Can it give guidance?
It is covered with gold and
silver;
there is no breath in it.
20 But the LORD is in his holy
temple;
let all the earth be silent
before him."

*Habakkuk's Prayer*

3 A prayer of Habakkuk the prophet. On *shigionoth.*[j]

2 LORD, I have heard of your
fame;
I stand in awe of your
deeds, O LORD.
Renew them in our day,
in our time make them
known;
in wrath remember mercy.

3 God came from Teman,
the Holy One from Mount
Paran. *Selah*[k]
His glory covered the heavens
and his praise filled the
earth.
4 His splendor was like the
sunrise;
rays flashed from his hand,
where his power was
hidden.
5 Plague went before him;
pestilence followed his steps.
6 He stood, and shook the earth;
he looked, and made the
nations tremble.
The ancient mountains
crumbled
and the age-old hills
collapsed.
His ways are eternal.
7 I saw the tents of Cushan in
distress,
the dwellings of Midian in
anguish.

8 Were you angry with the
rivers, O LORD?
Was your wrath against the
streams?
Did you rage against the sea
when you rode with your

*j*1 Probably a literary or musical term
*k*3 A word of uncertain meaning; possibly a musical term; also in verses 9 and 13

*3 Most mss have *mappiq* in the *he* (הּ־).

°4 ק עזו

עַל־סוּסֶיךָ מַרְכְּבֹתֶיךָ יְשׁוּעָה׃ עֶרְיָה תֵעוֹר קַשְׁתֶּךָ
bow-of-you she-is-uncovered uncovered (9) victory chariots-of-you horses-of-you with

שְׁבֻעוֹת מַטּוֹת אֹמֶר סֶלָה נְהָרוֹת תְּבַקַּע־אָרֶץ׃ רָאוּךָ
they-saw-you (10) earth you-split rivers selah calling arrows-of ones-being-sworn

יָחִילוּ הָרִים זֶרֶם מַיִם עָבָר נָתַן תְּהוֹם קוֹלוֹ
roar-of-him deep he-gave he-swept-by waters torrent-of mountains they-writhed

רוֹם יָדֵיהוּ נָשָׂא׃ שֶׁמֶשׁ יָרֵחַ עָמַד זְבֻלָה לְאוֹר
at-glint-of in-heaven he-stood-still moon sun (11) he-lifted waves-of-him on-high

חִצֶּיךָ יְהַלֵּכוּ לְנֹגַהּ בְּרַק חֲנִיתֶךָ׃ בְּזַעַם תִּצְעַד־
you-strode in-wrath (12) spear-of-you lightning-of at-flash-of they-flew arrows-of-you

אָרֶץ בְּאַף תָּדוּשׁ גּוֹיִם׃ יָצָאתָ לְיֵשַׁע עַמֶּךָ
people-of-you to-deliverance-of you-came-out (13) nations you-threshed in-anger earth

לְיֵשַׁע אֶת־מְשִׁיחֶךָ מָחַצְתָּ רֹּאשׁ מִבֵּית רָשָׁע
wickedness of-land-of leader you-crushed anointed-one-of-you *** to-deliverance-of

עָרוֹת יְסוֹד עַד־צַוָּאר סֶלָה׃ נָקַבְתָּ בְמַטָּיו רֹאשׁ
head with-spears-of-him you-pierced (14) selah head to foot to-be-stripped

פְּרָזָו יִסְעֲרוּ לַהֲפִיצֵנִי עֲלִיצֻתָם כְּמוֹ־לֶאֱכֹל
to-devour as gloating-of-them to-scatter-me they-stormed-out warriors-of-him

עָנִי בַּמִּסְתָּר׃ דָּרַכְתָּ בַיָּם סוּסֶיךָ חֹמֶר
churning-of horses-of-you on-the-sea you-trampled (15) in-the-hiding wretched

מַיִם רַבִּים׃ שָׁמַעְתִּי ׀ וַתִּרְגַּז בִּטְנִי לְקוֹל צָלֲלוּ
they-quivered at-sound heart-of-me and-she-trembled I-heard (16) great-ones waters

שְׂפָתַי יָבוֹא רָקָב בַּעֲצָמַי וְתַחְתַּי אֶרְגָּז אֲשֶׁר
yet I-trembled and-legs-of-me into-bones-of-me decay he-crept lips-of-me

אָנוּחַ לְיוֹם צָרָה לַעֲלוֹת לְעַם יְגוּדֶנּוּ׃
he-invades-us on-nation to-come calamity for-day-of I-will-wait-patiently

כִּי־תְאֵנָה לֹא־תִפְרָח וְאֵין יְבוּל בַּגְּפָנִים כִּחֵשׁ
he-fails on-the-vines grape and-there-is-no she-buds not fig-tree though (17)

מַעֲשֵׂה־זַיִת וּשְׁדֵמוֹת לֹא־עָשָׂה אֹכֶל גָּזַר מִמִּכְלָה צֹאן
sheep from-pen he-cuts-off food he-produces not and-fields olive crop-of

וְאֵין בָּקָר בָּרְפָתִים׃ וַאֲנִי בַּיהוָה אֶעְלוֹזָה
I-will-rejoice in-Yahweh yet-I (18) in-the-stalls cattle and-there-is-no

אָגִילָה בֵּאלֹהֵי יִשְׁעִי׃ יְהוִה אֲדֹנָי חֵילִי
strength-of-me Sovereign Yahweh (19) salvation-of-me in-God-of I-will-be-joyful

וַיָּשֶׂם רַגְלַי כָּאַיָּלוֹת וְעַל בָּמוֹתַי
heights-of-me and-to like-the-deers feet-of-me and-he-makes

יַדְרִכֵנִי לַמְנַצֵּחַ בִּנְגִינוֹתָי׃
on-stringed-instruments-of-me for-the-one-directing-music he-makes-go-me

horses
and your victorious chariots?
9 You uncovered your bow,
you called for many arrows. *Selah*
You split the earth with rivers;
10 the mountains saw you and writhed.
Torrents of water swept by;
the deep roared
and lifted its waves on high.
11 Sun and moon stood still in the heavens
at the glint of your flying arrows,
at the lightning of your flashing spear.
12 In wrath you strode through the earth
and in anger you threshed the nations.
13 You came out to deliver your people,
to save your anointed one.
You crushed the leader of the land of wickedness,
you stripped him from head to foot. *Selah*
14 With his own spear you pierced his head
when his warriors stormed out to scatter us,
gloating as though about to devour
the wretched who were in hiding.
15 You trampled the sea with your horses,
churning the great waters.
16 I heard and my heart pounded,
my lips quivered at the sound;
decay crept into my bones,
and my legs trembled.
Yet I will wait patiently for the day of calamity
to come on the nation invading us.
17 Though the fig tree does not bud
and there are no grapes on the vines,
though the olive crop fails
and the fields produce no food,
though there are no sheep in the pen
and no cattle in the stalls,
18 yet I will rejoice in the LORD,
I will be joyful in God my Savior.
19 The Sovereign LORD is my strength;
he makes my feet like the feet of a deer,
he enables me to go on the heights.
For the director of music. On my stringed instruments.

°*14* ק פרזיו

דְּבַר־ יְהוָה ׀ אֲשֶׁר הָיָה אֶל־ צְפַנְיָה בֶּן־ כּוּשִׁי בֶן־ גְּדַלְיָה
Gedaliah son-of Cushi son-of Zephaniah to he-came that Yahweh word-of (1:1)

בֶּן־ אֲמַרְיָה בֶּן־ חִזְקִיָּה בִּימֵי יֹאשִׁיָּהוּ בֶן־ אָמוֹן מֶלֶךְ יְהוּדָה׃
Judah king-of Amon son-of Josiah during-days-of Hezekiah son-of Amariah son-of

אָסֹף אָסֵף כֹּל מֵעַל פְּנֵי הָאֲדָמָה
the-earth faces-of from-upon everything I-will-sweep-away to-sweep-away (2)

נְאֻם־ יְהוָה׃ אָסֵף אָדָם וּבְהֵמָה אָסֵף
I-will-sweep-away and-animal man I-will-sweep-away (3) Yahweh declaration-of

עוֹף־ הַשָּׁמַיִם וּדְגֵי הַיָּם וְהַמַּכְשֵׁלוֹת אֶת־ הָרְשָׁעִים
the-wicked-ones with and-the-heaps-of-rubble the-sea and-fishes-of the-airs bird-of

וְהִכְרַתִּי אֶת־ הָאָדָם מֵעַל פְּנֵי הָאֲדָמָה נְאֻם־ יְהוָה׃
Yahweh declaration-of the-earth faces-of from-on the-man *** when-I-cut-off

וְנָטִיתִי יָדִי עַל־ יְהוּדָה וְעַל כָּל־ יוֹשְׁבֵי
ones-living-of all-of and-against Judah against hand-of-me and-I-will-stretch-out (4)

יְרוּשָׁלָםִ וְהִכְרַתִּי מִן־ הַמָּקוֹם הַזֶּה אֶת־ שְׁאָר הַבַּעַל אֶת־
*** the-Baal remnant-of *** the-this the-place from and-I-will-cut-off Jerusalem

שֵׁם הַכְּמָרִים עִם־ הַכֹּהֲנִים׃ וְאֶת־ הַמִּשְׁתַּחֲוִים עַל־
on the-ones-bowing-down and (5) the-idolatrous-priests and the-pagan-priests name-of

הַגַּגּוֹת לִצְבָא הַשָּׁמַיִם וְאֶת־ הַמִּשְׁתַּחֲוִים הַנִּשְׁבָּעִים לַיהוָה
by-Yahweh the-ones-swearing the-ones-bowing-down and-the-heavens to-host-of the-roofs

וְהַנִּשְׁבָּעִים בְּמַלְכָּם׃ וְאֶת־ הַנְּסוֹגִים מֵאַחֲרֵי יְהוָה
Yahweh from-after the-ones-turning-back and (6) by-Malcam also-the-ones-swearing

וַאֲשֶׁר לֹא־ בִקְשׁוּ אֶת־ יְהוָה וְלֹא דְרָשֻׁהוּ׃ הַס
silence! (7) they-inquire-of-him or-not Yahweh *** they-seek neither and-who

מִפְּנֵי אֲדֹנָי יְהוִה כִּי קָרוֹב יוֹם יְהוָה כִּי־ הֵכִין יְהוָה זֶבַח
sacrifice Yahweh he-prepared indeed Yahweh day-of near for Yahweh Sovereign at-before

הִקְדִּישׁ קְרֻאָיו׃ וְהָיָה בְּיוֹם זֶבַח
sacrifice-of on-day-of and-he-will-be (8) ones-being-invited-of-him he-consecrated

יְהוָה וּפָקַדְתִּי עַל־ הַשָּׂרִים וְעַל־ בְּנֵי הַמֶּלֶךְ וְעַל כָּל־
all-of and-to the-king sons-of and-to the-princes to then-I-will-punish Yahweh

הַלֹּבְשִׁים מַלְבּוּשׁ נָכְרִי׃ וּפָקַדְתִּי עַל כָּל־
all-of to and-I-will-punish (9) foreigner clothing-of the-ones-being-clad

הַדּוֹלֵג עַל־ הַמִּפְתָּן בַּיּוֹם הַהוּא הַמְמַלְאִים
the-ones-filling the-that on-the-day the-threshold on the-ones-avoiding-stepping

בֵּית אֲדֹנֵיהֶם חָמָס וּמִרְמָה׃ וְהָיָה בַיּוֹם הַהוּא
the-that on-the-day and-he-will-be (10) and-deceit violence gods-of-them temple-of

נְאֻם־ יְהוָה קוֹל צְעָקָה מִשַּׁעַר הַדָּגִים וִילָלָה מִן־
from and-wailing the-Fishes from-Gate-of cry sound-of Yahweh declaration-of

1 The word of the LORD that came to Zephaniah son of Cushi, the son of Gedaliah, the son of Amariah, the son of Hezekiah, during the reign of Josiah son of Amon king of Judah:

*Warning of Coming Destruction*

2 "I will sweep away everything
from the face of the earth,"
declares the LORD.
3 "I will sweep away both men
and animals;
I will sweep away the birds
of the air
and the fish of the sea.
The wicked will have only
heaps of rubble[a]
when I cut off man from the
face of the earth,"
declares the LORD.

*Against Judah*

4 "I will stretch out my hand
against Judah
and against all who live in
Jerusalem.
I will cut off from this place
every remnant of Baal,
the names of the pagan and
the idolatrous priests—
5 those who bow down on the
roofs
to worship the starry host,
those who bow down and
swear by the LORD
and who also swear by
Molech,[b]
6 those who turn back from
following the LORD
and neither seek the LORD
nor inquire of him.
7 Be silent before the Sovereign
LORD,
for the day of the LORD is
near.
The LORD has prepared a
sacrifice;
he has consecrated those he
has invited.
8 On the day of the LORD's
sacrifice
I will punish the princes
and the king's sons
and all those clad
in foreign clothes.
9 On that day I will punish
all who avoid stepping on
the threshold,[c]
who fill the temple of their
gods
with violence and deceit.
10 "On that day," declares the
LORD,
"a cry will go up from the
Fish Gate,

[a]3 The meaning of the Hebrew for this line is uncertain.
[b]5 Hebrew *Malcam,* that is, Milcom
[c]9 See 1 Samuel 5:5.

הַמִּשְׁנֶה וְשֶׁבֶר גָּדוֹל מֵהַגְּבָעוֹת׃ הֵילִילוּ יֹשְׁבֵי
ones-living-of wail! (11) from-the-hills loud and-crash the-New-Quarter

הַמַּכְתֵּשׁ כִּי נִדְמָה כָּל־ עַם כְּנַעַן
merchant people-of all-of he-will-be-wiped-out for the-market-district

נִכְרְתוּ כָּל־ נְטִילֵי כָסֶף׃ וְהָיָה בָּעֵת
at-the-time and-he-will-be (12) silver traders-of all-of they-will-be-ruined

הַהִיא אֲחַפֵּשׂ אֶת־ יְרוּשָׁלִַם בַּנֵּרוֹת וּפָקַדְתִּי עַל־הָאֲנָשִׁים
the-men to and-I-will-punish with-the-lamps Jerusalem *** I-will-search the-that

הַקֹּפְאִים עַל־ שִׁמְרֵיהֶם הָאֹמְרִים בִּלְבָבָם לֹא־
not in-heart-of-them the-ones-thinking dregs-of-them on the-ones-being-complacent

יֵיטִיב יְהוָה וְלֹא יָרֵעַ׃ וְהָיָה חֵילָם
wealth-of-them and-he-will-be (13) he-will-do-bad or-not Yahweh he-will-do-good

לִמְשִׁסָּה וּבָתֵּיהֶם לִשְׁמָמָה וּבָנוּ בָתִּים וְלֹא
but-not houses and-they-will-build for-demolishing and-houses-of-them for-plunder

יֵשֵׁבוּ וְנָטְעוּ כְרָמִים וְלֹא יִשְׁתּוּ אֶת־
*** they-will-drink but-not vineyards and-they-will-plant they-will-live-in

יֵינָם׃ קָרוֹב יוֹם־ יְהוָה הַגָּדוֹל קָרוֹב וּמַהֵר מְאֹד קוֹל יוֹם
day-of cry-of very and-quick near the-great Yahweh day-of near (14) wine-of-them

יְהוָה מַר צֹרֵחַ שָׁם גִּבּוֹר׃ יוֹם עֶבְרָה הַיּוֹם הַהוּא יוֹם
day-of the-that the-day wrath day-of (15) warrior there shouting bitter Yahweh

צָרָה וּמְצוּקָה יוֹם שֹׁאָה וּמְשׁוֹאָה יוֹם חֹשֶׁךְ וַאֲפֵלָה
and-gloom darkness day-of and-ruin trouble day-of and-anguish distress

יוֹם עָנָן וַעֲרָפֶל׃ יוֹם שׁוֹפָר וּתְרוּעָה עַל
against and-battle-cry trumpet day-of (16) and-blackness cloud day-of

הֶעָרִים הַבְּצֻרוֹת וְעַל הַפִּנּוֹת הַגְּבֹהוֹת׃
the-towers the-corners and-against the-ones-being-fortified the-cities

וַהֲצֵרֹתִי לָאָדָם וְהָלְכוּ כַּעִוְרִים
like-the-blind-men and-they-will-walk on-the-people and-I-will-bring-distress (17)

כִּי לַיהוָה חָטָאוּ וְשֻׁפַּךְ דָּמָם
blood-of-them and-he-will-be-poured-out they-sinned against-Yahweh because

כֶּעָפָר וּלְחֻמָם כַּגְּלָלִים׃ גַּם־ כַּסְפָּם גַּם־
or silver-of-them either (18) like-the-filths and-entrail-of-them like-the-dust

זְהָבָם לֹא־ יוּכַל לְהַצִּילָם בְּיוֹם עֶבְרַת יְהוָה
Yahweh wrath-of on-day-of to-save-them he-will-be-able not gold-of-them

וּבְאֵשׁ קִנְאָתוֹ תֵּאָכֵל כָּל־ הָאָרֶץ כִּי־
for the-world whole-of she-will-be-consumed jealousy-of-him and-in-fire-of

כָלָה אַךְ־ נִבְהָלָה יַעֲשֶׂה אֵת כָּל־ יֹשְׁבֵי הָאָרֶץ׃
the-earth ones-living-of all-of *** he-will-make being-sudden indeed end

wailing from the New Quarter,
and a loud crash from the hills.
11Wail, you who live in the market district[d];
all your merchants will be wiped out,
all who trade with[e] silver will be ruined.
12At that time I will search Jerusalem with lamps
and punish those who are complacent,
who are like wine left on its dregs,
who think, 'The LORD will do nothing,
either good or bad.'
13Their wealth will be plundered,
their houses demolished.
They will build houses
but not live in them;
they will plant vineyards
but not drink the wine.

*The Great Day of the LORD*

14"The great day of the LORD is near—
near and coming quickly.
Listen! The cry on the day of the LORD will be bitter,
the shouting of the warrior there.
15That day will be a day of wrath,
a day of distress and anguish,
a day of trouble and ruin,
a day of darkness and gloom,
a day of clouds and blackness,
16a day of trumpet and battle cry
against the fortified cities
and against the corner towers.
17I will bring distress on the people
and they will walk like blind men,
because they have sinned against the LORD.
Their blood will be poured out like dust
and their entrails like filth.
18Neither their silver nor their gold
will be able to save them
on the day of the LORD's wrath.
In the fire of his jealousy
the whole world will be consumed,
for he will make a sudden end
of all who live in the earth."

[d]11 Or *the Mortar*
[e]11 Or *in*

הִתְקוֹשְׁשׁוּ וָקוֹשּׁוּ הַגּוֹי לֹא נִכְסָף׃ בְּטֶרֶם
at-before (2) being-ashamed not the-nation and-gather-together! gather-together! (2:1)

לֶדֶת חֹק כְּמֹץ עָבַר יוֹם בְּטֶרֶם ׀ לֹא־ יָבוֹא עֲלֵיכֶם
upon-you he-comes not at-before day he-sweeps-on like-chaff appointed-time to-arrive

חֲרוֹן אַף־ יְהוָה בְּטֶרֶם לֹא־ יָבוֹא עֲלֵיכֶם יוֹם אַף־ יְהוָה׃
Yahweh wrath-of day-of upon-you he-comes not at-before Yahweh anger-of fierceness-of

בַּקְּשׁוּ אֶת־ יְהוָה כָּל־ עַנְוֵי הָאָרֶץ אֲשֶׁר מִשְׁפָּטוֹ פָּעָלוּ
they-do command-of-him who the-land humble-ones-of all-of Yahweh *** seek! (3)

בַּקְּשׁוּ־ צֶדֶק בַּקְּשׁוּ עֲנָוָה אוּלַי תִּסָּתְרוּ בְּיוֹם אַף־
anger-of on-day-of you-will-be-sheltered perhaps humility seek! righteousness seek!

יְהוָה׃ כִּי עַזָּה עֲזוּבָה תִהְיֶה וְאַשְׁקְלוֹן לִשְׁמָמָה אַשְׁדּוֹד
Ashdod in-ruin and-Ashkelon she-will-be being-abandoned Gaza indeed (4) Yahweh

בַּצָּהֳרַיִם יְגָרְשׁוּהָ וְעֶקְרוֹן תֵּעָקֵר׃ הוֹי
woe! (5) she-will-be-uprooted and-Ekron they-will-empty-her at-the-middays

יֹשְׁבֵי חֶבֶל הַיָּם גּוֹי כְּרֵתִים דְּבַר־ יְהוָה עֲלֵיכֶם
against-you Yahweh word-of Kerethites people-of the-sea land-of ones-living-of

כְּנַעַן אֶרֶץ פְּלִשְׁתִּים וְהַאֲבַדְתִּיךְ מֵאֵין
from-there-will-be-no indeed-I-will-destroy-you Philistines land-of Canaan

יוֹשֵׁב׃ וְהָיְתָה חֶבֶל הַיָּם נְוֺת כְּרֹת
Kerethite dwelling-places-of the-sea land-of and-she-will-be (6) one-being-left

רֹעִים וְגִדְרוֹת צֹאן׃ וְהָיָה חֶבֶל לִשְׁאֵרִית בֵּית
house-of to-remnant-of land and-he-will-be (7) sheep and-pens-of ones-being-shepherds

יְהוּדָה עֲלֵיהֶם יִרְעוּן בְּבָתֵּי אַשְׁקְלוֹן בָּעֶרֶב
in-the-evening Ashkelon in-houses-of they-will-find-pasture in-them Judah

יִרְבָּצוּן כִּי יִפְקְדֵם יְהוָה אֱלֹהֵיהֶם וְשָׁב
and-he-will-restore God-of-them Yahweh he-will-care-for-them indeed they-will-lie-down

שְׁבוּתָם׃ שָׁמַעְתִּי חֶרְפַּת מוֹאָב וְגִדּוּפֵי בְּנֵי עַמּוֹן אֲשֶׁר חֵרְפוּ
they-insulted who Ammon sons-of and-taunts-of Moab insult-of I-heard (8) fortune-of-them

אֶת־ עַמִּי וַיַּגְדִּילוּ עַל־ גְּבוּלָם׃ לָכֵן חַי־ אָנִי
I alive therefore (9) land-of-them against and-they-made-threats people-of-me ***

נְאֻם יְהוָה צְבָאוֹת אֱלֹהֵי יִשְׂרָאֵל כִּי־ מוֹאָב כִּסְדֹם תִּהְיֶה
she-will-become like-Sodom Moab surely Israel God-of Hosts Yahweh-of declaration-of

וּבְנֵי עַמּוֹן כַּעֲמֹרָה מִמְשַׁק חָרוּל וּמִכְרֵה־ מֶלַח וּשְׁמָמָה
and-wasteland salt and-pit-of weed place-of like-Gomorrah Ammon and-sons-of

עַד־ עוֹלָם שְׁאֵרִית עַמִּי יְבָזּוּם וְיֶתֶר
and-survivor-of they-will-plunder-them people-of-me remnant-of forever to

גּוֹיִ יִנְחָלוּם׃ זֹאת לָהֶם תַּחַת גְּאוֹנָם כִּי
for pride-of-them in-return-for for-them this (10) they-will-inherit-them nation-of-me

2 Gather together, gather together,
O shameful nation,
[2]before the appointed time arrives
and that day sweeps on like chaff,
before the fierce anger of the LORD comes upon you,
before the day of the LORD's wrath comes upon you.
[3]Seek the LORD, all you humble of the land,
you who do what he commands.
Seek righteousness, seek humility;
perhaps you will be sheltered
on the day of the LORD's anger.

*Against Philistia*

[4]Gaza will be abandoned
and Ashkelon left in ruins.
At midday Ashdod will be emptied
and Ekron uprooted.
[5]Woe to you who live by the sea,
O Kerethite people;
the word of the LORD is against you,
O Canaan, land of the Philistines.

"I will destroy you,
and none will be left."

[6]The land by the sea, where the Kerethites[f] dwell,
will be a place for shepherds and sheep pens.
[7]It will belong to the remnant of the house of Judah;
there they will find pasture.
In the evening they will lie down
in the houses of Ashkelon.
The LORD their God will care for them;
he will restore their fortunes.[g]

*Against Moab and Ammon*

[8]"I have heard the insults of Moab
and the taunts of the Ammonites,
who insulted my people
and made threats against their land.
[9]Therefore, as surely as I live,"
declares the LORD Almighty, the God of Israel,
"surely Moab will become like Sodom,
the Ammonites like Gomorrah—
a place of weeds and salt pits,
a wasteland forever.
The remnant of my people will plunder them;
the survivors of my nation will inherit their land."

[10]This is what they will get in return for their pride,

f6 The meaning of the Hebrew for this word is uncertain.
g7 Or *will bring back their captives*

°7 ק שביתם
°9 ק גויי

חֵרְפוּ וַיַּגְדִּלוּ עַל־ עַם יְהוָה צְבָאוֹת׃ נוֹרָא
being-awesome (11) Hosts Yahweh-of people-of against and-they-mocked they-insulted

יְהוָה עֲלֵיהֶם כִּי רָזָה אֵת כָּל־ אֱלֹהֵי הָאָרֶץ וְיִשְׁתַּחֲווּ־
then-they-will-worship the-land gods-of all-of *** he-destroys when to-them Yahweh

לוֹ אִישׁ מִמְּקוֹמוֹ כֹּל אִיֵּי הַגּוֹיִם׃ גַּם־אַתֶּם כּוּשִׁים
Cushites you too (12) the-nations shores-of every-of in-land-of-him everyone to-him

חַלְלֵי חַרְבִּי הֵמָּה׃ וְיֵט יָדוֹ עַל־
against hand-of-him and-he-will-stretch-out (13) they sword-of-me ones-slain-of

צָפוֹן וִיאַבֵּד אֶת־ אַשּׁוּר וְיָשֵׂם אֶת־ נִינְוֵה לִשְׁמָמָה
as-desolation Nineveh *** and-he-will-leave Assyria *** and-he-will-destroy north

צִיָּה כַּמִּדְבָּר׃ וְרָבְצוּ בְתוֹכָהּ עֲדָרִים כָּל־
every-of flocks in-midst-of-her and-they-will-lie-down (14) as-the-desert dryness

חַיְתוֹ־ גוֹי גַּם־ קָאַת גַּם־ קִפֹּד בְּכַפְתֹּרֶיהָ יָלִינוּ
they-will-roost on-columns-of-her screech-owl and desert-owl and herd creatures-of

קוֹל יְשׁוֹרֵר בַּחַלּוֹן חֹרֶב בַּסַּף כִּי אַרְזָה
cedar-beam indeed in-the-doorway rubble through-the-window he-will-echo call

עֵרָה׃ זֹאת הָעִיר הָעַלִּיזָה הַיּוֹשֶׁבֶת לָבֶטַח
in-safety the-one-living the-carefree-one the-city this (15) he-will-expose

הָאֹמְרָה בִּלְבָבָהּ אֲנִי וְאַפְסִי עוֹד אֵיךְ ׀ הָיְתָה לְשַׁמָּה
into-ruin she-became what! besides and-none I to-self-of-her the-one-saying

מַרְבֵּץ לַחַיָּה כֹּל עוֹבֵר עָלֶיהָ יִשְׁרֹק יָנִיעַ יָדוֹ׃
fist-of-him he-shakes he-scoffs by-her one-passing all-of for-wild-beast lair

הוֹי מֹרְאָה וְנִגְאָלָה הָעִיר הַיּוֹנָה׃
the-one-oppressing the-city and-one-being-defiled one-being-rebellious woe! (3:1)

לֹא שָׁמְעָה בְּקוֹל לֹא לָקְחָה מוּסָר בַּיהוָה לֹא בָטָחָה
she-trusts not in-Yahweh correction she-accepts not to-voice she-obeys not (2)

אֶל־ אֱלֹהֶיהָ לֹא קָרֵבָה׃ שָׂרֶיהָ בְקִרְבָּהּ אֲרָיוֹת
lions at-within-her officials-of-her (3) she-draws-near not God-of-her to

שֹׁאֲגִים שֹׁפְטֶיהָ זְאֵבֵי עֶרֶב לֹא גָרְמוּ לַבֹּקֶר׃
for-the-morning they-leave nothing evening wolves-of ones-ruling-her ones-roaring

נְבִיאֶיהָ פֹּחֲזִים אַנְשֵׁי בֹּגְדוֹת כֹּהֲנֶיהָ חִלְּלוּ־
they-profane priests-of-her treacheries men-of ones-being-arrogant prophets-of-her (4)

קֹדֶשׁ חָמְסוּ תּוֹרָה׃ יְהוָה צַדִּיק בְּקִרְבָּהּ לֹא יַעֲשֶׂה
he-does not at-within-her righteous Yahweh (5) law they-do-violence-to sanctuary

עַוְלָה בַּבֹּקֶר בַּבֹּקֶר מִשְׁפָּטוֹ יִתֵּן לָאוֹר לֹא
not on-the-new-day he-dispenses justice-of-him in-the-morning in-the-morning wrong

נֶעְדָּר וְלֹא־ יוֹדֵעַ עַוָּל בֹּשֶׁת׃ הִכְרַתִּי גוֹיִם נָשַׁמּוּ
they-are-demolished nations I-cut-off (6) shame unrighteous knowing yet-not he-fails

for insulting and mocking
the people of the LORD
Almighty.
11 The LORD will be awesome to
them
when he destroys all the
gods of the land.
The nations on every shore
will worship him,
every one in its own land.

*Against Cush*

12 "You too, O Cushites,[h]
will be slain by my sword."

*Against Assyria*

13 He will stretch out his hand
against the north
and destroy Assyria,
leaving Nineveh utterly
desolate
and dry as the desert.
14 Flocks and herds will lie down
there,
creatures of every kind.
The desert owl and the screech
owl
will roost on her columns.
Their calls will echo through
the windows,
rubble will be in the
doorways,
the beams of cedar will be
exposed.
15 This is the carefree city
that lived in safety.
She said to herself,
"I am, and there is none
besides me."
What a ruin she has become,
a lair for wild beasts!
All who pass by her scoff
and shake their fists.

*The Future of Jerusalem*

3 Woe to the city of
oppressors,
rebellious and defiled!
2 She obeys no one,
she accepts no correction.
She does not trust in the LORD,
she does not draw near to
her God.
3 Her officials are roaring lions,
her rulers are evening
wolves,
who leave nothing for the
morning.
4 Her prophets are arrogant;
they are treacherous men.
Her priests profane the
sanctuary
and do violence to the law.
5 The LORD within her is
righteous;
he does no wrong.
Morning by morning he
dispenses his justice,
and every new day he does
not fail,
yet the unrighteous know
no shame.
6 "I have cut off nations;

[h] 12 That is, people from the upper Nile region

פִּנּוֹתָם הֶחֱרַבְתִּי חוּצוֹתָם מִבְּלִי עוֹבֵר
one-passing-through from-no streets-of-them I-left-deserted strongholds-of-them

נִצְדּוּ עָרֵיהֶם מִבְּלִי־ אִישׁ מֵאֵין יוֹשֵׁב׃ אָמַרְתִּי
I-said (7) one-being-left from-no one from-no cities-of-them they-are-destroyed

אַךְ־ תִּירְאִי אוֹתִי תִּקְחִי מוּסָר וְלֹא־ יִכָּרֵת
he-would-be-cut-off then-not correction you-will-accept me you-will-fear surely

מְעוֹנָהּ כֹּל אֲשֶׁר־ פָּקַדְתִּי עָלֶיהָ אָכֵן הִשְׁכִּימוּ
they-were-eager but upon-her I-will-punish that all dwelling-of-her

הִשְׁחִיתוּ כֹּל עֲלִילוֹתָם׃ לָכֵן חַכּוּ־ לִי נְאֻם־
declaration-of for-me wait! therefore (8) deeds-of-them all-of they-acted-corruptly

יְהוָה לְיוֹם קוּמִי לְעַד כִּי מִשְׁפָּטִי לֶאֱסֹף
to-assemble decision-of-me indeed for-plunder to-stand-up-me on-day-of Yahweh

גּוֹיִם לְקָבְצִי מַמְלָכוֹת לִשְׁפֹּךְ עֲלֵיהֶם זַעְמִי כֹּל חֲרוֹן
fierceness-of all-of wrath-of-me on-them to-pour-out kingdoms to-gather-me nations

אַפִּי כִּי בְּאֵשׁ קִנְאָתִי תֵּאָכֵל כָּל־
whole-of she-will-be-consumed jealous-anger-of-me by-fire-of indeed anger-of-me

הָאָרֶץ׃ כִּי־ אָז אֶהְפֹּךְ אֶל־ עַמִּים שָׂפָה בְרוּרָה לִקְרֹא
to-call being-pure lip peoples to I-will-change then indeed (9) the-world

כֻלָּם בְּשֵׁם יְהוָה לְעָבְדוֹ שְׁכֶם אֶחָד׃ מֵעֵבֶר
from-beyond (10) one shoulder and-to-serve-him Yahweh on-name-of all-of-them

לְנַהֲרֵי־ כוּשׁ עֲתָרַי בַּת־ פוּצַי
peoples-being-scattered-of-me daughter-of worshipers-of-me Cush to-rivers-of

יוֹבִלוּן מִנְחָתִי׃ בַּיּוֹם הַהוּא לֹא תֵבוֹשִׁי
you-will-be-put-to-shame not the-that on-the-day (11) offering-of-me they-will-bring

מִכֹּל עֲלִילֹתַיִךְ אֲשֶׁר פָּשַׁעַתְּ בִּי כִּי־ אָז אָסִיר
I-will-remove then because to-me you-did-wrong that wrong-deeds-of-you for-all-of

מִקִּרְבֵּךְ עַלִּיזֵי גַּאֲוָתֵךְ וְלֹא־ תוֹסִפִי לְגָבְהָה
to-be-haughty you-will-repeat and-never pride-of-you rejoicers-of from-within-you

עוֹד בְּהַר קָדְשִׁי׃ וְהִשְׁאַרְתִּי בְקִרְבֵּךְ עַם עָנִי
meek people at-within-you but-I-will-leave (12) holiness-of-me on-hill-of again

וָדָל וְחָסוּ בְּשֵׁם יְהוָה׃ שְׁאֵרִית יִשְׂרָאֵל לֹא־ יַעֲשׂוּ
they-will-do not Israel remnant-of (13) Yahweh in-name-of that-they-trust and-humble

עַוְלָה וְלֹא־ יְדַבְּרוּ כָזָב וְלֹא־ יִמָּצֵא בְּפִיהֶם
in-mouth-of-them he-will-be-found or-not lie they-will-speak and-not wrong

לְשׁוֹן תַּרְמִית כִּי־ הֵמָּה יִרְעוּ וְרָבְצוּ
and-they-will-lie-down they-will-eat they indeed deceitfulness tongue-of

וְאֵין מַחֲרִיד׃ רָנִּי בַּת־ צִיּוֹן הָרִיעוּ
shout-aloud! Zion Daughter-of sing! (14) one-making-afraid and-there-will-be-no

their strongholds are
demolished.
I have left their streets
deserted,
with no one passing
through.
Their cities are destroyed;
no one will be left—no one
at all.
7 I said to the city,
'Surely you will fear me
and accept correction!'
Then her dwelling would not
be cut off,
nor all my punishments
come upon her.
But they were still eager
to act corruptly in all they
did.
8 Therefore wait for me,"
declares the LORD,
"for the day I will stand up
to testify.
I have decided to assemble the
nations,
to gather the kingdoms
and to pour out my wrath on
them—
all my fierce anger.
The whole world will be
consumed
by the fire of my jealous
anger.

9 "Then will I purify the lips of
the peoples,
that all of them may call on
the name of the LORD
and serve him shoulder to
shoulder.
10 From beyond the rivers of
Cush[j]
my worshipers, my scattered
people,
will bring me offerings.
11 On that day you will not be
put to shame
for all the wrongs you have
done to me,
because I will remove from
this city
those who rejoice in their
pride.
Never again will you be
haughty
on my holy hill.
12 But I will leave within you
the meek and humble,
who trust in the name of
the LORD.
13 The remnant of Israel will do
no wrong;
they will speak no lies,
nor will deceit be found in
their mouths.
They will eat and lie down
and no one will make them
afraid."

14 Sing, O Daughter of Zion;

i8 Septuagint and Syriac; Hebrew *will rise up to plunder*
j10 That is, the upper Nile region

יִשְׂרָאֵל שִׂמְחִי וְעָלְזִי בְּכָל־ לֵב בַּת יְרוּשָׁלָ͏ִם׃

Jerusalem Daughter-of heart with-all-of and-rejoice! be-glad! Israel

הֵסִיר יְהוָה מִשְׁפָּטַיִךְ פִּנָּה אֹיְבֵךְ

one-being-enemy-of-you he-turned-back punishments-of-you Yahweh he-took-away (15)

מֶלֶךְ יִשְׂרָאֵל ׀ יְהוָה בְּקִרְבֵּךְ לֹא־ תִירְאִי רָע עוֹד׃

again harm you-will-fear never at-within-you Yahweh Israel King-of

בַּיּוֹם הַהוּא יֵאָמֵר לִירוּשָׁלַ͏ִם אַל־ תִּירָאִי צִיּוֹן אַל־

not Zion you-fear not to-Jerusalem he-will-be-said the-that on-the-day (16)

יִרְפּוּ יָדָיִךְ׃ יְהוָה אֱלֹהַיִךְ בְּקִרְבֵּךְ* גִּבּוֹר

mighty at-within-you God-of-you Yahweh (17) hands-of-you let-them-hang-limp

יוֹשִׁיעַ יָשִׂישׂ עָלַיִךְ בְּשִׂמְחָה יַחֲרִישׁ בְּאַהֲבָתוֹ

with-love-of-him he-will-quiet with-joy in-you he-will-delight he-saves

יָגִיל עָלַיִךְ בְּרִנָּה׃ נוּגֵי

ones-being-sorrowful-of (18) with-singing over-you he-will-rejoice

מִמּוֹעֵד אָסַפְתִּי מִמֵּךְ הָיוּ מַשְׂאֵת עָלֶיהָ חֶרְפָּה׃

reproach to-you burden they-are from-you I-will-remove for-appointed-feast

הִנְנִי עֹשֶׂה אֶת־ כָּל־ מְעַנַּיִךְ בָּעֵת הַהִיא

the-that at-the-time ones-oppressing-you all-of with dealing see-I! (19)

וְהוֹשַׁעְתִּי אֶת־ הַצֹּלֵעָה וְהַנִּדָּחָה אֲקַבֵּץ

I-will-gather and-the-one-being-scattered the-one-being-lame *** and-I-will-rescue

וְשַׂמְתִּים לִתְהִלָּה וּלְשֵׁם בְּכָל־ הָאָרֶץ בָּשְׁתָּם׃

shame-of-them the-land in-every-of and-for-honor for-praise and-I-will-give-them

בָּעֵת הַהִיא אָבִיא אֶתְכֶם וּבָעֵת קַבְּצִי

to-bring-home-me and-at-the-time you I-will-gather the-that at-the-time (20)

אֶתְכֶם כִּי־ אֶתֵּן אֶתְכֶם לְשֵׁם וְלִתְהִלָּה בְּכֹל עַמֵּי

peoples-of among-all-of and-for-praise for-honor you I-will-give indeed you

הָאָרֶץ בְּשׁוּבִי אֶת־ שְׁבוּתֵיכֶם לְעֵינֵיכֶם אָמַר יְהוָה׃

Yahweh he-says before-eyes-of-you fortunes-of-you *** when-to-restore-me the-earth

---

shout aloud, O Israel!
Be glad and rejoice with all
your heart,
O Daughter of Jerusalem!
15 The LORD has taken away your
punishment,
he has turned back your
enemy.
The LORD, the King of Israel, is
with you;
never again will you fear
any harm.
16 On that day they will say to
Jerusalem,
"Do not fear, O Zion;
do not let your hands hang
limp.
17 The LORD your God is with
you,
he is mighty to save.
He will take great delight in
you,
he will quiet you with his
love,
he will rejoice over you with
singing."

18 "The sorrows for the
appointed feasts
I will remove from you;
they are a burden and a
reproach to you.[k]
19 At that time I will deal
with all who oppressed you;
I will rescue the lame
and gather those who have
been scattered.
I will give them praise and
honor
in every land where they
were put to shame.
20 At that time I will gather you;
at that time I will bring you
home.
I will give you honor and
praise
among all the peoples of the
earth
when I restore your fortunes[l]
before your very eyes,"
says the LORD.

[k] 18 Or *"I will gather you who mourn for the appointed feasts; / your reproach is a burden to you*

[l] 20 Or *I bring back your captives*

***17 Most mss have *sheva* under the *kaph* (ךְ).**

בִּשְׁנַת שְׁתַּיִם לְדָרְיָוֶשׁ הַמֶּלֶךְ בַּחֹדֶשׁ הַשִּׁשִּׁי בְּיוֹם אֶחָד
**one on-day the-sixth in-the-month the-king of-Darius two in-year-of (1:1)**

לַחֹדֶשׁ הָיָה דְבַר־ יְהוָה בְּיַד־ חַגַּי הַנָּבִיא אֶל־ זְרֻבָּבֶל
**Zerubbabel to the-prophet Haggai through-hand-of Yahweh word-of he-came of-the-month**

בֶּן־ שְׁאַלְתִּיאֵל פַּחַת יְהוּדָה וְאֶל־ יְהוֹשֻׁעַ בֶּן־ יְהוֹצָדָק הַכֹּהֵן
**the-priest Jehozadak son-of Joshua and-to Judah governor-of Shealtiel son-of**

הַגָּדוֹל לֵאמֹר׃ כֹּה אָמַר יְהוָה צְבָאוֹת לֵאמֹר הָעָם הַזֶּה אָמְרוּ
**they-say the-this the-people to-say Hosts Yahweh-of he-says this (2) to-say the-high**

לֹא עֶת־ בֹּא עֶת־ בֵּית יְהוָה לְהִבָּנוֹת׃ וַיְהִי דְּבַר־
**word-of then-he-came (3) to-be-built Yahweh house-of time-of to-come time-of not**

יְהוָה בְּיַד־ חַגַּי הַנָּבִיא לֵאמֹר׃ הַעֵת לָכֶם אַתֶּם
**yourselves for-you time? (4) to-say the-prophet Haggai through-hand-of Yahweh**

לָשֶׁבֶת בְּבָתֵּיכֶם סְפוּנִים וְהַבַּיִת הַזֶּה חָרֵב׃ וְעַתָּה
**and-now (5) ruin the-this while-the-house ones-being-paneled in-houses-of-you to-live**

כֹּה אָמַר יְהוָה צְבָאוֹת שִׂימוּ לְבַבְכֶם עַל־ דַּרְכֵיכֶם׃
**ways-of-you to thought-of-you make-careful! Hosts Yahweh-of he-says this**

זְרַעְתֶּם הַרְבֵּה וְהָבֵא מְעָט אָכוֹל וְאֵין־
**but-there-is-not to-eat little but-to-harvest to-be-much you-planted (6)**

לְשָׂבְעָה שָׁתוֹ וְאֵין־ לְשָׁכְרָה לָבוֹשׁ
**to-put-on-clothes to-have-fill but-there-is-not to-drink to-have-enough**

וְאֵין־ לְחֹם לוֹ וְהַמִּשְׂתַּכֵּר מִשְׂתַּכֵּר אֶל־צְרוֹר
**purse for earning-wage and-the-one-earning-wage to-him to-be-warm but-there-is-not**

נָקוּב׃ כֹּה אָמַר יְהוָה צְבָאוֹת שִׂימוּ לְבַבְכֶם עַל־
**to thought-of-you make-careful! Hosts Yahweh-of he-says this (7) having-hole**

דַּרְכֵיכֶם׃ עֲלוּ הָהָר וַהֲבֵאתֶם עֵץ וּבְנוּ הַבָּיִת
**the-house and-build! timber and-bring-down! the-mountain go-up! (8) ways-of-you**

וְאֶרְצֶה־ בּוֹ וְאֶכָּבְד אָמַר יְהוָה׃ פָּנֹה
**to-expect (9) Yahweh he-says and-I-may-be-honored in-him that-I-may-take-pleasure**

אֶל־ הַרְבֵּה וְהִנֵּה לִמְעָט וַהֲבֵאתֶם הַבַּיִת וְנָפַחְתִּי
**indeed-I-blew-away the-home when-you-brought to-little but-see! to-be-much to**

בוֹ יַעַן מֶה נְאֻם יְהוָה צְבָאוֹת יַעַן בֵּיתִי אֲשֶׁר־ הוּא
**he which house-of-me because-of Hosts Yahweh-of declaration-of why? for to-him**

חָרֵב וְאַתֶּם רָצִים אִישׁ לְבֵיתוֹ׃ עַל־ כֵּן עֲלֵיכֶם
**because-of-you this for (10) with-house-of-him each ones-being-busy while-you ruin**

כָּלְאוּ שָׁמַיִם מִטָּל וְהָאָרֶץ כָּלְאָה יְבוּלָהּ׃
**crop-of-her she-withheld and-the-earth from-dew heavens they-withheld**

וָאֶקְרָא חֹרֶב עַל־ הָאָרֶץ וְעַל־ הֶהָרִים וְעַל־ הַדָּגָן
**the-grain and-on the-mountains and-on the-field on drought and-I-called (11)**

### *A Call to Build the House of the Lord*

1 In the second year of King Darius, on the first day of the sixth month, the word of the LORD came through the prophet Haggai to Zerubbabel son of Shealtiel, governor of Judah, and to Joshua[a] son of Jehozadak, the high priest:
[2]This is what the LORD Almighty says: "These people say, 'The time has not yet come for the LORD's house to be built.' "
[3]Then the word of the LORD came through the prophet Haggai:
[4]"Is it a time for you yourselves to be living in your paneled houses, while this house remains a ruin?"
[5]Now this is what the LORD Almighty says: "Give careful thought to your ways. [6]You have planted much, but have harvested little. You eat, but never have enough. You drink, but never have your fill. You put on clothes, but are not warm. You earn wages, only to put them in a purse with holes in it."
[7]This is what the LORD Almighty says: "Give careful thought to your ways. [8]Go up into the mountains and bring down timber and build the house, so that I may take pleasure in it and be honored," says the LORD. [9]"You expected much, but see, it turned out to be little. What you brought home, I blew away. Why?" declares the LORD Almighty. "Because of my house, which remains a ruin, while each of you is busy with his own house. [10]Therefore, because of you the heavens have withheld their dew and the earth its crops. [11]I called for a drought on the fields and the mountains, on the grain,

[a]1 A variant of *Jeshua;* here and elsewhere in Haggai

°8 ק ואכבדה

וְעַל־ הַתִּירֹושׁ וְעַל־ הַיִּצְהָר וְעַל אֲשֶׁר תֹּוצִיא הָאֲדָמָה וְעַל־

and-on the-ground she-produces what and-on the-oil and-on the-new-wine and-on

הָאָדָם וְעַל־ הַבְּהֵמָה וְעַל כָּל־ יְגִיעַ כַּפָּיִם׃ וַיִּשְׁמַע

then-he-obeyed (12) hands labor-of all-of and-on the-cattle and-on the-man

זְרֻבָּבֶל ׀ בֶּן־ שַׁלְתִּיאֵל וִיהֹושֻׁעַ בֶּן־ יְהֹוצָדָק הַכֹּהֵן הַגָּדֹול

the-high the-priest Jehozadak son-of and-Joshua Shealtiel son-of Zerubbabel

וְכֹל ׀ שְׁאֵרִית הָעָם בְּקֹול יְהוָה אֱלֹהֵיהֶם וְעַל־ דִּבְרֵי

messages-of and-to God-of-them Yahweh to-voice-of the-people remnant-of and-whole-of

חַגַּי הַנָּבִיא כַּאֲשֶׁר שְׁלָחֹו יְהוָה אֱלֹהֵיהֶם וַיִּירְאוּ

and-they-feared God-of-them Yahweh he-sent-him because-that the-prophet Haggai

הָעָם מִפְּנֵי יְהוָה׃ וַיֹּאמֶר חַגַּי מַלְאַךְ יְהוָה

Yahweh messenger-of Haggai then-he-said (13) Yahweh at-before the-people

בְּמַלְאֲכוּת יְהוָה לָעָם לֵאמֹר אֲנִי אִתְּכֶם נְאֻם־ יְהוָה׃

Yahweh declaration-of with-you I to-say to-the-people Yahweh with-message-of

וַיָּעַר יְהוָה אֶת־ רוּחַ זְרֻבָּבֶל בֶּן־ שַׁלְתִּיאֵל פַּחַת

governor-of Shealtiel son-of Zerubbabel spirit-of *** Yahweh so-he-stirred-up (14)

יְהוּדָה וְאֶת־ רוּחַ יְהוֹשֻׁעַ בֶּן־ יְהוֹצָדָק הַכֹּהֵן הַגָּדֹול וְאֶת־ רוּחַ

spirit-of and the-high the-priest Jehozadak son-of Joshua spirit-of and Judah

כֹּל שְׁאֵרִית הָעָם וַיָּבֹאוּ וַיַּעֲשׂוּ מְלָאכָה בְּבֵית־ יְהוָה

Yahweh-of on-house-of work and-they-began and-they-came the-people remnant-of whole-of

צְבָאֹות אֱלֹהֵיהֶם׃ בְּיֹום עֶשְׂרִים וְאַרְבָּעָה לַחֹדֶשׁ בַּשִּׁשִּׁי

in-the-sixth of-the-month and-four twenty on-day-of (15) God-of-them Hosts

בִּשְׁנַת שְׁתַּיִם לְדָרְיָוֶשׁ הַמֶּלֶךְ׃ בַּשְּׁבִיעִי בְּעֶשְׂרִים וְאֶחָד לַחֹדֶשׁ

of-the-month and-one on-twenty in-the-seventh (2:1) the-king of-Darius two in-year-of

הָיָה דְּבַר־ יְהוָה בְּיַד־ חַגַּי הַנָּבִיא לֵאמֹר׃ אֱמָר־ נָא

now! speak! (2) to-say the-prophet Haggai through-hand-of Yahweh word-of he-came

אֶל־ זְרֻבָּבֶל בֶּן־ שַׁלְתִּיאֵל פַּחַת יְהוּדָה וְאֶל־ יְהוֹשֻׁעַ בֶּן־ יְהוֹצָדָק

Jehozadak son-of Joshua and-to Judah governor-of Shealtiel son-of Zerubbabel to

הַכֹּהֵן הַגָּדֹול וְאֶל־ שְׁאֵרִית הָעָם לֵאמֹר׃ מִי בָכֶם

of-you who? (3) to-ask the-people remnant-of and-to the-high the-priest

הַנִּשְׁאָר אֲשֶׁר רָאָה אֶת־ הַבַּיִת הַזֶּה בִּכְבֹודֹו הָרִאשֹׁון

the-former in-glory-of-him the-this the-house *** he-saw who the-one-being-left

וּמָה אַתֶּם רֹאִים אֹתֹו עַתָּה הֲלֹוא כָמֹהוּ כְּאַיִן בְּעֵינֵיכֶם׃

in-eyes-of-you like-nothing like-him not? now at-him ones-looking you and-how?

וְעַתָּה חֲזַק זְרֻבָּבֶל ׀ נְאֻם־ יְהוָה וַחֲזַק יְהוֹשֻׁעַ בֶּן־

son-of Joshua and-be-strong! Yahweh declaration-of Zerubbabel be-strong! but-now (4)

יְהוֹצָדָק הַכֹּהֵן הַגָּדֹול וַחֲזַק כָּל־ עַם הָאָרֶץ נְאֻם־

declaration-of the-land people-of all-of and-be-strong! the-high the-priest Jehozadak

the new wine, the oil and whatever the ground produces, on men and cattle, and on the labor of your hands."

12 Then Zerubbabel son of Shealtiel, Joshua son of Jehozadak, the high priest, and the whole remnant of the people obeyed the voice of the LORD their God and the message of the prophet Haggai, because the LORD their God had sent him. And the people feared the LORD.

13 Then Haggai, the LORD's messenger, gave this message of the LORD to the people: "I am with you," declares the LORD. 14 So the LORD stirred up the spirit of Zerubbabel son of Shealtiel, governor of Judah, and the spirit of Joshua son of Jehozadak, the high priest, and the spirit of the whole remnant of the people. They came and began to work on the house of the LORD Almighty, their God, 15 on the twenty-fourth day of the sixth month in the second year of King Darius.

*The Promised Glory of the New House*

2 On the twenty-first day of the seventh month, the word of the LORD came through the prophet Haggai: 2 "Speak to Zerubbabel son of Shealtiel, governor of Judah, to Joshua son of Jehozadak, the high priest, and to the remnant of the people. Ask them, 3 'Who of you is left who saw this house in its former glory? How does it look to you now? Does it not seem to you like nothing? 4 But now be strong, O Zerubbabel,' declares the LORD. 'Be strong, O Joshua son of Jehozadak, the high priest. Be strong, all you people of the land,' declares the LORD, 'and

יְהוָה וַעֲשׂוּ כִּי־אֲנִי אִתְּכֶם נְאֻם יְהוָה צְבָאוֹת׃ אֶת־הַדָּבָר
the-thing *** (5) Hosts Yahweh-of declaration-of with-you I for and-work! Yahweh

אֲשֶׁר־כָּרַתִּי אִתְּכֶם בְּצֵאתְכֶם מִמִּצְרַיִם וְרוּחִי
and-Spirit-of-me from-Egypt when-to-come-out-you with-you I-covenanted that

עֹמֶדֶת בְּתוֹכְכֶם אַל־תִּירָאוּ׃ כִּי כֹה אָמַר יְהוָה צְבָאוֹת עוֹד
more Hosts Yahweh-of he-says this indeed (6) you-fear not in-among-you remaining

אַחַת מְעַט הִיא וַאֲנִי מַרְעִישׁ אֶת־הַשָּׁמַיִם וְאֶת־הָאָרֶץ וְאֶת־הַיָּם וְאֶת־
and the-sea and the-earth and the-heavens *** shaking and-I she little-while one

הֶחָרָבָה׃ וְהִרְעַשְׁתִּי אֶת־כָּל־הַגּוֹיִם וּבָאוּ
and-they-will-come the-nations all-of *** and-I-will-shake (7) the-dry-land

חֶמְדַּת כָּל־הַגּוֹיִם וּמִלֵּאתִי אֶת־הַבַּיִת הַזֶּה כָּבוֹד
glory the-this the-house *** and-I-will-fill the-nations all-of one-desired-of

אָמַר יְהוָה צְבָאוֹת׃ לִי הַכֶּסֶף וְלִי הַזָּהָב נְאֻם
declaration-of the-gold and-to-me the-silver to-me (8) Hosts Yahweh-of he-says

יְהוָה צְבָאוֹת׃ גָּדוֹל יִהְיֶה כְּבוֹד הַבַּיִת הַזֶּה הָאַחֲרוֹן
the-present the-this the-house glory-of he-will-be great (9) Hosts Yahweh-of

מִן־הָרִאשׁוֹן אָמַר יְהוָה צְבָאוֹת וּבַמָּקוֹם הַזֶּה אֶתֵּן
I-will-grant the-this and-in-the-place Hosts Yahweh-of he-says the-former more-than

שָׁלוֹם נְאֻם יְהוָה צְבָאוֹת׃ בְּעֶשְׂרִים וְאַרְבָּעָה לַתְּשִׁיעִי
of-the-ninth and-four on-twenty (10) Hosts Yahweh-of declaration-of peace

בִּשְׁנַת שְׁתַּיִם לְדָרְיָוֶשׁ הָיָה דְּבַר־יְהוָה אֶל־חַגַּי הַנָּבִיא לֵאמֹר׃
to-say the-prophet Haggai to Yahweh word-of he-came of-Darius two in-year-of

כֹּה אָמַר יְהוָה צְבָאוֹת שְׁאַל־נָא אֶת־הַכֹּהֲנִים תּוֹרָה לֵאמֹר׃ הֵן
if (12) to-say law the-priests *** now! ask! Hosts Yahweh-of he-says this (11)

יִשָּׂא־אִישׁ בְּשַׂר־קֹדֶשׁ בִּכְנַף בִּגְדוֹ וְנָגַע
and-he-touches garment-of-him in-fold-of consecration meat-of person he-carries

בִּכְנָפוֹ אֶל־הַלֶּחֶם וְאֶל־הַנָּזִיד וְאֶל־הַיַּיִן וְאֶל־שֶׁמֶן וְאֶל־כָּל־
any-of or-to oil or-to the-wine or-to the-stew or-to the-bread to with-fold-of-him

מַאֲכָל הֲיִקְדָּשׁ וַיַּעֲנוּ הַכֹּהֲנִים וַיֹּאמְרוּ לֹא׃
no and-they-said the-priests and-they-answered does-he-become-consecrated? food

וַיֹּאמֶר חַגַּי אִם־יִגַּע טְמֵא־נֶפֶשׁ בְּכָל־אֵלֶּה
these to-any-of body one-defiled-of he-contacts if Haggai then-he-said (13)

הֲיִטְמָא וַיַּעֲנוּ הַכֹּהֲנִים וַיֹּאמְרוּ יִטְמָא׃
he-becomes-defiled and-they-said the-priests and-they-replied does-he-become-defiled?

וַיַּעַן חַגַּי וַיֹּאמֶר כֵּן הָעָם־הַזֶּה וְכֵן־הַגּוֹי
the-nation and-so the-this the-people so and-he-said Haggai then-he-replied (14)

הַזֶּה לְפָנַי נְאֻם־יְהוָה וְכֵן כָּל־מַעֲשֵׂה יְדֵיהֶם
hands-of-them deed-of all-of and-so Yahweh declaration-of in-sights-of-me the-this

work. For I am with you,' declares the LORD Almighty. [5]'This is what I covenanted with you when you came out of Egypt. And my Spirit remains among you. Do not fear.'

[6]"This is what the LORD Almighty says: 'In a little while I will once more shake the heavens and the earth, the sea and the dry land. [7]I will shake all nations, and the desired of all nations will come, and I will fill this house with glory,' says the LORD Almighty. [8]'The silver is mine and the gold is mine,' declares the LORD Almighty. [9]'The glory of this present house will be greater than the glory of the former house,' says the LORD Almighty. 'And in this place I will grant peace,' declares the LORD Almighty."

*Blessings for a Defiled People*

[10]On the twenty-fourth day of the ninth month, in the second year of Darius, the word of the LORD came to the prophet Haggai: [11]"This is what the LORD Almighty says: 'Ask the priests what the law says: [12]If a person carries consecrated meat in the fold of his garment, and that fold touches some bread or stew, some wine, oil or other food, does it become consecrated?' "

The priests answered, "No."

[13]Then Haggai said, "If a person defiled by contact with a dead body touches one of these things, does it become defiled?"

"Yes," the priests replied, "it becomes defiled."

[14]Then Haggai said, " 'So it is with this people and this nation in my sight,' declares the LORD. 'Whatever they do and whatever

וַאֲשֶׁר יַקְרִיבוּ שָׁם טָמֵא הוּא׃ וְעַתָּה שִׂימוּ־נָא לְבַבְכֶם
thought-of-you now! make-careful! and-now (15) he defiled there they-offer and-what

מִן־הַיּוֹם הַזֶּה וָמָעְלָה מִטֶּרֶם שׂוּם־אֶבֶן אֶל־אֶבֶן בְּהֵיכַל
in-temple-of stone on stone to-lay from-before and-onwards the-this the-day from

יְהוָה׃ מִהְיוֹתָם בָּא אֶל־עֲרֵמַת עֶשְׂרִים וְהָיְתָה עֲשָׂרָה בָּא אֶל־
to he-came ten but-she-was twenty heap-of to he-came when-to-be-them (16) Yahweh

הַיֶּקֶב לַחְשֹׂף חֲמִשִּׁים פּוּרָה וְהָיְתָה עֶשְׂרִים׃ הִכֵּיתִי אֶתְכֶם
you I-struck (17) twenty but-she-was measure fifty to-draw the-wine-vat

בַּשִּׁדָּפוֹן וּבַיֵּרָקוֹן וּבַבָּרָד אֵת כָּל־מַעֲשֵׂה יְדֵיכֶם
hands-of-you work-of all-of *** and-with-the-hail and-with-the-mildew with-the-blight

וְאֵין־אֶתְכֶם אֵלַי נְאֻם־יְהוָה׃ שִׂימוּ־נָא
now! make-careful! (18) Yahweh declaration-of to-me you yet-there-was-not

לְבַבְכֶם מִן־הַיּוֹם הַזֶּה וָמָעְלָה מִיּוֹם עֶשְׂרִים וְאַרְבָּעָה
and-four twenty from-day and-onwards the-this the-day from thought-of-you

לַתְּשִׁיעִי לְמִן־הַיּוֹם אֲשֶׁר־יֻסַּד הֵיכַל־יְהוָה שִׂימוּ
make-careful! Yahweh temple-of he-was-founded when the-day to-from of-the-ninth

לְבַבְכֶם׃ הַעוֹד הַזֶּרַע בַּמְּגוּרָה וְעַד־הַגֶּפֶן וְהַתְּאֵנָה
and-the-fig-tree the-vine and-until in-the-barn the-seed yet? (19) thought-of-you

וְהָרִמּוֹן וְעֵץ הַזַּיִת לֹא נָשָׂא מִן־הַיּוֹם הַזֶּה
the-this the-day from he-bore not the-olive and-tree-of and-the-pomegranate

אֲבָרֵךְ׃ וַיְהִי דְבַר־יְהוָה ׀ שֵׁנִית אֶל־חַגַּי
Haggai to second-time Yahweh word-of and-he-came (20) I-will-bless-you

בְּעֶשְׂרִים וְאַרְבָּעָה לַחֹדֶשׁ לֵאמֹר׃ אֱמֹר אֶל־זְרֻבָּבֶל פַּחַת־
governor-of Zerubbabel to tell! (21) to-day of-the-month and-four on-twenty

יְהוּדָה לֵאמֹר אֲנִי מַרְעִישׁ אֶת־הַשָּׁמַיִם וְאֶת־הָאָרֶץ׃ וְהָפַכְתִּי
and-I-will-overturn (22) the-earth and the-heavens *** shaking I to-say Judah

כִּסֵּא מַמְלָכוֹת וְהִשְׁמַדְתִּי חֹזֶק מַמְלְכוֹת הַגּוֹיִם
the-foreign-ones kingdoms-of power-of and-I-will-shatter royalties throne-of

וְהָפַכְתִּי מֶרְכָּבָה וְרֹכְבֶיהָ וְיָרְדוּ סוּסִים
horses and-they-will-fall and-ones-driving-her chariot and-I-will-overthrow

וְרֹכְבֵיהֶם אִישׁ בְּחֶרֶב אָחִיו׃ בַּיּוֹם הַהוּא
the-that on-the-day (23) brother-of-him by-sword-of each and-ones-riding-them

נְאֻם־יְהוָה צְבָאוֹת אֶקָּחֲךָ זְרֻבָּבֶל בֶּן־שְׁאַלְתִּיאֵל
Shealtiel son-of Zerubbabel I-will-take-you Hosts Yahweh-of declaration-of

עַבְדִּי נְאֻם־יְהוָה וְשַׂמְתִּיךָ כַּחוֹתָם
like-the-signet-ring and-I-will-make-you Yahweh declaration-of servant-of-me

כִּי־בְךָ בָחַרְתִּי נְאֻם יְהוָה צְבָאוֹת׃
Hosts Yahweh-of declaration-of I-chose to-you for

they offer there is defiled.

[15]" 'Now give careful thought to this from this day on[b]—consider how things were before one stone was laid on another in the LORD's temple. [16]When anyone came to a heap of twenty measures, there were only ten. When anyone went to a wine vat to draw fifty measures, there were only twenty. [17]I struck all the work of your hands with blight, mildew and hail, yet you did not turn to me,' declares the LORD. [18]'From this day on, from this twenty-fourth day of the ninth month, give careful thought to the day when the foundation of the LORD's temple was laid. Give careful thought: [19]Is there yet any seed left in the barn? Until now, the vine and the fig tree, the pomegranate and the olive tree have not borne fruit.

" 'From this day on I will bless you.' "

### *Zerubbabel the LORD's Signet Ring*

[20]The word of the LORD came to Haggai a second time on the twenty-fourth day of the month: [21]"Tell Zerubbabel governor of Judah that I will shake the heavens and the earth. [22]I will overturn royal thrones and shatter the power of the foreign kingdoms. I will overthrow chariots and their drivers; horses and their riders will fall, each by the sword of his brother.

[23]" 'On that day,' declares the LORD Almighty, 'I will take you, my servant Zerubbabel son of Shealtiel,' declares the LORD, 'and I will make you like my signet ring, for I have chosen you,' declares the LORD Almighty."

[b]15 *Or to the days past*

בַּחֹדֶשׁ הַשְּׁמִינִי בִּשְׁנַת שְׁתַּיִם לְדָרְיָוֶשׁ הָיָה דְבַר־יְהוָה אֶל־
to Yahweh word-of he-came of-Darius two of-year-of the-eighth in-the-month (1:1)

זְכַרְיָה בֶּן־בֶּרֶכְיָה בֶּן־עִדּוֹ הַנָּבִיא לֵאמֹר׃ קָצַף יְהוָה
Yahweh he-was-angry (2) to-say the-prophet Iddo son-of Berekiah son-of Zechariah

עַל־אֲבוֹתֵיכֶם קָצֶף׃ וְאָמַרְתָּ אֲלֵהֶם כֹּה אָמַר יְהוָה
Yahweh-of he-says this to-them therefore-you-tell (3) anger forefathers-of-you with

צְבָאוֹת שׁוּבוּ אֵלַי נְאֻם יְהוָה צְבָאוֹת וְאָשׁוּב אֲלֵיכֶם אָמַר
he-says to-you and-I-will-return Hosts Yahweh-of declaration-of to-me return! Hosts

יְהוָה צְבָאוֹת׃ אַל־תִּהְיוּ כַאֲבֹתֵיכֶם אֲשֶׁר קָרְאוּ־אֲלֵיהֶם
to-them they-proclaimed whom like-forefathers-of-you you-be not (4) Hosts Yahweh-of

הַנְּבִיאִים הָרִאשֹׁנִים לֵאמֹר כֹּה אָמַר יְהוָה צְבָאוֹת שׁוּבוּ נָא
now! turn! Hosts Yahweh-of he-says this to-say the-earlier-ones the-prophets

מִדַּרְכֵיכֶם הָרָעִים וּמַעֲלֵילֵיכֶם הָרָעִים וְלֹא
but-not the-evil-ones and-practices-of-you the-evil-ones from-ways-of-you

שָׁמְעוּ וְלֹא־הִקְשִׁיבוּ אֵלַי נְאֻם־יְהוָה׃
Yahweh declaration-of to-me they-would-pay-attention or-not they-would-listen

אֲבוֹתֵיכֶם אַיֵּה־הֵם וְהַנְּבִאִים הַלְעוֹלָם יִחְיוּ׃ אַךְ ׀
but (6) they-live to-forever? and-the-prophets they where? forefathers-of-you (5)

דְּבָרַי וְחֻקַּי אֲשֶׁר צִוִּיתִי אֶת־עֲבָדַי הַנְּבִיאִים
the-prophets servants-of-me *** I-commanded which and-decrees-of-me words-of-me

הֲלוֹא הִשִּׂיגוּ אֲבֹתֵיכֶם וַיָּשׁוּבוּ וַיֹּאמְרוּ כַּאֲשֶׁר
just-as and-they-said then-they-repented forefathers-of-you they-overtook not?

זָמַם יְהוָה צְבָאוֹת לַעֲשׂוֹת לָנוּ כִּדְרָכֵינוּ וּכְמַעֲלָלֵינוּ כֵּן
so and-as-practices-of-us as-ways-of-us to-us to-do Hosts Yahweh-of he-determined

עָשָׂה אִתָּנוּ׃ בְּיוֹם עֶשְׂרִים וְאַרְבָּעָה לְעַשְׁתֵּי־עָשָׂר חֹדֶשׁ הוּא־חֹדֶשׁ
month-of that month ten of-one-of and-four twenty on-day-of (7) to-us he-did

שְׁבָט בִּשְׁנַת שְׁתַּיִם לְדָרְיָוֶשׁ הָיָה דְבַר־יְהוָה אֶל־זְכַרְיָה בֶּן־בֶּרֶכְיָהוּ
Berekiah son-of Zechariah to Yahweh word-of he-came of-Darius two in-year-of Shebat

בֶּן־עִדּוֹא הַנָּבִיא לֵאמֹר׃ רָאִיתִי ׀ הַלַּיְלָה וְהִנֵּה־אִישׁ רֹכֵב
riding man and-see! the-night I-had-vision (8) to-say the-prophet Iddo son-of

עַל־סוּס אָדֹם וְהוּא עֹמֵד בֵּין הַהֲדַסִּים אֲשֶׁר בַּמְּצֻלָה
in-the-ravine that the-myrtle-trees among standing and-he red horse on

וְאַחֲרָיו סוּסִים אֲדֻמִּים שְׂרֻקִּים וּלְבָנִים׃ וָאֹמַר מָה־
what? and-I-asked (9) and-white-ones brown-ones red-ones horses and-behind-him

אֵלֶּה אֲדֹנִי וַיֹּאמֶר אֵלַי הַמַּלְאָךְ הַדֹּבֵר בִּי אֲנִי
I with-me the-one-talking the-angel to-me and-he-answered lord-of-me these

אַרְאֶךָּ מָה־הֵמָּה אֵלֶּה׃ וַיַּעַן הָאִישׁ הָעֹמֵד בֵּין־
among the-one-standing the-man then-he-explained (10) these they what I-will-show-you

°4 ק ומעלליכם

*A Call to Return to the LORD*

1 In the eighth month of the second year of Darius, the word of the LORD came to the prophet Zechariah son of Berekiah, the son of Iddo:

2"The LORD was very angry with your forefathers. 3Therefore tell the people: This is what the LORD Almighty says: 'Return to me,' declares the LORD Almighty, 'and I will return to you,' says the LORD Almighty. 4Do not be like your forefathers, to whom the earlier prophets proclaimed: This is what the LORD Almighty says: 'Turn from your evil ways and your evil practices.' But they would not listen or pay attention to me, declares the LORD. 5Where are your forefathers now? And the prophets, do they live forever? 6But did not my words and my decrees, which I commanded my servants the prophets, overtake your forefathers?

"Then they repented and said, 'The LORD Almighty has done to us what our ways and practices deserve, just as he determined to do.' "

*The Man Among the Myrtle Trees*

7On the twenty-fourth day of the eleventh month, the month of Shebat, in the second year of Darius, the word of the LORD came to the prophet Zechariah son of Berekiah, the son of Iddo.

8During the night I had a vision—and there before me was a man riding a red horse! He was standing among the myrtle trees in a ravine. Behind him were red, brown and white horses.

9I asked, "What are these, my lord?"

The angel who was talking with me answered, "I will show you what they are."

10Then the man standing among

הַהֲדַסִּים וַיֹּאמַר אֵלֶּה אֲשֶׁר שָׁלַח יְהוָה לְהִתְהַלֵּךְ בָּאָרֶץ׃
throughout-the-earth to-go Yahweh he-sent that these and-he-said the-myrtle-trees

וַיַּעֲנוּ אֶת־מַלְאַךְ יְהוָה הָעֹמֵד בֵּין הַהֲדַסִּים
the-myrtle-trees among the-one-standing Yahweh angel-of to and-they-reported (11)

וַיֹּאמְרוּ הִתְהַלַּכְנוּ בָאָרֶץ וְהִנֵּה כָל־הָאָרֶץ יֹשֶׁבֶת
being-at-rest the-world whole-of and-see! throughout-the-earth we-went and-they-said

וְשֹׁקָטֶת׃ וַיַּעַן מַלְאַךְ־יְהוָה וַיֹּאמַר יְהוָה צְבָאוֹת
Hosts Yahweh-of and-he-said Yahweh angel-of then-he-replied (12) and-being-in-peace

עַד־מָתַי אַתָּה לֹא־תְרַחֵם אֶת־יְרוּשָׁלַםִ וְאֵת עָרֵי יְהוּדָה
Judah towns-of and-to Jerusalem to you-will-show-mercy not you when? until

אֲשֶׁר זָעַמְתָּה זֶה שִׁבְעִים שָׁנָה׃ וַיַּעַן יְהוָה אֶת־הַמַּלְאָךְ
the-angel to Yahweh so-he-spoke (13) year seventy this you-were-angry which

הַדֹּבֵר בִּי דְּבָרִים טוֹבִים דְּבָרִים נִחֻמִים׃ וַיֹּאמֶר
then-he-said (14) comforting-ones words kind-ones words with-me the-one-talking

אֵלַי הַמַּלְאָךְ הַדֹּבֵר בִּי קְרָא לֵאמֹר כֹּה אָמַר יְהוָה
Yahweh-of he-says this to-say proclaim! to-me the-one-speaking the-angel to-me

צְבָאוֹת קִנֵּאתִי לִירוּשָׁלַםִ וּלְצִיּוֹן קִנְאָה גְדוֹלָה׃ וְקֶצֶף גָּדוֹל
great but-anger (15) great jealousy and-for-Zion for-Jerusalem I-am-jealous Hosts

אֲנִי קֹצֵף עַל־הַגּוֹיִם הַשַּׁאֲנַנִּים אֲשֶׁר אֲנִי קָצַפְתִּי מְּעָט
little I-was-angry I that the-secure-ones the-nations with being-angry I

וְהֵמָּה עָזְרוּ לְרָעָה׃ לָכֵן כֹּה־אָמַר יְהוָה שַׁבְתִּי
I-will-return Yahweh he-says this therefore (16) to-calamity they-added but-they

לִירוּשָׁלַםִ בְּרַחֲמִים בֵּיתִי יִבָּנֶה בָּהּ נְאֻם
declaration-of in-her he-will-be-rebuilt and-house-of-me with-mercies to-Jerusalem

יְהוָה צְבָאוֹת וְקָוֶה יִנָּטֶה עַל־יְרוּשָׁלָםִ׃
Jerusalem over he-will-be-stretched-out and-measuring-line Hosts Yahweh-of

עוֹד׀ קְרָא לֵאמֹר כֹּה אָמַר יְהוָה צְבָאוֹת עוֹד תְּפוּצֶינָה
they-will-overflow again Hosts Yahweh-of he-says this to-say proclaim! further (17)

עָרַי מִטּוֹב וְנִחַם יְהוָה עוֹד אֶת־צִיּוֹן
Zion *** again Yahweh and-he-will-comfort with-prosperity towns-of-me

וּבָחַר עוֹד בִּירוּשָׁלָםִ׃ וָאֶשָּׂא אֶת־עֵינַי
eyes-of-me *** then-I-lifted-up *(2:1[18]) to-Jerusalem again and-he-will-choose

וָאֵרֶא וְהִנֵּה אַרְבַּע קְרָנוֹת׃ וָאֹמַר אֶל־הַמַּלְאָךְ הַדֹּבֵר
the-one-speaking the-angel to and-I-asked (2[19]) horns four-of and-see! and-I-looked

בִּי מָה־אֵלֶּה וַיֹּאמֶר אֵלַי אֵלֶּה הַקְּרָנוֹת אֲשֶׁר זֵרוּ אֶת־
*** they-scattered that the-horns these to-me and-he-answered these what? to-me

יְהוּדָה אֶת־יִשְׂרָאֵל וִירוּשָׁלָם† ׃ וַיַּרְאֵנִי יְהוָה אַרְבָּעָה חָרָשִׁים׃
craftsmen four Yahweh then-he-showed-me (3[20]) and-Jerusalem Israel *** Judah

the myrtle trees explained, "They
are the ones the LORD has sent to
go throughout the earth."
[11]And they reported to the angel
of the LORD, who was standing
among the myrtle trees, "We have
gone throughout the earth and
found the whole world at rest and
in peace."
[12]Then the angel of the LORD
said, "LORD Almighty, how long
will you withhold mercy from
Jerusalem and from the towns of
Judah, which you have been angry with these seventy years?"
[13]So the LORD spoke kind and comforting words to the angel who
talked with me.
[14]Then the angel who was
speaking to me said, "Proclaim
this word: This is what the LORD
Almighty says: 'I am very jealous
for Jerusalem and Zion, [15]but I am
very angry with the nations that
feel secure. I was only a little angry, but they added to the calamity.'
[16]"Therefore, this is what the
LORD says: 'I will return to Jerusalem with mercy, and there my
house will be rebuilt. And the
measuring line will be stretched
out over Jerusalem,' declares the
LORD Almighty.
[17]"Proclaim further: This is what
the LORD Almighty says: 'My
towns will again overflow with
prosperity, and the LORD will
again comfort Zion and choose
Jerusalem.'"

*Four Horns and Four Craftsmen*

[18]Then I looked up—and there
before me were four horns! [19]I
asked the angel who was speaking
to me, "What are these?"
He answered me, "These are the
horns that scattered Judah, Israel
and Jerusalem."
[20]Then the LORD showed me four

***Heading, 1*** **The Hebrew numeration of chapter 2 begins with verse 18 of chapter 1 in English; the number in brackets indicates the English numeration.**

**†2 Most mss have *bireq* under the *mem* (לַם).**

°16 ק וקו

וָאֹמַר מָה אֵלֶּה בָאִים לַעֲשׂוֹת וַיֹּאמֶר לֵאמֹר אֵלֶּה
these to-say and-he-answered to-do ones-coming these what? and-I-asked (4[21])

הַקְּרָנוֹת אֲשֶׁר־ זֵרוּ אֶת־יְהוּדָה כְּפִי־ אִישׁ לֹא־ נָשָׂא
he-could-raise not one so-mouth-of Judah *** they-scattered that the-horns

רֹאשׁוֹ וַיָּבֹאוּ אֵלֶּה לְהַחֲרִיד אֹתָם לְיַדּוֹת אֶת־ קַרְנוֹת
horns-of *** to-throw-down them to-terrify these but-they-came head-of-him

הַגּוֹיִם הַנֹּשְׂאִים קֶרֶן אֶל־ אֶרֶץ יְהוּדָה לְזָרוֹתָהּ׃
to-scatter-her Judah land-of against horn the-ones-lifting-up the-nations

וָאֶשָּׂא עֵינַי וָאֵרֶא וְהִנֵּה־ אִישׁ וּבְיָדוֹ
and-in-hand-of-him man and-see! and-I-looked eyes-of-me then-I-lifted-up (5[2:1])

חֶבֶל מִדָּה׃ וָאֹמַר אָנָה אַתָּה הֹלֵךְ וַיֹּאמֶר אֵלַי
to-me and-he-answered going you to-where? and-I-asked (6[2]) measure line-of

לָמֹד אֶת־ יְרוּשָׁלִַם לִרְאוֹת כַּמָּה־ רָחְבָּהּ וְכַמָּה אָרְכָּהּ׃
length-of-her and-as-how width-of-her as-how to-find-out Jerusalem *** to-measure

וְהִנֵּה הַמַּלְאָךְ הַדֹּבֵר בִּי יֹצֵא וּמַלְאָךְ אַחֵר יֹצֵא
coming another and-angel leaving to-me the-one-speaking the-angel then-see! (7[3])

לִקְרָאתוֹ׃ וַיֹּאמֶר אֵלָו רֻץ דַּבֵּר אֶל־ הַנַּעַר הַלָּז לֵאמֹר
to-say that the-young-man to tell! run! to-him and-he-said (8[4]) to-meet-him

פְּרָזוֹת תֵּשֵׁב יְרוּשָׁלִַם מֵרֹב אָדָם וּבְהֵמָה
and-livestock man because-of-greatness-of Jerusalem she-will-be unwalled-cities

בְּתוֹכָהּ׃ וַאֲנִי אֶהְיֶה־ לָּהּ נְאֻם־ יְהוָה חוֹמַת אֵשׁ סָבִיב
around fire wall-of Yahweh declaration-of to-her I-will-be and-I (9[5]) at-inside-her

וּלְכָבוֹד אֶהְיֶה בְתוֹכָהּ׃ הוֹי הוֹי וְנֻסוּ מֵאֶרֶץ
from-land-of and-flee! come! come! (10[6]) at-within-her I-will-be and-for-glory

צָפוֹן נְאֻם־ יְהוָה כִּי כְּאַרְבַּע רוּחוֹת הַשָּׁמַיִם פֵּרַשְׂתִּי אֶתְכֶם
you I-scattered the-heavens winds-of to-four-of for Yahweh declaration-of north

נְאֻם־ יְהוָה׃ הוֹי צִיּוֹן הִמָּלְטִי יוֹשֶׁבֶת בַּת־ בָּבֶל׃
Babylon Daughter-of one-living-of escape! Zion come! (11[7]) Yahweh declaration-of

כִּי כֹה אָמַר יְהוָה צְבָאוֹת אַחַר כָּבוֹד שְׁלָחַנִי אֶל־ הַגּוֹיִם
the-nations against he-sent-me honor after Hosts Yahweh-of he-says this for (12[8])

הַשֹּׁלְלִים אֶתְכֶם כִּי הַנֹּגֵעַ בָּכֶם נֹגֵעַ בְּבָבַת עֵינוֹ׃
eye-of-him to-apple-of touching to-you the-one-touching for you the-ones-plundering

כִּי הִנְנִי מֵנִיף אֶת־ יָדִי עֲלֵיהֶם וְהָיוּ שָׁלָל
plunder so-they-will-be against-them hand-of-me *** raising see-I! surely (13[9])

לְעַבְדֵיהֶם וִידַעְתֶּם כִּי־ יְהוָה צְבָאוֹת שְׁלָחָנִי׃ רָנִּי
shout! (14[10]) he-sent-me Hosts Yahweh-of that then-you-will-know for-slaves-of-them

וְשִׂמְחִי בַּת־ צִיּוֹן כִּי הִנְנִי־ בָא וְשָׁכַנְתִּי בְתוֹכֵךְ
in-among-you and-I-will-live coming see-I! for Zion Daughter-of and-be-glad!

craftsmen.
21 I asked, "What are
these coming to do?"

He answered, "These are the horns that scattered Judah so that no one could raise his head, but the craftsmen have come to terrify them and throw down these horns of the nations who lifted up their horns against the land of Judah to scatter its people."

*A Man With a Measuring Line*

2 Then I looked up—and there before me was a man with a measuring line in his hand!
2 I
asked, "Where are you going?"

He answered me, "To measure Jerusalem, to find out how wide and how long it is."

3 Then the angel who was speaking to me left, and another
angel came to meet him
4 and said
to him: "Run, tell that young man, 'Jerusalem will be a city without walls because of the great number of men and livestock in it.
5 And I
myself will be a wall of fire around it,' declares the LORD, 'and I will be its glory within.'

6 "Come! Come! Flee from the land of the north," declares the LORD, "for I have scattered you to the four winds of heaven," declares the LORD.

7 "Come, O Zion! Escape, you who live in the Daughter of Babylon!"
8 For this is what the LORD
Almighty says: "After he has honored me and has sent me against the nations that have plundered you—for whoever touches you touches the apple of his eye—
9 I
will surely raise my hand against them so that their slaves will plunder them.[a] Then you will know that the LORD Almighty has sent me.

10 "Shout and be glad, O Daughter of Zion. For I am coming, and I will live among you," declares

[a] 8,9 Or *says after . . . eye:* 9 "*I . . . plunder them.*"

**Heading* See the first note on page 563.

°8 ק אליו

נְאֻם־ יְהוָה: וְנִלְווּ גוֹיִם רַבִּים אֶל־ יְהוָה
Yahweh with many-ones nations and-they-will-be-joined (15[11]) Yahweh declaration-of

בַּיּוֹם הַהוּא וְהָיוּ לִי לְעָם וְשָׁכַנְתִּי בְתוֹכֵךְ
in-among-you and-I-will-live as-people to-me and-they-will-become the-that in-the-day

וְיָדַעַתְּ כִּי־ יְהוָה צְבָאוֹת שְׁלָחַנִי אֵלָיִךְ: (16[12]) וְנָחַל
and-he-will-inherit (16[12]) to-you he-sent-me Hosts Yahweh-of that and-you-will-know

יְהוָה אֶת־ יְהוּדָה חֶלְקוֹ עַל אַדְמַת הַקֹּדֶשׁ וּבָחַר
and-he-will-choose the-holiness land-of in portion-of-him Judah *** Yahweh

עוֹד בִּירוּשָׁלָ͏ִם: (17[13]) הַס כָּל־ בָּשָׂר מִפְּנֵי יְהוָה כִּי
because Yahweh at-before mankind all-of be-still! (17[13]) to-Jerusalem again

נֵעוֹר מִמְּעוֹן קָדְשׁוֹ: (3:1) וַיַּרְאֵנִי אֶת־יְהוֹשֻׁעַ
Joshua *** then-he-showed-me (3:1) holiness-of-him from-dwelling-of he-roused-himself

הַכֹּהֵן הַגָּדוֹל עֹמֵד לִפְנֵי מַלְאַךְ יְהוָה וְהַשָּׂטָן עֹמֵד עַל־
at standing and-the-Satan Yahweh angel-of before standing the-high the-priest

יְמִינוֹ לְשִׂטְנוֹ: (2) וַיֹּאמֶר יְהוָה אֶל־ הַשָּׂטָן יִגְעַר
may-he-rebuke the-Satan to Yahweh and-he-said (2) to-accuse-him right-side-of-him

יְהוָה בְּךָ הַשָּׂטָן וְיִגְעַר יְהוָה בְּךָ הַבֹּחֵר
the-one-choosing to-you Yahweh indeed-may-he-rebuke the-Satan to-you Yahweh

בִּירוּשָׁלָ͏ִם הֲלוֹא זֶה אוּד מֻצָּל מֵאֵשׁ: (3) וִיהוֹשֻׁעַ
now-Joshua (3) from-fire being-snatched burning-stick this not? to-Jerusalem

הָיָה לָבֻשׁ בְּגָדִים צוֹאִים וְעֹמֵד לִפְנֵי הַמַּלְאָךְ:
the-angel before while-standing filthy-ones clothes being-dressed he-was

וַיַּעַן וַיֹּאמֶר אֶל־ הָעֹמְדִים לְפָנָיו לֵאמֹר הָסִירוּ
take-off! to-say before-him the-ones-standing to and-he-said then-he-spoke (4)

הַבְּגָדִים הַצֹּאִים מֵעָלָיו וַיֹּאמֶר אֵלָיו רְאֵה הֶעֱבַרְתִּי
I-took-away see! to-him then-he-said from-on-him the-filthy-ones the-clothes

מֵעָלֶיךָ עֲוֺנֶךָ וְהַלְבֵּשׁ אֹתְךָ מַחֲלָצוֹת: וָאֹמַר יָשִׂימוּ
let-them-put then-I-said (5) rich-garments you and-to-put-on sin-of-you from-on-you

צָנִיף טָהוֹר עַל־ רֹאשׁוֹ וַיָּשִׂימוּ הַצָּנִיף הַטָּהוֹר עַל רֹאשׁוֹ
head-of-him on the-clean the-turban so-they-put head-of-him on clean turban

וַיַּלְבִּשֻׁהוּ בְּגָדִים וּמַלְאַךְ יְהוָה עֹמֵד: (6) וַיָּעַד
then-he-gave-charge (6) standing Yahweh while-angel-of clothes and-they-put-on-him

מַלְאַךְ יְהוָה בִּיהוֹשֻׁעַ לֵאמֹר: (7) כֹּה־ אָמַר יְהוָה צְבָאוֹת אִם־ בִּדְרָכַי
in-ways-of-me if Hosts Yahweh-of he-says this (7) to-say to-Joshua Yahweh angel-of

תֵּלֵךְ וְאִם אֶת־ מִשְׁמַרְתִּי תִשְׁמֹר וְגַם־ אַתָּה
you then-also you-will-keep requirements-of-me *** and-if you-will-walk

תָדִין אֶת־ בֵּיתִי וְגַם תִּשְׁמֹר אֶת־ חֲצֵרָי
courts-of-me *** you-will-have-charge and-also house-of-me *** you-will-govern

---

the LORD. [11]"Many nations will be joined with the LORD in that day and will become my people. I will live among you and you will know that the LORD Almighty has sent me to you. [12]The LORD will inherit Judah as his portion in the holy land and will again choose Jerusalem. [13]Be still before the LORD, all mankind, because he has roused himself from his holy dwelling."

*Clean Garments for the High Priest*

**3** Then he showed me Joshua[b] the high priest standing before the angel of the LORD, and Satan[c] standing at his right side to accuse him. [2]The LORD said to Satan, "The LORD rebuke you, Satan! The LORD, who has chosen Jerusalem, rebuke you! Is not this man a burning stick snatched from the fire?"

[3]Now Joshua was dressed in filthy clothes as he stood before the angel. [4]The angel said to those who were standing before him, "Take off his filthy clothes."

Then he said to Joshua, "See, I have taken away your sin, and I will put rich garments on you."

[5]Then I said, "Put a clean turban on his head." So they put a clean turban on his head and clothed him, while the angel of the LORD stood by.

[6]The angel of the LORD gave this charge to Joshua: [7]"This is what the LORD Almighty says: 'If you will walk in my ways and keep my requirements, then you will govern my house and have charge of

---

[b]1 A variant of *Jeshua*; here and elsewhere in Zechariah
[c]1 *Satan* means *accuser*.

*Heading See the first note on page 563.

וְנָתַתִּי לְךָ מַהְלְכִים בֵּין הָעֹמְדִים הָאֵלֶּה׃ שְׁמַע־ נָא
now! listen! (8) the-these the-ones-standing among places to-you and-I-will-give

יְהוֹשֻׁעַ ׀ הַכֹּהֵן הַגָּדוֹל אַתָּה וְרֵעֶיךָ הַיֹּשְׁבִים לְפָנֶיךָ
before-you the-ones-sitting and-associates-of-you you the-high the-priest Joshua

כִּֽי־ אַנְשֵׁי מוֹפֵת הֵמָּה כִּֽי־ הִנְנִי מֵבִיא אֶת־ עַבְדִּי צֶמַח׃
Branch servant-of-me *** bringing see-I! indeed they symbol men-of that

כִּי ׀ הִנֵּה הָאֶבֶן אֲשֶׁר נָתַתִּי לִפְנֵי יְהוֹשֻׁעַ עַל־ אֶבֶן אַחַת
one stone on Joshua in-front-of I-set that the-stone see! indeed (9)

שִׁבְעָה עֵינָיִם הִנְנִי מְפַתֵּחַ פִּתֻּחָהּ נְאֻם יְהוָה צְבָאוֹת
Hosts Yahweh-of declaration-of inscription-of-her engraving see-I! eyes seven

וּמַשְׁתִּי אֶת־ עֲוֺן הָאָרֶץ־ הַהִיא בְּיוֹם אֶחָד׃ בַּיּוֹם
in-the-day (10) single in-day the-this the-land sin-of *** and-I-will-remove

הַהוּא נְאֻם יְהוָה צְבָאוֹת תִּקְרְאוּ אִישׁ לְרֵעֵהוּ אֶל־
to to-neighbor-of-him each you-will-invite Hosts Yahweh-of declaration-of the-that

תַּחַת גֶּפֶן וְאֶל־ תַּחַת תְּאֵנָה׃ וַיָּשָׁב הַמַּלְאָךְ הַדֹּבֵר
the-one-talking the-angel then-he-returned (4:1) fig-tree under and-to vine under

בִּי וַיְעִירֵנִי כְּאִישׁ אֲשֶׁר־ יֵעוֹר מִשְּׁנָתוֹ׃ וַיֹּאמֶר
and-he-asked (2) from-sleep-of-him he-is-wakened who as-man and-he-wakened-me with-me

אֵלַי מָה אַתָּה רֹאֶה וַיֹּאמֶר° רָאִיתִי ׀ וְהִנֵּה מְנוֹרַת זָהָב כֻּלָּהּ
all-of-her gold lampstand-of and-look! I-see and-I-answered seeing you what? to-me

וְגֻלָּהּ עַל־ רֹאשָׁהּ וְשִׁבְעָה נֵרֹתֶיהָ עָלֶיהָ שִׁבְעָה וְשִׁבְעָה מוּצָקוֹת
channels and-seven seven on-her lights-of-her and-seven top-of-her at with-bowl

לַנֵּרוֹת אֲשֶׁר עַל־ רֹאשָׁהּ׃ וּשְׁנַיִם זֵיתִים עָלֶיהָ אֶחָד מִימִין
on-right-of one by-her olive-trees also-two (3) top-of-her at that to-the-lights

הַגֻּלָּה וְאֶחָד עַל־ שְׂמֹאלָהּ׃ וָאַעַן וָאֹמַר אֶל־ הַמַּלְאָךְ
the-angel to and-I-said and-I-asked (4) left-of-her on and-one the-bowl

הַדֹּבֵר בִּי לֵאמֹר מָה־ אֵלֶּה אֲדֹנִי׃ וַיַּעַן הַמַּלְאָךְ
the-angel and-he-answered (5) lord-of-me these what? to-say with-me the-one-talking

הַדֹּבֵר בִּי וַיֹּאמֶר אֵלַי הֲלוֹא יָדַעְתָּ מָה־ הֵמָּה אֵלֶּה
these they what? you-know not? to-me and-he-said with-me the-one-talking

וָאֹמַר לֹא אֲדֹנִי׃ וַיַּעַן וַיֹּאמֶר אֵלַי לֵאמֹר זֶה
this to-say to-me and-he-said so-he-answered (6) lord-of-me no and-I-replied

דְּבַר־ יְהוָה אֶל־ זְרֻבָּבֶל לֵאמֹר לֹא בְחַיִל וְלֹא בְכֹחַ כִּי אִם־
rather but by-power or-not by-might not to-say Zerubbabel to Yahweh word-of

בְּרוּחִי אָמַר יְהוָה צְבָאוֹת׃ מִי־ אַתָּה הַר־ הַגָּדוֹל
the-mighty-one mountain-of you who? (7) Hosts Yahweh-of he-says by-Spirit-of-me

לִפְנֵי זְרֻבָּבֶל לְמִישֹׁר וְהוֹצִיא אֶת־ הָאֶבֶן הָרֹאשָׁה
the-cap the-stone *** then-he-will-bring-out to-level-ground Zerubbabel before

°2 ק ואמר

my courts, and I will give you a place among these standing here.

8" 'Listen, O high priest Joshua and your associates seated before you, who are men symbolic of things to come: I am going to bring my servant, the Branch. 9See, the stone I have set in front of Joshua! There are seven eyes[d] on that one stone, and I will engrave an inscription on it,' says the LORD Almighty, 'and I will remove the sin of this land in a single day.

10" 'In that day each of you will invite his neighbor to sit under his vine and fig tree,' declares the LORD Almighty."

*The Gold Lampstand and the Two Olive Trees*

4 Then the angel who talked with me returned and wakened me, as a man is wakened from his sleep. 2He asked me, "What do you see?"

I answered, "I see a solid gold lampstand with a bowl at the top and seven lights on it, with seven channels to the lights. 3Also there are two olive trees by it, one on the right of the bowl and the other on its left."

4I asked the angel who talked with me, "What are these, my lord?"

5He answered, "Do you not know what these are?"

"No, my lord," I replied.

6So he said to me, "This is the word of the LORD to Zerubbabel: 'Not by might nor by power, but by my Spirit,' says the LORD Almighty.

7"What[e] are you, O mighty mountain? Before Zerubbabel you will become level ground. Then he will bring out the capstone to

[d]9 Or *facets* [e]7 Or *Who*

תְּשֻׁאוֹת חֵן חֵן לָהּ׃ וַיְהִי דְבַר־יְהוָה אֵלַי לֵאמֹר׃
to-say to-me Yahweh word-of then-he-came (8) to-her blessing blessing shouts-of

יְדֵי זְרֻבָּבֶל יִסְּדוּ הַבַּיִת הַזֶּה וְיָדָיו
also-hands-of-him the-this the-temple they-laid-foundation Zerubbabel hands-of (9)

תְּבַצַּעְנָה וְיָדַעְתָּ כִּי־יְהוָה צְבָאוֹת שְׁלָחַנִי אֲלֵיכֶם׃
to-you he-sent-me Hosts Yahweh-of that then-you-will-know they-will-complete

כִּי מִי בַז לְיוֹם קְטַנּוֹת וְשָׂמְחוּ
and-they-will-rejoice small-things to-day-of he-despises who? indeed (10)

וְרָאוּ אֶת־הָאֶבֶן הַבְּדִיל בְּיַד זְרֻבָּבֶל שִׁבְעָה־אֵלֶּה עֵינֵי
eyes-of these seven Zerubbabel in-hand-of the-tin the-plumb-line *** when-they-see

יְהוָה הֵמָּה מְשׁוֹטְטִים בְּכָל־הָאָרֶץ׃ וָאַעַן וָאֹמַר
and-I-said then-I-asked (11) the-earth throughout-all-of ones-ranging they Yahweh

אֵלָיו מַה־שְּׁנֵי הַזֵּיתִים הָאֵלֶּה עַל־יְמִין הַמְּנוֹרָה וְעַל־
and-on the-lampstand right-of on the-these the-olive-trees two-of what? to-him

שְׂמֹאולָהּ׃ וָאַעַן שֵׁנִית וָאֹמַר אֵלָיו מַה־שְּׁתֵּי שִׁבֲּלֵי
branches-of two-of what? to-him and-I-said again and-I-asked (12) left-of-her

הַזֵּיתִים אֲשֶׁר בְּיַד שְׁנֵי צַנְתְּרוֹת הַזָּהָב הַמְרִיקִים
the-ones-pouring-out the-gold pipes-of two-of at-side-of that the-olive-trees

מֵעֲלֵיהֶם הַזָּהָב׃ וַיֹּאמֶר אֵלַי לֵאמֹר הֲלוֹא יָדַעְתָּ מָה־אֵלֶּה
these what? you-know not? to-say to-me and-he-replied (13) the-gold at-upon-them

וָאֹמַר לֹא אֲדֹנִי׃ וַיֹּאמֶר אֵלֶּה שְׁנֵי בְנֵי־הַיִּצְהָר
the-anointing-oil sons-of two-of these so-he-said (14) lord-of-me no and-I-said

הָעֹמְדִים עַל־אֲדוֹן כָּל־הָאָרֶץ׃ וָאָשׁוּב וָאֶשָּׂא
and-I-lifted and-I-did-again (5:1) the-earth all-of Lord-of to the-ones-serving

עֵינַי וָאֶרְאֶה וְהִנֵּה מְגִלָּה עָפָה׃ וַיֹּאמֶר אֵלַי מָה
what? to-me and-he-asked (2) one-flying scroll and-see! and-I-looked eyes-of-me

אַתָּה רֹאֶה וָאֹמַר אֲנִי רֹאֶה מְגִלָּה עָפָה אָרְכָּהּ עֶשְׂרִים
twenty length-of-her one-flying scroll seeing I and-I-answered seeing you

בָּאַמָּה וְרָחְבָּהּ עֶשֶׂר בָּאַמָּה׃ וַיֹּאמֶר אֵלַי זֹאת הָאָלָה
the-curse this to-me and-he-said (3) by-the-cubit ten and-width-of-her by-the-cubit

הַיּוֹצֵאת עַל־פְּנֵי כָל־הָאָרֶץ כִּי כָל־הַגֹּנֵב
the-one-being-thief every-of for the-land whole-of surfaces-of over the-one-going-out

מִזֶּה כָּמוֹהָ נִקָּה וְכָל־הַנִּשְׁבָּע
the-one-swearing-falsely and-every-of he-will-be-banished according-to-her on-this

מִזֶּה כָּמוֹהָ נִקָּה׃ הוֹצֵאתִיהָ נְאֻם
declaration-of I-will-send-out-her (4) he-will-be-banished according-to-her on-this

יְהוָה צְבָאוֹת וּבָאָה אֶל־בֵּית הַגַּנָּב וְאֶל־בֵּית
house-of and-into the-thief house-of into and-she-will-enter Hosts Yahweh-of

*11 Most mss have *dagesh* in the *lamed* (־לֵּה).

shouts of 'God bless it! God bless it!' "

8 Then the word of the LORD came to me: 9 "The hands of Zerubbabel have laid the foundation of this temple; his hands will also complete it. Then you will know that the LORD Almighty has sent me to you.

10 "Who despises the day of small things? Men will rejoice when they see the plumb line in the hand of Zerubbabel.

"(These seven are the eyes of the LORD, which range throughout the earth.)"

11 Then I asked the angel, "What are these two olive trees on the right and the left of the lampstand?"

12 Again I asked him, "What are these two olive branches beside the two gold pipes that pour out golden oil?"

13 He replied, "Do you not know what these are?"

"No, my lord," I said.

14 So he said, "These are the two who are anointed to[f] serve the Lord of all the earth."

*The Flying Scroll*

5 I looked again—and there before me was a flying scroll!

2 He asked me, "What do you see?"

I answered, "I see a flying scroll, thirty feet long and fifteen feet wide.[g]"

3 And he said to me, "This is the curse that is going out over the whole land; for according to what it says on one side, every thief will be banished, and according to what it says on the other, everyone who swears falsely will be banished. 4 The LORD Almighty declares, 'I will send it out, and it will enter the house of the thief

f14 Or *two who bring oil and*
g2 Hebrew *twenty cubits long and ten cubits wide* (about 9 meters long and 4.5 meters wide)

הַנִּשְׁבָּע בִּשְׁמִי לַשָּׁקֶר וְלָנָה בְּתוֹךְ

in-inside-of and-she-will-remain for-the-falsehood by-name-of-me the-one-swearing

בֵּיתוֹ וְכִלַּתּוּ וְאֶת־ עֵצָיו וְאֶת־ אֲבָנָיו׃

stones-of-him and timbers-of-him and and-she-will-destroy-him house-of-him

וַיֵּצֵא הַמַּלְאָךְ הַדֹּבֵר בִּי וַיֹּאמֶר אֵלַי שָׂא

lift-up! to-me and-he-said to-me the-one-speaking the-angel then-he-came-forward (5)

נָא עֵינֶיךָ וּרְאֵה מָה הַיּוֹצֵאת הַזֹּאת׃ וָאֹמַר

and-I-asked (6) the-this the-one-appearing what? and-look! eyes-of-you now!

מַה־ הִיא וַיֹּאמֶר זֹאת הָאֵיפָה הַיּוֹצֵאת וַיֹּאמֶר

and-he-added the-one-appearing the-measuring-basket this and-he-replied she what?

זֹאת עֵינָם בְּכָל־ הָאָרֶץ׃ וְהִנֵּה כִּכַּר עֹפֶרֶת

lead cover-of then-see! (7) the-land throughout-all-of appearance-of-them this

נִשֵּׂאת וְזֹאת אִשָּׁה אַחַת יוֹשֶׁבֶת בְּתוֹךְ הָאֵיפָה׃ וַיֹּאמֶר

and-he-said (8) the-basket in-inside-of sitting one woman and-this being-raised

זֹאת הָרִשְׁעָה וַיַּשְׁלֵךְ אֹתָהּ אֶל־ תּוֹךְ הָאֵיפָה וַיַּשְׁלֵךְ אֶת־

*** and-he-pushed the-basket inside-of into her and-he-pushed the-wickedness this

אֶבֶן הָעֹפֶרֶת אֶל־ פִּיהָ׃ וָאֶשָּׂא עֵינַי וָאֵרֶא

and-I-looked eyes-of-me then-I-lifted-up (9) mouth-of-her over the-lead cover-of

וְהִנֵּה שְׁתַּיִם נָשִׁים יוֹצְאוֹת וְרוּחַ בְּכַנְפֵיהֶם וְלָהֵנָּה כְנָפַיִם

wings and-to-them in-wings-of-them with-wind ones-appearing women two and-see!

כְּכַנְפֵי הַחֲסִידָה וַתִּשֶּׂאנָה אֶת־ הָאֵיפָה בֵּין הָאָרֶץ

the-earth between the-basket *** and-they-lifted-up the-stork like-wings-of

וּבֵין הַשָּׁמָיִם׃ וָאֹמַר אֶל־ הַמַּלְאָךְ הַדֹּבֵר בִּי

to-me the-one-speaking the-angel to and-I-asked (10) the-heavens and-between

אָנָה הֵמָּה מוֹלִכוֹת אֶת־ הָאֵיפָה׃ וַיֹּאמֶר אֵלַי לִבְנוֹת־ לָהּ

for-her to-build to-me and-he-replied (11) the-basket *** ones-taking they to-where?

בַיִת בְּאֶרֶץ שִׁנְעָר וְהוּכַן וְהֻנִּיחָה שָּׁם עַל־ מְכֻנָתָהּ׃

place-of-her in there then-she-will-be-set when-he-is-ready Shinar in-land-of house

וָאָשֻׁב וָאֶשָּׂא עֵינַי וָאֶרְאֶה וְהִנֵּה אַרְבַּע מַרְכָּבוֹת

chariots four-of and-see! and-I-looked eyes-of-me and-I-lifted-up and-I-did-again (6:1)

יֹצְאוֹת מִבֵּין שְׁנֵי הֶהָרִים וְהֶהָרִים הָרֵי

mountains-of and-the-mountains the-mountains two-of from-between ones-coming-out

נְחֹשֶׁת׃ בַּמֶּרְכָּבָה הָרִאשֹׁנָה סוּסִים אֲדֻמִּים וּבַמֶּרְכָּבָה הַשֵּׁנִית

the-second and-to-the-chariot red-ones horses the-first to-the-chariot (2) bronze

סוּסִים שְׁחֹרִים׃ וּבַמֶּרְכָּבָה הַשְּׁלִשִׁית סוּסִים לְבָנִים

white-ones horses the-third and-to-the-chariot (3) black-ones horses

וּבַמֶּרְכָּבָה הָרְבִעִית סוּסִים בְּרֻדִּים אֲמֻצִּים׃ וָאַעַן

and-I-asked (4) powerful-ones dappled-ones horses the-fourth and-to-the-chariot

and the house of him who swears falsely by my name. It will remain in his house and destroy it, both its timbers and its stones.' "

*The Woman in a Basket*

5 Then the angel who was speaking to me came forward and said to me, "Look up and see what this is that is appearing."

6 I asked, "What is it?"

He replied, "It is a measuring basket.[h]" And he added, "This is the iniquity[i] of the people throughout the land."

7 Then the cover of lead was raised, and there in the basket sat a woman! 8 He said, "This is wickedness," and he pushed her back into the basket and pushed the lead cover down over its mouth.

9 Then I looked up—and there before me were two women, with the wind in their wings! They had wings like those of a stork, and they lifted up the basket between heaven and earth.

10 "Where are they taking the basket?" I asked the angel who was speaking to me.

11 He replied, "To the country of Babylonia[j] to build a house for it. When it is ready, the basket will be set there in its place."

*Four Chariots*

6 I looked up again—and there before me were four chariots coming out from between two mountains—mountains of bronze! 2 The first chariot had red horses, the second black, 3 the third white, and the fourth dappled—all of them powerful. 4 I asked the angel

[h] 6 Hebrew *an ephah;* also in verses 7-11
[i] 6 Or *appearance*
[j] 11 Hebrew *Shinar*

וָאֹמַר אֶל־ הַמַּלְאָךְ הַדֹּבֵר בִּי מָה־ אֵלֶּה אֲדֹנִי׃
lord-of-me these what? to-me the-one-speaking the-angel to and-I-said

וַיַּעַן הַמַּלְאָךְ וַיֹּאמֶר אֵלָי אֵלֶּה אַרְבַּע רֻחוֹת הַשָּׁמַיִם
the-heavens spirits-of four-of these to-me and-he-said the-angel and-he-answered (4)

יוֹצְאוֹת מֵהִתְיַצֵּב עַל־ אֲדוֹן כָּל־ הָאָרֶץ׃ אֲשֶׁר־ בָּהּ
to-her that (6) the-world whole-of Lord-of before from-to-stand ones-going-out

הַסּוּסִים הַשְּׁחֹרִים יֹצְאִים אֶל־ אֶרֶץ צָפוֹן וְהַלְּבָנִים
and-the-white-ones north country-of toward the-ones-going the-black-ones the-horses

יָצְאוּ אֶל־ אַחֲרֵיהֶם וְהַבְּרֻדִּים יָצְאוּ אֶל־ אֶרֶץ הַתֵּימָן׃
the-south country-of toward they-go and-the-dappled-ones west-of-them toward they-go

וְהָאֲמֻצִּים יָצְאוּ וַיְבַקְשׁוּ לָלֶכֶת לְהִתְהַלֵּךְ*
to-go-around to-go then-they-strained they-went-out when-the-powerful-ones (7)

בָּאָרֶץ וַיֹּאמֶר לְכוּ הִתְהַלְּכוּ בָאָרֶץ וַתִּתְהַלַּכְנָה
so-they-went throughout-the-earth go-around! go! and-he-said throughout-the-earth

בָּאָרֶץ׃ וַיַּזְעֵק אֹתִי וַיְדַבֵּר אֵלַי לֵאמֹר רְאֵה
look! to-say to-me and-he-said me then-he-called (8) throughout-the-earth

הַיּוֹצְאִים אֶל־ אֶרֶץ צָפוֹן הֵנִיחוּ אֶת־ רוּחִי בְּאֶרֶץ
in-land-of Spirit-of-me *** they-gave-rest north country-of toward the-ones-going

צָפוֹן׃ וַיְהִי דְבַר־ יְהוָה אֵלַי לֵאמֹר׃ לָקוֹחַ מֵאֵת הַגּוֹלָה
the-exile from-with to-take (10) to-say to-me Yahweh word-of and-he-came (9) north

מֵחֶלְדַּי וּמֵאֵת טוֹבִיָּה וּמֵאֵת יְדַעְיָה וּבָאתָ אַתָּה בַּיּוֹם
on-the-day you and-you-go Jedaiah and-from-with Tobijah and-from-with from-Heldai

הַהוּא וּבָאתָ בֵּית יֹאשִׁיָּה בֶן־ צְפַנְיָה אֲשֶׁר־ בָּאוּ מִבָּבֶל׃
from-Babylon they-arrived who Zephaniah son-of Josiah house-of and-you-go the-same

וְלָקַחְתָּ כֶסֶף־ וְזָהָב וְעָשִׂיתָ עֲטָרוֹת וְשַׂמְתָּ בְּרֹאשׁ יְהוֹשֻׁעַ
Joshua on-head-of and-you-put crowns and-you-make and-gold silver and-you-take (11)

בֶּן־ יְהוֹצָדָק הַכֹּהֵן הַגָּדוֹל׃ וְאָמַרְתָּ אֵלָיו לֵאמֹר כֹּה אָמַר
he-says this to-say to-him and-you-tell (12) the-high the-priest Jehozadak son-of

יְהוָה צְבָאוֹת לֵאמֹר הִנֵּה־ אִישׁ צֶמַח שְׁמוֹ וּמִתַּחְתָּיו
and-from-place-of-him name-of-him Branch man here! to-say Hosts Yahweh-of

יִצְמָח וּבָנָה אֶת־ הֵיכַל יְהוָה׃ וְהוּא יִבְנֶה
he-will-build and-he (13) Yahweh temple-of *** and-he-will-build he-will-branch-out

אֶת־ הֵיכַל יְהוָה וְהוּא־ יִשָּׂא הוֹד וְיָשַׁב
and-he-will-sit majesty he-will-be-clothed and-he Yahweh temple-of ***

וּמָשַׁל עַל־ כִּסְאוֹ וְהָיָה כֹהֵן עַל־ כִּסְאוֹ
throne-of-him on priest and-he-will-be throne-of-him on and-he-will-rule

וַעֲצַת שָׁלוֹם תִּהְיֶה בֵּין שְׁנֵיהֶם׃ וְהָעֲטָרֹת
and-the-crowns (14) two-of-them between she-will-be harmony and-advice-of

who was speaking to me, "What are these, my lord?"

5The angel answered me, "These are the four spirits[k] of heaven, going out from standing in the presence of the Lord of the whole world. 6The one with the black horses is going toward the north country, the one with the white horses toward the west,[l] and the one with the dappled horses toward the south."

7When the powerful horses went out, they were straining to go throughout the earth. And he said, "Go throughout the earth!" So they went throughout the earth.

8Then he called to me, "Look, those going toward the north country have given my Spirit[m] rest in the land of the north."

*A Crown for Joshua*

9The word of the LORD came to me: 10"Take ⌞silver and gold⌟ from the exiles Heldai, Tobijah and Jedaiah, who have arrived from Babylon. Go the same day to the house of Josiah son of Zephaniah. 11Take the silver and gold and make a crown, and set it on the head of the high priest, Joshua son of Jehozadak. 12Tell him this is what the LORD Almighty says: 'Here is the man whose name is the Branch, and he will branch out from his place and build the temple of the LORD. 13It is he who will build the temple of the LORD, and he will be clothed with majesty and will sit and rule on his throne. And he will be a priest on his throne. And there will be harmony between the two.' 14The

k5 Or *winds* l6 Or *horses after them*
m8 Or *spirit*

*7 Most mss have *sheva* in the *kaph* (ךְ).

תִּהְיֶה לְחֵלֶם וּלְטוֹבִיָּה וְלִידַעְיָה וּלְחֵן בֶּן־ צְפַנְיָה
Zephaniah son-of and-to-Hen and-to-Jedaiah and-to-Tobijah to-Helem she-will-be

לְזִכָּרוֹן בְּהֵיכַל יְהוָה׃ וּרְחוֹקִים ׀ יָבֹאוּ
they-will-come and-ones-far-away (15) Yahweh in-temple-of as-memorial

וּבָנוּ בְּהֵיכַל יְהוָה וִידַעְתֶּם כִּי־ יְהוָה צְבָאוֹת
Hosts Yahweh-of that and-you-will-know Yahweh to-temple-of and-they-will-build

שְׁלָחַנִי אֲלֵיכֶם וְהָיָה אִם־ שָׁמוֹעַ תִּשְׁמְעוּן בְּקוֹל יְהוָה
Yahweh to-voice-of you-obey to-obey if and-he-will-happen to-you he-sent-me

אֱלֹהֵיכֶם׃ וַיְהִי בִּשְׁנַת אַרְבַּע לְדָרְיָוֶשׁ הַמֶּלֶךְ הָיָה דְבַר־
word-of he-came the-king of-Darius four in-year-of and-he-was (7:1) God-of-you

יְהוָה אֶל־ זְכַרְיָה בְּאַרְבָּעָה לַחֹדֶשׁ הַתְּשִׁעִי בְּכִסְלֵו׃ וַיִּשְׁלַח
and-he-sent (2) in-Kislev the-ninth of-the-month on-four Zechariah to Yahweh

בֵּית־אֵל שַׂר־אֶצֶר וְרֶגֶם מֶלֶךְ וַאֲנָשָׁיו לְחַלּוֹת אֶת־ פְּנֵי יְהוָה׃
Yahweh faces-of *** to-entreat with-men-of-him Melech and-Regem Ezer Shar El Beth

לֵאמֹר אֶל־ הַכֹּהֲנִים אֲשֶׁר לְבֵית־ יְהוָה צְבָאוֹת וְאֶל־ הַנְּבִיאִים
the-prophets and-to Hosts Yahweh-of of-house-of who the-priests to to-ask (3)

לֵאמֹר הַאֶבְכֶּה בַּחֹדֶשׁ הַחֲמִשִׁי הִנָּזֵר כַּאֲשֶׁר עָשִׂיתִי זֶה כַּמֶּה
so-many! this I-did as-that to-fast the-fifth in-the-month should-I-mourn? to-say

שָׁנִים׃ וַיְהִי דְּבַר־ יְהוָה צְבָאוֹת אֵלַי לֵאמֹר׃ אֱמֹר אֶל־כָּל־
all-of to ask! (5) to-say to-me Hosts Yahweh-of word-of then-he-came (4) years

עַם הָאָרֶץ וְאֶל־ הַכֹּהֲנִים לֵאמֹר כִּי־ צַמְתֶּם וְסָפוֹד
and-to-mourn you-fasted when to-say the-priests and-to the-land people-of

בַּחֲמִישִׁי וּבַשְּׁבִיעִי וְזֶה שִׁבְעִים שָׁנָה הֲצוֹם צַמְתֻּנִי
did-you-fast-for-me to-fast? year seventy for-this and-in-the-seventh in-the-fifth

אָנִי׃ וְכִי תֹאכְלוּ וְכִי תִשְׁתּוּ הֲלוֹא אַתֶּם הָאֹכְלִים וְאַתֶּם
and-you the-ones-eating you not? you-drank and-when you-ate and-when (6) I

הַשֹּׁתִים׃ הֲלוֹא אֶת־הַדְּבָרִים אֲשֶׁר קָרָא יְהוָה בְּיַד
through-hand-of Yahweh he-proclaimed that the-words *** not? (7) the-ones-drinking

הַנְּבִיאִים הָרִאשֹׁנִים בִּהְיוֹת יְרוּשָׁלַםִ יֹשֶׁבֶת וּשְׁלֵוָה
and-prosperous one-resting Jerusalem when-to-be the-earlier-ones the-prophets

וְעָרֶיהָ סְבִיבֹתֶיהָ וְהַנֶּגֶב וְהַשְּׁפֵלָה יֹשֵׁב׃
being-settled and-the-western-foothill and-the-Negev ones-around-her and-towns-of-her

וַיְהִי דְּבַר־ יְהוָה אֶל־זְכַרְיָה לֵאמֹר׃ כֹּה אָמַר יְהוָה
Yahweh-of he-says this (9) to-say Zechariah to Yahweh word-of then-he-came (8)

צְבָאוֹת לֵאמֹר מִשְׁפַּט אֱמֶת שְׁפֹטוּ וְחֶסֶד וְרַחֲמִים עֲשׂוּ
show! and-compassions and-mercy administer-justice! truth justice-of to-say Hosts

אִישׁ אֶת־ אָחִיו׃ וְאַלְמָנָה וְיָתוֹם גֵּר וְעָנִי אַל־ תַּעֲשֹׁקוּ
you-oppress not or-poor alien or-fatherless and-widow (10) another-of-him *** one

crown will be given to Heldai,[n]
Tobijah, Jedaiah and Hen[o] son of
Zephaniah as a memorial in the
temple of the LORD.
15 Those who
are far away will come and help to
build the temple of the LORD, and
you will know that the LORD Almighty has sent me to you. This
will happen if you diligently obey
the LORD your God."

*Justice and Mercy, Not Fasting*

7 In the fourth year of King
Darius, the word of the LORD
came to Zechariah on the fourth
day of the ninth month, the
month of Kislev.
2 The people of
Bethel had sent Sharezer and
Regem-Melech, together with
their men, to entreat the LORD
3 by
asking the priests of the house of
the LORD Almighty and the prophets, "Should I mourn and fast in
the fifth month, as I have done for
so many years?"
4 Then the word of the LORD Almighty came to me:
5 "Ask all the
people of the land and the priests,
'When you fasted and mourned in
the fifth and seventh months for
the past seventy years, was it
really for me that you fasted?
6 And
when you were eating and drinking, were you not just feasting for
yourselves?
7 Are these not the
words the LORD proclaimed
through the earlier prophets when
Jerusalem and its surrounding
towns were at rest and prosperous, and the Negev and the western foothills were settled?' "
8 And the word of the LORD came
again to Zechariah:
9 "This is what
the LORD Almighty says: 'Administer true justice; show mercy and
compassion to one another.
10 Do
not oppress the widow or the fatherless, the alien or the poor. In

n14 Syriac; Hebrew *Helem*
o14 Or *and the gracious one, the*

וְרָעַת֙ אִ֣ישׁ אָחִ֔יו אַֽל־ תַּחְשְׁב֖וּ בִּלְבַבְכֶ֑ם וַיְמָאֲנ֣וּ

but-they-refused (11) in-heart-of-you you-think not other-of-him each and-evil-of

לְהַקְשִׁ֗יב וַיִּתְּנ֤וּ כָתֵף֙ סֹרָ֔רֶת וְאָזְנֵיהֶ֖ם הִכְבִּ֥ידוּ

they-stopped-up and-ears-of-them being-stubborn back and-they-turned to-pay-attention

מִשְּׁמֽוֹעַ׃ וְלִבָּ֞ם שָׂ֣מוּ שָׁמִ֗יר מִשְּׁמ֙וֹעַ֙ אֶת־הַתּוֹרָ֔ה

the-law to from-to-listen flint they-made and-heart-of-them (12) from-to-listen

וְאֶת־הַדְּבָרִ֗ים אֲשֶׁ֨ר שָׁלַ֜ח יְהוָ֤ה צְבָאוֹת֙ בְּרוּח֔וֹ בְּיַ֖ד

through-hand-of by-Spirit-of-him Hosts Yahweh he-sent that the-words or-to

הַנְּבִיאִ֣ים הָרִֽאשֹׁנִ֑ים וַֽיְהִי֙ קֶ֣צֶף גָּד֔וֹל מֵאֵ֖ת יְהוָ֥ה צְבָאֽוֹת׃

Hosts Yahweh-of from-with great anger so-he-was the-earlier-ones the-prophets

וַיְהִ֥י כַאֲשֶׁר־ קָרָ֖א וְלֹ֣א שָׁמֵ֑עוּ כֵּ֤ן יִקְרְאוּ֙ וְלֹ֣א

then-not they-called when they-listened then-not he-called as-when and-he-was (13)

אֶשְׁמָ֔ע אָמַ֖ר יְהוָ֥ה צְבָאֽוֹת׃ וְאֵ֣סָעֲרֵ֗ם עַ֤ל

among and-I-scattered-with-whirlwind-them (14) Hosts Yahweh-of he-says I-would-listen

כָּל־ הַגּוֹיִם֙ אֲשֶׁ֣ר לֹֽא־ יְדָע֔וּם וְהָאָ֙רֶץ֙ נָשַׁ֣מָּה אַחֲרֵיהֶ֔ם

behind-them she-was-desolate and-the-land they-knew-them not where the-nations all-of

מֵֽעֹבֵ֖ר וּמִשָּׁ֑ב וַיָּשִׂ֧ימוּ אֶֽרֶץ־ חֶמְדָּ֖ה לְשַׁמָּֽה׃

to-desolation pleasantness land-of so-they-made or-from-one-coming from-one-going

וַֽיְהִ֛י דְּבַר־ יְהוָ֥ה צְבָא֖וֹת לֵאמֹֽר׃ כֹּ֤ה אָמַר֙ יְהוָ֣ה צְבָא֔וֹת

Hosts Yahweh-of he-says this (2) to-say Hosts Yahweh-of word-of and-he-came (8:1)

קִנֵּ֧אתִי לְצִיּ֛וֹן קִנְאָ֥ה גְדוֹלָ֖ה וְחֵמָ֣ה גְדוֹלָ֑ה קִנֵּ֖אתִי לָֽהּ׃

for-her I-am-jealous great and-burning great jealousy for-Zion I-am-jealous

כֹּ֚ה אָמַ֣ר יְהוָ֔ה שַׁ֚בְתִּי אֶל־ צִיּ֔וֹן וְשָׁכַנְתִּ֖י בְּת֣וֹךְ יְרוּשָׁלָ֑͏ִם

Jerusalem in-midst-of and-I-will-dwell Zion to I-will-return Yahweh he-says this (3)

וְנִקְרְאָ֤ה יְרֽוּשָׁלַ֙͏ִם֙ עִיר־ הָֽאֱמֶ֔ת וְהַר־ יְהוָ֥ה צְבָא֖וֹת

Hosts Yahweh-of and-mountain-of the-Truth City-of Jerusalem and-she-will-be-called

הַ֥ר הַקֹּֽדֶשׁ׃ כֹּ֤ה אָמַר֙ יְהוָ֣ה צְבָא֔וֹת עֹ֤ד יֵֽשְׁבוּ֙

they-will-sit again Hosts Yahweh-of he-says this (4) the-Holiness Mountain-of

זְקֵנִ֣ים וּזְקֵנ֔וֹת בִּרְחֹב֖וֹת יְרוּשָׁלָ֑͏ִם וְאִ֧ישׁ מִשְׁעַנְתּ֛וֹ בְּיָד֖וֹ

in-hand-of-him cane-of-him and-each Jerusalem in-streets-of and-old-women old-men

מֵרֹ֥ב יָמִֽים׃ וּרְחֹב֤וֹת הָעִיר֙ יִמָּ֣לְא֔וּ יְלָדִ֖ים

boys they-will-be-filled the-city and-streets-of (5) days because-of-many-of

וִֽילָד֑וֹת מְשַׂחֲקִ֖ים בִּרְחֹֽבֹתֶ֑יהָ׃ כֹּ֤ה אָמַר֙ יְהוָ֣ה צְבָא֔וֹת כִּ֣י

indeed Hosts Yahweh-of he-says this (6) in-streets-of-her ones-playing and-girls

יִפָּלֵ֗א בְּעֵינֵי֙ שְׁאֵרִית֙ הָעָ֣ם הַזֶּ֔ה בַּיָּמִ֖ים הָהֵ֑ם

the-those at-the-days the-this the-people remnant-of to-eyes-of he-may-be-marvelous

גַּם־ בְּעֵינַ֖י יִפָּלֵ֑א נְאֻ֖ם יְהוָ֥ה צְבָא֑וֹת כֹּ֤ה

this (7) Hosts Yahweh-of declaration-of will-he-be-marvelous in-eyes-of-me but

your hearts do not think evil of each other.'

[11] "But they refused to pay attention; stubbornly they turned their backs and stopped up their ears. [12] They made their hearts as hard as flint and would not listen to the law or to the words that the LORD Almighty had sent by his Spirit through the earlier prophets. So the LORD Almighty was very angry. [13] " 'When I called, they did not listen; so when they called, I would not listen,' says the LORD Almighty. [14] "I scattered them with a whirlwind among all the nations, where they were strangers. The land was left so desolate behind them that no one could ccme or go. This is how they made the pleasant land desolate.' "

*The LORD Promises to Bless Jerusalem*

8 Again the word of the LORD Almighty came to me. [2] This is what the LORD Almighty says: "I am very jealous for Zion; I am burning with jealousy for her."

[3] This is what the LORD says: "I will return to Zion and dwell in Jerusalem. Then Jerusalem will be called the City of Truth, and the mountain of the LORD Almighty will be called the Holy Mountain."

[4] This is what the LORD Almighty says: "Once again men and women of ripe old age will sit in the streets of Jerusalem, each with cane in hand because of his age. [5] The city streets will be filled with boys and girls playing there."

[6] This is what the LORD Almighty says: "It may seem marvelous to the remnant of this people at that time, but will it seem marvelous to me?" declares the LORD Almighty.

אָמַר יְהוָה צְבָאוֹת הִנְנִי מוֹשִׁיעַ אֶת־ עַמִּי מֵאֶרֶץ מִזְרָח
east from-country-of people-of-me *** saving see-I! Hosts Yahweh-of he-says

וּמֵאֶרֶץ מְבוֹא הַשָּׁמֶשׁ׃ וְהֵבֵאתִי אֹתָם וְשָׁכְנוּ
and-they-will-live them and-I-will-bring (8) the-sun setting-of and-from-country-of

בְּתוֹךְ יְרוּשָׁלָםִ וְהָיוּ־ לִי לְעָם וַאֲנִי אֶהְיֶה לָהֶם
to-them I-will-be and-I as-people to-me and-they-will-be Jerusalem in-midst-of

לֵאלֹהִים בֶּאֱמֶת וּבִצְדָקָה׃ כֹּה־ אָמַר יְהוָה צְבָאוֹת
Hosts Yahweh-of he-says this (9) and-in-righteousness in-faithfulness as-God

תֶּחֱזַקְנָה יְדֵיכֶם הַשֹּׁמְעִים בַּיָּמִים הָאֵלֶּה אֵת הַדְּבָרִים
the-words *** the-these in-the-days the-ones-hearing hands-of-you let-them-be-strong

הָאֵלֶּה מִפִּי הַנְּבִיאִים אֲשֶׁר בְּיוֹם יֻסַּד בֵּית־ יְהוָה
Yahweh-of house-of he-was-founded on-day-of who the-prophets from-mouth-of the-these

צְבָאוֹת הַהֵיכָל לְהִבָּנוֹת׃ כִּי לִפְנֵי הַיָּמִים הָהֵם שְׂכַר הָאָדָם
the-man wage-of the-those the-days before indeed (10) to-be-built the-temple Hosts

לֹא נִהְיָה וּשְׂכַר הַבְּהֵמָה אֵינֶנָּה וְלַיּוֹצֵא
and-to-the-one-going there-was-not-her the-beast or-wage-of he-was not

וְלַבָּא אֵין־ שָׁלוֹם מִן־ הַצָּר וַאֲשַׁלַּח אֶת־
*** for-I-turned the-enemy because-of safety there-was-no and-to-the-one-coming

כָּל־ הָאָדָם אִישׁ בְּרֵעֵהוּ׃ וְעַתָּה לֹא כַיָּמִים
as-the-days not but-now (11) against-neighbor-of-him each the-man every-of

הָרִאשֹׁנִים אֲנִי לִשְׁאֵרִית הָעָם הַזֶּה נְאֻם יְהוָה צְבָאוֹת׃
Hosts Yahweh-of declaration-of the-this the-people with-remnant-of I the-past-ones

כִּי־ זֶרַע הַשָּׁלוֹם הַגֶּפֶן תִּתֵּן פִּרְיָהּ
fruit-of-her she-will-yield the-vine the-well-being seed-of indeed (12)

וְהָאָרֶץ תִּתֵּן אֶת־ יְבוּלָהּ וְהַשָּׁמַיִם יִתְּנוּ
they-will-drop and-the-heavens crop-of-her *** she-will-produce and-the-ground

טַלָּם וְהִנְחַלְתִּי אֶת־ שְׁאֵרִית הָעָם הַזֶּה אֶת־
*** the-this the-people remnant-of to and-I-will-give-as-inheritance dew-of-them

כָּל־ אֵלֶּה׃ וְהָיָה כַּאֲשֶׁר הֱיִיתֶם קְלָלָה בַּגּוֹיִם בֵּית
house-of among-the-nations curse you-were as-that and-he-will-be (13) these all-of

יְהוּדָה וּבֵית יִשְׂרָאֵל כֵּן אוֹשִׁיעַ אֶתְכֶם וִהְיִיתֶם בְּרָכָה אַל־
not blessing and-you-will-be you I-will-save so Israel and-house-of Judah

תִּירָאוּ תֶּחֱזַקְנָה יְדֵיכֶם׃ כִּי כֹה אָמַר יְהוָה צְבָאוֹת
Hosts Yahweh-of he-says this indeed (14) hands-of-you let-them-be-strong you-be-afraid

כַּאֲשֶׁר זָמַמְתִּי* לְהָרַע לָכֶם בְּהַקְצִיף אֲבֹתֵיכֶם אֹתִי
me fathers-of-you when-to-anger upon-you to-bring-disaster I-determined just-as

אָמַר יְהוָה צְבָאוֹת וְלֹא נִחָמְתִּי׃ כֵּן שַׁבְתִּי זָמַמְתִּי
I-determined I-did-again so (15) I-showed-pity and-not Hosts Yahweh-of he-says

7This is what the LORD Almighty says: "I will save my people from the countries of the east and the west. 8I will bring them back to live in Jerusalem; they will be my people, and I will be faithful and righteous to them as their God."

9This is what the LORD Almighty says: "You who now hear these words spoken by the prophets who were there when the foundation was laid for the house of the LORD Almighty, let your hands be strong so that the temple may be built. 10Before that time there were no wages for man or beast. No one could go about his business safely because of his enemy, for I had turned every man against his neighbor. 11But now I will not deal with the remnant of this people as I did in the past," declares the LORD Almighty.

12"The seed will grow well, the vine will yield its fruit, the ground will produce its crops, and the heavens will drop their dew. I will give all these things as an inheritance to the remnant of this people. 13As you have been an object of cursing among the nations, O Judah and Israel, so will I save you, and you will be a blessing. Do not be afraid, but let your hands be strong."

14This is what the LORD Almighty says: "Just as I had determined to bring disaster upon you and showed no pity when your fathers angered me," says the LORD Almighty, 15"so now I have determined to do good again to

*14 Most mss have the accent over the first *mem* (זִמַּמְתִּי).

בַּיָּמִים הָאֵלֶּה לְהֵיטִיב אֶת־ יְרוּשָׁלַםִ וְאֶת־ בֵּית יְהוּדָה אַל־
not Judah house-of and-to Jerusalem to to-do-good the-these in-the-days

תִּירָאוּ׃ אֵלֶּה הַדְּבָרִים אֲשֶׁר תַּעֲשׂוּ דַּבְּרוּ אֱמֶת אִישׁ אֶת־
to each truth speak! you-must-do that the-things these (16) you-be-afraid

רֵעֵהוּ אֱמֶת וּמִשְׁפַּט שָׁלוֹם שִׁפְטוּ בְּשַׁעֲרֵיכֶם׃
in-courts-of-you render-judgment! soundness and-judgment-of truth other-of-him

וְאִישׁ ׀ אֶת־ רָעַת רֵעֵהוּ אַל־תַּחְשְׁבוּ בִּלְבַבְכֶם וּשְׁבֻעַת
and-swearing-of in-heart-of-you you-plot not neighbor-of-him evil-of *** and-each (17)

שֶׁקֶר אַל־תֶּאֱהָבוּ כִּי אֶת־ כָּל־ אֵלֶּה אֲשֶׁר שָׂנֵאתִי נְאֻם־ יְהוָה׃
Yahweh declaration-of I-hate that these all-of *** indeed you-love not falseness

וַיְהִי דְּבַר־ יְהוָה צְבָאוֹת אֵלַי לֵאמֹר׃ כֹּה־ אָמַר יְהוָה
Yahweh-of he-says this (19) to-say to-me Hosts Yahweh-of word-of and-he-came (18)

צְבָאוֹת צוֹם הָרְבִיעִי וְצוֹם הַחֲמִישִׁי וְצוֹם הַשְּׁבִיעִי
the-seventh and-fast-of the-fifth and-fast-of the-fourth fast-of Hosts

וְצוֹם הָעֲשִׂירִי יִהְיֶה לְבֵית־ יְהוּדָה לְשָׂשׂוֹן וּלְשִׂמְחָה
and-for-gladness for-joy Judah for-house-of he-will-become the-tenth and-fast-of

וּלְמֹעֲדִים טוֹבִים וְהָאֱמֶת וְהַשָּׁלוֹם אֱהָבוּ׃ כֹּה
this (20) love! and-the-peace therefore-the-truth happy-ones and-for-festivals

אָמַר יְהוָה צְבָאוֹת עֹד אֲשֶׁר יָבֹאוּ עַמִּים וְיֹשְׁבֵי
and-ones-inhabiting-of peoples they-will-come that yet Hosts Yahweh-of he-says

עָרִים רַבּוֹת׃ וְהָלְכוּ יֹשְׁבֵי אַחַת אֶל־ אַחַת לֵאמֹר
to-say another to one ones-inhabiting-of and-they-will-go (21) many-ones cities

נֵלְכָה הָלוֹךְ לְחַלּוֹת אֶת־ פְּנֵי יְהוָה וּלְבַקֵּשׁ אֶת־ יְהוָה צְבָאוֹת
Hosts Yahweh-of *** and-to-seek Yahweh faces-of *** to-entreat to-go let-us-go

אֵלְכָה גַּם־ אָנִי׃ וּבָאוּ עַמִּים רַבִּים וְגוֹיִם
and-nations many-ones peoples and-they-will-come (22) myself indeed I-am-going

עֲצוּמִים לְבַקֵּשׁ אֶת־ יְהוָה צְבָאוֹת בִּירוּשָׁלָםִ וּלְחַלּוֹת אֶת־
*** and-to-entreat in-Jerusalem Hosts Yahweh-of *** to-seek powerful-ones

פְּנֵי יְהוָה׃ כֹּה אָמַר יְהוָה צְבָאוֹת בַּיָּמִים הָהֵמָּה אֲשֶׁר
that the-those in-the-days Hosts Yahweh-of he-says this (23) Yahweh faces-of

יַחֲזִיקוּ עֲשָׂרָה אֲנָשִׁים מִכֹּל לְשֹׁנוֹת הַגּוֹיִם וְהֶחֱזִיקוּ
and-they-will-hold the-nations languages-of from-all-of men ten they-will-take-hold

בִּכְנַף אִישׁ יְהוּדִי לֵאמֹר נֵלְכָה עִמָּכֶם כִּי שָׁמַעְנוּ אֱלֹהִים
God we-heard because with-you let-us-go to-say Jew one by-hem-of-robe-of

עִמָּכֶם׃ מַשָּׂא דְבַר־ יְהוָה בְּאֶרֶץ חַדְרָךְ וְדַמֶּשֶׂק
and-Damascus Hadrach against-land-of Yahweh word-of oracle (9:1) with-you

מְנֻחָתוֹ כִּי לַיהוָה עֵין אָדָם וְכֹל שִׁבְטֵי יִשְׂרָאֵל׃
Israel tribes-of and-all-of man eye-of on-Yahweh for resting-place-of-him

Jerusalem and Judah. Do not be afraid. [16]These are the things you are to do: Speak the truth to each other, and render true and sound judgment in your courts; [17]do not plot evil against your neighbor, and do not love to swear falsely. I hate all this," declares the LORD.

[18]Again the word of the LORD Almighty came to me. [19]This is what the LORD Almighty says: "The fasts of the fourth, fifth, seventh and tenth months will become joyful and glad occasions and happy festivals for Judah. Therefore love truth and peace."

[20]This is what the LORD Almighty says: "Many peoples and the inhabitants of many cities will yet come, [21]and the inhabitants of one city will go to another and say, 'Let us go at once to entreat the LORD and seek the LORD Almighty. I myself am going.' [22]And many peoples and powerful nations will come to Jerusalem to seek the LORD Almighty and to entreat him."

[23]This is what the LORD Almighty says: "In those days ten men from all languages and nations will take firm hold of one Jew by the hem of his robe and say, 'Let us go with you, because we have heard that God is with you.' "

*Judgment on Israel's Enemies*

An Oracle

9 The word of the LORD is
against the land of
Hadrach
and will rest upon
Damascus—
for the eyes of men and all the
tribes of Israel
are on the LORD—[p]

[p]1 *Or Damascus. / For the eye of the LORD is on all mankind, / as well as on the tribes of Israel,*

וְגַם־ חֲמָת תִּגְבָּל־ בָּהּ צֹר וְצִידוֹן כִּי חָכְמָה מְאֹד׃
**very she-is-skillful though and-Sidon Tyre on-her she-borders Hamath and-too (2)**

וַתִּבֶן צֹר מָצוֹר לָהּ וַתִּצְבָּר־ כֶּסֶף כֶּעָפָר
**like-the-dust silver and-she-heaped-up for-her stronghold Tyre and-she-built (3)**

וְחָרוּץ כְּטִיט חוּצוֹת׃ הִנֵּה אֲדֹנָי יוֹרִשֶׁנָּה
**he-will-take-away-possessions-of-her Lord see! (4) streets like-dirt-of and-gold**

וְהִכָּה בַיָּם חֵילָהּ וְהִיא בָּאֵשׁ תֵּאָכֵל׃
**she-will-be-consumed by-fire and-she power-of-her on-the-sea and-he-will-destroy**

תֵּרֶא אַשְׁקְלוֹן וְתִירָא וְעַזָּה וְתָחִיל מְאֹד
**greatly and-she-will-writhe-in-agony and-Gaza and-she-will-fear Ashkelon she-will-see (5)**

וְעֶקְרוֹן כִּי־ הֹבִישׁ מֶבָּטָהּ וְאָבַד מֶלֶךְ מֵעַזָּה
**from-Gaza king and-he-will-be-lost hope-of-her he-will-wither for and-Ekron**

וְאַשְׁקְלוֹן לֹא תֵשֵׁב׃ וְיָשַׁב מַמְזֵר בְּאַשְׁדּוֹד
**in-Ashdod foreigner and-he-will-occupy (6) she-will-be-inhabited not and-Ashkelon**

וְהִכְרַתִּי גְּאוֹן פְּלִשְׁתִּים׃ וַהֲסִרֹתִי דָמָיו
**bloods-of-him and-I-will-take (7) Philistines pride-of and-I-will-cut-off**

מִפִּיו וְשִׁקֻּצָיו מִבֵּין שִׁנָּיו
**teeth-of-him from-between and-forbidden-foods-of-him from-mouth-of-him**

וְנִשְׁאַר גַּם־ הוּא לֵאלֹהֵינוּ וְהָיָה כְּאַלֻּף בִּיהוּדָה
**in-Judah as-leader and-he-will-become to-God-of-us he also and-he-will-be-left**

וְעֶקְרוֹן כִּיבוּסִי׃ וְחָנִיתִי לְבֵיתִי מִצָּבָה
**from-force to-house-of-me but-I-will-defend (8) like-Jebusite and-Ekron**

מֵעֹבֵר וּמִשָּׁב וְלֹא־ יַעֲבֹר עֲלֵיהֶם עוֹד
**again over-them he-will-overrun and-never and-from-one-coming from-one-marauding**

נֹגֵשׂ כִּי עַתָּה רָאִיתִי בְעֵינָי׃ גִּילִי מְאֹד בַּת־
**Daughter-of greatly rejoice! (9) with-eyes-of-me I-keep-watch now for one-oppressing**

צִיּוֹן הָרִיעִי בַּת יְרוּשָׁלִַם הִנֵּה מַלְכֵּךְ יָבוֹא לָךְ צַדִּיק
**righteous to-you he-comes king-of-you see! Jerusalem Daughter-of shout! Zion**

וְנוֹשָׁע הוּא עָנִי וְרֹכֵב עַל־ חֲמוֹר וְעַל־ עַיִר בֶּן־ אֲתֹנוֹת׃
**donkeys foal-of colt even-on donkey on and-riding gentle he and-having-salvation**

וְהִכְרַתִּי־ רֶכֶב מֵאֶפְרַיִם וְסוּס מִירוּשָׁלִַם
**from-Jerusalem and-horse from-Ephraim chariot and-I-will-take-away (10)**

וְנִכְרְתָה קֶשֶׁת מִלְחָמָה וְדִבֶּר שָׁלוֹם לַגּוֹיִם
**to-the-nations peace and-he-will-proclaim battle bow-of and-she-will-be-broken**

וּמָשְׁלוֹ מִיָּם עַד־ יָם וּמִנָּהָר עַד־ אַפְסֵי־ אָרֶץ׃ גַּם־ אַתְּ
**you also (11) earth ends-of to and-from-River sea to from-sea and-rule-of-him**

בְּדַם־ בְּרִיתֵךְ שִׁלַּחְתִּי אֲסִירַיִךְ מִבּוֹר
**from-pit prisoners-of-you I-will-free covenant-of-you because-of-blood-of**

2 and upon Hamath too, which borders on it,
and upon Tyre and Sidon, though they are very skillful.
3 Tyre has built herself a stronghold;
she has heaped up silver like dust,
and gold like the dirt of the streets.
4 But the Lord will take away her possessions
and destroy her power on the sea,
and she will be consumed by fire.
5 Ashkelon will see it and fear;
Gaza will writhe in agony,
and Ekron too, for her hope will wither.
Gaza will lose her king
and Ashkelon will be deserted.
6 Foreigners will occupy Ashdod,
and I will cut off the pride of the Philistines.
7 I will take the blood from their mouths,
the forbidden food from between their teeth.
Those who are left will belong to our God
and become leaders in Judah,
and Ekron will be like the Jebusites.
8 But I will defend my house against marauding forces.
Never again will an oppressor overrun my people,
for now I am keeping watch.

*The Coming of Zion's King*

9 Rejoice greatly, O Daughter of Zion!
Shout, Daughter of Jerusalem!
See, your king[q] comes to you,
righteous and having salvation,
gentle and riding on a donkey,
on a colt, the foal of a donkey.
10 I will take away the chariots from Ephraim
and the war-horses from Jerusalem,
and the battle bow will be broken.
He will proclaim peace to the nations.
His rule will extend from sea to sea
and from the River[r] to the ends of the earth.[s]
11 As for you, because of the blood of my covenant with you,
I will free your prisoners from the waterless pit.

q9 Or *King* r10 That is, the Euphrates
s10 Or *the end of the land*

אֵין מַיִם בּוֹ׃ שׁוּבוּ לְבִצָּרוֹן אֲסִירֵי הַתִּקְוָה גַּם־
even the-hope prisoners-of to-fortress return! (12) in-him waters there-are-no

הַיּוֹם מַגִּיד מִשְׁנֶה אָשִׁיב לָךְ׃ כִּי־ דָרַכְתִּי לִי
for-me I-will-bend-bow indeed (13) to-you I-will-restore twice announcing the-day

יְהוּדָה קֶשֶׁת מִלֵּאתִי אֶפְרַיִם וְעוֹרַרְתִּי בָנַיִךְ צִיּוֹן עַל־
against Zion sons-of-you and-I-will-rouse Ephraim I-will-fill bow Judah

בָּנַיִךְ יָוָן וְשַׂמְתִּיךְ כְּחֶרֶב גִּבּוֹר׃ וַיהוָה
then-Yahweh (14) warrior like-sword-of and-I-will-make-you Greece sons-of-you

עֲלֵיהֶם יֵרָאֶה וְיָצָא כַבָּרָק חִצּוֹ
arrow-of-him like-the-lightning and-he-will-flash he-will-appear over-them

וַאדֹנָי יְהוִה בַּשּׁוֹפָר יִתְקָע וְהָלַךְ בְּסַעֲרוֹת
in-storms-of and-he-will-march he-will-sound on-the-trumpet Yahweh and-Sovereign

תֵּימָן׃ יְהוָה צְבָאוֹת יָגֵן עֲלֵיהֶם וְאָכְלוּ
and-they-will-destroy over-them he-will-shield Hosts Yahweh-of (15) south

וְכָבְשׁוּ אַבְנֵי־ קֶלַע וְשָׁתוּ הָמוּ כְּמוֹ־ יָיִן
wine as they-will-roar and-they-will-drink sling stones-of and-they-will-overcome

וּמָלְאוּ כַּמִּזְרָק כְּזָוִיּוֹת מִזְבֵּחַ׃ וְהוֹשִׁיעָם
and-he-will-save-them (16) altar like-corners-of like-the-bowl and-they-will-be-full

יְהוָה אֱלֹהֵיהֶם בַּיּוֹם הַהוּא כְּצֹאן עַמּוֹ כִּי אַבְנֵי־
jewels-of indeed people-of-him as-flock-of the-that on-the-day God-of-them Yahweh

נֵזֶר מִתְנוֹסְסוֹת עַל־ אַדְמָתוֹ׃ כִּי מַה־ טּוּבוֹ וּמַה־
and-how! attractiveness-of-him how! indeed (17) land-of-him in ones-sparkling crown

יָפְיוֹ דָּגָן בַּחוּרִים וְתִירוֹשׁ יְנוֹבֵב בְּתֻלוֹת׃
young-women he-will-make-thrive and-new-wine young-men grain beauty-of-him

שַׁאֲלוּ מֵיְהוָה מָטָר בְּעֵת מַלְקוֹשׁ יְהוָה עֹשֶׂה חֲזִיזִים
storm-clouds making Yahweh spring in-time-of rain from-Yahweh ask! (10:1)

וּמְטַר־ גֶּשֶׁם יִתֵּן לָהֶם לְאִישׁ עֵשֶׂב בַּשָּׂדֶה׃ כִּי
indeed (2) of-the-field plant to-everyone to-them he-gives rain and-shower-of

הַתְּרָפִים דִּבְּרוּ־ אָוֶן וְהַקּוֹסְמִים חָזוּ שֶׁקֶר וַחֲלֹמוֹת
and-dreams-of lie they-see-vision and-the-ones-divining deceit they-speak the-idols

הַשָּׁוְא* יְדַבֵּרוּ הֶבֶל יְנַחֵמוּן עַל־ כֵּן נָסְעוּ כְמוֹ־ צֹאן
sheep like they-wander this for they-give-comfort in-vain they-tell the-falseness

יַעֲנוּ כִּי־ אֵין רֹעֶה׃ עַל־ הָרֹעִים
the-ones-shepherding against (3) one-shepherding there-is-no for they-are-oppressed

חָרָה אַפִּי וְעַל־ הָעַתּוּדִים אֶפְקוֹד כִּי־ פָקַד יְהוָה
Yahweh-of he-will-care for I-will-punish the-leaders and-against anger-of-me he-burns

צְבָאוֹת אֶת־ עֶדְרוֹ אֶת־ בֵּית יְהוּדָה וְשָׂם אוֹתָם כְּסוּס
like-horse-of them and-he-will-make Judah house-of for flock-of-him for Hosts

12 Return to your fortress, O
prisoners of hope;
even now I announce that I
will restore twice as much
to you.
13 I will bend Judah as I bend
my bow
and fill it with Ephraim.
I will rouse your sons, O Zion,
against your sons, O Greece,
and make you like a
warrior's sword.

*The LORD Will Appear*

14 Then the LORD will appear
over them;
his arrow will flash like
lightning.
The Sovereign LORD will sound
the trumpet;
he will march in the storms
of the south,
15 and the LORD Almighty will
shield them.
They will destroy
and overcome with
slingstones.
They will drink and roar as
with wine;
they will be full like a bowl
used for sprinkling[†] the
corners of the altar.
16 The LORD their God will save
them on that day
as the flock of his people.
They will sparkle in his land
like jewels in a crown.
17 How attractive and beautiful
they will be!
Grain will make the young
men thrive,
and new wine the young
women.

*The LORD Will Care for Judah*

10 Ask the LORD for rain in
the springtime;
it is the LORD who makes
the storm clouds.
He gives showers of rain to
men,
and plants of the field to
everyone.
2 The idols speak deceit,
diviners see visions that lie;
they tell dreams that are false,
they give comfort in vain.
Therefore the people wander
like sheep
oppressed for lack of a
shepherd.

3 "My anger burns against the
shepherds,
and I will punish the
leaders;
for the LORD Almighty will
care
for his flock, the house of
Judah,
and make them like a proud

[†]15 Or *bowl, / like*

***2 Most mss have *sheva* under the *vav* (וְא־).**

הוֹדוֹ בַּמִּלְחָמָה׃ מִמֶּנּוּ פִנָּה מִמֶּנּוּ יָתֵד מִמֶּנּוּ
from-him tent-peg from-him cornerstone from-him (4) in-the-battle pride-of-him

קֶשֶׁת מִלְחָמָה מִמֶּנּוּ יֵצֵא כָל־ נוֹגֵשׂ יַחְדָּו׃ וְהָיוּ
and-they-will-be (5) together one-ruling every-of he-will-come from-him battle bow-of

כְגִבֹּרִים בּוֹסִים בְּטִיט חוּצוֹת בַּמִּלְחָמָה וְנִלְחֲמוּ
and-they-will-fight in-the-battle streets in-mud-of ones-trampling like-mighty-men

כִּי יְהוָה עִמָּם וְהֹבִישׁוּ רֹכְבֵי סוּסִים׃
horses ones-riding-of and-they-will-overthrow with-them Yahweh because

וְגִבַּרְתִּי ׀ אֶת־ בֵּית יְהוּדָה וְאֶת־ בֵּית יוֹסֵף אוֹשִׁיעַ
I-will-save Joseph house-of and Judah house-of *** and-I-will-strengthen (6)

וְהוֹשְׁבוֹתִים כִּי רִחַמְתִּים וְהָיוּ
and-they-will-be I-have-compassion-on-them because and-I-will-restore-them

כַּאֲשֶׁר לֹא־ זְנַחְתִּים כִּי אֲנִי יְהוָה אֱלֹהֵיהֶם וְאֶעֱנֵם׃
and-I-will-answer-them God-of-them Yahweh I for I-rejected-them not as-though

וְהָיוּ כְגִבּוֹר אֶפְרַיִם וְשָׂמַח לִבָּם
heart-of-them and-he-will-be-glad Ephraim like-mighty-man and-they-will-become (7)

כְּמוֹ־ יָיִן וּבְנֵיהֶם יִרְאוּ וְשָׂמֵחוּ יָגֵל
he-will-rejoice and-they-will-be-joyful they-will-see and-children-of-them wine as

לִבָּם בַּיהוָה׃ אֶשְׁרְקָה לָהֶם וַאֲקַבְּצֵם
and-I-will-gather-in-them for-them I-will-signal (8) in-Yahweh heart-of-them

כִּי פְדִיתִים וְרָבוּ כְּמוֹ רָבוּ׃
they-were-numerous as and-they-will-be-numerous I-will-redeem-them surely

וְאֶזְרָעֵם בָּעַמִּים וּבַמֶּרְחַקִּים
yet-in-the-distant-lands among-the-peoples though-I-scatter-them (9)

יִזְכְּרוּנִי וְחָיוּ אֶת־ בְּנֵיהֶם וָשָׁבוּ׃
and-they-will-return children-of-them with and-they-will-survive they-will-remember-me

וַהֲשֵׁיבוֹתִים מֵאֶרֶץ מִצְרַיִם וּמֵאַשּׁוּר אֲקַבְּצֵם
I-will-gather-them and-from-Assyria Egypt from-land-of and-I-will-bring-back-them (10)

וְאֶל־ אֶרֶץ גִּלְעָד וּלְבָנוֹן אֲבִיאֵם וְלֹא יִמָּצֵא לָהֶם׃
for-them he-will-be-found and-not I-will-bring-them and-Lebanon Gilead land-of and-to

וְעָבַר בַּיָּם צָרָה וְהִכָּה בַיָּם גַּלִּים
surges to-the-sea and-he-will-subdue trouble through-the-sea and-he-will-pass (11)

וְהֹבִישׁוּ כֹּל מְצוּלוֹת יְאֹר וְהוּרַד גְּאוֹן
pride-of and-he-will-be-brought-down Nile depths-of all-of and-they-will-dry-up

אַשּׁוּר וְשֵׁבֶט מִצְרַיִם יָסוּר׃ וְגִבַּרְתִּים
and-I-will-strengthen-them (12) he-will-pass-away Egypt and-scepter-of Assyria

בַּיהוָה וּבִשְׁמוֹ יִתְהַלָּכוּ נְאֻם יְהוָה׃
Yahweh declaration-of they-will-walk and-in-name-of-him in-Yahweh

horse in battle.
4From Judah will come the cornerstone,
from him the tent peg,
from him the battle bow,
from him every ruler.
5Together they[a] will be like mighty men
trampling the muddy streets in battle.
Because the LORD is with them,
they will fight and overthrow the horsemen.

6"I will strengthen the house of Judah
and save the house of Joseph.
I will restore them
because I have compassion on them.
They will be as though
I had not rejected them,
for I am the LORD their God
and I will answer them.
7The Ephraimites will become like mighty men,
and their hearts will be glad as with wine.
Their children will see it and be joyful;
their hearts will rejoice in the LORD.
8I will signal for them
and gather them in.
Surely I will redeem them;
they will be as numerous as before.
9Though I scatter them among the peoples,
yet in distant lands they will remember me.
They and their children will survive,
and they will return.
10I will bring them back from Egypt
and gather them from Assyria.
I will bring them to Gilead and Lebanon,
and there will not be room enough for them.
11They will pass through the sea of trouble;
the surging sea will be subdued
and all the depths of the Nile will dry up.
Assyria's pride will be brought down
and Egypt's scepter will pass away.
12I will strengthen them in the LORD
and in his name they will walk,"
declares the LORD.

[a]4,5 *Or ruler, all of them together. / 5They*

פְּתַח לְבָנוֹן דְּלָתֶיךָ וְתֹאכַל אֵשׁ בַּאֲרָזֶיךָ׃
to-cedars-of-you fire that-she-may-devour doors-of-you Lebanon open! (11:1)

הֵילֵל בְּרוֹשׁ כִּי־ נָפַל אֶרֶז אֲשֶׁר אַדִּרִים שֻׁדָּדוּ הֵילִילוּ
wail! they-are-ruined stately-ones that cedar he-fell for pine-tree wail! (2)

אַלּוֹנֵי בָשָׁן כִּי יָרַד יַעַר הַבָּצוּר׃ קוֹל
sound-of (3) the-one-being-dense forest-of he-came-down for Bashan oaks-of

יִלְלַת הָרֹעִים כִּי שֻׁדְּדָה אַדַּרְתָּם קוֹל
sound-of richness-of-them she-is-destroyed for the-ones-shepherding wailing-of

שַׁאֲגַת כְּפִירִים כִּי שֻׁדַּד גְּאוֹן הַיַּרְדֵּן׃ כֹּה אָמַר יְהוָה
Yahweh he-says this (4) the-Jordan lushness-of he-is-destroyed for lions roar-of

אֱלֹהָי רְעֵה אֶת־ צֹאן הַהֲרֵגָה׃ אֲשֶׁר קֹנֵיהֶן
ones-buying-them that (5) the-slaughter flock-of *** pasture! God-of-me

יַהַרְגֻן וְלֹא יֶאְשָׁמוּ וּמֹכְרֵיהֶן יֹאמַר
they-say and-ones-selling-them they-are-punished and-not they-slaughter-them

בָּרוּךְ יְהוָה וַאעְשִׁר וְרֹעֵיהֶם לֹא יַחְמוֹל עֲלֵיהֶן׃
to-them they-spare not and-ones-shepherding-them for-I-am-rich Yahweh being-praised

כִּי לֹא אֶחְמוֹל עוֹד עַל־ יֹשְׁבֵי הָאָרֶץ נְאֻם־
declaration-of the-land ones-being-peoples-of on longer I-will-have-pity not for (6)

יְהוָה וְהִנֵּה אָנֹכִי מַמְצִיא אֶת־ הָאָדָם אִישׁ בְּיַד־ רֵעֵהוּ
neighbor-of-him into-hand-of each the-everyone *** giving-over I and-see! Yahweh

וּבְיַד מַלְכּוֹ וְכִתְּתוּ אֶת־ הָאָרֶץ וְלֹא אַצִּיל
I-will-rescue and-not the-land *** and-they-will-oppress king-of-him and-into-hand-of

מִיָּדָם׃ וָאֶרְעֶה אֶת־ צֹאן הַהֲרֵגָה לָכֵן
particularly the-slaughter flock-of *** so-I-pastured (7) from-hand-of-them

עֲנִיֵּי הַצֹּאן וָאֶקַּח־ לִי שְׁנֵי מַקְלוֹת לְאַחַד קָרָאתִי נֹעַם
Favor I-called to-one staffs two-of for-me then-I-took the-flock oppressed-ones-of

וּלְאַחַד קָרָאתִי חֹבְלִים וָאֶרְעֶה אֶת־ הַצֹּאן׃ וָאַכְחִד אֶת־
*** and-I-got-rid (8) the-flock *** and-I-pastured Unions I-called and-to-other

שְׁלֹשֶׁת הָרֹעִים בְּיֶרַח אֶחָד וַתִּקְצַר נַפְשִׁי בָּהֶם
of-them self-of-me and-she-grew-weary one in-month the-ones-shepherding three-of

וְגַם־ נַפְשָׁם בָּחֲלָה בִי׃ וָאֹמַר לֹא אֶרְעֶה אֶתְכֶם
you I-will-shepherd not and-I-said (9) to-me she-detested self-of-them and-also

הַמֵּתָה תָמוּת וְהַנִּכְחֶדֶת תִּכָּחֵד וְהַנִּשְׁאָרוֹת
and-the-ones-being-left let-her-perish and-the-one-perishing let-her-die the-one-dying

תֹּאכַלְנָה אִשָּׁה אֶת־ בְּשַׂר רְעוּתָהּ׃ וָאֶקַּח אֶת־ מַקְלִי אֶת־
*** staff-of-me *** then-I-took (10) other-of-her flesh-of *** each let-them-eat

נֹעַם וָאֶגְדַּע אֹתוֹ לְהָפֵיר אֶת־ בְּרִיתִי אֲשֶׁר כָּרַתִּי אֶת־ כָּל־ הָעַמִּים׃
the-nations all-of with I-made that covenant-of-me *** to-revoke him and-I-broke Favor

°2 ק הבציר

11 Open your doors, O Lebanon,
so that fire may devour your cedars!
2 Wail, O pine tree, for the cedar has fallen;
the stately trees are ruined!
Wail, oaks of Bashan;
the dense forest has been cut down!
3 Listen to the wail of the shepherds;
their rich pastures are destroyed!
Listen to the roar of the lions;
the lush thicket of the Jordan is ruined!

*Two Shepherds*

4 This is what the LORD my God says: "Pasture the flock marked for slaughter. 5 Their buyers slaughter them and go unpunished. Those who sell them say, 'Praise the LORD, I am rich!' Their own shepherds do not spare them. 6 For I will no longer have pity on the people of the land," declares the LORD. "I will hand everyone over to his neighbor and his king. They will oppress the land, and I will not rescue them from their hands."

7 So I pastured the flock marked for slaughter, particularly the oppressed of the flock. Then I took two staffs and called one Favor and the other Union, and I pastured the flock. 8 In one month I got rid of the three shepherds.

The flock detested me, and I grew weary of them 9 and said, "I will not be your shepherd. Let the dying die, and the perishing perish. Let those who are left eat one another's flesh."

10 Then I took my staff called Favor and broke it, revoking the covenant I had made with all the nations. 11 It was revoked on that day,

וַתֻּפַר בַּיּוֹם הַהוּא וַיֵּדְעוּ כֵן עֲנִיֵּי
afflicted-ones-of thus so-they-knew the-that on-the-day and-she-was-revoked (11)

הַצֹּאן הַשֹּׁמְרִים אֹתִי כִּי דְבַר־ יְהוָה הוּא׃ וָאֹמַר אֲלֵיהֶם אִם־
if to-them and-I-told (12) he Yahweh word-of that me the-ones-watching the-flock

טוֹב בְּעֵינֵיכֶם הָבוּ שְׂכָרִי וְאִם־ לֹא ׀ חֲדָלוּ וַיִּשְׁקְלוּ אֶת־ שְׂכָרִי
pay-of-me *** so-they-gave keep! not but-if pay-of-me give! in-eyes-of-you best

שְׁלֹשִׁים כָּסֶף׃ וַיֹּאמֶר יְהוָה אֵלַי הַשְׁלִיכֵהוּ אֶל־ הַיּוֹצֵר
the-one-being-potter to throw-him! to-me Yahweh and-he-said (13) silver thirty

אֶדֶר הַיְקָר אֲשֶׁר יָקַרְתִּי מֵעֲלֵיהֶם וָאֶקְחָה שְׁלֹשִׁים
thirty so-I-took from-with-them I-was-priced which the-price handsomeness-of

הַכֶּסֶף וָאַשְׁלִיךְ אֹתוֹ בֵּית יְהוָה אֶל־ הַיּוֹצֵר׃ וָאֶגְדַּע
then-I-broke (14) the-one-being-potter to Yahweh house-of him and-I-threw the-silver

אֶת־ מַקְלִי הַשֵּׁנִי אֵת הַחֹבְלִים לְהָפֵר אֶת־ הָאַחֲוָה בֵּין
between the-brotherhood *** to-break the-Unions *** the-second staff-of-me ***

יְהוּדָה וּבֵין יִשְׂרָאֵל׃ וַיֹּאמֶר יְהוָה אֵלַי עוֹד קַח־ לְךָ
for-you take! again to-me Yahweh then-he-said (15) Israel and-between Judah

כְּלִי רֹעֶה אֱוִלִי׃ כִּי הִנֵּה־אָנֹכִי מֵקִים רֹעֶה
one-shepherding raising-up I see! for (16) foolish one-shepherding equipment-of

בָּאָרֶץ הַנִּכְחָדוֹת לֹא־ יִפְקֹד הַנַּעַר לֹא־ יְבַקֵּשׁ
he-will-seek not the-young he-will-care-for not the-ones-being-lost over-the-land

וְהַנִּשְׁבֶּרֶת לֹא יְרַפֵּא הַנִּצָּבָה לֹא יְכַלְכֵּל
he-will-feed not the-one-being-healthy he-will-heal not and-the-one-being-injured

וּבְשַׂר הַבְּרִיאָה יֹאכַל וּפַרְסֵיהֶן יְפָרֵק׃
he-will-tear-off and-hoofs-of-them he-will-eat the-choice-one but-meat-of

הוֹי רֹעִי הָאֱלִיל עֹזְבִי הַצֹּאן חֶרֶב עַל־
to sword the-flock one-deserting-of the-worthlessness one-shepherding-of woe! (17)

זְרוֹעוֹ וְעַל־ עֵין יְמִינוֹ זְרֹעוֹ יָבוֹשׁ תִּיבָשׁ
may-she-be-withered to-be-withered arm-of-him right-of-him eye-of and-to arm-of-him

וְעֵין יְמִינוֹ כָּהֹה תִכְהֶה׃ מַשָּׂא דְבַר־
word-of oracle (12:1) may-she-be-blind to-be-blind right-of-him and-eye-of

יְהוָה עַל־ יִשְׂרָאֵל נְאֻם־ יְהוָה נֹטֶה שָׁמַיִם
heavens one-stretching-out Yahweh declaration-of Israel concerning Yahweh

וְיֹסֵד אֶרֶץ וְיֹצֵר רוּחַ־ אָדָם בְּקִרְבּוֹ׃ הִנֵּה
see! (2) at-within-him man spirit-of and-one-forming earth and-one-laying-foundation

אָנֹכִי שָׂם אֶת־ יְרוּשָׁלַםִ סַף־ רַעַל לְכָל־ הָעַמִּים סָבִיב
surrounding the-peoples for-all-of reeling cup-of Jerusalem *** making I

וְגַם עַל־ יְהוּדָה יִהְיֶה בַמָּצוֹר עַל־ יְרוּשָׁלָםִ׃
Jerusalem against with-the-siege he-will-be Judah against and-also

and so the afflicted of the flock
who were watching me knew it
was the word of the LORD.
[12]I told them, "If you think it
best, give me my pay; but if not,
keep it." So they paid me thirty
pieces of silver.
[13]And the LORD said to me,
"Throw it to the potter"—the
handsome price at which they
priced me! So I took the thirty
pieces of silver and threw them
into the house of the LORD to the
potter.
[14]Then I broke my second staff
called Union, breaking the brotherhood between Judah and Israel.
[15]Then the LORD said to me,
"Take again the equipment of a
foolish shepherd. [16]For I am going
to raise up a shepherd over the
land who will not care for the lost,
or seek the young, or heal the injured, or feed the healthy, but will
eat the meat of the choice sheep,
tearing off their hoofs.

[17]"Woe to the worthless
shepherd,
who deserts the flock!
May the sword strike his arm
and his right eye!
May his arm be completely
withered,
his right eye totally
blinded!"

*Jerusalem's Enemies to Be Destroyed*

An Oracle

12 This is the word of the
LORD concerning Israel.
The LORD, who stretches out the
heavens, who lays the foundation
of the earth, and who forms the
spirit of man within him, declares: [2]"I am going to make
Jerusalem a cup that sends all the
surrounding peoples reeling.
Judah will be besieged as well as

וְהָיָה בַיּוֹם־ הַהוּא אָשִׂים אֶת־יְרוּשָׁלִַם אֶבֶן מַעֲמָסָה
immovability rock-of Jerusalem *** I-will-make the-that on-the-day and-he-will-be (3)

לְכָל־ הָעַמִּים כָּל־ עֹמְסֶיהָ שָׂרוֹט יִשָּׂרֵטוּ
they-will-be-injured to-injure ones-trying-to-move-her all-of the-nations for-all-of

וְנֶאֶסְפוּ עָלֶיהָ כֹּל גּוֹיֵי הָאָרֶץ׃ בַּיּוֹם הַהוּא
the-that on-the-day (4) the-earth nations-of all-of against-her when-they-are-gathered

נְאֻם־ יְהוָה אַכֶּה כָל־ סוּס בַּתִּמָּהוֹן וְרֹכְבוֹ
and-one-riding-him with-the-panic horse every-of I-will-strike Yahweh declaration-of

בַּשִּׁגָּעוֹן וְעַל־ בֵּית יְהוּדָה אֶפְקַח אֶת־ עֵינַי וְכֹל
but-all-of eyes-of-me *** I-will-keep-watch Judah house-of and-over with-the-madness

סוּס הָעַמִּים אַכֶּה בַּעִוָּרוֹן׃ וְאָמְרוּ
then-they-will-say (5) with-the-blindness I-will-strike the-nations horse-of

אַלֻּפֵי יְהוּדָה בְּלִבָּם אַמְצָה לִי יֹשְׁבֵי יְרוּשָׁלִַם
Jerusalem ones-being-peoples-of to-me strength in-heart-of-them Judah leaders-of

בַּיהוָה צְבָאוֹת אֱלֹהֵיהֶם׃ בַּיּוֹם הַהוּא אָשִׂים אֶת־
*** I-will-make the-that on-the-day (6) God-of-them Hosts because-Yahweh-of

אַלֻּפֵי יְהוּדָה כְּכִיּוֹר אֵשׁ בְּעֵצִים וּכְלַפִּיד אֵשׁ בְּעָמִיר
among-sheaf flame and-like-torch-of in-woods fire like-pot-of Judah leaders-of

וְאָכְלוּ עַל־ יָמִין וְעַל־שְׂמֹאול אֶת־כָּל־ הָעַמִּים סָבִיב
surrounding the-peoples all-of *** left and-to right to and-they-will-consume

וְיָשְׁבָה יְרוּשָׁלִַם עוֹד תַּחְתֶּיהָ בִּירוּשָׁלִָם׃ וְהוֹשִׁיעַ
and-he-will-save (7) in-Jerusalem in-place-of-her still Jerusalem but-she-will-remain

יְהוָה אֶת־ אָהֳלֵי יְהוּדָה בָּרִאשֹׁנָה לְמַעַן לֹא־ תִגְדַּל
she-will-be-great not so-that at-the-first Judah dwellings-of *** Yahweh

תִּפְאֶרֶת בֵּית־ דָּוִיד וְתִפְאֶרֶת יֹשֵׁב יְרוּשָׁלִַם עַל־ יְהוּדָה׃
Judah more-than Jerusalem one-inhabiting-of and-honor-of David house-of honor-of

בַּיּוֹם הַהוּא יָגֵן יְהוָה בְּעַד יוֹשֵׁב יְרוּשָׁלִַם
Jerusalem one-living-of to-over Yahweh he-will-shield the-that on-the-day (8)

וְהָיָה הַנִּכְשָׁל בָּהֶם בַּיּוֹם הַהוּא כְּדָוִיד
like-David the-that on-the-day among-them the-one-being-feeble so-he-will-be

וּבֵית דָּוִיד כֵּאלֹהִים כְּמַלְאַךְ יְהוָה לִפְנֵיהֶם׃ וְהָיָה
and-he-will-be (9) before-them Yahweh like-Angel-of like-God David and-house-of

בַּיּוֹם הַהוּא אֲבַקֵּשׁ לְהַשְׁמִיד אֶת־ כָּל־ הַגּוֹיִם
the-nations all-of *** to-destroy I-will-set-out the-that on-the-day

הַבָּאִים עַל־ יְרוּשָׁלִָם׃ וְשָׁפַכְתִּי עַל־ בֵּית דָּוִיד וְעַל
and-on David house-of on and-I-will-pour-out (10) Jerusalem to the-ones-attacking

יוֹשֵׁב יְרוּשָׁלִַם רוּחַ חֵן וְתַחֲנוּנִים וְהִבִּיטוּ
and-they-will-look and-supplications grace spirit-of Jerusalem one-inhabiting-of

Jerusalem. 3On that day, when all
the nations of the earth are gathered against her, I will make
Jerusalem an immovable rock for
all the nations. All who try to
move it will injure themselves.
4On that day I will strike every
horse with panic and its rider
with madness," declares the LORD.
"I will keep a watchful eye over
the house of Judah, but I will blind
all the horses of the nations. 5Then
the leaders of Judah will say in
their hearts, 'The people of Jerusalem are strong, because the LORD
Almighty is their God.'
6"On that day I will make the
leaders of Judah like a firepot in a
woodpile, like a flaming torch
among sheaves. They will consume right and left all the surrounding peoples, but Jerusalem
will remain intact in her place.
7"The LORD will save the dwellings of Judah first, so that the hon-
or of the house of David and of
Jerusalem's inhabitants may not
be greater than that of Judah. 8On
that day the LORD will shield those
who live in Jerusalem, so that the
feeblest among them will be like
David, and the house of David
will be like God, like the Angel of
the LORD going before them. 9On
that day I will set out to destroy all
the nations that attack Jerusalem.

### *Mourning for the One They Pierced*

10"And I will pour out on the
house of David and the inhabitants of Jerusalem a spirit[v] of grace
and supplication. They will look

[v]10 Or *the Spirit*

אֵלַי אֵת אֲשֶׁר־ דָּקָרוּ וְסָפְדוּ עָלָיו כְּמִסְפֵּד עַל־
for as-mourning for-him and-they-will-mourn they-pierced whom *** on-me

הַיָּחִיד וְהָמֵר עָלָיו כְּהָמֵר עַל־
for as-to-grieve-bitterly for-him and-to-grieve-bitterly the-only-child

הַבְּכוֹר׃ בַּיּוֹם הַהוּא יִגְדַּל הַמִּסְפֵּד בִּירוּשָׁלִַם
in-Jerusalem the-weeping he-will-be-great the-that on-the-day (11) the-firstborn-son

כְּמִסְפַּד הֲדַדְ־ רִמּוֹן בְּבִקְעַת מְגִדּוֹן׃ וְסָפְדָה הָאָרֶץ
the-land and-she-will-mourn (12) Megiddo in-plain-of Rimmon Hadad like-weeping-of

מִשְׁפָּחוֹת מִשְׁפָּחוֹת לְבָד מִשְׁפַּחַת בֵּית־ דָּוִיד לְבָד וּנְשֵׁיהֶם
and-wives-of-them by-self David house-of clan-of by-self clans clans

לְבָד מִשְׁפַּחַת בֵּית־ נָתָן לְבָד וּנְשֵׁיהֶם לְבָד׃ מִשְׁפַּחַת
clan-of (13) by-self and-wives-of-them by-self Nathan house-of clan-of by-self

בֵּית־ לֵוִי לְבָד וּנְשֵׁיהֶם לְבָד מִשְׁפַּחַת הַשִּׁמְעִי לְבָד
by-self the-Shimei clan-of by-self and-wives-of-them by-self Levi house-of

וּנְשֵׁיהֶם לְבָד׃ כֹּל הַמִּשְׁפָּחוֹת הַנִּשְׁאָרוֹת מִשְׁפָּחֹת
clans the-ones-being-left the-clans all-of (14) by-self and-wives-of-them

מִשְׁפָּחֹת לְבָד וּנְשֵׁיהֶם לְבָד׃ בַּיּוֹם הַהוּא יִהְיֶה
he-will-be the-that on-the-day (13:1) by-self and-wives-of-them by-self clans

מָקוֹר נִפְתָּח לְבֵית דָּוִיד וּלְיֹשְׁבֵי יְרוּשָׁלִָם
Jerusalem and-to-ones-inhabiting-of David to-house-of being-opened fountain

לְחַטָּאת וּלְנִדָּה׃ וְהָיָה בַיּוֹם הַהוּא נְאֻם ׀
declaration-of the-that on-the-day and-he-will-be (2) and-for-impurity for-sin

יְהוָה צְבָאוֹת אַכְרִית אֶת־ שְׁמוֹת הָעֲצַבִּים מִן־ הָאָרֶץ וְלֹא
and-not the-land from the-idols names-of *** I-will-banish Hosts Yahweh-of

יִזָּכְרוּ עוֹד וְגַם אֶת־ הַנְּבִיאִים וְאֶת־ רוּחַ הַטֻּמְאָה
the-impurity spirit-of and the-prophets *** and-both more they-will-be-remembered

אַעֲבִיר מִן־ הָאָרֶץ׃ וְהָיָה כִּי־ יִנָּבֵא אִישׁ עוֹד
still anyone he-prophesies if and-he-will-be (3) the-land from I-will-remove

וְאָמְרוּ אֵלָיו אָבִיו וְאִמּוֹ יֹלְדָיו לֹא
not ones-bearing-him and-mother-of-him father-of-him to-him then-they-will-say

תִחְיֶה כִּי שֶׁקֶר דִּבַּרְתָּ בְּשֵׁם יְהוָה וּדְקָרֻהוּ
and-they-will-stab-him Yahweh in-name-of you-told lie because you-must-live

אָבִיהוּ וְאִמּוֹ יֹלְדָיו בְּהִנָּבְאוֹ׃
when-to-prophesy-him ones-bearing-him and-mother-of-him father-of-him

וְהָיָה ׀ בַּיּוֹם הַהוּא יֵבֹשׁוּ הַנְּבִיאִים אִישׁ
each the-prophets they-will-be-ashamed the-that on-the-day and-he-will-be (4)

מֵחֶזְיֹנוֹ בְּהִנָּבְאֹתוֹ וְלֹא יִלְבְּשׁוּ אַדֶּרֶת שֵׂעָר
hair garment-of they-will-put-on and-not when-to-prophesy-him of-vision-of-him

on[w] me, the one they have pierced, and they will mourn for him as one mourns for an only child, and grieve bitterly for him as one grieves for a firstborn son. 11On that day the weeping in Jerusalem will be great, like the weeping of Hadad Rimmon in the plain of Megiddo. 12The land will mourn, each clan by itself, with their wives by themselves: the clan of the house of David and their wives, the clan of the house of Nathan and their wives, 13the clan of the house of Levi and their wives, the clan of Shimei and their wives, 14and all the rest of the clans and their wives.

*Cleansing From Sin*

13 "On that day a fountain will be opened to the house of David and the inhabitants of Jerusalem, to cleanse them from sin and impurity.

2"On that day, I will banish the names of the idols from the land, and they will be remembered no more," declares the LORD Almighty. "I will remove both the prophets and the spirit of impurity from the land. 3And if anyone still prophesies, his father and mother, to whom he was born, will say to him, 'You must die, because you have told lies in the LORD's name.' When he prophesies, his own parents will stab him.

4"On that day every prophet will be ashamed of his prophetic vision. He will not put on a prophet's garment of hair in order

*w10* Or *to*

לְמַעַן כַּחֵשׁ׃ וְאָמַר לֹא נָבִיא אָנֹכִי אִישׁ־ עֹבֵד אֲדָמָה
land working-of man I prophet not and-he-will-say (5) to-deceive in-order-to

אָנֹכִי כִּי אָדָם הִקְנַנִי מִנְּעוּרָי׃ וְאָמַר אֵלָיו מָה הַמַּכּוֹת
the-wounds what? to-him if-he-asks (6) in-youths-of-me he-sold-me man indeed I

הָאֵלֶּה בֵּין יָדֶיךָ וְאָמַר אֲשֶׁר הֻכֵּיתִי בֵּית
house-of I-was-wounded that then-he-will-answer hands-of-you between the-these

מְאַהֲבָי׃ חֶרֶב עוּרִי עַל־ רֹעִי
one-being-shepherd-of-me against awake! sword (7) ones-being-friends-of-me

וְעַל־ גֶּבֶר עֲמִיתִי נְאֻם יְהוָה צְבָאוֹת הַךְ אֶת־
*** strike! Hosts Yahweh-of declaration-of close-one-of-me man even-against

הָרֹעֶה וּתְפוּצֶיןָ הַצֹּאן וַהֲשִׁבֹתִי יָדִי
hand-of-me and-I-will-turn the-sheep and-they-will-be-scattered the-one-shepherding

עַל־ הַצֹּעֲרִים׃ וְהָיָה בְכָל־ הָאָרֶץ נְאֻם־
declaration-of the-land in-whole-of and-he-will-be (8) the-ones-being-little against

יְהוָה פִּי־ שְׁנַיִם בָּהּ יִכָּרְתוּ יִגְוָעוּ וְהַשְּׁלִשִׁית
yet-the-third they-will-perish they-will-be-struck-down in-her two portion-of Yahweh

יִוָּתֶר בָּהּ׃ וְהֵבֵאתִי אֶת־ הַשְּׁלִשִׁית בָּאֵשׁ
into-the-fire the-third *** and-I-will-bring (9) in-her he-will-be-left

וּצְרַפְתִּים כִּצְרֹף אֶת־ הַכֶּסֶף וּבְחַנְתִּים
and-I-will-test-them the-silver *** like-to-refine and-I-will-refine-them

כִּבְחֹן אֶת־ הַזָּהָב הוּא יִקְרָא בִשְׁמִי וַאֲנִי אֶעֱנֶה אֹתוֹ
him I-will-answer and-I on-name-of-me he-will-call he the-gold *** like-to-test

אָמַרְתִּי עַמִּי הוּא וְהוּא יֹאמַר יְהוָה אֱלֹהָי׃ הִנֵּה
see! (14:1) God-of-me Yahweh he-will-say and-he he people-of-me and-I-will-say

יוֹם־ בָּא לַיהוָה וְחֻלַּק שְׁלָלֵךְ בְּקִרְבֵּךְ׃
in-among-you plunder-of-you when-he-will-be-divided of-Yahweh coming day

וְאָסַפְתִּי אֶת־ כָּל־ הַגּוֹיִם אֶל־ יְרוּשָׁלִַם לַמִּלְחָמָה
for-the-fight Jerusalem to the-nations all-of *** and-I-will-gather (2)

וְנִלְכְּדָה הָעִיר וְנָשַׁסּוּ הַבָּתִּים וְהַנָּשִׁים
and-the-women the-houses and-they-will-be-ransacked the-city and-she-will-be-captured

תִּשָּׁגַלְנָה° וְיָצָא חֲצִי הָעִיר בַּגּוֹלָה וְיֶתֶר
but-rest-of into-the-exile the-city half-of and-he-will-go *they-will-be-raped

הָעָם לֹא יִכָּרֵת מִן־ הָעִיר׃ וְיָצָא יְהוָה
Yahweh then-he-will-go-out (3) the-city from he-will-be-taken not the-people

וְנִלְחַם בַּגּוֹיִם הָהֵם כְּיוֹם הִלָּחֲמוֹ בְּיוֹם
in-day-of to-fight-him as-day-of the-those against-the-nations and-he-will-fight

קְרָב׃ וְעָמְדוּ רַגְלָיו בַּיּוֹם־ הַהוּא עַל־ הַר הַזֵּתִים
the-Olives Mount-of on the-that on-the-day feet-of-him and-they-will-stand (4) battle

to deceive. 5 He will say, 'I am not a prophet. I am a farmer; the land has been my livelihood since my youth.[x]' 6 If someone asks him, 'What are these wounds on your body[y]?' he will answer, 'The wounds I was given at the house of my friends.'

*The Shepherd Struck, the Sheep Scattered*

7 "Awake, O sword, against my shepherd,
against the man who is close to me!"
declares the LORD Almighty.
"Strike the shepherd,
and the sheep will be scattered,
and I will turn my hand against the little ones.
8 In the whole land," declares the LORD,
"two-thirds will be struck down and perish;
yet one-third will be left in it.
9 This third I will bring into the fire;
I will refine them like silver
and test them like gold.
They will call on my name
and I will answer them;
I will say, 'They are my people,'
and they will say, 'The LORD is our God.' "

*The LORD Comes and Reigns*

14 A day of the LORD is coming when your plunder will be divided among you.

2 I will gather all the nations to Jerusalem to fight against it; the city will be captured, the houses ransacked, and the women raped. Half of the city will go into exile, but the rest of the people will not be taken from the city.

3 Then the LORD will go out and fight against those nations, as he fights in the day of battle. 4 On that day his feet will stand on the

[x]5 Or *farmer; a man sold me in my youth*
[y]6 Or *wounds between your hands*

***2 The *Qere* word is a less graphic synonym of the *Ketbib*.**

°2 ק תשכבנה

אֲשֶׁר עַל־ פְּנֵי יְרוּשָׁלַםִ מִקֶּדֶם וְנִבְקַע הַר הַזֵּיתִים
the-Olives Mount-of and-he-will-be-split on-east Jerusalem faces-of to that

מֵחֶצְיוֹ מִזְרָחָה וָיָמָּה גֵּיא גְּדוֹלָה מְאֹד וּמָשׁ חֲצִי
half-of and-he-will-move very great valley and-to-west from-to-east in-two-of-him

הָהָר צָפוֹנָה וְחֶצְיוֹ־ נֶגְבָּה׃ וְנַסְתֶּם גֵּיא־
valley-of and-you-will-flee (5) to-south and-half-of-him to-north the-mountain

הָרַי כִּי־ יַגִּיעַ גֵּי־ הָרִים אֶל־ אָצַל וְנַסְתֶּם
and-you-will-flee Azel to mountains valley-of he-will-extend for mountains-of-me

כַּאֲשֶׁר נַסְתֶּם מִפְּנֵי הָרַעַשׁ בִּימֵי עֻזִּיָּה מֶלֶךְ־ יְהוּדָה
Judah king-of Uzziah in-days-of the-earthquake from-before you-fled as-that

וּבָא יְהוָה אֱלֹהַי כָּל־ קְדֹשִׁים עִמָּךְ׃ וְהָיָה
and-he-will-be (6) with-you holy-ones all-of God-of-me Yahweh then-he-will-come

בַּיּוֹם הַהוּא לֹא־ יִהְיֶה אוֹר יְקָרוֹת יְקִפָּאוֹן׃ וְהָיָה
and-he-will-be (7) or-frost cold-ones light he-will-be not the-that on-the-day

יוֹם־ אֶחָד הוּא יִוָּדַע לַיהוָה לֹא־ יוֹם וְלֹא־ לָיְלָה וְהָיָה
and-he-will-be nighttime or-no daytime no to-Yahweh he-is-known he unique day

לְעֵת־ עֶרֶב יִהְיֶה־ אוֹר׃ וְהָיָה׀ בַּיּוֹם הַהוּא
the-that on-the-day and-he-will-be (8) light he-will-be evening at-time-of

יֵצְאוּ מַיִם־ חַיִּים מִירוּשָׁלַםִ חֶצְיָם אֶל־ הַיָּם
the-sea to half-of-them from-Jerusalem living-ones waters they-will-flow-out

הַקַּדְמוֹנִי וְחֶצְיָם אֶל־ הַיָּם הָאַחֲרוֹן בַּקַּיִץ וּבָחֹרֶף
and-in-the-winter in-the-summer the-western the-sea to and-half-of-them the-eastern

יִהְיֶה׃ וְהָיָה יְהוָה לְמֶלֶךְ עַל־ כָּל־ הָאָרֶץ בַּיּוֹם
on-the-day the-earth whole-of over for-king Yahweh and-he-will-be (9) he-will-be

הַהוּא יִהְיֶה יְהוָה אֶחָד וּשְׁמוֹ אֶחָד׃ יִסּוֹב
he-will-become (10) only and-name-of-him one Yahweh he-will-be the-that

כָּל־ הָאָרֶץ כָּעֲרָבָה מִגֶּבַע לְרִמּוֹן נֶגֶב יְרוּשָׁלַםִ
Jerusalem south-of to-Rimmon from-Geba like-the-Arabah the-land whole-of

וְרָאֲמָה וְיָשְׁבָה תַחְתֶּיהָ לְמִשַּׁעַר בִּנְיָמִן
Benjamin at-from-Gate-of in-place-of-her and-she-will-remain but-she-will-be-raised-up

עַד־ מְקוֹם שַׁעַר הָרִאשׁוֹן עַד־ שַׁעַר הַפִּנִּים וּמִגְדַּל חֲנַנְאֵל עַד
to Hananel and-Tower-of the-Corners Gate-of and-to the-First Gate-of site-of to

יִקְבֵי הַמֶּלֶךְ׃ וְיָשְׁבוּ בָהּ וְחֵרֶם לֹא
never and-destruction in-her and-they-will-inhabit (11) the-royalty winepresses-of

יִהְיֶה־ עוֹד וְיָשְׁבָה יְרוּשָׁלַםִ לָבֶטַח׃ וְזֹאת׀ תִּהְיֶה
she-will-be and-this (12) in-security Jerusalem and-she-will-dwell again he-will-be

הַמַּגֵּפָה אֲשֶׁר יִגֹּף יְהוָה אֶת־ כָּל־ הָעַמִּים אֲשֶׁר צָבְאוּ
they-fought that the-nations all-of *** Yahweh he-will-strike which the-plague

Mount of Olives, east of Jerusalem, and the Mount of Olives will be split in two from east to west, forming a great valley, with half of the mountain moving north and half moving south. [5]You will flee by my mountain valley, for it will extend to Azel. You will flee as you fled from the earthquake[z] in the days of Uzziah king of Judah. Then the LORD my God will come, and all the holy ones with him.

[6]On that day there will be no light, no cold or frost. [7]It will be a unique day, without daytime or nighttime—a day known to the LORD. When evening comes, there will be light.

[8]On that day living water will flow out from Jerusalem, half to the eastern sea[a] and half to the western sea,[b] in summer and in winter.

[9]The LORD will be king over the whole earth. On that day there will be one LORD, and his name the only name.

[10]The whole land, from Geba to Rimmon, south of Jerusalem, will become like the Arabah. But Jerusalem will be raised up and remain in its place, from the Benjamin Gate to the site of the First Gate, to the Corner Gate, and from the Tower of Hananel to the royal winepresses. [11]It will be inhabited; never again will it be destroyed. Jerusalem will be secure.

[12]This is the plague with which the LORD will strike all the nations that fought against Jerusalem:

z5 Or [5]*My mountain valley will be blocked and will extend to Azel. It will be blocked as it was blocked because of the earthquake*
a8 That is, the Dead Sea
b8 That is, the Mediterranean

°6 ק וקפאון

עַל־ יְרוּשָׁלַ͏ִם הָמֵק ׀ בְּשָׂרוֹ וְהוּא עֹמֵד עַל־ רַגְלָיו
feet-of-him on standing while-he flesh-of-him to-rot Jerusalem against

וְעֵינָיו תִּמַּקְנָה בְחֹרֵיהֶן וּלְשׁוֹנוֹ תִּמַּק
she-will-rot and-tongue-of-him in-sockets-of-them they-will-rot and-eyes-of-him

בְּפִיהֶם׃ (13) וְהָיָה בַּיּוֹם הַהוּא תִּהְיֶה מְהוּמַת־ יְהוָה
Yahweh panic-of she-will-be the-that on-the-day and-he-will-be (13) in-mouth-of-them

רַבָּה בָּהֶם וְהֶחֱזִיקוּ אִישׁ יַד רֵעֵהוּ וְעָלְתָה
and-she-will-attack another-of-him hand-of each and-they-will-seize to-them great

יָדוֹ עַל־ יַד רֵעֵהוּ׃ (14) וְגַם־ יְהוּדָה תִּלָּחֵם
she-will-fight Judah and-too (14) another-of-him hand-of to hand-of-him

בִּירוּשָׁלָ͏ִם וְאֻסַּף חֵיל כָּל־ הַגּוֹיִם סָבִיב
surrounding the-nations all-of wealth-of and-he-will-be-collected at-Jerusalem

זָהָב וָכֶסֶף וּבְגָדִים לָרֹב מְאֹד׃ (15) וְכֵן תִּהְיֶה
she-will-be and-similar (15) very to-great-quantity and-clothes and-silver gold

מַגֵּפַת הַסּוּס הַפֶּרֶד הַגָּמָל וְהַחֲמוֹר וְכָל־ הַבְּהֵמָה
the-animal and-all-of and-the-donkey the-camel the-mule the-horse plague-of

אֲשֶׁר יִהְיֶה בַּמַּחֲנוֹת הָהֵמָּה כַּמַּגֵּפָה הַזֹּאת׃ (16) וְהָיָה
then-he-will-be (16) the-this like-the-plague the-those in-the-camps he-is that

כָּל־ הַנּוֹתָר מִכָּל־ הַגּוֹיִם הַבָּאִים עַל־
against the-ones-attacking the-nations from-all-of the-one-surviving all-of

יְרוּשָׁלָ͏ִם וְעָלוּ מִדֵּי שָׁנָה בְשָׁנָה לְהִשְׁתַּחֲוֹת
to-worship after-year year from-sufficiency-of and-they-will-go-up Jerusalem

לְמֶלֶךְ יְהוָה צְבָאוֹת וְלָחֹג אֶת־ חַג הַסֻּכּוֹת׃
the-Tabernacles Feast-of *** and-to-celebrate Hosts Yahweh-of to-King

(17) וְהָיָה אֲשֶׁר לֹא־ יַעֲלֶה מֵאֵת מִשְׁפְּחוֹת הָאָרֶץ אֶל־ יְרוּשָׁלַ͏ִם
Jerusalem to the-earth peoples-of from he-goes-up not if and-he-will-be (17)

לְהִשְׁתַּחֲוֹת לְמֶלֶךְ יְהוָה צְבָאוֹת וְלֹא עֲלֵיהֶם יִהְיֶה הַגָּשֶׁם׃
the-rain he-will-be for-them then-not Hosts Yahweh-of to-King to-worship

(18) וְאִם־ מִשְׁפַּחַת מִצְרַיִם לֹא־ תַעֲלֶה וְלֹא בָאָה וְלֹא עֲלֵיהֶם
for-them then-not taking-part and-not she-goes-up not Egypt people-of and-if (18)

תִּהְיֶה הַמַּגֵּפָה אֲשֶׁר יִגֹּף יְהוָה אֶת־ הַגּוֹיִם אֲשֶׁר לֹא
not that the-nations on Yahweh he-inflicts that the-plague she-will-be

יַעֲלוּ לָחֹג אֶת־ חַג הַסֻּכּוֹת׃ (19) זֹאת תִּהְיֶה
she-will-be this (19) the-Tabernacles Feast-of *** to-celebrate they-go-up

חַטַּאת מִצְרָיִם וְחַטַּאת כָּל־ הַגּוֹיִם אֲשֶׁר לֹא יַעֲלוּ
they-go-up not that the-nations all-of and-punishment-of Egypt punishment-of

לָחֹג אֶת־ חַג הַסֻּכּוֹת׃ (20) בַּיּוֹם הַהוּא יִהְיֶה
he-will-be the-that on-the-day (20) the-Tabernacles Feast-of *** to-celebrate

Their flesh will rot while they a
still standing on their feet, the
eyes will rot in their sockets, ar
their tongues will rot in the
mouths. [13]On that day men will b
stricken by the LORD with grea
panic. Each man will seize th
hand of another, and they will a
tack each other. [14]Judah too wi
fight at Jerusalem. The wealth c
all the surrounding nations will b
collected—great quantities of gol
and silver and clothing. [15]A simi
lar plague will strike the horse
and mules, the camels and don
keys, and all the animals in those
camps.

[16]Then the survivors from all the
nations that have attacked Jerusalem will go up year after year to
worship the King, the LORD Almighty, and to celebrate the Feast
of Tabernacles. [17]If any of the peoples of the earth do not go up to
Jerusalem to worship the King,
the LORD Almighty, they will have
no rain. [18]If the Egyptian people
do not go up and take part, they
will have no rain. The LORD[c] will
bring on them the plague he inflicts on the nations that do not go
up to celebrate the Feast of Tabernacles. [19]This will be the punishment of Egypt and the punishment of all the nations that do not
go up to celebrate the Feast of Tabernacles.

[c]18 *Or part, then the* LORD

| הַסִּירוֹת | וְהָיָה | לַיהוָה | קֹדֶשׁ | הַסּוּס | מְצִלּוֹת | עַל־ |
|---|---|---|---|---|---|---|
| the-cooking-pots | and-he-will-be | to-Yahweh | holy | the-horse | bells-of | on |

| הַמִּזְבֵּחַ׃ | לִפְנֵי | כַּמִּזְרָקִים | יְהוָה | בְּבֵית |
|---|---|---|---|---|
| the-altar | in-front-of | like-the-sacred-bowls | Yahweh | in-house-of |

| לַיהוָה | קֹדֶשׁ | וּבִיהוּדָה | בִּירוּשָׁלַםִ | סִיר | כָּל־ | וְהָיָה | |
|---|---|---|---|---|---|---|---|
| to-Yahweh-of | holy | and-in-Judah | in-Jerusalem | pot | every-of | and-he-will-be | (21) |

| וְלָקְחוּ | הַזֹּבְחִים | כָּל־ | וּבָאוּ | צְבָאוֹת |
|---|---|---|---|---|
| and-they-will-take | the-ones-sacrificing | all-of | and-they-will-come | Hosts |

| כְנַעֲנִי | יִהְיֶה | וְלֹא־ | בָהֶם | וּבִשְּׁלוּ | מֵהֶם |
|---|---|---|---|---|---|
| Canaanite | he-will-be | and-not | in-them | and-they-will-cook | from-them |

| הַהוּא׃ | בַּיּוֹם | צְבָאוֹת | יְהוָה | בְּבֵית־ | עוֹד |
|---|---|---|---|---|---|
| the-that | on-the-day | Hosts | Yahweh-of | in-house-of | longer |

20 On that day HOLY TO THE LORD
will be inscribed on the bells of
the horses, and the cooking pots
in the LORD's house will be like the
sacred bowls in front of the altar.
21 Every pot in Jerusalem and Judah
will be holy to the LORD Almighty,
and all who come to sacrifice will
take some of the pots and cook in
them. And on that day there will
no longer be a Canaanite[d] in the
house of the LORD Almighty.

[d] 21 Or *merchant*

מַשָּׂא דְבַר־ יְהוָה אֶל־יִשְׂרָאֵל בְּיַד מַלְאָכִי׃ אָהַבְתִּי אֶתְכֶם
you I-loved (2) Malachi through-hand-of Israel to Yahweh word-of oracle (1:1)

אָמַר יְהוָה וַאֲמַרְתֶּם בַּמָּה אֲהַבְתָּנוּ הֲלוֹא־ אָח עֵשָׂו לְיַעֲקֹב
to-Jacob Esau brother not? you-loved-us by-how? but-you-ask Yahweh he-says

נְאֻם־ יְהוָה וָאֹהַב אֶת־יַעֲקֹב׃ וְאֶת־ עֵשָׂו שָׂנֵאתִי וָאָשִׂים
and-I-turned I-hated Esau but (3) Jacob *** yet-I-loved Yahweh declaration-of

אֶת־ הָרָיו שְׁמָמָה וְאֶת־ נַחֲלָתוֹ לְתַנּוֹת מִדְבָּר׃
desert to-jackals-of inheritance-of-him and wasteland mountains-of-him ***

כִּי־ תֹאמַר אֱדוֹם רֻשַּׁשְׁנוּ וְנָשׁוּב וְנִבְנֶה
and-we-will-rebuild but-we-will-return we-were-crushed Edom she-may-say indeed (4)

חֳרָבוֹת כֹּה אָמַר יְהוָה צְבָאוֹת הֵמָּה יִבְנוּ וַאֲנִי אֶהֱרוֹס
I-will-demolish but-I they-may-rebuild they Hosts Yahweh-of he-says this ruins

וְקָרְאוּ לָהֶם גְּבוּל רִשְׁעָה וְהָעָם אֲשֶׁר־ זָעַם
he-shows-wrath that even-the-people Wickedness Land-of to-them and-they-will-call

יְהוָה עַד־ עוֹלָם׃ וְעֵינֵיכֶם תִּרְאֶינָה וְאַתֶּם תֹּאמְרוּ
you-will-say and-you they-will-see and-eyes-of-you (5) forever to Yahweh

יִגְדַּל יְהוָה מֵעַל לִגְבוּל יִשְׂרָאֵל׃ בֵּן יְכַבֵּד אָב
father he-honors son (6) Israel to-border-of even-beyond Yahweh he-is-great

וְעֶבֶד אֲדֹנָיו וְאִם־ אָב אָנִי אַיֵּה כְבוֹדִי וְאִם־
and-if honor-of-me where? I father now-if masters-of-him and-servant

אֲדוֹנִים אָנִי אַיֵּה מוֹרָאִי אָמַר יְהוָה צְבָאוֹת לָכֶם הַכֹּהֲנִים
the-priests to-you Hosts Yahweh-of he-says respect-of-me where? I masters

בּוֹזֵי שְׁמִי וַאֲמַרְתֶּם בַּמֶּה בָזִינוּ אֶת־
for we-showed-contempt by-how? but-you-ask name-of-me ones-showing-contempt-of

שְׁמֶךָ׃ מַגִּישִׁים עַל־ מִזְבְּחִי לֶחֶם מְגֹאָל וַאֲמַרְתֶּם בַּמֶּה
by-how? but-you-ask being-defiled food altar-of-me on ones-placing (7) name-of-you

גֵאַלְנוּךָ בֶּאֱמָרְכֶם שֻׁלְחַן יְהוָה נִבְזֶה הוּא׃ וְכִי־
and-when (8) he being-contemptible Yahweh table-of by-to-say-you we-defiled-you

תַגִּשׁוּן עִוֵּר לִזְבֹּחַ אֵין רָע וְכִי תַגִּישׁוּ
you-sacrifice and-when wrong is-there-not to-sacrifice blind-animal you-bring

פִּסֵּחַ וְחֹלֶה אֵין רָע הַקְרִיבֵהוּ נָא
now! offer-him! wrong is-there-not or-one-being-diseased crippled-animal

לְפֶחָתֶךָ הֲיִרְצְךָ אוֹ הֲיִשָּׂא
would-he-accept? or would-he-be-pleased-with-you? to-governor-of-you

פָּנֶיךָ אָמַר יְהוָה צְבָאוֹת׃ וְעַתָּה חַלּוּ־ נָא פְנֵי־ אֵל
God faces-of now! implore! and-now (9) Hosts Yahweh-of he-says faces-of-you

וִיחָנֵנוּ* מִיֶּדְכֶם הָיְתָה זֹּאת הֲיִשָּׂא מִכֶּם
of-you will-he-accept? this she-is from-hand-of-you that-he-may-be-gracious-to-us

1 An oracle: The word of the LORD to Israel through Malachi.[a]

*Jacob Loved, Esau Hated*

2 "I have loved you," says the LORD.

"But you ask, 'How have you loved us?'

"Was not Esau Jacob's brother?" the LORD says. "Yet I have loved Jacob, 3 but Esau I have hated, and I have turned his mountains into a wasteland and left his inheritance to the desert jackals."

4 Edom may say, "Though we have been crushed, we will rebuild the ruins."

But this is what the LORD Almighty says: "They may build, but I will demolish. They will be called the Wicked Land, a people always under the wrath of the LORD. 5 You will see it with your own eyes and say, 'Great is the LORD—even beyond the borders of Israel!'

*Blemished Sacrifices*

6 "A son honors his father, and a servant his master. If I am a father, where is the honor due me? If I am a master, where is the respect due me?" says the LORD Almighty. "It is you, O priests, who show contempt for my name.

"But you ask, 'How have we shown contempt for your name?'

7 "You place defiled food on my altar.

"But you ask, 'How have we defiled you?'

"By saying that the LORD's table is contemptible. 8 When you bring blind animals for sacrifice, is that not wrong? When you sacrifice crippled or diseased animals, is that not wrong? Try offering them to your governor! Would he be pleased with you? Would he accept you?" says the LORD Almighty.

9 "Now implore God to be gracious to us. With such offerings from your hands, will he accept

[a]1 Malachi means *my messenger*.

***2 Most mss have *dagesh* in the first *nun* (־נּנו).**

פָּנִים אָמַר יְהוָה צְבָאוֹת׃ מִי גַם־בָּכֶם וְיִסְגֹּר דְּלָתַיִם
doors that-he-would-shut of-you indeed who? (10) Hosts Yahweh-of he-says faces

וְלֹא־תָאִירוּ מִזְבְּחִי חִנָּם אֵין־לִי חֵפֶץ בָּכֶם
with-you pleasure to-me there-is-not uselessly altar-of-me you-would-light-fire so-not

אָמַר יְהוָה צְבָאוֹת וּמִנְחָה לֹא־אֶרְצֶה מִיֶּדְכֶם׃ כִּי
indeed (11) from-hand-of-you I-will-accept not and-offering Hosts Yahweh-of he-says

מִמִּזְרַח־שֶׁמֶשׁ וְעַד־מְבוֹאוֹ גָּדוֹל שְׁמִי בַּגּוֹיִם
among-the-nations name-of-me great setting-of-him and-to sun from-rising-of

וּבְכָל־מָקוֹם מֻקְטָר מֻגָּשׁ לִשְׁמִי וּמִנְחָה טְהוֹרָה כִּי־
because pure and-offering to-name-of-me being-brought incense place and-in-every-of

גָדוֹל שְׁמִי בַּגּוֹיִם אָמַר יְהוָה צְבָאוֹת׃ וְאַתֶּם מְחַלְּלִים
ones-profaning but-you (12) Hosts Yahweh-of he-says among-the-nations name-of-me great

אוֹתוֹ בֶּאֱמָרְכֶם שֻׁלְחַן אֲדֹנָי מְגֹאָל הוּא וְנִיבוֹ נִבְזֶה
being-contemptible and-fruit-of-him he being-defiled Lord table-of by-to-say-you him

אָכְלוֹ׃ וַאֲמַרְתֶּם הִנֵּה מַתְּלָאָה וְהִפַּחְתֶּם אוֹתוֹ
him and-you-sniff-contemptuously burden what! and-you-say (13) food-of-him

אָמַר יְהוָה צְבָאוֹת וַהֲבֵאתֶם גָּזוּל וְאֶת־הַפִּסֵּחַ וְאֶת־
and the-crippled and one-being-injured when-you-bring Hosts Yahweh-of he-says

הַחוֹלֶה וַהֲבֵאתֶם אֶת־הַמִּנְחָה הַאֶרְצֶה אוֹתָהּ
her should-I-accept? the-sacrifice *** and-you-offer the-one-being-diseased

מִיֶּדְכֶם אָמַר יְהוָה׃ וְאָרוּר נוֹכֵל וְיֵשׁ
and-there-is one-cheating indeed-being-cursed (14) Yahweh he-says from-hand-of-you

בְּעֶדְרוֹ זָכָר וְנֹדֵר וְזֹבֵחַ מָשְׁחָת לַאדֹנָי
to-Lord one-being-blemished but-one-sacrificing and-one-vowing male in-flock-of-him

כִּי מֶלֶךְ גָּדוֹל אָנִי אָמַר יְהוָה צְבָאוֹת וּשְׁמִי נוֹרָא
being-feared and-name-of-me Hosts Yahweh-of he-says I great king for

בַגּוֹיִם׃ וְעַתָּה אֲלֵיכֶם הַמִּצְוָה הַזֹּאת הַכֹּהֲנִים׃
the-priests the-this the-admonition for-you and-now (2:1) among-the-nations

אִם־לֹא תִשְׁמְעוּ וְאִם־לֹא תָשִׂימוּ עַל־לֵב לָתֵת כָּבוֹד לִשְׁמִי
to-name-of-me honor to-give heart in you-set not and-if you-listen not if (2)

אָמַר יְהוָה צְבָאוֹת וְשִׁלַּחְתִּי בָכֶם אֶת־הַמְּאֵרָה וְאָרוֹתִי
and-I-will-curse the-curse *** upon-you then-I-will-send Hosts Yahweh-of he-says

אֶת־בִּרְכוֹתֵיכֶם וְגַם אָרוֹתִיהָ כִּי אֵינְכֶם שָׂמִים עַל־לֵב׃
heart in ones-setting not-you because I-cursed-her yes-indeed blessings-of-you ***

הִנְנִי גֹעֵר לָכֶם אֶת־הַזֶּרַע וְזֵרִיתִי פֶרֶשׁ עַל־
on offal and-I-will-spread the-descendant *** because-of-you rebuking see-I! (3)

פְּנֵיכֶם פֶּרֶשׁ חַגֵּיכֶם וְנָשָׂא אֶתְכֶם אֵלָיו׃
with-him you and-he-will-carry-off festival-sacrifices-of-you offal-of faces-of-you

you?"—says the LORD Almighty.
[10]"Oh, that one of you would shut the temple doors, so that you would not light useless fires on my altar! I am not pleased with you," says the LORD Almighty, "and I will accept no offering from your hands. [11]My name will be great among the nations, from the rising to the setting of the sun. In every place incense and pure offerings will be brought to my name, because my name will be great among the nations," says the LORD Almighty.

[12]"But you profane it by saying of the Lord's table, 'It is defiled,' and of its food, 'It is contemptible.' [13]And you say, 'What a burden!' and you sniff at it contemptuously," says the LORD Almighty.

"When you bring injured, crippled or diseased animals and offer them as sacrifices, should I accept them from your hands?" says the LORD. [14]"Cursed is the cheat who has an acceptable male in his flock and vows to give it, but then sacrifices a blemished animal to the Lord. For I am a great king," says the LORD Almighty, "and my name is to be feared among the nations.

*Admonition for the Priests*

2 "And now this admonition is for you, O priests. [2]If you do not listen, and if you do not set your heart to honor my name," says the LORD Almighty, "I will send a curse upon you, and I will curse your blessings. Yes, I have already cursed them, because you have not set your heart to honor me.

[3]"Because of you I will rebuke[b] your descendants[c]; I will spread on your faces the offal from your festival sacrifices, and you will be carried off with it. [4]And you will

[b]3 Or *cut off* (see Septuagint)
[c]3 Or *will blight your grain*

וִידַעְתֶּ֗ם כִּ֚י שִׁלַּ֣חְתִּי אֲלֵיכֶ֔ם אֵ֖ת הַמִּצְוָ֣ה הַזֹּ֑את לִהְי֣וֹת

to-continue the-this the-admonition *** to-you I-sent that and-you-will-know (4)

בְּרִיתִ֣י אֶת־לֵוִ֔י אָמַ֖ר יְהוָ֣ה צְבָאֽוֹת: בְּרִיתִ֣י ׀ הָיְתָ֣ה אִתּ֗וֹ

with-him she-was covenant-of-me (5) Hosts Yahweh-of he-says Levi with covenant-of-me

הַֽחַיִּים֙ וְהַשָּׁל֔וֹם וָאֶתְּנֵֽם־ל֥וֹ מוֹרָ֖א וַיִּֽירָאֵ֑נִי

and-he-revered-me reverence to-him and-I-gave-them and-the-peace the-lives

וּמִפְּנֵ֥י שְׁמִ֖י נִחַ֥ת הֽוּא: תּוֹרַ֤ת אֱמֶת֙

truth instruction-of (6) he he-stood-in-awe name-of-me and-in-presences-of

הָיְתָ֣ה בְּפִ֔יהוּ וְעַוְלָ֖ה לֹא־נִמְצָ֣א בִשְׂפָתָ֑יו בְּשָׁל֤וֹם

in-peace on-lips-of-him he-was-found not and-falsehood in-mouth-of-him she-was

וּבְמִישׁוֹר֙ הָלַ֣ךְ אִתִּ֔י וְרַבִּ֖ים הֵשִׁ֥יב מֵעָוֺֽן: כִּֽי־

for (7) from-sin he-turned and-many-ones with-me he-walked and-in-uprightness

שִׂפְתֵ֤י כֹהֵן֙ יִשְׁמְרוּ־דַ֔עַת וְתוֹרָ֖ה יְבַקְשׁ֣וּ

they-should-seek and-instruction knowledge they-should-preserve priest lips-of

מִפִּ֑יהוּ כִּ֛י מַלְאַ֥ךְ יְהוָֽה־צְבָא֖וֹת הֽוּא: וְאַתֶּם֙ סַרְתֶּ֣ם

you-turned but-you (8) he Hosts Yahweh-of messenger-of because from-mouth-of-him

מִן־הַדֶּ֔רֶךְ הִכְשַׁלְתֶּ֥ם רַבִּ֖ים בַּתּוֹרָ֑ה שִֽׁחַתֶּם֙ בְּרִ֣ית

covenant-of you-violated by-the-teaching many-ones you-made-stumble the-way from

הַלֵּוִ֔י אָמַ֖ר יְהוָ֥ה צְבָאֽוֹת: וְגַם־אֲנִ֞י נָתַ֧תִּי אֶתְכֶ֛ם נִבְזִ֥ים

ones-being-despised you I-made I so-also (9) Hosts Yahweh-of he-says the-Levi

וּשְׁפָלִ֖ים לְכָל־הָעָ֑ם כְּפִ֗י אֲשֶׁ֤ר אֵֽינְכֶם֙

not-you that because-of-matter-of the-people before-all-of and-ones-humiliated

שֹׁמְרִ֣ים אֶת־דְּרָכַ֔י וְנֹשְׂאִ֥ים פָּנִ֖ים בַּתּוֹרָֽה: הֲל֨וֹא

not? (10) in-the-law faces but-ones-showing-partiality ways-of-me *** ones-following

אָ֤ב אֶחָד֙ לְכֻלָּ֔נוּ הֲל֛וֹא אֵ֥ל אֶחָ֖ד בְּרָאָ֑נוּ מַדּ֗וּעַ נִבְגַּד֙ אִ֣ישׁ

one do-we-break-faith why? he-created-us one God not? to-all-of-us one Father

בְּאָחִ֔יו לְחַלֵּ֖ל בְּרִ֥ית אֲבֹתֵֽינוּ: בָּגְדָ֣ה יְהוּדָ֔ה

Judah she-broke-faith (11) fathers-of-us covenant-of to-profane with-another-of-him

וְתוֹעֵבָ֛ה נֶעֶשְׂתָ֥ה בְיִשְׂרָאֵ֖ל וּבִירֽוּשָׁלָ֑͏ִם כִּ֣י ׀ חִלֵּ֣ל

he-desecrated indeed and-in-Jerusalem in-Israel she-was-committed and-detestable-thing

יְהוּדָ֗ה קֹ֤דֶשׁ יְהוָה֙ אֲשֶׁ֣ר אָהֵ֔ב וּבָעַ֖ל בַּת־אֵ֥ל נֵכָֽר:

foreign god daughter-of when-he-married he-loves that Yahweh sanctuary-of Judah

יַכְרֵ֨ת יְהוָ֜ה לָאִ֤ישׁ אֲשֶׁ֣ר יַעֲשֶׂ֔נָּה עֵ֖ר וְעֹנֶ֑ה

and-answering being-roused he-does-her who to-the-man Yahweh may-he-cut-off (12)

מֵאָהֳלֵ֖י יַעֲקֹ֑ב וּמַגִּ֣ישׁ מִנְחָ֔ה לַֽיהוָ֖ה צְבָאֽוֹת: וְזֹאת֙ שֵׁנִ֣ית

another and-this (13) Hosts to-Yahweh-of offering though-bringing Jacob from-tents-of

תַּעֲשׂ֔וּ כַּסּ֤וֹת דִּמְעָה֙ אֶת־מִזְבַּ֣ח יְהוָ֔ה בְּכִ֖י וַֽאֲנָקָ֑ה מֵאֵ֣ין ע֔וֹד

longer because-not and-wailing weeping Yahweh altar-of *** tear to-flood you-do

know that I have sent you this admonition so that my covenant with Levi may continue," says the LORD Almighty. [5]"My covenant was with him, a covenant of life and peace, and I gave them to him; this called for reverence and he revered me and stood in awe of my name. [6]True instruction was in his mouth and nothing false was found on his lips. He walked with me in peace and uprightness, and turned many from sin.

[7]"For the lips of a priest ought to preserve knowledge, and from his mouth men should seek instruction—because he is the messenger of the LORD Almighty. [8]But you have turned from the way and by your teaching have caused many to stumble; you have violated the covenant with Levi," says the LORD Almighty. [9]"So I have caused you to be despised and humiliated before all the people, because you have not followed my ways but have shown partiality in matters of the law."

*Judah Unfaithful*

[10]Have we not all one Father[d]? Did not one God create us? Why do we profane the covenant of our fathers by breaking faith with one another?

[11]Judah has broken faith. A detestable thing has been committed in Israel and in Jerusalem: Judah has desecrated the sanctuary the LORD loves, by marrying the daughter of a foreign god. [12]As for the man who does this, whoever he may be, may the LORD cut him off from the tents of Jacob[e]—even though he brings offerings to the LORD Almighty.

[13]Another thing you do: You flood the LORD's altar with tears. You weep and wail because he no

---

d10 Or *father*
e12 Or [12]*May the* LORD *cut off from the tents of Jacob anyone who gives testimony in behalf of the man who does this*

פְּנוֹת אֶל־ הַמִּנְחָה וְלָקַחַת רָצוֹן מִיֶּדְכֶם׃

from-hand-of-you pleasure or-to-accept the-offering to to-pay-attention

וַאֲמַרְתֶּם עַל־ מָה עַל כִּי־ יְהוָה הֵעִיד בֵּינְךָ

between-you he-acts-as-witness Yahweh that because why? for and-you-ask (14)

וּבֵין | אֵשֶׁת נְעוּרֶיךָ אֲשֶׁר אַתָּה בָּגַדְתָּה בָּהּ וְהִיא

though-she with-her you-broke-faith you because youths-of-you wife-of and-between

חֲבֶרְתְּךָ וְאֵשֶׁת בְּרִיתֶךָ׃ וְלֹא־ אֶחָד עָשָׂה וּשְׁאָר

and-rest-of he-made one and-not (15) covenant-of-you and-wife-of partner-of-you

רוּחַ לוֹ וּמָה הָאֶחָד מְבַקֵּשׁ זֶרַע אֱלֹהִים וְנִשְׁמַרְתֶּם

so-you-guard-yourself God offspring-of seeking the-one and-why? to-him spirit

בְּרוּחֲכֶם וּבְאֵשֶׁת נְעוּרֶיךָ אַל־ יִבְגֹּד׃ כִּי־

indeed (16) let-him-break-faith not youths-of-you and-with-wife-of in-spirit-of-you

שָׂנֵא שַׁלַּח אָמַר יְהוָה אֱלֹהֵי יִשְׂרָאֵל וְכִסָּה חָמָס עַל־

over violence and-he-covers Israel God-of Yahweh he-says to-divorce he-hates

לְבוּשׁוֹ אָמַר יְהוָה צְבָאוֹת וְנִשְׁמַרְתֶּם בְּרוּחֲכֶם

in-spirit-of-you so-you-guard-yourself Hosts Yahweh-of he-says garment-of-him

וְלֹא תִבְגֹּדוּ׃ הוֹגַעְתֶּם יְהוָה בְּדִבְרֵיכֶם וַאֲמַרְתֶּם

but-you-ask with-words-of-you Yahweh you-wearied (17) you-break-faith and-not

בַּמָּה הוֹגָעְנוּ בֶּאֱמָרְכֶם כָּל־ עֹשֵׂה רָע טוֹב | בְּעֵינֵי יְהוָה

Yahweh in-eyes-of good evil one-doing-of all-of by-to-say-you we-wearied by-how?

וּבָהֶם הוּא חָפֵץ אוֹ אַיֵּה אֱלֹהֵי הַמִּשְׁפָּט׃ הִנְנִי שֹׁלֵחַ

sending see-I! (3:1) the-justice God-of where? or he-is-pleased he and-with-them

מַלְאָכִי וּפִנָּה־ דֶרֶךְ לְפָנָי וּפִתְאֹם יָבוֹא אֶל־

to he-will-come then-suddenly before-me way and-he-will-prepare messenger-of-me

הֵיכָלוֹ הָאָדוֹן | אֲשֶׁר־אַתֶּם מְבַקְשִׁים וּמַלְאַךְ הַבְּרִית אֲשֶׁר־

whom the-covenant even-messenger-of ones-seeking you whom the-Lord temple-of-him

אַתֶּם חֲפֵצִים הִנֵּה־ בָא אָמַר יְהוָה צְבָאוֹת׃ וּמִי מְכַלְכֵּל

enduring but-who? (2) Hosts Yahweh-of he-says coming see! ones-desiring you

אֶת־ יוֹם בּוֹאוֹ וּמִי הָעֹמֵד בְּהֵרָאוֹתוֹ כִּי־הוּא

he for when-to-appear-him the-one-standing and-who? to-come-him day-of ***

כְּאֵשׁ מְצָרֵף וּכְבֹרִית מְכַבְּסִים׃ וְיָשַׁב

and-he-will-sit (3) ones-being-launderers or-like-soap-of one-refining like-fire-of

מְצָרֵף וּמְטַהֵר כֶּסֶף וְטִהַר אֶת־ בְּנֵי־ לֵוִי

Levi sons-of *** and-he-will-purify silver and-one-purifying one-refining

וְזִקַּק אֹתָם כַּזָּהָב וְכַכָּסֶף וְהָיוּ

then-they-will-be and-like-the-silver like-the-gold them and-he-will-refine

לַיהוָה מַגִּישֵׁי מִנְחָה בִּצְדָקָה׃ וְעָרְבָה

and-she-will-be-acceptable (4) in-righteousness offering men-bringing-of to-Yahweh

longer pays attention to your offerings or accepts them with pleasure from your hands. [14]You ask, "Why?" It is because the LORD is acting as the witness between you and the wife of your youth, because you have broken faith with her, though she is your partner, the wife of your marriage covenant.

[15]Has not ⌞the LORD⌟ made them one? In flesh and spirit they are his. And why one? Because he was seeking godly offspring.[f] So guard yourself in your spirit, and do not break faith with the wife of your youth.

[16]"I hate divorce," says the LORD God of Israel, "and I hate a man's covering himself[g] with violence as well as with his garment," says the LORD Almighty.

So guard yourself in your spirit, and do not break faith.

*The Day of Judgment*

[17]You have wearied the LORD with your words.

"How have we wearied him?" you ask.

By saying, "All who do evil are good in the eyes of the LORD, and he is pleased with them" or "Where is the God of justice?"

3 "See, I will send my messenger, who will prepare the way before me. Then suddenly the Lord you are seeking will come to his temple; the messenger of the covenant, whom you desire, will come," says the LORD Almighty.

[2]But who can endure the day of his coming? Who can stand when he appears? For he will be like a refiner's fire or a launderer's soap. [3]He will sit as a refiner and purifier of silver; he will purify the Levites and refine them like gold and silver. Then the LORD will have men who will bring offerings in righteousness, [4]and the offerings of Judah and Jerusalem

f15 Or [15]*But the one ⌞who is our father⌟ did not do this, not as long as life remained in him. And what was he seeking? An offspring from God*

g16 Or *his wife*

לַיהוָה מִנְחַת יְהוּדָה וִירוּשָׁלִָם כִּימֵי עוֹלָם וּכְשָׁנִים

and-as-years time-gone-by as-days-of and-Jerusalem Judah offering-of to-Yahweh

קַדְמֹנִיּוֹת׃ וְקָרַבְתִּי אֲלֵיכֶם לַמִּשְׁפָּט וְהָיִיתִי ׀ עֵד

testifier and-I-will-be for-the-judgment to-you so-I-will-come-near (5) former-ones

מְמַהֵר בַּמְכַשְּׁפִים וּבַמְנָאֲפִים

and-against-the-ones-committing-adultery against-the-ones-being-sorcerers being-quick

וּבַנִּשְׁבָּעִים לַשָּׁקֶר וּבְעֹשְׁקֵי

and-against-ones-defrauding-of by-the-falsehood and-against-the-ones-swearing

שְׂכַר־ שָׂכִיר אַלְמָנָה וְיָתוֹם וּמַטֵּי־ גֵר וְלֹא

but-not alien and-ones-depriving-justice-of and-fatherless widow laborer wage-of

יְרֵאוּנִי אָמַר יְהוָה צְבָאוֹת׃ כִּי אֲנִי יְהוָה לֹא שָׁנִיתִי וְאַתֶּם

so-you I-change not Yahweh I indeed (6) Hosts Yahweh-of he-says they-fear-me

בְּנֵי־ יַעֲקֹב לֹא כְלִיתֶם׃ לְמִימֵי אֲבֹתֵיכֶם

forefathers-of-you at-since-days-of (7) you-are-destroyed not Jacob descendants-of

סַרְתֶּם מֵחֻקַּי וְלֹא שְׁמַרְתֶּם שׁוּבוּ אֵלַי וְאָשׁוּבָה

and-I-will-return to-me return! you-kept and-not from-decrees-of-me you-turned-away

אֲלֵיכֶם אָמַר יְהוָה צְבָאוֹת וַאֲמַרְתֶּם בַּמֶּה נָשׁוּב׃

shall-we-return by-how? but-you-ask Hosts Yahweh-of he-says to-you

הֲיִקְבַּע אָדָם אֱלֹהִים כִּי אַתֶּם קֹבְעִים אֹתִי וַאֲמַרְתֶּם בַּמֶּה

by-how? but-you-ask me ones-robbing you yet God man will-he-rob? (8)

קְבַעֲנוּךָ הַמַּעֲשֵׂר וְהַתְּרוּמָה׃ בַּמְּאֵרָה אַתֶּם נֵאָרִים

ones-being-cursed you under-the-curse (9) and-the-offering the-tithe do-we-rob-you

וְאֹתִי אַתֶּם קֹבְעִים הַגּוֹי כֻּלּוֹ׃ הָבִיאוּ אֶת־ כָּל־

whole-of *** bring! (10) whole-of-him the-nation ones-robbing you because-me

הַמַּעֲשֵׂר אֶל־ בֵּית הָאוֹצָר וִיהִי טֶרֶף בְּבֵיתִי

in-house-of-me food that-he-may-be the-storage house-of into the-tithe

וּבְחָנוּנִי נָא בָּזֹאת אָמַר יְהוָה צְבָאוֹת אִם־לֹא אֶפְתַּח לָכֶם

for-you I-throw-open not if Hosts Yahweh-of he-says in-this now! indeed-test-me!

אֵת אֲרֻבּוֹת הַשָּׁמַיִם וַהֲרִיקֹתִי לָכֶם בְּרָכָה עַד־ בְּלִי־

not until blessing upon-you and-I-pour-out the-heavens floodgates-of ***

דָי׃ וְגָעַרְתִּי לָכֶם בָּאֹכֵל וְלֹא־

and-not from-the-one-devouring for-you and-I-will-prevent (11) room-enough

יַשְׁחִת לָכֶם אֶת־ פְּרִי הָאֲדָמָה וְלֹא־ תְשַׁכֵּל לָכֶם

of-you she-will-cast-fruit and-not the-land crop-of *** of-you he-will-destroy

הַגֶּפֶן בַּשָּׂדֶה אָמַר יְהוָה צְבָאוֹת׃ וְאִשְּׁרוּ

then-they-will-call-blessed (12) Hosts Yahweh-of he-says in-the-field the-vine

אֶתְכֶם כָּל־ הַגּוֹיִם כִּי־ תִהְיוּ אַתֶּם אֶרֶץ חֵפֶץ אָמַר יְהוָה

Yahweh-of he-says delight land-of you you-will-be for the-nations all-of you

will be acceptable to the LORD, as in days gone by, as in former years.

[5]"So I will come near to you for judgment. I will be quick to testify against sorcerers, adulterers and perjurers, against those who defraud laborers of their wages, who oppress the widows and the fatherless, and deprive aliens of justice, but do not fear me," says the LORD Almighty.

*Robbing God*

[6]"I the LORD do not change. So you, O descendants of Jacob, are not destroyed. [7]Ever since the time of your forefathers you have turned away from my decrees and have not kept them. Return to me, and I will return to you," says the LORD Almighty.

"But you ask, 'How are we to return?'

[8]"Will a man rob God? Yet you rob me.

"But you ask, 'How do we rob you?'

"In tithes and offerings. [9]You are under a curse—the whole nation of you—because you are robbing me. [10]Bring the whole tithe into the storehouse, that there may be food in my house. Test me in this," says the LORD Almighty, "and see if I will not throw open the floodgates of heaven and pour out so much blessing that you will not have room enough for it. [11]I will prevent pests from devouring your crops, and the vines in your fields will not cast their fruit," says the LORD Almighty. [12]"Then all the nations will call you blessed, for yours will be a delightful land," says the LORD Almighty.

צְבָאוֹת׃ חִזְקוּ עָלַי דִּבְרֵיכֶם אָמַר יְהוָה וַאֲמַרְתֶּם
yet-you-ask Yahweh he-says words-of-you against-me you-made-harsh (13) Hosts

מַה־ נִּדְבַּרְנוּ עָלֶיךָ׃ אֲמַרְתֶּם שָׁוְא עֲבֹד אֱלֹהִים וּמַה־ בֶּצַע
gain and-what? God to-serve futile you-said (14) against-you we-said what?

כִּי שָׁמַרְנוּ מִשְׁמַרְתּוֹ וְכִי הָלַכְנוּ קְדֹרַנִּית מִפְּנֵי
at-before like-mourner we-went-about and-when requirement-of-him we-carried-out when

יְהוָה צְבָאוֹת׃ וְעַתָּה אֲנַחְנוּ מְאַשְּׁרִים זֵדִים גַּם־
certainly arrogant-ones ones-calling-blessed we but-now (15) Hosts Yahweh-of

נִבְנוּ עֹשֵׂי רִשְׁעָה גַּם בָּחֲנוּ אֱלֹהִים וַיִּמָּלֵטוּ׃
and-they-escape God they-challenge even evil ones-doing-of they-prosper

אָז נִדְבְּרוּ יִרְאֵי יְהוָה אִישׁ אֶת־ רֵעֵהוּ
other-of-him with each Yahweh ones-fearing-of they-talked-together then (16)

וַיַּקְשֵׁב יְהוָה וַיִּשְׁמָע וַיִּכָּתֵב סֵפֶר זִכָּרוֹן
remembrance scroll-of and-he-was-written and-he-heard Yahweh and-he-listened

לְפָנָיו לְיִרְאֵי יְהוָה וּלְחֹשְׁבֵי
and-concerning-ones-honoring-of Yahweh concerning-ones-fearing-of in-presences-of-him

שְׁמוֹ׃ וְהָיוּ לִי אָמַר יְהוָה צְבָאוֹת לַיּוֹם אֲשֶׁר
when in-the-day Hosts Yahweh-of he-says to-me and-they-will-be (17) name-of-him

אֲנִי עֹשֶׂה סְגֻלָּה וְחָמַלְתִּי עֲלֵיהֶם כַּאֲשֶׁר יַחְמֹל
he-spares just-as to-them and-I-will-spare treasured-possession making-up I

אִישׁ עַל־ בְּנוֹ הָעֹבֵד אֹתוֹ׃ וְשַׁבְתֶּם וּרְאִיתֶם
and-you-will-see and-you-will-do-again (18) him the-one-serving son-of-him to man

בֵּין צַדִּיק לְרָשָׁע בֵּין עֹבֵד אֱלֹהִים לַאֲשֶׁר לֹא עֲבָדוֹ׃
he-serves-him not from-whom God one-serving between from-wicked righteous between

כִּי־ הִנֵּה הַיּוֹם בָּא בֹּעֵר כַּתַּנּוּר וְהָיוּ
and-they-will-be like-the-furnace burning coming the-day see! surely *(19[4:1])

כָל־ זֵדִים וְכָל־ עֹשֵׂה רִשְׁעָה קַשׁ וְלִהַט
and-he-will-set-on-fire stubble evil one-doing-of and-every-of arrogant-ones all-of

אֹתָם הַיּוֹם הַבָּא אָמַר יְהוָה צְבָאוֹת אֲשֶׁר לֹא־ יַעֲזֹב
he-will-be-left not that Hosts Yahweh-of he-says the-one-coming the-day them

לָהֶם שֹׁרֶשׁ וְעָנָף׃ וְזָרְחָה לָכֶם יִרְאֵי
ones-revering-of for-you but-she-will-rise (20[2]) or-branch root to-them

שְׁמִי שֶׁמֶשׁ צְדָקָה וּמַרְפֵּא בִּכְנָפֶיהָ וִיצָאתֶם
and-you-will-go-out in-wings-of-her with-healing righteousness sun-of name-of-me

וּפִשְׁתֶּם כְּעֶגְלֵי מַרְבֵּק׃ וְעַסּוֹתֶם
then-you-will-trample-down (21[3]) stall like-calves-of and-you-will-leap

רְשָׁעִים כִּי־ יִהְיוּ אֵפֶר תַּחַת כַּפּוֹת רַגְלֵיכֶם בַּיּוֹם אֲשֶׁר
when on-the-day feet-of-you soles-of under ash they-will-be indeed wicked-ones

13 "You have said harsh things against me," says the LORD.

"Yet you ask, 'What have we said against you?'

14 "You have said, 'It is futile to serve God. What did we gain by carrying out his requirements and going about like mourners before the LORD Almighty? 15 But now we call the arrogant blessed. Certainly the evildoers prosper, and even those who challenge God escape.' "

16 Then those who feared the LORD talked with each other, and the LORD listened and heard. A scroll of remembrance was written in his presence concerning those who feared the LORD and honored his name.

17 "They will be mine," says the LORD Almighty, "in the day when I make up my treasured possession.[h] I will spare them, just as in compassion a man spares his son who serves him. 18 And you will again see the distinction between the righteous and the wicked, between those who serve God and those who do not.

*The Day of the LORD*

4 "Surely the day is coming; it will burn like a furnace. All the arrogant and every evildoer will be stubble, and that day that is coming will set them on fire," says the LORD Almighty. "Not a root or a branch will be left to them. 2 But for you who revere my name, the sun of righteousness will rise with healing in its wings. And you will go out and leap like calves released from the stall. 3 Then you will trample down the wicked; they will be ashes under the soles of your feet on the day

[h] 17 *Or Almighty, "my treasured possession, in the day when I act*

***Heading, 19*** **Verses 19 through 24 of chapter 3 in Hebrew correspond to verses 1 through 6 of chapter 4 in English. The number in brackets is the English numeration of chapter 4.**

אֲנִי עֹשֶׂה אָמַר יְהוָה צְבָאוֹת׃ זִכְרוּ תּוֹרַת מֹשֶׁה
Moses law-of remember! (22[4]) Hosts Yahweh-of he-says doing I

עַבְדִּי אֲשֶׁר צִוִּיתִי אוֹתוֹ בְחֹרֵב עַל־ כָּל־ יִשְׂרָאֵל חֻקִּים וּמִשְׁפָּטִים׃
and-laws decrees Israel all-of for at-Horeb him I-gave that servant-of-me

הִנֵּה אָנֹכִי שֹׁלֵחַ לָכֶם אֵת אֵלִיָּה הַנָּבִיא לִפְנֵי בּוֹא
to-come before the-prophet Elijah *** to-you sending I see! (23[5])

יוֹם יְהוָה הַגָּדוֹל וְהַנּוֹרָא׃ וְהֵשִׁיב
and-he-will-turn (24[6]) and-the-one-being-dreadful the-great Yahweh day-of

לֵב־ אָבוֹת עַל־ בָּנִים וְלֵב בָּנִים עַל־ אֲבוֹתָם
fathers-of-them to children and-heart-of children to fathers heart-of

פֶּן־ אָבוֹא וְהִכֵּיתִי אֶת־ הָאָרֶץ חֵרֶם׃
curse the-land *** and-I-will-strike I-will-come or

when I do these things," says the
Lord Almighty.
4 "Remember the law of my servant Moses, the decrees and laws
I gave him at Horeb for all Israel.
5 "See, I will send you the
prophet Elijah before that great
and dreadful day of the Lord
comes. 6 He will turn the hearts of
the fathers to their children, and
the hearts of the children to their
fathers; or else I will come and
strike the land with a curse."

**Heading* See the note on page 590.